Jane's Fighting Ships 2009-2010

Commodore Stephen Saunders RN

One Hundred and Twelfth Edition

Founded in 1897 by Fred T Jane

Bookmark jfs.janes.com today!

The title is also available on online/CD-rom (New Gen), JDS (Jane's Data Services), IntraSpex (offline), and Intel centres. Online gives the capability of real-time editing, permitting frequent updating. We trust our readers will use these facilities to keep abreast of the latest changes as and when they occur.
Updates online: Any update to the content of this product will appear online as it occurs.

Jane's Fighting Ships online site gives you details of the additional information that is unique to online subscribers and the many benefits of upgrading to an online subscription. Don't delay, visit jfs.janes.com today and view the list of the latest updates to this online service.

ISBN 978 0 7106 2888 6
"Jane's" is a registered trademark

IHS Jane's, IHS (Global) Limited, Sentinel House, 163 Brighton Road, Coulsdon, Surrey, CR5 2YH, UK

In the US and its dependencies
Jane's Information Group Inc., 110 N. Royal Street, Suite 200, Alexandria, Virginia 22314, US

Copyright enquiries
e-mail: copyright@janes.com

This book was produced using FSC certified paper

Printed and bound in Great Britain by the MPG Books Group

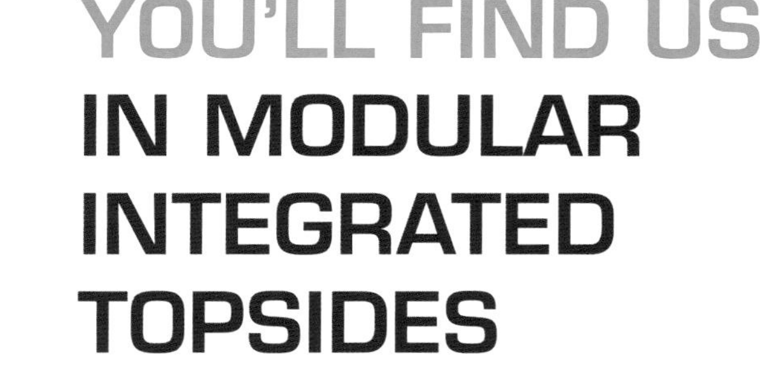

Contents

Glossary ....[7]

How to use *Jane's Fighting Ships* ....[10]

Alphabetical list of advertisers ....[15]

Ensigns and flags of the world's navies ....[17]

Executive overview ....[26]

Acknowledgements ....[36]

Ranks and insignia of the world's navies ....[37]

Pennant list of major surface ships ....[65]

World navies 1

Albania 2
Algeria 4
Angola 9
Anguilla 9
Antigua and Barbuda 9
Argentina 10
Australia 25
Azerbaijan 42
Bahamas 45
Bahrain 47
Bangladesh 52
Barbados 61
Belgium 61
Belize 66
Benin 66
Bermuda 67
Bolivia 67
Brazil 69
British Indian Ocean Territory 87
Brunei 87
Bulgaria 89
Cambodia 96
Cameroon 96
Canada 98
Cape Verde 113
Cayman Islands 114
Chile 115
China 127
Colombia 168
Comoros 177
Democratic Republic of Congo 177
Congo-Brazzaville 178
Cook Islands 178
Costa Rica 178
Côte d'Ivoire 180
Croatia 180
Cuba 184
Cyprus 186
Denmark 188
Djibouti 199
Dominica 200
Dominican Republic 201
East Timor 204
Ecuador 204
Egypt 213
El Salvador 224
Equatorial Guinea 227
Eritrea 227
Estonia 228
Falkland Islands 232
Faroe Islands 232
Fiji 233
Finland 234
France 242
Gabon 277
Gambia 278
Georgia 279
Germany 280
Ghana 298
Greece 299
Grenada 314
Guatemala 315
Guinea 316
Guinea-Bissau 316
Guyana 317
Honduras 317
Hong Kong 319
Hungary 322
Iceland 323
India 324
Indonesia 352
Iran 368
Iraq 380
Ireland 381
Israel 383
Italy 388
Jamaica 412
Japan 414
Jordan 447
Kazakhstan 448
Kenya 449
Kiribati 451
Korea, North 452
Korea, South 458
Kuwait 475
Latvia 479
Lebanon 482
Libya 483
Lithuania 486
Macedonia 490
Madagascar 490
Malawi 491
Malaysia 492
Maldives 506
Malta 508
Marshall Islands 509
Mauritania 509
Mauritius 511
Mexico 512
Federated States of Micronesia 526
Montenegro 527
Morocco 530
Mozambique 538
Myanmar 538
Namibia 544
NATO 545
Netherlands 546
New Zealand 559
Nicaragua 562
Nigeria 563
Norway 566
Oman 575
Pakistan 582
Palau 591
Panama 592
Papua New Guinea 595
Paraguay 595
Peru 598
Philippines 608
Poland 616
Portugal 628
Qatar 637
Romania 640
Russian Federation 648
St Kitts and Nevis 707
St Lucia 708
St Vincent and the Grenadines 709
Samoa 709
Saudi Arabia 710
Senegal 717
Serbia 720
Seychelles 721
Sierra Leone 722
Singapore 723
Slovenia 732
Solomon Islands 733
South Africa 733
Spain 739
Sri Lanka 761
Sudan 767
Suriname 767
Sweden 768
Switzerland 783
Syria 783
Taiwan 785
Tanzania 799
Thailand 800
Togo 820
Tonga 820
Trinidad and Tobago 821
Tunisia 823
Turkey 827
Turkmenistan 847
Tuvalu 848
Ukraine 848
United Arab Emirates 856
United Kingdom 865
United States 903
Uruguay 974
Vanuatu 978
Venezuela 979
Vietnam 986
Virgin Islands 992
Yemen 993
Zimbabwe 995

Indexes
Country abbreviations 999
Named ships 999
Named classes 1017
Aircraft by countries 1022

Jane's Fighting Ships website: jfs.janes.com

EDITORIAL AND ADMINISTRATION

Managing Director, IHS Jane's: Michael Dell, e-mail: michael.dell@janes.com

Group Publishing Director: Sean Howe, e-mail: sean.howe@janes.com

Publisher: Sara Morgan, e-mail: sara.morgan@janes.com

Compiler/Editor: Welcomes information and comments from users who should send material to:
Research and Information Services
IHS Jane's, IHS (Global) Limited, Sentinel House, 163 Brighton Road, Coulsdon, Surrey CR5 2YH, UK
Tel: (+44 20) 87 00 38 11 Fax: (+44 20) 87 00 39 59
e-mail: yearbook@janes.com

SALES OFFICES

Europe and Africa
IHS Jane's, IHS (Global) Limited, Sentinel House, 163 Brighton Road, Coulsdon, Surrey CR5 2YH, UK
Tel: (+44 20) 87 00 37 50 Fax: (+44 20) 87 00 37 51
e-mail: customer.servicesuk@janes.com

North/Central/South America
Jane's Information Group Inc., 110 N Royal Street, Suite 200 Alexandria, Virginia 22314, US
Tel: (+1 703) 683 21 34 Fax: (+1 703) 836 02 97
Tel: (+1 800) 824 07 68 Fax: (+1 800) 836 02 97
e-mail: customer.servicesus@janes.com

Asia
IHS Jane's, IHS (Global) Limited, 78 Shenton Way, #12–01, Singapore 079120, Singapore
Tel: (+65) 65 76 53 00 Fax: (+65) 62 26 11 85
e-mail: asiapacific@janes.com

Oceania
IHS Jane's, IHS (Global) Limited, Level 3, 33 Rowe Street, Eastwood, NSW 2122, Australia
Tel: (+61 2) 85 87 79 00 Fax: (+61 2) 85 87 79 01
e-mail: oceania@janes.com

Middle East
IHS Jane's, IHS (Global) Limited, PO Box 502138, Dubai, United Arab Emirates
Tel: (+971 4) 390 23 36 Fax: (+971 4) 390 88 48
e-mail: mideast@janes.com

Japan
IHS Jane's, IHS (Global) Limited, CERA51 Bldg, 1-21-8 Ebisu, Shibuya-ku, Tokyo 150-0013, Japan
Tel: (+81 3) 57 91 96 63 Fax: (+81 3) 54 20 64 02
e-mail: japan@janes.com

ADVERTISEMENT SALES OFFICES

(Head Office)
IHS Jane's, IHS (Global) Limited
Sentinel House, 163 Brighton Road,
Coulsdon, Surrey CR5 2YH, UK
Tel: (+44 20) 87 00 37 00 Fax: (+44 20) 87 00 38 59/37 44
e-mail: defadsales@janes.com

Janine Boxall, Global Advertising Sales Director,
Tel: (+44 20) 87 00 38 52 Fax: (+44 20) 87 00 38 59/37 44
e-mail: janine.boxall@janes.com

Richard West, Senior Key Accounts Manager
Tel: (+44 1892) 72 55 80 Fax: (+44 1892) 72 55 81
e-mail: richard.west@janes.com

Carly Litchfield, Advertising Sales Manager
Tel: (+44 20) 87 00 39 63 Fax: (+44 20) 87 00 37 44
e-mail: carly.litchfield@janes.com

Kevin Lyons, Advertising Sales Executive
Tel: (+44 20) 87 00 38 53 Fax: (+44 20) 87 00 37 44
e-mail: kevin.lyons@janes.com

(US/Canada office)
Jane's Information Group Inc.
110 N Royal Street, Suite 200,
Alexandria, Virginia 22314, US
Tel: (+1 703) 683 37 00 Fax: (+1 703) 836 55 37
e-mail: defadsales@janes.com

US and Canada
Janet Berta, US Advertising Sales Director,
Tel: (+1 703) 236 24 10 Fax: (+1 703) 836 55 37
e-mail: janet.berta@janes.com

Sean Fitzgerald, Southeast Region Advertising Sales Manager
Tel: (+1 703) 836 24 46 Fax: (+1 703) 836 55 37
e-mail: sean.fitzgerald@janes.com

Linda Hewish, Northeast Region Advertising Sales Manager
Tel: (+1 703) 836 24 13 Fax: (+1 703) 836 55 37
e-mail: linda.hewish@janes.com

Janet Murphy, Central Region Advertising Sales Manager
Tel: (+1 703) 836 31 39 Fax: (+1 703) 836 55 37
e-mail: janet.murphy@janes.com

Richard L Ayer
127 Avenida del Mar, Suite 2A, San Clemente, California 92672, US
Tel: (+1 949) 366 84 55 Fax: (+1 949) 366 92 89
e-mail: ayercomm@earthlink.com

Rest of the World
Australia: *Richard West* (UK Head Office)

Benelux: *Kevin Lyons* (UK Head Office)

Eastern Europe (excl. Poland): MCW Media & Consulting Wehrstedt
Dr Uwe H Wehrstedt
Hagenbreite 9, D-06463 Ermsleben, Germany
Tel: (+49 03) 47 43/620 90 Fax: (+49 03) 47 43/620 91
e-mail: info@Wehrstedt.org

Germany and Austria: *MCW Media & Consulting Wehrstedt* (see Eastern Europe)

Greece: *Carly Litchfield* (UK Head Office)

Hong Kong: *Carly Litchfield* (UK Head Office)

India: *Carly Litchfield* (UK Head Office)

Israel: *Oreet International Media*
15 Kinneret Street, IL-51201 Bene Berak, Israel
Tel: (+972 3) 570 65 27 Fax: (+972 3) 570 65 27
e-mail: admin@oreet-marcom.com
Defence: Liat Heiblum
e-mail: liat_h@oreet-marcom.com

Italy and Switzerland: *Ediconsult Internazionale Srl*
Piazza Fontane Marose 3, I-16123 Genoa, Italy
Tel: (+39 010) 58 36 84 Fax: (+39 010) 56 65 78
e-mail: genova@ediconsult.com

Japan: *Carly Litchfield* (UK Head Office)

Middle East: *Kevin Lyons* (UK Head Office)

Pakistan: *Kevin Lyons* (UK Head Office)

Poland: *Kevin Lyons* (UK Head Office)

Russia: Anatoly Tomashevich
1/3, appt 108, Zhivopisnaya Str, Moscow, 123103, Russia
Tel/Fax: (+7 495) 942 04 65
e-mail: to-anatoly@tochka.ru

Scandinavia: *Falsten Partnership*
23, Walsingham Road, Hove, East Sussex BN41 2XA, UK
Tel: (+44 1273) 77 10 20 Fax: (+ 44 1273) 77 00 70
e-mail: sales@falsten.com

Singapore: *Richard West* (UK Head Office)

South Africa: *Richard West* (UK Head Office)

Spain: Macarena Fernandez
VIA Exclusivas S.L., Virato, 69 - Sotano C, E-28010, Madrid, Spain
Tel: (+34 91) 448 76 22 Fax: (+34 91) 446 02 14
e-mail: macarena@viaexclusivas.com

Turkey: *Richard West* (UK Head Office)

ADVERTISING COPY
Kate Gibbs (UK Head Office)
Tel: (+44 20) 87 00 37 42 Fax: (+44 20) 87 00 38 59/37 44
e-mail: kate.gibbs@janes.com

For North America, South America and Caribbean only:
Tel: (+1 703) 683 37 00 Fax: (+1 703) 836 55 37
e-mail: us.ads@janes.com

Glossary: Jane's Fighting Ships

Type abbreviations are listed at head of Pennant List

AAW Anti-Air Warfare
ACDS Advanced Combat Direction System
ADCAP ADvanced CAPabilities
AEW Airborne Early Warning
AIP Air Independent Propulsion
ALSC Afloat Logistics and Sealift Capability
ARCI Acoustic Rapid COTS Insertion
ARM Anti-Radiation Missile
ASDS Advanced Swimmer Delivery System
A/S, ASW Anti-Submarine (Warfare)
ASM Air-to-Surface Missile
ASROC Rocket assisted torpedo, part of whose trajectory is in the air
ASV Air-to-Surface Vessel
AUV Autonomous Underwater Vehicle
BPDMS Base Point Defence Missile System
Cal Calibre - the diameter of a gun barrel; also used for measuring length of the barrel for example a 6 in gun 50 calibres long (6 in/50) would be 25 ft long
CEC Co-operative Engagement Capability
CIWS Close-In Weapon System
CODAG, CODOG, CODAGE CODLAG, CODLAG, COGOG, COSAG, COGAL Descriptions of mixed propulsion systems: combined diesel and gas turbine electric, diesel or gas turbine, gas turbine and gas turbine, gas diesel and gas turbine, diesel-electric and gas turbine, turbine or gas turbine, steam and gas turbine, gas turbine and electricity
COTS Commercial Off-The-Shelf
cp controllable pitch (propellers)
DDS Dry Dock Shelter
DP Dual Purpose (gun) for surface or AA use
Displacement Basically the weight of water displaced by a ship's hull when floating:
(a) Light: without fuel, water or ammunition
(b) Normal: used for Japanese MSA ships. Similar to 'standard'
(c) Standard: as defined by Washington Naval Conference 1922 - fully manned and stored but without fuel or reserve feed-water
(d) Full load: fully laden with all stores, ammunition, fuel and water
dwt deadweight tonnage (see tonnage)
EARS Electromagnetic Aircraft Recovery System
ECM Electronic countermeasures, for example, jamming
ECCM Electronic counter-countermeasures
EEZ Exclusive Economic Zone
EHF Extreme High Frequency
ELF Extreme Low Frequency radio
ELINT Electronic intelligence, for example, recording radar, W/T and so on
EMALS Electromagnetic Aircraft Launching System
ERGM Extended-Range Guided Munitions
ESM Electronic Support Measures for example, intercept
ESSM Evolved Sea Sparrow Missile
EW Electronic Warfare
FLIR Forward-Looking Infra-Red
FRAM Fleet Rehabilitation And Modernisation programme
GCCS Global Command and Control System
GFCS Gun Fire-Control System
GPS Global Positioning System
grt gross registered tonnage (see tonnage)
HDTI High Definition Thermal Imager
HIFR Helicopter In-Flight Refuelling
HF High Frequency
Horsepower (hp) or (hp(m)) Power developed or applied:
(a) bhp: brake horsepower = power available at the crankshaft
(b) shp: shaft horsepower = power delivered to the propeller shaft
(c) ihp: indicated horsepower = power produced by expansion of gases in the cylinders of reciprocating steam engines
(d) 1 kW = 1.341 hp = 1.360 metric hp
1 hp = 0.746 kW = 1.014 metric hp
1 metric hp = 0.735 kW = 0.968 hp
(e) Sustained horsepower may be different for similar engines in different conditions
IFF Identification Friend/Foe
IRST Infra-Red Search and Track
JMCIS Joint Maritime Command Information System
JTIDS Joint Tactical Information Distribution System
kT kiloton
kW kilowatt
LAMPS Light Airborne Multipurpose System
LAMS Local Area Missile System
Length Expressed in various ways:
(a) oa: overall = length between extremities
(b) pp: between perpendiculars = between fore side of the stem and after side of the rudderpost
(c) wl: waterline = between extremities on the water-line

SOHN WON-IL

10/2008, P Froud* / 1353685

LF	Low Frequency
MAD	Magnetic Anomaly Detector
MDF	Maritime Defence Force
Measurement	See Tonnage
MF	Medium Frequency
MFCS	Missile Fire-Control System
MG	Machine Gun
MIDAS	Mine and Ice Detection Avoidance System
MIRV	Multiple, Independently targetable Re-entry Vehicle
MPA	Maritime Patrol Aircraft
MSA	Japan Maritime Safety Agency
MSC	US Military Sealift Command
MW	Megawatt
NBC	Nuclear, Biological and Chemical (warfare)
net	net registered tonnage (see tonnage)
n mile	nautical mile (mean value 1.8532 km)
NMRS	Near-term Mine Reconnaissance System
NTDS	Naval Tactical Direction System
oa	overall length
OTC	Officer in Tactical Command
OTHT	Over The Horizon Targeting
PAAMS	Principal Anti-Air Missile System
PAP	Poisson Auto Propulse
PDMS	Point Defence Missile System
PWR	Pressurised Water Reactor
QRCC	Quick Reaction Combat Capability
RAIDS	Rapid Anti-ship missile Integrated Defence System
RAM	Radar Absorbent Material
RAM	Rolling Airframe Missile
RAS	Replenishment At Sea
RAST	Recovery, Assist, Secure and Traverse system
RBU	Anti-submarine rocket launcher
RCS	Radar Cross Section
RIB	Rigid Inflatable Boat
Ro-Ro	Roll-on/Roll-off
ROV	Remote Operated Vehicle
rpm	revolutions per minute
SAM	Surface-to-Air Missile
SAR	Search And Rescue
SATCOM	SATellite COMmunications
SAWCS	Submarine Acoustic Warfare Countermeasures System
SES	Surface Effect Ship
SHF	Super High Frequency
SINS	Ship's Inertial Navigation System
SLBM	Submarine-Launched Ballistic Missile
SLCM	Ship-Launched Cruise Missile
SLEP	Service Life Extension Programme
SMCS	Submarine Command System
SRBOC	Super Rapid Blooming Offboard Chaff
SSDE/SSE	Submerged Signal and Decoy Ejector
SSDS	Ship Self-Defence System
SSM	Surface-to-Surface Missile
SSTDS	Surface Ship Torpedo Defence System
STIR	Surveillance Target Indicator Radar
STOBAR	Short Take Off and Barrier Arrested Recovery
STOVL	Short Take Off and Vertical Landing
SUM	Surface-to-Underwater Missile
SURTASS	Surface Towed Array Surveillance System
SWATH	Small Waterplane Area Twin Hull
TACAN	TACtical Air Navigation beacon
TACTASS	TACtical Towed Acoustic Sensor System
TAINS	Tercom Aided Inertial Navigation System
TAS	Target Acquisition System
TASM	Tomahawk Anti-Ship Missile
TASS	Towed Array Surveillance System
TBMD	Theatre Ballistic Missile Defence
Tercom	Terrain Contour Matching
TLAM	Tomahawk Land Attack Missile
Tonnage	Measurement tons, computed on capacity of a ship's hull rather than its 'displacement' (see above): (a) Gross: the internal volume of all spaces within the hull and all permanently enclosed spaces above decks that are available for cargo, stores and accommodation. The result in cubic feet divided by 100 = gross tonnage (b) Net: gross minus all those spaces used for machinery, accommodation and so on ('non-earning' spaces) (c) Deadweight (dwt): the amount of cargo, bunkers, stores and so on, that a ship can carry at her load draught
Tonne	1,000 kilos = 2,204.6 lb Imperial (long) ton = 1.016 tonne or 2,240 lb US (short) ton = 0.9072 tonne or 2,000 lb
UAV	Unmanned Aerial Vehicle
UCAV	Unmanned Combat Aerial Vehicle
UHF	Ultra-High Frequency
USM	Underwater-to-surface missile
USV	Unmanned Surface Vehicle
UUV	Unmanned Undersea Vehicle
VDS	Variable Depth Sonar, can be lowered to best listening depth. In helicopters called 'dunking sonar'.
Vertrep	Vertical replenishment
VLF	Very Low Frequency radio
VLS	Vertical Launch System
VSTOL	Vertical or Short Take-Off/Landing
VSV	Very Slender Vessel
VTOL	Vertical Take-Off/Landing
wl	waterline length

FRIDTJOF NANSEN *1/2008*, Michael Nitz* / 1353686

How to use: Jane's Fighting Ships

(see also Glossary and Type abbreviations)

(1) Details of major warships are grouped under six separate non-printable headings. These are:-

(a) **Number and Class name**. Totals of vessels per class are listed as 'in service + building (proposed)' or 'in service + transfer (proposed)'.

(b) **Building programme**. This includes builders' names and key dates. In general the 'laid down' column reflects keel laying but modern shipbuilding techniques make it difficult to be specific about the start date of actual construction. Launching and christening can be similarly confusing, now that many ships are lowered into the water and formally christened some time later. Some nations commission their ships on completion of building, others after the ships have completed trials. In this hardcopy edition any date after April 2009 is projected or estimated and therefore liable to change.

(c) **Hull**. This section tends to have only specification and performance parameters and contains little free text. Hull related details such as **Military lift** and **Cargo capacity** may be included when appropriate. **Displacement** and **Measurement** tonnages, **Dimensions, Horsepower** and so on, are defined in the Glossary. Throughout the life of a ship its displacement tends to creep upwards as additional equipment is added and redundant fixtures and fittings are left in place. For the same reasons, ships of the same class, active in different navies, frequently have different displacements and other dissimilar characteristics. Unless otherwise stated the lengths and widths given are overall and the draught is at full load. Sustained maximum horsepower is given where the information is available and may not be the same for similar engines operating in different hulls under different conditions. **Speed** is the maximum obtainable under trials conditions.

(d) **Weapon systems**. This section contains operational details and some free text on weapons and sensors which are laid out in a consistent order using the same subheadings throughout the book. The titles are:- **Missiles** (subdivided into SLBM, SSM, SAM, A/S); **Guns** (numbers of barrels are given and the rate of fire is 'per barrel' unless stated otherwise); **Torpedoes**; **A/S mortars**; **Depth charges**; **Mines**; **Countermeasures**; **Combat data systems**; **Weapons control**; **Electro-optic systems**; **Radars**; **Sonars**. The Weapons control heading is used for weapons' direction equipment. In most cases the performance specifications are those of the manufacturer and may therefore be considered to be at the top end of the spectrum of effective performance. So-called 'operational effectiveness' is difficult to define, depends upon many variables and in the context of range may be considerably less than the theoretical maximum. Numbers inserted in the text refer to similar numbers included on line drawings.

(e) **Aircraft**. Only the types and numbers are included here. Where appropriate each country has a separate section listing overall numbers and operational parameters of front-line shipborne and land-based maritime aircraft, normally included after the Frigate section if there is one.

(f) **General comments**. A maximum of six sub-headings are used to sweep up the variety of additional information which is available but has no logical place in the other sections. These headings are: **Programmes**; **Modernisation**; **Structure**; **Operational**; **Sales** and **Opinion**. The last of these allows space for informed comment. Some ships remain theoretically in the order of battle in some navies even though they never go to sea and could be more accurately described as in reserve. Where this is known comment is made under **Operational**.

(2) Minor or less important ship entries follow the same format except that there is often much less detail in the first four headings and all additional remarks are put together under the single heading of **Comment**. The distinction between major and minor depends upon editorial judgement and is primarily a function of firepower. The age of the ship or class and its relative importance within the Navy concerned is also taken into account.

(3) The space devoted to front-line maritime aircraft reflects the importance of air power as an addition to the naval weapon systems armoury, but the format used is necessarily brief and covers only numbers, roles and operational characteristics. Greater detail can be found in *Jane's All the World's Aircraft* and the appropriate volume of the *Jane's Weapon Systems* series.

(4) Other than for coastal navies, tables are included at the front of each country section with such things as strength of the fleet, senior appointments, personnel numbers, bases and so on. There is also a list of pennant numbers and a deletions column covering the previous three years. If you cannot find your favourite ship, always look in the **Deletions** list first.

(5) No addenda is included because modern typesetting technology allows changes to the main text to be made up to a few weeks before publication.

(6) Shipbuilding companies and weapons manufacturers frequently change their names by merger or takeover. As far as possible the published name shows the title when the ship was built or weapon system installed. It is therefore historically accurate.

(7) Like many descriptive terms in international naval nomenclature, differences between Coast Guards, Maritime Police, Customs and other paramilitary maritime forces are often indistinct and particular to an individual nation. Such vessels are usually included if they have a paramilitary function and are armed.

(8) When selecting photographs for inclusion, priority is given to those that have been taken most recently. A glossy picture five years old may look nice but often does not show the ship as it is now.

(9) The Navies by country section is geared to the professional user who needs to be able to make an assessment of the fighting characteristics of a Navy or class of ship without having to cross refer to other Navies and sections of the book. Much effort has also been made to prevent entries spilling across from one page to another.

(10) Regular updates can be found online at jfs.janes.com.

(11) Photographs are dated and where * appears a new or re-scanned photograph has been substituted or added. Many are followed by a seven digit number to ease identification.

British Library Cataloguing-in-Publication Data.
A catalogue record for this book is available from the British Library.

Quality Policy

IHS Jane's is the world's leading unclassified information integrator for military, government and commercial organisations worldwide. To maintain this position, the Company will strive to meet and exceed customers' expectations in the design, production and fulfilment of goods and services.

Information published by IHS Jane's is renowned for its accuracy, authority and impartiality, and the Company is committed to seeking ongoing improvement in both products and processes.

IHS Jane's will at all times endeavour to respond directly to market demands and will also ensure that customer satisfaction is measured and employees are encouraged to question and suggest improvements to working practices.

IHS Jane's will continue to invest in its people through training and development to meet the Investor in People standards and changing customer requirements.

www.janes.com

IHS Jane's Users' Charter

This publication is brought to you by IHS Jane's, a global company drawing on more than 100 years of history and an unrivalled reputation for impartiality, accuracy and authority.

Our collection and output of information and images is not dictated by any political or commercial affiliation. Our reportage is undertaken without fear of, or favour from, any government, alliance, state or corporation.

We publish information that is collected overtly from unclassified sources, although much could be regarded as extremely sensitive or not publicly accessible.

Our validation and analysis aims to eradicate misinformation or disinformation as well as factual errors; our objective is always to produce the most accurate and authoritative data.

In the event of any significant inaccuracies, we undertake to draw these to the readers' attention to preserve the highly valued relationship of trust and credibility with our customers worldwide.

If you believe that these policies have been breached by this title, you are invited to contact the editor.

A copy of IHS Jane's Code of Conduct for its editorial teams is available from the publisher.

www.janes.com

Alphabetical list of advertisers

D

Daewoo Shipbuilding & Marine Engineering Co Ltd
85 Da-dong, Jung-gu, Seoul, 100-180 Korea .... [13]

H

Hanjin Heavy Industries & Construction Co Ltd
168-23 Sam sung-dong, Kangham-gu, Seoul,
Korea .... [9]

L

Lürssen Werft GmbH & Co
Friedrich-Klippert-Str. 1, D-28759 Bremen,
Germany .... *Opposite title page*

N

NAVANTIA SA
Velazquez 132, E-28006 Madrid, Spain .... [6]

T

Thales Nederland BV ta v. de
Postbus 42, NL-7550 GD Hengelo, Netherlands .... [2]

ThyssenKrupp Marine Systems
Oeffentlichkeisarbeit, PO Box 10 07 20, D-20005
Hamburg, Germany .... *Facing inside front cover*

Z

Zorya-Mashproekt
Prospekt Oktyabrsky 42a, Nikolaev UA-54018,
Ukraine .... [4]

FREE ENTRY/CONTENT IN THIS PUBLICATION

Having your products and services represented in our titles means that they are being seen by the professionals who matter - both by those involved in the procurement and by those working for the companies that are likely to affect your business. We therefore feel that it is very much in the interest of your organisation, as well as IHS Jane's, to ensure your data is current and accurate.

- **Don't forget** - You may be missing out on business if your entry in an IHS Jane's product is incorrect because you have not supplied the latest information to us.
- **Ask yourself** - Can you afford not to be represented in IHS Jane's printed and electronic products? And if you are listed, can you afford for your information to be out of date?
- **And most importantly** - The best part of all is that your entries in IHS Jane's products are TOTALLY FREE OF CHARGE.

Please provide (using a photocopy of this form or by email to the below address) the information on the following categories where appropriate:

1. Organisation name: ____________________
2. Division name: ____________________
3. Location address: ____________________
____
4. Mailing address if different: ____________________
____
5. Telephone (please include switchboard and main departmental contact numbers, for example Public Relations, Sales, and so on):
____
6. Facsimile: ____________________
7. E-mail: ____________________
8. Web sites: ____________________
9. Contact name and job title: ____________________
____
10. A brief description of your organisation's activities, products and services: ____________________
____
____
11. IHS Jane's publications in which you would like to be included: ____________________
____

Please send this information to:
Sarah Brooker, Research and Information Services, IHS Jane's,
Sentinel House, 163 Brighton Road, Coulsdon, Surrey CR5 2YH, UK
Tel: (+44 20) 87 00 38 11
Fax: (+44 20) 87 00 39 59
e-mail: yearbook@janes.com

Copyright enquiries:
e-mail: copyright@janes.com

Please tick this box if you do not wish your organisation's staff to be included in IHS Jane's mailing lists ☐

JFS

Ensigns and flags of the world's navies

In cases where countries do not have ensigns their warships normally fly the national flag.

Albania
Ensign

Algeria
Ensign

Angola
National Flag and Ensign

Anguilla
National Flag

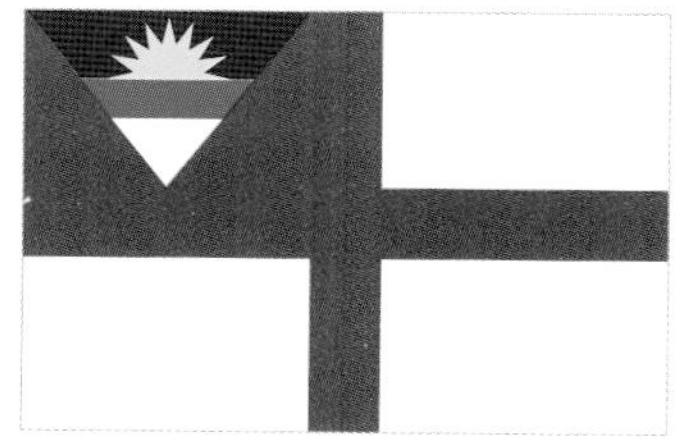

Antigua and Barbuda
Ensign

Argentina
National Flag and Ensign

Australia
Ensign

Azerbaijan
Ensign

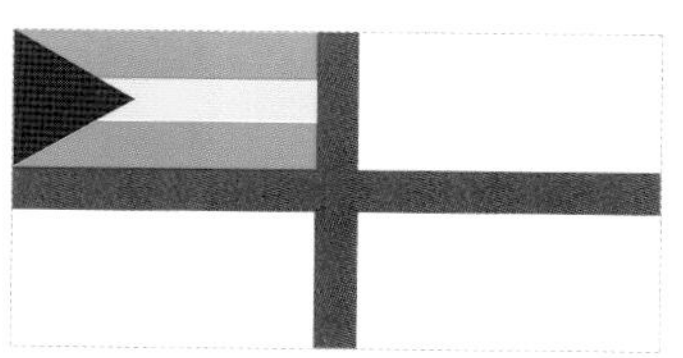

Bahamas
Ensign

Bahrain
National Flag and Ensign

Bangladesh
Ensign

Barbados
Ensign

Belgium
Ensign

Belize
National Flag and Ensign

Benin
National Flag and Ensign

Bermuda
Ensign

Bolivia
Ensign

Brazil
National Flag and Ensign

British Indian Ocean Territory
National Flag

Brunei
Ensign

Bulgaria
Ensign

Cambodia
National Flag and Ensign

China
Ensign

Costa Rica
Ensign

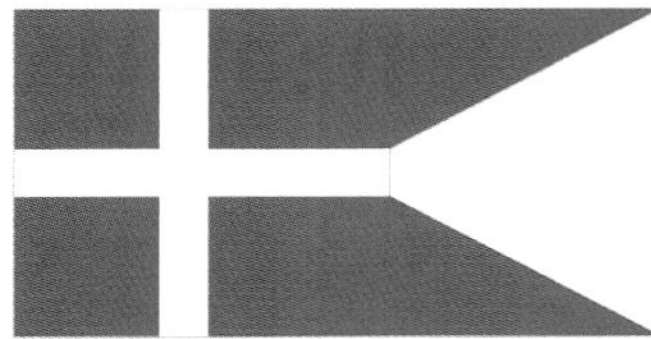
Denmark
Ensign

Cameroon
National Flag and Ensign

Colombia
Ensign

Côte d'Ivoire
National Flag and Ensign

Djibouti
National Flag and Ensign

Canada
National Flag and Ensign

Comoros
National Flag and Ensign

Croatia
Ensign

Dominica
National Flag and Ensign

Cape Verde
National Flag

Congo-Brazzaville
National Flag and Ensign

Cuba
National Flag and Ensign

Dominican Republic
Ensign

Cayman Islands
National Flag

Democratic Republic of Congo
National Flag and Ensign

Cyprus
National Flag and Ensign

East Timor
National Flag and Ensign

Chile
National Flag and Ensign

Cook Islands
National Flag

Cyprus, Turkish Republic of Northern (Not recognised by United Nations)
National Flag and Ensign

Ecuador
Ensign

Egypt
Ensign

Falkland Islands
Falkland Islands Flag

Gambia
National Flag and Ensign

Guatemala
National Flag and Ensign

El Salvador
National Flag and Ensign

Faroe Islands
Territory Flag

Georgia
Ensign

Guinea
National Flag and Ensign

Equatorial Guinea
National Flag and Ensign

Fiji
Ensign

Germany
Ensign

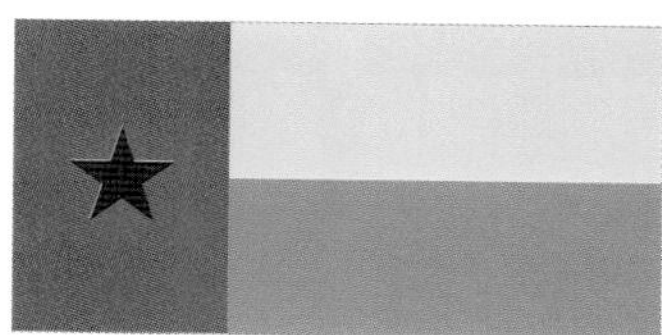

Guinea-Bissau
National Flag and Ensign

Eritrea
National Flag and Ensign

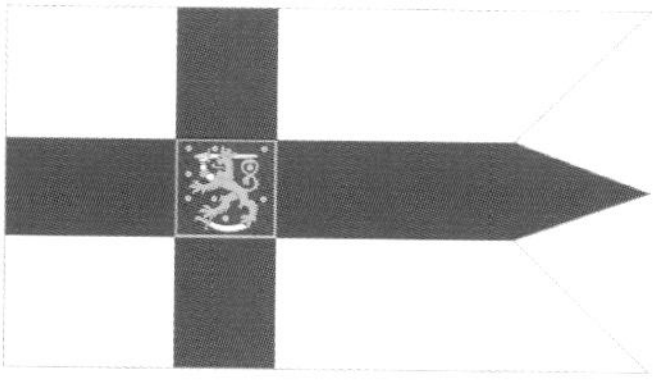

Finland
Ensign

Ghana
Ensign

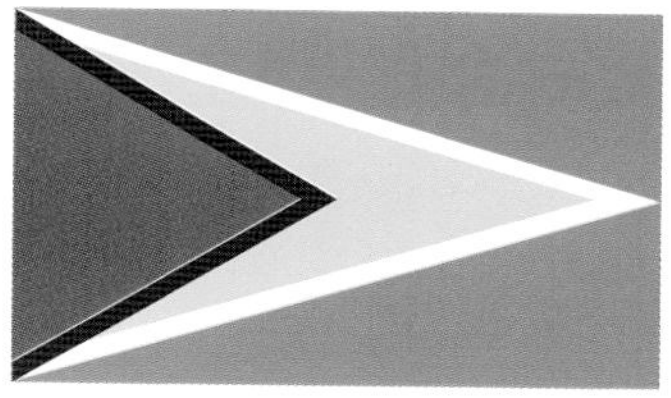

Guyana
National Flag and Ensign

Estonia
Ensign

France
National Flag and Ensign

Greece
National Flag and Ensign

Honduras
Ensign

European Union
Flag of the European Union

Gabon
National Flag and Ensign

Grenada
Ensign

Hong Kong
Regional Flag and Ensign

Hungary
National Flag

Ireland
National Flag and Ensign

Jordan
Ensign

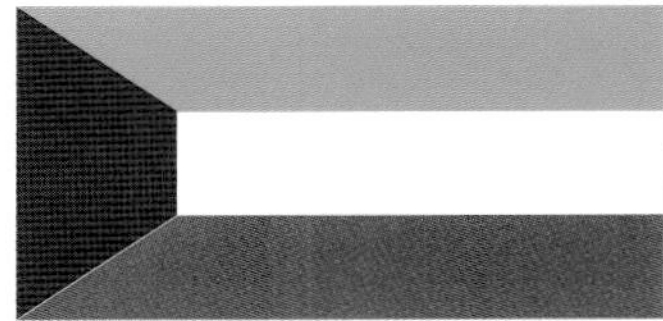

Kuwait
National Flag and Ensign

Iceland
Ensign

Israel
Ensign

Kazakhstan
Ensign

Latvia
Ensign

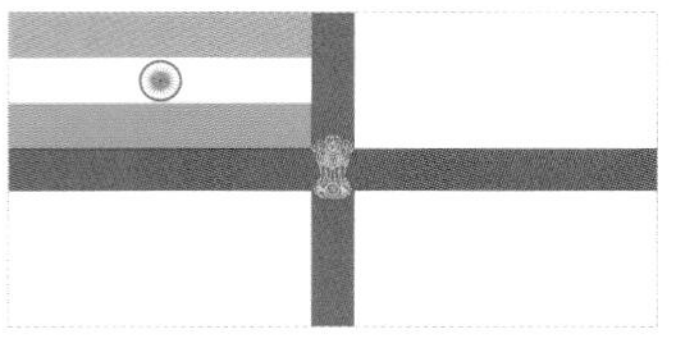

India
Ensign

Italy
Ensign

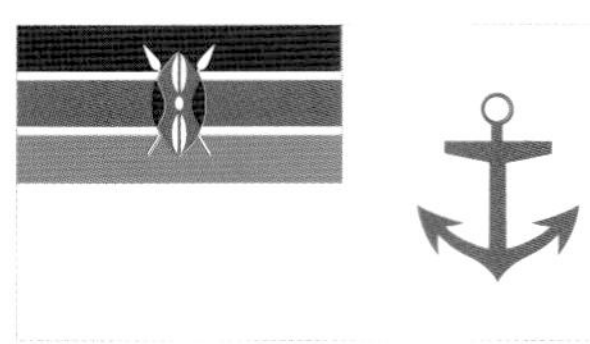

Kenya
Ensign

Lebanon
National Flag and Ensign

Indonesia
National Flag and Ensign

Jamaica
Ensign

Kiribati
National Flag and Ensign

Liberia
National Flag and Ensign

Iran
National Flag and Ensign

Japan
Japan (Navy) Ensign

Korea, North
National Flag and Ensign

Libya
Ensign

Iraq
National Flag

Japan
Japan (MSA) Ensign

Korea, South
National Flag and Ensign

Lithuania
Ensign

Macedonia, Former Yugoslav Republic of
National Flag

Madagascar
National Flag and Ensign

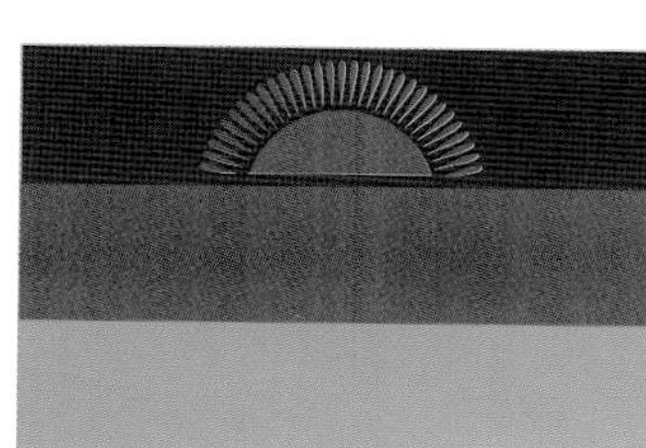

Malawi
National Flag

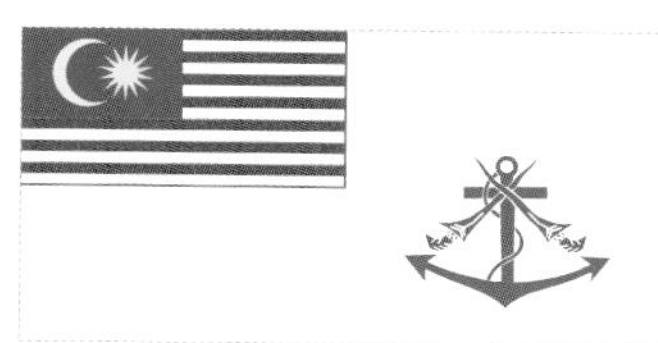

Malaysia
Ensign

Maldives
National Flag and Ensign

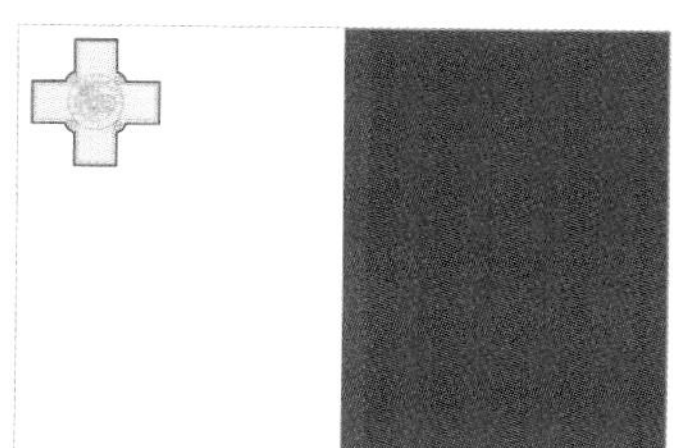

Malta
National Flag and Ensign

Marshall Islands
National Flag and Ensign

Mauritania
National Flag and Ensign

Mauritius
Ensign

Mexico
National Flag and Ensign

Federated States of Micronesia
Flag of the Federation

Montenegro
National Flag

Morocco
Ensign

Mozambique
National Flag and Ensign

Myanmar
Ensign

Namibia
National Flag and Ensign

NATO
Flag of the North Atlantic Treaty Organisation

Netherlands
National Flag and Ensign

New Zealand
Ensign

Nicaragua
National Flag and Ensign

Nigeria
Ensign

Norway
Ensign

Oman
Ensign

Pakistan
Ensign

Palau
National Flag and Ensign

Panama
National Flag and Ensign

Papua New Guinea
Ensign

Paraguay
National Flag and Ensign

Paraguay
National Flag and Ensign (reverse)

Peru
National Flag and Ensign

Philippines
National Flag and Ensign

Poland
Ensign

Portugal
National Flag and Ensign

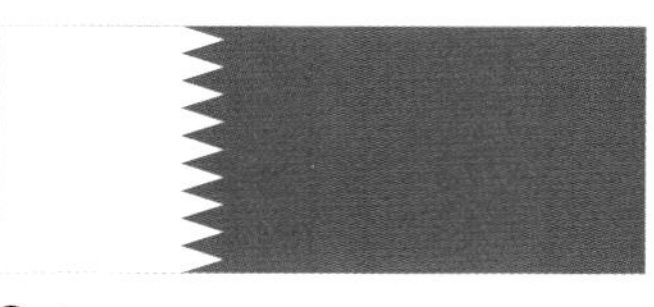

Qatar
National Flag and Ensign

Romania
National Flag and Ensign

Russian Federation
Ensign

Russian Federation
Border Guard Ensign

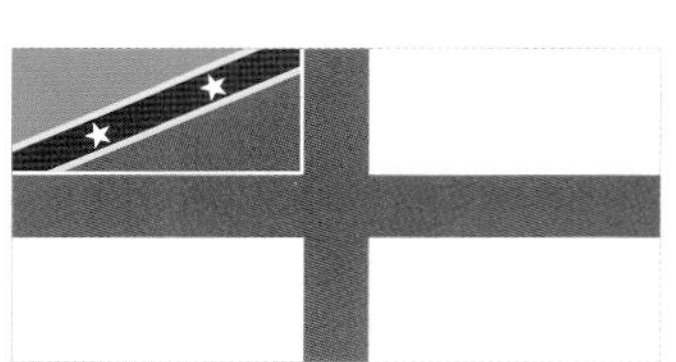

St Kitts and Nevis
Ensign

St Lucia
Ensign

St Vincent and the Grenadines
National Flag and Ensign

Samoa
National Flag and Ensign

Saudi Arabia
National Flag and Ensign

Senegal
National Flag and Ensign

Serbia
Naval Ensign

Seychelles
National Flag

Sierra Leone
Ensign

Singapore
Ensign

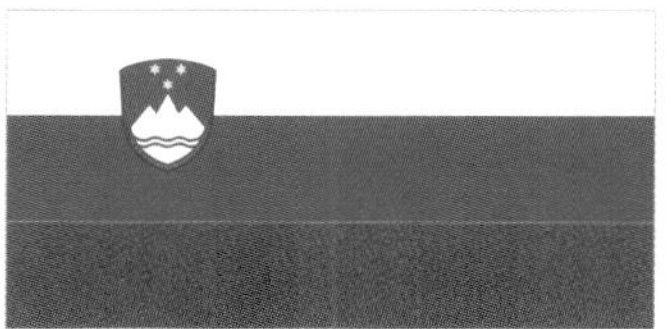

Slovenia
National Flag and Ensign

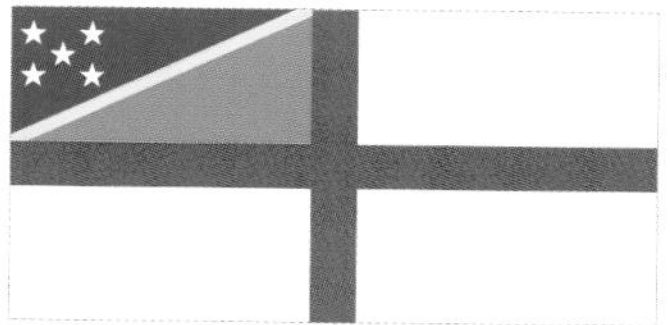

Solomon Islands
Ensign

South Africa
Ensign

Spain
National Flag and Ensign

Sri Lanka
Ensign

Sudan
National Flag and Ensign

Suriname
National Flag and Ensign

Sweden
Ensign

Switzerland
National Flag

Syria
National Flag and Ensign

Taiwan
National Flag and Ensign

Tanzania
National Flag and Ensign

Thailand
Ensign

Togo
National Flag and Ensign

Tonga
Ensign

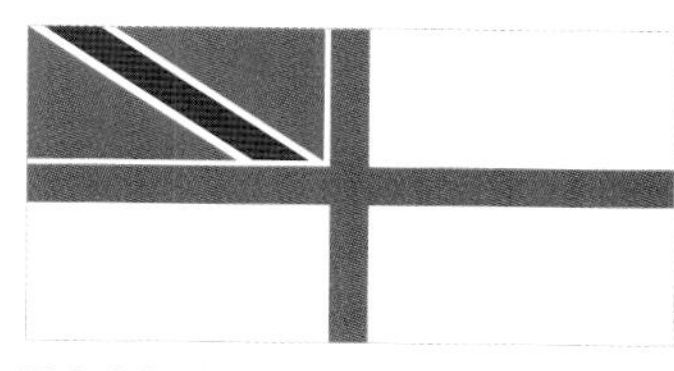

Trinidad and Tobago
Ensign

Tunisia
National Flag and Ensign

Turkey
National Flag and Ensign

Turkmenistan
National Flag

Tuvalu
National Flag and Ensign

Ukraine
Ensign

United Arab Emirates
National Flag and Ensign

United Kingdom
Ensign

United Nations
Flag of the United Nations Organisation

United States
National Flag and Ensign

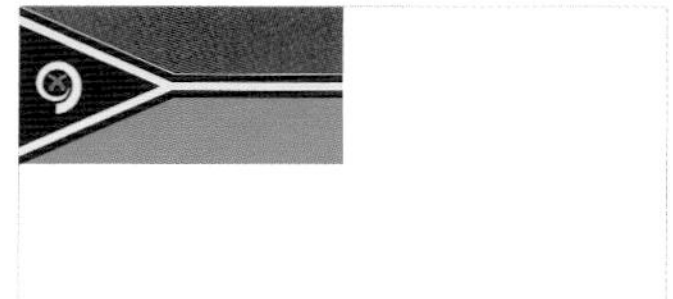

Vanuatu
Ensign

Vietnam
National Flag and Ensign

Yemen
National Flag and Ensign

Uruguay
National Flag and Ensign

Venezuela
Ensign

Virgin Islands (UK)
National Flag

Zimbabwe
National Flag

DARING

8/2007*, BAE Systems Marine / 1353677

Executive overview: Fighting Ships

Introduction

The hijacking of *Sirius Star* on 15 November 2008 was one of the most noteworthy of many incidents of piracy over the last year. Fully laden with oil, the ship was captured approximately 450 n miles southeast of the Kenyan coast while en route to the United States via the Cape of Good Hope. While the ship was later released after the payment of a ransom, the incident symbolises the sophistication, boldness and ruthlessness of the Somali pirates, the difficulties in combating them faced by maritime forces and the lack of a suitable international system within which pirates can be brought to justice.

The world's navies have not been inactive; indeed there has been a welcome commonality of purpose demonstrated by nations, not all of whom are natural military partners. Multilateral efforts have included NATO and EU task groups as well as ships from Australia, China, India, Japan, South Korea, Russia and Singapore. Nor has there been any lack of robustness when forced to take self-defensive measures. Two assumed pirates were killed when a team from the British frigate, *Cumberland*, returned fire on a dhow that it was attempting to board, while the Indian frigate, *Tabar*, sank a Thai fishing vessel when fired upon by hijackers who had boarded the ship. Despite these efforts, the frequency of hijacking incidents has continued to rise.

According to the International Maritime Bureau, 51 vessels were attacked in the first three months of 2009 compared with 111 in the whole of 2008. This figure was a 200 per cent increase on the previous year. The capture of two ships up to 500 n miles offshore during late March and the *Maersk Alabama* incident in April 2009 demonstrated that their audacity and willingness to operate at long distances from land remain undiminished.

Three steps are required to mitigate the problem. First, the legal framework that covers military operations against pirates and the prosecution of suspects is in need of revision. Second, there is a need to improve maritime domain awareness. The 'horizon' of a single ship is limited by the performance of its sensors, and those of its embarked aircraft. While these could be augmented by land-based maritime patrol aircraft, the use of long dwell-time UAVs offer greater potential to build a reliable picture in which irregular or suspicious activity can be spotted. Third, tougher military measures are required both ashore and afloat. Surprise, which has been the most effective weapon in the pirates' armoury, needs to be turned against them by using pre-emptive measures. Deterrence across a huge area of ocean is unlikely to succeed if ships are constrained to wait for the initiation of a hijacking which can take as little as 15 minutes. Ultimately, the solution to the problem lies in Somalia itself but, as restoration of the rule of law in that country remains a distant prospect, the problems of piracy in the region are destined to continue.

United States and Canada

US Africa Command (AFRICOM) became operational as a unified command on 1st October 2008 although its initial reception from African nations has been somewhat chilly due, it has been suggested, to American failure to gain prior support from key nations or from the African Union. For this reason, AFRICOM headquarters is likely to remain at Stuttgart, Germany, for the time being while Camp Lemonier in Djibouti, established in 2002 as a base for counterterrorism and humanitarian missions in the Horn of Africa, is to continue as the only US base on the continent. Despite lack of progress on land, a less politically sensitive sea-based approach is beginning to take effect.

The aim of the Africa Partnership Station (APS), modelled on the Global Fleet Stations concept, is both to provide a military presence in selected areas and to improve maritime security. This is achieved by the deployment of international training teams to build the skills, expertise and professionalism of African maritime forces. Typically, these are faced with problems of piracy, trafficking in drugs, humans and weapons, oil theft and illegal fishing. The first APS deployment to the Gulf of Guinea region was conducted by *Fort McHenry* and *Swift* from November 2007 to April 2008 and a further visit to the same area during February–May 2009 was made by *Nashville*. Time between major deployments is covered by shorter exercises and visits by ships, maritime patrol aircraft and mobile training teams. In the future, APS deployments are likely to expand into other regions of Africa. Overall the programme's relatively low profile is well suited to confidence-building and winning 'hearts and minds' and, in time, it could prove to be one of the US Navy's more enduring and productive initiatives.

The revival on 1 July 2008 of the US Fourth Fleet, originally established in 1943 and later disbanded in 1950, has also been controversial. Changing

GREEN BAY *6/2008*, US Navy* / 1353678

attitudes to the US in South and Central America have evolved into outright hostility from some nations (Venezuela and Bolivia) to at best equivocation elsewhere in the continent. This has been a surprising trend in an area which, since the declaration of the Monroe Doctrine in 1823, has been regarded as part of the United States' backyard. A good example of deteriorating relationships has been the decision by the Ecuadorian government not to renew the lease of Manta airfield with a consequent loss of a conveniently located forward operating base for US maritime patrol and AWACS aircraft. Therefore, an underlying aim of the re-established fleet is to build relationships as well as to rationalise the various maritime missions conducted by US Southern Command. These include counter-terrorism and drug operations, security co-operation and training as well as humanitarian assistance and disaster relief.

The revival of the fleet is also recognition of the increasing strategic importance of the region, based on rising economic and military power; Latin America has been the United States' fastest growing regional trade partner in recent years. As with AFRICOM, the current aims and ethos of the new fleet are more about the exercise of 'soft' power than power projection. Ships and submarines are assigned on a temporary rather than permanent basis and recent activities have included exercises such as UNITAS and PANAMAX, both part of the Partnership of the Americas initiative. A notable achievement was the treatment of almost one hundred thousand patients during the 2008 deployment of the hospital ship Comfort to 12 nations in the region.

Notwithstanding these organisational and, to some extent, cultural changes, the US Navy is faced with hard decisions at a time when the future size and shape of the fleet is being scrutinised and debated by the new Obama administration and by Congress. Perhaps the only certainty about the new shipbuilding plan is that it is to be very different from its predecessor. In particular, aspirations to achieve a 313-ship navy are destined to be abandoned in favour of a more modest total, reflecting a possible cut of approximately 50 ships. Not only is there likely to be a reduction in numbers, but there could also be a shift of emphasis as a high-tech, high-cost approach is modified by a lower risk and more affordable plan. The carrier force is already planned to reduce from 11 to 10 during the two-year plus gap between the decommissioning of *Enterprise* in 2013 and the commissioning of *Gerald R Ford* in 2015. Adjustment to a five-year carrier build cycle means that this will become the permanent size of the force by 2040. The DDG 1000 programme has been reduced to three ships, although this is still subject to the successful negotiation of contracts. All of them are now likely to be built at Bath Iron Works rather than being shared between two shipyards. The future cruiser CGX programme has been delayed to allow time for a fundamental review of the requirement which could include consideration of nuclear propulsion. If so, overall numbers may be reduced from 19 ships to a possible eight and the design may not now be a derivative of DDG 1000.

It is unclear whether the resultant shortfall is to be compensated by the construction of other ships. In the short term, the DDG-51 building programme is to be re-started and this may be followed by an as yet undefined Future Surface Combatant. Plans for amphibious shipping and sea-basing programmes are also to be re-evaluated. Despite a somewhat checkered history, the Littoral Combat Ship programme looks to be one of the few to survive in its present form. Trials of *Freedom* were reported to have been successful and *Independence* is to sail for the first time in 2009. Meanwhile, the names of the next two ships were announced in March 2009 and construction of two competing designs looks set to continue. Ultimately, a class of 55 ships is planned. The Virginia-class submarine programme also remains unaffected; a building rate of two per year is expected to start in 2011.

The Canadian Navy's efforts to re-shape the fleet to undertake expeditionary operations continue to be frustrated by funding difficulties. In 2007, plans to establish a Standing Contingency Force were put 'on hold' but encouragement was taken at the time from the government's continuing commitment to the Joint Support Ship project. These three ships were to be capable of sealift and afloat support while also being equipped with a hospital and facilities for a Joint Task Force headquarters. Unfortunately, the bidders for the project were unable to meet the requirement within the allotted budget and so a review of the project was initiated in 2008. The extent to which the requirement is to be 'de-scoped' remains to be seen. However, it is possible that the whole concept will be abandoned in favour of solving the most pressing issue: replacement of the afloat support capability currently provided by the 40-year-old *Protecteur* and *Preserver*.

Not all Canadian news has been bad. The Halifax class modernisation programme is to get underway in 2010 with a view of extending ships' lives into the 2020s. These ships and the ageing Iroquois-class destroyers are to be replaced by the Canadian Surface Combatant programme which is to use a common hull and a modular approach. The Arctic Patrol Ship programme remains intact and there are plans to procure a new maritime patrol aircraft to enter service in about 2020. In the immediate future, the submarine flotilla is to be boosted by the return of *Victoria* and *Windsor* to operational duties in 2010, the same year in which the new Sikorsky Cyclone helicopter is to start entering service.

China

Future historians may come to regard 2009 as the year that the Chinese Navy finally came of age. The deployment to the Gulf of Aden of the modern destroyers, *Wuhan* and *Haikou*, supported by a supply ship, was the first overseas naval operational mission to be conducted since 1949. The opportunity to contribute to international efforts to suppress piracy in the region must have seemed heaven-sent to the Chinese Navy leadership which, with a well-developed eye for image, has increased the tempo of naval diplomacy and of participation in minor exercises with foreign navies in recent years. The mission to protect shipping against Somali pirates certainly has all the key ingredients: it is a relatively straightforward and uncontroversial operation; it involves international co-operation in a good cause and generates a lot of positive publicity both at home and abroad. It quickly became clear that this was not just a photo-opportunity. The ships got down to business and, soon after arrival in theatre, began merchant-ship escort duties on 12 January. All of this is in marked contrast to a series of incidents in early March 2009 in which the two US Navy surveillance vessels were apparently harassed by a frigate and a fisheries patrol vessel. Both *Impeccable* and *Victorious* were reportedly located about 100 miles from the Chinese coast in the South China Sea and, if so, were entitled to conduct their operations in international waters. Aggressive manoeuvring and/or the use of threatening language are both dangerous and unproductive; such incidents in the Cold War achieved little except to raise tensions.

The pace of underwater operations has increased as the submarine service begins to emerge from a period of major change that has included the decommissioning of older coastal submarines and the introduction into service of a new generation of nuclear-powered and conventional boats. These have not been without their teething problems and, as has been observed on these pages before, it would have been surprising if the build-up of the necessary levels of training and experience had not proved to be difficult. According to the Federation of American Scientists (FAS), the number of out-of-area submarine deployments, which had dipped to two in 2006, recovered to seven in 2007 and reached a total of 12 in 2008. This rising trend probably reflects the introduction into service of the Type 093 Shang-class nuclear-powered attack boats to supplement the ageing Han class and while, in overall terms, the scale of operations remains comparatively low, a pattern of increasing activity is likely to continue. More extensive use of the 25 modern conventional submarines is expected and, in particular, the Yuan class, probably equipped with Air-Independent Propulsion (AIP), offers the potential for the conduct of covert operations. Meanwhile, the Jin-class ballistic missile submarines have yet to undertake a deterrent patrol. A test-firing of the JL-2 missile reportedly took place in June 2008 but there have been no indications that it has yet proved capable of operational deployment.

The sixth (since 1998) in the series of biannual Defence White Papers, 'China's National Defence in 2008' was published on 20 January 2009. The overall tone of the paper is measured and reasonable as it seeks to soothe international concerns about the rationale behind China's military build-up. "China pursues a national defense policy which is purely defensive in nature" and "China will never seek hegemony or engage in military expansion now or in the future, no matter how developed it becomes" are typical statements. Even the vexed question of Taiwan is treated in emollient terms. Following a change of government on the island, "The attempts of the separatist forces for "Taiwan independence" to seek "*de jure* Taiwan independence" have been thwarted, and the situation across the Taiwan Straits has taken a significantly positive turn". Nevertheless, the data provided in the White Paper does give cause for concern. According to the figures, the Chinese defence budget rose by a massive 19.3 per cent in 2007 and has more than doubled in five years to 355.4 billion Renminbi Yuan (USD52 billion). While the paper goes to some lengths to demonstrate that this is merely a reflection of increased Gross Domestic Product (GDP), which also more than doubled during the same period, and that defence expenditure remains low (about 1.4 per cent of GDP) in comparison with other countries, the rate of change has been very marked.

One of the interesting facts published in the paper was that the number of naval overseas visits decreased from 13 to five in 2008. This perhaps reflects a shift from a diplomatic offensive in 2007 to a more operational posture. Otherwise, the treatment of maritime matters was disappointing; the chapter on naval forces was particularly bland and did little more than to record the evolution of the PLA(N) from a coastal defence force into one capable of "offshore defensive operations". Future programmes were summarised as follows: "efforts are being made to build new types of submarines, destroyers, frigates and aircraft". The Chinese government should not be surprised that such opaque statements only increase suspicion that published expenditure data does not tell the whole story. The

HOUBEI CLASS *1/2008*, A Sheldon-Duplaix* / 1353679

programme that frequently gives rise to intense speculation, the building of an aircraft carrier, was not even mentioned and remains something of an enigma. However, the refurbishment of the ex-Russian ship, *Varyag*, continues and, following the move of the ship to a drydock on 27 April 2009, it is possible that the ship will emerge from Dalian in 2010 to perform, initially, a training role. It has been difficult to gauge progress in this project, given the lack of information about the original material state of the ship, but there seems little doubt that refit work has proved to be more technically demanding and time-consuming than originally intended, a situation which many other navies will find familiar. Therefore, it is reasonable to assume that any indigenous programme will have been similarly delayed. As yet there are no firm indications of building at any of the major dockyards and it is quite possible that the initiation of such a prestigious project would be publicised at the time.

In other areas of the fleet, the pace of shipbuilding has been quieter than in previous years; construction of the Yuan class of diesel submarines has resumed, suggesting that problems with the first of class have been overcome, while building of the Jiangkai II-class frigates also continues at two shipyards. No doubt a great deal is going on behind the scenes; the Chinese Navy still contains a number of increasingly obsolescent ships, incapable of conducting the networked operations to which it aspires. The transformation process is set to continue.

United Kingdom

For the Royal Navy, it has been another mixed year in which positive steps in some areas have been marred by setbacks in others.

To begin with the good news, the first Type 45 destroyer, *Daring*, arrived in her home port Portsmouth for the first time on 28 January 2009. She is to be followed by a further five ships, the seventh and eighth ships of the programme having been cancelled in 2008 as had been previously feared. Unquestionably, the new class of ships is to be highly capable and, in the words of *Daring*'s Commanding Officer, marks the start of a new era for the service. Designed to provide a high level of protection to a force operating within a 3.5 n mile radius against up to eight supersonic sea-skimming missiles, the newly named Sea Viper system is certainly one of the best of its type in the world. It also has the potential to be adapted in the future for an anti-ballistic missile defence role, although this would probably require an improved missile. For the time being, much remains to be done to get the first-of-class into service. An extensive programme of Stage 2 trials, including system integration and weapon acceptance, must be completed before the ship is commissioned in late 2009 or early 2010. Following test firings of the missile in the Mediterranean from the trials platform, *Longbow*, the first firing from a ship is to be conducted by second-of-class, *Dauntless*, in October 2010.

The future aircraft carrier project survived measures in late 2008 to solve the 'funding gap' in the defence budget, although the building programme is now to be lengthened by 1–2 years as a result. Perversely, this approach could well add to the eventual overall cost rather than reduce it. Nevertheless, the programme has developed considerable momentum. In a revised manufacturing strategy announced in March 2009, much of the building work has been allocated; the ships are still to be assembled at Rosyth, where work to extend and modernise No 1 Dock is underway, and construction of Block 3 is now to be undertaken on the Clyde rather than at Barrow. A number of major contracts have also been let. While commissioning dates have not been declared, it is probable that *Queen Elizabeth* will enter service in 2015 and *Prince of Wales* in 2018, 20 years after the intention to procure the ships was announced in the 1998 Defence Review. One of the reasons cited for the delay in the ship programme was to align the production of the ship with the procurement of the Joint Combat Aircraft (F-35B Joint Strike Fighter). Plans to move ahead with this programme were confirmed in March 2009 when the UK MOD committed to the procurement of three initial production aircraft which are to be used in the initial operational test and evaluation phase; the F-35B made its maiden flight on 28 June 2008.

The future of the destroyer/frigate force remains uncertain. The ageing Type 42 destroyers, of which only five now remain operational, are to be decommissioned over the next four years as the Type 45s enter service. However, the overall number of destroyers and frigates will only be 23 once the transition to the new class has been accomplished in 2013. The Future Surface Combatant (FSC) programme was supposed to have been brought forward as a result of the cut in Type 45 numbers but there is little confidence that this will happen. This is despite the fact that BVT Surface Fleet was awarded a contract in February 2009 to assist with preparation for the next phase of development. Although it is known that there are likely to be three variants (high-capability multimission; low-capability general purpose and ocean capable patrol ship), there is no commitment to overall numbers or timescale. Neither does it augur well that the lives of the Type 23 frigates, the workhorses of the fleet, have been extended to up to twice their original design intent. It was also discouraging to read the comment in the RUSI Journal by the Shadow Defence Minister, Dr Julian Lewis, that "if the Royal Navy is to have any chance of restoring the escort fleet, it must make the FSC as 'cheap as chips' ". There is always a balance to be struck between quantity and quality but experience in recent and ongoing conflicts suggests that the answer lies in spending more money on Defence, not cutting corners.

Another area of concern is the future of the afloat support replacement programme MARS. It had been expected that a contract for the construction of up to six fleet tankers, to enter service 2013–18, would be let in 2009.

KENT 8/2008*, Kazumasa Watanabe / 1353687

This segment of the programme had been given priority because the current Leaf- and Rover-class single-hull tankers are both reaching the end of their lives and no longer comply with regulations that require such ships to have double-hulls. It now seems likely that these ships, and subsequent plans for two fleet support and three logistics vessels, have been deferred by up to three years.

The situation for the submarine flotilla is also depressing. The number of hulls has been dwindling steadily over the years and current plans point to a force of just seven boats. The last of the Swiftsure class and first of the Trafalgar class are due to decommission in 2009 and, taking into account submarine refit periods, operational availability is likely to be about four boats. Meanwhile, the Astute class programme continues to struggle. Sea-trials of the first-of-class are not to begin until at least mid-2009 and the follow-on boat, *Ambush*, is not to be 'rolled out' until the end of 2009 or early 2010. While the keel of the fourth boat, *Audacious*, was formally laid in March 2009, and long-lead items have been ordered for hulls five and six, there is no commitment to an eighth boat. Construction of the later Astute class at Barrow is to run concurrently with that of the 'Trident II' boats whose building programme is to start in 2014 if the first boat is to be delivered in 2022 and to become operational in 2024 as planned. While the size of these boats has not been confirmed, it was announced in March 2009 that the successor SSBN is to have 12 missile tubes, rather than the 16 of the Vanguard class. This probably points to a smaller boat although one of the principal determinants of the design is to be a common US/UK missile compartment, scaled to accommodate a successor missile to Trident. Overall, given the record of the Astute class, it is not surprising that the Public Accounts Committee described the timetable for replacement as "extremely tight".

The UK's 40-year record of undetected deterrent patrols came to an abrupt end on about 3 February 2009 when *Vanguard* collided with the French ballistic missile submarine *Le Triomphant*. Both boats are thought to have been on patrol or in transit at the time. It is stating the obvious to say that submarines of allied nations should not have been in the same area at the same time, not least because there are established procedures precisely to avoid such a situation. While the locations of submarine patrol areas in general and deterrent areas in particular are highly classified and France may not have been a full participant in NATO waterspace management arrangements, it should have been possible at least to have agreed to operate in different general areas of the Atlantic Ocean. If this sort of discussion had not taken place, it reflects poorly on those concerned. Neither is it good enough to say that it was a 'one in a million' chance. The integrity of the nuclear deterrent and the safety of the crews of both countries were unnecessarily put at risk. Perhaps the only good thing to emerge from this unhappy incident is that the boats are almost impossible to detect.

Europe and the Mediterranean

NATO's 60th anniversary summit was held on 4 April 2009 at the French border city of Strasbourg and its neighbouring German town, Kehl. Co-hosted by the German Chancellor Angela Merkel and French President Nicolas Sarkozy, the highlights included the admission of Albania and Croatia into the Alliance and France's return to the integrated military structure. Contrary to popular belief, France did not leave the Alliance itself in 1966 and, during its absence from inner decision-making circles, continued to work quietly alongside NATO countries at a military level. This has particularly been the case at sea where ships and aircraft have been able to co-operate without causing political embarrassment.

It is to be hoped that France's renewed membership will lead to a resolution of at least some of the issues that have bedevilled EU/NATO relations over the last few years. While the two organisations ought to have a lot in common, competition has tended to hinder co-operation. However, the deployment of anti-piracy forces to the Gulf of Aden has provided the opportunity to work together, particularly over such crucial issues as Rules of Engagement. NATO carried out its first such mission in the region between October and December 2008. In Operation Allied Provider, four Standing NATO Maritime Group 2 (SNMG2) warships deployed in response to a UN request to conduct deterrence patrols and to provide escort to vessels delivering humanitarian aid to Somalia. An EU force, Operation Atalanta, took up station as the NATO ships completed their task. This operation is to be sustained throughout 2009 and command of the force is to be exercised in rotation by the Greek, Spanish and Dutch navies respectively. This force was boosted by a second NATO deployment in March–July 2009.

While one of the main outcomes of France's 2008 Defence White Paper was the renovation of transatlantic relations, some re-shaping of the naval force structure is to be implemented to reflect a re-appraisal of defence priorities. One major finding was that "protection of our population and territory calls for a major overhaul" and, as a result, a greater distinction is now to be made between forces required for this task and those required for intervention operations. The naval component of France's intervention capability is to continue to be spearheaded by the air group and naval combat aircraft are to be merged with those of the air force to form a pool of 300 aircraft from both services. However, the decision on whether to proceed with the construction of a second aircraft carrier has been deferred until 2011–12. Nevertheless, force projection capabilities are to be boosted

OLDENBURG *7/2008*, Michael Nitz* / 1353680

by the procurement of two further Mistral-class amphibious vessels; the first of which began construction at Saint-Nazaire in April 2009. Both are to be in service by 2020. The main effect of the redrawn balance between intervention and national protection forces is a reduction in Anti-Air Warfare (AAW) capability (from six to four specialised ships) while assets required for national protection are to be boosted by the conversion of the five Brest-based 'Avisos' to a patrol ship role. Submarine forces remain unchanged as a result of continued commitment to an independent nuclear deterrent and to a force of six cruise-missile carrying nuclear-powered attack boats.

The EU's Operation Atalanta is to be boosted in 2009 by the deployment of two Swedish Stockholm-class corvettes, supported by the logistic support ship, *Trosso*. While it is not the first time that Swedish naval forces have been deployed for out-of-area operations, the despatch of such ships, originally built for coastal defence duties, highlights their unsuitability for long-distance transits and for operations in ocean waters. Recognition that the Swedish Navy is not best equipped to contribute to this sort of operation is reflected in the Combat Support Ship (L 10) programme for two multipurpose ships. These are to be capable of conducting replenishment at sea, amphibious support, repair and maintenance, medical support and transport of about 170 troops. The requirement could be met by a modified Ro-Ro ferry design but the preference is likely to be for a purpose-built design, tailored to support the Visby class and built to commercial standards. Meanwhile, the Visby class programme will at last reach fruition in 2009 when, after a difficult and frustrating proving period, the first ships become available for operational service.

Looking ahead, thoughts are now turning to the procurement of less complex patrol ships better suited to tasks around the world. Sweden has been one of the pioneers of Air-Independent Propulsion (AIP) which is now fitted to all five of its submarines. The Södermanland class, which were retrofitted with this capability 2000–05, are due to be replaced by two next-generation A 26 class from about 2017. Few details have been released about the new boats but the design is likely to be required to meet a much broader requirement than their predecessors. Much will have been learned from the two-years spent by *Götland* in San Diego as an anti-submarine training target for the US Navy. Meanwhile, despite current emphasis on overseas operations, home defence has not been neglected. The refit and modernisation of the first two Koster (modified Landsort)-class minehunters was completed in early 2009 and the remaining three are expected to be completed in 2010.

Procurement of submarines by the Hellenic Navy has been in a state of flux for the last two years due to delays in the Type 214 submarine programme. Despite the launch in Germany of the first-of-class *Papanikolis*, in 2004, her commissioning is still awaited, pending resolution of alleged technical difficulties. Meanwhile construction of the other three boats at Hellenic Shipyards is at various stages of completion although it is not clear if and when they will enter operational service. In contrast, the Neptune II upgrade programme for the last three Glavkos (Type 209/1200) submarines has taken a dramatic turn. Following completion in early 2009 of *Okeanos*' refit, which included the installation of AIP, the upgrade programme for the other two boats was abandoned in favour of the construction of two new AIP-equipped Type 209/1400s. These are also to be built at Hellenic Shipyards. A decision on the way ahead for the acquisition of six new frigates is expected in 2009. The leading contender appears to be the French FREMM class, following the announcement by the Greek Minister of Defence, Mr Evangelos Meimarakis, on 22 January 2009 that negotiations had started. The ships are likely to be the air-defence (FREDA) variant featuring an A70 vertical launcher capable of firing both air-defence and land-attack missiles. Meanwhile, the mid-life upgrade of the first six Elli (Kortenaer)-class frigates is due to be completed in 2010 at which time a major upgrade of the Hydra (Meko 200) class is due to begin.

Developments on one side of the Aegean tend to be inextricably linked with those on the other, despite a welcome reduction in tensions in recent years. In spite of problems in the Greek Type 214 programme, the Turkish Navy opted to start contract negotiations in 2008 for the acquisition of six similar submarines, also to be equipped with AIP. The boats are to be built at Gölcük Shipyard with the first of class to enter service in 2015. The principal naval surface ship programme is the Ada (Milgem) class project for up to 12 anti-submarine warfare and offshore patrol vessels. The first-of-class, *Heybeliada*, was launched on 27 September 2008 on the same day that the second of class, *Büyükada*, was laid down. There are also 16 smaller Dearsan anti-submarine and littoral patrol craft to be built in batches of four. The principal Coast Guard programme is for the construction of four offshore vessels required for SAR and EEZ patrol duties. The design of the ships is based on the Italian Sirio (Comandante) class. Other Coast Guard programmes include continuing construction of the Kaan 33 class. These are being built by the Yonca-Onuk Shipyard which has achieved export success over the last few years with sales to Georgia, Malaysia and Pakistan.

The Israeli Navy is poised for expansion over the next few years with both submarine and surface ship programmes in progress or planned.

The first of a second batch of two Dolphin-class submarines is expected to be launched in Germany in 2009–10. Although few details of this project have been released, the boats are reported to be equipped with AIP and are planned to enter service in 2012. The other major programme is for a class of three surface combatants. These are likely to be based on the Lockheed Martin variant of the Littoral Combat Ship although the ships are to be more powerfully armed than the US versions. Weapons will almost certainly include an area air-defence system such as Standard or Barak 8. The geographical focus of Israeli naval operations is likely to remain the Mediterranean Sea. Although deployments to the Red Sea and beyond are possible, operations are constrained by the availability of only one small base (Eilat) and the need to rely on other nations for shore-based and/or afloat support facilities.

Russia

It has been a busy year for the Russian Navy, which has committed a number of its major units to operations and deployments. During the conflict with Georgia in August 2008, the Navy played a supporting role in what was overwhelmingly a land/air operation. While the primary Russian aim was to secure the regions of South Ossetia and Abkhazia, a key element of the plan was to destroy all Georgian military capabilities. This included the naval base at Poti in which most of the Georgian Navy was destroyed alongside. The only reported action at sea was the sinking of an unknown vessel by an SS-N-9 missile fired by the corvette, *Mirazh*. Apart from this, the principal role of the Russian Navy was to blockade Georgia's ports in order to deter/prevent arms shipments or reinforcements from entering the country. The Black Sea Fleet certainly did not take any chances. Led by the guided-missile cruiser *Moskva*, the task group included the destroyer *Smetlivy*, three Grisha-class frigates, one Nanuchka- and two Tarantul-class corvettes and three amphibious vessels. Although there was speculation that amphibious landings had been conducted in the vicinity of Ochamchire, it is more likely that the landing ships were employed in a ferry role and that troops were offloaded at the port without vehicles and equipment. Conclusions from the conflict are difficult to draw and are perhaps more political than military. The Russians seemed well-prepared, suggesting good intelligence, and responded quickly with overwhelming force. However, what the military leadership will wish to hear from the analysts is just how effective these joint operations might have been against a more powerful and well-organised enemy.

In well-publicised attempts to raise operational tempo and to 'show the flag', deployments of other warships, notably by the capital ships *Admiral Kuznetsov* and *Pyotr Velikiy*, also caught the headlines. As in 2007, the carrier departed in December from Severomorsk to visit the Mediterranean where exercises were conducted with the Black Sea Fleet and visits made to Turkey and Syria. The trip was relatively uneventful except for a fire, which led to the unfortunate death of a sailor, and a large oil spill which allegedly occurred while the ship was operating south of Ireland.

The deployment of the battle-cruiser *Pyotr Velikiy*, leading another group of ships, was the highest-profile diplomatic mission by the Russian Navy for many years. The flotilla visited the Caribbean to participate in exercises with the Venezuelan Navy and subsequently, for the first time since the end of the Cold War, to make a port-call to Cuba. The destroyer, *Admiral Chabanenko*, made a symbolic transit of the Panama Canal, the first by a Russian warship since the Second World War, to visit Balboa. Making its way back across the South Atlantic, *Pyotr Velikiy* visited Cape Town in January 2009 before proceeding to Mormugao in the Indian state of Goa. During this period, the ship was joined by the destroyers *Admiral Vinogradov* (Pacific Fleet) and *Admiral Levchenko* (Northern Fleet) for INDRA-2009, a biannual Russian-Indian exercise. The Indian Navy was represented on this occasion by the destroyer *Delhi* and the frigate *Tabar*. A feature of the exercise was that its second phase was dedicated to anti-piracy operations and conducted off the Somali coast.

All this activity has been superficially impressive and there has almost been a whiff of nostalgia as Russian ships once more ply the world's oceans. However, it is premature to talk about a Russian resurgence and/or the establishment of sustained presence in various regions of the world. It would take years to achieve such a posture and it is worth remembering that even at the height of the Soviet Navy's strength, ships were forced to spend much of the time at anchor due to lack of supporting infrastructure. It is also obvious today that while a few reliable ships are very busy, many others do not seem to venture very far. Nevertheless, the Russian Navy will have gained enormous benefit from the more frequent and ambitious operations of the last few years. A new generation of officers and sailors, both ashore and afloat, are learning about the difficulties of maintaining morale, operational effectiveness and a sound material state during long deployments. The experience gained will pay dividends in the future.

It is against this background that aspirations to build a force of five or six aircraft carrier groups must be viewed. To be fair to the Commander-in-Chief, Admiral Vysototsky, his announcement in July 2008 seemed to be a long-term vision, to be achieved in perhaps 50 years, and did not appear to be a commitment to a short-term programme. Despite the fact that there are a number of existing carrier designs, including those of the Ulyanovsk, Kuznetsov and smaller Kiev classes, a considerable amount of development work would be needed to bring these up to date. Even if this could be done relatively quickly, the requirement to design and build a next-generation VSTOL or CTOL carrier-borne aircraft needs to be taken into account. There are also industrial considerations. The last generation of carriers was built at Nikolayev in Ukraine so the facilities at Severodvinsk will need to

NEUSTRASHIMY

6/2008, Michael Nitz* / 1353681

be upgraded to handle ships of this size; construction of a new 420 m dry dock is under consideration. Therefore, even if a firm decision has already been taken, it could be many years before the first ship is commissioned. Furthermore, procurement of a carrier force needs to be balanced against other competing priorities. The destroyer force now averages about 21 years old and a replacement programme has not been announced. The frigate force is even older and, despite the long-awaited emergence in early 2009 of the second Neustrashimy-class frigate, *Yaroslav Mudryy*, from Yantar shipyard at Kaliningrad, construction of both the Steregushchiy- and Gorshkov-class frigates seems to be taking longer than expected.

Replacement of the submarine force is also proving troublesome. Sea trials of the first of a new class of ballistic-missile submarines, *Yuri Dolgorukiy*, did not start until 2009 while its Bulava missile is yet to be proven. There are also delays in the construction of the next generation attack submarine, *Severodvinsk*, and of the conventional Lada-class boats. Taken overall, most if not all naval programmes are experiencing serious problems and, after 20 years of neglect, it will take a long time and a great deal of money to put things right.

Indian Ocean, Gulf and Caspian

The golden anniversary of the commissioning of the carrier *Viraat* (ex-*Hermes*) on 18 November 2009 is likely to be celebrated by former ship's companies of two navies who have served in her; she is one of those ships that inspires particular affection. While her longevity is a testament to the robustness of the original design, the requirement for expenditure on a third major refit since transfer from the Royal Navy in 1987, necessitated by delays in future carrier programmes, will be exasperating for the Indian naval high command. The aim of the latest work is to extend the life of the ship until 2012 when *Vikramaditya*, which has been undergoing refurbishment at Severodvinsk since 2004, is planned to enter service. Fortunately, there are now grounds for optimism that this project, which had generated a somewhat acrimonious dispute, is at last making some progress.

The ship was re-launched in December 2008 at about the same time as agreement was reached between the Russian and Indian governments on the funding of cost overruns. As a result, the way-ahead now looks clear for the final purchase agreement to be signed in 2009 with a view to starting sea trials in 2011. Meanwhile, progress was also made in the other major surface ship contract. The keel of the Indigenous Aircraft Carrier was formally laid by the Defence Minister at Kochi Shipyard on 28 February 2009. The ship, which is going to be nearly 40,000 tons, is to be the largest warship ever built in the country and is likely to be followed by at least one further unit in order to realise the ambition of a three-carrier force. It remains to be seen whether the mating of some 872 blocks, some 400 of which have already been fabricated, can be achieved within the planned construction timescale. The ship is planned to be commissioned by 2015.

There could be a number of other highlights for the Indian Navy during 2009. Lease of the nuclear submarine *Chakra* (ex-*Nerpa*) is expected to start in September following certification by the Russian Navy, although the programme may have been delayed by the unfortunate accident in which 20 people were killed by the release of fire-suppressant gas during sea trials in November 2008. Meanwhile, launch of the indigenous nuclear submarine, the so-called Advanced Technology Vessel, is planned to take place at Vishakapatnam during the year. The project has been clothed in secrecy and even the formal confirmation of its existence in December 2007 did little more than fuel speculation about its design and capability. The submarine is likely to have a ballistic missile capability but, limited to one boat and (probably) less than 10 launch tubes, it is expected that its operating pattern will be different to the continuous at sea policy adopted by most other SSBN operators.

There was also good news from some of the surface ship programmes. Sea trials of *Shivalik*, the first of a new class of frigate, are due to begin in 2009 at about the same time as the first of the Batch 2 Talwar class, under construction at Yantar Shipyard, Kaliningrad, is due to be launched. Reportedly, negotiations for the procurement of a third batch of these ships began in early 2009. The spirited performance of *Tabar* during an anti-piracy patrol off Somalia will have done much to enhance the reputation of this class. The reach of the navy is also to be augmented by the procurement of eight Boeing Poseidon maritime patrol aircraft, for which a contract was signed in December 2008. Unfortunately, the transformation of the Indian Navy continues to be frustrated by setbacks. Construction of the Scorpene class conventional submarines had not begun by early 2009 and the first indigenous refit of a Kilo class, *Sindhukirti*, which began at Hindustan Shipyard, Vishakapatnam in 2006, could take as long as nine years to complete.

Following a review of coastal security in the wake of terrorist attacks on Mumbai in November 2008, there is to be a major overhaul of India's maritime defence organisation and infrastructure. The principal actions that have arisen are to designate the navy as the responsible authority for overall maritime security; to establish a command and intelligence network linking naval and Coast Guard operations centres; the improvement of port and inshore defence; the establishment of a new 'Coastal Command' and the establishment of a coastal radar and AIS chain to improve situational awareness.

In neighbouring Pakistan the third Khalid-class submarine, *Hamza*, the first to be entirely completed in Karachi, was commissioned on 26 September 2008. She is also the first to be equipped with AIP and the

ZULFIQUAR *10/2008*, Chris Sattler* / 1353682

first two boats of the class, commissioned in 1999 and 2003 respectively, are now to be similarly upgraded. Meanwhile, a further submarine programme is likely to be initiated in 2009. The principal contenders are widely considered to be the French Scorpene class and the German Type 214 class but procurement of a Chinese submarine, for example the Yuan class, should not be ruled out. China and Pakistan have been strategic allies for many years and naval ties have grown stronger recently. The Karachi Shipyard and Engineering Works are being modernised to facilitate construction of the fourth and final F22P frigate and licences to construct further similar, or possibly larger, vessels may also be obtained. There are also plans to expand ship construction and refit facilities at other ports such as Gwadar and Omara.

In the Gulf, the United Arab Emirates has been making much of the news. The first Baynunah-class corvette is to be launched at Cherbourg during 2009 while Abu Dhabi Shipbuilding (ADSB) is making progress on the construction of the five follow-on vessels. The shipyard is due to deliver its first ship eight months after the first-of-class with the others to follow at six-month intervals. ADSB is also to build 12 further 26-m Ghannatha class in a missile-armed interception craft configuration while the 12 existing craft are to be modified as troop carriers and mortar platforms. Meanwhile, a Comandante class anti-submarine corvette has been ordered from Italian shipbuilder Fincantieri. Six such ships entered Italian Navy service in 2001-03 and four of the Coast Guard configuration are currently under construction in Turkey. This 1,500-ton ship, and any follow-on vessels, is effectively a substitute for the rarely used Kortenaer frigates, transferred from the Netherlands in 1996–97.

The rejuvenation of the South African Navy over the last 10 years has gone remarkably smoothly in view of the challenges posed by the transition from an underfunded coastal force to a blue-water navy capable of exerting regional influence. Four new frigates and three new submarines have entered service and the navy is now poised to take a further major step, the acquisition of two Strategic Support Ships. These multirole ships are to enter service from about 2014 while a third unit, configured as a replenishment ship (to replace *Drakensberg*), is to be commissioned in about 2017.

The primary function of the new vessels is to transport, land and support a battalion group of some 1,500 troops with up to 350 vehicles. This is in addition to the capability to act as a mobile base and offshore headquarters, to conduct disaster and emergency relief missions and to provide logistic and medical support. An LHD design, which includes both a well-deck for operating small landing craft and a flight deck with six spots for medium helicopters, is a strong possibility.

Other contracts in the offing are for an initial batch of six offshore patrol vessels, to be built in a South African Shipyard, and for a new hydrographic survey ship to replace *Protea*. It is not surprising that the expansion of the navy poses a considerable recruitment, training and retention problem and this is linked to the need for a change of culture as the navy comes to terms with a period of profound change. As the Commander of the Navy, Admiral Johannes Mudimu, stated, "we must now move from force preparation to force employment".

East Asia and Australasia

A new Australian Defence White Paper, due to be published in 2009, is almost certain to be affected by the global financial crisis. However, all the indications are that the government will try to stick to its election pledge to increase defence spending by three per cent per year and, in view of the Prime Minister's comments in September 2008 that Australia would need to become a more serious maritime power, the Royal Australian Navy could be a beneficiary. The challenge now will be to translate political aspirations into firm contracts. While approval for a fourth Hobart-class air warfare destroyer is not now expected, endorsement of a new submarine programme is likely to go ahead. These boats are not only to replace the Collins class from about 2020, but also to double the size of the flotilla to about 12 boats. This is despite the fact that current manning problems restrict operational availability to three out of six boats.

Work on a successor class began in December 2007 and, while initially all options are likely to be examined, it is probable that the solution will be to adopt a recent European design equipped with predominantly American weapons and sensors. The geography of Australia suggests that nuclear power might at least bear some consideration. However, the submarines are more likely to be equipped with AIP in view of public and political opposition to nuclear energy. Other projects to be considered are the acquisition of a strategic sealift ship, to complement the Canberra-class LHDs, and the replacement of the current amphibious watercraft capability. Procurement of the F-35B variant of the Joint Strike Fighter, to operate from the LHDs, is also a possibility. Thoughts will also no doubt be turning to the size and shape of the future frigate force. The ANZAC class, about to begin the ASMD upgrade programme, is not due for replacement until about 2025 but, as other nations are discovering, a like-for-like replacement approach may not deliver the number of hulls required.

Following the announcement by the Japanese government that it intended to send units of the Japanese Navy to join international anti-piracy operations off the coast of Somalia, the destroyers *Sazanami* and *Samidare* sailed from Kure on 14 March 2009. Japanese Coast Guard officers were

TUNKU ABDUL RAHMAN

3/2008, Guy Toremans* / 1353683

embarked to handle any law-enforcement matters. The deployment of any MSDF forces outside Japan's borders tends to be controversial in view of the constraints placed on their use by the Self-Defence Forces Law. Therefore, despite the fact that this mission is not as politically sensitive as Japan's Indian Ocean refuelling operation, which has supported coalition forces in Afghanistan since 2001, further legislation is likely to be required. Initially, the deployment is to be conducted under the maritime police-action provision of the law. This already covers a fairly wide spectrum which includes the protection of Japanese ships, ships managed by Japanese companies or vessels carrying Japanese crew members or cargo for Japan. However, a new law on anti-piracy is expected to enable Japanese forces to assist in combating pirate attacks on foreign ships. This would mark another important step in extending the limits within which the Japanese Navy is mandated to operate. In a world in which defence can start a long way from home, it should be possible for it to participate in international, global operations without compromising the basic tenets of Japanese Defence policy.

If any ship is likely to 'push the boundaries' in the future, a prime candidate is the new helicopter-carrier, *Hyuga*, commissioned on 18 March 2009. She is to be followed by a second unit which is to enter service in 2011. The new ships, much larger than the Haruna class which they replace, call for a new concept of operations to exploit not just their primary ASW role but also their flexibility and utility to undertake a wide range of tasks. It is likely that they will be centrepiece of many future overseas operations, whether military or in response to a civilian emergency.

Meanwhile work progresses on the next generation of destroyers and submarines. The 5,000 ton 19DD–class destroyers, the first of which is to be laid down in July 2009, are to be a follow-on to the Takanami class to which they bear a resemblance. Their principal armament is expected to be Evolved Sea Sparrow and Type 90 surface-to-surface missiles. The Souryu-class submarines are now beginning to enter service; the first-of-class was commissioned in March 2009 and the second-of-class *Unryu* was launched in October 2008. These boats, fitted with AIP, are also likely to prompt new operating patterns to exploit their enhanced capability. A similarly equipped submarine, the German U32, successfully conducted a submerged transit of some 1,500 n miles in 2006.

There has also been less welcome news. A test-firing of a Standard SM-3 anti-ballistic missile on 20 November from the destroyer *Choukai*, the second ship of the class to be converted to the BMD role, was a failure. Given the 80 per cent success rate of these missiles, it is more likely that this was due to an individual missile fault rather than systemic failure. Finally, the official investigation into the pre-dawn collision on 19 February 2008 between the destroyer *Atago* and a fishing boat, which resulted in two fatalities, concluded that the ship was mainly at fault. This unfortunate incident is a reminder that keeping a good watch is as important today as it ever was.

Elsewhere in the region, the Malaysian Navy made an historic step forward when it took delivery of its first submarine on 29 January 2009. *Tunku Abdul Rahman* is a Scorpene-class boat which is to be stationed at a new submarine base at Sepanggar, near Kota Kinabalu in Sabah. The location of the base will enable the submarines to operate both in the South China and Sulu seas. The second-of-class, *Tun Razak*, is to be delivered in late 2009. Before the boats become operational, it will be necessary to establish a submarine rescue capability. The likely host ships are *Mahsuri* and *Setia Sekal* but there were no indications, as of early 2009, that Malaysia is planning to join the International Submarine Escape and Rescue Liaison Office, which co-ordinates submarine rescue activities worldwide.

Progress in other Malaysian programmes has been mixed. The decision to procure two new improved Lekiu-class frigates was made in 2006 but an order is not now expected until 2010. The Kedah-class corvettes have had something of a troubled history but the programme now appears to be proceeding satisfactorily. *Pahang* has taken part in anti-piracy operations in the Gulf of Aden, the first Malaysian-built ship, *Perak*, was commissioned in late 2008 and the remaining three ships are to enter service by 2010. The next major procurement initiative is likely to be the acquisition of up to three multirole ships capable of both military and civilian emergency roles.

In common with Malaysia and a number of other nations worldwide, the Royal Thai Navy (RTN) has also decided that there is a requirement for a multirole ship; approval for the project was given by the Thai cabinet on 9 September 2008. The amphibious ship (LPD) is to be designed and built by ST Marine of Singapore and is almost certainly based on the Endurance class that entered Singapore service from 2000. Delivery is expected in 2012 and the contract also includes the construction of two LCMs and two LCVPs. Unfortunately, progress in this project has probably resulted in cut-backs in others. The main casualty of the LPD order appears to have been the new frigate programme. Instead of buying two such ships, which were going to be based on the Malaysian Lekiu class, the programme has now been scaled down to the procurement of offshore patrol ships. A number of designs, including proposals from BVT Surface Fleet and Fassmer, are believed to be in the running but, as of early 2009, no decision had been taken. The order, when it comes, will follow a number of steady, if not spectacular, improvements to the surface fleet in recent years. Two new Chinese-built corvettes entered service in 2006 and the patrol force inventory has been augmented by the introduction into service of the first three of nine modified T 91 (T 991) class. In addition a new survey ship, based on the Dutch Snellius class, was commissioned in August 2008.

The Singapore Navy has also reached some important milestones. Following the decommissioning of the six 1970s vintage Sea Wolf-class fast attack craft in May 2008, the final two of the six Formidable-class frigates were commissioned on 16 January 2009. This class ushers in a new era of surface ship operations not only as very capable individual units but also as key nodes in the Singapore Armed Forces command-and-control network which integrates the information and responses of all the uniformed services. This is particularly important in a region where warning time is likely to be short. *Intrepid* successfully completed a first Aster 15 firing test off Toulon in April 2008 but it has also emerged that the frigates could, in the future, be equipped with the 100 km Aster 30. It had been reported that the ships were equipped with four eight-cell Sylver A43 vertical launch modules but it is now believed that two of the four modules are of the deeper A50 variant, capable of accommodating the longer area-defence missile. While acquisition of these weapons is not thought to be imminent, Singapore could become the first country in the region to have such a capability.

Next on the navy's agenda is the introduction into service from about 2010 of two submarines of the Västergötland class. Their pre-transfer refits are likely to be similar to those undertaken by two sister-ships that remain in Swedish service. Both of these were modernised with AIP, involving the insertion of a 12 m 'plug', improved optronics and a divers' lock-out to facilitate Special Forces operations. The two refitted boats are to replace at least two of the Challenger class that entered Singapore service in 2000 but which are now 40 years old.

Latin America

After many years of stagnation, 2008 proved to be a landmark year for the Brazilian Navy. Following endorsement of the nuclear-submarine (SSN) programme by President Lula in 2007, the project developed momentum in September 2008 when it was formally re-launched by the Commander of the Brazilian Navy. The aim is to complete South America's first SSN by 2020. The announcement followed a Franco-Brazilian arms package which confirmed France as Brazil's strategic partner in the development of its future submarine force. In the SSN project, there is to be French design support (provided by DCNS) on the hull and propulsion while nuclear aspects are to be taken forward by the Brazilian Navy. A prototype reactor, under development at the Aramar Experimental Centre, is to serve as a basis for the power-plant which is expected to be of the order of 48 MW. In addition, Brazil is to acquire four Scorpene or Marlin class conventional boats which are to be built at a new shipyard at Sepetiba Bay.

Meanwhile, in a separate contract, the five Tupi/Tikuna-class boats are to be upgraded by Lockheed Martin in parallel with the acquisition of the Mk 48 heavyweight torpedo from the United States. There have also been developments in the surface fleet. The corvette *Barroso*, which was laid down in 1994, was finally commissioned on 19 August 2008 and it is possible that a further three vessels will be built. In the meantime, a modernisation programme for the Inhaúma-class corvettes has been initiated. The last of the 1960s vintage Garcia-class frigates, *Pará*, was decommissioned in 2008, but the intention to procure six French FREMM-class frigates was announced later in the year; Brazil's current frigate inventory of Broadsword and Niterói classes is already over 30 years old. Plans to procure up to five new 1.800-ton Offshore Patrol Vessels have not yet been finalised but a Fassmer design, already used by both Chile and Argentina, is likely to be a strong contender. Meanwhile, a further four Vigilante class 500 ton patrol vessels were ordered in October 2008 and a class of 12 is expected. Elsewhere in the fleet, a second ex-UK LSL *Almirante Saboía* (ex-*Sir Bedivere*) is to enter service in 2009, following the transfer of *Garcia d'Ávila* (ex-*Sir Galahad*) in 2007, an Antarctic support ship *Almirante Maximiano* is to enter service in 2009, following conversion in a German shipyard, and a disaster response ship may be acquired in co-operation with Argentina.

Procurement of such a ship was one direct result of the closer defence co-operation that is to be developed between Brazil and Argentina, following a summit between Brazilian President Lula and Argentinian President Kirchner in September 2008. Naval collaboration is also likely to include the construction of (unspecified) ocean patrol vessels for the Brazilian Navy, the joint procurement of civilian polar research ships and an Antarctic support ship (possibly *Almirante Maximiano*). Repairs to the icebreaker and support ship, *Almirante Irizar*, which was badly damaged by a fire in 2007, did not begin until late 2008 and the ship is not expected to become operational again until 2012.

DEFENSORA

3/2008, M Declerck* / 1353684

The principal Argentine surface fleet programme is for up to five offshore patrol vessels which are likely to be similar to the Chilean Fassmer-designed vessels; construction of the first-of-class is expected to start in 2009. Elsewhere in the surface fleet, the Almirante Brown-class frigates have completed a refit programme and major modification of the fast attack craft, *Indomita*, started in January 2008. Her sister ship, *Intrepida*, is expected to follow. The outlook for the submarine flotilla is uncertain. There are no known plans to replace the current inventory and, if a new programme is not initiated in the next few years, it is possible that the capability will be lost altogether.

A major refit programme for the two most modern boats, the TR 1700 class, will be completed in 2010 when *San Juan* is expected to emerge from Domecq Garcia dockyard. However, the future of the Type 209 class *Salta* is more in doubt. Although she completed a refit in 2005, she is now 27 years old and her sister ship, *San Luis*, hitherto used as spares, is likely to be converted to a museum ship. There was better news for the Fleet Air Arm. Replacement Agave radars were reportedly acquired in 2008 with the result that operational availability of the Super Etendard aircraft may be raised from five to nine out of 11.

In Venezuela, the modernisation of the navy will begin to take effect in 2009 when the first of four 1,500-ton patrol vessels, *Guiacamacuto*, enters service in 2009. Launched in October 2008 at Navantia, San Fernando, she is the first of four such ships to be commissioned. The other major surface ship programme is for four larger 2,500 ton offshore patrol vessels, also under construction in Spain, the first of which is to be commissioned in 2010. It had been expected that an order for three Project 636 Kilo-class submarines would be made when the Russian cruiser, *Pyotr Velikiy*, visited Venezuela in November 2008. However, the lack of a formal announcement suggests that the project remains 'on hold', possibly as a result of the global economic downturn. A key feature of the contract would have been a substantial loan to finance the deal and, with a fall in oil prices affecting both countries, it may have been considered too risky an undertaking at the moment. Meanwhile, both of Venezuela's Type 209 boats are believed to be non-operational.

In contrast, the Type 209 submarines operated by the Ecuador Navy are planned to be refitted in Chile 2009–2012. Both boats, *Shyri* and *Huancavilca*, were commissioned in the mid-1970s and have already received two major refits, in the 1980s and 1990s. The latest modernisation work, to include a new combat system and sonar suite, is expected to extend life until at least 2020. Chile has also been involved in the renewal of the surface fleet. Having decommissioned two ex-British Leander-class frigates, originally built in the 1960s, two ex-Chilean Leanders were transferred in 2008, following an overhaul. These ships also are expected to remain in service until about 2020.

In Conclusion

The pirates of Somalia have performed at least one useful service over the last year: they have provided a much needed reminder of the importance of the sea and of potential maritime threats to global security. The vast majority of world trade, including critical supplies of energy and raw materials, travels by sea. Some 95 per cent of this travels through nine principal chokepoints including the Strait of Hormuz, the Malacca Strait and Bab El Mandab. It is a dangerous assumption that a relatively benign era, during which unprotected ships could proceed safely throughout much of the world, will necessarily prevail in the future. If anything, success in the Indian Ocean will not only have emboldened the pirates of Somalia but may also have encouraged other groups to adopt similar tactics elsewhere.

Neither are maritime threats confined to piracy. The terrorist attacks on Mumbai in November 2008, probably launched from mother-ships, could be replicated in other areas of the world; there is no reason why a ship-load of militants should not be able to strike at high-profile targets many hundreds of miles away. So far, there has been no apparent link between piracy and maritime terrorism but the readiness of pirates to take enormous risks for money should be a warning against complacency. The use of large ships for some kind of terrorist action cannot be discounted.

Another valuable lesson reinforced by experience in the waters off Somalia is that quantity is an important component of capability. That an international group of warships has found it difficult to police such a huge area of ocean gives substance to the claim that 'ships cannot be in two places at once'. This is an argument too easily forgotten, or ignored, despite the fact that the equivalent 'boots on the ground' has been such a critical factor in the Iraq and Afghanistan land campaigns. There are also dangers that the wrong conclusions could be drawn from anti-piracy operations. The constabulary nature of this task should not be allowed to dilute the need to concentrate on the capability and readiness to conduct high-intensity warfare. The lessons of history are that such contingencies can materialise with very little warning, and it would be dangerous to ignore these in a complex, uncertain world in which the balance of power appears to be shifting.

Stephen Saunders **May 2009**

Acknowledgements

The business of collecting information and recording change has always been a continuous process, but up to a few years ago its presentation had been cyclical. *Jane's Fighting Ships* hard-copy book remains annual, but for those users more impatient for change as it happens, the Online product, which is updated regularly, is ideal. The *Jane's Fighting Ships* microsite (http://jfs.janes.com) offers a dedicated portal into the electronic environment. Amongst the many offerings on the microsite is the NewsEdge service providing a regular feed of naval related news from hundreds of sources around the world. Feedback on the microsite is always useful and amongst refinements made over the last three years, ship silhouettes are in the process of being re-introduced for Online customers.

To the many anonymous people in government and industry who make data collection such a pleasure, my warmest thanks. We are not interested in secrets, but only in ensuring that open discussion on defence is based on reliable facts.

Thanks are due also to the many people who send colour photographs, whether every year or as the opportunity offers. While not every one can be published, any image, including those that are seemingly insignificant or of doubtful value, has the potential to be useful by corroborating other information about the ship(s) in question. Ideally, images should be at 300 dpi resolution although, exceptionally, lower quality images of rarely photographed ships will be considered for printing. Images should be sent by email or on a CD-ROM, preferably as soon as possible after they have been taken. For those who have not changed to the digital medium, colour prints are of course still gratefully received.

Ian Sturton's excellent scale line drawings have long been a major feature of the publication while changes to Ranks and Insignia have been given a major update this year by Dr Nigel Thomas, an international expert. Similarly, updates to Ensigns and Flags are required each year and these have been provided by Graham Bartram, General Secretary of the Flag Institute, one of the world's main research and documentation centres for flags and vexicology. The importance of the US Navy in maritime affairs merits a special contributor in Tom Philpott who is the editor of *Military Update* in Washington DC.

Other individual contributors who are at the heart of the updating process, and who wish to be acknowledged include:

Captain M Annati, Mr G de Bakker, Mr D Boey, Mr J Brodie, Señor C Busquets i Vilanova, Señor A Campanera i Rovira, Mr M Carneiro, Herr H Carstens, Mr R Cheung,Mr J Ciślak, Mr W Clements, Mr G Davies, Mr M Declerck, Herr H Ehlers, Mr R Fildes, Herr F Findler, Mr P Ford, Mr D Fox, Dr Z Freivogel, Señor A E Galarce, Signor M Ghiglino, Signor G Ghiglione, Colonel W Globke, Rear Admiral J Goldrick, Mr E Hooton, Captain Shaun Jones, Mr M Kadota, Mr Tohru Kizu, Mr P Körnefeldt, Mr A A de Kruijf, Colonel J Kürsener, Mr E Laursen, Mr M Laursen, Mr B Lemachko, Mr C D Maginley, Mr D Mahadzir, Mr M Mazumdar, Mr A Mevlutoglu, Mr M Mokrus, Mr R Montchai, Mr J Montes, Mr S Morison, Mr J Mortimer, Mr H Nakai, Mr L-G Nilsson, Herr M Nitz, Mr J Noot, Mr T Okano, Señor A Ortigueira Gil, Mr R Pabst, Mr F Philips, Mr I J Plokker, Mr M Prendergast, Captain B Prézelin, Señor D Quevedo Carmona, Mr A J R Risseeuw, Monsieur J Y Robert, Mr F Sadek, Mr S San, Mr C Sattler, Captain R Sharpe, Monsieur A Sheldon-Duplaix, Mr B Sullivan, Captain T Tamura, Mr D Thomas, Mr G Toremans, Prof A Wessels, Herr M Winter, Mr J Wise, Mr C D Yaylali, Mr T Yüksel.

It is with great sadness that I record the deaths of two longstanding contributors. Paolo Marsan died after a long illness on 22 May 2008 and Harry Steele, for many years a Jane's photographer, died suddenly on 16 March 2009.

Jane's staff at Coulsdon ease the production process, and no praise can be high enough for Emma Donald (content editor); Jack Brenchley (senior compositor) and the composition team at Amnet in Chennai, India; Kevan Box, Wayne Sudbury and Harriet Harding (scanning team); Jo Agius, Kate Whitehead, Mike Johnson and Leah Butson (image archiving); Martyn Buchanan (production controller) and Sara Morgan (publisher). Closer to home, my wife Ann is an indispensable member of the year-round editorial and administrative effort.

Cross referencing to other Jane's publications is made easy by Jane's Online service which includes, inter alia: *Jane's All the World's Aircraft, Jane's Amphibious and Special Forces, Jane's Air-Launched Weapons, Jane's C4I Systems, Jane's Electro-Optic Systems, Jane's International Defence Directory, Jane's Marine Propulsion, Jane's Naval Weapon Systems, Jane's Naval Construction and Retrofit Markets, Jane's Radar and Electronic Warfare Systems, Jane's Strategic Weapon Systems, Jane's Underwater Warfare Systems, Jane's Unmanned Maritime Vehicles and Systems, Jane's Unmanned Aerial Vehicles and Targets* and *Jane's World Air Forces. Jane's Sentinel Security Assessments* are an excellent source of politico-military information while *Jane's Defence Forecasts - Military Vessel Programmes*, is an online business tool for tracking and projecting military vessel upgrade and procurement programmes around the world. Jane's magazines provide up to the minute reports on defence issues. These include *Jane's Defence Weekly, Jane's International Defence Review, Jane's Foreign Report, Jane's Intelligence Review, Jane's Defence Industry, Jane's Missiles and Rockets* and *Jane's Navy International.* Amongst many other publications the Japanese magazine *Ships of the World* is also a source of useful data.

The focus of *Jane's Fighting Ships* remains seagoing personnel, whether on the bridge or in the operations room. The aim is to provide the operational capabilities of a ship or navy in a consistent and concise format. Individual entries are composed so that there is no need to turn a page or cross-refer to other sections. It is always a pleasure to get feedback from those at sea.

All updating material should be sent to:

Commodore Stephen Saunders
IHS Jane's
Sentinel House
163 Brighton Road
Coulsdon
Surrey CR5 2YH
Fax number: (+44 20) 87 00 39 59
e-mail: yearbook@janes.com

Stephen Saunders

During a 32-year career in the Royal Navy, Stephen Saunders travelled extensively and worked with many different navies. A surface ship officer and anti-submarine warfare specialist, he served in most classes of warship from Mine Countermeasures vessels to Aircraft Carriers. He commanded the frigate HMS *Sirius* and, as Captain 1st Frigate Squadron, HMS *Coventry*; in the latter role he also commanded the Royal Navy's Armilla patrol when deployed to the Gulf. His broad staff experience included attachment to the NATO staff of Commander US 6th Fleet and several tours in the Ministry of Defence, London. Appointments in Naval Operational Requirements and Defence Concepts led to his final job as Director Force Development within the Defence Policy Division. He graduated from the National Defence College, Latimer, in 1982 and the Royal College of Defence Studies in 1994. Since leaving the Royal Navy in 1998, he has worked in the shipbuilding industry and as a defence consultant.

Ranks and insignia of the world's navies

This section portrays the rank insignia worn by commissioned officers of the world's navies and coast guards on formal occasions. The rank titles are described in the language of the relevant country followed by the Royal Navy equivalent.

The traditional uniform pattern has been the very dark blue double-breasted service tunic introduced by the Royal Navy in the 19th Century, with rank insignia worn as thin, medium and wide gold braid rings, with a loop or 'curl' on the uppermost ring, around both cuffs. Other navies and coast guards have changed the tunic colour to black or a lighter shade of dark blue, varied the widths and order of the rings, or replaced the 'curl' with a star or other symbol. Some Middle East, African, Caribbean or Pacific states wear Army insignia or Navy cuff rings on cloth shoulder-straps only, whilst others, especially from the former Warsaw Pact, wear rank insignia simultaneously on the shoulder-straps and cuffs of the tunic.

Similarly most states imitate the Royal Navy by wearing cuff rings on the shoulder-straps of greatcoats or white tropical dress tunics, with 'Flag-Officers' (admirals and sometimes commodores) having gold braid shoulder-straps with a national device above 5 – 1 silver wire Army-style stars. On shirts, pullovers or camouflage field uniforms officers wear their cuff rings on cloth shoulder-loops slipped into cloth shoulder-straps or breast-loops, as metal badges on collars or rectangular breast-patches.

Albania (Forcat e Mbrojtjes Detare Shqipetare)

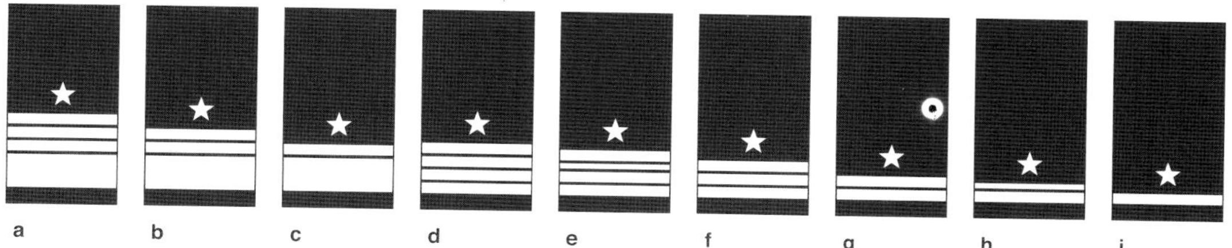

Gold wire stars and gold braid rings on very dark blue cuffs. Rank titles are in Albanian. The Albanian Border Guard includes a Coast Guard (Roja Bregdetare).
a: *Admiral*, Admiral *(rank not currently held)* **b:** *Nënadmiral*, Vice Admiral *(rank not currently held)*
c: *Kundëradmiral*, Rear Admiral *(rank not currently held)* **d:** *Kapiten i rangut 1 (të pare)*, Captain *(Commandant, Navy)*
e: *Kapiten i rangut 2 (të dytë)*, Commander **f:** *Kapiten i rangut 3 (të tretë)*, Lieutenant Commander **g:** *Kapiten Lejtnant*, Lieutenant
h: *Lejtnant*, Sub Lieutenant **i:** *Nënlejtnant*, Acting Sub Lieutenant

Algeria (Al-Quwwat Al-Bahria Al-Djaza'eria)

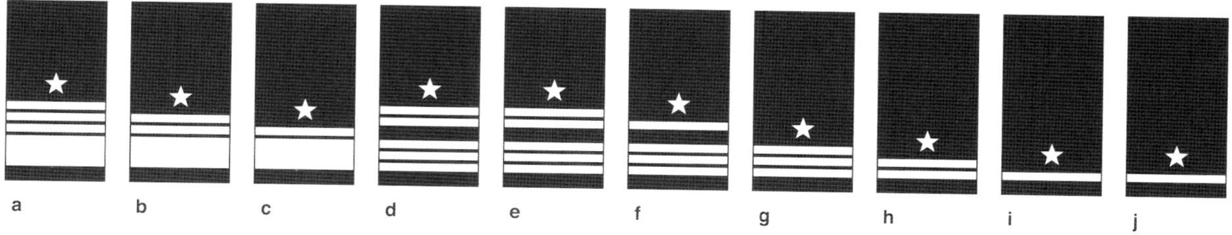

Gold braid stars and rings on dark blue cloth cuffs; a Commander (e) has silver braid second and fourth rings; a Midshipman (j) has a silver braid star. Rank insignia is worn simultaneously on shoulder-straps. Brass buttons. Algerian Army rank titles are used and written here in romanised Arabic. Algeria maintains a small Coast Guard.
a: *Farīq*, Vice Admiral *(rank not currently held)* **b:** *Liwā'*, Rear Admiral *(Commander, Navy)* **c:** *'Amid*, Commodore **d:** *'Aqīd*, Captain
e: *Muqaddam*, Commander **f:** *Rā'id*, Lieutenant Commander **g:** *Naqīb*, Lieutenant **h:** *Mulāzim Awwal*, Sub Lieutenant
i: *Mulāzim Thāni*, Acting Sub Lieutenant **j:** *Murashshah*, Midshipman

Angola (Marinha de Guerra Angolana)

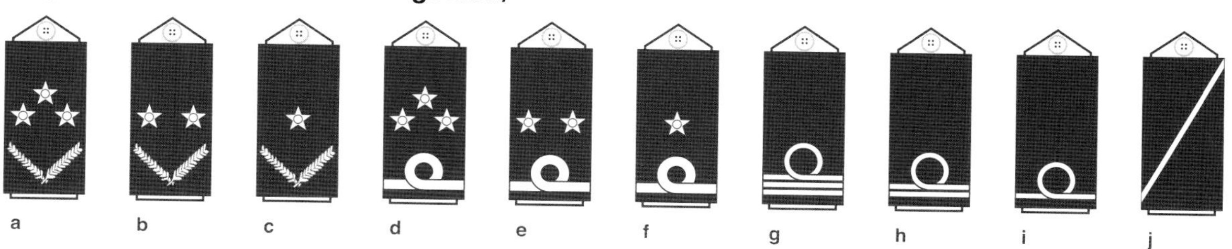

Gold stars, wreaths, rings and stripes on dark blue cloth shoulder-loops on white cloth shoulder-straps; white bone buttons. Rank titles are in Portuguese.
a: *Almirante*, Admiral *(Chief of Naval Staff)* **b:** *Vice-Almirante*, Vice Admiral **c:** *Contra-Almirante*, Rear Admiral **d:** *Capitão-de-Mar-e-Guerra*, Captain
e: *Capitão-de-Fragata*, Commander **f:** *Capitão-de-Corveta*, Lieutenant Commander **g:** *Tenente-de-Navio*, Lieutenant
h: *Tenente-de-Fragata*, Sub Lieutenant **i:** *Tenente-de-Corveta*, Acting Sub Lieutenant **j:** *Aspirante*, Midshipman

Argentina (Armada Argentina)

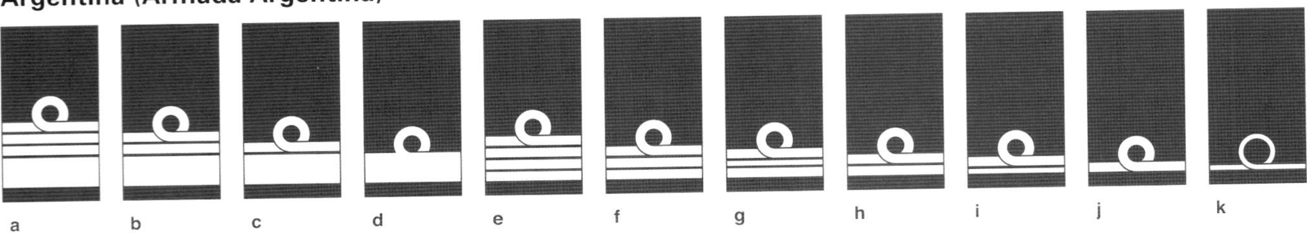

Gold braid rings with 'curl' on navy blue cloth cuffs. Rank titles are in Spanish.
a: *Almirante*, Admiral *(Chief of Naval Staff)* **b**: *Vicealmirante*, Vice Admiral **c**: *Contraalmirante*, Rear Admiral **d**: *Comodoro de Marina*, Commodore
e: *Capitán de Navío*, Captain **f**: *Capitán de Fragata*, Commander **g**: *Capitán de Corbeta*, Lieutenant Commander **h**: *Teniente de Navío*, Lieutenant
i: *Teniente de Fragata*, (Senior) Sub Lieutenant **j**: *Teniente de Corbeta*, Sub Lieutenant **k**: *Guardiamarina*, Acting Sub Lieutenant

Argentina Coast Guard (Prefectura Naval Argentina)

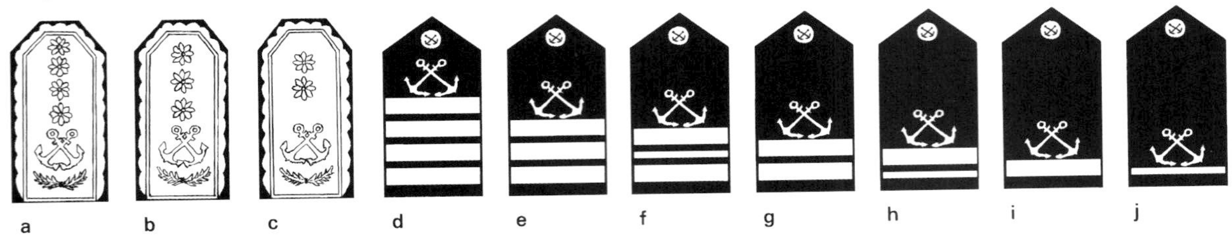

Silver suns, anchors and wreaths on gold braid shoulder-straps edged in very dark blue cloth (a–c); gold braid anchors and rings on very dark blue cloth shoulder-straps; brass buttons. Rank titles are in Spanish.
a: *Prefecto Nacional*, Admiral *(Prefect-General, PNA)* **b**: *Subprefecto Nacional*, Vice Admiral **c**: *Prefecto General*, Rear Admiral
d: *Prefecto Major*, Captain **e**: *Prefecto Principal*, Commander **f**: *Prefecto*, Lieutenant Commander **g**: *Subprefecto*, Lieutenant
h: *Oficial Principal*, (Senior) Sub Lieutenant **i**: *Oficial Auxiliar*, Sub Lieutenant **j**: *Oficial Ayudante*, Acting Sub Lieutenant

Australia (Royal Australian Navy)

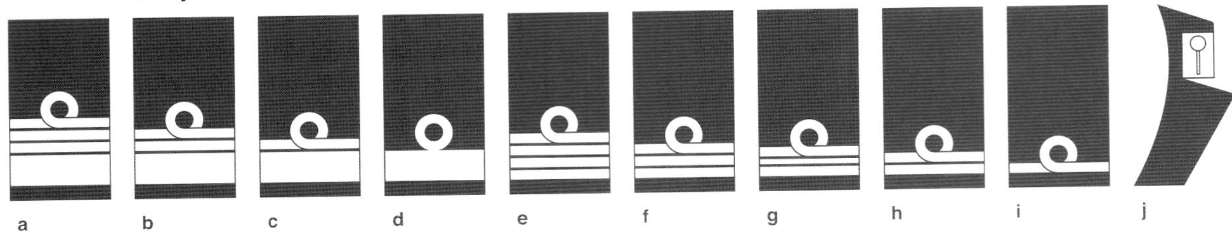

Gold braid rings with 'curl' on very dark blue cloth cuffs; brass button and white cord on white cloth collar-patch (j). Royal Navy rank titles are used. The Australian Volunteer Coast Guard is a civilian organisation.
a: Admiral *(rank not currently held)* **b**: Vice Admiral *(Chief of Navy)* **c**: Rear Admiral **d**: Commodore **e**: Captain **f**: Commander
g: Lieutenant Commander **h**: Lieutenant **i**: Sub Lieutenant **j**: Midshipman

Azerbaijan (Azerbycan herbi deniz qüvveleri)

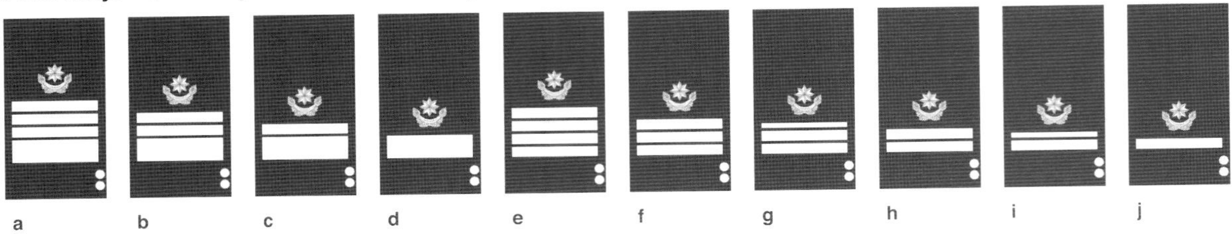

Gold wire stars and wreaths and gold braid rings on black cloth cuffs; brass buttons. Rank titles are in Azeri. The Azerbaijan Border Guard includes a small Coast Guard.
a: *Admiral*, Admiral *(rank not currently held)* **b**: *Vitse-admiral*, Vice Admiral *(Commander-in-Chief, Navy)* **c**: *Kontr-admiral*, Rear Admiral
d: *1 (Birinci) dereceli kapitan*, Captain **e**: *2 (Ikinci) dereceli kapitan*, Commander **f**: *3 (Üçüncü) dereceli kapitan*, Lieutenant Commander
g: *Kapitan-leytenant*, Lieutenant **h**: *Baş leytenant*, (Senior) Sub Lieutenant **i**: *Leytenant*, Sub Lieutenant **j**: *Kiçik leytenant*, Acting Sub Lieutenant

Bahamas (Royal Bahamas Defence Force)

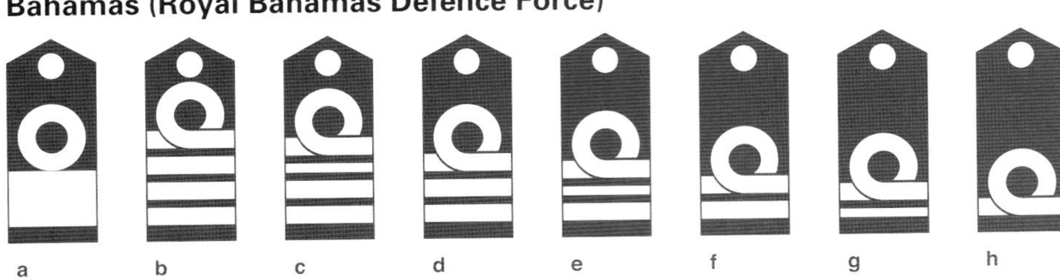

Gold braid rings with 'curl' on very dark blue cloth cuffs. Rank titles are in English.
a: *Commodore*, Commodore *(Commander, RBDF)* **b**: *Captain*, Captain *(rank not currently held)* **c**: *Senior Commander*, (Senior) Commander
d: *Commander*, Commander **e**: *Lieutenant Commander*, Lieutenant Commander **f**: *Senior Lieutenant*, Lieutenant **g**: *Lieutenant*, Sub Lieutenant
h: *Sub Lieutenant*, Acting Sub Lieutenant

Bahrain (Royal Bahrain Navy)

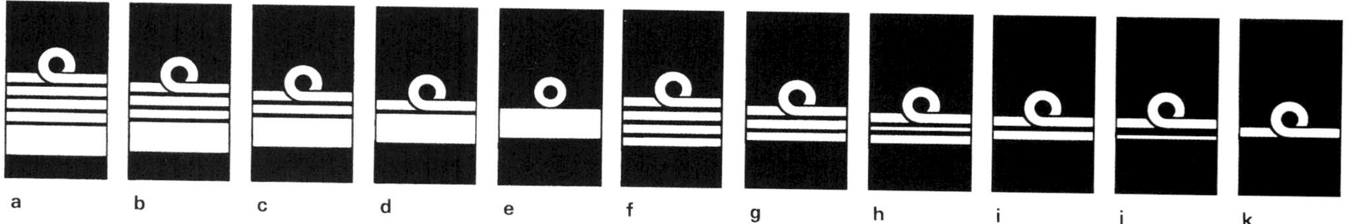

Gold braid rings with 'curl' on very dark blue cloth cuffs. Arabic Bahrain Army rank titles are used and written here in romanised script.
a: *Mushīr*, Admiral of the Fleet *(King of Bahrain)* **b**: *Farīq Awwal*, Admiral *(rank not currently held)* **c**: *Farīq*, Vice Admiral *(rank not currently held)*
d: *Liwā'*, Rear Admiral *(rank not currently held)* **e**: *'Amid*, Commodore *(Commander, RBNF)* **f**: *'Aqīd*, Captain **g**: *Muqaddam*, Commander
h: *Rā'id*, Lieutenant Commander **i**: *Naqīb*, Lieutenant **j**: *Mulāzim Awwal*, Sub Lieutenant **k**: *Mulāzim Thāni*, Acting Sub Lieutenant

Bangladesh (Nou Bahini)

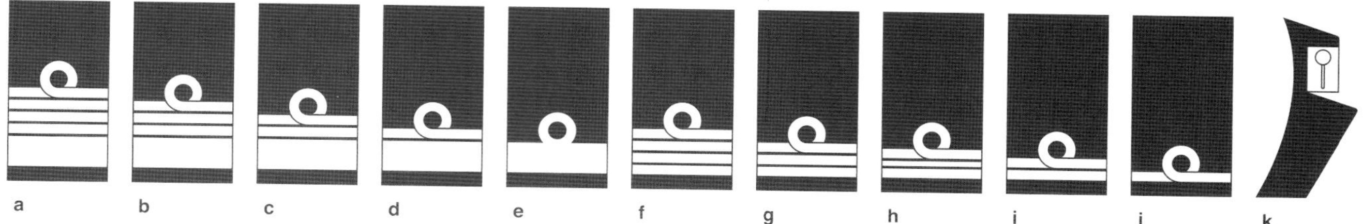

Gold braid rings with 'curl' on very dark blue cloth cuffs; brass button and white cord on white cloth collar-patch (k). Royal Navy rank titles are used. The Bangladesh Coast Guard forms part of the Ministry of Home Affairs. Personnel wear naval uniforms and insignia with a Commodore as the Director General.
a: Admiral of the Fleet *(rank not currently held)* **b**: Admiral *(rank not currently held)* **c**: Vice Admiral *(Chief of Naval staff)* **d**: Rear Admiral
e: Commodore **f**: Captain **g**: Commander **h**: Lieutenant Commander **i**: Lieutenant **j**: Sub Lieutenant & Acting Sub Lieutenant **k**: Midshipman

Barbados Coast Guard

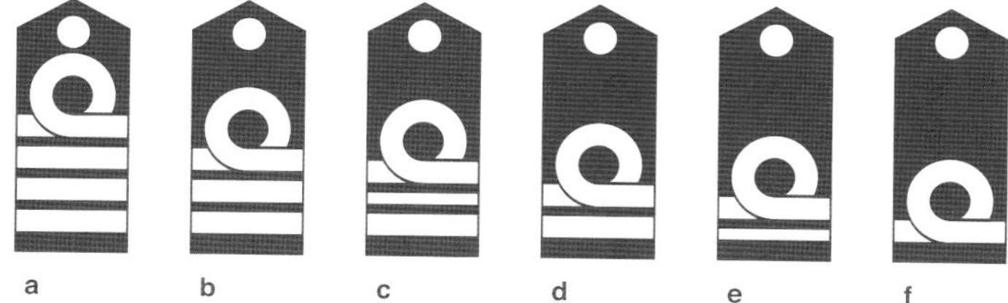

Gold braid rings with 'curl' on very dark blue cloth shoulder-straps; brass buttons. Rank titles are in English.
a: *Captain*, Captain *(rank not currently held)* **b**: *Commander*, Commander *(rank not currently held)*
c: *Lieutenant Commander*, Lieutenant Commander *(Commanding Officer, BCG)* **d**: *Lieutenant*, Lieutenant **e**: *Junior Lieutenant*, Sub Lieutenant
f: *Sub Lieutenant*, Acting Sub Lieutenant

Belgium (Naval Component) (Zeemacht/Force Navale)

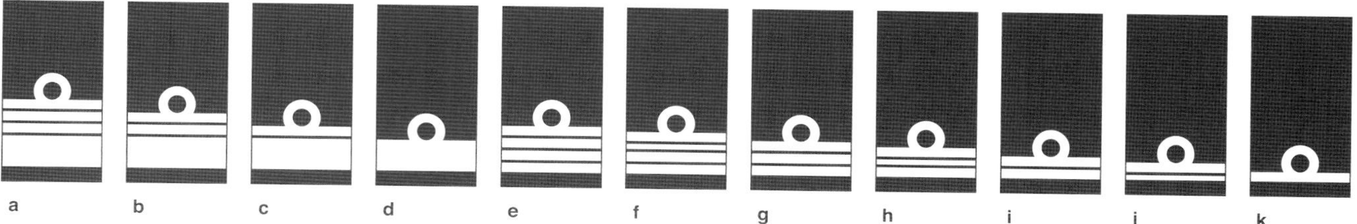

Gold braid rings on very dark blue cloth cuffs. Rank titles are in Flemish/French.
a: *Admiraal/Amiral*, Admiral *(King Albert II)* **b**: *Vice-admiraal/Vice amiral*, Vice Admiral *(Chief of Court Protocol)*
c: *Divisie-admiraal/Amiral de division*, Rear Admiral *(Commandant, Naval Component)* **d**: *Flottieljeadmiraal/Amiral de flottille*, Commodore
e: *Kapitein-ter-zee/Capitaine de vaisseau*, Captain **f**: *Fregatkapitein/Capitaine de frégate*, Commander
g: *Korvetkapitein/Capitaine de corvette*, Lieutenant Commander
h: *Luitenant-ter-zee 1ste (eerste) klasse/Lieutenant de vaisseau 1ère (première) classe*, (Senior) Lieutenant
i: *Luitenant-ter-zee/Lieutenant de vaisseau*, Lieutenant **j**: *Vaandrig-ter-zee/Enseigne de vaisseau*, Sub Lieutenant
k: *Vaandrig-ter-zee 2de (tweede) klasse/Enseigne de vaisseau 2e (deuxième) classe*, Acting Sub Lieutenant

Benin (Forces Navales Béninoises)

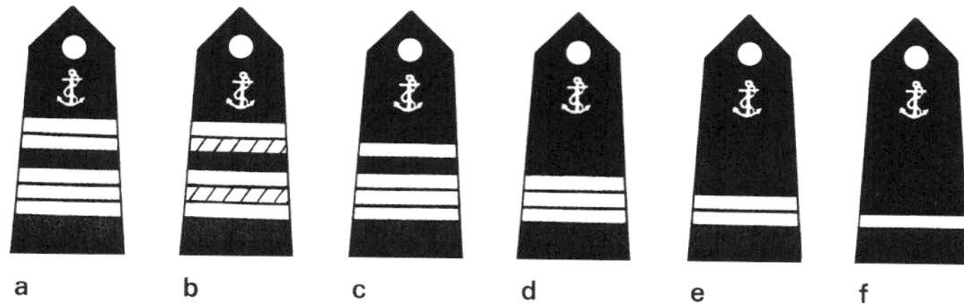

Gold braid anchor and rings on very dark blue cloth shoulder-straps; a Commander (b) has silver second and fourth rings; brass buttons. Rank titles are in French.
a: *Capitaine de vaisseau*, Captain *(rank not currently held)* **b**: *Capitaine de frégate*, Commander *(Commander, Navy)*
c: *Capitaine de corvette*, Lieutenant Commander **d**: *Lieutenant de vaisseau*, Lieutenant **e**: *Enseigne de vaisseau 1ère (première) classe*, Sub Lieutenant
f: *Enseigne de Vaisseau 2e (deuxième) classe*, Acting Sub Lieutenant

Bolivia (Armada Boliviana)

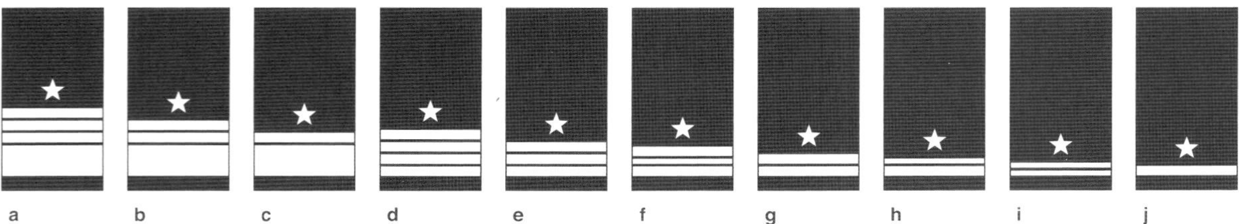

Gold wire stars and gold braid rings on very dark blue cloth cuffs. Rank titles are in Spanish.
a: *Almirante*, Admiral *(Commander-in-Chief, Armed Forces)* **b**: *Vicealmirante*, Vice Admiral *(Commandant General, Navy)* **c**: *Contralmirante*, Rear Admiral
d: *Capitán de Navío*, Captain **e**: *Capitán de Fragata*, Commander **f**: *Capitán de Corbeta*, Lieutenant Commander **g**: *Teniente de Navío*, Lieutenant
h: *Teniente de Fragata*, (Senior) Sub Lieutenant **i**: *Teniente de Corbeta*, Sub Lieutenant **j**: *Alférez*, Acting Sub Lieutenant

Brazil (Marinha do Brasil)

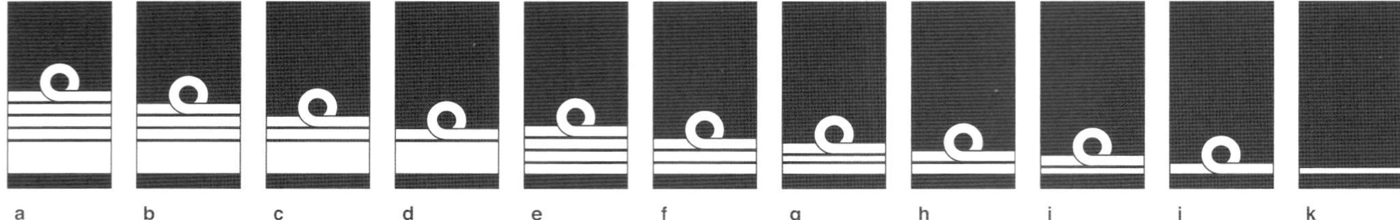

Gold braid stars and gold braid rings on very dark blue cloth cuffs. Rank titles are in Portuguese.
a: *Almirante*, Admiral of the fleet *(rank not currently held)* **b**: *Almirante de Esquadra*, Admiral *(Commander of the Navy)* **c**: *Vice-Almirante*, Vice Admiral
d: *Contra-Almirante*, Rear Admiral **e**: *Capitão-de-Mar-e-Guerra*, Captain **f**: *Capitão-de-Fragata*, Commander
g: *Capitão-de-Corveta*, Lieutenant Commander **h**: *Capitão-Tenente*, Lieutenant **i**: *1o (Primeiro) Tenente*, Sub Lieutenant
j: *2o (Segundo) Tenente*, Acting Sub Lieutenant **k**: *Guarda-Marinha*, Midshipman

Brunei (Royal Brunei Navy) (Angkatan Tentera Laut Diraja Brunei)

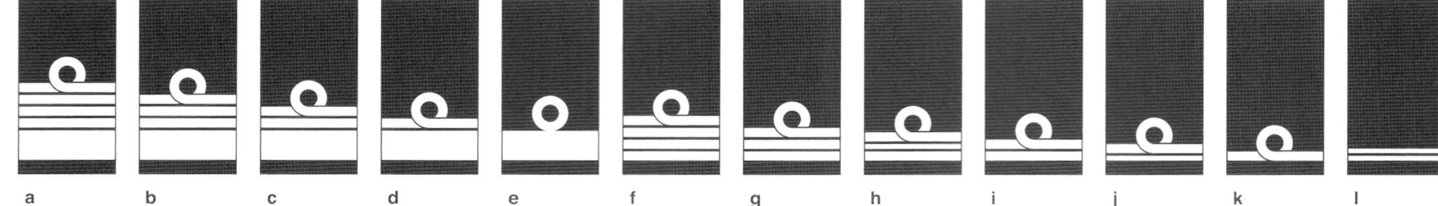

Gold braid rings with 'curl' and national title on very dark blue cloth shoulder-straps; brass buttons. Rank titles are in Malay.
a: *Fil Marsyal (L)*, Admiral of the Fleet *(Sultan Haji Hassanal Bolkiah Mu'izzaddin Waddaulah)* **b**: *Jeneral (L)*, Admiral *(rank not currently held)*
c: *Leftenan Jeneral (L)*, Vice Admiral *(rank not currently held)* **d**: *Mejar Jeneral (L)*, Rear Admiral *(rank not currently held)*
e: *Brigedier Jeneral (L)*, Commodore *(rank not currently held)* **f**: *Kolonel (L)*, Captain *(Commander, Navy)* **g**: *Leftenan Kolonel (L)*, Commander
h: *Mejar (L)*, Lieutenant Commander **i**: *Kapten (L)*, Lieutenant **j**: *Leftenan (L)*, Sub Lieutenant **k**: *Leftenan Muda (L)*, Acting Sub Lieutenant
l: *Kadet Kanan (L)*, Midshipman

Bulgaria (Voennomorski sili)

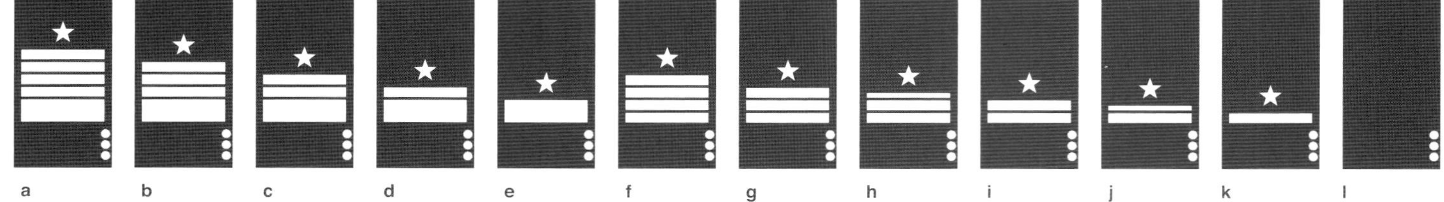

Gold wire stars and gold braid bars on black cuffs; brass buttons. Rank insignia is also worn simultaneously on gold braid shoulder-straps. Rank titles are in romanised Bulgarian. The Bulgarian Border Police (Granichna Politsiya) includes a small Coast Guard wearing dark-blue police uniforms and insignia.
a: *Admiral*, Admiral *(rank not currently held)* **b**: *Vitseadmiral*, Vice Admiral *(Commander-in-Chief, Navy)* **c**: *Kontraadmiral*, Rear Admiral
d: *Brigaden admiral*, Commodore **e**: *Kapitan I (parvi) rang*, Captain **f**: *Kapitan II (vtori) rang*, Commander
g: *Kapitan III (treti) rang*, Lieutenant Commander **h**: *Kapitan-leytenant*, Lieutenant **i**: *Starshi leytenant*, (Senior) Sub Lieutenant
j: *Leytenant*, Sub Lieutenant **k**: *Mladshi Leytenant*, Acting Sub Lieutenant **l**: *Ofitserski kandidat*, Midshipman

Cambodia (Royal Cambodian Navy)

Gold wire anchors, stars, branches and gold braid rings on navy blue cloth shoulder-straps; a Commander (e) has silver second and fourth rings; brass buttons. Cambodian Army rank titles are used.
a: *Udon-Nearvey-Ek*, Vice Admiral *(Commander, Navy)* **b**: *Udon-Nearvey-Tor*, Rear Admiral **c**: *Udon-Nearvey-Trey*, Commodore
d: *Vorak-Nearvey-Ek*, Captain **e**: *Vorak-Nearvey-Tor*, Commander **f**: *Vorak-Nearvey-Trey*, Lieutenant Commander **g**: *Aknouk-Nearvey-Ek*, Lieutenant
h: *Aknouk-Nearvey-Tor*, Sub Lieutenant **i**: *Aknouk-Nearvey-Trey*, Acting Sub Lieutenant

Cameroon (Marine Nationale du Cameroun)

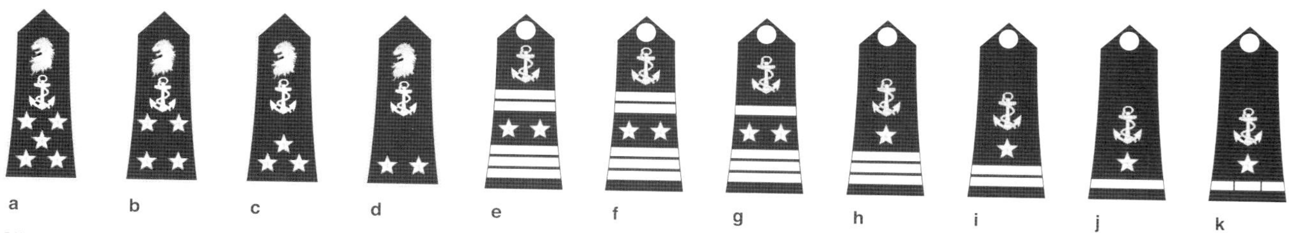

Silver lions, anchors and stars on very dark blue cloth shoulder-straps edged gold (a–d); gold anchors, stars and rings on very dark blue cloth shoulder-straps (e–k), brass buttons; a Commander (f) has silver braid first and second rings, a Midshipman (k) a gold braid ring with two mid-blue 'breaks'. Rank titles are in French.

a: *Amiral d'escadre*, Admiral *(rank not currently held)* **b**: *Vice-amiral d'escadre*, Vice Admiral *(rank not currently held)*
c: *Vice-amiral*, Rear Admiral *(Chief of Naval Staff)* **d**: *Contre-amiral*, Commodore **e**: *Capitaine de vaisseau*, Captain **f**: *Capitaine de frégate*, Commander
g: *Capitaine de corvette*, Lieutenant Commander **h**: *Lieutenant de vaisseau*, Lieutenant **i**: *Enseigne de vaisseau de 1ère (première) classe*, Sub Lieutenant
j: *Enseigne de vaisseau de 2e (deuxième) classe*, Acting Sub Lieutenant **k**: *Aspirant*, Midshipman

Canada

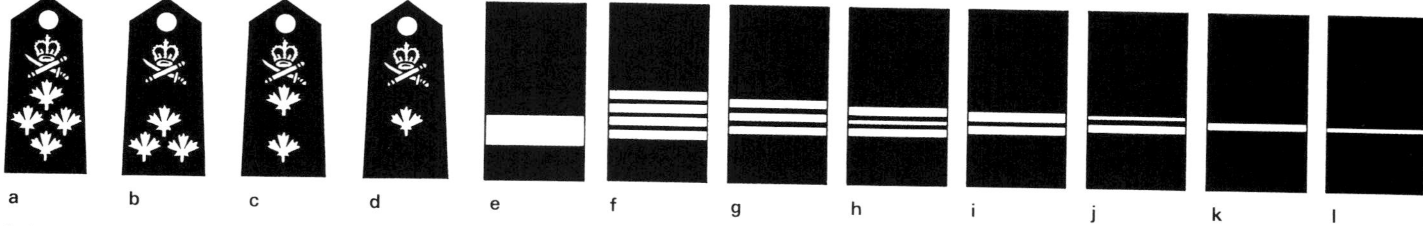

Gold embroidered crowns, crossed batons and scimitars and maple-leaves on very dark blue cloth shoulder-straps, brass buttons (a–d); gold braid rings on very dark blue cloth cuffs (e–l). Rank titles are in English/French.

a: *Admiral/Amiral*, Admiral *(rank not currently held)* **b**: *Vice Admiral/Vice-amiral*, Vice Admiral *(Chief of Maritime Staff)*
c: *Rear Admiral/Contre-amiral*, Rear Admiral **d**: *Commodore/Commodore*, Commodore **e**: Flag Officers **f**: *Captain/Capitaine de vaisseau*, Captain
g: *Commander/Capitaine de frégate*, Commander **h**: *Lieutenant Commander/Capitaine de corvette*, Lieutenant Commander
i: *Lieutenant/Lieutenant de vaisseau*, Lieutenant **j**: *Sub Lieutenant/Enseigne de vaisseau de 1ère (première) classe*, Sub Lieutenant
k: *Acting Sub Lieutenant/Enseigne de vaisseau de 2e (deuxième) classe*, Acting Sub Lieutenant **l**: *Officer Cadet/Aspirant de marine*, Midshipman

Canada (Canadian Coast Guard/Garde côtière canadienne)

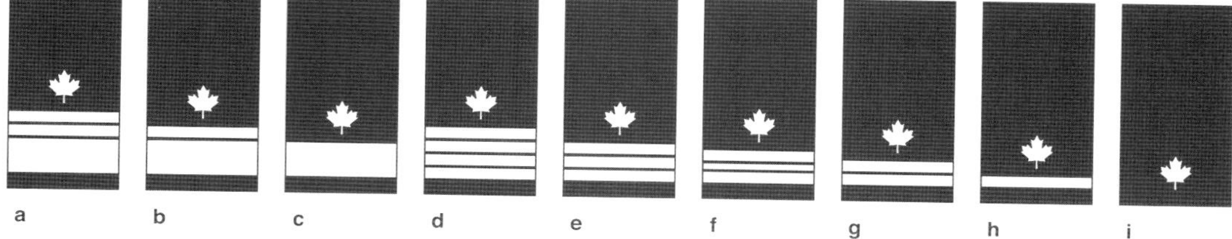

Gold wire maple-leaves and gold braid rings on very dark blue cloth cuffs. Rank titles are in English/French.

a: *Commissioner/Commissaire*, Vice Admiral *(Commissioner, CCG)* **b**: *Deputy Commissioner/Sous-commissaire*, Rear Admiral
c: *Assistant Commissioner/Commissaire adjoint* **d**: *Commanding Officer/Commandant*, Captain **e**: *Chief Officer/Capitaine en 2e (Second)*, Commander
f: *1st (First) Officer/1er (Premier) Officier*, Lieutenant Commander **g**: *2nd (Second) Officer/2e (Deuxième) Officier*, Lieutenant
h: *3rd (Third) Officer/3e (Troisième) Officier*, Sub Lieutenant **i**: *Officer Cadet/Élève-officier*, Midshipman

Chile (Armada de Chile)

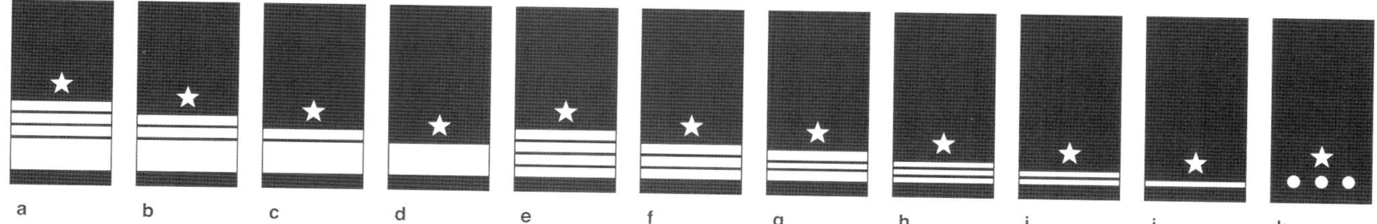

Gold wire, gold braid rings and brass buttons on very dark blue cloth cuffs. Rank titles are in Spanish.

a: *Almirante*, Admiral *(Commander-in Chief, Navy)* **b**: *Vicealmirante*, Vice Admiral **c**: *Contraalmirante*, Rear Admiral **d**: *Comodoro*, Commodore
e: *Capitán de Navío*, Captain **f**: *Capitán de Fragata*, Commander **g**: *Capitán de Corbeta*, Lieutenant Commander **h**: *Teniente 1° (Primero)*, Lieutenant
i: *Teniente 2° (Segundo)*, Sub Lieutenant **j**: *Subteniente*, Acting Sub Lieutenant **k**: *Guardiamarina*, Midshipman

China (People's Liberation Army Navy) (Zhōngguó Rénmín Jiěfàngjūn Hǎijūn)

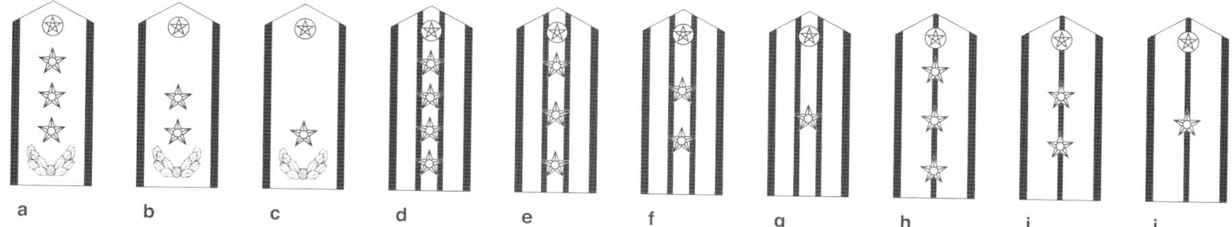

Gold metal stars (a–c), silver metal stars (d–j) and gold metal oak-leaves on gold braid shoulder-straps with black edging and centre-stripes; brass buttons. Rank titles are in romanised Mandarin Chinese written in 'Hanyu Pinyin'. The Chinese Border Guard includes a Coast Guard.

a: *Hǎijūn Shangjiang*, Admiral *(Commander-in-Chief, Navy)* **b**: *Hǎijūn Zhōngjiang*, Vice Admiral **c**: *Hǎijūn Shaojiang*, Rear Admiral
d: *Hǎijūn Daxiao*, Commodore **e**: *Hǎijūn Shangxiao*, Captain **f**: *Hǎijūn Zhōngxiao*, Commander **g**: *Hǎijūn Shaoxiao*, Lieutenant Commander
h: *Hǎijūn Shangwei*, Lieutenant **i**: *Hǎijūn Zhōngwei*, Sub Lieutenant **j**: *Hǎijūn Shaowei*, Acting Sub Lieutenant

Colombia (Armada Nacional de Colombia)

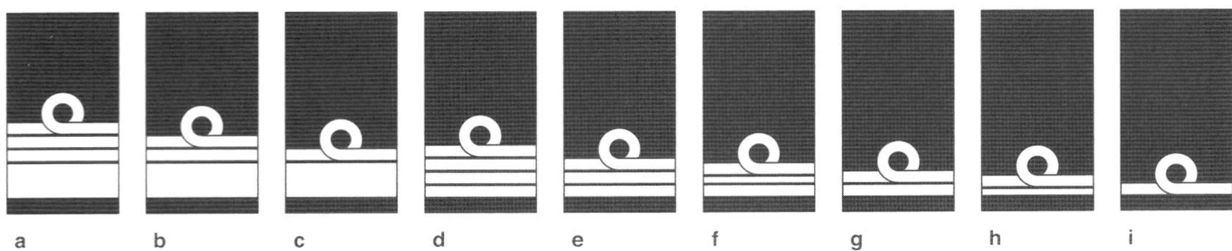

Gold braid rings with 'curl' on very dark blue cloth cuffs. Rank titles are in Spanish. The Colombian Navy maintains a small Coast Guard (Guardacosta).
a: *Almirante*, Admiral *(Commander, Navy)* **b**: *Vicealmirante*, Vice Admiral **c**: *Contralmirante*, Rear Admiral **d**: *Capitán de Navío*, Captain
e: *Capitán de Fragata*, Commander **f**: *Capitán de Corbeta*, Lieutenant Commander **g**: *Teniente de Navío*, Lieutenant
h: *Teniente de Fragata*, Sub Lieutenant **i**: *Teniente de Corbeta*, Acting Sub Lieutenant

Democratic Republic of Congo (Marine Nationale Congolaise)

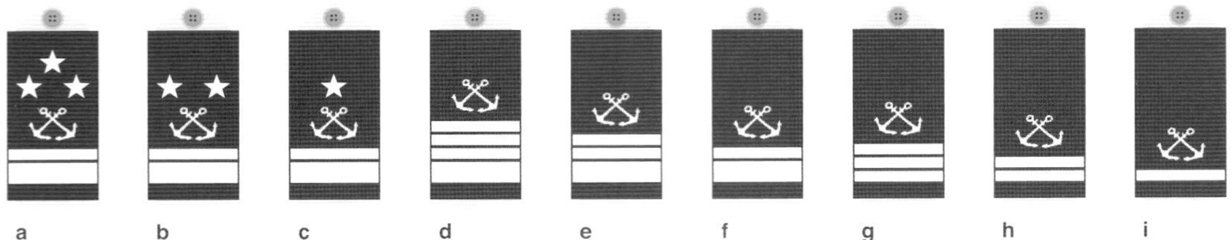

Silver braid stars and gold braid crossed anchors and rings on very dark blue cloth shoulder-loops. Rank titles are in French.
a: *Lieutenant Général*, Admiral **b**: *Général-Major*, Vice Admiral *(Commander, Navy)* **c**: *Général de Brigade*, Rear Admiral
d: *Capitaine de vaisseau*, Captain **e**: *Capitaine de frégate*, Commander **f**: *Capitaine de corvette*, Lieutenant Commander
g: *Lieutenant de vaisseau*, Lieutenant **h**: *Enseigne de vaisseau de 1ère (première) classe*, Sub Lieutenant
i: *Enseigne de vaisseau de 2e (deuxième) classe*, Acting Sub Lieutenant

Costa Rica (Coast Guard) (Servicio Nacional de Guardacostas)

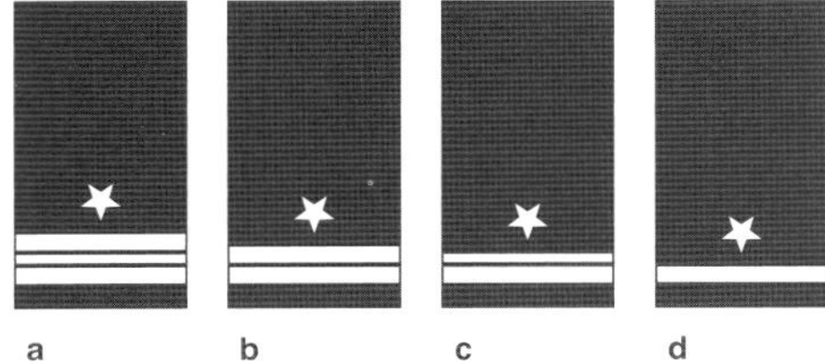

Gold wire stars and gold braid rings on very dark blue cuffs. Army rank titles in Spanish are used.
a: *Major*, Lieutenant Commander *(Commander, Coast Guard)* **b**: *Capitán*, Lieutenant **c**: *Teniente*, Sub Lieutenant
d: *Sub Teniente*, Acting Sub Lieutenant

Côte d'Ivoire (Marine Nationale de la Côte d'Ivoire)

Gold metal stars and anchors with ship's wheels and gold braid diagonal and vertical stripes on very dark blue cloth shoulder-straps, brass buttons; a Commander (f) has silver braid second and fourth vertical stripes, a Midshipman (k) a gold braid vertical stripe with two mid-blue 'breaks'. Rank titles are in French.
a: *Amiral*, Admiral *(rank not currently held)* **b**: *Vice-amiral d'escadre*, Vice Admiral *(rank not currently held)*
c: *Vice-amiral*, Rear Admiral *(rank not currently held)* **d**: *Contre-amiral*, Commodore (Commander, Navy) **e**: *Capitaine de vaisseau*, Captain
f: *Capitaine de frégate*, Commander **g**: *Capitaine de corvette*, Lieutenant Commander **h**: *Lieutenant de vaisseau*, Lieutenant
i: *Enseigne de vaisseau de 1ère (première) classe*, Sub Lieutenant **j**: *Enseigne de vaisseau de 2e (deuxième) classe*, Acting Sub Lieutenant
k: *Aspirant*, Midshipman

Croatia (Hrvatska Ratna Mornarica)

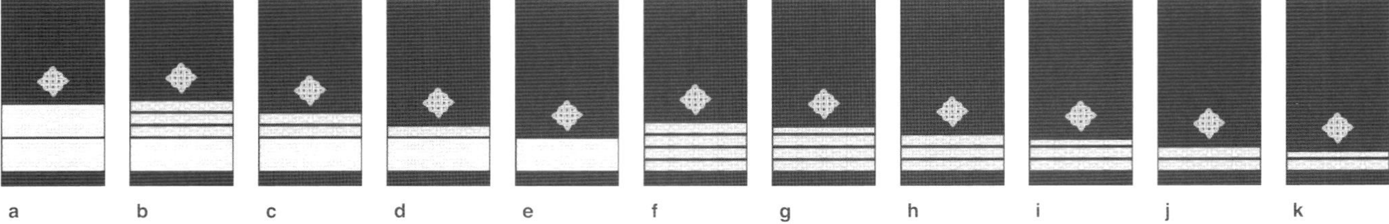

Gold wire rhomboids and gold braid rings on very dark blue cuffs. Rank titles are in Croatian.
a: *Stožerni Admiral*, Admiral of the Fleet *(rank not currently held)* **b**: *Admiral*, Admiral *(rank not currently held)*
c: *Viceadmiral*, Vice Admiral *(rank not currently held)* **d**: *Kontraadmiral*, Rear Admiral *(Commander, Navy)* **e**: *Komodor*, Commodore
f: *Kapetan bojnog broda*, Captain **g**: *Kapetan fregate*, Commander **h**: *Kapetan korvete*, Lieutenant Commander **i**: *Poručnik bojnog broda*, Lieutenant
j: *Poručnik fregate*, Sub Lieutenant **k**: *Poručnik korvete*, Acting Sub Lieutenant

Cuba (Marina de Guerra Revolucionaria)

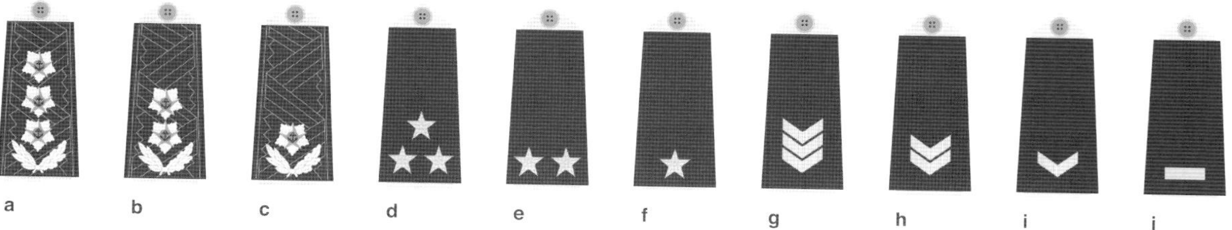

a b c d e f g h i j

Large gold stars with black anchors on red bosses and silver rays on black braid shoulder-loops (a–c); gold stars, chevrons and bars on black cloth shoulder-loops on white shoulder-straps; white bone buttons. Rank titles are in Spanish. The Cuban Border Guard includes a small Coast Guard.
a: *Almirante*, Vice Admiral *(rank not currently held)* **b**: *Vicealmirante*, Rear Admiral *(Commander, Navy)* **c**: *Contralmirante*, Commodore
d: *Capitán de Navío*, Captain **e**: *Capitán de Fragata*, Commander **f**: *Capitán de Corbeta*, Lieutenant Commander **g**: *Teniente de Navío*, Lieutenant
h: *Teniente de Fragata*, (Senior) Sub Lieutenant **i**: *Teniente de Corbeta*, Sub Lieutenant **j**: *Alférez*, Acting Sub Lieutenant

Cyprus (National Guard Naval Command)

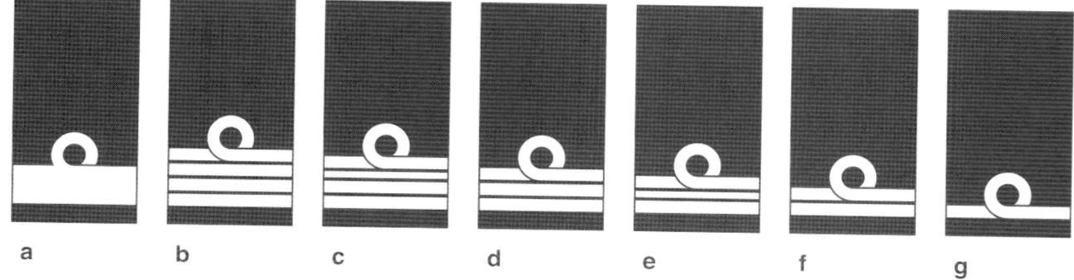

a b c d e f g

Gold braid rings with 'curl' on very dark blue cloth cuffs. Rank titles in romanised Greek. Cyprus also maintains a small Coast Guard entitled the Cyprus Port and Marine Police (Limeniki & Nautiki Astinomia) wearing dark blue Cyprus Police uniforms and insignia.
a: *Archiploiarchos*, Commodore *(rank not currently held)* **b**: *Ploiarchos*, Captain *(Commander, Navy)* **c**: *Antiploiarchos*, Commander
d: *Plotarchis*, Lieutenant Commander **e**: *Ipoploiarchos*, Lieutenant **f**: *Antipoploiarchos*, Sub Lieutenant **g**: *Simaioforos*, Acting Sub Lieutenant

Denmark (Kongelige Danske Marine)

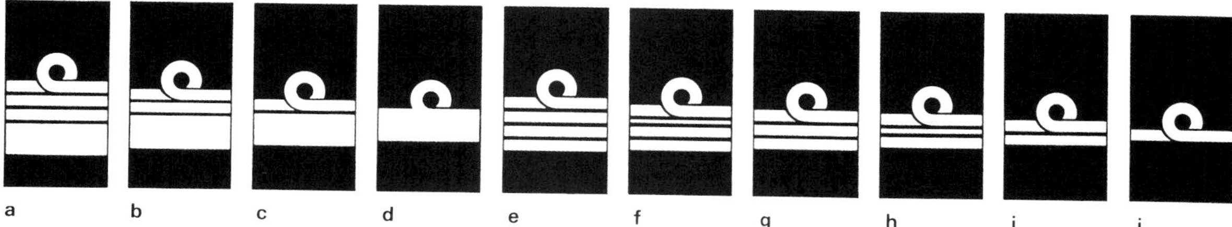

a b c d e f g h i j

Gold braid rings with 'curl' on black cuffs. Rank titles are in Danish. The Danish Coast Guard (Farlandsvæsenet) is commanded by a Director-General.
a: *Admiral*, Admiral *(rank not currently held)* **b**: *Viceadmiral*, Vice Admiral *(rank not currently held)* **c**: *Kontreadmiral*, Rear Admiral *(Chief of the Navy)*
d: *Flotilleadmiral*, Commodore **e**: *Kommandør*, Captain **f**: *Kommandørkaptajn*, Commander **g**: *Orlogskaptajn*, Lieutenant Commander
h: *Kaptajnløjtnant*, Lieutenant **i**: *Premierløjtnant*, Sub Lieutenant **j**: *Løjtnant*, Acting Sub Lieutenant

Djibouti (Marine Nationale Djiboutienne)

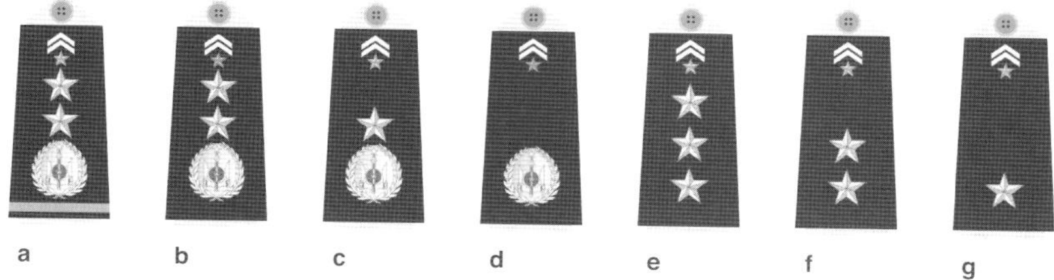

a b c d e f g

Gold wire chevrons and red cloth star above gold embroidered stars and crest and red cloth bar on very dark blue cloth shoulder-loops. Army rank titles are used and are in French.
a: *Colonel-Major*, Commodore *(Commander of the Navy)* **b**: *Colonel*, Captain **c**: *Lieutenant Colonel*, Commander
d: *Commandant*, Lieutenant Commander **e**: *Capitaine*, Lieutenant **f**: *Lieutenant*, Sub Lieutenant **g**: *Sous-lieutenant*, Acting Sub Lieutenant

Dominican Republic (Marina de Guerra Dominicana)

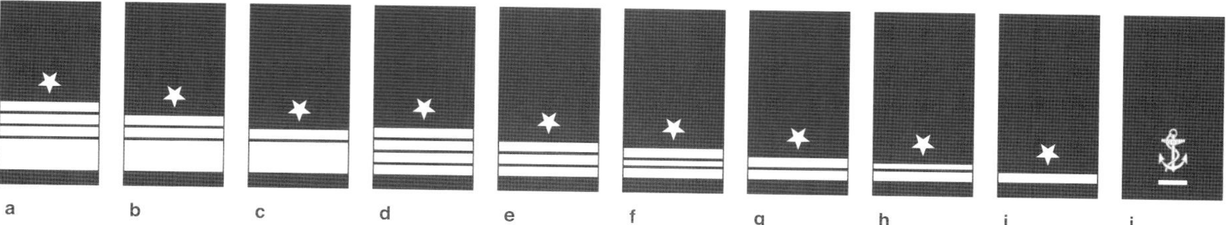

a b c d e f g h i j

Gold wire stars and anchor and gold braid rings and bar on very dark blue cuffs. Rank titles are in Spanish.
a: *Almirante*, Admiral *(rank not currently held)* **b**: *Vicealmirante*, Vice Admiral *(Chief of Naval Staff)* **c**: *Contralmirante*, Rear Admiral
d: *Capitán de Navío*, Captain **e**: *Capitán de Fragata*, Commander **f**: *Capitán de Corbeta*, Lieutenant **g**: *Teniente de Navío*, Lieutenant
h: *Alférez de Navío*, Sub Lieutenant **i**: *Alférez de Fragata*, Acting Sub Lieutenant
j: *Guardiamarina*, Midshipman, 1st Year of training *(higher ranks 2–5 bars)*

Ecuador (Armada de Ecuador)

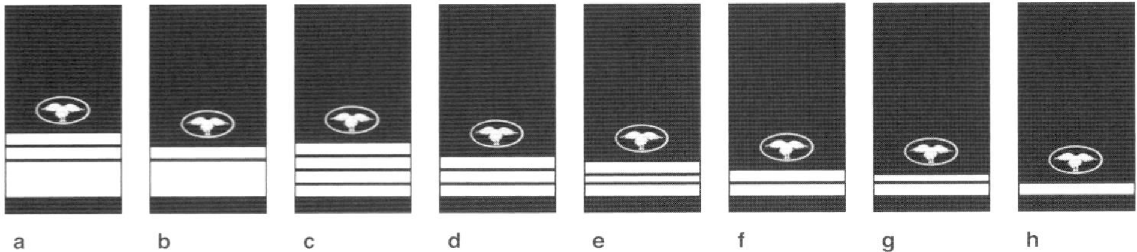

Gold wire condor in a very dark blue cloth oval edged in gold wire and gold braid rings on very dark blue cuffs. Rank titles are in Spanish.
a: *Vicealmirante*, Vice Admiral *(Commandant-General)* **b**: *Contralmirante*, Rear Admiral **c**: *Capitán de Navío*, Captain
d: *Capitán de Fragata*, Commander **e**: *Capitán de Corbeta*, Lieutenant Commander **f**: *Teniente de Navío*, Lieutenant
g: *Teniente de Fragata*, Sub Lieutenant **h**: *Teniente de Corbeta*, Acting Sub Lieutenant

Egypt

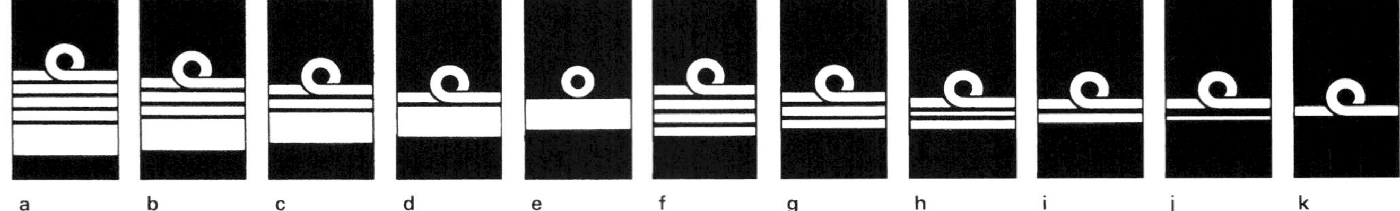

Gold braid rings with 'curl' on navy blue cloth cuffs. Arabic Egyptian Army rank titles are used and written here in romanised script.
a: *Mushīr*, Admiral of the Fleet *(rank not currently held)* **b**: *Farīq Awwal*, Admiral *(rank not currently held)* **c**: *Farīq*, Vice Admiral *(Commander, Navy)*
d: *Liwā'*, Rear Admiral **e**: *'Amid*, Commodore **f**: *'Aqīd*, Captain **g**: *Muqaddam*, Commander **h**: *Rā'id*, Lieutenant Commander **i**: *Naqīb*, Lieutenant
j: *Mulāzim Awwal*, Sub Lieutenant **k**: *Mulāzim Thāni*, Acting Sub Lieutenant

El Salvador (Fuerza Naval de El Salvador)

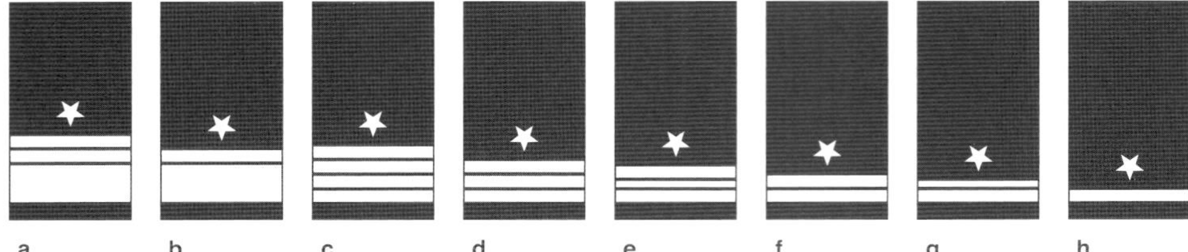

Gold wire stars and gold braid rings on very dark blue cuffs. Rank titles are in Spanish.
a: *Vice Almirante*, Vice Admiral *(rank not currently held)* **b**: *Contraalmirante*, Rear Admiral *(Commander, Naval Force)* **c**: *Capitán de Navío*, Captain
d: *Capitán de Fragata*, Commander **e**: *Capitán de Corbeta*, Lieutenant Commander **f**: *Teniente de Navío*, Lieutenant
g: *Teniente de Fragata*, Sub Lieutenant **h**: *Teniente de Corbeta*, Acting Sub Lieutenant

Estonia (Eesti Merevägi)

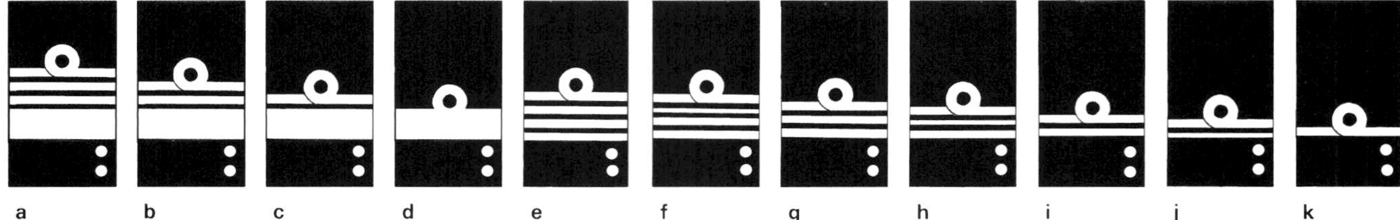

Gold braid rings with 'curl' on very dark blue cloth cuffs; brass buttons. Rank titles are in Estonian.
a: *Admiral*, Admiral *(rank not currently held)* **b**: *Viitseadmiral*, Vice Admiral *(Chief of the Defence Forces)*
c: *Kontradmiral*, Rear Admiral *(rank not currently held)* **d**: *Kommodoor*, Commodore *(rank not currently held)*
e: *Mereväekapten*, Captain *(Commander, Navy)* **f**: *Kaptenleitnant*, Commander **g**: *Kaptenmajor*, Lieutenant Commander **h**: *Vanemleitnant*, Lieutenant
i: *Leitnant*, (Senior) Sub Lieutenant **j**: *Nooremleitnant*, Sub Lieutenant **k**: *Lipnik*, Acting Sub Lieutenant

Fiji

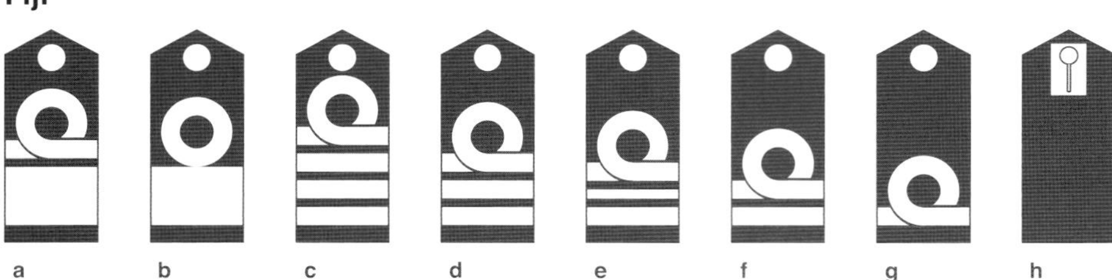

Gold braid rings with 'curl' on very dark blue cloth cuffs; brass button and white cord on white cloth collar-patch (h). Royal Navy rank titles are used.
a: Rear Admiral *(rank not currently held)* **b**: Commodore *(Commander, Royal Fiji Military Forces)* **c**: Captain *(Deputy Commander, RFMF)*
d: Commander *(Commanding Officer, Navy)* **e**: Lieutenant Commander **f**: Sub Lieutenant **g**: Midshipman

Finland (Suomen Merivoimat/Finska Marinen)

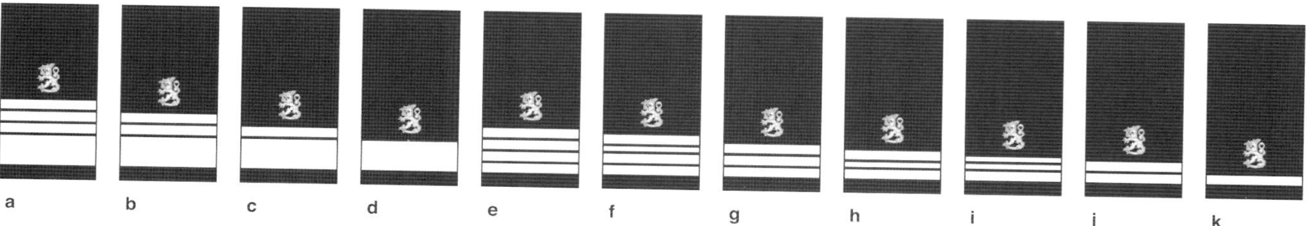

Gold wire Finnish heraldic lions and gold braid rings on navy blue cuffs. Rank titles are in Finnish/Swedish. The Finnish Coast Guard *(Merivartiosto/Sjöbevakning)* forms part of the Interior Ministry. Personnel wear naval uniforms and insignia with Captain *(Kommodori/Kommodor)* as the highest rank.

a: *Amiraali/Amiral*, Admiral *(Chief of Defence Staff)* **b:** *Vara-amiraali/Viceamiral*, Vice Admiral *(Commander, Navy)*
c: *Kontra-amiraali/Konteramiral*, Rear Admiral **d:** *Lippueamiraali/Flottiljamiral*, Commodore **e:** *Kommodori/Kommodor*, Captain
f: *Komentaja/Kommendör*, Commander **g:** *Komentajakapteeni/Kommendörkapten*, Lieutenant Commander
h: *Kapteeniluutnantti/Kaptenlöjtnant*, Lieutenant **i:** *Yliluutnantti/Premiärlöjtnant*, (Senior) Sub Lieutenant **j:** *Luutnantti/Löjtnant*, Sub Lieutenant
k: *Aliluutnantti/Underlöjtnant*, Acting Sub Lieutenant

France (Marine Nationale)

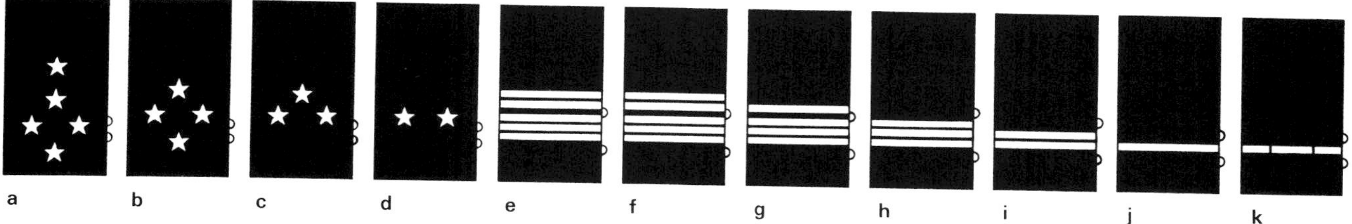

Silver metal stars and gold braid rings on very dark blue cloth cuffs, brass buttons; a Commander (f) has silver braid second and fourth rings, a Midshipman (k) a gold braid ring with two mid-blue 'breaks'. Rank titles are in French.

a: *Amiral*, Admiral (Chief of Naval Staff) **b:** *Vice-amiral d'escadre*, Vice Admiral **c:** *Vice-amiral*, Rear Admiral **d:** *Contre-amiral*, Commodore
e: *Capitaine de vaisseau*, Captain **f:** *Capitaine de frégate*, Commander **g:** *Capitaine de corvette*, Lieutenant Commander
h: *Lieutenant de vaisseau*, Lieutenant **i:** *Enseigne de vaisseau de 1ère (première) classe*, Sub Lieutenant
j: *Enseigne de vaisseau de 2e (deuxième) classe*, Acting Sub Lieutenant **k:** *Aspirant*, Midshipman

Gabon (Marine Gabonaise)

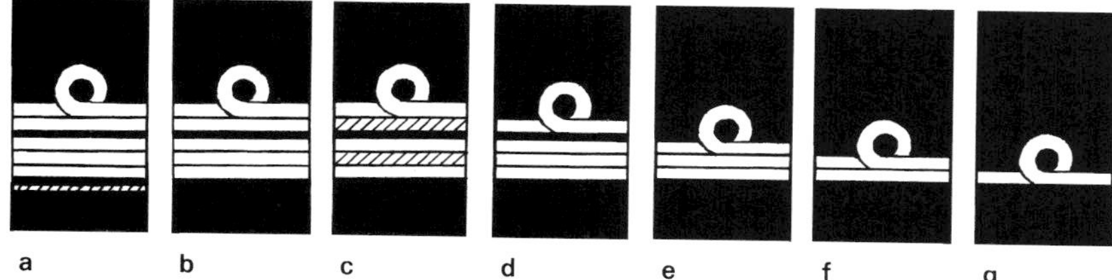

Gold braid rings with 'curl' on very dark blue cloth cuffs; a Commodore (a) has a silver braid bottom ring, a Commander (c) silver braid second and fourth rings. Rank titles are in French.

a: *Capitaine de vaisseau major*, Commodore *(Chief of Naval Staff)* **b:** *Capitaine de vaisseau*, Captain **c:** *Capitaine de frégate*, Commander
d: *Capitaine de corvette*, Lieutenant Commander **e:** *Lieutenant de vaisseau*, Lieutenant **f:** *Enseigne de vaisseau de 1ère (première) classe*, Sub Lieutenant
g: *Enseigne de vaisseau de 2e (deuxième) classe*, Acting Sub Lieutenant

Georgia (Sak'art'velos samkhedro-sazghvao dzalebi)

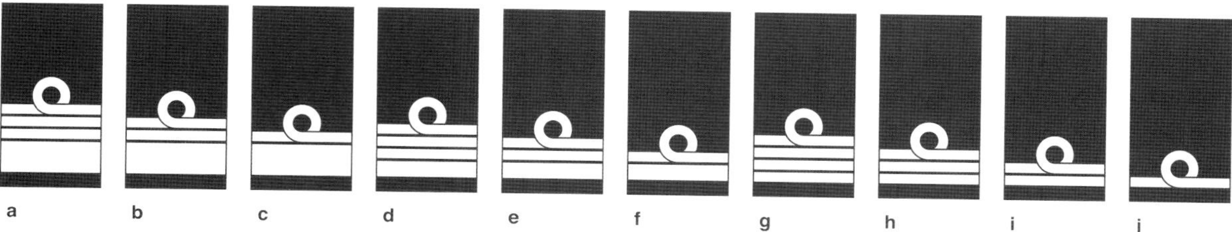

Gold braid rings with 'curl' on very dark blue cloth cuffs. Rank titles are in Georgian written here in romanised script. The Georgian Border Guard includes a small Coast Guard.

a: *Admirali*, Vice-Admiral *(rank not currently held)* **b:** *Vits'e admirali*, Rear Admiral *(rank not currently held)*
c: *Kontr-admirali*, Commodore *(rank not currently held)* **d:** *1 (Pirveli) rangis kapitani*, Captain *(Commander, Navy)*
e: *2 (Meore) rangis kapitani*, Commander **f:** *3 (Mesame) rangis kapitani*, Lieutenant Commander **g:** *Kapitani-leytenanti*, Lieutenant
h: *Up'rosi leytenanti*, (Senior) Sub Lieutenant **i:** *Leytenanti*, Sub Lieutenant **j:** *Michmani-leytenanti*, Acting Sub Lieutenant

Germany (Deutsche Marine)

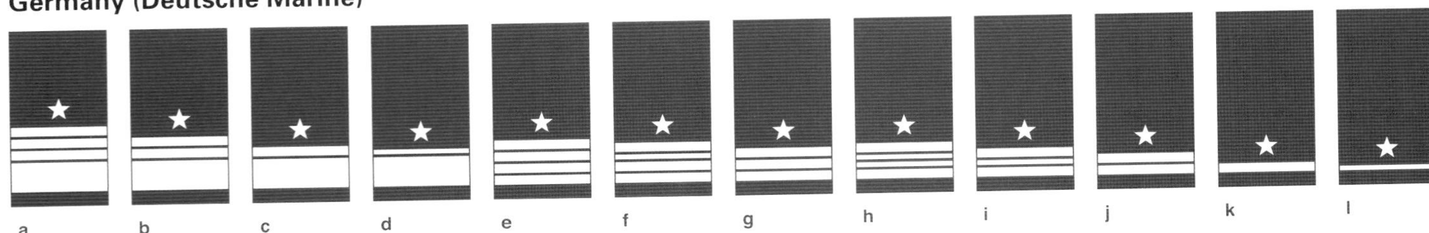

Gold wire stars and gold braid rings on very dark blue cloth cuffs. Rank titles are in German.
a: *Admiral*, Admiral *(rank not currently held)* **b**: *Vizeadmiral*, Vice Admiral *(Naval Inspector)* **c**: *Konteradmiral*, Rear Admiral
d: *Flottillenadmiral*, Commodore **e**: *Kapitän zur See*, Captain **f**: *Fregattenkapitän*, Commander **g**: *Korvettenkapitän*, Lieutenant Commander
h: *Stabskapitänleutnant*, (Senior) Lieutenant **i**: *Kapitänleutnant*, Lieutenant **j**: *Oberleutnant zur See*, Sub Lieutenant
k: *Leutnant zur See*, Acting Sub Lieutenant **l**: *Oberfähnrich zur See*, Midshipman

Germany Coast Guard (Küstenwache - Bundespolizeiamt See)

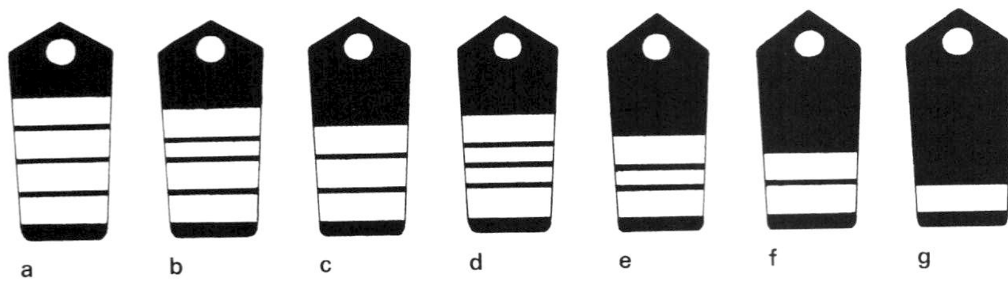

Gold braid rings on dark blue cloth shoulder-straps. Rank titles are in German.
a: *Polizeidirektor*, Captain *(Director, Coast Guard)* **b**: *Polizeioberrat*, Commander **c**: *Polizeirat*, Lieutenant Commander
d: *1. (Erster) Polizeihauptkommissar*, (Senior) Lieutenant **e**: *Polizeihauptkommissar*, Lieutenant **f**: *Polizeioberkommissar*, Sub Lieutenant
g: *Polizeikommissar*, Acting Sub Lieutenant

Ghana

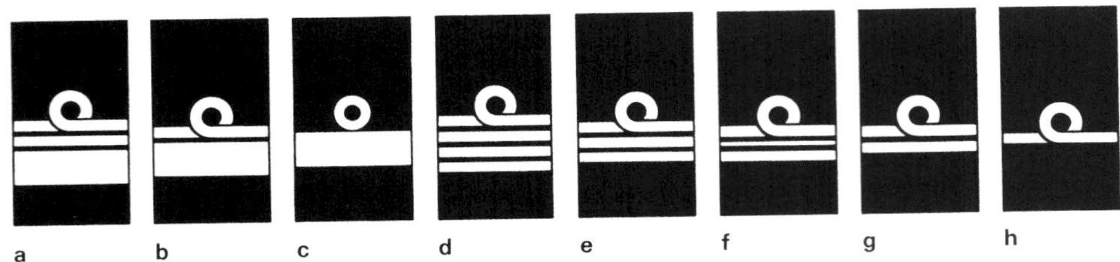

Gold braid rings with 'curl' on very dark blue cloth cuffs. British Royal Navy rank titles are used.
a: Vice Admiral *(rank not currently held)* **b**: Rear Admiral *(Chief of Naval Staff)* **c**: Commodore **d**: Captain **e**: Commander **f**: Lieutenant Commander
g: Lieutenant **h**: Sub Lieutenant

Greece (Hellenic Navy) (Elliniko Polemiko Nautiko)

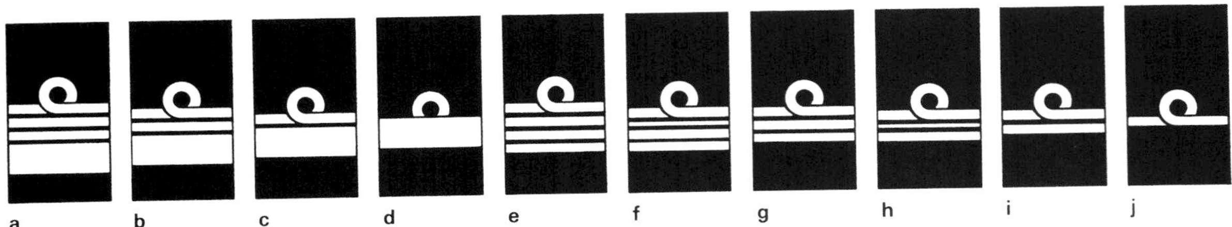

Gold braid rings with 'curl' on very dark blue cloth cuffs. Rank titles are in romanised Greek.
a: *Navarchos*, Admiral *(Honorary Chief of Naval Staff)* **b**: *Antinavarchos*, Vice Admiral *(Chief of Naval Staff)* **c**: *Iponavarchos*, Rear Admiral
d: *Archiploiarchos*, Commodore **e**: *Ploiarchos*, Captain **f**: *Antiploiarchos*, Commander **g**: *Plotarchis*, Lieutenant Commander
h: *Ipoploiarchos*, Lieutenant **i**: *Antipoploiarchos*, Sub Lieutenant **j**: *Simaioforos*, Acting Sub Lieutenant

Greece (Hellenic Coast Guard) (Limenikon Soma)

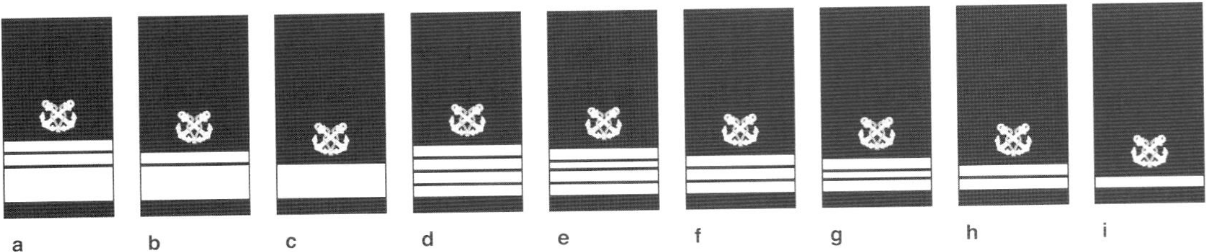

Gold wire crossed anchors and gold braid rings on very dark blue cloth cuffs. Hellenic Navy rank titles are used and written in romanised Greek.
a: *Antinavarchos*, Vice Admiral *(Commandant, Coast Guard)* **b**: *Iponavarchos*, Rear Admiral **c**: *Archiploiarchos*, Commodore **d**: *Ploiarchos*, Captain
e: *Antiploiarchos*, Commander **f**: *Plotarchis*, Lieutenant Commander **g**: *Ipoploiarchos*, Lieutenant **h**: *Antipoploiarchos*, Sub Lieutenant
i: *Simaioforos*, Acting Sub Lieutenant

Guatemala (Fuerza de Mar de Guatemala)

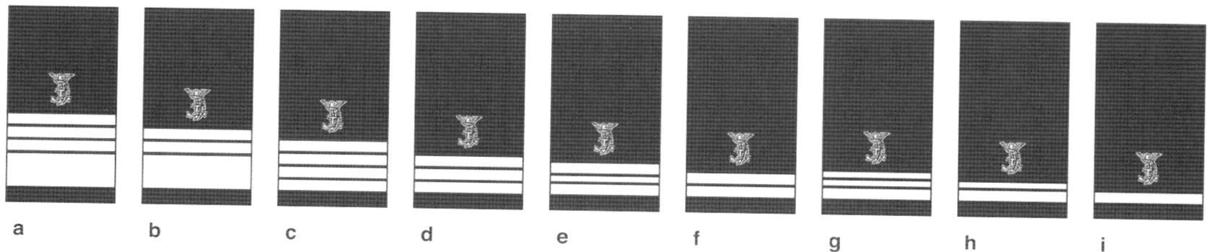

Gold wire Quetzal bird and anchor and gold braid rings on black cloth cuffs. Rank titles are in Spanish.
a: *Almirante*, Vice Admiral *(rank not currently held)* **b**: *Vicealmirante*, Rear Admiral *(rank not currently held)*
c: *Capitán de Navío*, Captain *(Commanding Officer, Navy)* **d**: *Capitán de Fragata*, Commander **e**: *Capitán de Corbeta*, Lieutenant Commander
f: *Teniente de Navío*, (Senior) Lieutenant **g**: *Teniente de Fragata*, Lieutenant **h**: *Alférez de Navío*, Sub Lieutenant
i: *Alférez de Fragata*, Acting Sub Lieutenant

Guinea (Marine de Guinée)

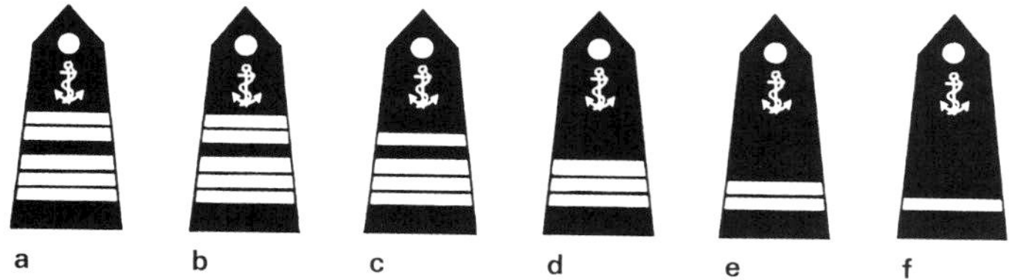

Gold wire anchors and gold braid rings on very dark blue cloth shoulder-straps; a Commander (b) has silver braid second and fourth rings; brass buttons. Rank titles are in French.
a: *Capitaine de vaisseau*, Captain *(Chief of Naval Staff)* **b**: *Capitaine de frégate*, Commander **c**: *Capitaine de corvette*, Lieutenant Commander
d: *Lieutenant de vaisseau*, Lieutenant **e**: *Enseigne de vaisseau 1ère (première) classe*, Sub Lieutenant
f: *Enseigne de vaisseau de 2e (deuxième) classe*, Acting Sub Lieutenant

Guinea-Bissau (Marinha de Guerra de Guiné-Bissau)

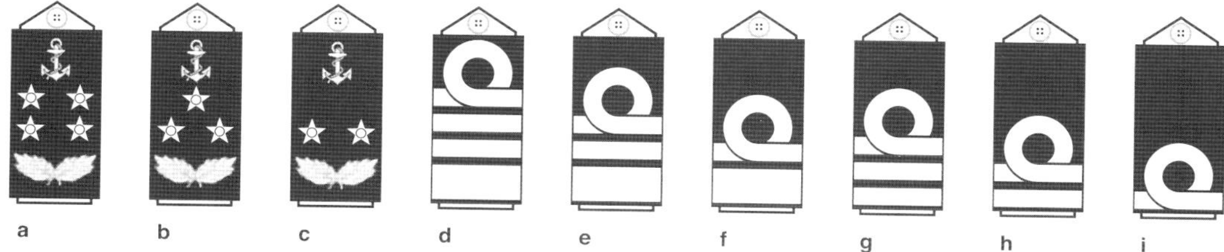

Gold anchors, stars, wreaths and rings on dark blue cloth shoulder-loops on white cloth shoulder-straps; white bone buttons. Rank titles are in Portuguese.
a: *Almirante*, Admiral *(rank not currently held)* **b**: *Vice-Almirante*, Vice Admiral *(rank not currently held)*
c: *Contra-Almirante*, Rear Admiral *(Commander, Navy)* **d**: *Capitão-de-Mar-e-Guerra*, Captain **e**: *Capitão-de-Fragata*, Commander
f: *Capitão-tenente*, Lieutenant Commander **g**: *Primeiro-tenente*, Lieutenant **h**: *Segundo-tenente*, Sub Lieutenant **i**: *Subtenente*, Acting Sub Lieutenant

Honduras (Fuerza Naval de Honduras)

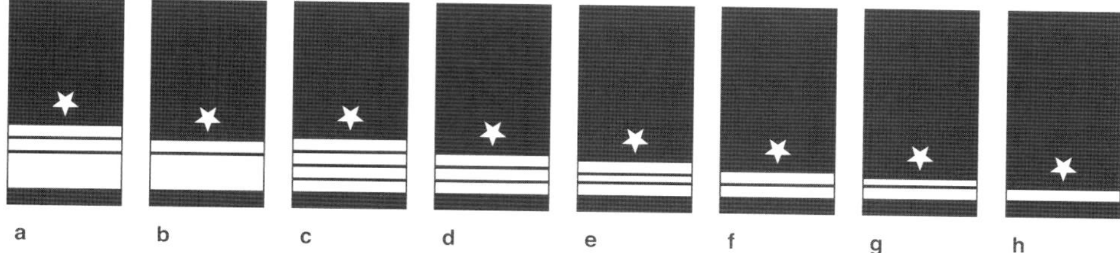

Gold wire stars and gold braid rings on very dark blue cuffs. Rank titles are in Spanish.
a: *Vicealmirante*, Admiral **b**: *Contraalmirante*, Rear Admiral **c**: *Capitán de Navío*, Captain *(Commanding Officer, Navy)*
d: *Capitán de Fragata*, Commander **e**: *Capitán de Corbeta*, Lieutenant Commander **f**: *Teniente de Navío*, Lieutenant
g: *Teniente de Fragata*, Sub Lieutenant **h**: *Alférez de Fragata*, Acting Sub Lieutenant

Hong Kong (Marine Police Region)

Silver-plated metal crossed tipstaves, wreaths, orchid-tree flowers in wreaths, Bath stars, bar, HKP shoulder-titles and buttons on dark blue cloth shoulder-straps. British Police Service rank titles are used.
a: *Assistant Commissioner*, Commodore *(C-in-C Marine Region)* **b**: *Chief Superintendent*, Captain **c**: *Senior Superintendent*, Commander
d: *Superintendent*, Lieutenant Commander **e**: *Chief Inspector*, Lieutenant **f**: *Senior Inspector*, (Senior) Sub Lieutenant **g**: *Inspector*, Sub Lieutenant
h: *Probationary Inspector*, Acting Sub Lieutenant

Iceland Coast Guard (Landhelgisgæslan)

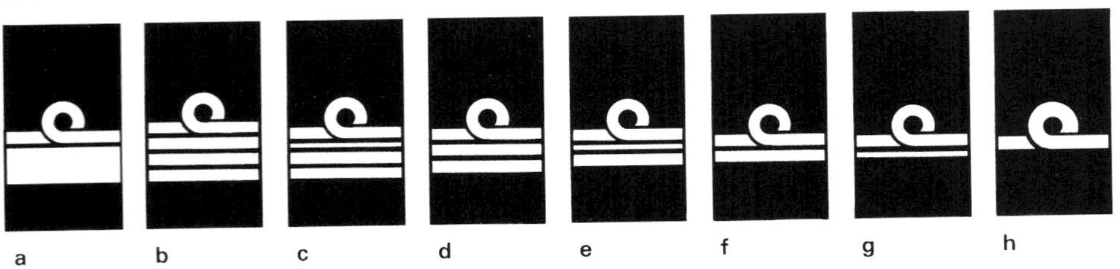

Gold braid rings with 'curl' on black cloth shoulder-straps. Rank titles are in Icelandic.
a: *Forstjóri Lanhelgisgæslunnar*, Rear Admiral *(Director-General, Coast Guard)* **b**: *Yfirmaður Gæsluframkvæmda*, Captain
c: *Skipherra (24 years seniority)*, Commander **d**: *Skipherra*, Lieutenant Commander **e**: *Yfirstýrimaður*, Lieutenant **f**: *1. Stýrimaður*, Sub Lieutenant
g: *2. Stýrimaður (2 years seniority)*, (Senior) Acting Sub Lieutenant **h**: *2. Stýrimaður*, Acting Sub Lieutenant

India (Bharatiya Nau Sena)

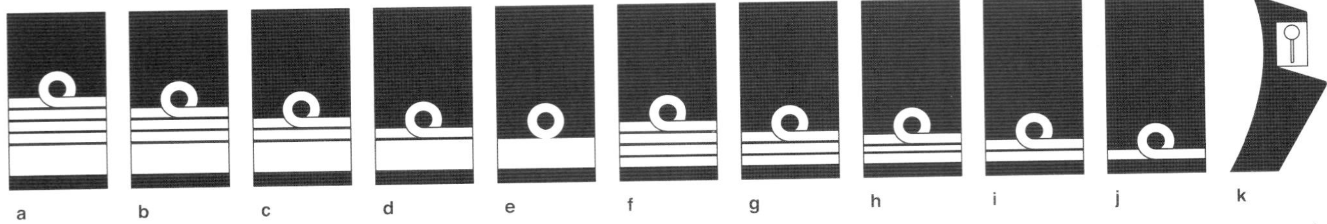

Gold braid rings with 'curl' on very dark blue cloth cuffs; brass button and white cord on white cloth collar-patch (k). Royal Navy rank titles are used.
a: Admiral of the Fleet *(honorary rank not currently held)* **b**: Admiral *(Chief of Naval Staff)* **c**: Vice Admiral **d**: Rear Admiral **e**: Commodore **f**: Captain
g: Commander **h**: Lieutenant Commander **i**: Lieutenant **j**: Sub Lieutenant **k**: Midshipman

India Coast Guard (Bharatiya Thatrakshak)

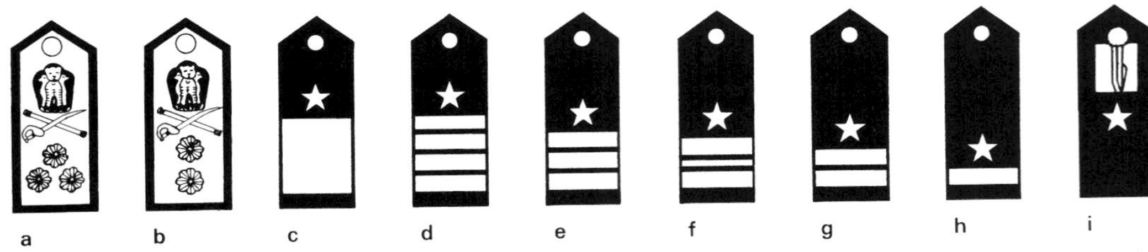

Gold wire 'Lions of Ashoka' on red cloth backing above silver wire crossed swords and scimitars and stars, all on gold braid shoulder-straps edged in dark blue cloth (a-b); gold wire stars and gold braid rings on very dark blue cloth shoulder-straps (c-h), brass button and white cord on white cloth collar-patch (i); brass buttons. Rank titles are in English.
a: *Director General*, Vice Admiral *(Director General, Coast Guard)* **b**: *Inspector General*, Rear Admiral
c: *Deputy Inspector General (3 years seniority)*, Commodore **d**: *Deputy Inspector General*, Captain **e**: *Commandant*, Commander
f: *Deputy Commandant*, Lieutenant Commander **g**: *Assistant Commandant*, Lieutenant
h: *Assistant Commandant (under training after completion of Phase III afloat training)*, Sub Lieutenant
i: *Assistant Commandant (under training after completion of Phase II afloat training)*, Midshipman

Indonesia (Tentara Nasional Indonesia - Tentara Laut)

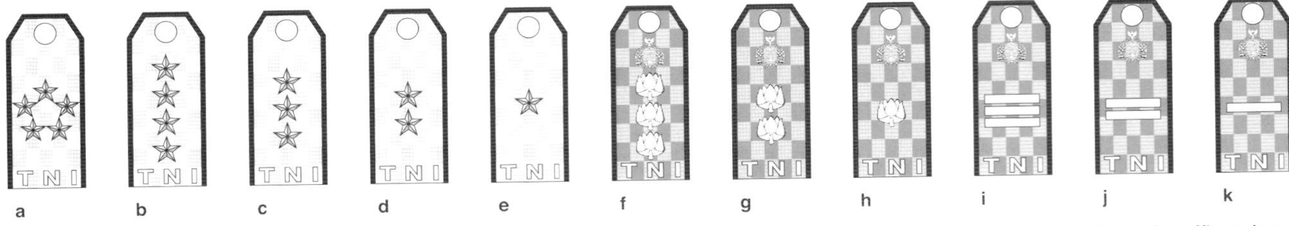

Gold wire stars, flowers, bars, Navy badge and Armed Forces title on gold braid (a–e) or brown braid shoulder-straps piped in red for officers in command positions. Gold buttons. Rank titles are in Indonesian. Indonesia maintains a Coast Guard.
a: *Laksamana Besar*, Admiral of the Fleet *(wartime rank not currently held)* **b**: *Laksamana, Admiral (Chief of Navy Staff)*
c: *Laksamana Madya*, Vice Admiral **d**: *Laksamana Muda*, Rear Admiral **e**: *Laksamana Pertama*, Commodore **f**: *Kolonel*, Captain
g: *Letnan Kolonel*, Commander **h**: *Mayor*, Lieutenant Commander **i**: *Kapten*, Lieutenant **j**: *Letnan Satu*, Sub Lieutenant
k: *Letnan Dua*, Acting Sub Lieutenant

Iran

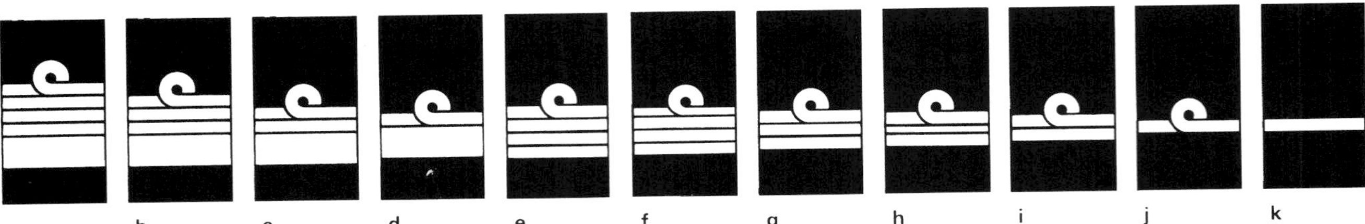

Gold braid rings with 'curl' on navy blue cloth cuffs. Rank titles are in romanised Farsi.
a: *Darybod*, Admiral *(rank not currently held)* **b**: *Darysaklar*, Vice Admiral *(rank not currently held)* **c**: *Daryban*, Rear Admiral *(Commander-in-Chief)*
d: *Darydar*, Commodore **e**: *Nakhoda Yekom*, Captain **f**: *Nakhoda Dovom*, Commander **g**: *Nakhoda Sevom*, Lieutenant Commander
h: *Navsarvan*, Lieutenant **i**: *Navban Yekom*, Sub Lieutenant **j**: *Navban Dovom*, Acting Sub Lieutenant **k**: *Navban Sevom*, Midshipman

Iraq

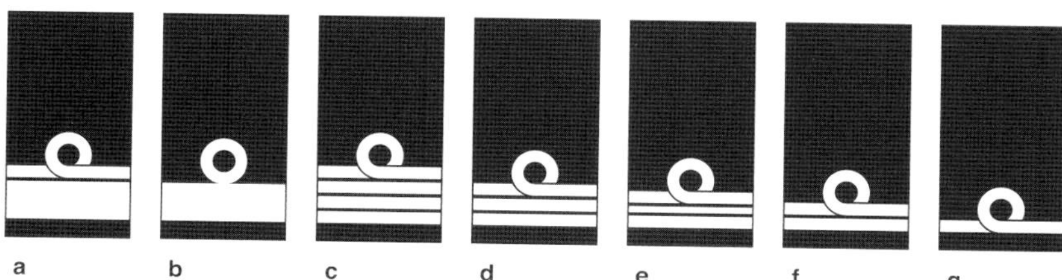

Gold braid rings with 'curl' on very dark blue cloth cuffs. Arabic Iraqi Army rank titles are used and written here in romanised script.
a: *Liwā'*, Rear Admiral *(Commander, Navy)* **b:** *'Amid*, Commodore **c:** *'Aqīd*, Captain **d:** *Muqaddam*, Commander **e:** *Rā'id*, Lieutenant Commander **f:** *Naqīb*, Lieutenant **g:** *Mulāzim Awwal*, Sub Lieutenant

Ireland (An Seirbhís Chabhlaigh na hÉireann)

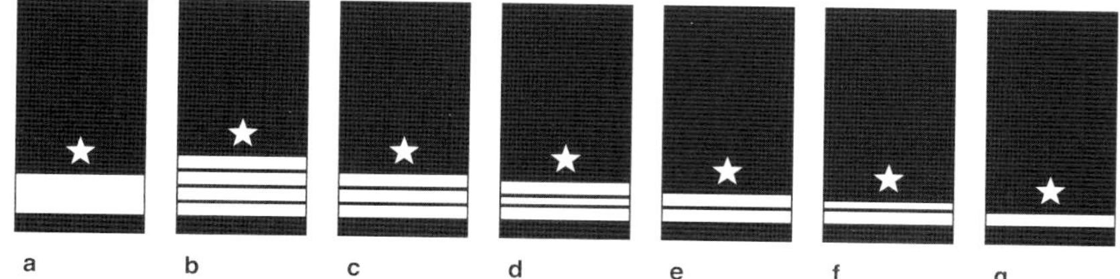

Gold wire stars and gold braid rings on very dark blue cuffs. Rank titles are in Irish/English.
a: *Ceannasoir/Commodore*, Commodore *(Flag Officer Commanding Naval Service)* **b:** *Captaen/Captain*, Captain **c:** *Ceannasai/Commander*, Commander **d:** *Lefteanant-Ceannasai/Lieutenant Commander*, Lieutenant Commander **e:** *Lefteanant/Lieutenant*, Lieutenant **f:** *Fo-Lefteanant/Sub Lieutenant*, Sub Lieutenant **g:** *Meirgire/Ensign*, Acting Sub Lieutenant

Israel (Heyl Hayam)

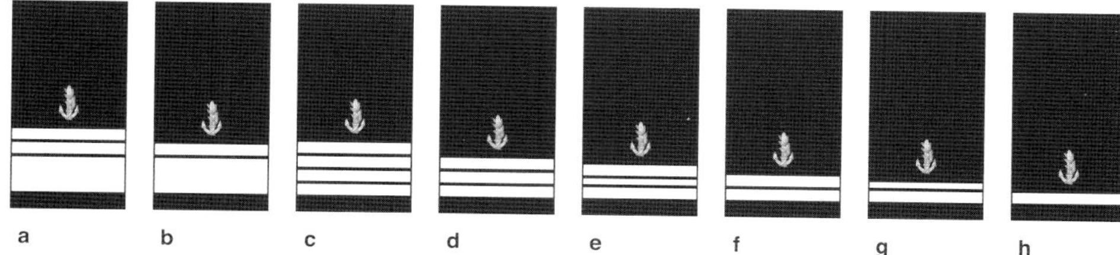

Gold wire anchor and leaf on very dark blue cloth cuffs. Israeli Army rank titles are used and the Hebrew is written here in romanised script.
a: *Alúf*, Vice Admiral *(Commander of the Navy)* **b:** *Tat alúf*, Rear Admiral **c:** *Alúf mishné*, Captain **d:** *Sgan alúf*, Commander **e:** *Rav séren*, Lieutenant Commander **f:** *Séren*, Lieutenant **g:** *Ségen*, Sub Lieutenant **h:** *Ségen mishné*, Acting Sub Lieutenant

Italy (Marina Militare)

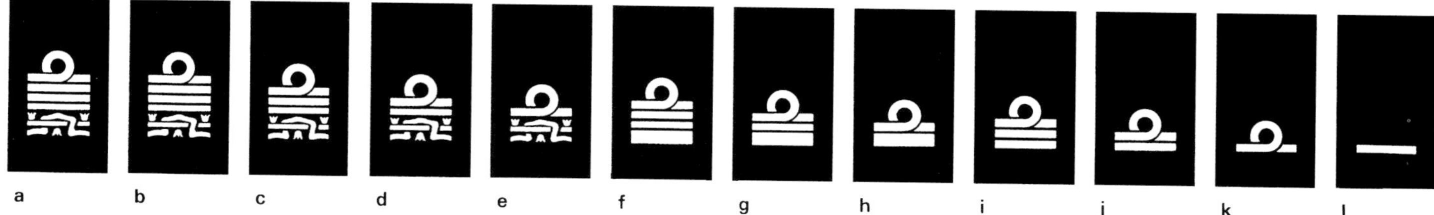

Gold braid bars with 'curl' and 'Greca' design on very dark blue cloth cuffs; upper and lower edges of top bar (but not the 'curl') edged in red cloth (b). Rank titles are in Italian. The Italian Coast Guard (Capitanerie di Porto - Guardia Costiera) forms part of the Navy. Personnel wear naval uniforms and insignia with the Commandant holding the rank of Vice-Admiral (Ammiraglio di Squadra).
a: *Ammiraglio*, Admiral *(Chief of Defence Staff)* **b:** *Ammiraglio di Squadra con Incarichi Speciali*, (Senior) Vice-Admiral *(Chief of Naval Staff)* **c:** *Ammiraglio di Squadra*, Vice-Admiral **d:** *Ammiraglio di Divisione*, Rear Admiral **e:** *Contrammiraglio*, Commodore **f:** *Capitano di Vascello*, Captain **g:** *Capitano di Fregata*, Commander **h:** *Capitano di Corvetta*, Lieutenant Commander **i:** *Tenente di Vascello*, Lieutenant **j:** *Sottotenente di Vascello*, Sub Lieutenant **k:** *Guardiamarina*, Acting Sub Lieutenant **l:** *Aspirante Guardiamarina*, Midshipman

Jamaica (Defence Force Coast Guard)

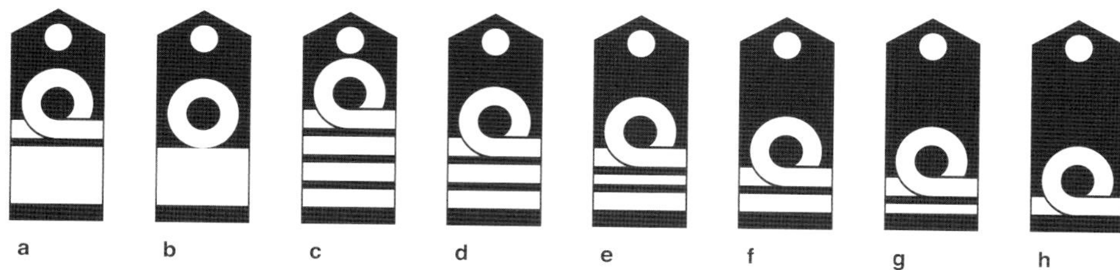

Gold braid rings with 'curl' on very dark blue cloth shoulder-straps. Rank titles are in English.
a: *Rear Admiral*, Rear Admiral *(rank not currently held)* **b:** *Commodore*, Commodore *(rank not currently held)* **c:** *Captain*, Captain *(Inspector General, JDF)* **d:** *Commander*, Commander *(Commander, Coast Guard)* **e:** *Lieutenant Commander*, Lieutenant Commander **f:** *Lieutenant*, Lieutenant **g:** *Junior Lieutenant*, Sub Lieutenant **h:** *Sub Lieutenant*, Acting Sub Lieutenant

Japan (Maritime Self Defence Force) (Nihon Kaijō Jieitai)

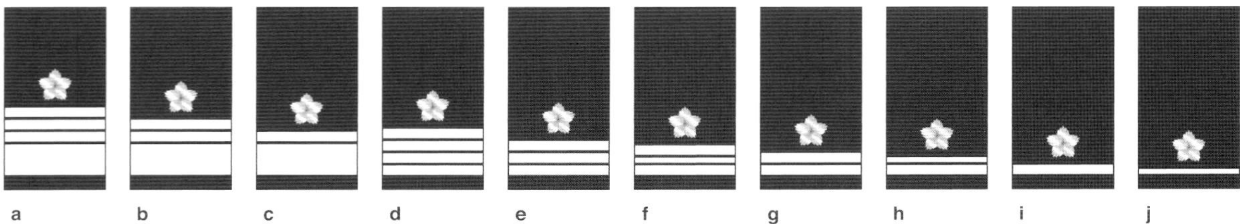

Gold wire cherry blossoms and gold braid rings on very dark blue cloth cuffs. Rank titles are in romanised Japanese.
a: *Kai-jō Baku-ryō-chō*, Admiral *(Maritime Chief of Staff)* **b**: *Kai-shō*, Vice Admiral **c**: *Kai-shō-ho*, Rear Admiral **d**: *1 (Ittō) Kai-sa*, Captain
e: *2 (Nitō) Kai-sa*, Commander **f**: *3 (Santō) Kai-sa*, Lieutenant Commander **g**: *1 (Ittō) Kai-i*, Lieutenant **h**: *2 (Nitō) Kai-i*, Sub Lieutenant
i: *3 (Santō) Kai-i*, Acting Sub Lieutenant **j**: *Jun Kai-i*, Warrant Officer

Japan (Coast Guard) (Kaijō Ho'an-chō)

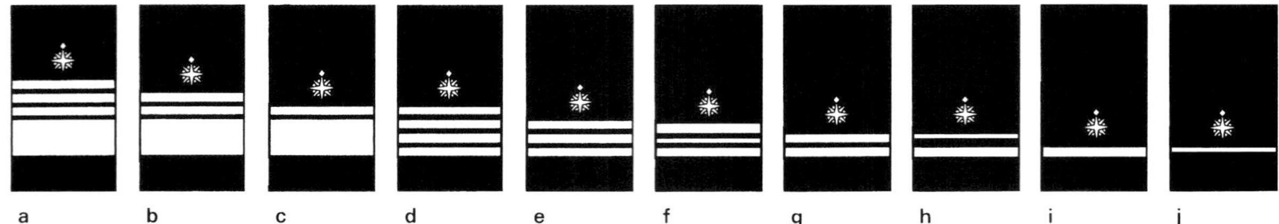

Gold wire compass devices and gold braid rings on very dark blue cloth cuffs. Japanese Navy rank titles are used and written in romanised Japanese.
a: *Ryō-chō*, Admiral *(Commandant, Coast Guard)* **b**: *Kai-shō*, Vice Admiral **c**: *Kai-shō-ho*, Rear Admiral **d**: *1 (Ittō) Kai-sa*, Captain
e: *2 (Nitō) Kai-sa*, Commander **f**: *3 (Santō) Kai-sa*, Lieutenant Commander **g**: *1 (Ittō) Kai-i*, Lieutenant **h**: *2 (Nitō) Kai-i*, Sub Lieutenant
i: *3 (Santō) Kai-i*, Acting Sub Lieutenant **j**: *Jun Kai-i*, Warrant Officer

Jordan (Royal Jordan Naval Force)

Brass crowns, stars and titles on dark blue cloth shoulder-straps; brass buttons. Jordanian Army rank titles are used and written here in romanised Arabic.
a: *Liwā'*, Rear Admiral *(Commander, RJNF)* **b**: *'Amid*, Commodore **c**: *'Aqīd*, Captain **d**: *Muqaddam*, Commander **e**: *Rā'id*, Lieutenant Commander
f: *Naqīb*, Lieutenant **g**: *Mulāzim Awwal*, Sub Lieutenant **h**: *Mulāzim*, Acting Sub Lieutenant

Kazakhstan

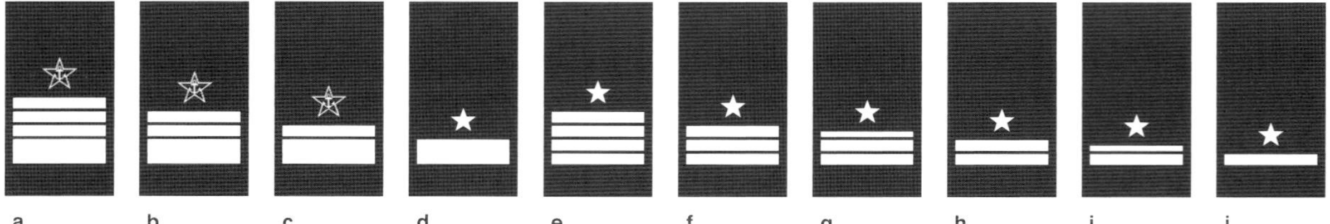

Black cloth stars edged in gold wire with a gold wire anchor, gold stars and gold braid bars on black cloth cuffs. Rank titles are in romanised Russian.
a: *Admiral*, Admiral *(rank not currently held)* **b**: *Vitse-admiral*, Vice Admiral *(rank not currently held)*
c: *Kontr-admiral*, Navy Rear Admiral *(Commander-in-Chief, Navy)* **d**: *Kapitan 1 (pervogo) ranga*, Captain **e**: *Kapitan 2 (vtorogo) ranga*, Commander
f: *Kapitan 3 (tretyego) ranga*, Lieutenant Commander **g**: *Kapitan-leytenant*, Lieutenant **h**: *Starshyi leytenant*, (Senior) Sub Lieutenant
i: *Leytenant*, Sub Lieutenant **j**: *Mladshiy leytenant*, Acting Sub Lieutenant

Kenya

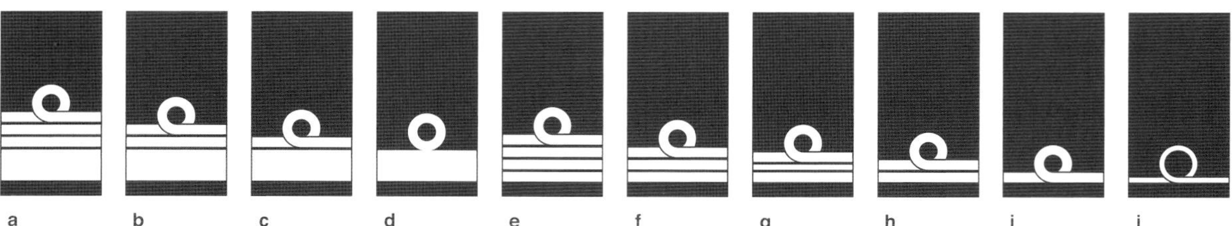

Gold braid rings with 'curl' on very dark blue cloth cuffs. Kenyan Army rank titles are used and written in English.
a: *General*, Admiral *(rank not currently held)* **b**: *Lieutenant General*, Vice Admiral *(rank not currently held)*
c: *Major General*, Rear Admiral *(Commander, Navy)* **d**: *Brigadier*, Commodore **e**: *Colonel*, Captain **f**: *Lieutenant Colonel*, Commander
g: *Major*, Lieutenant Commander **h**: *Captain*, Lieutenant **i**: *Lieutenant*, Sub Lieutenant **j**: *2nd (Second) Lieutenant*, Acting Sub Lieutenant

Korea, North (People's Democratic Republic)

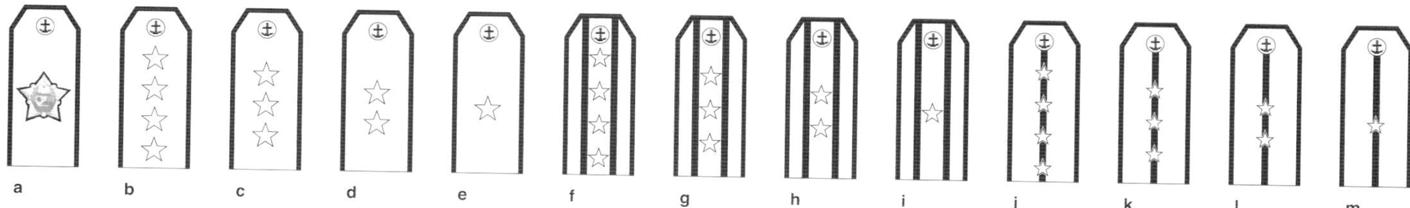

A large silver metal star with a coloured enamel boss and black underlay (a); silver metal stars on gold braid shoulder-straps with black edging and centre-stripes; brass buttons. North Korean Army rank titles are used and written here in romanised Korean.
a: *Cha-su*, Admiral of the Fleet **b:** *Tae-jang*, Admiral **c:** *Sang-jang*, Vice Admiral **d:** *Chung-jang*, Rear Admiral **e:** *So-jang*, Commodore
f: *Tae-chwa*, (Senior) Captain **g:** *Sang-chwa*, Captain **h:** *Chung-chwa*, Commander **i:** *So-chwa*, Lieutenant Commander **j:** *Tae-wi*, (Senior) Lieutenant
k: *Sang-wi*, Lieutenant **l:** *Chung-wi*, Sub Lieutenant **m:** *So-wi*, Acting Sub Lieutenant

Korea (Republic of Korea Navy) (Dee-han-min-guk Hae-gun)

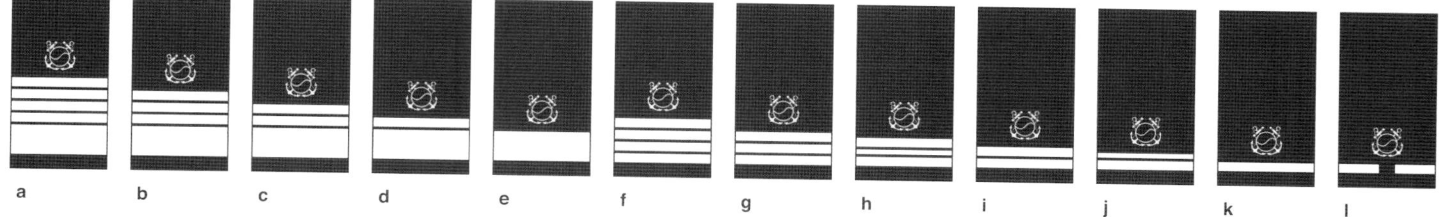

Gold wire Yin-Yang device on crossed anchors and gold braid rings on very dark blue cloth cuffs. Republic of Korea Army rank titles are used and written here in romanised Korean. The Republic of Korea Coast Guard (Haeyang-gyeongchal-cheong) forms part of the Armed Forces and is commanded by a Director. Personnel wear blue police uniforms and insignia.
a: *Won-su*, Admiral of the Fleet *(wartime rank not currently held)* **b:** *Tae-jang*, Admiral *(Chief of Naval Operations)* **c:** *Chung-jang*, Vice Admiral
d: *So-jang*, Rear Admiral **e:** *Chun-jang*, Commodore **f:** *Tae-ryong*, Captain **g:** *Chung-ryong*, Commander **h:** *So-ryong*, Lieutenant Commander
i: *Tae-wi*, Lieutenant **j:** *Chung-wi*, Sub Lieutenant **k:** *So-wi*, Acting Sub Lieutenant **l:** *Jun-wi*, Warrant Officer

Kuwait (Kuwaiti Naval Force)

Gold stars, crowns and swords and red 'staff' rings on very dark blue cloth shoulder-straps; brass buttons. Kuwaiti Army rank titles are used and written here in romanised Arabic.
a: *Liwā'*, Rear Admiral *(Chief of KNF)* **b:** *'Amid*, Commodore **c:** *'Aqīd*, Captain **d:** *Muqaddam*, Commander **e:** *Rā'id*, Lieutenant Commander
f: *Naqīb*, Lieutenant **g:** *Mulāzim Awwal*, Sub Lieutenant **h:** *Mulāzim*, Acting Sub Lieutenant

Latvia (Latvijas Jūras Spēki)

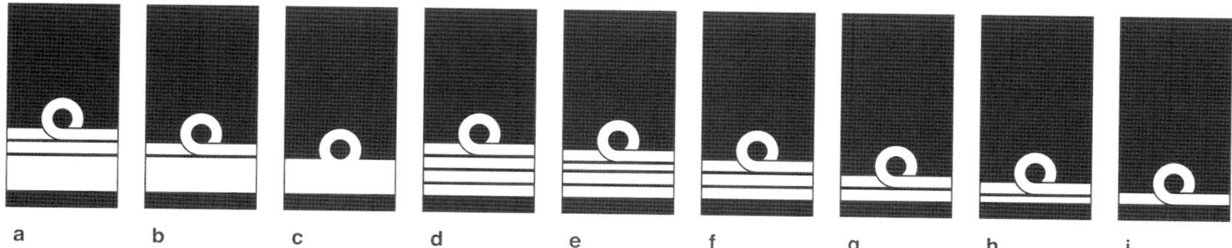

Gold braid rings with 'curl' on very dark blue cloth cuffs. Rank titles are in Latvian.
a: *Viceadmirālis*, Vice Admiral *(rank not currently held)* **b:** *Kontradmirālis*, Rear Admiral *(rank not currently held)*
c: *Flotiles admirālis*, Commodore *(rank not currently held)* **d:** *Jūras kapteinis*, Captain *(Commander-in-Chief, Naval Forces)*
e: *Komandkapteinis*, Commander **f:** *Komandleitnants*, Lieutenant Commander **g:** *Kapteiņleitnants*, Lieutenant **h:** *Virsleitnants*, Sub Lieutenant
i: *Leitnants*, Acting Sub Lieutenant

Lebanon (Al-Quwa'at al-bahriya al-Lubna'a)

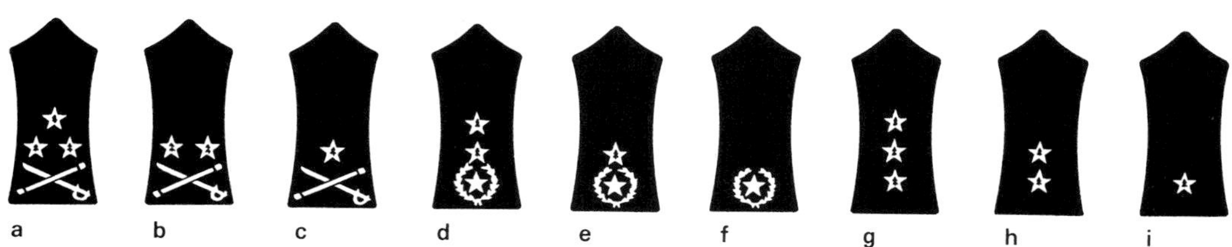

Gold stars, crossed swords and batons and wreaths on dark blue cloth shoulder-straps. Arabic Lebanese Army rank titles are used and written here in romanised script.
a: *'Imad*, Vice Admiral *(rank not currently held)* **b:** *Liwā'*, Rear Admiral *(Commander, Navy)* **c:** *'Amid*, Commodore **d:** *'Aqīd*, Captain
e: *Muqaddam*, Commander **f:** *Rā'id*, Lieutenant Commander **g:** *Ra'īs*, Lieutenant **h:** *Mulāzim Awwal*, Sub Lieutenant
i: *Mulāzim*, Acting Sub Lieutenant

Libya

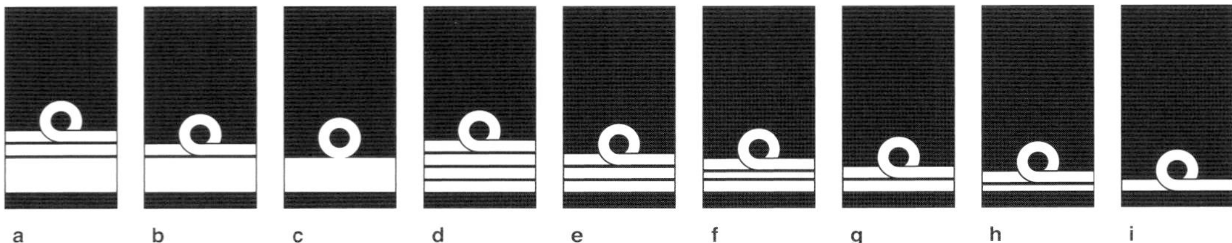

Gold braid rings with 'curl' on very dark blue cloth cuffs. Arabic Libyan Army rank titles are used and written here in romanised script.
a: *Farīq*, Vice Admiral *(rank not currently held)* **b**: *Liwā'*, Rear Admiral *(Chief of Naval Staff)* **c**: *'Amid*, Commodore **d**: *'Aqīd*, Captain
e: *Muqaddam*, Commander **f**: *Rā'id*, Lieutenant Commander **g**: *Naqīb*, Lieutenant **h**: *Mulāzim Awwal*, Sub Lieutenant
i: *Mulāzim*, Acting Sub Lieutenant

Lithuania (Karinės jūrų pajėgos)

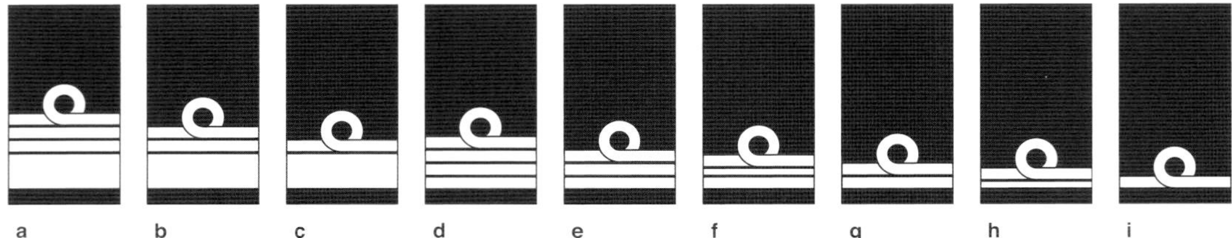

Gold braid rings with 'curl' on dark blue cloth cuffs. Rank titles are in Lithuanian.
a: *Viceadmirolas*, Vice Admiral *(rank not currently held)* **b**: *Kontradmirolas*, Rear Admiral *(rank not currently held)*
c: *Flotilės admirolas*, Commodore *(rank not currently held)* **d**: *Jūrų kapitonas*, Captain *(Commander, Naval Force)* **e**: *Komandoras*, Commander
f: *Komandoras leitenantas*, Lieutenant Commander **g**: *Kapitonas leitenantas*, Lieutenant **h**: *Vyresnysis leitenantas*, Sub Lieutenant
i: *Leitenantas*, Acting Sub Lieutenant

Madagascar

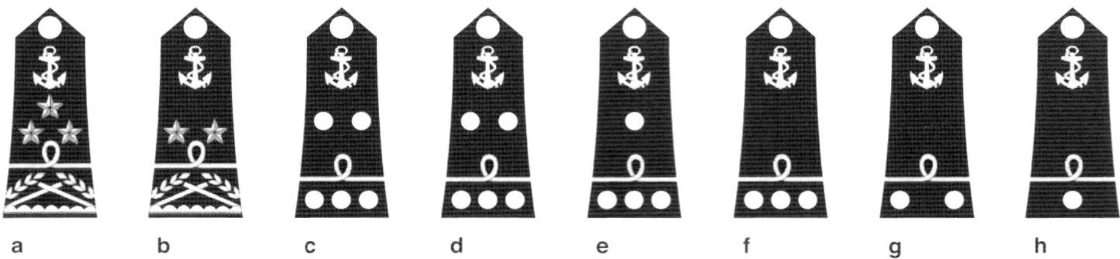

Gold anchors, stars, braids and discs on very dark blue cloth shoulder-straps; a Commander (d) has two silver discs immediately below the anchor; brass buttons. Rank titles are in French.
a: *Vice-amiral*, Rear Admiral **b**: *Contre-amiral*, Commodore *(Chief of Staff, Navy)* **c**: *Capitaine de vaisseau*, Captain **d**: *Capitaine de frégate*, Commander
e: *Capitaine de corvette*, Lieutenant Commander **f**: *Lieutenant de vaisseau*, Lieutenant **g**: *Enseigne de vaisseau de 1ère (première) classe*, Sub Lieutenant
h: *Enseigne de vaisseau de 2e (deuxième) classe*, Acting Sub Lieutenant

Malawi (Army Naval Detachment)

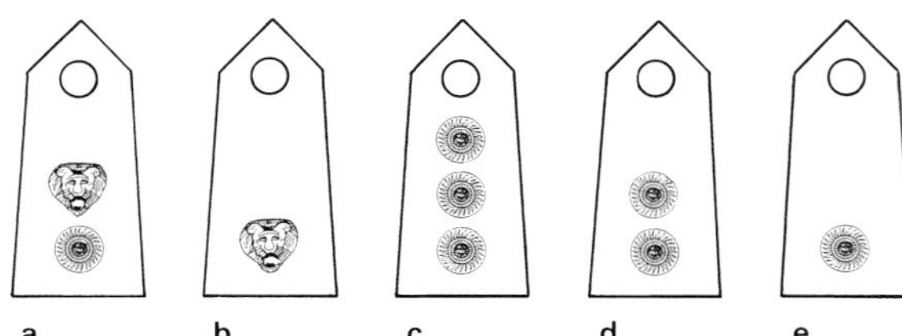

Red metal lion's heads and discs on very dark blue cloth backing on khaki cloth shoulder-straps; brown buttons. Malawi Army rank titles are used and written in English.
a: *Lieutenant Colonel*, Commander *(Commanding Officer, Naval Detachment)* **b**: *Major*, Lieutenant Commander **c**: *Captain*, Lieutenant
d: *Lieutenant*, Sub Lieutenant **e**: *Second Lieutenant*, Acting Sub Lieutenant

Malaysia - Royal Malaysian Navy (Tentera Laut DiRaja Malaysia)

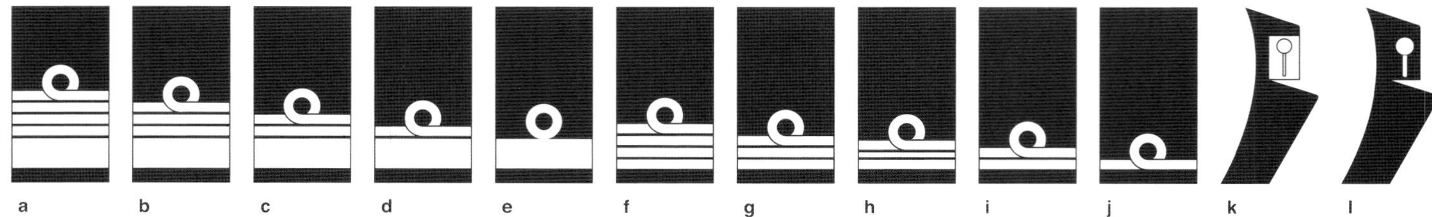

Gold braid rings with 'curl' on very dark blue cloth cuffs; brass buttons and white cords and white cloth collar-patch (l-m). Rank titles are in Malayan. The Malaysian Coast Guard – the Malaysian Maritime Enforcement Agency *(Agensi Penguatkuasaan Maritim Malaysia)* wears naval uniforms and insignia with a gold MMEA badge worn above gold braid rings without the 'curl'. The Director-General is an Admiral, RMN.
a: *Laksamana Armada Laut*, Admiral of the Fleet *(King, Malaysia, Sultan Mizan Zainal Abidin)*
b: *Laksamana*, Admiral *(Chief of Armed Forces and Chief of Navy)* **c**: *Laksamana Madya*, Vice Admiral **d**: *Laksamana Muda*, Rear Admiral
e: *Laksamana Pertama*, Commodore **f**: *Kapten*, Captain **g**: *Komander*, Commander **h**: *Leftenan Komander*, Lieutenant Commander
i: *Leftenan*, Lieutenant **j**: *Leftenan Madya, Sub Lieutenant & Leftenan Muda*, Acting Sub Lieutenant **k**: *Pegawai Kadet Kanan*, Midshipman
l: *Kadet*, Naval Cadet

Maldives (National Defence Force Coast Guard)

a b c d e f

Gold coats of arms, stars and rings on black cloth shoulder-straps with a white inner piping and gold outer piping. Army rank titles are used and written in English.
a: *Colonel*, Commander *(Director-General, Coast Guard)* **b:** *Lieutenant Colonel*, Commander **c:** *Major*, Lieutenant Commander **d:** *Captain*, Lieutenant
e: *First Lieutenant*, Sub Lieutenant **f:** *Lieutenant*, Acting Sub Lieutenant

Malta (Maritime Squadron, Armed Forces of Malta)

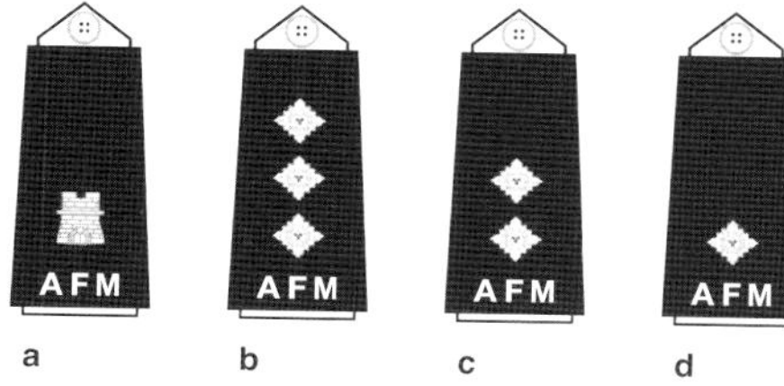

a b c d

White thread tower, stars and titles on dark blue shoulder-loops on white cotton shoulder-straps; white bone buttons. British Army rank titles are used.
a: *Major*, Lieutenant Commander *(Commanding Officer, Maritime Squadron)* **b:** *Captain*, Lieutenant **c:** *Lieutenant*, Sub Lieutenant
d: *2nd (Second) Lieutenant*, Acting Sub Lieutenant

Mauritania (Marine Mauritanienne)

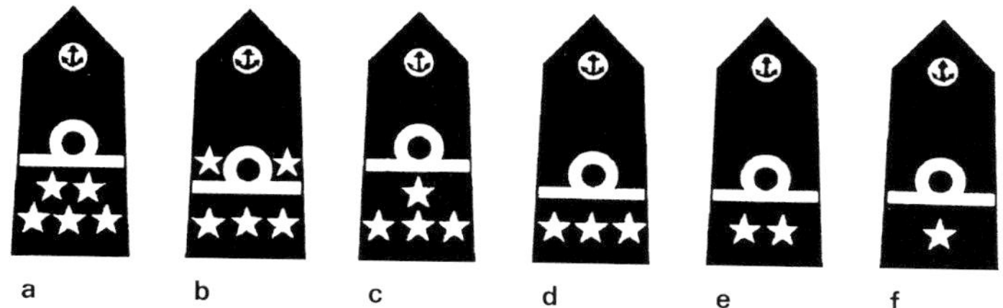

a b c d e f

Gold metal stars and gold braid rings on very dark blue cloth shoulder-straps; a Commander (b) has two silver metal stars above the braid ring; brass buttons. Arabic Mauritanian Army rank titles are used and written here in romanised script.
a: *'Aqīd*, Captain *(Chief of Naval Staff)* **b:** *Muqaddam*, Commander **c:** *Rā'id*, Lieutenant Commander **d:** *Naqīb*, Lieutenant
e: *Mulāzim Awwal*, Sub Lieutenant **f:** *Mulāzim Thāni*, Acting Sub Lieutenant

Mexico (Armada de México)

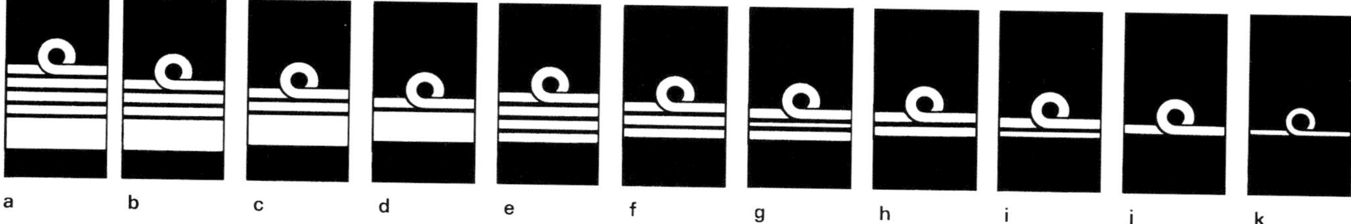

a b c d e f g h i j k

Gold braid rings with 'curl' on very dark blue cloth cuffs. Rank titles are in Spanish.
a: *Almirante, Secretario de Marina*, (Senior) Admiral *(Secretary of the Navy)* **b:** *Almirante*, Admiral *(Commander of the Navy)*
c: *Vicealmirante*, Rear Admiral **d:** *Contralmirante*, Commodore **e:** *Capitán de Navío*, Captain **f:** *Capitán de Fragata*, Commander
g: *Capitán de Corbeta*, Lieutenant Commander **h:** *Teniente de Navío*, (Senior) Lieutenant **i:** *Teniente de Fragata*, Lieutenant
j: *Teniente de Corbeta*, Sub Lieutenant **k:** *Guardiamarina*, Acting Sub Lieutenant

Montenegro (Ratna Mornarica)

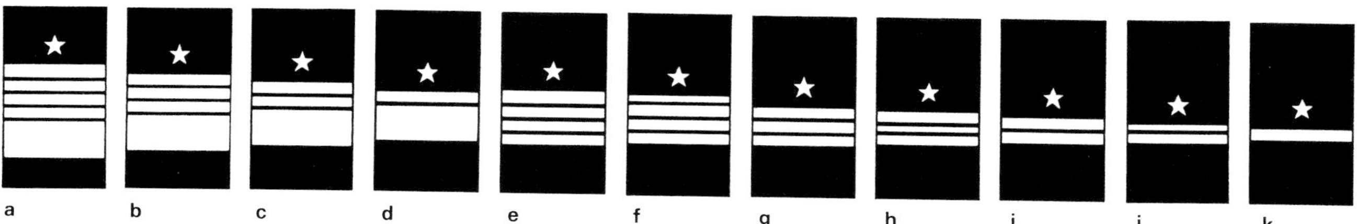

a b c d e f g h i j k

New rank insignia was prescribed in 2007 but former Serbian and Montenegrin Navy rank insignia are still being worn. Gold wire stars and gold braid rings on very dark blue cloth cuffs. Rank titles are in Serbian.
a: *Admiral flote*, Admiral *(rank not currently held)* **b:** *Admiral*, Vice Admiral *(rank not currently held)* **c:** *Viceadmiral*, Rear Admiral *(Chief of Defence Staff)*
d: *Kontraadmiral*, Commodore *(rank not currently held)* **e:** *Kapetan bojnog broda*, Captain *(Commander, Navy)* **f:** *Kapetan fregate*, Commander
g: *Kapetan korvete*, Lieutenant Commander **h:** *Poručnik bojnog broda*, (Senior) Lieutenant **i:** *Poručnik fregate*, Lieutenant
j: *Poručnik korvete*, Sub Lieutenant **k:** *Potporučnik*, Acting Sub Lieutenant

Morocco (Marine Royale Marocaine)

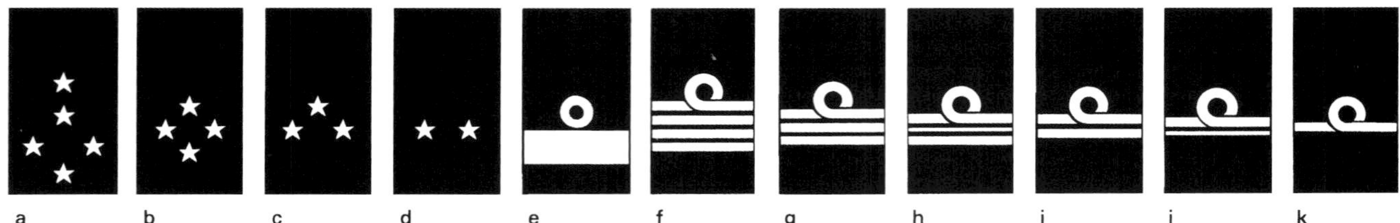

Silver metal stars and gold braid rings with 'curl' on very dark blue cloth cuffs; a Commander (f) has silver braid second and fourth rings, a Midshipman (k) a gold braid ring with two mid-blue 'breaks'. Rank titles are in French.
a: *Amiral*, Admiral *(rank not currently held)* **b**: *Amiral d'escadre*, Vice Admiral *(rank not currently held)*
c: *Vice-amiral*, Rear Admiral *(rank not currently held)* **d**: *Contre-amiral*, Commodore *(Inspector, Navy)* **e**: *Capitaine de vaisseau major*, (Senior) Captain
f: *Capitaine de vaisseau*, Captain **g**: *Capitaine de frégate*, Commander **h**: *Capitaine de corvette*, Lieutenant Commander
i: *Lieutenant de vaisseau*, Lieutenant **j**: *Enseigne de vaisseau de 1ère (première) classe*, Sub Lieutenant
k: *Enseigne de vaisseau de 2e (deuxième) classe*, Acting Sub Lieutenant

Mozambique (Marinha Moçambique)

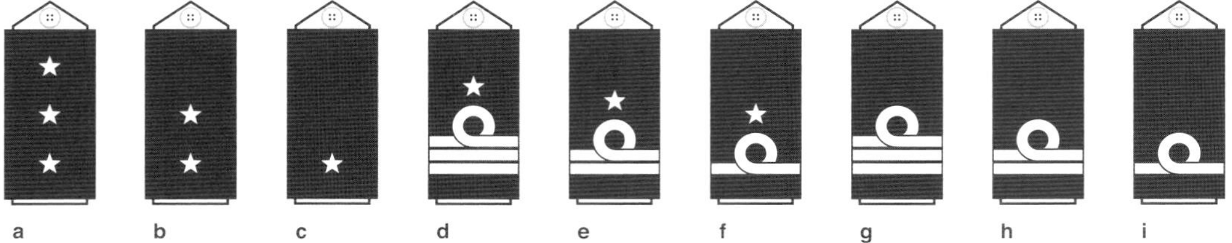

Gold metal stars and gold braid rings on very dark blue cloth shoulder-loops on white cotton shoulder-straps; white bone buttons. Rank titles are in Portuguese.
a: *Almirante*, Admiral *(rank not currently held)* **b**: *Vice-almirante*, Vice Admiral *(rank not currently held)* **c**: *Contra-almirante*, Rear Admiral *(C-in-C Navy)*
d: *Capitão-de-mar-e-guerra*, Captain **e**: *Capitão-de-fragata*, Commander **f**: *Capitão-tenente, Lieutenant Commander* **g**: *1o (Primeiro) tenente*, Lieutenant
h: *2o (Segundo) tenente*, Sub Lieutenant **i**: *Guarda-marinha*, Midshipman

Myanmar (Tatmadaw Yay)

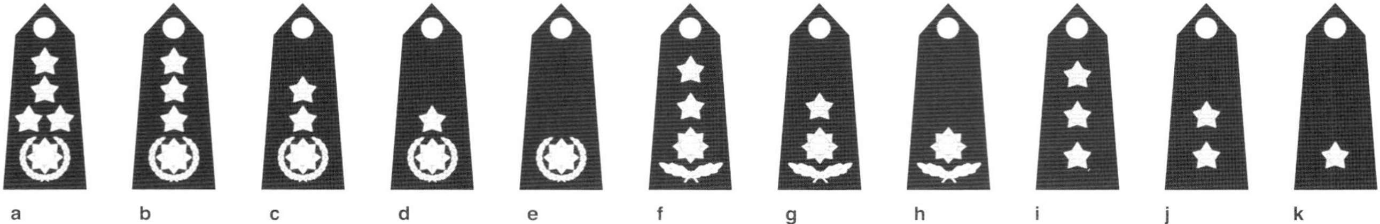

Large and small gold metal stars, wreaths and branches on very dark blue cloth shoulder-straps. Myanmar Army rank titles are used and written here in romanised Burmese.
a: *Bogyokhmugyi*, (Senior) Admiral *(rank not currently held)* **b**: *Dutiya Bogyokhmugyi*, Admiral *(rank not currently held)*
c: *Dutiya Bogyokgyi*, Vice Admiral *(Commander-in-Chief, Navy)* **d**: *Bogyoke*, Rear Admiral **e**: *Bohmugyoke*, Commodore **f**: *Bohmugyi*, Captain
g: *Dutiya Bohmugyi*, Commander **h**: *Bohmu*, Lieutenant Commander **i**: *Bogyi*, Lieutenant **j**: *Bo*, Sub Lieutenant **k**: *Dutiya Bo*, Acting Sub Lieutenant

Netherlands (Koninklijke Marine)

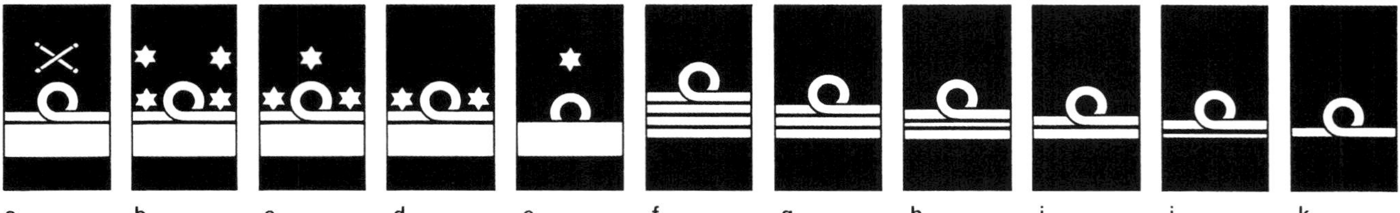

Silver wire batons and stars and gold braid rings with 'curl' on very dark blue cloth cuffs. Rank titles are in Dutch.
a: *Admiraal*, Admiral of the Fleet *(rank not currently held)* **b**: *Luitenant-admiraal*, Admiral *(rank not currently held)* **c**: *Vice-Admiraal*, Vice Admiral
d: *Schout-bij-nacht*, Rear Admiral **e**: *Commandeur*, Commodore **f**: *Kapitein-ter-zee*, Captain **g**: *Kapitein-luitenant-ter-zee*, Commander
h: *Luitenant-ter-zee 1e (eerste) klasse*, Lieutenant Commander **i**: *Luitenant-ter-zee 2e (tweede) klasse oudste kategorie*, Lieutenant
j: *Luitenant-ter-zee 2e (tweede) klasse*, Sub Lieutenant **k**: *Luitenant-ter-zee 3e (derde) klasse*, Acting Sub Lieutenant

New Zealand

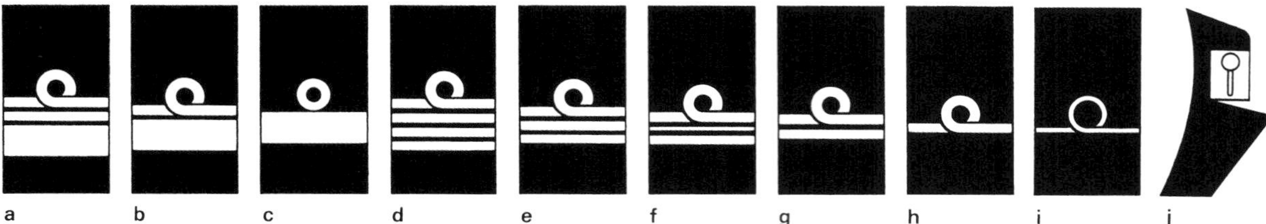

Gold braid rings with 'curl' on very dark blue cloth cuffs; brass button and white cord on white cloth collar-patch (j). Rank titles are in English.
a: *Vice Admiral*, Vice Admiral *(rank not currently held)* **b**: *Rear Admiral*, Rear Admiral *(Chief of Navy)* **c**: *Commodore*, Commodore **d**: *Captain*, Captain
e: *Commander*, Commander **f**: *Lieutenant Commander*, Lieutenant Commander **g**: *Lieutenant*, Lieutenant **h**: *Sub Lieutenant*, Sub Lieutenant
i: *Ensign*, Acting Sub Lieutenant **j**: *Midshipman*, Midshipman

Nicaragua (Fuerza Naval de Nicaragua)

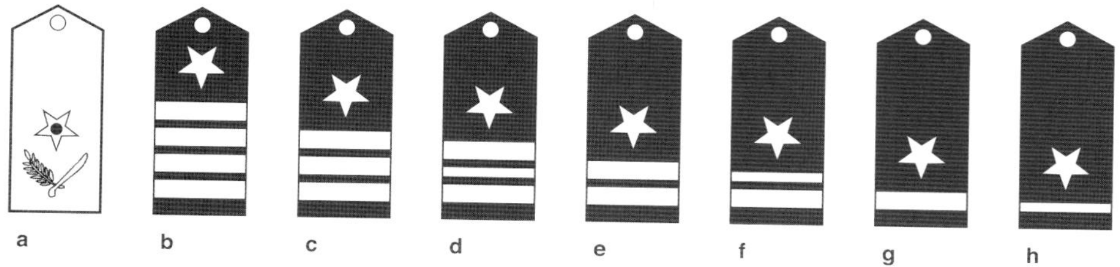

Gold metal buttons, gold wire stars and gold braid rings on very dark blue cloth shoulder-straps. A Rear Admiral (a) has a silver braid star with a red boss and a silver braid crossed palm branch and machete on a gold braid shoulder-strap. Rank titles are in Spanish.
a: *Contralmirante*, Rear Admiral **b:** *Capitán de Navío*, Captain **c:** *Capitán de Fragata*, Commander **d:** *Capitán de Corbeta*, Lieutenant Commander
e: *Teniente de Navío*, Lieutenant **f:** *Teniente de Fragata*, Sub Lieutenant **g:** *Teniente de Corbeta*, Acting Sub Lieutenant **h:** *Alférez*, Midshipman

Nigeria

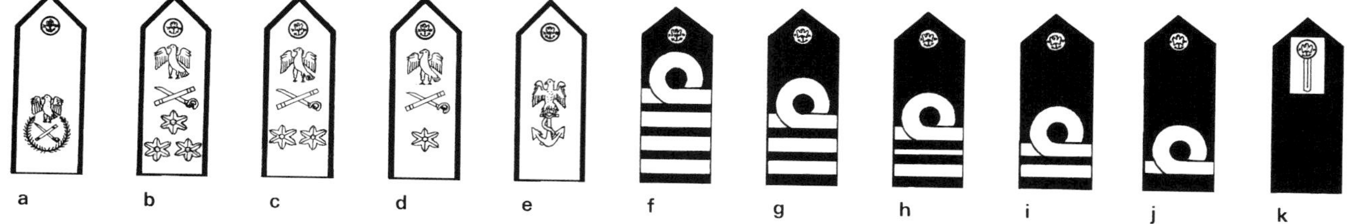

Silver wire eagles, batons, swords, wreaths and anchor on gold braid shoulder-straps edged in very dark blue cloth (a–e); gold braid rings with 'curl' on very dark blue cloth shoulder-straps (f–j), brass button and white cord on white cloth collar-patch (k); brass buttons. Royal Navy rank titles are used.
a: Admiral of the Fleet *(rank not currently held)* **b:** Admiral *(rank not currently held)* **c:** Vice Admiral *(Chief of Naval Staff)* **d:** Rear Admiral
e: Commodore **f:** Captain **g:** Commander **h:** Lieutenant Commander **i:** Lieutenant **j:** Sub Lieutenant **k:** Midshipman

Norway (Sjøforsvaret)

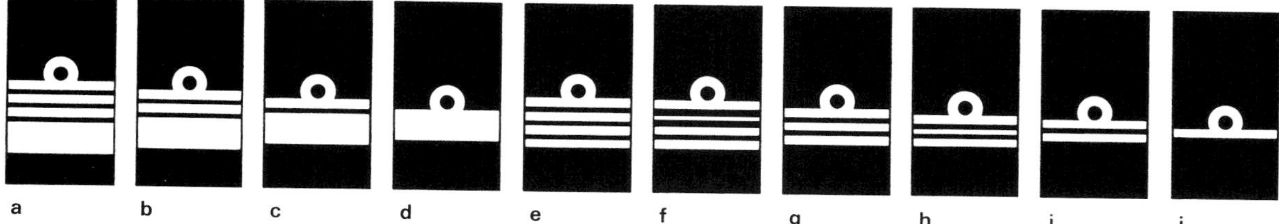

Gold braid rings with 'curl' on very dark blue cloth cuffs. Rank titles are in Norwegian.
a: *Admiral*, Admiral *(rank not currently held)* **b:** *Viseadmiral*, Vice Admiral *(Commander, National Joint HQ)*
c: *Kontreadmiral*, Rear Admiral *(Inspector-General, Navy)* **d:** *Flaggkommandør*, Commodore **e:** *Kommandør*, Captain
f: *Kommandørkaptein*, Commander **g:** *Orlogskaptein*, Lieutenant Commander **h:** *Kapteinløytnant*, Lieutenant **i:** *Løytnant*, Sub Lieutenant
j: *Fenrik*, Acting Sub Lieutenant

Oman (Royal Navy of Oman)

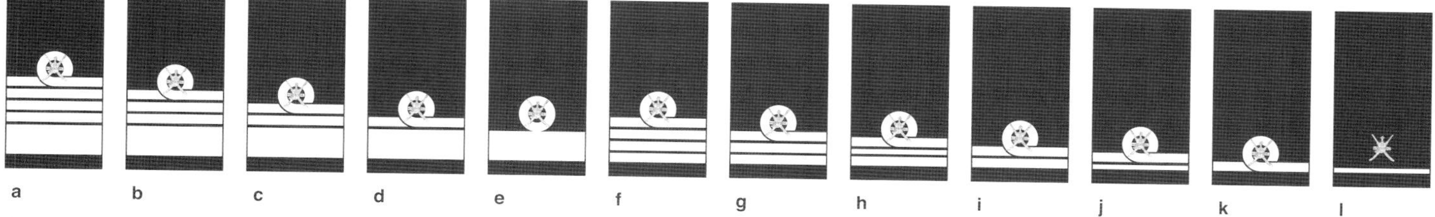

Gold wire dagger and crossed swords and gold braid rings with 'curl' on very dark blue cloth cuffs; a Midshipman (l) has a thin white ring. Arabic Oman Army rank titles are used and written here in romanised script. The Royal Oman Police Coast Guard is forms part of the Royal Oman Police wearing ROP uniforms and insignia.
a: *Mushīr*, Admiral of the Fleet *(Sultan Qabus ibn Sa'id)* **b:** *Farīq Awwal*, Admiral *(rank not currently held)* **c:** *Farīq*, Vice Admiral *(rank not currently held)*
d: *Liwā'*, Rear Admiral *(commander RNO)* **e:** *'Amid*, Commodore **f:** *'Aqīd*, Captain **g:** *Muqaddam*, Commander **h:** *Rā'id*, Lieutenant Commander
i: *Naqīb*, Lieutenant **j:** *Mulāzim Awwal*, Sub Lieutenant **k:** *Mulāzim Thāni*, Acting Sub Lieutenant **l:** *Dābit Murashshah*, Midshipman

Pakistan

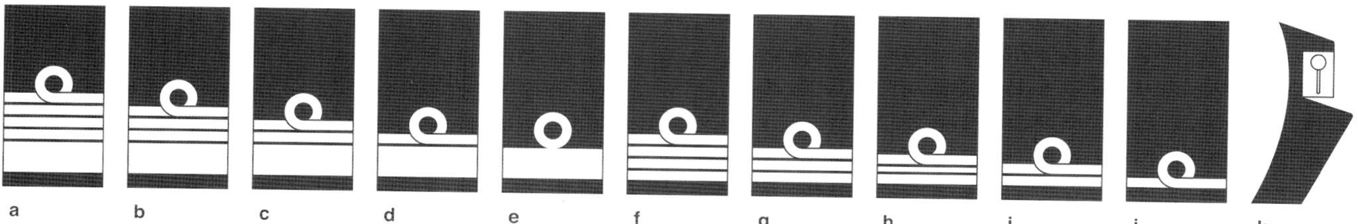

Gold braid rings with 'curl' on very dark blue cloth cuffs; brass button and white cord on white cloth collar-patch (k). Royal Navy rank titles are used. The Pakistan Coast Guard is organised as a Pakistan Army reinforced brigade. Personnel wear Army uniforms and insignia with a seconded Army Brigadier as Director-General.
a: Admiral of the Fleet *(rank not currently held)* **b:** Admiral *(Chief of the Naval Staff)* **c:** Vice Admiral **d:** Rear Admiral **e:** Commodore **f:** Captain
g: Commander **h:** Lieutenant Commander **i:** Lieutenant **j:** Sub Lieutenant **k:** Midshipman

Panama (Coast Guard) (Servicio Maritímo Nacional)

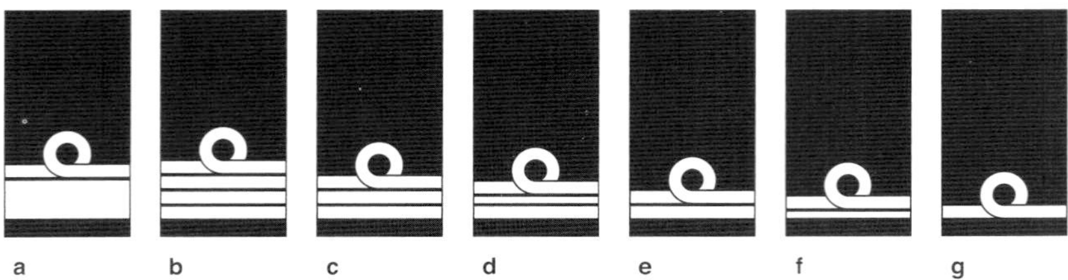

Gold braid rings with 'curl' on very dark blue cloth cuffs. Rank titles are in Spanish.
a: *Director General*, Rear Admiral *(Commander, SMN)* **b**: *Capitán de Navío*, Captain **c**: *Capitán de Fragata*, Commander
d: *Capitán de Corbeta*, Lieutenant Commander **e**: *Teniente de Navío*, Lieutenant **f**: *Teniente de Fragata*, Lieutenant
g: *Alférez de Navío*, Acting Sub Lieutenant

Paraguay (Armada Nacional Paraguaya)

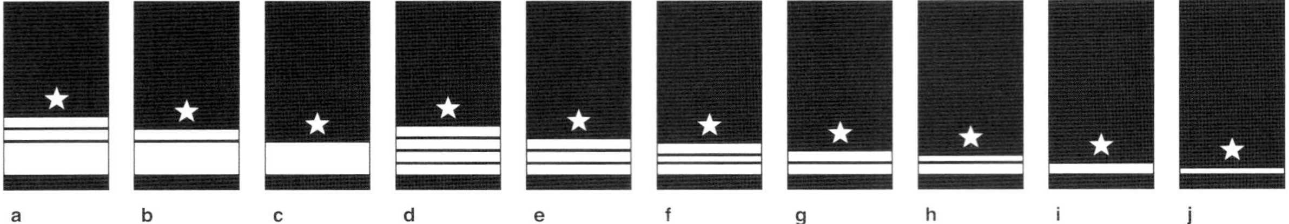

Gold wire stars and gold braid rings on very dark blue cuffs. Rank titles are in Spanish. The Paraguayan Coast Guard (Prefectura General Naval) forms part of the Navy and PGN personnel are led by serving naval officers.
a: *Vicealmirante*, Vice Admiral *(rank not currently held)* **b**: *Contralmirante*, Rear Admiral *(Commander of the Navy)*
c: *Contraalmirante Medio Inferior*, Commodore **d**: *Capitán de Navío*, Captain **e**: *Capitán de Fragata*, Commander
f: *Capitán de Corbeta*, Lieutenant Commander **g**: *Teniente de Navío*, Lieutenant **h**: *Teniente de Fragata*, (Senior) Sub Lieutenant
i: *Teniente de Corbeta*, Sub Lieutenant **j**: *Guardiamarina*, Acting Sub Lieutenant

Peru (Marina de Guerra del Perú)

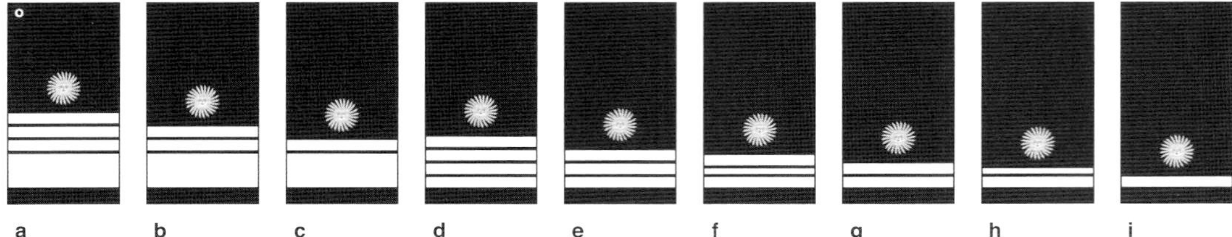

Gold wire suns and gold braid rings on very dark blue cuffs. Rank titles are in Spanish. There is a Peruvian Coast Guard (Dirección General de Capitanías y Guardacostas).
a: *Almirante*, Admiral *(Commandant-General)* **b**: *Vicealmirante*, Vice Admiral **c**: *Contralmirante*, Rear Admiral **d**: *Capitán de Navío*, Captain
e: *Capitán de Fragata*, Commander **f**: *Capitán de Corbeta*, Lieutenant Commander **g**: *Teniente 1º (Primero)*, Lieutenant
h: *Teniente 2º (Segundo)*, Sub Lieutenant **i**: *Alférez de Fragata*, Acting Sub Lieutenant

Philippines (Philippine Navy/Hukbong Dagat ng Pilipinas)

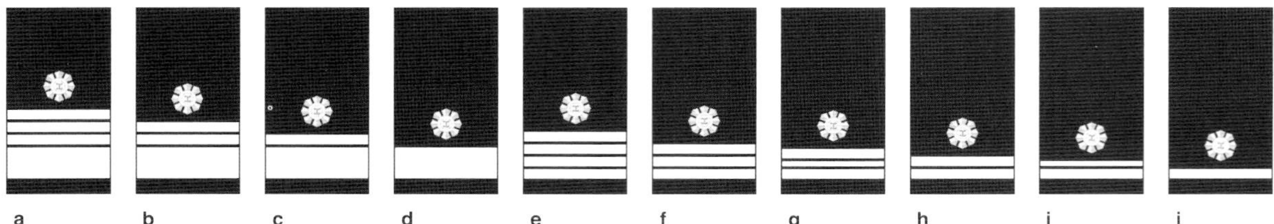

Gold wire suns and gold braid rings on very dark blue cuffs. The Navy title is in English/Tagalog, the rank titles in English only.
a: *Admiral*, Admiral *(rank not currently held)* **b**: *Vice Admiral*, Vice Admiral *(Flag-Officer-In-Command PN)* **c**: *Rear Admiral*, Rear Admiral
d: *Commodore*, Commodore **e**: *Captain*, Captain **f**: *Commander*, Commander **g**: *Lieutenant Commander*, Lieutenant Commander
h: *Lieutenant*, Lieutenant **i**: *Lieutenant Junior Grade*, Sub Lieutenant **j**: *Ensign*, Acting Sub Lieutenant

Philippines - Coast Guard/Tanurag Baybayin ng Pilipinas

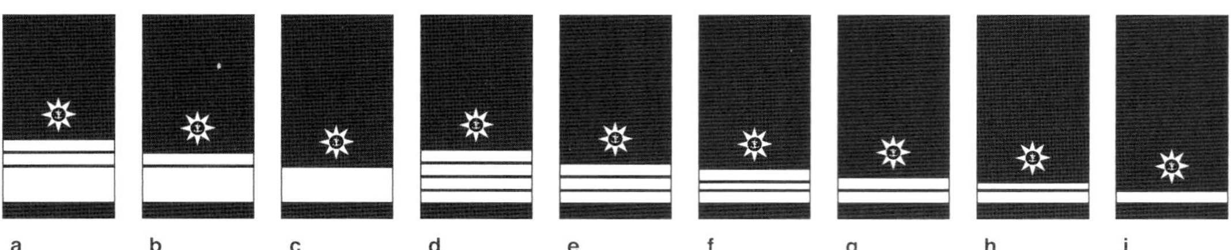

Gold wire suns with anchors and gold braid rings on very dark blue cuffs. The Coast Guard title is in English/Tagalog, the rank titles in English only.
a: *Vice Admiral*, Vice Admiral *(Commandant PCG)* **b**: *Rear Admiral*, Rear Admiral **c**: *Commodore*, Commodore **d**: *Captain*, Captain
e: *Commander*, Commander **f**: *Lieutenant Commander*, Lieutenant Commander **g**: *Lieutenant*, Lieutenant **h**: *Lieutenant Junior Grade*, Sub Lieutenant
i: *Ensign*, Acting Sub Lieutenant

Poland (Marynarka Wojenna)

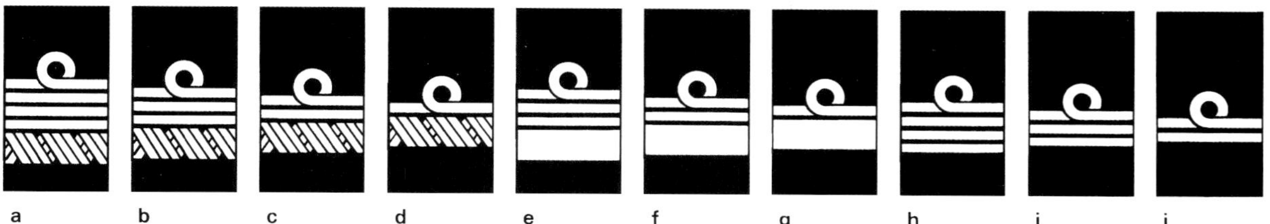

Gold braid rings with 'curl' and traditional Polish generals' embroidery on very dark blue cloth cuffs. Rank titles are in Polish.
a: *Admirał*, Admiral *(rank not currently held)* **b**: *Admirał floty*, Vice Admiral *(Commander of the Navy)* **c**: *Wiceadmirał*, Rear Admiral
d: *Kontradmirał*, Commodore **e**: *Komandor*, Captain **f**: *Komandor porucznik*, Commander **g**: *Komandor podporucznik*, Lieutenant Commander
h: *Kapitan marynarki*, Lieutenant **i**: *Porucznik marynarki*, Sub Lieutenant **j**: *Podporucznik marynarki*, Acting Sub Lieutenant

Portugal (Marinha de Guerra Portuguesa)

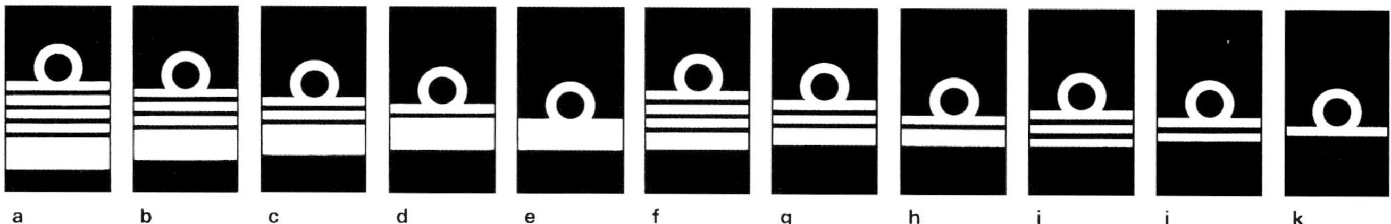

Gold braid rings with 'curl' on very dark blue cloth cuffs. Rank titles are in Portuguese.
a: *Almirante da Armada (rank not currently held)* **b**: *Almirante*, Admiral *(Chief of Naval Staff)* **c**: *Vice-almirante*, Vice Admiral
d: *Contra-almirante*, Rear Admiral **e**: *Comodoro*, Commodore **f**: *Capitão-de-mar-e-guerra*, Captain **g**: *Capitão-de-fragata*, Commander
h: *Capitão-tenente*, Lieutenant Commander **i**: *Primeiro-tenente*, Lieutenant **j**: *Segundo-tenente*, Sub Lieutenant
k: *Subtenente, Acting Sub Lieutenant & Guarda-marinha*, Midshipman

Qatar (Qatari Amiri Navy)

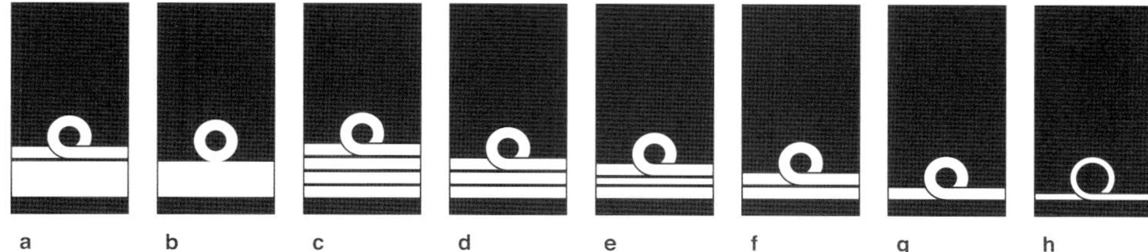

Gold braid rings with 'curl' on very dark blue cloth cuffs. Arabic Qatari Army rank titles are used and written here in romanised script. There is a Qatari Coast Guard, commanded by a Colonel.
a: *Liwā'*, Rear Admiral *(rank not currently held)* **b**: *'Amid*, Commodore *(Chief of Naval Staff)* **c**: *'Aqīd*, Captain **d**: *Muqaddam*, Commander
e: *Rā'id*, Lieutenant Commander **f**: *Naqīb*, Lieutenant **g**: *Mulāzim Awwal*, Sub Lieutenant **h**: *Mulāzim Thāni*, Acting Sub Lieutenant

Romania (Forţele Navale Române)

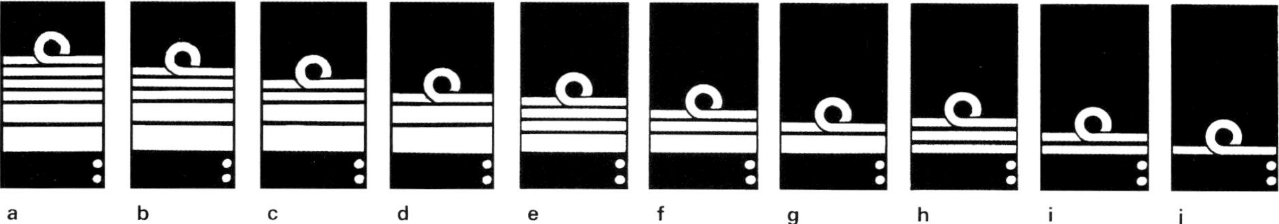

Gold braid rings with 'curl' on very dark blue cloth cuffs; brass buttons. Rank titles are in Romanian.
a: *Amiral*, Admiral *(Chief of Defence Staff)* **b**: *Viceamiral*, Vice Admiral *(rank not currently held)* **c**: *Contraamiral*, Rear Admiral *(Chief of Naval Staff)*
d: *Amiral de flotilă*, Commodore **e**: *Comandor*, Captain **f**: *Căpitan-comandor*, Commander **g**: *Locotenent comandor*, Lieutenant Commander
h: *Căpitan*, Lieutenant **i**: *Locotenent*, Sub Lieutenant **j**: *Aspirant*, Acting Sub Lieutenant

Russian Federation (Rossiskiy Voennomorsky Flot)

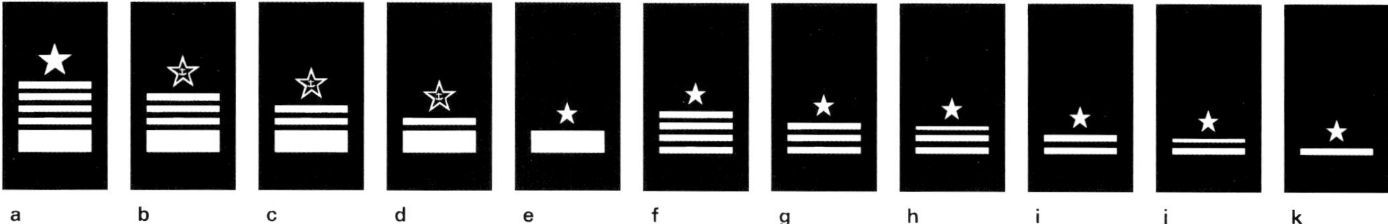

Gold wire large star (a) and small stars, black cloth stars edged in gold wire with a gold wire anchor (b-d) and gold braid bars on black cloth cuffs. Rank insignia is worn simultaneously on gold braid or black shoulder-straps. Rank titles are in romanised Russian. The Russian Federal Border Guard, which forms part of the Interior Ministry, includes a Coast Guard wearing naval-style uniforms.
a: *Admiral flota*, Admiral of the Fleet *(rank not currently held)* **b**: *Admiral*, Admiral *(Commander-in-Chief, Navy)* **c**: *Vitse-admiral*, Vice Admiral
d: *Kontr-admiral*, Rear Admiral **e**: *Kapitan 1 (pervogo) ranga*, Captain **f**: *Kapitan 2 (vtorogo) ranga*, Commander
g: *Kapitan 3 (tretyego) ranga*, Lieutenant Commander **h**: *Kapitan-leytenant*, Lieutenant **i**: *Starshiy leytenant*, (Senior) Sub Lieutenant
j: *Leytenant*, Sub Lieutenant **k**: *Mladshiy leytenant*, Acting Sub Lieutenant

Saudi Arabia (Royal Saudi Naval Forces)

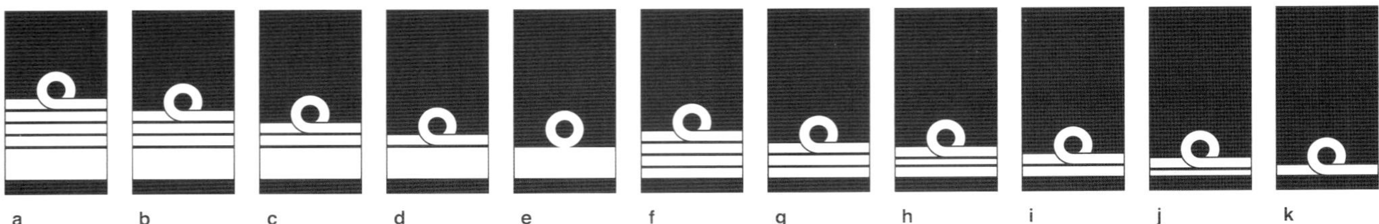

a b c d e f g h i j k

Gold braid rings with 'curl' on very dark blue cloth cuffs. Arabic Saudi Arabian Army rank titles are used and written here in romanised script. There is a Saudi Arabian Coast Guard, commanded by a Lieutenant-General.
a: *Mushīr*, Admiral of the Fleet **b**: *Farīq Awwal*, Admiral *(rank not currently held)* **c**: *Farīq*, Vice Admiral *(Commander, RSNF)* **d**: *Liwā'*, Rear Admiral
e: *'Amid*, Commodore **f**: *'Aqīd*, Captain **g**: *Muqaddam*, Commander **h**: *Rā'id*, Lieutenant Commander **i**: *Naqīb*, Lieutenant
j: *Mulāzim Awwal*, Sub Lieutenant **k**: *Mulāzim*, Acting Sub Lieutenant

Senegal (Marine Sénégalaise)

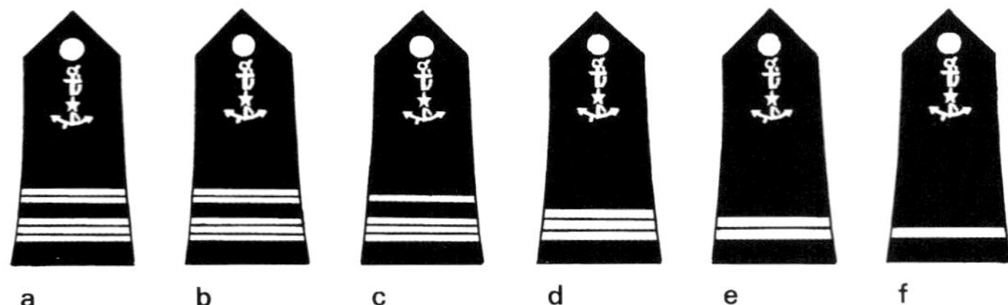

a b c d e f

Gold wire anchors with stars and gold braid rings on very dark blue cloth shoulder-straps; a Commander (b) has silver second and fourth rings; brass buttons. Rank titles are in French.
a: *Capitaine de vaisseau*, Captain *(Chief of Naval Staff)* **b**: *Capitaine de frégate*, Commander **c**: *Capitaine de corvette*, Lieutenant Commander
d: *Lieutenant de vaisseau*, Lieutenant **e**: *Enseigne de vaisseau de 1ère (première) classe*, Sub Lieutenant
f: *Enseigne de vaisseau de 2e (deuxième) classe*, Acting Sub Lieutenant

Seychelles (Coast Guard)

a b c d e f

Gold wire Seychelles coats of arms and gold braid rings on very dark blue cloth shoulder-straps; brass buttons. Seychelles Army rank titles are used and written in English.
a: *Colonel*, Captain *(rank not currently held)* **b**: *Lieutenant Colonel*, Commander *(Commanding Officer, Coast Guard)* **c**: *Major*, Lieutenant Commander
d: *Captain*, Lieutenant **e**: *First Lieutenant*, Sub Lieutenant **f**: *Lieutenant*, Acting Sub Lieutenant

Singapore (Republic of Singapore Navy)

a b c d e f g h i

Gold embroidered stars, crossed branches, coats of arms, bars and national titles on very dark blue cloth shoulder-straps; brass buttons. Rank titles are in English. The Singapore Police Coast Guard forms part of the Singapore Police. Personnel wear police uniforms and insignia with Deputy Assistant Commissioner (Commodore) as the highest rank.
a: *Vice Admiral*, Vice Admiral *(rank not currently held)* **b**: *Rear Admiral (2 stars)*, Rear Admiral *(Chief of Navy)* **c**: *Rear Admiral (1 star)*, Commodore
d: *Colonel*, Captain **e**: *Lieutenant Colonel*, Commander **f**: *Major*, Lieutenant Commander **g**: *Captain*, Lieutenant **h**: *Lieutenant*, Sub Lieutenant
i: *2nd (Second) Lieutenant*, Acting Sub Lieutenant

Slovenia (Slovenska Mornarica)

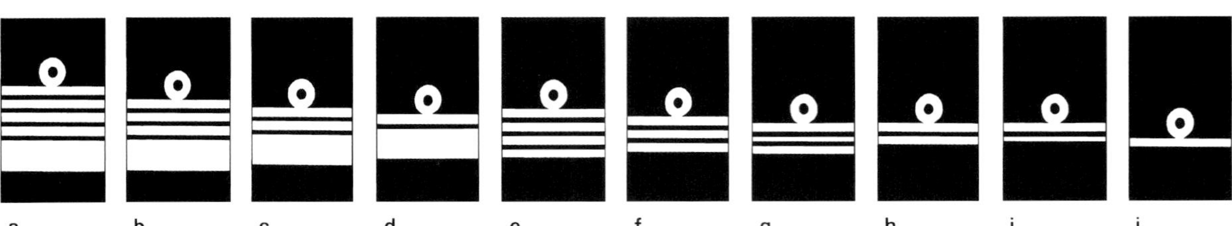

a b c d e f g h i j

Gold braid rings with 'curl' on very dark blue cloth cuffs. Rank titles are in Slovene.
a: *Admiral*, Admiral *(rank not currently held)* **b**: *Viceadmiral*, Vice Admiral *(rank not currently held)*
c: *Kontraadmiral*, Rear Admiral *(rank not currently held)* **d**: *Kapitan*, Commodore *(Commander, Armed Forces Command)* **e**: *Kapitan bojne ladje*, Captain
f: *Kapitan fregate*, Commander *(Commander, 430th Naval Detachment)* **g**: *Kapitan korvete*, Lieutenant Commander **h**: *Poročnik bojne ladje*, Lieutenant
i: *Poročnik fregate*, Sub Lieutenant **j**: *Poročnik korvete*, Acting Sub Lieutenant

South Africa

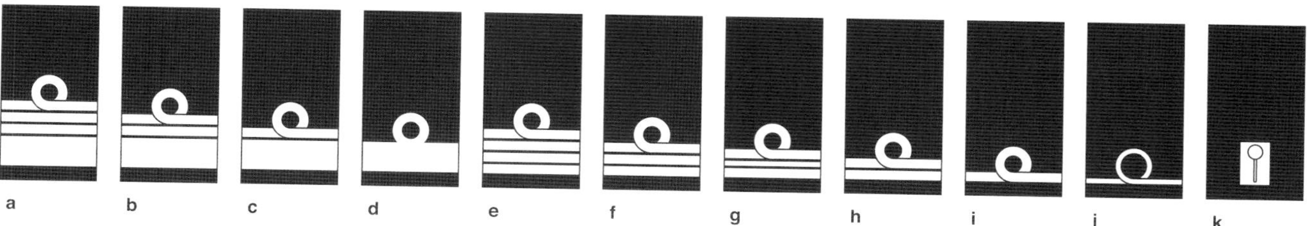

Gold braid rings on black cloth cuffs; brass button on white cord on white cloth cuff-patch (k); brass buttons. Rank titles are in English.
a: *Admiral*, Admiral *(rank not currently held)* **b:** *Vice Admiral*, Vice Admiral *(Chief of the Navy)* **c:** *Rear Admiral*, Rear Admiral
d: *Rear Admiral (Junior Grade)*, Commodore **e:** *Captain*, Captain **f:** *Commander*, Commander **g:** *Lieutenant Commander*, Lieutenant Commander
h: *Lieutenant*, Lieutenant **i:** *Sub-Lieutenant*, Sub Lieutenant **j:** *Ensign*, Acting Sub Lieutenant **k:** *Midshipman*, Midshipman

Spain (Armada Española)

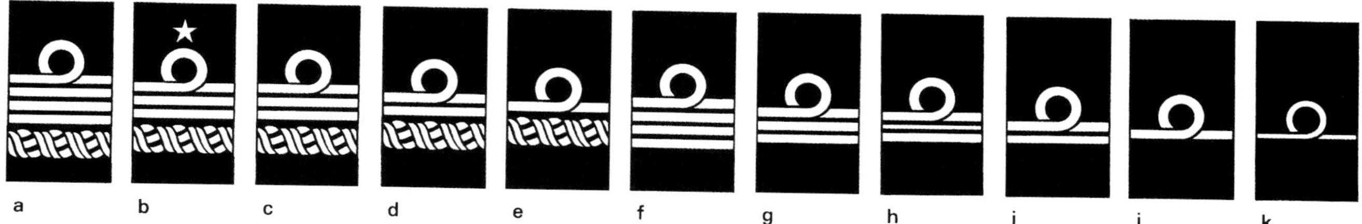

Gold wire star and gold braid rings with 'curl' and traditional Spanish generals' embroidery on very dark blue cloth cuffs. Rank titles are in Spanish.
a: *Capitán General*, Admiral of the Fleet *(King Juan Carlos II)* **b:** *Almirante General*, Admiral *(Chief of Naval Staff)* **c:** *Almirante*, Vice Admiral
d: *Vicealmirante*, Rear Admiral **e:** *Contraalmirante*, Commodore **f:** *Capitán de Navío*, Captain **g:** *Capitán de Fragata*, Commander
h: *Capitán de Corbeta*, Lieutenant Commander **i:** *Teniente de Navío*, Lieutenant **j:** *Alférez de Navío*, Sub Lieutenant
k: *Alférez de Fragata*, Acting Sub Lieutenant

Sri Lanka

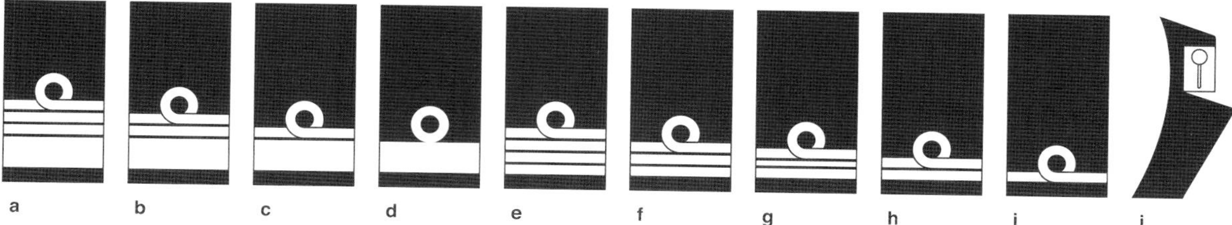

Gold braid rings with 'curl' on very dark blue cloth cuffs; brass button and white cord on white cloth collar-patch (j). Royal Navy rank titles are used.
a: Admiral *(rank not currently held)* **b:** Vice Admiral *(Commander of the Navy)* **c:** Rear Admiral **d:** Commodore **e:** Captain **f:** Commander
g: Lieutenant Commander **h:** Lieutenant **i:** Sub Lieutenant **j:** Midshipman

Sudan

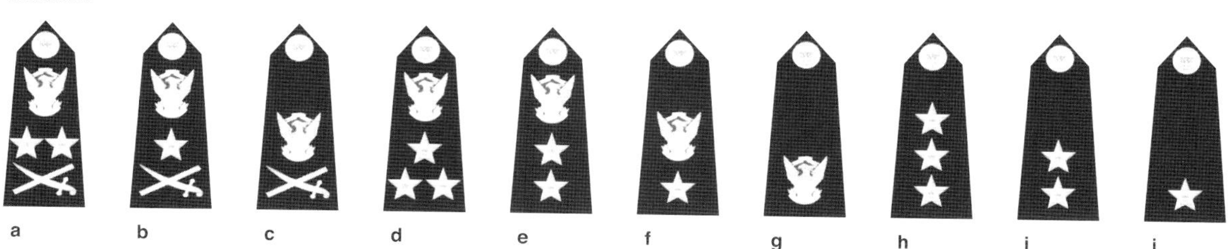

Gold eagles, stars and crossed swords and batons on very dark blue cloth shoulder-straps; brass buttons. Arabic Sudan Army rank titles are used and written here in romanised script.
a: *Farīq Awwal*, Admiral *(rank not currently held)* **b:** *Farīq*, Vice Admiral *(rank not currently held)* **c:** *Liwā'*, Rear Admiral *(rank not currently held)*
d: *'Amid*, Commodore *(Commander, Navy)* **e:** *'Aqīd*, Captain **f:** *Muqaddam*, Commander **g:** *Rā'id*, Lieutenant Commander **h:** *Naqīb*, Lieutenant
i: *Mulāzim Awwal*, Sub Lieutenant **j:** *Mulāzim Thāni*, Acting Sub Lieutenant

Suriname

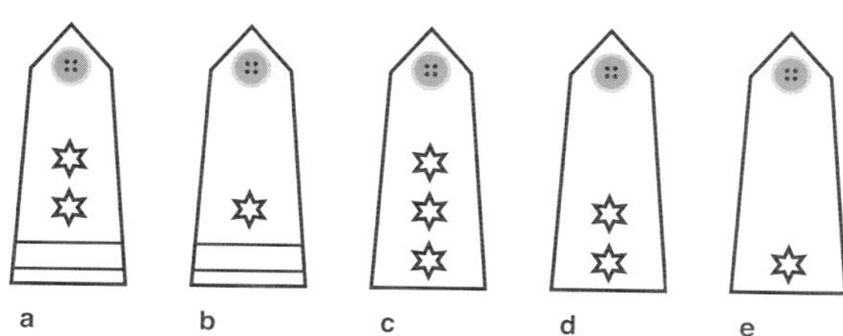

Gold stars and rings on white cotton shoulder-straps; white bone buttons. Rank titles are in Dutch.
a: *Kapitein-luitenant-ter-zee*, Commander *(Commander, Navy)* **b:** *Luitenant-ter-zee 1e (eerste) klasse*, Lieutenant Commander
c: *Luitenant-ter-zee 2e (tweede) klasse oudste kategorie*, Lieutenant **d:** *Luitenant-ter-zee 2e (tweede) klasse*, Sub Lieutenant
e: *Luitenant-ter-zee 3e (derde) klasse*, Acting Sub Lieutenant

Sweden (Svenska Marinen)

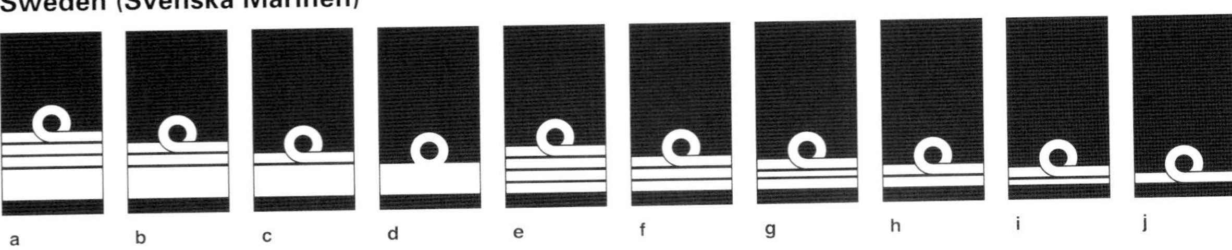

Gold braid rings with 'curl' on very dark blue cloth cuffs. Rank titles are in Swedish.
a: *Amiral*, Admiral *(King Carl Gustaf XVI)* **b:** *Viceamiral*, Vice Admiral *(rank not currently held)* **c:** *Konteramiral*, Rear Admiral *(Naval Inspector)*
d: *Flottiljamiral*, Commodore **e:** *Kommendör*, Captain **f:** *Kommendörkapten*, Commander **g:** *Örlogskapten*, Lieutenant Commander
h: *Kapten, Lieutenant* **i:** *Löjnant*, Sub Lieutenant **j:** *Fänrik*, Acting Sub Lieutenant

Sweden Coast Guard (Kustbevakning)

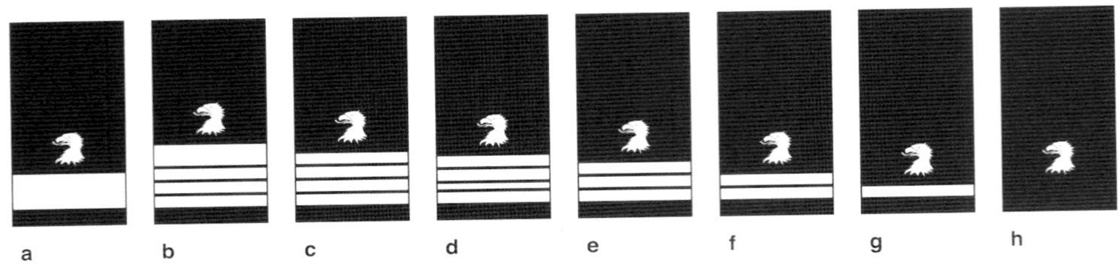

Gold metal eagles' heads and gold braid stripe and rings on very dark blue cloth shoulder-loops on light blue cloth shoulder-straps; blue bone buttons. Rank titles are in Swedish.
a: *Generaldirektör*, Rear Admiral *(Director General, Coast Guard)* **b:** *Kustbevakningsdirektör*, Commodore **c:** *Kustbevakningsöverinspektör*, Captain
d: *1. (Förste) Kustbevakningsinspektör*, Commander **e:** *Kustbevakningsinspektör*, Lieutenant Commander **f:** *Kustbevakningassistent*, Lieutenant
g: *Kustuppsyningsman*, Sub Lieutenant **h:** *Kustbevakningsaspirant*, Acting Sub Lieutenant

Syria (Syrian Arab Navy)

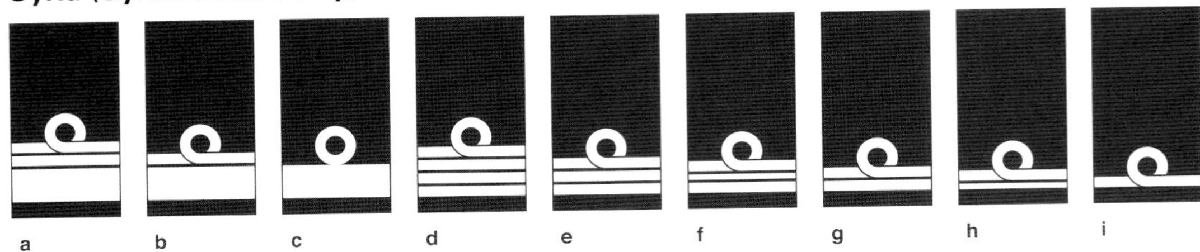

Gold braid rings with 'curl' on very dark blue cloth cuffs. Syrian Army rank titles are used and written here in romanised Arabic.
a: *Farīq*, Vice Admiral *(Commander, SAN)* **b:** *Liwā'*, Rear Admiral **c:** *'Amid*, Commodore **d:** *'Aqīd*, Captain **e:** *Muqaddam*, Commander
f: *Rā'id*, Lieutenant Commander **g:** *Naqīb*, Lieutenant **h:** *Mulāzim Awwal*, Sub Lieutenant **i:** *Mulāzim*, Acting Sub Lieutenant

Taiwan (Republic of China) (Zhōnghuá Mínguó Hǎijūn)

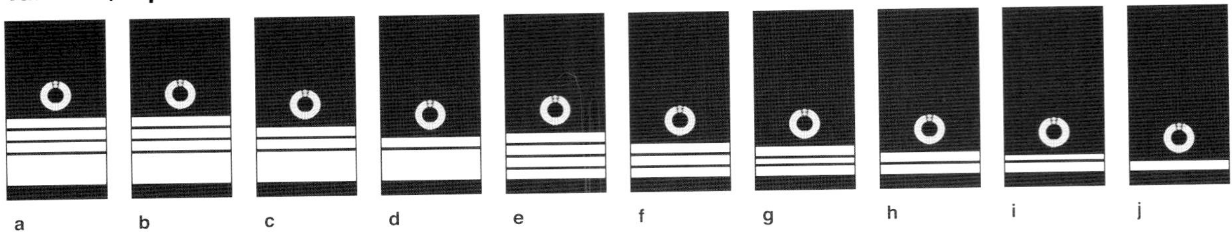

A gold wire cornsheaf on very dark blue cloth cuffs. Rank titles are in romanised Mandarin Chinese written in 'Hanyu Pinyin'. The Taiwanese Coast Guard is designated the 'Republic of China Coast Guard Administration'.
a: *Hǎijūn Yi-chi Shangjiang*, (Senior) Admiral *(4 shoulder-strap stars) (Commander-in-Chief of the Navy)*
b: *Hǎijūn Erh-chi Shangjiang*, Admiral *(3 shoulder-strap stars)* **c:** *Hǎijūn Zhōngjiang*, Vice Admiral **d:** *Hǎijūn Shaojiang*, Rear Admiral
e: *Hǎijūn Shangxiao*, Captain **f:** *Hǎijūn Zhōngxiao*, Commander **g:** *Hǎijūn Shaoxiao*, Lieutenant Commander **h:** *Hǎijūn Shangwei*, Lieutenant
i: *Hǎijūn Zhōngwei*, Sub Lieutenant **j:** *Hǎijūn Shaowei*, Acting Sub Lieutenant

Tanzania

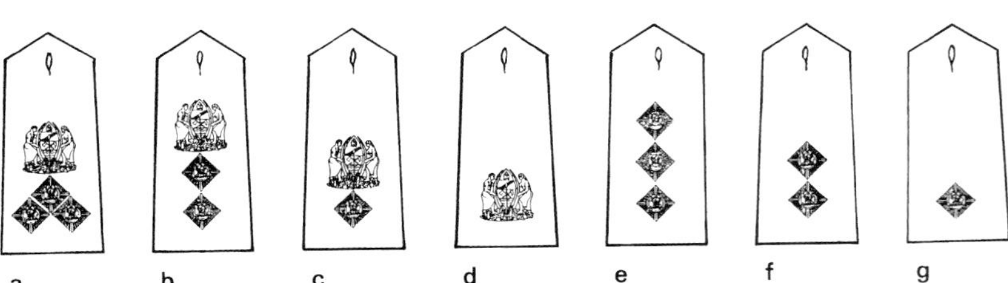

Gold wire national coats of arms and stars on light tan cotton shoulder-straps; brown buttons. Tanzanian Army rank titles are used and written in Swahili.
a: *Brigedia Jenerali*, Commodore *(Chief of the Navy)* **b:** *Kanali*, Captain **c:** *Luteni Kanali*, Commander **d:** *Meja*, Lieutenant Commander
e: *Kapteni*, Lieutenant **f:** *Luteni wa Kwanza*, Sub Lieutenant **g:** *Luteni wa Pili*, Acting Sub Lieutenant

Thailand (Royal Thai Navy)

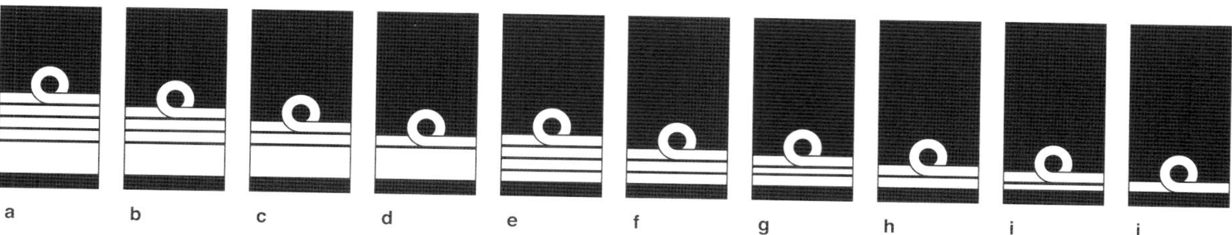

Gold braid rings with 'curl' on very dark blue cloth cuffs. Rank titles are in romanised Thai.
a: *Chom Phon Rua*, Admiral of the Fleet *(King Bhumibol Adulyadej)* **b**: *Phon Rua Eg*, Admiral *(Commander-in-Chief, Navy)* **c**: *Phon Rua Tho*, Vice Admiral **d**: *Phon Rua Tri*, Rear Admiral **e**: *Nawa Eg*, Captain **f**: *Nawa Tho*, Commander **g**: *Nawa Tri*, Lieutenant Commander **h**: *Rua Eg*, Lieutenant **i**: *Rua Tho*, Sub Lieutenant **j**: *Rua Tri*, Acting Sub Lieutenant

Togo (Marine Togolaise)

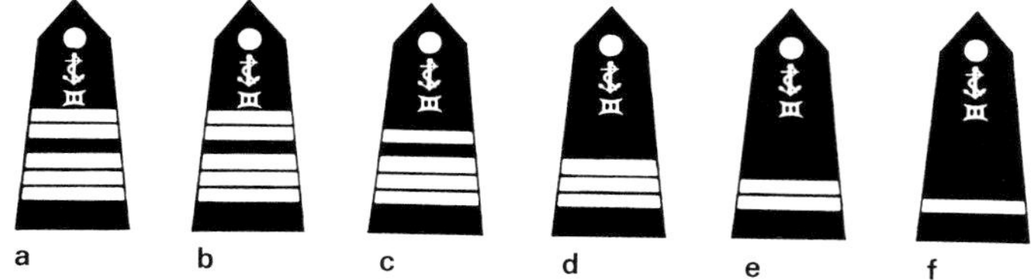

Gold wire anchors and monograms and gold braid rings on very dark blue cloth shoulder-straps; a Commander (b) has silver second and fourth rings; brass buttons. Rank titles are in French.
a: *Capitaine de vaisseau*, Captain *(Commander, Navy)* **b**: *Capitaine de frégate*, Commander **c**: *Capitaine de corvette*, Lieutenant Commander **d**: *Lieutenant de vaisseau*, Lieutenant **e**: *Enseigne de vaisseau de 1ère (première) classe*, Sub Lieutenant **f**: *Enseigne de vaisseau de 2e (deuxième) classe*, Acting Sub Lieutenant

Tonga

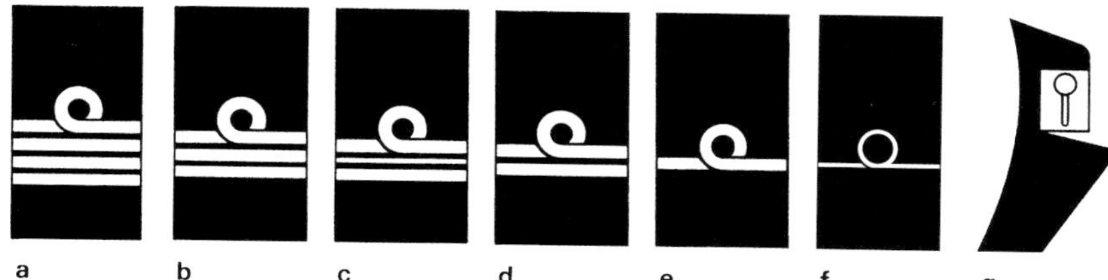

Gold braid rings with 'curl' on very dark blue cloth cuffs; brass button and white cord on white cloth collar-patch (g). Rank titles are in English.
a: *Captain*, Captain *(rank not currently held)* **b**: *Commander*, Commander *(Commander, Navy)* **c**: *Lieutenant Commander*, Lieutenant Commander **d**: *Lieutenant*, Lieutenant **e**: *Sub Lieutenant*, Sub Lieutenant **f**: *Ensign*, Acting Sub Lieutenant **g**: *Midshipman*, Midshipman

Trinidad and Tobago Coast Guard

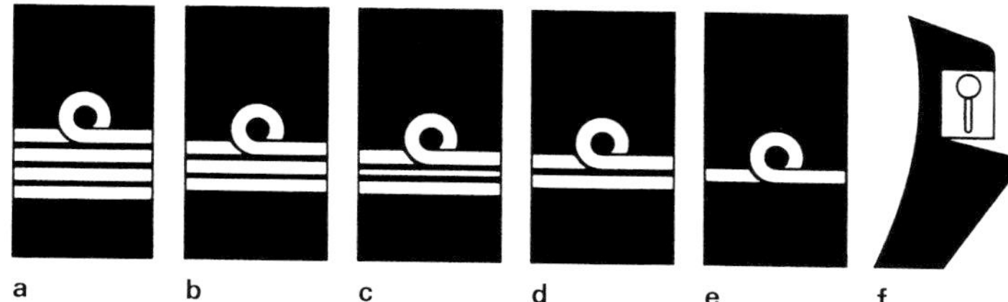

Gold braid rings with 'curl' on very dark blue cloth cuffs; brass button and white cord on white cloth collar-patch (f). Royal Naval rank titles are used.
a: Captain *(Commanding Officer, Coast Guard)* **b**: Commander **c**: Lieutenant Commander **d**: Lieutenant **e**: Sub Lieutenant **f**: Midshipman

Tunisia

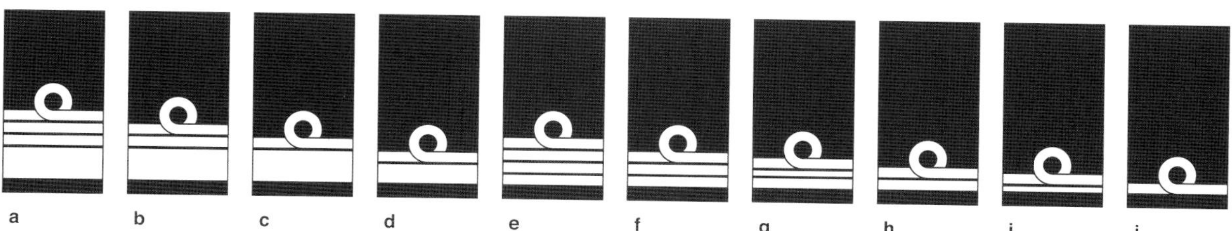

Gold braid rings with 'curl' on very dark blue cloth cuffs. Arabic Tunisian Army rank titles are used and written here in French. There is a Tunisian Coast Guard.
a: *Vice-amiral d'escadre*, Vice Admiral **b**: *Vice-amiral*, Rear Admiral *(Chief of Naval Staff)* **c**: *Contre-amiral*, Commodore **d**: *Capitaine de vaisseau major*, (Senior) Captain **e**: *Capitaine de vaisseau*, Captain **f**: *Capitaine de frégate*, Commander **g**: *Capitaine de corvette*, Lieutenant Commander **h**: *Lieutenant de vaisseau*, Lieutenant **i**: *Enseigne de vaisseau de 1ère (première) classe*, Sub Lieutenant **j**: *Enseigne de vaisseau de 2e (deuxième) classe*, Acting Sub Lieutenant

Turkey (Türk Deniz Kuvvetleri)

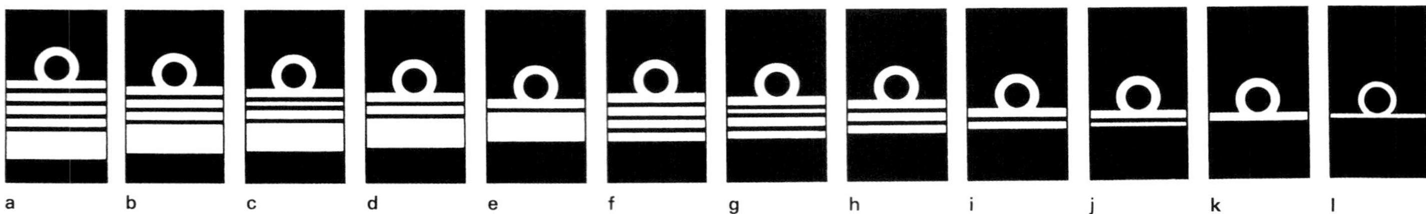

Gold braid rings with 'curl' on very dark blue cloth shoulder-straps; brass buttons. Rank titles are in Turkish. The Turkish Coast Guard *(Sahil Güvenlik Kiliği)* is manned by seconded naval personnel and is commanded by a Rear Admiral *(Tümamiral)*. Personnel wear naval uniforms and insignia with the distinguishing shoulder-title 'Sahil Güvenlik'.
a: *Büyük amiral*, Admiral of the Fleet *(rank not currently held)* **b**: *Oramiral*, Admiral *(C-in-C Navy)* **c**: *Koramiral*, Vice Admiral
d: *Tümamiral*, Rear Admiral **e**: *Tuğamiral*, Commodore **f**: *Albay*, Captain **g**: *Yarbay*, Commander **h**: *Binbaşi*, Lieutenant Commander
i: *Yüzbaşi*, Lieutenant **j**: *Üsteğmen*, Sub Lieutenant **k**: *Teğmen*, Acting Sub Lieutenant **l**: *Asteğmen*, (Junior) Acting Sub Lieutenant

Ukraine (Viys'kogo-Morskoy Sil)

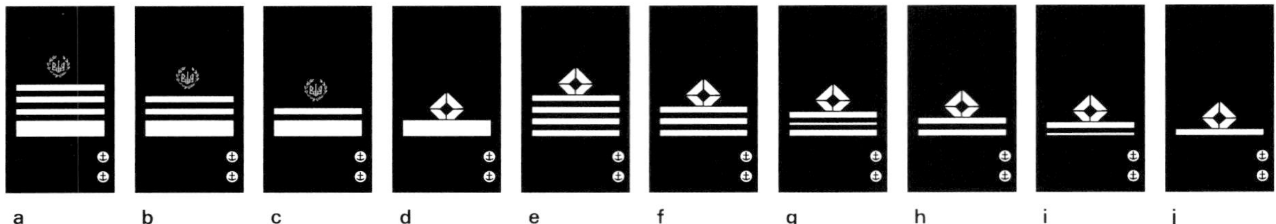

Gold wire tridents and wreaths and gold braid rings with square 'curl' on black cloth cuffs. Rank insignia is worn simultaneously on gold or black braid shoulder-straps. Rank titles are in romanised Ukrainian.
a: *Admiral*, Admiral *(C-in-C, Navy)* **b**: *Vitse-admiral*, Vice Admiral **c**: *Kontr-admiral*, Rear Admiral **d**: *Kapitan 1 rangy*, Captain
e: *Kapitan 2 rangy*, Commander **f**: *Kapitan 3 rangy*, Lieutenant Commander **g**: *Kapitan-leytenant*, Lieutenant
h: *Starshiy-leytenant*, (Senior) Sub Lieutenant **i**: *Leytenant*, Sub Lieutenant **j**: *Molodshiy leytenant*, Acting Sub Lieutenant

United Arab Emirates

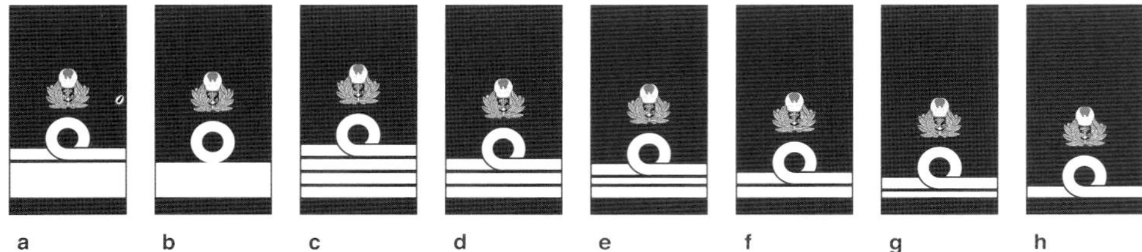

Gold wire cap-badge (gold eagle on red cloth, silver anchor, gold wreath) above gold braid rings with 'curl' on very dark blue cloth cuffs. Arabic UAE Army rank titles are used and written here in romanised script. The United Arab Emirates maintains a Coast Guard commanded by a Director-General.
a: *Liwā'*, Rear Admiral *(Commander, UAENF)* **b**: *'Amid*, Commodore **c**: *'Aqīd*, Captain **d**: *Muqaddam*, Commander **e**: *Rā'id*, Lieutenant Commander
f: *Naqīb*, Lieutenant **g**: *Mulāzim Awwal*, Sub Lieutenant **h**: *Mulāzim*, Acting Sub Lieutenant

United Kingdom (Royal Navy)

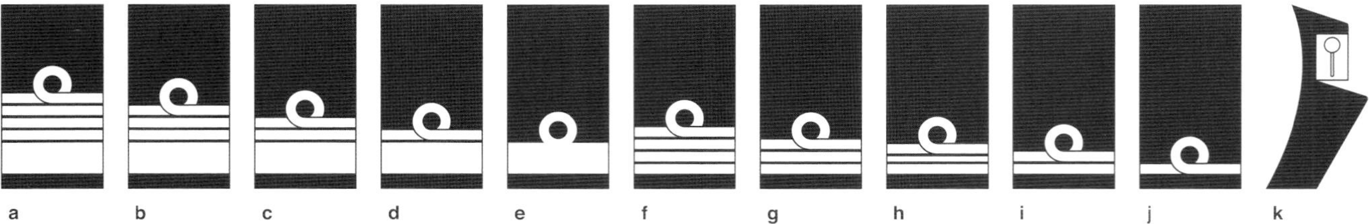

Gold braid rings with 'curl' on very dark blue cloth cuffs; brass button and white cord on white cloth collar-patch (k). Her Majesty's Coast Guard is a government agency. Personnel wear naval-style uniforms and insignia.
a: Admiral of the Fleet *(promotions to this rank discontinued March 1995)* **b**: Admiral *(First Sea Lord & Chief of the Naval Staff)* **c**: Vice Admiral
d: Rear Admiral **e**: Commodore **f**: Captain **g**: Commander **h**: Lieutenant Commander **i**: Lieutenant **j**: Sub Lieutenant & Acting Sub Lieutenant
k: Midshipman

United Kingdom (Royal Fleet Auxiliary Service)

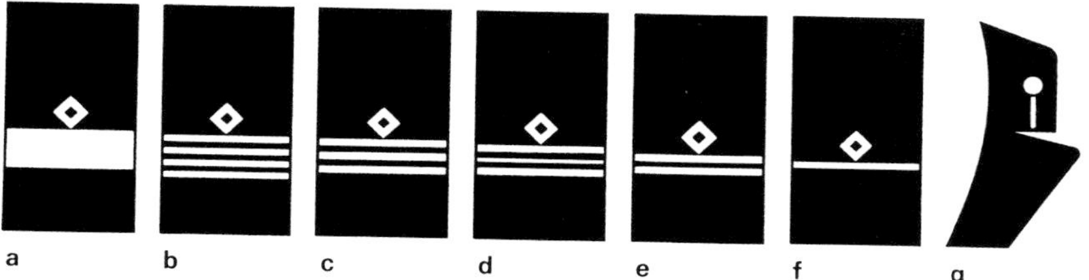

a b c d e f g

Gold braid rings and 'diamonds' on very dark blue cloth cuffs; brass button and white cord on collar (g). British Merchant Navy rank titles are used.
a: *Commodore*, Commodore *(Commanding Officer, RFA)* **b:** *Captain*, Captain **c:** *Chief Officer*, Commander **d:** *1st (First) Officer*, Lieutenant Commander
e: *2nd (Second) Officer*, Lieutenant **f:** *3rd (Third) Officer*, Sub Lieutenant **g:** *Deck Cadet*, Midshipman

United States

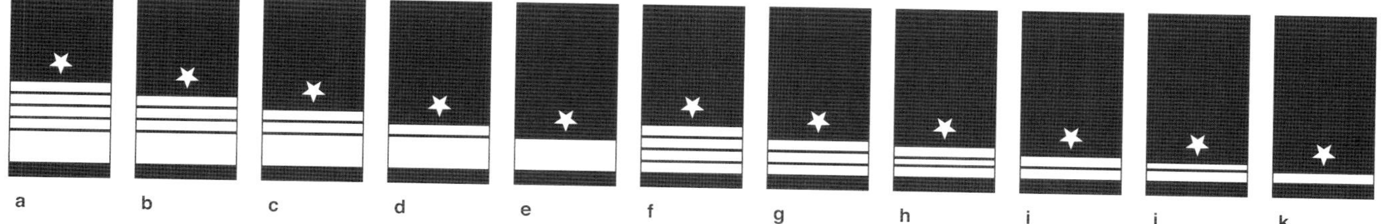

a b c d e f g h i j k

Gold wire stars and gold braid rings on very dark blue cloth cuffs. Rank titles are in English.
a: *Fleet Admiral*, Admiral of the Fleet *(rank not currently held)* **b:** *Admiral*, Admiral *(Chief of Naval Operations)* **c:** *Vice Admiral*, Vice Admiral
d: *Rear Admiral (Upper Half)*, Rear Admiral **e:** *Rear Admiral (Lower Half)*, Commodore **f:** *Captain*, Captain **g:** *Commander*, Commander
h: *Lieutenant Commander*, Lieutenant Commander **i:** *Lieutenant*, Lieutenant **j:** *Lieutenant Junior Grade*, Sub Lieutenant
k: *Ensign*, Acting Sub Lieutenant

United States Coast Guard

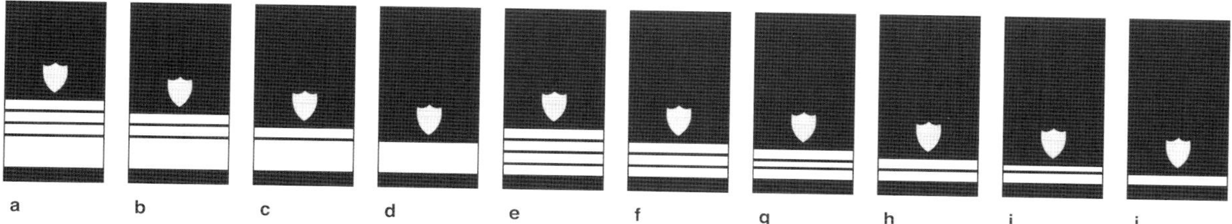

a b c d e f g h i j

Gold wire shields and gold braid rings on very dark blue cloth cuffs. Rank titles are in English.
a: *Admiral*, Admiral *(Commandant, USCG)* **b:** *Vice Admiral*, Vice Admiral **c:** *Rear Admiral (Upper Half)*, Rear Admiral
d: *Rear Admiral (Lower Half)*, Commodore **e:** *Captain*, Captain **f:** *Commander*, Commander **g:** *Lieutenant Commander*, Lieutenant Commander
h: *Lieutenant*, Lieutenant **i:** *Lieutenant Junior Grade*, Sub Lieutenant **j:** *Ensign*, Acting Sub Lieutenant

Uruguay (Armada Nacional)

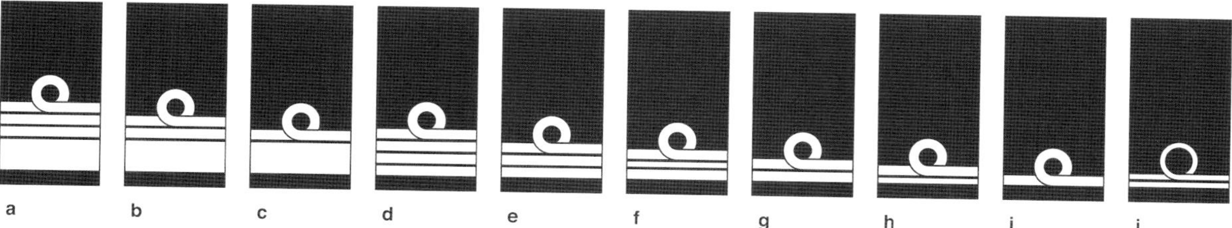

a b c d e f g h i j

Gold braid rings with 'curl' on very dark blue cloth cuffs. Rank titles are in Spanish. The Uruguayan Coast Guard *(Prefectura Nacional Naval)* forms part of the Navy. Personnel wear naval uniforms and insignia with a Rear Admiral *(Contra Almirante)* as the commanding officer *(Prefecto Nacional Naval)*.
a: *Almirante*, Admiral *(Commander-in-Chief, Navy)* **b:** *Vice Almirante*, Vice Admiral **c:** *Contra Almirante*, Rear Admiral **d:** *Capitán de Navío*, Captain
e: *Capitán de Fragata*, Commander **f:** *Capitán de Corbeta*, Lieutenant Commander **g:** *Teniente de Navio*, Lieutenant **h:** *Alférez de Navio*, Sub Lieutenant
i: *Alférez de Fragata*, Acting Sub Lieutenant **j:** *Guardiamarina*, Midshipman

Venezuela (Armada Bolivariana de Venezuela)

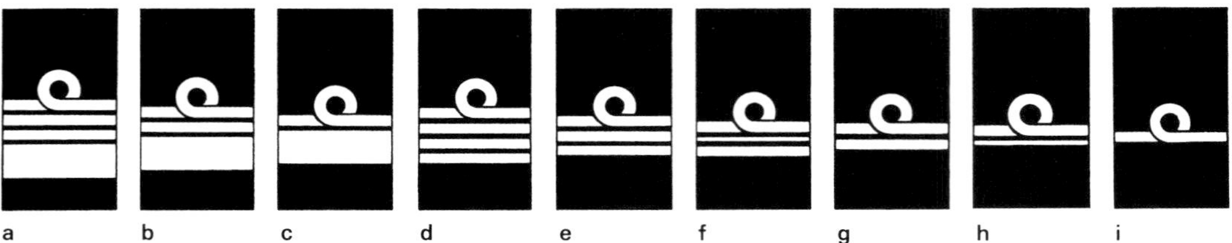

Gold braid rings with 'curl' on very dark blue cloth cuffs. Rank titles are in Spanish. The Coast Guard (Comando de Guardacostas) forms part of the Navy. Personnel wear naval uniforms and insignia with a Rear Admiral as the commanding officer.
a: *Almirante*, Admiral *(rank not currently held)* **b**: *Vicealmirante*, Vice Admiral *(Commander, Navy)* **c**: *Contralmirante*, Rear Admiral
d: *Capitán de Navío*, Captain **e**: *Capitán de Fragata*, Commander **f**: *Capitán de Corbeta*, Lieutenant Commander **g**: *Teniente de Navío*, Lieutenant
h: *Teniente de Fragata*, Sub Lieutenant **i**: *Alférez de Navío*, Acting Sub Lieutenant

Vietnam (Hai quan Nhan dan Viet Nam)

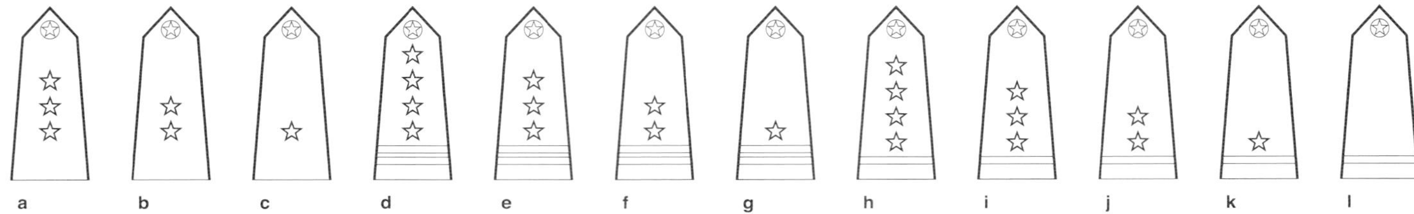

Gold metal stars and buttons (a–d), silver metal stars, bars and buttons (e–l) on gold braid shoulder-straps piped black. Rank titles are in Vietnamese. There is also the Vietnam People's Coast Guard (Canh sat bien) wearing the same rank insignia.
a: *Do Doc*, Admiral *(rank not currently held)* **b**: *Pho Do Doc*, Vice Admiral *(Commander, VPN)* **c**: *Chuan Do Doc*, Rear Admiral **d**: *Da Ta*, Commodore
e: *Thuong Ta*, Captain **f**: *Trung Ta*, Commander **g**: *Thieu Ta*, Lieutenant Commander **h**: *Da Uy*, (Senior) Lieutenant **i**: *Thuong Uy*, Lieutenant
j: *Trung Uy*, Sub Lieutenant **k**: *Thieu Uy* Acting Sub Lieutenant **l**: *Chuan Uy*, Midshipman

Yemen

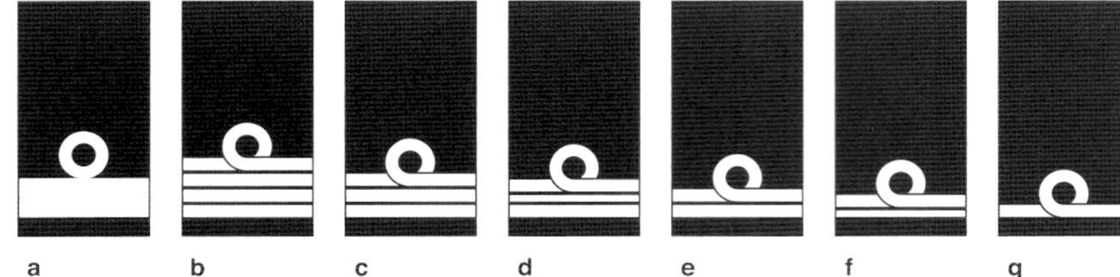

Gold braid rings with 'curl' on very dark blue cloth cuffs. Arabic Yemen Army rank titles are used and written here in romanised script.
a: *'Amid*, Commodore *(Commander, Navy)* **b**: *'Aqid*, Captain **c**: *Muqaddam*, Commander **d**: *Rā'id*, Lieutenant Commander **e**: *Naqīb*, Lieutenant
f: *Mulāzim Awwal*, Sub Lieutenant **g**: *Mulāzim Thāni*, Acting Sub Lieutenant

Pennant list of major surface ships

Type abbreviations

Notes: Designations specific to one nationality are followed by Country abbreviations.
The prefix W denotes a vessel of the Coastguard Service. Suffixes to type indicators are as follows:
F denotes a vessel capable of speeds in excess of 35 kt.
G denotes a vessel with a force guided missile system, including SAM, USM and SUM, usually with a range exceeding 20 miles.
H denotes a vessel equipped with a helicopter, or with a platform for operating one.
J denotes an air cushion or surface effect design.
K denotes a vessel equipped with hydrofoils.
M denotes a Combatant vessel with a close-range guided missile system.
N denotes a ship or submarine using nuclear propulsion.

Submarines

AGSS	Submarine, auxiliary, nuclear-powered (US)
DSRV	Deep submergence rescue vehicle
DSV	Deep submergence vehicle
SDV	Swimmer delivery vehicle
SNA	Submarine, attack, nuclear-powered (Fra)
SNLE	Ballistic missile nuclear-powered submarine (Fra)
SS	Submarine, general
SSA(N)	Submarine, auxiliary, nuclear-powered
SSA	Submarine with ASW capability (Jpn)
SSB	Ballistic missile submarine (CPR)
SSBN	Ballistic missile nuclear-powered submarine
SSC	Submarine, coastal
SSGN	Submarine, surface-to-surface missile, nuclear-powered
SSK	Patrol submarine with ASW capability
SSW	Submarine, midget
SSN	Submarine, attack, nuclear-powered

Aircraft Carriers

CV (M)	Aircraft carrier (guided missile system)
CVH (G)	Helicopter carrier (guided missile system)
CVN (M)	Aircraft carrier, nuclear-powered guided missile system)
PAN	Aircraft carrier, nuclear-powered (Fra)

Cruisers

CG	Guided missile cruiser
CGH	Guided missile cruiser with helicopter
CGN	Guided missile cruiser, nuclear-powered
CLM	Guided missile cruiser (Per)

Destroyers

DD	Destroyer
DDG (M)	Guided missile destroyer
DDGH (M)	Guided missile destroyer with helicopter, or helicopter platform
DDK	Destroyer (Jpn)

Frigates

DE	Destroyer escort (Jpn)
FF (L) (H)	Frigate (Light) (Helicopter)
FFG (M)	Guided missile frigate
FFGH (M)	Guided missile frigate with helicopter, or helicopter platform
FS (G) (H) (M)	Corvette (guided missile) (helicopter) (missile)

Patrol Forces

CF	River gunboat (Per)
CM	Corvette (guided missile) (Per)
HSIC	High Speed Interception Craft with speeds in excess of 55 kt
PB	Coastal patrol vessel under 45 m without heavy armament
PB (F) (I) (R)	Patrol boat (fast) (inshore) (river)
PBO (H)	Offshore patrol vessel between 45 and 60 m (helicopter)
PC	Vessel 35–55 m primarily for ASW role
PCK	As for PC but fitted with hydrofoils
PG	Vessel 45–85 m equipped with at least 76 mm (3-in) gun
PGG	As for PG but with force guided missile system
PGGJ	As for PGG but air cushion or ground effect design
PGGK	As for PGG but fitted with hydrofoils
PSO (H)	Offshore patrol vessel over 60 m (helicopter)
PTK	Attack boat torpedo fitted with hydrofoils
PTGK	Attack boat guided missile fitted with hydrofoils
SOC	Special operations craft (US)

Landing Ships

AAAV	Advanced Amphibious Assault Vehicle
ACV	Landing craft air cushion (Rus)
AGC	Amphibious command ship (RoC)
ASDS	Advanced Swimmer-Seal Delivery System
EDCG	Landing craft, utility (Brz)
LCA	Landing craft, assault
LCAC	Landing craft air cushion
LCC	Amphibious command ship
LCH	Landing craft, heavy (Aust)
LCM	Landing craft, mechanised
LCP (L)	Landing craft, personnel (large)
LCT	Landing craft, tank
LCU	Landing craft, utility
LCVP	Landing craft, vehicle/personnel with bow ramp
LHA	Amphibious assault ship general purpose with flooded well
LDW	Swimmer delivery vehicle
LHD (M)	Amphibious assault ship (multipurpose), can operate VSTOL aircraft and helicopters
LKA	Amphibious cargo ship with own landing craft
LLP	Assault ship, personnel
LPD	Amphibious transport, dock with own LCMs and helicopter deck
LPH	Amphibious assault ship, helicopter
LSD (H)	Landing ship dock with own landing craft, helicopter
LSL (H)	Landing ship logistic (Aust, UK, Sin), helicopter
LSM (H)	Landing ship medium with bow doors and/or landing ramp, helicopter
LST (H)	Landing ship tank with bow doors and/or landing ramp, helicopter
LSV	Landing ship vehicle with bow doors and/or landing ramp
RCL	Ramped craft, logistic (UK)
TCD	Landing ship, dock (Fra)
UCAC	Utility craft air cushion

Mine Warfare Ships

MCAC	Mine clearance air cushion
MCD	Mine countermeasures vessel, diving support
MCDV	Maritime coast defence vessel (Can)
MCMV	Mine countermeasures vessel
MCS	Mine countermeasures support ship
MH (I) (C) (O)	Minehunter (inshore) (coastal) (ocean)
MHCD	Minehunter coastal with drone
MHSC	Minehunter/sweeper coastal
ML (I) (C) (A)	Minelayer (inshore) (coastal) (auxiliary)
MS (I) (C) (R)	Minesweeper (inshore) (coastal) (river)
MSA (T)	Minesweeper, auxiliary (tug)
MSB	Minesweeper, boat
MSCD	Coastal minesweeper capable of controlling drones
MSD	Minesweeper, drone
MSO	Minesweeper, ocean
SRMH	Single role minehunter (UK)

Auxiliaries

ABU (H)	Buoy tender (helicopter)
AD	Destroyer tender
ADG	Degaussing/deperming ship
AE (L)	Ammunition ship capable of underway replenishment (small)
AEM	Missile support ship
AET (L)	Ammunition transport (small)
AF (L)	Stores ship (small)
AFS	Combat stores ship, capable of underway replenishment
AG (H)	Auxiliary miscellaneous (helicopter)
AGB	Icebreaker
AGDS	Deep submergence support ship
AGE (H)	Research ship (helicopter)
AGF (H)	Auxiliary Flag or command ship (helicopter)
AGI (H)	Intelligence collection ship (helicopter)
AGM (H)	Missile range instrumentation ship (helicopter)
AGOB	Polar research ship
AGOR (H)	Oceanographic research ship (helicopter)
AGOS (H)	Ocean surveillance ship (helicopter)
AGP	Patrol craft tender
AGS (C) (H)	Surveying ship (coastal) (helicopter)
AH	Hospital ship
AK (L) (R) (H)	Cargo ship (light) (Ro-Ro) (helicopter)
AKE	Armament stores carrier
AKR	Roll on/roll off sealift ship
AKS (L) (H)	Stores ship (light) (helicopter)
ANL	Boom defence/cable/netlayer
AO	Replenishment oiler (US)
AOE	Fast combat support ship, primarily for POL replenishment
AOR (L) (H)	Replenishment oiler (small) (helicopter)
AOT (L)	Transport oiler (small)
AP (H)	Personnel transport (helicopter)
APB	Barracks ship
APCR	Primary casualty receiving ship
AR (L)	Repair ship (small)
ARC	Submarine cable repair ship
ARS (D) (H)	Salvage ship (heavy lift) (helicopter)
AS (L)	Submarine tender (small)
ASE	Research ship (Jpn)
ASR	Submarine rescue ship
ATA	Auxiliary ocean tug
ATF	Fleet ocean tug and supply ship
ATR	Fleet ocean tug (firefighting and rescue)
ATS	Salvage and rescue ship
AVB	Aviation support ship
AVM	Aviation and missile support
AWT (L)	Water tanker (small)
AX (L) (H)	Training ship (small) (helicopter)
AXS	Sail training ship
AXT	Training tender
HSS	Helicopter support ship
HSV	High speed logistic support vessel (catamaran)
TV	Training ship (Jpn)

Service Craft

ASY	Auxiliary yacht (Jpn)
SAR	Search and rescue vessel
WFL	Water/fuel lighter (Aust)
YAC	Royal yacht
YAG	Service craft, miscellaneous
YAGK	Surface effect craft, experimental
YDG	Degaussing vessel
YDT	Diving tender
YE	Ammunition lighter
YF	Covered personnel transport under 40 m
YFB (H)	Ferry (helicopter)
YFL	Launch
YFRT	Range safety vesel
YFU	Former LCU used for cargo
YGS	Survey launch
YH	Ambulance boat
YM	Dredging craft
YO (G)	Fuel barge (gasolene)
YP	Harbour patrol craft
YPB	Floating barracks
YPC	Oil pollution control vessel
YPT	Torpedo recovery vessel
YT (B) (M) (L)	Harbour tug (large) (medium) (small)
YTR	Harbour fire/rescue craft with several monitors
YTT	Torpedo trials craft
YW	Water barge

Pennant numbers of major surface ships in numerical order

Number	*Ship's name*	*Type*	*Country*	*Page*
001	Guria	LCU	Georgia	279
001	President H I Remeliik	PB	Palau	591
001	San Juan	WPBO	Philippines	614
LRG 001	Constancia	PBR	Venezuela	985
LSM 001	Punta Macolla	PB	Venezuela	985
002	Edsa II	WPBO	Philippines	614
LRG 002	Perseverancia	PBR	Venezuela	985
LSM 002	Farallón Centinela	PB	Venezuela	985
003	Pampanga	WPBO	Philippines	614
AF 003	Amougna	PBR	Cote d'Ivoire	180
LRG 003	Honestidad	PBR	Venezuela	985
LSM 003	Charagato	PB	Venezuela	985
004	Batangas	WPBO	Philippines	614
AF 004	Monsekela	PBR	Cote d'Ivoire	180
LRG 004	Tenacidad	PBR	Venezuela	985
LSM 004	Bajo Brito	PB	Venezuela	985
LRG 005	Integridad	PBR	Venezuela	985
LSM 005	Bajo Araya	PB	Venezuela	985
LRG 006	Lealtad	PBR	Venezuela	985
LSM 006	Carecare	PB	Venezuela	985
LSM 007	Vela de Cobo	PB	Venezuela	985
LSM 008	Cayo Macereo	PB	Venezuela	985
01	Pohjanmaa	ML	Finland	236
01	Rabaul	PB	Papua New Guinea	595
A 01	Contramaestre Casado	APH	Spain	755
A 01	Paluma	AGSC	Australia	36
A 01	Salema	WPB	Spain	758
ADR 01	Banderas	YM	Mexico	525
AMP 01	Huasteco	APH/AK/AH	Mexico	526
ARE 01	Otomi	ATF	Mexico	526
ATQ 01	Aguascalientes	YOG/YO	Mexico	526
ATR 01	Maya	AKS	Mexico	525
ASV 01	Wyatt Earp	YGS	Australia	36
BE 01	Cuauhtémoc	AXS	Mexico	525
BI 01	Alejandro de Humboldt	AGOR	Mexico	524
BL 01	Manuel José Arce	AGP	El Salvador	226
CSL 01	Wattle	YE	Australia	39
F 01	Abu Dhabi	FFGHM	UAE	857
FL 01	Hiryu	FL/YTR	Japan	445
FM 01	Presidente Eloy Alfaro	FFGHM	Ecuador	206
FSM 01	Palikir	PB	Micronesia	527
G 01	Mazzei	PB/YXT	Italy	410
HL 01	Shoyo	AGS	Japan	445
KA 01	Kristaps	WPB	Latvia	481
LC 01	Yopito	LCM	Venezuela	985
LF 01	Cacine	PC	Guinea-Bissau	316
LL 01	Tsushima	AKSL	Japan	446
LP 01	Marlim	PB	Brazil	78
LPH 01	Suboficial Rogelio Lesme	YGS	Paraguay	597
M 01	Al Hasbah	MHC	UAE	860
MRF 01	Sökaren	MSD	Sweden	777
MS 01	Kinugasa	YPC	Japan	447
NGPWB 01	Bundeena	YFL/YDT	Australia	40
P 01	Alphonse Reynolds	PB	St Lucia	708
P 01	Bar	PB	Montenegro	530
P 01	Capitán Cabral	PBR	Paraguay	596
P 01	Jarabakka	PB	Suriname	767
P 01	Liberta	PB	Antigua and Barbuda	10
P 01	Oryx	PBO	Namibia	545
P 01	Salamis	PBM	Cyprus	187
P 01	Trident	PB	Barbados	61
P 01	Zibens	PB	Latvia	479
PB 01	Tyrrel Bay	PB	Grenada	314
PC 01	Matsunami	PC/PB	Japan	443
PL 01	Oki	PL/PSOH	Japan	438
PLH 01	Soya	PLH/PSOH	Japan	438
PM 01	Natsui	PM/PSO	Japan	441
PS 01	Shinzan	PS/PBF	Japan	442
PT 01	Fatimah I	PB	Gambia	278
Q 01	Damsah	PGGF	Qatar	639
S 01	Gladan	AXS	Sweden	778
SVG 01	Captain Mulzac	PB	St Vincent	709
TNBH 01	Xavier Pinto Telleria	–	Bolivia	69
TNR 01	Jose Manuel Pando	YAG	Bolivia	69
02	Dreger	PB	Papua New Guinea	595
02	Hämeenmaa	ML	Finland	236
02	Tukoro	PB	Vanuatu	978
A 02	Mermaid	AGSC	Australia	36
A 02	Rio Guadiaro	WPB	Spain	758
ADR 02	Magdalena	YM	Mexico	525
AMP 02	Zapoteco	APH/AK/AH	Mexico	526
ARE 02	Yaqui	ATF	Mexico	526
ATQ 02	Tlaxcala	YOG/YO	Mexico	526
BI 02	Onjuku	AGS	Mexico	524
CSL 02	Boronia	YE	Australia	39
FL 02	Shoryu	FL/YTR	Japan	445
FM 02	Moran Valverde	FFGHM	Ecuador	206
FSM 02	Micronesia	PB	Micronesia	527
G 02	Vaccaro	PB/YXT	Italy	410
HL 02	Takuyo	AGS	Japan	446
KAL-IV-02	Baruna Jaya I	AGS/AGOR	Indonesia	363
LF 02	Cacheu	PC	Guinea-Bissau	316
M 02	Al Murjan	MHC	UAE	860
MS 02	Saikai	YPC	Japan	447
NGPWB 02	Elouera	YFL/YDT	Australia	40
P 02	Defender	PB	St Lucia	708
P 02	Leonard C Banfield	PB	Barbados	61
P 02	Palmetto	PB	Antigua and Barbuda	10
P 02	Spari	PB	Suriname	767
P 02	Waspada	PTG	Brunei	88
P 02	Kyrenia	PBM	Cyprus	187
P 02	Lode	PB	Latvia	479
P 02	Nanawa	PBR	Paraguay	596
PB 02	Levera	PB	Grenada	314
PL 02	Erimo	PL/PSOH	Japan	438
PLH 02	Tsugaru	PLH/PSOH	Japan	438
PM 02	Kitakami	PM/PSO	Japan	441
PS 02	Saroma	PS/PBF	Japan	442
PT 02	Sulayman Jun-Kung	PB	Gambia	278
Q 02	Al Ghariyah	PGGF	Qatar	639
S 02	Falken	AXS	Sweden	778
TNR 02	Nicolas Suarez	YAG	Bolivia	69
03	Lata	PB	Solomon Islands	733
03	Seeadler	PB	Papua New Guinea	595
03	Sydney	FFGHM	Australia	30
A 03	Rio Pisuerga	WPB	Spain	758
A 03	Shepparton	AGSC	Australia	36
ADR 03	Kino	YM	Mexico	525
ARE 03	Seri	ATF	Mexico	526
ATR 03	Tarasco	AK	Mexico	525
BI 03	Altair	AGOR	Mexico	523
CSL 03	Telopea	YE	Australia	39
FL 03	Nanryu	FL/YTR	Japan	445
G 03	Di Bartolo	PB/YXT	Italy	410
HL 03	Meiyo	AGS	Japan	446
KAL-IV-03	Baruna Jaya II	AGS/AGOR	Indonesia	363
MS 03	Katsuren	YPC	Japan	447
NGPWB 03	Shoalhaven	YFL/YDT	Australia	40
P 03	Commander Tsomakis	PB	Cyprus	187
P 03	Giovanni Denaro	PB	Italy	410
P 03	Gramorgu	PB	Suriname	767
P 03	Herceg Novi	PB	Montenegro	530
P 03	Pejuang	PTG	Brunei	88
P 03	Rudyard Lewis	PB	Barbados	61
P 03	Yellow Elder	PB	Bahamas	46
P 03	Zarrar	PGGF	Pakistan	588
P 03	Linga	PB	Latvia	479
PL 03	Kudaka	PL/PSOH	Japan	438
PLH 03	Oosumi	PLH/PSOH	Japan	438
PM 03	Bihoro	PM/PSO	Japan	441
PS 03	Inasa	PS/PBF	Japan	442
Q 03	Rbigah	PGGF	Qatar	639
04	Auki	PB	Solomon Islands	733
04	Darwin	FFGHM	Australia	30
04	Moresby	PB	Papua New Guinea	595
A 04	Benalla	AGSC	Australia	36
A 04	Kahu	AXL	New Zealand	561
A 04	Martín Posadillo	AKRH	Spain	755
A 04	Rio Nalon	WPB	Spain	758
ADR 04	Yavaros	YM	Mexico	525
ARE 04	Cora	ATF	Mexico	526
BI 04	Antares	AGOR	Mexico	523
FL 04	Kairyu	FL/YTR	Japan	445
FM 04	Shiraito	FM/YTR	Japan	445
G 04	Avallone	PB/YXT	Italy	410
HL 04	Tenyo	AGS	Japan	446
KAL-IV-04	Baruna Jaya III	AGS/AGOR	Indonesia	363
M 04	Carlskrona	AG	Sweden	778
M 04	Imanta	MHC	Latvia	480
NGPWB 04	Sea Dragon	YFL/YDT	Australia	40
P 04	Bulta	PB	Latvia	479
P 04	Commander Georgiu	PB	Cyprus	187
P 04	Karrar	PGGF	Pakistan	588
P 04	Protector	PB	St Lucia	708
P 04	Seteria	PTG	Brunei	88
P 04	Teniente Farina	PBR	Paraguay	596
PL 04	Yahiko	PL/PSOH	Japan	438
PLH 04	Hayato	PLH/PSOH	Japan	438
PM 04	Tokachi	PM/PSO	Japan	441
PS 04	Kirishima	PS/PBF	Japan	442
Q 04	Barzan	PGGFM	Qatar	638
SVG 04	Hairoun	PB	St Vincent	709
TNR 04	Max Paredes	YAG	Bolivia	69
05	Almirante Cochrane	FFGHM	Chile	118
05	Melbourne	FFGHM	Australia	30
05	Uusimaa	ML	Finland	236
A 05	Adventure	YGS	New Zealand	561
A 05	El Camino Español	AKR	Spain	755
A 05	Rio Palma	WPB	Spain	758
ADR 05	Chamela	YM	Mexico	525
ARE 05	Iztaccihuatl	YTL	Mexico	526
BI 05	Rio Suchiate	AKS	Mexico	523
D 05	Ukale	PB	Dominica	200
FL 05	Suiryu	FL/YTR	Japan	445
FSM 05	Independence	PB	Micronesia	527
G 05	Oltramonti	PB/YXT	Italy	410
HL 05	Kaiyo	AGS	Japan	446
KAL-IV-05	Baruna Jaya IV	AGS/AGOR	Indonesia	363
L 05	President El Hadj Omar Bongo	LSTH	Gabon	278
M 05	Viesturs	MHC	Latvia	480
NGPWB 05	Ethel Joy	YFL/YDT	Australia	40
P 05	Enterprise	PB	Barbados	61
P 05	Itaipú	PBR	Paraguay	596
PL 05	Dejima	PL/PSOH	Japan	438
PLH 05	Zao	PLH/PSOH	Japan	438
PM 05	Hitachi	PM/PSO	Japan	441
PS 05	Kamui	PS/PBF	Japan	442
Q 05	Huwar	PGGFM	Qatar	638
TNR 05	Julio Olmos	YAG	Bolivia	69
06	Almirante Condell	FFGHM	Chile	118
06	Newcastle	FFGHM	Australia	30
A 06	Rio Andarax	WPB	Spain	758
ADR 06	Tepoca	YM	Mexico	525
ARE 06	Popocateptl	YTL	Mexico	526
BI 06	Rio Hondo	AGS	Mexico	524
G 06	Barbariso	PB/YXT	Italy	410
KA 06	Gaisma	WPB	Latvia	481
KAL-IV-06	Baruna Jaya VIII	AGOR	Indonesia	363
M 06	Talivaldis	MHC	Latvia	480

Number	Ship's name	Type	Country	Page
NGPWB 06	Reliance	YFL/YDT	Australia	40
P 06	Capitán Ortiz	PBF	Paraguay	597
P 06	Excellence	PB	Barbados	61
PL 06	Kurikoma	PL/PSOH	Japan	438
PLH 06	Chikuzen	PLH/PSOH	Japan	438
PM 06	Okitsu	PM/PSO	Japan	441
PS 06	Raizan	PS/PBF	Japan	442
Q 06	Al Udeid	PGGFM	Qatar	638
R 06	Illustrious	CV	UK	872
TNBTL-06	Horacio Ugarteche	YAG	Bolivia	69
07	Almirante Lynch	FFGHM	Chile	118
A 07	Rio Guadalope	WPB	Spain	758
ADR 07	Todo Santos	YM	Mexico	525
ARE 07	Citlaltepl	YTL	Mexico	526
BI 07	Moctezuma II	AGSC	Mexico	524
G 07	Paolini	PB/YXT	Italy	410
KA 07	Ausma	WPB	Latvia	481
M 07	Visvaldis	MHC	Latvia	480
NGPWB 07	Patonga	YFL/YDT	Australia	40
P 07	Général d'Armée Ba-Oumar	PBO	Gabon	277
P 07	Teniente Robles	PBF	Paraguay	597
PL 07	Satauma	PL/PSOH	Japan	438
PLH 07	Settsu	PLH/PSOH	Japan	438
PM 07	Isazu	PM/PSO	Japan	441
PS 07	Ashitaki	PS/PBF	Japan	442
Q07	Al Deebel	PGGFM	Qatar	638
R 07	Ark Royal	CV	UK	872
TNR 07	Thames Crespo	YAG	Bolivia	69
A 08	Rio Almanzora	WPB	Spain	758
ADR 08	Asuncion	YM	Mexico	525
ARE 08	Xinantecatl	YTL	Mexico	526
BI 08	Alacran	YGS	Mexico	523
FM 08	Minoo	FM/YTR	Japan	445
G 08	Greco	PB/YXT	Italy	410
KA 08	Saule	WPB	Latvia	481
L 08	Pono	LCU	Tanzania	800
M 08	Rūsiņš	MHC	Latvia	480
NGPWB 08	Bilgola	YFL/YDT	Australia	40
P 08	Colonel Djoue-Dabany	PBO	Gabon	277
P 08	Yhaguy	PBR	Paraguay	597
PL 08	Tosa	PL/PSOH	Japan	438
PLH 08	Echigo	PLH/PSOH	Japan	438
PM 08	Chitose	PM/PSO	Japan	441
PS 08	Kariba	PS/PBF	Japan	442
A 09	Manawanui	YDT	New Zealand	562
A 09	Rio Nervion	WPB	Spain	758
ADR 09	Almejas	YM	Mexico	525
ARE 09	Matlalcueye	YTL	Mexico	526
BI 09	Rizo	YGS	Mexico	523
FM 09	Ryusei	FM/YTR	Japan	445
G 09	Cinuli	PB/YXT	Italy	410
KA 09	Klints	WPB	Latvia	481
L 09	Kibua	LCU	Tanzania	800
NGPWB 09	Sea Witch	YFL/YDT	Australia	40
P 09	Tebicuary	PBR	Paraguay	597
PLH 09	Ryukyu	PLH/PSOH	Japan	438
PM 09	Kuwano	PM/PSO	Japan	441
PS 09	Arase	PS/PBF	Japan	442
010	Amur	PBO	Russian Federation	701
010	General Paraschiv Vasilescu	PB	Romania	644
011	Chukotka	PBO	Russian Federation	701
011	Varyag	CGHM	Russian Federation	666
012	Astrakhan	PG	Russian Federation	680
012	Olenegorskiy Gorniak	LSTM	Russian Federation	681
012	Rais Hadj Mubarek	SSK	Algeria	4
013	El Hadj Slimane	SSK	Algeria	4
013	PSKR 55	PBR	Russian Federation	705
014	PSKR-714	PTF	Russian Federation	703
016	Georgiy Pobedonosets	LSTM	Russian Federation	681
016	Ural	PBO	Russian Federation	701
017	Podolsk	PGM	Russian Federation	703
018	Murmansk	PGH	Russian Federation	701
021	Tolyatti	PCM	Russian Federation	702
022	Tver	PBO	Russian Federation	701
023	Nakhodka	PCM	Russian Federation	702
023	Nevelsk	PGM	Russian Federation	703
024	Kaliningrad	PCM	Russian Federation	702
024	Lieutenant Remus Lepri	MSC	Romania	645
025	Lieutenant Lupu Dunescu	MSC	Romania	645
026	Yuzhno-Sakhalinsk	PGM	Russian Federation	703
027	Kondopoga	LSTM	Russian Federation	681
027	Pter. Almaz	PGM	Russian Federation	703
028	Sochi	PGM	Russian Federation	703
029	Lieutenant Dimitrie Nicolescu	MSC	Romania	645
030	Sub Lieutenant Alexandru Axente	MSC	Romania	645
031	Alexander Otrakovskiy	LSTM	Russian Federation	681
031	Salamaua	LSM	Papua New Guinea	595
031	Yaroslavl	PCM	Russian Federation	702
032	Buna	LSM	Papua New Guinea	595
035	Victor Kingisepp	PBO	Russian Federation	701
037	Yastreb	PCM	Russian Federation	702
038	Zapolarye	PBO	Russian Federation	701
LP 039	Miguel Ela Edjodjomo	PB	Equatorial Guinea	227
040	Sarych	PCM	Russian Federation	702
041	Grif	PCM	Russian Federation	702
LP 041	Hipolito Micha	PB	Equatorial Guinea	227
042	Orlan	PCM	Russian Federation	702
042	Madeleine	PB	Lithuania	489
043	Amur	PBO	Russian Federation	701
043	Novorossiysk	PCM	Russian Federation	702
044	Magadnets	PBO	Russian Federation	701
044	PSKR-660	PTF	Russian Federation	703
045	Mikhail Kogalniceanu	PGR	Romania	644
046	I C Bratianu	PGR	Romania	644
047	Lascar Catargiu	PGR	Romania	644
047	PSKR-700	PTF	Russian Federation	703
048	PSKR-715	PTF	Russian Federation	703
052	Cheboksary	PCM	Russian Federation	702
053	Povorino	FFLM	Russian Federation	674
053	PSKR-718	PTF	Russian Federation	703
054	Eisk	FFLM	Russian Federation	674
054	MAK 160	FSGM	Russian Federation	677
055	BDK-98	LSTM	Russian Federation	681
055	Kasimov	FFLM	Russian Federation	674
055	Marshal Ustinov	CGHM	Russian Federation	666
BA 055	Dorado I	YAG	Panama	594
BA 056	Dorado II	YAG	Panama	594
057	Groza	PGR	Russian Federation	706
BA 057	Aguacero	YAG	Panama	594
058	Ladoga	PBO	Russian Federation	701
058	PSKR 57	PBR	Russian Federation	705
BA 058	Portobelo	YAG	Panama	594
059	Aleksandrovets	FFLM	Russian Federation	674
BA 059	Fantasma Azul	YAG	Panama	594
060	Vladimirets	PGK	Russian Federation	680
060	Anadyr	FFHM	Russian Federation	700
LS 060	Fournoi	PB	Greece	312
061	Chang Bogo	SSK	Korea, South	459
062	Yi Chon	SSK	Korea, South	459
063	Admiral Kuznetsov	CVGM	Russian Federation	664
063	Choi Muson	SSK	Korea, South	459
063	Nikolay Sipyagin	AK	Russian Federation	706
063	Sokol	PCM	Russian Federation	702
063	Sokol	PGM	Russian Federation	703
064	Muromets	FFLM	Russian Federation	674
065	Briz	PGM	Russian Federation	703
065	Minsk	PCM	Russian Federation	702
065	Park Wi	SSK	Korea, South	459
065	PSKR 53	PBR	Russian Federation	705
066	Blagoveshchensk	PGR	Russian Federation	705
066	Lee Jongmu	SSK	Korea, South	459
066	Oslyabya	LSTM	Russian Federation	681
067	Jung Woon	SSK	Korea, South	459
068	Lee Sunsin	SSK	Korea, South	459
069	Na Daeyong	SSK	Korea, South	459
LS 070	Ro	PB	Greece	312
071	Lee Eokgi	SSK	Korea, South	459
071	Suzdalets	FFLM	Russian Federation	674
072	Sohn Won-II	SSK	Korea, South	460
073	Jeongji	SSK	Korea, South	460
075	Ahn Jung-Geun	SSK	Korea, South	460
075	Grigore Antipa	AGOR	Romania	645
076	Storochevik	PGM	Russian Federation	703
077	Neptun	PGM	Russian Federation	703
077	Nikolay Kaplunov	PCM	Russian Federation	702
077	Peresvet	LSTM	Russian Federation	681
078	Kobchik	PCM	Russian Federation	702
078	PSKR-717	PTF	Russian Federation	703
079	Predanyy	FFLM	Russian Federation	699
LS 080	Agios Efstathios	PB	Greece	312
SSV 080	Pribaltika	AGIM	Russian Federation	688
081	Nikolay Vilkov	LSTM	Russian Federation	681
C 087	Rover I	PBF	St Kitts and Nevis	708
088	Cholmsk	PGM	Russian Federation	703
C 088	Rover II	PBF	St Kitts and Nevis	708
093	PSKR 56	PBR	Russian Federation	705
099	Krechet	PCM	Russian Federation	702
099	Pyotr Velikiy	CGHMN	Russian Federation	665
099	Siktivkar	PGM	Russian Federation	703
1	Uruguay	FF	Uruguay	974
A 1	Al Munassir	LCT	Oman	578
A 1	Comandante General Irigoyen	PSO	Argentina	17
AFDL 1	Hay Tan	YFD	Taiwan	795
B 1	Patagonia	AORH	Argentina	20
C 1	Paraguay	PGR	Paraguay	596
DF 1	Endeavor	YFD	Dominican Republic	203
FSF-1	Sea Fighter	AGE	US	949
H 1	HARAS 1-5	PB	Oman	581
KV 1	Titran	WPSOH	Norway	574
LCC 1	Kao Hsiung	AGF	Taiwan	793
LCS 1	Freedom	–	US	928
LHD 1	Wasp	LHDM	US	940
LSV 1	Gen Frank S Besson Jr	LSV-ARMY	US	947
MCM 1	Avenger	MCM/MHSO	US	948
PCL 1	Ning Hai	PCF	Taiwan	792
RM 1	Guarocuya	YTM/YTL	Dominican Republic	203
RSV 1	Safaga	MSI	Egypt	221
S 1	Shabab Oman	AXS	Oman	578
SB 1	Ho Chie	LCU	Taiwan	793
T 1	Teniente Herreros	AKL	Paraguay	598
T 1	Al Sultana	AKS	Oman	579
T-ACS 1	Keystone State	AK	US	961
T-AKE 1	Lewis and Clark	AKEH	US	954
Z 1	Al Bushra	PBO	Oman	577
Z 1	Baltyk	AORL	Poland	625
Z 1	Dheeb Al Bahar 1	PB	Oman	580
2	Pedro Campbell	FF	Uruguay	974
2	Uruguay	PBR	Uruguay	976
2-508	Al Hirasa	FFL	Syria	783
A 2	Nasr Al Bahr	LSTH	Oman	578
A 2	Teniente Olivieri	PBO	Argentina	17
AFDL 2	Kim Men	YFD	Taiwan	795
H 2	Haras 2	PB	Oman	581
HD 2	Viken	YPT/YDT	Norway	573
HSV-2	Swift	HSV/MCS	US	950
LCS 2	Independence	–	US	932
LHD 2	Essex	LHDM	US	940
LSV 2	CW 3 Harold C Clinger	LSV-ARMY	US	947
LSV-2	Cutthroat	DSV	US	951
MCM 2	Defender	MCM/MHSO	US	948
PCL 2	An Hai	PCF	Taiwan	792
Q 2	Libertad	AXS	Argentina	20
R 2	Querandi	YTB/YTL	Argentina	21
RM 2	Guarionex	YTM/YTL	Dominican Republic	203
RSV 2	Abu El Ghoson	MSI	Egypt	221

PENNANT LIST

Number	Ship's name	Type	Country	Page
SB 2	Ho Ten	LCU	Taiwan	793
T-ACS 2	Gem State	AK	US	961
T-AKE 2	Sacagawea	AKEH	US	954
Z 2	Al Mansoor	PBO	Oman	577
Z 2	Dheeb al bahar 2	PB	Oman	581
03	Lomor	PB	Marshall Islands	509
3	Uruguay	PBR	Uruguay	976
A 3	Francisco de Gurruchaga	PSO	Argentina	17
AFDL 3	Han Jih	YFD	Taiwan	795
B 3	Canal Beagle	AKS	Argentina	20
H 3	Haras 3	PB	Oman	581
HM 3	Torpen	YPT/YDT	Norway	573
HT 3	Karlsøy	YPT/YDT	Norway	573
LCS 3	Fort Worth	–	US	928
LHD 3	Kearsarge	LHDM	US	940
LSV 3	Gen Brehon B Somervell	LSV-ARMY	US	947
MCM 3	Sentry	MCM/MHSO	US	948
PC 3	Hurricane	PBFM	US	937
R 3	Tehuelche	YTB/YTL	Argentina	21
RM 3	Guaroa	YTM/YTL	Dominican Republic	203
RM 3	Enriquillo	ATA	Dominican Republic	203
SB 3	Ayanka	ARS/ATA	Russian Federation	698
T-ACS 3	Grand Canyon State	AK	US	961
T-AKE 3	Alan Shepard	AKEH	US	954
T-AVB 3	Wright	AVB	US	961
YAC 3	Oriole	AXS	Canada	104
Z 3	Al Najah	PBO	Oman	577
Z 3	Dheeb al bahar 3	PB	Oman	581
4	General Artigas	ARL	Uruguay	978
4	Uruguay	PBR	Uruguay	976
ARDM 4	Shippingport	ARDM	US	953
B 4	Bahia San Blas	AKS	Argentina	20
D 4	Melville	PB	Dominica	200
H 4	Haras 4	PB	Oman	581
HS 4	Sleipner	YPT/YDT	Norway	573
LCS 4	Coronado	–	US	932
LHA 4	Nassau	LHAM	US	943
LHD 4	Boxer	LHDM	US	940
LSV 4	LTG William B Bunker	LSV-ARMY	US	947
MCM 4	Champion	MCM/MHSO	US	948
R 4	Triunfo	YTM/YTL	Paraguay	598
RM 4	Magua	YTM/YTL	Dominican Republic	203
SI 4	Puerto Buenos Aires	YTL/YTR	Argentina	24
T-ACS 4	Gopher State	AK	US	961
T-AKE 4	Richard E Byrd	AKEH	US	954
T-AVB 4	Curtiss	AVB	US	961
5	15 de Noviembre	PBO	Uruguay	975
5	Uruguay	PBR	Uruguay	976
A 5	Ketam	YTM/YTL	Malaysia	502
ARD 5	Fo Wu 5	YFD	Taiwan	795
ARDM 5	ARCO	ARDM	US	953
B 5	Cabo de Hornos	AKS	Argentina	20
H 5	Haras 5	PB	Oman	581
HS 5	Mjølner	YPT/YDT	Norway	573
LHA 5	Peleliu	LHAM	US	943
LHD 5	Bataan	LHDM	US	940
LSV 5	MG Charles P Gross	LSV-ARMY	US	947
MCM 5	Guardian	MCM/MHSO	US	948
MSD 5	Hirsholm	MSD/AXL/AGSC	Denmark	194
PC 5	Typhoon	PBFM	US	937
Q 5	Almirante Irizar	AGB/AGOB	Argentina	21
R 5	Angostura	YTM/YTL	Paraguay	598
R 5	Mocovi	YTB/YTL	Argentina	21
T-AFS 5	Concord	AFSH	US	954
T-ACS 5	Flickertail State	AK	US	961
T-AKE 5	Robert E Peary	AKEH	US	954
6	25 de Agosto	PBO	Uruguay	975
6	Uruguay	PBR	Uruguay	976
A 6	Sotong	YTM/YTL	Malaysia	502
A 6	Suboficial Castillo	PSO	Argentina	17
AFDL 6	Dynamic	AFDL	US	953
ARD 6	Fo Wu 6	YFD	Taiwan	795
CG 6	Cascadura	PB	Trinidad and Tobago	821
H 6	Haras 6	PB	Oman	580
KV 6	Garsøy	WPSOH	Norway	574
LHA 6	America	LHA	US	946
LHD 6	Bonhomme Richard	LHDM	US	940
LSV 6	Sp/4 James A Loux	LSV-ARMY	US	947
MCM 6	Devastator	MCM/MHSO	US	948
MSD 6	Saltholm	MSD/AXL/AGSC	Denmark	194
PC 6	Sirocco	PBFM	US	937
R 6	Calchaqui	YTB/YTL	Argentina	21
SB 6	Moshchny	ARS/ATA	Russian Federation	698
T-AKE 6	Amelia Earhart	AKEH	US	954
T-ACS 6	Cornhusker State	AK	US	961
T-AOE 6	Supply	AOEH	US	954
7	Uruguay	PBR	Uruguay	976
A 7	Kupang	YTM/YTL	Malaysia	502
A 7	Al Neemran	LSTH	Oman	578
CG 7	Corozal Point	PB	Trinidad and Tobago	821
H 7	Haras 7	PB	Oman	580
HM 7	Kjeøy	YPT/YDT	Norway	573
KV 7	Åhav	WPSOH	Norway	574
LHD 7	Iwo Jima	LHDM	US	940
LPD 7	Cleveland	LPD	US	944
LSV 7	SSGT Robert T Kuroda	LSV-ARMY	US	947
MCM 7	Patriot	MCM/MHSO	US	948
PC 7	Squall	PBFM	US	937
R 7	Esperanza	YTM/YTL	Paraguay	598
R 7	Ona	YTB/YTL	Argentina	21
T-AKE 7	Carl M Brashear	AKEH	US	954
T-AOE 7	Rainier	AOEH	US	954
T-AFS 7	San Jose	AFSH	US	954
T-ARC 7	Zeus	ARC	US	956
8	Uruguay	PBR	Uruguay	976
A 8	Kepah	YTM/YTL	Malaysia	502
A 8	Saba Al Bahr	LSTH	Oman	578
CG 8	Crown Point	PB	Trinidad and Tobago	821
FFG 8	McInerney	FFH	US	930
H 8	Haras 8	PB	Oman	580
LHD 8	Makin Island	LHDM	US	940
LPD 8	Dubuque	LPD	US	944
LSV 8	MG Robert Smalls	LSV-ARMY	US	947
MCM 8	Scout	MCM/MHSO	US	948
P 8	Paul Bogle	PB	Jamaica	413
R 8	Toba	YTB/YTL	Argentina	21
SB 8	Canal Emilio Mitre	YTL/YTR	Argentina	24
T-AOE 8	Arctic	AOEH	US	954
T-AKE 8	Wally Schirra	AKEH	US	954
WPB 8	Zephyr	WPC/PB	US	967
Z 8	Meduza	AOTL	Poland	625
9	Uruguay	PBR	Uruguay	976
A 9	Alferez Sobral	PBO	Argentina	17
A 9	Siput	YTM/YTL	Malaysia	502
A 9	Al Doghas	LSTH	Oman	578
CG 9	Galera Point	PB	Trinidad and Tobago	821
H 9	Haras 9	PB	Oman	580
LPD 9	Denver	LPD	US	944
MCM 9	Pioneer	MCM/MHSO	US	948
PC 9	Chinook	PBFM	US	937
SB 9	Canal Costanero	YTL/YTR	Argentina	24
T-AKE 9	Matthew Perry	AKEH	US	954
10	Al Riffa	PB	Bahrain	49
10	Colonia	PB	Uruguay	975
10	Uruguay	PBR	Uruguay	976
A 10	Al Temsah	LSTH	Oman	578
A 10	Rio Guadalaviar	WPB	Spain	758
A 10	Teritup	YTM/YTL	Malaysia	502
ACV 10	Roebuck Bay	PB	Australia	41
ADR 10	Chacagua	YM	Mexico	525
ARE 10	Tlaloc	YTL	Mexico	526
BI 10	Cabezo	YGS	Mexico	523
CG 10	Barcolet Point	PB	Trinidad and Tobago	821
D 10	Almirante Brown	DDGHM	Argentina	12
FM 10	Kiyotaki	FM/YTR	Japan	445
H 10	Haras 10	PB	Oman	580
L 10	Guarapari	EDCG/LCU	Brazil	81
MCM 10	Warrior	MCM/MHSO	US	948
NGPWB 10	Brutus	YFL/YDT	Australia	40
P 10	Général Nazaire Boulingui	PTM	Gabon	278
P 10	Piratini	PB	Brazil	80
PC 10	Firebolt	PBFM	US	937
PK 10	Sailfish	PBF	Singapore	731
PLH 10	Daisen	PLH/PSOH	Japan	438
PM 10	Sorachi	PM/PSO	Japan	441
PS 10	Sanbe	PS/PBF	Japan	442
R 10	Chulupi	YTB/YTL	Argentina	21
SVG 10	H K Tannis	PB	Grenadines	709
T-AOE 10	Bridge	AOEH	US	954
T-AKR 10	Cape Island	AKR	US	961
T-AKE 10	Charles Drew	AKEH	US	954
T-AFS 10	Saturn	AFSH	US	955
U 10	Aspirante Nascimento	AXL	Brazil	84
WAGB 10	Polar Star	WAGBH	US	968
YTT 10	Battle Point	YTT	US	952
Z 10	Dhofar	PGGF	Oman	577
11	Capitán Prat	FFGM	Chile	117
11	Hawar	PB	Bahrain	49
11	Mahamiru	MHC	Malaysia	500
11	Rio Negro	PB	Uruguay	975
11	Smeli	FFLM	Bulgaria	90
11	Uruguay	PBR	Uruguay	976
A 11	Belankas	YTM/YTL	Malaysia	502
A 11	Endeavour	AORH	New Zealand	561
A 11	Marqués de la Ensenada	AORLH	Spain	756
A 11	Rio Cabriel	WPB	Spain	758
ADR 11	Coyuca	YM	Mexico	525
AGS 11	Sunjin	AGE	Korea, South	472
BE 11	Simón Bolívar	AXS	Venezuela	983
BI 11	Anegagada de Adentro	YGS	Mexico	523
BO 11	Punta Brava	AGOR	Venezuela	982
C 11	Lieutenant General Dimo Hamaambo	PB	Namibia	544
CF 11	Amazonas	CF/PGR	Peru	603
CM 11	Esmeraldas	FSGHM	Ecuador	206
D 11	La Argentina	DDGHM	Argentina	12
K 11	Felinto Perry	ASRH	Brazil	85
K 11	Stockholm	FSG	Sweden	773
L 11	Tambaú	EDCG/LCU	Brazil	81
LG 11	Los Taques	YAG	Venezuela	984
LH 11	Gabriela	AGSC	Venezuela	983
LL 11	Hokuto	ABU	Japan	446
M 11	Diana	PSOH/MCS/FSGM	Spain	747
M 11	Styrsö	MHSDI/YDT	Sweden	777
MCM 11	Gladiator	MCM/MHSO	US	948
P 11	Žemaitis	PBO	Lithuania	488
P 11	Barceló	PB	Spain	749
P 11	Mont Arreh	PB	Djibouti	200
P 11	Pirajá	PB	Brazil	80
PC 11	Constitución	PBG/PG	Venezuela	981
PC 11	Hayanami	PC/PB/YTR	Japan	444
PC 11	Whirlwind	PBFM	US	937
PF 11	Rajah Humabon	FF	Philippines	608
PL 11	Dionysos	PB	Cyprus	187
PM 11	Yubari	PM/PSO	Japan	441
PS 11	Mizuki	PS/PBF	Japan	442
Q 11	Comodoro Rivadavia	AGOR	Argentina	19
R 11	Príncipe de Asturias	CV	Spain	742
RA 11	General Francisco De Miranda	ATA	Venezuela	983
RTOP 11	Kralj Petar Kresimir IV	FSG	Croatia	182
SD 11	Wrona	YDG	Poland	625
SVK 11	Östhammar	PB	Sweden	774
T-AKR 11	Cape Intrepid	AKR	US	961
T-AKE 11	Washington Chambers	AKEH	US	954
U 11	Guarda Marinha Jansen	AXL	Brazil	84
WAGB 11	Polar Sea	WAGBH	US	968
YTT 11	Discovery Bay	YTT	US	952
Z 11	Al Sharqiyah	PGGF	Oman	577

Number	Ship's name	Type	Country	Page
12	Jerai	MHC	Malaysia	500
12	Paysandu	PB	Uruguay	976
12	Uruguay	PBR	Uruguay	976
12-64	Al Whada	SAR	Morocco	537
12-65	Sebou	SAR	Morocco	537
A 12	Rio Cervantes	WPB	Spain	758
A 12	São Paulo	CVM	Brazil	72
ADR 12	Farrallon	YM	Mexico	525
BI 12	Rio Tuxpan	AGS	Mexico	524
CF 12	Loreto	CF/PGR	Peru	603
CM 12	Manabi	FSGHM	Ecuador	206
D 12	Heroina	DDGHM	Argentina	12
F 12	Aukštaitis	FFLM	Lithuania	487
GC 12	General José Trinidad Moran	WFS	Venezuela	984
K 12	Malmö	FSG	Sweden	773
L 12	Camboriú	EDCG/LCU	Brazil	81
L 12	Ocean	LPH	UK	884
LG 12	Los Cayos	YAG	Venezuela	984
LH 12	Lely	AGSC	Venezuela	983
M 12	Spårö	MHSDI/YDT	Sweden	777
MCM 12	Ardent	MCM/MHSO	US	948
P 12	Djukas	PBO	Lithuania	488
P 12	Laya	PB	Spain	749
P 12	Pampeiro	PB	Brazil	80
PC 12	Federación	PBG/PG	Venezuela	981
PC 12	Setogiri	PC/PB/YTR	Japan	444
PC 12	Thunderbolt	PBFM	US	937
PL 12	Kourion	PB	Cyprus	187
PM 12	Motoura	PM/PSO	Japan	441
PS 12	Kouya	PS/PBF	Japan	442
R 12	Mataco	YTB/YTL	Argentina	21
RTOP 12	Kralj Dmitar Zvonimir	FSG	Croatia	182
T-AKE 12	William Mclean	AKEH	US	954
U 12	Guarda Marinha Brito	AXL	Brazil	84
YDT 12	Granby	YDT	Canada	105
Z 12	Al Bat'nah	PGGF	Oman	577
13	Ledang	MHC	Malaysia	500
13	Reshitelni	FSM	Bulgaria	91
13	Uruguay	PBR	Uruguay	976
A 13	Rio Ara	WPB	Spain	758
A 13	Tunas Samudera	AXS	Malaysia	501
ADR 13	Chairel	YM	Mexico	525
B 13	Ingeniero Julio Krause	AKS/AOTL	Argentina	20
CF 13	Marañon	CF/PGR	Peru	602
CM 13	Los Rios	FSGHM	Ecuador	206
D 13	Sarandi	DDGHM	Argentina	12
GC 13	Delfin	WPSO	Argentina	22
LL 13	Ginga	ABU	Japan	446
LPD 13	Nashville	LPD	US	944
M 13	Skaftö	MHSDI/YDT	Sweden	777
MCM 13	Dextrous	MCM/MHSO	US	948
P 13	Parati	PB	Brazil	80
PC 13	Independencia	PBG/PG	Venezuela	981
PC 13	Mizunami	PC/PB/YTR	Japan	444
PL 13	Ilarion	PB	Cyprus	187
PM 13	Kano	PM/PSO	Japan	441
PS 13	Tsukuba	PS/PBF	Japan	442
WPC 13	Shamal	WPC/PB	US	967
14	Almirante Latorre	FFGM	Chile	117
14	Bodri	FSM	Bulgaria	91
14	Kinabalu	MHC	Malaysia	500
14	Uruguay	PBR	Uruguay	976
A 14	Patiño	AORH	Spain	755
A 14	Resolution	AGS	New Zealand	561
A 14	Rio Adaja	WPB	Spain	758
ADR 14	San Andres	YM	Mexico	525
AGOR 14	Melville	AGOR	US	950
CF 14	Ucayali	CF/PGR	Peru	602
CM 14	El Oro	FSGHM	Ecuador	206
J 14	Nirupak	AGSH	India	346
KA 14	Astra	WPB	Latvia	481
L 14	Albion	LPD	UK	885
M 14	Sturkö	MHSDI/YDT	Sweden	777
MCM 14	Chief	MCM/MHSO	US	948
P 14	Bolong Kanta	PB	Gambia	278
P 14	Ordóñez	PB	Spain	749
P 14	Penedo	PB	Brazil	80
P 14	Perwira	PB	Brunei	89
PC 14	Iyonami	PC/PB/YTR	Japan	444
PC 14	Libertad	PBG/PG	Venezuela	981
PL 14	Karpasia	PB	Cyprus	187
PM 14	Sendai	PM/PSO	Japan	441
PS 14	Akagi	PS/PBF	Japan	442
R 14	Zbyszko	ARS	Poland	625
WPC 14	Tornado	WPC/PB	US	967
Z 14	Mussandam	PGGF	Oman	577
Z 14	Zahra 14	PBI	Oman	581
15	Almirante Blanco Encalada	FFGHM	Chile	118
15	Grundsund	YAG	Sweden	779
15	Uruguay	PBR	Uruguay	976
A 15	Cantabria	AORH	Spain	755
A 15	Nireekshak	ASR	India	348
A 15	Rio Duero	WPB	Spain	758
ADR 15	San Ignacio	YM	Mexico	525
AGOR 15	Knorr	AGOR	US	950
CM 15	Los Galapágos	FSGHM	Ecuador	206
DF 15	Recalada	WAGH/AHH	Argentina	24
F 15	Abu Bakr	FF/FFT	Bangladesh	55
G 15	Paraguassú	AP	Brazil	85
HP 15	Hitra	YPT/YDT	Norway	573
J 15	Investigator	AGSH	India	346
L 15	Bulwark	LPD	UK	885
L 15	Kesari	LSTH	India	345
LPD 15	Ponce	LPD	US	944
M 15	Aratu	MSC	Brazil	82
M 15	Tineycheide	WPBF	Spain	758
P 15	Acevedo	PB	Spain	749
P 15	Pemburu	PB	Brunei	89
P 15	Poti	PB	Brazil	80
PC 15	Kurinami	PC/PB/YTR	Japan	444
PC 15	Patria	PBG/PG	Venezuela	981
PL 15	Akamas	PB	Cyprus	187
PM 15	Teshio	PM/AGOB	Japan	441
Q 15	Cormoran	AGSC	Argentina	19
R 15	Macko	ARS	Poland	625
U 15	Pará	YFB	Brazil	84
V 15	Imperial Marinheiro	PG/ATR	Brazil	79
Z 15	Zahra 15	PBI	Oman	581
16	Uruguay	PBR	Uruguay	976
A 16	Rio Guadiana	WPB	Spain	758
ADR 16	Terminos	YM	Mexico	525
CF 16	Manuel Clavero	CF/PGR	Peru	603
CM 16	Loja	FSGHM	Ecuador	206
F 16	Umar Farooq	FF	Bangladesh	54
J 16	Jamuna	AGSH	India	346
L 16	Absalon	AGF/AKR/AH	Denmark	197
L 16	Nombre de Dios	YAG	Panama	594
L 16	Shardul	LSTH	India	345
M 16	Almirante Diaz Pimienta	WPBF	Spain	758
M 16	Anhatomirim	MSC	Brazil	82
P 16	Cándido Pérez	PB	Spain	749
P 16	Penyerang	PB	Brunei	89
PC 16	Hamanami	PC/PB/YTR	Japan	444
PC 16	Victoria	PBG/PG	Venezuela	981
R 16	Capayán	YTB/YTL	Argentina	21
U 16	Doutor Montenegro	AH	Brazil	85
17	Uruguay	PBR	Uruguay	976
A 17	Rio Francoli	WPB	Spain	758
ADR 17	Teculapa	YM	Mexico	525
CF 17	Putumayo	CF/PGR	Peru	603
F 17	Ali Haider	FF/FFT	Bangladesh	55
G 17	Potengi	AG	Brazil	86
J 17	Sutlej	AGSH	India	346
L 17	Esbern Snare	AGF/AKR/AH	Denmark	197
L 17	Sharabh	LSM/LSMH	India	345
LPD 17	San Antonio	LPDM	US	942
M 17	Atalaia	MSC	Brazil	82
M 17	Rio Arba	PB	Spain	758
PC 17	Shinonome	PC/PB/YTR	Japan	444
U 17	Parnaiba	PGRH	Brazil	79
Z 17	Zahra 17	PBI	Oman	581
18	Almirante Riveros	FFGHM	Chile	118
18	Fårösund	YAG	Sweden	779
18	Uruguay	PBR	Uruguay	976
A 18	Perkons	ATA	Latvia	480
F 18	Osman	FFG	Bangladesh	54
H 18	Comandante Varella	ABU	Brazil	83
J 18	Sandhayak	AGSH	India	346
L 18	Cheetah	LSM/LSMH	India	345
LPD 18	New Orleans	LPDM	US	942
M 18	Araçatuba	MSC	Brazil	82
M 18	Rio Caudal	PB	Spain	758
P 18	Armatolos	PG	Greece	306
PC 18	Harunami	PC/PB/YTR	Japan	444
R 18	Chiquilyán	YTB/YTL	Argentina	21
U 18	Oswaldo Cruz	AHH	Brazil	85
Z 18	Zahra 18	PBI	Oman	581
19	Almirante Williams	FFHM	Chile	119
19	Uruguay	PBR	Uruguay	976
GS 19	Zhigulevsk	AGIM	Russian Federation	688
H 19	Tenente Castelo	ABU	Brazil	83
J 19	Nirdeshak	AGSH	India	346
L 19	Mahish	LSM/LSMH	India	345
LCC 19	Blue Ridge	LCCH/AGFH	US	939
LPD 19	Mesa Verde	LPDM	US	942
M 19	Abrolhos	MSC	Brazil	82
M 19	Rio Bernesga	PB	Spain	758
P 19	Navmachos	PG	Greece	306
P 19	Ngunguri	PB	Tanzania	799
PC 19	Kiyozuki	PC/PB/YTR	Japan	444
PS 19	Miguel Malvar	FS	Philippines	610
R 19	Morcoyán	YTB/YTL	Argentina	21
T-AGOS 19	Victorious	AGOS	US	957
T-AH 19	Mercy	AHH	US	955
U 19	Carlos Chagas	AHH	Brazil	85
V 19	Caboclo	PG/ATR	Brazil	79
20	Ahmad El Fateh	PGGF	Bahrain	49
20	Capitán Miranda	AXS	Uruguay	977
20	Furusund	ARS	Sweden	779
20	Thomson	SSK	Chile	117
20	Uruguay	PBR	Uruguay	976
A 20	Moawin	AORH	Pakistan	589
A 20	Neptuno	ATF/AGDS	Spain	756
ACV 20	Holdfast Bay	PB	Australia	41
CG 20	Nelson	PBO	Trinidad and Tobago	821
F 20	Godavari	FFGHM	India	335
H 20	Comandante Manhães	ABU	Brazil	83
L 20	Magar	LSTH	India	345
LCC 20	Mount Whitney	LCCH/AGFH	US	939
LPD 20	Green Bay	LPDM	US	942
M 20	Albardão	MSC	Brazil	82
M 20	Rio Martin	PB	Spain	758
P 20	Anthypoploiarchos Laskos	PGGF/PGG	Greece	305
P 20	Mamba	PB	Tanzania	799
P 20	Murature	AX	Argentina	20
P 20	Pedro Teixeira	PBR	Brazil	79
PC 20	Ayanami	PC/PB/YTR	Japan	444
PK 20	Spearfish	PBF	Singapore	731
PS 20	Magat Salamat	FS	Philippines	610
PT 20	Manta Ray	WPB	Singapore	730
PV 20	Poseidon	PBF	Cyprus	188
Q 20	Puerto Deseado	AGOB	Argentina	19
S 20	Astute	SSN	UK	867
ST 20	Intrépido	SSW	Colombia	169
T-AGOS 20	Able	AGOS	US	957
T-AH 20	Comfort	AHH	US	955
U 20	Cisne Branco	AXS	Brazil	84

Number	Ship's name	Type	Country	Page
WAGB 20	Healy	WAGBH	US	968
Z 20	Seeb	PB	Oman	578
21	Al Jabiri	PGGF	Bahrain	49
21	Cheong Hae Jin	ARS	Korea, South	471
21	Haixun	PBOH	China	167
21	Hejaz	LST	Iran	378
21	Kuha 21	MSI	Finland	236
21	Simpson	SSK	Chile	117
21	Sirius	ABU	Uruguay	977
21	Sour	LCT	Lebanon	483
21	Vigilant	PSOH	Mauritius	511
A 21	Kalmat	AOTL	Pakistan	589
BP 21	Bredstedt	WPSO	Germany	296
CG 21	Gasper Grande	PBO	Trinidad and Tobago	822
CM 21	Velarde	CM/PGGFM	Peru	602
F 21	Gomati	FFGHM	India	335
F 21	Mariscal Sucre	FFGHM	Venezuela	980
G 21	Ary Parreiras	AKSH	Brazil	85
GC 21	Guaicamacuto	PSOH	Venezuela	982
GC 21	Lynch	WPB	Argentina	22
H 21	Sirius	AGSH	Brazil	83
HPL 21	Ankaran	PBF	Slovenia	732
HS 21	Hamashio	YGS	Japan	446
J 21	Darshak	AGSH	India	346
L 21	Guldar	LSM/LSMH	India	345
L 21	Isla Paridas	YAG	Panama	594
LC 21	Curiapo	LCM	Venezuela	985
LG 21	Polaris	PBF	Venezuela	984
LM 21	Quito	–	Ecuador	208
LPD 21	New York	LPDM	US	942
M 21	Rio Guadalobon	PB	Spain	758
P 21	Anaga	PB	Spain	750
P 21	Bendeharu	PB	Brunei	89
P 21	Emer	PSO	Ireland	382
P 21	King	AX	Argentina	20
P 21	Plotarchis Blessas	PGGF/PGG	Greece	305
P 21	Raposotavares	PBR	Brazil	79
PC 21	Tokinami	PC/PB/YTR	Japan	444
PF 21	Manaure	PBR	Venezuela	983
PK 21	White Marlin	PBF	Singapore	731
PL 21	Kojima	PL/PSOH	Japan	438
PLH 21	Mizuho	PLH/PSOH	Japan	437
PM 21	Tokara	PM/PBO	Japan	442
PV 21	Evagoras	PBF	Cyprus	188
R 21	Tritão	ATA	Brazil	86
RP 21	Fernando Gomez	AKSL	Venezuela	985
RTOP 21	Šibenik	PTGF	Croatia	181
S 21	Ambush	SSN	UK	867
SSN 21	Seawolf	SSN	US	913
ST 21	Indomable	SSW	Colombia	169
T-AGOS 21	Effective	AGOS	US	957
Z 21	Shinas	PB	Oman	578
Z 21	Zahra 21	PBI	Oman	581
22	Abdul Rahman Al Fadel	PGGF	Bahrain	49
22	Carrera	SSK	Chile	116
22	Damour	LCT	Lebanon	483
22	Karabala	LST	Iran	378
22	Kuha 22	MSI	Finland	236
22	Oyarvide	AGS	Uruguay	976
AM 22	Óbuda	MSR	Hungary	322
BP 22	Neustrelitz	WPBO	Germany	297
CG 22	Chacachacare	PBO	Trinidad and Tobago	822
CM 22	Santillana	CM/PGGFM	Peru	602
F 22	Almirante Brión	FFGHM	Venezuela	980
F 22	Ganga	FFGHM	India	335
GC 22	Toll	WPB	Argentina	22
GC 22	Yavire	PSOH	Venezuela	982
HS 22	Isoshi	YGS	Japan	446
J 22	Sarvekshak	AGSH	India	346
K 22	Gövle	FSG	Sweden	772
L 22	Kumbhir	LSM/LSMH	India	345
LG 22	Sirius	PBF	Venezuela	984
LPD 22	San Diego	LPDM	US	942
M 22	Rio Cedenta	PB	Spain	758
P 22	Aoife	PSO	Ireland	382
P 22	Ayety	WPBO	Georgia	280
P 22	Maharajalela	PB	Brunei	89
P 22	Tagomago	PB	Spain	750
P 22	Ypoploiarchos Mikonios	PGGF/PGG	Greece	305
PC 22	Hamagumo	PC/PB/YTR	Japan	444
PF 22	Mara	PBR	Venezuela	983
PK 22	Silver Marlin	PBF	Singapore	731
PL 22	Miura	PL/PSOH	Japan	438
PLH 22	Yashima	PLH/PSOH	Japan	437
PM 22	Fukue	PM/PBO	Japan	442
PS 22	Sultan Kudarat	FS	Philippines	610
PV 22	Odysseus	PBF	Cyprus	188
R 22	Tridente	ATA	Brazil	86
R 22	Viraat	CVM	India	329
S 22	Artful	SSN	UK	867
SSN 22	Connecticut	SSN	US	913
T-AGOS 22	Loyal	AGOS	US	957
Z 22	Sadh	PB	Oman	578
23	Al Taweelah	PGGF	Bahrain	49
23	Kuha 23	MSI	Finland	236
23	Maldonado	PBO/AG	Uruguay	975
23	O'Higgins	SSK	Chile	116
A 23	Antares	AGS	Spain	753
AFDL 23	Adept	AFDL	US	953
AGOR-23	Thomas G Thompson	AGOR	US	950
BP 23	Bad Düben	WPBO	Germany	297
CM 23	De Los Heros	CM/PGGFM	Peru	602
F 23	General Urdaneta	FFGHM	Venezuela	980
G 23	Almirante Gastão Motta	AOR	Brazil	86
GC 23	Naiguata	PSOH	Venezuela	982
H 23	Lokys	PB	Lithuania	489
HS 23	Uzushio	YGS	Japan	446
L 23	Gharial	LSTH	India	345
LG 23	Rigel	PBF	Venezuela	984
LM 23	Guayaquil	–	Ecuador	208
LPD 23	Anchorage	LPDM	US	942
M 23	Rio Ladra	PB	Spain	758
P 23	Aisling	PSO	Ireland	382
P 23	Kemaindera	PB	Brunei	89
P 23	Marola	PB	Spain	750
P 23	Ypoploiarchos Troupakis	PGGF/PGG	Greece	305
PC 23	Awanami	PC/PB/YTR	Japan	444
PF 23	Guaicaipuro	PBR	Venezuela	983
PK 23	Striped Marlin	PBF	Singapore	731
PM 23	Oirase	PM/PBO	Japan	442
PS 23	Datu Marikudo	FS	Philippines	610
PV 23	Thexas	PB	Cyprus	187
R 23	Triunfo	ATA	Brazil	86
S 23	Audacious	SSN	UK	867
SSN 23	Jimmy Carter	SSN	US	913
T-AGM 23	Observation Island	AGM	US	956
T-AGOS 23	Impeccable	AGOS	US	956
Z 23	Khassab	PB	Oman	578
24	Farsi	LST	Iran	378
24	Kuha 24	MSI	Finland	236
A 24	Rigel	AGS	Spain	753
AGOR-24	Roger Revelle	AGOR	US	950
BP 24	Bad Bramstedt	WPSO	Germany	296
CM 24	Herrera	CM/PGGFM	Peru	602
F 24	General Soublette	FFGHM	Venezuela	980
GC 24	Mantilla	WPSO	Argentina	22
GC 24	Tamanaco	PSOH	Venezuela	982
HS 24	Okishio	YGS	Japan	446
K 24	Sundsvall	FSG	Sweden	772
LG 24	Aldebaran	PBF	Venezuela	984
LM 24	Cuenca	–	Ecuador	208
LPD 24	Arlington	LPDM	US	942
M 24	Rio Cervera	PB	Spain	758
P 24	Mouro	PB	Spain	750
P 24	Simeoforos Kavaloudis	PGGF/PGG	Greece	305
P 24	Sokhumi	PBF	Georgia	279
PC 24	Uranami	PC/PB/YTR	Japan	444
PF 24	Tamanaco	PBR	Venezuela	983
PK 24	Black Marlin	PBF	Singapore	731
PM 24	Fuji	PM/PBO	Japan	442
PV 24	Onisilos	PB	Cyprus	187
R 24	Almirante Guilhem	ATF	Brazil	86
T-AGM 24	Invincible	T-AGM	US	957
25	Kasturi	FSGH	Malaysia	495
25	Kuha 25	MSI	Finland	236
25	Sardasht	LST	Iran	378
AGOR-25	Atlantis	AGOR	US	950
AT 25	Ang Pangulo	AP	Philippines	613
BP 25	Bayreuth	WPSO	Germany	296
CM 25	Larrea	CM/PGGFM	Peru	602
F 25	General Salom	FFGHM	Venezuela	980
F 25	Khalid Bin Walid	–	Bangladesh	53
G 25	Almirante Saboía	LSLH	Brazil	82
GC 25	Azopardo	WPSO	Argentina	22
H 25	Tenente Boanerges	ABU	Brazil	83
HS 25	Iseshio	YGS	Japan	446
LG 25	Antares	PBF	Venezuela	984
LPD 25	Somerset	LPDM	US	942
M 25	Rio Jucar	PB	Spain	758
P 25	Grosa	PB	Spain	750
PC 25	Shikinami	PC/PB/YTR	Japan	444
PK 25	Blue Marlin	PBF	Singapore	731
PM 25	Echizen	PM/PBO	Japan	442
R 25	Almirante Guillobel	ATF	Brazil	86
T-AGM 25	Howard O Lorenzen	AGM	US	958
26	Kuha 26	MSI	Finland	236
26	Lekir	FSGH	Malaysia	495
26	Sab Sahel	LST	Iran	378
26	Vanguardia	ARS	Uruguay	977
AGOR 26	Kilo Moana	AGOR	US	950
BP 26	Eschwege	WPSO	Germany	296
CM 26	Sanchez Carrión	CM/PGGFM	Peru	602
F 26	Almirante Garcia	FFGHM	Venezuela	980
GC 26	Thompson	WPSO	Argentina	22
H 26	Faroleiro Mário Seixas	ABU	Brazil	84
HS 26	Hayashio	YGS	Japan	446
KV 26	Thorsteinson	WPSOH	Norway	574
LG 26	Canopus	PBF	Venezuela	984
M 26	Rio Gallo	PB	Spain	758
P 26	Dzata	PBO	Ghana	299
P 26	Medas	PB	Spain	750
P 26	Ypoploiarchos Degiannis	PGGF/PGG	Greece	305
PK 26	Jumping Marlin	PBF	Singapore	731
PM 26	Kikuchi	PM/PBO	Japan	442
27	Banco Ortiz	YTB	Uruguay	978
27	Pyong Taek	ATS	Korea, South	471
CG 27	Plymouth	PB	Trinidad and Tobago	821
G 27	Marajo	AOR	Brazil	86
GC 27	Prefecto Fique	WPSO	Argentina	22
HS 27	Kurushima	YGS	Japan	446
LG 27	Altair	PBF	Venezuela	984
M 27	Rio Jiloca	PB	Spain	758
P 27	Inagua	PB	Bahamas	46
P 27	Izaro	PB	Spain	750
P 27	Sebo	PBO	Ghana	299
P 27	Simeoforos Xenos	PGGF/PGG	Greece	305
PM 27	Yoshino	PM/PBO	Japan	442
PN 27	Sipa	AOTL	Montenegro	530
U 27	Brasil	AXH	Brazil	84
28	Kwang Yang	ATS	Korea, South	471
28	Nakhoda Ragam	FSGH	Brunei	88
CG 28	Caroni	PB	Trinidad and Tobago	821
FFG 28	Boone	FFH	US	930
G 28	Mattoso Maia	LSTH	Brazil	80
GC 28	Prefecto Derbes	WPSO	Argentina	22
M 28	Rio Alfambra	PB	Spain	758
P 28	Achimota	PG	Ghana	299
P 28	Simeoforos Simitzopoulos	PGGF/PGG	Greece	305

Number	Ship's name	Type	Country	Page
P 28	Tabarca	PB	Spain	750
PM 28	Isuzu	PM/PBO	Japan	442
PS 28	Cebu	FS	Philippines	610
PX 28	Sangitan	PBF	Malaysia	505
S 28	Vanguard	SSBN	UK	870
SO 28	Pijao	SS	Colombia	169
29	Bendahara Sakam	FSGH	Brunei	88
29	Jebat	–	Malaysia	494
CG 29	Galeota	PB	Trinidad and Tobago	821
FFG 29	Stephen W Groves	FFH	US	930
G 29	Garcia D'Ávila	LSL	Brazil	81
M 29	Rio Santa Eulalia	PB	Spain	758
P 29	Simeoforos Starakis	PGGF/PGG	Greece	305
P 29	Yogaga	PG	Ghana	299
PM 29	Yamakuni	PM/PBO	Japan	442
PS 29	Negros Occidental	FS	Philippines	610
PX 29	Sabahan	PBF	Malaysia	505
S 29	Victorious	SSBN	UK	870
SO 29	Tayrona	SS	Colombia	169
U 29	Piraim	YFBH	Brazil	85
30	Al Jarim	PB	Bahrain	49
30	Jerambak	FSGH	Brunei	88
30	Lekiu	–	Malaysia	494
30	Vishwast	WPSOH	India	350
ACV 30	Botany Bay	PB	Australia	41
CG 30	Moruga	PB	Trinidad and Tobago	821
F 30	Guaicaipuro	PSOH	Venezuela	981
G 30	Ceará	LSDH	Brazil	81
LM 30	Casma	PGG	Chile	121
M 30	Ledbury	MHSC/PP	UK	887
M 30	Rio Ulla	PB	Spain	758
P 30	Anzone	PBO	Ghana	299
P 30	Bergantín	PB	Spain	750
P 30	Roraima	PBR	Brazil	79
PK 30	Billfish	PBF	Singapore	731
PT 30	Eagle Ray	WPB	Singapore	730
PX 30	Dungun	PBF	Malaysia	505
Q 30	Al Mabrukah	FSH/AXL/AGS	Oman	575
RPB 30	Kozara	PBR	Serbia	720
S 30	Tupi	SSK	Brazil	71
S 30	Vigilant	SSBN	UK	870
V 30	Inhaúma	FSGH	Brazil	76
WLBB 30	Mackinaw	WLBB	US	968
31	Al Jasrah	PB	Bahrain	49
31	Drummond	FFG	Argentina	14
31	Iskar	MSC	Bulgaria	94
31	Temerario	MSC	Uruguay	976
A 31	Malaspina	AGS	Spain	754
A 31	Ras El Hilal	YTB	Libya	486
AM 31	Dunaújváros	MSR	Hungary	322
BB 31	Gorgona	AGSC	Colombia	176
BG 31	Bukovina	PCF	Ukraine	855
C 31	Qahir Al Amwaj	FSGMH	Oman	576
CG 31	Kairi	PB	Trinidad and Tobago	822
F 31	Brahmaputra	FFGHM	India	336
G 31	Rio de Janeiro	LSDH	Brazil	81
GS 31	Tchusovoy	AGE	Russian Federation	687
K 31	Visby	FSGH	Sweden	771
L 31	Damuan	YFU	Brunei	89
LD 31	Neyba	LCU	Dominican Republic	203
LG 31	Chichiriviche	PB	Venezuela	985
LG 31	Isla Isabela	WPB	Ecuador	211
LM 31	Chipana	PGG	Chile	121
M 31	Cattistock	MHSC/PP	UK	887
M 31	Corvo Marino	PB	Spain	759
M 31	Segura	MHC	Spain	753
P 31	Bonsu	PBO	Ghana	299
P 31	Conejera	PB	Spain	749
P 31	Eithne	PSOH	Ireland	381
P 31	Rondônia	PBR	Brazil	79
P 31	Ureca	PB	Equatorial Guinea	227
PF 31	Terepaima	PBR	Venezuela	983
PG 31	Petrel	WPB	Venezuela	983
PL 31	Izu	PL/PSOH	Japan	437
PLH 31	Shikishima	PLH/PSOH	Japan	437
PS 31	Pangasinan	FS	Philippines	610
PX 31	Tioman	PBF	Malaysia	505
S 31	Sábalo	SSK	Venezuela	979
S 31	Salta	SSK	Argentina	12
S 31	Tamoio	SSK	Brazil	71
S 31	Vengeance	SSBN	UK	870
SS 31	Angamos	SSK	Peru	599
V 31	Jaceguai	FSGH	Brazil	76
32	Guerrico	FFG	Argentina	14
32	Tsibar	MHC	Bulgaria	93
32	Zibar	MSC	Bulgaria	94
A 32	Al Ahweirif	YTB	Libya	486
A 32	Tofiño	AGS	Spain	754
AM 32	Dunafoldvar	MSR	Hungary	322
BG 32	Donbas	PCF	Ukraine	855
C 32	Al Mua'zzar	FSGMH	Oman	576
CG 32	Moriah	PB	Trinidad and Tobago	822
D 32	Daring	DDGHM	UK	877
FFG 32	John L Hall	FFH	US	930
K 32	Helsingborg	FSGH	Sweden	771
L 32	Puni	YFU	Brunei	89
LG 32	Caruanta	PB	Venezuela	985
LG 32	Isla Seymour	WPB	Ecuador	210
M 32	Sella	MHC	Spain	753
P 32	Amapá	PBR	Brazil	79
P 32	David Hansen	PBI	Ghana	299
P 32	Dragonera	PB	Spain	749
P 32	Selis	PB	Lithuania	488
PG 32	Alcatraz	WPB	Venezuela	983
PS 32	Iloilo	FS	Philippines	610
PX 32	Tumpat	PBF	Malaysia	505
S 32	Caribe	SSK	Venezuela	979
S 32	Timbira	SSK	Brazil	71
SS 32	Antofagasta	SSK	Peru	599
T-AE 32	Flint	AEH	US	955
V 32	Julio de Noronha	FSGH	Brazil	76
33	Dobrotich	MSC	Bulgaria	94
33	Fortuna	MSC	Uruguay	976
33	Granville	FFG	Argentina	14
33	Teraban	LCU	Brunei	89
33	Vikram	WPSOH	India	350
A 33	Hespérides	AGOBH	Spain	753
AW 33	Lake Bulusan	AWT	Philippines	613
CG 33	Matelot	PB	Trinidad and Tobago	822
D 33	Dauntless	DDGHM	UK	877
FFG 33	Jarrett	FFH	US	930
J 33	Meen	AGS	India	347
K 33	Härnösand	FSGH	Sweden	771
K 33	Juang	PB	Malaysia	506
LG-33	Isla Santa Cruz	WPB	Ecuador	211
M 33	Brocklesby	MHSC/PP	UK	887
M 33	Tambre	MHC	Spain	753
P 33	Abhay	FSM	India	341
P 33	Espalmador	PB	Spain	749
P 33	Skalvis	PB	Lithuania	488
PF 33	Yaracuy	PBR	Venezuela	983
PG 33	Albatros	WPB	Venezuela	983
PX 33	Segama	PBF	Malaysia	505
S 33	Tapajó	SSK	Brazil	71
SS 33	Pisagua	SSK	Peru	599
T-AE 33	Shasta	AEH	US	955
V 33	Frontin	FSGH	Brazil	76
34	Audaz	MSC	Uruguay	976
34	Evstati Vinarov	MSC	Bulgaria	94
34	Novi Sad	FFGM	Montenegro	528
34	Serasa	LCU	Brunei	89
34	Vijaya	WPSOH	India	350
AW 34	Lake Paoay	AWT	Philippines	613
D 34	Diamond	DDGHM	UK	877
H 34	Almirante Graça Aranha	ABUH	Brazil	83
K 34	Nyköping	FSGH	Sweden	771
K 34	Pulai	PB	Malaysia	506
LG-34	Isla San Cristóbal	WPB	Ecuador	211
LM 34	Angamos	PGG	Chile	121
M 34	Canal Bocayna	PB	Spain	759
M 34	Middleton	MHSC/PP	UK	887
M 34	Turia	MHC	Spain	753
P 34	Ajay	FSM	India	341
P 34	Alcanada	PB	Spain	749
PF 34	Sorocaima	PBR	Venezuela	983
PG 34	Pelícano	WPB	Venezuela	983
S 34	Tikuna	SSK	Brazil	70
SS 34	Chipana	SSK	Peru	599
T-AE 34	Mount Baker	AEH	US	955
V 34	Barroso	FSGH	Brazil	76
35	Veera	WPSOH	India	350
D 35	Dragon	DDGHM	UK	877
H 35	Amorim Do Valle	AGS	Brazil	83
K 35	Karlstad	FSGH	Sweden	771
LG 35	Isla Santa Rosa	WPB	Ecuador	210
M 35	Duero	MHC	Spain	753
M 35	Pico Del Teide	PB	Spain	759
P 35	Akshay	FSM	India	341
PS 35	Emilio Jacinto	FS	Philippines	609
SS 35	Islay	SSK	Peru	599
T-AE 35	Kiska	AEH	US	955
Y 35	Mesaha 1	AGSC	Turkey	839
36	Varuna	WPSOH	India	350
36-1	Puerto Quepos	PB	Costa Rica	179
D 36	Defender	DDGHM	UK	877
F 36	Dunagiri	FFH	India	337
FFG 36	Underwood	FFH	US	930
H 36	Taurus	AGS	Brazil	83
K 36	Perak	PB	Malaysia	506
LG 36	Isla Puná	WPB	Ecuador	210
LM 36	Riquelme	PGG	Chile	121
M 36	Rio Guadalquivir	PB	Spain	759
M 36	Tajo	MHC	Spain	753
P 36	Agray	FSM	India	341
PS 36	Apolinario Mabini	FS	Philippines	609
RSRB 36	Sabac	YDG	Serbia	721
SS 36	Arica	SSK	Peru	599
Y 36	Mesaha 2	AGSC	Turkey	839
37	Vajra	WPSOH	India	350
D 37	Duncan	DDGHM	UK	877
F 37	Beas	FFGHM	India	336
FFG 37	Crommelin	FFH	US	930
H 37	Garnier Sampaio	AGS	Brazil	83
K 37	Bayu	PB	Malaysia	506
LG 37	Isla de la Plata	WPBF	Ecuador	210
LM 37	Orella	PGG	Chile	121
M 37	Chiddingfold	MHSC/PP	UK	887
M 37	Rio Tordera	PB	Spain	759
PS 37	Artemio Ricarte	FS	Philippines	609
38	Vivek	WPSOH	India	350
FFG 38	Curts	FFH	US	930
H 38	Cruzeiro Do Sul	AGS	Brazil	84
K 38	Hijau	PB	Malaysia	506
L 38	Galana	LCM	Kenya	451
LG 38	Isla Santa Clara	WPBF	Ecuador	210
LM 38	Serrano	PGG	Chile	121
M 38	Atherstone	MHSC/PP	UK	887
M 38	Rio Pas	PB	Spain	759
PS 38	General Mariano Alvares	PB	Philippines	609
Y 38	Yüzbaşi Naşit Öngören	YPB	Turkey	842
39	Hobart	DDGHM	Australia	27
39	Vigraha	WPSOH	India	350
AS 39	Emory S Land	ASH	US	958
F 39	Betwa	FFGHM	India	336
FFG 39	Doyle	FFH	US	930
GS 39	Syzran	AGIM	Russian Federation	688
L 39	Tana	LCM	Kenya	451
LG 39	Isla Fernandina	PBO	Ecuador	210
LM 39	Uribe	PGG	Chile	121

Number	Ship's name	Type	Country	Page
M 39	Hurworth	MHSC/PP	UK	887
M 39	Rio Guadalentin	PB	Spain	759
WMEC 39	Alex Haley	PSOH/WMEC	US	965
Y 39	Binbaşi Metin Sülüş	YPB	Turkey	842
40	Al Zubara	LCU	Bahrain	50
40	Carlos Manuel de Cespedes	AXT	Cuba	186
40	Varad	WPSOH	India	350
A 40	Attock	AOTL	Pakistan	589
ACV 40	Hervey Bay	PB	Australia	41
AS 40	Frank Cable	ASH	US	958
F 40	Niterói	FFGHM	Brazil	75
F 40	Talwar	FFGHM	India	334
FFG 40	Halyburton	FFH	US	930
H 40	Antares	AGS	Brazil	83
K 40	Veer	FSGM	India	340
LG 40	Isla Española	PBO	Ecuador	210
P 40	Grajaú	PBO	Brazil	78
PK 40	Swordfish	PBF	Singapore	731
S 40	Vela	SS	India	325
41	Ajeera	YFU	Bahrain	50
41	Brisbane	DDGHM	Australia	27
41	Drazki	FFGM	Bulgaria	90
41	Espora	FFGH	Argentina	15
A 41	Warnow	YFL	Germany	295
AP 41	Aquiles	APH	Chile	123
BP 41	Kustrin-Kiez	WPBR	Germany	297
F 41	Defensora	FFGHM	Brazil	75
F 41	Taragiri	FFH	India	337
FFG 41	McClusky	FFH	US	930
K 41	Nirbhik	FSGM	India	340
L 41	Hernán Cortés	LSTH	Spain	750
L 41	Jalashwa	LPD	India	346
LG 41	Isla San Salvador	PBO	Ecuador	210
LSD 41	Whidbey Island	LSD	US	945
M 41	Quorn	MHSC/PP	UK	887
P 41	Guaiba	PBO	Brazil	78
P 41	Meteoro	PSO	Spain	750
P 41	Orla	PSO	Ireland	382
PL 41	Aso	PL/PSO	Japan	439
PO 41	Espartana	PBO	Colombia	172
RTOP 41	Vukovar	PTGM	Croatia	182
S 41	Santa Cruz	SSK	Argentina	11
42	Mashtan	LCU	Bahrain	50
42	Merino	AGP/ASH	Chile	124
42	Rosales	FFGH	Argentina	15
42	Samar	WPSOH	India	350
42	Sydney	DDGHM	Australia	27
42	Verni	FFGM	Bulgaria	90
BP 42	Schwedt	WPBR	Germany	297
F 42	Constituição	FFGHM	Brazil	75
F 42	Vindhyagiri	FFH	India	337
FFG 42	Klakring	FFH	US	930
K 42	Nipat	FSGM	India	340
L 42	Umm Al Narr	LCU	UAE	861
L 42	Pizarro	LSTH	Spain	750
LSD 42	Germantown	LSD	US	945
N 42	Jotvingis	MCCS/AG	Lithuania	489
P 42	Ciara	PSO	Ireland	382
P 42	Graúna	PBO	Brazil	78
P 42	Rayo	PSO	Spain	750
PL 42	Dewa	PL/PSO	Japan	439
PO 42	Capitán Pablo José de Porto	PBO	Colombia	171
RTOP 42	Dubrovnik	PTGM	Croatia	182
S 42	San Juan	SSK	Argentina	11
S 42	Vagli	SS	India	325
43	Gaspar Obiang Esono	PBR	Equatorial Guinea	227
43	Gordi	FFGM	Bulgaria	90
43	Mulnaya	FSGM	Bulgaria	91
43	Rubodh	LCU	Bahrain	50
43	Sangram	WPSOH	India	350
43	Spiro	FFGH	Argentina	15
BE 43	Esmeralda	AXS	Chile	123
BP 43	Frankfurt/oder	WPBR	Germany	297
F 43	Liberal	FFGHM	Brazil	75
F 43	Trishul	FFGHM	India	334
FFG 43	Thach	FFH	US	930
GC 43	Mandubi	WAX	Argentina	22
K 43	Nishank	FSGM	India	340
LSD 43	Fort McHenry	LSD	US	945
P 43	Goiana	PBO	Brazil	78
P 43	Relámpago	PSO	Spain	750
PL 43	Hakusan	PL/PSO	Japan	439
PO 43	Capitán Jorge enrique Marquez Duran	PBO	Colombia	171
44	Parker	FFGH	Argentina	15
44	Sarang	WPSOH	India	350
44	Suwad	LCU	Bahrain	50
A 44	Bholu	YTB	Pakistan	590
BP 44	Aurith	WPBR	Germany	297
F 44	Independência	FFGHM	Brazil	75
F 44	Tabar	FFGHM	India	334
H 44	Ary Rongel	AGOBH	Brazil	82
K 44	Nirghat	FSGM	India	340
LSD 44	Gunston Hall	LSD	US	945
P 44	Guajará	PBO	Brazil	78
P 44	Kirpan	FSGHM	India	339
P 44	Torna	PSO	Spain	750
PO 44	Valle Del Cauca	–	Colombia	171
S 44	Shishumar	SSK	India	327
45	Fernando Nuara Engonda	PBR	Equatorial Guinea	227
45	Jaradah	LCU	Bahrain	50
45	Robinson	FFGH	Argentina	15
45	Sagar	WPSOH	India	350
A 45	Gama	YTB	Pakistan	590
F 45	União	FFGHM	Brazil	75
FFG 45	De Wert	FFH	US	930
H 45	Almirante Maximiano	AGOBH	Brazil	82
K 45	Vibhuti	FSGM	India	340
LSD 45	Comstock	LSD	US	945
P 45	Guaporé	PBO	Brazil	78
PO 45	San Andres	PSO	Colombia	172
S 45	Shankush	SSK	India	327
T-AG 45	Waters	AGS	US	957
46	Gomez Roca	FFGH	Argentina	15
46	Sankalp	WPSOH	India	350
46	Tighatlib	YFL	Bahrain	49
AE 46	Cape Bojeador	ABU	Philippines	614
AP 46	Contre-Almirante Oscar Viel Toro	AGS/AGOBH	Chile	122
F 46	Greenhalgh	FFGHM	Brazil	74
F 46	Krishna	AXH	India	347
FFG 46	Rentz	FFH	US	930
K 46	Vipul	FSGM	India	340
LSD 46	Tortuga	LSD	US	945
P 46	Gurupá	PBO	Brazil	78
P 46	Kuthar	FSGHM	India	339
S 46	Shalki	SSK	India	327
47	Samrat	WPSOH	India	350
47	Sri Perlis	PB	Malaysia	499
A 47	Nasr	AORH	Pakistan	589
AFDL 47	Reliance	AFDL	US	953
FFG 47	Nicholas	FFH	US	930
GC 47	Tonina	WARS	Argentina	22
K 47	Vinash	FSGM	India	340
LSD 47	Rushmore	LSD	US	945
P 47	Gurupi	PBO	Brazil	78
P 47	Khanjar	FSGHM	India	339
S 47	Shankul	SSK	India	327
F 48	Bosisio	FFGHM	Brazil	74
FFG 48	Vandegrift	FFH	US	930
GC 48	Estrellemar	WPB	Argentina	23
K 48	Vidyut	FSGM	India	340
LSD 48	Ashland	LSD	US	945
P 48	Brendan Simbwaye	PBO	Namibia	544
P 48	Guanabara	PBO	Brazil	78
SV 48	Behr Paima	AGS/AGOR	Pakistan	589
49	Sri Johor	PB	Malaysia	499
A 49	Gwadar	AOTL	Pakistan	589
F 49	Rademaker	FFGHM	Brazil	74
FFG 49	Robert G Bradley	FFH	US	930
GC 49	Remora	WPB	Argentina	23
LSD 49	Harpers Ferry	LSD	US	945
P 49	Guarujá	PBO	Brazil	78
P 49	Khukri	FSGHM	India	339
50	Al Manama	FSGH	Bahrain	48
50	Kiisla	PB	Finland	234
50	Rv	YDT	Netherlands	557
A 50	Alster	AGI	Germany	293
ACV 50	Corio Bay	PB	Australia	41
B 50	Sawahil	AGH	Kuwait	479
BG 50	Grigory Kuropiatnikov	PC	Ukraine	855
FFG 50	Taylor	FFH	US	930
GC 50	Congrio	WPB	Argentina	23
L 50	Tobruk	LSLH	Australia	34
LSD 50	Carter Hall	LSD	US	945
N 50	Tyr	AGDS	Norway	573
P 50	Guaratuba	PBO	Brazil	78
P 50	Sukanya	PSOH	India	344
PH 50	Hammerhead Shark	WPB	Singapore	730
PK 50	Spikefish	PBF	Singapore	731
T-ARS 50	Safeguard	ARS	US	955
Y 50	Gölcük	YO	Turkey	841
51	Al Muharraq	FSGH	Bahrain	48
51	Kurki	PB	Finland	234
A 51	Gaj	YTM/YTL	India	349
A 51	Mahón	ATA	Spain	757
A 51	Temsah	YTM	UAE	862
BG 51	Poltava	PC	Ukraine	855
BP 51	Vogtland	WPB	Germany	297
D 51	Rajput	DDGHM	India	331
DDG 51	Arleigh Burke	DDGHM	US	924
FFG 51	Gary	FFH	US	930
FL 51	Almirante Padilla	FLGHM	Colombia	170
FM 51	Carvajal	FFGHM	Peru	601
GC 51	Mero	WPB	Argentina	23
L 51	Al Feyi	LCU	UAE	861
L 51	Galicia	LPD	Spain	751
L 51	Kanimbla	LCCH/LLP	Australia	32
LM 51	Korcula	MHI	Croatia	183
LSD 51	Oak Hill	LSD	US	945
M 51	Kuršis	MHC	Lithuania	488
P 51	Gravataí	PBO	Brazil	78
P 51	Roisin	PSO	Ireland	382
P 51	Subhadra	PSOH	India	344
PC 51	Yodo	PC/YTR	Japan	443
PH 51	Mako Shark	WPB	Singapore	730
PL 51	Hida	PL/PSO	Japan	438
T-ARS 51	Grasp	ARS	US	955
T-AGS 51	John McDonnell	AGS	US	957
Y 51	Söndüren 1	YTB/YTM/YTL	Turkey	843
A 52	Las Palmas	AGOB	Spain	753
A 52	Oste	AGI	Germany	293
A 52	Ugaab	YTM	UAE	862
B 52	Hercules	LCC	Argentina	19
BG 52	Grigory Gnatenko	PC	Ukraine	855
BP 52	Rhön	WPB	Germany	297
CG 52	Bunker Hill	CGHM	US	921
D 52	Rana	DDGHM	India	331
DDG 52	Barry	DDGHM	US	924
FFG 52	Carr	FFH	US	930
FL 52	Caldas	FLGHM	Colombia	170
FM 52	Villavisencio	FFGHM	Peru	601
GC 52	Marsopa	WPB	Argentina	23
L 52	Castilla	LPD	Spain	751
L 52	Dayyinah	LCU	UAE	861
L 52	Manoora	LCCH/LLP	Australia	32
LSD 52	Pearl Harbor	LSD	US	945

Number	Ship's name	Type	Country	Page
M 52	Sūduvis	MHC	Lithuania	488
MB 52	Sputnik	ARS/ATA	Russian Federation	698
P 52	Niamh	PSO	Ireland	382
P 52	Suvarna	PSOH	India	344
PC 52	Kotobiki	PC/YTR	Japan	443
PH 52	White Shark	WPB	Singapore	730
PL 52	Akaishi	PL/PSO	Japan	438
T-ARS 52	Salvor	ARS	US	955
Y 52	Doğanarslan	YTB/YTM/YTL	Turkey	843
A 53	La Graña	ATA	Spain	757
A 53	Matanga	ATA/ATR	India	349
A 53	Oker	AGI	Germany	293
A 53	Virsaitis	MCCS/AG	Latvia	480
AO 53	Araucano	AOR	Chile	124
BP 53	Spreewald	WPB	Germany	297
CG 53	Mobile Bay	CGHM	US	921
D 53	Ranjit	DDGHM	India	331
DDG 53	John Paul Jones	DDGHM	US	924
FFG 53	Hawes	FFH	US	930
FL 53	Antioquia	FLGHM	Colombia	170
FM 53	Montero	FFGHM	Peru	601
GC 53	Petrel	WPB	Argentina	23
L 53	Jananah	LCU	UAE	861
P 53	Savitri	PSOH	India	344
PC 53	Nachi	PC/YTR	Japan	443
PH 53	Blue Shark	WPB	Singapore	730
PL 53	Kiso	PL/PSO	Japan	438
T-ARS 53	Grapple	ARS	US	955
Y 53	Kuvvet	YTB/YTM/YTL	Turkey	843
BP 54	Oderbruch	WPB	Germany	297
CG 54	Antietam	CGHM	US	921
D 54	Ranvir	DDGHM	India	331
DDG 54	Curtis Wilbur	DDGHM	US	924
FFG 54	Ford	FFH	US	930
FL 54	Independiente	FLGHM	Colombia	170
FM 54	Mariategui	FFGHM	Peru	601
GC 54	Salmon	WPB	Argentina	23
PC 54	Nunobiki	PC/YTR	Japan	443
PH 54	Tiger Shark	WPB	Singapore	730
55	Orca	AXL	Canada	104
BG 55	Galichina	PCK	Ukraine	856
CG 55	Leyte Gulf	CGHM	US	921
D 55	Ranvijay	DDGHM	India	331
DDG 55	Stout	DDGHM	US	924
FFG 55	Elrod	FFH	US	930
FM 55	Aguirre	FFGHM	Peru	600
FV 55	Indaw	PBO	Myanmar	540
GC 55	Bigua	WPB	Argentina	23
P 55	Sharada	PSOH	India	344
P 55	Wellington	PBO	New Zealand	560
PH 55	Basking Shark	WPB	Singapore	730
S 55	Sindhughosh	SSK	India	326
Y 55	Atil	YTB/YTM/YTL	Turkey	843
56	Kajava	AX	Finland	237
56	Raven	AXL	Canada	104
CG 56	San Jacinto	CGHM	US	921
DDG 56	John S McCain	DDGHM	US	924
FFG 56	Simpson	FFH	US	930
FM 56	Palacios	FFGHM	Peru	600
GC 56	Foca	WPB	Argentina	23
P 56	Sujata	PSOH	India	344
PH 56	Sandbar Shark	WPB	Singapore	730
S 56	Sindhudhvaj	SSK	India	326
Y 56	Pendik	YTB/YTM/YTL	Turkey	843
57	Caribou	AXL	Canada	104
57	Chun Jee	AORH	Korea, South	472
57	Lokki	AX	Finland	237
BG 57	Mikolaiv	PCF	Ukraine	855
CG 57	Lake Champlain	CGHM	US	921
DDG 57	Mitscher	DDGHM	US	924
FFG 57	Reuben James	FFH	US	930
FM 57	Bolognesi	FFGHM	Peru	600
FV 57	Inya	PBO	Myanmar	540
GC 57	Tiburon	WPB	Argentina	23
P 57	Kasos	PG	Greece	306
PH 57	Thresher Shark	WPB	Singapore	730
S 57	Sindhuraj	SSK	India	326
Y 57	Aksaz	YTB/YTM/YTL	Turkey	843
58	Dae Chung	AORH	Korea, South	472
58	Renard	AXL	Canada	104
A 58	Jyoti	AORH	India	347
CG 58	Philippine Sea	CGHM	US	921
DDG 58	Laboon	DDGHM	US	924
FFG 58	Samuel B Roberts	FFH	US	930
FM 58	Quiñónes	FFGHM	Peru	600
GC 58	Melva	WPB	Argentina	23
PH 58	Whitetip Shark	WPB	Singapore	730
S 58	Sindhuvir	SSK	India	326
59	Hwa Chun	AORH	Korea, South	472
59	Rajkiran	WPB	India	351
59	Wolf	AXL	Canada	104
A 59	Aditya	AORH/AS	India	348
CG 59	Princeton	CGHM	US	921
DDG 59	Russell	DDGHM	US	924
FFG 59	Kauffman	FFH	US	930
GC 59	Lenguado	WPB	Argentina	23
PH 59	Blacktip Shark	WPB	Singapore	730
S 59	Sindhuratna	SSK	India	326
60	Grizzly	AXL	Canada	104
A 60	Gorch Fock	AXS	Germany	293
ACV 60	Arnhem Bay	PB	Australia	41
AGOR 60	Vidal Gormaz	AGOR	Chile	123
CG 60	Normandy	CGHM	US	921
D 60	Mysore	DDGHM	India	332
DDG 60	Paul Hamilton	DDGHM	US	924
FFG 60	Rodney M Davis	FFH	US	930
GC 60	Orca	WPB	Argentina	23
P 60	Bahamas	PB	Bahamas	45
P 60	Bracui	PBO	Brazil	80
PH 60	Goblin Shark	WPB	Singapore	730
S 60	Sindhukesari	SSK	India	326
T-AGS 60	Pathfinder	AGS	US	957
61	Ashdod	LCT	Israel	387
61	Briz	MSC	Bulgaria	93
61	Cougar	AXL	Canada	104
61	Rajkamal	WPB	India	351
BG 61	Odessa	PCF	Ukraine	855
BP 61	Prignitz	WPB	Germany	297
CG 61	Monterey	CGHM	US	921
D 61	Delhi	DDGHM	India	332
DDG 61	Ramage	DDGHM	US	924
FFG 61	Ingraham	FFH	US	930
GC 61	Pinguino	WPB	Argentina	23
L 61	Rey Juan Carlos I	LHD	Spain	752
M 61	Evniki	MHC	Greece	308
OB 61	Novigrad	PCM	Croatia	181
P 61	Baradero	PB	Argentina	18
P 61	Benevente	PBO	Brazil	80
P 61	Chilreu	PSO	Spain	749
P 61	Kora	FSGHM	India	338
P 61	Nassau	PB	Bahamas	45
P 61	Polemistis	PG	Greece	306
PG 61	Agusan	PB	Philippines	615
PH 61	School Shark	WPB	Singapore	730
PL 61	Hateruma	PL/PSO	Japan	439
Q 61	Ciudad de Zarate	ABU	Argentina	21
S 61	Sindhukirti	SSK	India	326
T 61	Capana	LSTH	Venezuela	982
T 61	Trinkat	PBO	India	344
T-AGS 61	Sumner	AGS	US	957
62	Moose	AXL	Canada	104
62	Shkval	MSC	Bulgaria	93
BG 62	Podilliya	PCF	Ukraine	855
BP 62	Uckermark	WPB	Germany	297
CG 62	Chancellorsville	CGHM	US	921
D 62	Mumbai	DDGHM	India	332
DDG 62	Fitzgerald	DDGHM	US	924
M 62	Evropi	MHSC	Greece	308
OB 62	Šolta	PCM	Croatia	181
P 62	Alboran	PSOH	Spain	749
P 62	Barranqueras	PB	Argentina	18
P 62	Bocaina	PBO	Brazil	80
P 62	Kirch	FSGHM	India	338
P 62	Niki	PG	Greece	307
PG 62	Catanduanes	PB	Philippines	615
PL 62	Hakata	PL/PSO	Japan	439
Q 62	Ciudad de Rosario	ABU	Argentina	21
S 62	Sindhuvijay	SSK	India	326
T 62	Esequibo	LSTH	Venezuela	982
T-AGS 62	Bowditch	AGS	US	957
TR 62	Calicuchima	AETL	Ecuador	209
63	Priboy	MSC	Bulgaria	93
BG 63	Pavel Derzhavin	PCF	Ukraine	855
BP 63	Altmark	WPB	Germany	297
BRS 63	George Slight Marshall	ABU	Chile	123
CG 63	Cowpens	CGHM	US	921
DDG 63	Stethem	DDGHM	US	924
M 63	Bedi	MSO	India	346
M 63	Kallisto	MHSC	Greece	308
OB 63	Cavtat	PCM	Croatia	181
P 63	Arnomendi	PSOH	Spain	749
P 63	Babitonga	PBO	Brazil	80
P 63	Clorinda	PB	Argentina	18
P 63	Doxa	PG	Greece	307
P 63	Kulish	FSGHM	India	338
PG 63	Romblon	PB	Philippines	615
PL 63	Yonakuni	PL/PSO	Japan	439
Q 63	Punta Alta	ABU	Argentina	21
S 63	Sindhurakshak	SSK	India	326
T 63	Goajira	LSTH	Venezuela	982
T 63	Tarasa	PBO	India	344
T-AGS 63	Henson	AGS	US	957
TR 63	Atahualpa	AWT	Ecuador	209
64	Jija Bai	WPBO	India	351
64	Shtorm	MSC	Bulgaria	93
BP 64	Börde	WPB	Germany	297
CG 64	Gettysburg	CGHM	US	921
DDG 64	Carney	DDGHM	US	924
GC 64	Mar Del Plata	WPB	Argentina	22
M 64	Bhavnagar	MSO	India	346
M 64	Calypso	MHC	Greece	308
OB 64	Hrvatska Kostajnica	PCM	Croatia	181
P 64	Concepción Del Uruguay	PB	Argentina	18
P 64	Eleftheria	PG	Greece	307
P 64	Karmukh	FSGHM	India	338
P 64	Tarifa	PSOH	Spain	749
PG 64	Palawan	PB	Philippines	615
PL 64	Motobu	PL/PSO	Japan	439
T 64	Los Llanos	LSTH	Venezuela	982
T-AGS 64	Bruce C Heezen	AGS	US	957
TR 64	Quisquis	AWT	Ecuador	209
Y 64	Ersev Bayrak	YTB/YTM/YTL	Turkey	843
65	Chand Bibi	WPBO	India	351
65-3	Cabo Blanco	PB	Costa Rica	179
65-4	Isla Burica	PB	Costa Rica	179
A 65	Marinero Jarano	AWT	Spain	756
BP 65	Rhoen	WPB	Germany	297
CG 65	Chosin	CGHM	US	921
CVN 65	Enterprise	CVNM	US	916
DDG 65	Benfold	DDGHM	US	924
GC 65	Martin Garcia	WPB	Argentina	22
M 65	Alleppey	MSO	India	346
P 65	Punta Mogotes	PB	Argentina	18
PL 65	Kunigami	PL/PSO	Japan	439
S 65	Sindhushastra	SSK	India	326
T 65	Bangaram	PBO	India	344
T-AGS 65	Mary Sears	AGS	US	957
TR 65	Taurus	AOTL	Ecuador	209
66	Kittur Chennamma	WPBO	India	351
A 66	Condestable Zaragoza	AWT	Spain	756

Number	Ship's name	Type	Country	Page
ATF 66	Galvarino	ATF	Chile	124
CG 66	Hue City	CGHM	US	921
DDG 66	Gonzalez	DDGHM	US	924
GC 66	Rio Lujan	WPB	Argentina	22
M 66	Ratnagiri	MSO	India	346
P 66	Rio Santiago	PB	Argentina	18
T 66	Bitra	PBO	India	344
67	Rani Jindan	WPBO	India	351
ATF 67	Lautaro	ATF	Chile	124
CG 67	Shiloh	CGHM	US	921
DDG 67	Cole	DDGHM	US	924
GC 67	Rio Uruguay	WPB	Argentina	22
M 67	Karwar	MSO	India	346
P 67	Mzizi	PB	Tanzania	799
P 67	Ypoploiarchos Roussen	PGG	Greece	304
T 67	Batti Malv	PBO	India	344
68	Formidable	FFGHM	Singapore	725
68	Habbah Khatun	WPBO	India	351
CG 68	Anzio	CGHM	US	921
CVN 68	Nimitz	CVNM	US	917
DDG 68	The Sullivans	DDGHM	US	924
GC 68	Rio Paraguay	WPB	Argentina	22
M 68	Cannanore	MSO	India	346
P 68	Mzia	PB	Tanzania	799
P 68	Ypoploiarchos Daniolos	PGG	Greece	304
T 68	Baratang	PBO	India	344
69	Intrepid	FFGHM	Singapore	725
69	Ramadevi	WPBO	India	351
CG 69	Vicksburg	CGHM	US	921
CVN 69	Dwight D Eisenhower	CVNM	US	917
DDG 69	Milius	DDGHM	US	924
GC 69	Rio Parana	WPB	Argentina	22
M 69	Cuddalore	MSO	India	346
P 69	Ypoploiarchos Kristallidis	PGG	Greece	304
T 69	Car Nicobar	PBO	India	345
70	Avvaiyyar	WPBO	India	351
70	Rauma	PTGM	Finland	235
70	Steadfast	FFGHM	Singapore	725
ACV 70	Dame Roma Mitchell	PB	Australia	41
CG 70	Lake Erie	CGHM	US	921
CVN 70	Carl Vinson	CVNM	US	917
DDG 70	Hopper	DDGHM	US	924
GC 70	Rio de la Plata	WPB	Argentina	22
M 70	Kakinada	MSO	India	346
P 70	Ypoploiarchos Grigoropoulos	PGG	Greece	304
PS 70	Quezon	FS	Philippines	610
RA 70	Chimborazo	ATF	Ecuador	209
T 70	Chetlat	PBO	India	345
71	Alvand	FFG	Iran	371
71	Raahe	PTGM	Finland	235
71	Tara Bai	WPBO	India	351
71	Tenacious	FFGHM	Singapore	725
A 71	Juan Sebastián de Elcano	AXS	Spain	754
AT 71	Mangyan	ABU	Philippines	614
CG 71	Cape St George	CGHM	US	921
CVN 71	Theodore Roosevelt	CVNM	US	917
DDG 71	Ross	DDGHM	US	924
GC 71	La Plata	WPB	Argentina	22
M 71	Kozhikode	MSO	India	346
M 71	Landsort	MHSCDM	Sweden	776
P 71	Anthypoploiarchos Ritsos	PGG	Greece	304
P 71	Serviola	PSOH	Spain	748
PSG 71	Micalvi	PB/AEM	Chile	121
S 71	Galerna	SSK	Spain	741
T 71	Cinque	PBO	India	345
T 71	Margarita	LCU	Venezuela	982
72	Ahalya Bai	WPBO	India	351
72	Alborz	FFG	Iran	371
72	Porvoo	PTGM	Finland	235
72	Stalwart	FFGHM	Singapore	725
A 72	Arosa	AXS	Spain	754
AF 72	Lake Taal	YO	Philippines	613
BS 72	Andrija Mohorovičić	AX	Croatia	183
CG 72	Vella Gulf	CGHM	US	921
CVN 72	Abraham Lincoln	CVNM	US	917
DDG 72	Mahan	DDGHM	US	924
GC 72	Buenos Aires	WPB	Argentina	22
M 72	Arholma	MHSCDM	Sweden	776
M 72	Konkan	MSO	India	346
P 72	Centinela	PSOH	Spain	748
P 72	Ypoploiarchos Votsis	PGFG	Greece	305
PC 72	Urayuki	PC/SAR	Japan	443
PSG 72	Ortiz	PB/AEM	Chile	121
RB 72	Sangay	YTM/YTL	Ecuador	209
S 72	Siroco	SSK	Spain	741
T 72	Cheriyam	PBO	India	345
T 72	La Orchila	LCU	Venezuela	982
73	Collins	SSK	Australia	26
73	Lakshmi Bai	WPBO	India	351
73	Naantali	PTGM	Finland	235
73	Sabalan	FFG	Iran	371
73	Supreme	FFGHM	Singapore	725
BS 73	Faust Vrančić	ASR	Croatia	184
CG 73	Port Royal	CGHM	US	921
CVN 73	George Washington	CVNM	US	917
DDG 73	Decatur	DDGHM	US	924
GC 73	Cabo Corrientes	WPB	Argentina	22
M 73	Koster	–	Sweden	777
P 73	Anthypoploiarchos Pezopoulos	PGFG	Greece	305
P 73	Vigía	PSOH	Spain	748
PSG 73	Isaza	PB/AEM	Chile	121
RB 73	Cotopaxi	YTM/YTL	Ecuador	209
S 73	Mistral	SSK	Spain	741
74	Akka Devi	WPBO	India	351
74	Farncomb	SSK	Australia	26
A 74	La Graciosa	AXS	Spain	754
A 74	Sagardhwani	–	India	346
CVN 74	John C Stennis	CVNM	US	917
DDG 74	McFaul	DDGHM	US	924
GC 74	Rio Quequen	WPB	Argentina	22
M 74	Kullen	–	Sweden	777
P 74	Atalaya	PSOH	Spain	748
P 74	Plotarchis Vlahavas	PGFG	Greece	305
PC 74	Asoyuki	PC/PB	Japan	444
PMD 74	Videla	PB/AEM	Chile	121
PS 74	Rizal	FS	Philippines	610
S 74	Tramontana	SSK	Spain	741
75	Naiki Devi	WPBO	India	351
75	Waller	SSK	Australia	26
A 75	Sisargas	AXS	Spain	754
A 75	Tarangini	AXS	India	347
AU 75	Bessang Pass	PB	Philippines	615
CVN 75	Harry S Truman	CVNM	US	917
DDG 75	Donald Cook	DDGHM	US	924
GC 75	Bahia Blanca	WPB	Argentina	22
M 75	Vinga	–	Sweden	777
P 75	Plotarchis Maridakis	PGFG	Greece	305
P 75	Descubierta	PSOH/MCS/FSGM	Spain	747
PC 75	Hatagumo	PC/SAR	Japan	443
RB 75	Iliniza	YTM/YTL	Ecuador	209
RM 75	Andagoya	YTL	Colombia	177
76	Dechaineux	SSK	Australia	26
76	Ganga Devi	WPBO	India	351
76	Hang Tuah	FFH/AX	Malaysia	501
A 76	Giralda	AXS	Spain	754
CVN 76	Ronald Reagan	CVNM	US	917
DDG 76	Higgins	DDGHM	US	924
GC 76	Ingeniero White	WPB	Argentina	22
M 76	Ven	–	Sweden	777
P 76	Infanta Elena	PSOH/MCS/FSGM	Spain	747
P 76	Ypoploiarchos Tournas	PGFG	Greece	305
PC 76	Makigumo	PC/SAR	Japan	443
RB 76	Altar	YTM/YTL	Ecuador	209
RB 76	Josué Alvarez	YTL	Colombia	177
77	Huvudskär	PBR	Sweden	774
77	Sheean	SSK	Australia	26
A 77	Sálvora	AXS	Spain	754
CVN 77	George H W Bush	CVNM	US	917
DDG 77	O'Kane	DDGHM	US	924
F 77	Te Kaha	FFHM	New Zealand	559
GC 77	Golfo San Matias	WPB	Argentina	22
M 77	Ulvön	–	Sweden	777
P 77	Infanta Cristina	PSOH/MCS/FSGM	Spain	747
P 77	Plotarchis Sakipis	PGFG	Greece	305
PC 77	Hamazuki	PC/SAR	Japan	443
PSH 77	Cabrales	PB/AEM	Chile	121
RB 77	Don Vizo	YTL	Colombia	177
78	Rankin	SSK	Australia	26
A 78	Peregrina	AXS	Spain	754
AF 78	Lake Buhi	YO	Philippines	613
CVN 78	Gerald R Ford	CVN	US	920
DDG 78	Porter	DDGHM	US	924
F 78	Kent	FFGHM	UK	878
G 78	Ottonelli	PB	Italy	410
GC 78	Madryn	WPB	Argentina	22
P 78	Cazadora	PSOH/MCS/FSGM	Spain	747
PC 78	Isozuki	PC/SAR	Japan	443
PM 78	Ishikari	PM/PSO	Japan	441
PSG 78	Sibbald	PB/AEM	Chile	121
RB 78	Portete	YTL	Colombia	177
RB 78	Quilotoa	YTM/YTL	Ecuador	209
AE 79	Limasawa	ABU	Philippines	614
DDG 79	Oscar Austin	–	US	926
F 79	Portland	FFGHM	UK	878
G 79	Barletta	PB	Italy	410
GC 79	Rio Deseado	WPB	Argentina	22
P 79	Vencedora	PSOH/MCS/FSGM	Spain	747
PC 79	Shimanami	PC/SAR	Japan	443
PM 79	Abukuma	PM/PSO	Japan	441
RB 79	Maldonado	YTL	Colombia	177
80	Hamina	PTGM	Finland	235
ACV 80	Storm Bay	PB	Australia	41
BG 80	Dunai	AGF	Ukraine	855
DDG 80	Roosevelt	–	US	926
G 80	Bigliani	PB	Italy	410
GC 80	Ushuaia	WPB	Argentina	22
PC 80	Yuzuki	PC/SAR	Japan	443
PM 80	Isuzu	PM/PSO	Japan	441
RB 80	Cienaga de San Juan	YTL	Colombia	177
81	Bayandor	FS	Iran	372
81	Tapper	PBR	Sweden	774
81	Tornio	PTGM	Finland	235
81	Zhenghe	AXH	China	159
BG 81	Lubny	PGR	Ukraine	856
CLM 81	Almirante Grau	CG/CLM	Peru	600
DBM 81	Cetina	LCT/ML	Croatia	182
DDG 81	Winston S Churchill	–	US	926
F 81	Santa María	FFGHM	Spain	745
F 81	Sutherland	FFGHM	UK	878
G 81	Cavaglia	PB	Italy	410
GC 81	Canal de Beagle	WPB	Argentina	22
P 81	Toralla	PB	Spain	749
PC 81	Tamanami	PC/SAR	Japan	443
PZM 81	Piloto Pardo	PSO	Chile	125
RF 81	Capitán Castro	YTL	Colombia	177
T 81	Ciudad Bolívar	AORH	Venezuela	983
82	Djärv	PBR	Sweden	774
82	Hanko	PTGM	Finland	235
82	Huon	MHC	Australia	35
82	Naghdi	FS	Iran	372
82	Resilience	PCM/PGM	Singapore	727
82	Shichang	HSS/AHH	China	159
82-2	Santamaria	PB	Costa Rica	179
82-3	Juan Rafael Mora	PB	Costa Rica	179
82-4	Pancha Carrasco	PB	Costa Rica	179
A 82	Contramaestre Navarrete	AXL	Spain	754

Number	Ship's name	Type	Country	Page
BG 82	Kaniv	PGR	Ukraine	856
DBV 82	Krka	LCT/ML	Croatia	182
DDG 82	Lassen	–	US	926
DF 82	Rio Napo	YFD	Ecuador	209
F 82	Somerset	FFGHM	UK	878
F 82	Victoria	FFGHM	Spain	745
G 82	Galiano	PB	Italy	410
P 82	Formentor	PB	Spain	749
PC 82	Awagiri	PC/SAR	Japan	443
PZM 82	Comandante Toro	PSO	Chile	125
83	Armidale	PB	Australia	35
83	Dristig	PBR	Sweden	774
83	Hawkesbury	MHC	Australia	35
83	Pori	PTGM	Finland	235
83	Shi Lang	CVGM	China	134
83	Unity	PCM/PGM	Singapore	727
A 83	Contramaestre Sánchez Fernández	AXL	Spain	754
BG 83	Nizyn	PGR	Ukraine	856
DDG 83	Howard	–	US	926
F 83	Numancia	FFGHM	Spain	745
F 83	St Albans	FFGHM	UK	878
G 83	Macchi	PB	Italy	410
K 83	Nashak	FSGM	India	340
PC 83	Shimagiri	PC/PB	Japan	444
PM 83	Horobetsu	PM/PSO	Japan	441
RF 83	Joves Fiallo	YTL	Colombia	177
84	Händig	PBR	Sweden	774
84	Larrakia	PB	Australia	35
84	Norman	MHC	Australia	35
84	Sovereignty	PCM/PGM	Singapore	727
A 84	Contramaestre Antero	AXL	Spain	754
BG 84	Izmayl	PGR	Ukraine	856
DDG 84	Bulkeley	–	US	926
F 84	Enymiri	FSM	Nigeria	564
F 84	Reina Sofía	FFGHM	Spain	745
G 84	Smalto	PB	Italy	410
PC 84	Okinami	PC/PB	Japan	444
PM 84	Shirakami	PM/PSO	Japan	441
85	Bathurst	PB	Australia	35
85	Gascoyne	MHC	Australia	35
85	Justice	PCM/PGM	Singapore	727
85	Trygg	PBR	Sweden	774
A 85	Contramaestre Lamadrid	AXL	Spain	754
DDG 85	McCampbell	–	US	926
F 85	Cumberland	FFGHM	UK	880
F 85	Navarra	FFGHM	Spain	745
G 85	Fortuna	PB	Italy	410
P 85	Intrepida	PGGF	Argentina	18
PC 85	Hayagiri	PC/PB	Japan	444
PM 85	Matsuura	PM/PSO	Japan	441
RF 85	Miguel Silva	YTL	Colombia	177
86	Albany	PB	Australia	35
86	Diamantina	MHC	Australia	35
86	Freedom	PCM/PGM	Singapore	727
86	Modig	PBR	Sweden	774
A 86	Tir	AXH	India	347
DDG 86	Shoup	–	US	926
F 86	Campbeltown	FFGHM	UK	880
F 86	Canarias	FFGHM	Spain	745
G 86	Buonocore	PB	Italy	410
H 86	Gleaner	YGS	UK	888
LT 86	Zamboanga Del Sur	LST	Philippines	612
P 86	Indomita	PGGF	Argentina	18
PC 86	Natsugiri	PC/PB	Japan	444
RF 86	Capitan Rigoberto Giraldo	YTL	Colombia	177
87	Hurtig	PBR	Sweden	774
87	Independence	PCM/PGM	Singapore	727
87	Pirie	PB	Australia	35
87	Yarra	MHC	Australia	35
DDG 87	Mason	–	US	926
F 87	Chatham	FFGHM	UK	880
G 87	Squitieri	PB	Italy	410
H 87	Echo	AGSH	UK	888
LT 87	South Cotabato	LST	Philippines	612
PC 87	Suganami	PC/PB	Japan	444
PM 87	Misasa	PM/PSO	Japan	441
RF 87	Vladimir Valek	YTL	Colombia	177
S 87	Turbulent	SSN	UK	868
88	Maitland	PB	Australia	35
88	Rapp	PBR	Sweden	774
DDG 88	Preble	–	US	926
G 88	La Malfa	PB	Italy	410
GC 88	Medusa	WPB	Argentina	23
H 88	Enterprise	AGSH	UK	888
P 88	Victory	FSGM	Singapore	726
RF 88	Teniente Luis Bernal	YTL	Colombia	177
S 88	Tireless	SSN	UK	868
89	Ararat	PB	Australia	35
89	Stolt	PBR	Sweden	774
AG 89	Kalinga	AKLH	Philippines	614
DDG 89	Mustin	–	US	926
F 89	Aradu	FFGHM	Nigeria	564
G 89	Rosati	PB	Italy	410
GC 89	Perca	WPB	Argentina	23
P 89	Valour	FSGM	Singapore	726
PM 89	Takatori	PM/PBO	Japan	441
90	Ärlig	PBR	Sweden	774
90	Broome	PB	Australia	35
90	Elicura	LSM	Chile	122
90	Sabha	FFGHM	Bahrain	47
A 90	Varonis	AKS/AXL	Latvia	480
AC 90	Mactan	AK	Philippines	613
DDG 90	Chaffee	–	US	926
GC 90	Calamar	WPB	Argentina	23
P 90	Vigilance	FSGM	Singapore	726
PM 90	Chikugo	PM/PSO	Japan	441
S 90	Torbay	SSN	UK	868
Y 90	Deney	YTB/YTM/YTL	Turkey	843
91	Bundaberg	PB	Australia	35
91	Munter	PBR	Sweden	774
A 91	Astrolabio	YGS	Spain	754
ASY 91	Hashidate	ASY/YAC	Japan	436
BE 91	Guayas	AXS	Ecuador	208
BI 91	Orion	YGS	Ecuador	208
D 91	Nottingham	DDGH	UK	875
DDG 91	Pinckney	–	US	926
GC 91	Hipocampo	WPB	Argentina	23
K 91	Pralaya	FSGM	India	340
M 91	Sagar	MSO	Bangladesh	58
P 91	Valiant	FSGM	Singapore	726
PM 91	Yamakuni	PM/PSO	Japan	441
PO 91	Lubin	AKR	Montenegro	530
R 91	Charles de Gaulle	CVNM/PAN	France	248
RF 91	Teniente Alejandro Baldomero Salgado	YTL	Colombia	177
S 91	Trenchant	SSN	UK	868
92	Orädd	PBR	Sweden	774
92	Putsaari	ANL	Finland	240
92	Rancagua	LSTH	Chile	122
92	Wollongong	PB	Australia	35
A 92	Escandallo	YGS	Spain	754
D 92	Liverpool	DDGH	UK	875
DDG 92	Momsen	–	US	926
G 92	Alberti	PBF	Italy	410
GC 92	Robaldo	WPB	Argentina	23
K 92	Prabal	FSGM	India	340
MHV 92	Holger Danske	PB	Denmark	195
P 92	Vigour	FSGM	Singapore	726
PM 92	Katsura	PM/PSO	Japan	441
S 92	Talent	SSN	UK	868
93	Childers	PB	Australia	35
93	Valdivia	LSTH	Chile	122
DDG 93	Chung-Hoon	–	US	926
G 93	Angelini	PBF	Italy	410
GC 93	Camaron	WPB	Argentina	23
P 93	Vengeance	FSGM	Singapore	726
RF 93	Sejeri	YTL	Colombia	177
S 93	Triumph	SSN	UK	868
94	Fearless	PCM/PGM	Singapore	727
94	Launceston	PB	Australia	35
94	Orompello	LSM	Chile	122
DDG 94	Nitze	–	US	926
G 94	Cappelletti	PBF	Italy	410
GC 94	Gaviota	WPB	Argentina	23
LH 94	Rigel	YFS	Ecuador	208
PM 94	Kumano	PM/PBO	Japan	441
95	Brave	PCM/PGM	Singapore	727
95	Chacabuco	LSTH	Chile	122
95	Maryborough	PB	Australia	35
D 95	Manchester	DDGH	UK	876
DDG 95	James E Williams	–	US	926
G 95	Ciorlieri	PBF	Italy	410
GC 95	Abadejo	WPB	Argentina	23
M 95	Shapla	MHSC/PBO/AGS	Bangladesh	58
PM 95	Amami	PM/PBO	Japan	441
Y 95	Torpido Tenderi	YPT	Turkey	842
96	Glenelg	PB	Australia	35
96	Pikkala	YFB	Finland	240
D 96	Gloucester	DDGH	UK	876
DDG 96	Bainbridge	–	US	926
G 96	D'Amato	PBF	Italy	410
M 96	Saikat	MHSC/PBO/AGS	Bangladesh	58
PM 96	Kurokami	PM/PBO	Japan	441
RF 96	Inirida	YTL	Colombia	177
97	Gallant	PCM/PGM	Singapore	727
D 97	Edinburgh	DDGH	UK	876
DDG 97	Halsey	–	US	926
G 97	Fais	PBF	Italy	410
M 97	Surovi	MHSC/PBO/AGS	Bangladesh	58
PM 97	Kunashiri	PM/PBO	Japan	441
R 97	Jeanne d'Arc	CVHG	France	250
98	Daring	PCM/PGM	Singapore	727
98	Mursu	AKSL	Finland	238
D 98	York	DDGH	UK	876
DDG 98	Forrest Sherman	–	US	926
G 98	Feliciani	PBF	Italy	410
M 98	Shaibal	MHSC/PBO/AGS	Bangladesh	58
PM 98	Minabe	PM/PBO	Japan	441
Y 98	Takip 1	YPT	Turkey	842
99	Dauntless	PCM/PGM	Singapore	727
DDG 99	Farragut	–	US	926
F 99	Cornwall	FFGHM	UK	880
G 99	Garzoni	PBF	Italy	410
Y 99	Takip 2	YPT	Turkey	842
100	Stavropol	PGM	Russian Federation	703
AU 100	Tirad Pass	PB	Philippines	615
BG 100	Sivas	PB	Ukraine	856
DDG 100	Kidd	–	US	926
G 100	Lippi	PBF	Italy	410
101	Al Hussein	PB	Jordan	448
101	Fouque	LSL	Iran	378
101	General Matrosov	PBO	Russian Federation	701
101	Ho Hsing	WPSO	Taiwan	796
101	Levuka	PB	Fiji	234
101	Lilian	PB	Lithuania	489
101	Raif Denktaş	WPBI	Turkey	846
A 101	Mar Caribe	ATF/AGDS	Spain	756
DD 101	Murasame	DDGHM	Japan	422
DDG 101	Gridley	–	US	926
F 101	Alvaro de Bazán	FFGHM	Spain	744
FNH 101	Guaymuras	PB	Honduras	317
G 101	Lombardi	PBF	Italy	410
GC 101	Aries	PB	Dominican Republic	202
GC 101	Dorado	WPB	Argentina	23
LM 101	Zuiun	AKSL	Japan	447
LP 101	Paz Zamora	PBR	Bolivia	68
M 101	Almirante Grau	YFL	Bolivia	68
P 101	Kagitingan	PB	Philippines	611

PENNANT LIST

Number	Ship's name	Type	Country	Page
P 101	Panama	PB	Panama	593
P 101	Oecussi	PB	East Timor	204
PC 101	Asogiri	PC/PB	Japan	445
PL 101	Shiretoko	PL/PSO	Japan	439
S 101	Manthatisi	SSK	South Africa	734
S 101	Shyri	SSK	Ecuador	205
SHV 101	Hårek	PB	Norway	571
WTGB 101	Katmai Bay	TUGS-WTGB	US	969
102	Akhmeta	PB	Georgia	279
102	Al Hassan	PB	Jordan	448
102	Derbent	PGM	Russian Federation	703
102	Kaliningrad	LSTM	Russian Federation	681
102	Kihu	PB	Lithuania	489
102	Lautoka	PB	Fiji	234
102	Sovetskiy Pogranichnik	AO	Russian Federation	706
102	Uragon	PTFG	Bulgaria	92
102	Wei Hsung	WPSO	Taiwan	796
BG 102	Obolon	PB	Ukraine	856
D 102	Netzahualcoyotl	DDH	Mexico	513
DD 102	Harusame	DDGHM	Japan	422
DDG 102	Sampson	–	US	926
F 102	Almirante Don Juan de Borbón	FFGHM	Spain	744
FNH 102	Honduras	PB	Honduras	317
G 102	Miccoli	PBF	Italy	410
P 102	Atauro	PB	East Timor	204
P 102	Calamar	PB	Panama	593
P 102	Shetgang	PB	Bangladesh	58
PC 102	Murozuki	PC/PB	Japan	445
PG 102	Bagong Lakas	PB	Philippines	611
PM 102	Rafael Del Castillo Y Rada	PB	Colombia	173
PO 102	Juan de la Barrera	PG/PGH	Mexico	520
S 102	Charlotte Maxeke	SSK	South Africa	734
S 102	Huancavilca	SSK	Ecuador	205
SHV 102	Hvasser	PB	Norway	571
WTGB 102	Bristol Bay	TUGS-WTGB	US	969
103	Al Maks	ATA	Egypt	223
103	Burya	PTFG	Bulgaria	92
103	Karelia	PBO	Russian Federation	701
103	Kedrov	FFHM	Russian Federation	700
103	King Abdullah	PB	Jordan	448
BG 103	Darnitsya	PB	Ukraine	856
DD 103	Yuudachi	DDGHM	Japan	422
DDG 103	Truxtun	–	US	926
F 103	Blas de Lezo	FFGHM	Spain	744
FNH 103	Hibueras	PB	Honduras	317
G 103	Trezza	PBF	Italy	410
GC 103	Procion	PB	Dominican Republic	202
H 103	Guama	ABU	Cuba	186
M 103	Comandante Arandia	YFL	Bolivia	68
P 103	L'Audacieux	PBO	Cameroon	96
P 103	Miguel Sotoa	PBR	Paraguay	597
PC 103	Wakagumo	PC/PB	Japan	445
PL 103	Wakasa	PL/PSO	Japan	439
PM 103	José Maria Palas	PB	Colombia	173
PO 103	Mariano Escobedo	PG/PGH	Mexico	520
PS 103	Kongou	PS/PB	Japan	442
PVL 103	Pikker	PB	Estonia	230
S 103	Queen Modjadji I	SSK	South Africa	734
SHV 103	Hekkingen	PB	Norway	571
WTGB 103	Mobile Bay	TUGS-WTGB	US	969
104	Grum	PTFG	Bulgaria	92
DD 104	Kirisame	DDGHM	Japan	422
DDG 104	Sterett	–	US	926
F 104	Mendez Nuñez	FFGHM	Spain	744
FNH 104	Tegucigalpa	PB	Honduras	318
G 104	Apruzzi	PBF	Italy	410
GC 104	Aldebarán	PB	Dominican Republic	202
M 104	Walney	MHC/SRMH	UK	888
P 104	Bakassi	PBO	Cameroon	97
PC 104	Kagayuki	PC/PB	Japan	445
PG 104	Bagong Silang	PB	Philippines	611
PL 104	Kii	PL/PSO	Japan	439
PM 104	Medardo Monzon Coronado	PB	Colombia	173
PO 104	Manuel Doblado	PG/PGH	Mexico	520
PS 104	Katsuragi	PS/PB	Japan	442
S 104	Sceptre	SSN	UK	867
SHV 104	Kvitsøy	PB	Norway	571
WTGB 104	Biscayne Bay	TUGS-WTGB	US	969
105	Al Agami	ATA	Egypt	223
105	Baykal	PBO	Russian Federation	701
105	Ivan Yevteyev	AK	Russian Federation	706
105	Mou Hsing	WPSO	Taiwan	796
105-1	Isla Del Coco	PB	Costa Rica	179
DD 105	Inazuma	DDGHM	Japan	422
DDG 105	Dewey	–	US	926
F 105	Roger de Lauria	FFGHM	Spain	744
G 105	Ballali	PBF	Italy	410
GC 105	Antares	PB	Dominican Republic	202
L 105	Arromanches	RCL	UK	900
M 105	Bedok	MHC	Singapore	730
PB 105	Sir Milton	PB	Sierra Leone	722
PC 105	Hayagumo	PC/PBF	Japan	443
PM 105	Jaime Gómez Castro	PB	Colombia	173
PS 105	Bizan	PS/PB	Japan	442
PVL 105	Torm	PB	Estonia	231
SHV 105	Slotterøy	PB	Norway	571
WTGB 105	Neah Bay	TUGS-WTGB	US	969
106	Brest	PBO	Russian Federation	701
106	Fu Hsing	WPSO	Taiwan	796
106	MPK 197	FFLM	Russian Federation	674
106	Nirolhu	PB	Maldives	507
106	Shkval	PGR	Russian Federation	705
DD 106	Samidare	DDGHM	Japan	422
DDG 106	Stockdale	–	US	926
G 106	Bovienzo	PBF	Italy	410
GC 106	Bellatrix	PB	Dominican Republic	202
M 106	Kallang	MHC	Singapore	730
M 106	Penzance	MHC/SRMH	UK	888
P 106	Akwayafe	PB	Cameroon	97
P 106	Manuel Trujillo	PBR	Paraguay	597
PC 106	Murakumo	PC/PBF	Japan	443
PM 106	Juan Nepomuceno Peña	PB	Colombia	173
PO 106	Santos Degollado	PG/PGH	Mexico	520
PS 106	Shizuki	PS/PB	Japan	442
PVL 106	Maru	PB	Estonia	230
SHV 106	Halten	PB	Norway	571
WTGB 106	Morro Bay	TUGS-WTGB	US	969
107	Al Antar	ATA	Egypt	223
107	Smerch	PTFG	Bulgaria	92
107	Yinchuan	DDGM/DDGHM	China	139
107	Yusup Akaev	MHSC/MHSCM	Russian Federation	684
DD 107	Ikazuchi	DDGHM	Japan	422
DDG 107	Gravely	–	US	926
G 107	Carreca	PBF	Italy	410
GC 107	Canopus	PB	Dominican Republic	202
L 107	Andalsnes	RCL	UK	900
M 107	German Busch	YFL	Bolivia	68
M 107	Katong	MHC	Singapore	730
M 107	Pembroke	MHC/SRMH	UK	888
P 107	Jabanne	PB	Cameroon	97
PC 107	Izunami	PC/PBF	Japan	443
PPVL 107	Kou	PBO	Estonia	230
PS 107	Takachiho	PS/PB	Japan	442
S 107	Trafalgar	SSN	UK	868
WTGB 107	Penobscot Bay	TUGS-WTGB	US	969
108	Chin Hsing	WPSO	Taiwan	796
108	Xining	DDGM/DDGHM	China	139
DD 108	Akebono	DDGHM	Japan	422
DDG 108	Wayne E Meyer	–	US	926
G 108	Conversano	PBF	Italy	410
GC 108	Capella	PB	Dominican Republic	202
M 108	Grimsby	MHC/SRMH	UK	888
M 108	Punggol	MHC	Singapore	730
PC 108	Yamagumo	PC/PBF	Japan	443
PO 108	Juan N Alvares	PG/PGH	Mexico	520
PS 108	Takatsuki	PS/PBF	Japan	442
WTGB 108	Thunder Bay	TUGS-WTGB	US	969
109	Al Dekheila	ATA	Egypt	223
109	Kaifeng	DDG	China	140
109	Teh Hsing	WPSO	Taiwan	796
A 109	Bayleaf	AOT	UK	890
DD 109	Ariake	DDGHM	Japan	422
DDG 109	Jason Dunham	–	US	926
G 109	Inzerilli	PBF	Italy	410
GC 109	Orion	PB	Dominican Republic	202
L 109	Akyab	RCL	UK	900
M 109	Bangor	MHC/SRMH	UK	888
PC 109	Natsugumo	PC/PBF	Japan	443
PL 109	Shikine	PL/PSO	Japan	439
PO 109	Manuel Gutierrez Zamora	PG/PGH	Mexico	520
PS 109	Nobaru	PS/PBF	Japan	442
PVL 109	Valvas	AGF	Estonia	230
WTGB 109	Sturgeon Bay	TUGS-WTGB	US	969
110	Alexander Shabalin	LSTM	Russian Federation	681
110	Dalian	DDG	China	140
A 110	Orangeleaf	AOT	UK	890
ACV 110	Ashmore Guardian	PBO	Australia	41
BG 110	Ljubomir	PB	Ukraine	856
DD 110	Takanami	DDGHM	Japan	421
DDG 110	William P Lawrence	–	US	926
G 110	Letizia	PBF	Italy	410
GC 110	Sirius	PB	Dominican Republic	202
L 110	Aachen	RCL	UK	900
M 110	Ramsey	MHC/SRMH	UK	888
PC 110	Akigumo	PC/PBF	Japan	443
PG 110	Tomas Batilo	PBF	Philippines	611
PL 110	Suruga	PL/PSO	Japan	439
PO 110	Valentin Gomez Farias	PG/PGH	Mexico	520
S 110	Glavkos	SSK	Greece	300
111	Al Iskandarani	ATA	Egypt	223
111	Dareen	YTB/YTM	Saudi Arabia	716
111	Marasesti	FFGH	Romania	642
A 111	Alerta	AGI/AGOR	Spain	753
ACA 111	Caloyeras	YW/YO	Peru	604
D 111	Comodoro Manuel Azueta	FF/AX	Mexico	525
DD 111	Oonami	DDGHM	Japan	421
DDG 111	Spruance	–	US	926
F 111	Te Mana	FFHM	New Zealand	559
G 111	Mazzarella	PBF	Italy	410
L 111	Arezzo	RCL	UK	900
LG 111	Rio Puyango	WPBR	Ecuador	211
M 111	Blyth	MHC/SRMH	UK	888
MS 111	Guns	PB	Pakistan	591
P 111	Ladse	PBF	Slovenia	732
P 111	Pabna	PBR	Bangladesh	58
PC 111	Tatsugumo	PC/PBF	Japan	443
PG 111	Bonny Serrano	PBF	Philippines	611
PVL 111	Vapper	PB	Estonia	231
S 111	Nereus	SSK	Greece	300
112	Harbin	DDGHM	China	138
DD 112	Makinami	DDGHM	Japan	421
DDG 112	Michael Murphy	–	US	926
G 112	Nioi	PBF	Italy	410
GC 112	Altair	PB	Dominican Republic	202
LG 112	Rio Mataje	WPBR	Ecuador	211
M 112	Shoreham	MHC/SRMH	UK	888
MS 112	Sur	PB	Pakistan	591
P 112	Noakhali	PBR	Bangladesh	58
PC 112	Ikigumo	PC/PBF	Japan	443
PG 112	Bienvenido Salting	PBF	Philippines	611
PM 112	Quitasueño	PGF	Colombia	173
S 112	Triton	SSK	Greece	300
T-AKR 112	Cape Texas	AKR	US	961
Y 112	Pinar 2	YW	Turkey	841
113	Dozornyy	FFLM	Russian Federation	699

Number	Ship's name	Type	Country	Page
113	Menzhinsky	FFHM	Russian Federation	700
113	PSKR-665	PTF	Russian Federation	703
113	Qingdao	DDGHM	China	138
113	Tuwaig	YTB/YTM	Saudi Arabia	716
113	Yunga	FFLM	Russian Federation	674
DD 113	Sazanami	DDGHM	Japan	421
G 113	Partipilo	PBF	Italy	410
L 113	Audemer	RCL	UK	900
LG 113	Rio Zarumilla	WPBR	Ecuador	211
MS 113	Malan	PB	Pakistan	591
P 113	Patuakhali	PBR	Bangladesh	58
PC 113	Natsuzuki	PC/PBF	Japan	443
PM 113	José Maria Garcia Y Toledo	PB	Colombia	173
PO 113	Ignacio L Vallarta	PG/PGH	Mexico	520
S 113	Proteus	SSK	Greece	300
T-AKR 113	Cape Taylor	AKR	US	961
Y 113	Pinar 3	YW	Turkey	841
DD 114	Suzunami	DDGHM	Japan	421
G 114	Puleo	PBF	Italy	410
GC 114	Arcturus	PB	Dominican Republic	202
LG 114	Rio Chone	WPBR	Ecuador	211
P 114	Akhisar	PBO	Turkey	836
P 114	Rangamati	PBR	Bangladesh	58
PG 114	Salvador Abcede	PBF	Philippines	611
PM 114	Juan Nepomuceno Eslava	PB	Colombia	173
PO 114	Jesus Gonzalez Ortega	PG/PGH	Mexico	520
Y 114	Pinar 4	YW	Turkey	841
YFB 114	Grumete Perez	YFB	Chile	124
115	Burevi	PB	Maldives	507
115	Emil Racovita	AGS	Romania	645
115	Ivan Lednev	AK	Russian Federation	706
115	Shenyang	DDGHM	China	134
G 115	Zannotti	PBF	Italy	410
LG 115	Rio Daule	WPBR	Ecuador	211
P 115	Bogra	PBR	Bangladesh	58
PG 115	Ramon Aguirre	PBF	Philippines	611
PL 115	Noto	PL/PSO	Japan	439
PM 115	Tecim Jaime E Cárdenas Gomez	PB	Colombia	173
116	Pisagua	AKSL	Chile	124
116	Shijiazhuang	DDGHM	China	134
116	Taipei	WPSO	Taiwan	797
G 116	Laganà	PB	Italy	410
LG 116	Rio Babahoyo	WPBR	Ecuador	211
PG 116	Nicolas Mahusay	PBF	Philippines	611
S 116	Poseidon	SSK	Greece	300
Y 116	Pinar 6	YW	Turkey	841
117	PSKR 52	PBR	Russian Federation	705
117	Ras Al Fulaijah	MSO	Libya	485
117	Taichung	WPSO	Taiwan	797
BG 117	Batutinets	PB	Ukraine	856
G 117	Sanna	PB	Italy	410
PL 117	Rebun	PL/PSO	Japan	439
PO 117	Mariano Matamoros	PG/PGH	Mexico	520
S 117	Amphitrite	SSK	Greece	300
118	Keelung	WPSO	Taiwan	797
118	Korsakov	PGM	Russian Federation	703
ACP 118	Noguera	YW/YO	Peru	604
BG 118	Arabat	PB	Ukraine	856
G 118	Inzucchi	PB	Italy	410
GC 118	Alumine	PB	Argentina	23
PL 118	Shimokita	PL/PSO	Japan	439
S 118	Okeanos	SSK	Greece	300
119	Hualien	WPSO	Taiwan	797
119	Nikolay Starshinov	AK	Russian Federation	706
119	Ras Al Qula	MSO	Libya	485
ACP 119	Gauden	YW/YO	Peru	604
G 119	Vitali	PB	Italy	410
GC 119	Traful	PB	Argentina	23
PL 119	Suzuka	PL/PSO	Japan	439
S 119	Pontos	SSK	Greece	300
120	Penhu	WPSO	Taiwan	797
G 120	Calabrese	PB	Italy	410
GC 120	Lacar	PB	Argentina	23
PL 120	Kunisaki	PL/PSO	Japan	439
S 120	Papanikolis	SSK	Greece	301
U 120	Skadovsk	PB	Ukraine	851
121	Moskva	CGHM	Russian Federation	666
121	Vahakari	AKSL	Finland	238
A 121	Guardiamarina Barrutia	AXT	Spain	754
G 121	Bakinets	FFL	Azerbaijan	42
G 121	Urso	PB	Italy	410
GC 121	Fontana	PB	Argentina	23
LG121	Rio Esmeraldas	WPBR	Ecuador	210
P 121	AB 21	PC	Turkey	836
PF 121	Diligente	PBR	Colombia	174
PO 121	Cadete Virgilio Uribe	PSOH	Mexico	520
S 121	Pipinos	SSK	Greece	301
Y 121	Havuz 1	YAC	Turkey	843
122	Nantou	WPSO	Taiwan	797
A 122	Guardiamarina Chereguini	AXT	Spain	754
DD 122	Hatsuyuki	DDGHM	Japan	424
G 122	La Spina	PB	Italy	410
GC 122	Mascardi	PB	Argentina	23
LG 122	Rio Santiago	WPBR	Ecuador	210
P 122	AB 22	PC	Turkey	836
PF 122	Juan Lucio	PBR	Colombia	174
PL 122	Iwami	PL/PSO	Japan	439
PO 122	Teniente José Azueta	PSOH	Mexico	520
S 122	Matrozos	SSK	Greece	301
Y 122	Havuz 2	YAC	Turkey	843
123	Kinmen	WPSO	Taiwan	796
123	PSKR 58	PBR	Russian Federation	705
123	Ras Al Massad	MSO	Libya	485
A 123	Guardiamarina Rull	AXT	Spain	754
ARB 123	Guardian Rios	ATS	Peru	605
DD 123	Shirayuki	DDGHM	Japan	424
G 123	Salone	PB	Italy	410
GC 123	Viedna	PB	Argentina	23
NL 123	Sarucabey	LSTH/ML	Turkey	837
P 123	AB 23	PC	Turkey	836
PF 123	Alfonso Vargas	PBR	Colombia	174
PL 123	Koshiki	PL/PSO	Japan	439
PO 123	Capitán de Fragata Pedro Sáinz de Baranda	PSOH	Mexico	520
S 123	Katsonis	SSK	Greece	301
Y 123	Havuz 3	YAC	Turkey	843
124	Neon Antonov	AK	Russian Federation	706
A 124	Guardiamarina Salas	AXT	Spain	754
DD 124	Mineyuki	DDGHM	Japan	424
G 124	Cavatorto	PB	Italy	410
GC 124	San Martin	PB	Argentina	23
NL 124	Karamürselbey	LSTH/ML	Turkey	837
P 124	AB 24	PC	Turkey	836
PF 124	Fritz Hagale	PBR	Colombia	174
PO 124	Comodoro Carlos Castillo Bretón	PSOH	Mexico	520
Y 124	Havuz 4	YAC	Turkey	843
125	Lienchiang	WPSO	Taiwan	796
125	Ras Al Hani	MSO	Libya	485
DD 125	Sawayuki	DDGHM	Japan	424
G 125	Fusco	PB	Italy	410
GC 125	Buenos Aires	PB	Argentina	23
NL 125	Osman Gazi	LSTH/ML	Turkey	837
PF 125	Vengadora	PBR	Colombia	174
PL 125	Katori	PL/PSO	Japan	439
PO 125	Vicealmirante Othón P Blanco	PSOH	Mexico	520
Y 125	Havuz 5	YAC	Turkey	843
126	PSKR-657	PTF	Russian Federation	703
DD 126	Hamayuki	DDGHM	Japan	424
G 126	De Rosa	PB	Italy	410
GC 126	Musters	PB	Argentina	23
L 126	Balikpapan	LCH/LSM	Australia	34
PF 126	Humberto Cortez	PBR	Colombia	174
PL 126	Kunigami	PL/PSO	Japan	439
PO 126	Contralmirante Angel Ortiz Monasterio	PSOH	Mexico	520
127	Minsk	LSTM	Russian Federation	681
DD 127	Isoyuki	DDGHM	Japan	424
G 127	Zaccola	PB	Italy	410
L 127	Brunei	LCH/LSM	Australia	34
P 127	AB 27	PC	Turkey	836
PL 127	Etomo	PL/PSO	Japan	439
DD 128	Haruyuki	DDGHM	Japan	424
G 128	Stanisci	PB	Italy	410
L 128	Labuan	LCH/LSM	Australia	34
P 128	AB 28	PC	Turkey	836
PF 128	Carlos Galindo	PBR	Colombia	174
PL 128	Esan	PL/PSO	Japan	439
Y 128	Havuz 8	YAC	Turkey	843
129	MPK 139	FFLM	Russian Federation	674
129	PSKR-690	PTF	Russian Federation	703
DD 129	Yamayuki	DDGHM	Japan	424
G 129	Sottile	PB	Italy	410
GC 129	Colhue	PB	Argentina	23
L 129	Tarakan	LCH/LSM	Australia	34
P 129	AB 29	PC	Turkey	836
PB-129	Merjen	WPB	Turkmenistan	847
PF 129	Capitán Jaime Rook	PBR	Colombia	174
Y 129	Havuz 9	YAC	Turkey	843
130	Korolev	LSTM	Russian Federation	681
DD 130	Matsuyuki	DDGHM	Japan	424
G 130	De Falco	PB	Italy	410
GC 130	Maria L Pendo	PB	Argentina	23
H 130	Roebuck	AGS	UK	889
L 130	Wewak	LCH/LSM	Australia	34
PF 130	Manuela Saenz	PBR	Colombia	174
U 130	Hetman Sagaidachny	FFHM	Ukraine	849
Y 130	Havuz 10	YAC	Turkey	843
131	Ingeniero Mery	YFD	Chile	123
131	Nanjing	DDGM/DDGHM	China	139
ATC 131	Mollendo	AOR	Peru	604
DD 131	Setoyuki	DDGHM	Japan	424
GC 131	Roca	PB	Argentina	23
H 131	Scott	AGSH	UK	888
P 131	AB 31	PC	Turkey	836
P 131	Iliria	PB	Albania	3
PO 131	Capitán de Navio Sebastian José Holzinger	PSOH	Mexico	518
SB 131	Nicolay Chiker	ATS	Russian Federation	697
132	Hefei	DDGM/DDGHM	China	139
132	Ibn Ouf	LSTH	Libya	485
132	Mutilla	YFD	Chile	123
132	PSKR-712	PTF	Russian Federation	703
A 132	Diligence	ARH	UK	892
DD 132	Asayuki	DDGHM	Japan	424
GC 132	Puelo	PB	Argentina	23
PO 132	Capitán de Navio Blas Godinez	PSOH	Mexico	518
133	Chongqing	DDGM/DDGHM	China	139
133	Havouri	AKSL	Finland	238
133	Kaani	PB	Maldives	507
133	PSKR-641	PTF	Russian Federation	703
133	Talcahuano	YFD	Chile	123
GC 133	Futalaufquen	PB	Argentina	23
L 133	Betano	LCH/LSM	Australia	34
PO 133	Brigadier José Mariá de la Vega	PSOH	Mexico	518
134	Ibn Haritha	LSTH	Libya	485
134	PSKR-725	PTF	Russian Federation	703
134	Zunyi	DDGM/DDGHM	China	139
F 134	Laksamana Hang Nadim	FSGM	Malaysia	497
GC 134	Falkner	PB	Argentina	23
PO 134	General Felipe B Berriozábal	PSOH	Mexico	518
Y 134	Havuz 11	YAC	Turkey	843

Number	Ship's name	Type	Country	Page
A 135	Argus	APCR	UK	892
F 135	Laksamana Tun Abdul Jamil	FSGM	Malaysia	497
GC 135	Hess	PB	Argentina	23
P 135	AB 35	PC	Turkey	836
PF 135	Riohacha	PBR	Colombia	172
S 135	Hashmat	SSK	Pakistan	582
SB 135	Fotiy Krylov	ATS	Russian Federation	697
136	Hangzhou	DDGHM	China	135
F 136	Laksamana Muhammad Amin	FSGM	Malaysia	497
GC 136	Colhue Huapi	PB	Argentina	23
P 136	AB 36	PC	Turkey	836
PF 136	Leticia	PBR	Colombia	172
S 136	Hurmat	SSK	Pakistan	582
Y 136	Havuz 13	YAC	Turkey	843
137	Anatoly Korolev	PGM	Russian Federation	703
137	Fuzhou	DDGHM	China	135
137	Khabarovsk	PGR	Russian Federation	706
137	PSKR-631	PTF	Russian Federation	703
F 137	Laksamana Tan Pusmah	FSGM	Malaysia	497
GC 137	Cormoran	WPB	Argentina	23
PF 137	Arauca	PBR	Colombia	172
S 137	Khalid	SSK	Pakistan	583
138	Naryan-Mar	FFLM	Russian Federation	674
138	Shkval	PGR	Russian Federation	706
138	Taizhou	DDGHM	China	135
GC 138	Cisne	WPB	Argentina	23
S 138	Saad	SSK	Pakistan	583
139	Kizljar	PGM	Russian Federation	703
139	Ningbo	DDGHM	China	135
139	PSKR-659	PTF	Russian Federation	703
GC 139	Pejerrey	WPB	Argentina	23
S 139	Hamza	SSK	Pakistan	583
Y 139	Yakit	YFB/YE	Turkey	842
GC 140	Yehuin	PB	Argentina	23
P 140	Rajshahi	PB	Pakistan	587
PG 140	Emilio Aguinaldo	PBO	Philippines	611
Y 140	H 500	YW	Turkey	841
141	Vyborg	PGM	Russian Federation	703
DT 141	Paitá	LSTH	Peru	603
GC 141	Quillen	PB	Argentina	23
P 141	Mubarraz	PGGFM	UAE	860
PC 141	Cabo Corrientes	PB	Colombia	172
PG 141	Antonio Luna	PBO	Philippines	611
PO 141	Justo Sierra Mendez	PSOH	Mexico	518
Y 141	H 501	YW	Turkey	841
142	Bug	PBO	Russian Federation	701
DDH 142	Hiei	DDHM	Japan	426
DT 142	Pisco	LSTH	Peru	603
GC 142	Surel	WPBF	Argentina	23
P 142	Makasib	PGGFM	UAE	860
PC 142	Cabo Manglares	PB	Colombia	172
Y 142	H 502	YW	Turkey	841
143	Almaz	PGM	Russian Federation	703
143	PSKR-723	PTF	Russian Federation	703
143	Sergey Sudetsky	AK	Russian Federation	706
DDH 143	Shirane	DDHM	Japan	425
DT 143	Callao	LSTH	Peru	603
GC 143	Surubi	WPB	Argentina	23
PC 143	Cabo Tiburon	PB	Colombia	172
PO 143	Guillermo Prieto	PSOH	Mexico	518
DDH 144	Kurama	DDHM	Japan	425
DT 144	Eten	LSTH	Peru	603
GC 144	Boga	WPB	Argentina	23
PC 144	Cabo de la Vella	PB	Colombia	172
PO 144	Matias Romero	PSOH	Mexico	518
F 145	Amatola	FFGHM	South Africa	735
GC 145	Sabalo	WPB	Argentina	23
146	PSKR 54	PBR	Russian Federation	705
146	Storm	PGR	Russian Federation	706
F 146	Isandlwana	FFGHM	South Africa	735
GC 146	Huala	WPB	Argentina	23
F 147	Spioenkop	FFGHM	South Africa	735
GC 147	Pacu	WPB	Argentina	23
148	ORSK	LSTM	Russian Federation	681
F 148	Mendi	FFGHM	South Africa	735
GC 148	Manduruyu	WPB	Argentina	23
P 148	Otago	PBO	New Zealand	560
149	Kuban	PCM	Russian Federation	702
GC 149	Corvina	WPB	Argentina	23
150	Anzac	FFGHM	Australia	28
150	Saratov	LSTM	Russian Federation	681
GC 150	Fagnano	PB	Argentina	23
V 150	Jägaren	PC	Sweden	775
151	Arunta	FFGHM	Australia	28
151	Azov	LSTM	Russian Federation	681
151	Midhili	PB	Maldives	507
151	Perantau	AGS	Malaysia	501
GC 151	Nahuel Huapi	PB	Argentina	23
LR 151	Hamal	PB	Dominican Republic	202
P 151	Espadarte	PB	Cape Verde	113
P 151	Ban Yas	PGGF	UAE	860
PO 151	Durango	PSOH	Mexico	519
152	Berkut	PCM	Russian Federation	702
152	Nikolay Filchenkov	LSTM	Russian Federation	681
152	Warramunga	FFGHM	Australia	28
LR 152	Vega	PB	Dominican Republic	202
P 152	Marban	PGGF	UAE	860
PO 152	Sonora	PSOH	Mexico	519
153	Stuart	FFGHM	Australia	28
BH 153	Quindio	–	Colombia	176
DD 153	Yuugiri	DDGHM	Japan	423
LR 153	Deneb	PB	Dominican Republic	202
P 153	Rodqm	PGGF	UAE	860
PO 153	Guanajuato	PSOH	Mexico	519
U 153	Priluki	PGGK	Ukraine	851
154	Parramatta	FFGHM	Australia	28
154	Vasiliy Suntzov	AK	Russian Federation	706
ATP 154	Bayóvar	AOT	Peru	605
DD 154	Amagiri	DDGHM	Japan	423
LR 154	Acamar	PB	Dominican Republic	202
P 154	Shaheen	PGGF	UAE	860
PO 154	Veracruz	PSOH	Mexico	519
U 154	Kahovka	PGGK	Ukraine	851
155	Ballarat	FFGHM	Australia	28
ATP 155	Zorritos	AOT	Peru	605
BO 155	Providencia	AGOR	Colombia	175
DD 155	Hamagiri	DDGHM	Japan	423
LR 155	Pollux	PBF	Dominican Republic	203
P 155	Sagar	PGGF	UAE	860
U 155	Pridneprovye	FSGM	Ukraine	851
156	Orel	FFHM	Russian Federation	700
156	Toowoomba	FFGHM	Australia	28
156	Yamal	LSTM	Russian Federation	681
BO 156	Malpelo	AGOR	Colombia	175
D 156	Nazim	DD	Pakistan	590
DD 156	Setogiri	DDGHM	Japan	423
LR 156	Castor	PBF	Dominican Republic	203
P 156	Tarif	PGGF	UAE	860
U 156	Kremenchuk	FSGM	Ukraine	851
157	Perth	FFGHM	Australia	28
DD 157	Sawagiri	DDGHM	Japan	423
LR 157	Shaula	PBF	Dominican Republic	203
P 157	Larkana	PB	Pakistan	588
158	Dzerzhinsky	FFHM	Russian Federation	700
158	Tsesar Kunikov	LSTM	Russian Federation	681
158	Yung Chuan	MSC	Taiwan	794
DD 158	Umigiri	DDGHM	Japan	423
LR 158	Atria	PBF	Dominican Republic	203
160	Vorovsky	FFHM	Russian Federation	700
BE 160	Gloria	AXS	Colombia	176
Y 160	Önder	YTB/YTM/YTL	Turkey	843
161	Aisberg	PGH	Russian Federation	701
161	Changsha	DDGM/DDGHM	China	139
161	Korshun	PCM	Russian Federation	702
BL 161	Cartagena de Indias	AGP	Colombia	176
LG-161	Rio Coangos	WPBR	Ecuador	212
P 161	Muray Jib	FSGHM	UAE	858
PO 161	Oaxaca	PSOH	Mexico	519
Y 161	Öncü	YTB/YTM/YTL	Turkey	843
162	Nanning	DDGM/DDGHM	China	139
162	Yung Fu	MSC	Taiwan	794
BL 162	Buenaventura	AGP	Colombia	176
LG-162	Rio Muisne	WPBR	Ecuador	212
P 162	Das	FSGHM	UAE	858
PO 162	Baja California	PSOH	Mexico	519
Y 162	Özgen	YTB/YTM/YTL	Turkey	843
163	Nanchang	DDGM/DDGHM	China	139
163	Voron	PCM	Russian Federation	702
LG-163	Rio Tangare	WPBR	Ecuador	212
M 163	Muhafiz	MHSC	Pakistan	588
P 163	Express	PB/AXL	UK	883
PO 163	Bicentenario	PSOH	Mexico	519
Y 163	Ödev	YTB/YTM/YTL	Turkey	843
164	Guilin	DDGM/DDGHM	China	139
164	Onega	FFLM	Russian Federation	674
M 164	Mujahid	MHSC	Pakistan	588
P 164	Explorer	PB/AXL	UK	883
PO 164	Independencia	PSOH	Mexico	519
S 164	Barracuda	SSK	Portugal	629
Y 164	Özgür	YTB/YTM/YTL	Turkey	843
165	Zhanjiang	DDG	China	140
MB 165	Serdity	ARS/ATA	Russian Federation	698
P 165	Example	PB/AXL	UK	883
166	Zhuhai	DDG	China	140
M 166	Munsif	MHSC	Pakistan	588
167	Shenzhen	DDGHM	China	137
167	Yung Ren	MSC	Taiwan	794
L 167	Ios	LCU	Greece	308
P 167	Exploit	PB/AXL	UK	883
WMEC 167	Acushnet	PSO/WMEC	US	965
168	Guangzhou	DDGHM	China	136
168	Yung Sui	MSC	Taiwan	794
T-ATF 168	Catawba	ATF	US	956
169	Wuhan	DDGHM	China	136
L 169	Irakleia	LCU	Greece	308
MB 169	Pochetnyy	ARS/ATA	Russian Federation	698
SSV 169	Tavriya	AGIM	Russian Federation	688
T-ATF 169	Navajo	ATF	US	956
170	Lanzhou	DDGHM	China	137
170	Neva	PGH	Russian Federation	701
170	Zorkiy	FFLM	Russian Federation	699
DDG 170	Sawakaze	DDGM	Japan	425
DF 170	Mayor Jaime Arias Arango	ASL	Colombia	177
L 170	Folegandros	LCU	Greece	308
S 170	Tridente	SSK	Portugal	630
171	Haikou	DDGHM	China	137
171	Kedah	FSGHM	Malaysia	496
171	MPK 113	FFLM	Russian Federation	674
A 171	Endurance	AGOBH	UK	883
AH 171	Carrasco	AGSC/EH	Peru	604
DDG 171	Hatakaze	DDGHM	Japan	420
LG-171	Rio Tena	WPBR	Ecuador	212
MB 171	Loksa	ARS/ATA	Russian Federation	698
S 171	Arpão	SSK	Portugal	630
T-ATF 171	Sioux	ATF	US	956
172	Pahang	FSGHM	Malaysia	496
172	Primorye	PBO	Russian Federation	701
AGOR 172	Quest	AGORH	Canada	104
AH 172	Stiglich	AGSC/AH	Peru	604
DDG 172	Shimakaze	DDGHM	Japan	420
LG-172	Rio Puyo	WPBR	Ecuador	212
S 172	U 23	SSK	Germany	283
T-ATF 172	Apache	ATF	US	956
173	Anadyr	PGH	Russian Federation	701
173	Perak	FSGHM	Malaysia	496
DDG 173	Kongou	DDGHM	Japan	419
L 173	Chios	LSTH	Greece	307

Number	Ship's name	Type	Country	Page
LG-173	Rio Portoviejo	WPBR	Ecuador	212
S 173	U 24	SSK	Germany	283
174	Terengganu	FSGHM	Malaysia	496
AEH 174	Macha	AGSC/EH	Peru	603
DDG 174	Kirishima	DDGHM	Japan	419
L 174	Samos	LSTH	Greece	307
LG-174	Rio Manta	WPBR	Ecuador	212
175	Kelantan	FSGHM	Malaysia	496
175	Pskov	FFHM	Russian Federation	700
AH 175	Carrillo	AGSC/EH	Peru	604
DDG 175	Myoukou	DDGHM	Japan	419
L 175	Ikaria	LSTH	Greece	307
SSV 175	Viktor Leonov	AGIM	Russian Federation	688
176	Kala 6	LCU/AKSL	Finland	238
176	Rahova	PGR	Romania	644
176	Selangor	FSGHM	Malaysia	496
176	Vyacheslav Denisov	AK	Russian Federation	706
AH 176	Melo	AGSC/EH	Peru	604
DDG 176	Choukai	DDGHM	Japan	419
L 176	Lesbos	LSTH	Greece	307
177	Opanez	PGR	Romania	644
DDG 177	Atago	DDGHM	Japan	418
L 177	Rodos	LSTH	Greece	307
178	Smardan	PGR	Romania	644
178	Smelyy	FFLM	Russian Federation	699
DDG 178	Ashigara	DDGHM	Japan	418
L 178	Naxos	LCU	Greece	308
MB 178	Saturn	ARS/ATA	Russian Federation	698
P 178	Ekpe	PGF	Nigeria	565
179	Posada	PGR	Romania	644
L 179	Paros	LCU	Greece	308
P 179	Damisa	PGF	Nigeria	565
180	Rovine	PGR	Romania	644
L 180	Kefallinia	LCUJ	Greece	307
P 180	Agu	PGF	Nigeria	565
D 181	Tariq	FFHM/FFGH	Pakistan	584
DDH 181	Hyuga	CVHG	Japan	417
L 181	Ithaki	LCUJ	Greece	307
LG-181	Rio Zamora	WPBR	Ecuador	212
P 181	Siri	PGGF	Nigeria	565
S 181	U 31	SSK	Germany	282
D 182	Babur	FFHM/FFGH	Pakistan	584
L 182	Kerkira	LCUJ	Greece	307
LG-182	Rio Palora	WPBR	Ecuador	212
P 182	Ayam	PGGF	Nigeria	565
S 182	U 32	SSK	Germany	282
183	Volga	PGH	Russian Federation	701
D 183	Khaibar	FFHM/FFGH	Pakistan	584
L 183	Zakynthos	LCUJ	Greece	307
P 183	Ekun	PGGF	Nigeria	565
S 183	U 33	SSK	Germany	282
SFP 183	Akademik Seminikhin	AGS	Russian Federation	686
184	Mikhail Konovalov	AK	Russian Federation	706
D 184	Badr	FFHM/FFGH	Pakistan	584
S 184	U 34	SSK	Germany	282
185	Sakhalin	PBO	Russian Federation	701
D 185	Tippu Sultan	FFHM/FFGH	Pakistan	584
S 185	U 35	SSK	Germany	282
D 186	Shahjahan	FFHM/FFGH	Pakistan	584
S 186	U 36	SSK	Germany	282
T-AO 187	Henry J Kaiser	AOH	US	955
188	Zborul	FSG	Romania	645
189	Pescarusul	FSG	Romania	645
189	PSKR 59	PBR	Russian Federation	705
T-AO 189	John Lenthall	AOH	US	955
190	Lastunul	FSG	Romania	645
190	Monchegorsk	FFLM	Russian Federation	674
191	Chung Cheng	LSDM	Taiwan	792
LSD 193	Shiu Hai	LSDH	Taiwan	792
T-AO 193	Walter S Diehl	AOH	US	955
S 194	U 15	SSK	Germany	283
T-AO 194	John Ericsson	AOH	US	955
L 195	Serifos	LCU	Greece	308
S 195	U 16	SSK	Germany	283
T-AO 195	Leroy Grumman	AOH	US	955
196	Sneznogorsk	FFLM	Russian Federation	674
196	Zabaykalye	PBO	Russian Federation	701
P 196	Andromeda	PB	Greece	305
S 196	U 17	SSK	Germany	283
T-AO 196	Kanawha	AOH	US	955
S 197	U 18	SSK	Germany	283
T-AO 197	Pecos	AOH	US	955
198	Kamchatka	PBO	Russian Federation	701
P 198	Kyknos	PB	Greece	305
T-AO 198	Big Horn	AOH	US	955
199	Brest	FFLM	Russian Federation	674
199	Dvina	AK	Russian Federation	706
P 199	Pigasos	PB	Greece	305
T-AO 199	Tippecanoe	AOH	US	955
200	Oljevern 01	AGS	Norway	572
200	Oljevern 02	AGS	Norway	572
200	Oljevern 03	AGS	Norway	572
200	Oljevern 04	AGS	Norway	572
200	Perekop	–	Russian Federation	689
G 200	Buratti	PB	Italy	411
T-AO 200	Guadalupe	AOH	US	955
201	Chung Hai	LST	Taiwan	793
201	Iveria	PB	Georgia	279
201	Kayvan	PB	Iran	374
201	Kujang	WPB	Indonesia	367
201	Kula	PB	Fiji	233
A 201	Orion	AGIH	Sweden	777
F 201	Nicolas Bravo	FFH	Mexico	515
G 201	De Ianni	PB	Italy	411
P 201	Cabo Fradera	PBR	Spain	750
P 201	Istiklal	PB	Tunisia	824
P 201	Neiafu	PB	Tonga	820
P 201	Ruposhi Bangla	PB	Bangladesh	57
PS 201	Tsuruugi	PS/PBOF	Japan	442
SSV 201	Priazove	AGIM	Russian Federation	688
T-AO 201	Patuxent	AOH	US	955
UAM 201	Creoula	AXS	Portugal	635
VS 201	Idabato	PB	Cameroon	97
WLB 201	Juniper	WLB/ABU	US	969
202	Kikau	PB	Fiji	233
202	Parang	WPB	Indonesia	367
202	Tiran	PB	Iran	374
F 202	Hermenegildo Galeana	FFH	Mexico	515
G 202	Salerno	PB	Italy	411
LM 202	Seiun	AKSL	Japan	447
P 202	Joumhouria	PB	Tunisia	824
P 202	Pangai	PB	Tonga	820
PC 202	Kitagumo	PC/PB	Japan	443
PC 202	Matias de Cordova	PB	Mexico	521
PS 202	Hotaka	PS/PBOF	Japan	442
T-AO 202	Yukon	AOH	US	955
VS 202	Isongo	PB	Cameroon	97
WLB 202	Willow	WLB/ABU	US	969
203	Celurit	WPB	Indonesia	367
203	El Wacil	PB	Morocco	535
203	Kiro	PB	Fiji	233
203	Mestia	PB	Georgia	279
G 203	Rossi	PB	Italy	411
LDG 203	Bacamarte	LCU	Portugal	635
LM 203	Sekiun	AKSL	Japan	447
P 203	Al Jala	PB	Tunisia	824
P 203	Cacique Nome	PB	Panama	593
P 203	Savea	PB	Tonga	820
PC 203	Yukigumo	PC/PB	Japan	443
PM 203	Tortuguero	ABU	Dominican Republic	201
PS 203	Norikura	PS/PBOF	Japan	442
T-AO 203	Laramie	AOH	US	955
VS 203	Mouanco	PB	Cameroon	97
WLB 203	Kukui	WLB/ABU	US	969
204	Apsheron	AKH/AGF	Russian Federation	690
204	Cundrik	WPB	Indonesia	367
204	El Jail	PB	Morocco	535
204	Mahan	PB	Iran	374
BH 204	El Idrissi	AGS	Algeria	7
G 204	Garulli	PB	Italy	411
LM 204	Houun	AKSL	Japan	447
P 204	3 de Noviembre	PB	Panama	593
P 204	Remada	PB	Tunisia	824
PM 204	Capotillo	ABU	Dominican Republic	201
PS 204	Kaimon	PS/PBOF	Japan	442
T-AO 204	Rappahannock	AOH	US	955
VS 204	Campo	PB	Cameroon	97
WLB 204	Elm	WLB/ABU	US	969
205	Belati	WPB	Indonesia	367
205	Chung Chien	LST	Taiwan	793
205	El Mikdam	PB	Morocco	535
G 205	Sanges	PB	Italy	411
LM 205	Reiun	AKSL	Japan	447
PS 205	Asama	PS/PBOF	Japan	442
T 205	Kassir	PBR	Kuwait	477
U 205	Lutsk	FFLM	Ukraine	850
WLB 205	Walnut	WLB/ABU	US	969
206	El Khafir	PB	Morocco	535
206	Golok	WSAR	Indonesia	367
206	Kapitan 1st Rank Dimitri Dobrev	ADG/AX	Bulgaria	95
206	RT 249	MHC	Russian Federation	684
G 206	Corrias	PB	Italy	411
LM 206	Genun	AKSL	Japan	447
P 206	10 de Noviembre	PB	Panama	593
PC 206	Ignacio López Rayón	PB	Mexico	521
PS 206	Houou	PS/PBOF	Japan	442
U 206	Vinnitsa	FFLM	Ukraine	850
WLB 206	Spar	WLB/ABU	US	969
207	El Haris	PB	Morocco	535
207	Endurance	LPDM	Singapore	729
207	Panan	WSAR	Indonesia	367
F 207	Bremen	FFGHM	Germany	286
G 207	Cortile	PB	Italy	411
LM 207	Ayabane	AKSL	Japan	447
P 207	28 de Noviembre	PB	Panama	593
P 207	Utique	PB	Tunisia	823
U 207	Uzhgorod	PCM	Ukraine	851
WLB 207	Maple	WLB/ABU	US	969
208	Chung Shun	LST	Taiwan	793
208	El Essahir	PB	Morocco	535
208	Pedang	WSAR	Indonesia	367
208	Resolution	LPDM	Singapore	729
F 208	Niedersachsen	FFGHM	Germany	286
G 208	Casotti	PB	Italy	411
LM 208	Koun	AKSL	Japan	447
P 208	Jerba	PB	Tunisia	823
P 208	4 de Noviembre	PB	Panama	593
PC 208	Juan Antonio de La Fuente	PB	Mexico	521
SSV 208	Kurily	AGIM	Russian Federation	688
U 208	Khmelnitsky	PCM	Ukraine	851
WLB 208	Aspen	WLB/ABU	US	969
209	Erraid	WPB	Morocco	537
209	Kapak	WSAR	Indonesia	367
209	Persistence	LPDM	Singapore	729
F 209	Rheinland-Pfalz	FFGHM	Germany	286
G 209	Prata	PB	Italy	411
P 209	Kuriat	PB	Tunisia	823
P 209	5 de Noviembre	PB	Panama	593
PC 209	Leon Guzman	PB	Mexico	521
U 209	Ternopil	FFLM	Ukraine	850
WLB 209	Sycamore	WLB/ABU	US	969
210	Ayeda 4	AOTL/AWTL	Egypt	222
210	Endeavour	LPDM	Singapore	729
210	Erraced	WPB	Morocco	537
210	RT 273	MHC	Russian Federation	684
210	Smolny	–	Russian Federation	689
F 210	Emden	FFGHM	Germany	286

Number	Ship's name	Type	Country	Page
G 210	Marra	PB	Italy	411
P 210	Tsotne Dadiani	WPB	Georgia	280
PC 210	Ignacio Ramirez	PB	Mexico	521
PC 210	Kawagiri	PC/PB	Japan	443
T 210	Dastoor	PBR	Kuwait	477
WLB 210	Cypress	WLB/ABU	US	969
211	El Kaced	WPB	Morocco	537
211	Parvin	PC	Iran	374
F 211	Ignacio Allende	FFHM	Mexico	514
F 211	Köln	FFGHM	Germany	286
G 211	Gottardi	PB	Italy	411
M 211	Alkyon	MSC	Greece	308
P 211	General Mazniashvili	WPB	Georgia	280
P 211	Meghna	PB	Bangladesh	57
PC 211	Ignacio Mariscal	PB	Mexico	521
PC 211	Tosagiri	PC/PB	Japan	443
WLB 211	Oak	WLB/ABU	US	969
212	Al Qiaq	YFU	Saudi Arabia	715
212	Atabarah	AOTL/AWTL	Egypt	222
212	Bahram	PC	Iran	374
212	Essaid	WPB	Morocco	537
A 212	Ägir	YDT/AGF	Sweden	779
DCB 212	Máncora	PBR	Peru	607
F 212	Karlsruhe	FFGHM	Germany	286
F 212	Mariano Abasolo	FFHM	Mexico	514
G 212	La Piccirella	PB	Italy	411
P 212	Jamuna	PB	Bangladesh	57
PC 212	Heriberto Jara Corona	PB	Mexico	521
PF 212	Al Hani	FFGM	Libya	484
WLB 212	Hickory	WLB/ABU	US	969
213	Nahid	PC	Iran	374
DCB 213	Huaura	PBR	Peru	607
F 213	Augsburg	FFGHM	Germany	286
F 213	Guadaloupe Victoria	FFHM	Mexico	514
G 213	Perissinotto	PB	Italy	411
PF 213	Al Qirdabiyah	FFGM	Libya	484
WLB 213	Fir	WLB/ABU	US	969
214	Akdu	AOTL/AWTL	Egypt	222
214	Al Sulayel	YFU	Saudi Arabia	715
214	Ghazee	PB	Maldives	507
A 214	Belos III	ARSH	Sweden	779
DCB 214	Quilca	PBR	Peru	607
F 214	Francisco Javier Mina	FFHM	Mexico	514
F 214	Lübeck	FFGHM	Germany	286
G 214	Rocca	PB	Italy	411
M 214	Avra	MSC	Greece	308
PC 214	Colima	PB	Mexico	521
PC 214	Nijigumo	PC/PB	Japan	443
WLB 214	Hollyhock	WLB/ABU	US	969
215	RT 233	MHC	Russian Federation	684
F 215	Brandenburg	FFGHM	Germany	284
G 215	Bertoldi	PB	Italy	411
PC 215	Pucusana	PBR	Peru	607
PC 215	Jose Joaquin Fernandez de Lizardi	PB	Mexico	521
T 215	Mahroos	PBR	Kuwait	477
WLB 215	Sequoia	WLB/ABU	US	969
216	Al Ula	YFU	Saudi Arabia	715
216	Ayeda 3	AOTL/AWTL	Egypt	222
216	Chung Kuang	LST	Taiwan	793
F 216	Schleswig-Holstein	FFGHM	Germany	284
G 216	Verdecchia	PB	Italy	411
PC 216	Chicama	PBR	Peru	606
PC 216	Francisco J Mugica	PB	Mexico	521
PC 216	Iseyuki	PC/PB	Japan	443
WLB 216	Alder	WLB/ABU	US	969
217	Chung Suo	LST	Taiwan	793
F 217	Bayern	FFGHM	Germany	284
G 217	De Santis	PB	Italy	411
PC 217	Huanchaco	PBR	Peru	606
PC 217	Isonami	PC/PB	Japan	443
218	Afif	YFU	Saudi Arabia	715
218	Aleksin	FFLM	Russian Federation	675
218	Chung Chi	LST	Taiwan	793
218	Maryut	AOTL/AWTL	Egypt	222
F 218	Mecklenburg-Vorpommern	FFGHM	Germany	284
G 218	Piccinni Leopardi	PB	Italy	411
PC 218	Chorrillos	PBR	Peru	606
PC 218	Nagozuki	PC/PB	Japan	443
PC 218	Jose Maria Del Castillo Velazco	PB	Mexico	521
219	RT 231	MHC	Russian Federation	684
F 219	Sachsen	FFGHM	Germany	287
G 219	Bianco	PB	Italy	411
PC 219	Chancay	PBR	Peru	606
PC 219	Yaezuki	PC/PB	Japan	443
220	Al Nil	AOTL/AWTL	Egypt	222
220	Dheba	YFU	Saudi Arabia	716
F 220	Hamburg	FFGHM	Germany	287
G 220	Starace	PB	Italy	411
PC 220	Camana	PBR	Peru	606
PC 220	Hamayuki	PC/PB	Japan	443
PC 220	Jose Natividad Macias	PB	Mexico	521
221	Chung Chuan	LST	Taiwan	793
221	Priyadarshini	WPBO	India	351
221	Regele Ferdinand	FFHM	Romania	641
221	Sobat	AFL	Sudan	767
F 221	Hessen	FFGHM	Germany	287
G 221	Cultrona	PB	Italy	411
P 221	Kaman	PGGF	Iran	373
PC 221	Chala	PBR	Peru	606
PC 221	Komayuki	PC/PB	Japan	443
PR 221	Capitán Palomeque	PBR	Bolivia	68
222	Dinder	AFL	Sudan	767
222	Razia Sultana	WPBO	India	351
222	Regina Maria	FFHM	Romania	641
222	Umlus	YFU	Saudi Arabia	716
G 222	Benvenuti	PB	Italy	411
P 222	Zoubin	PGGF	Iran	373
PC 222	Umigiri	PC/PB	Japan	443
PC 222	Zorritos	PBR	Peru	606
223	Annie Besant	WPBO	India	351
223	Iskandhar	PB	Maldives	507
M 223	Libertador	YFL	Bolivia	68
P 223	Araz	PB	Azerbaijan	42
P 223	Khadang	PGGF	Iran	373
PC 223	Asagiri	PC/PB	Japan	443
PC 223	Tamaulipas	PB	Mexico	521
PM 223	Rio Chira	PB	Peru	606
224	Al Furat	AOTL/AWTL	Egypt	222
224	Al Leeth	YFU	Saudi Arabia	716
224	Kamla Devi	WPBO	India	351
224	Proteo	ARS	Bulgaria	95
M 224	Trinidad	YFL	Bolivia	68
P 224	Peykan	PGGF	Iran	373
PC 224	Punta Arenas	PBR	Peru	606
PC 224	Yucatan	PB	Mexico	521
225	Amrit Kaur	WPBO	India	351
P 225	Joshan	PGGF	Iran	373
PC 225	Santa Rosa	PBR	Peru	606
PC 225	Tabasco	PB	Mexico	521
226	Al Quonfetha	YFU	Saudi Arabia	716
226	Chung Chih	LST	Taiwan	793
226	Kanak Lata Baura	WPBO	India	351
P 226	Falakhon	PGGF	Iran	373
PC 226	Pacasmayo	PBR	Peru	606
PC 226	Cochimie	PB	Mexico	521
227	Bhikaji Cama	WPBO	India	351
227	Chung Ming	LST	Taiwan	793
DE 227	Yuubari	FFG/DE	Japan	427
P 227	Shamshir	PGGF	Iran	373
PC 227	Barranca	PBR	Peru	606
228	Sucheta Kripalani	WPBO	India	351
DE 228	Yuubetsu	FFG/DE	Japan	427
P 228	Gorz	PGGF	Iran	373
P 228	Toxotis	PB	Greece	305
PC 228	Coishco	PBR	Peru	606
PC 228	Puebla	PB	Mexico	521
229	Sarojini Naidu	WPBO	India	351
DE 229	Abukuma	FFGM/DE	Japan	426
F 229	Lancaster	FFGHM	UK	878
P 229	Gardouneh	PGGF	Iran	373
P 229	Tolmi	PG	Greece	306
PC 229	Independencia	PBR	Peru	606
230	Chung Pang	LST	Taiwan	793
230	Durgabai Deshmukh	WPBO	India	351
230	Shaladein	ARL	Egypt	222
A 230	Admiral Pitka	FFLH/AGFH/AGE	Estonia	228
DE 230	Jintsu	FFGM/DE	Japan	426
P 230	Khanjar	PGGF	Iran	373
P 230	Ormi	PG	Greece	306
PC 230	San Nicolas	PBR	Peru	606
PC 230	Leona Vicario	PB	Mexico	521
231	Chung Yeh	LST	Taiwan	793
231	Halaib	AEL	Egypt	222
231	Kasturba Gandhi	WPBO	India	351
DE 231	Ooyodo	FFGM/DE	Japan	426
F 231	Argyll	FFGHM	UK	878
GC 231	El Mounkid I	SAR	Algeria	8
P 231	Neyzeh	PGGF	Iran	373
PC 231	Josefa Ortiz de Dominguez	PB	Mexico	521
PC 231	Río Cañete	PBR	Peru	607
SSV 231	Vassily Tatischev	AGIM	Russian Federation	688
232	Aruna Asaf Ali	WPBO	India	351
232	Chung Ho	LSTH	Taiwan	792
232	Hauki	AKSL	Finland	238
232	Kalmykia	FFLM	Russian Federation	675
DE 232	Sendai	FFGM/DE	Japan	426
GC 232	El Mounkid II	SAR	Algeria	8
P 232	Tabarzin	PGGF	Iran	373
PC 232	Río Santa	PBR	Peru	607
233	Chung Ping	LSTH	Taiwan	792
233	Subhadra Kumari Chauhan	WPBO	India	351
A 233	Maistros	AXS	Greece	309
DE 233	Chikuma	FFGM/DE	Japan	426
GC 233	El Mounkid III	SAR	Algeria	8
P 233	Derafsh	PGGF	Iran	373
PC 233	Río Majes	PBR	Peru	607
234	Meera Behan	WPBO	India	351
A 234	Sorokos	AXS	Greece	309
DE 234	Tone	FFGM/DE	Japan	426
F 234	Iron Duke	FFGHM	UK	878
GC 234	El Mounkid IV	SAR	Algeria	8
PC 234	Matarani	PBR	Peru	606
235	Hirsala	AKSL	Finland	238
235	Savitri Bai Phule	WPBO	India	351
F 235	Monmouth	FFGHM	UK	878
PC 235	Río Viru	PBR	Peru	607
F 236	Montrose	FFGHM	UK	878
PC 236	Río Lurin	PBR	Peru	607
237	Hila	AKSL	Finland	239
F 237	Westminster	FFGHM	UK	878
238	Haruna	AKSL	Finland	239
A 238	Zefiros	AXS	Greece	309
F 238	Northumberland	FFGHM	UK	878
PC 238	Sama	PBR	Peru	606
239	RT 252	MHC	Russian Federation	684
F 239	Richmond	FFGHM	UK	878
240	Kaszub	FSM	Poland	620
F 240	Yavuz	FFGHM	Turkey	831
LD 240	Bahia Zapzurro	–	Colombia	175
M 240	Aidon	MSC	Greece	308
U 240	Feodosiya	YDT/YFL/YPT	Ukraine	854
241	Askeri	YFB	Finland	239
F 241	Turgutreis	FFGHM	Turkey	831
M 241	Kichli	MSC	Greece	308
PC 241	Démocrata	PBO	Mexico	521

Number	Ship's name	Type	Country	Page
F 242	Fatih	FFGHM	Turkey	831
M 242	Kissa	MSC	Greece	308
PC 242	Rio Piura	PBR	Peru	606
243	MPK 227	FFLM	Russian Federation	675
F 243	Yildirim	FFGHM	Turkey	831
PC 243	Rio Nepeña	WPB	Peru	606
F 244	Barbaros	FFGHM	Turkey	830
PC 244	Rio Tambo	WPB	Peru	606
245	MPK 105	FFLM	Russian Federation	675
A 245	Leeuwin	AGS	Australia	36
F 245	Orucreis	FFGHM	Turkey	830
PC 245	Rio Ocoña	WPB	Peru	606
A 246	Melville	AGS	Australia	36
F 246	Salihreis	FFGHM	Turkey	830
LD 246	Morrosquillo	LCU	Colombia	175
PC 246	Rio Huarmey	WPB	Peru	606
A 247	Pelikanen	YPT	Sweden	779
F 247	Kemalreis	FFGHM	Turkey	830
PC 247	Rio Zaña	WPB	Peru	606
LD 248	Bahía Honda	LCU	Colombia	175
M 248	Pleias	MSC	Greece	308
LD 249	Bahía Portete	LCU	Colombia	175
PF 250	Contamana	PBR	Peru	607
251	Wodnik	AXTH	Poland	624
251	Zulfiquar	FFGH	Pakistan	586
GC 251	El Mouderrib I	AXL	Algeria	8
LD 251	Bahía Solano	LCU	Colombia	175
PF 251	Nueva Reqena	PBR	Peru	607
252	Shamsheer	FFGH	Pakistan	586
GC 252	El Mouderrib II	AXL	Algeria	8
LD 252	Bahía Cupica	LCU	Colombia	175
PF 252	Atalaya	PBR	Peru	607
253	Iskra	AXS	Poland	624
253	Saif	FFGH	Pakistan	586
C 253	Stalwart	PB	St Kitts and Nevis	707
F 253	Zafer	FFGH	Turkey	833
GC 253	El Mouderrib III	AXL	Algeria	8
LD 253	Bahía Utria	LCU	Colombia	175
PF 253	Zorrillos	PBR	Peru	607
GC 254	El Mouderrib IV	AXL	Algeria	8
LD 254	Bahía Malaga	LCU	Colombia	175
PF 254	Poyeni	PBR	Peru	607
255	Mutiara	AGSH	Malaysia	500
GC 255	El Mouderrib V	AXL	Algeria	8
PF 255	Aguaytia	PBR	Peru	607
GC 256	El Mouderrib VI	AXL	Algeria	8
PF 256	Puerto Inca	PBR	Peru	607
GC 257	El Mouderrib VII	AXL	Algeria	8
P 257	Clyde	PSOH	UK	884
PF 257	San Alejandro	PBR	Peru	607
260	Admiral Petre Barbuneanu	FS	Romania	643
F 260	Braunschweig	FSGHM	Germany	288
M 260	Edincik	MHC	Turkey	838
PF 260	Río Huallaga	PBR	Peru	607
F 261	Magdeburg	FSGHM	Germany	288
GC 261	El Mourafek	WARL	Algeria	7
M 261	Edremit	MHC	Turkey	838
PF 261	Río Santiago	PBR	Peru	607
262	Nawigator	AGI	Poland	624
F 262	Erfurt	FSGHM	Germany	288
M 262	Enez	MHC	Turkey	838
P 262	Tainha	PB	Cape Verde	114
PF 262	Río Putumayo	PBR	Peru	607
263	Hydrograf	AGI	Poland	624
263	Vice Admiral Eugeniu Rosca	FS	Romania	643
F 263	Oldenburg	FSGHM	Germany	288
M 263	Erdek	MHC	Turkey	838
PF 263	Río Nanay	PBR	Peru	607
264	Contre Admiral Eustatiu Sebastian	FSH	Romania	643
A 264	Trossö	AGP	Sweden	778
F 264	Ludwigshafen	FSGHM	Germany	288
LIF 264	Rio Napo	PBR	Peru	607
M 264	Erdemli	MHC	Turkey	838
P 264	Archer	PB/AXL	UK	883
265	Admiral Horia Macelariu	FSH	Romania	643
265	Heweliusz	AGS	Poland	623
A 265	Visborg	AKH	Sweden	778
LIF 265	Rio Yavari	PBR	Peru	607
M 265	Alanya	MHSC	Turkey	838
266	Arctowski	AGS	Poland	623
LIF 266	Rio Matador	PBR	Peru	607
M 266	Amasra	MHSC	Turkey	838
O 266	Sirius	AORH	Australia	38
P 266	Machitis	PG	Greece	306
M 267	Ayvalik	MHSC	Turkey	838
P 267	Nikiforos	PG	Greece	306
M 268	Akçakoca	MHSC	Turkey	838
P 268	Aittitos	PG	Greece	306
M 269	Anamur	MHSC	Turkey	838
P 269	Krateos	PG	Greece	306
LIF 270	Rio Itaya	PBR	Peru	607
M 270	Akçay	MHSC	Turkey	838
P 270	Biter	PB/AXL	UK	883
A 271	Gold Rover	AORLH	UK	891
LIF 271	Rio Patayacu	PBR	Peru	607
PC 271	Cabo Corrientes	PB	Mexico	521
272	Generał Kazimierz Pułaski	FFGHM	Poland	619
LIF 272	Rio Zapote	PBR	Peru	607
P 272	Smiter	PB/AXL	UK	883
PC 272	Cabo Corzo	PB	Mexico	521
273	Generał Tadeusz Kościuszko	FFGHM	Poland	619
A 273	Black Rover	AORLH	UK	891
LIF 273	Rio Chambira	PBR	Peru	607
P 273	Pursuer	PB/AXL	UK	883
PC 273	Cabo Catoche	PB	Mexico	521
274	Vice Admiral Constantin Balescu	ML/MCS	Romania	645
P 274	Tracker	PB/AXL	UK	883
PF 274	Rio Tambopata	PBR	Peru	607
P 275	Raider	PB/AXL	UK	883
278	Bukhansan	PBO	Korea, South	473
279	Chulmasan	PBO	Korea, South	473
P 279	Blazer	PB/AXL	UK	883
280	Iroquois	DDGH	Canada	102
P 280	Dasher	PB/AXL	UK	883
281	Constanta	AETLMH	Romania	646
281	Piast	ARS	Poland	625
P 281	Tyne	PSO	UK	883
PC 281	Punta Morro	PB	Mexico	521
282	Athabaskan	DDGH	Canada	102
282	Lech	ARS	Poland	625
P 282	Severn	PSO	UK	883
PC 282	Punta Mastun	PB	Mexico	521
283	Algonquin	DDGH	Canada	102
283	Midia	AETLMH	Romania	646
P 283	Mersey	PSO	UK	883
P 284	Scimitar	PB	UK	883
P 285	Sabre	PB	UK	883
P 286	Diopos Antoniou	PB	Greece	306
P 287	Kelefstis Stamou	PB	Greece	306
T-AKR 287	Algol	AKRH	US	962
288	Mircea	AXS	Romania	646
T-AKR 288	Bellatrix	AKRH	US	962
T-AKR 289	Denebola	AKRH	US	962
PL 290	Rio Ramis	PBR	Peru	607
T-AKR 290	Pollux	AKRH	US	962
291	Orzeł	SSK	Poland	618
P 291	Puncher	PB/AXL	UK	883
PL 291	Rio Ilave	PBR	Peru	607
T-AKR 291	Altair	AKRH	US	962
P 292	Charger	PB/AXL	UK	883
T-AKR 292	Regulus	AKRH	US	962
P 293	Ranger	PB/AXL	UK	883
PL 293	Juli	PBR	Peru	607
T-AKR 293	Capella	AKRH	US	962
294	Sokół	SSK	Poland	617
P 294	Trumpeter	PB/AXL	UK	883
PL 294	Moho	PBR	Peru	607
T-AKR 294	Antares	AKRH	US	962
295	Sęp	SSK	Poland	617
T-AKR 295	Shughart	AKR	US	958
296	Bielik	SSK	Poland	617
296	Electronica	ADG/AGI	Romania	646
T-AKR 296	Gordon	AKR	US	958
297	Kondor	SSK	Poland	617
T-AKR 297	Yano	AKR	US	958
298	Magnetica	ADG/AGI	Romania	646
T-AKR 298	Gilliland	AKR	US	958
Y 298	Bandicoot	MSCD/YTB	Australia	35
Y 299	Wallaroo	MSCD/YTB	Australia	35
P 300	Rayyan	PB	Kuwait	477
S 300	Ula	SSK	Norway	567
T-AKR 300	Bob Hope	AKR	US	958
301	Denden	LST	Eritrea	228
301	Huracan	PTG	Mexico	517
301	Jebel Antar	PB	Algeria	8
301	Teanoai	PB	Kiribati	451
301	Tripoli	PB	Lebanon	482
A 301	Drakensberg	AORH	South Africa	738
M 301	Rio Guaporé	YFL	Bolivia	68
MSO 301	Yaeyama	MSO	Japan	431
P 301	Bizerte	PBOM	Tunisia	824
P 301	Inttisar	PB	Kuwait	477
P 301	Kozlu	PBO/AGS	Turkey	836
P 301	Panquiaco	PB	Panama	592
PA 301	Almirante Didiez Burgos	PBO/WMEC	Dominican Republic	201
PR 301	General Banzer	PBR	Bolivia	68
S 301	Utsira	SSK	Norway	567
T-AKR 301	Fisher	AKR	US	958
302	Atiya	AORL	Bulgaria	95
302	Jebel Hando	PB	Algeria	8
302	Jounieh	PB	Lebanon	482
302	Okba	PG	Morocco	533
302	Tormenta	PTG	Mexico	517
ABH 302	Morona	ABH	Peru	605
MSO 302	Tsushima	MSO	Japan	431
P 302	Aman	PB	Kuwait	477
P 302	Horria	PBOM	Tunisia	824
P 302	Kuşadasi	PBO/AGS	Turkey	836
P 302	Ligia Elena	PB	Panama	592
PA 302	Almirante Juan Alexandro Acosta	PBO/WMEC	Dominican Republic	201
PR 302	Antofagasta	PBR	Bolivia	68
S 302	Utstein	SSK	Norway	567
T-AKR 302	Seay	AKR	US	958
303	Akin	AOTL	Bulgaria	95
303	Batroun	PB	Lebanon	482
303	Saku	PB	Fiji	233
303	Triki	PG	Morocco	533
MSO 303	Hachijyo	MSO	Japan	431
P 303	Maimon	PB	Kuwait	477
P 303	Naos	PB	Panama	592
S 303	Utvaer	SSK	Norway	567
T-AKR 303	Mendonca	AKR	US	958
W 303	Svalbard	WPSOH	Norway	574
304	Al Riyadh	WPBF	Saudi Arabia	716
304	Byblos	PB	Lebanon	482
304	Commandant El Khattabi	PGG	Morocco	534
304	MPK 192	FFLM	Russian Federation	675
304	Ras Djenad	PB	Algeria	8
304	Saqa	PB	Fiji	233
OR 304	Success	AORH	Australia	38
P 304	Mobark	PB	Kuwait	477
P 304	Monastir	PBOM	Tunisia	824
S 304	Uthaug	SSK	Norway	567

Number	Ship's name	Type	Country	Page
T-AKR 304	Pililaau	AKR	US	958
305	Beirut	PB	Lebanon	482
305	Commandant Boutouba	PGG	Morocco	534
305	Ras Tenes	PB	Algeria	8
305	Zulurab	WPBF	Saudi Arabia	716
P 305	AG 5	ABU	Turkey	842
P 305	Al Shaheed	PB	Kuwait	477
P 305	Escudo de Veraguas	PB	Panama	592
S 305	Uredd	SSK	Norway	567
T-AKR 305	Brittin	AKR	US	958
306	Commandant El Harty	PGG	Morocco	534
306	Ras Tekkouch	PB	Algeria	8
306	Sidon	PB	Lebanon	482
ABH 306	Puno	AH	Peru	605
P 306	AG 6	ABU	Turkey	842
P 306	Bayan	PB	Kuwait	477
P 306	Taboga	PB	Panama	592
T-AKR 306	Benavidez	AKR	US	958
307	Commandant Azouggarh	PGG	Morocco	534
307	Ras Sisli	PB	Algeria	8
307	Sarafand	PB	Lebanon	482
A 307	Thetis	YNT	Greece	310
P 307	Dasman	PB	Kuwait	477
P 307	Karamürsel	PBO/AGS	Turkey	836
308	El Hahiq	PBO	Morocco	534
308	Ras Nouh	PB	Algeria	8
308	Zelenodolsk	FFLM	Russian Federation	675
P 308	Subahi	PB	Kuwait	477
P 308	Kerempe	PBO/AGS	Turkey	836
309	El Tawfiq	PBO	Morocco	534
309	Ras Bougaroni	PB	Algeria	8
P 309	Jaberi	PB	Kuwait	477
P 309	Kilimli	PBO/AGS	Turkey	836
310	L V Rabhi	PBO	Morocco	534
310	Ras Tamentfoust	PB	Algeria	8
F 310	Fridtjof Nansen	FFGHM	Norway	568
P 310	Saad	PB	Kuwait	477
T-AKR 310	Watson	AKR	US	959
U 310	Chernigiv	MSO	Ukraine	852
311	Errachiq	PBO	Morocco	534
311	Kazanets	FFLM	Russian Federation	675
311	Prabparapak	PTFG	Thailand	809
311	Ras Oullis	PB	Algeria	8
F 311	Roald Amundsen	FFGHM	Norway	568
P 311	Ahmadi	PB	Kuwait	477
P 311	Bishkhali	PB	Bangladesh	58
P 311	Weeraya	PB	Sri Lanka	762
T-AKR 311	Sisler	AKR	US	959
U 311	Cherkasy	MSO	Ukraine	852
312	El Akid	PBO	Morocco	534
312	Hanhak Sattru	PTFG	Thailand	809
F 312	Otto Sverdrup	FFGHM	Norway	568
P 312	MTB 2	YAG/YDT	Turkey	839
P 312	Naif	PB	Kuwait	477
P 312	Padma	PB	Bangladesh	57
T-AKR 312	Dahl	AKR	US	959
W 312	Ålesund	WPBO	Norway	573
313	El Maher	PBO	Morocco	534
313	Suphairin	PTFG	Thailand	809
ALY 313	Marte	AXS	Peru	605
F 313	Helge Ingstad	FFGHM	Norway	568
M 313	Admiral Cowan	MHC	Estonia	229
P 313	MTB 3	YAG/YDT	Turkey	839
P 313	Surma	PB	Bangladesh	57
P 313	Thafir	PB	Kuwait	477
P 313-1	Shahid Mehdavi	PTFG	Iran	373
P 313-2	Shahid Kord	PTFG	Iran	373
P 313-3	Shahid Shafihi	PTFG	Iran	373
P 313-4	Shahid Towsali	PTFG	Iran	373
P 313-5	Shahid Hejat Zadeh	PTFG	Iran	373
P 313-6	Shahid Dara	PTFG	Iran	373
P 313-7	Shahid Absalan	PTFG	Iran	373
P 313-8	Shahid Rahisi Raisi	PTFG	Iran	373
P 313-9	Shahid Golzam	PTFG	Iran	373
P 313-10	Shahid Sahrabi	PTFG	Iran	373
T-AKR 313	Red Cloud	AKR	US	959
WLI 313	Bluebell	WLI/ABU	US	969
314	El Majid	PBO	Morocco	534
F 314	Thor Heyerdahl	FFGHM	Norway	568
M 314	Sakala	MHC	Estonia	229
P 314	Karnaphuli	PC	Bangladesh	57
P 314	Marzoug	PB	Kuwait	477
P 314	MTB 4	YAG/YDT	Turkey	839
T-AKR 314	Charlton	AKR	US	959
W 314	Stålbas	WPBO	Norway	573
315	Al Khyber	SS	Libya	483
315	El Bachir	PBO	Morocco	534
C 315	Late	–	Tonga	820
M 315	Ugandi	MHC	Estonia	229
P 315	Jagatha	PB	Sri Lanka	762
P 315	Mash'noor	PB	Kuwait	477
P 315	MTB 5	YAG/YDT	Turkey	839
P 315	Tista	PC	Bangladesh	57
T-AKR 315	Watkins	AKR	US	959
WLIC 315	Smilax	WLIC	US	971
316	Al Hunain	SS	Libya	483
316	El Hamiss	PBO	Morocco	534
316	RT 57	MHC	Russian Federation	684
P 316	Abeetha II	PB	Sri Lanka	762
P 316	MTB 6	YAG/YDT	Turkey	839
P 316	Wadah	PB	Kuwait	477
T-AKR 316	Pomeroy	AKR	US	959
317	Assir	WPB	Saudi Arabia	716
317	El Karib	PBO	Morocco	534
P 317	Edithara II	PB	Sri Lanka	762
P 317	MTB 7	YAG/YDT	Turkey	839
T-AKR 317	Soderman	AKR	US	959
318	Aldhahran	WPB	Saudi Arabia	716
318	Raïs Bargach	PSO	Morocco	534
P 318	MTB 8	YAG/YDT	Turkey	839
P 318	Wickrama II	PB	Sri Lanka	762
W 318	Harstad	ARS	Norway	574
319	Alkahrj	WPB	Saudi Arabia	716
319	Raïs Britel	PSO	Morocco	534
P 319	MTB 9	YAG/YDT	Turkey	839
W 319	Leikvin	WPBO	Norway	573
320	Arar	WPB	Saudi Arabia	716
320	Raïs Charkaoui	PSO	Morocco	534
W 320	Nordkapp	WPSOH	Norway	574
321	Raïs Maaninou	PSO	Morocco	534
321	Ratcharit	PGGF	Thailand	809
P 321	Denizkuşu	PTGF	Turkey	835
W 321	Senja	WPSOH	Norway	574
322	Raïs Al Mounastiri	PSO	Morocco	534
322	Witthayakhom	PGGF	Thailand	809
A 322	Heros	YTM	Sweden	780
ART 322	San Lorenzo	YPT	Peru	604
P 322	Atmaca	PTGF	Turkey	835
P 322	Ranarisi	PB	Sri Lanka	762
W 322	Andenes	WPSOH	Norway	574
323	Metel	FFLM	Russian Federation	674
323	Udomdet	PGGF	Thailand	809
P 323	Şahin	PTGF	Turkey	835
A 324	Hera	YTM	Sweden	780
A 324	Protea	AGSH	South Africa	737
P 324	Kartal	PTGF	Turkey	835
GC 325	El Hamil	PBF	Algeria	8
GC 326	El Assad	PBF	Algeria	8
P 326	Pelikan	PTGF	Turkey	835
GC 327	Markhad	PBF	Algeria	8
P 327	Albatros	PTGF	Turkey	835
WIX 327	Eagle	WIX/AXS	US	970
GC 328	Etair	PBF	Algeria	8
P 328	Şimşek	PTGF	Turkey	835
P 329	Kasirga	PTGF	Turkey	835
330	Halifax	FFGHM	Canada	100
F 330	Vasco Da Gama	FFGH	Portugal	631
P 330	Kiliç	PGGF	Turkey	835
P 330	Ranajaya	PB	Sri Lanka	762
U 330	Melitopol	MHSC	Ukraine	852
W 330	Nornen	PBO	Norway	575
331	Chon Buri	PG	Thailand	810
331	Requin	PB	Algeria	8
331	RT 341	MHC	Russian Federation	684
331	Sri Gaya	AP	Malaysia	500
331	Vancouver	FFGHM	Canada	100
331	Wallaby	WFL/AOTL	Australia	39
F 331	Alvares Cabral	FFGH	Portugal	631
P 331	Kalkan	PGGF	Turkey	835
P 331	Ranadeera	PB	Sri Lanka	762
U 331	Mariupol	MHSC	Ukraine	852
W 331	Farm	PBO	Norway	575
332	MPK 107	FFLM	Russian Federation	674
332	Songkhla	PG	Thailand	810
332	Sri Tiga	AP	Malaysia	500
332	Ville de Québec	FFGHM	Canada	100
332	Wombat	WFL/AOTL	Australia	39
F 332	Corte Real	FFGH	Portugal	631
M 332	Motajica	MSR	Serbia	720
P 332	Mizrak	PGGF	Turkey	835
P 332	Ranawickrama	PB	Sri Lanka	762
W 332	Heimdal	PBO	Norway	575
333	Marsouin	PB	Algeria	8
333	Phuket	PG	Thailand	810
333	Toronto	FFGHM	Canada	100
333	Warrigal	WFL/AOTL	Australia	39
F 333	Bartolomeu Dias	FFGHM	Portugal	630
P 333	Tufan	PGGF	Turkey	835
W 333	Njord	PBO	Norway	575
334	Hankoniemi	AKSL	Finland	238
334	Murene	PB	Algeria	8
334	Regina	FFGHM	Canada	100
334	Wyulda	WFL/AOTL	Australia	39
F 334	D. Francisco Da Almeida	FFGHM	Portugal	630
P 334	Meltem	PGGF	Turkey	835
W 334	Tor	PBO	Norway	575
335	Calgary	FFGHM	Canada	100
M 335	Vučedol	MSR	Serbia	720
P 335	Imbat	PGGF	Turkey	835
336	Montreal	FFGHM	Canada	100
M 336	Djerdap	MSR	Serbia	720
P 336	Zipkin	PGGF	Turkey	835
337	Fredericton	FFGHM	Canada	100
P 337	Atak	PGGF	Turkey	835
338	Winnipeg	FFGHM	Canada	100
P 338	Bora	PGGF	Turkey	835
339	Charlottetown	FFGHM	Canada	100
340	RT 210	MHC	Russian Federation	684
340	St John's	FFGHM	Canada	100
P 340	Doğan	PGGF	Turkey	835
P 340	Prathpa	PB	Sri Lanka	762
W 340	Barentshav	ARS	Norway	574
341	El Yadekh	PG	Algeria	6
341	Ottawa	FFGHM	Canada	100
M 341	Ingeniero Gumucio	YFL	Bolivia	68
M 341	Karmøy	MHCM/MSCM	Norway	572
M 341	Novi Sad	MSR	Serbia	720
P 341	Marti	PGGF	Turkey	835
P 341	Udara	PB	Sri Lanka	762
W 341	Bergen	ARS	Norway	574
342	El Mourakeb	PG	Algeria	6
342	Martadinata	FF	Indonesia	353
M 342	Jorge Villarroel	YFL	Bolivia	68
M 342	Måløy	MHCM/MSCM	Norway	572
P 342	Tayfun	PGGF	Turkey	835
W 342	Sortland	ARS	Norway	574
343	El Kechef	PG	Algeria	6
A 343	Sleipner	AKR	Sweden	778
M 343	Hinnøy	MHCM/MSCM	Norway	572
P 343	Volkan	PGGF	Turkey	835

Number	Ship's name	Type	Country	Page
344	El Moutarid	PG	Algeria	6
A 344	Loke	AKL	Sweden	780
P 344	Rüzgar	PGGF	Turkey	835
Y 344	Arvak	YTL	Denmark	199
345	El Rassed	PG	Algeria	6
P 345	Poyraz	PGGF	Turkey	835
Y 345	Alsin	YTL	Denmark	199
346	El Djari	PG	Algeria	6
P 346	Gurbet	PGGF	Turkey	835
347	El Saher	PG	Algeria	6
P 347	Firtina	PGGF	Turkey	835
S 347	Atilay	SSK	Turkey	829
348	El Moukadem	PG	Algeria	6
348	RT 248	MHC	Russian Federation	684
P 348	Yildiz	PGGF	Turkey	835
S 348	Saldiray	SSK	Turkey	829
349	El Tinai	PG	Algeria	6
P 349	Karayel	PGGF	Turkey	835
S 349	Batiray	SSK	Turkey	829
350	El Kanass	PG	Algeria	6
350	Sovetskaya Gavani	FFLM	Russian Federation	674
DCB 350	La Cruz	PBR	Peru	606
M 350	Alta	MHCM/MSCM	Norway	572
S 350	Yildiray	SSK	Turkey	829
351	Ahmad Yani	FFGHM	Indonesia	354
351	Al Jouf	WPBF	Saudi Arabia	716
351	Djebel Chenoua	FSG	Algeria	5
DCB 351	Cabo Blanco	PBR	Peru	606
LP 351	Raider	PBR	Bolivia	68
M 351	Otra	MHCM/MSCM	Norway	572
S 351	Doğanay	SSK	Turkey	829
352	El Chihab	FSG	Algeria	5
352	Slamet Riyadi	FFGHM	Indonesia	354
352	Turaif	WPBF	Saudi Arabia	716
DCB 352	Colán	PBR	Peru	606
M 352	Rauma	MHCM/MSCM	Norway	572
S 352	Dolunay	SSK	Turkey	829
353	Al Kirch	FSG	Algeria	5
353	Hail	WPBF	Saudi Arabia	716
353	Yos Sudarso	FFGHM	Indonesia	354
DCB 353	Samanco	PBR	Peru	606
S 353	Preveze	SSK	Turkey	828
354	El Mahir	PG	Algeria	6
354	Najran	WPBF	Saudi Arabia	716
354	Oswald Siahaan	FFGHM	Indonesia	354
354	Stelyak	FFLM	Russian Federation	674
DCB 354	Besique	PBR	Peru	606
F 354	Niels Juel	FFGM	Denmark	190
S 354	Sakarya	SSK	Turkey	828
355	Abdul Halim Perdanakusuma	FFGHM	Indonesia	354
DCB 355	Salinas	PBR	Peru	606
F 355	Olfert Fischer	FFGM	Denmark	190
S 355	18 Mart	SSK	Turkey	828
356	El Azoum	PG	Algeria	6
356	Karel Satsuitubun	FFGHM	Indonesia	354
DCB 356	Ancón	PBR	Peru	606
F 356	Peter Tordenskiold	FFGM	Denmark	190
S 356	Anafartalar	SSK	Turkey	828
357	El Djasur	PG	Algeria	6
DCB 357	Paracas	PBR	Peru	606
F 357	Thetis	FFHM	Denmark	189
S 357	Gür	SSK	Turkey	828
358	El Hamis	PG	Algeria	6
DCB 358	La Punta	PBR	Peru	606
F 358	Triton	FFHM	Denmark	189
P 358	Hessa	AXL	Norway	572
S 358	Çanakkale	SSK	Turkey	828
A 359	Ostria	AXS	Greece	309
F 359	Vaedderen	FFHM	Denmark	189
P 359	Vigra	AXL	Norway	572
S 359	Burakreis	SSK	Turkey	828
F 360	Hvidbjørnen	FFHM	Denmark	189
P 360	Viana Do Castelo	PSOH	Portugal	633
S 360	1. Inönü	SSK	Turkey	828
U 360	Genichesk	MHC	Ukraine	852
361	Fatahillah	FFG/FFGH	Indonesia	355
F 361	Ivar Huitfeldt	FFGHM	Denmark	192
P 361	Figueira Da Foz	PSOH	Portugal	633
362	Malahayati	FFG/FFGH	Indonesia	355
362	MPK 17	FFLM	Russian Federation	674
F 362	Peter Willemoes	FFGHM	Denmark	192
P 362	Ponta Delgada	PSOH	Portugal	633
363	Nala	FFG/FFGH	Indonesia	355
F 363	Niels Juel	FFGHM	Denmark	192
P 363	Sines	PSOH	Portugal	633
364	Geofjord	AGS	Norway	572
364	Ki Hajar Dewantara	FFGH/FFT	Indonesia	364
365	Diponegoro	FS	Indonesia	357
366	Sultan Hasanuddin	FS	Indonesia	357
367	Sultan Iskandar Muda	FS	Indonesia	357
368	Frans Kaisiepo	FS	Indonesia	357
369	MPK 191 III	FFLM	Russian Federation	674
P 370	Rio Minho	PBR	Portugal	634
PG 370	José Andrada	PB	Philippines	611
371	Kapitan Patimura	FS	Indonesia	356
M 371	Ohue	MHSC	Nigeria	566
PG 371	Enrique Jurado	PB	Philippines	611
372	Untung Suropati	FS	Indonesia	356
M 372	Barama	MHSC	Nigeria	566
PG 372	Alfredo Peckson	PB	Philippines	611
373	Nuku	FS	Indonesia	356
A 373	Gregos	AXS	Greece	309
374	Lambung Mangkurat	FS	Indonesia	356
A 374	Prometheus	AORH/MCCS	Greece	309
PG 374	Simeon Castro	PB	Philippines	611
375	Cut Nyak Dien	FS	Indonesia	356
375	MPK 82	FFLM	Russian Federation	674
A 375	Zeus	AOTL	Greece	310
PG 375	Carlos Albert	PB	Philippines	611
376	Sultan Thaha Syaifuddin	FS	Indonesia	356
A 376	Orion	AOTL	Greece	310
PG 376	Heracleo Alano	PB	Philippines	611
377	Sutanto	FS	Indonesia	356
PG 377	Liberato Picar	PB	Philippines	611
378	Sutedi Senoputra	FS	Indonesia	356
PG 378	Hilario Ruiz	PB	Philippines	611
379	Wiratno	FS	Indonesia	356
PG 379	Rafael Pargas	PB	Philippines	611
380	Memet Sastrawiria	FS	Indonesia	356
PG 380	Nestor Reinoso	PB	Philippines	611
381	Tjiptadi	FS	Indonesia	356
DLS 381	Punta Malpelo	DLS/PBF	Peru	603
PG 381	Dioscoro Papa	PB	Philippines	611
382	Hasan Basri	FS	Indonesia	356
DLS 382	Punta Mero	DLS/PBF	Peru	603
383	Iman Bonjol	FS	Indonesia	356
DLS 383	Punta Sal	DLS/PBF	Peru	603
PG 383	Ismael Lomibao	PB	Philippines	611
384	Pati Unus	FS	Indonesia	356
PG 384	Leovigildo Gantioque	PB	Philippines	611
385	Teuku Umar	FS	Indonesia	356
A 385	Fort Rosalie	AFSH	UK	891
PG 385	Federico Martir	PB	Philippines	611
386	Silas Papare	FS	Indonesia	356
A 386	Fort Austin	AFSH	UK	891
PG 386	Filipino Flojo	PB	Philippines	611
A 387	Fort Victoria	AORH	UK	891
PG 387	Anastacio Cacayorin	PB	Philippines	611
A 388	Fort George	AORH	UK	891
PG 388	Manuel Gomez	PB	Philippines	611
Y 388	Tulugaq	PB	Denmark	194
A 389	Wave Knight	AORH	UK	890
PG 389	Testimo Figuracion	PB	Philippines	611
390	Korets	FFLM	Russian Federation	674
A 390	Wave Ruler	AORH	UK	890
PG 390	José Loor Sr	PB	Philippines	611
392	MPK 178 III	FFLM	Russian Federation	674
PG 392	Juan Magluyan	PB	Philippines	611
PG 393	Florenca Nuno	PB	Philippines	611
PG 394	Alberto Navaret	PB	Philippines	611
PG 395	Felix Apolinario	PB	Philippines	611
PG 396	Brigadier Abraham Campo	PB	Philippines	611
400	Vitse Admiral Kulakov	DDGHM	Russian Federation	669
401	Admiral Branimir Ormanov	AGS	Bulgaria	94
401	Cakra	–	Indonesia	353
401	Ho Chi	LCU	Taiwan	793
A 401	Independencia	PBO	Panama	592
L 401	Al Soumood	LCU	Kuwait	478
L 401	Ertuğrul	LSTH/ML	Turkey	837
M 401	Coati	YFL	Bolivia	68
P 401	Cassiopea	PSOH	Italy	401
PG 401	Gavion	WPB	Venezuela	984
TNBH 401	Julian Apaza	–	Bolivia	69
U 401	Kirovograd	LSM	Ukraine	852
402	Daoud Ben Aicha	LSMH	Morocco	536
402	Ho Huei	LCU	Taiwan	793
402	Nanggala	–	Indonesia	353
402	Polyarny	MHSC/MHSCM	Russian Federation	684
A 402	Flamenco	YO	Panama	594
A 402	Manzanillo	AP	Mexico	522
L 402	Al Tahaddy	LCU	Kuwait	478
L 402	Serdar	LSTH/ML	Turkey	837
M 402	Cobija	YFL	Bolivia	68
P 402	Libra	PSOH	Italy	401
PG 402	Alca	WPB	Venezuela	984
U 402	Konstantin Olshansky	LST	Ukraine	852
403	Ahmed Es Sakali	LSMH	Morocco	536
403	Ho Yao	LCU	Taiwan	793
ASR 403	Chihaya	ASRH	Japan	435
L 403	Saffar	LCU	Kuwait	478
P 403	Spica	PSOH	Italy	401
PG 403	Bernacla	WPB	Venezuela	984
Y 403W	RP 101	YTM	Italy	409
404	Abou Abdallah El Ayachi	LSMH	Morocco	536
P 404	Vega	PSOH	Italy	401
PG 404	Chaman	WPB	Venezuela	984
Y 404	RP 102	YTM	Italy	409
405	El Aigh	AKS	Morocco	536
405	Jordan Nikolov Orce	PTFG	Montenegro	528
405	Vologda	SSK	Russian Federation	661
AS 405	Chiyoda	AS/ASRH	Japan	435
P 405	Esploratore	PB	Italy	401
PG 405	Cormoran	WPB	Venezuela	984
406	Ante Banina	PTFG	Montenegro	528
406	Gremyashchiy	DDGHM	Russian Federation	670
406	Ho Chao	LCU	Taiwan	793
406	Xia	SSBN	China	128
LP 406	General Bejar	PBR	Bolivia	68
P 406	Sentinella	PB	Italy	401
PG 406	Colimbo	WPB	Venezuela	984
Y 406	RP 103	YTM	Italy	409
407	Sidi Mohammed Ben Abdallah	LSTH	Morocco	535
P 407	Vedetta	PB	Italy	401
PG 407	Fardela	WPB	Venezuela	984
Y 407	RP 104	YTM	Italy	409
408	Dakhla	AKS	Morocco	536
P 408	Staffetta	PB	Italy	401
PG 408	Fumarel	WPB	Venezuela	984
Y 408	RP 105	YTM	Italy	409
409	Magneto-Gorsk	SSK	Russian Federation	661
409	Moroz	FSG	Russian Federation	678
LP 409	Mariscal de Zapita	PBR	Bolivia	68
P 409	Sirio	PSOH	Italy	400
PG 409	Negron	WPB	Venezuela	984
A 410	Atromitos	YTM/YTL	Greece	311

Number	Ship's name	Type	Country	Page
LP 410	Capitán Bretel	PBR	Bolivia	68
P 410	Orione	PSOH	Italy	400
PG 410	Pigargo	WPB	Venezuela	984
Y 410	RP 106	YTM	Italy	409
411	Kangan	AWT	Iran	378
A 411	Adamastos	YTM/YTL	Greece	311
A 411	Rio Papaloapan	LSTH	Mexico	523
LP 411	Teniente Soliz	PBR	Bolivia	68
P 411	El Nasr	PB	Mauritania	510
P 411	Shaheed Daulat	PC	Bangladesh	56
PG 411	Pagaza	WPB	Venezuela	984
412	Taheri	AWT	Iran	378
A 412	Aias	YTM/YTL	Greece	311
A 412	Usumacinta	LSTH	Mexico	523
MSC 412	Addriyah	MHSC	Saudi Arabia	715
P 412	Shaheed Farid	PC	Bangladesh	56
PG 412	Serreta	WPB	Venezuela	984
413	Pin Klao	FFT	Thailand	815
A 413	Pilefs	YTM/YTL	Greece	311
P 413	Shaheed Mohibullah	PC	Bangladesh	56
Y 413	Porto Fossone	YTB	Italy	409
LA 414	Guaqui	PBR	Bolivia	68
MSC 414	Al Quysumah	MHSC	Saudi Arabia	715
P 414	Shaheed Aktheruddin	PC	Bangladesh	56
A 415	Evros	AEL	Greece	310
M 415	Olev	MSI	Estonia	229
416	Tariq Ibn Ziyad	FSGM	Libya	484
A 416	Ouranos	AOTL	Greece	310
LP 416	Independencia	PBR	Bolivia	68
M 416	Vaindlo	MSI	Estonia	229
MSC 416	Al Wadeeah	MHSC	Saudi Arabia	715
Y 416	Porto Torres	YTB	Italy	409
A 417	Hyperion	AOTL	Greece	310
Y 417	Porto Corsini	YTB	Italy	409
418	Buevlyanin	MHSC/MHSCM	Russian Federation	684
418	Inej	FSG	Russian Federation	678
MSC 418	Safwa	MHSC	Saudi Arabia	715
SSV 418	Ekvator	AGI/AGIM	Russian Federation	688
A 419	Pandora	AP	Greece	310
420	Al Jawf	MHC	Saudi Arabia	715
A 420	Pandrosos	AP	Greece	310
U 420	Donetsk	ACV/LCUJM	Ukraine	852
421	Bandar Abbas	AORLH	Iran	379
421	Cornwall	PB	Jamaica	412
421	Naresuan	FFGHM	Thailand	802
421	Orkan	FSGM	Poland	620
C 421	Ardent	PB	St Kitts and Nevis	707
L 421	Canterbury	AKRH/AX	New Zealand	562
Y 421	Porto Empedocle	YTB	Italy	409
422	Bushehr	AORLH	Iran	379
422	Middlesex	PB	Jamaica	412
422	Piorun	FSGM	Poland	620
422	Shaqra	MHC	Saudi Arabia	715
422	Taksin	FFGHM	Thailand	802
A 422	Kadmos	YTM/YTL	Greece	311
AOE 422	Towada	AOE/AORH	Japan	435
Y 422	Porto Pisano	YTB	Italy	409
423	Grom	FSGM	Poland	620
423	Smerch	FSG	Russian Federation	678
423	Surrey	PB	Jamaica	412
A 423	Heraklis	YTM/YTL	Greece	311
AOE 423	Tokiwa	AOE/AORH	Japan	435
Y 423	Porto Conte	YTB	Italy	409
424	Al Kharj	MHC	Saudi Arabia	715
424	Daylam	AEL/AKL/AWT	Iran	379
A 424	Jason	YTM/YTL	Greece	311
AOE 424	Hamana	AOE/AORH	Japan	435
425	Jaroslavl	SSK	Russian Federation	661
425	Kolomna	MHSC/MHSCM	Russian Federation	684
A 425	Odisseus	YTM/YTL	Greece	311
AOE 425	Mashuu	AOE/AORH	Japan	434
Y 425	Porto Ferraio	YTB	Italy	409
426	Mineralny Vodi	MHSC/MHSCM	Russian Federation	684
AOE 426	Oumi	AOE/AORH	Japan	434
Y 426	Porto Venere	YTB	Italy	409
A 428	Nestor	YTM/YTL	Greece	311
Y 428	Porto Salvo	YTB	Italy	409
429	Lipetsk	SSK	Russian Federation	661
A 429	Perseus	YTM/YTL	Greece	311
430	Al Nour	PC	Egypt	219
431	Kharg	AORH	Iran	379
431	Tapi	FS	Thailand	807
431	Vladikavkaz	SSK	Russian Federation	661
A 431	Ahti	YDT	Estonia	229
432	Khirirat	FS	Thailand	807
A 432	Gigas	YTM/YTL	Greece	311
A 432	Tasuja	MLC	Estonia	229
433	Al Hadi	PC	Egypt	219
433	Makut Rajakumarn	FFH	Thailand	804
A 433	Kerkini	YW	Greece	310
434	Admiral Ushakov	DDGHM	Russian Federation	670
A 434	Prespa	YW	Greece	310
A 435	Kekrops	YTM/YTL	Greece	311
436	Al Hakim	PC	Egypt	219
A 436	Minos	YTM/YTL	Greece	311
A 437	Pelias	YTM/YTL	Greece	311
438	Leytenant Ilin	MHSC/MHSCM	Russian Federation	684
A 438	Aegeus	YTM/YTL	Greece	311
439	Al Wakil	PC	Egypt	219
A 439	Atrefs	YTM/YTL	Greece	311
440	Novosibirsk	SSK	Russian Federation	661
A 440	Diomidis	YTM/YTL	Greece	311
441	Rattanakosin	FSGM	Thailand	806
A 441	Theseus	YTM/YTL	Greece	311
442	Al Qatar	PC	Egypt	219
442	Sukhothai	FSGM	Thailand	806
442	Yan Myat Aung	PC	Myanmar	541
A 442	Romaleos	YTM/YTL	Greece	311
443	Kotelnich	MHSC/MHSCM	Russian Federation	684
443	Yan Nyein Aung	PC	Myanmar	541
444	Yan Khwin Aung	PC	Myanmar	541
445	Al Gabbar	PC	Egypt	219
445	Yan Ye Aung	PC	Myanmar	541
446	Yan Min Aung	PC	Myanmar	541
447	Yan Paing Aung	PC	Myanmar	541
448	Al Salam	PC	Egypt	219
448	Yan Win Aung	PC	Myanmar	541
449	Yan Aye Aung	PC	Myanmar	541
450	Razliv	FSG	Russian Federation	678
450	Yan Zwe Aung	PC	Myanmar	541
F 450	Elli	FFGH	Greece	303
451	Al Rafa	PC	Egypt	219
F 451	Limnos	FFGH	Greece	303
F 452	Hydra	FFGH	Greece	302
Y 452	RP 108	YTM	Italy	409
F 453	Spetsai	FFGH	Greece	302
454	Yelnya	MHSC/MHSCM	Russian Federation	684
F 454	Psara	FFGH	Greece	302
455	Chao Phraya	FFG/FFGH	Thailand	803
F 455	Salamis	FFGH	Greece	302
456	Bangpakong	FFG/FFGH	Thailand	803
Y 456	RP 109	YTM	Italy	409
457	Kraburi	FFG/FFGH	Thailand	803
458	Saiburi	FFG/FFGH	Thailand	803
Y 458	RP 110	YTM	Italy	409
F 459	Adrias	FFGH	Greece	303
A 460	Evrotas	YPT	Greece	311
F 460	Aegeon	FFGH	Greece	303
Y 460	RP 111	YTM	Italy	409
461	Phuttha Yotfa Chulalok	FFGHM	Thailand	804
A 461	Arachthos	YPT	Greece	311
F 461	Navarinon	FFGH	Greece	303
462	Phuttha Loetla Naphalai	FFGHM	Thailand	804
F 462	Kountouriotis	FFGH	Greece	303
Y 462	RP 112	YTM	Italy	409
A 463	Nestos	YPT	Greece	311
F 463	Bouboulina	FFGH	Greece	303
MST 463	Uraga	MSTH/ML	Japan	430
Y 463	RP 113	YTM	Italy	409
A 464	Axios	ARL/AOR/MCCS	Greece	310
F 464	Kanaris	FFGH	Greece	303
MST 464	Bungo	MSTH/ML	Japan	430
Y 464	RP 114	YTM	Italy	409
F 465	Themistocles	FFGH	Greece	303
Y 465	RP 115	YTM	Italy	409
466	Avangard	MHSC/MHSCM	Russian Federation	684
A 466	Trichonis	YW	Greece	310
F 466	Nikiforos Fokas	FFGH	Greece	303
Y 466	RP 116	YTM	Italy	409
A 467	Doirani	YW	Greece	310
Y 467	RP 123	YTM	Italy	409
468	Kaluga	SSK	Russian Federation	661
A 468	Kalliroe	YW	Greece	310
Y 468	RP 118	YTM	Italy	409
469	Vyborg	SSK	Russian Federation	661
469	Yadryn	MHSC/MHSCM	Russian Federation	684
A 469	Stimfalia	YW	Greece	310
A 470	Aliakmon	ARL/AOR/MCCS	Greece	310
Y 470	RP 119	YTM	Italy	409
471	Delvar	AEL/AKL/AWT	Iran	379
471	Maga	PTG	Myanmar	540
F 471	Antonio Enes	FSH	Portugal	632
Y 471	RP 120	YTM	Italy	409
472	Kalaat Beni Hammad	LSTH	Algeria	6
472	Saittra	PTG	Myanmar	540
472	Sirjan	AEL/AKL/AWT	Iran	379
Y 472	RP 121	YTM	Italy	409
473	Duwa	PTG	Myanmar	540
473	Kalaat Beni Rached	LSTH	Algeria	6
Y 473	RP 122	YTM	Italy	409
474	Zeyda	PTG	Myanmar	540
A 474	Pytheas	AGOR	Greece	309
F 475	João Coutinho	FSH	Portugal	632
A 476	Strabon	AGSC	Greece	309
F 476	Jacinto Candido	FSH	Portugal	632
477	Saint Petersburg	SSK	Russian Federation	660
F 477	General Pereira d'Eça	FSH	Portugal	632
Y 477	RP 124	YTM	Italy	409
A 478	Naftilos	AGS	Greece	309
Y 478	RP 125	YTM	Italy	409
A 479	I Karavoyiannos Theophilopoulos	ABUH	Greece	311
Y 479	RP 126	YTM	Italy	409
Y 480	RP 127	YTM	Italy	409
481	Charak	AEL/AKL/AWT	Iran	379
481	Ho Shun	LCU	Taiwan	793
A 481	St Lykoudis	ABUH	Greece	311
Y 481	RP 128	YTM	Italy	409
482	Chiroo	AEL/AKL/AWT	Iran	379
ARC 482	Muroto	ARC	Japan	435
Y 482	RP 129	YTM	Italy	409
483	Soroo	AEL/AKL/AWT	Iran	379
Y 483	RP 130	YTM	Italy	409
484	Ho Chung	LCU	Taiwan	793
Y 484	RP 131	YTM	Italy	409
Y 485	RP 132	YTM	Italy	409
F 486	Baptista de Andrade	FSH	Portugal	632
Y 486	RP 133	YTM	Italy	409
487	B 806	SSK	Russian Federation	661
F 487	João Roby	FSH	Portugal	632
Y 487	RP 134	YTM	Italy	409
488	Ho Shan	LCU	Taiwan	793
F 488	Afonso Cerqueira	FSH	Portugal	632
489	Ho Chuan	LCU	Taiwan	793
490	Ho Seng	LCU	Taiwan	793
F 490	Gaziantep	FFGHM	Turkey	832
P 490	Comandante Cigala Fulgosi	PSOH	Italy	400
491	Ho Meng	LCU	Taiwan	793
F 491	Giresun	FFGHM	Turkey	832

Number	Ship's name	Type	Country	Page
P 491	Comandante Borsini	PSOH	Italy	400
492	Ho Mou	LCU	Taiwan	793
F 492	Gemlik	FFGHM	Turkey	832
P 492	Comandante Bettica	PSOH	Italy	400
493	Ho Shou	LCU	Taiwan	793
F 493	Gelibolu	FFGHM	Turkey	832
P 493	Comandante Foscari	PSOH	Italy	400
494	Ho Chun	LCU	Taiwan	793
F 494	Gökçeada	FFGHM	Turkey	832
495	Ho Yung	LCU	Taiwan	793
F 495	Gediz	FFGHM	Turkey	832
F 496	Gokova	FFGHM	Turkey	832
F 497	Göksu	FFGHM	Turkey	832
LCU 497	Ho Fong	LCU	Taiwan	793
A 498	Lana	AGS	Nigeria	566
LCU 498	Ho Hu	LCU	Taiwan	793
Y 498	Mario Marino	YDT	Italy	401
A 499	Commander Apayi Joe	YTB/YTL	Nigeria	566
Y 499	Alcide Pedretti	YDT	Italy	401
500	Grozavu	ATA	Romania	647
F 500	Bozcaada	FFGM	Turkey	834
M 500	Foça	MSI	Turkey	838
U 500	Donbas	AGF/AR	Ukraine	853
501	Eilat	FSGHM	Israel	384
501	German Ugryumov	MHSC/MHSCM	Russian Federation	684
501	Hercules	ATA	Romania	647
501	La Galité	PGGF	Tunisia	823
501	Lieutenant Colonel Errhamani	FFGM	Morocco	532
501	Teluk Langsa	LST	Indonesia	361
A 501	Altair	YXT	Sweden	778
A 501	Kyanwa	PBO	Nigeria	565
F 501	Bodrum	FFGM	Turkey	834
HQ 501	Tran Khanh Du	LST	Vietnam	991
HTS 501	Bronzewing	YTL	Australia	39
LT 501	Laguna	LST	Philippines	612
M 501	Fethiye	MSI	Turkey	838
PR 501	Santa Cruz de la Sierra	PBR	Bolivia	68
SS 501	Souryu	SSK	Japan	415
TM 501	Bocachica	–	Colombia	176
502	Kurmuk	PBR	Sudan	767
502	Lahav	FSGHM	Israel	384
502	Teluk Bayur	LST	Indonesia	361
502	Tunis	PGGF	Tunisia	823
A 502	Antares	YXT	Sweden	778
A 502	Ologbo	PBO	Nigeria	565
F 502	Bandirma	FFGM	Turkey	834
HQ 502	Vung Tau	LST	Vietnam	991
HTS 502	Currawong	YTL	Australia	39
M 502	Fatsa	MSI	Turkey	838
SS 502	Unryu	SSK	Japan	415
TM 502	Arturus	–	Colombia	176
503	Carthage	PGGF	Tunisia	823
503	Hanit	FSGHM	Israel	384
503	Qaysan	PBR	Sudan	767
503	Teluk Amboina	–	Indonesia	361
A 503	Arcturus	YXT	Sweden	778
A 503	Nwamba	PBO	Nigeria	565
F 503	Beykoz	FFGM	Turkey	834
HQ 503	Qui Nonh	LST	Vietnam	991
M 503	Finike	MSI	Turkey	838
TM 503	Pedro David Salas	–	Colombia	176
504	Chita	SSK	Russian Federation	661
504	Qeshm	LSL	Iran	378
504	Rumbek	PBR	Sudan	767
504	Teluk Kau	LST	Indonesia	361
A 504	Argo	YXT	Sweden	778
A 504	Obula	PBO	Nigeria	565
F 504	Bartin	FFGM	Turkey	834
HTS 504	Mollymawk	YTL	Australia	39
LT 504	Lanao Del Norte	LST	Philippines	612
TM 504	Sirius	–	Colombia	176
505	Aleksey Lebedev	MHSC/MHSCM	Russian Federation	684
505	Hamilcar	PG	Tunisia	824
505	Hormuz	LSL	Iran	378
505	Mayom	PBR	Sudan	767
A 505	Astrea	YXT	Sweden	778
F 505	Bafra	FFGM	Turkey	834
506	Dauriya	AKH/AGF	Russian Federation	690
506	Forur	LSL	Iran	378
506	Hannon	PG	Tunisia	824
507	Daqhiliya	MSO	Egypt	221
507	Himilcon	PG	Tunisia	824
507	Mogochey	SSK	Russian Federation	661
TM 507	Calima	–	Colombia	176
508	Hannibal	PG	Tunisia	824
508	Teluk Tomini	LST	Indonesia	361
TM 508	Bahía Santa Catalina	–	Colombia	176
509	Hasdrubal	PG	Tunisia	824
509	Teluk Ratai	LST	Indonesia	361
AOR 509	Protecteur	AORH	Canada	104
TM 509	Móvil I	–	Colombia	176
510	BT 230	MHSC/MHSCM	Russian Federation	684
510	Giscon	PG	Tunisia	824
510	Teluk Saleh	LST	Indonesia	361
AOR 510	Preserver	AORH	Canada	104
TM 510	Móvil II	–	Colombia	176
U 510	Slavutich	AGFHM	Ukraine	854
511	Al Siddiq	PGGF	Saudi Arabia	714
511	Hengam	LSLH	Iran	377
511	Jymy	YFB	Finland	239
511	Kontradmiral X Czernicki	AKHM/ APHM/AGI	Poland	624
511	Nantong	FFG	China	144
511	Pattani	PBOH	Thailand	805
511	Teluk Bone	LST	Indonesia	361
A 511	Elbe	ARLHM	Germany	293
A 511	Shaheed Ruhul Amin	PBO/AX	Bangladesh	55
F 511	Heybeliada	FSG	Turkey	833
U 511	Simferopol	AGS	Ukraine	853
512	Larak	LSLH	Iran	377
512	Narathiwat	PBOH	Thailand	805
512	Raju	YFB	Finland	239
512	Teluk Semangka	LSTH	Indonesia	361
512	Wuxi	FFG	China	144
A 512	Mosel	ARLHM	Germany	293
A 512	Shahayak	YR	Bangladesh	59
SSV 512	Kildin	AGI/AGIM	Russian Federation	688
513	Al Farouq	PGGF	Saudi Arabia	714
513	Al Zuara	PTFG	Libya	485
513	BT 48	MHSC/MHSCM	Russian Federation	684
513	Huayin	FFG	China	144
513	Sinai	MSO	Egypt	221
513	Teluk Penyu	LSTH	Indonesia	361
513	Tonb	LSLH	Iran	377
A 513	Rhein	ARLHM	Germany	293
A 513	Shahjalal	AG	Bangladesh	59
514	Burgas	PB	Bulgaria	93
514	Lavan	LSLH	Iran	377
514	Teluk Mandar	LSTH	Indonesia	361
514	Zhenjiang	FFG	China	144
A 514	Werra	ARLHM	Germany	293
M 514	Silifke	MSC	Turkey	839
515	Abdul Aziz	PGGF	Saudi Arabia	714
515	Al Ruha	PTFG	Libya	485
515	Teluk Sampit	LSTH	Indonesia	361
515	Xiamen	FFG	China	144
A 515	Khan Jahan Ali	AOTL	Bangladesh	59
A 515	Main	ARLHM	Germany	293
M 515	Saros	MSC	Turkey	839
516	Assiyut	MSO	Egypt	221
516	Jiujiang	FFG	China	144
516	Teluk Banten	LSTH	Indonesia	361
A 516	Donau	ARLHM	Germany	293
A 516	Iman Gazzali	AOTL	Bangladesh	59
LT 516	Kalinga Apayao	LST	Philippines	612
M 516	Sigacik	MSC	Turkey	839
517	Faisal	PGGF	Saudi Arabia	714
517	Nanping	FFG	China	144
517	Teluk Ende	LSTH	Indonesia	361
M 517	Sapanca	MSC	Turkey	839
518	Jian	FFG	China	144
M 518	Sariyer	MSC	Turkey	839
519	Changzhi	FFG	China	144
519	Khalid	PGGF	Saudi Arabia	714
520	Bisma	PBO	Indonesia	368
520	Rassvet	FSG	Russian Federation	678
A 520	Sagres	AXS	Portugal	635
P 520	Diana	PB	Denmark	194
SSV 520	Feodor Golovin	AGIM	Russian Federation	688
521	Al Siddiq	MHC	Egypt	220
521	Amyr	PGGF	Saudi Arabia	714
521	Baladewa	PBO	Indonesia	368
521	Jiaxin	FFGHM	China	142
521	Kiiski 1	MSI	Finland	237
521	Krasnokamensk	SSK	Russian Federation	661
521	Sattahip	PG	Thailand	810
A 521	Schultz Xavier	ABU	Portugal	636
P 521	Freja	PB	Denmark	194
P 521	Vigilante	PBO	Cape Verde	113
522	Kiiski 2	MSI	Finland	237
522	Klongyai	PG	Thailand	810
522	Lianyungang	FFGHM	China	142
522	Sergei Kolbassev	MHSC/MHSCM	Russian Federation	684
522	Shehab	PGGF	Libya	485
A 522	D. Carlos I	AGS	Portugal	635
P 522	Havfruen	PB	Denmark	194
S 522	Salvatore Pelosi	SSK	Italy	390
523	Al Fikah	PTFG	Libya	485
523	Kiiski 3	MSI	Finland	237
523	Putian	FFGHM	China	142
523	Takbai	PG	Thailand	810
523	Tariq	PGGF	Saudi Arabia	714
A 523	Almirante Gago Coutinho	AGS	Portugal	635
P 523	Najaden	PB	Denmark	194
S 523	Giuliano Prini	SSK	Italy	390
524	Al Farouk	MHC	Egypt	220
524	Balchik	PB	Bulgaria	92
524	Kantang	PG	Thailand	810
524	Kiiski 4	MSI	Finland	237
524	Sanming	FFGHM	China	142
524	Wahag	PGGF	Libya	485
524	Yuen Feng	AKM	Taiwan	795
S 524	Primo Longobardo	SSK	Italy	390
525	Al Mathur	PTFG	Libya	485
525	BT 232	MHSC/MHSCM	Russian Federation	684
525	Kiiski 5	MSI	Finland	237
525	Maanshan	FFGHM	China	140
525	Oqbah	PGGF	Saudi Arabia	714
525	Sozopol	PB	Bulgaria	92
525	Thepha	PG	Thailand	810
525	Wu Kang	AKM	Taiwan	795
S 525	Gianfranco Gazzana Priaroggia	SSK	Italy	390
526	Hsin Kang	AKM	Taiwan	795
526	Kiiski 6	MSI	Finland	237
526	Nakat	FSG	Russian Federation	678
526	Nesebar	PB	Bulgaria	92
526	Taimuang	PG	Thailand	810
526	Wenzhou	FFGHM	China	140
S 526	Salvatore Todaro	SSK	Italy	389
527	Abu Obaidah	PGGF	Saudi Arabia	714
527	Kiiski 7	MSI	Finland	237
527	Luoyang	FFGHM	China	142
S 527	Scirè	SSK	Italy	389
528	Mianyang	FFGHM	China	142
528	Shouaiai	PGGF	Libya	485
M 528	Suarez Arana	YFL	Bolivia	68
529	B 187	SSK	Russian Federation	661

Number	Ship's name	Type	Country	Page
529	Xuzhou	FFGHM	China	141
530	Giza	MSO	Egypt	220
530	Steregushchiy	FFGHM	Russian Federation	673
530	Wu Yi	AOEHM	Taiwan	795
530	Zhoushan	FFGHM	China	141
531	Kavarna	PB	Bulgaria	93
531	Khamronsin	FS	Thailand	806
531	Syöksy	YFB	Finland	239
531	Teluk Gilimanuk	LSM	Indonesia	362
P 531	Terme	PBO/AGI	Turkey	836
532	Shoula	PGGF	Libya	485
532	Teluk Celukan Bawang	LSM	Indonesia	362
532	Thayanchon	FS	Thailand	806
532	Tulcea	AOT	Romania	647
533	Aswan	MSO	Egypt	220
533	Longlom	FS	Thailand	806
533	Taizhou	FFG	China	144
533	Teluk Cendrawasih	LSM	Indonesia	362
A 533	Norge	YAC	Norway	573
534	Jinhua	FFG	China	144
534	Shafak	PGGF	Libya	485
534	Teluk Berau	LSM	Indonesia	362
534	Varna	PB	Bulgaria	93
535	Aysberg	FSG	Russian Federation	678
535	Huangshi	FFG	China	146
535	Teluk Peleng	LSM	Indonesia	362
A 535	Valkyrien	–	Norway	573
536	Qina	MSO	Egypt	220
536	Teluk Sibolga	LSM	Indonesia	362
536	Wuhu	FFG	China	146
537	Cangzhou	FFG	China	146
537	Teluk Manado	LSM	Indonesia	362
538	Rad	PGGF	Libya	485
538	Teluk Hading	LSM	Indonesia	362
539	Anqing	FFGHM	China	142
539	Sohag	MSO	Egypt	220
539	Teluk Parigi	LSM	Indonesia	362
540	Huainan	FFGHM	China	142
540	Priboy	FSG	Russian Federation	678
540	Teluk Lampung	LSM	Indonesia	362
A 540	Dannebrog	YAC	Denmark	198
A 540	Hansaya	LCP	Sri Lanka	766
U 540	Chigirin	AXL	Ukraine	853
541	Hua Hin	PSO	Thailand	809
541	Huaibei	FFGHM	China	142
541	Teluk Jakarta	LSM	Indonesia	362
541	Vinha	YFB	Finland	239
A 541	Birkholm	MSD/AXL/AGSC	Denmark	194
P 541	Aboubekr Ben Amer	PBO	Mauritania	510
U 541	Smila	AXL	Ukraine	853
542	BT 114	MHSC/MHSCM	Russian Federation	684
542	Dat Assawari	MHC	Egypt	221
542	Klaeng	PSO	Thailand	809
542	Laheeb	PGGF	Libya	485
542	Teluk Sangkuring	LSM	Indonesia	362
542	Tongling	FFGHM	China	142
542-051	Ercsi	PBR	Hungary	323
542-054	Baja	PBR	Hungary	323
A 542	Fyrholm	MSD/AXL/AGSC	Denmark	194
TG 542	Playa Blanca	–	Colombia	176
U 542	Nova Kahovka	AXL	Ukraine	853
543	Dandong	FFG	China	144
543	Marshal Shaposhnikov	DDGHM	Russian Federation	669
543	Si Racha	PSO	Thailand	809
543	Teluk Cirebon	AKL/ARL	Indonesia	365
A 543	Ertholm	MSD/AXL/AGSC	Denmark	194
TG 543	Tierra Bomba	–	Colombia	176
544	Siping	FFGH	China	147
544	Teluk Sabang	AKL/ARL	Indonesia	365
A 544	Alholm	MSD/AXL/AGSC	Denmark	194
TG 544	Bell Salter	–	Colombia	176
545	B 439	SSK	Russian Federation	661
545	Linfen	FFG	China	144
545	Navarin	MHC	Egypt	221
TG 546	Orion	–	Colombia	176
547	Ust-Kamshats	SSK	Russian Federation	661
TG 547	Pegasso	–	Colombia	176
548	Admiral Panteleyev	DDGHM	Russian Federation	669
548	Burullus	MHC	Egypt	221
549	Ust-Bolsheretsk	SSK	Russian Federation	661
C 550	Cavour	CV	Italy	391
LC 550	Bacolod City	LSVH	Philippines	612
551	Liven	FSG	Russian Federation	678
551	Maoming	FFG	China	144
A 551	Danbjørn	AGB	Denmark	199
ATF 551	Ta Wan	ATF/ARS	Taiwan	795
B 551	Voum-Legleita	PBO	Mauritania	510
C 551	Giuseppe Garibaldi	CVGM	Italy	392
F 551	Minerva	FSM	Italy	398
LC 551	Dagupan City	LSVH	Philippines	612
P 551	Sadd	PBF	Pakistan	591
WLM 551	Ida Lewis	WLM/ABU	US	969
552	Ta Hu	ARS	Taiwan	795
552	Yibin	FFG	China	144
A 552	Isbjørn	AGB	Denmark	199
F 552	Urania	FSM	Italy	398
P 552	Havkatten	PGGM/MHCD/ MLC/AGSC	Denmark	193
P 552	Shabhaz	PBF	Pakistan	591
WLM 552	Katherine Walker	WLM/ABU	US	969
553	Shaoguan	FFG	China	144
A 553	Thorbjørn	AGB/AGS	Denmark	199
ATF 553	Ta Han	ATF/ARS	Taiwan	795
D 553	Andrea Doria	DDGHM	Italy	394
F 553	Danaide	FSM	Italy	398
P 553	Laxen	PGGM/MHCD/ MLC/AGSC	Denmark	193
P 553	Vaqar	PBF	Pakistan	591
WLM 553	Abigail Burgess	WLM/ABU	US	969
554	Alrosa	SSK	Russian Federation	661
554	Anshun	FFG	China	144
ATF 554	Ta Kang	ATF/ARS	Taiwan	795
D 554	Caio Duilio	DDGHM	Italy	394
F 554	Sfinge	FSM	Italy	398
P 554	Burq	PBF	Pakistan	591
P 554	Makrelen	PGGM/MHCD/ MLC/AGSC	Denmark	193
WLM 554	Marcus Hanna	WLM/ABU	US	969
555	Geyzer	FSG	Russian Federation	678
555	Zhaotong	FFG	China	144
ATF 555	Ta Fung	ATF/ARS	Taiwan	795
F 555	Driade	FSM	Italy	398
P 555	Støren	PGGM/MHCD/ MLC/AGSC	Denmark	193
WLM 555	James Rankin	WLM/ABU	US	969
YTM 555	Tillicum	YTB/YTL/YTR/YTM	Canada	105
F 556	Chimera	FSM	Italy	398
TG 556	Lancha Ambulancia	–	Colombia	176
WLM 556	Joshua Appleby	WLM/ABU	US	969
557	Jishou	FFG	China	144
F 557	Fenice	FSM	Italy	398
P 557	Glenten	PGGM/MHCD/ MLC/AGSC	Denmark	193
TG 557	Armada I	–	Colombia	176
WLM 557	Frank Drew	WLM/ABU	US	969
558	Zigong	FFG	China	144
F 558	Sibilla	FSM	Italy	398
P 558	Gribben	PGGM/MHCD/ MLC/AGSC	Denmark	193
TG 558	Juanchaco	–	Colombia	176
WLM 558	Anthony Petit	WLM/ABU	US	969
559	Beihai	FFG	China	144
A 559	Sleipner	AKS	Denmark	198
WLM 559	Barbara Mabrity	WLM/ABU	US	969
560	BT 256	MHSC/MHSCM	Russian Federation	684
560	Dongguan	FFG	China	144
560	Won San	MLH	Korea, South	470
560	Zyb	FSG	Russian Federation	678
A 560	Gunnar Thorson	YPC/ABU	Denmark	198
D 560	Luigi Durand de la Penne	DDGHM	Italy	395
P 560	Ravnen	PGGM/MHCD/ MLC/AGSC	Denmark	193
WLM 560	William Tate	WLM/ABU	US	969
561	BT 115	MHSC/MHSCM	Russian Federation	684
561	Kang Kyeong	MHSC	Korea, South	470
561	Multatuli	AGFH	Indonesia	365
561	Shantou	FFG	China	144
A 561	Gunnar Seidenfaden	YPC/ABU	Denmark	198
D 561	Francesco Mimbelli	DDGHM	Italy	395
P 561	Skaden	PGGM/MHCD/ MLC/AGSC	Denmark	193
WLM 561	Harry Claiborne	WLM/ABU	US	969
YTR 561	Firebird	YTB/YTL/ YTR/YTM	Canada	105
562	Jiangmen	FFG	China	144
562	Kang Jin	MHSC	Korea, South	470
A 562	Mette Miljø	AKL	Denmark	199
P 562	Viben	PGGM/MHCD/ MLC/AGSC	Denmark	193
WLM 562	Maria Bray	WLM/ABU	US	969
YTR 562	Firebrand	YTB/YTL/ YTR/YTM	Canada	105
563	BT 44	MHSC/MHSCM	Russian Federation	684
563	Foshan	FFG	China	144
563	Ko Ryeong	MHSC	Korea, South	470
A 563	Marie Miljø	AKL	Denmark	199
ATF 563	Ta Tai	ATF/ARS	Taiwan	795
P 563	Søløven	PGGM/MHCD/ MLC/AGSC	Denmark	193
WLM 563	Henry Blake	WLM/ABU	US	969
564	Admiral Tributs	DDGHM	Russian Federation	669
564	Magamed Gadgiev	MHSC/MHSCM	Russian Federation	684
564	Yichang	FFGHM	China	142
WLM 564	George Cobb	WLM/ABU	US	969
565	BT 100	MHSC/MHSCM	Russian Federation	684
565	Kim Po	MHSC	Korea, South	470
565	Yulin	FFGHM	China	142
566	Huaihua	FFGHM	China	142
566	Ko Chang	MHSC	Korea, South	470
567	Kum Wha	MHSC	Korea, South	470
567	Xiangfan	FFGHM	China	142
568	Chaohu	FFGHM	China	141
570	Huangshan	FFGHM	China	141
570	Passat	FSG	Russian Federation	678
A 570	Taşkizak	AOTL	Turkey	840
F 570	Maestrale	FFGHM	Italy	396
P 570	Knud Rasmussen	PGBH	Denmark	193
571	Yang Yang	MSC/MHC	Korea, South	471
A 571	Albay Hakki Burak	AOT	Turkey	840
F 571	Grecale	FFGHM	Italy	396
P 571	Ejnar Mikkelsen	PGBH	Denmark	193
SSV 571	Belomore	AGIM	Russian Federation	688
572	Admiral Vinogradov	DDGHM	Russian Federation	669
572	Ongjin	MSC/MHC	Korea, South	471
A 572	Yuzbasi Ihsan Tolunay	AOT	Turkey	840
F 572	Libeccio	FFGHM	Italy	396
573	Hae Nam	MSC/MHC	Korea, South	471
A 573	Binbaşi Sadettin Gürcan	AORL	Turkey	841
F 573	Scirocco	FFGHM	Italy	396
F 574	Aliseo	FFGHM	Italy	396
575	DKA 144	LCU	Russian Federation	682
F 575	Euro	FFGHM	Italy	396
A 576	Değirmendere	ATA	Turkey	843
F 576	Espero	FFGHM	Italy	396
A 577	Sokullu Mehmet Paşa	AG/AX	Turkey	840
F 577	Zeffiro	FFGHM	Italy	396
A 578	Darica	ATR	Turkey	844
A 579	Cezayirli Gazi Hasan Paşa	AG/AX	Turkey	840

Number	Ship's name	Type	Country	Page
580	Dore	LCU	Indonesia	361
A 580	Akar	AORH	Turkey	840
A 581	Çinar	AWT	Turkey	841
A 581	Darshak	LCU/LCP	Bangladesh	60
582	Kupang	LCU	Indonesia	361
A 582	Kemer	PBO/AGS	Turkey	836
A 582	Tallashi	LCU/LCP	Bangladesh	60
F 582	Artigliere	FFGHM	Italy	397
583	Dili	LCU	Indonesia	361
A 583	Agradoot	AGS	Bangladesh	59
F 583	Aviere	FFGHM	Italy	397
SS 583	Harushio	SSK	Japan	416
584	Nusa Utara	LCU	Indonesia	361
A 584	LCT 101	LCU/LCP	Bangladesh	60
F 584	Bersagliere	FFGHM	Italy	397
SS 584	Natsushio	SSK	Japan	416
A 585	Akin	ASR	Turkey	842
A 585	LCT 102	LCU/LCP	Bangladesh	60
F 585	Granatiere	FFGHM	Italy	397
A 586	Akbaş	YTB/YTM/YTL	Turkey	843
SFP 586	Akademik Isanin	AGS	Russian Federation	686
SS 586	Arashio	SSK	Japan	416
A 587	Gazal	ATF	Turkey	843
A 587	LCT 104	LCU/LCP	Bangladesh	60
SS 587	Wakashio	SSK	Japan	416
A 588	Çandarli	AGS	Turkey	839
SS 588	Fuyushio	SSK	Japan	416
A 589	Işin	ARS	Turkey	841
590	Makassar	LPD/APCR	Indonesia	360
A 590	Inebolu	ATF	Turkey	843
SS 590	Oyashio	SSK	Japan	415
YTL 590	Lawrenceville	YTB/YTL/ YTR/YTM	Canada	105
591	Surabaya	LPD/APCR	Indonesia	360
SS 591	Michishio	SSK	Japan	415
YTL 591	Parksville	YTB/YTL/ YTR/YTM	Canada	105
A 592	Karadeniz Ereğli	AKS/AWT	Turkey	842
SS 592	Uzushio	SSK	Japan	415
YTL 592	Listerville	YTB/YTL/ YTR/YTM	Canada	105
593	BT 215	MHSC/MHSCM	Russian Federation	684
SS 593	Makishio	SSK	Japan	415
YTL 593	Merrickville	YTB/YTL/ YTR/YTM	Canada	105
A 594	Çubuklu	AGS	Turkey	839
SS 594	Isoshio	SSK	Japan	415
YTL 594	Granville	YTB/YTL/ YTR/YTM	Canada	105
A 595	Yarbay Kudret Güngör	AORH	Turkey	840
SS 595	Narushio	SSK	Japan	415
A 596	Ulubat	AWT	Turkey	841
SS 596	Kuroshio	SSK	Japan	415
A 597	Van	AWT	Turkey	841
SS 597	Takashio	SSK	Japan	415
A 598	Sögüt	AWT	Turkey	841
SS 598	Yaeshio	SSK	Japan	415
A 599	Çesme	AGS	Turkey	839
SS 599	Setoshio	SSK	Japan	415
600	Zvezdochka	AGE/ASR	Russian Federation	687
A 600	Kavak	AWT	Turkey	841
SS 600	Mochishio	SSK	Japan	415
601	23 of July	PGGF	Egypt	217
601	Lung Chiang	PGGF	Taiwan	791
601	Ras El Blais	PBO	Tunisia	826
A 601	Monge	AGMH	France	267
LG-601	Rio Jubones	WPBR	Ecuador	212
MSC 601	Hirashima	MHSC	Japan	431
NF 601	Filigonio Hichamón	YTD/YAG	Colombia	177
P 601	Élorn	PB	France	276
P 601	Jayasagara	PB	Sri Lanka	761
P 601	Limam El Hadrami	PB	Mauritania	510
S 601	Rubis	SSN/SNA	France	244
U 601	Alchevsk	AGS	Ukraine	853
602	6 of October	PGGF	Egypt	217
602	Junon	PB	Seychelles	721
602	Nizhny Novgorod	SSN	Russian Federation	658
602	Ras Ajdir	PBO	Tunisia	826
602	Sui Chiang	PGGF	Taiwan	791
MSC 602	Yakushima	MHSC	Japan	431
NF 602	SSIM Manuel A Moyar	YTD/YAG	Colombia	177
P 602	Verdon	PB	France	276
S 602	Saphir	SSN/SNA	France	244
603	21 of October	PGGF	Egypt	217
603	Aiyar Lulin	–	Myanmar	542
603	Jin Chiang	PCG	Taiwan	791
603	Ras El Edrak	PBO	Tunisia	826
MSC 603	Takashima	MHSC	Japan	431
NF 603	Igaraparaná	YTD/YAG	Colombia	177
P 603	Adour	PB	France	276
S 603	Casabianca	SSN/SNA	France	244
Y 603	Nymphea	YFL	France	272
604	18 of June	PGGF	Egypt	217
604	Aiyar Mai	LCU	Myanmar	543
604	Fortune	PB	Seychelles	721
604	Ras El Manoura	PBO	Tunisia	826
NF 604	SSIM Julio Correa Hernández	YTD/YAG	Colombia	177
P 604	Scarpe	PB	France	276
S 604	Émeraude	SSN/SNA	France	244
Y 604	Fuchsia	YFL	France	272
605	25 of April	PGGF	Egypt	217
605	Admiral Levchenko	DDGHM	Russian Federation	669
605	Aiyar Maung	LCU	Myanmar	543
605	Andromache	PB	Seychelles	722
605	Ras Enghela	PBO	Tunisia	826
605	Tan Chiang	PCG	Taiwan	791
NF 605	Manacacías	YTD/YAG	Colombia	177
P 605	Vertonne	PB	France	276
S 605	Améthyste	SSN/SNA	France	244
Y 605	Gendarme Perez	YFL	France	272
606	Aiyar Minthamee	LCU	Myanmar	543
606	Hsin Chiang	PCG	Taiwan	791
606	Ras Ifrikia	PBO	Tunisia	826
606	Topaz	PBO	Seychelles	722
NF 606	Cotuhe	YTD/YAG	Colombia	177
P 606	Dumbea	PB	France	276
S 606	Perle	SSN/SNA	France	244
Y 606	Lavande	YFL	France	272
607	Aiyar Minthar	LCU	Myanmar	543
607	Feng Chiang	PCG	Taiwan	791
A 607	Meuse	AORHM	France	269
NF 607	SSCIM Senen Alberto Arango	PBR	Colombia	172
P 607	Yser	PB	France	276
608	MDK 18	ACV/LCUJ	Russian Federation	682
608	Tseng Chiang	PCG	Taiwan	791
A 608	Var	AORHM	France	269
NF 608	CPCIM Guillermo Londoño Vargas	PBR	Colombia	172
P 608	Argens	PB	France	276
609	Kao Chiang	PCG	Taiwan	791
609	MDK 88	ACV/LCUJ	Russian Federation	682
NF 609	Ariarí	YTD/YAG	Colombia	177
P 609	Hérault	PB	France	276
610	Jing Chiang	PCG	Taiwan	791
610	Nastoychivy	DDGHM	Russian Federation	670
D 610	Tourville	DDGHM	France	255
NF 610	Mario Villegas	PBR	Colombia	172
P 610	Gravona	PB	France	276
YDT 610	Sechelt	YTT/YPT/YDT	Canada	105
611	Hsian Chiang	PCG	Taiwan	791
611	Mohammed V	FFGHM	Morocco	531
611	Phosamton	AXL	Thailand	815
LG 611	Rio Verde	WPBF	Ecuador	212
M 611	Vulcain	MCD	France	266
NF 611	Tony Pastrana Contreras	PBR	Colombia	172
P 611	Odet	PB	France	276
P 611	Tawheed	PC	Bangladesh	56
Y 611	MDLC Richard	PB	France	276
YPT 611	Sikanni	YTT/YPT/YDT	Canada	105
612	Badr	–	Saudi Arabia	713
612	Bangkeo	MSC	Thailand	814
612	Hassan LI	FFGHM	Morocco	531
612	Tsi Chiang	PCG	Taiwan	791
D 612	De Grasse	DDGHM	France	255
LG 612	Rio Bulu Bulu	WPBF	Ecuador	212
NF 612	CTCIM Jorge Moreno Salazar	PBR	Colombia	172
P 612	Maury	PB	France	276
P 612	Tawfiq	PC	Bangladesh	56
YDT 612	Sooke	YTT/YPT/YDT	Canada	105
613	Donchedi	MSC	Thailand	814
A 613	Achéron	MCD	France	266
LG 613	Rio Macara	WPBF	Ecuador	212
NF 613	Juan Ricardo Oyola Vera	PBR	Colombia	172
P 613	Charente	PB	France	276
P 613	Tamjeed	PC	Bangladesh	56
YPT 613	Stikine	YTT/YPT/YDT	Canada	105
614	Al Yarmook	–	Saudi Arabia	713
614	Po Chiang	PCG	Taiwan	791
D 614	Cassard	DDGHM	France	252
LG 614	Rio Yaguachi	WPBF	Ecuador	212
M 614	Styx	MCD	France	266
P 614	Tanveer	PC	Bangladesh	56
P 614	Tech	PB	France	276
615	Bora	PGGJM	Russian Federation	676
615	Chan Chiang	PCG	Taiwan	791
D 615	Jean Bart	DDGHM	France	252
LG 615	Rio Cañar	WPBF	Ecuador	212
P 615	Penfeld	PB	France	276
WMEC 615	Reliance	PSOH/WMEC	US	964
616	Hitteen	–	Saudi Arabia	713
616	Samum	PGGJM	Russian Federation	676
A 616	Le Malin	YDT	France	270
LG 616	Rio San Miguel	WPBF	Ecuador	212
P 616	Trieux	PB	France	276
S 616	Le Triomphant	SSBN/SNLE-NG	France	246
WMEC 616	Diligence	PSOH/WMEC	US	964
617	Chu Chiang	PCG	Taiwan	791
617	Mirazh	FSG	Russian Federation	678
AD 617	Yakal	ARL	Philippines	613
LG 617	Rio Quinindé	WPBF	Ecuador	212
P 617	Vésubie	PB	France	276
S 617	Le Téméraire	SSBN/SNLE-NG	France	246
WMEC 617	Vigilant	PSOH/WMEC	US	964
618	Obninsk	SSN	Russian Federation	659
618	Tabuk	–	Saudi Arabia	713
LG 618	Rio Catamayo	WPBF	Ecuador	212
P 618	Escaut	PB	France	276
S 618	Le Vigilant	SSBN/SNLE-NG	France	246
WMEC 618	Active	PSOH/WMEC	US	964
619	Severomorsk	DDGHM	Russian Federation	669
P 619	Huveaune	PB	France	276
S 619	Le Terrible	SSBN/SNLE-NG	France	246
WMEC 619	Confidence	PSOH/WMEC	US	964
620	Bespokoiny	DDGHM	Russian Federation	670
620	Shtyl	FSG	Russian Federation	678
D 620	Forbin	DDGHM	France	251
P 620	Sayura	PSOH	Sri Lanka	761
P 620	Sévre	PB	France	276
WMEC 620	Resolute	PSOH/WMEC	US	964
621	Flaming	MHCM	Poland	622
621	Mandau	PTFG	Indonesia	358
621	Thalang	MCS	Thailand	813
D 621	Chevalier Paul	DDGHM	France	251
P 621	Aber-Wrach	PB	France	276
P 621	Samudura	PSOH	Sri Lanka	761
WMEC 621	Valiant	PSOH/WMEC	US	964
622	Rencong	PTFG	Indonesia	358

Number	Ship's name	Type	Country	Page
M 622	Pluton	MCD	France	266
P 622	Estéron	PB	France	276
P 622	Sagara	PSOH	Sri Lanka	765
623	Badik	PTFG	Indonesia	358
623	Mewa	MHCM	Poland	622
P 623	Mahury	PB	France	276
WMEC 623	Steadfast	PSOH/WMEC	US	964
624	Czajka	MHCM	Poland	622
624	Keris	PTFG	Indonesia	358
P 624	Organabo	PB	France	276
WMEC 624	Dauntless	PSOH/WMEC	US	964
WMEC 625	Venturous	PSOH/WMEC	US	964
WMEC 626	Dependable	PSOH/WMEC	US	964
WMEC 627	Vigorous	PSOH/WMEC	US	964
WMEC 629	Decisive	PSOH/WMEC	US	964
630	Goplo	MHC	Poland	622
A 630	Marne	AORHM	France	269
WMEC 630	Alert	PSOH/WMEC	US	964
Y 630	Bonite	YTL	France	273
631	Bang Rachan	MHSC	Thailand	814
631	Gardno	MHC	Poland	622
A 631	Somme	AORHM	France	269
632	Bukowo	MHC	Poland	622
632	Nongsarai	MHSC	Thailand	814
633	Dabie	MHC	Poland	622
633	Lat Ya	MHSC	Thailand	814
A 633	Taape	AG/ATS/YDT/ YPC/YPT	France	269
634	Jamno	MHC	Poland	622
634	Tha Din Daeng	MHSC	Thailand	814
Y 634	Rouget	YTL	France	273
635	Mielno	MHC	Poland	622
A 635	Revi	AFL	France	270
U 635	Skvyra	YDT/YFL/YPT	Ukraine	854
636	Wicko	MHC	Poland	622
A 636	Maïto	YTM	France	273
637	Resko	MHC	Poland	622
A 637	Maroa	YTM	France	273
638	Sarbsko	MHC	Poland	622
A 638	Manini	YTM	France	273
Y 638	Lardier	YTM	France	273
639	Necko	MHC	Poland	622
Y 639	Giens	YTM	France	273
640	DKA 704	LCMS	Russian Federation	682
640	Naklo	MHC	Poland	622
D 640	Georges Leygues	DDGHM	France	253
Y 640	Mengam	YTM	France	273
YTB 640	Glendyne	YTB/YTL/ YTR/YTM	Canada	105
641	Druzno	MHC	Poland	622
A 641	Esterel	YTM	France	272
D 641	Dupleix	DDGHM	France	253
M 641	Éridan	MHC	France	266
Y 641	Balaguier	YTM	France	273
YTB 641	Glendale	YTB/YTL/ YTR/YTM	Canada	105
642	Hancza	MHC	Poland	622
A 642	Lubéron	YTM	France	272
D 642	Montcalm	DDGHM	France	253
M 642	Cassiopée	MHC	France	266
UAM 642	Calmaria	YP	Portugal	637
WLI 642	Buckthorn	WLI/ABU	US	969
Y 642	Taillat	YTM	France	273
YTB 642	Glenevis	YTB/YTL/ YTR/YTM	Canada	105
643	Mamry	MHSCM	Poland	623
D 643	Jean de Vienne	DDGHM	France	253
M 643	Androméde	MHC	France	266
UAM 643	Cirro	YP	Portugal	637
Y 643	Nividic	YTM	France	273
YTB 643	Glenbrook	YTB/YTL/ YTR/YTM	Canada	105
644	Wigry	MHSCM	Poland	623
D 644	Primauguet	DDGHM	France	254
M 644	Pégase	MHC	France	266
UAM 644	Vendaval	YP	Portugal	637
YTB 644	Glenside	YTB/YTL/ YTR/YTM	Canada	105
645	Sniardwy	MHSCM	Poland	623
A 645	Alizé	YDT	France	269
D 645	La Motte-Picquet	DDGHM	France	254
M 645	Orion	MHC	France	266
UAM 645	Moncão	YP	Portugal	637
646	Wdzydze	MHSCM	Poland	623
D 646	Latouche-Tréville	DDGHM	France	254
M 646	Croix Du Sud	MHC	France	266
UAM 646	Suão	YP	Portugal	637
M 647	Aigle	MHC	France	266
UAM 647	Macareu	YP	Portugal	637
Y 647	Le Four	YTM	France	273
648	Kostroma	SSN	Russian Federation	657
M 648	Lyre	MHC	France	266
UAM 648	Preia-Mar	YP	Portugal	637
A 649	L'Étoile	AXS	France	268
M 649	Persée	MHC	France	266
UAM 649	Baixa-Mar	YP	Portugal	637
Y 649	Port Cros	YTM	France	273
650	Admiral Chabanenko	DDGHM	Russian Federation	668
A 650	La Belle Poule	AXS	France	268
M 650	Sagittaire	MHC	France	266
651	Singa	PBO	Indonesia	359
FNH 651	Nacaome	PB	Honduras	318
GC 651	Tecun Uman	PB	Guatemala	315
M 651	Verseau	MHC	France	266
A 652	Mutin	AXS	France	269
FNH 652	Goascoran	PB	Honduras	318
GC 652	Kaibil Balan	PB	Guatemala	315
M 652	Céphée	MHC	France	266
653	Ajak	PBO	Indonesia	359
A 653	La Grand Hermine	AXS	France	268
FNH 653	Patuca	PB	Honduras	318
GC 653	Azumanche	PB	Guatemala	315
M 653	Capricorne	MHC	France	266
654	Snezhnogorsk	SSN	Russian Federation	659
FNH 654	Ulua	PB	Honduras	318
GC 654	Tzacol	PB	Guatemala	315
FNH 655	Choluteca	PB	Honduras	318
GC 655	Bitol	PB	Guatemala	315
656	Orienburg	SSAN	Russian Federation	663
BH 656	Gucumaz	PB	Guatemala	315
FNH 656	Rio Coco	PB	Honduras	318
Y 656	Phaéton	YAG	France	271
Y 657	Machaon	YAG	France	271
659	DK-143	ACV	Russian Federation	707
661	Tambov	SSN	Russian Federation	659
663	Pskov	SSN	Russian Federation	658
A 664	Malabar	ATA	France	272
665	DK-259	ACV	Russian Federation	707
668	DK-453	ACV	Russian Federation	707
A 669	Tenace	ATA	France	272
670	DK-323	ACV	Russian Federation	707
670	Ramadan	PGGF	Egypt	218
MSC 670	Awashima	MHSC	Japan	432
P 671	Glaive	PB	France	275
672	Khyber	PGGF	Egypt	218
MSC 672	Uwajima	MHSC	Japan	432
MSC 673	Ieshima	MHSC	Japan	432
674	El Kadessaya	PGGF	Egypt	218
MSC 674	Tsukishima	MHSC	Japan	432
A 675	Fréhel	YTM	France	273
MSC 675	Maejima	MHSC	Japan	432
P 675	Arago	PBO	France	261
676	El Yarmouk	PGGF	Egypt	218
A 676	Saire	YTM	France	273
MSC 676	Kumejima	MHSC	Japan	432
P 676	Flamant	PBO	France	262
UAM 676	Guia	ABU	Portugal	636
677	DKA 70	LCMS	Russian Federation	682
677	Su Yong	LST	Korea, South	468
A 677	Armen	YTM	France	273
MSC 677	Makishima	MHSC	Japan	432
P 677	Cormoran	PBO	France	262
678	Admiral Kharlamov	DDGHM	Russian Federation	669
678	Badr	PGGF	Egypt	218
678	Buk Han	LST	Korea, South	468
A 678	La Houssaye	YTM	France	273
MSC 678	Tobishima	MHSC	Japan	432
P 678	Pluvier	PBO	France	262
A 679	Kéréon	YTM	France	273
MSC 679	Yugeshima	MHSC	Japan	432
P 679	Grèbe	PBO	France	262
680	DK-285	ACV	Russian Federation	707
680	Hettein	PGGF	Egypt	218
A 680	Siciè	YTM	France	273
MSC 680	Nagashima	MHSC	Japan	432
P 680	Sterne	PBO	France	261
681	Kojoon Bong	LSTH	Korea, South	468
A 681	Taunoa	YTM	France	273
MSC 681	Sugashima	MHC	Japan	431
P 681	Albatros	PSO	France	262
682	Biro Bong	LSTH	Korea, South	468
A 682	Rascas	YTM	France	273
MSC 682	Notojima	MHC	Japan	431
P 682	L'Audacieuse	PBO	France	262
683	Hyangro Bong	LSTH	Korea, South	468
MSC 683	Tsunoshima	MHC	Japan	431
P 683	La Boudeuse	PBO	France	262
684	Danil Moskovskiy	SSN	Russian Federation	659
MSC 684	Naoshima	MHC	Japan	431
P 684	La Capricieuse	PBO	France	262
685	Seongin Bong	LSTH	Korea, South	468
MSC 685	Toyoshima	MHC	Japan	431
P 685	La Fougueuse	PBO	France	262
MSC 686	Ukushima	MHC	Japan	431
P 686	La Glorieuse	PBO	France	262
MSC 687	Izushima	MHC	Japan	431
P 687	La Gracieuse	PBO	France	262
688	DK-458	ACV	Russian Federation	707
MSC 688	Aishima	MHC	Japan	431
P 688	La Moqueuse	PBO	France	262
SSN 688	Los Angeles	SSN	US	914
MSC 689	Aoshima	MHC	Japan	431
P 689	La Railleuse	PBO	France	262
690	Fabian Wrede	AX	Finland	238
MSC 690	Miyajima	MHC	Japan	431
P 690	La Rieuse	PBO	France	262
SSN 690	Philadelphia	SSN	US	914
691	Tatarstan	FFGM	Russian Federation	673
691	Wilhelm Carpelan	AX	Finland	238
MSC 691	Shishijima	MHC	Japan	431
P 691	La Tapageuse	PBO	France	262
SSN 691	Memphis	SSN	US	914
692	Axel Von Fersen	AX	Finland	238
MSC 692	Kuroshima	MHC	Japan	431
Y 692	Telenn Mor	ABU	France	270
A 693	Acharné	YTM	France	273
A 695	Bélier	YTB	France	272
A 696	Buffle	YTB	France	272
A 697	Bison	YTB	France	272
SSN 698	Bremerton	SSN	US	914
699	DK-447	ACV	Russian Federation	707
SSN 699	Jacksonville	SSN	US	914
700	Kingston	MM	Canada	103
A 700	Khaireddine	AGS	Tunisia	825
SSN 700	Dallas	SSN	US	914
SSV 700	Temryuk	AGS/AGI/AGE	Russian Federation	685
U 700	Netisin	YDT	Ukraine	854
701	Glace Bay	MM	Canada	103
701	Karachejevo-Cherkessia	PGGK	Russian Federation	680
701	Sirius	LSM	Bulgaria	93

Number	Ship's name	Type	Country	Page
701	Thar	WPB	Egypt	224
A 701	N N O Salammbo	AGOR/AX	Tunisia	825
P 701	Nandimithra	PGG	Sri Lanka	761
SSN 701	La Jolla	SSN	US	914
702	Antares	LSM	Bulgaria	93
702	Budenovsk	PGGK	Russian Federation	680
702	Madina	FFGHM	Saudi Arabia	712
702	Nanaimo	MM	Canada	103
702	Pylky	FFM	Russian Federation	671
L 702	Chikoko I	LCU	Malawi	491
P 702	Suranimala	PGG	Sri Lanka	761
703	Edmonton	MM	Canada	103
703	Nur	WPB	Egypt	224
P 703	Kasungu	PB	Malawi	491
Y 703	Lilas	YFL	France	272
Y 703	Lilas	PB	France	276
704	Hofouf	FFGHM	Saudi Arabia	712
704	Shawinigan	MM	Canada	103
P 704	Kaning'a	PB	Malawi	491
705	Stupinets	FSGM	Russian Federation	677
705	Whitehorse	MM	Canada	103
SSN 705	City of Corpus Christi	SSN	US	914
U 705	Kremenets	ATA/YTM	Ukraine	855
Y 705	Pivoine	YFL	France	272
706	Abha	FFGHM	Saudi Arabia	712
706	Borovsk	PGGK	Russian Federation	680
706	Yellowknife	MM	Canada	103
SSN 706	Albuquerque	SSN	US	914
U 706	Izyaslav	ATA/YTM	Ukraine	855
Y 706	Chimère	AXL	France	268
707	Goose Bay	MM	Canada	103
708	Moncton	MM	Canada	103
708	Taif	FFGHM	Saudi Arabia	712
709	Saskatoon	MM	Canada	103
710	Brandon	MM	Canada	103
F 710	La Fayette	FFGHM	France	256
Y 710	General Delfosse	YFL	France	272
711	Pulau Rengat	MHSC	Indonesia	363
711	Summerside	MM	Canada	103
711	Yoon Young-Ha	PGGF	Korea, South	467
F 711	Surcouf	FFGHM	France	256
P 711	Barkat	PC	Bangladesh	57
SSN 711	San Francisco	SSN	US	914
Y 711	Farfadet	AXL	France	268
712	Chang	LST	Thailand	812
712	Neustrashimy	FFHM	Russian Federation	672
712	Pulau Rupat	MHSC	Indonesia	363
A 712	Athos	YFRT	France	270
F 712	Courbet	FFGHM	France	256
P 712	Salam	PB	Bangladesh	57
713	Kerch	CGHM	Russian Federation	667
713	Nisr	WPB	Egypt	224
713	Pangan	LST	Thailand	812
A 713	Aramis	YFRT	France	270
F 713	Aconit	FFGHM	France	256
P 713	Capitaine Moulié	PB	France	276
P 713	Sangu	PBO/AX	Bangladesh	55
SSN 713	Houston	SSN	US	914
714	Lanta	LST	Thailand	812
F 714	Guépratte	FFGHM	France	256
P 714	Turag	PBO/AX	Bangladesh	55
SSN 714	Norfolk	SSN	US	914
715	Bystry	DDGHM	Russian Federation	670
715	Prathong	LST	Thailand	812
SSN 715	Buffalo	SSN	US	914
WHEC 715	Hamilton	PSOH/WHEC	US	963
P 716	MDLC Jacques	PB	France	276
WHEC 716	Dallas	PSOH/WHEC	US	963
SSN 717	Olympia	SSN	US	914
WHEC 717	Mellon	PSOH/WHEC	US	963
718	MT 265	MSOM	Russian Federation	683
WHEC 718	Chase	PSOH/WHEC	US	963
719	Nimr	WPB	Egypt	224
SSN 719	Providence	SSN	US	914
WHEC 719	Boutwell	PSOH/WHEC	US	963
P 720	Géranium	PB	France	275
SSN 720	Pittsburgh	SSN	US	914
WHEC 720	Sherman	PSOH/WHEC	US	963
721	Pulau Rote	MSC	Indonesia	362
721	Sichang	LSTH	Thailand	812
A 721	Khadem	ATA	Bangladesh	60
P 721	Jonquille	PB	France	275
SSN 721	Chicago	SSN	US	914
WHEC 721	Gallatin	PSOH/WHEC	US	963
722	Al Munjed	ARS	Libya	486
722	Pulau Raas	MSC	Indonesia	362
722	Surin	LSTH	Thailand	812
722	Vaarlahti	AKSL	Finland	238
A 722	Sebak	YTM	Bangladesh	60
P 722	Violette	PB	France	275
SSN 722	Key West	SSN	US	914
U 722	Borsziv	YTR	Ukraine	855
WHEC 722	Morgenthau	PSOH/WHEC	US	963
723	Pulau Romang	MSC	Indonesia	362
723	Vänö	AKSL	Finland	238
A 723	Rupsha	YTM	Bangladesh	60
P 723	Jasmin	PB	France	275
SSN 723	Oklahoma City	SSN	US	914
WHEC 723	Rush	PSOH/WHEC	US	963
724	Pulau Rimau	MSC	Indonesia	362
A 724	Shibsha	YTM	Bangladesh	60
SSN 724	Louisville	SSN	US	914
WHEC 724	Munro	PSOH/WHEC	US	963
SSN 725	Helena	SSN	US	914
WHEC 725	Jarvis	PSOH/WHEC	US	963
726	Pulau Rusa	MSC	Indonesia	362
MCL 726	Ogishima	MCSD	Japan	431
SSGN 726	Ohio	SSGN	US	911
WHEC 726	Midgett	PSOH/WHEC	US	963
727	Pulau Rangsang	MSC	Indonesia	362
727	Yaroslav Mudryy	FFHM	Russian Federation	672
MCL 727	Sakushima	MCSD	Japan	431
SSGN 727	Michigan	SSGN	US	911
SSGN 728	Florida	SSGN	US	911
U 728	Evpatoriya	YTR	Ukraine	855
729	Pulau Rempang	MSC	Indonesia	362
SSGN 729	Georgia	SSGN	US	911
730	Haukipää	YTM	Finland	240
F 730	Floréal	FFGHM	France	258
SSBN 730	Henry M Jackson	SSBN	US	910
731	Hakuni	AKSL	Finland	238
731	Neukrotimy	FFM	Russian Federation	671
F 731	Prairial	FFGHM	France	258
SSBN 731	Alabama	SSBN	US	910
F 732	Nivôse	FFGHM	France	258
SSBN 732	Alaska	SSBN	US	910
F 733	Ventôse	FFGHM	France	258
SSBN 733	Nevada	SSBN	US	910
F 734	Vendémiaire	FFGHM	France	258
SSBN 734	Tennessee	SSBN	US	910
F 735	Germinal	FFGHM	France	258
SSBN 735	Pennsylvania	SSBN	US	910
SSBN 736	West Virginia	SSBN	US	910
SSBN 737	Kentucky	SSBN	US	910
738	MT 264	MSOM	Russian Federation	683
SSBN 738	Maryland	SSBN	US	910
739	Hästö	AKSL	Finland	239
SSBN 739	Nebraska	SSBN	US	910
P 740	Fulmar	PB	France	276
SSBN 740	Rhode Island	SSBN	US	910
741	Prab	–	Thailand	812
SSBN 741	Maine	SSBN	US	910
742	Satakut	–	Thailand	812
SSBN 742	Wyoming	SSBN	US	910
A 743	Denti	AETL	France	268
SSBN 743	Louisiana	SSBN	US	910
747	DKA 67	LCU	Russian Federation	682
A 748	Léopard	AXL	France	268
A 749	Panthére	AXL	France	268
A 750	Jaguar	AXL	France	268
SSN 750	Newport News	SSN	US	914
WMSL 750	Bertholf	PSOH/WMSL	US	963
751	Dong Hae	FS	Korea, South	467
751	Lohi	LCU	Finland	239
A 751	Lynx	AXL	France	268
SSN 751	San Juan	SSN	US	914
WMSL 751	Waesche	PSOH/WMSL	US	963
752	Lohm	LCU	Finland	239
752	Su Won	FS	Korea, South	467
A 752	Guépard	AXL	France	268
SSN 752	Pasadena	SSN	US	914
WMSL 752	Stratton	PSOH/WMSL	US	963
753	Kang Reung	FS	Korea, South	467
A 753	Chacal	AXL	France	268
SSN 753	Albany	SSN	US	914
754	Bezboyaznennyy	DDGHM	Russian Federation	670
A 754	Tigre	AXL	France	268
SSN 754	Topeka	SSN	US	914
Y 754	Taina	YFL	France	271
755	An Yang	FS	Korea, South	467
A 755	Lion	AXL	France	268
SSN 755	Miami	SSN	US	914
756	Po Hang	FS/FSG	Korea, South	466
SSN 756	Scranton	SSN	US	914
U 756	Sudak	AWT	Ukraine	853
757	Kun San	FS/FSG	Korea, South	466
SSN 757	Alexandria	SSN	US	914
758	Kyong Ju	FS/FSG	Korea, South	466
A 758	Beautemps-Beaupré	AGOR	France	266
SSN 758	Asheville	SSN	US	914
Y 758	Kermeur	YFB	France	271
759	Mok Po	FS/FSG	Korea, South	466
A 759	Dupuy de Lôme	AGIH	France	267
SSN 759	Jefferson City	SSN	US	914
Y 759	Kernaleguen	YFB	France	271
SSN 760	Annapolis	SSN	US	914
761	Kim Chon	FS/FSG	Korea, South	466
761	Mataphon	LCM/LCVP/LCP	Thailand	813
P 761	Kara	PB	Togo	820
P 761	Mimosa	PB	France	276
SSN 761	Springfield	SSN	US	914
762	Chung Ju	FS/FSG	Korea, South	466
762	Rawi	LCM/LCVP/LCP	Thailand	813
L 762	Lachs	LCU	Germany	291
P 762	Mono	PB	Togo	820
SSN 762	Columbus	SSN	US	914
Y 762	L'Etoile de Mer	YFL	France	271
763	Adang	LCM/LCVP/LCP	Thailand	813
763	Jin Ju	FS/FSG	Korea, South	466
SSN 763	Santa Fe	SSN	US	914
Y 763	Dharuba	YFL	France	271
YTB 763	Muskegon	YTB	US	954
764	Phetra	LCM/LCVP/LCP	Thailand	813
SSN 764	Boise	SSN	US	914
765	Kolam	LCM/LCVP/LCP	Thailand	813
765	Yo Su	FS/FSG	Korea, South	466
L 765	Schlei	LCU	Germany	291
SSN 765	Montpelier	SSN	US	914
Y 765	Avel Mor	YFL	France	271
766	Jin Hae	FS/FSG	Korea, South	466
766	Talibong	LCM/LCVP/LCP	Thailand	813
SSN 766	Charlotte	SSN	US	914
767	Sun Chon	FS/FSG	Korea, South	466
SSN 767	Hampton	SSN	US	914
768	Yee Ree	FS/FSG	Korea, South	466
A 768	Élan	AG/ATS/YDT/YPC/YPT	France	269
SSN 768	Hartford	SSN	US	914
769	Won Ju	FS/FSG	Korea, South	466
SSN 769	Toledo	SSN	US	914

Number	Ship's name	Type	Country	Page
770	Valentin Pikul	MSOM	Russian Federation	683
770	Yangjiang	PTG	China	150
770	Yevgeniy Kocheshkov	ACVM/LCUJM	Russian Federation	681
A 770	Glycine	AXL	France	268
M 770	Antarès	MHI	France	265
SSN 770	Tucson	SSN	US	914
Y 770	Morse	YT	France	273
771	An Dong	FS/FSG	Korea, South	466
771	Anawrahta	FSG	Myanmar	539
771	Kampela 1	LCU/AKSL	Finland	238
771	Shunde	PTG	China	150
771	Thong Kaeo	LCU	Thailand	813
A 771	Eglantine	AXL	France	268
M 771	Altaïr	MHI	France	265
SSN 771	Columbia	SSN	US	914
Y 771	Otarie	YT	France	273
YTB 771	Keokuk	YTB	US	954
772	Bayintnaung	FSG	Myanmar	539
772	Chon An	FS/FSG	Korea, South	466
772	Kampela 2	LCU/AKSL	Finland	238
772	Nanhai	PTG	China	150
772	Thong Lang	LCU	Thailand	813
M 772	Aldébaran	MHI	France	265
SSN 772	Greeneville	SSN	US	914
Y 772	Loutre	YT	France	273
773	Panyu	PTG	China	150
773	Song Nam	FS/FSG	Korea, South	466
773	Wang Nok	LCU	Thailand	813
P 773	Njambuur	PBO	Senegal	718
SSN 773	Cheyenne	SSN	US	914
Y 773	Phoque	YT	France	273
774	Lianjiang	PTG	China	150
774	Wang Nai	LCU	Thailand	813
A 774	Chevreuil	AG/ATS/YDT/ YPC/YPT	France	269
SSN 774	Virginia	SSN	US	912
775	Bu Chon	FS/FSG	Korea, South	466
775	Xinhui	PTG	China	150
A 775	Gazelle	AG/ATS/YDT/ YPC/YPT	France	269
SSN 775	Texas	SSN	US	912
776	Jae Chon	FS/FSG	Korea, South	466
SSN 776	Hawaii	SSN	US	912
777	Dae Chon	FS/FSG	Korea, South	466
777	Porkkala	MLI	Finland	236
SSN 777	North Carolina	SSN	US	912
Y 777	Palangrin	YFL	France	271
778	Burny	DDGHM	Russian Federation	670
778	Sok Cho	FS/FSG	Korea, South	466
P 778	Réséda	PB	France	276
SSN 778	New Hampshire	SSN	US	912
779	Yong Ju	FS/FSG	Korea, South	466
SSN 779	New Mexico	SSN	US	912
SSN 780	Missouri	SSN	US	912
781	Man Nok	LCU	Thailand	812
781	Nam Won	FS/FSG	Korea, South	466
SSN 781	California	SSN	US	912
782	Kwan Myong	FS/FSG	Korea, South	466
782	Man Klang	LCU	Thailand	812
782	Mordoviya	ACVM/LCUJM	Russian Federation	681
SSN 782	Mississippi	SSN	US	912
U 782	Sokal	YH/TFL	Ukraine	854
YTB 782	Manistee	YTB	US	954
783	Man Nai	LCU	Thailand	812
783	Sin Hung	FS/FSG	Korea, South	466
SSN 783	Minnesota	SSN	US	912
U 783	Illichivsk	YDT/YFL/YPT	Ukraine	854
Y 783	Avel Aber	YTR	France	271
SSN 784	North Dakota	SSN	US	912
Y 784	La Loude	YTR	France	271
785	Kong Ju	FS/FSG	Korea, South	466
A 785	Thétis	MCD/BEGM	France	267
SSN 785	Jack Warner	SSN	US	912
Y 785	La Divette	YTR	France	271
Y 786	Auté	YFL	France	271
Y 787	Tiaré	YFL	France	271
YTB 787	Kittanning	YTB	US	954
A 789	Melia	PB	France	276
F 789	Lieutenant de Vaisseau Le Hénaff	FFGM	France	257
A 790	Coralline	AGE	France	271
F 790	Lieutenant de Vaisseau Lavallée	FFGM	France	257
Y 790	Dionée	YDT	France	270
791	Hai Shih	SS	Taiwan	787
A 791	Lapérouse	AGS	France	267
F 791	Commandant L'herminier	FFGM	France	257
P 791	Hortensia	PB	France	276
Y 791	Myosotis	YDT	France	270
792	Hai Bao	SS	Taiwan	787
792	Träskö	YFB	Finland	239
A 792	Borda	AGS	France	267
F 792	Premier Maître l'Her	FFGM	France	257
Y 792	Gardénia	YDT	France	270
793	Hai Lung	SSK	Taiwan	786
A 793	Laplace	AGS	France	267
F 793	Commandant Blaison	FFGM	France	257
Y 793	Liseron	YDT	France	270
794	Hai Hu	SSK	Taiwan	786
F 794	Enseigne de Vaisseau Jacoubet	FFGM	France	257
Y 794	Magnolia	YDT	France	270
F 795	Commandant Ducuing	FFGM	France	257
Y 795	Ajonc	YDT	France	270
F 796	Commandant Birot	FFGM	France	257
Y 796	Genêt	YDT	France	270
F 797	Commandant Bouan	FFGM	France	257
Y 797	Giroflée	YDT	France	270
798	Matelot Brice Kpomasse	PB	Benin	66
Y 798	Acanthe	YDT	France	270
YTB 798	Opelika	YTB	US	954
799	DKA 325	LCMS	Russian Federation	682
799	Hylje	YPC	Finland	240
799	La Sota	PB	Benin	66
L 800	Rotterdam	LPD	Netherlands	552
WLIC 800	Pamlico	WLIC	US	970
801	Ladny	FFM	Russian Federation	671
801	Pandrong	PBO	Indonesia	359
801	Pusan	AGOR	Korea, South	471
801	Rais Hamidou	PTGM	Algeria	5
801	Te Mataili	PB	Tuvalu	848
L 801	Johan de Witt	LPD	Netherlands	553
MHV 801	Aldebaran	PB	Denmark	195
TRV 801	Tuna	YPT	Australia	38
UAM 801	Coral	YGS	Portugal	635
WLIC 801	Hudson	WLIC	US	970
802	Abu Al Barakat Al Barbari	AGOR	Morocco	536
802	Hamzah	AGG	Iran	379
802	Pusan	AGOR	Korea, South	471
802	Salah Rais	PTGM	Algeria	5
802	Sura	PBO	Indonesia	359
A 802	Sidi Bou Said	ABU	Tunisia	825
A 802	Snellius	AGSH	Netherlands	554
F 802	De Zeven Provincien	FFGHM	Netherlands	548
MHV 802	Carina	PB	Denmark	195
S 802	Walrus	SSK	Netherlands	547
TRV 802	Trevally	YPT	Australia	38
UAM 802	Atlanta	YGS	Portugal	635
WLIC 802	Kennebec	WLIC	US	970
803	Pusan	AGOR	Korea, South	471
803	Rais Ali	PTGM	Algeria	5
803	Todak	PBO	Indonesia	358
A 803	Luymes	AGSH	Netherlands	554
F 803	Tromp	FFGHM	Netherlands	548
MHV 803	Aries	PB	Denmark	195
S 803	Zeeleeuw	SSK	Netherlands	547
TRV 803	Tailor	YPT	Australia	38
WLIC 803	Saginaw	WLIC	US	970
804	Hiu	PBO	Indonesia	358
804	Huoqiu	MCMV	China	156
A 804	Pelikaan	AP	Netherlands	556
A 804	Tabarka	ABU	Tunisia	825
F 804	De Ruyter	FFGHM	Netherlands	548
MHV 804	Andromeda	PB	Denmark	195
805	Layang	PBO	Indonesia	358
805	Pusan	AGOR	Korea, South	471
805	Tula	SSBN	Russian Federation	651
A 805	Taguermess	ABU	Tunisia	825
F 805	Evertsen	FFGHM	Netherlands	548
MHV 805	Gemini	PB	Denmark	195
UAM 805	Fisalia	YGS	Portugal	635
806	Lemadang	PBO	Indonesia	358
806	Motorist	MSOM	Russian Federation	683
806	Pusan	AGOR	Korea, South	471
806	Severstal	SSBN	Russian Federation	650
MHV 806	Dubhe	PB	Denmark	195
807	Boa	PB	Indonesia	360
807	Ekaterinburg	SSBN	Russian Federation	651
807	Phraongkamrop	PB	Thailand	818
807	Yay Bo	AGSC	Myanmar	543
BG 807	Matros Mikola Mushnirov	PBR	Ukraine	856
MHV 807	Jupiter	PB	Denmark	195
YTB 807	Massapequa	YTB	US	954
808	Picharnpholakit	PB	Thailand	818
808	Pytlivy	FFM	Russian Federation	671
808	Welang	PB	Indonesia	360
MHV 808	Lyra	PB	Denmark	195
S 808	Dolfijn	SSK	Netherlands	547
YTB 808	Wenatchee	YTB	US	954
809	Raminthra	PB	Thailand	818
809	Suluh Pari	PB	Indonesia	360
MHV 809	Antares	PB	Denmark	195
810	Katon	PB	Indonesia	360
810	Pusan	AGOR	Korea, South	471
810	Smetlivy	DDGM	Russian Federation	667
MHV 810	Luna	PB	Denmark	195
P 810	Jaguar	PB	Netherlands	558
S 810	Bruinvis	SSK	Netherlands	547
811	Chanthara	AGS	Thailand	815
811	Kakap	PBOH	Indonesia	359
811	V Gumanenko	MHOM	Russian Federation	683
MHV 811	Apollo	PB	Denmark	195
P 811	Panter	PB	Netherlands	558
U 811	Balta	ADG	Ukraine	854
Y 811	Knurrhahn	APB	Germany	294
812	Al Riyadh	FFGHM	Saudi Arabia	710
812	Kerapu	PBOH	Indonesia	359
812	Suk	AGOR	Thailand	815
812	Voronezh	SSGN	Russian Federation	654
MHV 812	Hercules	PB	Denmark	195
P 812	Nirbhoy	PC	Bangladesh	56
P 812	Poema	PB	Netherlands	558
Y 812	Lütje Hörn	YTM	Germany	296
YTB 812	Acconac	YTB	US	954
813	Burespadoongkit	PB	Thailand	818
813	Pharuehatsabodi	AGSH	Thailand	814
813	Tongkol	PBOH	Indonesia	359
MHV 813	Baunen	PB	Denmark	195
UAM 813	Bellatrix	AXS	Portugal	636
814	Barakuda	PBOH	Indonesia	359
814	Liaoyang	ML/MST	China	155
814	Makkah	FFGHM	Saudi Arabia	710
MHV 814	Budstikken	PB	Denmark	195
UAM 814	Canopus	AXS	Portugal	636
Y 814	Knechtsand	YTM	Germany	296
815	Sanca	PB	Indonesia	360
MHV 815	Kureren	PB	Denmark	195

Number	Ship's name	Type	Country	Page
Y 815	Scharhörn	YTM	Germany	296
YTB 815	Neodesha	YTB	US	954
816	Al Dammam	FFGHM	Saudi Arabia	710
816	Smolensk	SSGN	Russian Federation	654
816	Warakas	PB	Indonesia	360
MHV 816	Patrioten	PB	Denmark	195
Y 816	Vogelsand	YTM	Germany	296
817	Panana	PB	Indonesia	360
MHV 817	Partisan	PB	Denmark	195
Y 817	Nordstrand	YTM	Germany	296
818	Kalakae	PB	Indonesia	360
MHV 818	Sabotøren	PB	Denmark	195
819	R 47	FSGM	Russian Federation	677
819	Tedong Naga	PB	Indonesia	360
Y 819	Langeness	YTM	Germany	296
820	Briansk	SSBN	Russian Federation	651
820	Viper	PB	Indonesia	360
YTB 820	Wanamassa	YTB	US	954
821	Ch'ungnam	AGOR	Korea, South	471
821	Lublin	LST/ML	Poland	622
821	Piton	PB	Indonesia	360
821	Suriya	ABU	Thailand	816
822	Gniezno	LST/ML	Poland	622
822	Weling	PB	Indonesia	360
823	Krakow	LST/ML	Poland	622
823	Matacora	PB	Indonesia	360
823	Misairutei-San-Gou	PTGK	Japan	428
YTB 823	Canonchet	YTB	US	954
824	Dmitriy Donskoy	SSBN	Russian Federation	650
824	Hayabusa	PGGF	Japan	428
824	Poznan	LST/ML	Poland	622
824	Tedung Selar	PB	Indonesia	360
SSV 824	Liman	AGI/AGIM	Russian Federation	688
YTB 824	Santaquin	YTB	US	954
825	Boiga	PB	Indonesia	360
825	Dimitrovgrad	FSGM	Russian Federation	677
825	Torun	LST/ML	Poland	622
825	Wakataka	PGGF	Japan	428
826	Isku	MLI	Finland	239
826	Kelabang	MSC	Indonesia	362
826	Ootaka	PGGF	Japan	428
827	Krait	PB	Indonesia	360
827	Kumataka	PGGF	Japan	428
827	Verchoture	SSBN	Russian Federation	651
828	Arkhangelsk	SSBN	Russian Federation	650
828	Kala Hitam	MSC	Indonesia	362
828	Umitaka	PGGF	Japan	428
F 828	Van Speijk	FFGHM	Netherlands	550
YTB 828	Catahecassa	YTB	US	954
829	Shirataka	PGGF	Japan	428
829	Tarihu	PB	Indonesia	360
830	Alkura	PB	Indonesia	360
830	Högsåra	AKSL	Finland	239
U 830	Korets	ATA/YTM	Ukraine	855
831	Chula	AORL	Thailand	816
831	Kallanpää	YTM	Finland	240
831	Kangwon	AGOR	Korea, South	471
831	Komendor	MSOM	Russian Federation	683
F 831	Van Amstel	FFGHM	Netherlands	550
U 831	Kovel	ATA/YTM	Ukraine	855
YTB 831	Dekanawida	YTB	US	954
832	Samui	YO	Thailand	816
A 832	Zuiderkruis	AORH	Netherlands	556
833	Prong	YO	Thailand	816
833	R 125	FSGM	Russian Federation	677
834	Proet	YO	Thailand	816
835	Gepard	SSN	Russian Federation	656
835	Samed	YO	Thailand	816
Y 835	Todendorf	YFRT	Germany	295
YTB 835	Skenandoa	YTB	US	954
836	Houtskär	AKSL	Finland	238
A 836	Amsterdam	AORH	Netherlands	555
L 836	Ranavijaya	LCM	Sri Lanka	765
Y 836	Putlos	YFRT	Germany	295
YTB 836	Pokagon	YTB	US	954
Y 837	Baumholder	YFRT	Germany	295
839	Karelia	SSBN	Russian Federation	651
L 839	Ranagaja	LCM	Sri Lanka	765
Y 839	Munster	YFRT	Germany	295
P 840	Holland	PSO	Netherlands	551
PG 840	Conrado Yap	PBF	Philippines	612
841	Chuang	YW	Thailand	816
841	Karabane	LCT	Senegal	719
P 841	Chiriqui	PB	Panama	593
P 841	Zeeland	PSO	Netherlands	551
842	Chik	YO	Thailand	816
P 842	Friesland	PSO	Netherlands	551
P 842	Veraguas	PB	Panama	593
PG 842	Tedorico Dominado Jr	PBF	Philippines	612
Y 842	Schwimmdock 3	–	Germany	295
P 843	Bocas Del Toro	PB	Panama	593
P 843	Groningen	PSO	Netherlands	551
PG 843	Cosme Acosta	PBF	Philippines	612
PG 844	José Artiaga Jr	PBF	Philippines	612
PG 846	Nicanor Jimenez	PBF	Philippines	612
847	Orel	SSGN	Russian Federation	654
847	Sibarau	PB	Indonesia	359
PG 847	Leopoldo Regis	PBF	Philippines	612
848	Siliman	PB	Indonesia	359
PG 848	Leon Tadina	PBF	Philippines	612
849	Novomoskovsk	SSBN	Russian Federation	651
PG 849	Loreto Danipog	PBF	Philippines	612
851	Dongdiao	AGM/AGI	China	157
851	KD 11	LCU	Poland	622
851	Klueng Badaan	YTL	Thailand	817
A 851	Cerberus	YDT	Netherlands	557
GC 851	Utatlan	PB	Guatemala	315
PG 851	Apollo Tiano	PBF	Philippines	612
852	KD 12	LCU	Poland	622
852	Marn Vichai	YTL	Thailand	817

Number	Ship's name	Type	Country	Page
852	R 257	FSGM	Russian Federation	677
A 852	Argus	YDT	Netherlands	557
GC 852	Subteniente Osorio Saravia	PB	Guatemala	315
U 852	Shostka	ABU	Ukraine	854
853	KD 13	LCU	Poland	622
853	Rin	YTB	Thailand	817
853	Tigr	SSN	Russian Federation	656
A 853	Nautilus	YDT	Netherlands	557
M 853	Haarlem	MHC	Netherlands	554
PG 853	Sulpicio Fernandez	PBF	Philippines	612
U 853	Shulyavka	YDT/YFL/YPT	Ukraine	854
854	Rang	YTB	Thailand	817
A 854	Hydra	YDT	Netherlands	557
855	Kontradmiral Vlasov	MSOM	Russian Federation	683
855	R 187	FSGM	Russian Federation	677
855	Samaesan	YTR	Thailand	817
856	Raet	YTR	Thailand	817
M 856	Maassluis	MHC	Netherlands	554
857	Sigalu	PB	Indonesia	359
M 857	Makkum	MHC	Netherlands	554
858	Silea	PB	Indonesia	359
M 858	Middelburg	MHC	Netherlands	554
859	Siribua	PB	Indonesia	359
M 859	Hellevoetsluis	MHC	Netherlands	554
M 860	Schiedam	MHC	Netherlands	554
Y 860	Schwedeneck	AG	Germany	292
861	Changxingdao	ASRH	China	161
861	Kled Keo	AKS	Thailand	816
M 861	Urk	MHC	Netherlands	554
Y 861	Kronsort	AG	Germany	292
862	Chongmingdao	ASRH	China	161
862	Ryazan	SSBN	Russian Federation	652
862	Siada	PB	Indonesia	359
M 862	Zierikzee	MHC	Netherlands	554
Y 862	Helmsand	AG	Germany	292
863	Sikuda	PB	Indonesia	359
863	Yongxingdao	ASRH	China	161
M 863	Vlaardingen	MHC	Netherlands	554
Y 863	Stollergrund	AG	Germany	292
864	Sigurot	PB	Indonesia	359
M 864	Willemstad	MHC	Netherlands	554
Y 864	Mittelgrund	AG	Germany	292
866	Cucut	PB	Indonesia	360
Y 866	Breitgrund	AG	Germany	292
867	Kobra	PB	Indonesia	360
867	Volk	SSN	Russian Federation	656
868	Anakonda	PB	Indonesia	360
869	Patola	PB	Indonesia	360
870	R 2	FSGM	Russian Federation	677
870	Taliwangsa	PB	Indonesia	360
871	Similan	AORH	Thailand	815
872	Leopard	SSN	Russian Federation	656
874	Kala 4	LCU/AKSL	Finland	238
874	Morshansk	FSGM	Russian Federation	677
A 874	Linge	YTM	Netherlands	557
875	Pyhäranta	MLI	Finland	236
A 875	Regge	YTM	Netherlands	557
Y 875	Hiev	–	Germany	295
876	Pansio	MLI	Finland	236
876	Victoria	SSK	Canada	98
A 876	Hunze	YTM	Netherlands	557
Y 876	Griep	–	Germany	295
877	Kampela 3	LCU/AKSL	Finland	238
877	Windsor	SSK	Canada	98
A 877	Rotte	YTM	Netherlands	557
878	Corner Brook	SSK	Canada	98
878	Pantera	SSN	Russian Federation	656
A 878	Gouwe	YTM	Netherlands	557
879	Chicoutimi	SSK	Canada	98
879	Valas	AKSL	Finland	238
L 880	Shakthi	LSM	Sri Lanka	765
881	Hongzhu	AORH	China	160
882	Fengcang	AORH	China	160
885	Qinghai Hu	AORH	China	160
886	Qiandao Hu	AORH	China	160
887	Weishan Hu	AORH	China	160
888	Fuxian Hu	AF	China	163
890	Vepr	SSN	Russian Federation	656
891	Bi Sheng	AGOR/AGE	China	157
AG 891	Corregidor	ABU	Philippines	616
U 891	Kherson	YDT/YFL/YPT	Ukraine	854
Y 891	Altmark	APB	Germany	294
892	Hua Luogeng	AGOR/AGE	China	157
894	Alskär	YFB	Finland	239
Y 895	Wische	APB	Germany	294
899	Halli	YPC	Finland	240
900	Beidiao	AGI	China	157
A 900	Mercuur	ASL/YTT	Netherlands	555
L 900	Shah Amanat	LSL	Bangladesh	60
901	A Zheleznyakov	MHOM	Russian Federation	683
901	Balikpapan	AOTL	Indonesia	365
901	Mourad Rais	FFLM	Algeria	4
901	Sharm El Sheikh	FFGHM	Egypt	214
901	Sriyanont	PB	Thailand	818
901	Tareq	SSK	Iran	369
CP 901	Saettia	SAR	Italy	412
L 901	Shah Poran	LCU	Bangladesh	60
MHV 901	Enø	PB	Denmark	194
WMEC 901	Bear	PSOH/WMEC	US	964
902	Boraida	AORH	Saudi Arabia	715
902	Noor	SSK	Iran	369
902	Rais Kellich	FFLM	Algeria	4
902	Sambu	AOTL	Indonesia	365
902	Tomsk	SSGN	Russian Federation	654
A 902	Van Kinsbergen	AXL	Netherlands	555
CP 902	Ubaldo Diciotti	SAR	Italy	412
L 902	Shah Makhdum	LCU	Bangladesh	60
MHV 902	Manø	PB	Denmark	194
P 902	Liberation	PBR/YFLB	Belgium	64

Number	Ship's name	Type	Country	Page
WMEC 902	Tampa	PSOH/WMEC	US	964
903	Arun	AORLH	Indonesia	365
903	Rais Korfou	FFLM	Algeria	4
903	Yunes	SSK	Iran	369
CP 903	Luigi Dattilo	SAR	Italy	412
MHV 903	Hjortø	PB	Denmark	194
WMEC 903	Harriet Lane	PSOH/WMEC	US	964
904	Cheliabinsk	SSGN	Russian Federation	654
904	Yunbou	AORH	Saudi Arabia	715
CP 904	Michele Fiorillo	SAR	Italy	412
MHV 904	Lyø	PB	Denmark	194
WMEC 904	Northland	PSOH/WMEC	US	964
CP 905	Antonio Peluso	SAR	Italy	412
MHV 905	Askø	PB	Denmark	194
WMEC 905	Spencer	PSOH/WMEC	US	964
906	Toushka	FFGHM	Egypt	214
CP 906	Orazio Corsi	SAR	Italy	412
MHV 906	Faenø	PB	Denmark	194
WMEC 906	Seneca	PSOH/WMEC	US	964
MHV 907	Hvidsten	PB	Denmark	194
WMEC 907	Escanaba	PSOH/WMEC	US	964
908	Vitse-Admiral Zakharin	MSOM	Russian Federation	683
908	Yandanshang	LSTH	China	153
MHV 908	Brigaden	PB	Denmark	194
WMEC 908	Tahoma	PSOH/WMEC	US	964
909	Jiuhuashan	LSTH	China	153
909	Vitseadmiral Zhukov	MSOM	Russian Federation	683
MHV 909	Speditøren	PB	Denmark	194
WMEC 909	Campbell	PSOH/WMEC	US	964
910	Huanggangshan	LSTH	China	153
MHV 910	Ringen	PB	Denmark	194
WMEC 910	Thetis	PSOH/WMEC	US	964
911	Chakri Naruebet	CVM	Thailand	801
911	Ivan Golubets	MSOM	Russian Federation	683
911	Mubarak	FFGHM	Egypt	214
911	Sorong	AOTL	Indonesia	365
911	Tianzhushan	LSTH	China	153
MHV 911	Bopa	PB	Denmark	194
P 911	Madhumati	PSO	Bangladesh	55
WMEC 911	Forward	PSOH/WMEC	US	964
912	Daqingshan	LSTH	China	153
912	Turbinist	MSOM	Russian Federation	683
912	Zelenograd	SSBN	Russian Federation	652
P 912	Kapatakhaya	PBO/AX	Bangladesh	55
WMEC 912	Legare	PSOH/WMEC	US	964
913	Baxianshan	LSTH	China	153
913	Kovrovets	MSOM	Russian Federation	683
P 913	Karatoa	PBO/AX	Bangladesh	55
WMEC 913	Mohawk	PSOH/WMEC	US	964
P 914	Gomati	PBO/AX	Bangladesh	55
915	Podolsk	SSBN	Russian Federation	652
M 915	Aster	MHC/AEL	Belgium	64
916	R 29	FSGM	Russian Federation	677
916	Taba	FFGHM	Egypt	214
M 916	Bellis	MHC/AEL	Belgium	64
M 917	Crocus	MHC/AEL	Belgium	64
PVM 917	Al Manoud	YDT	Libya	486
919	Krasnoyarsk	SSGN	Russian Federation	654
920	Vilyachinsk	SSGN	Russian Federation	654
921	El Fateh	AXT	Egypt	221
921	R 20	FSGM	Russian Federation	677
M 921	Lobelia	MHC/AEL	Belgium	64
SB 921	Paradoks	ATS	Russian Federation	698
SB 922	Shakhter	ATS	Russian Federation	698
923	Soputan	ATF	Indonesia	366
M 923	Narcis	MHC/AEL	Belgium	64
924	Leuser	ATF	Indonesia	366
924	R 14	FSGM	Russian Federation	677
M 924	Primula	MHC/AEL	Belgium	64
927	Yuntaishan	LST	China	153
928	Wufengshan	LST	China	153
929	Zijinshan	LST	China	153
930	Lingyanshan	LST	China	153
F 930	Leopold 1	FFGHM	Belgium	62
931	Burujulasad	AGORH	Indonesia	364
931	Dongtingshan	LST	China	153
F 931	Louise-Marie	FFGHM	Belgium	62
932	Chin Yang	FFGH	Taiwan	790
932	Dewa Kembar	AGSH	Indonesia	363
932	Helanshan	LST	China	153
933	Fong Yang	FFGH	Taiwan	790
933	Jalanidhi	AGOR	Indonesia	364
933	Liupanshan	LST	China	153
934	Danxiashan	LSTH	China	153
934	Feng Yang	FFGH	Taiwan	790
934	Lampo Batang	YTM	Indonesia	365
935	Lan Yang	FFGH	Taiwan	790
935	Tambora	YTM	Indonesia	365
935	Xuefengshan	LSTH	China	153
936	Bromo	YTM	Indonesia	365
936	Hae Yang	FFGH	Taiwan	790
936	Haiyangshan	LSTH	China	153
937	Hwai Yang	FFGH	Taiwan	790
937	Qingchengshan	LSTH	China	153
937	R 18	FSGM	Russian Federation	677
937	Soummam	AXH	Algeria	7
938	Ning Yang	FFGH	Taiwan	790
938	Petropavlosk Kamchatsky	SSBN	Russian Federation	652
939	Putuoshan	LSTH	China	153
939	Yi Yang	FFGH	Taiwan	790
940	R 11	FSGM	Russian Federation	677
940	Tiantaishan	LSTH	China	153
941	Shengshan	LSM	China	154
F 941	Abu Qir	FFGM	Egypt	215
942	Lushan	LSM	China	154
944	Yushan	LSM	China	154
945	Huashan	LSM	China	154
946	R 24	FSGM	Russian Federation	677
946	Songshan	LSM	China	154

Number	Ship's name	Type	Country	Page
F 946	El Suez	FFGM	Egypt	215
947	Blåtunga	LCPFM	Sweden	775
947	Omsk	SSGN	Russian Federation	654
U 947	Krasnoperekopsk	ATA/YTM	Ukraine	855
948	Xueshan	LSM	China	154
949	Hengshan	LSM	China	154
950	Taishan	LSM	China	154
A 950	Valcke	YTM	Belgium	65
951	Kuzbass	SSN	Russian Federation	656
951	Najim Al Zaffer	FFG	Egypt	216
951	Ulsan	FFG	Korea, South	464
952	R 109	FSGM	Russian Federation	677
952	Seoul	FFG	Korea, South	464
A 952	Wesp	YTL	Belgium	65
953	Chung Nam	FFG	Korea, South	464
953	R 239	FSGM	Russian Federation	677
U 953	Dubno	ATA/YTM	Ukraine	855
954	Ivanovets	FSGM	Russian Federation	677
954	R 297	FSGM	Russian Federation	677
A 954	Zeemeeuw	YTL	Belgium	65
955	Masan	FFG	Korea, South	464
955	R 60	FSGM	Russian Federation	677
A 955	Mier	YTL	Belgium	65
956	El Nasser	FFG	Egypt	216
956	Kyong Buk	FFG	Korea, South	464
957	Chon Nam	FFG	Korea, South	464
958	Che Ju	FFG	Korea, South	464
A 958	Zenobe Gramme	AXS	Belgium	64
959	Pusan	FFG	Korea, South	464
A 960	Godetia	AGFH	Belgium	65
P 960	Skjold	PTGMF	Norway	570
961	Chung Ju	FFG	Korea, South	464
961	Damyat	FFGH	Egypt	215
961	Wagio	AKL	Indonesia	365
P 961	Storm	PTGMF	Norway	570
962	R 71	FSGM	Russian Federation	677
A 962	Belgica	AGOR/PBO	Belgium	64
P 962	Skudd	PTGMF	Norway	570
A 963	Stern	AGFH	Belgium	65
P 963	Steil	PTGMF	Norway	570
P 964	Glimt	PTGMF	Norway	570
P 965	Gnist	PTGMF	Norway	570
966	Rasheed	FFGH	Egypt	215
966	Volgocherensk	PGGK	Russian Federation	680
HQ 966	Truong	AKL	Vietnam	992
970	Samara	SSN	Russian Federation	656
971	Kwanggaeto Daewang	DDGHM	Korea, South	463
971	R 298	FSGM	Russian Federation	677
971	Tanjung Kambani	AP	Indonesia	362
972	Dr Soeharso	LPD/APCR	Indonesia	360
972	Euljimundok	DDGHM	Korea, South	463
973	Tanjung Nusanive	AP	Indonesia	360
973	Yangmanchun	DDGHM	Korea, South	463
974	Tanjung Fatagar	AP	Indonesia	360
975	Chungmugong Yi Sun-Shin	DDGHM	Korea, South	461
976	Moonmu Daewang	DDGHM	Korea, South	461
977	Daejoyoung	DDGHM	Korea, South	461
978	R 19	FSGM	Russian Federation	677
978	Wang Geon	DDGHM	Korea, South	461
979	Gang Gam Chan	DDGHM	Korea, South	461
981	Choi Young	DDGHM	Korea, South	461
981	Karang Pilang	AP	Indonesia	361
982	Karang Tekok	AP	Indonesia	361
983	Karang Banteng	AP	Indonesia	361
984	Karang Galang	AP	Indonesia	361
985	Karang Unarang	AP	Indonesia	361
985	Kashalot	SSN	Russian Federation	656
990	Wudangshan	LSM	China	151
991	Emeishan	LSTH	China	153
991	Sejong Daewang	DDGHM	Korea, South	462
992	Huadingshan	LSTH	China	153
992	R 5	FSGM	Russian Federation	677
992	Yi I	DDGHM	Korea, South	462
993	Luoxiaoshan	LSTH	China	153
993	Syvatoy Giorgiy Pobedonosets	SSBN	Russian Federation	652
993	Torsö	YFB	Finland	239
994	Daiyunshan	LSTH	China	153
995	R 79	FSGM	Russian Federation	677
995	Wanyang-Shan	LSTH	China	153
996	Laotieshan	LSTH	China	153
A 996	Albatros	YTM	Belgium	65
997	Magadan	SSN	Russian Federation	656
997	Yunwashan	LSTH	China	153
998	Kunlunshan	LHD	China	152
DDG 1000	Zumwalt	DDGH	US	928
DDG 1001	Michael Mansoor	DDGH	US	928
T-AKR 1001	Adm Wm H Callaghan	AKR	US	961
1005	Fantome	YGS	Australia	36
PC 1005	Han Kang	PG	Korea, South	472
1006	Meda	YGS	Australia	36
PC 1006	Sumjinkang	PSO	Korea, South	474
1008	Duyfken	YGS	Australia	36
1009	Tom Thumb	YGS	Australia	36
1010	John Gowlland	YGS	Australia	36
1011	Geographe	YGS	Australia	36
P 1011	Titas	PTF	Bangladesh	56
1012	Casuarina	YGS	Australia	36
P 1012	Kusiyara	PTF	Bangladesh	56
P 1013	Chitra	PTF	Bangladesh	56
P 1014	Dhansiri	PTF	Bangladesh	56
1021	Conder	YGS	Australia	36
1023	Jurrat	PTG	Pakistan	587
1026	Essequibo	PBO	Guyana	317
1028	Quwwat	PTG	Pakistan	587
1029	Jalalat	PTG	Pakistan	587
1030	Shujaat	PTG	Pakistan	587
D 1051	Al Gaffa	YDT	UAE	862
GC 1051	Kukulkán	PB	Guatemala	315

Number	Ship's name	Type	Country	Page
M 1058	Fulda	MHC	Germany	291
M 1059	Weilheim	MHC	Germany	291
1060	Barkat	PBO	Pakistan	590
1061	Rehmat	PBO	Pakistan	590
M 1061	Rottweil	MCD	Germany	292
1062	Nusrat	PBO	Pakistan	590
M 1062	Sulzbach-Rosenberg	MHC	Germany	291
1063	Vehdat	PBO	Pakistan	590
M 1063	Bad Bevensen	MHC	Germany	291
M 1064	Grömitz	MHC	Germany	291
M 1065	Dillingen	MHC	Germany	291
P 1066	Subqat	PB	Pakistan	590
M 1067	Bad Rappenau	MHC	Germany	291
M 1068	Datteln	MHC	Germany	291
P 1068	Rafaqat	PB	Pakistan	590
M 1069	Homburg	MHC	Germany	291
P 1069	Sadaqat	PB	Pakistan	590
M 1090	Pegnitz	MHCD	Germany	291
M 1091	Kulmbach	MHC	Germany	291
M 1092	Hameln	MHCD	Germany	291
M 1093	Auerbach	MHCD	Germany	291
M 1094	Ensdorf	MHCD	Germany	291
M 1095	Überherrn	MHC	Germany	291
M 1096	Passau	MHC	Germany	291
M 1097	Laboe	MHC	Germany	291
M 1098	Siegburg	MHCD	Germany	291
M 1099	Herten	MHC	Germany	291
1101	Chasanyabadee	PB	Thailand	817
1101	Cheng Kung	FFGHM	Taiwan	788
PI 1101	Polaris	PBF	Mexico	520
1102	Chawengsak Songkram	PB	Thailand	818
PI 1102	Sirius	PBF	Mexico	520
1103	Cheng Ho	FFGHM	Taiwan	788
1103	Phromyothee	PB	Thailand	817
PI 1103	Capella	PBF	Mexico	520
PI 1104	Canopus	PBF	Mexico	520
1105	Chi Kuang	FFGHM	Taiwan	788
1105	Kaoh Chhlam	PBR	Cambodia	96
PI 1105	Vega	PBF	Mexico	520
1106	Kaoh Rong	PBR	Cambodia	96
1106	Yueh Fei	FFGHM	Taiwan	788
PI 1106	Achernar	PBF	Mexico	520
1107	Tzu-i	FFGHM	Taiwan	788
PI 1107	Rigel	PBF	Mexico	520
1108	Pan Chao	FFGHM	Taiwan	788
PI 1108	Arcturus	PBF	Mexico	520
1109	Chang Chien	FFGHM	Taiwan	788
PI 1109	Alpheratz	PBF	Mexico	520
1110	Tien Tan	FFGHM	Taiwan	788
PI 1110	Procyón	PBF	Mexico	520
PI 1111	Avior	PBF	Mexico	520
PI 1112	Deneb	PBF	Mexico	520
PI 1113	Fomalhaut	PBF	Mexico	520
PI 1114	Pollux	PBF	Mexico	520
PI 1115	Régulus	PBF	Mexico	520
PI 1116	Acrux	PBF	Mexico	520
PI 1117	Spica	PBF	Mexico	520
PI 1118	Hadar	PBF	Mexico	520
PI 1119	Shaula	PBF	Mexico	520
PI 1120	Mirfak	PBF	Mexico	520
PI 1121	Ankaa	PBF	Mexico	520
PI 1122	Bellatrix	PBF	Mexico	520
T-AOT 1122	Paul Buck	AOT	US	959
PI 1123	Elnath	PBF	Mexico	520
T-AOT 1123	Samuel L Cobb	AOT	US	959
PI 1124	Alnilán	PBF	Mexico	520
T-AOT 1124	Richard G Matthiesen	AOT	US	959
PI 1125	Peacock	PBF	Mexico	520
T-AOT 1125	Lawrence H Gianella	AOT	US	959
PI 1126	Betelgeuse	PBF	Mexico	520
PI 1127	Adhara	PBF	Mexico	520
PI 1128	Alioth	PBF	Mexico	520
PI 1129	Rasalhague	PBF	Mexico	520
PI 1130	Nunki	PBF	Mexico	520
1131	Mondolkiri	PBF	Cambodia	96
PI 1131	Hamal	PBF	Mexico	520
PI 1132	Suhail	PBF	Mexico	520
PI 1133	Dubhe	PBF	Mexico	520
1134	Ratanakiri	PBF	Cambodia	96
PI 1134	Denebola	PBF	Mexico	520
PI 1135	Alkaid	PBF	Mexico	520
PI 1136	Alphecca	PBF	Mexico	520
PI 1137	Eltanin	PBF	Mexico	520
PI 1138	Kochab	PBF	Mexico	520
PI 1139	Enif	PBF	Mexico	520
P 1140	Cacine	PBO	Portugal	633
PI 1140	Schedar	PBF	Mexico	520
PI 1141	Markab	PBF	Mexico	520
M 1142	Umzimkulu	MHC	South Africa	737
PI 1142	Megrez	PBF	Mexico	520
PI 1143	Mizar	PBF	Mexico	520
P 1144	Quanza	PBO	Portugal	633
PI 1144	Phekda	PBF	Mexico	520
PI 1145	Acamar	PBF	Mexico	520
P 1146	Zaire	PBO	Portugal	633
PI 1146	Diphda	PBF	Mexico	520
PI 1147	Menkar	PBF	Mexico	520
PI 1148	Sabik	PBF	Mexico	520
P 1150	Argos	PBR	Portugal	634
P 1151	Dragão	PBR	Portugal	634
P 1152	Escorpião	PBR	Portugal	634
P 1153	Cassiopeia	PBR	Portugal	634
P 1154	Hidra	PBR	Portugal	634
P 1155	Centauro	PBR	Portugal	634
P 1156	Orion	PBR	Portugal	634
P 1157	Pégaso	PBR	Portugal	634
P 1158	Sagitario	PBR	Portugal	634
1161	Maroub	PBR	Sudan	767
P 1161	Save	PBO	Portugal	633
1162	Fijab	PBR	Sudan	767
1163	Salak	PBR	Sudan	767
1164	Halote	PBR	Sudan	767
P 1165	Aguia	PBR	Portugal	634
P 1167	Cisne	PBR	Portugal	634
1201	Baklan	HSIC	Yemen	993
PI 1201	Isla Coronado	PBF	Mexico	521
1202	Kang Ding	FFGHM	Taiwan	789
1202	Siyan	HSIC	Yemen	993
PI 1202	Isla Lobos	PBF	Mexico	521
1203	Si Ning	FFGHM	Taiwan	789
1203	Zuhrab	HSIC	Yemen	993
PI 1203	Isla Guadalupe	PBF	Mexico	521
1204	Akissan	HSIC	Yemen	993
PI 1204	Isla Cozumel	PBF	Mexico	521
1205	Hunaish	HSIC	Yemen	993
1205	Kun Ming	FFGHM	Taiwan	789
1206	Di Hua	FFGHM	Taiwan	789
1206	Zakr	HSIC	Yemen	993
1207	Wu Chang	FFGHM	Taiwan	789
1208	Chen Te	FFGHM	Taiwan	789
M 1212	Umhloti	MHC	South Africa	737
1301	Yung Feng	MHC	Taiwan	794
PI 1301	Acuario	PBF	Mexico	522
WPB 1301	Farallon	WPB	US	966
1302	Yung Chia	MHC	Taiwan	794
PI 1302	Aguila	PBF	Mexico	522
1303	Yung Ting	MHC	Taiwan	794
PI 1303	Aries	PBF	Mexico	522
PI 1304	Auriga	PBF	Mexico	522
WPB 1304	Maui	WPB	US	966
1305	Yung Shun	MHC	Taiwan	794
PI 1305	Cancer	PBF	Mexico	522
1306	Yung Yang	MSO	Taiwan	794
PI 1306	Capricorno	PBF	Mexico	522
1307	Yung TZU	MSO	Taiwan	794
PI 1307	Centauro	PBF	Mexico	522
WPB 1307	Ocracoke	WPB	US	966
1308	Yung Ku	MSO	Taiwan	794
PI 1308	Geminis	PBF	Mexico	522
1309	Yung Teh	MSO	Taiwan	794
WPB 1309	Aquidneck	WPB	US	966
WPB 1310	Mustang	WPB	US	966
1311	Pengawal 11	PB	Malaysia	505
WPB 1311	Naushon	WPB	US	966
1312	Pengawal 12	PB	Malaysia	505
LST 1312	Ambe	LST	Nigeria	565
WPB 1312	Sanibel	WPB	US	966
WPB 1313	Edisto	WPB	US	966
WPB 1314	Sapelo	WPB	US	966
WPB 1315	Matinicus	WPB	US	966
WPB 1316	Nantucket	WPB	US	966
WPB 1318	Baranof	WPB	US	966
WPB 1319	Chandeleur	WPB	US	966
WPB 1320	Chincoteague	WPB	US	966
WPB 1321	Cushing	WPB	US	966
WPB 1322	Cuttyhunk	WPB	US	966
WPB 1323	Drummond	WPB	US	966
WPB 1324	Key Largo	WPB	US	966
WPB 1326	Monomoy	WPB	US	966
WPB 1327	Orcas	WPB	US	966
WPB 1329	Sitkinak	WPB	US	966
WPB 1330	Tybee	WPB	US	966
WPB 1331	Washington	WPB	US	966
WPB 1332	Wrangell	WPB	US	966
WPB 1333	Adak	WPB	US	966
WPB 1334	Liberty	WPB	US	966
WPB 1335	Anacapa	WPB	US	966
WPB 1336	Kiska	WPB	US	966
WPB 1337	Assateague	WPB	US	966
WPB 1338	Grand Isle	WPB	US	966
WPB 1339	Key Biscayne	WPB	US	966
WPB 1340	Jefferson Island	WPB	US	966
WPB 1341	Kodiak Island	WPB	US	966
WPB 1342	Long Island	WPB	US	966
WPB 1343	Bainbridge Island	WPB	US	966
WPB 1344	Block Island	WPB	US	966
WPB 1345	Staten Island	WPB	US	966
WPB 1346	Roanoke Island	WPB	US	966
WPB 1347	Pea Island	WPB	US	966
WPB 1348	Knight Island	WPB	US	966
WPB 1349	Galveston Island	WPB	US	966
AM 1353	Coral Snake	–	Australia	40
1401	Hendijan	PBO	Iran	379
PI 1401	Miaplacidus	PBF	Mexico	522
1402	Sirik	PBO	Iran	379
PI 1402	Algol	PBF	Mexico	522
1403	Konarak	PBO	Iran	379
PI 1403	Beaver	PBF	Mexico	522
1404	Gavatar	PBO	Iran	379
PI 1404	Merak	PBF	Mexico	522
1405	Mooam	PBO	Iran	379
PI 1405	Caph	PBF	Mexico	522
1406	Bahregan	PBO	Iran	379
PI 1406	Mirach	PBF	Mexico	522
1407	Kalat	PBO	Iran	379
1408	Genaveh	PBO	Iran	379
1409	Rostani	PBO	Iran	379
A 1409	Wilhelm Pullwer	YAG	Germany	292
1410	Nayband	PBO	Iran	379
1411	Pengawal 1	PB	Malaysia	505
A 1411	Berlin	AFSH	Germany	293
1412	Pengawal 2	PB	Malaysia	505
A 1412	Frankfurt Am Main	AFSH	Germany	293
1413	Pengawal 3	PB	Malaysia	505
1414	Pengawal 4	PB	Malaysia	505
1415	Pengawal 5	PB	Malaysia	505
1416	Pengawal 6	PB	Malaysia	505
1417	Pengawal 7	PB	Malaysia	505
1418	Pengawal 8	PB	Malaysia	505
A 1425	Ammersee	AOL	Germany	294

Number	Ship's name	Type	Country	Page
A 1426	Tegernsee	AOL	Germany	294
A 1435	Westerwald	AEL	Germany	294
A 1437	Planet	AGE	Germany	292
A 1439	Baltrum	ATS/YDT	Germany	296
A 1440	Juist	ATS/YDT	Germany	296
A 1441	Langeoog	ATS/YDT	Germany	296
A 1442	Spessart	AOL	Germany	294
A 1443	Rhön	AOL	Germany	294
A 1451	Wangerooge	ATS/YDT	Germany	296
A 1452	Spiekeroog	ATS/YDT	Germany	296
A 1456	Alliance	AGOR	NATO	546
A 1458	Fehmarn	ATR	Germany	295
FNH 1491	Punta Caxinas	LCU	Honduras	319
M 1499	Umkomaas	MHC	South Africa	737
1501	Jaemin I	ARSH	Korea, South	473
1502	Jaemin II	ARS	Korea, South	474
1503	Jaemin III	ARSH	Korea, South	474
1503	Sri Indera Sakti	AOR/AE/AXH	Malaysia	500
1504	Mahawangsa	AOR/AE/AXH	Malaysia	500
1505	Sri Inderapura	LSTH	Malaysia	499
1507	Jaemin VII	ARSH	Korea, South	475
1508	Jaemin VIII	ARSH	Korea, South	475
A 1531	E 1	AXL	Turkey	840
A 1532	E 2	AXL	Turkey	840
A 1533	E 3	AXL	Turkey	840
A 1534	E 4	AXL	Turkey	840
A 1535	E 5	AXL	Turkey	840
A 1536	E 6	AXL	Turkey	840
A 1537	E 7	AXL	Turkey	840
A 1538	E 8	AXL	Turkey	840
A 1542	Söndüren 2	YTB/YTM/YTL	Turkey	843
A 1543	Söndüren 3	YTB/YTM/YTL	Turkey	843
A 1544	Söndüren 4	YTB/YTM/YTL	Turkey	843
P 1552	Tobie	PB	South Africa	737
P 1553	Tern	PB	South Africa	737
P 1554	Tekwane	PB	South Africa	737
P 1565	Isaac Dyobha	PG	South Africa	736
P 1567	Galeshewe	PG	South Africa	736
1571	Penyelamat 1	PB	Malaysia	504
1572	Penyelamat 2	PB	Malaysia	504
1573	Penyelamat 3	PB	Malaysia	504
1574	Penyelamat 4	PB	Malaysia	504
A 1600	Iskenderun	AK	Turkey	840
1601	Ta Kuan	AGOR	Taiwan	794
LEP 1601	Ona	WPB	Chile	125
LEP 1602	Yagan	WPB	Chile	125
LEP 1603	Alacalufe	WPB	Chile	125
LEP 1604	Hallef	WPB	Chile	125
LSG 1609	Aysén	WPB	Chile	125
LSG 1610	Corral	WPB	Chile	125
LSG 1611	Conceptión	WPB	Chile	125
LSG 1612	Caldera	WPB	Chile	125
LSG 1613	San Antonio	WPB	Chile	125
LSG 1614	Antofagasta	WPB	Chile	125
LSG 1615	Arica	WPB	Chile	125
LSG 1616	Coquimbo	WPB	Chile	125
LSG 1617	Puerto Natales	WPB	Chile	125
LSG 1618	Valparaíso	WPB	Chile	125
LSG 1619	Punta Arenas	WPB	Chile	125
LSG 1620	Talcahuano	WPB	Chile	125
LSG 1621	Quintero	WPB	Chile	125
LSG 1622	Chiloé	WPB	Chile	125
LSG 1623	Puerto Montt	WPB	Chile	125
LSG 1624	Iquique	WPB	Chile	125
Y 1643	Bottsand	YPC	Germany	295
Y 1644	Eversand	YPC	Germany	295
Y 1656	Wustrow	YTM	Germany	296
Y 1658	Dranske	YTM	Germany	296
Y 1671	AK 1	YFL	Germany	294
Y 1675	AM 8	YFL	Germany	295
Y 1676	MA 2	YFL	Germany	294
Y 1677	MA 3	YFL	Germany	294
Y 1678	MA 1	YFL	Germany	294
Y 1679	AM 7	YFL	Germany	295
Y 1683	AK 6	YFL	Germany	295
Y 1685	Aschau	YFL	Germany	294
Y 1686	AK 2	YFL	Germany	295
Y 1687	Borby	YFL	Germany	294
Y 1689	Bums	YAG	Germany	293
LSR 1700	Tokerau	SAR	Chile	125
1701	Peninjau	PB	Malaysia	504
LSR 1703	Pelluhue	WPB	Chile	125
LSR 1704	Arauco	WPB	Chile	125
LSR 1705	Chacao	WPB	Chile	125
LSR 1706	Queitao	WPB	Chile	125
LSR 1707	Guaiteca	WPB	Chile	125
LSR 1708	Curaumila	WPB	Chile	125
1801	Keelung	DDGHM	Taiwan	787
1801	Penggalang 1	PB	Malaysia	504
DT 1801	Quokka	YTL	Australia	39
1802	Damrong Rachanuphap	PBO	Thailand	817
1802	Penggalang 2	PB	Malaysia	504
1802	Suao	DDGHM	Taiwan	787
1803	Lopburi Rames	PBO	Thailand	817
1803	Tsoying	DDGHM	Taiwan	787
1804	Srinakarin	PSO	Thailand	817
1805	Makung	DDGHM	Taiwan	787
1814	Diaz	PB	Chile	121
1815	Bolados	PB	Chile	121
1816	Salinas	PB	Chile	121
1817	Tellez	PB	Chile	121
1818	Bravo	PB	Chile	121
1820	Machado	PB	Chile	121
1822	Troncoso	PB	Chile	121
1823	Hudson	PB	Chile	121
LPM 1901	Maule	WPB	Chile	126
LPM 1902	Rapel	WPB	Chile	126
LPM 1903	Aconcagua	WPB	Chile	126
LPM 1904	Lauca	WPB	Chile	126
LPM 1905	Isluga	WPB	Chile	126
LPM 1907	Maullín	WPB	Chile	126
LPM 1908	Copiapó	WPB	Chile	126
LPM 1909	Cau-Cau	WPB	Chile	126
LPM 1910	Pudeto	WPB	Chile	126
LPM 1911	Robinson Crusoe	WPB	Chile	126
2001	Seal	YDT/PB	Australia	39
LCU 2001	Runnymede	LCU-ARMY	US	947
LCU 2001	Yusoutei-Ichi-Gou	LCU	Japan	430
LCU 2002	Kennesaw Mountain	LCU-ARMY	US	947
LCU 2002	Yusoutei-Ni-Gou	LCU	Japan	430
2003	Malu Baizam	YDT/PB	Australia	39
LCU 2003	Macon	LCU-ARMY	US	947
2004	Shark	YDT/PB	Australia	39
LCU 2004	Aldie	LCU-ARMY	US	947
LCU 2005	Brandy Station	LCU-ARMY	US	947
LCU 2006	Bristoe Station	LCU-ARMY	US	947
LCU 2007	Broad Run	LCU-ARMY	US	947
LCU 2008	Buena Vista	LCU-ARMY	US	947
LCU 2009	Calaboza	LCU-ARMY	US	947
LCU 2010	Cedar Run	LCU-ARMY	US	947
LCU 2011	Chickahominy	LCU-ARMY	US	947
LCU 2012	Chickasaw Bayou	LCU-ARMY	US	947
2013	Almaty	PB	Kazakhstan	449
LCU 2013	Churubusco	LCU-ARMY	US	947
LCU 2014	Coamo	LCU-ARMY	US	947
LCU 2015	Contreras	LCU-ARMY	US	947
LCU 2016	Corinth	LCU-ARMY	US	947
LCU 2017	El Caney	LCU-ARMY	US	947
LCU 2018	Five Forks	LCU-ARMY	US	947
LCU 2019	Fort Donelson	LCU-ARMY	US	947
LCU 2020	Fort Mchenry	LCU-ARMY	US	947
LCU 2021	Great Bridge	LCU-ARMY	US	947
LCU 2022	Harpers Ferry	LCU-ARMY	US	947
2023	Aktau	PB	Kazakhstan	449
LCU 2023	Hobkirk	LCU-ARMY	US	947
LCU 2024	Homigueros	LCU-ARMY	US	947
LCU 2025	Malvern Hill	LCU-ARMY	US	947
LCU 2026	Matamoros	LCU-ARMY	US	947
LCU 2027	Mechanicsville	LCU-ARMY	US	947
LCU 2028	Missionary Bridge	LCU-ARMY	US	947
LCU 2029	Molino Del Ray	LCU-ARMY	US	947
LCU 2030	Monterrey	LCU-ARMY	US	947
LCU 2031	New Orleans	LCU-ARMY	US	947
LCU 2032	Palo Alto	LCU-ARMY	US	947
2033	Atyrau	PB	Kazakhstan	449
LCU 2033	Paulus Hook	LCU-ARMY	US	947
LCU 2034	Perryville	LCU-ARMY	US	947
LCU 2035	Port Hudson	LCU-ARMY	US	947
2043	Schambyl	PB	Kazakhstan	449
T-AKR 2044	Cape Orlando	AKR	US	961
LCAC 2101	Air Cushion-tei - 1 - Gou	LCAC	Japan	430
LCAC 2102	Air Cushion-tei - 2 - Gou	LCAC	Japan	430
LCAC 2103	Air Cushion-tei - 3 - Gou	LCAC	Japan	430
LCAC 2104	Air Cushion-tei - 4 - Gou	LCAC	Japan	430
LCAC 2105	Air Cushion-tei - 5 - Gou	LCAC	Japan	430
LCAC 2106	Air Cushion-tei - 6 - Gou	LCAC	Japan	430
2161	Sembilang	PB	Malaysia	504
2162	Alu-Alu	PB	Malaysia	504
2163	Mersuji	PB	Malaysia	504
2164	Siakap	PB	Malaysia	504
2201	Nusa	PB	Malaysia	504
2202	Rentap	PB	Malaysia	504
GN 2301	Utique	PB	Tunisia	826
2344	Al Amane	SAR	Morocco	537
2345	Ait Baâmrane	SAR	Morocco	537
2551	Malawali	PB	Malaysia	504
2552	Serasan	PB	Malaysia	504
2553	Manjung	PB	Malaysia	504
2554	Tebrau	PB	Malaysia	504
2601	Rhu	PB	Malaysia	504
DT 2601	Tammar	YTL	Australia	39
2602	Stapa	PB	Malaysia	504
T-AK 3000	CPL Louis J Hauge, Jr	AKRH	US	960
3001	Tae Pung Yang I	ARSH	Korea, South	473
3002	Tae Pung Yang II	ARSH	Korea, South	475
T-AK 3002	PFC James Anderson, Jr	AKRH	US	960
T-AK 3003	1st Lt Alex Bonnyman	AKRH	US	960
T-AK 3005	SGT Matej Kocak	AKH	US	961
3006	Tae Pung Yang VI	ARSH	Korea, South	475
L 3006	Largs Bay	LSD	UK	893
T-AK 3006	PFC Eugene A Obregon	AKH	US	961
3007	Tae Pung Yang VII	ARSH	Korea, South	475
L 3007	Lyme Bay	LSD	UK	893
T-AK 3007	MAJ Stephen W Pless	AKH	US	961
3008	Tae Pung Yang VIII	ARSH	Korea, South	475
L 3008	Mounts Bay	LSD	UK	893
T-AK 3008	2nd Lt John P Bobo	AKRH	US	961
L 3009	Cardigan Bay	LSD	UK	893
T-AK 3009	PFC Dewayne T Williams	AKRH	US	961
T-AK 3010	1st Lt Baldomero Lopez	AKRH	US	961
T-AK 3011	1st Lt Jack Lummus	AKRH	US	961
T-AK 3012	SGT William R Button	AKRH	US	961
T-AK 3015	1st Lt Harry L Martin	AK	US	960
T-AK 3016	L/CPL Roy M Wheat	AK	US	960
T-AK 3017	GYSGT Fred W Stockham	AKR	US	960
P 3100	Mamba	PB	Kenya	450
P 3126	Nyayo	PGGF	Kenya	450
P 3127	Umoja	PGGF	Kenya	450
P 3130	Shujaa	PBO	Kenya	450
3131	Sipadan	PB	Malaysia	503
P 3131	Shupavu	PBO	Kenya	450
3132	Lang	PB	Malaysia	503
3133	Segantang	PB	Malaysia	503
3134	Jarak	PB	Malaysia	503
3135	Kukup	PB	Malaysia	503
3136	Sempadi	PB	Malaysia	503
3137	Labas	PB	Malaysia	503
3138	Nyireh	PB	Malaysia	503
3139	Kuraman	PB	Malaysia	503
3140	Siamil	PB	Malaysia	503

Number	Ship's name	Type	Country	Page
3141	Pemanggil	PB	Malaysia	503
3142	Bidong	PB	Malaysia	503
3143	Satang	PB	Malaysia	503
3144	Rumbia	PB	Malaysia	503
3145	Ligitan	PB	Malaysia	503
3221	Ramunia	PB	Malaysia	504
3222	Marudu	PB	Malaysia	504
3223	Danga	PB	Malaysia	504
3224	Siangin	PB	Malaysia	504
3225	Kimanis	PB	Malaysia	504
P 3301	Ardhana	PB	UAE	859
P 3302	Zurara	PB	UAE	859
P 3303	Murban	PB	UAE	859
P 3304	Al Ghullan	PB	UAE	859
P 3305	Radoom	PB	UAE	859
P 3306	Ghanadhah	PB	UAE	859
3501	Ilocos Norte	PB	Philippines	614
3501	Perdana	PTFG	Malaysia	499
A 3501	Annad	YTB	UAE	862
3502	Nueva Vizcaya	PB	Philippines	614
3502	Serang	PTFG	Malaysia	499
3503	Ganas	PTFG	Malaysia	499
3503	Romblon	PB	Philippines	614
3504	Davao Del Norte	PB	Philippines	614
3504	Ganyang	PTFG	Malaysia	499
3505	Jerong	PB	Malaysia	499
3506	Todak	PB	Malaysia	499
3507	Paus	PB	Malaysia	499
3508	Yu	PB	Malaysia	499
TV 3508	Kashima	AXH/TV	Japan	433
3509	Baung	PB	Malaysia	499
3510	Pari	PB	Malaysia	499
3511	Handalan	PTFG	Malaysia	498
3512	Perkasa	PTFG	Malaysia	498
3513	Pendekar	PTFG	Malaysia	498
TV 3513	Shimayuki	AXGHM/TV	Japan	433
3514	Gempita	PTFG	Malaysia	498
TV 3515	Yamagiri	AX/TV	Japan	434
TV 3516	Asagiri	AX/TV	Japan	434
P 3568	Pukaki	PBO	New Zealand	560
P 3569	Rotoiti	PBO	New Zealand	560
P 3570	Taupo	PBO	New Zealand	560
P 3571	Hawea	PBO	New Zealand	560
TSS 3601	Asashio	SSK	Japan	416
TSS 3606	Hayashio	SSK	Japan	416
P 3711	Um Almaradim	PBM	Kuwait	476
P 3713	Ouha	PBM	Kuwait	476
P 3715	Failaka	PBM	Kuwait	476
P 3717	Maskan	PBM	Kuwait	476
P 3719	Al-Ahmadi	PBM	Kuwait	476
P 3721	Alfahaheel	PBM	Kuwait	476
P 3723	Al-Yarmouk	PBM	Kuwait	476
P 3725	Garoh	PBM	Kuwait	476
3901	Gagah	PBF	Malaysia	504
3902	Tabah	PBF	Malaysia	504
3903	Cekal	PBF	Malaysia	504
3904	Berani	PBF	Malaysia	504
3905	Setia	PBF	Malaysia	504
3906	Amanah	PBF	Malaysia	504
3907	Jujur	PBF	Malaysia	504
3908	Ikhlas	PBF	Malaysia	504
3909	Budiman	PBF	Malaysia	504
3910	Tegas	PBF	Malaysia	504
3911	Mulia	PBF	Malaysia	504
3912	Bijak	PBF	Malaysia	504
3913	Adil	PBF	Malaysia	504
3914	Pintar	PBF	Malaysia	504
3915	Bistari	PBF	Malaysia	504
4001	Marlin	AX	Malaysia	505
LST 4001	Oosumi	LPD/LSTH	Japan	429
LST 4002	Shimokita	LPD/LSTH	Japan	429
LST 4003	Kunisaki	LPD/LSTH	Japan	429
LSU 4171	Yura	LSU/LCU	Japan	430
LSU 4172	Noto	LSU/LCU	Japan	430
ATS 4202	Kurobe	AVM/TV	Japan	434
ATS 4203	Tenryu	AVHM/TV	Japan	434
T-AK 4296	Capt Steven L Bennett	AK	US	960
AMS 4301	Hiuchi	YTT	Japan	436
AMS 4302	Suou	YTT	Japan	436
AMS 4303	Amakusa	YTT	Japan	436
AMS 4304	Genkai	YTT	Japan	436
AMS 4305	Enshuu	YTT	Japan	436
T-AK 4396	Maj Bernard F Fisher	AK	US	959
P 4505	Al Sanbouk	PGGF	Kuwait	475
L 4510	Trondenes	LCP	Norway	571
L 4511	Hysnes	LCP	Norway	571
L 4512	Hellen	LCP	Norway	571
L 4513	Torås	LCP	Norway	571
L 4514	Møvik	LCP	Norway	571
L 4520	Skrolsvik	LCP	Norway	571
L 4521	Kråkenes	LCP	Norway	571
L 4522	Stangnes	LCP	Norway	571
L 4523	Kjøkøy	LCP	Norway	571
L 4524	Mørvika	LCP	Norway	571
L 4525	Kopås	LCP	Norway	571
L 4526	Tangen	LCP	Norway	571
L 4527	Oddane	LCP	Norway	571
L 4528	Malmøya	LCP	Norway	571
L 4529	Brettingen	LCP	Norway	571
L 4530	Løkhaug	LCP	Norway	571
L 4531	Søviknes	LCP	Norway	571
L 4532	Osternes	LCP	Norway	571
L 4533	Fjell	LCP	Norway	571
L 4534	Lerøy	LCP	Norway	571
T-AK 4543	LTC John U D Page	AK	US	960
T-AK 4544	SSGT Edward A Carter	AK	US	960
HSV 4676	Westpac Express	HSV	US	951
5001	Sambongho	PSO	Korea, South	474
T-AG 5001	VADM K R Wheeler	AG	US	959
AGB 5003	Shirase	AGBH	Japan	436
T-AK 5029	Cape Jacob	AK/AKR/AE	US	961
T-AK 5051	Cape Gibson	AK/AKR/AE	US	961
T-AKR 5051	Cape Ducato	AKR	US	961
T-AKR 5052	Cape Douglas	AKR	US	961
T-AKR 5053	Cape Domingo	AKR	US	961
T-AKR 5054	Cape Decision	AKR	US	961
T-AKR 5055	Cape Diamond	AKR	US	961
T-AKR 5062	Cape Isabel	AKR	US	961
T-AKR 5063	Cape May	AK/AKR	US	962
T-AKR 5065	Cape Mohican	AK/AKR	US	962
T-AKR 5066	Cape Hudson	AKR	US	961
T-AKR 5067	Cape Henry	AKR	US	961
T-AKR 5068	Cape Horn	AKR	US	961
T-AKR 5069	Cape Edmont	AKR	US	961
T-AK 5070	Cape Flattery	AK/AKR	US	962
T-AK 5073	Cape Farewell	AK/AKR	US	962
T-AKR 5076	Cape Inscription	AKR	US	961
T-AKR 5082	Cape Knox	AKR	US	961
T-AKR 5083	Cape Kennedy	AKR	US	961
AGS 5102	Futami	AGS	Japan	432
AGS 5103	Suma	AGS	Japan	432
AGS 5104	Wakasa	AGS	Japan	432
AGS 5105	Nichinan	AGS	Japan	432
AOS 5201	Hibiki	AGOSH	Japan	432
AOS 5202	Harima	AGOSH	Japan	432
A 5203	Andromeda	AGSC	Portugal	635
A 5204	Polar	AXS	Portugal	636
A 5205	Auriga	AGSC	Portugal	635
A 5210	Bérrio	AORLH	Portugal	636
A 5302	Caroly	AXS	Italy	405
A 5303	Ammiraglio Magnaghi	AGSH	Italy	404
A 5304	Aretusa	AGS	Italy	404
A 5308	Galatea	AGS	Italy	404
A 5309	Anteo	ARSH	Italy	407
A 5311	Palinuro	AXS	Italy	405
A 5312	Amerigo Vespucci	AXS	Italy	404
A 5313	Stella Polare	AXS	Italy	405
A 5315	Raffaele Rossetti	AG/AGOR	Italy	404
A 5316	Corsaro II	AXS	Italy	405
A 5318	Prometeo	ATR	Italy	408
A 5319	Ciclope	ATR	Italy	408
A 5320	Vincenzo Martellotta	AG/AGE	Italy	404
A 5322	Capricia	AXS	Italy	405
A 5323	Orsa Maggiore	AXS	Italy	405
A 5324	Titano	ATR	Italy	408
A 5325	Polifemo	ATR	Italy	408
A 5326	Etna	AORH	Italy	406
A 5327	Stromboli	AORH	Italy	406
A 5328	Gigante	ATR	Italy	408
A 5329	Vesuvio	AORH	Italy	406
A 5330	Saturno	ATR	Italy	408
A 5340	Elettra	AGORH/ AGE/AGI	Italy	404
A 5347	Gorgona	AKL	Italy	407
A 5348	Tremiti	AKL	Italy	407
A 5349	Caprera	AKL	Italy	407
A 5351	Pantelleria	AKL	Italy	407
A 5352	Lipari	AKL	Italy	407
A 5353	Capri	AKL	Italy	407
A 5359	Bormida	AWT	Italy	407
A 5364	Ponza	ABU	Italy	407
A 5365	Tenace	ATR	Italy	408
A 5366	Levanzo	ABU	Italy	407
A 5367	Tavolara	ABU	Italy	407
A 5368	Palmaria	ABU	Italy	407
A 5370	Panarea	AWT	Italy	406
A 5371	Linosa	AWT	Italy	406
A 5372	Favignana	AWT	Italy	406
A 5373	Salina	AWT	Italy	406
A 5376	Ticino	AWT	Italy	407
A 5377	Tirso	AWT	Italy	407
A 5379	Astice	AXL	Italy	405
A 5380	Mitilo	AXL	Italy	405
A 5382	Porpora	AXL	Italy	405
A 5383	Procida	ABU	Italy	407
A 5390	Leonardo	AGOR(C)	NATO	546
S 5509	Al Dorrar	SS	Kuwait	476
M 5550	Lerici	MHSC	Italy	403
M 5551	Sapri	MHSC	Italy	403
M 5552	Milazzo	MHSC	Italy	403
M 5553	Vieste	MHSC	Italy	403
M 5554	Gaeta	MHSC	Italy	403
M 5555	Termoli	MHSC	Italy	403
M 5556	Alghero	MHSC	Italy	403
M 5557	Numana	MHSC	Italy	403
M 5558	Crotone	MHSC	Italy	403
M 5559	Viareggio	MHSC	Italy	403
M 5560	Chioggia	MHSC	Italy	403
M 5561	Rimini	MHSC	Italy	403
P 5702	Istiqlal	PGGF	Kuwait	476
ASE 6101	Kurihama	ASE/AGE	Japan	433
ASE 6102	Asuka	AGEH	Japan	433
6111	Dokdo	LPD	Korea, South	469
P 6121	Gepard	PGGFM	Germany	290
P 6122	Puma	PGGFM	Germany	290
P 6123	Hermelin	PGGFM	Germany	290
P 6124	Nerz	PGGFM	Germany	290
P 6125	Zobel	PGGFM	Germany	290
P 6126	Frettchen	PGGFM	Germany	290
P 6127	Dachs	PGGFM	Germany	290
P 6128	Ozelot	PGGFM	Germany	290
P 6129	Wiesel	PGGFM	Germany	290
P 6130	Hyäne	PGGFM	Germany	290
7501	Langkawi	PSOH	Malaysia	503
7502	Banggi	PSOH	Malaysia	503
Y 8005	Nieuwediep	YFL	Netherlands	557
Y 8018	Breezand	YTL	Netherlands	557
Y 8019	Balgzand	YTL	Netherlands	557
Y 8050	Urania	AXS	Netherlands	555
Y 8055	Schelde	YTL	Netherlands	557

Number	Ship's name	Type	Country	Page
Y 8056	Wierbalg	YTL	Netherlands	557
Y 8057	Malzwin	YTL	Netherlands	557
Y 8058	Zuidwal	YTL	Netherlands	557
Y 8059	Westwal	YTL	Netherlands	557
P 8111	Durbar	PTFG	Bangladesh	56
P 8112	Duranta	PTFG	Bangladesh	56
P 8113	Durvedya	PTFG	Bangladesh	56
P 8114	Durdam	PTFG	Bangladesh	56
P 8125	Durdharsha	PTFG	Bangladesh	56
P 8126	Durdanta	PTFG	Bangladesh	56
8127	Sir William Roe	YFRT	UK	894
P 8128	Dordanda	PTFG	Bangladesh	56
P 8131	Anirban	PTFG	Bangladesh	56
P 8141	Uttal	PTFG	Bangladesh	56
A 8201	Punta Barima	PB	Venezuela	986
A 8202	Punta Mosquito	PB	Venezuela	986
A 8203	Punta Mulatos	PB	Venezuela	986
A 8204	Punta Perret	PB	Venezuela	986
A 8205	Punta Cardon	PB	Venezuela	986
A 8206	Punta Playa	PB	Venezuela	986
P 8221	TB 1	PTL	Bangladesh	58
P 8222	TB 2	PTL	Bangladesh	58
P 8223	TB 3	PTL	Bangladesh	58
P 8224	TB 4	PTL	Bangladesh	58
P 8235	TB 35	PTK	Bangladesh	56
P 8236	TB 36	PTK	Bangladesh	56
P 8237	TB 37	PTK	Bangladesh	56
P 8238	TB 38	PTK	Bangladesh	56
A 8307	Punta Macoya	PB	Venezuela	986
A 8308	Punta Moron	PB	Venezuela	986
A 8309	Punta Unare	PB	Venezuela	986
A 8310	Punta Ballena	PB	Venezuela	986
A 8311	Punta Macuro	PB	Venezuela	986
A 8312	Punta Mariusa	PB	Venezuela	986
B 8421	Rio Arauca II	PB	Venezuela	986
B 8422	Rio Catatumbo II	PB	Venezuela	986
B 8423	Rio Apure II	PB	Venezuela	986
B 8424	Rio Negro II	PB	Venezuela	986
B 8425	Rio Meta II	PB	Venezuela	986
B 8426	Rio Portuguesa II	PB	Venezuela	986
B 8427	Rio Sarare	PB	Venezuela	986
B 8428	Rio Uribante	PB	Venezuela	986
B 8429	Rio Sinaruco	PB	Venezuela	986
B 8430	Rio Icabaru	PB	Venezuela	986
B 8431	Rio Guarico II	PB	Venezuela	986
B 8432	Rio Yaracuy	PB	Venezuela	986
FNH 8501	Chamelecon	PB	Honduras	318
Y 8760	Patria	AOTL	Netherlands	556
L 9011	Foudre	LSDH/TCD 90	France	264
L 9012	Siroco	LSDH/TCD 90	France	264
L 9013	Mistral	LHDM/BPC	France	263
L 9014	Tonnerre	LHDM/BPC	France	263
L 9031	Francis Garnier	LSTH	France	265
L 9032	Dumont d'Urville	LSTH	France	265
L 9033	Jacques Cartier	LSTH	France	265
L 9034	La Grandière	LSTH	France	265
L 9051	Sabre	LCT	France	265
L 9052	Dague	LCT	France	265
L 9061	Rapière	LCT	France	265
L 9062	Hallebarde	LCT	France	265
L 9090	Gapeau	LSL	France	270
T-AOT 9109	Petersburg	AOT	US	961
9423	Nesbitt	YGS	UK	889
9424	Pat Barton	YGS	UK	889
9425	Cook	YGS	UK	889
9426	Owen	YGS	UK	889
T-AKR 9666	Cape Vincent	AKR	US	961
T-AKR 9678	Cape Rise	AKR	US	961
T-AKR 9679	Cape Ray	AKR	US	961
T-AKR 9701	Cape Victory	AKR	US	961
T-AKR 9711	Cape Trinity	AKR	US	961
L 9892	San Giorgio	LPD	Italy	402
L 9893	San Marco	LPD	Italy	402
L 9894	San Giusto	LPD	Italy	402
T-AKR 9960	Cape Race	AKR	US	961
T-AKR 9961	Cape Washington	AKR	US	961
T-AKR 9962	Cape Wrath	AKR	US	961
21689	Dugong	YDT/PB	Australia	39
WLI 65400	Bayberry	WLI/ABU	US	970
WLI 65401	Elderberry	WLI/ABU	US	970
WLR 65501	Ouachita	WLR	US	970
WLR 65502	Cimarron	WLR	US	970
WLR 65503	Obion	WLR	US	970
WLR 65504	Scioto	WLR	US	970
WLR 65505	Osage	WLR	US	970
WLR 65506	Sangamon	WLR	US	970
WYTL 65601	Capstan	WYTL	US	971
WYTL 65602	Chock	WYTL	US	971
WYTL 65604	Tackle	WYTL	US	971
WYTL 65607	Bridle	WYTL	US	971
WYTL 65608	Pendant	WYTL	US	971
WYTL 65609	Shackle	WYTL	US	971
WYTL 65610	Hawser	WYTL	US	971
WYTL 65611	Line	WYTL	US	971
WYTL 65612	Wire	WYTL	US	971
WYTL 65614	Bollard	WYTL	US	971
WYTL 65615	Cleat	WYTL	US	971
WLIC 75301	Anvil	WLIC	US	971
WLIC 75302	Hammer	WLIC	US	971
WLIC 75303	Sledge	WLIC	US	971
WLIC 75304	Mallet	WLIC	US	971
WLIC 75305	Vise	WLIC	US	971
WLIC 75306	Clamp	WLIC	US	971
WLR 75307	Wedge	WLR	US	970
WLIC 75309	Hatchet	WLIC	US	971
WLIC 75310	Axe	WLIC	US	971
WLR 75401	Gasconade	WLR	US	970
WLR 75402	Muskingum	WLR	US	970
WLR 75403	Wyaconda	WLR	US	970
WLR 75404	Chippewa	WLR	US	970
WLR 75405	Cheyenne	WLR	US	970
WLR 75406	Kickapoo	WLR	US	970
WLR 75407	Kanawha	WLR	US	970
WLR 75408	Patoka	WLR	US	970
WLR 75409	Chena	WLR	US	970
WLR 75500	Kankakee	WLR	US	970
WLR 75501	Greenbrier	WLR	US	970
87301	Barracuda	WPB	US	967
87302	Hammerhead	WPB	US	967
87303	Mako	WPB	US	967
87304	Marlin	WPB	US	967
87305	Stingray	WPB	US	967
87306	Dorado	WPB	US	967
87307	Osprey	WPB	US	967
87308	Chinook	WPB	US	967
87309	Albacore	WPB	US	967
87310	Tarpon	WPB	US	967
87311	Cobia	WPB	US	967
87312	Hawksbill	WPB	US	967
87313	Cormorant	WPB	US	967
87314	Finback	WPB	US	967
87315	Amberjack	WPB	US	967
87316	Kittiwake	WPB	US	967
87317	Blackfin	WPB	US	967
87318	Bluefin	WPB	US	967
87319	Yellowfin	WPB	US	967
87320	Manta	WPB	US	967
87321	Coho	WPB	US	967
87322	Kingfisher	WPB	US	967
87323	Seahawk	WPB	US	967
87324	Steelhead	WPB	US	967
87325	Beluga	WPB	US	967
87326	Blacktip	WPB	US	967
87327	Pelican	WPB	US	967
87328	Ridley	WPB	US	967
87329	Cochito	WPB	US	967
87330	Manowar	WPB	US	967
87331	Moray	WPB	US	967
87332	Razorbill	WPB	US	967
87333	Adelie	WPB	US	967
87334	Gannet	WPB	US	967
87335	Narwhal	WPB	US	967
87336	Sturgeon	WPB	US	967
87337	Sockeye	WPB	US	967
87338	Ibis	WPB	US	967
87339	Pompano	WPB	US	967
87340	Halibut	WPB	US	967
87341	Bonito	WPB	US	967
87342	Shrike	WPB	US	967
87343	Tern	WPB	US	967
87344	Heron	WPB	US	967
87345	Wahoo	WPB	US	967
87346	Flyingfish	WPB	US	967
87347	Haddock	WPB	US	967
87348	Brant	WPB	US	967
87349	Shearwater	WPB	US	967
87350	Petrel	WPB	US	967
87352	Sea Lion	WPB	US	967
87353	Skipjack	WPB	US	967
87354	Dolphin	WPB	US	967
87355	Hawk	WPB	US	967
87356	Sailfish	WPB	US	967
87357	Sawfish	WPB	US	967
87358	Swordfish	WPB	US	967
87359	Tiger Shark	WPB	US	967
87360	Blue Shark	WPB	US	967
87361	Sea Horse	WPB	US	967
87362	Sea Otter	WPB	US	967
87363	Manatee	WPB	US	967
87364	Ahi	WPB	US	967
87365	Pike	WPB	US	967
87366	Terrapin	WPB	US	967
87367	Sea Dragon	WPB	US	967
87368	Sea Devil	WPB	US	967
87369	Crocodile	WPB	US	967
87370	Diamondback	WPB	US	967
87371	Reef Shark	WPB	US	967
87372	Alligator	WPB	US	967
87373	Sea Dog	WPB	US	967
87374	Sea Fox	WPB	US	967

WORLD NAVIES

A-Z

Albania

FORCE DETAR

Country Overview

After being governed by a communist regime since 1946, democratic elections in the Republic of Albania took place in 1991 although since then there have been periods of instability. Situated in western part of the Balkan Peninsula, the country has an area of 11,100 square miles and is bordered to the north by Montenegro and Serbia, to the east by FYRO Macedonia and to the south by Greece. There is a coastline of 195 n miles with the Adriatic Sea on which Durrës and Vlorë are the principal ports. The capital and largest city is Tirana. Territorial waters (12 n miles) are claimed but an EEZ has not been claimed. Italy provides strong operational, training and administrative support. Joint Coast Guard and Customs patrols are mounted within territorial waters while other personnel training is conducted in Italy.

Headquarters Appointments

Commander of the Navy:
Captain Gerveni Kristaq

Personnel

2009: 1,156 approximately

Bases

HQ: Durrës
Districts: Durrës (1st), Vlorë (2nd).
Bases: Shengyin, Himarë, Saranda, Sazan Island, Porto Palermo, Vlorë.

PATROL FORCES

Notes: (1) Pennant numbers beginning with '1' indicate units from the Durrës district. Those beginning with '2' are from the Vlorë district.
(2) There are six inshore patrol craft of 12-15 m length.

1 SHANGHAI II CLASS (FAST ATTACK CRAFT—GUN) (PC)

P 115

Displacement, tons: 113 standard; 134 full load
Dimensions, feet (metres): 127.3 × 17.7 × 5.6 *(38.8 × 5.4 × 1.7)*
Main machinery: 2 Type L-12V-180 diesels; 2,400 hp(m) *(1.76 MW)* (forward)
2 Type 12-D-6 diesels; 1,820 hp(m) *(1.34 MW)* (aft); 4 shafts
Speed, knots: 30
Range, n miles: 700 at 16.5 kt
Complement: 34
Guns: 4 China 37 mm/63 (2 twin); 180 rds/min to 8.5 km *(4.6 n miles)*; weight of shell 1.42 kg.
4 USSR 25 mm/60 (2 twin); 270 rds/min to 3 km *(1.6 n miles)*; weight of shell 0.34 kg.
Torpedoes: 2—21 in *(533 mm)* tubes; Yu-1; 9.2 km *(5 n miles)* at 39 kt; warhead 400 kg.
Depth charges: 2 projectors; 8 depth charges in lieu of torpedo tubes.
Mines: Rails can be fitted; probably only 10 mines.
Radars: Surface search/fire control: Pot Head; I-band.
Sonars: Hull-mounted set probably fitted.

Comment: Four transferred from China in mid-1974 and two in 1975. One ship escaped to Italy in early 1997, returned in early 1998 and was reported repaired in 2000. Has torpedo tubes on the stern taken from deleted Huchuan class. Seldom seen at sea.

SHANGHAI II (China colours) *6/1992* / 0081445

2 PO 2 (PROJECT 501) CLASS (COASTAL PATROL CRAFT) (PB)

A 120 **A 212**

Displacement, tons: 56 full load
Dimensions, feet (metres): 70.5 × 11.5 × 3.3 *(21.5 × 3.5 × 1)*
Main machinery: 1 Type 3-D-12 diesel; 300 hp(m) *(220 kW)* sustained; 1 shaft
Speed, knots: 12
Complement: 8
Guns: 2—12.7 mm MGs. At least one of the class has a twin 25 mm/60.
Radars: Surface search: I-band.

Comment: Two survive from a total of 11 transferred from USSR 1957-60. Previous minesweeping gear has been removed and the craft are used for utility roles. All escaped to Italy in early 1997 and returned, two in early 1998 and one in late 1998. Two others were towed back as being beyond repair. One other *A 451* was sunk in a collision with an Italian corvette in March 1997. Seldom seen at sea.

PO 2 (old number) *7/1992, Terje Nilsen* / 0056447

MINE WARFARE FORCES

1 T 43 (PROJECT 254) CLASS (MINESWEEPER—OCEAN) (MSO)

M 111

Displacement, tons: 500 standard; 580 full load
Dimensions, feet (metres): 190.2 × 27.6 × 6.9 *(58 × 8.4 × 2.1)*
Main machinery: 2 Kolomna Type 9-D-8 diesels; 2,000 hp(m) *(1.47 MW)* sustained; 2 shafts
Speed, knots: 15
Range, n miles: 3,000 at 10 kt; 2,000 at 14 kt
Complement: 65
Guns: 4—37 mm/63 (2 twin); 160 rds/min to 9 km *(5 n miles)*; weight of shell 0.7 kg.
8—12.7 mm MGs.
Depth charges: 2 projectors.
Mines: 16.
Radars: Air/surface search: Ball End; E/F-band.
Navigation: Furuno; I-band.
Sonars: Stag Ear; hull-mounted set probably fitted.

Comment: Transferred from USSR in 1960. All escaped to Italy in early 1997 and were returned in 1998. *M 111* refitted in Italy in 2002 and *M 112* has been decommissioned.

T 43
5/1996, Piet Cornelis
1153014

AUXILIARIES

Notes: In addition there are a Project 368 Poluchat survey and torpedo recovery craft of 20 tons *(A 110)*, an old ex-USSR Shalanda class tender *Marinza* (A 210), a water-barge, two tugs and a floating dock *(Vlorë)*.

1 LCT 3 CLASS (REPAIR SHIP) (ARL)

A 223 (ex-MOC 1203)

Displacement, tons: 640 full load
Dimensions, feet (metres): 192 × 31 × 7 *(58.6 × 9.5 × 2.1)*
Main machinery: 2 diesels; 1,000 hp *(746 kW)*; 2 shafts
Speed, knots: 8
Complement: 24

Comment: 1943-built LCT converted in Italian use as a repair craft. Refitted in Italy, transferred in 1999 and used for moored technical support. To be decommissioned once improvements to naval base facilities have been made.

LCT 3 (Italian colours) *10/1998, Diego Quevedo* / 0017507

COAST GUARD (ROJA BREGDETARE)

Notes: (1) A Project 522 'Nyryat 1' diving tender (R 218) was transferred from the Navy in 2003.
(2) An Italian Coast Guard craft CP 224 transferred in 2008.

2 COASTAL PATROL CRAFT (PB)

R 117 **R 217**

Displacement, tons: 18 full load
Dimensions, feet (metres): 45.6 × 13 × 3 *(13.9 × 4 × 0.9)*
Main machinery: 2 diesels; 1,300 hp *(942 kW)*; 2 waterjets
Speed, knots: 34. **Range, n miles:** 200 at 30 kt
Complement: 4
Guns: 2—12.7 mm MGs.
Radars: Surface search: Raytheon; I-band.

Comment: Transferred from the US on 27 February 1999. Reported operational.

R 217 *6/2007, Massimo Annati* / 1166505

1 + 3 DAMEN STAN PATROL 4207 (PB)

ILIRIA P 131 **ORIK** **LISSUS** **BUTRINTI**

Displacement, tons: 205
Dimensions, feet (metres): 140.4 × 23.3 × 8.3 *(42.8 × 7.11 × 2.52)*
Main machinery: 2 Caterpillar 3516B DI-TA; 5,600 hp *(4.17 MW)*; 2 cp props
Speed, knots: 26
Complement: To be announced
Guns: To be announced.

Comment: Contract signed with Damen Shipyards, Gorinchem on 13 November 2007 for the acquisition of four Stan Patrol 4207 offshore patrol vessels. The first vessel was built in Holland whilst the remaining three are to be built at Pashaliman Shipyard near Vlorë. The contract also includes refurbishment of the shipyard, training and maintenance services. Details are based on those in UK Customs service and in Jamaica.

ILIRIA *7/2007, A A de Kruijf* / 1335320

8 V 4000 (FAST PATROL CRAFT) (PBF)

Displacement, tons: 27.3 full load
Dimensions, feet (metres): 54.1 × 14.8 × 2.6 *(16.5 × 4.5 × 0.8)*
Main machinery: 2 Isotta Fraschini ID 36 SS 16V diesels; 2,450 hp(m) *(1.8 MW)* sustained
Speed, knots: 48. **Range, n miles:** 420 at 35 kt
Complement: 5
Radars: Surface search: GEM DX 132; I-band.

Comment: Eight Drago craft transferred from the Italian Guardia di Finanza in 2006.

V 4000 CRAFT *6/2006, Guardia di Finanza* / 1164418

3 SEA SPECTRE MK III (PB)

R 118 **R 215** **R 216**

Displacement, tons: 41 full load
Dimensions, feet (metres): 65 × 18 × 5.9 *(19.8 × 5.5 × 1.8)*
Main machinery: 3 Detroit 8V-71 diesels; 690 hp *(515 kW)* sustained; 3 shafts
Speed, knots: 28. **Range, n miles:** 450 at 25 kt
Complement: 9
Guns: 2—25 mm. 2—12.7 mm MGs.
Radars: Surface search: Raytheon; I-band.

Comment: Transferred from the US on 27 February 1999.

R 215 *6/2008** / 1335319

4 TYPE 227 INSHORE PATROL CRAFT (PBR)

R 123 (ex-CP 229) **R 124** (ex-CP 235) **R 225** (ex-CP 234) **R 226** (ex-CP 236)

Displacement, tons: 16 full load
Dimensions, feet (metres): 44.0 × 15.7 × 4.3 *(13.4 × 4.8 × 1.3)*
Main machinery: 2 AIFO 8281-SRM diesels; 1,770 hp *(1.32 MW)*; 2 shafts
Speed, knots: 24. **Range, n miles:** 400 at 24 kt
Complement: 5
Radars: Surface search: I-band.

Comment: Wooden construction. Built in Italy 1966-69. Transferred from Italian Coast Guard to Albanian Coast Guard in 2002.

7 TYPE 2010 INSHORE PATROL CRAFT (PBR)

R 125 (ex-CP 2008) **R 127** (ex-CP 2021) **R 224** (ex-CP 2010) **R 228** (ex-CP 2023)
R 126 (ex-CP 2020) **R 128** (ex-CP 2034) **R 227** (ex-CP 2007)

Displacement, tons: 15 full load
Dimensions, feet (metres): 41.0 × 11.8 × 3.6 *(12.5 × 3.6 × 1.1)*
Main machinery: 2 AIFO diesels; 1,072 hp *(800 kW)*; 2 shafts
Speed, knots: 24. **Range, n miles:** 533 at 20 kt
Complement: 5
Radars: Surface search: I-band.

Comment: Former harbour launches built in Italy in the 1970s. GRP construction. One transferred from Italian Coast Guard to Albanian Coast Guard in 2002 and a further six in 2004.

1 TYPE 303 COASTAL PATROL CRAFT (PB)

R 122 (ex-CP 303)

Displacement, tons: 20 full load
Dimensions, feet (metres): 44.0 × 12.5 × 3.6 *(13.4 × 3.8 × 1.1)*
Main machinery: 2 GM6V53 diesels; 730 hp *(544 kW)*; 2 shafts
Speed, knots: 13. **Range, n miles:** 350 at 13 kt
Complement: 5
Radars: Surface search: I-band.

Comment: Built in US in 1965. Transferred from Italian Coast Guard to Albanian Coast Guard in 2002.

1 TYPE 246 CLASS (INSHORE PATROL CRAFT) (PBR)

- (ex-CP 249)

Displacement, tons: 22 full load
Dimensions, feet (metres): 49.2 × 15.9 × 5.4 *(15.0 × 4.85 × 1.65)*
Main machinery: 2 Isotta Fraschini ID 35 SS6V diesels; 1,350 hp(m) *(1.0 MW)*; 2 shafts
Speed, knots: 27
Complement: 7
Radars: Surface search: I-band.

Comment: Built in Italy in 1980. Transferred from the Italian Coast Guard in 2008.

Algeria

MARINE DE LA REPUBLIQUE ALGERIENNE

Country Overview

Formerly a French colony, the People's Democratic Republic of Algeria gained independence in 1962. Situated in north Africa, it has an area of 919,595 square miles and is bordered to the east by Tunisia and Libya, to the south by Niger, Mali, and Mauritania and to the west by Morocco. It has a 540 n mile coastline with the Mediterranean. The capital, largest city and principal port is Algiers. Territorial seas (12 n miles) and Fishery zones (32/52 n miles) have been claimed but an EEZ has not been claimed.

Headquarters Appointments

Commander of the Navy:
Lieutenant General Malek Necib
Inspector General of the Navy:
Major General Abdelmadjid Taright

Personnel

(a) 2009: 7,500 (500 officers) (Navy) (includes at least 600 naval infantry); 500 (Coast Guard)
(b) Voluntary service

Bases

Algiers (1st Region), Mers-el-Kebir (2nd Region), Jijel (3rd Region), Annaba (CG HQ)

Coast Defence

Four batteries of truck-mounted SS-C-3 Styx twin launchers. Permanent sites at Algiers, Mers-el-Kebir and Jijel linked by radar.

SUBMARINES

Notes: One decommissioned Romeo class is used for training.

2 + 2 KILO CLASS (PROJECT 877EKM/636) (SSK)

Name	*No*	*Builders*	*Laid down*	*Launched*	*Commissioned*
RAIS HADJ MUBAREK	012	Admiralty Yard, Leningrad	1985	1986	Oct 1987
EL HADJ SLIMANE	013	Admiralty Yard, Leningrad	1985	1987	Jan 1988
–	–	Admiralty Yard, Leningrad	2007	2009	2010
–	–	Admiralty Yard, Leningrad	2009	2011	2012

Displacement, tons: 2,325 surfaced; 3,076 dived
Dimensions, feet (metres): 238.2 × 32.5 × 21.7 *(72.6 × 9.9 × 6.6)*
Main machinery: Diesel-electric; 2 diesels; 3,650 hp(m) *(2.68 MW)*; 2 generators; 1 motor; 5,900 hp(m) *(4.34 MW)*; 1 shaft; 2 auxiliary MT-168 motors; 204 hp(m) *(150 kW)*; 1 economic speed motor; 130 hp(m) *(95 kW)*

Speed, knots: 17 dived; 10 surfaced; 9 snorting
Range, n miles: 6,000 at 7 kt snorting; 400 at 3 kt dived
Complement: 52 (13 officers)

Torpedoes: 6—21 in *(533 mm)* tubes. Combination of Russian TEST-71ME; anti-submarine active/passive homing to 15 km *(8.2 n miles)* at 40 kt; warhead 205 kg and 53–65; anti-surface ship passive wake homing to 19 km *(10.3 n miles)* at 45 kt; warhead 300 kg. Total of 18 weapons.
Mines: 24 in lieu of torpedoes.
Countermeasures: ESM: Brick Pulp; radar warning.
Weapons control: MVU 110 TFCS.
Radars: Surface search: Snoop Tray; I-band.
Sonars: MGK 400 Shark Teeth/Shark Fin; hull-mounted; passive/active search and attack; medium frequency.
MG 519 Mouse Roar; active attack; high frequency.

RAIS HADJ MUBAREK *3/1996* / 0056450

Programmes: The Project 877EKM were new construction hulls which replaced the Romeo class. A contract for the construction of two Project 636 boats was signed with Admiralty Shipyards in mid-2006 and construction of the first is reported to have begun in 2007.
Modernisation: Following refits in 1993-96, both submarines undergoing further two-year refits at Admiralty Yard, St Petersburg. Work on the first boat, which is reported to have included upgrade of the sonar system, began in November 2005 and completed in 2008. Refit of the second boat is expected.
Structure: Diving depth, 790 ft *(240 m)*. 9,700 kWh batteries. Pressure hull 169.9 ft *(51.8 m)*. May be fitted with SA-N-5/8 portable SAM launcher.
Operational: During the refit period until 2009, only one boat will be operational. Both based at Mers El Kebir.

FRIGATES

Notes: Acquisition of four new frigates is under consideration. A decision is expected in 2009.

3 MOURAD RAIS (KONI) CLASS (PROJECT 1159.2) (FFLM)

Name	*No*	*Builders*	*Commissioned*
MOURAD RAIS	901	Zelenodolsk Shipyard	20 Dec 1980
RAIS KELLICH	902	Zelenodolsk Shipyard	24 Mar 1982
RAIS KORFOU	903	Zelenodolsk Shipyard	3 Jan 1985

Displacement, tons: 1,440 standard; 1,900 full load
Dimensions, feet (metres): 316.3 × 41.3 × 11.5 *(96.4 × 12.6 × 3.5)*
Main machinery: CODAG; 1 SGW, Nikolayev, M8B gas turbine (centre shaft); 18,000 hp(m) *(13.25 MW)* sustained; 2 Russki B-68 diesels; 15,820 hp(m) *(11.63 MW)* sustained; 3 shafts
Speed, knots: 27 gas; 22 diesel
Range, n miles: 1,800 at 14 kt
Complement: 130

Missiles: SAM: SA-N-4 Gecko twin launcher ❶; semi-active radar homing to 15 km *(8 n miles)* at 2.5 Mach; height envelope 9–3,048 m *(29.5–10,000 ft)*; warhead 50 kg; 20 missiles. Some anti-surface capability.
Guns: 4—3 in *(76 mm)*/59 AK 726 (2 twin) ❷; 90 rds/min to 16 km *(8.5 n miles)*; weight of shell 5.9 kg.
4—30 mm/65 (2 twin) ❸; 500 rds/min to 5 km *(2.7 n miles)*; weight of shell 0.54 kg.
A/S mortars: 2—12-barrelled RBU 6000 ❹; range 6,000 m; warhead 31 kg.
Torpedoes: 4—533 mm (2 twin) (in 903 only) ❺.
Depth charges: 2 racks.
Mines: Rails; capacity 22.
Countermeasures: Decoys: 2 PK 16 chaff launchers (901, 902); 2 PJ 46 decoy launchers (903).
ESM: Watch Dog. Cross Loop D/F. NRJ-6A (903).
Weapons control: 3P-60 UE.
Radars: Air/surface search: Pozitiv-ME1.2 (903) ❻; I-band.
Strut Curve; E/F-band (901 and 902).
Navigation: Don 2; I-band.
Fire Control: Drum tilt ❼; H/I-band (for search/acquisition/FC).
Pop Group ❽; F/H/I-band (for missile control).
Hawk screech (901 and 902) ❾; I-band.
IFF: High Pole B. 2 Square Head.

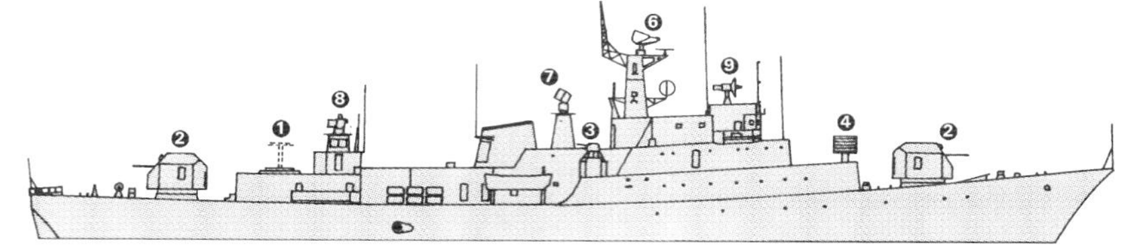

MOURAD RAIS *(Scale 1 : 900), Ian Sturton* / 0567433

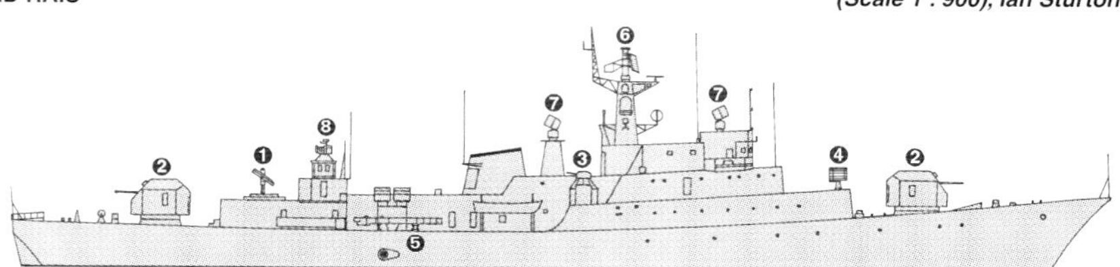

RAIS KORFOU *(Scale 1 : 900), Ian Sturton* / 0104159

Sonars: Hercules (MG 322) hull-mounted; active search and attack; medium frequency.

Programmes: New construction ships built in USSR with hull numbers 5, 7 and 10 in sequence. Others of the class built for Cuba, Yugoslavia, East Germany and Libya. Interest was shown in ex-GDR ships in 1991 but sale was rejected by the German government.
Modernisation: New generators fitted 1992–94. *Rais Korfou* in refit at Kronstadt from 1997 to November 2000. The refit included replacement of Strut Curve radar, removal of Hawk screech fire-control radar, fitting of torpedo tubes and a new electronic suite. Refit of *Mourad Rais* began in late 2007 and of *Rais Kellich* in late 2008.
Structure: The deckhouse aft in Type II Konis houses air conditioning machinery.
Operational: All have been used for Training cruises. All based at Mers El Kebir.

RAIS KORFOU *4/2005*. *Rafael Cabrera* / 1167851

RAIS KELLICH *11/2008**, *Michael Nitz* / 1335441

CORVETTES

3 + (1) DJEBEL CHENOUA (C 58) CLASS (PROJECT 802) (FSG)

Name	*No*	*Builders*	*Launched*	*Commissioned*
DJEBEL CHENOUA	351	ECRN, Mers-el-Kebir	3 Feb 1985	Nov 1988
EL CHIHAB	352	ECRN, Mers-el-Kebir	Feb 1990	June 1995
AL KIRCH	353	ECRN, Mers-el-Kebir	July 2000	2002

Displacement, tons: 496 standard; 540 full load
Dimensions, feet (metres): 191.6 × 27.9 × 8.5 *(58.4 × 8.5 × 2.6)*
Main machinery: 3 MTU 20V 538TB92 diesels; 12,800 hp(m) *(9.4 MW)*; 3 shafts
Speed, knots: 31
Complement: 52 (6 officers)

Missiles: SSM: 4 China C 802 (CSS-N-8 Saccade) (2 twin); active radar homing to 120 km *(66 n miles)* at 0.9 Mach; warhead 165 kg.
Guns: 1 Russian 3 in *(76 mm)*/59 AK 176; 120 rds/min to 15 km *(8 n miles)*; weight of shell 5.9 kg.
1—30 mm/65 AK 630; 6 barrels per mounting; 3,000 rds/min combined to 2 km.
Countermeasures: Decoys: 2 chaff launchers.
Electro-optic devices: Optronic director.
Radars: Surface search: E/F-band.
Navigation: Racal Decca 1226; I-band.
Fire control: I-band.

Programmes: Ordered July 1983. Project 802 built with Bulgarian assistance. First one completed trials in 1988. Work on the second of class was suspended in 1992 due to shipyard debt problems but the ship completed in 1995. Main guns were fitted at a later date. Construction of a fourth ship is reported to be under consideration.
Structure: Hull size suggests association with Bazán Cormoran class.

AL KIRCH *6/2005, Marian Ferrette* / 1127285

EL CHIHAB *7/2005, B Prézelin* / 1129990

3 NANUCHKA II (BURYA) CLASS (PROJECT 1234) (MISSILE CORVETTES) (PTGM)

Name	*No*	*Builders*	*Commissioned*
RAIS HAMIDOU	801	Petrovsky, Leningrad	4 July 1980
SALAH RAIS	802	Petrovsky, Leningrad	9 Feb 1981
RAIS ALI	803	Petrovsky, Leningrad	8 May 1982

Displacement, tons: 660 full load
Dimensions, feet (metres): 194.5 × 38.7 × 8.5 *(59.3 × 11.8 × 2.6)*
Main machinery: 6 M 504 diesels; 26,112 hp(m) *(19.2 MW)*; 3 shafts
Speed, knots: 33. **Range, n miles:** 2,500 at 12 kt; 900 at 31 kt
Complement: 42 (7 officers)

Missiles: SSM: 16 Zvezda SS-N-25 (in 802) (4 quad) (Kh 35E Uran); active radar homing to 130 km *(70.2 n miles)* at 0.9 Mach; warhead 145 kg; sea skimmer.
4 SS-N-2C (in 801 and 803); active radar or IR homing to 46 km *(25 n miles)* at 0.9 Mach; warhead 513 kg.
SAM: SA-N-4 Gecko twin launcher; semi-active radar homing to 15 km *(8 n miles)* at 2.5 Mach; height envelope 9-3,048 m *(29.5-10,000 ft)*; warhead 50 kg; 20 missiles. Some anti-surface capability.
Guns: 2—57 mm/75 AK 725 (twin); 120 rds/min to 12.7 km *(6.8 n miles)*; weight of shell 2.8 kg.
1—30 mm/65 AK 630 (in 802); 6 barrels per mounting; 3,000 rds/min combined to 2 km.
Countermeasures: Decoys 2 PK 16 16-barrelled chaff launchers (801, 803). 2 PJ 46 decoy launchers (802).
ESM: Bell Tap. Cross Loop; D/F (801, 803). NRJ-6A (802).
Radars: Surface search Square Tie (Radome) (801 and 803); I-band. Pozitiv-ME1.2 (802); I-band.
Navigation: Don 2; I-band.
Fire control: Pop Group; F/H/I-band (SA-N-4). Muff Cob or Drum Tilt (802); G/H-band. Plank Shave; E-band (SS-N-25).
IFF: Two Square Head. High Pole.

Programmes: Delivered as new construction.
Modernisation: *Salah Rais* refitted at Kronstadt 1997 to November 2000 with refurbished diesels, a replacement SSM system and electronic suite. Refit of *Rais Hamidou* began in late 2007 and of *Rais Ali* in late 2008.

SALAH RAIS (SS-N-25 not fitted) *12/2007, Diego Quevedo* / 1335235

RAIS ALI *9/2007, Diego Quevedo* / 1335234

LAND-BASED MARITIME AIRCRAFT

Numbers/Type: 2 Beechcraft Super King Air 200T.
Operational speed: 282 kt *(523 km/h)*.
Service ceiling: 35,000 ft *(10,670 m)*.
Range: 2,030 n miles *(3,756 km)*.
Role/Weapon systems: Operated by air force for crew training and for close-range EEZ operations. Sensors: Weather radar only. Weapons: Unarmed.

Numbers/Type: 3 Fokker F27-400/600.
Operational speed: 250 kt *(463 km/h)*.
Service ceiling: 25,000 ft *(7,620 m)*.
Range: 2,700 n miles *(5,000 km)*.
Role/Weapon systems: Visual reconnaissance duties in support of EEZ, particularly offshore platforms. Sensors: Weather radar and visual means only. Weapons: Limited armament.

Numbers/Type: 28/6 MiG-29SMT/MiG-29UBT Fulcrum
Operational speed: 750 kt *(1,400 km/h)*.
Service ceiling: 57,000 ft *(17,400 m)*.
Range: 1,186 n miles *(2,200 km)*.
Role/Weapon systems: Contract signed in early 2006 for the supply of 28 MiG-29 SMT single-seat all-weather fighters with attack capability and six two-seat MiG-29 UBT. There is an option for a further 20 aircraft. However, following reported refusal to accept the Flanker aircraft, up to 16 Su-30 Mk I fighters may be acquired in lieu. The MiG-29 SMT is an upgraded version of the original airframe with reduced radar signature and improved avionics. Sensors: Saphir-29 radar. Weapons: AAM: R77. ASM: two Kh-31 A/P (AS-17 Krypton). Conventional bombs; four KAB-500KR TV-guided bombs. 30 mm cannon.

Numbers/Type: 6 AugustaWestland AW 101.
Operational speed: 160 kt *(296 km/h)*.
Service ceiling: 15,000 ft *(4,572 m)*.
Range: 550 n miles *(1,019 km)*.
Role/Weapon systems: Contract reported in late 2007 for a total of six utility variants of the EH 101. All are to be configured for SAR duties although the aircraft design facilitates rapid role-change to a troop-carrying configuration. Delivery is expected to start in 2009 and to be completed in 2010. Military lift is 28 troops and up to 4 tonnes underslung. Sensors: Telephonics RDR-1600 SAR Weather Avoidance Radar.

Numbers/Type: 6 AugustaWestland Super Lynx 300.
Operational speed: 120 kt *(222 km/h)*.
Service ceiling: 10,000 ft *(3,048 m)*.
Range: 320 n miles *(593 km)*.
Role/Weapon systems: Contract reported in late 2007 for a total of six unarmed variants of the Super Lynx. Roles include maritime surveillance and SAR. Delivery is expected to start in 2009 and to be completed in 2010.

PATROL FORCES

15 KEBIR CLASS (FAST ATTACK CRAFT—GUN) (PG)

EL YADEKH 341
EL MOURAKEB 342
EL KECHEF 343
EL MOUTARID 344
EL RASSED 345
EL DJARI 346
EL SAHER 347
EL MOUKADEM 348
EL TINAI 349
EL KANASS 350
EL MAHIR 354
–355
EL AZOUM 356
EL DJASUR 357
EL HAMIS 358

Displacement, tons: 166 standard; 200 full load
Dimensions, feet (metres): 123 × 22.6 × 5.6 *(37.5 × 6.9 × 1.7)*
Main machinery: 2 MTU 12V 538TB92 diesels; 5,110 hp(m) *(3.8 MW)*; 2 shafts (see *Structure*)
Speed, knots: 27
Range, n miles: 3,300 at 12 kt; 2,600 at 15 kt
Complement: 27 (3 officers)

Guns: 1 OTO Melara 3 in *(76 mm)*/62 compact (341–342); 85 rds/min to 16 km *(9 n miles)* anti-surface; 12 km *(6.5 n miles)* anti-aircraft; weight of shell 6 kg.
4 USSR 25 mm/60 (2 twin) (remainder); 270 rds/min to 3 km *(1.6 n miles)*; weight of shell 0.34 kg.
2 USSR 14.5 mm (twin) (in first five).
Electro-optic devices: Lawrence Scott optronic director (in 341 and 342).
Radars: Surface search: Racal Decca 1226; I-band.

Programmes: Design and first pair ordered from Brooke Marine in June 1981. First left for Algeria without armament in September 1982, second arrived Algiers 12 June 1983. A further seven were then assembled or built at ECRN, Mers-el-Kebir. Of these, 346 commissioned 10 November 1985 and 347-349 delivered by 1993. After a delay two further craft were completed; 350 in late 1997 followed by 354 in 1998. 356-358 have since been added and original plans for a class of 15 look to have been achieved.
Structure: Same hull as Barbados *Trident*. There are some variations in armament.
Operational: Six of the class have been transferred to the Coast Guard.

EL HAMIS *9/2007, Diego Quevedo* / 1335233

EL MOURAKEB *3/2006, M Declerck* / 1159230

9 OSA II CLASS (PROJECT 205) (FAST ATTACK CRAFT—MISSILE) (PTGF)

644–652

Displacement, tons: 245 full load
Dimensions, feet (metres): 126.6 × 24.9 × 8.8 *(38.6 × 7.6 × 2.7)*
Main machinery: 3 Type M 504 diesels; 10,800 hp(m) *(7.94 MW)* sustained; 3 shafts
Speed, knots: 37. **Range, n miles**: 500 at 35 kt
Complement: 30

Missiles: SSM: 4 SS-N-2C; active radar or IR homing to 83 km *(43 n miles)* at 0.9 Mach; warhead 513 kg.
Guns: 4—30 mm/65 (2 twin); 500 rds/min to 5 km *(2.7 n miles)*; weight of shell 0.54 kg.
Radars: Surface search: Square Tie; I-band.
Fire control: Drum Tilt; H/I-band.
IFF: 2 Square Head. High Pole B.

Programmes: Osa II transferred 1976–77 (four), fifth in September 1978, sixth in December 1978, next pair in 1979 and one from the Black Sea on 7 December 1981.
Modernisation: Plans to re-engine were reported as starting in late 1992 but there has been no confirmation.
Operational: At least six Osa IIs are active. Based at Mers El Kebir.

OSA 651 *7/2008*, Diego Quevedo* / 1336042

AMPHIBIOUS FORCES

2 LANDING SHIPS (LOGISTIC) (LSTH)

Name	*No*	*Builders*	*Commissioned*
KALAAT BENI HAMMAD	472	Brooke Marine, Lowestoft	Apr 1984
KALAAT BENI RACHED	473	Vosper Thornycroft, Woolston	Oct 1984

Displacement, tons: 2,450 full load
Dimensions, feet (metres): 305 × 50.9 × 8.1 *(93 × 15.5 × 2.5)*
Main machinery: 2 MTU 16V 1163TB82 diesels; 8,880 hp(m) *(6.5 MW)* sustained; 2 shafts
Speed, knots: 15
Range, n miles: 3,000 at 12 kt
Complement: 81
Military lift: 240 troops; 7 MBTs and 380 tons other cargo; 2 ton crane with athwartships travel

Guns: 2 Breda 40 mm/70 (twin); 300 rds/min to 12.5 km *(6.8 n miles)*; weight of shell 0.96 kg.
4 USSR 25 mm/60 (2 twin); 270 rds/min to 3 km *(1.6 n miles)*; weight of shell 0.34 kg.
Countermeasures: Decoys: Wallop Barricade double layer chaff launchers.
ESM: Racal Cutlass; intercept.
ECM: Racal Cygnus; jammer.
Electro-optic devices: CSEE Naja optronic.
Radars: Navigation: Racal Decca TM 1226; I-band.
Fire control: Marconi S 800; J-band.

Helicopters: Platform only for one Sea King.

Programmes: First ordered in June 1981, and launched 18 May 1983; second ordered 18 October 1982 and launched 15 May 1984. Similar hulls to Omani *Nasr Al Bahr*.
Structure: These ships have a through tank deck closed by bow and stern ramps. The forward ramp is of two sections measuring length 18 m (when extended) × 5 m breadth, and the single section stern ramp measures 4.3 × 5 m with the addition of 1.1 m finger flaps. Both hatches can support a 60 ton tank and are winch operated. In addition, side access doors are provided on each side forward. The tank deck side bulkheads extend 2.25 m above the upper deck between the forecastle and the forward end of the superstructure, and provide two hatch openings to the tank deck below. Additional 25 mm guns have been fitted either side of the bridge.
Operational: Both are reported active. Based at Jijel.

KALAAT BENI HAMMAD *8/2004, B Prézelin* / 1044061

KALAAT BENI RACHED *11/2007, Frank Findler* / 1335231

1 POLNOCHNY B CLASS (PROJECT 771) (LSM)

471

Displacement, tons: 760 standard; 834 full load
Dimensions, feet (metres): 246.1 × 31.5 × 7.5 *(75 × 9.6 × 2.3)*
Main machinery: 2 Kolomna Type 40-D diesels; 4,400 hp(m) *(3.2 MW)* sustained; 2 shafts
Speed, knots: 18. **Range, n miles:** 1,000 at 18 kt
Complement: 42
Military lift: 180 troops; 350 tons including up to 6 tanks
Guns: 2—30 mm/65 (twin) AK 230; 500 rds/min to 5 km *(2.7 n miles)*; weight of shell 0.54 kg. 2—140 mm 18-tubed rocket launchers.
Radars: Navigation: Don 2; I-band.
Fire control: Drum Tilt; H/I-band.
IFF: Square Head. High Pole B.

Comment: Class built in Poland 1968–70. Transferred from USSR in August 1976. Tank deck covers 237 m^2. Operational and employed on training tasks. Based at Jijel.

POLNOCHNY 471 *1990, van Ginderen Collection* / 0505954

MINE WARFARE FORCES

Notes: (1) The Coast Guard support ship *El Mourafek* may have a minelaying capability.
(2) Two MCMV are expected to be out to tender in due course.

SURVEY SHIPS

1 SURVEY SHIP (AGS)

EL IDRISSI BH 204 (ex-A 673)

Displacement, tons: 540 full load
Complement: 28 (6 officers)

Comment: Built by Matsukara, Japan and delivered 17 April 1980. Based at Algiers.

EL IDRISSI *9/1990* / 0056453

2 SURVEY CRAFT (YFS)

RAS TARA **ALIDADE**

Comment: *Ras Tara* is of 16 tons displacement, built in 1980 and has a crew of four. *Alidade* is of 20 tons, built in 1983 and has a crew of eight.

AUXILIARIES

1 POLUCHAT I CLASS (PROJECT 638) (YPT)

A 641

Displacement, tons: 70 standard; 100 full load
Dimensions, feet (metres): 97.1 × 19 × 4.8 *(29.6 × 5.8 × 1.5)*
Main machinery: 2 Type M 50F diesels; 2,200 hp(m) *(1.6 MW)* sustained; 2 shafts
Speed, knots: 20. **Range, n miles:** 1,500 at 10 kt
Complement: 15

Comment: Transferred from USSR in early 1970s. Has been used for SAR. Based at Mers El Kebir.

POLUCHAT *1989* / 0506183

1 DAXIN CLASS (AXH)

Name	*No*	*Builders*	*Launched*	*Commissioned*
SOUMMAM	937	Hudong Shipyard, Shanghai	Mar 2005	2006

Displacement, tons: 5,470 full load
Dimensions, feet (metres): 426.5 × 52.5 × 15.7 *(130.0 × 16.0 × 4.8)*
Main machinery: 2 6PC2-5L diesels; 7,800 hp(m) *(5.73 MW)*; 2 shafts
Speed, knots: 15
Range, n miles: 5,000 at 15 kt
Complement: 170 plus 30 instructors plus 200 Midshipmen

Guns: 1—57 mm. 4—37 mm (2 twin). 2-30 mm/65 AK 630; 6 barrels per mounting; 3,000 rds/min combined to 2 km.
Countermeasures: Decoys: 2 PJ 46 decoy launchers.
ESM/ECM: NRJ-6A.
Radars: Air/surface search: Eye Shield; E-band.
Surface search: China Type 756; I-band.
Navigation: Racal Decca 1290; I-band.
Fire control: Round Ball; I-band.
Sonars: Echo Type 5; hull-mounted; active; high frequency.
Helicopters: Platform only.

Comment: Very similar to Chinese training ship of same class. Based at Mers-el-Kebir.

SOUMMAM *7/2008*, Camil Busquets i Vilanova* / 1335232

TUGS

Notes: There are a number of harbour tugs of about 265 tons. These include *Kader* A 210, *El Chadid* A 211 and *Mazafran* 1–4 Y 206–209.

MAZAFRAN 4 *6/1994* / 0056454

COAST GUARD

Notes: (1) Six Kebir class were transferred from the Navy for Coast Guard duties but may have naval crews.
(2) There are also up to 12 small fishery protection vessels in the GC 301 series.

1 SUPPORT SHIP (WARL)

EL MOURAFEK GC 261

Displacement, tons: 600 full load
Dimensions, feet (metres): 193.6 × 27.6 × 6.9 *(59 × 8.4 × 2.1)*
Main machinery: 2 diesels; 2,200 hp(m) *(1.6 MW)*; 2 shafts
Speed, knots: 14
Complement: 54
Guns: 2—12.7 mm MGs.
Radars: Surface search: I-band.

Comment: Delivered by transporter ship from China in April 1990. The design appears to be a derivative of the T43 minesweeper but with a stern gantry. May have a minelaying capability. Based at Algiers.

EL MOURAFEK *6/2007, B Prézelin* / 1167941

7 EL MOUDERRIB (CHUI-E) CLASS (AXL)

EL MOUDERRIB I-VII GC 251-GC 257

Displacement, tons: 388 full load
Dimensions, feet (metres): 192.8 × 23.6 × 7.2 *(58.8 × 7.2 × 2.2)*
Main machinery: 3 PCR/Kolomna diesels; 6,600 hp(m) *(4.92 MW)*; 3 shafts
Speed, knots: 24
Range, n miles: 1,400 at 15 kt
Complement: 42 including 25 trainees
Guns: 4 China 14.5 mm (2 twin).
Radars: Surface search: Type 756; I-band.

Comment: Two delivered by transporter ship from China in April 1990 and described as training vessels. Two more acquired in January 1991, the last three in July 1991. Hainan class hull with modified propulsion and superstructure similar to some Chinese paramilitary vessels. Used for training when boats are carried aft in place of the second 14.5 mm gun. GC 255 and 257 are reported non-operational.

EL MOUDERRIB IV *3/2006, M Declerck* / 1164475

4 BAGLIETTO TYPE 20 (PBF)

EL HAMIL GC 325 **EL ASSAD** GC 326 **MARKHAD** GC 327 **ETAIR** GC 328

Displacement, tons: 44 full load
Dimensions, feet (metres): 66.9 × 17.1 × 5.5 *(20.4 × 5.2 × 1.7)*
Main machinery: 2 CRM 18DS diesels; 2,660 hp(m) *(2 MW)*; 2 shafts
Speed, knots: 36
Range, n miles: 445 at 20 kt
Complement: 11 (3 officers)
Guns: 1 Oerlikon 20 mm.

Comment: The first pair delivered by Baglietto, Varazze in August 1976 and six further in pairs at two monthly intervals. Fitted with radar and optical fire control. Four others of the class cannibalised for spares.

BAGLIETTO 20 *3/2006, M Declerck* / 1164477

6 BAGLIETTO MANGUSTA CLASS (PB)

—323 —324 **REQUIN** 331 —332 **MARSOUIN** 333 **MURENE** 334

Displacement, tons: 91 full load
Dimensions, feet (metres): 98.4 × 19.0 × 7.2 *(30.0 × 5.8 × 2.2)*
Main machinery: 3 MTU diesels; 4,000 hp *(3.0 MW)*; 3 shafts
Speed, knots: 32.5
Range, n miles: 800 at 24 kt
Complement: 14 (3 officers)
Guns: 2—25 mm (1 twin). 1—12.7 mm MG.
Radars: Navigation: I-band.

Comment: One of six patrol craft first delivered to Algeria in early 1977 and thought to have been decommissioned between 1998 and 2001. One patrol craft brought back to service in 2006.

REQUIN *3/2006, M Declerck* / 1164476

4 EL MOUNKID CLASS (SAR)

EL MOUNKID I GC 231
EL MOUNKID II GC 232
EL MOUNKID III GC 233
EL MOUNKID IV GC 234

Comment: First three delivered by transporter ship from China which arrived in Algiers in April 1990, a fourth followed a year later. Used for SAR.

GC 231-233 *1991* / 0056457

12 JEBEL ANTAR CLASS (PB)

JEBEL ANTAR 301
JEBEL HANDO 302
—303
RAS DJENAD 304
RAS TENES 305
RAS TEKKOUCH 306
RAS SISLI 307
RAS NOUH 308
RAS BOUGARONI 309
RAS TAMENTFOUST 310
RAS OULLIS 311
—312

Displacement, tons: To be announced
Dimensions, feet (metres): 55.8 × ? × ? *(17.0 × ? × ?)*
Main machinery: 2 diesels; 2 shafts
Speed, knots: 15
Complement: To be announced
Guns: To be announced.
Radars: Navigation: I-band.

Comment: Patrol craft reported constructed at Mers-el-Kebir 1982–83.

0 + 21 OCEA FPB 98 CLASS (PATROL CRAFT) (PB)

Displacement, tons: 116 full load
Dimensions, feet (metres): 115.5 × 22.3 × 4.0 *(35.2 × 6.8 × 1.2)*
Main machinery: 2 MTU 12V M70 diesels; 4,600 hp *(3.43 MW)*; 2 Kamewa waterjets
Speed, knots: 32
Range, n miles: 300 at 28 kt
Complement: 11 (3 officers)
Guns: 3—12.7 mm MGs.
Radars: Navigation: Sperry Bridgemaster; I-band.

Comment: The contract with OCEA, reported to have been signed in 2007, for the construdtion of 21 patrol craft was announced in October 2008. Delivery of the first vessel is expected in late 2008 and the programme is to be completed in 2012. The vessels are to be built at St Nazaire. Details are based on those of similar craft in Kuwaiti service and may be different.

FPB 98 CLASS (Kuwaiti colours) *8/2004, B Prézelin* / 1133080

CUSTOMS

Notes: The Customs service is a paramilitary organisation employing a number of patrol craft armed with small MGs. These include *Bouzagza, Djurdjura, Hodna, Aures* and *Hoggar*. The first three are P 1200 class 39 ton craft capable of 33 kt. The next pair are P 802 class. They were built by Watercraft, Shoreham and delivered in November 1985.

Angola

MARINHA DE GUERRA

Country Overview

Formerly known as Portuguese West Africa, the Republic of Angola became independent in 1975 but has been ravaged by civil war ever since. With an area of 481,354 square miles it has borders to the south with Namibia, to the east with Zambia and to the north and east with the Democratic Republic of the Congo which separates a small exclave, Cabinda, from the rest of the country. Angola has a coastline with the south Atlantic Ocean of some 864 n miles. The capital, largest city and principal port is Luanda. Territorial seas (12 n miles) and a fisheries zone (200 n miles) are claimed. A 200 n mile Exclusive Economic Zone (EEZ) has been claimed but the limits have not been published.

Headquarters Appointments

Commander of the Navy: Admiral Augusto da Silva Cunha

Personnel

(a) 2009: 890
(b) Voluntary service

Bases

Luanda, Lobito, Namibe. (There are other good harbours available on the 1,000 mile coastline.) Naval HQ at Luanda on Ila de Luanda is in an old fort, as is Namibe.

Naval Aviation

Seven EADS-CASA C 212-300MP and one Fokker F27 maritime patrol aircraft are operated by the Air Force.

PATROL FORCES

2 NAMACURRA CLASS (INSHORE PATROL CRAFT) (PB)

Displacement, tons: 5 full load
Dimensions, feet (metres): 29.5 × 9 × 2.8 *(9 × 2.7 × 0.8)*
Main machinery: 2 Yamaha outboards; 380 hp(m) *(2.79 kW)*
Speed, knots: 32. **Range, n miles:** 180 at 20 kt
Complement: 4
Guns: 1—12.7 mm MG. 2—7.62 mm MGs.
Depth charges: 1 rack.
Radars: Surface search: Furuno; I-band.

Comment: Built in South Africa in 1980–81. Can be transported by road. Donated by South Africa in 2006.

NAMACURRA (South Africa colours) ***8/2001, van Ginderen Collection*** / 0132783

Anguilla

Country Overview

British dependency since 1971 following secession from associated state of St Kitts-Nevis-Anguilla. With an area of 35 square miles, the island is situated at the northern end of the Leeward Islands in the Lesser Antilles and bordered by the Caribbean to the west and Atlantic to the east. Territorial seas (3 n miles) and a fishery zone (200 n miles) are claimed.

Headquarters Appointments

Inspector of Marine:
Inspector Elliott Forbes

Personnel

2009: 79

POLICE

1 HALMATIC M160 CLASS (INSHORE PATROL CRAFT) (PB)

DOLPHIN

Displacement, tons: 18 light
Dimensions, feet (metres): 52.5 × 15.4 × 4.6 *(16 × 4.7 × 1.4)*
Main machinery: 2 MAN V10 diesels; 820 hp *(610 kW)* sustained; 2 shafts
Speed, knots: 34. **Range, n miles:** 575 at 23 kt
Complement: 8
Guns: 1—12.7 mm MG.
Radars: Surface search: JRC 2254; I-band.

Comment: Built by Halmatic and delivered 22 December 1989. Identical craft to Qatar. GRP hull. Rigid inflatable boat launched by gravity davit. Returned to service on 30 August 2004 after refit.

DOLPHIN ***6/2006, Anguilla Police*** / 1164311

1 BOSTON WHALER (INSHORE PATROL CRAFT) (PB)

LAPWING

Displacement, tons: 2.2 full load
Dimensions, feet (metres): 27 × 10 × 1.5 *(8.2 × 3 × 0.5)*
Main machinery: 2 Johnson outboards; 300 hp *(225 kW)*
Speed, knots: 38
Complement: 4

Comment: Delivered in 1990 and re-engined in 2005.

LAPWING ***6/2006, Anguilla Police*** / 1164310

Antigua and Barbuda

Country Overview

Independent since 1981, the British monarch, represented by a governor-general, is head of state. Situated at the southern end of the Leeward Islands in the Lesser Antilles chain, the country comprises Antigua (108 square miles), Barbuda to the north and uninhabited Redonda to the southwest. The capital, largest town, and main port is St John's. An archipelagic state, territorial seas (12 n miles) and a fishery zone (200 n miles) are claimed. A 200 n mile Exclusive Economic Zone (EEZ) has also been claimed but the limits are not defined. The Antigua Barbuda Defence Force (ABDF) took over the Coast Guard on 1 May 1995.

Headquarters Appointments

Commanding Officer, Coast Guard:
Lieutenant Auden Nicholas

Personnel

2009: 50 (3 officers)

Bases

HQ: Deepwater Harbour, St Johns
Maintenance: Camp Blizzard

COAST GUARD

Notes: (1) In addition there is a Hurricane RIB, *CG 081* with a speed of 35 kt and two Boston Whalers, *CG 071-2*, with speeds of 30 kt. All were acquired in 1988/90.
(2) A 920 Zodiac RHIB, CG 091, was donated by the US government in 2003. It is capable of over 40 kt.

CG 091 *9/2004, ABDFCG* / 0587690

CG 081 *9/2004, ABDFCG* / 0587691

1 SWIFT 65 ft CLASS (PB)

Name	*No*	*Builders*	*Commissioned*
LIBERTA	P 01	Swiftships, Morgan City	30 Apr 1984

Displacement, tons: 36 full load
Dimensions, feet (metres): 65.5 × 18.4 × 5 *(20 × 5.6 × 1.5)*
Main machinery: 2 Detroit Diesel 12V-71TA diesels; 840 hp *(616 kW)* sustained; 2 shafts
Speed, knots: 22
Range, n miles: 250 at 18 kt
Complement: 9
Guns: 1 — 12.7 mm MG. 2 — 7.62 mm MGs.
Radars: Surface search: Furuno; I-band.

Comment: Ordered in November 1983. Aluminium construction. Funded by US. Refitted in 2001.

LIBERTA *5/2003* / 0568341

1 DAUNTLESS CLASS (PB)

Name	*No*	*Builders*	*Commissioned*
PALMETTO	P 02	SeaArk Marine, Monticello	7 July 1995

Displacement, tons: 11 full load
Dimensions, feet (metres): 40 × 14 × 4.3 *(12.2 × 4.3 × 1.3)*
Main machinery: 2 Caterpillar 3208TA diesels; 870 hp *(650 kW)* sustained; 2 shafts
Speed, knots: 27
Range, n miles: 600 at 18 kt
Complement: 4
Guns: 1 — 7.62 mm MG.
Radars: Surface search: Raytheon R40; I-band.

Comment: Funded by USA. Similar craft delivered to several Caribbean countries in 1994–98.

PALMETTO *9/2004, ABDFCG* / 0587689

Argentina

ARMADA ARGENTINA

Country Overview

The Argentine Republic is in southern South America. With an area of 1,068,302 square miles it has borders to the north with Bolivia and Paraguay, to the east with Brazil and Uruguay and to the south and west with Chile. The country includes the Tierra del Fuego territory which comprises the eastern half of the Isla Grande de Tierra del Fuego and a number of adjacent islands to the east, including Isla de los Estados. It also claims sovereignty of the Falkland Islands. The capital, largest city and principal port is Buenos Aires. There are further ports at La Plata, Bahia Blanca, Comodoro Rivadavia and a river port at Rosario. There are some 5,940 n miles of navigable internal waterways. Territorial Seas (12 n miles) are claimed. An EEZ (200 n miles) is claimed but its limits are only partly defined by boundary agreements.

Headquarters Appointments

Chief of Naval General Staff:
Admiral Jorge Omar Godoy
Deputy Chief of Naval Staff:
Vice Admiral Benito Ítalo Rótolo
Director General Personnel:
Vice Admiral Enrique Salvador Olmedo
Naval Operations Commander:
Rear Admiral Luis Oscar Manino

Senior Appointments

Commander Fleet:
Rear Admiral Eduardo Raúl Castro Rivas
Commander, Marine Infantry:
Rear Admiral Captain Osvaldo Emilio Colombo
Commander Naval Aviation:
Rear Admiral Carlos Rodolfo Machetanz
Commander, Naval Area Austral:
Rear Admiral Daniel Alberto Enrique Mártin
Commander, Submarines:
Captain Gustavo Ricardo Grunschlager
Commander, Atlantic:
Rear Admiral Delfor Raúl Ferraris
Commander, Naval Area Fluvial:
Captain Alejandro Arturo Fernandez Löbbe

Personnel

2009: 18,249 (2,531 officers)

Organisation

Naval Area Austral covers coastal area from latitude 46° to 60° south.
Naval Area Atlantic covers coastal area from latitude 36° 18' to 46° south.
Naval Area Fluvial includes the rivers Paraná, Uruguay and Plate.
Naval Area Antarctica is activated when *Almirante Irizar* deploys.

Special Forces

Consists of tactical divers who operate from submarines and other naval units, and amphibious commandos who are trained in parachuting and behind the lines operations. Both groups consist of about 150.

Bases

Buenos Aires (Dársena Norte): Some naval training.
Rio Santiago (La Plata): Schools.
Mar del Plata: Submarine base plus Maritime Patrol Division and Hydrographic ships.
Puerto Belgrano: Main naval base, schools. Fleet Marine Force.
Ushuaia, Deseado, Dársena Sur, Zárate, Caleta Paula; Small naval bases.

Prefix to Ships' Names

ARA (Armada Republica Argentina)

Naval Aviation

Personnel: 2,500
The Naval Air Command is at Puerto Belgrano.
1st Naval Air Wing (Punta Indio Naval Air Base): Naval Reconnaissance Group with Beech 200s. Naval Aviation School with Beech T-34 Turbo Mentor.
2nd Naval Air Wing (Comandante Espora Naval Air Base): ASW Squadron with Grumman S-2T Trackers; 2nd Naval Helicopter Squadron with Agusta/Sikorsky SH-3H and AS-61D Sea Kings; 2nd Naval Attack Squadron with Super Etendards; 1st Naval Helicopter Squadron with Alouette III and Fennecs.
3rd Naval Air Wing (Almirante Zar Naval Air Base, Trelew): 6th Naval Reconnaissance and Surveillance Squadron with Lockheed P-3C Orions, Beechcraft B 200 and Pilatus PC-6B.
52 Logistic Support Flight (Almirante Izar Naval Air Base): Fokker F-28s.

Marine Corps

Personnel: 2,800
2nd Marine Infantry Battalion (Puerto Belgrano)
3rd Marine Infantry Battalion (Zarate)
4th Marine Infantry Battalion (Ushuaia)
5th Marine Infantry Battalion (Training) (Rio Grande)
Marine Field Artillery Battalion (Puerto Belgrano)
Command and Logistics Support Battalion (Puerto Belgrano)
Amphibious Vehicles Battalion (Puerto Belgrano)
Communications Battalion (Puerto Belgrano)
Marine A/A Battalion (Puerto Belgrano)
Amphibious Engineers Company (Puerto Belgrano)
Amphibious Commandos Group (Puerto Belgrano)
There are Marine Security Battalions at Naval Bases in Buenos Aires and Puerto Belgrano.
There are Marine Security Companies at Naval Bases in Mar del Plata, Trelew, Ushuaia, Punta Indio and Zarate.

Strength of the Fleet

Type	*Active (Reserve)*	*Building*
Patrol Submarines	3	–
Destroyers	4	–
Frigates	9	–
Patrol Ships	5	5
Fast Attack Craft (Gun/Missile)	2	–
Coastal Patrol Craft	6	–
Survey/Oceanographic Ships	4	–
Survey Launches	1	–
Transports/Tankers	8	–
Training Ships	8	–

PENNANT LIST

Submarines

S 31	Salta
S 41	Santa Cruz
S 42	San Juan

Destroyers

D 10	Almirante Brown
D 11	La Argentina
D 12	Heroina
D 13	Sarandi

Frigates

31	Drummond
32	Guerrico
33	Granville
41	Espora
42	Rosales
43	Spiro
44	Parker
45	Robinson
46	Gomez Roca

Patrol Forces

A 1	Comandante General Irigoyen
A 2	Teniente Olivieri
A 3	Francisco de Gurruchaga
A 6	Suboficial Castillo
A 9	Alferez Sobral
P 20	Murature
P 21	King
P 61	Baradero
P 62	Barranqueras
P 63	Clorinda
P 64	Concepción del Uruguay
P 65	Punta Mogotes
P 66	Rio Santiago
P 85	Intrepida
P 86	Indomita

Auxiliaries

B 1	Patagonia
B 3	Canal Beagle
B 4	Bahia San Blas
B 5	Cabo de Hornos
B 13	Ingeniero Julio Krause
B 52	Hercules
Q 2	Libertad
Q 5	Almirante Irizar
Q 11	Comodoro Rivadavia
Q 15	Cormoran
Q 20	Puerto Deseado
Q 61	Ciudad de Zarate
Q 62	Ciudad de Rosario
Q 63	Punta Alta
Q 73	Itati
Q 74	Fortuna I
Q 75	Fortuna II
Q 76	Fortuna III
R 2	Querandi
R 3	Tehuelche
R 5	Mocovi
R 6	Calchaqui
R 7	Ona
R 8	Toba
R 10	Chulupi
R 12	Mataco
R 16	Capayán
R 18	Chiquillán
R 19	Morcoyán

SUBMARINES

Notes: (1) Cosmos and Havas underwater chariots in service. Cosmos types are capable of carrying limpet or ground mines.
(2) There are no known plans to replace the current submarine force.

2 SANTA CRUZ (TR 1700) CLASS (SSK)

Name	*No*	*Builders*	*Laid down*	*Launched*	*Commissioned*
SANTA CRUZ	S 41	Thyssen Nordseewerke	6 Dec 1980	28 Sep 1982	18 Oct 1984
SAN JUAN	S 42	Thyssen Nordseewerke	18 Mar 1982	20 June 1983	19 Nov 1985

Displacement, tons: 2,116 surfaced; 2,264 dived
Dimensions, feet (metres): 216.5 × 23.9 × 21.3 *(66 × 7.3 × 6.5)*
Main machinery: Diesel-electric; 4 MTU 16V 6,720 hp diesels; 6,720 hp(m) *(4.94 MW)* sustained; 4 alternators; 4.4 MW; 1 Siemens Type 1HR4525 + 1HR 4525 4-circuit DC motor; 6.6 MW; 1 shaft
Speed, knots: 15 surfaced; 12 snorting; 26 dived
Range, n miles: 12,000 at 8 kt surfaced; 20 at 25 kt dived; 460 at 6 kt dived
Complement: 29 (5 officers)

Torpedoes: 6—21 in *(533 mm)* bow tubes. 22 AEG SST 4; wire-guided; active/passive homing to 12/28 km *(6.5/15 n miles)* at 35/23 kt; warhead 260 kg; automatic reload in 50 seconds or US Mk 37; wire-guided; active/passive homing to 8 km *(4.4 n miles)* at 24 kt; warhead 150 kg. Swim-out discharge. Mk 48 to replace Mk 37 in due course.
Mines: Capable of carrying 34 ground mines.
Countermeasures: ESM: Kollmorgen Sea Sentry III; radar warning.
Weapons control: Signaal Simbads; can handle 5 targets and 3 torpedoes simultaneously.
Radars: Navigation: Thomson-CSF Calypso IV; I-band.
Sonars: Atlas Elektronik CSU 3/4; active/passive search and attack; medium frequency.
Thomson Sintra DUUX 5; passive ranging.

Programmes: Contract signed 30 November 1977 with Thyssen Nordseewerke for two submarines to be built at Emden. Parts and technical oversight were also to be provided for the construction of four further boats in Argentina by Astilleros Domecq Garcia, Buenos Aires. Work on units three and four was initiated and S 43 *(Santa Fe)* was reported as 70 per cent complete by 2004. However, although completion of the boat is being kept under review, funding is likely to prove difficult in the current financial climate. Work on S 44 *(Santiago del Estero)* was reported as 30 per cent complete in 1996 but further work since then has not been reported. Equipment for numbers five and six has been used for spares.
Modernisation: Both completed refits between 1999–2002. Refit included new main motors and sonar upgrade. *Santa Cruz* underwent a two-year mid-life refit at Domecq Garcia 2005–07. She was followed by *San Juan* on 17 August 2007 and is expected to be completed in 2010. The scope of the upgrade is reported to include new MTU engines, new batteries and replacement of masts.
Structure: Diving depth, 270 m *(890 ft)*.
Operational: Maximum endurance is 70 days. Both can be used for Commando insertion operations. They are based at Mar del Plata.

SANTA CRUZ *7/2004, A E Galarce* / 1044064

SAN JUAN *5/2004, A E Galarce* / 1044065

1 SALTA (TYPE 209/1200) CLASS (SSK)

Name	*No*	*Builders*	*Laid down*	*Launched*	*Commissioned*
SALTA	S 31	Howaldtswerke, Kiel	30 Apr 1970	9 Nov 1972	7 Mar 1974

Displacement, tons: 1,140 surfaced; 1,248 dived
Dimensions, feet (metres): 183.4 × 20.5 × 17.9 *(55.9 × 6.3 × 5.5)*
Main machinery: Diesel-electric; 4 MTU 12V 493 AZ80 diesels; 2,400 hp(m) *(1.76 MW)* sustained; 4 alternators; 1.7 MW; 1 motor; 4,600 hp(m) *(3.36 MW);* 1 shaft
Speed, knots: 10 surfaced; 22 dived; 11 snorting
Range, n miles: 6,000 at 8 kt surfaced; 230 at 8 kt; 400 at 4 kt dived
Complement: 31 (5 officers)

Torpedoes: 8—21 in *(533 mm)* bow tubes. 14 AEG SST 4 Mod 1; wire-guided; active/passive homing to 12/28 km *(6.5/15 n miles)* at 35/23 kt; warhead 260 kg or US Mk 37; wire-guided; active/passive homing to 8 km *(4.4 n miles)* at 24 kt; warhead 150 kg. Swim-out discharge.
Mines: Capable of carrying ground mines.
Countermeasures: ESM: Thomson CSF DR 2000; radar warning.
Weapons control: Signaal M8 digital; computer-based; up to 3 targets engaged simultaneously.
Radars: Navigation: Thomson-CSF Calypso II.
Sonars: Atlas Elektronik CSU 3 (AN 526/AN 5039/41); active/passive search and attack; medium frequency.
Thomson Sintra DUUX 2C and DUUG 1D; passive ranging.

Programmes: Ordered in 1968. Built in sections by Howaldtswerke Deutsche Werft AG, Kiel from the IK 68 design of Ingenieurkontor, Lübeck. Sections were shipped to Argentina for assembly at Tandanor, Buenos Aires. Second of class *(San Luis)* has been used for spares since 1997 and, although re-activation remains a possibility, is likely to be converted into a museum ship.
Modernisation: *Salta* completed a mid-life modernisation at the Domecq Garcia Shipyard in May 1995. New engines, weapons and electrical systems fitted. Installation of new batteries began at Domecq Garcia in 2004 and completed in August 2005.
Structure: Diving depth, 250 m *(820 ft).*
Operational: Operational and based at Mar del Plata.

SALTA ***12/2002, A E Galarce*** / 0529819

DESTROYERS

4 ALMIRANTE BROWN (MEKO 360 H2) CLASS (DDGHM)

Name	*No*	*Builders*	*Laid down*	*Launched*	*Commissioned*
ALMIRANTE BROWN	D 10	Blohm + Voss, Hamburg	8 Sep 1980	28 Mar 1981	26 Jan 1983
LA ARGENTINA	D 11	Blohm + Voss, Hamburg	30 Mar 1981	25 Sep 1981	4 May 1983
HEROINA	D 12	Blohm + Voss, Hamburg	24 Aug 1981	17 Feb 1982	31 Oct 1983
SARANDI	D 13	Blohm + Voss, Hamburg	9 Mar 1982	31 Aug 1982	16 Apr 1984

Displacement, tons: 2,900 standard; 3,630 full load
Dimensions, feet (metres): 413.1 × 46 × 19 (screws) *(125.9 × 14 × 5.8)*
Main machinery: COGOG; 2 RR Olympus TM3B gas turbines; 50,000 hp *(37.4 MW)* sustained
2 RR Tyne RM1C gas turbines; 9,900 hp *(7.4 MW)* sustained; 2 shafts; cp props
Speed, knots: 30; 20.5 cruising
Range, n miles: 4,500 at 18 kt
Complement: 200 (26 officers)

ALMIRANTE BROWN ***(Scale 1 : 1,200), Ian Sturton*** / 0569252

Missiles: SSM: 8 Aerospatiale MM 40 Exocet (2 quad) launchers ❶; inertial cruise; active radar homing to 70 km *(40 n miles);* warhead 165 kg; sea-skimmer.
SAM: Selenia/Elsag Albatros octuple launcher ❷; 24 Aspide; semi-active homing to 13 km *(7 n miles)* at 2.5 Mach; height envelope 15–5,000 m *(49.2–16,405 ft);* warhead 30 kg.
Guns: 1 OTO Melara 5 in *(127 mm)*/54 automatic ❸; 45 rds/min to 23 km *(12.42 n miles)* anti-surface; 7 km *(3.6 n miles)* anti-aircraft; weight of shell 32 kg; also fires chaff and illuminants.
8 Breda/Bofors 40 mm/70 (4 twin) ❹; 300 rds/min to 12.6 km *(6.8 n miles)* anti-surface; 4 km *(2.2 n miles)* anti-aircraft; weight of shell 0.96 kg; 2 Oerlikon 20 mm.
Torpedoes: 6—324 mm ILAS 3 (2 triple) tubes ❺. Whitehead A 244; anti-submarine; active/passive homing to 7 km *(3.8 n miles)* at 33 kt; warhead 34 kg (shaped charge); 18 reloads.
Countermeasures: Decoys: CSEE Dagaie double mounting; Graseby G1738 towed torpedo decoy system.
2 Breda 105 mm SCLAR chaff rocket launchers; 20 tubes per launcher; can be trained and elevated; chaff to 5 km *(2.7 n miles);* illuminants to 12 km *(6.6 n miles).*
ESM/ECM: Sphinx/Scimitar.
Combat data systems: Signaal SEWACO; Link 10/11. SATCOMs can be fitted.
Electro-optic systems: 2 Signaal LIROD radar/optronic systems ❻ each controlling 2 twin 40 mm mounts.
Radars: Air/surface search: Signaal DA08A ❽; F-band; range 204 km *(110 n miles)* for 2 m² target.
Surface search: Signaal ZW06 ❾; I-band.
Navigation: Decca 1226; I-band.
Fire control: Signaal STIR ❿; I/J/K-band; range 140 km *(76 n miles);* Signaal WM25 ❼; I/J-band.
Sonars: Atlas Elektronik 80 (DSQS-21BZ); hull-mounted; active search and attack; medium frequency.

Helicopters: AS 555 Fennec or SH-3D Sea King (D 11, D 13) ⓫.

Programmes: Six were originally ordered in 1978, but later restricted to four when Meko 140 frigates were ordered in 1979. Similar to Nigerian frigate *Aradu.*
Modernisation: Block II Exocet MM 40 may be fitted when funds are available. *La Argentina* completed 2 year refit in 2006. Upgrades included extension of the flight deck to facilitate Sea King operations. *Sarandi* is undergoing a similar refit during 2008–10. *Heroina* completed refit in 2008 but did not receive the flight deck extension.
Operational: *Almirante Brown* took part in allied Gulf operations in late 1990. Fennec helicopters delivered in 1996 provide over the horizon targeting for SSMs and have the potential to improve ASW capability. All are active and form 2nd Destroyer Squadron based at Puerto Belgrano. All can be used as Flagships.

LA ARGENTINA

11/2002, Mario R V Carneiro / 0528303

ALMIRANTE BROWN

10/2005, Mario R V Carneiro / 1151089

FRIGATES

3 DRUMMOND (TYPE A 69) CLASS (FFG)

Name	*No*	*Builders*	*Laid down*	*Launched*	*Commissioned*
DRUMMOND (ex-*Good Hope*, ex-*Lieutenant de Vaisseau le Hénaff* F 789)	31	Lorient Naval Dockyard	12 Mar 1976	5 Mar 1977	Mar 1978
GUERRICO (ex-*Transvaal*, ex-*Commandant l'Herminier* F 791)	32	Lorient Naval Dockyard	1 Oct 1976	13 Sep 1977	Oct 1978
GRANVILLE	33	Lorient Naval Dockyard	1 Dec 1978	28 June 1980	22 June 1981

Displacement, tons: 950 standard; 1,170 full load
Dimensions, feet (metres): 262.5 × 33.8 × 9.8; 18 (sonar) *(80 × 10.3 × 3; 5.5)*
Main machinery: 2 SEMT-Pielstick 12 PC2.2 V 400 diesels; 12,000 hp(m) *(8.82 MW)* sustained; 2 shafts; LIPS cp props
Speed, knots: 23. **Range, n miles**: 4,500 at 15 kt; 3,000 at 18 kt
Complement: 93 (10 officers)

Missiles: SSM: 4 Aerospatiale MM 38 Exocet (2 twin) launchers ❶; inertial cruise; active radar homing to 42 km *(23 n miles)*; warhead 165 kg; sea-skimmer.
Guns: 1 Creusot-Loire 3.9 in *(100 mm)*/55 Mod 1953 ❷; 80° elevation; 60 rds/min to 17 km *(9 n miles)* anti-surface; 8 km *(4.4 n miles)* anti-aircraft; weight of shell 13.5 kg.
2 Breda 40 mm/70 (twin) ❸; 300 rds/min to 12.5 km *(6.8 n miles)*; weight of shell 0.96 kg; ready ammunition 736 (or 444) using AP tracer, impact or proximity fuzing.
2 Oerlikon 20 mm ❹. 2—12.7 mm MGs.
Torpedoes: 6—324 mm Mk 32 (2 triple) tubes ❺. Whitehead A 244; anti-submarine; active/passive homing to 7 km *(3.8 n miles)* at 33 kt; warhead 34 kg.
Countermeasures: Decoys: CSEE Dagaie double mounting; 10 or 6 replaceable containers; trainable; chaff to 12 km *(6.5 n miles)*; illuminants to 4 km *(2.2 n miles)*; decoys in H- to J-bands or Corvus sextuple launchers for chaff.
ESM: DR 2000/DALIA 500; radar warning.
ECM: Thomson-CSF Alligator; jammer.

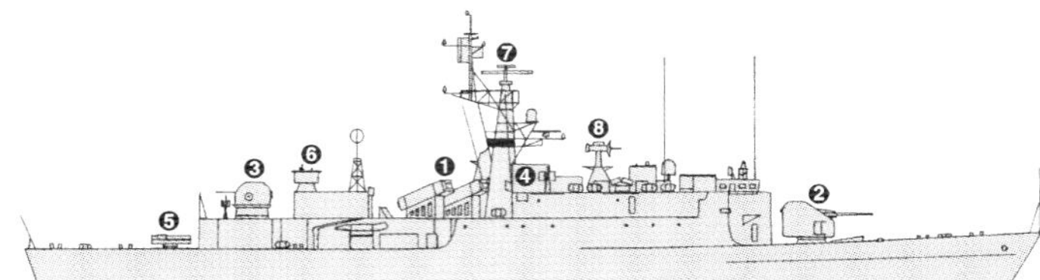

GRANVILLE *(Scale 1 : 900), Ian Sturton* / 0506262

Combat data systems: MINIACO C 31.
Weapons control: Thomson-CSF Vega system. CSEE Panda Mk 2 optical director ❻. Naja optronic director (for 40 mm guns).
Radars: Air/surface search: Thomson-CSF DRBV 51A ❼ with UPX12 IFF; G-band.
Navigation: Decca 1226; I-band.
Fire control: Thomson-CSF DRBC 32E ❽; I/J-band (for 100 mm gun).
Sonars: Thomson Sintra Diodon; hull-mounted; active search and attack.

Programmes: The first pair was originally built for the French Navy and sold to the South African Navy in 1976 while under construction. As a result of a UN embargo on arms sales to South Africa this sale was cancelled. Purchased by Argentina in Autumn 1978. Both arrived in Argentina 2 November 1978 (third ship being ordered shortly afterwards) and all have proved very popular ships in the Argentine Navy. The transfer of a further three of the class from the French Navy is very unlikely.
Modernisation: *Drummond* has had her armament updated to the same standard as the other two, replacing the Bofors 40/60. All three ships fitted with MINIACO C 31 combat data system by 2008.
Operational: Endurance, 15 days. Very economical in fuel consumption. Employed on EEZ patrol operations. All based at Mar del Plata.

GRANVILLE *12/2002, A E Galarce* / 0529818

DRUMMOND *5/2004, A E Galarce* / 1044066

6 ESPORA (MEKO 140 A16) CLASS (FFGH)

Name	*No*	*Builders*	*Laid down*	*Launched*	*Commissioned*
ESPORA	41	AFNE, Rio Santiago	3 Oct 1980	23 Jan 1982	5 July 1985
ROSALES	42	AFNE, Rio Santiago	1 July 1981	4 Mar 1983	14 Nov 1986
SPIRO	43	AFNE, Rio Santiago	4 Jan 1982	24 June 1983	24 Nov 1987
PARKER	44	AFNE, Rio Santiago	2 Aug 1982	31 Mar 1984	17 Apr 1990
ROBINSON	45	AFNE, Rio Santiago	8 June 1983	15 Feb 1985	28 Aug 2000
GOMEZ ROCA	46	AFNE, Rio Santiago	1 Dec 1983	14 Nov 1986	20 May 2004

Displacement, tons: 1,470 standard; 1,850 full load
Dimensions, feet (metres): 299.1 × 36.4 × 11.2 *(91.2 × 11.1 × 3.4)*
Main machinery: 2 SEMT-Pielstick 16 PC2-5 V 400 diesels; 20,400 hp(m) *(15 MW)* sustained; 2 shafts
Speed, knots: 28
Range, n miles: 4,000 at 18 kt
Complement: 93 (11 officers)

Missiles: SSM: 4 Aerospatiale MM 38 Exocet ❶ inertial cruise; active radar homing to 42 km *(23 n miles)*; warhead 165 kg; sea-skimmer.
Guns: 1 OTO Melara 3 in *(76 mm)*/62 compact ❷; 85 rds/min to 16 km *(8.7 n miles)* anti-surface; 12 km *(6.5 n miles)* anti-aircraft; weight of shell 6 kg; also fires chaff and illuminants.
4 Breda 40 mm/70 (2 twin) ❸; 300 rds/min to 12.5 km *(6.8 n miles)*; weight of shell 0.96 kg; ready ammunition 736 (or 444) using AP tracer, impact or proximity fuzing.
2—12.7 mm MGs.
Torpedoes: 6—324 mm ILAS 3 (2 triple) tubes ❹. Whitehead A 244/S; anti-submarine; active/passive homing to 7 km *(3.8 n miles)* at 33 kt; warhead 34 kg (shaped charge).
Countermeasures: Decoys: CSEE Dagaie double mounting; 10 or 6 replaceable containers; trainable; chaff to 12 km *(6.5 n miles)*; illuminants to 4 km *(2.2 n miles)*; decoys in H- to J-bands.
ESM: Elettronica RQN-3B; radar warning.
ECM: Elettronica TQN-2X; jammer.
Combat data systems: Signaal SEWACO.
Electro-optic systems: 1 LIROD 8 optronic director ❺.
Radars: Air/surface search: Signaal DA05 ❻; E/F-band; range 137 km *(75 n miles)* for 2 m² target.
Navigation: Decca TM 1226 (41–45); I-band.
Concilium Celestar (46); I-band.
Fire control: Signaal WM28 ❼; I/J-band; range 46 km *(25 n miles)*.
Signaal WM 22/41; I/J-band.
IFF: Mk 10.
Sonars: Atlas Elektronik ASO 4; hull-mounted; active search and attack; medium frequency.

Helicopters: 1 SA 319B Alouette III or AS 555 Fennec ❽ (in 44–46).

Programmes: A contract was signed with Blohm + Voss on 1 August 1979 for this group of ships which are scaled down Meko 360s. All have been fabricated in AFNE, Rio Santiago. The last pair were to have been scrapped, but on 8 May 1997 a decision was taken to complete them some 14 years after each was first launched. A formal restart ceremony was held on 18 July 1997 and *Robinson* became operational in 2001. *Gomez Roca* became operational in late 2005.
Modernisation: Plans to fit MM 40 Exocet from Meko 360. Flight deck extensions for AS 555 helicopters. *Robinson* and *Gomez Roca* equipped with different EW suite.
Structure: The last three ships were fitted on build with a telescopic hangar. The first three ships may be retro-fitted at a later date.
Operational: Mostly used for offshore patrol and fishery protection duties but *Spiro* and *Rosales* sent to the Gulf in 1990–91. Form 2nd Frigate Squadron based at Puerto Belgrano.

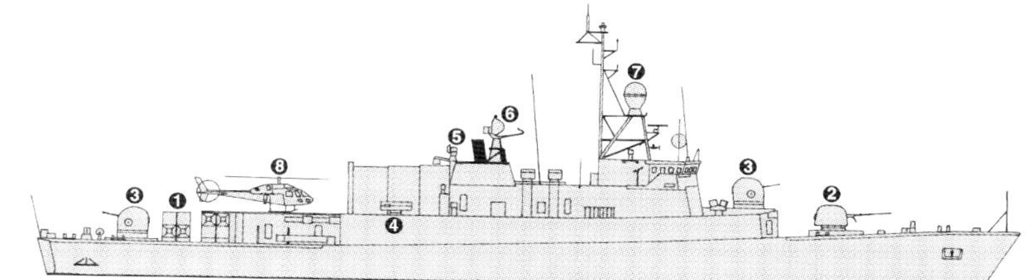

PARKER (Scale 1 : 900), Ian Sturton / 0012007

ROBINSON 5/2008*, Guy Toremans / 1335603

ROSALES 5/2008*, M Declerck / 1335607

ROBINSON 6/2008*, Robert Pabst / 1335602

SHIPBORNE AIRCRAFT

Numbers/Type: 5 Aerospatiale SA 316B Alouette III.
Operational speed: 113 kt *(210 km/h).*
Service ceiling: 10,500 ft *(3,200 m).*
Range: 290 n miles *(540 km).*
Role/Weapon systems: ASW Helicopter; used for liaison in peacetime; wartime role includes commando assault and ASW/ASVW. Sensors: Nose-mounted search radar. Weapons: ASW; 2 × Mk 44 torpedoes. ASV; 2 × AS12 missiles.

ALOUETTE III *5/2008*, Guy Toremans* / 1335606

Numbers/Type: 4 Aerospatiale AS 555 SN Fennec.
Operational speed: 121 kt *(225 km/h).*
Service ceiling: 13,125 ft *(4,000 m).*
Range: 389 n miles *(722 km).*
Role/Weapon systems: Principal role OTHT with potential ASW capability. Delivered in 1996. More are wanted. Sensors: Bendix RDR 1500 radar; Mk 3 MAD. Weapons: ASW; 2 × A 244 torpedoes or 4 depth bombs may be fitted.

FENNEC *7/2004, A E Galarce* / 1044071

Numbers/Type: 2/1/4 Agusta-Sikorsky ASH-3H/ASH-3D/UH-3D Sea King.
Operational speed: 120 kt *(222 km/h).*
Service ceiling: 12,205 ft *(3,720 m).*
Range: 630 n miles *(1,165 km).*
Role/Weapon systems: Seven aircraft: Two ASH-3H armed with Exocet AM-39; one ASH-3D ASW aircraft and four UH-3D utility/transport aircraft acquired from the US Navy in 2008. The latter for Antarctic operations and to replace UH-1H aircraft. Sensors (ASH variants): APS-705 search radar, Bendix AQS 18 sonar. Weapons: ASW; up to 4 × A 244 torpedoes or 4 × depth bombs. ASV: 1 AM 39 Exocet ASM (ASH-3H).

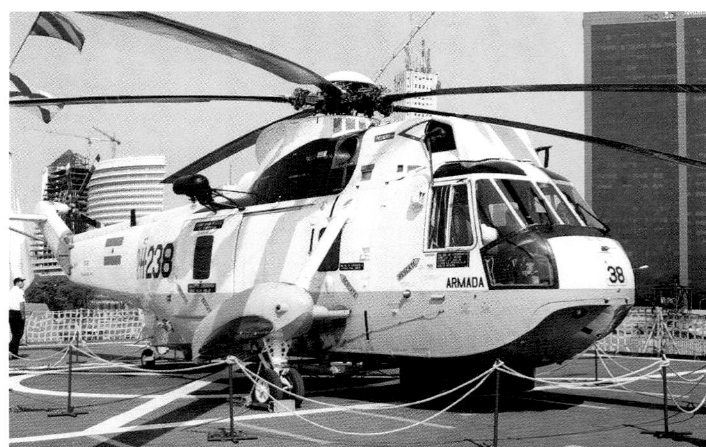

SEA KING *8/2002, A E Galarce* / 0529816

Numbers/Type: 5 + (6) Dassault-Breguet Super Etendard.
Operational speed: Mach 1.
Service ceiling: 44,950 ft *(13,700 m).*
Range: 920 n miles *(1,700 km).*
Role/Weapon systems: Strike Fighter with anti-shipping ability. In the past have flown from US or Brazilian aircraft carriers. Five aircraft are operational out of a total of 11. Five replacement Agave radars reportedly received in 2008. This may increase operational availability to eight or nine aircraft. Strike, air defence and ASV roles. Hi-lo-hi combat radius 460 n miles *(850 km).* Sensors: Thomson-CSF Agave multimode radar, ECM. Weapons: Strike; 2.1 tons of 'iron' bombs. ASVW; 1 AM 39 Exocet or 1 × Martin Pescador missiles. Self-defence; 2 × Magic AAMs. Standard; 2 × 30 mm cannon.

SUPER ETENDARD *10/2007, Argentine Navy* / 1335605

Numbers/Type: 5 Grumman S-2ET Tracker.
Operational speed: 130 kt *(241 km/h).*
Service ceiling: 25,000 ft *(7,620 m).*
Range: 1,350 n miles *(2,500 km).*
Role/Weapon systems: Used for MR and EEZ patrol. One shipped to Israel in 1989 for Garrett turboprop installation. Prototype for fleet conversion in Argentina when completed in 2000. Sensors: EL/M-2022 search radar up to 32 sonobuoys, ALD-2B or AES 210/E ESM, echo-ranging depth charges. Weapons: ASW; A 244 torpedoes, bombs and depth charges.

S-2 TRACKER (landing on São Paulo) *5/2002, Walter Lastra/Fuerzas Navales* / 0528430

Numbers/Type: 7 Aermacchi MB-326GB.
Operational speed: 468 kt *(867 km/h).*
Service ceiling: 47,000 ft *(14,325 m).*
Range: 1,320 n miles *(2,446 km).*
Role/Weapon systems: Light Attack; supplements anti-shipping/strike; also has training role. Weapons: ASV; 1.8 tons of 'iron' bombs. Strike; 6 × rockets. Recce; underwing camera pod.

AERMACCHI 326 *4/2004* / 0051048

Numbers/Type: 4 Beechcraft B 200M Cormoran.
Operational speed: 260 kt *(482 km/h).*
Service ceiling: 31,000 ft *(9,448 m).*
Range: 2,000 n miles *(3,705 km).*
Role/Weapon systems: Multipurpose converted to Cormoran version for maritime patrol. There are three other unconverted aircraft. Sensors: Search radar. Weapons: Unarmed.

BEECH CORMORAN *5/2004* / 0570789

LAND-BASED MARITIME AIRCRAFT

Notes: (1) In addition there are three Fokker F28 for Logistic Support; one Pilatus PC-6B for reconnaissance and nine Beech T-34 Turbo Mentor training aircraft. The four Lockheed Electra L-188 are no longer in service.
(2) Thirty-six ex-US Navy A4M Skyhawk with radar APG-66 acquired by the Air Force by July 1998. First 18 delivered in crates in 1995–96 and remainder modernised before delivery in 1997–98.
(3) Acquisition of second-hand Mirage 2000 aircraft is reported to be under consideration.
(4) There are plans to acquire at least six LMAASA AT-63 Pampa training/light attack aircraft to replace the MB-326 fleet.

Numbers/Type: 6 Lockheed P-3B Orion.
Operational speed: 410 kt *(760 km/h)*.
Service ceiling: 28,300 ft *(8,625 m)*.
Range: 4,000 m *(7,410 km)*.
Role/Weapon systems: Two acquired in 1997 from US; four more in 1998, and two for spares in 1999. Sensors: APS-115 radar; ESM. Weapons: Three aircraft modified by 2007 under Gran Explorador programme. Upgrades are likely to have included restoration of ASW capabilities, addition of AM-39 Exocet and radar modifications. FLIR may also be added. A fourth aircraft is to be modified in 2009.

ORION *6/2002, Argentine Navy / 0528429*

PATROL FORCES

0 + 5 OFFSHORE PATROL VESSELS (PSO)

Displacement, tons: 1,850 full load
Dimensions, feet (metres): 262.5 × 42.6 × 12.5 *(80.0 × 13.0 × 3.8)*
Main machinery: 2 Wärtsilä 12V26 diesels; 10,950 hp *(8.2 MW)*; 2 shafts; LIPS cp props; 2 bow thrusters
Speed, knots: 21
Range, n miles: 8,600 at 12 kt
Complement: 30 + 30 passengers
Guns: 1—40 mm.
Radars: Surface search: To be announced.
Navigation: To be announced.
Fire control: To be announced.
Helicopters: Platform for one medium.

Programmes: Project POM (Patrullero Oceánico Multipropósito) is for five offshore patrol vessels. The ships are expected to be to a Fassmer design and generally similar to ships procured under the Chilean Danubio IV programme. Approval for the project was given in mid-2007 and constructionis expected to start at Astillero Rio Santiago Shipyard in February 2009. The first ship is to be delivered in 2010 and subsequent units are to follow at about six month intervals.
Structure: Steel construction. The design includes stealth features. Upper-deck layout features a helicopter launching platform, crane, two 7 m RIBs, container storage and a special rescue zone.

OPV *6/2005, Fassmer GmbH / 1116081*

3 CHEROKEE CLASS (PATROL SHIPS) (PSO)

Name	*No*	*Builders*	*Commissioned*
COMANDANTE GENERAL IRIGOYEN (ex-*Cahuilla*)	A 1	Charleston SB and DD Co	10 Mar 1945
FRANCISCO DE GURRUCHAGA (ex-*Luiseno* ATF 156)	A 3	Charleston SB and DD Co	16 June 1945
SUBOFICIAL CASTILLO (ex-*Takelma* ATF 113)	A 6	United Engineering Co, Alameda	3 Aug 1944

Displacement, tons: 1,235 standard; 1,731 full load
Dimensions, feet (metres): 205 × 38.5 × 17 *(62.5 × 11.7 × 5.2)*
Main machinery: Diesel-electric; 4 GM 12—278 diesels; 4,400 hp *(3.28 MW)*; 4 generators; 1 motor; 3,000 hp *(2.24 MW)*; 1 shaft
Speed, knots: 16
Range, n miles: 6,500 at 15 kt; 15,000 at 8 kt
Complement: 85
Guns: 4 Bofors 40 mm/60 (2 twin) (A 1); 2 Bofors 40 mm/60 (A 3); 1 Bofors 40 mm/60 (A 6); 2 Oerlikon 20 mm/70 (A 1); 4 Oerlikon 20 mm (A 3, A 6); 2—12.7 mm MGs (A 6).
Radars: Surface search: Racal Decca 626; I-band.
Navigation: Racal Decca 1230; I-band.

Comment: Fitted with powerful pumps and other salvage equipment. *Comandante General Irigoyen* transferred by the US at San Diego, California, on 9 July 1961. Classified as a tug until 1966 when she was rerated as patrol ship. *Francisco De Gurruchaga* transferred on 24 July 1975 by sale, *Suboficial Castillo* on 30 September 1993 by grant aid. *Gurruchaga* fitted with two new diesel engines in 2008. The ships appear to be fitted for but not with armament. All operational and based at Mar del Plata.

SUBOFICIAL CASTILLO *11/2007, A E Galarce / 1335601*

1 OLIVIERI CLASS (PATROL SHIP) (PBO)

Name	*No*	*Builders*	*Commissioned*
TENIENTE OLIVIERI (ex-*Marsea 10*)	A 2	Quality SB, Louisiana	1981

Displacement, tons: 1,640 full load
Dimensions, feet (metres): 184.8 × 40 × 14 *(56.3 × 12.2 × 4.3)*
Main machinery: 2 GM/EMD 16-645 E6; 3,230 hp *(2.4 MW)* sustained; 2 shafts; bow thruster
Speed, knots: 14
Range, n miles: 2,800 at 10 kt
Complement: 15 (4 officers)
Guns: 2—12.7 mm MGs.

Comment: Built by Quality Shipyards, New Orleans, as an oilfield support ship but rated as an Aviso. Acquired from US Maritime Administration 15 November 1987. Capable of carrying 600 tons of stores and 800 tons of liquids. Based at Puerto Belgrano.

TENIENTE OLIVIERI *3/2000 / 0104168*

1 SOTOYOMO CLASS (PATROL SHIP) (PBO)

Name	*No*	*Builders*	*Commissioned*
ALFEREZ SOBRAL (ex-*Salish* ATA 187)	A 9	Levingstone, Orange	9 Sep 1944

Displacement, tons: 800 full load
Dimensions, feet (metres): 143 × 33.9 × 13 *(43.6 × 10.3 × 4)*
Main machinery: Diesel-electric; 2 GM 12-278A diesels; 2,200 hp *(1.64 MW)*; 2 generators; 1 motor; 1,500 hp *(1.12 MW)*; 1 shaft
Speed, knots: 12.5
Range, n miles: 16,500 at 8 kt
Complement: 49
Guns: 1 Bofors 40 mm/60. 2 Oerlikon 20 mm.
Radars: Surface search: Decca 1226; I-band.

Comment: Former US ocean tug transferred on 10 February 1972. Paid off in 1987 but back in service by 1996. Armament has been reduced.

ALFEREZ SOBRAL *2/2001, Eric Grove / 1127024*

2 INTREPIDA CLASS (TYPE TNC 45)
(FAST ATTACK CRAFT—GUN/MISSILE) (PGGF)

Name	*No*	*Builders*	*Launched*	*Commissioned*
INTREPIDA	P 85	Lürssen, Bremen	2 Dec 1973	20 July 1974
INDOMITA	P 86	Lürssen, Bremen	8 Apr 1974	12 Dec 1974

Displacement, tons: 268 full load
Dimensions, feet (metres): 147.3 × 24.3 × 7.9 *(44.9 × 7.4 × 2.4)*
Main machinery: 4 MTU MD 16V 538TB90 diesels; 12,000 hp(m) *(8.82 MW)*; 4 shafts
Speed, knots: 25
Range, n miles: 1,450 at 20 kt
Complement: 39 (5 officers)
Missiles: SSM: 2 Aerospatiale Exocet MM 38 *(Intrepida)*; active radar homing to 42 km *(23 n miles)*; warhead 165 kg.
Guns: 1 OTO Melara 3 in *(76 mm)*/62 compact; 85 rds/min to 16 km *(9 n miles)* anti-surface; 12 km *(6.5 n miles)* anti-aircraft; weight of shell 6 kg.
1 or 2 Bofors 40 mm/70; 330 rds/min to 12 km *(6.5 n miles)* anti-surface; 4 km *(2.2 n miles)* anti-aircraft; weight of shell 0.89 kg.
2—12.7 mm MGs.
2 Oerlikon 81 mm rocket launchers for illuminants.
Torpedoes: 2—21 in *(533 mm)* launchers. AEG SST-4; wire-guided; active/passive homing to 28 km *(15 n miles)* at 23 kt; warhead 250 kg.
Countermeasures: ESM: Racal RDL 1; radar warning.
Weapons control: Signaal WM22 optronic for guns/missiles. Signaal M11 for torpedo guidance and control.
Radars: Surface search: Decca 626; I-band.

Comment: These two vessels were ordered in 1970. Both are painted with a brown/green camouflage. Camouflage netting can also be fitted. Exocet SSM fitted vice the forward of the two Bofors guns in *Intrepida* in 1998. *Indomita* started refit at Domeq Garcia shipyard in January 2008. Upgrades are expected to include new diesel engines, modification of WM22, to include FLIR and laser rangefinder, replacement of surface search radar and unspecified changes to armament. *Intrepida* is likely to start a similar refit in 2009.

INTREPIDA *6/2001, Argentine Navy* / 0130735

INTREPIDA (with camouflage netting) *3/2001* / 0126381

4 BARADERO (DABUR) CLASS
(COASTAL PATROL CRAFT) (PB)

Name	*No*	*Builders*	*Commissioned*
BARADERO	P 61	Israel Aircraft Industries	1978
BARRANQUERAS	P 62	Israel Aircraft Industries	1978
CLORINDA	P 63	Israel Aircraft Industries	1978
CONCEPCIÓN DEL URUGUAY	P 64	Israel Aircraft Industries	1978

Displacement, tons: 33.7 standard; 39 full load
Dimensions, feet (metres): 64.9 × 18 × 5.8 *(19.8 × 5.5 × 1.8)*
Main machinery: 2 GM 12V-71TA diesels; 840 hp *(627 kW)* sustained; 2 shafts
Speed, knots: 19
Range, n miles: 450 at 13 kt
Complement: 9
Guns: 2 Oerlikon 20 mm. 4—12.7 mm MGs.
Depth charges: 2 portable rails.
Radars: Navigation: I-band.

Comment: Of all-aluminium construction. Employed in 1991 and 1992 as part of the UN Central American peacekeeping force. Based at Ushuaia.

BARADERO CLASS *12/2000, Eric Grove* / 1044073

2 POINT CLASS (PB)

Name	*No*	*Builders*	*Commissioned*
PUNTA MOGOTES (ex-*Point Hobart*)	P 65 (ex-82377)	J Martinac, Tacoma	13 July 1970
RIO SANTIAGO (ex-*Point Carrew*)	P 66 (ex-82374)	USCG Yard, Curtis Bay	18 May 1970

Displacement, tons: 67 full load
Dimensions, feet (metres): 83 × 17.2 × 15.8 *(25.3 × 5.2 × 1.8)*
Main machinery: 2 Caterpillar diesels; 1,600 hp *(1.19 MW)*; 2 shafts
Speed, knots: 22
Range, n miles: 1,200 at 8 kt
Complement: 10
Guns: 2—12.7 mm MGs.
Radars: Surface search: Raytheon SPS 64; I-band.

Comment: *Punta Mogotes* transferred from US Coast Guard on 8 July 1999 and is based at Mar del Plata. *Rio Santiago* transferred 22 August 2000.

RIO SANTIAGO *4/2007, A E Galarce* / 1167920

AMPHIBIOUS FORCES

Notes: (1) Marine Corps acquired two Guardian craft in October 1999 and two more in February 2000. Powered by twin 150 hp Johnson outboards. Carry 1—12.7 mm MG and 4—7.62 mm MGs, Raytheon radar.
(2) The first two of a new class of eight indigenously built LCVPs entered service in 2007. Their names are reported to be *Corbeta Uruguay* and *Rompehielos General San Martin*.
(3) The acquisition of a multirole ship, possibly in co-operation with Brazil is under consideration. The design (possibly LPD) would probably be tailored to both military and humanitarian roles.

GUARDIAN 35 *5/2004, A E Galarce* / 1044075

1 HERCULES (TYPE 42) CLASS (LCC)

Name	*No*	*Builders*	*Laid down*	*Launched*	*Commissioned*
HERCULES	B 52 (ex-D 1, ex-28)	Vickers, Barrow	16 June 1971	24 Oct 1972	12 July 1976

Displacement, tons: 3,150 standard; 4,100 full load
Dimensions, feet (metres): 412 × 47 × 19 (screws) *(125.6 × 14.3 × 5.8)*
Flight deck, feet (metres): 85.3 × 42.66 *(26 × 13)*
Main machinery: COGOG; 2 RR Olympus TM3B gas turbines; 50,000 hp *(37.3 MW)* sustained
2 RR Tyne RM1A gas-turbines; 9,900 hp *(7.4 MW)* sustained; 2 shafts; cp props
Speed, knots: 29; 18 (Tynes). **Range, n miles:** 4,000 at 18 kt
Complement: 180 plus (238 marines)

Missiles: SAM: British Aerospace Sea Dart Mk 30 twin launcher ❶; semi-active radar homing to 40 km *(21.5 n miles)* at 2 Mach; height envelope 100–18,300 m *(328–60,042 ft)*; 22 missiles; limited anti-ship capability.
Guns: 1 Vickers 4.5 in *(115 mm)*/55 Mk 8 automatic ❷; 25 rds/min to 22 km *(12 n miles)*; weight of shell 21 kg; also fires chaff and illuminants.
2 Oerlikon 20 mm Mk 7 ❸. 4—12.7 mm MGs.
Countermeasures: Decoys: Graseby towed torpedo decoy. Knebworth Corvus 8-tubed trainable launchers for chaff.
ESM: Racal RDL 257; radar intercept.
ECM: Racal RCM 2; jammer.
Combat data systems: Plessey-Ferranti ADAWS-4; Link 10.
Radars: Air search: Marconi Type 965P with double AKE2 array and 1010/1011 IFF ❹; A-band.
Surface search: Marconi Type 992Q ❺; E/F-band.
Navigation, HDWS and helicopter control: Kelvin Hughes Type 1006; I-band.
Fire control: Marconi Type 909 ❻; I/J-band (for Sea Dart missile control).
Sonars: Graseby Type 184M; hull-mounted; active search and attack; medium frequency 6–9 kHz.
Kelvin Hughes Type 162M classification set; sideways looking; active; high frequency.

Helicopters: 2 Sea King ❼.

Programmes: Contract signed 18 May 1970 between the Argentine government and Vickers Ltd.

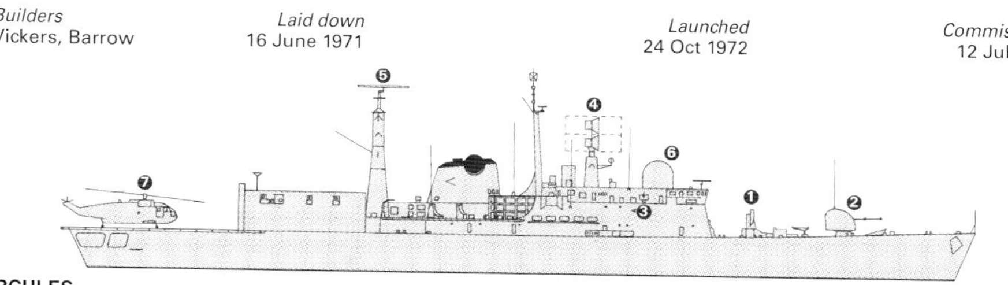

HERCULES

(Scale 1 : 1,200), Ian Sturton / 0528400

HERCULES

6/2001, Argentine Navy / 0130745

Modernisation: Combat Data System has been improved with local modifications. Refitted in Chile from November 1999 to July 2000 to make flight deck and hanger Sea King capable. Further modifications included removal of MM38 launchers to be replaced by assault boats and, in a refit which began in 2008, the Sea Dart launcher is likely to be removed and the missile magazine adapted to accommodate a company of marines. The Type 965 radar is to be replaced by LW-08 (ex-*25 de Mayo*). The second of class, *Santisima Trinidad*, has been decommissioned and is to be converted into a museum.
Operational: Based at Puerto Belgrano. Seadart SAM and Type 909 fire-control radar are probably non-operational. Officially described as an Amphibious command and control ship.

16 LCVPS

EDVP 30–37 **+8**

Displacement, tons: 13 full load
Dimensions, feet (metres): 35.8 × 10.5 × 3.4 *(10.9 × 3.2 × 1.1)*
Main machinery: 1 Gray 64 HN9 diesel; 165 hp *(123 kW)* sustained; 1 shaft
Speed, knots: 9. **Range, n miles:** 110 at 9 kt
Military lift: 3.5 tons
Guns: 2—12.7 mm MGs.

Comment: Details are for the eight LCVPs acquired from the US in 1970. There is a smaller variant built locally since 1971.

LCVP 1 and 4

9/2007, A E Galarce / 1167921

SURVEY AND RESEARCH SHIPS

Notes: (1) There are also two Fisheries Research Ships employed by the government. These are *Oca Balda* and *Eduardo Holmberg*.
(2) Two 10 m hydrographic launches, *Monte Blanco* and *Kualchink* entered service in 2004.

1 RESEARCH SHIP (AGOR)

Name	*No*	*Builders*	*Commissioned*
COMODORO RIVADAVIA	Q 11	Mestrina, Tigre	6 Dec 1974

Displacement, tons: 820 full load
Dimensions, feet (metres): 171.2 × 28.9 × 9.5 *(52.2 × 8.8 × 2.9)*
Main machinery: 2 Stork Werkspoor RHO-218K diesels; 1,160 hp(m) *(853 kW)*; 2 shafts; cp props
Speed, knots: 12. **Range, n miles:** 6,000 at 12 kt
Complement: 34 (8 officers)

Comment: Laid down on 17 July 1971 and launched on 2 December 1972. Used for research. To be re-engined in 2009.

COMODORO RIVADAVIA

3/2001 / 0126380

1 SURVEY SHIP (AGOB)

Name	*No*	*Builders*	*Commissioned*
PUERTO DESEADO	Q 20 (ex-Q 8)	Astarsa, San Fernando	26 Feb 1979

Displacement, tons: 2,133 standard; 2,400 full load
Dimensions, feet (metres): 251.9 × 51.8 × 21.3 *(76.8 × 15.8 × 6.5)*
Main machinery: 2 MAN 9L20/27 diesels; 2,450 hp *(1.8 MW)*; 2 shafts
Speed, knots: 14. **Range, n miles:** 12,000 at 12 kt
Complement: 61 (12 officers) plus 20 scientists
Radars: Navigation: Decca 1629; I-band.

Comment: Laid down on 17 March 1976 for Consejo Nacional de Investigaciones Tecnicas y Scientificas. Launched on 4 December 1976. For survey work fitted with: four Hewlett-Packard 2108-A, gravimeter, magnetometer, seismic systems, high-frequency sonar, geological laboratory. Omega and NAVSAT equipped. Painted with an orange hull in late 1996 for Antarctic deployments.

PUERTO DESEADO

11/2004, A E Galarce / 1151098

1 SURVEY CRAFT (AGSC)

Name	*No*	*Builders*	*Commissioned*
CORMORAN	Q 15	AFNE, Rio Santiago	20 Feb 1964

Displacement, tons: 102 full load
Dimensions, feet (metres): 83 × 16.4 × 5.9 *(25.3 × 5 × 1.8)*
Main machinery: 2 GM 6-71 diesels; 440 hp(m) *(323 kW)*; 2 shafts
Speed, knots: 11
Complement: 19 (3 officers)
Radars: Navigation: Decca TM1226; I-band.

Comment: Launched 10 August 1963. Classified as a coastal launch.

CORMORAN

5/2003, A E Galarce / 0572406

TRAINING SHIPS

Notes: (1) There are also three small yachts: *Itati* (Q 73), *Fortuna I* (Q 74) and *Fortuna II* (Q 75) plus a 25 ton yawl *Tijuca* acquired in 1993. *Fortuna III* was commissioned in 2004. A further yacht, *Irene* was acquired in 2005.
(2) Construction of a new sail-training vessel *Santa Maria de los Buenos Aires* was started at Domecq Garcia (renamed CINAR) on 15 October 2008. The ship is to be completed in 2010 although it is not clear whether the vessel is to be civilian or naval operated.

1 SAIL TRAINING SHIP (AXS)

Name	*No*	*Builders*	*Commissioned*
LIBERTAD	Q 2	AFNE, Rio Santiago	28 May 1963

Displacement, tons: 3,025 standard; 3,765 full load
Dimensions, feet (metres): 262 wl; 301 oa × 45.3 × 21.8 *(79.9; 91.7 × 13.8 × 6.6)*
Main machinery: 2 Sulzer diesels; 2,400 hp(m) *(1.76 MW);* 2 shafts
Speed, knots: 13.5 under power
Range, n miles: 12,000 at 8 kt
Complement: 200 crew plus 150 cadets
Guns: 4 Hotchkiss 47 mm saluting guns.
Radars: Navigation: Decca; I-band.

Comment: Launched 30 May 1956. She set record for crossing the North Atlantic under sail in 1966. Sail area, 26,835 m². Based at Puerto Belgrano. Mid-life refit at Rio Santiago Shipyard completed in 2006. The refit is reported to have included new engines.

LIBERTAD *9/2008*, Chris Sattler* / 1335604

2 KING CLASS (AX)

Name	*No*	*Builders*	*Launched*	*Commissioned*
MURATURE	P 20	Base Nav Rio Santiago	5 July 1943	12 Apr 1945
KING	P 21	Base Nav Rio Santiago	2 Nov 1943	28 July 1946

Displacement, tons: 913 standard; 1,000 normal; 1,032 full load
Dimensions, feet (metres): 252.7 × 29.5 × 13.1 *(77 × 9 × 4)*
Main machinery: 2 Werkspoor diesels; 2,500 hp(m) *(1.8 MW);* 2 shafts
Speed, knots: 18
Range, n miles: 9,000 at 12 kt
Complement: 130
Guns: 3 Vickers 4 in *(105 mm)*/45; 16 rds/min to 19 km *(10 n miles);* weight of shell 16 kg.
3 Bofors 40 mm/60 (1 twin, 2 single); 120 rds/min/barrel to 10 km *(5.5 n miles);* weight of shell 0.89 kg.
5—12.7 mm MGs.
Radars: Surface search: Racal Decca 1226; I-band.

Comment: Named after Captain John King, an Irish follower of Admiral Brown, who distinguished himself in the war with Brazil, 1826–28; and Captain Jose Murature, who performed conspicuous service against the Paraguayans at the Battle of Cuevas in 1865. *King* laid down June 1938. *Murature* March 1940. Both used for cadet training.

MURATURE *9/2007, A E Galarce* / 1167919

AUXILIARIES

Notes: (1) The acquisition of an Antarctic support vessel, possibly as part of a joint programme with Brazil, has been initiated.
(2) There is a fishery protection vessel *Luisito* Q 51. Painted yellow, it is based at Mar del Plata.

1 CHARTERED SHIP (AKS/AOTL)

Name	*No*	*Builders*	*Commissioned*
INGENIERO JULIO KRAUSE	B 13	Astarsa, Tigre	1981

Displacement, tons: 8,346 full load
Dimensions, feet (metres): 366.8 × 56.4 × 22.0 *(111.8 × 17.2 × 6.7)*
Main machinery: 1 Sulzer diesel; 5,800 hp *(4.3 MW);* 1 shaft
Speed, knots: 14
Complement: 32
Cargo capacity: 7,500 tons fuel

Comment: Chartered by the navy on 5 March 1993. Capable of stern replenishment at sea. Has been employed as a fleet oiler 2007–08.

1 DURANCE CLASS (AORH)

Name	*No*	*Builders*	*Launched*	*Commissioned*
PATAGONIA (ex-*Durance*)	B 1 (ex-A 629)	Brest Naval Dockyard	6 Sep 1975	1 Dec 1976

Displacement, tons: 17,800 full load
Dimensions, feet (metres): 515.9 × 69.5 × 38.5 *(157.3 × 21.2 × 10.8)*
Main machinery: 2 SEMT-Pielstick 16 PC2.5 V 400 diesels; 20,800 hp(m) *(15.3 MW)* sustained; 2 shafts; LIPS cp props
Speed, knots: 15. **Range, n miles:** 9,000 at 15 kt
Complement: 164 (10 officers) plus 29 spare
Cargo capacity: 9,000 tons fuel; 500 tons Avcat; 140 distilled water; 170 victuals; 150 munitions; 50 naval stores
Guns: 2 Bofors 40 mm/60. 4—12.7 mm MGs.
Radars: Navigation: 2 Racal Decca 1226; I-band.
Helicopters: 1 Alouette III.

Comment: Acquired from France on 12 July 1999 having been in reserve for two years. Entered Argentine Navy service in July 2000 after short refit.

PATAGONIA *5/2000, A E Galarce* / 0104175

3 COSTA SUR CLASS (TRANSPORT) (AKS)

Name	*No*	*Builders*	*Commissioned*
CANAL BEAGLE	B 3	Astillero Principe y Menghi SA	29 Apr 1978
BAHIA SAN BLAS	B 4	Astillero Principe y Menghi SA	27 Nov 1978
CABO DE HORNOS (ex-*Bahia Camarones*)	B 5	Astillero Principe y Menghi SA	28 June 1979

Displacement, tons: 10,894 full load
Dimensions, feet (metres): 390.3 × 57.4 × 24.6 *(119 × 17.5 × 7.5)*
Main machinery: 2 AFNE-Sulzer diesels; 6,400 hp(m) *(4.7 MW);* 2 shafts
Speed, knots: 16.5
Complement: 40

Comment: Three ships ordered December 1975. Laid down 10 January 1977 (B 3), 11 April 1977 (B 4) and 29 April 1978 (B 5). Launched 19 October 1977 (B 3), 29 April 1978 (B 4) and 4 November 1978 (B 5). Used to supply offshore research installations in Naval Area South. *Bahia San Blas* painted grey in 1998 indicating an active naval role in amphibious support operations. Capable of carrying up to eight LCVPs on deck. 132 troops can be accommodated in containers. The ship has been fitted with a helicopter (light) landing deck near the bow. *Cabo de Hornos* entered refit at Astillero Rio Santiago in late 2007 but was not adapted for an amphibious role.

BAHIA SAN BLAS *7/2007, A E Galarce* / 1167922

CANAL BEAGLE *8/1999, P Marsan* / 0081446

1 FLOATING DOCK

Number	*Dimensions, feet (metres)*	*Capacity, tons*
3	215.8 × 46 × 45.5 *(65.8 × 14 × 13.7)*	750

Comment: Based at Puerto Belgrano. All other docks have been sold.

3 RED CLASS (BUOYTENDERS) (ABU)

Name	*No*	*Builders*	*Commissioned*
PUNTA ALTA (ex-*Red Birch*)	Q 63 (ex-WLM 687)	CG Yard, Maryland	19 Feb 1965
CIUDAD DE ZARATE (ex-*Red Cedar*)	Q 61 (ex-WLM 688)	CG Yard, Maryland	1 Aug 1970
CIUDAD DE ROSARIO (ex-*Red Wood*)	Q 62 (ex-WLM 685)	CG Yard, Maryland	4 Apr 1964

Displacement, tons: 525 full load
Dimensions, feet (metres): 161.1 × 33 × 6 *(49.1 × 10.1 × 1.8)*
Main machinery: 2 Caterpillar D398 diesels; 1,800 hp *(1.34 MW)*; 2 shafts; cp props; bow thruster
Speed, knots: 12. **Range, n miles:** 2,248 at 11 kt
Complement: 31 (6 officers)
Guns: 2—12.7 mm MGs.

Comment: Ex-USCG buoy tenders. First one transferred on 10 June 1998 and recommissioned on 17 November 1998. Two more transferred 30 July 1999. Strengthened hull for light ice breaking. Equipped with a 10 ton boom. *Punta Alta* used as supply ship in the southern archipelago. The other pair are used as river supply ships.

CIUDAD DE ROSARIO *7/2008*, A E Galarce* / 1335600

ICEBREAKERS

Notes: During the repair of *Almirante Irizar*, ships are being leased as required to support Antarctic operations. These include the Russian icebreaker *Vasily Golovnin* and the Chinese icebreaker, *Xue Long*.

1 SUPPORT SHIP (AGB/AGOB)

Name	*No*	*Builders*	*Launched*	*Commissioned*
ALMIRANTE IRIZAR	Q 5	Wärtsilä, Helsinki	3 Feb 1978	15 Dec 1978

Displacement, tons: 14,900 full load
Dimensions, feet (metres): 398.1 × 82 × 31.2 *(121.3 × 25 × 9.5)*
Main machinery: Diesel-electric; 4 Wärtsilä-SEMT-Pielstick 8 PC2.5 L diesels; 18,720 hp(m) *(13.77 MW)* sustained; 4 generators; 2 Stromberg motors; 16,200 hp(m) *(11.9 MW)*; 2 shafts
Speed, knots: 17
Complement: 135 ship's company plus 45 passengers
Radars: Air/surface search: Plessey AWS 2; E/F-band.
Navigation: 2 Decca; I-band.
Helicopters: 2 ASH-3H Sea King.

Comment: Fitted for landing craft with two 16 ton cranes, fin stabilisers, Wärtsilä bubbling system and a 60 ton towing winch. RAST helicopter securing system. Designed for Antarctic support operations and able to remain in polar regions throughout the Winter with 210 people aboard. Used as a transport to South Georgia in December1981 and as a hospital ship during the Falklands war April to June 1982. Has been used as a Patagonian supply ship, and for other activities associated with the Navy in the region. The ship completed a refit including the installation of Satcom, by early 2005. 40 mm guns have been removed. Following a generator-room fire on 11 April 2007, the ship requires substantial repair work. This began on 1 October 2008 and is expected to be completed in 2012.

ALMIRANTE IRIZAR *3/2006, A E Galarce* / 1040738

TUGS

11 TUGS (YTB/YTL)

QUERANDI R 2, **TEHUELCHE** R 3, **MOCOVI** R 5, **CALCHAQUI** R 6, **ONA** R 7, **TOBA** R 8, **CHULUPI** R 10, **MATACO** R 12, **CAPAYÁN** R 16, **CHIQUILYÁN** R 18, **MORCOYÁN** R 19

Comment: R 2-3 and R 7-8 and R 12 are coastal tugs of about 250 tons. The remainder are harbour tugs transferred from the USA.

MATACO
5/2000, A E Galarce
0104177

PREFECTURA NAVAL ARGENTINA – COAST GUARD

Headquarters Appointments

Commander:
Prefecto General Oscar Adolfo Arce
Vice Commander:
Prefecto General Enrique Julio Cingolani
Director of Operations:
Prefecto General Norberto Venerini

Personnel

2009: 11,900 (1,600 officers)

Tasks

Under the General Organisation Act the PNA is charged with:
1. Enforcement of Federal Laws on the high seas and waters subject to the Argentine Republic.
2. Enforcement of environmental protection laws in Federal waters.
3. Safety of ships in EEZ. Search and Rescue.
4. Security of waterfront facilities and vessels in port.
5. Operation of certain Navaids.
6. Operation of some Pilot Services.
7. Management and operation of Aviation Service; Coastguard Vessels; Salvage, Fire and Anti-Pollution Service; Yachtmaster School; National Diving School; several Fire Brigades and Anti-Narcotics Department.
8. Operation of some Customs activities.

Organisation

Formed in 10 districts; High Parana River, Upper Parana and Paraguay Rivers, Lower Parana River, Upper Uruguay River, Lower Uruguay River, Delta, River Plate, Northern Argentine Sea, Southern Argentine Sea, Lakes and Comahue.

History

The Spanish authorities in South America established similar organisations to those in Spain. In 1756 the Captainship of the Port came into being in Buenos Aires-in 1810 the Ship Registry office was added to this title. On 29 October 1896 the title of Capitania General de Puertos was established by Act of Congress, the beginning of the PNA. Today, as a security and safety force, it has responsibilities throughout the rivers of Argentina, the ports and harbours as well as within territorial waters out to the 200 mile EEZ. An attempt was made in January 1992 to restrict operations to a 12 mile limit but the legislation was cancelled. The Coast Guard was placed under the Interior Ministry in 1996.

Identity markings

Two unequal blue stripes with, superimposed, crossed white anchors followed by the title Prefectura Naval.

Strength of Prefectura

Patrol Ships	6
Large Patrol Craft	3
Coastal Patrol Craft	20
Inshore Patrol Craft	77
Training Ships	4
Pilot Stations	1
Pilot and Patrol Craft	5

PATROL FORCES

Notes: In addition to the ships and craft listed below the PNA operates 400 craft, including floating cranes, run abouts and inflatables of all types. Six Zodiac Hurricanes SR 9201–9206 entered service in 2004.

1 PATROL SHIP (WPSO)

Name	*No*	*Builders*	*Commissioned*
DELFIN	GC 13	Ijsselwerf, Netherlands	14 May 1957

Displacement, tons: 700 standard; 1,000 full load
Dimensions, feet (metres): 193.5 × 29.8 × 13.8 *(59 × 9.1 × 4.2)*
Main machinery: 2 MAN diesels; 2,300 hp(m) *(1.69 MW)*; 2 shafts
Speed, knots: 15 **Range, n miles**: 6,720 at 10 kt
Complement: 27
Guns: 1 Oerlikon 20 mm (fitted for). 2—12.7 mm Browning MGs.
Radars: Navigation: Decca; I-band.

Comment: Whaler acquired for PNA in 1969. Commissioned 23 January 1970.

DELFIN *7/2003, **A E Galarce*** / 0572409

2 LYNCH CLASS (LARGE PATROL CRAFT) (WPB)

Name	*No*	*Builders*	*Commissioned*
LYNCH	GC 21	AFNE, Rio Santiago	20 May 1964
TOLL	GC 22	AFNE, Rio Santiago	7 July 1966

Displacement, tons: 100 standard; 117 full load
Dimensions, feet (metres): 98.4 × 21 × 6.9 *(30 × 6.4 × 2.1)*
Main machinery: 2 MTU Maybach diesels; 2,700 hp(m) *(1.98 MW)*; 2 shafts
Speed, knots: 22. **Range, n miles**: 2,000
Complement: 14 (3 officers)
Guns: 1 Oerlikon 20 mm (can be carried). 1—7.62 mm MG.
Radars: Surface search: Decca; I-band.

LYNCH *1/1997, **Prefectura Naval*** / 0012018

5 HALCON (TYPE B 119) CLASS (WPSO)

Name	*No*	*Builders*	*Commissioned*
MANTILLA	GC 24	Bazán, El Ferrol	20 Dec 1982
AZOPARDO	GC 25	Bazán, El Ferrol	28 Apr 1983
THOMPSON	GC 26	Bazán, El Ferrol	20 June 1983
PREFECTO FIQUE	GC 27	Bazán, El Ferrol	29 July 1983
PREFECTO DERBES	GC 28	Bazán, El Ferrol	20 Nov 1983

Displacement, tons: 910 standard; 1,084 full load
Dimensions, feet (metres): 219.9 × 34.4 × 13.8 *(67 × 10.5 × 4.2)*
Main machinery: 2 Bazán-MTU 16V 956TB91 diesels; 7,500 hp(m) *(5.52 MW)* sustained; 2 shafts
Speed, knots: 20. **Range, n miles**: 5,000 at 18 kt
Complement: 33 (10 officers)
Guns: 1 Breda 40 mm/70; 300 rds/min to 12.5 km *(7 n miles)*; weight of shell 0.96 kg. 2—12.7 mm MGs.
Radars: Navigation: Decca 1226 ARPA; I-band.
Helicopters: Platform for 1 Dauphin 2.

Comment: Ordered in 1979 from Bazán, El Ferrol, Spain. All have Magnavox MX 1102 SATNAV. Hospital with four beds. Carry one rigid rescue craft *(6 m)* with a 90 hp MWM diesel powering a Hamilton water-jet and a capacity for 12 and two inflatable craft *(4.1 m)* with Evinrude outboard. Refits of these ships started in 2005.

MANTILLA *6/2005, **A E Galarce*** / 1151095

1 LARGE PATROL CRAFT (WAX)

Name	*No*	*Builders*	*Commissioned*
MANDUBI	GC 43	Base Naval Rio Santiago	1940

Displacement, tons: 270 full load
Dimensions, feet (metres): 108.9 × 20.7 × 6.2 *(33.2 × 6.3 × 1.9)*
Main machinery: 2 MAN G6V-23.5/33 diesels; 500 hp(m) *(367 kW)*; 1 shaft
Speed, knots: 14.
Range, n miles: 800 at 14 kt; 3,400 at 10 kt
Complement: 12
Guns: 2—12.7 mm Browning MGs.
Radars: Surface search: Decca; I-band.

Comment: Since 1986 has acted as training craft for PNA Cadets School carrying 20 cadets.

MANDUBI *8/1994, **Mario Diaz*** / 0056488

1 RIVER PATROL SHIP (WARS)

Name	*No*	*Builders*	*Commissioned*
TONINA	GC 47	SANYM SA San Fernando, Argentina	30 June 1978

Displacement, tons: 103 standard; 153 full load
Dimensions, feet (metres): 83.8 × 21.3 × 10.1 *(25.5 × 6.5 × 3.3)*
Main machinery: 2 GM 16V-71TA diesels; 1,000 hp *(746 kW)* sustained; 2 shafts
Speed, knots: 10. **Range, n miles**: 2,800 at 10 kt
Complement: 11 (3 officers)
Guns: 1 Oerlikon 20 mm.
Radars: Navigation: Decca 1226; I-band.

Comment: Served as training ship for PNA Cadets School until 1986. Now acts as salvage ship with salvage pumps and recompression chamber. Capable of operating divers and underwater swimmers. Also used as a patrol ship.

TONINA *1/1998, **Hartmut Ehlers*** / 0017541

18 MAR DEL PLATA (Z-28) CLASS (COASTAL PATROL CRAFT) (WPB)

MAR DEL PLATA GC 64
MARTIN GARCIA GC 65
RIO LUJAN GC 66
RIO URUGUAY GC 67
RIO PARAGUAY GC 68
RIO PARANA GC 69
RIO DE LA PLATA GC 70
LA PLATA GC 71
BUENOS AIRES GC 72
CABO CORRIENTES GC 73
RIO QUEQUEN GC 74
BAHIA BLANCA GC 75
INGENIERO WHITE GC 76
GOLFO SAN MATIAS GC 77
MADRYN GC 78
RIO DESEADO GC 79
USHUAIA GC 80
CANAL DE BEAGLE GC 81

Displacement, tons: 81 full load
Dimensions, feet (metres): 91.8 × 17.4 × 5.2 *(28 × 5.3 × 1.6)*
Main machinery: 2 MTU 8V-331-TC92 diesels; 1,770 hp(m) *(1.3 MW)* sustained; 2 shafts
Speed, knots: 22. **Range, n miles**: 1,200 at 12 kt; 780 at 18 kt
Complement: 14 (3 officers)
Guns: 1 Oerlikon 20 mm. 2—12.7 mm Browning MGs.
Radars: Navigation: Decca 1226; I-band.

Comment: Ordered 24 November 1978 from Blohm + Voss to a Z-28 design. First delivered in June 1979 and then at monthly intervals. Steel hulls. GC 82 and 83 were captured by the British Forces in 1982.

CABO CORRIENTES *4/2008*, **A E Galarce*** / 1335599

1 COASTAL PATROL CRAFT (WPB)

Name	*No*	*Builders*	*Commissioned*
DORADO	GC 101	Base Naval, Rio Santiago	17 Dec 1939

Displacement, tons: 43 full load
Dimensions, feet (metres): 69.5 × 14.1 × 4.9 *(21.2 × 4.3 × 1.5)*
Main machinery: 2 GM 6071-6A diesels; 360 hp *(268 kW)*; 1 shaft
Speed, knots: 12
Range, n miles: 1,550
Complement: 7 (1 officer)
Radars: Navigation: Furuno; I-band.

DORADO *12/1999, R O Rivero* / 0056490

35 SMALL PATROL CRAFT (WPB)

ESTRELLEMAR GC 48, **REMORA** GC 49, **CONGRIO** GC 50, **MERO** GC 51, **MARSOPA** GC 52, **PETREL** GC 53, **SALMON** GC 54, **BIGUA** GC 55, **FOCA** GC 56, **TIBURON** GC 57, **MELVA** GC 58, **LENGUADO** GC 59, **ORCA** GC 60, **PINGUINO** GC 61, **MEDUSA** GC 88, **PERCA** GC 89, **CALAMAR** GC 90, **HIPOCAMPO** GC 91, **ROBALDO** GC 92, **CAMARON** GC 93, **GAVIOTA** GC 94, **ABADEJO** GC 95, **GC 102-114**

Displacement, tons: 15 full load
Dimensions, feet (metres): 41 × 11.8 × 3.6 *(12.5 × 3.6 × 1.1)*
Main machinery: 2 GM diesels; 514 hp *(383 kW)*; 2 shafts
Speed, knots: 20
Range, n miles: 400 at 18 kt
Complement: 3
Guns: 12.7 mm Browning MG.
Radars: Navigation: I-band.

Comment: First delivered September 1978. First 14 built by Cadenazzi, Tigre 1977–79, most of the remainder by Ast Belen de Escobar 1984–86. *GC 102-114* are slightly smaller.

PERCA *11/2004, A E Galarce* / 1151093

1 BAZAN TYPE (WPBF)

SUREL GC 142

Displacement, tons: 14.5 full load
Dimensions, feet (metres): 39 × 12.4 × 2.2 *(11.9 × 3.8 × 0.7)*
Main machinery: 2 MAN D2848 LXE diesels; 1,360 hp(m) *(1 MW)* sustained; 2 Hamilton 362 waterjets
Speed, knots: 38
Range, n miles: 300 at 25 kt
Complement: 4
Guns: 1 — 12.7 mm MG.
Radars: Navigation: Furuno; I-band.

Comment: Acquired in 1997 from Bazán, San Fernando. Similar to Spanish Bazán 39 class for Spanish Maritime Police. Plans to acquire further craft were not fulfilled.

SUREL *12/2001, A E Galarce* / 0529809

10 ALUCAT 1050 CLASS (WPB)

CORMORAN GC 137, **CISNE** GC 138, **PEJERREY** GC 139, **SURUBI** GC 143, **BOGA** GC 144, **SABALO** GC 145, **HUALA** GC 146, **PACU** GC 147, **MANDURUYU** GC 148, **CORVINA** GC 149

Displacement, tons: 9 full load
Dimensions, feet (metres): 37.7 × 12.5 × 2 *(11.5 × 3.8 × 0.6)*
Main machinery: 2 Volvo 61 ALD; 577 hp(m) *(424 kW)*; 2 Hamilton 273 waterjets
Speed, knots: 18
Complement: 4
Radars: Navigation: Furuno 12/24; I-band.

Comment: First three delivered in September 1994. Seven more ordered in 1999.

HUALA *4/2000, Hartmut Ehlers* / 0104180

33 ALUCAT 850 CLASS (WPB)

GC 152–184 (ex-LS 9201-9233)

Displacement, tons: 7 full load
Dimensions, feet (metres): 30.2 × 10.8 × 2 *(9.2 × 3.3 × 0.6)*
Main machinery: 2 Volvo TAMD 41B; 400 hp(m) *(294 kW)*; 2 waterjets
Speed, knots: 26
Complement: 4
Radars: Navigation: Furuno; I-band.

Comment: Alucat 850 class built by Damen. First six delivered in 1995, six more in February 1996, five more in December 1996 and five in December 1997. Five more ordered in 1999.

GC 181 *10/2005, A E Galarce* / 1151092

36 FAST INTERVENTION CRAFT (WPB)

Displacement, tons: To be announced
Dimensions, feet (metres): 28.5 × 6.9 × 1.97 *(8.7 × 2.1 × 0.6)*
Main machinery: 1 diesel; waterjet propulsion
Speed, knots: 33
Complement: 10
Guns: 1 — 7.62 mm MG.

Comment: Built to a local design. Began entering service in 2007.

22 PATROL CRAFT (PB)

ALUMINE GC 118 (ex-SP 14), **TRAFUL** GC 119 (ex-SP 15), **LACAR** GC 120 (ex-SP 24), **MASCARDI** GC 122 (ex-SP 17), **FONTANA** GC 121 (ex-SP 32), **VIEDNA** GC 123 (ex-SP 20), **SAN MARTIN** GC 124 (ex-SP 21), **BUENOS AIRES** GC 125 (ex-SP 22), **MUSTERS** GC 126 (ex-SP 26), **COLHUE** GC 129 (ex-SP 16), **MARIA L PENDO** GC 130 (ex-SP 18), **ROCA** GC 131 (ex-SP 28), **PUELO** GC 132 (ex-SP 29), **FUTALAUFQUEN** GC 133 (ex-SP 30), **FALKNER** GC 134 (ex-SP 31), **HESS** (ex-*Huechulafquen*) GC 135 (ex-SP 34), **COLHUE HUAPI** GC 136 (ex-SP 33), **YEHUIN** GC 140 (ex-SP 30, ex-SP 35), **QUILLEN** GC 141 (ex-SP 27), **FAGNANO** GC 150 (ex-SP 23), **NAHUEL HUAPI** GC 151 (ex-SP 19), **CARDIEL** - (ex-SP 25)

(All names preceded by **LAGO**)

Comment: There are three main types of craft. Eight 23 m Stan Tender 2200 were built by Damen, Gorinchem (GC 122-125, 129, 130, 150, 151); three 16 m Stan Tender 1750 were built by Damen, Gorinchem (GC 118, 119, 133); six 11 m CAT 1100 were built by Damen, Gorinchem (GC 120, 126, 131, 132, 141 and *Cardiel*); five 11 m CAT 1100 were built by Astillero Mestrina, Tigre (GC 121, G 134-136, GC 140). GC 133, 141, 150, 151 and *Cardiel* are employed as pilot craft.

VIEDNA *4/2007, A E Galarce* / 1167924

4 TRAINING SHIPS (WAXL/WAXS)

ESPERANZA **ADHARA II** **TALITA II** **DR BERNARDO HOUSSAY** (ex-*El Austral*)

Displacement, tons: 33.5 standard
Dimensions, feet (metres): 62.3 × 14.1 × 8.9 *(19 × 4.3 × 2.7)*
Main machinery: 1 VM diesel; 90 hp(m) *(66 kW)*; 1 shaft
Speed, knots: 6; 15 sailing
Complement: 6 plus 6 cadets

Comment: Details given are for *Esperanza* built by Ast Central de la PNA. Launched and commissioned 20 December 1968 as a sail training ship. The 30 ton training craft *Adhara II* and *Talita II* are of similar dimensions. *Dr Bernardo Houssay* isa Danish-built ketch built in 1930. Displacement 460 tons and has a crew of 25 (five officers). Acquired by the PNA in 1996 and underwent refit at Tandanor Shipyard in 2007.

TALITA II *6/1998, **Prefectura Naval*** / 0017545

DR BERNARDO HOUSSAY *5/2000, **Harald Carstens*** / 0104181

6 SERVICE CRAFT (YTL/YTR)

PUERTO BUENOS AIRES SI 4 –SB 5 **CANAL EMILIO MITRE** SB 8
–SB 3 **CANAL COSTANERO** SB 9 –SB 10

Comment: *Canal Emilio Mitre* is a small tug of 53 tons full load, it has a speed of 10 kt and was built by Damen Shipyard, Netherlands in 1982.

PILOT VESSELS

1 PILOT STATION (WAGH/AHH)

Name	*No*	*Builders*	*Commissioned*
RECALADA (ex-*Rio Limay*)	DF 15	Astillero Astarsa	30 May 1972

Displacement, tons: 10,070 full load
Dimensions, feet (metres): 482.3 × 65.6 × 28 *(147 × 20 × 8.5)*
Speed, knots: 13
Complement: 28 (3 officers)

Comment: Commissioned as a Coast Guard ship 24 December 1991. Painted red with a white superstructure. Has a helicopter deck forward and a 20 bed hospital. After an extensive conversion and refit the ship replaced *Lago Lacar* in 1995.

RECALADA *8/1994, **Marcelo Campodonico*** / 0056494

LAND-BASED MARITIME AIRCRAFT

Notes: In addition to the aircraft listed, there are two Piper Warrior II/Archer II training aircraft and five Schweizer 300C training helicopters.

Numbers/Type: 2/3 Casa C-212 S 68/C-212 A 68 Aviocar.
Operational speed: 190 kt *(353 km/h)*.
Service ceiling: 24,000 ft *(7,315 m)*.
Range: 1,650 n miles *(3,055 km)*.
Role/Weapon systems: Two S 68 acquired in 1989, three A 68 in 1990. Medium-range reconnaissance and coastal surveillance duties in EEZ. Sensors: Bendix RDS 32 surface search radar. Omega Global GNS-500. Weapons: ASW; can carry torpedoes, depth bombs or mines. ASV; 2 × rockets or machine gun pods not normally fitted.

CASA C-212 *6/2002, **CASA/EADS*** / 0528295

Numbers/Type: 1 Aerospatiale SA 330 Super Puma.
Operational speed: 151 kt *(279 km/h)*.
Service ceiling: 15,090 ft *(4,600 m)*.
Range: 335 n miles *(620 km)*.
Role/Weapon systems: Support and SAR helicopter for patrol work. Updated in France in 1996. Sensors: Omera search radar. Weapons: Can carry pintle-mounted machine guns but is usually unarmed.

SUPER PUMA *11/1996, **Luis O Zunino*** / 0056495

Numbers/Type: 3 Aerospatiale AS 365 Dauphin 2.
Operational speed: 150 kt *(278 km/h)*.
Service ceiling: 15,000 ft *(4,575 m)*.
Range: 410 n miles *(758 km)*.
Role/Weapon systems: Acquired in 1995–96 to replace the Super Puma during the latter's update but have been retained. Sensors: Agrion search radar. Weapons: Unarmed.

DAUPHIN 2 *10/1996, **Prefectura Naval*** / 0012022

Australia

Country Overview

The Commonwealth of Australia comprises the island continent and the island of Tasmania which are separated by the Bass Strait. The British monarch, represented by a governor-general, is head of state. With an overall area of 2,966,151 square miles, it has a 13,910 n mile coastline with the Pacific (Coral and Tasman Seas) and Indian Oceans, the Timor Sea, Arafura Sea and the Torres Strait. External dependencies are the Australian Antarctic Territory, Christmas Island, the Cocos Islands, the Territory of Heard Island and McDonald Islands, Norfolk Island, the Ashmore and Cartier Islands and the Coral Sea Islands Territory. Canberra is the capital while Sydney is the largest city and a major port. There are further ports at Melbourne, Fremantle, Newcastle, Port Kembla, Geelong, Brisbane, Gladstone, Port Hedland and Port Walcott. Territorial Seas (12 n miles) are claimed. An EEZ (200 n miles) is also claimed.

Headquarters Appointments

Chief of Navy:
Vice Admiral R H Crane, AM, CSM
Deputy Chief of Navy:
Rear Admiral D R Thomas, AM, CSC
Fleet Commander, Australia:
Rear Admiral N S Coates, AM
Commander Australian Navy Systems Command:
Commodore S Gilmore, AM, CSC

Senior Appointments

Chief Capability Development Group:
Vice Admiral M J Tripovich, AM, CSC
Head of Maritime Systems Division:
Rear Admiral B C Robinson, AM
Commander Border Protection Command:
Rear Admiral A K Du Toit, AM
Head of Information and Capability Management Division:
Rear Admiral P D Jones, DSC, AM
Commander Australian Defence College:
Rear Admiral J V P Goldrick, AM, CSC

Diplomatic Representation

Head Australian Defence Staff, Washington:
Air Vice Marshall K Osley, AM, CSC
Head Australian Defence Staff, London:
Air Commodore S Martin, AM
Naval Attaché in Washington:
Commodore V di Pietro, CSC
Defence Attaché in Riyadh:
Captain B Gorringe
Naval Attaché in Jakarta:
Captain R Plath
Naval Adviser in London:
Captain W Martin
Defence Attaché in Wellington:
Captain M C Kellam
Defence Attaché, NATO/EU:
Commander C Dunchue
Defence Adviser in Dili:
Captain D Micheal
Defence Adviser in Islamabad:
Captain M Schmidt

Diplomatic Representation – *continued*

Defence Adviser in Manila:
Captain V Jones
Defence Adviser in New Delhi:
Captain J Mead

Personnel

(a) 2009: Permanent 13,219 officers and sailors
(b) Reserve: 8,599 (4,274 active, 4,325 standby)

RAN Reserve

The Naval Reserve is integrated into the Permanent Force. Personnel are either Active Reservists with regular commitments or Inactive Reservists with periodic or contingent duty. The missions undertaken by the Reserve include Coordination and Guidance of Psychology, Public Relations, Intelligence, Diving and patrol boat/landing craft operations. In addition, members of the Ready Reserve (a component of the Active Reserve) are shadow posted to selected major fleet units.

Border Protection Command

Border Protection Command (BPC), established on 30 March 2005 as the Joint Offshore Protection Command and renamed on 23 October 2006, coordinates and manages offshore maritime security within Australia's Offshore Maritime Domain. BPC integrates the resources of the Department of Defence and the Australian Customs Service (ACS) and includes personnel from the Australian Fisheries Management Agency and the Australia Quarantine Inspection Service. BPC has responsibility for offshore counter-terrorism prevention, interdiction and response capabilities and activities, including the protection of offshore oil and gas facilities, and civil maritime surveillance and response. The Commander is jointly accountable to the Chief of the Defence Force and the Chief Executive Officer of Customs.

BPC also manages the developing Australian Maritime Identification System. This system will bring together all the information held across government agencies on vessels operating in Australia's maritime area of interest. The aim is to be capable of identifying and assessing all vessels, other than recreational boats, within the 200 n mile EEZ.

Principal day-to-day assets of the Command include: one major fleet unit (FFG/FFH/LPA/AOR/HS); Armidale-class patrol boats; ACS surface units including the Bay class, contracted vessels *Triton* and *Oceanic Viking*; contracted Coastwatch surveillance aircraft and RAAF AP-3C maritime patrol aircraft.

Shore Establishments

Canberra: Navy Headquarters, Navy Systems Command Headquarters, *Harman* (Communications, Administration).
Sydney: Fleet Headquarters, Fleet Base East (Garden Island), *Waterhen* (Mine Warfare and Clearance Diving), *Watson* (Warfare Training), *Penguin* (Diving, Hospital), *Kuttabul* (Administration).
Wollongong Hydrographic Headquarters.
Jervis Bay Area: *Albatross* (Air Station), *Creswell* (Leadership and Management Training and Fleet Support), Jervis Bay Range Facility.
Cockburn Sound (WA): Fleet Base West, *Stirling* (Administration and Maintenance Support, Submarines, Communications).
Darwin: Minor warship base, *Coonawarra* (Administration).
Cairns: *Cairns* (Administration), Minor Warship Base.
Adelaide: Regional Naval Headquarters, South Australia.
Brisbane: Regional Naval Headquarters, South Queensland.
Hobart: Regional Naval Headquarters, Tasmania.

Fleet Deployment

Fleet Base East (and other Sydney bases): 4 FFG, 3 FFH, 1 AOR, 2 LPA, 1 LSH, 1 ASR, 6 MHC, 2 MSA.
Fleet Base West: 6 SS, 1 DSRV, 5 FFH, 1 AORH.
Darwin Naval Base: 10 PB, 2 LCH.
Cairns: 4 PB, 4 LCH, 2 AGS, 4 AGSC.

Fleet Air Arm (see *Shipborne Aircraft* section).

Squadron	*Aircraft*
723	Squirrel AS 350B, Utility, SAR
817	Sea King Mk 50, Utility
816	Seahawk S-70B-2, ASW, ASST

Prefix to Ships' Names

HMAS. Her Majesty's Australian Ship

Strength of the Fleet

Type	*Active*	*Building (Projected)*
Patrol Submarines	6	–
Destroyers	–	(3)
Frigates (FFG)	12	–
Minehunters (Coastal)	6	–
Minesweepers (Auxiliary)	2	–
Large Patrol Craft	14	–
Assault Ships	–	(2)
Amphibious Heavy Lift Ship	1	–
Amphibious Transports	2	(1)
Landing Craft	10	–
Survey Ships	6	–
Replenishment Ships	2	–
Training Ships	7	–

DELETIONS

Frigates

2008	*Adelaide*

Patrol Forces

2006	*Wollongong, Gawler, Geelong, Fremantle, Launceston, Bendigo, Geraldton*
2007	*Dubbo, Gladstone, Townsville, Ipswich*

Auxiliaries

2006	*Westralia*

PENNANT LIST

Submarines

73	Collins
74	Farncomb
75	Waller
76	Dechaineux
77	Sheean
78	Rankin

Destroyers

39	Hobart (bldg)
41	Brisbane (bldg)
42	Sydney (bldg)

Frigates

03	Sydney
04	Darwin
05	Melbourne
06	Newcastle
150	Anzac
151	Arunta
152	Warramunga
153	Stuart
154	Parramatta
155	Ballarat
156	Toowoomba
157	Perth

Mine Warfare Forces

M 82	Huon
M 83	Hawkesbury
M 84	Norman
M 85	Gascoyne
M 86	Diamantina
M 87	Yarra
Y 298	Bandicoot
Y 299	Wallaroo

Patrol Forces

83	Armidale
84	Larrakia
85	Bathurst
86	Albany
87	Pirie
88	Maitland
89	Ararat
90	Broome
91	Bundaberg
92	Wollongong
93	Childers
94	Launceston
95	Maryborough
96	Glenelg

Amphibious Forces

L 50	Tobruk
L 51	Kanimbla
L 52	Manoora
L 126	Balikpapan
L 127	Brunei
L 128	Labuan
L 129	Tarakan
L 130	Wewak
L 133	Betano

Survey Ships

A 01	Paluma
A 02	Mermaid
A 03	Shepparton
A 04	Benalla
A 245	Leeuwin
A 246	Melville

Auxiliaries

O 266	Sirius
OR 304	Success

SUBMARINES

Notes: Feasibility studies on the next generation of submarines were initiated in December 2007. Initial (First Pass) approval is likely to be sought in about 2011 with a view to (Second Pass) approval of construction and contracts following by 2015. Entry into service is expected in about 2022. The capability mix is likely to include greater emphasis on land attack. While nuclear propulsion is an option, it is unlikely to be selected.

DECHAINEUX

1/2006, Mick Prendergast / 1167937

6 COLLINS CLASS (SSK)

Name	*No*	*Builders*	*Laid down*	*Launched*	*Commissioned*
COLLINS	73	Australian Submarine Corp, Adelaide	14 Feb 1990	28 Aug 1993	27 July 1996
FARNCOMB	74	Australian Submarine Corp, Adelaide	1 Mar 1991	15 Dec 1995	31 Jan 1998
WALLER	75	Australian Submarine Corp, Adelaide	19 Mar 1992	14 Mar 1997	10 July 1999
DECHAINEUX	76	Australian Submarine Corp, Adelaide	4 Mar 1993	12 Mar 1998	23 Feb 2001
SHEEAN	77	Australian Submarine Corp, Adelaide	17 Feb 1994	1 May 1999	23 Feb 2001
RANKIN	78	Australian Submarine Corp, Adelaide	12 May 1995	7 Nov 2001	29 Mar 2003

Displacement, tons: 3,051 surfaced; 3,353 dived
Dimensions, feet (metres): 255.2 × 25.6 × 23 *(77.8 × 7.8 × 7)*
Main machinery: Diesel-electric; 3 Hedemora/Garden Island Type V18B/14 diesels; 6,020 hp *(4.42 MW)*; 3 Jeumont Schneider generators; 4.2 MW; 1 Jeumont Schneider motor; 7,344 hp(m) *(5.4 MW)*; 1 shaft; 1 MacTaggart Scott DM 43006 hydraulic motor for emergency propulsion
Speed, knots: 10 surfaced; 10 snorting; 20 dived
Range, n miles: 9,000 at 10 kt (snort); 11,500 at 10 kt (surfaced) 400 at 4 kt (dived)
Complement: 45 (8 officers)

Missiles: SSM: McDonnell Douglas Sub Harpoon Block 1B (UGM 84C); active radar homing to 92 km *(50 n miles)* at 0.9 Mach; warhead 227 kg.
Torpedoes: 6—21 in *(533 mm)* fwd tubes. Gould Mk 48 Mod 4/6/7; dual purpose; wire-guided; active/passive homing to 38 km *(21 n miles)* at 55 kt or 50 km *(27 n miles)* at 40 kt; warhead 295 kg. Air turbine pump discharge. Total of 22 weapons including Mk 48 and Sub Harpoon.
Mines: 44 in lieu of torpedoes.
Countermeasures: Decoys: 2 SSE.
ESM: Condor CS-5600; intercept and warning.
Weapons control: AN-BYG 1. Link 11.
Radars: Navigation: Kelvin Hughes Type 1007; I-band.
Sonars: Thomson Sintra Scylla active/passive bow array and passive flank, intercept and ranging arrays.
Thales SHORTASS retractable, passive.

Programmes: Contract signed on 3 June 1987 for construction of six Swedish-designed Kockums Type 471. Fabrication work started in June 1989; bow and midships (escape tower) sections of the first submarines built in Sweden.
Structure: Stirling air independent propulsion (AIP) has been tested on a shore rig. Scylla is an updated Eledone sonar suite. Diving depth, 250 m *(820 ft)*. Anechoic tiles are fitted during build to all but *Collins* which is retrofitted. Pilkington Optronics CK 43 search and CH 93 attack periscopes fitted. Plans for an external mine belt have been abandoned.
Modernisation: The Replacement Combat System AN-BYG 1 is based on Raytheon's CCS Mk 2. The shore facilities version was established in mid-2005 and the first seagoing system in *Waller* in 2006. The other boats are to follow by 2010. Meanwhile, following trials in *Collins* to improve the performance of the current combat system, the systems in *Dechaineux*, *Sheean*, *Rankin* and *Farncomb* have been augmented. In parallel, significant improvements to noise signature have been achieved following modifications to propellers and casing sections and improvements to the hydraulics system and engine reliability. These have been made to all six boats. Collaborative development of the US Mk 48 Mod 7 ADCAP torpedo is being progressed and the first firing was conducted by *Waller* during RIMPAC 08 in July 2008. All boats have been fitted with the Condor CS 5600 ESM system. *Collins* has received a set of modifications to facilitate the deployment and recovery of special forces. Further upgrades under the Collins Continuous Improvement Programme are to include improvements to communications and EW capabilities, a periscope system upgrade and sonar upgrades.
Operational: All submarines are based at Fleet Base West with one or two deploying regularly to the east coast.

RANKIN *1/2008*, Chris Sattler* / 1335626

COLLINS *1/2008*, Chris Sattler* / 1335624

WALLER

5/2008, Chris Sattler* / 1335625

DESTROYERS

0 + 3 HOBART CLASS (DESTROYERS) (DDGHM)

Name	*No*	*Builders*	*Laid down*	*Launched*	*Commissioned*
HOBART	39	ASC, Osborne, South Australia	2011	2013	2014
BRISBANE	41	ASC, Osborne, South Australia	2012	2014	2016
SYDNEY	42	ASC, Osborne, South Australia	2014	2015	2017

Displacement, tons: 6,250 full load
Dimensions, feet (metres): 481.3 oa; 437 pp × 61 × 16.1 *(146.7; 133.2 × 18.6 × 4.9)*
Flight deck, feet (metres): 86.6 × 56 *(26.4 × 17)*
Main machinery: CODOG; 2 GE LM 2500 gas turbines; 47,328 hp(m) *(34.8 MW)* sustained; 2 Bazan/Caterpillar diesels; 12,240 hp(m) *(9 MW)* sustained; 2 shafts; LIPS cp props
Speed, knots: 28
Range, n miles: 4,500 at 18 kt
Complement: 202 (accommodation for 234)

Missiles: SSM: 8 Boeing Harpoon Block 2; active radar homing to 124 km *(67 n miles)* at 0.9 Mach; warhead 227 kg.
SAM: Mk 41 VLS (48 cells); 32 Raytheon SM2-MR (Block IIIA); command/inertial guidance; semi-active radar homing to 167 km *(90 n miles)* at 2.5 Mach. 64 Evolved Sea Sparrow RIM 162B (in quadpacks); semi-active radar homing to 18 km *(9.7 n miles)* at 3.6 Mach; warhead 38 kg.
Guns: 1 FMC 5 in *(127 mm)*/54 Mk 45 Mod 4; 20 rds/min to 100 km *(54 n miles)* for extended range munitions; weight of shell 32 kg.
1 Raytheon 20 mm Vulcan Phalanx Block 2B; 6 barrels per launcher; 4,500 rds/min combined to 1.5 km. 2 Rafael Typhoon 25 mm.
Torpedoes: 4—323 mm (2 twin) Mk 32 Mod 9 fixed launchers. Eurotorp MU 90; anti-submarine; active/passive homing to 25 km *(13.5 n miles)* at 29/50 kt; warhead 32 kg.
Countermeasures: Decoys: G & D Aircraft SRBOC Mk 36 Mod 1 decoy launchers for SRBOC/NATO Sea Gnat. Nulka expendable decoy launchers.
ESM: To be announced.
ECM: To be announced.
Combat data systems: Lockheed Aegis Baseline 7.1; Link 11/16.
Weapons control: GFCS to be announced.
Radars: Air/surface search: Aegis SPY-1D. E/F-band.
Surface search: Sperry Marine AN/SPQ-9B; I-band.
Fire control: 2 Raytheon SPG-62 Mk 99 (for SAM). I/J-band.
Navigation: To be announced.
Sonars: Ultra integrated sonar suite comprising Type 2150 hull mounted sonar, towed array and torpedo detection.

Helicopters: 1 Sikorsky S-70B Seahawk or MRH 90.

Programmes: The Navantia F-100 was selected by the Australian government as the platform for the Hobart class Air Warfare Destroyers on 20 June 2007. The contract to build the ships was signed on 4 October 2007. The Combat System is to be an Australian version of Aegis; subsystems yet to be selected include communications and electronic warfare. The project is to be executed under an alliance arrangement between the Australian government, ASC AWD Shipbuilder Pty Ltd and Raytheon Australia Pty Ltd. The headquarters of the Alliance is the AWD Systems Centre in Adelaide. Hull blocks are to be manufactured around Australia and consolidated at the ASC Shipyard in Osborne, South Australia. There is an option for a fourth ship.

HOBART CLASS

10/2007, Royal Australian Navy / 1292470

FRIGATES

8 ANZAC (MEKO 200) CLASS (FFGHM)

Name	*No*	*Builders*	*Laid down*	*Launched*	*Commissioned*
ANZAC	150	Transfield, Williamstown	5 Nov 1993	16 Sep 1994	18 May 1996
ARUNTA (ex-*Arrernte*)	151	Transfield, Williamstown	22 July 1995	28 June 1996	12 Dec 1998
WARRAMUNGA (ex-*Warumungu*)	152	Tenix Defence Systems, Williamstown	26 July 1997	23 May 1998	31 Mar 2001
STUART	153	Tenix Defence Systems, Williamstown	25 July 1998	17 Apr 1999	17 Aug 2002
PARRAMATTA	154	Tenix Defence Systems, Williamstown	4 June 1999	17 June 2000	4 Oct 2003
BALLARAT	155	Tenix Defence Systems, Williamstown	4 Aug 2000	25 May 2002	26 June 2004
TOOWOOMBA	156	Tenix Defence Systems, Williamstown	26 July 2002	16 May 2003	8 Oct 2005
PERTH	157	Tenix Defence Systems, Williamstown	24 July 2003	20 Mar 2004	26 Aug 2006

Displacement, tons: 3,700 full load
Dimensions, feet (metres): 387.1 oa; 357.6 wl × 48.6 × 14.3 *(118; 109 × 14.8 × 4.35)*
Main machinery: CODOG: 1 GE LM 2500 gas turbine; 30,172 hp *(22.5 MW)* sustained; 2 MTU 12V 1163 TB83 diesels; 8,840 hp(m) *(6.5 MW)* sustained; 2 shafts; cp props
Speed, knots: 27
Range, n miles: 6,000 at 18 kt
Complement: 174 (24 officers)

ARUNTA ***(Scale 1 : 1,200), Ian Sturton*** / 1153838

Missiles: SSM: 8 McDonnell Douglas Harpoon Block 2 ❶; active radar homing to 124 km *(67 n miles)* at 0.9 Mach; warhead 227 kg.
SAM: Lockheed Martin Mk 41 Mod 5 octuple vertical launcher ❷. Quadpack Evolved Sea Sparrow RIM-162 for 32 missiles; semi-active homing to 18.0 km *(9.7 n miles)* at 3.6 Mach; warhead 38 kg.
Guns: 1 United Defense 5 in (127 mm)/54/62 Mk 45 Mod 2 ❸; 20 rds/min to 23 km *(12.6 n miles)*; weight of shell 32 kg.
4—12.7 mm MGs.
2 Rafael Mini Typhoon 12.7 mm remote-controlled guns (for selected deployments).
Torpedoes: 6—324 mm (2 triple) Mk 32 Mod 5 tubes ❹. Eurotorp MU 90; active/passive homing to 25 km *(13.5 n miles)* at 29/50 kt.
Countermeasures: Decoys: G & D Aircraft SRBOC Mk 36 Mod 1 decoy launchers ❺ for SRBOC/NATO Sea Gnat.
4 BAe Nulka quad expendable decoy launchers.
FEL SLQ-25A towed torpedo decoy.
RESM: Thales Centaur; radar intercept. CESM Telefunken PST-1720 Telegon 10; comms intercept.
Combat data systems: Saab Systems 9LV 453 Mk 3 (Mk 3E in 157). Link 11. Link 16.
Weapons control: Saab Systems Ceros 200 optronic director with CEA SSCWI (for RIM-162).

Radars: Air search: Raytheon SPS-49(V)8 ANZ ❻; C-band.
Air/surface search: Ericsson Sea Giraffe ❼; G/H-band.
Navigation: Atlas Elektronik 9600 ARPA; I-band.
Fire control: CelsiusTech Ceros 200 ❽; J-band.
IFF: Cossor AIMS Mk XII.
Sonars: Thomson Sintra Spherion B Mod 5; hull-mounted; active search and attack; medium frequency. Thales UMS 5424 Petrel; active mine avoidance; very high frequency.

Helicopters: 1 S-70B-2 Seahawk ❾.

Programmes: Contract signed with Australian Marine Engineering Consolidated (now Tenix Defence) on 10 November 1989 to build eight Blohm + Voss designed MEKO 200 ANZAC frigates for Australia and two for New Zealand. First ship started construction 27 March 1992. Modules were constructed at Whangarei and shipped to Williamstown for assembly. The second and fourth ships of the class were delivered to New Zealand.
Modernisation: Evolved Seasparrow missile (ESSM) was integrated in *Warramunga*, the world's first warship to be so fitted (first missile launched 21 January 2003). All remaining ships have since been similarly equipped. Petrel MOAS (Mine Obstacle Avoidance Sonar) was introduced in 2005, the MU 90 torpedo in 2008 and Harpoon has now been progressively installed across the entire class. F157 is the first of class to be fitted with the 9LV Mk 3E Combat Management System, which forms the foundation of the ASMD Upgrade programme to be implemented 2010–16. Other key elements of the upgrade include replacement of Sea Giraffe radar with CEAFAR active phased array radar; installation of the Sagem Vampir IRST (Infra-Red Search and Track) system, replacement of the navigation radar with a dual Kelvin Hughes Sharp Eye system and a significant modernisation and upgrade to the Operations Room. A major communications upgrade will also be completed.
Structure: Space and weight have been reserved for the installation of Mini Typhoon, an additional octuple VLS, additional channels of fire for VLS, towed array sonar, offboard active ECM, extended ESM frequency coverage, Helo datalink and SATCOM. The installation of CEAFAR phased array radar involves removal of the lattice mast and replacement with an enclosed cupola mast structure.
Operational: Two RHIBs are carried on all ships. 153, 154 and 155 are based at Sydney; the remainder at Perth.

STUART ***1/2008*, Chris Sattler*** / 1335623

TOOWOOMBA ***7/2008*, John Mortimer*** / 1335622

PERTH

*2/2008**, **Chris Sattler** / 1335621*

PARRAMATTA

6/2008*, Mick Prendergast / 1335610

BALLARAT

5/2008*, Chris Sattler / 1353672

4 ADELAIDE (OLIVER HAZARD PERRY) CLASS (FFGHM)

Name	*No*	*Builders*	*Laid down*	*Launched*	*Commissioned*
SYDNEY	03	Todd Pacific Shipyard Corporation, Seattle, US	16 Jan 1980	26 Sep 1980	29 Jan 1983
DARWIN	04	Todd Pacific Shipyard Corporation, Seattle, US	3 July 1981	26 Mar 1982	21 July 1984
MELBOURNE	05	Australian Marine Eng (Consolidated), Williamstown	12 July 1985	5 May 1989	15 Feb 1992
NEWCASTLE	06	Australian Marine Eng (Consolidated), Williamstown	21 July 1989	21 Feb 1992	11 Dec 1993

Displacement, tons: 4,200 full load
Dimensions, feet (metres): 453 × 45 × 24.5 (sonar); 14.8 (keel) *(138.1 × 13.7 × 7.5; 4.5)*
Main machinery: 2 GE LM 2500 gas turbines; 41,000 hp *(30.6 MW)* sustained; 1 shaft; cp prop; 2 auxiliary electric retractable propulsors fwd; 650 hp *(484 kW)*
Speed, knots: 29 (4 on propulsors)
Range, n miles: 4,500 at 20 kt
Complement: 184 (15 officers) plus aircrew

Missiles: SSM: 8 McDonnell Douglas Harpoon Block 2; active radar homing to 124 km *(67 n miles)* at 0.9 Mach; warhead 227 kg.
SAM: GDC Pomona Standard SM-1MR Block VI; Mk 13 Mod 4 launcher for both SAM and SSM systems ❶; command guidance; semi-active radar homing to 38 km *(20.5 n miles)* at 2 Mach; 40 missiles (combined SSM and SAM).
32 Raytheon RIM-162 ESSM; Mk 41 8-cell VLS launcher ❷; semi-active radar homing to 18.5 km *(10 n miles)* at 3.6 Mach; warhead 227 kg.
Guns: 1 OTO Melara 3 in *(76 mm)*/62 US Mk 75 compact ❸; 85 rds/min to 16 km *(9 n miles)* anti-surface; 12 km *(6.5 n miles)* anti-aircraft; weight of shell 6 kg.
1 General Electric/GDC 20 mm Mk 15 Vulcan Phalanx ❹; anti-missile system with 6 barrels; 4,500 rds/min combined to 1.5 km.
Up to 6—12.7 mm MGs.
2 Rafael Mini-Typhoon 12.7 mm remote-controlled guns (for selected deployments).
Torpedoes: 6—324 mm Mk 32 (2 triple) tubes ❺. Eurotorp MU 90; active/passive homing to 25 km *(13.5 n miles)* at 29/50 kt.
Countermeasures: Decoys: 4 Loral Hycor SRBOC Mk 36 chaff and IR decoy launchers; fixed 6-barrelled system; range 1–4 km. 4 BAe Nulka quad expendable decoy launchers.
2 Rafael long-range chaff rocket launchers (fixed 2-barrel system). LESCUT torpedo countermeasures.

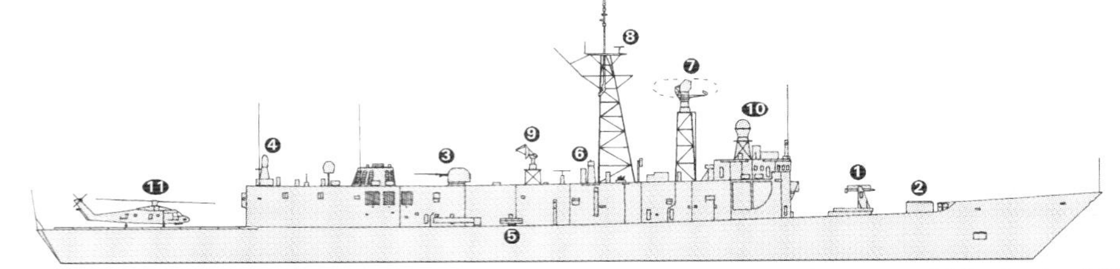

SYDNEY *(Scale 1 : 1,200), Ian Sturton* / 1153837

ESM/ECM: Elbit EA-2118 jammer. Rafael C-Pearl ❻; intercept.
Combat data systems: ADACS. OE-2 SATCOM; Link 11. Link 16.
Weapons control: Sperry Mk 92 Mod 12 gun and missile control (Signaal derivative). Radamec 2500 optronic director with TV, laser and IR imager.
Radars: Air search: Raytheon SPS-49 A(V)1 ❼; C-band.
Surface search/navigation: ISC Cardion SPS-55 ❽; I-band.
Fire control: Lockheed SPG-60 ❾; I/J-band; range 110 km *(60 n miles)*; Doppler search and tracking.
Sperry Mk 92 Mod 12 ❿; I/J-band.
IFF: AIMS Mk XII.
Sonars: Thales Spherion (TMS 4131); active search and attack; medium frequency; hull mounted. Petrel (TMS 5424) high frequency mine-avoidance, Albatros (TMS 4350) towed-array torpedo-warning system.

Helicopters: 2 Sikorsky S-70B-2 Seahawks ⓫ or 1 Seahawk and 1 Squirrel.

Programmes: US numbers: *Sydney* FFG 35; *Darwin* FFG 44.
Modernisation: The original ship design was modified to provide improved helicopter facilities. The improvements resulted in angling the transom, increasing the ship's overall length by 8 ft and fitting the RAST helo recovery system. The modifications also included longitudinal strengthening and buoyancy upgrades. The FFG Upgrade Program (FFG-UP) was delivered by Project Sea 1390. The lead ship *Sydney* returned to service in April 2006. Work on *Melbourne* completed in 2007 and *Darwin* and *Newcastle* completed in 2008. All four ships are to return to full operational service in 2009. The modification included major upgrades to the combat system and sensors including installation of the Mk 41 VLS and integration of ESSM. The first firing of ESSM from an FFG was conducted by *Sydney* on 20 August 2007. SM-1 missiles are to be replaced by SM-2 Block IIIA from 2010.
Operational: *Canberra* decommissioned on 12 November 2005 and *Adelaide* on 19 January 2008. The four remaining upgraded ships of the class are based at Fleet Base East. For operational tasking the ships are fitted with enhanced communications, TopLite Electro-Optical sights and the Mini Typhoon weapon system. All ships are fighter and air control capable.

DARWIN *6/2008*, Mick Prendergast* / 1335609

SYDNEY *6/2008*, Chris Sattler* / 1335620

SHIPBORNE AIRCRAFT

Numbers/Type: 6 Westland Sea King HAS 50/50A.
Operational speed: 125 kt *(230 km/h)*.
Service ceiling: 14,500 ft *(4,400 m)*.
Range: 490 n miles *(908 km)*.
Role/Weapon systems: Utility helicopter; embarked periodically for operations from *Success*, *Tobruk* and the LPAs. Life extension completed in November 1996 for six aircraft. To be replaced by MRH 90 from 2010. One more acquired from UK in 1996 and upgraded to 50LEP (Mk 50) standard. Sensors: AW 391(A) radar. Weapons: MAG 58 7.62 mm MG.

SEA KING *2/2005, Paul Jackson* / 1153848

Numbers/Type: 16 Sikorsky S-70B-2 Seahawk.
Operational speed: 135 kt *(250 km/h)*.
Service ceiling: 10,000 ft *(3,050 m)*.
Range: 600 n miles *(1,110 km)*.
Role/Weapon systems: Seahawk SH-60F derivative aircraft designed by Sikorsky to meet RAN specifications for ASW and ASuW operations. Eight assembled by ASTA in Victoria. Helicopters embarked in FFG-7 and in ANZAC frigates. Fully NVG compatible cockpit. Upgrades from 2004 (expected to complete in 2009) include Raytheon AAQ 27 FLIR, Tracor ALE 47 countermeasures Northrop Grumman AN/AAR-54 MAWS and Elisra AES 210 ESM. A two-phase Seahawk Capability Assurance Programme is in progress; obsolescent parts are to be replaced in the first phase and systems capability to be upgraded in the second. Sensors: Thales Super Searcher Surface surveillance radar, CDC Sonobuoy Processor and Barra Side Processor, and CAE Magnetic Anomaly Detector Set controlled by a Rockwell Collins Tactical Data System. Weapons: ASW; two Mk 46 Mod 5 (replacement by MU 90 is under review) torpedoes. ASV; one Mag 58 MG.

SEAHAWK *9/2006, Royal Australian Navy* / 1167434

Numbers/Type: 6 Eurocopter MRH-90.
Operational speed: 165 kt *(305 km/h)*.
Service ceiling: 10,000 ft *(3,050 m)*.
Range: 648 n miles *(1,200 km)*.
Role/Weapon systems: Contract let with Australian Aerospace to provide a total of 46 MRH-90 to the Australian Defence Force (ADF). The Army is to be allocated 40 while six MSH (Maritime Support Helicopters) are to enter RAN service in 2011 to replace the Sea King fleet. They are to be capable of operating from *Kanimbla*, *Manoora* and future amphibious ships. Primary missions are to be afloat logistics support, SAR and MEDIVAC and boarding party operations. Sensors: Honeywell PRIMUS 701A weather radar, piloting FLIR, EW Self Protection System (Thales RWR, EADS Laser Warner System, LFK AN/AAR-60 Missile Launch Detection System (MILDS), MBDA Saphir-M chaff/flare dispenser system), Thales 'Top Owl' Helmet Mounted Sight and Display (HMSD) with integrated night vision device. Weapons: 2—7.62 mm MGs.

MRH 90 *12/2007, RAN* / 1335611

LAND-BASED MARITIME AIRCRAFT

Notes: (1) Replacement of the AP-3C maritime patrol aircraft fleet from around 2015 is being taken forward under Project Air 7000. The Boeing P-8A Poseidon is a potential platform. The same project includes procurement of a Maritime Unmanned Aerial System (MUAS) to augment the AP-3C replacement platform.
(2) Australia joined the System Design and Development phase of the Joint Strike Fighter in October 2002. Up to 100 aircraft are required to replace the F/A-18 Hornet and F/A-18F Super Hornet fleets by 2020.

Numbers/Type: 6 Boeing 737 AEW&C 'Wedgetail'.
Operational speed: to be confirmed.
Service ceiling: 41,000 ft *(12,500 m)*.
Range: to be confirmed.
Role/Weapon systems: Contract for four aircraft (adaptation of Boeing Business Jet) signed on 20 December 2000. Two additional aircraft, under option, were added in 2004. Delivery of first two aircraft was originally scheduled for November 2006 but these have been delayed. The aircraft are planned to be delivered from mid-2009. AAR capable. Sensors: Details unconfirmed but likely to include Northrop Grumman ESSD L-band multirole electronically scanned array (MESA) radar (fuselage mounted); electronic warfare self-protection (EWSP) system (including IR countermeasures, chaff and flares); Links 11 and 16; Satcom.

BOEING WEDGETAIL *7/2004, Boeing* / 0566617

Numbers/Type: 17/4 General Dynamics F-111C/RF-111C.
Operational speed: 793 kt *(1,469 km/h)*.
Service ceiling: 60,000 ft *(18,290 m)*.
Range: 2,540 n miles *(4,700 km)*.
Role/Weapon systems: Air Force operates the F-111 for maritime and land strike. Four are designated RF-111 and are employed as photo reconnaissance aircraft. Upgraded F/A-18A/Bs and 24 F/A-18F Block 2 Super Hornets will replace the F-111 from late 2010. Sensors: AN/APQ-169 radar, Elta EL-8222 ECM pod, AN/AVQ-26 Pave Track targeting pod. Weapons: 4 Harpoon missiles, 2 AGM-142 stand-off missiles, combinations of Mk 82 and Mk 84 bombs or Paveway II laser guided bombs, AIM-9 Sidewinder AAM.

F-111C *2/2003, Paul Jackson* / 0552764

Numbers/Type: 18 Lockheed P-3C/AP-3C Orion.
Operational speed: 410 kt *(760 km/h)*.
Service ceiling: 28,300 ft *(8,625 m)*.
Range: 4,000 n miles *(7,410 km)*.
Role/Weapon systems: Operated by Air Force for long-range maritime patrol, ASW, maritime strike and ISR. Three more aircraft (plus one for spare parts) without armament or sensors acquired for training. All aircraft upgraded to AP-3C standard by late 2004. Sensors: Elta EL/M-2022A(V)3 radar, GDC UYS-503 acoustic system, Star Safire III electro-optics, ELTA ALR-2001 ESM, up to 84 sonobuoys. Weapons: eight Mk 46(V)5 torpedoes (replacement by MU 90 is under review), up to six Harpoon missiles.

ORION AP-3C *2/2005, Paul Jackson* / 1153868

Numbers/Type: 68 McDonnell Douglas F/A-18 Hornet.
Operational speed: 1,032 kt *(1,910 km/h)*.
Service ceiling: 50,000 ft *(15,240 m)*.
Range: 1,000 n miles *(1,829 km)*.
Role/Weapon systems: Air defence and strike aircraft operated by Air Force but with fleet defence and anti-shipping secondary roles. An upgrade programme is being conducted in three phases. Phase 1 modifications, completed in 2002, included new radios, upgraded mission computers, EW upgrade and GPS. Phase 2-1, completed in 2003, included installation of the AN/APG-73 radar and upgraded aircraft software. In Phase 2-2, completed by late 2007, the aircraft are to be equipped with Link 16, improved avionics and helmet mounted sight. In Phase 2-3, the EW suite (RWR and jammer) is to be upgraded and in Phase 2-4, a new target designation system (HDTS) is to be installed. Phase 3, structural modifications, is to be completed by 2010. Upgraded F/A-18A/Bs are 24 F/A-18F Block 2 Super Hornets are to replace the F-111 from late 2010. Sensors: APG-73 attack radar, Litening Pod radar warning receiver. Weapons: ASV; 4 × Harpoon missiles. Strike; 1 × 20 mm cannon, up to 7.7 tons of 'iron' bombs. Fleet defence; 4 × AAMRAM and 4 × ASRAAM.

F/A-18 Hornet *6/1997, Jane's* / 0581750

Numbers/Type: 13 Aerospatiale AS 350B Squirrel.
Operational speed: 125 kt *(232 km/h).*
Service ceiling: 10,000 ft *(3,050 m).*
Range: 275 n miles *(510 km).*
Role/Weapon systems: Support helicopter for utility tasks and training duties. No longer deployed as shipborne aircraft. Sensors: None. Weapons: ASV; two Mag 58 MGs.

SQUIRREL *9/2006, Royal Australian Navy* / 1167433

Numbers/Type: 24 Boeing F/A-18F Super Hornet.
Operational speed: 930 kt *(1,721 km/h).*
Service ceiling: 50,000 ft *(15,240 m).*
Range: 1,320 n miles *(2,376 km).*
Role/Weapon systems: Acquisition of 24 aircraft confirmed on 17 March 2008. To enter service in 2010, they are to act as an interim replacement for the F-111 from 2010. Details are for those in US Navy service. Sensors: APG-73 radar, APG-79 AESA radar, ALR-67(V)3 RWR. ECM: ALQ-165 ASPJ, ALQ-214 RFCM, towed decoys. Weapons: 11 wing stations for 8,680 kg of weapons (same armament as C/D) plus 20 mm guns.

F/A-18F *9/2005, US Navy* / 1154040

AMPHIBIOUS FORCES

Notes: Replacements for the current amphibious capability are being procured under Joint Project (JP) 2048. *Tobruk* and one of the LPA amphibious transports (*Kanimbla* and *Manoora*) are to be replaced by the Canberra-class LHDs and the second LPA is to be replaced by a 'strategic sealift' capability by 2018. JP 2048 is also to delivery replacement of the watercraft capability represented by the Balikpapan class LCH, LCM 8 and LCVP and other ship-to-shore assets required to integrate with the new LHDs.

2 KANIMBLA (NEWPORT) CLASS (LCCH/LLP)

Name	*No*	*Builders*	*Laid down*	*Launched*	*Commissioned*	*Recommissioned*
KANIMBLA (ex-*Saginaw*)	L 51 (ex-1188)	National Steel & Shipbuilding	24 May 1969	7 Feb 1970	23 Jan 1971	29 Aug 1994
MANOORA (ex-*Fairfax County*)	L 52 (ex-1193)	National Steel & Shipbuilding	28 Mar 1970	19 Dec 1970	16 Oct 1971	25 Nov 1994

Displacement, tons: 4,975 light; 8,450 full load
Dimensions, feet (metres): 552 × 69.5 × 17.5 (aft) *(168.2 × 21.2 × 5.3)*
Main machinery: 6 ALCO 16-251 diesels; 16,500 hp *(12.3 MW)* sustained; 2 shafts; cp props; bow thruster
Speed, knots: 20. **Range, n miles:** 23,500 at 15 kt
Complement: 213 (12 officers)
Military lift: 450 troops (25 officers); 229 lane-metres of vehicles; 2 LCM 8; 250 tons aviation fuel

Guns: 1 General Electric/General Dynamics 20 mm Vulcan Phalanx Mk 15 can be fitted ❶. 4—12.7 mm MGs. Fitted for but not with army-operated RBS 70 launchers.
2 Mini Typhoon 12.7 mm guns. 2 Typhoon 25 mm guns.
Countermeasures: 2 SRBOC Mk 36 chaff and IR launchers.
Radars: Surface search: Kelvin Hughes 1007 ❷; I-band.
Navigation: Kelvin Hughes ❸; I-band.

Helicopters: 4 Army Black Hawks ❹ or 3 Sea Kings or 1 Chinook.

Programmes: Acquired by sale from US on 25 August and 27 September 1994.

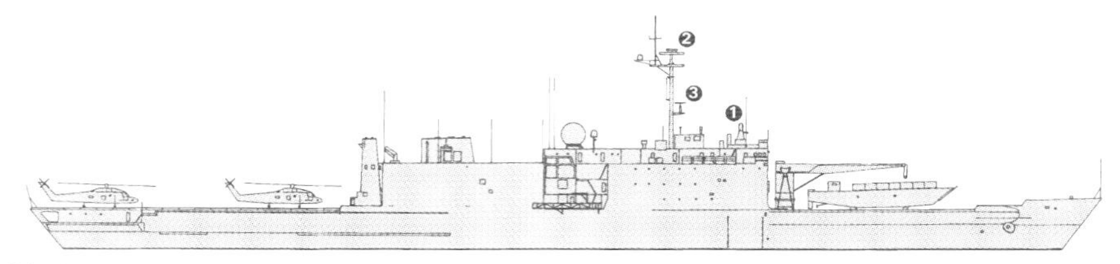

MANOORA *(Scale 1 : 1,500), Ian Sturton* / 0569257

Modernisation: Conversion contract let to Forgacs Shipbuilding, Newcastle in May 1995. Both ships modified by fitting a hangar to take four Black Hawk helicopters, to incorporate a third landing spot forward, to increase aviation fuel capacity and to dispense with the bow landing ramp. The after flight deck is Chinook capable. A stern gate to the tank deck is retained. The ships' carrying capacity includes the M1A1 tank as well as other wheeled and tracked vehicles and artillery. Two LCM 8 are carried on the deck forward when the third landing spot is not used. Installation of communications and command support system to support a deployable JTFHQ was undertaken in both ships in 2001. The ships have a Joint Operations Room and an enhanced medical and surgical fit which can provide Level 3 clinical capacity when a Primary Care Reception Facility is embarked.
Operational: Both based at Sydney. To be replaced in 2013 and 2016.

MANOORA *5/2008*, Chris Sattler* / 1335618

KANIMBLA

11/2008, Chris Sattler* / 1353673

MANOORA

6/2008, Mick Prendergast* / 1335608

KANIMBLA

11/2008, Chris Sattler* / 1335619

1 HEAVY LIFT SHIP (LSLH)

Name	*No*	*Builders*	*Laid down*	*Launched*	*Commissioned*
TOBRUK	L 50	Carrington Slipways Pty Ltd	7 Feb 1978	1 Mar 1980	23 Apr 1981

Displacement, tons: 3,300 standard; 5,700 full load
Dimensions, feet (metres): 417 × 60 × 16 *(127 × 18.3 × 4.9)*
Main machinery: 2 Mirrlees Blackstone KDMR8 diesels; 9,600 hp *(7.2 MW)*; 2 shafts
Speed, knots: 18. **Range, n miles:** 8,000 at 15 kt
Complement: 148 (13 officers)
Military lift: 314 troops (prolonged embarkation); 1,300 tons cargo or 330 lane-metres of vehicles; 70 tons capacity derrick; 2—4.25 ton cranes; 2 LCVP; 2 LCM 8
Guns: 2—12.7 mm MGs. 2 Mini Typhoon 12.7 mm guns. 2 Mini Typhoon 25 mm guns.
Radars: Surface search: Kelvin Hughes Type 1006; I-band. Navigation: Kelvin Hughes 1007; I-band.

Helicopters: Platform for one Sea King. Second Chinook capable spot on forward flight deck (clear of cargo).
Structure: The design is an update of the British Sir Bedivere class and provides facilities for the operation of helicopters, landing craft, amphibians for ship-to-shore movement. A special feature is the ship's heavy lift derrick system for handling heavy loads. Able to embark a squadron of M1A1 tanks plus a number of wheeled vehicles and artillery in addition to its troop lift. Bow and stern ramps are fitted. Two LCM 8 carried on deck and two LCVPs at davits.
Operational: A basic communications fit enables participation in amphibious operations but not in command role. Based at Sydney. To be replaced in 2012.

TOBRUK ***3/2007, Chris Sattler*** / 1167905

TOBRUK ***6/2008*, Chris Sattler*** / 1335617

6 LANDING CRAFT (HEAVY) (LCH/LSM)

Name	*No*	*Builders*	*Commissioned*
BALIKPAPAN	L 126	Walkers Ltd, Queensland	8 Dec 1971
BRUNEI	L 127	Walkers Ltd, Queensland	5 Jan 1973
LABUAN	L 128	Walkers Ltd, Queensland	9 Mar 1973
TARAKAN	L 129	Walkers Ltd, Queensland	15 June 1973
WEWAK	L 130	Walkers Ltd, Queensland	10 Aug 1973
BETANO	L 133	Walkers Ltd, Queensland	8 Feb 1974

Displacement, tons: 358 light; 509 full load
Dimensions, feet (metres): 146 × 33 × 6.5 *(44.5 × 10.1 × 2)*
Main machinery: 2 Caterpillar 3406E diesels; 442 hp *(330 kW)* sustained; 2 shafts
Speed, knots: 10. **Range, n miles:** 3,000 at 10 kt
Complement: 16 (2 officers)
Military lift: 2 M1A1
Guns: 2—12.7 mm MGs.
Radars: Navigation: Racal Decca Bridgemaster; I-band.

Comment: Originally this class was ordered for the Army but only *Balikpapan* saw Army service until being commissioned into the Navy on 27 September 1974. The remainder were built for the Navy. *Balikpapan* and *Betano* based at Darwin. The remainder are based at Cairns. All have been given a life extension refit, which started with *Wewak* in 2000, and completed with *Brunei* in 2002. All were re-engined with Caterpillar diesels 2005–07. *Buna* and *Salamaua* transferred to Papua New Guinea Defence Force in November 1974.

TARAKAN ***8/2008*, Chris Sattler*** / 1335616

4 LANDING CRAFT (LIGHT) (LCVP)

T 4-7

Displacement, tons: 6.5 full load
Dimensions, feet (metres): 43.3 × 11.5 × 2.3 *(13.2 × 3.5 × 0.7)*
Main machinery: 2 Volvo Penta Sterndrives; 400 hp(m) *(294 kW)*
Speed, knots: 22; 15 (fully laden)
Complement: 3
Military lift: 4.5 tons cargo or 1 Land Rover or 36 troops

Comment: Prototype built by Geraldton, Western Australia. Trials conducted in late 1992. Three more delivered in July 1993. Two for *Tobruk*, one for *Success* and one spare attached to Defence Maritime Services at Garden Island, Sydney.

T5 ***8/1999, van Ginderen Collection*** / 0104188

0 + 2 CANBERRA CLASS (AMPHIBIOUS ASSAULT SHIPS) (LHD)

Name	*Builders*	*Laid down*	*Launched*	*Commissioned*
CANBERRA	Navantia, Ferrol/Tenix, Williamstown	2009	2011	2013
ADELAIDE	Navantia, Ferrol/Tenix, Williamstown	2010	2012	2014

Displacement, tons: 25,790 full load
Dimensions, feet (metres): 757.2 × 105.0 × 19.7 *(230.8 × 32.0 × 6.0)*
Flight deck, feet (metres): 663.9 × 105.0 *(202.3 × 32.0)*
Main machinery: Diesel-electric; 4 diesels; 35,000 hp *(26 MW)*; 2 podded propulsors
Speed, knots: 19
Range, n miles: 9,000 at 15 kt
Complement: 243 (plus 978 embarked forces)
Guns: To be announced.
Countermeasures: To be announced.
Combat data systems: To be announced.

Helicopters: Landing spots for 6 NH90 TTH or S-70 Blackhawk or Eurocopter Tiger ARH.

Programmes: Tenix/Navantia announced on 20 June 2007 as the preferred tenderer for Project 2048, the procurement of two helicopter-capable assault ships. A contract for the design and build of the ships was signed on 9 October 2007. The design of the ships is based on the Navantia Strategic Projection Ship under construction for the Spanish Navy. It is planned that the ships' hulls from keel to flight deck are to be built at Ferrol, Spain. Once built, they are to be transported to Tenix's Williamstown shipyard in Melbourne where the locally built superstructure will be joined to the hull. *Canberra* is planned to arrive in Australia in 2011 and *Adelaide* in 2013. The majority of combat system design and integration work is to take place at Adelaide.
Structure: The hangar (1,000 m²) is to be capable of accommodating 11 NH90s. Below the hangar, there is to be a 2,000 m² 'garage' to accommodate 150 vehicles (including main battle tanks), provisions or containers. The landing dock (69.3 × 16 m) is to be capable of operating four LCM-8 landing craft or at least one landing craft air cushion. Medical facilities will include operating rooms, intensive care unit and sick bay. The 'ski jump' deck is also suitable for launching fixed-wing UAVs and will also enable cross-decking of STOVL aircraft operated by allies.
Operational: The principal roles are amphibious, strategic projection of land forces and disaster relief. The ships are to replace the capabilities of *Tobruk* and *Kanimbla* or *Manoora*.

LHD — *6/2007*, **TENIX MARINE** / 1167961

PATROL FORCES

14 ARMIDALE CLASS (PATROL CRAFT) (PB)

Name	*No*	*Builders*	*Commissioned*
ARMIDALE	83	Austal Ships, Fremantle	24 June 2005
LARRAKIA	84	Austal Ships, Fremantle	10 Feb 2006
BATHURST	85	Austal Ships, Fremantle	10 Feb 2006
ALBANY	86	Austal Ships, Fremantle	15 July 2006
PIRIE	87	Austal Ships, Fremantle	29 July 2006
MAITLAND	88	Austal Ships, Fremantle	29 Sep 2006
ARARAT	89	Austal Ships, Fremantle	10 Nov 2006
BROOME	90	Austal Ships, Fremantle	10 Feb 2007
BUNDABERG	91	Austal Ships, Fremantle	3 Mar 2007
WOLLONGONG	92	Austal Ships, Fremantle	23 June 2007
CHILDERS	93	Austal Ships, Fremantle	10 July 2007
LAUNCESTON	94	Austal Ships, Fremantle	22 Sep 2007
MARYBOROUGH	95	Austal Ships, Fremantle	8 Dec 2007
GLENELG	96	Austal Ships, Fremantle	22 Feb 2008

Displacement, tons: 270
Dimensions, feet (metres): 184.6 × 31.8 × 8.8 *(56.8 × 9.7 × 2.7)*
Main machinery: 2 MTU 4000 16V diesels; 6,225 hp *(4.64 MW)*; 2 shafts
Speed, knots: 25. **Range, n miles:** 3,000 at 12 kt
Complement: 21
Guns: 1—25 mm Rafael M242 Bushmaster. 2—12.7 mm MGs.
Countermeasures: RESM; BAE Systems Prism III; intercept.
Electro-optic systems: Rafael Toplite optronic director.
Radars: Surface search/navigation: Bridgemaster E; E/F/I-band.

Comment: Austal Ships in conjunction with Defence Maritime Services (DMS) contracted on 17 December 2003 to supply patrol boats to replace the Fremantle class under Project Sea 1444. The craft are of monohull design and are capable of carrying two RHIBs. DMS is contracted to provide through-life logistics and maintenance support over 15 years. The craft are named after Australian cities and towns. Ten of the craft are based at Darwin, Northern Territory and four at Cairns, Queensland. The ships are operated by 21 crews under a multicrewing regime to maximise operational availability of the hulls.

WOLLONGONG — *8/2008**, **Chris Sattler** / 1335615

MINE WARFARE FORCES

6 HUON (GAETA) CLASS (MINEHUNTERS—COASTAL) (MHC)

Name	*No*	*Builders*	*Launched*	*Commissioned*
HUON	82	Intermarine/ADI, Newcastle	25 July 1997	15 May 1999
HAWKESBURY	83	ADI, Newcastle	24 Apr 1998	12 Feb 2000
NORMAN	84	ADI, Newcastle	3 May 1999	26 Aug 2000
GASCOYNE	85	ADI, Newcastle	11 Mar 2000	2 June 2001
DIAMANTINA	86	ADI, Newcastle	2 Dec 2000	4 May 2002
YARRA	87	ADI, Newcastle	19 Jan 2002	1 Mar 2003

Displacement, tons: 720 full load
Dimensions, feet (metres): 172.2 × 32.5 × 9.8 *(52.5 × 9.9 × 3.0)*
Main machinery: 1 Fincantieri GMT diesel; 1,986 hp(m) *(1.46 MW)*; 1 shaft; LIPS cp prop; 3 Isotta Fraschini 1300 diesels; 1,440 hp(m) *(1,058 kW)*; 3 electrohydraulic motors; 506 hp(m) *(372 kW)*; Riva Calzoni retractable/rotatable APUs
Speed, knots: 14 diesel; 6 APUs
Range, n miles: 1,600 at 12 kt
Complement: 40 (6 officers) plus 9 spare

Guns: 1 MSI DS 30B 30 mm/75. 650 rds/min to 10 km *(5.4 n miles)* anti-surface; 3 km *(1.6 n miles)* anti-aircraft; weight of shell 0.36 kg.
Countermeasures: MCM: 2 Bofors SUTEC Double-Eagle Mk 2 mine disposal vehicles with DAMDIC charges; ADI double Oropesa mechanical sweep and capable of towing the Australian developed Mini-Dyad influence sweep.
Decoys: 2 MEL Aviation Super Barricade; chaff launchers.
ESM: AWADI Prism.
Combat data systems: GEC-Marconi Nautis 2M with Link 11 receive only.
Weapons control: Radamec 1400N optronic surveillance system.
Radars: Navigation: Kelvin Hughes 1007; I-band.
Sonars: GEC-Marconi Type 2093; VDS; VLF-VHF multifunction with five arrays; mine search and classification.

Programmes: The Force Structure Review of May 1991 recommended the acquisition of coastal minehunters of proven design. A contract was signed with Australian Defence Industries (ADI) on 12 August 1994 to build six Intermarine designed Gaeta class derivatives. The hull of the first ship was constructed at Intermarine's Sarzana Shipyard in Italy and arrived in Australia as deck cargo on 31 August 1995 for fitting out in Newcastle, where the remaining five ships were built at ADI's Throsby Basin. Local content for this project was about 69 per cent.
Structure: Monocoque GRP construction. A recompression chamber, one RIB and an inflatable diving boat are carried to support a six-man diving team.
Operational: This class which is named after Australian rivers, is based at HMAS *Waterhen* in Sydney. *Huon* and *Hawkesbury* are tasked on a rotational basis to meet border security requirements.

ALBANY — *7/2008**, **John Mortimer** / 1335614

2 MINESWEEPERS AUXILIARY (TUGS) (MSCD/YTB)

BANDICOOT (ex-*Grenville VII*) Y 298 — **WALLAROO** (ex-*Grenville V*) Y 299

Displacement, tons: 412 full load
Dimensions, feet (metres): 95.8 × 28 × 11.3 *(29.6 × 8.5 × 3.4)*
Main machinery: 2 Stork Werkspoor diesels; 2,400 hp(m) *(1.76 MW)*; 2 shafts
Speed, knots: 11
Range, n miles: 6,300 at 10 kt
Complement: 10
Radars: Navigation: Furuno 7040D; I-band.

Comment: Built in Singapore 1982 and operated by Maritime (PTE) Ltd. Purchased by the RAN and refurbished prior to delivery 11 August 1990. Used for minesweeping trials towing large AMASS influence and mechanical sweeps. No side scan sonar. Also used as berthing tugs. Bollard pull, 30 tons. Both are expected to decommission in 2010.

BANDICOOT — *5/2007*, **Chris Sattler** / 1167900

3 MINESWEEPING DRONES (MSD)

MSD 02–04

Dimensions, feet (metres): 24 × 9.2 × 2 *(7.3 × 2.8 × 0.6)*
Main machinery: 2 Yamaha outboards; 300 hp(m) *(221 kW)*
Speed, knots: 45; 8 (sweeping)

Comment: Built by Hamil Haven in 1991–92. Remote-controlled drones. GRP hulls made by Hydrofield. Used for sweeping ahead of the MSA craft. Differential GPS navigation system with Syledis Vega back-up.

MSD 02 *10/2007, Royal Australian Navy* / 1167888

SURVEY SHIPS (HYDROGRAPHIC SURVEY)

Notes: In addition to the ships listed below, there are three civilian survey capable vessels; *Southern Surveyor*, *Solander* and *Cape Fergusson*. The Australian Antarctic Division also lease-operates the Antarctic supply ship *Aurora Australis*. This ship commenced operations in the Antarctic in 1990, is capable of carrying 70 scientists and is fitted with a helicopter hangar.

AURORA AUSTRALIS *4/2007, Bob Fildes* / 1167899

2 LEEUWIN CLASS (AGS)

Name	*No*	*Builders*	*Launched*	*Commissioned*
LEEUWIN	A 245	NQEA, Cairns	19 July 1997	27 May 2000
MELVILLE	A 246	NQEA, Cairns	23 June 1998	27 May 2000

Displacement, tons: 2,170 full load
Dimensions, feet (metres): 233.6 × 49.9 × 14.1 *(71.2 × 15.2 × 4.3)*
Main machinery: Diesel-electric; 4 GEC Alsthom 6RK 215 diesel generators; 4,290 hp *(3.2 MW)* sustained; 2 Alsthom motors; 1.94 MW; 2 shafts; 1 Schottel bow thruster
Speed, knots: 14
Range, n miles: 18,000 at 9 kt
Complement: 56 (10 officers) plus 5 trainees
Radars: Navigation: STN Atlas 9600 ARPA; I-band.
Sonars: C-Tech CMAS 36/39; hull mounted; high frequency active.

Helicopters: 1 AS 350B (not permanently embarked).

Comment: Contract awarded 2 April 1996 to North Queensland Engineers & Agents (NQEA). Fitted with Atlas Fansweep-20 multibeam echo sounder and one Atlas Hydrographic Deso single beam echo sounder. Also fitted with Klein 2000 towed light-weight sidescan sonar. The ships are capable of various small boat configurations utilising the three SMB davits. The ships are also fitted with an additional RHIB and two light utility boats. Based at Cairns.

MELVILLE *11/2003, John Mortimer* / 0569143

4 PALUMA CLASS (AGSC)

Name	*No*	*Builders*	*Commissioned*
PALUMA	A 01	Eglo, Adelaide	27 Feb 1989
MERMAID	A 02	Eglo, Adelaide	4 Dec 1989
SHEPPARTON	A 03	Eglo, Adelaide	24 Jan 1990
BENALLA	A 04	Eglo, Adelaide	20 Mar 1990

Displacement, tons: 320 full load
Dimensions, feet (metres): 118.9 × 42.0 × 8.6 *(36.6 × 12.8 × 2.65)*.
Main machinery: 2 Detroit 12V-92TA diesels; 1,100 hp *(820 kW)* sustained; 2 shafts
Speed, knots: 11
Range, n miles: 3,600 at 11 kt
Complement: 14 (3 officers)
Radars: Navigation: Kelvin Hughes 1007; I-band.
Sonars: Skipper S113; hull-mounted; active; high frequency.

Comment: Catamaran design based on Prince class ro-ro passenger ferries. Steel hulls and aluminium superstructure. Contract signed in November 1987. Fitted with two ELAC LAX 4700 dual-frequency echo sounders and Knudsen 320B high frequency hull-mounted side-scan sonar. The ships are to be upgraded to multibeam echo-sounder systems 2008–10. All ships based at Cairns and normally operate in pairs when undertaking survey operations.

MERMAID *7/2008*, John Mortimer* / 1335613

9 SURVEY MOTOR BOATS (YGS)

FANTOME 1005	**TOM THUMB** 1009	**CASUARINA** 1012
MEDA 1006	**JOHN GOWLLAND** 1010	**CONDER** 1021
DUYFKEN 1008	**GEOGRAPHE** 1011	**WYATT EARP** ASV 01

Dimensions, feet (metres): 35.1 × 9.5 × 5.6 *(10.7 × 2.9 × 1.7)*
Main machinery: 2 Volvo Penta AQAD-41A diesel stern drives; 400 hp(m) *(294 kW)*; 2 props
Speed, knots: 24
Range, n miles: 300 at 12 kt
Complement: 4 (1 officer)
Radars: Navigation: JRC; I-band.

Comment: Six Survey Motor Boats (SMB) built by Pro Marine, Victoria 1992–1993. Two additional SMBs (CAS and GEO) were built in 1997 to supplement the Leeuwin-class AGS. One SMB has been taken out of service. The remaining seven SMBs are fitted with an Atlas Hydrographic Fansweep 20 multibeam echo sounder and Atlas Hydrographic Deso 15 single beam echo sounder. Three SMBs are fitted for the Klein 2000 towed lightweight side scan sonar. SMB *Conder* built by North Queensland Engineers and Agents in 2003 as a prototype replacement SMB is fitted with an Atlas Hydrographic Fansweep 20 multibeam echo sounder and Atlas Hydrographic Deso 15 single beam echo sounder. Six SMBs are allocated to the Leeuwin-class AGS in Cairns and two to the hydrographic school at HMAS *Penguin*. The Antarctic Survey Vessel (ASV) *Wyatt Earp*, a 9 m craft purpose built by Pro Marine, Victoria in 1992 for operations in the Antarctic. ASV *Wyatt Earp* is allocated to the Deployable Geospatial Support Team (DGST 1) in Wollongong and is fitted with ODOM Hydrotrac single beam echo sounder. The ASV is also fitted for a C-MAX CM2 towed lightweight side scan sonar or JW Fishers, Proton 4 marine magnetometer.

TOM THUMB *8/2008*, Chris Sattler* / 1335612

DEEP SUBMERGENCE VEHICLES

1 RESCUE SUBMERSIBLE (DSRV)

REMORA

Displacement, tons: 16.5
Dimensions, feet (metres): 19.7 × 7.9 × 13.4 (with skirt); 7.9 (without skirt) *(6.0 × 2.4 × 4.1; 2.4)*
Main machinery: 2 electric motors; 150 hp *(112 kW)*; 4 axial thrusters; 4 vertical thrusters; 2 transverse thrusters
Speed, knots: 3 dived
Complement: 1 operator and 6 survivors

Comment: Manufactured in 1995 by Can Dive Marine Services, Canada for Australian Submarine Corporation and subsequently in 2001 wholly owned by the RAN, *Remora* is operated and maintained (at 12 h notice) by a contractor. Capable of operating to depths in excess of 500 m in a current of 3 kt, it can evacuate six personnel at a time and transfer them under pressure of up to 5 Bar directly to two 36-man decompression chambers for medical and hyperbaric treatment. A Remotely Operated Vehicle (ROV), *Remora* is flown and powered from the surface giving it unlimited endurance (emergency life support onboard is 240 man-hours). It is launchable from a craft of opportunity in up to Sea State 5 using a Launch And Recovery System (LARS) that is part of the deployable suite. The skirt on the vehicle can be remotely manipulated to achieve mating angles up to 60°.
Communications are by fibre-optic cable. The entire suite of *Remora*, LARS and all associated equipment can be fitted into ISO containers to facilitate rapid worldwide deployment. The USN replacement system, SRDRS, is based on the Remora system. Following an accident on 5 December 2006, the DSRV was stranded on the seabed until it was recovered on 24 April 2007. However, safety certification for the system had not been obtained by early 2008 and alternative options are under consideration.

REMORA *6/2002, K Bristow, RAN / 0528408*

TRAINING SHIPS

Notes: In addition to *Young Endeavour* (navy operated) and *Salthorse* there are five Fleet class yachts. Of 36.1 ft *(11 m)*. GRP yachts named *Charlotte of Cerberus, Friendship of Leeuwin, Scarborough of Cerberus, Lady Penrhyn of Nirimba* and *Alexander of Creswell*. The names are a combination of Australia's first colonising fleet and the training base to which each yacht is allocated.

1 SAIL TRAINING SHIP (AXS)

Name	*Builders*	*Launched*	*Commissioned*
YOUNG ENDEAVOUR	Brooke Yachts, Lowestoft	2 June 1987	25 Jan 1988

Displacement, tons: 239 full load
Dimensions, feet (metres): 144 × 26 × 13 *(44 × 7.8 × 4)*
Main machinery: 2 Perkins V8 diesels; 334 hp *(294 kW)*; 2 shafts
Speed, knots: 14 sail; 10 diesel
Range, n miles: 2,500 at 7 kt
Complement: 33 (9 RAN, 24 youth)

Comment: Built to Lloyds 100 AI LMC yacht classification by Brooke Yachts, Lowestoft. Sail area 707.1 m². Presented to Australia by UK Government as a bicentennial gift. Operated by RAN on behalf of the Young Endeavour Youth Scheme.

YOUNG ENDEAVOUR *5/2007, Chris Sattler / 1167902*

1 SAIL TRAINING SHIP (AXS)

SALTHORSE

Displacement, tons: 32 full load
Dimensions, feet (metres): 65.0 × 16.7 × 7.5 *(19.8 × 5.1 × 2.3)*
Main machinery: 2 Ford Lehman diesel; 120 hp *(89 kW)*
Speed, knots: 8
Range, n miles: 1,400 at 6 kt
Complement: 1 JRC JMA-2253; I-band

Comment: Ketch with steel hull and aluminium masts. Acquired in 1999 for officer training at HMAS *Creswell*.

SALTHORSE *6/2002, Royal Australian Navy / 0528411*

1 TRAINING SHIP (AXL)

Name	*Builders*	*Launched*
SEAHORSE MERCATOR	Tenix Shipbuilding, Henderson WA	15 Oct 1998

Displacement, tons: 165 full load.
Dimensions, feet (metres): 103.3 × 26.9 × 7.9 *(31.5 × 8.2 × 2.4)*
Main machinery: 2 Caterpillar 3412 diesels; 2 shafts
Speed, knots: 16
Range, n miles: 2,700 at 10 kt
Complement: 8 plus 18 trainees

Comment: Operated by Defence Maritime Services as a Navigation training ship based at Sydney. Similar to Pacific class patrol craft.

SEAHORSE MERCATOR *11/2008*, Chris Sattler / 1335634*

AUXILIARIES

Notes: (1) Only *Sirius* and *Success* are navy operated. The rest have been contracted to the Defence Maritime Services. These craft have blue hulls and buff superstructures, and are chartered as required.
(2) In addition to the vessels listed there are some 24 workboats (AWB and NWB numbers), a VIP launch *Tresco II* and an admiral's barge *Admiral Hudson*.

1 SIRIUS CLASS (REPLENISHMENT TANKER) (AORH)

Name	*No*	*Builders*	*Launched*	*Commissioned*
SIRIUS (ex-*Delos*)	O 266	Hyundai Mipo Dockyard, Korea	12 Apr 2004	16 Sep 2006

Displacement, tons: 46,017 full load
Measurement, tons: 8,585 light
Dimensions, feet (metres): 621.7 × 101.7 × 34.5 *(189.5 × 31.0 × 10.5)*
Main machinery: 1 Hyundai B&W 6S 50MC diesel; 1 shaft; bow thruster
Speed, knots: 16.5
Range, n miles: 16,000 at 14 kt
Complement: 56 (8 officers)
Cargo capacity: Total volume in excess of 36,000 m³. Dry cargo capacity 240 tonnes
Guns: 5 — 12.7 mm MGs (Rafael Mini Typhoon 12.7 mm from 2010).
Radars: 2 Sperry Marine Bridgemaster-E; E/F/I-bands.

Helicopter: Platform for day/night operations.

Comment: Acquired as the replacement for the single-hulled *Westralia*, *Sirius* is a double-hulled ship built to Lloyd's standard. Bought new in June 2004 as *MT Delos* and subsequently leased for use as an oil tanker until September 2005. Contract for the conversion of the ship to military use awarded to Tenix Defence on 15 March 2005. The conversion included the addition of a flight deck and RAS equipment. The first RAN ship to carry the name *Sirius*, she is named after the flagship of the First Fleet which arrived in Australia in 1788. To remain in service until 2020.

SIRIUS *2/2007, Chris Sattler* / 1167903

2 TRIALS AND SAFETY VESSELS (ASR)

Name	*Builders*	*Commissioned*
SEAHORSE STANDARD (ex-*British Viking*)	Marystown Shipyard, Newfoundland	1980
SEAHORSE SPIRIT (ex-*British Magnus*)	Marystown Shipyard, Newfoundland	1980

Measurement, tons: 2,090 grt; 1,635 dwt
Dimensions, feet (metres): 236.2 × 52.5 × 17.4 *(72 × 16 × 5.3)*
Main machinery: 2 MLW-ALCO Model 251 V-12 diesels; 5,480 hp(m) *(4.03 MW)*; 1 shaft; cp prop; 2 stern and 2 bow thrusters
Speed, knots: 9
Complement: 20 plus 44 spare

Comment: Acquired 2 December 1998 by Defence Maritime Services to support RAN trials in Western and Southern Australian waters. Dynamic Positioning system. These ships are also used for weapon recovery and can embark the 'Remora' submarine rescue suite.

SEAHORSE SPIRIT *8/2008*, Chris Sattler* / 1335632

1 TRIALS AND SAFETY VESSEL (ASR)

Name	*No*	*Builders*	*Commissioned*
SEAHORSE HORIZON (ex-*Protector*, ex-*Blue*, *Nabilla*, ex-*Osprey*)	– (ex-ASR 241)	Stirling Marine Services, WA	1984

Displacement, tons: 670 full load
Dimensions, feet (metres): 140.1 × 31.2 × 9.8 *(42.7 × 9.5 × 3)*
Main machinery: 2 Detroit 12V-92TA diesels; 2,440 hp *(1.82 MW)* sustained; 2 Heimdal cp props
Speed, knots: 11.5
Range, n miles: 10,000 at 11 kt
Complement: 6 civilian or 9 navy (for training)
Radars: Navigation: JRC 310; I-band. Decca RM 970BT; I-band.
Sonars: Klein; side scan; high frequency.

Helicopters: Platform for 1 light.

Comment: A former National Safety Council of Australia vessel commissioned into the Navy in November 1990. Used to support contractor's sea trials of the Collins class submarines, and for mine warfare trials and diving operations. LIPS dynamic positioning, two ROVs and a recompression chamber. Helicopter deck and a submersible were removed in 1992. Based at Jervis Bay. Decommissioned in early 1998 and run as part of the commercial support programme. Also used for junior officer training.

SEAHORSE HORIZON *10/2006, Chris Sattler* / 1164787

3 FISH CLASS (TORPEDO RECOVERY VESSELS) (YPT)

TUNA TRV 801 **TREVALLY** TRV 802 **TAILOR** TRV 803

Displacement, tons: 91.6 full load
Dimensions, feet (metres): 88.5 × 20.9 × 4.5 *(27 × 6.4 × 1.4)*
Main machinery: 3 GM diesels; 890 hp *(664 kW)*; 3 shafts
Speed, knots: 13
Complement: 9
Radars: Navigation: I-band.

Comment: All built at Williamstown completed between January 1970 and April 1971. Can transport eight torpedoes. Based at Jervis Bay, Sydney and Fleet Base West respectively. Run as part of the commercial support programme from 1997. Blue hulls and buff superstructures.

TREVALLY *5/2006, Bob Fildes* / 1159952

1 DURANCE CLASS (UNDERWAY REPLENISHMENT TANKER) (AORH)

Name	*No*	*Builders*	*Laid down*	*Launched*	*Commissioned*
SUCCESS	OR 304	Cockatoo Dockyard, Sydney	9 Aug 1980	3 Mar 1984	19 Feb 1986

Displacement, tons: 17,933 full load
Dimensions, feet (metres): 515.7 × 69.5 × 30.6 *(157.2 × 21.2 × 8.6)*
Main machinery: 2 SEMT-Pielstick 16 PC2.5 V 400 diesels; 20,800 hp(m) *(15.3 MW)* sustained; 2 shafts; LIPS cp props
Speed, knots: 20
Range, n miles: 8,616 at 15 kt
Complement: 237 (25 officers)
Cargo capacity: 10,200 tons: 8,707 dieso; 975 Avcat; 116 distilled water; 57 victuals; 250 munitions including SM1 missiles and Mk 46 torpedoes; 95 naval stores and spares
Guns: 1 Vulcan Phalanx Mk 15 CIWS. 7 — 12.7 mm MGs. Rafael Mini Typhoon 12.7 mm guns from 2010.
Radars: Navigation: 2 Kelvin Hughes Type 1006; I-band.

Helicopters: 1 AS 350B Squirrel, Sea King or Seahawk.

Comment: Based on French Durance class design. Replenishment at sea from four beam positions (two having heavy transfer capability) and vertrep. One LCVP is carried on the starboard side aft. Hangar modified to take Sea Kings. Phalanx gun fitted aft in 1997. The ship is to be replaced in about 2015.

SUCCESS *4/2008*, Chris Sattler* / 1335633

4 SELF-PROPELLED LIGHTERS (WFL/AOTL)

WARRIGAL 333 (ex-WFL 8001)
WALLABY 331 (ex-WFL 8002)
WOMBAT 332 (ex-WFL 8003)
WYULDA 334 (ex-WFL 8004)

Displacement, tons: 265 light; 1,206 full load
Dimensions, feet (metres): 124.6 × 33.5 × 12.5 *(38 × 10.2 × 3.8)*
Main machinery: 2 Harbourmaster outdrives (1 fwd, 1 aft)
Speed, knots: 8
Cargo capacity: 560 tons dieso and 200 tons water

Comment: First three were laid down at Williamstown in 1978. The fourth, for HMAS *Stirling*, was ordered in 1981 from Williamstown Dockyard. Used for water/fuel transport. Steel hulls with twin, swivelling, outboard propellers. *Warrigal* at Darwin; *Wombat* and *Wallaby* at Fleet Base East; *Wyulda* at Fleet Base West.

WALLABY *9/2007, Chris Sattler* / 1167895

3 WATTLE CLASS STORES LIGHTERS (YE)

WATTLE CSL 01 **BORONIA** CSL 02 **TELOPEA** CSL 03

Displacement, tons: 147 full load
Dimensions, feet (metres): 79.4 × 32.8 × 5.4 *(24.2 × 10.0 × 1.66)*
Main machinery: 2 Caterpillar D333C diesels; 600 hp *(447 kW)*
Speed, knots: 8
Range, n miles: 320 at 8 kt
Radars: Navigation: 1 JRC JMA-2253; I-band.

Comment: Built by Cockatoo DY, Sydney and delivered in 1972. Employed to transport ammunition and stores. Equipped with 3-ton electric crane. CSL 02 and 03 based at Sydney and CSL 01 at Darwin.

TELOPEA *10/2006, Chris Sattler* / 1164784

4 DIVING TENDERS (YDT/PB)

SEAL 2001 **MALU BAIZAM** 2003 **SHARK** 2004 **DUGONG** 21689

Displacement, tons: 22 full load
Dimensions, feet (metres): 65.5 × 18.5 × 4.6 *(20 × 5.6 × 1.4)*
Main machinery: 2 MTU 8V 183 diesels; 2 shafts
Speed, knots: 26
Range, n miles: 450 at 20 kt
Complement: 6 plus 16 divers

Comment: Built by Geraldton Boat Builders, Western Australia and completed in August 1993. Carry 2 tons of diving equipment to support 24 hour diving operations in depths of 54 m. *Shark* based at *Stirling*, *Seal* at *Waterhen* and *Dugong* at Sydney, *Malu Baizam* is based at Thursday Island in the Torres Strait and is navy manned. *Porpoise* grounded in 1995 and was assessed as being beyond economical repair. Replacement built in 1996. Run as part of the commercial support operation from 1997. Sister craft *Coral Snake* and *Red Viper* are operated by the Army.

SEAL *3/2007, John Mortimer* / 1335631

TUGS

Notes: In addition the two MSCD are used as tugs. Details under Mine Warfare Forces.

7 HARBOUR TUGS (YTL)

TAMMAR DT 2601
QUOKKA DT 1801
SEAHORSE QUENDA
BRONZEWING HTS 501 (152)
CURRAWONG HTS 502 (153)
MOLLYMAWK HTS 504 (154)
SEAHORSE CHUDITCH

Comment: *Tammar* has a bollard pull of 35 tons and is based at *Stirling*; *Quokka* bollard pull 8 tons, is based at Darwin. The three HTS vessels have a bollard pull of 5 tons. Run as part of the commercial support programme from 1997. *Seahorse Chuditch* and *Seahorse Quenda* were built in Malaysia and delivered in 2003. 23 m long they have a bollard pull of 16 tons.

CURRAWONG *8/2008*, Chris Sattler* / 1335630

QUOKKA *8/2008*, Chris Sattler* / 1335629

ARMY

Notes: (1) Operated by Royal Australian Army Corps of Transport. Personnel: About 300 as required.
(2) In addition to the craft listed below there are 159 assault boats 16.4 ft *(5 m)* in length and capable of 30 kt. Can carry 12 troops or 1,200 kg of equipment. Also there are 12 ex-US Army LARC-V amphibious wheeled lighters can operate with *Manoora* and *Kanimbla* and have limited capability tooperate with *Tobruk* and LCHs. They will be able to operate with LHDs.
(3) All LCM are to be replaced in about 2016 by new amphibious watercraft (JP 2048).

6 AMPHIBIOUS WATERCRAFT (LCM)

AB 2000–2005

Displacement, tons: 135 full load
Dimensions, feet (metres): 83.3 × 24.9 × 3.3 *(25.4 × 7.6 × 1.0)*
Main machinery: 2 Detroit 6062 diesels; 2 Doen waterjets
Speed, knots: 11
Range, n miles: 720 at 10 kt
Complement: 5
Guns: 2—12.7 mm MGs.

Comment: Contract signed with ADI in June 2002 to provide watercraft to operate in conjunction with the LPAs. Two carried by each ship. Of aluminium construction, they have through-deck, roll-on/roll-off design and bow and stern ramps. With 65 tonne cargo capacity, the craft can carry five armoured vehicles.

AB 2000 *12/2004, Bob Fildes* / 1153864

14 LCM 8 CLASS

AB 1050–1051, 1053, 1056, 1058–1067

Displacement, tons: 107 full load
Dimensions, feet (metres): 73.5 × 21 × 5.2 *(22.4 × 6.4 × 1.6)*
Main machinery: 2 8V92GM diesels; 720 hp *(547 kW)*; 2 shafts
Speed, knots: 11
Range, n miles: 290 at 10 kt
Complement: 4
Military lift: 55 tons
Guns: 2—12.7 mm MGs.

Comment: Built by North Queensland Engineers, Cairns and Dillinghams, Fremantle to US design. Based at Townsville and Darwin. *AB 1057* transferred to Tonga 1982, *AB 1052* and *AB 1054* soldto civilian use in 1992. All upgraded to Mod 2 standard by late 1999 with new engines and with endurance increased.

AB 1056 — *10/2002, John Mortimer* / 0528383

2 SAFCOL CRAFT

CORAL SNAKE AM 1353 **RED VIPER**

Displacement, tons: 22 full load
Dimensions, feet (metres): 65.5 × 20.0 × 4.6 *(20 × 6.1 × 1.4)*
Main machinery: 2 General Motors Detroit 8V92 diesels; 1,800 hp *(1.34 MW)*
Speed, knots: 28
Range, n miles: 350 at 25 kt
Complement: 3

Comment: Sister to Seal class built at Geraldton Boat Builders. *Coral Snake* delivered in 1994 and *Red Viper* in 1996. Used as Special Action Forces Craft Offshore Large (SAFCOL) to support dives and transport of stores and personnel.

RED VIPER — *7/2007, Mick Prendergast* / 1167934

9 EXPRESS SHARK CAT CLASS (PB)

AM 237–244 **AM 428**

Comment: Built by NoosaCat, Queensland and delivered by 1995. Trailer transportable. Similar craft in service with Navy and Police. Multihulls 30.8 ft *(9.4 m)* in length overall with twin Johnson outboards; 450 hp *(336 kW)* total power output, giving 40 kt maximum speed.

AM 243 — *11/1997, van Ginderen Collection* / 0012946

NON-NAVAL PATROL CRAFT

Notes: (1) In addition to the commercial support craft already listed, various State and Federal agencies, including some fishery departments, have built offshore patrol craft up to 25 m and 26 kt.
(2) Cocos Island patrol carried out by *Sir Zelman Cowan* of 47.9 × 14 ft *(14.6 × 4.3 m)* with two Cummins diesels; 20 kt, range 400 n miles at 17 kt, complement 13 (3 officers). Operated by West Australian Department of Harbours and Lights.
(3) All previously listed RAAF craft have been sold for civilian use.

4 SHARK CAT 800 CLASS (WORKBOATS) (YFL)

0801–0803 **0805**

Displacement, tons: 13.7 full load
Dimensions, feet (metres): 27.4 × 9.2 × 3.3 *(8.35 × 2.8 × 1.0)*
Main machinery: 2 Mercury outboard engines
Speed, knots: 30
Complement: 1 plus 11 passengers

Comment: Built by Shark Cat, Noosaville, Queensland and delivered in 1980s. GRP construction. Used for target-towing, naval police and range clearance duties. *0801* and *0802* based at Fleet Base East; *0803* and *0805* at HMAS *Creswell*.

SHARK CAT 0801 — *9/2006, Chris Sattler* / 1164782

4 NOOSACAT 930 WORKBOATS (YFL)

0901–0904

Dimensions, feet (metres): 30.5 × 11.5 × 2.3 *(9.3 × 3.5 × 0.7)*
Main machinery: 2 Volvo Penta ADQ41DP diesels; 2 props
Speed, knots: 30. **Range, n miles**: 240 at 20 kt

Comment: Built by Noosacat, Queensland and delivered in 1994. GRP hulled craft for general purpose stores and personnel transport. *0903* and *0904* based at Sydney, *0902* at HMAS *Creswell* and 0901 at HMAS *Cerberus*.

NOOSACAT 0904 — *6/2002, Royal Australian Navy* / 0528412

10 STEBER CLASS WORKBOATS (YFL/YDT)

BUNDEENA NGPWB 01
ELOUERA NGPWB 02
SHOALHAVEN NGPWB 03
SEA DRAGON NGPWB 04
ETHEL JOY NGPWB 05
RELIANCE NGPWB 06
PATONGA NGPWB 07
BILGOLA NGPWB 08
SEA WITCH NGPWB 09
BRUTUS NGPWB 10

Displacement, tons: 13.7 full load
Dimensions, feet (metres): 43.3 × 15.4 × 4.4 *(13.2 × 4.7 × 1.3)*
Main machinery: 2 diesels (01-06). 1 diesel (07-10)
Speed, knots: 25 (01-06). 20 (07-10)

Comment: Built by Steber craft and delivered in 1997. GRP hulled craft for general purpose stores and personnel transport and for use as diving tenders. Most have radars 01, 02, 07 and 08 based at Sydney, 03 at HMAS *Cresswell*, 04 and 09 at Fleet Base West and 06 at HMAS *Cerberus*.

ELOUERA — *3/2008*, Chris Sattler* / 1335628

CUSTOMS

Notes: (1) Surface Vessels: The Australian Customs Service (ACS) has initiated a study of a replacement vessel for the Bay class.
(2) Aircraft: The ACS manages its civil aerial surveillance programme through commercial contracts with Surveillance Australia (fixed wing), Australian Helicopters (Torres Strait) and Helicopters Australia (Gove). The new fixed-wing aircraft fleet consists of six De Havilland Dash 8-202 and four Dash 8-315 equipped with radar, IR and EO sensors. These aircraft are either new or have been upgraded under Project Sentinel which provided the Dash 8 with new electro-optics and the Raytheon 2022 SAR/ISAR radar, as well as an integrated information management system and a range of other electronic sensors. The aircraft are based in Broome (WA), Darwin (NT), Horn Island (QLD – Torres Strait), Weipa (QLD) and Cairns (QLD). The ACS helicopter surveillance fleet consists of a Bell 412 and an AS350 Squirrel (Australian Helicopters) which are both based in the Torres Strait. A Eurocopter-145 helicopter is based in Gove (NT) in a rapid response and surveillance role.

DASH 8-200 *6/2005, Massimo Annati* / 1153871

8 BAY CLASS (PB)

ROEBUCK BAY ACV 10
HOLDFAST BAY ACV 20
BOTANY BAY ACV 30
HERVEY BAY ACV 40
CORIO BAY ACV 50
ARNHEM BAY ACV 60
DAME ROMA MITCHELL ACV 70
STORM BAY ACV 80

Displacement, tons: 134
Dimensions, feet (metres): 125.3 × 23.6 × 7.9 *(38.2 × 7.2 × 2.4)*
Main machinery: 2 MTU 16V 2000M 70 diesels; 2,856 hp(m) *(2.1 MW)* sustained; 2 shafts. 1 Vosper Thornycroft bow thruster
Speed, knots: 24
Range, n miles: 1,000 at 20 kt
Complement: 12
Radars: Surface search: Racal Decca; E/F- and I-band.
Sonars: Wesmar SS 390E dipping sonar.

Comment: Built by Austal Ships and delivered from February 1999 to August 2000. The craft carry two RIBs capable of 35 kt.

CORIO BAY *7/2008*, John Mortimer* / 1335627

1 OFFSHORE PATROL VESSEL (PSO)

Name	*Builders*	*Commissioned*
OCEANIC VIKING	Flekkefjord Slip & Maskinfabrikk AS, Norway	1996

Displacement, tons: 12,698 full load
Measurement, tons: 9,075 grt
Dimensions, feet (metres): 346.4 × 72.2 × 22.3 *(105.6 × 22.0 × 6.8)*
Main machinery: 2 Wärtsilä 12V 28 B diesels; 10,770 hp *(7.9 MW)*; 2 shafts; bow and stern thrusters; bow and midships azimuth propellers
Speed, knots: 18
Range, n miles: 33,800 at 12 kt
Complement: 20 plus 35 government officials
Guns: 2—12.7 mm MGs.
Radars: Surface search: Kelvin Hughes 5000R/2/S-U; E/F-band.
Navigation: Kelvin Hughes 6000A/1/6-U; I-band.

Comment: Originally built as a cable-laying vessel. Chartered by the Customs Service to conduct patrols in the Southern Ocean particularly in the vicinity of Australian waters surrounding Heard Island and McDonald Islands. Also available for general border protection tasks. Usually carries fisheries officers and an armed boarding party. Equipped with infra-red camera for low-light and night vision. Carries three high-speed craft for boarding, interception and surveillance.

OCEANIC VIKING *1/2007, ACS* / 1167432

1 OFFSHORE PATROL VESSEL (PSOH)

Name	*Builders*	*Commissioned*
TRITON	Vosper Thornycroft, Woolston	Sep 2000

Displacement, tons: 1,100 full load
Measurement, tons: 2,236 grt
Dimensions, feet (metres): 323.8 × 73.8 × 10.5 *(98.7 × 22.5 × 3.2)*
Main machinery: Diesel-electric; 2 Paxman 12V 185 diesel generators; 5,364 hp *(4 MW)*; 1 HMA motor; 4,700 hp *(3.5 MW)*; 1 shaft (centreline); 2 HMA motors; 938 hp (700 kW); 2 Schottel propulsors (outer hulls)
Speed, knots: 20; 8 (outer propulsors)
Range, n miles: 17,000 at 10 kt
Complement: 14 plus 30 government officials
Guns: 2—12.7 mm MGs.
Radars: Surface search/navigation: Grumman Sperry Marine Bridgemaster E; E/F/I-bands.

Helicopters: Platform for 1 medium.

Comment: Originally built as trimaran hull demonstrator vessel for the UK MoD research agency. Following five years of trials, sold to Gardline Shipping in 2005 and thereafter acted as a hydrographic survey vessel for the UK Maritime and Coast Guard Agency. Contracted in early 2007 by the Australian Customs Service to act as an offshore patrol vessel in northern waters from Broome, West Australia, to Cairns, Queensland. It carries two 7 m high-speed interception craft.

TRITON *12/2006, Gardline Shipping Ltd* / 1167431

1 OFFSHORE PATROL VESSEL (PBO)

ASHMORE GUARDIAN ACV 110

Measurement, tons: 339 grt
Dimensions, feet (metres): 114.5 × 26.2 × ? *(34.9 × 8.0 × ?)*
Main machinery: 2 diesels; 2 shafts
Speed, knots: 10
Complement: 6 plus 10 government officials
Radars: Surface search/navigation: To be announced.

Comment: Modified commercial fleet support ship chartered by Border Defence Command to protect offshore maritime areas off north-western Australia. Priority tasks are environmental protection and the prevention of illegal fishing and people smuggling. The vessel is stationed at the Ashmore Reef National Nature Reserve and Cartier Island Marine Reserves. The ship is equipped with two 7 m RHIBs.

ASHMORE GUARDIAN *12/2008*, Australian Customs Service* / 1335635

Azerbaijan

Country Overview

Formerly part of the USSR, the Republic of Azerbaijan declared its independence in 1991. Situated in the Transcaucasia region of western Asia, the country, which includes the disputed region of Nagorno-Karabakh, has an area of 33,400 square miles and is bordered to the north by Russia and Georgia and to the south with Iran. Armenia to the west includes the exclave of Nakhichevan. Azerbaijan has a coastline of 398 n miles with the Caspian Sea on which Baku, the capital and largest city, is the principal port. Maritime claims in the Caspian Sea have yet to be resolved. Coast Guard formed in July 1992 with ships transferred from the Russian Caspian Flotilla and Border Guard. Operational control and maintenance was assumed by Russia 1995–99 but since then, the Azeri Navy has taken back full responsibility. During 2003 there were increasing signs of a drive to improve effectiveness, reflecting heightened tensions in the Caspian Sea. US assistance has been granted as part of the Caspian Guard initiative.

Headquarters Appointments

Commander of Navy:
Rear Admiral Shahin Sultanov

Personnel

2009: 2,200

Bases

Baku

FRIGATES

1 PETYA II (PROJECT 159A) CLASS (FFL)

BAKINETS (ex-SKR 16) G 121

Displacement, tons: 950 standard; 1,180 full load
Dimensions, feet (metres): 268.3 × 29.9 × 9.5 *(81.8 × 9.1 × 2.9)*
Main machinery: CODAG: 2 gas turbines; 30,000 hp(m) *(22 MW);* 1 Type 61V-3 diesel; 5,400 hp(m) *(3.97 MW)* sustained; centre shaft; 3 shafts
Speed, knots: 32
Range, n miles: 4,870 at 10 kt
Complement: 98 (8 officers)

Guns: 4—3 in *(76 mm)*/59 AK 726 (2 twin); 90 rds/min to 15 km *(8 n miles);* weight of shell 5.9 kg. 4—30 mm/65 (2 twin) AK 230; 500 rds/min to 5 km *(2.7 n miles);* weight of shell 0.54 kg.
A/S mortars: 2 RBU 6000 12-tubed trainable; range 6,000 m; warhead 31 kg.
Mines: Can carry 22.
Countermeasures: ESM.

Radars: Air/surface search: Strut Curve; F-band.
Navigation: I-band.

Comment: Probably transferred from the Russian Caspian Flotilla in 1992. The bridge superstructure has been extended aft to provide another deck at 01 level. The removal of the funnel suggests that there may be an underwater exhaust system. There appears not to be a fire-control radar.

BAKINETS *6/2008** / 1335330

PATROL FORCES

1 TURK (AB 25) CLASS (PB)

ARAZ (ex-AB 34) P 223

Displacement, tons: 170 full load
Dimensions, feet (metres): 132 × 21 × 5.5 *(40.2 × 6.4 × 1.7)*
Main machinery: 4 SACM-AGO V16CSHR diesels; 9,600 hp(m) *(7.06 MW);* 2 cruise diesels; 300 hp(m) *(220 kW);* 2 shafts
Speed, knots: 22
Complement: 31 (3 officers)
Guns: 1 or 2 Bofors 40 mm/70.
1 Oerlikon 20 mm (if only 1—40 mm fitted). 2—12.7 mm MGs.
Depth charges: 1 rack.
Radars: Surface search: Racal Decca; I-band.

Comment: Ex-AB 34 transferred from Turkey July 2000.

TURK CLASS (Turkish colours) *11/1998, Selim San* / 0050287

3 PETRUSHKA (UK-3) CLASS (PB/AXL)

P 213–215

Displacement, tons: 335 full load
Dimensions, feet (metres): 129.3 × 27.6 × 7.2 *(39.4 × 8.4 × 2.2)*
Main machinery: 2 Wola H12 diesels; 756 hp(m) *(556 kW);* 2 shafts
Speed, knots: 11
Range, n miles: 1,000 at 11 kt
Complement: 13 plus 30

Comment: Built as training ships at Wisla Shipyard, Poland. Probably operated both in the training and patrol ship role.

P 214 *7/2008*, M Globke* / 1335203

1 LUGA CLASS (PROJECT 888) (PB/AXT)

T 710 (ex-*Oka*)

Displacement, tons: 1,697 standard; 1,820 full load
Dimensions, feet (metres): 234.3 × 38.1 × 14.8 *(71.4 × 11.6 × 4.5)*
Main machinery: 2 Zgoda-Sulzer 6TD48 diesels; 2,650 hp(m) *(1.95 MW)* sustained; 2 shafts; cp props
Speed, knots: 16
Range, n miles: 7,200 at 11 kt
Complement: 56 (24 officers)
Guns: 4 ZU-23-2MR Wrobel 23 mm (2 twin).
Radars: Navigation: 2 Don 2; I-band.

Comment: Built at Gdansk, Poland in 1976–77. Of same general design as Polish Wodnik class ships with an extra deck and a larger superstructure. Probably employed in both training and patrol ship roles.

AMPHIBIOUS FORCES

2 POLNOCHNY B CLASS (PROJECT 771) (LSM)

D 432 (ex-MDK 36) **D 433** (ex-MDK 37)

Displacement, tons: 760 standard; 834 full load
Dimensions, feet (metres): 246.1 × 31.5 × 7.5 *(75 × 9.6 × 2.3)*
Main machinery: 2 Kolomna Type 40-D diesels; 4,400 hp(m) *(3.2 MW)* sustained; 2 shafts
Speed, knots: 18
Range, n miles: 1,000 at 18 kt
Complement: 42
Military lift: 180 troops; 350 tons including up to 6 tanks
Guns: 2—30 mm/65 (twin) AK 230; 500 rds/min to 5 km *(2.7 n miles)*; weight of shell 0.54 kg.
2—140 mm 18-tubed rocket launchers.
Radars: Navigation: Don 2; I-band.
Fire control: Drum Tilt; H/I-band.
IFF: Square Head. High Pole B.

Comment: Built in Poland 1968–70. Tank deck covers 237 m².

D 432 *6/2008** / 1335326

1 POLNOCHNY A (PROJECT 770) CLASS (LSM)

D 431 (ex-MDK 107)

Displacement, tons: 800 full load
Dimensions, feet (metres): 239.5 × 27.9 × 5.8 *(73 × 8.5 × 1.8)*
Main machinery: 2 Kolomna Type 40-D diesels; 4,400 hp(m) *(3.2 MW)* sustained; 2 shafts
Speed, knots: 19
Range, n miles: 1,000 at 18 kt
Complement: 40
Military lift: 6 tanks; 350 tons
Guns: 2 USSR 30 mm/65 (twin); 500 rds/min to 5 km *(2.7 n miles)*; weight of shell 0.54 kg.
2—140 mm rocket launchers; 18 barrels to 9 km *(4.9 n miles)*.
Radars: Surface search: Decca; I-band.
Fire control: Drum Tilt; H/I-band.

Comment: Built at Northern Shipyard, Gdansk in the late 1960s.

POLNOCHNY CLASS (Egyptian colours) *10/2000, F Sadek* / 0103742

2 T-4 (PROJECT 1785) CLASS (LCM)

D 437 **+1**

Displacement, tons: 35 light; 93 full load
Dimensions, feet (metres): 66.9 × 17.7 × 3.9 *(20.4 × 5.4 × 1.2)*
Main machinery: 2 diesels; 2 shafts
Speed, knots: 10
Complement: 2
Military lift: 50 tons cargo

Comment: Transferred from Russia in 1992.

1 VYDRA CLASS (LCU)

D 436

Displacement, tons: 425 standard; 600 full load
Dimensions, feet (metres): 179.7 × 25.3 × 6.6 *(54.8 × 7.7 × 2)*
Main machinery: 2 Type 3-D-12 diesels; 600 hp(m) *(440 kW)* sustained; 2 shafts
Speed, knots: 11
Range, n miles: 2,500 at 10 kt
Complement: 20
Military lift: 200 troops; 150 tons
Radars: Navigation: Decca; I-band.

Comment: Probably transferred from the Russian Caspian Flotilla in 1992.

D 436 *6/2008** / 1335325

MINE WARFARE FORCES

2 YEVGENYA CLASS (PROJECT 1258) (MINEHUNTERS) (MHC)

M 328 (ex-RT 136) **M 327** (ex-RT 473)

Displacement, tons: 77 standard; 90 full load
Dimensions, feet (metres): 80.7 × 18 × 4.9 *(24.6 × 5.5 × 1.5)*
Main machinery: 2 Type 3-D-12 diesels; 600 hp(m) *(440 kW)* sustained; 2 shafts
Speed, knots: 11
Range, n miles: 300 at 10 kt
Complement: 10
Guns: 2—14.5 mm (twin) MGs.
Countermeasures: Minehunting gear is lowered on a crane at the stern.
Radars: Navigation: Don 2; I-band.
Sonars: MG 7 lifted over the stern.

Comment: Ex-Russian craft built in the 1970s.

M 328 *6/2008** / 1335323

2 SONYA (YAKHONT) (PROJECT 12650) CLASS (COASTAL MINEHUNTER) (MHC)

M 325 (ex-BT 16) **M 326**

Displacement, tons: 450 full load
Dimensions, feet (metres): 157.4 × 28.9 × 6.6 *(48 × 8.8 × 2)*
Main machinery: 2 Kolomna Type 9-D-8 diesels; 2,000 hp(m) *(1.47 MW)* sustained; 2 shafts
Speed, knots: 15
Range, n miles: 3,000 at 10 kt
Complement: 43 (5 officers)
Missiles: 2 quad SA-N-5 launchers.
Guns: 2—30 mm/65 AK 630 or 2—30 mm/65 (twin) and 2—25 mm/80 (twin).
Mines: 8.
Radars: Don 2 or Kivach or Nayada; I-band.
IFF: 2 Square Head. High Pole B.
Sonars: MG 69/79; hull-mounted; active minehunting; high frequency.

Comment: Wooden hull with GRP sheath. Transferred from Russia in 1992. One further vessel is reported non-operational.

M 325 *6/2008** / 1335324

AUXILIARIES

Notes: A variety of auxiliary craft is reported to be in Azerbaijan service although operational status has not been confirmed. Vessels include a Shelon class torpedo recovery craft, an Emba class cable ship and four survey ships (one Kamenka, one Finik, one Vadim Popov and one Valeryan Uryvayev). There is also a Neftegaz (B 92) class salvage tug S 003, three Toplivo class coastal tankers, two Pozharny class firefighting craft, an SK-620 class A 343 and two Tamyr-class icebreakers *Kapitan Izmaylov* and *Kapitan A Radzhabov*.

1 VIKHR (IVA) (PROJECT B-99) CLASS (FIREFIGHTING TUG) (ARS)

S 703

Displacement, tons: 2,300 full load
Dimensions, feet (metres): 237.2 × 46.9 × 15.1 *(72.3 × 14.3 × 4.6)*
Main machinery: 2 diesels; 5,900 hp(m) *(4.4 MW)*; 2 shafts; cp props; 2 bow thrusters
Speed, knots: 16
Range, n miles: 2,500 at 12 kt
Complement: 25

Comment: Built in Gdansk, Poland, in mid-1980s.

S 703 *6/2008** / 1335322

1 RESEARCH SHIP (PROJECT 10470) (AGS)

A 671 (ex-*Svyaga*)

Displacement, tons: To be announced
Dimensions, feet (metres): 413.4 × 54.5 × 13.8 *(126 × 16.6 × 4.2)*
Main machinery: 2 diesels; 1,315 hp *(17.65 MW)*; 2 shafts
Speed, knots: To be announced
Complement: To be announced

Comment: Former civilian Project 1677 Oleg Koshevoy class river/sea tanker converted by the Soviet Union in 1985 to undertake underwater research. Taken over by the Azerbaijan Navy in 1992. Possibly used as a platform for the operation of submersibles.

A 671 *5/2008**, **M Globke** / 1335204

BORDER GUARD

3 STENKA (PROJECT 205P) CLASS (PBF)

S 005 **S 006** (ex-AK 374) **S 007** (ex-AK 234)

Displacement, tons: 253 full load
Dimensions, feet (metres): 129.3 × 25.9 × 8.2 *(39.4 × 7.9 × 2.5)*
Main machinery: 3 diesels; 14,100 hp(m) *(10.36 MW)*; 3 shafts
Speed, knots: 37
Range, n miles: 2,300 at 14 kt
Complement: 25
Guns: 4—30 mm/65 (2 twin) AK 230.
Radars: Surface search: Pot Drum; H/I-band.
Fire control: Drum Tilt; H/I-band.
Navigation: Palm Frond; I-band.

Comment: Ex-Russian craft built in the 1970s. Sonar and torpedo tubes removed. Operated by the Border Guard.

STENKA S 006 *6/2008** / 1335327

2 SILVER SHIPS 48 ft CLASS (PB)

S 11–12

Displacement, tons: 12.5
Dimensions, feet (metres): 48.0 × 12 × 3.5 *(14.6 × 3.7 × 1.1)*
Main machinery: 2 Caterpillar 3196D diesels; 1,140 hp *(850 kW)*; 2 surface piercing props
Speed, knots: 40
Range, n miles: 385 at 36 kt
Complement: 6
Radars: Surface search: I-band.

Comment: Constructed by Silver Ships of Theodore, Alabama. Acquired in 2001, although the details of the purchase are unclear.

S 11 and S 12 *6/2008** / 1335321

1 OSA II (PROJECT 205) CLASS (PB)

S 008

Displacement, tons: 245 full load
Dimensions, feet (metres): 126.6 × 24.9 × 8.8 *(38.6 × 7.6 × 2.7)*
Main machinery: 3 Type M 504 diesels; 10,800 hp(m) *(7.94 MW)* sustained; 3 shafts
Speed, knots: 37
Range, n miles: 500 at 35 kt
Complement: 30
Guns: 4 USSR 30 mm/65 AK 230 (2 twin); 500 rds/min to 5 km *(2.7 n miles)*; weight of shell 0.54 kg.
Radars: Surface search: I-band.
Fire control: Drum Tilt; H/I-band.

Comment: Probably transferred from the Russian Caspian Flotilla in 1992. SS-N-2B missiles have been removed.

OSA S 008 *6/2008** / 1335328

1 POINT CLASS (PB)

Name	*No*	*Builders*	*Commissioned*
– (ex-*Point Brower*)	S 14 (ex-S-201, ex-82372)	USCG Yard, Curtis Bay	21 Apr 1970

Displacement, tons: 67 full load
Dimensions, feet (metres): 83 × 17.2 × 5.8 *(25.3 × 5.3 × 1.8)*
Main machinery: 2 Caterpillar diesels; 1,600 hp *(1.19 MW)*; 2 shafts
Speed, knots: 22
Range, n miles: 1,200 at 8 kt
Complement: 10
Guns: 2 — 12.7 mm MGs.
Radars: Surface search: Hughes/Furuno SPS-73; I-band.

Comment: Transferred from US Coast Guard on 28 February 2003.

POINT CLASS *6/2008** / 1335329

1 ZHUK (GRIF) CLASS (PROJECT 1400M) (PB)

P 222 (ex-AK 55)

Displacement, tons: 39 full load
Dimensions, feet (metres): 78.7 × 16.4 × 3.9 *(24 × 5 × 1.2)*
Main machinery: 2 Type M 401B diesels; 2,200 hp(m) *(1.6 MW)* sustained; 2 shafts
Speed, knots: 30
Range, n miles: 1,100 at 15 kt
Complement: 13
Guns: 2 — 14.5 mm (twin). 1 — 12.7 mm MG.
Radars: Surface search: Spin Trough; I-band.

Comment: Ex-Russian craft built in the 1970s.

ZHUK CLASS (Ukraine colours) *7/2000, Hartmut Ehlers* / 0106655

Bahamas

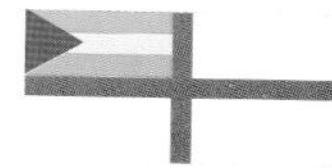

Country Overview

The Commonwealth of the Bahamas gained independence in 1971; the British monarch, represented by a governor-general, is head of state. Situated in the west Atlantic Ocean, it comprises about 700 islands and islets, and nearly 2,400 cays and rocks which stretch between Florida and Hispaniola. About 30 of the islands are inhabited. The capital, Nassau, is on New Providence Island which contains more than half of the total population. Grand Bahama, the most northerly of the group, is the second major island. An archipelagic regime, territorial seas (12 n miles) and a fishery zone (200 n miles) are claimed. A 200 n mile Exclusive Economic Zone (EEZ) has been claimed but the limits are not defined.

Headquarters Appointments

Commander Royal Bahamas Defence Force:
Commodore Clifford Scavella
Squadron Commanding Officer:
Commander Samuel Evans

Bases

HMBS *Coral Harbour* (New Providence Island)
HMBS *Matthew Town* (Great Inagua Island)

Personnel

2009: 922

Prefix to Ships' Names

HMBS (Her Majesty's Bahamian Ship)

PATROL FORCES

Notes: There are three interception craft P 121–123.

2 BAHAMAS CLASS

Name	*No*	*Builders*	*Commissioned*
BAHAMAS	P 60	Moss Point Marine, Escatawpa	27 Jan 2000
NASSAU	P 61	Moss Point Marine, Escatawpa	27 Jan 2000

Displacement, tons: 375 full load
Dimensions, feet (metres): 198.8 × 29.2 × 8.5 *(60.6 × 8.9 × 2.6)*
Main machinery: 3 Caterpillar 3516B diesels; 6,600 hp(m) *(4.85 MW)*; 3 shafts
Speed, knots: 24
Range, n miles: 3,000 at 10 kt
Complement: 35 plus 28 spare
Guns: 1 Bushmaster 25 mm. 3 — 12.7 mm MGs.
Radars: Surface search/Navigation: Decca Bridgemaster Type 656-14/CAB; I-band.

Comment: Order placed 14 March 1997 with Halter Marine Group. Aluminium superstructures fabricated at Equitable Shipyards while hulls built at Moss Point. The design is an adapted Vosper International Europatrol 250 with a RIB and launching crane at the stern. Based at Nassau.

BAHAMAS *6/2003, Marco Ghiglino* / 1129991

1 CHALLENGER CLASS (PB)

P 41

Displacement, tons: 8 full load
Dimensions, feet (metres): 27 × 5.5 × 1 *(8.2 × 1.7 × 0.3)*
Main machinery: 2 Evinrude outboards; 450 hp *(330 kW)*
Speed, knots: 26
Complement: 4
Guns: 1 — 7.62 mm MG.

Comment: Built by Boston Whaler Edgewater, Florida and delivered in September 1995. GRP hull.

P 41 *9/1996, RBDF* / 0056530

1 PROTECTOR CLASS (PB)

Name	*No*	*Builders*	*Commissioned*
YELLOW ELDER	P 03	Fairey Marine, Cowes	20 Nov 1986

Displacement, tons: 110 standard; 180 full load
Dimensions, feet (metres): 108.3 × 22 × 6.9 *(33 × 6.7 × 2.1)*
Main machinery: 3 Detroit 16V-149TI diesels; 3,483 hp *(2.6 MW)* sustained; 3 shafts
Speed, knots: 30
Range, n miles: 300 at 24 kt; 600 at 14 kt on 1 engine
Complement: 20 (3 officers) plus 5 spare
Guns: 1 Rheinmetall 20 mm. 3—7.62 mm MGs.
Radars: Surface search: Furuno; I-band.

Comment: Ordered December 1984. Steel hull. One RIB is carried and can be launched by a trainable crane. Based at Coral Harbour. *Port Nelson* and *Samana* decommissioned in 2007.

PROTECTOR CLASS *4/1996, **RBDF*** / 0056527

1 ELEUTHERA (KEITH NELSON) CLASS (PB)

Name	*No*	*Builders*	*Commissioned*
INAGUA	P 27	Vosper Thornycroft	10 Dec 1979

Displacement, tons: 30 standard; 37 full load
Dimensions, feet (metres): 60 × 15.8 × 4.6 *(18.3 × 4.8 × 1.4)*
Main machinery: 2 Caterpillar 3408BTA diesels; 1,070 hp *(800 kW)* sustained; 2 shafts
Speed, knots: 20
Range, n miles: 650 at 16 kt
Complement: 11
Guns: 3—7.62 mm MGs.
Radars: Surface search: Furuno; I-band.

Comment: The survivor of a class of five. Light machine guns mounted in sockets either side of the bridge. One more is used as a museum. Main engine replaced in 1990.

INAGUA *6/1998, **RBDF*** / 0017574

2 DAUNTLESS CLASS (INSHORE PATROL CRAFT) (PB)

P 42 **P 43**

Displacement, tons: 11 full load
Dimensions, feet (metres): 40.4 × 14 × 4.3 *(12.3 × 4.3 × 1.3)*
Main machinery: 2 Caterpillar 3208TA diesels; 870 hp *(650 kW)* sustained; 2 shafts
Speed, knots: 25
Range, n miles: 600 at 18 kt
Complement: 5
Guns: 2—7.62 mm MGs.
Radars: Furuno 1761; I-band.

Comment: Built by SeaArk Marine, Monticello, Arkansas and delivered in January 1996. Aluminium construction. Used primarily for medium-range search and rescue missions. Based at Coral Harbour.

P 43 *6/1999, **RBDF*** / 0081453

4 BOSTON WHALERS (PBF)

P 110–113

Displacement, tons: 1.5 full load
Dimensions, feet (metres): 20 × 7.2 × 1.1 *(6.1 × 2.2 × 0.4)*
Main machinery: 2 Evinrude outboards; 180 hp *(134 kW) (P 110-111)*; 2 Mariner outboards; 150 hp *(120 kW) (P 112-113)*
Speed, knots: 45 *(P 110-111)*; 38 *(P 112-113)*
Complement: 3

Comment: *P 110* and *111* are Impact designs commissioned 25 September 1995. *P 112* and *113* are Wahoo types commissioned 23 October 1995.

P 110 and P 111 *9/1997, **RBDF*** / 0012053

P 113 *6/1999, **RBDF*** / 0081454

2 SEA ARK 49 ft CUTTERS (PB)

P 48–49

Displacement, tons: 16.5 full load
Dimensions, feet (metres): 49.0 × 16.0 × 4.5 *(14.9 × 5.25 × 1.4)*
Main machinery: 2 Caterpillar C-12 diesels; 1,320 hp *(984 kW)*; 2 shafts
Speed, knots: 30
Range, n miles: 300 at 12 kt
Complement: 6
Radars: Navigation: Furuno; I-band.

Comment: Sea Ark Dauntless RAM design. Aluminium construction. Donated by the US on 26 May 2006. Delivered on 18 July 2008.

P 48 *6/2008*, **SeaArk Marine*** / 1298814

Bahrain

Country Overview

Formerly under British control from 1861, Bahrain gained its independence in 1971. Situated in the southern Gulf, with which it has a coastline of 87 n miles, the country comprises a group of 33 islands between the Qatar Peninsula to the east and Saudi Arabia to the west. The principal islands include Bahrain (217 square miles), Al Muharraq; Umm an Na'san; Sitrah; Jiddah and the Hawar group. The capital, largest city and principal port is Manama. Territorial seas (12 n miles) are claimed. An EEZ has not been claimed.

Headquarters Appointments

Chief of Staff:
Major General Shaikh Abdullah Bin Salman Bin Khalid Al Khalifa

Headquarters Appointments – *continued*

Commander of Navy:
Brigadier Abdulla al Mansoori
Director of Coast Guard:
Colonel Ala Abdulla Seyadi

Personnel

(a) 2009: 1,000 (Navy), 770 (Coast Guard 260 seagoing)
(b) Voluntary service

Bases

Mina Sulman (Navy)
Bandar-Dar (CG base)
Muharraq (CG HQ)

Coast Guard

This unit is under the direction of the Ministry of the Interior.

Prefix to Ships' Names

BRNS (Bahrain Royal Navy Ship)

FRIGATES

1 OLIVER HAZARD PERRY CLASS (FFGHM)

Name	*No*	*Builders*	*Laid down*	*Launched*	*Commissioned*	*Recommissioned*
SABHA (ex-*Jack Williams*)	90 (ex-FFG 24)	Bath Iron Works	25 Feb 1980	30 Aug 1980	19 Sep 1981	25 Feb 1997

Displacement, tons: 2,750 light; 3,638 full load
Dimensions, feet (metres): 445 × 45 × 14.8; 24.5 (sonar) *(135.6 × 13.7 × 4.5; 7.5)*
Main machinery: 2 GE LM 2500 gas turbines; 41,000 hp *(30.59 MW)* sustained; 1 shaft; cp prop
2 auxiliary retractable props; 650 hp *(484 kW)*
Speed, knots: 29. **Range, n miles:** 4,500 at 20 kt
Complement: 206 (13 officers) including 19 aircrew

Missiles: SSM: 4 McDonnell Douglas Harpoon; active radar homing to 90 km *(52 n miles)* at 0.9 Mach; warhead 227 kg.
SAM: 36 GDC Standard SM-1MR Block VI; command guidance; semi-active radar homing to 38 km *(20.5 n miles)* at 2 Mach.
1 Mk 13 Mod 4 launcher for both SSM and SAM missiles (1).
Guns: 1 OTO Melara 3 in *(76 mm)*/62 Mk 75 (2); 85 rds/min to 16 km *(8.7 n miles)* anti-surface; 12 km *(6.6 n miles)* anti-aircraft; weight of shell 6 kg.
1 General Electric/General Dynamics 20 mm/76 6-barrelled Mk 15 Vulcan Phalanx (3); 3,000 rds/min (4,500 in Block 1) combined to 1.5 km.
4 – 12.7 mm MGs.
Torpedoes: 6 – 324 mm Mk 32 Mod 7 (2 triple) tubes (4). 24 Honeywell Mk 46; anti-submarine; active/passive homing to 11 km *(5.9 n miles)* at 40 kt; warhead 44 kg.
Countermeasures: Decoys: 2 Loral Hycor SRBOC 6-barrelled fixed Mk 36 (5); IR flares and chaff to 4 km *(2.2 n miles)*.
SLQ-25 Nixie; torpedo decoy.

SABHA
(Scale 1 : 1,200), Ian Sturton / 0056532

ESM/ECM: SLQ-32(V)2 (6); radar warning. Sidekick modification adds jammer and deception system.
Combat data systems: NTDS with Link 14. INMARSAT.
Weapons control: SWG-1 Harpoon LCS. Mk 92 (Mod 4). The Mk 92 is the US version of the Signaal WM28 system. Mk 13 weapon direction system. 2 Mk 24 optical directors.
Radars: Air search: Raytheon SPS-49(V)4 (7); C-band; range 457 km *(250 n miles)*.
Surface search: ISC Cardion SPS-55 (8); I-band.
Fire control: Lockheed STIR (modified SPG-60) (9); I/J-band; range 110 km *(60 n miles)*.
Sperry Mk 92 (Signaal WM28) (10); I/J-band.
Tacan: URN 25.

Sonars: Raytheon SQS-56; hull-mounted; active search and attack; medium frequency.

Helicopters: 1 Eurocopter BO 105 (11). Space for 2 SH-2G.

Programmes: *Sabha* transferred from the US by grant 18 September 1996. Arrived in the Gulf in June 1997 for a work-up and training period. Transfer of a second ship is unlikely.
Structure: Apart from the removal of the US SATCOM aerials there are no visible changes from US service.
Operational: A transfer of helicopters is required if the ASW potential of the ship is to be realised.

SABHA
4/2000, Guy Toremans / 0104200

SABHA
6/2003, A Sharma / 0568881

CORVETTES

2 AL MANAMA (MGB 62) CLASS (FSGH)

Name	*No*	*Builders*	*Commissioned*
AL MANAMA	50	Lürssen	14 Dec 1987
AL MUHARRAQ	51	Lürssen	3 Feb 1988

Displacement, tons: 632 full load
Dimensions, feet (metres): 206.7 × 30.5 × 9.5 *(63 × 9.3 × 2.9)*
Main machinery: 4 MTU 20V 538TB92 diesels; 12,820 hp(m) *(9.42 MW)* sustained; 4 shafts
Speed, knots: 32. **Range, n miles**: 4,000 at 16 kt
Complement: 43 (7 officers)

Missiles: SSM: 4 Aerospatiale MM 40 Exocet launchers (2 twin) ❶; inertial cruise; active radar homing to 70 km *(40 n miles)* at 0.9 Mach; warhead 165 kg; sea-skimmer.
Guns: 1 OTO Melara 3 in *(76 mm)*/62 compact ❷; 85 rds/min to 16 km *(8.7 n miles)* anti-surface; 12 km *(6.5 n miles)* anti-aircraft; weight of shell 6 kg.
2 Breda 40 mm/70 (twin) ❸; 300 rds/min to 12.5 km *(6.8 n miles)*; weight of shell 0.96 kg.
2—7.62 mm MGs.
Countermeasures: Decoys: CSEE Dagaie ❹; chaff and IR flares.
ESM/ECM: Racal Decca Cutlass/Cygnus ❺; intercept and jammer.
Weapons control: CSEE Panda Mk 2 optical director. Philips TV/IR optronic director ❻.

AL MANAMA *(Scale 1 : 600)*, **Ian Sturton** / 0104201

Radars: Air/surface search: Philips Sea Giraffe 50 HC ❼; G-band.
Navigation: Racal Decca 1226; I-band.
Fire control: Philips 9LV 331 ❽; J-band.

Helicopters: 1 Eurocopter BO 105 ❾.

Programmes: Ordered February 1984.

Modernisation: Upgrade planned to include a SAM self-defence system.
Structure: Similar to Singapore and UAE designs. Steel hull, aluminium superstructure. Fitted with a helicopter platform which incorporates a lift to lower the aircraft into the hangar.
Operational: Planned SA 365F helicopters were not acquired.

AL MUHARRAQ *9/2008**, **Shaun Jones** / 1335640

AL MANAMA *11/2001*, **Royal Australian Navy** / 0526836

SHIPBORNE AIRCRAFT

Notes: SH-2G helicopters may be acquired for the frigate in due course.

Numbers/Type: 2 Eurocopter BO 105.
Operational speed: 113 kt *(210 km/h)*.
Service ceiling: 9,845 ft *(3,000 m)*.
Range: 407 n miles *(754 km)*.
Role/Weapon systems: Acquired in August 1994 as the first aircraft of a Naval Air Arm. Sensors: Bendix RDR 1500B radar. Weapons: Unarmed.

BO 105
6/1995
0056541

PATROL FORCES

4 AHMAD EL FATEH (TNC 45) CLASS (FAST ATTACK CRAFT—MISSILE) (PGGF)

Name	*No*	*Builders*	*Commissioned*
AHMAD EL FATEH	20	Lürssen	5 Feb 1984
AL JABIRI	21	Lürssen	3 May 1984
ABDUL RAHMAN AL FADEL	22	Lürssen	10 Sep 1986
AL TAWEELAH	23	Lürssen	25 Mar 1989

Displacement, tons: 228 half load; 259 full load
Dimensions, feet (metres): 147.3 × 22.9 × 8.2 *(44.9 × 7 × 2.5)*
Main machinery: 4 MTU 16V 538TB92 diesels; 13,640 hp(m) *(10 MW)* sustained; 4 shafts
Speed, knots: 40
Range, n miles: 1,600 at 16 kt
Complement: 36 (6 officers)

Missiles: SSM: 4 Aerospatiale MM 40 Exocet (2 twin); inertial cruise; active radar homing to 70 km *(40 n miles)* at 0.9 Mach; warhead 165 kg; sea-skimmer.
Guns: 1 OTO Melara 3 in *(76 mm)*/62; dual purpose; 85 rds/min to 16 km *(8.7 n miles)* anti-surface; 12 km *(6.5 n miles)* anti-aircraft; weight of shell 6 kg.
2 Breda 40 mm/70 (twin); 300 rds/min to 12.5 km *(6.8 n miles)*; weight of shell 0.96 kg.
3—7.62 mm MGs.
Countermeasures: Decoys: CSEE Dagaie launcher; trainable mounting; 10 containers firing chaff decoys and IR flares.
ESM: Thales Sealion.
ECM: Racal Cygnus (not in 20 and 21); jammer.
Weapons control: 1 Panda optical director for 40 mm guns.
Radars: Air/surface search: Philips Sea Giraffe 50 HC; G-band.
Fire control: Philips 9LV 226/231; J-band.
Navigation: Racal Decca 1226; I-band.

Programmes: First pair ordered in 1979, second pair in 1985. Similar craft in service with Ecuador, Kuwait and UAE navies.
Structure: Only the second pair have the communication radome on the after superstructure.
Operational: Refits from 2000 by Lürssen at Abu Dhabi.

AHMAD EL FATEH *4/2003, A Sharma / 0568844*

AL TAWEELAH *4/2000, Guy Toremans / 0104203*

2 AL JARIM (FPB 20) CLASS (FAST ATTACK CRAFT—GUN) (PB)

Name	*No*	*Builders*	*Commissioned*
AL JARIM	30	Swiftships, Morgan City	9 Feb 1982
AL JASRAH	31	Swiftships, Morgan City	26 Feb 1982

Displacement, tons: 33 full load
Dimensions, feet (metres): 63 × 18.4 × 6.5 *(19.2 × 5.6 × 2)*
Main machinery: 2 Detroit 12V-71TA diesels; 840 hp(m) *(627 kW)* sustained; 2 shafts
Speed, knots: 30
Range, n miles: 1,200 at 18 kt
Guns: 1 Oerlikon GAM-BO1 20 mm.
Radars: Surface search: Decca 110; I-band.

Comment: Aluminium hulls.

AL JARIM *5/2003, A Sharma / 0568879*

2 AL RIFFA (FPB 38) CLASS (FAST ATTACK CRAFT—GUN) (PB)

Name	*No*	*Builders*	*Commissioned*
AL RIFFA	10	Lürssen	3 Mar 1982
HAWAR	11	Lürssen	3 Mar 1982

Displacement, tons: 188 half load; 205 full load
Dimensions, feet (metres): 126.3 × 22.9 × 7.2 *(38.5 × 7 × 2.2)*
Main machinery: 2 MTU 16V 538TB92 diesels; 6,810 hp(m) *(5 MW)* sustained; 2 shafts
Speed, knots: 32. **Range, n miles:** 1,100 at 16 kt
Complement: 27 (3 officers)
Guns: 2 Breda 40 mm/70 (twin); dual purpose; 300 rds/min to 12 km *(6.5 n miles)* anti-surface; 4 km *(2.2 n miles)*; weight of shell 0.96 kg.
1—57 mm Starshell rocket launcher.
Mines: Mine rails fitted.
Countermeasures: Decoys: 1 Wallop Barricade chaff launcher.
ESM: Racal RDL-2 ABC; radar warning.
Weapons control: CSEE Lynx optical director with Philips 9LV 126 optronic system.
Radars: Surface search: Philips 9GR 600; I-band.
Navigation: Racal Decca 1226; I-band.

Comment: Ordered in 1979. *Al Riffa* launched April 1981. *Hawar* launched July 1981.

HAWAR *6/2003, A Sharma / 0568880*

AUXILIARIES

Notes: There are also two RTK Medevac boats and one Diving Boat (512).

1 PERSONNEL TRANSPORT CRAFT (YFL)

TIGHATLIB 46

Comment: Catamaran hulled transport craft. Details not known.

TIGHATLIB *6/2003, A Sharma / 0568877*

AMPHIBIOUS FORCES

0 + 2 LANDING CRAFT (LCU)

Displacement, tons: 380
Dimensions, feet (metres): 145.5 × 32.8 × 7.2 *(44.4 × 10.0 × 2.2)*
Main machinery: 2 Caterpillar CAT 3406TA diesels; 730 hp *(544 kW)*; 2 shafts
Speed, knots: 10
Range, n miles: 1,000 at 8.5 kt
Complement: 11 (3 officers) plus 40 troops
Military lift: military vehicles

Comment: Contract with Abu Dhabi Shipbuilding for the construction of two landing craft announced on 11 November 2008. The vessels, designed in the UAE, are to be of steel construction and based on those in service in the UAE Navy. Delivery of the first vessel is expected in 2010.

LCU (UAE colours) *6/2006, ADSB / 1159231*

1 AJEERA CLASS (SUPPLY SHIP) (YFU)

Name	*No*	*Builders*	*Commissioned*
AJEERA	41	Swiftships, Morgan City	21 Oct 1982

Displacement, tons: 420 full load
Dimensions, feet (metres): 129.9 × 36.1 × 5.9 *(39.6 × 11 × 1.8)*
Main machinery: 2 General Motors 16V-71 diesels; 1,800 hp *(1.34 MW)* sustained; 2 shafts
Speed, knots: 13
Range, n miles: 1,500 at 10 kt
Complement: 21
Guns: 2—12.7 mm MGs.
Radars: Navigation: Racal Decca; I-band.

Comment: Used as general purpose cargo ships and can carry up to 200 tons of fuel and water. Built to an LCU design with a bow ramp and 15 ton crane.

AJEERA *4/2003, A Sharma* / 0568843

4 LCU 1466 CLASS (LCU)

MASHTAN 42 **RUBODH** 43 **SUWAD** 44 **JARADAH** 45

Displacement, tons: 360 full load
Dimensions, feet (metres): 119 × 34 × 6 *(36.3 × 10.4 × 1.8)*
Main machinery: 3 Gray Marine 64YTL diesels; 675 hp *(504 kW)*; 3 shafts
Speed, knots: 8
Range, n miles: 800 at 8 kt
Complement: 15
Cargo capacity: 167 tons
Guns: 2—12.7 mm MGs.
Radars: Navigation: Racal Decca; I-band.

Comment: Transferred from US in 1991. Capable of carrying 150 tons of cargo.

RUBODH *4/2003, A Sharma* / 0568842

0 + 2 HALMATIC WORK BOATS (PB)

Displacement, tons: 13.3
Dimensions, feet (metres): 52.5 × 13.1 × 2.3 *(16.0 × 4.0 × 0.7)*
Main machinery: 2 diesels; 2 waterjets
Speed, knots: 24
Complement: 5
Radars: Navigation: I-band.

Comment: Contract with Abu Dhabi Shipbuilding for the construction of two work boats announced on 11 November 2008. Based on the VT Halmatic Sea Keeper design with an asymmetric catamaran hull, the craft are highly manoeuvrable and are capable of carrying a 10 tonne payload. Delivery is expected in 2010.

WORK BOAT *2/2007, Patrick Allen/Jane's* / 1321982

1 LANDING CRAFT (LCU)

AL ZUBARA (ex-*Sabha*) 40

Displacement, tons: 150 full load
Dimensions, feet (metres): 73.8 × 24.6 × 3.9 *(22.5 × 7.5 × 1.2)*
Main machinery: 2 General Motors 8V92N diesels; 780 hp *(575 kW)*; 2 shafts
Speed, knots: 6
Complement: 8
Radars: Navigation: I-band.

Comment: Fairey Marine Cowes, UK Loadmaster II class which entered service in 1981.

AL ZUBARA *4/2003, A Sharma* / 0568839

COAST GUARD

Notes: (1) Six 11.6 m Fountain Boats interceptor craft, capable of 55+ kt, are to be delivered in 2009.
(2) There are six 8 m coastal patrol craft, Haris 2, Haris 4-8.
(3) There are 10 interceptor craft. Jarada 1-2 (11 m, 35 kt); Jarada 3 (9.7 m, 42 kt); Jarada 4-5 (11 m, 36 kt) and Haris 10-15 (9.7 m, 42 kt).

JARADA 1 *11/2008*, John Fidler* / 1335636

1 WASP 30 METRE CLASS (WPB)

AL MUHARRAQ

Displacement, tons: 90 standard; 103 full load
Dimensions, feet (metres): 98.5 × 21 × 5.5 *(30 × 6.4 × 1.6)*
Main machinery: 2 Detroit 16V-149TI diesels; 2,322 hp *(1.73 MW)* sustained; 2 shafts
Speed, knots: 25
Range, n miles: 500 at 22 kt
Complement: 9
Guns: 2—7.62 mm MGs.
1 Hughes chain 7.62 mm.
Radars: Surface search: Racal Decca; I-band.

Comment: Ordered from Souters, Cowes, Isle of Wight in 1984. Laid down November 1984, launched 12 August 1985, shipped 21 October 1985. GRP hull.

AL MUHARRAQ *4/2003, A Sharma* / 0568841

4 HALMATIC 20 METRE CLASS (WPB)

DERA'A 2 **DERA'A 6** **DERA'A 7** **DERA'A 8**

Displacement, tons: 31.5 full load
Dimensions, feet (metres): 65.9 × 19.4 × 5.1 *(20.1 × 5.9 × 1.5)*
Main machinery: 2 MTU 8V 2000 M92 diesels; 2,170 hp *(1.6 MW)* sustained; 2 shafts
Speed, knots: 29
Range, n miles: 500 at 20 kt
Complement: 7
Guns: 1 – 12.7 mm MG. 2 – 7.62 mm MGs.

Comment: Three delivered in late 1991, the last in early 1992. GRP hulls. All four craft underwent a mid-life refit at Abu Dhabi shipbuilding 2008–09.

DERA'A 8 *11/2008*, John Fidler* / 1335639

2 WASP 20 METRE CLASS (WPB)

DERA'A 4 **DERA'A 5**

Displacement, tons: 36.3 full load
Dimensions, feet (metres): 65.6 × 16.4 × 4.9 *(20 × 5 × 1.5)*
Main machinery: 2 Detroit 12V-71TA diesels; 840 hp *(626 kW)* sustained; 2 shafts
Speed, knots: 24.5
Range, n miles: 500 at 20 kt
Complement: 8
Guns: 2 – 7.62 mm MGs.
Radars: Surface search: Racal Decca; I-band.

Comment: Built by Souters, Cowes, Isle of Wight. Delivered 1983. GRP hulls.

DERA'A 4 *6/2000, Bahrain Coast Guard* / 0104206

6 HALMATIC 160 CLASS (WPB)

SAIF 5–10

Displacement, tons: 17 full load
Dimensions, feet (metres): 47.2 × 12.8 × 3.9 *(14.4 × 3.9 × 1.2)*
Main machinery: 2 MTU S6062 06N04M diesels; 950 hp *(708 kW)* sustained; 2 shafts
Speed, knots: 27
Range, n miles: 500 at 20 kt
Complement: 4
Guns: 1 – 7.62 mm MG.
Radars: Surface search: Furuno; I-band.

Comment: Built by Halmatic, UK, and delivered in 1990–91. GRP hulls. All six craft underwent a mid-life refit at Abu Dhabi Shipbuilding 2008–09.

SAIF 10 *10/2008*, John Fidler* / 1335637

4 FAIREY SWORD CLASS (WPB)

SAIF 1–4

Displacement, tons: 15
Dimensions, feet (metres): 44.9 × 13.4 × 4.3 *(13.7 × 4.1 × 1.3)*
Main machinery: 2 GM 8V-71 diesels; 590 hp *(440 kW)* sustained; 2 shafts
Speed, knots: 22
Complement: 6
Radars: Navigation: Furuno; I-band.

Comment: Purchased in 1980. Built by Fairey Marine Ltd.

SAIF 3 *11/1999, Bahrain Coast Guard* / 0056543

2 HAWAR CLASS (PB)

HAWAR 1 **HAWAR 2**

Displacement, tons: 10.5 full load
Dimensions, feet (metres): 40.7 × 13.0 × 2.3 *(12.4 × 4.0 × 0.7)*
Main machinery: 2 Cummins 6CTA8.3 diesels
Speed, knots: 30
Guns: 1 – 7.62 mm MG.

Comment: Entered service in 2003.

HAWAR 1 *6/2003, John Fidler* / 0567903

1 SUPPORT CRAFT (YAG)

SAFRA 3

Displacement, tons: 165 full load
Dimensions, feet (metres): 85 × 25.9 × 5.2 *(25.9 × 7.9 × 1.6)*
Main machinery: 2 Detroit 16V-92TA diesels; 1,380 hp *(1.03 MW)*; 2 shafts
Speed, knots: 13. **Range, n miles:** 700 at 12 kt
Complement: 6
Radars: Navigation: Racal Decca; I-band.

Comment: Built by Halmatic, Havant and delivered in early 1992. Logistic support work boat equipped for towing and firefighting. Can carry 15 tons.

SAFRA 3 *4/2003, A Sharma* / 0568840

1 LANDING CRAFT (LCM)

SAFRA 2

Displacement, tons: 150 full load
Dimensions, feet (metres): 73.9 × 24.6 × 4 *(22.5 × 7.5 × 1.2)*
Main machinery: 2 General Motors 8V92N diesels; 780 hp *(575 kW)*; 2 shafts
Speed, knots: 6
Complement: 8
Radars: Navigation: Furuno; I-band.

Comment: Fairey Marine Loadmaster II class which was delivered in 1981. Based at Bandar-Dar. Similar to craft in naval service.

3 WASP 11 METRE CLASS (WPB)

SAHAM 1–3

Displacement, tons: 7 full load
Dimensions, feet (metres): 36.1 × 10.5 × 2.6 *(11 × 3.2 × 0.8)*
Main machinery: 2 Yamaha outboards; 400 hp(m) *(294 kW)*
Speed, knots: 25
Complement: 3
Radars: Navigation: I-band.

Comment: Built by Souters, Cowes in 1983.

SAHAM 2 *10/1997, Bahrain Coast Guard* / 0012061

4 RODMAN 20 M CLASS (PB)

DERA'A 11–14

Displacement, tons: 33 full load
Dimensions, feet (metres): 67.2 × 16.2 × 7.4 *(20.5 × 4.93 × 2.25)*
Main machinery: 2 MTU 8V 2000 M92 diesels; 2,170 hp *(1.6 MW)*; 2 shafts
Speed, knots: 30
Complement: 11
Guns: 1—12.7 mm MG. 2—7.62 mm MGs.
Radars: Navigation: I-band.

Comment: Built by Rodman, Spain, and delivered 2008–09.

DERA'A 11 *11/2008*, John Fidler* / 1335638

Bangladesh

Country Overview

The People's Republic of Bangladesh, formerly East Pakistan, proclaimed independence in 1971. Situated in south Asia and with an area of 55,598 square miles, most of its land border is with India (cutting off north-east India from the rest). There is a short border with Myanmar to the south-east. Its 313 n mile coastline is with the Bay of Bengal on which the principal port of Chittagong is situated. The capital and largest city is Dhaka. Territorial waters (12 n miles) are claimed. An EEZ (200 n miles) has been claimed but the limits have not been defined.

Headquarters Appointments

Chief of Naval Staff:
Vice Admiral Sarwar Jahan Nizam
Assistant Chief of Naval Staff (Operations):
Rear Admiral Abu Sayed Mohammed Abdul Awal
Assistant Chief of Naval Staff (Personnel):
Rear Admiral Mohammed Farid Habib
Assistant Chief of Naval Staff (Materials):
Commodore Abul Khair Chowdhury
Assistant Chief of Naval Staff (Logistics):
Commodore H Habibur Rahman Bhuiyan

Senior Appointments

Naval Administrative Authority, Dhaka:
Commodore Mudasser Nasir
Commodore Commanding BN Flotilla:
M Anwarul Islam
Commodore Commanding Chittagong:
Commodore Zahir Uddin Ahmed
Commodore Commanding Khulna:
Commodore M Mohiuddin Razib
Director General Coast Guard:
Commodore M A K Azad
Commodore Superintendent, Dockyard:
Commodore M M Jasimuddin Bhuiyan

Bases

Chittagong (BNS *Issa Khan*, BN Dockyard, Naval Stores Depot, Chittagong, BNS *Ulka*, Bangladesh. Naval Academy, BNS *Patenga*, BNS *Bhatiary*, Naval Units *Cox's Bazar*, *Chanua* and *St Martins*), Kaptai (BNS *Shaheed Moazzam*).
Dhaka (NHQ, BNS *Haji Mohsin* and Naval Unit *Pagla*).
Khulna (BNS *Titumir*, BNS *Mongla*, BNS *Upasham*, Forward Bases *Khepupara* and *Hiron Point*.

Personnel

(a) 2009: 12,150 (1,300 officers)
(b) Voluntary service

Strength of the Fleet

Type	*Active*	*Building*
Frigates	5	–
Fast Attack Craft (Missile)	9	–
Fast Attack Craft (Torpedo)	8	–
Fast Attack Craft (Gun)	13	–
Large Patrol Craft	7	–
Coastal Patrol Craft	9	–
Riverine Patrol Craft	5	–
Minesweepers	4	–
Training Ships	1	–
Repair Ship	1	–
Tankers	2	–
Survey Craft	4	–

Coast Guard

Formed on 19 December 1995 with two ships on loan from the Navy. Bases at Chittagong (East Zone) and Khulna (West Zone). Personnel 721 (54 officers). Colours thick red and thin blue diagonal stripes on hull with COAST GUARD on ships side.

Prefix to Ships' Names

Navy: BNS
Coast Guard: CGS

PENNANT LIST

Frigates

F 15 Abu Bakr
F 16 Umar Farooq
F 17 Ali Haider
F 18 Osman
F 25 Khalid Bin Walid

Patrol Forces

P 111 Pabna (CG)
P 112 Noakhali (CG)
P 113 Patuakhali (CG)
P 114 Rangamati (CG)
P 115 Bogra (CG)
P 201 Ruposhi Bangla (CG)
P 211 Meghna
P 212 Jamuna
P 311 Bishkhali
P 312 Padma
P 313 Surma
P 314 Karnaphuli
P 315 Tista
P 411 Shaheed Daulat
P 412 Shaheed Farid
P 413 Shaheed Mohibullah
P 414 Shaheed Aktheruddin
P 611 Tawheed (CG)
P 612 Tawfiq (CG)
P 613 Tamjeed (CG)
P 614 Tanveer (CG)
P 711 Barkat
P 712 Salam
P 713 Sangu
P 714 Turag
P 811 Nirbhoy
P 911 Madhumati
P 912 Kapatakhaya
P 913 Karatoa
P 914 Gomati
P 1011 Titas
P 1012 Kusiyara
P 1013 Chitra
P 1014 Dhansiri
P 8111 Durbar
P 8112 Duranta
P 8113 Durvedya
P 8114 Durdam
P 8125 Durdharsha
P 8126 Durdanta
P 8128 Dordanda
P 8131 Anirban
P 8141 Uttal
P 8221 TB 1
P 8222 TB 2
P 8223 TB 3
P 8224 TB 4
P 8235 TB 35
P 8236 TB 36
P 8237 TB 37
P 8238 TB 38

Mine Warfare Forces

M 91 Sagar
M 95 Shapla
M 96 Saikat
M 97 Surovi
M 98 Shaibal

Auxiliaries

A 511 Shaheed Ruhul Amin
A 512 Shahayak
A 513 Shahjalal
A 515 Khan Jahan Ali
A 516 Imam Gazzali
A 581 Darshak
A 582 Tallashi
A 583 Agradoot
A 584 LCT-101
A 585 LCT-102
A 587 LCT-104
A 711 Sundarban
A 721 Khadem
A 722 Sebak
A 723 Rupsha
A 724 Shibsha
A 731 Balaban
L 900 Shah Amanat
L 901 Shah Paran
L 902 Shah Makhdum

SUBMARINES

Notes: Plans to acquire a submarine service were announced by the Defence Minister in April 2004 but there has been little apparent development of the programme.

FRIGATES

Notes: Replacement of the Salisbury and Leopard class frigates is a high priority although timescales have not been announced.

1 MODIFIED ULSAN CLASS

Name	*No*	*Builders*	*Laid down*	*Launched*	*Commissioned*	*Recommissioned*
KHALID BIN WALID (ex-*Bangabandhu*)	F 25	Daewoo Heavy Industries	12 May 1999	29 Aug 2000	20 June 2001	12 July 2007

Displacement, tons: 2,170 standard; 2,370 full load
Dimensions, feet (metres): 340.3 × 41 × 12.5 *(103.7 × 12.5 × 3.8)*
Main machinery: CODAD: 4 SEMT-Pielstick 12V PA6V280 STC diesels; 22,501 hp *(16.78 MW)* sustained; 2 shafts
Speed, knots: 25
Range, n miles: 4,000 at 18 kt
Complement: 186 (16 officers)

Missiles: 4 Otomat Mk 2 ❶; command guidance; active radar homing to 180 km *(97.2 n miles)*, at 0.9 Mach; warhead 210 kg; sea-skimmer.
SAM: 1 HQ-7 (FM-90N); line of sight guidance to 13 km *(7 n miles)* at 2.4 Mach; warhead 14 kg.
Guns: 1 Otobreda 3 in *(76 mm)*/62 Super Rapid ❷; 120 rds/min to 16 km *(8.7 n miles)*; weight of shell 6 kg.
4 Otobreda 40 mm/70 (2 twin) compact ❸; 300 rds/min to 12.5 km *(6.8 n miles)*; weight of shell 0.96 kg.
Torpedoes: 6 – 324 mm B-515 (2 triple) tubes ❹; Whitehead A244S; anti-submarine; active/passive homing to 7 km *(3.8 n miles)*; warhead 34 kg (shaped charge).
Countermeasures: Decoys: 2 Super Barricade launchers ❺.
ESM: Racal Cutlass 242; intercept.
ECM: Racal Scorpion; jammer.
Combat data systems: Thales TACTICOS.

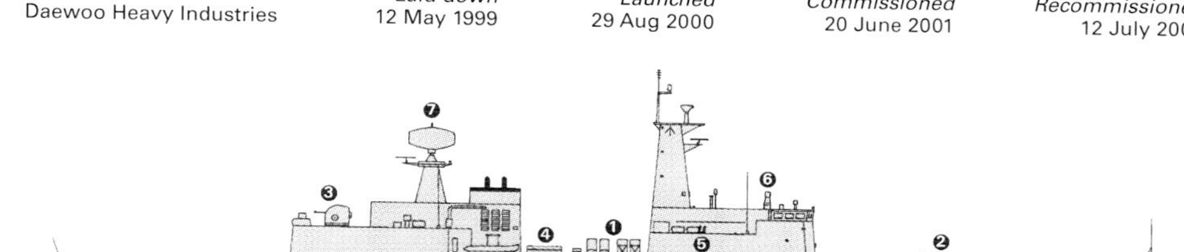

KHALID BIN WALID *(Scale 1 : 900), Ian Sturton* / 0130076

Weapons control: Signaal Mirador optronic director ❻.
Radars: Air search: Signaal DA08 ❼; F-band.
Surface search: Thales Variant; G-band.
Fire control: Signaal Lirod Mk 2; K-band.
Navigation: 2 KH-1007; I-band.
Sonars: STN Atlas ASO 90; hull-mounted; active search; medium frequency.

Helicopters: Hangar and platform for operation of 'Lynx' sized helicopter.

Programmes: Modified Ulsan class ordered from Daewoo in March 1998. Arrived at Chittagong on 16 June 2001.
Operational: The ship was decommissioned on 13 February 2002 for design modification, warranty repairs and capability upgrades. This included installation of FM-90N, the export version of the Chinese HQ-7 SAM system. A period of uncertainty, during which the ship's future was kept under review, followed. This ended on 12 July 2007 when the ship was recommissioned.

KHALID BIN WALID *6/2001* / 0111271

KHALID BIN WALID *6/2001, Daewoo* / 0094449

1 OSMAN (JIANGHU I) CLASS (TYPE 053 H1) (FFG)

Name	*No*	*Builders*	*Laid down*	*Launched*	*Commissioned*
OSMAN (ex-*Xiangtan*)	F 18 (ex-556)	Hudong Shipyard, Shanghai	1986	Dec 1988	4 Nov 1989

Displacement, tons: 1,425 standard; 1,702 full load
Dimensions, feet (metres): 338.6 × 35.4 × 10.2 *(103.2 × 10.7 × 3.1)*
Main machinery: 2 Type 12 E 390V diesels; 16,000 hp(m) *(11.9 MW)* sustained; 2 shafts
Speed, knots: 26
Range, n miles: 2,700 at 18 kt
Complement: 300 (27 officers)

Missiles: SSM: 8 C-802 (YK-83 (CSS-N-8 Saccade)) ❶ mid-course guidance and active radar homing to 150 km *(81 n miles)* at 0.9 Mach; warhead 165 kg.
Guns: 4 China 3.9 in *(100 mm)*/56 (2 twin) ❷; 25 rds/min to 22 km *(12 n miles)*; weight of shell 15.6 kg.
8 China 37 mm/76 (4 twin) ❸; 180 rds/min to 8.5 km *(4.6 n miles)* anti-aircraft; weight of shell 1.42 kg.
A/S mortars: 2 RBU 1200 5-tubed fixed launchers ❹; range 1,200 m; warhead 34 kg.
Depth charges: 2 BMB-2 projectors; 2 racks.
Mines: Can carry up to 60.
Countermeasures: Decoys: 2 Loral Hycor SRBOC Mk 36 6-barrelled chaff launchers.
ESM: Watchdog; radar warning.
Weapons control: Wok Won director (752A) ❺.

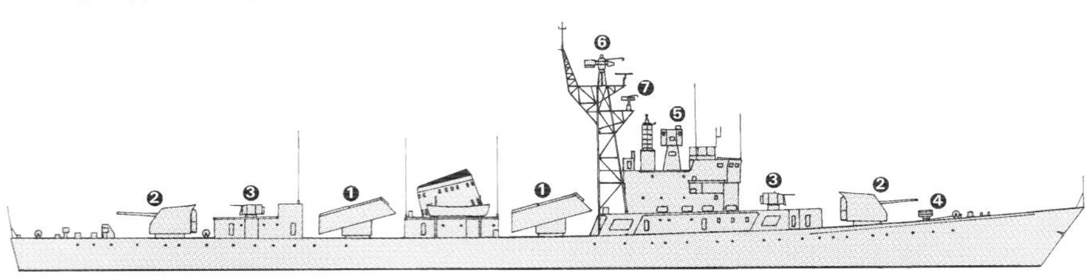

OSMAN (before conversion to C-802) ***(Scale 1 : 900), Ian Sturton*** / 0130383

Radars: Air/surface search: MX 902 Eye Shield (922-1) ❻; G-band.
Surface search/fire control: Square Tie (254) ❼; I-band.
Navigation: Fin Curve (352); I-band.
IFF: High Pole A.
Sonars: Echo Type 5; hull-mounted; active search and attack; medium frequency.

Programmes: Transferred 26 September 1989 from China, arrived Bangladesh 8 October 1989. Second order expected in 1991 was cancelled.

Modernisation: C-802 missiles replaced HY-2 (C-201) missiles in 2007.
Structure: This is a Jianghu Type I (version 4) hull with twin 100 mm guns (vice the 57 mm in the ships sold to Egypt), Wok Won fire-control system and a rounded funnel.
Operational: A test-firing of C-802 was carried out on 12 May 2008.

OSMAN (before conversion to C-802) ***10/2003, Hartmut Ehlers*** / 0569148

1 SALISBURY CLASS (TYPE 61) (FF)

Name	*No*	*Builders*	*Laid down*	*Launched*	*Commissioned*
UMAR FAROOQ (ex-*Llandaff*)	F 16	Hawthorn Leslie Ltd	27 Aug 1953	30 Nov 1955	11 Apr 1958

Displacement, tons: 2,170 standard; 2,408 full load
Dimensions, feet (metres): 339.8 × 40 × 15.5 (screws) *(103.6 × 12.2 × 4.7)*
Main machinery: 8 16 VTS ASR 1 diesels; 14,400 hp *(10.7 MW)* sustained; 2 shafts
Speed, knots: 24. **Range, n miles**: 2,300 at 24 kt; 7,500 at 16 kt
Complement: 237 (14 officers)

Guns: 2 Vickers 4.5 in *(115 mm)*/45 (twin) Mk 6 ❶; dual purpose; 20 rds/min to 19 km *(10 n miles)* anti-surface; 6 km *(3.3 n miles)* anti-aircraft; weight of shell 25 kg.
2 Bofors 40 mm/60 Mk 9 ❷; 120 rds/min to 3 km *(1.6 n miles)* anti-aircraft; 10 km *(5.5 n miles)* maximum.
A/S mortars: 1 triple-barrelled Squid Mk 4 ❸; fires pattern of 3 depth charges to 300 m ahead of ship.
Countermeasures: Decoys: Corvus chaff launchers.
Weapons control: 1 Mk 6M gun director.
Radars: Air search: Marconi Type 965 with double AKE 2 array ❹; A-band.
Air/surface search: Plessey Type 993 ❺; E/F-band.
Heightfinder: Type 278M ❻; E-band.

UMAR FAROOQ ***(Scale 1 : 900), Ian Sturton*** / 0505957

Surface search: Decca Type 978 ❼; I-band.
Navigation: Decca Type 978; I-band.
Fire control: Type 275 ❽; F-band.
Sonars: Type 174; hull-mounted; active search; medium frequency.
Graseby Type 170B; hull-mounted; active attack; 15 kHz.

Programmes: Transferred from UK at Royal Albert Dock, London 10 December 1976.
Operational: The radar Type 982 aerial is still retained on the after mast but the set is non-operational. The ship has been modified as a training ship and is expected to remain in service for some years.

UMAR FAROOQ ***3/2007, Paul Daly*** / 1166506

2 LEOPARD CLASS (TYPE 41) (FF/FFT)

Name	*No*	*Builders*	*Laid down*	*Launched*	*Commissioned*
ABU BAKR (ex-*Lynx*)	F 15	John Brown & Co Ltd, Clydebank	13 Aug 1953	12 Jan 1955	14 Mar 1957
ALI HAIDER (ex-*Jaguar*)	F 17	Wm Denny & Bros Ltd, Dumbarton	2 Nov 1953	30 July 1957	12 Dec 1959

Displacement, tons: 2,300 standard; 2,520 full load
Dimensions, feet (metres): 339.8 × 40 × 15.5 (screws) *(103.6 × 12.2 × 4.7)*
Main machinery: 8 16 VTS ASR 1 diesels; 14,400 hp *(10.7 MW)* sustained; 2 shafts; F 17 fitted with cp props
Speed, knots: 24
Range, n miles: 2,300 at full power; 7,500 at 16 kt
Complement: 235 (15 officers)

Guns: 4 Vickers 4.5 in *(115 mm)*/45 (2 twin) Mk 6 ❶; dual purpose; 20 rds/min to 19 km *(10 n miles)* anti-surface; 6 km *(3.3 n miles)* anti-aircraft; weight of shell 25 kg.
1 Bofors 40 mm/60 Mk 9 ❷; 120 rds/min to 3 km *(1.6 n miles)* anti-aircraft; 10 km *(5.5 n miles)*.
2—7.62 mm MGs.
Countermeasures: Decoys: Corvus chaff launchers.
ESM: Radar warning.
Weapons control: Mk 6M gun director.
Radars: Air search: Marconi Type 965 with single AKE 1 array ❸; A-band.
Air/surface search: Plessey Type 993 ❹; E/F-band.

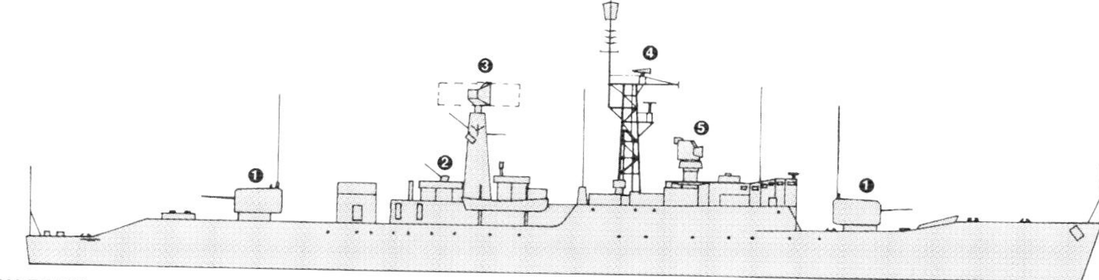

ABU BAKR

(Scale 1 : 900), Ian Sturton / 0505958

Navigation: Decca Type 978; Kelvin Hughes 1007; I-band.
Fire control: Type 275 ❺; F-band.

Programmes: *Ali Haider* transferred from UK 16 July 1978 and *Abu Bakr* on 12 March 1982. *Ali Haider* refitted at Vosper Thornycroft August–October 1978. *Abu Bakr* extensively refitted in 1982.

Structure: All welded. Fitted with stabilisers. Sonars removed while still in service with RN. Fuel tanks have a water compensation system to improve stability.
Operational: Both to remain in service until replacements have been acquired.

ALI HAIDER

2/2001, Michael Nitz / 0529082

PATROL FORCES

Notes: (1) Plans to acquire an offshore patrol vessel, four missile-firing craft and further patrol craft were announced by the Defence Minister in April 2004. Five patrol craft are to be constructed at Khulna Shipyard. They are to be operated by the navy.
(2) Six harbour patrol craft are being built at Khulna Shipyard for the Coast Guard. The first, *Atrai*, was commissioned in September 2007.

1 MADHUMATI (SEA DRAGON) CLASS (LARGE PATROL CRAFT) (PSO)

Name	*No*	*Builders*	*Commissioned*
MADHUMATI	P 911	Hyundai, Ulsan	18 Feb 1998

Displacement, tons: 635 full load
Dimensions, feet (metres): 199.5 × 26.2 × 8.9 *(60.8 × 8 × 2.7)*
Main machinery: 2 SEMT-Pielstick 12 PA6 diesels; 9,600 hp(m) *(7.08 MW)* sustained; 2 shafts
Speed, knots: 24
Range, n miles: 6,000 at 15 kt
Complement: 43 (7 officers)
Guns: 1 Bofors 57 mm/70 Mk 1; 220 rds/min to 17 km *(9.3 n miles)*; weight of shell 2.4 kg. 1 Bofors 40 mm/70. 2 Oerlikon 20 mm.
Weapons control: Optronic director.
Radars: Surface search: Kelvin Hughes KH 1007; I-band.
Navigation: GEM Electronics SPN 753B; I-band.

Comment: Ordered in 1995 and delivered in October 1997. Very similar to the South Korean Coast Guard vessels, but with improved fire-control equipment. Vosper stabilisers.

MADHUMATI

2/1998, Bangladesh Navy / 0017589

6 ISLAND CLASS (COASTAL PATROL CRAFT/TRAINING CRAFT) (PBO/AX)

Name	*No*	*Builders*	*Commissioned*	*Recommissioned*
SHAHEED RUHUL AMIN (ex-*Jersey*)	A 511 (ex-P 295)	Hall Russell, Aberdeen	15 Oct 1976	1994
KAPATAKHAYA (ex-*Shetland*)	P 912 (ex-P 298)	Hall Russell, Aberdeen	14 July 1977	4 May 2003
KARATOA (ex-*Alderney*)	P 913 (ex-P 278)	Hall Russell, Aberdeen	6 Oct 1979	4 May 2003
GOMATI (ex-*Anglesey*)	P 914 (ex-P 277)	Hall Russell, Aberdeen	1 June 1979	3 Oct 2004
SANGU (ex-*Guernsey*)	P 713 (ex-P 297)	Hall Russell, Aberdeen	28 Oct 1977	3 Oct 2004
TURAG (ex-*Lindisfarne*)	P 714 (ex-P 300)	Hall Russell, Aberdeen	3 Mar 1978	3 Oct 2004

Displacement, tons: 925 standard; 1,260 full load
Dimensions, feet (metres): 176 wl; 195.3 oa × 36 × 15 *(53.7; 59.5 × 11 × 4.5)*
Main machinery: 2 Ruston 12RKC diesels; 5,640 hp *(4.21 MW)* sustained; 1 shaft; cp prop
Speed, knots: 16.5
Range, n miles: 7,000 at 12 kt
Complement: 39
Guns: 1 Bofors 40 mm/60 Mk 3. 2 FN 7.62 mm MGs.
Countermeasures: ESM: Orange Crop; intercept.
Combat data systems: Racal CANE DEA-1 action data automation.
Radars: Navigation: Kelvin Hughes Type 1006; I-band.

Comment: *Shaheed Ruhul Amin* transferred as a training craft in 1993. Five further former UK Island class acquired as patrol craft. *Kapatakhaya* transferred 31 July 2002, *Karatoa* 31 October 2002, *Gomati* on 12 September 2003 and *Sangu* and *Turag* on 29 January 2004.

TURAG

3/2004, Derek Fox / 1042116

4 DURDHARSHA (HUANGFEN) CLASS (TYPE 021)
(FAST ATTACK CRAFT—MISSILE) (PTFG)

DURDHARSHA P 8125 **DURDANTA** P 8126 **DORDANDA** P 8128 **ANIRBAN** P 8131

Displacement, tons: 171 standard; 205 full load
Dimensions, feet (metres): 126.6 × 24.9 × 8.9 *(38.6 × 7.6 × 2.7)*
Main machinery: 3 diesels; 12,000 hp(m) *(8.8 MW)*; 3 shafts
Speed, knots: 35. **Range, n miles:** 800 at 30 kt
Complement: 35 (5 officers)
Missiles: SSM: 4 HY-2; active radar or IR homing to 80 km *(43.2 n miles)* at 0.9 Mach; warhead 513 kg.
Guns: 4 USSR 30 mm/65 (2 twin).
Radars: Surface search: Square Tie; I-band.
IFF: High Pole A.

Comment: Built in China. First four commissioned in Bangladesh Navy on 10 November 1988. Chinese equivalent of the Soviet Osa class which started building in 1985. All damaged in April 1991 typhoon but recovered and repaired (*Durnibar* was converted to a patrol craft). A fifth vessel *Anirban* was delivered in June 1992. Original main machinery replaced.

DORDANDA *6/2003, Bangladesh Navy* / 0572413

5 DURBAR (HEGU) CLASS (TYPE 024)
(FAST ATTACK CRAFT—MISSILE) (PTFG)

DURBAR P 8111 **DURANTA** P 8112 **DURVEDYA** P 8113 **DURDAM** P 8114 **UTTAL** P 8141

Displacement, tons: 68 standard; 79.2 full load
Dimensions, feet (metres): 88.6 × 20.7 × 4.3 *(27 × 6.3 × 1.3)*
Main machinery: 4 Type L-12V-180B diesels; 4,800 hp(m) *(3.57 MW)*; 4 shafts
Speed, knots: 37.5. **Range, n miles:** 400 at 30 kt
Complement: 17 (4 officers)
Missiles: SSM: 2 SY-1; active radar or IR homing to 45 km *(24.3 n miles)* at 0.9 Mach; warhead 513 kg.
Guns: 2—25 mm/80 (twin); 270 rds/min to 3 km *(1.6 n miles)*; weight of shell 0.34 kg.
Radars: Surface search: Square Tie; I-band.

Comment: Built in China. First pair commissioned in Bangladesh Navy on 6 April 1983, second pair on 10 November 1983. Two badly damaged in April 1991 typhoon but were repaired. *Uttal* was delivered in June 1992. Missiles are seldom embarked. All have been refitted with new versions of original engines.

UTTAL *3/1998* / 0017590

4 HUCHUAN CLASS (TYPE 026)
(FAST ATTACK CRAFT—TORPEDO) (PTK)

TB 35 P 8235 **TB 36** P 8236 **TB 37** P 8237 **TB 38** P 8238

Displacement, tons: 46 full load
Dimensions, feet (metres): 73.8 × 16.4 × 6.9 (foil) *(22.5 × 5 × 2.1)*
Main machinery: 3 Type L-12V-180 diesels; 3,600 hp(m) *(2.64 MW)*; 3 shafts
Speed, knots: 50. **Range, n miles:** 500 at 30 kt
Complement: 23 (3 officers)
Guns: 4 China 14.5 mm (2 twin); 600 rds/min to 7 km *(3.8 km)*.
Torpedoes: 2—21 in *(533 mm)* China YU-1; anti-ship; to 9.2 km *(5 n miles)* at 39 kt or 3.7 km *(2.1 n miles)* at 51 k.t; warhead 400 kg.
Radars: Surface search: China Type 753; I-band.

Comment: Chinese Huchuan class. Two damaged in April 1991 typhoon but were repaired. All reported operational.

TB 38 *6/2003, Bangladesh Navy* / 0572415

1 DURJOY (HAINAN) CLASS (TYPE 037)
(LARGE PATROL CRAFT) (PC)

NIRBHOY P 812

Displacement, tons: 375 standard; 392 full load
Dimensions, feet (metres): 192.8 × 23.6 × 7.2 *(58.8 × 7.2 × 2.2)*
Main machinery: 4 diesels; 4,000 hp(m) *(2.94 MW)* sustained; 4 shafts
Speed, knots: 30.5. **Range, n miles:** 1,300 at 15 kt
Complement: 70
Guns: 4 China 57 mm/70 (2 twin); 120 rds/min to 12 km *(6.5 n miles)*; weight of shell 6.31 kg.
4—25 mm/60 (2 twin); 270 rds/min to 3 km *(1.6 n miles)* anti-aircraft.
A/S mortars: 4 RBU 1200 fixed 5-barrelled launchers; range 1,200 m; warhead 34 kg.
Depth charges: 2 racks; 2 throwers. 18 DCs.
Mines: Fitted with rails for 12 mines.
Radars: Surface search: I-band.
IFF: High Pole.
Sonars: Tamir II; hull-mounted; short-range attack; high frequency.

Comment: Transferred from China and commissioned 1 December 1985. Forms part of Escort Squadron 81 at Chittagong. *Durjoy* damaged beyond repair by cyclone in 1991. *Nirbhoy* refitted with new main machinery.

NIRBHOY *6/2003, Bangladesh Navy* / 0572414

8 SHAHEED (SHANGHAI II) (TYPE 062) CLASS
(FAST ATTACK CRAFT—GUN) (PC)

SHAHEED DAULAT P 411 **SHAHEED FARID** P 412 **SHAHEED MOHIBULLAH** P 413 **SHAHEED AKTHERUDDIN** P 414 **TAWHEED** P 611 **TAWFIQ** P 612 **TAMJEED** P 613 **TANVEER** P 614

Displacement, tons: 113 standard; 134 full load
Dimensions, feet (metres): 127.3 × 17.7 × 5.6 *(38.8 × 5.4 × 1.7)*
Main machinery: 4 Type L 12-180 diesels; 4,400 hp(m) *(3.2 MW)* sustained; 4 shafts
Speed, knots: 30. **Range, n miles:** 800 at 16.5 kt
Complement: 36 (4 officers)
Guns: 4—37 mm/63 (2 twin); 180 rds/min to 8.5 km *(4.6 n miles)*; weight of shell 1.4 kg.
4—25 mm/80 (2 twin); 270 rds/min to 3 km *(1.6 n miles)* anti-aircraft.
Depth charges: 2 throwers; 8 charges.
Mines: 10 can be carried.
Radars: Surface search: Skin Head/Pot Head; E-band.
Sonars: Hull-mounted; active; short range; high frequency. Some reported to have VDS.

Comment: Transferred from China March 1982. Different engine arrangement from Chinese craft. P 411-414 form Patrol Squadron 41 based at Khulna. P 611 was handed over to the Coast Guard in March 2003 and P 612, P 613 and P 614 were lent to the Coast Guard 2005-2007. P 412 capsized in a storm on 20 September 2006 but is reported to have been salvaged.

TAMJEED *3/1998* / 0017591

4 SEA DOLPHIN CLASS (FAST ATTACK CLASS—GUN) (PTF)

TITAS P 1011 **KUSIYARA** P 1012 **CHITRA** P 1013 **DHANSIRI** P 1014

Displacement, tons: 143 full load
Dimensions, feet (metres): 107.9 × 22.6 × 7.9 *(32.9 × 6.9 × 2.4)*
Main machinery: 2 MTU MD 16V 538 TB90 diesels; 4,500 hp(m) *(3.35 MW)* sustained; 2 shafts
Speed, knots: 37. **Range, n miles:** 600 at 20 kt
Complement: 28 (4 officers)
Guns: 1—40 mm.
2—30 mm (1 twin).
2—20 mm.
Weapons control: Optical director.
Radars: Surface search: Raytheon 1645; I-band.

Comment: Built by Korea SEC in the 1980s and transferred from South Korea as a gift. First pair (P 1011, 1012) recommissioned on 27 May 2000 and second pair (P 1013, 1014) on 3 October 2004. All form 101 Patrol Squadron based at Chittagong.

TITAS *6/2001, Bangladesh Navy* / 0529005

1 RUPOSHI BANGLA CLASS (COASTAL PATROL CRAFT) (PB)

Name	*No*	*Builders*	*Launched*	*Commissioned*
RUPOSHI BANGLA	P 201	Hong Leong-Lürssen	28 June 1999	23 Jan 2000

Displacement, tons: 195 full load
Dimensions, feet (metres): 126.3 × 23 × 13.5 *(38.5 × 7 × 4.1)*
Main machinery: 2 Paxman 12VP 185 diesels; 6,729 hp(m) *(4.95 MW)* sustained; 2 shafts
Speed, knots: 30
Complement: 27 (5 officers)
Guns: 1 Oto Melara 25 mm KBA. 2—7.62 mm MGs.
Radars: Surface search: Furuno; I-band.

Comment: Ordered in June 1998 and laid down 11 August 1998. Based on the PZ design for the Malaysian Police. Operated by the Coast Guard.

RUPOSHI BANGLA *10/1999, Hong Leong-Lürssen* / 0064625

1 HAIZHUI (TYPE 062/1) CLASS (COASTAL PATROL CRAFT) (PC)

Name	*No*	*Commissioned*
BARKAT	P 711	4 Aug 1996

Displacement, tons: 139 full load
Dimensions, feet (metres): 134.5 × 17.4 × 5.9 *(40.9 × 5.3 × 1.8)*
Main machinery: 4 Chinese L12-180A diesels; 4,800 hp(m) *(35.3 MW)*; 4 shafts
Speed, knots: 28
Range, n miles: 750 at 17 kt
Complement: 43 (4 officers)
Guns: 4 China 37 mm/63 (2 twin); 180 rds/min to 8.5 km *(4.6 n miles)*; weight of shell 1.42 kg.
4 China 25 mm/80 (2 twin).
Depth charges: 2 rails.
Radars: Surface search: Anitsu 726; I-band.
Sonars: Stag Ear; active; high frequency.

Comment: Acquired from China in 1995. This is the Shanghai III, the larger and slower version of the Shanghai II which in Chinese service has anti-submarine mortars. An inclined pole mast and platform behind the bridge are distinguishing features.

BARKAT *3/1998* / 0017592

1 COASTAL PATROL CRAFT (PB)

Name	*No*	*Builders*	*Commissioned*
SALAM (ex-*Durnibar*)	P 712 (ex-P 8127)	Khulna Shipyard	19 Mar 2002

Displacement, tons: 185 standard; 216 full load
Dimensions, feet (metres): 126.6 × 24.9 × 8.9 *(38.6 × 7.6 × 2.7)*
Main machinery: 2 Paxman 12V 185 diesels; 4,800 hp *(3.6 MW)* sustained; 2 shafts
Speed, knots: 24
Range, n miles: 3,460 at 13 kt
Complement: 27 (5 officers)
Guns: 1 Bofors 40 mm/60; 120 rds/min 20 3 km (1.6 n miles).
2 GCM AO2 30 mm (twin).
Radars: Surface search: Furuno HR 2010; E/F-band.
Navigation: Anritsu; I-band.

Comment: Former Huangfen class missile craft transferred from China in 1988. Sunk in River Kamaphuli in 1991 during cyclone and later recovered. Renovated and converted to patrol craft role and recommissioned in 2002.

2 KARNAPHULI (KRALJEVICA) CLASS (LARGE PATROL CRAFT) (PC)

Name	*No*	*Builders*	*Commissioned*
KARNAPHULI (ex-*PBR 502*)	P 314	Yugoslavia	1956
TISTA (ex-*PBR 505*)	P 315	Yugoslavia	1956

Displacement, tons: 195 standard; 245 full load
Dimensions, feet (metres): 141.4 × 20.7 × 5.7 *(43.1 × 6.3 × 1.8)*
Main machinery: 2 Paxman 12V P185 (P 314); 2 MTU 12V 396TE84 (P 315); 2 shafts
Speed, knots: 24
Range, n miles: 1,500 at 12 kt
Complement: 44 (4 officers)
Guns: 2 Bofors 40 mm/70. 2 Oerlikon 20 mm. 2—128 mm rocket launchers (5 barrels per mounting).
Depth charges: 2 racks; 2 Mk 6 projectors.
Radars: Surface search: Decca 1229; I-band.
Sonars: QCU 2; hull-mounted; active; high frequency.

Comment: Transferred and commissioned 6 June 1975. *Karnaphuli* re-engined in 1995, *Tista* in 1998.

TISTA *6/1999, Bangladesh Navy* / 0056550

2 AKSHAY CLASS (COASTAL PATROL CRAFT) (PB)

Name	*No*	*Builders*	*Commissioned*
PADMA (ex-*Akshay*)	P 312	Hooghly D & E Co, Calcutta	4 Apr 1973
SURMA (ex-*Ajay*)	P 313	Hooghly D & E Co, Calcutta	26 July 1974

Displacement, tons: 120 standard; 150 full load
Dimensions, feet (metres): 117.2 × 20 × 5.5 *(35.7 × 6.1 × 1.7)*
Main machinery: 2 Paxman YHAXM diesels; 1,100 hp *(820 kW)*; 2 shafts
Speed, knots: 18
Range, n miles: 500 at 12 kt
Complement: 35 (3 officers)
Guns: 4 or 8 Oerlikon 20 mm 1 or (2 quad). 2 Bofors 40 mm/60 (twin) *(Surma)*.
Radars: Surface search: Racal Decca; I-band.

Comment: Built in 1962 and transferred from India in 1973–4. *Surma* has a 40 mm gun aft vice the second quad 20 mm.

PADMA *6/1997, Bangladesh Navy* / 0012065

2 MEGHNA CLASS (COASTAL PATROL CRAFT) (PB)

Name	*No*	*Builders*	*Launched*
MEGHNA	P 211	Vosper Private, Singapore	6 May 1984
JAMUNA	P 212	Vosper Private, Singapore	25 Sep 1984

Displacement, tons: 410 full load
Dimensions, feet (metres): 152.5 × 24.6 × 6.6 *(46.5 × 7.5 × 2)*
Main machinery: 2 Paxman Valenta 12CM diesels; 5,000 hp *(3.73 MW)* sustained; 2 shafts
Speed, knots: 20
Range, n miles: 2,000 at 16 kt
Complement: 47 (3 officers)
Guns: 1 Bofors 57 mm/70 Mk 1; 200 rds/min to 17 km *(9.3 n miles)*; weight of shell 2.4 kg.
1 Bofors 40 mm/70; 300 rds/min to 12 km *(6.5 n miles)*; weight of shell 0.96 kg.
2—7.62 mm MGs; launchers for illuminants on the 57 mm gun.
Weapons control: Selenia NA 18 B optronic system.
Radars: Surface search: Decca 1229; I-band.

Comment: Built for EEZ work under the Ministry of Agriculture. Both completed late 1984. Both damaged in April 1991 typhoon but have been repaired. P 212 damaged by container ship at Chittagong in September 2003.

MEGHNA *6/2003, Bangladesh Navy* / 0572416

4 TYPE 123K (CHINESE P4) CLASS (FAST ATTACK CRAFT—TORPEDO) (PTL)

TB 1 P 8221 **TB 2** P 8222 **TB 3** P 8223 **TB 4** P 8224

Displacement, tons: 25 full load
Dimensions, feet (metres): 62.3 × 10.8 × 3.3 *(19 × 3.3 × 1)*
Main machinery: 2 Type L-12V-180 diesels; 2,400 hp(m) *(1.76 MW)*; 2 shafts
Speed, knots: 50. **Range, n miles:** 410 at 30 kt
Complement: 12 (1 officer)
Guns: 2—14.5 mm (twin) MG.
Torpedoes: 2—17.7 in *(450 mm)*; anti-ship.
Radars: Surface search: Pot Head; I-band.

Comment: Transferred from China 6 April 1983. Three reported to be operational.

TB 4 — *6/2003, Bangladesh Navy* / 0572417

1 RIVER CLASS (COASTAL PATROL CRAFT) (PB)

Name	*No*	*Builders*	*Commissioned*
BISHKHALI (ex-*Jessore*)	P 311	Brooke Marine Ltd	20 May 1965

Displacement, tons: 115 standard; 143 full load
Dimensions, feet (metres): 107 × 20 × 6.9 *(32.6 × 6.1 × 2.1)*
Main machinery: 2 MTU 12V 538TB90 diesels; 4,500 hp(m) *(3.3 MW)* sustained; 2 shafts
Speed, knots: 24
Complement: 30
Guns: 2 Breda 40 mm/70; 300 rds/min to 12.5 km *(6.8 n miles)*; weight of shell 0.96 kg.
Radars: Surface search: Racal Decca; I-band.

Comment: PNS *Jessore*, which was sunk during the 1971 war, was salvaged and extensively repaired at Khulna Shipyard and recommissioned as *Bishkhali* on 23 November 1978.

BISHKHALI — *6/1996, Bangladesh Navy* / 0056554

5 PABNA CLASS (RIVERINE PATROL CRAFT) (PBR)

Name	*No*	*Builders*	*Commissioned*
PABNA	P 111	DEW Narayangonj, Dhaka	12 June 1972
NOAKHALI	P 112	DEW Narayangonj, Dhaka	10 July 1972
PATUAKHALI	P 113	DEW Narayangonj, Dhaka	27 Mar 1975
RANGAMATI	P 114	DEW Narayangonj, Dhaka	12 Feb 1977
BOGRA	P 115	DEW Narayangonj, Dhaka	15 July 1977

Displacement, tons: 69.5 full load
Dimensions, feet (metres): 75 × 20 × 3.5 *(22.9 × 6.1 × 1.1)*
Main machinery: 2 Cummins diesels; 2 shafts
Speed, knots: 10.8. **Range, n miles:** 700 at 8 kt
Complement: 33 (3 officers)
Guns: 1 Bofors 40 mm/60 or Oerlikon 20 mm.

Comment: The first indigenous naval craft built in Bangladesh. Form River Patrol Squadron 11 at Mongla. All operated by the Coast Guard from 2003.

PABNA — *6/2003, Bangladesh Navy* / 0572418

2 PATROL CRAFT (PB)

SHETGANG P 102 **PORTE GRANDE**

Dimensions, feet (metres): 102.3 × 17.7 × 4.6 *(31.2 × 5.4 × 1.4)*
Main machinery: 2 MTU diesels; 3,000 hp *(2.2 MW)*; 2 shafts
Speed, knots: 25
Complement: To be announced
Guns: To be announced.
Radars: To be announced.

Comment: Both ships constructed by Chittagong Port Authority and commissioned on 29 May 2006. Operated by the Coast Guard.

6 HIGH-SPEED INTERCEPTION CRAFT (HSIC)

Displacement, tons: 3.4 full load
Dimensions, feet (metres): 34.1 × 9.2 × 2.0 *(10.4 × 2.8 × 0.6)*
Main machinery: 2 VM diesels; 640 hp *(480 kW)*; 2 shafts
Speed, knots: 54. **Range, n miles:** 200 at 35 kt
Complement: 2 plus 8
Guns: 1—7.62 mm MG.

Comment: RIB33SC design by FB Design, Italy. Funded by UN for riverine and coastal patrol in southern Sudan. Craft in UN livery but commissioned in Bangladesh Navy in 2005.

INTERCEPTION CRAFT — *6/2007, Massimo Annati* / 1166507

MINE WARFARE FORCES

4 SHAPLA (RIVER) CLASS (MINESWEEPERS/PATROL CRAFT/SURVEY SHIPS) (MHSC/PBO/AGS)

Name	*No*	*Builders*	*Commissioned*
SHAPLA (ex-*Waveney*)	M 95	Richards, Lowestoft	12 July 1984
SAIKAT (ex-*Carron*)	M 96	Richards, Great Yarmouth	30 Sep 1984
SUROVI (ex-*Dovey*)	M 97	Richards, Great Yarmouth	30 Mar 1985
SHAIBAL (ex-*Helford*)	M 98	Richards, Great Yarmouth	7 June 1985

Displacement, tons: 890 full load
Dimensions, feet (metres): 156 × 34.5 × 9.5 *(47.5 × 10.5 × 2.9)*
Main machinery: 2 Ruston 6RKC diesels; 3,100 hp *(2.3 MW)* sustained; 2 shafts; cp props
Speed, knots: 14. **Range, n miles:** 4,500 at 10 kt
Complement: 30 (7 officers)
Guns: 1 Bofors 40 mm/60 Mk 3.
Radars: Navigation: 2 Racal Decca TM 1226C; I-band.

Comment: These ships are four of a class of 12 of which seven are in service with Brazil. Transferred from the UK on 3 October 1994 and recommissioned on 27 April 1995. Steel hulled for deep-armed team sweeping with wire sweeps, and intended for use both as minesweepers and as patrol craft. Fitted with Racal Integrated Minehunting System. *Shaibal* converted for hydrographic survey duties but retains minesweeping gear. Fitted with echo sounders, side-scan sonar and a laboratory.

SUROVI — *3/1998* / 0017593

1 SAGAR (T 43) CLASS (MINESWEEPER) (MSO)

Name	*No*	*Builders*	*Commissioned*
SAGAR	M 91	Wuhan Shipyard	27 Apr 1995

Displacement, tons: 520 standard; 590 full load
Dimensions, feet (metres): 196.8 × 27.6 × 6.9 *(60 × 8.8 × 2.3)*
Main machinery: 2 CXZ MAN B&W Type 9L 20-27 diesels; 2,400 hp *(1.8 MW)* sustained; 2 shafts; cp props
Speed, knots: 14. **Range, n miles:** 3,000 at 10 kt
Complement: 70 (10 officers)

Guns: 4 China 37 mm/63 (2 twin); 180 rds/min to 8.5 km *(4.6 n miles)*; weight of shell 1.42 kg.
4—25 mm/60 (2 twin); 270 rds/min to 3 km *(1.6 n miles)*.
4 China 14.5 mm/93 (2 twin); 600 rds/min to 7 km *(3.8 n miles)*.
Depth charges: 2 BMB-2 projectors; 20 depth charges.
Mines: Can carry 12-16.
Countermeasures: MCMV; MPT-1 paravanes; MPT-3 mechanical sweep; acoustic and magnetic gear.
Radars: Surface search: Fin Curve; I-band.
Sonars: Celcius Tech CMAS 36/39; active high frequency mine detection.

Comment: Ordered from China in 1993. Based on Type 010G minesweeper design. Used mostly as a patrol ship. New sonar fitted in 1998.

SAGAR — *3/1998* / 0017594

SURVEY AND RESEARCH SHIPS

1 SURVEY SHIP (AGS)

Name	*No*	*Builders*	*Commissioned*
AGRADOOT (ex-*Kodan*)	A 583	Khulna Shipyard	19 Mar 2002

Displacement, tons: 687 full load
Dimensions, feet (metres): 157.0 × 25.6 × 11.5 *(47.8 × 7.8 × 3.5)*
Main machinery: 2 Baudouin diesels
Speed, knots: 12.5
Complement: 70 (8 officers)
Guns: 1 Oerlikon 20 mm.
Radars: Furuno HR 2110. Kelvin Hughes HR-3000A.

Comment: Former Thai trawler converted into a Survey vessel by Khulna shipyard. Fitted with two dual frequency digital hydrographic echo sounders, side-scan sonar and laboratories. Carries a survey launch.

AGRADOOT *6/2003, Bangladesh Navy* / 0572419

AUXILIARIES

Notes: Floating Dock A 711 (*Sundarban*) acquired from Brodogradiliste Joso Lozovina-Mosor, Trogir, Yugoslavia in 1980; capacity 3,500 tons. Has a complement of 85 (5 officers). Floating crane A 731 (*Balaban*) is self-propelled at 9 kt and has a lift of 70 tons; built at Khulna Shipyard and commissioned 18 May 1988, she has a complement of 29 (two officers).

1 TANKER (AOTL)

Name	*No*	*Commissioned*
KHAN JAHAN ALI	A 515	14 July 1987

Displacement, tons: 2,900 full load
Measurement, tons: 1,343 gross
Dimensions, feet (metres): 250.8 × 37.5 × 18.4 *(76.4 × 11.4 × 5.6)*
Main machinery: 1 diesel; 1,350 hp(m) *(992 kW)*; 1 shaft
Speed, knots: 12
Complement: 26 (3 officers)
Cargo capacity: 1,500 tons
Guns: 2 Oerlikon 20 mm.

Comment: Completed in Japan in 1983. Can carry out stern replenishment at sea but is seldom used in this role. Replacement is under consideration.

KHAN JAHAN ALI *3/1998* / 0017595

1 TANKER (AOTL)

IMAN GAZZALI A 516

Displacement, tons: 213 full load
Dimensions, feet (metres): 146.8 × 23 × 11.2 *(44.8 × 7 × 3.4)*
Main machinery: 1 Cummins diesel; 1 shaft
Speed, knots: 8
Complement: 30 (2 officers)

Comment: An oil tanker of some 600,000 litres capacity acquired in 1994 and commissioned 6 May 1997.

IMAN GAZZALI *6/1999, Bangladesh Navy* / 0056556

1 REPAIR SHIP (YR)

SHAHAYAK A 512

Displacement, tons: 477 full load
Dimensions, feet (metres): 146.6 × 26.2 × 6.6 *(44.7 × 8 × 2)*
Main machinery: 1 Cummins 12 VTS 6 diesel; 425 hp *(317 kW)*; 1 shaft
Speed, knots: 11.5
Range, n miles: 3,800 at 11.5 kt
Complement: 45 (1 officer)
Guns: 1 Oerlikon 20 mm.

Comment: Re-engined and modernised at Khulna Shipyard and commissioned on 23 November 1978 to act as repair vessel.

SHAHAYAK *6/1996, Bangladesh Navy* / 0056557

1 TENDER (AG)

SHAHJALAL A 513

Displacement, tons: 600 full load
Dimensions, feet (metres): 131.8 × 29.7 × 12.6 *(40.2 × 9.1 × 3.8)*
Main machinery: 1 V 16-cyl type diesel; 1 shaft
Speed, knots: 12
Range, n miles: 7,000 at 12 kt
Complement: 55 (3 officers)
Guns: 1 Oerlikon 20 mm.

Comment: Ex-Thai fishing vessel SMS *Gold 4*. Probably built in Tokyo. Commissioned on 15 January 1987 and used as a diving/salvage tender.

SHAHJALAL *6/1996, Bangladesh Navy* / 0056558

1 HARBOUR TENDER (YAG)

SANKET

Displacement, tons: 80 full load
Dimensions, feet (metres): 96.5 × 20 × 5.9 *(29.4 × 6.1 × 1.8)*
Main machinery: 2 Deutz diesels; 2,400 hp(m) *(1.76 MW)*; 2 shafts
Speed, knots: 16
Range, n miles: 1,000 at 16 kt
Complement: 16 (1 officer)
Guns: 1 Oerlikon 20 mm.

Comment: Former harbour craft of the Chittagong Port Authority taken over by the navy in 1984. It is used as a utility harbour craft. No pennant number has been allocated.

SANKET *3/1996* / 0056559

1 LANDING CRAFT LOGISTIC (LSL)

SHAH AMANAT L 900

Displacement, tons: 366 full load
Dimensions, feet (metres): 154.2 × 34.1 × 8 *(47 × 10.4 × 2.4)*
Main machinery: 2 Caterpillar D 343 diesels; 730 hp *(544 kW)* sustained; 2 shafts
Speed, knots: 9.5
Complement: 31 (3 officers)
Military lift: 150 tons
Guns: 2 — 12.7 mm MGs.

Comment: Australian civil vessel confiscated by the Navy while engaged in smuggling in 1988. Transferred to the Navy and commissioned in 1990.

SHAH AMANAT *6/1996, Bangladesh Navy* / 0056562

2 LCU 1512 CLASS (LCU)

SHAH PORAN (ex-*Cerro Gordo*) L 901 **SHAH MAKHDUM** (ex-*Cadgel*) L 902

Displacement, tons: 375 full load
Dimensions, feet (metres): 134.9 × 29 × 6.1 *(41.1 × 8.8 × 1.9)*
Main machinery: 4 Detroit 6-71 diesels; 696 hp *(508 kW)* sustained; 2 shafts
Speed, knots: 11. **Range, n miles:** 1,200 at 8 kt
Complement: 14 (2 officers)
Military lift: 170 tons
Guns: 2 — 12.7 mm MGs.
Radars: Navigation: LN 66; I-band.

Comment: Ex-US Army landing craft transferred in April 1991 and commissioned 30 January 1993 after refit.

SHAH MAKHDUM *6/1996, Bangladesh Navy* / 0056563

5 YUCH'IN CLASS (TYPE 068/069) (LCU/LCP)

DARSHAK A 581 **TALLASHI** A 582 **LCT 101** A 584 **LCT 102** A 585 **LCT 104** A 587

Displacement, tons: 85 full load
Dimensions, feet (metres): 81.2 × 17.1 × 4.3 *(24.8 × 5.2 × 1.3)*
Main machinery: 2 Type 12V 150 diesels; 600 hp(m) *(440 kW)*; 2 shafts
Speed, knots: 11.5. **Range, n miles:** 450 at 11.5 kt
Complement: 23
Military lift: Up to 150 troops *(L 101-104)*
Guns: 4 China 14.5 mm (2 twin) MGs can be carried.

Comment: Named craft transferred from China in 1983 fitted with survey equipment and used as inshore survey craft. Second pair transferred 4 May 1986; third pair 1 July 1986. Probably built in the late 1960s. Two badly damaged in April 1991 typhoon and LCT 103 was subsequently scrapped.

TALLASHI (survey) *6/2003, Bangladesh Navy* / 0572421

LCT 101 *2/1992, Bangladesh Navy* / 0056561

3 LCVP

L 011 **L 012** **L 013**

Displacement, tons: 83 full load
Dimensions, feet (metres): 69.9 × 17.1 × 4.9 *(21.3 × 5.2 × 1.5)*
Main machinery: 2 Cummins diesels; 730 hp *(544 kW)*; 2 shafts
Speed, knots: 12
Complement: 10 (1 officer)

Comment: First two built at Khulna Shipyard and *013* at DEW Narayangong; all completed in 1984.

L 011 *6/1996, Bangladesh Navy* / 0056564

TUGS

1 HUJIU CLASS (OCEAN TUG) (ATA)

KHADEM A 721

Displacement, tons: 1,472 full load
Dimensions, feet (metres): 197.5 × 38 × 16.1 *(60.2 × 11.6 × 4.9)*
Main machinery: 2 LVP 24 diesels; 1,800 hp(m) *(1.32 MW)*; 2 shafts
Speed, knots: 14
Range, n miles: 7,200 at 14 kt
Complement: 56 (7 officers)
Guns: 2 — 12.7 mm MGs.
Radars: Navigation: China Type 756; I-band.

Comment: Commissioned 6 May 1984 after transfer from China.

KHADEM *6/1996, Bangladesh Navy* / 0056565

3 COASTAL TUGS (YTM)

SEBAK A 722 **RUPSHA** A 723 **SHIBSHA** A 724

Displacement, tons: 330 full load
Dimensions, feet (metres): 99.9 × 28.1 × 1.6 *(30.0 × 8.4 × 3.5)*
Main machinery: 2 Caterpillar 12V 3512B diesels; 2,700 hp *(2.0 MW)*; 2 shafts
Speed, knots: 12
Range, n miles: 1,800 at 12 kt
Complement: 23 (3 officers)
Guns: 2 — 7.62 mm MGs (fitted for).

Comment: Details are for *Rupsha* and *Shibsha* built to a Damen Stan Tug 3008 design by Khulna Shipyard. Construction started in 2001, completed in 2003 and commissioned on 3 October 2004. *Sebak* built in Narayangang Dockyard in 1993 and commissioned on 23 December 1993.

SHIBSHA *6/2003, Bangladesh Navy* / 0572422

Barbados

Country Overview

Barbados gained independence in 1966; the British monarch, represented by a governor-general, is head of state. The easternmost island of the Windward Islands of the Lesser Antilles chain, it consists of a single island of 166 square miles. The capital, largest town and principal port is Bridgetown, located on the southwestern coast. Territorial seas (12 n miles) are claimed. A 200 n mile Exclusive Economic Zone (EEZ) has also been claimed but the limits are not defined. A Coast Guard was formed in 1973 and became the naval arm of the Barbados Defence Force in 1979.

Headquarters Appointments

Chief of Staff, Barbados Defence Force:
Colonel Alvin Quintyne
Commanding Officer Coast Guard Squadron:
Lieutenant Commander Errington Shurland

Personnel

2009:
(a) 96 (11 officers)
(b) Voluntary service

Bases

Spring Garden, Bridgetown (HMBS *Pelican*).

Prefix to Ships' Names

HMBS

COAST GUARD

Notes: (1) Three 10 m Damen RIB 1000 capable of 35 kt were delivered in June 2007.
(2) A Zodiac 920 RHIB was donated by the US in 2004.

1 KEBIR CLASS (LARGE PATROL CRAFT) (PB)

Name	*No*	*Builders*	*Launched*	*Commissioned*
TRIDENT	P 01	Brooke Marine	14 Apr 1981	Nov 1981

Displacement, tons: 155.5 standard; 190 full load
Dimensions, feet (metres): 123 × 22.6 × 5.6 *(37.5 × 6.9 × 1.7)*
Main machinery: 2 Paxman Valenta 12CM diesels; 5,000 hp *(3.73 MW)* sustained; 2 shafts
Speed, knots: 29
Range, n miles: 3,000 at 12 kt
Complement: 18
Guns: 2—12.7 mm MGs. 2—7.62 mm MGs.
Radars: Surface search: Racal Decca Bridgemaster; I-band.

Comment: Refitted by Bender Shipyard in 1990 when the old guns were removed. Refitted again by Cable Marine in 1998 after a main engine seized. Same hull as Algerian Kebir class. To be decommissioned when third Damen 4207 enters service.

TRIDENT *4/2008*, Marco Ghiglino* / 1335332

3 DAMEN STAN PATROL 4207 (PB)

Name	*No*	*Builders*	*Commissioned*
LEONARD C BANFIELD	P 02	Damen Shipyard, Gorinchem	14 Sep 2007
RUDYARD LEWIS	P 03	Damen Shipyard, Gorinchem	13 Sep 2008
–	P 04	Damen Shipyard, Gorinchem	Apr 2009

Displacement, tons: 205
Dimensions, feet (metres): 140.4 × 23.3 × 8.3 *(42.8 × 7.11 × 2.52)*
Main machinery: 2 Caterpillar 3516B DI-TA; 5,600 hp *(4.17 MW)*; 2 cp props
Speed, knots: 26
Complement: 14
Guns: To be announced.

Comment: Contract signed with Damen Shipyards, Gorinchem for construction of a Damen Stan Patrol 4207 offshore patrol craft. *Leonard C Banfield* arrived Barbados on 6 September 2007. Steel hull with aluminium superstructure. Capable of carrying a 7 m RIB. Similar craft in service in Jamaica Coast Guard.

RUDYARD LEWIS *3/2008*, Marco Ghiglino* / 1335331

2 DAMEN STAN PATROL 1204 (PB)

ENTERPRISE P 05 **EXCELLENCE** P 06

Displacement, tons: To be announced
Dimensions, feet (metres): 39.3 × 12.1 × 2.2 *(11.98 × 3.7 × 0.66)*
Main machinery: 2 Caterpillar C7 diesels; 740 hp *(550 kW)*; 2 Hamilton waterjets
Speed, knots: 24
Complement: 4

Comment: Contract signed with Damen Shipyards, Gorinchem for construction of three Damen Stan Patrol 1204 patrol craft. Both commissioned on 13 September 2008. Aluminium hull with GRP superstructure.

EXCELLENCE *2/2008*, Damen Shipyards* / 1305301

Belgium

Country Overview

The Kingdom of Belgium is situated in north-western Europe. With an area of 11,787 square miles, it is bordered to the north by the Netherlands and to the south by France. It has a 35 n mile coastline with the North Sea. The capital and largest city is Brussels while the principal port is Antwerp which is accessible via the Schelde and Meuse estuaries, which lie within the Netherlands. Antwerp is also connected to an extensive canal system. Territorial seas (12 n miles) are claimed and an EEZ has also been claimed.

Headquarters Appointments

Commander, Maritime Command:
Rear Admiral Jean Paul Robyns

Headquarters Appointments — *continued*

Deputy Commander, Maritime Command:
Captain Georges Heeren

Personnel

(a) 2009: 2,566
(b) Voluntary service

Bases

Zeebrugge: Frigates, MCMV, Reserve Units, Training Ships, Logistics, Diving Centre. Mine Warfare Operational Sea Test centre (MOST).
Oostende: Belgium-Netherlands Mine-warfare school (EGUERMIN).
Koksijde: Naval aviation.
Brugge: Naval training centre.

Fleet Disposition

Operational control of Belgian and Netherlands surface forces is under Admiral Benelux Command at Den Helder.

DELETIONS

Frigates

2006	*Wielingen* (to Bulgaria)
2007	*Westdiep* (to Bulgaria)

FRIGATES

2 KAREL DOORMAN CLASS (FFGHM)

Name	*No*	*Builders*	*Laid down*	*Launched*	*Commissioned*	*Recommissioned*
LEOPOLD 1 (ex-*Karel Doorman*)	F 930 (ex-F 827)	Koninklijke Maatschappij De Schelde, Flushing	26 Feb 1985	20 Apr 1988	31 May 1991	26 Mar 2007
LOUISE-MARIE (ex-*Willem Van Der Zaan*)	F 931 (ex-F 829)	Koninklijke Maatschappij De Schelde, Flushing	6 Nov 1985	21 Jan 1989	28 Nov 1991	4 Apr 2008

Displacement, tons: 3,320 full load
Dimensions, feet (metres): 401.2 oa; 374.7 wl × 47.2 × 14.1 *(122.3; 114.2 × 14.4 × 4.3)*
Flight deck, feet (metres): 72.2 × 47.2 *(22 × 14.4)*
Main machinery: CODOG; 2 RR Spey SM1C; 33,800 hp *(25.2 MW)* sustained; 2 Stork-Wärtsilä 12SW280 diesels; 9,790 hp(m) *(7.2 MW)* sustained; 2 shafts; LIPS cp props
Speed, knots: 30 (Speys); 21 (diesels)
Range, n miles: 5,000 at 18 kt
Complement: 156 (16 officers) (accommodation for 163)

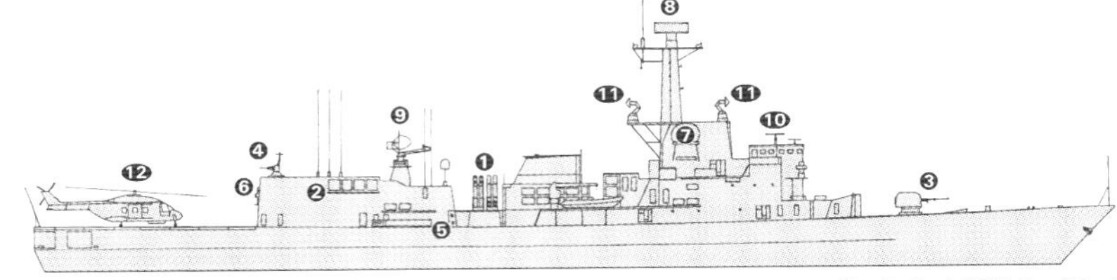

LEOPOLD I *(Scale 1 : 1,200), Ian Sturton* / 1335443

Missiles: SSM: 8 McDonnell Douglas Harpoon Block 1C (2 quad) launchers ❶; active radar homing to 124 km *(67 n miles)* at 0.9 Mach; warhead 227 kg.
SAM: Raytheon Sea Sparrow RIM 7P Mk 48 vertical launchers ❷; semi-active radar homing to 16 km *(8.5 n miles)* at 2.5 Mach; warhead 38 kg; 16 missiles. Canisters mounted on port side of hangar.
Guns: 1–3 in *(76 mm)*/62 OTO Melara compact Mk 100 ❸; 100 rds/min to 16 km *(8.6 n miles)* anti-surface; 12 km *(6.5 n miles)* anti-aircraft; weight of shell 6 kg. 1 Signaal SGE-30 Goalkeeper with General Electric 30 mm 7-barrelled ❹; 4,200 rds/min combined to 2 km. 2 Oerlikon 20 mm; 800 rds/min to 2 km.
Torpedoes: 4–324 mm US Mk 32 Mod 9 (2 twin) tubes (mounted inside the after superstructure) ❺. Honeywell Mk 46 Mod 5; anti-submarine; active/passive homing to 11 km *(5.9 n miles)* at 40 kt; warhead 44 kg.
Countermeasures: Decoys: 2 Loral Hycor SRBOC 6-tubed fixed Mk 36 quad launchers; IR flares and chaff to 4 km *(2.2 n miles)*.
SLQ-25 Nixie towed torpedo decoy.
ESM/ECM: Argo APECS II (includes AR 700 ESM) ❻; intercept and jammers.
Combat data systems: Signaal SEWACO VIIB action data automation; Link 11. SATCOM ❼. WSC-6 twin aerials.
Radars: Air/surface search: Signaal SMART ❽; 3D; F-band.
Air search: Signaal LW08 ❾; D-band.
Surface search: Signaal Scout ❿; I-band.
Navigation: Racal Decca 1226; I-band.
Fire control: 2 Signaal STIR ⓫; I/J/K-band; range 140 km *(76 n miles)* for 1 m^2 target.
Sonars: Signaal PHS-36; hull-mounted; active search and attack; medium frequency.
Thomson Sintra Anaconda DSBV 61; towed array; passive low frequency.

Helicopters: 1 NH 90 ⓬.

Programmes: The purchase of two ex-Netherlands frigates was approved by Belgium's Council of Ministers on 20 July 2005 and a contract for their supply, a support package, weapons transfer, joint upgrades and crew training was signed on 21 December 2005.
Modernisation: Modification of flight decks to operate the NH90 helicopter has been completed in F 931 and is to be undertaken in F 930 by 2009. In conjunction with the Netherlands programme, both ships are to undergo a mid-life modernisation period 2010–2012. Upgrades are to include replacement of the combat data system by Guardian MRF, addition of a Thales Seastar radar, installation of a low-frequency active sonar and replacement of SATCOM systems. Platform systems are also to be upgraded.
Structure: The VLS SAM is similar to Canadian Halifax and Greek MEKO classes. The ship is designed to reduce radar and IR signatures and has extensive NBCD arrangements. Full automation and roll stabilisation fitted. The APECS jammers are mounted starboard forward of the bridge and port aft corner of the hangar.

LEOPOLD 1 *5/2008*, A A de Kruijf* / 1335244

LEOPOLD I *10/2008*, M Declerck* / 1335442

LOUISE-MARIE *1/2008*, Piet Cornelis* / 1335243

SHIPBORNE AIRCRAFT

Numbers/Type: 3 Aerospatiale SA 316B Alouette III.
Operational speed: 113 kt *(210 km/h).*
Service ceiling: 10,500 ft *(3,200 m).*
Range: 290 n miles *(540 km).*
Role/Weapon systems: CG helicopter; used for close-range search and rescue and support for commando forces. Sensors: Carries Thomson-CSF search radar. Weapons: Unarmed. It is planned to upgrade these aircraft with new navigation and communications systems.

ALOUETTE III *7/2008*, Maritime Photographic* / 1335242

Numbers/Type: 10 NHIndustries NH90.
Operational speed: 157 kt *(291 km/h).*
Service ceiling: 13,940 ft *(4,250 m).*
Range: 621 n miles *(1,150 km).*
Role/Weapon systems: Two NFH shipborne aircraft, three SAR helicopters and five TTH (troop transport) to start entering service in mid-2011. Sensors and weapons to be announced.

NH90 *6/2001, NHIndustries* / 0094462

LAND-BASED MARITIME AIRCRAFT

Numbers/Type: 4 Westland Sea King Mk 48.
Operational speed: 140 kt *(260 km/h).*
Service ceiling: 10,500 ft *(3,200 m).*
Range: 630 n miles *(1,165 km).*
Role/Weapon systems: SAR helicopter; operated by air force; used for surface search and combat rescue tasks. Upgraded in 1995 with new radar, FLIR and GPS. One decommissioned in 2005 and two reported operational. Sensors: Bendix RDR 1500B search radar. FLIR 2000F. Weapons: Unarmed.

SEA KING *6/2008*, Michael Nitz* / 1335241

PATROL FORCES

Notes: (1) Three 7 m RIC were acquired in May 1994 from RIBTEC, Swanwick.
(2) A range safety craft A 998 has replaced the hovercraft *Barbara* A 999.
(3) There are plans to acquire three new Ready Duty Ships which are also to be used as training platforms. Their duties are to include fishery protection, immigration control, surveillance and SAR.

A 998 *6/2005, M Declerck* / 1151239

1 RIVER PATROL CRAFT (PBR/YFLB)

Name	*No*	*Builders*	*Launched*	*Commissioned*
LIBERATION	P 902	Hitzler, Regensburg	29 July 1954	4 Aug 1954

Displacement, tons: 45 full load
Dimensions, feet (metres): 85.5 × 13.1 × 3.2 *(26.1 × 4 × 1)*
Main machinery: 2 MWM diesels; 440 hp(m) *(323 kW)*; 2 shafts
Speed, knots: 10
Complement: 7
Guns: 2—12.7 mm MGs.
Radars: Navigation: Racal Decca; I-band.

Comment: Laid down 12 March 1954. Paid off 12 June 1987 but put back in active service 15 September 1989 after repairs. Last of a class of 10 used for patrol and personnel transport. Replacement planned when funds are available.

LIBERATION *6/2005, M Declerck* / 1151237

MINE WARFARE FORCES

6 FLOWER CLASS (TRIPARTITE) (MINEHUNTERS—COASTAL) (MHC/AEL)

Name	*No*	*Builders*	*Launched*	*Commissioned*
ASTER	M 915	Beliard, Ostend	6 June 1985	17 Dec 1985
BELLIS	M 916	Beliard, Ostend	14 Feb 1986	14 Aug 1986
CROCUS	M 917	Beliard, Ostend	6 Aug 1986	5 Feb 1987
LOBELIA	M 921	Beliard, Ostend	6 Jan 1988	9 May 1989
NARCIS	M 923	Beliard, Ostend	30 Mar 1990	27 Sep 1990
PRIMULA	M 924	Beliard, Ostend	17 Dec 1990	29 May 1991

Displacement, tons: 620 standard; 650 full load
Dimensions, feet (metres): 168.9 × 29.2 × 8.2 *(51.5 × 8.9 × 2.5)*
Main machinery: 1 Stork Wärtsilä A-RUB 215W-12 diesel; 1,860 hp(m) *(1.37 MW)* sustained; 1 shaft; LIPS cp prop; 2 motors; 240 hp(m) *(176 kW)*; 2 active rudders; 2 bow thrusters
Speed, knots: 15
Range, n miles: 3,000 at 12 kt
Complement: 46 (5 officers)

Guns: 1 DCN 20 mm/20; 720 rds/min to 10 km *(5.5 n miles)*. 2—12.7 mm MGs.
Countermeasures: MCM: 2 PAP 104 remote-controlled mine locators; 39 charges. Mechanical sweep gear (medium depth).
Combat data systems: Atlas Elektronic IMCMS.
Radars: Navigation: Racal Decca 1229; I-band.
Sonars: Thales TSM 2022 Mk III; hull-mounted; active minehunting; 100, 200 and 400 kHz.

Programmes: Developed in co-operation with France and the Netherlands. A 'ship factory' for the hulls was built at Ostend and the hulls were towed to Rupelmonde for fitting out. Each country built its own hulls but France provided all MCM gear and electronics, Belgium electrical installation and the Netherlands the engine room equipment.
Modernisation: Propulsion system upgrade completed in 1999 for all of the class. Capability upgrade to extend service life of six ships to 2020 is in progress at Zeebrugge. Modifications include an MCM command and control system, an Integrated Mine Countermeasures System (comprising hull-mounted and self-propelled variable-depth sonar (installed in Double Eagle Mk III Mod 1 ROV)) and a Mine-Identification and Disposal System (MIDS) based on the STN Atlas Seafox. Linked to the ship by a 3,000 m fibre optic tether, one variant (Seafox-C) is used for mine disposal and another (Seafox-I) is used for identification. The equipment was first installed in HrMS *Hellevoetsluis*. Completion dates for capability upgrades were: *Primula* (February 2006), *Aster* (October 2006), *Lobelia* (October 2007), *Bellis* (February 2008), *Crocus* (October 2008) and *Narcis* (February 2009).
Structure: GRP hull fitted with active tank stabilisation, full NBC protection and air conditioning. Has automatic pilot and buoy tracking.
Operational: A 5 ton container can be carried, stored for varying tasks-HQ support, research, patrol, extended diving, drone control. The ship's company varies from 33 to 46 depending on the assigned task. Six divers are carried when minehunting. All of the class are based at Zeebrugge.
Sales: Three of the class paid off for sale in July 1993 and were bought by France in 1997.

PRIMULA *6/2008*, Harald Carstens* / 1335240

BELLIS *7/2008*, Maritime Photographic* / 1335239

SURVEY SHIPS

Notes: In addition to *Belgica* there are five small civilian manned survey craft: *Ter Streep, Scheldewacht II, De Parel II, Veremans* and *Prosper*.

1 SURVEY SHIP (AGOR/PBO)

Name	*No*	*Builders*	*Launched*	*Commissioned*
BELGICA	A 962	Boelwerf, Temse	6 Jan 1984	5 July 1984

Displacement, tons: 1,085 full load
Dimensions, feet (metres): 167.6 × 32.8 × 14.4 *(51.1 × 10 × 4.4)*
Main machinery: 1 ABC 6M DZC diesel; 1,600 hp(m) *(1.18 MW)* sustained; 1 Kort nozzle prop
Speed, knots: 13.5
Range, n miles: 5,000 at 12 kt
Complement: 26 (11 civilian)
Radars: Navigation: Racal Decca 1229; I-band.

Comment: Ordered 1 December 1982. Laid down 17 October 1983. Used for hydrography, oceanography, meteorology and fishery control. Marisat fitted. Based at Zeebrugge. Painted white.

BELGICA *6/2004, B Prézelin* / 1044079

TRAINING SHIPS

1 SAIL TRAINING VESSEL (AXS)

Name	*No*	*Builders*	*Commissioned*
ZENOBE GRAMME	A 958	Boel and Zonen, Temse	27 Dec 1961

Displacement, tons: 149 full load
Dimensions, feet (metres): 92 × 22.5 × 7 *(28 × 6.8 × 2.1)*
Main machinery: 1 MWM diesel; 200 hp(m) *(147 kW)*; 1 shaft
Speed, knots: 10
Complement: 14 (2 officers)
Radars: Navigation: Racal Decca; I-band.

Comment: Auxiliary sail ketch. Laid down 7 October 1960 and launched 23 October 1961. Designed for scientific research but now only used as a training ship.

ZENOBE GRAMME *7/2007, Adolfo Ortigueira Gil* / 1167854

AUXILIARIES

Notes: It is planned to acquire a Command and Support Ship (MCS) to replace BNS *Godetia* in about 2015.

1 COMMAND AND SUPPORT SHIP (AGFH)

Name	*No*	*Builders*	*Launched*	*Commissioned*
GODETIA	A 960	Boelwerf, Temse	7 Dec 1965	23 May 1966

Displacement, tons: 2,000 standard; 2,260 full load
Dimensions, feet (metres): 301 × 46 × 11.5 *(91.8 × 14 × 3.5)*
Main machinery: 4 ACEC-MAN diesels; 5,400 hp(m) *(3.97 MW)*; 2 shafts; cp props
Speed, knots: 19
Range, n miles: 8,700 at 12.5 kt
Complement: 105 (8 officers)
Guns: 6—12.7 mm MGs.
Radars: Surface search: Racal Decca 1229; I-band.
Helicopters: 1 Alouette III.

Comment: Laid down 15 February 1965. Rated as Command and Logistic Support Ship. Refit (1979-80) and mid-life conversion (1981–82) included helicopter deck and replacement cranes. Refitted in 1992 and again in 2006. To be equipped with a mine-avoidance sonar in 2009. Minesweeping cables fitted either side of helo deck have been removed. Can also serve as a Royal Yacht. To be replaced by new ship in about 2015.

GODETIA *5/2007, M Declerck* / 1167853

1 SUPPORT SHIP (AGFH)

Name	*No*	*Builders*	*Commissioned*
STERN (ex-*KBV 171*)	A 963	Karlskronavarvet	3 Sep 1980

Displacement, tons: 375 full load
Dimensions, feet (metres): 164 × 27.9 × 7.9 *(50 × 8.5 × 2.4)*
Main machinery: 2 Hedemora V16A diesels; 4,480 hp(m) *(3.28 MW)* sustained; 2 shafts; cp props
Speed, knots: 18
Range, n miles: 3,000 at 12 kt
Complement: 13
Guns: 1—20 mm.
Radars: Navigation: 2 Kelvin Hughes; E/F- and I-band.
Helicopters: Platform for 1 light.

Comment: Transferred from Swedish Coast Guard on 6 October 1998. GRP hull indentical to Landsort class. In Swedish service the ship carried a 20 mm gun, and had a Subsea sonar. Known as a Ready Duty Ship and used for fishery protection and SAR duties.

STERN *6/2008*, Harald Carstens* / 1335238

TUGS

2 COASTAL TUGS (YTM)

Name	*No*	*Launched*
VALCKE (ex-*Steenbank*, ex-*Astroloog*)	A 950	1960
ALBATROS (ex-*Westgat*)	A 996	1967

Displacement, tons: 183 full load
Dimensions, feet (metres): 99.7 × 24.9 × 11.8 *(30.4 × 7.6 × 3.6)*
Main machinery: Diesel-electric; 2 Deutz diesel generators; 1,240 hp(m) *(911 kW)*; 1 shaft; 1 bow thruster
Speed, knots: 11
Complement: 8

Comment: Known as Ready Duty Ships. Details given are for A 950 which was launched in 1960. A 996 is 206 tons and was launched in 1967.

ALBATROS *5/2008*, A A de Kruijf* / 1335237

VALCKE *10/2006, M Declerck* / 1164728

3 HARBOUR TUGS (YTL)

WESP A 952 **ZEEMEEUW** A 954 **MIER** A 955

Displacement, tons: 195 full load
Dimensions, feet (metres): 86.5 × 24.7 × 10.7 *(26.23 × 7.5 × 3.25)*
Main machinery: 2 ABC 6 MDUS diesels; 1,000 hp *(746 kW)*
Speed, knots: 11
Complement: 4

Comment: Details given are for A 952 and A 955. A 954 is 146 tons.

WESP *7/2008*, Maritime Photographic* / 1335236

ZEEMEEUW *10/2006, M Declerck* / 1164726

Belize

Country Overview

Formerly known as British Honduras, Belize became an independent state in 1981. The British monarch, represented by a governor-general, is head of state. With an area of 8,867 square miles, it has borders with Mexico to the north and Guatemala to the west; its 208 n mile coastline is on the Caribbean Sea and fringed by numerous coral barrier reefs and cays. The capital city is Belmopan while the largest city and major port is Belize City. Territorial seas (12 n miles) are claimed. A 200 n mile Exclusive Economic Zone (EEZ) has been claimed but the limits are not defined. The Belize National Coast Guard Service was formed on 29 November 2005.

Headquarters Appointments

Commander of the Coast Guard: Brigadier Cedric Borland

Personnel

(a) 2009: 152 (2 officers)
(b) The Maritime Wing of the Belize Defence Force comprises volunteers from the Army.

Bases

Ladyville, Hunting Cay, Calabash Cay (Turneffe Atoll) (planned)

Maritime Patrol

Two Air Force operated Pilatus Britten-Norman Defenders are used for maritime surveillance.

PATROL FORCES

Notes: Current assets include:
1. Two Halmatic 22 ft RIBs with twin Yamaha 115 hp outboards. Names *Stingray Commando* and *Blue Marlin Ranger.*
2. Two Pelikan 35 ft craft with twin Yamaha 200 hp outboards. Built at Bradleys Boatyard in 1996 and called *Ocean Sentinel* and *Reef Sniper.*
3. Six Colombian 32 ft skiffs with twin Yamaha 200 hp outboards, confiscated and commissioned in service 1995–97.
4. One 36 ft skiff.
5. Two US donated craft Stinger I and Stinger II.

PELIKAN CRAFT *6/2001, Belize Defence Force* / 0109932

Benin

FORCES NAVALES

Country Overview

Formerly part of French West Africa, the republic gained full independence in 1960 as the Republic of Dahomey; it was renamed The Republic of Benin in 1975. With an area of 43,484 square miles it has borders to the east with Nigeria and to the west with Togo. Benin has a short coastline of 65 n miles with the Gulf of Guinea. The capital is Porto-Novo while Cotonou is the largest city and principal port. Benin has not claimed an Exclusive Economic Zone (EEZ) but is one of a few coastal states which claims a 200 n mile territorial sea. The naval force was established in 1978.

Headquarters Appointments

Commander of the Navy: Commander Maxime Ahoyo

Aircraft

Dornier Do 128 and a DHC-6 Twin Otter reconnaissance aircraft are used for surveillance.

Bases

Cotonou

Personnel

2009: 220 (30 officers)

PATROL FORCES

Notes: There are two French-built 6 m river patrol craft with hydrojet propulsion.

2 CHINESE 27 METRE CLASS (PATROL CRAFT) (PB)

MATELOT BRICE KPOMASSE 798 **LA SOTA** 799

Displacement, tons: 80 full load
Dimensions, feet (metres): 88.6 × 13.4 × 4.6 *(27 × 4.1 × 1.4)*
Main machinery: 2 diesels; 1,000 hp *(746 kW)*
Complement: 13
Guns: 4—14.5 mm (2 twin) MGs.
Radars: Navigation: I-band.

Comment: Understood to have been transferred from China in 2000. A similar craft is in service in Cape Verde.

KPOMASSE and SOTA
2001, Benin Navy
0114348

Bermuda

Country Overview

A British self-governing dependency, a Governor, appointed by the British Crown, is responsible for external affairs, internal security, defence, and the police. Situated in the north Atlantic Ocean some 650 n miles southeast of Cape Hatteras, the country consists of six principal islands, of which the largest is 14 miles long, linked by bridges and a causeway; there are some 150 other small islands, islets, and rocks, of which about 20 are inhabited. Hamilton is the capital, chief port and largest town. Territorial seas (12 n miles) and an Exclusive Economic Zone (EEZ) (200 n miles) are claimed.

Headquarters Appointments

Commanding Officer: Sergeant Keith Senior

Bases

Hamilton

POLICE

Notes: In addition to patrol craft, three tugs, *Powerful, Faithful* and *Refit* are operated by the Department of Marine and Port Services.

1 AUSTAL PATROL CRAFT (PB)

GUARDIAN

Displacement, tons: To be announced
Dimensions, feet (metres): 53.5 × 16.1 × 3.9 *(16.3 × 4.9 × 1.2)*
Main machinery: 2 Caterpillar C12 diesels; 1,300 hp *(970 kW)*; 2 shafts
Speed, knots: 28
Range, n miles: 400 at 25 kt
Complement: 3 plus 8 passengers

Comment: Contract with Austal Ships in August 2005 to build aluminium hull craft for operations up to 200 n miles from shore. Similar to craft operated by the New South Wales police. Delivery was made on 25 September 2006.

GUARDIAN *9/2006, Austal* / 1335333

4 PATROL CRAFT (PBI)

HERON I-IV

Comment: *Heron I*, delivered in July 1997 to replace the previous craft of the same name, and *Heron III* delivered in June 1992 are 22 ft Boston Whalers fitted with twin Yamaha 225 hp and twin Yamaha 115 hp outboards, respectively. *Heron II* delivered in August 1996 to replace the previous craft of the same name, is a 27 ft Boston Whaler with twin Yamaha 250 hp(m) outboard engines. *Heron IV*, delivered in 2001, is a further 22 ft Boston Whaler with twin 115 hp outboards.

HERON II *6/1997, Bermuda Police* / 0012079

2 SAR CRAFT (SAR)

RESCUE I RESCUE II

Comment: *Rescue I* replaced the craft of the same name in November 1998 and *Rescue II* replaced the craft of the same name in 2001. Both are Halmatic 24 ft Arctic RIBs with twin 200 hp Yamaha outboards and a complement of three.

HALMATIC ARCTIC RIB *2001, Bermuda Police* / 0109933

Bolivia

ARMADA BOLIVIANA

Country Overview

The Republic of Bolivia is one of two landlocked countries in South America; Paraguay is the other. With an area of 424,165 square miles, it has borders to the north and east with Brazil, to the southeast with Paraguay, to the south with Argentina, and to the west with Chile and Peru. It has a 211 n mile shoreline with Lake Titicaca. The constitutional capital is Sucre while the administrative capital and seat of government is La Paz which is connected by railway to the Chilean port of Antofagasta.

The Bolivian Navy was founded in 1963 and received its present name in 1982. Its purpose is to patrol some 10,000 miles in three geographical areas. The Amazon basin includes the rivers Ichilo, Mamore, Itenez, Yacuma, Orthon, Abuna, Beni and Madre de Dios. The central basin comprises Lake Titicaca while the Del Plata basin includes the rivers Paraguay and Bermejo. Most advanced training is carried out in Argentina and Peru.

Headquarters Appointments

Commandant General of the Navy:
Vice Admiral José Luis Cabas V

Headquarters Appointments —*continued*

Chief of the Naval Staff:
Rear Admiral Rafael Bandeira Arze
Inspector General:
Rear Admiral Armando Pacheco Gutierrez

Personnel

(a) 2009: 6,659 (including Marines)
(b) 12 months' selective military service

Organisation

The country is divided into six naval districts, three naval areas and a Fuerza de Tareas Especiales.
1st Naval District (Beni) (HQ Riberalta). River Beni.
2nd Naval District (Mamore) (HQ Trinidad). Rivers Ichilo and Mamore.
3rd Naval District (Madera) (HQ Puerto Guayamerin). Rivers Madera and Itenez.
4th Naval District (Titicaca) (HQ San Pedro de Tiquina). Lake Titicaca.
5th Naval District (Santa Cruz de la Sierra) (HQ Puerto Quijarro). River Paraguay.
6th Naval District (Pando) (HQ Cobija). Rivers Acre, Madre dos Dios and Tahuamanu.
1st Naval Area (Cochabamba) (Puerto Villarroel). Naval yard and oil transport.
2nd Naval Area (Santa Cruz). Support duties.
3rd Naval Area (Bermejo).
4th Naval Area (La Paz).
Fuerza de Tareas Especiales consists of five task groups (based at Guayamerin, Cobija, Riberalta, Puerto Suarez and Copacabana) to provide support in counter-drug operations.

Marine Corps

The Bolivian Navy has seven marine corps battalions (BIM I-VII). Two are located in 4th Naval District and one in each of the remainder.

Prefix to Ships' Names

ARB

PATROL FORCES

Notes: It is reported that an unknown number of assault craft were donated by China in 2007–08 and 18 RHIBs by Chile in 2008.

3 RIVER PATROL CRAFT (PBR)

CAPITÁN PALOMEQUE PR 221 **ANTOFAGASTA** PR 302 **GENERAL BANZER** PR 301

Displacement, tons: 8 full load
Dimensions, feet (metres): 42.7 × 10.5 × 1.6 *(13 × 3.2 × 0.5)*
Main machinery: 2 diesels; 2 shafts
Speed, knots: 27
Complement: 4
Guns: 1 — 7.62 mm MG.

Comment: Details given are for *Capitán Palomeque* acquired in 1993. The others are similar in appearance and all are less than ten years old. Operate in the 2nd and 3rd Districts.

CAPITÁN PALOMEQUE *1996, Bolivian Navy / 0056585*

1 SANTA CRUZ CLASS (PBR)

SANTA CRUZ DE LA SIERRA PR 501

Displacement, tons: 46 full load
Dimensions, feet (metres): 68.9 × 19 × 3.9 *(21 × 5.8 × 1.2)*
Main machinery: 2 Detroit diesels; 2 shafts
Speed, knots: 20
Range, n miles: 800 at 16 kt
Complement: 10
Guns: 2 — 12.7 mm MGs.
Radars: Surface search: Furuno; I-band.

Comment: Built by Hope Shipyards, Louisiana, in 1985. Used both as a patrol craft and supply ship. Operates in the 5th District on the river Paraguay.

SANTA CRUZ DE LA SIERRA (old number) *1996, Bolivian Navy / 0056584*

8 RIVER PATROL CRAFT (PBR)

PAZ ZAMORA LP 101
RAIDER LP 351
GENERAL BEJAR LP 406
MARISCAL DE ZAPITA LP 409
CAPITÁN BRETEL LP 410
TENIENTE SOLIZ LP 411
GUAQUI LA 414
INDEPENDENCIA LP 416

Displacement, tons: 5 full load
Dimensions, feet (metres): 42.3 × 12.7 × 3.3 *(12.9 × 3.9 × 1)*
Main machinery: 2 diesels; 2 shafts
Speed, knots: 15
Complement: 5
Guns: 1 — 12.7 mm MG.
Radars: Surface search: Raytheon; I-band.

Comment: Details given are for *Capitán Bretel, Teniente Soliz* and *Guaqui* which is used as a logistic craft. The remainder are Boston Whaler types. All operate in the 4th District except *Paz Zamora* (1st) and *Raider* (5th).

CAPITÁN BRETEL alongside TENIENTE SOLIZ *1996, Bolivian Navy / 0056587*

42 RIVER PATROL CRAFT (PBR)

LP 01–42

Comment: Thirty-two Piranas were delivered from 1992–96. Fitted with one 12.7 mm MG and has twin outboards. Ten more craft delivered by the US 1998–99.

PIRANA Mk II *1996, Bolivian Navy / 0056588*

LAND-BASED MARITIME AIRCRAFT

Notes: (1) One Cessna 402C is based at La Paz-El Alto.
(2) An agreement was reached in 2006 to acquire three ex-Spanish Army CASA C-212-100 aircraft. These are probably used as transport aircraft and/or for medevac.
(3) Two Cougar AS 532AC helicopters are on extended loan from Venezuela. They are used for transport and VIP purposes.

AUXILIARIES

Notes: (1) Approximately 30 Rodman craft are used for transport and logistic support. A mixture of craft was acquired from Spain in 1999. These include 15 craft of 6–8 m with pennant numbers BA 401-415. They are capable of carrying 20 troops or one medium tracked vehicle. There are five 11 m craft with pennant numbers FNM 400-404. There are two 17 m catamaran craft with pennant numbers FNM 342-343.
(2) *Guayamerin* (TNTB-01) is an LCM used as a transport vessel on Lake Titicaca. Built in Bolivia she was commissioned on 22 July 1998.
(3) A dredger *Pirai II* (FNDR-01) was commissioned on 11 August 2001.

11 RIVER TRANSPORTS (YFL)

ALMIRANTE GRAU M 101
COMANDANTE ARANDIA M 103
GERMAN BUSCH M 107
LIBERTADOR M 223
TRINIDAD M 224
RIO GUAPORÉ M 301
INGENIERO GUMUCIO M 341
JORGE VILLARROEL M 342
COATI M 401
COBIJA M 402
SUAREZ ARANA M 528 (ex-M 501)

Displacement, tons: 70 full load
Dimensions, feet (metres): 78.7 × 21.3 × 4.6 *(24 × 6.5 × 1.4)*
Speed, knots: 12
Range, n miles: 500 at 12 kt
Complement: 11
Radars: Navigation: Raytheon; I-band.

Comment: Details given are for *Ingeniero Gumucio* which is a troop transport and supply ship. The remainder are craft of various types, some acquired from China. *Suarez Arana* (M 528) sank in the Paraguay River in September 2006 but was salvaged on 4 October 2006.

INGENIERO GUMUCIO *1996, Bolivian Navy / 0056589*

6 LOGISTIC VESSELS (YAG)

JOSE MANUEL PANDO TNR 01
NICOLAS SUAREZ TNR 02
MAX PAREDES TNR 04
JULIO OLMOS TNR 05
HORACIO UGARTECHE TNBTL-06
THAMES CRESPO TNR 07

Comment: TNR-01 is a tug. The remainder are pusher/lighter combinations. There are eight lighters TNBTP-02A, -02B, -04A, -04B, -05A, -06A, -06B and -07A.

MAX PAREDES *6/2000, Bolivian Navy* / 0104222

2 HOSPITAL SHIPS

Name	*No*	*Tonnage*
JULIAN APAZA	TNBH 401	150
XAVIER PINTO TELLERIA	TNBH 01	–

Comment: *Julian Apaza* given by the US; assembled in 1972 and based at Lake Titicaca. *Telleria* was built in 1997 and is based at Puerto Villarod.

TELLERIA *6/2000, Bolivian Navy* / 0104223

1 TRAINING VESSEL

BUQUE ESCUELA NAVAL MILITAR

Displacement, tons: 80 full load
Dimensions, feet (metres): 117.3 × 29.5 × 3.9 *(35.7 × 9.0 × 1.2)*
Main machinery: 2 diesels; 1,300 hp *(969 kW)*
Speed, knots: 18
Complement: 15 plus 50 trainees

Comment: Catamaran design. Launched at Tiquina, Lake Titicaca on 9 May 2001. Following a donation by the Venezuelan government in 2007, the ship was launched in 2008 and is expected to be completed in 2009.

Brazil

MARINHA DO BRASIL

Country Overview

The Federal Republic of Brazil is the largest country in South America. With an area of 3,286,500 square miles it has borders to the north with Colombia, Venezuela, Guyana, Suriname and French Guiana, to the south with Uruguay and to the west with Argentina, Paraguay, Bolivia, and Peru. It has a coastline of 4,045 n miles with the south Atlantic Ocean. There are some 23,220 n miles of internal waterways that consist primarily of the Amazon and its tributaries; the river is navigable by ocean-going ships from its mouth to Iquitos in Peru. The capital is Brasilia while the largest city is São Paulo. The principal ports are the former capital, Rio de Janeiro, Santos, Paranaguá, Recife, and Vitória. Manaus is an important river port. Territorial seas (12 n miles) are claimed. An EEZ (200 n miles) is claimed and its limits have been partly defined by boundary agreements.

Headquarters Appointments

Commander of the Navy:
Admiral Júlio Soares de Moura Neto
Chief of Naval Staff:
Admiral Aurélio Ribeiro da Silva Filho
Commandant General Brazilian Marine Corps:
Admiral (Marine Corps) Alvaro Augusto Dias Monteiro
General Director of Personnel:
Admiral José Antonio de Castro Leal
General Director of Material:
Admiral Marcus Vinicius Oliveira dos Santos
General Secretary of Navy:
Admiral Marcos Martins Torres
Vice Chief of Naval Staff:
Vice Admiral Rodrigo Otávio Fernandes de Hônkis

Senior Officers

Commander-in-Chief, Fleet:
Vice Admiral Fernando Edourdo Studart Wiemer
Commander, Fleet Marine Force:
Vice Admiral (Marine Corps) Paulo César Stingelim Guimarães
Commander, I Naval District:
Vice Admiral Gilberto Max Roffé Hirschfeld
Commander, II Naval District:
Vice Admiral Arnon Lima Barbosa
Commander, III Naval District:
Vice Admiral Edison Lawrence Mariath Dantas
Commander, IV Naval District:
Vice Admiral Eduardo Monteiro Lopes
Commander, V Naval District:
Vice Admiral Arthur Pires Ramos
Commander, VI Naval District:
Rear Admiral Cesar Sidonio Daiha Moreira de Souza
Commander, VII Naval District:
Rear Admiral Edouardo Bacellar Leal Ferreira
Commander, VIII Naval District:
Vice Admiral Terenilton Sousa Santos

Senior Officers — *continued*

Commander, IX Naval District:
Vice Admiral Pedro Fava

Personnel

a) 2009: 38,800 (5,800 officers) Navy; (including 2,100 naval air)
15,800 (800 officers) Marines
b) One year's national service

Bases

Arsenal de Marinha do Rio de Janeiro – Rio de Janeiro (Naval shipyard with three dry docks and one floating dock with graving docks of up to 70,000 tons capacity)
Base Naval do Rio de Janeiro – Rio de Janeiro (Main Naval Base with two dry docks)
Base Almirante Castro e Silva – Rio de Janeiro (Naval Base for submarines)
Base Naval de Aratu – Bahia (Naval Base and repair yard with one dry dock and synchrolift)
Base Naval de Val-de-Cães – Pará (Naval River and repair yard with one dry dock)
Base Naval de Natal – Rio Grande do Norte (Small Naval Base and repair yard with one floating dock)
Base Fluvial de Ladário – Mato Grosso do Sul (Small Naval River Base and repair yard with one dry dock)
Base Aérea Naval de São Pedro d'Aldeia – Rio de Janeiro (Naval Air Station)
Estação Naval do Rio Negro – Amazonas (Small Naval River Station and repair yard with one floating dock)
Estação Naval do Rio Grande – Rio Grande do Sul (Small Naval Station and repair yard)

Organisation

Naval Districts as follows:
I Naval District (HQ Rio de Janeiro)
II Naval District (HQ Salvador)
III Naval District (HQ Natal)
IV Naval District (HQ Belém)
V Naval District (HQ Rio Grande)
VI Naval District (HQ Ladário)
VII Naval District (HQ Brasilia)
VIII Naval District (HQ São Paulo)
IX Naval District (HQ Manaus)

Naval Aviation

Squadrons: São Pedro da Aldeira; HA-1 Super Lynx; HS-1 Sea King; HI-1 JetRanger; HU-1 Ecureuil 1 and 2; HU-2 Super Puma/Cougar; VF 1 Skyhawk AF1.
Manaus; HU-3 Ecureuil.
Ladário; HU-4 Jet Ranger.
Rio Grande; HU-5 Ecureuil.

Prefix to Ships' Names

These vary, indicating the type of ship for example, N Ae = Aircraft Carrier; CT = Destroyer.

Marines (Corpo de Fuzileiros Navais)

Headquarters at Fort São José, Rio de Janeiro.
Divisão Anfibia: 3 Infantry Battalions (Riachuelo, Humaita and Paissandu), 1 Artillery Battalion, 1 C^2 Battalion, 1 Air Control and Air Defence Battalion, 1 Tank Battalion.
Tropa de Reforço: 1 Engineer Battalion, 1 Amphib Vehicles Battalion, 1 Logistic Battalion. 1 Police Company, 1 Disembarkation Support Company.
Special Forces Battalion (Tonelero).
Grupamentos Regionais: One security group in each naval district and command (Rio de Janeiro, Salvador, Natal, Belém, Rio Grande and Ladário). There is an amphibious river group at Manaus.

Strength of the Fleet

Type	*Active*	*Building (Planned)*
Submarines (Patrol)	5	(6)
Aircraft Carrier	1	–
Frigates	9	(6)
Corvettes	5	–
Patrol Forces	31	7 (13)
LSD/LST	4	1
Minesweepers (Coastal)	6	–
Survey and Research Ships	7	1
Buoy Tenders	17	–
S/M Rescue Ship	1	–
Tankers	2	–
Hospital Ships	3	–
Training Ships	8	–

DELETIONS

Frigates

2006 *Dodsworth*
2008 *Pará*

Patrol Forces

2006 *Piratini, Pirajá, Pampeiro, Parati, Penedo, Poti*

Auxiliaries

2008 *Trindade*

PENNANT LIST

Submarines

S 30 Tupi
S 31 Tamoio
S 32 Timbira
S 33 Tapajó
S 34 Tikuna

Aircraft Carriers

A 12 São Paulo

Destroyers/Frigates

F 40 Niteroi
F 41 Defensora
F 42 Constituição
F 43 Liberal
F 44 Independência
F 45 União
F 46 Greenhalgh
F 48 Bosisio
F 49 Rademaker

Corvettes

V 30 Inhaúma
V 31 Jaceguai
V 32 Julio de Noronha
V 33 Frontin
V 34 Barroso

Amphibious Forces

G 25 Almirante Saboia
G 28 Mattoso Maia
G 29 Garcia d'Avila
G 30 Ceará
G 31 Rio de Janeiro
L 10 Guarapari
L 11 Tambaú
L 12 Camboriú

Patrol Forces

V 15 Imperial Marinheiro
V 19 Caboclo
P 01 Marlim
P 10 Piratini
P 11 Pirajá
P 12 Pampeiro
P 13 Parati
P 14 Penedo
P 15 Poti
P 20 Pedro Teixeira
P 21 Raposo Tavares
P 30 Roraima
P 31 Rondônia
P 32 Amapá
P 40 Grajaú
P 41 Guaiba
P 42 Graúna
P 43 Goiana
P 44 Guajará
P 45 Guaporé
P 46 Gurupá
P 47 Gurupi
P 48 Guanabara
P 49 Guarujá
P 50 Guaratuba
P 51 Gravataí
P 60 Bracui
P 61 Benevente
P 62 Bocaina
P 63 Babitonga

Mine Warfare Forces

M 15 Aratú
M 16 Anhatomirim
M 17 Atalaia
M 18 Araçatuba
M 19 Abrolhos
M 20 Albardão

Survey Ships and Tenders

H 18 Comandante Varella
H 19 Tenente Castelo
H 20 Comandante Manhães
H 21 Sirius
H 25 Tenente Boanerges
H 26 Faroleiro Mário Seixas
H 34 Almirante Graça Aranha
H 35 Amorim do Valle
H 36 Taurus
H 37 Garnier Sampaio
H 38 Cruzeiro do Sul
H 40 Antares
H 44 Ary Rongel

Auxiliaries

G 15 Paraguassú
G 17 Potengi
G 21 Ary Parreiras
G 23 Almirante Gastao Motta
G 27 Marajo
K 11 Felinto Perry
R 21 Tritão
R 22 Tridente
R 23 Triunfo
R 24 Almirante Guilhem
R 25 Almirante Guillobel
U 10 Aspirante Nascimento
U 11 Guarda Marinha Jansen
U 12 Guarda Marinha Brito
U 15 Pará
U 16 Doutor Montenegro
U 17 Parnaiba
U 18 Oswaldo Cruz
U 19 Carlos Chagas
U 20 Cisne Branco
U 27 Brasil
U 29 Piraim

SUBMARINES

Notes: (1) Following the revival by President Lula in June 2007 of plans to acquire a nuclear-powered submarine, the programme was formally re-launched on 26 September 2008 by the Commander of the Brazilian Navy. The co-ordination office COGESN is to be based in Rio de Janeiro and is to be headed by Fleet Admiral (Reserve) José Alberto Accioly Fragelli who is to administer an annual budget of USD250 million. The 6,000 ton submarine is to enter service in 2020. An 11 MW prototype nuclear reactor is under development at the Aramar Experimental Centre in Sao Paulo state. A co-operative agreement with the French shipbuilder DCNS is expected to facilitate French design support on the hull and propulsion.
(2) As part of the Franco-Brazilian arms package signed between the Presidents of France and Brazil on 12 February 2008, it is likely that agreement will be reached to build up to four Marlin-class conventional submarines. The first boat is likely to be built in France while the remainder may be built at a new Brazilian Navy shipyard at Sepetiba Bay, Rio de Janeiro State. The existing submarine building shipyard at Arsenal de Marinha, Rio de Janeiro, is to remain available for the support and upgrade of the Tupi and Tikuna classes, both based on the German Type 209/1400 class.

1 TIKUNA (TYPE 209/1450) CLASS (SSK)

Name	*No*	*Builders*	*Laid down*	*Launched*	*Commissioned*
TIKUNA	S 34	Arsenal de Marinha, Rio de Janeiro	11 June 1996	9 Mar 2005	16 Dec 2005

Displacement, tons: 1,454 surfaced; 1,586 dived
Dimensions, feet (metres): 203.4 × 20.3 × 18 *(62.0 × 6.2 × 5.5)*
Main machinery: Diesel-electric; 4 MTU 12V 396 diesels; 3,760 hp(m) *(2.76 MW)*; 4 Siemens alternators; 1 Siemens motor; 1 shaft
Speed, knots: 11 surfaced/snorting; 22 dived
Range, n miles: 11,000 at 8 kt surfaced; 400 at 4 kt dived
Complement: 41 (8 officers)

Torpedoes: 8—21 in *(533 mm)* bow tubes. Marconi Mk 24 Tigerfish Mod 1 or 2; wire-guided; active homing to 13 km *(7 n miles)* at 35 kt; passive homing to 29 km *(15.7 n miles)* at 24 kt; warhead 134 kg. IPqM designed A/S torpedoes may also be carried; 18 km *(9.7 n miles)* at 45 kt. Total of 16 torpedoes.
Mines: 32 IPqM/Consub MCF-01/100 carried in lieu of torpedoes.
Countermeasures: ESM: Argos AR-900; radar warning.
Weapons control: STN Atlas Electronik ISUS 83-13; 2 Kollmorgen Mod 76 periscopes.
Radars: Navigation: Terma Scanter; I-band.
Sonars: Atlas Elektronik CSU-83/1; hull-mounted; passive/active search and attack; medium frequency. STN Atlas Elektronik FAS-3 flank array.

Programmes: Planned intermediate stage between Tupi class and the first SSN. Designed by the Naval Engineering Directorate. Contract effective with HDW in October 1995. Plans for a second of class have been cancelled.
Modernisation: Tigerfish torpedoes are likely to be replaced by Mk 48 Mod 6 and a Lockheed Martin integrated combat system AN/BYG-501 Mod 1D is to be installed. The upgrade is also likely to include a new flank array. Work is to be completed by 2011.
Structure: Improved Tupi design similar to Turkish Gur class. Diving depth, 300 m *(985 ft)*. Very high-capacity batteries with GRP lead-acid cells by Microlite. More powerful engines than *Tupi*. Fitted with two Kollmorgen Mod 76 non-penetrative optronic masts.
Operational: Endurance, 60 days. Sea trials began on 10 November 2005.

TIKUNA *10/2006, Brazilian Navy* / 1170093

TIKUNA

5/2006, Brazilian Navy / 1170092

4 TUPI (TYPE 209/1400) CLASS (SSK)

Name	*No*	*Builders*	*Laid down*	*Launched*	*Commissioned*
TUPI	S 30	Howaldtswerke-Deutsche Werft, Kiel	8 Mar 1985	28 Apr 1987	6 May 1989
TAMOIO	S 31	Arsenal de Marinha, Rio de Janeiro	15 July 1986	18 Nov 1993	17 July 1995
TIMBIRA	S 32	Arsenal de Marinha, Rio de Janeiro	15 Sep 1987	5 Jan 1996	16 Dec 1996
TAPAJÓ	S 33	Arsenal de Marinha, Rio de Janeiro	6 Aug 1992	5 June 1998	21 Dec 1999

Displacement, tons: 1,453 surfaced; 1,590 dived
Dimensions, feet (metres): 200.8 × 20.3 × 18 *(61.2 × 6.2 × 5.5)*
Main machinery: Diesel-electric; 4 MTU 12V 493 AZ80 GA31L diesels; 2,400 hp(m) *(1.76 MW)*; 4 Siemens alternators; 1.7 MW; 1 Siemens motor; 4,600 hp(m) *(3.36 MW)* sustained; 1 shaft
Speed, knots: 11 surfaced/snorting; 21.5 dived
Range, n miles: 8,200 at 8 kt surfaced; 400 at 4 kt dived
Complement: 36 (7 officers)

Torpedoes: 8—21 in *(533 mm)* bow tubes. 16 Marconi Mk 24 Tigerfish Mod 1 or 2; wire-guided; active homing to 13 km *(7 n miles)* at 35 kt; passive homing to 29 km *(15.7 n miles)* at 24 kt; warhead 134 kg. IPqM anti-submarine torpedoes may also be carried; range 18 km *(9.7 n miles)* at 45 kt. Swim-out discharge.

Countermeasures: ESM: IPqM/Elebra Defensor ET/SLR-1X; radar intercept.
Weapons control: Ferranti KAFS-A10 action data automation (to be replaced by UDS SUBTICS).
Radars: Navigation: Terma Scanter; I-band.
Sonars: Atlas Elektronik CSU-83/1; hull-mounted; passive/active search and attack; medium frequency. STN Atlas Elektronik FAS-3 flank array.

Programmes: Contract signed with Howaldtswerke in February 1984. Financial negotiations were completed with the West German Government in October 1984. Original plans included building four in Brazil followed by two improved Tupis for a total of six. In the end only three were constructed in Brazil.
Modernisation: A programme (Mod Sub) to upgrade auxiliary machinery, sonars, weapon control, countermeasures and navigation systems was announced in 2003. Refit work on S 31 was completed in June 2005 while work on S 32 was completed in January 2007. The programme is to be completed in 2008. Tigerfish torpedoes are to be replaced by Mk 48 Mod 6 and a Lockheed Martin integrated combat system AN/BYG-501 Mod 1D is to be installed. The upgrade is also likely to include a new flank array. Work on all four boats is to be completed by 2011.
Structure: Hull constructed of HY 80 steel. Single hull. Diving depth, 250 m *(820 ft)*. Equipped with Sperry Mk 29 Mod 3 SINS and two Kollmorgen Mod 76 periscopes.
Operational: Based at Niteroi, Rio de Janeiro.

TAPAJÓ

10/2005, Mario R V Carneiro / 1153025

TAMOIO

2/2006, Marco Ghiglino / 1167123

AIRCRAFT CARRIERS

1 CLEMENCEAU CLASS (CVM)

Name	*No*	*Builders*	*Laid down*	*Launched*	*Commissioned*
SÃO PAULO (ex-*Foch*)	A 12 (ex-R 99)	Chantiers de l'Atlantique, St. Nazaire	15 Feb 1957	23 July 1960	15 July 1963

Displacement, tons: 27,307 standard; 33,673 full load
Dimensions, feet (metres): 869.4 oa; 780.8 pp × 104.1 hull (168 oa) × 28.2 *(265; 238 × 31.7; 51.2 × 8.6)*
Flight deck, feet (metres): 850 × 154 *(259 × 47)*
Main machinery: 6 La Valle boilers; 640 psi *(45 kg/cm²)*; 840°F *(450°C)*; 2 GEC Alsthom turbines; 126,000 hp(m) *(93 MW)*; 2 shafts
Speed, knots: 30
Range, n miles: 7,000 at 18 kt; 4,800 at 24 kt; 3,500 at full power
Complement: 1,220 (80 officers); 358 (80 officers) aircrew

Missiles: SAM: 3 Matra Sadral; Mistral missiles; IR homing to 4 km *(2.2 n miles)* at 2.5 Mach; warhead 3 kg.
Guns: 5 – 12.7 mm MGs.
Countermeasures: 2 CSEE AMBL 2A Sagai (10 barrelled trainable launchers); chaff and IR flares.
Combat data systems: IPqM/Elebra SICONTA Mk 4 tactical system; Links YB and 14. Inmarsat.
Weapons control: 2 Sagem DMa optical directors.
Radars: Air search: Thomson-CSF DRBV 23B ❶; D-band.
Air/surface search: Thomson-CSF DRBV 15 ❷; E/F-band.
Heightfinder: 2 DRBI 10 ❸; E/F-band.
Navigation: Racal Decca 1226; I-band.
Fire control: 2 Thomson-CSF DRBC 32C.
Tacan: NRBP-2B.
Landing approach control: NRBA 51 ❹; I-band.

Fixed-wing aircraft: 10-15 A-4 Skyhawks.
Helicopters: 4-6 Agusta SH-3A/D Sea Kings; 3 Aerospatiale UH-12/13; 2 UH-14 Cougar.

Programmes: Acquired from France on 15 November 2000 and following modifications in Brest, arrived in Brazil in February 2001.
Modernisation: A foldable mini ski-jump has been fitted to both catapults. The jet deflectors are enlarged (this implies reducing the area of the forward lift). Crotale and Sadral systems disembarked before transfer. Refit in 2003 included re-tubing of boilers and refurbishment of catapults. A further refit 2005–08 included a full machinery overhaul, flight deck renovations and the installation of three twin Matra SAM. The combat data system was upgraded to SICONTA Mk 4.
Structure: Flight deck, island superstructure and bridges, hull (over machinery spaces and magazines) are all armour plated. There are three bridges: Flag, Command and Aviation.
Two Mitchell-Brown steam catapults; Mk BS 5; able to launch 20 ton aircraft at 110 kt. The flight deck is angled at 8°. Two lifts 52.5 × 36 ft *(16 × 10.97 m)* one of which is on the starboard deck edge. Dimensions of the hangar are 590.6 × 78.7 × 23 ft *(180 × 24 × 7 m)*.
Operational: Oil fuel capacity is 3,720 tons. Service life 2025.

SÃO PAULO *9/2003, S C Neto/Mario R V Carneiro* / 0569158

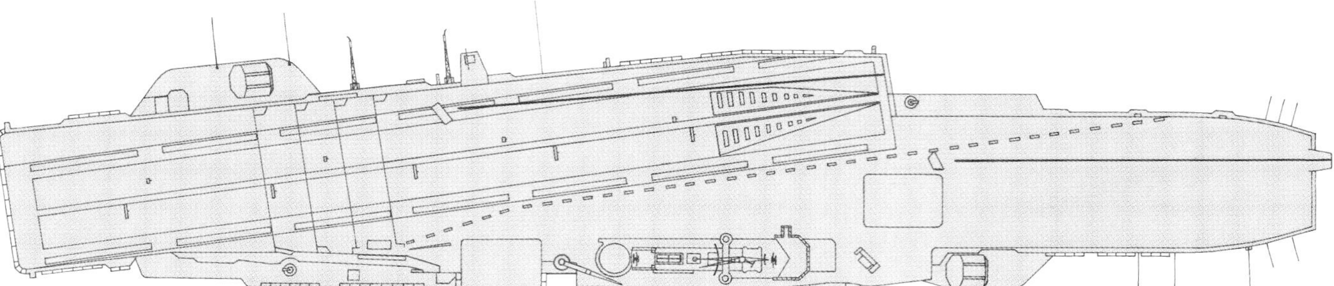

SÃO PAULO *(Scale 1 : 1,500), Ian Sturton* / 0529159

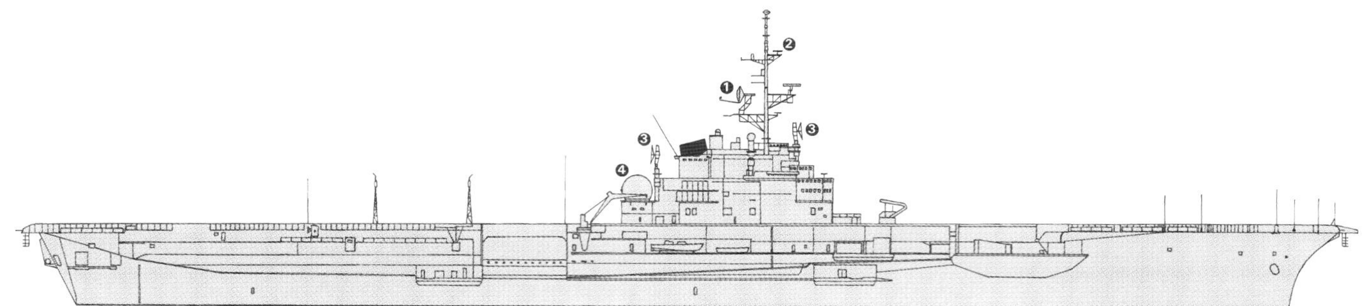

SÃO PAULO *(Scale 1 : 1,500), Ian Sturton* / 0130381

SÃO PAULO *2/2001, Mario R V Carneiro* / 0059752

SÃO PAULO *9/2007, Mario R V Carneiro* / 1335447

SÃO PAULO

9/2007, Mario R V Carneiro / 1335448

FRIGATES

Notes: Acquisition of up to six new frigates is reportedly under consideration. Following the Franco-Brazilian arms package of 12 February 2008, the French FREMM class is likely to be a strong contender.

3 BROADSWORD CLASS (TYPE 22) (FFGHM)

Name	*No*	*Builders*	*Laid down*	*Launched*	*Commissioned*	*Recommissioned*
GREENHALGH (ex-*Broadsword*)	F 46 (ex-F 88)	Yarrow Shipbuilders, Glasgow	7 Feb 1975	12 May 1976	3 May 1979	30 June 1995
BOSISIO (ex-*Brazen*)	F 48 (ex-F 91)	Yarrow Shipbuilders, Glasgow	18 Aug 1978	4 Mar 1980	2 July 1982	31 Aug 1996
RADEMAKER (ex-*Battleaxe*)	F 49 (ex-F 89)	Yarrow Shipbuilders, Glasgow	4 Feb 1976	18 May 1977	28 Mar 1980	30 Apr 1997

Displacement, tons: 3,500 standard; 4,731 full load
Dimensions, feet (metres): 430 oa; 410 wl × 48.5 × 19.9 (screws) *(131.2; 125 × 14.8 × 6)*
Main machinery: COGOG; 2 RR Olympus TM3B gas turbines; 50,000 hp *(37.3 MW)* sustained; 2 RR Tyne RM1C gas turbines; 9,900 hp *(7.4 MW)* sustained; 2 shafts; cp props
Speed, knots: 30; 18 on Tynes
Range, n miles: 4,500 at 18 kt on Tynes
Complement: 239 (17 officers)

Missiles: SSM: 4 Aerospatiale MM 38 Exocet ❶; inertial cruise; active radar homing to 42 km *(23 n miles)* at 0.9 Mach; warhead 165 kg; sea-skimmer.
SAM: 2 British Aerospace 6-barrelled Seawolf GWS 25 Mod 4 ❷; command line of sight (CLOS) TV/radar tracking to 5 km *(2.7 n miles)* at 2+ Mach; warhead 14 kg; 32 rounds.
Guns: 2 Bofors SAK 40 mm/L 70-350 A-3 ❸; 300 rds/min to 12 km (6.5 n miles)
2 Oerlikon BMARC 20 mm GAM-BO1; 1,000 rds/min to 2 km.
Torpedoes: 6—324 mm Plessey STWS Mk 2 (2 triple) tubes ❹. Honeywell Mk-46 Mod 5; active/passive homing to 11 km (5.9 n miles) at 40 kt; warhead 44 kg.
Countermeasures: Decoys: 4 Loral Hycor SRBOC Mk 36; 6-barrelled fixed launchers ❺; for chaff.
Graseby Type 182; towed torpedo decoy.

GREENHALGH — *(Scale 1 : 1,200), Ian Sturton* / 0012084

ESM: MEL UAA-2; intercept.
Combat data systems: CAAIS; Link YB being fitted. Inmarsat.
Weapons control: GWS 25 Mod 4 (for SAM); GWS 50 (Exocet).
Radars: Air/surface search: Marconi Type 967/968 ❻; D/E-band.
Navigation: Kelvin Hughes Type 1006; I-band.
Fire control: Two Marconi Type 910 ❼; I/Ku-band (for Seawolf).
Sonars: Plessey Type 2050; hull-mounted; search and attack; medium frequency.

Helicopters: 2 Westland Super Lynx AH-11A ❽.

Programmes: Contract signed on 18 November 1994 to transfer four Batch I Type 22 frigates from the UK, one in 1995, two in 1996 and one in 1997. It is not planned to buy more Type 22s.
Modernisation: Plans to fit a single 57 mm gun on the bow were shelved in favour of a 40 mm gun on each beam. These guns are being taken from the Niteroi class. A modernisation programme is planned to start in mid-2009. Upgrades are likely to include replacement of Exocet MM 38 with MM 40 and modernisation of the Seawolf SAM system.
Structure: Accommodation modified in UK service to take 65 officers under training.
Operational: Primary role is ASW. Form part of Second Escort Squadron at Niteroi, Rio de Janeiro. F 47 decommissioned in 2005.

BOSISIO — *10/2005, Mario R V Carneiro* / 1153024

GREENHALGH — *9/2007, Mario R V Carneiro* / 1335449

6 NITERÓI CLASS (FFGHM)

Name	No	Builders	Laid down	Launched	Commissioned
NITERÓI	F 40	Vosper Thornycroft Ltd	8 June 1972	8 Feb 1974	20 Nov 1976
DEFENSORA	F 41	Vosper Thornycroft Ltd	14 Dec 1972	27 Mar 1975	5 Mar 1977
CONSTITUIÇÃO	F 42	Vosper Thornycroft Ltd	13 Mar 1974	15 Apr 1976	31 Mar 1978
LIBERAL	F 43	Vosper Thornycroft Ltd	2 May 1975	7 Feb 1977	18 Nov 1978
INDEPENDÊNCIA	F 44	Arsenal de Marinha, Rio de Janeiro	11 June 1972	2 Sep 1974	3 Sep 1979
UNIÃO	F 45	Arsenal de Marinha, Rio de Janeiro	11 June 1972	14 Mar 1975	12 Sep 1980

Displacement, tons: 3,200 standard; 3,707 full load
Dimensions, feet (metres): 424 × 44.2 × 18.2 (sonar) *(129.2 × 13.5 × 5.5)*
Main machinery: CODOG; 2 RR Olympus TM3B gas turbines; 50,880 hp *(37.9 MW)* sustained; 4 MTU 16V 956 TB 91 diesels; 15,000 hp(m) *(11.0 MW)* sustained; 2 shafts; cp props
Speed, knots: 30 gas; 22 diesels
Range, n miles: 5,300 at 17 kt on 2 diesels; 4,200 at 19 kt on 4 diesels; 1,300 at 28 kt on gas
Complement: 209 (22 officers)

Missiles: SSM: 4 Aerospatiale MM 40 Exocet (2 twin) launchers (1); inertial cruise; active radar homing to 70 km *(40 n miles)* at 0.9 Mach; warhead 165 kg; sea-skimmer.
SAM: AESN Albatros (8 cell, 2 reloads) (2); Aspide 2000; semi-active radar homing to 21 km *(11 n miles)* at 2.5 Mach.
Guns: 1 Vickers 4.5 in *(115 mm)*/55 Mk 8 (3); 25 rds/min to 22 km *(12 n miles)* anti-surface; 6 km *(3.2 n miles)* anti-aircraft; weight of shell 21 kg.
2 Bofors SAK 40 mm/L 70-600 Mk 3 Sea Trinity (4); 330 rds/min to 4 km *(2.2 n miles)*.
Torpedoes: 6—324 mm Mk 32 (2 triple) tubes (5). Honeywell Mk 46 Mod 5; anti-submarine; active/passive homing to 11 km *(5.9 n miles)* at 40 kt; warhead 44 kg.
A/S mortars: 1 Bofors 375 mm trainable rocket launcher (twin-tube) (6); automatic loading; range 1,600 m.
Countermeasures: Decoys: 4 IPqM/Elebra MDLS 16-barrel chaff launchers (7).
ESM: Racal Cutlass B-1B; intercept.

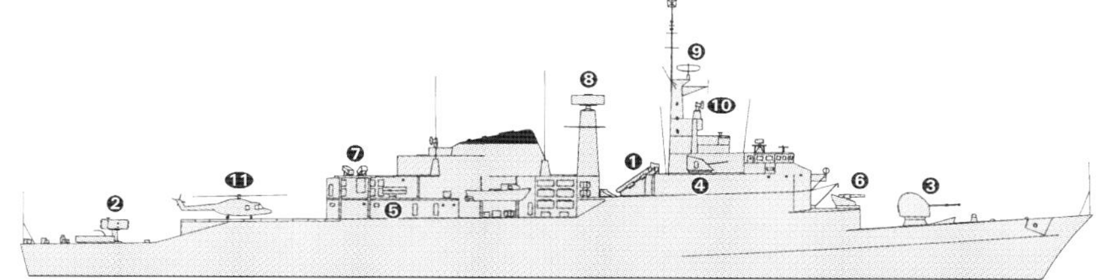

LIBERAL ***(Scale 1 : 1,200), Ian Sturton*** / 1170228

Combat data systems: IPqM/Elebra Siconta II. Link YB.
Weapons control: Saab/Combitech EOS-400/10B optronic director. WSA 401. FCS.
Radars: Air/surface search: AESN RAN 20 S (3L) (8); D-band.
Surface search: Terma Scanter 4100 (9); I-band.
Fire control: 2 AESN RTN 30X (10); I/J-band.
Navigation: Furuno FR-1942 Mk 2; I-band.
Sonars: EDO 997F; hull-mounted; active search and attack; medium frequency. EDO 700E VDS (F 40, F 41); active search and attack.

Helicopters: 1 Westland Super Lynx AH-11A (11).

Programmes: A contract announced on 29 September 1970 was signed between the Brazilian government and Vosper Thornycroft for the design and building of six Vosper Thornycroft Mark 10 frigates. Seventh ship with differing armament was ordered from Navy Yard, Rio de Janeiro in June 1981 and is used as a training ship.
Modernisation: The modernisation plan (Mod Frag) first signed in March 1995 included replacing Seacat by Aspide, Plessey AWS 2 radar by Alenia RAN 20S, RTN 10X by RTN 30X, ZW06 radar by Terma Scanter, new 40 mm mountings, new EW equipment, combat data system and hull-mounted sonar. Ikara removed. Work was undertaken by Elebra. *Liberal* completed 2001. *Defensora* (2002), *Independência* (2004) and *Niterói* (2004). *Constituição* and *União* were completed in 2005.
Structure: Originally F 40, 41, 44 and 45 were of the A/S configuration. F 42 and 43 general purpose design. Fitted with retractable stabilisers.
Operational: Endurance, 45 days' stores, 60 days' provisions. The helicopter has Sea Skua ASM. All are based at Niterói and form the First Escort Squadron.

DEFENSORA ***3/2008*, M Declerck*** / 1335338

INDEPENDÊNCIA ***5/2008*, Guy Toremans*** / 1335339

CORVETTES

1 + (3) BARROSO CLASS (FSGH)

Name	*No*	*Builders*	*Laid down*	*Launched*	*Commissioned*
BARROSO	V 34	Arsenal de Marinha, Rio de Janeiro	21 Dec 1994	20 Dec 2002	19 Aug 2008

Displacement, tons: 1,785 standard; 2,350 full load
Dimensions, feet (metres): 339.3 × 37.4 × 13.0; 17.4 (sonar) *(103.4 × 11.4 × 3.95; 5.3)*
Main machinery: CODOG; 1 GE LM 2500 gas turbine; 27,500 hp *(20.52 MW)* sustained; 2 MTU 20V 1163 TB83 diesels; 11,780 hp(m) *(8.67 MW)* sustained; 2 shafts; Kamewa cp props
Speed, knots: 29
Range, n miles: 4,000 at 12 kt
Complement: 145 (15 officers)

Missiles: SSM: 4 Aerospatiale MM 40 Exocet Block II ❶; inertial cruise; active radar homing to 70 km *(40 n miles)* at 0.90 Mach; warhead 165 kg; sea-skimmer.
Guns: 1 Vickers 4.5 in *(115 mm)* Mk 8 ❷; 55° elevation; 25 rds/min to 22 km *(12 n miles)*; weight of shell 21 kg.
1 Bofors SAK Sea Trinity CIWS 40 mm/70 Mk 3 ❸; 330 rds/min to 4 km *(2.2 n miles)*; anti-aircraft; 2.5 km *(1.4 n miles)* anti-missile; weight of shell 0.96 kg; with '3P' improved ammunition.
2—12.7 mm MGs.
Torpedoes: 6 ARES/DSAM SLT Mod 400 324 mm (2 triple) tubes ❹; Honeywell Mk 46 Mod 5; anti-submarine; active/passive homing to 11 km *(5.9 n miles)* at 40 kt; warhead 44 kg.
Countermeasures: Decoys: 2 IPqM/Elebra MDLS 101 12-tubed decoy launchers ❺.
ESM: IPqM/Elebra ET/SLR-1X ❻; radar warning.
ECM: IPqM/Elebra ET/SLQ-2 ❼; jammer.
Combat data systems: IPqM/Esca Siconta Mk III with Link YB.
Weapons control: Saab/Combitech EOS-400 FCS with optronic director ❽; two OFDLSE optical directors ❾.
Radars: Surface search: AESN RAN-20S ❿; F-band.
Navigation: Terma Scanter 4100; E/F/I-band.
Fire control: AESN RTN-30-X ⓫; I/J-band (for Albatross and guns).
Sonars: EDO 997(F); hull-mounted; active; medium frequency.

Helicopters: 1 AH-11A Westland Super Lynx ⓬.

Programmes: Ordered in 1994 as a follow-on to the Inhauma programme. The building programme has been beset by funding difficulties and although a class of six vessels was once projected, it is unlikely that more than a further three vessels will be built.
Structure: The hull is some 4.2 m longer than the Inhauma class to improve sea-keeping qualities and allow extra space in the engine room. The design allows the use of containerised equipment to aid modernisation. Efforts have been made to incorporate stealth technology. Vosper stabilisers.
Operational: To become operational in March 2009.

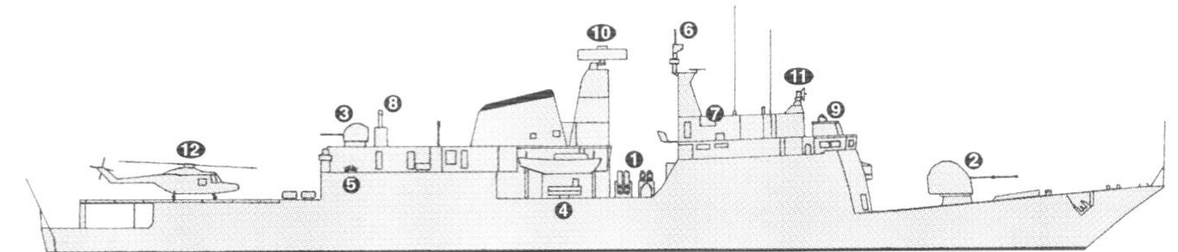

BARROSO *(Scale 1 : 900), Ian Sturton* / 0506270

BARROSO *6/2008** / 1335340

4 INHAÚMA CLASS (FSGH)

Name	*No*	*Builders*	*Laid down*	*Launched*	*Commissioned*
INHAÚMA	V 30	Arsenal de Marinha, Rio de Janeiro	23 Sep 1983	13 Dec 1986	12 Dec 1989
JACEGUAI	V 31	Arsenal de Marinha, Rio de Janeiro	15 Oct 1984	8 June 1987	2 Apr 1991
JULIO DE NORONHA	V 32	Verolme, Angra dos Reis	8 Dec 1986	15 Dec 1989	27 Oct 1992
FRONTIN	V 33	Verolme, Angra dos Reis	14 May 1987	6 Feb 1992	11 Mar 1994

Displacement, tons: 1,600 standard; 2,140 full load
Dimensions, feet (metres): 314.2 × 37.4 × 12.1; 17.4 (sonar) *(95.8 × 11.4 × 3.7; 5.3)*
Main machinery: CODOG; 1 GE LM 2500 gas turbine; 27,500 hp *(20.52 MW)* sustained; 2 MTU 16V 396 TB 91 diesels; 7,500 hp(m) *(5.5 MW)* sustained; 2 shafts; Kamewa cp props
Speed, knots: 27
Range, n miles: 4,000 at 15 kt
Complement: 145 (20 officers)

Missiles: SSM: 4 Aerospatiale MM 40 Exocet Block II ❶; inertial cruise; active radar homing to 70 km *(40 n miles)* at 0.9 Mach; warhead 165 kg; sea-skimmer.
Guns: 1 Vickers 4.5 in *(115 mm)* Mk 8 ❷; 55° elevation; 25 rds/min to 22 km *(12 n miles)*, weight of shell 21 kg.
2 Bofors 40 mm/70 ❸; 300 rds/min to 12 km *(6.5 n miles)* anti-surface; 4 km *(2.2 n miles)* anti-aircraft; weight of shell 0.96 kg. 2—12.7 mm MGs.
Torpedoes: 6—324 mm Mk 32 (2 triple) tubes ❹. Honeywell Mk 46 Mod 5; anti-submarine; active/passive homing to 11 km *(5.9 n miles)* at 40 kt; warhead 44 kg.
Countermeasures: Decoys: 2 Plessey Shield chaff launchers ❺; fires chaff and IR flares in distraction, decoy or centroid patterns.
ESM: IPqM/Elebra Defensor ET/SLR-1X; radar intercept.
ECM: IPqM/Elebra ET SLQ-1; jammer ❼.
Combat data systems: Ferranti CAAIS 450/WSA 421; Link YB.
Weapons control: Saab EOS-400 FCS with optronic director ❽ and two OFDLSE optical ❾ directors.
Radars: Surface search: Plessey AWS 4 ❿; E/F-band.
Navigation: Kelvin Hughes Type 1007; I/J-band.
Fire control: Selenia Orion RTN 10X ⓫; I/J-band.
Sonars: Atlas Elektronik DSQS-21C; hull-mounted; active; medium frequency.

Helicopters: 1 Westland Super Lynx ⓬ or UH-12/13 Ecureuil.

Programmes: Designed by Brazilian Naval Design Office with advice from West German private Marine Technik design company. Signature of final contract on 1 October 1981. First pair ordered on 15 February 1982 and second pair 9 January 1986. In mid-1986 the government approved, in principle, construction of a total of 16 ships but this was reduced to four.
Modernisation: A modernisation programme began in late 2008.
Operational: Form part of First Frigate Squadron based at Niterói, Rio de Janeiro.

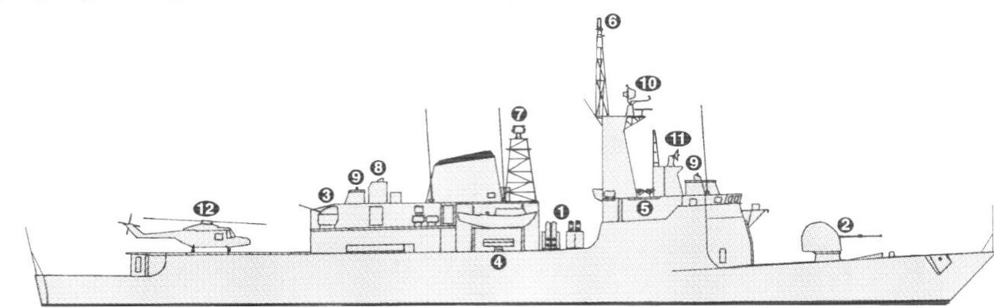

INHAÚMA *(Scale 1 : 900), Ian Sturton* / 0017617

INHAÚMA *9/2007, Mario R V Carneiro* / 1335446

JULIO DE NORONHA
10/2005, Mario R V Carneiro
1153018

SHIPBORNE AIRCRAFT (FRONT LINE)

Notes: It is planned to acquire up to three AEW aircraft by 2022.

Numbers/Type: 15/3 McDonnell Douglas AF-1/AF-1A Skyhawk.
Operational speed: 560 kt *(1,040 km/h).*
Service ceiling: 45,000 ft *(13,780 m).*
Range: 1,060 n miles *(1,965 km).*
Role/Weapon systems: Acquired from Kuwait Air Force in September 1998 to restore carrier fixed wing flying. A further five aircraft are kept as spares. An upgrade programme is under consideration. A Letter of Intent is expected in 2009. Sensors: APQ 145B radar; ESM/ECM. Weapons: AAM; 4 AIM 9H; 2 Colt 20 mm cannon; ASVW; bombs and rocket pods.

AF-1 ***10/2001, S C Neto/Mario R V Carneiro*** / 0569157

Numbers/Type: 4/1 Sikorsky SH-3A/SH-3B.
Operational speed: 125 kt *(230 km/h).*
Service ceiling: 12,200 ft *(3,720 m).*
Range: 400 n miles *(740 km).*
Role/Weapon systems: ASW helicopter; carrierborne and shore-based for medium-range ASW, ASVW and SAR. Sixteen delivered between 1970 and 1997. Three have been lost. Sensors: SMA APS-705(V)II or Northrop Grumman LN-66 HP search radar; Bendix AQS 13B or AQS 18(V) dipping sonar. Weapons: ASW; up to 2 × Mk 46 torpedoes, or 4 Mk II depth bombs. ASVW; 2 × AM 39 Exocet missiles.

Numbers/Type: 2/5 Aerospatiale UH-14 (AS 332F1 Super Puma)/UH-14 (AS 532 SC Cougar).
Operational speed: 120 kt *(222 km/h).*
Service ceiling: 12,000 ft *(3,657 m).*
Range: 445 n miles *(825 km).*
Role/Weapon systems: SAR, troop transport and ASVW. Sensors: Bendix RDR-1400C search radar. Weapons: None.

UH-14 ***6/2003, S C Neto/Mario R V Carneiro*** / 0569155

Numbers/Type: 4 Sikorsky S-70B Seahawk.
Operational speed: 135 kt *(250 km/h).*
Service ceiling: 10,000 ft *(3,050 m).*
Range: 600 n miles *(1,110 km).*
Role/Weapon systems: Four ex-US Navy aircraft ordered, under FMS funding arrangements, in June 2008. The aircraft are to have an ASW/ASUW role. Sensors: APS-124 search radar; Helras dipping sonar. Weapons: ASW: 2 Mk 46 torpedoes; Penguin ASM.

SEAHAWK S-70B (Turkish colours) ***6/2002, Selçuk Emre*** / 0533251

Numbers/Type: 12 AH-IIA Westland Super Lynx.
Operational speed: 125 kt *(232 km/h).*
Service ceiling: 12,000 ft *(3,650 m).*
Range: 130 n miles *(240 km).*
Role/Weapon systems: ASW/ASV roles. First batch upgraded in 1994–97 to Super Lynx standard with Mk 3 radar and Racal Kestrel EW suite. Sensors: Sea Spray Mk 1/Mk 3 radar; Racal MIR 2 ESM; Sea Star III FLIR. Weapons: ASW; 2 × Mk 46 torpedoes, or Mk II depth bombs. ASV; 4 × BAe/Ferranti Sea Skua missiles.

AH-IIA ***5/2008*, Guy Toremans*** / 1335337

Numbers/Type: 18 Aerospatiale UH-12 Esquilo (AS-350BA Ecureuil).
Operational speed: 147 kt *(272 km/h).*
Service ceiling: 10,000 ft *(3,050 m).*
Range: 240 n miles *(445 km).*
Role/Weapon systems: Support helicopters for Fleet liaison and Marine Corps transportation. Sensors: None. Weapons: 2 × axial 7.62 mm MGs or 1 × lateral MG or 1 × rocket pod.

UH-12 ***12/2002, Mario R V Carneiro*** / 0569156

Numbers/Type: 7 Aerospatiale UH-13 Esquilo (AS 355F2 Ecureuil 2).
Operational speed: 121 kt *(224 km/h).*
Service ceiling: 11,150 ft *(3,400 m).*
Range: 240 n miles *(445 km).*
Role/Weapon systems: SAR, liaison and utility in support of Marine Corps. One transferred to Uruguay in 2006. Sensors: Search radar. Weapons: 2 × axial 7.62 mm MGs or 1 × lateral MG or 1 × rocket pod.

UH-13 ***3/2008*, M Declerck*** / 1335336

Numbers/Type: 16 IH-6B (Bell JetRanger III).
Operational speed: 115 kt *(213 km/h).*
Service ceiling: 20,000 ft *(6,100 m).*
Range: 368 n miles *(682 km).*
Role/Weapon systems: Utility and training helicopters. One lost in June 2005. Sensors: None. Weapons: 2 × 7.62 mm MGs or 1 lateral 12.7 mm MG or 2 × rocket pods.

IH-6B ***12/2002, Mario R V Carneiro*** / 0569154

LAND-BASED MARITIME AIRCRAFT (FRONT LINE)

Numbers/Type: 8 Lockheed P-3BR Orion.
Operational speed: 411 kt *(761 km/h).*
Service ceiling: 28,300 ft *(8,625 m).*
Range: 4,000 m *(7,410 km).*
Role/Weapon systems: Twelve P-3 A/B acquired by the Air Force from the US Navy in 2002. Eight being upgraded to P-3BR standard by EADS/CASA. Contract awarded in April 2005 and aircraft to be delivered 2008–10. The remaining four aircraft are to be used for spare parts. Sensors: Raytheon AN/APS-137B(V)5 radar, ASQ-81 MAD, EADS/CASA FITS, AAR-47 warning receiver, AN/ALR-66(V)3 ESM, AN/ALQ-78A countermeasures suite. Weapons: ASW; eight Mk 46 torpedoes, eight Mk 14 depth charges. ASuW: 4 Aerospatiale AM-39 Exocet.

P-3BR *2002, Brazilian Navy* / 0536045

Numbers/Type: 10/9 Bandeirante P-95A/P-95B (EMB-111(B)).
Operational speed: 194 kt *(360 km/h).*
Service ceiling: 25,500 ft *(7,770 m).*
Range: 1,590 n miles *(2,945 km).*
Role/Weapon systems: Air Force operated for coastal surveillance role by four squadrons. Sensors: MEL Super Searcher (P-95B) or Eaton/AIL APS-28 Sea Searcher (P-95A) search radar, searchlight pod on starboard wing, EFIS-74 (electronic flight instrumentation) and Collins APS-65 (autopilot); ESM Thomson-CSF DR2000A/Dalia 1000A Mk II, GPS (Trimble). Weapons: 4 or 6 × 127 mm rockets, or up to 28 × 70 mm rockets.

EMB-111 *6/1995* / 0503428

Numbers/Type: 53 A-1 (Embraer/Alenia/Aermacchi) AMX.
Operational speed: 493 kt *(914 km/h).*
Service ceiling: 42,650 ft *(13,000 m).*
Range: 1,800 n miles *(3,336 km).*
Role/Weapon systems: Air Force operated for strike, reconnaissance and anti-shipping attack; shore-based for fleet air defence and ASV primary roles; operated by 3rd/10th Group at Santa Maria Air Base (KS) and Santa Cruz Air Base. Sensors: Tecnasa/SMA SCP-01 Scipio radar. ECM suite/ESM flares and chaffs; GPS and IFF. Weapons: Strike; up to 3,800 kg of 'IRON' bombs; Self-defence; AAM; 2 × MAA-1 Piranha or 2 × AIM-9 Sidewinder missiles; 2 DEFA 30 mm cannon.

AMX *6/1998* / 0013614

PATROL FORCES

Notes: (1) There are plans to acquire five offshore patrol ships of approximately 1,800 tons. Construction is expected to start in 2010.
(2) There are 114 LAEP series Instruction and Support craft. 24 LAEP-10 are 10 m long and 90 LAEP-7 are 7 m long.
(3) There are 174 LPN series River patrol craft of 3 to 15 m length.
(4) Fifteen 8 m aluminium hulled LAR (fast insertion craft) have entered service with the Brazilian Marines. Further orders are expected. There are two other variants of the class: LIN are operated by port authorities and LAM are ambulance craft.
(5) Four Tracker II (LPAN-21) 21 m patrol craft are employed as police patrol craft.
(6) There are plans to acquire two 200-ton river patrol ships.

1 + 5 (4) MARLIM (MEATINI) CLASS (PB)

MARLIM LP 01

Displacement, tons: 40 full load
Dimensions, feet (metres): 74.8 × 17.1 × 3.3 *(22.8 × 5.2 × 1)*
Main machinery: 2 CRM 18D/52 diesels; 2,500 hp(m) *(1.84 MW)*; 2 shafts
Speed, knots: 34
Range, n miles: 550 at 20 kt
Complement: 11 (1 officer)
Guns: 1 — 12.7 mm MG.
Radars: Surface search: 1 GEM 1210; I-band.

Comment: The first of a new class of patrol craft that entered service in 2005. Slightly longer version of Italian Meatini class design in service with Guardia di Finanzia. Built by Inace Shipyard, Brazil. Aluminium hull. Five further craft are to be delivered in 2009 and a class of 10 is expected. Details are for those in service in Italy and may be different.

MARLIM *6/2007, L Frangetto* / 1170090

12 GRAJAÚ CLASS (LARGE PATROL CRAFT) (PBO)

Name	*No*	*Builders*	*Launched*	*Commissioned*
GRAJAÚ	P 40	Arsenal de Marinha	21 May 1993	1 Dec 1993
GUAIBA	P 41	Arsenal de Marinha	10 Dec 1993	12 Sep 1994
GRAÚNA	P 42	Estaleiro Mauá, Niteroi	10 Nov 1993	15 Aug 1994
GOIANA	P 43	Estaleiro Mauá, Niteroi	26 Jan 1994	26 Feb 1997
GUAJARÁ	P 44	Peenewerft, Germany	24 Oct 1994	28 Apr 1995
GUAPORÉ	P 45	Peenewerft, Germany	23 Jan 1995	29 Aug 1995
GURUPÁ	P 46	Peenewerft, Germany	11 May 1995	8 Dec 1995
GURUPI	P 47	Peenewerft, Germany	6 Sep 1995	23 Apr 1996
GUANABARA	P 48	Inace, Fortalesa	5 Nov 1997	9 July 1999
GUARUJÁ	P 49	Inace, Fortalesa	24 Apr 1998	25 Nov 1999
GUARATUBA	P 50	Peenewerft, Germany	16 June 1999	1 Dec 1999
GRAVATAÍ	P 51	Peenewerft, Germany	26 Aug 1999	17 Feb 2000

Displacement, tons: 197 standard; 217 full load
Dimensions, feet (metres): 152.6 × 24.6 × 7.5 *(46.5 × 7.5 × 2.3)*
Main machinery: 2 MTU 16V 396 TB94 diesels; 5,800 hp(m) *(4.26 MW)* sustained; 2 shafts
Speed, knots: 26
Range, n miles: 2,200 at 12 kt
Complement: 29 (4 officers)
Guns: 1 Bofors 40 mm/70. 2 Oerlikon 20 mm (P 40-44). 2 Oerlikon BMARC 20 mm GAM-BO1 (P 45-51).
Weapons control: ARES/DSAM AO optronic director may be fitted in due course.
Radars: Surface search: Racal Decca 1290A; I-band.

Comment: Two ordered in late 1987 to a Vosper QAF design similar to Bangladesh Meghna class. Technology transfer in February 1988 and construction started in July 1988 for the first pair; second pair started construction in September 1990. Class name changed in 1993 when the first four were renumbered to reflect revised delivery dates. Building problems are also reflected in the replacing of the order for the third pair with Peenewerft in November 1993 and the fourth pair in August 1994. Two more ordered from Inace in September 1996 and from Peenewerft in 1998. Used for EEZ patrol duties and diver support. Carry one RIB and telescopic launching crane. A similar vessel has been built for Namibia.

GUAPORÉ *4/2006, A E Galarce* / 1040737

GUAJARÁ *2/2006, Marco Ghiglino* / 1167121

2 IMPERIAL MARINHEIRO CLASS (COASTAL PATROL SHIPS) (PG/ATR)

Name	No	Builders	Commissioned
IMPERIAL MARINHEIRO	V 15	Smit, Kinderdijk, Netherlands	8 June 1955
CABOCLO	V 19	Smit, Kinderdijk, Netherlands	5 Apr 1955

Displacement, tons: 911 standard; 1,025 full load
Dimensions, feet (metres): 184 × 30.5 × 11.7 *(56 × 9.3 × 3.6)*
Main machinery: 2 Sulzer 6TD36 diesels; 2,160 hp(m) *(1.59 MW)*; 2 shafts
Speed, knots: 16
Complement: 64 (6 officers)
Guns: 1—3 in *(76 mm)*/50 Mk 33; 50 rds/min to 12.8 km *(6.9 n miles)*; weight of shell 6 kg.
2 or 4 Oerlikon 20 mm.
Radars: Surface search: Racal Decca; I-band.

Comment: Fleet tugs classed as corvettes. Equipped for firefighting. *Imperial Marinheiro* has acted as a submarine support ship but gave up the role in 1990. V 21 and V 23 withdrawn from service in 2002, V 24 in 2003 and V 20 in 2004. V 19 has been re-engined and returned to service.

IMPERIAL MARINHEIRO CLASS *2/2000, van Ginderen Collection* / 0104229

2 PEDRO TEIXEIRA CLASS (RIVER PATROL SHIPS) (PBR)

Name	No	Builders	Launched	Commissioned
PEDRO TEIXEIRA	P 20	Arsenal de Marinha	14 Oct 1970	17 Dec 1973
RAPOSO TAVARES	P 21	Arsenal de Marinha	11 June 1972	17 Dec 1973

Displacement, tons: 690 standard; 900 full load
Dimensions, feet (metres): 208.7 × 31.8 × 5.6 *(63.6 × 9.7 × 1.7)*
Main machinery: 4 MAN V6 V16/18 TL diesels; 3,840 hp(m) *(2.82 MW)*; 2 shafts
Speed, knots: 16
Range, n miles: 5,000 at 13 kt
Complement: 58 (6 officers)
Guns: 1 Bofors 40 mm/60; 120 rds/min to 12 km *(6.5 n miles)*.
6—12.7 mm MGs. 2—81 mm Mk 2 mortars.
Radars: Surface search: 2 Racal Decca; I-band.
Helicopters: 1 Bell JetRanger or UH-12 Esquilo.

Comment: Built in Rio de Janeiro. Belong to Amazon Flotilla. Can carry two armed LCVPs and 85 marines in deck accommodation. Both ships to be re-engined.

PEDRO TEIXEIRA *6/1997, Brazilian Navy* / 0012091

3 RORAIMA CLASS (RIVER PATROL SHIPS) (PBR)

Name	No	Builders	Launched	Commissioned
RORAIMA	P 30	Maclaren, Niteroi	2 Nov 1972	21 Feb 1975
RONDÔNIA	P 31	Maclaren, Niteroi	10 Jan 1973	3 Dec 1975
AMAPÁ	P 32	Maclaren, Niteroi	9 Mar 1973	12 Jan 1976

Displacement, tons: 340 standard; 365 full load
Dimensions, feet (metres): 151.9 × 27.9 × 4.6 *(46.3 × 8.5 × 1.4)*
Main machinery: 2 Volvo-Penta D49A-MS diesels; 1,825 hp(m) *(1.36 MW)*; 2 shafts
Speed, knots: 17
Range, n miles: 6,000 at 15 kt
Complement: 48 (5 officers)
Guns: 1 Bofors 40 mm/60; 120 rds/min to 12 km *(6.5 n miles)*.
2 Oerlikon 20 mm. 2—81 mm mortars. 6—12.7 mm MGs.
Radars: Surface search: 2 Racal Decca; I-band.

Comment: Carry two armed LCVPs. Belong to Amazon Flotilla. All re-engined with Volvo engines.

RORAIMA *6/1998, Brazilian Navy* / 0017623

0 + 6 VIGILANTE (NAPA 500) CLASS (PBO)

Name	Builders	Laid down	Launched	Commissioned
–	INACE, Fortalesa	26 Nov 2006	2008	Oct 2009
–	INACE, Fortalesa	17 July 2007	2008	Mar 2010

Displacement, tons: 406 standard; 477 full load
Dimensions, feet (metres): 177.8 × 26.2 × 8.9 *(54.2 × 8.0 × 2.7)*
Main machinery: 2 MTU 16V 538TB93 diesels; 8,000 hp(m) *(5.9 MW)*; 2 shafts
Speed, knots: 24
Range, n miles: 2,400 at 15 kt
Complement: 43 (8 officers)
Guns: 1 Bofors SAK-40 mm/L70 Mk 3 Sea Trinity; 330 rds/min to 4 km *(2.2 n miles)*; weight of shell 0.96 kg.
2 Oerlikon/Royal Ordnance 20 mm GAM-BO1; 1,000 rds/min to 2 km.
Countermeasures: Decoys: 2 IPqM/Elebra MDLS 101 (12-tubed) launchers.
ESM: To be announced.
Weapons control: ARES/DSAM AO optical sight.
Radars: Surface search: To be announced.
Navigation: To be announced.

Comment: Following an invitation to tender in June 2006, contract awarded on 28 September 2006 to Indústria Naval do Ceará (INACE), Fortalesa, for the construction of two patrol ships in partnership with the French company CMN. The ships, designated NAPA 500, are to CMN's 54 m Vigilante 400CL 54 design and are to be similar in configuration to the three Al Bushra class in service in the Royal Navy of Oman. CMN is to provide technical assistance and integrated logistic support. Steel was first cut on 1 November 2006. The ships are to be employed on EEZ patrol duties. The contract for a further four vessels was let in October 2008 and a class of 12 is projected by 2016.

VIGILANTE 400 *6/2006, R Scott/NAVYPIX* / 1165269

1 PARNAIBA CLASS (RIVER MONITOR) (PGRH)

Name	No	Builders	Commissioned
PARNAIBA	U 17 (ex-P 2)	Arsenal de Marinha, Rio de Janeiro	6 Nov 1938

Displacement, tons: 620 standard; 720 full load
Dimensions, feet (metres): 180.5 × 33.3 × 5.1 *(55 × 10.1 × 1.6)*
Main machinery: 2 diesels; 2 shafts
Speed, knots: 12
Range, n miles: 1,350 at 10 kt
Complement: 74 (6 officers)
Guns: 1 US 76 mm. 2 Bofors 40 mm/70. 6 Oerlikon 20 mm.
Radars: Surface search: Racal Decca; I-band.
Navigation: Furuno 3600; I-band.
Helicopters: Platform for one IH-6B Jet Ranger.

Comment: Laid down 11 June 1936. Launched 2 September 1937. In Mato Grosso Flotilla. Re-armed with new guns in 1960. 3 in *(76 mm)* side armour and partial deck protection. Refitted in 1995/96 with improved armament, and with diesel engines replacing the steam reciprocating propulsion plant. Converted again in 1998 with Bofors 40 mm/70 guns taken from Niterói-class frigates and a helo deck at the stern. Facilities to refuel and re-arm a UH-12 helicopter. Recommissioned 6 May 1999.

PARNAIBA *5/2000, Hartmut Ehlers* / 0087859

4 BRACUI (RIVER) CLASS (COASTAL PATROL CRAFT) (PBO)

Name	*No*	*Builders*	*Commissioned*
BRACUI (ex-*Itchen*)	P 60 (ex-M 2009)	Richards, Lowestoft	12 Oct 1985
BENEVENTE (ex-*Blackwater*)	P 61 (ex-M 2008)	Richards, Great Yarmouth	5 July 1985
BOCAINA (ex-*Spey*)	P 62 (ex-M 2013)	Richards, Lowestoft	4 Apr 1986
BABITONGA (ex-*Arun*)	P 63 (ex-M 2014)	Richards, Lowestoft	29 Aug 1986

Displacement, tons: 770 standard; 890 full load
Dimensions, feet (metres): 156 × 34.5 × 9.5 *(47.5 × 10.5 × 2.9)*
Main machinery: 2 Ruston 6 RKC diesels; 3,100 hp(m) *(2.3 MW)* sustained; 2 shafts
Speed, knots: 14
Range, n miles: 4,500 at 10 kt
Complement: 32 (4 officers)
Guns: 1 Bofors 40 mm/60.
2—7.62 mm MGs.
Mines: Rails for up to 20.
Radars: Surface search: 2 Racal Decca TM 1226C; I-band.

Comment: Second batch of ex-UK River class minesweepers transferred in 1998. These four were converted as patrol craft in UK service. Recommissioned 6 April, 10 July, 10 July and 9 September respectively. Three others transferred in 1995 are listed as Survey Ships.

BOCAINA ***7/1998, Maritime Photographic*** / 0056608

6 PIRATINI CLASS (COASTAL PATROL CRAFT) (PB)

Name	*No*	*Builders*	*Commissioned*
PIRATINI (ex-PGM 109)	P 10	Arsenal de Marinha, Rio de Janeiro	30 Nov 1970
PIRAJÁ (ex-PGM 110)	P 11	Arsenal de Marinha, Rio de Janeiro	8 Mar 1971
PAMPEIRO (ex-PGM 118)	P 12	Arsenal de Marinha, Rio de Janeiro	16 June 1971
PARATI (ex-PGM 119)	P 13	Arsenal de Marinha, Rio de Janeiro	29 July 1971
PENEDO (ex-PGM 120)	P 14	Arsenal de Marinha, Rio de Janeiro	30 Sep 1971
POTI (ex-PGM 121)	P 15	Arsenal de Marinha, Rio de Janeiro	29 Oct 1971

Displacement, tons: 105 standard; 146 full load
Dimensions, feet (metres): 95 × 19 × 6.5 *(29 × 5.8 × 2)*
Main machinery: 4 Cummins VT-12M diesels; 1,100 hp *(820 kW)*; 2 shafts
Speed, knots: 17
Range, n miles: 1,700 at 12 kt
Complement: 16 (2 officers)
Guns: 1 Oerlikon 20 mm. 2—12.7 mm MGs.
Radars: Surface search: Racal Decca 1070; I-band.
Navigation: Furuno 3600; I-band.

Comment: Built under offshore agreement with the USA and similar to the US Cape class. 81 mm mortar removed in 1988. Carries an inflatable launch. P 10, P 11, P 14 and P 15 are based at Ladário Fluvial Base, Mato Grosso, the other two at Amazonas.

POTI ***6/1998, Brazilian Navy*** / 0017624

AMPHIBIOUS FORCES

Notes: (1) Replacement of the two Ceará-class LSDs is under consideration. Options include ex-US Navy Austin class.
(2) Construction of three EDCG 41 LCU began at AMRJ in 2008.
(3) There are six EDVP II class landing craft of 13 tons built by BFL, Ladario and capable of carrying 3.7 tons or 37 troops at 9 kt. These are based at Ladario.
(4) There are 32 RIBs for special operations.

1 NEWPORT CLASS (LSTH)

Name	*No*	*Builders*	*Laid down*	*Launched*	*Commissioned*	*Recommissioned*
MATTOSO MAIA (ex-*Cayuga*)	G 28 (ex-LST 1186)	National Steel & Shipbuilding Co	28 Sep 1968	12 July 1969	8 Aug 1970	30 Aug 1994

Displacement, tons: 5,159 standard; 8,757 full load
Dimensions, feet (metres): 522.3 (hull) × 69.5 × 17.5 (aft) *(159.2 × 21.2 × 5.3)*
Main machinery: 6 ALCO 16-251 diesels; 16,500 hp *(12.3 MW)* sustained; 2 shafts; cp props; bow thruster; 800 hp *(596 kW)*
Speed, knots: 20
Range, n miles: 14,250 at 14 kt
Complement: 267 (17 officers)

Military lift: 351 (33 officers); 500 tons vehicles; 3 LCVPs and 1 LCPL on davits

Guns: 1 General Electric/General Dynamics 20 mm Vulcan Phalanx Mk 15. 8—12.7 mm MGs.
Radars: Surface search: Raytheon SPS-10F; G-band.
Navigation: Raytheon SPS-64(V)6 and Furuno FR 2120; I-band.

Helicopters: Platform only.

Programmes: Transferred from the USN by lease 26 August 1994, arriving in Brazil in late October. Purchased outright on 19 September 2000.
Structure: The ramp is supported by twin derrick arms. A stern gate to the tank deck permits unloading of amphibious tractors into the water, or unloading of other vehicles into an LCU or onto a pier. Vehicle stowage covers 19,000 sq ft. Length over derrick arms is 562 ft *(171.3 m)*; full load draught is 11.5 ft forward and 17.5 ft aft.

MATTOSO MAIA ***6/2003, S C Neto/Mario R V Carneiro*** / 0569153

2 CEARÁ (THOMASTON) CLASS (LSDH)

Name	*No*	*Builders*	*Laid down*	*Launched*	*Commissioned*	*Recommissioned*
CEARÁ (ex-*Hermitage*)	G 30 (ex-LSD 34)	Ingalls, Pascagoula	11 Apr 1955	12 June 1956	14 Dec 1956	28 Nov 1989
RIO DE JANEIRO (ex-*Alamo*)	G 31 (ex-LSD 33)	Ingalls, Pascagoula	11 Oct 1954	20 Jan 1956	24 Aug 1956	21 Nov 1990

Displacement, tons: 6,880 standard; 12,150 full load
Dimensions, feet (metres): 510 × 84 × 19 *(155.5 × 25.6 × 5.8)*
Main machinery: 2 Babcock & Wilcox boilers; 580 psi *(40.8 kg/cm²)*; 2 GE turbines; 24,000 hp *(17.9 MW)*; 2 shafts
Speed, knots: 22.5. **Range, n miles:** 14,800 at 12 kt
Complement: 223 (21 officers)
Military lift: 340 troops; 3 EDCG-41 (LCU) or 6 EDVM-25 (LCM 8) or 50 amphibious tractors in tank-deck and 30 amphibious tractors on upper deck

Guns: 6 USN 3 in *(76 mm)*/50 (3 twin) Mk 33; 50 rds/min to 12.8 km *(7 n miles)*; weight of shell 6 kg.
4—12.7 mm MGs.
Radars: Surface search: Raytheon SPS-10F; G-band.
Air/surface search: Plessey AWS-2 (G 30); AWS-4 (G 31); E/F-band.
Navigation: Raytheon CRP 3100 (G 30); I-band. Furuno ARPA M-1942; E/F/I-band.

Helicopters: Platform for Super Puma.

Programmes: The original plan to build a 4,500 ton LST was overtaken by the acquisition of these two LSDs from the US initially on a lease and finally by purchase on 24 January 2001.
Structure: Has two 50 ton capacity cranes and a docking well of 391 × 48 ft *(119.2 × 14.6 m)*. Two LCVPs and two LCP(L)s on davits. Ice-strengthened bow. SATCOM fitted. Phalanx guns and SRBOC chaff launchers removed before transfer. Air search radars removed.

CEARÁ

9/2007, ***Mario R V Carneiro*** / 1335451

1 SIR GALAHAD CLASS (LSL)

Name	*No*	*Builders*	*Laid down*	*Launched*	*Commissioned*
GARCIA D'ÁVILA (ex-*Sir Galahad*)	G 29 (ex-L 3005)	Swan Hunter, Wallsend-on-Tyne	12 May 1985	13 Dec 1986	25 Nov 1987

Displacement, tons: 8,585 full load
Dimensions, feet (metres): 461.0 × 64.0 × 14.1 *(140.5 × 19.5 × 4.3)*
Main machinery: 2 Mirrlees-Blackstone diesels; 13,320 hp *(9.94 MW)*; 2 shafts; cp props; 1 bow thruster; 400 hp *(298 kW)*
Speed, knots: 18. **Range, n miles:** 13,000 at 15 kt
Complement: 49 (15 officers)
Military lift: 343 troops (537 overload); 16 MBT, 34 mixed vehicles

Guns: 2 Oerlikon/Royal Ordnance 20 mm GAM-BO3 (twin); 650 rds/min to 10 km *(5.4 n miles)*; weight of shell 0.36 kg. 2—7.62 mm MGs.
Countermeasures: Decoys: 2 Plessey Shield 200 (6-tubed launchers).
Combat data systems: Racal CANE data automation.
Radars: Navigation: Kelvin-Hughes Type 1007; I-band.

Helicopters: Platform for 1 medium.

Comment: Former UK Royal Fleet Auxiliary decommissioned in July 2006 and recommissioned into the Brazilian Navy on 4 December 2007 following a refit at Portsmouth. The work included overhaul of the engines and controllable-pitch propellers and upgrade of communications equipment. The ship is equipped with bow and stern ramps, a 25-tonne crane and three 8-tonne cranes. Up to four mexeflote pontoons can be attached to the hull.

GARCIA D'ÁVILA

*2/2008**, ***Maritime Photographic*** / 1335335

3 LCU 1610 CLASS (EDCG/LCU)

Name	*No*	*Builders*	*Commissioned*
GUARAPARI	L 10 (ex-GED 10)	Arsenal de Marinha, Rio de Janeiro	27 Mar 1978
TAMBAÚ	L 11 (ex-GED 11)	Arsenal de Marinha, Rio de Janeiro	27 Mar 1978
CAMBORIÚ	L 12 (ex-GED 12)	Arsenal de Marinha, Rio de Janeiro	6 Jan 1981

Displacement, tons: 390 full load
Dimensions, feet (metres): 134.5 × 27.6 × 6.6 *(41 × 8.4 × 2.0)*
Main machinery: 2 GM 12V-71 diesels; 874 hp *(650 kW)* sustained; 2 shafts; cp props
Speed, knots: 11
Range, n miles: 1,200 at 8 kt
Complement: 14 (2 officers)
Military lift: 172 tons
Guns: 3—12.7 mm MGs.
Radars: Navigation: Furuno 3600; I-band.

Comment: Original pennant numbers restored in 2004. Based at Niteroi.

CAMBORIÚ

6/2001, ***Brazilian Navy*** / 0130473

5 + 5 EDVM 25 CLASS (LCM)

801–805

Displacement, tons: 61 standard; 130 full load
Dimensions, feet (metres): 71 × 21 × 4.8 *(21.7 × 6.4 × 1.5)*
Main machinery: 2 Detroit diesels; 400 hp *(294 kW)* sustained; 2 shafts
Speed, knots: 9
Range, n miles: 95 at 9 kt
Complement: 5
Military lift: 150 troops plus 72 tons equipment

Comment: Five vessels constructed by Inace and delivered 1993–94. Construction of a further five craft started at AMRJ in 2008. LCM 8 type. Based at Niteroi.

801

6/2001, ***Brazilian Navy*** / 0130472

1 SIR BEDIVERE CLASS (LANDING SHIP LOGISTIC) (LSLH)

Name	*No*	*Builders*	*Laid down*	*Launched*	*Commissioned*
ALMIRANTE SABOÍA (ex-*Sir Bedivere*)	G 25 (ex-L 3004)	Hawthorn Leslie, Hebburn-on-Tyne	Oct 1965	20 July 1966	18 May 1967

Displacement, tons: 3,270 light; 6,700 full load
Dimensions, feet (metres): 441.1 × 59.8 × 13 *(134.4 × 18.2 × 4)*
Main machinery: 2 Mirrlees 10-ALSSDM diesels; 9,400 hp *(7.01 MW)* or 2 Wärtsilä 280 V12 diesels; 9,928 hp(m) *(7.3 MW)* sustained (SLEP); 2 shafts; bow thruster; 980 hp(m) *(720 kW)* (SLEP)
Speed, knots: 17
Range, n miles: 8,000 at 15 kt
Complement: 51 (18 officers); 49 (15 officers) (SLEP)
Military lift: 340 troops (534 hard lying); 18 MBTs; 34 mixed vehicles; 120 tons POL; 30 tons ammunition; 1–25 ton crane; 2–4.5 ton cranes. Capacity for 20 helicopters (11 tank deck and 9 vehicle deck)
Guns: 2 or 4 Oerlikon 20 mm. 4—7.62 mm MGs. 2 Mk 44 7.62 mm Miniguns.
Countermeasures: Decoys: 2 Plessey Shield chaff launchers.
Radars: Navigation: Kelvin Hughes Type 1006 or Racal Decca 2690; I-band.
Aircraft control: Kelvin Hughes Type 1007; I-band (SLEP).

Helicopters: Platform to operate Lynx, Chinook or Sea King.

Comment: Former UK Royal Fleet Auxiliary decommissioned on 18 February 2008 and to be recommissioned into the Brazilian Navy in May 2009. Fitted for bow and stern loading with drive-through facilities and deck-to-deck ramps. Facilities provided for onboard maintenance of vehicles and for laying out pontoon equipment. Mexeflote self-propelled floating platforms can be strapped one on each side. SLEP in Rosyth from December 1994 to January 1998 included lengthening by 29 ft an enlarged flight deck, new main engines and a new bridge. The helicopter platform was lowered by one deck, which has reduced the size of the stern ramp.

ALMIRANTE SABOÍA (UK colours) *4/2007, Shaun Jones* / 1170256

MINE WARFARE FORCES

6 ARATU (SCHÜTZE) CLASS (MINESWEEPERS—COASTAL) (MSC)

Name	*No*	*Builders*	*Commissioned*
ARATU	M 15	Abeking & Rasmussen, Lemwerder	5 May 1971
ANHATOMIRIM	M 16	Abeking & Rasmussen, Lemwerder	30 Nov 1971
ATALAIA	M 17	Abeking & Rasmussen, Lemwerder	13 Dec 1972
ARAÇATUBA	M 18	Abeking & Rasmussen, Lemwerder	13 Dec 1972
ABROLHOS	M 19	Abeking & Rasmussen, Lemwerder	25 Feb 1976
ALBARDÃO	M 20	Abeking & Rasmussen, Lemwerder	25 Feb 1976

Displacement, tons: 241 standard; 280 full load
Dimensions, feet (metres): 154.9 × 23.6 × 6.9 *(47.2 × 7.2 × 2.1)*
Main machinery: 2 MTU Maybach diesels; 4,500 hp(m) *(3.3 MW)*; 2 shafts; 2 Escher-Weiss cp props
Speed, knots: 24
Range, n miles: 710 at 20 kt
Complement: 32 (4 officers)
Guns: 1 Bofors SAK 40 mm/70; 300 rds/min to 12 km *(6.5 n miles)*; weight of shell 0.96 kg.
Radars: Surface search: Furuno M-1831; I-band.
Navigation: Furuno FR 1831; I-band.

Comment: Wooden hulled. First four ordered in April 1969 and last pair in November 1973. Same design as the now deleted German Schütze class. Can carry out wire, magnetic and acoustic sweeping. A life-extension refit programme started in 2001. M 15 completed in 2002 and M17, 18 and 19 by 2005. M16 completed in 2006 and M 20 completed in 2007. Modifications include replacement of the surface search radar, communications upgrade and hull preservation measures. Based at Aratu, Bahia.

ABROLHOS *3/1998, Brazilian Navy* / 0017625

SURVEY AND RESEARCH SHIPS

Notes: (1) Survey ships are painted white except for those operating in the Antarctic which have red hulls.
(2) There are also 24 buoy tenders of between 15 and 26 m: seven LB 15, two LB 17 (*Lufada* and *Piracema*), one LB 19, 10 LB 20 (*Achernar, Aldebaran, Betelgeuse, Capella, Denébola, Formalhaut, Regulus, Rigel, Vega* and *Pollux*), two LB 23 (*Suboficial Oliveira* and *Marco Zero*) and two LB 26 (*Tubarão* and *Boto*).
(3) There is one inshore survey craft, *Camocim*, based at Niteroi.

1 POLAR RESEARCH SHIP (AGOBH)

Name	*No*	*Builders*	*Commissioned*
ARY RONGEL (ex-*Polar Queen*)	H 44	Eides, Norway	22 Jan 1981

Displacement, tons: 1,928 standard; 3,628 full load
Dimensions, feet (metres): 247 × 42.7 × 17.4 *(75.3 × 13 × 5.3)*
Main machinery: 2 MAK 6M-453 diesels; 4,500 hp(m) *(3.3 MW)*; 1 shaft; cp prop; 2 bow thrusters; 1 stern thruster
Speed, knots: 14.5
Range, n miles: 17,000 at 12 kt
Complement: 70 (19 officers) + 22 scientists
Radars: Navigation: Sperry; I-band; Racal-Decca; I/J-band.
Cargo capacity: 2,400 m^3
Helicopters: Platform for UH-13 Esquilo.

Comment: Acquired by sale 19 April 1994. Ice-strengthened hull fitted with Simrad Albatross dynamic positioning system.

ARY RONGEL *6/2002, Carlos Veras, Brazilian Navy* / 0572424

0 + 1 POLAR RESEARCH SHIP (AGOBH)

Name	*No*	*Commissioned*
ALMIRANTE MAXIMIANO (ex-*Ocean Express*)	H 45	1974

Displacement, tons: 5,450 full load
Dimensions, feet (metres): 306.4 × 43.9 × ? *(93.4 × 13.4 × ?)*
Main machinery: to be announced
Speed, knots: to be announced
Complement: to be announced
Radars: Surface search: to be announced.
Navigation: to be announced.
Helicopters: 2 medium.

Comment: Reportedly acquired in 2008 and undergoing conversion to an Antarctic support ship role in Germany. The refit includes provision of a hangar and flight deck to operate two helicopters.

1 RESEARCH SHIP (AGS)

Name	*No*	*Builders*	*Commissioned*
ANTARES (ex-M/V *Lady Harrison*)	H 40	Mjellem and Karlsen A/S, Bergen	Aug 1984

Displacement, tons: 855 standard; 1,248 full load
Dimensions, feet (metres): 180.3 × 33.8 × 14.1 *(55 × 10.3 × 4.3)*
Main machinery: 1 Burmeister & Wain Alpha diesel; 1,860 hp(m) *(1.37 MW)*; 1 shaft; cp prop; bow thruster
Speed, knots: 13.5. **Range, n miles:** 10,000 at 12 kt
Complement: 58 (12 officers) + 12
Radars: Surface search: Racal Decca RMS 1230C; E/F-band.
Navigation: Racal Decca RM 914C; I-band.

Comment: Research vessel acquired from Racal Energy Resources. Equipped with side-scan sonar for route survey, Atlas Krupp deep echo sounder and Kongsberg/Simrad EA-500 deep echo sounder. Used for seismographic survey. Recommissioned 6 June 1988.

ANTARES *4/2000, Hartmut Ehlers / 0104233*

3 AMORIM DO VALLE (RIVER) CLASS (SURVEY SHIPS) (AGS)

Name	*No*	*Builders*	*Commissioned*
AMORIM DO VALLE (ex-*Humber*)	H 35 (ex-M 2007)	Richards Ltd, Lowestoft	7 June 1985
TAURUS (ex-*Helmsdale/ Jorge Leite*)	H 36 (ex-M 2010)	Richards Ltd, Lowestoft	1 Mar 1986
GARNIER SAMPAIO (ex-*Ribble*)	H 37 (ex-M-2012)	Richards, Great Yarmouth	19 Feb 1986

Displacement, tons: 770 standard; 890 full load
Dimensions, feet (metres): 156 × 34.5 × 9.5 *(47.5 × 10.5 × 2.9)*
Main machinery: 2 Ruston 6RKC diesels; 3,100 hp *(2.3 MW)* sustained; 2 shafts; cp props
Speed, knots: 14
Range, n miles: 4,500 at 10 kt
Complement: 36 (4 officers)
Radars: Navigation: 2 Racal Decca TM 1226C; I-band.

Comment: Three ships transferred from the UK on 31 January 1995. The contract was signed on 18 November 1994. Steel hulled. All minesweeping gear and the 40 mm gun removed on transfer. Used as hydrographic ships. H 35 and H 36 fitted with a stern gantry and second crane amidships for oceanographic research. Equipment includes multibeam echo-sounders. Four others of the class transferred in 1998 are listed under Patrol Forces. The class is also in service with the Bangladesh Navy.

AMORIM DO VALLE *6/1995, David Cullen / 1153035*

GARNIER SAMPAIO *6/2002, Brazilian Navy / 0529149*

1 SIRIUS CLASS (SURVEY SHIP) (AGSH)

Name	*No*	*Builders*	*Launched*	*Commissioned*
SIRIUS	H 21	Ishikawajima Co Ltd, Tokyo	30 July 1957	17 Jan 1958

Displacement, tons: 1,448 standard; 1,885 full load
Dimensions, feet (metres): 255.7 × 39.3 × 12.2 *(78 × 12.1 × 3.7)*
Main machinery: 2 Vilares-Burmeister & Wain diesels; 1,550 hp *(1.15 MW)*; 2 shafts; cp props
Speed, knots: 14. **Range, n miles:** 12,000 at 11 kt
Complement: 129 (16 officers) plus 14 scientists
Radars: Surface search: Racal Decca RMS 1230C; E/F-band.
Navigation: Furuno M 1942; E/F/I-band.
Furuno; I-band.
Helicopters: 1 Bell JetRanger or UH-12.

Comment: Laid down 1955–56. Special surveying apparatus, echo-sounders, Raydist equipment, sounding machines installed, and landing craft (LCVP), jeep, and survey launches carried. All living and working spaces are air conditioned.

SIRIUS *9/2007, Mario R V Carneiro / 1335445*

1 LIGHTHOUSE TENDER (ABUH)

Name	*No*	*Builders*	*Launched*	*Commissioned*
ALMIRANTE GRAÇA ARANHA	H 34	Ebin, Niteroi	23 May 1974	9 Sep 1976

Displacement, tons: 1,070 standard; 2,440 full load
Dimensions, feet (metres): 245.3 × 42.6 × 13.8 *(74.8 × 13 × 4.2)*
Main machinery: 1 diesel; 2,440 hp(m) *(1.8 MW)*; 1 shaft; bow thruster
Speed, knots: 14
Complement: 81 (13 officers)
Radars: Navigation: 2 Racal Decca; I-band.
Helicopters: 1 Bell JetRanger.

Comment: Laid down in 1971. Fitted with telescopic hangar, 10 ton crane, two landing craft, GP launch and two Land Rovers. Omega navigation system.

ALMIRANTE GRAÇA ARANHA *4/2000, Hartmut Ehlers / 0104234*

4 BUOY TENDERS (ABU)

Name	*No*	*Builders*	*Commissioned*
COMANDANTE VARELLA	H 18	Arsenal de Marinha, Rio de Janeiro	20 May 1982
TENENTE CASTELO	H 19	Estanave, Manaus	15 Aug 1984
COMANDANTE MANHÃES	H 20	Estanave, Manaus	15 Dec 1983
TENENTE BOANERGES	H 25	Estanave, Manaus	29 Mar 1985

Displacement, tons: 300 standard; 420 full load
Dimensions, feet (metres): 123 × 28.2 × 8.5 *(37.5 × 8.6 × 2.6)*
Main machinery: 2 MAN R8V16-18TL 8 cylinder diesels; 1,300 hp(m) *(955 kW)*; 2 shafts
Speed, knots: 12. **Range, n miles:** 2,880 at 9 kt
Complement: 22 (2 officers)
Radars: Navigation: Racal Decca TM 1226C; I-band.
Furuno; I-band.

Comment: Dual-purpose minelayers. *Comandante Varella* is based at Rio Grande, *Tenente Castelo* at São Luis, *Comandante Manhães* at Natal and *Tenente Boanerges* at Salvador.

COMANDANTE VARELLA *1/2000, van Ginderen Collection / 0104235*

1 BUOY TENDER (ABU)

FAROLEIRO MÁRIO SEIXAS (ex-*Mestre Jerânimo*) H 26

Displacement, tons: 234 standard; 294 full load
Dimensions, feet (metres): 116.4 × 21.8 × 11.8 *(35.5 × 6.6 × 3.6)*
Main machinery: 2 Scania DSI 14 MO3 diesels; 900 hp *(671 kW)*; 2 shafts
Speed, knots: 10
Complement: 19 (2 officers)
Radars: Navigation: Racal Decca RD 150; I-band.

Comment: Former fishing vessel built in Vigo, Spain. Acquired by Brazilian Navy in 1979 and rebuilt as a buoy tender. Commissioned 31 January 1984.

FAROLEIRO MÁRIO SEIXAS ***6/2002, Brazilian Navy*** / 0529148

1 RESEARCH SUPPORT VESSEL (AGS)

Name	*No*	*Builders*	*Laid down*	*Launched*	*Commissioned*
CRUZEIRO DO SUL (ex-*DSND Surveyor*)	H 38	Løngva Mek, Verksted	1 Mar 1986	1 July 1986	31 July 1986

Measurement, tons: 1,716 grt
Dimensions, feet (metres): 180.3 × 33.8 × 14.1 *(65.7 × 11.0 × 4.5)*
Main machinery: 1 Bergen KRMB-9 diesel; 1 shaft; Ulstein cp prop; 1 Ulstein forward thruster *(368 kW)*; 1 Brunvoll forward thruster *(600 kW)*; 1 Ulstein retractable azimuth thruster *(880 kW)*; 2 Ulstein bow thrusters (*552 kW* and *368 kW*)
Speed, knots: 13.5
Range, n miles: 10,000 at 12 kt
Complement: 53 (11 officers)
Radars: Surface search: Raytheon R 84; I-band.
Navigation: Raytheon R 81; I-band.

Comment: Originally built as a multirole inspection/survey vessel and converted in 1991 into a ROV support vessel. Acquired by the Brazilian Navy and commissioned on 28 February 2008. The ship is capable of performing a range of tasks including pipeline inspection, structural inspection, geophysical and geotechnical operations and other support services. The principal features of the ship include a 6-ton Hydralift crane, large survey/inspection and data processing offices, a wet and dry lab space and a photo lab. The ship has high station-keeping performance. There is a large work-deck area and a moontube for deploying survey transducers.

TRAINING SHIPS

Notes: (1) There are 10 small sail training ships.
(2) One training vessel *Braz de Aguiar* (ex-*Calha Norte*) is attached to the Naval Academy for merchant officers (CIABA) at Belém.
(3) There are three small training craft (*Rosca Fina, Voga Picada, Leva Arriba*).

1 MODIFIED NITERÓI CLASS (AXH)

Name	*No*	*Builders*	*Commissioned*
BRASIL	U 27	Arsenal de Marinha, Rio de Janeiro	21 Aug 1986

Displacement, tons: 2,548 light; 3,729 full load
Dimensions, feet (metres): 430.7 × 44.3 × 13.8 *(131.3 × 13.5 × 4.2)*
Main machinery: 2 Pielstick/Ishikawajima (Brazil) 6 PC2.5 L 400 diesels; 7,020 hp(m) *(5.17 MW)* sustained; 2 shafts
Speed, knots: 18
Range, n miles: 7,000 at 15 kt
Complement: 218 (27 officers) plus 201 midshipmen
Guns: 2 Bofors 40 mm/70. 4 saluting guns.
Countermeasures: Decoys: 2 CBV 50.8 mm flare launchers.
ESM: Racal RDL-2 ABC; radar intercept.
Weapons control: Saab Scania TVT 300 optronic director.
Radars: Surface search: Racal Decca RMS 1230C; E/F-band.
Navigation: Racal Decca TM 1226C and TMS 1230; I-band.
Helicopters: Platform for 1 Sea King.

Comment: A modification of the Vosper Thornycroft Mk 10 Frigate design ordered in June 1981. Laid down 18 September 1981, launched 23 September 1983. Designed to carry midshipmen and other trainees from the Naval and Merchant Marine Academies. Minimum electronics as required for training. There are two 51 mm launchers for flares and other illuminants.

BRASIL ***10/2008*, Kazumasa Watanabe*** / 1335452

3 NASCIMENTO CLASS (AXL)

Name	*No*	*Builders*	*Commissioned*
ASPIRANTE NASCIMENTO	U 10	Ebrasa, Santa Catarina	13 Dec 1980
GUARDA MARINHA JANSEN	U 11	Ebrasa, Santa Catarina	22 July 1981
GUARDA MARINHA BRITO	U 12	Ebrasa, Santa Catarina	22 July 1981

Displacement, tons: 108.5 standard; 136 full load
Dimensions, feet (metres): 91.8 × 21.3 × 5.9 *(28 × 6.5 × 1.8)*
Main machinery: 2 Mercedes Benz OM-352A diesels; 650 hp(m) *(484 kW)*; 2 shafts
Speed, knots: 10
Range, n miles: 700 at 10 kt
Complement: 6 (2 officers) + 10 midshipmen
Guns: 2 — 12.7 mm MGs.
Radars: Navigation: Racal Decca; I-band.

Comment: Can carry 10 trainees overnight. All of the class are attached to the Naval Academy at Rio de Janeiro.

GUARDA MARINHA JANSEN ***5/2003, A E Galarce*** / 0572425

1 SAIL TRAINING SHIP (AXS)

Name	*No*	*Builders*	*Launched*	*Commissioned*
CISNE BRANCO	U 20	Damen Shipyards, Gorinchem	4 Aug 1999	28 Feb 2000

Displacement, tons: 1,038 full load
Dimensions, feet (metres): 249.3 × 34.4 × 15.7 *(76 × 10.5 × 4.8)*
Main machinery: 1 Caterpillar 3508B DI-TA diesel; 1,015 hp(m) *(746 kW)* sustained; 1 shaft; Berg cp prop; bow thruster; 408 hp(m) *(300 kW)*
Speed, knots: 17 (sail); 11 (diesel)
Complement: 50 (10 officers) + 31 midshipmen
Radars: Navigation: Furuno FR 1510 Mk 3; I-band.

Comment: Ordered in 1998. Maximum sail area 2,195 m^2.

CISNE BRANCO ***7/2008*, Maritime Photographic*** / 1335334

AUXILIARIES

Notes: (1) There are four Rio Pardo class transport vessels (*Rio Pardo, Rio Negro, Rio Chuí* and *Rio Oiapoque*). Capable of carrying 600 passengers, they are all based at Rio de Janeiro.
(2) One Torpedo Recovery Craft, *Almirante Hess*, is based at Niteroí.
(3) Acquisition of a replenishment tanker, to replace *Marajo*, is under consideration. Options include an ex-US Navy Cimarron-class oiler.
(4) A new hospital ship, U 28, to be based at Ladário on the Paraguay River, is to enter service in 2009.

1 PARÁ CLASS (RIVER TRANSPORT SHIP) (YFB)

Name	*No*	*Builders*	*Commissioned*
PARÁ	U 15	Inconav/MacLaren, Niterói	19 Jan 2005

Displacement, tons: 1,064 standard; 1,327 full load
Dimensions, feet (metres): 184.1 × 70.2 × 13.0 *(56.1 × 21.4 × 3.97)*
Main machinery: 2 Ishibras-Daihatsu diesels; 2 shafts
Speed, knots: 10
Range, n miles: 2,380 at 10 kt
Complement: 66 (7 officers)
Guns: 4 Oerlikon 20 mm.
Radars: Navigation: Furuno 1830 and 1942; I-band.

Comment: Ex-civilian catamaran hull vessel capable of carrying 175 marines and 350 tons cargo.

1 SUBMARINE RESCUE SHIP (ASRH)

Name	*No*	*Builders*	*Commissioned*
FELINTO PERRY (ex-*Holger Dane*, ex-*Wildrake*)	K 11	Stord Verft, Norway	Dec 1979

Displacement, tons: 2,840 standard; 4,107 full load
Dimensions, feet (metres): 256.6 × 57.4 × 15.1 *(78.2 × 17.5 × 4.6)*
Main machinery: Diesel-electric; 2 BMK KVG B12 and 2 KVG B16 diesels; 11,400 hp(m) *(8.4 MW)*; 2 Daimler-Benz motors; 7,000 hp(m) *(5.15 MW)*; 2 shafts; cp props; 2 bow thrusters; 2 stern thrusters
Speed, knots: 14.5
Complement: 65 (9 officers)
Radars: Navigation: 2 Raytheon; I-band.
Helicopters: Platform only.

Comment: Former oilfield support ship acquired 28 December 1988. Has an octagonal heliport (62.5 ft diameter) above the bridge. Equipped with a moonpool for saturation diving, and rescue and recompression chambers as the submarine rescue ship. A DeepOcean Phantom DS4 ROV, capable of operating to 610 m, is also carried. Dynamic positioning system. Based at Niteroi, Rio de Janeiro.

FELINTO PERRY *2/2003, Mario R V Carneiro* / 0569152

1 BARROSO PEREIRA CLASS (TRANSPORT) (AKSH)

Name	*No*	*Builders*	*Commissioned*
ARY PARREIRAS	G 21	Ishikawajima, Tokyo	6 Mar 1957

Displacement, tons: 5,820 standard; 9,464 full load
Measurement, tons: 4,200 dwt; 4,879 gross (Panama)
Dimensions, feet (metres): 362 pp; 391.8 oa × 52.5 × 20.5 *(110.4; 119.5 × 16 × 6.3)*
Main machinery: 2 Ishikawajima boilers and turbines; 4,800 hp(m) *(3.53 MW)*; 2 shafts
Speed, knots: 15
Complement: 127 (15 officers)
Military lift: 1,972 troops (overload); 497 troops (normal)
Cargo capacity: 425 m³ refrigerated cargo space; 4,000 tons
Guns: 2—3 in *(76 mm)* Mk 33; 50 rds/min to 12.8 km *(6.9 n miles)* anti-aircraft; weight of shell 6 kg.
2 or 4 Oerlikon 20 mm.
Radars: Navigation: 2 Racal Decca; I-band.
Helicopters: Platform for one medium.

Comment: Transport and cargo vessel. Helicopter landing platform aft. Medical, hospital and dental facilities. Working and living quarters are mechanically ventilated with partial air conditioning. Refrigerated cargo space 15,500 cu ft. Operates commercially from time to time. Likely to be decommissioned in 2009, having been replaced in the transport role by *Garcia d'Ávila*.

ARY PARREIRAS *2/2006, Marco Ghiglino* / 1167120

1 RIVER TRANSPORT SHIP (AP)

Name	*No*	*Builders*	*Commissioned*
PARAGUASSÚ (ex-*Garapuava*)	G 15	Amsterdam Drydock	1951

Displacement, tons: 200 standard; 285 full load
Dimensions, feet (metres): 131.2 × 23 × 4.9 *(40 × 7 × 1.5)*
Main machinery: 3 diesels; 2,505 hp(m) *(1.84 MW)*; 1 shaft
Speed, knots: 13
Range, n miles: 2,500 at 10 kt
Complement: 35 (4 officers)
Military lift: 178 troops
Guns: 6—7.62 mm MGs.
Radars: Furuno 3600; I-band.

Comment: Passenger ship converted into a troop carrier in 1957 and acquired on 20 June 1972.

PARAGUASSÚ *5/2000, Hartmut Ehlers* / 0104240

1 RIVER TRANSPORT (YFBH)

Name	*No*	*Builders*	*Commissioned*
PIRAIM (ex-*Guaicuru*)	U 29	Estaleiro SNBP, Mato Grosso	10 Mar 1982

Displacement, tons: 73.3 standard; 91.5 full load
Dimensions, feet (metres): 82.0 × 18.0 × 3.2 *(25.0 × 5.5 × 0.97)*
Main machinery: 2 MWM diesels; 400 hp(m) *(294 kW)*; 2 shafts
Speed, knots: 7. **Range, n miles:** 700 at 7 kt
Complement: 17 (2 officers)
Guns: 4—7.62 mm MG.
Radars: Navigation: Furuno 3600; I-band.
Helicopters: Platform for UH-12.

Comment: Used as a logistics support ship for the Mato Grosso Flotilla. Can carry two platoons of marines and two rigid inflatable boats.

PIRAIM *6/1998, Brazilian Navy* / 0017635

2 HOSPITAL SHIPS (AHH)

Name	*No*	*Builders*	*Commissioned*
OSWALDO CRUZ	U 18	Arsenal de Marinha, Rio de Janeiro	29 May 1984
CARLOS CHAGAS	U 19	Arsenal de Marinha, Rio de Janeiro	7 Dec 1984

Displacement, tons: 360 standard; 490 full load
Dimensions, feet (metres): 154.2 × 26.9 × 5.9 *(47.2 × 8.5 × 1.8)*
Main machinery: 2 Volvo diesels; 714 hp(m) *(525 kW)*; 2 shafts
Speed, knots: 17. **Range, n miles:** 4,000 at 12 kt
Complement: 25 (4 officers) plus 21 medical (6 doctors/dentists)
Radars: Navigation: Racal Decca; I-band.
Helicopters: Platform for 1 UH-12/13 Esquilo.

Comment: *Oswaldo Cruz* launched 11 July 1983, and *Carlos Chagas* 16 April 1984. Has two sick bays, dental surgery, a laboratory, two clinics and X-ray centre. The design is a development of the Roraima class with which they operate in the Amazon Flotilla. Since 1992 both ships painted grey with dark green crosses on the hull.

OSWALDO CRUZ *6/2004, Brazilian Navy* / 1044086

1 HOSPITAL SHIP (AH)

Name	*No*	*Builders*	*Commissioned*
DOUTOR MONTENEGRO	U 16	CONAVE Shipyard, Manaus	17 May 2000

Displacement, tons: 300 standard; 347 full load
Dimensions, feet (metres): 134.5 × 36 × 7.9 *(41.0 × 11 × 2.4)*
Main machinery: 2 Cummins NT 855M diesels; 720 hp *(537 kW)*; 2 shafts
Speed, knots: 5
Complement: 50 (8 officers) plus 11 (8 doctors/dentists)
Radars: Navigation: Furuno 1942 Mk 2.

Comment: U 16 was built in January 1997 and belonged to the government of the Acre state before transfer to the Brazilian Navy. The ship has two wards, a pediatric ICU, an operating theatre, an X-ray room, a dentist office, a lab for clinical analysis, a trauma room and a pharmacy.

DOUTOR MONTENEGRO *6/2007, Brazilian Navy* / 1170088

1 REPLENISHMENT TANKER (AOR)

Name	*No*	*Builders*	*Commissioned*
ALMIRANTE GASTÃO MOTTA	G 23	Ishibras, Rio de Janeiro	26 Nov 1991

Displacement, tons: 4,471 standard; 10,320 full load
Dimensions, feet (metres): 442.9 × 62.3 × 24.6 *(135 × 19 × 7.5)*
Main machinery: Diesel-electric; 2 Wärtsilä 12V32 diesel generators; 11,700 hp(m) *(8.57 MW)* sustained; 1 motor; 1 shaft; Kamewa cp prop
Speed, knots: 20
Range, n miles: 9,000 at 15 kt
Complement: 121 (13 officers) + 12 spare
Cargo capacity: 5,920 tons dieso; 950 tons JP-5; 200 tons dry
Guns: 2—12.7 mm MGs.
Radars: 2 unknown; I-band.

Comment: Ordered March 1987. Laid down 11 December 1989 and launched 1 June 1990. Fitted for abeam and stern refuelling.

ALMIRANTE GASTÂO MOTTA *9/2007, Mario R V Carneiro* / 1335450

1 REPLENISHMENT TANKER (AOR)

Name	*No*	*Builders*	*Launched*	*Commissioned*
MARAJO	G 27	Ishikawajima do Brasil	31 Jan 1968	8 Jan 1969

Displacement, tons: 7,500 standard; 15,110 full load
Dimensions, feet (metres): 440.7 × 63.3 × 24 *(134.4 × 19.3 × 7.3)*
Main machinery: 1 Sulzer GRD 68 diesel; 8,000 hp(m) *(5.88 MW)*; 1 shaft
Speed, knots: 13
Range, n miles: 9,200 at 13 kt
Complement: 80 (13 officers)
Cargo capacity: 7,470 tons fuel
Radars: Surface search: Racal Decca TM 1226C; I-band.
Navigation: Racal Decca BT 503; I-band.

Comment: Fitted for abeam replenishment with two stations on each side. Was to have been replaced by *Gastão Motta* but is to be retained in service until 2009.

MARAJO *1/1999* / 0056623

1 RIVER TENDER (AG)

Name	*No*	*Builders*	*Commissioned*
POTENGI	G 17	Papendrecht, Netherlands	28 June 1938

Displacement, tons: 150 standard; 594 full load
Dimensions, feet (metres): 178.8 × 24.5 × 6 *(54.5 × 7.5 × 1.8)*
Main machinery: 2 Krohout diesels; 550 hp(m) *(404 kW)*; 2 shafts
Speed, knots: 10
Range, n miles: 600 at 8 kt
Complement: 19 (2 officers)
Cargo capacity: 460 tons of general cargo including fuel, frozen and dry stores
Guns: 4—7.62 mm MGs.
Radars: Furuno 3600; I-band.

Comment: Launched 16 March 1938. Employed in the Mato Grosso Flotilla on river service. Converted to logistic support ship and recommissioned 6 May 1999.

POTENGI *5/2000, Hartmut Ehlers* / 0104241

4 FLOATING DOCKS

CIDADE DE NATAL (ex-G 27, ex-AFDL 39)
ALMIRANTE SCHIECK
ALFONSO PENA (ex-ARD 14)
ALMIRANTE JERONIMO GONÇALVES (ex-G 26, ex-Goiaz AFDL 4)

Comment: The first two are floating docks loaned to Brazil by US Navy in the mid-1960s and purchased 11 February 1980. Ship lifts of 2,800 tons and 1,000 tons respectively. *Cidade de Natal* based at Natal and *Almirante Jeronimo Gonçalves* at Manaus. *Almirante Schieck* of 3,600 tons displacement was built by Arsenal de Marinha, Rio de Janeiro and commissioned 12 October 1989. *Alfonso Pena* acquired from US and based at Val-de-Caes (Para).

TUGS

Notes: (1) In addition to the vessels listed below there are eight harbour tugs: *Comandante Marroig* (BNRJ 03), *Comandante Didier* (BNRJ 04), *Tenente Magalhães* (BNA 06), *Cabo Schram* (BNVC 01), *Intrépido* (BNRJ 16), *Arrojado* (BNRJ 17), *Valente* (BNRJ 18) and *Impávido* (BNRJ 19).
(2) There are plans to procure six ocean tugs from 2009–22. These are also to serve as offshore patrol ships.

2 ALMIRANTE GUILHEM CLASS (FLEET OCEAN TUGS) (ATF)

Name	*No*	*Builders*	*Commissioned*
ALMIRANTE GUILHEM (ex-*Superpesa 4*)	R 24	Sumitomo, Uraga	1976
ALMIRANTE GUILLOBEL (ex-*Superpesa 5*)	R 25	Sumitomo, Uraga	1976

Displacement, tons: 2,393 standard; 2,735 full load
Dimensions, feet (metres): 207 × 44 × 14.8 *(63.2 × 13.4 × 4.5)*
Main machinery: 2 GM EMD 20-645F7B diesels; 7,120 hp *(5.31 MW)* sustained; 2 shafts; cp props; bow thruster
Speed, knots: 14
Range, n miles: 10,000 at 13 kt
Complement: 40 (4 officers)
Guns: 2 Oerlikon 20 mm (not always carried)
Radars: Racal Decca; I-band. Furuno; I-band.

Comment: Originally built as civilian tugs. Bollard pull, 84 tons. Commissioned into the Navy 22 January 1981.

ALMIRANTE GUILLOBEL *5/2003, A E Galarce* / 0572426

3 TRITÃO CLASS (FLEET OCEAN TUGS) (ATA)

Name	*No*	*Builders*	*Commissioned*
TRITÃO (ex-*Sarandi*)	R 21	Estanave, Manaus	19 Feb 1987
TRIDENTE (ex-*Sambaiba*)	R 22	Estanave, Manaus	8 Oct 1987
TRIUNFO (ex-*Sorocaba*)	R 23	Estanave, Manaus	5 July 1986

Displacement, tons: 819 standard; 1,680 full load
Dimensions, feet (metres): 181.8 × 38.1 × 11.2 *(55.4 × 11.6 × 3.4)*
Main machinery: 2 Vilares-Burmeister and Wain Alpha diesels; 2,480 hp(m) *(1.82 MW)*; 2 shafts; bow thruster
Speed, knots: 13
Complement: 44 (6 officers)
Guns: 2 Oerlikon 20 mm.
Radars: Navigation: 1 Racal Decca; I-band. 2 Furuno; I-band.

Comment: Offshore supply vessels acquired from National Oil Company of Brazil and converted for naval use. Assumed names of previous three ships of Sotoyomo class. Fitted to act both as tugs and patrol vessels. Bollard pull, 23.5 tons. Firefighting capability. Endurance, 45 days.

TRIDENTE *10/2004, A E Galarce* / 1153016

British Indian Ocean Territory

Country Overview

The British Indian Ocean Territory was established as a British dependency in 1965 and is administered by a Commissioner and Administrator who reside in the UK. Situated in the Indian Ocean, halfway between Africa and Indonesia, the territory comprises six atolls of the Chagos Archipelago which consist of the order of 1,000 uninhabited islands. The largest island is Diego Garcia (17 square miles) which was leased to the United States in 1971 in order to build an air and naval base. Adjacent to the small military port, the lagoon provides a protected anchorage for US pre-positioned forces while the island is also home to a number of communications and space-related facilities. Exclusively occupied by military (largely US) forces and contractors, the base includes a small British garrison, whose commanding officer represents the Commissioner. Territorial waters (12 n miles) are claimed as is a 200 n mile fishery zone.

PATROL FORCES

1 FISHERY PATROL SHIP (PSO)

PACIFIC MARLIN (ex-*Bigorange XI*)

Measurement, tons: 1,200 grt
Dimensions, feet (metres): 189.3 × 40.0 × 12.5 *(57.7 × 12.2 × 3.8)*
Main machinery: 2 Yanmar G250-E diesels; 2,600 hp *(1.9 MW)*; 2 shafts; 1 Kamome TF30DLN bow thruster; 300 hp *(225 kW)*
Speed, knots: 12.5
Complement: 20 (accommodation for 33)
Radars: Surface search/navigation: JRC JMA-3210; I-band.

Comment: Former Production Testing Vessel built by Teraoka Zosen, Japan in 1978. Converted for fishery protection duties and chartered from Swire Pacific Offshore until December 2009. Equipped with 32 ton deck crane and two fast rescue craft. Steel construction.

PACIFIC MARLIN
6/2008*, Swire Pacific Offshore
1336058

Brunei

ANGKATAN TENTERA LAUT DIRAJA BRUNEI

Country Overview

Formerly a British dependency, the Nation of Brunei is a sultanate that gained full independence in 1984. Situated on the northern coast of the island of Borneo, the country has a total area of 2,226 square miles and is bordered and divided into two halves by the Malaysian state of Sarawak. It has an 87 n mile coastline with the South China Sea. The capital and largest town is Bandar Seri Begawan which also has port facilities. There are further ports at Kuala Belait and Muara. Territorial seas (3 n miles) and an EEZ (200 n mile) are claimed.

Headquarters Appointments

Commander of the Navy:
Colonel Abd Halim bin Haji Mohd Hanifah
Fleet Commander:
Lieutenant Haji Aznan bin Haji Julaihi

Personnel

(a) 2009: 747 (58 officers)
(b) Voluntary service

Bases

Muara

Prefix to Ships' Names

KDB (Kapal Di-Raja Brunei)

CORVETTES

NAKHODA RAGAM (on trials)

6/2002, H M Steele / 0533228

3 BRUNEI CLASS (FSGH)

Name	*No*	*Builders*	*Laid down*	*Launched*
NAKHODA RAGAM	28	BAE System Marine (Scotstoun)	16 Mar 1999	13 Jan 2001
BENDAHARA SAKAM	29	BAE System Marine (Scotstoun)	15 Nov 1999	23 June 2001
JERAMBAK	30	BAE System Marine (Scotstoun)	5 Apr 2000	22 June 2002

Displacement, tons: 1,940 full load
Dimensions, feet (metres): 311.7 oa; 294.9 wl × 42 × 11.8 *(95; 89.9 × 12.8 × 3.6)*
Main machinery: CODAD; 4 MAN 20 RK270 diesels; 2 shafts; cp props
Speed, knots: 30. **Range, n miles:** 5,000 at 12 kt
Complement: 79 plus 24 spare

Missiles: SSM: 8 MBDA Exocet MM 40 Block II ❶; active radar homing to 70 km *(40 n miles)* at 0.9 Mach.
SAM: BAe 16 cell VLS ❷. BAe Sea Wolf; Command Line Of Sight (CLOS) radar/TV tracking to 6 km *(3.3 n miles)* at 2.5 Mach; warhead 14 kg; 16 missiles.
Guns: Otobreda 76 mm Super Rapid ❸. 120 rds/min to 16 km *(8.7 n miles)*; weight of shell 6 kg.
2 MSI 30 mm/75. 650 rds/min to 10 km *(5.4 n miles)* ❹.
Torpedoes: 6 Marconi 324 mm (2 triple) tubes ❺.
Countermeasures: Decoys: 2 Super Barricade chaff launchers ❻.
ECM: Thales Scorpion; jammer.
ESM: Thales Cutlass 242; intercept.
CESM: Falcon DS 300; intercept.
Combat data systems: Nautis Mk 2 with Link Y.
Weapons control: Radamec 2500 optronic director ❼.
Radars: Air/surface search: Plessey AWS 9 ❽; E/F-band.
Surface search: Kelvin Hughes 1007 ❾; I-band.
Fire control: 2 Marconi 1802 ❿; I/J-band.

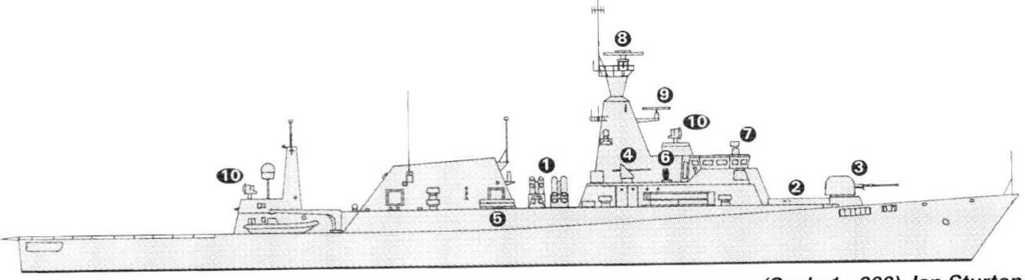

NAKHODA RAGAM *(Scale 1 : 900), Ian Sturton* / 0526842

Sonars: Thomson Marconi 4130C1; hull mounted.

Helicopters: Platform for 1 medium.

Programmes: Tenders requested on 28 April 1995. Yarrow Shipbuilders selected in August 1995. Detailed design done in 1996 with final contract signed 14 January 1998. Long-term support contract signed with BAE Systems in May 2002.
Structure: Scaled down version of Malaysian Lekiu class. Facilities to land and refuel S-70A and Bell 212 helicopters.

Operational: Sea trials of first of class began in January 2002. Training for all three crews provided by Flagship Training. *Jerambak* conducted acceptance trials in late 2004. Following settlement of a contractural dispute between the Brunei Procurement Agency and BAE Systems in early 2007, the Brunei government took formal possession of the vessels. Plans to commission the ships into naval service have been cancelled and it is planned to sell them to another navy. Meanwhile the ships remain under care and maintenance at Barrow.

BENDAHARA SAKAM *4/2004, John Brodie* / 1044352

PATROL FORCES

Notes: (1) There are also up to 15 Rigid Raider assault boats operated by the River Division for infantry battalions. These boats are armed with 1 — 7.62 mm MG.
(2) Plans to acquire new patrol craft have been reported.

3 WASPADA CLASS (FAST ATTACK CRAFT — MISSILE) (PTG)

Name	*No*	*Builders*	*Launched*	*Commissioned*
WASPADA	P 02	Vosper (Singapore)	3 Aug 1977	2 Aug 1978
PEJUANG	P 03	Vosper (Singapore)	15 Mar 1978	25 Mar 1979
SETERIA	P 04	Vosper (Singapore)	22 June 1978	22 June 1979

Displacement, tons: 206 full load
Dimensions, feet (metres): 121 × 23.5 × 6 *(36.9 × 7.2 × 1.8)*
Main machinery: 2 MTU 20V 538 TB91 diesels; 7,680 hp(m) *(5.63 MW)* sustained; 2 shafts
Speed, knots: 32
Range, n miles: 1,200 at 14 kt
Complement: 24 (4 officers)

Missiles: SSM: 2 Aerospatiale MM 38 Exocet; inertial cruise; active radar homing to 42 km *(23 n miles)* at 0.9 Mach; warhead 165 kg.
Guns: 2 Oerlikon 30 mm GCM-B01 (twin); 650 rds/min to 10 km *(5.5 n miles)*; weight of shell 1 kg.
2 — 7.62 mm MGs. 2 MOD(N) 2 in launchers for illuminants.
Countermeasures: ESM: Decca RDL; radar warning.
Weapons control: Sea Archer system with Sperry Co-ordinate Calculator and 1412A digital computer. Radamec 2500 optronic director.
Radars: Surface search: Kelvin Hughes Type 1007; I-band.

Modernisation: Started in 1988 and included improved gun fire control and ESM equipment. Further improvements in 1998–2000 included Type 1007 radar and a Radamec 2500 optronic director.
Structure: Welded steel hull with aluminium alloy superstructure. *Waspada* has an enclosed upper bridge for training purposes.
Operational: Reported active. All three vessels took part in Exercise Rajawali, in September 2006, during which MM 38 Exocet were fired.

SETERIA *6/2005* / 1167118

PEJUANG *7/2000* / 0104244

3 PERWIRA CLASS (COASTAL PATROL CRAFT) (PB)

Name	*No*	*Builders*	*Launched*	*Commissioned*
PERWIRA	P 14	Vosper (Singapore)	5 May 1974	9 Sep 1974
PEMBURU	P 15	Vosper (Singapore)	30 Jan 1975	17 June 1975
PENYERANG	P 16	Vosper (Singapore)	20 Mar 1975	24 June 1975

Displacement, tons: 38 full load
Dimensions, feet (metres): 71 × 20 × 5 *(21.7 × 6.1 × 1.2)*
Main machinery: 2 MTU MB 12V 331 TC81 diesels; 2,450 hp(m) *(1.8 MW)* sustained; 2 shafts
Speed, knots: 32. **Range, n miles:** 600 at 22 kt; 1,000 at 16 kt
Complement: 14 (2 officers)
Guns: 2 Oerlikon/BMARC 20 mm GAM-BO1; 800 rds/min to 2 km; weight of shell 0.24 kg. 2—7.62 mm MGs.
Radars: Surface search: Racal Decca RM 1290; I-band.

Comment: Of all-wooden construction on laminated frames. Fitted with enclosed bridges-modified July 1976. A high speed RIB is launched from a stern ramp. New guns fitted in mid-1980s. All three ships operational.

PEMBURU *6/2005* / 1167117

LAND-BASED MARITIME AIRCRAFT

Notes: (1) There are also six BO-105, four S-70A and ten Bell 212 utility helicopters.
(2) The requirement for maritime patrol aircraft was to have been met by three CN-235 MPA but these were not acquired. A decision on the way-ahead is awaited.

AUXILIARIES

2 TERABAN CLASS (LCU)

Name	*No*	*Builders*	*Commissioned*
TERABAN	33	Transfield, Perth	8 Nov 1996
SERASA	34	Transfield, Perth	8 Nov 1996

Displacement, tons: 220 full load
Dimensions, feet (metres): 119.8 × 26.2 × 4.9 *(36.5 × 8 × 1.5)*
Main machinery: 2 diesels; 2 shafts
Speed, knots: 12
Complement: 12
Military lift: 100 tons
Radars: Navigation: Racal; I-band.

Comment: Ordered in November 1995 and delivered in December 1996. Used as utility transports. Bow and side ramps are fitted. Reported active.

SERASA *6/2005* / 1167116

2 CHEVERTON LOADMASTERS (YFU)

Name	*No*	*Builders*	*Commissioned*
DAMUAN	L 31	Cheverton Ltd, Isle of Wight	May 1976
PUNI	L 32	Cheverton Ltd, Isle of Wight	Feb 1977

Displacement, tons: 60; 64 *(Puni)* standard
Dimensions, feet (metres): 65 × 20 × 3.6 *(19.8 × 6.1 × 1.1)* (length 74.8 *(22.8) Puni*)
Main machinery: 2 Detroit 6-71 diesels; 442 hp *(305 kW)* sustained; 2 shafts
Speed, knots: 9. **Range, n miles:** 1,000 at 9 kt
Complement: 8
Military lift: 32 tons
Radars: Navigation: Racal Decca RM 1216; I-band

DAMUAN *6/2005* / 1167115

POLICE

Notes: In addition to the vessels listed below there are two 12 m Rotork type *Behagia* 07 and *Selamat* 10 and four River Patrol Craft *Aman* 01, *Damai* 02, *Sentosa* 04 and *Sejahtera* 06.

7 INSHORE PATROL CRAFT

PDB 11–15 **PDB 63** **PDB 68**

Displacement, tons: 20 full load
Dimensions, feet (metres): 47.7 × 13.9 × 3.9 *(14.5 × 4.2 × 1.2)*
Main machinery: 2 MAN D 2840 LE diesels; 1,040 hp(m) *(764 kW)* sustained; 2 shafts
Speed, knots: 30. **Range, n miles:** 310 at 22 kt
Complement: 7
Guns: 1—7.62 mm MG.
Radars: Surface search: Furuno; I-band.

Comment: Built by Singapore SBEC. First three handed over in October 1987, second pair in 1988, last two in 1996. Aluminium hulls.

PDB 15 *3/1999, John Webber* / 0056631

3 BENDEHARU CLASS (PB)

BENDEHARU P 21 **MAHARAJALELA** P 22 **KEMAINDERA** P 23

Displacement, tons: 68 full load
Dimensions, feet (metres): 93.5 × 17.8 × 5.6 *(28.5 × 5.4 × 1.7)*
Main machinery: 2 MTU diesels; 2,260 hp *(1.7 MW)*; 2 shafts
Speed, knots: 29
Guns: 1—12.7 mm MG.
Radars: Navigation: I-band.

Comment: Constructed by PT Pal, Surabaya, and entered service in 1991.

Bulgaria

VOENNOMORSKI SILI

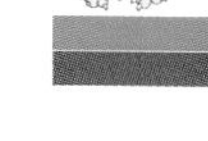

Country Overview

Situated in the Balkan Peninsula, the Republic of Bulgaria has an area of 42,823 square miles and is bordered to the north by Romania and to the south by Turkey and Greece. The River Danube forms much of the northern border. Bulgaria has a coastline of 191 n miles with the Black Sea on which Varna and Burgas are the principal ports. The capital is Sofia. Territorial waters (12 n miles) are claimed. An Exclusive Economic Zone (EEZ) was declared in 1987 but the precise limits have yet to be fully agreed and defined.

Headquarters Appointments

Commander of the Navy and Chief of Staff:
Rear Admiral Minko Slavov Kavaldzhiev

Diplomatic Representation

Defence Attaché, London:
Rear Admiral P I Manushev

Organisation

Four squadrons: Submarine, Surface, MCMV and Auxiliary, with Headquarters at Varna and Burgas. There is also a Border Guard Unit.

Personnel

(a) 2009: 4,140 (695 officers)
(b) Reserves 10,000

Bases

North Zone: HQ, Naval Base, Air Station and Higher Naval School (Nikola Yonkov Vaptsarov) at Varna.
South Zone: Burgas (HQ) and Atiya (naval base).
Danube: Vidin (naval base).

Coast Defence

One battalion with six truck-mounted SS-C-3 Styx twin launchers. Two Army regiments of coastal artillery with 100 mm and 130 mm guns. A coastal surveillance system, EKRAN, is planned to become operational in 2012.

DELETIONS

Submarines

2007 *Slava*

Corvettes

2006 *Letyashti, Bditelni, Bezstrashni, Khrabri*

Amphibious Forces

2006 Vydra 205

SUBMARINES

Notes: Procurement of two second-hand submarines from a NATO country is reported to be under consideration.

FRIGATES

1 KONI CLASS (PROJECT 1159) (FFLM)

SMELI (ex-*Delfin*) 11

Displacement, tons: 1,440 standard; 1,900 full load
Dimensions, feet (metres): 316.3 × 41.3 × 11.5 *(96.4 × 12.6 × 3.5)*
Main machinery: CODAG; 1 SGW, Nikolayev M8B gas turbine (centre shaft); 18,000 hp(m) *(13.25 MW)* sustained; 2 Russki B-68 diesels; 15,820 hp(m) *(11.63 MW)* sustained; 3 shafts
Speed, knots: 27 gas; 22 diesel
Range, n miles: 1,800 at 14 kt
Complement: 110

Missiles: SAM: SA-N-4 Gecko twin launcher ❶; semi-active radar homing to 15 km *(8 n miles)* at 2.5 Mach; warhead 50 kg; altitude 9.1-3,048 m *(30-10,000 ft)*; 20 missiles.
Guns: 4—3 in *(76 mm)*/59 AK 726 (2 twin) ❷; 90 rds/min to 15 km *(8 n miles)*; weight of shell 5.9 kg.
4—30 mm/65 (2 twin) ❸; 500 rds/min to 5 km *(2.7 n miles)*; weight of shell 0.54 kg.
A/S mortars: 2 RBU 6000 12-tubed trainable ❹; range 6,000 m; warhead 31 kg.
Depth charges: 2 racks.
Mines: Capacity for 22.

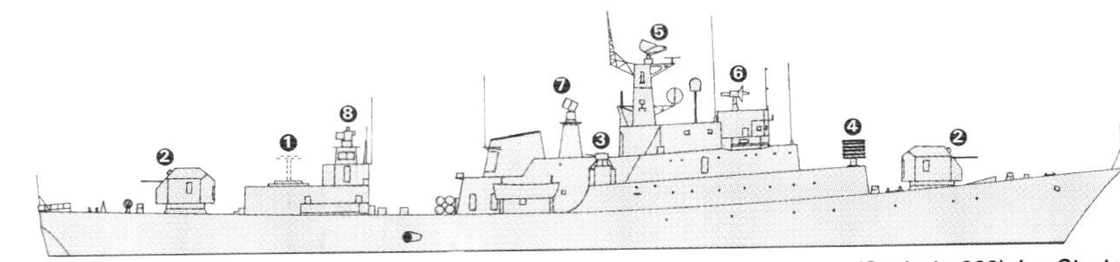

SMELI *(Scale 1 : 900), Ian Sturton* / 0114505

Countermeasures: Decoys: 2 PK 16 chaff launchers.
ESM: 2 Watch Dog; radar warning.
Radars: Air search: Strut Curve ❺; F-band; range 110 km *(60 n miles)* for 2 m² target.
Surface search: Don 2; I-band.
Fire control: Hawk Screech ❻; I-band (for 76 mm). Drum Tilt ❼; H/I-band (for 30 mm). Pop Group ❽; F/H/I-band (for SA-N-4).
IFF: High Pole B.
Sonars: Hercules (MG 322); hull-mounted; active search and attack; medium frequency.

Programmes: First reported in the Black Sea in 1976. Type I retained by the USSR for training foreign crews but transferred in February 1990 when the Koni programme terminated. Others of the class acquired by the former East German Navy (now deleted), Serbia (deleted but for sale), Algeria, Cuba (deleted) and Libya.
Modernisation: Marisat fitted in 1996. Reported to be RAS capable. Communications upgrade planned to achieve NATO interoperability.
Operational: Based at Varna. Decommissioning was expected when *Drazki* entered service but remains operational.

SMELI *6/2004, C D Yaylali* / 0587693

3 WIELINGEN CLASS (TYPE E-71) (FFGM)

Name	*No*	*Builders*	*Laid down*	*Launched*	*Commissioned*
DRAZKI (ex-*Wandelaar*)	41 (ex-F 912)	Boelwerf, Temse	28 Mar 1975	21 June 1977	27 Oct 1978
VERNI (ex-*Wielingen*)	42 (ex-F 910)	Boelwerf, Temse	5 Mar 1974	30 Mar 1976	20 Jan 1978
GORDI (ex-*Westdiep*)	43 (ex-F 911)	Cockerill, Hoboken	2 Sep 1974	8 Dec 1975	20 Jan 1978

Displacement, tons: 1,940 light; 2,430 full load
Dimensions, feet (metres): 349 × 40.3 × 18.4 *(106.4 × 12.3 × 5.6)*
Main machinery: CODOG; 1 RR Olympus TM3B gas-turbine; 25,440 hp *(19 MW)* sustained; 2 Cockerill 240 CO V 12 diesels; 6,000 hp(m) *(4.4 MW)*; 2 shafts; LIPS cp props
Speed, knots: 26; 15 on 1 diesel; 20 on 2 diesels
Range, n miles: 4,500 at 18 kt; 6,000 at 15 kt
Complement: 159 (13 officers)

Missiles: SSM: 4 Aerospatiale MM 38 (2 twin) launchers ❶; inertial cruise; active radar homing to 42 km *(23 n miles)* at 0.9 Mach; warhead 165 kg; sea-skimmer.
SAM: Raytheon Sea Sparrow RIM-7P; Mk 29 octuple launcher ❷; semi-active radar homing to 16 km *(8.5 n miles)* at 2.5 Mach; warhead 38 kg.
Guns: 1 Creusot-Loire 3.9 in *(100 mm)*/55 Mod 68 ❸; 80 rds/min to 17 km *(9 n miles)* anti-surface; 8 km *(4.4 n miles)* anti-aircraft; weight of shell 13.5 kg.
Torpedoes: 2—21 in *(533 mm)* launchers. ECAN L5 Mod 4; anti-submarine; active/passive homing to 9.5 km *(5 n miles)* at 35 kt; warhead 150 kg; depth to 550 m *(1,800 ft)*.
A/S mortars: 1 Creusot-Loire 375 mm 6-barrelled trainable launcher ❹; Bofors rockets to 1,600 m; warhead 107 kg.
Countermeasures: Decoys: 2 Tracor MBA SRBOC 6-barrelled Mk 36 launchers; chaff (Mk 214 Seagnat) and IR flares to 4 km *(2.2 n miles)*. Nixie SLQ-25; towed anti-torpedo decoy.
ESM: Argos AR 900; intercept.
Combat data systems: Signaal SEWACO IV action data automation; Link 11. SATCOM.

DRAZKI *(Scale 1 : 900), Ian Sturton* / 1164332

Weapons control: Sagem Vigy 105 optronic director ❺.
Radars: Air/surface search: Signaal DA05 ❻; E/F-band.
Surface search/fire control: Signaal WM25 ❼; I/J-band.
Navigation: Signaal Scout; I/J band.
IFF: Mk XII.
Sonars: Computing Devices Canada SQS 510; hull-mounted; active search and attack; medium frequency.

Programmes: A compact, well-armed class of frigate originally designed by and for the Belgian Navy. Following the signature of a letter of intent on 4 December 2004, the Bulgarian government gave final approval on 17 March 2005 for transfer of ex-*Wandelaar* to Bulgarian service in October 2005. The procurement of ex-*Westdiep* and ex-*Wielingen* was confirmed on 7 December 2007. Ex-*Westdiep* transferred on 22 August 2008 and ex-*Wielingen* in February 2009.
Modernisation: The ship completed a major upgrade programme before leaving Belgian service. This included update of Sea Sparrow to 7P, modification of WM25 radar to include improved ECCM and MTI capabilities and a new navigation radar and sonar. A new optronic director, IFF and communications facilities were also installed. Platform improvements included new diesel engines and alternators.
Structure: Fully air conditioned. Fin stabilisers fitted.
Operational: The ships are used for surveillance missions in the Black Sea, maritime interdiction and contributions to international peace-support operations, both under the NATO flag and as part of the Black Sea Naval Co-operation Task Group (BLACKSEAFOR).

GORDI *8/2008*, Guy Toremans* / 1335245

CORVETTES

1 TARANTUL II CLASS (PROJECT 1241.1M) (FSGM)

MULNAYA 43 (ex-101)

Displacement, tons: 385 standard; 455 full load
Dimensions, feet (metres): 184.1 × 37.7 × 8.2 *(56.1 × 11.5 × 2.5)*
Main machinery: COGAG; 2 Nikolayev Type DR 77 gas turbines; 16,016 hp(m) *(11.77 MW)* sustained; 2 Nikolayev Type DR 76 gas turbines with reversible gearboxes; 4,993 hp(m) *(3.67 MW)* sustained; 2 shafts
Speed, knots: 36 on 4 turbines
Range, n miles: 400 at 36 kt; 2,000 at 20 kt
Complement: 34 (5 officers)

Missiles: SSM: 4 Raduga SS-N-2C Styx (2 twin) launchers; active radar or IR homing to 83 km *(45 n miles)* at 0.9 Mach; warhead 513 kg; sea-skimmer.
SAM: SA-N-5 Grail quad launcher; manual aiming; IR homing to 6 km *(3.2 n miles)* at 1.5 Mach; altitude to 2,500 m *(8,000 ft)*; warhead 1.5 kg.
Guns: 1—3 in *(76 mm)*/59 AK 176; 120 rds/min to 15 km *(8.1 n miles)*; weight of shell 5.9 kg.
2—30 mm/65; 6 barrels per mounting; 3,000 rds/min to 2 km.
Countermeasures: Decoys: 2 PK 16 chaff launchers.
ESM: 2 Half Hat; intercept.
Weapons control: Hood Wink optronic director. Band Stand datalink for SSM.
Radars: Air/surface search: Plank Shave; E-band.
Navigation: Kivach; I-band.
Fire control: Bass Tilt; H/I-band.
Band Stand (Mineral ME); D-band (for SSN 2C).
IFF: Square Head. High Pole.

Comment: Built at Volodarski, Rybinsk. Transferred from USSR in December 1989. Name means Thunderbolt. Based at Atiya.

MULNAYA (old number) *7/2000, van Ginderen Collection* / 0104245

2 RESHITELNI (PAUK I) (PROJECT 1241P) CLASS (FSM)

RESHITELNI 13 **BODRI** 14

Displacement, tons: 440 full load
Dimensions, feet (metres): 195.2 × 33.5 × 10.8 *(59.5 × 10.2 × 3.3)*
Main machinery: 2 Type 521 diesels; 16,180 hp(m) *(11.9 MW)* sustained; 2 shafts
Speed, knots: 32
Range, n miles: 2,200 at 14 kt
Complement: 38

Missiles: SAM: SA-N-5 Grail quad launcher; manual aiming; IR homing to 6 km *(3.2 n miles)* at 1.5 Mach; altitude to 2,500 m *(8,000 ft)*; warhead 1.5 kg; 8 missiles.
Guns: 1—3 in *(76 mm)*/59 AK 176; 120 rds/min to 15 km *(8 n miles)*; weight of shell 5.9 kg.
1—30 mm/65; 6 barrels; 3,000 rds/min combined to 2 km.
Torpedoes: 4—16 in *(406 mm)* tubes. Type 40; anti-submarine; active/passive homing up to 15 km *(8 n miles)* at up to 40 kt; warhead 100–150 kg.
A/S mortars: 2 RBU 1200 5-tubed fixed; range 1,200 m; warhead 34 kg.
Depth charges: 2 racks (12).
Countermeasures: Decoys: 2 PK 16 chaff launchers.
ESM: 3 Brick Plug; intercept.
Radars: Air/surface search: Peel Cone; E-band.
Surface search: Spin Trough; I-band.
Fire control: Bass Tilt; H/I-band.
Sonars: Foal Tail VDS (mounted on transom); active attack; high frequency.

Comment: *Reshitelni* transferred from USSR in September 1989, *Bodri* in December 1990. Based at Varna.

BODRI *4/2007, C D Yaylali* / 1335246

0 + (2) GOWIND 200 CLASS (CORVETTES) (FS)

Displacement, tons: 1,950 full load
Dimensions, feet (metres): 337.9 × 46.6 × ? *(103.0 × 14.2 × ?)*
Main machinery: CODAD; 2 waterjets
Speed, knots: 30
Range, n miles: 2,970 at 12 kt
Complement: 70

Missiles: SSM: To be announced.
SAM: To be announced.
Guns: To be announced.
Countermeasures: To be announced.
Combat data systems: DCNS Setis.
Electro-optic systems: To be announced.
Radars: Air/surface search: To be announced.
Surface search: To be announced.
Fire control: To be announced.
Navigation: To be announced.

Comment: Following a meeting in October 2006 between French President Sarkozy and Bulgarian Prime Minister Stanishev, it was agreed in principle to proceed with negotiations to procure up to four corvettes. Although it had been hoped to finalise a contract by late 2007, progress was halted due to reported Bulgarian budgetary concerns until a further visit by President Sarkozy in 2008 appeared to revive the project. Negotiations continue. The design of the Gowind series of corvettes has drawn on experienced gained in the FREMM frigate project. Design features include an integrated mast structure, a flight deck and hangar and space for a 16-cell VLS system, eight surface-to-surface missiles and a medium calibre gun. Particular attention has been paid to Stealth features. IR signature is reduced by channelling exhaust gases through waterjets rather than a funnel. Subject to contract, the first ship is likely to be built at Lorient and the second at Varna. There is likely to be an option for a further two ships.

GOWIND 200 *10/2007, DCNS/Armaris* / 1169319

LAND-BASED MARITIME AIRCRAFT (FRONT LINE)

Numbers/Type: 3 Mil Mi-14PL 'Haze A'.
Operational speed: 120 kt *(222 km/h)*.
Service ceiling: 15,000 ft *(4,570 m)*.
Range: 240 n miles *(445 km)*.
Role/Weapon systems: Primary role as inshore/coastal ASW and Fleet support helicopter; one converted as transport. Based at Asparukhovo airport. Sensors: Search radar, MAD, sonobuoys, dipping sonar. Weapons: ASW; up to 2 × torpedoes, or mines, or depth bombs.

HAZE *6/2006, Bulgarian Navy* / 1164494

Numbers/Type: 6 Eurocopter AS 565MB Panther.
Operational speed: 150 kt *(278 km/h)*.
Service ceiling: 15,420 ft *(4,700 m)*.
Range: 464 n miles *(859 km)*.
Role/Weapon systems: Six aircraft ordered on 28 January 2005. Delivery is to begin in 2010. The aircraft are to be shore-based and are to be used for maritime surveillance, ASW, anti-surface and SAR roles. Sensors and weapons to be announced.

AS 565 PANTHER (French colours) *1/2007, B Prézelin* / 1305023

PATROL FORCES

Notes: Customs craft operate on the Danube. Vessels include three Boston Whalers donated by the US and RIBs given by the UK in 1992–93.

9 ZHUK (PROJECT 1400M) CLASS (COASTAL PATROL CRAFT) (PB)

511–513 521–523 531–533

Displacement, tons: 39 full load
Dimensions, feet (metres): 78.7 × 16.4 × 3.9 *(24 × 5 × 1.2)*
Main machinery: 2 Type M 401B diesels; 2,200 hp(m) *(1.6 MW)* sustained; 2 shafts
Speed, knots: 30
Range, n miles: 1,100 at 15 kt
Complement: 11 (3 officers)
Guns: 4 USSR 14.5 mm (2 twin) MGs.
Radars: Surface search: Spin Trough; I-band.

Comment: Transferred from USSR 1980–81. Belong to the Border Police under the Minister of the Interior and have 'Border Guard' insignia on the ships side. Based at Atiya and at Varna.

ZHUK 512 (and others) *6/1996, Bulgarian Navy* / 0506272

6 OSA (PROJECT 205) CLASS (FAST ATTACK CRAFT—MISSILE) (PTFG)

URAGON 102 – 105 (ex-111)
BURYA 103 (Osa I) – 106 (ex-112) (Osa 1)
GRUM 104 **SMERCH** 107 (ex-113)

Displacement, tons: 245 full load; 210 (Osa I)
Dimensions, feet (metres): 126.6 × 24.9 × 8.8 *(38.6 × 7.6 × 2.7)*
Main machinery: 3 Type M 504 diesels; 10,800 hp(m) *(7.94 MW)* sustained; 3 shafts (Osa II)
3 Type 503A diesels; 8,025 hp(m) *(5.9 MW)* sustained; 3 shafts (Osa I)
Speed, knots: 37 (Osa II); 35 (Osa I)
Range, n miles: 500 at 35 kt
Complement: 26 (3 officers)

Missiles: SSM: 4 SS-N-2A/B Styx; active radar/IR homing to 46 km *(25 n miles)* at 0.9 Mach; warhead 513 kg. SS-N-2A in Osa I.
Guns: 4 USSR 30 mm/65 (2 twin); 500 rds/min to 5 km *(2.7 n miles)*; weight of shell 0.54 kg.
Radars: Surface search/fire control: Square Tie; I-band.
Fire control: Drum Tilt; H/I-band.
IFF: High Pole. Square Head.

Comment: Four Osa IIs built between 1965 and 1970, and transferred from USSR between 1977 and 1982. Two Osa Is transferred in 1972 and survived longer than expected. Names: 102 Hurricane, 103 Storm, 104 Thunder, and 107 Tornado. All based at Sozopol and seldom go to sea.

GRUM *6/2002, A Sheldon-Duplaix* / 0524968

BURYA *6/2002, A Sheldon-Duplaix* / 0524970

3 NEUSTADT CLASS (PB)

SOZOPOL (ex-*Rosenheim*) 525 (ex-BG 18) **BALCHIK** (ex-*Duderstadt*) 524 (ex-BG 14)
NESEBAR (ex-*Neustadt*) 526 (ex-BG 11)

Displacement, tons: 218 full load
Dimensions, feet (metres): 127.1 × 23 × 5 *(38.5 × 7 × 2.2)*
Main machinery: 2 MTU MD diesels; 6,000 hp(m) *(4.41 MW)*; 1 MWM diesel; 685 hp(m) *(500 kW)*; 3 shafts
Speed, knots: 30
Range, n miles: 450 at 27 kt
Complement: 17
Guns: 2 — 7.62 mm MGs.
Radars: Surface search: Selenia ARP 1645; I-band.
Navigation: Racal Decca Bridgemaster MA 180/4; I-band.

Comment: Built in 1970 by Lürssen, Vegesack. 525 transferred from German Border Guard in June 2002, *526* on 16 April 2004 and *524* in December 2004. Operated by the Border Police.

NESEBAR *5/2004, Martin Mokrus* / 0587692

3 COASTAL PATROL CRAFT (PB)

BURGAS 514 **KAVARNA** 531 **VARNA** 534

Displacement, tons: 50 standard
Dimensions, feet (metres): 68.9 × 19.0 × 4.6 *(21.0 × 5.8 × 1.4)*
Main machinery: 2 Deutz MWM TBD 616 diesels; 2,970 hp(m) *(2.2 MW)*; 2 shafts
Speed, knots: 30

Comment: Contract awarded in November 2002 to Lürssen, Berne-Bardenfleth. Delivery of the first two craft made in 2003 and of the third in October 2005. Operated by Border Police.

KAVARNA (in foreground) *9/2005, Michael Nitz* / 1133236

AMPHIBIOUS FORCES

2 POLNOCHNY A (PROJECT 770) CLASS (LSM)

SIRIUS (ex-*Ivan Zagubanski*) 701 **ANTARES** 702

Displacement, tons: 750 standard; 800 full load
Dimensions, feet (metres): 239.5 × 27.9 × 5.8 *(73 × 8.5 × 1.8)*
Main machinery: 2 Kolomna Type 40-D diesels; 4,400 hp(m) *(3.2 MW)* sustained; 2 shafts
Speed, knots: 19
Range, n miles: 1,000 at 18 kt
Complement: 40
Military lift: 350 tons including 6 tanks; 180 troops
Guns: 2 USSR 30 mm (twin). 2—140 mm 18-barrelled rocket launchers.
Radars: Navigation: Spin Trough; I-band.

Comment: Built 1963 to 1968. Transferred from USSR 1986-87. Not fitted either with the SA-N-5 Grail SAM system or with Drum Tilt fire-control radars. Plans to convert them to minelayers have been shelved and both are now used as transports. Based at Atiya.

ANTARES *6/2006, Bulgarian Navy* / 1164493

6 VYDRA (PROJECT 106K) CLASS (LCU)

703–708

Displacement, tons: 425 standard; 550 full load
Dimensions, feet (metres): 179.7 × 25.3 × 6.6 *(54.8 × 7.7 × 2)*
Main machinery: 2 Type 3-D-12 diesels; 600 hp(m) *(440 kW)* sustained; 2 shafts
Speed, knots: 12
Range, n miles: 2,500 at 10 kt
Complement: 20
Military lift: 200 tons or 100 troops or 3 MBTs
Guns: 1—14.5 mm.
Radars: Navigation: Don 2; I-band.
IFF: High Pole.

Comment: Built 1963 to 1969. Ten transferred from the USSR in 1970, the remainder built in Bulgaria between 1974 and 1978. In 1992–93 *703-707* converted to be used as minelayers. Many deleted. All based at Atiya.

VYDRA 705 *6/2006, Bulgarian Navy* / 1164492

MINE WARFARE FORCES

Notes: (1) Six Vydra class (see *Amphibious Forces*) converted to minelayers in 1992-93. Some are in reserve.
(2) MCM long-term projects include:
acquisition of up to six second-hand MCM vessels
establishment of a mine-warfare data centre
the acquisition of route-survey and bottom surveillance systems
procurement of a shallow-water MCM capability.

4 BRIZ (SONYA) (PROJECT 12650) CLASS (MINESWEEPERS—COASTAL) (MSC)

BRIZ 61 **SHKVAL** 62 **PRIBOY** 63 **SHTORM** 64

Displacement, tons: 450 full load
Dimensions, feet (metres): 157.4 × 28.9 × 6.6 *(48 × 8.8 × 2)*
Main machinery: 2 Kolomna Type 9-D-8 diesels; 2,000 hp(m) *(1.47 MW)* sustained; 2 shafts
Speed, knots: 15
Range, n miles: 1,500 at 14 kt
Complement: 43 (5 officers)
Guns: 2 USSR 30 mm/65 (twin); 500 rds/min to 5 km *(2.7 n miles)*; weight of shell 0.54 kg.
2 USSR 25 mm/80 (twin); 270 rds/min to 3 km *(1.6 n miles)*; weight of shell 0.34 kg.
Mines: 5.
Radars: Surface search/navigation: Kivach; I-band.
IFF: Two Square Head. High Pole B.
Sonars: MG 69/79; hull-mounted; active minehunting; high frequency.

Comment: Wooden hulled ships transferred from USSR in 1981–84. Based at Atiya.

SHKVAL *6/2006, Bulgarian Navy* / 1164491

1 FLOWER (TRIPARTITE) CLASS (MINEHUNTER) (MHC)

Name	*No*	*Builders*	*Laid down*	*Launched*	*Commissioned*
TSIBAR (ex-*Myosotis*)	32 (ex-M 922)	Beliard, Ostend	6 July 1987	4 Aug 1988	14 Dec 1989

Displacement, tons: 562 standard; 595 full load
Dimensions, feet (metres): 168.9 × 29.2 × 8.5 *(51.5 × 8.9 × 2.6)*
Main machinery: 1 Stork Wärtsilä A-RUB 215X-12 diesel; 1,860 hp(m) *(1.35 MW)* sustained; 1 shaft; LIPS cp prop; 2 active rudders; 2 motors; 240 hp(m) *(179 kW)*; 2 bow thrusters
Speed, knots: 15 diesel; 7 electric
Range, n miles: 3,000 at 12 kt
Complement: 46
Guns: 1 DCN 20 mm/20; 720 rds/min to 10 km. 2—12.7 mm MGs.
Countermeasures: MCM: 2 PAP 104 remote-controlled mine locators; 39 charges. Mechanical minesweeping gear.
Radars: Navigation: Racal Decca TM 1229C; I-band.
Sonars: Thomson Sintra DUBM 21A; hull-mounted; minehunting; 100 kHz (±10 kHz).

Programmes: Originally procured for the Belgian Navy in co-operation with France and the Netherlands. The hull was built at Ostend and the ship was fitted out at Rupelmonde. It was subsequently modified to act as an ammunition transport. The ship was decommissioned from Belgian service in 2004 and, following an announcement on 7 December 2007 is to be re-actived and transferred to Bulgaria in early 2009. Details are based on the ships in Belgian service before modernisation.
Modernisation: The ship is to be overhauled before entering Bulgarian service.
Structure: GRP hull fitted with active tank stabilisation, full NBC protection and air conditioning. Has automatic pilot and buoy tracking. A 5-ton container can be carried for varying tasks.

TSIBAR (Belgian colours) *6/2001, Findler & Winter* / 0114697

4 ISCAR (VANYA) (PROJECT 257D) CLASS (MINESWEEPERS—COASTAL) (MSC)

ISKAR 31 **ZIBAR** 32 **DOBROTICH** 33 **EVSTATI VINAROV** 34

Displacement, tons: 245 full load
Dimensions, feet (metres): 131.2 × 23.9 × 5.9 *(40 × 7.3 × 1.8)*
Main machinery: 2 M 870 diesels; 2,502 hp(m) *(1.84 MW)*; 2 shafts; cp props
Speed, knots: 16
Range, n miles: 2,400 at 10 kt
Complement: 36
Guns: 2 USSR 30 mm/65 (twin); 500 rds/min to 5 km *(2.7 n miles)*; weight of shell 0.54 kg.
Mines: Can carry 8.
Radars: Surface search: Don 2; I-band.
Sonars: MG 69/79; hull-mounted; active minehunting; high frequency.

Comment: Built 1961 to 1973. Transferred from the USSR-two in 1970, two in 1971 and two in 1985. Can act as minehunters. Two paid off in 1992, but back in service in 1994 and then finally scrapped in 1995. Based at Varna.

ISKAR *6/2007, Maritime Photographic* / 1166832

2 YEVGENYA (PROJECT 1258) CLASS (MINESWEEPERS—COASTAL) (MSC)

65–66

Displacement, tons: 77 standard; 90 full load
Dimensions, feet (metres): 80.4 × 18 × 4.6 *(24.5 × 5.5 × 1.4)*
Main machinery: 2 Type 3-D-12 diesels; 600 hp(m) *(440 kW)* sustained; 2 shafts
Speed, knots: 11
Range, n miles: 300 at 10 kt
Complement: 10 (1 officer)
Guns: 2—25 mm/80 (twin).
Mines: 8 racks.
Radars: Surface search: Spin Trough; I-band.
IFF: High Pole.
Sonars: MG-7 lifted over stern; active; high frequency.

Comment: GRP hulls built at Kolpino. Transferred from USSR 1977. Based at Varna.

YEVGENYA 66 *6/2006, Bulgarian Navy* / 1164490

2 PO 2 (PROJECT 501) CLASS (MINESWEEPERS—INSHORE) (MSB)

218–219

Displacement, tons: 56 full load
Dimensions, feet (metres): 70.5 × 11.5 × 3.3 *(21.5 × 3.5 × 1)*
Main machinery: 1 Type 3-D-12 diesel; 300 hp(m) *(220 kW)* sustained; 2 shafts
Speed, knots: 12
Complement: 8

Comment: Built in Bulgaria. First units completed in early 1950s and last in early 1960s. Originally a class of 24 and these are the last two to survive. Occasionally carries a 12.7 mm MG, when used for patrol duties. Both based at Varna.

PO 2 *7/2000, van Ginderen Collection* / 0104252

6 OLYA (PROJECT 1259) CLASS (MINESWEEPERS—INSHORE) (MSB)

51–56

Displacement, tons: 64 full load
Dimensions, feet (metres): 84.6 × 14.9 × 3.3 *(25.8 × 4.5 × 1)*
Main machinery: 2 Type 3D 6S11/235 diesels; 471 hp(m) *(346 kW)* sustained; 2 shafts
Speed, knots: 12. **Range (miles)**: 300 at 10 kt
Complement: 15
Guns: 2—12.7 mm MGs (twin).
Radars: Navigation: Pechora; I-band.

Comment: First five built between 1988 and 1992 in Bulgaria to the Russian Olya design. *56* completed in 1996. Minesweeping equipment includes AT-6, SZMT-1 and 3 PKT-2 systems. *55* based at Varna, the remainder at Balchik.

OLYA 52 *7/2000, van Ginderen Collection* / 0104250

SURVEY SHIPS

1 MOMA (PROJECT 861) CLASS (AGS)

ADMIRAL BRANIMIR ORMANOV 401

Displacement, tons: 1,580 full load
Dimensions, feet (metres): 240.5 × 36.8 × 12.8 *(73.3 × 11.2 × 3.9)*
Main machinery: 2 Zgoda-Sulzer 6TD48 diesels; 3,300 hp(m) *(2.43 MW)* sustained; 2 shafts; cp props
Speed, knots: 17. **Range, n miles**: 9,000 at 12 kt
Complement: 37 (5 officers)
Radars: Navigation: 2 Don-2; I-band.

Comment: Built at Northern Shipyard, Gdansk, Poland in 1977. Based at Varna. Two others of the class belonging to Russia were refitted in Bulgaria in 1995–96.

ADMIRAL BRANIMIR ORMANOV *6/2007, Maritime Photographic* / 1166833

2 COASTAL SURVEY VESSELS (PROJECT 612) (AGSC)

231 **331**

Displacement, tons: 114 full load
Dimensions, feet (metres): 87.6 × 19 × 4.9 *(26.7 × 5.8 × 1.5)*
Main machinery: 2 Type 3-D-12 diesels; 600 hp(m) (440 kW) sustained; 2 shafts
Speed, knots: 12. **Range, n miles**: 600 at 10 kt
Complement: 9 (2 officers)
Radars: Navigation: I-band.

Comment: Built in Bulgaria in 1986 and 1988 respectively. Can carry 2 tons of equipment. *231* is based at Varna and *331* at Atiya.

AGSC 331 *6/1996, Bulgarian Navy* / 0506274

AUXILIARIES

1 SUPPORT TANKER (AOTL)

AKIN 303 (ex-203)

Displacement, tons: 1,250 full load
Dimensions, feet (metres): 181.8 × 36.1 × 11.5 *(55.4 × 11 × 3.5)*
Main machinery: 2 Sulzer 6AL-20-24 diesels; 1,500 hp(m) *(1.1 MW)*; 2 shafts
Speed, knots: 12. **Range, n miles:** 1,000 at 8 kt
Complement: 23
Cargo capacity: 650 tons fuel
Guns: 2 ZU-23-2F Wrobel 23 mm (twin).
Radars: Navigation: I-band.

Comment: Laid down 1989, launched 1993 and completed in 1994 at Burgas Shipyards, Burgas. Based at Varna.

AOT 303 *6/2006, Bulgarian Navy* / 1164488

1 MESAR CLASS (PROJECT 102) (SUPPORT TANKER) (AORL)

ATIYA 302

Displacement, tons: 3,240 full load
Dimensions, feet (metres): 319.8 × 45.6 × 16.4 *(97.5 × 13.9 × 5)*
Main machinery: 2 diesels; 12,000 hp(m) *(8.82 MW)*; 2 shafts
Speed, knots: 18. **Range, n miles:** 12,000 at 15 kt
Complement: 32 (6 officers)
Cargo capacity: 1,593 tons
Guns: 4 USSR 30 mm/65 (2 twin).
Radars: Navigation: 2 Don 2; I-band.

Comment: Built in Bulgaria in 1987. Abeam fuelling to port and astern fuelling. Mount 1.5 ton crane amidships. Also carries dry stores. Based at Atiya.

ATIYA *7/2002, S Breyer* / 0568845

2 DIVING TENDERS (PROJECT 245) (YDT)

223 **323**

Displacement, tons: 112 full load
Dimensions, feet (metres): 91.5 × 17.1 × 7.2 *(27.9 × 5.2 × 2.2)*
Main machinery: Diesel-electric; 2 MCK 83-4 diesel generators; 1 motor; 300 hp(m) *(220 kW)*; 1 shaft
Speed, knots: 10. **Range, n miles:** 400 at 10 kt
Complement: 6 + 7 divers
Radars: Navigation: Don 2; I-band.

Comment: Built in Bulgaria in mid-1980s. A twin 12.7 mm MG can be fitted. Capable of bell diving to 60 m. *223* based at Varna. *323* based at Atiya.

YDT 323 *6/2006, Bulgarian Navy* / 1164485

2 TYPE 215 (TORPEDO RECOVERY VESSELS) (ARS)

222 **+1**

Displacement, tons: 110 full load
Dimensions, feet (metres): 87.3 × 19.0 × 4.9 *(26.6 × 5.8 × 1.5)*
Main machinery: 1 diesel; 290 hp(m) *(216 kW)*; 1 shaft
Speed, knots: 12

Comment: Capable of carrying five torpedoes.

222 *6/2007, Maritime Photographic* / 1167807

1 BEREZA (PROJECT 130) CLASS (ADG/AX)

KAPITAN 1st RANK DIMITRI DOBREV 206

Displacement, tons: 2,051 full load
Dimensions, feet (metres): 228 × 45.3 × 13.1 *(69.5 × 13.8 × 4)*
Main machinery: 2 Zgoda-Sulzer 8 AL 25/30 diesels; 2,925 hp(m) *(2.16 MW)* sustained; 2 shafts; cp props
Speed, knots: 13. **Range, n miles:** 1,000 at 13 kt
Complement: 48
Radars: Navigation: Kivach; I-band.

Comment: New construction built in Poland and transferred July 1988. Used as a degaussing ship. Fitted with an NBC citadel and upper deck wash-down system. The ship has three laboratories. Has also been used as a training ship. Based at Varna.

KAPITAN 1st RANK DIMITRI DOBREV *7/2007, Bob Fildes* / 1166829

5 AUXILIARIES (ATS)

224 **312** **313** **321** **421**

Comment: *421* is a survey vessel converted to a training ship. *224* and *321* are firefighting vessels. *312* and *313* are tugs.

421 *6/2003, Schaeffer/Marsan* / 0567877

224 *6/2006, Bulgarian Navy* / 1164483

1 SALVAGE SHIP (ARS)

Name	*No*	*Builders*	*Commissioned*
PROTEO (ex-*Proteo*, ex-*Perseo*)	224 (ex-A 5310)	Cantieri Navali Riuniti, Ancona	24 Aug 1951

Displacement, tons: 1,865 standard; 2,147 full load
Dimensions, feet (metres): 248 × 38 × 21 *(75.6 × 11.6 × 6.4)*
Main machinery: 2 Fiat diesels; 4,800 hp(m) *(3.53 MW)*; 1 shaft
Speed, knots: 16. **Range, n miles:** 7,500 at 13 kt
Complement: 122 (8 officers)
Radars: Navigation: SMA-748; I-band.

Comment: Transferred to Bulgaria on 3 June 2004 having been decommissioned from the Italian Navy in 2002. Originally laid down in 1943, construction was suspended until restarted in 1949. Details are those of the ship when in Italian service.

PROTEO *7/2007, Bob Fildes* / 1166830

Cambodia

Country Overview

Formerly a French protectorate, the south-east Asian Kingdom of Cambodia was ravaged by the Vietnam War and then by the Khmer Rouge regime before relative stability followed the nation's first multiparty elections in 1993. With an overall land area of 69,898 square miles, the country is bordered to the north by Thailand and Laos and to the east by Vietnam. There is a 239 n mile coastline with the Gulf of Thailand. The capital and largest city is Phnom Penh while the principal port is Sihanoukville. There are extensive inland waterways. Territorial seas (12 n miles) are claimed. An EEZ (200 n miles) is claimed but the limits have not been fully defined.

Headquarters Appointments

Commander of Navy:
Vice Admiral Ung Samkhan
Chief of Naval Staff:
Rear Admiral Sao Sarin

Personnel

2009: 2,800 (780 officers) including marines

Bases

Ream (Sihanoukville) (ocean), Phnom Penh (river), Sihanoukville (civil)

Organisation

Ocean Division has nine battalions and the River Division seven battalions. Command HQ is at Phnom Penh.

PATROL FORCES

Notes: (1) There are also about 170 motorised and manual canoes.
(2) Six patrol craft of unknown type were donated by China on 9 January 2005. They may be operated by the Marine Police.
(3) Seven patrol craft and a landing craft were delivered by China on 7 November 2007. These included four 46 m and three 20 m craft. A 60 m floating dock was also delivered.

2 MODIFIED STENKA CLASS (PROJECT 205P) (FAST ATTACK CRAFT—PATROL) (PBF)

MONDOLKIRI 1131 **RATANAKIRI** 1134

Displacement, tons: 211 standard; 253 full load
Dimensions, feet (metres): 129.3 × 25.9 × 8.2 *(39.4 × 7.9 × 2.5)*
Main machinery: 3 Caterpillar diesels; 14,000 hp(m) *(10.29 MW)*; 3 shafts
Speed, knots: 37. **Range, n miles:** 800 at 24 kt; 500 at 35 kt
Complement: 25 (5 officers)
Guns: 2—23 mm/87 (twin). 1 Bofors 40 mm/70.
Radars: Surface search: Racal Decca Bridgemaster; I-band.
Fire control: Muff Cob; G/H-band.
Navigation: Racal Decca; I-band.
IFF: High Pole. 2 Square Head.

Comment: Four transferred from USSR in November 1987. Export model without torpedo tubes and sonar. One pair were modernised in Hong Leong Shipyard, Butterworth, from early 1995 to April 1996. New engines, guns and radars were fitted. The second pair similarly refitted by August 1997. By late 1998 only two were operational although it was reported in 2000 that a third may have undergone a further refit. Pennant numbers were changed for UN operations but changed back again in November 1993.

MONDOLKIRI *8/1997, Hong Leong Shipyard* / 0056666

2 KAOH CLASS (RIVER PATROL CRAFT) (PBR)

KAOH CHHLAM 1105 **KAOH RONG** 1106

Displacement, tons: 44 full load
Dimensions, feet (metres): 76.4 × 20 × 3.9 *(23.3 × 6.1 × 1.2)*
Main machinery: 2 Deutz/MWM TBD 616 V16 diesels; 2,992 hp(m) *(2.2 MW)*; 2 shafts
Speed, knots: 34
Range, n miles: 400 at 30 kt
Complement: 13 (3 officers)
Guns: 2—14.5 mm MG (twin). 2—12.7 mm MGs.
Radars: Surface search: Racal Decca Bridgemaster; I-band.

Comment: Ordered from Hong Leong Shipyard, Butterworth to a German design in 1995 and delivered 20 January 1997. Aluminium construction.

KAOH CHHLAM *1/1997, Hong Leong Shipyard* / 0056667

Cameroon

MARINE NATIONALE RÉPUBLIQUE

Country Overview

The Republic of Cameroon became a unitary republic in 1972 and replaced the federation of East Cameroon (formerly French Cameroons) and West Cameroon (formerly part of British Cameroons). With an area of 183,569 square miles, the country has borders to the west with Nigeria and to the south with Gabon and Equatorial Guinea. It has a 217 n mile coastline with Atlantic Ocean on the Bight of Bonny. The capital is Yaoundé while Douala is the principal port which also serves adjacent landlocked states. Kribi is the country's second port. Cameroon is the only coastal state to claim territorial seas of 50 n miles. It has not been declared an Exclusive Economic Zone (EEZ) and claims to jurisdiction would be complicated by the offshore islands of Bioko (Equatorial Guinea), São Tomé and Principe.

Headquarters Appointments

Chief of Naval Staff:
Vice Admiral Guillaume Ngouah Ngally

Personnel

2009: 1,250

Bases

Douala (HQ), Limbe, Kribi

PATROL FORCES

Notes: (1) Ten Rodman 6.5 m craft were delivered in 2000. All have speeds in excess of 25 kt.
(2) There are some eight Simmoneau 10 m craft in service and a further 15 12 m Raidco craft.

1 BIZERTE (TYPE PR 48) CLASS (LARGE PATROL CRAFT) (PBO)

Name	*No*	*Builders*	*Commissioned*
L'AUDACIEUX	P 103	SFCN, Villeneuve-La-Garenne	11 May 1976

Displacement, tons: 250 full load
Dimensions, feet (metres): 157.5 × 23.3 × 7.5 *(48 × 7.1 × 2.3)*
Main machinery: 2 SACM 195 V12 CZSHR diesels; 6,000 hp(m) *(4.41 MW)* sustained; 2 shafts; cp props
Speed, knots: 23. **Range, n miles:** 2,000 at 16 kt
Complement: 25 (4 officers)
Guns: 2 Bofors 40 mm/70; 300 rds/min to 12.8 km *(7 n miles)*; weight of shell 0.96 kg.

Comment: *L'Audacieux* ordered in September 1974. Laid down on 23 April 1975, launched on 31 October 1975. Similar to Bizerte class in Tunisia. Operational status doubtful and not reported at sea since 1995. Fitted for SS 12M missiles but these are not embarked.

BIZERTE CLASS (Tunisian colours) *1993, van Ginderen Collection* / 0056668

1 COASTAL PATROL CRAFT (PB)

QUARTIER MAÎTRE ALFRED MOTTO

Displacement, tons: 96 full load
Dimensions, feet (metres): 95.4 × 20.3 × 6.3 *(29.1 × 6.2 × 1.9)*
Main machinery: 2 Baudouin diesels; 1,290 hp(m) *(948 kW)*; 2 shafts
Speed, knots: 14
Complement: 17 (2 officers)
Guns: 2—7.62 mm MGs.
Radars: Surface search: I-band.

Comment: Built at Libreville, Gabon in 1974. Discarded as a derelict hulk in 1990 but refurbished and brought back into service with assistance from the French Navy in 1995–96.

QUARTIER MAÎTRE ALFRED MOTTO *2/1996, **French Navy*** / 0056670

1 BAKASSI (TYPE P 48S) CLASS (OFFSHORE PATROL CRAFT) (PBO)

Name	*No*	*Builders*	*Launched*	*Commissioned*
BAKASSI	P 104	SFCN, Villeneuve-La-Garenne	22 Oct 1982	9 Jan 1984

Displacement, tons: 308 full load
Dimensions, feet (metres): 172.5 × 23.6 × 7.9 *(52.6 × 7.2 × 2.4)*
Main machinery: 2 SACM 195 V16 CZSHR diesels; 8,000 hp(m) *(5.88 MW)* sustained; 2 shafts
Speed, knots: 25. **Range, n miles:** 2,000 at 16 kt
Complement: 39 (6 officers)
Guns: 2 Bofors 40 mm/70; 300 rds/min to 12.8 km *(7 n miles)*; weight of shell 0.96 kg.
Weapons control: 2 Naja optronic systems. Racal Decca Cane 100 command system.
Radars: 2 Furuno; I-band.

Comment: Ordered January 1981. Laid down 16 December 1981. Six month major refit by Raidco Marine (Lorient) in 1999. This included removing the Exocet missile system and EW equipment, and fitting new propellers and a funnel aft of the mainmast to replace the waterline exhausts. New radars were also installed. Two RIBs are carried.

BAKASSI *7/1999, **H M Steele*** / 0121304

2 SWIFT PBR CLASS (RIVER PATROL CRAFT) (PBR)

PR 001 **PR 005**

Displacement, tons: 12 full load
Dimensions, feet (metres): 38 × 12.5 × 3.2 *(11.6 × 3.8 × 1)*
Main machinery: 2 Stewart and Stevenson 6V-92TA diesels; 520 hp *(388 kW)* sustained; 2 shafts
Speed, knots: 32. **Range, n miles:** 210 at 20 kt
Complement: 4
Guns: 2—12.7 mm MGs. 2—7.62 mm MGs.

Comment: Last two survivors of 30 built by Swiftships and supplied under the US Military Assistance Programme. First 10 delivered in March 1987, second 10 in September 1987 and the remainder in March 1988. Several others have been cannibalised for spares.

PBR class ***4/1992*** / 0056671

2 RODMAN 101 (COASTAL PATROL CRAFT) (PB)

AKWAYAFE P 106 **JABANNE** P 107

Displacement, tons: 63 full load
Dimensions, feet (metres): 98.4 × 19 × 5.9 *(30 × 5.8 × 1.8)*
Main machinery: 2 Detroit diesels; 2,800 hp(m) *(2.06 MW)*; 2 shafts
Speed, knots: 26
Range, n miles: 800 at 18 kt
Complement: 9
Guns: 2—12.7 mm MGs.
Radars: Surface search: Furuno; I-band.

Comment: Delivered in late 2000.

AKWAYAFE *7/2001, **Adolfo Ortigueira Gil*** / 0524974

4 RODMAN 46 CLASS (PB)

IDABATO VS 201 **ISONGO** VS 202 **MOUANCO** VS 203 **CAMPO** VS 204

Displacement, tons: 12.5
Dimensions, feet (metres): 45.9 × 12.5 × 2.9 *(14.0 × 3.8 × 0.9)*
Main machinery: 2 MAN D 2842 diesels; 900 hp *(671 kW)*; 2 Hamilton waterjets
Speed, knots: 30
Complement: 4
Comment: GRP hull. Built in 2000 by Rodman, Vigo.

AMPHIBIOUS FORCES

2 YUNNAN CLASS (TYPE 067) (LCU)

DEBUNDSHA **KOMBO A JANEA**

Displacement, tons: 135 full load
Dimensions, feet (metres): 93.8 × 17.7 × 4.9 *(28.6 × 5.4 × 1.5)*
Main machinery: 2 diesels; 600 hp(m) *(441 kW)*; 2 shafts
Speed, knots: 12
Range, n miles: 500 at 10 kt
Complement: 22 (2 officers)
Military lift: 46 tons
Guns: 2—14.5 mm (1 twin) MGs.
Radars: Surface search: Fuji; I-band.

Comment: Acquired from China in 2002.

YUNNAN CLASS *8/2000, **Hachiro Nakai*** / 0103675

Canada

Country Overview

Canada is the world's second-largest country. The British monarch, represented by a governor-general, is head of state. With an area of 3,849,652 square miles, it occupies most of northern North America and is bordered to the south by the United States and to the west by the US state of Alaska. It has a coastline of 131,647 n miles with the Pacific, Arctic and Atlantic Oceans and with Baffin Bay and the Davis Strait. Numerous coastal islands include the Arctic Archipelago to the north, Newfoundland, Cape Breton, Prince Edward, and Anticosti to the east and Vancouver Island and the Queen Charlotte Islands to the west. Hudson Bay contains Southampton Island and many smaller islands. The 2,035 n mile St Lawrence-Great Lakes navigation system enables ocean-going vessels to sail between the Atlantic Ocean and the Great Lakes via the St Lawrence Seaway (opened 1959). Ottawa is the capital while Toronto is the largest city. Major ports include Vancouver, Montreal, Halifax, Sept-Îles, Port-Cartier, Quebec City, Saint John (New Brunswick), Thunder Bay, Prince Rupert, and Hamilton. Territorial seas (12 n miles) are claimed. A 200 n mile EEZ has been claimed but the limits have only been partly defined by boundary agreements.

Headquarters Appointments

Chief of Maritime Staff:
Vice Admiral D W Robertson, CMM, MSM, CD
Assistant Chief of Maritime Staff:
Commodore K E Williams, OMM, MSM, CD
Director General Maritime Personnel and Readiness:
Commodore L M Hickey, OMM, CD
Director General Maritime Force Development:
Captain J E T P Ellis, CD

Flag Officers

Commander, Maritime Forces, Atlantic:
Rear Admiral P A Maddison, OMM, MSM, CD
Commander, Maritime Forces, Pacific:
Rear Admiral T H W Pile, CMM, CD
Commander, Naval Reserves:
Commodore J J Bennett, OMM, CD

Diplomatic Representation

Defence Attaché, Washington:
Captain A L Garceau, CD
Naval Adviser, London:
Captain N H Jolin, OMM, CD
Defence Attaché, Tokyo:
Captain J E H A Langlois, CD

Establishment

The Royal Canadian Navy (RCN) was officially established on 4 May 1910, when Royal Assent was given to the Naval Service Act. On 1 February 1968 the Canadian Forces Reorganisation Act unified the three branches of the Canadian Forces and the title 'Royal Canadian Navy' was dropped.

Personnel

2009: 8,553 (Regular), 3,850 (Reserves)

Prefix to Ships' Names

HMCS

Bases

Halifax and Esquimalt

Fleet Deployment

Atlantic
Canadian Fleet Atlantic (destroyer, frigates, AOR)
Maritime Operations Group Five (maritime warfare forces, submarines, training ships)

Pacific
Canadian Fleet Pacific (destroyer, frigates, AOR)
Maritime Operations Group Four (maritime warfare forces, submarines, training ships)

Maritime Air Components (MAC)

1 Canadian Air Division HQ Detachment Regional Air Control Element Atlantic (Halifax)
1 Canadian Air Division HQ Detachment Regional Air Control Element Pacific (Esquimault)

Squadron/Unit	*Base*	*Aircraft*	*Function*
MP 404 (MP&T)	Greenwood, NS	Aurora/ Arcturus	LRMP/ Training
MP 405 (MP)	Greenwood, NS	Aurora	LRMP
HT 406 (M) OTS	Shearwater, NS	Sea King	Training
MP 407 (MP)	Comox, BC	Aurora	LRMP
MH 423 (MH)	Shearwater, NS	Sea King	General
MH 443 (MH)	Victoria, BC	Sea King	General
HOTEF	Shearwater, NS	Sea King	Test
MP & EU	Greenwood, NS	Aurora	Test

Notes

1. Detachments from 423 and 443 meet ships' requirements in Atlantic and Pacific Fleets respectively. Sea King helicopters are now classified as General Purpose vice the former ASW designation.
2. 413 Squadron based in Greenwood, NS, and 442 Squadron based in Comox, BC, are two maritime search and rescue squadrons under the command of 1 Canadian Air Division (CAD).
3. Combat training support provided by commercial contract from March 2002.

Strength of the Fleet

Type	*Active*	*Building*
Submarines	4	–
Destroyers	3	–
Frigates	12	–
Mine Warfare Forces	12	–
Survey Ships	1	–
Support Ships	2	(3)

PENNANT LIST

Submarines

876	Victoria
877	Windsor
878	Corner Brook
879	Chicoutimi

Destroyers

280	Iroquois
282	Athabaskan
283	Algonquin

Frigates

330	Halifax
331	Vancouver
332	Ville de Québec
333	Toronto
334	Regina
335	Calgary
336	Montreal
337	Fredericton
338	Winnipeg
339	Charlottetown
340	St John's
341	Ottawa

Mine Warfare Forces

700	Kingston
701	Glace Bay
702	Nanaimo
703	Edmonton
704	Shawinigan
705	Whitehorse
706	Yellowknife
707	Goose Bay
708	Moncton
709	Saskatoon
710	Brandon
711	Summerside

Training Ships

55	Orca
56	Raven
57	Caribou
58	Renard
59	Wolf
60	Grizzly
61	Cougar
62	Moose

Auxiliaries

172	Quest
509	Protecteur
510	Preserver
610	Sechelt
611	Sikanni
612	Sooke
613	Stikine

SUBMARINES

4 VICTORIA (UPHOLDER) CLASS (TYPE 2400) (SSK)

Name	*No*	*Builders*	*Start date*	*Launched*	*Commissioned*	*Recommissioned*
VICTORIA (ex-*Unseen*)	876 (ex-S 41)	Cammell Laird, Birkenhead	Jan 1986	14 Nov 1989	7 June 1991	2 Dec 2000
WINDSOR (ex-*Unicorn*)	877 (ex-S 43)	Cammell Laird, Birkenhead (VSEL)	Feb 1989	16 Apr 1992	25 June 1993	4 Oct 2003
CORNER BROOK (ex-*Ursula*)	878 (ex-S 42)	Cammell Laird, Birkenhead (VSEL)	Aug 1987	28 Feb 1991	8 May 1992	29 June 2003
CHICOUTIMI (ex-*Upholder*)	879 (ex-S 40)	Vickers Shipbuilding and Engineering, Barrow	Nov 1983	2 Dec 1986	9 June 1990	2 Oct 2004

Displacement, tons: 2,168 surfaced; 2,455 dived
Dimensions, feet (metres): 230.6 × 25 × 17.7 *(70.3 × 7.6 × 5.5)*
Main machinery: Diesel-electric; 2 Paxman Valenta 16SZ diesels; 3,620 hp *(2.7 MW)* sustained; 2 GEC alternators; 2.8 MW; 1 GEC motor; 5,400 hp *(4 MW)*; 1 shaft
Speed, knots: 12 surfaced; 20 dived; 12 snorting
Range, n miles: 8,000 at 8 kt snorting
Complement: 48 (7 officers) plus 11 spare

Torpedoes: 6—21 in *(533 mm)* bow tubes. 18 Raytheon Mk 48 Mod 4M; dual purpose; active/passive homing to 50 km *(27 n miles)*/38 km *(21 n miles)* at 40/55 kt; warhead 267 kg. Air turbine pump discharge.
Countermeasures: Decoys: 2 SSE launchers.
ESM: Sea Search II; intercept.
Weapons control: Lockheed Martin SFCS.
Radars: Navigation: Kelvin Hughes Type 1007; I-band.
Furuno (portable); I-band.
Sonars: Thomson Sintra Type 2040; hull-mounted; passive search and intercept; medium frequency.
BAE Type 2007; flank array; passive; low frequency.
Thales Type 2046; towed array; passive very low frequency.
Thales Type 2019; passive/active range and intercept (PARIS).

Programmes: First ordered 2 November 1983. Further three ordered on 2 January 1986. Laid up after post Cold War defence cuts in 1994 and acquired from the UK on 6 April 1998. Refitted at Vickers, Barrow, for delivery from June 2000.
Modernisation: A mid-life update is under consideration and there are plans to modernise the Mk 48 torpedo.

CORNER BROOK *8/2007, Blake Rodgers, RCN* / 1166835

Structure: Single-skinned NQ1 high tensile steel hull, tear dropped shape 9:1 ratio, five man lock-out chamber in fin. Fitted with elastomeric acoustic tiles. Diving depth, greater than 200 m *(650 ft)*. Fitted with Pilkington Optronics CK 35 search and CH 85 attack optronic periscopes.
Operational: *Victoria* is based in the Pacific Fleet at Esquimault, BC and the remaining three submarines are based in the Atlantic Fleet at Halifax, NS. *Victoria* arrived in Canada in October 2000 and transferred to the Pacific Fleet in August 2003, following an extended work period. Currently in an Extended Docking Work Period (EDWP), *Victoria* will resume operations in mid-2010. *Windsor* was accepted in 2002, completed several patrols and is undergoing EDWP at Halifax 2007–10. *Corner Brook* arrived in mid-2003 and is currently operational. While on passage to Canada in October 2004, *Chicoutimi* suffered a serious fire. Extensive repairs are required and will be carried out 2010–13 in conjunction with EDWP on the west coast.

WINDSOR

6/2006, Formation Imaging Services / 1335652

VICTORIA

10/2000, CDF / 0094514

FRIGATES

12 HALIFAX CLASS (FFGHM)

Name	*No*	*Builders*	*Laid down*	*Launched*	*Commissioned*
HALIFAX	330	Saint John SB Ltd, New Brunswick	19 Mar 1987	30 Apr 1988	29 June 1992
VANCOUVER	331	Saint John SB Ltd, New Brunswick	19 May 1988	8 July 1989	23 Aug 1993
VILLE DE QUÉBEC	332	Marine Industries Ltd, Sorel	17 Jan 1989	16 May 1991	14 July 1994
TORONTO	333	Saint John SB Ltd, New Brunswick	24 Apr 1989	18 Dec 1990	29 July 1993
REGINA	334	Marine Industries Ltd, Sorel	6 Oct 1989	25 Oct 1991	30 Sep 1994
CALGARY	335	Marine Industries Ltd, Sorel	15 June 1991	28 Aug 1992	12 May 1995
MONTREAL	336	Saint John SB Ltd, New Brunswick	8 Feb 1991	28 Feb 1992	21 July 1994
FREDERICTON	337	Saint John SB Ltd, New Brunswick	25 Apr 1992	13 Mar 1993	10 Sep 1994
WINNIPEG	338	Saint John SB Ltd, New Brunswick	19 Mar 1993	5 Dec 1993	23 June 1995
CHARLOTTETOWN	339	Saint John SB Ltd, New Brunswick	5 Dec 1993	10 July 1994	9 Sep 1995
ST JOHN'S	340	Saint John SB Ltd, New Brunswick	24 Aug 1994	12 Feb 1995	26 June 1996
OTTAWA	341	Saint John SB Ltd, New Brunswick	29 Apr 1995	22 Nov 1995	28 Sep 1996

Displacement, tons: 4,770 full load
Dimensions, feet (metres): 441.9 oa; 408.5 pp × 53.8 × 16.4; 23.3 (screws) *(134.7; 124.5 × 16.4 × 5; 7.1)*
Main machinery: CODOG; 2 GE LM 2500 gas turbines; 47,494 hp *(35.43 MW)* sustained
1 SEMT-Pielstick 20 PA6 V 280 diesel; 8,800 hp(m) *(6.48 MW)* sustained; 2 shafts; cp props
Speed, knots: 29
Range, n miles: 9,500 at 13 kt (diesel); 3,930 at 18 kt (gas)
Complement: 198 (17 officers) plus 17 (8 officers) aircrew

Missiles: SSM: 8 McDonnell Douglas Harpoon Block 1C (2 quad) launchers ❶; active radar homing to 130 km *(70 n miles)* at 0.9 Mach; warhead 227 kg.
SAM: Raytheon Sea Sparrow RIM-7P; 2 Mk 48 octuple vertical launchers ❷; semi-active radar homing to 16 km *(8.5 n miles)* at 2.5 Mach; warhead 38 kg; 16 missiles. Evolved Sea Sparrow RIM-162 (339, 340); semi-active homing to 18 km *(9.7 n miles)* at 3.6 Mach; warhead 38 kg.
Guns: 1 Bofors 57 mm/70 Mk 2 ❸; 220 rds/min to 17 km *(9 n miles)*; weight of shell 2.4 kg.
1 GE/GDC 20 mm Vulcan Phalanx Mk 15 Mod 1 ❹; anti-missile; 3,000 rds/min (6 barrels combined) to 1.5 km.
6—12.7 mm MGs.
Torpedoes: 4—324 mm Mk 32 Mod 9 (2 twin) tubes ❺. 24 Honeywell Mk 46 Mod 5; anti-submarine; active/passive homing to 11 km *(5.9 n miles)* at 40 kt; warhead 44 kg.
Countermeasures: Decoys: 4 Plessey Shield Mk 2 decoy launchers ❻; sextuple mountings; fires P8 chaff and P6 IR flares in distraction, decoy or centroid modes.
Nixie SLQ-25; towed acoustic decoy.
ESM: MEL/Lockheed Canews SLQ-501 ❼; radar intercept; (1–18 GHz). SRD 502; intercept. Sea Search AN/ULR 501.
ECM: MEL/Lockheed Ramses SLQ-503 ❽; jammer.
Combat data systems: UYC-501 SHINPADS action data automation with UYQ-504 and UYK-505 or 507 (336–341) processors. Links 11 and 14.
Weapons control: AHWCS for Harpoon. CDC UYS-503(V); sonobuoy processing system.
Radars: Air search: Raytheon SPS-49(V)5 ❾; C-band.
Air/surface search: Ericsson Sea Giraffe HC 150 ❿; G/H-band.
Fire control: Two Signaal SPG-503 (STIR 1.8) ⓫; K/I-band.
Navigation: Sperry Mk 340 being replaced by Kelvin Hughes 1007; I-band.
Tacan: URN 25. IFF Mk XII.
Sonars: Westinghouse SQS-510; hull-mounted; active search and attack; medium frequency.
General Dynamics SQR-501 CANTASS towed array (uses part of Martin Marietta SQR-19 TACTASS).

Helicopters: 1 CH-124A ASW ⓬.

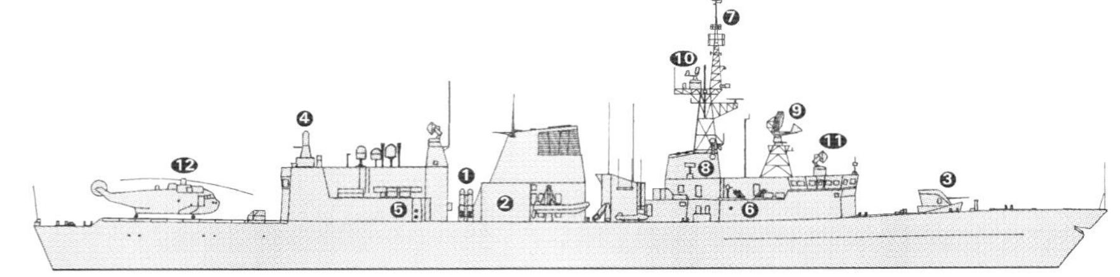

HALIFAX *(Scale 1 : 1,200), Ian Sturton* / 0528399

VILLE DE QUEBEC *8/2008*, RCN* / 1335650

Programmes: On 29 June 1983 Saint John Shipbuilding Ltd won the competition for the first six of a new class of patrol frigates. Combat system design and integration was subcontracted to Loral Canada (formerly Paramax, a subsidiary of Unisys). Three ships were subcontracted to Marine Industries Ltd in Lauzon and Sorel. On 18 December 1987 six additional ships of the same design were ordered from Saint John SB Ltd.
Modernisation: The Halifax Class Modernisation (HCM)/Frigate Life Extension (FELEX) programme subsumes all maintenance, sustainment and stand-alone projects planned to ensure the continued operation of the class for the duration of its life. In general, combat system enhancements are to reflect increasing emphasis on littoral operations in a joint force and a coalition. Major equipment acquisitions through HCM/FELEX include a modernised command and control system, multi-LINK, IFF Mode S/5, upgrade or replacement of SPS-49, Sea Giraffe and SPG-503 radars, a new ESM system, upgrades to the internal communications system, Harpoon to Block II, Bofors 57 mm gun to Mk 3 standard and an improvement of the degaussing system. In addition, a CTG capability is to be added to four ships. Projects already underway include modifications to receive Evolved Sea Sparrow (ESSM) (to be completed by 2010), the upgrade of the Vulcan Phalanx to Block 1B and the fitting of SEOSS and SIRIUS Infra-Red Search and Track (IRST). ASW projects include improvement of torpedo defence. Integration of the Cyclone helicopter will also make a significant contribution to ASW improvements. The HCM/FELEX Project will also be responsible for platform changes arising from the planned modifications. These include upper deck and operations room reconfiguration, power supplies, heating/ventilation/air-conditioning, chill water supplies, hull strength, and stability. All ships are being modified to achieve a common equipment and systems baseline before beginning the HCM/FELEX upgrade which is to begin with *Halifax* in 2010. Seven ships are to be refitted in Halifax Shipyard and five on the west coast at Victoria Shipyard.
Structure: Much effort has gone into stealth technology. Gas turbine engines are raft mounted. Dresball IR suppression is fitted. Indal RAST helicopter handling system.
Operational: Problems on first of class trials included higher than designed radiated noise levels which were reported as speed associated. These have been rectified and the ships are stable and quiet in all sea conditions. *Vancouver, Regina, Calgary, Winnipeg* and *Ottawa* are Pacific based.

FREDERICTON *8/2007, Blake Rodgers, RCN* / 1166834

ST JOHN'S

5/2007, **Frank Findler** / 1166765

CALGARY

*8/2008**, **RCN** / 1335648

TORONTO

*6/2008**, **M Declerck** / 1335649

DESTROYERS

Notes: The Canadian Surface Combatants (CSC) programme is for the construction of 15 ships to replace the current destroyer and frigate force. These vessels are to have a common hull and machinery, displace up to 7,500 tonnes, and are to employ modular concepts. The first batch of ships are to be optimised for air defence and command and control roles, as replacements for the Iroquois-class DDHGs, and later batches are to replace the Halifax-class frigates. It is planned that the first ships will become operational in the 2018–20 period.

3 IROQUOIS CLASS (DDGH)

Name	*No*	*Builders*	*Laid down*	*Launched*	*Commissioned*
IROQUOIS	280	Marine Industries Ltd, Sorel	15 Jan 1969	28 Nov 1970	29 July 1972
ATHABASKAN	282	Davie Shipbuilding, Lauzon	1 June 1969	27 Nov 1970	30 Sep 1972
ALGONQUIN	283	Davie Shipbuilding, Lauzon	1 Sep 1969	23 Apr 1971	3 Nov 1973

Displacement, tons: 5,300 full load
Dimensions, feet (metres): 398 wl; 426 oa × 50 × 15.5 keel/21.5 screws (121.4; 129.8 × 15.2 × 4.7/6.6)
Main machinery: COGOG; 2 Pratt & Whitney FT4A2 gas turbines; 50,000 hp (*37 MW*); 2 GM Allison 570-KF gas turbines; 12,700 hp (*9.5 MW*) sustained; 2 shafts; LIPS cp props
Speed, knots: 27
Range, n miles: 4,500 at 15 kt (cruise turbines)
Complement: 255 (23 officers) plus 30 (9 officers) aircrew

Missiles: SAM: 1 Martin Marietta Mk 41 VLS ❶ for 29 GDC Standard SM-2MR Block III/IIIA; command/inertial guidance; semi-active radar homing to 167 km *(90 n miles)* at Mach 2.5.
Guns: 1 OTO Melara 3 in *(76 mm)*/62 Super Rapid ❷; 120 rds/min to 16 km *(8.7 n miles)*; weight of shell 6 kg. 6–12.7 mm MGs.
1 GE/GDC 20 mm/76 6-barrelled Vulcan Phalanx Mk 15 ❸; 3,000 rds/min combined to 1.5 km.
Torpedoes: 6–324 mm Mk 32 (2 triple) tubes ❹. Honeywell Mk 46 Mod 5; anti-submarine; active/passive homing to 11 km *(5.9 n miles)* at 40 kt; warhead 44 kg.
Countermeasures: Decoys: 4 Plessey Shield Mk 2 6-tubed fixed launchers ❺. P 8 chaff or P 6 IR flares.
BAe Nulka offboard decoys in quad pack launchers.
SLQ-25 Nixie; torpedo decoy.
ESM: MEL SLQ-501 Canews ❻; radar warning.
ECM: BAe Nulka.
Combat data systems: SHINPADS, automated data handling with UYQ-504 and UYK-507 processors. Links 11, 14 and 16. JMCIS and Marconi Matra SHF SATCOM ❼.
Weapons control: Signaal LIROD 8 ❽ optronic director. UYS-503(V) sonobuoy processor.
Radars: Air search: Signaal SPQ-502 (LW08) ❾; D-band.

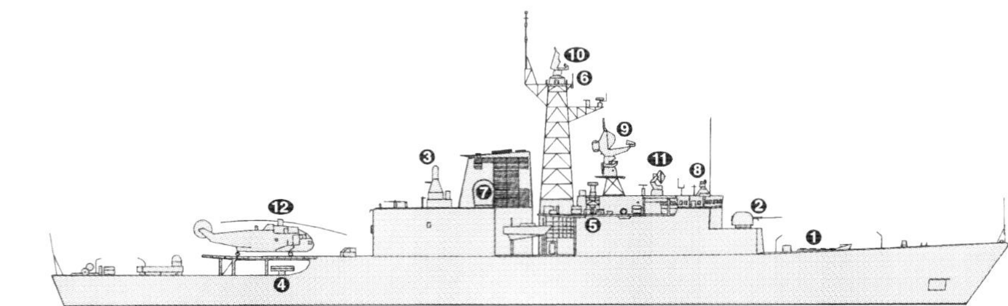

IROQUOIS ***(Scale 1 : 1,200), Ian Sturton*** / 0056677

Surface search: Signaal SPQ-501 (DA08) ❿; E/F-band.
Fire control: 2 Signaal SPG-501 (STIR 1.8) ⓫; I/J-band.
Navigation: 2 Raytheon Pathfinder; I-band.
Tacan: URN 26.
Sonars: General Dynamics SQS-510; combined VDS and hull-mounted; active search and attack; medium frequency.

Helicopters: 2 CH-124A Sea King ASW ⓬.

Modernisation: A contract for the Tribal Class Update and Modernisation Project (TRUMP) was awarded to Litton Systems Canada Limited in June 1986. The equipment reflected the changing role of the ship and replaced systems that did not meet the air defence requirement. *Algonquin* completed modernisation in October 1991, followed by *Iroquois* in May 1992 and *Athabaskan* in August 1994. Sonar upgraded from 1998. Nulka system replaced ULQ-6 in 1999. JMCIS has been fitted vice JOTS II, with SHF SATCOM in all three ships. Shipboard Electro-Optic Surveillance System (SEOSS) is being fitted in all ships. Vulcan Phalanx upgraded to Block 1B from 2003. A programme to upgrade/overhaul the SPQ-501, SPQ-502 and SPG-501 radarsand the LIROD 8 optronic director began in 2008.
Structure: These ships are also fitted with a landing deck equipped with double hauldown and Beartrap, pre-wetting system to counter NBC conditions, enclosed citadel and bridge control of machinery. The flume type anti-roll tanks have been replaced during modernisation with a water displaced fuel system. Design weight limit has been reached.
Operational: Helicopters can carry 12.7 mm MGs and ESM/FLIR instead of ASW gear. To remain in service until 2015.

IROQUOIS ***10/2006, Charles Barber, RCN*** / 1166839

ALGONQUIN ***10/2007, Michael Nitz*** / 1335651

SHIPBORNE AIRCRAFT

Notes: The five HELTAS Sea Kings have been converted to a battlefield/utility transport role. All acoustic systems have been removed.

Numbers/Type: 28 Sikorsky CH-148 Cyclone.
Operational speed: 165 kt *(305 km/h).*
Service ceiling: 11,320 ft *(3,450 m).*
Range: 444 n miles *(821 km).*
Role/Weapon systems: Contract for the acquisition of 28 helicopters to replace the Sea King (by 2012) made on 23 November 2004. Delivery of the aircraft is to begin in late 2010. Multimission maritime helicopter for ASW and ASUW and secondary missions of SAR, special forces operations, and Medevac. Sensors: L3 HELRAS sonar, Telephonics APS-143B(V)3 ISAR radar, GDC acoustic signal processor, FLIR Systems Star Safire III electro-optics system, Rockwell-Collins ARC-210 communications suite, ATK Alliant AN/ARR-47 MAWS, Lockheed Martin AN/ALQ-210 ESM/radar warning, Lockheed Martin AN/ALR-47 laser warning, BAE AN/ALQ-144 IR jammer, BAE AN/ALE-47 countermeasures dispenser system; Links 11 and 22. Weapons: Two Mk 46 torpedoes and C6 7.62 mm MG.

CH-148 *6/2005, Sikorsky* / 1123062

Numbers/Type: 22/5 Sikorsky CH-124A ASW/CH-124B SCF Utility Sea King.
Operational speed: 110 kt *(203 km/h)*
Service ceiling: 10,000 ft *(3,030 m)*
Range: 380 n miles *(705 km)*
Role/Weapon systems: ASW, surface surveillance and support, convertible for carriage of six troops; deployed from shore or from three classes of ships (Halifax class FFG (1 aircraft), Iroquois class DDG (2 aircraft) and 'Protecteur' AOR (3 aircraft)); Sensors: CH-124A/B: APS-503 radar, ASN-123 mission computer, GPS, ARA-5 direction finder, APX-77A IFF, HF/VHF/UHF comms (with secure voice capability), ALQ-144 IR countermeasures (fitted for but not with). CH-124A: AQS-502 dipping sonar, ARR-52A sono receiver and ARR-1047 OTPI. CH-124B: AN/ARC-210 communications, AN/AAR-47 MAWS, AN/ALQ-144 IR jammer and AN/ALE-47 CDS. Weapons: Two Mk 46 torpedoes and C6 7.62 mm MGs for both aircraft types.

CH-124A *10/2006, M Declerck* / 1164761

LAND-BASED MARITIME AIRCRAFT (FRONT LINE)

Notes: Procurement of a new maritime patrol aircraft to replace the Aurora from about 2020 is under consideration.

Numbers/Type: 18 Lockheed CP-140 Aurora.
Operational speed: 405 kt *(750 km/h)*
Service ceiling: 34,000 ft *(9,930 m)*
Range: 4,000 n miles *(7,410 km)*
Role/Weapon systems: Operated for long-range maritime surveillance over Atlantic, Pacific and Arctic Oceans; roles include ASW/ASV and SAR. Incremental modernisation (AIMP) programme to upgrade avionics and communications in up to 12 aircraft scheduled 2000–2013. Contract for update of navigation and flight instruments awarded to CMC Electronics in late 2000 and to MacDonald Dettwiler in January 2003 for replacement of AN/APS 506 radar by Telephonics AN/APS-143(V)3. In parallel, an ASLEP programme addresses airframe structural issues. Sensors: APS-506 radar, IFF, ALR-502 (to be replaced by AN/ALQ-217) ESM, ECM, FLIR OR 5008 (to be replaced by L-3 Wescam MX-20), ASQ-502 MAD, OL 5004 acoustic processor. Weapons: 8 Mk 46 Mod 5 torpedoes.

AURORA *10/2007, Michael Nitz* / 1335647

Numbers/Type: 2 Lockheed CP-140A Arcturus.
Operational speed: 405 kt *(750 km/h)*
Service ceiling: 34,000 ft *(9,930 m)*
Range: 4,000 n miles *(7,410 km)*
Role/Weapon systems: Arcturus operated for unarmed Arctic patrol, maritime surveillance, SAR and training. Fitted with same equipment as Aurora but without the ASW fit. To be withdrawn from service. Sensors: APS-507 radar, IFF.

PATROL FORCES

Notes: It was announced on 9 July 2007 that up to eight Arctic/Offshore Patrol Ships (AOPS) are to be acquired. The ships are to be tasked with maritime security duties in Canada's Exclusive Economic Zone, including the full length of the Northwest Passage in Summer and approaches in Winter. The broad requirement is for a 100 m ship of about 6,000 tons with an ice-strengthened steel hull capable of operating at 3 kt in ice up to 1 m thick. With a maximum speed of about 20 kt, the ships are to be armed (possibly with a 40 mm gun) and to be helicopter capable. The first ship is to be delivered in 2013. Naval support facilities are also to be constructed at the existing deep-water port of Nanisivik on Strathcona Sound, Nunavut. These are to be completed in 2015.

AMPHIBIOUS FORCES

Notes: The Standing Contingency Force concept was evolved in response to the need for a sea-based expeditionary capability for operations in the world's littorals. As part of the process to determine the required capabilities, an initial Integrated Tactical Effects (ITE) experiment was conducted in November 2006 using USS *Gunston Hall* as a trials platform. While development of a full SCF capability has since been placed in abeyance until at least 2011, conceptual development continues at the Maritime Warfare Centre.

MINE WARFARE FORCES

Notes: The Interim Remote Minehunting and Disposal System (IRMDS) is based on the Remote Minehunting System – Technology Demonstration (RMS-TD) system developed by Defence Research and Development Canada in conjunction with MDA Ltd of Richmond, BC, ISE Ltd of Port Moody, BC and DCNI of Paris, France. The production system is not expected to enter service until 2011 but, in the meantime, has been prepared for limited operation in an interim capacity. Initial Operating Capability was achieved on 1 April 2007. IRMDS, also known as Seakeeper, can be controlled from the Kingston class MCMVs and Sechelt class YDTs. French trials have been conducted from *Armorique* and *Taape*. The system consists of an 8.3 m long semi-submersible drone powered by a 375 hp diesel engine and capable of up to 16 kt transit speed and 10 kt minehunting. The Aurora towfish can deploy to depths of 15–200 m and is a mount for the L3/Klein K5500 multibeam side scan sonar and Reson 8125 echo sounder. Sonar operations can be conducted in up to Sea State 5. Missions are controlled from a C2 container embarked in a host ship or installed ashore.

12 KINGSTON CLASS (MM)

Name	*No*	*Builders*	*Laid down*	*Launched*	*Commissioned*
KINGSTON	700	Halifax Shipyards	15 Dec 1994	12 Aug 1995	21 Sep 1996
GLACE BAY	701	Halifax Shipyards	28 Apr 1995	22 Jan 1996	26 Oct 1996
NANAIMO	702	Halifax Shipyards	11 Aug 1995	17 May 1996	10 May 1997
EDMONTON	703	Halifax Shipyards	8 Dec 1995	16 Aug 1996	21 June 1997
SHAWINIGAN	704	Halifax Shipyards	26 Apr 1996	15 Nov 1996	14 June 1997
WHITEHORSE	705	Halifax Shipyards	26 July 1996	24 Feb 1997	17 Apr 1998
YELLOWKNIFE	706	Halifax Shipyards	7 Nov 1996	5 June 1997	18 Apr 1998
GOOSE BAY	707	Halifax Shipyards	22 Feb 1997	4 Sep 1997	26 July 1998
MONCTON	708	Halifax Shipyards	31 May 1997	5 Dec 1997	12 July 1998
SASKATOON	709	Halifax Shipyards	5 Sep 1997	30 Mar 1998	21 Nov 1998
BRANDON	710	Halifax Shipyards	6 Dec 1997	3 Sep 1998	5 June 1999
SUMMERSIDE	711	Halifax Shipyards	28 Mar 1998	4 Oct 1998	18 July 1999

Displacement, tons: 962 full load
Dimensions, feet (metres): 181.4 × 37.1 × 11.2 *(55.3 × 11.3 × 3.4)*
Main machinery: Diesel-electric; 4 Wärtsilä UD 23V12 diesels; 4 Jeumont ANR-53-50 alternators; 7.2 MW; 2 Jeumont CI 560L motors; 3,000 hp(m) *(2.2 MW)*; 2 LIPS Z drive azimuth thrusters
Speed, knots: 15; 10 sweeping
Range, n miles: 5,000 at 8 kt
Complement: 31 (Patrol); 37 (MCM)

Guns: 1 Bofors 40 mm/60 Mk 5C. 2—12.7 mm MGs.
Countermeasures: Three positions on the sweep deck can receive a variety of mission payloads on a 20 ft ISO footprint: (a) Indal Technologies AN/SLQ 38 deep mechanical minesweeping system (MMS) (2 systems); (b) MDA Ltd. AN/SQS 511 heavy-weight high-definition Route Survey System (RSS) (4 systems); (c) ISE Ltd. Trailblazer 25 bottom object inspection vehicle (BOIV) (1 system); (d) ISE Ltd. HYSUB 50 deep seabed intervention system (DSIS) (1 system); (e) Fullerton and Sherwood Ltd. 6-man, 2-compartment containerised diving system (CDS) (2 systems); (f) Naval engineered 6-person accommodation module (6 modules); and (g) MDA Ltd. Interim Remote Minehunting and Disposal System (IRMDS) control van (1 system). In addition, a number of light-weight systems, not normally fitted on 20 ft ISO bedplates or in containers, can be embarked: (a) L3/Klein K5500 high-definition side scan sonar (2 systems); (b) L3/Klein K 3000 dual frequency side scan sonar (4 systems); and (c) Deep Ocean Engineering Inc. Phantom 4 remotely operated vehicle (P4ROV) (2 systems).
Radars: Surface search: Kelvin Hughes 6000; E/F-band.
Navigation: Kelvin Hughes; I-band.

Programmes: Contract awarded to Fenco MacLaren on 15 May 1992. Halifax Shipyards is owned by Saint John Shipbuilding. Known as Maritime Coastal Defence Vessels (MCDV) combining MCM with general patrol duties.
Modernisation: Radars are to be replaced 2009–10.
Operational: Predominantly manned by reservists. Six on each coast (700, 701, 704, 707, 708 and 711 Atlantic, remainder Pacific). One ship per coast is kept at extended readiness on a rotational basis.

SASKATOON *10/2006, Michael Nitz* / 1166836

SURVEY AND RESEARCH SHIPS

1 RESEARCH SHIP (AGORH)

Name	*No*	*Builders*	*Launched*	*Commissioned*
QUEST	AGOR 172	Burrard, Vancouver	9 July 1969	21 Aug 1969

Displacement, tons: 2,130 full load
Dimensions, feet (metres): 252.0 × 42 × 18.4 *(76.8 × 12.8 × 5.6)*
Main machinery: Diesel-electric; 2 Fairbanks-Morse diesel generators; 2 GE motors; 2 shafts
Speed, knots: 14.5. **Range, n miles**: 10,000 at 12 kt
Complement: 24 plus 21 scientists

Comment: Used by Defence Research and Development Canada (DRDC) for acoustic, hydrographic and general oceanographic research activities. Designed with special acoustic quieting (anechoic tiles, rotating machinery on resilient mounts, propulsion and service diesels resiliently mounted and acoustically enclosed, various operational quiet states). Capable of operating in summer ice conditions (Ice Class I). Based in Halifax, NS, operates mainly in North and Mid Atlantic. Mid-life update in 1997–99 included new communications and navigation equipment, improved noise insulation, updated deck cranes and hardware, and modernised laboratories.

QUEST *6/2008*, Don Glencross* / 1335646

TRAINING SHIPS

8 ORCA CLASS (TRAINING SHIPS) (AXL)

ORCA 55	**CARIBOU** 57	**WOLF** 59	**COUGAR** 61
RAVEN 56	**RENARD** 58	**GRIZZLY** 60	**MOOSE** 62

Displacement, tons: 210 full load
Dimensions, feet (metres): 108.3 × 27.6 × 8.2 *(33.0 × 8.4 × 2.5)*
Main machinery: 2 Caterpillar 3516 diesels; 5,000 hp *(3.7 MW)*; 2 shafts
Speed, knots: 21
Range, n miles: 750 at 15 kt
Complement: 4 plus 16 trainees
Guns: 1 — 12.7 mm MG (fitted for).
Radars: 2 Raytheon NSC 1810; I-band.

Comment: Contract awarded to Victoria Shipyards, BC, on 8 November 2004 for the construction of six training vessels. The option to build a further two has been exercised. Based on the Australian *Seahorse Mercator* design. Construction of the first vessel began on 8 September 2005 with formal acceptance on 17 November 2006. The eighth and final vessel was delivered in late 2008. All vessels based at Esquimalt.

RENARD *5/2008*, RCN* / 1335645

1 SAIL TRAINING SHIP (AXS)

Name	*No*	*Builders*	*Launched*
ORIOLE	YAC 3	Owens	4 June 1921

Displacement, tons: 92 full load
Dimensions, feet (metres): 102 × 19 × 9 *(31.1 × 5.8 × 2.7)*
Main machinery: 1 Cummins diesel; 165 hp *(123 kW)*; 1 shaft
Speed, knots: 8
Complement: 6 (1 officer) plus 18 trainees

Comment: Commissioned in the Navy in 1948 and based at Esquimalt. Sail area (with spinnaker) 11,000 sq ft. Height of mainmast 94 ft *(28.7 m)*, mizzen 55.2 ft *(16.8 m)*.

ORIOLE *6/2008*, RCN* / 1335644

AUXILIARIES

Notes: Plans to procure three Joint Support Ships were cancelled on 22 August 2008 on cost grounds; it is reported that the Statement of Requirement could not be met with the funds allocated. While the requirement to replace the AORs remains a high priority, extension of the project definition stage is likely to result in a delay of at least two years and a contract is unlikely to be let until late 2010.

2 PROTECTEUR CLASS (AORH)

Name	*No*	*Builders*	*Laid down*	*Launched*	*Commissioned*
PROTECTEUR	AOR 509	St John Dry Dock Co, NB	17 Oct 1967	18 July 1968	30 Aug 1969
PRESERVER	AOR 510	St John Dry Dock Co, NB	17 Oct 1967	29 May 1969	30 July 1970

Displacement, tons: 9,259 light; 25,676 full load
Dimensions, feet (metres): 564 × 76 × 34.3 *(171.9 × 23.2 × 10.46)*
Main machinery: 2 Babcock & Wilcox boilers; 1 GE Canada turbine; 21,000 hp *(15.7 MW)*; 1 shaft; bow thruster
Speed, knots: 21
Range, n miles: 4,100 at 20 kt; 7,500 at 11.5 kt
Complement: 335 (38 officers) including 45 aircrew
Cargo capacity: 13,036 tons fuel; 506 tons aviation fuel; 352 tons dry cargo; 300 tons ammunition; 2 cranes (15 ton lift)

Guns: 2 GE/GDC 20 mm/76 6-barrelled Vulcan Phalanx Mk 15. 6 — 12.7 mm MGs.
Countermeasures: Decoys: 6 Loral Hycor SRBOC chaff launchers.
ESM: Racal Kestrel SLQ-504; radar warning.
Combat data systems: EDO Link 11; SATCOM WSC-3(V).
Radars: Surface search: Norden SPS-502 with Mk XII IFF.
Navigation: Racal Decca 1630 and 1629; I-band.
Tacan: URN 20.

Helicopters: 3 CH-124A or CH-124B Sea King.

Comment: Four replenishment positions. Both have been used as Flagships and troop carriers. They can carry military vehicles and bulk equipment for sealift purposes; also two LCVPs. For the Gulf deployment in 1991, the 76 mm gun was remounted, two Vulcan Phalanx and two Bofors 40/60 guns were fitted, four Plessey Shield chaff launchers and ESM equipment were provided for *Protecteur*. Bofors and 76 mm guns are unlikely to be fitted again. *Protecteur* transferred to the Pacific Fleet November 1992.

PROTECTEUR *10/2008*, Michael Nitz* / 1335643

4 SECHELT CLASS (YTT/YPT/YDT)

Name	*No*	*Builders*	*Commissioned*
SECHELT	YDT 610	West Coast Manly	10 Nov 1990
SIKANNI	YPT 611	West Coast Manly	10 Nov 1990
SOOKE	YDT 612	West Coast Manly	10 Nov 1990
STIKINE	YPT 613	West Coast Manly	10 Nov 1990

Displacement, tons: 290 full load
Dimensions, feet (metres): 108.5 × 27.8 × 7.8 *(33.1 × 8.5 × 2.4)*
Main machinery: 2 Caterpillar 3412T diesels; 1,080 hp *(806 kW)* sustained; 2 shafts
Speed, knots: 12.5
Complement: 4 or 12 (610 and 612)
Sonars: Fitted for (610 and 612) L3/Klein K 3000 or K 5500 side scan sonar.

Comment: *Sikanni* and *Stikine* based at the Nanoose Bay Maritime Experimental and Test Range. *Sechelt* and *Sooke* converted to diving tenders in 1997 with a 6 place recompression chamber embarked. Diving operations supported to 80 m. Both have been used as control platforms for IRMDS and are also fitted for the Phantom 4 ROV. *Sechelt* based at Halifax, Novia Scotia, *Sooke* at Esquimault, British Columbia.

SOOKE (with containerised diving system) ***6/2002, CDF*** / 0528415

2 GRANBY CLASS (GENERAL PURPOSE DIVING TENDERS) (YDT)

YDT 11 **GRANBY** YDT 12

Displacement, tons: 110
Dimensions, feet (metres): 99 × 20 × 8.5 *(27.3 × 6.2 × 2.6)*
Main machinery: Diesel; 228 hp (170 kW); 1 shaft
Speed, knots: 11
Complement: 13
Radars: Navigation: Racal Decca; I-band.
Sonars: Fitted for L3/Klein K 5500.

Comment: Built to provide platform for underwater engineering and 100 m surface supplied diving operations. Secondary role is support of MCM operations and maritime explosive ordnance disposal operations. The ships are equipped to deploy the Deep Ocean Engineering Phantom 4 ROV. Both ships are to be replaced by new construction ships in about 2010.

GRANBY ***11/1995, CDF*** / 0056682

TUGS AND TENDERS

13 COASTAL TUGS (YTB/YTL/YTR/YTM)

GLENDYNE YTB 640
GLENDALE YTB 641
GLENEVIS YTB 642
GLENBROOK YTB 643
GLENSIDE YTB 644
LAWRENCEVILLE YTL 590
PARKSVILLE YTL 591
LISTERVILLE YTL 592
MERRICKVILLE YTL 593
GRANVILLE (ex-*Marysville*) YTL 594
FIREBIRD YTR 561
FIREBRAND YTR 562
TILLICUM YTM 555

Comment: Glen class are 255 ton tugs built in the mid-1970s. Ville class are 70 ton tugs built in mid-1970s. The two YTRs are firefighting craft of 130 tons. The YTM is a 160 ton tug.

GLENDYNE ***11/2008*, RCN*** / 1335641

6 DIVING SUPPORT CRAFT (YDT)

FORTUNE
ABALONE
RESOLUTE
DUNGENESS
TONNERRE
SCULPIN

Displacement, tons: 2.2 full load
Dimensions, feet (metres): 39 × 12.5 × 2.3 *(11.9 × 3.8 × 0.7)*
Main machinery: 2 Caterpillar 3126TA diesels; 740 hp(m) *(548 kW)*; 2 WMC 357 waterjets
Speed, knots: 36
Range, n miles: 600 at 29 kt
Complement: 3 plus 14 divers
Sonars: Fitted for L3/Klein K 3000 and K 5500 side scan sonars.

Comment: Built by Celtic Shipyards and delivered in early 1997. Landing craft bows for launching unmanned submersibles (fitted for Phantom 4 ROV). Bollard pull 6,560 lb. 1,000 kg hydraulic crane. *Fortune, Resolute* and *Tonnerre* based at Halifax, Nova Scotia, and the remainder at Esquimault, British Columbia.

DIVING SUPPORT CRAFT ***11/2008*, RCN*** / 1335642

COAST GUARD

Administration

Commissioner Canadian Coast Guard:
George Da Pont
Deputy Commissioner:
Charles Gadula

Establishment

In January 1962, the ships owned and operated by the Department of Transport along with vessels operated by some other government agencies were amalgamated into a new organisation to be known as the Canadian Coast Guard. This reflected the increase in duties that had occurred since 1945, especially in the Arctic. Further expansion and diversification followed: notably of the dedicated search and rescue facilities, vessel traffic management and pollution prevention and response.

On 1 April 1995, the fleet of the Department of Fisheries and Oceans was merged with the Coast Guard under the direction of the Minister of Fisheries and Oceans. Its headquarters are in Ottawa while operations are administered from regional offices in Vancouver, British Columbia (Pacific Region); Sarnia, Ontario (Central and Arctic Region); Quebec, Quebec (Quebec Region); Dartmouth, Nova Scotia, (Maritimes Region) and St John's, Newfoundland (Newfoundland Region).

Missions

The Canadian Coast Guard carries out the following missions:

1. Provides services for the safe, economical and efficient movement of ships in Canadian waters through the provision of aids to navigation systems, marine communication and traffic management and channel maintenance.
2. Provides icebreaking services and vessel escort through ice in the Arctic and, in Winter, in the Gulf and River St Lawrence and the Great Lakes.
3. Contributes to the marine component of the Search and Rescue programme and participates with the Department of National Defence in Joint Rescue Coordination Centres in Victoria, British Columbia; Trenton, Ontario and Halifax, Nova Scotia. Sponsors a Coast Guard Auxiliary and promotes pleasure craft safety.
4. Participates (from April 2005) as a Special Operating Agency in joint patrols with the Royal Canadian Mounted Police to combat organised crime and terrorism.
5. Carries out fisheries patrols and enforcement of fishery regulations.
6. Provides and operates hydrographic survey, oceanographic and fisheries research vessels.
7. Supports other departments, boards and agencies of the government through the provision of ships, aircraft and other maritime services.

Shipborne Aircraft

A total of 22 helicopters can be operated from vessels equipped with flight decks. There are 15 MBB BO 105, four Bell 212 and three Bell 206L. One Sikorsky S 61N is based at Prince Rupert, BC, in the Pacific Region. This aircraft cannot operate from current vessels. Helicopters are painted in Canadian Coast Guard markings.

Small Craft

In addition to the ships listed there are numerous lifeboats, surfboats, self-propelled barges and other small craft which are carried on board the larger vessels. Also excluded are shore-based work boats, floating oil spill boats, oil slick-lickers or any of the small boats which are available for use at the various Canadian Coast Guard Bases and lighthouse stations.

DELETIONS

2006	*J E Bernier*
2007	*Simcoe*
2008	*Ile des Barques*

HEAVY ICEBREAKERS

Notes: The programme for a new heavy icebreaker, to replace *Louis St Laurent* was announced in February 2008. The new ship, to be named *John G Diefenbaker*, is to enter service in 2017.

1 GULF CLASS (TYPE 1300)

Name	*Builders*	*Launched*	*Commissioned*
LOUIS S ST LAURENT	Canadian Vickers Ltd, Montreal	3 Dec 1966	Oct 1969

Displacement, tons: 14,500 full load
Measurement, tons: 11,441 grt; 5,370 net
Dimensions, feet (metres): 392.7 × 80.1 × 32.2 *(119.7 × 24.4 × 9.8)*
Main machinery: Diesel-electric; 5 Krupp MaK 16 M 453C diesels; 39,400 hp(m) *(28.96 MW)*; 5 Siemens alternators; 3 GE motors; 27,000 hp(m) *(19.85 MW)*; 3 shafts; bow thruster
Speed, knots: 20
Range, n miles: 23,000 at 16 kt
Complement: 46 (13 officers) plus 38 scientists
Radars: Navigation: 3 Kelvin Hughes; I-band.
Helicopters: 2 BO 105 CBS.

Comment: Larger than any of the former Coast Guard icebreakers. Two 49.2 ft *(15 m)* landing craft embarked. Mid-life modernisation July 1988 to early 1993 included replacing main engines with a diesel-electric system, adding a more efficient *Henry Larsen* type icebreaking bow (adds 8 m to length) with an air bubbler system and improving helicopter facilities with a fixed hangar. In addition the complement was reduced. Based in the Maritimes Region at Dartmouth, NS but to re-deploy to the Newfoundland and Labrador region in 2009. On 22 August 1994 became the first Canadian ship to reach the North Pole, in company with USCG *Polar Sea*. To be decommissioned in 2017.

LOUIS S ST LAURENT *6/1998, Harald Carstens* / 0056691

LOUIS S ST LAURENT *6/1998, Harald Carstens* / 0017665

1 TERRY FOX CLASS (TYPE 1200)

Name	*Builders*	*Launched*	*Commissioned*
TERRY FOX	Burrard Yarrow, Vancouver	1982	1983

Displacement, tons: 7,100 full load
Measurement, tons: 4,233 gross; 1,955 net
Dimensions, feet (metres): 288.7 × 58.7 × 27.2 *(88 × 17.9 × 8.3)*
Main machinery: 4 Werkspoor 8-cyl 4SA diesels; 23,200 hp(m) *(17 MW)*; 2 shafts; cp props; bow and stern thrusters
Speed, knots: 16. **Range, n miles**: 1,920 at 15 kt
Complement: 24 (10 officers)
Radars: Navigation: 2 Racal Decca ARPA; 1 Furuno 1411; E/F- and I-bands.

Comment: Initially leased for two years from Gulf Canada Resources during the completion of *Louis S St Laurent* conversion but has now been retained. Commissioned in Coast Guard colours 1 November 1991 and purchased 1 November 1993. Based in the Newfoundland and Labrador region.

TERRY FOX *7/1997, M B MacKay* / 0012133

MEDIUM ICEBREAKERS

3 R CLASS (TYPE 1200)

Name	*Builders*	*Launched*	*Commissioned*
PIERRE RADISSON	Burrard, Vancouver	3 June 1977	June 1978
AMUNDSEN (ex-*Sir John Franklin*)	Burrard, Vancouver	10 Mar 1978	Mar 1979
DES GROSEILLIERS	Port Weller, Ontario	20 Feb 1982	Aug 1982

Displacement, tons: 6,400 standard; 8,180 (7,594, *Des Groseilliers*) full load
Measurement, tons: 5,910 gross; 1,678 net
Dimensions, feet (metres): 322 × 64 × 23.6 *(98.1 × 19.5 × 7.2)*
Main machinery: Diesel-electric; 6 Montreal Loco 251V-16F diesels; 17,580 hp *(13.1 MW)*; 6 GEC generators; 11.1 MW sustained; 2 motors; 13,600 hp *(10.14 MW)*; 2 shafts; bow thruster
Speed, knots: 16
Range, n miles: 15,000 at 13.5 kt
Complement: 38 (12 officers)
Radars: Navigation: Sperry; E/F- and I-band.
Helicopters: 1 Bell 212.

Comment: Based in the Quebec Region at Quebec. *Amundsen* underwent a major refit in 2003 to convert her to an Arctic research role.

AMUNDSEN *6/2003, P Dionne* / 0572428

1 MODIFIED R CLASS (TYPE 1200)

Name	*Builders*	*Launched*	*Commissioned*
HENRY LARSEN	Versatile Pacific SY, Vancouver, BC	3 Jan 1987	29 June 1988

Displacement, tons: 5,798 light; 8,290 full load
Measurement, tons: 6,172 gross; 1,756 net
Dimensions, feet (metres): 327.3 × 64.6 × 24 *(99.8 × 19.7 × 7.3)*
Main machinery: Diesel-electric; 3 Wärtsilä Vasa 16V32 diesel generators; 17.13 MW/60 Hz sustained; 3 motors; 16,320 hp(m) *(12 MW)*; 3 shafts
Speed, knots: 16
Range, n miles: 15,000 at 13.5 kt
Complement: 31 (11 officers) plus 20 spare berths
Radars: Navigation: Racal Decca Bridgemaster; I-band.
Helicopters: 1 Bell 212.

Comment: Contract date 25 May 1984, laid down 23 August 1985. Although similar in many ways to the R class she has a different hull form particularly at the bow and a very different propulsion system. Fitted with Wärtsilä air bubbling system. Based at St John's in the Newfoundland and Labrador Region. Engine room fire in 1998 put her out of commission for some time.

HENRY LARSEN *3/1999, Canadian Coast Guard* / 0056707

LIGHT ICEBREAKERS

6 MARTHA L BLACK CLASS (TYPE 1100)

Name	*Builders*	*Commissioned*
MARTHA L BLACK	Versatile Pacific, Vancouver, BC	30 Apr 1986
GEORGE R PEARKES	Versatile Pacific, Vancouver, BC	17 Apr 1986
EDWARD CORNWALLIS	Marine Industries Ltd, Tracy, Quebec	14 Aug 1986
SIR WILLIAM ALEXANDER	Marine Industries Ltd, Tracy, Quebec	13 Feb 1987
SIR WILFRID LAURIER	Canadian Shipbuilding Ltd, Ontario	15 Nov 1986
ANN HARVEY	Halifax Industries Ltd, Halifax, NS	29 June 1987

Displacement, tons: 4,662 full load
Measurement, tons: 3,818 *(Martha L Black)*; 3,809 *(George R Pearkes)*; 3,812 *(Sir Wilfrid Laurier)*; 3,727 *(Edward Cornwallis* and *Sir William Alexander)*; 3,823 *(Ann Harvey)* gross
Dimensions, feet (metres): 272.2 × 53.1 × 18.9 *(83 × 16.2 × 5.8)*
Main machinery: Diesel-electric; 3 Bombardier/Alco 12V-251 diesels; 8,019 hp *(6 MW)* sustained; 3 Canadian GE generators; 6 MW; 2 Canadian GE motors; 7,040 hp *(5.25 MW)*; 2 shafts; bow thrusters
Speed, knots: 15.5
Range, n miles: 6,500 at 15 kt
Complement: 25 (10 officers)
Radars: Navigation: Racal Decca Bridgemaster; I-band.
Helicopters: 1 light type, such as Bell 206L.

Comment: *Black* based in the Quebec Region at Quebec, *Cornwallis* and *Alexander* in the Maritimes Region at Dartmouth, *Ann Harvey* and *Pearkes* in the Newfoundland and Labrador Region at St Johns and *Laurier* in the Pacific Region at Victoria. The feasibility of converting *Cornwallis* to a survey ship was investigated but not taken forward.

GEORGE R PEARKES ***4/1996, van Ginderen Collection*** / 0056692

SIR WILLIAM ALEXANDER ***8/1998, M B MacKay*** / 0017668

1 GRIFFON CLASS (TYPE 1100)

Name	*Builders*	*Commissioned*
GRIFFON	Davie Shipbuilding, Lauzon	Dec 1970

Displacement, tons: 3,096 full load
Measurement, tons: 2,212 gross; 752 net
Dimensions, feet (metres): 233.9 × 49 × 15.5 *(71.3 × 14.9 × 4.7)*
Main machinery: Diesel-electric; 4 Fairbanks-Morse 38D8-1/8-12 diesel generators; 5.8 MW sustained; 2 motors; 3,982 hp(m) *(2.97 MW)*; 2 shafts
Speed, knots: 14
Range, n miles: 5,500 at 10 kt
Complement: 25 (9 officers)
Radars: Navigation: 2 Kelvin Hughes; I-band.
Helicopters: Platform for 1 light type, such as Bell 206L.

Comment: Based in the Central and Arctic Region at Prescott, Ontario.

GRIFFON ***7/1998, van Ginderen Collection*** / 0017669

MULTIROLE VESSELS

2 SAMUEL RISLEY CLASS (TYPE 1050)

Name	*Builders*	*Commissioned*
SAMUEL RISLEY	Vito Construction Ltd, Delta, BC	4 July 1985
EARL GREY	Pictou Shipyards Ltd, Pictou, NS	30 May 1986

Displacement, tons: 2,935 full load
Measurement, tons: 1,988 gross *(Grey)*; 1,967 gross *(Risley)*; 642 net *(Grey)*; 649.5 net *(Risley)*
Dimensions, feet (metres): 228.7 × 44.9 × 19 *(69.7 × 13.7 × 5.8)*
Main machinery: Diesel-electric; 4 Wärtsilä 4SA 12-cyl diesels; 8,644 hp(m) *(6.4 MW) (Samuel Risley)*; 4 Deutz 4SA 9-cyl diesels; 8,836 hp(m) *(6.5 MW) (Earl Grey)*; 2 shafts; cp props
Speed, knots: 13. **Range**: 18,000 at 12 kt
Complement: 22 (9 officers)
Radars: Navigation: 2 Racal Decca; I-band.

Comment: *Risley* based in the Central and Arctic Region at Pary Sound, Ontario, *Grey* in the Maritimes Region at Charlottetown, PEI.

SAMUEL RISLEY ***4/1993, Canadian Coast Guard*** / 0056694

2 PROVO WALLIS CLASS (TYPE 1000)

Name	*Builders*	*Commissioned*
BARTLETT	Marine Industries, Sorel	Dec 1969
PROVO WALLIS	Marine Industries, Sorel	Oct 1969

Displacement, tons: 1,620 full load *(Bartlett)*
Measurement, tons: 1,317 gross; 491 net
Dimensions, feet (metres): 189.3; 209 *(Provo Wallis)* × 42.5 × 15.4 *(57.7; 63.7 × 13 × 4.7)*
Main machinery: 2 National Gas 6-cyl diesels; 2,100 hp *(1.55 MW)*; 2 shafts; LIPS cp props
Speed, knots: 12.5. **Range, n miles**: 3,300 at 11 kt
Complement: 24 (9 officers)
Radars: Navigation: 2 Kelvin Hughes; I-band.

Comment: Both ships based in Pacific Region at Victoria. *Bartlett* was modernised in 1988 and *Provo Wallis* completed one year modernisation at Marystown, Newfoundland at the end of 1990. Work included lengthening the hull by 6 m, installing new equipment and improving accommodation.

PROVO WALLIS ***6/2008*, M Mazumdar*** / 1335247

1 TRACY CLASS (TYPE 1000)

Name	*Builders*	*Commissioned*
TRACY	Port Weller Drydocks, Ontario	17 Apr 1968

Displacement, tons: 1,300 full load
Measurement, tons: 963 gross; 290 net
Dimensions, feet (metres): 181.1 × 38 × 12.1 *(55.2 × 11.6 × 3.7)*
Main machinery: Diesel-electric; 2 Fairbanks-Morse 38D8-1/8-8 diesel generators; 1.94 MW sustained; 2 motors; 2,000 hp *(1.49 MW)*; 2 shafts
Speed, knots: 13. **Range, n miles**: 5,000 at 11 kt
Complement: 23 (8 officers)
Radars: Navigation: Kelvin Hughes; I-band.

Comment: Based in Quebec Region at Sorel.

TRACY ***4/1999, Canadian Coast Guard*** / 0056716

OFFSHORE PATROL VESSELS

1 SIR WILFRED GRENFELL (TYPE 600)

Name	*Builders*	*Commissioned*
SIR WILFRED GRENFELL	Marystown SY, Newfoundland	1987

Displacement, tons: 3,753 full load
Measurement, tons: 2,403 gross; 664.5 net
Dimensions, feet (metres): 224.7 × 49.2 × 16.4 *(68.5 × 15 × 5)*
Main machinery: 4 Deutz 4SA (2-16-cyl, 2-9-cyl) diesels; 12,862 hp(m) *(9.46 MW);* 2 shafts; cp props
Speed, knots: 16. **Range, n miles:** 11,000 at 14 kt
Complement: 20

Comment: Built on speculation in 1984–85. Modified to include an 85 tonne towing winch and additional SAR accommodation and equipment. Ice strengthened hull. Based in the Newfoundland Region and Labrador at St John's.

SIR WILFRED GRENFELL *8/1997, M B MacKay* / 0012137

1 LEONARD J COWLEY CLASS (TYPE 600)

Name	*Builders*	*Commissioned*
LEONARD J COWLEY	Manly Shipyard, RivTow Ind, Vancouver BC	June 1985

Displacement, tons: 2,080 full load
Measurement, tons: 2,244 grt; 655 net
Dimensions, feet (metres): 236.2 × 45.9 × 16.1 *(72 × 14 × 4.9)*
Main machinery: 2 Wärtsilä Nohab F 312A diesels; 2,325 hp(m) *(1.71 MW);* 1 shaft; bow thruster
Speed, knots: 12
Range, n miles: 12,000 at 12 kt
Complement: 19 (7 officers)
Guns: 2—12.7 mm MGs.
Radars: Surface search: Sperry 340; E/F-band.
Navigation: Sperry ARPA; I-band.
Helicopters: Capability for 1 light.

Comment: Based in Newfoundland and Labrador Region at St John's.

LEONARD J COWLEY *9/1996, D Maginley* / 0056698

2 CAPE ROGER CLASS (TYPE 600)

Name	*Builders*	*Commissioned*
CYGNUS	Marystown SY, Newfoundland	May 1981
CAPE ROGER	Ferguson Industries, Pictou NS	Aug 1977

Displacement, tons: 1,465 full load
Measurement, tons: 1,255 grt; 357 net
Dimensions, feet (metres): 205 × 40 × 13 *(62.5 × 12.2 × 4.1)*
Main machinery: 2 Wärtsilä Nohab F 212V diesels, 4,461 hp(m) *(3.28 MW);* 1 shaft; bow thruster
Speed, knots: 13. **Range, n miles:** 10,000 at 12 kt
Complement: 19
Guns: 2—12.7 mm MGs.
Helicopters: Capability for 1 light.

Comment: *Cygnus* based in Maritimes Region at Dartmouth and *Cape Roger* in Newfoundland and Labrador Region at St John's. Half-life refits completed in 1995–97.

CYGNUS *9/1999, Canadian Coast Guard* / 0056704

MIDSHORE PATROL VESSELS

Notes: The acquisition of 12 40 m mid-shore patrol vessels was approved in the 2007 budget. Eight of these vessels are to be used for conservation and protection duties in the Maritimes, Quebec and Pacific regions. The remaining four vessels are to be used for maritime security duties on the St Lawrence Seaway-Great Lakes system and are to be operated jointly by the Coast Guard and by the RCMP. Bids for the design were re-invited in September 2007 for submission by March 2008. A contract is expected in 2009.

1 TANU CLASS (TYPE 500)

Name	*Builders*	*Commissioned*
TANU	Yarrows Ltd, Victoria BC	Sep 1968

Displacement, tons: 925 full load
Measurement, tons: 746 grt; 203 net
Dimensions, feet (metres): 164.3 × 3.2 × 15.1 *(50.1 × 9.8 × 4.6)*
Main machinery: 2 Fairbanks-Morse diesels; 2,624 hp *(1.96 MW);* 1 shaft
Speed, knots: 11. **Range, n miles:** 5,000 at 11 kt
Complement: 16 (6 officers)
Guns: 2—12.7 mm MGs.

Comment: Based in Pacific Region at Patricia Bay.

TANU *7/2004, M K Mitchell* / 1042125

2 LOUISBOURG CLASS (TYPE 500)

Name	*Builders*	*Commissioned*
LOUISBOURG	Breton Industries, Port Hawkesbury, NS	1977
LOUIS M LAUZIER (ex-*Cape Harrison*)	Breton Industries, Port Hawkesbury, NS	1976

Displacement, tons: 460 full load
Measurement, tons: 295 grt; 65 net
Dimensions, feet (metres): 125 × 27.2 × 8.5 *(38.1 × 8.3 × 2.6)*
Main machinery: 2 MTU 12V 538 TB91 diesels; 4,600 hp(m) *(3.38 MW);* 2 shafts
Speed, knots: 13.5. **Range, n miles:** 3,840 at 10 kt
Complement: 14
Guns: 2—12.7 mm MGs.

Comment: Both based in the Quebec Region. *Louis M Lauzier* returned to service from charter (to Memorial University) in 2005.

LOUISBOURG *9/1999, Canadian Coast Guard* / 0056708

1 ARROW POST CLASS

Name	*Builders*	*Commissioned*
ARROW POST	Hike Metal Products, Wheatley, Ontario	1991

Measurement, tons: 228 gross; 93.1 net
Dimensions, feet (metres): 94.8 × 28.9 × ? *(28.9 × 8.8 × ?)*
Main machinery: 1 Caterpillar 3512 diesel; 711 hp *(954 kW);* 1 shaft
Speed, knots: 12. **Range, n miles:** 2,800 at 11 kt
Complement: 6 (3 officers)

Comment: Based in Pacific Region at Prince Rupert, British Columbia. To be replaced by new midshore patrol vessel.

ARROW POST *6/2004, M K Mitchell* / 1042124

1 CUTTER (TYPE 200)

Name	*Builders*	*Commissioned*
HARP	Georgetown SY, PEI	12 Dec 1986

Displacement, tons: 225 full load
Measurement, tons: 179 gross; 69 net
Dimensions, feet (metres): 76.1 × 24.9 × 8.2 *(23.2 × 7.6 × 2.5)*
Main machinery: 2 Caterpillar 3408 diesels; 850 hp *(634 kW)*; 2 Kort nozzle props
Speed, knots: 10. **Range, n miles:** 500 at 10 kt
Complement: 7 (3 officers)
Radars: Navigation: Sperry Mk 1270; I-band.

Comment: Ordered 26 April 1985. Ice strengthened hull. Based in Newfoundland and Labrador Region at St Anthony.

TYPE 200 CUTTER *3/1999, Canadian Coast Guard* / 0056706

1 GORDON REID CLASS (TYPE 500)

Name	*Builders*	*Commissioned*
GORDON REID	Versatile Pacific, Vancouver	Oct 1990

Measurement, tons: 836 gross; 247 net
Dimensions, feet (metres): 163.9 × 36.1 × 13.1 *(49.9 × 11 × 4)*
Main machinery: 4 Deutz SBV-6M-628 diesels; 2,475 hp(m) *(1.82 MW)* sustained; 2 shafts; bow thruster; 400 hp *(294 kW)*
Speed, knots: 15. **Range, n miles:** 2,500 at 15 kt
Complement: 14 (6 officers)

Comment: Designed for long-range patrols along the British Columbian coast out to 200 mile limit. Has a stern ramp for launching Zodiac Hurricane 733 rigid inflatables in up to Sea State 6. The Zodiac has a speed of 50 kt and is radar equipped. Based in the Pacific Region at Victoria.

GORDON REID *6/2004, M K Mitchell* / 1042122

NAVAIDS VESSELS

1 NAHIDIK CLASS (TYPE 700)

Name	*Builders*	*Commissioned*
NAHIDIK	Allied Shipbuilders Ltd, N Vancouver	1974

Displacement, tons: 1,125 full load
Measurement, tons: 856 gross; 392 net
Dimensions, feet (metres): 175.2 × 49.9 × 6.6 *(53.4 × 15.2 × 2)*
Main machinery: 2 Detroit diesels; 4,290 hp *(3.2 MW)*; 2 shafts
Speed, knots: 14. **Range, n miles:** 5,000 at 10 kt
Complement: 12 (6 officers)

Comment: Based in Central and Arctic Region at Hay River, North West Territories.

NAHIDIK *6/2004, Canadian Coast Guard* / 1042126

1 DUMIT CLASS (TYPE 700)

Name	*Builders*	*Commissioned*
DUMIT	Allied Shipbuilders Ltd, N Vancouver	July 1979

Displacement, tons: 629 full load
Measurement, tons: 569 gross; 176 net
Dimensions, feet (metres): 160.1 × 40 × 5.2 *(48.8 × 12.2 × 1.6)*
Main machinery: 2 Caterpillar 3512TA; 2,420 hp *(1.8 MW)* sustained; 2 shafts
Speed, knots: 13.5
Range, n miles: 7,700 at 11 kt
Complement: 10

Comment: Similar to *Eckaloo*. Based in Central and Arctic Region at Hay River, North West Territories.

DUMIT *7/1996, Canadian Coast Guard* / 0017671

1 TEMBAH CLASS (TYPE 700)

Name	*Builders*	*Commissioned*
TEMBAH	Allied Shipbuilders Ltd, N Vancouver	Oct 1963

Measurement, tons: 189 gross; 58 net
Dimensions, feet (metres): 123 × 25.9 × 3 *(37.5 × 7.9 × 0.9)*
Main machinery: 2 Cummins diesels; 500 hp *(373 kW)*; 2 shafts
Speed, knots: 12
Range, n miles: 1,300 at 10 kt
Complement: 9

Comment: Based in Central and Arctic Region at Hay River, North West Territories.

TEMBAH *4/1999, Canadian Coast Guard* / 0056714

1 ECKALOO CLASS (TYPE 700)

Name	*Builders*	*Commissioned*
ECKALOO	Vancouver SY Ltd	31 Aug 1988

Displacement, tons: 534 full load
Measurement, tons: 661 gross; 213 net
Dimensions, feet (metres): 160.8 × 44 × 4 *(49 × 13.4 × 1.2)*
Main machinery: 2 Caterpillar 3512TA; 2,420 hp *(1.8 MW)* sustained; 2 shafts
Speed, knots: 13
Range, n miles: 2,000 at 11 kt
Complement: 10
Helicopters: Platform for 1 Bell 206L/L-1.

Comment: Replaced vessel of the same name. Similar design to *Dumit*. Based in Central and Arctic Region at Hay River, North West Territories.

ECKALOO *9/1994, van Ginderen Collection* / 0056697

SPECIAL ROLE VESSELS

1 VAKTA CLASS

Name	*Builders*	*Commissioned*
VAKTA	Hike Metal Products Ltd, Wheatley, Ontario	2004

Measurement, tons: 34 gross; 26 net
Dimensions, feet (metres): 53.5 × 14.8 × 9.8 *(16.3 × 4.5 × 3.0)*
Main machinery: 2 Caterpillar diesels; 980 hp *(731 kW)*; 2 shafts
Speed, knots: 21
Complement: 3

Comment: Replaced *Namao* in 2005. Provides navigational aids and SAR services on Lake Winnipeg. Based in the Central and Arctic Region at Gimli, Manitoba.

VAKTA *6/2005, Canadian Coast Guard* / 1151242

5 COVE ISLAND CLASS (TYPE 800)

Name	*Builders*	*Commissioned*
COVE ISLE	Canadian D and D, Kingston, Ontario	1980
GULL ISLE	Canadian D and D, Kingston, Ontario	1980
TSEKOA II	Allied Shipbuilders, Vancouver	1984
ILE SAINT-OURS	Breton Industries, Port Hawkesbury, NS	15 May 1986
CARIBOU ISLE	Breton Industries, Port Hawkesbury, NS	16 June 1986

Displacement, tons: 138 full load
Measurement, tons: 92 gross; 36 net
Dimensions, feet (metres): 75.5 × 19.7 × 4.4 *(23 × 6 × 1.4)*
Main machinery: 2 Detroit 8V-92 diesels; 475 hp *(354 kW)*; 2 shafts
Speed, knots: 11
Range, n miles: 1,800 at 11 kt
Complement: 5
Radars: Navigation: Sperry 1270; I-band.

Comment: Details given are for the last two. *Cove Isle* and *Gull Isle* are 3 m shorter in length; *Tsekoa II* is 3.7 m longer. *Cove Isle, Gull Isle* and *Caribou Isle* are based in the Central and Arctic Region at Parry Sound, Amherstburg and *Prescott* respectively. *Tsekoa II* is based in the Pacific at Victoria. *Ile Saint-Ours* is based in the Quebec Region at Sorel. *Ile des Barques* was decommissioned in 2008.

ILE SAINT-OURS *9/1994, van Ginderen Collection* / 0056696

4 CUTTERS (TYPE 400)

Name	*Builders*	*Commissioned*
POINT HENRY	Breton Industrial and Machinery, Pt Hawkesbury, NS	1980
ISLE ROUGE	Breton Industrial and Machinery, Pt Hawkesbury, NS	1980
POINT RACE	Breton Industrial and Machinery, Pt Hawkesbury, NS	1982
CAPE HURD	Breton Industrial and Machinery, Pt Hawkesbury, NS	1982

Displacement, tons: 97 full load
Measurement, tons: 57 gross; 14 net
Dimensions, feet (metres): 70.8 × 18 × 5.6 *(21.6 × 5.5 × 1.7)*
Main machinery: 2 MTU 8V 396TC82 diesels; 1,740 hp(m) *(1.28 MW)* sustained; 2 shafts
Speed, knots: 20
Range, n miles: 950 at 12 kt
Complement: 5

Comment: Aluminium alloy hulls. *Point Henry* and *Point Race* based in Pacific Region at Prince Rupert and Campbell River respectively; *Cape Hurd* and *Isle Rouge* in Central and Arctic Region at Amherstburgh.

POINT RACE *6/2001, Canadian Coast Guard* / 0126356

3 POST CLASS

Name	*Builders*	*Commissioned*
ATLIN POST	Philbrooks Shipyard Ltd, Sidney, BC	1975
KITIMAT II	Philbrooks Shipyard Ltd, Sidney, BC	1974
SOOKE POST	Philbrooks Shipyard Ltd, Sidney, BC	1973

Measurement, tons: 57 gross; 15 net
Dimensions, feet (metres): 65.0 × 17.1 × ? *(19.8 × 5.2 × ?)*
Main machinery: 2 General Motors V12-71 diesels; 800 hp *(596 kW)*; 2 shafts
Speed, knots: 15
Range, n miles: 400 at 12 kt
Complement: 4 (3 officers)

Comment: *Atlin Post* based at Patricia Bay, British Columbia, *Kitimat II* at Prince Rupert, British Columbia and *Sooke Post* at Port Hardy, BC. To be replaced by new midshore patrol vessels.

ATLIN POST *6/2001, Canadian Coast Guard* / 0126355

1 CUMELLA CLASS

Name	*Builders*	*Commissioned*
CUMELLA	A F Theriault & Son, Meteghan, NS	1983

Measurement, tons: 80 gross; 19 net
Dimensions, feet (metres): 76.1 × 15.7 × ? *(23.2 × 4.8 × ?)*
Main machinery: 2 General Motors V6-24L diesels; 1,680 hp *(1.25 MW)*; 2 shafts
Speed, knots: 15
Range, n miles: 600 at 12 kt
Complement: 4 (2 officers)

Comment: Based in Maritimes Region at Grand Manaan, New Brunswick. To be replaced by new midshore patrol vessel.

CUMELLA *6/2001, Canadian Coast Guard* / 0126354

1 QUÉBÉCOIS CLASS

Name	*Builders*	*Commissioned*
E P LE QUÉBÉCOIS	Les Chantiers Maritimes, Paspebiac, Quebec	1968

Measurement, tons: 186 gross; 32 net
Dimensions, feet (metres): 78.1 × 23.3 × ? *(28.3 × 7.1 × ?)*
Main machinery: 1 Caterpillar 3509 diesel; 509 hp *(380 kW)*; 1 shaft
Speed, knots: 11. **Range, n miles:** 2,800 at 9 kt
Complement: 8 (4 officers)

Comment: Based at Sept Îles, Quebec. Refitted in 1994. To be replaced by new midshore patrol vessel.

E P LE QUÉBÉCOIS *6/2002, Canadian Coast Guard* / 0529823

5 SAR CRAFT (TYPE 100)

Name	*Builders*	*Commissioned*
CG 119	Eastern Equipment, Montreal	1973
MALLARD	Matsumoto Shipyard, Vancouver, BC	Feb 1986
SKUA	Matsumoto Shipyard, Vancouver, BC	Mar 1986
OSPREY	Matsumoto Shipyard, Vancouver, BC	May 1986
STERNE	Matsumoto Shipyard, Vancouver, BC	Mar 1987

Measurement, tons: 15 gross
Dimensions, feet (metres): 40.8 × 13.2 × 4.2 *(12.4 × 4.1 × 1.3)*
Main machinery: 2 Mitsubishi diesels; 637 hp *(475 kW)*; 2 shafts
Speed, knots: 26. **Range, n miles:** 300 at 18 kt
Complement: 6 (3 officers)

Comment: CG 119 (laid up) based in Central and Arctic Region at Prescott; *Sterne* (laid up) is based in Quebec Region at Quebec and *Mallard, Skua* (laid up) and *Osprey* in the Pacific Region at Powell River, Ganges and Kitsilano respectively. CG 119 is structurally different to and slower than the remainder.

CG 119 *1990, van Ginderen Collection* / 0505968

SAR LIFEBOATS

Notes: There are also at least 15 Inshore Rescue boats with CG numbers.

10 LIFEBOATS (TYPE 300A)

Name	*Builders*	*Commissioned*
BICKERTON	Halmatic, Havant	Aug 1989
SPINDRIFT	Georgetown, PEI	Oct 1993
SPRAY	Industrie Raymond, Quebec	Sep 1994
COURTENAY BAY (ex-*Spume*)	Industrie Raymond, Quebec	Oct 1994
W JACKMAN (ex-*Cap Aux Meules*)	Industrie Raymond, Quebec	Sep 1995
W G GEORGE	Industrie Raymond, Quebec	Sep 1995
CAP AUX MEULES	Hike Metal Products Ltd, Ontario	Oct 1996
CLARK'S HARBOUR	Hike Metal Products Ltd, Ontario	Sep 1996
SAMBRO	Hike Metal Products Ltd, Ontario	Jan 1997
WESTPORT	Hike Metal Products Ltd, Ontario	May 1997

Measurement, tons: 34 gross
Dimensions, feet (metres): 52 × 17.5 × 4.6 *(15.9 × 5.3 × 1.5)*
Main machinery: 2 Caterpillar 3408BTA diesels; 1,070 hp *(786 kW)* sustained; 2 shafts
Speed, knots: 16–20. **Range, n miles:** 200 at 12 kt
Complement: 4 (2 officers)
Radars: Navigation: Furuno; I-band.

Comment: Seven based in Martimes Region, two in Newfoundland and Labrador Region, one in Quebec Region. *Bickerton* has GRP hull, remainder aluminium.

CLARKS HARBOUR *8/1996, Kathy Johnson* / 0056702

31 LIFEBOATS (TYPE 300B)

Name	*Builders*	*Commissioned*
THUNDER CAPE	Metalcraft Marine, Kingston	Aug 2000
CAPE SUTIL	Metalcraft Marine, Kingston	Dec 1998
CAPE CALVERT	Metalcraft Marine, Kingston	Aug 1999
CAPE ST JAMES	Metalcraft Marine, Kingston	Nov 1999
CAPE MERCY	Metalcraft Marine, Kingston	Dec 2000
CAPE LAMBTON	Metalcraft Marine, Kingston	July 2001
CAPE STORM	Metalcraft Marine, Kingston	Nov 2002
CAPE FOX	Victoria Shipyard Co Ltd, Victoria, BC	May 2003
CAPE NORMAN	Victoria Shipyard Co Ltd, Victoria, BC	May 2003
CAP DE RABAST	Victoria Shipyard Co Ltd, Victoria, BC	Aug 2003
CAP ROZIER	Victoria Shipyard Co Ltd, Victoria, BC	Aug 2003
CAPE MUDGE	Victoria Shipyard Co Ltd, Victoria, BC	Nov 2003
CAPE FAREWELL	Victoria Shipyard Co Ltd, Victoria, BC	Nov 2003
CAPE COCKBURN	Victoria Shipyard Co Ltd, Victoria, BC	Jan 2004
CAPE SPRY	Victoria Shipyard Co Ltd, Victoria, BC	Apr 2004
CAP NORD	Victoria Shipyard Co Ltd, Victoria, BC	Apr 2004
CAP BRETON	Victoria Shipyard Co Ltd, Victoria, BC	Apr 2004
CAPE MCKAY	Victoria Shipyard Co Ltd, Victoria, BC	June 2004
CAPE CHAILLON	Victoria Shipyard Co Ltd, Victoria, BC	Oct 2004
CAPE PROVIDENCE	Victoria Shipyard Co Ltd, Victoria, BC	Oct 2004
CAPE COMMODORE	Victoria Shipyard Co Ltd, Victoria, BC	Oct 2004
CAPE ANN	Victoria Shipyard Co Ltd, Victoria, BC	Nov 2004
CAPE CAUTION	Victoria Shipyard Co Ltd, Victoria, BC	Dec 2004
CAPE DISCOVERY	Victoria Shipyard Co Ltd, Victoria, BC	Jan 2005
CAPE HEARNE	Victoria Shipyard Co Ltd, Victoria, BC	Feb 2005
CAPE DUNDAS	Victoria Shipyard Co Ltd, Victoria, BC	Mar 2005
CAP TOURMENTE	Victoria Shipyard Co Ltd, Victoria, BC	Apr 2005
CAP D'ESPOIR	Victoria Shipyard Co Ltd, Victoria, BC	June 2005
CAP PERCÉ	Victoria Shipyard Co Ltd, Victoria, BC	Aug 2005
CAPE EDENSAW	Victoria Shipyard Co Ltd, Victoria, BC	Sep 2005
CAPE KUPER	Victoria Shipyard Co Ltd, Victoria, BC	Oct 2005

Measurement, tons: 33.8 gross
Dimensions, feet (metres): 47.9 × 14 × 4.5 *(14.6 × 4.27 × 1.37)*
Main machinery: 2 Caterpillar 3196 diesels; 905 hp *(675 kW)* sustained; 2 shafts
Speed, knots: 22–25
Range, n miles: 200 n miles
Complement: 4
Radars: Navigation: Furuno 1942; I-band.

Comment: Multitask medium endurance lifeboat.

THUNDER CAPE *2000, Canadian Coast Guard* / 0104265

AIR CUSHION VEHICLES

Notes: Plans to acquire a new Air Cushion to replace *Waban Aki* were announced in 2007. The new craft, to enter service in 2009, is expected to be similar to the 28.5 m AP1-88/400 type that is already in service.

1 AP1-88/200 TYPE

Name	*Builders*	*Commissioned*
WABAN-AKI	Westland Aerospace	15 July 1987

Displacement, tons: 47.6 light
Dimensions, feet (metres): 80.4 × 36.7 × 19.6 *(24.5 × 11.2 × 6.6)* (height on cushion)
Main machinery: 4 Deutz diesels; 2,394 hp(m) *(1.76 MW)*
Speed, knots: 50; 35 cruising
Complement: 4 (3 officers)
Cargo capacity: 12 tons

Comment: *Waban-Aki* is based at Trois Rivières and capable of year round operation as a Navaid Tender for flood control operations in the St Lawrence. Fitted with a hydraulic crane. The name means People of the Dawn.

WABAN-AKI *4/1999, Canadian Coast Guard / 0056717*

2 AP1-88/400 TYPE

SIPU MUIN SIYAY

Displacement, tons: 69 full load
Dimensions, feet (metres): 93.5 × 39.4 *(28.5 × 12)*
Main machinery: 4 Caterpillar 3412 TTA diesels; 3,650 hp(m) *(2.68 MW)* sustained
Speed, knots: 50; 35 cruising
Complement: 4
Cargo capacity: 22.6 tons

Comment: Contract awarded to GKN Westland in May 1996. Built at Hike Metal Products, Wheatley, Ontario and completed in August and December 1998 respectively. Well-deck size 8.2 × 4.6 m. There is a 5,000 kg load crane. *Sipu Muin* is based at Trois Rivières and the second at Sea Island, BC.

SIPU MUIN *5/1998, Canada Coast Guard / 0017672*

1 AP1-88/100 TYPE (TRAINING SHIP) (AXL)

PENAC (ex-*Liv Viking*)

Displacement, tons: 45.5 full load
Dimensions, feet (metres): 80.4 × 39.0 *(24.5 × 11.9)*
Main machinery: 2 Deutz BF 12L513 diesels; 1,050 hp(m) *(785 kW)*. 2 MTU 12V 183TB32 diesels; 1,640 hp(m) *(1.25 MW)* sustained
Speed, knots: 50; 35 cruising
Complement: 7
Cargo capacity: 5.3 tons

Comment: Built by Hoverworks Ltd, Isle of Wight, UK in 1984. Procured by Canadian Coast Guard in 2004. Based in Vancouver, BC.

PENAC *6/2004, Canadian Coast Guard / 1042123*

FISHERY RESEARCH SHIPS

10 + 3 FISHERY RESEARCH SHIPS

Name	*Commissioned*	*Based*	*Measurement, tons*
ALFRED NEEDLER	Aug 1982	Dartmouth, NS	925 grt
WILFRED TEMPLEMAN	Mar 1982	St John's, NL	925 grt
W E RICKER (ex-*Callistratus*)	Dec 1978	Nanaimo, BC	1,040 grt
TELEOST	1996	St John's, NL	
PANDALUS III	1986	St Andrew's, NB	13 grt
SHAMOOK	1975	St John's, NL	187 grt
OPILIO	1989	Shippagan, NB	74 grt
CALANUS II	1991	Rimouski, QC	160 grt
NEOCALIGUS	2001	Nanaimbo, QC	98 grt

Comment: First four are classified as Offshore Fishery Science vessels, remainder as Near-shore Fishery Research vessels. *Shark* was decommissioned in 2006. Three new 67 m offshore fishery science vessels were funded in the 2006 and 2007 budgets. Bids for the design are expected to be sought in 2009 and the ships are to enter service 2011–12.

TELEOST *4/1999, Canadian Coast Guard / 0056713*

SURVEY AND RESEARCH SHIPS

7 + 1 RESEARCH SHIPS

Name	*Commissioned*	*Based*	*Displacement, tons*
MATTHEW	1990	Dartmouth, NS	950
F C G SMITH	1986	Quebec, QC	300
HUDSON	1963	Dartmouth, NS	3,740
JOHN P TULLY	1985	Patricia Bay, BC	1,800
VECTOR	1967	Patricia Bay, BC	520
LIMNOS	1968	Burlington, ON	
FREDERICK G CREED	1988	Rimouski, QC	81

Comment: *Hudson* and *Tully* are classified as Offshore Oceanographic Science vessels. *Hudson* is to be replaced by a new 90 m vessel in 2013. *Matthew, Frederick G Creed, Limnos* and *Vector* are classified as Hydrographic Survey Vessels. *F C G Smith* is classified as a Channel Survey and Sounding Vessel.

F C G SMITH *7/1998, C D Maginley / 0017673*

ROYAL CANADIAN MOUNTED POLICE

Notes: The Marine Branch of the Royal Canadian Mounted Police is responsible for enforcement of Customs, Immigration, Shipping and Drug regulations as well as for standard policing duties in areas that are difficult to access by land. *Simmonds*, a 17 m catamaran, is on loan to the Canadian Coast Guard in the Great Lakes region. In addition there are some 377 smaller craft for use on inland waterways.

2 PATROL CRAFT (PB)

INKSTER MURRAY

Measurement, tons: 64 gross; 48 net
Dimensions, feet (metres): 64.8 × 22.0 × ? *(19.75 × 6.7 × ?)*
Main machinery: *Inkster*: 2 Mann diesels 1,640 hp *(1.2 MW)*. *Murray*: 2 Caterpillar diesels 2,100 hp *(1.6 MW)*; 2 Arneson surface drives
Speed, knots: To be announced
Complement: 4

Comment: Catamaran design patrol craft. *Inkster* based on the Pacific Coast and *Murray* on the Atlantic coast.

INKSTER *6/2006, RCMP* / 1159227

3 PATROL CRAFT (PB)

NADON HIGGIT LINDSAY

Measurement, tons: 61 gross; 46 net
Dimensions, feet (metres): 58.0 × 22.0 × ? (17.7 × 6.7 × ?)
Main machinery: 2 Mann diesels 1,640 hp *(1.2 MW)*; 2 Arneson surface drives
Speed, knots: to be announced
Complement: 4

Comment: Catamaran design patrol craft. All three based on the Pacific coast.

LINDSAY *6/2006, RCMP* / 1159228

Cape Verde

Country Overview

A former Portuguese colony, the Republic of Cape Verde became independent in 1975. Situated in the Atlantic Ocean some 335 n miles due west of the western point of Africa, it has a land area of 1,557 square miles and consists of ten islands and a number of islets. These are divided into the northerly windward (Barlavento) and southerly leeward (Sotavento) groups. The windward group includes the islands of Santo Antão, São Vicente, Santa Luzia, São Nicolau, Sal and Boa Vista and the islets of Branco and Raso; the leeward group includes the islands of Santiago, Brava, Fogo and Maio and the islets of the Secos group. Mindelo, on São Vicente, is the principal port and economic centre while Praia on Santiago is the capital and largest town. An archipelagic state, territorial seas (12 n miles) are claimed. A 200 n mile Exclusive Economic Zone (EEZ) has been claimed but the limits are not fully defined.

Headquarters Appointments

Commander, Coast Guard:
Lieutenant Colonel Fernando Carvalho Pereira

Personnel

2009: 50

Bases

Praia, main naval base.
Mindelo (Isle de São Vicente), naval repair yard.

Maritime Aircraft

One Dornier 228-212 and one Embraer EMB 110 Bandeirante are used for maritime surveillance.

PATROL FORCES

1 KONDOR I CLASS (COASTAL PATROL CRAFT) (PBO)

Name	*No*	*Builders*	*Commissioned*
VIGILANTE (ex-*Kühlungsborn*)	P 521 (ex-BG 32, ex-GS 07)	Peenewerft, Wolgast	1970

Displacement, tons: 360 full load
Dimensions, feet (metres): 170.3 × 23.3 × 7.2 *(51.9 × 7.1 × 2.2)*
Main machinery: 2 Russki/Kolomna Type 40DM diesels; 4,408 hp(m) *(3.24 MW)* sustained; 2 shafts; cp props
Speed, knots: 18
Range, n miles: 1,800 at 15 kt
Complement: 19 (3 officers)
Guns: 2—25 mm (twin) (ZU 23).
Radars: Surface search: Kelvin Hughes Nucleus 2 5000A; I-band.

Comment: Former GDR minesweeper taken over by the German Coast Guard, and then acquired by Cape Verde in September 1998. Armament refitted in Cape Verde in 1999. Started refit in 2007.

KONDOR I (Malta colours) *6/1997, Robert Pabst* / 0017674

1 ESPADARTE CLASS (PETERSON MK 4 TYPE) (COASTAL PATROL CRAFT) (PB)

Name	*No*	*Builders*	*Commissioned*
ESPADARTE	P 151	Peterson Builders Inc	19 Aug 1993

Displacement, tons: 22 full load
Dimensions, feet (metres): 51.3 × 14.8 × 4.3 *(15.6 × 4.5 × 1.3)*
Main machinery: 2 Detroit 6V-92TA diesels; 520 hp *(388 kW)* sustained; 2 shafts
Speed, knots: 24
Range, n miles: 500 at 20 kt
Complement: 6 (1 officer)
Guns: 2—12.7 mm MGs (twin). 2—7.62 mm MGs.
Radars: Surface search: Raytheon; I-band.

Comment: Ordered from Peterson Builders Inc, under FMS programme on 25 September 1992. Option on three more not taken up. Aluminium hulls. The 12.7 mm mounting is aft with the smaller guns on the bridge roof.

Mk 4 CPC (US colours) *11/1993, Peterson Builders* / 0081500

1 CHINESE 27 METRE CLASS (PATROL CRAFT) (PB)

Name	*No*	*Commissioned*
TAINHA	P 262	2000

Displacement, tons: 55
Dimensions, feet (metres): 88.6 × 13.1 × 3.9 *(27 × 4 × 1.2)*
Main machinery: 2 diesels; 1,000 hp *(746 kW)*
Complement: 9 (1 officer)
Guns: 2—12.7 mm MGs. 2—7.62 mm MGs.
Radars: Surface search/navigation: R 770 UA; I-band.

Comment: Transferred from China in 2004. Similar craft in service in Benin.

TAINHA
6/2007, Cape Verde Coast Guard
1167966

Cayman Islands

Country Overview

A British dependency since 1962, the island group is situated south of Cuba in the Caribbean Sea. It comprises three islands: Grand Cayman, containing the capital George Town, Little Cayman and Cayman Brac, located about 80 miles northeast of Grand Cayman. Territorial seas (12 n miles) and a Fishery Zone (200 n miles) are claimed. A governor, appointed by the British Crown, is responsible for external affairs, internal security, defence and the police. The Marine section is a division of the Royal Cayman Islands Police (RCIP) and UK Customs Drugs Task Force. Its roles are Maritime Drug Interdiction, SAR, Safety, Conservation and Fishery Protection.

Headquarters Appointments

Commander Royal Cayman Islands Police (Marine):
Brad Ebanks

Personnel

2009: 15 (mixture of police and customs)

Bases

Grand Cayman (main), Little Cayman, Cayman Brac.

POLICE

Notes: (1) Two SAFE Boats 38 ft interceptors were delivered in January 2009.
(2) A Concept pursuit craft, *Derry's Pride*, with twin 225 hp Johnson outboards is based at Grand Cayman together with *Intrepid*, an 'Eduardono' Colombian craft, and *Typhoon*, a 24 ft RIB. Two Boston Whalers, *Lima 1* and *MissMolly*, are based at Little Cayman and Cayman Brac respectively.

DERRY'S PRIDE ***6/2001, RCIP*** / 0121307

LIMA 1 ***6/2001, RCIP*** / 0121306

1 DAUNTLESS CLASS (PB)

CAYMAN PROTECTOR

Displacement, tons: 17 full load
Dimensions, feet (metres): 47.9 × 14.1 × 3.3 *(14.6 × 4.3 × 1)*
Main machinery: 2 Caterpillar 3208TA diesels; 720 hp(m) *(529 kW)* sustained; 2 shafts
Speed, knots: 26. **Range, n miles**: 400 at 20 kt
Complement: 11
Guns: 2–7.62 mm MGs.
Radars: Raytheon R40; I-band.

Comment: Built by SeaArk Marine, Monticello and acquired in July 1994. Aluminium construction. Based at Grand Cayman.

CAYMAN PROTECTOR ***6/2001, RCIP*** / 0121305

1 SEA ARK 65 ft CUTTER (PB)

CAYMAN GUARDIAN

Displacement, tons: 27 standard
Dimensions, feet (metres): 65.0 × 18.0 × 5.5 *(19.8 × 5.5 × 1.7)*
Main machinery: 2 diesels; 2 shafts
Speed, knots: to be announced
Complement: 8
Radars: Navigation: Raymarine; I-band.

Comment: SeaArk Marine Dauntless RAM patrol craft acquired in December 2008. To be employed on border protection tasks. Aluminium construction.

CAYMAN GUARDIAN ***12/2008*, SeaArk Marine*** / 1335342

1 SEA ARK 38 ft CUTTER (PB)

CAYMAN DEFENDER

Displacement, tons: 10.1 full load
Dimensions, feet (metres): 38.0 × 13.0 × 3.7 *(11.6 × 4.0 × 1.1)*
Main machinery: 2 MAN diesels; 1,100 hp *(820 kW)*
Speed, knots: 33
Complement: 4
Radars: Navigation: Raymarine; I-band.

Comment: SeaArk Marine Dauntless RAM patrol craft acquired on 7 October 2008. To be employed on border protection tasks. Aluminium construction.

CAYMAN DEFENDER ***10/2008*, SeaArk Marine*** / 1335341

Chile

ARMADA DE CHILE

Country Overview

The Republic of Chile is situated in western South America. With an area of 292,135 square miles it has borders to the north with Peru and to the east with Bolivia and Argentina. Off the 2,305 n mile coastline with the Pacific Ocean lie the Chonos Archipelago, Wellington Island and the western portion of Tierra del Fuego. Chilean islands in the south Pacific include the Juan Fernández Islands, Easter Island, and Salas y Gómez. The capital and largest city is Santiago. Principal ports include Valparaiso, Talcahuano, Tomé, Antofagasta, San Antonio, Arica, Iquique, Coquimbo, San Vicente, Puerto Montt, and Punta Arenas. Territorial seas (12 n miles) and an EEZ (200 n miles) are claimed.

Headquarters Appointments

Commander-in-Chief:
Admiral Rodolfo Codina Diaz
Chief of Naval Staff:
Vice Admiral Sergio Robinson Prieto
Naval Operations Command:
Vice Admiral Gustavo Jordan Astaburuaga
Director General, Naval Personnel:
Vice Admiral Cristián Millar Drago
Director General, Naval Services:
Vice Admiral Cristián Gantes Young
Director General Maritime Territory and Merchant Marine:
Vice Admiral Edmundo Gonzales Robles
Flag Officer, Fleet:
Rear Admiral Federico Niemann Figari
Flag Officer, Submarines:
Rear Admiral Ellis Berg Pearce
Commander, Naval Infantry:
Rear Admiral Cristián del Real Pérez
Flag Officer, 1st Naval Zone:
Rear Admiral Robert Gibbons Hodgson
Flag Officer, 2nd Naval Zone:
Rear Admiral Eduardo Junge Pumpin
Flag Officer, 3rd Naval Zone:
Rear Admiral Felipe Ojeda Simons
Flag Officer, 4th Naval Zone:
Rear Admiral Francisco Guzmán Vial
Flag Officer, Aviation:
Rear Admiral Felipe Carvajal Carvallo

Diplomatic Representation

Naval Attaché in Ottawa:
Captain Alfredo Whittle Pinto
Naval Attaché in Beijing:
Captain Ivo Alexis Brito
Naval Attaché in London:
Captain José Miguel Romero Aguirre
Naval Attaché in Washington:
Rear Admiral Marcelo Barbieri Wiedmeier
Naval Attaché in Buenos Aires:
Captain Cristián Figari Oxley
Naval Attaché in Seoul:
Captain Jorge Eduardo Montenegro
Naval Attaché in Lima:
Captain Juan Carlos Pons
Naval Attaché in Madrid:
Captain Jorge Ugalde Jacques

Diplomatic Representation —*continued*

Naval Attaché in Brasilia:
Captain Hernan Miller
Naval Attaché in Quito:
Captain Alejandro Campos Calvo
Naval Attaché in Paris:
Captain Guillermo Luttges Mathieus
Naval Attaché in Panama City:
Captain Eduardo Felipe Encina

Personnel

(a) 2009: 16,500 (1,988 officers)
(b) 3,400 Marines
(c) 2 years' national service (1,300)

Command Organisation

1st Naval Zone. HQ at Valparaiso. From 26° 00' S to 34° 09' S.
2nd Naval Zone. HQ at Talcahuano. From 34° 09' S to 46° 00' S.
3rd Naval Zone. HQ at Punta Arenas. From 46° 00' S to South Pole.
4th Naval Zone. HQ at Iquique. From 18° 21' S to 26° 00' S.
Coast Guard is fully integrated with the Navy.

Naval Air Stations and Organisation

Having won the battle to own all military aircraft flying over the sea, a fixed-wing squadron of about 20 CASA/ENAER Halcón is envisaged when finances permit.
Viña del Mar (Valparaiso); *Almirante Von Schroeders* (Punta Arenas); *Guardiamarina Zañartu* (Puerto Williams).
Four Squadrons: VP1: EMB-111, P-3A and C-295
HA1: NAS 332C Cougar
VC1: EMB-111, CASA-212 and O-2A
HU1: BO 105C, Bell 206B, AS-365
VP1: PC 7

Infanteria de Marina

Organisation: 4 detachments each comprising Amphibious Warfare, Coast Defence and Local Security. Also embarked are detachments of commandos, engineering units and a logistic battalion.
1st Marine Infantry Detachment 'Patricio Lynch'. At Iquique.
2nd Marine Infantry Detachment 'Miller'. At Viña del Mar.
3rd Marine Infantry Detachment 'Sargento Aldea'. At Talcahuano.
4th Marine Infantry Detachment 'Cochrane'. At Punta Arenas.
51 Commando Group. At Valparaiso.
Some embarked units, commando and engineering units and a logistics battalion.

Bases

Valparaiso. Main naval base, schools, repair yard. HQ 1st Naval Zone. Air station.

Bases —*continued*

Talcahuano. Naval base, schools, major repair yard (two dry docks, three floating docks), two floating cranes. HQ 2nd Naval Zone. Submarine base.
Punta Arenas. Naval base. Dockyard with slipway having building and repair facilities. HQ 3rd Naval Zone. Air station.
Iquique. Small naval base. HQ 4th Naval Zone.
Puerto Montt. Small naval base.
Puerto Williams (Beagle Channel). Small naval base. Air station.
Dawson Island (Magellan Straits). Small naval base.

Strength of the Fleet (including Coast Guard)

Type	*Active*	*Building*
Patrol Submarines	4	–
Frigates	8	–
Landing Ships (Tank)	3	–
Landing Craft	2	–
Fast Attack Craft (Missile)	7	–
Large Patrol Craft	7	1
Coastal Patrol Craft	50	–
Survey Ships	3	–
Training Ships	1	–
Transports	1	–
Tankers	1	–
Tenders	4	–

DELETIONS

Destroyers

2006 *Capitán Prat* (old), *Almirante Cochrane* (old)

Frigates

2006 *Ministro Zenteno*
2007 *Almirante Condell* (old), *Almirante Lynch* (old)

Patrol Forces

2006 *Fresia, Campos, Johnson*

Tugs

2007 *Leucoton*

PENNANT LIST

Notes: From 1997 pennant numbers have been painted on major warship hulls.

Submarines

20 Thomson
21 Simpson
22 Carrera
23 O'Higgins

Frigates

05 Almirante Cochrane
06 Almirante Condell
07 Almirante Lynch
11 Capitán Prat
14 Almirante Latorre
15 Almirante Blanco Encalada
18 Almirante Riveros
19 Almirante Williams

Patrol Forces

30 Casma
31 Chipana
34 Angamos
36 Riquelme
37 Orella
38 Serrano
39 Uribe
73 Isaza
74 Videla
77 Cabrales
78 Sibbald
1601 Ona (CG)
1602 Yagan (CG)
1603 Alacalufe (CG)
1604 Hallef (CG)
1609 Aysen (CG)
1610 Corral (CG)
1611 Concepcion (CG)
1612 Caldera (CG)
1613 San Antonio (CG)
1614 Antofagasta (CG)
1615 Arica (CG)
1616 Coquimbo [1616] (CG)
1617 Natales (CG)
1618 Valparaiso (CG)
1619 Punta Arenas (CG)
1620 Talcahuano (CG)
1621 Quintero (CG)
1622 Chiloe (CG)
1623 Puerto Montt (CG)
1624 Iquique
1814 Diaz
1815 Bolados
1816 Salinas
1817 Tellez
1818 Bravo
1820 Machado
1822 Troncoso
1823 Hudson
1901 Maule (CG)
1902 Rapel (CG)
1903 Aconcagua (CG)
1904 Lauca (CG)
1905 Isluga (CG)
1907 Maullín (CG)
1908 Copiapó (CG)
1909 Cau-Cau (CG)
1910 Pudeto (CG)
1911 Robinson Crusoe (CG)

Survey Ships

46 Contre-almirante Oscar Viel Toro
60 Vidal Gormaz
63 George Slight Marshall

Training Ships

43 Esmeralda

Amphibious Forces

90 Elicura
92 Rancagua
93 Valdivia
94 Orompello
95 Chacabuco

Auxiliaries

41 Aquiles
42 Merino
53 Araucano
71 Micalvi
72 Ortiz
YFB 114 Grumete Perez
116 Pisagua

Tugs/Supply Ships

ATF 66 Galvarino
ATF 67 Lautaro

SUBMARINES

Notes: There are some Swimmer Delivery Vehicles French Havas Mk 8 in service. This is the two-man version.

2 SCORPENE CLASS (SSK)

Name	*No*	*Builders*	*Laid down*	*Launched*	*Commissioned*
O'HIGGINS	23	DCN Cherbourg/IZAR	18 Nov 1999	1 Nov 2003	8 Sep 2005
CARRERA	22	IZAR, Cartagena/DCN	Nov 2000	24 Nov 2004	20 July 2006

Displacement, tons: 1,577 surfaced; 1,711 dived
Dimensions, feet (metres): 217.8 × 20.3 × 19 *(66.4 × 6.2 × 5.8)*
Main machinery: Diesel electric; 4 MTU 16V 396 SE84 diesels; 2,992 hp(m) *(2.4 MW)*; 1 Jeumont Schneider motor; 3,808 hp(m) *(2.8 MW)*; 1 shaft
Speed, knots: 20 dived; 12 surfaced
Range, n miles: 550 at 4 kt dived; 6,500 at 8 kt surfaced
Complement: 31 (6 officers)

Missiles: MBDA Exocet SM39 Block 2; launched from 21 in *(533 mm)* tubes; inertial cruise; active terminal homing to 50 km *(27 n miles)* at 0.9 Mach; warhead 165 kg.
Torpedoes: 6—21 in *(533 mm)* tubes. 18 WASS Black Shark torpedoes; wire (fibre-optic cable) guided; active/passive homing to 50 km *(27 n miles)* at 50 kt; warhead 250 kg.
Countermeasures: ESM; Argos AR 900; intercept.
Weapons control: UDS International SUBTICS.
Radars: Navigation: Sagem; I-band.
Sonars: Hull mounted; active/passive search and attack, medium frequency.

Programmes: Project Neptune. Contract awarded to DCN and Bazán on 18 December 1997 and became effective in April 1998. The bows of both boats were built at Cherbourg and the sterns at Cartagena. First steel cut for *O'Higgins* on 22 July 1998 and final assembly by DCN began on 15 November 2002 when the stern arrived at Cherbourg. Final assembly of *Carrera* began on 22 March 2004 when the bow arrived at Cartagena. *O'Higgins* arrived at Valparaiso on 10 December 2005 and *Carrera* at Talcahuano on 13 December 2006.
Modernisation: Procurement of Exocet SM 39 is reportedly under consideration.
Structure: Equipped with Sagem APS attack periscope, an SMS optronic search periscope and SISDEF datalink terminal. Diving depth more than 300 m *(984 ft)*. AIP is not fitted.
Operational: Based at Talcahuano.

O'HIGGINS — *3/2007, Ships of the World* / 1305003

CARRERA — *7/2006, Diego Quevedo* / 1164536

2 THOMSON (TYPE 209/1300) CLASS (SSK)

Name	*No*	*Builders*	*Laid down*	*Launched*	*Commissioned*
THOMSON	20	Howaldtswerke	1 Nov 1980	28 Oct 1982	31 Aug 1984
SIMPSON	21	Howaldtswerke	15 Feb 1982	29 July 1983	18 Sep 1984

Displacement, tons: 1,260 surfaced; 1,390 dived
Dimensions, feet (metres): 195.2 × 20.3 × 18 *(59.5 × 6.2 × 5.5)*
Main machinery: Diesel-electric; 4 MTU 12V 493 AZ80 GA31L diesels; 2,400 hp(m) *(1.76 MW)* sustained; 4 Piller alternators; 1.7 MW; 1 Siemens motor; 4,600 hp(m) *(3.38 MW)* sustained; 1 shaft
Speed, knots: 11 surfaced; 21.5 dived
Range, n miles: 400 at 4 kt dived; 16 at 21.5 kt dived; 8,200 at 8 kt snorkel
Complement: 32 (5 officers)

Missiles: MBDA Exocet SM 39 Block 2; launched from 21 in *(533 mm)* torpedo tubes; inertial cruise; active terminal homing to 50 km *(27 n miles)* at 0.9 Mach; warhead 165 kg.
Torpedoes: 8—21 in *(533 mm)* bow tubes. 14 WASS Black Shark torpedoes; wire (fibre-optic cable) guided; active/passive homing to 50 km *(27 n miles)* at 50 kt; warhead 250 kg.
Countermeasures: ESM: Thomson-CSF DR 2000U; radar warning.
Weapons control: UDS International SUBTICS.
Radars: Surface search: Thomson-CSF Calypso II; I-band.
Sonars: Atlas Elektronik CSU 3; hull-mounted; active/passive search and attack; medium frequency.

Programmes: Ordered from Howaldtswerke, Kiel in 1980.

Modernisation: *Thomson* refit completed at Talcahuano in late 1990, *Simpson* in 1991. Refit duration about 10 months each. A major programme to upgrade and extend the service life of both boats to 2025 has been initiated. The work is to include the fitting of a UDS Subtics combat management system and a new fire-control system. Torpedo tubes are to be upgraded to enable the Whitehead Black Shark torpedoes and anti-ship missiles to be fired while platform improvements are likely to include a new engine-control system and battery set. Work on *Simpson* started in 2006 and is to complete by early 2008. Modernisation of *Thomson* is to be undertaken 2008–10.
Structure: Fin and associated masts lengthened by 50 cm to cope with wave size off Chilean coast.

SIMPSON *10/2007, Michael Nitz* / 1170096

FRIGATES

2 LATORRE CLASS (FFGM)

Name	*No*	*Builders*	*Laid down*	*Launched*	*Commissioned*
ALMIRANTE LATORRE (ex-*Jacob van Heemskerck*)	14 (ex-F 812)	Koninklijke Maatschappij De Schelde, Flushing	21 Jan 1981	5 Nov 1983	15 Jan 1986
CAPITÁN PRAT (ex-*Witte de With*)	11 (ex-F 813)	Koninklijke Maatschappij De Schelde, Flushing	15 Dec 1981	25 Aug 1984	17 Sep 1986

Displacement, tons: 3,750 full load
Dimensions, feet (metres): 428 × 47.9 × 14.1 (20.3 screws) *(130.5 × 14.6 × 4.3; 6.2)*
Main machinery: COGOG; 2 RR Olympus TM3B gas turbines; 50,880 hp *(37.9 MW)* sustained
2 RR Tyne RM1C gas turbines; 9,900 hp *(7.4 MW)* sustained; 2 shafts; LIPS cp props
Speed, knots: 30
Range, n miles: 4,700 at 16 kt on Tynes
Complement: 197 (23 officers)

Missiles: SSM: 4 McDonnell Douglas Harpoon Block 2 ❶; active radar homing to 130 km *(70 n miles)* at 0.9 Mach; warhead 227 kg.
SAM: 40 GDC Pomona Standard SM-1MR; Block VI; Mk 13 Mod 1 launcher ❷; command guidance; semi-active radar homing to 38 km *(20.5 n miles)* at 2 Mach.
Raytheon RIM-7P Sea Sparrow Mk 29 octuple launcher ❸; semi-active radar homing to 16 km *(8.5 n miles)* at 2.5 Mach; warhead 38 kg; 24 missiles.
Guns: 1 Signaal SGE-30 Goalkeeper ❹ with General Electric 30 mm 7-barrelled; 4,200 rds/min combined to 2 km.
2 Oerlikon 20 mm.
Torpedoes: 4—324 mm US Mk 32 (2 twin) tubes ❺. Honeywell Mk 46 Mod 5; anti-submarine; active/passive homing to 11 km *(5.9 n miles)* at 40 kt; warhead 44 kg.
Countermeasures: Decoys: 2 Loral Hycor Mk 36 SRBOC 6-tubed fixed quad launchers ❻; IR flares and chaff to 4 km *(2.2 n miles)*. SLQ-25 Nixie towed torpedo decoy.
ESM/ECM: Sphinx and Ramses; intercept and jammer.
Combat data systems: Signaal SEWACO VI action data automation; Link 11. SHF SATCOM ❼. JMCIS.
Radars: Air search: Signaal LW08 ❽; D-band; range 264 km *(145 n miles)* for 2 m² target.
Air/surface search: Signaal Smart; 3D ❾; F-band.
Surface search: Signaal Scout ❿; I-band.
Fire control: 2 Signaal STIR 240 ⓫; I/J/K-band; range 140 km *(76 n miles)* for 1 m² target.
Signaal STIR 180 ⓬; I/J/K-band.
Sonars: Westinghouse SQS-509; hull-mounted; active search and attack; medium frequency.

Programmes: Contract signed on 26 March 2004 for the acquisition of two air-defence frigates. *Latorre* transferred on 16 December 2005 and arrived in Chile on 3 March 2006. *Prat* transferred on 17 July 2006 and arrived in Chile on 26 October 2006. 200 SM-1 missiles also reported acquired. Harpoon Block II missiles procured separately from the US.
Operational: Command facilities for a task group commander and his staff.

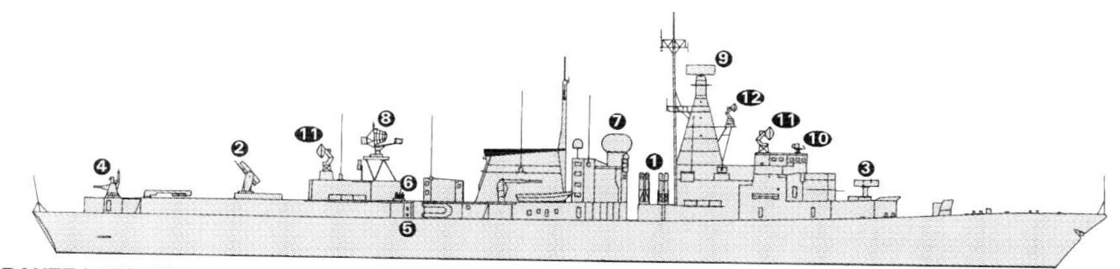

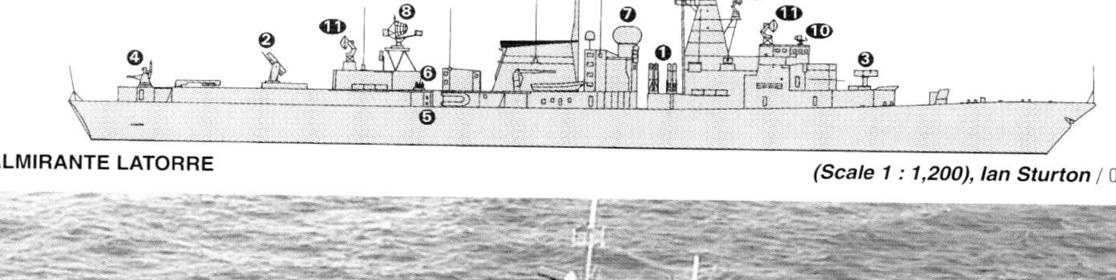

ALMIRANTE LATORRE *(Scale 1 : 1,200), Ian Sturton* / 0114748

ALMIRANTE LATORRE *12/2005, Piet Cornelis* / 1153044

CAPITÁN PRAT *7/2006, A A de Kruijf* 1164534

2 BLANCO ENCALADA (KAREL DOORMAN) CLASS (FFGHM)

Name	*No*	*Builders*	*Laid down*	*Launched*	*Commissioned*
ALMIRANTE BLANCO ENCALADA (ex-*Abraham van der Hulst*)	15 (ex-F 832)	Koninklijke Maatschappij De Schelde, Flushing	8 Feb 1989	7 Sep 1991	15 Dec 1993
ALMIRANTE RIVEROS (ex-*Tjerk Hiddes*)	18 (ex-F 830)	Koninklijke Maatschappij De Schelde, Flushing	28 Oct 1986	9 Dec 1989	3 Dec 1992

Displacement, tons: 3,320 full load
Dimensions, feet (metres): 401.2 oa; 374.7 wl × 47.2 × 14.1 *(122.3; 114.2 × 14.4 × 4.3)*
Flight deck, feet (metres): 72.2 × 47.2 *(22 × 14.4)*
Main machinery: CODOG; 2 RR Spey SM1C; 33,800 hp *(25.2 MW)* sustained (early ships of the class will initially only have SM1A gas generators and 30,800 hp *(23 MW)* sustained available); 2 Stork-Wärtsilä 12SW280 diesels; 9,790 hp(m) *(7.2 MW)* sustained; 2 shafts; LIPS cp props
Speed, knots: 30 (Speys); 21 (diesels)
Range, n miles: 5,000 at 18 kt
Complement: 156 (16 officers) (accommodation for 163)

Missiles: SSM: 4 McDonnell Douglas Harpoon Block II launchers ❶; active radar homing to 130 km *(70 n miles)* at 0.9 Mach; warhead 227 kg.
SAM: Raytheon RIM-7P Sea Sparrow Mk 48 vertical launchers ❷; semi-active radar homing to 16 km *(8.5 n miles)* at 2.5 Mach; warhead 38 kg; 16 missiles. Canisters mounted on port side of hangar.
Guns: 1—3 in *(76 mm)*/62 OTO Melara compact Mk 100 ❸; 100 rds/min to 16 km *(8.6 n miles)* anti-surface; 12 km *(6.5 n miles)* anti-aircraft; weight of shell 6 kg. This is the version with an improved rate of fire.
Torpedoes: 4—324 mm US Mk 32 Mod 9 (2 twin) tubes (mounted inside the after superstructure) ❹. Honeywell Mk 46 Mod 5; anti-submarine; active/passive homing to 11 km *(5.9 n miles)* at 40 kt; warhead 44 kg.
Countermeasures: Decoys: 2 Loral Hycor SRBOC 6-tubed fixed Mk 36 quad launchers; IR flares and chaff to 4 km *(2.2 n miles)*.
SLQ-25 Nixie towed torpedo decoy.
ESM/ECM: Argo APECS II (includes AR 700 ESM) ❺; intercept and jammers.
Combat data systems: Signaal SEWACO VIIB action data automation; Link 11. WSC-6 twin aerials.
Weapons control: Signaal IRSCAN infra-red detector (fitted in F 829 for trials and may be retrofitted in all in due course). Signaal VESTA helo transponder.
Radars: Air/surface search: Signaal SMART ❻; 3D; F-band.
Air search: Signaal LW08 ❼; D-band.
Surface search: Signaal Scout ❽; I-band.
Navigation: Racal Decca 1226; I-band.
Fire control: 2 Signaal STIR 180 ❾; I/J/K-band; range 140 km *(76 n miles)* for 1 m² target.

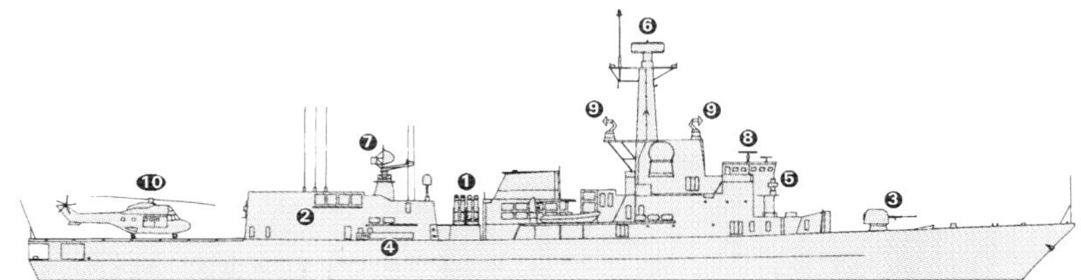

ALMIRANTE BLANCO ENCALADA *(Scale 1 : 1,200), Ian Sturton* / 1164333

ALMIRANTE RIVEROS *3/2007, Piet Cornelis* / 1335345

Sonars: Signaal PHS-36; hull-mounted; active search and attack; medium frequency.
Thomson Sintra Anaconda DSBV 61; towed array; passive low frequency. LFAS may be fitted in due course.

Helicopters: 1 NAS 332SC Cougar ❿.

Programmes: Contract signed on 26 March 2004 for the acquisition of two frigates. *Blanco Encalada* transferred on 16 December 2005 and arrived in Chile on 3 March 2006. *Riveros* was handed over on 18 April 2007 and arrived in Chile on 1 August 2007.
Structure: The VLS SAM is similar to Canadian Halifax and Greek MEKO classes. Both ships modified to operate Cougar helicopters. This includes lengthening and partly raising the helicopter hangar and replacement of the flight-deck grid with the ASIST system which includes 35 m traverse rails. A new horizon bar has also been installed.

3 COCHRANE CLASS (TYPE 23) (FFGHM)

Name	*No*	*Builders*	*Laid down*	*Launched*	*Commissioned*
ALMIRANTE COCHRANE (ex-*Norfolk*)	05 (ex-F 230)	Yarrow Shipbuilders, Glasgow	14 Dec 1985	10 July 1987	1 June 1990
ALMIRANTE CONDELL (ex-*Marlborough*)	06 (ex-F 233)	Swan Hunter Shipbuilder, Wallsend-on-Tyne	22 Oct 1987	21 Jan 1989	14 June 1991
ALMIRANTE LYNCH (ex-*Grafton*)	07 (ex-F 80)	Yarrow Shipbuilders, Glasgow	13 May 1993	5 Nov 1994	29 May 1997

Displacement, tons: 3,500 standard; 4,200 full load
Dimensions, feet (metres): 436.2 × 52.8 × 18 (screws); 24 (sonar) *(133 × 16.1 × 5.5; 7.3)*
Main machinery: CODLAG; 2 RR Spey SM1A (ex-F 230 and F 233) or SM1C (ex-F 80) gas turbines (see *Structure*); 31,100 hp *(23.2 MW)* sustained; 4 Paxman 12CM diesels; 8,100 hp *(6 MW)*; 2 GEC motors; 4,000 hp *(3 MW)*; 2 shafts
Speed, knots: 28; 15 on diesel-electric
Range, n miles: 7,800 miles at 15 kt
Complement: 181 (13 officers)

Missiles: SSM: 8 McDonnell Douglas Harpoon (2 quad) launchers ❶; active radar homing to 130 km *(70 n miles)* at 0.9 Mach; warhead 227 kg (84C). 4 normally carried.
SAM: British Aerospace Seawolf GWS 26 Mod 1 VLS ❷; Command Line Of Sight (CLOS) radar/TV tracking to 6 km *(3.3 n miles)* at 2.5 Mach; warhead 14 kg; 32 canisters.
Guns: 1 Vickers 4.5 in *(114 mm)*/55 Mk 8 Mod 1 ❸; 25 rds/min to 27.5 km *(14.8 n miles)* anti-surface; weight of shell 21 kg. Mk 8 Mod 1 being progressively fitted.
2 DES/MSI DS 30B 30 mm/75 ❹; 650 rds/min to 10 km *(5.4 n miles)* anti-surface; 3 km *(1.6 n miles)* anti-aircraft; weight of shell 0.36 kg.
Torpedoes: 4 Cray Marine 324 mm fixed (2 twin) tubes ❺. Honeywell Mk 46 Mod 5; anti-submarine; active/passive homing to 11 km *(5.9 n miles)* at 40 kt; warhead 44 kg.
Countermeasures: Decoys: Outfit DLH; 4 Sea Gnat 6-barrelled 130 mm/102 mm launchers ❻. DLF 2/3 offboard decoys.
ESM: Racal UAT ❼; intercept.

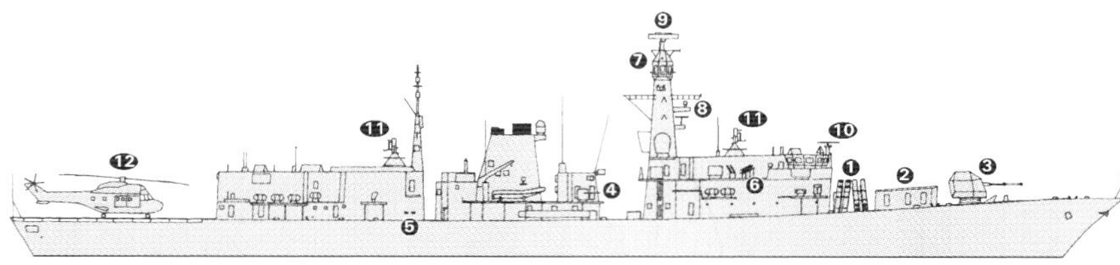

ALMIRANTE COCHRANE *(Scale 1 : 1,200), Ian Sturton* / 1164334

Combat data systems: BAeSEMA Surface Ship Command System (DNA); Link 11.
Weapons control: BAe GSA 8B/GPEOD optronic director ❽. GWS 60 (for SSM). GWS 26 (for SAM).
Radars: Air/surface search: Plessey Type 996(I) ❾; 3D; E/F-band.
Surface search: Racal Decca Type 1008 ❿; E/F-band.
Navigation: Kelvin Hughes Type 1007; I-band.
Fire control: 2 Marconi Type 911 ⓫; I/Ku-band.
IFF: 1010/1011 or 1018/1019.
Sonars: Ferranti/Thomson Sintra Type 2050; bow-mounted; active search and attack.

Helicopters: 1 NAS 332C Cougar ⓬.

Programmes: Formerly in UK Royal Navy service, letter of intent for purchase of the three ships signed by Chilean government in December 2004 followed by formal agreement on 7 September 2005. The contract includes purchase of the three ships, pre-sale sanitisation and maintenance and a package of operator and maintainer training. BAE Systems to act as lead contractor with Fleet Support Limited to undertake overhauls in Portsmouth. Work started on *Cochrane* in late 2005; she was recommissioned on 22 November 2006, *Lynch* was recommissioned on 28 March 2007 and *Condell* on 28 May 2008.
Modernisation: Most of the pre-transfer work was focused on the ships' power plants, with both diesel engines and gas turbines being removed for scheduled maintenance. Main gearwheel changes were also being effected on *Condell* and *Lynch*. Mk 46 torpedoes are to be replaced by Eurotorp MU 90.
Structure: Incorporates stealth technology to minimise acoustic, magnetic, radar and IR signatures. The design includes a 7° slope to all vertical surfaces, rounded edges, reduction of IR emissions and a hull bubble system to reduce radiated noise.

ALMIRANTE LYNCH *7/2007, J Brodie* / 1305002

ALMIRANTE CONDELL

7/2008*, Ian Harris / 1335344

1 BROADSWORD CLASS (TYPE 22) (FFHM)

Name	*No*	*Builders*	*Laid down*	*Launched*	*Commissioned*
ALMIRANTE WILLIAMS (ex-*Sheffield*)	19 (ex-F 96)	Swan Hunter Shipbuilders, Wallsend-on-Tyne	29 Mar 1984	26 Mar 1986	26 July 1988

Displacement, tons: 4,100 standard; 4,800 full load
Dimensions, feet (metres): 480.5 × 48.5 × 21 *(146.5 × 14.8 × 6.4)*
Main machinery: COGOG: 2 RR Olympus TM3B gas turbines; 50,000 hp *(37.3 MW)* sustained; 2 RR Tyne RM1C gas turbines; 9,900 hp *(7.4 MW)*; 2 shafts; cp props
Speed, knots: 30; 18 on Tynes
Complement: 273 (30 officers) (accommodation for 296)

Missiles: SSM: 4 McDonnell Douglas Harpoon Block II; active radar homing to 130 km *(70 n miles)* at 0.9 Mach; warhead 227 kg.
SAM: 2 British Aerospace Seawolf Block II (GWS 25 Mod 3 launcher); Command Line Of Sight (CLOS) with 2 channel radar tracking to 5 km *(2.7 n miles)* at 2+ Mach; warhead 14 kg.

Guns: 1 Vickers 4.5 in *(114 mm)* 55 Mk 8; 25 rds/min to 22 km *(11.9 n miles)*; weight of shell 21 kg. 2 Oerlikon 20 mm.
Torpedoes: 6—324 mm tubes.
Countermeasures: Decoys: Outfit DLJ Sea Gnat.
ESM: UAT intercept.
ECM: Type 670.
Combat data systems: CACS 1.
Weapons control: To be announced.
Radars: Air/surface search: Marconi Type 967/968; D/E-band.
Surface search: Racal Decca Type 2008; E/F-band.
Navigation: Kelvin Hughes Type 1008; I-band.
Fire control: 2 Marconi Type 911; I-Ku-band (for Seawolf).
Sonars: Ferranti/Thomson Sintra Type 2050; hull-mounted; active search and attack.

Helicopters: 1 NAS 332SC Cougar.

Programmes: Originally successors to the UK Leander class, these ships entered RN service in 1987 but were withdrawn, half-way through their ships' lives, as a result of the 1998 UK Defence Review. Agreement for transfer to Chile ratified by the Chilean government in April 2003.
Modernisation: The ship is to undergo a modernisation programme which started in March 2008 at ASMAR-Talcahuano Yard. This is to include installation of a new combat data system, Harpoon surface-to-surface missiles, and a 114 mm gun. The hangar and flightdeck are to be adapted to operate Cougar.
Structure: Broadsword Batch 2 ships were stretched versions of Batch 1.
Operational: The ship entered service on 5 September 2003.

ALMIRANTE WILLIAMS

9/2003, B Sullivan / 0567435

SHIPBORNE AIRCRAFT

Numbers/Type: 8 Aerospatiale Dauphin AS-365N2.
Operational speed: 150 kt *(388 km/h)*.
Service ceiling: 15,000 ft *(4,575 m)*.
Range: 410 n miles *(758 km)*.
Role/Weapon systems: Multipurpose aircraft which replaced Bell 412 in SAR and surveillance roles. Three new aircraft were received in 2006 to replace older aircraft and a further four AS-365F (ex-Irish Corps) acquired in 2008.

AS-365 *6/2006, Chilean Navy* / 1164415

Numbers/Type: 5 Nurtanio (Aerospatiale) NAS 332C Cougar.
Operational speed: 151 kt *(279 km/h)*.
Service ceiling: 15,090 ft *(4,600 m)*.
Range: 335 n miles *(620 km)*.
Role/Weapon systems: ASV/ASW helicopters; surface search and SAR secondary roles. All five aircraft undergoing modernisation and refurbishment from 2007 to extend service life until 2022. Two further new aircraft and one second-hand may be acquired. Sensors: Thomson-CSF Varam radar and Thomson Sintra HS-312 dipping sonar. DR 2000 ESM. Weapons: ASW; 2 × Alliant Mk 46 Mod 2 torpedoes or depth bombs. ASV; 1 or 2 × Aerospatiale AM 39 Exocet missiles.

COUGAR *7/2001, Maritime Photographic* / 0121314

Numbers/Type: 4 MBB BO105C.
Operational speed: 113 kt *(210 km/h)*.
Service ceiling: 9,845 ft *(3,000 m)*.
Range: 407 n miles *(754 km)*.
Role/Weapon systems: Coastal patrol helicopter for patrol, training and liaison duties; SAR as secondary role. Sensors: Bendix search radar. Weapons: Unarmed.

BO 105C *11/2001, Freddie Philips* / 0534054

Numbers/Type: 4 Bell 206B JetRanger.
Operational speed: 115 kt *(213 km/h)*.
Service ceiling: 13,500 ft *(4,115 m)*.
Range: 368 n miles *(682 km)*.
Role/Weapon systems: Some tasks and training carried out by torpedo-armed liaison helicopter; emergency war role for ASW. To be replaced by Bell 412. Weapons: ASW; 1 × Mk 46 torpedo or 2 depth bombs.

JETRANGER *7/2001, Maritime Photographic* / 0121315

LAND-BASED MARITIME AIRCRAFT (FRONT LINE)

Notes: (1) In addition there are one EMB-110 and three Casa Aviocar 212/300 support aircraft.
(2) The Air Force has one Boeing 707 converted for AEW duties.

Numbers/Type: 3 Embraer EMB-111 Bandeirante.
Operational speed: 194 kt *(360 km/h)*.
Service ceiling: 25,500 ft *(7,770 m)*.
Range: 1,590 n miles *(2,945 km)*.
Role/Weapon systems: Designated EMB-111N for peacetime EEZ and wartime MR. Sensors: Eaton-AIL AN/APS-128 search radar, Thomson-CSF DR 2000 ESM, searchlight. Weapons: Strike; 6 × 127 mm or 28 × 70 mm rockets.

Numbers/Type: 7 Pilatus PC-7 Turbo-Trainer.
Operational speed: 270 kt *(500 km/h)*.
Service ceiling: 32,000 ft *(9,755 m)*.
Range: 1,420 n miles *(2,630 km)*.
Role/Weapon systems: Training includes simulated attacks to exercise ships' AA defences; emergency war role for strike operations. Sensors: None. Weapons: 4 × 127 mm or similar rockets and machine gun pods.

Numbers/Type: 3 Lockheed P-3A Orion.
Operational speed: 410 kt *(760 km/h)*.
Service ceiling: 28,300 ft *(8,625 m)*.
Range: 4,000 n miles *(7,410 km)*.
Role/Weapon systems: Long-range MR for surveillance and SAR. First one delivered from US in March 1993 followed by seven more of which one has been modified for transport, two are in reserve and two are used for spares. Sensors: Three aircraft upgraded with new radar, ESM and FLIR. APS-115 radar. Weapons: Armed with Harpoon from mid-2007.

ORION *6/2003, Chilean Navy* / 0569794

Numbers/Type: 9 Cessna 0-2A Skymaster.
Operational speed: 130 kt *(241 km/h)*.
Service ceiling: 5,000 ft *(1,524 m)*.
Range: 550 n miles *(1,019 km)*.
Role/Weapon systems: Maritime coastal patrol and training acquired in 1998/99. Sensors: None. Weapons: May be equipped with 4 weapons stations in due course.

SKYMASTER *6/1999, Chilean Navy* / 0056723

Numbers/Type: 3 EADS CASA C-295 Persuader.
Operational speed: 260 kt *(482 km/h)*.
Service ceiling: 13,540 ft *(4,125 m)*.
Range: 840 n miles *(1,555 km)*.
Role/Weapon systems: Three maritime surveillance aircraft (stretched versions of CN-235) ordered on 18 October 2007. There is an option for a further five aircraft. To be equipped with Fully Integrated Tactical System (FITS). Sensors to be announced.

EADS CASA C-295 *10/2007, EADS* / 1170095

PATROL FORCES

Notes: It is planned to procure three new corvettes, possibly derived from the Fassmer OPV (Coast Guard) design. Such ships would be more heavily armed and would replace the Casma class fast attack craft.

3 CASMA (SAAR 4) CLASS (FAST ATTACK CRAFT—MISSILE) (PGG)

Name	*No*	*Builders*	*Commissioned*
CASMA (ex-*Romah*)	LM 30	Haifa Shipyard	Mar 1974
CHIPANA (ex-*Keshet*)	LM 31	Haifa Shipyard	Oct 1973
ANGAMOS (ex-*Reshef*)	LM 34	Haifa Shipyard	Apr 1973

Displacement, tons: 415 standard; 450 full load
Dimensions, feet (metres): 190.7 × 24.9 × 9.2 *(58.1 × 7.6 × 2.8)*
Main machinery: 4 MTU 16V 396 diesels; 13,029 hp(m) *(9.58 MW)* (30 and 31); 4 MTU 16V 596TB91 diesels; 15,000 hp(m) *(11.3 MW)* (34); 4 shafts
Speed, knots: 32. **Range, n miles:** 1,650 at 30 kt; 3,700 at 18 kt
Complement: 46 (8 officers)

Missiles: SSM: 4 IAI Gabriel I or II; radar or optical guidance; semi-active radar homing to 20 km *(10.8 n miles)* (I) or 36 km *(20 n miles)* (II); at 0.7 Mach; warhead 75 kg HE.
Guns: 2 OTO Melara 3 in *(76 mm)*/62 compact; 85 rds/min to 16 km *(8.7 n miles)* anti-surface; 12 km *(6.5 n miles)* anti-aircraft; weight of shell 6 kg.
2 Oerlikon 20 mm; 800 rds/min to 2 km.
2—12.7 mm MGs.
Countermeasures: Decoys: 4 Rafael LRCR chaff decoy launchers.
ESM: Elta Electronics MN-53; intercept.
ECM: Elta Rattler; jammer.
Radars: Surface search: Elta EL-2208C; E/F-band.
Navigation: Raytheon 20X; I-band.
Fire control: Selenia Orion RTN 10X; I/J-band.

Programmes: One transferred from Israel December 1979 and second in January 1981. Two more acquired from Israel 1 June 1997 but one (ex-*Tarshish*) was cannibalised for spares in 1998.
Modernisation: New engines fitted in the first pair in 2000. Weapons control systems have been upgraded in LM 30 and LM 34. Similar refit of LM 31 completed by 2003.
Operational: All operate in Third Naval Zone (Beagle Channel).

CASMA *9/2000*, **MTU** / 0094035

4 RIQUELME (TIGER) CLASS (TYPE 148) (FAST ATTACK CRAFT—MISSILE) (PGG)

Name	*No*	*Builders*	*Commissioned*
RIQUELME (ex-*Wolf*)	LM 36 (ex-P 6149)	CMN Cherbourg	26 Feb 1974
ORELLA (ex-*Elster*)	LM 37 (ex-P 6154)	CMN Cherbourg	14 Nov 1974
SERRANO (ex-*Tiger*)	LM 38 (ex-P 6141)	CMN Cherbourg	30 Oct 1972
URIBE (ex-*Luchs*)	LM 39 (ex-P 6143)	CMN Cherbourg	9 Apr 1973

Displacement, tons: 234 standard; 265 full load
Dimensions, feet (metres): 154.2 × 23 × 8.9 *(47 × 7 × 2.7)*
Main machinery: 4 MTU 16V 396 diesels; 13,029 hp(m) *(9.58 MW)* sustained; 4 shafts
Speed, knots: 31. **Range, n miles:** 570 at 30 kt; 1,600 at 15 kt
Complement: 30 (4 officers)

Missiles: SSM: 4 Aerospatiale MM 38 Exocet (2 twin) launchers; inertial cruise; active radar homing to 42 km *(23 n miles)* at 0.9 Mach; warhead 165 kg; sea-skimmer.
Guns: 1 OTO Melara 3 in *(76 mm)*/62 compact; 85 rds/min to 16 km *(8.6 n miles)* anti-surface; 12 km *(6.5 n miles)* anti-aircraft; weight of shell 6 kg.
1 Bofors 40 mm/70; 330 rds/min to 12 km *(6.5 n miles)* anti-surface; 4 km *(2.2 n miles)* anti-aircraft; weight of shell 0.96 kg; fitted with GRP dome (1984).
2—12.7 mm MGs.
Mines: Laying capability.
Countermeasures: Decoys: Wolke chaff launcher.
Combat data systems: PALIS and Link 11.
Weapons control: CSEE Panda optical director. Thomson-CSF Vega PCET system, controlling missiles and guns.
Radars: Air/surface search: Thomson-CSF Triton; G-band; range 33 km *(18 n miles)* for 2 m^2 target.
Navigation: SMA 3 RM 20; I-band; range 73 km *(40 n miles)*.
Fire control: Thomson-CSF Castor; I/J-band.

Programmes: First pair transferred from Germany on 27 August 1997 and sailed in a transport ship on 2 September 1997. Four more transferred on 22 September 1998 and sailed 11 October. These four were all damaged during a storm in transit, and the two best were taken into service, with the other pair *(Pelikan* and *Kranich)* being used for spares. The ship names have prefixed ranks but these are not used.
Modernisation: New engines fitted in 2000. Speed reduced to 31 kt.
Structure: Similar to Combattante II craft. EW equipment was removed prior to transfer.
Operational: Operate in 4th Naval Zone (Iquique). Exocet missiles were not part of the transfer but have been acquired separately.

URIBE *7/2001*, **Maritime Photographic** / 0121316

SERRANO *7/2001*, **Maritime Photographic** / 0121317

8 GRUMETE DIAZ (DABUR) CLASS (COASTAL PATROL CRAFT) (PB)

DIAZ 1814	**TELLEZ** 1817	**TRONCOSO** 1822
BOLADOS 1815	**BRAVO** 1818	**HUDSON** 1823
SALINAS 1816	**MACHADO** 1820	

Displacement, tons: 39 full load
Dimensions, feet (metres): 64.9 × 18 × 5.9 *(19.8 × 5.5 × 1.8)*
Main machinery: 2 Detroit 12V 71TA diesels; 840 hp *(627 kW)* sustained; 2 shafts
Speed, knots: 19
Range, n miles: 450 at 13 kt
Complement: 8 (2 officers)
Guns: 2 Oerlikon 20 mm or 2—12.7 mm MGs.
Radars: Surface search: Racal Decca Super 101 Mk 3; I-band.

Comment: All have LPC numbers and Grumete precedes the ships' names. First six transferred from Israel and commissioned 3 January 1991. Second batch of four more transferred and commissioned 17 March 1995. A RIB inspection boat is carried on the stern. Deployed in 4th Naval Zone (Iquique) and in 2nd Naval Zone and operate in the Chiloé area. All underwent life extension refits in 2001–02 at Valparaiso and Puerto Montt. Two craft deleted in 2006. Service lives end by 2012.

HUDSON *7/2001*, **Maritime Photographic** / 0121321

6 MICALVI CLASS (LARGE PATROL CRAFT) (PB/AEM)

Name	*No*	*Builders*	*Launched*	*Commissioned*
MICALVI	PSG 71	ASMAR, Talcahuano	12 Sep 1992	30 Mar 1993
ORTIZ	PSG 72	ASMAR, Talcahuano	23 July 1993	15 Dec 1993
ISAZA	PSG 73	ASMAR, Talcahuano	7 Jan 1994	31 May 1994
VIDELA (ex-*Morel*)	PMD 74	ASMAR, Talcahuano	21 Apr 1994	11 Aug 1994
CABRALES	PSH 77	ASMAR, Talcahuano	4 Apr 1996	29 June 1996
SIBBALD	PSG 78	ASMAR, Talcahuano	5 June 1996	29 Aug 1996

Displacement, tons: 518 full load
Dimensions, feet (metres): 139.4 × 27.9 × 9.5 *(42.5 × 8.5 × 2.9)*
Main machinery: 2 Caterpillar 3512TA diesels; 2,560 hp(m) *(1.88 MW)* sustained; 2 shafts
Speed, knots: 15. **Range, n miles:** 4,200 at 12 kt
Complement: 23 (5 officers) plus 10 spare
Guns: 1 Bofors 40 mm/60. 2 Oerlikon 20 mm.
Radars: Surface search: Racal Decca; I-band.

Comment: First four built under design project Taitao. Last pair built for export but bought by the Navy. Multipurpose patrol vessels with a secondary mission of transport and servicing navigational aids. Provision for bow thruster, sonar and mine rails. Can carry 35 tons cargo in holds and 18 tons in containers. Crane lift of 2.5 tons. The ships' names all have prefixed ranks but these are not used. *Micalvi* and *Ortiz* were classified as missile tenders in 1999 but reclassified as patrol craft in 2004. *Cabrales* has been converted for use as a survey vessel. *Videla* has been modified to provide medical support.

ORTIZ *7/2001*, **Maritime Photographic** / 0534129

MICALVI *11/2001*, **Freddie Philips** / 0534131

AMPHIBIOUS FORCES

Notes: There are plans to acquire a multipurpose vessel capable of force-projection and disaster-relief roles. The broad requirement is for a ship of up to 10,000 tons with a flightdeck capable of operating four medium lift helicopters, a dock and Ro-Ro capabilities. The ship is likely to be procured on the second-hand market and would replace *Valdivia*.

1 NEWPORT CLASS (LSTH)

Name	*No*	*Builders*	*Laid down*	*Launched*	*Commissioned*	*Recommissioned*
VALDIVIA (ex-*San Bernardino*)	93 (ex-LST 1189)	National Steel & Shipbuilding Co	12 July 1969	28 Mar 1970	27 Mar 1971	30 Sep 1995

Displacement, tons: 4,975 light; 8,450 full load
Dimensions, feet (metres): 522.3 (hull) × 69.5 × 17.5 (aft) *(159.2 × 21.2 × 5.3)*
Main machinery: 6 ALCO 16-251 diesels; 16,500 hp *(12.3 MW)* sustained; 2 shafts; cp props; bow thruster
Speed, knots: 20. **Range, n miles:** 14,250 at 14 kt
Complement: 257 (13 officers)
Military lift: 400 troops; 500 tons vehicles; 3 LCVPs and 1 LCPL on davits
Radars: Surface search: Raytheon SPS-67; G-band.
Navigation: Marconi LN66; I/J-band.

Helicopters: Platform only.

Programmes: Transferred from the US by lease on 30 September 1995. A second of class was offered but not accepted due to its poor condition.
Structure: The hull form required to achieve 20 kt would not permit bow doors, thus these ships unload by a 112 ft ramp over their bow. The ramp is supported by twin derrick arms. A ramp just forward of the superstructure connects the lower tank deck with the main deck and a vehicle passage through the superstructure provides access to the parking area amidships. A stern gate to the tank deck permits unloading of amphibious tractors into the water, or unloading of other vehicles into an LCU or on to a pier. Vehicle stowage covers 19,000 sq ft. Length over derrick arms is 562 ft *(171.3 m)*; full load draught is 11.5 ft forward and 17.5 ft aft. Bow thruster fitted to hold position offshore while unloading amphibious tractors.
Operational: Damaged by grounding in mid-1997, but subsequently repaired.

VALDIVIA — *1/1999, van Ginderen Collection* / 0056726

2 MAIPO (BATRAL) CLASS (LSTH)

Name	*No*	*Builders*	*Launched*	*Commissioned*
RANCAGUA	92	ASMAR, Talcahuano	6 Mar 1982	8 Aug 1983
CHACABUCO	95 (ex-93)	ASMAR, Talcahuano	16 July 1985	15 Apr 1986

Displacement, tons: 873 standard; 1,409 full load
Dimensions, feet (metres): 260.4 × 42.7 × 8.2 *(79.4 × 13 × 2.5)*
Main machinery: 2 Caterpillar diesels; 4,012 hp(m) *(2.95 MW)* sustained; 2 shafts; cp props
Speed, knots: 16. **Range, n miles:** 3,500 at 13 kt
Complement: 43 (5 officers)
Military lift: 180 troops; 12 vehicles; 350 tons
Guns: 2 Bofors 40 mm/60. 1 Oerlikon 20 mm. 2—81 mm mortars.
Radars: Navigation: Decca 1229; I/J-band.
Helicopters: Platform for 1 Bell 206B or BO 105C.

Comment: First laid down in 1980 to standard French design with French equipment. Have 40 ton bow ramps and vehicle stowage above and below deck. Both ships underwent life-extension refits in 2002–03.

CHACABUCO — *12/2004, Globke Collection* / 1047869

2 ELICURA CLASS (LSM)

Name	*No*	*Builders*	*Commissioned*
ELICURA	90	Talcahuano	10 Dec 1968
OROMPELLO	94	Dade Dry Dock Co, MI	15 Sep 1964

Displacement, tons: 290 light; 750 full load
Dimensions, feet (metres): 145 × 34 × 12.8 *(44.2 × 10.4 × 3.9)*
Main machinery: 2 Cummins VT-17-700M diesels; 900 hp *(660 kW)*; 2 shafts
Speed, knots: 10.5. **Range, n miles:** 2,900 at 9 kt
Complement: 20
Military lift: 350 tons
Guns: 3 Oerlikon 20 mm (can be carried).
Radars: Navigation: Raytheon 1500B; I/J-band.

Comment: Two of similar class operated by Chilean Shipping Co. Oil fuel, 77 tons.

ELICURA — *10/2001, Freddie Philips* / 0534132

SURVEY SHIPS

Notes: Replacement of the Antarctic support ship *Oscar Viel Toro* is under consideration.

1 TYPE 1200 CLASS (AGS/AGOBH)

Name	*No*	*Builders*	*Commissioned*
CONTRE-ALMIRANTE OSCAR VIEL TORO (ex-*Norman McLeod Rogers*)	AP 46	Canadian Vickers, Montreal	Oct 1960

Displacement, tons: 6,320 full load
Measurement, tons: 4,179 gross; 1,847 net
Dimensions, feet (metres): 294.9 × 62.5 × 20 *(89.9 × 19.1 × 6.1)*
Main machinery: 4 Fairbanks-Morse 38D8-1/8-12 diesels; 8,496 hp *(6.34 MW)* sustained; 4 GE generators; 4.8 MW; 2 Ruston RK3CZ diesels; 7,250 hp *(5.6 MW)* sustained; 2 GE generators; 2.76 MW; 2 GE motors; 12,000 hp *(8.95 MW)*; 2 shafts
Speed, knots: 15
Range, n miles: 12,000 at 12 kt
Complement: 33
Guns: 2 Oerlikon 20 mm.
Helicopters: 1 BO 105C.

Comment: Acquired from the Canadian Coast Guard on 16 February 1995. The ship was formerly based on the west coast at Victoria, BC, and was laid up in 1993. Replaced the deleted *Piloto Pardo* as the Antarctic patrol and survey ship.

CONTRE-ALMIRANTE OSCAR VIEL TORO — *6/2004, Chilean Navy* / 1044093

1 ROBERT D CONRAD CLASS (AGOR)

Name	*No*	*Builders*	*Commissioned*
VIDAL GORMAZ (ex-*Thomas Washington*)	AGOR 60 (ex-AGOR 10)	Marinette Marine, WI	27 Sep 1965

Displacement, tons: 1,490 full load
Dimensions, feet (metres): 208.9 × 40 × 15.3 *(63.7 × 12.2 × 4.7)*
Main machinery: Diesel-electric; 2 FBM diesel generators; 1 Reliance motor; 1,000 hp *(746 kW)*; 1 shaft
Speed, knots: 12
Range, n miles: 14,500 at 10 kt
Complement: 46 (10 officers and 17 scientists)
Guns: 2 Oerlikon 20 mm.
Radars: Navigation: Decca 252/6; I-band. Raytheon R-84; I-band.

Comment: Transferred from US on 28 September 1992. This is the first class of ships designed and built by the US Navy for oceanographic research. Fitted with instrumentation and laboratories to measure gravity and magnetism, water temperature, sound transmission in water, and the profile of the ocean floor. Special features include 10 ton capacity boom and winches for handling over-the-side equipment; 620 hp gas turbine (housed in funnel structure) for providing 'quiet' power when conducting experiments; can propel the ship at 6.5 kt. Ships of this class are in service with several other navies. To be replaced by a new vessel in about 2010.

VIDAL GORMAZ *6/2008*, Chilean Navy* / 1335350

1 BUOY TENDER (ABU)

Name	*No*	*Builders*	*Commissioned*
GEORGE SLIGHT MARSHALL (ex-*M V Vigilant*)	BRS 63	Netherlands	July 1978

Displacement, tons: 1,100 full load
Dimensions, feet (metres): 173.9 × 36.7 × 11.5 *(53 × 11.2 × 3.5)*
Main machinery: 2 Ruston 6AP230 diesels; 1,360 hp *(1 MW)*; 2 shafts; bow thruster
Speed, knots: 10
Range, n miles: 4,600 at 5 kt
Complement: 20
Guns: 2 Oerlikon 20 mm.
Radars: Navigation: Decca 252/6; I-band.

Comment: Acquired from the UK Mersey Harbour Board and recommissioned 5 February 1997. Carries a 15 ton derrick.

GEORGE SLIGHT MARSHALL *6/2008*, Chilean Navy* / 1335349

0 + 1 OCEANOGRAPHIC RESEARCH SHIP (AGOR)

Name	*No*	*Builders*	*Laid down*	*Launched*	*Commissioned*
–	–	ASMAR, Talcahuano	2008	2009	Nov 2010

Measurement, tons: 3,020 grt
Dimensions, feet (metres): 243.1 × 51.2 × 17.7 *(74.1 × 15.6 × 5.4)*
Main machinery: Diesel electric; 3 Wärtsilä 8L20 diesel generators; 6,435 hp *(4.8 MW)*; 2 Ansaldo motors; 4,023 hp *(3.0 MW)*; 1 shaft; 1 bow thruster (450 kW); 1 stern thruster (450 kW)
Speed, knots: 14.5
Range, n miles: 10,000 at 12 kt
Complement: 43 (9 officers) plus 25 scientists
Radars: Surface search: To be announced.
Navigation: To be announced.

Comment: Project Medusa: Contract signed with ASMAR Talcahuano on 28 December 2007 for the construction of an oceanographic and fisheries research vessel to replace *Vidal Gormaz*. The ST-367 design was developed by Skipsteknisk of Norway. The ship is equipped with four laboratories while the hydroacoustic research and positioning equipment is to be provided by Kongsberg Simrad. This includes: multibeam echosounders for deep and medium depth water, singlebeam echosounder for deep water, sub-bottom profiler, omni-directional sonar for biomass, surface sound velocity profiler and an acoustic Doppler current profiler.

ST-367 *1/2008*, Skipsteknisk* / 1294329

TRAINING SHIPS

1 SAIL TRAINING SHIP (AXS)

Name	*No*	*Builders*	*Commissioned*
ESMERALDA (ex-*Don Juan de Austria*)	BE 43	Bazán, Cadiz	15 June 1954

Displacement, tons: 3,420 standard; 3,754 full load
Dimensions, feet (metres): 371.0 × 44.6 × 23 *(113.1 × 13.1 × 7)*
Main machinery: 1 Burmeister & Wain diesel; 1,400 hp(m) *(1.03 MW)*; 1 shaft
Speed, knots: 13. **Range, n miles:** 11,600 at 10 kt
Complement: 306 (23 officers and 79 cadets)
Guns: 4 Hotchkiss saluting guns.

Comment: Four-masted schooner originally intended for the Spanish Navy. Near sister ship of *Juan Sebastian de Elcano* in the Spanish Navy. Refitted Saldanha Bay, South Africa, 1977. Sail area, 26,910 sq ft.

ESMERALDA *6/2007, Chris Sattler* / 1170094

AUXILIARIES

Notes: Plans to replace the replenishment ship *Araucano* are under consideration. The most likely option is procurement on the second-hand market. Contenders include ex-US Navy Henry J Kaiser class *Andrew Higgins* AO 190.

3 FLOATING DOCKS (YFD)

Name	*No*	*Commissioned*	*Lift*
INGENIERO MERY (ex-*ARD 25*)	131	1944 (1973)	3,000 tons
MUTILLA (ex-*ARD 32*)	132	1944 (1960)	3,000 tons
TALCAHUANO (ex-*ARD 5*)	133	1944 (1999)	3,000 tons

Comment: There is also a Floating Dock *Marinero Gutierrez* with a 1,200 ton lift. Built in 1991.

1 TRANSPORT SHIP (APH)

Name	*No*	*Builders*	*Launched*	*Commissioned*
AQUILES	AP 41	ASMAR, Talcahuano	4 Dec 1987	15 July 1988

Displacement, tons: 2,767 light; 4,550 full load
Dimensions, feet (metres): 337.8 × 55.8 × 18 *(103 × 17 × 5.5; max)*
Main machinery: 2 Krupp MaK 8 M 453B diesels; 7,080 hp(m) *(5.10 MW)* sustained; 1 shaft; bow thruster
Speed, knots: 18
Complement: 80
Military lift: 250 troops
Helicopters: Platform for up to Cougar size.

Comment: Ordered 4 October 1985. Can be converted rapidly to act as hospital ship.

AQUILES *7/2001, Maritime Photographic* / 0121327

1 ÄLVSBORG CLASS (SUPPORT SHIP) (AGP/ASH)

Name	*No*	*Builders*	*Launched*	*Commissioned*
MERINO (ex-*Älvsborg*)	42 (ex-A 234, ex-M 02)	Karlskronavarvet	11 Nov 1969	6 Apr 1971

Displacement, tons: 2,660 full load
Dimensions, feet (metres): 303.1 × 48.2 × 13.2 *(92.4 × 14.7 × 4)*
Main machinery: 2 Nohab-Polar 112 VS diesels; 4,200 hp(m) *(3.1 MW)*; 1 shaft; cp prop; bow thruster; 350 hp(m) *(257 kW)*
Speed, knots: 16
Complement: 52 (accommodation for 205)
Guns: 3 Bofors 40 mm/70 SAK 48.
Countermeasures: Decoys: 2 Philax chaff/IR launchers.
Radars: Raytheon; E/F-band.
Surface search: Philips 9GR 600; I-band.
Fire control: Philips 9LV 200 Mk 2; I/J-band.
Navigation: Terma Scanter 009; I-band.
Helicopters: Platform for 1 medium.

Comment: Ordered in 1968 as a minelayer. Transferred from the Swedish Navy in November 1996, having been paid off in 1995. Recommissioned 7 February 1997. Originally designed as a minelayer with a capacity of 300 mines. Converted to act as a general support ship with improved accommodation and workshops. Acts as a depot ship for submarines and attack craft. The full name is *Almirante José Toribio Merino Castro.*

MERINO *7/2001, Maritime Photographic* / 0121328

1 REPLENISHMENT SHIP (AOR)

Name	*No*	*Builders*	*Commissioned*
ARAUCANO	AO 53	Burmeister & Wain, Copenhagen	10 Jan 1967

Displacement, tons: 23,000 full load
Dimensions, feet (metres): 497.6 × 74.9 × 28.8 *(151.7 × 22.8 × 8.8)*
Main machinery: 1 Burmeister & Wain Type 62 VT 2BF140 diesel; 10,800 hp(m) *(7.94 MW)*; 1 shaft
Speed, knots: 17. **Range, n miles:** 12,000 at 15.5 kt
Complement: 130 (14 officers)
Cargo capacity: 21,126 m^3 liquid; 1,444 m^3 dry
Guns: 4 Bofors 40 mm/60 (2 twin).
Radars: Navigation: Racal Decca; I-band.

Comment: Launched on 21 June 1966. Single-hulled design.

ARAUCANO *7/2001, Chilean Navy* / 0121329

1 HARBOUR TRANSPORT (YFB)

Name	*No*	*Builders*	*Commissioned*
GRUMETE PEREZ	YFB 114	ASMAR, Talcahuano	12 Dec 1975

Displacement, tons: 165 full load
Dimensions, feet (metres): 80 × 22 × 8.5 *(24.4 × 6.7 × 2.6)*
Main machinery: 1 diesel; 370 hp(m) *(272 kW)*; 1 shaft
Speed, knots: 10
Complement: 6
Guns: 1 Oerlikon 20 mm can be carried.
Radars: Navigation: Furuno; I-band.

Comment: Transferred to Seaman's School as harbour transport. Modified fishing boat design.

GRUMETE PEREZ *8/1997, Chilean Navy* / 0012168

1 SUPPLY SHIP (AKSL)

Name	*No*	*Builders*	*Commissioned*
PISAGUA	116	SIMAR, Santiago	11 July 1995

Displacement, tons: 195 full load
Dimensions, feet (metres): 73.2 × 19.7 × 4.9 *(22.3 × 6 × 1.5)*
Main machinery: 1 diesel; 1 shaft
Speed, knots: 8. **Range, n miles:** 500 at 8 kt
Cargo capacity: 50 tons
Radars: Navigation: Furuno; I-band.

Comment: LCU design operated by the Seaman's School, Quiriquina Island as a general purpose stores ship.

PISAGUA *8/1997, Chilean Navy* / 0012169

TUGS

Notes: Small harbour tugs *Reyes, Cortés* (both 100 tons and built in 1960) and *Galvez* (built in 1975), and the small personnel transport *Buzo Sobenes* BRT 112 are also in commission.

BUZO SOBENES *7/1997, Chilean Navy* / 0012170

2 VERITAS CLASS (TUG/SUPPLY VESSELS) (ATF)

Name	*No*	*Builders*	*Commissioned*
GALVARINO (ex-*Maersk Traveller*)	ATF 66	Aukra Bruk, Aukra	1974
LAUTARO (ex-*Maersk Tender*)	ATF 67	Aukra Bruk, Aukra	1973

Displacement, tons: 941 light; 2,380 full load
Dimensions, feet (metres): 191.3 × 41.4 × 12.8 *(58.3 × 12.6 × 3.9)*
Main machinery: 2 Krupp MaK 8 M 453AK diesels; 6,400 hp(m) *(4.7 MW)*; 2 shafts; cp props; bow thruster
Speed, knots: 14
Complement: 11 plus 12 spare berths
Cargo capacity: 1,400 tons
Guns: 1 Bofors 40 mm/70 can be carried.
Radars: Navigation: Terma Pilot 7T-48; Furuno FR 240; I-band.

Comment: *Janequero* and *Galvarino* delivered from Maersk and commissioned into Navy 26 January 1988. *Lautaro* delivered in 1991. *Janequero* since deleted. Bollard pull, 70 tonnes; towing winch, 100 tons. Fully air conditioned. Designed for towing large semi-submersible platform in extreme weather conditions. Ice strengthened. *Lautaro* underwent refit at ASMAR October 2006 to January 2007.

GALVARINO *7/2001, Maritime Photographic* / 0121330

COAST GUARD

Notes: There are also large numbers of harbour and SAR craft.

1 + 1 (2) OFFSHORE PATROL VESSELS (PSO)

Name	*No*	*Builders*	*Launched*	*Commissioned*
PILOTO PARDO	PZM 81	ASMAR, Talcahuano	14 June 2007	13 June 2008
COMANDANTE TORO	PZM 82	ASMAR, Talcahuano	15 Oct 2008	June 2009

Displacement, tons: 1,728 full load
Dimensions, feet (metres): 264.4 × 42.6 × 12.5 *(80.6 × 13.0 × 3.8)*
Main machinery: 2 Wärtsilä 12V26 diesels; 10,950 hp *(8.2 MW)*; 2 shafts; LIPS cp props; 2 bow thrusters
Speed, knots: 20
Range, n miles: 8,600 at 12 kt
Complement: 35 + 30 passengers
Guns: 1 — 40 mm/70. 6 — 12.7 mm MGs.
Radars: Surface search/navigation: Sperry Marine Bridgemaster E; E/F/I-bands.
Fire control: To be announced.
Helicopters: AS 365 or BO 105.

Programmes: Project Danubio IV. Contract signed on 20 May 2005 with Fassmer GmbH & Co. and Astilleros y Maestranzas de la Armada (ASMAR) for the design and construction of two patrol vessels. Fassmer is providing the design and construction assistance for the vessels which are under construction at Talcahuano Yard. Two further units are planned for delivery in 2010 and 2011.
Structure: Steel construction. The design includes stealth features. Upper-deck layout features a hangar, flight deck, crane, two 7 m RIBs, container storage and a special rescue zone.
Operational: PZM 81 based at Talcahuano.

PILOTO PARDO *6/2008*, Chilean Navy* / 1335348

18 PROTECTOR CLASS (WPB)

ALACALUFE LEP 1603
HALLEF LEP 1604
AYSÉN LSG 1609
CORRAL LSG 1610
CONCEPTIÓN LSG 1611
CALDERA LSG 1612
SAN ANTONIO LSG 1613
ANTOFAGASTA LSG 1614
ARICA LSG 1615
COQUIMBO LSG 1616
PUERTO NATALES LSG 1617
VALPARAÍSO LSG 1618
PUNTA ARENAS LSG 1619
TALCAHUANO LSG 1620
QUINTERO LSG 1621
CHILOÉ LSG 1622
PUERTO MONTT LSG 1623
IQUIQUE LSG 1624

Displacement, tons: 120 full load
Dimensions, feet (metres): 107.3 × 22 × 6.6 *(33.1 × 6.6 × 2)*
Main machinery: 2 MTU MDEC 2,000 diesels; 5,200 hp(m) *(3.82 MW)*; 2 shafts
Speed, knots: 22
Range, n miles: 800 at 16 kt
Complement: 10 (2 officers)
Guns: 1 — 12.7 mm MG.
Radars: Navigation: Raytheon R-84; I-band.

Comment: All built under licence from FBM at ASMAR, Talcahuano, in conjunction with FBM Marine. There are minor differences between LEP 1603-4 and the rest. First commissioned 24 June 1989 and last on 10 March 2004. A class of 19 (Project Danube) is envisaged. All conduct coastal patrols between Arica and Puerto Williams.

ARICA *12/2004, Globke Collection* / 1047868

ALACALUFE *6/2003, Chilean Navy* / 0569805

1 ASMAR 1160 (SEARCH AND RESCUE CRAFT) (SAR)

TOKERAU LSR 1700

Displacement, tons: 7.8 standard; 10 full load
Dimensions, feet (metres): 41.5 × 12.8 × 2.1 *(12.7 × 3.9 × 0.65)*
Main machinery: 2 Volvo Penta TAMD-61A diesels; 612 hp *(456 kW)*; 2 Hamilton waterjets
Speed, knots: 20
Range, n miles: 310 at 17 kt
Complement: 4 plus 32 survivors
Radars: Navigation: Raytheon R-84; I-band.

Comment: Built by Asmar Talcahuano and entered service in 1992. GRP hull and superstructure with inflatable surrounding bulwark. Carries extensive naviation, diving and first-aid equipment.

TOKERAU *6/2008*, Chilean Navy* / 1335347

6 TYPE 44 CLASS (WPB)

PELLUHUE LSR 1703
ARAUCO LSR 1704
CHACAO LSR 1705
QUEITAO LSR 1706
GUAITECA LSR 1707
CURAUMILA LSR 1708

Displacement, tons: 18 full load
Dimensions, feet (metres): 44 × 12.8 × 3.6 *(13.5 × 3.9 × 1.1)*
Main machinery: 2 Detroit 6V-38 diesels; 185 hp *(136 kW)*; 2 shafts
Speed, knots: 14
Range, n miles: 215 at 10 kt
Complement: 3

Comment: Acquired from the US and recommissioned on 31 May 2001.

QUEITAO *6/2008*, Chilean Navy* / 1335346

2 COASTAL PATROL CRAFT (WPB)

ONA LEP 1601 **YAGAN** LEP 1602

Displacement, tons: 79 full load
Dimensions, feet (metres): 80.7 × 17.4 × 5.6 *(24.6 × 5.3 × 1.7)*
Main machinery: 2 MTU 8V 331TC82 diesels; 1,300 hp(m) *(960 kW)* sustained; 2 shafts
Speed, knots: 18
Range, n miles: 415 at 15 kt
Complement: 5
Guns: 2 — 12.7 mm MGs.
Radars: Navigation: Raytheon R-84; I-band.

Comment: Built by Asenav and commissioned in 1980.

YAGAN *6/2003, Chilean Navy* / 0569804

10 INSHORE PATROL CRAFT (WPB)

MAULE LPM 1901
RAPEL LPM 1902
ACONCAGUA LPM 1903
LAUCA LPM 1904
ISLUGA LPM 1905
MAULLÍN LPM 1907
COPIAPÓ LPM 1908
CAU-CAU LPM 1909
PUDETO LPM 1910
ROBINSON CRUSOE LPM 1911

Displacement, tons: 14 full load
Dimensions, feet (metres): 43.3 × 11.5 × 3.5 *(13.2 × 3.5 × 1.1)*
Main machinery: 2 MTU D-2566 MTE diesels; 470 hp(m) *(350 kW)* sustained; 2 shafts
Speed, knots: 18
Range, n miles: 280 at 14 kt
Guns: 1 — 12.7 mm MG.
Radars: Navigation: Raytheon; I-band.

Comment: LPM 1901–1910 ordered in August 1981. Completed by Asenav 1982–83. LPM 1911 is a smaller 12 m craft built by Ast Sitecna, Puerto Montt, and commissioned 19 July 2000.

ACONCAGUA *12/2004, Globke Collection* / 1047867

4 + 11 DEFENDER CLASS (RESPONSE BOATS) (PBF)

PM 2050 **PM 2052–2054**

Displacement, tons: 2.7 full load
Dimensions, feet (metres): 25.0 × 8.5 × 3.6 *(7.6 × 2.6 × 1.1)*
Main machinery: 2 Honda outboard motors; 450 hp *(335 kW)*
Speed, knots: 46
Range, n miles: 175 at 35 kt
Complement: 4
Guns: 2 — 7.62 mm MGs.
Radars: Navigation: Furuno 1834; I-band.

Comment: High-speed inshore patrol craft of aluminium construction and foam collar built by SAFE Boats International, Port Orchard, Washington. Four delivered 2007–08 and a further 11 are to be delivered 2009–14.

PM 2050 *6/2007, Chilean Navy* / 1292774

1 + 19 ARCHANGEL CLASS (RESPONSE BOAT) (PBF)

LPM 4201

Displacement, tons: 12.6
Dimensions, feet (metres): 42.5 × 13.3 × 7.2 *(12.9 × 4.1 × 2.3)*
Main machinery: 2 Caterpillar C9 diesels; 550 hp *(409 kW)*; 2 Hamilton 322 waterjets
Speed, knots: 36
Range, n miles: 300 at 25 kt
Complement: 6
Guns: 2 — 7.62 mm MGs.
Radars: Navigation: Furuno; I-band.

Comment: High-speed inshore patrol craft of aluminium construction and foam collar built by SAFE Boats International, Port Orchard, Washington. First delivered in 2008 and 19 further to be delivered 2009–14.

ARCHANGEL CLASS *6/2008*, Chilean Navy* / 1335343

15 RODMAN 800 CLASS (WPB)

PM 2031–2045

Displacement, tons: 4 full load
Dimensions, feet (metres): 29.2 × 9.8 × 3.6 *(8.9 × 3 × 1.1)*
Main machinery: 2 Volvo diesels; 300 hp(m) *(220 kW)*; 2 shafts
Speed, knots: 28
Range, n miles: 150 at 25 kt
Complement: 3
Guns: 1 — 12.7 mm MG.
Radars: Navigation: Raytheon; I-band.

Comment: Built by Rodman Polyships, Vigo and all delivered by 17 May 1996.

PM 2034 *7/2001, Maritime Photographic* / 0121331

China

PEOPLE'S LIBERATION ARMY NAVY (PLAN)

Country Overview

The People's Republic of China, proclaimed on 1 October 1949, is the world's third-largest country by area (3,695,000 square miles) and the largest by population. It is bordered to the north by Kyrgyzstan, Kazakhstan, Mongolia and Russia, to the south by Vietnam, Laos, Myanmar, India, Bhutan, Nepal and North Korea and to the west by Pakistan, Afghanistan and Tajikistan. It has a 7,830 n mile coastline with the Yellow, East China and South China seas. There are more than 3,400 offshore islands of which Hainan is the largest. Sovereignty over Taiwan, still formally a province of China, is also claimed. Ownership of some or all of the Spratly Islands is disputed between China, Brunei, Taiwan, Vietnam, Malaysia and the Philippines although a code of conduct was mutually brokered in 2002. The principal ports are Shanghai (largest city), Fuzhou, Qingdao, Tianjin, Guangzhou and Hangzhou which is linked to the capital Beijing by the Grand Canal. Overall there are 54,000 n miles of navigable inland waterways including the Yangtze River on which the port of Wuhan is situated. Territorial seas (12 n miles) are claimed. A 200 n mile EEZ has also been claimed but the limits have not been defined.

Headquarters Appointments

Commander-in-Chief of the Navy:
Admiral Wu Shengli
Political Commissar of the Navy:
Admiral Liu Xiaojiang
Deputy Commanders-in-Chief of the Navy:
Vice Admiral Zhao Xingfa
Vice Admiral Zhang Yongyi
Vice Admiral Zhang Zhannan
Vice Admiral Ding Yiping
Vice Admiral Wang Yucheng

Fleet Commanders

North Sea Fleet:
Rear Admiral Tian Zhong
East Sea Fleet:
Rear Admiral Xu Hongmeng
South Sea Fleet:
Vice Admiral Su Shiliang

Personnel

(a) 2009: 250,000 officers and men, including 25,000 naval air force, 8–10,000 marines (28,000 in time of war) and 28,000 for coastal defence
(b) 2 years' national service for sailors afloat; 3 years for those in shore service. Some stay on for up to 15 years. 41,000 conscripts

Operational Numbers

Because numbers of vessels are kept in operational reserve, the Chinese version of the order of battle tends to show fewer ships than are counted by Western observers.

Organisation

Each of the North, East and South Sea Fleets has two submarine divisions, three DD/FF divisions and one MCMV division. The North also has one Amphibious Division, and the other Fleets have two each. The South has two Marine Infantry Brigades.

Bases

North Sea Fleet. Major bases: Qingdao (HQ), Huludao, Jianggezhuang, Guzhen Bay, Lushun, Xiaopingdao. Minor bases: Weihai Wei, Qingshan, Luda, Lianyungang, Ling Shan, Ta Ku Shan, Changshandao, Liuzhuang, Dayuanjiadun, Dalian
East Sea Fleet. Major bases: Ningbo (HQ), Zhoushan, Shanghai, Daxie, Fujan. Minor bases: Zhenjiangguan, Wusong, Xinxiang, Wenzhou, Sanduao, Xiamen, Xingxiang, Quandou, Wen Zhou SE, Wuhan, Dinghai, Jiaotou
South Sea Fleet. Major bases: Zhanjiang (HQ), Yulin (Hainan Island), Huangfu, Hong Kong, Yalong (Hainan Island), Guangzhou (Canton). Minor bases: Haikou, Shantou, Humen, Kuanchuang, Tsun, Kuan Chung, Mawai, Beihai, Ping Tan, San Chou Shih, Tang-Chiah Huan, Longmen, Bailong, Dongcun, Baimajing, Xiachuandao, Yuchi

Coast Defence

A large number of HY-2 (CSSC-3) and HY-3 (CSSC-301) SSMs in 20 semi-fixed armoured sites. 35 Coastal Artillery regiments.

Equipment Procurement

Although often listed under the name of the designer, equipment has not necessarily been supplied direct from the parent company. It may have been acquired from a third party or by reverse engineering.

Training

The main training centres are:

Dalian: Naval Vessel Academy
Guangzhou (Canton): Naval Arms Command College
Qingdao: Submarine Academy
Wuhan: Naval Engineering University
Nanjing: Naval Staff College
Yan Tai: Aviation Engineering College

Marines

There are two brigades based at Heieu and subordinate to the Navy. Each has three Infantry regiments and one Artillery regiment.

Naval Air Force

With 25,000 officers and men and over 800 aircraft, this is a considerable naval air force primarily land-based. There is a total of eight Divisions with 27 Regiments split between the three Fleets. Some aircraft are laid up unrepaired.

Air bases include:

North Sea Fleet: Dalian, Qingdao, Jinxi, Jiyuan, Laiyang, Jiaoxian, Xingtai, Laishan, Anyang, Changzhi, Liangxiang and Shan Hai Guan
East Sea Fleet: Danyang, Daishan, Shanghai (Dachang), Ningbo, Luqiao, Feidong and Shitangqiao
South Sea Fleet: Foluo, Haikou, Lingshui, Sanya, Guiping, Jialaishi and Lingling

Strength of the Fleet

Type	*Active (Reserve)*	*Building (Planned)*
SSBN	1	5 (1)
SSB	1	–
SSN	6	(3)
Patrol Submarines	46	2 (2)
Aircraft carriers	0	1 (1)
Destroyers	27	–
Frigates	49	2
Fast Attack Craft (Missile)	94	5
Patrol Craft	181	–
Minesweepers (Ocean)	27 (22)	–
Mine Warfare Drones	4 (42)	–
Minelayer	1	–
Hovercraft	10	–
LPD	1	–
LSTs	27	–
LSMs	54	–
LCMs-LCUs	175	–
Training Ships	2	–
Troop Transports (AP/AH)	6	–
Submarine Support Ships	11	–
Salvage and Repair Ships	1	–
Supply Ships	19	–
Fleet Replenishment Ships	5	–
Support Tankers	77	–
Hospital Ship	1	(1)
Icebreakers	4	–

DELETIONS

Submarines

2006 8 Romeo, 1 Ming
2008 7 Romeo, 1 Mod Romeo

Destroyers

2007 *Xian*

Frigates

2007 *Change De* (to CG), *Shaoxing* (to CG)

PENNANT LIST

Submarines

406 Xia

Destroyers

107 Yinchuan
108 Xining
109 Kaifeng
110 Dalian
112 Harbin
113 Qingdao
115 Shenyang
116 Shijiazhuang
131 Nanjing
132 Hefei
133 Chongqing
134 Zunyi
136 Hangzhou
137 Fuzhou
138 Taizhou
139 Ningbo
161 Changsha
162 Nanning
163 Nanchang
164 Guilin
165 Zhanjiang
166 Zhuhai
167 Shenzhen
168 Guangzhou
169 Wuhan
170 Lanzhou
171 Haikou

Frigates

511 Nantong
512 Wuxi
513 Huayin
514 Zhenjiang
515 Xiamen
516 Jiujiang
517 Nanping
518 Jian
519 Changzhi
521 Jiaxing
522 Lianyungang
523 Putian
524 Sanming
525 Maanshan
526 Wenzhou
527 Luoyang
528 Mianyang
529 Xuzhou
530 Zhoushan
533 Taizhou
534 Jinhua
535 Huangshi
536 Wuhu
537 Cangzhou
539 Anqing
540 Huainan
541 Huaibei
542 Tongling
543 Dandong
544 Siping
545 Linfen
551 Maoming
552 Yibin
553 Shaoguan
554 Anshun
555 Zhaotong
557 Jishou
558 Zigong
559 Beihai
560 Dongguan
561 Shantou
562 Jiangmen
563 Foshan
564 Yichang
565 Yulin
566 Huaihua
567 Xiangfan
568 Chaohu
570 Huangshan

Patrol Forces

770 Yangjiang
771 Shunde
772 Nanhai
773 Panyu
774 Lianjiang
775 Xinhui

Amphibious Forces

908 Yandanshan
909 Jiuhuashan
910 Huangganshan
911 Tianzhushan
912 Daqingshan
913 Baxianshan
918 –
927 Yuntaishan
928 Wufengshan
929 Zijinshan
930 Lingyanshan
931 Dongtingshan
932 Helanshan
933 Liupanshan
934 Danxiashan
935 Xuefengshan
936 Haiyangshan
937 Qingchengshan
939 Putuoshan
940 Tiantaishan
941 Shengshan
942 Lushan
943 –
944 Yushan
945 Huashan
946 Songshan
947 –
948 Xueshan
949 Hengshan
950 Taishan
990 Wudangshan
992 Huadingshan
993 Luoxiaoshan
994 Daiyunshan
995 Wangyangshan
996 Laotieshan
997 Yunwashan
998 Kunlunshan

Survey and Research Ships

851 Dongdiao
891 Bi Sheng
892 Hua Luogeng
900 Beidiao

Training Ships

81 Zhenghe
82 Shichang

Principal Auxiliaries

506 Yongxingdao
861 Changxingdao
862 Chongmingdao
863 Yongxingdao
881 Hongzhu
882 Fengcang
885 Qinghai Hu
886 Qiandao Hu
887 Weishan Hu
888 Fuxian Hu
920 Dazhi

SUBMARINES

Strategic Missile Submarines

Notes: The fourth test flight of a JL-2 missile was successfully accomplished on about 12 June 2005. The firing was made from a submarine, probably the Golf class SSB, off Qingdao and impacted in the western desert. The first launch from a Jin-class submarine is expected once missile flight testing has been completed, probably in 2009.

0 + 5 (1) JIN CLASS (TYPE 094) (SSBN)

Name	*No*	*Builders*	*Laid down*	*Launched*	*Commissioned*
–	–	Bohai Shipyard, Huludao	2001	28 July 2004	Mar 2007
–	–	Bohai Shipyard, Huludao	2003	2006	2009
–	–	Bohai Shipyard, Huludao	2004	2009	2011
–	–	Bohai Shipyard, Huludao	2006	2011	2013
–	–	Bohai Shipyard, Huludao	2007	2012	2014

Displacement, tons: 8,000
Dimensions, feet (metres): 449.5 × 38.7 × 7.5 *(137.0 × 11.8 × 2.3)*
Main machinery: Nuclear: 2 PWR; 150 MW; 2 turbines; 1 shaft
Speed, knots: To be announced
Complement: 140

Missiles: SLBM; 12 JL-2 (CSS-NX-5); 3-stage solid-fuel rocket; stellar inertial guidance to over 8,000 km *(4,320 n miles)*; single nuclear warhead of 1 MT or 3-8 MIRV of smaller yield. CEP 300 m approx.
Torpedoes: 6–21 in (533 mm tubes).
Countermeasures: Decoys: ESM.
Radars: Surface search.
Sonars: Hull mounted passive/active; flank and towed arrays.

Programmes: The first of class became operational as a submarine in mid-2007 and as a ballistic-missile submarine in about 2009–10, depending on the successful introduction into service of the JL-2 missile. Four further boats are thought to be under construction and are likely to commission at two year intervals. A class of six is expected.
Structure: Likely to be based on the Type 093 SSN design which in turn is believed to be derived from the Russian Victor III design. The dimensions of the hull assume the incorporation of a 30 m 'missile plug' of 12 tubes for the 42 ton JL-2 missiles.
Operational: Likely to be based at Yalong, Hainan Island. While the performance of the missile is speculative, its range may prompt a change in operating concept to a 'bastion' patrol approach. The second of class began sea trials in 2008.

JIN CLASS *12/2006* / 1167755

JIN CLASS *10/2007* 1166717

1 XIA CLASS (TYPE 092) (SSBN)

Name	*No*	*Builders*	*Laid down*	*Launched*	*Commissioned*
XIA	406	Bohai Shipyard, Huludao	1978	30 Apr 1981	1987

Displacement, tons: 6,500 dived
Dimensions, feet (metres): 393.6 × 33 × 26.2 *(120 × 10 × 8)*
Main machinery: Nuclear; turbo-electric; 1 PWR; 90 MW; 1 shaft
Speed, knots: 22 dived
Complement: 140

Missiles: SLBM: 12 JL-1 (CSS-N-3); inertial guidance to 2,150 km *(1,160 n miles)*; warhead single nuclear 250 kT.
Torpedoes: 6–21 in *(533 mm)* bow tubes. Yu-3 (SET-65E); active/passive homing to 15 km *(8.1 n miles)* at 40 kt; warhead 205 kg.
Countermeasures: ESM: Type 921-A; radar warning.
Radars: Surface search: Snoop Tray; I-band.
Sonars: Trout Cheek; hull-mounted; active/passive search and attack; medium frequency.

Programmes: A second of class was reported launched in 1982 and an unconfirmed report suggests that one of the two was lost in an accident in 1985.
Modernisation: Started major update in late 1995 at Huludao, thought to include fitting improved JL-1A missile with increased range but this has not been confirmed.
Structure: Diving depth 300 m *(985 ft)*.

Operational: First test launch of the JL-1 missile took place on 30 April 1982 from a submerged pontoon near Huludao (Yellow Sea). Second launched on 12 October 1982, from the Golf class trials submarine. The first firing from *Xia* was in 1985 and was unsuccessful (delaying final acceptance into service of the submarine) and it was not until 27 September 1988 that a satisfactory launch took place. Based in the North Sea Fleet at Jianggezhuang. Following a refit which completed in late 1998, was reported to be operational as a submarine in 2003 although firing of a JL-1 missile has not been reported and its status as a ballistic-missile submarine is uncertain.

XIA *2002, Ships of the World* / 0529138

1 GOLF CLASS (TYPE 031) (SSB)

200

Displacement, tons: 2,350 surfaced; 2,950 dived
Dimensions, feet (metres): 319.9 × 28.2 × 21.7 *(97.5 × 8.6 × 6.6)*
Main machinery: Diesel-electric; 3 Type 37-D diesels; 6,000 hp(m) *(4.41 MW)*; 3 motors; 5,500 hp(m) *(4 MW)*; 3 shafts
Speed, knots: 17 surfaced; 13 dived
Range, n miles: 6,000 surfaced at 15 kt
Complement: 86 (12 officers)

Missiles: SLBM: 1 JL-2 (CSS-NX-5); 3-stage solid fuel; stellar inertial guidance to 8,000 km *(4,320 n miles)*; single nuclear warhead of 1 MT or 3-8 MIRV of smaller yield. CEP 300 m approx.
Torpedoes: 10-21 in *(533 mm)* tubes (6 bow, 4 stern). 12 Type Yu-4 (SAET-50); passive homing to 15 km *(8.1 n miles)* at 30 kt; warhead 309 kg.
Radars: Navigation: Snoop Plate; I-band.
Sonars: Pike Jaw; hull-mounted; active/passive search; medium frequency.

Programmes: Ballistic missile submarine similar but not identical to the deleted USSR Golf class. Built at Dalian and launched in September 1966.
Modernisation: Refitted in 1995 to take the JL-2 missile.
Operational: This was the trials submarine for the JL-1 ballistic missile which was successfully launched to 1,800 km in October 1982. Continues to be available as a trials platform for the successor missile JL-2 and probably conducted a test firing on 12 June 2005. Based in the North Sea Fleet.

GOLF 200 — *2002, Ships of the World* / 0529137

Attack Submarines

Notes: Following the entry into service of two units of the Shang class, it is believed that further attack submarines are under consideration. These are likely to be to a modified evolutionary design, possibly to be known as the Type 095 class.

2 SHANG CLASS (TYPE 093) (SSN)

Name	*No*	*Builders*	*Laid down*	*Launched*	*Commissioned*
–	–	Bohai Shipyard, Huludao	1994	24 Dec 2002	Dec 2006
–	–	Bohai Shipyard, Huludao	2000	Dec 2003	June 2007

Displacement, tons: 6,000 dived
Dimensions, feet (metres): 351 × 36 × 24.6 *(107 × 11 × 7.5)*
Main machinery: Nuclear: 2 PWR; 150 MW; 2 turbines; 1 shaft
Speed, knots: 30 dived
Complement: 100

Missiles: SSM: YJ-82 (C-801A); radar active homing to 40 km *(22 n miles)* at 0.9 Mach; warhead 165 kg.
Torpedoes: 6—21 in *(533 mm)* bow tubes; combination of Yu-3 (SET-65E); active/passive homing to 15 km *(8.1 n miles)* at 40 kt; warhead 205 kg and Yu-4; active/passive homing to 15 km *(8.1 n miles)* at 30 kt; warhead 309 kg. Yu-6 wake-homing torpedo may also be carried.
Countermeasures: Decoys: ESM.
Radars: Surface search.
Sonars: Hull mounted passive/active; flank and towed arrays.

Programmes: Designed in conjunction with Russian experts. Prefabrication started in late 1994 and the first launch took place in late 2002. The boats entered service in 2006 and 2007 respectively.
Structure: Performance is likely to be similar to the double-hulled Russian Victor III design.
Operational: Sea trials of the first of class began in 2005 and of the second boat in 2006. Both based at Yalong, Hainan Island.

SHANG CLASS — *6/2007* / 1166715

SHANG CLASS — *6/2007* / 1166716

4 HAN CLASS (TYPE 091/091G) (SSN)

No	*Builders*	*Laid down*	*Launched*	*Commissioned*
402	Bohai Shipyard, Huludao	1974	1977	Jan 1980
403	Bohai Shipyard, Huludao	1980	1983	21 Sep 1984
404	Bohai Shipyard, Huludao	1984	1987	Nov 1988
405	Bohai Shipyard, Huludao	1987	8 Apr 1990	Dec 1990

Displacement, tons: 4,500 surfaced; 5,550 dived
Dimensions, feet (metres): 314.9; 331.4 (*404* onwards) × 32.8 × 24.2 *(96.0; 101.0 × 10 × 7.4)*
Main machinery: Nuclear; turbo-electric; 1 PWR; 90 MW; 1 shaft
Speed, knots: 25 dived; 12 surfaced
Complement: 75

Missiles: SSM: YJ-82 (C-801A); inertial cruise; active radar homing to 40 km *(22 n miles)* at 0.9 Mach; warhead 165 kg.
Torpedoes: 6–21 in *(533 mm)* bow tubes; combination of Yu-3 (SET-65E); active/passive homing to 15 km *(8.1 n miles)* at 40 kt; warhead 205 kg and Yu-4; active/passive homing to 15 km *(8.1 n miles)* at 36 kt; warhead 309 kg.
Mines: 36 in lieu of torpedoes.
Countermeasures: ESM: Type 921-A; radar warning.
Radars: Surface search: Snoop Tray; I-band.
Sonars: Trout Cheek; hull-mounted; active/passive search and attack; medium frequency.
DUUX-5; passive ranging and intercept; low frequency.

Programmes: First of this class delayed by problems with the power plant. Although completed in 1974 she was not fully operational until the 1980s.
Modernisation: The basic Russian ESM equipment was replaced by a French design. A French intercept sonar set has been fitted.
Structure: From *404* onwards the hull has been extended by some 5 m although this was not to accommodate missile tubes as previously reported. SSMs may be fired from the torpedo tubes. Diving depth 300 m *(985 ft)*.
Operational: Three based in North Sea Fleet at Jianggezhuang, one based at the new submarine base at Yalong, Hainan Island, in 2005. *403* and *404* started mid-life refits in 1998 which completed in early 2000. *405* started mid-life refit in 2000 and was reported completed in 2002. Torpedoes are a combination of older straight running and more modern Russian homing types. The first of class *401* was reported to have been decommissioned in 2003 and it is expected that others will follow now that the Type 093 has entered service.

HAN 404 — ***5/1996, Ships of the World*** / 0506277

HAN 402 — ***1990*** / 0506276

Patrol Submarines

Notes: An unknown number of midget submarines are reported in service.

2 + 2 (2) YUAN CLASS (TYPE 041) (SSG)

Name	*No*	*Builders*	*Laid down*	*Launched*	*Commissioned*
–	330	Wuhan Shipyard	–	31 May 2004	2006
–	–	Wuhan Shipyard	–	31 Aug 2007	2009
–	–	Wuhan Shipyard	–	Nov 2007	2010
–	–	Wuhan Shipyard	–	Apr 2008	2011

Displacement, tons: To be announced
Dimensions, feet (metres): 236.2 × 27.5 × ? *(72.0 × 8.4 × ?)*
Main machinery: Diesel-electric; 4 diesels; 1 motor; 2 Stirling AIP (to be confirmed); 1 shaft
Speed, knots: To be announced
Complement: To be announced

Missiles: SSM: YJ-82 (C-801A); inertial cruise; active radar homing to 40 km *(22 n miles)* at 0.9 Mach; warhead 165 kg.
Torpedoes: 6–21 in *(533 mm)* bow tubes. Combination of Yu-4 (SAET-50); active/passive homing to 15 km *(8.1 n miles)* at 30 kt; warhead 309 kg and Yu-3 (SET-65E); active/passive homing to 15 km *(8.1 n miles)* at 40 kt; warhead 205 kg. Yu-6 wake-homing torpedoes may also be fitted.
Countermeasures: To be announced.
Weapons control: To be announced.
Radars: To be announced.
Sonars: Bow-mounted; active/passive search and attack; medium; medium frequency. Flank array; passive search; low frequency.

Programmes: A new class of submarine of which the first of class was launched in May 2004. Production of the second of class was delayed by trials of the first of class. Series production is expected to proceed.
Structure: The boat appears to be a Chinese indigenous design. Shorter and broader than the Song class, it exhibits some of the features of the Russian Kilo class design including a teardrop-shaped hull with a distinctive 'hump' and large fin. The teardrop shape suggests a pressurised double hull construction. The stern of the boat resembles the Song class; the single shaft has a seven-bladed propeller. The submarine is covered with anechoic tiles. The submarine is believed to incorporate air-independent propulsion using Stirling engine technology.
Operational: Sea trials of the first of class started in 2005.

YUAN CLASS — ***1/2008**** / 1335696

YUAN CLASS — ***4/2005, Ships of the World*** / 1127027

13 SONG CLASS (TYPE 039/039G) (SSG)

No	*Builders*	*Laid down*	*Launched*	*Commissioned*
320	Wuhan Shipyard	1991	25 May 1994	June 1999
321	Wuhan Shipyard	1995	11 Nov 1999	Apr 2001
322	Wuhan Shipyard	1996	28 June 2000	Dec 2001
323	Wuhan Shipyard	1998	May 2002	Nov 2003
324	Wuhan Shipyard	1999	28 Nov 2002	Dec 2003
325	Wuhan Shipyard	2001	3 Dec 2002	2004
314	Wuhan Shipyard	2001	19 May 2003	2004
315	Wuhan Shipyard	2002	29 Sep 2003	2004
316	Wuhan Shipyard	2002	28 Aug 2004	2005
326	Wuhan Shipyard	2002	July 2004	2005
328	Jiangnan Shipyard, Shanghai	2002	Aug 2004	2005
327	Wuhan Shipyard	2003	Sep 2004	2006
329	Jiangnan Shipyard, Shanghai	2003	Nov 2004	2006

Displacement, tons: 1,700 surfaced; 2,250 dived
Dimensions, feet (metres): 246 × 24.6 × 17.5 *(74.9 × 7.5 × 5.3)*
Main machinery: Diesel-electric; 4 MTU 16V 396 SE; 6,092 hp(m) *(4.48 MW)* diesels; 4 alternators; 1 motor; 1 shaft
Speed, knots: 15 surfaced; 22 dived
Complement: 60 (10 officers)

Missiles: SSM: YJ-82 (C-801A); radar active homing to 40 km *(22 n miles)* at 0.9 Mach; warhead 165 kg.
Torpedoes: 6—21 in *(533 mm)* tubes. Combination of Yu-4 (SAET-50); passive homing to 15 km *(8.1 n miles)* at 30 kt; warhead 309 kg and Yu-3 (SET-65E); active/passive homing to 15 km *(8.1 n miles)* at 40 kt; warhead 205 kg. Yu-6 wake-homing torpedoes may also be fitted.
Mines: In lieu of torpedoes.
Countermeasures: ESM: Type 921-A; radar warning.
Radars: Surface search: I-band.
Sonars: Bow-mounted; passive/active search and attack; medium frequency.
Flank array; passive search; low frequency.

Programmes: First of class (Type 039) started sea trials in August 1995, as a result of which substantial modifications were made. Second of class (Type 039G) trials started in early 2000 and third in early 2001. Fourth commissioned in 2003 while fifth and sixth conducted trials in late 2003. Construction of the seventh hull is understood to have started in 2001 and of the eighth, ninth and tenth hulls in 2002. The twelfth hull is reported to have started construction at Wuhan in 2003. The building programme appears to have been switched to Jiangnan Shipyard, Shanghai, where the eleventh and thirteenth boats were built. Further units of the class are not expected.
Structure: Comparable in size to Ming class but with a single skew propeller and an integrated spherical bow sonar. The forward hydroplanes are mounted below the bridge, which is on a step lower than the part of the fin that contains the masts in earlier boats. The fin is of a different shape (no cutaway) in later boats. Some of the details are speculative and the latest hulls of the class may have benefited from experience gained with the Kilos. The diesel engines are likely to be reverse engineered. Sonars are reported to be of French design.

SONG CLASS *4/2004, Ships of the World* / 1042142

SONG CLASS *1/2007, Ships of the World* / 1166772

SONG CLASS 315 and 316 *6/2005, Hachiro Nakai* / 1153050

SONG CLASS *6/2004* / 1042169

12 KILO CLASS (PROJECT 877EKM/636) (SSG)

No	*Builders*	*Laid down*	*Launched*	*Commissioned*
364 (ex-B 171)	Nizhny Novgorod	–	–	Feb 1995
365 (ex-B 177)	Nizhny Novgorod	–	31 Mar 1985	Aug 1995
366	Admiralty, St Petersburg	–	24 Apr 1997	6 Jan 1998
367	Admiralty, St Petersburg	–	18 June 1998	11 Dec 1998
368	Admiralty, St Petersburg	–	27 May 2004	20 Oct 2004
369	Admiralty, St Petersburg	–	19 Aug 2004	5 May 2005
370	Severodvinsk Shipyard	29 May 2003	21 May 2005	22 Dec 2005
371	Admiralty, St Petersburg	–	28 Feb 2005	18 July 2005
372	Nizhny Novgorod	1991	17 May 2004	Oct 2005
373	Admiralty, St Petersburg	–	24 May 2005	Oct 2005
374	Severodvinsk Shipyard	29 May 2003	27 July 2005	27 Dec 2005
375	Admiralty, St Petersburg	–	26 Aug 2005	30 May 2006

Displacement, tons: 2,325 surfaced; 3,076 dived
Dimensions, feet (metres): 238.2; 242.1 (Project 636) × 32.5 × 21.7 *(72.6; 73.8 × 9.9 × 6.6)*
Main machinery: Diesel-electric; 2 diesels; 3,650 hp(m) *(2.68 MW)*; 2 generators; 1 motor; 5,900 hp(m) *(4.34 MW)*; 1 shaft; 2 auxiliary motors; 204 hp(m) *(150 kW)*; 1 economic speed motor; 130 hp(m) *(95 kW)*
Speed, knots: 17 dived; 10 surfaced
Complement: 52 (13 officers)

Missiles: SLCM: Novator Alfa Klub SS-N-27 (3M-54E1); active radar homing to 180 km *(97.2 n miles)* at 0.7 Mach (cruise) and 2.5 Mach (attack); warhead 450 kg.
Torpedoes: 6–21 in *(533 mm)* tubes. 18 torpedoes. Combination of TEST 71/96; wire-guided; active/passive homing to 15 km *(8.1 n miles)* at 40 kt; warhead 205 kg and 53-65; passive wake homing to 19 km *(10.3 n miles)* at 45 kt; warhead 300 kg.
Mines: 24 in lieu of torpedoes.
Countermeasures: ESM: Squid Head or Brick Pulp; radar warning.
Weapons control: MVU-119 EM Murena TFCS.
Radars: Surface search: Snoop Tray; I-band.
Sonars: Shark Teeth; hull-mounted; passive/active search and attack; medium frequency.
Mouse Roar; hull-mounted; active attack; high frequency.

Programmes: The first four boats were ordered in mid-1993. The first two are Project 877 hulls built for a former Warsaw Pact country and subsequently cancelled. The first one departed the Baltic in December 1994 and arrived by transporter ship in February 1995. The second was delivered by the same method in November 1995. The third and fourth are of the newer Project 636 design. The first of these two left the Baltic by transporter in November 1997 and arrived in January 1998. The second followed in December 1998 arriving on 1 February 1999. A contract for a further eight 636 or 636M variants armed with SS-N-27 was signed on 3 May 2002. The first of these was originally laid down at Nizhny Novgorod for the Russian Navy, but was never completed due to lack of funding. She is likely to be the last submarine to have been built at the shipyard. Five of the boats were built by Admiralty Yard, St Petersburg and the remaining two boats at Severodvinsk. The programme was completed in 2006.
Modernisation: The first four submarines are to be refitted in Russian shipyards. Upgrades are likely to include installation of the Klub (3M54) (SS-N-27) anti-ship missile system.
Structure: Latest export version of the elderly Kilo design and has better weapon systems co-ordination and improved accommodation than the earlier ships of the class. Double-hull construction with six watertight compartments. Normal diving depth is 240 m with 300 m available in emergency. At least two torpedo tubes can fire wire-guided weapons. An SA-N-8 SAM launcher may be fitted on top of the fin. Some modifications have been carried out after arrival in China including a possible new ESM.
Operational: The first four based at Xiangshan in the East Sea Fleet. Of the remaining eight boats, four are likely to be based in the East Sea Fleet and four in the South Sea Fleet.

KILO CLASS *1/2008**, **A Sheldon-Duplaix** / 1335695

KILO CLASS (in transit) *6/2006* / 1164401

19 MING CLASS (TYPE 035) (SS)

352–354 | 356–363 | 305–308 | 310–313

Displacement, tons: 1,584 surfaced; 2,113 dived
Dimensions, feet (metres): 249.3 × 24.9 × 16.7
(76 × 7.6 × 5.1)
Main machinery: Diesel-electric; 2 diesels; 5,200 hp(m) *(3.82 MW)*; 2 shafts
Speed, knots: 15 surfaced; 18 dived; 10 snorting
Range, n miles: 8,000 at 8 kt snorting; 330 at 4 kt dived
Complement: 57 (10 officers)

Torpedoes: 8—21 in *(533 mm)* (6 fwd, 2 aft) tubes. Combination of Yu-4 (SAET-50); passive homing to 15 km *(8.1 n miles)* at 30 kt; warhead 309 kg, and Yu-1 (53-51) to 9.2 km *(5 n miles)* at 39 kt or 3.7 km *(2.1 n miles)* at 51 kt; warhead 400 kg; 16 weapons.
Mines: 32 in lieu of torpedoes.

Radars: Surface search: Snoop Tray; I-band.
Sonars: Pike Jaw; hull-mounted; active/passive search and attack; medium frequency
DUUX 5; passive ranging and intercept; low frequency

Programmes: First three completed between 1971 and 1979 one of which was scrapped after a fire and another *(232)* has been decommissioned. These were Type ES5C/D. Building resumed at Wuhan Shipyard in 1987 at the rate of one per year to a modified design ES5E. The programme was thought to have ended with hull number 14 *(363)* launched in May 1996, but *305* was launched in June 1997 followed by *306* in September 1997, *307* in May 1998, *308* in October 1998, *310* in June 2000, *311* in September 2000, *312* in May 2001 and *313* in April 2002. The expected launch of a further boat in 2003 did not take place and, in view of the 'Kilo' programme, this programme has probably been discontinued.
Structure: Diving depth, 300 m *(985 ft)*. Only the later models have the DUUX 5 sonar. Hull 20 is reported to have a 2 m extension to its machinery space.
Operational: Thirteen are based in the North Sea Fleet at Lushun, Qingdao and Xiapingdao. From *305* onwards, based in the South Sea Fleet. Some have moved to Xiachuandao. Fitted with Magnavox SATNAV. All onboard *361* (70 officers and men) killed in an accident in April 2003. The cause of the accident is believed to have been carbon monoxide poisoning. After repairs at Dalian, the submarine became operational again in 2004.

MING CLASS ***3/2008**** / 1335661

MING CLASS ***3/2006, Lemachko Collection*** / 1166769

AIRCRAFT CARRIERS

Notes: (1) The former Russian aircraft carrier *Minsk* is a tourist attraction at Shenzhen.
(2) Building of an indigenous aircraft carrier is expected to start by 2010 with a view to entering service in about 2015.

0 + 1 KUZNETSOV (OREL) (PROJECT 1143.5/6) CLASS (CVGM)

Name	*No*	*Builders*	*Laid down*	*Launched*	*Commissioned*
SHI LANG (ex-*Varyag*, ex-*Riga*)	83	Nikolayev South, Ukraine	6 Dec 1985	6 Dec 1988	2008

Displacement, tons: 45,900 standard; 58,500 full load
Dimensions, feet (metres): 999 oa; 918.6 wl × 229.7 oa; 121.4 wl × 34.4 *(304.5; 280 × 70; 37 × 10.5)*
Flight deck, feet (metres): 999 × 229.7 *(304.5 × 70)*
Main machinery: 8 boilers; 4 turbines; 200,000 hp(m) *(147 MW)*; 4 shafts
Speed, knots: 30
Range, n miles: 3,850 at 29 kt; 8,500 at 18 kt
Complement: 1,960 (200 officers plus 626 aircrew plus 40 Flag staff

Missiles: SAM: To be announced.
Guns: To be announced.
A/S mortars: To be announced.
Countermeasures: Decoys: ESM/ECM: To be announced.
Weapons control: To be announced.
Radars: Air search: To be announced.
Air/surface search: To be announced.
Surface search: To be announced.
Navigation: To be announced.
Fire control: To be announced.
Aircraft control: To be announced.
Tacan: To be announced.
IFF: To be announced.
Sonars: To be announced.

Fixed-wing aircraft: 18 Su-33 Flanker D.
Helicopters: To be announced.

SHI LANG — ***2/2008**** / 1335660

Programmes: Procurement of an aircraft carrier capability has been a high priority for the Chinese Navy since the 1990s. Ex-*Varyag*, the second of the Kuznetsov class (the first of class, *Admiral Kuznetsov*, remains in service in the Russian Navy) was between 70 and 80 per cent complete by early 1993 when building was terminated after an unsuccessful attempt by the Russian Navy to fund completion. Subsequently the ship was bought by China and, having been towed through the Bosporus on 2 November 2001, arrived at Dalian in March 2002. Since then, there have been conflicting reports about Chinese plans for the ship but, following its emergence from dock in mid-2005 painted in military colours, it is likely that it is intended to bring the ship into operational service. Work in 2006 included the apparent application of a non-skid surface to the flight deck and, by mid-2008, the exterior of the ship was looking relatively shipshape. However the overall project appears to be taking longer than expected. A further 2-3 months docking period is probably required to fit shafts and/or propellers. In November 2008, it was reported that Chinese negotiations to acquire an initial batch of 14 Su-33 for training were nearing completion. A further 36 modernised aircraft may be acquired at a later date.
Structure: The hangar is 183 × 29.4 × 7.5 m and can hold up to 18 Flanker aircraft. There are two starboard side lifts, a ski jump of 14° and angled deck of 7°. There are four arrester wires. The ship has some 16.5 m of freeboard.
Operational: Initial sea trials could start in 2009 after which an extensive period of trials and training is likely to follow. It is unlikely that the ship will begin operational flying training until at the earliest 2010. The ships (unconfirmed) pennant number suggests that her initial status will be as a training ship. The aircraft inventory is not yet known but is likely to comprise a mixture of Russian-built fixed-wing aircraft and helicopters. The ship's name has also not been confirmed; Admiral Shi Lang was commander-in-chief of the Manchu fleets which conquered Taiwan in 1681.

DESTROYERS

2 LUZHOU CLASS (TYPE 051C) (DDGHM)

Name	*No*	*Builders*	*Laid down*	*Launched*	*Commissioned*
SHENYANG	115	Dalian Shipyard	2002	28 Dec 2004	Oct 2006
SHIJIAZHUANG	116	Dalian Shipyard	2003	26 July 2005	Mar 2007

Displacement, tons: 7,000 full load
Dimensions, feet (metres): 508.5 × 55.8 × 19.7 *(155.0 × 17.0 × 6.0)*
Main machinery: To be announced.
Speed, knots: To be announced
Complement: To be announced

Missiles: SSM: 8 C-802 (YJ-83) 2 quad ❶; active radar homing to 160 km *(86 n miles)* at 0.9 Mach; warhead 165 kg; sea skimmer.
SAM: 6 (2 forward, 4 aft) SA-N-20 Grumble (Rif-M) ❷ circular vertical launchers; 8 rounds per launcher; command guidance; semi-active radar homing to 150 km *(81 n miles)*; warhead 90 kg; altitude 27,432 m *(90,000 ft)*. 48 missiles.
Guns: 1—3.9 in *(100 mm)*/56 ❸; 25 rds/min to 22 km *(12 n miles)*; weight of shell 15.6 kg.
2 Type 730 ❹ 30 mm 7 barrels per mounting; 4,200 rds/min combined to 1.5 km.
A/S mortars: To be announced.
Countermeasures: Decoys: 2—18 tube launchers. 2—10 tube launchers.
Combat data systems: To be announced. SATCOM.
Weapons control: Band Stand ❺; I-band (datalink for C-802).
Radars: Air search: Top Plate (Fregat MAE-3) ❻; 3D; E-band.
Air/surface search: Type 364 Seagull C ❼; G-band.

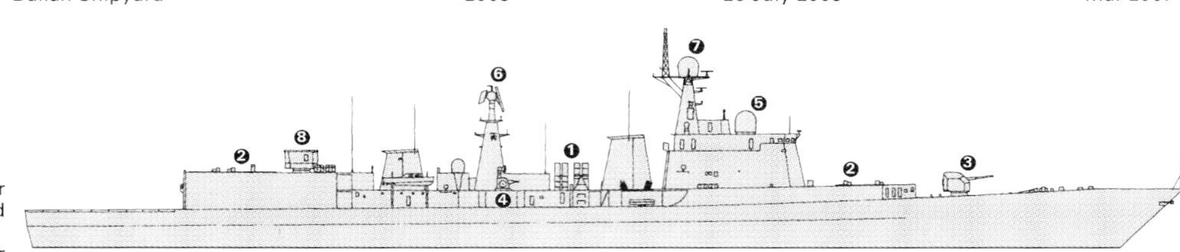

SHENYANG — ***(Scale 1 : 1,200), Ian Sturton*** / 1164337

Fire control: Tomb Stone (Volna); I/J-band (for Rif-M) ❽. Band Stand (Mineral ME) ❺; I-band (for C-802). Type 344 (MR 34); I-band (for 100 mm).
Type 347G(2) (LR 66); I-band (for Type 730).
Navigation: To be announced.
Sonars: Bow mounted, to be announced.

Helicopters: Platform only.

Programmes: The requirement for these ships arose from a need to address AAW deficiencies. It may predate the Luyang programmes and could have been delayed by procurement of the SAM system.

Structure: Design appears to be based on the Type 051B/ Luhai DDG but to be less stealthy than the Luyang classes, although the dimensions are similar. Two VLS launchers are installed in the platform in front of the bridge and four in the aft superstructure. The AAW system is controlled by a Tomb Stone (Flap Lid) phased-array radar installed on a structure behind the aft mast. The number of SSMs is limited to eight due to lack of space between the forward funnel and aft mast.
Operational: Both ships conducted sea trials in 2006. Based in the North Sea Fleet.

SHENYANG — ***1/2008*, Ships of the World*** / 1335656

4 SOVREMENNY CLASS (PROJECT 956E/956EM) (DDGHM)

Name	*No*	*Builders*	*Laid down*	*Launched*	*Commissioned*
HANGZHOU (ex-*Vazhny*, ex-*Yekaterinburg*)	136 (ex-698)	North Yard, St Petersburg	4 Nov 1988	23 May 1994	25 Dec 1999
FUZHOU (ex-*Alexandr Nevsky*)	137	North Yard, St Petersburg	22 Feb 1989	16 Apr 1999	16 Jan 2001
TAIZHOU	138	North Yard, St Petersburg	27 June 2002	27 Apr 2004	28 Dec 2005
NINGBO	139	North Yard, St Petersburg	2003	23 July 2004	28 Sep 2006

Displacement, tons: 7,940 full load
Dimensions, feet (metres): 511.8 × 56.8 × 21.3 *(156 × 17.3 × 6.5)*
Main machinery: 4 KVN boilers; 2 GTZA-674 turbines; 99,500 hp(m) *(73.13 MW)* sustained; 2 shafts; bow thruster
Speed, knots: 32. **Range, n miles:** 2,400 at 32 kt; 4,000 at 14 kt
Complement: 296 (25 officers) plus 60 spare

Missiles: SSM: 8 Raduga SS-N-22 Sunburn (Moskit 3M-80E) (2 quad) launchers ❶; active/passive radar homing to 160 km (240 in 138, 139) *(87 (130) n miles)* at 2.5 (4.5 for attack) Mach; warhead 300 kg; sea-skimmer.
SAM: 2 SA-N-7 Gadfly (Uragan) ❷ 9M38M1 Smerch: command/semi-active radar and IR homing to 25 km *(13.5 n miles)* at 3 Mach; warhead 70 kg; altitude 15-14,020 m *(50-46,000 ft)*; 44 missiles. Multiple channels of fire.
2 CADS-N-1 (Kashtan) (138, 139) ❸; each has 30 mm gatling combined with 8 SA-N-11 (Grisson) and Hot Flash/Hot Spot radar/optronic director. Laser beam guidance for missiles to 8 km *(4.4 n miles)*; warhead 9 kg; 9,000 rds/min to 1.5 km for guns.
Guns: 4 (2 (138, 139)) 130 mm/56 (2 (1) twin) AK 130 ❹; 70 rds/min to 22 km *(12 n miles)*; weight of shell 33.4 kg.
4—30 mm/65 AK 630 (136, 137) ❺; 6 barrels per mounting; 3,000 rds/min combined to 2 km.
Torpedoes: 4—21 in *(533 mm)* (2 twin) tubes ❻.
A/S mortars: 2 RBU 1000 6-barrelled ❼; range 1,000 m; warhead 55 kg; 120 rockets carried. Torpedo countermeasure.
Mines: Mine rails for up to 40.
Countermeasures: Decoys: 8 PK 10 and 2 PK 2 chaff launchers.
ESM/ECM: 4 Foot Ball. 6 Half Cup laser warner.
Weapons control: 1 China optronic director and laser rangefinder ❽. Band Stand ❾; I-band datalink for SS-N-22. Bell Nest, 2 Light Bulb and 2 Tee Pump datalinks.
Radars: Air search: Top Plate (Fregat MAE-3) ❿; 3D; E-band.
Surface search: 3 Palm Frond ⓫; I-band.
Fire control: 6 Front Dome (MR-90) ⓬; H/I-band (for SA-N-7). Band Stand (Mineral ME) ❾; I-band (for SS-N-22). Kite Screech ⓭; H/I/K-band (for 130 mm guns). 2 Bass Tilt ⓮; H/I-band (for 30 mm guns).
Sonars: Bull Horn (Platina) and Whale Tongue; hull-mounted; active search and attack; medium frequency.

Helicopters: 1 Harbin Zhi-9C Haitun ⓯ or Kamov Ka-28 Helix.

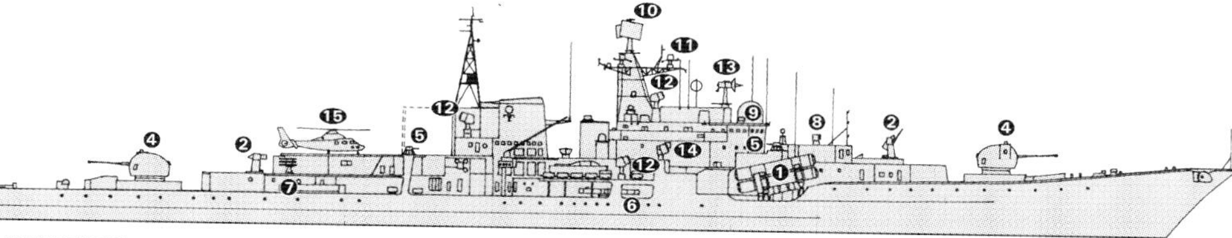

HANGZHOU

(Scale 1 : 1,200), Ian Sturton / 1164870

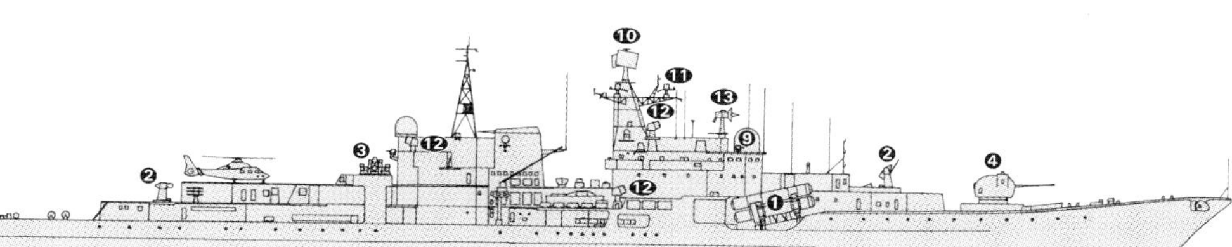

TAIZHOU

(Scale 1 : 1,200), Ian Sturton / 1164871

FUZHOU

12/2005, Ships of the World / 1153060

Programmes: After prolonged negotiations, a contract was signed in September 1996 for two uncompleted Russian Sovremenny class destroyers. These were hulls 18 and 19. Progress was held up for a time because China wanted KA-28 helicopters included, and the Russians demanded extra payment for the aircraft. Deleted Russian units of the class may have been cannibalised for some equipment. A contract for the procurement of two more ships was signed on 3 January 2002. The keel of the first modified Sovremenny class was laid down on 27 June 2002. An option for two further ships is unlikely to be taken up.

Structure: These are the first Chinese warships to have a data system link. The optronic director is probably a Chinese version of Squeeze Box. The second two ships (Project 956EM) are to a modified design which include variations in weapon fit including replacement of the AK 630 system with 'Kashtan' (with associated Cross Dome target indication radar) CIWS and a reduction to one forward AK 130 turret. The flight deck has been extended. Two single-armed launchers for SA-N-7 are retained. An uprated SS-N-22 system with 240 km range is also fitted.

Operational: 136 arrived in China on 16 February 2000 and 137 in February 2001. SS-N-22 test fired on 15 September 2001. 138 was delivered on 28 December 2005 and 139 in late 2006. All four ships are based in the East Sea Fleet.

Opinion: The main role of these ships is anti-surface warfare although they also possess a good AAW capability. Together with the new AAW destroyers, they represent a step-change in Chinese naval capabilities.

SOVREMENNY 139

12/2006, Ships of the World / 1166770

SOVREMENNY 139

10/2006, B Prézelin / 1164322

2 LUYANG I (TYPE 052B) CLASS (DDGHM)

Name	*No*	*Builders*	*Laid down*	*Launched*	*Commissioned*
GUANGZHOU	168	Jiangnan Shipyard, Shanghai	2001	25 May 2002	18 July 2004
WUHAN	169	Jiangnan Shipyard, Shanghai	2001	9 Sep 2002	18 July 2004

Displacement, tons: 7,000 full load
Dimensions, feet (metres): 508.5 × 55.8 × 19.7 *(155 × 17 × 6)*
Main machinery: CODOG: 2 Ukraine DA80 gas turbines; 48,600 hp(m) *(35.7 MW)*; 2 diesels; 8,840 hp(m) *(6.5 MW)*; 2 shafts; cp props
Speed, knots: 29
Range, n miles: 4,500 at 15 kt
Complement: 280 (40 officers)

Missiles: SSM: 16 C-802 (YJ-83/C SS-N-8 Saccade) 4 quad ❶; mid-course guidance and active radar homing to 150 km *(81 n miles)* at 0.9 Mach; warhead 165 kg; sea skimmer.
SAM: SA-N-12 Grizzly (Shtil-1) 9M38M2 ❷; command/semi-active radar and IR homing to 35 km *(18.9 n miles)* at 3 Mach; warhead 70 kg; 2 magazines (forward and aft). 48 missiles.
Guns: 1—3.9 in *(100 mm)*/56 ❸; 25 rds/min to 22 km *(12 n miles)*; weight of shell 15.6 kg.
2–30 mm Type 730 ❹; 7 barrels per mounting; 4,200 rds/min combined to 1.5 km.
Torpedoes: 6–324 mm B 515 (2 triple) tubes ❺; Yu-2/5/6; active/passive homing to 11 km *(5.9 n miles)* at 40 kt; warhead 44 kg.
A/S mortars: 4 multiple rocket launchers (possibly multirole) ❻.
Countermeasures: Decoys: 4–18 tube 100 mm launchers ❼.
ESM: SRW 210A.
ECM: Type 984 (I-band jammer). Type 985 (E/F-band jammer).
Combat data systems: To be announced. SATCOM.
Weapons control: Band Stand (Mineral ME) ❽; I-band; datalink (for C-803).
Radars: Air search: Top Plate (Fregat MAE-3); 3D; ❾; E/F-band.
Air/surface search: Type 364 Seagull C ❿; G-band.
Fire control: 4 Front Dome (Orekh) ⓫; H/I-band (for SA-N-12).
Band Stand (Mineral ME) ❽; I-band (for C-802).
Type 344 (MR 34) ⓬; I-band (for 100 mm).
2 Type 347G(2) (LR 66); I-band (for Type 730).
Navigation: To be announced.

GUANGZHOU *(Scale 1 : 1,200), Ian Sturton* / 1170050

WUHAN *6/2007* / 1166873

Sonars: Bow mounted. To be announced.

Helicopters: 1 Harbin Zhi-9A Haitun or Kamov KA-28 Helix ⓭.

Programmes: Construction of new multirole destroyers with medium-range air defence capability started in 2001.

Structure: Based on 'Luhai' design but with more advanced stealth features. The aft superstructure contains the hangar on the port side and aft missile magazine to starboard.
Operational: Based in the South Sea Fleet.

GUANGZHOU *9/2007, R G Sharpe* / 1166778

GUANGZHOU *9/2007, B Prézelin* / 1166780

2 LUYANG II (TYPE 052C) CLASS (DDGHM)

Name	*No*	*Builders*	*Laid down*	*Launched*	*Commissioned*
LANZHOU	170	Jiangnan Shipyard, Shanghai	June 2002	29 Apr 2003	18 July 2004
HAIKOU	171	Jiangnan Shipyard, Shanghai	Nov 2002	29 Oct 2003	20 July 2005

Displacement, tons: 7,000 full load
Dimensions, feet (metres): 508.5 × 55.8 × 19.7 *(155 × 17 × 6)*
Main machinery: CODOG: 2 Ukraine DA80 gas turbines; 48,600 hp(m) *(35.7 MW)*; 2 diesels; 8,840 hp(m) *(6.5 MW)*; 2 shafts; cp props
Speed, knots: 29
Range, n miles: 4,500 at 15 kt
Complement: 280 (40 officers)

Missiles: SSM: 8 C-602 (YJ-62) ❶ 2 quad; inertial-GPS guidance and terminal active radar homing to 280 km *(151 n miles)* at 0.8 Mach; warhead 300 kg.
SAM: HHQ-9 ❷; 8 vertical fixed sextuple launchers (6 forward, 2 aft); command guidance; semi-active radar homing to 100 km *(54 n miles)* at 3 Mach; warhead 90 kg; 48 missiles.
Guns: 1—3.9 in *(100 mm)*/56 ❸; 25 rds/min to 22 km *(12 n miles)*; weight of shell 15.6 kg.
2–30 mm Type 730 ❹; 7 barrels per mounting; 4,200 rds/min combined to 1.5 km.
Torpedoes: 6—324 mm B 515 (2 triple) tubes ❺; Yu-2/5/6; active/passive homing to 11 km *(5.9 n miles)* at 40 kt; warhead 44 kg.
A/S mortars: 4 multiple rocket launchers (possibly multirole) ❻.
Countermeasures: ESM/ECM: NRJ-6A.
Combat data systems: To be announced. SATCOM.
Weapons control: Band Stand (Mineral ME) ❼; I-band; datalink for YJ-62.
Radars: Air search: Type 517 Knife Rest ❽; A-band.
Air search/fire control: Type 346 phased arrays ❾; 3D; G-band.
Air/surface search: Type 364 Seagull C ❿; G-band.
Fire control: Type 344 (MR 34) ⓫; I-band (for 100 mm).
Band Stand ❼; I-band (for YJ-62).
2 Type 347G(2) (LR 66); I-band (for Type 730).
Navigation: To be announced.
Sonars: Bow mounted. To be announced.

Helicopters: 2 Harbin Zhi-9A Haitun or Kamov KA-28 Helix ⓬.

Programmes: The second phase of the destroyer construction programme which introduces the long-range HHQ-9 missile system into service.
Structure: Appears to share the same basic hull design as the Type 052B destroyers which in turn are based on the Luhai class. As well as incorporating stealth features, the design includes a taller forward superstructure in which the four phased array antennas are installed. The helicopter hangar is on the port side of the aft superstructure. Details are speculative and firm details of both the SAM and SSM systems are yet to be confirmed. The CIWS systems are on raised platforms forward and on top of the hangar.
Operational: Based in the South Sea Fleet.

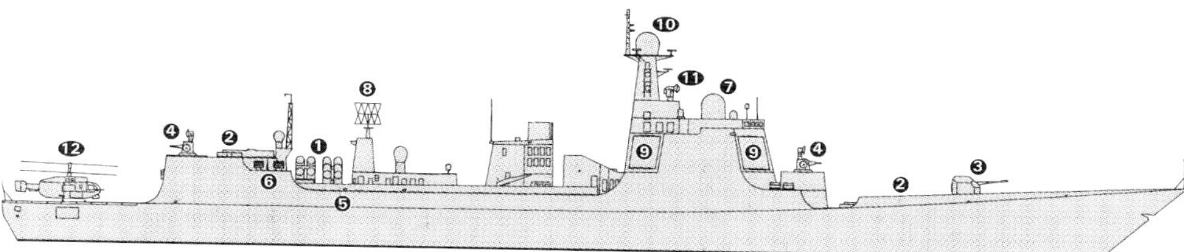

LANZHOU *(Scale 1 : 1,200), Ian Sturton* / 1170051

HAIKOU *1/2007, Ships of the World* / 1167731

HAIKOU *6/2007* 1335694

1 LUHAI CLASS (TYPE 051B) (DDGHM)

Name	*No*	*Builders*	*Laid down*	*Launched*	*Commissioned*
SHENZHEN	167	Dalian Shipyard	July 1996	16 Oct 1997	4 Jan 1999

Displacement, tons: 6,000 full load
Dimensions, feet (metres): 505 × 52.5 × 19.7 *(154 × 16 × 6)*
Main machinery: CODOG: 2 Ukraine gas turbines; 48,600 hp(m) *(35.7 MW)*; 2 MTU 12V 1163 TB 83 diesels; 8,840 hp(m) *(6.5 MW)* sustained; 2 shafts; cp props
Speed, knots: 29. **Range, n miles:** 4,500 at 14 kt
Complement: 250 (42 officers)

Missiles: SSM: 16 C-802 (YJ-83/CSS-N-8 Saccade) ❶; mid-course guidance and active radar homing to 150 km *(81 n miles)* at 0.9 Mach; warhead 165 kg; sea skimmer.
SAM: 1 HQ-7 (Crotale) octuple launcher ❷; CSA-N-4 line of sight guidance to 13 km *(7 n miles)* at 2.4 Mach; warhead 14 kg. Possible reloading hatch aft of the HQ-7 launcher.
Guns: 2—3.9 in *(100 mm)*/56 (twin) ❸; 25 rds/min to 22 km *(12 n miles)*; weight of shell 15.6 kg.
8—37 mm/63 Type 76A (4 twin) ❹; 180 rds/min to 8.5 km *(4.6 n miles)* anti-aircraft; weight of shell 1.42 kg.
Torpedoes: 6—324 mm B515 (2 triple) tubes ❺ Yu-2/5/6; active/passive homing to 11 km *(5.9 n miles)* at 40 kt; warhead 44 kg.
Countermeasures: Decoys: 2 Type 946 15-tube 100 mm chaff launchers ❻.
2 Type 947 10-tube 130 mm chaff launchers.
ESM: Type 826.
ECM: Type 984; I-band jammer; Type 985; E/F-band jammer.
Combat data systems: Thomson-CSF Tavitac; SATCOM.
Weapons control: 2 GDG 776 optronic directors.
Radars: Air search: Type 517 Knife Rest ❼; A-band.
Air search: Type 381C Rice Shield ❽; G-band.
Air/surface search: Type 360 Seagull S ❾; E/F-band.
Fire control: Type 344 (MR 34) ❿; I-band (for SSM and 100 mm).
2 Type 347G(1) Rice Bowl ⓫; I-band (for 37 mm).
Type 345 (MR 35) ⓬; I/J-band (for HQ-7).
Navigation: Racal/Decca 1290; I-band.
Sonars: DUBV-23; hull mounted; active search and attack; medium frequency.

Helicopters: 2 Harbin Zhi-9C Haitun ⓭ or Kamov Ka-28 Helix.

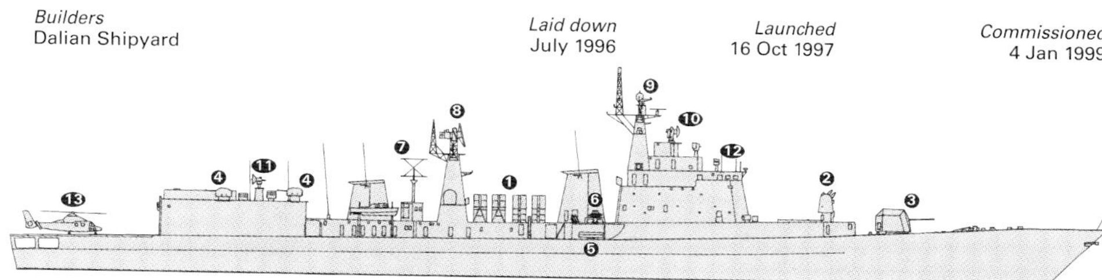

SHENZHEN *(Scale 1 : 1,200), Ian Sturton* / 0569249

SHENZHEN *12/2007, Hachiro Nakai* / 1166774

Programmes: Follow-on from the Luhu class. Although the only ship of its class, it would appear to be the baseline design for the Type 051C destroyers.
Structure: Apart from the second funnel and octuple SSM launchers, there are broad similarities with the smaller Luhu. Anti-aircraft guns are all mounted aft allowing more space in front of the bridge which seems to show a reloading hatch for HQ-7.
Operational: Based at Zhanjiang in South Sea Fleet. Out of area deployment to Europe in 2001.

2 LUHU (TYPE 052) CLASS (DDGHM)

Name	*No*	*Builders*	*Laid down*	*Launched*	*Commissioned*
HARBIN	112	Jiangnan Shipyard, Shanghai	Nov 1990	Oct 1991	July 1994
QINGDAO	113	Jiangnan Shipyard, Shanghai	Jan 1993	Oct 1993	Mar 1996

Displacement, tons: 4,600 full load
Dimensions, feet (metres): 472.4 × 52.5 × 16.7 *(144 × 16 × 5.1)*
Main machinery: CODOG: 2 GE LM 2500 gas turbines (112); 55,000 hp *(41 MW)* sustained or 2 Ukraine gas turbines (113) 48,600 hp(m) *(35.7 MW)*; 2 MTU 12V 1163 TB83 diesels; 8,840 hp(m) *(6.5 MW)* sustained; 2 shafts; cp props
Speed, knots: 31
Range, n miles: 5,000 at 15 kt
Complement: 266 (38 officers)

Missiles: SSM: 16 C-802 (YJ 83/CSS-N-8) Saccade ❶; mid-course guidance and active radar homing to 150 km *(81 n miles)* at 0.9 Mach; warhead 165 kg; sea-skimmer.
SAM: 1 HQ-7 (Crotale) octuple launcher ❷; CSA-4; line of sight guidance to 13 km *(7 n miles)* at 2.4 Mach; warhead 14 kg. 32 missiles.
Guns: 2—3.9 in *(100 mm)*/56 (twin) ❸; 25 rds/min to 22 km *(12 n miles)*; weight of shell 15.6 kg.
8—37 mm/63 Type 76A (4 twin) ❹; 180 rds/min to 8.5 km *(4.6 n miles)* anti-aircraft; weight of shell 1.42 kg.
Torpedoes: 6—324 mm Whitehead B515 (2 triple) tubes ❺. Yu-2 (Mk 46 Mod 1); active/passive homing to 11 km *(5.9 n miles)* at 40 kt; warhead 44 kg.
A/S mortars: 2 FQF 2500 ❻ 12-tubed fixed launchers; range 1,200 m; warhead 34 kg. 120 rockets.
Countermeasures: Decoys: 2 Type 946; 15 barrelled 100 mm chaff launchers.
ESM: Rapids.
ECM: Scimitar.
Combat data systems: Thomson-CSF Tavitac action data automation. SATCOM. Link W.
Weapons control: 2 GDG-775 optronic directors ❼.
Radars: Air search: Type 518 (navalised REL-2) ❽; D-band.
Air/surface search: Type 363S Sea Tiger ❾; E/F-band.
Surface search: Type 362 (ESR 1) ❿; I-band.
Fire control: Type 344 (MR 34) ⓫; I-band (for SSM and 100 mm).
2 Type 347G(1) Rice Bowl ⓬; I-band (for 37 mm).
Type 345 (MR 35) ⓭; I/J-band (for HQ-7).
Navigation: Racal Decca 1290; I-band.
Sonars: DUBV-23; Hull-mounted; active search and attack; medium frequency.
DUBV-43 VDS; active attack; medium frequency.

Helicopters: 2 Harbin Zhi-9C Haitun ⓮.

Programmes: Class of two ordered in 1985 but delayed by priority being given to export orders for Thailand.
Modernisation: *Harbin* completed refit in early 2003. *Qingdao* completed similar refit in 2005. Both fitted with a new low radar profile 100 mm gun turret.
Structure: The most notable features are the SAM launcher, improved radar and fire-control systems and a modern 100 mm gun. Gas turbines for the second of class came from the Ukraine. The HQ-7 launcher is a Chinese copy of Crotale. DCN Samahe 110N helo handling system. *Harbin* has a dome-shaped radome on the superstructure while *Qingdao* has cylindrical antennae in the same position. Both are likely to be ECM systems.
Operational: Both based in North Sea Fleet.

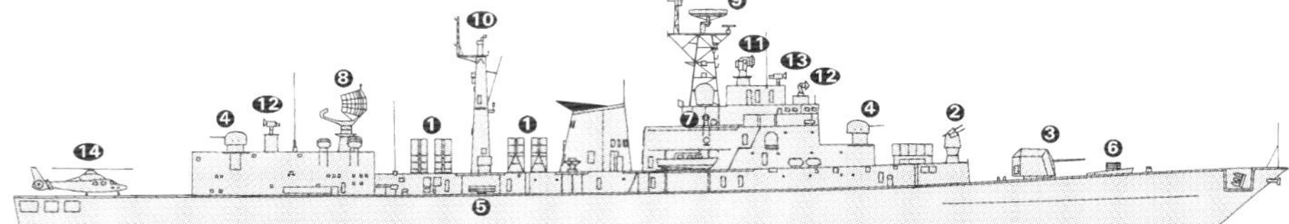
HARBIN ***(Scale 1 : 1,200), Ian Sturton*** / 0569255

QINGDAO ***9/2007*** / 1335692

HARBIN ***10/2008*, Michael Nitz*** / 1335693

HARBIN ***10/2007, Chris Sattler*** / 1166842

10 LUDA (TYPES 051/051D/051Z) CLASS (DDGM/DDGHM)

YINCHUAN	107	**CHONGQING**	133	**NANCHANG**	163
XINING	108	**ZUNYI**	134	**GUILIN**	164
NANJING	131	**CHANGSHA**	161		
HEFEI	132	**NANNING**	162		

Displacement, tons: 3,250 standard; 3,670 full load
Dimensions, feet (metres): 433.1 × 42 × 15.1
(132 × 12.8 × 4.6)
Main machinery: 2 or 4 boilers; 2 turbines; 72,000 hp(m) *(53 MW)*; 2 shafts
Speed, knots: 32
Range, n miles: 2,970 at 18 kt
Complement: 280 (45 officers)

Missiles: SSM: 6 HY-2 (C-201) (CSS-C-3A Seersucker) (2 triple) launchers ❶; active radar or IR homing to 95 km *(51 n miles)* at 0.9 Mach; warhead 513 kg.
Guns: 4 USSR 5.1 in *(130 mm)*/58 (2 twin) ❷; 20 rds/min to 28 km *(15 n miles)*; weight of shell 33.4 kg.
8 China 57 mm/70 (4 twin); 120 rds/min to 12 km *(6.5 n miles)*; weight of shell 6.31 kg or 8 China 37 mm/63 (4 twin) ❸; 180 rds/min to 8.5 km *(4.6 n miles)*; weight of shell 1.42 kg.
8 USSR 25 mm/60 (4 twin) ❹; 270 rds/min to 3 km *(1.6 n miles)* anti-aircraft; weight of shell 0.34 kg.
Torpedoes: 6—324 mm Whitehead B515 (2 triple tubes) (fitted in some); Yu-2 (Mk 46 Mod 1); active/passive homing to 11 km *(5.9 n miles)* at 40 kt; warhead 44 kg.
A/S mortars: 2 FQF 2500 12-tubed fixed launchers ❺; 120 rockets; range 1,200 m; warhead 34 kg. Similar in design to the RBU 1200.
Depth charges: 2 or 4 BMB projectors; 2 or 4 racks.
Mines: 38.
Combat data systems: ZKJ-1 (132).
Radars: Air search: Type 515 Bean Sticks ❻; A-band.
Type 381 Rice Shield ❼ (132); 3D; G-band. Similar to Hughes SPS-39A.
Surface search: Type 354 Eye Shield ❽; G-band.
Type 352 Square Tie (not in all); I-band.
Navigation: Fin Curve or Racal Decca 1290; I-band.
Fire control: Wasp Head (also known as Wok Won) or Type 343 Sun Visor B (series 2) ❾; I-band.
2 Type 347G Rice Bowl ❿; I-band.
IFF: High Pole.
Sonars: Pegas 2M and Tamir 2; hull-mounted; active search and attack; high frequency.

Programmes: The first Chinese-designed destroyers of such a capability to be built. First of class completed in 1971. 107 to 108 built at Luda; 131 to 134 at Shanghai and 161 to 164 at Guangzhou. Similar to the deleted USSR Kotlin class. The programme was much retarded after 1971 by drastic cuts in the defence budget. In early 1977 building of series two of this class was put in hand and includes those after 108, with the latest 164 completed in April 1990. The order of completion was 160 (scrapped), 161, 107, 162, 131, 108, 132, 163, 133, 134 and 164.
Modernisation: Equipment varies considerably from ship to ship. The original Type 051 ships are 107, 131, 161 and 162. Type 051D ships are 108, 133, 134, 163 and 164. 132 is a command ship (Type 051Z) fitted with ZKJ-1 command system and Rice Screen (Type 381A) 3-D radar.
Structure: Electronics vary in later ships. Some ships have 57 mm guns, others 37 mm. SAM is fitted in *Kaifeng* and *Dalian* in X gun position.
Operational: Capable of foreign deployment, although command and control is limited. Underway refuelling is practised. Basing: 107, 108 in North Sea Fleet; 161-164 in South Sea Fleet and 131-134 in East Sea Fleet. 160 was damaged by an explosion in 1978, and was scrapped. 106 decommissioned on 11 October 2007 and 105 in December 2007.

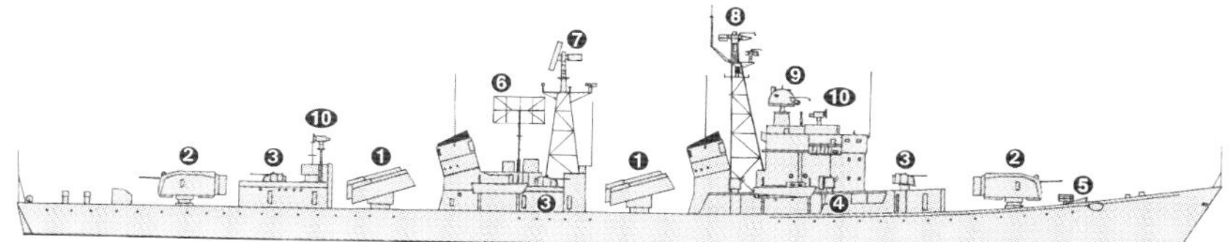

HEFEI *(Scale 1 : 1,200), Ian Sturton* / 0056749

ZUNYI *12/2007, Chris Sattler* / 1335691

ZUNYI *5/2007* / 1166871

YINCHUAN *6/2007* / 1166870

4 LUDA (TYPE 051DT/051G/051G II) CLASS (DDG)

Name	*No*	*Builders*	*Laid down*	*Launched*	*Commissioned*
KAIFENG	109	Dalian Shipyard	–	–	–
DALIAN	110	Dalian Shipyard	–	–	–
ZHANJIANG	165	Dalian Shipyard	1988	1990	1991
ZHUHAI	166	Dalian Shipyard	1988	1990	1991

Displacement, tons: 3,250 standard; 3,730 full load
Dimensions, feet (metres): 433.1 × 42 × 15.3 *(132 × 12.8 × 4.7)*
Main machinery: 2 boilers; 2 turbines; 72,000 hp(m) *(53 MW);* 2 shafts
Speed, knots: 32
Range, n miles: 2,970 at 18 kt
Complement: 280 (45 officers)

Missiles: SSM: 16 C 801A (YJ 81/CSS-N-4) (Sardine) ❶; active radar homing to 95 km *(51 n miles)* at 0.9 Mach; warhead 165 kg; sea-skimmer.
SAM: 1 HQ-7 (Crotale) octuple launcher ❷; line of sight guidance to 13 km *(7 n miles)* at 2.4 Mach; warhead 14 kg.
Guns: 2 USSR 5.1 in *(130 mm)*/54 (109, 110) ❸; 20 rds/min to 28 km *(15 n miles);* weight of shell 33.4 kg.
4—3.9 in *(100 mm)*/56 (2 twin) (165, 166) ❹; 18 rds/min to 22 km *(12 n miles);* weight of shell 15 kg.
6 China 57 mm/63 (3 twin) (109,110) ❺; 120 rds/min to 12 km *(6.5 n miles);* weight of shell 6.31 kg.
6 China 37 mm/63 Type 76A (3 twin) (165, 166) ❻; 180 rds/min to 8.5 km *(4.6 n miles);* weight of shell 1.42 kg.
Torpedoes: 6—324 mm Whitehead B515 (2 triple tubes) ❼; Yu-2 (Mk 46 Mod 1); active/passive homing to 11 km *(5.9 n miles)* at 40 kt; warhead 44 kg.
A/S mortars: 2 FQF 2500 12-tubed fixed launchers ❽; 120 rockets; range 1,200 m; warhead 34 kg. Similar in design to the RBU 1200.
Countermeasures: Decoys: 2 Type 946; 15 barrelled 100 mm chaff launchers.
ESM: Type 825; intercept.
ECM: Type 981; jammer.
Combat data systems: Thomson-CSF Tavitac with Vega FCS (109); ZKJ-1 (110); ZKJ 4A (165); ZKJ 4B (166).
Radars: Air search: Type 517 Knife Rest ❾; A-band.
Surface search: Type 363 Sea Tiger S (109). Type 354 Eye Shield (165, 166) ❿; E/F-band.
Navigation: Racal Decca 1290; I-band.
Fire control: Type 344 (MR 34) (165, 166) ⓫; I-band (for SSM and 100 mm).
Type 343G Sun Visor (109, 110) ⓬; I-band.
Type 347G(1) Rice Bowl ⓭; I-band (for 57/37 mm).
Type 345 (MR 35) ⓮; I/J-band (for HQ-7).
IFF: High Pole.
Sonars: DUBV 23 (165, 166); hull-mounted; active search and attack; medium frequency.

Programmes: Updated Luda designs sometimes known collectively as the Luda III class.
Modernisation: 109 redesignated Type 051DT after being fitted with Tavitac, Sea Tiger radar and HQ-7 (Crotale). In 1999, she was further modified to receive 16 C0801A missiles, Type 825 ESM, Type 981 ECM and Type 946 chaff launchers. 110 subsequently modernised with ZKJ-1 command system and an otherwise similar configuration as 109. 166 underwent extensive modernisation 2001–03. Principal enhancements include the replacement of YJ-1 by four quadruple YJ-81 missiles, the installation of an octuple HQ-7 SAM launcher in place of the aft (X turret) 37 mm gun and the replacement of the 130 mm guns with twin 100 mm guns fore and aft. 165 is reported to have undergone a similar upgrade.
Structure: The VDS sonar is a copy of DUBV 43.
Operational: Basing: 109 and 110 in North Sea Fleet; 165 and 166 in South Sea Fleet.

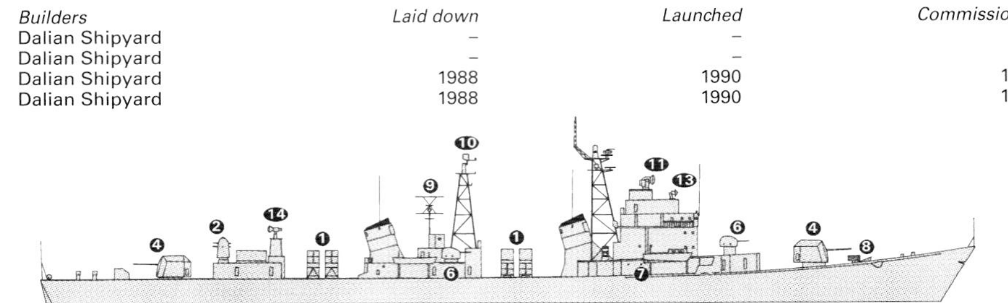
ZHANJIANG *(Scale 1 : 1,200), Ian Sturton* / 0572402

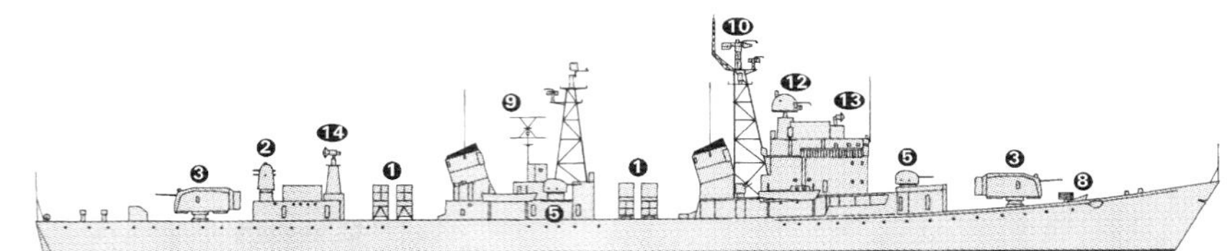
KAIFENG *(Scale 1 : 1,200), Ian Sturton* / 0126350

DALIAN *6/2007* / 1166869

FRIGATES

2 JIANGKAI I (TYPE 054) CLASS (FFGHM)

Name	*No*	*Builders*	*Laid down*	*Launched*	*Commissioned*
MAANSHAN	525	Hudong-Zhonghua Shipyard, Shanghai	Dec 2001	11 Sep 2003	18 Feb 2005
WENZHOU	526	Huangpu Shipyard, Guangzhou	Feb 2002	13 Nov 2003	26 Sep 2006

Displacement, tons: 3,500 standard; 3,900 full load
Dimensions, feet (metres): 433.2 × 49.2 × 16.4 *(132.0 × 15.0 × 5.0)*
Main machinery: CODAD; 4 SEMT-Pielstick diesels; 2 shafts
Speed, knots: 27. **Range, n miles:** 3,800 at 18 kt
Complement: 190

Missiles: SSM: 8 C-802 (YJ-83/CSS-N-8 Saccade) ❶; mid-course guidance and active radar homing to 150 km *(81 n miles)* at 0.9 Mach; warhead 165 kg; sea skimmer.
SAM: 1 HQ-7 (Crotale) ❷; CSA-N-4 line-of-sight guidance to 13 km *(7 n miles)* at 2.4 Mach; warhead 14 kg.
Guns: 1—3.9 in *(100 mm)*/56 ❸; 25 rds/min to 22 km *(12 n miles);* weight of shell 15.6 kg.
4—300 mm/65 AK 630 ❹; 6 barrels per mounting; 3,000 rds/min combined to 2 km.
Torpedoes: 6—324 mm B515 (2 triple) tubes; Yu-2/6/7; active/passive homing to 11 km *(5.9 n miles)* at 40 kt; warhead 44 kg.
Countermeasures: to be announced.
Combat data systems: to be announced.
Radars: Air/surface search: Type 360 Seagull S ❺; E/F-band.
Surface search: Type 364 Seagull C ❻; G-band.
Fire control: Type 344 (MR 34) ❼; I-band (for SSM and 100 mm).
Type 345 (MR 35) ❽; I/J-band (for HQ-7).
Type 347G(1) Rice Bowl ❾; I-band (for AK 630).
Navigation: RM-1290; I-band.
Sonars: to be announced.

Helicopters: 1 Harbin Zhi-9C Haitun ❿.

Programmes: Two vessels of a new general-purpose frigate class which followed the Jiangwei II class. Further ships are unlikely.
Structure: A new design incorporating stealth features.
Operational: Assigned to the East Sea Fleet.

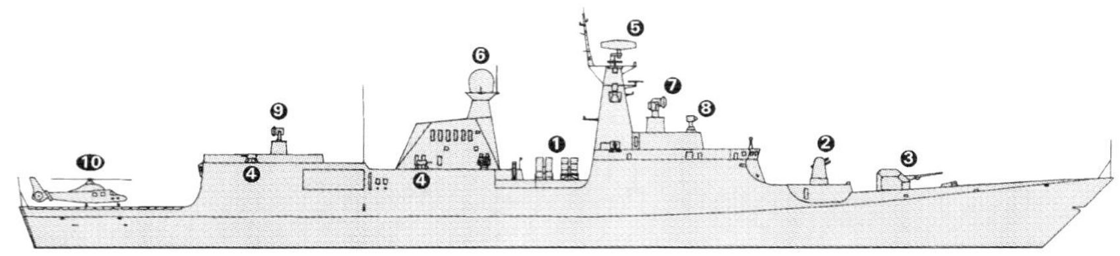
MAANSHAN *(Scale 1 : 1,200), Ian Sturton* / 1164338

WENZHOU *1/2007, Ships of the World* / 1167733

WENZHOU

1/2007, Ships of the World / 1167734

4 + 2 JIANGKAI II (TYPE 054A) CLASS (FFGHM)

Name	*No*	*Builders*	*Laid down*	*Launched*	*Commissioned*
ZHOUSHAN	530	Huangpu Shipyard, Guangzhou	2005	30 Sep 2006	29 Jan 2008
XUZHOU	529	Hudong-Zhonghua Shipyard, Shanghai	2006	21 Dec 2006	2008
HUANGSHAN	570	Huangpu Shipyard, Guangzhou	2006	18 Mar 2007	2008
CHAOHU	568	Hudong-Zhonghua Shipyard, Shanghai	2006	23 May 2007	9 July 2008
–	–	Huangpu Shipyard, Guangzhou	2007	2008	2009
–	–	Hudong-Zhonghua Shipyard, Shanghai	2007	2010	2011

Displacement, tons: 3,500 standard; 3,900 full load
Dimensions, feet (metres): 433.2 × 52.5 × 16.4 *(134.0 × 16.0 × 5.0)*
Main machinery: CODAD; 4 SEMT Pielstick 16PA 6V 280 STC; 28,200 hp *(20.7 MW)*; 2 shafts
Speed, knots: 27
Range, n miles: 3,800 at 18 kt
Complement: To be announced

Missiles: SSM: 8 C-802 (YJ-83/CSS-N-8 Saccade) ❶; mid-course guidance and active radar homing to 150 km *(81 n miles)* at 0.9 Mach; warhead 165 kg; sea skimmer.
SAM: HHQ-16 ❷. 1 (forward) 32 cell vertical launch system (possible cold launch).
Guns: 1—3 in *(76 mm)* ❸.
2—30 mm Type 730 ❹; 7 barrels per mounting; 4,200 rds/min combined to 1.5 km.
Torpedoes: 6—324 mm B515 (2 triple) tubes; Yu-2/6/7; active/passive homing to 11 km *(5.9 n miles)* at 40 kt; warhead 44 kg.
Countermeasures: Decoys: 2—24 barrelled launchers.
Combat data systems: To be announced.
Weapons control: Band Stand (Mineral ME) ❺; I-band; datalink for C-803.

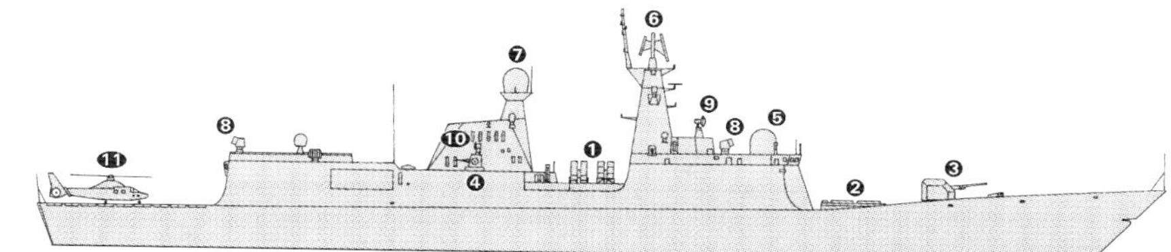

JIANGKAI II

(Scale 1 : 1,200), Ian Sturton / 1335659

Radars: Air search: Top Plate (Fregat MAE-3) ❻; 3D; E/F-band.
Air/surface search: Type 364 Seagull C ❼; G-band.
Fire control: 4 Front Dome (Orekh) ❽; H/I-band for HHQ-16.
Band Stand (Mineral ME) ❺; I-band (for YJ-83).
Type 344 (MR 34) ❾; I-band (for 76 mm gun).
2 Type 347G(2) (LR 66) ❿; I-band for Type 730.
Navigation: RM-1290; I-band.
Sonars: To be announced.

Helicopters: 1 Harbin Zhi-9A Haitun ⓫.

Programmes: Follow-on ships to the two ships of the Jiangkai I class. The modified design includes a VLS launcher for the SAM system. Under construction at two shipyards, it is likely that this design will be built in sufficient numbers to replace the ageing Jianghu class frigates. The construction of hull 6 at Hudong Shipyard has been delayed by up to a year by the collapse of a crane in 2008.
Operational: *Zhoushan* and *Xuzhou* based in East Sea Fleet and *Huangshan* and *Chaohu* in South Sea Fleet.

JIANGKAI II

6/2007 / 1166849

JIANGKAI II

2/2008, Ships of the World* / 1335655

4 JIANGWEI I (TYPE 053 H2G) CLASS (FFGHM)

Name	*No*	*Builders*	*Laid down*	*Launched*	*Commissioned*
ANQING	539	Hudong Shipyard, Shanghai	Nov 1990	July 1991	Dec 1991
HUAINAN	540	Hudong Shipyard, Shanghai	Jan 1991	Oct 1991	July 1992
HUAIBEI	541	Hudong Shipyard, Shanghai	July 1992	Apr 1993	Aug 1993
TONGLING	542	Hudong Shipyard, Shanghai	Dec 1992	Sep 1993	Apr 1994

Displacement, tons: 2,250 full load
Dimensions, feet (metres): 366.5 × 40.7 × 15.7 *(111.7 × 12.4 × 4.8)*
Main machinery: 2 Type 18E 390 diesels; 24,000 hp(m) *(17.65 MW)* sustained; 2 shafts
Speed, knots: 27. **Range, n miles:** 4,000 at 18 kt
Complement: 170

Missiles: SSM: 6 YJ-1 (Eagle Strike) (C-801) (CSS-N-4 Sardine) or C-802 (YJ-83) (2 triple) launchers ❶; active radar homing to 40 km *(22 n miles)* or 150 km *(81 n miles)* (C-802) at 0.9 Mach; warhead 165 kg; sea-skimmer.
SAM: 1 HQ-61 sextuple launcher ❷; RF 61 (CSA-N-2); semi-active radar homing to 10 km *(5.5 n miles)* at 2 Mach. Similar to Sea Sparrow. May be replaced in due course.
Guns: 2 China 3.9 in *(100 mm)*/56 (twin) ❸; 25 rds/min to 22 km *(12 n miles)*; weight of shell 15.6 kg.
8 China 37 mm/63 Type 76A (4 twin) ❹; 180 rds/min to 8.5 km *(4.6 n miles)* anti-aircraft; weight of shell 1.42 kg.
A/S mortars: 2 Type 87 ❺ 6-tubed launchers.
Countermeasures: Decoys: 2 China Type 945 26-barrelled chaff launchers ❻.
ESM: RWD8; intercept.
ECM: NJ81-3; jammer. Similar to Scimitar.

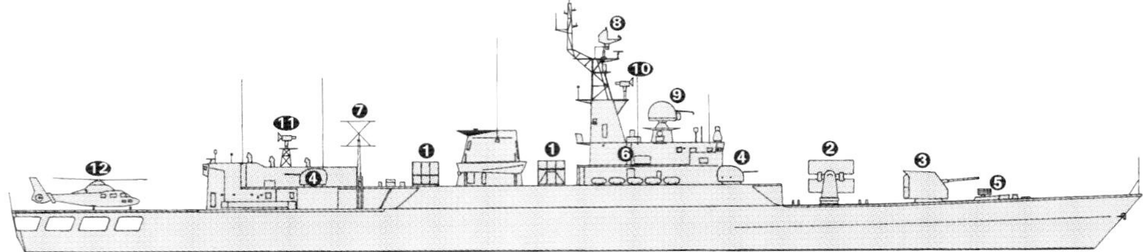

HUAIBEI (*Scale 1 : 900*), *Ian Sturton* / 0130723

Radars: Air search: Type 517 Knife Rest ❼; A-band.
Air/surface search: Type 360 Seagull S ❽; E/F-band.
Fire control: Type 343 (Wok Won) (Wasp Head) ❾; I-band (for 100 mm).
Type 342 (Fog Lamp) ❿; I/J-band (for SAM).
Type 347G(1) Rice Bowl ⓫; I/J-band (for 37 mm).
Navigation: Racal Decca 1290; I-band.
Sonars: Echo Type 5; hull-mounted; active search and attack; medium frequency.

Helicopters: 2 Harbin Z-9C (Dauphin) ⓬.

Programmes: Programme started in 1988. First one conducted sea trials in late 1991. Four of the class built before the design moved on to the Jiangwei II.
Modernisation: SAM system has been unsatisfactory and may be replaced in due course.
Structure: The sextuple launcher is a multiple launch SAM system using the CSA-N-2 missile.
Operational: All based in the East Sea Fleet at Dinghai.

HUAIBEI *4/2000, Ships of the World* / 0103659

10 JIANGWEI II (TYPE 053H3) CLASS (FFGHM)

Name	*No*	*Builders*	*Laid down*	*Launched*	*Commissioned*
JIAXIN	521 (ex-597)	Hudong Shipyard, Shanghai	Oct 1996	10 Aug 1997	Nov 1998
LIANYUNGANG	522	Hudong Shipyard, Shanghai	Dec 1996	8 Aug 1997	Feb 1999
PUTIAN	523	Hudong Shipyard, Shanghai	June 1997	10 Aug 1998	Oct 1999
SANMING	524	Hudong Shipyard, Shanghai	Dec 1997	Dec 1998	Nov 1999
YICHANG	564	Huangpu Shipyard, Guangzhou	Dec 1997	Oct 1998	Dec 1999
YULIN	565	Huangpu Shipyard, Guangzhou	May 1998	Apr 1999	Mar 2000
HUAIHUA (ex-*Yuxi*)	566	Hudong Shipyard, Shanghai	May 2000	Jan 2001	Mar 2002
XIANGFAN	567	Huangpu Shipyard, Guangzhou	Mar 2001	Aug 2001	Sep 2002
LUOYANG	527	Hudong Shipyard, Shanghai	2003	1 Oct 2004	2005
MIANYANG	528	Huangpu Shipyard, Guangzhou	2003	30 May 2004	2005

Displacement, tons: 2,250 full load
Dimensions, feet (metres): 366.5 × 40.7 × 15.7 *(111.7 × 12.4 × 4.8)*
Main machinery: 2 Type 18E 390 diesels; 24,000 hp(m) *(17.65 MW)* sustained; 2 shafts
Speed, knots: 27
Range, n miles: 4,000 at 18 kt
Complement: 170

Missiles: SSM: 8 YJ-1 (Eagle Strike) (C-801) (CSS-N-4 Sardine) or C-802 (YJ-83) (2 quad) launchers ❶; active radar homing to 40 km *(22 n miles)* or 150 km *(81 n miles)* (C-802) at 0.9 Mach; warhead 165 kg; sea-skimmer.
SAM: 1 HQ-7 (Crotale) octuple launcher ❷; CSA-N-4 line of sight guidance to 13 km *(7 n miles)* at 2.4 Mach; warhead 14 kg.
Guns: 2 China 3.9 in *(100 mm)*/56 (twin) ❸; 25 rds/min to 22 km *(12 n miles)*; weight of shell 15.6 kg.
8 China 37 mm/63 Type 76A (4 twin) ❹; 180 rds/min to 8.5 km *(4.6 n miles)* anti-aircraft; weight of shell 1.42 kg.
A/S mortars: 2 RBU 1200 ❺; 5-tubed fixed launchers; range 1,200 m; warhead 34 kg.
Countermeasures: Decoys 2 SRBOC Mk 36 6-barrelled chaff launchers ❻; 2 China 26-barrelled chaff launchers ❼.
ESM: SR-210; intercept.
ECM: 981-3 noise jammer. RWD-8 deception jammer.

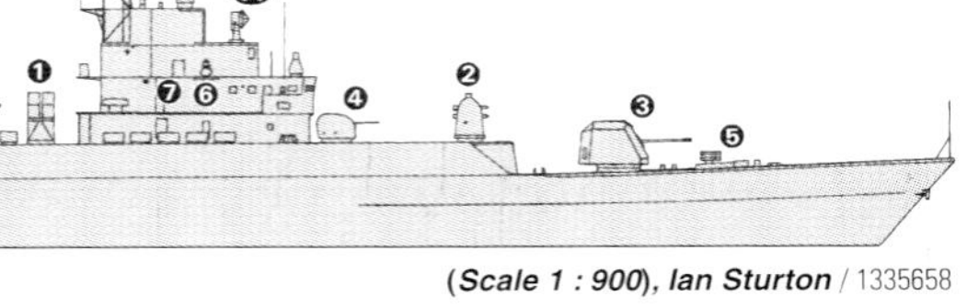

JIANGWEI II (*Scale 1 : 900*), *Ian Sturton* / 1335658

Combat data systems: ZKJ 3C. SATCOM.
Weapons control: JM-83H optronic director.
Radars: Air search: Type 517 Knife Rest ❽; A-band.
Air/surface search: Type 360 Seagull S ❾; E/F-band.
Fire control: Type 343G (Wok Won). Type 344 (MR 34) (527, 528) ❿; I-band (for SSM and 100 mm).
Type 345 (MR 35) ⓫; I/J-band (for HQ-7).
Type 347G(1) Rice Bowl ⓬; I/J-band (for 37 mm).
Navigation: 2 RM-1290; I-band.
Sonars: Echo Type 5; hull-mounted; active search and attack; medium frequency.

Helicopters: 2 Harbin Z-9C (Dauphin) ⓭.

Programmes: Follow-on to the Jiangwei class, building some four years later. The building programme appeared to have been terminated after eight ships but reports indicate that two further ships are under construction. Further units are possible.
Structure: An improved SAM system, updated fire-control radars and a redistribution of the after anti-aircraft guns are the obvious differences from the original Jiangwei. New Type 99 turret fitted in 522 and to be retro-fitted to the remainder of the class.
Operational: Basing: 521-524 and 527-528 in East Sea Fleet; 564-567 in South Sea Fleet.
Sales: Four under construction for Pakistan.

LUOYANG

10/2008, Guy Toremans* / 1335690

LIANYUNGANG

3/2007, Paul Daly / 1166845

SANMING

3/2007, Paul Daly / 1166844

25 JIANGHU I//II/V (TYPE 053H/053H1/053H1G) CLASS (FFG)

Name	No	Name	No	Name	No
NANTONG	511	TAIZHOU (II)	533	ZHAOTONG (II)	555
WUXI	512	JINHUA (II)	534	JISHOU (II)	557
HUAYIN	513	DANDONG (II)	543	ZIGONG (V)	558
ZHENJIANG	514	LINFEN	545	BEIHAI (V)	559
XIAMEN	515	MAOMING	551	DONGGUAN (V)	560
JIUJIANG	516	YIBIN	552	SHANTOU (V)	561
NANPING	517	SHAOGUAN (II)	553	JIANGMEN (V)	562
JIAN	518	ANSHUN (II)	554	FOSHAN (V)	563
CHANGZHI	519				

Displacement, tons: 1,425 standard; 1,702 full load
Dimensions, feet (metres): 338.5 × 35.4 × 10.2 *(103.2 × 10.8 × 3.1)*
Main machinery: 2 Type 12E 390V diesels; 14,400 hp(m) *(10.6 MW)* sustained; 2 shafts
Speed, knots: 26
Range, n miles: 4,000 at 15 kt; 2,700 at 18 kt
Complement: 200 (30 officers)

Missiles: SSM: 4 HY-2 (C-201) (CSSC-3 Seersucker) (2 twin) launchers ❶; active radar or IR homing to 80 km *(43.2 n miles)* at 0.9 Mach; warhead 513 kg.
Guns: 2 or 4 China 3.9 in *(100 mm)*/56 (2 single ❷ or 2 twin ❸); 25 rds/min to 22 km *(12 n miles)*; weight of shell 15.6 kg.
12 China 37 mm/63 (6 twin) ❹ (8 (4 twin), in some); 180 rds/min to 8.5 km *(4.6 n miles)* anti-aircraft; weight of shell 1.42 kg.
A/S mortars: 2 RBU 1200 5-tubed fixed launchers (4 in some) ❺; range 1,200 m; warhead 34 kg.
Depth charges: 2 BMB-2 projectors; 2 racks (in some).
Mines: Can carry up to 60.
Countermeasures: Decoys: 2 RBOC Mk 33 6-barrelled chaff launchers or 2 China 26-barrelled launchers.
ESM: Jug Pair or Watchdog; radar warning.
Weapons control: Wok Won director (in some) ❻.
Radars: Air search: Type 517 Knife Rest ❼; A-band.
Air/surface search: Type 354 Eye Shield (MX 902) ❽; G-band.
Type (unknown) ❾; I-band.
Surface search/fire control: Type 352 Square Tie ❿; I-band.
Navigation: Don 2 or Fin Curve or Racal Decca; I-band.
Fire control: Type 347G Rice Bowl (in some) ⓫; I/J-band.
Type 343 (Wok Won) (Wasp Head) (in some) ⓬; I-band.
IFF: High Pole A. Yard Rake or Square Head.
Sonars: Echo Type 5; hull-mounted; active search and attack; medium frequency.

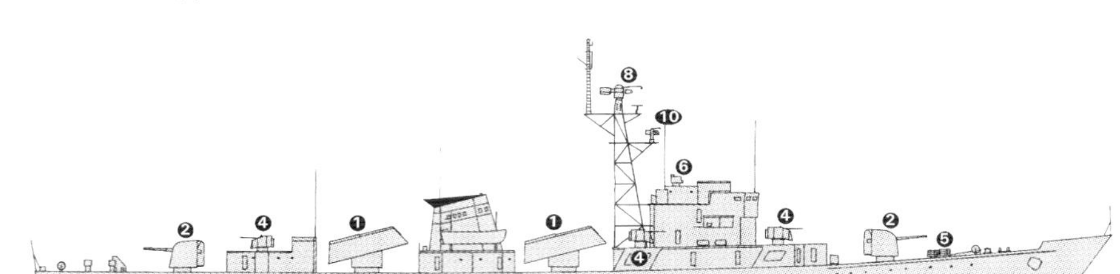
ZHENJIANG (TYPE 053H) *(Scale 1 : 900)*, *Ian Sturton* / 0529151

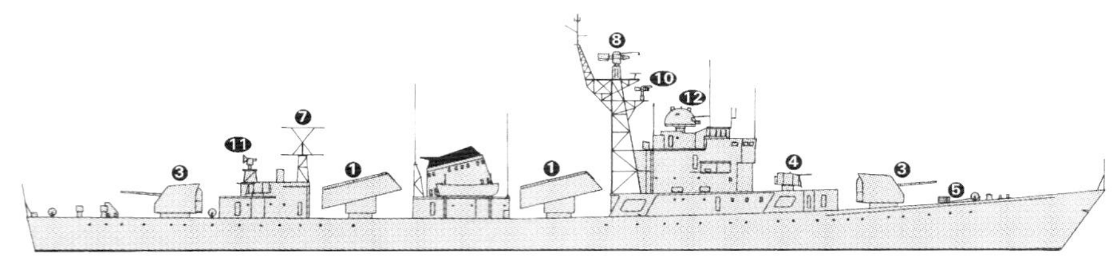
TAIZHOU (TYPE 053H1) *(Scale 1 : 900)*, *Ian Sturton* / 0130728

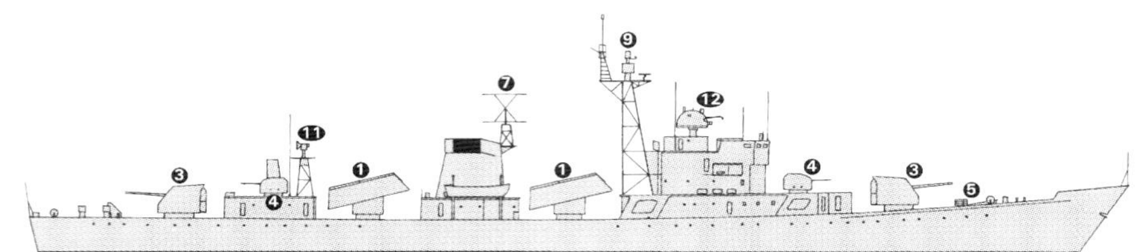
DONGGUAN (TYPE 053H1G) *(Scale 1 : 900)*, *Ian Sturton* / 0130727

Programmes: Pennant numbers changed in 1979. All built in Shanghai starting in the mid-1970s at the Hudong, Jiangnan and Huangpu shipyards. Ships were completed in the following order: 515, 516, 517, 511, 512, 513, 514, 518, 519, 520, 551, 552, 533, 534, two for Egypt, 543, 553, 554, 555, 545, 556 (to Bangladesh), 557, 544, 558, 560, 561, 559, 562 and 563. The last of class 563 completed in February 1996. Reports that construction had restarted in 1997 were incorrect.
Modernisation: Equipment varies considerably from ship to ship. The Type 053H ships are 511-519 and 551 and 552. These are equipped with SY-1 or SY-2 SSM, single 100 mm guns and SJD-3 sonar. Type 053H1 ships are 533, 534, 543, 553, 554, 555 and 557. These are similar to Type 053H but are equipped with twin 100 mm guns and SJD-5 (Echo 5) sonar. Type 053H1G ships are 558-563. These are similar to Type 053H1 but are equipped with 37 mm enclosed gun mounts. A larger bridge structure suggests a possible CIC compartment. The designation of the Air/Surface search radar in Type 053H1G is not yet known but it bears similarities to the I-band MR-36A which has been promoted as a replacement for Type 352 'Square Tie'. 516 appears to have been modified for a shore bombardment role having been fitted with a new twin 100 mm mounting and seven 122 mm MLRs. 559 may also be similarly converted. 509 and 510 have been converted to a Coast Guard role.
Structure: All of the class have the same hull dimensions. Previously reported Type numbers have been superseded by the following designations:
Type I has at least five versions. Version 1 has an oval funnel and square bridge wings; version 2 a square funnel with bevelled bridge face; version 3 an octagonal funnel; version 4 reverts back to the oval funnel and version 5 has a distinctive fluting arrangement with cowls on the funnel, as well as gunhouses on the 37 mm guns. Some have bow bulwarks.
Type II. See separate entry.
Types III and IV. See separate entry.

HUAYIN (TYPE 053H) *12/2007*, *Chris Sattler* / 1170059

Operational: 520 paid off in 1993. Basing: 511-519, 543 and 545 in North Sea Fleet, 533-534 in East Sea Fleet and 551-555 and 557-563 in the South Sea Fleet.
Sales: Two have been transferred to Egypt, one in September 1984, the other in March 1985, and one, *Xiangtan* 556, to Bangladesh in November 1989.

WUXI (TYPE 053H) *1/2008**, *A Sheldon-Duplaix* / 1335687

HUAYIN (TYPE 053H)

10/2008, Chris Sattler* / 1335689

SHANTOU (TYPE 053H1G)

9/2000 / 0103662

ZIGONG (TYPE 053H1G)

4/2008* / 1335688

3 JIANGHU III (TYPE 053 H2) CLASS (FFG)

HUANGSHI 535 **WUHU** 536 **CANGZHOU** 537

Displacement, tons: 1,924 full load
Dimensions, feet (metres): 338.5 × 35.4 × 10.2 *(103.2 × 10.8 × 3.1)*
Main machinery: 2 Type 18E 390V diesels; 14,400 hp(m) *(10.6 MW)* sustained; 2 shafts
Speed, knots: 26. **Range, n miles:** 4,000 at 15 kt; 2,700 at 18 kt
Complement: 200 (30 officers)

Missiles: SSM: 8 YJ-1 (Eagle Strike) (C-801) (CSS-N-4 Sardine) ❶; active radar homing to 40 km *(22 n miles)* at 0.9 Mach; warhead 165 kg. *Cangzhou* is fitted with C-802 (YJ-83) (CSS-N-8 Saccade) with an extended range to 150 km *(81 n miles)*.
Guns: 4 China 3.9 in *(100 mm)*/56 (2 twin) ❷; 25 rds/min to 22 km *(12 n miles)*; weight of shell 15.6 kg.
8 China 37 mm/63 (4 twin) ❸; 180 rds/min to 8.5 km *(4.6 n miles)* anti-aircraft; weight of shell 1.42 kg.
A/S mortars: 2 RBU 1200 5-tubed fixed launchers ❹; range 1,200 m; warhead 34 kg.
Depth charges: 2 BMB-2 projectors; 2 racks.
Mines: Can carry up to 60.
Countermeasures: Decoys: 2 China 26-barrelled chaff launchers.
ESM: Elettronica Newton; radar warning.
ECM: Elettronica 929 (Type 981); jammer.
Combat data systems: ZKJ-3.

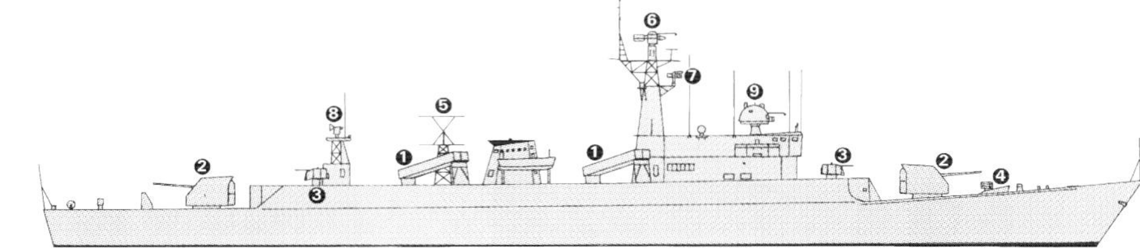

CANGZHOU *(Scale 1 : 900), Ian Sturton* / 0130726

Radars: Air search: Type 517 Knife Rest ❺; A-band.
Air/surface search: Type 354 Eye Shield (MX 902) ❻; G-band.
Surface search/fire control: Type 352 Square Tie ❼; I-band.
Navigation: Fin Curve; I-band.
Fire control: Type 347G Rice Bowl ❽; I/J-band.
Type 343G (Wok Won) (Wasp Head) ❾; I-band.
IFF: High Pole A. Square Head.
Sonars: Echo Type 5; hull-mounted; active search and attack; medium frequency.

Programmes: These ships are Jianghu hulls 27, 28 and 30 and are referred to as New Missile Frigates. Built at Hudong, Shanghai. *Huangshi* commissioned 14 December 1986, *Wuhu* in 1987, and *Cangzhou* completed in 1989. They were the first Chinese warships to be equipped with a computerised combat system.
Structure: The main deck is higher in the midships section and the lower part of the mast is solid. The arrangement of the launchers is side by side, as opposed to the staggered pairings in the first two ships. These were the first all-enclosed, air conditioned ships built in China.
Operational: Based in East Sea Fleet at Dinghai.
Sales: Four modified Type III to Thailand in 1991–92.

CANGZHOU *10/1992, Ships of the World* / 0056766

HUANGSHI *2/2001, Ships of the World* / 0126362

1 JIANGHU IV (TYPE 053HTH) CLASS (FFGH)

Name	*No*	*Builders*	*Laid down*	*Launched*	*Commissioned*
SIPING	544	Hudong Shipyard, Shanghai	1984	Sep 1985	Nov 1986

Displacement, tons: 1,550 standard; 1,865 full load
Dimensions, feet (metres): 338.5 × 35.4 × 10.2 *(103.2 × 10.8 × 3.1)*
Main machinery: 2 Type 12E 390V diesels; 14,400 hp(m) *(10.6 MW)* sustained; 2 shafts
Speed, knots: 26
Range, n miles: 4,000 at 15 kt; 2,700 at 18 kt
Complement: 185 (30 officers)

Missiles: SSM: 2 HY-2 (C-201) (CSSC-3 Seersucker) (twin) launchers ❶; active radar or IR homing to 80 km *(43.2 n miles)* at 0.9 Mach; warhead 513 kg.
Guns: 1 Creusot-Loire 3.9 in *(100 mm)*/55 ❷; 60–80 rds/min to 17 km *(9.3 n miles)*; weight of shell 13.5 kg.
8 China 37 mm/63 (4 twin) ❸; 180 rds/min to 8.5 km *(4.6 n miles)* anti-aircraft; weight of shell 1.42 kg.
Torpedoes: 6–324 mm ILAS (2 triple) tubes ❹. Yu-2 (Mk 46 Mod 1) active/passive homing to 11 km *(5.9 n miles)* at 40 kt; warhead 44 kg.
A/S mortars: 2 RBU 1200 5-tubed fixed launchers ❺; range 1,200 m; warhead 34 kg.
Countermeasures: Decoys: 2 SRBOC Mk 33 6-barrelled chaff launchers or 2 China 26-barrelled launchers.
ESM: Jug Pair or Watchdog; radar warning.
Weapons control: CSEE Naja optronic director for 100 mm gun.
Radars: Air/surface search: Type 354 Eye Shield (MX 902) ❻; G-band.
Surface search/fire control: Type 352 Square Tie ❼; I-band.
Navigation: Don 2 or Fin Curve; I-band.
IFF: High Pole A. Yard Rake or Square Head.
Sonars: Echo Type 5; hull-mounted; active search and attack; medium frequency.

Helicopters: Harbin Z-9C (Dauphin) ❽.

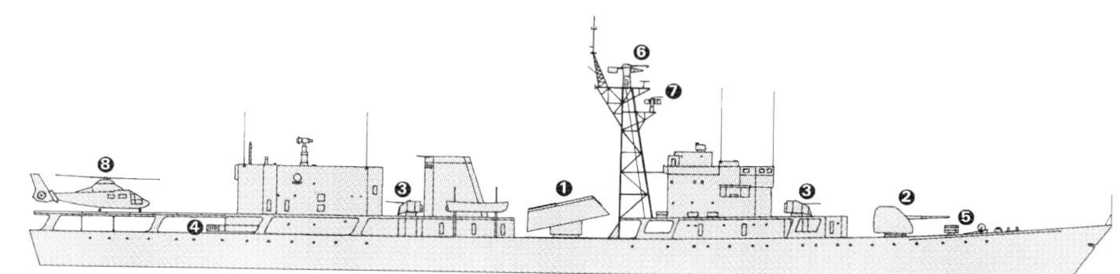

SIPING *(Scale 1 : 900), Ian Sturton* / 0572397

SIPING *6/2003* / 0569166

Programmes: Built as a standard Jianghu I and then converted, probably as a helicopter trials ship for the Luhu and Jiangwei classes, before being commissioned.
Structure: The after part of the ship has been rebuilt to take a hangar and flight deck for a single helicopter. Alcatel 'Safecopter' landing aid. This ship also has a French 100 mm gun and optronic director, and Italian triple torpedo tubes mounted on the quarterdeck.
Operational: Based in North Sea Fleet at Guzhen Bay. Acts as a training ship for Dalian Naval Academy.

SHIPBORNE AIRCRAFT

Notes: It has been reported that negotiations are in progress to procure up to 50 Sukhoi Su-33 Flanker D naval fighters from Russia. A derivative of the Sukhoi Su-27, Su-33s can operate from aircraft carriers, using a ski-jump for launch, and are capable of in-flight refuelling. In November 2008, it was reported that acquisition of an initial batch of 14 aircraft, to be used in a training role, was nearing completion. A further 36 modernised aircraft are likely to follow.

Numbers/Type: 15 Changhe Z-8 Super Frelon.
Operational speed: 134 kt *(248 km/h)*.
Service ceiling: 10,000 ft *(3,100 m)*.
Range: 440 n miles *(815 km)*.
Role/Weapon systems: ASW helicopter; Eight SA 321G delivered from France in 1977 but supplemented by 12 locally built Zhi-8, of which the first operational aircraft was delivered in late 1991. Thomson Sintra HS-12 in four SA 321Gs for SSBN escort role. Sensors: HS-12 dipping sonar and processor, some have French-built search radar. Weapons: ASW; Whitehead A244 or Yu-2 (Mk 46 Mod 1) torpedo. ASV; C-802K ASM.

Z-8 *9/2002, Paul Jackson* / 0525833

Numbers/Type: 11 Hai Z-9C Haitun (Panther).
Operational speed: 140 kt *(260 km/h)*.
Service ceiling: 15,000 ft *(4,575 m)*.
Range: 410 n miles *(758 km)*.
Role/Weapon systems: Eurocopter AS 365 Panther 2 aircraft built under licence. All delivered by about 2000. An anti-ship missile variant, Z-9D, was rolled out in mid-2008. The missile is believed to be the 4-15 km range TL-10, similar to the Iranian Kosar. Sensors: Thomson-CSF Agrion; HS-12 dipping sonar; Crouzet MAD. Weapons: ASV; Whitehead A244 torpedoes or Yu-2 (Mk 46 Mod 1).

Z-9C *12/2007, Hachiro Nakai* / 1166773

Numbers/Type: 6/4 Kamov Ka 28PL/28PS Helix A.
Operational speed: 135 kt *(250 km/h)*.
Service ceiling: 19,685 ft *(6,000 m)*.
Range: 432 n miles *(800 km)*.
Role/Weapon systems: First pair are (Ka 28PL) ASW helicopters acquired in 1997 for evaluation. Four more ASW versions and four (Ka 28PS) for SAR delivered in late 1999. Sensors: Splash Drop radar; VGS-3 dipping sonar; MAD; ESM. Weapons: three torpedoes or depth bombs or mines.

Ka-28 *6/2004* / 1042165

LAND-BASED MARITIME AIRCRAFT (FRONT LINE)

Notes: In addition to those listed there are about 170 training and transport aircraft.

Numbers/Type: 2 KJ-2000 AWACS.
Operational speed: 425 kt *(785 km/h)*.
Service ceiling: 34,440 ft *(10,500 m)*.
Range: 2,753 n miles *(5,100 km)*.
Role/Weapon systems: Airborne Warning And Control System (AWACS) aircraft based on the Russian-made A-50 (Mainstay) airframe which itself is based on the Ilyushin Il-76 transport aircraft. The non-rotating radome houses three Chinese-made (ESA) phased array antennas in a triangular configuration. A SATCOM antenna may be installed inside a fairing on top of forward cabin. At least three further prototypes have been built since 2002 and are undergoing tests at China Flight Test Establishment (CFTE) in Yanliang, Shaanxi Province and Nanjing, Jiangsu Province where the main contractor for the radar system, Nanjing Research Institute of Electronic Technology (also known as 14 Institute), is based.

KJ-2000 *8/2005, Jane's* / 1046316

Numbers/Type: 24 Sukhoi Su-30 MK 2 Flanker.
Operational speed: 1,345 kt *(2,500 km/h)*.
Service ceiling: 59,000 ft *(18,000 m)*.
Range: 2,160 n miles *(4,000 km)*.
Role/Weapon systems: 24 delivered in 2004. The air force operates at least 150 of the similar Su-27 which also might be used for fleet air-defence. Sensors: Doppler radar. Weapons: One 30 mm cannon; 10 AAMs. Kh-35 anti-ship missiles may be fitted to some aircraft in due course.

Su-27 ***5/2003*** / 0114638

Numbers/Type: 54 XAC JH-7.
Operational speed: 653 kt *(1,210 km/h)*.
Service ceiling: 51,180 ft *(15,600 m)*.
Range: 891 n miles *(1,650 km)*.
Role/Weapon systems: All-weather dual seat 'Flounder' type attack fighter first delivered in 1998. A second batch of 18 JH-7A was delivered in 2004. Sensors: Letri JL-10A Shen-Ying pulse Doppler fire-control radar capable of tracking four targets to 29 n miles *(54 km)* in look-down mode simultaneously. Weapons: AAM; PL-5b, PL-7 and 23 mm gun. ASM; Two C-801 or C-802 anti-ship missiles; C-701 anti-ship missile and 500 kg LGBs. AS-17 (Kh-31) may be fitted in due course.

JH-7 ***5/2003*** / 0114641

Numbers/Type: 4 Harbin SH-5.
Operational speed: 243 kt *(450 km/h)*.
Service ceiling: 23,000 ft *(7,000 m)*.
Range: 2,563 n miles *(4,750 km)*.
Role/Weapon systems: Multipurpose amphibian introduced into service in 1986. Final total of about 20 planned with ASW and avionics upgrade. Sensors: Doppler radar; MAD; sonobuoys. Weapons: ASV; four C 101, two gun turret, bombs. ASW; Yu-2 (Mk 46 Mod 1) torpedoes, mines, depth bombs.

SH-5 ***9/2007*** / 1335686

Numbers/Type: 4 SAC Y-8X (Cub).
Operational speed: 351 kt *(650 km/h)*.
Service ceiling: 34,120 ft *(10,400 m)*.
Range: 3,020 n miles *(5,600 km)*.
Role/Weapon systems: Maritime patrol version of An-12 Cub transport; first flown 1985. There are reported to be two Y-8J variants equipped with Searchwater radar in a dropped nose radome. In addition there are two Y-8DZ Elint variants in service. Sensors: Litton APSO-504(V)3 search radar in undernose radome. Two Litton LTN 72R INS and Omega/Loran. Weapons: No weapons carried.

Y-8X ***7/1997*** / 0012195

Numbers/Type: 30 Harbin H-5 (Il-28 Beagle).
Operational speed: 487 kt *(902 km/h)*.
Service ceiling: 40,350 ft *(12,300 m)*.
Range: 1,175 n miles *(2,180 km)*.
Role/Weapon systems: Overwater strike aircraft with ASW/ASVW roles. Numbers are doubtful as some have been phased out and others moved into second line roles such as target towing and ECM training. Weapons: ASW; two torpedoes or four depth bombs. ASVW; one torpedo + mines. Standard; four 23 mm cannon.

H-5 (Romanian colours) ***2002, Lindsay Peacock*** / 0524583

Numbers/Type: 70/20/20 SAC J-8-I Finback A/SAC J-8-II Finback B/SAC J-8-IV Finback D.
Operational speed: 701 kt *(1,300 km/h)*.
Service ceiling: 65,620 ft *(20,000 m)*.
Range: 1,187 n miles *(2,200 km)*.
Role/Weapon systems: Dual role, all-weather fighter introduced into service in 1990 and production continues. There are at least 170 more in service with the Air Force. Weapons: 23 mm twin-barrel cannon; PL-2/7 AAM; ASM. PL-2 has some ASM capability.

Numbers/Type: 35 Nanchang Q-5 (Fantan-A).
Operational speed: 643 kt *(1,190 km/h)*.
Service ceiling: 52,500 ft *(16,000 m)*.
Range: 650 n miles *(1,188 km)*.
Role/Weapon systems: Strike aircraft developed from Shenyang J-6; operated in the beachhead and coastal shipping attack role. A-5M version adapted to carry two torpedoes or C-801 ASM. Weapons: Two 23 mm cannon, two cluster bombs, one or two air-to-air missiles. Capable of carrying 1 ton warload.

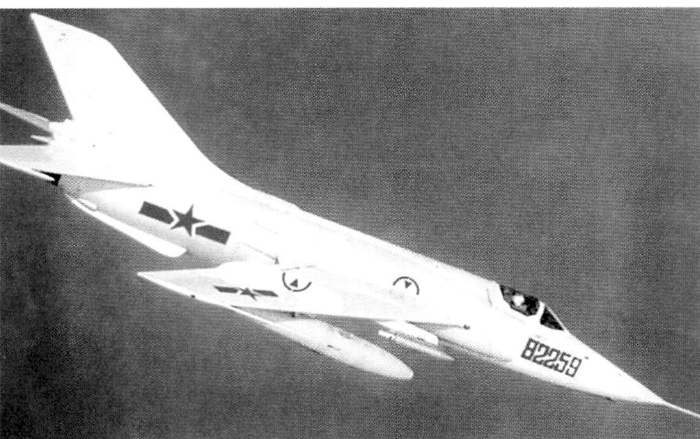

FANTAN-A ***6/2002, Ships of the World*** / 0554726

Numbers/Type: 30/1 XAC H-6D/XAC H-6X (Tu-16 Badger).
Operational speed: 535 kt *(992 km/h)*.
Service ceiling: 40,350 ft *(12,300 m)*.
Range: 2,605 n miles *(4,800 km)*.
Role/Weapon systems: Three regiments of H-6D bomber and maritime reconnaissance aircraft. Some converted as tankers. H-6s now believed to be out of service and deliveries of new version H-6X, armed with ASM, have begun. Sensors: Search/attack radar; ECM. Weapons: ASV; two underwing anti-shipping missiles of local manufacture, including C-801. Up to five 23 mm cannon; bombs.

H-6X ***6/2004*** / 1042161

Numbers/Type: 69 CAC J-7.
Operational speed: 1,175 kt *(2,175 km/h)*.
Service ceiling: 61,680 ft *(18,800 m)*.
Range: 804 n miles *(1,490 km)*.
Role/Weapon systems: Land-based Fleet air defence fighter with limited strike role against enemy shipping or beachhead. There are some 40 J-7B and 29 J-7E. Sensors: Search attack radar, some ECM. Weapons: ASV; 500 kg bombs or 36 rockets. Standard; two 30 mm cannon. AD; two 'Atoll' AAMs.

J-7E ***6/2002, Ships of the World*** / 0554725

PATROL FORCES

Notes: (1) Many patrol craft carry the HN-5 shoulder-launched Chinese version of the SA-N-5 SAM.
(2) More Patrol Craft are listed under Paramilitary vessels at the end of the Chinese section.

60 + 5 HOUBEI (TYPE 022) CLASS (FAST ATTACK CRAFT—MISSILE) (PGGF)

2208–2211 **+56**

Displacement, tons: 220 full load
Dimensions, feet (metres): 139.7 × 40.0 × 4.9 *(42.6 × 12.2 × 1.5)*
Main machinery: 2 diesels; 6,865 hp *(5.1 MW)*; 4 waterjet propulsors
Speed, knots: 36
Complement: 12

Missiles: 8 C-802 (YJ-83/CSS-N-8) Saccade; mid-course guidance and active radar homing to 150 km *(81 n miles)* at 0.9 Mach; warhead 165 kg; sea skimmer.
Guns: 1—30 mm/65 AK 630; 6 barrels; 3,000 rds/min combined to 2 km; 12 missiles.
Weapons control: Optronic director.
Radars: Surface search: Type 348 (LR 66); I-band.
Navigation: I-band.

Comment: A new fast attack craft, the first of which was launched at Qiuxin Shipyard, Shanghai in April 2004. The design is believed to be based on a 42 m hull developed by AMD Marine Consulting, Sydney. This was further progressed by its joint venture company in Guangzhou, Sea Bus International (SBI), into a patrol boat configuration which was selected by the Chinese Navy after a five-yearinvestigation into various platform contenders. The craft has a wave-piercing catamaran hull form and a centre bow. Likely to be of aluminium alloy construction, the design clearly incorporates RCS reduction measures. Following extensive first of class trials, full production was reported to have taken place in at least six shipyards. Although production slowed in 2008, up to 100 craft are required to replace the ageing patrol boat inventory. Dimensions are based on the original AMD design. The installation of C-802 missiles suggests that there may be a datalink to facilitate over-the-horizon targeting. The craft are based in all three fleets and are likely to use a sector-defence concept.

HOUBEI *1/2008** / 1335685

HOUBEI *12/2007, Chris Sattler* / 1335684

HOUBEI CLASS *6/2007* / 1166866

16 HOUXIN (TYPE 037/1G) CLASS (FAST ATTACK CRAFT—MISSILE) (PTG)

751–760 **764–769**

Displacement, tons: 478 full load
Dimensions, feet (metres): 203.4 × 23.6 × 7.5 *(62.8 × 7.2 × 2.4)*
Main machinery: 4 China PR 230ZC diesels; 4,000 hp(m) *(2.94 MW)*; 4 shafts
Speed, knots: 28
Range, n miles: 750 at 18 kt
Complement: 71

Missiles: SSM: 4 YJ-1 (Eagle Strike) (C-801) (CSS-N-4 Sardine) (2 twin); active radar homing to 40 km *(22 n miles)* at 0.9 Mach; warhead 165 kg; sea-skimmer. C-802 in due course.
Guns: 4—37 mm/63 (Type 76A) (2 twin); 180 rds/min to 8.5 km *(4.6 n miles)* anti-aircraft; weight of shell 1.42 kg.
4—14.5 mm (Type 69) (2 twin); 600 rds/min to 7 km *(3.8 n miles)*.
Countermeasures: ESM/ECM: Intercept and jammer.
Radars: Surface search: Type 352 (Square Tie); I-band.
Fire control: Type 341 (Rice Lamp); I-band.
Navigation: Anritsu Type 723; I-band.

Programmes: First seen in 1991 and built at the rate of up to three per year at Qiuxin and Huangpu Shipyards to replace the Houku class and for export. Building may have stopped in mid-1999.
Structure: This is a missile armed version of the Hainan class. There are some variations in the bridge superstructure in later ships of the class.
Operational: Split between the East and South Sea Fleets.
Sales: Two to Burma in December 1995, two in July 1996 and two in late 1997.

HOUXIN 758 *3/2003, Bob Fildes* / 0569184

HOUXIN 765 *5/2004* / 1042140

3 HAIJIU (TYPE 037/1) CLASS (LARGE PATROL CRAFT) (PC)

688 **693** **697**

Displacement, tons: 490 full load
Dimensions, feet (metres): 210 × 23.6 × 7.2 *(64 × 7.2 × 2.2)*
Main machinery: 4 diesels; 8,800 hp(m) *(6.47 MW)*; 4 shafts
Speed, knots: 28
Range, n miles: 750 at 18 kt
Complement: 72
Guns: 4 China 57 mm/70 (2 twin); 120 rds/min to 12 km *(6.5 n miles)*; weight of shell 6.31 kg.
2 USSR 30 mm/65 (1 twin); 500 rds/min to 5 km *(2.7 n miles)* anti-aircraft; weight of shell 0.54 kg.
A/S mortars: 4 RBU 1200 5-tubed fixed launchers; range 1,200 m; warhead 34 kg.
Depth charges: 2 rails.
Radars: Surface search: Pot Head; I-band.
Fire control: Round Ball; I-band.
Sonars: Stag Ear or Thomson Sintra SS 12 (688, 693).

Comment: A lengthened version of the Hainan class probably used as a prototype for the Houxin class. Based in East Sea Fleet. One other has been scrapped.

HAIJIU 688 *6/2008** / 1335706

6 HOUJIAN (OR HUANG) (TYPE 037/2) CLASS
(FAST ATTACK CRAFT—MISSILE) (PTG)

Name	*No*	*Builders*	*Launched*	*Commissioned*
YANGJIANG	770	Huangpu Shipyard	Jan 1991	May 1991
SHUNDE	771	Huangpu Shipyard	July 1994	Feb 1995
NANHAI	772	Huangpu Shipyard	Feb 1995	Apr 1995
PANYU	773	Huangpu Shipyard	May 1995	July 1995
LIANJIANG	774	Huangpu Shipyard	Sep 1998	Feb 1999
XINHUI	775	Huangpu Shipyard	Apr 1999	Nov 1999

Displacement, tons: 520 standard
Dimensions, feet (metres): 214.6 × 27.6 × 7.9 *(65.4 × 8.4 × 2.4)*
Main machinery: 3 SEMT-Pielstick 12 PA6 280 diesels; 15,840 hp(m) *(11.7 MW)* sustained; 3 shafts
Speed, knots: 32
Range, n miles: 1,800 at 18 kt
Complement: 75

Missiles: SSM: 6 YJ-1 (Eagle Strike) (C-801) (CSS-N-4 Sardine) (2 triple); inertial cruise; active radar homing to 40 km *(22 n miles)* at 0.9 Mach; warhead 165 kg or C-802 (CSS-N-8 Saccade); range 120 km *(66 n miles)*.
Guns: 2—37 mm/63 (twin) Type 76A; 180 rds/min to 8.5 km *(4.6 n miles)* anti-aircraft; weight of shell 1.42 kg.
4—30 mm/65 (2 twin) Type 69; 500 rds/min to 5 km *(2.7 n miles)*; weight of shell 0.54 kg.
Countermeasures: Decoys: 2 Type 945G 26-barrelled launcher.
ESM: Type 928; intercept.
Weapons control: Type JM-83 optronic director.
Radars: Surface search: Type 348 (MR 36); I-band.
Fire control: Type 347G Rice Bowl; I-band.
Navigation: Type 765; I-band.

Programmes: First of class laid down in 1989 and built in a very short time. Sometimes called the Huang class.
Modernisation: Some may be fitted with Type 363 search radar and Type 344 (MR 34) fire-control radar rather than Type 347G.
Operational: Based in South Sea Fleet at Hong Kong from mid-1997. One possibly sunk in late 1997. *Lianjiang* severely damaged in a collision with a freighter on 26 June 2006 but was later repaired at Guangdong Shipyard in 2008.

SHUNDE *6/2007* / 1166848

93 HAINAN (TYPE 037) CLASS
(FAST ATTACK CRAFT—PATROL) (PC)

275–285, 290, 302, 305, 609–610, 618–622, 626–629, 636–643, 646–650, 657–681, 683–687 689–692, 695–699, 701, 707, 723–733, 740–742

Displacement, tons: 375 standard; 392 full load
Dimensions, feet (metres): 192.8 × 23.6 × 7.2 *(58.8 × 7.2 × 2.2)*
Main machinery: 4 PCR/Kolomna Type 9-D-8 diesels; 4,000 hp(m) *(2.94 MW)* sustained; 4 shafts
Speed, knots: 30.5
Range, n miles: 1,300 at 15 kt
Complement: 78

Missiles: Can be fitted with 4 YJ-1 launchers in lieu of the after 57 mm gun.
Guns: 4 China 57 mm/70 (2 twin); 120 rds/min to 12 km *(6.5 n miles)*; weight of shell 6.31 kg.
4 USSR 25 mm/60 (2 twin); 270 rds/min to 3 km *(1.6 n miles)* anti-aircraft; weight of shell 0.34 kg.
A/S mortars: 4 RBU 1200 5-tubed fixed launchers; range 1,200 m; warhead 34 kg.
Depth charges: 2 BMB-2 projectors; 2 racks. 18 DCs.
Mines: Rails fitted for 12.
Radars: Surface search: Pot Head or Skin Head; E/F-band.
IFF: High Pole.
Sonars: Stag Ear; hull-mounted; active search and attack; high frequency.
Thomson Sintra SS 12 (in some); VDS.

Programmes: A larger Chinese-built version of the former Soviet SO 1. Low freeboard. Programme started 1963–64 and continued with new hulls replacing the first ships of the class. There are at least six variants with minor differences.
Structure: Later ships have a tripod or solid foremast in place of a pole and a short stub mainmast. Two trials SS 12 sonars fitted in 1987.
Operational: Divided between the three Fleets.
Sales: Two to Bangladesh, one in 1982 and one in 1985; eight to Egypt in 1983–84; six to North Korea 1975–78; four to Pakistan, two in 1976 and two in 1980; six to Burma in 1991 and four in 1993.

HAINAN 686 *10/2008*, Chris Sattler* / 1335682

HAINAN 686 *10/2006, E & M Laursen* / 1164869

11 HUANGFEN (TYPE 021) (OSA I TYPE)
(FAST ATTACK CRAFT—MISSILE) (PTGF)

3113–3114 3130–3131 6106–6107 6119–6120 6122–6123 7119

Displacement, tons: 171 standard; 205 full load
Dimensions, feet (metres): 126.6 × 24.9 × 8.9 *(38.6 × 7.6 × 2.7)*
Main machinery: 3 Type 42-160 diesels; 12,000 hp(m) *(8.8 MW)* sustained; 3 shafts
Speed, knots: 35
Range, n miles: 800 at 30 kt
Complement: 28

Missiles: SSM: 4 HY-2 (CSS-N-3 Seersucker) (2 twin) launchers; active radar or IR homing to 80 km *(43.2 n miles)* at 0.9 Mach; warhead 513 kg.
Guns: 4 USSR 25 mm/60 (2 twin); 270 rds/min to 3 km *(1.6 n miles)* anti-aircraft.
Replaced in some by 4 USSR 30 mm/65 (2 twin) AK 230.
Radars: Surface search: Square Tie; I-band.
Fire control: Round Ball or Rice Lamp; H/I-band.
IFF: 2 Square Head; High Pole A.

Programmes: First reported in 1985.
Operational: China credits this class with a speed of 39 kt. Split between the Fleets. Numbers continue to be reduced.
Sales: Four to North Korea, 1980; four to Pakistan, 1984; four to Bangladesh, 1988; and one more in 1992. Three of a variant were transferred to Yemen in June 1995, delivery having been delayed by the Yemen civil war. A variant called the Houdong class has been built for Iran. Five delivered to Iran in September 1994, five more in March 1996.

HUANGFEN 6120 *3/2002, Ships of the World* / 0529118

25 HAIQING (TYPE 037/1S) CLASS
(FAST ATTACK CRAFT—PATROL) (PC)

710–717 743–744 761–763 786–797

Displacement, tons: 478 full load
Dimensions, feet (metres): 206 × 23.6 × 7.9 *(62.8 × 7.2 × 2.4)*
Main machinery: 4 Chinese PR 230ZC diesels; 4,000 hp(m) *(2.94 MW)* sustained; 4 shafts
Speed, knots: 28
Range, n miles: 1,300 at 15 kt
Complement: 71
Guns: 4 China 37 mm/63 (2 twin) Type 76. 4 China 14.5 mm (2 twin) Type 69.
A/S mortars: 2 Type 87 6-tubed launchers.
Radars: Surface search: Anritsu RA 723; I-band.
Sonars: Hull mounted; active search and attack; medium frequency Thomson Sintra SS 12; VDS.

Programmes: Starting building at Qiuxin Shipyard in 1992 and replaced the Hainan class programme. First one completed in November 1993. Production continued at Qingdao, Chongqing and Huangpu as well as Qiuxin.
Structure: Based on the Hainan class, but the large A/S mortars suggest a predominantly ASW role, and this may explain the rapid building rate.
Operational: In service in all three Fleets. Some pennant numbers may have changed.
Sales: One to Sri Lanka in December 1995.

HAIQING 743 *6/2008** / 1335705

25 HAIZHUI/SHANGHAI III (TYPE 062/1) CLASS (COASTAL PATROL CRAFT) (PC)

1201–1208 **1236** **1239–1240** **2326–2329** **4339–4348**

Displacement, tons: 170 full load
Dimensions, feet (metres): 134.5 × 17.4 × 5.9 *(41 × 5.3 × 1.8)*
Main machinery: 4 Chinese L12-180A diesels; 4,400 hp(m) *(3.22 MW)* sustained; 4 shafts
Speed, knots: 25. **Range, n miles:** 750 at 17 kt
Complement: 43

Guns: 4 China 37 mm/63 (2 twin); 180 rds/min to 8.5 km *(4.6 n miles)*; weight of shell 1.42 kg. 4 China 14.5 mm (2 twin) Type 69 or 4 China 25 mm (2 twin).
Radars: Surface search: Pot Head or Anritsu 726; I-band.
Sonars: Stag Ear; hull-mounted; active search; high frequency (in some).

Programmes: First seen in 1992 and built for Chinese use and for export. Sometimes referred to as Shanghai III class when not fitted with ASW equipment.
Structure: Lengthened Shanghai II hull. Inclined pole mast and a pronounced step at the back of the bridge superstructure are recognition features. Much reduced top speed. Some may be equipped with RBU 1200 launchers in place of other armament.
Operational: Based in the North and East Sea Fleets.
Sales: Three of a variant to Tunisia in 1994, three to Sri Lanka in August 1995, three more in May 1996 and three more in August 1998. One to Bangladesh in mid-1996. One to Sierra Leone in 1997.

HAIZHUI 1208 *10/2005, Flor Van Otterdyk* / 1164395

HAIZHUI 1202 *3/2007* / 1166862

35 SHANGHAI II (TYPE 062) CLASS (FAST ATTACK CRAFT—GUN) (PC)

Displacement, tons: 113 standard; 134 full load
Dimensions, feet (metres): 127.3 × 17.7 × 5.6 *(38.8 × 5.4 × 1.7)*
Main machinery: 2 Type L-12V-180 diesels; 2,400 hp(m) *(1.76 MW)* (forward); 2 Type 12-D-6 diesels; 1,820 hp(m) *(1.34 MW)* (aft); 4 shafts
Speed, knots: 30. **Range, n miles:** 700 at 16.5 kt on 1 engine
Complement: 38

Guns: 4 China 37 mm/63 (2 twin); 180 rds/min to 8.5 km *(4.6 n miles)*; weight of shell 1.42 kg. 4 USSR 25 mm/60 (2 twin); 270 rds/min to 3 km *(1.6 n miles)* anti-aircraft; weight of shell 0.34 kg.
Some are fitted with a twin 57 mm/70, some have a twin 75 mm Type 56 recoilless rifle mounted forward and some have a twin 14.5 mm MG.
Depth charges: 2 projectors; 8 weapons.
Mines: Mine rails can be fitted for 10 mines.
Radars: Surface search: Skin Head; E/F-band or Pot Head; I-band.
IFF: High Pole.
Sonars: Hull-mounted active sonar or VDS in some.

Programmes: Construction began in 1961 and continued at Shanghai and other yards at rate of about 10 a year for 30 years before being replaced by the Type 062/1G Haizhui class.
Structure: The five versions of this class vary slightly in the outline of their bridges. A few of the class have been reported as fitted with RBU 1200 anti-submarine mortars.
Operational: Evenly divided between the three Fleets. Reported but not confirmed that up to 20 have been converted to sweep mines. Numbers continue to decline.
Sales: Eight to North Vietnam in May 1966, plus Romanian craft of indigenous construction. Seven to Tanzania in 1970–71, six to Guinea, 12 to North Korea, 12 to Pakistan, five to Sri Lanka in 1972, two to Tunisia in 1977, six to Albania, eight to Bangladesh in 1980–82, three to Congo, four to Egypt in 1984, three to Sri Lanka in 1991, two to Tanzania in 1992. Many of the earlier craft have since been deleted.

SHANGHAI II (Sri Lankan colours) *1992* / 0012772

4 HARBOUR PATROL CRAFT (PBI)

7358–7361

Displacement, tons: 80 full load
Dimensions, feet (metres): 82 × 13.3 × 4.5 *(25 × 4.1 × 1.4)*
Main machinery: 2 diesels; 2 shafts
Speed, knots: 28
Guns: 2—14.5 mm (twin).
Radars: Surface search: I-band.

Comment: Four new patrol craft arrived at Hong Kong on 1 July 1997. There may be more of the class, which are similar to some of the paramilitary patrol craft, but much faster.

HARBOUR PATROL CRAFT 7360 *6/1999, Ships of the World* / 0056772

AMPHIBIOUS FORCES

Notes: (1) In addition to the ships listed below there are up to 500 minor LCM/LCVP types used to transport stores and personnel.
(2) Eight Yuchai class (USSR T 4 design) and ten T4 LCMs are still in reserve in the South Sea Fleet.
(3) A 20 m WIG (wing-in-ground effect) craft assembled at Shanghai and completed in late 1997. Resembles Russian Volga II passenger ferry and may enter naval service if it proves to be reliable.

1 YUDENG (TYPE 073) CLASS (LSM)

Name	*No*	*Builders*	*Launched*	*Commissioned*
WUDANGSHAN	990	Zhonghua Shipyard	Mar 1991	Aug 1994

Displacement, tons: 1,850 full load
Dimensions, feet (metres): 285.4 × 42.7 × 12.5 *(87 × 13 × 3.8)*
Main machinery: 2 diesels; 2 shafts
Speed, knots: 14
Complement: 35
Military lift: 500 troops; 9 tanks
Guns: 2 China 57 mm/50 (twin). 4—25 mm (2 twin).
Radars: Navigation: China Type 753; I-band.

Comment: The only one of the class. Based in the South Sea Fleet. Production may have been for export or the design was overtaken by the smaller Wuhu-A class.

WUDANGSHAN *4/2008** / 1335681

1 YUZHAO (TYPE 071) CLASS (ASSAULT SHIP) (LHD)

Name	*No*	*Builders*	*Laid down*	*Launched*	*Commissioned*
KUNLUNSHAN	998	Hudong-Zhonghua Shipyard, Shanghai	June 2006	21 Dec 2006	2008

Displacement, tons: 17,600 approx
Dimensions, feet (metres): 689.0 × 91.9 × 23.0 *(210.0 × 28.0 × 7.0)*
Main machinery: CODAD; 4 SEMT Pielstick 16 PC2.6 V 400 diesels; 47,000 hp *(35.2 MW)*; 2 shafts
Speed, knots: 20
Complement: 120
Military lift: Four air-cushion vehicles plus vehicles and troops
Guns: 1—76 mm ❶.
4—30 mm/65 AK 630 ❷.
Countermeasures: Decoys: 2 launchers ❸.
Radars: Air search: Type 363 (Sea Tiger) ❹; E/F-band.
Air/surface search: Type 364 Seagull C ❺; G-band.
Fire control: Type 347G(2) (LR 66) ❻; J-band for 76 mm.
Type 347G(1) (Rice Bowl) ❼; J-band for AK 630.
Navigation: Type NR 2000 ❽; I-band.

Helicopters: 2 Z-8 Super Frelon.

Programmes: After several years' speculation, the existence of the programme was confirmed when construction of a ship was initiated in mid-2006. The programme constitutes a key component of the PLA(N)'s plan to improve its sealift and power projection capabilities. Further ships are expected once evaluation trials have been completed.

Structure: The principal features of the ship include a large well deck area to accommodate four Air Cushion Vehicles (ACV) in the aft two-thirds of the ship. The ACVs are likely to access the ship through a stern gate. The ship may have to ballast down for operation. There is a large stern helicopter flight deck and a hangar. An internal garage deck for vehicles may be accessed via side ramps (port and starboard). There is space for the HQ7 launcher which may be fitted at a later date. Two LCVPs are carried.
Opinion: This ship represents a major enhancement of amphibious capability. Based at Zhanjiang (South Sea Fleet).

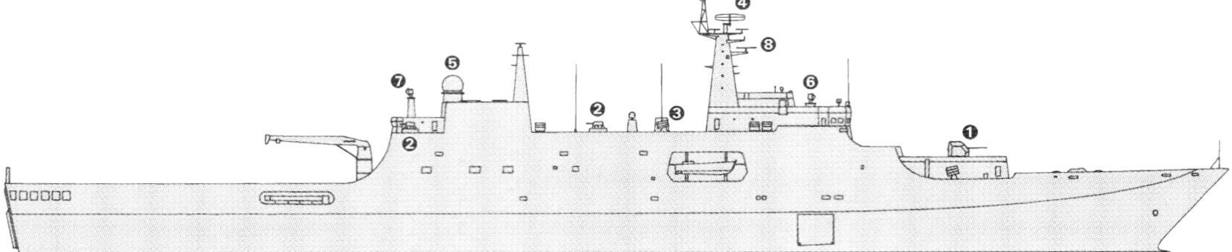

KUNLUNSHAN *(Scale 1 : 1,500), Ian Sturton* / 1166825

KUNLUNSHAN *9/2007* / 1166865

KUNLUNSHAN *9/2007* / 1166864

KUNLUNSHAN *9/2007* / 1166863

10 YUTING I (TYPE 072 II) CLASS (LSTH)

Name	*No*	*Builders*	*Launched*	*Commissioned*
EMEISHAN	991	Zhonghua Shipyard, Shanghai	Sep 1991	Sep 1992
DANXIASHAN	934	Zhonghua Shipyard, Shanghai	Apr 1995	Sep 1995
XUEFENGSHAN	935	Zhonghua Shipyard, Shanghai	July 1995	Dec 1995
HAIYANGSHAN	936	Zhonghua Shipyard, Shanghai	Dec 1995	May 1996
QINGCHENGSHAN	937	Zhonghua Shipyard, Shanghai	Apr 1996	Aug 1996
YANDANSHANG	908 (ex-938)	Zhonghua Shipyard, Shanghai	Aug 1996	Jan 1997
JIUHUASHAN	909 (ex-939)	Zhonghua Shipyard, Shanghai	Nov 1999	Apr 2000
HUANGGANGSHAN	910	Zhonghua Shipyard, Shanghai	May 2000	Dec 2001
PUTUOSHAN	939	Zhonghua Shipyard, Shanghai	Apr 2001	Aug 2001
TIANTAISHAN	940	Zhonghua Shipyard, Shanghai	Dec 2001	Apr 2002

Displacement, tons: 3,770 standard; 4,800 full load
Dimensions, feet (metres): 393.7 × 52.5 × 10.5 *(120 × 16 × 3.2)*
Main machinery: 2 diesels; 2 shafts
Speed, knots: 17. **Range, n miles:** 3,000 at 14 kt
Complement: 120
Military lift: 250 troops; 10 tanks; 4 LCVP
Guns: 6 China 37 mm/63 (3 twin); 180 rds/min to 8.5 km *(4.6 n miles)*; weight of shell 1.42 kg.
Radars: Navigation: 2 China Type 753; I-band.
Helicopters: Platform for 2 medium.

Comment: To augment amphibious lift capabilities and provide helicopter lift. Bow and bridge structures are very similar to the Yukan class but there is a large helicopter deck. 934-937 and 991 based in South Sea Fleet. 908-910 and 939-940 based in East Sea Fleet.

HUANGGANGSHAN *1/2008*, A Sheldon-Duplaix* / 1335683

PUTUOSHAN *6/2007* / 1166861

10 YUTING II (TYPE 072 III) CLASS (LSTH)

Name	*No*	*Builders*	*Launched*	*Commissioned*
BAXIANSHAN	913	Zhonghua Shipyard, Shanghai	23 Apr 2003	Oct 2003
TIANZHUSHAN	911	Dalian Shipyard	1 July 2003	2004
HUADINGSHAN	992	Wuhan Shipyard	June 2003	2004
–	918	Wuhan Shipyard	Apr 2004	2004
LUOXIAOSHAN	993	Zhonghua Shipyard, Shanghai	18 July 2003	Jan 2004
DAQINGSHAN	912	Dalian Shipyard	Sep 2003	2004
DAIYUNSHAN	994	Wuhan Shipyard	16 Dec 2003	2004
WANYANG-SHAN	995	Zhonghua Shipyard, Shanghai	26 Nov 2003	2004
LAOTIESHAN	996	Dalian Shipyard	1 Jan 2004	2004
YUNWASHAN	997	Wuhan Shipyard	2004	2005

Displacement, tons: 3,770 standard; 4,800 full load
Dimensions, feet (metres): 393.7 × 53.8 × 10.5 *(120 × 16.4 × 3.2)*
Main machinery: 2 diesels; 2 shafts
Speed, knots: 17. **Range, n miles:** 3,000 at 14 kt
Complement: 120
Military lift: 250 troops; 10 tanks; 4 LCVP
Guns: 2—57 mm.
Radars: Navigation: 2 China Type 753; I-band.
Helicopters: Platform for 2 medium.

Comment: Details are speculative but reported to be an improved version of the Yuting I class with similar dimensions. Design differences include modifications to the stern, including the ramp and a taller funnel. A tunnel in the centre of the superstructure connects the main and after decks. With construction undertaken at three shipyards, a pause in the programme after 10 ships may be temporary. 992-996 based in the South Sea Fleet; 911 and 912 in the North and 913 and 918 in the East.

BAXIANSHAN *10/2008*, Chris Sattler* / 1335680

DAQINGSHAN *6/2007* / 1166854

7 YUKAN (TYPE 072) CLASS (LST)

YUNTAISHAN 927
WUFENGSHAN 928
ZIJINSHAN 929
LINGYANSHAN 930
DONGTINGSHAN 931
HELANSHAN 932
LIUPANSHAN 933

Displacement, tons: 3,110 standard; 4,170 full load
Dimensions, feet (metres): 393.6 × 50 × 9.5 *(120 × 15.3 × 2.9)*
Main machinery: 2 Type 12E 390 diesels; 14,400 hp(m) *(10.6 MW)* sustained; 2 shafts
Speed, knots: 18
Range, n miles: 3,000 at 14 kt
Complement: 109
Military lift: 200 troops; 10 tanks; 2 LCVP; total of 500 tons
Guns: 2 China 57 mm/50 (1 twin); 120 rds/min to 12 km *(6.5 n miles)*; weight of shell 6.31 kg.
4, 6 or 8—37 mm (2, 3 or 4 twin); 180 rds/min to 8.5 km *(4.6 n miles)*; weight of shell 1.42 kg.
4—25 mm/60 (2 twin) (some also have 4—25 mm (2 twin) mountings amidships above the tank deck); 270 rds/min to 3 km *(1.6 n miles)*.
Radars: Navigation: 2 China Type 753; I-band.

Comment: First completed in 1980 at Wuhan Shipyard. Building appeared to terminate in November 1995. Bow and stern ramps fitted. Carry two LCVPs. Bow ramp maximum load 50 tons, stern ramp 20 tons. Five based in the East and two in South Sea Fleets.

HELANSHAN *12/2007, Chris Sattler* / 1170057

LINGYANSHAN *3/2001, Ships of the World* / 0126363

32 YULIANG (TYPE 079) CLASS (LSM)

957–988

Displacement, tons: 1,100 full load
Dimensions, feet (metres): 206.7 × 32.8 × 7.9 *(63 × 10 × 2.4)*
Main machinery: 2 diesels; 2 shafts
Speed, knots: 14
Complement: 60
Military lift: 3 tanks
Guns: 4—25 mm/60 (2 twin); 270 rds/min to 3 km *(1.6 n miles)*.
2 BM 21 MRL rocket launchers; range about 9 km *(5 n miles)*.
Radars: Navigation: Fin Curve; I-band.

Comment: Production started in 1980 in three or four smaller shipyards. Numbers have been overestimated in the past and production stopped in favour of Yuhai class. Four in the North Sea Fleet, remainder based in the South Sea Fleet.

YULIANG 986 *6/2008** / 1335702

10 YUNSHU CLASS (LSM)

Name	No	Builders	Launched	Commissioned
SONGSHAN	946	Hudong Zhonghua Shipyard, Shanghai	June 2003	2004
–	947	Qingdao Naval Dockyard	1 Aug 2003	2004
XUESHAN	948	Lushun Shipyard	Sep 2003	2004
YUSHAN	944	Lushun Shipyard	20 Mar 2004	2004
HUASHAN	945	Wuhu Shipyard	1 July 2003	2004
SHENGSHAN	941	Hudong Zhonghua Shipyard, Shanghai	Dec 2003	2004
HENGSHAN	949	Lushun Shipyard	Feb 2004	2004
LUSHAN	942	Wuhu Shipyard	2004	2004
–	943	Qingdao Naval Dockyard	2004	2004
TAISHAN	950	Hudong Zhonghua Shipyard, Shanghai	Mar 2004	2004

Displacement, tons: 1,460 standard; 1,850 full load
Dimensions, feet (metres): 285.4 × 41.3 × 7.4 *(87.0 × 12.6 × 2.25)*
Main machinery: 2 diesels; 2 shafts
Speed, knots: 17
Range, n miles: 1,500 at 14 kt
Complement: 70
Military lift: 6 tanks or 12 trucks or 250 tons dry stores
Guns: 2—57 mm.
Radars: Navigation: I-band.

Comment: A new class of LSM, based on the Yudeng class, built at Zhonghua, Wuhu, Qingdao and Lushun. Series production at four shipyards suggests that further ships may be built. 941-944 based in the East Sea Fleet and 945-950 in the South Sea Fleet.

YUSHAN *6/2008** / 1335704

10 YUBEI (TYPE 074A) CLASS (LCU)

No	Builders	Launched	Commissioned
3128	Qingdao Naval Dockyard	Sep 2003	2004
3315	Zhanjiang Shipyard North	2003	2004
3232	Shanghai Shipyard International	Sep 2003	2004
3129	Qingdao Naval Dockyard	Dec 2003	2004
3316	Dinghai Naval Dockyard	Sep 2003	2004
3317	Dinghai Naval Dockyard	Nov 2003	2004
3318	Dinghai Naval Dockyard	Jan 2004	2004
3233	Qingdao Naval Dockyard	2004	2004
3234	–	2004	2005
3235	–	2004	2005

Displacement, tons: 900 standard; 1,200 full load
Dimensions, feet (metres): 213.2 × 36.1 × 88.6 *(65.0 × 11.0 × 2.7)*
Main machinery: 2 diesels; 2 shafts
Speed, knots: To be announced
Complement: To be announced
Military lift: 10 tanks; 150 troops
Guns: 4—14.5 mm (2 twin).
Radars: To be announced.

Comment: Built at Qingdao, Zhanjiang, Shanghai and Dinghai. Catamaran hull with superstructure on the starboard side. Basing: *3128* and *3129* in the North Sea Fleet; *3232-35* in the South Sea Fleet; *3315-3318* in the East Sea Fleet.

YUBEI 3315 *8/2003* / 1042164

10 YUHAI (TYPE 074) (WUHU-A) CLASS (LSM)

3111 3113 3115–3117 3229 3244 7593–7595

Displacement, tons: 799 full load
Dimensions, feet (metres): 191.6 × 34.1 × 8.9 *(58.4 × 10.4 × 2.7)*
Main machinery: 2 MAN-8L 20/27 diesels; 4,900 hp(m) *(3.6 MW)*; 2 shafts
Speed, knots: 14
Complement: 56
Military lift: 2 tanks; 250 troops
Guns: 2—25 mm/80 (1 twin). 4—14.5 mm (2 twin).
Radars: Navigation: I-band.

Comment: First one completed in Wuhu Shipyard in 1995. One sold to Sri Lanka in December 1995. Basing: *3111, 3113, 3115-3117* in the North Sea Fleet; *3229* and *3244* in the East Sea Fleet and *7593-7597* in the South Sea Fleet.

YUHAI CLASS *2/1999* / 0056780

120 YUNNAN CLASS (TYPE 067) (LCU)

Displacement, tons: 85 standard; 135 full load
Dimensions, feet (metres): 93.8 × 17.7 × 4.9 *(28.6 × 5.4 × 1.5)*
Main machinery: 2 diesels; 600 hp(m) *(441 kW)*; 2 shafts
Speed, knots: 12
Range, n miles: 500 at 10 kt
Complement: 12
Military lift: 46 tons
Guns: 4—14.5 mm (2 twin) MGs.
Radars: Navigation: Fuji; I-band.

Comment: Built in China 1968–72 although a continuing programme was reported in 1982. Pennant numbers in 3000 series (3313, 3321, 3344 seen). 5000 series (5526 seen) and 7000 series (7566 and 7568 seen). The majority of the operational hulls are based in the South Sea Fleet. One to Sri Lanka in 1991 and a second in 1995. Estimation of numbers is difficult but most are believed to be in reserve or in non-naval service. Some may have 12.7 mm MGs. Twelve in the East Sea Fleet, remainder in the South.

YUNNAN 3221 *6/2008** / 1335701

1 YUDAO CLASS (TYPE 073) (LSM)

965

Displacement, tons: 1,650 full load
Dimensions, feet (metres): 253.9 × 34.1 × 9.8 *(77.4 × 10.4 × 3)*
Speed, knots: 18
Range, n miles: 1,000 at 16 kt
Complement: 60
Guns: 4—25 mm/60 (2 twin); 270 rds/min to 3 km *(1.6 n miles)*.
Radars: Navigation: Fin Curve; I-band.

Comment: First entered service in early 1980s. *965* is the only one left and is in the East Fleet.

YUDAO 965 *6/1995* / 0056781

20 YUCH'IN (TYPE 068/069) CLASS (LCM)

Displacement, tons: 58 standard; 85 full load
Dimensions, feet (metres): 81.2 × 17.1 × 4.3 *(24.8 × 5.2 × 1.3)*
Main machinery: 2 Type 12V 150C diesels; 600 hp(m) *(441 kW)*; 2 shafts
Speed, knots: 11.5. **Range, n miles:** 450 at 11.5 kt
Complement: 12
Military lift: Up to 150 troops
Guns: 4—14.5 mm (2 twin) MGs.

Comment: Built in Shanghai 1962–72. Smaller version of Yunnan class with a shorter tank deck and longer poop deck. Primarily intended for personnel transport. Based in South Sea Fleet. Six sold to Bangladesh and two to Tanzania in 1995.

YUCH'IN 3201 *10/2008*, Chris Sattler* / 1335679

10 JINGSAH II CLASS (HOVERCRAFT) (UCAC)

452 **+9**

Displacement, tons: 70 standard; 78 full load
Dimensions, feet (metres): 72.2 × 26.2 *(22 × 8)*
Main machinery: 2 propulsion motors; 2 lift motors
Speed, knots: 55
Military lift: 15 tons
Guns: 4—14.5 mm (2 twin) MGs.

Comment: The prototype was built at Dagu in 1979. This may now have been scrapped and been superseded by this improved version which has a bow door for disembarkation. Numbers are uncertain and may be conditional on progress with WIG craft.

JINGSAH II ***1993, Ships of the World*** / 0056783

25 TYPE 271 (LANDING CRAFT) (LCU)

Displacement, tons: 610 standard; 800 full load
Dimensions, feet (metres): 185.4 × 34.1 × 7.5 *(56.5 × 10.4 × 2.3)*
Main machinery: 2 diesels; 2,250 hp *(1.7 MW)*; 2 shafts
Speed, knots: 13
Complement: 25
Military lift: 150 tons
Guns: 4—14.5 mm (2 twin).
Radars: Navigation: I-band.

Comment: Utility landing craft widely used for the transport of troops, vehicles and stores. The first variant (Type 271-I) entered service in about 1970 and this was followed in the late 1970s by Type 270-II and in the late 1980s by Type 271-III. Building continued in the 1990s to replace decommissioned craft but current numbers are approximate. Details are based on the latest generation of craft.

TYPE 271 ***10/2008*, Chris Sattler*** / 1335678

1 + 3 YUYI CLASS (LANDING CRAFT—AIR CUSHION) (LCAC)

Displacement, tons: To be announced
Dimensions, feet (metres): To be announced
Main machinery: 4 gas turbines for propulsion and lift
Speed, knots: To be announced. **Range, n miles:** To be announced
Complement: To be announced
Military lift: Armoured Fighting Vehicle plus troops or 60–70 tons approx
Radars: To be announced.

Comment: The first of a new class of air cushion landing craft design, probably intended for operation from the Yuzhao (Type 071) class LHD. The craft appears to be similar to but smaller than the US Navy LCAC. The vehicle is expected to be capable of transporting an armoured fighting vehicle and troops. In contrast to the US Navy LCAC, the driving/command module is located on the port side instead of the starboard side. The main cargo deck is about 6 m wide and there are bow and stern ramps. Propulsion is provided by two 4 m shrouded reversible-pitch propellers, probably powered by four gas turbines. Built at Qiuxin Shipyard, the first vessel was launched in January 2008.

LCAC ***6/2008**** / 1335703

MINE WARFARE FORCES

Notes: There are also some 50 auxiliary minesweepers of various types including trawlers and motor-driven junks. Up to 20 Shanghai II class, known as the Fushun class, may be used.

1 WOLEI CLASS (MINELAYER) (ML/MST)

LIAOYANG 814

Displacement, tons: 2,300 standard; 3,100 full load
Dimensions, feet (metres): 311.3 × 47.2 × 13.1 *(94.9 × 14.4 × 4)*
Main machinery: 2 diesels; 4,300 hp *(3.2 MW)*; 2 shafts
Speed, knots: 18. **Range, n miles:** 7,000 at 14 kt
Complement: 180
Guns: 2 China 57 mm/50 (twin).
6 China 37 mm/63 (3 twin); 180 rds/min to 8.5 km *(4.6 n miles)*; weight of shell 1.42 kg.
Mines: 300.
Radars: Surface search. Fire control. Navigation.

Comment: Built at Dalian Shipyard and completed successful sea trials in 1988. Resembles the deleted Japanese Souya class and may be used as a support ship as well as a minelayer. Based in the North Sea Fleet.

WOLEI 814 ***6/2002*** / 0529145

4 WOSAO (TYPE 082) CLASS (MINESWEEPERS—COASTAL) (MSC)

800–803

Displacement, tons: 290 standard; 320 full load
Dimensions, feet (metres): 147 × 22.3 × 7.5 *(44.8 × 6.8 × 2.3)*
Main machinery: 2 diesels; 2,000 hp *(1.5 MW)*; 2 shafts
Speed, knots: 15. **Range, n miles:** 500 at 8 kt
Complement: 28
Guns: 4 China 25 mm/60 (2 twin); 270 rds/min to 3 km *(1.6 n miles)*.
Mines: 6.
Countermeasures: Acoustic, magnetic and mechanical sweeps.
Radars: Navigation: China Type 753; I-band.
Sonars: Hull-mounted; active minehunting.

Comment: Building started in 1986. First of class commissioned in 1988 but second, with modified bridge structure, not seen until 1997. There are further craft but numbers have not been confirmed. Steel hull with low magnetic properties. Equipped with mechanical (Type 316), magnetic (Type 317), acoustic (Type 318) and infrasonic (Type 319) sweeps. Based in the East Sea Fleet.

WOSAO ***10/2008*, Chris Sattler*** / 1335675

6 WOCHI CLASS (MCMV)

328–329 **438** **805** **810** **840**

Displacement, tons: To be announced
Dimensions, feet (metres): 219.8 × 32.8 × ? *(67.0 × 10.0 × ?)*
Main machinery: To be announced
Speed, knots: To be announced
Complement: To be announced
Guns: 1—57 mm.
Countermeasures: To be announced.
Combat data systems: To be announced.
Radars: To be announced.
Sonars: To be announced.

Comment: A new class of mine-countermeasures vessel which, although outwardly similar to the T43 class is approximately 5 m longer. Construction has taken place at Qiuxin Shipyard, Shanghai, and at Wuhan. Little is known about the details or capabilities of the vessel.

WOCHI 810 ***11/2007*** / 1166860

1 WOZANG CLASS (MCMV)

Name	*No*	*Builders*	*Launched*	*Commissioned*
HUOQIU	804	Qiuxin Shipyard, Shanghai	Apr 2004	July 2005

Displacement, tons: 575 full load
Dimensions, feet (metres): 180.4 × 30.5 × 8.5 *(55.0 × 9.3 × 2.6)*
Main machinery: 2 diesels; 2 shafts
Speed, knots: To be announced
Complement: To be announced
Guns: 2—25 mm (twin).
Countermeasures: To be announced.
Combat data systems: To be announced.
Radars: To be announced.
Sonars: To be announced.

Comment: A new class of mine-countermeasures vessel which was thought to be a successor to the T43 class before the appearance of the Wochi class. Little is known about the capabilities of the vessel. Based in the East Sea Fleet.

WOZANG 804 *1/2008*, A Sheldon-Duplaix* / 1335677

16 T 43 CLASS (TYPE 6610) (MINESWEEPERS—OCEAN) (MSO)

807–809 811–813 830–838 850

Displacement, tons: 520 standard; 590 full load
Dimensions, feet (metres): 196.8 × 27.6 × 6.9 *(60 × 8.8 × 2.3)*
Main machinery: 2 PCR/Kolomna Type 9-D-8 diesels; 2,000 hp(m) *(1.47 MW)*; 2 shafts
Speed, knots: 14. **Range, n miles**: 3,000 at 10 kt
Complement: 70 (10 officers)

Guns: 2 or 4 China 37 mm/63 (1 or 2 twin) (3 of the class have a 65 mm/52 forward instead of one twin 37 mm/63); dual purpose; 180 rds/min to 8.5 km *(4.6 n miles)*; weight of shell 1.42 kg.
4 USSR 25 mm/60 (2 twin); 270 rds/min to 3 km *(1.6 n miles)*.
4 China 14.5 mm/93 (2 twin); 600 rds/min to 7 km *(3.8 n miles)*.
Some also carry 1—85 mm/52 Mk 90K; 18 rds/min to 15 km *(8 n miles)*; weight of shell 9.6 kg.
Depth charges: 2 BMB-2 projectors; 20 depth charges.
Mines: Can carry 12-16.
Countermeasures: MCMV; MPT-1 paravanes; MPT-3 mechanical sweep; acoustic and magnetic gear.
Radars: Surface search: Fin Curve or Type 756; F-band.
IFF: High Pole or Yard Rake.
Sonars: Tamir II; hull-mounted; active search and attack; high frequency.

Programmes: Started building in 1956 and continued intermittently until about 1987 at Wuhan and at Guangzhou.
Structure: Based on the USSR T 43s, some of which transferred in the mid-1950s but have all now been deleted.
Operational: Some are used as patrol ships with sweep gear removed. Three units reported as having a 65 mm/52 gun forward. Basing: *811-813* in the North Sea Fleet; *807, 808, 830-834* in the East Sea Fleet; *809, 835-838* and *850* in the South Sea Fleet. There are approximately 22 of the class in reserve.
Sales: One to Bangladesh in 1995.

T 43 832 *10/2008*, Chris Sattler* / 1335676

T 43 833 *12/2005, Massimo Annati* / 1153106

4 (+ 42 RESERVE) FUTI CLASS (TYPE 312) (DRONE MINESWEEPERS) (MSD)

Displacement, tons: 47 standard
Dimensions, feet (metres): 68.6 × 12.8 × 6.9 *(20.9 × 3.9 × 2.1)*
Main machinery: Diesel-electric; 1 Type 12V 150C diesel generator; 300 hp(m) *(220 kW)*; 1 motor; cp prop
Speed, knots: 12. **Range, n miles**: 144 at 12 kt
Complement: 3

Comment: A large number of these craft, similar to the German Troikas, has been built since the early 1970s. Fitted to carry out magnetic and acoustic sweeping under remote control up to 5 km *(2.7 n miles)* from shore control station. Most are kept in reserve.

DRONE Type 312 *1988, CSSC* / 0056775

SURVEY AND RESEARCH SHIPS

Notes: (1) In addition to the naval ships shown in this section there are large numbers of civilian marine survey ships. The majority belong to the **National Marine Bureau** and have funnel markings of a red star with light blue wave patterns on either side. There are about 37 ships with names *Zhong Guo Hai Jian* or *Xiang Yang Hong* followed by a pennant number. The **National Land Resources Department** has two Geological Survey Squadrons and these ships have a red star and light blue ring on a white or yellow background. The **State Education Department** Science section owns ships with funnel markings of yellow and blue lines either side of a circular blue design. Also there are a few nationalised companies such as the **China Marine Oil Company** which have a band of light blue round the top of the funnel.
(2) There is a large number of ocean surveillance fishing trawlers. These sometimes engage in fishing activities and are not easily distinguishable from civilian fishing vessels.
(3) There is a 130 m survey ship with pennant number 871.

AGI 201 (converted trawler) *6/1997, A Sharma* / 0017746

XIANG YANG HONG 14 (National Marine Bureau) *4/2004, Ships of the World* / 1042141

ZHONG GUO HAI JIAN 71 *4/2008** / 1335674

FENDOU SHIHAO (National Land Resources) *6/1999, Ships of the World* / 0056795

DONG FANG HONG 2 (State Education Department) *4/2004, Ships of the World* / 1042130

HAI YING 12 HAO (China Marine Oil Company) *6/1997, A Sharma* / 0006690

2 DAHUA CLASS (AGOR/AGE)

BI SHENG 891 (ex-970, ex-909) **HUA LUOGENG** 892

Displacement, tons: 6,000 full load
Dimensions, feet (metres): 426.5 × 57.4 × 23 *(130.0 × 17.5 × 7)*
Main machinery: 2 diesels; 2 shafts
Speed, knots: 20
Complement: 80
Helicopters: Platform for one medium.

Comment: First ship launched on 9 March 1997 with pennant number 909 at Zhonghua, and completed in August 1997 with new pennant number which has also been superseded. There is a helicopter deck aft. This is a key unit which has been involved in a number of trials including those for the HQ-9 phased array radar. It is currently fitted with Top Plate air search radar and Front Dome missile fire-control radars. A second unit, also constructed by Hudong-Zhonghua Shipyard, was launched on 30 March 2006.

DAHUA 891 *6/2007, Ships of the World* / 1166771

DAHUA 892 *10/2006, E & M Laursen* / 1164861

2 SPACE EVENT SHIPS (AGMH/AGI)

YUAN WANG 1 **YUAN WANG 2**

Displacement, tons: 17,100 standard; 21,000 full load
Dimensions, feet (metres): 610.2 × 74.1 × 24.6 *(186 × 22.6 × 7.5)*
Main machinery: 1 Sulzer diesel; 17,400 hp(m) *(12.78 MW)*; 1 shaft
Speed, knots: 20
Range, n miles: 18,000 at 20 kt
Complement: 470

Comment: Built by Shanghai Jiangnan Yard and entered service in December 1979. Both equipped with helicopter decks but no hangar. Extensive communications, SATNAV and meteorological equipment were installed in 1986–87. In the late 1990s, both ships refitted to support manned spacecraft missions.

YUAN WANG 1 *6/1995* / 0056799

1 SPACE EVENT SHIP (AGM/AGI)

DONGDIAO 851 (ex-232)

Displacement, tons: 6,000 full load
Dimensions, feet (metres): 426.5 × 53.8 × 21.3 *(130 × 16.4 × 6.5)*
Main machinery: 2 diesels; 2 shafts
Speed, knots: 20
Complement: 250
Guns: 1—37 mm. 2—14.5 mm.
Helicopters: Platform for one medium.

Comment: First seen fitting out in 1999. A larger version of Dadie class. Two radar (possibly missile tracking) arrays have been replaced by three radomes. In service in March 2000.

DONGDIAO *6/2008** / 1335699

1 DADIE CLASS (AGI)

BEIDIAO 900 (ex-841)

Displacement, tons: 2,550 full load
Dimensions, feet (metres): 308.4 × 37.1 × 13.1 *(94 × 11.3 × 4)*
Main machinery: 2 diesels; 2 shafts
Speed, knots: 17
Complement: 170 (18 officers)
Guns: 4—14.5 mm (2 twin)
Radars: Navigation: 2 Type 753; I-band.

Comment: Built at Wuhan shipyard, Wuchang and commissioned in 1986. North Sea Fleet and seen regularly in Sea of Japan and East China Sea.

BEIDAO 900 *4/2008** / 1335671

2 KAN CLASS (AGOR)

101 **102**

Displacement, tons: 1,100 full load
Dimensions, feet (metres): 225 × 22.5 × 9 *(68.6 × 6.9 × 2.7)*
Main machinery: 2 diesels; 2 shafts
Speed, knots: 18
Complement: 150
Radars: Navigation: Fin Curve; I-band.

Comment: Details given are for *102* which is believed built in 1985–87, possibly at Shanghai. Large open stern area. Aft main deck area covered and may have cable reel system. *101* is similar but slightly larger and may have been built in 1965 as an ASR. Operate in East China Sea and Sea of Japan.

KAN 101 *5/2000, van Ginderen Collection* / 0103684

1 SHUGUANG CLASS (ex-T 43) (AGOR/AGS)

203

Displacement, tons: 500 standard; 570 full load
Dimensions, feet (metres): 190.3 × 28.9 × 11.5 *(58 × 8.8 × 3.5)*
Main machinery: 2 PRC/Kolomna Type 9-D-8 diesels; 2,000 hp(m) *(1.47 MW)* sustained; 2 shafts
Speed, knots: 15
Range, n miles: 5,300 at 8 kt
Complement: 55-60

Comment: Converted from ex-Soviet T 43 minesweeper in late 1960s. Painted white. This last survivor is based in the North Sea Fleet.

SHUGUANG 203 *10/1997, van Ginderen Collection* / 0012980

1 BIN HAI CLASS (AGOR)

HAI 521

Displacement, tons: 550 full load
Dimensions, feet (metres): 164 × 32.8 × 11.5 *(50 × 10 × 3.5)*
Main machinery: 2 Niigata Type 6M26KHHS diesels; 1,600 hp(m) *(1.18 MW)*; 2 shafts; bow thruster
Speed, knots: 14. **Range, n miles**: 5,000 at 11 kt
Complement: 15 (7 officers) plus 25 scientists
Radars: Navigation: Japanese AR-M31; I-band.

Comment: A purpose-built research ship built by Niigata Engineering Co, Niigata (Japan) in 1974–75. Launched 10 March 1975. Commissioned July 1975. First operated by the China National Machinery Export-Import Corporation on oceanographic duties. Operates on East and South China research projects but based in North Sea Fleet. For small vessel, has cruiser stern with raked bow and small funnel well aft. Capability to operate single DSRV and the Chinese Navy has a number of Japanese-built KSWB-300 submersibles. Painted white. This ship may belong to the China Marine Oil Company and further vessels may be in service.

1 GANZHU CLASS (AGS)

420

Displacement, tons: 1,000 full load
Dimensions, feet (metres): 213.2 × 29.5 × 9.7 *(65 × 9 × 3)*
Main machinery: 4 diesels; 4,400 hp(m) *(3.23 MW)*; 2 shafts
Speed, knots: 20
Complement: 125
Guns: 4—37 mm/63 (2 twin); 8—14.5 mm (4 twin).

Comment: Built at Zhujiang in 1973–75. Long refit in 1996 for up to two years.

GANZHU 420 *8/1998* / 0056802

5 YENLAI CLASS (AGS)

226–227 **420** **427** **943**

Displacement, tons: 1,040 full load
Dimensions, feet (metres): 241.8 × 32.1 × 9.7 *(73.7 × 9.8 × 3)*
Main machinery: 2 PRC/Kolomna Type 9-D-8 diesels; 2,000 hp(m) *(1.47 MW)* sustained; 2 shafts
Speed, knots: 16
Range, n miles: 4,000 at 14 kt
Complement: 25
Guns: 4 China 37 mm/63 (2 twin). 4—25 mm/80 (2 twin).
Radars: Navigation: Fin Curve; I-band.

Comment: Built at Zhonghua Shipyard, Shanghai in early 1970s. Carries four survey motor boats.

YENLAI 226 *6/2005, Hachiro Nakai* / 1153052

1 SPACE EVENT SHIP (AGMH)

YUAN WANG 3

Displacement, tons: 16,790 full load
Dimensions, feet (metres): 590.5 × 72.8 × 26.2 *(180 × 22.2 × 8.0)*
Main machinery: 1 diesel; 1 shaft
Speed, knots: 20. **Range, n miles**: 18,000 at 12 kt
Complement: 470
Helicopters: Platform for 1 medium.

Comment: A second-generation space tracking ship launched in 1994 and commissioned in April 1995. Equipped with E/F-band tracking radar. The ship is normally positioned in the South Atlantic off the West African coast for ShenZhou flight missions.

YUAN WANG 3 *6/2008** / 1335673

1 SPACE EVENT SHIP (AGMH)

YUAN WANG 4

Displacement, tons: 13,000 full load
Dimensions, feet (metres): 512.5 × 67.6 × 25.4 *(156.2 × 20.6 × 7.75)*
Main machinery: 2 diesels; 2 shafts
Speed, knots: 20
Range, n miles: 18,000 at 12 kt
Complement: 200
Helicopters: 1 medium.

Comment: Ex-survey ship *(Xiangyanghong 10)* originally constructed in the late 1970s. Converted into a space tracking ship and renamed *Yuan Wang 4* in 1998 to support manned space flight missions, mainly for spacecraft tracking and communications relay roles. Normally positioned in the South Pacific for spacecraft missions.

YUAN WANG 4 *6/2008** / 1335672

2 SPACE EVENT SHIPS (AGMH)

YUAN WANG 5 **YUAN WANG 6**

Measurement, tons: 24,966 dwt
Dimensions, feet (metres): 729.0 × 82.7 × 26.9 *(222.2 × 25.2 × 8.2)*
Main machinery: To be announced
Speed, knots: 20
Range, n miles: 20,000 at 12 kt
Complement: To be announced
Helicopters: 1 medium.

Comment: Two new third-generation space tracking ships built at Jiangnan Shipyard in Shanghai. *Yuan Wang 5* was launched on 15 September 2006 and started undergoing sea trials in early 2007. The ship entered service in early 2008. The second ship was originally named *Yuan Wang 6* but may be allocated another number to reflect replacement of earlier ships. *Yuan Wang 6* reportedly differs from *Yuan Wang 5* in that it includes a large mission control hall occupying two decks. This ship entered service in late 2008.

YUAN WANG 5 *2/2008*, Ships of the World* / 1335657

1 RESEARCH SHIP (AGE)

HAIYANG 20

Displacement, tons: To be announced
Dimensions, feet (metres): 426.5 × ? × ? *(130.0 × ? × ?)*
Main machinery: To be announced
Speed, knots: To be announced
Complement: To be announced
Radars: To be announced.
Helicopters: 1 medium.

Comment: Naval manned research ship first reported in 2005. The details and capabilities of the ship are not yet known.

HAIYANG 20 *12/2005, Massimo Annati* / 1153098

1 SURVEY SHIP (AGS)

852

Displacement, tons: To be announced
Dimensions, feet (metres): 367.4 × ? × ? *(112.0 × ? × ?)*
Main machinery: To be announced
Speed, knots: To be announced
Complement: To be announced
Radars: To be announced.

Comment: Naval manned hydrographic ship first reported in 2005. The details and capabilities of the ship are not yet known.

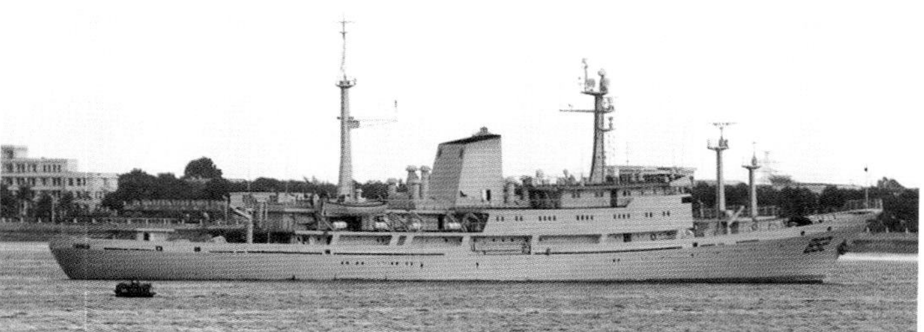

SURVEY SHIP 852 *8/2007* / 1166859

DEEP SUBMERGENCE VEHICLES

0 + 1 RESCUE SUBMERSIBLE

LR 7

Displacement, tons: 26.5
Dimensions, feet (metres): 31.5 × 10.5 × 11.1 *(9.6 × 3.2 × 3.4)*
Main machinery: 2 electric motors; 26.8 hp *(20 kW)*; 4 tiltable side thrusters; 16 hp *(12 kW)*
Speed, knots: 3
Complement: 2 pilots and 1 rescue chamber operator

Comment: Powered by two external lead-acid battery pods, the Perry Slingsby LR 7 is a development of the LR 5 rescue submersible, originally built for North Sea commercial operations and subsequently purchased by the Royal Navy for submarine rescue operations. Capable of operating down to 500 m depth, it can be deployed anywhere in the world and operated from the deck of any suitable mother ship. Its role is to rescue up to 18 survivors at a time from a disabled submarine on the seabed and bring them back to the surface. This can be done at normal atmospheric pressure and at increased pressue up to 5 bar. Mating with the disabled submarine can be achieved at up to 60° bow up. LR 7 is complemented by an ROV, Scorpio 45, which is attached to a 1,000 m umbilical. This is used to locate the disabled submarine, clear obstructions from the escape hatches and replenish life support stores. Following tests in Scotland, LR 7 is due to enter service in the Chinese Navy in 2009.

2 DSRV (SALVAGE SUBMARINES) (DSRV)

Displacement, tons: 35 full load
Dimensions, feet (metres): 48.9 × 8.5 × 8.5 *(14.9 × 2.6 × 2.6)*
Main machinery: 2 silver-zinc batteries; 1 mortar; 1 shaft
Speed, knots: 4. **Range, n miles**: 40 at 2 kt
Complement: 3

Comment: First tested in 1986 and can be carried on large salvage ships. Capable of 'wet' rescue at 200 m and of diving to 600 m. Capacity for six survivors. Underwater TV, high-frequency active sonar and a manipulator arm are all fitted. Life support duration is 1,728 man-hours. An upgrade of submarine rescue capabilities may be planned following attendance at international conferences in 2001 and talks with industry. Up to three modern DSRV may be required.

DSRV *1991, CSSC* / 0056786

TRAINING SHIPS

1 DAXIN CLASS (AXH)

Name	*No*	*Builders*	*Launched*	*Commissioned*
ZHENGHE	81	Qiuxin, Shanghai	12 July 1986	27 Apr 1987

Displacement, tons: 5,470 full load
Dimensions, feet (metres): 426.5 × 52.5 × 15.7 *(130.0 × 16.0 × 4.8)*
Main machinery: 2 SEMT Pielstick 6PC2-5L diesels; 7,800 hp(m) *(5.73 MW)*; 2 shafts
Speed, knots: 15
Range, n miles: 5,000 at 15 kt
Complement: 170 plus 30 instructors plus 200 Midshipmen
Guns: 4 China 57 mm/70 (2 twin). 4—30 mm AK 230 (2 twin). 4—12.7 mm MGs.
A/S mortars: 2 FQF 2500 fixed 12-tubed launchers; range 1,200 m; warhead 34 kg.
Radars: Air/surface search: Eye Shield; E-band.
Surface search: China Type 756; I-band.
Navigation: Racal Decca 1290; I-band.
Fire control: Round Ball; I-band.
Sonars: Echo Type 5; hull-mounted; active; high frequency.
Helicopters: Platform only.

Comment: Resembles a small cruise liner. Subordinate to the Naval Academy and replaced *Huian*. Based in the North Sea Fleet. A similar ship sold to Algeria in 2006.

ZHENGHE *9/2000, B Lemachko* / 0126258

1 SHICHANG CLASS (HSS/AHH)

Name	*No*	*Builders*	*Launched*	*Commissioned*
SHICHANG	82	Qiuxin, Shanghai	Apr 1996	27 Jan 1997

Displacement, tons: 10,000 full load
Dimensions, feet (metres): 393.7 × 59.1 × 23 *(120 × 18 × 7)*
Main machinery: 2 diesels; 2 shafts
Speed, knots: 17.5
Range, n miles: 8,000 at 17 kt
Complement: 170 plus 200 trainees
Military lift: 300 containers
Helicopters: 2 Zhi-9A Haitun.

Comment: China's first air training ship described officially as a defence mobilisation vessel which can be used for civilian freight, for helicopter or navigation training, or as a hospital ship. The vessel looks like a scaled down version of the UK *Argus* with the bridge superstructure forward and an after funnel on the starboard side of the flightdeck. There are two landing spots. Based in the South Sea Fleet.

SHICHANG *5/1998, Sattler/Steele* / 0017738

SHICHANG *5/1998, RAN* / 0017739

AUXILIARIES

Notes: (1) There is a water-tanker with similar characteristics to the Fuzhou class with pennant number *1101*.
(2) There are two water tankers of unknown dimensions with pennant numbers *1102* and *1104*.
(3) There are two 70 m Kansha class salvage ships which carry French-supplied 7 m salvage submersibles capable of operating to depths of 300 m.
(4) There are two tankers *637* and *960*. Both of unknown type.

2 FUQING CLASS (REPLENISHMENT SHIPS) (AORH)

HONGZHU (ex-*Taicang*) 881 (ex-575) **FENGCANG** (ex-*Dongyun*) 882 (ex-615)

Displacement, tons: 7,500 standard; 21,750 full load
Dimensions, feet (metres): 552 × 71.5 × 30.8 *(168.2 × 21.8 × 9.4)*
Main machinery: 1 Sulzer 8RL B66 diesel; 15,000 hp(m) *(11 MW)* sustained; 1 shaft
Speed, knots: 18
Range, n miles: 18,000 at 14 kt
Complement: 130 (24 officers)
Cargo capacity: 10,550 tons fuel; 1,000 tons dieso; 200 tons feed water; 200 tons drinking water; 4 small cranes
Guns: 8—37 mm (4 twin) (fitted for but not with).
Radars: Navigation: Fin Curve or Racal Decca 1290; I-band.
Helicopters: Platform for 1 medium.

Comment: Operational in late 1979. This is the first class of ships built for underway replenishment in the Chinese Navy. Helicopter platform but no hangar. Both built at Dalian. Two liquid replenishment positions each side with one solid replenishment position each side by the funnel. A third of the class *Hongcang* (X 950) was converted to merchant use in 1989 and renamed *Hai Lang*, registered at Dalian. A fourth (X 350) was sold to Pakistan in 1987. 882 based in the North and 881 in the East. *Fengcang* appears to have a command role.

HONGZHU *10/2007, Chris Sattler* / 1166841

FENGCANG *3/2004, L-G Nilsson* / 1042154

1 NANYUN CLASS (REPLENISHMENT SHIP) (AORH)

Name	*No*	*Builders*	*Launched*	*Commissioned*
QINGHAI HU (ex-*Nancang*, ex-*Vladimir Peregudov*)	885 (ex-953)	Kherson/Dalian	Apr 1992	2 June 1996

Displacement, tons: 37,000 full load
Measurement, tons: 28,750 dwt
Dimensions, feet (metres): 586.9 × 83 × 36.1 *(178.9 × 25.3 × 11)*
Main machinery: 1 B&W diesel; 11,600 hp(m) *(8.53 MW)*; 1 shaft
Speed, knots: 16
Complement: 125
Cargo capacity: 9,630 tons fuel
Helicopters: 1 Super Frelon.

Comment: Sometimes referred to as Fusu class. One of a class of 11 built at Kherson Shipyard, Crimea. Laid down in January 1989. Sailed from Ukraine to Dalian Shipyard in 1993. Completed fitting out in China and joined the South Sea Fleet. RAS rigs on both sides and stern refuelling. Similar to Indian *Jyoti* but with better helicopter facilities.

QINGHAI HU (old number) *8/2000, Robert Pabst* / 0103677

QINGHAI HU *6/2005, A Sheldon-Duplaix* / 1153101

2 FUCHI CLASS (REPLENISHMENT SHIPS) (AORH)

Name	*No*	*Builders*	*Laid down*	*Launched*	*Commissioned*
QIANDAO HU (ex-*Fuchi*)	886	Hudong Shipyard, Shanghai	2002	29 Mar 2003	30 Apr 2004
WEISHAN HU	887	Guangzou Shipyard	–	June 2003	2004

Displacement, tons: 23,000 full load
Dimensions, feet (metres): 585.6 × 81.4 × 28.5 *(178.5 × 24.8 × 8.7)*
Main machinery: 2 SEMT-Pielstick diesels; 24,000 hp *(17.9 MW)*; 2 shafts
Speed, knots: 19
Range, n miles: 10,000 at 14 kt
Complement: 130
Cargo capacity: 10,500 tons fuel, 250 tons of water, 680 tons of ammunition and stores
Guns: 8—37 mm (4 twin).
Radars: To be announced.
Helicopters: Platform for 1 medium.

Comment: Ships which bear a marked resemblance to Type R22T Similan class tanker built for Thailand in 1996. Fitted with two RAS stations (one liquids, one solids) on each side. Basing: 886 in the East Sea Fleet and 887 in the South Sea Fleet.

QIANDAO HU *2/2006, Lemachko Collection* / 1166766

WEISHAN HU *9/2007, R G Sharpe* / 1166779

6 QIONGSHA CLASS (4 AP + 2 AH)

Y 830–Y 835

Displacement, tons: 2,150 full load
Dimensions, feet (metres): 282.1 × 44.3 × 13.1 *(86 × 13.5 × 4)*
Main machinery: 3 SKL 8 NVD 48 A-2U diesels; 3,960 hp(m) *(2.91 MW)* sustained; 3 shafts
Speed, knots: 16
Complement: 59
Military lift: 400 troops; 350 tons cargo
Guns: 8 China 14.5 mm/93 (4 twin); 600 rds/min to 7 km *(3.8 n miles)*.
Radars: Navigation: Fin Curve; I-band.

Comment: Personnel attack transports begun about 1980. Previous numbers of this class were overestimated. All South Sea Fleet. Has four sets of davits, light cargo booms serving forward and aft. No helicopter pad. Twin funnels. Carries a number of LCAs. *Y 832* and *Y 833* converted to Hospital Ships (AH) and painted white.

QIONGSHA 832 *6/2008** / 1335698

2 DADONG (TYPE 946) CLASS (SALVAGE SHIPS) (ARS)

304

Displacement, tons: 1,500 full load
Dimensions, feet (metres): 269 × 36.1 × 8.9 *(82 × 11 × 2.7)*
Main machinery: 2 diesels; 7,400 hp(m) *(5.44 MW)*; 2 shafts
Speed, knots: 18
Complement: 150
Guns: 4—25 mm/80 (2 twin).
Radars: Navigation: Type 756; F-band.

Comment: Built at Hudong Shipyard, Shanghai. Has a large and conspicuous crane aft. Principal role is wreck location and salvage. Based in the East Sea Fleet.

3 DAJIANG (TYPE 925) CLASS (SUBMARINE SUPPORT SHIPS) (ASRH)

CHANGXINGDAO 861 (ex-J 121) **YONGXINGDAO** 863 (ex-J 506)
CHONGMINGDAO 862 (ex-J 302)

Displacement, tons: 11,975 full load
Dimensions, feet (metres): 512.5 × 67.6 × 22.3 *(156.2 × 20.6 × 6.8)*
Main machinery: 2 MAN K9Z60/105E diesels; 9,000 hp(m) *(6.6 MW)*; 2 shafts
Speed, knots: 20
Complement: 308
Guns: Light MGs. Can carry 6—37 mm (3 twin).
Radars: Surface search: Eye Shield; E-band.
Navigation: 2 Fin Curve; I-band.
Helicopters: 2 Aerospatiale SA 321G Super Frelon.

Comment: Submarine support and salvage ships built at Shanghai. First launched in mid-1973, operational in 1976. *Yongxingdao* has a smoke deflector on funnel. Provision for DSRV on forward well-deck aft of launching crane. Foremast on *Yongxingdao* suggests long-range communications capability, possibly for submarine command. Basing: 861 in the North Sea Fleet; 862 in the East Sea Fleet; 863 in the South Sea Fleet.

CHANGXINGDAO *6/2007* / 1166858

5 DALANG (TYPE 922 II/III) CLASS (SUBMARINE SUPPORT SHIPS) (ASL)

305 (ex-503) **122** **332** **138**

Displacement, tons: 3,700 standard; 4,200 full load
Dimensions, feet (metres): 367 × 47.9 × 14.1 *(111.9 × 14.6 × 4.3)*
Main machinery: 2 diesels; 4,000 hp(m) *(2.94 MW)*; 2 shafts
Speed, knots: 16
Range, n miles: 8,000 at 14 kt
Complement: 180
Guns: 2—25 mm/80 (1 twin) or 2—14.5 mm/93 (1 twin).
Radars: Navigation: Fin Curve; I-band.

Comment: Construction of the first Type 922-II class *305* (ex-*503*) began at Guangzhou Shipyard in September 1971. It was commissioned in November 1975. As a result of experience gained, development of an improved Type 922-III version began in 1978. Construction of the first of these ships *(122)* began in December 1982 at Wuchang Shipyard, Wuhan, and the ship later commissioned in 1986. Subsequently, three further modified ships were built: *332* (1989), *138* (1992) and *510* (1995). These modifications include changes to upper deck design and the possible incorporation of a decompression chamber.

DALANG 332 *5/2000, M Declerck* / 0103679

2 DAZHOU (TYPE 946) CLASS (SUBMARINE TENDERS) (ASL)

502 **137** (ex-504)

Displacement, tons: 1,100 full load
Dimensions, feet (metres): 259.2 × 31.2 × 8.5 *(79 × 9.5 × 2.6)*
Main machinery: 2 diesels; 2 shafts
Speed, knots: 18
Complement: 130
Guns: 2 China 37 mm/63 (twin). 4—14.5 mm/93 (2 twin).
Radars: Navigation: Fin Curve; I-band.

Comment: The first, *502*, commissioned in 1977; the second in 1978. Both built at Guangzhou Shipyard. *502* based in the South Sea Fleet and *137* in the North Sea Fleet. Both have been used as AGIs.

DAZHOU 502 *6/2008** / 1335697

3 YANTAI CLASS (SUPPLY SHIPS) (AK)

800 **801** **938**

Displacement, tons: 3,330 full load
Dimensions, feet (metres): 255.9 × 37.7 × 9.8 *(78.0 × 11.5 × 3.0)*
Main machinery: 2 diesels; 9,600 hp(m) *(7.06 MW)*; 2 shafts
Speed, knots: 17
Range, n miles: 3,000 at 16 kt
Complement: 100
Guns: 2 China 37 mm/63 (twin).
Radars: Navigation: Type 756; I-band.

Comment: First seen in 1992. Appears to be based on a landing ship design but without a bow door. Fitted with cargo-handling cranes fore and aft. A ship with pennant number 938 has also been reported unloading missile containers. It is not known whether this is an additional ship or a change of pennant number. Based in South Sea Fleet.

YANTAI 938 *6/2007* / 1166855

2 DAYUN (TYPE 904) CLASS SUPPLY SHIPS (AKH)

883 (ex-951) **884** (ex-952)

Displacement, tons: 8,500 standard; 10,975 full load
Dimensions, feet (metres): 407.5 × 42 × 12.5 *(124.2 × 12.8 × 3.8)*
Main machinery: 2 diesels; 9,000 hp(m) *(6.6 MW)*; 2 shafts
Speed, knots: 22
Complement: 240
Guns: 4—37 mm/63 (2 twin). 4—25 mm/80 (2 twin).
Radars: Navigation: 2 Type 756; I-band.
Helicopters: 2 SA 321 Super Frelon.

Comment: First of class completed at Hudong Shipyard in March 1992, second in August 1992. Four landing craft are embarked. Both based in South Sea Fleet. A reported third of class was in fact the first of the larger Nanyun class. Pennant numbers may have changed.

DAYUN CLASS *6/2005, A Sheldon-Duplaix* / 1153100

13 DANLIN CLASS SUPPLY SHIPS (AK/AOT)

531 **592** **794** **834** **972** +3
591 **594** **827** **835** **975**

Displacement, tons: 1,290 full load
Dimensions, feet (metres): 198.5 × 29.5 × 13.1 *(60.5 × 9 × 4)*
Main machinery: 1 USSR/PRC Type 6DRN 30/50 diesel; 750 hp(m) *(551 kW)*; 1 shaft
Speed, knots: 15
Complement: 35
Cargo capacity: 750–800 tons
Guns: 4—25 mm/80 (2 twin). 4—14.5 mm (2 twin).
Radars: Navigation: Fin Curve or Skin Head; I-band.

Comment: Built in China in early 1960–62. The six AKs have refrigerated stores capability and serve in the South Sea Fleet. The seven AOTs are split between the Fleets. Not all are armed.

DANLIN 794 *5/1992, Henry Dodds* / 0056790

13 DANDAO CLASS (AK/AOT)

201	485	599	757	759	802	841
484	529	629	758	791	803	

Displacement, tons: 1,600 full load
Dimensions, feet (metres): 215.6 × 41 × 13 *(65.7 × 12.5 × 4)*
Main machinery: 1 diesel; 1 shaft
Speed, knots: 12
Complement: 40
Guns: 4 China 37 mm/63 (2 twin). 4 China 14.5 mm/93 (2 twin).
Radars: Navigation: Fin Curve; I-band.

Comment: Built in the late 1970s. Similar to the Danlin class. Two in the North and one in the East Sea Fleet.

DANDAO 529 — *9/2007* / 1335667

6 HONGQI CLASS (AK)

443 528 755 756 771 836

Displacement, tons: 1,950 full load
Dimensions, feet (metres): 203.4 × 39.4 × 14.4 *(62 × 12 × 4.4)*
Main machinery: 1 diesel; 1 shaft
Speed, knots: 14. **Range, n miles:** 2,500 at 11 kt
Complement: 35
Guns: 4 China 25/80 (2 twin).

Comment: Used to support offshore military garrisons. A further ship, L 202, appears to be similar but carries no armament. Others of this type in civilian use. Three in the North, two in the East Sea Fleet.

HONGQI 755 — *3/2003, Bob Fildes* / 0569175

4 SUPPLY TANKERS (AOL)

565 631 633 641

Displacement, tons: To be announced
Dimensions, feet (metres): To be announced
Main machinery: To be announced
Speed, knots: To be announced
Complement: To be announced
Radars: To be announced.

Comment: Two supply tankers of an unknown type.

AOL 641 — *10/2008*, Chris Sattler* / 1335668

2 SHENGLI CLASS (AOT)

620 621

Displacement, tons: 3,300 standard; 4,950 full load
Dimensions, feet (metres): 331.4 × 45.3 × 18 *(101 × 13.8 × 5.5)*
Main machinery: 1 6 ESDZ 43/82B diesel; 2,600 hp(m) *(1.91 MW)*; 1 shaft
Speed, knots: 14. **Range, n miles:** 2,400 at 11 kt
Complement: 48
Cargo capacity: 3,400 tons dieso
Guns: 2—37 mm/63 (twin). 4—25 mm/80 (2 twin).
Radars: Navigation: Fin Curve; I-band.

Comment: Built at Hudong SY, Shanghai in late 1970s. Others of the class in commercial service.

9 LEIZHOU CLASS (AWT/AOT)

412 555 558 736 755 792 793 823 826

Displacement, tons: 900 full load
Dimensions, feet (metres): 173.9 × 32.2 × 10.5 *(53 × 9.8 × 3.2)*
Main machinery: 1 diesel; 500 hp(m) *(367 kW)*; 1 shaft
Speed, knots: 12
Range, n miles: 1,200 at 10 kt
Complement: 25–30
Cargo capacity: 450 tons
Guns: 4—14.5 mm/93 (2 twin).
Radars: 2 navigation; I-band.

Comment: Built in late 1960s at Qingdao and Wudong. Split between the Fleets. Some have been converted to carry water, others carry oil. Many deleted or in civilian use.

LEIZHOU 755 — *10/2006, E & M Laursen* / 1164863

23 FULIN CLASS (REPLENISHMENT SHIPS) (AOT)

560	583	607	626	630	634	639	924
563	589	609	628	632	635	922	941
582	606	623	629	633	638	923	

Displacement, tons: 2,300 standard
Dimensions, feet (metres): 216.5 × 42.6 × 13.1 *(66 × 13 × 4)*
Main machinery: 1 diesel; 600 hp(m) *(441 kW)*; 1 shaft
Speed, knots: 10
Range, n miles: 1,500 at 8 kt
Complement: 30
Guns: 4—14.5 mm/93 (2 twin).
Radars: Navigation: Fin Curve; I-band.

Comment: A total of 20 of these ships built at Hudong, Shanghai, beginning in 1972. *630, 632, 633* and *635* are to a slightly modified design. Naval ships painted grey. Many others of the class are civilian but may carry pennant numbers.

FULIN 639 — *6/2007* / 1166853

1 + (1) ANWEI (TYPE 920) CLASS (HOSPITAL SHIP) (AHH)

Name	*No*	*Builders*	*Laid down*	*Launched*	*Commissioned*
–	866	Guangzhou Shipyard International	2006	29 Aug 2007	2008

Displacement, tons: 23,000 full load
Dimensions, feet (metres): 590.5 × 80.7 × 29.5 *(180 × 24.6 × 9)*
Main machinery: 2 diesels; 2 shafts
Speed, knots: 19
Range, n miles: 10,000 at 14 kt
Complement: 130
Radars: To be announced.
Helicopters: 1 medium.

Comment: The first purpose-built hospital ship for the Chinese Navy was launched in August 2007 and commissioned in 2008. The design seems to be based on the Fuchi class replenishment ships. Details of the ship's medical facilities have not yet been made available but the ship is fitted with a flight deck and hangar capable of operating a medium size helicopter. Based in the South Sea Fleet. A second ship is expected.

ANWEI CLASS — *8/2007* / 1166856

3 JINYOU CLASS (AOT)

622 625 675

Displacement, tons: 4,800 full load
Dimensions, feet (metres): 324.8 × 104.3 × 187.0 *(99.0 × 31.8 × 5.7)*
Main machinery: 1 SEMT-Pielstick 8PC2.2L diesel; 3,000 hp *(2.24 MW)*; 1 shaft
Speed, knots: 15. **Range, n miles:** 4,000 at 10 kt
Complement: 40
Radars: Navigation: I-band.

Comment: Built by Kanashashi Shipyard, Japan and entered service 1989–90.

27 FUZHOU CLASS (AOT/AWT)

570	**608**	**903**	**909**	**920**	**933**	**939**
573	**629**	**904**	**910**	**926**	**935**	**940**
580	**637**	**906**	**912**	**927**	**937**	**945**
581	**644**	**907**	**913**	**930**	**938**	

Displacement, tons: 2,100 full load
Dimensions, feet (metres): 208.3 × 41.3 × 12.5 *(63.5 × 12.6 × 3.8)*
Main machinery: 1 diesel; 600 hp(m) *(441 kW)*; 1 shaft
Speed, knots: 11
Complement: 35
Cargo capacity: 600 tons
Guns: 4—25 mm/80 (2 twin). 4—14.5 mm/93 (2 twin).
Radars: Navigation: Fin Curve; I-band.

Comment: Built 1964–70. Transport ships for liquids, 18 for oil and nine for water.

FUZHOU 629 *6/2007* / 1166852

23 GUANGZHOU CLASS (AOTL/AWTL)

555 558 590 593 924 645 646 647 +15

Displacement, tons: 530 full load
Dimensions, feet (metres): 160.8 × 24.6 × 9.8 *(49 × 7.5 × 3)*
Main machinery: 1 diesel; 1 shaft
Speed, knots: 10
Complement: 19
Guns: 4—14.5 mm/93 (2 twin).

Comment: Coastal tankers built in the 1970s and 1980s. At least 18 of the class are civilian but may carry pennant numbers.

GUANGZHOU 645 *10/2008*, Chris Sattler* / 1335669

9 YANNAN CLASS (BUOY TENDERS) (ABU)

124 263 463 982 983 B-21 B-22 B-24 B-25

Displacement, tons: 1,750 standard
Dimensions, feet (metres): 237.2 × 38.7 × 13.1 *(72.3 × 11.8 × 4)*
Main machinery: 2 diesels; 2,640 hp(m) *(1.94 MW)*; 2 shafts
Speed, knots: 12
Complement: 95
Radars: Navigation: Fin Curve; I-band.

Comment: Built 1978–79; commissioned 1980. Ships with 'B' pennant numbers are probably in Coast Guard service.

YANNAN B-25 *3/2004, L-G Nilsson* / 1042153

9 YEN PAI CLASS (ADG)

202 203 735 736 745 746 860 863 864

Displacement, tons: 746 standard
Dimensions, feet (metres): 213.3 × 29.5 × 8.5 *(65 × 9 × 2.6)*
Main machinery: Diesel-electric; 2 12VE 230ZC diesels; 2,200 hp(m) *(1.62 MW)*; 2 ZDH-99/57 motors; 2 shafts
Speed, knots: 16
Range, n miles: 800 at 15 kt
Complement: 55
Guns: 4—37 mm/63 (2 twin). 4—25 mm/80 (2 twin).
Radars: Navigation: Type 756; I-band.

Comment: Enlarged version of T 43 MSF with larger bridge and funnel amidships. Reels on quarterdeck for degaussing function. Not all the guns are embarked.

YEN PAI 864 *10/2008*, Chris Sattler* / 1335666

1 DANYAO CLASS (SUPPORT SHIP) (AF)

FUXIAN HU 888

Displacement, tons: 15,000 full load
Dimensions, feet (metres): 498.7 × 62.3 × ? *(152 × 19 × ?)*
Main machinery: 2 SEMT Pielstick 16PC V 400 diesels; 24,000 hp *(17.9 MW)*; 2 shafts
Speed, knots: To be announced
Complement: To be announced
Guns: 2—37 mm (twin).
Helicopters: Platform for one medium.

Comment: Support ship under construction at Guangzhou, and launched on 28 December 2006. The ship is equipped with two pairs of davits, capable of handling small landing craft, and a flight deck for medium helicopters. Potential roles for the ship include resupply of the Spratly and Paracel Islands in the South China Sea. Following sea trials in 2007, the ship is reported to have been commissioned in late 2007. Based in the South Sea Fleet.

FUXIAN HU *6/2008*, Ships of the World* / 1335654

1 TYPE 648 SUBMARINE TENDER (ASL)

911

Displacement, tons: 3,500 standard; 4,000 full load
Dimensions, feet (metres): 282.1 × 45.9 × 13.1 *(86.0 × 14.0 × 4.0)*
Main machinery: 2 diesels; 2 shafts
Speed, knots: 16
Guns: 8—25 mm (4 twin).
Radars: Navigation: I-band.
Helicopters: Platform for one medium.

Comment: The first and only hull of its class was commissioned in 1985. The role of the ship is to provide conventional submarines with repair and maintenance facilities in addition to fuel and water. Based in the East Sea Fleet.

TYPE 648 911 *10/2008*, Chris Sattler* / 1335670

1 DACHOU CLASS (YPT)

Name	*No*	*Builders*	*Commissioned*
–	846	Wuzhou Shipyard	Nov 2006

Displacement, tons: To be announced
Dimensions, feet (metres): 219.8 × 32.8 × ? *(67.0 × 10.0 × ?)*
Main machinery: To be announced
Speed, knots: To be announced
Complement: To be announced
Guns: To be announced.
Countermeasures: To be announced.
Combat data systems: To be announced.
Radars: To be announced.
Sonars: To be announced.

Comment: A new class of torpedo recovery vessel which appears very similar in design to that of the Wochi class mine countermeasures vessels on which outline details are based. Based at Zhanjiang, South Sea Fleet.

DACHOU 846 — *6/2008*, Ships of the World* / 1335653

ICEBREAKERS

1 YANBING (MOD YANHA) CLASS (AGB/AGI)

723

Displacement, tons: 4,420 full load
Dimensions, feet (metres): 334.6 × 56 × 19.5 *(102 × 17.1 × 5.9)*
Main machinery: Diesel-electric; 2 diesel generators; 2 motors; 2 shafts
Speed, knots: 17
Complement: 95
Guns: 8—37 mm/63 Type 61/74 (4 twin).
Radars: Navigation: 2 Fin Curve; I-band.

Comment: Enlarged version of Yanha class icebreaker, built in 1982, with greater displacement, longer and wider hull, added deck level and curved upper funnel. In October 1990, painted white while operating in Sea of Japan. Used as an AGI in the North Sea Fleet.

YANBING 723 — *12/2001, Ships of the World* / 0529115

3 YANHA CLASS (AGB/AGI)

519 **721** **722**

Displacement, tons: 3,200 full load
Dimensions, feet (metres): 290 × 53 × 17 *(88.4 × 16.2 × 5.2)*
Main machinery: Diesel-electric; 2 diesel generators; 1 motor; 1 shaft
Speed, knots: 17.5
Complement: 90
Guns: 8—37 mm/63 Type 61/74 (4 twin). 4—25 mm/80 Type 61.
Radars: Navigation: Fin Curve; I-band.

Comment: *721* and *722* built in 1969–70. *519* commissioned in 1989. Used as AGIs in the North Sea Fleet.

519 — *10/1991, G Jacobs* / 0505974

TUGS

Notes: (1) The vessels below represent a cross-section of the craft available.
(2) There is a salvage ship of unknown type. The pennant number is 181.

SALVAGE VESSEL — *12/2007, Chris Sattler* / 1170055

4 TUZHONG CLASS (ATF)

154 **710** **830** **890**

Displacement, tons: 3,600 full load
Dimensions, feet (metres): 278.5 × 46 × 18 *(84.9 × 14 × 5.5)*
Main machinery: 2 10 ESDZ 43/82B diesels; 8,600 hp(m) *(6.32 MW)*; 2 shafts
Speed, knots: 18.5
Complement: 120
Radars: Navigation: Fin Curve; I-band.

Comment: Built in late 1970s. Can be fitted with twin 37 mm AA armament and at least one of the class *(710)* has been fitted with a Square Tie radar. 35 ton towing winch. One in each Fleet and one in reserve.

TUZHONG — *11/1996, A Sharma* / 0012228

1 DAOZHA CLASS (ATF)

Displacement, tons: 4,000 full load
Dimensions, feet (metres): 275.6 × 41.3 × 17.7 *(84 × 12.6 × 5.4)*
Main machinery: 2 diesels; 8,600 hp(m) *(6.32 MW)*; 2 shafts
Speed, knots: 18
Complement: 125

Comment: Built in 1993–94 probably as a follow-on to the Tuzhong class. Based in South Sea Fleet.

DAOZHA — *9/1993, Hachiro Nakai* / 0506142

10 HUJIU CLASS (ATF)

147	**622**	**717**	**842**	**875**
155	**711**	**837**	**843**	**877**

Displacement, tons: 1,470 full load
Dimensions, feet (metres): 197.5 × 38.1 × 14.4 *(60.2 × 11.6 × 4.4)*
Main machinery: 2 LVP 24 diesels; 1,800 hp(m) *(1.32 MW)*; 2 shafts
Speed, knots: 15
Range, n miles: 7,200 at 14 kt
Complement: 56
Radars: Navigation: Fin Curve or Type 756; I-band.

Comment: Built at Wuhu in 1980s. One sold to Bangladesh in 1984 and a second in 1995. Three based in the North and East, three in the South Sea Fleet.

HUJIU 877 — *10/2006, E & M Laursen* / 1164866

17 GROMOVOY CLASS (ATF)

149	**167**	**684**	**809**	**814**	**824**
156	**680**	**716**	**811**	**817**	**827**
166	**683**	**802**	**813**	**822**	

Displacement, tons: 795 standard; 890 full load
Dimensions, feet (metres): 149.9 × 31.2 × 15.1 *(45.7 × 9.5 × 4.6)*
Main machinery: 2 diesels; 1,300 hp(m) *(956 kW)*; 2 shafts
Speed, knots: 11. **Range, n miles:** 7,000 at 7 kt
Complement: 25-30 (varies)
Guns: 4—14.5 mm (2 twin) or 12.7 mm (2 twin) MGs.
Radars: Navigation: Fin Curve or OKI X-NE-12 (Japanese); I-band.

Comment: Built at Luda Shipyard and Shanghai International, 1958–62. Four in North Sea Fleet, nine in East Sea Fleet and four in South Sea Fleet.

GROMOVOY 716 *9/2007* / 1335664

20 ROSLAVL CLASS (ATA/ARS)

153	**168**	**613**	**704**	**853**	**863**
159	**518**	**618**	**707**	**854**	**867**
161–164	**604**	**646**	**852**	**862**	

Displacement, tons: 670 full load
Dimensions, feet (metres): 149.9 × 31 × 15.1 *(45.7 × 9.5 × 4.6)*
Main machinery: Diesel-electric; 2 diesel generators; 1,200 hp(m) *(882 kW)*; 1 motor; 1 shaft
Speed, knots: 12
Range, n miles: 6,000 at 11 kt
Complement: 28
Guns: 4—14.5 mm (2 twin) MGs.

Comment: Built in China in mid-1960s to the USSR design. One carries diving bell and submarine rescue gear on stern and is classified as ARS. Split evenly between the fleets.

ROSLAVL 852 *10/2008*, Chris Sattler* / 1335665

MARITIME MILITIA (MBDF)

Notes: (1) China has four regular paramilitary maritime Security Forces: the Customs Service *(Hai Guan)*; the maritime section of the Public Security Bureau *(Hai Gong)*; the maritime command *(Gong Bian)* of the Border Security Force (which is itself a part of the PLA-subordinated People's Armed Police); and the Border Defence Coast Guard *(Bian Jian)*.
These four organisations patrol extensively with a variety of vessels. In recent years the better disciplined and centrally controlled *Hai Guan* has received a significant number of new vessels, many of them with offshore capabilities. A number of Haitun helicopters are also in service.
(2) Types of vessels vary from Huxins, Shanghai IIs and Huludaos to a number of other designs spread across all forces. For example Huxin and Huludao classes can show the markings of all four services.
(3) From December 1999 pennant numbers have been standardised to show the vessels' legitimate operating area. This is an attempt to crack down on illegal activities by making it easier for merchant ships to report violations to the Maritime Police (Hai Gong), who have taken overall responsibility.

a. 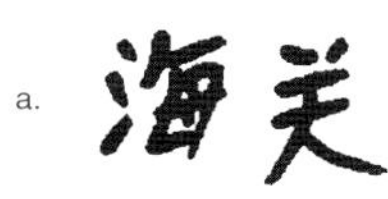

HAI GUAN (HOI KWAN) – CUSTOMS

b. 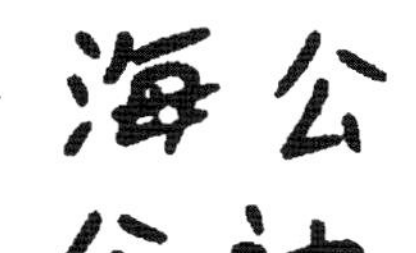

HAI GONG (HOI KUNG) – MARITIME POLICE

c. 公边 GONG BIAN (KUNG BIN) – BORDER SECURITY

d. 

BIAN JIAN (PIN KAM) – BORDER DEFENCE

CUSTOMS (HAI GUAN)

Notes: A new class of 20-24 Qui-M class offshore patrol craft is reported to have entered service. Armed with twin 30 mm guns, a distinguishing feature is a stern ramp to facilitate the handling of high-speed interceptor craft. At 100 m length, they are substantially larger than previous Customs vessels and, despite appearances, there has been some speculation as to whether these craft are manned by naval personnel.

HULUDAO CLASS (TYPE 206) (FAST ATTACK CRAFT—PATROL) (PC)

Displacement, tons: 180 full load
Dimensions, feet (metres): 147.6 × 21 × 5.6 *(45 × 6.4 × 1.7)*
Main machinery: 3 MWM TBD604BV12 diesels; 5,204 hp(m) *(3.82 MW)* sustained; 3 shafts
Speed, knots: 29. **Range, n miles:** 1,000 at 15 kt
Complement: 24 (6 officers)
Guns: 6 China 14.5 mm Type 82 (3 twin); 600 rds/min to 7 km *(3.8 n miles)*; weight of shell 1.42 kg.

Comment: EEZ patrol craft first seen at Wuxi Shipyard in 1988. The craft is sometimes referred to as the Wuting class.

HAI GONG HULUDAO *6/1995* / 0056810

7 TYPE P 58E (COMMAND SHIPS) (AGF)

901–907

Displacement, tons: 435 full load
Dimensions, feet (metres): 190.3 × 24.9 × 7.5 *(58 × 7.6 × 2.3)*
Main machinery: 4 MTU diesels; 8,720 hp(m) *(6.4 MW)* sustained; 4 shafts
Speed, knots: 27. **Range, n miles:** 1,500 at 12 kt
Complement: 50
Guns: 2 China 14.5 mm/93 (twin) MGs.
Radars: Surface search: I-band.

Comment: First one built at Guangzhou in 1990, last one in 1998. Less well armed but similar to those in service with Pakistan's MSA. Used as command ships.

HAI GUAN 901 *1993, T Hollingsbee* / 0056811

42 COASTAL PATROL CRAFT (NEW) (PB)

801–842

Displacement, tons: 98 full load
Dimensions, feet (metres): 101.7 × 15.4 × 4.6 *(31 × 4.7 × 1.4)*
Main machinery: 2 diesels; 2 shafts
Speed, knots: 32
Complement: 15
Guns: 2 China 14.5 mm/93 (twin).
Radars: Surface search: Racal Decca ARPA; I-band.

Comment: Building in Shanghai at about six a year since 1992. More may follow.

HAI GUAN 812 *1993, T Hollingsbee* / 0506223

COASTAL PATROL CRAFT (OLD) (PB)

Comment: Shanghai type hull but with a different superstructure. Two twin 14.5 mm MGs. Being phased out and replaced by the 800 series of patrol craft.

HAI GUAN 62 *6/1995* / 0056812

2 COMBATBOAT 90E (PBF)

Displacement, tons: 9 full load
Dimensions, feet (metres): 39 × 9.5 × 2.3 *(11.9 × 2.9 × 0.7)*
Main machinery: 1 Scania AB DSI 14 diesel; 398 hp(m) *(293 kW)*; waterjet
Speed, knots: 40
Complement: 2

Comment: Two delivered to Hai Guan in April 1997. This is the transport version of the Swedish raiding craft and can lift two tons of stores or 6-10 troops.

COMBATBOAT 90E (Swedish colours) *5/1999, Per Körnefeldt* / 0056813

COAST GUARD (GONG BIAN)

Notes: The 2006 Defence White Paper gave prominence to improvement to border and maritime security affairs and, in that context, the emergence of a Coast Guard as a distinct force is a logical result of that process. It is unclear whether the force is controlled by a national command structure or whether forces are commanded at the local (provincial) level. It is likely that the new organisation will have subsumed some, if not all, of the functions and seagoing units of the Gong Bian (Border Security Force) but this has not been confirmed. Neither is it clear to what extent other constituents of the Maritime Militia (Customs, Maritime Police and Border Defence) have been affected. While details of major units are given, there is reported also to be a large number of smaller inshore craft.

CG 33031 *6/2007* / 1166846

CG 31021 and 31011 *7/2007* / 1170053

1 OFFSHORE PATROL SHIP (PSO)

HAIJING 1001

Displacement, tons: 1,000 approx
Dimensions, feet (metres): To be announced
Main machinery: To be announced
Speed, knots: To be announced
Complement: To be announced
Guns: 1 — 37 mm.
Radars: Surface search: E/F-band.
Navigation: I-band.

Comment: Coastal patrol ship, possibly called *Pudong*, built for the China Coast Guard.

HAIJING 1001 *6/2007* / 1166851

2 JIANGHU CLASS (PSOH)

HAIJING 1002 (ex-509) **HAIJING 1003** (ex-510)

Displacement, tons: 1,425 standard; 1,702 full load
Dimensions, feet (metres): 338.5 × 35.4 × 10.2 *(103.2 × 10.8 × 3.1)*
Main machinery: 2 Type 12E 390V diesels; 14,400 hp(m) *(10.6 MW)* sustained; 2 shafts
Speed, knots: 26
Range, n miles: 4,000 at 15 kt
Complement: To be announced
Guns: 1 — 37 mm. 4 — 14.5 (2 twin) MGs.
Radars: Surface search: E/F-band.
Navigation: I-band.
Helicopters: 1 medium.

Comment: Two former Jianghu-class frigates transferred from the PLAN to the Coast Guard in March 2007 and recommissioned in July 2007. The ships were originally built in the 1970s. Modifications to the ships include removal of all the previous missile and gun armament and changes to the superstructure to include an upper deck at 01-deck level and two sets of davits aft for high-speed interception craft. The new armament includes a single-barrel 37 mm gun forward and two twin 14.5 mm machine guns aft of the funnel. There are also two water cannons forward.

HAIJING 1002 *7/2007* / 1166850

HUXIN CLASS (PB)

Displacement, tons: 165 full load
Dimensions, feet (metres): 91.9 × 13.8 × 5.2 *(28 × 4.2 × 1.6)*
Main machinery: 2 diesels; 1,000 hp(m) *(735 kW)*; 2 shafts
Speed, knots: 17
Range, n miles: 400 at 10 kt
Complement: 26
Guns: 2 China 14.5 mm/93 (twin).
Radars: Surface search: Skin Head; I-band.

Comment: This is a class of modified Huangpu design with a greater freeboard and a slightly larger displacement. First seen in 1989 and now in series production. Huxin 178 is a modified command vessel with a forward superstructure extension.

HUXIN 44091 *6/2005* / 1164340

COASTAL PATROL CRAFT (NEW) (PB)

Displacement, tons: 58 full load
Dimensions, feet (metres): 73.8 × 15.7 × 5.2 *(22.5 × 4.8 × 1.6)*
Main machinery: 2 diesels; 1,600 hp(m) *(1.18 MW)*; 2 shafts
Speed, knots: 22. **Range, n miles:** 850 at 11 kt
Complement: 13
Guns: 2—14.5 mm (twin).
Radars: Surface search: I-band.

Comment: Large numbers of this type in all Fleet areas. Armaments vary.

GONG BIAN 4401 *6/1999* / 0056807

GONG BIAN 4407 *6/1997* / 0017754

COASTAL PATROL CRAFT (OLD) (PB)

Displacement, tons: 82 full load
Dimensions, feet (metres): 82 × 13.5 × 4.6 *(25 × 4.1 × 1.4)*
Main machinery: 2 diesels; 900 hp(m) *(662 kW)*; 2 shafts
Speed, knots: 14
Range, n miles: 900 at 11 kt
Complement: 12
Guns: 4—14.5 mm/93 2 (twin).
Radars: Surface search: Fin Curve; I-band.

Comment: Large numbers of this type still extensively used although numbers are declining in favour of Huxin and the newer CPC design.

GONG BIAN 1301 *3/1995, van Ginderen Collection* / 0056808

STEALTH CRAFT (PBF)

Comment: Since 1996 large numbers of low profile stealth craft have been active in the South Sea areas, and have been reported as far away as the Philippines. Sizes vary from 30 to 60 m in length and many are capable of speeds in excess of 30 kt. Most are paramilitary vessels but some may be privately owned.

STEALTH *8/1996* / 0012232

INSHORE PATROL CRAFT (PBI)

Displacement, tons: 32 full load
Dimensions, feet (metres): 62 × 13.1 × 3.6 *(18.9 × 4 × 1.1)*
Main machinery: 2 diesels; 900 hp(m) *(662 kW)*; 2 shafts
Speed, knots: 15
Complement: 5
Guns: 1—12.7 mm MG.

Comment: Details given are for the standard small patrol craft. In addition there are a number of speedboats confiscated from smugglers and used for interception duties.

GONG BIAN 3110 *4/1998* / 0017755

GONG BIAN SPEEDBOAT *2/1995, T Hollingsbee* / 0056809

MARITIME SAFETY ADMINISTRATION

Notes: The China Coast Guard (Maritime Safety Administration), part of the Ministry of Communications, was established in 1998 and is responsible for safety at sea, security and pollution control in Chinese offshore waters, ports and inland rivers. The agency reportedly operates some 150 vessels which are painted white with a large diagonal red stripe and four thin blue stripes.

MSA 1015 *12/2007, Chris Sattler* / 1335663

MSA 1005 *10/2008*, Chris Sattler* / 1335662

1 HAIXUN 21 CLASS (PBOH)

HAIXUN 21

Displacement, tons: 1,500 full load
Dimensions, feet (metres): 305.8 × 40.0 × 17.7 *(93.2 × 12.2 × 5.4)*
Main machinery: 2 diesels; 2 shafts
Speed, knots: 22
Radars: Navigation.
Helicopters: Platform for one medium.

Comment: Commissioned in 2003. Conducted joint exercises with the Japanese Coast Guard in May 2004.

HAIXUN 21 *5/2004, Hachiro Nakai* / 0589002

1 + 1 HAIXUN 31 CLASS (PBOH)

HAIXUN 31

Displacement, tons: 3,000 full load
Dimensions, feet (metres): 367.4 × 45.9 × 16.4 *(112.0 × 14.0 × 5.0)*
Main machinery: 2 diesels; 2 shafts
Speed, knots: 18
Radars: Navigation.
Helicopters: 1 medium.

Comment: Commissioned on 22 February 2005. The ship is equipped with a hangar and flight deck. A second ship is reported to be under construction.

Colombia

ARMADA DE LA REPUBLICA

Country Overview

The Republic of Colombia is the only South American country that fronts both the Caribbean Sea and the Pacific Ocean with coastlines of 950 n miles and 782 n miles respectively. With an area of 440,831 square miles, it is bordered to the north by Panama, to the east by Venezuela and Brazil and to the south by Peru and Ecuador. The capital and largest city is Bogotá. Buenaventura and Tumaco are the main Pacific ports while Cartagena, Santa Marta and Barranquilla, which is near the mouth of the principal river and transport artery, the Magdalena, are on the Caribbean side. Territorial seas (12 n miles) are claimed but while it has claimed a 200 n mile EEZ, its limits have not been fully defined.

Headquarters Appointments

Commander of the Navy:
Admiral Guillermo Enrique Barrera Hurtado
Deputy Commander and Chief of Staff of the Navy:
Vice Admiral Carlos Humberto Pineda Gallo
Inspector General:
Vice Admiral Jaime Parra Cifuentes
Chief of Naval Operations:
Vice Admiral Guillermo Edgar Augusto Cely Nuñez
Chief of Naval Intelligence:
Rear Admiral Cesar Augusto Narvaez Arciniegas
Commander Caribbean Force:
Rear Admiral Roberto García Marquez
Chief of Logistics:
Rear Admiral Hugo de Jesus Garcia Nursery
Commander Marine Corps:
Brigadier General Fernando Ortiz Poland
Commander Pacific Force:
Rear Admiral Flaminio Orlando Malaver Calderon
Commander South Force:
Colonel Luis Jesús Suarez Castillo

Personnel

(a) 2009: 12,000 (Navy); 9,000 (Marines); 200 (Coast Guard); 100 (Aircrew)
(b) 2 years' national service (few conscripts in the Navy)

Organisation

Caribbean Force Command: HQ at Cartagena.
Pacific Force Command: HQ at Bahia Malaga.
Naval Force South: HQ at Puerto Leguízamo.
Riverine Brigade: HQ at Bogotá, DC.
Coast Guard: HQ at Bogotá.

Bases

ARC Bolivar, Cartagena, Main naval base (floating dock, 1 slipway), schools.
ARC Bahia Málaga: Major Pacific base.
ARC Barranquilla: Naval training base.
ARC Puerto Leguízamo: Putumayo River base.
Turbo: Minor River base.
Puerto López: Minor River base.
Puerto Carreño: Minor River base.
Inrida: Minor River base.
San Andrés y Providencia: Specific Command

Marine Corps

Organisation: First Brigade (Corozal):
BAFIM 1 (San Andrés)
BAFIM 2 (Cartagena)
BAFIM 3 (Malagana)
BAFIM 4 (Corozal)
CFENIM Training Battalion (Coveñas)
Second Riverine Brigade (Bogotá)
BASFLIM 3 (Bahia Solano)
BASFLIM 4 (Bahía Málaga)
No. 70 Battalion (Tumaco)
No. 80 Battalion (Buenaventura)
No. 10 Battalion (Guapí)

Strength of the Fleet

Type	*Active*	*Building (planned)*
Patrol Submarines	2	–
Midget Submarines	2	–
Frigates	4	–
Patrol Ships and Fast Attack Craft (Gun)	9	2
Coast Patrol Craft	36	–
Amphibious Forces	8	–
River Patrol Craft	51	50
River Patrol Craft Support	6	–
River Assault Boats	169	–
Survey Vessels	7	–
Auxiliaries	26	–
Training Ships	6	–

Prefix to Ships' Names

ARC (Armada Republica de Colombia)

Dimar

Maritime authority in charge of hydrography and navigational aids.

Coast Guard and Customs (DIAN)

The Coast Guard was established in 1979 but then gave way to the Customs Service before being re-established in January 1992 under the control of the Navy. Headquarters at Bogotá. Main bases are Cartagena, Buenaventura y Turbo and Valle. Ships have a red and yellow diagonal stripe on the hull and patrol craft have a PM number. Customs craft were absorbed into the Coast Guard but by 1995 were again independent as part of the DIAN (Direccion de Impuestos y Aduanas Nacionales). Customs craft have Aduana written on the ship's side, a thick and two thin diagonal stripes and have AN numbers.

PENNANT LIST

Submarines

SO 28	Pijao
SO 29	Tayrona
ST 20	Intrépido
ST 21	Indomable

Frigates

FL 51	Almirante Padilla
FL 52	Caldas
FL 53	Antioquia
FL 54	Independiente

Patrol Forces

PC 141	Cabo Corrientes
PC 142	Cabo Manglares
PC 143	Cabo Tiburon
PC 144	Cabo de la Vella
PO 41	Espartana
PO 42	Capitán Pablo José de Porto
PO 43	Capitán Jorge Enrique Marques Duran
PO 44	Valle del Cauca
PO 45	San Andrés
PM 102	Rafael del Castillo y Rada
PM 103	TN José María Palas
PM 104	CN Medardo Monzon Coronado
PM 105	S2 Jaime Gómez Castro
PM 106	S2 Juan Nepomuceno Peña
PM 112	Quitasueño
PM 113	José María García y Toledo
PM 114	Juan Nepomuceno Eslava
PM 115	TECIM Jaime E Cárdenas Gomez
PB 446	Capella
PF 121	Diligente
PF 122	Juan Lucio
PF 123	Alfonso Vargas
PF 124	Fritz Hagale
PF 125	Vengadora
PF 126	Humberto Cortez
PF 128	Carlos Galindo
PF 129	Capitán Jaime Rook
PF 130	Manuela Saenz
PF 135	Riohacha
PF 136	Leticia
PF 137	Arauca
PRF 189	Mitú

Amphibious Forces

LD 240	Bahía Zapzurro
LD 246	Morrosquillo
LD 248	Bahía Honda
LD 249	Bahía Portete
LD 251	Bahía Solano
LD 252	Bahía Cupica
LD 253	Bahía Utría
LD 254	Bahía Málaga

Auxiliaries

BL 161	Cartagena de Indias
BL 162	Buenaventura
TM 501	Bocachica
TM 502	Arturus
TM 503	Pedro David Salas
TM 504	Sirius
TM 507	Calima
TM 508	Bahí Santa Catalina
TM 509	Móvil I
TM 510	Móvil II
TG 542	Playa Blanca
TG 543	Tierra Bouba
TG 544	Bell Salter
TG 546	Orion
TG 547	Pegasso
DF 170	Mayor Jaime Arias Arango
NF 601	Filigonio Hichamón
NF 602	SSIM Manuel Antonio Moyar
NF 603	Igaraparaná
NF 604	SSIM Julio Correa Hernández
NF 605	Manacacías
NF 606	Cotuhe
NF 607	SSCIM Senen Alberto Araujo
NF 608	CPCIM Guillermo Londoño Vargas
NF 609	Ariarí
NF 610	Mario Villegas
NF 611	Tony Pastrana Contreras
NF 612	CTCIM Jorge Moreno Salazar
NF 613	Juan Ricardo Oyola Vera

Survey Vessels

BO 155	Providencia
BO 156	Malpelo
BH 153	Quindio
BB 31	Gorgona
BB 33	Abadía Médez
BB 34	Ciénaga de Mayorquin
BB 35	Isla Palma

Training Ships

BE 160	Gloria
YT 230	Comodoro
YT 231	Tridente
YT 232	Cristina
YT 233	Albatros
YT 234	Poseidon

Tugs

RB 77	Don Vizo
RB 78	Portete
RB 79	Maldonado
RB 80	Cienaga de San Juan
RF 81	Capitán Castro
RF 83	Joves Fiallo
RF 85	Miguel Silva
RF 86	Capitán Rigoberto Giraldo
RF 87	Vladimir Valek
RF 88	Teniente Luis Bernal
RF 91	TN Alejandro Baldomero Salgado
RF 93	Sejeri
RF 96	Inirida
RM 75	Andagoya
RM 76	Josué Alvarez

SUBMARINES

Notes: (1) Three Swimmer Delivery Vehicles were acquired in 1970: *Defensora* (LS 15), *Poderosa* (LS 16) and *Protectora* (LS 17).
(2) Replacement of the Cosmos midget submarines is under consideration. Procurement of ex-German 206A class is a possibility.

2 PIJAO (TYPE 209/1200) CLASS (SS)

Name	*No*	*Builders*	*Laid down*	*Launched*	*Commissioned*
PIJAO	SO 28	Howaldtswerke, Kiel	1 Apr 1972	10 Apr 1974	18 Apr 1975
TAYRONA	SO 29	Howaldtswerke, Kiel	1 May 1972	16 July 1974	16 July 1975

Displacement, tons: 1,180 surfaced; 1,285 dived
Dimensions, feet (metres): 183.4 × 20.5 × 17.9 *(55.9 × 6.3 × 5.4)*
Main machinery: Diesel-electric; 4 MTU 12V 493 AZ80 diesels; 2,400 hp(m) *(1.76 MW)* sustained; 4 AEG alternators; 1.7 MW; 1 Siemens motor; 4,600 hp(m) *(3.38 MW)* sustained; 1 shaft
Speed, knots: 22 dived; 11 surfaced
Range, n miles: 8,000 at 8 kt surfaced; 4,000 at 4 kt dived
Complement: 34 (7 officers)

Torpedoes: 8—21 in *(533 mm)* bow tubes. 14 AEG SUT; dual purpose; wire-guided; active/passive homing to 12 km *(6.5 n miles)* at 35 kt; 28 km *(15 n miles)* at 23 kt; warhead 250 kg. Swim-out discharge.
Countermeasures: ESM: Thomson-CSF DR 2000; intercept.
Weapons control: Signaal M8/24 TFCS.
Radars: Surface search: Thomson-CSF Calypso II; I-band.
Sonars: Krupp Atlas PSU 83-55; hull-mounted; active/passive search and attack; medium frequency.
Atlas Elektronik PRS 3-4; passive ranging; integral with CSU 3.

Programmes: Ordered in 1971.
Modernisation: Both boats were refitted by HDW at Kiel 1990–91; main batteries were replaced. Further refits were carried out at Cotecmar; *Pijao* 1999–2002 and *Tayrona* 2003–06. Further modernisation at Cotecmar is planned, possibly with ADW assistance.
Structure: Single-hulled. Diving depth, 820 ft *(250 m)*.
Operational: Both boats employed on counter-drug operations.

PIJAO

4/2008*, Marco Ghiglino / 1335712

2 MIDGET SUBMARINES (SSW)

Name	*No*	*Builders*	*Launched*	*Commissioned*
INTRÉPIDO	ST 20	Cosmos, Livorno	1 Jan 1972	17 Apr 1973
INDOMABLE	ST 21	Cosmos, Livorno	1 Jan 1972	17 Apr 1973

Displacement, tons: 58 surfaced; 70 dived
Dimensions, feet (metres): 75.5 × 13.1 *(23 × 4)*
Main machinery: Diesel-electric; 1 diesel; 1 motor; 300 hp(m) *(221 kW)*; 1 shaft
Speed, knots: 11 surfaced; 6 dived

Range, n miles: 1,200 surfaced; 60 dived
Complement: 8
Mines: 6 Mk 21 with 300 kg warhead. 8 Mk 11 with 50 kg warhead.

Comment: They can carry eight swimmers with 2 tons of explosive as well as two swimmer delivery vehicles (SDVs). Built by Cosmos, Livorno and commissioned at 40 tons, but subsequently enlarged in the early 1980s. Listed by the Navy as 'Tactical Submarines'.

INTRÉPIDO

2000, Colombian Navy / 0103690

FRIGATES

Notes: Replacement of the Almirante Padilla class from about 2025 is under consideration.

4 ALMIRANTE PADILLA CLASS (TYPE FS 1500) (FLGHM)

Name	*No*	*Builders*	*Laid down*	*Launched*	*Commissioned*
ALMIRANTE PADILLA	FL 51	Howaldtswerke, Kiel	17 Mar 1981	6 Jan 1982	31 Oct 1983
CALDAS	FL 52	Howaldtswerke, Kiel	14 June 1981	23 Apr 1982	14 Feb 1984
ANTIOQUIA	FL 53	Howaldtswerke, Kiel	22 June 1981	28 Aug 1982	30 Apr 1984
INDEPENDIENTE	FL 54	Howaldtswerke, Kiel	22 June 1981	21 Jan 1983	24 July 1984

Displacement, tons: 1,500 standard; 2,100 full load
Dimensions, feet (metres): 325.1 × 37.1 × 12.1 *(99.1 × 11.3 × 3.7)*
Main machinery: 4 MTU 20V 1163 TB92 diesels; 23,400 hp(m) *(17.2 MW)* sustained; 2 shafts; cp props
Speed, knots: 27; 18 on 2 diesels
Range, n miles: 7,000 at 14 kt; 5,000 at 18 kt
Complement: 94

Missiles: SSM: 4 Aerospatiale MM 40 Exocet ❶; inertial cruise; active radar homing to 70 km *(40 n miles)* at 0.9 Mach; warhead 165 kg; sea-skimmer.
SAM: 2 Matra Simbad twin launchers ❷; Mistral; IR homing to 4 km *(2.2 n miles)*; warhead 3 kg; anti-sea-skimmer.
Guns: 1 OTO Melara 3 in *(76 mm)*/62 compact ❸; 85 rds/min to 16 km *(8.7 n miles)*; weight of shell 6 kg.
2 Breda 40 mm/70 (twin) ❹; 300 rds/min to 12.5 km *(6.8 n miles)* anti-surface; weight of shell 0.96 kg.
2—12.7 mm MGs.
Torpedoes: 6–324 mm ILAS 3 (2 triple) tubes ❺; Whitehead A244S; anti-submarine; active/passive homing to 7 km *(3.8 n miles)*; warhead 38 kg (shaped charge).
Countermeasures: Decoys: 1 CSEE Dagaie double mounting; IR flares and chaff decoys (H- to J-band).
ESM: Argo AC672; radar warning.
ECM: Racal Scimitar; jammer.

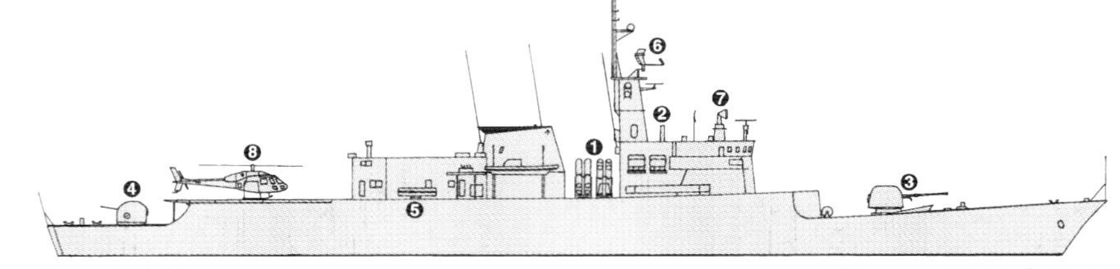

ALMIRANTE PADILLA *(Scale 1 : 900), Ian Sturton* / 0056815

Combat data systems: Thomson-CSF TAVITAC action data automation. Possibly Link Y fitted.
Weapons control: 2 Canopus optronic directors. Thomson-CSF Vega II GFCS.
Radars: Air/surface search: Thomson-CSF Sea Tiger ❻; E/F-band; range 110 km *(60 n miles)* for 2 m^2 target.
Navigation: Furuno; I-band.
Fire control: Castor II B ❼; I/J-band; range 15 km *(8 n miles)* for 1 m^2 target.
IFF: Mk 10.
Sonars: Atlas Elektronik ASO 4-2; hull-mounted; active attack; medium frequency.

Helicopters: 1 MBB BO 105 CB ❽ or 1 Bell 412.

Programmes: Order for four Type FS 1500 placed late 1980. Reclassified as light frigates in 1999. Similar to Malaysian Kasturi class frigates.
Modernisation: Mistral SAM system fitted. Helicopter deck lengthened by 2 m to take Bell 412 aircraft. There have also been minor modifications to ship systems and superstructure. A major modernisation period began at Cotecmar in 2008. *Antioquia* is to receive new engines and new radars are also reported to be part of the package.

ALMIRANTE PADILLA *8/2008*, Ships of the World* / 1335707

INDEPENDIENTE *3/2008*, Marco Ghiglino* / 1335711

SHIPBORNE AIRCRAFT

Numbers/Type: 2 MBB BO 105CB.
Operational speed: 113 kt *(210 km/h).*
Service ceiling: 9,854 ft *(3,000 m).*
Range: 407 n miles *(754 km).*
Role/Weapon systems: Surface search and limited ASW helicopter. Sensors: Search/weather radar. Weapons: ASW; provision to carry depth bombs. ASV; light attack role with machine gun pods.

BO 105 *2000, Colombian Navy* / 0103692

Numbers/Type: 2 Eurocopter AS 555 Fennec.
Operational speed: 121 kt *(225 km/h).*
Service ceiling: 13,125 ft *(4,000 m).*
Range: 389 n miles *(722 km).*
Role/Weapon systems: OTHT capability for surface-to-surface role. Also used for logistic support. More are being acquired. Sensors: Bendix RDR 1500B radar. Weapons: Torpedoes may be fitted in due course.

AS 555 *6/2000, Colombian Navy* / 0103693

Numbers/Type: 4 Bell 412.
Operational speed: 122 kt *(226 km/h).*
Service ceiling: 10,000 ft *(3,300 m).*
Range: 500 n miles *(744 km).*
Role/Weapon systems: Multipurpose used mostly for surveillance, troop transport and logistic support. Sensors: Weather radar. Weapons: ASV 7.62 mm MG can be carried.

BELL 412 *6/1999, Colombian Navy* / 0056820

Numbers/Type: 1 Bell UH-1N Twin Huey.
Operational speed: 110 kt *(204 km/h).*
Service ceiling: 10,000 ft *(3,048 m).*
Range: 230 n miles *(426 km).*
Role/Weapon systems: Light Utility platform for all-weather assault, transport, airborne command and control, armed reconnaissance and SAR. Can carry eight marines. To enter service in 2009. Sensors: BRITE Star FLIR. Weapons: Can be armed with 12.7 mm or 7.62 mm machine guns and 2.75 in rockets.

UH-1N (US Navy colours) *5/1999, A Sharma* / 0084120

LAND-BASED MARITIME AIRCRAFT

Notes: The Navy operates the following fixed-wing aircraft for maritime surveillance and transport: four RC690, six Navajo PA-31, six Cessna 206, one Cessna 150, two Cessna 208B, one Beech B-350, two Gavillan 358, one Gulfstream I and two PA-28 Cherokee. There are also two Bell 212 and one Eurocopter BK-117.

Numbers/Type: 4 Casa CN-235 200.
Operational speed: 210 kt *(384 km/h).*
Service ceiling: 24,000 ft *(7,315 m).*
Range: 2,000 n miles *(3,218 km).*
Role/Weapon systems: EEZ surveillance. First two delivered in 2003. Two further aircraft ordered in 2007 for delivery in 2009. Sensors: Search radar Bendix APS 504(V)5; FLIR. Weapons: Unarmed.

CN-235 *6/2003, CASA* / 0587695

PATROL FORCES

Notes: (1) Three Orca class 12 m fast intercept craft, capable of 40 kt, entered service in 2003. (2) Two Bravo 36 patrol craft, capable of 35 kt, are based at Covenas.

1 RELIANCE CLASS

Name	*No*	*Builders*	*Commissioned*
VALLE DEL CAUCA (ex-*Durable*)	PO 44 (ex-WMEC 628)	Coast Guard Yard, Baltimore	8 Dec 1967

Displacement, tons: 1,129 full load
Dimensions, feet (metres): 210.5 × 34 × 10.5 *(64.2 × 10.4 × 3.2)*
Main machinery: 2 Alco 16V-251 diesels; 6,480 hp *(4.83 MW)* sustained; 2 shafts; LIPS cp props
Speed, knots: 18. **Range, n miles:** 6,100 at 14 kt; 2,700 at 18 kt
Complement: 75 (12 officers)
Guns: 1 Boeing 25 mm/87 Mk 38 Bushmaster; 200 rds/min to 6.8 km *(3.4 n miles).* 2 — 12.7 mm MGs.
Radars: Surface search: Hughes/Furuno SPS-73; I-band.
Helicopters: Platform for one medium.

Comment: Transferred to Colombia on 4 September 2003. During 34 years in USCG service, underwent Major Maintenance Availability (MMA) in 1989. The exhausts for main engines, ship service generators and boilers were run in a vertical funnel which reduced flight deck size. Capable of towing ships up to 10,000 tons. Based in the Pacific.

VALLE DEL CAUCA *6/2008** / 1335710

2 LAZAGA CLASS (FAST ATTACK CRAFT — GUN) (PBO)

Name	*No*	*Builders*	*Commissioned*
CAPITÁN PABLO JOSÉ DE PORTO (ex-*Recalde*)	PO 42 (ex-PM 116, ex-P 06)	Bazán, La Carraca	17 Dec 1977
CAPITÁN JORGE ENRIQUE MARQUEZ DURAN (ex-*Cadarso*)	PO 43 (ex-PM 117, ex-P 03)	Bazán, La Carraca	10 July 1976

Displacement, tons: 393 full load
Dimensions, feet (metres): 190.6 × 24.9 × 8.5 *(58.1 × 7.6 × 2.6)*
Main machinery: 2 MTU/Bazán 16V 956 TB 91 diesels; 7,500 hp(m) *(5.5 MW)* sustained; 2 shafts
Speed, knots: 26. **Range, n miles:** 2,400 at 15 kt
Complement: 40 (4 officers)
Guns: 1 Breda 40 mm/70. 1 Oerlikon 20 mm L85. 1 — 12.7 mm MG.
Weapons control: CSEE optical director.
Radars: Surface search: Furuno; E/F-band.
Navigation: Furuno; I-band.

Comment: Paid off from the Spanish Navy in 1993 and put into reserve. Acquired by Colombia in March 1997 for extensive refurbishment at Bazán, San Fernando. Recommissioned 25 April 1998 and 25 June 1998 respectively. Radars have been changed and the 76 mm gun replaced by a 20 mm cannon. These ships may be used to carry troops. Four more of the class are available and more may be acquired in due course.

CAPITÁN JORGE ENRIQUE MARQUEZ DURAN *6/2001, Maritime Photographic* / 0114510

1 CORMORAN CLASS (FAST ATTACK CRAFT—GUN) (PBO)

Name	*No*	*Builders*	*Commissioned*
ESPARTANA (ex-*Cormoran*)	PO 41	Bazán, San Fernando	27 Oct 1989

Displacement, tons: 358 full load
Dimensions, feet (metres): 185.7 × 24.7 × 6.5 *(56.6 × 7.5 × 2)*
Main machinery: 3 MTU-Bazán 16V 956 TB91 diesels; 11,250 hp(m) *(8.27 MW)* sustained; 3 shafts
Speed, knots: 32. **Range, n miles:** 2,500 at 15 kt
Complement: 31 (5 officers)
Guns: 1 Bofors 40/70 SP 48. 1 Oerlikon 20 mm.
Weapons control: Alcor C optronic director.
Radars: Surface search: Raytheon; I-band.

Comment: Built with overseas sales in mind, this ship was launched in October 1985, but from 1989 served in the Spanish Navy until April 1994 when she was laid up at Cartagena. Transferred in September 1995, she was then refitted at Cadiz, before sailing for Colombia in mid-1996. Based at San Andres Island and belongs to the Coast Guard.

ESPARTANA *6/2008** / 1335709

1 BALSAM CLASS (PSO)

Name	*No*	*Builders*	*Commissioned*
SAN ANDRES (ex-*Gentian*)	PO 45 (ex-WIX 290)	Zenith Dredge Corporation, Duluth	3 Nov 1942

Displacement, tons: 1,034 full load
Dimensions, feet (metres): 180 × 37 × 12 *(54.9 × 11.3 × 3.8)*
Main machinery: Diesel electric; 2 diesels; 1,402 hp *(1.06 MW)*; 1 motor; 1,200 hp *(895 kW)*; 1 shaft; bow thruster
Speed, knots: 13. **Range, n miles:** 8,000 at 12 kt
Complement: 53
Guns: To be announced.
Radars: Navigation: Raytheon SPS-64(V)1.

Comment: Following overhaul at Boston, transferred from the US Coast Guard on 15 October 2007.

BALSAM CLASS (Estonian colours) *6/2003, Hartmut Ehlers* / 0561492

4 POINT CLASS (PB)

Name	*No*	*Builders*	*Commissioned*
CABO CORRIENTES (ex-*Point Warde*)	PC 141 (ex-82368)	J M Martinac, Tacoma	14 Aug 1967
CABO MANGLARES (ex-*Point Wells*)	PC 142 (ex-82343)	USCG Yard, Curtis Bay	20 Nov 1963
CABO TIBURON (ex-*Point Estero*)	PC 143 (ex-82344)	USCG Yard, Curtis Bay	11 Dec 1963
CABO DE LA VELLA (ex-*Point Sal*)	PC 144 (ex-82352)	J M Martinac, Tacoma	5 Dec 1966

Displacement, tons: 66; 69 full load
Dimensions, feet (metres): 83 × 17.2 × 5.8 *(25.3 × 5.2 × 1.8)*
Main machinery: 2 Caterpillar 3412 diesels; 1,600 hp *(1.19 MW)*; 2 shafts
Speed, knots: 23.5. **Range, n miles:** 1,500 at 8 kt
Complement: 10 (1 officer)
Guns: 2—12.7 mm MGs.
Radars: Surface search: Hughes/Furuno SPS-73; I-band.

Comment: Steel hulled craft with aluminium superstructure built in United States 1960–70. *Cabo Corrientes* transferred on 29 June 2000 followed by *Cabo Manglares* on 13 October 2000. *Cabo Tiburon* and *Cabo de la Vella* transferred on 8 February 2001 and 29 May 2001 respectively.

CABO DE LA VELLA *6/2008** / 1335714

0 + 1 OFFSHORE PATROL VESSELS (PSO)

Displacement, tons: 1,790 full load
Dimensions, feet (metres): 272.0 × 42.6 × 13.1 *(82.9 × 13.0 × 4.0)*
Main machinery: 2 diesels; 10,940 hp *(8.2 MW)*; 2 shafts
Speed, knots: 20. **Range, n miles:** 7,500 at 12 kt
Complement: 40
Guns: 1—18 mm. 2—12.7 mm MGs.
Radars: Surface search: Hughes/Furuno SPS-73; I-band.
Helicopters: Platform for one medium.

Comment: Damen designed offshore patrol ship to be built at Cotecmar. Construction is to begin in 2009.

3 ARAUCA CLASS (RIVER GUNBOATS) (PBR)

Name	*No*	*Builders*	*Commissioned*
RIOHACHA	PF 135 (ex-35)	Union Industrial de Barranquilla	6 Sep 1956
LETICIA	PF 136 (ex-36)	Union Industrial de Barranquilla	6 Sep 1956
ARAUCA	PF 137 (ex-37)	Union Industrial de Barranquilla	6 Sep 1956

Displacement, tons: 275 full load
Dimensions, feet (metres): 163.5 × 27.2 × 8.9 *(49.9 × 8.3 × 2.7)*
Main machinery: 2 Caterpillar diesels; 916 hp *(683 kW)*; 2 shafts
Speed, knots: 14. **Range, n miles:** 1,890 at 14 kt
Complement: 43; 39 plus 6 orderlies
Guns: 2 USN 3 in *(76 mm)*/50 Mk 26. 4 Oerlikon 20 mm (*Riohacha* and *Arauca*). 1—40 mm; 4—20 mm *(Leticia)*.

Comment: Launched in 1955. Based in Naval Force South.

ARAUCA *1991, Colombian Navy* / 0056821

6 + 1 (3) NORDRIZA CLASS (PATROL SUPPORT VESSELS) (PBR)

SSCIM SENEN ALBERTO ARANGO NF 607 (ex-NF 147)
CPCIM GUILLERMO LONDOÑO VARGAS NF 608 (ex-NF 146)
MARIO VILLEGAS NF 610
TONY PASTRANA CONTRERAS NF 611 (ex-NF 149)
CTCIM JORGE MORENO SALAZAR NF 612
JUAN RICARDO OYOLA VERA NF 613

Displacement, tons: 260
Dimensions, feet (metres): 126.0 × 31.2 × 3.1 *(38.4 × 9.5 × 0.95)*
Main machinery: Diesels
Speed, knots: 9
Complement: 18 plus 82 troops
Guns: 8—12.7 mm MGs (4 twin). 1 Mk 19 grenade launcher.
Helicopters: Platform (NF 612, 613) for 1 small.

Comment: Powerfully armed river patrol vessels. Built to an innovative design by Cotecmar, Cartagena, in three batches: Batch I (NF 607, 608); Batch II (NF 610, 611) and Batch III (NF 612, 613). Batch III ships have a helicopter deck. A seventh and eighth ship were under construction in 2008 and two further ships are expected.

OYOLA VERA *6/2008** / 1335708

3 + 47 LPR-40 CLASS (RIVER PATROL CRAFT) (PB)

Displacement, tons: 13.7 full load
Dimensions, feet (metres): 41.7 × 9.2 × 2.3 *(12.72 × 2.8 × 0.7)*
Main machinery: 2 Caterpillar C9 diesels; 503 hp *(375 kW)*; 2 waterjets
Speed, knots: 29. **Range, n miles:** 513 at 25 kt
Complement: 4
Guns: 3—12.7 mm MGs.
Radars: Surface search: Raytheon R70; I-band.

Comment: New class of inshore patrol craft designed by Cotecmar. Aluminium construction. Transportable on a C-130 aircraft. The construction programme at Cotecmar began in 2007 and the first three are to enter service in 2009. Some 50 of the class are expected.

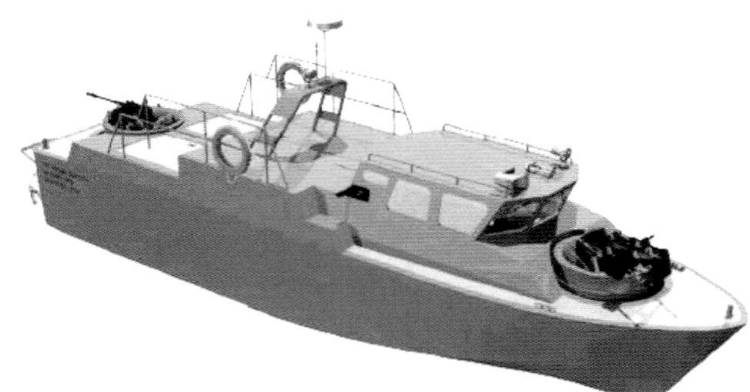

LPR 40 (artist's impression) *10/2006, COTECMAR* / 1164347

2 JOSÉ MARIA PALAS (SWIFT 110) CLASS (LARGE PATROL CRAFT) (PB)

Name	*No*	*Builders*	*Commissioned*
JOSÉ MARIA PALAS	PM 103 (ex-GC 103)	Swiftships Inc, Berwick	Sep 1989
MEDARDO MONZON CORONADO	PM 104 (ex-GC 104)	Swiftships Inc, Berwick	July 1990

Displacement, tons: 99 full load
Dimensions, feet (metres): 109.9 × 24.6 × 6.6 *(33.5 × 7.5 × 2)*
Main machinery: 4 Detroit 12V-71TI diesels; 2,400 hp *(1.79 MW)*; 4 shafts
Speed, knots: 25. **Range, n miles:** 2,250 at 15 kt
Complement: 19 (3 officers)
Guns: 1 Bofors 40 mm/70. 1 – 12.7 mm MG. 2 – 7.62 mm MGs.
Radars: Surface search: Furuno FR 8100D; I-band.

Comment: Acquired under US FMS programme. These ships belong to the Coast Guard.

JOSÉ MARIA PALAS *1/1996, van Ginderen Collection* / 0056824

1 ASHEVILLE CLASS (FAST ATTACK CRAFT – GUN) (PGF)

Name	*No*	*Builders*	*Commissioned*
QUITASUEÑO (ex-*Tacoma*)	PM 112	Tacoma Boat Building	14 July 1969

Displacement, tons: 225 standard; 245 full load
Dimensions, feet (metres): 164.5 × 23.8 × 9.5 *(50.1 × 7.3 × 2.9)*
Main machinery: CODOG; 2 Cummins VT12-875M diesels; 1,450 hp *(1.08 MW)*; 1 GE LM 1500 gas turbine; 13,300 hp *(9.92 MW)*; 2 shafts; cp props
Speed, knots: 40
Range, n miles: 1,700 at 16 kt on diesels; 325 at 37 kt
Complement: 24
Guns: 1 US 3 in *(76 mm)*/50 Mk 34; 50 rds/min to 12.8 km *(7 n miles)*; weight of shell 6 kg. 1 Bofors 40 mm/56; 160 rds/min to 11 km *(5.9 n miles)* anti-aircraft; weight of shell 0.96 kg. 2 – 12.7 mm (twin) MGs.
Radars: Surface search: Raytheon 3100; I-band.

Comment: Transferred from US by lease 16 May 1983 and recommissioned 6 September 1983 and by sale August 1989. Fire-control system removed. Unreliable propulsion system prevented further transfers of this class and it is unlikely the gas turbine is operational, which reduces the top speed to 16 kt. Belongs to the Coast Guard.

QUITASUEÑO *2000, Colombian Navy* / 0103696

2 TOLEDO CLASS (LARGE PATROL CRAFT) (PB)

Name	*No*	*Builders*	*Commissioned*
JOSÉ MARIA GARCIA Y TOLEDO	PM 113	Bender Marine, Mobile	15 July 1994
JUAN NEPOMUCENO ESLAVA	PM 114	Bender Marine, Mobile	25 May 1994

Displacement, tons: 142 full load
Dimensions, feet (metres): 116 × 24.9 × 7 *(35.4 × 7.6 × 2.1)*
Main machinery: 2 MTU 12V 396TE94 diesels; 8,240 hp(m) *(6.1 MW)*; 2 shafts
Speed, knots: 25. **Range, n miles:** 1,200 at 15 kt
Complement: 25 (5 officers)
Guns: 1 Bushmaster 25 mm/87 Mk 96. 2 – 12.7 mm MGs.
Radars: Surface search: Furuno FR 151OD; I-band.

Comment: Acquired under US FMS programme. These ships belong to the Coast Guard.

JUAN NEPOMUCENO ESLAVA *6/2001, Maritime Photographic* / 0114511

2 RAFAEL DEL CASTILLO Y RADA (SWIFT 105) CLASS (LARGE PATROL CRAFT) (PB)

Name	*No*	*Builders*	*Commissioned*
RAFAEL DEL CASTILLO Y RADA	PM 102 (ex-GC 102, ex-AN 202)	Swiftships Inc, Berwick	28 Feb 1983
TECIM JAIME E CÁRDENAS GOMEZ (ex-*Olaya Herrera*)	PM 115 (ex-AN 21, ex-AN 201)	Swiftships Inc, Berwick	16 Oct 1981

Displacement, tons: 115 full load
Dimensions, feet (metres): 105 × 22 × 7 *(31.5 × 6.7 × 2.1)*
Main machinery: 4 MTU 12V 331 TC92 diesels; 5,320 hp(m) *(3.97 MW)* sustained; 4 shafts
Speed, knots: 25. **Range, n miles:** 1,200 at 18 kt
Complement: 19 (3 officers)
Guns: 1 Bofors 40 mm/60 Mk 3 (PM 102). 2 – 12.7 mm MGs.
Weapons control: 1 COAR optronic director.
Radars: Surface search: Raytheon; I-band.

Comment: Delivered for the Customs service. PM 102 is part of the Coast Guard. PM 115 was paid off, but returned unarmed as part of the resurrected Customs service until being transferred back to the Coast Guard in 1997.

RAFAEL DEL CASTILLO Y RADA *6/1999, Colombian Navy* / 0056826

2 JAIME GÓMEZ (MK III PB) CLASS (COASTAL PATROL CRAFT) (PB)

Name	*No*	*Builders*	*Commissioned*
JAIME GÓMEZ CASTRO	PM 105 (ex-GC 105)	Peterson Builders	1975
JUAN NEPOMUCENO PEÑA	PM 106 (ex-GC 106)	Peterson Builders	1977

Displacement, tons: 34 full load
Dimensions, feet (metres): 64.9 × 18 × 5.1 *(19.8 × 5.5 × 1.6)*
Main machinery: 3 Detroit 8V-71 diesels; 690 hp *(515 kW)* sustained; 3 shafts
Speed, knots: 28. **Range, n miles:** 450 at 26 kt
Complement: 7 (1 officer)
Guns: 2 – 12.7 mm MGs. 2 – 7.62 mm MGs. 1 Mk 19 grenade launcher.
Radars: Surface search: 2 Furuno FR 1510D; I-band.

Comment: Acquired from the USA. Recommissioned in December 1989 and February 1990 respectively. Original 40 mm and 20 mm guns replaced by lighter armament. Both based at Leticia, Rio Amazonas, under coast guard control.

JAIME GÓMEZ CASTRO *2000, Colombian Navy* / 0103697

3 SWIFTSHIPS CLASS (RIVER PATROL CRAFT) (PBR)

PRF 320–322

Displacement, tons: 17 full load
Dimensions, feet (metres): 45.5 × 11.8 × 1.8 *(13.9 × 3.6 × 0.6)*
Main machinery: 2 Detroit 6V-92TA diesels; 900 hp *(671 kW)*; 2 Hamilton water-jets
Speed, knots: 22. **Range, n miles:** 600 at 22 kt
Complement: 4
Guns: 2 M2HB 12.7 mm MGs; 2 M60D 7.62 mm MGs.
Radars: Surface search: Raytheon 40; I-band.

Comment: Acquired in 2000. Hard chine modified V hull form. Can carry up to eight troops.

SWIFTSHIPS CLASS *6/2001, Ecuador Coast Guard* / 0114516

2 ROTORK 412 CRAFT (RIVER PATROL CRAFT) (PBR)

CAPITÁN JAIME ROOK PF 129 (ex-PM 107)
MANUELA SAENZ PF 130 (ex-PM 108)

Displacement, tons: 9 full load
Dimensions, feet (metres): 41.7 × 10.5 × 2.3 *(12.7 × 3.2 × 0.7)*
Main machinery: 2 Caterpillar diesels; 240 hp *(179 kW)*; 2 shafts
Speed, knots: 25
Complement: 4
Military lift: 4 tons or 8 marines
Guns: 1 – 12.7 mm MG. 2 – 7.62 mm MGs.
Radars: Surface search: Raytheon; I-band.

Comment: Acquired in 1989–90. Capable of transporting eight fully equipped marines but used as river patrol craft.

CAPITÁN JAIME ROOK *1990, Colombian Navy* / 0056828

9 TENERIFE CLASS (RIVER PATROL CRAFT) (PBR)

PF 305–313

Displacement, tons: 12 full load
Dimensions, feet (metres): 40.7 × 9.5 × 2 *(12.4 × 2.9 × 0.6)*
Main machinery: 2 Caterpillar 3208TA diesels; 850 hp *(634 kW)* sustained; 2 shafts
Speed, knots: 29
Range, n miles: 530 at 15 kt
Complement: 5 plus 12 troops
Guns: 3 – 12.7 mm MGs (1 twin, 1 single). 1 Mk 19 grenade launcher. 1 – 7.62 mm MGs.
Radars: Surface search: Raytheon 1900; I-band.

Comment: Built by Bender Marine, Mobile, Alabama. Acquired in October 1993 for anti-narcotics patrols. Aluminium hulls. Can be transported by aircraft. Names were dropped and new pennants numbers assigned in 2006.

MITÚ *2000, Colombian Navy* / 0103698

15 INSHORE PATROL CRAFT

BP 401 **BP 430** **BP 433** **BP 443** **BP 445** **BP 462–471**

Comment: Miscellaneous patrol craft capable of about 10 kt. *BP 401* is a former US LCPL acquired in 1993. Names were dropped and new BP pennant numbers assigned in 2006.

BP 401 *6/1999, Colombian Navy* / 0056830

11 ANDRÓMEDA CLASS (INSHORE PATROL CRAFT) (PBI)

BP 451–461

Comment: Names were dropped and BP pennant numbers assigned in 2006.

ANDROMEDA *2000, Colombian Navy* / 0103699

10 RIO CLASS (RIVER PATROL CRAFT) (PBR)

PRF 301–304 **PRF 314–319**

Displacement, tons: 7 full load
Dimensions, feet (metres): 31 × 11.1 × 2 *(9.8 × 3.5 × 0.6)*
Main machinery: 2 Detroit 6V-53 diesels; 296 hp *(221 kW)* sustained; 2 water-jets
Speed, knots: 24. **Range, n miles**: 150 at 22 kt
Complement: 4
Guns: 2 – 12.7 mm (twin) MGs. 1 – 7.62 mm MG. 1 – 60 mm mortar.
Radars: Surface search: Raytheon 1900; I-band.

Comment: Acquired in 1989–90. Ex-US PBR Mk II built by Uniflite in 1970. All recommissioned in September 1990. GRP hulls. Names were dropped and new pennant numbers assigned in 2006.

PRF 301 (old number) *2000, Colombian Navy* / 0103700

7 RIVER PATROL CRAFT (PBR)

DILIGENTE PF 121 (ex-LR 121)
JUAN LUCIO PF 122
ALFONSO VARGAS PF 123
FRITZ HAGALE PF 124
VENGADORA PF 125 (ex-LR 125)
HUMBERTO CORTEZ PF 126
CARLOS GALINDO PF 128

Comment: All between 31 and 40 tons. Various designs and ages, but all are armed with two 12.7 mm MGs and most have 7.62 mm MGs as well.

VENGADORA (old number) *2000, Colombian Navy* / 0103701

20 DELFIN CLASS (INSHORE PATROL CRAFT) (PBI)

BP 421–429 **BP 431** **BP 434–442** **BP 446**

Displacement, tons: 5.4 full load
Dimensions, feet (metres): 25.9 × 8.5 × 3.1 *(7.9 × 2.6 × 0.9)*
Main machinery: 2 Evinrude outboards; 400 hp *(294 kW)*
Speed, knots: 40
Complement: 4
Guns: 1 – 12.7 mm MG. 2 – 7.62 mm MGs.
Radars: Surface search: Raytheon; I-band.

Comment: First two built by Mako Marine, Miami and delivered in December 1992. Remainder acquired locally from 1993–94. Names were dropped and BP pennant numbers assigned in 2006.

DELFIN CLASS *6/2001, Maritime Photographic* / 0114512

0 + 4 DAMEN STAN PATROL 4207 (PB)

Name	*No*	*Builders*	*Commissioned*
–	–	Cotecmar, Cartagena	2011
–	–	Cotecmar, Cartagena	2012
–	–	Cotecmar, Cartagena	2013
–	–	Cotecmar, Cartagena	2014

Displacement, tons: 205
Dimensions, feet (metres): 140.4 × 23.3 × 8.3 *(42.8 × 7.11 × 2.52)*
Main machinery: 2 Caterpillar 3516B DI-TA; 5,600 hp *(4.17 MW)*; 2 cp props
Speed, knots: 26
Complement: 14
Guns: To be announced.

Comment: Contract expected to be signed with Damen Shipyards, Gorinchem for construction of four Damen Stan Patrol 4207 offshore patrol craft. Likely to be built under licence by Cotecmar, Cartagena. Steel hull with aluminium superstructure. Capable of carrying a 7 m RIB. Similar craft in service in Barbados and Jamaica Coast Guards.

STAN PATROL 4207 (Jamaica colours) ***11/2006, Martyn Westers*** / 1164414

4 + 10 MIDNIGHT EXPRESS INTERCEPT CRAFT (PBF)

Displacement, tons: 6 full load
Dimensions, feet (metres): 39.2 × 9.5 × 1.7 *(11.9 × 2.9 × 0.5)*
Main machinery: 3 outboard motors; 1,050 hp *(782 kW)*
Speed, knots: 55
Complement: 4
Guns: 1—7.62 mm MG.

Comment: Glass-fibre construction. First four ordered from Midnight Express, Fort Lauderdale, on 20 December 2006. A further 10 likely to be ordered in 2009. The detailed configuration has not been confirmed; propulsion may be inboard diesel engines with surface drives.

AMPHIBIOUS FORCES

Notes: Procurement of a new class of LCUs to replace the current inventory is under consideration.

169 RIVER ASSAULT BOATS (RAB) (PBR)

Comment: There are about 250 river assault craft. These include some 100 Eduardoño 7.8 m E26A and E23B class, an unknown number of 6.8 m Boston Whaler craft and approximately 125 Pirañas 7.5 m craft. Typical armament includes 1—12.7 mm MG and 2—7.62 mm MGs.

ASSAULT BOAT ***2000, Colombian Navy*** / 0103703

1 LCM 8

BAHÍA ZAPZURRO LD 240

Displacement, tons: 125 full load
Dimensions, feet (metres): 71.9 × 20.7 × 9.9 *(21.9 × 6.3 × 3)*
Main machinery: 1 diesel; 285 hp *(213 kW)*; 1 shaft
Speed, knots: 12
Complement: 5
Military lift: 60 tons or 150 troops

Comment: Transferred in 1993.

BAHÍA ZAPZURRO ***6/1999, Colombian Navy*** / 0056832

7 MORROSQUILLO (LCU 1466A) CLASS (LCU)

MORROSQUILLO LD 246
BAHÍA HONDA LD 248
BAHÍA PORTETE LD 249
BAHÍA SOLANO LD 251
BAHÍA CUPICA LD 252
BAHÍA UTRIA LD 253
BAHÍA MALAGA LD 254

Displacement, tons: 347 full load
Dimensions, feet (metres): 119 × 34 × 6 *(36.3 × 10.4 × 1.8)*
Main machinery: 3 Detroit 6-71 diesels; 522 hp *(389 kW)* sustained; 3 shafts
Speed, knots: 7. **Range, n miles:** 700 at 7 kt
Complement: 14
Cargo capacity: 167 tons or 300 troops
Guns: 2—12.7 mm MGs.
Radars: Navigation: Raytheon; I-band.

Comment: Former US Army craft built in 1954 and transferred in 1991 and 1992 with new engines. Used as inshore transports. Speed quoted is fully laden. Numbers split between each coast.

MORROSQUILLO ***1/1993*** / 0056833

SURVEY SHIPS

Notes: There are also three small buoy tenders: *Abadía Médez* BB 33, *Ciénaga de Mayorquin* BB 34, and *Isla Palma* BB 35.

2 PROVIDENCIA CLASS (AGOR)

Name	*No*	*Builders*	*Commissioned*
PROVIDENCIA	BO 155	Martin Jansen SY, Leer	24 July 1981
MALPELO	BO 156	Martin Jansen SY, Leer	24 July 1981

Displacement, tons: 1,157 full load
Dimensions, feet (metres): 164.3 × 32.8 × 13.1 *(50.3 × 10 × 4)*
Main machinery: 2 MAN-Augsburg diesels; 1,570 hp(m) *(1.15 MW)*; 1 Kort nozzle prop; bow thruster
Speed, knots: 13. **Range, n miles:** 15,000 at 12 kt
Complement: 48 (5 officers) plus 6 scientists
Radars: Navigation: Raytheon; I-band.

Comment: Both launched in January 1981. *Malpelo* employed on fishery research and *Providencia* on geophysical research. Both are operated by DIMAR, the naval authority in charge of hydrographic, pilotage, navigational and ports services. Painted white.

MALPELO ***2000, Colombian Navy*** / 0103704

1 BUOY TENDER

Name	*No*	*Builders*	*Commissioned*
QUINDIO (ex-YFR 443)	BH 153	Niagara SB Corporation	11 Nov 1943

Displacement, tons: 600 full load
Dimensions, feet (metres): 131 × 29.8 × 9 *(40 × 9.1 × 2.7)*
Main machinery: 2 Union diesels; 600 hp *(448 kW)*; 2 shafts
Speed, knots: 10
Complement: 17 (2 officers)

Comment: Transport ship transferred by lease from the US in July 1964 and by sale on 31 March 1979. Used as a buoy tender.

QUINDIO ***2000, Colombian Navy*** / 0103705

1 SURVEY SHIP (AGSC)

Name	*No*	*Builders*	*Commissioned*
GORGONA	BB 31 (ex-BO 154, ex-BO 161, ex-FB 161)	Lidingoverken, Sweden	28 May 1954

Displacement, tons: 574 full load
Dimensions, feet (metres): 135 × 29.5 × 9.3 *(41.2 × 9 × 2.8)*
Main machinery: 2 Wärtsilä Nohab diesels; 910 hp(m) *(669 kW)*; 2 shafts
Speed, knots: 13
Complement: 45 (2 officers)

Comment: Paid off in 1982 but after a complete overhaul at Cartagena naval base was back in service in late 1992. A further major refit took place 2005–06. This included work on the hull and possible changes to the superstructure.

GORGONA (old number) ***1993, Colombian Navy*** / 0056835

TRAINING SHIPS

Notes: There are also five sail training yachts *Comodoro* YT 230, *Tridente* YT 231 and *Cristina* YT 232, *Albatros* YT 233, *Poseidon* YT 234.

1 SAIL TRAINING SHIP (AXS)

Name	*No*	*Builders*	*Launched*	*Commissioned*
GLORIA	BE 160	AT Celaya, Bilbao	6 Sep 1966	16 May 1969

Displacement, tons: 1,250 full load
Dimensions, feet (metres): 249.3 oa; 211.9 wl; × 34.8 × 21.7 *(76; 64.6 × 10.6 × 6.6)*
Main machinery: 1 auxiliary diesel; 530 hp(m) *(389 kW)*; 1 shaft
Speed, knots: 10.5
Complement: 51 (10 officers) plus 88 trainees

Comment: Sail training ship. Barque rigged. Hull is entirely welded. Sail area, 1,675 sq yds *(1,400 sq m)*. Endurance, 60 days. Similar to Ecuador, Mexico and Venezuelan vessels.

GLORIA ***9/2006, Camil Busquets i Vilanova*** / 1164399

AUXILIARIES

Notes: (1) There are nine ex-US 11 m armoured troop carriers TNT 381–389.
(2) Eleven craft are employed on general administrative duties: *Orca* BA 03, *Halcon* BA 04, *Ara* BA 05, *Almirante III* BA 06, *Cano del Oro* BA 07, BA 08, *Escafandra* BA 11, BA 12–15.

2 LUNEBURG CLASS (TYPE 701) (SUPPORT SHIPS) (AGP)

Name	*No*	*Builders*	*Commissioned*
CARTAGENA DE INDIAS (ex-*Luneburg*)	BL 161 (ex-A 1411)	Flensburger	31 Jan 1966
BUENAVENTURA (ex-Nienburg)	BL 162 (ex-A 1416)	Bremer Vulcan	1 Aug 1968

Displacement, tons: 3,483 full load
Dimensions, feet (metres): 341.2 × 43.3 × 13.8 *(104 × 13.2 × 4.2)*
Main machinery: 2 MTU MD 16V 538 TB90 diesels; 6,000 hp(m) *(4.1 MW)* sustained; 2 shafts; cp props; bow thruster
Speed, knots: 16. **Range, n miles:** 3,200 at 14 kt
Complement: 70 (9 officers)
Cargo capacity: 1,100 tons
Guns: 4 Bofors 40 mm/70 (2 twin).
Radars: Navigation: I-band.

Comment: BL 161 paid off from the German Navy in 1994. Taken in hand for refit by HDW, Kiel in August 1997. Recommissioned on 2 November 1997. Guns were cocooned in German service. The ship acts as a depot ship for patrol craft. BL 162 paid off and was transferred the same day on 27 March 1998. She is now based at Málaga. Both ships are to be refitted with helicopter decks in orderto operate Bell 412 helicopters.

BUENAVENTURA ***9/2007, US Navy*** / 1335713

8 TRANSPORTS

BOCACHICA TM 501
ARTURUS TM 502
PEDRO DAVID SALAS TM 503 (ex-TM 101)
SIRIUS TM 504 (ex-TM 62)
CALIMA TM 507 (ex-TM 49)
BAHÍA SANTA CATALINA TM 508
MÓVIL I TM 509
MÓVIL II TM 510

Comment: Small supply ships of various characteristics from 30 tons to 3 tons. Some have transferred to an inshore patrol craft role.

CALIMA (old number) ***6/1999, Colombian Navy*** / 0056838

8 BAY SUPPORT CRAFT

PLAYA BLANCA TG 542
TIERRA BOMBA TG 543
BELL SALTER TG 544
ORION TG 546
PEGASSO TG 547
LANCHA AMBULANCIA TG 556
ARMADA I TG 557
JUANCHACO TG 558

Comment: Mostly small craft of less than 10 tons. The largest is TG 544 which is 87 tons and has previously been listed as an Admiral's Yacht.

BELL SALTER ***6/1999, Colombian Navy*** / 0056840

7 RIVER SUPPORT CRAFT (YTD/YAG)

FILIGONIO HICHAMÓN NF 601 (ex-NF 141)
SSIM MANUEL A MOYAR NF 602 (ex-NF 144)
IGARAPARANÁ NF 603 (ex-RR 92, LR 92)
SSIM JULIO CORREA HERNÁNDEZ NF 604 (ex-NF 143)
MANACACÍAS NF 605 (ex-RR 95, LR 95)
COTUHE NF 606 (ex-RR 98)
ARIARÍ NF 609 (ex-PF-127, RR 97)

Comment: Miscellaneous service craft of unknown characteristics.

1 FLOATING DOCK (ASL)

MAYOR JAIME ARIAS ARANGO DF 170 (ex-DF 41, ex-170)

Comment: Capacity of 165 tons, length 140 ft *(42.7 m)*, displacement 700 tons. Used as a non-self-propelled depot ship for the midget submarines.

MAYOR JAIME ARIAS ARANGO *6/2001, Maritime Photographic* / 0114513

TUGS

15 TUGS (YTL)

ANDAGOYA RM 75
JOSUÉ ALVAREZ RB 76
DON VIZO RB 77
PORTETE RB 78
MALDONADO RB 79
CIENAGA DE SAN JUAN RB 80
CAPITÁN CASTRO RF 81
JOVES FIALLO RF 83
MIGUEL SILVA RF 85
CAPITAN RIGOBERTO GIRALDO RF 86
VLADIMIR VALEK RF 87
TENIENTE LUIS BERNAL RF 88
TENIENTE ALEJANDRO BALDOMERO SALGADO RF 91
SEJERI RF 93
INIRIDA RF 96

Comment: River craft of various types described as 'Remolcador Bahia (RB), Fluvial (RF) or Mar (RM)'. Used for transport and ferry duties in harbours and rivers. RF 86 modified as a support vessel and armed with 12.7 mm MGs.

JOSUÉ ALVAREZ *6/1999, Colombian Navy* / 0056841

Comoros

Country Overview

A former French Overseas Territory, the Union of the Comoros declared independence on 6 July 1975. The islands are situated at the northern entrance to the Mozambique Channel, between the African mainland and the island of Madagascar. There are three islands: Njazidja (formerly known as Grande Comore), Mwali (Mohéli), and Nzwani (Anjouan). A fourth island in the archipelago, Mayotte (Mahoré), is formally claimed by Comoros but chose to remain a French dependency. The nation has been beset by instability during most of its life and, despite broad acceptance in 2002 of a new constitution, which proposed a degree of autonomy for the three islands and resolution of political differences with Anjouan, re-unification remains fragile. The largest town, capital and principal port is Moroni on south-western Njazidja. An archipelagic state, territorial seas (12 n miles) are claimed. A 200 n mile EEZ has been claimed but the limits are not fully defined.

Bases

Moroni.

PATROL FORCES

2 YAMAYURI CLASS (PBI)

Name	*No*	*Builders*	*Commissioned*
KARTHALA	–	Ishihara Dockyard Co Ltd	Oct 1981
NTRINGUI	–	Ishihara Dockyard Co Ltd	Oct 1981

Displacement, tons: 26.5 standard; 41 full load
Dimensions, feet (metres): 59 × 14.1 × 3.6 *(18 × 4.3 × 1.1)*
Main machinery: 2 Nissan RD10TA06 diesels; 900 hp(m) *(661 kW)* maximum; 2 shafts
Speed, knots: 20
Complement: 6
Guns: 2—12.7 mm (twin) MGs.
Radars: Surface search: FRA 10; I-band.

Comment: These two patrol vessels of the Coast Guard type (steel-hulled), supplied under Japanese government co-operation plan. Used for fishery protection services. Operational status doubtful.

KARTHALA *10/1981, Ishihara DY* / 0056842

Democratic Republic of Congo

Country Overview

Formerly known as the Belgian Congo until it became independent in 1960, the Democratic Republic of the Congo was known as Zaire from 1971–97. With an area of 905,568 square miles, it has borders to the north with the Republic of the Congo. A 22 n mile coastline with the Atlantic Ocean separates Angola, to the south, from its Cabinda province. The capital and largest city is Kinshasa (formerly Léopoldville) while the principal ports are Matadi and Boma, on the lower Congo, and Banana, at its mouth. Territorial seas (12 n miles) are claimed. An EEZ has reportedly been claimed but the details have not been published. A cease fire in the civil war was declared in September 1999 although some fighting continued until January 2001. In July 2003, the Transitional National Government was established as part of the evolving peace process.

Headquarters Appointments

Chief of the Navy:
Vice Admiral Didier Etumba Longila

Personnel

(a) 2009: 6,700 (1,000 officers)
(b) Voluntary service

Organisation and Bases

There are five regional commands and 19 naval bases as follows:
1 Region (Lakes Tanganyika and Mweru): Kalemie (11 NB) (HQ), Moliro (12 NB), Pweto (13 NB), Uvira (14 NB)
2 Region(Middle Congo and tributaries): Kinshasha (21 NB) (HQ), Bolobo (22 NB), Bandundu (23 NB), Ilebo (24 NB)
3 Region (Lower Congo): Banana (31 NB) (HQ), Boma (32 NB), Matadi (33 NB)
4 Region (Higher Congo and tributaries): Mbandaka (41 NB) (HQ), Zongo (42 NB), Bumba (43 NB), Kisangani (44 NB)
5 Region (Lakes Kivu, Edward and Albert): Goma (51 NB) (HQ), Bukavu (52 NB), Vitshumbi (53 NB), Mahagi (54 NB)

PATROL FORCES

Notes: Some barges and small patrol craft have been mounted with guns.

1 SHANGHAI II (TYPE 062) CLASS (FAST ATTACK CRAFT—GUN) (PC)

102

Displacement, tons: 113 standard; 134 full load
Dimensions, feet (metres): 127.3 × 17.7 × 5.6 *(38.8 × 5.4 × 1.7)*
Main machinery: 2 Type L-12V-180 diesels; 2,400 hp(m) *(1.76 MW)* (forward); 2 Type 12-D-6 diesels; 1,820 hp(m) *(1.34 MW)* (aft); 4 shafts
Speed, knots: 30. **Range, n miles:** 700 at 16.5 kt on 1 engine
Complement: 38
Guns: 4 China 37 mm/63 (2 twin); 180 rds/min to 8.5 km *(4.6 n miles)*; weight of shell 1.42 kg.
4 USSR 25 mm/60 (2 twin); 270 rds/min to 3 km *(1.6 n miles)* anti-aircraft; weight of shell 0.34 kg.
Radars: Surface search: Furuno; I-band.

Comment: Four craft were originally delivered from China 1976–78. Two of these were replaced in 1987. All craft were reported derelict after the civil war but, following the refurbishment of *102*, more may be restored to operational use.

SHANGHAI II 102 *3/2005, M Declerck* / 1151082

Congo-Brazzaville

Country Overview

Formerly known as the Middle Congo, part of a French colony, the Republic of Congo gained independence in 1960. An unstable political period followed, culminating in civil war between 1997 and 2000 when a Transitional Council was created. A new constitution was approved by referendum in 2002. With an area of 132,000 square miles, it is situated in west-central Africa and has borders to the north with Cameroon and the Central African Republic, to the south-west with Angola (Cabinda enclave) and to the west with Gabon. The River Congo, a major transport artery, provides the southern and much of the eastern border with the Democratic Republic of Congo (formerly Zaire). It has a 91 n mile coastline with the Atlantic Ocean. Brazzaville is the capital and largest city while Pointe Noire is the principal port and centre of the offshore oil industry. Congo has not claimed an EEZ but is one of a few coastal states which claims a 200 n mile territorial sea. The navyconsists mainly of riverine craft but acquisition of offshore patrol vessels to protect offshore resources is a possibility.

Headquarters Appointments

Chief of the Navy:
Capitaine de Vaisseau Andre Bouagnabea Moundanza

Organisation

There are two commands: Brazzaville (riverine) and Pointe Noire (coastal).

Bases

Pointe Noire, Brazzaville, Impfondo.

Cook Islands

Country Overview

The Cook Islands are a South Pacific island group which became self-governing in 1965; defence and external affairs remain the responsibility of the New Zealand government. Situated some 2,430 n miles south of Hawaii, they comprise two groups of widely scattered islands. The Southern Group includes Rarotonga, Aitutaki, Atiu, Mangaia, Mauke, Mitiaro, Manuae and Takutea. The Northern Group is composed of low-lying coral islands and includes Pukapuka, Tongareva (also called Penrhyn), Manihiki, Palmerston, Rakahanga, Suwarrow and Nassau. The port of Avarua on the island of Rarotonga is the administrative centre. Territorial seas (12 n miles) are claimed. An Exclusive Economic Zone (EEZ) (200 n miles) is claimed but limits have not been fully defined by boundary agreements.

Headquarters Appointments

Maritime Commander:
Superintendent Taivero Isamaela

Bases

Avatiu Wharf, Rarotonga

PATROL FORCES

1 PACIFIC CLASS (LARGE PATROL CRAFT) (PB)

Name	*Builders*	*Commissioned*
TE KUKUPA	Australian Shipbuilding Industries	1 Sep 1989

Displacement, tons: 162 full load
Dimensions, feet (metres): 103.3 × 26.6 × 6.9 *(31.5 × 8.1 × 2.1)*
Main machinery: 2 Caterpillar 3516TA diesels; 2,820 hp *(2.1 MW)* sustained; 2 shafts
Speed, knots: 20
Range, n miles: 2,500 at 12 kt
Complement: 17 (3 officers)
Radars: Surface search: Furuno 1011; I-band.

Comment: Laid down 16 May 1988 and launched 27 January 1989. Cost, training and support provided by Australia under defence co-operation. Acceptance date was 9 March 1989 but the handover was deferred another six months because of the change in local government. Has Furuno D/F equipment, SATNAV and a Stressl seaboat with a 40 hp outboard engine. A half-life refit was conducted in 1997 and, following the announcement by the Australian government to extend the Pacific Patrol Boat programme to a 30 year ship life, *Te Kukupa* undertook a life extension refit at Townsville in 2006.

TE KUKUPA *8/2007, John Mortimer* / 1166718

Costa Rica

SERVICIO NACIONAL GUARDACOSTAS

Country Overview

The Republic of Costa Rica is an independent Central American State which lies between Nicaragua to the north and Panama to the south-east. With an area of 19,652 square miles, it has a 584 n mile coastline with the North Pacific Ocean and of 112 n miles with the Caribbean. The uninhabited Cocos Island, about 290 n miles southwest of Burrica Point, is also under Costa Rican sovereignty. The country's capital is San José while other important cities are the Caribbean port of Limón and the Pacific port of Puntarenas. Territorial seas (12 n miles) are claimed. While a 200 n mile EEZ has been claimed, the limits have only been partly defined by boundary agreements.

Personnel

(a) 2009: 350 officers and men
(b) Voluntary service

Bases

Pacific: Golfito, Punta Arenas, Cuajiniquil, Quepos.
Atlantic: Limon, Moin.

PATROL FORCES

Notes: Three Boston Whalers, *Tauro* (20-1), *Villa Mar* (20-2) and *Cocori* (22-1) are operational. The first of six Costa Rican-built Apex RIBs, *Escorpion* (24-1), entered service in 2001.

APEX RIB *5/2001, Julio Montes* / 0109935

1 SWIFT 105 ft CLASS (FAST PATROL CRAFT) (PB)

Name	*No*	*Builders*	*Commissioned*
ISLA DEL COCO	105-1 (ex-1055)	Swiftships, Morgan City	Feb 1978

Displacement, tons: 118 full load
Dimensions, feet (metres): 105 × 23.3 × 7.2 *(32 × 7.1 × 2.2)*
Main machinery: 3 MTU 12V 1163 TC92 diesels; 10,530 hp(m) *(7.74 MW)*; 3 shafts
Speed, knots: 33. **Range, n miles:** 1,200 at 18 kt; 2,000 at 12 kt
Complement: 17 (3 officers)
Guns: 1—12.7 mm MG. 4—7.62 mm (2 twin) MGs. 1—60 mm mortar.
Radars: Navigation: Furuno; I-band.

Comment: Aluminium construction. Refitted in 1985–86 under FMS funding. The twin MGs are fitted abaft the bridge and the mortar is on the stern. Based at Punta Arenas.

ISLA DEL COCO (old number) *2/1989* / 0056844

3 POINT CLASS (COASTAL PATROL CRAFT) (PB)

Name	*No*	*Builders*	*Commissioned*
SANTAMARIA (ex-*Point Camden*)	82-2 (ex-82373)	J Martinac, Tacoma	4 May 1970
JUAN RAFAEL MORA (ex-*Point Chico*)	82-3 (ex-82339)	US Coast Guard Yard, Curtis Bay	29 Oct 1962
PANCHA CARRASCO (ex-*Point Bridge*)	82-4 (ex-82338)	US Coast Guard Yard, Curtis Bay	10 Oct 1962

Displacement, tons: 67 full load
Dimensions, feet (metres): 83 × 17.2 × 5.8 *(25.3 × 5.2 × 1.8)*
Main machinery: 2 Caterpillar 3412 diesels; 1,600 hp *(1.19 MW)*; 2 shafts
Speed, knots: 23. **Range, n miles:** 1,200 at 8 kt
Complement: 10
Guns: 2—12.7 mm MGs.
Radars: Navigation: Raytheon SPS-64/Hughes SPS-73; I-band.

Comment: First transferred from USCG on 15 December 1999. A second transferred on 22 June 2001 and third on 28 September 2001.

SANTAMARIA *2/2000, Julio Montes* / 0109937

2 SWIFT 65 ft CLASS (COASTAL PATROL CRAFT) (PB)

CABO BLANCO 65-3 **ISLA BURICA** 65-4

Displacement, tons: 35 full load
Dimensions, feet (metres): 65.5 × 18.4 × 6.6 *(20 × 5.6 × 2)*
Main machinery: 2 MTU 8V 331 TC92 diesels; 1,770 hp(m) *(1.3 MW)*; 2 shafts
Speed, knots: 23
Range, n miles: 500 at 18 kt
Complement: 7 (2 officers)
Guns: 1—12.7 mm MG. 4—7.62 mm (2 twin) MGs. 1—60 mm mortar.
Radars: Navigation: Furuno; I-band.

Comment: Built by Swiftships, Morgan City in 1979. Refitted 1985–86 under FMS funding. 65-3 is based at Limon.

CABO BLANCO *2/2008*, Marco Ghiglino* / 1335715

1 SWIFT 36 ft CLASS (INSHORE PATROL CRAFT) (PB)

PUERTO QUEPOS (ex-*Telamanca*) 36-1

Displacement, tons: 11 full load
Dimensions, feet (metres): 36 × 10 × 2.6 *(11 × 3.1 × 0.8)*
Main machinery: 2 Detroit diesels; 500 hp *(373 kW)*; 2 shafts
Speed, knots: 24
Range, n miles: 250 at 18 kt
Complement: 4 (1 officer)
Guns: 1—12.7 mm MG. 1—60 mm mortar.
Radars: Navigation: Raytheon 1900; I-band.

Comment: Built by Swiftships, Morgan City and completed in March 1986.

PUERTO QUEPOS *2/2000, Julio Montes* / 0109936

1 SWIFT 42 ft CLASS (INSHORE PATROL CRAFT) (PB)

PRIMERA DAMA (ex-*Donna Margarita*, ex-*Puntarena* 42-1)

Displacement, tons: 11 full load
Dimensions, feet (metres): 42.0 × 14.1 × 2.95 *(12.8 × 4.3 × 0.9)*
Main machinery: 2 Detroit diesels; 700 hp *(520 kW)*; 2 shafts
Speed, knots: 33
Range, n miles: 450 at 18 kt
Complement: 4 (1 officer)

Comment: Completed in 1986. Formerly used as a hospital craft.

Cote d'Ivoire

MARINE CÔTE D'IVOIRE

Country Overview

Formerly a French colony, The Republic of Côte d'Ivoire gained full independence in 1960. Located in west Africa, the country has an area of 133,425 square miles and a 281 n mile coastline with the Gulf of Guinea. It is bordered to the east by Ghana and to the west by Liberia and Guinea. The capital is Yamoussoukro while the former capital, Abidjan, is the largest city, principal port and commercial centre. A further port at San Pedro is linked to Mali by rail. Territorial seas (12 n miles) are claimed. A 200 n mile EEZ has been claimed but the limits have not been defined by boundary agreements.

Following the rebellion of September 2002, a Government of National Conciliation has restored a level of stability although internal tensions continue. While the navy remains unchanged, operational effectiveness is likely to have suffered.

Headquarters Appointments

Chief of Naval Staff:
Rear Admiral Vagba Faussignaux

Bases

Use made of ports at Locodjo (Abidjan), Sassandra, Tabouand San-Pédro

Personnel

2009: 950 (75 officers)

PATROL FORCES

1 PATRA CLASS (LARGE PATROL CRAFT) (PBO)

Name	*No*	*Builders*	*Launched*	*Commissioned*
L'INTRÉPIDE	–	Auroux, Arcachon	21 July 1978	6 Oct 1978

Displacement, tons: 147.5 full load
Dimensions, feet (metres): 132.5 × 19.4 × 5.2 *(40.4 × 5.9 × 1.6)*
Main machinery: 2 SACM AGO 195 V12 CZSHR diesels; 4,340 hp(m) *(3.19 MW)* sustained; 2 shafts; cp props
Speed, knots: 26. **Range, n miles**: 1,750 at 10 kt; 750 at 20 kt
Complement: 19 (2 officers)
Guns: 1 Breda 40 mm/70. 1 Oerlikon 20 mm. 2—7.62 mm MGs.
Radars: Surface search: Racal Decca 1226; I-band.

Comment: Of similar design to French Patra class. Laid down 7 July 1977. Patrol endurance of five days. SS-12M missiles are no longer carried. Sister ship *L'Ardent* decommissioned in 2003 to provide spares. Operational status doubtful.

PATRA CLASS *3/1994* / 0080123

CTM (French colours) *6/1995* / 0012960

AUXILIARIES

Notes: (1) There are also some Rotork 412 craft supplied in 1980. Some are naval, some civilian.
(2) Two French harbour tugs *Merisier* and *Meronnior* were acquired in September 1999.
(3) A Yunnan class LCM *Atchan* may still be in limited service.

2 CTM (LCM)

ABY (ex-*CTM 15*) **TIAGHA** (ex-*CTM 16*)

Displacement, tons: 150 full load
Dimensions, feet (metres): 78 × 21 × 4.2 *(23.8 × 6.4 × 1.3)*
Main machinery: 2 Poyaud 520 V8 diesels; 225 hp(m) *(165 kW)*; 2 shafts
Speed, knots: 9.5. **Range, n miles**: 350 at 8 kt
Complement: 6
Military lift: 48 tons

Comment: Transferred from France in March 1999. Built in about 1968. Bow ramps are fitted. Probably not operational.

AFFAIRES MARITIMES

2 RODMAN 890 (PBR)

AMOUGNA AF 003 **MONSEKELA** AF 004

Dimensions, feet (metres): 29.2 × 9.8 × 3.6 *(8.9 × 3 × 0.8)*
Main machinery: 2 Volvo diesels; 300 hp(m) *(220 kW)*; 2 shafts
Speed, knots: 28. **Range, n miles**: 150 at 25 kt
Complement: 3
Guns: 1—7.62 mm MG.
Radars: Surface search: I-band.

Comment: Two craft delivered by Rodman in 1997. Employed on Fishery Protection duties.

AMOUGNA *6/1997, Rodman* / 0583296

Croatia

HRVATSKA RATNA MORNARICA

Country Overview

Formerly a constituent republic of the Federal Republic of Yugoslavia, Croatia declared its independence in 1991. With an area of 21,829 square miles, it is situated in south-east Europe in the Balkan Peninsula and bordered to the north by Slovenia and Hungary, to the east and south by Bosnia and Herzegovina and to the east by Montenegro. There are some 1,100 offshore islands and there is an overall coastline of 3,127 n miles with the Adriatic Sea on which Dubrovnik, Split, Ploče and Rijeka are the principal ports. The capital and largest city is Zagreb. Territorial waters (12 n miles) are claimed and an Ecological and Fishery Zone was declared in 2004.

Headquarters Appointments

Commander of the Navy: Commodore Ante Urlić
Commander, Fleet: Captain Marin Stošić

Personnel

2009: 1,850 (620 officers)

General

The Navy was established on 12 September 1991. The law to establish a Coast Guard, as a component of the navy, was passed on 3 October 2007. Its roles are to include fishery protection, counter-drugs and smuggling operations and environmental protection. Some naval units will almost certainly be transferred to the new force.

Bases and Organisation

Headquarters: Lora-Split.
Main base: Split.
Minor bases: Sibenik, Pula, Ploče, Lastovo, Vis.
River Patrol Flotillas: Osijek (Drava) and Sisak (Sava).

The future organisation of the Croatian Navy is to include the naval flotilla, a coastguard and a battalion of marine infantry.

Coast Defence

Three mobile RBS 15 batteries on trucks are likely to be decommissioned. Total of 10 coastal artillery batteries. Jadran command system for coastal defence using Italian (Gem) built and US (More) radars installed in 2003. Sites include the islands of Vis, Lastovo, Dugi Otok and Mljet.

Naval Infantry

Headquarters in Split. A move to Dubrovnik is under consideration.

SUBMARINES

2 R-2 MALA CLASS
(TWO-MAN SWIMMER DELIVERY VEHICLES) (LDW)

Displacement, tons: 1.4
Dimensions, feet (metres): 16.1 × 4.6 × 4.3 *(4.9 × 1.4 × 1.3)*
Main machinery: 1 motor; 4.7 hp(m) *(3.5 kW)*; 1 shaft
Speed, knots: 4.4
Range, n miles: 18 at 4.4 kt; 23 at 3.7 kt
Complement: 2
Mines: 250 kg of limpet mines.

Comment: Free-flood craft with the main motor, battery, navigation pod and electronic equipment housed in separate watertight cylinders. Instrumentation includes aircraft type gyrocompass, magnetic compass, depth gauge (with 0 to 100 m scale), echo-sounder, sonar and two searchlights. Constructed of light aluminium and plexiglass, it is fitted with fore and after-hydroplanes,the tail being a conventional cruciform with a single rudder abaft the screw. Large perspex windows give a good all-round view. Operating depth, 60 m *(196.9 ft)*, maximum. Two reported sold to Syria and one to Sweden.

Notes: There is also an R-1 craft which is 3.7 m long and capable of 2.8 kt down to 50 m. It has a range of 4 n miles. There may also be some locally built SDVs.

R-2 *2/2002, RH-Alan* / 0528428

R-1 *2/2002, RH-Alan* / 0528427

LAND-BASED MARITIME AIRCRAFT

Notes: Six Pilatus aircraft, four Mi-8 helicopters and one unmanned aircraft are used for fishery protection and counter-pollution tasks.

PATROL FORCES

Notes: (1) Procurement of four new offshore patrol vessels remains under consideration. The broad requirement is for a 78 m, 1,000 ton vessel capable of 25 kt.
(2) Two RHIBs were acquired in 2008 for special forces. Their names are *Bljesak* and *Oluja*.

1 RIVER PATROL CRAFT (PBR)

OB 93

Displacement, tons: 48 full load
Dimensions, feet (metres): 63.6 × 14.4 × 3.3 *(19.4 × 4.4 × 1.0)*
Main machinery: 2 Torpedo B 536RM diesels; 280 hp *(206 kW)*; 2 shafts
Speed, knots: 12
Complement: 9
Guns: 1—20 mm.
Radars: Surface search/navigation: Furuno M 1942 Mk 2; I-band.

Comment: Former minesweeper launched in 1971 at Mačvanska Mitrovica. Used as a river patrol vessel. Based in Osijek on River Drava.

OB 93 *10/2007, Croatian Navy* / 1170102

1 KONČAR (TYPE R-02) CLASS
(FAST ATTACK CRAFT—MISSILE) (PTGF)

Name	*No*	*Builders*	*Launched*	*Commissioned*
ŠIBENIK (ex-*Vlado Četković*)	RTOP 21 (ex-402)	Tito SY, Kraljevica	20 Aug 1977	Mar 1978

Displacement, tons: 264 full load
Dimensions, feet (metres): 150.3 × 27.6 × 9.8 *(45.8 × 8.4 × 3.0)*
Main machinery: CODAG; 2 RR Proteus 52-M558 gas turbines; 7,200 hp *(5.37 MW)* sustained; 2 MTU 16V 538 TB91 diesels; 7,200 hp(m) *(5.29 MW)* sustained; 4 shafts; cp props
Speed, knots: 38; 23 (diesels)
Range, n miles: 500 at 35 kt; 880 at 23 kt (diesels)
Complement: 31 (5 officers)

Missiles: SSM: 4 Saab RBS 15B; active radar homing to 70 km *(37.8 n miles)* at 0.8 Mach; warhead 83 kg.
Guns: 1 Bofors 57 mm/70; 200 rds/min to 17 km *(9.3 n miles)*; weight of shell 2.4 kg. 128 mm rocket launcher for illuminants.
1—30 mm/65 AK 630M; 6 barrels; 3,000 rds/min to 4 km.
Countermeasures: Decoys: 2 Wallop Barricade double layer chaff launchers.
Weapons control: PEAB 9LV 202 GFCS.
Radars: Surface search: Decca 1226; I-band.
Fire control: Philips TAB; I/J-band.

Programmes: Type name, Raketna Topovnjaca. Recommissioned into the Croatian Navy on 28 September 1991. Others of the class serve with the Yugoslav Navy.
Modernisation: The original Styx missiles have been replaced by RBS 15 and the after 57 mm gun by a 30 mm AK 630. Fire-control radar was updated in 1994 and a new surface search radar is to be acquired in 2008.
Structure: Aluminium superstructure. Designed by the Naval Shipping Institute in Zagreb based on Swedish Spica class with bridge amidships like Malaysian boats.
Operational: Based at Split. Reported operational.

ŠIBENIK *10/2004, Croatian Navy* / 1170103

4 MIRNA (TYPE 140) CLASS
(FAST ATTACK CRAFT—PATROL) (PCM)

Name	*No*	*Builders*	*Launched*
NOVIGRAD (ex-*Biokovo*)	OB 61 (ex-171)	Kraljevica Shipyard	18 Dec 1980
ŠOLTA (ex-*Mukos*)	OB 62 (ex-176)	Kraljevica Shipyard	11 Nov 1982
CAVTAT (ex-*Vrlika*, ex-*Cer*)	OB 63 (ex-180)	Kraljevica Shipyard	27 Sep 1984
HRVATSKA KOSTAJNICA (ex-*Durmitor*)	OB 64 (ex-181)	Kraljevica Shipyard	10 Jan 1985

Displacement, tons: 142 full load
Dimensions, feet (metres): 106.9 × 22 × 7.5 *(32.6 × 6.7 × 2.3)*
Main machinery: 2 SEMT-Pielstick 12 PA4 200 VGDS diesels; 5,292 hp(m) *(3.89 MW)* sustained; 2 shafts
Speed, knots: 25
Range, n miles: 600 at 24 kt
Complement: 19 (3 officers)

Missiles: SAM: 1 SA-N-5 Grail quad mounting; manual aiming; IR homing to 6 km *(3.2 n miles)* at 1.5 Mach; altitude to 2,500 m *(8,000 ft)*; warhead 1.5 kg.
Guns: 1 Bofors 40 mm/70. 4 Hispano 20 mm (quad) Type M75. 2—128 mm illuminant launchers.
Depth charges: 8 DCs.
Countermeasures: Decoys: chaff launcher (PB 62).
Radars: Surface search: Racal Decca 1216C; I-band.
Sonars: Simrad SQS-3D/SF; active high frequency.

Comment: An electric outboard motor has been removed. Two were captured after sustaining heavy damage, one by a missile and the other by a torpedo fired from the island of Brač. Both fully repaired and all four are operational and display coast guard markings.

SOLTA *5/2007, Marco Ghiglino* / 1167916

2 HELSINKI CLASS (FAST ATTACK CRAFT—MISSILE) (PTGM)

Name	*No*	*Builders*	*Commissioned*
VUKOVAR (ex-*Oulu*)	RTOP 41 (ex-62)	Wärtsilä, Helsinki	1 Oct 1985
DUBROVNIK (ex-*Kotka*)	RTOP 42 (ex-63)	Wärtsilä, Helsinki	16 June 1986

Displacement, tons: 280 standard; 300 full load
Dimensions, feet (metres): 147.6 × 29.2 × 9.9 *(45 × 8.9 × 3)*
Main machinery: 3 MTU 16V 538 TB92 diesels; 10,230 hp(m) *(7.52 MW)* sustained; 3 shafts
Speed, knots: 30
Complement: 30

Missiles: SSM: 8 Saab RBS 15 ❶; inertial guidance; active radar homing to 70 km *(37.8 n miles)* at 0.8 Mach; warhead 150 kg; sea-skimmer.
Guns: 1 Bofors 57 mm/70 ❷; 200 rds/min to 17 km *(9.3 n miles)*; weight of shell 2.4 kg.
6—103 mm rails for rocket illuminants.
2 Sako 23 mm/87 (twin) ❸.
Depth charges: 2 rails.
Countermeasures: Decoys: Philax chaff and IR flare launcher.
ESM: Argo; radar intercept.
Weapons control: Saab EOS 400 optronic director.
Radars: Surface search: 9GR 600 ❹; I-band.
Fire control: Philips 9LV 225 ❺; J-band.
Navigation: Raytheon ARPA; I-band.
Sonars: Simrad Marine SS 304; high-resolution active scanning.
Finnyards Sonac/PTA towed array; low frequency.

Programmes: Both ordered for the Finnish Navy on 13 January 1983. Decommissioned in 2007 and sold to Croatia in 2008. Details are as for ships in Finnish service and may be different.
Modernisation: A Sako barbette can take either twin 23 mm guns or a Sadral SAM launcher. The Sako mounting has replaced the original ZU version.
Structure: The light armament can be altered to suit the planned role. Missile racks can also be replaced by mine rails. Hull and superstructure of light alloy.

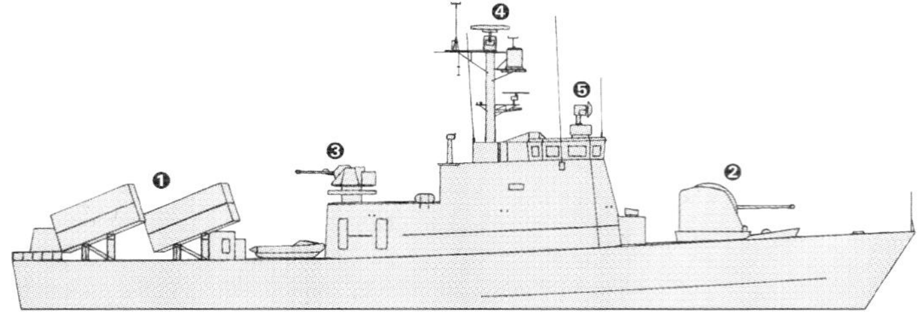

VUKOVAR *(Scale 1 : 600), Ian Sturton* / 1335453

VUKOVAR *6/2008*, Croatian Navy* / 1294947

2 KRALJ (TYPE R-03) CLASS (FSG)

Name	*No*	*Builders*	*Launched*	*Commissioned*
KRALJ PETAR KRESIMIR IV	RTOP 11	Kraljevica Shipyard	21 Mar 1992	7 July 1992
KRALJ DMITAR ZVONIMIR	RTOP 12	Kraljevica Shipyard	30 Mar 2001	16 Sep 2001

Displacement, tons: 382 (11), 390 (12) full load
Dimensions, feet (metres): 177.8 × 28.2 × 11.8 *(54.2 × 8.6 × 3.6)*
Main machinery: 3 M 504B-2 diesels; 12,500 hp(m) *(9.2 MW)* sustained; 3 shafts
Speed, knots: 32. **Range, n miles**: 1,700 at 18 kt
Complement: 32 (5 officers)

Missiles: SSM: 4 or 8 Saab RBS 15B (2 or 4 twin) ❶; active radar homing to 70 km *(37.8 n miles)* at 0.8 Mach; warhead 83 kg.
Guns: 1 Bofors 57 mm/70 ❷; 200 rds/min to 17 km *(9.3 n miles)*; weight of shell 2.4 kg. Launchers for illuminants on side of mounting.
1—30 mm/65 AK 630M ❸; 6 barrels; 3,000 rds/min combined to 4 km.
Mines: 4 AIM-70 magnetic or 6 SAG-1 acoustic in lieu of SSMs.
Countermeasures: Decoys: 2 Wallop Barricade chaff/IR launchers.
Weapons control: PEAB 9LV 249 Mk 2 director.
Kolonka for AK 630M.
Radars: Surface search: Racal BT 502 ❹; E/F-band.
Fire control: PEAB 9LV 249 Mk 2 ❺; I/J-band.
Navigation: Racal 1290A; I-band.
Sonars: RIZ PP10M; hull-mounted; active search; high frequency.

Programmes: The building of this class (formerly called Kobra by NATO) was officially announced as 'suspended' in 1989 but was restarted in 1991. Designated as a missile Gunboat.
Modernisation: Both ships are to be modernised with new diesel engines, probably of German origin. The RBS 15 missiles are to be overhauled.
Structure: Derived from the Koncar class with a stretched hull and a new superstructure. Either missiles or mines may be carried. The second of class is 0.6 m longer than the first ship and incorporates modifications to the bridge structure.
Operational: Based at Split. The future of RTOP 12 is under consideration.

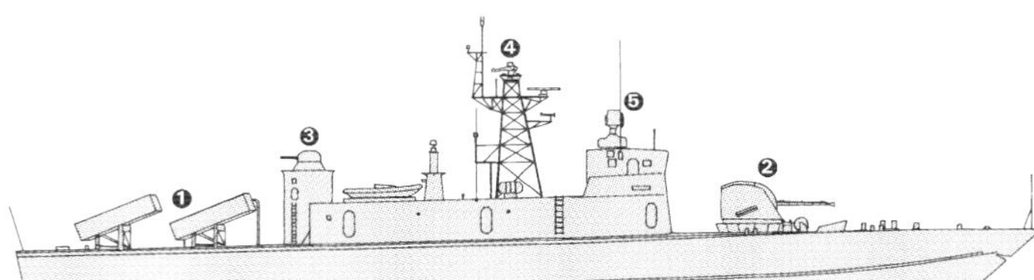

KRALJ DMITAR ZVONIMIR *(Scale 1 : 600), Ian Sturton* / 1044094

KRALJ PETAR KRESIMIR IV *2/2002, Hrvatski Vojnik* / 0528426

KRALJ PETAR KRESIMIR IV *10/2007, Croatian Navy* / 1170104

KRALJ DMITAR ZVONIMIR *10/2007, Croatian Navy* / 1170105

AMPHIBIOUS FORCES

Notes: The former landing craft DSM 110, decommissioned in 2004, is reported to be undergoing refit at Marina Punat. It is likely to be re-activated as a transport ship although it is unclear whether this is to be under naval or civilian ownership.

2 CETINA (SILBA) CLASS (LCT/ML)

Name	*No*	*Builders*	*Launched*	*Commissioned*
CETINA	DBM 81	Brodosplit, Split	18 July 1992	19 Feb 1993
KRKA	DBV 82	Brodosplit, Split	17 Sep 1994	9 Mar 1995

Displacement, tons: 880 full load
Dimensions, feet (metres): 163.1 oa; 144 wl × 33.5 × 10.5 *(49.7; 43.9 × 10.2 × 3.2)*
Main machinery: 2 Alpha 10V23L-VO diesels; 3,100 hp(m) *(2.28 MW)* sustained; 2 shafts; cp props
Speed, knots: 12. **Range, n miles**: 1,200 at 12 kt
Complement: 27 (5 officers)
Military lift: 460 tons or 6 medium tanks or 7 APCs or 4—130 mm guns plus towing vehicles or 300 troops with equipment
Missiles: SAM: 1 SA-N-5 Grail quad mounting *(Cetina)*.
Guns: 4—30 mm/65 (2 twin) AK 230 *(Cetina)*.
2 *(Krka)* Hispano 20 mm M71.
Mines: SAG-2 (152 DBM 81, 114 DBM 82); MNS 90 (124 DBM 81, 92 DBM 82); AIM M70 (72 DBM 81, 52 DBM 82).
Radars: Surface search: Racal Decca 1290A; I-band.

Comment: Ro-ro design with bow and stern ramps. *Cetina*'s two 30 mm guns are either side of the bridge. Can be used for minelaying, transporting weapons or equipment and personnel. *Krka* is being used as a water carrier. Both are operational and based at Split.

CETINA *9/2005, Croatian Navy* / 1170106

KRKA *6/2007, Freivogel Collection* / 1167948

3 TYPE 21 (LCVP)

DJB 103 **DJB 104** **DJB 107**

Displacement, tons: 38 full load
Dimensions, feet (metres): 69.9 × 14.1 × 5.2 *(21.3 × 4.3 × 1.1)*
Main machinery: 1 (2 in *103*) MTU 12V 331 TC81 diesel; 1,450 hp(m) *(1.07 MW)*; 1 shaft (2 waterjets in *103*)
Speed, knots: 21
Range, n miles: 320 at 18 kt
Complement: 6
Military lift: 6 tons or 40 troops
Guns: 1—20 mm M71. 1—30 mm grenade launcher.
Radars: Navigation: Decca 1213; I-band.

Comment: Built at Greben Shipyard 1987–88. *DJB 103* upgraded with new main machinery in 1991.

DJB 103 ***5/1997, Dario Vuljanič*** / 0012246

1 TYPE 22 (LCVPF)

DJC 106 (ex-624)

Displacement, tons: 42 full load
Dimensions, feet (metres): 73.2 × 15.7 × 3.3 *(22.3 × 4.8 × 1)*
Main machinery: 2 MTU MWM 604TDV8 diesels; 1,740 hp(m) *(1.28 MW)*; 2 waterjets
Speed, knots: 35. **Range, n miles:** 320 at 22 kt
Complement: 8
Military lift: 40 troops or 15 tons cargo
Guns: 2 Hispano 20 mm. 1—30 mm grenade launcher.
Radars: Navigation: Decca 150; I-band.

Comment: Built at Greben Shipyard in 1987 of polyester and glass fibre.

DJC 106 ***8/1998, N A Sifferlinger*** / 0038489

MINE WARFARE FORCES

1 MPMB CLASS (MINEHUNTER—INSHORE) (MHI)

Name	*No*	*Builders*	*Launched*	*Commissioned*
KORCULA	LM 51	Greben, Vela Luka	22 Apr 2006	20 Apr 2007

Displacement, tons: 173 full load
Dimensions, feet (metres): 84.3 × 22.3 × 8.5 (25.7 × 6.8 × 2.6)
Main machinery: 2 MTU 8V 183TE62 diesels; 993 hp(m) (730 kW); 2 Holland Roerpropeler stern azimuth thrusters; bow thruster; 190 hp(m) (140 kW)
Speed, knots: 11. **Range, n miles:** 1,000 at 9 kt
Complement: 14 (3 officers)
Missiles: SAM: SA-N-10 (Igla).
Guns: 1—20 mm M71.
Countermeasures: Minehunting: 1 Super Sea Rover (Benthos); Minesweeping: MDL3 mechanical sweep.
Radars: Navigation: Kelvin Hughes 5000 ARPA, NINAS Mod.
Sonars: Reson mine avoidance; active; high frequency.
Klein 2000 side scan; active for route survey; high frequency.

Comment: Ordered in 1995. The ship has a trawler appearance with a gun on the forecastle and a hydraulic crane on the sweep deck. GRP hull. Due to a shortage of funds, building had stopped by late 1999 but was later revived. Became fully operational in mid-2008. Further ships, possibly to a modified design, are under consideration.

KORCULA ***9/2007, Croatian Navy*** / 1170101

TRAINING SHIPS

Notes: A sail training ship is under construction at Greben Shipyard. Of GRP construction, the vessel is to replace *Jadran* (in Montenegro) and is to be available for both naval and maritime schools. The name is likely to be *Vila Velebita*.

1 MOMA (PROJECT 861) CLASS (AX)

Name	*No*	*Builders*	*Commissioned*
ANDRIJA MOHOROVIČIĆ	BS 72 (ex-PH 33)	Northern Shipyard, Gdansk	1972

Displacement, tons: 1,514 full load
Dimensions, feet (metres): 240.5 × 36.7 × 12.8 *(73.3 × 11.2 × 3.9)*
Main machinery: 2 Zgoda-Sulzer 6TD48 diesels; 3,300 hp(m) *(2.4 MW)* sustained; 2 shafts; cp props
Speed, knots: 17
Range, n miles: 9,000 at 11 kt
Complement: 27 (4 officers)
Radars: Navigation: Racal Decca BT 502; I-band.

Comment: Built in 1971 for the Yugoslav Navy as a survey vessel. Based at Split. Has a 5 ton crane and carries a launch. Used as the Naval Academy training ship.

ANDRIJA MOHOROVIČIĆ ***1/2007, Croatian Navy*** / 1170100

AUXILIARIES

Notes: In addition there are two harbour tugs *LR-71* and *LR-73*, two diving tenders *BRM-81* and *BRM-83*, auxiliary transport ship *PDS-713*, five harbour transport boats *BMT-1/5*, and two yachts *Učka* (ex-*Podgorka*) and *Jadranka* (ex-civilian *Smile*). *Jadranka* was involved in a grounding incident in April 2006.

LR 71 ***12/2006, Croatian Navy*** / 1170099

BRM 83 ***2/2007, Croatian Navy*** / 1335354

1 SPASILAC CLASS (ASR)

Name	*No*	*Builders*	*Commissioned*
FAUST VRANČIĆ (ex-*Spasilac*)	BS 73 (ex-PS 12)	Tito Shipyard, Belgrade	10 Sep 1976

Displacement, tons: 1,590 full load
Dimensions, feet (metres): 182 × 39.4 × 12.5 *(55.5 × 12 × 3.8)*
Main machinery: 2 diesels; 4,340 hp(m) *(3.19 MW)*; 2 shafts; Kort nozzle props; bow thruster
Speed, knots: 13
Range, n miles: 4,000 at 12 kt
Complement: 28 (4 officers)
Cargo capacity: 350 tons fuel; 300 tons deck cargo
Guns: 2—20 mm M 71.
Radars: Navigation: Kelvin Hughes Nucleus 5000R; I-band.

Comment: Former salvage ship now employed as a training and command unit. All salvage equipment has been removed. Underwent refit during 2005. Based at Split.

FAUST VRANČIĆ *12/2006, Croatian Navy* / 1170098

1 PT 71 TYPE (TRANSPORT) (AKL)

PT 71 (ex-*Meduza*)

Displacement, tons: 710 full load
Dimensions, feet (metres): 152.2 × 23.6 × 17.1 *(46.4 × 7.2 × 5.2)*
Main machinery: 1 Burmeister & Wain diesel; 930 hp(m) *(684 kW)*; 1 shaft
Speed, knots: 10
Complement: 16 (2 officers)
Guns: 1 Bofors 40 mm/60. 2 Hispano 20 mm M71 can be carried.
Radars: Navigation: Racal Decca 1216A; I-band.

Comment: Built in 1953. Underwent refit at Marina Punat in 2007. Water capacity 320 tons.

PT 71 *2/2007, Croatian Navy* / 1170097

MINISTRY OF INTERIOR

Notes: (1) A Ministry of Interior maritime force polices inshore waters. These vessels are in five types:
Type 1: 3—24 m craft capable of 30 kt; P-1 *(Srd)*, P-2 *(Marino)*, P-101 *(Sveti Mihovic)*
Type 2: 6—13 m craft capable of 23 kt; P-11 to P-16
Type 3: 6—11 m craft capable of 23 kt; P-111 to P-116
Type 4: 4—14 m craft capable of 30 kt; P-201, P 202, P 203 and P 207
Type 5: Numerous small craft under 10 m; RIB or inflatable construction
(2) In addition there are civilian registered base port craft with PU (Pula), SB (Sibenic), ST (Split) and so on markings.

P 207 *9/2008*, Per Körnefeldt* / 1335352

SVETI MIHOVIC *9/2008*, Per Körnefeldt* / 1335353

P 114 *9/2008*, Per Körnefeldt* / 1335351

Cuba

MARINA DE GUERRA REVOLUCIONARIA

Country Overview

The Republic of Cuba is an independent republic located in the Caribbean Sea with which it has a 2,020 n mile coastline. The most westerly of the Greater Antilles group, the country comprises two main islands, Cuba (40,519 square miles) and Isla de la Juventud (849 square miles), and more than 1,600 small coral cays and islets. To the west, Cuba commands the approaches to the Gulf of Mexico; the Straits of Florida and the Yucatán Channel separate the country from Florida and Mexico respectively. To the east, the Windward Passage separates the island from Hispaniola (Haiti and the Dominican Republic). Jamaica lies to the south and the Bahamas to the north-east. Havana is the capital, largest city and principal port. Territorial seas (6 n miles) are claimed. A 200 n mile EEZ has been claimed but the limits have not been defined.

The Navy is in a parlous state and has no capability to sustain operations beyond territorial waters.

Headquarters Appointments

Chief of Naval Staff:
Vice Admiral Pedro Perez Miguel Betancourt

Personnel

2009: 2,000 (approximately) (including 500 marines)

Command Organisation

Western Naval District (HQ Cabanas).
Eastern Naval District (HQ Holguin).

Naval Aviation

Four Kamov Ka-28 and 14 Mi-14PL Haze A have been reported but operational status is not known.

Coast Defence

Truck mounted SS-N-2B Styx.

Bases

Cabanas, Nicaro, Cienfuegos, Havana, Santiago de Cuba, Banes.
The Naval Academy is at Punta Santa Ana.

DELETIONS

Notes: Some vessels have been disposed of. Others are decaying alongside in harbour.

CORVETTES

1 PAUK II CLASS (PROJECT 1241PE) (FSM)

321

Displacement, tons: 440 full load
Dimensions, feet (metres): 191.9 × 33.5 × 11.2 *(58.5 × 10.2 × 3.4)*
Main machinery: 2 Type M 521 diesels; 16,184 hp(m) *(11.9 MW)* sustained; 2 shafts
Speed, knots: 32. **Range, n miles:** 2,400 at 14 kt
Complement: 32
Missiles: SAM: SA-N-5 quad launcher; manual aiming, IR homing to 10 km *(5.4 n miles)* at 1.5 Mach; warhead 1.1 kg.
Guns: 1 USSR 76 mm/59 AK 176; 120 rds/min to 15 km *(8 n miles)*; weight of shell 5.9 kg.
1—30 mm/65; 6 barrels; 3,000 rds/min combined to 2 km.
4—25 mm (2 twin).
A/S mortars: 2 RBU 1200 5-tubed fixed; range 1,200 m; warhead 34 kg.
Countermeasures: 2 PK 16 chaff launchers.
Radars: Air/surface search: Positive E; E/F-band.
Navigation: Pechora; I-band.
Fire control: Bass Tilt; H/I-band.
Sonars: Rat Tail; VDS (on transom); attack; high frequency.

Comment: Built at Yaroslav Shipyard in the USSR and transferred in May 1990. Similar to the ships built for India. Has a longer superstructure than the Pauk I and electronics with a radome similar to the Parchim II class. Torpedo tubes removed. Two twin 25 mm guns fitted on the stern. Based at Havana. Operational status doubtful.

PAUK II

2/2001, **Michael Nitz** / 0534082

PATROL FORCES

6 OSA II CLASS (PROJECT 205) (FAST ATTACK CRAFT—MISSILE) (PTGF)

261 262 267 268 271 274

Displacement, tons: 171 standard; 245 full load
Dimensions, feet (metres): 126.6 × 24.9 × 8.8 *(38.6 × 7.6 × 2.7)*
Main machinery: 3 Type M 504 diesels; 10,800 hp(m) *(7.94 MW)* sustained; 3 shafts
Speed, knots: 37.
Range, n miles: 500 at 35 kt
Complement: 30
Missiles: SSM: 4 SS-N-2B Styx; active radar or IR homing to 46 km *(25 n miles)* at 0.9 Mach; warhead 513 kg.
Guns: 4—30 mm/65 (2 twin); 500 rds/min to 5 km *(2.7 n miles)*; weight of shell 0.54 kg.
Radars: Surface search: Square Tie; I-band.
Fire control: Drum Tilt; H/I-band.
IFF: Square Head. High Pole B.

Comment: One Osa II delivered in mid-1976, one in January 1977 and one in March 1978. Further two delivered in December 1978, one in April 1979, one in October 1979, two from Black Sea November 1981, four in February 1982. While a few may be seagoing, most have been cannibalised for spares and all have had their missiles disembarked for use in shore batteries. One was sunk as a tourist attraction in 1998. Based at Nicaro and Cabanas.

OSA II (Bulgarian colours)

8/1998, **E & M Laursen** / 0017645

MINE WARFARE FORCES

2 SONYA CLASS (PROJECT 1265) (MINESWEEPERS/HUNTERS) (MSC/MH)

570 578

Displacement, tons: 450 full load
Dimensions, feet (metres): 157.4 × 28.9 × 6.6 *(48 × 8.8 × 2)*
Main machinery: 2 Kolomna Type 9-D-8 diesels; 2,000 hp(m) *(1.47 MW)* sustained; 2 shafts
Speed, knots: 15
Range, n miles: 3,000 at 10 kt
Complement: 43
Guns: 2—30 mm/65 (twin); 500 rds/min to 5 km *(2.7 n miles)*; weight of shell 0.54 kg.
2—25 mm/80 (twin); 270 rds/min to 3 km *(1.6 n miles)*.
Mines: Can carry 8.
Radars: Navigation: Don 2; I-band.
IFF: 2 Square Head. High Pole B.
Sonars: MG 69/79; hull-mounted; active minehunting; high frequency.

Comment: Transferred from USSR in January and December 1985. Two others are non-operational and these two have not been reported at sea since 1999.

SONYA (Russian colours)

5/1990 / 0056851

3 YEVGENYA CLASS (PROJECT 1258) (MINEHUNTERS) (MHC)

501 **510** **511**

Displacement, tons: 77 standard; 90 full load
Dimensions, feet (metres): 80.7 × 18 × 4.9 *(24.6 × 5.5 × 1.5)*
Main machinery: 2 Type 3-D-12 diesels; 600 hp(m) *(440 kW)* sustained; 2 shafts
Speed, knots: 11. **Range, n miles:** 300 at 10 kt
Complement: 10
Guns: 2—14.5 mm (twin) MGs.
Countermeasures: Minehunting gear is lowered on a crane at the stern.
Radars: Navigation: Don 2; I-band.
Sonars: MG 7 lifted over the stern.

Comment: First pair transferred from USSR in November 1977, one in September 1978, two in November 1979, two in December 1980, two from the Baltic on 10 December 1981, one in October 1982 and four on 1 September 1984. There are two squadrons, based at Cabanas and Nicaro although these last three are the only seaworthy units.

YEVGENYA (Ukraine colours) *6/2003, Ships of the World* / 0572652

AUXILIARIES

Notes: In addition there are two other vessels: *Siboney* H 101 of 535 tons and used for cadet training, and a buoy tender *Taino* H 102 of 1,123 tons. Neither are active.

1 PELYM (PROJECT 1799) CLASS (AXT)

CARLOS MANUEL DE CESPEDES 40

Displacement, tons: 1,050 full load
Dimensions, feet (metres): 210.3 × 38.4 × 11.5 *(64.1 × 11.7 × 3.5)*
Main machinery: 1 diesel; 1,540 hp *(1.1 MW)*; 1 shaft
Speed, knots: 13.5. **Range, n miles:** 1,000 at 13 kt
Complement: 40
Radars: Navigation: Don; I-band.

Comment: Transferred from the USSR in 1982 equipped as deperming vessel. Deperming gear deleted and converted to use as a training ship since about 1999. Based at Havana.

PELYM *4/2006, Göran Olsson* / 1164744

1 BIYA (PROJECT 871) CLASS (ABU)

GUAMA H 103

Displacement, tons: 766 full load
Dimensions, feet (metres): 180.4 × 32.1 × 8.5 *(55 × 9.8 × 2.6)*
Main machinery: 2 diesels; 1,200 hp(m) *(882 kW)*; 2 shafts; cp props
Speed, knots: 13. **Range, n miles:** 4,700+ at 11 kt
Complement: 29 (7 officers)
Radars: Navigation: Don 2; I-band.

Comment: Has laboratory facilities, one survey launch and a 5 ton crane. Built in Poland and acquired from USSR in November 1980. Subordinate to Institute of Hydrography. Last deployed in 1993, but is used locally as a buoy tender and is based at Havana.

BIYA CLASS (Russian colours) *10/1993, van Ginderen Collection* / 0506283

BORDER GUARD

Notes: (1) A 5,000 strong force which operates under the Ministry of the Interior at a higher state of readiness than the Navy. Pennant numbers painted in red.
(2) A 17 m patrol craft *Flecha* and an auxiliary craft 040 have been reported.

2 STENKA (TARANTUL) CLASS (PROJECT 205P) (FAST ATTACK CRAFT—PATROL) (PB)

801 **816**

Displacement, tons: 211 standard; 253 full load
Dimensions, feet (metres): 129.3 × 25.9 × 8.2 *(39.4 × 7.9 × 2.5)*
Main machinery: 3 M 583A diesels; 12,172 hp(m) *(8.95 MW)*; 3 shafts
Speed, knots: 34. **Range, n miles:** 2,250 at 14 kt
Complement: 25 (5 officers)
Guns: 4—30 mm/65 (2 twin) AK 230; 500 rds/min to 5 km *(2.7 n miles)*; weight of shell 0.54 kg.
Radars: Surface search: Pot Drum; H/I-band.
Fire control: Muff Cob; G/H-band.
IFF: High Pole. Square Head.

Comment: Similar to class operated by Russian border guard with torpedo tubes and sonar removed. Transferred from USSR in February 1985 (two) and August 1985 (one). These two reported to be operational.

STENKA *1990* / 0056852

18 ZHUK (GRIF) CLASS (PROJECT 1400M) (COASTAL PATROL CRAFT) (PB)

589 **+17**

Displacement, tons: 39 full load
Dimensions, feet (metres): 78.7 × 16.4 × 3.9 *(24 × 5 × 1.2)*
Main machinery: 2 Type M 401B diesels; 2,200 hp(m) *(1.6 MW)* sustained; 2 shafts
Speed, knots: 30. **Range, n miles:** 1,100 at 15 kt
Complement: 11 (3 officers)
Guns: 4—14.5 mm (2 twin) MGs.
Radars: Surface search: Spin Trough; I-band.

Comment: A total of 40 acquired since 1971. Last batch of two arrived December 1989. Some transferred to Nicaragua. The total has been reduced to allow for wastage. In some of the class the after gun has been removed. Most of the remaining vessels are still active.

ZHUK 589 *4/2006, Göran Olsson* / 1164743

Cyprus

Country Overview

Formerly a British colony, the Republic of Cyprus gained independence in 1960. The United Kingdom retained sovereignty over two military bases on the south coast. The total area of the country is 3,572 square miles but, since 1974, the northern third of the country has been occupied by Turkish troops and has formed, de facto, a separate (not UN recognised) state called the Turkish Republic of Northern Cyprus. Situated in the eastern Mediterranean Sea, with which it has a 351 n mile coastline, the island lies west of Syria and south of Turkey. Nicosia is the capital and largest city while Limassol and Larnaca are the principal ports. Territorial seas (12 n miles) are claimed. A 200 n mile EEZ was claimed in 2004.

Headquarters Appointments

Commander Navy Command of the National Guard:
Captain Andreas Ioannides

General

Raif Denktas KKTCSG 101, two 40 m craft (KKTCSG 01-02), two Kaan 15 (KKTCSG 11-12), two 14 m craft (KKTCSG 102-103) and a converted cabin cruiser KKTCSG 104 are patrol craft permanently based at Kyrenia (Girne) in northern Cyprus. For details of these vessels see Turkey Coast Guard section.

Bases

Limassol
Mari

Coast Defence

Twenty-four Exocet MM 40 Block 2. Truck-mounted in batteries of four.

PATROL FORCES

Notes: There are also three launches and a number of RIBs in use by the Underwater Diving section of the Navy.

1 MODIFIED PATRA CLASS (PBM)

Name	*No*	*Builders*	*Commissioned*
SALAMIS	P 01	Chantiers de l'Esterel	24 May 1983

Displacement, tons: 92 full load
Dimensions, feet (metres): 105.3 × 21.3 × 5.9 *(32.1 × 6.5 × 1.8)*
Main machinery: 2 SACM 195 CZSHRY12 diesels; 4,680 hp(m) *(3.44 MW)* sustained; 2 shafts
Speed, knots: 30. **Range, n miles**: 1,200 at 15 kt
Complement: 22
Missiles: SAM: 1 Matra Simbad twin launcher; Mistral; IR homing to 4 km *(2.2 n miles)*; warhead 3 kg.
Guns: 1 Otobreda 40 mm/70. 1 Rheinmetall Wegmann 20 mm.
Radars: Surface search: Decca 1226; I-band.

Comment: Laid down in December 1981 for Naval Command of National Guard.

SALAMIS *10/1999, E & M Laursen* / 0056854

1 DILOS CLASS (COASTAL PATROL CRAFT) (PBM)

Name	*No*	*Builders*	*Commissioned*
KYRENIA (ex-*Knossos*)	P 02 (ex-P 268)	Hellenic Shipyards, Skaramanga	1979

Displacement, tons: 92 full load
Dimensions, feet (metres): 95.1 × 16.2 × 5.6 *(29 × 5 × 1.7)*
Main machinery: 2 MTU 12V 331TC81 diesels; 2,700 hp(m) *(1.97 MW)* sustained; 2 shafts
Speed, knots: 26
Range, n miles: 1,600 at 24 kt
Complement: 17 (4 officers)
Missiles: 1 Matra Simbad twin launcher; Mistral; IR homing to 4 km *(2.2 n miles)*; warhead 3 kg
Guns: 1 Rheinmetall Wegmann 20 mm.
Radars: Surface search: Racal Decca 914C; I-band.

Comment: Ordered in May 1976 to a design by Abeking & Rasmussen. Transferred from Greece in March 2000 and used mainly for SAR. Others of the class are in service in Georgia, and with the Hellenic Coast Guard and Customs services.

KYRENIA (Greek colours) *61/1998, E M Cornish* / 0052296

2 RODMAN 55HJ CLASS (PBF)

PANAGOS AGATHOS

Displacement, tons: 15.7 full load
Dimensions, feet (metres): 57.1 × 12.5 × 2.3 *(17.4 × 3.8 × 0.7)*
Main machinery: 2 MAN diesels; 2 waterjets
Speed, knots: 48
Range, n miles: 300 at 35 kt
Complement: 7
Guns: 1—12.7 mm MG. 2—7.62 mm MGs.
Radars: Surface search: Furuno; I-band.

Comment: GRP hulls built by Rodman, Vigo and commissioned on 8 June 2002.

PANAGOS *9/2002, van Ginderen Collection* / 1044096

2 VITTORIA CLASS (COASTAL PATROL CRAFT) (PB)

Name	*No*	*Builders*	*Commissioned*
COMMANDER TSOMAKIS	P 03	Cantiere Navale Vittoria, Adria	Aug 2004
COMMANDER GEORGIU	P 04	Cantiere Navale Vittoria, Adria	Aug 2004

Displacement, tons: 95 full load
Dimensions, feet (metres): 88.6 × 21.0 × 4.3 *(27.0 × 6.4 × 1.3)*
Main machinery: 2 MTU diesels; 5,440 hp *(4.05 MW)*; 2 waterjets
Speed, knots: 46. **Range, n miles**: 800 at 35 kt
Complement: 12
Guns: 1 Breda 25 mm. 2—12.7 mm MGs.

Comment: Built by Cantiere Navale Vittoria, Italy. Two similar craft are in service with the Police Force.

LAND-BASED MARITIME AIRCRAFT

Notes: There are also three Bell 206 utility helicopters.

Numbers/Type: 1 Pilatus Britten-Norman Maritime Defender BN-2A.
Operational speed: 150 kt *(280 km/h)*.
Service ceiling: 18,900 ft *(5,760 m)*.
Range: 1,500 n miles *(2,775 km)*.
Role/Weapon systems: Operated around southern coastline of Cyprus to prevent smuggling and terrorist activity. Sensors: Search radar, searchlight mounted on wings. Weapons: ASV; various machine gun pods and rockets.

POLICE

Notes: (1) In addition there are six speed boats, *Astrapi* 30–35, of 5.3 m with 280 hp engines built in Cyprus in 1999–2000.
(2) Personnel numbers are approximately 330 Maritime Police.

2 VITTORIA CLASS (COASTAL PATROL CRAFT) (PB)

Name	*No*	*Builders*	*Commissioned*
THEXAS	PV 23	Cantiere Navale Vittoria, Adria	2004
ONISILOS	PV 24	Cantiere Navale Vittoria, Adria	2004

Displacement, tons: 95 full load
Dimensions, feet (metres): 88.9 × 13.4 × 1.0 *(27.6 × 4.1 × 0.3)*
Main machinery: 2 MTU diesels; 5,440 hp *(4.05 MW)*; 2 waterjets
Speed, knots: 45. **Range, n miles**: 800 at 35 kt
Complement: 12
Guns: 2—12.7 mm MGs.

Comment: Built by Cantiere Navale Vittoria, Italy and delivered in 2004. *Thexas* based at Limassol, *Onisilos* at Larnaca.

THEXAS *4/2006, Paolo Marsan* / 1166781

5 SAB 12 TYPE (PB)

DIONYSOS PL 11 (ex-G 55/GS 12)
KOURION PL 12 (ex-G 54/GS 27)
ILARION PL 13 (ex-G 52/GS 25)
KARPASIA PL 14 (ex-G 50/GS 10)
AKAMAS PL 15 (ex-G 57/GS 28)

Displacement, tons: 14 full load
Dimensions, feet (metres): 41.3 × 13.1 × 3.6 *(12.6 × 4 × 1.1)*
Main machinery: 2 Volvo Penta diesels; 700 hp(m) *(520 kW)*; 2 shafts
Speed, knots: 16
Range, n miles: 300 at 15 kt
Complement: 5
Guns: 1—7.62 mm MG.
Radars: Surface search: Raytheon; I-band.

Comment: Built in 1979 by Veb Yachwerft, Berlin. Harbour patrol craft of the former GDR MAB 12 class transferred in December 1992. New radars fitted. *Dionysos* based at Latsi, *Kourion* at Larnaca, *Ilarion* at Napa, *Karpasia* at Limassol and *Akamar* at Paphos.

DIONYSOS *8/2006, Marco Ghiglino* / 1164745

1 SHALDAG CLASS (PBF)

Name	*No*	*Builders*	*Commissioned*
ODYSSEUS	PV 22	Israel Shipyards	4 Sep 1997

Displacement, tons: 56 full load
Dimensions, feet (metres): 81.4 × 19.7 × 3.9 *(24.8 × 6 × 1.2)*
Main machinery: 2 MTU 12V 396TE diesels; 4,500 hp(m) *(3.3 MW)* sustained; 2 Kamewa waterjets
Speed, knots: 45
Range, n miles: 850 at 16 kt
Complement: 15
Guns: 1 Oerlikon 20 mm; 2—7.62 mm MGs.
Weapons control: Optronic director.
Radars: Surface search: Raytheon; I-band.

Comment: Similar to craft in service with Sri Lankan Navy. Based at Limassol.

ODYSSEUS *3/2005, Joly/Marsan* / 1133387

2 POSEIDON CLASS (PBF)

Name	*No*	*Builders*	*Commissioned*
POSEIDON	PV 20	Brodotehnika SY, Belgrade	21 Nov 1991
EVAGORAS	PV 21	Brodotehnika SY, Belgrade	21 Nov 1991

Displacement, tons: 58 full load
Dimensions, feet (metres): 80.7 × 18.7 × 3.9 *(24.6 × 5.7 × 1.2)*
Main machinery: 2 MTU 12V 396 TE94 diesels; 4,280 hp(m) *(3.2 MW)* sustained; 2 Kamewa 56 water-jets
Speed, knots: 42. **Range, n miles:** 600 at 20 kt
Complement: 9
Guns: 1 Breda KVA 25 mm; ISBRS rocket launcher. 2—12.7 mm MGs.
Radars: Surface search: JRC; I-band.

Comment: Designated as FAC-23 Jets. Aluminium construction. New radars fitted. *Poseidon* based at Latsi and *Evagoras* at Larnaca.

EVAGORAS *4/2006, Paolo Marsan* / 1166782

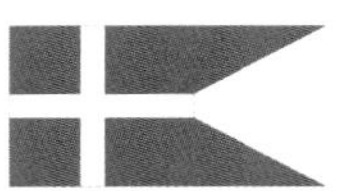

Denmark

DEN KONGELIGE DANSKE MARINE

Country Overview

The Kingdom of Denmark is a constitutional monarchy. The southernmost of the Scandinavian countries, it comprises most of the Jutland peninsula and more than 400 islands, the principal of which are Sjaelland (the largest), Fyn, Lolland, Falster, Langeland and Møn. The island of Bornholm lies in the Baltic about 70 n miles east of Sjaelland. With an area of 16,639 square miles, the country is bordered to the south by Germany. Its 1,825 n mile coastline is with the North Sea to the west, the Skagerrak to the north and the Kattegatt, which is linked to the Baltic Sea by the Øresund, to the east. The capital, largest city and principal port is Copenhagen. There are further ports at Århus, Odense and Ålborg. Territorial seas (12 n miles) are claimed. It has claimed a 200 n mile EEZ for the mainland and 200 n mile Fishery Zones for the external territories of the Faroes and Greenland.

Headquarters Appointments

Admiral Fleet:
Rear Admiral Nils Wang
Inspector Naval Home Guard:
Captain K R Andersen

Diplomatic Representation

Defence Attaché, Washington and Ottawa:
Brigadier P J Larsen
Defence Attaché, London, Dublin and The Hague:
Captain N A K Olsen
Defence Attaché, Paris:
Colonel C J D Dirksen
Defence Attaché, Berlin and Prague:
Colonel F Rytter
Defence Attaché, Moscow and Minsk:
Brigadier S B Bojesen
Defence Attaché, Warsaw:
Colonel K H Lawes
Defence Attaché, Vilnius:
Commander Senior Grade C V Rasmussen
Defence Attaché, Cairo:
Colonel K Winther
Defence Attaché, Kiev:
Lieutenant Colonel O B Hansen
Defence Attaché, Tagreb:
Lieutenant Colonel S Knudsen

Personnel

(a) 2009: 3,770 (874 officers) including 450 national service
Reserves: 4,000.
Naval Home Guard: 4,800.
(b) 4 months' national service

Bases

Korsør (Corvettes, Patrol Craft Stanflex), Frederikshavn (Inspection ships, MCMV, Support Ships), Copenhagen, Grønnedal (Greenland)

Naval Air Arm

Naval helicopters owned and operated by Navy in naval squadron based at Karup, Jutland. All servicing and maintenance by Air Force. LRMP are flown by the Air Force.

Naval Home Guard

Established in 1952 as a separate service under the operational control of the navy. Duties include surveillance, harbour control, search and rescue and the guarding of naval installations ashore. Following the Defence Agreement 2004, the service is to play a greater role in home defence and further tasks include environmental survey, pollution control and support of the police and customs services.

Coast Defence

The coastal radar system, known as Kyra, is being upgraded. The system is based on the Terma Scanter 2001 and 4000 radars in conjunction with electro-optical camera equipped lookout stations. The 28 sites were completed in 2008. The system is operated from the maritime headquarters at Aarhus and from two naval reporting centres at Fredrikshavn and on Bornhölm Island.

Command and Control

The Royal Danish Navy, on behalf of the Ministry of Defence, runs and maintains the icebreakers. Likewise, the Navy runs and maintains two environmental protection divisions based in Copenhagen and Korsør respectively. Responsibility for environmental survey, protection and pollution fighting in maritime areas around Denmark is executed by the Royal Danish Navy. Survey ships are run by the Farvandsvæsenet Nautisk Afdeling (Administration of Navigation and Hydrography) under the Ministry of Defence, and the Directorate of Fisheries has four rescue vessels.

Appearance

Ships are painted in six different colours as follows:
Grey: frigates, corvettes and patrol frigates.
Orange: survey vessels.
White: Royal Yacht and the sail training yawls.
Black/yellow: service vessels, tugs and ferryboats.

Strength of the Fleet

Type	*Active*	*Building (Projected)*
Frigates	7	3
Large Patrol Craft	12	–
Patrol Craft	41	4
Minehunters and Drones	12	–
Support Ships	2	–
Training Ships	4	–
Research Ships	1	–
Transport Ship	1	–
Icebreakers	3	–
Royal Yacht	1	–

Prefix to Ships' Names

HDMS

DELETIONS

Patrol Forces

2006 *Svaerdfisken, Vejrø*
2007 *Romsø*
2008 *Flyvefisken* (to Lithuania), *Hajen* (to Lithuania), *Farø, Barsø, Drejø, Agdlek,* MHV 91, MHV 93, MHV 95
2009 *Lonmen* (to Lithuania), *Romø, Samsø, Laesø, Thurø, Agpa,* MHV 90, MHV 94, *Lunden*

Survey Ships

2006 SKA 15

PENNANT LIST

Frigates

F 354 Niels Juel
F 355 Olfert Fischer
F 356 Peter Tordenskiold
F 357 Thetis
F 358 Triton
F 359 Vaedderen
F 360 Hvidbjørnen
F 361 Ivar Huitfeldt (bldg)
F 362 Peter Willemoes (bldg)
F 363 Niels Juel (bldg)

Patrol Forces

P 520 Diana
P 521 Freja
P 522 Havfruen
P 523 Najaden
P 552 Havkatten
P 553 Laxen
P 554 Makrelen
P 555 Støren
P 557 Glenten
P 558 Gribben
P 560 Ravnen
P 561 Skaden
P 562 Viben
P 563 Søløven
P 570 Knud Rasmussen
P 571 Ejnar Mikkelsen
Y 388 Tulugaq

Auxiliaries

A 540 Dannebrog
A 541 Birkholm
A 542 Fyrholm
A 543 Ertholm
A 544 Alholm
A 551 Danbjørn
A 552 Isbjørn
A 553 Thorbjørn
A 559 Sleipner
A 560 Gunnar Thorson
A 561 Gunnar Seidenfaden
A 562 Mette Miljø
A 563 Marie Miljø
L 16 Absalon
L 17 Esbern Snare
MSD 5 Hirsholm
MSD 6 Saltholm
Y 101 Svanen
Y 102 Thyra
Y 344 Arvak
Y 345 Alsin

FRIGATES

4 THETIS CLASS (FFHM)

Name	*No*	*Builders*	*Laid down*	*Launched*	*Commissioned*
THETIS	F 357	Svenborg Vaerft	10 Oct 1988	14 July 1989	1 July 1991
TRITON	F 358	Svenborg Vaerft	27 June 1989	16 Mar 1990	2 Dec 1991
VAEDDEREN	F 359	Svenborg Vaerft	19 Mar 1990	21 Dec 1990	9 June 1992
HVIDBJØRNEN	F 360	Svenborg Vaerft	2 Jan 1991	11 Oct 1991	30 Nov 1992

Displacement, tons: 2,600 standard; 3,500 full load
Dimensions, feet (metres): 369.1 oa; 327.4 wl × 47.2 × 19.7 *(112.5; 99.8 × 14.4 × 6.0)*
Main machinery: 3 MAN/Burmeister & Wain Alpha 12V 28/32A diesels; 10,800 hp(m) *(7.94 MW)* sustained; 1 shaft; Kamewa cp prop; bow and azimuth thrusters; 880 hp(m) *(647 kW)*, 1,100 hp(m) *(800 kW)*
Speed, knots: 20; 8 on thrusters
Range, n miles: 8,500 at 15.5 kt
Complement: 60 (12 officers) plus 30 spare berths

Missiles: SAM: 4 Stinger mountings (2 twin) on hangar roof near mast.
Guns: 1 OTO Melara 3 in *(76 mm)*/62; Super Rapid ❶; dual purpose; 120 rds/min to 16 km *(8.7 n miles)*; SAPOMER round weight 12.7 kg.
2—12.7 mm MGs.
Depth charges: 1 rail (door in stern).
Countermeasures: Decoys: 2 Sea Gnat DL-12T 12-barrelled launchers for chaff and IR flares.
ESM: Racal Sabre; intercept.
Combat data systems: Terma TDS; SATCOM ❷.
Weapons control: Bofors 9LV 200 Mk 3 director. FSI Safire surveillance director ❸.
Radars: Air/surface search: Plessey AWS 6 ❹; G-band.
Surface search: Furuno 2135; E/F-band.
Navigation: Furuno 2115; I-band.
Fire control: CelsiusTech 9LV Mk 3 ❺; I/J-band.
Sonars: Thomson Sintra TSM 2640 Salmon; VDS; active search and attack; medium frequency.
C-Teck; hull-mounted; active search; medium frequency.

Helicopters: 1 Westland Lynx Mk 90B ❻.

Programmes: Preliminary study by YARD in 1986 led to Dwinger Marine Consultants being awarded a contract for a detailed design completed in mid-1987. All four ordered in October 1987.
Modernisation: There are plans for a new air search radar and SAM in due course.
Structure: The hull is some 30 m longer than the decommissioned Hvidbjørnen class to improve sea-keeping qualities and allow considerable extra space for additional armament. The design allows the use of containerised equipment to be shipped depending on role and there is some commonality with the Flex 300 ships. The hull is ice strengthened to enable penetration of 1 m thick ice and efforts have been made to incorporate stealth technology, for instance by putting anchor equipment, bollards and winches below the upper deck. There is a double skin up to 2 m below the waterline. A rigid inflatable boarding craft plumbed by a hydraulic crane is fitted alongside the fixed hangar. The bridge and ops room are combined. *Thetis* was modified in the stern for seismological survey. Since these operations have terminated, the stern has been remodified to facilitate the ability to act as a command ship and to conduct training. Modifications to *Vaedderen* for Galathea III have been removed.
Operational: Primary role is sovereignty patrol and fishery protection in the North Atlantic. *Vaedderen* supported the Galathea III oceanographic project in 2006-07.

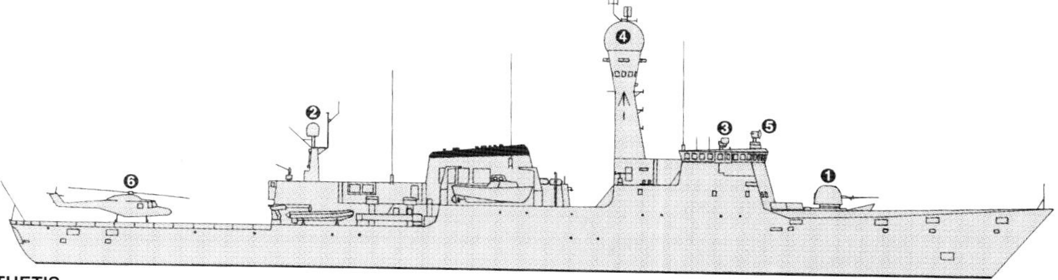

THETIS
(Scale 1 : 900), Ian Sturton / 0012258

THETIS
9/2005, Guy Toremans / 1133412

THETIS
9/2006, M Declerck
1164778

THETIS
8/2007, Per Körnefeldt / 1335459

3 NIELS JUEL CLASS (FFGM)

Name	No	Builders	Laid down	Launched	Commissioned
NIELS JUEL	F 354	Aalborg Vaerft	20 Oct 1976	17 Feb 1978	26 Aug 1980
OLFERT FISCHER	F 355	Aalborg Vaerft	6 Dec 1978	10 May 1979	16 Oct 1981
PETER TORDENSKIOLD	F 356	Aalborg Vaerft	3 Dec 1979	30 Apr 1980	2 Apr 1982

Displacement, tons: 1,320 full load
Dimensions, feet (metres): 275.5 × 33.8 × 10.2 *(84 × 10.3 × 3.1)*
Main machinery: CODOG; 1 GE LM 2500 gas turbine; 24,600 hp *(18.35 MW)* sustained; 1 MTU 20 V 956 TB82 diesel; 5,210 hp(m) *(3.83 MW)* sustained; 2 shafts
Speed, knots: 28, gas; 20, diesel
Range, n miles: 2,500 at 18 kt
Complement: 94 (15 officers)

Missiles: SSM: 8 McDonnell Douglas Harpoon (2 quad) launchers ❶; active radar homing to 130 km *(70 n miles)* at 0.9 Mach; warhead 227 kg.
SAM: 12 (2 sextuple) Raytheon Sea Sparrow Mk 48 Mod 3 VLS (12 missiles) or Mk 56 Mod O VLS (24 missiles) modular launchers ❷; semi-active radar homing to 14.6 km *(8 n miles)* at 2.5 Mach; warhead 39 kg; 12 missiles.
4 Stinger mountings (2 twin) ❸.
Guns: 1 OTO Melara 3 in *(76 mm)*/62 compact ❹; 85 rds/min to 16 km *(8.7 n miles)* anti-surface; 12 km *(6.6 n miles)* anti-aircraft; SAPOMER round weight 12.7 kg.
4—12.7 mm MGs.
Depth charges: 1 rack.
Countermeasures: Decoys: 2 DL-12T Sea Gnat 12-barrelled chaff launchers ❺.

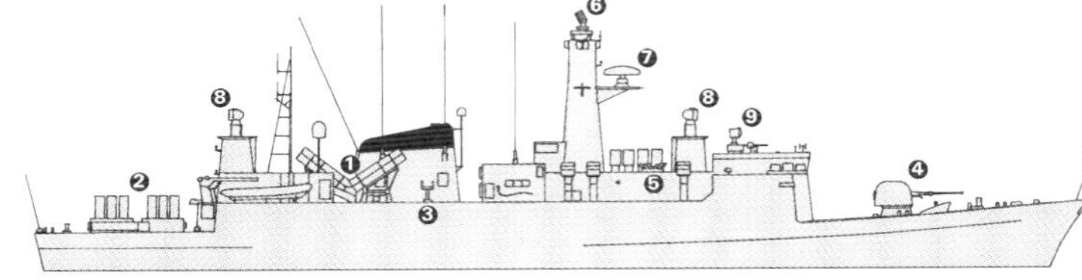

PETER TORDENSKIOLD *(Scale 1 : 900), Ian Sturton* / 1047859

Combat data systems: CelciusTech 9LV Mk 3. Link 11. SATCOMs (can be fitted forward or aft of the funnel).
Weapons control: Philips 9LV 200 Mk 3 GFCS with TV tracker. Raytheon Mk 91 Mod 1 MFCS with two directors. Harpoon to 1A(V) standard.
Radars: Air search: DASA TRS-3D ❻; G/H-band.
Surface search: Philips 9GR 600 ❼; I-band.
Fire control: 2 Mk 95 ❽; I/J-band (for SAM).
Philips 9LV 200 Mk 1 Rakel 203C ❾; J-band (for guns and SSM).
Navigation: Terma Scanter Mil; I-band.
Sonars: Plessey PMS 26; hull-mounted; active search and attack; 10 kHz.

Programmes: YARD Glasgow designed the class to Danish order.
Modernisation: Mid-life update from 1996, including a NATO Sea Sparrow VLS, and new communications. Air search radar replaced by TST TRS-3D. Improved combat data system fitted. F 356 completed in May 1998, F 354 in April 1999, F 355 in December 2001. Stinger SAM mounted each side of the funnel.
Operational: Normally only one sextuple SAM launcher is carried, but the second set can be embarked in a few hours. To be replaced by new frigates from 2011.

OLFERT FISCHER *6/2008*, Michael Nitz* / 1335363

NIELS JUEL *11/2005, Martin Mokrus* / 1159963

NIELS JUEL

4/2005, Per Körnefeldt / 1133391

PETER TORDENSKIOLD

6/2007, Michael Nitz / 1166534

NIELS JUEL

9/2005, Per Körnfeldt / 1159930

0 + 3 IVAR HUITFELDT CLASS (FFGHM)

Name	*No*	*Builders*	*Laid down*	*Launched*	*Commissioned*
IVAR HUITFELDT	F 361	Odense Shipyard, Lindø	2 June 2008	2010	2011
PETER WILLEMOES	F 362	Odense Shipyard, Lindø	17 Mar 2009	2011	2012
NIELS JUEL	F 363	Odense Shipyard, Lindø	Dec 2009	2012	2013

Displacement, tons: 5,850
Dimensions, feet (metres): 452.5 × 64.0 × 20.7 *(138.7 × 19.8 × 6.3)*
Main machinery: CODAD; 4 MTU 20V M70 diesels; 44,000 hp *(32.8 MW)*; 2 shafts; cp props; bow thruster
Speed, knots: 28
Complement: 100 (accommodation for 165)

Missiles: SSM: 16 Boeing Harpoon Block 2 (2 octuple AHWCS VLS launchers) ❶; active radar homing to 124 km *(67 n miles)* at 0.9 Mach; warhead 227 kg.
SAM: 32 GDC Standard SM-2 MR Block IIIA ❷; command/inertial guidance; semi-active radar homing to 167 km *(90 n miles)* at 2.5 Mach. Lockheed Martin Mk 41 VLS (32 cells). 24 Evolved Sea Sparrow RIM 162B ❸; semi-active radar homing to 18 km *(9.7 n miles)* at 3.6 Mach; warhead 38 kg. 2 Raytheon Mk 56 VLS (2 × 12 cells).
6 twin Sea Stinger launchers.
Guns: 2 OTO Melara 76 mm ❹. 1 Oerlikon Contraves 35 mm ❺.
Torpedoes: 4—324 mm (2 twin) launchers ❻; Eurotorp MU 90 Impact; active/passive homing to 15 km *(8 n miles)* at 29/50 kt.
Countermeasures: Decoys: Terma 130 mm Decoy Launching System; 2 DL-12T and 2 DL-6T launchers (36 barrels).
ESM: To be announced.
Combat data systems: Terma C-Flex Combat Management System.
Weapons control: To be announced.

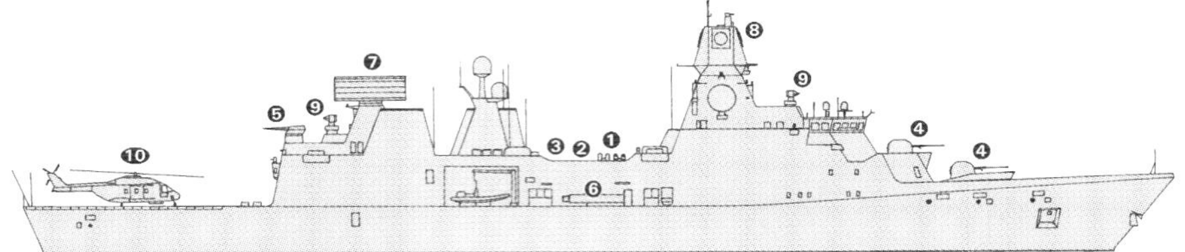

IVAR HUITFELDT *(Scale1 : 1,200), Ian Sturton* / 1335454

Radars: Air/surface search: Thales Smart-L; 3D ❼; D-band.
Fire control (SAM): Thales APAR phased array ❽; I/J-band.
Fire control (guns): Saab Ceros 200 ❾; J/K-band.
Navigation: Furuno; E/F/I-bands.
Sonars: Atlas ASO 94 hull mounted. VDS/DTAS/ATAS to be decided.

Helicopters: 1 medium or 2 Lynx ❿.

Programmes: Construction of three frigates was approved in the 2004 Defence Agreement. The contract for construction was signed with Odense Shipyard on 20 December 2006. The blocks of the ships are under construction at Klaipeda, Lithuania, and at Loksa, Estonia. The first four blocks were delivered to Odense on 20 May 2008.

Structure: Built to DNV standards. The design is based on the Absalon class Flexible Support Ships and utilises the same hull (with one fewer deck) and the majority of equipment. There are to be dedicated staff facilities for national or NATO task group commanders. Four Stanflex container positions are to be located on the weapons deck and one at B-position. There is to be cargo space for four 20 ft TEU containers. The flight deck is to be capable of operating 20 ton helicopters and prepared to operate UAVs. 'A' gun position is suitable for upgrade to a 127 mm gun if and when required.
Operational: The ships are to have a global, expeditionary role and to be capable of providing area air-defence and support of land forces.

SHIPBORNE AIRCRAFT

Notes: The Defence Agreement of 10 June 2004 (covering 2005–09) provided for the procurement of four maritime helicopters and a project to update Lynx helicopters. These projects have been superseded by a study to acquire a new maritime helicopter capability to replace Lynx. The new aircraft are to operate from the Ivar Huitfeldt-class frigates, and the Thetis, Absalon and Knud Rasmussen classes.

Numbers/Type: 8 Westland Lynx Mk 90B.
Operational speed: 125 kt *(232 km/h)*.
Service ceiling: 12,500 ft *(3,810 m)*.
Range: 320 n miles *(593 km)*.
Role/Weapon systems: Shipborne helicopter for EEZ and surface search tasks. All upgraded to Super Lynx standard with first delivered November 2000. Sensors: Ferranti Seaspray; Racal Kestrel ESM; FLIR 2000. Weapons: Unarmed.

LYNX *9/2006, M Declerck* / 1164767

Numbers/Type: 4 Sikorsky S-61A-1 Sea King.
Operational speed: 118 kt *(219 km/h)*.
Service ceiling: 14,700 ft *(4,480 m)*.
Range: 542 n miles *(1,005 km)*
Role/Weapon systems: Land-based SAR helicopter for combat rescue and surface search. To be replaced by EH 101 in 2009. Sensors: Bendix weather radar; GEC Avionics FLIR. Weapons: unarmed.

SEA KING *5/1999, H M Steele* / 0056867

Numbers/Type: 8 AgustaWestland EH 101 Mk 512.
Operational speed: 160 kt *(296 km/h)*.
Service ceiling: 15,000 ft *(4,572 m)*.
Range: 550 n miles *(1,019 km)*.
Role/Weapon systems: Contract on 7 December 2001 for a total of 14 utility variants of the EH 101. Eight are configured for SAR duties and six for troop-carrying although the aircraft are designed for rapid role-change. By agreement with the UK, the delivery of six aircraft has been delayed in order to meet a high-priority UK operational requirement. Military lift is 28 troops and up to four tonnes underslung. Sensors: Telephonics RDR-1600 SAR Weather Avoidance Radar.

EH 101 *7/2006, Jane's/Patrick Allen* / 1184189

LAND-BASED MARITIME AIRCRAFT

Numbers/Type: 3 Challenger 604.
Operational speed: 470 kt *(870 km/h)*.
Service ceiling: 41,000 ft *(12,497 m)*.
Range: 3,769 n miles *(6,980 km)*.
Role/Weapon systems: Maritime reconnaissance for EEZ patrol in the Baltic and off Greenland. Sensors: Terma SLAR radar; IR/UV scanner. Weapons: unarmed.

CHALLENGER 604 *6/2005, Massimo Annati* / 1153495

PATROL FORCES

10 FLYVEFISKEN CLASS (LARGE PATROL/ATTACK CRAFT AND MINEHUNTERS/LAYERS) (PGGM/MHCD/MLC/AGSC)

Name	*No*	*Builders*	*Commissioned*
HAVKATTEN	P 552	Danyard A/S, Aalborg	1 Nov 1990
LAXEN	P 553	Danyard A/S, Aalborg	22 Mar 1991
MAKRELEN	P 554	Danyard A/S, Aalborg	1 Oct 1991
STØREN	P 555	Danyard A/S, Aalborg	24 Apr 1992
GLENTEN	P 557	Danyard A/S, Aalborg	29 Apr 1993
GRIBBEN	P 558	Danyard A/S, Aalborg	1 July 1993
RAVNEN	P 560	Danyard A/S, Aalborg	17 Oct 1994
SKADEN	P 561	Danyard A/S, Aalborg	10 Apr 1995
VIBEN	P 562	Danyard A/S, Aalborg	15 Jan 1996
SØLØVEN	P 563	Danyard A/S, Aalborg	28 May 1996

Displacement, tons: 480 full load
Dimensions, feet (metres): 177.2 × 29.5 × 8.2 *(54 × 9 × 2.5)*
Main machinery: CODAG; 1 GE LM 500 gas turbine (centre shaft) (P 557, 560, 561 and 562); 5,450 hp *(4.1 MW)* sustained; 2 MTU 16V 396 TB94 diesels (outer shafts); 5,800 hp(m) *(4.26 MW)* sustained; 3 shafts; cp props on outer shafts; bow thruster. Auxiliary propulsion by hydraulic motors on outer gearboxes; hydraulic pumps driven by 1 GM 12V-71 diesel; 500 hp *(375 kW)*
Speed, knots: 30; 20 on diesels; 10 on hydraulic propulsion
Range, n miles: 2,400 at 18 kt
Complement: 19-29 (depending on role) (4 officers)

Missiles: SSM: 8 McDonnell Douglas Harpoon; active radar homing to 130 km *(70 n miles)* at 0.9 Mach; warhead 227 kg. Attack role only. Block II from 2004 gives land attack option.
SAM: Raytheon Sea Sparrow RIM 7P; Mk 48 Mod 3 VLS (6 missiles); semi-active radar homing to 16 km *(8.5 n miles)* at 2.5 Mach; warhead 38 kg. Fitted for Attack, MCM and Minelaying roles. In MCM role one Stinger twin launcher can be fitted instead of Sea Sparrow.
Guns: 1 OTO Melara 3 in *(76 mm)*/62 Super Rapid; dual purpose; 120 rds/min to 16 km *(8.7 n miles)*; SAPOMER round weight 12.7 kg.
2—12.7 mm MGs.
Torpedoes: 4—324 mm tubes; Eurotorp MU 90 Impact.
Depth charges: 4.
Mines: 60. Minelaying role only.
Countermeasures: MCMV: Ibis 43 minehunting system with Thomson Sintra 2061 tactical system and 2054 side scan sonar towed by MSF class drones (see *Mine Warfare Forces* section). Bofors Double Eagle ROV Mk II. Minehunting role only.
Decoys: 2 Sea Gnat 130 mm DL-6T 6-barrelled launcher for chaff and IR flares.
ESM: Racal Sabre; radar warning.
Combat data systems: Terma/CelsiusTech TDS. Link 11.
Weapons control: CelsiusTech 9LV Mk 3 optronic director. Harpoon to 1A(V) standard or AHWCS with Block II.
Radars: Air/surface search: Plessey AWS 6 (552-555); G-band; or EADS TRS-3D (557-563); G/H-band.
Surface search: Terma Scanter Mil; I-band.
Navigation: Furuno; I-band.
Fire control: CelsiusTech 9LV 200 Mk 3; J-band.
Sonars: CelsiusTech CTS-36/39; hull-mounted; active search; high frequency.
Thomson Sintra TSM 2640 Salmon; VDS; medium frequency. For ASW only.

Programmes: Standard Flex 300 replaced Daphne class (seaward defence craft), Søløven class (fast attack craft torpedo), and Sund (MCM) class. First batch of seven with option on a further nine contracted with Danyard on 27 July 1985. Second batch of six ordered 14 June 1990 and last one authorised in 1993 to a total of 14, two less than originally planned.
Modernisation: Mk 48 Mod 3 SAM launchers replaced by Mk 56 launchers. Harpoon launchers upgraded to AHWCS version 2 capable of firing Block II missiles. Link 11 fitted. The combat data system is to be replaced by Terma C-Flex.
Structure: GRP sandwich hulls. Four positions prepared to plug in armament and equipment containers in combinations meeting the requirements of the various roles. Torpedo tubes and minerails detachable. Combat data system modular with standard consoles of which three to six are embarked depending on the role. SAV control aerials are mounted on the bridge. TRS-3D radar fitted inlast seven.
Operational: Following an operational review of the class, the original concept, to be able to re-role by the interchange of mission-specific containers for different taskings (ASUW, ASW, MCM and Patrol) has been abandoned. Under a revised concept of employment, the class is to be reduced to ten ships. Of these, four ships are to be permanently roled for MCM *(Laxen, Makrelen, Havkatten, Støren)*, four for a combat role (ASW or ASUW) *(Glenten, Skaden, Viben, Ravnen)* and two (*Gribben* and *Søløven*) for Patrol duties. Of the four ships decommissioned *Svaerdfisken* has been scrapped and *Flyvefisken* and *Hajen* have been sold to Lithuania. *Lommen* having served as a test platform for the Terma C-Flex combat system, is to be decommissioned in 2008 and is also to be sold to Lithuania. Gas turbines are not fitted in MCM and patrol ships.

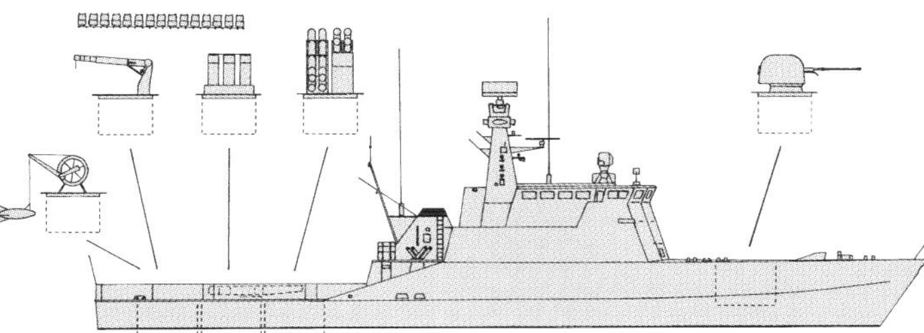
FLYVEFISKEN (composite fit) ***(Scale 1 : 600), Ian Sturton*** / 0103718

STØREN (MCM) ***8/2007, Maritime Photographic*** / 1166519

GRIBBEN (patrol) ***6/2007, Michael Nitz*** / 1166517

VIBEN (combat) ***6/2008*, Michael Nitz*** / 1335360

2 KNUD RASMUSSEN CLASS (ARCTIC PATROL SHIPS) (PGBH)

Name	*No*	*Builders*	*Laid down*	*Launched*	*Commissioned*
KNUD RASMUSSEN	P 570	Karstensens Skibsvaerft, Skagen	21 Nov 2005	19 Oct 2006	18 Feb 2008
EJNAR MIKKELSEN	P 571	Karstensens Skibsvaerft, Skagen	2005	1 July 2007	16 Jan 2009

Displacement, tons: 1,720
Dimensions, feet (metres): 235.6 × 47.9 × 16.2 *(71.8 × 14.6 × 4.95)*
Main machinery: 2 MAN B&W ALPHA 8L 27/38 diesels; 7,300 hp *(5.4 MW)*; 1 shaft; cp prop
Speed, knots: 17
Complement: 18 (accommodation for 43)
Guns: 2—12.7 mm MGs.
Countermeasures: To be announced.
Combat data systems: Terma C-Flex.
Radars: Surface/air search: Terma Scanter 4100; I-band.
Navigation: Furuno; E/F/I-bands.
Sonars: Reson; hull mounted (retractable).

Helicopters: Platform for 1 medium.

Programmes: Contract for the construction of two ships let in December 2004. Production started in September 2005. The hulls and propulsion were manufactured/installed by the Stocznia Pólnocna (Northern) Shipyard in Gdansk and the ships subsquently completed at Skagen. Installation of military equipment was undertaken by Naval Material Command.
Structure: Built to DNV Navy ICE 1A standards. A high-speed long-range rescue craft, an ice-strengthened version of the Combat Boat 90E, can be launched from a bay in the stern. Fitted with four Stanflex container positions for equipment and weapons, the design has the flexibility to operate in its (lightly armed) primary role or in a more heavily armed secondary role. The ships are to be equipped with SeaFLIR infrared imaging system.
Operational: Have replaced Agdlek class. The principal role is sovereignty patrol in the arctic waters off Greenland while secondary roles, such as command and control of a small force, might be exercised globally. Containerised weapons including a 76 mm gun, a Mk 56 launcher with evolved Sea Sparrow missiles and MU 90 torpedoes may be fitted.

KNUD RASMUSSEN ***7/2008*, MOD Denmark*** / 1294588

2 VTS CLASS (COASTAL PATROL CRAFT) (PB)

VTS 3 **VTS 4**

Displacement, tons: 34 full load
Dimensions, feet (metres): 55.8 × 16.1 × 6.9 *(17 × 4.9 × 2.1)*
Main machinery: 2 MWM TBD 616 V12 diesels; 979 hp(m) *(720 kW)*; 2 waterjets
Speed, knots: 33. **Range, n miles:** 300 at 30 kt
Complement: 3
Guns: 1 – 7.62 mm MG can be carried.
Radars: Surface search: Furuno FR-1831; I-band.
Navigation: Furuno M1831; I-band.

Comment: Built by Mulder & Rijke, Netherlands. Completed in 1997 and 1998 to replace Botved type.

VTS 3 *6/1999, Royal Danish Navy* / 0056874

1 AGDLEK CLASS (LARGE PATROL CRAFT) (PB)

Name	*No*	*Builders*	*Commissioned*
TULUGAQ	Y 388	Svendborg Vaerft	26 June 1979

Displacement, tons: 394 full load
Dimensions, feet (metres): 103 × 25.3 × 11.2 *(31.4 × 7.7 × 3.4)*
Main machinery: 1 Burmeister & Wain Alpha A08-26 VO diesel; 800 hp(m) *(588 kW)*; 1 shaft
Speed, knots: 12
Complement: 14 (3 officers)
Guns: 2 – 12.7 mm MGs.
Radars: Surface search: Furuno 2135; E/F-band.
Navigation: Furuno 1510; I-band.

Comment: Ice strengthened. SATCOM fitted. *Agdlek* decommissioned in 2008 and replaced by *Knud Rasmussen*. *Agpa* decommissioned in 2009. Last remaining craft, *Tulugaq*, stationed in Greenland.

TULUGAQ *10/2004, Per Körnefeldt* / 1044106

4 + 2 DIANA (SF MK II) CLASS (LARGE PATROL CRAFT) (PB)

DIANA P 520 **FREJA** P 521 **HAVFRUEN** P 522 **NAJADEN** P 523 — P 524 — P 525

Displacement, tons: 276 full load
Dimensions, feet (metres): 141.1 × 26.9 × 7.2 *(43.0 × 8.2 × 2.2)*
Main machinery: 2 MTU 396 16V TB94 diesels; 2,700 hp *(2 MW)*; 2 shafts; cp props
Speed, knots: 25
Complement: 9 (accommodation for 15)
Guns: 2 – 12.7 mm MGs.
Radars: Navigation: Furuno FR-2117; I-band.

Comment: GRP vessels to replace the Ø class. Ordered on 3 December 2004 from Faaborg Vaerft, Denmark, the hull, superstructure and machinery are to be built by Kockums, Karlskrona. Fitted with one Stanflex container position. The first delivered on 12 December 2007, the second on 4 April 2008, the third on 25 September 2008 and the fourth on 11 December 2008.

FREJA *9/2008*, L-G Nilsson* / 1335361

6 HOLM CLASS (MULTIROLE CRAFT) (MSD/AXL/AGSC)

BIRKHOLM A 541 **FYRHOLM** A 542 **ERTHOLM** A 543 **ALHOLM** A 544 **HIRSHOLM** MSD 5 **SALTHOLM** MSD 6

Displacement, tons: 138 full load
Dimensions, feet (metres): 94.8 × 21.0 × 6.6 *(28.9 × 6.4 × 2.0)*
Main machinery: 2 Scania DC 16 diesels; 1,005 hp(m) *(750 kW)*; 2 azimuth thrusters
Speed, knots: 12
Complement: 3 (accommodation for 9)
Radars: Navigation: Furuno FR-2117; I-band.

Comment: Multirole GRP vessels constructed by Danish Yacht A/S, Skagen. One Stanflex container position. Two vessels (A 541 and A 542) are inshore survey craft to replace *SKA 11* and *SKA 15*, two (A 543 and *A 544*) are training vessels. Two MCM drones were delivered by late 2007.

BIRKHOLM *6/2008*, Frank Findler* / 1335458

ALHOLM *8/2008*, Michael Nitz* / 1335362

10 + 1 (1) MHV 900 CLASS (COASTAL PATROL CRAFT) (PB)

Name	*No*	*Builders*	*Commissioned*
ENØ	MHV 901	Søby Shipyard	10 Oct 2003
MANØ	MHV 902	Søby Shipyard	8 May 2004
HJORTØ	MHV 903	Søby Shipyard	29 Jan 2005
LYØ	MHV 904	Søby Shipyard	30 Sep 2005
ASKØ	MHV 905	Søby Shipyard	5 July 2006
FAENØ	MHV 906	Søby Shipyard	14 Apr 2007
HVIDSTEN	MHV 907	Søby Shipyard	8 Mar 2008
BRIGADEN	MHV 908	Søby Shipyard	15 June 2008
SPEDITØREN	MHV 909	Søby Shipyard	18 Jan 2009
RINGEN	MHV 910	Søby Shipyard	Apr 2009
BOPA	MHV 911	Søby Shipyard	Nov 2009

Displacement, tons: 95 full load
Dimensions, feet (metres): 89.3 × 18.7 × 8.2 *(27.2 × 5.7 × 2.5)*
Main machinery: 2 Saab Scania DI 16V8 diesels; 980 hp(m) *(730 kW)*; 2 shafts
Speed, knots: 13
Complement: 10
Guns: 2 – 7.62 mm MGs.
Radars: Navigation: Furuno FR-2117.

Comment: Similar to but 3.5 m longer than the MHV 800 class. Steel construction. Eleven vessels ordered and there is an option for a twelfth. Operated by the Naval Home Guard.

MANØ *7/2008*, Martin Mokrus* / 1335456

18 MHV 800 CLASS (COASTAL PATROL CRAFT) (PB)

Name	*No*	*Builders*	*Commissioned*
ALDEBARAN	MHV 801	Soby Shipyard	9 July 1992
CARINA	MHV 802	Soby Shipyard	30 Sep 1992
ARIES	MHV 803	Soby Shipyard	30 Mar 1993
ANDROMEDA	MHV 804	Soby Shipyard	30 Sep 1993
GEMINI	MHV 805	Soby Shipyard	28 Feb 1994
DUBHE	MHV 806	Soby Shipyard	1 July 1994
JUPITER	MHV 807	Soby Shipyard	30 Nov 1994
LYRA	MHV 808	Soby Shipyard	30 May 1995
ANTARES	MHV 809	Soby Shipyard	30 Nov 1995
LUNA	MHV 810	Soby Shipyard	30 May 1996
APOLLO	MHV 811	Soby Shipyard	30 Nov 1996
HERCULES	MHV 812	Soby Shipyard	28 May 1997
BAUNEN	MHV 813	Soby Shipyard	17 Dec 1997
BUDSTIKKEN	MHV 814	Soby Shipyard	30 Aug 1998
KUREREN	MHV 815	Soby Shipyard	30 May 1999
PATRIOTEN	MHV 816	Soby Shipyard	25 Feb 2000
PARTISAN	MHV 817	Soby Shipyard	29 Nov 2000
SABOTØREN	MHV 818	Soby Shipyard	13 Oct 2001

Displacement, tons: 83 full load
Dimensions, feet (metres): 77.8 × 18.4 × 6.6 *(23.7 × 5.6 × 2)*
Main machinery: 2 Saab Scania DSI-14 diesels; 900 hp(m) *(661 kW)*; 2 shafts
Speed, knots: 13
Range, n miles: 990 at 11 kt
Complement: 8 + 4 spare
Guns: 2 — 7.62 mm MGs. 2 — 12.7 mm MGs (can be fitted).
Radars: Navigation: Furuno FR-1505; I-band.

Comment: First six ordered in April 1991, second six in July 1992, six more in 1997. Steel hulls with a moderate ice capability. Operated by the Naval Home Guard.

BUDSTIKKEN *6/2008*, A A de Kruijf* / 1335358

ALDEBARAN *6/2006, Harald Carstens* / 1159948

ANDROMEDA *7/2007, Michael Nitz* / 1166509

6 LCP CLASS (COASTAL PATROL CRAFT) (PB)

LCP 1–4 SAR 1–2

Displacement, tons: 6.5 full load
Dimensions, feet (metres): 39.0 × 9.5 × 2.3 *(11.9 × 2.9 × 0.7)*
Main machinery: 1 Scania DSI 14 V8 diesel; 625 hp *(465 kW)*; 1 Kamewa water-jet
Speed, knots: 38
Complement: 3
Guns: 1 — 12.7 mm or 7.62 mm MG.

Comment: Based on the Swedish Combatboat 90E, these craft were developed as a joint venture between Forsvarets Materielverk and Storebro by whom LCP 1-4 were constructed and completed in 2004. Used as fast landing craft from the Absalon class support ships, they can carry 10 fully equipped soldiers or four stretchers. Two ice-strengthened variants are to be operated bythe Arctic Patrol Ships. Painted orange, they were delivered in 2006.

LCP 1 *4/2005, Martin Mokrus* / 1133403

1 MHV 90 CLASS (COASTAL PATROL CRAFT) (PB)

HOLGER DANSKE MHV 92

Displacement, tons: 85 full load
Dimensions, feet (metres): 64.9 × 18.7 × 8.2 *(19.8 × 5.7 × 2.5)*
Main machinery: 1 Burmeister & Wain diesel; 400 hp(m) *(294 kW)*; 1 shaft
Speed, knots: 11
Complement: 12
Guns: 2 — 7.62 mm MGs.
Radars: Navigation: Furuno 1505; I-band.

Comment: Built between 1973 and 1975. New radars fitted. MHV 90 class being progressively replaced by MHV 900 class. This last one expected to decommission in 2009. Operated by Naval Home Guard.

MHV 90 CLASS *6/2006, Martin Mokrus* / 1159964

MINE WARFARE FORCES

Notes: See also Flyvefisken class under *Patrol Forces.*

4 MSF CLASS (MRD)

MSF 1–4

Displacement, tons: 125 full load
Dimensions, feet (metres): 86.9 × 23 × 6.9 *(26.5 × 7 × 2.1)*
Main machinery: 2 Scania DSI 14 diesels; 1,000 hp(m) *(736 kW)*; 2 Schottel waterjets or 2 Schottel azimuth thrusters
Speed, knots: 12
Complement: 4
Combat data systems: IN-SNEC/INFOCOM.
Radars: Navigation: Raytheon 40 or Terma; I-band.
Sonars: Thomson Marconi STS 2054 side scan active; high frequency.

Comment: MSF (Minor Standard Vessel). Ordered in January 1997 from Danyard, Aalborg, and five delivered June 1998 to January 1999. Used primarily as MCM drones although built as multipurpose platform (with one Stanflex container position). Fitted with containerised MCM gear for working in conjunction with Flyvefisken class minehunters. GRP hulls. IN-SNEC is a high data rate sonar/TV link. INFOCOM is a low data rate command link. Plans for further craft are under consideration. One transferred to Sweden in 2001.

MSF 3 *6/2008*, M Declerck* / 1335359

6 SAV CLASS (MINEHUNTER—DRONES) (MSD)

MRD 1 (ex-MRF 1) **MRD 2** (ex-MRF 2) **MRD 3–6**

Displacement, tons: 32 full load
Dimensions, feet (metres): 59.7 × 15.6 × 3.9 *(18.2 × 4.8 × 1.2)*
Main machinery: 2 Detroit diesels; 350 hp(m) *(257 kW)*; 2 Schottel waterjet propulsors
Speed, knots: 12
Complement: 4
Combat data systems: Terma link to Flyvefisken class (in MCMV configuration).
Radars: Navigation: Furuno; I-band.
Sonars: Thomson Sintra: TSM 2054 side scan; active minehunting; high frequency.

Comment: Built by Danyard with GRP hulls. First one completed in March 1991, second in December 1991. Four more ordered in mid-1994 and delivered in 1996. The vessels are robot drones (or Surface Auxiliary Vessels (SAV)) operated in pairs by the Flyvefisken class in MCMV configuration. Hull is based on the Hugin class TRVs with low noise propulsion. The towfish with side scan sonar is lowered and raised from the stern-mounted gantry. The first two craft have slightly different funnel designs. *MRD 4* is used as a station vessel at Korsør and the remainder are laid-up.

MRD 4 *5/2008*, E & M Laursen* / 1335367

1 RESEARCH SHIP (AGE)

DANA

Displacement, tons: 3,700 full load
Dimensions, feet (metres): 257.5 × 48.6 × 19.7 *(78.5 × 14.8 × 6)*
Main machinery: 2 Burmeister and Wain Alpha 16V23-LU diesels; 4,960 hp(m) *(3.65 MW)*; 1 shaft cp prop; bow and stern thrusters
Speed, knots: 15
Range, n miles: 8,000 at 14 kt
Complement: 27 plus 12 scientists

Comment: Built by Dannebrog, Aarhus in 1982. Used mostly for Fisheries survey and research. Has an ice-strengthened hull and three 6 ton cranes.

DANA *6/2002, Royal Danish Navy* / 0533223

SURVEY SHIPS

4 SURVEY LAUNCHES (YGS)

SKA 12-14 **SKA 16**

Displacement, tons: 52 full load
Dimensions, feet (metres): 65.6 × 17.1 × 6.9 *(20 × 5.2 × 2.1)*
Main machinery: 1 GM diesel; 540 hp *(403 kW)*; 1 shaft
Speed, knots: 12
Complement: 6 (1 officer)
Radars: Navigation: Furuno; I-band.

Comment: GRP hulls. Built 1981–84 by Rantsausminde. *SKA 12* has strengthened hull and is permanently deployed to Naval Station Grønnedal (Greenland) for surveying of Greenland waters. *SKA 11* was lost off Greenland on 3 May 2006. Multibeam echo sounders are fitted. *SKA 13* and *14* have been modified for other tasks at the Naval Bases. *SKA 11* and *15* were replaced by two Holm class. The survey launches can work alone, in pairs or in conjunction with Flyvefisken class vessels. All have red hulls and white superstructures.

SKA 16 *9/2006, E & M Laursen* / 1159935

TRAINING SHIPS

Notes: There are two small Sail Training Ships, *Svanen* Y 101 and *Thyra* Y 102. Of 32 tons they have a sail area of 480 m² and an auxiliary diesel of 72 hp(m) *(53 kW)*. Built in 1960 by Molich yacht builders, Hundested. Used to train midshipmen before attending the naval academy.

THYRA *6/2008*, Frank Findler* / 1335457

AUXILIARIES

Notes: (1) The OPLOG organisation consists of the former Mobile Logistic Unit and parts of the maintenance and supply facilities of the naval bases at Fredeickshavn and Korsör. The mobile capability includes containerised workshops, stores, accommodation and helicopter refuelling facilities carried on approximately 40 trucks and trailers.

(2) Sealift: The ARK project, to secure availability of strategic sealift to NATO, was launched by Denmark in 2003. Germany became a full partner in 2006. Full time charter of the 171 m *Tor Anglia* (2,450 lane-metres + 627 TEU) was arranged in 2003, of the 183 m *Tor Futura* (2,308 lane-metres + 644 TEU) in 2004, of the 182 m *Ark Forwarder* (2,715 lane-metres) in 2006 and of the 193 m *Tor Dania* (2,240 lane-metres) in 2007. The ships are on call for the NATO Response Force and also for Danish and German national operations.

2 ABSALON CLASS (COMBAT SUPPORT SHIPS) (AGF/AKR/AH)

Name	*No*	*Builders*	*Laid down*	*Launched*	*Commissioned*
ABSALON	L 16	Odense Shipyard, Lindø	28 Nov 2003	25 Feb 2004	19 Oct 2004
ESBERN SNARE	L 17	Odense Shipyard, Lindø	2004	21 June 2004	18 Apr 2005

Displacement, tons: 6,300 full load
Dimensions, feet (metres): 449.6 × 64.0 × 20.7 *(137.0 × 19.5 × 6.3)*
Main machinery: CODAD. 2 MTU 8000 M 70 diesels; 22,300 hp *(16.63 MW)*; 2 shafts; CP propellers; bow thruster
Speed, knots: 23
Range, n miles: 11,500 at 14 kt
Complement: 99 + 70 staff

Missiles: SSM: 16 Boeing Harpoon Block II ❶ (2 octuple AHWCS VLS launchers); active radar homing to 124 km *(67 n miles)* at 0.9 Mach; warhead 227 kg.
SAM: 36 Evolved Sea Sparrow RIM 162B ❷; semi-active radar homing to 18 km *(9.7 n miles)* at 3.6 Mach; warhead 38 kg. 3 Raytheon Mk 56 VLS (3 × 12 cells).
4 twin Sea Stinger launchers.
Guns: United Defense 5 in *(127 mm)*/62 Mk 45 Mod 4 ❸; 20 rds/min to 23 km *(12.6 n miles)*; weight of shell 32 kg. Prepared for extended range capable munitions.
2 Oerlikon Contraves 35 mm GDM08 Millenium guns ❹.
4—12.7 mm MGs.
Torpedoes: 6—324 mm (2 triple) launchers ❺; Eurotorp Mu 90 Impact; active/passive homing to 15 km *(8 n miles)* at 29/50 kt.
Countermeasures: Decoys: Terma 130 mm Decoy Launching System 2 DL-12T and 2 DL-6T launchers (36 barrels).
ESM: EDO ES 3701.

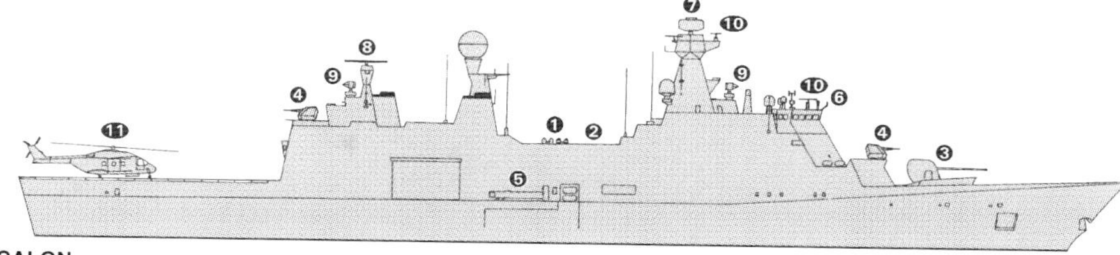

ABSALON *(Scale 1 : 1,200), Ian Sturton* / 1166532

Combat data systems: Terma C-Flex.
Electro-optic systems: FLIR Systems Sea Star Safire III ❻.
Radars: Air/surface search: Thales SMART-S 3D ❼; E/F-band.
Surface search/navigation: Terma Scanter 2001 ❽; I-band.
Fire control: 2 SaabTech Ceros 200 Mk 3 ❾; J/K-band.
Navigation: 2 FR-2135 ❿; E/F/I-band.
Sonars: Atlas ASO 94 hull mounted. VDS/DTAS/ATAS to be decided.
Helicopter: 2 EH 101 ⓫.

Programmes: Contract on 16 October 2001 for detailed design and construction of two multirole support ships. Construction of first of class started on 30 April 2003.
Structure: Built to DNV Navy standards with five Stanflex container positions. Ro-Ro ramp aft gives access to 900 m² of multipurpose deck (vehicles (including 62 ton MBT), logistics, ammunition, up to 34 TEU containers). 2 Combat Boat 90E high-speed insertion craft carried on cargo deck. Flight deck capable of operating 20 ton helicopters.
Operational: To be capable of acting as a command platform, transporting up to 200 personnel and equipment, provision of joint logistic support, and as a hospital ship. *Absalon* achieved full operational capability in 2007 and *Esbern Snare* in mid-2008.

ABSALON *9/2007, Royal Danish Navy* / 1166513

ABSALON *9/2007, B Moultrie* / 1166512

ESBERN SNARE *5/2008*, B Moultrie* / 1335357

1 TRANSPORT SHIP (AKS)

Name	*No*	*Builders*	*Commissioned*
SLEIPNER	A 559	Åbenrå Vaerft og A/S	18 July 1986

Displacement, tons: 465 full load
Dimensions, feet (metres): 119.6 × 24.9 × 8.8 *(36.5 × 7.6 × 2.7)*
Main machinery: 1 Callesen diesel; 575 hp(m) *(423 kW)*; 1 shaft
Speed, knots: 11
Range, n miles: 2,400 at 11 kt
Complement: 7 (1 officer)
Cargo capacity: 150 tons
Radars: Navigation: Furuno FR-2115; I-band.

SLEIPNER *4/2007, E & M Laursen* / 1335455

1 ROYAL YACHT (YAC)

Name	*No*	*Builders*	*Commissioned*
DANNEBROG	A 540	R Dockyard, Copenhagen	20 May 1932

Displacement, tons: 1,130 full load
Dimensions, feet (metres): 246 × 34 × 12.1 *(75 × 10.4 × 3.7)*
Main machinery: 2 Burmeister & Wain Alpha T23L-KVO diesels; 1,800 hp(m) *(1.32 MW)*; 2 shafts; cp props
Speed, knots: 14
Complement: 54 (12 officers)
Guns: 2—40 mm saluting guns.
Radars: Navigation: Furuno FR-2115; I-band.

Comment: Laid down 2 January 1931, launched on 10 October 1931. Major refit 1980 included new engines and electrical gear. Marisat fitted in 1992.

DANNEBROG *4/2008*, E & M Laursen* / 1335365

2 POLLUTION CONTROL CRAFT (YPC)

MILJØ 101–102

Displacement, tons: 16 full load
Dimensions, feet (metres): 53.8 × 14.4 × 7.1 *(16.2 × 4.2 × 2.2)*
Main machinery: 1 MWM TBD232V12 diesel; 454 hp(m) *(334 kW)* sustained; 1 shaft
Speed, knots: 15
Range, n miles: 350 at 8 kt
Complement: 3 (1 officer)

Comment: Built by Ejvinds Plastikbodevaerft, Svendborg. Carry derricks and booms for framing oil slicks and dispersant fluids. Naval manned. Delivered 1 November and 1 December 1977.

MILJØ 102 *7/2008** / 1335356

4 RESCUE VESSELS (PBO)

NORDSØEN **VESTKYSTEN** **HAVØRNEN** **VIBEN**

Measurement, tons: 594 gwt *(Nordsøen)*; 657 gwt *(Vestkysten)*; 188 gwt *(Havørnen)*; 23 gwt *(Viben)*
Dimensions, feet (metres): 174.6 × 33.8 × 10.8 *(53.2 × 10.3 × 3.3) (Nordsøen)*
163.7 × 32.8 × 13.8 *(49.9 × 10 × 4.2) (Vestkysten)*
101.4 × 21.6 × ? *(30.9 × 6.6 × ?)* (Havørnen)
56.4 × 11.8 × 5.2 *(17.2 × 3.6 × 1.6)* (Viben)

Comment: Non-naval ships operated by the Ministry of Food and Fisheries. *Nordsøen* and *Vestkysten* operate primarily in the North Sea and Kattegat area, *Havørnen* in the Baltic Sea around Bornholm and *Viben* in shallow waters. Capable of 14–18 kt.

NORDSØEN *1/1999, Harald Carstens* / 0056889

2 OIL POLLUTION CRAFT (YPC/ABU)

GUNNAR THORSON A 560 **GUNNAR SEIDENFADEN** A 561

Displacement, tons: 750 full load
Dimensions, feet (metres): 183.7 × 40.3 × 12.8 *(56 × 12.3 × 3.9)*
Main machinery: 2 Burmeister and Wain Alpha 8V23L-VO diesels; 2,320 hp(m) *(1.7 MW)*; 2 shafts; cp props; bow thruster
Speed, knots: 12.5
Complement: 16 (7 officers)

Comment: Built by Ørnskov Stålskibsvaerft, Frederikshavn. Delivered 8 May and 2 July 1981 respectively. *G Thorson* at Copenhagen, *G Seidenfaden* at Korsør. Carry firefighting equipment. Large hydraulic crane fitted in 1988 for the secondary task of buoy tending. Orange painted hulls.

GUNNAR THORSON *8/2007, Michael Nitz* / 1166510

GUNNAR SEIDENFADEN *5/2002, L-G Nilsson* / 0526823

2 SEA TRUCKS (AKL)

METTE MILJØ A 562 **MARIE MILJØ** A 563

Displacement, tons: 157 full load
Dimensions, feet (metres): 97.7 × 26.2 × 5.2 *(29.8 × 8 × 1.6)*
Main machinery: 2 Grenaa diesels; 660 hp(m) *(485 kW)*; 2 shafts
Speed, knots: 10
Complement: 9 (1 officer)

Comment: Built by Carl B Hoffmann A/S, Esbjerg and Søren Larsen & Sønners Skibsvaerft A/S, Nykøbing Mors. Delivered 22 February 1980. Have orange and yellow superstructure.

METTE MILJØ *7/2008** / 1335355

2 ARVAK CLASS (HARBOUR TUGS) (YTL)

ARVAK Y 344 **ALSIN** Y 345

Displacement, tons: 79 full load
Dimensions, feet (metres): 52.5 × 21.7 × 8.2 *(16.0 × 6.6 × 2.5)*
Main machinery: 1 MTU 12V 183TE62 diesel; 737 hp(m) *(550 kW)*
Speed, knots: 10

Comment: Built by Hvide Sande Skibs & Baadebyggeri and delivered on 18 November 2002. In service at Korsør and Frederikshavn. Fitten with Stanflex container position aft to facilitate transport of containerised stores and equipment between naval bases.

ALSIN *5/2008*, E & M Laursen* / 1335366

ICEBREAKERS

Notes: Icebreakers, are controlled by the Navy but have a combined naval and civilian crew. Maintenance is done at Frederikshavn in Summer. Surveying is no longer conducted by these vessels.

1 THORBJØRN CLASS (AGB/AGS)

Name	*No*	*Builders*	*Commissioned*
THORBJØRN	A 553	Svendborg Vaerft	June 1981

Displacement, tons: 2,344 full load
Dimensions, feet (metres): 221.4 × 50.2 × 15.4 *(67.5 × 15.3 × 4.7)*
Main machinery: Diesel-electric; 4 Burmeister & Wain Alpha 16U28L-VO diesels; 6,800 hp(m) *(5 MW)*; 2 motors; 2 shafts
Speed, knots: 16.5
Range, n miles: 22,000 at 16 kt
Complement: 22 (7 officers)

Comment: No bow thruster. Side rolling tanks. Fitted for surveying duties in non-ice periods.

THORBJØRN *9/2006, M Declerck* / 1164771

2 DANBJØRN CLASS (AGB)

Name	*No*	*Builders*	*Commissioned*
DANBJØRN	A 551	Lindø Vaerft, Odense	1965
ISBJØRN	A 552	Lindø Vaerft, Odense	1966

Displacement, tons: 3,685 full load
Dimensions, feet (metres): 252 × 56 × 20 *(76.8 × 17.1 × 6.1)*
Main machinery: Diesel-electric; 6 Burmeister and Wain 12-26MT-40V diesels; 10,500 hp(m) *(7.72 MW)*; 8 motors; 5,240 hp(m) *(38.5 MW)*; 4 shafts
Speed, knots: 14
Range, n miles: 11,500 at 14 kt
Complement: 25 (9 officers)

Comment: Two of the four propellers are positioned forward, two aft.

ISBJØRN *9/2008*, E & M Laursen* / 1335364

Djibouti

MARINE NATIONALE DJIBOUTIENNE

Country Overview

Formerly the French territory of French Somaliland and later the Afars and the Issas, Djibouti became independent in 1977. With an area of 8,957 square miles and a coastline of 170 n miles, the country is situated in a strategic position on the Bab el Mandeb, the strait that links the Red Sea with the Gulf of Aden. It is bordered to the north by Eritrea, to the west by Ethiopia and to the south by Somalia. The largest town and capital is also called Djibouti whose port serves as an international transhipment and refuelling centre. It also provides Ethiopia with its only rail link to the sea. Territorial seas (12 n miles) are claimed. A 200 n mile Exclusive Economic Zone (EEZ) has been claimed but the limits are not fully defined.

Headquarters Appointments

Commander of Navy:
Colonel Abdourahman Aden Cher

Personnel

2009: 380

Bases

Djibouti

French Navy

The permanent French naval contingent usually includes up to three frigates and a repair ship.

PATROL FORCES

Notes: (1) Up to six RIBs are in use. Zodiac and Avon types.
(2) One LCM (ex-CTM 14) transferred from France in 1999.
(3) There is a small patrol craft *P 02*.
(4) Two Cantieri del Golfo 500L class were acquired in 2006. The 10 m craft are capable of 37 kt.

1 PLASCOA CLASS (COASTAL PATROL CRAFT) (PB)

Name	*No*	*Builders*	*Commissioned*
MONT ARREH	P 11	Plascoa, Cannes	16 Feb 1986

Displacement, tons: 35 full load
Dimensions, feet (metres): 75.5 × 18 × 4.9 *(23 × 5.5 × 1.5)*
Main machinery: 2 SACM Poyaud V12-520 M25 diesels; 1,700 hp(m) *(1.25 MW)*; 2 shafts
Speed, knots: 25
Range, n miles: 750 at 12 kt
Complement: 15
Guns: 1 Giat 20 mm. 1—12.7 mm MG.
Radars: Navigation: Decca 36; I-band.

Comment: Ordered in October 1984 and transferred as a gift from France. GRP hulls. Refitted in 1988 and 1994. *Moussa Ali* decommissioned in 2001.

MONT ARREH *1986, Plascoa* / 0056896

1 SWARI CLASS (INSHORE PATROL CRAFT) (PBR)

P 13

Comment: 21 m craft acquired from Iraq in 1989. Can be armed with MGs and rocket launchers. Outboard engines give speeds up to 25 kt in calm conditions. Four further craft are no longer operational.

2 BATTALION 17 (PBF)

P 16 **P 17**

Displacement, tons: 35.5 full load
Dimensions, feet (metres): 55.9 × 17 × 5.2 *(17.05 × 5.2 × 1.6)*
Main machinery: 2 MTU 12V 183 TE 92 diesels
Speed, knots: 35.2
Range, n miles: 680 at 30 kt
Complement: 9
Guns: 2—14.5 mm MGs (1 twin).
Radars: Surface search: Raytheon; I-band.

Comment: Australian design craft built by Harena Boat Yard at Assab, Eritrea and delivered in 2001. Five similar craft in service in Eritrea.

BATTALION 17 (Eritrean colours) *6/2000, Eritrean Navy* / 0103788

4 PATROL CRAFT (PC)

Displacement, tons: 17.7 full load
Dimensions, feet (metres): 44.0 × 12.5 × 3.9 *(13.4 × 3.8 × 1.2)*
Main machinery: 2 General Motors Detroit 6V53 diesels; 2 shafts
Speed, knots: 13
Range, n miles: 200 at 11 kt
Complement: 4

Comment: Former US Coast Guard lifeboats constructed in the 1960s. Four were delivered in June 2006 under FMS funding arrangements. A further craft was transferred as spares.

Dominica

Country Overview

Formerly a British colony, the Commonwealth of Dominica became an independent republic in 1978. With an area of 290 sq miles and coastline of 80 n miles, it is the largest and most northerly of the Windward Islands in the Lesser Antilles chain and is situated in the Caribbean Sea between the French possessions of Guadeloupe to the north and Martinique to the south. The capital, major town, and port is Roseau. Territorial seas (12 n miles) are claimed. A 200 n mile Exclusive Economic Zone (EEZ) has been claimed but the limits are not fully defined.

Headquarters Appointments

Head of Police Coast Guard:
Inspector Eric Elizee

Personnel

2009: 35

Bases

Roseau

COAST GUARD

1 SWIFT 65 FT CLASS (PB)

Name	*No*	*Builders*	*Commissioned*
MELVILLE	D 4	Swiftships, Morgan City	1 May 1984

Displacement, tons: 33 full load
Dimensions, feet (metres): 64.9 × 18.4 × 6.6 *(19.8 × 5.6 × 2)*
Main machinery: 2 Detroit 12V-71TA diesels; 840 hp *(616 kW)* sustained; 2 shafts
Speed, knots: 23. **Range, n miles:** 250 at 18 kt
Complement: 10
Guns: 1—7.62 mm MG.
Radars: Furuno; I/J-band.

Comment: Donated by US government. Similar craft supplied to Antigua and St Lucia. Aluminium construction.

MELVILLE *11/1993, Maritime Photographic* / 0506143

1 DAUNTLESS CLASS (PB)

Name	*No*	*Builders*	*Commissioned*
UKALE	D 05	SeaArk Marine	8 Nov 1995

Displacement, tons: 11 full load
Dimensions, feet (metres): 40 × 14 × 4.3 *(12.2 × 4.3 × 1.3)*
Main machinery: 2 Caterpillar 3208TA diesels; 870 hp *(650 kW)* sustained; 2 shafts
Speed, knots: 27
Range, n miles: 600 at 18 kt
Complement: 6
Guns: 1—7.62 mm MG (can be carried).
Radars: Raytheon; I-band.

Comment: Similar to craft delivered by the US to many Caribbean coast guards under FMS. Aluminium construction.

UKALE *11/1995, SeaArk* / 0056897

3 PATROL CRAFT (PBR)

VIGILANCE	OBSERVER	RESCUER

Displacement, tons: 2.4 full load
Dimensions, feet (metres): 27 × 8.4 × 1 *(8.2 × 2.6 × 0.3)*
Main machinery: 1 Evinrude outboard; 225 hp *(168 kW)* sustained or 2 Johnson outboards *(Rescuer)*; 280 hp *(205 kW)*
Speed, knots: 28 or 45 *(Rescuer)*
Complement: 3

Comment: First two are Boston Whalers acquired in 1988. *Rescuer* is of similar size but is an RHIB acquired in 1994.

OBSERVER
11/1993
Maritime Photographic
0506227

Dominican Republic

MARINA DE GUERRA

Country Overview

The Dominican Republic is an independent state whose constitution was promulgated in 1966. With an area of 18,816 square miles, it occupies the eastern two thirds of the island of Hispaniola, which it shares with Haiti to the west. There are also a number of adjacent islands, notably Beata and Saona. It has a 697 n mile coastline and is bordered to the north by the Atlantic Ocean, to the east by the Mona Passage, which separates it from Puerto Rico, and to the south by the Caribbean Sea. Santo Domingo is the capital, largest city and principal port. Territorial seas (6 n miles) are claimed. A 200 n mile EEZ has been claimed but the limits have not been defined by boundary agreements.

Headquarters Appointments

Chief of Naval Staff:
Vice Admiral Julio C Ventura Bayonet

Personnel

(a) 2009: 3,800 officers and men (including naval infantry)
(b) Selective military service

Bases

27 de Febrero, Santo Domingo: HQ of CNS, Naval School. Supply base.
Las Calderas, Las Calderas, Bañi: Naval dockyard, 700 ton synchrolift. Training centre. Supply base.
Haina: Dockyard facility. Supply base.
Puerto Plata. Small naval base.

Organisation

There are three naval zones:
North: Haitian border east to the Mona passage.
South: Mona passage west to the Haitian border.
Santo Domingo: Naval establishments in the capital and its environs.

DELETIONS

Notes: *Melia* still flies an ensign as a museum ship.

Auxiliaries

2006 *Capitán Beotegui*

PATROL FORCES

2 BALSAM CLASS (PBO/WMEC)

Name	*No*	*Builders*	*Commissioned*
ALMIRANTE JUAN ALEXANDRO ACOSTA (ex-*Citrus*)	PA 302 (ex-C 456, ex-WMEC 300)	Marine Iron, Duluth	30 May 1943
ALMIRANTE DIDIEZ BURGOS (ex-*Buttonwood*)	PA 301 (ex-C 457, ex-WLB 306)	Duluth Shipyard, Minnesota	24 Sep 1943

Displacement, tons: 1,034 full load
Dimensions, feet (metres): 180 × 37 × 12 *(54.9 × 11.3 × 3.8)*
Main machinery: Diesel-electric; 2 Cooper Bessemer diesels; 1,402 hp *(1.06 MW)*; 2 motors; 1,200 hp *(895 kW)*; 1 shaft; bow thruster
Speed, knots: 13
Complement: 54 (4 officers)
Guns: 1—4 in; 2—20 mm (456). 2—20 mm; 2—12.7 MGs (457).
Radars: Surface search: Raytheon SPS-64(V)1; I-band.

Comment: C 456 built as a buoy tender but served as a US Coast Guard cutter from 1979 to 1994. Transferred by gift on 16 September 1995 and recommissioned in January 1996 after a short refit. C 457 transferred from US Coast Guard on 30 June 2001.

ALMIRANTE JUAN ALEXANDRO ACOSTA ***8/2002, A Sheldon-Duplaix*** / 0534105

2 WHITE SUMAC CLASS (ABU)

Name	*No*	*Builders*	*Commissioned*
TORTUGUERO (ex-*White Pine*)	PM 203 (ex-BA 1, ex-WLM 547)	Erie Concrete and Steel, Erie	11 July 1944
CAPOTILLO (ex-*White Sumac*)	PM 204 (ex-BA 2, ex-WLM 504)	Niagara Shipbuilding	1943

Displacement, tons: 485 full load
Dimensions, feet (metres): 133 × 31 × 9 *(40.5 × 9.5 × 2.7)*
Main machinery: 2 Caterpillar 353 diesels; 600 hp *(448 kW)*; 2 shafts
Speed, knots: 9
Complement: 24

Comment: PM 203 transferred from US Coast Guard in 1999 and PM 204 on 20 September 2002. Fitted with a 10 ton capacity boom. Reclassified as patrol ships in 2006.

TORTUGUERO ***12/1999, A Sheldon-Duplaix*** / 0056903

2 CANOPUS (SWIFTSHIPS 110 ft) CLASS (LARGE PATROL CRAFT) (PB)

Name	*No*	*Builders*	*Commissioned*
CANOPUS (ex-*Cristobal Colon*)	GC 107	Swiftships, Morgan City	June 1984
ORION	GC 109	Swiftships, Morgan City	Aug 1984

Displacement, tons: 93.5 full load
Dimensions, feet (metres): 109.9 × 23.9 × 5.9 *(33.5 × 7.3 × 1.8)*
Main machinery: 3 Caterpillar 3412E diesels; 1,700 hp *(1.3 MW)* sustained; 3 shafts
Speed, knots: 23
Range, n miles: 1,500 at 12 kt
Complement: 19 (3 officers)
Guns: 1—20 mm or 2—12.7 mm MGs.
Radars: Surface search: Raytheon; I-band.

Comment: Built of aluminium. GC 107 completely rebuilt and reconditioned by Swiftships in 2003. GC 109 was similarly refitted in 2004.

CANOPUS *1/2004, Swiftships* / 0587700

3 POINT CLASS (PB)

Name	*No*	*Builders*	*Commissioned*
ARIES (ex-*Point Martin*) (ex-*Point Baton*)	GC 101 (ex-82379)	USCG Yard, Curtis Bay, MD	20 Aug 1970
ANTARES	GC 105 (ex-82340)	J Martinac, Tacoma	20 Aug 1970
SIRIUS (ex-*Point Spencer*)	GC 110 (ex-82349)	J Martinac, Tacoma	25 Oct 1966

Displacement, tons: 67 full load
Dimensions, feet (metres): 83 × 17.2 × 5.8 *(25.3 × 5.2 × 1.8)*
Main machinery: 2 Caterpillar D3412 diesels; 1,600 hp *(1.19 MW)*; 2 shafts
Speed, knots: 22
Range, n miles: 1,200 at 8 kt
Complement: 10
Guns: 2—12.7 mm MGs.
Radars: Surface search: Hughes/Furuno SPS-73; I-band.

Comment: *Antares* transferred from US Coast Guard 1 October 1999 and *Sirius* transferred 12 December 2000. *Aries* reported decommissioned in 2005 but returned to service after refit in 2007.

SIRIUS *6/2004, A Sheldon-Duplaix* / 0587698

4 BELLATRIX CLASS (COASTAL PATROL CRAFT) (PB)

Name	*No*	*Builders*	*Commissioned*
PROCION	GC 103	Sewart Seacraft Inc, Berwick, LA	1967
ALDEBARÁN	GC 104	Sewart Seacraft Inc, Berwick, LA	1972
BELLATRIX	GC 106	Sewart Seacraft Inc, Berwick, LA	1967
CAPELLA	GC 108	Sewart Seacraft Inc, Berwick, LA	1968

Displacement, tons: 60 full load
Dimensions, feet (metres): 85 × 18 × 5 *(25.9 × 5.5 × 1.5)*
Main machinery: 2 Caterpillar 3412E diesels; 1,700 hp *(1.3 MW)* sustained; 2 shafts
Speed, knots: 18.7
Range, n miles: 800 at 15 kt
Complement: 12
Guns: 3—12.7 mm MGs.
Radars: Surface search: Raytheon SPS-64; I-band.

Comment: Transferred to the Dominican Navy by the US. *Procion* was taken out of service in 1995 but returned in 1997 after a long refit. GC 103 and GC 106 completely rebuilt and reconditioned by Swiftships, Morgan City, in 2003. GC 104 and GC 108 were similarly refitted in 2004.

CAPELLA *8/2002, A Sheldon-Duplaix* / 0534085

BELLATRIX *6/2004, A Sheldon-Duplaix* / 0587699

2 SWIFTSHIPS 35 M CLASS (LARGE PATROL CRAFT) (PB)

Name	*No*	*Builders*	*Commissioned*
ALTAIR	GC 112	Swiftships, Morgan City	Oct 2003
ARCTURUS	GC 114	Swiftships, Morgan City	Mar 2004

Displacement, tons: 95 standard
Dimensions, feet (metres): 115.1 × 24.0 × 5.0 *(35.1 × 7.3 × 1.5)*
Main machinery: 3 CAT 3412 diesels; 3,600 hp *(2.7 MW)*; 3 Hamilton HM 651 waterjets
Speed, knots: 25
Range, n miles: To be announced
Complement: To be announced
Guns: 1—25 mm. 2—12.7 mm MGs.

Comment: Two craft ordered from Swiftships, Morgan City, LA as part of wider programme to increase capability to conduct counter-smuggling and drug-trafficking operations. Fitted with launching ramp for 4.7 m RIB.

ALTAIR *12/2003, A Sheldon-Duplaix* / 0569189

4 DAMEN 1505 PATROL CRAFT (LARGE PATROL CRAFT) (PB)

Name	*No*	*Builders*	*Commissioned*
HAMAL	LR 151	Astilleros Navales de la Bahia de las Calderas	Dec 2004
VEGA	LR 152	Astilleros Navales de la Bahia de las Calderas	Dec 2004
DENEB	LR 153	Astilleros Navales de la Bahia de las Calderas	14 Apr 2005
ACAMAR	LR 154	Astilleros Navales de la Bahia de las Calderas	14 Apr 2005

Displacement, tons: 16
Dimensions, feet (metres): 49.5 × 14.8 × 3.3 *(15.1 × 4.5 × 1.0)*
Main machinery: 2 Caterpillar 2406 diesels; 1,800 hp *(1.3 MW)*
Speed, knots: 34. **Range, n miles:** To be announced
Complement: 6
Guns: 1—7.62 mm MG (fitted for).

Comment: Damen Stan Patrol 1505 design craft constructed in the Dominican Republic. Aluminium construction. Employed as patrol craft on counter-drugs and illegal immigration duties.

VEGA *6/2006, Damen Shipyards* / 1164479

4 INTERCEPTOR CRAFT (PBF)

POLLUX LR 155 **CASTOR** LR 156 **SHAULA** LR 157 **ATRIA** LR 158

Displacement, tons: To be announced
Dimensions, feet (metres): 44.0 × 9.0 × 3.0 *(13.4 × 2.75 × 0.9)*
Main machinery: 3 Yanmar DE 315 diesels; 945 hp *(704 kW)*; Bravo X drives
Speed, knots: 60
Range, n miles: 600 at 25 kt
Complement: 6

Comment: Manufactured by Nor-Tech, Fort Myers, Florida. Composite and glass fibre V-bottomed hull. The first two donated by the US Southern Command on 13 July 2007 and the second two on 6 September 2007. Employed on counter drugs, arms trafficking and illegal immigration duties.

INTERCEPTOR CRAFT ***6/2007, US Southern Command*** / 1167968

LAND-BASED MARITIME AIRCRAFT

Numbers/Type: 2 Bell OH-58 Kiowa.
Operational speed: 102 kt *(188 km/h)*
Service ceiling: 14,000 ft *(4,267 m)*
Range: 260 n miles *(481 km)*
Role/Weapon systems: Light observation helicopters. The first was acquired in November 2003 and two further were received from the US in 2006. Two remain in service. Fitted for 7.62 mm MG.

OH-58 (Australian colours) ***6/1996, Rockwell Australia*** / 1164548

AUXILIARIES

Notes: (1) There are also two dredgers manned by the Navy. *Puerto Plata* BD 11, *San Pedro* BD 12.
(2) There are eight auxiliary craft: *Nizao* LA 1, *Soco* LA 2, *Chavon* LA 3, *Yuma* LA 4, *Cayo Arena* LA 5, *Rio Ozama* LA 7, *Beata* LA 8, *Cayo Levantado* LA 9.

DREDGER ***10/1998, A Sheldon-Duplaix*** / 0056902

1 FLOATING DOCK (YFD)

ENDEAVOR DF 1 (ex-AFDL 1)

Comment: Lift, 1,000 tons. Commissioned in 1943. Transferred from US on loan 8 March 1986 and approved for transfer 10 June 1997. DF 2 (ex-AFDM 2), previously reported, was not acquired.

1 LCU 1600 CLASS (UTILITY LANDING CRAFT) (LCU)

NEYBA (ex-*Commando*) LD 31 (ex-LDM 4, ex-LCU 1675)

Displacement, tons: 200 light; 375 full load
Dimensions, feet (metres): 134.9 × 29 × 6.1 *(41.1 × 8.8 × 1.9)*
Main machinery: 4 Detroit 6-71 diesels; 696 hp *(519 kW)* sustained; 2 shafts; Kort nozzles
2 Detroit 12V-71 diesels (LCU 1680-1681); 680 hp *(508 kW)* sustained; 2 shafts; Kort nozzles
Speed, knots: 11
Range, n miles: 1,200 at 8 kt
Complement: 14 (2 officers)
Military lift: 134 tons or 400 troops
Guns: 2 — 12.7 mm MGs.
Radars: Navigation: Furuno; I-band.

Comment: Steel hulled construction. Built by General Ship and Engineering Works in 1978. Formerly operated by the US Army and transferred in 2004.

LCU 1600 CLASS (US colours) ***8/2004, Hachiro Nakai*** / 1043687

1 SOTOYOMO CLASS (ATA)

Name	*No*	*Builders*	*Commissioned*
ENRIQUILLO	RM 3 (ex-RM 22)	Levington SB Co, Orange TX	26 Feb 1945

Displacement, tons: 534 standard; 860 full load
Dimensions, feet (metres): 143 × 33.9 × 13 *(43.6 × 10.3 × 4.0)*
Main machinery: Diesel-electric; 2 GM 12-278A diesels; 2,200 hp *(1.64 MW)*; 2 generators; 1 motor; 1,500 hp *(1.12 MW)*; 1 shaft
Speed, knots: 13
Range, n miles: 8,000 at 10 kt
Complement: 45
Radars: Surface search: Raytheon SPS-5D; G/H-band.

Comment: Leased from the US on 30 October 1980 and transferred on 10 June 1997. Reported decommissioned in 2005 but returned to service in 2007. Employed as afloat support ship.

ENRIQUILLO (old number) ***8/2002, A Sheldon-Duplaix*** / 0534084

TUGS

4 COASTAL/HARBOUR TUGS (YTM/YTL)

GUAROCUYA RM 1 **GUAROA** RM 3
GUARIONEX RM 2 **MAGUA** RM 4

Displacement, tons: 265 full load
Dimensions, feet (metres): 85.6 × 26.0 × 13.3 *(26.1 × 7.9 × 4.05)*
Main machinery: 2 Caterpillar 3512B diesels; 3,500 hp *(2.6 MW)*; 2 shafts
Speed, knots: 12.7
Complement: 6

Comment: Details given are for RM 1 and RM 2, Damen Stantug 2608, built at Astilleros Navales de la Bahia de las Calderas and commissioned in April 2004 and June 2005 respectively. The details of RM 3 and RM 4 are not known.

East Timor

Country Overview

The Democratic Republic of Timor-Leste (also known as East Timor) has an area of 7,400 square miles and lies in the eastern part of Timor island, the largest and easternmost of the Lesser Sunda Islands in the Malay Archipelago. Originally settled in the early 16th century, the Portuguese and Dutch competed for influence until boundaries became established. Dutch Timor, in the west, later became part of the Republic of Indonesia in 1950. Portuguese Timor, comprising the region of Dili, in the east, and the small area of Oecussi in the north-west, was annexed by Indonesia in 1975. Following an armed conflict and two and a half years of UN administration (UNTAET), East Timor gained independence on 20 May 2002 and became a UN member on 27 September 2002. There has been a succession of further UN missions. UNMISET was withdrawn on 20 May 2005 and was succeeded by a political mission, UNOTIL. Following internal security problems, an expanded mission, UNMIT,was established on 25 August 2006. This includes police personnel and military advisers. The capital, principal city and port is Dili. Maritime claims are not known.

The role of the Naval Component of The East Timor Defence Force is to conduct Fishery Protection duties in the East Timorese EEZ and to safeguard the only direct access to the enclave of Oecussi which is by sea.

Headquarters Appointments

Commander in Chief Defence Forces: Brigadier General Taur Matan Ruak

Personnel

2009: 150 (under training)

Bases

Hera Harbour

PATROL FORCES

2 ALBATROZ CLASS (RIVER PATROL CRAFT) (PB)

Name	*No*	*Builders*	*Commissioned*
OECUSSI (ex-*Açor*)	P 101 (ex-P 1163)	Arsenal do Alfeite	9 Dec 1974
ATAURO (ex-*Albatroz*)	P 102 (ex-P 1162)	Arsenal do Alfeite	9 Dec 1974

Displacement, tons: 45 full load
Dimensions, feet (metres): 77.4 × 18.4 × 5.2 *(23.6 × 5.6 × 1.6)*
Main machinery: 2 Cummins diesels; 1,100 hp *(820 kW)*; 2 shafts
Speed, knots: 20. **Range, n miles:** 2,500 at 12 kt
Complement: 8 (1 officer)
Guns: 1 Oerlikon 20 mm/65. 2—12.7 mm MGs.
Radars: Surface search: Decca RM 316P; I-band.

Comment: Transferred by Portugal in 2001 to establish the Naval Component of the ETDF.

0 + 2 SHANGHAI II CLASS (FAST ATTACK CRAFT—GUN) (PB)

Displacement, tons: 134 full load
Dimensions, feet (metres): 127.3 × 17.7 × 5.6 *(38.8 × 5.4 × 1.7)*
Main machinery: 2 Type L12-180 diesels; 2,400 hp(m) *(1.76 MW)* (forward); 2 Type 12-D-6 diesels; 1,820 hp(m) *(1.34 MW)* (aft); 4 shafts
Speed, knots: 30
Range, n miles: 700 at 16.5 kt
Complement: 38
Guns: 4—37 mm/63 (2 twin). 4—25 mm/80 (2 twin).
Radars: Surface search: Skin Head; E/F-band.

Comment: Agreement by the East Timor government for the transfer of two Chinese Shanghai II-class patrol craft was reached in April 2008. The date of the transfer has not been confirmed. The contract is reported to include upgrade of shore infrastructure.

OECUSSI *4/2008*, John Mortimer* / 1305302

Ecuador

ARMADA DEL ECUADOR

Country Overview

The Republic of Ecuador is situated in northwestern South America. With an area of 105,037 square miles it straddles the equator and has borders to the north with Colombia and to the south with Peru. It has a coastline of 1,210 n miles with the Pacific Ocean. The country also includes the Galápagos Islands about 520 n miles west of the mainland. The capital is Quito while Guayaquil is the principal port and commercial centre. Ecuador has not claimed an EEZ but is oneof a few coastal states which claims a 200 n mile territorial sea.

Headquarters Appointments

Commander-in-Chief of the Navy:
Rear Admiral Livio Espinoza
Chief of Naval Staff:
Rear Admiral Aland Molestina
Chief of Naval Operations:
Rear Admiral Milton Lalama

Headquarters Appointments—*continued*

Flag Officer Fleet:
Captain Oswaldo Zambrano

Diplomatic Representation

Naval Attaché in Rome:
Captain Renan Ruiz
Naval Attaché in London and Paris:
Captain Carlos Rivera
Naval Attaché in Washington:
Captain Javier Ricaurte
Naval Attaché in Santiago:
Captain Manolo Alava
Naval Attaché in Bogota:
Captain Francisco Recaurte
Naval Attaché in Caracas:
Captain Miguel Quelal
Naval Attaché in Lima:
Captain Alejandro Vela
Naval Attaché in Brasilia:
Captain Ronald Munoz

Personnel

(a) 2009: 7,283 (including naval aviation, marines and Coast Guard)
(b) 1 year's selective national service

Organisation

1st Naval Zone: HQ at Guayaquil. Provinces of El Oro, Guayas and Manabi.
2nd Naval Zone: HQ at San Cristobal. Provinces of Galapagos Islands.
3rd Naval Zone: HQ at Esmeraldas. Provinces of Esmeraldas and Amazonas.

Prefix to Ships' Names

BAE (Buque de Armada de Ecuador)

Bases

Guayaquil (Fleet HQ and main naval base), Jaramijo, San Cristobal, Esmeraldas. Guayaquil (rotary wing) and Manta (fixed wing) air bases.

Establishments

The Naval Academy and Merchant Navy Academy in Salinas; Naval War College in Guayaquil.

Naval Infantry

There are four battalions each comprising amphibious warfare, coastal defence, local security and special forces elements. They are based at: Guayaquil (HQ), Esmeraldas (1st Battalion), Jaramijo (2nd Battalion), San Eduardo (3rd Battalion) and Jambeli (4th Battalion).

Coast Guard

Small force formed in 1980. Hull markings include diagonal thick and thin red stripes on the hull.

PENNANT LIST

Submarines

S 101	Shyri
S 102	Huancavilca

Frigates

FM 01	Presidente Alfaro
FM 02	Moran Valverde

Corvettes

CM 11	Esmeraldas
CM 12	Manabi
CM 13	Los Rios
CM 14	El Oro
CM 15	Los Galápagos
CM 16	Loja

Patrol Forces

LM 21	Quito
LM 23	Guayaquil
LM 24	Cuenca

Survey/Research Vessels

BI 91	Orion
LH 94	Rigel

Tugs

RA 70	Chimborazo
RB 72	Sangay
RB 73	Cotopaxi
RB 75	Iliniza
RB 76	Altar
RB 78	Quilotoa

Auxiliaries

TR 62	Calicuchima
TR 63	Atahualpa
TR 64	Quisquis
TR 65	Taurus
BE 91	Guayas
DF 82	Rio Napo

Coast Guard

LG 31	Isla Isabela
LG 32	Isla Seymour
LG 33	Isla Santa Cruz
LG 34	Isla San Cristóbal
LG 35	Isla Santa Rosa
LG 36	Isla Puná
LG 37	Isla de la Plata
LG 38	Isla Santa Clara
LG 39	Isla Fernandina
LG 40	Isla Española
LG 41	Isla San Salvador
LG 111	Rio Puyango
LG 112	Rio Mataje
LG 113	Rio Zarumilla
LG 114	Rio Chone
LG 115	Rio Daule
LG 116	Rio Babahoyo
LG 121	Rio Esmeraldas
LG 122	Rio Santiago

SUBMARINES

2 SHYRI (TYPE 209/1300) CLASS (SSK)

Name	*No*	*Builders*	*Laid down*	*Launched*	*Commissioned*
SHYRI	S 101 (ex-S 11)	Howaldtswerke, Kiel	5 Aug 1974	5 Oct 1976	5 Nov 1977
HUANCAVILCA	S 102 (ex-S 12)	Howaldtswerke, Kiel	2 Jan 1975	15 Mar 1977	16 Mar 1978

Displacement, tons: 1,285 surfaced; 1,390 dived
Dimensions, feet (metres): 195.1 × 20.5 × 17.9 *(59.5 × 6.3 × 5.4)*
Main machinery: Diesel-electric; 4 MTU 12V 493 AZ80 GA31L diesels; 2,400 hp(m) *(1.76 MW)* sustained; 4 Siemens alternators; 1.7 MW; 1 Siemens motor; 4,600 hp(m) *(3.38 MW)* sustained; 1 shaft
Speed, knots: 10 surfaced/snorting; 20 dived
Complement: 45 (10 officers)

Torpedoes: 8—21 in *(533 mm)* bow tubes. Whitehead A 184 Mod 3; dual purpose; wire-guided; active/passive homing to 25 km *(13.7 n miles)* at 24 kt; 17 km *(9.2 n miles)* at 38 kt; warhead 250 kg. AEG SST 4; anti-surface; wire-guided; active/passive homing to 12.7 km *(6.8 n miles)* at 33 kt; 28 km *(15.0 n miles)* at 23 kt; warhead 260 kg. Total of 14 weapons.
Countermeasures: ESM: Thomson-CSF DR 2000U; intercept.
Weapons control: Signaal M8 Mod 24.
Radars: Surface search: Furuno 1832; I-band.
Sonars: Atlas Elektronik CSU 3; hull-mounted; active/passive search and attack; medium frequency.
Thomson Sintra DUUX 2; passive ranging.

Programmes: Ordered in March 1974.
Modernisation: *Shyri* underwent major refit in West Germany in 1983; *Huancavilca* in 1984. Second refits by Astinave, Ecuador; *Shyri* in 1994 and *Huancavilca* in 1996. Batteries were changed in both boats 2006–07. the contract for modernisation of both submarines was signed with ASMAR, Talcahuano, on 10 January 2008. DCNS subsequently sub-contracted to modernise the combat systems and technical assistance. The upgrade is to include replacement of the combat system with SUBTICS, replacement of the sonar system with Thales S-Cube multimission suite (including passive bow cylindrical array, passive flank array), Velox M8 intercept array, and a self-noise monitoring system), replacement of the batteries and improvements to the periscopes, machinery control and navigation systems. Work on *Shyri* began on 5 September 2008 and is to be completed in 2010. *Huancavilca* is to be refitted 2010–12. The refits are to extend service lives until about 2030.
Operational: Based at Guayaquil.

TYPE 209 ***6/2001, Maritime Photographic*** / 0114670

SHYRI ***6/1998*** / 0017796

FRIGATES

0 + 2 (1) LEANDER CLASS (FFGHM)

Name	*No*	*Builders*	*Laid down*	*Launched*	*Commissioned*
PRESIDENTE ELOY ALFARO (ex-*Almirante Condell*)	FM 01 (ex-06)	Yarrow & Co, Scotstoun	5 June 1971	12 June 1972	21 Dec 1973
MORAN VALVERDE (ex-*Almirante Lynch*)	FM 02(ex-07)	Yarrow & Co, Scotstoun	6 Dec 1971	6 Dec 1972	25 May 1974

Displacement, tons: 2,500 standard; 3,200 full load
Dimensions, feet (metres): 372 oa; 360 wl × 43 × 18 (screws) *(113.4; 109.7 × 13.1 × 5.5)*
Main machinery: 2 Babcock & Wilcox boilers; 550 psi *(38.7 kg/cm²)*; 850°F *(450°C)*; 2 White/English Electric turbines; 30,000 hp *(22.4 MW)*; 2 shafts
Speed, knots: 27
Range, n miles: 4,500 at 12 kt
Complement: 248 (20 officers)

Missiles: SSM: 2 Aerospatiale MM 38 Exocet; inertial cruise; active radar homing to 42 km *(23 n miles)* at 0.9 Mach; warhead 165 kg.
SAM 3 twin Matra Simbad launchers for Mistral (may be fitted); IR homing to 4 km *(2.2 n miles)*; warhead 3 kg.
Guns: 2 Vickers 4.5 in *(115 mm)*/45 Mk 6 (twin) semi-automatic; 20 rds/min to 19 km *(10 n miles)* anti-surface; 6 km *(3.2 n miles)* anti-aircraft; weight of shell 25 kg.
4 Oerlikon 20 mm Mk 9 (2 twin); 800 rds/min to 2 km.
Torpedoes: 6—324 mm Mk 32 (2 triple) tubes; Whitehead A 244; anti-submarine; pattern running to 7 km *(3.8 n miles)* at 33 kt; warhead 34 kg.
Countermeasures: Decoys 2 Corvus 8-barrelled trainable chaff rocket launchers; distraction or centroid patterns to 1 km. Wallop Barricade double layer chaff launchers.
ESM/ECM: Elta EW system; intercept and jammer.
Combat data systems: Sisdef Imagen SP 100 includes datalink. Link 11 receive.
Weapons control: Maiten-1/CH for gunnery.
Radars: Air search: Marconi Type 965/966; A-band.
Surface search: Marconi Type 992 Q; E/F-band.
Navigation: Liton Type 1006; I-band.
Fire control: Selenia; I-band (for guns).
Sonars: Graseby Type 184 M/P; hull-mounted; active search and attack; medium frequency (6/9 kHz).

Helicopters: 1 Bell 230.

Programmes: Following service in the Chilean Navy, both ships were decommissioned in 2007 and subsequently acquired by the Ecuador Navy. Following overhaul and modification in Chilean yards, they were transferred on 18 April 2008 (FM 01) and 15 October 2008 (FM 02). They replaced two ex-British Leanders (*Penelope* and *Danae*) originally built in the 1960s and acquired in 1991. The acquisition of a third ship (ex-*Ministro Zenteno* (ex-*Achilles*)) is also under consideration.
Modernisation: While in Chilean service, *Lynch* (1989) and *Condell* (1993) were both modernised by ASMAR, Talcahuano. Upgrades included enlargement of the hangar and flight deck, the fitting of the Indal Assist helicopter recovery system, mounting of two twin MM 40 Exocet launchers on each side of the hangar and moving the torpedo tubes down one deck. Other modifications included a new combat data system, improvements to the fire-control radars and the installation of Israeli EW systems. *Lynch* was further modernised in 2002. Upgrades included complete overhaul of propulsion and machinery systems. Phalanx close-in weapon systems have been removed and it is assumed that SSM, SAM and torpedoes have been transferred from the decommissioned ships.

PRESIDENTE ELOY ALFARO — ***4/2008*, Ecuador Navy*** / 1335375

CORVETTES

6 ESMERALDAS CLASS (FSGHM)

Name	*No*	*Builders*	*Laid down*	*Launched*	*Commissioned*
ESMERALDAS	CM 11	Fincantieri Muggiano	27 Sep 1979	1 Oct 1980	7 Aug 1982
MANABI	CM 12	Fincantieri Ancona	19 Feb 1980	9 Feb 1981	21 June 1983
LOS RIOS	CM 13	Fincantieri Muggiano	5 Dec 1979	27 Feb 1981	9 Oct 1983
EL ORO	CM 14	Fincantieri Ancona	20 Mar 1980	9 Feb 1981	11 Dec 1983
LOS GALAPÁGOS	CM 15	Fincantieri Muggiano	4 Dec 1980	4 July 1981	26 May 1984
LOJA	CM 16	Fincantieri Ancona	25 Mar 1981	27 Feb 1982	26 May 1984

Displacement, tons: 685 full load
Dimensions, feet (metres): 204.4 × 30.5 × 8 *(62.3 × 9.3 × 2.5)*
Main machinery: 4 MTU 20V 956 TB92 diesels; 22,140 hp(m) *(16.27 MW)* sustained; 4 shafts
Speed, knots: 37. **Range, n miles:** 4,400 at 14 kt
Complement: 51

Missiles: SSM: 6 Aerospatiale MM 40 Exocet (2 triple) launchers ❶; inertial cruise; active radar homing to 70 km *(40 n miles)* at 0.9 Mach; warhead 165 kg; sea-skimmer.
SAM: Selenia Elsag Albatros quad launcher ❷; Aspide; semi-active radar homing to 13 km *(7 n miles)* at 2.5 Mach; warhead 30 kg.
Guns: 1 OTO Melara 3 in *(76 mm)*/62 compact ❸; 85 rds/min to 16 km *(8.7 n miles)*; weight of shell 6 kg.
2 Breda 40 mm/70 (twin) ❹; 300 rds/min to 12.5 km *(6.8 n miles)* anti-surface; weight of shell 0.96 kg.
Torpedoes: 6—324 mm ILAS-3 (2 triple) tubes ❺; Whitehead Motofides A244; anti-submarine; self-adaptive patterns to 7 km *(3.8 n miles)* at 33 kt; warhead 34 kg shaped charge. Not fitted in all.
Countermeasures: Decoys: 1 Breda 105 mm SCLAR launcher; chaff to 5 km *(2.7 n miles)*; illuminants to 12 km *(6.6 n miles)*.
ESM/ECM: Elettronika Gamma ED; radar intercept and jammer.
Combat data systems: Selenia IPN 10 action data automation. Link Y.

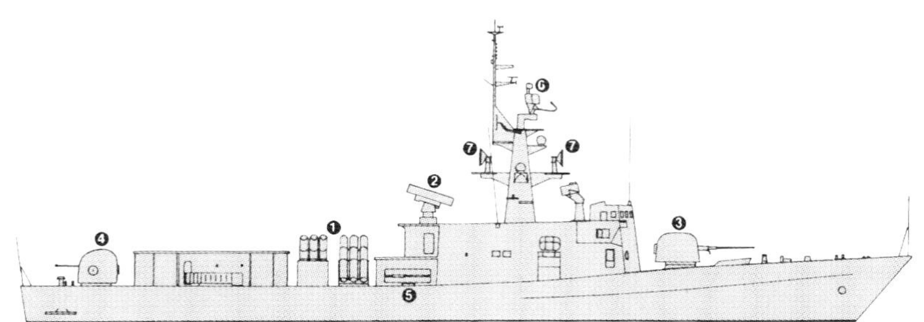

ESMERALDAS — ***(Scale 1 : 600), Ian Sturton*** / 0505980

Weapons control: 2 Selenia NA21 with C03 directors.
Radars: Air/surface search: Selenia RAN 10S ❻; E/F-band; range 155 km *(85 n miles)*.
Navigation: Furuno 2115; I-band.
Fire control: 2 Selenia Orion 10X ❼; I/J-band; range 40 km *(22 n miles)*.
Sonars: Thomson Sintra Diodon; hull-mounted; active search and attack; 11, 12 or 13 kHz.

Helicopters: Platform for 1 Bell 206B.

Programmes: Ordered in 1979.
Modernisation: A modernisation programme began in 2006. *Esmeraldas* was reportedly fitted with new Israeli systems, including the combat data system; the engines were also refurbished. The other five ships are expected to be similarly upgraded.
Operational: Torpedo tubes removed from two of the class to refit in frigates. CM 16 took part in Exercise Unitas during 2008.

EL ORO

2/2000 / 0103731

MANABI

6/2002, Ecuador Navy / 0533898

SHIPBORNE AIRCRAFT

Numbers/Type: 2 Bell 230T.
Operational speed: 145 kt *(269 km/h)*.
Service ceiling: 18,000 ft *(5,500 m)*.
Range: 307 n miles *(568 km)*.
Role/Weapon systems: Support helicopter for afloat reconnaissance and SAR. Navalised Bell 230s acquired in 1995. Sensors: Surveillance radar. Weapons: None.

BELL 230

6/2003, Ecuador Navy / 0568886

Numbers/Type: 3/3 Bell 206 Jet Ranger/206TH 57 Sea Ranger.
Operational speed: 115 kt *(213 km/h)*.
Service ceiling: 13,500 ft *(4,115 m)*.
Range: 368 n miles *(682 km)*.
Role/Weapon systems: Support helicopter for afloat reconnaissance and SAR. Sensors: None. Weapons: Depth bombs, 7.62 mm MG.

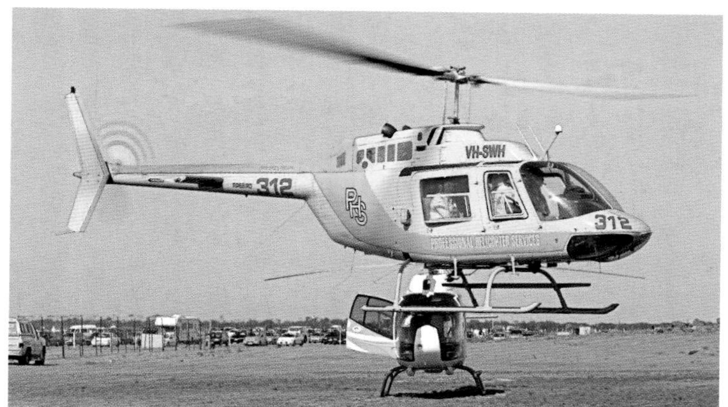

BELL 206

5/2004, Paul Jackson / 0569619

LAND-BASED MARITIME AIRCRAFT (FRONT LINE)

Notes: (1) The Navy operates one CASA CN-235M-100 transport aircraft, four ENAER T-35 Pillan training aircraft, one Beech King Air B-300, one Beech King Air B-350 and two Beech T-34C.
(2) Up to two Unmanned Air Vehicles (UAV) are to be procured for surveillance of maritime areas. The UAVs are to be equipped with synthetic aperture radar and electro-optic sensors.

Numbers/Type: 1 Casa CN-235-300MP Persuader.
Operational speed: 210 kt *(384 km/h)*.
Service ceiling: 24,000 ft *(7,315 m)*.
Range: 2,000 n miles *(3,218 km)*.
Role/Weapon systems: EEZ surveillance. Delivered in 2005/06. Sensors: surveillance radar. Weapons: unarmed.

CN 235-300MP *6/2008*, Ecuador Navy* / 1335374

Numbers/Type: 3 Beech King Air B-200.
Operational speed: 239 kt *(443 km/h)*.
Service ceiling: 9,144 m *(30,000 ft)*.
Range: 2,000 n miles *(3,218 km)*.
Role/Weapon systems: Maritime Patrol aircraft delivered in January and June 1997. Sensors: Bottom-mounted surveillance radar and ESM.

B-200 *6/1999, Ecuador Navy* / 0054061

PATROL FORCES

Notes: There are plans to acquire an offshore patrol ship of 1,500-1,800 tons.

3 QUITO (LÜRSSEN 45) CLASS

Name	*No*	*Builders*	*Launched*	*Commissioned*
QUITO	LM 21	Lürssen, Vegesack	20 Nov 1975	13 July 1976
GUAYAQUIL	LM 23	Lürssen, Vegesack	5 Apr 1976	22 Dec 1977
CUENCA	LM 24	Lürssen, Vegesack	6 Dec 1976	17 July 1977

Displacement, tons: 255
Dimensions, feet (metres): 147.6 × 23 × 8.1 *(45 × 7 × 2.5)*
Main machinery: 4 MTU 16V 396 diesels; 13,600 hp(m) *(10 MW)* sustained; 4 shafts
Speed, knots: 40. **Range, n miles:** 700 at 40 kt; 1,800 at 16 kt
Complement: 35

Missiles: SSM: 4 Aerospatiale MM 38 Exocet; inertial cruise; active radar homing to 42 km *(23 n miles)* at 0.9 Mach; warhead 165 kg; sea-skimmer.
Guns: 1 OTO Melara 3 in *(76 mm)*/62 compact; 85 rds/min to 16 km *(8.7 n miles)*; weight of shell 6 kg.
2 Oerlikon 35 mm/90 (twin); 550 rds/min to 6 km *(3.3 n miles)*; weight of shell 1.55 kg.
Countermeasures: ESM: ELISRA NS-9010; intercept.
Weapons control: Thomson-CSF Vega system.
Radars: Air/surface search: Thomson-CSF Triton; G-band; range 33 km *(18 n miles)* for 2 m² target.
Fire control: Thomson-CSF Pollux; I/J-band; range 31 km *(17 n miles)* for 2 m² target.
Navigation: Furuno 2115; I-band.

Modernisation: New engines fitted during refits in 1994–95 at Guayaquil. A further modernisation programme was initiated in 2005. Upgrades are to include replacement of the Oerlikon 35 mm gun with a new Breda 40 mm/70 twin turret and a new combat data system.
Operational: *Quito* may be laid up.

CUENCA *2/2000* / 0103732

SURVEY AND RESEARCH SHIPS

1 SURVEY CRAFT (YFS)

Name	*No*	*Builders*	*Commissioned*
RIGEL	LH 94 (ex-LH 92)	Halter Marine	1975

Displacement, tons: 50 full load
Dimensions, feet (metres): 64.5 × 17.1 × 3.6 *(19.7 × 5.2 × 1.1)*
Main machinery: 2 diesels; 2 shafts
Speed, knots: 10
Complement: 10 (2 officers)

Comment: Used for inshore oceanographic work.

RIGEL (old number) *6/2005, Ecuador Navy* / 1151078

1 SURVEY SHIP (YGS)

Name	*No*	*Builders*	*Commissioned*
ORION (ex-*Dometer*)	BI 91 (ex-HI 91, ex-HI 92)	Ishikawajima, Tokyo	10 Nov 1982

Measurement, tons: 1,105 gross
Dimensions, feet (metres): 210.6 pp × 35.1 × 11.8 *(64.2 × 10.7 × 3.6)*
Main machinery: Diesel-electric; 3 Caterpillar 3412 diesel generators; 2,380 hp *(1.77 MW)* sustained; 2 motors; 1,900 hp *(1.42 MW)*; 1 shaft
Speed, knots: 12.6. **Range, n miles:** 6,000 at 12 kt
Complement: 45 (6 officers) plus 14 civilians
Radars: Surface search/Navigation: Furuno 2837; E/F-band.
Navigation: Sperry Marine Bridgemaster; I-band.

Comment: Research vessel for oceanographic, hydrographic and meteorological work. A refit 2007–08 included installation of a flight deck and new engines.

ORION *6/2008*, Ecuador Navy* / 1335373

TRAINING SHIPS

1 SAIL TRAINING SHIP (AXS)

Name	*No*	*Builders*	*Commissioned*
GUAYAS	BE 91 (ex-BE 01)	Ast Celaya, Spain	23 July 1977

Measurement, tons: 234 dwt; 934 gross
Dimensions, feet (metres): 264 × 33.5 × 13.4 *(80 × 10.2 × 4.2)*
Main machinery: 1 GM 12V-149T diesel; 875 hp *(652 kW)* sustained; 1 shaft
Speed, knots: 11.3
Complement: 50 plus 80 trainees

Comment: Three masted. Launched 23 September 1976. Has accommodation for 180. Similar to ships in service with Colombia, Mexico and Venezuela. Modernised 2006–07.

GUAYAS *7/2008*, Kazumasa Watanabe* / 1335460

AUXILIARIES

Notes: A new dredger, *Francisco de Orellana*, was commissioned in July 2008.

1 YW CLASS (WATER TANKER) (AWT)

Name	*No*	*Builders*	*Commissioned*
ATAHUALPA (ex-*YW 131*)	TR 63	Leatham D Smith SB Co	17 Sep 1945

Displacement, tons: 460 light; 1,481 full load
Dimensions, feet (metres): 174 × 32 × 15 *(53.1 × 9.8 × 4.6)*
Main machinery: 1 GM 8V-278A diesel; 640 hp *(477 kW)*; 2 shafts
Speed, knots: 8
Complement: 25 (5 officers)
Cargo capacity: 930 tons

Comment: Acquired from the US on 2 May 1963. Purchased on 1 December 1977. Paid off in 1988 but back in service in 1990 to provide water for the Galapagos Islands.

ATAHUALPA *6/2005, Ecuador Navy* / 1151077

1 OIL TANKER (AOTL)

Name	*No*	*Builders*	*Commissioned*
TAURUS	TR 65 (ex-T 66)	Astinave, Guayaquil	1985

Measurement, tons: 1,175 dwt; 1,110 gross
Dimensions, feet (metres): 174.2 × 36 × 14.4 *(53.1 × 11 × 4.4)*
Main machinery: 2 GM diesels; 1,050 hp *(783 kW)*; 1 shaft
Speed, knots: 11
Complement: 20

Comment: Acquired for the Navy in 1987.

TAURUS *6/2003, Ecuador Navy* / 0568887

1 ARMAMENT STORES CARRIER (AETL)

Name	*No*	*Builders*	*Commissioned*
CALICUCHIMA (ex-*Throsk*)	TR 62 (ex-A 379)	Cleland SB Co, Wallsend	20 Sep 1977

Displacement, tons: 2,184 full load
Dimensions, feet (metres): 231.2 × 39 × 15 *(70.5 × 11.9 × 4.6)*
Main machinery: 2 General Motors diesels; 2,100 hp *(1.56 MW)*; 1 shaft
Speed, knots: 11
Range, n miles: 4,000 at 11 kt
Complement: 29 (5 officers)
Cargo capacity: 785 tons
Radars: Navigation: Decca 926; I-band.

Comment: Acquired from the UK in November 1991. Recommissioned 24 March 1992.

CALICUCHIMA *11/2004, Globke Collection* / 1129995

1 WATER CLASS (WATER TANKER) (AWT)

Name	*No*	*Builders*	*Commissioned*
QUISQUIS (ex-*Waterside*)	TR 64 (ex-Y 20)	Drypool Engineering, Hull	1968

Measurement, tons: 519 gross
Dimensions, feet (metres): 131.5 × 25.7 × 11.7 *(40.1 × 7.7 × 3.5)*
Main machinery: 1 Lister-Blackstone ERS-8-MCR diesel; 660 hp *(492 kW)*; 1 shaft
Speed, knots: 10
Range, n miles: 1,585 at 9 kt
Complement: 20 (4 officers)
Cargo capacity: 150 tons
Radars: Navigation: Furuno; I-band.

Comment: Acquired from the UK in November 1991.

QUISQUIS *2/1992, A J Moorey* / 0056909

2 ARD 12 CLASS (FLOATING DOCKS) (YFD)

Name	*No*	*Builders*	*Commissioned*
RIO NAPO (ex-*ARD 24*)	DF 82	USA	1944
CENEPA (ex-*ARD 26*)		USA	1944

Dimensions, feet (metres): 492 × 81 × 17.7 *(150 × 24.7 × 5.4)*

Comment: *Napo* bought from the US in 1988. Suitable for docking ships up to 3,200 tons. *Cenepa* is 48 ft longer and was transferred from US service in 2000.

1 SUPPLY SHIP (AKL)

Name	*No*	*Builders*	*Commissioned*
GALAPAGOS (ex-*Arca Foz*, ex-*Riveira*)	–	Astilleros de Huelva, Spain	1982

Measurement, tons: 2,617 grt
Dimensions, feet (metres): 245 × 47.6 × 15.1 *(74.7 × 14.2 × 4.6)*
Main machinery: 1 diesel; 2,100 hp *(1.56 MW)*; 1 cp prop
Speed, knots: 12
Complement: To be announced

Comment: Spanish-built refrigerated cargo ship acquired in July 2008. The ship is used to supply the Galapagos Islands.

TUGS

5 HARBOUR TUGS (YTM/YTL)

SANGAY RB 72	**ILINIZA** RB 75	**QUILOTOA** RB 78
COTOPAXI RB 73	**ALTAR** RB 76	

Comment: Mostly built in the 1950s and 1960s.

1 CHEROKEE CLASS (ATF)

Name	*No*	*Builders*	*Commissioned*
CHIMBORAZO (ex-*Chowanoc* ATF 100)	RA 70 (ex-R 710, ex-R 71, ex-R 105)	Charleston SB & DD Co	21 Feb 1945

Displacement, tons: 1,235 standard; 1,640 full load
Dimensions, feet (metres): 205 × 38.5 × 17 *(62.5 × 11.7 × 5.2)*
Main machinery: Diesel-electric; 4 Caterpillar D 399 diesels; 4 generators; 1 motor; 3,000 hp *(2.24 MW)*; 1 shaft
Speed, knots: 12
Range, n miles: 7,000 at 15 kt
Complement: 67 (5 officers)
Guns: 1 — 40 mm. 2 — 12.7 mm MGs.
Radars: Navigation: Simrad; I-band.

Comment: Launched 20 August 1943 and transferred 1 October 1977.

CHIMBORAZO *6/2001, Maritime Photographic* / 0114524

COAST GUARD

Notes: In addition to the vessels listed below, there are up to 40 river patrol launches operated by both the Coast Guard and the Army.

3 ISLA FERNANDINA (VIGILANTE) CLASS (OFFSHORE PATROL CRAFT) (PBO)

Name	*No*	*Builders*	*Commissioned*
ISLA FERNANDINA (ex-*6 de Diciembre*)	LG 39	Astilleros de Murueta, Spain	Jan 2006
ISLA ESPAÑOLA (ex-*11 de Noviembre*)	LG 40	Astilleros de Murueta, Spain	Jan 2006
ISLA SAN SALVADOR (ex-*11 de Abril*)	LG 41	Astilleros de Murueta, Spain	Jan 2006

Displacement, tons: 320
Dimensions, feet (metres): 147.7 × 32.1 × 8.0 *(45.0 × 9.8 × 2.5)*
Main machinery: 2 MTU 16V 4000 M90; 1 MTU 12V 4000 M80; 3 shafts
Speed, knots: 25
Range, n miles: 3,000 at 12 kt
Complement: 27 (4 officers)
Guns: 1—12.7 mm MG. 2—7.62 mm MGs.
Radars: Navigation: I-band.

Comment: Contract for three craft for the coast Guard let to FBM Babcock Marine in partnership with Astilleros de Murueta, Spain, on 4 March 2004. The steel-hulled craft, to be built in Spain, is based on the FBM Marine Protector 45 class. Propulsion arrangements allow for the use of two main engines or a smaller central engine for loiter. A 5 m interception craft is carried on the aft work deck. LG 39 based at Esmeraldas, LG 40 at Manta and LG 41 in the Galapagos Islands.

ISLA ESPAÑOLA *1/2006*, ***Ecuador Coast Guard*** / 1158715

2 MANTA CLASS (LARGE PATROL CRAFT) (WPBF)

Name	*No*	*Builders*	*Commissioned*
ISLA DE LA PLATA (ex-*9 de Octubre*, ex-*Manta*)	LG 37 (ex-LM 25)	Lürssen, Vegesack	11 June 1971
ISLA SANTA CLARA (ex-*27 de Octubre*, ex-*Nuevo Rocafuerte*)	LG 38 (ex-LM 27)	Lürssen, Vegesack	23 June 1971

Displacement, tons: 119 standard; 134 full load
Dimensions, feet (metres): 119.4 × 19.1 × 6 *(36.4 × 5.8 × 1.8)*
Main machinery: 2 MTU 392TE 94 diesels; 4,370 hp(m) *(3.26 MW)*; 2 shafts
Speed, knots: 30
Range, n miles: 700 at 30 kt; 1,500 at 15 kt
Complement: 19 (3 officers)
Guns: 1—20 mm. 1—12.7 mm MG.
Radars: Navigation: I-band.

Structure: Similar design to the Chilean Guacolda class with an extra diesel, 3 kt faster.
Operational: A third of class sank in September 1998 after a collision with a tug. Transferred from the Navy in 2000. Refitted and modernised in 2003–04 at Astinane, Guayaquil.

ISLA DE LA PLATA *6/2001*, ***Ecuador Coast Guard*** / 0114527

2 ESPADA CLASS (LARGE PATROL CRAFT) (WPB)

Name	*No*	*Builders*	*Commissioned*
ISLA SANTA ROSA (ex-*5 de Agosto*)	LG 35	Moss Point Marine, Escatawpa	May 1991
ISLA PUNÁ (ex-*27 de Febrero*)	LG 36	Moss Point Marine, Escatawpa	Nov 1991

Displacement, tons: 190 standard; 220 full load
Dimensions, feet (metres): 119.4 × 19.0 × 5.9 *(36.4 × 5.8 × 1.8)*
Main machinery: 2 Detroit 16V-149TI diesels; 2,322 hp *(1.73 MW)* sustained; 1 Detroit 16V-92TA; 690 hp *(514 kW)* sustained; 3 shafts
Speed, knots: 18
Range, n miles: 1,500 at 14 kt
Complement: 19 (3 officers)
Guns: 1—20 mm GAM-BO1. 2—12.7 mm MGs.
Radars: Surface search: Furuno Marine; I-band.

Comment: Built under FMS programme. Steel hulls and aluminium superstructure. Accommodation is air conditioned. Carry a 10-man RIB and launching crane on the stern. Both modernised 2007–08.

ISLA SANTA ROSA *6/2002*, ***Ecuador Coast Guard*** / 0533896

2 SWIFTSHIPS CLASS (RIVER PATROL CRAFT) (WPBR)

Name	*No*	*Builders*	*Commissioned*
RIO ESMERALDAS (ex-*9 de Octubre*)	LG121 (ex-LG 47, ex-LG 37)	Swiftships, Morgan City	1 Oct 1992
RIO SANTIAGO (ex-*27 de Octubre*)	LG 122 (ex-LG 48, ex-LG 38)	Swiftships, Morgan City	1 Oct 1992

Displacement, tons: 17 full load
Dimensions, feet (metres): 45.5 × 11.8 × 1.8 *(13.9 × 3.6 × 0.6)*
Main machinery: 2 Detroit 6V-92TA diesels; 900 hp *(671 kW)*; 2 Hamilton water-jets
Speed, knots: 20
Range, n miles: 600 at 22 kt
Complement: 4 (1 officer)
Guns: 2 M2HB 12.7 mm MGs; 2 M60D 7.62 mm MGs.
Radars: Surface search: Raytheon 40; I-band.

Comment: Transferred from US under MAP to the Navy and thence to the Coast Guard. Hard chine modified V hull form. Can carry up to eight troops. Used as command craft for river flotillas.

RIO SANTIAGO *6/2005*, ***Ecuador Coast Guard*** / 1151076

1 POINT CLASS (COASTAL PATROL CRAFT) (WPB)

Name	*No*	*Builders*	*Commissioned*
ISLA SEYMOUR (ex-*24 de Mayo*, ex-*Point Richmond*)	LG 32 (ex-82370)	CG Yard, Curtis Bay	25 Aug 1967

Displacement, tons: 54 standard; 66 full load
Dimensions, feet (metres): 83 × 17.2 × 5.8 *(25.3 × 5.2 × 1.8)*
Main machinery: 2 Caterpillar 3412 diesels; 1,600 hp *(1.19 MW)*; 2 shafts
Speed, knots: 18
Range, n miles: 1,500 at 8 kt
Complement: 10 (2 officers)
Guns: 2—12.7 mm MGs.
Radars: Navigation: Raytheon SPS 64(V)1; I-band.

Comment: Transferred from US Coast Guard on 22 August 1997.

ISLA SEYMOUR *6/2001*, ***Ecuador Coast Guard*** / 0114515

4 PIRAÑA CLASS (RIVER PATROL CRAFT) (WPBR)

LG 131 (ex-LG 51) **LG 132** (ex-LG 52) **LG 133** (ex-LG 53) **LG 134** (ex-LG 54)

Main machinery: 2 outboard motors; 300 hp *(224 kW)*
Speed, knots: 35
Complement: 6
Guns: 1 Ametralladora MAG 7.62 mm.

Comment: Built by Astinave and commissioned 1994–95.

LG 134 (old number) *6/2001, Ecuador Coast Guard* / 0114517

1 PGM-71 CLASS (LARGE PATROL CRAFT) (WPB)

Name	*No*	*Builders*	*Commissioned*
ISLA ISABELA (ex-25 *de Julio*, ex-*Quito*)	LG 31 (ex-LGC 31, ex-LC 71)	Peterson, USA	30 Nov 1965

Displacement, tons: 150 standard; 180 full load
Dimensions, feet (metres): 101.5 × 21 × 5 *(30.9 × 6.4 × 1.5)*
Main machinery: 2 Detroit diesels; 1,500 hp *(1.1 MW)*; 2 shafts
Speed, knots: 15. **Range, n miles:** 1,000 at 12 kt
Complement: 21 (3 officers)
Guns: 1 Oerlikon 20 mm. 2 — 12.7 mm MGs.
Radars: Surface search: Furuno Marine; I-band.

Comment: Transferred from US to the Navy under MAP on 30 November 1965 and then to the Coast Guard in 1980. Paid off into reserve in 1983 and deleted from the order of battle. Refitted with new engines in 1988–89. Second of class deleted in 1997.

ISLA ISABELA *6/2005, Ecuador Coast Guard* / 1151075

2 10 DE AGOSTO CLASS (LARGE PATROL CRAFT) (WPB)

Name	*No*	*Builders*	*Commissioned*
ISLA SANTA CRUZ (ex-*10 de Agosto*)	LG-33 (ex-LGC-33)	Bremen, Germany	1954
ISLA SAN CRISTÓBAL (ex-*3 de Noviembre*)	LG-34 (ex-LGC-34)	Bremen, Germany	1955

Displacement, tons: 35 standard; 45 full load
Dimensions, feet (metres): 76.75 × 15.7 × 4.6 *(23.4 × 4.8 × 1.4)*
Main machinery: 2 Detroit diesels
Speed, knots: 10. **Range, n miles:** 450 at 12 kt
Complement: 11 (1 officer)
Radars: Surface search: Raytheon; I-band.
Guns: 2 Ametralladora .30.

Comment: Transferred from Coopno-Coopin to the coast guard on 12 January 1992 and 4 June 1992. Were to have been replaced by the Vigilante class but remain in service.

ISLA SAN CRISTÓBAL *11/2004, Globke Collection* / 1129994

6 RIO PUYANGO CLASS (RIVER PATROL CRAFT) (WPBR)

Name	*No*	*Builders*	*Commissioned*
RIO PUYANGO	LG 111 (ex-LG 41, ex-LGC 40)	Halter Marine, New Orleans	15 June 1986
RIO MATAJE	LG 112 (ex-LG 42, ex-LGC 41)	Halter Marine, New Orleans	15 June 1986
RIO ZARUMILLA	LG 113 (ex-LG 43, ex-LGC 42)	Astinave, Guayaquil	11 Mar 1988
RIO CHONE	LG 114 (ex-LG 44, ex-LGC 43)	Astinave, Guayaquil	11 Mar 1988
RIO DAULE	LG 115 (ex-LG 45, ex-LGC 44)	Astinave, Guayaquil	17 June 1988
RIO BABAHOYO	LG 116 (ex-LG 46, ex-LGC 45)	Astinave, Guayaquil	17 June 1988

Displacement, tons: 17
Dimensions, feet (metres): 44 × 13.5 × 3.5 *(13.4 × 4.1 × 1.1)*
Main machinery: 2 Detroit 8V-71 diesels; 460 hp *(343 kW)* sustained; 2 shafts
Speed, knots: 26. **Range, n miles:** 500 at 18 kt
Complement: 5 (1 officer)
Guns: 1 — 12.7 mm MG. 2 — 7.62 mm MGs.
Radars: Surface search: Furuno 2400; I-band.

Comment: Two delivered by Halter Marine in June 1986. Four more ordered in February 1987; assembled under licence at Astinave shipyard, Guayaquil. Used mainly for drug interdiction.

RIO BABAHOYO (old number) *6/2002, Ecuador Coast Guard* / 0533895

3 NAPO CLASS (PBF)

LG 151 (ex-LG 59) **LG 152** (ex-LG 60) **LG 153** (ex-LG 61)

Main machinery: 2 inboard motors; 300 hp *(224 kW)*
Speed, knots: 40
Complement: 6
Guns: 1 Ametralladora MAG 7.62 mm MG.

Comment: Built by Astinave, Guayaquil. Entered service in 2002.

LG 151 (old number) *6/2003, Ecuador Coast Guard* / 0568885

2 RINKER CLASS (PBF)

LG 191 (ex-LG 57) **LG 192** (ex-LG 58)

Main machinery: 2 outboard motors; 300 hp *(224 kW)*
Speed, knots: 40
Complement: 5
Guns: 1 Ametralladora MAG 7.62 mm MG.

Comment: Built in US. Entered service in 2002.

RINKER CLASS *6/2003, Ecuador Coast Guard* / 0568884

2 ALBATROS CLASS (WPBR)

LG 63–64

Main machinery: 1 outboard motor; 115 hp *(85 kW)*
Speed, knots: 40
Complement: 5
Guns: 1 Ametralladora MAG 7.62 mm MG.

Comment: Built in Chile. Entered service in 2004.

ALBATROS CLASS ***6/2005, Ecuador Coast Guard*** / 1151074

8 FAST INTERCEPT CRAFT (WPBF)

Name	*No*	*Builders*	*Commissioned*
RIO VERDE	LG 611	FB Design shipyard, Italy	Jan 2008
RIO BULU BULU	LG 612	FB Design shipyard, Italy	Jan 2008
RIO MACARA	LG 613	FB Design shipyard, Italy	Jan 2008
RIO YAGUACHI	LG 614	FB Design shipyard, Italy	Jan 2008
RIO CAÑAR	LG 615	FB Design shipyard, Italy	Jan 2008
RIO SAN MIGUEL	LG 616	FB Design shipyard, Italy	Jan 2008
RIO QUININDÉ	LG 617	FB Design shipyard, Italy	Jan 2008
RIO CATAMAYO	LG 618	FB Design shipyard, Italy	Jan 2008

Displacement, tons: 6 full load
Dimensions, feet (metres): 37.5 × 9.2 × 2.8 *(11.43 × 2.81 × 0.84)*
Main machinery: 2 Cummins diesels; 710 hp *(530 kW)*; 2 surface drives
Speed, knots: 52
Complement: 4
Guns: 1 chainsaw MAG 7.62 mm MG.
Radars: Navigation: Furuno; I-band.

Comment: Fabio Buzzi FB 38 STAB design. The principal feature of the design is a rigid hull of cored sandwich construction stabilised by two torpedo-shaped inflatable sections on the side of the stern sections to improve stability and safety in rough seas.

RIO VERDE ***6/2008*, Ecuador Coast Guard*** / 1335372

1 ALBATROS 1100 CLASS (WPBR)

Name	*No*	*Builders*	*Commissioned*
RIO JUBONES	LG-601	Astilleros SITECNA, Chile	2008

Displacement, tons: To be announced
Dimensions, feet (metres): 36.1 × 10.5 × 4.9 *(11.00 × 3.20 × 1.50)*
Main machinery: 3 outboard motors
Speed, knots: 40
Complement: 5

Comment: Delivered in 2008.

RIO JUBONES ***6/2008*, Ecuador Coast Guard*** / 1335371

3 ALBATROS 830 CLASS (WPBR)

Name	*No*	*Builders*	*Commissioned*
RIO COANGOS	LG-161	Astilleros SITECNA, Chile	2008
RIO MUISNE	LG-162	Astilleros SITECNA, Chile	2008
RIO TANGARE	LG-163	Astilleros SITECNA, Chile	2008

Displacement, tons: To be announced
Dimensions, feet (metres): 27.2 × 7.9 × 3.8 *(8.3 × 2.4 × 1.15)*
Main machinery: 2 outboard motors
Speed, knots: 40
Complement: 4

Comment: Delivered in 2008.

RIO COANGOS ***6/2008*, Ecuador Coast Guard*** / 1335370

4 ALBATROS 730 CLASS (WPBR)

Name	*No*	*Builders*	*Commissioned*
RIO TENA	LG-171	Astilleros SITECNA, Chile	2008
RIO PUYO	LG-172	Astilleros SITECNA, Chile	2008
RIO PORTOVIEJO	LG-173	Astilleros SITECNA, Chile	2008
RIO MANTA	LG-174	Astilleros SITECNA, Chile	2008

Displacement, tons: To be announced
Dimensions, feet (metres): 20.7 × 7.5 × 3.8 *(6.3 × 2.3 × 1.15)*
Main machinery: 1 outboard motor
Speed, knots: 35
Complement: 5

Comment: Delivered in 2008.

RIO TENA ***6/2008*, Ecuador Coast Guard*** / 1335369

2 ALBATROS 630 CLASS (WPBR)

Name	*No*	*Builders*	*Commissioned*
RIO ZAMORA	LG-181	Astilleros SITECNA, Chile	2008
RIO PALORA	LG-182	Astilleros SITECNA, Chile	2008

Displacement, tons: To be announced
Dimensions, feet (metres): 20.7 × 7.2 × 3.9 *(6.3 × 2.2 × 1.2)*
Main machinery: 1 outboard motor
Speed, knots: 30
Complement: 4

Comment: Delivered in 2008.

RIO ZAMORA ***6/2008*, Ecuador Coast Guard*** / 1335368

Egypt

Country Overview

The Arab Republic of Egypt was established in 1953. The country was united with Syria as the United Arab Republic 1958–61. Located in north-eastern Africa and the Sinai Peninsula, the country has an area of 385,229 square miles and is bordered to the east by Israel, to the south by Sudan and to the west by Libya. It has a 1,323 n mile coastline with the Mediterranean and Red Seas. Cairo is the capital and largest city while Alexandria is the principal port. Port Said and Port Suez are at the northern and southern ends of the 88 n mile long Suez Canal respectively. Territorial seas (12 n miles) are claimed. An EEZ (200 n miles) has been claimed but the limits have not been defined.

Headquarters Appointments

Commander in Chief, Navy:
Vice Admiral Mohamed Hussein Mameesh
Chief of Naval Staff:
Rear Admiral Mostafa Mohamed Ezz El-Din Wahba
Chief of Operations:
Rear Admiral Usama Ahmed Ahmed El-Gendy
Chief of Armaments:
Commodore Mohamed Mohamed Abd-el-Aziz

Personnel

(a) 2009: 18,500 officers and men, including 2,000 Coast Guard and 10,000 conscripts (Reserves of 14,000)
(b) 1-3 years' national service (depending on educational qualifications)

Bases

Alexandria (HQ), Port Said, Mersa Matru, Abu Qir, Suez. Safaqa and Hurghada on the Red Sea.
Naval Academy: Abu Qir.

Coast Defence

There are three batteries of Border Guard Otomat truck-mounted SSMs (two twin launchers each) with targeting by Plessey radars (fixed) and Thomson-CSF radars (mobile). Two Artillery brigades, under naval co-operative control, are armed with 100, 130 and 152 mm guns.

Maritime Air

Although the Navy has no air arm the Air Force has a number of E-2Cs, ASW Sea Kings and Gazelles with an ASM capability (see *Land-based Maritime Aircraft* section). The Sea Kings and Seasprite helicopters are controlled by the Anti-Submarine Brigade, based at Alexandria, and have some naval aircrew.

Prefix to Ships' Name

ENS

Strength of the Fleet

Type	*Active*	*Building (Projected)*
Submarines (Patrol)	4	–
Frigates	10	(2)
Fast Attack Craft (Missile)	31	3
Fast Attack Craft (Gun)	9	–
Fast Attack Craft (Patrol)	8	–
LSMs/LST	3	(2)
LCUs	9	–
Minesweepers (Ocean)	7	–
Minehunters (Coastal)	5	–
Route Survey Vessels	2	–

PENNANT LIST

Frigates

901	Sharm el Sheikh
906	Toushka
911	Mubarak
916	Taba
951	Najim al Zaffer
956	El Nasser
961	Damyat
966	Rasheed
F 941	Abu Qir
F 946	El Suez

Patrol Forces

430	Al Nour
433	Al Hadi
436	Al Hakim
439	Al Wakil
442	Al Qatar
445	Al Gabbar
448	Al Salam
451	Al Rafa
601	23 of July
602	6 of October
603	21 of October
604	18 of June
605	25 of April
670	Ramadan
672	Khyber
674	El Kadessaya
676	El Yarmouk
678	Badr
680	Hettein

Mine Warfare Forces

507	Daqhiliya
513	Sinai
516	Assiyut
521	Al Siddiq
524	Al Farouk
530	Giza
533	Aswan
536	Qina
539	Sohag
542	Dat Assawari
545	Navarin
548	Burullus
RSV 1	Safaga
RSV 2	Abu el Ghoson

Auxiliaries

210	Ayeda 4
212	Atabarah
214	Akdu
216	Ayeda 3
218	Maryut
220	Al Nil
224	Al Furat
230	Shaladein
231	Halaib
103	Al Maks
105	Al Agami
107	Al Antar
109	Al Dekheila
111	Al Iskandarani

Training Ships

P 91	Al Kousser
921	El Fateh

SUBMARINES

Notes: (1) Preliminary negotiations for the acquisition of Type 206A boats from Germany took place in December 2004. Up to four submarines might be acquired but there have been no firm reports of progress.
(2) Some two-man Swimmer Delivery Vehicles (SDVs) of Italian CF2 FX 100 design are in service.

4 IMPROVED ROMEO CLASS (PROJECT 033) (SSK)

849 **852** **855** **858**

Displacement, tons: 1,475 surfaced; 1,830 dived
Dimensions, feet (metres): 251.3 × 22 × 16.1 *(76.6 × 6.7 × 4.9)*
Main machinery: Diesel-electric; 2 Type 37-D diesels; 4,000 hp(m) *(2.94 MW)*; 2 motors; 2,700 hp(m) *(1.98 MW)*; 2 creep motors; 2 shafts
Speed, knots: 16 surfaced; 13 dived
Range, n miles: 9,000 at 9 kt surfaced
Complement: 54 (8 officers)

Missiles: SSM: McDonnell Douglas Sub Harpoon; active radar homing to 130 km *(70 n miles)* at 0.9 Mach; warhead 227 kg.
Torpedoes: 8—21 in *(533 mm)* tubes (6 bow, 2 stern). 14 Alliant Mk 37F Mod 2; wire-guided; active/passive homing to 18 km *(9.7 n miles)* at 32 kt; warhead 148 kg.
Mines: 28 in lieu of torpedoes.
Countermeasures: ESM: Argo Phoenix AR-700-S5; radar warning.
Weapons control: Singer Librascope Mk 2. Datalink.
Radars: Surface search: I-band.
Sonars: Atlas Elektronik CSU 83; bow-mounted; active/passive; medium frequency.
Loral; hull-mounted; active attack; high frequency.

Programmes: Two transferred from China 22 March 1982. Second pair arrived from China 3 January 1984, commissioned 21 May 1984.

ROMEO 849 *3/2006, M Declerck* / 1167114

Modernisation: In early 1988 a five year contract was signed with Tacoma, Washington to retrofit Harpoon, and Mk 37 wire-guided torpedoes; weapon systems improvements to include Loral active sonar, Atlas Elektronik passive sonar and fire-control system. New air conditioning was also installed. The US Congress did not give approval to start work until July 1989 and then Tacoma went bankrupt and the work was not taken over by Loral/Lockheed Martin until April 1992. Towed communications wire and GPS are fitted. Kollmorgen 76 and 86 periscopes. Plans to fit optronic masts have not been confirmed. Plans to install an inertial navigation system were announced in 2003.
Operational: *855* was the first to complete modernisation and the remainder completed by mid-1996. All four are reported to have completed machinery overhauls in the last few years and are based at Alexandria. There has been very little activity and operational status is doubtful. Of remaining submarines, *831*, *840* and *843* are non-operational and *846* has been scrapped.

ROMEO 852 and 855 *3/2007, Marco Ghiglino* / 1166536

FRIGATES

Notes: Acquisition of two Koni-class frigates, one as spares, from Montenegro was reportedly discussed in 2004 but there have been no further reports of progress.

4 OLIVER HAZARD PERRY CLASS (FFGHM)

Name	*No*	*Builders*	*Laid down*	*Launched*	*Commissioned*
MUBARAK (ex-*Copeland*)	911 (ex-FFG 25)	Todd Shipyards, San Pedro	24 Oct 1979	26 July 1980	7 Aug 1982
TABA (ex-*Gallery*)	916 (ex-FFG 26)	Bath Iron Works	17 May 1980	20 Dec 1980	5 Dec 1981
SHARM EL SHEIKH (ex-*Fahrion*)	901 (ex-FFG 22)	Todd Shipyards, Seattle	1 Dec 1978	24 Aug 1979	16 Jan 1982
TOUSHKA (ex-*Lewis B Puller*)	906 (ex-FFG 23)	Todd Shipyards, San Pedro	23 May 1979	15 Mar 1980	17 Apr 1982

Displacement, tons: 2,750 light; 3,638 full load
Dimensions, feet (metres): 445 × 45 × 14.8; 24.5 (sonar) *(135.6 × 13.7 × 4.5; 7.5)*
Main machinery: 2 GE LM 2500 gas turbines; 41,000 hp *(30.59 MW)* sustained; 1 shaft; cp prop
2 auxiliary retractable props; 650 hp *(484 kW)*
Speed, knots: 29. **Range, n miles:** 4,500 at 20 kt
Complement: 206 (13 officers) including 19 aircrew

Missiles: SSM: 4 McDonnell Douglas Harpoon Block 1B; active radar homing to 92 km *(50 n miles)* at 0.9 Mach; warhead 227 kg.
SAM: 36 GDC Standard SM-1MR Block VI; command guidance; semi-active radar homing to 38 km *(20.5 n miles)* at 2 Mach.
1 Mk 13 Mod 4 launcher for both SSM and SAM missiles ❶.
Guns: 1 OTO Melara 3 in *(76 mm)*/62 Mk 75 ❷; 85 rds/min to 16 km *(8.7 n miles)* anti-surface; 12 km *(6.6 n miles)* anti-aircraft; weight of shell 6 kg.
1 General Electric/General Dynamics 20 mm/76 6-barrelled Mk 15 Vulcan Phalanx ❸; 3,000 rds/min combined to 1.5 km.
4—12.7 mm MGs.
Torpedoes: 6—324 mm Mk 32 (2 triple) tubes ❹. 24 Alliant Mk 46 Mod 5; anti-submarine; active/passive homing to 11 km *(5.9 n miles)* at 40 kt; warhead 44 kg.
Countermeasures: Decoys: 2 Loral Hycor SRBOC 6-barrelled fixed Mk 36 ❺; IR flares and chaff to 4 km *(2.2 n miles)*.
T-Mk-6 Fanfare/SLQ-25 Nixie; torpedo decoy.
ESM/ECM: Raytheon SLQ-32 ❻; radar warning.
Combat data systems: NTDS with Link Y.
Weapons control: SWG-1 Harpoon LCS. Mk 92 (Mod 4). Mk 13 weapon direction system. 2 Mk 24 optical directors.
Radars: Air search: Raytheon SPS-49(V)4 ❼; C/D-band.
Surface search: ISC Cardion SPS-55 ❽; I-band.
Fire control: Lockheed STIR (modified SPG-60) ❾; I/J-band; range 110 km *(60 n miles)*.
Sperry Mk 92 (Signaal WM28) ❿; I/J-band.
Navigation: Furuno; I-band ⓫; JRC; I-band.
Tacan: URN 25. IFF Mk XII AIMS UPX-29.
Sonars: Raytheon SQS-56; hull-mounted; active search and attack; medium frequency.

Helicopters: 2 Kaman SH-2G Seasprite ⓬.

Programmes: First one acquired from US on 18 September 1996, second on 28 September 1996, third on 31 March 1998, and fourth on 30 September 1998.
Modernisation: JRC radar fitted on hangar roof.
Operational: First pair arrived in Egypt in mid-1997 after working up, third in late 1998 and fourth in 1999. All reported active, at least one in the Red Sea.

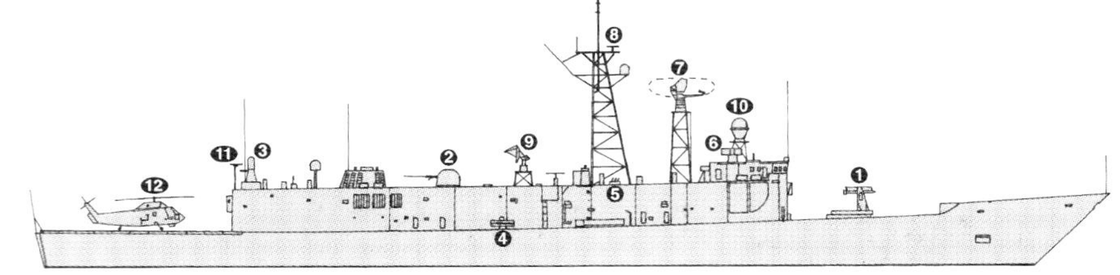

MUBARAK *(Scale 1 : 1,200), Ian Sturton* / 0103734

TABA *6/2006* / 1167111

TABA *6/2006* / 1167112

TABA *6/2006* / 1167113

2 KNOX CLASS (FFGH)

Name	*No*	*Builders*	*Laid down*	*Launched*	*Commissioned*	*Recommissioned*
DAMYAT (ex-*Jesse L Brown*)	961 (ex-FF 1089)	Avondale Shipyard	8 Apr 1971	18 Mar 1972	17 Feb 1973	1 Oct 1994
RASHEED (ex-*Moinester*)	966 (ex-FF 1097)	Avondale Shipyard	25 Aug 1972	12 May 1973	2 Nov 1974	1 Oct 1994

Displacement, tons: 3,011 standard; 4,260 full load
Dimensions, feet (metres): 439.6 × 46.8 × 15; 24.8 (sonar) *(134 × 14.3 × 4.6; 7.8)*
Main machinery: 2 Combustion Engineering/Babcock & Wilcox boilers; 1,200 psi *(84.4 kg/cm^2)*; 950°F *(510°C)*; 1 turbine; 35,000 hp *(26 MW)*; 1 shaft
Speed, knots: 27
Range, n miles: 4,000 at 22 kt on 1 boiler
Complement: 288 (17 officers)

Missiles: SSM: 8 McDonnell Douglas Harpoon; active radar homing to 130 km *(70 n miles)* at 0.9 Mach; warhead 227 kg.
A/S: Honeywell ASROC Mk 16 octuple launcher with reload system (has 2 cells modified to fire Harpoon) ❶; inertial guidance to 1.6–10 km *(1–5.4 n miles)*; payload Mk 46.
Guns: 1 FMC 5 in *(127 mm)*/54 Mk 42 Mod 9 ❷; 20–40 rds/min to 24 km *(13 n miles)* anti-surface; 14 km *(7.7 n miles)* anti-aircraft; weight of shell 32 kg.
1 General Electric/General Dynamics 20 mm/76 6-barrelled Mk 15 Vulcan Phalanx ❸; 3,000 rds/min combined to 1.5 km.
Torpedoes: 4—324 mm Mk 32 (2 twin) fixed tubes ❹. 22 Alliant Mk 46 Mod 5; anti-submarine; active/passive homing to 11 km *(5.9 n miles)* at 40 kt; warhead 44 kg.
Countermeasures: Decoys: 2 Loral Hycor SRBOC 6-barrelled fixed Mk 36 ❺; IR flares and chaff to 4 km *(2.2 n miles)*.
T Mk 6 Fanfare/SLQ-25 Nixie; torpedo decoy. Prairie Masker hull and blade rate noise suppression.
ESM/ECM: Elettronica ❻ intercept and jammer.
Combat data systems: FFISTS mini NTDS with Link Y.
Weapons control: SWG-1A Harpoon LCS. Mk 68 GFCS. Mk 114 ASW FCS. Mk 1 target designation system.
Radars: Air search: Lockheed SPS-40B ❼; B-band; range 320 km *(175 n miles)*.
Surface search: Raytheon SPS-10 or Norden SPS-67 ❽; G-band.
Navigation: Marconi LN66; I-band.
Fire control: Western Electric SPG-53A/D/F ❾; I/J-band.
Tacan: SRN 15.
Sonars: EDO/General Electric SQS-26 CX; bow-mounted; active search and attack; medium frequency.

Helicopters: 1 Kaman SH-2G Seasprite ❿.

Programmes: Lease agreed from USA in mid-1993 and signed 27 July 1994 when both ships sailed for Egypt. Two others were transferred for spares in 1996. Ships of this class have been transferred to Greece, Taiwan, Turkey and Thailand.
Modernisation: Vulcan Phalanx fitted in the mid-1980s. There are plans to fit quadruple Harpoon launchers and possibly to remove the ASROC launcher. EW suite replaced.
Structure: Four torpedo tubes are fixed in the midship superstructure, two to a side, angled out at 45°. A lightweight anchor is fitted on the port side and an 8,000 lb anchor fits in to the after section of the sonar dome.
Operational: These ships have had boiler problems in Egyptian service. Refits may be undertaken with US assistance if and when funds become available.

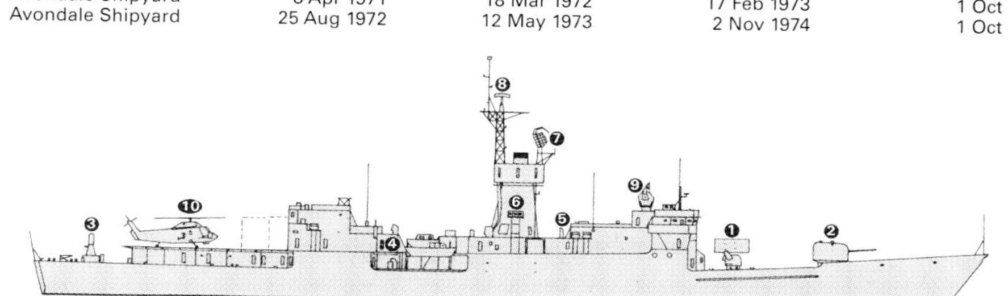
DAMYAT
(Scale 1 : 1,200), Ian Sturton / 0506185

RASHEED
3/2007, Marco Ghiglino / 1166535

2 DESCUBIERTA CLASS (FFGM)

Name	*No*	*Builders*	*Laid down*	*Launched*	*Commissioned*
EL SUEZ (ex-*Serviola*)	F 946	Bazán, Ferrol	28 Feb 1979	20 Dec 1979	27 Oct 1984
ABU QIR (ex-*Centinela*)	F 941	Bazán, Ferrol	31 Oct 1978	6 Oct 1979	21 May 1984

Displacement, tons: 1,233 standard; 1,479 full load
Dimensions, feet (metres): 291.3 × 34 × 12.5 *(88.8 × 10.4 × 3.8)*
Main machinery: 4 MTU-Bazán 16V 956 TB91 diesels; 15,000 hp(m) *(11 MW)* sustained; 2 shafts; cp props
Speed, knots: 25.5; 28 trials
Range, n miles: 4,000 at 18 kt
Complement: 116 (10 officers)

Missiles: SSM: 8 McDonnell Douglas Harpoon (2 quad) launchers ❶; active radar homing to 130 km *(70 n miles)* at 0.9 Mach; warhead 227 kg.
SAM: Selenia Elsag Albatros octuple launcher ❷; 24 Aspide; semi-active radar homing to 13 km *(7 n miles)* at 2.5 Mach; height envelope 15–5,000 m *(49.2–16,405 ft)*; warhead 30 kg.
Guns: 1 OTO Melara 3 in *(76 mm)*/62 compact ❸; 85 rds/min to 16 km *(8.7 n miles)*; weight of shell 6 kg.
2 Bofors 40 mm/70 ❹; 300 rds/min to 12.5 km *(6.8 n miles)*; weight of shell 0.96 kg.
Torpedoes: 6—324 mm Mk 32 (2 triple) tubes ❺. MUSL Stingray; anti-submarine; active/passive homing to 11 km *(5.9 n miles)* at 45 kt; warhead 35 kg (shaped charge); depth to 750 m *(2,460 ft)*.
A/S mortars: 1 Bofors 375 mm twin-barrelled trainable launcher ❻; automatic loading; range 1,600 or 3,600 m depending on type of rocket.
Countermeasures: ESM/ECM: Elettronica SpA Beta; intercept and jammer.
Prairie Masker; acoustic signature suppression.
Combat data systems: Signaal SEWACO action data automation. Link Y.
Radars: Air/surface search: Signaal DA05 ❼; E/F-band; range 137 km *(75 n miles)* for 2 m^2 target.
Navigation: Signaal ZW06; I-band.
Fire control: Signaal WM25 ❽; I/J-band.
Sonars: Raytheon 1160B; hull-mounted; active search and attack; medium frequency.
Raytheon 1167 ❾; VDS; active search; 12-7.5 kHz.

Programmes: Ordered September 1982 from Bazán, Spain. The two Spanish ships *Centinela* and *Serviola* were sold to Egypt prior to completion and transferred after completion at Ferrol and modification at Cartagena. *El Suez* completed 28 February 1984 and *Abu Qir* on 31 July 1984.
Modernisation: The combat data system, air search and fire-control radars were updated in 1995–96.
Operational: Stabilisers fitted. Modern noise insulation of main and auxiliary machinery. *Abu Qir* reported operational.

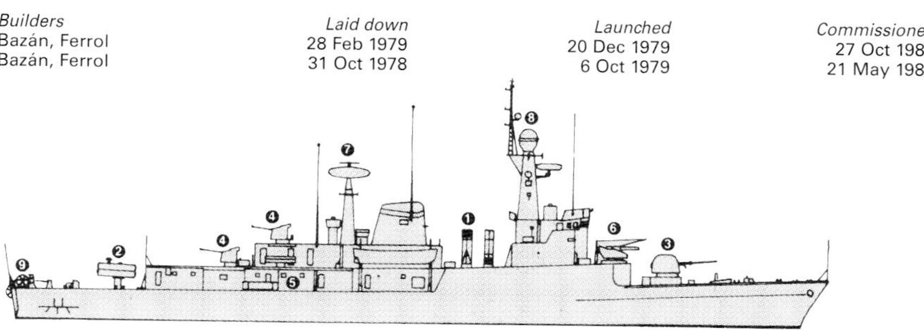
EL SUEZ
(Scale 1 : 900), Ian Sturton / 0505984

EL SUEZ
10/1999 / 0085001

2 JIANGHU I CLASS (FFG)

Name	*No*	*Builders*	*Commissioned*
NAJIM AL ZAFFER	951	Hudong, Shanghai	27 Oct 1984
EL NASSER	956	Hudong, Shanghai	16 Apr 1985

Displacement, tons: 1,425 standard; 1,702 full load
Dimensions, feet (metres): 338.5 × 35.4 × 10.2 *(103.2 × 10.8 × 3.1)*
Main machinery: 2 Type 12 E 390V diesels; 14,400 hp(m) *(10.6 MW)* sustained; 2 shafts
Speed, knots: 26
Range, n miles: 4,000 at 15 kt
Complement: 195

Missiles: SSM: 4 HY-2 (C-201) (2 twin) ❶; active radar or passive IR homing to 80 km *(43.2 n miles)* at 0.9 Mach; warhead 513 kg.
Guns: 4 China 57 mm/70 (2 twin) ❷; 120 rds/min to 12 km *(6.5 n miles)*; weight of shell 6.31 kg.
12 China 37 mm/63 (6 twin) ❸; 180 rds/min to 8.5 km *(4.6 n miles)*; weight of shell 1.42 kg.
A/S mortars: 4 RBU 1200 5-tubed fixed launchers ❹; range 1,200 m; warhead 34 kg.
Depth charges: 4 projectors.
Mines: Up to 60.
Countermeasures: ESM/ECM: Elettronica SpA Beta or Litton Triton; intercept and jammer.
Radars: Air search: Type 765 ❺; A-band.
Surface search: Eye Shield ❻; G-band.
Surface search/gun direction: Square Tie; I-band.
Fire control: Fog Lamp.
Navigation: Decca RM 1290A; I-band.
Sonars: China Type E5; hull-mounted; active search and attack; high frequency.

Programmes: Ordered from China in 1982. This is a Jianghu I class modified with 57 mm guns vice the standard 100 mm. These were the 17th and 18th hulls of the class.

Modernisation: Combat data system to be fitted together with CSEE Naja optronic fire-control directors. There are also plans, confirmed in October 1994, to remove the after superstructure and guns and build a flight deck for an SH-2G Seasprite helicopter. Although a refit programme is reported to have been proposed by China, there is still no sign yet of work being done.
Structure: The funnel is the rounded version of the Jianghu class.
Operational: Both ships are active.

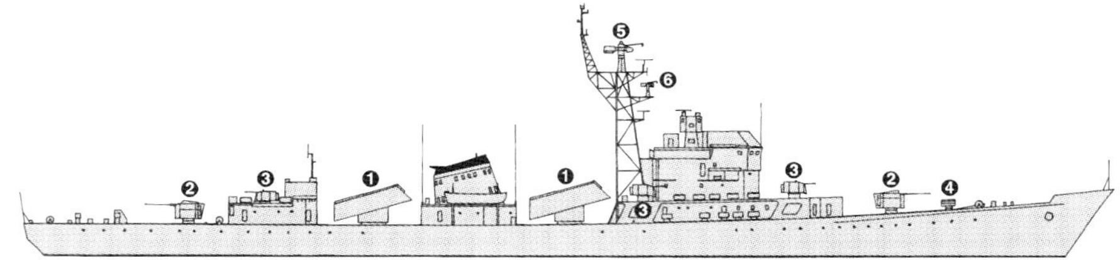

NAJIM AL ZAFFER *(Scale 1 : 900), Ian Sturton* / 0056914

EL NASSER *5/2006, B Prézelin* / 1040733

NAJIM AL ZAFFER *5/2007, Camil Busquets i Vilanova* / 1166549

SHIPBORNE AIRCRAFT

Numbers/Type: 10 Kaman SH-2G(E) Seasprite.
Operational speed: 130 kt *(241 km/h).*
Service ceiling: 22,500 ft *(6,860 m).*
Range: 367 n miles *(679 km).*
Role/Weapon systems: Total of 10 upgraded SH-2F aircraft transferred under FMS by September 1998. New engines and avionics. A further avionics upgrade was reportedly under consideration in 2004. Sensors: LN66/HP radar; ALR-66 ESM; ALE-39 ECM; ARN-118 Tacan; Ocean Systems AQS-18A dipping sonar. Possible mine detection optronic sensor. Weapons: 2 × Mk 46 torpedoes or a depth bomb.

SEASPRITE *1/2004, Kaman* / 0566188

LAND-BASED MARITIME AIRCRAFT (FRONT LINE)

Notes: There are also 2/4 Westland Commando Mk 2B/2E helicopters. Some refitted in 1997/98.

Numbers/Type: 9 Aerospatiale SA 342L Gazelle.
Operational speed: 142 kt *(264 km/h).*
Service ceiling: 14,105 ft *(4,300 m).*
Range: 407 n miles *(755 km).*
Role/Weapon systems: Air Force helicopter for coastal anti-shipping strike, particularly against FAC and insurgents. Sensors: SFIM sight. Weapons: ASV; 2 × AS-12 wire-guided missiles.

Numbers/Type: 6 Grumman E-2C Hawkeye 2000.
Operational speed: 323 kt *(598 km/h).*
Service ceiling: 37,000 ft *(11,278 m).*
Range: 1,540 n miles *(2,852 km).*
Role/Weapon systems: Air Force airborne early warning and control tasks; capable of handling up to 30 tracks over water or land. A sixth Hawkeye 2000 aircraft ordered in June 2001. Sensors: APS-138 search/warning radar being replaced by APS-145 from October 2002 as part of major upgrade programme. The first upgraded aircraft delivered in February 2003, second in early 2004, third in August 2004, fourth in May 2005 and fifth in December 2006. A request for an additional two aircraft was made in October 2007. Various ESM/ECM systems. Weapons: Unarmed.

HAWKEYE 2000 *3/2003, Northrop Grumman* / 0530203

Numbers/Type: 2 Westland Sea King Mk 47.
Operational speed: 112 kt *(208 km/h).*
Service ceiling: 14,700 ft *(4,480 m).*
Range: 664 n miles *(1,230 km).*
Role/Weapon systems: Air Force helicopter for ASW and surface search; secondary role as SAR helicopter. Airframe and engine refurbishment in 1990. Seven more are in reserve and out of service. Sensors: MEL search radar. Weapons: ASW; 4 × Mk 46 or Stingray torpedoes or depth bombs. ASV; Otomat.

Numbers/Type: 2 Beechcraft 1900C.
Operational speed: 267 kt *(495 km/h).*
Service ceiling: 25,000 ft *(7,620 m).*
Range: 1,569 n miles *(2,907 km).*
Role/Weapon systems: Two (of six) Air Force aircraft acquired in 1988 and used for maritime surveillance. Sensors: Litton search radar; Motorola multimode SLAMMR radar; Singer S-3075 ESM; Datalink Y. Weapons: Unarmed.

PATROL FORCES

5 TIGER CLASS (TYPE 148)
(FAST ATTACK CRAFT—MISSILE) (PGGF)

Name	*No*	*Builders*	*Commissioned*
23 OF JULY (ex-*Alk*)	601 (ex-P 6155)	CMN, Cherbourg	7 Jan 1975
6 OF OCTOBER (ex-*Fuchs*)	602 (ex-P 6146)	CMN, Cherbourg	17 Oct 1973
21 OF OCTOBER (ex-*Löwe*)	603 (ex-P 6148)	CMN, Cherbourg	9 Jan 1974
18 OF JUNE (ex-*Dommel*)	604 (ex-P 6156)	CMN, Cherbourg	12 Feb 1975
25 OF APRIL (ex-*Weihe*)	605 (ex-P 6157)	CMN, Cherbourg	3 Apr 1975

Displacement, tons: 234 standard; 265 full load
Dimensions, feet (metres): 154.2 × 23 × 8.9 *(47 × 7 × 2.7)*
Main machinery: 4 MTU MD 16V 538 TB90 diesels; 12,000 hp(m) *(8.82 MW)* sustained; 4 shafts
Speed, knots: 36
Range, n miles: 570 at 30 kt; 1,600 at 15 kt
Complement: 30 (4 officers)

Missiles: SSM: 4 Aerospatiale MM 38 Exocet (2 twin) launchers; inertial cruise; active radar homing to 42 km *(23 n miles)* at 0.9 Mach; warhead 165 kg; sea-skimmer.
Guns: 1 OTO Melara 3 in *(76 mm)*/62 compact; 85 rds/min to 16 km *(8.6 n miles)* anti-surface; 12 km *(6.5 n miles)* anti-aircraft; weight of shell 6 kg.
1 Bofors 40 mm/70; 330 rds/min to 12 km *(6.5 n miles)* anti-surface; 4 km *(2.2 n miles)* anti-aircraft; weight of shell 0.96 kg; fitted with GRP dome (1984) (see *Modernisation*).
Mines: Laying capability.
Countermeasures: Decoys: Wolke chaff launcher. Hot Dog IR launcher.
Combat data systems: PALIS and Link 11.
Weapons control: CSEE Panda optical director. Thomson-CSF Vega PCET system, controlling missiles and guns.
Radars: Air/surface search: Thomson-CSF Triton; G-band; range 33 km *(18 n miles)* for 2 m² target.
Navigation: SMA 3 RM 20; I-band; range 73 km *(40 n miles).*
Fire control: Thomson-CSF Castor; I/J-band.

Programmes: 601 transferred from Germany in July 2002 and the remainder in March 2003. Weapons and sensors have also been transferred with the possible exception of EW equipment.
Modernisation: Triton search and Castor fire-control radars fitted to the whole class.
Structure: Steel-hulled craft. Similar to Combattante II craft.

21 OF OCTOBER *4/2003, Michael Nitz* / 0552773

25 OF APRIL *4/2003, Michael Nitz* / 0552771

18 OF JUNE *4/2003, Michael Nitz* / 0552772

0 + 3 AMBASSADOR III CLASS (FAST ATTACK CRAFT—MISSILE) (PCFG)

Displacement, tons: 550 full load
Dimensions, feet (metres): 198.8 × 29.2 × 8.5 *(60.6 × 8.9 × 2.6)*
Main machinery: 3 MTU diesels; 30,400 hp(m) *(22.7 MW)* sustained; 3 shafts
Speed, knots: 41. **Range, n miles:** 2,000 at 15 kt
Complement: 36 (8 officers)

Missiles: SSM: 8 (2 quad) McDonnell Douglas Harpoon Block II; active radar homing to 130 km *(76 n miles)* at 0.9 Mach; warhead 227 kg.
SAM: 1 Raytheon Mk 49 RAM (RIM-116) launcher; 21 RAM block 1A missile; passive IR/anti-radiation homing to 9.6 km *(5.2 n miles)* at 2 Mach; warhead 9.1 kg.
Guns: 1 OTO Melara 3 in *(76 mm)*/62 Super Rapid; 120 rds/min to 16 km *(8.6 n miles)* anti-surface; 12 km *(6.6 n miles)* anti-aircraft; weight of shell 6 kg.
1 Raytheon Mk 15 Mod 21 (block 1B) Phalanx; 300 rds/min combined to 1.5 km.
2—7.62 mm MGs.
Countermeasures: Decoys: To be announced.
ESM: To be announced.
ECM: To be announced.
Combat data systems: To be announced.
Weapons control: Thales STING optronic director.
Radars: Air/surface search: EADS TRS-3D; C-band.
Fire control: Thales STING; I-band.
Navigation: Thales Scout; I-band.

Comment: Following responses to an ITT issued in 1999, the Egyptian Navy placed an order in January 2001 for four Fast Attack Craft (Missile). These craft were to have been built by Halter Marine. However, following suspension of the project in 2002 and the subsequent purchase of the shipbuilder by Singapore Technologies, the project was revived in 2004 and a contract for the design of a new craft was then let to VT Halter Marine in late 2005. This was followed on 22 November 2006 by a contract (modified in September 2008) for the construction of three craft. The vessels are to be sold to Egypt under US FMS funding arrangements. Delivery of the first craft is expected in 2012.

AMBASSADOR III (artist's impression) *6/2001, Halter Marine* / 0073895

6 RAMADAN CLASS (FAST ATTACK CRAFT—MISSILE) (PGGF)

Name	*No*	*Builders*	*Launched*	*Commissioned*
RAMADAN	670	Vosper Thornycroft	6 Sep 1979	20 July 1981
KHYBER	672	Vosper Thornycroft	31 Jan 1980	15 Sep 1981
EL KADESSAYA	674	Vosper Thornycroft	19 Feb 1980	6 Apr 1982
EL YARMOUK	676	Vosper Thornycroft	12 June 1980	18 May 1982
BADR	678	Vosper Thornycroft	17 June 1981	17 June 1982
HETTEIN	680	Vosper Thornycroft	25 Nov 1980	28 Oct 1982

Displacement, tons: 307 full load
Dimensions, feet (metres): 170.6 × 25 × 7.5 *(52 × 7.6 × 2.3)*
Main machinery: 4 MTU 20V 538 TB91 diesels; 15,360 hp(m) *(11.29 MW)* sustained; 4 shafts
Speed, knots: 40. **Range, n miles:** 1,600 at 18 kt
Complement: 30 (4 officers)

Missiles: SSM: 4 OTO Melara/Matra Otomat Mk 2; active radar homing to 160 km *(86.4 n miles)* at 0.9 Mach; warhead 210 kg.
Guns: 1 OTO Melara 3 in *(76 mm)* compact; 85 rds/min to 16 km *(8.7 n miles)*; weight of shell 6 kg.
2 Breda 40 mm/70 (twin); 300 rds/min to 12.5 km *(6.8 n miles)* anti-surface; weight of shell 0.96 kg.
Countermeasures: Decoys: 4 Protean fixed launchers each with 4 magazines containing 36 chaff decoy and IR flare grenades.
ESM: Racal Cutlass; radar intercept.
ECM: Racal Cygnus; jammer.
Combat data systems: AMS Nautis 3.
Weapons control: Marconi Sapphire System with 2 radar/TV and 2 optical directors.
Radars: Air/surface search: Marconi sS 820; E/F-band; range 73 km *(40 n miles)*.
Navigation: Marconi S 810; I-band.
Fire control: 2 Marconi ST 802; I-band.

Programmes: The contract was carried out at the Porchester yard of Vosper Thornycroft Ltd with some hulls built at Portsmouth Old Yard, being towed to Porchester for fitting out.
Modernisation: Contracts for the modernisation of these craft was let in 2001. Alenia Marconi Systems upgraded the Otomat missiles to Mk 2, renovated the S 820 and ST 802 radars and replaced the CAAIS combat system by NAUTIS 3. Work carried out 2002–2007.
Operational: Portable SAM SA-N-5 sometimes carried.

EL YARMOUK *3/2006, M Declerck* / 1167109

12 OSA I (PROJECT 205) CLASS (FAST ATTACK CRAFT—MISSILE) (PTFG)

631	**643**	**651** (ex-306)	– (ex-304)	– (ex-11)	– (ex-14)
633	**649** (ex-305)	**653** (ex-307)	– (ex-308)	– (ex-12)	– (ex-15)

Displacement, tons: 171 standard; 210 full load
Dimensions, feet (metres): 126.6 × 24.9 × 8.9 *(38.6 × 7.6 × 2.7)*
Main machinery: 3 MTU diesels; 12,000 hp(m) *(8.82 MW)*; 3 shafts
Speed, knots: 35
Range, n miles: 400 at 34 kt
Complement: 30

Missiles: SSM: 4 SS-N-2A Styx; active radar or IR homing to 46 km *(25 n miles)* at 0.9 Mach; altitude preset up to 300 m *(984.3 ft)*; warhead 513 kg.
SAM: SA-N-5 Grail; manual aiming; IR homing to 6 km *(3.2 n miles)* at 1.5 Mach; altitude to 2,500 m *(8,000 ft)*; warhead 1.5 kg.
Guns: 4 USSR 30 mm/65 (2 twin); 500 rds/min to 5 km *(2.7 n miles)* anti-aircraft; weight of shell 0.54 kg.
2—12.7 mm MGs.
Countermeasures: ESM: Thomson-CSF DR 875; radar warning.
ECM: Racal; jammer.
Radars: Air/surface search: Kelvin Hughes; I-band.
Navigation: Racal Decca 916; I-band.
Fire control: Drum Tilt; H/I-band.
IFF: High Pole. Square Head.

Programmes: Of the 13 reported to have been delivered to Egypt by the Soviet Navy in 1966–68, three remained in service in 2003. Acquisition of additional craft has been reported from two sources. Five Osa I class, originally acquired by the Yugoslav Navy in the 1960s, were delivered by May 2007. *651* and *653* were reported commissioned on 28 October 2007. Also, four Osa II were transferred from Finland in late 2006. These were originally acquired from the then Soviet Union by Finland in 1974; subsequently converted in 1993 to a minelaying role and decommissioned in 2000.
Modernisation: Refitted with MTU diesels, two machine guns, improved radars and EW equipment.
Operational: Three more *637* and *639* and *641* are laid up. The operational status of *631*, *633* and *643* is doubtful. It is unclear whether the ex-Yugoslav and Finnish craft are to have an operational role or to be used as spares.

OSA 643 *3/2007, Marco Ghiglino* / 1166520

OSA 649 *5/2007, Freivogel Collection* / 1166529

OSA 653 *5/2007, Freivogel Collection* / 1166530

4 OCTOBER CLASS (FAST ATTACK CRAFT—MISSILE) (PTFG)

781 783 787 789

Displacement, tons: 82 full load
Dimensions, feet (metres): 84 × 20 × 5 *(25.5 × 6.1 × 1.3)*
Main machinery: 4 CRM 12 D/SS diesels; 5,000 hp(m) *(3.67 MW)* sustained; 4 shafts
Speed, knots: 38. **Range, n miles:** 400 at 30 kt
Complement: 20

Missiles: SSM: 2 OTO Melara/Matra Otomat Mk 2; active radar homing to 160 km *(86.4 n miles)* at 0.9 Mach; warhead 210 kg; can be carried.
Guns: 4 BMARC/Oerlikon 30 mm/75 (2 twin); 650 rds/min to 10 km *(5.5 n miles)* anti-surface; 3 km *(1.6 n miles)* anti-aircraft; weight of shell 1 kg and 0.36 kg mixed.
Countermeasures: Decoys: 2 Protean fixed launchers each with 4 magazines containing 36 chaff decoy and IR flare grenades.
ESM: Racal Cutlass; radar warning.
Weapons control: Marconi Sapphire radar/TV system.
Radars: Air/surface search: Marconi S 810; range 48 km *(25 n miles)*.
Fire control: Marconi/ST 802; I-band.

Programmes: Built in Alexandria 1975–76. Hull of same design as USSR Komar class. Refitted by Vosper Thornycroft, completed 1979–81. *791* was washed overboard on return trip, recovered and returned to Portsmouth for refit. Left UK after repairs on 12 August 1982. Probably Link fitted.
Modernisation: Alenia Marconi systems to upgrade Otomat missiles to Mk 2 between 2002–2007.
Operational: *791* reported non-operational and *785* is laid up.

OCTOBER 783 — *2/2004* / 1044123

5 SHERSHEN CLASS (FAST ATTACK CRAFT—GUN) (PTFM)

753 755 757 759 761

Displacement, tons: 145 standard; 170 full load
Dimensions, feet (metres): 113.8 × 22 × 4.9 *(34.7 × 6.7 × 1.5)*
Main machinery: 3 Type M 503A diesels; 8,025 hp(m) *(5.9 MW)* sustained; 3 shafts
Speed, knots: 45. **Range, n miles:** 850 at 30 kt
Complement: 23

Missiles: SAM: SA-N-5 Grail *(755-761)*; manual aiming; IR homing to 6 km *(3.2 n miles)* at 1.5 Mach; warhead 1.5 kg.
Guns: 4 USSR 30 mm/65 (2 twin); 500 rds/min to 5 km *(2.7 n miles)*; weight of shell 0.54 kg.
2 USSR 122 mm rocket launchers (*755-761* in lieu of torpedo tubes); 20 barrels per launcher; range 9 km *(5 n miles)*.
Depth charges: 12.
Countermeasures: ESM: Thomson-CSF DR 875; radar warning.
Radars: Surface search: Pot Drum; H/I-band.
Fire control: Drum Tilt, H/I-band (in some).
IFF: High Pole.

Programmes: Five delivered from USSR in 1967 and two more in 1968. One deleted. *753* completed an extensive refit at Ismailia in 1987; *751* in 1988.
Structure: The last four have had their torpedo tubes removed to make way for multiple BM21 rocket launchers and one SA-N-5 Grail, which are not always carried. Some have Drum Tilt radars removed. *753* has also had its torpedo tubes removed but these may be replaced.
Operational: Based at Alexandria, Port Said and Mersa Matru. *751* reported non-operational.

SHERSHEN 757 — *3/2007, Marco Ghiglino* / 1166522

4 HEGU CLASS (FAST ATTACK CRAFT—MISSILE) (PTFG)

609 611 613 615

Displacement, tons: 68 standard; 79.2 full load
Dimensions, feet (metres): 88.6 × 20.7 × 4.3 *(27 × 6.3 × 1.3)*
Main machinery: 4 Type L-12V-180 diesels; 4,800 hp(m) *(3.53 MW)*; 4 shafts
Speed, knots: 37.5. **Range, n miles:** 400 at 30 kt
Complement: 17 (2 officers)

Missiles: SSM: 2 SY-1; active radar or passive IR homing to 40 km *(22 n miles)* at 0.9 Mach; warhead 513 kg.
Guns: 2—23 mm (twin); locally constructed to fit 25 mm mounting.
Countermeasures: ESM: Litton Triton; radar intercept.
Radars: Surface search/fire control: Square Tie; I-band or Decca; I-band.
IFF: High Pole A.

Programmes: Acquired from China and commissioned in Egypt on 27 October 1984. The Hegu is the Chinese version of the deleted Komar.
Modernisation: ESM: fitted in 1995–96.
Operational: *619* and *617* are reported laid up.

HEGU 609 — *3/2000* / 0103740

HEGU 609 and 611 — *3/2007, Marco Ghiglino* / 1166521

8 HAINAN CLASS (FAST ATTACK CRAFT—PATROL) (PC)

AL NOUR 430	**AL HADI** 433	**AL HAKIM** 436	**AL WAKIL** 439
AL QATAR 442	**AL GABBAR** 445	**AL SALAM** 448	**AL RAFA** 451

Displacement, tons: 375 standard; 392 full load
Dimensions, feet (metres): 192.8 × 23.6 × 7.2 *(58.8 × 7.2 × 2.2)*
Main machinery: 4 PRC/Kolomna Type 9-D-8 diesels; 4,000 hp *(2.94 MW)* sustained; 4 shafts
Speed, knots: 30.5
Range, n miles: 1,300 at 15 kt
Complement: 69

Guns: 4 China 57 mm/70 (2 twin); 120 rds/min to 12 km *(6.5 n miles)*; weight of shell 6.31 kg.
4—23 mm (2 twin); locally constructed to fit the 25 mm mountings.
Torpedoes: 6—324 mm (2 triple) tubes (in two of the class). Mk 44 or MUSL Stingray.
A/S mortars: 4 RBU 1200 fixed 5-tubed launchers; range 1,200 m; warhead 34 kg.
Depth charges: 2 projectors; 2 racks. 18 DCs.
Mines: Rails fitted. 12 mines.
Radars: Surface search: Pot Head or Skin Head; I-band.
Navigation: Decca; I-band.
IFF: High Pole.
Sonars: Stag Ear; hull-mounted; active search and attack; high frequency.

Programmes: First pair transferred from China in October 1983, next three in February 1984 (commissioned 21 May 1984) and last three late 1984.
Modernisation: Two fitted with torpedo tubes and with Singer Librascope fire control. No sign of the remainder being similarly equipped. New sonar reported being fitted.
Operational: Based at Alexandria.

AL WAKIL — *4/2007, Marco Ghiglino* / 1166523

4 SHANGHAI II CLASS (FAST ATTACK CRAFT—GUN) (PB)

793 795 797 799

Displacement, tons: 113 standard; 131 full load
Dimensions, feet (metres): 127.3 × 17.7 × 5.6 *(38.8 × 5.4 × 1.7)*
Main machinery: 2 Type L12-180 diesels; 2,400 hp(m) *(1.76 MW)* (forward); 2 Type L12-180Z diesels; 1,820 hp(m) *(1.34 MW)* (aft); 4 shafts
Speed, knots: 30. **Range, n miles:** 700 at 16.5 kt
Complement: 34

Guns: 4 China 37 mm/63 (2 twin); 180 rds/min to 8.5 km *(4.6 n miles)*; weight of shell 1.42 kg.
2—23 mm (1 twin); locally constructed to fit the 25 mm mountings.
Mines: Rails can be fitted for 10 mines.
Countermeasures: ESM: Thomson-CSF; radar warning.
Radars: Surface search: Decca; I-band.
IFF: High Pole.

Programmes: Transferred from China in 1984.
Operational: Three based at Suez and one *(799)* at Mersa Matru. *795* refitted in 1998.

SHANGHAI 797 — *6/1997, J W Currie* / 0012295

AMPHIBIOUS FORCES

Notes: (1) Acquisition of LSTs is a high priority.
(2) Ro-Ro ferries are chartered for amphibious exercises.
(3) Rigid Raiders with Johnson outboards are also in service.
(4) Three small hovercraft similar to Slingsby SAH 2200 reported to be in service.

3 POLNOCHNY A (PROJECT 770) CLASS (LSM)

301 **303** **305**

Displacement, tons: 800 full load
Dimensions, feet (metres): 239.5 × 27.9 × 5.8 *(73 × 8.5 × 1.8)*
Main machinery: 2 Kolomna Type 40-D diesels; 4,400 hp(m) *(3.2 MW)* sustained; 2 shafts
Speed, knots: 19
Range, n miles: 1,000 at 18 kt
Complement: 40
Military lift: 6 tanks; 350 tons
Guns: 2 USSR 30 mm/65 (twin); 500 rds/min to 5 km *(2.7 n miles)*; weight of shell 0.54 kg. 2—140 mm rocket launchers; 18 barrels to 9 km *(4.9 n miles)*.
Radars: Surface search: Decca; I-band.
Fire control: Drum Tilt; H/I-band.

Comment: Built at Northern Shipyard, Gdansk and transferred from USSR 1973–74. All used for Gulf logistic support in 1990–91. SA-N-5 may be carried. Radar updated. All are active.

POLNOCHNY 303 *10/2000, F Sadek* / 0103742

5 SEAFOX TYPE (SWIMMER DELIVERY CRAFT) (LDW)

21 **23** **26** **27** **28**

Displacement, tons: 11.3 full load
Dimensions, feet (metres): 36.1 × 9.8 × 2.6 *(11 × 3 × 0.8)*
Main machinery: 2 GM 6V-92TA diesels; 520 hp *(388 kW)* sustained; 2 shafts
Speed, knots: 30
Range, n miles: 200 at 20 kt
Complement: 3
Guns: 2—12.7 mm MGs. 2—7.62 mm MGs.
Radars: Surface search: LN66; I-band.

Comment: Ordered from Uniflite, Washington in 1982. GRP construction painted black. There is a strong underwater team in the Egyptian Navy which is also known to use commercial two-man underwater chariots. Based at Abu Qir. 26 and 28 are not fully operational and others of the class are in various states of repair. RIBs are also in service.

SEAFOX *1999* / 0056917

9 VYDRA CLASS (LCU)

330 **332** **334** **336** **338** **340** **342** **344** **346**

Displacement, tons: 425 standard; 600 full load
Dimensions, feet (metres): 179.7 × 25.3 × 6.6 *(54.8 × 7.7 × 2)*
Main machinery: 2 Type 3-D-12 diesels; 600 hp(m) *(440 kW)* sustained; 2 shafts
Speed, knots: 11
Range, n miles: 2,500 at 10 kt
Complement: 20
Military lift: 200 troops; 250 tons.
Guns: 2 or 4—37 mm/63 (1 or 2 twin) (may be fitted).
Radars: Navigation: Decca; I-band.

Comment: Built in late 1960s, transferred from USSR 1968–69. For a period after the Israeli war of October 1973 several were fitted with rocket launchers and two 37 or 40 mm guns, some of which have now been removed. All still in service.

VYDRA 332 *3/2007, Marco Ghiglino* / 1166524

MINE WARFARE FORCES

2 OSPREY CLASS (MINEHUNTERS—COASTAL) (MHC)

Name	*No*	*Builders*	*Launched*	*Commissioned*
AL SIDDIQ (ex-*Cardinal*)	521 (ex-MHC 60)	Intermarine, Savannah	9 Mar 1996	18 Oct 1997
AL FAROUK (ex-*Raven*)	524 (ex-MHC 61)	Intermarine, Savannah	28 Sep 1996	5 Sep 1998

Displacement, tons: 930 full load
Dimensions, feet (metres): 187.8 × 35.9 × 9.5 *(57.2 × 11 × 2.9)*
Main machinery: 2 Isotta Fraschini ID 36 SS 8V AM diesels; 1,600 hp(m) *(1.18 MW)* sustained; 2 Voith-Schneider props; 3 Isotta Fraschini ID 36 diesel generators; 984 kW
Speed, knots: 13
Range, n miles: 1,500 at 10 kt
Complement: 51 (5 officers)

Guns: 2—12.7 mm MGs.
Countermeasures: MCM: Alliant SLQ-48 mine neutralisation system ROV (with 1,070 m cable). Degaussing DGM-4.
Combat data systems: Unisys SYQ 13 and SYQ 109; integrated combat and machinery control system. USQ-119E(V), UHF Dama, and OTCIXS provide GCCS connectivity.
Radars: Surface search: Raytheon SPS-64(V)9; I-band.
Navigation: R41XX; I-band.
Sonars: Raytheon/Thomson Sintra SQQ-32(V)3; VDS; active minehunting; high frequency.

Programmes: Original design contract for Lerici-class minehunters was awarded in August 1986 to Intermarine USA which built eight of the 12 ships of the class for the US Navy. Transferred to Egypt on 7 January 2007 and recommissioned on 28 October 2007.
Structure: Construction is of monocoque GRP throughout hull, with frames eliminated. Main machinery is mounted on GRP cradles and provided with acoustic enclosures. SQQ-32 is deployed from a central well forward. Fitted with Voith cycloidal propellers which eliminate need for forward thrusters during station keeping.

AL SIDDIQ and AL FAROUK *3/2007, Paul Daly* / 1167736

4 YURKA CLASS (MINESWEEPERS—OCEAN) (MSO)

GIZA 530 **ASWAN** 533 **QINA** 536 **SOHAG** 539

Displacement, tons: 540 full load
Dimensions, feet (metres): 171.9 × 30.8 × 8.5 *(52.4 × 9.4 × 2.6)*
Main machinery: 2 Type M 503 diesels; 5,350 hp(m) *(3.91 MW)* sustained; 2 shafts
Speed, knots: 17
Range, n miles: 1,500 at 12 kt
Complement: 45
Guns: 4 USSR 30 mm/65 (2 twin); 500 rds/min to 5 km *(2.7 n miles)*; weight of shell 0.54 kg.
Mines: Can lay 10.
Radars: Navigation: Don; I-band.
Sonars: Stag Ear; hull-mounted; active search; high frequency.

Comment: Steel-hulled minesweepers transferred from the USSR in 1969. Built 1963–69. Egyptian Yurka class do not carry Drum Tilt radar and have a number of ship's-side scuttles. The plan to equip them with VDS sonar has been shelved. At least one operates an ROV.

SOHAG *3/2007, Marco Ghiglino* / 1166525

2 SWIFTSHIPS TYPE (ROUTE SURVEY VESSELS) (MSI)

Name	*No*	*Builders*	*Commissioned*
SAFAGA	RSV 1 (ex-610)	Swiftships	1 Oct 1994
ABU EL GHOSON	RSV 2 (ex-613)	Swiftships	1 Oct 1994

Displacement, tons: 165 full load
Dimensions, feet (metres): 90 × 24.8 × 8 *(27.4 × 7.6 × 2.4)*
Main machinery: 2 MTU 12V 183TA61 diesels; 928 hp(m) *(682 kW)*; 2 shafts; bow thruster; 60 hp(m) *(44 kW)*
Speed, knots: 12
Range, n miles: 1,500 at 10 kt
Complement: 16 (2 officers)
Guns: 1—12.7 mm MG.
Radars: Navigation: Furuno 2020; I-band.
Sonars: EG & G side scan; active; high frequency.

Comment: Route survey vessels ordered from Swiftships in November 1990 and delivered in September 1993. Two more are planned to be built in Egyptian yards in due course. Unisys improved SYQ-12 command system. Provision for both shallow and deep towed bodies. The names have been taken from the obsolete K 8 class.

ABU EL GHOSON *3/2006, M Declerck* / 1167106

3 SWIFTSHIPS TYPE (COASTAL MINEHUNTERS) (MHC)

Name	*No*	*Builders*	*Launched*	*Commissioned*
DAT ASSAWARI	542 (ex-CMH 1)	Swiftships, Morgan City	4 Oct 1993	13 July 1997
NAVARIN	545 (ex-CMH 2)	Swiftships, Morgan City	13 Nov 1993	13 July 1997
BURULLUS	548 (ex-CMH 3)	Swiftships, Morgan City	4 Dec 1993	13 July 1997

Displacement, tons: 203 full load
Dimensions, feet (metres): 111 × 27 × 8 *(33.8 × 8.2 × 2.3)*
Main machinery: 2 MTU 12V 183TE61 diesels; 1,068 hp(m) *(786 kW)*; 2 Schottel steerable props; 1 White Gill thruster; 300 hp *(224 kW)*
Speed, knots: 12.4
Range, n miles: 2,000 at 10 kt
Complement: 25 (5 officers)
Guns: 2—12.7 mm MGs.
Radars: Navigation: Sperry; I-band.
Sonars: Thoray/Thomson Sintra TSM 2022; hull-mounted; active minehunting; high frequency.

Comment: MCM vessels with GRP hulls ordered from Swiftships in December 1990 with FMS funding. First one acceptance trials in June 1994 and completion in August. Fitted with a Unisys command data handling system which is an improved version of SYQ-12. GPS and line of sight navigation system. Dynamic positioning. A side scan sonar body and Gaymarine Pluto ROV can be streamed from a deck crane. Portable decompression chamber carried. Two delivered 29 November 1995 and the third in April 1996. All were finally commissioned after delays caused by problems with the minehunting equipment.

DAT ASSAWARI *3/2006, M Declerck* / 1167107

3 T 43 CLASS (MINESWEEPERS—OCEAN) (MSO)

DAQHILIYA 507 **SINAI** 513 **ASSIYUT** 516

Displacement, tons: 580 full load
Dimensions, feet (metres): 190.2 × 27.6 × 6.9 *(58 × 8.4 × 2.1)*
Main machinery: 2 Kolomna Type 9-D-8 diesels; 2,000 hp(m) *(1.47 MW)* sustained; 2 shafts
Speed, knots: 15
Range, n miles: 3,000 at 10 kt
Complement: 65
Guns: 4—37 mm/63 (2 twin); 160 rds/min to 9 km *(5 n miles)*; weight of shell 0.7 kg. 8—12.7 mm (4 twin) MGs.
Mines: Can carry 20.
Radars: Navigation: Don 2; I-band.
Sonars: Stag Ear; hull-mounted; active search; high frequency.

Comment: Delivered in the early 1970s from the USSR. Others of the class have been sunk or used as targets or cannibalised for spares. The plan to fit them with VDS sonars and ROVs has been shelved.

DAQAHLIYA *3/2000* / 0103745

TRAINING SHIPS

Notes: (1) *Al Kousser* P 91 is a 1,000 ton vessel belonging to the Naval Academy. *Intishat* is a 500 ton training ship. Pennant number 160 is a USSR Sekstan class used as a cadet training ship. Two YSB training craft acquired from the US in 1989. A 3,300 ton training ship *Aida IV* presented by Japan in 1988 for delivery in March 1992 belongs to the Arab Maritime Transport Academy.
(2) The campaign to transfer the Black Swan-class sloop *Tariq*, formerly HMS *Whimbrel*, to Liverpool, to become a floating memorial to the Battle of the Atlantic, faltered in 2008 due to a disagreement over price.

1 PRESIDENTIAL YACHT (YAC/AX)

Name	*Builders*	*Commissioned*
EL HORRIYA (ex-*Mahroussa*)	Samuda, Poplar	1865

Displacement, tons: 4,560 full load
Dimensions, feet (metres): 479 × 42.6 × 17.4 *(146 × 13 × 5.3)*
Main machinery: 3 boilers; 3 turbines; 5,500 hp *(4.1 MW)*; 3 shafts
Speed, knots: 16
Complement: 160

Comment: Became a museum in 1987 but was reactivated in 1992. Used as a training ship as well as a Presidential Yacht.

EL HORRIYA *3/2007, Marco Ghiglino* / 1166526

1 Z CLASS (AXT)

Name	*No*	*Builders*	*Laid down*	*Launched*	*Commissioned*
EL FATEH (ex-*Zenith*, ex-*Wessex*)	921	Wm Denny & Bros, Dumbarton	19 May 1942	5 June 1944	22 Dec 1944

Displacement, tons: 1,730 standard; 2,575 full load
Dimensions, feet (metres): 362.8 × 35.7 × 16 *(110.6 × 10.9 × 4.9)*
Main machinery: 2 Admiralty boilers; 2 Parsons turbines; 40,000 hp *(30 MW)*; 2 shafts
Speed, knots: 24
Range, n miles: 2,800 at 20 kt
Complement: 186
Radars: Air/surface search: Marconi SNW 10; D-band.
Navigation: Racal Decca 916; I-band.
Fire control: Marconi Type 275; F-band.

Programmes: Purchased from the UK in 1955.
Operational: Used primarily for harbour training, and the intention is to keep the ship in service. Last seen at sea in 1994. The last survivor of its class, the ship may be preserved as a museum. The ship has been disarmed.

EL FATEH *3/2006, M Declerck* / 1167102

AUXILIARIES

Notes: (1) There are also two survey launches *Misaha 1* and *2* with a crew of 14. Both were commissioned in 1991.
(2) A small barge *Amira Rama* was donated to the Navy in 1987 and is used as lighthouse tender.
(3) *Al Hurreya 1*, a 6,000 ton 139 m transport ship, was launched at Alexandria on 27 January 2004 and delivered on 7 April 2005. A second ship *Al Hurreya 2* was launched on 24 June 2006. This is being followed by a larger 10,000 ton 173 m vessel which is expected to be launched in 2009.

AL HURREYA 2 *6/2006, F Sadek* / 1040740

7 TOPLIVO 2 CLASS (TANKERS) (AOTL/AWTL)

AYEDA 4 210 **MARYUT** 218 **AL NIL** 220 **AL FURAT** 224
ATABARAH 212 **AKDU** 214 **AYEDA 3** 216

Displacement, tons: 1,029 full load
Dimensions, feet (metres): 176.2 × 31.8 × 10.5 *(53.7 × 9.7 × 3.2)*
Main machinery: 1 6DR 30/50-5 diesel; 600 hp(m) *(441 kW)*; 1 shaft
Speed, knots: 10
Range, n miles: 400 at 7 kt
Complement: 16
Cargo capacity: 500 tons diesel or water (211–215)
Radars: Navigation: Spin Trough; I-band.

Comment: Built in Alexandria in 1972–77 to a USSR design. Another of the class 217 is laid up.

AYEDA 4 *3/2006, M Declerck* / 1167105

1 LÜNEBURG CLASS (TYPE 701) (SUPPORT SHIP) (ARL)

Name	*No*	*Builders*	*Commissioned*
SHALADEIN (ex-*Glücksburg*)	230 (ex-A 1414)	Bremer Vulkan/ Flensburger Schiffbau	9 July 1968

Displacement, tons: 3,709 full load
Dimensions, feet (metres): 374.9 × 43.3 × 13.8 *(114.3 × 13.2 × 4.2)*
Main machinery: 2 MTU MD 16V 538 TB90 diesels; 6,000 hp(m) *(4.1 MW)* sustained; 2 shafts; cp props; bow thruster
Speed, knots: 17
Range, n miles: 3,200 at 14 kt
Complement: 71 (9 officers)
Cargo capacity: 1,100 tons
Guns: 4 Bofors 40 mm/70 (2 twin).
Countermeasures: Decoys: 2 Breda 105 mm SCLAR chaff launchers.

Comment: Transferred from Germany in early 2003 to act as support ship, including missile maintenance, of Type 148 patrol craft.

SHALADEIN *4/2003, Frank Findler* / 0552746

1 WESTERWALD CLASS (TYPE 760) (AMMUNITION TRANSPORT) (AEL)

Name	*No*	*Builders*	*Commissioned*
HALAIB (ex-*Odenwald*)	231 (ex-A 1436)	Orenstein and Koppel, Lübeck	23 Mar 1967

Displacement, tons: 3,460 standard; 4,042 full load
Dimensions, feet (metres): 344.4 × 46 × 15.1 *(105 × 14 × 4.6)*
Main machinery: 2 MTU MD 16V 538 TB90 diesels; 6,000 hp(m) *(4.1 MW)* sustained; 2 shafts; cp props; bow thruster
Speed, knots: 17. **Range, n miles:** 3,500 at 17 kt
Complement: 31
Cargo capacity: 1,080 tons ammunition
Guns: 2 Bofors 40 mm.
Radars: Navigation: Kelvin Hughes; I-band.

Comment: Transferred from Germany in early 2003.

HALAIB *4/2003, Frank Findler* / 0552745

2 POLUCHAT 1 CLASS (YPT)

936 **937**

Displacement, tons: 100 full load
Dimensions, feet (metres): 97.1 × 19 × 4.8 *(29.6 × 5.8 × 1.5)*
Main machinery: 2 Type M 50 diesels; 2,200 hp(m) *(1.6 MW)* sustained; 2 shafts
Speed, knots: 20. **Range, n miles:** 1,500 at 10 kt
Complement: 15
Radars: Surface search: Spin Trough; I-band.

Comment: Used as Torpedo Recovery Vessels. Unarmed.

POLUCHAT *3/2000* / 0103779

2 NYRYAT I (PROJECT 522) CLASS (DIVING TENDERS) (YDT)

P 001 **P 002**

Displacement, tons: 116 full load
Dimensions, feet (metres): 93.8 × 17.1 × 5.6 *(28.6 × 5.2 × 1.7)*
Main machinery: 1 diesel; 450 hp(m) *(331 kW)* sustained; 1 shaft
Speed, knots: 12.5
Range, n miles: 1,500 at 10 kt
Complement: 15
Radars: Surface search: Spin Trough; I-band.

Comment: Transferred in 1964.

TUGS

Notes: (1) There are also four Coast Guard harbour tugs built by Damen in 1982. Names *Khoufou, Khafra, Ramses* and *Kreir*. Two other harbour tugs were delivered in 1998. Names *Ajmi* and *Jihad*.
(2) Two former oilfield supply vessels 113 and 115 are probably employed as tugs. They are also fitted with firefighting equipment.
(3) A large Chinese built tug *El Alamein* is reported to be in service.

115 *3/2007, Marco Ghiglino* / 1166527

5 OKHTENSKY CLASS (ATA)

AL MAKS 103	**AL ANTAR** 107	**AL ISKANDARANI** 111
AL AGAMI 105	**AL DEKHEILA** 109	

Displacement, tons: 930 full load
Dimensions, feet (metres): 156.1 × 34 × 13.4 *(47.6 × 10.4 × 4.1)*
Main machinery: Diesel-electric; 2 BM diesel generators; 1 motor; 1,500 hp(m) *(1.1 MW)*; 1 shaft
Speed, knots: 13
Range, n miles: 6,000 at 13 kt
Complement: 38

Comment: Two transferred from USSR in 1966, others assembled at Alexandria. Replacements are needed.

AL AGAMI *3/2007, Marco Ghiglino* / 1166528

COAST GUARD

Notes: (1) The Coast Guard is controlled by the Navy.
(2) There are four obsolete P 6 craft; pennant numbers 222, 246, 253 and 201.
(3) There is also a minimum of four ex-USN Bollinger type harbour security craft of 3.9 tons capable of 22 kt. Twin diesel engines. Carry a 7.62 mm MG.
(4) There is an unknown number of RIBs for inshore patrols.
(5) A fast patrol craft, donated by Italy in 2007, is operated by the Ports Police for counter-smuggling and illegal immigration operations.

3 TYPE 83 CLASS (LARGE PATROL CRAFT) (WPB)

46 47 54

Displacement, tons: 85 full load
Dimensions, feet (metres): 83.7 × 21.3 × 5.6 *(25.5 × 6.5 × 1.7)*
Main machinery: 2 diesels; 2 shafts
Speed, knots: 24
Complement: 12
Guns: 4—23 mm (2 twin). 1 Oerlikon 20 mm.
Radars: Surface search: Furuno; I-band.

Comment: Two of this class commissioned 13 July 1997. Built locally, these craft are similar to the Swiftships 93 ft class. Three are operational.

TYPE 83 CLASS *10/1995* / 0056923

6 CRESTITALIA MV 70 CLASS (COASTAL PATROL CRAFT) (WPBF)

Displacement, tons: 36 full load
Dimensions, feet (metres): 68.9 × 17.4 × 3 *(21 × 5.3 × 0.9)*
Main machinery: 2 MTU 12V 331 TC92 diesels; 2,660 hp(m) *(1.96 MW)* sustained; 2 shafts
Speed, knots: 35
Range, n miles: 500 at 32 kt
Complement: 10 (1 officer)
Guns: 2 Oerlikon 30 mm A32 (twin). 1 Oerlikon 20 mm.
Radars: Surface search: Racal Decca; I-band.

Comment: Ordered 1980-GRP hulls. Naval manned but still employed on Coast Guard duties.

CRESTITALIA 70 ft *1980, Crestitalia* / 0505986

21 TIMSAH CLASS (LARGE PATROL CRAFT) (WPB)

01–02 04–22

Displacement, tons: 106 full load
Dimensions, feet (metres): 101.8 × 17 × 4.8 *(30.5 × 5.2 × 1.5)*
Main machinery: 2 MTU 8V 331 TC92 diesels; 1,770 hp *(1.3 MW)* sustained; 2 shafts *(01–06)*; 2 MTU 12V 331 TC92 diesels; 2,660 hp(m) *(1.96 MW)* sustained; 2 shafts *(07–19)*
Speed, knots: 25
Range, n miles: 600 at 18 kt
Complement: 13
Guns: 2 Oerlikon 30 mm (twin) or 2—14.5 mm MGs.
Radars: Surface search: Racal Decca; I-band.

Comment: First three Timsah I completed December 1981, second three Timsah I December 1982 at Timsah SY, Ismailia. These all have funnels but there appear to be minor structural differences. *03* sunk in late 1993. Further six Timsah II ordered in January 1985 and completed in 1988–89 with a different type of engine and with waterline exhaust vice a funnel. Last of this batch in service in 1992, followed by ten more by 1999.

TIMSAH 17 *4/2002, A Sharma* / 0528333

TIMSAH 16 *7/2006, Marco Ghiglino* / 1164998

TIMSAH 19 *4/2005, Queun/Marsan* / 1151174

9 SWIFTSHIPS 93 ft CLASS (LARGE PATROL CRAFT) (WPB)

35–43

Displacement, tons: 102 full load
Dimensions, feet (metres): 93.2 × 18.7 × 4.9 *(28.4 × 5.7 × 1.5)*
Main machinery: 2 MTU 12V 331 TC92 diesels; 2,660 hp(m) *(1.96 MW)* sustained; 2 shafts
Speed, knots: 27
Range, n miles: 900 at 12 kt
Complement: 14 (2 officers)
Guns: 4—23 mm (2 twin); 1 Oerlikon 20 mm or 2—14.5 mm MG.
Radars: Surface search: Furuno; I-band.

Comment: Ordered November 1983. First three built in US, remainder assembled by Osman Shipyard, Ismailia. First four commissioned 16 April 1985, five more in 1986. Armament upgraded with 23 mm guns fitted forward in some of the class.

SWIFTSHIPS 42 *3/2006, M Declerck* / 1164997

12 SEA SPECTRE PB MK III CLASS (COASTAL PATROL CRAFT) (WPB)

Displacement, tons: 37 full load
Dimensions, feet (metres): 64.9 × 18 × 5.9 *(19.8 × 5.5 × 1.8)*
Main machinery: 3 GM 8V-71TI diesels; 1,800 hp *(1.3 MW)*; 3 shafts
Speed, knots: 29. **Range, n miles:** 450 at 25 kt
Complement: 9 (1 officer)
Guns: 2—12.7 mm MGs.
Radars: Surface search: Raytheon; I-band.

Comment: PB Mk III type built by Peterson, Sturgeon Bay and delivered in 1980–81. Used for Customs duties.

SPECTRE *1981, Peterson Builders* / 0056924

9 PETERSON TYPE (COASTAL PATROL CRAFT) (WPB)

71–79

Displacement, tons: 18 full load
Dimensions, feet (metres): 45.6 × 13 × 3 *(13.9 × 4 × 0.9)*
Main machinery: 2 MTU 8V 183 TE92 diesels; 1,314 hp(m) *(966 kW)* sustained; Hamilton 362 water-jets
Speed, knots: 34. **Range, n miles:** 200 at 30 kt
Complement: 4
Guns: 2—12.7 mm MGs.
Radars: Surface search: Raytheon; I-band.

Comment: Built by Peterson Shipbuilders, Sturgeon Bay and delivered between June and October 1994 under FMS. Replaced Bertram type and used as pilot boats.

PETERSON 72 (US colours) *6/1994, PBI* / 0056925

5 NISR CLASS (LARGE PATROL CRAFT) (WPB)

THAR 701	**NUR** 703	**NISR** 713	**NIMR** 719	**AL BAHR**

Displacement, tons: 110 full load
Dimensions, feet (metres): 102 × 18 × 4.9 *(31 × 5.2 × 1.5)*
Main machinery: 2 Maybach diesels; 3,000 hp(m) *(2.2 MW)*; 2 shafts
Speed, knots: 24
Complement: 15
Guns: 2 or 4—23 mm (twin). 1 BM 21 122 mm 8-barrelled rocket launcher.
Radars: Surface search: Racal Decca 1230; I-band.

Comment: Built by Castro, Port Said on P6 hulls. First three launched in May 1963. Two more completed 1983. The rocket launcher and after 23 mm guns are interchangeable. 701 and 703 were refitted in 1998. Naval manned but employed on Coast Guard duties.

3 PETERSON TYPE (COASTAL PATROL CRAFT) (WPBF)

80–82

Displacement, tons: 20 full load
Dimensions, feet (metres): 51 × 12 × 3 *(15.5 × 3.7 × 0.9)*
Main machinery: 2 MTU diesels; 2,266 hp(m) *(1.66 MW)*; Hamilton 391 water-jets
Speed, knots: 45. **Range, n miles:** 320 at 30 kt
Complement: 5
Guns: 2—12.7 mm MGs.
Radars: Surface search: Raytheon; I-band.

Comment: Built by Peterson Shipbuilders, Sturgeon Bay and delivered between October and December 1996 under FMS. Aluminium construction. Used mostly as pilot boats.

PETERSON 81 *3/2000* / 0103781

29 DC 35 TYPE (YFL)

Displacement, tons: 4 full load
Dimensions, feet (metres): 35.1 × 11.5 × 2.6 *(10.7 × 3.5 × 0.8)*
Main machinery: 2 Perkins T6-354 diesels; 390 hp *(287 kW)*; 2 shafts
Speed, knots: 25
Complement: 4

Comment: Built by Dawncraft, Wroxham, UK, from 1977. Harbour launches. One destroyed in September 1994. About half are laid up at Port Said.

DC 35 *8/1994, F Sadek* / 0056927

6 + (12) SWIFTSHIPS PROTECTOR CLASS (LARGE PATROL CRAFT) (WPB)

90 +5

Displacement, tons: 116 full load
Dimensions, feet (metres): 85.0 × 20.0 × 4.9 *(26.1 × 6.1 × 1.5)*
Main machinery: 2 Caterpillar 3512B diesels; 2 Hamilton HM651 waterjets
Speed, knots: 40
Complement: 12
Radars: Navigation: I-band.

Comment: Contract awarded 24 September 2004 to Swiftships, Morgan City, LA, for the construction of six patrol craft under the US government's Foreign Military Sales programme. The contract includes a training package. With an aluminium hull and superstructure and a high-speed RIB launching well, the craft are designed for SAR, law enforcement, and local patrol operations. Details of weapons and sensors have not been confirmed but up to a 30 mm gun with associated fire-control system may be fitted. A FLIR system may also be installed. Delivery of the first craft was made in June 2006 and completed in February 2007. A further 12 craft may be procured.

PROTECTOR 90 *1/2006* / 1041657

El Salvador

FUERZA NAVAL DE EL SALVADOR

Country Overview

The Republic of El Salvador is an independent Central American State whose current constitution was established in 1983. With an area of 8,124 square miles, it has a 166 n mile coastline with the Pacific Ocean and is bounded to the north by Honduras and to the west by Guatemala. The country's capital is San Salvador while Acajutla, La Libertad and La Unión are the principal ports. El Salvador has not claimed an Exclusive Economic Zone (EEZ) but is one of a few coastal states which claims a 200 n mile territorial sea.

Senior Officer

Commander of the Navy:
Captain Walter Ricardo Rivero Alemán

Personnel

(a) 2009: 1,077 (including 160 naval infantry)
(b) Voluntary service

Bases

Acajutla, La Libertad, El Triunfo y La Union

Air Bases

El Tamarindo Air Station is reported to have been improved to enable the Third Air Brigade to provide air support to naval patrols. The US may donate fixed-wing aircraft and helicopters to assist in this task.

PATROL FORCES

Notes: (1) There are two high-speed RHIBs donated by Taiwan and US.
(2) Three Boston Whaler craft were acquired in February 2007.
(3) There are plans to replace the Camcraft with similar vessels.

3 CAMCRAFT TYPE (COASTAL PATROL CRAFT) (PB)

PM 6 (ex-*CG 6*) **PM 7** (ex-*CG 7*) **PM 8** (ex-*CG 8*)

Displacement, tons: 100 full load
Dimensions, feet (metres): 100 × 21 × 4.9 *(30.5 × 6.4 × 1.5)*
Main machinery: 3 Detroit 12V-71TA diesels; 1,260 hp *(939 kW)* sustained; 3 shafts
Speed, knots: 25. **Range, n miles:** 780 at 24 kt
Complement: 10
Guns: 1—20 mm Oerlikon or 1—12.7 mm MG. 2—7.62 mm MGs. 1—81 mm mortar.
Radars: Surface search: Furuno; I-band.

Comment: Aluminium hulled. Delivered 24 October, 8 November and 3 December 1975. Refitted in 1986 at Lantana Boatyard. Sometimes carry a combined 12.7 mm MG/81 mm mortar mounting in the stern. New radars fitted in 1995.

PM 7 *10/2003, Julio Montes* / 1166724

1 POINT CLASS (PB)

No	*Builders*	*Commissioned*
PM 12 (ex-GC 12, ex-82358)	J Martinac, Tacoma	17 Mar 1967

Displacement, tons: 67 full load
Dimensions, feet (metres): 83 × 17.2 × 5.8 *(25.3 × 5.2 × 1.8)*
Main machinery: 2 Caterpillar diesels; 1,600 hp *(1.19 MW)*; 2 shafts
Speed, knots: 22. **Range, n miles:** 1,200 at 8 kt
Complement: 10
Guns: 2—12.7 mm MGs.
Radars: Surface search: Hughes/Furuno SPS-73; I-band.

Comment: Ex-*Point Stuart* transferred from US Coast Guard on 27 April 2001.

PM 12 *11/2001, Julio Montes* / 0130481

1 SWIFTSHIPS 77 ft CLASS (COASTAL PATROL CRAFT) (PB)

PM 11 (ex-GC 11)

Displacement, tons: 48 full load
Dimensions, feet (metres): 77.1 × 20 × 4.9 *(23.5 × 6.1 × 1.5)*
Main machinery: 3 Detroit 12V-71TA diesels; 1,260 hp *(939 kW)* sustained; 3 shafts
Speed, knots: 26
Complement: 7
Guns: 2—12.7 mm MGs. Aft MG combined with 81 mm mortar.
Radars: Surface search: Furuno; I-band.

Comment: Aluminium hull. Delivered by Swiftships, Morgan City 6 May 1985.

PM 11 *10/2003, Julio Montes* / 1166723

1 SWIFTSHIPS 65 ft CLASS (COASTAL PATROL CRAFT) (PB)

PM 10 (ex-*GC 10*)

Displacement, tons: 36 full load
Dimensions, feet (metres): 65.6 × 18.3 × 5 *(20 × 6 × 1.5)*
Main machinery: 2 Detroit 12V-71TA diesels; 840 hp *(626 kW)* sustained; 2 shafts
Speed, knots: 23
Range, n miles: 600 at 18 kt
Complement: 6
Guns: 1 Oerlikon 20 mm. 1 or 2—12.7 mm MGs. 1—81 mm mortar.
Radars: Surface search: Furuno; I-band.

Comment: Aluminium hull. Delivered by Swiftships, Morgan City 14 June 1984. Was laid up for a time in 1989–90 but became operational again in 1991. Refitted in 1996.

PM 10 *6/2003, El Salvador Navy* / 0568340

4 TYPE 44 CLASS (PBI)

PRM 01–04

Displacement, tons: 18 full load
Dimensions, feet (metres): 44 × 12.8 × 3.6 *(13.5 × 3.9 × 1.1)*
Main machinery: 2 Detroit 6V-38 diesels; 185 hp *(136 kW)*; 2 shafts
Speed, knots: 14
Range, n miles: 215 at 10 kt
Complement: 3

Comment: Ex-USCG craft similar to those transferred to Uruguay.

PRM 04 *11/2001, Julio Montes* / 0130482

6 PIRANHA CLASS (RIVER PATROL CRAFT) (PBR)

PF 01–06 (ex-LOF 021–026)

Displacement, tons: 8.2 full load
Dimensions, feet (metres): 36 × 10.1 × 1.6 *(11 × 3.1 × 0.5)*
Main machinery: 2 Caterpillar 3208TA diesels; 680 hp *(507 kW)* sustained; 2 shafts
Speed, knots: 26
Complement: 5
Guns: 2—12.7 mm (twin) MGs. 2—7.62 mm (twin) MGs.
Radars: Surface search: Furuno 3600; I-band.

Comment: Riverine craft with Kevlar hulls used by the Naval Infantry. Completed in March 1987 by Lantana Boatyard, Florida. Same type supplied to Honduras. Five craft reported operational.

PF 05 — *4/2005, Julio Montes* / 1166722

9 PROTECTOR CLASS (RIVER PATROL CRAFT) (PBR)

PC 01–09

Displacement, tons: 9 full load
Dimensions, feet (metres): 40.4 × 13.4 × 1.4 *(12.3 × 4 × 0.4)*
Main machinery: 2 Caterpillar 3208TA diesels; 680 hp *(507 kW)* sustained; 2 shafts
Speed, knots: 28. **Range, n miles:** 350 at 20 kt
Complement: 4
Guns: 2—12.7 mm MGs. 2—7.62 mm MGs.
Radars: Surface search: Furuno 3600; I-band.

Comment: Ordered in December 1987 from SeaArk Marine (ex-MonArk). Four delivered in December 1988 and four in February and March 1989. Seven reported operational, one in maintenance and one non-operational.

PC 03 — *3/2006, Julio Montes* / 1166721

8 AIR PATROL BOATS (PBI)

PFR 1–8

Comment: Purchased in Miami for SAR on inland waters.

PFR 04 — *4/2005, Julio Montes* / 1166720

2 MERCOUGAR INTERCEPT CRAFT (PBR)

PA 01 **PA 02**

Comment: Two remaining of five 40 ft craft delivered by Mercougar in 1988. Powered by two Ford Merlin diesels; 600 hp *(448 kW)* giving speeds of up to 40 kt and range of 556 km *(300 n miles)*. Radar fitted.

PA 02 — *5/2001, Julio Montes* / 0109938

1 BALSAM CLASS (AGP)

Name	*No*	*Builders*	*Commissioned*
MANUEL JOSÉ ARCE (ex-*Madrona*)	BL 01 (ex-WLB 302)	Zenith Dredge, Duluth, MN	30 May 1943

Displacement, tons: 1,034 full load
Dimensions, feet (metres): 180 × 37 × 12 *(54.9 × 11.3 × 3.8)*
Main machinery: Diesel electric; 2 diesels; 1,402 hp *(1.06 MW)*; 1 motor; 1,200 hp *(895 kW)*; 1 shaft; bow thruster
Speed, knots: 13. **Range, n miles:** 8,000 at 12 kt
Complement: 53
Guns: 2—12.7 mm MGs.
Radars: Navigation: Raytheon SPS-64(V)1.

Comment: Transferred from the US Coast Guard on 14 June 2002. Used as a mother ship for coastal patrol craft.

ARCE — *5/2003, Julio Montes* / 1166719

AUXILIARIES

3 LCM 8 CLASS

BD 02 (ex-LD 02) **BD 04** (ex-LD 04) **BD 05** (ex-LD 05)

Displacement, tons: 45 full load
Dimensions, feet (metres): 64.7 × 14 × 5 *(21.5 × 4.6 × 1.6)*
Main machinery: 2 Detroit 12V 71TA diesels; 840 hp *(626 kW)* sustained; 2 shafts
Speed, knots: 15
Complement: 6
Guns: 2—12.7 mm MGs. 2—7.62 mm MGs.
Radars: Navigation: Furuno; I-band.

Comment: First one delivered by SeaArk Marine in January 1987, second pair in May 1996.

BD 04 — *6/2003, El Salvador Navy* / 0568336

POLICE

Notes: Ten jet-skis are reported to have been delivered in 2002 for SAR.

20 RODMAN 890 (PBR)

L-01-01–L-01-20

Displacement, tons: 3.1 full load
Dimensions, feet (metres): 29.2 × 9.8 × 3.6 *(8.9 × 3 × 0.8)*
Main machinery: 2 Volvo diesels; 300 hp(m) *(220 kW)*; 2 shafts
Speed, knots: 28. **Range, n miles:** 150 at 25 kt
Complement: 3
Guns: 1—7.62 mm MG.
Radars: Surface search: I-band.

Comment: Eleven craft delivered by Rodman in 1998. Operational availability is reported to be constrained by lack of spares.

RODMAN L-01-07 — *6/1998, Rodman* / 0576109

Equatorial Guinea

Country Overview

The Republic of Equatorial Guinea became independent in 1968 as a federation of the two former Spanish provinces of Fernando Po and Río Muni. It became a unitary state in 1973. Located in west Africa, the country has an overall area of 10,831 square miles and includes a mainland section which is bordered to the north by Cameroon and to the east and south by Gabon. It has a 160 n mile coastline with the Gulf of Guinea in which lie the islands of Bioko (formerly Fernando Po), Annobón, Corisco, Elobey Grande and Elobey Chico. The administrative capital on the mainland is Bata while Malabo, on the north coast of Bioko, is capital of the republic, largest city and prinicpal port. Territorial waters (12 n miles) are claimed. A 200 n mile Exclusive Economic Zone (EEZ) has been claimed but the boundaries have not been agreed.

Personnel

2009: 120 officers and men

Bases

Malabo, Bata.

PATROL FORCES

Notes: (1) The Lantana 68 class *Isla de Bioko* and 20 m patrol craft *Riowele* are believed to be non-operational.
(2) Two Shaldag II patrol craft were delivered from Israel in August 2005. They are named *Isla de Corisco* and *Isla de Annobon*.
(3) There is a patrol craft *Estuario de Muni*. Of possible Ukrainian origin, the 75 m craft is armed with a twin 30 m AK 230 gun forward and two twin 14.5 mm aft.

ESTUARIO DE MUNI *6/2008** / 1335440

1 DAPHNE CLASS (PB)

Name	*No*	*Builders*	*Commissioned*
URECA (ex-*Nymfen*)	P 31 (ex-P 535)	Royal Dockyard, Copenhagen	4 Oct 1963

Displacement, tons: 170 full load
Dimensions, feet (metres): 121 × 20 × 6.5 *(36.9 × 6.1 × 2.0)*
Main machinery: 3 diesels; 3 shafts
Speed, knots: 20
Complement: 23
Guns: 2—14.5 mm.
Radars: Navigation: Furuno; I-band.

Comment: Acquired in 1999.

2 ZHUK (GRIF) CLASS (PROJECT 1400M) (PB)

MIGUEL ELA EDJODJOMO LP 039 **HIPOLITO MICHA** LP 041

Displacement, tons: 39 full load
Dimensions, feet (metres): 78.7 × 16.4 × 3.9 *(24 × 5 × 1.2)*
Main machinery: 2 diesels; 2 shafts
Speed, knots: 30. **Range, n miles:** 1,100 at 15 kt
Complement: 13 (1 officer)
Guns: 2—14.5 mm (twin, fwd) MGs. 1—12.7 mm (aft) MG.
Radars: Surface search: Furuno; I-band.

Comment: Reported to have been transferred from Ukraine in 2000.

2 KALKAN (PROJECT 50030) M CLASS (INSHORE PATROL CRAFT) (PBR)

GASPAR OBIANG ESONO 43 **FERNANDO NUARA ENGONDA** 45

Displacement, tons: 8.5 full load
Dimensions, feet (metres): 38.1 × 10.8 × 2.0 *(11.6 × 3.3 × 0.6)*
Main machinery: 1 Type 475K diesel; 496 hp *(370 kW)*; 1 waterjet
Speed, knots: 34
Complement: 2

Comment: Built by Morye Feodosiya and reportedly acquired in 2001.

KALKAN CLASS (Ukraine colours) *6/2003, Morye* / 0572655

Eritrea

Country Overview

A British protectorate from 1941, The State of Eritrea was federated with Ethiopia in 1952 and incorporated as a province in 1962. The following war of liberation culminated in independence in 1993. The country is situated on the southwest shore of the Red Sea with which it has a 621 n mile coastline with an area of 46,842 square miles, it is bordered to the north by Sudan, to the west by Ethiopia and to the south by Djibouti. The largest town and capital is Asmara and the principal port is Massawa. There are no claims to maritime jurisdiction over territorial seas or Exclusive Economic Zone (EEZ).

All vessels of the former Ethiopian Navy were put up for sale at Djibouti from 16 September 1996. All were either taken over by Eritrea, sold to civilian firms or scrapped.

Headquarters Appointments

Commander Eritrean Navy:
Major General Hummed Mohammed Karikare
Chief of Staff:
Brigadier General Fitsum Gebrehiwet

Personnel

2009: 1,100 including 500 conscripts

Bases

Assab, Massawa, Dahlak.

PATROL FORCES

Notes: (1) There are also about 50 rigid raiding craft.
(2) The Osa II class FMB 161 is reported non-operational.

4 SUPER DVORA CLASS (FAST ATTACK CRAFT—GUN) (PTF)

P 101–104

Displacement, tons: 58 full load
Dimensions, feet (metres): 82 × 18.7 × 3 *(25 × 5.7 × 0.9)*
Main machinery: 2 MTU 8V 396 TE 94 diesels; 3,046 hp(m) *(2.24 MW)*; 2 shafts; ASD 14 surface drives
Speed, knots: 40. **Range, n miles:** 1,200 at 17 kt
Complement: 10 (1 officer)
Guns: 2—23 mm (twin). 2—12 mm MGs.
Depth charges: 1 rail.
Weapons control: Optronic sight.
Radars: Surface search: Raytheon; I-band.

Comment: Built by Israel Aircraft Industries and delivered from July 1993 to a modified Super Dvora design. The original order may have been for six of the class. All are based at Massawa and all are active.

SUPER DVORA P 104 *6/2000, Eritrean Navy* / 0103787

5 BATTALION 17 (PBF)

P 084–088

Displacement, tons: 35.5 full load
Dimensions, feet (metres): 55.9 × 17 × 5.2 *(17.05 × 5.2 × 1.6)*
Main machinery: 2 MTU 12V 183TE 92 diesels
Speed, knots: 35.2
Range, n miles: 680 at 30 kt
Complement: 9
Guns: 2—14.5 mm MGs (1 twin).
Radars: Surface search: Raytheon; I-band.

Comment: Australian design craft built by Harena Boat Yard at Assab, Eritrea. Five craft delivered in 2000 with possible further orders since then.

P 086 *6/2000, Eritrean Navy* / 0103788

3 SWIFTSHIPS 105 ft CLASS (LARGE PATROL CRAFT) (PB)

P 151–153

Displacement, tons: 118 full load
Dimensions, feet (metres): 105 × 23.6 × 6.5 *(32 × 7.2 × 2)*
Main machinery: 2 MTU MD 16V 538 TB90 diesels; 6,000 hp(m) *(4.41 MW)* sustained; 2 shafts
Speed, knots: 30. **Range, n miles:** 1,200 at 18 kt
Complement: 21
Guns: 4 Emerlec 30 mm (2 twin) *(P 151)*; 600 rds/min to 6 km *(3.3 n miles)*; weight of shell 0.35 kg.
4—23 mm/60 (2 twin) *(P 152/153)*. 2—12.7 mm (twin).
Radars: Surface search: Decca RM 916; I-band.

Comment: Six ordered in 1976 of which four were delivered in April 1977 before the cessation of US arms sales to Ethiopia. Built by Swiftships, Louisiana. One deserted to Somalia and served in that Navy for a time. Based at Massawa and in reasonable condition. All are active.

P 153 *1/1998* / 0017825

AMPHIBIOUS FORCES

Notes: (1) Two obsolete ex-USSR T4 LCUs (LST-63 and 64) are in harbour service at Massawa.
(2) The passenger vessel *Harat* arrived at Massawa on 10 February 2006. The 118 m vessel has a helicopter landing deck and accommodation for 2,800. Inspected by the commander of the navy on arrival, the ship may have a military role.

1 CHAMO CLASS (LST)

DENDEN 301

Displacement, tons: 884 full load
Dimensions, feet (metres): 197.5 × 39.3 × 4.7 *(60.2 × 12 × 1.44)*
Main machinery: 2 MTU 6V 396TB 63; 1,350 hp(m) *(1 MW)*; 2 shafts
Speed, knots: 10
Complement: 23
Guns: 2—23 mm (1 twin); 2—12.7 mm MGs.

Comment: German built former Ethiopian commercial LST taken over by Eritrea in 1997 and subsequently transferred to the Navy. Reported operational.

1 ASHDOD CLASS (LST)

P 63 (ex-302)

Displacement, tons: 400 standard; 730 full load
Dimensions, feet (metres): 205.5 × 32.8 × 5.8 *(62.7 × 10 × 1.8)*
Main machinery: 3 MWM diesels; 1,900 hp(m) *(1.4 MW)*; 3 shafts
Speed, knots: 10.5
Complement: 20
Guns: 2—23 mm (1 twin). 2—12.7 mm MGs.

Comment: Former Ethiopian commercial LST acquired from Israel in 1993, taken over by Eritrea in 1997 and subsequently transferred to the Navy. Reported operational.

P 63 (Israeli pennant number) *1995, Eritrean Navy* / 0103789

Estonia

EESTI MEREVÄGI

Country Overview

The Republic of Estonia regained independence in 1991 after 51 years as a Soviet republic. Situated in northeastern Europe, the country includes more than 1,500 islands, the largest of which are Saaremaa and Hiiumaa. With an area of 17,462 square miles it has borders to the east with Russia and to the south with Latvia. It has a 750 n mile coastline with the Baltic Sea and Gulf of Finland. Tallinn is the capital, largest city and principal port. Territorial seas (12 n miles) are claimed but while it has claimed a 200 n mile Exclusive Economic Zone (EEZ), its limits have not been fully defined by boundary agreements.

The Navy was founded in 1918 and re-established on 22 April 1994. The Border Guard comes under the Ministry of Internal Affairs and is responsible for SAR and Pollution Prevention.

Headquarters Appointments

Commander of the Navy and Chief of Staff:
Captain Igor Schvede

Personnel

(a) 2009: 644 (70 officers)
(b) 8-11 months' national service
(c) Border Guard: 300

Bases

Major: Miinisadam (Tallinn)
Minor: Kopli (Tallinn) (Border Guard)

FRIGATES

1 MODIFIED HVIDBJØRNEN CLASS (FFLH/AGFH/AGE)

Name	*No*	*Builders*	*Laid down*	*Launched*	*Commissioned*
ADMIRAL PITKA (ex-*Beskytteren*)	A 230 (ex-F 340)	Aalborg Vaerft	11 Dec 1974	29 May 1975	27 Feb 1976

Displacement, tons: 1,970 full load
Dimensions, feet (metres): 245 × 40 × 17.4 *(74.7 × 12.2 × 5.3)*
Main machinery: 3 MAN/Burmeister & Wain Alpha diesels; 7,440 hp(m) *(5.47 MW)*; 1 shaft; cp prop
Speed, knots: 18. **Range, n miles:** 4,500 at 16 kt on 2 engines; 6,000 at 13 kt on 1 engine
Complement: 43 (9 officers)
Guns: 1 USN 3 in *(76 mm)*/50; Mk 22.
Countermeasures: ESM: Racal Cutlass; radar warning.
Radars: Navigation: 2 Litton Decca E; I-band.
Helicopters: Platform for 1 Lynx type.

Programmes: Transferred by gift from Denmark in July 2000 and formally recommissioned on 21 November 2000.
Structure: Strengthened for ice operations.
Operational: Flagship of the Estonian Navy, its primary role is as a Command and Support ship and its secondary role is as a research ship. The vessel was refitted prior to being transferred. Modifications included the replacement of the military radars with Litton Marine radars, and the removal of PMS 26 sonar.

ADMIRAL PITKA *5/2007, Per Körnefeldt* / 1170107

MINE WARFARE FORCES

2 FRAUENLOB (TYPE 394) CLASS (MSI)

Name	*No*	*Builders*	*Commissioned*
OLEV (ex-*Diana*)	M 415 (ex-M 2664)	Krogerwerft, Rendsburg	21 Sep 1967
VAINDLO (ex-*Undine*)	M 416 (ex-M 2662)	Krogerwerft, Rendsburg	20 Mar 1967

Displacement, tons: 246 full load
Dimensions, feet (metres): 124.6 × 26.9 × 6.6 *(38 × 8.2 × 2)*
Main machinery: 2 MTU MB 12V 493 TY70 diesels; 2,200 hp(m) *(1.62 MW)* sustained; 2 shafts
Speed, knots: 14. **Range, n miles:** 400 at 12 kt
Complement: 23 (5 officers)
Guns: 1 Bofors 40 mm/70.
Mines: Laying capability.
Radars: Navigation: Atlas Elektronik; I-band.

Comment: *Olev* transferred in June 1997 and *Vaindlo*, which replaced *Kalev*, on 8 October 2002 having paid off from the German Navy in 1995. Capable of influence and mechanical minesweeping.

VAINDLO **9/2005, Guy Toremans** / 1129997

OLEV **6/2000, Findler & Winter** / 0103792

3 SANDOWN CLASS (MINEHUNTERS) (MHC)

Name	*No*	*Builders*	*Launched*	*Commissioned*
ADMIRAL COWAN (ex-*Sandown*)	M 313 (ex-M 101)	Vosper Thornycroft, Woolston	16 Apr 1988	9 June 1989
SAKALA (ex-*Inverness*)	M 314 (ex-M 102)	Vosper Thornycroft, Woolston	27 Feb 1990	24 Jan 1991
UGANDI (ex-*Bridport*)	M 315 (ex-M 105)	Vosper Thornycroft, Woolston	20 July 1992	6 Nov 1993

Displacement, tons: 450 standard; 484 full load
Dimensions, feet (metres): 172.2 × 34.4 × 7.5 *(52.5 × 10.5 × 2.3)*
Main machinery: 2 Paxman-Valenta 6RP200E/M diesels; 1,523 hp *(1.14 MW)* sustained; Voith-Schneider propulsion; 2 Schottel bow thrusters
Speed, knots: 13 diesels; 6.5 electric drive. **Range, n miles:** 2,500 at 12 kt
Complement: 34 (5 officers) plus 6 spare berths

Guns: 1 DES/MSI DS 30B 30 mm/75; 650 rds/min to 10 km *(5.4 n miles)* anti-surface; 3 km *(1.6 n miles)* anti-aircraft; weight of shell 0.36 kg.
Dillon Aero M 134 7.62 mm Minigun; 6 barrels; 3,000 rds/min.
Countermeasures: MCM: Seafox C expendable mine-disposal system.
Combat data systems: BAE Insyte Nautis 3.
Radars: Navigation: Kelvin Hughes Type 1007; I-band.
Sonars: Marconi Type 2093; VDS; VLF-VHF multifunction with 5 arrays; mine search and classification.

Programmes: Single-role minehunter originally designed for deep water operations and built by Vosper Thornycroft for the UK Royal Navy. All three ships withdrawn from RN service following force-level reductions announced in 2004. Preliminary agreement for the regeneration and transfer of the three ships made between the UK and Estonian governments in late 2005. Following a letter of intent on 11 April 2006, a final agreement was signed on 14 September 2006. *Admiral Cowan* handed over on 26 April 2007 and *Sakala* on 28 January 2008. *Ugandi* was handed over in January 2009 and is to undertake navigation and training roles.
Modernisation: The modernisation package is expected to upgrade the two operational ships to the similar equipment standards as those in service in the RN. Principal components include Sonar Type 2093, Seafox C submersibles, Drumgrange Precise Fixing System and Nautis 3 combat data system. Armament options include 30 mm guns and M 134 Minigun CIWS.
Structure: GRP hull. Combines vectored thrust units with bow thrusters and remote-control submersibles. The sonar is deployed from a well in the hull.
Operational: The ships are expected to replace the two Landau class MHC.

ADMIRAL COWAN **11/2008*, Michael Nitz** / 1335716

AUXILIARIES

1 MAAGEN CLASS (YDT)

Name	*No*	*Builders*	*Commissioned*
AHTI (ex-*Mallemukken*)	A 431 (ex-Y 385)	Helsingor Dockyard	19 May 1960

Displacement, tons: 190 full load
Dimensions, feet (metres): 88.6 × 23.6 × 9.5 *(27 × 7.2 × 2.9)*
Main machinery: 1 diesel; 385 hp(m) *(283 kW)*; 1 shaft
Speed, knots: 10
Complement: 11
Guns: 2 — 12.7 mm MGs.
Radars: Surface search: Pechora; I-band.
Navigation: Skanter 009; I-band.
Sonars: Sidescan.

Comment: Handed over at Tallinn on 29 March 1994, having decommissioned from the Danish Navy in 1992. Serves as a diving tender and for route surveillance.

AHTI **6/2003, Hartmut Ehlers** / 0561497

1 LINDORMEN CLASS (COASTAL MINELAYER) (MLC)

Name	*No*	*Builders*	*Launched*	*Commissioned*
TASUJA (ex-*Lindormen*)	A 432 (ex-N 43)	Svendborg Vaerft	7 June 1977	16 Feb 1978

Displacement, tons: 570 full load
Dimensions, feet (metres): 146 × 29.5 × 8.0 *(44.5 × 9.0 × 2.6)*
Main machinery: 2 Frichs diesels; 1,600 hp *(1.2 MW)*; 2 shafts
Speed, knots: 14
Complement: 27 (4 officers)
Guns: 2 — 12.7 mm MGs.
Radars: Navigation: I-band.

Comment: Former Danish minelayer handed over on 12 April 2006. Ex-*Lossen* was also procured as a civilian training ship for the Estonian Maritime Academy.

TASUJA **6/2006, Frank Findler** / 1305005

BORDER GUARD (EESTI PIIRIVALVE)

Notes: (1) *Director General:* Colonel Harry Hein
(2) The letters PV are visible on the national flag which is defaced with green and yellow markings.
(3) Three vessels are used for anti-pollution duties. *Triin* (PVL-200) (ex-*Bester*) and *Reet* (PVL-201) (ex-*EVA-200)* are both 34 m vessels which entered Border Guard service in May 2001. *Kati* (PVL-202) (ex-*KBV-003*) is a 40 m vessel transferred from Sweden in May 2002.
(4) PVL-110 is a Slavyanka class LCM acquired in 1997 and used as a harbour utility craft.
(5) *Tiir* (PVL-104) is an ex-Russian Serna class 26 m LCM used as a utility craft.
(6) The Border Guard Aviation Group was formed in February 1993 and includes two L-410 maritime patrol aircraft and two Mi-8 helicopters.

REET *6/2003, Hartmut Ehlers* / 0561496

PVL-110 *6/2003, Hartmut Ehlers* / 0561495

L-410 *7/2004, Paul Jackson* / 0589739

1 BALSAM CLASS (AGF)

Name	*No*	*Builders*	*Commissioned*
VALVAS (ex-*Bittersweet*)	PVL 109 (ex-WLB 389)	Duluth Shipyard, Minnesota	11 May 1944

Displacement, tons: 1,034 full load
Dimensions, feet (metres): 180 × 37 × 12 *(54.9 × 11.3 × 3.8)*
Main machinery: Diesel electric; 2 diesels; 1,402 hp *(1.06 MW)*; 1 motor; 1,200 hp *(895 kW)*; 1 shaft; bow thruster
Speed, knots: 13
Range, n miles: 8,000 at 12 kt
Complement: 53
Guns: 2—25 mm/L80 (1 twin). 2—12.7 mm MGs.
Radars: Navigation: Raytheon SPS-64(V)1.

Comment: Transferred from the US Coast Guard and recommissioned as a Border Guard Headquarters ship on 5 September 1997.

VALVAS *6/2003, Hartmut Ehlers* / 0561492

1 SILMÄ CLASS (LARGE PATROL CRAFT) (PBO)

Name	*No*	*Builders*	*Commissioned*
KOU (ex-*Silmä*)	PPVL 107	Laivateollisuus, Turku	19 Aug 1963

Displacement, tons: 530 full load
Dimensions, feet (metres): 158.5 × 27.2 × 14.1 *(48.3 × 8.3 × 4.3)*
Main machinery: 1 Werkspoor diesel; 1,800 hp(m) *(1.32 MW)*; 1 shaft
Speed, knots: 15
Complement: 10
Guns: 2—25 mm/80 (twin).
Radars: Surface search: I-band.
Sonars: Simrad SS105; active scanning; 14 kHz.

Comment: Transferred from Finland Frontier Guard in January 1995.

KOU *4/2007, E & M Laursen* / 1305004

1 VIIMA CLASS (COASTAL PATROL CRAFT) (PB)

Name	*No*	*Builders*	*Commissioned*
MARU (ex-*Viima*)	PVL 106	Laivateollisuus, Turku	12 Oct 1964

Displacement, tons: 134 full load
Dimensions, feet (metres): 117.1 × 21.7 × 7.5 *(35.7 × 6.6 × 2.3)*
Main machinery: 3 MTU MB diesels; 4,050 hp(m) *(2.98 MW)*; 3 shafts; cp props
Speed, knots: 23
Complement: 9
Guns: 2—25 mm/L 80 (1 twin). 2—14.5 mm MGs (twin). 1—7.62 mm MG.
Radars: Surface search: I-band.

Comment: Acquired from Finland Frontier Guard in January 1995.

MARU *6/2003, Hartmut Ehlers* / 0589736

1 PIKKER CLASS (COASTAL PATROL CRAFT) (PB)

Name	*No*	*Builders*	*Launched*	*Commissioned*
PIKKER	PVL 103	Talinn	23 Dec 1995	Apr 1996

Displacement, tons: 90 full load
Dimensions, feet (metres): 91.9 × 19 × 4.9 *(28.0 × 5.8 × 1.5)*
Main machinery: 2 12YH 18/20 diesels; 2,700 hp(m) *(1.98 MW)* sustained; 2 shafts
Speed, knots: 23
Complement: 5
Guns: 1—14.5 mm MG.
Radars: Surface search: Kelvin Hughes nucleus; I-band.

Comment: Steel hull and superstructure. Carries a RIB with a hydraulic launch crane aft.

PIKKER *6/2003, Hartmut Ehlers* / 0561494

1 VAPPER CLASS (COASTAL PATROL CRAFT) (PB)

Name	*No*	*Builders*	*Commissioned*
VAPPER	PVL 111	Baltic Ship Repairers, Tallinn	1 June 2000

Displacement, tons: 117 full load
Dimensions, feet (metres): 103 × 19.7 × 5.9 *(31.4 × 6.0 × 1.8)*
Main machinery: 2 Deutz TBD 620 V12 diesels; 4,087 hp(m) *(3.1 MW)*; 2 shafts
Speed, knots: 27
Complement: 7
Guns: 2—25 mm (1 twin). 1—14.5 mm.
Radars: Navigation: Furuno; I-band.

Comment: Launched in April 2000. Steel hull and aluminium superstructure. Carries one RIB for SAR and inspection.

VAPPER *8/2000* / 0114351

1 STORM CLASS (PB)

Name	*No*	*Builders*	*Launched*
TORM (ex-*Arg*)	PVL 105 (ex-P968)	Bergens Mek, Verksteder	24 May 1966

Displacement, tons: 100 standard; 135 full load
Dimensions, feet (metres): 120 × 20 × 5 *(36.5 × 6.1 × 1.5)*
Main machinery: 2 MTU MB 16V 538 TB90 diesels; 6,000 hp(m) *(4.41 MW)* sustained; 2 shafts
Speed, knots: 32
Range, n miles: 800 at 25 kt
Complement: 8
Guns: 2—25 mm/80 (twin). 2—14.5 mm MGs (twin).
Radars: Surface search: Racal Decca TM 1226; I-band.

Comment: Built in 1966 and paid off from the Norwegian Navy in 1991. Transferred 16 December 1994 stripped of all weapons and associated sensors. Rearmed in 1995 with light guns. No further transfers are expected.

TORM *6/1999, Estonian Border Guard* / 0056948

3 KBV 236 CLASS (PB)

PVK 001 (ex-*KBV 257*) **PVK 002** (ex-*KBV 259*) **PVK 003** (ex-*KBV 246*)

Displacement, tons: 17 full load
Dimensions, feet (metres): 63 × 13.1 × 4.3 *(19.2 × 4 × 1.3)*
Main machinery: 2 Volvo Penta TAMD120A diesels; 700 hp(m) *(515 kW)*; 2 shafts
Speed, knots: 22
Complement: 5
Guns: 1—7.62 mm MG.

Comment: Transferred on 4 April 1992, 20 October 1993 and 6 December 1993. Former Swedish Coast Guard vessel built in 1970. Similar craft to Latvia and Lithuania.

PVK 003 *8/1995, Erki Holm* / 0056949

11 INSHORE PATROL CRAFT (PBI)

PVK 006 **PVK 008** **PVK 010–013** **PVK 016–017** **PVK 020–021** **PVK 025**

Comment: *PVK 010* is a 15 m patrol craft built in 1997, *PVK 011* was commissioned in 1999, *PVK 017* (ex-EVA 203) is a 44 ton MFV type of vessel built in Finland in 1963. *PVK 018* (ex-EVA 204) is a 22 kt craft built in Finland in1993 and *PVK 008* and *013* are 13.7 ton icebreaking launches acquired from Finland and based on Lake Peipus. There is also a Jet Combi 10 power boat based on Lake Peipus. Further craft under 12 m have numbers *PVK 004, 006, 012, 016, 020-021. PVK 025* is an ex-Swedish craft (KBV 275) acquired in January 1997.

PVK 010 *6/2002, Baltic Ship Repairers* / 0526817

1 GRIFFON 2000 TDX MK II (HOVERCRAFT) (UCAC)

PVH 1

Displacement, tons: 6.8 full load
Dimensions, feet (metres): 36.1 × 15.1 *(11 × 4.6)*
Main machinery: 1 Deutz BF8L 513 diesel; 320 hp *(293 kW)* sustained
Speed, knots: 33
Range, n miles: 300 at 25 kt
Complement: 2
Military lift: 16 troops or 2 tons
Guns: 1—7.62 mm MG.

Comment: Similar to craft supplied to Finland. Acquired in 1999.

PVH 1 *9/1999, Nick Hall* / 0103794

MARITIME ADMINISTRATION (EESTI VEETEDE AMET (EVA))

Notes: The Maritime Administration (EVA) was re-established in 1990 and is responsible for hydrographic work, aids to navigation, ice-breaking and control of shipping. The main base is at Tallin. Ships are painted with a blue hull and white superstructure and are as follows:

Tarmo, icebreaker built in 1963 and acquired from Finland in 1992. Fleet flagship.
EVA 010, port control launch built in Finland in 1991
EVA 017, port control launch built in Finland in 1995
EVA 019, port control launch built in Estonia in 1997
EVA 300 (ex-*Tormilind*), hydrographic ship built in Russia in 1983
EVA 303 (ex-*Kaater*), buoy ship built in Poland in 1988
EVA 305, hydrographic launch built in Russia in 1979
EVA 308 (ex-GS-108-93), buoy ship built in Poland in 1968
EVA 309 (ex-BGK-117-93), buoy ship built in Russia in 1967
EVA 316 (ex-*Lonna*), buoy ship built in Finland in 1980
EVA 317-318, buoy ships built in Finland in 1994
EVA 319, buoy ship built in Finland in 1996
EVA 320, hydrographic ship built in Finland in 1997
EVA 321, buoy ship built in Estonia in 1999
EVA 322, launch built in Finland in 1997
EVA 323, launch built in Finland in 1994
EVA 324, workboat built in Japan in 1996
EVA 325, hydrographic ship built in Finland in 2002

TARMO *6/2003, Hartmut Ehlers* / 0561491

EVA-318 *6/2003, Hartmut Ehlers* / 0589737

EVA-308 *6/2003, Hartmut Ehlers* / 0589738

Falkland Islands

Country Overview

The Falkland Islands are a self-governing British dependency administered by a Governor and a legislative council. Situated in the south Atlantic Ocean 323 n miles northeast of Cape Horn, approximately 200 islands are divided into two main groups on the east and west by the narrow Falkland Sound. The two largest islands are West Falkland Island (2,090 square miles) and East Falkland Island (2,610 square miles) on which the capital, largest town and principal port, Stanley, is situated. Territorial waters (12 n miles) are claimed as is a 200 n mile fishery zone.

Maritime Aircraft

There are two Pilatus Britten-Norman Defender unarmed maritime surveillance aircraft.

PATROL FORCES

Notes: (1) The ex-Northern Lighthouse Board vessel *Pharos*, renamed *Pharos SG* has been on charter since November 2006, to the Government of South Georgia and the South Sandwich Islands as a fishery patrol and logistics support vessel. The Falkland Islands government continues to provide the fishery officer and support facilities.
(2) The Fisheries Patrol Vessel *Dorada* was temporarily replaced by *Protegat* in May 2008. A permanent replacement is expected to enter service in 2009.

1 FISHERY PATROL SHIP (PSO)

PROTEGAT (ex-*Sumiyoshi Maru 35*, ex-*Chokyo Moru 35*)

Measurement, tons: 1,174 grt
Dimensions, feet (metres): 230.2 × 34.8 × 18.4 *(70.17 × 10.6 × 5.6)*
Main machinery: 1 Niigata NHP30AH diesel; 1,800 hp *(1.3 MW)*; 1 shaft; 1 Kamome bow thruster; 200 hp *(150 kW)*
Speed, knots: 13.5
Range, n miles: 19,000 at 10 kt
Complement: 16 plus accommodation for 5 augmentees
Guns: 1—20 mm Oerlikon (to be fitted if charter extended).
Radars: Surface search/navigation: 1 JRC JMA 527; 1 Furuno FR 2135; 1 Furuno FR 1525; E/F/I-bands.

Comment: Former fishing vessel built by Miho Zoshenko KK-Shimizu in 1987. Converted for fishery protection duties and first chartered in May 2008. The current charter will expire in January 2014. Steel construction with bulbous bow.

PROTEGAT *6/2008*, Falkland Island Fisheries* / 1335206

Faroe Islands

Country Overview

The Faroe Islands are a self-governing island group that is an integral part of Denmark which retains control of foreign relations. Located in the North Atlantic Ocean, about midway between the Shetland Islands and Iceland, there are 18 islands, of which the most important are Østerø, Suderø, Sandø, Vagø, Bordø and Strømø, on which the capital and principal port, Tórshavn, is situated. Territorial waters (12 n miles) are claimed. A 200 n mile fishery zone has also been claimed although the limits have only been partly defined by boundary agreements.

The Coast Guard and Fisheries come under the Landsstyri which is the islands' local government. Vessels work closely with the Danish Navy.

Headquarters Appointments

Head of Coast Guard:
Captain Elmar Hojgaard

Personnel

2009: 60

Bases

Tórshavn (Isle of Streymoy)

COAST GUARD

Notes: There is also an inshore patrol vessel *Spogsvin*.

1 PATROL SHIP (PBO)

TJALDRID

Displacement, tons: 650 full load
Dimensions, feet (metres): 146 × 33.1 × 10.5 *(44.5 × 10.1 × 3.2)*
Main machinery: 2 MWM diesels; 2,400 hp(m) *(1.76 MW)*; 2 shafts
Speed, knots: 14.5
Complement: 18 plus 4 divers
Guns: 1 Oerlikon 20 mm can be carried.
Radars: Surface search: Raytheon TM/TCPA; I-band.

Comment: Originally a commercial tug built in 1976 by Svolvaer, Verksted and acquired by the local government in 1987. The old 57 mm gun has been replaced. A decompression chamber can be carried.

TJALDRID ***12/1999, Faroes Coast Guard*** / 0080652

1 PATROL SHIP (PSO)

BRIMIL

Displacement, tons: 2,000 full load
Dimensions, feet (metres): 208.71 × 41.3 × 14.1 *(63.6 × 12.6 × 4.3)*
Main machinery: 2 Bergen diesels; 5,452 hp *(4.06 MW)*
Speed, knots: 17
Complement: 12 with accommodation for 30 including 3 divers
Radars: Surface search: 2 Furuno.

Comment: Built for Faroese government as a patrol vessel by Myclebust Mek. Verksted, Norway. Entered service in April 2001.

BRIMIL ***7/2008*, Marco Ghiglino*** / 1353022

Fiji

Country Overview

A former British colony, the Republic of Fiji gained independence in 1970. Part of Melanesia, it is situated in the south Pacific Ocean some 972 n miles north of New Zealand and comprises more than 300 islands and islets, 100 of which are inhabited. The largest and most important of these are Viti Levu and Vanua Levu, which together contain more than 85 per cent of the total land area. To the southeast lie Taveuni, Kandavu, Koro and the Lau group while to the northwest lie Rotuma and the Yasawa group. The capital, largest town and principal port is Suva. An archipelagic state, territorial seas (12 n miles) are claimed. An Exclusive Economic Zone (EEZ) (200 n miles) is also claimed but limits have yet to be fully defined by boundary agreements.

Headquarters Appointments

Commander, Navy:
To be announced

Personnel

2009: 300

Bases

RFNS *Viti*, at Togalevu (Training).
RFNS *Stanley Brown*.
Operation base at Walu Bay, Suva.
Forward base at Lautoka.

Prefix to Ships' Names

RFNS (Republic of Fiji naval ship)

PATROL FORCES

3 PACIFIC CLASS (LARGE PATROL CRAFT) (PB)

Name	*No*	*Builders*	*Commissioned*
KULA	201	Transfield Shipbuilding	28 May 1994
KIKAU	202	Transfield Shipbuilding	27 May 1995
KIRO	203	Transfield Shipbuilding	14 Oct 1995

Displacement, tons: 162 full load
Dimensions, feet (metres): 103.3 × 26.6 × 6.9 *(31.5 × 8.1 × 2.1)*
Main machinery: 2 Caterpillar 3516TA diesels; 2,820 hp *(2.09 MW)* sustained; 2 shafts
Speed, knots: 20. **Range, n miles:** 2,500 at 12 kt
Complement: 17 (4 officers)
Guns: 1—20 mm Oerlikon. 2—12.7 mm MGs.
Radars: Surface search: Furuno; I-band.

Comment: Ordered in December 1992. These are hulls 17, 19 and 20 of the class offered by the Australian government under Defence Co-operation Programme. *Kikau* underwent a half-life refit at Gladstone in 2001 followed by *Kula* and *Kiro* in 2002. Following the decision by the Australian government to extend the Pacific Patrol Boat project until 2025, life extension refits will be required for *Kikau* in 2011 and for *Kula* and Kiro in 2012.

KIRO ***9/1998, van Ginderen Collection*** / 0017831

2 VAI (DABUR) CLASS (COASTAL PATROL CRAFT) (PB)

SAKU 303 **SAQA** 304

Displacement, tons: 39 full load
Dimensions, feet (metres): 64.9 × 18 × 5.8 *(19.8 × 5.5 × 1.8)*
Main machinery: 4 GM 12V-71TA diesels; 1,680 hp *(1.25 MW)* sustained; 2 shafts
Speed, knots: 19
Range, n miles: 450 at 13 kt
Complement: 9 (2 officers)
Guns: 2—20 mm Oerlikon. 2—12.7 mm MGs.
Radars: Surface search: Racal Decca Super 101 Mk 3; I-band.

Comment: Built in mid-1970s by Israel Aircraft Industries and transferred from Israel 22 November 1991. ASW equipment is not fitted. Reported as being no longer required by the Navy and may be used by other government departments.

SAQA ***6/1995*** / 0056954

2 COASTAL PATROL CRAFT (PB)

Name	*No*	*Builders*	*Recommissioned*
LEVUKA	101	Beaux's Bay Craft, Louisiana	22 Oct 1987
LAUTOKA	102	Beaux's Bay Craft, Louisiana	28 Oct 1987

Displacement, tons: 97 full load
Dimensions, feet (metres): 110 × 24 × 5 *(33.8 × 7.4 × 1.5)*
Main machinery: 4 GM 12V-71TA diesels; 1,680 hp *(1.25 MW)* sustained; 4 shafts
Speed, knots: 12
Complement: 12 (2 officers)
Guns: 1 — 12.7 mm MG.
Radars: Surface search: Racal Decca; I-band.

Comment: Built in 1979–80 as oil rig support craft. Purchased in September 1987. All aluminium construction.

LAUTOKA
8/1996, Fiji Navy
0056953

Finland

SUOMEN MERIVOIMAT

Country Overview

The Republic of Finland is situated in northern Europe. Nearly one third of the country lies north of the Arctic Circle. With an area of 130,559 square miles, which includes some 60,000 lakes, it has borders to the north with Norway and to the east with Russia. It has a 675 n mile coastline with the Baltic Sea and Gulf of Finland. The Ahvenanmaa archipelago (Åland Islands), consisting of some 6,500 islands, lies southwest of the mainland. Helsinki is the capital, largest city and principal port. Territorial Seas and a Fishing Zone, both of 12 n miles, have been claimed but not an EEZ.

Headquarters Appointments

Commander-in-Chief Finnish Navy:
Vice Admiral Hans Holström
Chief of Staff FNHQ:
Captain Veli-Jukka Pennala

Diplomatic Representation

Defence Attaché in London:
Captain K Varsio

Personnel

(a) 2009: 2,200 regulars
(b) 3,650 conscripts (6–12 months' national service)

Fleet Organisation

Naval Headquarters: Turku
Gulf of Finland Naval Command; main base Upinniemi, Helsinki.
Archipelago Sea Naval Command; main base at Pansio, near Turku.
Kotka Coastal Command at Kotka.
Uusimaa Jaeger Brigade at Dragsvik.
Not all ships are fully manned all the time but all are rotated on a regular basis.

Coast Defence

Coastal Artillery and naval infantry troops. RBS 15 truck-mounted quadruple SSM launchers. 155 mm, 130 mm and 100 mm fixed and mobile guns.

Frontier Guard

All Frontier Guard vessels come under the Ministry of the Interior. The ships have dark green hulls with a thick red diagonal stripe superimposed by a thin white stripe. Superstructure is painted grey. Personnel numbers: 600.

DELETIONS

Patrol Forces

2007 *Oulu, Kotka* (both to Croatia)

PENNANT LIST

Patrol Forces

50	Kiisla
51	Kurki
70	Rauma
71	Raahe
72	Porvoo
73	Naantali
80	Hamina
81	Tornio
82	Hanko
83	Pori

Mine Warfare Forces

01	Pohjanmaa
02	Hämeenmaa
05	Uusimaa
21-26	Kuha 21-26
521-527	Kiiski 1-7
777	Porkkala
875	Pyhäranta
876	Pansio

Auxiliaries

56	Kajava
57	Lokki
92	Putsaari
96	Pikkala
98	Mursu
99	Kustaanmiekka
121	Vahakari
133	Havouri
176	Kala 6
232	Hauki
235	Hirsala
237	Hila
238	Haruna
241	Askeri
334	Hankoniemi
511	Jymy
512	Raju
531	Syöksy
541	Vinha
722	Vaarlahti
723	Vänö
730	Haukipää
731	Hakuni
739	Hästö
751	Lohi
752	Lohm
771	Kampela 1
772	Kampela 2
792	Träskö
799	Hylje
826	Isku
830	Högsåra
831	Kallanpää
836	Houtskär
874	Kala 4
877	Kampela 3
879	Valas
894	Alskär
899	Halli
993	Torsö

PATROL FORCES

2 KIISLA CLASS (COASTAL PATROL CRAFT) (PB)

Name	*No*	*Builders*	*Commissioned*
KIISLA	50	Hollming, Rauma	25 May 1987
KURKI	51	Hollming, Rauma	Nov 1990

Displacement, tons: 270 full load
Dimensions, feet (metres): 158.5 × 28.9 × 7.2 *(48.3 × 8.8 × 2.2)*
Main machinery: 2 MTU 16V 538TB93 diesels; 7,510 hp(m) *(6.9 MW)* sustained; 2 Kamewa 90 waterjets
Speed, knots: 25
Complement: 10
Guns: 2 USSR 23 mm/60 (twin) or 1 Madsen 20 mm.
Weapons control: Radamec 2100 optronic director.
Sonars: Simrad SS304 hull-mounted and VDS; active search; high frequency.

Comment: First ordered on 23 November 1984 and second on 22 November 1988. Plans for two further craft were cancelled. The design allows for rapid conversion to attack craft, ASW craft, minelayer, minesweeper or minehunter. A central telescopic crane over the engine room casing is used to launch a 5.7 m rigid inflatable sea boat. A fire monitor is mounted in the bows. The Kamewa steerable water-jets extend the overall hull length by 2 m. Transferred from the Frontier Guard in 2004.

KIISLA ***6/2004, Finnish Navy*** / 0587710

4 RAUMA CLASS (FAST ATTACK CRAFT—MISSILE) (PTGM)

Name	*No*	*Builders*	*Commissioned*
RAUMA	70	Hollming, Rauma	18 Oct 1990
RAAHE	71	Hollming, Rauma	20 Aug 1991
PORVOO	72	Finnyards, Rauma	27 Apr 1992
NAANTALI	73	Finnyards, Rauma	23 June 1992

Displacement, tons: 215 standard; 248 full load
Dimensions, feet (metres): 157.5 × 26.2 × 4.5 *(48 × 8 × 1.5)*
Main machinery: 2 MTU 16V 538 TB93 diesels; 7,510 hp(m) *(5.52 MW)* sustained; 2 Riva Calzoni IRC 115 water-jets
Speed, knots: 30
Complement: 19 (5 officers)

Missiles: SSM: 6 Saab RBS 15SF (could embark 8); active radar homing to 150 km *(80 n miles)* at 0.8 Mach; warhead 200 kg.
SAM: 1 sextuple launcher; Matra Mistral; IR homing to 4 km *(2.2 n miles)*; warhead 3 kg.
Guns: 1 Bofors 40 mm/70; 300 rds/min to 12 km *(6.6 n miles)*; weight of shell 0.96 kg. 6—103 mm rails for rocket illuminants. 2—12.7 mm MGs.
2 Sako 23 mm/87 (twin); can be fitted instead of Mistral launcher.
A/S mortars: 4 Saab Elma LLS-920 9-tubed launchers; range 300 m; warhead 4.2 kg shaped charge.
Depth charges: 1 rail.
Countermeasures: Decoys: Philax chaff and IR flares.
ESM/ECM: Thales SIEWS.
Weapons control: Bofors Electronic 9LV Mk 3 optronic director with TV camera; infra-red and laser telemetry.
Radars: Surface search: 9GA 208; I-band.
Fire control: Bofors Electronic 9LV 225; J-band.
Navigation: Raytheon ARPA; I-band.
Sonars: Simrad Subsea Toadfish sonar; search and attack; active high frequency.
Finnyards Sonac/PTA towed array; low frequency.

Programmes: Ordered 27 August 1987.
Structure: Developed from Helsinki class. Hull and superstructure of light alloy. SAM and 23 mm guns are interchangeable within the same Sako barbette which has replaced the ZU mounting.
Operational: Primary function is the anti-ship role but there is some ASW capability. Mine rails can be fitted in place of the missile launchers. Towed array cable is 78 m with 24 hydrophones and can be used at speeds between 3 and 12 kt.

NAANTALI *10/2007, Michael Nitz* / 1170110

4 HAMINA CLASS (FAST ATTACK CRAFT—MISSILE) (PTGM)

Name	*No*	*Builders*	*Commissioned*
HAMINA	80 (ex-74)	Aker Finnyards, Rauma	24 Aug 1998
TORNIO	81	Aker Finnyards, Rauma	12 May 2003
HANKO	82	Aker Finnyards, Rauma	22 June 2005
PORI	83	Aker Finnyards, Rauma	19 June 2006

Displacement, tons: 270 full load
Dimensions, feet (metres): 164 × 26.2 × 6.2 *(50.8 × 8.3 × 2)*
Main machinery: 2 MTU 16V 538 TB93 diesels; 7,510 hp(m) *(5.52 MW)* sustained; 2 Kamewa 90SII waterjets
Speed, knots: 32
Range, n miles: 500 at 30 kt
Complement: 29 (5 officers)

Missiles: SSM: 4 Saab RBS 15SF; active radar homing to 100 km *(54 n miles)* at 0.8 Mach; warhead 200 kg.
SAM: Denel Umkhonto 8 cell VLS; inertial guidance with mid-course guidance and IR homing to 12 km *(6.5 n miles)* at 2.4 Mach; warhead 23 kg.
Guns: Bofors 57 mm/L 70 Mk 3; 220 rds/min to 17 km *(9.2 n miles)*; weight of shell 2.6 kg. 2—12.7 mm MGs.
Depth charges: 1 rail.
Mines: 1 rail for 10 mines.
Countermeasures: Decoys: 2 Rheinmetall MASS-2L; decoy launchers.
ESM/ECM: Thales SIEWS; radar intercept.
Combat data systems: EADS Advanced Naval Combat System (ANCS SQ 2000).
Weapons control: Saab Ceros electro-optic director. Sagem EOMS IR scanner.
Radars: Air/surface search: EADS TRS-3D; G-band.
Fire control: SAAB Ceros 200; J-band.
Navigation: Furuno; I-band.
Sonars: Simrad Subsea Toadfish sonar; search and attack; active high frequency.
Finnyards Sonac/PTA towed array; low frequency.

Programmes: First ordered on 31 December 1996, second in February 2000, third on 3 December 2003 and a fourth on 15 February 2005 for delivery in 2006.
Structure: A continuation of the Rauma design with aluminium hull, composite superstructure and RAM coating. Signature reduction is aided by RAM coatings on the superstructure, submerged engine exhausts, upper deck pre-wetting, resilient mountings for all machinery, waterjet propulsion and conductive sealings on doors and hatches to prevent electromagnetic leakage.
Operational: Umkhonto missile fired from *Hanko* on 26 May 2006. The squadron is based at Upinniemi and became operational in 2008.

TORNIO *10/2007, Frank Findler* / 1305007

TORNIO *10/2007, Michael Nitz* / 1170109

MINE WARFARE FORCES

0 + 3 MCMV 2010 CLASS (MINEHUNTERS) (MHSC)

Name	*Builders*	*Laid down*	*Launched*	*Commissioned*
–	Intermarine, Sarzana	July 2007	2009	2010
–	Intermarine, Sarzana	Mar 2008	2009	2011
–	Aker Finnyards, Rauma	2009	2011	2012

Displacement, tons: 697 full load
Dimensions, feet (metres): 172.1 × 32.5 × 10.2 *(52.5 × 9.9 × 3.1)*
Main machinery: 2 MTU 8V 396 TE74K diesels (for transit); 2,680 hp *(2 MW)*; 2 motors (for minehunting); 2 Voith Schneider cycloidal propellers
Speed, knots: 13 diesel
Range, n miles: 1,500 at 12 kt
Complement: 36 (6 officers)

Guns: 1 Bofors 40 mm/70.
Countermeasures: MCM: Atlas Sea Fox C MIDS.
Combat data systems: Atlas Integrated mine countermeasure system (IMCMS).
Radars: Navigation: I-band.
Sonars: Atlas Elektronik SQS-12M hull-mounted; LF/HF/VHF minehunting sonar; Double Eagle Mk 3 dual-frequency UDS.

Programmes: Contract signed with Intermarine SPA on 23 November 2006 for the construction of three MCMVs. The first two ships are to be built at Sarzana; the third ship is to be built by Intermarine and completed at Aker Shipyards, Rauma. The contract includes training and logistic support. The principal components of the minehunting combat system are: a command system, a hull-mounted sonar and self-propelled variable depth sonar (installed in Saab Double Eagle Mk III ROV), a Mine Identification and Disposal System (MIDS) based on the Atlas Sea Fox; both Hydroid Remus and Kongsberg Hugin 1000 AUVs are used for seabed survey and reconnaissance.
Structure: Monocoque GRP construction. The design is similar to the Gaeta class built for the Italian and Australian navies. A new superstructure accommodates the command-and-control suite in the forward-central superstructure and mine-detection and hunting housing and recovery equipment in the central and stern sections.
Operational: The three vessels are expected to become operational by 2014.

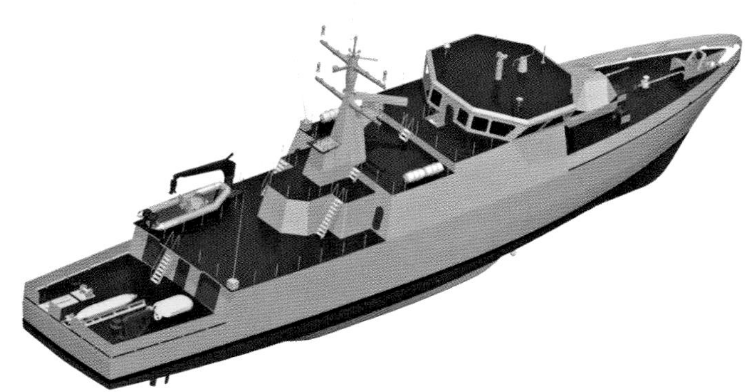
MCMV 2010 *7/2008*, INTERMARINE* / 1294572

2 HÄMEENMAA CLASS (MINELAYERS) (ML)

Name	*No*	*Builders*	*Laid down*	*Launched*	*Commissioned*
HÄMEENMAA	02	Finnyards, Rauma	2 Apr 1991	11 Nov 1991	15 Apr 1992
UUSIMAA	05	Finnyards, Rauma	12 Nov 1991	June 1992	2 Dec 1992

Displacement, tons: 1,450 full load
Dimensions, feet (metres): 255.2 oa; 228.3 wl × 38.1 × 10.5 *(77.8; 69.6 × 11.6 × 3.2)*
Main machinery: 2 Wärtsilä 16V22 diesels; 6,300 hp(m) *(4.64 MW)* sustained; 2 Kamewa cp props; bow thruster; 247 hp(m) *(184 kW)*
Speed, knots: 20
Complement: 66

Missiles: SAM: Denel Umkhonto 8 cell VLS; inertial guidance with mid-course guidance and IR homing to 12 km *(6.5 n miles)* at 2.4 Mach; warhead 23 kg.
Guns: 1 Bofors 57 mm/70 Mk 1; 220 rds/min to 17 km *(9.2 n miles)*; weight of shell 2.6 kg. 2—40 mm grenade launchers. 2—12.7 mm MGs.
A/S mortars: 2 RBU 1200 fixed 5-tubed launchers; range 1,200 m; warhead 34 kg.
Depth charges: 2 racks for 8 DCs.
Mines: 4 rails for 200 contact (S 43-55, 541, 558) or influence (Seamine 2004 and PM 90) mines.
Countermeasures: Decoys: 2 Rheinmetall MASS-2L; decoy launchers.
ESM/ECM: Thales SIEW.
Combat data systems: EADS ANCS 2000.
Weapons control: Saab Ceros electro-optic director. Sagem EOMS IR scanner.
Radars: Air/surface search: EADS TRS-3D; G-band.
Surface search and Navigation: 3 Furuno 2827/2837S; E/F/I-bands.
Sonars: Simrad; hull-mounted; active mine detection; high frequency.

Helicopters: Platform for 1 light.

Programmes: First one ordered 29 December 1989 after the original order in July from Wärtsilä had been cancelled. Second ordered 13 February 1991.
Modernisation: A contract for the mid-life upgrade of both vessels was awarded to EADS Defence and Security Division in April 2006. Modernisation, undertaken by Aker Shipyards, included EADS ANCS 2000 combat data system, EADS TRS 3D radar, Sagem EOMS and Umkhonto point defence missile system. *Hämeenmaa* completed upgrade on 13 April 2007 and *Uusimaa* in September 2007. Both vessels became fully operational in 2008.
Structure: Steel hull and alloy superstructure. Ice strengthened (Ice class 1A) and capable of breaking up to 40 mm ice. During the modernisation period (2006–07), a new fixed bow, stabilisers, two new masts and a new combat information system were added. The flight deck can operate light helicopters.
Operational: Dual role as a transport and support ship.

UUSIMAA *6/2008*, M Declerck* / 1335718

1 MINELAYER (ML)

Name	*No*	*Builders*	*Laid down*	*Launched*	*Commissioned*
POHJANMAA	01	Wärtsilä, Helsinki	4 May 1978	28 Aug 1978	8 June 1979

Displacement, tons: 1,000 standard; 1,100 full load
Dimensions, feet (metres): 255.8 × 37.7 × 9.8 *(78.2 × 11.6 × 3)*
Main machinery: 2 Wärtsilä Vasa 16V22 diesels; 6,300 hp(m) *(4.64 MW)* sustained; 2 shafts; cp props; bow thruster
Speed, knots: 19
Range, n miles: 3,500 at 15 kt
Complement: 90

Missiles: SAM: 2 sextuple launchers; Matra Mistral; IR homing to 4 km *(2.2 n miles)*; warhead 3 kg.
Guns: 1 Bofors 57 mm/70; 200 rds/min to 17 km *(9.3 n miles)*; weight of shell 2.4 kg.
6—103 mm launchers for illuminants fitted to the mounting.
2 Bofors 40 mm/70; 300 rds/min to 12 km *(6.6 n miles)*; weight of shell 0.96 kg.
4 Sako 23 mm/87 (2 twin). 2—12.7 mm MGs.
A/S mortars: 2 RBU 1200 fixed 5-tubed launchers; range 1,200 m; warhead 34 kg.
Depth charges: 2 rails.
Mines: 120 including UK Stonefish.
Countermeasures: Decoys: Philax chaff and IR flare launcher.
ESM: Argo; radar intercept.
Radars: Air search: Signaal DA05; E/F-band.
Surface search: Philips 9GR 600; I-band.
Fire control: Phillips 9LV 220; J-band.
Navigation: I-band.
Sonars: Simrad; hull-mounted; active search and attack; high frequency.
Bottom classification; search; high frequency.

Programmes: Design completed 1976. Ordered late 1977.
Modernisation: In 1992 the forward 23 mm guns were replaced by 12.7 mm MGs. Major refit in 1996–98 to replace the main gun, improve air defences and minelaying capability. The SAM mounting is interchangeable with 23 mm guns.
Operational: Also serves as training ship. Carries 70 trainees accommodated in Portakabins on the mine deck. Helicopter area on quarterdeck but no hangar.

POHJANMAA *5/2008*, Michael Nitz* / 1335717

3 PANSIO CLASS (MINELAYERS—LCU TYPE) (MLI)

Name	*No*	*Builders*	*Commissioned*
PANSIO	876 (ex-576)	Olkiluoto Shipyard	25 Sep 1991
PYHÄRANTA	875 (ex-575, ex-475)	Olkiluoto Shipyard	26 May 1992
PORKKALA	777	Olkiluoto Shipyard	29 Oct 1992

Displacement, tons: 450 standard
Dimensions, feet (metres): 144.3 oa; 128.6 wl × 32.8 × 6.6 *(44; 39.2 × 10 × 2)*
Main machinery: 2 MTU 12V 183 TE62 diesels; 1,500 hp(m) *(1.1 MW)*; 2 shafts; bow thruster
Speed, knots: 10
Complement: 12
Guns: 2 ZU 23 mm/87 (twin). 1—12.7 mm MG.
Mines: 50.
Radars: Navigation: Raytheon ARPA; I-band.

Comment: Ordered in May 1990. Used for inshore minelaying and transport with a capacity of 100 tons. Ice strengthened with ramps in bow and stern. Has a 15 ton crane fitted aft.

PYRÄRANTA *4/2007, Guy Toremans* / 1170108

6 KUHA CLASS (MINESWEEPERS—INSHORE) (MSI)

Name	*No*	*Builders*	*Commissioned*
KUHA 21	21	Laivateollisuus, Turku	1974–75
KUHA 22	22	Laivateollisuus, Turku	1974–75
KUHA 23	23	Laivateollisuus, Turku	1974–75
KUHA 24	24	Laivateollisuus, Turku	1974–75
KUHA 25	25	Laivateollisuus, Turku	1974–75
KUHA 26	26	Laivateollisuus, Turku	1974–75

Displacement, tons: 90 full load
Dimensions, feet (metres): 87.2 wl; 104 oa × 22.7 × 6.6 *(26.6; 31.7 × 6.9 × 2)*
Main machinery: 2 Cummins MT-380M diesels; 600 hp(m) *(448 kW)*; 1 shaft; cp prop; active rudder
Speed, knots: 12
Complement: 15 (3 officers)
Guns: 2 ZU 23 mm/60 (twin). 1—12.7 mm MG.
Radars: Navigation: Decca; I-band.
Sonars: Reson Seabat 6012 mine avoidance; active high frequency.

Comment: All ordered 1972. First one completed 28 June 1974, and last on 13 November 1975. Fitted for magnetic, acoustic and pressure-mine clearance. Hulls are of GRP. May carry a Pluto ROV. Four of the class were lengthened in 1997/98 and remaining two by 2000 to take a new minesweeping control system, and new magnetic and acoustic sweeps. New sonars installed. Armament not fittedin all of the class.

KUHA 21 *6/2001, Finnish Navy* / 0114724

7 KIISKI CLASS (MINESWEEPERS—INSHORE) (MSI)

Name	*No*	*Builders*	*Commissioned*
KIISKI 1	521	Fiskars, Turku	1983–84
KIISKI 2	522	Fiskars, Turku	1983–84
KIISKI 3	523	Fiskars, Turku	1983–84
KIISKI 4	524	Fiskars, Turku	1983–84
KIISKI 5	525	Fiskars, Turku	1983–84
KIISKI 6	526	Fiskars, Turku	1983–84
KIISKI 7	527	Fiskars, Turku	1983–84

Displacement, tons: 20 full load
Dimensions, feet (metres): 49.9 × 13.4 × 3.3 *(15.2 × 4.1 × 1.2)*
Main machinery: 2 Valmet 611 CSMP diesels; 340 hp(m) *(250 kW)*; 2 Hamilton water-jets
Speed, knots: 11
Range, n miles: 260 at 11 kt
Complement: 4

Comment: Ordered January 1983. All completed by 24 May 1984. GRP hull. Built to be used with Kuha class for unmanned teleguided sweeping, but this was not successful and they are now used for manned magnetic and acoustic sweeping operations with crew of four.

KIISKI 5 — *6/2001, Finnish Navy* / 0114725

LAND-BASED MARITIME AIRCRAFT

Numbers/Type: 2 Agusta AB 412 Griffon.
Operational speed: 122 kt *(226 km/h)*.
Service ceiling: 17,000 ft *(5,180 m)*.
Range: 354 n miles *(656 km)*.
Role/Weapon systems: Operated by Coast Guard/Frontier force for patrol and SAR. Sensors: Radar and FLIR. Weapons: Unarmed at present but mountings for machine guns.

AB 412 — *6/2005, Finnish Navy* / 1133422

Numbers/Type: 3 Eurocopter AS 332L1 Super Puma.
Operational speed: 130 kt *(240 km/h)*.
Service ceiling: 15,090 ft *(4,600 m)*.
Range: 672 n miles *(1,245 km)*.
Role/Weapon systems: Coastal patrol, surveillance and SAR helicopters. Sensors: Surveillance radar, FLIR, tactical navigation systems and SAR equipment. Weapons: Unarmed.

AS 332 — *6/2005, Finnish Navy* / 1133423

Numbers/Type: 2 Agusta AB 206B JetRanger.
Operational speed: 116 kt *(215 km/h)*.
Service ceiling: 13,500 ft *(4,120 m)*.
Range: 364 n miles *(674 km)*.
Role/Weapon systems: Coastal patrol and inshore surveillance helicopters. Sensors: Visual means only. FLIR may be fitted in due course. Weapons: Unarmed.

AB 206 (Swedish colours) — *6/2000, Andreas Karlsson, Swedish Defence Image* / 0106563

Numbers/Type: 2 Dornier Do 228-212.
Operational speed: 223 kt *(413 km/h)*.
Service ceiling: 29,600 ft *(9,020 m)*.
Range: 939 n miles *(1,740 km)*.
Role/Weapon systems: Maritime surveillance, SAR and pollution control. Acquired in 1995. Sensors: GEC-Marconi Seaspray radar; Terma Side scan radar; FLIR/TV, SLAR and IR/UV scanner. Weapons: Unarmed.

DORNIER 228 (German colours) — *9/2002, Frank Findler* / 0528878

TRAINING SHIPS

2 LOKKI CLASS (AX)

Name	*No*	*Builders*	*Commissioned*
LOKKI	57	Valmet/Lavateollisuus	28 Aug 1986
KAJAVA	56	Valmet/Lavateollisuus	3 Oct 1981

Displacement, tons: 59 *(Lokki)*; 64
Dimensions, feet (metres): 87.9 × 18 × 6.2 *(26.8 × 5.5 × 1.9)*
87.9 × 17.1 × 8.5 *(26.8 × 5.2 × 2.1) (Lokki)*
Main machinery: 2 MTU 8V 396TB82 diesels; 1,740 hp(m) *(1.28 MW)* sustained *(Lokki)*
2 MTU 8V 396 TB84 diesels; 2,100 hp(m) *(1.54 MW)* sustained; 2 shafts
Speed, knots: 25
Complement: 6
Guns: 2 ZU 23 mm/60 can be carried.
Sonars: Simrad SS 242; hull-mounted; active search; high frequency.

Comment: Transferred from the Frontier Guard to the Navy in 1999 and used as training vessels. Built in light metal alloy. *Lokki* has a V-shaped hull. A third of class to Lithuania in 1997 and a fourth to Latvia in 2001.

LOKKI — *6/2001, Finnish Navy* / 0114723

3 FABIAN WREDE CLASS (AX)

Name	*No*	*Builders*	*Commissioned*
FABIAN WREDE	690	UKI Workboat, Usikaupunki	15 Aug 2006
WILHELM CARPELAN	691	UKI Workboat, Usikaupunki	14 June 2007
AXEL VON FERSEN	692	UKI Workboat, Usikaupunki	30 June 2008

Displacement, tons: 65 full load
Dimensions, feet (metres): 64.9 × 19.0 × 6.2 *(19.8 × 5.8 × 1.9)*
Main machinery: 1 Caterpillar C 18 diesel; 670 hp *(500 kW)*; 1 shaft
Speed, knots: 12
Complement: 2 plus 8 trainees
Radars: Navigation: I-band.

Comment: Naval Academy training ships.

FABIAN WREDE *6/2008** / 1335719

AUXILIARIES

5 VALAS CLASS (GP TRANSPORTS) (AKSL)

VALAS 879 **MURSU** 98 **VAHAKARI** 121 **VAARLAHTI** 722 **VÄNÖ** 723

Displacement, tons: 285 full load
Dimensions, feet (metres): 100.4 × 26.5 × 10.4 *(30.6 × 8.1 × 3.2)*
Main machinery: 1 Wärtsilä Vasa 8V22 diesel; 1,576 hp(m) *(1.16 MW)* sustained; 1 shaft
Speed, knots: 12
Complement: 11
Military lift: 35 tons or 150 troops
Guns: 2—23 mm/60 (twin). 1—12.7 mm MG.
Mines: 28 can be carried.
Radars: Navigation: Decca 1226; I-band.

Comment: Completed 1979–80. *Mursu* acts as a diving tender. Funnel is offset to starboard. Can be used as minelayers or transport/cargo carriers and are capable of breaking thin ice.

VALAS (old number) *7/1998, van Ginderen Collection* / 0069878

3 KAMPELA CLASS (LCU TRANSPORTS) (LCU/AKSL)

Name	*No*	*Builders*	*Commissioned*
KAMPELA 1	771	Enso Gutzeit	29 July 1976
KAMPELA 2	772	Enso Gutzeit	21 Oct 1976
KAMPELA 3	877	Finnmekano	23 Oct 1979

Displacement, tons: 90 light; 260 full load
Dimensions, feet (metres): 106.6 × 26.2 × 4.9 *(32.5 × 8 × 1.5)*
Main machinery: 2 Scania diesels; 460 hp(m) *(338 kW)*; 2 shafts
Speed, knots: 9
Complement: 10
Guns: 2 or 4 ZU 23 mm/60 (1 or 2 twin).
Mines: About 20 can be carried.

Comment: Can be used as amphibious craft, transports, minelayers or for shore support. Armament can be changed to suit role.

KAMPELA 2 (old number) *6/2000, Finnish Navy* / 0103800

2 KALA CLASS (LCU TRANSPORTS) (LCU/AKSL)

KALA 4 874 **KALA 6** 176

Displacement, tons: 60 light; 200 full load
Dimensions, feet (metres): 88.6 × 26.2 × 6 *(27 × 8 × 1.8)*
Main machinery: 2 Valmet diesels; 360 hp(m) *(265 kW)*; 2 shafts
Speed, knots: 9
Complement: 10
Guns: 2 Oerlikon 20 mm (not in all).
Mines: 34.
Radars: Navigation: Decca 1226; I-band.

Comment: Completed between 1956 and 4 December 1959 *(Kala 6)*. Can be used as coastal transports, amphibious craft, minelayers or for shore support. Armament can be changed to suit role.

KALA 6 *6/2001, Finnish Navy* / 0114729

6 HAUKI CLASS (TRANSPORTS) (AKSL)

HAVOURI 133 **HIRSALA** 235 **HAKUNI** 731
HAUKI 232 **HANKONIEMI** 334 **HOUTSKÄR** 836

Displacement, tons: 45 full load
Dimensions, feet (metres): 47.6 × 15.1 × 7.2 *(14.5 × 4.6 × 2.2)*
Main machinery: 2 Valmet 611 CSM diesels; 586 hp(m) *(431 kW)*; 1 shaft
Speed, knots: 12
Complement: 4
Cargo capacity: 6 tons or 40 passengers
Radars: Navigation: I-band.

Comment: Completed 1979. Ice strengthened; two serve isolated island defences. Four converted in 1988 as tenders to the Marine War College, but from 1990 back in service as light transports.

HOUTSKÄR (old number) *9/1997, Finnish Navy* / 0587703

4 HILA CLASS (TRANSPORTS) (AKSL)

HILA 237 **HARUNA** 238 **HÄSTÖ** 739 **HÖGSÅRA** 830

Displacement, tons: 50 full load
Dimensions, feet (metres): 49.2 × 13.1 × 5.9 *(15 × 4 × 1.8)*
Main machinery: 2 diesels; 416 hp(m) *(306 kW)*; 2 shafts
Speed, knots: 12
Complement: 4

Comment: Ordered from Kotkan Telakka in August 1990. Second pair completed in 1994. Ice strengthened.

HILA *6/2000, Finnish Navy* / 0103801

1 TRIALS SHIP (MLI)

Name	*No*	*Builders*	*Launched*	*Commissioned*
ISKU	826 (ex-829, ex-16)	Reposaaron Konepaja	4 Dec 1969	1970

Displacement, tons: 180 full load
Dimensions, feet (metres): 108.5 × 28.5 × 5.9 *(33 × 8.7 × 1.8)*
Main machinery: 4 Type M 50 diesels; 4,400 hp(m) *(3.3 MW)* sustained; 4 shafts
Speed, knots: 18
Complement: 25
Radars: Navigation: Raytheon ARPA; I-band.

Comment: Formerly a missile experimental craft, now used for various equipment trials. Modernised in 1989–90 by Uusikaupunki Shipyard and lengthened by 7 m. Can quickly be converted to a minelayer.

ISKU *6/2000, Finnish Navy* / 0103798

2 LOHI CLASS (LCU TRANSPORTS) (LCU)

LOHI 751 (ex-351) **LOHM** 752

Displacement, tons: 38 full load
Dimensions, feet (metres): 65.6 × 19.7 × 3 *(20 × 6 × 0.9)*
Main machinery: 2 WMB diesels; 1,200 hp(m) *(882 kW)*; 2 water-jets
Speed, knots: 20
Range, n miles: 240 at 20 kt
Complement: 4
Guns: 2 ZU 23 mm/60 (twin). 1 — 14.5 mm MG.

Comment: Commissioned September 1984. Used as troop carriers and for light cargo. Guns not always carried.

LOHI (old number) *6/2000, Finnish Navy* / 0103802

1 TRANSPORT AND COMMAND LAUNCH (YFB)

ASKERI 241

Displacement, tons: 25 full load
Dimensions, feet (metres): 52.6 × 14.5 × 4.5 *(16 × 4.4 × 1.4)*
Main machinery: 2 Volvo Penta diesels; 1,100 hp(m) *(808 kW)*; 2 shafts
Speed, knots: 22
Complement: 6
Radars: Surface search: I-band.
Navigation: Raytheon; I-band.

Comment: Completed in 1992. Closely resembles Spanish PVC II class.

COMMAND LAUNCH *6/2000, Finnish Navy* / 0103804

7 VIHURI CLASS (COMMAND LAUNCHES) (YFB)

JYMY 511 **SYÖKSY** 531 **TRÄSKÖ** 792 **ALSKÄR** 894
RAJU 512 **VINHA** 541 **TORSÖ** 993

Displacement, tons: 13 full load
Dimensions, feet (metres): 42.7 × 13.1 × 3 *(13 × 4 × 0.9)*
Main machinery: 2 diesels; 772 hp(m) *(567 kW)*; 2 water-jets
Speed, knots: 30
Complement: 6
Radars: Surface search: I-band.

Comment: First of class *Vihuri* delivered in 1988, the next five in 1991 and the last pair in 1993. *Träskö, Torsö* and *Alskär* act as fast transports. The remainder are command launches for Navy squadrons. *Vihuri* was destroyed by fire in late 1991.

VINHA *5/1993, van Ginderen Collection* / 0069883

30 MERIUISKO CLASS (LCP)

U 201–211 **U 301–312** **U 400 series**

Displacement, tons: 10 full load
Dimensions, feet (metres): 36 × 11.5 × 1.6 *(11 × 3.5 × 0.5)*
Main machinery: 2 Volvo TAMD70E diesels; 418 hp(m) *(307 kW)* sustained; 2 Hamilton waterjets
Speed, knots: 36; 30 full load
Complement: 3
Military lift: 25 troops or 2.5 tons equipment
Radars: Navigation (U 401 series): I-band.

Comment: First batch of 11 completed by Alumina Varvet from 1983 to 1986. A further four ordered in 1989. Constructed of light alloy. Fitted with small bow ramp. Two of the class equipped with cable handling system for boom defence work. Batch one has smaller cabins.

U 304 *6/2000, Finnish Army* / 0103805

36 JURMO CLASS (LCP)

U 601–636

Displacement, tons: 10 full load
Dimensions, feet (metres): 46.9 × 12.1 × 2.5 *(14.3 × 3.7 × 0.75)*
Main machinery: 2 Caterpillar diesels; 2 FF-jet 375 waterjets
Speed, knots: 30+
Complement: 2
Military lift: 21 troops with equipment or 2.5 tons cargo
Guns: 2—12.7 mm MGs.
Radars: Navigation: I-band.

Comment: Developed from Meriusko class for troop carrying role. Prototype built by Alutech Ltd and delivered in 1999. Delivered by 2005. Cargo hatch of composite material to provide armoured protection. Trials with the German AFS *Berlin* were carried out in July 2007. Trials of the Kongsberg Sea Protector 12.7 mm remotely controlled gun conducted in *U 634* in 2008.

U 603 *8/2002*, ***E & M Laursen*** / 0534066

23 RAIDING CRAFT (LCVP)

G 100 series

Displacement, tons: 3 full load
Dimensions, feet (metres): 26.2 × 6.9 × 1 *(8 × 2.1 × 0.3)*
Main machinery: 1 Yanmar 4LHA-STE diesel; 240 hp *(179 kW)*; 1 RR FF-jet 240 waterjet
Speed, knots: 30
Complement: 1
Military lift: 9 troops with equipment

Comment: First batch of 23 units ordered in February 2001. Based on Swedish Gruppbåt and built by Alutech Ltd. Delivered late 2001.

RAIDING CRAFT ***6/2001, Finnish Navy*** / 0114721

1 CABLE SHIP (ANL)

PUTSAARI 92

Displacement, tons: 430 full load
Dimensions, feet (metres): 149.5 × 28.6 × 8.2 *(45.6 × 8.7 × 2.5)*
Main machinery: 1 Wärtsilä diesel; 510 hp(m) *(375 kW)*; 1 shaft; active rudder; bow thruster
Speed, knots: 10
Complement: 20

Comment: Built by Rauma-Repola, Rauma, launched on 15 December 1965 and commissioned in 1966. Modernised by Wärtsilä in 1987. Fitted with two 10 ton cable winches. Strengthened for ice operations.

PUTSAARI ***6/2001, Finnish Navy*** / 0114720

1 SUPPORT CRAFT (YFB)

PIKKALA (ex-*Fenno*) 96

Displacement, tons: 66 full load
Dimensions, feet (metres): 75.5 × 14.4 × 6.6 *(23 × 4.4 × 2)*
Main machinery: 1 Valmet diesel; 177 hp(m) *(130 kW)*; 1 shaft
Speed, knots: 10
Complement: 5

Comment: Used for utility and transport roles at Helsinki. Commissioned in June 1946 at Turhu.

PIKKALA ***6/2000, Finnish Navy*** / 0103806

2 POLLUTION CONTROL VESSELS (YPC)

HYLJE 799 **HALLI** 899

Displacement, tons: 1,500 *(Hylje)*; 1,600 *(Halli)* full load
Dimensions, feet (metres): 164; 198.5 *(Halli)* × 41 × 9.8 *(50; 60.5 × 12.5 × 3)*
Main machinery: 2 Saab diesels; 680 hp(m) *(500 kW)*; 2 shafts; active rudders; bow thruster *(Hylje)*
2 Wärtsilä diesels; 2,650 hp(m) *(19.47 MW)*; 2 shafts; active rudders *(Halli)*
Speed, knots: 7 *(Hylje)*; 13 *(Halli)*

Comment: Painted grey. Strengthened for ice. Owned by Ministry of Environment, civilian-manned but operated by Navy from Turku. *Hylje* commissioned 3 June 1981, *Halli* in January 1987. Capacity is about 550 m^3 *(Hylje)* and 1,400 m^3 *(Halli)* of contaminated seawater. The ships have slightly different superstructure lines aft.

HYLJE ***10/2006, J Ciślak*** / 1164996

TUGS

2 HARBOUR TUGS (YTM)

HAUKIPÄÄ 730 **KALLANPÄÄ** 831

Displacement, tons: 38 full load
Dimensions, feet (metres): 45.9 × 16.4 × 7.5 *(14 × 5 × 2.3)*
Main machinery: 2 diesels; 360 hp(m) *(265 kW)*; 2 shafts
Speed, knots: 9
Complement: 2

Comment: Delivered by Teijon Telakka Oy in December 1985. Similar to Hauki class. Also used as utility craft.

HAUKIPÄÄ (old number) ***6/2000, Finnish Navy*** / 0103813

FRONTIER GUARD

1 IMPROVED TURSAS CLASS (OFFSHORE PATROL VESSEL) (WPBO)

MERIKARHU

Displacement, tons: 1,100 full load
Dimensions, feet (metres): 189.6 × 36.1 × 15.1 *(57.8 × 11 × 4.6)*
Main machinery: 2 Wärtsilä Vasa 8R26 diesels; 3,808 hp(m) *(2.8 MW)* sustained; 1 shaft; cp prop; bow and stern thrusters
Speed, knots: 15. **Range, n miles:** 2,000 at 15 kt
Complement: 30
Guns: 2—23 mm/87 (twin) can be carried.
Radars: Surface search. Navigation.

Comment: Ordered 17 June 1993 from Finnyards, and completed 28 October 1994. Capable of 5 kt in 50 cm of ice. Used as an all-weather patrol ship in the Baltic, capable of Command, SAR, tug work with 30 ton bollard pull, and environmental pollution cleaning up. Carries an RIB launched from a hydraulic crane.

MERIKARHU *6/2005, Finnish Navy* / 1133421

2 TURSAS CLASS (OFFSHORE PATROL VESSELS) (WPBO)

TURSAS **UISKO**

Displacement, tons: 1,250 full load
Dimensions, feet (metres): 201.6 × 33.5 × 15.9 *(61.45 × 10.2 × 4.85)*
Main machinery: Diesel electric; 2 Rolls-Royce azimuth thrusters; 4,360 hp *(3.2 MW)*
Speed, knots: 14
Complement: 32
Guns: 2 Sako 23 mm/60 (twin).
Sonars: Simrad SS105; active scanning; 14 kHz.

Comment: First ordered from Rauma-Repola on 21 December 1984, launched 31 January 1986 and delivered 6 June 1986. Second ordered 20 March 1986, launched 19 June 1986 and delivered 27 January 1987. Both ships underwent conversion at Uusikaupunki Workboat Ltd 2004–06. The ships were lengthened by 12 m and modified to conduct anti-pollution operations.

UISKO (before conversion) *6/2005, Finnish Navy* / 1133420

3 TELKKÄ CLASS (WPBO)

TELKKÄ **TAVI** **TIIRA**

Displacement, tons: 400 full load
Dimensions, feet (metres): 160.8 × 24.6 × 11.8 *(49 × 7.5 × 3.6)*
Main machinery: 2 diesels; 6,120 hp(m) *(4.5 MW)*; 2 shafts
Speed, knots: 20
Complement: 17
Guns: 1—20 mm.
Sonars: Sonac PTA; towed array; low frequency.

Comment: *Telkkä* entered service in July 1999, *Tavi* in 2003 and *Tiira* on 27 May 2004.

TAVI *6/2005, Finnish Navy* / 1133419

4 SLINGSBY SAH 2200 (HOVERCRAFT) (UCAC)

Displacement, tons: 5.5 full load
Dimensions, feet (metres): 34.8 × 13.8 *(10.6 × 4.2)*
Main machinery: 1 Cummins 6CTA-8-3M-1 diesel; 300 hp *(224 kW)*
Speed, knots: 40
Range, n miles: 400 at 30 kt
Complement: 2
Military lift: 2.2 tons or 12 troops
Guns: 1—12.7 mm MG.
Radars: Navigation: Raytheon R41; I-band.

Comment: First one acquired from Slingsby Amphibious Hovercraft Company in March 1993. Three more ordered in February 1998 and delivered in late 1999.

SLINGSBY 2200 *6/1993, Slingsby* / 0069892

3 GRIFFON 2000 TDX(M) (HOVERCRAFT) (UCAC)

Displacement, tons: 6.8 full load
Dimensions, feet (metres): 36.1 × 15.1 *(11 × 4.6)*
Main machinery: 1 Deutz BF8L513 diesel; 320 hp *(239 kW)* sustained
Speed, knots: 33
Range, n miles: 300 at 25 kt
Complement: 2
Military lift: 16 troops or 2 tons
Guns: 1—7.62 mm MG.
Radars: Navigation: I-band.

Comment: First two acquired from Griffon, UK and commissioned 1 December 1994; third one bought in June 1995. Can be embarked in an LCU. Speed indicated is at Sea State 3 with a full load. Similar to those in service with the UK Navy.

GRIFFON 2000 *6/1994, P Felstead* / 0080653

39 INSHORE PATROL CRAFT AND TENDERS (PB)

Class	*Total*	*Tonnage*	*Speed*	*Commissioned*
RV-37	7	20	12	1978–85
RV-150	10	25	12	1992–96
RV-113	14	10	28	1984–90

RV-113 class *6/1993* / 0069894

France

MARINE NATIONALE

Country Overview

The French Republic, which includes the island of Corsica, is situated in western Europe. With an area of 210,026 square miles, the mainland is bordered to the north by Belgium, Luxembourg and Germany, to the south-east by Switzerland and Italy and to the south-west by Spain. It has a 1,852 n mile coastline with the Atlantic Ocean, Mediterranean Sea, North Sea and English Channel. Overseas departments are French Guiana, Martinique, Guadeloupe and Réunion. Dependencies include St Pierre and Miquelon, Mayotte, New Caledonia, French Polynesia, the French Southern and Antarctic Territories, and Wallis and Futuna Islands. The capital and largest city is Paris while the principal ports are Marseille, Le Havre, Dunkirk, St Nazaire and Rouen. Strasbourg is a port on the Rhine. Territorial seas (12 n miles) are claimed. An EEZ (200 n miles) has also been claimed but not all the large number of boundaries have been defined by agreements.

Headquarters Appointments

Chief of the Naval Staff:
Amiral Pierre-François Forissier
Inspector General of the Armies:
Amiral Christian Penillard
Director of Personnel:
Vice-Amiral Benoit Chomel de Jarnieu
Major General of the Navy:
Vice-Amiral d'Escadre Alain Launay
Inspector General of the Navy:
Commissaire Général Jean Fillon

Senior Appointments

C-in-C Atlantic Theatre (CECLANT):
Vice-Amiral d'Escadre Anne-François de Bourdoncle de Saint Salvy
C-in-C Mediterranean Theatre (CECMED):
Vice-Amiral d'Escadre Jean Tandonnet
Flag Officer, French Forces Polynesia (ALPACI):
Contre-Amiral Jean-Louis Vichot
Flag Officer, Naval Forces Indian Ocean (ALINDIEN):
Vice-Amiral Gérard Valin
Flag Officer, Antilles:
Contre-Amiral Philippe Arnould
Flag Officer, Cherbourg:
Vice-Amiral Philippe Périssé
Flag Officer, Submarines (ALFOST):
Vice-Amiral d'Escadre Jean François Baud
Flag Officer, Naval Action Force (ALFAN):
Vice-Amiral d'Escadre Bertrand Ambriot
Deputy Flag Officer, Naval Action Force (TOULON):
Contre-Amiral Alain Hinden
Deputy Flag Officer, Naval Action Force (BREST):
Contre-Amiral Pierre Labonne
Flag Officer Naval Aviation (ALAVIA):
Vice-Amiral Olivier de Rostolan
Flag Officer Lorient and Commandant Marines (Alfusco):
Contre-Amiral Marin Gillier

Diplomatic Representation

Defence Attaché in London:
Vice-Amiral Yann Tainguy
Naval Attaché in London:
Capitaine de Vaisseau Henri-François Piot
Naval Attaché in Washington:
Capitaine de Vaisseau Bruno Demeocq
Defence and Naval Attaché in Riyad:
Capitaine de Vaisseau Bruno Thomé
Head of French Military Delegation to the European Union:
to be announced
Head of French Military Mission to HQ SACT:
Contre-Amiral Christian Canova
Head of French Military Mission to Joint Force Command Naples: to be announced
Naval Attaché in Washington:
Capitaine de Vaisseau Philippe Alquier

Personnel

(a) 2009: 38,713 (4,508 officers)
(b) 2009: civilians in direct support: 7,368

Bases

Brest: Main Atlantic base. SSBN base
Toulon: Mediterranean Command base
Cherbourg: Channel base
Bayonne: Landes firing range
Small bases at Papeete (Tahiti), Fort-de-France (Martinique), Nouméa (New Caledonia), Degrad-des-Cannes (French Guiana), Port-des-Galets (La Réunion), Dakar-Cap Vert (Senegal) and Abu Dhabi.

Shipyards (Naval)

All former naval shipbuilding facilities are privatised and are operated by DCNS. Main facilities are at:
Cherbourg: Submarines and Fast Attack Craft (private shipyard)
Brest: Major warships and refitting
Lorient: Destroyers and Frigates, MCMVs, Patrol Craft
Toulon: Major refits.

Dates

Armement pour essais: After launching when the ship is sufficiently advanced to allow a crew to live on board, and the commanding officer has joined. From this date the ship hoists the French flag and is ready to undertake her first harbour trials.

Armement définitif: On this date the ship has received her full complement and is able to undergo sea trials.

Clôture d'armement: Trials are completed and the ship is now able to undertake her first endurance cruise.

Croisière de longue durée or *traversée de longue durée:* The endurance cruise follows the *clôture d'armement* and lasts until the ship is accepted with all systems fully operational.

Admission au service actif: Commissioning date.

Reserve

A ship in 'Reserve Normale' has no complement but is available at short notice. 'Reserve Speciale' means that a refit will be required before the ship can go to sea again. 'Condamnation' is the state before being broken up or sold; at this stage a Q number is allocated.

Prefix to Ships' Names

FS is used in NATO communications but is not official.

Strength of the Fleet

Type	*Active (Reserve)*	*Building (Projected)*
Submarines (SSBN)	3	1
Submarines (SSN)	6	(6)
Aircraft Carriers	1	(1)
Helicopter Carrier	1	–
Destroyers	12	2
Frigates	19 (1)	2 (9)
Public Service Force	8	–
Patrol Craft	10	–
LPH/LSDs	4	–
LST/LCT	9	–
LCMs	17	–
Route Survey Vessels	3	–
Minehunters	13	–
Diving Tenders	6	–
Survey/Research Ships	7	2
Tankers (AOR)	4	–
Maintenance Ships	2	(2)
Supply Tenders	7	–
Transports	9	–
Training Ships	16	–

DELETIONS

Submarines

2008 *L'Inflexible*

Destroyers

2007 *Duquesne*

Patrol Forces

2006 *Stenia, Camelia, Bellis*
2008 *Epée*

Amphibious Forces

2006 *Ouragan*
2007 *Orage*

Auxiliaries

2006 *Isard, La Persévérante, Poséidon, Faune*
2007 *Néreide*
2008 *Bougainville, D'Entrecasteaux, Rari*
2009 *Loire, Jules Verne*

Tugs

2007 *Martinet*

Fleet Air Arm Bases

Notes: (1) In addition to the following squadrons, there are three other squadrons operating with mixed Air Force and Navy crews on behalf of both services:

- Helicopter Squadron EH-1/67 "Pyrénées", based at Cazaux AFB, for the combat SAR (CSAR) role, operating eight specialised Aerospatiale SA-330 Puma helicopters and four Eurocopter EC 725 R2 Cougar Mk 2 Plus Resco delivered in 2005–06. These helicopters regularly embark on *Charles de Gaulle*.
- Army special operations helicopter flight EOS 3 based at Pau, equipped with Aerospatiale AS 532 Cougar helicopters to be replaced from 2006 by eight new Eurocopter EC 725 R2 Cougar Mk 2 Plus HUS. Roles include counter-terrorism and they can embark on *Charles de Gaulle*, LSDs and eventually on La Fayette and Floréal-class frigates.
- Training Squadron EAT-319, based at Avord AFB, with Embraer 121 Xingu light transport (some coming from the Navy) for pilot basic training.

(2) There are also naval sections within various Air Force training units where trainees fly CAP 231 light aircraft, Aerospatiale TB-30 Epsilon or Embraer Tucano basic and Dassault/Dornier Alphajet advanced trainers. Basic helicopter training is performed within the Army Aviation at Dax with Aerospatiale Gazelles and Ecureuils.
(3) Fighter pilots are trained to carrier operations in the US at NAS Meridian, flying BAE Systems/MDD (Boeing) T-45C Goshawk.

Embarked Squadrons

Base/Squadron No	*Aircraft*	*Task*
Lann Bihoué/4F	E-2C Hawkeye	AEW
Landivisiau/11F	Super Étendard	Assault, Recce
Landivisiau/12F	Rafale M	Air Defence
Landivisiau/17F	Super Étendard	Assault, Recce
Hyères/31F	Lynx	ASW
Lanvéoc-Poulmic/34F	Lynx	ASW
Hyères/36F	Panther	Surveillance

Support Squadrons

Base/Squadron No	*Aircraft*	*Task*
Hyères/CEPA/10S	Various	Research, trials
Lanvéoc-Poulmic/22S (detachments on ships)	Alouette III	Training, Support Atlantic Region
Lanvéoc-Poulmic/32F (detachment at Hyères)	Super Frelon,	Transport, SAR
Hyères/35F (detachments at various locations and ships)	Dauphin 2, Alouette III	Surveillance, SAR, Carrier-borne SAR
Landivisiau/57S	Falcon 10 MER	Support, Training

Maritime Patrol Squadrons

Base/Squadron No	*Aircraft*	*Task*
Nîmes-Garons/21F	Atlantique Mk 2	MP
Lann Bihoué/23F	Atlantique Mk 2	MP
Lann Bihoué/24F	Falcon 50M/Xingu	Surveillance, SAR
Faaa (Papeete)/25F (detachment at Tontouta, New Caledonia)	Gardian	Surveillance, SAR
Nîmes-Garons/28F	Nord 262E/Xingu	Surveillance, SAR, Flying School, liaison

Training Squadrons

Base/Squadron No	*Aircraft*	*Task*
Lanvéoc-Poulmic/EIP/50S	MS 880 Rallye/CAP 10	Initial Flying School, Recreational

Approximate Fleet Dispositions 1 May 2009

		Channel	*Atlantic*	*Mediterranean*	*Indian Ocean**	*Pacific*	*Antilles F. Guiana*
Carriers	FAN	–	1 (hel)	1	–	–	–
SSBN	FOST	–	3	–	–	–	–
SSN	FOST	–	–	6	–	–	–
DDG/DDH	FAN	–	6	5	–	–	–
FFG	FAN	–	5	10	2	2	1
MCMV (incl tenders)	FAN	1	14	5	–	–	–
Patrol Forces**	FAN/GM	5	4	2	5	4	4
LPD/LSD	FAN	–	–	4	–	–	–
LST/LCT	FAN	–	1	2	2	2	1
AOR	FAN	–	–	3	1	–	–

FAN = Force d'Action Navale (HQ at Toulon). All surface ships based at Toulon, Brest or overseas.
FOST = Force Océanique Stratégique (HQ at Brest). SSBNs based at l'Île Longue near Brest. All SSNs based at Toulon.
GM = Gendarmerie Maritime
*Plus one or two DDG/DDH/FFG regularly deployed from Toulon.
**Patrol forces include vessels manned by the Navy and major craft from the Gendarmerie Maritime

PENNANT LIST

Submarines

S 601	Rubis
S 602	Saphir
S 603	Casabianca
S 604	Émeraude
S 605	Améthyste
S 606	Perle
S 616	Le Triomphant
S 617	Le Téméraire
S 618	Le Vigilant
S 619	Le Terrible (bldg)

Aircraft and Helicopter Carriers

R 91	Charles de Gaulle
R 97	Jeanne d'Arc

Destroyers

D 610	Tourville
D 612	De Grasse
D 614	Cassard
D 615	Jean Bart
D 620	Forbin (bldg)
D 621	Chevalier Paul (bldg)
D 640	Georges Leygues
D 641	Dupleix
D 642	Montcalm
D 643	Jean de Vienne
D 644	Primauguet
D 645	La Motte-Picquet
D 646	Latouche-Tréville

Frigates

F 710	La Fayette
F 711	Surcouf
F 712	Courbet
F 713	Aconit
F 714	Guépratte
F 730	Floréal
F 731	Prairial
F 732	Nivôse
F 733	Ventôse
F 734	Vendémiaire
F 735	Germinal
F 789	Lieutenant de Vaisseau le Hénaff
F 790	Lieutenant de Vaisseau Lavallée
F 791	Commandant l'Herminier
F 792	Premier Maître l'Her
F 793	Commandant Blaison
F 794	Enseigne de Vaisseau Jacoubet
F 795	Commandant Ducuing
F 796	Commandant Birot
F 797	Commandant Bouan

Mine Warfare Forces

M 611	Vulcain
M 614	Styx
M 622	Pluton
M 641	Éridan
M 642	Cassiopée
M 643	Andromède
M 644	Pégase
M 645	Orion
M 646	Croix du Sud
M 647	Aigle
M 648	Lyre
M 649	Persée
M 650	Sagittaire
M 651	Verseau
M 652	Céphée
M 653	Capricorne
M 770	Antarès
M 771	Altaïr
M 772	Aldébaran

Patrol Forces

A 789	Melia (GM)
P 601	Elorn (GM)
P 602	Verdon (GM)
P 603	Adour (GM)
P 604	Scarpe (GM)
P 605	Vertonne (GM)
P 606	Dumbéa (GM)
P 607	Yser (GM)
P 608	Argens (GM)
P 609	Hérault (GM)
P 610	Gravona (GM)
P 611	Odet (GM)
P 612	Maury (GM)
P 613	Charente (GM)
P 614	Tech (GM)
P 615	Penfeld (GM)
P 616	Trieux (GM)
P 617	Vésubie (GM)
P 618	Escaut (GM)
P 619	Huveaune (GM)
P 620	Sèvre (GM)
P 621	Aber Wrach (GM)
P 622	Estéron (GM)
P 623	Mahury (GM)
P 624	Organabo (GM)
P 671	Glaive (GM)
P 675	Arago
P 676	Flamant
P 677	Cormoran
P 678	Pluvier
P 679	Grèbe
P 680	Sterne
P 681	Albatros
P 682	L'Audacieuse
P 683	La Boudeuse
P 684	La Capricieuse
P 685	La Fougueuse
P 686	La Glorieuse
P 687	La Gracieuse
P 688	La Moqueuse
P 689	La Railleuse
P 690	La Rieuse
P 691	La Tapageuse
P 720	Géranium (GM)
P 721	Jonquille (GM)
P 722	Violette (GM)
P 723	Jasmin (GM)
P 740	Fulmar (GM)
P 778	Réséda (GM)

GM = Gendarmerie Maritime

Amphibious Forces

L 9011	Foudre
L 9012	Siroco
L 9013	Mistral
L 9014	Tonnerre
L 9031	Francis Garnier
L 9032	Dumont D'Urville
L 9033	Jacques Cartier
L 9034	La Grandière
L 9051	Sabre
L 9052	Dague
L 9061	Rapière
L 9062	Hallebarde
L 9090	Gapeau

Major Auxiliaries Survey and Support Ships

A 601	Monge
A 607	Meuse
A 608	Var
A 613	Achéron
A 616	Le Malin
A 630	Marne
A 631	Somme
A 633	Taape
A 635	Revi
A 636	Maito
A 637	Maroa
A 638	Manini
A 649	L'Étoile
A 641	Esterel
A 642	Lubéron
A 645	Alizé
A 650	La Belle Poule
A 652	Mutin
A 653	La Grand Hermine
A 664	Malabar
A 669	Tenace
A 675	Fréhel
A 676	Saire
A 677	Armen
A 678	La Houssaye
A 679	Kéréon
A 680	Sicié
A 681	Taunoa
A 682	Rascas
A 693	Acharné
A 695	Bélier
A 696	Buffle
A 697	Bison
A 712	Athos
A 713	Aramis
A 748	Léopard
A 749	Panthère
A 750	Jaguar
A 751	Lynx
A 752	Guépard
A 753	Chacal
A 754	Tigre
A 755	Lion
A 758	Beautemps-Beaupré
A 759	Dupuy de Lôme
A 768	Élan
A 770	Glycine
A 771	Églantine
A 774	Chevreuil
A 775	Gazelle
A 785	Thétis
A 790	Coralline
A 791	Lapérouse
A 792	Borda
A 793	Laplace
Y 638	Lardier
Y 639	Giens
Y 640	Mengam
Y 641	Balaguier
Y 642	Taillat
Y 643	Nividic
Y 647	Le Four
Y 649	Port Cros
Y 692	Telenn Mor
Y 706	Chimère
Y 711	Farfadet
Y 758	Kermeur
Y 759	Kernaleguen
Y 770	Morse
Y 771	Otarie
Y 772	Loutre
Y 773	Phoque

SUBMARINES

Attack Submarines

Notes: (1) The Agosta class submarine *Ouessant* was re-introduced into service on 5 August 2005 following a refit. It is used as a training vessel by DCNS to support submarine sales to Malaysia.
(2) France signed an MoU with Norway and UK on 5 August 2003 for the procurement of the NATO Submarine Rescue System (NSRS). Based in UK, the system entered service in November 2008.

0 + 6 SUFFREN (BARRACUDA) CLASS (SSN)

Name	*No*	*Builders*	*Laid down*	*Launched*	*Commissioned*
SUFFREN	–	DCN, Cherbourg	Apr 2008	2015	2017
DUGAY TROUIN	–	DCN, Cherbourg	2010	2013	2019
DUPETIT THOUARS	–	DCN, Cherbourg	2012	2015	2021
DUQUESNE	–	DCN, Cherbourg	2014	2017	2023
TOURVILLE	–	DCN, Cherbourg	2016	2019	2025
DE GRASSE	–	DCN, Cherbourg	2018	2021	2027

Displacement, tons: 4,765 surfaced; 5,300 dived
Dimensions, feet (metres): 326.4 × 28.9 × 23.9 *(99.5 × 8.8 × 7.3)*
Main machinery: Nuclear; 1 PWR (derivative of K-15); 50 MW; turbo-electric; 2 motors; 1 shaft; pump jet propulsor
Speed, knots: 25 dived
Complement: 60 (12 officers)

Missiles: SLCM: Up to 12 MBDA Scalp-Naval land-attack missile launched in capsule from torpedo tubes; inertial cruise and tercom, electro-optic homing to 1,000 km *(540 n miles)* at 0.9 Mach; warhead 300 kg.
SSM: Aerospatiale SM 39 Exocet Block 2 Mod 2 launched from 21 in *(533 mm)* torpedo tubes; inertial cruise; active radar homing to 50 km *(27 n miles)* at 0.9 Mach; warhead 165 kg.
Torpedoes: 4—21 in *(533 mm)* bow tubes. Future heavyweight torpedo. Total of 24 torpedoes/missiles in mixed load.
Mines: Type FG 29. In lieu of torpedoes.
Countermeasures: ESM.
Combat data systems: SYCOBS, Link 22, Syracuse satcom, ELF comms.
Radars: Surface search: I-band.
Sonars: Thales UMS 3000 comprising bow sonar, wide aperture flank array and a reelable thin-line towed array.

Programmes: Studies for a new generation SSN (Project Barracuda) funded under the 1997–2002 budget. Programme launched on 14 October 1998 and development phase in November 2002. *Suffren* was ordered on 22 December 2006 and first steel was cut at Cherbourg on 19 December 2007. The contract includes a 6-year integrated support package. Subsequent boats are to be built at 24-month intervals.
Structure: Much of the technology emanates from the Le Triomphant design as well as new features developed for the Scorpene design. A high level of automation is planned to reduce complement to 60. Diving depth is over 350 m. A hybrid propulsion system uses electric propulsion at cruise speeds and turbo-mechanical propulsion for higher speeds. The boats are to have dry dock hangar capability. A SAGEM-SAFRAN optronic mast is to be installed instead of a periscope.
Operational: Sea trials for *Suffren* are scheduled for 2016 and entry into service in 2017. The submarines are to be available for 240 days per year and refits are planned at 10-year intervals. Diving depth 350 m.

SUFFREN CLASS (artist's impression) *11/2004, DCN* / 0590253

6 RUBIS AMÉTHYSTE CLASS (SSN/SNA)

Name	*No*	*Builders*	*Laid down*	*Launched*	*Commissioned*
RUBIS	S 601	Cherbourg Naval Dockyard	11 Dec 1976	7 July 1979	23 Feb 1983
SAPHIR	S 602	Cherbourg Naval Dockyard	1 Sep 1979	1 Sep 1981	6 July 1984
CASABIANCA	S 603	Cherbourg Naval Dockyard	19 Sep 1981	22 Dec 1984	21 Apr 1987
ÉMERAUDE	S 604	Cherbourg Naval Dockyard	4 Mar 1983	12 Apr 1986	15 Sep 1988
AMÉTHYSTE	S 605	Cherbourg Naval Dockyard	31 Oct 1984	14 May 1988	3 Mar 1992
PERLE	S 606	Cherbourg Naval Dockyard	27 Mar 1987	22 Sep 1990	7 July 1993

Displacement, tons: 2,410 surfaced; 2,670 dived
Dimensions, feet (metres): 241.5 × 24.9 × 21 *(73.6 × 7.6 × 6.4)*
Main machinery: Nuclear; turbo-electric; 1 PWR CAS 48; 48 MW; 2 turbo-alternators; 1 motor; 9,500 hp(m) *(7 MW)*; SEMT-Pielstick/Jeumont Schneider 8 PA4 V 185 SM diesel-electric auxiliary propulsion; 450 kW; 1 emergency motor; 1 pump jet propulsor
Speed, knots: 25
Complement: 68 (8 officers) (2 crews)

Missiles: SSM: Aerospatiale SM 39 Exocet; launched from 21 in *(533 mm)* torpedo tubes; inertial cruise; active radar homing to 50 km *(27 n miles)* at 0.9 Mach; warhead 165 kg.
Torpedoes: 4—21 in *(533 mm)* tubes. ECAN F17 Mod 2; wire-guided; active/passive homing to 20 km *(10.8 n miles)* at 40 kt; warhead 250 kg; depth 600 m *(1,970 ft)*. Total of 14 torpedoes and missiles carried in a mixed load.
Mines: Up to 32 FG 29 in lieu of torpedoes.
Countermeasures: ESM: Thomson-CSF ARUR 13/DR 3000U; intercept.
Combat data systems: TIT (Traitement des Informations Tactiques) data system (to be replaced by TITLAT); OPSMER command support system; Syracuse 2 SATCOM. Link 11 (receive only).
Weapons control: LAT (Lancement des Armes Tactiques) system (to be combined with TIT as TITLAT).
Radars: Navigation: 1 Thomson-CSF DRUA-33A; I-band; 1 Kelvin Hughes 1007; I-band.
Sonars: Thomson Sintra DMUX 20 multifunction; passive search; low frequency.
DSUV 62C; towed passive array; very low frequency.
DSUV 22 *(Saphir)*; listening suite.
DUUG 7A sonar intercept.

Programmes: The programme was terminated early by defence economies with the seventh of class *Turquoise* and eighth of class *Diamant* being cancelled.
Modernisation: Between 1989 and 1995 the first four of this class converted under operation Améthyste (AMÉlioration Tactique HYdrodynamique Silence Transmission Ecoute) to bring them to the same standard of ASW (included new sonars) efficiency as *Améthyste* and *Perle* rather than that required for the original anti-surface ship role. Two F17 torpedoes can be guided simultaneously against separate targets. *Saphir* recommissioned 1 July 1991, *Rubis* in February 1993; *Casabianca* in June 1994 and *Émeraude* in March 1996. A new radar added on a telescopic mast. A modernisation programme began in 2004. Upgrades include improvements to the tactical system (TITLAT programme) installation of a pump jet propulsor and a new ESM suite. The installation of new reactor cores in two boats, to extend life, is under consideration.
Structure: Diving depth, greater than 300 m *(984 ft)*. There has been a marked reduction in the size of the reactor compared with the L'Inflexible class. On completion of the modernisation programme, all six of the class are virtually identical.
Operational: All operational SSNs are assigned to Escadrille des Sous-Marins nucléaires d'attaque (ESNA) based at Toulon but frequently deploy to the Atlantic or overseas. Endurance rated at 45 days, limited by amount of food carried. *Rubis* had an underwater collision on 30 March 2007. Repairs at Brest were completed in July 2008. *Émeraude* had a bad steam leak on 30 March 1994 which caused casualties amongst the crew. *Saphir* undertook a refit/refuel in September 2000 following reactor problems. The submarine returned to service in late 2001. Modernisation refits completed for *Améthyste* (January 2006). *Saphir* was refitted 2006–07. Service life of all boats extended to 35 years. To be replaced by the Suffren class from 2017.

RUBIS *8/2008*, B Prézelin* / 1335766

AMÉTHYSTE *8/2008*, B Prézelin* / 1335765

CASABIANCA *2/2008*, B Prézelin* / 1335764

RUBIS

8/2008, B Prézelin* / 1353708

AMETHYST

11/2008, Maritime Photographic* / 1353707

CASABIANCA

9/2007, B Prézelin / 1305053

Strategic Missile Submarines

3 + 1 LE TRIOMPHANT CLASS (SSBN/SNLE-NG)

Name	*No*	*Builders*	*Laid down*	*Launched*	*Commissioned*
LE TRIOMPHANT	S 616	DCN, Cherbourg	9 June 1989	13 July 1993	21 Mar 1997
LE TÉMÉRAIRE	S 617	DCN, Cherbourg	18 Dec 1993	8 Aug 1997	23 Dec 1999
LE VIGILANT	S 618	DCN, Cherbourg	1997	12 Apr 2003	26 Nov 2004
LE TERRIBLE	S 619	DCN, Cherbourg	Nov 2002	21 Mar 2008	July 2010

Displacement, tons: 12,640 surfaced; 14,335 dived
Dimensions, feet (metres): 453 × 41; 55.8 (aft planes) × 41 *(138 × 12.5; 17 × 12.5)*
Main machinery: Nuclear; turbo-electric; 1 PWR Type K15 (enlarged CAS 48); 150 MW; 2 turbo-alternators; 1 motor; 41,500 hp(m) *(30.5 MW)*; diesel-electric auxiliary propulsion; 2 SEMT-Pielstick 8 PA4 V 200 SM diesels; 900 kW; 1 emergency motor; 1 shaft; pump jet propulsor
Speed, knots: 25 dived
Complement: 111 (15 officers) (2 crews)

Missiles: SLBM: 16 Aerospatiale M45/TN 75; 3-stage solid fuel rockets; inertial guidance to 6,000 km *(3,240 n miles)*; thermonuclear warhead with 6 MRV each of 100 kT. To be replaced by M51.1/TN 75 which has a planned range of 9,000 km *(4,860 n miles)* and 6 MRVs (to be fitted first in S 619 in 2010) and from 2015 by M51.2 (to be fitted first in S 618) with the new TNO (Tête Nucléaire Océanique) warhead.
SSM: Aerospatiale SM 39 Exocet; launched from 21 in *(533 mm)* torpedo tubes; inertial cruise; active radar homing to 50 km *(27 n miles)* at 0.9 Mach; warhead 165 kg.
Torpedoes: 4—21 in *(533 mm)* tubes. ECAN L5 Mod 3; dual purpose; active/passive homing to 9.5 km *(5.1 n miles)* at 35 kt; warhead 150 kg; depth to 550 m *(1,800 ft)*; total of 18 torpedoes and SSM carried in a mixed load.
Countermeasures: ESM: Thomson-CSF ARUR 13/DR 3000U; intercept.
Weapons control: SAD (Système d'Armes de Dissuasion) strategic data system (for SLBMs) SAD M5I will be fitted in S 619; SAT (Système d'Armes Tactique) tactical data system and DLA 4A weapon control system (for SSM and torpedoes). SYCOBS to be fitted in S 619.
Radars: Search: Dassault; I-band.
Sonars: Thomson Sintra DMUX 80 'multifunction' passive bow and flank arrays (S 616-618). Thales UMS 300 (S 619) comprising bow, flank and towed arrays. DUUX 5; passive ranging and intercept; low frequency.
DSUV 61 (S 616-618); towed array; very low frequency.

Programmes: *Le Triomphant* ordered 10 March 1986. *Le Téméraire* ordered 18 October 1989. *Le Vigilant* ordered 27 May 1993. *Le Terrible* ordered 28 July 2000. Class of six originally planned, but reduced to four after the end of the Cold War. Sous-marins Nucléaires Lanceurs d'Engins-Nouvelle Génération (SNLE-NG).
Modernisation: Development of the M5 missile discontinued in favour of the less expensive M51 which is planned to equip S 619 (M 51.1) in 2010 and the first three submarines between 2010 and 2015. *Le Vigilant* first to be fitted 2010–11. Three batches of M 51 missiles ordered by 2008. Warhead TN O on (M 51.2) is to replace TN 75 (on M 51.1) by 2015.
Structure: Built of HLES 100 steel capable of withstanding pressures of more than 100 kg/mm². Diving depth 500 m *(1,640 ft)*. Height from keel to top of fin is 21.3 m *(69.9 ft)*. Plans to lengthen the hull in later ships of the class have been shelved.
Operational: First sea cruise of *Le Triomphant* 16 July to 22 August 1995. First submerged M45 launch on 14 February 1995, second on 19 September 1996. *Le Triomphant* completed 30 month refit in April 2005 and conducted test launch of M45 missile on 2 February 2005. *Le Triomphant* is to undergo her second refit, including conversion to fire the M 51 missile, in 2012. *Le Téméraire* official trials started April 1998, first submerged M 45 launch 4 May 1999. *Le Téméraire* completed 22-month refit in October 2007. *Le Vigilant* is to be refitted, including M 51 conversion, in 2010 following the commissioning of *Le Terrible*. The first underwater test launch of the M 51.1 missile is to be conducted from *Le Terrible* in 2009, following ten land-based tests the first of which was made on 9 November 2006. An underwater launch from a submerged caisson was conducted on 13 November 2008. All submarines based at Ile Longue, Brest.

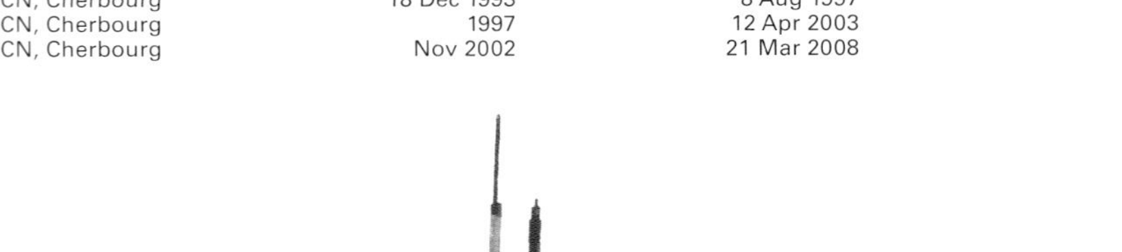

LE VIGILANT *7/2008*, B Prézelin* / 1335768

LE TRIOMPHANT *5/2008*, B Prézelin* / 1335767

LE TÉMÉRAIRE *6/2002, French Navy* / 0529140

AIRCRAFT CARRIERS

0 + (1) FUTURE AIRCRAFT CARRIER CLASS (CV)

Name	*No*	*Builders*	*Laid down*	*Launched*	*Commissioned*
–	–	Aker Shipyards, St Nazaire	2013	2015	2018

Displacement, tons: 70,000 full load
Dimensions, feet (metres): 928.5 × 127.9 × 37.7 *(283.0 × 39.0 × 11.5)*
Flight deck, feet (metres): 928.5 × 255.9 *(283.0 × 78.0)*
Main machinery: Integrated Full Electric Propulsion; 2 Rolls Royce MT 30 gas turbine alternators; 4 electric motors
Speed, knots: 26
Range, n miles: 10,000 at 25 kt
Complement: 900 approx plus 620 aircrew plus further 100

Missiles: SAM: ASTER 15.
Guns: To be announced.
Countermeasures: To be announced.
Combat data systems: Link 11, Link 16, Link 22 and JSAT datalinks; Syracuse 3 SATCOM.
Electro-optic systems: To be announced.
Radars: Air search: To be announced.
Surface search: To be announced.
Navigation: To be announced.
Fire control: To be announced.
Tacan: To be announced.

Fixed-wing aircraft: Up to 40. A typical mix might include 32 Rafale M, three E-2C Hawkeye and 5 NH-90 helicopters.
Helicopters: Up to five NH 90.

Programmes: A second aircraft carrier (PA2) was planned under the 2003–08 Defence Programming Law but, according to the 2009–14 Defence Programming Law, a decision to proceed with construction is not expected until 2011–2012. It was announced on 13 February 2004 that the ship was to be built in co-operation with the UK carrier programme and DCN and Thales established a joint venture company, MO PA2 to manage the project at industry level. Studies in 2005 concluded that the British CVF design could be adapted and a contract for a preliminary definition study, based on CVF, was awarded to MO PA2 on 12 December 2005. Chantiers de l'Atlantique and EADS also took part in the work. Formal agreement to share design costs reached between French and UK governments on 24 January 2006 and an MoU was signed on 6 March 2006. The construction timetable is speculative.
Structure: The CVF-FR, has been adapted from the UK CVF design. The main differences between UK CVF and CVF-FR are the requirement to install two 90 m C-13 steam catapults and a four-wire arrester system, the installation of national combat and data and weapons systems and facilities for the storage of nuclear weapons. A potential requirement to incorporate nuclear propulsion is also being studied.

PA 2 *8/2006, MO-PA2* / 1167147

PA 2 *8/2006, MO-PA2* / 1167148

PA 2 *8/2006, MO-PA2* / 1167146

1 CHARLES DE GAULLE CLASS (CVNM/PAN)

Name	*No*	*Builders*	*Laid down*	*Launched*	*Commissioned*
CHARLES DE GAULLE	R 91	DCN, Brest	14 Apr 1989	7 May 1994	18 May 2001

Displacement, tons: 37,085 standard; 42,500 full load
Dimensions, feet (metres): 857.7 oa; 780.8 wl × 211.3 oa; 103.3 wl × 30.9 *(261.5; 238 × 64.4; 31.5 × 9.4)*
Flight deck, feet (metres): 857.7 × 211.3 *(261.5 × 64.4)*
Main machinery: Nuclear; 2 PWR Type K15; 300 MW; 2 GEC Alsthom turbines; 83,000 hp(m) *(61 MW)* sustained; 2 shafts
Speed, knots: 27
Complement: 1,256 ship's company (94 officers) plus 610 aircrew plus 42 flag staff (accommodation for 1,950) (plus temporary 800 marines)

Missiles: SAM: EUROSAAM SAAM/F system with 4 (2 port, 2 starboard) DCN Sylver A43 octuple VLS launchers ❶; MBDA ASTER 15; inertial guidance and mid-course update; active radar homing at 3 Mach to 30 km *(16.2 n miles)*; warhead 13 kg. 32 weapons.
2 Matra Sadral PDMS sextuple launchers ❷; Mistral; IR homing to 4 km *(2.2 n miles)*; warhead 3 kg; anti-sea-skimmer; able to engage targets down to 10 ft above sea level.
Guns: 4 Giat 20F2 20 mm; 720 rds/min to 8 km *(4.3 n miles)*; weight of shell: 0.25 kg.
Countermeasures: Decoys: 4 CSEE Sagaie AMBL-2A 10-barrelled trainable launchers ❸; medium range; chaff to 8 km *(4.3 n miles)*; IR flares to 3 km *(1.6 n miles)*. Dassault LAD offboard decoys. SLAT torpedo decoys from 2006.
ESM: Thomson-CSF ARBR 21; intercept. 1 DIBV 2A Vampir MB; (IRST) ❹.
ECM: 2 ARBB 33B ❺; jammers.
Combat data systems: SENIT 8; Links 11, 14 and 16. Syracuse 3 and FLEETSATCOM ❻. AIDCOMER and MCCIS command support systems.
Electro-optic systems: 2 DIBC 2A (Sagem VIGY-105) optronic directors.
Radars: Air search: Thomson-CSF DRBJ 11B ❼; 3D; E/F-band; range 366 km *(200 n miles)* for aircraft.
Thales DRBV 26D Jupiter ❽; D-band; range 183 km *(100 n miles)* for 2 m² target.
Air/surface search: Thomson-CSF DRBV 15C Sea Tiger Mk 2 ❾; E/F-band; range 110 km *(60 n miles)* for 2 m² target.
Navigation: 2 Racal 1229 (DRBN 34A) ❿; I-band.
Fire control: Thomson-CSF Arabel 3D ⓫; I/J-band (for SAAM); range 70 km *(38 n miles)* for 2 m² target.
Tacan: NRBP 20A ⓬.
Sonars: SLAT torpedo attack warning.

Fixed-wing aircraft: 20 Super Étendard, 2 E-2C Hawkeye. 12 Rafale F2 and F3.
Helicopters: 2 AS 565 Panther or 2 AS 322 Cougar (AF) or 2 Super Frelon plus 2 Dauphin SAR.

Programmes: On 23 September 1980 the Defence Council decided to build two nuclear-propelled carriers to replace *Clemenceau* in 1996 and *Foch* some years later. First of class ordered 4 February 1986, first metal cut 24 November 1987. Hull floated for technical trials on 19 December 1992, and back in dock on 8 January 1993. A 19.8 m *(65 ft)* long one-twelfth scale model was used for hydrodynamic trials. Building programme delayed three years due to defence budget cuts.
Modernisation: From October 1999 to March 2000 modifications included additional radiation shielding, and lengthening of angled flight deck by 4.4 m. A 43 launchers to be replaced by A 50 (for ASTER 15 and ASTER 30) in due course. During her IPER 2007–08, she was fitted with new propellers, Syracuse 3 Satcom, and modifications to operate Rafale F2 and F3. The next IPER is planned 2016–17.

CHARLES DE GAULLE *6/2005, Per Körnefeldt* / 1153174

CHARLES DE GAULLE *6/2005, B Sullivan* / 1153155

Structure: Two lifts 62.3 × 41 ft *(19 × 12.5 m)* of 36 tons capacity. Hangar for 20-25 aircraft; dimensions 454.4 × 96.5 × 20 ft *(138.5 × 29.4 × 6.1 m)*. Angled deck 8.5° and 655.7 ft *(200 m)* overall length. Catapults: 2 USN Type C13-3; length 246 ft *(75 m)* for Super Étendards and up to 23 tonne aircraft. Enhanced weight capability of flight deck to allow operation of AEW aircraft. Island placed well forward so that both lifts can be protected from the weather. CSEE Dallas (Deck Approach and Landing Laser System) fitted, later to be replaced by MLS system. Active fin stabilisers. Bunkerage of 3,000 cum of avgas and 1,500 cum dieso.

Operational: Seven years continuous steaming at 25 kt available before refuelling (same reactors as *Le Triomphant*). Both reactors self-sustaining by 10 June 1998. Sea trials started 26 January 1999 and continued until 9 November 2000 when a large section of the port propeller was lost while steaming at high speed. Trials resumed on 26 March 2001 with spare propellers from decommissioned *Clemenceau*. A 15-month refuel/refit (IPER) at Toulon was completed in November 2008. Based at Toulon.

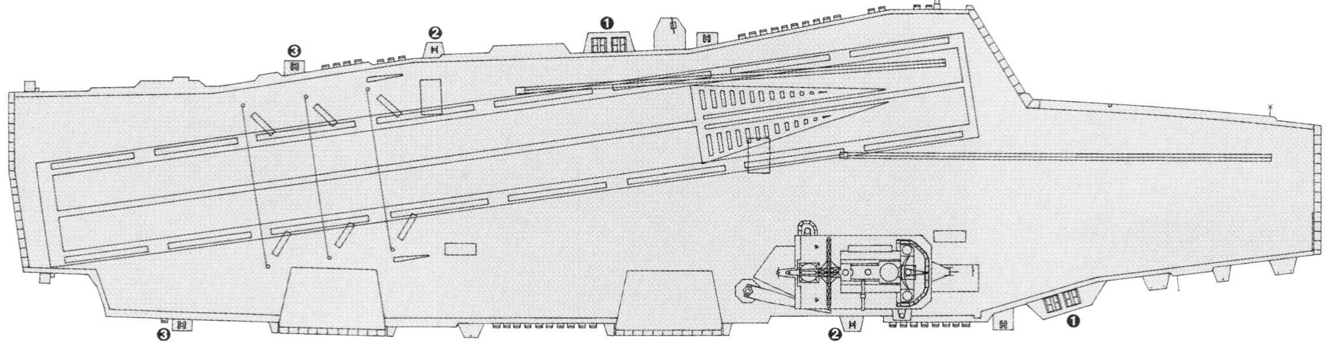

CHARLES DE GAULLE *(Scale 1 : 1,500), Ian Sturton* / 0104438

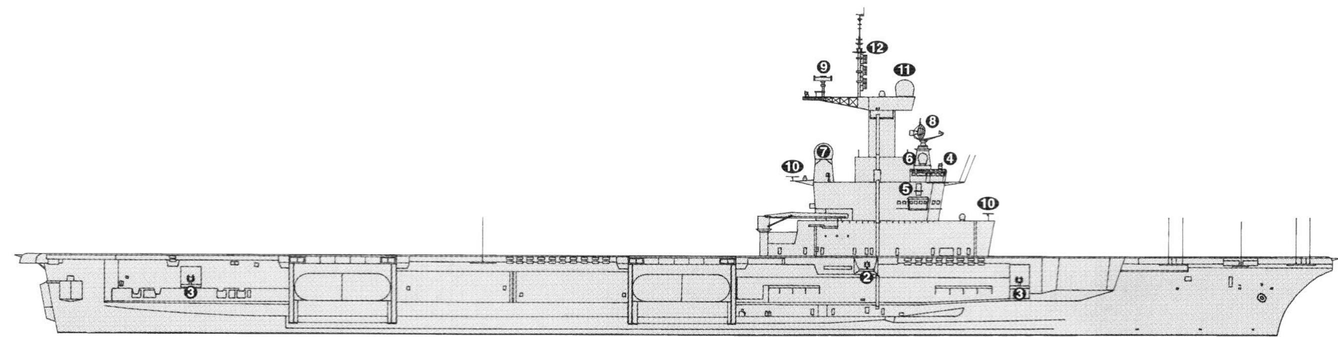

CHARLES DE GAULLE *(Scale 1 : 1,500), Ian Sturton* / 0069903

CHARLES DE GAULLE

3/2006 / 1167143

CHARLES DE GAULLE

4/2006, Guy Toremans / 1167142

CHARLES DE GAULLE

10/2006, H M Steele / 1040771

HELICOPTER CARRIERS

1 JEANNE D'ARC CLASS (CVHG)

Name	*No*	*Builders*	*Laid down*	*Launched*	*Commissioned*
JEANNE D'ARC (ex-*La Résolue*)	R 97	Brest Naval Dockyard	7 July 1960	30 Sep 1961	16 July 1964

Displacement, tons: 10,575 standard; 13,270 full load
Dimensions, feet (metres): 597.1 × 78.7 hull × 24.6 *(182 × 24 × 7.5)*
Flight deck, feet (metres): 203.4 × 68.9 *(62 × 21)*
Main machinery: 4 boilers; 640 psi *(45 kg/cm²)*; 840°F *(450°C)*; 2 Rateau-Bretagne turbines; 40,000 hp(m) *(29.4 MW)*; 2 shafts
Speed, knots: 26.5
Range, n miles: 6,500 at 16 kt
Complement: 506 (33 officers) plus 13 instructors and 150 cadets

Missiles: SSM: 6 Aerospatiale MM 38 Exocet (2 triple) ❶; inertial cruise; active radar homing to 42 km *(23 n miles)* at 0.9 Mach; warhead 165 kg; sea-skimmer.
Guns: 2 DCN 3.9 in *(100 mm)*/55 Mod 53 CADAM automatic ❷; 60 rds/min to 17 km *(9 n miles)* anti-surface; 8 km *(4.4 n miles)* anti-aircraft; weight of shell 13.5 kg. 4—12.7 mm MGs.
Countermeasures: Decoys: 2 CSEE/VSEL Syllex 8-barrelled trainable launchers for chaff (may not be fitted). 1 AN/SQL-25A Nixie torpedo decoy.
ESM: Thomson-CSF ARBR 16/ARBX 10; intercept.
Combat data systems: ACOM/OPSMER command support system; Link 11 (receive only). SATCOM. INMARSAT.
Weapons control: 2 CT Analogical; 2 Sagem DMAa optical sights. SATCOM ❸.
Radars: Air search: Thomson-CSF DRBV 22D ❹; D-band; range 366 km *(200 n miles)*.
Air/surface search: DRBV 51 ❺; G-band.
Navigation: 2 DRBN 34A (Racal-Decca); I-band.
Fire control: 2 (+1 unused) Thomson-CSF DRBC 32A; I-band.
Tacan: SRN-6.
Sonars: Thomson Sintra DUBV 24C; hull-mounted; active search; medium frequency; 5 kHz.

Helicopters: 2 Pumas and 2 Gazelles from the Army and 3 Navy Alouette III for annual training cruises. Up to 8 Super Frelon or 10 mixed heavy/light aircraft in war time.

Modernisation: Refits during 1989–90 extended ship life by about 20 years. SENIT 2 combat data system was to have been fitted but this was cancelled as a cost-saving measure. Extensive propulsion machinery repairs were conducted 1997–98. Two 100 mm guns were removed from quarterdeck in 2000. A life-extension refit was undertaken in 2006. A new SATCOM radome was installed in a radome aft of the funnel.
Structure: Flight deck lift has a capacity of 12 tons. Some of the hangar space is used to accommodate officers under training. The ship is almost entirely air conditioned. Carries two LCVPs. Topmast can be removed for passing under bridges or other obstructions.
Operational: Based at Brest and used for training officer cadets. After rapid modification, she could be used as a commando ship, helicopter carrier or troop transport with commando equipment and a battalion of 700 men. Flagship of the Training Squadron for an Autumn/Spring cruise with Summer refit. Army helicopters Super Puma/Cougar and Gazelle are embarked during training cruises. Service life has been extended to at least 2010. She is not likely to be replaced in her training role by a new or chartered ship and, in future, a training squadron, based on an LHD/BPC, may occasionally be constituted.

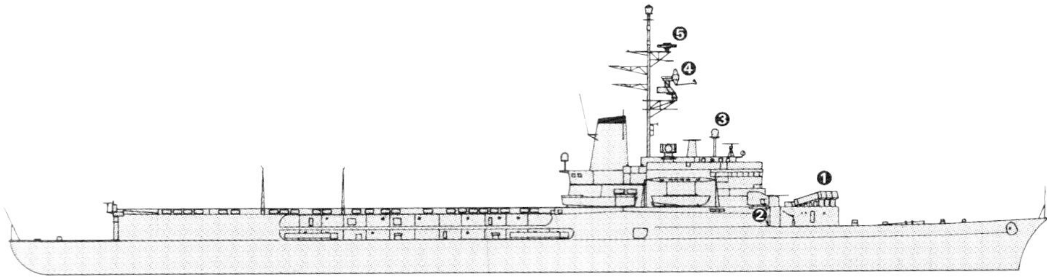

JEANNE D'ARC *(Scale 1 : 1,500), Ian Sturton* / 1167436

JEANNE D'ARC *11/2007, B Prézelin* / 1305055

JEANNE D'ARC *5/2008*, Camil Busquets i Vilanova* / 1335776

DESTROYERS

1 + 1 FORBIN (HORIZON) CLASS (DDGHM)

Name	*No*	*Builders*	*Laid down*	*Launched*	*Commissioned*
FORBIN	D 620	DCN, Lorient	16 Jan 2004	10 Mar 2005	June 2009
CHEVALIER PAUL	D 621	DCN, Lorient	13 Jan 2005	12 July 2006	Dec 2009

Displacement, tons: 5,700 standard; 7,050 full load
Dimensions, feet (metres): 501.6 oa; 464.9 wl × 66.6 × 26.2 *(152.9; 141.7 × 20.3 × 8.0)*
Main machinery: CODOG: 2 Fiat/GE LM 2500 gas turbines; 63,030 hp *(47 MW)*; 2 SEMT-Pielstick 12PA 6STC; 11,700 hp(m) *(9.4MW)*; 2 shafts; cp props; bow thruster (550 kW)
Speed, knots: 31 (18 on diesels)
Range, n miles: 7,000 at 18 kt
Complement: 195 (27 officers)

Missiles: SSM: 8 MBDA Exocet MM 40 Block 3 ❶; inertial cruise; active radar homing to 180 km *(97 n miles)* at 0.9 Mach; warhead 165 kg; sea-skimmer.
SAM: EUROPAAMS PAAMS with DCN Sylver A50 VLS ❷ for Aerospatiale Matra Aster 15 (16 missiles) and Aster 30 (32 missiles); 48 cells (six octuple launcher modules); inertial guidance, mid-course update and active homing; range (Aster 15) 30 km *(16.2 n miles)* at 3 Mach; (Aster 30) 100 km *(54 n miles)* at 4.5 Mach.
1 MBDA Tetral quadruple launcher (fitted for but not with) ❸ for Mistral SR SAMs; IR homing to 6 km; warhead 3 kg; anti-sea-skimmer; able to engage targets down to 10 ft above sea level.
Guns: 2 OTO Melara 76 mm/62 Super Rapid ❹; 120 rds/min to 16 km *(8.7 n miles)*; weight of shell 6 kg. 2 Giat 20F2 20 mm ❺; 720 rds/min to 2 km.
Torpedoes: 2 EUROTORP TLS 324 mm fixed launchers ❻. Up to 24 Eurotorp Mu 90 Impact torpedoes; active/passive homing to 25 km *(13.5 n miles)* at 29 kt or 12 km *(6.5 n miles)* at 50 kt; warhead 32 kg.
Countermeasures: SIGEN EW suite comprising 2 EADS NGDS multifunction decoy launchers ❼, radar warning equipment, a high-power jammer ❽ and an ESM/ECM support aid. SLAT torpedo defence system.
Combat data systems: EUROSYSNAV; 2 Link 11 (Link 22 in the future) and Link 16; OPSMER or SIC 21 follow-on command support system; Syracuse 3 SATCOM ❾.
Electro-optic systems: Sagem Vampir optronic director ❿.
Radars: Air/surface search: Thales/Marconi DRBV 27 (S 1850M) Astral ⓫; D-band.
Surveillance/fire control: Alenia Marconi EMPAR ⓬; G-band; multifunction.
Surface search: 2 SPN 753 ⓭; I-band.
Fire control: Alenia Marconi NA 25 ⓮; J-band.
Sonars: Thales TUS-WASS 4110CL; hull-mounted; active search and attack; medium frequency.

Helicopters: 1 NHI NH90 ⓯.

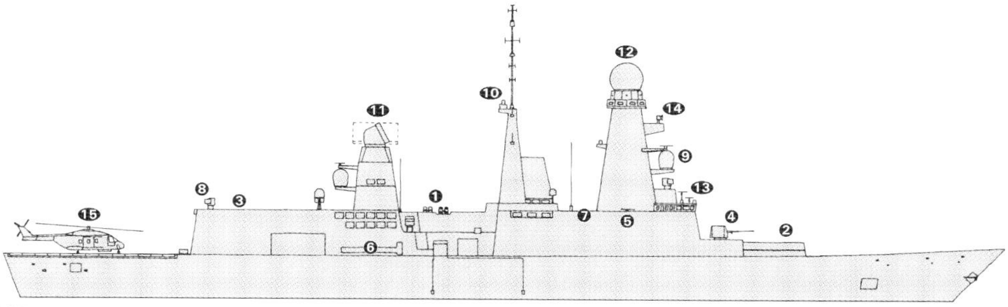

FORBIN *(Scale 1 : 1,200), Ian Sturton* / 1167437

FORBIN *6/2007, B Prézelin* / 1305052

Programmes: Classified as 'Frégates de défense aérienne' (FDA). Initially a three-nation project with Italy and UK. Joint project office established in 1993. After UK withdrew in April 1999, an agreement was signed on 7 September 1999 between France and Italy to continue. Following a French/Italian MoU on 22 September 2000 to build four destroyers, the French government ordered two ships to be built by DCN Lorient and delivered in December 2006 and April 2008. They are planned to replace *Suffren* and *Duquesne*. Plans to build a second pair of ships, to replace *Cassard* and *Jean Bart*, have been shelved in favour of two AAW variants of the FREMM design.
Structure: Details given are subject to change. Space available for two additional missile launcher modules, possibly with Sylver A70 VLS.
Operational: Sea trials for *Forbin* started in July 2006 and for *Chevalier Paul* on 15 October 2007. Commissioning has been delayed by integration of the combat management system and PAAMS. Both based at Toulon.

CHEVALIER PAUL *6/2008*, B Prézelin* / 1335763

FORBIN *6/2008*, Cor Van Nierkerken* / 1335775

2 CASSARD CLASS (TYPE F 70 (A/A)) (DDGHM)

Name	*No*	*Builders*	*Laid down*	*Launched*	*Commissioned*
CASSARD	D 614	Lorient Naval Dockyard	3 Sep 1982	6 Feb 1985	28 July 1988
JEAN BART	D 615	Lorient Naval Dockyard	12 Mar 1986	19 Mar 1988	21 Sep 1991

Displacement, tons: 4,230 standard; 5,000 full load
Dimensions, feet (metres): 455.9 × 45.9 × 21.3 (sonar) *(139 × 14.0 × 6.5)*
Main machinery: 4 SEMT-Pielstick 18 PA6 V 280 BTC diesels; 43,200 hp(m) *(31.75 MW)* sustained; 2 shafts
Speed, knots: 29.5
Range, n miles: 8,000 at 17 kt.
Complement: 250 (25 officers) accommodation for 253

Missiles: SSM: 8 (4 carried in peacetime) Aerospatiale MM 40 Exocet Block 2 ❶; inertial cruise; active radar homing to 70 km *(40 n miles)* at 0.9 Mach; warhead 165 kg; sea-skimmer.
SAM: 40 GDC Pomona Standard SM-1MR Block VI; semi-active radar homing to 38 km *(20.5 n miles)* at 2 Mach; height envelope 45-18,288 m *(150-60,000 ft)*. Mk 13 Mod 5 launchers ❷ taken from T 47 (DDG) ships.
2 Matra Sadral PDMS sextuple launchers ❸; 39 Mistral; IR homing to 4 km *(2.2 n miles)*; warhead 3 kg; anti-sea-skimmer; able to engage targets down to 10 ft above sea level.
Guns: 1 DCN/Creusot-Loire 3.9 in *(100 mm)*/55 Mod 68 CADAM automatic ❹; 78 rds/min to 17 km *(9 n miles)* anti-surface; 8 km *(4.4 n miles)* anti-aircraft; weight of shell 13.5 kg.
2 Giat 20F2 20 mm ❺; 720 rds/min to 2 km *(1.1 n miles)*.
4—12.7 mm MGs.
Torpedoes: 2 fixed launchers model KD 59E ❻. 10 ECAN L5 Mod 4; anti-submarine; active/passive homing to 9.5 km *(5.1 n miles)* at 35 kt; warhead 150 kg; depth to 550 m *(1,800 ft)*.
Countermeasures: Decoys: 2 CSEE AMBL 1B Dagaie ❼ and 2 AMBL 2A (D 614) or 2B (D 615) Sagaie 10-barrelled trainable launchers ❽; fires a combination of chaff and IR flares. Dassault LAD offboard decoys.
ESM: Thomson-CSF ARBR 17B (DR 4000) ❾; radar intercept. DIBV 1A Vampir ❿; IR detector (integrated with search radar for active/passive tracking in all weathers). ARBG-1A (Saigon) comms intercept at masthead.

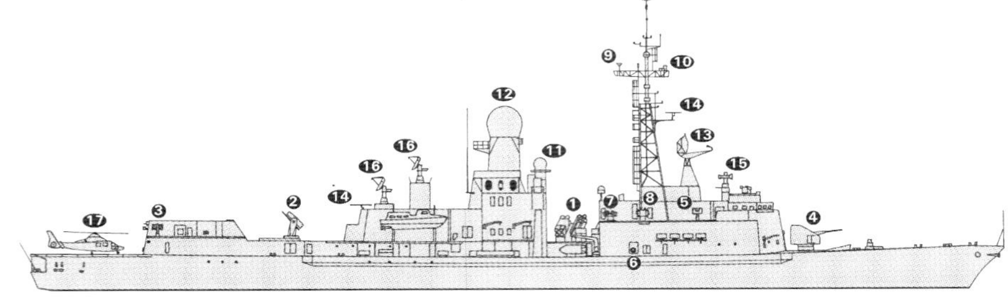
CASSARD *(Scale 1 : 1,200), Ian Sturton* / 0569909

ECM: 2 Dassault Electronique ARBB 33; jammers; H-, I- and J-bands.
Torpedo defence: SLQ-25A Nixie.
Combat data systems: SENIT 6/8; Links 11, 14 and 16. Syracuse 2 SATCOM ⓫. OPSMER command support system.
Electro-optic systems: DCN CTMS optronic/radar system with DIBC 1A Piranha II IR/TV tracker; CSEE Najir optronic secondary director.
Radars: Air search: Thomson-CSF DRBJ 11B ⓬; 3D; E/F-band; range 366 km *(200 n miles)*.
Air/surface search: Thomson-CSF DRBV 26C ⓭; D-band.
Navigation: 2 Racal DRBN 34A; I-band (1 for close-range helicopter control ⓮).
Fire control: Thomson-CSF DRBC 33A ⓯; I-band (for guns). 2 Raytheon SPG-51C ⓰; G/I-band (for missiles).
Sonars: Thomson Sintra DUBA 25A (13 kHz) (D 614); DUBA 24C (5 kHz) (D 615); hull-mounted; active search and attack; medium frequency.

Helicopters: 1 AS 565SA Panther ⓱.

Programmes: The building programme was considerably slowed down by finance problems and doubts about the increasingly obsolescent Standard SM 1 missile system and was curtailed at two units. Re-rated F 70 (ex-C 70) on 6 June 1988, officially 'frégates anti-aériennes (FAA)'.
Modernisation: DRBJ 15 radar initially fitted in *Cassard* but this was replaced in 1992 by DRBJ 11. Panther has replaced Lynx helicopter. *Cassard* refitted 2000–2001. Upgrade included hull strengthening, fitting of new propellers and SENIT 68 combat direction system (SENIT 6 core augmented by SENIT 8 data-link processing component (for Link 16 and data forwarding). *Jean Bart* similarly refitted October 2002 to September 2003. Plans to fit ASTER 30 have been abandoned.
Structure: Samahe 210 helicopter handling system.
Operational: Helicopter used for third party targeting for the SSM. Both ships are based at Toulon. Service lives: *Cassard*, 2018; *Jean Bart*, 2021. To be replaced by FREDA (AAW variants of FREMM) rather than by a second batch of Forbin class.

CASSARD *1/2007, B Prézelin* / 1305056

CASSARD *2/2008*, B Prézelin* / 1335761

4 GEORGES LEYGUES CLASS (TYPE F 70 (ASW)) (DDGHM)

Name	No	Builders	Laid down	Launched	Commissioned
GEORGES LEYGUES	D 640	Brest Naval Dockyard	16 Sep 1974	17 Dec 1976	10 Dec 1979
DUPLEIX	D 641	Brest Naval Dockyard	17 Oct 1975	2 Dec 1978	13 June 1981
MONTCALM	D 642	Brest Naval Dockyard	5 Dec 1975	31 May 1980	28 May 1982
JEAN DE VIENNE	D 643	Brest Naval Dockyard	26 Oct 1979	17 Nov 1981	25 May 1984

Displacement, tons: 3,880 standard; 4,830 full load
Dimensions, feet (metres): 455.9 × 45.9 × 19.35 *(139 × 14 × 5.9)*
Main machinery: CODOG; 2 RR Olympus TM3B gas turbines; 52,000 hp *(38.2 MW)* sustained; 2 SEMT-Pielstick 16 PA6 V280 diesels; 11,200 hp(m) *(8.3 MW)* sustained; 2 shafts; LIPS cp props
Speed, knots: 30; 20 on diesels
Range, n miles: 8,000 at 15 kt on diesels; 2,500 at 28 kt
Complement: 235 (22 officers) (D 641-643); 183 (18 officers) plus 36 cadets (D 640)

Missiles: SSM: 4 MBDA Exocet MM 38 (D 640 and D 641) or 8 Exocet MM 40 (D 642 and D 643) ❶; inertial cruise; active radar homing to 42 km *(23 n miles)* (MM 38) or 70 km *(40 n miles)* (MM 40) at 0.9 Mach; warhead 165 kg; sea-skimmer. 4 additional Exocet MM 40 missiles can be carried as a warload (D 642 and D 643).
SAM: Thomson-CSF Crotale Naval EDIR octuple launcher ❷; command line of sight guidance; radar/IR homing to 13 km *(7 n miles)* at 2.4 Mach; warhead 14 kg; 26 missiles.
2 Matra Sadral sextuple launchers (D 641-643) or 2 MBDA Simbad twin launchers (D 640) for Mistral SR SAMs; IR homing to 6 km *(3.2 n miles)*; warhead 3 kg.
Guns: 1 DCN/Creusot-Loire 3.9 in *(100 mm)*/55 Mod 68 CADAM automatic ❸; dual purpose; 78 rds/min to 17 km *(9 n miles)* anti-surface; 8 km *(4.4 n miles)* anti-aircraft; weight of shell 13.5 kg.
2 Breda/Mauser 30 mm (D 641-643) ❹. 800 rds/min to 3 km; weight of shell 0.37 kg.
2 (D 641-643) or 4 (D 640) M2HB 12.7 mm MGs.
Torpedoes: 2 DCN KD-59E fixed tubes for 533 mm *(21 in)* DCN L5 Mod 4 torpedoes; active/passive homing to 7 km *(3.8 n miles)*; 8 to 10 torpedoes.
Honeywell Mk 46 mod 2 or EuroTorp MU 90 Impact lightweight torpedoes for helicopters (D 641-643).
Countermeasures: Decoys: CSEE/VSEL Syllex (D 640); two 8-barrel trainable launchers. EADS AMBL-1C (Dagaie Mk 2) (D 641-643) ❺; 2 10-barrel trainable launchers; chaff and IR flares. 4 AMBL-3A (Replica) (D 641-643); offboard decoys.
ESM: Thomson-CSF ARBR-10X and ARBR-16B (DR 2000) or (D 643) ARBR-17 (DR 4000) ❻ radar intercept; Sagem DIBV-2A (Vampir MB) IRST (D 641-643).
ECM: Dassault Electronique ARBB-32B (D 640) or Thales ARBB-36A (D 641-643) jammer.
Torpedo defence: AN/SLQ-25A Nixie (2 towed decoys); Prairie-Masker noise suppression system.
Combat data systems: DCN SENIT 4 CDS and (D 641-643) STIDAV/SENIT 8-01 added for anti-air/anti-missile defence; Link 11. ACOM/Opsmer command support system. Syracuse ❼ and Inmarsat satcomms.

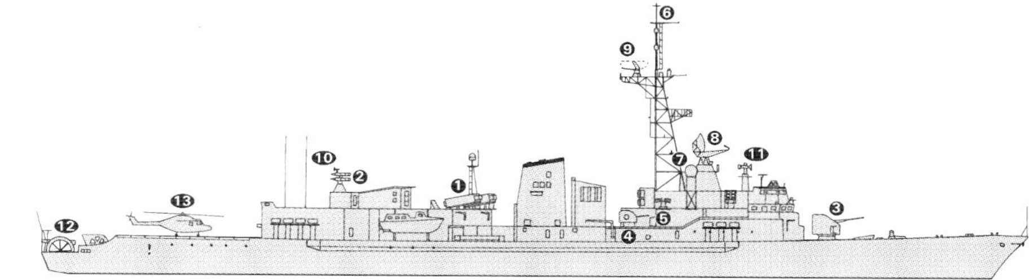

DUPLEIX *(Scale 1 : 1,200), Ian Sturton* / 0581795

Electro-optic systems: Thomson-CSF CTH (Vega) radar/optronic FCS and CSEE DM-Ab (Panda) optical director for 100 mm guns; 2 Sagem DIBC-2A (VIGY 105) optronic FCSs for 30 mm guns (D 641-643).
Radars: Air search: Thomson-CSF DRBV 26A (Jupiter) ❽; D-band.
Air/surface search: Thomson-CSF DRBV-51C (D 640); G-band; Thales DRBV-15A or -15B (Sea Tiger) ❾ (D 641-643); E/F-band.
Navigation: 1 DRBN-34A (RM 1290) (D 641) or Kelvin Hughes DRBN 37 (KH 1007 Nucleus) (D 640, D 642, D 643); I-band; one for helo control.
Fire control: Thomson-CSF Castor 2J ❿ for Crotale Naval SAM; J-band.
Thomson-CSF DRBC-32E ⓫ (Castor 2B) for gun FCS; I-band.
Sonars: Thomson-Sintra DUBV-23D (D 641) bow mounted; active search and attack; 5 kHz.
1 UMS 4110 CL (D 640, D 642, D 643).
Thomson-Sintra DUBV-43B (D 640-642) or -43C (D 643) VDS ⓬; active search and attack; 5 kHz; paired with DUBV-23D; tows at up to 24 kt down to 300 m *(985 ft)* for DUBV-43B or 700 m *(2,300 ft)* for -43C.
TUS DSBV-62C (D 641) (Lamproie) passive linear towed array with URDT-1A torpedo warning equipment (D 641-643); very low frequency.

Helicopters: 2 Westland WG 13 Lynx Mk 4 (FN) ⓭ (D 641-643; one normally carried in peacetime); 1 Aerospatiale Alouette III (D 640).

Programmes: Design of a new ASW escort vessel approved in December 1971 under the designation of 'Corvette anti-sous-marine type 1970 (C 70)'. Re-rated 'Frégate anti-sous-marinetype1970(FASM70orF70)' on6June1988. First four ships on the 1970–75 Defence Programming Law. To be replaced by FREMM/ASM 2012–13.
Modernisation: Ships of this class, except *Georges Leygues*, have received regular upgrades. Most important was the Opération programmée amélioration autodéfense antimissiles (OP3A, air defence upgrade programme) completed in March 1996 for *Jean de Vienne*, April 1999 for *Dupleix* and April 2000 for *Montcalm*; large command structure fitted above the bridge, SENIT 8-01 CDS package added to current CDS to command and control air-defence weapons and systems, 2 MBDA Sadral SAM launchers and 2 OTO Melara/Mauser 30 mm gun mounts (controlled by Sagem VIGY 105 optronic directors) added; new ESM suite, new ECM equipment and Replica offboard decoys. Plans to fit MBDA Milas ASW missiles have been shelved. Due to her new role (see below), *Georges Leygues* has had only limited upgrades and will not be modernised further. All four ships modified (or being modified) to receive female crew.
Structure: Hull and main deck have been strengthened to cope with fatigue problems; to restore seaworthiness, 235 tonnes of ballast have been embarked and two fuel tanks turned into water-ballasts; completed 2002–03 on all four ships. DCN SPHEX helicopter handling system.
Operational: From June 1999 *Georges Leygues* has been assigned to a training role as a tender to *Jeanne d'Arc*; accommodation for 36 cadets and classrooms (partially in the helicopter hangar); based at Brest. Exocet not routinely carried by *George Leygues*. The three other ships are based at Toulon. Endurance 45 days. Service lives: *Georges Leygues* 2017; *Dupleix* 2015; *Montcalm* 2016 and *Jean de Vienne* 2018. Camcopter S-100 UAV recovered to *Montcalm* on 10 October 2008.

DUPLEIX *2/2008*, B Prézelin* / 1335762

JEAN DE VIENNE *6/2008*, B Prézelin* / 1335759

3 MODIFIED GEORGES LEYGUES CLASS (TYPE F 70 (ASW)) (DDGHM)

Name	*No*	*Builders*	*Laid down*	*Launched*	*Commissioned*
PRIMAUGUET	D 644	Brest Naval Dockyard	17 Nov 1981	17 Mar 1984	5 Nov 1986
LA MOTTE-PICQUET	D 645	Brest Naval Dockyard/Lorient	12 Feb 1982	6 Feb 1985	18 Feb 1988
LATOUCHE-TRÉVILLE	D 646	Brest Naval Dockyard/Lorient	15 Feb 1984	19 Mar 1988	16 July 1990

Displacement, tons: 4,010 standard; 4,910 full load
Dimensions, feet (metres): 455.9 × 49.2 × 18.7 *(139 × 15.0 × 5.7)*
Main machinery: CODOG; 2 RR Olympus TM3B gas turbines; 52,000 hp *(38.2 MW)* sustained; 2 SEMT-Pielstick 16 PA6 V280 diesels; 11,200 hp(m) *(8.3 MW)* sustained; 2 shafts; LIPS cp props
Speed, knots: 30; 21 on diesels
Range, n miles: 8,000 at 15 kt on diesels; 2,500 at 28 kt
Complement: 233 (21 officers)

Missiles: SSM: 8 MBDA Exocet MM 40 (only 4 in peacetime) ❶; inertial cruise and active radar homing to 72 km *(39 n miles)* at 0.93 Mach; warhead 165 kg.
SAM: Thomson-CSF Crotale Naval EDIR system ❷; octuple launcher; radar/IR command to line-of-sight to 13 km *(7 n miles)* at 2.4 Mach; warhead 14 kg; total of 26 V5S missiles carried.
2 MBDA Simbad twin launchers for Mistral SR SAMs; IR homing to 6 km *(3.2 n miles)*; warhead 3 kg.
Guns: 1 DCN 100 mm/55 *(3.9 in/55)* Modèle 68 CADAM automatic ❸; dual purpose; 78 rds/min to 17 km *(9 n miles)* anti-surface; 6 km *(3.2 n miles)* anti-aircraft; weight of shell 13.5 kg.
2 Giat 20F2 20 mm ❹; 720 rds/min to 2 km; 4—12.7 mm MGs.
Torpedoes: Two 324 mm EuroTorp B515/1H/F fixed torpedo tubes for EuroTorp MU 90 Impact lightweight ASW torpedoes; active/passive homing to 25 km *(13.5 n miles)* at 29 kt or 12 km *(6.5 n miles)* at 50 kt; warhead 32 kg of TATB explosive (shaped charge); depth to 1,000 m; same torpedoes for the helicopters.
Countermeasures: EADS AMBL-1C (Dagaie Mk 2); two 10-barrel trainable launchers ❺; chaff and IR flares. Four AMBL-3A (Replica) (D 645); offboard decoys.
ESM: Thales ARBR-17 ❻ (DR 4000) radar intercept; ARBG-1A (Saigon) comms intercept; Sagem DIBV-2A (Vampir MB) IRST.
ECM: Thales ARBV-36A jammer.
Torpedo defence: AN/SLQ-25A Nixie (two torpedo decoys); Prairie-Masker noise suppression system.
Combat data systems: DCN SENIT 4 CDS; Link 11 (Link 22 in due course). ACOM/Opsmer command support system; Syva ASW decision aid. Syracuse ❼ and Inmarsat satcomms.
Electro-optic systems: DCN CTMS radar/optronic FCS (with DRBC-33A radar, DIBC-1A Pirana IR tracker, TV tracker) and CSEE DM-Ab (Panda) optical director for 100 mm gun. Alcatel DLT-L5 for torpedoes.
Radars: Air/surface search: Thomson-CSF DRBV-15A (D 645) or -15B (Sea Tiger) (D 644, D 646) ❽; E/F-band.
Navigation: 2 DRBN 34A (D 646); 2 DRBN 37 (D 644, D 645); I-band.
Fire control: Thomson-CSF Castor 2J ❾ for Crotale Naval SAM; J-band.
Thomson-CSF DRBC-33A (Castor 2C) ❿ for gun FCS; I-band.
Sonars: Thomson-Sintra DUBV-24C bow-mounted; active search and attack; 5 kHz Thomson-Sintra DUBV-43C VDS ⓫; active search and attack; 5 kHz; paired with DUBV-24C; tows at up to 24 kt down to 700 m *(2,300 ft)*.
TUS DSBV-61B passive linear towed array with URDT-1A torpedo warning equipment; very low frequency.
PAF sonobuoy data processing system.

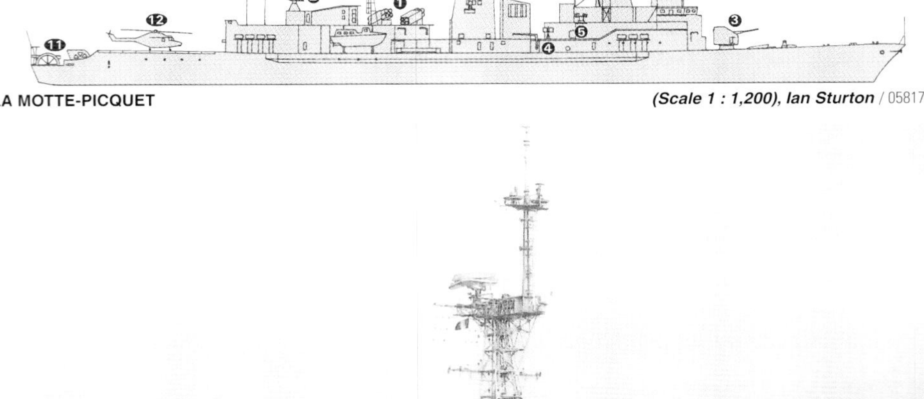

LA MOTTE-PICQUET *(Scale 1 : 1,200), Ian Sturton* / 0581796

LA MOTTE-PICQUET *5/2008*, B Prézelin* / 1335760

Helicopters: 2 Westland WG 13 Lynx Mk 4 (FN) ⓬ (one normally carried in peacetime).

Programmes: 'Frégates anti-sous-marines type 1970' (FASM 70 or F 70). Authorised on the 1975–80 Defence Programming Law. Fourth unit cancelled before construction had started. *La Motte-Picquet* and *Latouche-Tréville* started building at Brest and towed to Lorient for outfitting. To be replaced by FREMM/ASM in the late 2010s.
Modernisation: The ships have been upgraded by the OP3A (Opération programmée amélioration autodéfense antimissiles) air defence upgrade programme, limited to the upgrade of sensors and ESM equipment and the installation of two MBDA Simbad twin launchers for Mistral SR SAMs; completed 1997–99. In 2004–06, further modernisation include the replacement of the two KD-59E launchers for 533 mm *(21 in)* L 5 torpedoes by two 324 mm B 515 fixed tubes for EuroTorp MU 90 Impact lightweight torpedoes. Plans to fit MBDA Milas ASW missiles have been shelved. All vessels modified to receive female crew. Might receive the LFTASS (ATBF 2) very low frequency towed active sonar.
Structure: Bridge raised one deck as compared to first four ships of the class. Hull and main deck have been strengthened to cope with fatigue problems; to restore seaworthiness, 235 tonnes of ballast have been embarked and two fuel tanks turned into water-ballasts; completed 2002–03 on all ships. DCN SPHEX helicopter handling system.
Operational: All based at Brest. Service lives: 2021–23.

LATOUCHE-TRÉVILLE *2/2008*, France* / 1335758

2 TOURVILLE CLASS (TYPE F 67) (DDGHM)

Name	*No*	*Builders*	*Laid down*	*Launched*	*Commissioned*
TOURVILLE	D 610	Lorient Naval Dockyard	16 Mar 1970	13 May 1972	21 June 1974
DE GRASSE	D 612	Lorient Naval Dockyard	25 July 1972	30 Nov 1974	1 Oct 1977

Displacement, tons: 4,650 standard; 6,100 full load
Dimensions, feet (metres): 501.6 × 51.8 × 21.6 *(152.8 × 15.8 × 6.6)*
Main machinery: 4 boilers; 640 psi *(45 kg/cm²)*; 840°F *(450°C)*; 2 Rateau turbines; 58,000 hp(m) *(43 MW)*; 2 shafts
Speed, knots: 31
Range, n miles: 4,500 at 18 kt
Complement: 298 (24 officers)

Missiles: SSM: 6 Aerospatiale MM 38 Exocet ❶; inertial cruise; active radar homing to 42 km *(23 n miles)* at 0.9 Mach; warhead 165 kg; sea-skimmer.
SAM: Thomson-CSF Crotale Naval EDIR octuple launcher ❷; command line of sight guidance; radar/IR homing to 13 km *(7 n miles)* at 2.4 Mach; warhead 14 kg. 26 missiles.
Guns: 2 DCN/Creusot-Loire 3.9 in *(100 mm)*/55 Mod 68 CADAM automatic ❸; dual purpose; 78 rds/min to 17 km *(9 n miles)* anti-surface; 8 km *(4.4 n miles)* anti-aircraft; weight of shell 13.5 kg.
2 Oerlikon Mk 10 20 mm ❹.
4—12.7 mm MGs.
Torpedoes: 2 DCN KD-59E 533 mm fixed launchers ❺; for DCN L5; anti-submarine; active/passive homing to 9.5 km *(5.1 n miles)* at 35 kt; warhead 150 kg; depth to 550 m *(1,800 ft)*. Honeywell Mk 46 or Eurotorp Mu 90 Impact torpedoes for helicopters.
Countermeasures: Decoys: 2 CSEE/VSEL Syllex 8-barrelled trainable launcher (to be replaced by 2 Dagaie systems) ❻; chaff to 1 km in centroid and distraction patterns.
RESM: ARBR 16; radar intercept.
CESM: Thomson-CSF Altesse (D 610); comms intercept.
ECM: ARBB 32B; jammer.
Torpedo defence: Prairie Masker noise suppression system.
Combat data systems: SENIT 3 action data automation; Links 11 and 14. Syracuse 2 SATCOM ❼. OPSMER command support system. Inmarsat and Syracuse SATCOM.

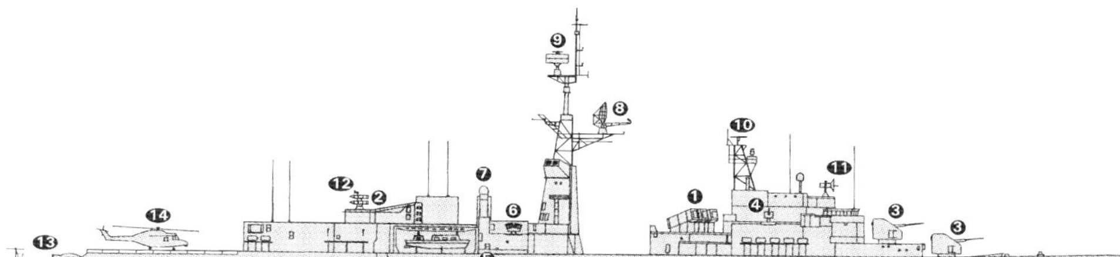

TOURVILLE

(Scale 1 : 1,200), Ian Sturton / 0569912

Electro-optic systems: SENIT 3 radar/TV tracker (possibly SAT Murène in due course). 2 Sagem DMAa optical directors.
Radars: Air search: Thomson-CSF DRBV 26A ❽; D-band; range 182 km *(100 n miles)* for 2 m² target.
Air/surface search: Thomson-CSF DRBV 51B ❾; G-band; range 29 km *(16 n miles)*.
Navigation: 2 DRBN 34 ❿; (Racal Decca Type 1226); I-band (1 for helicopter control).
Fire control: Thomson-CSF DRBC 32D (Castor 2B) ⓫; I-band. Crotale ⓬; J-band (for SAM).
Sonars: Thomson Sintra DUBV 23D; bow-mounted; active search and attack; medium frequency.
Thomson Sintra DSBX 1A (ATBF) VDS (SLASM) (D 610) ⓭; active 1 kHz transmitter and 5 kHz transceiver in same 10 tonne towed body.
Thomson Sintra DSBV 62C; passive linear towed array; very low frequency.

Helicopters: 2 Westland Lynx Mk 4 ⓮.

Programmes: Originally rated as corvettes but reclassified as 'frégates anti-sous-marins (FASM)' on 8 July 1971 and given D pennant numbers.
Modernisation: Major communications and combat data systems updates. The SLASM ASW combat suite installed in *Tourville* from March 1994 to April 1995, *De Grasse* from May 1995 to September 1996. This included new signal processing for the bow sonar, plus LF and MF towed active sonar with separate towed passive array including torpedo warning. Acoustic processor for helo borne sonobuoys. Milas ASW missile cancelled. Passive towed arrays fitted in 1990. Malafon removed from *Tourville* in 1994 and *De Grasse* in 1996. *De Grasse* refitted at Brest in 2003.
Structure: Hulls have been strengthened with side support beams.
Operational: Assigned to ALFAN Brest. Helicopters are now used primarily in the ASW role with sonar or sonobuoy dispenser, and ASW weapons. Service lives: *Tourville* 2012; *De Grasse* 2014. To be replaced by first two FREMM.

TOURVILLE

9/2005, H M Steele / 1153156

TOURVILLE

3/2007, Paul Daly / 1170116

FRIGATES

5 LA FAYETTE CLASS (FFGHM)

Name	*No*	*Builders*	*Laid down*	*Launched*	*Commissioned*
LA FAYETTE	F 710	DCN, Lorient	15 Dec 1990	13 June 1992	23 Mar 1996
SURCOUF	F 711	DCN, Lorient	3 July 1992	3 July 1993	7 Feb 1997
COURBET	F 712	DCN, Lorient	15 Sep 1993	12 Mar 1994	1 Apr 1997
ACONIT (ex-*Jauréguiberry*)	F 713	DCN, Lorient	1 Aug 1996	8 June 1997	3 June 1999
GUÉPRATTE	F 714	DCN, Lorient	1 Oct 1998	3 Mar 1999	27 Oct 2001

Displacement, tons: 3,300 standard; 3,750 full load
Dimensions, feet (metres): 407.5 oa; 377.3 pp × 50.5 × 19.0 (screws) *(124.2; 115 × 15.4 × 5.8)*
Main machinery: CODAD; 4 SEMT-Pielstick 12 PA6 V 280 STC diesels; 21,107 hp(m) *(15.52 MW)* sustained; 2 shafts; LIPS cp props; bow thruster
Speed, knots: 25
Range, n miles: 7,000 at 15 kt; 9,000 at 12 kt
Complement: 153 (15 officers) plus 25 marines

Missiles: SSM: 8 Aerospatiale MM 40 Block 2 Exocet ❶; inertial cruise; active radar homing to 70 km *(40 n miles)* at 0.9 Mach; warhead 165 kg; sea-skimmer.
SAM: Thomson-CSF Crotale Naval CN 2 octuple launcher ❷; command line of sight guidance; radar/IR homing to 13 km *(7 n miles)* at 3.5 Mach; warhead 14 kg. 26 missiles. Space for 2 × 8 cell VLS ❸.
Guns: 1 DCN 3.9 in *(100 mm)*/55 TR ❹; 78 rds/min to 17 km *(9 n miles)*; weight of shell 13.5 kg.
2 Giat 20F2 20 mm ❺; 720 rds/min to 10 km *(5.5 n miles)*.
Countermeasures: Decoys: 2 CSEE AMBL-1C (Dagaie Mk 2) ❻; 10-barrelled trainable launchers; chaff and IR flares.
ESM: Thomson-CSF ARBR 21A (DR 3000-S) ❼; radar intercept. ARBG-1 (Saigon) (F 710-712) or ARBG 2A (F 713-714) (Maigret); comms intercept.
DIBV 10 Vampir ❽; IR detector (can be fitted).
ECM: Dassault ARBB 33; jammer (can be fitted).
Torpedo defence: SLQ-25A Nixie.
Combat data systems: Thomson-CSF TAVITAC 2000. Link 11. Syracuse 2 SATCOM ❾. OPSMER command support system. INMARSAT.
Electro-optic systems: Sagem TDS 90 VIGY optronic system.
Radars: Air/surface search: Thales DRBV-15C (Sea Tiger 2) ❿; E/F-band; range 110 km *(60 n miles)* for 2 m^2 target.
Navigation: 2 Racal Decca 1229 (DRBN 34B) ⓫; I-band. One set for helicopter control.
Fire control: Thomson-CSF Castor 2J/C ⓬; J-band; range 17 km *(9.2 n miles)* for 1 m^2 target.
Crotale ⓭; J-band (for SAM).

Helicopters: 1 Aerospatiale AS 565MA Panther ⓮; or platform for 1 Super Frelon. NH90 in due course.

Programmes: Originally described as 'Frégates Légères' but this was changed in 1992 to 'Frégates type La Fayette'. First three ordered 25 July 1988; three more 24 September 1992 but the last of these was cancelled in May 1996. The construction timetable was delayed by several months because of funding problems.
Modernisation: Exocet MM40 Block 3 missiles may be fitted.
Structure: Constructed from high-tensile steel with a double skin from waterline to upperdeck. 10 mm plating protects vital spaces. External equipment and upper deck fittings are concealed or placed in low positions. Superstructure inclined at 10° to vertical to reduce REA. Extensive use of radar absorbent paint. DCN Samahe helicopter handling system. RHIB assault craft fitted-these are launched and recovered from a stern access. The design includes potential to install new and/or replace old weapon systems in the future. This includes the SAAM/F system to replace Crotale (space is available forward of the bridge to install Sylver A43 octuple VLS launchers for Aster 15 missiles). This upgrade is not believed to be funded.
Operational: *La Fayette* started sea trials 27 September 1993, *Surcouf* 4 July 1994, *Courbet* 14 September 1995, *Aconit* 14 April 1998 and *Guépratte* on 16 January 2001. These frigates are designed for out of area operations on overseas stations. Super Frelon helicopters can land on the flight deck. NH 90 prototype trials in *Courbet* in 1998. The ship can launch inflatable boats from a hatch in the stern which hinges upwards. The Vampir IR detector and ARBB 33 jammer are fitted 'for but not with'. *Courbet* refitted 2005. All based at Toulon.
Sales: Three of an improved design to Saudi Arabia, six for Taiwan, and six for Singapore.

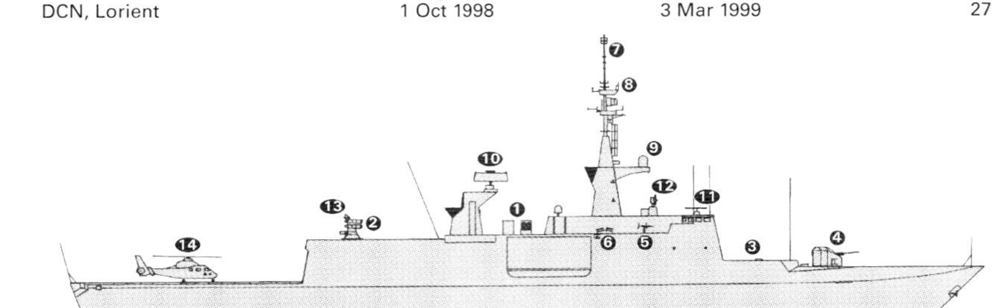

LA FAYETTE *(Scale 1 : 1,200), Ian Sturton* / 0581797

GUÉPRATTE *3/2008*, Guy Toremans* / 1335774

COURBET *2/2008*, B Prézelin* / 1335757

SURCOUF *10/2008*, Peter Ford* / 1335773

9 D'ESTIENNE D'ORVES (TYPE A 69) CLASS (FFGM)

Name	*No*	*Builders*	*Laid down*	*Launched*	*Commissioned*
LIEUTENANT DE VAISSEAU LE HÉNAFF	F 789	Lorient Naval Dockyard	21 Mar 1977	16 Sep 1978	13 Feb 1980
LIEUTENANT DE VAISSEAU LAVALLÉE	F 790	Lorient Naval Dockyard	30 Nov 1977	12 May 1979	8 Oct 1980
COMMANDANT L'HERMINIER	F 791	Lorient Naval Dockyard	29 May 1979	7 Mar 1981	19 Jan 1986
PREMIER MAÎTRE L'HER	F 792	Lorient Naval Dockyard	15 Dec 1978	28 June 1980	5 Dec 1981
COMMANDANT BLAISON	F 793	Lorient Naval Dockyard	15 Nov 1979	7 Mar 1981	28 Apr 1982
ENSEIGNE DE VAISSEAU JACOUBET	F 794	Lorient Naval Dockyard	8 July 1980	26 Sep 1981	23 Oct 1982
COMMANDANT DUCUING	F 795	Lorient Naval Dockyard	1 Oct 1980	26 Sep 1981	17 Mar 1983
COMMANDANT BIROT	F 796	Lorient Naval Dockyard	23 Mar 1981	22 May 1982	14 Mar 1984
COMMANDANT BOUAN	F 797	Lorient Naval Dockyard	12 Oct 1981	23 Apr 1983	31 Oct 1984

Displacement, tons: 1,175 standard; 1,250 (F 789-791), 1,290 (F 792-793), 1,330 (F 794-797) full load
Dimensions, feet (metres): 264.1 × 33.8 × 18 (sonar) *(80.5 × 10.3 × 5.5)*
Main machinery: 2 SEMT-Pielstick 12 PC2 V 400 diesels; 12,000 hp(m) *(8.82 MW)*; 2 shafts; LIPS cp props
2 SEMT-Pielstick 12 PA6 V 280 BTC diesels; 14,400 hp(m) *(10.6 MW)* sustained; 2 shafts; LIPS cp props *(Commandant L'Herminier)*
Speed, knots: 24; 25 (F 791). **Range, n miles:** 4,500 at 15 kt
Complement: 90 (7 officers) plus 18 marines (in some)

Missiles: SSM: 4 Aerospatiale MM 40 (MM 38 in F 789–791) Exocet ❶; inertial cruise; active radar homing to 70 km *(40 n miles)* (or 42 km *(23 n miles)*) at 0.9 Mach (MM 40); warhead 165 kg; sea-skimmer; active radar homing to 42 km *(23 n miles)* at 0.9 Mach (MM 38).
SAM: Matra Simbad twin launcher for Mistral ❷; IR homing to 4 km *(2.2 n miles)*; warhead 3 kg.
Guns: 1 DCN/Creusot-Loire 3.9 in *(100 mm)*/55 Mod 68 CADAM automatic ❸; 80 rds/min to 17 km *(9 n miles)* anti-surface; 8 km *(4.4 n miles)* anti-aircraft; weight of shell 13.5 kg.
2 Giat 20 mm ❹; 720 rds/min to 10 km *(5.5 n miles)*.
4—12.7 mm MGs.
Torpedoes: 4 fixed tubes ❺. ECAN L5; dual purpose; active/passive homing to 9.5 km *(5.1 n miles)* at 35 kt; warhead 150 kg; depth to 550 m *(1,800 ft)*.
A/S mortars: 1 Creusot-Loire 375 mm Mk 54 6-tubed trainable launcher (F 789, F 790, F 791); range 1,600 m; warhead 107 kg. Removed from others.
Countermeasures: Decoys: 2 CSEE AMBL-1A (Dagaie) 10-barrelled trainable launchers ❻; chaff and IR flares; H- to J-band.
SLQ-25 Nixie torpedo decoy.
ESM: ARBR 16; radar warning.
Combat data systems: Syracuse 2 SATCOM (F 792, F 793, F 794, F 795, F 796, F 797) ❼. OPSMER command support system with Link 11 (receive only) in MM 40 ships. INMARSAT.
Weapons control: Thomson-CSF Vega system; CSEE DM-Ab (Panda) optical secondary director.
Radars: Air/surface search: Thomson-CSF DRBV 51A ❽; G-band.
Navigation: Kelvin Hughes 1007; I-band.
Fire control: Thomson-CSF DRBC 32E ❾; I-band.
Sonars: Thomson Sintra DUBA 25; hull-mounted; search and attack; medium frequency.

Programmes: Classified as 'Avisos'.
Modernisation: In 1985 *Commandant L'Herminier*, F 791, fitted with 12PA6 BTC Diesels Rapides as trial for Type F 70. Most have dual MM 38/MM 40 ITL (Installation de Tir Légère) capability. Weapon fit depends on deployment and operational requirement. Those without ITL are fitted with ITS (Installation de Tir Standard). Syracuse 2 SATCOM fitted in F 792-797, vice the A/S mortar, and accommodation provided for commandos. Matra Simbad launchers have been fitted aft of the A/S mortar/Syracuse SATCOM for operations. Fast raiding craft fitted to *Commandant Birot* and to others in due course.
Operational: Endurance, 30 days and primarily intended for coastal A/S operations. Also available for overseas patrols. All assigned to FAN with F 794, F 795, F 796 and F 797 based at Toulon; the remainder at Brest. Decommissioning plans are under review. It is likely that the Toulon-based ships will be reduced to a patrol ship role following the removal of ASW systems (sonar, torpedoes, mortars) and remain in service until 2017–20. The Brest-based ships are to retain their ASW capability and are likely to be decommissioned 2014–18.
Sales: The original *Lieutenant de Vaisseau Le Hénaff* and *Commandant l'Herminier* sold to South Africa in 1976 while under construction. As a result of the UN embargo on arms sales to South Africa, they were sold to Argentina in September 1978 followed by a third, specially built. Six ships were sold to Turkey in October 2000. All delivered by July 2002 after refit at Brest. The last one, *Second Maître Le Bihan*, decommissioned from the French Navy on 26 June 2002. No further sales are planned.

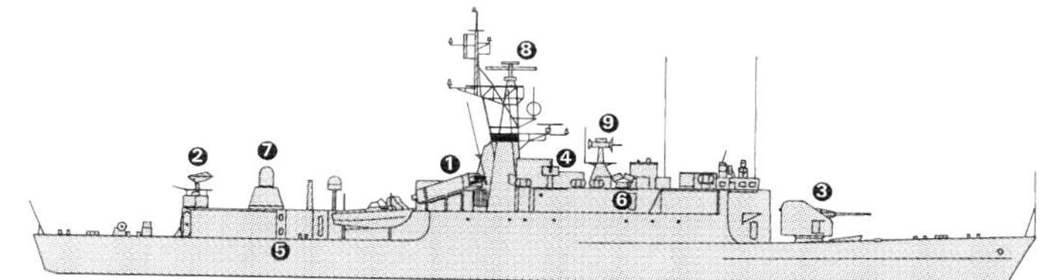

PREMIER MAÎTRE L'HER *(Scale 1 : 900)*, **Ian Sturton** / 0535887

COMMANDANT L'HERMINIER *5/2008**, **B Prézelin** / 1335756

ENSEIGNE DE VAISSEAU JACOUBET *9/2008**, **B Prézelin** / 1335755

PREMIER MAÎTRE L'HER *9/2008**, **B Prézelin** / 1335754

6 FLORÉAL CLASS (FFGHM)

Name	*No*	*Builders*	*Laid down*	*Launched*	*Commissioned*
FLORÉAL	F 730	Chantiers de l'Atlantique, St Nazaire	2 Apr 1990	6 Oct 1990	27 May 1992
PRAIRIAL	F 731	Chantiers de l'Atlantique, St Nazaire	11 Sep 1990	16 Mar 1991	20 May 1992
NIVÔSE	F 732	Chantiers de l'Atlantique, St Nazaire	16 Jan 1991	10 Aug 1991	16 Oct 1992
VENTÔSE	F 733	Chantiers de l'Atlantique, St Nazaire	28 June 1991	14 Mar 1992	5 May 1993
VENDÉMIAIRE	F 734	Chantiers de l'Atlantique, St Nazaire	17 Jan 1992	23 Aug 1992	21 Oct 1993
GERMINAL	F 735	Chantiers de l'Atlantique, St Nazaire	17 Aug 1992	14 Mar 1993	18 May 1994

Displacement, tons: 2,600 standard; 2,950 full load
Dimensions, feet (metres): 306.8 × 45.9 × 14.1 *(93.5 × 14 × 4.3)*
Main machinery: CODAD; 4 SEMT-Pielstick 6 PA6 L 280 BTC diesels; 8,820 hp(m) *(6.5 MW)* sustained; 2 shafts; LIPS cp props; 272 hp *(200 kW)* bow thruster; 340 hp(m) *(250 kW)*
Speed, knots: 20
Range, n miles: 9,000 at 15 kt
Complement: 90 (11 officers) (including aircrew) plus 24 Marines + 13 spare

Missiles: SSM: 2 Aerospatiale MM 38 Exocet ❶; inertial cruise; active radar homing to 42 km *(23 n miles)* at 0.9 Mach; warhead 165 kg; sea-skimmer.
SAM: 1 or 2 Matra Simbad twin launchers can replace 20 mm guns or Dagaie launcher.
Guns: 1 DCN 3.9 in *(100 mm)*/55 Mod 68 CADAM ❷; 78 rds/min to 17 km *(9 n miles)*; weight of shell 13.5 kg.
2 Giat 20 F2 20 mm ❸; 720 rds/min to 10 km *(5.5 n miles)*.
Countermeasures: Decoys (fitted for but not with): 2 CSEE AMBL-1C (Dagaie Mk II); 10-barrelled trainable launchers ❹; chaff and IR flares.
ESM: Thomson-CSF ARBR 16A (F 735) ❺; radar intercept.
ARBG 1A (Saigon); comms intercept (F 730 and F 733).
Combat data systems: ACOM/OPSMER command support system (F 735). Syracuse (F 730 and F 733) and INMARSAT ❼ SATCOM.
Electro-optic systems: CSEE Najir optronic director ❻.
Radars: Air/surface search: Thomson-CSF Mars DRBV 21C ❽; D-band.
Navigation: 2 Racal Decca 1229 (DRBN 34A); I-band (1 for helicopter control ❾).

Helicopters: 1 AS 565MA Panther or platform for 1 AS 332F Super Puma ❿.

Programmes: Officially described as 'Frégates de Surveillance' or 'Ocean capable patrol vessel' and designed to operate in the offshore zone in low-intensity operations. First two ordered on 20 January 1989; built at Chantiers de l'Atlantique, St Nazaire, with weapon systems fitted by DCAN Lorient. Second pair ordered 9 January 1990; third pair in January 1991. Named after the months of the Revolutionary calendar.

Structure: Built to merchant passenger marine standards with stabilisers and air conditioning. New funnel design improves air flow over the flight deck. Has one freight bunker aft for about 100 tons cargo. Second-hand Exocet MM 38 has been fitted instead of planned MM 40.
Operational: Endurance, 50 days. Able to operate a helicopter up to Sea State 5. Stations as follows: *Ventose* in Antilles, *Germinal* at Toulon, *Prairial* in Tahiti. *Floréal* and *Nivôse* at La Réunion and *Vendémiaire* at Noumea (New Caledonia). *Floréal* refitted in floating dry-dock at Papeete in 2003. Service life 2022–24.
Sales: Two delivered to Morocco in 2002 and 2003.

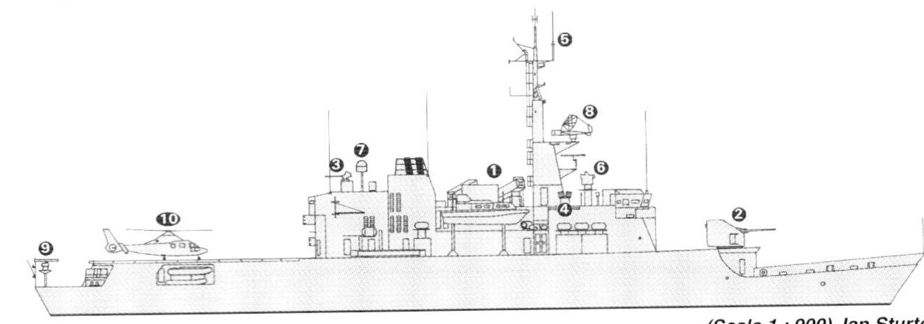

PRAIRIAL — *(Scale 1 : 900), Ian Sturton* / 0529161

PRAIRIAL — *6/2008*, Chris Sattler* / 1335772

VENDÉMIAIRE — *5/2005, Chris Sattler* / 1153139

0 + 8 (3) AQUITAINE CLASS (FFGHM)

Name	*Builders*	*Laid down*	*Launched*	*Commissioned*
AQUITAINE	DCN, Lorient	Dec 2007	Dec 2009	Jan 2012
NORMANDIE	DCN, Lorient	2009	2011	2013
PROVENCE	DCN, Lorient	2010	2012	2014
BRETAGNE	DCN, Lorient	2011	2013	2015
AUVERGNE	DCN, Lorient	2012	2014	2016
LANGUEDOC	DCN, Lorient	2013	2015	2017
ALSACE	DCN, Lorient	2014	2016	2018
LORRAINE	DCN, Lorient	2015	2017	2019

Displacement, tons: 5,135 standard; 6,000 full load (approx)
Dimensions, feet (metres): 466.5 oa; 449.8 wl × 64.6 × 17.7 *(142.2; 137.1 × 19.7 × 5.4)*
Main machinery: CODLOG; 1 Fiat/GE LM 2500+ G4 gas turbine; 47,370 hp(m) *(34.8 MW)*; 2 Jeumont motors; 2 shafts
Speed, knots: 27.5 (16 on motors)
Range, n miles: 6,000 at 15 kt
Complement: 108 (22 officers) (accommodation for 145)

Missiles: SLCM: 16 (2 octuple) cell Sylver A70 VLS ❶ for MBDA Scalp-Naval; inertial/terrain following navigation with GPS and high precision IIR terminal guidance to 1,000 km *(540 n miles)*; warhead 300 kg.
SAM: 16 (2 octuple) cell Sylver A43 VLS for MBDA Aster 15 ❶; inertial guidance, mid-course update and final active homing to 30 km *(16.2 n miles)* at 3 Mach
SSM: 8 MBDA Exocet MM 40 Block 3 ❷; inertial cruise; active radar homing to 180 km *(100 n miles)* at 0.9 Mach; warhead 165 kg.
Guns: 1-OTO Melara 76 mm/62SR ❸. 2 — 20 mm.
Torpedoes: 2 twin 324 mm Eurotorp B 515/2H/F fixed launchers for Eurotorp MU 90; active/passive homing to 25 km *(13.5 n miles)* at 29 kt or 12 km *(6.5 n miles)* at 50 kt; warhead 32 kg. 19 weapons (F-ASM); 4 weapons (F-AVT).
Countermeasures: Decoys: 2 EADS NGDS 12-barrelled chaff, IR and anti-torpedo decoy launchers.
ESM/ECM: Sigen CESM and RESM suite.
Torpedo defence: SLAT (Thales TUS WASSB 525/12) and Alto torpedo warning system.
Combat data systems: DCN/Thales SETIS CMS. Links 11 and 16, 22 and JSAT.
Electro-optic systems: 1 optronic FCS. Thales Artémis IRST.
Radars: Air/surface search: Thales Herakles 3-D multifunction ❹; E/F-band.

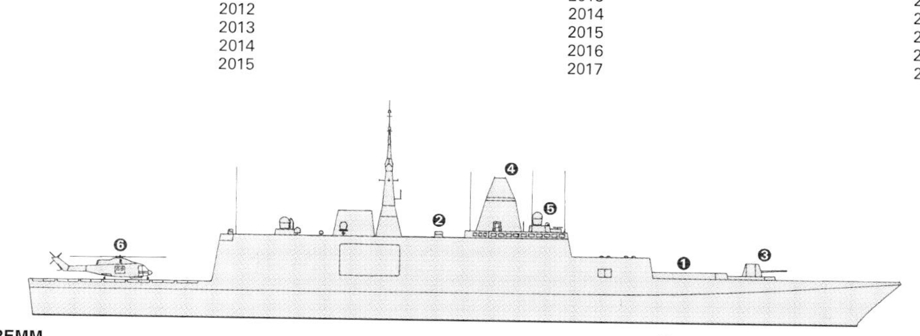

FREMM *(Scale 1 : 1,200), Ian Sturton* / 1170136

Fire control: Alenia Marconi NA-25XP ❺; J-band.
Navigation: 2 to be decided.
Sonars: Thales TUS 4110CL; hull mounted (bow dome); active search and attack. Thales Captas UMS-4249 active/passive towed array (F-ASM).

Helicopters: 1 NH-90 ❻. ASW aircraft in ASW variant. Transport aircraft and tactical UAV in land attack variant.

Programmes: Agreement reached on 7 November 2002 for a 27-ship collaborative programme with Italy. The original French requirement was for 17 FREMM of which there would be eight ASW (F-ASM) variants and nine land-attack (F-AVT). This plan was later modified by the 2009–14 Defence Programming Law in which the total number of ships was reduced to 11, the F-AVT variants were dropped and two AAW variants (FREDA) were included. Contract for the first phase awarded on 16 November 2005 to Armaris (DCN/Thales joint venture) for the construction of a first batch of eight ships. This comprises six F-ASM and two FREDA (formerly F-AVT) (*Auvergne* and *Alsace*). A second batch of three ships is to be funded by the 2009 budget.
Structure: FREMM has a conventional hull design. The main engine room contains the gas turbine and two diesel generators while the aft machinery space contains the motors. Particular attention has been paid to signature reduction. The radar signature is expected to be comparable to that of the La Fayette class while exhaust cooling measures are expected to achieve a comparatively low IR signature. Acoustic quietening is to be achieved by the rafting of engines and motors and the use of electric propulsion. The original design for a single integrated mast has been abandoned in favour of a two mast configuration. The Herakles radar is housed in the foremast and communications and IFF in the after mast. F-AVT will have accommodation for 30 marines and will be able to launch/recover 9.5 m raiding craft through a stern access. FREDA are to include 2–16 cell launchers for Aster 15 and 30.
Operational: Sea trials for *Aquitaine* are planned to start in 2010.

SHIPBORNE AIRCRAFT

Notes: The naval drone concepts for the French Navy have moved to a common navy/army project for a VTOL drone that could perform both tactical and long-range missions. It should be able to operate from the flight deck of a frigate. Contenders contracted on 10 November 2006 are Thales, Boeing Little Bird, Sagem/Bell/Rheinmetall with an Eagle Eye derivative and EADS/Vertivision with Orka 2000. Following a feasibility study, a demonstration phase will test a UAV operationally. Up to 50 UAV may be required in due course. On 1 December 2005, a contract was awarded to DCN to study and develop the integration of UAVs on board naval ships (with the objective of deck trials at sea on a frigatein 2009).

Numbers/Type: 26 Dassault Aviation ACM Rafale M.
Operational speed: Mach 2.
Service ceiling: 50,000 ft *(15,240 m)*.
Range: 2,000 n miles *(3,700 km)*.
Role/Weapon systems: Total procurement of 58 Rafale M single-seaters (air superiority and ground/surface attack). First of two Rafale M naval prototypes (single seaters) flown 12 December 1992. First deck trials in *Foch* in 1993. First production Rafale M flown 7 July 1999 and assigned to development trials. Second aircraft delivered to the Navy 19 July 2000 and 14 more delivered by 2007 to form Flottile 12F. All aircraft at standard F1 (air superiority role; crash programme carried out to enable tanker role). Further aircraft at standard F2 with limited air-to-ground capabilities. Prototype M2 brought to this standard for carrier trials in December 2005; first production aircraft delivered in March 2006, seven more delivered in 2007, and last seven in 2008 to replace Super Etendards in Flotille 11F. Standard F3 true multirole variant to enter service from 2009 (with full air superiority, air-to-ground, air-to-surface, nuclear strike and reconnaissance capabilities). All 15 Rafale F2 being converted to F3 standard by September 2009. This is to be followed by nine F1 by 2015. Sensors: Thales/Dassault Electronique RBE2 multirole radar; Thales/Dassault Electronique/MBDA SPECTRA integrated EW/IR countermeasure suite; Thales/Sagem OSF optronic surveillance and target acquisition equipment (from standard F2); MIDSCO MIDS-LVT terminal for Link 16 (from standard F2); Thales Reco NG optronic reconnaissance pod (for eight specially wired standard F3 Rafales). Weapons: Giat M791 30 mm cannon; up to eight AAMs (air defence role), including MBDA Magic 2 short range and MBDA Mica EM medium range AAMs (standard F1); MBDA Mica IR replacing Magic 2 from standard F2 (later, MBDA Meteor to replace Mica EM); MBDA SCALP-EG stand-off precision guided ASM (from standard F2); Sagem AASM general purpose precision ammunition (from standard F2); MBDA Exocet AM 39 Block 2 Mod 2 ASM (one carried) and ASMP-A nuclear strike missile (standard F3); nacelle for air-to-air refuelling. Up to 8 tons of military load on 13 hardpoints.

RAFALE M *6/2008*, Ships of the World* / 1335749

Numbers/Type: 43 Dassault-Bréguet Super Étendard.
Operational speed: Mach 1.
Service ceiling: 45,000 ft *(13,700 m)*.
Range: 1,460 n miles *(2,700 km)*.
Role/Weapon systems: Carrierborne all-weather strike fighter with nuclear strike capabilities and limited air defence role; tactical recce role to be added. All aircraft still in inventory modernised 1994–1999 to Standard F3. Standard F4 for all the fleet from mid-2000 to early 2005; tactical recce role added; standard 5 upgrade for a total of 35 aircraft by 2008. Service life extended to 2015. Sensors: Dassault Electronique Anémone radar, DRAX (standard3) or Thales-Detexis Sherloc-F ESM (standard 4), SAGEM UAT 90 computer, Thomson-CSF Barracuda jammer, Phimat chaff dispenser, Alkan IR decoy dispenser; Thales Optrosys photo/optronic chassis (with Omera 40 panoramic camera and SDS-250 digital camera) in a ventral bay (Standard F4); Thales Improved Damocles day/night FLIR/designator (Standard F4 and F5). Weapons: air defence and self protection: two Matra BAe Dynamic Magic 2 short range AAMs and two DEFA 30 mm cannon; nuclear strike: one Aerospatiale ASMP nuclear ASM; air-to-surface: one Aerospatiale AM 39 Exocet anti-ship missile; air-to-ground: bombs and MBDA CEMB/BANG 125 or 250 bombs with Raytheon Enhanced Paveway 2 precision guidance (Standard 4 and 5) or one Aerospatiale AS 30L laser guided missile. 7 hardpoints (from standard 4).

SUPER ÉTENDARD *6/2005, Paul Jackson* / 1153141

Numbers/Type: 3 Grumman E-2C Hawkeye Group 2.
Operational speed: 320 kt *(593 km/h)*.
Service ceiling: 37,000 ft *(11,278 m)*.
Range: 1,540 n miles *(2,852 km)*.
Role/Weapon systems: Used for AEW, and direction of AD and strike operations. First pair ordered in May 1995 and delivered in April and December 1998 respectively. Third delivered in December 2003. First two aircraft completed upgrade programme (including eight-bladed propellers) in 2006. Procurement of a fourth aircraft was discontinued in December 2007. Sensors: APS-145 radar, ESM, ALR-73 PDS, ALQ-108 airborne tactical data system with Links 11 and 16. Weapons: Unarmed.

E-2C *1/2007, B Prézelin* / 1305021

Numbers/Type: 4/10 Eurocopter EC 725 R2 Cougar Mk 2 Plus Resco/EC 725 HUS.
Operational speed: 154 kt *(285 km/h).*
Service ceiling: 13,120 ft *(4,000 m).*
Range: 421 n miles *(780 km).*
Role/Weapon systems: Cougar Resco perform the Combat SAR (C-SAR) mission with AF Squadron EH 1/67 'Pyrénées' (with mixed Air Force/Navy crews). One or two to embark in *Charles de Gaulle* for every deployment. A total of 14 such aircraft is expected. Cougar HUS (Hélicoptère Unite Spéciale) are operated by Army Aviation Flight no 3 for special operations, including maritime counter-terrorism, and could be embarked in *Charles de Gaulle*, LHDs, LSDs, FREMM/AVT, La Fayette and Floréal class frigates. Sensors: Bendix 1400C radar; Thales Chlio FLIR; Thales Sherloc radar warning; Thales MWS 20 Damien missile warning; Marconi laser detector; Alkan Elips chaff dispenser; Link 16 in due course (Resco helicopters). Weapons: 2 FN 7.62 mm MGs (possibly 12.7 mm MGs or 20 mm cannons on HUS variant). Capable of carrying 29 passengers or 11 stretchers.

EC 725 HUS *1/2007, **B Prézelin*** / 1305022

EC 725 RESCO *1/2007, **B Prézelin*** / 1305024

Numbers/Type: 3/6/15 Eurocopter (Aerospatiale) SA 365F Dauphin 2/SA 365N Dauphin 2/AS 565MA Panther.
Operational speed: 165 kt *(305 km/h).*
Service ceiling: 16,700 ft *(5,100 m).*
Range: 486 n miles *(900 km).*
Role/Weapon systems: New-built SA 365F Dauphin 2s acquired to replace Alouette IIIs for carrierborne SAR. They feature the same ORB-32 radars as Panthers. SA 365Ns are second-hand helicopters purchased for SAR, general surveillance and public service roles from various locations in metropolitan France. They do not have any radar. Fifteen AS 565 Panthers purchased in several batches to operate from Cassard class DDGs, La Fayette and Floréal class frigates. 16th aircraft acquired from the Armée de l'Air (French Air Force). All Panthers to be modernised to Standard 2 2008–2012 with new avionics, comprehensive countermeasures suite (laser, radar and missile warning systems, decoy dispenser), FLIR and datalink. Follow-on Standard 3 are to feature a new surveillance radar and lightweight anti-ship missiles. Service life to 2025 (AS 565MA). Sensors: (AS 565MA and SA 365F) Thales ORB-32 radar and (AS 565MA) Thales Chlio FLIR on some helicopters (all fitted for); Titus tactical situation management aid (with encrypted data link). Weapons: (AS 565MA) provision for internally mounted 7.62 mm MG.

SA 365F DAUPHIN 2 *2/2008*, **B Prézelin*** / 1335752

AS 565 PANTHER *2/2008*, **B Prézelin*** / 1335753

Numbers/Type: 1 NH Industries NH 90 NFH.
Operational speed: 162 kt *(300 km/h).*
Service ceiling: 13,940 ft *(4,250 m).*
Range: 621 n miles *(1,150 km).*
Role/Weapon systems: Total of 27 NH-90 ordered 30 June 2000 for the French Navy in two variants: 13 NHS support helicopters with secondary ASuW role; 14 NHC combat helicopters for ASW and ASuW. First production aircraft flown on 12 May 2006. Delivery programme: Two NHS by November 2009, all NHC by 2013. Sensors: both variants: Thales ENR surveillance radar; Sagem OLOSP tactical FLIR; MBDA Saphir decoy dispenser; Link 11; NHC: TUS FLASH dipping sonar, and UMS 2000-TSM 8203 sonobuoy processing system. Weapons: ASM (NHC and NHS); 2 MU 90 Impact torpedoes (NHC).

NH 90 *3/2004, **NHI*** / 0062373

Numbers/Type: 100 Aerospatiale SA 330Ba Puma.
Operational speed: 139 kt *(257 km/h).*
Service ceiling: 15,750 ft *(4,800 m).*
Range: 297 n miles *(550 km).*
Role/Weapon systems: Troop carrying helicopter owned by French Army and operable from amphibious ships.

SA 330 *6/2005, **FAP*** / 0589661

Numbers/Type: 7 Aerospatiale SA 321G Super Frelon.
Operational speed: 135 kt *(250 km/h).*
Service ceiling: 10,170 ft *(3,100 m).*
Range: 420 n miles *(778 km).* 594 n miles *(1,100 km)* with auxiliary tank.
Role/Weapon systems: Formerly ASW helicopter; used for assault and support tasks embarked on carriers and LSDs; radar updated; provision for 27 passengers. Service life extended to 2012 to allow replacement by NH 90. Assigned to Flotille 32F. Sensors: Omera ORB search radar. Thales Chlio FLIR fitted to one aircraft. Weapons: Provision for 20 mm gun.

SUPER FRELON *7/2008*, **B Prézelin*** / 1335751

Numbers/Type: 27 Westland Lynx Mk 4 (FN).
Operational speed: 125 kt *(232 km/h).*
Service ceiling: 12,500 ft *(3,810 m).*
Range: 320 n miles *(593 km).*
Role/Weapon systems: Sole French ASW helicopter, all now of the Mk 4 variant; embarked in destroyers and deployed on training tasks. Service life to 2015. To be replaced by NH 90. A limited modernisation (Link 11 and Thales Chlio FLIR) programme will be applied to a small number of aircraft. Sensors: Omera 31 search radar, Alcatel (DUAV 4) dipping sonar, sonobuoys, Sextant Avionique MAD. Weapons: ASW; two Mk 46 Mod 1 (all aircraft being modified to launch EuroTorp Mu 90 Impact) torpedoes, or depth charges. ASV: 1—7.62 mm MG.

LYNX *2/2008*, **B Prézelin*** / 1335750

Numbers/Type: 27 Aerospatiale SA 319B Alouette III.
Operational speed: 113 kt *(210 km/h).*
Service ceiling: 10,500 ft *(3,200 m).*
Range: 327 n miles *(605 km).*
Role/Weapon systems: General purpose helicopter SA 316B with Turboméca Artouste engine; SA 319B with Astazou engine; replaced by Lynx for ASW; now used for trials, surveillance and training tasks. Sensors: Some radar. Weapons: Unarmed.

ALOUETTE III *6/2008*, **Chris Sattler*** / 1335771

LAND-BASED MARITIME AIRCRAFT (FRONT LINE)

Notes: In addition to frontline aircraft, the naval inventory includes 11 Embraer EMB-121 Xingu executive aircraft used for communications (Flotilles 24F and 28F) and eight CAP 10 and nine Morane-Saulnier (SOCATA) Rallye for initial in-flight training with EIP/Escadrille 50S.

Numbers/Type: 4 Dassault Falcon 50M.
Operational speed: 475 kt *(880 km/h)*.
Service ceiling: 49,000 ft *(14,930 m)*.
Range: 3,500 n miles *(6,480 km)*.
Role/Weapon systems: Maritime reconnaissance and SAR roles in the Atlantic and overseas stations (replaced deleted Atlantic Mk 1). First aircraft delivered in December 1999 (for Opeval), second in March 2000, third in March 2001; fourth and last one late 2002. Being fitted with a Spationav VI terminal to share common picture with maritime surveillance assets. A Standard 2 modernisation programme is to be implemented from 2007. Allocated to Flotille 24F (Lann-Bihoué). Sensors: Thales/DASA Ocean Master 100(V) search radar, Thales Chlio FLIR, Inmarsat C. Weapons: Unarmed (two SAR chains). Endurance: six hours 30 minutes at 100 n miles *(185 km)* from base, four hours at 500 n miles *(926 km)* or one hour at 1,200 n miles *(2,222 km)*.

FALCON 50M *1/2007, B Prézelin* / 1305025

Numbers/Type: 4 Boeing E-3F Sentry AWACS.
Operational speed: 460 kt *(853 km/h)*.
Service ceiling: 30,000 ft *(9,145 m)*.
Range: 870 n miles *(1,610 km)*.
Role/Weapon systems: Air defence early warning aircraft with secondary role to provide coastal AEW for the Fleet; 6 hours endurance at the range given above. Modernised 2003–06 under the Radar System Improvement Programme (RSIP). Sensors: Westinghouse APY-2 surveillance radar, Bendix weather radar, Mk XII IFF, Yellow Gate, ESM, ECM. Weapons: Unarmed. Operated by the Air Force.

E-3F *6/2002, Armée de l'Air* / 0118289

Numbers/Type: 27 Dassault Aviation Atlantique Mk 2.
Operational speed: 355 kt *(658 km/h)*.
Service ceiling: 32,800 ft *(10,000 m)*.
Range: 11 hours patrol at 600 n miles from base; 8 hours patrol at 1,000 n miles from base; 4 hours patrol at 1,500 n miles from base.
Role/Weapon systems: Maritime reconnaissance. ASW, ASV, COMINT/ELINT roles. Last one delivered in January 1998. Assigned to Flottilles 21F and 23F. Six aircraft are in long-term storage. Sensors: Thomson-CSF Iguane radar, ARAR 13 ESM, ECM, FLIR, MAD, sonobuoys (with DSAX-1 Thomson-CSF Sadang processing equipment). Link 11 (being fitted in all). COMINT/ELINT equipment optional. Integrated sensor/weapon system built around a CIMSA 15/125X computer. Weapons: Two AM 39 Exocet ASMs in ventral bay, or up to eight lightweight torpedoes (Mk 46 and later Mu 90), or depth charges, mines or bombs. Limited modernisation programme planned to adapt aircraft to Mu 90 torpedoes. More extensive modernisation planned for 18 aircraft 2008–2015. Four other aircraft are likely to be limited to a reconnaissance role. One withdrawn from service in 2007. Aircraft deployed to Dakar, Djibouti and (occasionally) Chad.

ATLANTIQUE II *3/2006, M Declerck* / 1167138

Numbers/Type: 10 Aerospatiale N262E.
Operational speed: 226 kt *(420 km/h)*.
Service ceiling: 26,900 ft *(8,200 m)*.
Role/Weapon systems: Crew training and EEZ surveillance role. All allocated to Flotilla 28F for surveillance, SAR and Flying School. Modified N262A aircraft. Service life 2014. Partial replacement by further Falcon 50M is under consideration. Sensors: Omera ORB 32 radar; photo pod. Weapons: Unarmed. Target towing capability.

Numbers/Type: 6 Dassault-Aviation Falcon 10MER.
Operational speed: 492 kt *(912 km/h)*.
Service ceiling: 35,500 ft *(10,670 m)*.
Range: 1,920 n miles *(3,560 km)*.
Role/Weapon systems: Primary aircrew/ECM training role but also has overwater surveillance role. Avionics upgrade (Standard 2) programme started in 2006. Sensors: Search radar. Weapons: Unarmed. Allocated to Flottille 57S (Landivisiau).

FALCON 10MER *7/2003, Paul Jackson* / 0569996

Numbers/Type: 5 Dassault-Aviation Falcon 200/Gardian.
Operational speed: 470 kt *(870 km/h)*.
Service ceiling: 45,000 ft *(13,715 m)*.
Range: 2,425 n miles *(4,490 km)*.
Role/Weapon systems: Assigned to Flotilla 25F based at Tahiti with permanent detachments at Tontouta (New Caledonia) and Martinique. Maritime reconnaissance role. Service life 2015; modernisation/replacement is under consideration. Sensors: Thomson-CSF Varan radar, Omega navigation, ECM/ESM pods. Weapons: Unarmed.

PATROL FORCES

Notes: (1) 'Sauvegarde Maritime' is the organisation that encompasses the surveillance and traffic control of all maritime approaches around continental France and overseas territories. It also includes pollution control. Although all naval ships could participate in surveillance tasks, specialised vessels include the OPVs manned by the navy, patrol vessels and patrol craft of the 'Gendarmarie Maritime', French Customs and 'Affaires Maritimes'. In addition there are merchant support vessels on long-term charter (see *Government Maritime Forces*). All these ships, including specialised naval ships, display blue/white/red stripes on hull sides.
(2) Naval patrol ships (OPVs) are referred to as 'Patrouilleurs de Service Public' (PSP, Public Service Special Patrol Vessel). All PSPs and other government service craft are to be fitted with Spationev VI terminals to share a common maritime picture.
(3) The potential use of Unmanned Surface Vehicles (USV) is under investigation.
(4) There are some 60 RHIBs in service for harbour and ship protection.

1 LAPÉROUSE CLASS (PBO)

Name	*No*	*Builders*	*Launched*	*Commissioned*
ARAGO	P 675 (ex-*A 795*)	Lorient Naval Dockyard	9 Sep 1990	9 July 1991

Displacement, tons: 830 standard; 980 full load
Dimensions, feet (metres): 193.5 × 35.8 × 11.9 *(59 × 10.9 × 3.6)*
Main machinery: 2 Wärtsilä UD 30 V12 M6D diesels; 2,500 hp(m) *(1.84 MW)*; 2 cp props; bow thruster; 160 hp(m) *(120 kW)*
Speed, knots: 15. **Range, n miles:** 5,200 at 12 kt
Complement: 30 (3 officers)
Guns: 2—12.7 mm MGs.
Radars: Navigation: 1 Decca E 250 (DRBN 38A); 1 Furuno; I-band.

Comment: Ex-survey ship converted in 2002 for patrol duties. Based at Toulon. Equipped with raiding craft.

ARAGO *1/2008*, B Prézelin* / 1335748

1 STERNE CLASS (PBO)

Name	*No*	*Builders*	*Commissioned*
STERNE	P 680	La Perrière, Lorient	20 Oct 1980

Displacement, tons: 250 standard; 380 full load
Dimensions, feet (metres): 160.7 × 24.6 × 9.2 *(49 × 7.5 × 2.8)*
Main machinery: 2 SACM-Wärtsilä UD33V 12M5 diesels; 3,600 hp(m) *(2.65 MW)* sustained; electrohydraulic auxiliary propulsion on starboard shaft; 150 hp(m) *(110 kW)*; 2 shafts
Speed, knots: 20; 6 on auxiliary propulsion. **Range, n miles:** 4,900 at 12 kt; 1,500 at 20 kt
Complement: 20 (3 officers); 2 crews
Guns: 2—12.7 mm MGs.
Radars: Navigation: 1 Racal Decca; 1 Furuno; I-band.

Comment: *Sterne* was the first ship for the FSMC. Has active tank stabilisation. Launched 31 October 1979 and completed 18 July 1980 for the 'Affaires Maritimes' but then transferred and is now manned and operated by the Navy from Brest. Service life 2009.

STERNE *11/2004, B Prézelin* / 1042236

10 P 400 CLASS (LARGE PATROL CRAFT) (PBO)

Name	*No*	*Builders*	*Commissioned*
L'AUDACIEUSE	P 682	CMN, Cherbourg	18 Sep 1986
LA BOUDEUSE	P 683	CMN, Cherbourg	15 Jan 1987
LA CAPRICIEUSE	P 684	CMN, Cherbourg	13 Mar 1987
LA FOUGUEUSE	P 685	CMN, Cherbourg	13 Mar 1987
LA GLORIEUSE	P 686	CMN, Cherbourg	18 Apr 1987
LA GRACIEUSE	P 687	CMN, Cherbourg	17 July 1987
LA MOQUEUSE	P 688	CMN, Cherbourg	18 Apr 1987
LA RAILLEUSE	P 689	CMN, Cherbourg	16 May 1987
LA RIEUSE	P 690	CMN, Cherbourg	13 June 1987
LA TAPAGEUSE	P 691	CMN, Cherbourg	11 Feb 1988

Displacement, tons: 406 standard; 480 full load
Dimensions, feet (metres): 179.8 × 26.2 × 8.5 *(54.8 × 8 × 2.5)*
Main machinery: 2 SEMT-Pielstick 16 PA4 200 VGDS diesels; 8,000 hp(m) *(5.88 MW)* sustained; 2 shafts
Speed, knots: 23. **Range, n miles:** 4,200 at 15 kt
Complement: 26 (3 officers) plus 20 passengers
Guns: 1 Bofors 40 mm/60; 1 Giat 20F2 20 mm; 2—7.62 mm MGs.
Radars: Surface search: 1 Racal Decca DRBN-38A (Bridgemaster E 250); I-band.

Programmes: First six ordered in May 1982, with further four in March 1984. The original propulsion system was unsatisfactory. Modifications were ordered and construction slowed. This class relieved the Patra fast patrol craft which have all transferred to the Gendarmerie.
Structure: Steel hull and superstructure protected by an upper deck bulwark. Design modified from original missile craft configuration. Now capable of transporting personnel with appropriate store rooms. Of more robust construction than previously planned and used as overseas transports. Can be converted for missile armament (MM 38) with dockyard assistance and Simbad PDMS is under consideration. *L'Audacieuse* has done trials with a VDS-12 sonar. Twin funnels replaced the unsatisfactory submerged diesel exhausts in 1990–91. P 682 fitted with new propellers in 2003. If successful the rest of the class will be fitted.
Modernisation: A modernisation programme started in 2002. P 682, 683, 689, 690 and 691 have been refitted. The remainder completed by 2006.
Operational: Deployments: Antilles; P 685, French Guiana; P 682, 684. Nouméa; P 686, 688. La Réunion; P 683 and 690. Tahiti; P 689 and P 691. P 687 completed refit at Lorient in 2006 and subsequently based at Brest. Endurance, 15 days with 45 people aboard. Replacement is under consideration. P 685 to be deleted in 2009.
Sales: To Gabon and Oman.

LA GRACIEUSE *9/2008*, J Brodie* / 1335747

LA GRACIEUSE *6/2006, B Prézelin* / 1040716

1 TRAWLER TYPE (PSO)

Name	*No*	*Builders*	*Commissioned*
ALBATROS (ex-*Névé*)	P 681	Ch de la Seine Maritime	1967

Displacement, tons: 1,940 standard; 2,800 full load
Dimensions, feet (metres): 278.9 × 44.3 × 19.7 *(85.0 × 13.5 × 6.0)*
Main machinery: Diesel-electric; 2 SACM UD 33 V12 S4 diesel generators; 3,050 hp(m) *(2.24 MW)* sustained; 2 motors; 2,200 hp(m) *(1.62 MW)*; 1 shaft
Speed, knots: 15. **Range, n miles:** 14,700 at 14 kt
Complement: 50 (8 officers) plus 15 passengers
Guns: 1 Bofors 40 mm/60. 2—12.7 mm MGs.
Countermeasures: ESM: ARBR 16 radar detector.
Radars: Surface search: 2 DRBN 38A; I-band.

Comment: Former trawler bought in April 1983 from Compagnie Nav. Caennaise for conversion into a patrol ship. Commissioned 19 May 1984. Conducts patrols from Réunion to Kerguelen, Crozet, St Paul and Amsterdam Islands with occasional deployments to South Pacific. Vertrep facilities. Can carry 200 tons cargo, and has 4 tonne telescopic crane. Hospital with six berths and operating room. Major refit in Lorient from June 1990 to March 1991 included new diesel-electric propulsion. A further major overhaul was undertaken in France August 2001-April 2002. Maintenance now carried out in Indian Ocean Shipyards. Service life: 2015.

ALBATROS *4/2002, B Prézelin* / 0528841

1 GRÈBE CLASS (PBO)

Name	*No*	*Builders*	*Commissioned*
GRÈBE	P 679	SFCN, Villeneuve La Garenne	6 Apr 1991

Displacement, tons: 300 standard; 410 full load
Dimensions, feet (metres): 170.6 × 32.2 × 9 *(52 × 9.8 × 2.8)*
Main machinery: 2 Wärtsilä UD 33 V12 M6D diesels; 4,800 hp(m) *(3.53 MW)*; diesel-electric auxiliary propulsion; 245 hp(m) *(180 kW)*; 2 shafts; cp props
Speed, knots: 18; 7.5 on auxiliary propulsion
Range, n miles: 4,500 at 12 kt
Complement: 19 (4 officers); accommodation for 24
Guns: 2—12.7 mm MGs.
Radars: Navigation: Racal Decca; I-band.

Comment: Type Espadon 50 ordered 17 July 1988 and launched 16 November 1989. Serter 'Deep V' hull; stern ramp for craft storage and handling. Large deck area (8 × 8 m) for Vertrep operations. Pollution control equipment and remotely operated water-jet gun for firefighting. Based at Toulon from November 1997. Service life 2016.

GRÈBE *6/2007, Per Körnefeldt* / 1170133

3 FLAMANT (OPV 54) CLASS (PBO)

Name	*No*	*Builders*	*Launched*	*Commissioned*
FLAMANT	P 676	CMN, Cherbourg	24 Apr 1995	18 Dec 1997
CORMORAN	P 677	Leroux & Lotz, Lorient	15 May 1995	29 Oct 1997
PLUVIER	P 678	CMN, Cherbourg	2 Dec 1996	18 Dec 1997

Displacement, tons: 314 standard; 390 full load
Dimensions, feet (metres): 179.8 × 32.8 × 9.2 *(54.8 × 10 × 2.8)*
Main machinery: CODAD; 2 Deutz/MWM 16V TBD 620 diesels and 2 MWM 12V TBD 234 diesels; 7,230 hp(m) *(5.32 MW)* sustained; 2 shafts; LIPS cp props
Speed, knots: 22 (7 loitering)
Range, n miles: 4,500 at 14 kt
Complement: 20 (3 officers)
Guns: 2—12.7 mm MGs.
Radars: Surface search: 1 Racal Decca Bridgemaster 250 (DRBN 38A); I-band.
Navigation: Racal Decca 20V90 (DRBN 34B); I-band. Racal Decca DRBN 34A (Bridgemaster E 250); I-band.

Comment: Authorised in July 1992 and ordered in August 1993 to a Serter Deep V design. Has a stern door for a 7 m EDL 700 fast assault craft or a Zodiac Hurricane RIB, capable of 30 kt. Two passive stabilisation tanks are fitted, and a remotely operated water-jet gun for firefighting. Deck area of 12 × 9 m for Vertrep. Similar to craft built for Mauritania in 1994. Hulls of all three ships strengthened by DCN Brest by late 2004. Service life: 2022. All based at Cherbourg.

FLAMANT *7/2008*, Maritime Photographic* / 1335770

AMPHIBIOUS FORCES

Notes: (1) There are plans to acquire new EDA (Engins de Débarquement Amphibie) landing craft to replace CTMs and operate with Mistral class LHDs and Foudre class LSDs. They will be faster than current CTMs and LCMs. L-Cat from CNIM is a candidate.
(2) About 25 LCVPs are still in service (from 59 built). Most are used on board LSDs (Foudre class), Batral LCTs and AORs.
(3) Replacement of the Batral class LSTs is under consideration. Options include new Ro-Ro vessels.
(4) Evaluation of a new 30 m landing craft began in October 2008. The L-Cat demonstrator was built by the Gemelin Shipyard at La Rochelle and has the potential to act as a ship-to-shore connector, combining the attributes of a catamaran for transit and, by deploying a movable pontoon deck, a landing craft in beaching mode.

L-Cat demonstrator *11/2008*, CNIM* / 1294795

2 + 1 (1) MISTRAL CLASS (AMPHIBIOUS ASSAULT SHIPS) (LHDM/BPC)

Name	*No*	*Builders*	*Laid down*	*Launched*	*Commissioned*
MISTRAL	L 9013	DCN Brest	10 July 2003	6 Oct 2004	15 Dec 2006
TONNERRE	L 9014	DCN Brest	26 Aug 2003	26 July 2005	1 Aug 2007

Displacement, tons: 16,529 standard; 21,600 full load; 22,300 flooded
Dimensions, feet (metres): 653 × 105 × 20.3 *(199 × 32 × 6.2)*
Flight deck, feet (metres): 653 × 105 (199 × 32)
Main machinery: Electric propulsion: 4 (3 Wärtsilä 16V32 and 1 Wärtsilä 18V200) diesel generators provide total of 20.8 MW for propulsion and services. 2 Alstom Mermaid podded propulsors trainable through 360°; 19,040 hp(m) *(14 MW)* sustained; 1 bow thruster; 2,040 hp(m) *(1.5 MW)*
Speed, knots: 19
Range, n miles: 11,000 at 15 kt; 6,000 at 18 kt
Complement: 177 (20 officers)
Military lift: 450 (up to 900 in austerity conditions) troops and 60 armoured vehicles/(13 MBTs) (approx 1,200 tons of cargo). 4 CTM (LCU) or 2 LCACs.

Missiles: SAM: 2 MBDA Simbad twin PDMS launchers for Matra BAE Dynamics Mistral; IR homing to 6 km (3.2 n miles); warhead 3 kg; anti-sea-skimmer.
Guns: 2 Breda Mauser 30 mm/70; 800 rds/min to 3 km; weight of shell 0.36 kg. 4—12.7 mm MGs.
Countermeasures: ESM: ARBR 21; intercept.
Torpedo defence: SLAT system.
Combat data systems: SENIT 9 combat data system, SIC 21 command support system for joint operations; space available for afloat CJTF command; Syracuse III, Fleetsatcom and Inmarsat. Link 11, Link 16.
Weapons control: 2 Sagem VIGY-20 optronic systems.
Radars: Air/surface search: Thales MRR; 3-D; G-band.
Navigation: 2 Racal-Decca Bridgemaster E 250 (DRBN 38A); I-band.

Helicopters: Up to 16 NH90 or SA 330 Puma or AS 532U2 Cougar or AS 665 Tigre attack helicopters.

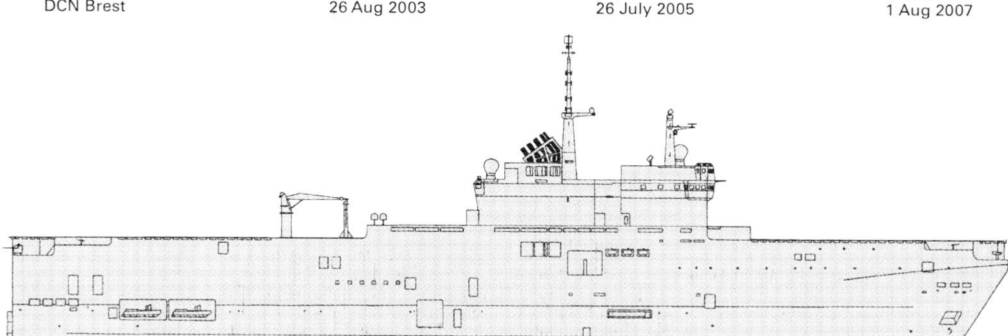

MISTRAL *(Scale 1 : 1,500), Ian Sturton* / 1042093

MISTRAL *10/2008*, Peter Ford* / 1335787

Programmes: Designated BPC (Bâtiment de Projection et de Commandement, support and command ship for force projection), ex-NTCD (new LHDs); which have replaced *Ouragan* and *Orage*. Design and definition phase launched 12 November 1999; building contract notified 22 December 2000; ordered from DCN (prime contractor) and Alstom Marine-Chantiers de l'Atlantique. Forward sections built at St Nazaire, and middle and aft blocks at Brest where final construction and outfitting took place. Sixty per cent of the aft section subcontracted to Stocznia Remontowa, Gdansk, and shipped to Brest by barge. Two further ships are planned to replace the Foudre-class LSDs. While delivery was not expected until about 2020, the order for the third ship is now expected in 2009.
Modernisation: Measures to improve self-defence capabilities are under consideration.
Structure: Built to merchant marine standards. Flight deck has 6 spots, one of which calibrated for CH-53 or MV-22 operations. One 1,800 m² hangar for helicopters or vehicles (2 lifts), one 2,650 m² hangar for vehicles only (1 lift); up to 1,200 tons load on vehicle deck. Well dock 885 m². Hospital: 69 beds; additional modular field hospital may be embarked for humanitarian missions. Other modular facilities could also be embarked according to missions.
Operational: Roles: forward presence, force projection, logistic support for deployed force (ashore or at sea), humanitarian aid, disaster relief, command ship for combined operations. Endurance: 45 days. Sea trials of *Mistral* began 7 March 2005 and of *Tonnerre* on 13 December 2005. Both base at Toulon.

MISTRAL *6/2006, Ships of the World* / 1305010

2 FOUDRE CLASS (LANDING SHIPS DOCK) (LSDH/TCD 90)

Name	*No*	*Builders*	*Laid down*	*Launched*	*Commissioned*
FOUDRE	L 9011	DCN, Brest	26 Mar 1986	19 Nov 1988	7 Dec 1990
SIROCO	L 9012	DCN, Brest	9 Oct 1994	14 Dec 1996	21 Dec 1998

Displacement, tons: 8,190 *(Foudre)*, 8,230 *(Siroco)* light; 12,400 full load; 17,200 flooded
Dimensions, feet (metres): 551 × 77.1 × 17 (30.2 flooded) *(168 × 23.5 × 5.2; 9.2)*
Main machinery: 2 SEMT-Pielstick 16 PC2.5 V 400 diesels; 20,800 hp(m) *(15.3 MW)* sustained; 2 shafts; LIPS cp props; bow thruster; 1,000 hp(m) *(735 kW)*
Speed, knots: 21. **Range, n miles:** 11,000 at 15 kt
Complement: 218 (18 officers)
Military lift: 470 (up to 2,000 for 3 days) troops plus 1,880 tons load; 1 EDIC/CDIC plus 4 CTMs (typical) or 2 CDIC or 10 CTMs or 20 LARC XV amphibious vehicles; 150 vehicles

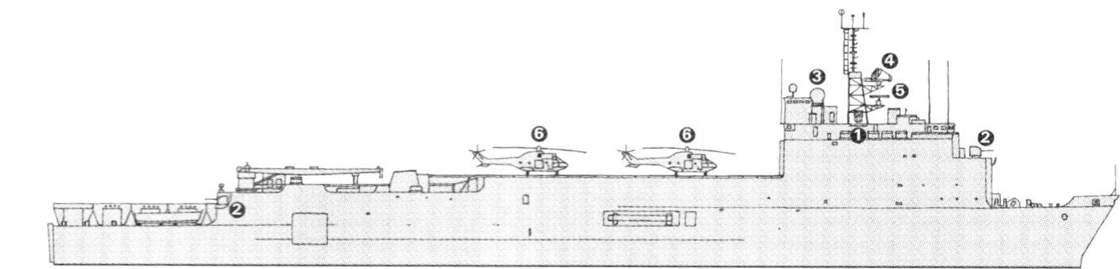

SIROCO *(Scale 1 : 1,500), Ian Sturton* / 0529157

Missiles: SAM: 2 *(Siroco)* or 3 *(Foudre)* MBDA Matra Simbad twin launchers ❶; Mistral; IR homing to 4 km *(2.2 n miles)*; warhead 3 kg.
Guns: 3 Breda/Mauser 30 mm/70 ❷. 800 rds/min to 3 km *(1.6 n miles)*; weight of shell 0.36 kg. 4—12.7 mm MGs.
Countermeasures: ECM: 2 Thales ARBB 36A jammers. SLQ-25 Nixie towed torpedo decoy.
Combat data systems: STIDAV/SENIT 8-01 for close range air defence; Syracuse SATCOM ❸. OPSMER command support system. Link 11 (receive only). INMARSAT.
Weapons control: 2 Sagem DIBC-2A VIGY-105 optronic systems (for 30 mm guns).
Radars: Air/surface search: Thomson-CSF DRBV 21A Mars ❹; D-band.
Surface search: Racal Decca 2459 *(Foudre)*; I-band.
Navigation: 2 Racal-Decca DRBN 34A *(Siroco)* or Racal-Decca 1229 *(Foudre)*; I-band (1 for helo control) ❺.

Helicopters: 4 AS 532UL Cougar or SA 330B Puma ❻ or 2 Super Frelon.

Programmes: First ordered 5 November 1984, second 11 April 1994. Transports de Chalands de Débarquement (TCD).
Modernisation: Sadral SAM replaced by two lightweight Simbad SAMs either side of bridge. New air search radar. 30 mm guns to replace 40 mm and 20 mm in *Foudre* and fitted on build in *Siroco*. Sagem optronic fire control fitted in 1997.
Structure: Designed to take a mechanised regiment of the Rapid Action Force and act as a logistic support ship. Extensive command (OPSMER and other systems) and hospital facilities (500 m²) include two operating suites and 47 beds. Modular field hospital may be embarked on *Siroco*. Well dock of 122 × 14.2 m *(1,732 m²)* which can be used to dock a 400 tons ship. Crane of 37 tons and lift of 52 tons *(Foudre)* or 38 tons *(Siroco)*. Flight deck of *Foudre* 1,450 m² with two landing spots (the landing grid and SAMAHE helo handling system have been removed). Additional landing spot on the (removable) well rolling cover. *Siroco* landing deck extendedaft up to the lift to give a 1,740 m² area. Flume stabilisation fitted in 1993 to *Foudre*.
Operational: Two landing spots on flight deck plus one on deck well rolling cover. Can operate Super Frelons or Super Pumas. Could carry up to 1,600 troops in emergency. Endurance, 30 days (with 700 persons aboard). Assigned to FAN and based at Toulon. Typical loads: one CDIC, four CTM, 10 AMX 10RC armoured cars and 50 vehicles or total of 180 to 200 vehicles (without landing craft).

SIROCO *6/2002, French Navy* / 0529144

FOUDRE *8/2004, B Prézelin* / 1042219

4 BATRAL TYPE (LIGHT TRANSPORTS AND LANDING SHIPS) (LSTH)

Name	*No*	*Builders*	*Commissioned*
FRANCIS GARNIER	L 9031	Brest Naval Dockyard	21 June 1974
DUMONT D'URVILLE	L 9032	Français de l'Ouest	5 Feb 1983
JACQUES CARTIER	L 9033	Français de l'Ouest	28 Sep 1983
LA GRANDIÈRE	L 9034	Français de l'Ouest	20 Jan 1987

Displacement, tons: 750 standard; 1,580 full load
Dimensions, feet (metres): 262.4 × 42.6 × 7.9 *(80 × 13 × 2.4)*
Main machinery: 2 SACM AGO 195 V12 diesels; 3,600 hp(m) *(2.65 MW)* sustained; 2 shafts; cp props
Speed, knots: 14.5. **Range, n miles**: 4,500 at 13 kt
Complement: 52 (5 officers)
Military lift: 180 troops; 12 vehicles; 350 tons load; 10 ton crane
Missiles: SAM: 2 Matra Simbad twin launchers (may be fitted).
Guns: 2 Bofors 40 mm/60 (L 9031). 2 Giat 20F2 20 mm (L 9032-L 9034). 2—12.7 mm MGs.
Radars: Navigation: DRBN 32; I-band.

Helicopters: Platform for Lynx or Panther.

Programmes: Classified as Batral 3F. Bâtiments d'Assaut et deTRAnsport Légers (BATRAL). First two launched 17 November 1973. *Dumont D'Urville* floated out 27 November 1981. *Jacques Cartier* launched 28 April 1982 and *La Grandière* 15 December 1985. *F Garnier* refitted at Brest 2000.
Structure: 40 ton bow ramp; stowage for vehicles above and below decks. One LCVP and one LCPS carried. Helicopter landing platform. Last three of class have bridge one deck higher, a larger helicopter platform and a crane replaces the boom on the cargo deck.
Operational: Deployment: *F Garnier*, Martinique; *D D'Urville*, Papeete; *J Cartier*, New Caledonia; *La Grandière*, Indian Ocean. Service lives of *F Garnier* (2011), *Dumont D'Urville* (2012), *J Cartier* (2013) and *La Grandière* (2014) extended. *Champlain* placed in reserve in Martinique 2004 and later sunk as a target. Deletion of *F Garnier* in 2009 is expected.
Sales: Ships of this class built for Chile, Gabon, Ivory Coast and Morocco. *La Grandière* was also built for Gabon under Clause 29 arrangements but funds were not available.

FRANCIS GARNIER *5/2006, M Declerck* / 1167137

2 CDIC CLASS (LCT)

Name	*No*	*Builders*	*Commissioned*
RAPIÈRE	L 9061	SFCN, Villeneuve la Garenne	28 July 1988
HALLEBARDE	L 9062	SFCN, Villeneuve la Garenne	2 Mar 1989

Displacement, tons: 380 standard; 750 full load
Dimensions, feet (metres): 194.9 × 39 × 5.9 *(59.4 × 11.9 × 1.8)*
Main machinery: 2 SACM Uni Diesel UD 30 V12 M1 diesels; 1,200 hp(m) *(882 kW)* sustained; 2 shafts
Speed, knots: 10.5. **Range, n miles**: 1,000 at 10 kt
Complement: 18 (1 officer) plus 230 passengers
Military lift: 340 tons
Guns: 2 Giat 20F2 20 mm. 2—12.7 mm MGs.
Radars: Navigation: Racal Decca 1229; I-band.

Comment: CDIC (Chaland de Débarquement d'Infanterie et de Chars) built to work with Foudre class. The wheelhouse can be lowered to facilitate docking manoeuvres in the LPDs. Assigned to FAN at Toulon. Given names on 21 July 1997. Replacement of these ships is under consideration. Service lives: 2012.

HALLEBARDE *1/2007, B Prézelin* / 1305028

2 EDIC 700 CLASS (LCT)

Name	*No*	*Builders*	*Commissioned*
SABRE	L 9051	SFCN, Villeneuve la Garenne	13 June 1987
DAGUE	L 9052	SFCN, Villeneuve la Garenne	19 Dec 1987

Displacement, tons: 365 (L 9051), 325 (L 9052) standard; 736 full load
Dimensions, feet (metres): 193.6 × 38.1 × 5.8 *(59 × 11.6 × 1.7)*
Main machinery: 2 SACM Uni Diesel UD 30 V12 M3 diesels; 1,400 hp(m) *(1 MW)* sustained; 2 shafts
Speed, knots: 12. **Range, n miles**: 1,800 at 12 kt
Complement: 10 plus 180 passengers
Military lift: 200 tons, 11 trucks or 5 AMX 30
Guns: 2 Giat 20F2 20 mm. 2—12.7 mm MGs.
Radars: Navigation: Racal Decca 1229; I-band.

Comment: Ordered 10 March 1986. Given names on 29 April 1999. Rated as Engins de Débarquement d'Infanterie et Chars (EDIC III). Based at Dakar-Cap Vert (L 9051) and Djibouti (L 9052). L 9051 refitted in 2004. Similar craft to Lebanon and Senegal. Service lives: 2011.

SABRE *6/2008*, Cor Van Nierkerken* / 1335786

15 CTMS (LCM)

CTM 17–31

Displacement, tons: 59 standard; 150 full load
Dimensions, feet (metres): 78 × 21 × 4.2 *(23.8 × 6.4 × 1.3)*
Main machinery: 2 Poyaud V8520NS diesels; 450 hp(m) *(331 kW)*; 2 shafts
Speed, knots: 9.5
Range, n miles: 380 at 8 kt
Complement: 4 + 200 passengers
Military lift: 90 tons (maximum); 48 tons (normal)
Guns: 2—12.7 mm MGs.
Radars: Navigation: I-band.

Comment: First series of 16 built 1966–70 and all have been deleted. Second series *CTM 17-18* built by Auroux, Arachon; *CTM 19-31* built at CMN, Cherbourg 1982–92. All have a bow ramp. Chalands de Transport de Matériel (CTM). *CTM 17* based at Lorient, *CTM 18* at Mayotte, *CTM 24, 25* at Djibouti, *CTM 26* at Dakar and 10 at Toulon. Six others of the class, CTM 12-16, are based at La Rochelle and operated by the French Army Transport Corps (BTI). The Army *CTM 17* is based at Dakar-Cap Vert.

CTM 27 *2/2008*, B Prézelin* / 1335745

MINE WARFARE FORCES

Notes: Replacement of the capabilities of the current mine-countermeasures force is under consideration. The new system, to be introduced from about 2018, is likely to be based on unmanned underwater vehicles.

3 ANTARÈS (BRS) CLASS (ROUTE SURVEY VESSELS) (MHI)

Name	*No*	*Builders*	*Commissioned*
ANTARÈS	M 770	Socarenam, Boulogne	15 Dec 1993
ALTAÏR	M 771	Socarenam, Boulogne	9 July 1994
ALDÉBARAN	M 772	Socarenam, Boulogne	10 Mar 1995

Displacement, tons: 250 standard; 340 full load
Dimensions, feet (metres): 92.8 × 25.3 × 13.1 *(28.3 × 7.7 × 4)*
Main machinery: 1 Baudouin 12P15-2SR diesel; 800 hp(m) *(590 kW)*; 1 shaft; cp prop; bow thruster
Speed, knots: 12. **Range, n miles**: 3,600 at 10 kt
Complement: 25 (1 officer)
Guns: 1—12.7 mm MG.
Radars: Navigation: 1 Racal-Decca Bridgemaster C 180; I-band.
Sonars: 1 TUS DUBM-44 towed sidescan.

Comment: The vessels' role is to conduct surveillance operations in the approaches to Brest in support of the SSBN fleet. BRS Bâtiments Remorqueurs de Sonars. Trawler type similar to Glycine class (see *Training Ships* section). The DUBM 41B towed bodies have been replaced by TUS DUBM-44 Synthetic Aperture Sonar. A mechanical sweep is also carried. There are two 4.5 ton hydraulic cranes. Original dual navigation training role has been lost.

ALTAIR *7/2008*, B Prézelin* / 1335744

13 ÉRIDAN (TRIPARTITE) CLASS (MINEHUNTERS) (MHC)

Name	*No*	*Laid down*	*Launched*	*Commissioned*
ÉRIDAN	M 641	20 Dec 1977	2 Feb 1979	16 Apr 1984
CASSIOPÉE	M 642	26 Mar 1979	26 Sep 1981	5 May 1984
ANDROMÈDE	M 643	6 Mar 1980	22 May 1982	18 Oct 1984
PÉGASE	M 644	22 Dec 1980	23 Apr 1983	30 May 1985
ORION	M 645	17 Aug 1981	6 Feb 1985	14 Jan 1986
CROIX DU SUD	M 646	22 Apr 1982	6 Feb 1985	14 Nov 1986
AIGLE	M 647	2 Dec 1982	8 Mar 1986	1 July 1987
LYRE	M 648	13 Oct 1983	14 Nov 1986	16 Dec 1987
PERSÉE	M 649	30 Oct 1984	19 Apr 1988	4 Nov 1988
SAGITTAIRE	M 650	1 Feb 1993	14 Jan 1995	2 Apr 1996
VERSEAU (ex-*Iris*)	M 651	20 May 1986	21 June 1987	6 Oct 1988
CÉPHÉE (ex-*Fuchsia*)	M 652	28 Oct 1985	23 Oct 1987	18 Feb 1988
CAPRICORNE (ex-*Dianthus*)	M 653	17 Apr 1985	26 Feb 1987	14 Aug 1987

Displacement, tons: 562 standard; 615 full load
Dimensions, feet (metres): 168.9 × 29.2 × 12.5 *(51.5 × 8.9 × 3.8)*
Main machinery: 1 Stork Wärtsilä A-RUB 215V-12 diesel; 1,860 hp(m) *(1.37 MW)* sustained; 1 shaft; LIPS cp prop
Auxiliary propulsion; 2 motors; 240 hp(m) *(179 kW)*; 2 active rudders; 120 hp *(90 kW)*; 1 bow thruster
Speed, knots: 18; 7 on auxiliary propulsion
Range, n miles: 3,000 at 12 kt
Complement: 49 (5 officers)

Guns: 1 Giat 20F2 20 mm; 720 rds/min to 2 km; 1—12.7 mm MG. 2—7.62 mm MGs.
Countermeasures: MCM: 2 ECA PAP 104 Mod 4 ROVs; Bofors Double Eagle Mk 2 ROV.
Combat data systems: TSM 2061.
Radars: Navigation: Racal Decca DRBN-38A (Bridgemaster E 250); I-band.
Sonars: 1 DUBM 21E (TUS 2022 Mk III) sonar (hull-mounted) and one SPIV PVDS on Bofors Double Eagle Mk 2 ROV; dual frequency.

Programmes: All French ships built in Lorient. Belgium, France and the Netherlands each agreed to build 15 (10 in Belgium with option on five more). Subsequently the French programme was cut to 10. Belgium provided all the electrical installations, France all the minehunting gear and some electronics and the Netherlands the propulsion systems. Replacement for the last of class (sold to Pakistan) was ordered in January 1992. Three Belgian ships of the class acquired between March and August 1997 after being in reserve since 1990.
Modernisation: A modernisation programme started in 2001 and was completed in December 2005. Modernisation included replacement of sonar by TUS 2022 Mk III, fitting of a Bofors Double Eagle Mk 2 ROV, a new tactical data system and upgrade of radar and comms.
Structure: GRP hull. Equipment includes: autopilot and hovering; automatic radar navigation; navigation aids by Loran and Syledis.
Operational: Minehunting, minesweeping, patrol, training, directing ship for unmanned mine-sweeping, HQ ship for diving operations and pollution control. Prepacked 5 ton modules of equipment embarked for separate tasks. M 645, 651 and 653 based at Toulon, remainder at Brest. M 651 and M 649 to be deleted in 2009.
Sales: The original tenth ship of the class, completed in 1989, was transferred to Pakistan 24 September 1992 as part of an order for three; the second built in Lorient, the third in Karachi.

ÉRIDAN *6/2008*, Martin Mokrus* / 1335743

CÉPHÉE *5/2008*, Michael Nitz* / 1335785

CROIX DU SUD *6/2008*, Harald Carstens* / 1335784

4 MCM DIVING TENDERS (MCD)

Name	*No*	*Builders*	*Launched*	*Commissioned*
VULCAIN	M 611	La Perrière, Lorient	17 Jan 1986	11 Oct 1986
PLUTON	M 622	La Perrière, Lorient	13 May 1986	12 Dec 1986
ACHÉRON	A 613	CMN, Cherbourg	19 Nov 1986	21 Apr 1987
STYX	M 614	CMN, Cherbourg	3 Mar 1987	22 July 1987

Displacement, tons: 409 standard; 505 full load
Dimensions, feet (metres): 136.5 × 24.6 × 12.5 *(41.6 × 7.5 × 3.8)*
Main machinery: 2 SACM MGO 175 V16 ASHR diesels; 2,200 hp(m) *(1.62 MW)*; 2 shafts; bow thruster; 70 hp(m) *(51 kW)*
Speed, knots: 13.7
Range, n miles: 2,800 at 13 kt; 7,400 at 9 kt
Complement: 14 (1 officer) plus 12 divers
Guns: 1—12.7 mm MG. 2—7.62 mm MGs.
Radars: Navigation: Decca DRBN-38; I-band.

Comment: First pair ordered in December 1984. Second pair ordered July 1985. Designed to act as support ships for clearance divers. (Bâtiments Bases pour Plongeurs Démineurs – BBPD). *Vulcain* based at Cherbourg, *Pluton* at Toulon, *Achéron* at Toulon as a divingschool tender and *Styx* at Brest. Modified Chamois (BSR) class design. 5 ton hydraulic crane.

VULCAIN *4/2008*, Derek Fox* / 1335742

SURVEY AND RESEARCH SHIPS

Notes: (1) These ships are painted white. A total of about 100 officers and technicians with oceanographic and hydrographic training is employed in addition to the ships' companies listed here. They occupy the extra billets marked as 'scientists'.
(2) In addition to the ships listed below there is a civilian-manned 25 m trawler *L'Aventurière II* (launched July 1986) operated by GESMA, Brest for underwater research which comes under DCN.
(3) Two 9 m survey launches, *Matthew* and *Hunter* were built in 1980.
(4) In New Caledonia, there is a 30 m buoy-tender *Louis Hénin* and a 7 m survey launch *Chambeyron*.
(5) There are three ROVs used for research and salvage: *Erato* can operate to a depth of 1,200 m; *Achille* to 400 m; *Ulisse* to 1,000 m.

1 BEAUTEMPS-BEAUPRÉ CLASS (BHO HYDROGRAPHIC AND OCEANOGRAPHIC SURVEY SHIP) (AGOR)

Name	*No*	*Builders*	*Laid down*	*Launched*	*Commissioned*
BEAUTEMPS-BEAUPRÉ	A 758	Alstom Marine, Lorient	17 July 2001	26 Apr 2002	13 Dec 2003

Displacement, tons: 2,125 standard; 3,330 full load
Dimensions, feet (metres): 264.5 × 48.9 × 23.0 *(80.6 × 14.9 × 7)*
Main machinery: Diesel-electric; four 1,500 hp(m) *(1.1 MW)* Mitsubishi diesels; 2 Alstom electric motors; 2,950 hp *(2.2 MW)*; 1 shaft; 3,000 hp(m) *(2.2 MW)*.
2 active rudders 300 hp(m) *(220 kW)* each; bow thruster 600 hp(m) *(440 kW)*.
Speed, knots: 14
Range, n miles: 8,300 at 12 kt
Complement: 26 (5 officers) (two crews) plus 25 to 30 scientists
Guns: 2—7.62 mm MGs.
Radars: Navigation: 2 Kongsberg; I-band
Sonars: EG & G side looking towed sonar; Kongsberg/Simrad EM 120 deep multipath echo sounder (12 kHz); Kongsberg/Simrad EA 600 deep echo sounder (12 kHz); Kongsberg/Simrad EM 1002S shallow waters multipath echo-sounder (95 kHz); Kongsberg/Simrad EA 400-210 shallow waters echo sounder (33 kHz); Kongsber/Simrad SBP 120 (3 to 7 kHz) narrow beam and SHOM 9TR 109 (3.5 kHz) wide beam sediment echo sounders. Bodenseewerk KSS31 gravimeter; Thales SMM II magnetometer; acoustic current profiler. Most sensor transducers mounted on a removable chassis fixed underneath the hull. Oceanographic buoys; Sippican Mk 21.

Comment: Contracted to Alstom-Leroux Naval 13 March 2001. Derived from the civilian research ship *Thalassa* built in 1995 by Leroux & Lotz (now part of Alstom Marine) for the French government civilian agency IFREMER. 95 per cent funded by the MoD and 5 per cent by the Ministry of civilian research on behalf of IFREMER that will use the ship 10 days per year. First steel cut 17 July 2001. Started builder sea trials 17 October 2002 and official acceptance trials late December. Two VH 8 survey launches. 10 tonne stern gantry and 10 tonne crane; up to 5 shelters can be shipped and bolted on the deck to increase lab surfaces; up to 4 vehicles can be stored in the hold. Endurance 45 days. Bâtiment hydrographique et océanographique (BHO, hydrographic and oceanographic survey ship).

BEAUTEMPS-BEAUPRÉ *8/2008*, B Prézelin* / 1335741

1 DUPUY DE LÔME INTELLIGENCE COLLECTION SHIP (AGIH)

Name	*No*	*Builders*	*Laid down*	*Launched*	*Commissioned*
DUPUY DE LÔME	A 759	Royal Niestern Sander, Delfzijl	1 Dec 2002	27 Mar 2004	23 June 2006

Displacement, tons: 3,100 standard; 4,000 full load
Dimensions, feet (metres): 333.8 × 51.7 × 16.1 *(101.7 × 15.8 × 4.9)*
Main machinery: 2 MaK 9M25 diesels; 7,965 hp *(5.94 MW)*; 2 shafts; 2 bow thrusters
Speed, knots: 16. **Range, n miles:** 3,400 at 16 kt
Complement: 32 + 78 specialists
Guns: 2—12.7 mm MGs.
Radars: Navigation: 2 Racal-Decca DRBN-38A; I-band.

Programmes: Programme initiated 29 October 2001. Contract awarded 14 January 2002 to Thales Naval France (for the mission system) and Compagnie Nationale de Navigation to procure and maintain the vessel for initial five year period. Installation of the MINREM mission system started at Toulon in January 2005. After trials, the ship was delivered to the navy on 15 December 2005 and replaced *Bougainville* in April 2006.
Structure: The ship has a design life of 30 years and is fitted with a flight deck and underway replenishment facilities.
Operational: Fitted with both COMINT and ELINT equipment. The ship is to be available for 350 days a year and active for 240 days. There are two complements. Based at Brest.

DUPUY DE LÔME *8/2008*, Ships of the World* / 1335740

1 POURQUOI PAS? CLASS (OCEANOGRAPHIC SURVEY SHIP) (AGOR)

Name	*No*	*Builders*	*Laid down*	*Launched*	*Commissioned*
POURQUOI PAS?	–	Alstom Marine, St Nazaire	20 Jan 2004	14 Oct 2004	27 Sep 2005

Displacement, tons: 5,000 standard; 6,600 full load
Dimensions, feet (metres): 353.0 × 65.6 × 22.6 *(107.6 × 20 × 6.9)*
Main machinery: Diesel-electric; four Wärtsilä 8L 20C diesel generators 7,725 hp *(5.8 MW)*; two Alstom electric motors; 4,500 hp(m) *(3.3 MW)*; 2 shafts; LIPS cp props
Speed, knots: 14.5. **Range, n miles:** 16,000 at 11 kt
Complement: 33 + 40 scientists
Radars: Navigation: 2 Kongsberg; I-band.
Sonars: Reason Seabat 7111 (100 kHz) and Seabat 7150 (12/24 kHz) multipath echo sounders; Simrad EA 600 (12/38/200 kHz) deep echo sounder; RDI Ocean Surveyor current profiler (38/150 kHz); Eramer/Triton Elics sediment echo sounder (2-8 kHz); most sensor transducers mounted on a removable chassis fixed underneath the hull; also optional towed sonars.

Comment: Contract awarded 17 December 2002 to Alstom Marine. Funded 55 per cent by the Ministry of Research and Education, and 45 per cent by the MoD which will use the ship 150 days per year; civilian manned (operated by Genavir on behalf of IFREMER research agency — see Government Maritime Forces), with navy specialists when operating for military campaigns. First steel cut 1 September 2003. Trials in February 2005 and delivery in March 2005. Optional additional labs in containers; helo deck. Able to operate the *Nautile* mini sub, the *Victor 6000* ROV or the future NATO Submarine Rescue System (NSRS); can embark up to three navy VH 8 survey launches (two under davits); stern gantry to handle equipments up to 22 tonnes. Space allocated to embark up to 20 20 ft containers. Endurance 60 days. *Pourquoi Pas?* (Why not?) is the name given by the famous explorer and oceanographer Jean-Baptiste Charcot (1867–1936) to several of his research vessels.

POURQUOI PAS? *9/2005, B Prézelin* / 1153176

3 LAPÉROUSE (BH2) CLASS (AGS)

Name	*No*	*Builders*	*Launched*	*Commissioned*
LAPÉROUSE	A 791	Lorient Naval Dockyard	14 Nov 1986	20 Apr 1988
BORDA	A 792	Lorient Naval Dockyard	14 Nov 1986	16 June 1988
LAPLACE	A 793	Lorient Naval Dockyard	9 Nov 1988	5 Oct 1989

Displacement, tons: 850 standard; 980 full load
Dimensions, feet (metres): 193.5 × 35.8 × 13.8 *(59 × 10.9 × 4.2)*
Main machinery: 2 Unidiesel UD 30 175V12RVR diesels; 2,500 hp(m) *(1.84 MW)*; 2 cp props; auxiliary propulsion; electric motor and 160 hp(m) *(120 kW)* bow thruster
Speed, knots: 15. **Range, n miles:** 6,000 at 12 kt
Complement: 31 (3 officers) plus 11–18 scientists
Guns: 2—7.62 mm MGs
Radars: Navigation: Decca Bridgemaster (DRBN 38A) (A 791, 792); Furuno (A 793); I-band.
Sonars: Thomson Sintra DUBM 42 (A 792, A 793); active search; high frequency.
DUBM 21C (A 791); active search; high frequency.
EG & G towed sidescan sonar.
Kongsberg/Simrad EM 1002 S shallow water multipath echo sounder (95 kHz); Thales SMM II magnetometer; sediment echo sounder. Atlas DESO 20 echo sounder (A 791) (100 kHz).

Comment: Ordered under 1982 and 1986 estimates, first two on 24 July 1984, third 22 January 1986 and fourth (*Arago* – converted in 2002 to patrol craft) on 12 April 1988. BH2 (Bâtiments Hydrographiques de 2e classe). Carry 2-3 VH 8 survey launches. Based at Brest.

BORDA *6/2007, B Prézelin* / 1305032

1 RESEARCH SHIP (AGMH)

Name	*No*	*Builders*	*Launched*	*Commissioned*
MONGE	A 601	Chantiers de l'Atlantique, St Nazaire	6 Oct 1990	5 Nov 1992

Displacement, tons: 17,760 standard; 21,040 full load
Dimensions, feet (metres): 740.1 × 81.4 × 25.3 *(225.6 × 24.8 × 7.7)*
Main machinery: 2 SEMT-Pielstick 8 PC2.5 L 400 diesels; 10,400 hp(m) *(7.65 MW)* sustained; 1 shaft; LIPS cp props; bow thruster; 1,360 hp(m) *(1 MW)*
Speed, knots: 16. **Range, n miles:** 15,000 at 15 kt
Complement: 115 (9 officers) plus 90 military and civilian technicians
Guns: 2—20 mm. 2—12.7 mm MGs.
Combat data systems: Tavitac 2000 for trials.
Radars: Air search: Thomson-CSF DRBV 15C (Sea Tiger Mk 2); E/F-band.
Missile tracking: 1 Gascogne; C-band. 2 Amor; C-band. 1 Savoie; C-band. 1 Stratus (for trajectography); L-band. 6 Antares (telemetry); E/F-band.
Navigation: Two Racal Decca (DRBN 34A) (one for helo control); I-band.
Helicopters: 1 Alouette III.

Comment: Ordered 25 November 1988. Rated as a BEM (Bâtiment d'Essais et de Mesures). Laid down 26 March 1990, and launched 6 October 1990. She has 14 telemetry antennas; optronic tracking unit; LIDAR; Syracuse SATCOM and Inmarsat. Flume tank stabilisation restricts the ship to a maximum of 9° roll at slow speed in Sea State 6. Flagship of the Trials Squadron. Used for space surveillance by the French Space Agency (CNES) and for M 45 and M 51 ballistic missile tests. Hangar space for two Super Frelon or NH 90. To be equipped a single Stratus with two aerials, to replace Savoie and Stratus, by 2009. Based at Brest.

MONGE *5/2008*, B Prézelin* / 1335739

1 LAPÉROUSE CLASS (MCD/BEGM)

Name	*No*	*Builders*	*Launched*	*Commissioned*
THÉTIS (ex-*Nereide*)	A 785	Lorient Naval Dockyard	14 Dec 1986	9 Nov 1988

Displacement, tons: 900 standard; 1,050 full load
Dimensions, feet (metres): 193.5 × 35.8 × 12.5 *(59.0 × 10.9 × 3.8)*
Main machinery: 2 Uni Diesel UD 30 V16 M4 diesels; 2,710 hp(m) *(1.99 MW)* sustained; 1 shaft; cp prop
Speed, knots: 15. **Range, n miles:** 6,000 at 12 kt
Complement: 38 (2 officers) plus 7 passengers
Guns: 2—12.7 mm MGs.
Radars: Navigation: Racal Decca Bridgemaster (DRBN 38A); I-band.
Sonars: VDS; Thomson Sintra DUBM 42 and DUBM 60A; active search; high frequency. TUS TSM 2022 Mk 3 PVDS (fitted to Double Eagle ROV); active search and classification.

Comment: Same hull as Lapérouse class. Classified as Bâtiment Experimental Guerre de Mines (BEGM). Operated by the Centre d'Études, d'Instruction et d'Entraînement de la Guerre des Mines (CETIEGM) in Brest. Launched 19 March 1988. Renamed to avoid confusion with Y 700. Equipped to conduct trials on all underwater weapons and sensors for mine warfare. Can lay mines. Can support six divers.

THÉTIS *7/2008*, B Prézelin* / 1335738

7 TYPE VH 8 FASSMER SURVEY LAUNCHES (YGS)

Displacement, tons: 4.5
Dimensions, feet (metres): 25.9 × 7.9 × 1.6 *(7.9 × 2.4 × 0.5)*
Main machinery: 1 Volvo Penta Aquamatic Duotrop (41 TD) diesel; Z-drive; 1 shaft; 237 hp(m) *(174 kW)*
Speed, knots: 17. **Range, n miles:** 109
Complement: 6

Comment: Built by Fr. Fassmer GmbH & Co (Germany); first craft delivered October 2002 and based at Toulon since July 2003. Last craft delivered October 2003. Carried by *Beautemps-Beaupré* and Lapérouse-class survey vessels. Vedette hydrographique de 8m (VH 8). Fitted with two echo sounders, one multipath echo sounder (Simrad EM 3200), side-scan towed sonar and towed magnetometer. Unofficial names: *Albatros, Cormoran, Goeland, Guillemot, Macareux, Pelican, Phaeton.*

1 RESEARCH SHIP (AETL)

Name	No	Builders	Launched	Commissioned
DENTI	A 743	DCAN Toulon	7 Oct 1975	15 July 1976

Displacement, tons: 190 full load
Dimensions, feet (metres): 113.8 × 21.6 × 7.5 *(34.7 × 6.6 × 2.3)*
Main machinery: 2 Baudouin DP8 diesels; 960 hp(m) *(706 kW)*; 2 shafts; cp props
Speed, knots: 12. **Range, n miles:** 800 at 12 kt
Complement: 6 (2 officers) plus 6 scientists
Radars: Navigation: Decca; I-band.

Comment: Employed on ammunition trials for DCN off Toulon. Service life extended to 2010.

DENTI *6/2007, B Prézelin* / 1305035

TRAINING SHIPS

Notes: The incomplete hulk of *Narvik*, the first type BAMO catamaran minehunter (project cancelled), has been adapted to act as a training hulk for marines to conduct ship assault operations. Laid up at Lorient.

2 CHIMERE CLASS (TRAINING SHIPS) (AXL)

CHIMÈRE Y 706 **FARFADET** Y 711

Displacement, tons: 100 full load
Dimensions, feet (metres): 100.1 × 17.1 × 5.7 *(30.5 × 5.2 × 1.75)*
Main machinery: 2 Baudouin DK4 M diesels; 400 hp *(300 kW)*; 1 shaft
Speed, knots: 11
Complement: 7
Radars: Navigation: Decca 1226; I-band.

Comment: Naval school tenders built at Bayonne and which entered service in 1970 (Y 706) and 1971 (Y 711). Due to be decommissioned in 2010.

CHIMÈRE *11/2006, B Prézelin* / 1040701

8 LÉOPARD CLASS (AXL)

Name	No	Builders	Commissioned
LÉOPARD	A 748	ACM, St Malo	4 Dec 1982
PANTHÈRE	A 749	ACM, St Malo	4 Dec 1982
JAGUAR	A 750	ACM, St Malo	18 Dec 1982
LYNX	A 751	La Perrière, Lorient	18 Dec 1982
GUÉPARD	A 752	ACM, St Malo	1 July 1983
CHACAL	A 753	ACM, St Malo	10 Sep 1983
TIGRE	A 754	La Perrière, Lorient	1 July 1983
LION	A 755	La Perrière, Lorient	10 Sep 1983

Displacement, tons: 335 standard; 470 full load
Dimensions, feet (metres): 141 × 27.1 × 10.5 *(43 × 8.3 × 3.2)*
Main machinery: 2 SACM MGO 175 V16 ASHR diesels; 2,200 hp(m) *(1.62 MW)*; 2 shafts; cp props
Speed, knots: 15. **Range, n miles:** 4,800 at 12 kt
Complement: 15 plus 22 trainees
Guns: 2—12.7 mm MGs.
Radars: Navigation: Racal Decca DRBN-38A (Bridgemaster E 250); I-band.

Comment: First four ordered May 1980. Further four ordered April 1981. Form 20ème Divec (Training division) for shiphandling training and occasional EEZ patrols. Based at Brest. To be decommissioned 2010–14.

PANTHÈRE *6/2008*, Michael Nitz* / 1335783

2 GLYCINE CLASS (AXL)

Name	No	Builders	Commissioned
GLYCINE	A 770	Socarenam, Boulogne	11 Apr 1992
EGLANTINE	A 771	Socarenam, Boulogne	9 Sep 1992

Displacement, tons: 250 standard; 295 full load
Dimensions, feet (metres): 92.8 × 25.3 × 12.5 *(28.3 × 7.7 × 3.8)*
Main machinery: 1 Baudouin 12P15-2SR diesel; 800 hp(m) *(588 kW)*; 1 shaft; cp prop
Speed, knots: 10. **Range, n miles:** 3,600 at 10 kt
Complement: 10 + 16 trainees
Radars: Navigation: 4 Furuno; I-band.

Comment: Trawler type training ships. Three more built in 1995–96 as route survey craft (included under *Mine Warfare Forces* section). Based at Brest.

EGLANTINE *8/2007, B Prézelin* / 1305037

2 LA BELLE POULE CLASS (AXS)

L'ÉTOILE A 649 **LA BELLE POULE** A 650

Displacement, tons: 275 full load
Dimensions, feet (metres): 127 × 24.3 × 12.1 *(37.5 × 7.4 × 3.7)*
Main machinery: 1 Baudouin DNP 8 diesel; 245 hp(m) *(180 kW)*; 1 shaft
Speed, knots: 9 (diesel)
Complement: 20 (1 officer) plus 20 trainees

Comment: Auxiliary sail vessels. Built by Chantiers de Normandie (Fécamp) and launched 7 July 1932 and 8 February 1932 respectively. Accommodation for three officers, 30 cadets, five petty officers, 12 men. Sail area 450 m². Attached to Naval School. A 650 refitted in 2006.

LA BELLE POULE *6/2008*, B Prézelin* / 1335737

1 SAIL TRAINING SHIP (AXS)

LA GRAND HERMINE (ex-*La Route est Belle*, ex-*Ménestrel*) A 653

Displacement, tons: 13 full load
Dimensions, feet (metres): 45.9 × 13.5 × 6.6 *(14.0 × 4.1 × 2.0)*
Main machinery: 1 MWM D 225A diesel; 55 hp *(41 kW)*; 1 shaft
Speed, knots: 7
Complement: 7
Radars: Navigation: 1 Furuno DRBN 39; I-band.

Comment: Training yawl built in Marseille in 1932. Procured by the French Navy in 1963 and based at Brest.

LA GRAND HERMINE *2/2005, B Prézelin* / 1153158

1 SAIL TRAINING SHIP (AXS)

Name	*No*	*Builders*	*Launched*
MUTIN	A 652	Florimond-Guignardeau, Les Sables d'Olonne	18 Mar 1927

Displacement, tons: 57 full load
Dimensions, feet (metres): 108.3 × 21 × 11.2 *(33 × 6.4 × 3.4)*
Main machinery: 1 diesel; 112 hp(m) *(82 kW)*; 1 auxiliary prop
Speed, knots: 6 (diesel)
Range, n miles: 860 at 6 kt
Complement: 12 + 6 trainees
Radars: Navigation: Furuno; I-band.

Comment: Attached to the Navigation School. Has a sail area of 312 m^2. This is the oldest ship in the French Navy. Used by the SOE during the Second World War.

MUTIN *7/2005, B Prézelin* / 1153159

AUXILIARIES

Notes: (1) The programme to procure up to eight 'Bâtiments de Soutien et d'assistance hauturiers' (BSAH) has been delayed due to funding difficulties and may have been overtaken by plans (announced in July 2008) to charter two 'Bâtiments de Soutien, d'assistance et de dépollution' (BSAP) from Bourbon Offshore.
(2) 30–40 harbour service craft are to be procured to replace older series of harbour tenders and service craft. With the same basic hull and machinery, the class should comprise pilot boats, diving support tenders and fire-fighting craft. Entry into service is planned by 2010.
(3) Inshore transport duties at Brest and Toulon have been chartered to civilian companies. At Brest, Société Morbihannaise de Navigation (SMN) awarded a five-year contract from 1 July 2004 to transport 2,300 daily passengers from Brest to and from Lanvéoc-Poulmic and I'Ile Longue. The company has progressively introduced five purposely-built light transports; *Bindy, Tibidy, Trébéron, Arun* and *Térénez* built 2004–05 by Gamelin, La Rochelle (aluminium hull and superstructure, 35.4 × 9 × 1.7 m, 20 kt, 400 passengers).
(4) There are plans to acquire four new AOR to replace the Durance class from about 2017.

4 CHAMOIS CLASS (SUPPLY TENDERS) (AG/ATS/YDT/YPC/YPT)

Name	*No*	*Builders*	*Commissioned*
TAAPE	A 633	La Perrière, Lorient	2 Nov 1983
ÉLAN	A 768	La Perrière, Lorient	7 Apr 1978
CHEVREUIL	A 774	La Perrière, Lorient	7 Oct 1977
GAZELLE	A 775	La Perrière, Lorient	13 Jan 1978

Displacement, tons: 315 (375 A 633) light; 505 full load
Dimensions, feet (metres): 136.1 × 24.6 × 10.5 *(41.5 × 7.5 × 3.2)*
Main machinery: 2 SACM AGO 175 V16 diesels; 2,850 hp(m) *(2.06 MW)*; 2 shafts; cp props; bow thruster
Speed, knots: 14.5
Range, n miles: 7,200 (6,000 A 633) at 12 kt
Complement: 20 plus 12 spare berths
Radars: Navigation: Racal Decca 1226; I-band.

Comment: Similar to the standard fish oil rig support ships. Can act as tugs, oil pollution vessels, salvage craft (two 30 ton and two 5 ton winches), coastal and harbour controlled minelaying, torpedo recovery, diving tenders and a variety of other tasks. Bollard pull 25 tons. Can carry 100 tons of stores on deck or 125 tons of fuel and 40 tons of water or 65 tons of fuel and 120 tons of water. *Taape* ordered in March 1982 from La Perrière-of improved design but basically similar with bridge one deck higher. *Elan* based at Cherbourg, remainder at Toulon. Three paid off so far, one of which (ex-*Chamois*) transferred to Madagascar in May 1996. *Élan, Chevreuil* and *Gazelle* to be decommissioned in late 2009 and *Taape* in 2013.

CHEVREUIL *4/2008*, B Prézelin* / 1335736

4 DURANCE CLASS (UNDERWAY REPLENISHMENT TANKERS) (AORHM)

Name	*No*	*Builders*	*Laid down*	*Launched*	*Commissioned*
MEUSE	A 607	Brest Naval Dockyard	2 June 1977	2 Dec 1978	21 Nov 1980
VAR	A 608	Brest Naval Dockyard	8 May 1979	1 June 1981	29 Jan 1983
MARNE	A 630	Brest Naval Dockyard	4 Aug 1982	2 Feb 1985	16 Jan 1987
SOMME	A 631	Normed, la Seyne	3 May 1985	3 Oct 1987	7 Mar 1990

Displacement, tons: 7,600 (A 607); 7,800 (others) standard; 17,900 (A 607); 18,500 (others) full load
Dimensions, feet (metres): 515.9 × 69.5 × 38.5 *(157.3 × 21.2 × 10.8)*
Main machinery: 2 SEMT-Pielstick 16 PC2.5 V 400 diesels; 20,800 hp(m) *(15.3 MW)* sustained; 2 shafts; LIPS cp props
Speed, knots: 19
Range, n miles: 9,000 at 15 kt
Complement: 162 (11 officers) plus 29 spare
Cargo capacity: 1,300 tons FFO; 5,200 diesel; 3,000 TR5 Avcat; 130 distilled water; 170 victuals; 150 munitions; 50 naval stores *(Meuse)*. 1,300 tons FFO; 8,400 diesel; 1,090 TR5 Avcat; 260 distilled water; 170 munitions; 250 tons spare parts *(Var, Somme* and *Marne)*

Missiles: SAM: 3 (1 in A 607) Matra Simbad twin launchers; Mistral; IR homing to 4 km *(2.2 n miles)*; warhead 3 kg.
Guns: 1 Bofors 40 mm/L 60.
2 Oerlikon Mk 10 20 mm.
4—12.7 mm MGs.
Countermeasures: ESM/ECM.
Combat data systems: AIDCOMER command support system (fitted for BCR ships). Syracuse and INMARSAT SATCOM.
Radars: Navigation: 2 Racal Decca Bridgemaster (DRBN 38A); I-band.

Helicopters: 1 SA 319B Alouette III.

Programmes: One classed as Pétrolier Ravitailleur d'Escadres (PRE). Other three classed as Bâtiments de Commandement et de Ravitaillement (BCR; Command and Replenishment Ships).
Modernisation: EW equipment fitted to improve air defences under the 3A programme in 1996–99. Simbad SAM may be carried at bridge deck level. Oerlikon 20 mm to be replaced by 12.7 mm MGs.
Structure: Four beam transfer positions and two astern, two of the beam positions having heavy transfer capability. *Var, Marne* and *Somme* differ from *Meuse* in several respects. The bridge extends further aft, boats are located either side of the funnel and a crane is located between the gantries. Also fitted with Syracuse 3 SATCOM.
Operational: *Var, Marne* and *Somme* are designed to carry a Maritime Zone staff or Commander of a Logistic Formation and a commando unit of up to 45 men. Capable of accommodating 250 men. Assigned to FAN with one of the three BCR ships deployed to the Indian Ocean as a Flagship. *Somme* replaced *Var* in that role for two years from August 2009. To be replaced after 2015 by new ships.
Sales: One to Australia built locally; two of similar but smaller design to Saudi Arabia. One to Argentina in July 1999.

MEUSE *2/2008*, B Prézelin* / 1335735

MARNE *3/2007, Paul Daly* / 1170126

1 ALIZE CLASS (DIVING TENDER) (YDT)

Name	*No*	*Builders*	*Commissioned*
ALIZÉ	A 645	Socarénam, Boulogne	8 Nov 2005

Displacement, tons: 1,100 standard; 1,700 full load
Dimensions, feet (metres): 196.8 × 45.3 × 16.4 *(60.0 × 13.8 × 5.0)*
Main machinery: 2 ABC diesels; 3,800 hp *(2.8 MW)*; 2 shafts; bow thruster
Speed, knots: 14. **Range, n miles:** 7,500 at 12 kt
Complement: 17 (3 officers) plus 30 passengers
Guns: 2—12.7 mm MGs.
Radars: Navigation: Racal Decca Bridgemaster (DRBN 38A); I-band.
Helicopters: Platform for one medium.

Comment: Ordered in November 2003. Replaced *Isard* in diving support role in 2006. Equipped with recompression chamber and medical facilities. Based at Toulon.

ALIZÉ *6/2007, Per Körnefeldt* / 1170123

1 LE MALIN CLASS (YDT)

LE MALIN (ex-*Apache*) A 616

Displacement, tons: 1,100 full load
Dimensions, feet (metres): 177.2 × 36.1 × ? *(54.0 × 11.0 × ?)*
Main machinery: 1 diesel; 2,550 hp *(1.9 MW)*; 1 shaft
Speed, knots: 14
Complement: 16 (2 officers)
Radars: Navigation: 2 Furuno; I-band.

Comment: Ex-fishing vessel built in Gdansk in 1997, seized on 23 June 2004 and acquired by the French Navy on 7 September 2005 at Port des Galets (La Réunion). Refitted at Toulon in 2006 and entered French naval service as a diving tender replacing *Poséidon* in that role in April 2006. Based at Toulon.

LE MALIN *10/2006, B Prézelin* / 1040705

1 RR 4000 TYPE (SUPPLY TENDERS) (AFL)

Name	*No*	*Builders*	*Commissioned*
REVI	A 635	Breheret, Couëron	9 Mar 1985

Displacement, tons: 1,035 light; 1,577 full load
Dimensions, feet (metres): 167.3 × 41.3 × 13.1 *(51 × 12.6 × 4)*
Main machinery: 2 SACM-Wärtsilä AGO 195 V12 M6 diesels; 4,410 hp(m) *(3.24 MW)*; 2 shafts; cp props; 2 bow thrusters; 400 hp *(300 kW)*
Speed, knots: 14.5
Range, n miles: 5,800 at 12 kt
Complement: 26 (2 officers) plus 8 passengers
Radars: Navigation: Racal Decca Bridgemaster (DRBN 38A); I-band.

Comment: 'Remorqueurs ravitailleurs' built for le Centre d'Expérimentation du Pacifique. Can carry 400 tons of cargo or six 20 ft containers. 50 ton gantry and 18 ton crane. Two water cannons on deck. Bollard pull 47 tons. Based at Papeete.

RR 4000 CLASS *4/2007, B Prézelin* / 1305040

1 TRANSPORT LANDING SHIP (LSL)

Name	*No*	*Builders*	*Commissioned*
GAPEAU	L 9090	Chantier Serra, la Seyne	2 Oct 1987

Displacement, tons: 563 standard; 1,090 full load
Dimensions, feet (metres): 216.5 × 41.0 × 11.2 *(66 × 12.5 × 3.4)*
Main machinery: 2 diesels; 550 hp(m) *(404 kW)*; 2 shafts
Speed, knots: 11
Range, n miles: 1,900 at 10 kt
Complement: 6 + 30 scientists
Cargo capacity: 460 tons
Radars: Navigation: Racal Decca 1226 and Furuno FRS 1000; I-band.

Comment: Supply ship with bow doors. Operates for Centre d'Essais de la Mediterranée. Conducts transfers between Toulon or Port Pothuau and Levant Island (missile range).

GAPEAU *5/2003, Per Körnefeldt* / 0569982

1 MOORING VESSEL (ABU)

TELENN MOR Y 692

Displacement, tons: 392 standard; 520 full load
Dimensions, feet (metres): 135.8 × 29.9 × 6.2 *(41.4 × 9.1 × 1.9)*
Main machinery: 2 Baudouin diesels; 900 hp(m) *(670 kW)*
Speed, knots: 8
Radars: 1 Racal Decca; I-band.

Comment: Commissioned on 16 January 1986 and based at Brest. Equipped with 18 ton hydraulic crane.

TELENN MOR *8/2006, B Prézelin* / 1040706

2 RANGE SUPPORT VESSELS (YFRT)

ATHOS A 712 **ARAMIS** A 713

Displacement, tons: 89 standard; 108 full load
Dimensions, feet (metres): 105.3 × 21.3 × 6.2 *(32.1 × 6.5 × 1.9)*
Main machinery: 2 SACM UD 33V12 M5 diesels; 3,950 hp(m) *(2.94 MW)*; 2 shafts
Speed, knots: 28
Range, n miles: 1,200 at 15 kt
Complement: 13 plus 6 passengers
Guns: 1 – 12.7 mm MG.
Radars: Navigation: Racal Decca 1226 (A 712); Furuno (A 713); I-band.

Comment: Built by Chantiers Navals de l'Esterel for Missile Trials Centre of des Landes (CELM). Based at Bayonne, forming Groupe des Vedettes de l'Adour. A 712 commissioned 20 November 1979 and A 713 on 9 September 1980. Classified as Range Safety Craft from July 1995. *Athos* completed refit at Cherbourg in April 2003. Service life extended to 2010.

ATHOS *5/2008*, B Prézelin* / 1335734

9 VIP 21 DIVING TENDERS (YDT)

DIONÉE Y 790 **LISERON** Y 793 **GENÊT** Y 796
MYOSOTIS Y 791 **MAGNOLIA** Y 794 **GIROFLÉE** Y 797
GARDÉNIA Y 792 **AJONC** Y 795 **ACANTHE** Y 798

Displacement, tons: 35 standard; 49 full load
Dimensions, feet (metres): 71.2 × 16.1 × 5.2 *(21.7 × 4.9 × 1.6)*
Main machinery: 2 Baudouin 12F11M or V6 TI 330 diesels; 530 hp(m) *(390 kW)*; 3 shafts (1 for loitering)
Speed, knots: 13. **Range, n miles:** 500 at 12 kt
Complement: 4 plus 14 divers
Radars: Navigation: Racal Decca RD 170.

Comment: Diving tenders built at Lorient. First one delivered in February 1990. *Y 794* and *Y 798* based at Cherbourg. *Y 790, Y 791, Y 792, Y 795* and *Y 797* based at Toulon. *Y 793* and *Y 796* based at Brest. Rated as 'Vedettes d'Instruction Plongée de 21 m (VIP 21)', divers training craft, and 'Vedettes d'Intervention Plongeurs-Démineurs (VIPD 21)', clearance diving team support craft.

GENÊT *5/2008*, B Prézelin* / 1335733

10 TYPE V14 (HARBOUR CRAFT) (YFL)

TAINA Y 754	**PALANGRIN** Y 777	**AUTÉ** Y 786
L'ETOILE DE MER Y 762	**Y 779**	**TIARÉ** Y 787
DHARUBA Y 763	**Y 780**	
AVEL MOR Y 765	**Y 781**	

Displacement, tons: 14.5 standard; 19.5 full load
Dimensions, feet (metres): 47.9 × 15.1 × 6.2 *(14.6 × 4.6 × 1.9)*
Main machinery: 2 Baudouin diesels; 1,000-750 hp(m) *(735-551 kW)*; 2 shafts
Speed, knots: 25
Range, n miles: 400 at 11 kt
Complement: 4

Comment: Y 754, Y 786 (both at Brest) and Y 787 (Nouméa) are small personnel transport craft. Y 762 (Toulon) and Y 765 (Brest) VIP transport craft. Y 763 and P 790 patrol boats (the latter having been used by the Gendarmerie Maritime), both based at Mayotte, Indian Ocean. Y 777 (Brest) radiologial monitoring craft. Y 779 (Cherbourg), Y 780 (Brest) and Y 781 (Toulon) pilot craft. Design by DCN Cherbourg. Same hull and similar arrangement as for PBs manned by the Gendarmerie Maritime (see *Government forces*). Built under control of DCN Lorient by Stento Shipyard, Balaruc-les-Bains in 1987–88, or by Chantiers Alan Sibiril, Carantec, in 1990–93.

Y 786 *9/2007, B Prézelin* / 1305042

Y 777 *9/2007, B Prézelin* / 1305045

2 VTP CLASS (TRANSPORTS) (YFB)

KERMEUR Y 758 **KERNALEGUEN** Y 759

Displacement, tons: 15 standard; 21 full load
Dimensions, feet (metres): 45.9 × ? × ? *(14.0 × ? × ?)*
Main machinery: 2 MAN diesels; 800 hp *(600 kW)*; 2 shafts
Speed, knots: 8
Complement: 3 + 45 passengers
Radars: Navigation: Furuno; I-band.

Comment: Built by Raidco Marine and delivered 19 September 2006. GRP hull and superstructure. Used as transport craft at l'Ile Longue.

KERMEUR *8/2007, B Prézelin* / 1305044

6 FLOATING REPAIR FACILITIES

Comment: There is one 150 × 33 m floating dock of 3,800 tons capacity, built at Brest in 1975. Based at Papeete. There are five floating cranes: three 15 ton cranes at Toulon (GFA 1, 3 and 4), one at Brest (GFA 6 *Alpaga*) and one 60 ton crane at Cherbourg.

2 PHAÉTON CLASS (TOWED ARRAY TENDERS) (YAG)

PHAÉTON Y 656 **MACHAON** Y 657

Displacement, tons: 69 standard; 75 full load
Dimensions, feet (metres): 63.0 × 22.3 × 3.9 *(19.2 × 6.8 × 1.2)*
Main machinery: 2 SACM diesel; 720 hp(m) *(530 kW)*; waterjet
Speed, knots: 8. **Range, n miles:** 300 at 8 kt
Complement: 4

Comment: 18.6 m catamarans built in 1993–94 at Brest. Water-jet propulsion, speed 8 kt. Hydraulic crane and winch to handle submarine towed arrays. *Phaéton* based at Toulon, *Machaon* at Brest.

MACHAON *6/2008*, B Prézelin* / 1335732

42 + 5 HARBOUR SUPPORT CRAFT

Comment: There are 11 oil barges (CICGH), one of which is of 1,200 tonnes and the rest between 100 and 800 tonnes, eight 400 tonne oily bilge barges (CIEM), three anti-pollution barges (800 tonne BAPM, and two 400 tonne CIEP), and seven water barges (CIE, 120 to 400 tonnes). Some self-propelled. Also 10 self-propelled YFUs (CHA 27-30, 32, 34-38), and one 15 m Sea Truck craft *(Anthias)*.

CHA 30 *10/1999, van Ginderen Collection* / 0069961

1 RADIOLOGICAL MONITORING CRAFT (AGE)

CORALLINE A 790

Displacement, tons: 41 standard; 49 full load
Dimensions, feet (metres): 71.2 × 16.1 × 5.2 *(21.7 × 4.9 × 1.6)*
Main machinery: 2 Baudouin 12F11M diesels; 530 hp *(390 kW)*; 2 shafts
Speed, knots: 13. **Range, n miles:** 500 at 12 kt
Complement: 7
Radars: Navigation: Furuno 1832; I-band.

Comment: Built by DCN Lorient and delivered 1 December 1990. Similar to VIP 21 diving tenders but with different superstructure. Employed on radiation monitoring tasks at Cherbourg.

3 VIR FIREFIGHTING CRAFT (YTR)

AVEL ABER (ex-*Elorn*) Y 783 **LA LOUDE** Y 784 **LA DIVETTE** Y 785

Displacement, tons: 14 standard; 23 full load
Dimensions, feet (metres): 47.9 × 15.1 × 6.2 *(14.6 × 4.6 × 1.9)*
Main machinery: 2 Baudouin V6 TI450 diesels; 750 hp *(550 kW)*; 2 shafts
Speed, knots: 17. **Range, n miles:** 110 at 12 kt
Complement: 4
Radars: Navigation: Furuno 1832; I-band.

Comment: Firefighting craft built by Alan Sibril, Carantec, and delivered in 1993–94. Similar to V 14 craft. Equipped with two water cannons.

AVEL ABER *8/2008*, B Prézelin* / 1335731

5 COUACH-PLASCOA 980 (SERVICE CRAFT) (YFL)

NYMPHEA Y 603 (ex-P706)
FUCHSIA Y 604 (ex-P712)
GENDARME PEREZ Y 605 (ex-P 708)
PIVOINE Y 705 (ex-P705)
GENERAL DELFOSSE Y 710 (ex-P 710)

Displacement, tons: 6 standard; 7 full load
Dimensions, feet (metres): 32.5 × 12.2 × 3.3 *(9.9 × 3.73 × 1.0)*
Main machinery: 2 Volvo Penta TAMD 61 diesels; 500 hp *(370 kW)*; 2 shafts
Speed, knots: 28. **Range, n miles:** 200 at 15 kt
Complement: 4
Radars: Navigation: Furuno 2400; I-band.

Comment: Former Gendarmerie Maritime craft built in 1985 and transferred in 2004–05. Based at Brest *(Nymphea, General Delfosse)*, Toulon *(Pivoine)*, Saint Mandrier *(Fuchsia, Gendarme Perez)*.

PIVOINE *10/2006, B Prézelin* / 1040711

6 ARCOR 34 (SERVICE CRAFT) (YFL)

LAVANDE Y 606 (ex-P 717)
LILAS Y 703 (ex-P 703)
GENTIANE – (ex-P 711)
BEGONIA – (ex-P 704)
STERDEN
AN HEOL

Displacement, tons: 7 standard; 8 full load
Dimensions, feet (metres): 33.8 × 12.3 × 3.34 *(10.3 × 3.7 × 1.0)*
Main machinery: 2 Volvo Penta TAMD 61 diesels; 500 hp *(370 kW)*; 2 shafts
Speed, knots: 26. **Range, n miles:** 200 at 20 kt
Complement: 3
Radars: Navigation: Furuno 1830; I-band.

Comment: Built in 1989–90 by CN d'Aquitaine. *Sterden* and *An Heol* are used as transport craft in the submarine base at l'Ile Longue. The others are former Gendarmerie Maritime craft transferred in 2004–05. Based at Brest *(Begonia)*, l'EcoleNavale *(Lilas)*, Saint Mandrier *(Lavande)* and Hyères *(Gentiane)*.

5 SELF-PROPELLED FLOATING CRANES (YD)

Y 675–679

Displacement, tons: To be announced
Dimensions, feet (metres): 70.2 × 37.7 × 5.6 *(21.4 × 9.9 × 1.7)*
Main machinery: 2 diesels; 300 hp *(220 kW)*; 2 shafts
Speed, knots: 6
Complement: 3

Comment: Ordered from Socarenam, Boulogne-sur-Mer on 16 January 2007 and delivered in March 2008. Equipped with a crane with a capacity of 8.3 tonnes to 8.5 metres and a winch with a capacity of 12 tonnes. Capable of carrying 24 tonnes of cargo. One based at Cherbourg and two each at Brest and Toulon.

Y 677 *5/2008*, B Prézelin* / 1335730

TUGS

2 ESTEREL (TYPE RPC 50) CLASS (COASTAL/HARBOUR TUGS) (YTM)

ESTEREL A 641 (ex-Y 601)
LUBÉRON A 642 (ex-Y 602)

Displacement, tons: 510 standard; 670 full load
Dimensions, feet (metres): 119.1 oa; 116.5 wl × 38.1 × 16.4 *(36.3; 35.5 × 11.6 × 5)*
Main machinery: 2 ABC 8 DZ 1000. 179 diesels; 2 Voith-Schneider 28 GII propulsors; 5,120 hp(m) *(3,812 kW)*
Speed, knots: 14. **Range, n miles:** 1,500 at 12 kt
Complement: 8
Radars: Navigation: Furuno DRBN 39; I-band.

Comment: Ordered 15 December 2000; built by SOCARENAM, Boulogne. *Esterel* delivered 27 March 2002 and *Lubéron* 4 July 2002. Based at Toulon to assist *Charles de Gaulle* in harbour. Bollard pull 52 tonnes; 1,350 kN towing winch; fire fighting equipment; 20 cubic metre tank for pollution control dispersal agent. Classified as 'Remorqueurs portuaires et côtiers de 50 tonnes de traction' (RPC 50, 50 tonne bollard pull harbour tugs).

ESTEREL *6/2008*, B Prézelin* / 1335729

2 OCEAN TUGS (ATA)

MALABAR A 664
TENACE A 669

Displacement, tons: 1,080 light; 1,454 full load
Dimensions, feet (metres): 167.3 × 37.8 × 18.6 *(51 × 11.5 × 5.7)*
Main machinery: 2 Krupp MaK 9 M 452 AK diesels; 4,600 hp(m) *(3.38 MW)*; 1 shaft; Kort nozzle
Speed, knots: 15
Range, n miles: 9,500 at 13 kt
Complement: 56 (2 officers)
Radars: Navigation: Racal Decca RM 1226 (A 669); Racal Decca 060 (A 664); I-band. Racal Decca 060; I-band.

Comment: *Malabar* and *Tenace* built by J. Oelkers, Hamburg. *Tenace* commissioned 15 November 1973, and *Malabar* on 3 February 1976. Based at Brest. Can carry firefighting and oil-pollution control equipment. Bollard pull, 60 tons. One of the class to Turkey in 1999. To be decommissioned in 2011.

MALABAR *7/2006, B Prézelin* / 1040712

3 BÉLIER CLASS (YTB)

BÉLIER A 695
BUFFLE A 696
BISON A 697

Displacement, tons: 356 light; 500 full load
Dimensions, feet (metres): 104.3 × 30.2 × 13.8 *(31.8 × 9.2 × 4.2)*
Main machinery: 2 SACM-Wärtsilä UD 33V12 M4 diesels; 2,600 hp(m) *(1.91 MW)*; 2 Voith-Schneider props
Speed, knots: 11
Complement: 12
Radars: Navigation: Racal-Decca C 810; I-band.

Comment: Built by DCN at Cherbourg. *Bélier* commissioned 10 July 1980, *Buffle* on 19 July 1980, *Bison* on 16 April 1981. A 695 and 697 based at Toulon and A 696 at Brest. Bollard pull, 25 tons. Service life: 2015.

BISON *6/2008*, Cor Van Nierkerken* / 1335782

3 MAÏTO CLASS (YTM)

MAÏTO A 636 **MAROA** A 637 **MANINI** A 638

Displacement, tons: 228 standard; 280 full load
Dimensions, feet (metres): 90.5 × 27.2 × 11.5 *(27.6 × 8.3 × 3.5)*
Main machinery: 2 SACM-Wärtsilä UD 30 L6 M6 diesels; 1,280 hp(m) *(940 kW)*; 2 Voith-Schneider propulsors
Speed, knots: 11
Range, n miles: 1,200 at 11 kt
Complement: 6 + 4 passengers
Radar: Navigation: Racal-Decca 1226; I-band.

Comment: Built by SFCN, Villeneuve-La-Garenne, and formerly used at the CEP Nuclear Test Range. *Maïto* commissioned 25 July 1984 and is based at Martinique. *Maroa* (commissioned 28 July 1984) and *Manini* (commissioned 12 September 1985) are both based at Papeete, Tahiti. Bollard pull, 12 tons. Fire-fighting water cannon.

MAÏTO *11/2006, M Declerck* / 1167128

16 FRÉHEL CLASS (COASTAL TUGS) (YTM)

LARDIER Y 638	**TAILLAT** Y 642	**FRÉHEL** A 675	**KÉRÉON** (ex-*Sicie*) A 679
GIENS Y 639	**NIVIDIC** Y 643	**SAIRE** A 676	**SICIÉ** A 680
MENGAM Y 640	**LE FOUR** Y 647	**ARMEN** A 677	**TAUNOA** A 681
BALAGUIER Y 641	**PORT CROS** Y 649	**LA HOUSSAYE** A 678	**RASCAS** A 682

Displacement, tons: 220 standard; 259 full load
Dimensions, feet (metres): 82 × 27.6 × 11.2 *(25 × 8.4 × 3.4)*
Main machinery: 2 SACM-Wärtsilä UD 30 V12 M3 diesels (A 675 and 676); 2 Baudouin P 15 25 (others); 2 Voith-Schneider propulsors; 1,280 hp(m) (941 kW); 1,360 hp(m) *(1 MW)* in later vessels
Speed, knots: 11
Range, n miles: 800 at 10 kt
Complement: 8 (coastal); 5 (harbour)
Radars: 1 Racal Decca RM 170 or Bridgemaster C 181; I-band.

Comment: Built at Lorient Naval et Industries shipyard (formerly Chantiers et Ateliers de la Perrière, now part of Leroux et Lotz) and at Boulogne by SOCARENAM. *Fréhel* in service 23 May 1989, based at Cherbourg, *Saire* 6 October 1989 at Cherbourg, *Armen* 6 December 1991 at Brest, *La Houssaye* 30 October 1992 at Brest, *Kéréon* 5 December 1992 at Brest. *Mengam* 6 October 1994 at Brest and Sicié 6 October 1994 at Toulon, *Giens* 2 December 1994 at Toulon, *Lardier* 12 March 1995 at Toulon, *Balaguier* 8 July 1995 at Toulon, *Taillat* 18 October 1995 at Toulon. *Taunoa* completed 9 March 1996 at Brest, *Nividic* on 13 February 1996 at Brest, *Port Cros* on 21 June 1997 at Toulon, *Le Four* on 13 March 1998 at Brest and *Rascas* on 22 November 2003 at Toulon. Bollard pull 12 tons. Type RPC 12 coastal tugs, with 'A' pennant numbers and a crew of eight. Type RP12 harbour tugs with 'Y' pennant numbers and a crew of five. A further order for six craft has been abandoned.

LARDIER *6/2008*, Cor Van Nierkerken* / 1335781

4 TYPE RP 10 HARBOUR TUGS/PUSHERS (YT)

MORSE Y 770 **OTARIE** Y 771 **LOUTRE** Y 772 **PHOQUE** Y 773

Displacement, tons: 83 standard; 97 full load
Dimensions, feet (metres): 47.2 × 21.0 × 6.9 *(14.4 × 6.4 × 2.1)*
Main machinery: 2 Baudouin 6R123S diesels; 800 hp *(588 kW)*; 2 shafts
Speed, knots: 8
Range, n miles: 160 at 7 kt
Complement: 4
Radars: Navigation: Furuno M 1832; I-band.

Comment: Ordered on 21 November 2003. All entered service on 5 October 2005. Built by SOCARENAM, Boulogne. Bollard pull 10 tons. *Morse* based at Mayotte and the remainder at Toulon.

OTARIE *4/2008*, B Prézelin* / 1335728

1 ACTIF CLASS (YTM)

ACHARNÉ A 693

Displacement, tons: 218 standard; 293 full load
Dimensions, feet (metres): 89.9 × 24.6 × 14.8 *(27.4 × 7.5 × 4.5)*
Main machinery: 1 SACM MGO V16 diesel; 1,050 hp(m) *(773 kW)*; 1 shaft; prop in Kort nozzle
Speed, knots: 11. **Range, n miles:** 4,100 at 10 kt
Complement: 15
Radars: Navigation: 1 Decca; I-band.

Comment: Last of 12 coastal tugs commissioned 5 July 1974. Bollard pull 13 tons. Based at Cherbourg. To be decommissioned in 2010.

ACHARNÉ *6/2003, Schaeffer/Marsan* / 0569968

2 BONITE (TYPE RP 380) CLASS (HARBOUR TUGS) (YTL)

BONITE Y 630 **ROUGET** Y 634

Displacement, tons: 95 full load
Dimensions, feet (metres): 68.2 × 20.3 × 8.5 *(20.8 × 6.2 × 2.6)*
Main machinery: 1 Poyaud UD 1215 diesel; 380 hp *(280 kW)*; 1 shaft
Speed, knots: 10
Complement: 7

Comment: Both built by Schneider, Châlons-sur-Saone, and commissioned in 1975. Attached to the Naval Academy and Training Centre. Based at Lanvéoc-Poulmic, near Brest. Service life 2010.

4 TYPE PSS 10 PUSHER TUGS (YTL)

P 101–104

Displacement, tons: 44 standard; 69 full load
Dimensions, feet (metres): 57.4 × 21.0 × 6.6 *(17.5 × 6.4 × 2.0)*
Main machinery: 2 Poyaud UD 25 L06 M4D diesels; 800 hp *(588 kW)*; 2 shafts in Kort nozzles
Speed, knots: 10. **Range, n miles:** 480 at 6 kt
Complement: 3

Comment: Built by Leroux Naval Industrie, Lorient, and commissioned in 1993. Designed to handle Le Triomphant class SSBNs. *P 101* and *P 102* based at Brest and *P 103* and *P 104* at Cherbourg.

P 101 *8/2008*, B Prézelin* / 1335727

26 TYPE P4 PUSHER TUGS (YTL)

P 6 **P 13–24** **P 26–38**

Displacement, tons: 28 standard; 30 full load
Dimensions, feet (metres): 39.0 × 14.4 × 6.9 *(11.9 × 4.4 × 2.1)*
Main machinery: 2 Poyaud UD 6 *(P 6)*; 430 hp *(316 kW)* or Poyaud UD 18 *(P 13-30)*; 440 hp *(324 kW)* or Baudouin V6 TI 330 *(P 31-38)*; 480 hp *(353 kW)* diesels; 2 shafts
Speed, knots: 9
Range, n miles: 540 at 8 kt
Complement: 3

Comment: Built by shipyards at Brest and Lorient. *P 6* entered service in 1973, *P 13-18* 1982–83 and the remainder 1989–97. Based at naval bases in France and overseas. Bollard pull 5 tons.

P 17 *5/2008*, B Prézelin* / 1335726

GOVERNMENT MARITIME FORCES

Notes: (1) 'Action de l'Etat en Mer (AEM)' encompasses all activities regarding maritime surveillance and sea traffic control, fishery protection and policing, SAR, safety of navigation, pollution control and so on. It involves the Marine Nationale (navy), the Gendarmerie Maritime, the Affaires Maritimes, the Douanes françaises (customs), the Administration des Phares et Balises (lighthouses and navigation aids management organisation) and some local police forces. The organisation is for French mainland as well as for overseas territories. In homeland waters, it is under the direct control of the flag officers (C-in-Cs) at Cherbourg, Brest and Toulon. All ships and craft involved in AEM tasks display 'AEM markings' (inclined blue/white/red stripes on their hull sides). This also applies to naval manned patrol vessels (patrouilleurs de service public, PSP) and to the Eurocopter SA 365N Dauphin 2 helicopters acquired by the naval air arm for SAR duties.
(2) For the 'Sauvegarde maritime' (maritime approaches surveillance organisation), most AEM tasked vessels (including naval OPVs) and coastal VTS are connected, through a dedicated datalink, to the Spationav common maritime picture network. Spationav display terminals are also being fitted to the Dassault Falcon 50M land-based maritime surveillance aircraft.

AUXILIARIES

Notes: (1) Permanently chartered vessels for AEM tasks include four salvage and rescue tugs, and four support and pollution fighting vessels. They perform civilian tasks such as safety of navigation, SAR, pollution control, and military missions in support of the fleet: torpedo recovery, diving operation support, submarine crew rescue, experiments, and so on.
(2) In addition, the UK tug *Anglian Monarch* is chartered from Klyne Tugs Ltd, under a share agreement with the UK Maritime and Coast Guard Agency. Based at Dover.
(3) A contract was renewed with Abeilles International in July 2002 for emergency use of a large fleet of harbour tugs. Similar contracts are concluded with local fishing associations.
(4) The DGA (Directorate General for Armament) charters the 67 m *Langevin* for submarine associated trials.
(5) On 29 November 2005, the European Maritime Safety Agency (EMSA) contracted Louis Dreyfus Armateurs (LDA) for the standby charter of the cable repair vessel *Ile de Bréhat* (built 2001, 14,960 UMS, 140 m, 15 kt) for oil recovery during emergencies. Currently chartered for the maintenance and repairs of transatlantic submarine cables, this ship is based at Brest. It will receive some modifications to be classified as '(standby) oil recovery vessel'; it will be capable of recovering and storing up to 4,000 m^3 of polluted water and of deploying a ROV.

2 ULSTEIN UT 515 (SALVAGE AND RESCUE TUGS) (ARS)

ABEILLE BOURBON **ABEILLE LIBERTÉ**

Displacement, tons: 3,200 standard; 4,000 full load
Dimensions, feet (metres): 262.5 × 54.1 × 21.3 *(80.0 × 16.5 × 6.5)*
Main machinery: 4 MaK 8M32C diesels; 21,700 hp(m) *(16 MW)*; 2 shafts; 2 cp props; 2 bow and 2 stern thrusters
Speed, knots: 19.5
Complement: 12
Radars: Navigation: 2 Furuno; I-band.

Comment: Contract awarded in November 2003 to Abeilles International for the procurement and operation (over eight years) of two Ulstein 515 salvage tugs, classified as Remorques d'Intervention, d'Assistance et de Sauvetage (RIAS). Equipped with a 500 ton towing winch and with extensive fire-fighting and pollution control equipment. Vessels built by Maritim, Gdansk and outfitted by Myklebust, Norway. The first ship, *Abeille Bourbon*, entered service on 21 May 2005 and is based at Brest. She was fitted with a reinforced bow in November 2007. *Abeille Liberté* entered service on 25 October 2005 and is based at Cherbourg. There are two crews of 12 per ship.

ABEILLE BOURBON *8/2008*, B Prézelin* / 1335725

1 ULSTEIN UT 710 (SALVAGE AND RESCUE TUG) (ARS)

ARGONAUTE (ex-*Island Patriot*)

Displacement, tons: 2,371 standard; 4,420 full load
Dimensions, feet (metres): 226.0 × 50.8 × 23.0 *(68.9 × 15.5 × 7)*
Main machinery: 2 Rolls Royce Bergen BRM-9 diesels; 10,800 hp(m) *(8.1 MW)*; 2 shafts; 2 cp props with Kort nozzles; 2 bow and 1 stern thrusters
Speed, knots: 16
Range, n miles: 19,000 at 10 kt
Complement: 9 plus 22 passengers
Radars: Navigation: 2 Raytheon; I-band.

Comment: Built by Aker-Brevik Construction AS, Norway, the ship was launched on 7 July 2003 and entered service with Island Offshore on 12 December 2003. Chartered by the French government from 1 January 2004 and modified in June 2004 to meet naval requirements. Based at Brest. Fitted for pollution control and with fire-fighting equipment. Capable of operating an ROV.

ARGONAUTE *6/2008*, Richard Scott* / 1335780

2 ULSTEIN UT 507 CLASS (SALVAGE TUGS) (ARS)

ABEILLE FLANDRE (ex-*Neptun Suecia*) **ABEILLE LANGUEDOC** (ex-*Neptun Gothia*)

Displacement, tons: 3,000 standard; 3,500 full load
Dimensions, feet (metres): 207.7 × 47.2 × 23.9 *(63.4 × 14.4 × 7.3)*
Main machinery: 4 MaK 8M453AK diesels; 23,000 hp *(16.9 MW)*; 2 cp props; 2 Ulstein bow thrusters
Speed, knots: 17
Range, n miles: 36,000 at 10 kt
Complement: 12
Radars: Navigation: 1 Racal Decca Bridgemaster; 1 Racal Decca Bright Track 90; E/F-band.

Comment: Built by Ulstein Hatho A/S, Norway and entered service in 1978 and 1979. On long-term charter from Abeilles International since 14 December 1979. Bollard pull 160 tons. *Abeille Flandre* based at Toulon since 30 May 2005 and *Abeille Languedoc* at La Pallice, near La Rochelle, since 25 October 2005. Both ships refitted in 2005.

ABEILLE FLANDRE *6/2008*, B Prézelin* / 1335724

2 ULSTEIN UT 711 CLASS (BUOY TENDERS) (ABU)

ALCYON (ex-*Bahram*) **AILETTE** (ex-*Cyrus*)

Displacement, tons: 1,210 standard; 1,900 full load
Dimensions, feet (metres): 173.9 × 43.6 × 22.3 *(53.0 × 13.3 × 6.8)*
Main machinery: 2 Bergens-Normo KVMB-12 diesels; 5,200 hp *(3.9 MW)*; 2 cp props; 1 Ulstein 90 bow thruster; 500 hp *(370 kW)*; 1 Rolls Royce bow thruster (*Ailette* only); 400 hp *(300 kW)*
Speed, knots: 14.5. **Range, n miles:** 5,400 at 14 kt
Complement: 7 plus 15 passengers
Radars: Navigation: Racal-Decca Bridgemaster 252C and Furuno FR 2120; I-band.

Comment: Built by A & C de la Manche, Dieppe and entered service in 1981 and 1982. On long-term charter from SURF (Groupe Bourbon). Former oil-field supply vessels both modernised in 2002–03 by Chantiers Piriou, Concarneau, for limited oil-pollution control activities: TRANSREC 250 sea skimming system and polluted water storage capacity of 500 m³. New 23 ton hydraulic deck crane fitted; dynamic positioning system fitted to *Ailette*. Deck capacity 480 tons and bollard pull of 64 tons. *Alcyon* based at Brest and *Ailette* at Toulon.

AILETTE *2/2008*, B Prézelin* / 1335723

1 ULSTEIN UT 704 CLASS (SALVAGE AND RESCUE TUG) (ARS)

CARANGUE (ex-*Pilot Fish*, ex-*Smit Lloyd 119*, ex-*Maersk Handler*)

Displacement, tons: 1,300 standard; 2,000 full load
Dimensions, feet (metres): 212.3 × 45.3 × 19.7 *(64.7 × 13.8 × 6.0)*
Main machinery: 2 Nohars-Nohab F2 16V-D diesels; 7,050 hp *(5.2 MW)*; 2 cp props; bow thruster
Speed, knots: 16. **Range, n miles:** 21,000 at 10 kt
Complement: 8
Radars: Navigation: 2 Furuno; I-band.

Comment: Built by Samsung SB, Koje, South Korea and entered service in 1980. On long-term charter from Abeilles International since 1994. Equipped with two fire-pumps, two water cannons, anti-pollution equipment and a hydraulic crane. Based at Toulon.

CARANGUE *2/2008*, B Prézelin* / 1335722

1 AQUITAINE EXPLORER CLASS (SALVAGE VESSEL) (ARS)

AQUITAINE EXPLORER (ex-*Abeille Supporter*, ex-*Seaway Hawk*, ex-*Seaway Devon*)

Displacement, tons: 2,500 full load
Dimensions, feet (metres): 208.7 × 44.0 × 18.9 *(63.6 × 13.4 × 5.75)*
Main machinery: 2 MaK 12M453AK diesels; 8,800 hp *(5.9 MW)*; 2 cp props; bow and stern lateral thrusters
Speed, knots: 14
Complement: 11 + 27
Radars: Navigation: I-band.

Comment: Built by Aukra Bruk, Norway and entered service in 1975. Acquired in 1982 by DGA (Armaments Directorate) for support of undersea activities in conjunction with CEL (Landes Launch Centre) (Abyssub ROV operates to 5,000 m). Operated by Abeilles International until 30 June 2000 and thereafter by NTA/ABC Maritime. Bollard pull 100 tons. Also used in support of pollution control. Based at Bayonne.

AQUITAINE EXPLORER *1/2005, B Prézelin* / 1153165

RESEARCH SHIPS

Note: Several government agencies use research vessels for various purposes. Most of them are operated by GENAVIR on their behalf. Main agency is IFREMER (Institut Français de Recherche pour l'Exploitation de la Mer) that operates four large ocean-going vessels; *Pourquoi Pas?* (2005, 6,600 tons), *Thalassa* (1996, 3,022 tons), *L'Atalante* (1989, 3,550 tons), *Le Suroît* (1975, modernised 1999, 1,132 tons); and three coastal operations vessels: *L'Europe* (1993, 264 tons catamaran), *Thalia* (1978, 135 grt, trawler type) and *Gwen Drez* (1976, 249 tons, trawler type). IRD (Institut de Recherche pour le Développement, ex-ORSTOM) operates in the Pacific two research vessels: *Antéa* (1995, 421 grt, catamaran) and *Alis* (1987, 198 grt UMS, trawler type), and two smaller craft. INSU (Institut National des Sciences de l'Univers) operates five coastal vessels (12.5 to 24.9 m) along the French coasts. TAAF (Administration des Terres Australes et Antarctiques Françaises) uses *Marion Dufresne* (1995, 9,403 GRT UMS, 120 m long), a large support ship for Antarctic operations also fitted for scientific research work, *L'Astrolabe*, (ex-*Austral Fish*, 1986, 1,370 grt) and *La Curieuse* (1989, 150 grt UMS, trawler type).

POLICE (GENDARMERIE MARITIME)

Note: The Gendarmerie Maritime is a force of 1,050 officers and men belonging to the Gendarmerie Nationale but acting under the operational control of the Marine Nationale. The Force is tasked to safeguard, supervise and control shipping traffic.

1 PATRA CLASS (COASTAL PATROL CRAFT) (PB)

Name	*No*	*Builders*	*Commissioned*
GLAIVE	P 671	Auroux, Arcachon	2 Apr 1977

Displacement, tons: 115 standard; 147.5 full load
Dimensions, feet (metres): 132.5 × 19.4 × 5.2 *(40.4 × 5.9 × 1.6)*
Main machinery: 2 SACM AGO 195 V12 diesels; 4,410 hp(m) *(3.24 MW)*; 2 shafts; cp props
Speed, knots: 26
Range, n miles: 1,750 at 10 kt; 750 at 20 kt
Complement: 18 (1 officer)
Guns: 1 Bofors 40 mm/60. 2—7.5 mm MGs.
Radars: Surface search: Racal Decca 1226; I-band.

Comment: Based at Cherbourg. Service life extended to 2010.

PATRA CLASS *6/2006, B Prézelin* / 1040756

4 GERANIUM CLASS (PB)

Name	*No*	*Builders*	*Commissioned*
GÉRANIUM	P 720	DCN, Lorient	19 Feb 1997
JONQUILLE	P 721	Chantiers Guy Couach Plascoa	15 Nov 1997
VIOLETTE	P 722	DCN, Lorient	4 Dec 1997
JASMIN	P 723	Chantiers Guy Couach Plascoa	15 Nov 1997

Displacement, tons: 80 (P 270, P 722); 82 (P 721, P 723) standard; 100 full load
Dimensions, feet (metres): 105.7 × 20 × 6.2 *(32.2 × 6.1 × 1.9)*
Main machinery: 2 Deutz/MWM TBD 516 V16; 1 Deutz/MWM TBD 516 V12; 3,960 hp *(2.95 MW)*; 2 shafts; 1 Hamilton 422 water-jet
Speed, knots: 30
Range, n miles: 1,500 at 15 kt
Complement: 15 (2 officers)
Guns: 1—12.7 mm MG. 1—7.62 mm MG.
Radars: Navigation: Racal-Decca CH 180/6; E/F-band.

Comment: There are some minor differences between the DCN (details shown) and the Plascoa craft. *Géranium* based at Cherbourg; *Jonquille* at Réunion Island (to Toulon in September 2008); *Violette* at Pointe-à-Pitre, Guadeloupe; *Jasmin* at Papeete, Tahiti. Two similar craft built for Affaires Maritimes.

JONQUILLE *10/2008*, Peter Ford* / 1335777

4 VSC 14 CLASS (PB)

MIMOSA P 761 **RÉSÉDA** P 778 **MELIA** A 789 **HORTENSIA** P 791

Displacement, tons: 21 full load
Dimensions, feet (metres): 47.9 × 15.1 × 6.2 *(14.6 × 4.6 × 1.9)*
Main machinery: 2 Baudouin 12 F11 SM diesels; 800 hp(m) *(588 kW)*; 2 shafts
Speed, knots: 20
Range, n miles: 360 at 18 kt
Complement: 7
Guns: 1 — 12.7 mm MG. 1 — 7.62 mm MG.
Radars: Navigation: Furuno; I-band.

Comment: Type V14 SC. P 761, P 789 and P 778 built 1987–88 and P 791 1990–92. Similar to naval tenders with Y pennant numbers. P 778 and P 791 at Brest and A 789 and P 761 at Toulon. Being replaced in service by VCSM craft.

RÉSÉDA *7/2008*, B Prézelin* / 1335721

1 FULMAR CLASS (COASTAL PATROL CRAFT) (PB)

FULMAR (ex-*Jonathan*) P 740

Displacement, tons: 550 standard; 680 full load
Dimensions, feet (metres): 120.7 × 27.9 × 15.4 *(36.8 × 8.5 × 4.7)*
Main machinery: 1 Stork Wärtsilä 8 FDH 240G diesel; 1,200 hp(m) *(882 kW)*; 1 shaft. Bow thruster
Speed, knots: 13
Range, n miles: 3,500 at 12 kt
Complement: 9 (1 officer)
Guns: 1 — 12.7 mm MG.
Radars: Surface search: 2 Furuno; I-band.

Comment: Former trawler built in 1990, acquired in October 1996 and converted for patrol duties by April 1997. Recommissioned 28 October 1997 and is based at St Pierre and Miquelon for western Atlantic Fishery Protection duties.

FULMAR *2000, French Navy* / 0104486

24 TYPE VCSM (PATROL CRAFT) (PB)

ÉLORN P 601	**YSER** P 607	**CHARENTE** P 613	**HUVEAUNE** P 619
VERDON P 602	**ARGENS** P 608	**TECH** P 614	**SÈVRE** P 620
ADOUR P 603	**HÉRAULT** P 609	**PENFELD** P 615	**ABER-WRACH** P 621
SCARPE P 604	**GRAVONA** P 610	**TRIEUX** P 616	**ESTÉRON** P 622
VERTONNE P 605	**ODET** P 611	**VÉSUBIE** P 617	**MAHURY** P 623
DUMBEA P 606	**MAURY** P 612	**ESCAUT** P 618	**ORGANABO** P 624

Displacement, tons: 42
Dimensions, feet (metres): 65.6 × 17.1 × 4.9 *(20.0 × 5.2 × 1.5)*
Main machinery: 2 MAN V12 diesels; 2 shafts; 2,000 hp(m) *(1,470 kW)*
Speed, knots: 28
Range, n miles: 530 at 15 kt
Complement: 5
Guns: 2 — 7.62 mm MG.
Radars: Navigation: Furuno; I-band.

Comment: Designated 'Vedette Côtière de Surveillance Maritime' (VCSM), coastal surveillance craft. Raidco RPB 20. Ordered in two batches of 11 on 6 Dec 2001 and 6 June 2002. Built at l'Herbaudière by Raidco Marine with the co-operation of Chantiers Beneteau. Bear names of rivers. First of class (P 601) entered service on 20 June 2003 followed by P 602-604 in 2003, P 605-610 in 2004 and P 611-615 in 2005. The remainder entered service by March 2007. Replace VSC 14 and VSC 10 craft. GRP hull and superstructure. One 4.9 m RIB fitted aft on an inclined ramp. Also fitted with water-cannon. P 606 based at Noumea, New Caledonia, P 623 and P 624 in French Guiana and P 602 at Mayotte. Two similar craft in service in Morocco and two in Senegal.

ESTÉRON *5/2008*, Marco Ghiglino* / 1335778

2 ARCOR 34 (PATROL CRAFT) (PB)

CAPITAINE MOULIÉ P 713 **MDLC JACQUES** P 716

Displacement, tons: 7 standard; 8 full load
Dimensions, feet (metres): 33.8 × 12.3 × 3.34 *(10.3 × 3.7 × 1.0)*
Main machinery: 2 Volvo Penta TAMD 61 diesels; 500 hp *(370 kW)*; 2 shafts
Speed, knots: 26
Range, n miles: 200 at 20 kt
Complement: 3
Radars: Navigation: Furuno 1830; I-band.

Comment: Built in 1989–90 by CN d'Aquitaine. Being replaced.

MDLC JACQUES *10/2008*, Peter Ford* / 1335779

1 COUACH-PLASCOA 980 (PATROL CRAFT) (PB)

MDLC RICHARD Y 611 (ex-P 709)

Displacement, tons: 6 standard; 7 full load
Dimensions, feet (metres): 32.5 × 12.2 × 3.3 *(9.9 × 3.73 × 1.0)*
Main machinery: 2 Volvo Penta TAMD 61 diesels; 500 hp *(370 kW)*; 2 shafts
Speed, knots: 28
Range, n miles: 200 at 15 kt
Complement: 4
Radars: Navigation: Furuno 2400; I-band.

Comment: Built in 1985. *MDLC Richard* is a training craft for the Gendarmerie Maritime at Toulon.

MDLC RICHARD (old number) *6/2007, B Prézelin* / 1305011

CUSTOMS (DOUANES FRANÇAISES)

Notes: The French customs service has a number of tasks not normally associated with such an organisation. In addition to the usual duties of dealing with ships entering either its coastal area or ports it also has certain responsibilities for rescue at sea, control of navigation, fishery protection and pollution protection. Operated by about 650 personnel, the fleet comprises 12 large patrol vessels (28 to 35 m), 16 patrol boats (15 to 27 m) and 27 smaller craft. The larger vessels include DF 48 *Arafenua* (105 tons), DF 41 *Avel Gwalarn* (67 tons), DF 42 *Suroît* (67 tons), DF 31 Alizé (64 tons), DF 37 *Vent d'Aval* (64 tons), DF 43 *Haize Hegoa* (64 tons), DF 44 *Mervent* (64 tons), DF 45 *Vent d'Autan* (64 tons), DF 46 *Avel Sterenn* (64 tons), DF 47 *Lissero* (64 tons), DF 36 *Kan Avel* (64 tons) and DF 40 *Vent d'Amont* (61 tons). In addition, two 400 ton patrol ships *Jacques Oudart Fourmentin* and *Kermovan* (ex-*Tevennec*), entered service in 2007 and 2008 respectively. All vessels have DF numbers painted on the bow and 'AEM markings' (blue/white/red inclined stripes). There are also 13 Reims-Cessna F406 lightweight patrol aircraft, including three equipped for pollution control and six Eurocopter AS 350B1 Ecureuil helicopters. On 20 December 2005, the Customs ordered, through the Directorate General for Armament (DGA), five Eurocopter EC 135 helicopters specially equipped for the maritime surveillance role (FLIR) and SAR. They will be delivered in 2007 to replace some of the Ecureuils.

KERMOVAN *8/2008*, B Prézelin* / 1335720

IRIS *10/2008*, Adolfo Ortigueira Gil* / 1335769

HAUTS DE FRANCE *5/2004, Schaeffer/Marsan* / 1042222

AFFAIRES MARITIMES

Notes: The Affaires Maritimes is a force administered and funded by the Ministry of Transport to enforce safety of navigation, SAR, fishery protection and pollution control. The force also contributes to surveillance against terrorist activities. Operational control is vested locally in Préfet Maritimes who are naval flag officers. SAR is coordinated through a network of Maritime Rescue Coordination Centres (MRCC) at Gris Nez (Dover Strait), Jobourg (Western Channel), Corsen (Brittany), Etel (Bay of Biscay), La Garde (Mediterranean, Gulf of Lion), Aspretto (Corsica), Port des Galets (La Réunion), Fort-de-France (Caribbean). CROSS Etel is responsible for monitoring all fishing activity in French waters. Vessels operated by Affaires Maritimes are usually unarmed and manned by civilians. They are painted with grey/blue hulls, grey superstructure and display the AEM blue/white/red stripes, PM pennant numbers and 'Affaires Maritimes' written on the superstructure. The fleet comprises:

- Five large patrol vessels (30–52 m): PM 41 *Themis* (400 tons), PM 40 *Iris* (230 tons), PM 32 *Armoise* (91 tons), PM 30 *Gabian* (76 tons), PM 29 *Mauve* (65 tons); *Osiris*, a seized fishing trawler, is based at La Réunion.
- 19 patrol launches (8–17 m): Most recent are four Callisto class 16 m FPB 50 Mk II patrol boats built 2000–01 by OCEA, Les Sables d'Olonne.
- Service craft which may be identified by 'Phares & Balises' written on the superstructure. Larger vessels include: *Armorique* (500 tons), *Hauts de France* (450 tons), *Gascogne*, *Provence* (326 tons), *Chef de Caux* (128 tons), *Louis Henin* (73 tons) and *Le Kahouanne* (73 tons).

THEMIS *7/2007, B Prézelin* / 1305048

Gabon

MARINE GABONAISE

Country Overview

A former French colony, the Gabonese Republic achieved independence in 1960. Located astride the Equator, the country has an area of 103,347 square miles and has borders to the north with Cameroon and Equatorial Guinea and to the east and south with Congo. It has a 480 n mile coastline with the Atlantic Ocean. The capital, largest city and principal port is Libreville and there is a further port at Port-Gentil. Territorial seas (12 n miles) are claimed. A 200 n mile Exclusive Economic Zone (EEZ) has been claimed but the limits are not defined; jurisdiction is complicated by the offshore islands of Isla de Annobon (Equatorial Guinea) and São Tomé and Principe.

Headquarters Appointments

Chief of Naval Staff:
Captain Paul Bivigou Nziengui

Bases

Port Gentil, Mayumba

Personnel

2009: 600 (65 officers)

PATROL FORCES

2 P 400 CLASS (LARGE PATROL CRAFT) (PBO)

Name	*No*	*Builders*	*Commissioned*
GÉNÉRAL d'ARMÉE BA-OUMAR	P 07	CMN, Cherbourg	27 June 1988
COLONEL DJOUE-DABANY	P 08	CMN, Cherbourg	14 Sep 1990

Displacement, tons: 446 full load
Dimensions, feet (metres): 179 × 26.2 × 8.5 *(54.6 × 8 × 2.5)*
Main machinery: 2 Wärtsilä UD 33 V16 diesels; 8,000 hp(m) *(5.88 MW)* sustained; 2 shafts; cp props
Speed, knots: 24. **Range, n miles:** 4,200 at 15 kt
Complement: 32 (4 officers)
Military lift: 20 troops
Guns: 1 Bofors 57 mm/70 SAK 57 Mk 2 (P 07); 220 rds/min to 17 km *(9 n miles)*; weight of shell 2.4 kg. Not in P 08 which has a second Oerlikon 20 mm.
2 Giat F2 20 mm (P 08).
Weapons control: CSEE Naja optronic director (P 07).
Radars: Racal Decca 1226C; I-band.

Programmes: Contract signed May 1985 with CMN Cherbourg. First laid down 2 July 1986, launched 18 December 1987 and arrived in Gabon 6 August 1988 for a local christening ceremony. Second ordered in February 1989 and launched 29 March 1990.
Structure: There is space on the quarterdeck for two MM 40 Exocet surface-to-surface missiles. These craft are similar to the French vessels but with different engines. *Djoue-Dabany* had twin funnels fitted in 1992, similar to French P 400 class conversions.

COLONEL DJOUE-DABANY *6/2000, Gabon Navy* / 0104491

1 PATRA CLASS (FAST ATTACK CRAFT—MISSILE) (PTM)

Name	*No*	*Builders*	*Commissioned*
GÉNÉRAL NAZAIRE BOULINGUI (ex-*Président Omar Bongo*)	P 10	Chantiers Naval de l'Estérel	7 Aug 1978

Displacement, tons: 160 full load
Dimensions, feet (metres): 138 × 25.3 × 6.5 *(42 × 7.7 × 1.9)*
Main machinery: 3 SACM 195 V12 CSHR diesels; 5,400 hp(m) *(3.97 MW)* sustained; 3 shafts
Speed, knots: 32. **Range, n miles:** 1,500 at 15 kt
Complement: 20 (3 officers)
Missiles: SSM: 4 Aerospatiale SS 12M; wire-guided to 5.5 km *(3 n miles)* subsonic; warhead 30 kg.
Guns: 1 Bofors 40 mm/60. 1 DCN 20 mm.
Radars: Surface search: Racal Decca RM1226; I-band.

Comment: Re-activated in 2000.

GÉNÉRAL NAZAIRE BOULINGUI *6/2000, Gabon Navy* / 0104492

LAND-BASED MARITIME AIRCRAFT

Numbers/Type: 1 Embraer Emb-111 Bandeirante.
Operational speed: 194 kt *(360 km/h).*
Service ceiling: 25,500 ft *(7,770 m).*
Range: 1,590 n miles *(2,945 km).*
Role/Weapon systems: Air Force coastal surveillance and EEZ protection tasks are primary roles. Sensors: APS-128 search radar, limited ECM, searchlight. Weapons: ASV; 8 × 127 mm rockets or 28 × 70 mm rockets.

AMPHIBIOUS FORCES

12 LANDING CRAFT PERSONNEL (LCVP)

Comment: Two 12 m craft built by Tanguy Marine, Le Havre in 1985. Equipped with two Volvo Penta 165 hp(m) *(121 kW)* engines. There are also 10 Simonneau craft: one of 12 m, two of 8 m and seven of 7 m.

1 BATRAL TYPE (LSTH)

Name	*No*	*Builders*	*Launched*	*Commissioned*
PRESIDENT EL HADJ OMAR BONGO	L 05	Français de l'Ouest, Rouen	16 Apr 1984	26 Nov 1984

Displacement, tons: 770 standard; 1,336 full load
Dimensions, feet (metres): 262.4 × 42.6 × 7.9 *(80 × 13 × 2.4)*
Main machinery: 2 SACM Type 195 V12 CSHR diesels; 3,600 hp(m) *(2.65 MW)*; 2 shafts; cp props
Speed, knots: 16
Range, n miles: 4,500 at 13 kt
Complement: 39
Military lift: 188 troops; 12 vehicles; 350 tons cargo
Guns: 1 Bofors 40 mm/60; 300 rds/min to 12 km *(6.5 n miles)*; weight of shell 0.89 kg. 2—81 mm mortars. 2 Browning 12.7 mm MGs. 1—7.62 mm MG.
Radars: Surface search: Racal Decca 1226; I-band.
Helicopters: Capable of operating up to SA 330 Puma size.

Comment: Sister to French *La Grandière*. Carries one LCVP and one LCP. Started refit by Denel, Cape Town in April 1996, and returned to service in 1997 with bow doors welded shut. Completed repair and cleaning at Abidjan during 2000.

PRESIDENT EL HADJ OMAR BONGO *6/1993, Gabon Navy* / 0069977

POLICE

Notes: (1) Four Rodman 20 m craft were delivered in January 2006. Their names are: *Awore* P 01, *Mangoye* P 02, *Betseng* P 03 and *Mendene* P 04.
(2) Two Rodman 14 m craft were delivered in January 2006. Their names are: *Mbanie* and *Kouango*.

Gambia

Country Overview

The Republic of Gambia was a British protectorate until 1965 when it gained independence. With an area of 4,361 square miles, it has a short 43 n mile coastline with the Atlantic Ocean but is otherwise completely surrounded by Senegal. The two countries united in 1981 to form the confederation of Senegambia but this collapsed in 1989 when the countries reverted to being separate states. The capital, largest city and principal port is Banjul (formerly Bathurst). Territorial seas (12 n miles) and a 200 n mile fishing zone are claimed. The patrol craft came under 3 Marine Company of the National Army until 1996 when a navy was established.

Headquarters Appointments

Commander, Navy:
Lieutenant Commander Sarjo Fofana

Personnel

(a) 2009: 150
(b) Voluntary service

Bases

Banjul

PATROL FORCES

Notes: Two ex-Guardia Civil 16 m Rodman 55M craft were reported transferred by Spain on 9 July 2007.

2 PATROL CRAFT (PB)

FATIMAH I PT 01 **SULAYMAN JUN-KUNG** PT 02

Displacement, tons: 25
Dimensions, feet (metres): 52.8 × 14.8 × 5.3 *(16.1 × 4.5 × 1.6)*
Main machinery: Caterpillar diesel; 800 hp *(596 kW)*
Speed, knots: 40
Guns: 3—7.62 mm MGs.
Radars: Surface search: Furuno; I-band.

Comment: Procured from Taiwan in 1999.

FATIMAH *6/2000, Gambian Navy* / 0104493

1 PETERSON MK 4 CLASS (PB)

Name	*No*	*Builders*	*Commissioned*
BOLONG KANTA	P 14	Peterson Builders, Sturgeon Bay	15 Oct 1993

Displacement, tons: 24 full load
Dimensions, feet (metres): 50.9 × 14.8 × 4.3 *(15.5 × 4.5 × 1.3)*
Main machinery: 2 Detroit 6V-92A diesels; 520 hp *(388 kW)* sustained; 2 shafts
Speed, knots: 24. **Range, n miles:** 500 at 20 kt
Complement: 6
Guns: 2—12.7 mm MGs.
Radars: Raytheon R41X; I-band.

Comment: Reported seaworthy. Agreement with US government in September 2005 to assist with maintenance and spares. Similar craft in service in Egypt, Cape Verde and Senegal.

PETERSON Mk 4 (Senegal colours) *1/1998* / 0050096

Georgia

Country Overview

Formerly part of the USSR, the Republic of Georgia declared independence in 1991. Situated in the Transcaucasia region of western Asia, the country has an area of 26,900 square miles and is bordered to the north by Russia and to the south by Turkey, Armenia and Azerbaijan. It has a coastline of 167 n miles with the Black Sea on which Poti and Batumi are the principal ports. T'bilisi is the capital and largest city. The country includes two autonomous republics, Abkhazia and Ajaria, and one autonomous region, South Ossetia. USSR legislation appears still to apply to maritime claims. Territorial waters (12 n miles) are claimed, as is an EEZ (200 n miles) although the limits of the latter are not defined. Naval and Coast Guard Forces (part of the Border Guard) formed 7 July 1993. While merger of the two forces has been considered, they are likely to remain different commands.

Much of the Georgian Navy and Coast Guard was destroyed during the Georgia-Russia conflict in August 2008. It is likely that remaining units will be merged into a single Coast Guard force.

Headquarters Appointments

Commander of the Navy:
Captain Besik Shengelia

Personnel

2009: 710 (184 officers)

Bases

Poti (HQ), Batumi.

PATROL FORCES

Notes: In addition to the vessels listed below, the following vessels are on the Navy List:
(1) A former fishing vessel *Gantiadi* (016) is used as a patrol craft and tender. It is armed with two 23 mm guns and 2—12.7 mm MGs.
(2) Three 'Aist' (Project 1398) class patrol launches (10, 12, 14). 14 is active with the Hydrographic Service and has a blue hull.
(3) A 'Nyryat' (DHK-81) and 'Flamingo' (DHK-82) are active with the Hydrographic service and are civilian manned.
(4) A Project 371U patrol launch *Gali* (04).
(5) There are ten 9 m 'Black Shark' RHIBs built by Batumi Shipyard in 2006–07. Powered by two Mercury 250 hp outboard engines, they are capable of 48 kt and of carrying about 10 troops.
(6) There are two 7.5 m RHIBs A 24 and A 28. They are capable of 38 kt.

1 POLUCHAT 1 CLASS (PB)

AKHMETA 102

Displacement, tons: 86 standard; 100 full load
Dimensions, feet (metres): 97.1 × 19 × 4.8 *(29.6 × 5.8 × 1.5)*
Main machinery: 2 Type M 50 diesels; 2,200 hp(m) *(1.6 MW)* sustained; 2 shafts
Speed, knots: 20
Range, n miles: 1,500 at 10 kt
Complement: 15
Guns: 2—37 mm/L 68. 1—140 mm 17 round rocket launcher.
Radars: Surface search: Spin Trough; I-band.

Comment: Acquired in a disarmed state from commercial sources in Ukraine. Refitted at Metallist Ship Repair Yard, Balaklava 2000–02.

P 102 *8/2000, Hartmut Ehlers* / 0104494

2 DILOS CLASS (PB)

Name	*No*	*Builders*	*Commissioned*
IVERIA (ex-*Lindos*)	201 (ex-P 269)	Hellenic Shipyard, Skaramanga	1978
MESTIA (ex-*Dilos*)	203 (ex-P 267)	Hellenic Shipyard, Skaramanga	1978

Displacement, tons: 74.5 standard; 86 full load
Dimensions, feet (metres): 95.1 × 16.2 × 5.6 *(29 × 5 × 1.7)*
Main machinery: 2 MTU 12V 331TC92 diesels; 2,660 hp(m) *(1.96 MW)* sustained; 2 shafts
Speed, knots: 27
Range, n miles: 1,600 at 24 kt
Complement: 15
Guns: 4—23 mm ZSU (2 twin). 2—12.7 mm MGs.
Radars: Surface search: Racal Decca 1226C; I-band.

Comment: First one transferred from the Greek Navy in February 1998, second in September 1999. Reported to have been refitted in Greece in 2004.

IVERIA and MESTIA *10/2002, Hartmut Ehlers* / 0552757

1 KAAN 33 (FAST ATTACK CRAFT) (PBF)

SOKHUMI P 24

Displacement, tons: 120 full load
Dimensions, feet (metres): 116.8 × 22.0 × 4.7 *(35.6 × 6.7 × 1.4)*
Main machinery: 2 MTU 12V 4000 M90 diesels; 7,396 hp(m) *(5.44 MW)*; 2MJP 753 DD waterjets
Speed, knots: 47
Range, n miles: 970 at 15 kt
Complement: 18 (2 officers)
Guns: 1—12.7 mm MG (stabilised).

Comment: With advanced composites structure, the craft are modified versions of those in service in the Turkish Coast Guard. The craft are suitable for use as the patrol of littoral waters, maritime interdiction and special forces operations. The vessel was delivered in mid-2008.

SOKHUMI *6/2008*, Yonca-Onuk* / 1335376

LAND-BASED MARITIME AIRCRAFT

Notes: While there is no naval air arm, two Mi-14 helicopters were reported delivered in April 2004 after five years undergoing refitting in Ukraine. They are believed to be for patrol and SAR duties and to be unarmed.

AMPHIBIOUS FORCES

1 VYDRA (PROJECT 106K) CLASS (LCU)

GURIA 001

Displacement, tons: 425 standard; 550 full load
Dimensions, feet (metres): 179.7 × 26.6 × 6.6 *(54.8 × 8.1 × 2)*
Main machinery: 2 Type 3-D-12 diesels; 600 hp(m) *(440 kW)* sustained; 2 shafts
Speed, knots: 12
Range, n miles: 2,500 at 10 kt
Complement: 20
Military lift: 200 tons or 100 troops or 3 MBTs
Guns: 4—23 mm ZSU (2 twin).
Radars: Navigation: Don 2; I-band.
IFF: High Pole.

Comment: Built at Burgas Shipyard 1974–75. Transferred to Georgia on 6 July 2001.

VYDRA CLASS *10/2002, Hartmut Ehlers* / 0552747

COAST GUARD

Notes: In addition to the vessels listed below, the following vessels are on the Coast Guard list:
(1) A former fishing vessel *P 101*.
(2) Three Aist (Project 1398) class patrol launches *(P 0212, 702, 703)*.
(3) One Strizh (Project 1390) class launch *P 0116*.
(4) One 44 m tug *Poti* (ex-*Zorro*) acquired from Ukraine in 1999 for salvage purposes.
(5) Six patrol craft *(P 0112-0116, P 105)*. *P 0111* reported destroyed in August 2008.

1 LINDAU (TYPE 331) CLASS (WPBO)

Name	*No*	*Builders*	*Commissioned*
AYETY (ex-*Minden*)	P 22 (ex-M1085)	Burmester, Bremen	22 Jan 1960

Displacement, tons: 463 full load
Dimensions, feet (metres): 154.5 × 27.2 × 9.8 *(47.1 × 8.3 × 2.8)*
Main machinery: 2 MTU MD diesels; 4,000 hp(m) *(2.94 MW)*; 2 shafts
Speed, knots: 16. **Range, n miles:** 850 at 16 kt
Complement: 43
Guns: 1 Bofors 40 mm/70. 2—12.7 mm MGs.
Radars: Surface search: Atlas Elektronik TRS; I-band.

Comment: Paid off from German Navy in 1997 and transferred 15 November 1998 to the Coast Guard. Former minehunter refitted as a patrol craft in Germany before transfer. Reported destroyed in August 2008.

AYETY *10/2002, Hartmut Ehlers* / 0552749

2 DAUNTLESS CLASS (WPB)

P 106 (ex-P 208) **P 209**

Displacement, tons: 11 full load
Dimensions, feet (metres): 40 × 14 × 4.3 *(12.2 × 4.3 × 1.3)*
Main machinery: 2 Caterpillar 3208TA diesels; 870 hp *(650 kW)*; 2 shafts
Speed, knots: 27
Range, n miles: 600 at 18 kt
Complement: 5
Guns: 1—12.7 mm MG.
Radars: Surface search: Raytheon; I-band.

Comment: Aluminium construction. Acquired in July 1999 from SeaArk Marine.

P 209 *10/2002, Hartmut Ehlers* / 0552751

2 POINT CLASS (WPB)

Name	*No*	*Builders*	*Commissioned*
TSOTNE DADIANI (ex-*Point Countess*)	P 210 (ex-82335)	USCG Yard, Curtis Bay	8 Aug 1962
GENERAL MAZNIASHVILI (ex-*Point Baker*)	P 211 (ex-82342)	USCG Yard, Curtis Bay	30 Oct 1963

Displacement, tons: 66; 69 full load
Dimensions, feet (metres): 83.0 × 17.2 × 5.8 *(25.3 × 5.3 × 1.8)*
Main machinery: 2 Caterpillar 3412 diesels; 1,600 hp *(1.19 MW)*; 2 shafts
Speed, knots: 23.5. **Range, n miles:** 1,500 at 8 kt
Complement: 10 (1 officer)
Guns: 2—12.7 mm MGs.
Radars: Surface search: Hughes/Furuno SPS-73; I-band.

Comment: Steel hulled craft with aluminium superstructure. First transferred from United States in June 2000 and second on 12 February 2002.

GENERAL MAZNIASHVILI *10/2002, Hartmut Ehlers* / 0589740

8 ZHUK CLASS (WPB)

P 102–104 **P 203–207**

Displacement, tons: 25 full load
Dimensions, feet (metres): 49 × 14.8 × 2.4 *(14.9 × 4.5 × 0.7)*
Main machinery: 2 GM diesels; 450 hp *(335 kW)*; 2 shafts
Speed, knots: 12
Range, n miles: 200 at 12 kt
Complement: 7
Guns: 2—23 mm (1 twin) *(P 204, P 205)*.
2—12.7 mm MGs *(P 203)*.

Comment: P 102-104 constructed at Batumi 1997–99. P 203 transferred from Ukraine in April 1997. P 204-205 acquired from Ukraine and P 206-207 transferred from Georgian Navy in 1998. Two craft had been modernised under the 'Orbi' programme by late 2007.

P 203 *10/2002, Hartmut Ehlers* / 0552753

Germany

DEUTSCHE MARINE

Country Overview

The Federal Republic of Germany (FRG) is situated in central Europe. The country was re-unified in 1990 when the German Democratic Republic became part of the FRG. With an area of 137,823 square miles, it is bordered to the north by Denmark, to the east by Poland and the Czech Republic, to the south by Austria and Switzerland and to the west by France, Luxembourg, Belgium and the Netherlands. It has a 1,290 n mile coastline with the North and Baltic Seas which are linked by the Kiel Canal. The capital and largest city is Berlin. North Sea ports include Hamburg, Wilhelmshaven, Bremen, Nordenham and Emden, while the main Baltic ports are Lübeck, Wismar, Rostock and Stralsund. The Rhine is the principal inland waterway on which Duisburg is the largest port. Territorial seas (12 n miles) are claimed. An EEZ (200 n miles) has also been claimed.

Headquarters Appointments

Chief of Naval Staff:
Vice Admiral Wolfgang Nolting
Chief of Staff:
Rear Admiral Hans-Jochen Witthauer

Commander-in-Chief

Commander-in-Chief, Fleet:
Vice Admiral Hans-Joachim Stricker

Diplomatic Representation

Defence Attaché in Paris:
Rear Admiral George Von Maltzan
Defence Attaché in Rome:
Captain J Schamong

Diplomatic Representation—*continued*

Naval Attaché in London:
Captain Uwe Hovorka
Naval Attaché in Washington:
Captain R Schmitt-Raiser
Naval Attaché in Moscow:
Captain G Hamann
Defence Attaché in Pretoria:
Captain Hans-Uwe Mergener
Defence Attaché in Kuala-Lumpur:
Commander Heinz Udo Schindt
Defence Attaché in Abu Dhabi:
Commander H Weis
Defence Attaché in Tunis:
Commander J Giese
Defence Attaché in Copenhagen:
Commander T Papenroth

Diplomatic Representation—*continued*

Naval Attaché in Tel Aviv:
Commander W Knipprath
Defence Attaché in Mexico City:
Commander H P Lochbaum
Naval Attaché in Ankara:
Commander G Pichel
Naval Attaché in Bangkok:
Commander Joachim Schumacher
Defence Attaché in The Hague:
Commander L Stellmann
Defence Attaché in Lisbon:
Commander J H Mandt

Personnel

(a) 2009: 21,300 (5,192 officers) (including naval air arm) plus 3,700 conscripts
(b) 9 months' national service

Fleet Disposition

1st Flotilla (Kiel)
1st Corvette Squadron (Warnemünde); Type 130
7th FPB Squadron (Warnemünde); Type 143A
3rd and 5th Mine Warfare Squadron (Kiel); Type 332, 333 and 352
1st Submarine Squadron (Eckernförde); Type 206A and Type 212
Fleet Service Ships; Type 423
2nd Flotilla (Wilhelmshaven)
2nd Frigate Squadron; Type 123 and 124
4th Frigate Squadron; Type 122
Auxiliary Squadron; Type 702 (AORH), 703 (AOL), 704 (AOL), 720 (ATR), 722 (ATS), 760 (AEL)

Bases

C-in-C Fleet: Glücksburg, Naval Command: Rostock.
Baltic: Kiel, Warnemünde, Eckernförde.
North Sea: Wilhelmshaven.
Naval Arsenal: Wilhelmshaven, Kiel.
Training (other than in bases above): Bremerhaven.

Naval Air Arm

AG 51 (Tactical Air Support of Maritime Operations) (GAF Schleswig)
MFG 3 'Graf Zeppelin' (LRMP Wing at Nordholz)
P-3C Orion, remaining 2 Breguet Atlantic converted for Sigint; Sea Lynx (landbased for embarkation and maintenance). Dornier Do 228 (for pollution control)
MFG 5 (land-based SAR and Fleet Support with embarked helos) Sea King Mk 41.

Strength of the Fleet

Type	*Active*	*Building (Projected)*
Submarines—Patrol	10	2
Frigates	15	4
Corvettes	5	(8)
Fast Attack Craft—Missile	10	–
LCM/LCU	2	–
Minehunters	14	–
Minesweepers—Coastal	5	–
Minesweepers—Drones	18	–
Tenders	6	–
Replenishment Ships	6	1
Ammunition Transports	1	–
Tugs—Icebreaking	1	–
AGIs	3	–
Sail Training Ships	1	–
Diver Support Vessel	1	–

Prefix to Ships' Names

Prefix FGS is used in communications.

Hydrographic Service

This service, under the direction of the Ministry of Transport, is civilian-manned with HQ at Hamburg. Survey ships are listed at the end of the section.

DELETIONS

Submarines

2006	U 30
2007	U 29
2008	U 22, U 25

Mine Warfare Vessels

2006	*Weiden, Frankenthal*
2007	*Mühlhausen*

Survey and Research Ships

2004	*Planet* (old), *Kalkgrund*

Auxiliaries

2006	*Eisvogel, Nordwind*
2007	*Muschel*
2008	*Bergen* (to Lebanon), TF 5

PENNANT LIST

Submarines

S 172	U 23
S 173	U 24
S 181	U 31
S 182	U 32
S 183	U 33
S 184	U 34
S 194	U 15
S 195	U 16
S 196	U 17
S 197	U 18

Frigates

F 207	Bremen
F 208	Niedersachsen
F 209	Rheinland-Pfalz
F 210	Emden
F 211	Köln
F 212	Karlsruhe
F 213	Augsburg
F 214	Lübeck
F 215	Brandenburg
F 216	Schleswig-Holstein
F 217	Bayern
F 218	Mecklenburg-Vorpommern
F 219	Sachsen
F 220	Hamburg
F 221	Hessen

Corvettes

F 260	Braunschweig
F 261	Magdeburg
F 262	Erfurt
F 263	Oldenburg
F 264	Ludwigshafen

Patrol Forces

P 6121	S 71 Gepard
P 6122	S 72 Puma
P 6123	S 73 Hermelin
P 6124	S 74 Nerz
P 6125	S 75 Zobel
P 6126	S 76 Frettchen
P 6127	S 77 Dachs
P 6128	S 78 Ozelot
P 6129	S 79 Wiesel
P 6130	S 80 Hyäne

Mine Warfare Forces

M 1058	Fulda
M 1059	Weilheim
M 1061	Rottweil
M 1062	Sulzbach-Rosenberg
M 1063	Bad Bevensen
M 1064	Grömitz
M 1065	Dillingen
M 1067	Bad Rappenau
M 1068	Datteln
M 1069	Homburg
M 1090	Pegnitz
M 1091	Kulmbach
M 1092	Hameln
M 1093	Auerbach
M 1094	Ensdorf
M 1095	Überherrn
M 1096	Passau
M 1097	Laboe
M 1098	Siegburg
M 1099	Herten

Amphibious Forces

L 762	Lachs
L 765	Schlei

Auxiliaries

A 50	Alster
A 52	Oste
A 53	Oker
A 60	Gorch Fock
A 511	Elbe
A 512	Mosel
A 513	Rhein
A 514	Werra
A 515	Main
A 516	Donau
A 1409	Wilhelm Pullwer
A 1411	Berlin
A 1412	Frankfurt Am Main
A 1425	Ammersee
A 1426	Tegernsee
A 1435	Westerwald
A 1437	Planet
A 1439	Baltrum
A 1440	Juist
A 1441	Langeoog
A 1442	Spessart
A 1443	Rhön
A 1451	Wangerooge
A 1452	Spiekeroog
A 1458	Fehmarn
Y 811	Knurrhahn
Y 812	Lütje Hörn
Y 814	Knechtsand
Y 815	Scharhörn
Y 816	Vogelsand
Y 817	Nordstrand
Y 819	Langeness
Y 835	Todendorf
Y 836	Putlos
Y 837	Baumholder
Y 839	Munster
Y 842	Schwimmdock A
Y 860	Schwedeneck
Y 861	Kronsort
Y 862	Helmsand
Y 863	Stollergrund
Y 864	Mittelgrund
Y 866	Breitgrund
Y 875	Hiev
Y 876	Griep
Y 891	Altmark
Y 895	Wische
Y 1643	Bottsand
Y 1644	Eversand
Y 1656	Wustrow
Y 1658	Dranske
Y 1671	AK 1
Y 1675	AM 8
Y 1676	MA 2
Y 1677	MA 3
Y 1678	MA 1
Y 1679	AM 7
Y 1683	AK 6
Y 1685	Aschau
Y 1686	AK 2
Y 1687	Borby
Y 1689	Bums

SUBMARINES

4 + 2 TYPE 212A (SSK)

Name	*No*	*Builders*	*Laid down*	*Launched*	*Commissioned*
U 31	S 181	HDW, Kiel	Feb 2000	20 Mar 2002	19 Oct 2005
U 32	S 182	TNSW, Emden	Jan 2002	4 Dec 2003	19 Oct 2005
U 33	S 183	HDW, Kiel	Oct 2002	13 Sep 2004	13 June 2006
U 34	S 184	TNSW, Emden	June 2003	1 July 2005	3 May 2007
U 35	S 185	HDW, Kiel	Aug 2007	2009	2013
U 36	S 186	HDW, Kiel	Aug 2008	2010	2013

Displacement, tons: 1,450 surfaced; 1,830 dived
Dimensions, feet (metres): 183.4; (187.3 Batch 2) × 23 × 19.7 *(55.9; (57.1) × 7 × 6)*
Main machinery: Diesel-electric; 1 MTU 16V 396 diesel; 4,243 hp(m) *(3.12 MW)*; 1 alternator; 1 Siemens Permasyn motor; 3,875 hp(m) *(2.85 MW)*; 1 shaft; 9 Siemens/HDW PEM fuel cell (AIP) modules; 306 kW; sodium sulphide high-energy batteries
Speed, knots: 20 dived; 12 surfaced
Range, n miles: 8,000 at 8 kt surfaced
Complement: 28 (8 officers)

Torpedoes: 6–21 in *(533 mm)* bow tubes; water ram discharge; Atlas Elektronik DM 2 A4 torpedoes; wire guided active/passive homing to 50 km *(27 n miles)* at 50 kt; warhead 250 kg. Total 12 weapons.
Countermeasures: DASA FL 1800U or EADS MRBR 800 (Batch 2); radar warning.
Weapons control: Kongsberg MSI-90U (Batch 1). Atlas Elektronik ISUS (Batch 2).
Radars: Navigation: Kelvin Hughes 1007; I-band.
Sonars: STN Atlas Elektronik DBQS-40; passive ranging and intercept; FAS-3 flank and passive towed array.
STN Atlas Elektronik MOA 3070 or Allied Signal ELAK; mine detection; active; high frequency.

Programmes: Design phase first completed in 1992 by ARGE 212 (HDW/TNSW) in conjunction with IKL. Authorisation for the first four of the class was given on 6 July 1994, but the first steel cut was delayed to 1 July 1998 because of modifications needed to achieve commonality with the Italian Navy. The order for Batch 2 of two modified boats was made on 22 September 2006 and steel for *U 35* was cut on 21 August 2007. The submarines are to enter service in 2012 and 2013.
Modernisation: The fifth and sixth boats are to include EFAS flank array sonar, Carl Zeiss SERO 400 periscope and OMS 100 non-penetrating optronic mast. There will be a lock-in lock-out system for special forces and the PEM fuel-cell system is to be brought to the latest standard. IDAS, a missile system under evaluation, was fired from *U 33* on 29 May 2008. The system has both an anti-aircraft and land-attack capability and may be deployed from about 2014.
Structure: Equipped with a hybrid fuel cell/battery propulsion based on the Siemens PEM fuel cell technology. The submarine is designed with a partial double hull which has a larger diameter forward. This is joined to the after end by a short conical section which houses the fuel cell plant. Two LOX tanks and hydrogen stored in metal cylinders are carried around the circumference of the smaller hull section. Zeiss search and attack periscopes.
Operational: Maximum speed on AIP is 8 kt without use of main battery. *U 32* conducted a submerged transit from the German Bight to the Bay of Cadiz 11–25 April 2006. The entire passage was conducted using air-independent propulsion and without snorkelling, a speed of advance of 4–6 kt. Based at Eckernförde as part of the First Submarine Squadron.
Sales: Two identical submarines have been built in Italy and two further are under contract.

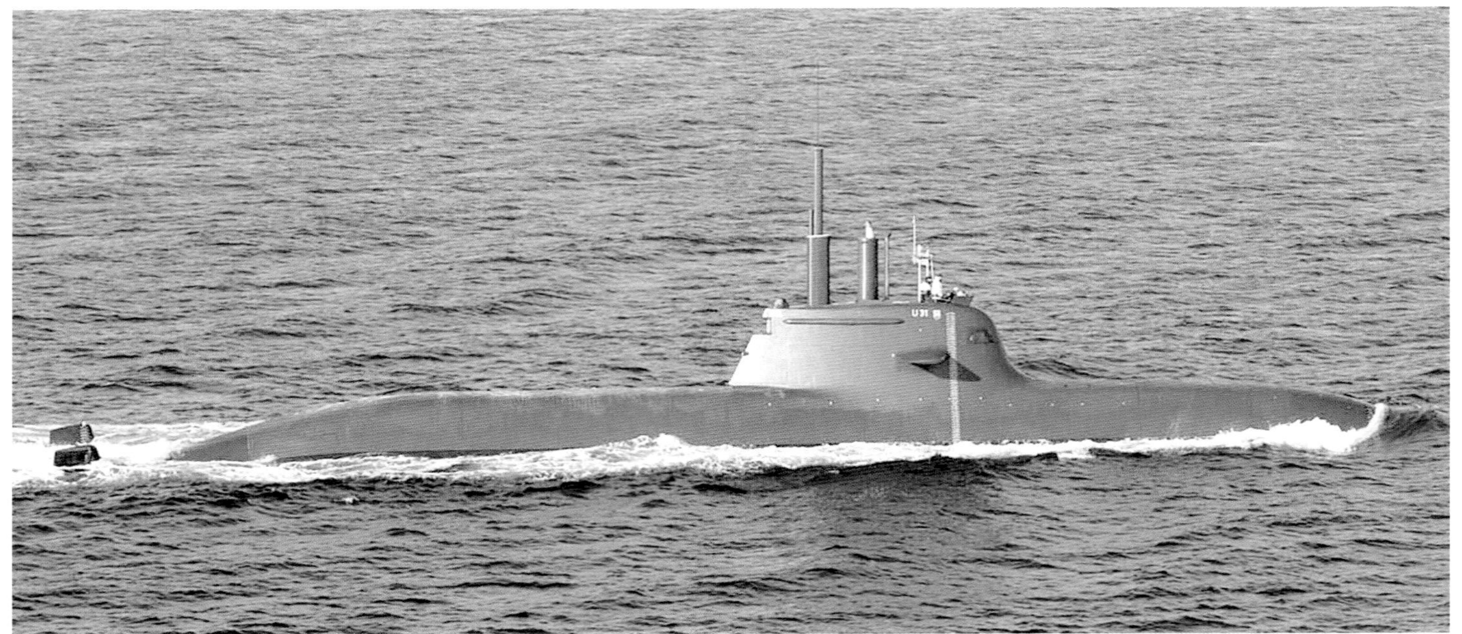

U 31 — ***2/2005, Michael Nitz*** / 1133424

U 34 — ***5/2007, Michael Nitz*** / 1166726

6 TYPE 206A (SSK)

Name	No	Builders	Laid down	Launched	Commissioned
U 15	S 194	Howaldtswerke, Kiel	1 June 1970	15 June 1972	17 July 1974
U 16	S 195	Rheinstahl Nordseewerke, Emden	1 Nov 1970	29 Aug 1972	9 Nov 1973
U 17	S 196	Howaldtswerke, Kiel	1 Oct 1970	10 Oct 1972	28 Nov 1973
U 18	S 197	Rheinstahl Nordseewerke, Emden	1 Apr 1971	31 Oct 1972	19 Dec 1973
U 23	S 172	Rheinstahl Nordseewerke, Emden	5 Mar 1973	25 May 1974	2 May 1975
U 24	S 173	Rheinstahl Nordseewerke, Emden	20 Mar 1972	26 June 1973	16 Oct 1974

Displacement, tons: 450 surfaced; 498 dived
Dimensions, feet (metres): 159.4 × 15.1 × 14.8 *(48.6 × 4.6 × 4.5)*
Main machinery: Diesel-electric; 2 MTU 12V 493 AZ80 GA 31L diesels; 1,200 hp(m) *(882 kW)* sustained; 2 alternators; 810 kW; 1 Siemens motor; 1,800 hp(m) *(1.32 MW)* sustained; 1 shaft
Speed, knots: 10 surfaced; 17 dived
Range, n miles: 4,500 at 5 kt surfaced
Complement: 22 (4 officers)

Torpedoes: 8—21 in *(533 mm)* bow tubes. STN Atlas DM 2A3; wire-guided; active homing to 13 km *(7 n miles)* at 35 kt; passive homing to 28 km *(15 n miles)* at 23 kt; warhead 260 kg.
Mines: GRP container secured outside hull each side. Each container holds 12 mines, carried in addition to the normal torpedo or mine armament (16 in place of torpedoes).
Countermeasures: ESM: Thomson-CSF DR 2000U with THORN EMI Sarie 2; intercept.
Weapons control: SLW 83 (TFCS).
Radars: Surface search: Thomson-CSF Calypso II; I-band.
Sonars: Atlas Elektronik DBQS-21D; passive/active search and attack; medium frequency.
Thomson Sintra DUUX 2; passive ranging.

Programmes: Authorised on 7 June 1969.
Modernisation: Mid-life conversion of the class was a very extensive one, including the installation of new sensors (sonar DBQS-21D with training simulator STU-5), periscopes, weapon control system (LEWA), ESM, weapons (torpedo Seeal), GPS navigation, and a comprehensive refitting of the propulsion system, as well as habitability improvements. Conversion work was shared between Thyssen Nordseewerke *(U 23, 24, 15)* at Emden and HDW *(U 16, 17, 18)* at Kiel. The work started in mid-1987 and completed in February 1992.
Structure: Hulls are built of high-tensile non-magnetic steel.
Operational: First squadron based at Eckernförde.
Sales: Two unmodernised (Type 206) were to have been acquired by Indonesia but the sale was cancelled in late 1998.

U 18

7/2008*, B Sullivan / 1353048

U 15

5/2008*, Michael Nitz / 1353049

FRIGATES

4 BRANDENBURG CLASS (TYPE 123) (FFGHM)

Name	*No*	*Builders*	*Laid down*	*Launched*	*Commissioned*
BRANDENBURG	F 215	Blohm + Voss, Hamburg	11 Feb 1992	28 Aug 1992	14 Oct 1994
SCHLESWIG-HOLSTEIN	F 216	Howaldtswerke, Kiel	1 July 1993	8 June 1994	2 Nov 1995
BAYERN	F 217	Thyssen Nordseewerke, Emden	16 Dec 1993	30 June 1994	15 June 1996
MECKLENBURG-VORPOMMERN	F 218	Bremer Vulkan/Thyssen Nordseewerke	23 Nov 1993	8 July 1995	6 Dec 1996

Displacement, tons: 5,400 full load
Dimensions, feet (metres): 455.7 oa; 416.3 wl × 54.8 × 22.3 *(138.9; 126.9 × 16.7 × 6.8)*
Main machinery: CODOG: 2 GE 7LM2500SA-ML gas turbines; 51,000 hp *(38 MW)* sustained; 2 MTU 20V 956 TB92 diesels; 11,070 hp(m) *(8.14 MW)* sustained; 2 shafts; Escher Wyss; cp props
Speed, knots: 29; 21 on diesels
Range, n miles: 4,000 at 18 kt
Complement: 229 (31 officers) plus 14

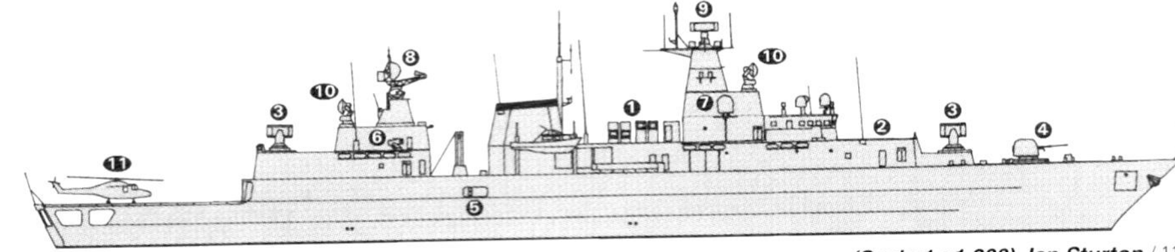

BRANDENBURG *(Scale 1 : 1,200), Ian Sturton* / 1153487

Missiles: SSM: 4 Aerospatiale MM 38 Exocet (2 twin) ❶ (from Type 101A); inertial cruise; active radar homing to 42 km *(23 n miles)* at 0.9 Mach; warhead 165 kg; sea-skimmer.
SAM: Martin Marietta VLS Mk 41 Mod 3 ❷ for 16 NATO Sea Sparrow RIM-7P; semi-active radar homing to 16 km *(8.5 n miles)* at 2.5 Mach; warhead 38 kg.
2 Raytheon RAM RIM-116 21 cell Mk 49 launchers ❸; passive IR/anti-radiation homing to 9.6 km *(5.2 n miles)* at 2.5 Mach; warhead 9.1 kg; 42 missiles.
Guns: 1 OTO Melara 3 in *(76 mm)*/62 Mk 75 ❹; 105 rds/min to 16 km *(8.6 n miles)* anti-surface; 12 km *(6.5 n miles)* anti-aircraft; weight of shell 6 kg.
2 Rheinmetall 20 mm Rh 202 to be replaced by Mauser 27 mm.
Torpedoes: 4—324 mm Mk 32 Mod 9 (2 twin) tubes ❺; anti-submarine. Honeywell Mk 46 Mod 2; anti-submarine; active/passive homing to 11 km *(5.9 n miles)* at 40 kt; warhead 44 kg. To be replaced by Eurotorp MU 90 Impact in due course.
Countermeasures: Decoys: 4 Rheinmetall MASS-4L decoy launchers ❻.
ESM/ECM: EADS FL 1800S Stage II; intercept and jammers.
Combat data systems: Atlas Elektronik/Paramax SATIR action data automation with Unisys UYK 43 computer; Link 11. Link 16. SATCOM ❼.
Weapons control: Thales MWCS. 2 optical sights. STN Atlas Elektronic WBA optronic sensor.
Radars: Air search: Thales LW08 ❽; D-band.
Air/surface search: Thales SMART ❾; 3D; F-band.
Fire control: 2 Thales STIR 180 trackers ❿.
Navigation: 2 Sperry Bridgemaster E; I-band.
Sonars: Atlas Elektronik DSQS-23BZ; hull-mounted; active search and attack; medium frequency.
Towed array (provision only); active; low frequency.

Helicopters: 2 Westland Sea Lynx Mk 88A ⓫.

MECKLENBURG-VORPOMMERN *10/2004, B Sullivan* / 0587753

Programmes: Four ordered 28 June 1989. Developed by Blohm + Voss whose design was selected in October 1988. Replaced deleted Hamburg class.
Modernisation: SCOT 3 SATCOM and STN optronic sensor fitted from 1998. All four ships are to undergo a major modernisation programme to extend service life to at least 2025. A contract was signed on 21 September 2005 for Phase 1 (2007–11), the replacement of the combat data system by the Thales SABRINA 21 system, which incorporates Tacticos-NC and Sewaco-DDS technology. In Phase 2 (2008–14), ASW capabilities are to be upgraded with the installation of the Eurotorp MU 90 lightweight torpedo. Low Frequency Towed Active Sonar (LFTAS) is being trialled in *Bayern* from 2006–2009. Phase 2 is also likely to include upgrade of the IFF system. Phase 3 (2012–16) will improve AAW and ASUW capabilities by installation and integration of RIM-162 Evolved Sea Sparrow (ESSM) and a new surface-to-surface missile. In a separate contract the DSQS-23BZ bow sonar is to be upgraded 2005–09.
Structure: The design is a mixture of MEKO and improved serviceability Type 122 having the same propulsion as the Type 122. Contemporary stealth features. All steel. Fin stabilisers. Space allocated for a Task Group Commander and Staff.
Operational: 2nd Frigate Squadron based at Wilhelmshaven. One RIB is carried for boarding operations.

BAYERN *6/2008*, A A de Kruijf* / 1353053

BRANDENBURG *9/2008*, B Sullivan* / 1353052

BRANDENBURG *9/2008*, J Brodie* / 1353047

MECKLENBURG-VORPOMMERN *5/2008*, Michael Nitz* / 1353054

MECKLENBURG-VORPOMMERN *9/2004, John Brodie* / 0587720

8 BREMEN CLASS (TYPE 122) (FFGHM)

Name	No	Builders	Laid down	Launched	Commissioned
BREMEN	F 207	Bremer Vulkan	9 July 1979	27 Sep 1979	7 May 1982
NIEDERSACHSEN	F 208	AG Weser/Bremer Vulkan	9 Nov 1979	9 June 1980	15 Oct 1982
RHEINLAND-PFALZ	F 209	Blohm + Voss/Bremer Vulkan	29 Sep 1979	3 Sep 1980	9 May 1983
EMDEN	F 210	Thyssen Nordseewerke, Emden/Bremer Vulkan	23 June 1980	17 Dec 1980	7 Oct 1983
KÖLN	F 211	Blohm + Voss/Bremer Vulkan	16 June 1980	29 May 1981	19 Oct 1984
KARLSRUHE	F 212	Howaldtswerke, Kiel/Bremer Vulkan	10 Mar 1981	8 Jan 1982	19 Apr 1984
AUGSBURG	F 213	Bremer Vulkan	4 Apr 1987	17 Sep 1987	3 Oct 1989
LÜBECK	F 214	Thyssen Nordseewerke, Emden/Bremer Vulkan	1 June 1987	15 Oct 1987	19 Mar 1990

Displacement, tons: 3,680 full load
Dimensions, feet (metres): 426.4 × 47.6 × 21.3 *(130 × 14.5 × 6.5)*
Main machinery: CODOG; 2 GE LM 2500 gas turbines; 51,000 hp *(38 MW)* sustained; 2 MTU 20V 956TB92 diesels; 11,070 hp(m) *(8.14 MW)* sustained; 2 shafts; cp props
Speed, knots: 30; 20 on diesels
Range, n miles: 4,000 at 18 kt
Complement: 219 (26 officers)

Missiles: SSM: 8 McDonnell Douglas Harpoon (2 quad) launchers ❶; active radar homing to 130 km *(70 n miles)* at 0.9 Mach; warhead 227 kg.
SAM: 8 Raytheon NATO Sea Sparrow RIM-7P; Mk 29 octuple launcher ❷; semi-active radar homing to 16 km *(8.5 n miles)* at 2.5 Mach; warhead 38 kg.
2 Raytheon RAM RIM-116 21 cell Mk 49 launchers ❸; passive IR/anti-radiation homing to 9.6 km *(5.2 n miles)* at 2.5 Mach; warhead 9.1 kg.
Guns: 1 OTO Melara 3 in *(76 mm)*/62 Compact ❹; 108 rds/min to 16 km *(8.6 n miles)* anti-surface; 12 km *(6.5 n miles)* anti-aircraft; weight of shell 6 kg.
2 Mauser 27 mm.
4—12.7 mm MGs.
Torpedoes: 4—324 mm Mk 32 (2 twin) tubes ❺. 8 Honeywell Mk 46 Mod 2; anti-submarine; active/passive homing to 11 km *(5.9 n miles)* at 40 kt; warhead 44 kg. To be replaced by Eurotorp MU 90.
Countermeasures: Decoys: 4 Loral Hycor SRBOC ❻ 6-barrelled fixed Mk 36; chaff and IR flares to 4 km *(2.2 n miles)*.
SLQ-25 Nixie; towed torpedo decoy. Prairie bubble noise reduction.
ESM/ECM: EADS FL 1800 Stage II ❼; intercept and jammer.
Combat data systems: SATIR action data automation; Link 11; Link 16; Matra Marconi SCOT 1A SATCOM ❽ (3 sets for the class).
Weapons control: Thales WM25/STIR. STN Atlas Elektronic WBA optronic sensor.
Radars: Air/surface search: DASA TRS-3D/32 ❾; C-band.
Navigation: Kelvin Hughes Nucleus 2 5000A; I-band.
Fire control: Thales WM25 ❿; I/J-band.
Thales STIR ⓫; I/J/K-band; range 140 km *(76 n miles)* for 1 m² target.
Sonars: Atlas Elektronik DSQS-21BZ (BO); hull-mounted; active search and attack; medium frequency.

Helicopters: 2 Westland Sea Lynx Mk 88A ⓬.

Programmes: Approval given in early 1976 for first six of this class, a modification of the Netherlands Kortenaer class. Replaced the deleted Fletcher and Köln classes. Equipment ordered February 1986 after order placed 6 December 1985 for last pair. Hulls and some engines provided in the five building yards. Ships were then towed to the prime contractor Bremer Vulkan where weapon systems and electronics were fitted and trials conducted. The three names for F 210-212 were changed from the names of Länder to take the well known town names of the Köln class as they were paid off.
Modernisation: RAM fitted from 1993–1996: Updated EW fit from 1994. 20 mm guns, taken from Type 520 LCUs, fitted aft of the bridge on each side. TRS-3D/32 radar has replaced DA 08 in all ships. STN optronic sensor fitted from 1998. 27 mm guns to replace 20 mm in due course. All eight ships are to undergo a modernisation programme to extend service life to at least 2015. A contract was signed on 21 September 2005 for the replacement of the combat data system by the Thales SABRINA 21 system, which incorporates Tacticos-NC and Sewaco-DDS technology. The work is to include integration of Link 16 which is currently being fitted throughout the class. The modernisation is also likely to include upgrade of the IFF system and installation of the Rheinmetall MSP 500 optronic director. The first ship to be refitted was *Bremen*, which completed in 2008. The programme will be completed when *Köln* returns to the fleet in 2011.
Operational: Form 4th Frigate Squadron based at Wilhelmshaven. Three containerised SCOT 1A terminals acquired in 1988 and when fitted are mounted on the hangar roof.

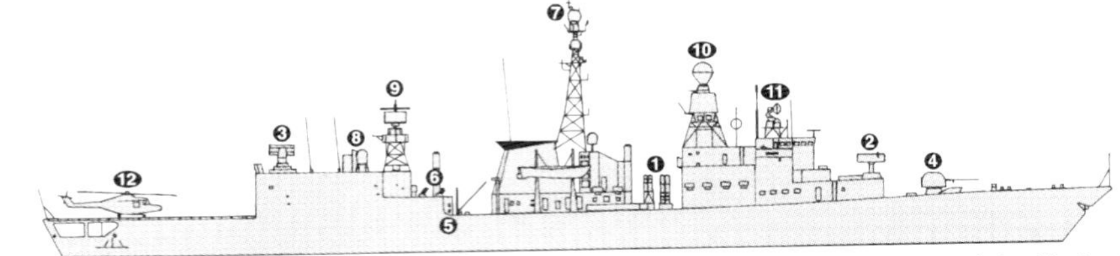

EMDEN *(Scale 1 : 1,200), Ian Sturton* / 0012400

KÖLN *3/2008*, Guy Toremans* / 1353057

RHEINLAND-PFALZ *3/2008*, Michael Nitz* / 1353055

LÜBECK *5/2008*, Michael Nitz* / 1353056

3 SACHSEN CLASS (TYPE 124) (FFGHM)

Name	*No*	*Builders*	*Laid down*	*Launched*	*Commissioned*
SACHSEN	F 219	Blohm + Voss, Hamburg	1 Feb 1999	1 Dec 1999	4 Nov 2004
HAMBURG	F 220	Howaldtswerke, Kiel	1 Sep 2000	16 Aug 2002	13 Dec 2004
HESSEN	F 221	Thyssen Nordseewerke, Emden	14 Sep 2002	27 June 2003	15 Dec 2005

Displacement, tons: 5,600 full load
Dimensions, feet (metres): 469.2 oa; 433.7 wl × 57.1 × 22.7 *(143; 132.2 × 17.4 × 6.9)*
Main machinery: CODAG; 1 GE LM 2500 gas turbine; 31,514 hp *(23.5 MW)*; 2 MTU 20V 1163 TB 93 diesels; 20,128 hp(m) *(14.8 MW)*; 2 shafts; cp props
Speed, knots: 29
Range, n miles: 4,000 at 18 kt
Complement: 255 (39 officers)

Missiles: SSM: 4 McDonnell Douglas Harpoon Block 1D ❶ 2 (twin); active radar homing to 95 km *(51 n miles)* at 0.9 Mach; warhead 227 kg.
SAM: Mk 41 VLS (32 cells) ❷ 24 Raytheon Standard SM-2 Block IIIA; command/inertial guidance; semi-active radar homing to 167 km *(90 n miles)* at 2.5 Mach. 32 Evolved Sea Sparrow RIM 162B; semi-active radar homing to 18 km *(9.7 n miles)* at 3.6 Mach; warhead 39 kg.
2 RAM RIM-116 launchers ❸. 21 cell Mk 49 launchers; passive IR/anti-radiation homing to 9.6 km *(5.2 n miles)* at 2.5 Mach; warhead 9.1 kg. 42 missiles.
Guns: 1 Otobreda 76 mm/62 IROF ❹; 108 rds/min to 16 km (8.6 n miles) anti-surface; 12 km *(6.5 n miles)* anti-aircraft; weight of shell 6 kg.
2 Mauser 27 mm ❺.
4—12.7 mm MGs.
Torpedoes: 6—324 mm (2 triple) Mk 32 Mod 7 tubes ❻. Eurotorp Mu 90 Impact.
Countermeasures: Decoys: 6 SRBOC 130 mm chaff launchers ❼.
ESM/ECM: EADS FI 1800S-II; intercept ❽ and jammer.
Combat data systems: CDS F 124; Link 11/16.
Electro-optic systems: MSP optronic director ❾.
Radars: Air search: SMART L ❿ 3D; D-band.
Air/surface search: Thales APAR phased array ⓫; I/J-band.
Navigation: 2 SAM 9600M ⓬; E/I-band.
IFF: Mk XII.
Sonars: Atlas DSQS-21B (Mod); bow-mounted; active search; medium frequency.

Helicopters: 2 NH90 NFH ⓭ or 2 Lynx 88A.

Programmes: Type 124 air defence ships built to replace the Lütjens class. A collaborative design with the Netherlands. A Memorandum of Understanding (MoU) was signed in October 1993 between Blohm + Voss, Royal Schelde and Bazán shipyards. A contract to build three ships was authorised on 12 June 1996. An option for a fourth is not likely to be exercised. *Hessen* started sea trials on 21 January 2005.
Modernisation: SRBOC chaff launchers are to be replaced with MASS from 2010.
Structure: Based on the Type 123 hull with improved stealth features. MBB-FHS helo handling system.
Operational: Successful sea-firings of Standard SM-2 and ESSM conducted at USN range off southern California in July/August 2004. Part of 2nd Frigate Squadron based at Wilhelmshaven.

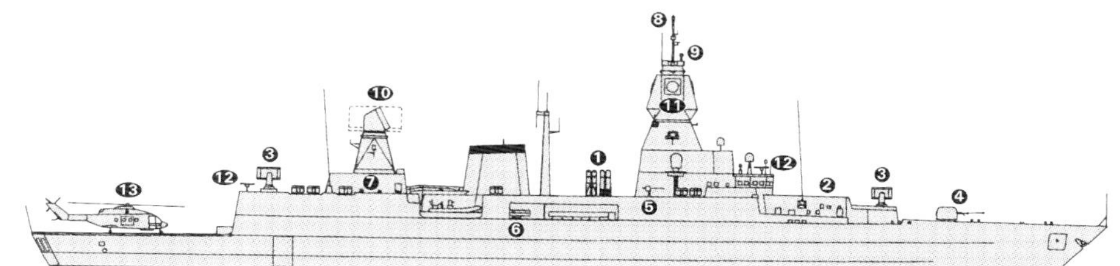

SACHSEN ***(Scale 1 : 1,200), Ian Sturton*** / 1353058

SACHSEN ***6/2007, Maritime Photographic*** / 1166746

HAMBURG ***11/2007, B Sullivan*** / 1166751

HESSEN ***10/2007, Michael Nitz*** / 1166732

0 + 4 BADEN-WÜRTTEMBERG (TYPE 125) CLASS (FFGHM)

Name	No	Builders	Laid down	Launched	Commissioned
BADEN-WÜRTTEMBERG	–	–	2009	2012	2014
NORDRHEIN-WESTFALEN	–	–	2010	2013	2015
–	–	–	2011	2014	2016
–	–	–	2012	2015	2017

Displacement, tons: 6,800 full load
Dimensions, feet (metres): 477.7 × 60.4 × 16.4 *(145.6 × 18.4 × 5.0)*
Main machinery: CODLAG: 1 gas turbine; 26,820 hp *(20 MW)*; 4 diesels; 16,100 hp *(12 MW)*; 2 motors; 12,100 hp *(9.0 MW)*; 2 shafts; cp props; bow thruster
Speed, knots: 26
Range, n miles: 4,000 at 18 kt
Complement: 110 (accommodation for 190)

Missiles: SSM: 8 McDonnell Douglas Harpoon ❶.
SAM: 2 Raytheon RAM 21-cell Mk 49 launchers ❷.
Guns: 1 OTO Melara 5 in *(127 mm)*/64 LW ❸.
2 Rheinmetall/Mauser MLG 27 mm. 5—12.7 mm remote-controlled MGs; 2—12.7 mm MGs.
Countermeasures: 4 Rheinmetall MASS decoy launchers; anti-torpedo defence system.
Combat data systems: Atlas Elektronik. Links 11, 16 and 22.
Weapons control: 2 multisensor. 1 EO surveillance system ❹.
Radars: Air/EADS TRS-3D/NR ❺; C-band.
Navigation: To be announced ❻.
Sonars: One diver detection (HF).

Helicopters: 2 MH 90 ❼.

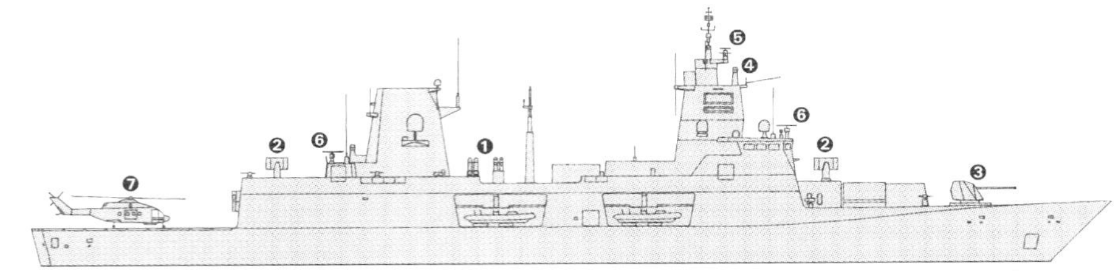

BADEN-WÜRTTEMBERG CLASS ***(Scale 1 : 1,200), Ian Sturton*** / 1166826

Programmes: The contract for the design and construction of four F 125 frigates was signed on 26 June 2007. The building consortium includes ThyssenKrupp Marine Systems and Lürssen Werft. The principal role of the ship is to conduct long-endurance crisis-management operations, particularly tactical naval gunfire support and support of special forces. The details of the ship are based on current planning assumptions and could change.
Structure: The ships are to be equipped with an 'innovative damage control concept'. There is to be accommodation for up to 50 special forces for whom there will be a dedicated operations room. The ship is to carry four high speed 10 m craft. A VLS launcher may also be incorporated. A water cannon is to be fitted.
Operational: The ships will be designed to be able to deploy for up to two years without return to home-base. This will include a 50 per cent reduced manning concept featuring two crews of about 100 each (plus 20 for the aviation detachment). These would relieve each other on a regular, four-month, rotating schedule.

CORVETTES

Notes: The K 131 programme is for a medium-size surface combatant, to replace the Type 122 frigates and the Type 143A fast attack craft. Up to eight ships, built to a modular design, are likely to be required to enter service from about 2017.

5 BRAUNSCHWEIG (K130) CLASS (FSGHM)

Name	No	Builders	Laid down	Launched	Commissioned
BRAUNSCHWEIG	F 260	Blohm + Voss, Hamburg	2005	19 Apr 2006	16 Apr 2008
MAGDEBURG	F 261	Lürssen, Vegesack	2005	6 Sep 2006	22 Sep 2008
ERFURT	F 262	Thyssen Nordseewerke, Emden	2006	29 Mar 2007	Apr 2009
OLDENBURG	F 263	Blohm + Voss, Hamburg	2006	28 June 2007	Apr 2009
LUDWIGSHAFEN	F 264	Lürssen, Vegesack	2006	26 Sep 2007	May 2009

Displacement, tons: 1,840 full load
Dimensions, feet (metres): 291.3 × 43.4 × 15.7 *(88.8 × 13.2 × 4.8)*
Main machinery: 2 MTU diesels; total of 19,850 hp(m) *(14.8 MW)*; 2 shafts
Speed, knots: 26. **Range, n miles:** 2,500 at 15 kt
Complement: 58 (8 officers)

Missiles: SSM: 4 Saab RBS-15 Mk 3 ❶; active radar homing to 200 km *(108 n miles)* at 0.9 Mach; warhead 200 kg.
SAM: 2 Raytheon RAM RIM-116 21 cell Mk 49 launchers ❷; passive IR/anti-radiation homing to 9.6 km *(5.2 n miles)* at 2.5 Mach; warhead 9.1 kg; 42 missiles.
Guns: 1 Otobreda 76 mm/62 ❸; 108 rds/min to 16 km *(8.6 n miles)* anti-surface; weight of shell 6 kg; 2 Mauser 27 mm ❹.
Countermeasures: Decoys: 2 Rheinmetall MASS ❺; decoy launchers.
ESM/ECM: EADS UL 5000K; intercept and jammer.
Combat data systems: SEWACO; Link 11/16.
Electro-optic systems: 2 Thales Mirador Trainable Electro-Optical Observation System (TEOOS) ❻.
Radars: Air/surface search: EADS TRS-3D ❼; C-band.
Navigation: 2 Raymarine Pathfinder/ST 34 ❽; E/F/I-bands.
Fire control: EADS TRS-3D; C-band.

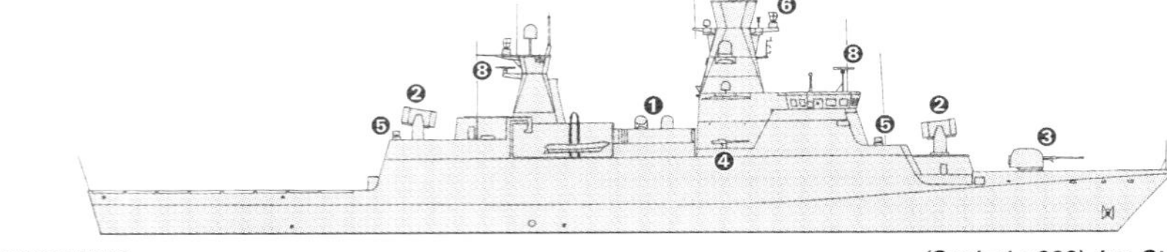

BRAUNSCHWEIG ***(Scale 1 : 900), Ian Sturton*** / 1166827

Helicopters: Platform for 1 medium and for UAV (possibly Schiebel Camcopter).

Programmes: Invitations to tender accepted at the end of 1998. Blohm + Voss selected as consortium leader 18 July 2000. Consortium includes Thyssen Nordseewerke and Lürssen. Batch of five ships ordered on 14 December 2001 and first steel cut for the first of class on 19 July 2004. The bow section of the first ship was launched on 6 September 2005. All bow sections are being constructed at Emden, the aft sections at Lürssen and the superstructure at Blohm+Voss. There will be no further ships of this class.
Modernisation: All five ships are to be fitted with bow-thrusters.
Structure: Measures to reduce radar, IR (water-cooled surface exhaust system) and noise signatures have been included in the design.
Operational: The ships form the 1st Corvette Squadron based at Rostock-Warnemünde.

BRAUNSCHWEIG ***4/2008*, Michael Nitz*** / 1353059

BRAUNSCHWEIG *4/2008*, Michael Nitz* / 1353060

OLDENBURG *7/2008*, Michael Nitz* / 1353061

SHIPBORNE AIRCRAFT

Numbers/Type: 30 NH Industries MH-90.
Operational speed: 165 kt *(305 km/h)*.
Service ceiling: 9,720 ft *(2,960 m)*.
Range: 430 n miles *(796 km)*.
Role/Weapon systems: 30 MH-90 helicopters, to replace the Sea King inventory, are planned to be delivered from 2015. Sensors: ENR 90 radar, Thales FLASH dipping sonar, FLIR. Weapons: Eurotorp Mu-90 torpedoes, ASM (to be confirmed).

MH 90 *6/2001, NH Industries* / 0062373

Numbers/Type: 21 Westland Sea King Mk 41 KWS.
Operational speed: 140 kt *(260 km/h)*.
Service ceiling: 10,500 ft *(3,200 m)*.
Range: 630 n miles *(1,165 km)*.
Role/Weapon systems: Used in shipborne role for Berlin class AFSH. Land-based roles include SAR, area surveillance and transport. Sensors: Ferranti Sea Spray Mk 3 radar, FLIR, RWR, chaff and flare dispenser. Weapons: 1—12.7 mm MG.

SEA KING *6/2008*, Harald Carstens* / 1353062

Numbers/Type: 22 Westland Super Lynx Mk 88A.
Operational speed: 125 kt *(232 km/h)*.
Service ceiling: 12,500 ft *(3,010 m)*.
Range: 320 n miles *(593 km)*.
Role/Weapon systems: Shipborne ASW/ASV role. Sensors: GEC Marine Sea Spray 3000 FLIR and Bendix AQS-18 dipping sonar. Weapons: ASW; up to two Mk 46 Mod 2 (or Eurotorp MU 90 Impact in due course) torpedoes. ASV; BAe Sea Skua, 1—12.7 mm MG.

LYNX MK 88A — *3/2008*, Frank Findler / 1353046*

LAND-BASED MARITIME AIRCRAFT (FRONT LINE)

Numbers/Type: 8 Lockheed P-3C Orion CUP.
Operational speed: 405 kt *(750 km/h)*.
Service ceiling: 30,000 ft *(9,145 m)*.
Range: 4,875 n miles *(9,030 km)*.
Role/Weapon systems: Long-range maritime reconnaissance aircraft procured from the Netherlands 2005–06 and became fully operational in 2008. Aircraft updated under CUP programme. Sensors: AN/APS-137B(V)5 radar, AAQ 22 Safire FLIR, AN/ALR 95 ESM, AN/ALE 47 chaff dispenser, AN/AAR 47 missile warning system, AN/SSQ 227 central processor, AN/ASQ-78B acoustic processor, AQS 81 MAD. Weapons: 8 Mk 46 torpedoes (or Eurotorp MU 90 Impact in due course).

P-3C — *7/2006, Michael Winter / 1159960*

Numbers/Type: 2 Dornier DO 228-212.
Operational speed: 156 kt *(290 km/h)*.
Service ceiling: 20,700 ft *(6,300 m)*.
Range: 667 n miles *(1,235 km)*.
Role/Weapon systems: Pollution control. Sensors: Weather radar; SLAR, IR/UR scanner, microwave radiometer, LLTV camera and data downlink. Weapons: Unarmed.

DORNIER 228 — *8/2006, Frank Findler / 1159886*

Numbers/Type: 2 Breguet Atlantic 1.
Operational speed: 355 kt *(658 km/h)*.
Service ceiling: 32,800 ft *(10,000 m)*.
Range: 4,850 n miles *(8,990 km)*.
Role/Weapon systems: Long-range Sigint aircraft.

ATLANTIC — *5/2006, Michael Nitz / 1164831*

Numbers/Type: 50 Panavia Tornado IDS.
Operational speed: Mach 2.2.
Service ceiling: 80,000 ft *(24,385 m)*.
Range: 1,500 n miles *(2,780 km)*.
Role/Weapon systems: Swing-wing strike and recce; shore-based for fleet tactical support (recce, ASUW, limited air defence). Former naval aircraft transferred to the German Air Force in 2005. Sensors: Texas Instruments nav/attack system, MBB/Alenia multisensor recce pod. Weapons: ASV; four Kormoran 2 missiles. Fleet AD; two 27 mm cannon, four AIM-9L Sidewinder.

TORNADO — *9/2004, Frank Findler / 1044258*

PATROL FORCES

Notes: Vessels in this section have an 'S' number as part of their name as well as a 'P' pennant number. The 'S' number is shown in the Pennant List at the front of this country.

10 GEPARD CLASS (TYPE 143 A) (FAST ATTACK CRAFT—MISSILE) (PGGFM)

Name	*No*	*Builders*	*Launched*	*Commissioned*
GEPARD	P 6121	AEG/Lürssen	25 Sep 1981	13 Dec 1982
PUMA	P 6122	AEG/Lürssen	8 Feb 1982	24 Feb 1983
HERMELIN	P 6123	AEG/Kröger	8 Dec 1981	5 May 1983
NERZ	P 6124	AEG/Lürssen	18 Aug 1982	14 July 1983
ZOBEL	P 6125	AEG/Kröger	30 June 1982	25 Sep 1983
FRETTCHEN	P 6126	AEG/Lürssen	26 Jan 1983	15 Dec 1983
DACHS	P 6127	AEG/Kröger	14 Dec 1982	22 Mar 1984
OZELOT	P 6128	AEG/Lürssen	7 June 1983	3 May 1984
WIESEL	P 6129	AEG/Lürssen	8 Aug 1983	12 July 1984
HYÄNE	P 6130	AEG/Lürssen	5 Oct 1983	13 Nov 1984

Displacement, tons: 391 full load
Dimensions, feet (metres): 190 × 25.6 × 8.5 *(57.6 × 7.8 × 2.6)*
Main machinery: 4 MTU MA 16V 956 SB80 diesels; 13,200 hp(m) *(9.7 MW)* sustained; 4 shafts
Speed, knots: 40. **Range, n miles**: 2,600 at 16 kt; 600 at 33 kt
Complement: 34 (4 officers)

Missiles: SSM: 4 Aerospatiale MM 38 Exocet; inertial cruise; active radar homing to 42 km *(23 n miles)* at 0.9 Mach; warhead 165 kg; sea-skimmer.
SAM: 1 Raytheon RAM RIM-116 21 cell Mk 49 launcher; passive IR/anti-radiation homing to 9.6 km *(5.2 n miles)* at 2.5 Mach; warhead 9.1 kg.
Guns: 1 Otobreda 3 in *(76 mm)*/62 compact; 85 rds/min to 16 km *(8.6 n miles)* anti-surface; 12 km *(6.5 n miles)* anti-aircraft; weight of shell 6 kg. 2—12.7 mm MGs.
Mines: Can lay mines.
Countermeasures: Decoys: Buck-Wegmann Hot Dog/Silver Dog; IR/chaff dispenser.
ESM/ECM: Dasa FL 1800 Mk 2; radar intercept and jammer.
Combat data systems: AGIS with Signaal update; Link 11.
Electro-optic systems: STN Atlas WBA optronic sensor.
Radars: Surface search/fire control: Signaal WM27; I/J-band; range 46 km *(25 n miles)*.
Navigation: Sperry Bridgemaster; I-band.

Programmes: Ordered mid-1978 from AEG-Telefunken with subcontracting to Lürssen (P 6121, 6122, 6124-6128) and Kröger (P 6123, 6129, 6130).
Modernisation: Updated EW fit in 1994–95. RAM fitted in *Puma* in 1992, and to the rest from 1993–98. Combat data system update completed in 1999. Improved EW aerials fitted from 1999.
Structure: Wooden hulls on aluminium frames.
Operational: Form 7th Squadron based on the tender *Elbe* at Warnemünde. To remain in commission until 2015+.

PUMA — *6/2008*, Michael Nitz / 1353063*

HYÄNE — *6/2008*, A A de Kruijf / 1353065*

NERZ — *4/2008*, Ian Harris / 1353064*

AMPHIBIOUS FORCES

Notes: Procurement of a Joint Support Ship, possibly using an LHD/LPD design, is under consideration. Up to three units may be acquired with entry into service from 2020.

2 TYPE 520 (LCU)

LACHS L 762 **SCHLEI** L 765

Displacement, tons: 430 full load
Dimensions, feet (metres): 131.2 × 28.9 × 7.2 *(40 × 8.8 × 2.2)*
Main machinery: 2 MWM 12-cyl diesels; 1,020 hp(m) *(750 kW)*; 2 shafts
Speed, knots: 11
Complement: 17
Military lift: 150 tons
Radars: Navigation: Kelvin-Hughes; I-band.

Comment: Similar to the US LCU (Landing Craft Utility) type. Provided with bow and stern ramp. Built by Howaldtswerke, Hamburg, 1965–66. Two sold to Greece in November 1989 and six more in 1992. Based at Eckenförde. Guns have been removed.

SCHLEI *6/2008*, Michael Nitz* / 1353066

MINE WARFARE FORCES

9 FRANKENTHAL CLASS (TYPE 332) (MINEHUNTERS—COASTAL) (MHC)

Name	*No*	*Builders*	*Launched*	*Commissioned*
BAD BEVENSEN	M 1063	Lürssenwerft	21 Jan 1993	9 Dec 1993
BAD RAPPENAU	M 1067	Abeking & Rasmussen	3 June 1993	19 Apr 1994
GRÖMITZ	M 1064	Krögerwerft	29 Apr 1993	23 Aug 1994
DATTELN	M 1068	Lürssenwerft	27 Jan 1994	8 Dec 1994
DILLINGEN	M 1065	Abeking & Rasmussen	26 May 1994	25 Apr 1995
HOMBURG	M 1069	Krögerwerft	21 Apr 1994	26 Sep 1995
SULZBACH-ROSENBERG	M 1062	Lürssenwerft	27 Apr 1995	23 Jan 1996
FULDA	M 1058	Abeking & Rasmussen	29 Sep 1997	16 June 1998
WEILHEIM	M 1059	Lürssenwerft	26 Feb 1998	3 Dec 1998

Displacement, tons: 650 full load
Dimensions, feet (metres): 178.8 × 30.2 × 8.5 *(54.5 × 9.2 × 2.6)*
Main machinery: 2 MTU 16V 396 TB84 diesels; 5,550 hp(m) *(4.08 MW)* sustained; 2 shafts; cp props; 1 motor (minehunting)
Speed, knots: 18
Complement: 37 (5 officers)

Missiles: SAM: 2 Stinger quad launchers.
Guns: 1 Mauser 27 mm. 3—12.7 mm MGs.
Combat data systems: STN MWS 80-4.
Radars: Navigation: Raytheon SPS-64 or Sperry Bridgemaster; I-band.
Sonars: Atlas Elektronik DSQS-11M; hull-mounted; high frequency.

Programmes: First 10 ordered in September 1988 with STN Systemtechnik Nord as main contractor. M 1066 laid down at Lürssen 6 December 1989. Two ordered 16 October 1995.
Structure: Same hull, similar superstructure and high standardisation as Type 332 and 352. Built of amagnetic steel. Two STN Systemtechnik Nord Pinguin-B3 drones with sonar, TV cameras and two countermining charges, but not Troika control and minelaying capabilities.
Sales: Six of the class built for Turkey from late 1999. M 1060 and M 1066 decommissioned in 2006 and have been sold to the UAE. M 1061 converted to diving support role in 2007.

WEILHEIM *5/2008*, Michael Nitz* / 1353067

5 KULMBACH CLASS (TYPE 333) (MINEHUNTERS—COASTAL) (MHC)

Name	*No*	*Builders*	*Launched*	*Commissioned*
ÜBERHERRN	M 1095	Abeking & Rasmussen	30 Aug 1988	19 Sep 1989
LABOE	M 1097	Krögerwerft	13 Sep 1988	7 Dec 1989
KULMBACH	M 1091	Abeking & Rasmussen	15 June 1989	24 Apr 1990
PASSAU	M 1096	Abeking & Rasmussen	1 Mar 1990	18 Dec 1990
HERTEN	M 1099	Krögerwerft	22 Dec 1989	26 Feb 1991

Displacement, tons: 635 full load
Dimensions, feet (metres): 178.5 × 30.2 × 8.2 *(54.4 × 9.2 × 2.5)*
Main machinery: 2 MTU 16V 538 TB91 diesels; 6,140 hp(m) *(4.5 MW)* sustained; 2 shafts; cp props
Speed, knots: 18
Complement: 37 (4 officers)

Missiles: SAM: 2 Stinger quad launchers.
Guns: 1 Mauser 27 mm. 3—12.7 mm MGs.
Mines: 60.
Countermeasures: Decoys: 2 Silver Dog chaff rocket launchers (to be replaced by Rheinmetall MASS).
ESM: Thomson-CSF DR 2000 (to be replaced by SAAB Avitronic SME 100); radar warning.
Combat data systems: PALIS with Link 11.
Radars: Surface search/fire control: Signaal WM20/2; I/J-band.
Navigation: Raytheon SPS-64 or Sperry Bridgemaster; I-band.
Sonars: Atlas Elektronik DSQS-11M; hull-mounted; high frequency.

Programmes: On 3 January 1985 an STN Systemtechnik Nord-headed consortium was awarded the order. The German designation of 'Schnelles Minenkampfboot' was changed in 1989 to 'Schnelles Minensuchboot'. After modernisation redesignated 'Minenjagdboote'.
Modernisation: Five ships of Hameln class converted to minehunters 1999–2001 and redesignated Kulmbach class (Type 333). Eight to ten disposable ROV Sea Fox I are carried for inspection and up to 30 Sea Fox C for mine disposal. It has a range of 500 m at 6 kt and uses a shaped charge.
Structure: Ships built of amagnetic steel adapted from submarine construction. Signaal M 20 System removed from the deleted Zobel class fast attack craft. PALIS active link.

LABOE *7/2008*, B Prézelin* / 1353044

5 ENSDORF CLASS (TYPE 352) (MINESWEEPERS—COASTAL) (MHCD)

Name	*No*	*Builders*	*Launched*	*Commissioned*
HAMELN	M 1092	Lürssenwerft	15 Mar 1988	29 June 1989
PEGNITZ	M 1090	Lürssenwerft	13 Mar 1989	9 Mar 1990
SIEGBURG	M 1098	Krögerwerft	14 Apr 1989	17 July 1990
ENSDORF	M 1094	Lürssenwerft	8 Dec 1989	25 Sep 1990
AUERBACH	M 1093	Lürssenwerft	18 June 1990	7 May 1991

Displacement, tons: 635 full load
Dimensions, feet (metres): 178.5 × 30.2 × 8.2 *(54.4 × 9.2 × 2.5)*
Main machinery: 2 MTU 16V 538 TB91 diesels; 6,140 hp(m) *(4.5 MW)* sustained; 2 shafts; cp props
Speed, knots: 18
Complement: 38 (4 officers)

Missiles: SAM: 2 Stinger quad launchers.
Guns: 1 Mauser 27 mm. 3—12.7 mm MGs.
Mines: 60.
Countermeasures: Decoys: 2 Silver Dog chaff rocket launchers (to be replaced by Rheinmetall MASS).
ESM: Thomson-CSF DR 2000 (to be replaced by SAAB Avitronic SME 100); radar warning.
Combat data systems: PALIS with Link 11. STN C2 remote-control system for minesweeping drone Seehund.
Radars: Surface search/fire control: Signaal WM20/2; I/J-band.
Navigation: Raytheon SPS-64 or Sperry Bridgemaster; I-band.
Sonars: STN ADS DSQS 15A mine-avoidance; active high frequency.

Programmes: On 3 January 1985 an STN Systemtechnik Nord-headed consortium was awarded the order. The German designation of 'Schnelles Minenkampfboot' was changed in 1989 to 'Schnelles Minensuchboot'. After modernisation redesignated 'Hohlstablenkboote'.
Modernisation: Five minesweepers of Hameln class converted 2000–2001 to control up to four remotely controlled minesweeping drones (Seehund). ROV Sea Fox I carried for inspection. ROV Sea Fox C for mine disposal. Double oropesa system for mechanical sweeping.
Structure: Ships built of amagnetic steel adapted from submarine construction. Signaal M 20 System removed from the deleted Zobel class fast attack craft. PALIS active link.

ENSDORF *4/2008*, Martin Mokrus* / 1353045

18 SEEHUND (MINESWEEPERS—DRONES) (MSD)

SEEHUND 1–18

Displacement, tons: 95 full load
Dimensions, feet (metres): 78.1 × 15 × 6.9 *(23.8 × 4.6 × 2.1)*
Main machinery: 1 Deutz MWM D602 diesel; 446 hp(m) *(328 kW)*; 1 shaft
Speed, knots: 9. **Range, n miles:** 520 at 8 kt
Complement: 3 (passage crew)

Comment: Built by MaK, Kiel and Blohm + Voss, Hamburg between August 1980 and May 1982. Modernised in conjunction with the Type 352 conversion programme 2000–2001.

SEEHUND 17 *5/2008*, Michael Nitz* / 1353068

1 DIVER SUPPORT SHIP (TYPE 332B) (MCD)

Name	*No*	*Builders*	*Launched*	*Commissioned*
ROTTWEIL	M 1061	Krögerwerft	12 Mar 1992	7 July 1993

Displacement, tons: 650 full load
Dimensions, feet (metres): 178.8 × 30.2 × 8.5 *(54.5 × 9.2 × 2.6)*
Main machinery: 2 MTU 16V 396TB84 diesels; 5,550 hp(m) *(4.08 MW)* sustained; 2 shafts; cp props; 1 motor (minehunting)
Speed, knots: 18
Complement: 27 (5 officers)

Missiles: SAM: 2 Stinger quad launchers.
Guns: 1 Mauser 27 mm.
Combat data systems: STN MWS 80-4.
Radars: Navigation: Sperry Bridgemaster SPS-64; I-band.
Sonars: Atlas Elektronik DSQS-11M; hull-mounted; high frequency.

Comment: Built and operated as minehunter until 2007 when it was converted to a diving support role. Carries three diving teams. Capable of laying 24 mines. Amagnetic steel construction. Based at Eckernförde.

ROTTWEIL *4/2002, H M Steele* / 0068085

SURVEY AND RESEARCH SHIPS

Notes: A 12 ton midget submarine *Narwal* was recommissioned in April 1996 for research. Originally built by Krupp Atlas as an SDV.

1 TYPE 751 (AGE)

Name	*No*	*Builders*	*Commissioned*
PLANET	A 1437	Thyssen Nordseewerke, Emden	31 May 2005

Displacement, tons: 3,500 full load
Dimensions, feet (metres): 239.5 × 89.26 × 22.3 *(73 × 27.2 × 6.8)*
Main machinery: Diesel electric; 2 permanent magnet motors; 6,034 hp(m) *(4.5 MW)*; 2 shafts
Speed, knots: 15. **Range, n miles:** 5,000 at 15 kt
Complement: 25 plus 20 trials personnel

Comment: Ex-Type 752 SWATH design which replaced the old *Planet*. The roles of the ship include both research and trials. It is run by Wehrtechnische Dienstelle (WTD 71) in Eckenförde. It supports both WTD 71 and Forschungsanstalt für Wasserschall und Geophysik (FWG) in Kiel. First authorised in April 1998 and contract placed with TNSW, Emden. After a delay of over two years, firm order finally made in December 2000. Launched on 12 August 2003, the ship has a sonar well, torpedo tubes and can carry five 20 ft containers.

PLANET *3/2007, Michael Nitz* / 1166735

3 SCHWEDENECK CLASS (TYPE 748) (MULTIPURPOSE) (AG)

Name	*No*	*Builders*	*Commissioned*
SCHWEDENECK	Y 860	Krögerwerft, Rendsburg	20 Oct 1987
KRONSORT	Y 861	Elsflether Werft	2 Dec 1987
HELMSAND	Y 862	Krögerwerft, Rendsburg	4 Mar 1988

Displacement, tons: 1,018 full load
Dimensions, feet (metres): 185.3 × 35.4 × 17 *(56.5 × 10.8 × 5.2)*
Main machinery: Diesel-electric; 3 MTU 6V 396 TB53 diesel generators; 1,485 kW 60 Hz sustained; 1 motor; 1 shaft
Speed, knots: 13
Range, n miles: 2,400 at 13 kt
Complement: 13 plus 10 trials parties
Radars: Navigation: 2 Raytheon; I-band.

Comment: Order for first three placed in mid-1985. One more was planned after 1995 but was not funded. Based at Eckernförde.

HELMSAND *6/2007, Frank Findler* / 1166806

3 STOLLERGRUND CLASS (TYPE 745) (MULTIPURPOSE) (AG)

Name	*No*	*Builders*	*Commissioned*
STOLLERGRUND	Y 863	Krögerwerft	31 May 1989
MITTELGRUND	Y 864	Elsflether Werft	21 Sep 1989
BREITGRUND	Y 866	Elsflether Werft	23 Feb 1990

Displacement, tons: 450 full load
Dimensions, feet (metres): 109.9 × 30.2 × 10.5 *(33.5 × 9.2 × 3.2)*
Main machinery: 1 Deutz-MWM SBV6M628 diesel; 1,690 hp(m) *(1.24 MW)* sustained; 1 shaft; bow thruster
Speed, knots: 12. **Range, n miles:** 1,000 at 12 kt
Complement: 7 plus 6 trials personnel

Comment: Five ordered from Lürssen in November 1987; two subcontracted to Elsflether. Equipment includes two I-band radars and an intercept sonar. Based at the Armed Forces Technical Centre, Eckernförde. *Bant* decommissioned in 2003 and *Kalkgrund* in 2004. Both ships transferred to Israel.

STOLLERGRUND *6/2006, A A de Kruijf* / 1164825

1 TRIALS SHIP (TYPE 741) (YAG)

Name	*No*	*Builders*	*Commissioned*
WILHELM PULLWER	A 1409 (ex-Y 838)	Schürenstadt, Bardenfleth	18 July 1967

Displacement, tons: 160 full load
Dimensions, feet (metres): 103.3 × 24.6 × 7.2 *(31.5 × 7.5 × 2.2)*
Main machinery: 2 MTU MB diesels; 700 hp(m) *(514 kW)*; 2 Voith-Schneider props
Speed, knots: 12.5
Complement: 17

Comment: Wooden hulled trials ship for barrage systems. To be decommissioned in 2012.

WILHELM PULLWER *9/2004, Hartmut Ehlers* / 1044260

1 TRIALS BOAT (TYPE 740) (YAG)

Name	*No*	*Builders*	*Commissioned*
BUMS	Y 1689	Howaldtswerke, Kiel	16 Feb 1970

Dimensions, feet (metres): 86.6 × 22.3 × 4.9 *(26.4 × 6.8 × 1.5)*

Comment: Single diesel engine. Has a 3 ton crane. Based at Eckernförde. To be decommissioned in 2012.

BUMS *8/1997, N Sifferlinger* / 0012437

INTELLIGENCE VESSELS

3 OSTE CLASS (TYPE 423) (AGI)

Name	*No*	*Builders*	*Commissioned*
ALSTER	A 50	Schiffsbaugesellschaft, Flensburg	5 Oct 1989
OSTE	A 52	Schiffsbaugesellschaft, Flensburg	30 June 1988
OKER	A 53	Schiffsbaugesellschaft, Flensburg	10 Nov 1988

Displacement, tons: 3,200 full load
Dimensions, feet (metres): 273.9 × 47.9 × 13.8 *(83.5 × 14.6 × 4.2)*
Main machinery: 2 Deutz-MWM BV16M628 diesels; 8,980 hp(m) *(6.6 MW)* sustained; 2 shafts; 2 motors (for slow speed)
Speed, knots: 21 (diesels); 8 (motors)
Complement: 36 plus 40 specialists or 51 plus 36 specialists
Missiles: SAM: 2 Stinger launchers.
Guns: 2—12.7 mm Mauser MGs.

Comment: Ordered in March 1985 and December 1986 and replaced the Radar Trials Ships of the same name (old *Oker* and *Alster* transferred to Greece and Turkey respectively). *Oste* launched 15 May 1987, *Oker* 24 September 1987, *Alster* 4 November 1988. Carry Atlas Elektronik passive sonar and optical ELAM and electronic surveillance equipment. Particular attention given to accommodation standards. Fitted for but not with light armaments.

ALSTER *6/2008*, Harald Carstens* / 1353069

TRAINING SHIPS

Notes: In addition to the one listed below there are 54 other sail training vessels (Types 910-915).

1 SAIL TRAINING SHIP (AXS)

Name	*No*	*Builders*	*Commissioned*
GORCH FOCK	A 60	Blohm + Voss, Hamburg	17 Dec 1958

Displacement, tons: 2,006 full load
Dimensions, feet (metres): 293 × 39.2 × 16.1 *(89.3 × 12 × 4.9)*
Main machinery: Auxiliary 1 Deutz MWM BV6M628 diesel; 1,690 hp(m) *(1.24 MW)* sustained; 1 shaft; Kamewa cp prop
Speed, knots: 11 power; 15 sail. **Range, n miles**: 1,990 at 10 kt
Complement: 206 (10 officers, 140 cadets)

Comment: Sail training ship of the improved Horst Wessel type. Barque rig. Launched on 23 August 1958. Sail area, 21,141 sq ft. Major modernisation in 1985 at Howaldtswerke. Second major refit in 1991 at Motorenwerke, Bremerhaven included a new propulsion engine and three diesel generators, which increased displacement. Third major refit at Elsfleth-Werft in 2000–2001 included modernisation of electrical distribution system.

GORCH FOCK *5/2008*, Michael Nitz* / 1353070

AUXILIARIES

2 + 1 BERLIN CLASS (TYPE 702) (AFSH)

Name	*No*	*Builders*	*Launched*	*Commissioned*
BERLIN	A 1411	Flensburger	30 Apr 1999	11 Apr 2001
FRANKFURT AM MAIN	A 1412	Flensburger	5 Jan 2001	27 May 2002

Displacement, tons: 20,240 full load
Dimensions, feet (metres): 570.8 oa; 527.6 wl × 79.7 × 24.3 *(174.0; 160.8 × 24.3 × 7.4)*
Main machinery: 2 MAN 12V 32/40 diesels; 14,388 hp(m) *(10.58 MW)* sustained; 2 shafts; cp props; bow thruster; 1,000 hp(m) *(735 kW)*
Speed, knots: 20
Complement: 139 (12 officers) plus 94 for embarked staff
Cargo capacity: 9,540 tons fuel; 450 tons water; 280 tons cargo; 160 tons ammunition
Missiles: SAM: 2 RAM launchers fitted for but not with.
Guns: 4 Mauser 27 mm. 4—12.7 mm MGs.
Radars: Navigation: and aircraft control: Sperry Bridgemaster; E/F/I-bands.
Helicopters: 2 Sea King Mk 41.

Comment: First ship ordered 15 October 1997, and second 3 July 1998. Hulls built by FSG, superstructure by Kröger and electronics by Lürssen. MBB-FHS helo handling system. Two RAS beam stations and stern refuelling. Two portable SAM launchers are carried. EW equipment may be fitted. These ships are designed to support UN type operations abroad. Trials with the Finnish 14 m Jurmo class landing craft were conducted in A 1412 during 2007. There can be 26 containers mounted in two layers on the upper deck. This could include a containerised hospital unit for 50. A 1411 based at Wilhelmshaven and A 1412 at Kiel. Approval for construction of a third ship, to enter service in 2012, was given on 3 December 2008. The ship will incorporate improvements based on experience of the first two ships. These include increased power and accommodation.

FRANKFURT AM MAIN *5/2008*, Michael Nitz* / 1353071

FRANKFURT AM MAIN *3/2007, A A de Kruijf* / 1166749

6 ELBE CLASS (TYPE 404) (TENDERS) (ARLHM)

Name	*No*	*Builders*	*Launched*	*Commissioned*
ELBE	A 511	Bremer Vulkan	24 June 1992	28 Jan 1993
MOSEL	A 512	Bremer Vulkan	22 Apr 1993	22 July 1993
RHEIN	A 513	Flensburger Schiffbau	11 Mar 1993	22 Sep 1993
WERRA	A 514	Flensburger Schiffbau	17 June 1993	9 Dec 1993
MAIN	A 515	Lürssen/Krögerwerft	15 June 1993	23 June 1994
DONAU	A 516	Lürssen/Krögerwerft	24 Mar 1994	22 Nov 1994

Displacement, tons: 3,114 full load
Dimensions, feet (metres): 329.7 oa; 295.3 wl × 50.5 × 13.5 *(100.5; 90.0 × 15.4 × 4.1)*
Main machinery: 1 Deutz MWM 8V 12M 628 diesel; 3,335 hp(m) *(2.45 MW)*; 1 shaft; bow thruster
Speed, knots: 15. **Range, n miles**: 2,000 at 15 kt
Complement: 40 (4 officers) plus 12 squadron staff plus 38 maintainers
Cargo capacity: 450 tons fuel; 150 tons water; 11 tons luboil; 130 tons ammunition
Missiles: SAM: 2 Stinger (Fliegerfaust 2) quad launchers.
Guns: 2 Mauser 27 mm. 4—12.7 mm MGs.
Radars: Navigation: I-band.
Helicopters: Platform for 1 Sea King.

Comment: Funds released in November 1990 for the construction of six ships to replace the Rhein class. Containers for maintenance and repairs, spare parts and supplies for fast attack craft and minesweepers. Waste disposal capacity: 270 m³ liquids, 60 m³ solids. Allocated as follows: *Elbe* to 7th Squadron FPBs, *Mosel* to 5th Squadron MSC, *Rhein* and *Werra* to 3rd Squadron MSC, *Donau* to 1st Squadron corvettes. *Main* underwent conversion to submarine depot ship from November 2006 to November 2007. Mauser 27 mm guns are fitted at the break of the forecastle. Converted with helicopter refuelling facilities from July 1996 to July 1997.

DONAU *6/2008*, Frank Findler* / 1353043

2 REPLENISHMENT TANKERS (TYPE 704) (AOL)

Name	*No*	*Builders*	*Commissioned*
SPESSART (ex-*Okapi*)	A 1442	Kröger, Rendsburg	1974
RHÖN (ex-*Okene*)	A 1443	Kröger, Rendsburg	1974

Displacement, tons: 14,169 full load
Measurement, tons: 6,103 grt; 10,800 dwt
Dimensions, feet (metres): 427.1 × 63.3 × 28.5 *(130.2 × 19.3 × 8.7)*
Main machinery: 1 MaK 12-cyl diesel; 8,000 hp(m) *(5.88 MW)*; 1 shaft; cp prop
Speed, knots: 16
Range, n miles: 3,250 at 12 kt
Complement: 42
Cargo capacity: 11,000 m^3 fuel; 400 m^3 water
Radars: Navigation: Sperry Bridgemaster; E/F/I-bands.

Comment: Completed for Terkol Group as tankers. Acquired in 1976 for conversion (*Spessart* at Bremerhaven, *Rhön* at Kröger). The former commissioned for naval service on 5 September 1977 and the latter on 23 September 1977. Has two portable SAM positions. Civilian manned.

SPESSART *6/2008*, Michael Nitz* / 1353072

2 WALCHENSEE CLASS (TYPE 703) (REPLENISHMENT TANKERS) (AOL)

Name	*No*	*Builders*	*Commissioned*
AMMERSEE	A 1425	Lindenau, Kiel	2 Mar 1967
TEGERNSEE	A 1426	Lindenau, Kiel	23 Mar 1967

Displacement, tons: 2,174 full load
Dimensions, feet (metres): 235.9 × 36.7 × 13.8 *(71.9 × 11.2 × 4.2)*
Main machinery: 2 MWM 12-cyl diesels; 1,370 hp(m) *(1 MW)*; 1 Kamewa prop
Speed, knots: 12
Range, n miles: 3,250 at 12 kt
Complement: 21
Radars: Navigation: Sperry Bridgemaster; E/F/I-bands.

Comment: Civilian manned.

TEGERNSEE *10/2007, Michael Nitz* / 1166745

1 KNURRHAHN CLASS (TYPE 730) (APB)

Name	*No*	*Builders*	*Commissioned*
KNURRHAHN	Y 811	Sietas, Hamburg	Nov 1989

Displacement, tons: 1,424 full load
Dimensions, feet (metres): 157.5 × 45.9 × 5.9 *(48 × 14 × 1.8)*

Comment: Accommodation for 200 people.

KNURRHAHN *4/2008*, Michael Nitz* / 1353073

1 WESTERWALD CLASS (TYPE 760) (AMMUNITION TRANSPORT) (AEL)

Name	*No*	*Builders*	*Commissioned*
WESTERWALD	A 1435	Orenstein and Koppel, Lübeck	11 Feb 1967

Displacement, tons: 3,460 standard; 4,032 full load
Dimensions, feet (metres): 344.4 × 46 × 15.5 *(105 × 14 × 4.7)*
Main machinery: 2 MD 16V 872 TB90 diesels; 6,000 hp(m) *(4.1 MW)* sustained; 2 shafts; cp props; bow thruster
Speed, knots: 16
Range, n miles: 3,500 at 17 kt
Complement: 63
Cargo capacity: 1,080 tons ammunition
Guns: 2 Bofors 40 mm (cocooned).
Countermeasures: Decoys: 2 Breda SCLAR 105 mm chaff launchers are carried in A 1436.
Radars: Navigation: Sperry Bridgemaster; I-band.

Comment: Based at Wilhelmshaven. Civilian manned. *Odenwald* transferred to Egypt in 2003.

WESTERWALD *8/2003, Martin Mokrus* / 0570617

2 OHRE CLASS (ACCOMMODATION SHIPS) (APB)

ALTMARK Y 891 (ex-H 11) **WISCHE** (ex-*Harz*) Y 895 (ex-H 31)

Displacement, tons: 1,320 full load
Dimensions, feet (metres): 231 × 39.4 × 5 *(70.4 × 12 × 1.6)*

Comment: Ex-GDR Type 162 built by Peenewerft, Wolgast. One hydraulic 8 ton crane fitted. First commissioned 1985. Classified as 'Schwimmende Stuetzpunkte'. Propulsion and armament has been removed and they are used as non-self-propelled accommodation ships for crews of vessels in refit. Civilian manned. Both modernised at Wilhelmshaven and to remain in service until further notice. Two others paid off in 2000 later than expected.

ALTMARK *9/2006, Frank Findler* / 1159915

6 LAUNCHES (TYPE 946/945) (YFL)

AK 1 Y 1671 **MA 2** Y 1676 **MA 3** Y 1677 **MA 1** Y 1678 **ASCHAU** Y 1685 **BORBY** Y 1687

Dimensions, feet (metres): 39.4 × 12.8 × 6.2 *(12.0 × 3.9 × 1.9)*
Main machinery: 1 MAN D2540MTE diesel; 366 hp(m) *(269 kW)*; 1 shaft

Comment: Built by Hans Boost, Trier. All completed in 1985 except *MA 1* and *Aschau* which are larger at 16.2 m and completed in 1992. AK prefix indicates Kiel, and MA Wilhelmshaven and Neustadt.

AK 1 *6/2008*, Frank Findler* / 1353037

5 LAUNCHES (TYPES 743, 744, 744A, 1344) (YFL)

AM 7 Y 1679 | **AK 2** Y 1686 | **WARNOW** A 41
AM 8 Y 1675 | **AK 6** Y 1683

Dimensions, feet (metres): 62.3 × 13.1 × 3.9 *(19 × 4 × 1.2)* approx
Main machinery: 1 or 2 diesels

Comment: For personnel transport and trials work. Types 744 *(AK 6)* and 744A *(AK 2)* are radio calibration craft. AM prefix indicates Eckernförde, and AK Kiel. *Warnow* A 41 is a former GDR tug (Type1344) used as a diving boat at Warnemünde.

WARNOW *5/2007, Michael Nitz* / 1166738

4 RANGE SAFETY CRAFT (TYPE 905) (YFRT)

Name	*No*	*Builders*	*Commissioned*
TODENDORF	Y 835	Lürssen, Vegesack	25 Nov 1993
PUTLOS	Y 836	Lürssen, Vegesack	24 Feb 1994
BAUMHOLDER	Y 837	Lürssen, Vegesack	30 Mar 1994
MUNSTER	Y 839	Lürssen, Vegesack	14 July 1994

Displacement, tons: 126 full load
Dimensions, feet (metres): 91.2 × 19.7 × 4.6 *(27.8 × 6 × 1.4)*
Main machinery: 2 KHD TBD 234 diesels; 2,054 hp(m) *(1.51 MW)*; 2 shafts
Speed, knots: 16
Complement: 6

Comment: Replaced previous Types 369 and 909 craft. Funded by the Army and civilian manned.

TODENDORF *3/2008*, Martin Mokrus* / 1353039

2 OIL RECOVERY SHIPS (TYPE 738) (YPC)

Name	*No*	*Builders*	*Commissioned*
BOTTSAND	Y 1643	Lühring, Brake	24 Jan 1985
EVERSAND	Y 1644	Lühring, Brake	11 June 1988

Measurement, tons: 500 gross; 650 dwt
Dimensions, feet (metres): 151.9 × 39.4 (137.8, bow opened) × 10.2 *(46.3 × 12; 42 × 3.1)*
Main machinery: 1 Deutz BA12M816 diesel; 1,000 hp(m) *(759 kW)* sustained; 2 shafts
Speed, knots: 10
Complement: 6

Comment: Built with two hulls which are connected with a hinge in the stern. During pollution clearance the bow is opened. Ordered by Ministry of Transport but taken over by West German Navy. Normally used as tank cleaning vessels and harbour oilers. Civilian manned. *Bottsand* based at Warnemünde, *Eversand* at Wilhelmshaven. A third of class *Thor* belongs to the Ministry of Transport.

EVERSAND *6/2008*, Martin Mokrus* / 1353040

21 PERSONNEL TENDERS (TYPES 934 AND GDR 407) (YFL)

V 3–8 | **V 10–20** | **B 11** | **B 33–34** | **B 83**

Comment: *V 3-20* built in 1987–88 by Hatecke. The B series are ex-GDR craft built by Yachtwerft, Berlin.

V 18 *6/2008*, Michael Winter* / 1353038

FLOATING REPAIR FACILITIES

5 FLOATING REPAIR FACILITIES

SCHWIMMDOCK 3 Y 842 | **DOCK A** | **GRIEP** Y 876
DRUCKDOCK (DOCK C) | **HIEV** Y 875

Comment: There are three floating docks: Schwimmdock 3 is 8,000 tons while Dock C is used for submarine pressure tests. Dock A is 1,000 tons and is to be replaced by a new Dock B in 2009. Y 875 and Y 876 are self-propelled floating cranes with a 100 ton crane.

DOCK 3 *7/2008*, Frank Findler* / 1353041

TUGS

1 HELGOLAND CLASS (TYPE 720B) (ATR)

Name	*No*	*Builders*	*Commissioned*
FEHMARN	A 1458	Unterweser, Bremerhaven	1 Feb 1967

Displacement, tons: 1,310 standard; 1,643 full load
Dimensions, feet (metres): 223.1 × 41.7 × 14.4 *(68 × 12.7 × 4.4)*
Main machinery: Diesel-electric; 4 MWM 12-cyl diesel generators; 2 motors; 3,300 hp(m) *(2.43 MW)*; 2 shafts
Speed, knots: 17
Range, n miles: 6,400 at 16 kt
Complement: 34
Mines: Laying capacity.
Radars: Navigation: Raytheon; I-band.
Sonars: High definition, hull-mounted for wreck search.

Comment: Launched on 9 April 1965. Carry firefighting equipment and has an ice-strengthened hull. Employed as safety ship for the submarine training group. Twin 40 mm guns removed. One of the class to Uruguay in 1998.

FEHMARN *5/2008*, Michael Nitz* / 1353075

8 HARBOUR TUGS (TYPES 725, 724, 660) (YTM)

Name	*No*	*Builders*	*Commissioned*
VOGELSAND	Y 816	Orenstein und Koppel, Lübeck	14 Apr 1987
NORDSTRAND	Y 817	Orenstein und Koppel, Lübeck	20 Jan 1987
LANGENESS	Y 819	Orenstein und Koppel, Lübeck	5 Mar 1987
LÜTJE HÖRN	Y 812	Husumer Schiffswerft	31 May 1990
KNECHTSAND	Y 814	Husumer Schiffswerft	16 Nov 1990
SCHARHÖRN	Y 815	Husumer Schiffswerft	1 Oct 1990
WUSTROW (ex-*Zander*)	Y 1656	VEB Yachtwerft, Berlin	25 May 1989
DRANSKE (ex-*Kormoran*)	Y 1658	VEB Yachtwerft, Berlin	12 Dec 1989

Displacement, tons: 445 full load
Dimensions, feet (metres): 99.3 × 29.8 × 8.5 *(30.3 × 9.1 × 2.6)*
Main machinery: 2 Deutz MWM SBV6M628 diesels; 3,360 hp(m) *(2.47 MW)* sustained; 2 Voith-Schneider props
Speed, knots: 12
Complement: 4

Comment: Details given are for the Type 725 (Y 812-819) which have a bollard pull of 23 tons. Y 1656 and Y 1658 are Type 660 former GDR vessels of 320 tons. Y 823 to Greece in 1998.

SCHARHÖRN *6/2008*, Frank Findler* / 1353042

WUSTROW *6/2008*, Michael Nitz* / 1353074

5 WANGEROOGE CLASS (3 TYPE 722 AND 3 TYPE 754) (ATS/YDT)

Name	*No*	*Builders*	*Commissioned*
WANGEROOGE	A 1451	Schichau, Bremerhaven	9 Apr 1968
SPIEKEROOG	A 1452	Schichau, Bremerhaven	14 Aug 1968
BALTRUM	A 1439	Schichau, Bremerhaven	8 Oct 1968
JUIST	A 1440	Schichau, Bremerhaven	1 Oct 1971
LANGEOOG	A 1441	Schichau, Bremerhaven	14 Aug 1968

Displacement, tons: 854 standard; 1,024 full load
Dimensions, feet (metres): 170.6 × 39.4 × 12.8 *(52 × 12.1 × 3.9)*
Main machinery: Diesel-electric; 4 MWM 16-cyl diesel generators; 2 motors; 2,400 hp(m) *(1.76 MW)*; 2 shafts
Speed, knots: 14
Range, n miles: 5,000 at 10 kt
Complement: 24 plus 33 trainees (A 1439-1441)
Guns: 1 Bofors 40 mm/70 (cocooned in some, not fitted in all).

Comment: First two are salvage tugs with firefighting equipment and ice-strengthened hulls. *Wangerooge* sometimes used for pilot training and *Spiekeroog* as submarine safety ship. The other three were converted 1974–78 to training ships with *Baltrum* and *Juist* being used as diving training vessels at Neustadt, with recompression chambers and civilian crews. A 1455 sold to Uruguay in 2002.

SPIEKEROOG *4/2007, Frank Findler* / 1166801

COAST GUARD (KÜSTENWACHE)

Notes: The Coast Guard was formed on 1 July 1974 and is a loose affiliation of the forces of several organisations including: seagoing units of the Border Guard (Bundespolizei); Fishery Protection (Fischereischutz); Maritime Police (Wasserschutzpolizei); Water and Navigation Board (Schiffahrtspolizei); Customs (Zoll). These organisations have responsibility for the operation and maintenance of their own craft but all have the inscription *Küstenwache* on the side.

BORDER GUARD (Bundespolizei)

Notes: (1) The force consists of about 600 men. Headquarters at Neustadt and bases at Warnemunde and Cuxhaven. There are three Flotillas; one each at Neustadt, Cuxhaven and Warnemunde. The name of the force was changed from Bundesgrenzschutz-See to Bundespolizei on 1 July 2005.
(2) The force is augmented by a maritime section of the anti-terrorist force GSG 9.
(3) Craft have dark blue hulls and white superstructures with a black, red and yellow diagonal stripe and the inscription Küstenwache painted on the ship's side and Bundespolizei insignia.
(4) There is a total of some 60 helicopters including 13 Eurocopter EC 155, 9 EC 135, 13 Bell UH-1D, 8 Bell 212, 17 BO-105 and a number of AS 330 Puma.
(5) All 40 mm guns removed in 1997.

3 BAD BRAMSTEDT CLASS (WPSO)

Name	*No*	*Builders*	*Commissioned*
BAD BRAMSTEDT	BP 24 (ex-BG 24)	Abeking and Rasmussen, Lemwerder	8 Nov 2002
BAYREUTH	BP 25 (ex-BG 25)	Abeking and Rasmussen, Lemwerder	2 May 2003
ESCHWEGE	BP 26 (ex-BG 26)	Abeking and Rasmussen, Lemwerder	18 Dec 2003

Displacement, tons: 800 standard
Dimensions, feet (metres): 216.3 × 34.8 × 10.5 *(65.9 × 10.6 × 3.2)*
Main machinery: 1 MTU 16V 1163 diesel; 7,000 hp(m) *(5.2 MW)*; 1 shaft; fixed propeller
Speed, knots: 21.5
Complement: 14 + 10 in temporary accommodation
Radars: Surface search: I-band.
Navigation: I-band.
Helicopters: Platform for 1 light.

Comment: Contract awarded in 2000 to Prime Contractor Abeking and Rasmussen for three craft to replace six ships of Neustadt class. Hulls constructed by Yantar, Kaliningrad and completed at Lemwerder. Steel hull with aluminium superstructure. The Russian Federal Border Guard Sprut class offshore patrol vessels is based on this design.

ESCHWEGE *7/2008*, Maritime Photographic* / 1353076

1 BREDSTEDT CLASS (TYPE PB 60) (WPSO)

Name	*No*	*Builders*	*Commissioned*
BREDSTEDT	BP 21 (ex-BG 21)	Elsflether Werft	24 May 1989

Displacement, tons: 673 full load
Dimensions, feet (metres): 214.6 × 30.2 × 10.5 *(65.4 × 9.2 × 3.2)*
Main machinery: 1 MTU 20V 1163 TB93 diesel; 8,325 hp(m) *(6.12 MW)* sustained; 1 shaft; bow thruster; 1 auxiliary diesel generator; 1 motor
Speed, knots: 25 (12 on motor). **Range, n miles:** 2,000 at 25 kt; 7,000 at 10 kt
Complement: 17 plus 4 spare
Guns: 1 — 40 mm MGs.
Radars: Surface search: Racal AC 2690 BT; I-band.
Navigation: 2 Racal ARPA; I-band.
Helicopters: Platform for 1 light.

Comment: Ordered 27 November 1987, laid down 3 March 1988 and launched 18 December 1988. An Avon Searider rigid inflatable craft can be lowered by a stern ramp. A second RIB on the port side is launched by crane. Based at Cuxhaven.

BREDSTEDT *11/2008*, Michael Nitz* / 1353077

3 EUROPA CLASS (WPBR)

EUROPA 1–3

Displacement, tons: 10
Dimensions, feet (metres): 47.2 × 12.5 × 3.1 *(14.4 × 3.8 × 0.9)*
Main machinery: 2 MAN diesels; 240 hp(m) *(180 kW)*
Speed, knots: 22
Radars: Kelvin Hughes; I-band

Comment: River patrol craft built by Schless Werft in 1975.

2 SASSNITZ CLASS (TYPE PB 50 ex-TYPE 153) (WPBO)

Name	No	Builders	Commissioned
NEUSTRELITZ (ex-*Sassnitz*)	BP 22 (ex-BG 22, ex-P 6165, ex-591)	Peenewerft, Wolgast	31 July 1990
BAD DÜBEN (ex-*Binz*)	BP 23 (ex-BG 23, ex-593)	Peenewerft, Wolgast	23 Dec 1990

Displacement, tons: 369 full load
Dimensions, feet (metres): 160.4 oa; 147.6 wl × 28.5 × 7.2 *(48.9; 45 × 8.7 × 2.2)*
Main machinery: 2 MTU 12V 595 TE90 diesels; 8,800 hp(m) *(6.48 MW)* sustained; 2 shafts
Speed, knots: 25. **Range, n miles**: 2,400 at 20 kt
Complement: 33 (7 officers)
Guns: 2—7.62 mm MGs.
Radars: Surface search: Racal AC 2690 BT; I-band (BG 22 and 23).
Navigation: Racal ARPA; I-band (BG 22 and 23).

Comment: Ex-GDR designated Balcom 10 and seen for the first time in the Baltic in August 1988. The original intention was to build up to 50 for the USSR, Poland and the GDR. In 1991 the first three were transferred to the Border Guard, based at Neustadt. *Neustrelitz* fitted with German engines and electronics in 1992–93 and accommodation improved. *Bad Düben* similarly modified at Peenewerft in 1995–96. The original design had the SS-N-25 SSM and three engines. The third of class, *Sellin*, had been on loan to WTD 71 (weapons trials) at Eckernförde but was sold in 1999.

BAD DÜBEN (old number) *4/2003, Frank Findler* / 0570608

4 SCHWEDT CLASS (WPBR)

SCHWEDT BP 42 (ex-BG 42)
KUSTRIN-KIEZ BP 41 (ex-BG 41)
FRANKFURT/ODER BP 43 (ex-BG 43)
AURITH BP 44 (ex-BG 44)

Displacement, tons: 6 full load
Dimensions, feet (metres): 33.5 × 10.5 × 2.6 *(10.2 × 3.2 × 0.8)*
Main machinery: 2 Volvo Penta TAMD 42 WJ; 462 hp(m) *(340 kW)*; 2 Hamilton 211 waterjets
Speed, knots: 32. **Range, n miles**: 200 at 25 kt
Complement: 3
Guns: 1—7.62 mm MG.
Radars: Navigation: I-band.

Comment: River patrol craft which belong to the BGSAMT-Frankfurt/Oder since 1994.

FRANKFURT/ODER (old number) *12/1998, BGSAMT* / 0056996

4 TYPE SAB 12 (WPB)

VOGTLAND BP 51 (ex-BG 51, ex-G 56, ex-GS 17)
RHÖN BP 52 (ex-BG 52, ex-G 53, ex-GS 26)
SPREEWALD BP 53 (ex-BG 53, ex-G 51, ex-GS 16)
ODERBRUCH BP 54 (ex-BG 54)

Displacement, tons: 14 full load
Dimensions, feet (metres): 41.3 × 13.1 × 3.6 *(12.6 × 4 × 1.1)*
Main machinery: 2 Volvo Penta diesels; 539 hp(m) *(396 kW)*; 2 shafts
Speed, knots: 16
Complement: 5

Comment: Ex-GDR MAB 12 craft based at Karnin, Stralsund and Frankfurt/Oder. Five sold to Cyprus in 1992. Belong to BGSAMT-Rostock.

SPREEWALD *4/2007, Hartmut Ehlers* / 1166788

5 PRIGNITZ CLASS (WPB)

PRIGNITZ BP 61 **UCKERMARK** BP 62 **ALTMARK** BP 63 **BÖRDE** BP 64 **RHOEN** BP 65

Displacement, tons: 38 full load
Dimensions, feet (metres): 68.9 × 17.0 × 8.5 *(21.0 × 5.2 × 2.6)*
Main machinery: 2 diesels; 1,580 hp(m) *(1.2 MW)*; 1 shaft; fixed propeller
Speed, knots: 23

Comment: Built by Schiffs-und-Entwicklungsgesellschaft 2006–08.

PRIGNITZ *11/2008*, Michael Nitz* / 1353078

FISHERY PROTECTION SHIPS (Fischereischutz)

Notes: Operated by Ministry of Food and Agriculture.

3 PATROL SHIPS

MEERKATZE 77 m vessel of 2,250 tons and 15 kt. Completed December 1977
SEEFALKE 83 m vessel of 2,400 tons and 20 kt. Completed August 1981
SEEADLER 72 m vessel of 2,000 tons and 19 kt. Completed 2000

Comment: Fishery Protection Ships. Black hulls with grey superstructure and black, red and yellow diagonal stripes. An order for two 72 m vessels to replace *Seefalke* and *Meerkatze* was made in December 2006. Being built by Peenewerft, they are to be delivered in 2009.

SEEADLER *7/2008*, Maritime Photographic* / 1353079

MARITIME POLICE (Wasserschutzpolizei)

Notes: (1) Under the control of regional governments. Most have Küstenwache markings but colours vary from region to region.
(2) There are 14 seaward patrol craft: *WSP 1, 4, 5* and *7, Bremen 3* and *6, Helgoland, Sylt, Fehmarn, Birknack, Eider, Falshöft, Bürgermeister Brauer* and *Bürgermeister Weichmann*.
(3) Harbour craft include *Stegnitz, Greif, Glücksburg, Stoltera, Schwansen, Vossbrook, Brunswick, Trave, Wagrien, Bussard, Habicht, Gernsheim, Hoben, Koblenz* and *Breitling*.

BÜRGERMEISTER BRAUER *5/2008*, Frank Findler* / 1353035

BREMEN 3 *8/2008*, Frank Findler* / 1353036

CUSTOMS (Zoll)

Notes: (1) Operated by Ministry of Finance with a total of over 100 craft. Green hulls with grey superstructure and sometimes carry machine guns. Some have Küstenwache markings.
(2) Seaward patrol craft include *Usedom, Hamburg, Bremerhaven, Schleswig-Holstein, Emden, Hohwacht, Glückstadt, Hiddensee, Rügen, Kalkgrund* and *Priwall.*

SCHLESWIG-HOLSTEIN *5/2008*, Michael Nitz* / 1353080

WALTER HERWIG III *12/2006, Frank Findler* / 1166799

WATER AND NAVIGATION BOARD (SCHIFFAHRTSPOLIZEI)

Notes: (1) Comes under the Ministry of Transport. Most ships have black hulls with black/red/yellow stripes. Some have Küstenwache markings.
(2) Eight buoy tenders: *Gustav Meyer, Bruno Illing, Norden, Baumrönne, Vilm, Knechtsand, Strelasund, Triton.*
(3) Five oil recovery ships: *Scharhörn, Arkona, Nordsee, Mellum, Neuwerk.*
(4) Two SKB 64 and 601 types (ex-GDR). *Vogelsand, Ranzow.*
(5) One launch: *Friedrich Voss.*

NORDSEE *5/2008*, Frank Findler* / 1353034

KOMET *4/2007, Frank Findler* / 1166800

SCHARHÖRN *5/2008*, Michael Nitz* / 1353081

POSEIDON *6/2008*, Michael Nitz* / 1353082

CIVILIAN SURVEY AND RESEARCH SHIPS

Notes: The following ships operate for the Bundesamt für Seeschiffahrt und Hydrographie (BSH), either under the Ministry of Transport or the Ministry of Research and Technology (*Polarstern, Meteor, Poseidon, Sonne* and *Alkor*).
KOMET (survey and research) 1,590 tons completed by Krögerwerft in October 1998.
ATAIR (survey), **DENEB** (survey), **WEGA** (survey) 1,050 tons, diesel-electric, 11.5 kt. Complement 16 plus 6 scientists. Built by Krögerwerft and Peenewerft *(Deneb)*, completed 3 August 1987, 24 November 1994 and 26 October 1990 respectively.
METEOR (research) 3,500 tons, diesel-electric, 14 kt, range 10,000 n miles. Complement 33 plus 29 research staff. Completed by Schlichting, Travemünde 15 March 1986.
WALTHER HERWIG III 2,400 tons. Completed 1993.
CAPELLA 455 tons. Completed by Fassmerwerft in 2003.
POLARSTERN (polar research) 10,878 grt. Completed 1982.
SONNE (research) 1,200 grt. Completed by Rickmerswerft 1990.
ALKOR and **HEINKE** 1,200 tons. Completed 1990.
SOLEA 770 tons. Completed by Fassmer 2004.
MARIA S MERIAN 6,050 tons. Completed by Kröger in 2005.
POSEIDON 1,700 tons. Completed by Schichau in 1976.

ALKOR *6/2008*, Michael Nitz* / 1353083

Ghana

Country Overview

Formerly a British colony known as the Gold Coast, Ghana gained independence in 1957. Located in west Africa, the country has an area of 92,100 square miles and a 292 n mile coastline with the Gulf of Guinea. It is bordered to the east by Togo and to the west by Ivory Coast. The capital and largest city is Accra which has links to a deep-water port at Tema. There is a second port at Sekondi-Takoradi. Territorial seas (12 n miles) are claimed. A 200 n mile Exclusive Economic Zone (EEZ) has been claimed but the limits are not defined.

Headquarters Appointments

Commander, Navy: Rear Admiral A R S Nuno
Eastern Naval Command: Commodore M Quashie
Western Naval Command: Commodore F Daley

Personnel

(a) 2009: 2,100 (150 officers)
(b) Voluntary service

Bases

Burma Camp, Accra (Headquarters)
Sekondi (Western Naval Command)
Tema (near Accra) (Eastern Naval Command)

Maritime Aircraft

Two Fokker F27 are operated for Coastal Surveillance, SAR and shipping control.

PATROL FORCES

2 BALSAM CLASS (PBO)

Name	*No*	*Builders*	*Commissioned*
ANZONE (ex-*Woodrush*)	P 30 (ex-WLB 407)	Duluth Shipyard, Minnesota	22 Sep 1944
BONSU (ex-*Sweetbrier*)	P 31 (ex-WLB 405)	Duluth Shipyard, Minnesota	26 July 1944

Displacement, tons: 935 standard; 1,025 full load
Dimensions, feet (metres): 180 × 37 × 12 *(54.9 × 11.3 × 3.8)*
Main machinery: Diesel electric; 2 diesels; 1,710 hp *(1.28 MW)*; 1 motor; 1,200 hp *(895 kW)*; 1 shaft; bow thruster
Speed, knots: 13. **Range, n miles:** 8,000 at 12 kt
Complement: 60 (5 officers)
Guns: 1 — 14.5 mm.
Radars: Navigation: Raytheon SPS-64(V)1.

Comment: Formed USCG buoy tenders. *Anzone* transferred from the US Coast Guard on 4 May 2001 and *Bonsu* on 27 August 2001. Both received new engines 1988–91. Employed on EEZ patrol, fishery protection and troop support duties.

BONSU *6/2007, Ghana Navy* / 1335248

2 LÜRSSEN FPB 45 CLASS (FAST ATTACK CRAFT—GUN) (PBO)

Name	*No*	*Builders*	*Commissioned*
DZATA	P 26	Lürssen, Vegesack	4 Dec 1979
SEBO	P 27	Lürssen, Vegesack	2 May 1980

Displacement, tons: 269 full load
Dimensions, feet (metres): 147.3 × 23 × 8.9 *(44.9 × 7 × 2.7)*
Main machinery: 2 MTU 16V 538TB91 diesels; 6,140 hp(m) *(4.5 MW)* sustained; 2 shafts
Speed, knots: 27. **Range, n miles:** 1,800 at 16 kt; 700 at 25 kt
Complement: 45 (5 officers)
Guns: 2 Breda 40 mm/70; 300 rds/min to 12.5 km *(6.8 n miles)*; weight of shell 0.96 kg.
Radars: Surface search: Decca Type 978; I-band.

Comment: Ordered in 1976. *Dzata* completed a major overhaul at Swan Hunter's Wallsend, Tyneside yard on 8 May 1989. *Sebo* started a similar refit at CMN Cherbourg in May 1991 which completed in August 1992. Employed in Fishery Protection role.

DZATA *5/2002* / 0533318

2 LÜRSSEN PB 57 CLASS (FAST ATTACK CRAFT—GUN) (PG)

Name	*No*	*Builders*	*Commissioned*
ACHIMOTA	P 28	Lürssen, Vegesack	27 Mar 1981
YOGAGA	P 29	Lürssen, Vegesack	27 Mar 1981

Displacement, tons: 389 full load
Dimensions, feet (metres): 190.6 × 25 × 9.2 *(58.1 × 7.6 × 2.8)*
Main machinery: 3 MTU 16V 538 TB91 diesels; 9,210 hp(m) *(6.78 MW)* sustained; 3 shafts
Speed, knots: 30
Complement: 55 (5 officers)
Guns: 1 OTO Melara 3 in *(76 mm)* compact; 85 rds/min to 16 km *(8.6 n miles)* anti-surface; 12 km *(6.5 n miles)* anti-air; weight of shell 6 kg; 250 rounds.
1 Breda 40 mm/70; 300 rds/min to 12.5 km *(6.8 n miles)* anti-surface; weight of shell 0.96 kg.
Weapons control: LIOD optronic director.
Radars: Surface search/fire control: Thomson-CSF Canopus A; I/J-band.
Navigation: Decca TM 1226C; I-band.

Comment: Ordered in 1977. *Yogaga* completed a major overhaul at Swan Hunter's Wallsend, Tyneside yard 8 May 1989. *Achimota* started a similar refit at CMN Cherbourg in May 1991 and was joined by *Yogaga* for repairs in late 1991. Both completed by August 1992. Employed on Fishery Protection duties.

ACHIMOTA *6/2007, Ghana Navy* / 1167861

1 INSHORE PATROL CRAFT (PBI)

DAVID HANSEN P 32

Displacement, tons: 31.5 light; 41.25 full load
Dimensions, feet (metres): 64.9 × 18.0 × 5.9 *(19.8 × 5.5 × 1.8)*
Main machinery: 3 Detroit 8V 71 diesel; 690 hp *(515 kW)* sustained; 3 shafts
Speed, knots: 28. **Range, n miles:** 450 at 26 kt
Complement: 10 (1 officer)
Guns: 1 — 14.5 mm MG.

Comment: Ex-US Navy PB Mk III Series built by Peterson Builders, Wisconsin in 1975–76. Aluminium construction. The design includes a pilot house offset to starboard to provide space to port for the installation of additional weapons. Transferred to the Ghana Navy in 2001 and employed on harbour and anchorage surveillance and security patrols.

DAVID HANSEN *6/2007, Ghana Navy* / 1167860

Greece

HELLENIC NAVY

Country Overview

The Hellenic Republic is situated in south-eastern Europe and occupies the southernmost part of the Balkan Peninsula. It includes more than 3,000 islands, most of which are in the Aegean Sea. With an area of 50,949 square miles, it has borders to north-west with Albania, to the north with the Former Yugoslav Republic of Macedonia and with Bulgaria and to the north-east with Turkey. It has a 7,387 n mile coastline with the Aegean, Mediterranean and Ionian Seas. The capital and largest city is Athens whose seaport, Piraeus, is also the largest. Other major ports include Thessaloníki, Patras and Iráklion. Territorial seas (6 n miles) are claimed but an EEZ is not claimed.

Headquarters Appointments

Chief of the Hellenic Navy:
Vice Admiral G Karamalikis
Deputy Chief of Staff:
Rear Admiral N Vazaios
Commander, Navy Training Command:
Rear Admiral D Papagiannidis
Inspector General:
Rear Admiral E Mitrou

Fleet Command

Commander of the Fleet:
Vice Admiral K Karaiskos
Deputy Commander of the Fleet:
Rear Admiral G Dimitriadis

Personnel

(a) 2009: 20,200 (4,200 officers) including 3,800 conscripts
(b) 12 months' national service

Bases

Salamis and Souda Bay

Naval Commands

Commander of the Fleet has under his flag all combatant ships. Navy Logistic Command is responsible for the bases at Salamis and Souda Bay, the Supply Centre and all auxiliary ships. Navy Training Command is in charge of the Petty Officers' School, the naval staff and commanding officers course and two training centres.

Naval Districts

Aegean, Ionian and Northern Greece

Naval Aviation

Alouette III helicopters (Training).
AB 212ASW helicopters (No 1 Squadron).
S-70B-6 Seahawk (No 2 Squadron).
P-3B Orions are operated under naval command by mixed Air Force and Navy crews.

Prefix to Ships' Names

HS (Hellenic Ship)

Strength of the Fleet

Type	Active	Building (Planned)
Patrol Submarines	8	4
Frigates	14	–
Corvettes	3	–
Fast Attack Craft—Missile	18	2
Offshore Patrol Craft	8	–
Coastal Patrol Craft	8	–
LST/LSD/LSM	5	–
LCU/LCM	4	–

Strength of the Fleet—*continued*

Type	Active	Building (Planned)
Hovercraft	4	–
Minesweepers—Coastal	8	–
Survey and Research Ships	4	–
Support Ships	2	–
Training Ships	5	–
Tankers	6	–
Auxiliary Transports	4	–
Ammunition Ship	1	–

DELETIONS

Notes: Some of the deleted ships are in unmaintained reserve in anchorages.

Mine Warfare Forces

2006 *Klio, Erato*

PENNANT LIST

Submarines

S 110	Glavkos
S 111	Nereus
S 112	Triton
S 113	Proteus
S 116	Poseidon
S 117	Amphitrite
S 118	Okeanos
S 119	Pontos
S 120	Papanikolis
S 121	Pipinos (bldg)
S 122	Matrozos (bldg)
S 123	Katsonis (bldg)

Frigates

F 450	Elli
F 451	Limnos
F 452	Hydra
F 453	Spetsai
F 454	Psara
F 455	Salamis
F 459	Adrias
F 460	Aegeon
F 461	Navarinon
F 462	Kountouriotis
F 463	Bouboulina
F 464	Kanaris
F 465	Themistocles
F 466	Nikiforos Fokas

Patrol Forces

P 18	Armatolos
P 19	Navmachos
P 20	Anthyploiarchos Laskos
P 21	Plotarchis Blessas
P 22	Ypoploiarchos Mikonios
P 23	Ypoploiarchos Troupakis
P 24	Simeoforos Kavaloudis
P 26	Ypoploiarchos Degiannis
P 27	Simeoforos Xenos
P 28	Simeoforos Simitzopoulos
P 29	Simeoforos Starakis
P 57	Kasos
P 61	Polemistis
P 62	Niki
P 63	Doxa
P 64	Eleftheria
P 67	Ypoploiarchos Roussen
P 68	Ypoploiarchos Daniolos
P 69	Ypoploiarchos Kristallidis
P 70	Ypoploiarchos Grigoropoulos (bldg)
P 71	Anthypoploiarchos Ritsos (bldg)
P 72	Ypoploiarchos Votsis
P 73	Anthyploiarchos Pezopoulos
P 74	Plotarchis Vlahavas
P 75	Plotarchis Maridakis
P 76	Ypoploiarchos Tournas
P 77	Plotarchis Sakipis
P 196	Andromeda
P 198	Kyknos
P 199	Pigasos
P 228	Toxotis
P 229	Tolmi
P 230	Ormi
P 266	Machitis
P 267	Nikiforos
P 268	Aittitos
P 269	Krateos
P 286	Diopos Antoniou
P 287	Kelefstis Stamou

Amphibious Forces

L 167	Ios
L 169	Irakleia
L 170	Folegandros
L 173	Chios
L 174	Samos
L 175	Ikaria
L 176	Lesbos
L 177	Rodos
L 178	Naxos
L 179	Paros
L 180	Kefallinia
L 181	Ithaki
L 182	Kerkira
L 183	Zakynthos
L 195	Serifos

Minesweepers/Hunters

M 61	Evniki
M 62	Evropi
M 63	Kallisto
M 64	Calypso
M 211	Alkyon
M 214	Avra
M 240	Aidon
M 241	Kichli
M 242	Kissa
M 248	Pleias

Auxiliaries, Training and Survey Ships

A 233	Maistros
A 234	Sorokos
A 238	Zefiros
A 307	Thetis
A 359	Ostria
A 373	Gregos
A 374	Prometheus
A 375	Zeus
A 376	Orion
A 410	Atromitos
A 411	Adamastos
A 412	Aias
A 413	Pilefs
A 415	Evros
A 416	Ouranos
A 417	Hyperion
A 419	Pandora
A 420	Pandrosos
A 422	Kadmos
A 423	Heraklis
A 424	Iason
A 425	Odisseus
A 428	Nestor
A 429	Perseus
A 432	Gigas
A 433	Kerkini
A 434	Prespa
A 435	Kekrops
A 436	Minos
A 437	Pelias
A 438	Aegeus
A 439	Atrefs
A 440	Diomidis
A 441	Theseus
A 442	Romaleos
A 460	Evrotas
A 461	Arachthos
A 463	Nestos
A 464	Axios
A 466	Trichonis
A 467	Doirani
A 468	Kalliroe
A 469	Stimfalia
A 470	Aliakmon
A 474	Pytheas
A 476	Strabon
A 478	Naftilos
A 479	I Karavoyiannos Theophilopoulos
A 481	St Lykoudis

SUBMARINES

8 + 2 GLAVKOS CLASS (TYPE 209/1100/1200) (SSK)

Name	No	Builders	Laid down	Launched	Commissioned
GLAVKOS	S 110	Howaldtswerke, Kiel	1 Sep 1968	15 Sep 1970	6 Sep 1971
NEREUS	S 111	Howaldtswerke, Kiel	15 Jan 1969	7 June 1971	10 Feb 1972
TRITON	S 112	Howaldtswerke, Kiel	1 June 1969	14 Oct 1971	8 Aug 1972
PROTEUS	S 113	Howaldtswerke, Kiel	1 Oct 1969	1 Feb 1972	8 Aug 1972
POSEIDON	S 116	Howaldtswerke, Kiel	15 Jan 1976	21 Mar 1978	22 Mar 1979
AMPHITRITE	S 117	Howaldtswerke, Kiel	26 Apr 1976	14 June 1978	14 Sep 1979
OKEANOS	S 118	Howaldtswerke, Kiel	1 Oct 1976	16 Nov 1978	15 Nov 1979
PONTOS	S 119	Howaldtswerke, Kiel	25 Jan 1977	21 Mar 1979	29 Apr 1980

Displacement, tons: 1,125 surfaced; 1,235 dived (S 110-113) 1,200 surfaced; 1,285 dived (S 116, 117, 119). 1,430 (approx) (S 118)
Dimensions, feet (metres): 179.5 × 20.3 × 18.5 *(54.4 × 6.2 × 5.6)* (S 110-113)
183.4 × 20.3 × 18.8 *(55.9 × 6.2 × 5.7)* (S 116, 117, 119)
204.7 × 20.3 × 18.8 *(62.4 × 6.2 × 5.7)* (S 118)
Main machinery: Diesel-electric; 4 MTU 12V 493 AZ80 diesels; 2,400 hp(m) *(1.76 MW)* sustained; 4 Siemens alternators; 1.7 MW; 1 Siemens motor; 4,600 hp(m) *(3.38 MW)* sustained; 1 shaft; 2 HDW PEM fuel cells (S 118); 240 kW
Speed, knots: 11 surfaced; 21.5 dived
Complement: 38 (6 officers)

Missiles: McDonnell Douglas Sub Harpoon; active radar homing to 130 km *(70 n miles)* at 0.9 Mach; warhead 258 kg. Can be discharged from 4 tubes only (S 110-113).
Torpedoes: 8—21 in *(533 mm)* bow tubes. 14 AEG SUT Mod 0; wire-guided; active/passive homing to 12 km *(6.5 n miles)* at 35 kt; warhead 250 kg. Swim-out discharge.
Countermeasures: ESM: Argos AR-700-S5; radar warning (S 110-113).
Thomson Arial DR 2000; radar warning (S 116-119).
Weapons control: Signaal Sinbads (S 116, 117, 119). Atlas Elektronik ISUS-90 (S 118). Unisys/Kanaris with UYK-44 computers (S 110-113).
Radars: Surface search: Thomson-CSF Calypso II (S 116-119). Thomson MILNAV (S 110-113); I-band.
Sonars: Atlas Elektronik CSU 83-90 (DBQS-21); (S 110-113); Atlas Elektronik CSU 3-4 (S 116-119); hull-mounted; active/passive search and attack; medium frequency.
Atlas Elektronik PRS-3-4; passive ranging. STN Atlas flank array (S 118); passive low frequency.

POSEIDON *11/2005, M Declerck* / 1164522

Programmes: Designed by Ingenieurkontor, Lübeck for construction by Howaldtswerke, Kiel and sale by Ferrostaal, Essen all acting as a consortium.
Modernisation: Contract signed 5 May 1989 with HDW and Ferrostaal to implement a Neptune I update programme to bring first four up to an improved standard and along the same lines as the German S 206A class. Included Sub Harpoon, flank array sonar, Unisys FCS, Sperry Mk 29 Mod 3 inertial navigation system, GPS and Argos ESM. *Triton* completed refitat Kiel in May 1993, *Proteus* at Salamis in December 1995, *Glavkos* in November 1997, and *Nereus* in March 2000. A contract signed 31 May 2002 with Hellenic Shipyards (main sub-contractor HDW) for a Neptune II modernisation programme for S 117-119. S 116 is not to be modernised. *Okeanos* started refit in December 2004 and was completed in 2009. A 'plug-in' extension of 6.5 m was required to incorporate AIP (Siemens PEM fuel cell system). In addition an STN Atlas ISUS-90 combat management system, flank array sonar, electro-optic mast, SATCOM, Link II and Sub Harpoon were fitted. Plans to upgrade *Pontos* and *Amphritite*, have been superseded by plans to build two new Type 209/1400 class.
Structure: A single-hull design with two ballast tanks and forward and after trim tanks. Fitted with snort and remote machinery control. The single screw is slow revving. Very high-capacity batteries with GRP lead-acid cells and battery cooling by Wilh Hagen and VARTA. Diving depth, 250 m *(820 ft)*. Fitted with two periscopes.
Operational: Endurance, 50 days. A mining capability is reported but not confirmed. The four Type 209/1100 boats are likely to be decommissioned as the new Type 214 boats enter service.

1 + 3 PAPANIKOLIS (TYPE 214) CLASS (SSK)

Name	*No*	*Builders*	*Laid down*	*Launched*	*Commissioned*
PAPANIKOLIS	S 120	Howaldtswerke, Kiel	27 Feb 2001	22 Apr 2004	2009
PIPINOS	S 121	Hellenic Shipyards, Skaramanga	15 Oct 2002	Apr 2007	2009
MATROZOS	S 122	Hellenic Shipyards, Skaramanga	1 Apr 2003	Mar 2008	2009
KATSONIS	S 123	Hellenic Shipyards, Skaramanga	1 Apr 2004	Dec 2008	2010

Displacement, tons: 1,700 (surfaced); 1,800 (dived)
Dimensions, feet (metres): 213.3 × 20.7 × 21.6 *(65 × 6.3 × 6.6)*
Main machinery: 2 MTU 16V 396 diesels; 5,600 hp(m) *(4.17 MW)*; 1 Siemens Permasyn motor; 1 shaft; 2 HDW PEM fuel cells; 240 kW
Speed, knots: 20 dived; 11 surfaced
Complement: 40 (6 officers)

Missiles: SSM: Boeing Sub Harpoon.
Torpedoes: 8—21 in *(533 mm)* bow tubes (4 fitted for Sub Harpoon discharge); Atlas Elektronik DM2A4 torpedoes; wire-guided; active/passive homing to 50 km *(27 n miles)* at 50 kt; warhead 250 kg. Total of 16 weapons.
Countermeasures: Decoys: CIRCE torpedo countermeasures. ESM. Elbit TIMNEX II.
Weapons control: STN Atlas ISUS-90.
Radars: Surface search: Thales Sphynx; I-band.
Sonars: Bow and flank arrays. To be fitted for but not with towed array.

Programmes: Decision taken on 24 July 1998 and announced on 9 October to order three HDW designed submarines with an option for a fourth. The first of class is being built at Kiel and subsequent hulls at Hellenic Shipyards. Contracts to build signed 15 February 2000 and the fourth was ordered in 2002. Acceptance of the first of class was declined in November 2006 due to contractural disagreements. The implications for the other three boats and the timescale of the overall programme are not known.
Structure: Diving depth 400 m *(1,300 ft)*. To be equipped with Zeiss optronic mast and SATCOM.
Operational: *Papanikolis* started initial sea trials on 2 February 2005 and further trials were completed in September 2008.

PAPANIKOLIS *6/2008*, Michael Winter* / 1335464

PAPANIKOLIS *7/2008*, A A de Kruijf* / 1335377

FRIGATES

Notes: Procurement of a class of up to six multipurpose frigates is a high priority and a decision on the way ahead is expected in 2009. The requirement is for an air-defence capable ship with additional ASW and ASUW roles. Competing designs are likely to include: FREMM (DCNS); MEKO D (Hellenic Shipyards); LCF (Royal Schelde); F-100 (Navantia).

4 HYDRA CLASS (MEKO 200 HN) (FFGH)

Name	*No*	*Builders*	*Laid down*	*Launched*	*Commissioned*
HYDRA	F 452	Blohm + Voss, Hamburg	17 Dec 1990	25 June 1991	15 Oct 1992
SPETSAI	F 453	Hellenic Shipyards, Skaramanga	11 Aug 1992	9 Dec 1993	24 Oct 1996
PSARA	F 454	Hellenic Shipyards, Skaramanga	12 Dec 1993	20 Dec 1994	30 Apr 1998
SALAMIS	F 455	Hellenic Shipyards, Skaramanga	20 Dec 1994	15 May 1997	16 Dec 1998

Displacement, tons: 2,710 light; 3,350 full load
Dimensions, feet (metres): 383.9; 357.6 (wl) × 48.6 × 19.7 *(117; 109 × 14.8 × 6)*
Main machinery: CODOG; 2 GE LM 2500 gas turbines; 60,000 hp *(44.76 MW)* sustained; 2 MTU 20V 956 TB82 diesels; 10,420 hp(m) *(7.66 MW)* sustained; 2 shafts; cp props
Speed, knots: 31 gas; 20 diesel
Range, n miles: 4,100 at 16 kt
Complement: 199 (27 officers) plus 16 flag staff

Missiles: SSM: 8 McDonnell Douglas Harpoon Block 1C; 2 quad launchers ❶; active radar homing to 130 km *(70 n miles)* at 0.9 Mach; warhead 227 kg.
SAM: Raytheon NATO Sea Sparrow RIM-7P (F 452, 453, 454) Mk 48 Mod 2 vertical launcher ❷; 16 missiles; semi-active radar homing to 16 km *(8.5 n miles)* at 2.5 Mach; warhead 38 kg. Raytheon ESSM RIM-162 (F 455); Mk 38 Mod 5 launcher; 16 missiles; semi-active radar homing to 18.5 km *(10 n miles)* at 3.6 Mach; warhead 38 kg.
Guns: 1 FMC 5 in *(127 mm)*/54 Mk 45 Mod 2A ❸ 20 rds/min to 24 km *(13 n miles)* anti-surface; 14 km *(7.7 n miles)* anti-aircraft; weight of shell 32 kg.
2 GD/GE Vulcan Phalanx 20 mm Mk 15 Mod 12 ❹; 6 barrels per mounting; 3,000 rds/min combined to 1.5 km.
Torpedoes: 6—324 mm Mk 32 Mod 5 (2 triple) tubes ❺. Honeywell Mk 46 Mod 5; anti-submarine; active/passive homing to 11 km *(5.9 n miles)* at 40 kt; warhead 44 kg.
Countermeasures: Decoys: 4 Mk 36 Mod 2 SRBOC chaff launchers ❻.
SLQ-25 Nixie; torpedo decoy.
ESM: Argo AR 700; Telegon 10; intercept.
ECM: Argo APECS II; jammer.
Combat data systems: Signaal STACOS Mod 2; Links 11 and 14.
Weapons control: 2 Signaal Mk 73 Mod 1 (for SAM). Vesta Helo transponder with datalink for OTHT. SAR-8 IR search. SWG 1 A(V) Harpoon LCS.
Radars: Air search: Signaal MW08 ❼; 3D; F/G-band.
Air/surface search: Signaal/Magnavox; DA08 ❽; G-band.
Navigation: Racal Decca 2690 BT; ARPA; I-band.
Fire Control: 2 Signaal STIR ❾; I/J/K-band.
IFF: Mk XII Mod 4.
Sonars: Raytheon SQS-56/DE 1160; hull-mounted and VDS.

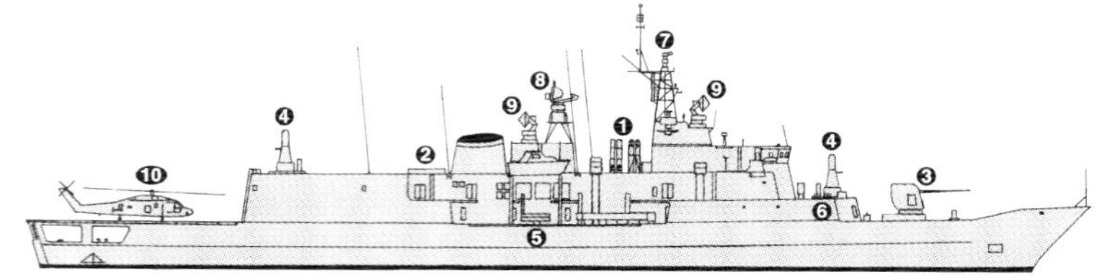

HYDRA *(Scale 1 : 1,200), Ian Sturton* / 0052282

PSARA *10/2008*, M Declerck* / 1335381

Helicopters: 1 Sikorsky S-70B-6 Aegean Hawk ❿.

Programmes: Decision to buy four Meko 200 HN announced on 18 April 1988. The first ship ordered 10 February 1989 built by Blohm + Voss, Hamburg and the remainder ordered 10 May 1989 at Hellenic Shipyards, Skaramanga. Programme was delayed by financial problems at Hellenic Shipyards in 1992 and some of the prefabrication of *Spetsai* was done in Hamburg.
Modernisation: A mid-life upgrade programme is planned 2010–14. Enhancements are to include upgrades and replacement of sensors and trackers in addition to platform improvements. As a separate programme Mk 48 launcher systems are being upgraded to Mod 5 to accommodate ESSM. This programme is to be completed by late 2009.
Structure: The design follows the Portuguese Vasco da Gama class. All steel fin stabilisers.
Operational: Aegean Hawk carried from 1995. *Hydra* and *Salamis* are part of the 1st Frigate Squadron and *Spetsai* and *Psara* part of the 2nd Frigate Squadron.

HYDRA *6/2005, Michael Winter* / 1133492

SALAMIS *6/2006, Marco Ghiglino* / 1164520

10 ELLI (KORTENAER) CLASS (FFGH)

Name	*No*	*Builders*	*Laid down*	*Launched*	*Commissioned*
ELLI (ex-*Pieter Florisz*)	F 450 (ex-F 812)	Koninklijke Maatschappij de Schelde, Flushing	1 July 1977	15 Dec 1979	10 Oct 1981
LIMNOS (ex-*Witte de With*)	F 451 (ex-F 813)	Koninklijke Maatschappij de Schelde, Flushing	13 June 1978	27 Oct 1979	18 Sep 1982
AEGEON (ex-*Banckert*)	F 460 (ex-F 810)	Koninklijke Maatschappij de Schelde, Flushing	25 Feb 1976	13 July 1978	29 Oct 1980
ADRIAS (ex-*Callenburgh*)	F 459 (ex-F 808)	Koninklijke Maatschappij de Schelde, Flushing	30 June 1975	12 Mar 1977	26 July 1979
NAVARINON (ex-*Van Kinsbergen*)	F 461 (ex-F 809)	Koninklijke Maatschappij de Schelde, Flushing	2 Sep 1975	16 Apr 1977	24 Apr 1980
KOUNTOURIOTIS (ex-*Kortenaer*)	F 462 (ex-F 807)	Koninklijke Maatschappij de Schelde, Flushing	8 Apr 1975	18 Dec 1976	26 Oct 1978
BOUBOULINA (ex-*Pieter Florisz*, ex-*Willem van der Zaan*)	F 463 (ex-F 826)	Koninklijke Maatschappij de Schelde, Flushing	21 Jan 1981	8 May 1982	1 Oct 1983
KANARIS (ex-*Jan van Brakel*)	F 464 (ex-F-825)	Koninklijke Maatschappij de Schelde, Flushing	16 Nov 1979	16 May 1981	14 Apr 1983
THEMISTOCLES (ex-*Philips Van Almonde*)	F 465 (ex-F-823)	Dok en Werfmaatschappij-Fijenoord	3 Oct 1977	11 Aug 1979	2 Dec 1981
NIKIFOROS FOKAS (ex-*Bloys van Treslong*)	F 466 (ex-F 824)	Dok en Werfmaatschappij-Fijenoord	27 Apr 1978	15 Nov 1980	25 Nov 1982

Displacement, tons: 3,050 standard; 3,630 full load
Dimensions, feet (metres): 428 × 47.9 × 20.3 (screws) *(130.5 × 14.6 × 6.2)*
Main machinery: COGOG; 2 RR Olympus TM3B gas turbines; 50,880 hp *(39.7 MW)* sustained; 2 RR Tyne RM1C gas turbines; 9,900 hp *(7.4 MW)* sustained; 2 shafts; LIPS cp props
Speed, knots: 30
Range, n miles: 4,700 at 16 kt
Complement: 172 (26 officers)

Missiles: SSM: 8 McDonnell Douglas Harpoon (2 quad) launchers ❶; active radar homing to 130 km *(70 n miles)* at 0.9 Mach; warhead 227 kg.
SAM: Raytheon NATO Sea Sparrow RIM-7P ❷; Mk 29 octuple launcher; 8 missiles; semi-active radar homing to 16 km *(8.5 n miles)* at 2.5 Mach; warhead 38 kg.
Portable Redeye; shoulder-launched; short range.
Guns: 1 (F 459-466) or 2 (F 450, 451) OTO Melara 3 in *(76 mm)*/62 compact ❸; 85 rds/min to 16 km *(8.6 n miles)* anti-surface; 12 km *(6.5 n miles)* anti-aircraft; weight of shell 6 kg.
1 (F 459, 460, 461, 462) or 2 (F 450, 451) GE/GD Vulcan Phalanx 20 mm Mk 15 6-barrelled ❹; 3,000 rds/min combined to 1.5 km.
Torpedoes: 4—324 mm Mk 32 (2 twin) tubes ❺. 16 Honeywell Mk 46 Mod 5; anti-submarine; active/passive homing to 11 km *(5.9 n miles)* at 40 kt; warhead 44 kg. Can be fitted.
Countermeasures: Decoys: 2 Loral Hycor Mk 36 SRBOC chaff launchers (Sippican ALEX in F 459, F 461, F 462).
ESM: Elettronika Sphinx and MEL Scimitar; intercept.
EDO CS-3701 (F 459, F 461, F 462); intercept.
ECM: ELT 715; jammer.
Combat data systems: Signaal SEWACO II action data automation; Thales Tacticos (F 459, F 461, F 462); Links 10, 11 and 14, SHF Satcom.
Electro-optic systems: Thales Mirador Trainable Electrical-Optical Observation System (TEOOS) (F 459, F, 461, F 462).
Radars: Air search: Signaal LW08 ❻; D-band; range 264 km *(145 n miles)* for 2 m² target.
Surface search: Signaal ZW06 ❼; Thales Scout Mk 2 (F 459, F 461, F 462); I-band.
Fire control: Signaal WM25 ❽; I/J-band; range 46 km *(25 n miles)*.
Signaal STIR ❾; I/J/K-band; range 39 km *(21 n miles)* for 1 m² target.
Sonars: Canadian Westinghouse SQS-505; hull-mounted; active search and attack; 7 kHz.

Helicopters: 2 AB 212ASW ❿.

Programmes: A contract was signed with the Netherlands on 15 September 1980 for the purchase of *Elli*, a Kortenaer class, building for the Netherlands' Navy. An option for a second ship *Limnos* was exercised on 7 June 1981. On 9 November 1992, agreement was reached to transfer further ships of the class from the Netherlands Navy: *Aegeon* recommissioned on 14 May 1993, *Adrias* on 30 March 1994, *Navarinon* on 1 March 1995 and *Kountouriotis* on 15 December 1997. The first four ships are known as Batch I and the next two as Batch II. Four Batch III ships were later acquired on decommissioning from the Netherlands Navy: *Bouboulina* recommissioned on 14 December 2001, *Kanaris*, on 29 November 2002, *Themistocles* on 24 October 2003 and *Nikiforos Fokas* on 17 December 2003.
Modernisation: Mid-life modernisation programme (MLM) is planned for the six Batch I and II ships to extend life to 2020. The upgrade is being undertaken by Hellenic Shipyards with Thales Nederland acting as main sub-contractor. The MLM includes replacement of the combat data system with Tacticos, replacement of ZW06 surface search radar with Scout, improvements to the tracking performance of LW08 and WM25/STIR and installation of the Mirador optronic director. Upgrades to the EW capability are to include EDO CS-3701 ESM receiver and upgrade of SRBOC. Upgrade of the Sea Sparrow system to RIM 162 ESSM has been postponed indefinitely. *Kountouritis*, the first modernised frigate, was handed back to the Hellenic Navy on 12 September 2006 the second, *Adrias*, in February 2007 and the third *Navarinon* in late 2007. *Limnos* is to be completed in 2009 and *Elli* and *Aegeon* in 2010.
Structure: Hangar is 2 m longer than in the original Netherlands-designed ships to accommodate AB 212ASW helicopters.
Operational: Assignments; 1st FS *(Elli, Adrias, Kountouriotis, Bouboulina, Themistocles)*. 2nd FS *(Limnos, Aegeon, Navarinon, Kanaris, Nikiforos Fokas)*.

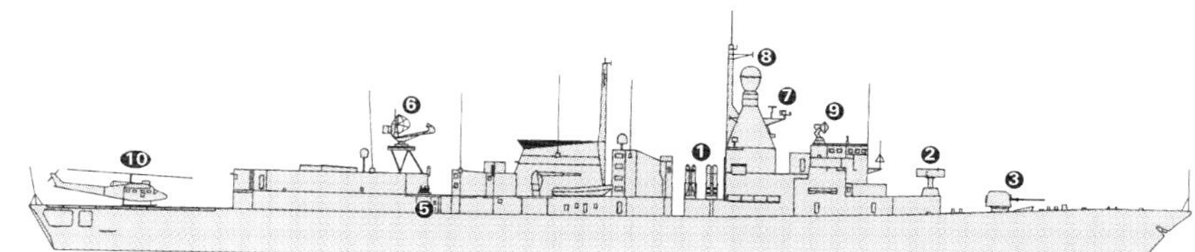

KANARIS *(Scale 1 : 1,200), Ian Sturton* / 1044255

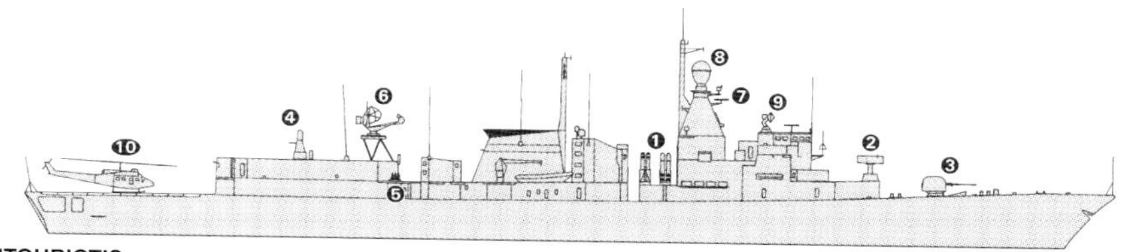

ELLI *(Scale 1 : 1,200), Ian Sturton* / 0126346

KOUNTOURIOTIS *(Scale 1 : 1,200), Ian Sturton* / 1335461

ELLI *2/2007, Camil Busquets i Vilanova* / 1170148

NIKIFOROS FOKAS *8/2007, Michael Nitz* / 1170146

KOUNTOURIOTIS *6/2008*, Giorgio Ghiglione* / 1335463

SHIPBORNE AIRCRAFT

Notes: There are also two Alouette IIIs used for SAR and training.

Numbers/Type: 11 Sikorsky S-70B-6 Aegean Hawk.
Operational speed: 135 kt *(250 km/h)*.
Service ceiling: 10,000 ft *(3,050 m)*.
Range: 600 n miles *(1,110 km)*.
Role/Weapon systems: Five ordered 17 August 1991. First one delivered 14 October 1994, remainder in July 1995. The option was taken up on three more of which one was delivered in 1997, and two more in 1998. Three further more modern aircraft ordered June 2000, all of which have been delivered (differences are indicated in brackets). All of the original eight aircraft are to be similarly upgraded. Sensors: Telephonica APS 143(V)3 search radar and AAQ-22 (or AAS 44) FLIR, AlliedSignal AQS18(V)3 (or Ocean Systems HELRAS) dipping sonar, MAD, Litton ALR 606(V)2 (or LR 100) ESM, Litton ASN 150(V) tactical data system with CD22 or Link 11. Weapons: ASV; Kongsberg Penguin Mk 2 Mod 7, two AS 12 (or four AGM-114K Hellfire). ASW; two (or three) Mk 46 torpedoes.

AEGEAN HAWK *10/2001, Diego Quevedo* / 0126292

Numbers/Type: 8 Agusta AB 212ASW.
Operational speed: 106 kt *(196 km/h)*.
Service ceiling: 14,200 ft *(4,330 m)*.
Range: 230 n miles *(425 km)*.
Role/Weapon systems: Shipborne ASW and surface search role from escorts. Sensors: Selenia APS-705 radar, AlliedSignal AQS-18 dipping sonar (ASW version). Weapons: ASV; two AS 12. ASW; two Mk 46 or two A244/S homing torpedoes.

AB 212ASW *6/2003, Adolfo Ortigueira Gil* / 0568866

LAND-BASED MARITIME AIRCRAFT

Notes: (1) A squadron of Air Force Mirage 2000 EG fighters is assigned to the naval strike role using Exocet AM 39 ASMs.
(2) Replacement of the six P-3B Orions is under consideration. Options include the Embraer P-99, ATR 72/500, EADS CASA CN-235 and Beriev Be-200.

Numbers/Type: 6 Lockheed P-3B Orion.
Operational speed: 410 kt *(760 km/h)*.
Service ceiling: 28,300 ft *(8,625 m)*.
Range: 4,000 n miles *(7,410 km)*.
Role/Weapon systems: Four P-3A transferred from the USN in 1992–93 as part of the Defence Co-operation. Four P-3B acquired in 1996 plus two more P-3A. Two more P-3B in 1997. The six P-3B are operational; two P-3A are used for ground training only and the remainder for spares. Sensors: APS 80 radar; sonobuoys; ESM. Weapons: ASW; Mk 46 torpedoes, depth bombs and mines.

ORION *6/1997, Hellenic Navy* / 0012468

PATROL FORCES

Notes: Eight coastal patrol craft ordered on 24 September 2002 from Motomarine Shipyards. The first was planned to enter service in 2003. Eight further craft ordered by the Hellenic Coast Guard and delivered in 2004.

3 + 4 ROUSSEN (SUPER VITA) CLASS (FAST ATTACK CRAFT—MISSILE) (PGG)

Name	*No*	*Builders*	*Commissioned*
YPOPLOIARCHOS ROUSSEN	P 67	Elefsis Shipyard	20 Dec 2005
YPOPLOIARCHOS DANIOLOS	P 68	Elefsis Shipyard	22 Feb 2006
YPOPLOIARCHOS KRISTALLIDIS	P 69	Elefsis Shipyard	8 May 2006
YPOPLOIARCHOS GRIGOROPOULOS	P 70	Elefsis Shipyard	2009
ANTHYPOPLOIARCHOS RITSOS	P 71	Elefsis Shipyard	2010
–	–	Elefsis Shipyard	2012
–	–	Elefsis Shipyard	2012

Displacement, tons: 660 full load
Dimensions, feet (metres): 203.1 × 31.2 × 8.5 *(61.9 × 9.5 × 2.6)*
Main machinery: 4 MTU 16V 595TE 90 diesels; 23,170 hp *(17.3 MW)*; 4 shafts
Speed, knots: 34
Range, n miles: 1,800 at 12 kt
Complement: 45 (8 officers)

Missiles: SSM: 8 MBDA Exocet MM 40 Block 2 (Block 3 in P 70 and P 71) ❶; inertial cruise; active radar homing to 70 km *(40 n miles)* at 0.9 Mach; warhead 165 kg; sea skimmer.
SAM: 1 RAM RIM-116 ❷; Mk 49 launcher; passive IR/anti-radiation homing to 9.6 km *(5.2 n miles)* at 2.5 Mach; warhead 9.1 kg.
Guns: 1 Oto Melara 76 mm/62 Super Rapid ❸; 120 rds/min to 16 km *(8.7 n miles)*; weight of shell 6 kg.
2 Otobreda 30 mm ❹.
Countermeasures: Decoys: 2 Loral Hycor Mk 36 SRBOC chaff launchers ❺.
ESM: Thales DR 3000 ❻; intercept.
Combat data systems: Thales Tacticos. Link 11.
Electro-optic systems: Thales Mirador Trainable Electro-Optical Observation System (TEOOS) ❼.
Radars: Air/surface search: Thales MW-08 ❽; G-band.
Surface search: Thales Scout Mk 2 LPI; I-band.
Navigation: Litton Marine Bridgemaster; I-band.
Fire control: Thales Sting ❾; I/J-band.
IFF: Mk XII.

Programmes: Design selected 21 September 1999 based on Vosper Thornycroft Vita corvettes in service in Qatar. Contract signed 7 January 2000 for the building of first three vessels which started in March 2000. *Roussen* launched on 13 November 2002, *Daniolos* on 8 July 2003, *Kristallidis* on 5 April 2004. A contract for the construction of two further ships was signed on 23 August 2003. *Grigoropoulos* was launched on 20 December 2005 and *Ritsos* on 9 October 2006. The contract for the sixth and seventh vessels was signed on 25 September 2008.
Structure: A rigid inflatable boat is carried amidships.

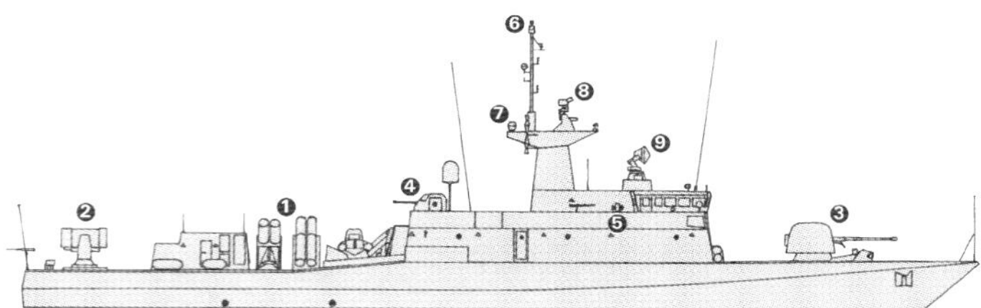

YPOPLOIARCHOS ROUSSEN *(Scale 1 : 900), Ian Sturton* / 0126344

DANIOLOS *7/2006, Richard Scott* / 1159225

ROUSSEN *6/2006* / 1164517

9 LASKOS (LA COMBATTANTE III) CLASS (FAST ATTACK CRAFT—MISSILE) (PGGF/PGG)

Name	*No*	*Builders*	*Commissioned*
ANTHYPOPLOIARCHOS LASKOS	P 20	CMN Cherbourg	20 Apr 1977
PLOTARCHIS BLESSAS	P 21	CMN Cherbourg	7 July 1977
YPOPLOIARCHOS MIKONIOS	P 22	CMN Cherbourg	10 Feb 1978
YPOPLOIARCHOS TROUPAKIS	P 23	CMN Cherbourg	8 Nov 1977
SIMEOFOROS KAVALOUDIS	P 24	Hellenic Shipyards, Skaramanga	14 July 1980
YPOPLOIARCHOS DEGIANNIS	P 26	Hellenic Shipyards, Skaramanga	Dec 1980
SIMEOFOROS XENOS	P 27	Hellenic Shipyards, Skaramanga	31 Mar 1981
SIMEOFOROS SIMITZOPOULOS	P 28	Hellenic Shipyards, Skaramanga	June 1981
SIMEOFOROS STARAKIS	P 29	Hellenic Shipyards, Skaramanga	12 Oct 1981

Displacement, tons: 359 standard; 425 full load (P 20-23)
329 standard; 429 full load (P 24-29)
Dimensions, feet (metres): 184 × 26.2 × 7 *(56.2 × 8 × 2.1)*
Main machinery: 4 MTU 20V 538TB92 diesels; 17,060 hp(m) *(12.54 MW)* sustained; 4 shafts (P 20-23)
4 MTU 20V 538TB91 diesels; 15,360 hp(m) *(11.29 MW)* sustained; 4 shafts (P 24-29)
Speed, knots: 36 (P 20-23); 32.5 (P 24-29)
Range, n miles: 700 at 32 kt; 2,700 at 15 kt
Complement: 43 (6 officers)

Missiles: SSM: 4 Aerospatiale MM 38 Exocet (P 20-P 23); inertial cruise; active radar homing to 42 km *(23 n miles)* at 0.9 Mach; warhead 165 kg.
6 Kongsberg Penguin Mk 2 Mod 3 (P 24-P 29); inertial/IR homing to 27 km *(15 n miles)* at 0.8 Mach; warhead 120 kg.
Guns: 2 OTO Melara 3 in *(76 mm)*/62 compact; 85 rds/min to 16 km *(8.6 n miles)* anti-surface; 12 km *(6.5 n miles)* anti-aircraft; weight of shell 6 kg.
4 Emerson Electric 30 mm (2 twin); multipurpose; 1,200 rds/min combined to 6 km *(3.2 n miles)*; weight of shell 0.35 kg.
Torpedoes: 2—21 in *(533 mm)* aft tubes. AEG SST-4; anti-surface; wire-guided; active homing to 12 km *(6.5 n miles)* at 35 kt; passive homing to 28 km *(15 n miles)* at 23 kt; warhead 250 kg.
Countermeasures: Decoys: Wegmann chaff launchers.
ESM: Thomson CSF DR 2000S (P 20-23); intercept.
Combat data systems: Tacticos (P 20-23). Link 11 (P 20-23).
Weapons control: 2 CSEE Panda optical directors for 30 mm guns. Mirador optronic director (P 20-P 23). NFT PFCS-2 (P 24-P 29).
Radars: Surface search: Thomson-CSF Triton (P 24-29); Thales Variant (P 20-23); G-band.
Thales Scout (P 20-23); I-band.
Navigation: Decca 1226C (P 24-29); I-band.
Sperry Bridgemaster (P 20-23); E/F/I-band.
Fire control: Thomson-CSF Castor II; I/J-band.
Thomson-CSF Pollux; I/J-band.

Programmes: First four ordered in September 1974. Second group of six ordered 1978.
Modernisation: P 24-29 upgraded to fire Penguin Mk 2 Mod 3 missiles. A contract for the upgrade of P 20-23 was signed on 31 October 2003. Modernisation began in 2005 and is to be completed in 2009. The programme includes installation of the Tacticos Combat Management System, the MIRADOR optronic director, SRBOC launchers, Thales DR 3000 ESM, Link 11 and Variant, Scout Mk 2 and Bridgemaster radars. P 20 was completed in April 2008 and P 22 in September 2008. P 21 and P 23 are to be completed in February 2009 and August 2009 respectively.
Structure: First four fitted with SSM Exocet; remainder have Penguin.
Operational: P 25 sunk after collision with a ferry in November 1996.

SIMEOFOROS SIMITZOPOULOS (with Penguin) *9/2000, A Sharma* / 0126333

PLOTARCHIS BLESSAS (with Exocet) *7/2006, Marco Ghiglino* / 1164515

SIMEOFOROS STARAKIS *11/2008*, M Declerck* / 1335380

6 VOTSIS (LA COMBATTANTE IIA) (TYPE 148) CLASS (FAST ATTACK CRAFT—MISSILE) (PGFG)

Name	*No*	*Builders*	*Commissioned*
YPOPLOIARCHOS VOTSIS (ex-*Iltis*)	P 72 (ex-P 51)	CMN, Cherbourg	8 Jan 1973
ANTHYPOPLOIARCHOS PEZOPOULOS (ex-*Storch*)	P 73 (ex-P 30)	CMN, Cherbourg	17 July 1974
PLOTARCHIS VLAHAVAS (ex-*Marder*)	P 74	CMN, Cherbourg	14 June 1973
PLOTARCHIS MARIDAKIS (ex-*Häher*)	P 75	CMN, Cherbourg	12 June 1974
YPOPLOIARCHOS TOURNAS (ex-*Leopard*)	P 76	CMN, Cherbourg	21 Aug 1973
PLOTARCHIS SAKIPIS (ex-*Jaguar*)	P 77	CMN, Cherbourg	13 Nov 1973

Displacement, tons: 265 full load
Dimensions, feet (metres): 154.2 × 23 × 8.9 *(47 × 7 × 2.7)*
Main machinery: 4 MTU MD 16V 538 TB90 diesels; 12,000 hp(m) *(8.82 MW)* sustained; 4 shafts
Speed, knots: 36
Range, n miles: 570 at 30 kt; 1,600 at 15 kt
Complement: 41 (6 officers)

Missiles: SSM: 4 Aerospatiale MM 38 Exocet (2 twin) launchers (P 72-73 and P 76-77); inertial cruise; active radar homing to 42 km *(23 n miles)* at 0.9 Mach; warhead 165 kg; sea-skimmer.
4 McDonnell Douglas Harpoon (2 twin) launchers (P 74-75); active radar homing to 130 km *(70 n miles)* at 0.9 Mach; warhead 227 kg.
Guns: 1 OTO Melara 3 in *(76 mm)*/62 compact; 85 rds/min to 16 km *(8.6 n miles)* anti-surface; 12 km *(6.5 n miles)* anti-aircraft; weight of shell 6 kg.
1 Bofors 40 mm/70; 330 rds/min to 12 km *(6.5 n miles)* anti-surface; 4 km *(2.2 n miles)* anti-aircraft; weight of shell 0.96 kg; fitted with GRP dome (1984).
Mines: Laying capability.
Countermeasures: Decoys: Wolke chaff launcher.
ESM: Thomson-CSF DR 2000S; intercept.
Combat data systems: PALIS and Link 11.
Weapons control: CSEE Panda optical director. Thomson-CSF Vega PCET system, controlling missiles and guns.
Radars: Air/surface search: Thomson-CSF Triton; G-band; range 33 km *(18 n miles)* for 2 m^2 target.
Navigation: SMA 3 RM 20; I-band.
Fire control: Thomson-CSF Castor; I/J-band.

Programmes: First pair transferred from Germany in September 1993 and recommissioned 17 February 1994. Two more transferred 16 March 1995 and recommissioned 30 June 1995. Third pair transferred from Germany and recommissioned on 27 October 2000.
Modernisation: Mid-life updates in 1980s. P 74-75 fitted with Harpoon. New ESM fitted after transfer. P 76-77 modernised at Lamda Shipyards in 2003–2004.
Structure: Steel hulls. Similar to Combattante II class. Spray rails have been fitted to improve hydrodynamic performance.

YPOPLOIARCHOS TOURNAS *11/2004, M Declerck* / 1133495

4 NASTY CLASS (PATROL CRAFT) (PB)

Name	*No*	*Builders*	*Commissioned*
ANDROMEDA	P 196	Mandal, Norway	Nov 1966
KYKNOS	P 198	Mandal, Norway	Feb 1967
PIGASOS	P 199	Mandal, Norway	Apr 1967
TOXOTIS	P 228	Mandal, Norway	May 1967

Displacement, tons: 72 full load
Dimensions, feet (metres): 80.4 × 24.6 × 6.9 *(24.5 × 7.5 × 2.1)*
Main machinery: 2 MTU 12V 331TC92 diesels; 2,660 hp(m) *(1.96 MW)* sustained; 2 shafts
Speed, knots: 25
Range, n miles: 676 at 17 kt
Complement: 20 (2 officers)
Guns: 1 Bofors 40 mm/70. 1 Rheinmetall 20 mm.
Radars: Surface search: Decca 1226; I-band.

Comment: Six of the class acquired from Norway in 1967 and paid off into reserve in the early 1980s. Four re-engined and brought back into service in 1988. These craft continue to be active although top speed has been markedly reduced. Torpedo tubes have been removed.

PIGASOS *7/2004, C D Yaylali* / 0587756

2 ARMATOLOS (OSPREY 55) CLASS (LARGE PATROL CRAFT) (PG)

Name	*No*	*Builders*	*Commissioned*
ARMATOLOS	P 18	Hellenic Shipyards, Skaramanga	27 Mar 1990
NAVMACHOS	P 19	Hellenic Shipyards, Skaramanga	15 July 1990

Displacement, tons: 555 full load
Dimensions, feet (metres): 179.8; 166.7 (wl) × 34.4 × 8.5 *(54.8; 50.8 × 10.5 × 2.6)*
Main machinery: 2 MTU 16V 1163TB63 diesels; 10,000 hp(m) *(7.3 MW)* sustained; 2 shafts; Kamewa cp props
Speed, knots: 25
Range, n miles: 500 at 25 kt, 2,800 at 12 kt
Complement: 48 (7 officers)
Guns: 1 OTO Melara 3 in *(76 mm)*/62 compact; 85 rds/min to 16 km *(8.6 n miles)* anti-surface; 12 km *(6.6 n miles)* anti-aircraft; weight of shell 6 kg.
1 Bofors 40 mm/70.
Mines: Rails.
Countermeasures: Decoys: 2 chaff launchers.
ESM: Thomson-CSF DR 2000S; intercept.
Weapons control: Selenia Elsag NA 21.
Radars: Surface search: Thomson-CSF Triton; G-band.
Fire control: Selenia RTNX; I/J-band.

Comment: Built in co-operation with Danyard A/S. Ordered in March 1988. First one laid down 8 May 1989 and launched 19 December 1989. Second laid down 9 November 1989 and launched 16 May 1990. Armament is of modular design and therefore can be changed. 76 mm guns replaced the forward Bofors 40 mm in 1995, after being taken from decommissioned Gearing-class destroyers. Options on more of the class were shelved in favour of the Hellenic 56 design.

NAVMACHOS *7/2002, Ptisi* / 0525871

2 KASOS (HELLENIC 56) CLASS (BATCH 1) (LARGE PATROL CRAFT) (PG)

Name	*No*	*Builders*	*Commissioned*
KASOS (ex-*Pyrpolitis*)	P 57	Hellenic Shipyard, Skaramanga	4 May 1993
POLEMISTIS	P 61	Hellenic Shipyard, Skaramanga	16 June 1994

Displacement, tons: 555 full load
Dimensions, feet (metres): 185.4 × 32.8 × 8.9 *(56.5 × 10 × 2.7)*
Main machinery: 2 Wärtsilä Nohab 16V25 diesels; 9,200 hp(m) *(6.76 MW)* sustained; 2 shafts
Speed, knots: 24
Range, n miles: 2,470 at 15 kt; 900 at 24 kt
Complement: 48 (7 officers)
Guns: 1 OTO Melara 3 in *(76 mm)*/62 compact; 85 rds/min to 16 km *(8.6 n miles)* anti-surface; 12 km *(6.6 n miles)* anti-aircraft; weight of shell 6 kg.
1 Bofors 40 mm/70. 2 Rheinmetall 20 mm.
Mines: 2 rails.
Countermeasures: ESM: Thomson-CSF DR 2000S; intercept.
Weapons control: Selenia Elsag NA 21.
Radars: Surface search: Thomson-CSF Triton; I-band.

Comment: First pair ordered 20 February 1990. This is a design by the Hellenic Navy which uses the modular concept so that weapons and sensors can be changed as required. Appearance is similar to Osprey 55 class. First of class *Pyrpolitis* (renamed *Kasos* in 2006) launched 16 September 1992, *Polemistis* 21 June 1993. Completion delayed by the shipyard's financial problems. Alternative guns and Harpoon SSM can be fitted. 25 fully equipped troops can be carried. Engines are resiliently mounted.

POLEMISTIS *5/2004, Martin Mokrus* / 0587755

POLEMISTIS *8/2000, van Ginderen Collection* / 0104560

4 MACHITIS CLASS (LARGE PATROL CRAFT) (PG)

Name	*No*	*Builders*	*Commissioned*
MACHITIS	P 266	Hellenic Shipyards, Skaramanga	29 Oct 2003
NIKIFOROS	P 267	Hellenic Shipyards, Skaramanga	30 Mar 2004
AITTITOS	P 268	Hellenic Shipyards, Skaramanga	5 Aug 2004
KRATEOS	P 269	Hellenic Shipyards, Skaramanga	20 Oct 2005

Displacement, tons: 575 full load
Dimensions, feet (metres): 185.4 × 32.8 × 8.9 *(56.5 × 10 × 2.7)*
Main machinery: 2 Wärtsilä Nohab 16V25 diesels; 9,200 hp(m) *(6.76 MW)* sustained; 2 shafts
Speed, knots: 24. **Range, n miles**: 2,000 at 15 kt; 900 at 24 kt
Complement: 49 (8 officers)
Guns: 1 Otobreda 3 in *(76 mm)*/62 compact; 85 rds/min to 16km *(8.6 n miles)* anti-surface; 12 km *(6.6 n miles)* anti-aircraft; weight of shell 6 kg.
1 Otobreda 40 mm/70-520R. 2 Rheinmetall 20 mm.
Mines: 2 rails.
Countermeasures: ESM: Thomson-CSF DR 3000.
Combat data systems: TACTICOS with Link 11.
Weapons control: Thales Lirod Mk 2.
Radars: Air/surface search: Signaal Variant; E/F-band.
Surface search: Thales Scout Mk 2; I-band.
Fire control: Thales Lirod Mk 2; K-band.
Navigation: Bridgemaster I-band.

Comment: Contract to build four improved Pyrpolitis class given to Hellenic Shipyard on 21 December 1999. Building started in February 2000 *Machitis* launched in June 2002, *Nikiforos* on 13 December 2002, *Aititos* on 26 February 2003 and *Krateos* on 30 October 2003. An option for a fifth vessel is unlikely to be exercised.

MACHITIS *12/2004, Marco Ghiglino* / 1170145

2 TOLMI (ASHEVILLE) CLASS (LARGE PATROL CRAFT) (PG)

Name	*No*	*Builders*	*Commissioned*
TOLMI (ex-*Green Bay*)	P 229	Peterson, Wisconsin	5 Dec 1969
ORMI (ex-*Beacon*)	P 230	Peterson, Wisconsin	21 Nov 1969

Displacement, tons: 225 standard; 245 full load
Dimensions, feet (metres): 164.5 × 23.8 × 9.5 *(50.1 × 7.3 × 2.9)*
Main machinery: 2 MTU 12V 596TE94 diesels; 4,500 hp *(3.3 MW)*; 2 shafts
Speed, knots: 20. **Range, n miles**: 1,700 at 16 kt
Complement: 32 (6 officers)
Guns: 2 Bofors 40 mm/70 Mk 10. 4—12.7 mm (2 twin) MGs.
Weapons control: Mk 63 GFCS.
Radars: Surface search: Sperry SPS-53; I/J-band.
Fire control: Western Electric SPG-50; I/J-band.

Comment: Transferred from the USA in mid-1990 after a refit and recommissioned 18 June 1991. Both were in reserve from April 1977 having originally been built for the Cuban crisis. Similar craft in Turkish, Colombian and South Korean navies. Original gas-turbine propulsion engine was removed prior to transfer and both craft reported re-engined in 2004.

TOLMI *8/2006, Marco Ghiglino* / 1164516

2 ANTONIOU CLASS (PB)

Name	*No*	*Builders*	*Commissioned*
DIOPOS ANTONIOU	P 286	Ch N de l'Esterel	4 Dec 1975
KELEFSTIS STAMOU	P 287	Ch N de l'Esterel	28 July 1975

Displacement, tons: 115 full load
Dimensions, feet (metres): 105 × 19 × 5.3 *(32 × 5.8 × 1.6)*
Main machinery: 2 MTU 12V 331TC81 diesels; 2,610 hp(m) *(1.92 MW)* sustained; 2 shafts
Speed, knots: 30. **Range, n miles**: 1,500 at 15 kt
Complement: 20 (2 officers)
Guns: 1 Rheinmetall 20 mm. 1—12.7 mm MG.
Radars: Surface search: Decca 1226; I-band.

Comment: Originally ordered for Cyprus, later transferred to Greece. Wooden hulls. Fast RIB carried on the stern. Surface-to-surface missiles no longer carried.

DIOPOS ANTONIOU *7/2007, A A de Kruijf* / 1170144

11 SPECIAL WARFARE CRAFT (PBF)

SAP 1–11

Displacement, tons: 6.6 full load
Dimensions, feet (metres): 44.3 × 11.6 × 2.3 *(13.2 × 3.55 × 0.7)*
Main machinery: 2 Caterpillar; 840 hp *(625 kW)*; surface-piercing propeller
Speed, knots: 60+
Complement: 4
Guns: 1—12.7 mm MG. 2—7.62 mm MGs.

Comment: Details are for *SAP 7-9*, donated by Angelopoulos family to Hellenic Navy for use by special forces. RIB42SC rigid inflatable monohull with removable synthetic armour panels. Built by Italian shipyard Fabio Buzzi.

SPECIAL WARFARE CRAFT *6/2006* / 1164514

3 NIKI (THETIS) (TYPE 420) CLASS (PATROL SHIPS) (PG)

Name	*No*	*Launched*	*Commissioned*
NIKI (ex-*Thetis*)	P 62 (ex-P 6052)	1 July 1961	6 Sep 1991
DOXA (ex-*Najade*)	P 63 (ex-P 6054)	12 May 1962	6 Sep 1991
ELEFTHERIA (ex-*Triton*)	P 64 (ex-P 6055)	10 Nov 1962	7 Sep 1992

Displacement, tons: 575 standard; 732 full load
Dimensions, feet (metres): 229.7 × 26.9 × 8.6 *(70 × 8.2 × 2.7)*
Main machinery: 2 MAN V84V diesels; 6,800 hp(m) *(5 MW)*; 2 shafts
Speed, knots: 19.5
Range, n miles: 2,760 at 15 kt
Complement: 65 (7 officers)

Guns: 4 Breda 40 mm/70 (2 twin); 300 rds/min to 12.5 km *(6.7 n miles)*; weight of shell 0.96 kg. 2 Rheinmetall 20 mm.
Torpedoes: 6—324 mm Mk 32 (2 triple) tubes; 6 Honeywell Mk 46 Mod 5; active/passive homing to 11 km *(5.9 n miles)* at 40 kt; warhead 44 kg.
Depth charges: 2 rails.
Countermeasures: ESM: Thomson-CSF DR 2000S; intercept.
Weapons control: Signaal Mk 9 TFCS.
Radars: Surface search: Thomson-CSF TRS 3001; E/F-band.
Navigation: Decca BM-E; I-band.
Sonars: Atlas Elektronik ELAC 1 BV; hull-mounted; active search and attack; high frequency.

Programmes: All built by Rolandwerft, Bremen, and transferred from Germany.
Modernisation: The A/S mortars have been replaced by a second 40 mm gun and single torpedo tubes by triple mountings (to be confirmed). Upgrades started in 2000 and completed in 2002 included new diesel generators, two Rheinmetall 20 mm guns to replace the MGs and a new navigation suite.
Structure: *Doxa* has a deckhouse before bridge for sick bay.

ELEFTHERIA *7/2006, Marco Ghiglino* / 1164518

AMPHIBIOUS FORCES

Notes: (1) There is a number of paid off LSTs and LSMs in unmaintained reserve at Salamis.
(2) Procurement of a landing platform dock is under consideration.

59 LANDING CRAFT

Displacement, tons: 56 full load
Dimensions, feet (metres): 56 × 14.4 × 3.9 *(17 × 4.4 × 1.2)*
Main machinery: 2 Gray Marine 64 HN9 diesels; 330 hp *(264 kW)*; 2 shafts
Speed, knots: 10
Range, n miles: 130 at 10 kt
Military lift: 30 tons

Comment: Details given are for the 11 LCMs transferred from the USA in 1956–58. Twenty-nine LCVPs were also transferred from the USA 1956–71 and the remainder (12 LCPs and 7 LCAs) were built in Greece from 1977.

5 CHIOS (JASON) CLASS (LSTH)

Name	*No*	*Builders*	*Launched*	*Commissioned*
CHIOS	L 173	Eleusis Shipyard	16 Dec 1988	30 May 1996
SAMOS	L 174	Eleusis Shipyard	6 Apr 1989	20 May 1994
LESBOS	L 176	Eleusis Shipyard	5 July 1990	25 Feb 1999
IKARIA	L 175	Eleusis Shipyard	22 Oct 1998	6 Oct 1999
RODOS	L 177	Eleusis Shipyard	6 Oct 1999	30 May 2000

Displacement, tons: 4,400 full load
Dimensions, feet (metres): 380.5 × 50.2 × 11.3 *(116 × 15.3 × 3.4)*
Main machinery: 2 Wärtsilä Nohab 16V25 diesels; 9,200 hp(m) *(6.76 MW)* sustained; 2 shafts
Speed, knots: 16
Complement: 112 (12 officers)
Military lift: 300 troops plus vehicles; 4 LCVPs
Guns: 1 OTO Melara 76 mm/62 Mod 9 compact; 100 rds/min to 16 km *(8.6 n miles)* anti-surface; 12 km *(6.5 n miles)* anti-aircraft; weight of shell 6 kg.
2 Breda 40 mm/70; 300 rds/min to 12 km *(6.5 n miles)*; weight of shell 0.96 kg.
4 Rheinmetall 20 mm (2 twin).
Weapons control: 1 CSEE Panda optical director. Thomson-CSF Canopus GFCS.
Radars: Thomson-CSF Triton; G-band.
Fire control: Thomson-CSF Pollux; I/J-band.
Navigation: Kelvin Hughes Type 1007; I-band.
Helicopters: Platform for one medium.

Comment: Contract for construction of five LSTs by Eleusis Shipyard signed 15 May 1986. Bow and stern ramps, drive through design. First laid down 18 April 1987, second in September 1987, third in May 1988, fourth April 1989 and fifth November 1989. Completion of all five and in particular the last three, severely delayed by shipyard financial problems which were later overcome, following privatisation. Combat data system is a refurbished German system.

SAMOS *9/2003, Schaeffer/Marsan* / 0568865

LESBOS *11/2005, M Declerck* / 1164513

4 KEFALLINIA (ZUBR) CLASS (PROJECT 1232) (HOVERCRAFT) (LCUJ)

Name	*No*	*Builders*	*Commissioned*
KEFALLINIA	L 180 (ex-717)	Almaz, St Petersburg	22 Jan 2001
ITHAKI	L 181 (ex-U 421)	Morye Shipyard, Ukraine	2 Mar 2001
ZAKYNTHOS	L 183	Almaz, St Petersburg	5 Oct 2001
KERKIRA	L 182	Almaz, St Petersburg	4 Jan 2005

Displacement, tons: 550 full load
Dimensions, feet (metres): 189 × 84 *(57.6 × 25.6)*
Main machinery: 5 Type DP-71L gas-turbines; 2 for lift, 20,000 hp(m) *(14.7 MW)* nominal; 3 for drive, 30,000 hp(m) *(22.1 MW)* nominal
Speed, knots: 60
Range, n miles: 300 at 55 kt
Complement: 40 (5 officers)
Military lift: 3 MBT or 10 APC plus 230 troops (total 130 tons)
Guns: 2—30 mm/65 AK 630; 6 barrels per mounting.
2 retractable 122 mm rocket launchers.
Mines: 2 rails can be carried for 80.
Countermeasures: ESM: intercept.
Weapons control: Optronic director.
Radars: Air/surface search: Cross Dome; I-band.
Fire control: Bass Tilt; H/I-band.

Comment: Two ordered from Russia and two from Ukraine on 24 January 2000. First delivered late December 2000, the remainder in 2001. L 180 was second-hand, L 181 was completion of a half-built vessel and L 183 was new build. The second Ukrainian ship was not accepted into service and a replacement (L 182) was ordered from Russia on 30 September 2002 and launched on 24 June 2004. There are no plans for further craft.

KEFALLINIA *1/2001, T L Valmas* / 0034713

6 TYPE 520 (LCU)

NAXOS (ex-*Renke*) L 178 **SERIFOS** (ex-*Rochen*) L 195 **IRAKLEIA** (ex-*Forelle*) L 169
PAROS (ex-*Salm*) L 179 **IOS** (ex-*Barbe*) L 167 **FOLEGANDROS** (ex-*Delphin*) L 170

Displacement, tons: 430 full load
Dimensions, feet (metres): 131.2 × 28.9 × 7.2 *(40 × 8.8 × 2.2)*
Main machinery: 2 MWM 12-cyl diesels; 1,020 hp(m) *(750 kW)*; 2 shafts
Speed, knots: 11. **Range, n miles:** 1,200 at 11 kt
Complement: 17
Military lift: 150 tons
Guns: 2 Rheinmetall 20 mm (not all fitted).
Radars: Navigation: Kelvin Hughes; I-band.

Comment: First two transferred from Germany 16 November 1989, remainder on 31 January 1992. Built by HDW, Hamburg in 1966. Bow and stern ramps similar to US Type. One other (ex-*Murane*) used for spares. Both L 178 and L 195 modified to act as auxiliary transport.

PAROS *7/2007, Bob Fildes* / 1170143

FOLEGANDROS *11/2004, M Declerck* / 1133499

2 + (3) EVNIKI (OSPREY) CLASS (MINEHUNTERS—COASTAL) (MHC)

Name	*No*	*Builders*	*Launched*	*Commissioned*
EVNIKI (ex-*Pelican*)	M 61 (ex-MHC 53)	Avondale Industries	27 Feb 1993	18 Nov 1995
CALYPSO (ex-*Heron*)	M 64 (ex-MHC 52)	Intermarine, Savannah	21 Mar 1992	6 Aug 1994

Displacement, tons: 930 full load
Dimensions, feet (metres): 187.8 × 35.9 × 9.5 *(57.2 × 11 × 2.9)*
Main machinery: 2 Isotta Fraschini ID 36 SS 8V AM diesels; 1,600 hp(m) *(1.18 MW)* sustained; 2 Voith-Schneider props; 3 Isotta Fraschini ID 36 diesel generators; 984 kW
Speed, knots: 10. **Range, n miles:** 1,500 at 10 kt
Complement: 49 (9 officers)

Guns: 2—12.7 mm MGs.
Countermeasures: MCM: Alliant SLQ-48 mine neutralisation system ROV (with 1,070 m cable). Degaussing DGM-4.
Combat data systems: Unisys SYQ 13 and SYQ 109; integrated combat and machinery control system. USQ-119E(V), UHF Dama, and OTCIXS provide GCCS connectivity.
Radars: Surface search: Raytheon SPS-64(V)9; I-band.
Navigation: R41XX; I-band.
Sonars: Raytheon/Thomson Sintra SQQ-32(V)3; VDS; active minehunting; high frequency.

Programmes: Original design contract for Lerici class minehunters was awarded in August 1986 to Intermarine USA which built eight of the 12 ships of the class for the US Navy. Ex-*Heron* transferred free of charge and ex-*Pelican* acquired through FMS funding. Both recommissioned on 16 March 2007. The procurement of three further ships is under consideration.
Structure: Construction is of monocoque GRP throughout hull, with frames eliminated. Main machinery is mounted on GRP cradles and provided with acoustic enclosures. SQQ-32 is deployed from a central well forward. Fitted with Voith cycloidal propellers which eliminate need for forward thrusters during station keeping.

OSPREY CLASS (US colours) *4/2004, US Navy* / 1043630

MINE WARFARE FORCES

6 ALKYON (MSC 294) CLASS (MINESWEEPERS—COASTAL) (MSC)

Name	*No*	*Builders*	*Commissioned*
ALKYON (ex-*MSC 319*)	M 211	Peterson Builders	3 Dec 1968
AVRA (ex-*MSC 318*)	M 214	Peterson Builders	3 Oct 1968
AIDON (ex-*MSC 314*)	M 240	Peterson Builders	22 June 1967
KICHLI (ex-*MSC 308*)	M 241	Peterson Builders	14 July 1964
KISSA (ex-*MSC 309*)	M 242	Peterson Builders	1 Sep 1964
PLEIAS (ex-*MSC 310*)	M 248	Peterson Builders	13 Oct 1964

Displacement, tons: 320 standard; 370 full load
Dimensions, feet (metres): 144 × 28 × 8.2 *(43.3 × 8.5 × 2.5)*
Main machinery: 2 GM-268A diesels; 1,760 hp *(1.3 MW)*; 2 shafts
Speed, knots: 13
Range, n miles: 2,500 at 10 kt
Complement: 37 (6 officers)
Guns: 2 Oerlikon 20 mm (twin).
Radars: Navigation: Decca; I-band.
Sonars: UQS-1D; active; high frequency.

Comment: Built in the USA for Greece, wooden hulls. Modernisation programme from 1990 to 1995 with replacement main engines and navigation radar. Two decommissioned in 2005 and 2006 respectively.

AVRA *7/2006, Marco Ghiglino* / 1164512

2 EVROPI (HUNT) CLASS (MHSC)

Name	*No*	*Builders*	*Commissioned*
EVROPI (ex-*Bicester*)	M 62 (ex-M 36)	Vosper Thornycroft	20 Mar 1986
KALLISTO (ex-*Berkeley*)	M 63 (ex-M 40)	Vosper Thornycroft	14 Jan 1988

Displacement, tons: 750 full load
Dimensions, feet (metres): 197 × 34.1 × 10.5 *(60 × 10.4 × 3.2)*
Main machinery: 2 MTU diesels; 1,900 hp *(1.42 MW)*; 1 Deltic Type 9-55B diesel for pulse generator and auxiliary drive; 780 hp *(582 kW)*; 2 shafts; bow thruster
Speed, knots: 15 diesels; 8 hydraulic drive
Range, n miles: 1,500 at 12 kt
Complement: 46 (9 officers)
Guns: 1 DES/MSI DS 30B 30 mm/75; 650 rds/min to 10 km *(5.4 n miles)* anti-surface; 3 km *(1.6 n miles)* anti-aircraft; weight of shell 0.36 kg.
Countermeasures: MCM: 2 PAP 104 remotely controlled submersibles, MS 14 magnetic loop, Sperry MSSA Mk 1 Towed Acoustic Generator and conventional Mk 8 Oropesa sweeps.
ESM: MEL Matilda UAR 1.
Combat data systems: CAAIS DBA 4 action data automation.
Radars: Navigation: Kelvin Hughes Type 1006; I-band.
Sonars: Plessey 193M Mod 1; hull-mounted; minehunting; 100/300 kHz.
Mil Cross mine avoidance sonar; hull-mounted; active; high frequency.
Type 2059 to track PAP 104.

Comment: First one transferred from UK 31 July 2000, second one 28 February 2001. Main machinery replaced by MTU units between May 2004 and January 2005. There are no further plans for upgrades.

EVROPI *2/2007, Adolfo Ortigueira Gil* / 1170142

SURVEY AND RESEARCH SHIPS

1 SURVEY SHIP (AGS)

Name	*No*	*Builders*	*Commissioned*
NAFTILOS	A 478	Annastadiades Tsortanides, Perama	3 Apr 1976

Displacement, tons: 1,470 full load
Dimensions, feet (metres): 207 × 38 × 13.8 *(63.1 × 11.6 × 4.2)*
Main machinery: 2 Burmeister & Wain SS28LM diesels; 2,640 hp(m) *(1.94 MW)*; 2 shafts
Speed, knots: 15
Complement: 43 (5 officers)

Comment: Launched 19 November 1975. Of similar design to the two lighthouse tenders.

NAFTILOS *9/1999, van Ginderen Collection* / 0079497

1 RESEARCH SHIP (AGOR)

Name	*No*	*Builders*	*Commissioned*
PYTHEAS	A 474	Annastadiades Tsortanides, Perama	15 Dec 1983

Displacement, tons: 670 standard; 840 full load
Dimensions, feet (metres): 164.7 × 31.5 × 21.6 *(50.2 × 9.6 × 6.6)*
Main machinery: 2 Detroit 12V-92TA diesels; 1,020 hp *(760 kW)* sustained; 2 shafts
Speed, knots: 14
Complement: 43 (5 officers)

Comment: *Pytheas* ordered in May 1982. Launched 19 September 1983. A similar ship, *Aegeon*, was constructed to Navy specification in 1984 but now belongs to the Maritime Research Institute.

PYTHEAS *7/2007, A A de Kruijf* / 1170141

1 HISTORIC SHIP (YXR)

OLYMPIAS

Dimensions, feet (metres): 121.4 × 17.1 × 4.9 *(37 × 5.2 × 1.5)*
Main machinery: 170 oars (85 each side in three rows)
Speed, knots: 8
Complement: 180

Comment: Construction started in 1985 and completed in 1987. Made of Oregon pine. Built for historic research and as a reminder of the naval hegemony of ancient Greeks. Part of the Hellenic Navy. Refit in 1992–93.

OLYMPIAS *6/1996, Hellenic Navy* / 0079500

1 SURVEY SHIP (AGSC)

Name	*No*	*Builders*	*Commissioned*
STRABON	A 476	Emanuil-Maliris, Perama	27 Feb 1989

Displacement, tons: 252 full load
Dimensions, feet (metres): 107.3 × 20 × 8.2 *(32.7 × 6.1 × 2.5)*
Main machinery: 1 MAN D2842LE; 571 hp(m) *(420 kW)* sustained; 1 shaft
Speed, knots: 12.5
Complement: 27 (4 officers)

Comment: Ordered in 1987, launched September 1988. Used as coastal survey vessel.

STRABON *6/2000, Hellenic Navy* / 0104567

TRAINING SHIPS

5 SAIL TRAINING SHIPS (AXS)

MAISTROS A 233
SOROKOS A 234
ZEFIROS A 238
OSTRIA A 359
GREGOS A 373

Displacement, tons: 12 full load (A 233 and 234)
Dimensions, feet (metres): 48.6 × 12.8 × 6.9 *(14.8 × 3.9 × 2.1)*

Comment: Sail training ships acquired in 1983–84 (A 233-234) and 1989 (A 359). A 359 is slightly smaller at 12.1 × 3.6 m. There are two further craft A 238 and A 373.

AUXILIARIES

Notes: Procurement of a submarine rescue ship is under consideration.

7 FLOATING REPAIR FACILITIES

Comment: There are two floating docks. One is 45 m *(147.6 ft)* in length and has a 6,000 ton lift. Built at Eleusis with Swedish assistance and launched 5 May 1988; delivered 1989. The second is the ex-US AFDM 2 transferred in 1999. This dock was built in 1942 and has a 12,000 ton lift. There are five floating cranes that were all built in Greece.

1 PROMETHEUS (ETNA) CLASS (AORH/MCCS)

Name	*No*	*Builders*	*Commissioned*
PROMETHEUS	A 374	Elefsis Shipyard	4 July 2003

Displacement, tons: 13,400 full load
Dimensions, feet (metres): 480.6 × 68.9 × 24.3 *(146.5 × 21 × 7.4)*
Flight deck, feet (metres): 91.9 × 68.9 *(28 × 21)*
Main machinery: 2 Sulzer 12 ZAV 40S diesels; 22,400 hp(m) *(16.46 MW)* sustained; 2 shafts; cp props; bow thruster
Speed, knots: 21
Range, n miles: 7,600 at 18 kt
Complement: 140 (19 officers) plus 119 spare including flag staff

Cargo capacity: 6,350 tons gas oil; 1,200 tons JP5; 2,100 m^3 ammunition and stores
Missiles: SAM: 2 Stinger mountings.
Guns: 1 GD/GE Vulcan Phalanx 20 mm; 6 barrels per mounting; 3,000 rds/min combined to 1 km.
4—20 mm guns.
Countermeasures: SLQ-25 Nixie; torpedo decoy.
Radars: Surface search: Raytheon SPS-10D; G-band.
Navigation: GEM LD-1825; I-band.
Helicopters: Aegean Hawk or AB 212.

Comment: Ordered in August 1999 from Fincantieri and from Elefsis on 7 January 2000. First steel cut July 2000, launched 18 February 2002. Almost identical to the Italian Etna class. One Phalanx CIWS has been fitted. There is one RAS station on each side and one astern station. Has a secondary role as a mine countermeasures command and support ship.

PROMETHEUS *8/2007, Michael Nitz* / 1170140

2 AXIOS (LÜNEBURG) (TYPE 701) CLASS (SUPPORT SHIPS) (ARL/AOR/MCCS)

Name	*No*	*Builders*	*Commissioned*	*Recommissioned*
AXIOS (ex-*Coburg*)	A 464 (ex-A 1412)	Bremer Vulcan	9 July 1968	30 Sep 1991
ALIAKMON (ex-*Saarburg*)	A 470 (ex-A 1415)	Blohm + Voss	30 July 1968	19 Oct 1994

Displacement, tons: 3,709 full load
Dimensions, feet (metres): 374.9 × 43.3 × 13.8 *(114.3 × 13.2 × 4.2)*
Main machinery: 2 MTU MD 16V 538 TB90 diesels; 6,000 hp(m) *(4.41 MW)* sustained; 2 shafts; cp props; bow thruster
Speed, knots: 17. **Range, n miles:** 3,200 at 14 kt
Complement: 89 (12 officers)
Cargo capacity: 1,400 tons fuel; 200 tons ammunition; 130 tons water
Guns: 4 Bofors 40 mm/70 (2 twin); 300 rds/min to 12 km *(6.5 n miles)*; weight of shell 0.96 kg.
Radars: Navigation: Decca; I-band.

Comment: Both ships converted to Fleet oilers by Hellenic Shipyards. Contract signed 21 December 1999. *Axios* completed September 2000 and *Aliakmon* in December 2002. Have secondary role as mine countermeasures and support ships.

AXIOS *4/2006, B Prézelin* / 1164324

4 OURANOS CLASS (AOTL)

Name	*No*	*Builders*	*Commissioned*
OURANOS	A 416	Kinosoura Shipyard	27 Jan 1977
HYPERION	A 417	Kinosoura Shipyard	27 Apr 1977
ZEUS	A 375 (ex-A 490)	Hellenic Shipyards	21 Feb 1989
ORION	A 376	Hellenic Shipyards	5 May 1989

Displacement, tons: 2,100 full load
Dimensions, feet (metres): 219.8; 198.2 (wl) × 32.8 × 13.8 *(67; 60.4 × 10 × 4.2)*
Main machinery: 1 MAN-Burmeister & Wain 12V 20/27 diesel; 1,632 hp(m) *(1.2 MW)* sustained; 1 shaft
Speed, knots: 11
Complement: 33 (5 officers)
Cargo capacity: 1,300 tons oil or petrol
Guns: 2 Rheinmetall 20 mm.

Comment: First two are oil tankers. The others were ordered from Hellenic Shipyards, Skaramanga in December 1986 and are used as petrol tankers. There are some minor superstructure differences between the first two and the last two which have a forward crane instead of kingposts.

OURANOS *7/2006, Marco Ghiglino* / 1164507

HYPERION *9/2001, A Sharma* / 0126326

6 WATER TANKERS (YW)

KERKINI (ex-German *FW 3*) A 433
PRESPA A 434
TRICHONIS (ex-German *FW 6*) A 466
DOIRANI A 467
KALLIROE A 468
STIMFALIA A 469

Comment: All built between 1964 and 1990. Capacity, 600 tons except A 433 and A 466 which can carry 300 tons and A 469 which can carry 1,000 tons. Three in reserve. *Stimfalia* is similar to *Ouranos*. A 433 damaged in collision on 15 April 2002.

KALLIROE *11/2004, M Declerck* / 1133497

1 NET TENDER (YNT)

Name	*No*	*Builders*	*Commissioned*
THETIS (ex-*AN 103*)	A 307	Kröger, Rendsburg	Apr 1960

Displacement, tons: 680 standard; 805 full load
Dimensions, feet (metres): 169.5 × 33.5 × 11.8 *(51.7 × 10.2 × 3.6)*
Main machinery: Diesel-electric; 1 MAN GTV-40/60 diesel generator; 1 motor; 1,470 hp(m) *(1.08 MW)*; 1 shaft
Speed, knots: 12. **Range, n miles:** 6,500 at 10 kt
Complement: 58 (4 officers)
Guns: 1 Bofors 40 mm/60. 3 Rheinmetall 20 mm.
Radars: Navigation: Decca; I-band.

Comment: US offshore order. Launched in 1959. Some guns not always embarked.

THETIS *9/1998, A Sharma* / 0052305

1 AMMUNITION SHIP (AEL)

Name	*No*	*Builders*	*Commissioned*
EVROS (ex-*Schwarzwald*, ex-*Amaltheé*)	A 415	Ch Dubigeon Nantes	7 June 1956

Displacement, tons: 2,400 full load
Measurement, tons: 1,667 gross
Dimensions, feet (metres): 263.1 × 39 × 15.1 *(80.2 × 11.9 × 4.6)*
Main machinery: 1 Sulzer 6SD60 diesel; 3,000 hp(m) *(2.2 MW)*; 1 shaft
Speed, knots: 15. **Range, n miles:** 4,500 at 15 kt
Complement: 55 (7 officers)
Guns: 4 Bofors 40 mm/60.

Comment: Bought by FDR from Société Navale Caënnaise in February 1960. Transferred to Greece 6 June 1976.

EVROS *6/2005, Hellenic Navy* / 1133500

2 AUXILIARY TRANSPORTS (AP)

Name	*No*	*Builders*	*Commissioned*
PANDORA	A 419	Perama Shipyard	26 Oct 1973
PANDROSOS	A 420	Perama Shipyard	1 Dec 1973

Displacement, tons: 390 full load
Dimensions, feet (metres): 153.5 × 27.2 × 6.2 *(46.8 × 8.3 × 1.9)*
Main machinery: 2 diesels; 2 shafts
Speed, knots: 12
Military lift: 500 troops
Radars: Navigation: Racal Decca; I-band.

Comment: Launched 1972 and 1973.

PANDORA *10/2007, Martin Mokrus* / 1335462

3 TYPE 430A (TORPEDO RECOVERY CRAFT) (YPT)

EVROTAS (ex-*TF 106*) A 460 (ex-Y 872)
ARACHTHOS (ex-*TF 108*) A 461 (ex-Y 874)
NESTOS (ex-*TF 4*) A 463 (ex-Y 854)

Comment: First two acquired from Germany on 16 November 1989, second pair on 5 March 1991. Of about 56 tons with stern ramps for torpedo recovery. Built in 1966. A 461 ran aground on 20 June 2002.

TYPE 430A (German colours) *6/1998, Michael Nitz* / 0052255

2 BUOY TENDERS (ABUH)

Name	*No*	*Builders*	*Commissioned*
I KARAVOYIANNOS THEOPHILOPOULOS	A 479	Perama Shipyard	17 Mar 1976
ST LYKOUDIS	A 481	Perama Shipyard	2 Jan 1976

Displacement, tons: 1,450 full load
Dimensions, feet (metres): 207.3 × 38 × 13.1 *(63.2 × 11.6 × 4)*
Main machinery: 1 Deutz MWM TBD5008UD diesel; 2,400 hp(m) *(1.76 MW)*; 1 shaft
Speed, knots: 15
Complement: 53 (6 officers)
Radars: Navigation: Racal Decca; I-band.
Helicopters: Platform for 1 light.

Comment: Similar to *Naftilos*, the survey ship.

ST LYKOUDIS *8/2006, Marco Ghiglino* / 1164503

TUGS

19 HARBOUR TUGS (YTM/YTL)

Name	*No*	*Commissioned*
ATROMITOS	A 410	1968
ADAMASTOS	A 411	1968
AIAS (ex-*Ankachak* YTM 767)	A 412	1972
PILEFS (ex-*Lütje Horn*)	A 413	1991
KADMOS	A 422	1989
HERAKLIS	A 423	1978
JASON	A 424	1978
ODISSEUS	A 425	1978
NESTOR (ex-*Wahpeton*)	A 428	1989
PERSEUS	A 429	1989
GIGAS	A 432	1961
KEKROPS	A 435	1989
MINOS (ex-*Mellum*)	A 436	1991
PELIAS (ex-*Knechtsand*)	A 437	1991
AEGEUS (ex-*Schärhorn*)	A 438	1991
ATREFS (ex-*Ellerbek*)	A 439	1971
DIOMIDIS (ex-*Neuwerk*)	A 440	1963
THESEUS (ex-*Heppens*)	A 441	2000
ROMALEOS	A 442	2000

Comment: Some may be armed.

GIGAS *11/2005, M Declerck* / 1164501

PELIAS *1/2002, M Declerck* / 0525884

COAST GUARD (LIMENIKON SOMA)

Senior Officers

Commander-in-Chief:
Vice Admiral Theodoros Rentzeperis
Deputy Commander-in-Chief:
Rear Admiral Athanassios Bouskos
Inspector General:
Rear Admiral Galanis Panagiotis

Personnel

2009: 4,000 (1,055 officers)

Bases

HQ: Piraeus
Main bases: Piraeus, Eleusis, Thessalonika, Volos, Patra, Corfu, Rhodes, Mytilene, Heraklion (Crete), Chios, Kavala, Chalcis, Igoumenitsa, Rafina
Minor bases: Every port and island of Greece

Ships and Craft

In general very similar in appearance to naval ships, being painted grey. Since 1990 pennant numbers have been painted white and on both sides of the hull they carry a blue and white band with two crossed anchors. From 1993 ships have been given grey hulls and white superstructures.

General

This force consists of about 150 patrol craft and anti-pollution vessels including 24 inflatables for the 48 man Underwater Missions Squad and 12 anti-pollution vessels. Administration in peacetime is by the Ministry of Merchant Marine. In wartime it would be transferred to naval command.

Officers are trained at the Naval Academy and ratings at two special schools.

The pennant numbers are all preceded as in the accompanying photographs by Greek 'Lambda Sigma' for Limenikon Soma.

Duties

The policing of all Greek harbours, coasts and territorial waters, navigational safety, SAR operations, anti-pollution surveillance and operations, supervision of port authorities, merchant navy training, inspection of Greek merchant ships worldwide.

Coast Guard Air Service

In October 1981 the Coast Guard acquired two Cessna Cutlass 172 RG aircraft and in July 1988 two Socata TB 20s. Maintenance and training by the Air Force. Based at Dekelia air base. Four Eurocopter Super Pumas AS 322C1 ordered in August 1998. First pair delivered in December 1999, second pair in May 2000. Being operated by mixed Air Force and Coast Guard crews. Bendix radar fitted. Three Reims Cessna Vigilant maritime patrol aircraft ordered in July 1999. First (F 406) delivered on 7 March 2001 and the other two in 2002. Six AS 365N3 Dauphin 2 helicopters were delivered in mid-2004.

Notes: (1) Three 8 m Boston Whalers were donated by the US government on 26 June 2004.
(2) A tender for an offshore patrol vessel was issued on 3 April 2007. The ship is to be of about 60 m and capable of operating a Dauphin 2 helicopter.

3 + (1) SAAR 4 CLASS (LARGE PATROL CRAFT) (PB)

FOURNOI LS 060 **RO** LS 070 **AGIOS EFSTATHIOS** LS 080

Displacement, tons: 415 standard; 450 full load
Dimensions, feet (metres): 190.6 × 25 × 8 *(58.0 × 7.8 × 2.4)*
Main machinery: 4 MTU 16V956 TB91 diesels; 15,000 hp(m) *(11.03 MW)* sustained; 4 shafts
Speed, knots: 32
Range, n miles: 1,650 at 30 kt; 4,000 at 17.5 kt
Complement: 30
Guns: 1—30 mm. 2—12.7 mm MGs.
Weapons control: Rafael DAFCO.
Radars: Air/surface search: SIGNAAL variant; E/F-band.
Navigation: Bridgemaster; I-band.

Comment: Three vessels ordered in November 2002. The first two (probably ex-Israeli Navy) built at Israel Shipyards while the third assembled at Hellenic Shipyards, Skaramanga. The first vessel delivered 23 December 2003, the second in February 2004 and the third in April 2004. A fourth vessel may be ordered. The ships are named after Greek islands.

AGIOS EFSTATHIOS *7/2004, C D Yaylali* / 0583669

RO *4/2005, P Marsan* / 1164325

1 VOSPER EUROPATROL 250 MK 1 (PBF)

LS 050

Displacement, tons: 240 full load
Dimensions, feet (metres): 155.2 × 24.6 × 7.9 *(47.3 × 7.5 × 2.4)*
Main machinery: 3 GEC/Paxman Valenta 16CM diesels; 13,328 hp(m) *(9.8 MW)*; 3 shafts
Speed, knots: 40
Range, n miles: 2,000 at 16 kt
Complement: 21
Radars: Surface search: Racal Decca; I-band.

Comment: Ordered from McTay Marine, Bromborough in July 1993 and completed in November 1994. This is a Vosper International design with a steel hull and aluminium superstructure. Replenishment at sea facilities are provided by light jackstay and the ship carries a 45 kt RIB with water-jet propulsion. A continuous patrol speed of 4 kt is achievable using the centre shaft. Air conditioned accommodation. Similar craft built for the Bahamas. Fitted for a 40 mm gun but this is not carried. Transferred to the Coast Guard in 2004.

LS 050 *5/2004, Martin Mokrus* / 0587762

7 DILOS CLASS (WPB)

LS 010 **LS 015** **LS 020** **LS 025** **LS 030** **LS 035** **LS 040**

Displacement, tons: 86 full load
Dimensions, feet (metres): 95.1 × 16.2 × 5.6 *(29 × 5 × 1.7)*
Main machinery: 2 MTU 12V 331 TC92 diesels; 2,660 hp(m) *(1.96 MW)* sustained; 2 shafts
Speed, knots: 27. **Range, n miles:** 1,600 at 24 kt
Complement: 18
Guns: 2 Rheinmetall 20 mm.
Radars: Surface search: Racal Decca 1226C; I-band.

Comment: Same Abeking and Rasmussen design as the three naval craft and built at Hellenic Shipyards in the early 1980s. Three former Customs craft transferred to the Coast Guard in 2004.

LS 040 *7/2007, A A de Kruijf* / 1170139

14 GUARDIAN 53 CRAFT (WPB)

LS 114–119 **LS 121–123** **LS 125–128** **LS 133**

Displacement, tons: 24 full load
Dimensions, feet (metres): 54.1 × 15.4 × 4.6 *(16.5 × 4.7 × 1.4)*
Main machinery: 2 MAN D2840 LE 401 diesels; 1,644 hp(m) *(1.21 MW)* sustained; 2 shafts
Speed, knots: 34. **Range, n miles:** 500 at 25 kt
Complement: 5 (1 officer)
Guns: 1—12.7 mm MG. 1—7.62 mm MG.
Radars: Surface search: Raytheon; I-band.

Comment: Ordered from Colvic Craft, Colchester in 1993. Shipped to Motomarine, Glifada for engine and electronics installation. Completed in mid-1994. GRP hulls with a stern platform for recovery of divers.

LS 119 *11/2004, M Declerck* / 1133490

3 COMBATBOAT 90HEX (WPBF)

LS 134–136

Displacement, tons: 19 full load
Dimensions, feet (metres): 52.2 × 12.5 × 2.6 *(15.9 × 3.8 × 0.8)*
Main machinery: 2 Volvo Penta TAMD 163P diesels; 1,500 hp(m) *(1.1 MW)*; 2 waterjets
Speed, knots: 45
Range, n miles: 240 at 30 kt
Complement: 3
Guns: 3—12.7 mm MGs.
Radars: Surface search: I-band.

Comment: Built by Dockstavarvet in Sweden and delivered 6 July 1998. Same design as Swedish naval craft but with more powerful engines. GRP construction with armoured protection for cockpit.

LS 136 *7/2004, A Campanera i Rovira* / 0587761

4 INTERMARINE CRAFT (WPB)

LS 129–132

Displacement, tons: 25 full load
Dimensions, feet (metres): 53.8 × 14.8 × 7.5 *(16.4 × 4.5 × 2.3)*
Main machinery: 2 MAN diesels; 2,000 hp(m) *(1.47 MW)* sustained; 2 shafts
Speed, knots: 36

Comment: Constructed by Intermarine, La Spezia and delivered 1996–97.

16 OL 44 CLASS (WPB)

LS 55	**LS 84–88**	**LS 97**	**LS 103**	**LS 109–110**
LS 65	**LS 95**	**LS 101**	**LS 106–107**	**LS 112**

Displacement, tons: 14 full load
Dimensions, feet (metres): 44.9 × 14.4 × 2 *(13.7 × 4.4 × 0.6)*
Main machinery: 2 diesels; 630 hp(m) *(463 kW)*; 2 shafts
Speed, knots: 23
Complement: 4
Guns: 1 – 7.62 mm MG.
Radars: Surface search: JRC; I-band.

Comment: Built by Olympic Marine. GRP hulls.

LS 101 *5/2000, van Ginderen Collection* / 0104571

15 MOTOMARINE PANTHER 57 MK II CRAFT (WPB)

LS 601–615

Displacement, tons: 27
Dimensions, feet (metres): 63.0 × 15.4 × 3.0 *(19.2 × 4.7 × 0.9)*
Main machinery: 2 MTU 12V2000 M 91 diesels; 2 surface piercing propellers
Speed, knots: 50

Comment: Constructed by Motomarine, Koropi, Greece. *LS 601* delivered November 2003 and remainder by August 2004. LS 609-615 delivered between February 2005 and March 2006.

LS 601 *7/2007, Bob Fildes* / 1170137

16 LS 51 CLASS (WPB)

LS 51–52 **LS 155–157** **+11**

Displacement, tons: 13 full load
Dimensions, feet (metres): 44 × 11.5 × 3.3 *(13.4 × 3.5 × 1)*
Main machinery: 2 diesels; 630 hp(m) *(463 kW)*; 2 shafts
Speed, knots: 25
Range, n miles: 400 at 18 kt
Complement: 4
Guns: 1 – 7.62 mm MG.
Radars: Surface search: Racal Decca; I-band.

Comment: Built by Olympic Marine. GRP hulls.

82 COASTAL CRAFT

Comment: Included in the total are 20 of 8.2 m, 17 of 7.9 m, 26 of 5.8 m and 19 ex-US Criss craft. In addition the Coast Guard operates 24 Inflatable craft, and 10 SAR craft *(LS 509-518)*.

LS 130 *10/2002, E & M Laursen* / 0533891

LS 214 *7/2004, C D Yaylali* / 0587760

4 POLLUTION CONTROL SHIPS (YPC)

LS 401 **LS 413–415**

Displacement, tons: 230 full load
Dimensions, feet (metres): 95.1 × 20.3 × 8.2 *(29 × 6.2 × 2.5)*
Main machinery: 2 CAT 3512 DITA diesels; 2,560 hp(m) *(1.88 MW)* sustained; 2 shafts
Speed, knots: 15
Range, n miles: 500 at 13 kt
Complement: 12
Radars: Navigation: Furuno; I-band.

Comment: Details given are for *LS 413-415*. Built by Astilleros Gondan, Spain in collaboration with Motomarine. Delivered in 1993–94. *LS 401* is an older pollution control ship.

LS 414 *11/2005, M Declerck* / 1164499

10 ARUN 60 CLASS (LIFEBOATS) (SAR)

SAR 12–14 **SAR 17–19** **SAR 511** **SAR 515–516** **SAR 520**

Displacement, tons: 34 full load
Dimensions, feet (metres): 59.0 × 17.4 × 4.9 *(18.0 × 5.3 × 1.5)*
Main machinery: 2 Caterpillar 3408 diesels; 2 shafts
Speed, knots: 18
Complement: 5

Comment: Built by Motormarine, Koropi, Greece. GRP hull moulded by Halmatic, UK. A stretched version of the lifeboat used in the UK and Canada. Entered service 1997–98.

SAR 516 *5/2006, Marco Ghiglino* / 1164498

35 MOTOMARINE PANTHER 57 MK 1 CRAFT (WPB)

LS 137–172

Displacement, tons: 28 full load
Dimensions, feet (metres): 59.7 × 15.3 × 3.0 *(18.2 × 4.68 × 0.92)*
Main machinery: 2 MAN diesels; 2 shafts
Speed, knots: 44
Guns: 1 — 12.7 mm MG.

Comment: A development of the Guardian class. Constructed by Motomarine and delivered between about 1997 and 2006.

LS 149
5/2008*, Jurg Kürsener
1335378

CUSTOMS

Notes: The Customs service also operates large numbers of coastal and inshore patrol. The craft have a distinctive Alpha Lambda (Α/(GL)) on the hull and are sometimes armed with 7.62 mm MGs.

AL 20 ***6/2002, C D Yaylali*** / 0525874

Grenada

Country Overview

Grenada gained independence in 1974; the British monarch, represented by a governor-general, is the head of state. The southernmost of the Windward Islands in the Lesser Antilles chain, the country comprises the island of Grenada (311 square miles) and some of the southern Grenadines including Carriacou and Petit Martinique. The capital, largest town, and main port is St George's. Territorial seas (12 n miles) are claimed. A 200 n mile Exclusive Economic Zone (EEZ) has been claimed but the limits are not defined. The Coast Guard craft are operated under the direction of the Commissioner of Police.

Personnel
2009: 30

Bases
Prickly Bay

COAST GUARD

Notes: A 920 Zodiac RHIB, donated by the US government, entered service in 2004.

1 GUARDIAN CLASS (COASTAL PATROL CRAFT) (PB)

Name	*No*	*Builders*	*Commissioned*
TYRREL BAY	PB 01	Lantana, Florida	21 Nov 1984

Displacement, tons: 90 full load
Dimensions, feet (metres): 105 × 20.6 × 7 *(32 × 6.3 × 2.1)*
Main machinery: 3 Detroit 12V-71TA diesels; 1,260 hp *(939 kW)* sustained; 3 shafts
Speed, knots: 24
Range, n miles: 1,500 at 18 kt
Complement: 15 (2 officers)
Guns: 2 — 12.7 mm MGs. 2 — 7.62 mm MGs.
Radars: Furuno 1411 Mk II; I-band.

Comment: Similar to Jamaican and Honduras vessels. Aluminium construction. Refit in 1995/96.

TYRREL BAY ***11/1990, Bob Hanlon*** / 0064681

1 DAUNTLESS CLASS (PB)

Name	*No*	*Builders*	*Commissioned*
LEVERA	PB 02	SeaArk Marine	8 Sep 1995

Displacement, tons: 11 full load
Dimensions, feet (metres): 40 × 14 × 4.3 *(12.2 × 4.3 × 1.3)*
Main machinery: 2 Caterpillar 3208TA diesels; 870 hp *(650 kW)* sustained; 2 shafts
Speed, knots: 27
Range, n miles: 600 at 18 kt
Complement: 5
Guns: 1 — 7.62 mm MG.
Radars: Raytheon R40X; I-band.

Comment: One of many of this type, provided by the US, throughout the Caribbean navies. Aluminium construction.

LEVERA ***9/1995, SeaArk Marine*** / 0064683

2 BOSTON WHALERS (PB)

Displacement, tons: 1.3 full load
Dimensions, feet (metres): 22.3 × 7.4 × 1.2 *(6.7 × 2.3 × 0.4)*
Main machinery: 2 outboards; 240 hp *(179 kW)*
Speed, knots: 40+
Complement: 4
Guns: 1 — 12.7 mm MG.

Comment: Acquired in 1988–89.

BOSTON WHALER ***11/1990, Bob Hanlon*** / 0064682

Guatemala

Country Overview

The Republic of Guatemala is situated in Central America between Mexico to the north, Belize to the east and Honduras and El Salvador to the south-east. With an area of 42,042 square miles, it has an 83 n mile coastline with the Caribbean and a 133 n mile coastline with the Pacific Ocean. The capital city is Guatemala City while the principal Caribbean ports are Puerto Barrios and Santo Tomás de Castilla and Pacific ports are Puerto Quetzal, San José and Champerico. Territorial seas (12 n miles) are claimed. A 200 n mile EEZ has been claimed but the limits are not defined.

Headquarters Appointments

Commander of the Navy:
Rear Admiral Carlos Roberto Campos Sanchez
Commander Caribbean Naval Region:
Captain Luis Alfredo Monterroso de la Moro
Commander Pacific Naval Region:
Captain Rafael Alfonso Renau Franco

Personnel

(a) 2009: 1,250 (130 officers) including 500 Marines (2 battalions) (mostly volunteers)
(b) 2¼ years' national service

Bases

Pacific: Puerto Quetzal (HQ), Puerto San Jose, Champerico
Atlantic: Santo Tomás de Castilla (HQ), Puerto Barrios, Livingston

PATROL FORCES

Notes: (1) There is also a naval manned Ferry *15 de Enero* (T 691) and a 69 ft launch *Orca* which was built locally in 1996/97.
(2) Three sail training craft, *Mendieta, Margarita* and *Ostuncalco* are based at Santo Thomás de Castilla.
(3) Two launches were reported donated by the Guatemalan government and the US Embassy in 2005.
(4) There are two 11 m personnel landing craft *Picuda* D 361 and *Barracuda* D 362.
(5) The acquisition of 10 small patrol craft from Brazil was announced in April 2008.

1 BROADSWORD CLASS (COASTAL PATROL CRAFT) (PB)

Name	*No*	*Builders*	*Commissioned*
KUKULKÁN	GC 1051 (ex-P 1051)	Halter Marine	4 Aug 1976

Displacement, tons: 90.5 standard; 110 full load
Dimensions, feet (metres): 105 × 20.4 × 6.3 *(32 × 6.2 × 1.9)*
Main machinery: 2 Detroit 8V 92TA Model 91; 1,300 hp *(970 kW)*; 2 shafts
Speed, knots: 22
Range, n miles: 1,150 at 20 kt
Complement: 20 (5 officers)
Guns: 2 Oerlikon GAM/204 GK 20 mm. 2—7.62 mm MGs.
Radars: Surface search: Furuno; I-band.

Comment: As the flagship she used to rotate between Pacific and Atlantic bases every two years but has remained in the Pacific since 1989. Rearmed with 20 mm guns in 1989. These were replaced by GAM guns in 1990–91 when the ship received a new radar. Refitted again in 1996 with new engines.

KUKULKÁN *12/2004, Julio Montes* / 1129555

2 SEWART CLASS (COASTAL PATROL CRAFT) (PB)

Name	*No*	*Builders*	*Commissioned*
UTATLAN	GC 851 (ex-P 851)	Sewart, Louisiana	May 1967
SUBTENIENTE OSORIO SARAVIA	GC 852 (ex-P 852)	Sewart, Louisiana	Nov 1972

Displacement, tons: 54 full load
Dimensions, feet (metres): 85 × 18.7 × 7.2 *(25.9 × 5.7 × 2.2)*
Main machinery: 2 Detroit 8V 92TA Model 91; 1,300 hp *(970 kW)*; 2 shafts
Speed, knots: 22
Range, n miles: 400 at 12 kt
Complement: 17 (4 officers)
Guns: 1 Oerlikon GAM/204 GK 20 mm. 2—7.62 mm MGs.
Radars: Surface search: Furuno; I-band.

Comment: Aluminium superstructure. Both rearmed with 20 mm guns, and 75 mm recoilless removed in 1990. P 851 is based in the Atlantic; P 852 in the Pacific. Refitted in 1995–96 with new engines.

SUBTENIENTE OSORIO SARAVIA *12/2004, Julio Montes* / 1129556

6 CUTLASS CLASS (5 COASTAL PATROL CRAFT AND 1 SURVEY CRAFT) (PB)

Name	*No*	*Builders*	*Commissioned*
TECUN UMAN	GC 651 (ex-P 651)	Halter Marine	26 Nov 1971
KAIBIL BALAN	GC 652 (ex-P 652)	Halter Marine	8 Feb 1972
AZUMANCHE	GC 653 (ex-P 653)	Halter Marine	8 Feb 1972
TZACOL	GC 654 (ex-P 654)	Halter Marine	10 Mar 1976
BITOL	GC 655 (ex-P 655)	Halter Marine	4 Aug 1976
GUCUMAZ	BH 656 (ex-GC 656)	Halter Marine	15 May 1981

Displacement, tons: 45 full load
Dimensions, feet (metres): 64.5 × 17 × 3 *(19.7 × 5.2 × 0.9)*
Main machinery: 2 Detroit 8V 92TA Model 91 diesels; 1,300 hp *(970 kW)*; 2 shafts
Speed, knots: 25. **Range, n miles:** 400 at 15 kt
Complement: 10 (2 officers)
Guns: 2 Oerlikon GAM/204 GK 20 mm. 2 or 3—12.7 mm MGs.
Radars: Surface search: Furuno; I-band.

Comment: First five rearmed with 20 mm guns in 1991. P 651, 654 and 655 are in the Atlantic, remainder in the Pacific. Aluminium hulls. *Gucumaz* was used as a survey craft but by 1996 was again serving as a patrol craft with three MGs. Reverted to survey craft in 2004. 654 and 656 refitted in 1994–95, remainder in 1995–97. New engines fitted.

GUCUMAZ *12/2004, Julio Montes* / 1129558

AZUMANCHE *12/2004, Julio Montes* / 1129557

1 DAUNTLESS CLASS (PB)

IXIMCHE

Displacement, tons: 11 full load
Dimensions, feet (metres): 40 × 12.66 × 2.3 *(12.19 × 3.86 × 0.69)*
Main machinery: 2 Caterpillar 3208TA diesels; 850 hp *(635 kW)*; 2 shafts
Speed, knots: 28. **Range, n miles:** 400 at 22 kt
Complement: 5
Guns: 1—7.62 mm MG.
Radars: Surface search: Raytheon R40X; I-band.

Comment: Built by SeaArk, Monticello, of aluminium construction. Donated by US government as foreign aid in 1997.

DAUNTLESS CLASS (Cayman Islands colours) *6/2001, RCIS* / 0121305

6 VIGILANTE CLASS (PBI)

GC 271–276

Displacement, tons: 3.5 full load
Dimensions, feet (metres): 26.6 × 10 × 1.8 *(8.1 × 3 × 0.5)*
Main machinery: 2 Evinrude outboards; 600 hp *(448 kW)*
Speed, knots: 40+
Complement: 4
Guns: 1 — 12.7 mm MG.
Radars: Surface search: Furuno; I-band.

Comment: Ordered in 1993 from Boston Whaler. Delivered in 1994 and divided three to each coast.

GC 275 — *12/1999* / 0104574

20 RIVER PATROL CRAFT (PBR)

Group A	Group B	Group C	Group D
DENEB	LAGO DE ATITLAN	CHOCHAB	MERO
SIRIUS	MAZATENANGO	ALIOTH	SARDINA
PROCYON	RETALHULEU	MIRFA	PAMPANA
VEGA	ESCUINTLA	SCHEDAR	MAVRO-I
POLLUX		COMAMEFA	
SPICA			
STELLA MARIS			

Comment: Group A are wooden hull craft with a speed of 19 kt. Group B have aluminium hulls and a speed of 28 kt. Group C are probably of Israeli design and Group D are commercial craft caught smuggling and confiscated. All can be armed with 7.62 mm MGs and are used by Marine battalions as well as the Navy.

CHOCHAB AND COMAMEFA — *2/1996, Julio Montes* / 0064686

Guinea

Country Overview

A former French colony, The Republic of Guinea became independent in 1958. Located in west Africa, the country has an area of 94,926 square miles, a 173 n mile coastline with the Atlantic Ocean and includes the Iles de Los. It is bordered to the north by Guinea-Bissau and Senegal and to the south by Liberia and Sierra Leone. The capital, largest city and principal port is Conakry. Territorial seas (12 n miles) are claimed. A 200 n mile Exclusive Economic Zone (EEZ) has been claimed but the limits have not been formally agreed. Fishery Protection may be provided by civilian contractors.

Personnel

(a) 2009: 400 officers and men
(b) 2 years' conscript service

Bases

Conakry, Kakanda

Notes: (1) A number of craft, including two Zhuk, two Bogomol, two Stinger and two Swiftships *(Vigilante* P 300 and *Intrepide* P 328*)* are laid up alongside. Some of these might be resurrected to combat piracy problems in the region. A Damen 13 m patrol boat, *Matakang*, is reported to have been delivered in 1999 and there are two MonArk 8 m Stinger craft, P 30 and P 35, which were delivered in 1985.
(2) Development of the port of Conakry is under consideration.

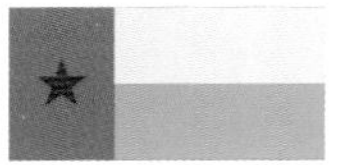

Guinea-Bissau

Country Overview

A former Portuguese colony, The Republic of Guinea-Bissau gained independence in 1974. Located in west Africa, the country has an area of 13,948 square miles, a 189 n mile coastline with the Atlantic Ocean and includes about 60 offshore islands, among them the Bijagós (Bissagos) Islands. It is bordered to the north by Senegal and to the south by Guinea. The capital, largest city and principal port is Bissau. Other ports include Cacheu and Bolama. Territorial seas (12 n miles) are claimed. A 200 n mile Exclusive Economic Zone (EEZ) has been claimed and has been partially defined by boundary agreements.

Headquarters Appointments

Head of Navy: Commander Americo Bubo Na Tchute

Personnel

(a) 2009: 310 officers and men
(b) Voluntary service

Base

Bissau

Maritime Aircraft

A Cessna 337 patrol aircraft is used for offshore surveillance, when serviceable.

PATROL FORCES

Notes: (1) One Rodman R 800 8.7 m patrol craft with a speed of 28 kt acquired in 1999.
(2) One 15 m Peterson Mk 4 class, *Ilha de Caio*, is reported unserviceable.

2 ALFEITE TYPE (COASTAL PATROL CRAFT) (PC)

Name	*No*	*Builders*	*Commissioned*
CACINE	LF 01	Arsenal do Alfeite	9 Mar 1994
CACHEU	LF 02	Arsenal do Alfeite	9 Mar 1994

Displacement, tons: 55 full load
Dimensions, feet (metres): 64.6 × 19 × 10.6 *(19.7 × 5.8 × 3.2)*
Main machinery: 3 MTU 12V 183 TE92 diesels; 3,000 hp(m) *(2.2 MW)* maximum; 3 Hamilton MH 521 water-jets
Speed, knots: 28
Complement: 9 (1 officer)
Radars: Navigation: Furuno FR 2010; I-band.

Comment: Ordered from Portugal in 1991. GRP hulls. Used for fishery protection patrols and customs duties. Operational status doubtful.

CACHEU — *3/1994, Arsenal do Alfeite* / 0064688

Guyana

Country Overview

Formerly known as British Guiana, the Cooperative Republic of Guyana became an independent state in 1966. With an area of 83,000 square miles it has borders to the east with Suriname, to the west with Venezuela and to the south with Brazil; its 270 n mile coastline is on the Atlantic Ocean. The capital, largest city and chief port is Georgetown. Territorial seas (12 n miles) and a fisheries zone (200 n miles) are claimed. A 200 n mile Exclusive Economic Zone (EEZ) has also been claimed but the limits are not defined. Rebuilding of the Coast Guard started in 2001.

Headquarters Appointments

Commanding Officer, Coast Guard:
Commander John Flores

Personnel

(a) 2009: 180
(b) Voluntary service

Bases

Georgetown (HQ), Benab (Corentyne), Morawhanna

PATROL FORCES

1 RIVER CLASS (COASTAL PATROL CRAFT) (PBO)

Name	*No*	*Builders*	*Commissioned*
ESSEQUIBO (ex-*Orwell*)	1026 (ex-M 2011)	Richards, Great Yarmouth	27 Nov 1985

Displacement, tons: 890 full load
Dimensions, feet (metres): 156 × 34.5 × 9.5 *(47.5 × 10.5 × 2.9)*
Main machinery: 2 Ruston 6 RKC diesels; 3,100 hp(m) *(2.3 MW)* sustained; 2 shafts
Speed, knots: 14. **Range, n miles:** 4,500 at 10 kt
Complement: 32 (4 officers)
Guns: 1—20 mm.
2—7.62 mm MGs.
Radars: Surface search: 2 Racal Decca TM 1226C; I-band.

Comment: Ex-UK River class transferred on 22 June 2001 having previously been employed as patrol ship and then officers' training ship.

ESSEQUIBO *7/2001, Derek Fox* / 0114272

4 TYPE 44 CLASS (WPB)

BARRACUDA **HYMARA** **PIRAI** **TIRAPUKA**

Displacement, tons: 18 full load
Dimensions, feet (metres): 44 × 12.8 × 3.6 *(13.5 × 3.9 × 1.1)*
Main machinery: 2 Detroit 6V-38 diesels; 185 hp *(136 kW)*; 2 shafts
Speed, knots: 14
Range, n miles: 215 at 10 kt
Complement: 3

Comment: Acquired from the US and recommissioned on 9 August 2001.

TYPE 44 (Uruguay Colours) *5/2000, Hartmut Ehlers* / 0105801

Honduras

FUERZA NAVAL REPUBLICA

Country Overview

The Republic of Honduras is one of the largest Central American republics. With an area of 43,433 square miles, it is situated between El Salvador and Guatemala to the west and Nicaragua to the south and east. It has a 350 n mile coastline with the Caribbean and a 93 n mile coastline with the Pacific Ocean. The capital and largest city is Tegucigalpa while the principal Caribbean ports are La Ceiba and Puerto Cortés and Pacific port is Amapala. Territorial seas (12 nmiles) are claimed. A 200 n mile EEZ is claimed and has been partly defined by boundary agreements.

Headquarters Appointments

Commanding Officer, General HQ:
Capitan de Navio Don Juan Pablo Rodríguez Rodríguez

Personnel

2009: 1,100 including 450 marines

Bases

Tegucigalpa (General HQ)
Puerto Cortés, Puerto Castilla (Atlantic HQ), Amapala (Pacific HQ), La Ceiba, Puerto Trujillo

PATROL FORCES

Notes: (1) In addition there may be three Piranha river craft still in limited service.
(2) Five 23 m catamarans reported to have been ordered in 2004.
(3) Two 11 m personnel landing craft are used for anti-drug operations.
(4) Four interceptor craft, capable of 60 kt, were donated by the United States in 2007.

3 SWIFT 105 ft CLASS (FAST ATTACK CRAFT—GUN) (PB)

GUAYMURAS FNH 101 **HONDURAS** FNH 102 **HIBUERAS** FNH 103

Displacement, tons: 111 full load
Dimensions, feet (metres): 105 × 23.6 × 7 *(32 × 7.2 × 2.1)*
Main machinery: 2 MTU 16V 538TB90 diesels; 6,000 hp(m) *(4.4 MW)* sustained; 2 shafts
Speed, knots: 30
Range, n miles: 1,200 at 18 kt
Complement: 17 (3 officers)
Guns: 6 Hispano-Suiza 20 mm (2 triple). 2—12.7 mm MGs.
Weapons control: Kollmorgen 350 optronic director.
Radars: Surface search: Furuno; I-band.

Comment: First delivered by Swiftships, Morgan City in April 1977 and last two in March 1980. Aluminium hulls. Armament changed 1996–98.

HONDURAS and HIBUERAS *12/2004, Julio Montes* / 1129559

1 GUARDIAN CLASS (COASTAL PATROL CRAFT) (PB)

TEGUCIGALPA FNH 104 (ex-FNH 107)

Displacement, tons: 94 full load
Dimensions, feet (metres): 106 × 20.6 × 7 *(32.3 × 6.3 × 2.1)*
Main machinery: 3 Detroit 16V-92TA diesels; 2,070 hp *(1.54 MW)* sustained; 3 shafts
Speed, knots: 30
Range, n miles: 1,500 at 18 kt
Complement: 17 (3 officers)
Guns: 1 General Electric Sea Vulcan 20 mm Gatling.
3 Hispano Suiza 20 mm (1 triple). 2—12.7 mm MGs.
Weapons control: Kollmorgen 350 optronic director.
Radars: Surface search: Furuno; I-band.

Comment: Delivered by Lantana Boatyard, Florida August 1986. Second of class, *Copan*, no longer in service. A third of the class, completed in May 1984, became the Jamaican *Paul Bogle*. Aluminium hulls. Operational status doubtful.

GUARDIAN CLASS *7/1986, Giorgio Arra* / 0506000

6 SWIFT 65 ft CLASS (COASTAL PATROL CRAFT) (PB)

NACAOME (ex-*Aguan*, ex-*Gral*) FNH 651
GOASCORAN (ex-*General J T Cabanas*) FNH 652
PATUCA FNH 653
ULUA FNH 654
CHOLUTECA FNH 655
RIO COCO FNH 656

Displacement, tons: 33 full load
Dimensions, feet (metres): 69.9 × 17.1 × 5.2 *(21.3 × 5.2 × 1.6)*
Main machinery: 2 GM 12V-71TA diesels; 840 hp *(627 kW)* sustained; 2 shafts (FNH 651-2)
2 MTU 8V 396 TB93 diesels; 2,180 hp(m) *(1.6 MW)* sustained; 2 shafts (FNH 653-5)
Speed, knots: 25 (FNH 651-2); 36 (FNH 653-6)
Range, n miles: 2,000 at 22 kt (FNH 651-2)
Complement: 9 (2 officers)
Guns: 2—12.7 mm MGs. 3—7.62 MGs.
Radars: Surface search: Racal Decca; I-band.

Comment: First pair built by Swiftships, Morgan City originally for Haiti. Contract cancelled and Honduras bought the two that had been completed in 1973–74. Delivered in 1977. Last four ordered in 1979 and delivered 1980.

PATUCA *5/1993* / 0064690

1 SWIFT 85 ft CLASS (COASTAL PATROL CRAFT) (PB)

CHAMELECON (ex-*Rio Kuringwas*) FNH 8501

Displacement, tons: 60 full load
Dimensions, feet (metres): 85 × 20 × 5 *(25.9 × 6.1 × 1.8)*
Main machinery: 2 Detroit diesels; 2 shafts
Speed, knots: 25
Complement: 10 (2 officers)
Radars: Surface search: Racal/Decca; I-band.

Comment: Built by Swiftships, Morgan City in about 1967 for Nicaragua from where it was transferred in 1979.

CHAMELECON *2000, Honduran Navy* / 0105811

5 OUTRAGE CLASS (RIVER PATROL CRAFT) (PBR)

Displacement, tons: 2.2 full load
Dimensions, feet (metres): 24.9 × 7.9 × 1.3 *(7.6 × 2.4 × 0.4)*
Main machinery: 2 Evinrude outboards; 300 hp *(224 kW)*
Speed, knots: 30
Range, n miles: 200 at 30 kt
Complement: 4
Guns: 1—12.7 mm MG. 2—7.62 mm MGs.
Radars: Navigation: Furuno 3600; I-band.

Comment: Built by Boston Whaler in 1982. Seven deleted so far. Radar is sometimes embarked.

OUTRAGE *10/1997, Julio Montes* / 0012491

4 TYPE 44 CLASS (WPB)

GUANAJA (ex-4434)
ROATAN (ex-44390)
UTILA (ex-44351)
CAYO COCHINAS (ex-44365)

Displacement, tons: 18 full load
Dimensions, feet (metres): 44 × 12.8 × 3.6 *(13.5 × 3.9 × 1.1)*
Main machinery: 2 Detroit 6V-38 diesels; 185 hp *(136 kW)*; 2 shafts
Speed, knots: 14
Range, n miles: 215 at 10 kt
Complement: 3

Comment: Acquired from the US in December 2005.

PREFECTURA 442 (Uruguay colours) *6/2005, A E Galarce* / 1133602

15 RIVER CRAFT (PBR)

Comment: 4.6 m craft acquired from Taiwan in 1996. Nine based at Castilla, three at Cortes and three at Amapala. Single Mercury outboard engine. Carry a 7.62 mm MG. Three sunk in 1998.

PBR *10/1997, R Torrento* / 0012492

AUXILIARIES

Notes: In addition there are two ex-US LCM 8 (*Warunta* FNH 7401, *Tansin* FNH 7402) transferred in 1987. Both are used as transport vessels.

LCM 8 *2000, Honduran Navy* / 0105812

1 LANDING CRAFT (LCU)

PUNTA CAXINAS FNH 1491

Displacement, tons: 625 full load
Dimensions, feet (metres): 149 × 33 × 6.5 *(45.4 × 10 × 2)*
Main machinery: 3 Caterpillar 3412 diesels; 1,821 hp *(1.4 MW)* sustained; 3 shafts
Speed, knots: 14
Range, n miles: 3,500 at 12 kt
Complement: 18 (3 officers)
Cargo capacity: 100 tons equipment or 50,000 gallons dieso plus 4 standard containers
Radars: Navigation: Furuno 3600; I-band.

Comment: Ordered in 1986 from Lantana, Florida, and commissioned in May 1988.

PUNTA CAXINAS *12/2004, Julio Montes* / 1129560

Hong Kong

POLICE MARINE REGION

Country Overview

Formerly a British colony, the Hong Kong Special Administrative Region of China reverted to Chinese sovereignty on 30 June 1997. While China has assumed responsibility for foreign affairs and defence, the territory is to maintain its own legal, social, and economic systems until at least 2047. Hong Kong comprises three main regions, Hong Kong Island (29 sq miles), Kowloon Peninsula and Stonecutters Island (6 sq miles) and the New Territories (380 sq miles). As with the remainder of China, territorial seas (12 n miles) are claimed. An EEZ (200 n mile) is also claimed but the limits have not been defined by boundary agreements. The role of the Marine Police is to maintain the integrity of the sea boundary and territorial waters of Hong Kong, enforce the laws of Hong Kong in territorial waters, prevent illegal immigration by sea, SAR in territorial and adjacent waters, and casualty evacuation.

Headquarters Appointments

Regional Commander (Marine):
Chang Mo See
Deputy Regional Commander (Marine):
J A Cox

Organisation

Marine Police Regional HQ, Sai Wan Ho
Bases at Ma Liu Shui, Tui Min Hoi, Tai Lam Chung, Aberdeen, Sai Wan Ho

Personnel

(a) 2009: 2,600
(b) Voluntary service

POLICE

4 SURVEILLANCE BARGES (YAG)

PB 1–4

Displacement, tons: 227
Dimensions, feet (metres): 98.4 × 42.6 × 2.6 *(30.0 × 13 × 0.8)*
Main machinery: 2 Cummins 75 MDG DB diesels
Complement: 10
Radars: Surface search: Decca; I-band.

Comment: Steel-hulled barges. PB 1-2 (built by Guangzhou Waterway Bureau Shipyards) delivered in June 2002 and PB 3-4 (built by Leung Wan Kee Shipyards) in October 2007. PB 1-2 are moored in Deep Bay, PB 3 in Rocky Harbour and PB 4 at Kat O (Crooked Island).

PB 1 *6/2004, Hong Kong Police* / 0589752

1 TRAINING VESSEL (WAX)

PL 3

Displacement, tons: 420 full load
Dimensions, feet (metres): 131.2 × 28.2 × 10.5 *(40 × 8.6 × 3.2)*
Main machinery: 2 Caterpillar 3512TA diesels; 2,350 hp *(1.75 MW)* sustained; 2 shafts
Speed, knots: 14. **Range, n miles:** 1,500 at 14 kt
Complement: 7
Radars: Surface search: 2 Racal Decca ARPA C342/8; I-band.

Comment: Built by Hong Kong SY in 27 July 1987 and commissioned 1 February 1988. Steel hull. Racal ARPA and GPS Electronic Chart system. 12.7 mm MGs removed in mid-1996. Can carry up to 30 armed police for short periods. Former command vessel converted to a training role.

PL 3 *6/2004, Hong Kong Police* / 0589753

6 KEKA CLASS (PATROL CRAFT) (WPB)

PL 60–65

Displacement, tons: 105
Dimensions, feet (metres): 98.4 × 20.7 × 7.2 *(30.0 × 6.3 × 2.2)*
Main machinery: 2 MTU 12V-396TE 84 diesels
Speed, knots: 25. **Range, n miles:** 360 at 15 kt
Complement: 14
Radars: Surface search: Decca; I-band.

Comment: Aluminium-hulled craft built by Cheoy Lee Shipyards Ltd to replace Damen Mk1 class patrol craft. Delivered in 2002, 2004 and 2005.

PL 64 *12/2007, Chris Sattler* / 1170158

10 DAMEN MK III CLASS (PATROL CRAFT) (WPB)

PL 70–73 **PL 75** **PL 77** **PL 79–80** **PL 82–83**

Displacement, tons: 96 full load
Dimensions, feet (metres): 91.2 × 19.0 × 7.2 *(27.8 × 5.8 × 2.2)*
Main machinery: 2 MTU 12V 396 TB83 diesels; 2,965 hp(m) *(2.2 MW)* sustained; 2 shafts
1 Mercedes-Benz OM 424A 12V diesel; 465 hp(m) *(347 kW)* sustained; 1 Kamewa 45 water-jet
Speed, knots: 25 on 3 diesels; 8 on water-jet and cruising diesel
Range, n miles: 600 at 14 kt
Complement: 14
Radars: Surface search: Racal Decca; I-band.

Comment: Steel-hulled craft constructed by Chung Wah SB & Eng Co Ltd, 1985–86. 12.7 mm MGs removed in mid-1996.

PL 82 *12/2007, Chris Sattler* / 1170157

6 PROTECTOR (ASI 315) CLASS (COMMAND/PATROL CRAFT) (WPB)

PL 51–56

Displacement, tons: 150 full load
Dimensions, feet (metres): 107 × 26.9 × 8.2 *(32.6 × 8.2 × 2.5)*
Main machinery: 2 Caterpillar 3516TA diesels; 5,600 hp *(4.17 MW)* sustained; 2 shafts; 1 Caterpillar 3412TA; 764 hp *(570 kW)* sustained; Hamilton HM 521 waterjet (centreline)
Speed, knots: 30. **Range, n miles:** 600 at 18 kt
Complement: 19
Weapons control: GEC V3901 optronic director.
Radars: Surface search: Racal Decca; I-band.

Comment: Built by Transfield Australian Shipbuilding Industries and completed in 1993. As well as patrol work, the craft provide command platforms for Divisional commanders. 12.7 mm guns removed in 1996 and the optronic director is used for surveillance only.

PL 54 *12/2007, Chris Sattler* / 1170156

5 HARBOUR PATROL CRAFT (WPB)

PL 11–17

Displacement, tons: 35 full load
Dimensions, feet (metres): 52.5 × 15.1 × 4.9 *(16 × 4.6 × 1.5)*
Main machinery: 2 Cummins NTA-855-M diesels; 700 hp *(522 kW)* sustained; 2 shafts
Speed, knots: 12
Complement: 6
Radars: Surface search: Racal Decca; I-band.

Comment: Built by Chung Wah SB & Eng Co Ltd in 1987–88.

PL 17 *12/2007, Chris Sattler* / 1335253

5 SEA STALKER 1500 CLASS (INTERCEPTOR CRAFT) (HSIC)

PL 85–89

Displacement, tons: 8.7 full load
Dimensions, feet (metres): 48.6 × 9.5 × 2.6 *(14.8 × 2.7 × 1.2)*
Main machinery: 3 Innovation Marine Sledge Hammers; 1,590 hp(m) *(1.2 MW)*; 3 shafts
Speed, knots: 60; 45 in Sea State 3
Complement: 5
Radars: Surface search: Raytheon; I-band.

Comment: Built by Damen, Gorinchem in 1999. Used by the Small Boat Division.

PL 86 *6/2004, Hong Kong Police* / 0589746

4 SEASPRAY CLASS (LOGISTIC CRAFT) (YFB)

PL 46–49

Displacement, tons: 10.7 full load
Dimensions, feet (metres): 37.4 × 13.8 × 3.9 *(11.4 × 4.2 × 1.2)*
Main machinery: 2 Caterpillar 3208TA diesels; 700 hp *(522 kW)* sustained; 2 shafts
Speed, knots: 25
Complement: 4
Radars: Navigation: Koden; I-band.

Comment: Built by Seaspray Boats, Fremantle in 1992. Catamaran hulls capable of carrying 16 police officers.

PL 47 *12/2007, Chris Sattler* / 1170154

11 SEASPRAY CLASS (INSHORE PATROL CRAFT) (WPB)

PL 22–32

Displacement, tons: 8.7 full load
Dimensions, feet (metres): 32.5 × 13.8 × 3.9 *(9.9 × 4.2 × 1.2)*
Main machinery: 2 Caterpillar 3208TA diesels (Caterpillar C7 diesels PL 25 and 29); 700 hp (908 PL 25, 29) *(522 kW)* (677 PL 25, 29); 2 shafts
Speed, knots: 35
Complement: 4
Radars: Surface search: Koden; I-band.

Comment: Built by Seaspray Boats, Fremantle in 1992–93.

PL 28 *12/2007, Chris Sattler* / 1170152

9 INSHORE PATROL CRAFT (WPB)

PL 20–21 **PL 90–96**

Displacement, tons: 2.3
Dimensions, feet (metres): 26.2 × 10.2 × 3.3 *(8.1 × 3.1 × 1.0)*
Main machinery: 2 outboards; 540 hp *(403 kW)*
Speed, knots: 42
Complement: 3
Radars: Surface search: Koden; I-band.

Comment: Details given are for *PL 20-21* which are Sharkcat class of catamaran construction, commissioned in October 1988. *PL 90-92* are Boston Whaler Guardians with 2 Johnson 115 hp outboards, and *PL 93-96* are Boston Whaler Vigilants with 2 Johnson 250 hp outboards. The Whalers were all delivered in 1997 and are capable of speeds in excess of 33 kt.

PL 93 *12/2007, Chris Sattler* / 1335252

6 CHEOY LEE CLASS (INSHORE PATROL CRAFT) (WPB)

PL 40–45

Displacement, tons: 19.4
Dimensions, feet (metres): 42.9 × 13.2 × 2.6 *(13.07 × 4.0 × 0.8)*
Main machinery: 2 MAN D2842LE403 diesels; 1,420 hp *(1.06 MW)* sustained; 2 Hamilton water-jets
Speed, knots: 35
Complement: 4
Radars: Surface search: Bridgemaster E 180; I-band.

Comment: Based upon a design from Peterson Shipbuilders, these shallow draft vessels were constructed by Cheoy Lee Shipyards Ltd and delivered in 2000.

PL 42 *12/2007, Chris Sattler* / 1335251

8 HIGH SPEED INTERCEPTORS (HSIC)

PV 30–37

Displacement, tons: 2.7 full load
Dimensions, feet (metres): 28.3 × 8.7 × 2.4 *(8.5 × 2.6 × 0.7)*
Main machinery: 2 Mercury outboards; 500 hp *(373 kW)*
Speed, knots: 51
Complement: 3

Comment: Built by Queensland Ships in 1997. Used by the Small Boat Division.

PV 35 *12/2007, Chris Sattler* / 1170151

6 + 11 LUNG-TEH CLASS (PATROL CRAFT) (PBF)

PL 5–10

Displacement, tons: 39
Dimensions, feet (metres): 62.3 × 16.4 × 3.3 *(19.0 × 5.0 × 1.0)*
Main machinery: 3 Caterpillar C32 diesels; 3,345 hp *(2.5 MW)*; 3 Hamilton waterjets
Speed, knots: 45
Complement: 8

Comment: Contract for the construction of 17 patrol craft signed with Lung-Teh Shipyard, Taiwan on 19 September 2006. Aluminium construction. The first six entered service in November 2007 with the remainder to follow by 2009.

PL 5 *12/2007, Chris Sattler* / 1170153

6 HIGH-SPEED INTERCEPTORS (PBF)

PV 5–10

Displacement, tons: To be announced
Dimensions, feet (metres): 32.4 × 8.4 × 2.0 *(9.88 × 2.55 × 0.6)*
Main machinery: 2 Mercury Verado outboards; 550 hp *(410 kW)*
Speed, knots: 50
Complement: 3

Comment: Constructed by Brisbane Ship Constructions Ltd in 2007.

PV 6 *6/2007, Hong Kong Police* / 1335250

3 FB 55SC CLASS (INSHORE PATROL CRAFT) (PBF)

Displacement, tons: 10.2
Dimensions, feet (metres): 53.9 × 9.3 × 2.75 *(16.43 × 2.85 × 0.84)*
Main machinery: 3 Seatek diesels; 2,250 hp *(1.7 MW)*; surface piercing propeller
Speed, knots: 65 approx
Complement: 8

Comment: Designed by FB design of Italy. Delivered in 2003. Kevlar monohull fast inshore patrol craft for maritime law enforcement tasks. Eight seats in forward compartment.

FB 55SC *12/2007, Chris Sattler* / 1170150

1 FB RIB 42SC CLASS (INSHORE PATROL CRAFT) (PB)

Displacement, tons: 6 approx
Dimensions, feet (metres): 43.3 × 11.6 × 2.3 *(13.2 × 3.55 × 0.7)*
Main machinery: 2 Caterpillar diesels; 1,400 hp *(1.04 MW)*; surface piercing propeller
Speed, knots: 63
Complement: 3

Comment: Designed by FB design, Italy. Rigid inflatable Kevlar monohull for maritime law enforcement tasks. Delivered 2004.

RIB 42SC *12/2007, Chris Sattler* / 1170149

CUSTOMS

Headquarters Appointments

Senior Superintendent Ports and Marine Command:
Li Chun-fai

Notes: The Marine Enforcement Group is based at Stonecutters Island. There are five Sector Command launches of which there are Damen 26 m craft completed in 1986 by Chung Wah SB & Eng Co Ltd, Kowloon. In all essentials these craft are sisters of the 10 operated by the Hong Kong Police with the exception of the latter's slow speed waterjet. Names: *Sea Glory* (CE 6), *Sea Guardian* (CE 5), *Sea Leader* (CE 2). Two 32 m Challenger launches, *Sea Reliance* (CE 8) and *Sea Fidelity* (CE 9) were commissioned in October 2000. With a gross tonnage of 125 tonnes, the craft have a maximum speed of 28 kt. Equipped with a 'sea-rider' they are also fitted with night vision aids and narcotics and explosives scanning devices. There are also four 17 m FB design high-speed pursuit craft (CE 15-18), capable of 49 kt, and two Boston Whaler 10 m shallow-water launches (CE 12-13) capable of 39 kt.

CE 2 *6/2007, Chris Sattler* / 1335249

CE 16 *6/2007, Ports and Maritime Command* / 1167810

CE 13 *6/2007, Ports and Maritime Command* / 1167809

LAND-BASED MARITIME AIRCRAFT

Notes: All aircraft belong to the Government Flying Service based at Hong Kong International Airport.

Numbers/Type: 3 Eurocopter AS 332 L2 Super Puma.
Operational speed: 130 kt *(240 km/h).*
Service ceiling: 15,090 ft *(4,600 m).*
Range: 672 n miles *(1,245 km).*
Role/Weapon systems: SAR/coastal surveillance, Medevac and transport. Sensors: radar, Spectrolab searchlight. Weapons: Unarmed. Medical equipment and up to six stretchers. Ordered on 17 September 1999. The aircraft entered service in April 2002.

AS 332 *6/2005, Government Flying Service* / 1127922

Numbers/Type: 2 BAE Jetstream J 41.
Operational speed: 260 kt *(482 km/h).*
Service ceiling: 26,000 ft *(7,925 m).*
Range: 774 n miles *(1,433 km).*
Role/Weapon systems: SAR (command and control), airborne surveillance, survey and photography. Sensors: Radar, FLIR, survey camera, VHF/UHF/DF.

Jetstream *6/2005, Government Flying Service* / 1127924

Numbers/Type: 4 Eurocopter EC 155B1.
Operational speed: 140 kt *(260 km/h).*
Service ceiling: 16,760 ft *(5,110 m).*
Range: 432 n miles *(800 km).*
Role/Weapon systems: SAR, Medevac, VIP transport; enlarged variant of 'Dauphin'. Sensors: Radar, FLIR, searchlight, siren, loudspeaker. Weapons: Unarmed. Two stretchers. Ordered on 17 September 1999; aircraft delivered in late 2002.

EC 155 *6/2005, Government Flying Service* / 1127923

Hungary

Country Overview

A landlocked central European country, the Republic of Hungary has an area of 35,919 square miles and is bordered by Slovakia, Ukraine, Romania, Serbia, Croatia, Slovenia and Austria. Budapest is the country's capital and largest city. The country is divided into two general regions by the principal river, the Danube, which flows for 145 n miles north-south through the centre of the country and serves as a major artery of the transport system.

Diplomatic Representation

Defence Attaché in London:
Lieutenant Colonel Árpád Ibolya

Bases

Budapest.

Personnel

(a) 2009: 100
(b) National service replaced by a professional army on 3 November 2004.

MINE WARFARE FORCES

3 NESTIN CLASS (RIVER MINESWEEPERS) (MSR)

ÓBUDA AM 22 **DUNAÚJVÁROS** AM 31 **DUNAFOLDVAR** AM 32

Displacement, tons: 72.3 full load
Dimensions, feet (metres): 87.1 × 21.3 × 3.9 *(26.5 × 6.5 × 1.2)*
Main machinery: 2 Torpedo 12-cyl diesels; 520 hp(m) *(382 kW)*; 2 shafts
Speed, knots: 15. **Range, n miles:** 810 at 11 kt
Complement: 17 (1 officer)
Guns: 6 Hispano 20 mm (1 quad M75 fwd, 2 single M70 aft).
Mines: 24 ground mines.
Radars: Navigation: Decca 101; I-band.

Comment: Built by Brodotehnika, Belgrade in 1980–82. Full magnetic/acoustic and wire sweeping capabilities. Kram minesweeping system employs a towed sweep at 200 m. The ships form the first 'Honved' Ordnance Disposal and Warship Regiment.

ÓBUDA *10/1998, Hungary Maritime Wing* / 0064703

2 AN-2 CLASS (RIVER PATROL VESSELS) (PBR)

ERCSI 542-051 **BAJA** 542-054

Displacement, tons: 10.5 full load
Dimensions, feet (metres): 44.0 × 12.5 × 1.97 *(13.4 × 3.8 × 0.6)*
Main machinery: 2 Volvo Penta diesels; 380 hp(m) *(283 kW)* sustained; 2 shafts
Speed, knots: 19
Complement: 7 (1 officer)

Comment: Last survivors of an original 45 units built at Duna Shipyard in 1953. Refitted 2005. Employed on river patrol, diving support and disaster relief duties.

AN-2 CLASS *6/2007, Hungary Maritime Wing* / 1170159

Iceland

LANDHELGISGAESLAN

Country Overview

An island republic, the Republic of Iceland lies just south of the Arctic Circle in the North Atlantic Ocean about 162 n miles southeast of Greenland and 432 n miles northwest of Scotland. With an area of 39,769 square miles, the country has a 2,695 n mile coastline. Reykjavik is the capital, largest city and principal port. Territorial waters (12 n miles) are claimed. A 200 n mile Exclusive Economic Zone (EEZ) has also been claimed although the limits are not fully defined by boundary agreements. The Coast Guard Service deals with fishery protection, salvage, rescue, security, pollution control, hydrographic research, lighthouse duties and bomb disposal.

Headquarters Appointments

Director General of Coast Guard:
Commodore Georg K Lárusson

Personnel

2009: 145 officers and men

Colours

Since 1990 vessels have been marked with red, white and blue diagonal stripes on the ships' side and the Coast Guard name (Landhelgisgaeslan).

Bases

Reykjavík

Research Ships

A number of government Research Ships bearing RE pennant numbers operate off Iceland.

Maritime Patrol Aircraft

Maritime aircraft include a Fokker Friendship plus two AS 332 Super Puma and one SA 365 Dauphin. The Fokker Friendship is to be replaced in mid-2009 by a Bombardier Dash-8 maritime surveillance aircraft.

COAST GUARD

2 AEGIR CLASS (PSOH)

Name	*No*	*Builders*	*Commissioned*
AEGIR	–	Aalborg Vaerft, Denmark	1968
TYR	–	Dannebrog Vaerft, Denmark	15 Mar 1975

Displacement, tons: 1,128 (1,214 *Tyr*) standard; 1,500 full load
Dimensions, feet (metres): 229.1 (233.4 *Tyr*) × 32.8 × 15.1 *(69.8 (71.1) × 10.0 × 4.6)*
Main machinery: 2 MAN/Burmeister & Wain 8L 40/54 diesels; 13,200 hp(m) *(9.68 MW)* sustained; 2 shafts; cp props
Speed, knots: 19 *(Aegir)*; 20 *(Tyr)*. **Range, n miles**: 9,000 at 18 kt
Complement: 19
Guns: 1 Bofors 40 mm/60 Mk 3.
Radars: Surface search/navigation: Sperry; E/F/I-band.

Comment: Similar ships but *Tyr* has a slightly improved design and *Aegir* has no sonar. The hangar is between the funnels. In 1994 a large crane was fitted on the starboard side at the forward end of the flight deck. In 1997 the helicopter deck was extended and a radome fitted on the top of the tower. *Aegir* refitted in Poland in 2005 and *Tyr* in 2006. Work included extension and modernisation of the bridge, upgrade of accommodation and the installation of helicopter-in-flight refuelling equipment.

TYR *9/2008*, Adolfo Ortigueira Gil* / 1335788

1 BALDUR CLASS (AGS/PB)

Name	*No*	*Builders*	*Commissioned*
BALDUR	–	Velsmidja Seydisfjardar	8 May 1991

Displacement, tons: 54 full load
Dimensions, feet (metres): 67.9 × 17.1 × 5.6 *(20.7 × 5.2 × 1.7)*
Main machinery: 2 Caterpillar 3406TA diesels; 640 hp *(480 kW)*; 2 shafts
Speed, knots: 12
Complement: 5
Radars: Navigation: Furuno; I-band.

Comment: Built in an Icelandic Shipyard. Used for survey work and patrol duties.

BALDUR *6/2005, Iceland Coast Guard* / 1153888

1 ODINN CLASS (PSOH)

Name	*No*	*Builders*	*Commissioned*
ODINN	–	Aalborg Vaerft, Denmark	Jan 1960

Displacement, tons: 910 standard; 1,200 full load
Dimensions, feet (metres): 209.0 × 33 × 13 *(63.7 × 10 × 4)*
Main machinery: 2 MAN/Burmeister & Wain diesels; 5,700 hp(m) *(4.19 MW)*; 2 shafts
Speed, knots: 18. **Range, n miles**: 9,500 at 17 kt
Complement: 19
Guns: 1 Bofors 40 mm/60 Mk 3.
Radars: Surface search/navigation: Sperry; E/F/I-band.

Comment: Refitted in Denmark in late 1975 by Aarhus Flydedock AS with a hangar and helicopter deck which was later adapted in 1989 for the operation of RHIB inspection craft; a crane was fitted at the starboard forward end of the flight deck. The original 57 mm gun was replaced in 1990. To be replaced in 2009 by a new vessel. Ulstein UT 512L under construction in Chile.

ODINN *2/2002, L-G Nilsson* / 0561502

0 + 1 ULSTEIN UT 512L (OFFSHORE PATROL SHIP) (PSO)

Name	*No*	*Builders*	*Commissioned*
–	–	ASMAR, Talcahuano	2009

Displacement, tons: 4,000 full load
Dimensions, feet (metres): 307.1 × 50.8 × 16.1 *(93.6 × 15.5 × 4.9)*
Main machinery: 2 Bergen B 32: 40L diesels; 10,730 hp *(8 MW)*; 2 Kamewa Ulstein cp props; two bow thrusters; 1 Kamewa Ulstein 736 kW tunnel thruster; 1 Ulstein Aquamaster swing-up 883 kW azimuth thruster
Speed, knots: 19.5
Complement: 48

Comment: Contract awarded on 1 December 2006 for the construction of a replacement vessel for *Odinn*. The ship, designated UT 512L, is an enlarged design of the Norwegian Coast Guard ship *Harstad*. The Rolls Royce design is for a variety of coastguard and EEZ management roles including offshore standby and rescue, firefighting, salvage, pollution prevention, general law enforcement operations and fishery control. The ship is under construction at ASMAR shipyard in Chile. Further ships may be ordered to replace Iceland's ageing inventory of ships.

UT 512L (artist's impression) *6/2007, Iceland Coast Guard* / 1305270

India

Country Overview

The Republic of India is a federal democracy which gained independence in 1947. It consists of the entire Indian peninsula and parts of the Asian mainland. With an area of 1,269,219 square miles, it is bordered to the north by Pakistan, Tibet, Nepal, China, and Bhutan and to the east by Burma and Bangladesh, which almost separates north-east India from the rest of the country. The status of Jammu and Kashmir is disputed with Pakistan. It has a 4,104 n mile coastline with the Arabian Sea, the Gulf of Mannar (which separates it from Sri Lanka) and the Bay of Bengal. The capital is New Delhi while the largest city is Mumbai. The principal ports include Mumbai, Calcutta, Madras and Vishakapatnam. Territorial waters (12 n miles) are claimed. A 200 n mile EEZ has been claimed although the limits have only been partly defined by boundary agreements.

Headquarters Appointments

Chief of Naval Staff:
Admiral Sureesh Mehta, AVSM, PVSM
Vice Chief of Naval Staff:
Vice Admiral Raman Prem Suthan, AVSM, VSM
Deputy Chief of Naval Staff:
Vice Admiral Anup Singh, AVSM, NM
Chief of Personnel:
Vice Admiral Dalip Kumar Dewan, AVSM
Chief of Material:
Vice Admiral B S Randhawa, AVSM, VSM
Controller Warship Production and Acquisition:
Vice Admiral Dilip Deshpande, VSM

Senior Appointments

Flag Officer Commanding Western Naval Command:
Vice Admiral Jagjit Singh Bedi, PVSM, UYSM, AVSM, VSM
Flag Officer Commanding Eastern Naval Command:
Vice Admiral Nirmal Verma, PVSM, AVSM
Flag Officer Commanding Southern Naval Command:
Vice Admiral Sunil Krishnaji Damle, AVSM, NM, VSM
Commander-in-Chief, Andaman and Nicobar:
Vice Admiral Vijay Shankar
Flag Officer Commanding Western Fleet:
Rear Admiral S P S Cheema
Flag Officer Commanding Eastern Fleet:
Rear Admiral A B Thapliyal
Flag Officer, Naval Aviation and Goa Area (at Goa):
Rear Admiral Sudhir Pillai
Flag Officer, Submarines (Vishakapatnam):
Rear Admiral Titus Moraes
Flag Officer, Sea Training:
Rear Admiral S Lanba

Personnel

(a) 2009: 53,000 (7,500 officers) (including 5,000 Naval Air Arm and 2,000 Marines)
(b) Voluntary service
(c) The Marine Commando Force was formed in 1986.

Naval Air Arm

Squadron	*Aircraft*	*Role*
300 (Goa)	Sea Harrier FRS. Mk 51	Fighter/Strike
310 (Goa)	Dornier 228	MRMP
312 (Chennai)	Tu-142M 'Bear F'	LRMP/ASW
315 (Goa)	Il-38 May	LRMP/ASW
318 (Port Blair)	Dornier 228, HAL Chetak	MRMP
321 (Mumbai)	HAL Chetak	Utility/SAR
330 (Mumbai)	Sea King Mk 42B	ASW
333 (ships) (Vizag)	Kamov Ka-28 'Helix'	ASW
336 (Kochi)	Sea King Mk 42A/42B	ASW
339 (Mumbai)	Ka-28 'Helix', Ka-31	ASW/ASVW/AEW
342 (Kochi)	Heron, Searcher II	UAV
550 (Kochi)	Dornier 228, PBN Defender, Deepak	Training
551 A (Goa)	Kiran Mk I/II	Training
551 B (Goa)	Sea Harrier T Mk 60	Training
552 (Goa)	Sea Harrier T Mk 60	Training
561 (Chennai)	HAL Chetak, Hughes 300	Training

Naval Air Arm—*continued*

Air Stations

Name	*Location*	*Role*
INS *Kunjali*	Mumbai	Helicopters
INS *Garuda*	Willingdon Island, Kochi	Helicopters
INS *Hansa*	Goa	HQ Flag Officer Naval Air Stations, LRMP, Strike/Fighter
INS *Utkrosh*	Port Blair, Andaman Isles	Maritime Patrol Maritime Patrol Maritime Patrol
INS *Dega*	Vishakapatnam	Fleet support and maritime patrol
INS *Rajali*	Arakonam	LRMP, Helo Training
NAS *Ramnad*	Bangalore	LRMP Naval Air Technical School
NAS *Uchipili*	Tamil Nadu	UAV

Prefix to Ships' Names

INS

Colour Scheme

Surface ship colour scheme was changed from dark grey to light grey in 2004.

Bases and Establishments

New Delhi, Integrated HQ of Ministry of Defence (Navy).
Mumbai, C-in-C **Western Command**, barracks and main Dockyard; with one 'Carrier' dock. Submarine base (INS *Vajrabahu*). Supply school (INS *Hamla*). The region includes Mazagon and Goa shipyards.
Vishakapatnam, C-in-C **Eastern Command**, submarine base (INS *Virbahu*), submarine school (INS *Satyavahana*) and major dockyard built with Soviet support and being extended. Naval Air Station (INS *Dega*). Marine Gas Turbine maintenance facility (INS *Eksila*). New entry training (INS *Chilka*). At Thirunelveli is the submarine VLF W/T station completed in September 1986. The region includes Hindustan and Garden Reach shipyards.
Kochi, C-in-C **Southern Command**, Naval Air Station, and professional schools (INS *Venduruthy*) (all naval training comes under Southern Command). Ship repair yard. Gunnery Training establishment (INS *Dronacharya*).
There are also limited support facilities including a floating dock at Port Blair in the Andaman Islands.
Goa is HQ Flag Officer Naval Aviation.
Karwar (near Goa) is the site for a new naval base; first phase was opened on 31 May 2005 and operations began on 15 December 2005. Phase 2 is to include expansion of the berthing facilities to accommodate aircraft carriers and the construction of a naval air station with a 6,000 ft runway. There is a small base at Minicoy Island, one of the Lakshadweep archipelago. Plans to build a new base on the east coast, 50 km south of Vishakapatnam, were announced in 2006.
Shipbuilding: Mumbai (submarines, destroyers, frigates, corvettes); Calcutta (frigates, corvettes, LSTs, auxiliaries); Goa (patrol craft, LCU, MCMV facility planned). Vishakapatnam (corvettes, patrol craft).

Marine Commando Force (MCF)

The MCF was formed in 1987. Known as MARCOS, elements are based in the three regional commands. The force is trained in counter-terrorism operations.

Coast Defence

Truck-mounted SS-3-C Styx missiles. Several fixed sites.

Strength of the Fleet

Type	*Active*	*Building (Projected)*
Attack Submarine (SSN)	–	2
Patrol Submarines	16	6 (6)
Aircraft Carriers	1	2
Destroyers	8	3 (3)
Frigates	12	6 (7)
Corvettes	24	4 (8)
Patrol Ships	6	5 (3)
Patrol Craft	18	–
LPD	1	–
LST	3	2
LSM/LCM	14	–
Minesweepers-Ocean	10	–
Minehunters	–	(8)
Research and Survey Ships	10	–
Training Ships	4	–
Diving Support/Rescue Ship	1	–
Replenishment Tankers	2	1 (1)
Transport Ships	3	–
Support Tankers	6	–
Water Carriers	2	–
Ocean Tugs	1	–

DELETIONS

Frigates

2007 *Udaygiri*

Patrol Forces

2006 *Prahar* (sunk), T 54

Mine Warfare Forces

2006 *Malpe*
2007 *Mahe*

Amphibious Forces

2008 *Ghorpad*

Auxiliaries

2006 *Amba*
2007 *Shakti*

Survey Ships

2007 *Mithun*

PENNANT LIST

Submarines

S 40	Vela
S 42	Vagli
S 44	Shishumar
S 45	Shankush
S 46	Shalki
S 47	Shankul
S 55	Sindhughosh
S 56	Sindhudhvaj
S 57	Sindhuraj
S 58	Sindhuvir
S 59	Sindhuratna
S 60	Sindhukesari
S 61	Sindhukirti
S 62	Sindhuvijay
S 63	Sindhurakshak
S 65	Sindhushastra

Aircraft Carriers

R 22	Viraat

Destroyers

D 51	Rajput
D 52	Rana
D 53	Ranjit
D 54	Ranvir
D 55	Ranvijay
D 60	Mysore
D 61	Delhi
D 62	Mumbai

Frigates

F 20	Godavari
F 21	Gomati
F 22	Ganga
F 31	Brahmaputra
F 36	Dunagiri
F 37	Beas
F 39	Betwa
F 40	Talwar
F 41	Taragiri
F 42	Vindhyagiri
F 43	Trishul
F 44	Tabar
F 46	Krishna (training)

Corvettes

P 33	Abhay
P 34	Ajay
P 35	Akshay
P 36	Agray
P 44	Kirpan
P 46	Kuthar
P 47	Khanjar
P 49	Khukri
P 61	Kora
P 62	Kirch
P 63	Kulish
P 64	Karmukh
K 40	Veer
K 41	Nirbhik
K 42	Nipat
K 43	Nishank
K 44	Nirghat
K 45	Vibhuti
K 46	Vipul
K 47	Vinash
K 48	Vidyut
K 83	Nashak
K 91	Pralaya
K 92	Prabal

Patrol Forces

P 50	Sukanya
P 51	Subhadra
P 52	Suvarna
P 53	Savitri
P 55	Sharada
P 56	Sujata

Mine Warfare Forces

M 63	Bedi
M 64	Bhavnagar
M 65	Alleppey
M 66	Ratnagiri
M 67	Karwar
M 68	Cannanore
M 69	Cuddalore
M 70	Kakinada
M 71	Kozhikode
M 72	Konkan

Amphibious Forces

L 15	Kesari
L 16	Shardul
L 17	Sharabh
L 18	Cheetah
L 19	Mahish
L 20	Magar
L 21	Guldar
L 22	Kumbhir
L 23	Gharial
L 32	–
L 33	–
L 34	Vasco da Gama
L 35	–
L 36	–
L 37	–
L 38	Midhur
L 39	Mangala
L 41	Jalashwa

Auxiliaries and Survey Ships

–	Nicobar
–	Andamans
–	Swaraj Deep
A 15	Nireekshak
A 53	Matanga
A 58	Jyoti
A 59	Aditya
A 72	Torpedo Recovery Vessel
A 74	Sagardhwani
A 75	Tarangini
A 86	Tir
J 14	Nirupak
J 15	Investigator
J 16	Jamuna
J 17	Sutlej
J 18	Sandhayak
J 19	Nirdeshak
J 21	Darshak
J 22	Sarvekshak
J 33	Meen

Seaward Defence Forces

T 55	–
T 56	–
T 57	–
T 58	–
T 59	–
T 61	Trinkat
T 63	Tarasa
T 65	Bangaram
T 66	Bitra
T 67	Batti Malv
T 68	Baratang

SUBMARINES

Notes: (1) The Advanced Technology Vessel (ATV) project was initiated in the 1980s. In addition to traditional SSN/SSGN functions, the boat is likely to have a strategic role and, to this end, may also be capable of deploying nuclear-tipped ballistic missiles in addition to torpedo-tube launched conventional anti-ship and land-attack missiles. The delayed Project K-15 Sagarika 750 km range ballistic missile is a possibility. A test-firing of the missile was made from a submerged pontoon on 26 February 2008. Currently led by Vice Admiral D S P Varma, the ATV project has facilities in Delhi, Hyderabad, Vishakapatnam (where the boat is reported to be under construction) and Kalpakkam (where the PWR reactor reportedly became fully operational in 2006). Companies in support of the project are reported to be Larsen and Toubro at Hazira, Mazagon Dock Ltd and Bharat Electronics. It is believed that the submarine is a development of a Russian design, derived either from the Project 885 Severodvinsk class SSGN or more probably from the Victor/Akula class generation. The nuclear propulsion system is understood to be an Indo-Russian PWR although reports that it may be a Russian supplied VM-5 PWR have also circulated. It was announced in December 2007 that sea trials of the ATV are to begin in 2009.
(2) A request for proposals for a class of six submarines, to follow the Scorpene programme, is expected in 2009. Contenders include further Scorpene class, German Type 214 and Russian Amur 1650 class.
(3) India operates up to 11 Cosmos CE2F/FX100 swimmer delivery vehicles, delivered in 1991.
(4) Procurement of at least two Deep Sea Rescue Vehicles (DSRV) was reported to be in progress in 2005. The new DRSV would be operated from *Nireekshak* or a vessel of opportunity.

Attack Submarines

0 + 1 AKULA (SCHUKA-B) CLASS (PROJECT 971) (SSN)

Name	*No*	*Builders*	*Laid down*	*Launched*	*Commissioned*
CHAKRA (ex-*Nerpa*)	–	Komsomolsk Shipyard	1986	24 June 2006	2009

Displacement, tons: 7,500 surfaced; 9,100 dived
Dimensions, feet (metres): 360.1 oa; 337.9 wl × 45.9 × 34.1 *(110; 103 × 14.0 × 10.4)*
Main machinery: Nuclear; 1 VM-5 PWR; 190 MW; 2 GT3A turbines; 47,600 hp(m) *(35 MW)*; 2 emergency propulsion motors; 750 hp(m) *(552 kW)*; 1 shaft; 2 spinners; 1,006 hp(m) *(740 kW)*
Speed, knots: 28 dived; 10 surfaced
Complement: 62 (31 officers)

Missiles: SLCM/SSM: Novator Alfa Klub SS-N-27 (3m-54E-1 anti-ship); active radar homing to 180 km *(97.2 n miles)* at 0.7 Mach (cruise) and 2.5 Mach (attack); warhead 450 kg.
Torpedoes: 4—21 in *(533 mm)* and 4—25.6 in *(650 mm)* tubes.
Countermeasures: ESM: Rim Hat; intercept.
Radars: Surface search: Snoop Pair or Snoop Half with back to back aerials on ESM mast; I-band.
Sonars: Shark Gill (Skat MGK 503); hull-mounted; passive/active search and attack; low/medium frequency.
Mouse Roar; hull-mounted; active attack; high frequency.
Skat 3 towed array; passive; very low frequency.

Programmes: The construction of *Nerpa* (K 152) began at Komsomolsk in 1986 but, following the collapse of the Soviet Union in 1991, work was suspended. Negotiations for the 10-year lease of the boat by the Indian Navy started in about 1996 and terms were subsequently agreed in September 2001 when construction, likely to have been at least partly financed by India, was restarted. The boat was subsequently launched in 2006 and, following sea trials and certification by the Russian Navy, is likely to be handed over in September 2009. The contract included a training package and three crews are reported to have been trained at Sosnovy Bor near St Petersburg. The weapons and sensors of the submarine in Indian service are speculative and have not been confirmed.
Structure: The very long fin is particularly notable. Diving depth 450 m approximately.
Operational: *Chakra* bears the same name as the Charlie class SSN leased from the Soviet Union 1988–91. Initially, the principal role of the submarine is to be training of both sea-going and shore-based personnel in nuclear submarine operations and support. The boat is likely to carry a number of Russian crew which may place some restrictions on the boat's operational use. As experience is gained, the submarine is likely to be deployed on a broader range of SSN operations.

AKULA CLASS *6/2007*, ***Ships of the World*** / 1305156

Patrol Submarines

2 FOXTROT (PROJECT 641) CLASS (SS)

Name	*No*	*Builders*	*Commissioned*
VELA	S 40	Sudomekh, Leningrad	Aug 1973
VAGLI	S 42	Sudomekh, Leningrad	Aug 1974

Displacement, tons: 1,952 surfaced; 2,475 dived
Dimensions, feet (metres): 299.5 × 24.6 × 19.7 *(91.3 × 7.5 × 6)*
Main machinery: Diesel-electric; 3 Type 37-D diesels; 6,000 hp(m) *(4.4 MW)*; 3 motors (1 × 2,700 and 2 × 1,350); 5,400 hp(m) *(3.97 MW)*; 3 shafts; 1 auxiliary motor; 140 hp(m) *(103 kW)*
Speed, knots: 16 surfaced; 15 dived
Range, n miles: 20,000 at 8 kt surfaced; 380 at 2 kt dived
Complement: 75 (8 officers)

Torpedoes: 10—21 in *(533 mm)* (6 fwd, 4 aft) tubes. 22 SET-65E/SAET-60; active/passive homing to 15 km *(8.1 n miles)* at 40 kt; warhead 205 kg.
Mines: 44 in lieu of torpedoes.
Countermeasures: ESM: Stop Light; radar warning.
Radars: Surface search: Snoop Tray; I-band.
Sonars: Herkules/Fenik; bow-mounted; passive search and attack; medium frequency.

Structure: Diving depth 250 m *(820 ft)*, reducing with age.
Operational: Survivors of an original eight of the class. *Vagli* completed refit in 2004 and *Vela* was reportedly in refit in 2006. Both based at Vishakapatnam.

FOXTROT *2/2001*, ***Guy Toremans*** / 0105814

10 SINDHUGHOSH (KILO) (PROJECT 877EM/8773) CLASS (SSK)

Name	*No*	*Builders*	*Commissionec*
SINDHUGHOSH	S 55	Sudomekh, Leningrad	30 Apr 1986
SINDHUDHVAJ	S 56	Sudomekh, Leningrad	12 June 1987
SINDHURAJ	S 57	Sudomekh, Leningrad	20 Oct 1987
SINDHUVIR	S 58	Sudomekh, Leningrad	16 May 1988
SINDHURATNA	S 59	Sudomekh, Leningrad	19 Nov 1988
SINDHUKESARI	S 60	Sudomekh, Leningrad	19 Dec 1988
SINDHUKIRTI	S 61	Sudomekh, Leningrad	9 Dec 1990
SINDHUVIJAY	S 62	Sudomekh, Leningrad	17 Dec 1990
SINDHURAKSHAK	S 63	Sudomekh, St Petersburg	24 Dec 1997
SINDHUSHASTRA	S 65	Sudomekh, St Petersburg	19 July 2000

Displacement, tons: 2,325 surfaced; 3,076 dived
Dimensions, feet (metres): 238.2 × 32.5 × 21.7 *(72.6 × 9.9 × 6.6)*
Main machinery: Diesel-electric; 2 Model 4-2AA-42M diesels; 3,650 hp(m) *(2.68 MW)*; 2 generators; 1 motor; 5,900 hp(m) *(4.34 MW)*; 1 shaft; 2 MT-168 auxiliary motors; 204 hp(m) *(150 kW)*; 1 economic speed motor; 130 hp(m) *(95 kW)*
Speed, knots: 10 surfaced; 17 dived; 9 snorting
Range, n miles: 6,000 at 7 kt snorting; 400 at 3 kt dived
Complement: 52 (13 officers)

Missiles: SLCM: Novator Alfa Klub SS-N-27 (3M-54 anti-ship missiles) (S 55, 57, 59, 60, 62 and 65); active radar homing to 180 km *(97.2 n miles)* at 0.7 Mach (cruise) and 2.5 Mach (attack); warhead 450 kg.
Novator Klub SS-N-30 (3M 14) land-attack missiles (S 55, S 62); terrain following/SATNAV guidance to 300 km *(162 n miles)* at 0.7 Mach; warhead 450 kg.
SAM: SA-N-8 portable launcher; IR homing to 3.2 n miles *(6 km)*.
Torpedoes: 6—21 in *(533 mm)* tubes. Combination of Type 53-65; passive wake homing to 19 km *(10.3 n miles)* at 45 kt; warhead 305 kg and TEST 71/96; anti-submarine; active/passive homing to 15 km *(8.1 n miles)* at 40 kt or 20 km *(10.8 n miles)* at 25 kt; warhead 220 kg. Total of 18 weapons. Wire-guided on 2 tubes.
Mines: 24 DM-1 in lieu of torpedoes.
Countermeasures: ESM: Squid Head; radar warning.
Weapons control: Uzel MVU-119EM TFCS.
Radars: Navigation: Snoop Tray; I-band.
Sonars: Shark Teeth/Shark Fin; MGK-400; or Bel Ushus (S 55, 62); hull-mounted; active/passive search and attack; medium frequency.
Mouse Roar; MG-519; hull-mounted; active search; high frequency.

Programmes: The Kilo class was launched in the former Soviet Navy in 1979 and although India was the first country to acquire one they have since been transferred to Algeria, Poland, Romania, Iran and China. Because of the slowness of the S 209 programme, the original order in 1983 for six Kilo class expanded to 10 but was then cut back again to eight. Two further orders were confirmed in May 1997. S 63 was a spare Type 877 hull built for the Russian Navy, but never purchased. S 65 is a Type 8773 and was fitted for SLCM on build. She was launched on 14 October 1999.
Modernisation: *Sindhuvir* completed major refit at Severodvinsk from May 1997 to July 1999. *Sindhuraj* and *Sindhukesari* completed similar refits at Admiralty Yard, St Petersburg from May 1999 to November 2001. *Sindhuratna* completed a two-year refit at Severodvinsk in 2002. *Sindhughosh*, following refit work at Vishakapatnam from 1999, started modernisatior at Severodvinsk in September 2002 which completec on 22 April 2005. *Sindhuvijay* started a two-year refi at Severodvinsk in May 2005 which was completed or 8 May 2007 although acceptance of the boat was delayed until August 2008 due to reported defects ir the missile system. She became the sixth boat to be fitted with SS-N-27. Both *Sindhughosh* and *Sindhuvijay* are equipped with the SS-N-30 (3M 14) land-attack missiles. *Sindhukirti* began refit at Hindustan Shipyard Vishakapatnam, in January 2006 but may not rejoin the fleet until 2015.
Structure: Diving depth, 300 m *(985 ft)*. Reported tha from *Sindhuvir* onwards these submarines have ar SA-N-8 SAM capability. The launcher is shoulder held anc stowed in the fin for use when the submarine is surfaced Two torpedo tubes can fire wire-guided torpedoes anc four tubes have automatic reloading. Anechoic tiles are fitted on casings and fins.
Operational: First four form the 11th Submarine Squadron Based at Vishakapatnam and the remainder of the 12th Squadron based at Mumbai. There are doubts abou the operational status of *Sindhudhvaj* which has no been included in the refit cycle. She is reported to be at Vishakapatnam and, while she may be under repair there has been speculation that she may be modified to fire Brahmos cruise missiles.

SINDHUVIJAY — ***9/2008*, Diego Quevedo*** / 1353085

SINDHURAKSHAK — ***12/2007, Michael Nitz*** / 1353084

0 + 6 SCORPENE CLASS (SSK)

Name	*No*	*Builders*	*Laid down*	*Launched*	*Commissioned*
–	–	Mazagon Dock Ltd, Mumbai	2009	2012	2013

Displacement, tons: 1,705 dived
Dimensions, feet (metres): 217.8 × 20.3 × 19 *(66.4 × 6.2 × 5.8)*
Main machinery: Diesel electric; 4 MTU 16V 396 SE84 diesels; 2,992 hp(m) *(2.2 MW)*; 1 Jeumont Schneider motor; 3,808 hp(m) *(2.8 MW)*; 1 shaft
Speed, knots: 20 dived; 11 surfaced
Range, n miles: 550 at 4 kt dived; 6,500 at 8 kt surfaced
Complement: 31 (6 officers)

Missiles: MBDA Exocet SM 39. Block 2 launched from 21 in *(533 mm)* tubes; inertial cruise, active terminal homing to 50 km *(27 n miles)* at 0.9 Mach; warhead 165 kg.
Torpedoes: 6—21 in *(533 mm)* tubes.
Countermeasures: ESM.
Weapons control: UDS International SUBTICS.
Radars: Navigation: Sagem; I-band.
Sonars: Hull mounted; active/passive search and attack, medium frequency.

Programmes: Project 75. Following protracted negotiations which began in 2002, a contract for the licensed production of six submarines at Mazagon Dock Ltd, Mumbai, was signed on 6 October 2005. The agreement is reported to include an option for a further nine boats. DCNS is to supply technical advisers and provide prefabricated hull elements and the combat systems, including the command system, underwater sensors, optronics, and communications. MBDA is to supply Exocet SM39 missiles as part of the package.

SCORPENE (computer graphic) ***1998, DCN*** / 0017689

Details are based on the boats built for Chile. AIP is not to be installed in the first two boats but a reassessment for the remaining submarines will be made at a later date. Delivery of all six boats was to have begun in 2012 and to have been completed in about 2018 but this programme is likely to have been delayed by at least a year.
Structure: Diving depth more than 300 m *(984 ft)*. AIP would require the addition of an 8 m 'plug' to incorporate the MESMA system.

4 SHISHUMAR (TYPE 209/1500) CLASS (SSK)

Name	*No*	*Builders*	*Laid down*	*Launched*	*Commissioned*
SHISHUMAR	S 44	Howaldtswerke, Kiel	1 May 1982	13 Dec 1984	22 Sep 1986
SHANKUSH	S 45	Howaldtswerke, Kiel	1 Sep 1982	11 May 1984	20 Nov 1986
SHALKI	S 46	Mazagon Dock Ltd, Mumbai	5 June 1984	30 Sep 1989	7 Feb 1992
SHANKUL	S 47	Mazagon Dock Ltd, Mumbai	3 Sep 1989	21 Mar 1992	28 May 1994

Displacement, tons: 1,450 standard; 1,660 surfaced; 1,850 dived
Dimensions, feet (metres): 211.2 × 21.3 × 19.7 *(64.4 × 6.5 × 6)*
Main machinery: Diesel-electric; 4 MTU 12V 493 AZ80 GA31L diesels; 2,400 hp(m) *(1.76 MW)* sustained; 4 Siemens alternators; 1.8 MW; 1 Siemens motor; 4,600 hp(m) *(3.38 MW)* sustained; 1 shaft
Speed, knots: 11 surfaced; 22 dived
Range, n miles: 8,000 snorting at 8 kt; 13,000 surfaced at 10 kt
Complement: 40 (8 officers)

Torpedoes: 8—21 in *(533 mm)* tubes. 14 AEG SUT Mod 1; wire-guided; active/passive homing to 28 km *(15.3 n miles)* at 23 kt; 12 km *(6.6 n miles)* at 35 kt; warhead 250 kg.
Mines: External 'strap-on' type for 24 mines.
Countermeasures: Decoys: C 303 acoustic decoys.
ESM: Argo Phoenix II AR 700 or Kollmorgen Sea Sentry; radar warning.
Weapons control: Singer Librascope Mk 1.
Radars: Surface search: Thomson-CSF Calypso; I-band.
Sonars: Atlas Elektronik CSU 83; active/passive search and attack; medium frequency. TSM 2272 to be fitted.
Thomson Sintra DUUX-5; passive ranging and intercept.

Programmes: Howaldtswerke concluded an agreement with the Indian Navy on 11 December 1981. This was in four basic parts: the building in West Germany of two Type 1500 submarines; the supply of 'packages' for the building of two more boats at Mazagon, Mumbai; training of various groups of specialists for the design and construction of the Mazagon pair; logistic services during the trials and early part of the commissions as well as consultation services in Mumbai. In 1984 it was announced that a further two submarines would be built at Mazagon for a total of six but this was overtaken by events in 1987–88 and the agreement with HDW terminated at four. This was reconsidered in 1992 and again in 1997. Government approval was given in mid-1999 for the construction of further submarines.

SHANKUL ***2/2006, Ships of the World*** / 1164317

Modernisation: Thomson Sintra Eledone sonars may be fitted in due course. Trials for integration of indigenous Panchendriya ATAS developed by NPOL are in progress in Karanj.
Structure: The Type 1500 has a central bulkhead and an IKL designed integrated escape sphere which can carry the full crew of up to 40 men, has an oxygen supply for 8 hours, and can withstand pressures at least as great as those that can be withstood by the submarine's pressure hull. Diving depth 260 m *(853 ft)*.
Operational: Form 10th Submarine Squadron based at Mumbai. *Shishumar* mid-life refit started in 1999 and had been completed by 2001. She undertook a further repair period in 2004 following a collision. *Shankul* underwent refit 2001–2005 and *Shankush* is reported to have started refit in 2001. *Shalki* started refit in early 2007.

SHISHUMAR ***2/2001, Guy Toremans*** / 0105813

AIRCRAFT CARRIERS

Notes: The Maritime Capability Perspective Plan includes proposals to achieve a three-carrier force by 2022. Construction of a second indigenously built carrier is expected to start in about 2017.

0 + 1 MODIFIED KIEV CLASS (PROJECT 1143.4) (CVGM)

Name	*Builders*	*Laid down*	*Launched*	*Commissioned*
VIKRAMADITYA (ex-*Admiral Gorshkov*, ex-*Baku*)	Nikolayev South	17 Feb 1978	1 Apr 1982	11 Jan 1987

Displacement, tons: 45,400 full load
Dimensions, feet (metres): 928.5 oa; 818.6 wl × 167.3 oa; 107.3 wl × 32.8 *(283; 249.5 × 51; 32.7 × 10)*
Main machinery: 8 KWG4 boilers; 4 GTZA 674 turbines; 200,000 hp(m) *(147 MW)*; 4 shafts
Speed, knots: 29
Range, n miles: 13,800 at 18 kt
Complement: 1,200 plus aircrew

Missiles: SAM/Guns: To be announced.
Countermeasures: Decoys: 2 PK2 chaff launchers; 2 towed torpedo decoys.
ESM/ECM: Bharat intercept and jammers.
Combat data systems: Lesorub E.
Radars: Air search: Plate Steer.
Surface search: 2 Strut Pair.
Navigation: Aircraft control.
Sonars: Horse Jaw (MG 355); hull-mounted; active search; medium frequency.

Fixed-wing aircraft: 12 MiG 29K.
Helicopters: 6 Helix 27/28/31.

Programmes: Last of the four Project 1143.4 aircraft carriers built for the Soviet Navy. First offered for sale to India by Russia in 1994. By 1999 the proposal was to gift the ship as long as India pays for the refit. Following a Government to Government agreement on 4 October 2000 and protracted negotiations, contract signed on 20 January 2004 for a five-year refit at a cost estimated to be USD625 million. However, it was announced in August 2007 that the refit had been delayed by three years and that the ship would not enter service until 2012. This may still prove to be optimistic. Agreement to fund cost overruns was reached in December 2008.
Modernisation: New propulsion, power and air conditioning systems to be fitted. All the original Russian weapons systems removed and to be replaced by six Kashtan SAM/gun systems. The flight deck is to be converted to a STOBAR configuration with a 14.3° ski-jump.
Structure: The ship has a 198 m angled deck with three arrestor wires. Flight deck lifts are 19.2 × 10.3 m and 18.5 × 4.7 m, and can lift 30 tons (aft) and 20 tons (midships) respectively. The hangar is 130 × 22.5 m.
Operational: The ship was re-launched on 4 December 2008. Sea trials are expected to start in 2011. The ship is to be based at Karwar.

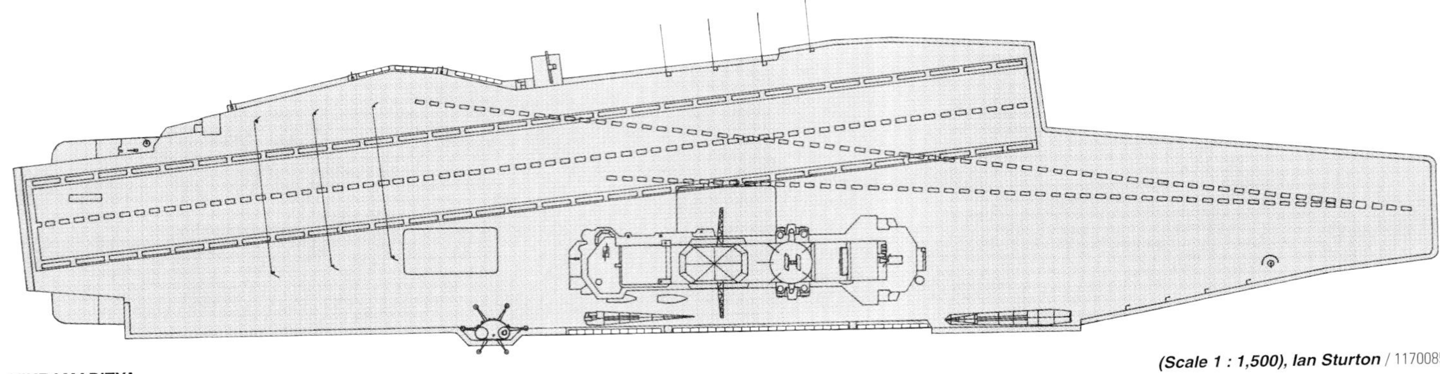

VIKRAMADITYA ***(Scale 1 : 1,500), Ian Sturton*** / 1170085

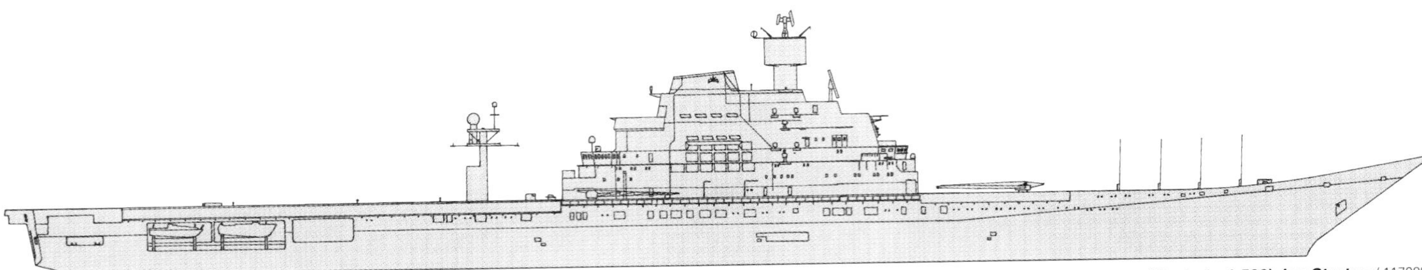

VIKRAMADITYA ***(Scale 1 : 1,500), Ian Sturton*** / 1170086

VIKRAMADITYA (artist's impression) ***10/2004, Nevskoye Design Bureau*** / 1042276

1 HERMES CLASS (CVM)

Name	*No*	*Builders*	*Laid down*	*Launched*	*Commissioned*
VIRAAT (ex-*Hermes*)	R 22	Vickers Shipbuilding Ltd, Barrow-in-Furness	21 June 1944	16 Feb 1953	18 Nov 1959

Displacement, tons: 23,900 standard; 28,700 full load
Dimensions, feet (metres): 685 wl; 744.3 oa × 90; 160 oa × 28.5 *(208.8; 226.9 × 27.4; 48.8 × 8.7)*
Main machinery: 4 Admiralty boilers; 400 psi *(28 kg/cm²)*; 700°F *(370°C)*; 2 Parsons geared turbines; 76,000 hp *(57 MW)*; 2 shafts
Speed, knots: 28
Complement: 1,350 (143 officers)

Missiles: SAM/Guns: 2 Octuple IAI/Rafael Barak 1 VLS ❶, command line of sight radar or optical guidance to 10 km *(5.5 n miles)* at 2 Mach; warhead 22 kg.
Guns: 4—30 mm/65 (2 twin) AK 230 ❷; 500 rds/min to 5 km *(2.7 n miles)*; weight of shell 0.54 kg.
Countermeasures: Decoys: 2 Knebworth Corvus chaff launchers ❸.
ESM: Bharat Ajanta; intercept ❹.
Combat data systems: CAAIS action data automation. SATCOM.
Radars: Air search: Bharat RAWL-02 Mk 3 (LW08) ❺; D-band.
Air/surface search: Bharat RAWS (PFN 513) ❻; E/F-band.
Fire control: IAI/Elta EL/M-2221 ❼; Ka-band.
Navigation: 2 Bharat Rashmi ❽; I-band.
Tacan: FT 13-S/M.
Sonars: Graseby Type 184M; hull-mounted; active search and attack; 6–9 kHz.

Fixed-wing aircraft: 12 Sea Harriers FRS Mk 51 ❾ (capacity for 30).
Helicopters: 7 Sea King Mk 42B/C ❿ ASW/ASV/Vertrep and Ka-27 Helix. Ka-31 Helix.

Programmes: Purchased in May 1986 from the UK, thence to an extensive refit in Devonport Dockyard. Commissioned in Indian Navy 20 May 1987.
Modernisation: UK refit included new fire-control equipment, navigation radars and deck landing aids. Boilers were converted to take distillate fuel and the ship was given improved NBC protection. New search radar in 1995. Further modernisation in 1999–2001 refit, improved indigenous RAWL 02 (Mk II) and Rashmi radars for CCA/navigation, EW equipment and new communications systems. A further refit, completed in December 2004, included installation of Barak CIWS. This has replaced the previously fitted 40 mm guns. A further refit, to extend ship-life to 2012, was completed in 2008.
Structure: Fitted with 12° ski jump. Reinforced flight deck (0.75 in); 1 to 2 in of armour over magazines and machinery spaces. Four LCVP on after davits. Magazine capacity includes 80 lightweight torpedoes. Barak launchers are recessed in the starboard side of the flight deck, aft of the island.
Operational: The Sea Harrier complement is likely to be of the order of six aircraft leaving room for a greater mix of Sea King and Helix helicopters. Based at Mumbai.

VIRAAT *10/2005, Ships of the World* / 1153836

VIRAAT
10/2007, Ships of the World
1170082

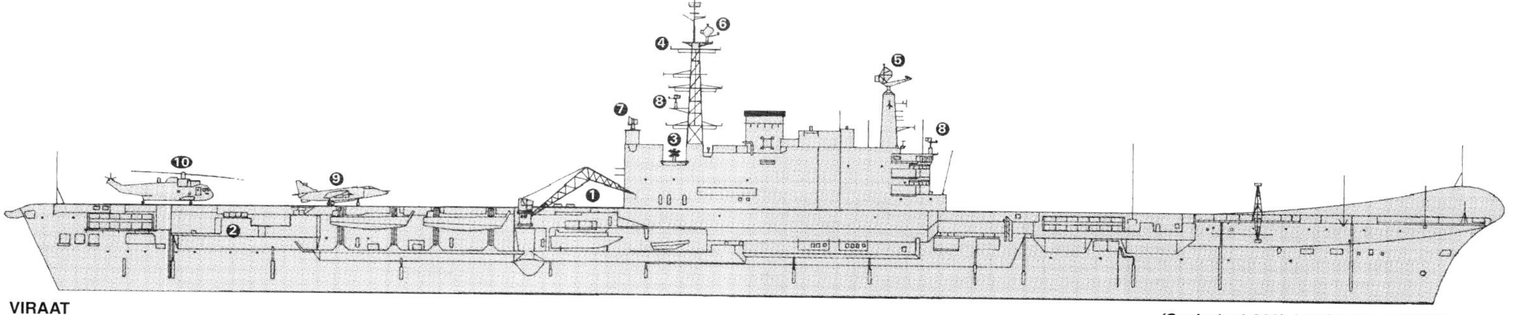

VIRAAT *(Scale 1 : 1,200), Ian Sturton* / 1303034

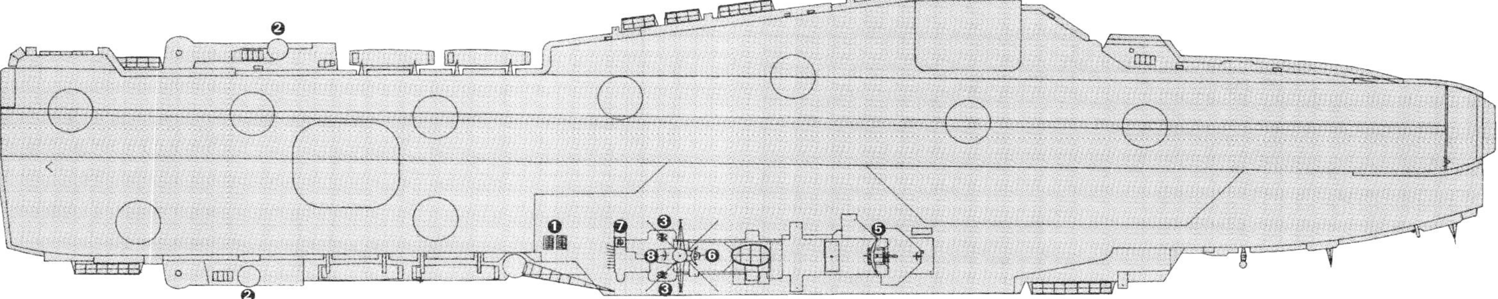

VIRAAT *(Scale 1 : 1,200), Ian Sturton* / 1166562

0 + 1 INDIGENOUS AIRCRAFT CARRIER CLASS (PROJECT 71) (CVM)

Name	*No*	*Builders*	*Laid down*	*Launched*	*Commissioned*
VIKRANT	–	Kochi Shipyard Ltd	28 Feb 2009	2013	2015

Displacement, tons: 37,500 standard
Dimensions, feet (metres): 826.8 × 190.3 × 27.5 *(252.0 × 58.0 × 8.4)*
Main machinery: COGAG: 4 General Electric LM 2500 gas turbines; 120,000 hp *(89.5 MW)*; 2 shafts; cp props
Speed, knots: 28
Range, n miles: 7,500 at 18 kt
Complement: 1,400 (160 officers)

Missiles: SAM: To be announced.
Guns: CIWS: To be announced.
Radars: Air search; surface search; fire control.
Sonars: Hull mounted.

Fixed-wing aircraft: 12 MiG-29K.

Helicopters: 10 Ka-31 and ALH.

Programmes: The plan announced in 1989 was to build two new aircraft carriers. The Indigenous Aircraft Carrier (IAC), formerly the Air Defence Ship (ADS), is to replace the former *Vikrant* (and will probably receive the same name) while *Vikramaditya* (ex-*Admiral Gorshkov*) is to replace *Viraat* in 2012. A number of international companies including DCN, IZAR and Fincantieri are believed to have been involved in conceptual and design work of the ADS and it is understood that the shipbuilder, Cochin Shipyard Ltd (CSL), has sub-contracted specialist 'task forces' to collaborate in building the ship. Two contracts signed in mid-2004 with Fincantieri to finalise the ADS design and its ancillary propulsion systems and main power plants. Fincantieri is likely to provide further assistance during the vessel's construction, tests and sea trials. First steel cut on 11 April 2005 and construction of building blocks started thereafter. However the project has been afflicted by delays, including reported problems in acquiring sufficient high-quality steel.
Structure: All details are still speculative and the diagrams show an indicative design including a short take off (with 14° ski jump) and arrested recovery (STOBAR) system. The ADS is to have a similar propulsion system as the *Cavour* being built for the Italian Navy.
Operational: The ship is to be based on the east coast possibly at a new base.

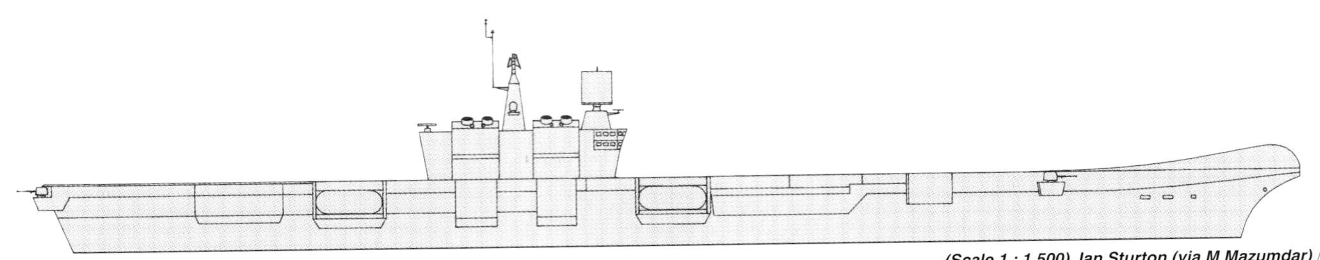

PROJECT 71 ***(Scale 1 : 1,500), Ian Sturton (via M Mazumdar)*** / 0529540

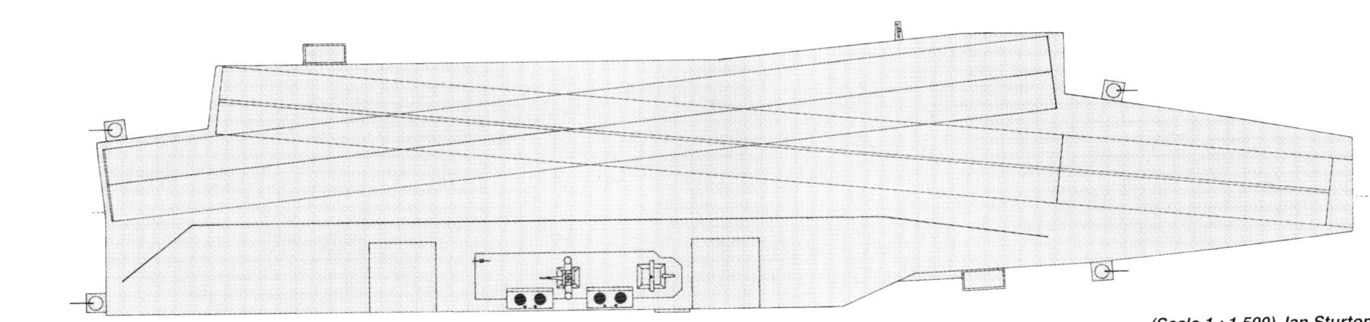

PROJECT 71 ***(Scale 1 : 1,500), Ian Sturton*** / 1353093

DESTROYERS

0 + 3 (4) KOLKATA (PROJECT 15A) CLASS (DDGHM)

Name	*No*	*Builders*	*Laid down*	*Launched*	*Commissioned*
KOLKATA	–	Mazagon Dock Ltd, Mumbai	26 Sep 2003	30 Mar 2006	2011
–	–	Mazagon Dock Ltd, Mumbai	25 Oct 2005	2009	2012
–	–	Mazagon Dock Ltd, Mumbai	2006	2011	2013

Displacement, tons: 7,000 full load
Dimensions, feet (metres): 534.8 × 57.1 × 21.3 *(163 × 17.4 × 6.5)*
Main machinery: 4 Zorya/Mashprockt DT-59 gas turbines; 82,820 hp(m) *(61.7 MW)*; 2 shafts; cp props
Speed, knots: 32. **Range, n miles:** 4,500 at 18 kt
Complement: 360 (40 officers)

Missiles: SSM: 16 Brahmos PJ-10 (2 octuple VLS) ❶; active/passive radar homing to 290 km *(157 n miles)* at 2.6 Mach; warhead 200 kg; sea skimmer in terminal phase.
SAM: IAI/Rafael Barak 2/8 ❷. 1 × 16 cell VLS launcher (forward), 1 × 32 cell VLS launcher (aft); total of 48 missiles.
4 octuple IAI/Rafael Barak 1 VLS; command line of sight or optical guidance to 10 km *(5.5 n miles)* at 2 Mach; warhead 22 kg.
SAM/Guns: 2 CADS-N-1 (Kashtan) (may replace AK 630); each has twin 30 mm Gatling combined with 8 SA-N-11 (Grisson) and Hot Flash/Hot Spot radar/optronic director. Laser beam guidance for missiles to 8 km *(4.4 n miles)*; warhead 9 kg; 9,000 rds/min (combined) to 1.5 km for guns.
Guns: 1—3.9 in *(100 mm)*/59 A 190E ❸; 60 rds/min to 21.5 km *(11.6 n miles)*; weight of shell 16 kg.
2—30 mm/AK 630 ❹; 6 barrels per mounting; 3,000 rds/min combined to 2 km.
Torpedoes: 5 PTA 21 in *(533 mm)* (quin) tubes ❺. Combination of SET 65E; anti-submarine; active/passive homing to 15 km *(8.1 n miles)* at 40 kt; warhead 205 kg and Type 53-65; passive wake homing to 19 km *(10.3 n miles)* at 45 kt; warhead 305 kg.
A/S mortars: 2 RBU 6000 ❻; 12 tubed trainable; range 6,000 m; warhead 31 kg.
Countermeasures: Decoys: 2 PK2 chaff launchers ❼. Towed torpedo decoy.
ESM: Bharat Ajanta Mk 2; intercept.
ECM: Elettronica TQN-2; jammer.
Combat data systems: CAIO-15A.
Radars: Air search: Bharat RAWL-02 Mk 3 (LW08) ❽; D-band.
Air/surface search: EL/M-2238 STAR; 3D; E/F-band ❾.
Fire control: ELTA EL-M 2221 STGR; I/J/K-band (for SAM) ❿; Ratep 5P-10E Puma; I-band (for 100 mm); Plank Shave (Granit Garpun B) (for SSM) ⓫; I/J-band.
Navigation: Kelvin Hughes Nucleus 6000; E/F-band. 2 Nyada MR-212/201; I-band.
Sonars: Bharat HUMSA; hull-mounted; medium frequency. Towed array (to be confirmed).

Helicopters: 2 Westland Sea Kings Mk 42B ⓬ or 2 Hindustan Aeronautics ALH.

Programmes: The first of three modified Delhi class was laid down in 2003 but progress since her launch in 2006 has been very slow. Four further ships are to be ordered under Project 15B.
Structure: Designed by the Indian Naval Design Bureau, the design appears to be a development of the Delhi class incorporating some features of both the Talwar and Project 17 frigates.

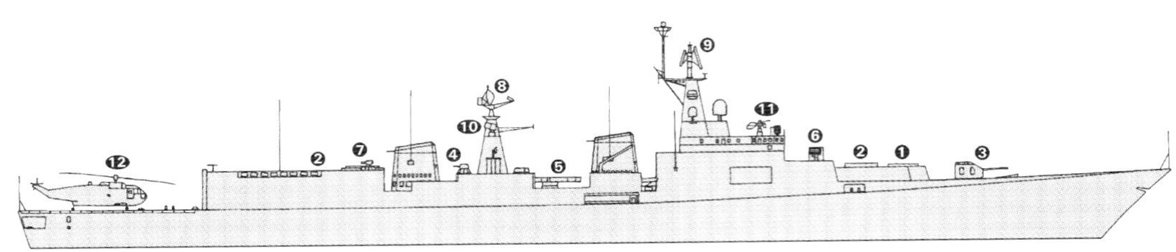

PROJECT 15A ***(Scale 1 : 1,200), Ian Sturton*** / 1042090

5 RAJPUT (KASHIN II) CLASS (PROJECT 61ME) (DDGHM)

Name	*No*	*Builders*	*Laid down*	*Launched*	*Commissioned*
RAJPUT (ex-*Nadezhniy*)	D 51	Nikolayev North (61 Kommuna)	11 Sep 1976	17 Sep 1977	4 May 1980
RANA (ex-*Gubitelyniyy*)	D 52	Nikolayev North (61 Kommuna)	29 Nov 1976	27 Sep 1978	19 Feb 1982
RANJIT (ex-*Lovkiyy*)	D 53	Nikolayev North (61 Kommuna)	29 June 1977	16 June 1979	24 Nov 1983
RANVIR (ex-*Tverdyy*)	D 54	Nikolayev North (61 Kommuna)	24 Oct 1981	12 Mar 1983	21 Apr 1986
RANVIJAY (ex-*Tolkoviyy*)	D 55	Nikolayev North (61 Kommuna)	19 Mar 1982	1 Feb 1986	21 Dec 1987

Displacement, tons: 3,950 standard; 4,974 full load
Dimensions, feet (metres): 480.5 × 51.8 × 15.7 *(146.5 × 15.8 × 4.8)*
Main machinery: COGAG; 4 Ukraine gas turbines; 72,000 hp(m) *(53 MW)*; 2 shafts
Speed, knots: 35
Range, n miles: 4,500 at 18 kt; 2,600 at 30 kt
Complement: 320 (35 officers)

Missiles: SSM: 2 (D 51) or 4 SS-N-2D Mod 2 Styx (D 52, 53) ❶; IR homing to 83 km *(45 n miles)* at 0.9 Mach; warhead 513 kg; sea-skimmer.
4 (D 51) or 8 (D 54, 55) Brahmos PJ-10; active/passive radar terminal homing to 290 km *(157 n miles)* at 2.6 Mach; warhead 200 kg.
SAM: 2 (D 51, 52, 53) or 1 (D 54, 55) SA-N-1 Goa twin launchers ❷; command guidance to 31.5 km *(17 n miles)* at 2 Mach; height 91–22, 860 m *(300–75,000 ft)*; warhead 60 kg; 44 missiles. Some SSM capability.
2 octuple IAI/Rafael Barak 1 VLS (D 54, D 55); command line of sight radar or optical guidance to 10 km *(5.5 n miles)* at 2 Mach; warhead 22 kg.
Guns: 2—3 in *(76 mm)*/59 AK 726 (twin, fwd) ❸; 90 rds/min to 16 km *(8.5 n miles)*; weight of shell 5.9 kg.
8—30 mm/65 (4 twin) AK 230 (D 51, 52, 53) ❹; 500 rds/min to 5 km *(2.7 n miles)*; weight of shell 0.54 kg.
2—30 mm/65 AK 630 (6 barrels per mounting) (D 54, 55); 3,000 rds/min combined to 2 km.
Torpedoes: 5—21 in *(533 mm)* (quin) tubes ❺. Combination of SET-65E; anti-submarine; active/passive homing to 15 km *(8.1 n miles)* at 40 kt; warhead 205 kg and Type 53-65; passive wake homing to 19 km *(10.3 n miles)* at 45 kt; warhead 305 kg.
A/S mortars: 2 RBU 6000 12-tubed trainable ❻; range 6,000 m; warhead 31 kg.
Countermeasures: 4 PK 16 chaff launchers for radar decoy and distraction.
ESM: Bharat Ajanta Mk 2; intercept.
ECM: Elettronica TQN-2; jammer.
Radars: Air search: Big Net A (D 51, 54-55) ❼; C-band; range 183 km *(100 n miles)* for 2 m^2 target.
Bharat/Signaal RAWL-02 Mk 2 (LW04) (D 52, 53); D-band.
Air/surface search: Head Net C (D 51-54) ❽; 3D; E-band.
EL/M-2238 STAR (D 54, 55); 3D; E/F-band.
Navigation: 2 Bharat Rashmi; I-band.
Fire control: 2 Peel Group ❾; H/I-band; range 73 km *(40 n miles)* for 2 m^2 target.
Owl Screech ❿; G-band.
2 Drum Tilt ⓫ or 2 Bass Tilt; H/I-band or 2 EL/M-2221 STGR; I/J/K-band.
IFF: 2 High Pole B.
Sonars: Vycheda MG 311 (D 51, 52, 55); hull-mounted; active search and attack; medium frequency.
Mare Tail VDS; active search; medium frequency.

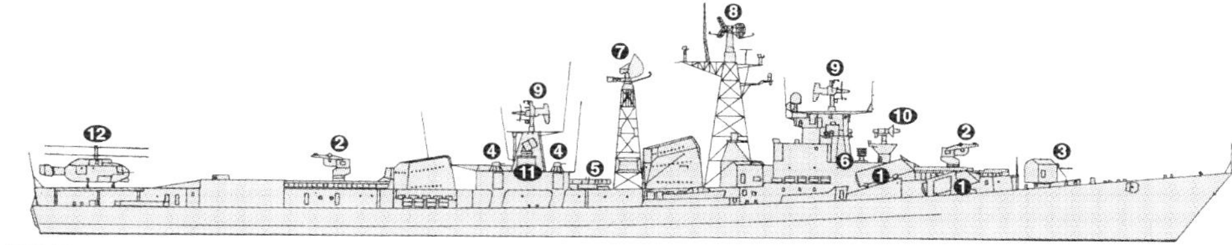

RANA *(Scale 1 : 1,200), Ian Sturton* / 0506295

RANJIT *10/2004, Toshiyuki Hanta* / 1042266

Bharat Humsa (D 53, 54); hull-mounted; medium frequency.

Helicopters: 1 Ka-28 Helix ⓬.

Programmes: First batch of three ordered in the mid-1970s. *Ranvir* was the first of the second batch ordered on 20 December 1982.
Modernisation: New EW equipment installed on all ships refitted since 1993. It is possible that an Italian combat data system compatible with Selenia IPN-10 has been installed. D 51, 54 and 55 have undergone extensive modernisation since 2003. This includes installation of Brahmos SSM and Barak SAM. EL/M-2238 STAR search radar has replaced Head Net C in D 55 and is likely to be fitted to other ships. All ships are Inmarsat fitted.
Structure: Originally built to a modified Kashin-class design, the ships are equipped with a helicopter hangar, reached by a lift from the flight deck, to replace the after 76 mm twin mount. Recent modifications have led to some differences in structure. While D 52 and D 53 remain unmodified, four Brahmos missile launchers have replaced the forward SS-N-2D mountings in D 51 while, in D 54 and D 55, an 8-cell Brahmos VLS system has been installed in lieu of the aft SA-N-1 launcher. D 54 and D 55 have also been fitted (port and starboard) with two octuple VLS silos for Barak SAM and associated EL/M-2221 STGR fire-control radars. These silos are in place of the forward AK-630 mountings. D 52 and D 53 may be similarly fitted in due course.
Operational: All based at Vishakapatnam. Dhanush (Prithvi) ballistic missile test launched from *Rajput* on 28 December 2005. Vertical launch of Brahmos was conducted from *Ranvir* on 18 December 2008.

RANVIJAY *10/2004, Ships of the World* / 1042265

RANA *10/2008*, US Navy* / 1353086

3 DELHI CLASS (PROJECT 15) (DDGHM)

Name	*No*	*Builders*	*Laid down*	*Launched*	*Commissioned*
DELHI	D 61	Mazagon Dock Ltd, Mumbai	14 Nov 1987	1 Feb 1991	15 Nov 1997
MYSORE	D 60	Mazagon Dock Ltd, Mumbai	2 Feb 1991	4 June 1993	2 June 1999
MUMBAI	D 62	Mazagon Dock Ltd, Mumbai	14 Dec 1992	20 Mar 1995	22 Jan 2001

Displacement, tons: 6,700 full load
Dimensions, feet (metres): 534.8 × 57.1 × 21.3 *(163 × 17.4 × 6.5)*
Main machinery: 4 Zorya/Mashprockt DT-59 gas turbines; 82,820 hp(m) *(61.7 MW)*; 2 shafts; cp props
Speed, knots: 32
Range, n miles: 4,500 at 18 kt
Complement: 360 (40 officers)

Missiles: SSM: 16 Zvezda SS-N-25 (4 quad) (KH 35E Uran) (1) active radar homing to 130 km *(70.2 n miles)* at 0.9 Mach; warhead 145 kg; sea skimmer.
SAM: 2 SA-N-7 Gadfly (Kashmir/Uragan) (2) command, semi-active radar and IR homing to 25 km *(13.5 n miles)* at 3 Mach; warhead 70 kg. Total of 48 missiles.
4 Octuple IAI/Rafael Barak 1 VLS (D 60, D 61) (3); command line of sight radar or optical guidance to 10 km *(5.5 n miles)* at 2 Mach; warhead 22 kg.
Guns: 1 USSR 3.9 in *(100 mm)*/59 (4). AK 100; 60 rds/min to 21.5 km *(11.5 n miles)*; weight of shell 15.6 kg.
4 (2 in D 61) USSR 30 mm/65 (5) AK 630; 6 barrels per mounting; 3,000 rds/min combined to 2 km.
Torpedoes: 5 PTA 21 in *(533 mm)* (quin) tubes (6). Combination of SET 65E; anti-submarine; active/passive homing to 15 km *(8.1 n miles)* at 40 kt; warhead 205 kg and Type 53-65; passive wake homing to 19 km *(10.3 n miles)* at 45 kt; warhead 305 kg.
A/S mortars: 2 RBU 6000 (7); 12 tubed trainable; range 6,000 m; warhead 31 kg.
Depth charges: 2 rails.
Countermeasures: Decoys: 2 PK2 chaff launchers (8). Towed torpedo decoy.
ESM: Bharat Ajanta Mk 2; intercept.
Combat data systems: Bharat IPN Shikari (IPN 10).
Radars: Air search: Bharat RAWL-02 Mk 3 (LW08) (D 60); Bharat RAWL-02 Mk 2 (LW04) (D 61, D 62) (9); D-band.
Air/surface search: Half Plate (10); E-band.
Fire control: 6 Front Dome (11); H/I-band (for SAM); Kite Screech (12); I/J-band (for 100 mm); 2 Bass Tilt (MR-123) (D 62); I/J-band (for AK 630); EL/M-2221 STGR (D 60, D 61) (13) (for Barak); I/J/K-band; Plank Shave (Granit Garpun B) (14) (for SSM); I/J-band.
Navigation: 3 Nyada MR-212/201; I-band.
Sonars: Bharat HUMVAD; hull-mounted; active search; medium frequency.
Bharat HUMSA; hull-mounted; medium frequency (D 62).
Indal/Garden Reach Model 15-750 VDS.
Thales ATAS; active towed array (D 62).

Helicopters: 2 Westland Sea Kings Mk 42B (15) or 2 Hindustan Aeronautics ALH.

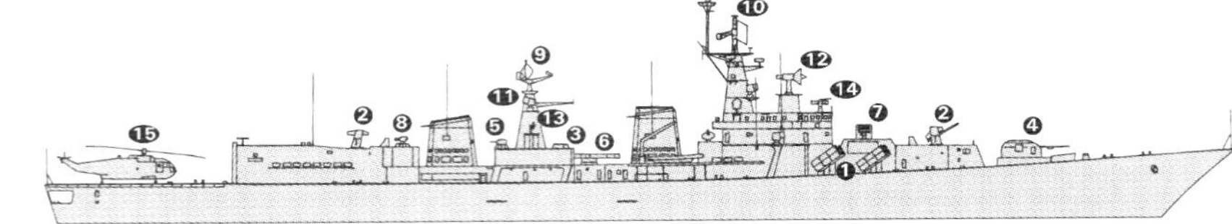

DELHI ***(Scale 1 : 1,500), Ian Sturton*** / 057239

DELHI (before being fitted with Barak) ***2/2001, Sattler/Steele*** / 012136

Programmes: Built with Russian Severnoye Design Bureau assistance. *Delhi* ordered in March 1986. Programme was called Project 15. Much delay was caused by the breakdown in the central control of Russian export equipment.
Structure: The design is described as a 'stretched *Rajput*' with some *Godavari* features. A combination of Russian and Indian weapon systems fitted. Missile blast deflectors indicate an original intention to fit SS-N-22 Sunburn. Samahé helo handling system. Forward funnel offset to port and after funnel to starboard.
Modernisation: Barak has replaced the forward AK-630 mountings in D 60 and D 61. The two Bass Tilt radar have also been replaced by EL/M-2221 STGR. D 62 is to be similarly refitted. SS-N-25 may be replaced by Brahmos.
Operational: Based at Mumbai. Have Flag facilities.

MYSORE ***4/2007, Hachiro Nakai*** / 116653

MUMBAI

6/2005, Maritime Photographic / 1151257

MUMBAI

7/2005, A A de Kruijf / 1151116

MYSORE

4/2007, Mitsuhiro Kadota / 1166561

FRIGATES

Notes: Project 17A is for a new class of warships to complement or succeed the Project 17 Shivalik class. A Request for Information (RFI) was issued to European and Russian shipyards in December 2006 for the procurement of seven frigates, one or more of which might be built in a foreign shipyard and remaining ships in India. The initiative is reported to have been prompted by concerns about the ability of Indian shipyards to meet projected force levels.

3 + 3 (3) TALWAR (PROJECT 1135.6) CLASS (FFGHM)

Name	*No*	*Builders*	*Laid down*	*Launched*	*Commissioned*
TALWAR	F 40	Baltic Shipyard, St Petersburg	10 Mar 1999	12 May 2000	18 June 2003
TRISHUL	F 43	Baltic Shipyard, St Petersburg	24 Sep 1999	24 Nov 2000	25 June 2003
TABAR	F 44	Baltic Shipyard, St Petersburg	26 May 2000	25 May 2001	19 Apr 2004
–	–	Yantar Shipyard, Kaliningrad	27 July 2007	2009	2011
–	–	Yantar Shipyard, Kaliningrad	28 Nov 2007	2010	2012
–	–	Yantar Shipyard, Kaliningrad	11 June 2008	2010	2012

Displacement, tons: 3,620 standard; 4,035 full load
Dimensions, feet (metres): 409.6 × 49.9 × 15.1 *(124.8 × 15.2 × 4.6)*
Main machinery: COGAG; 2 Zorya DN-59 gas turbines; 43,448 hp/m *(34.2 MW)*; 2 Zorya UGT 6000 gas turbines; 16,628 hp(m) *(12.4 MW)*; 2 shafts; fixed propellers
Speed, knots: 32
Range, n miles: 4,850 at 14 kt; 1,600 at 30 kt
Complement: 180 (18 officers)

Missiles: SSM: 8 SS-N-27 Novator Alfa Klub-N (Batch 1) (3K-54-TE) ❶ active radar homing to 180 km *(97.2 n miles)* at 0.7 Mach (cruise) and 2.5 Mach (attack); warhead 450 kg. 8 Brahmos PJ-10 (Batch 2); active/passive radar terminal homing to 290 km *(157 n miles)* at 0.9 Mach; warhead 513 kg. VLS silo.
SAM: SA-N-7 Gadfly (Kashmir/Uragan) single launcher ❷ command, semi-active radar and IR homing to 25 km *(13.5 n miles)* at 3 Mach; warhead 70 kg. 24 9M 317 missiles.
SAM/Guns: 2 CADS-N-1 (Kashtan) ❸ each has twin 30 mm Gatling combined with 8 SA-N-11 (Grisson) and Hot Flash/Hot Spot radar/optronic director. Laser beam guidance for missiles to 8 km *(4.4 n miles)* warhead 9 kg; 9,000 rds/min (combined) to 1.5 km for guns.
Guns: 1—3.9 in *(100 mm)*/70 A 190E ❹; 80 rds/min to 21.5 km *(11.6 n miles)*; weight of shell 15.6 kg.
Torpedoes: 4 DTA-53 21 in *(533 mm)* (2 twin) fixed launchers ❺.
A/S mortars: 1 RBU 6000 12-barrelled launcher ❻ range 6 km; warhead 31 kg.
Countermeasures: Decoys: 2 PK 2 chaff launchers (to be fitted).
ESM: ASOR (TK-25E-5); jammer.
Combat data systems: Trebovaniye-M.
Radars: Air search: Top Plate (Fregat-M2EM) ❼ 3D; E/F-band.
Air/surface search: Cross Dome (Positiv-E) ❽; E/F-band.
Fire control: 4 Front Dome (MR-90) ❾; H/I-band (for SA-N-7). Plank Shave (Garpun-B) ❿; I/J-band (for SSM); Ratep 5P-10E Puma ⓫; I-band (for 100 mm gun).
Navigation: Kelvin Hughes Nucleus 6000 ⓬; E/F-band. 2 Nyada MR 212/201 (Palm Frond) ⓭; I-band.
Sonars: HUMSA; hull mounted; active/passive medium frequency.
VDS (may be fitted in future).

Helicopters: 1 Ka-28/Ka-31 Helix ⓮ or ALH.

Programmes: Contract placed in 1997 and confirmed 21 July 1998 for the first batch of three modified Krivak IIIs. Mutual interference difficulties reportedly delayed entry into service of first of class by one year. An option for a second batch of three ships was exercised on 14 July 2006. Construction at Yantar Shipyard, Kaliningrad, started in July 2007. The first ship is to be delivered after five years and the other two ships at six-month intervals thereafter. Negotiations for the procurement of three Batch 3 ships began in early 2009.
Structure: Batch 1 are the first surface units to be fitted with the SS-N-27 missile. This may be replaced by the Brahmos missile in Batch 2.

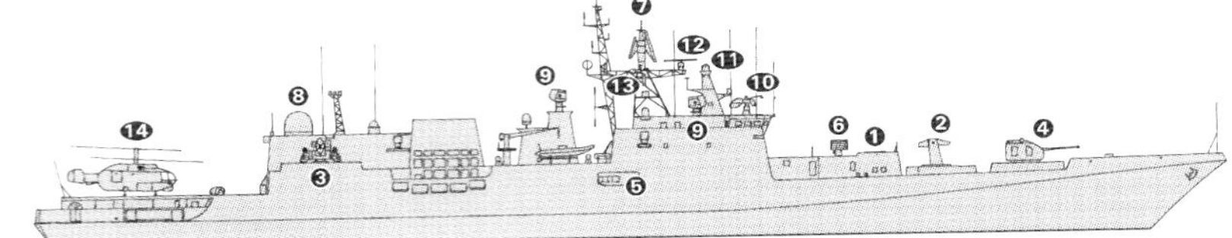

TALWAR I *(Scale 1 : 1,200), Ian Sturton* / 1166541

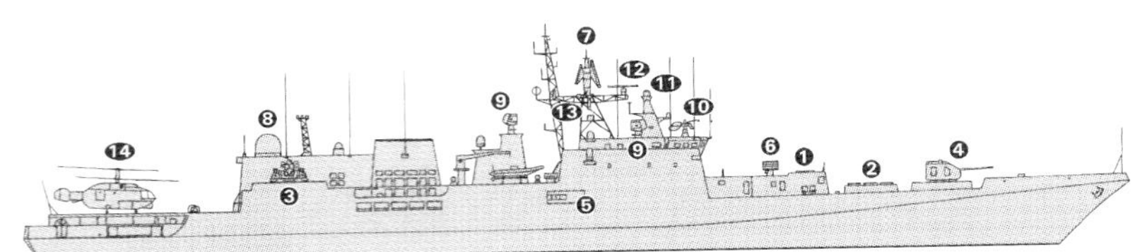

TALWAR II *(Scale 1 : 1,200), Ian Sturton* / 1166540

TABAR *6/2006, Chris Sattler* / 1164473

TABAR *5/2004, Harald Carstens* / 1042274

0 + 3 SHIVALIK (PROJECT 17) CLASS (FFGHM)

Name	*No*	*Builders*	*Laid down*	*Launched*	*Commissioned*
SHIVALIK	–	Mazagon Dock Ltd, Mumbai	11 July 2001	18 Apr 2003	2009
SATPURA	–	Mazagon Dock Ltd, Mumbai	Oct 2002	4 June 2004	2009
SAHYADRI	–	Mazagon Dock Ltd, Mumbai	17 Mar 2003	27 May 2005	2010

Displacement, tons: 4,600 standard; 5,300 full load
Dimensions, feet (metres): 469.3 × 55.5 × 17.4 *(143.0 × 16.9 × 5.3)*
Main machinery: CODOG; 2 GE LM 2,500 gas turbines; 44,000 hp *(32.8 MW)*; 2 SEMT-Pielstick PA6 STC diesels; 15,200 hp *(11.3 MW)*; 2 cp propellers.
Speed, knots: 30
Range, n miles: 4,500 at 18 kt; 1,600 at 30 kt
Complement: 257 (35 officers)

Missiles: SSM: 8 SS-N-27 Novator Alfa Klub-N (3K-54-TE) ❶; active radar homing to 180 km *(97.2 n miles)* at 0.7 Mach (cruise) and 2.5 Mach (attack); warhead 450 kg; VLS silo.
SAM: SA-N-7 Gadfly (Kashmir/Uragan) single launcher 6 ❷ command, semi-active radar and IR homing to 25 km *(13.5 n miles)* at 3 Mach; warhead 70 kg. 24 9M38M1 missiles.
SAM/Guns: 1 octuple Barak VLS ❸; command line-of-sight radar or optical guidance to 10 km *(5.5 n miles)* at 2 Mach; warhead 22 kg.
Guns: 1 OTO Melara 3 in *(76 mm)*/62 Super Rapid ❹; 120 rds/min to 16 km *(8.7 n miles)*; weight of shell 6 kg.
Torpedoes: 6–324 mm ILAS 3 (2 triple) ❺.
A/S mortars: 2 RBU 6000 12-barrelled launcher ❻ range 6 km; warhead 31 kg.
Countermeasures: Decoys: 2 PK 2 chaff launchers.
ESM: Bharat Ajanta; intercept.

SHIVALIK *(Scale 1 : 1,200), Ian Sturton* / 0569247

ECM: ASOR (TK-25E-5); jammer.
Combat data systems: BEL EMCCA.
Radars: Air search: Bharat RAWL-02 Mk 3 (LW08) ❼; E/F-band
Air/surface search: Top Plate (Fregat-M2EM) ❽ 3D; D/E-band.
Fire control: 2 BEL Shikari (based on Contraves Seaguard) ❾ (for 76 mm); I/K-bands.
1 Bharat Aparna (modified Plank Shave/Garpun B) ❿ (for SSMs); I/J-bands.
4 Front Dome (MR 90) ⓫ (for SA-N-7); H/I-band.
Navigation: 1 BEL Rashmi; I-band.
Sonars: Bharat HUMSA; hull-mounted; active search and attack; medium frequency.
VDS; active search; medium frequency.

Helicopters: 1 Sea King Mk 42B ⓬.

Programmes: Three Project 17 ships approved in June 1999 and construction of the first of class began in 2001. Initially, building was rapid but the production process has taken much longer than first estimates. While Project 17A for seven follow-on ships has been initiated, these may be to a different design.
Structure: An enlarged and modified version of the Talwar class, the aft section resembles the Delhi class. Signature reduction (IR and RCS) features are believed to be incorporated. Details are speculative.
Operational: Sea trials of *Shivalik* are planned to have started by mid-2009.

3 GODAVARI CLASS (PROJECT 16) (FFGHM)

Name	*No*	*Builders*	*Laid down*	*Launched*	*Commissioned*
GODAVARI	F 20	Mazagon Dock Ltd, Mumbai	2 June 1978	15 May 1980	10 Dec 1983
GOMATI	F 21	Mazagon Dock Ltd, Mumbai	1981	19 Mar 1984	16 Apr 1988
GANGA	F 22	Mazagon Dock Ltd, Mumbai	1980	21 Oct 1981	30 Dec 1985

Displacement, tons: 4,209 full load
Dimensions, feet (metres): 414.9 × 47.6 × 14.8 (29.5 sonar) *(126.5 × 14.5 × 4.5; 9)*
Main machinery: 2 Babcock & Wilcox boilers; 550 psi *(38.7 kg/cm²)*; 850°F *(450°C)*; 2 turbines; 30,000 hp *(22.4 MW)*; 2 shafts
Speed, knots: 28
Range, n miles: 4,500 at 12 kt
Complement: 313 (40 officers including 13 aircrew)

Missiles: SSM: 4 SS-N-2D Styx ❶; active radar (Mod 1) or IR (Mod 2) homing to 83 km *(45 n miles)* at 0.9 Mach; warhead 513 kg; sea-skimmer at end of run. Indian designation.
SAM: 1 Octuple IAI/Rafael Barak VLS ❷; command line of sight radar or optical guidance to 10 km *(5.5 n miles)* at 2 Mach; warhead 22 kg.
Guns: 1 OTO Melara 76 mm/62 Super Rapid ❸; 120 rds/min to 16 km *(8.7 n miles)*; weight of shell 6kg.
8–30 mm/65 (4 twin) AK 230 ❹; 500 rds/min to 5 km *(2.7 n miles)*; weight of shell 0.54 kg.
2–7.63 mm MGs.
Torpedoes: 6–324 mm ILAS 3 (2 triple) tubes ❺. Whitehead A244S; anti-submarine; active/passive homing to 7 km *(3.8 n miles)* at 33 kt; warhead 34 kg (shaped charge). *Godavari* has tube modifications for the Indian NST 58 version of A244S.
Countermeasures: Decoys: 2 chaff launchers (Super Barricade). Graseby G738 towed torpedo decoy.
ESM/ECM: Selenia INS-3 (Bharat Ajanta and Elettronica TQN-2); intercept and jammer.
Combat data systems: Selenia IPN-10 action data automation. Inmarsat communications (JRC) ❻.
Weapons control: MR 301 MFCS. MR 103 GFCS.
Radars: Air search: Bharat RAWL-02 Mk 3 (LW08) ❼; D-band.
Air/surface search: EL/M-2238 STAR ❽; 3D; E/F-band.
Navigation/helo control: 2 Signaal ZW06 ❾; or Don Kay; I-band.
Fire control: 2 Drum Tilt ❿; H/I-band (for 30 mm).
EL/M-2221 STGR ⓫; I/J/K-band.
Bel Lynx ⓬; I-band (for 76 mm).
Sonars: Bharat APSOH; hull-mounted; active panoramic search and attack; medium frequency.

GANGA *(Scale 1 : 1,200), Ian Sturton* / 1166539

GANGA *2/2006, M Mazumdar* / 1164474

Fathoms Oceanic VDS.
Thomson Sintra DSBV 62 (in *Ganga*); passive towed array; very low frequency.
Type 162M; bottom classification; high frequency.

Helicopters: 2 Sea King or 1 Sea King and 1 Chetak ⓭.

Modernisation: Barak launchers have replaced SA-N-4 in all three ships. 57 mm gun has been replaced by OTO Melara 76 mm.

Structure: A further modification of the original Leander design with an indigenous content of 72 per cent and a larger hull. Poor welding is noticeable in *Godavari*. *Gomati* is the first Indian ship to have digital electronics in her combat data system.
Operational: French Samahé helicopter handling equipment is fitted. Usually only one helo is carried with more than one crew. These ships have a unique mixture of Russian, Western and Indian weapon systems which has inevitably led to some equipment compatibility problems.

GODAVARI *10/2008*, US Navy* / 1353087

3 BRAHMAPUTRA CLASS (PROJECT 16A) (FFGHM)

Name	No	Builders	Laid down	Launched	Commissioned
BRAHMAPUTRA	F 31	Garden Reach SY, Kolkata	1989	29 Jan 1994	14 Apr 2000
BETWA	F 39	Garden Reach SY, Kolkata	22 Aug 1994	26 Feb 1998	7 July 2004
BEAS	F 37	Garden Reach SY, Kolkata	26 Feb 1998	2002	11 July 2005

Displacement, tons: 4,450 full load
Dimensions, feet (metres): 414.9 × 47.6 × 14.8 (29.5 sonar) *(126.5 × 14.5 × 4.5; 9)*
Main machinery: 2 boilers; 550 psi *(38.7 kg/cm²)*; 850°F *(450°C)*; 2 Bhopal turbines; 30,000 hp *(22.4 MW)*; 2 shafts
Speed, knots: 27. **Range, n miles:** 4,500 at 12 kt
Complement: 351 (31 officers and 13 aircrew)

Missiles: SSM: 16 SS-N-25 (4 quad) (KH-35E Uran) ❶; active radar homing to 130 km *(70.2 n miles)* at 0.9 Mach; warhead 145 kg; sea skimmer.
SAM: 1 Octuple IAI/Rafael Barak VLS ❷; command line of sight radar or optical guidance to 10 km *(5.5 n miles)* at 2 Mach; warhead 22 kg.
Guns: OTO Melara 76 mm/62 ❸; 85 rds/min to 16 km *(8.6 n miles)* weight of shell 6 kg.
4—30 mm/65 AK 630 ❹; 6 barrels per mounting; 3,000 rds/min combined to 2 km.
Torpedoes: 6—324 mm ILAS 3 (2 triple) tubes ❺. Whitehead A244S; anti-submarine; active/passive homing to 7 km *(3.8 n miles)* at 33 kt; warhead 34 kg (shaped charge).
Countermeasures: Decoys: 2 chaff launchers (Super Barricade in due course). Graseby G738 towed torpedo decoy.
ESM: Selenia INS-3 (Bharat Ajanta) ❻; intercept.
Combat data systems: BEL EMCCA. Inmarsat communications (JRC).

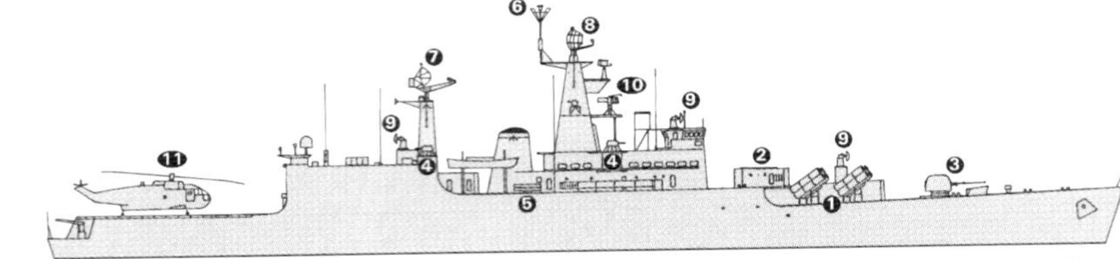

BRAHMAPUTRA *(Scale 1 : 1,200), Ian Sturton* / 0121334

Weapons control: MR 103 GFCS.
Radars: Air search: Bharat RAWL-02 Mk 3 (LW08) ❼; D-band.
Air/surface search: Bharat RAWS-03 (using DA 08 antenna) (PFN 513) ❽; E/F-band.
Navigation/helo control: Decca Bridgemaster; I-band. BEL Rashmi (PIN 524) (using ZW 06 antenna); I-band.
Fire control: 2 BEL Shikari (based on Contraves Seaguard) ❾ (for 76 mm and Ak 630); I/K-bands.
EL/M-2221 STGR (for Barak); I/J/K-bands.
Bharat Aparna (modified Plank Shave/Garpun B) ❿ (for SSM); I/J-band.
Selenia RAN (for SAM); I-band.

Sonars: Bharat HUMSA (APSOH); hull-mounted; active panoramic search and attack; medium frequency.
Thales towed array.

Helicopters: 2 Sea King or 1 Sea King and 1 Chetak ⓫.

Programmes: Project 16A. Progress has been very slow.
Structure: The main difference is the replacement of the Godavari SS-N-2 by SS-N-25. Following the cancellation of the Trishul SAM programme, Barak has been fitted in its place. Gun armament has also improved.

BETWA *3/2006* / 1164472

BEAS *3/2008*, Michael Nitz* / 130530

3 NILGIRI (LEANDER) CLASS (FFH)

Name	*No*	*Builders*	*Laid down*	*Launched*	*Commissioned*
DUNAGIRI	F 36	Mazagon Dock Ltd, Mumbai	25 Jan 1973	9 Mar 1974	5 May 1977
TARAGIRI	F 41	Mazagon Dock Ltd, Mumbai	15 Oct 1975	25 Oct 1976	16 May 1980
VINDHYAGIRI	F 42	Mazagon Dock Ltd, Mumbai	5 Nov 1976	12 Nov 1977	8 July 1981

Displacement, tons: 2,962 full load (F 35-F 36). 3,039 full load (F 41-F 42)
Dimensions, feet (metres): 372 × 36.1 (F 35-F 36); 44.3 (F 41 and F 42) × 18 *(113.5 × 11; 13.5 × 5.5)*
Main machinery: 2 Babcock & Wilcox boilers; 550 psi *(38.7 kg/cm²)*; 850°F *(450°C)*; 2 turbines; 30,000 hp *(22.4 MW)*; 2 shafts
Speed, knots: 27; 28 (F 41 and F 42)
Range, n miles: 4,500 at 12 kt
Complement: 267 (17 officers). 300 (20 officers) (F 41 and F 42)

Guns: 2 Vickers 4.5 in *(114 mm)*/45 (twin) Mk 6 ❶; 20 rds/min to 19 km *(10.4 n miles)* anti-surface; 6 km *(3.3 n miles)* anti-aircraft; weight of shell 25 kg.
4—30 mm/65 (2 twin) AK 230 ❷; 500 rds/min to 5 km *(2.7 n miles)*; weight of shell 0.54 kg.
2 Oerlikon 20 mm/70 ❸; 800 rds/min to 2 km.
Torpedoes: 6—324 mm ILAS 3 (2 triple) tubes (F 41 and F 42) ❹. Whitehead A244S or Indian NST 58 version; anti-submarine; active/passive homing to 7 km *(3.8 n miles)* at 33 kt; warhead 34 kg (shaped charge).
A/S mortars: 1 Bofors 375 mm twin-tubed launcher (F 41 and F 42) ❺; range 1,600 m.
1 Limbo Mk 10 triple-tubed launcher (remainder); range 1,000 m; warhead 92 kg.
Countermeasures: Decoys: Graseby 738; towed torpedo decoy.
ESM: Bharat Ajanta; intercept. FH5 Telegon D/F.
ECM: Racal Cutlass; jammer.
Combat data systems: Signaal DS-22.

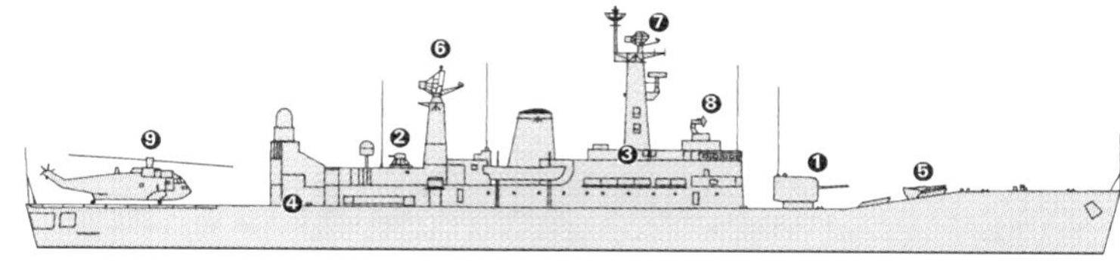

VINDHYAGIRI ***(Scale 1 : 1,200), Ian Sturton*** / 1042089

Radars: Air search: Bharat RAWL-02 Mk 2 (LW04) ❻; D-band.
Air/surface search: Signaal DA 05 ❼; E/F-band.
Navigation: Signaal ZW 06; I-band.
Fire control: Signaal M 45 ❽; I/J-band.
IFF: Type 944; 954M.
Sonars: Westinghouse SQS-505; hull-mounted; active search and attack; medium frequency. Type 170; active attack; high frequency.
Westinghouse VDS (F 36 only); active; medium frequency.
Thomson Diodon VDS in F 41 and F 42.

Helicopters: 1 Chetak or 1 Sea King Mk 42 (in *Taragiri* and *Vindhyagiri*) ❾.

Programmes: The first major warships built in Indian yards to a UK design with a 60 per cent indigenous component. An ex-UK Leander class was acquired in 1995 and is listed under Training Ships.

Modernisation: The VDS arrays are installed inside towed bodies built by Fathom Oceanology Ltd of Canada. The transducer elements in both cases are identical. AK 230 guns have replaced the obsolete Seacat. *Vindhyagiri* modified with UAV control stations above the hangar in order to operate Heron II UAVs.
Structure: In the first two the hangar was provided with telescopic extension to take the Alouette III helicopter while in the last pair, a much-changed design, the Mk 10 Mortar has been removed as well as VDS and the aircraft space increased to make way for a Sea King helicopter with a telescopic hangar and Canadian Beartrap haul-down gear. In these two an open deck has been left below the flight deck for handling mooring gear and there is a cut-down to the stern.
Operational: *Himgiri* was decommissioned on 6 May 2005 and *Udaygiri* in 2007.

VINDHYAGIRI ***11/2003*** / 1042277

DUNAGIRI ***2/2001, Michael Nitz*** / 0534080

CORVETTES

4 KORA CLASS (PROJECT 25A) (FSGHM)

Name	*No*	*Builders*	*Laid down*	*Launched*	*Commissioned*
KORA	P 61	Garden Reach SY, Kolkata	10 Jan 1990	23 Sep 1992	10 Aug 1998
KIRCH	P 62	Garden Reach SY, Kolkata/Mazagon Dock	31 Jan 1990	28 Sep 1995	22 Jan 2001
KULISH	P 63	Garden Reach SY, Kolkata	4 Oct 1995	18 Aug 1997	20 Aug 2001
KARMUKH	P 64	Garden Reach SY, Kolkata/Mazagon Dock	27 Aug 1997	6 Apr 2000	4 Feb 2004

Displacement, tons: 1,460 full load
Dimensions, feet (metres): 298.9 × 34.4 × 14.8 *(91.1 × 10.5 × 4.5)*
Main machinery: 2 SEMT-Pielstick/Kirloskar 18 PA6 V 280 diesels; 14,400 hp(m) *(10.58 MW)* sustained; 2 shafts; LIPS cp props
Speed, knots: 25
Range, n miles: 4,000 at 16 kt
Complement: 134 (14 officers)

Missiles: SSM: 8 Zvezda SS-N-25 (2 quad) (Kh 35E Uran) ❶; active radar homing to 130 km *(70.2 n miles)* at 0.9 Mach; warhead 145 kg; sea skimmer.
SAM: 2 SA-N-5 Grail ❷; manual aiming; IR homing to 6 km *(3.2 n miles)* at 1.5 Mach; altitude to 2,500 m *(8,000 ft)*; warhead 1.5 kg.
Guns: 1 USSR 3 in *(76 mm)*/59 AK 176 (P 61) ❸; 120 rds/min to 15 km *(8.0 n miles)*; weight of shell 5.9 kg. 1 Otobreda 76 mm/62 (P 62, P 63 and P 64).
2—30 mm/65 AK 630 ❹; 6 barrels per mounting; 3,000 rds/min to 2 km.
Countermeasures: Decoys: 2 PK 10 chaff launchers ❺. 2 BEL TOTED; towed torpedo decoys.
ESM: Bharat Ajanta P Mk II intercept ❻.

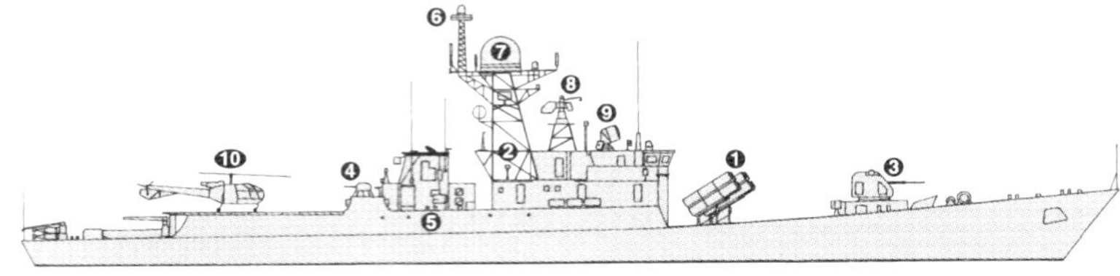

KORA (Scale 1 : 900), Ian Sturton / 0064715

Combat data systems: Bharat Vympal IPN-10.
Radars: Air search: Cross Dome ❼; E/F-band; range 130 km *(70 n miles)*.
Air/surface search: Plank Shave (Granit Harpun B) ❽; I/J-band.
Fire control: Bass Tilt (P 61) ❾; H/I-band; BEL Lynx (P62-64); I-band.
Navigation: Bharat 1245; I-band.
IFF: Square Head.

Helicopters: Platform only ❿ for Chetak (to be replaced by Hindustan Aeronautics ALH in due course).

Programmes: First pair ordered in April 1990 and second pair in October 1994. Programme slowed by delays in provision of Russian equipment and it is not clear whether further vessels are to be built.
Structure: Very similar to the original Khukri class except that SS-N-25 has replaced SS-N-2. Stabilisers fitted.
Operational: Sea trials for *Kirch* and *Kulish* probably took place in 2000. All 16 SS-N-25 can be fired in one salvo.

KIRCH 3/2004, Bob Fildes / 1042273

KULISH 10/2008*, Michael Nitz / 1353086

4 KHUKRI CLASS (PROJECT 25) (FSGHM)

Name	*No*	*Builders*	*Laid down*	*Launched*	*Commissioned*
KHUKRI	P 49	Mazagon Dock Ltd, Mumbai	27 Sep 1985	3 Dec 1986	23 Aug 1989
KUTHAR	P 46	Mazagon Dock Ltd, Mumbai	13 Sep 1986	15 Apr 1989	7 June 1990
KIRPAN	P 44	Garden Reach SY, Kolkata	15 Nov 1985	16 Aug 1988	12 Jan 1991
KHANJAR	P 47	Garden Reach SY, Kolkata	15 Nov 1985	16 Aug 1988	22 Oct 1991

Displacement, tons: 1,423 full load
Dimensions, feet (metres): 298.9 × 34.4 × 13.1 *(91.1 × 10.5 × 4)*
Main machinery: 2 SEMT-Pielstick/Kirloskar 18 PA6 V 280 diesels; 14,400 hp(m) *(10.58 MW)* sustained; 2 shafts; LIPS cp props
Speed, knots: 24
Range, n miles: 4,000 at 16 kt
Complement: 112 (12 officers)

Missiles: SSM: 4 SS-N-2D Mod 1 Styx (2 twin) launchers ❶; IR homing to 83 km *(45 n miles)* at 0.9 Mach; warhead 513 kg.
SAM: SA-N-5 Grail ❷; manual aiming; IR homing to 6 km *(3.2 n miles)* at 1.5 Mach; altitude to 2,500 m *(8,000 ft)*; warhead 1.5 kg.
Guns: 1 USSR 3 in *(76 mm)*/59 AK 176 ❸; 120 rds/min to 15 km *(8.0 n miles)*; weight of shell 5.9 kg.
2—30 mm/65 AK 630 ❹; 6 barrels per mounting; 3,000 rds/min to 2 km.
Countermeasures: Decoys: 2 PK 16 chaff launchers ❺.
ESM: Bharat Ajanta P; intercept.
Combat data systems: Selenia IPN-10 *(Khukri)*; Bharat Vympal IPN-10 (remainder).

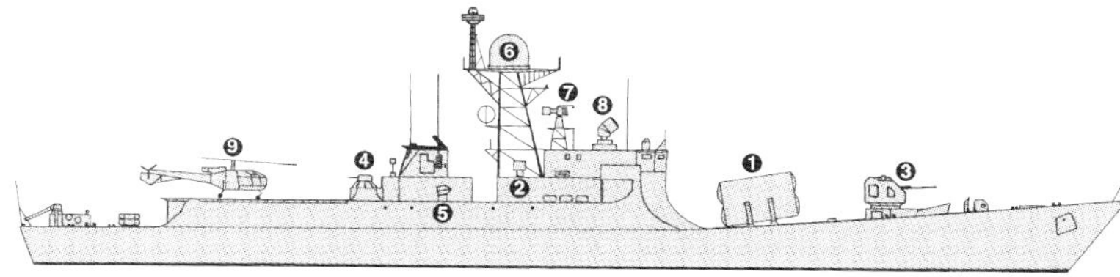

KHUKRI *(Scale 1 : 900), Ian Sturton* / 0064713

Radars: Air search: Cross Dome ❻; E/F-band; range 130 km *(70 n miles)*.
Air/surface search: Plank Shave ❼; I-band.
Fire control: Bass Tilt ❽; H/I-band.
Navigation: Bharat 1245; I-band.

Helicopters: Platform only ❾ for Chetak (to be replaced by HAL Dhruv in due course).

Programmes: First two ordered December 1983, two in 1985. The diesels were assembled in India under licence by Kirloskar. Indigenous content of the whole ship is about 65 per cent.
Structure: The reported plan was to make the first four ASW ships, and the remainder anti-aircraft or general purpose. However *Khukri* has neither torpedo tubes nor a sonar (apart from an Atlas Elektronik echo-sounder), so if the plan is correct these ships will rely on an ALH helicopter which has dunking sonar and ASW torpedoes and depth charges. All have fin stabilisers and full air conditioning.
Operational: All based at Vishakapatnam.

KUTHAR *2/2006, M Mazumdar* / 1164471

KIRPAN *2/2001, Michael Nitz* / 0534081

KUTHAR *4/2007, Mitsuhiro Kadota* / 1166560

0 + 4 (8) PROJECT 28 (CORVETTES) (FFG)

Name	No	Builders	Laid down	Launched	Commissioned
–	–	Garden Reach Shipbuilding & Engineering, Kolkata	18 Nov 2006	2009	2010
–	–	Garden Reach Shipbuilding & Engineering, Kolkata	27 Sep 2007	2010	2011

Displacement, tons: 2,500 full load
Dimensions, feet (metres): 358.3 × 46.5 × 7.0 *(109.2 × 14.17 × 3.72)*
Main machinery: CODAD: 4 Pielstick 12PA 6 STC diesels; 22,030 hp *(16.2 MW)*; 2 shafts; cp props
Speed, knots: 25
Range, n miles: 4,000 at 12 kt
Complement: 123

Missiles: SSM: SS-N-27 Novator Alfa Klub-N (3K-54-TE); active radar homing to 220 km *(119 n miles)* at 0.7 Mach (cruise) and 2.5 Mach (dive); warhead 450 kg; VLS silo.
SAM: 1-16 cell IAI/Rafael Barak VLS; command line of sight radar or optical guidance to 10 km *(5.5 n miles)* at 2.0 Mach; warhead 22 kg.
Guns: 1 Otobreda 3 in *(76 mm)*/62 Super Rapid; 120 rds/min to 16 km *(8.7 n miles)*; weight of shell 6 kg.
2–30 mm/65 AK 630; 6 barrels per mounting; 3,000 rds/min combined to 2 km.
Torpedoes: 6–324 or 533 mm ILAS (2 triple); Eurotorp MU-90.
A/S mortars: 2 RBU 6000 12-barrelled launchers; range 6 km; warhead 31 kg.
Countermeasures: Decoys: 4 Kavach chaff/flare decoy launchers. Towed torpedo decoy.
ESM: To be announced.
ECM: To be announced.
Combat data systems: BEL CMS-28. Datalinks. Satcom.

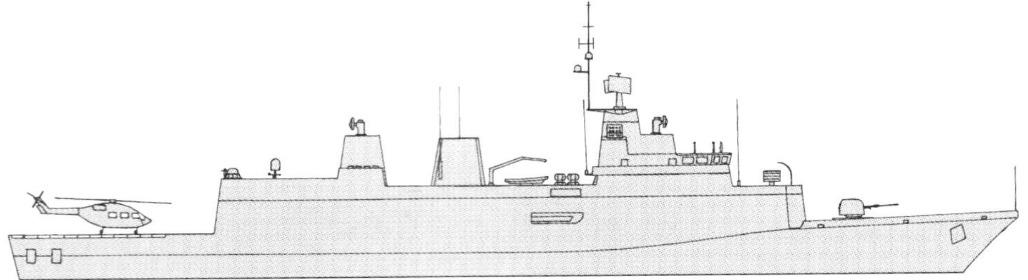

PROJECT 28 — *(Scale 1 : 900), Ian Sturton* / 1353092

Weapons control: EO director.
Radars: Surveillance: Bharat Revathi; 3D; E/F-band.
Fire control: Plank Shave (Garpun B); I-band (for SSM).
Bel Lynx (for 76 mm); I-band.
2 Elta EL/M-2221 STGR; I/J/K-band (for Barak).
Navigation: Decca Bridgemaster; I-band.
Sonars: Hull-mounted sonar. Active/passive towed array.

Helicopters: 1 Ka-28PL or HAL Dhruv.

Programmes: Multipurpose corvette designed to operate in Indian offshore waters. First four units ordered in 2003 and first steel cut for first of class on 12 August 2005. The first of class was reportedly laid-down in 2006 and further ships are likely to follow at 18-month intervals. A class of 12 is planned.
Structure: The design is understood to be the result of a joint venture by the Indian Navy's DGND SSG (Directorate General Naval Design Surface Ship Group) and Garden Reach Shipbuilder's in-house design team. Details have not been formally released and are speculative. Measures to reduce acoustic, magnetic, IR and radar cross-section signatures are reported to have been incorporated. The hull may use amagnetic steel.

12 VEER (TARANTUL I) CLASS (PROJECT 1241RE) (FSGM)

Name	No	Builders	Laid down	Launched	Commissioned
VEER	K 40	Volodarski, Rybinsk	1984	Oct 1986	26 Mar 1987
NIRBHIK	K 41	Volodarski, Rybinsk	1985	Oct 1987	21 Dec 1987
NIPAT	K 42	Volodarski, Rybinsk	1986	Nov 1988	5 Dec 1988
NISHANK	K 43	Volodarski, Rybinsk	1987	June 1989	2 Sep 1989
NIRGHAT	K 44	Volodarski, Rybinsk	1988	Mar 1990	4 June 1990
VIBHUTI	K 45	Mazagon Dock, Mumbai	28 Sep 1987	26 Apr 1990	3 June 1991
VIPUL	K 46	Mazagon Dock, Mumbai	29 Feb 1988	3 Jan 1991	16 Mar 1992
VINASH	K 47	Goa Shipyard	30 Jan 1989	24 Jan 1992	20 Nov 1993
VIDYUT	K 48	Goa Shipyard	27 May 1990	12 Dec 1992	16 Jan 1995
NASHAK	K 83	Mazagon Dock, Mumbai	21 Jan 1991	12 Nov 1993	29 Dec 1994
PRABAL	K 92	Mazagon Dock, Mumbai	31 Aug 1998	28 Sep 2000	11 Apr 2002
PRALAYA	K 91	Goa Shipyard	14 Nov 1998	14 Dec 2000	18 Dec 2002

Displacement, tons: 455 full load; 477 full load (K 92 and K 91)
Dimensions, feet (metres): 184.1 × 37.7 × 8.2 *(56.1 × 11.5 × 2.5)*
Main machinery: COGAG (M15E); 2 Nikolayev Type DR 77 (DS 71 in K 92) gas turbines; 16,016 hp(m) *(11.77 MW)* sustained; 2 Nikolayev Type DR 76 gas turbines with reversible gearboxes; 4,993 hp(m) *(3.67 MW)* sustained; 2 shafts
Speed, knots: 36. **Range, n miles:** 2,000 at 20 kt; 400 at 36 kt
Complement: 41 (5 officers)

Missiles: SSM: 4 SS-N-2D Mod 1 Styx; IR homing to 83 km *(45 n miles)* at 0.9 Mach; warhead 513 kg; sea-skimmer at end of run. 16 (4 quad) SS-N-25 (Kh 35 Uran) in K 91 and K 92; active radar homing to 130 km *(70.2 n miles)* at 0.9 Mach; warhead 145 kg; sea skimmer.
SAM: SA-N-5 Grail quad launcher; manual aiming; IR homing to 6 km *(3.2 n miles)* at 1.5 Mach; warhead 1.5 kg.
Guns: 1 USSR 3 in *(76 mm)*/59 AK 176; 120 rds/min to 15 km *(8 n miles)*; weight of shell 5.9 kg.
1 OTO Melara 3 in *(76 mm)*/62 Super Rapid (K 91 and K 92); 120 rds/min to 16 km (8.7 n miles); weight of shell 6 kg.
2–30 mm/65 AK 630; 6 barrels per mounting; 3,000 rds/min combined to 2 km. 2–7.62 mm MGs.
Countermeasures: Decoys: PK 16 chaff launcher.
ESM: Bharat Ajanta P Mk II; intercept.
Weapons control: Hood Wink optronic director.
Radars: Air/surface search: Plank Shave; E-band.
Cross Dome (K 91 and K 92); E/F-band.

PRALAYA — *3/2008*, Guy Toremans* / 1305305

Navigation: Mius; I-band.
Fire control: Bass tilt: H/I-band.
BEL Lynx (K 91 and K 92) (for guns); I-band; Bharat Aparna (modified Plank Shave/Harpun B) (for SSM); I/J-band.
IFF: Salt Pot, Square Head A.

Programmes: First five are USSR Tarantul I class built for export. Six further of the same type built in India. Two further craft, armed with the SS-N-25 missile were delivered in 2002. It is not clear whether there are to be further vessels.
Structure: K 92 and K 91 are to a modified design to accommodate the SS-N-25 missile. Principal differences are the bridge and mast configurations.
Operational: All form the 22nd Missile Vessel Squadron at Mumbai although K 41, 43 and 47 are reported to have moved to Vishakapatnam. *Prahar* sunk after a collision on 21 April 2006.

PRABAL — *3/2007, Marco Ghiglino* / 1166559

4 ABHAY (PROJECT 1241 PE) (PAUK II) CLASS (FSM)

Name	*No*	*Builders*	*Commissioned*
ABHAY	P 33	Volodarski	10 Mar 1989
AJAY	P 34	Volodarski	24 Jan 1990
AKSHAY	P 35	Volodarski	10 Dec 1990
AGRAY	P 36	Volodarski	30 Jan 1991

Displacement, tons: 485 full load
Dimensions, feet (metres): 191.9 × 33.5 × 11.2 *(58.5 × 10.2 × 3.4)*
Main machinery: 2 Type M 521 diesels; 16,184 hp(m) *(11.9 MW)* sustained; 2 shafts
Speed, knots: 28
Range, n miles: 2,400 at 14 kt
Complement: 32 (6 officers)

Missiles: SAM: SA-N-5/8 Grail quad launcher; manual aiming, IR homing to 6 km *(3.2 n miles)* at 1.5 Mach; warhead 1.5 kg.
Guns: 1 USSR 3 in *(76 mm)*/59 AK 176; 120 rds/min to 15 km *(8 n miles)*; weight of shell 5.9 kg.
1—30 mm/65 AK 630; 6 barrels; 3,000 rds/min combined to 2 km.
Torpedoes: 4—21 in *(533 mm)* (2 twin) tubes. SET-65E; active/passive homing to 15 km *(8.1 n miles)* at 40 kt; warhead 205 kg.
A/S mortars: 2 RBU 1200 5-tubed fixed; range 1,200 m; warhead 34 kg.
Countermeasures: 2 PK 16 chaff launchers.
Radars: Air/surface search: Cross Dome; E/F-band.
Navigation: Pechora; I-band.
Fire control: Bass Tilt; H/I-band.
Sonars: Rat Tail VDS (on transom); attack; high frequency.

AJAY *3/2007, Marco Ghiglino* / 1166558

Programmes: Modified Pauk II class built in the USSR at Volodarski, Rybinsk for export. Original order in late 1983 but completion of the first delayed by lack of funds and the order for the others was not reinstated until 1987. Names associated with former coastal patrol craft.
Modernisation: There are plans to re-engine all four ships.
Structure: Has a longer superstructure than the Pauk I, larger torpedo tubes and improved electronics.
Operational: Classified as ASW ships. Comprise 23rd Patrol Boat Squadron based at Mumbai. *Agray* was damaged by an onboard explosion on 6 February 2004 but is reportedly under repair at Mumbai.

SHIPBORNE AIRCRAFT

Notes: (1) Plans to procure up to eight second-hand Sea Harriers from the UK were abandoned in late 2006.
(2) Replacement of the Sea King fleet was initiated in January 2006 when Requests for Proposals were issued to eight overseas suppliers. Following evaluation, a contract is expected in 2009. In the meantime six UH-3H Sea Kings are reported to have been acquired for operation from *Jalashwa* following transfer in 2007. The aircraft are to be used for commando assault, vertrep and general patrol duties.
(3) The maiden flight of the naval version of the HAL Tejas light combat aircraft is expected in 2009. While the Indian Navy has expressed interest, there is no commitment to procure the aircraft.

Numbers/Type: 12/4 MIG 29K Fulcrum/29 KUB.
Operational speed: 750 kt *(1,400 km/h)*.
Service ceiling: 57,000 ft *(17,400 m)*.
Range: 1,400 n miles *(2,600 km)*.
Role/Weapon systems: All-weather single-seat fighter with attack capability, optimised for ski-jump take off, is to be main weapon of *Admiral Gorshkov* aircraft carrier. Initial order for 12 aircraft and four trainers to be delivered from 2009 following the maiden flight of a twin-seat MiG 29KUB on 20 January 2007. Agreement in principle to acquire a further 29 aircraft was reached in September 2008. Sensors: Phazotron-NIIR Zhuk-ME radar; Elta EL/M-8222 jammer; OLS IR search and track. Weapons: AAM; RVV-AE and R-73. ASM: Kh-35 (possibly Club). Conventional bombs: KAB-500 Kr. 30 mm cannon.

MiG 29KUB *1/2007, Piotr Butowski* / 1184939

Numbers/Type: 14/2 British Aerospace Sea Harrier FRS. Mk 51/Mk 60.
Operational speed: 640 kt *(1,186 km/h)*.
Service ceiling: 51,200 ft *(15,600 m)*.
Range: 800 n miles *(1,480 km)*.
Role/Weapon systems: Fleet air defence, strike and reconnaissance STOVL fighter. Three more acquired from UK in 1999 to make good losses. Of total numbers, only about one third are operational. Sensors: Ferranti Blue Fox air interception radar, limited ECM/RWR (Elta 8420 in due course). Weapons: Air defence; two Magic AAMs (possibly ASRAAM in due course), two 30 mm Aden cannon. Plans for a mid-life upgrade have been abandoned. Avionics are to be improved to extend life of aircraft to 2020.

SEA HARRIER *1994, Indian Navy* / 0012970

Numbers/Type: 2/15/5 Westland Sea King Mk 42A/Mk 42B/Mk 42C.
Operational speed: 112 kt *(208 km/h)*.
Service ceiling: 11,500 ft *(3,500 m)*.
Range: 664 n miles *(1,230 km)*.
Role/Weapon systems: Mk 42A has primary ASW and 42B primary ASV capability; Mk 42C for commando assault/vertrep. Not all aircraft are operational. Sensors: MEL Super Searcher radar, Thomson Sintra H/S-12 dipping sonar (Mk 42A and B), AQS 902B acoustic processor (Mk 42B); Marconi Hermes ESM (Mk 42B); Bendix weather radar (Mk 42C). Weapons: ASW; 2 Whitehead A244S or USSR APR-2 torpedoes; Mk 11 depth bombs, mines (Mk 42B only). ASV; two Sea Eagle (Mk 42B only). Unarmed (Mk 42C).

SEA KING 42B *8/2002, Arjun Sarup* / 0569194

Numbers/Type: 12 Kamov Ka-28 Helix A.
Operational speed: 110 kt *(204 km/h)*.
Service ceiling: 12,000 ft *(3,660 m)*.
Range: 270 n miles *(500 km)*.
Role/Weapon systems: ASW helicopter embarked in large escorts. Has replaced Ka-25. Sensors: Splash Drop search radar; VGS-3 dipping sonar, sonobuoys. Weapons: ASW; two Whitehead A244S or USSR APR-2 torpedoes or four depth bombs.

Ka-28 *6/2006, Chris Sattler* / 1164470

Numbers/Type: 9 Kamov Ka-31 Helix B.
Operational speed: 119 kt *(220 km/h)*.
Service ceiling: 11,480 ft *(3,500 m)*.
Range: 325 n miles *(600 km)*.
Role/Weapon systems: AEW helicopter. First two delivered late 2002 with remainder in 2003. Radar antenna folds beneath fuselage. Sensors: OKO E-80/M radar.

Ka-31 *6/2005, Patrick Allen/Jane's* / 1136991

Numbers/Type: 23 Aerospatiale (HAL) SA 319B Chetak (Alouette III).
Operational speed: 113 kt *(210 km/h)*.
Service ceiling: 10,500 ft *(3,200 m)*.
Range: 290 n miles *(540 km)*.
Role/Weapon systems: Several helicopter roles performed including embarked ASW and carrier-based SAR, utility and support to commando forces. 15 aircraft are operated by Coast Guard. Weapons: ASW; two Whitehead A244S torpedoes.

CHETAK *4/2007* / 1305304

Numbers/Type: 20 HAL Dhruv.
Operational speed: 156 kt *(290 km/h)*.
Service ceiling: 9,850 ft *(3,000 m)*.
Range: 216 n miles *(400 km)*.
Role/Weapon systems: Formerly known as Advanced Light Helicopter (ALH), full production was delayed by thrust and vibration problems which have now been overcome. The naval variant started trials in March 1995 and the first two were delivered in 2003. Sensors: Dipping sonar, ECM. Weapons: ASW; torpedoes, depth charges. ASV; Sea Eagle ASM.

Dhruv *2/2001, HAL* / 0095088

LAND-BASED MARITIME AIRCRAFT (FRONT LINE)

Numbers/Type: 2 Fokker F27 Friendship.
Operational speed: 250 kt *(463 km/h)*.
Service ceiling: 29,500 ft *(8,990 m)*.
Range: 2,700 n miles *(5,000 km)*.
Role/Weapon systems: Operated by coast guard for long-range patrol. Search radar only. Unarmed.

Numbers/Type: 14 Dornier 228.
Operational speed: 200 kt *(370 km/h)*.
Service ceiling: 28,000 ft *(8,535 m)*.
Range: 940 n miles *(1,740 km)*.
Role/Weapon systems: Coastal surveillance and EEZ protection duties for Navy and Coast Guard. Sensors: MEL Marec or THORN EMI Super Marec search radar with FLIR, cameras and searchlight. Weapons: Unarmed, but may carry anti-ship missiles in due course.

DORNIER 228 *12/2000* / 0121342

Numbers/Type: 5 Ilyushin Il-38 (May).
Operational speed: 347 kt *(645 km/h)*.
Service ceiling: 32,800 ft *(10,000 m)*.
Range: 3,887 n miles *(7,200 km)*.
Role/Weapon systems: Shore-based long-range ASW reconnaissance into Indian Ocean. Following the loss of two aircraft in a mid-air collision in 2002, two replacement aircraft were donated by Russia. All five aircraft upgraded to Il-38SD standard with improved avionics, radar, ASM (probably Brahmos) and ASW capabilities. The first three aircraft had been delivered by 2008. Delivery of the final two is expected by 2010. Sensors: Leninets Sea Dragon/Novella radar, MAD, sonobuoys, ESM. Weapons: ASW; various torpedoes, mines and depth bombs.

MAY *2/2001, Wingman Aviation* / 0121338

Numbers/Type: 6 Pilatus Britten-Norman Maritime Defender.
Operational speed: 150 kt *(280 km/h)*.
Service ceiling: 18,900 ft *(5,760 m)*.
Range: 1,500 n miles *(2,775 km)*.
Role/Weapon systems: Coastal and short-range reconnaissance tasks undertaken in support of Navy (6) and Coast Guard. Six upgraded with turboprop engines 1996–97. Sensors: Search radar, camera. Weapons: Unarmed.

DEFENDER *2/2001, Wingman Aviation* / 0121339

Numbers/Type: 4 Tupolev Tu-142M (Bear F).
Operational speed: 500 kt *(925 km/h)*.
Service ceiling: 45,000 ft *(13,720 m)*.
Range: 6,775 n miles *(12,550 km)*.
Role/Weapon systems: First entered service in April 1988 for long-range surface surveillance and ASW. Air Force manned. Sensors: Wet Eye search and attack radars, MAD, cameras. 75 active and passive sonobuoys. Weapons: ASW; 12 torpedoes, depth bombs. ASV; two 23 mm cannon. Avionics, ASM (possibly SS-N-25) and ASW package upgraded in mid-life update from 2001.

BEAR F *2/2001* / 0121345

Numbers/Type: 8 SEPECAT/HAL Jaguar International.
Operational speed: 917 kt *(1,699 km/h)* (max).
Service ceiling: 36,000 ft *(11,000 m)*.
Range: 760 n miles *(1,408 km)*.
Role/Weapon systems: A maritime strike squadron. Air Force operated. Sensors: Thomson-CSF Agave radar. Weapons: ASV; 2 BAe Sea Eagle; 2 DEFA 30 mm cannon or up to 8-1,000 lb bombs. Can carry 2 Magic AAM overwing.

JAGUAR *2/2001, Wingman Aviation* / 0121340

Numbers/Type: 8 Boeing P-8I Poseidon.
Operational speed: 490 kt *(907 km/h)*.
Service ceiling: 41,000 ft *(12,500 m)*.
Range: 1,380 n miles *(2,555 km)*.
Role/Weapon systems: Contract for eight aircraft signed on 31 December 2008. Deliveries to begin in 2013 and to be completed by 2016. To replace Tu-142 (Bear F). Design based on Boeing 737-800ERX. Crew of nine. Sensors: To be equipped with modern ASW, ASUW and intelligence, surveillance and reconnaissance (ISR) sensors. Weapons: To be announced.

BOEING P-8A Poseidon demonstrator *6/2004, US Navy* / 1043653

UNMANNED AIR VEHICLES

Numbers/Type: 4 Israel Aircraft Industries Heron.
Operational speed: 125 kt *(231 km/h)*.
Service ceiling: 26,500 ft *(8,075 m)*.
Range: 108 n miles *(200 km)*.
Role/Weapon systems: Capable of performing a variety of missions but primarily a real-time system for intelligence collection, surveillance, target acquisition/tracking, and communications/data relay. Several payloads can be carried simultaneously including real-time TV/FLIR, synthetic aperture radar or camera. Can be controlled from ground station via direct LOS data/command link. Part of UAV squadron commissioned on 6 January 2006. Based at Kochi but operated from other bases. Has conducted sea trials with INS *Vindhyagiri*. Endurance 50 hours.

HERON UAV *12/2005, IAI* / 1116200

Numbers/Type: 8 Israel Aircraft Industries Searcher II.
Operational speed: 105 kt *(194 km/h)*.
Service ceiling: 20,000 ft *(6,100 m)*.
Range: 92 n miles *(170 km)*.
Role/Weapon systems: Can be configured for tactical surveillance or as communications relay aircraft. Several payloads can be carried simultaneously including real-time TV/FLIR, synthetic aperture radar or camera. Can be controlled from ground station via direct LOS data/command link. Part of UAV squadron commissioned on 6 January 2006. Based at Kochi but operated from other bases. Endurance 18 hours.

Searcher II *6/2003, C Hoyle/Jane's* / 0531011

PATROL FORCES

0 + 4 OFFSHORE PATROL VESSEL (PSOH)

Name	*No*	*Builders*	*Laid down*	*Launched*	*Commissioned*
–	–	Goa Shipyard	2006	2009	Mar 2010
–	–	Goa Shipyard	25 Sep 2007	2009	Sep 2010
–	–	Goa Shipyard	7 May 2008	2010	Dec 2010
–	–	Goa Shipyard	2008	2011	June 2011

Displacement, tons: 2,215 full load
Dimensions, feet (metres): 344.5 × 42.3 × 11.8 *(105.0 × 12.9 × 3.6)*
Main machinery: 2 Pielstick PA 6B STC diesels; 20,900 hp(m) *(15.58 MW)*; 2 shafts; cp props
Speed, knots: 25
Range, n miles: 6,000 at 16 kt
Complement: 118 (16 officers)
Guns: 1 OTO Melara 3 in *(76 mm)*/62 Super Rapid; 120 rds/min to 16 km *(8.7 n miles)*; weight of shell 6 kg.
2—30 mm/65 AK 630 (6 barrels per mounting); 3,000 rds/min combined to 2 km.
Radars: Surface search: To be announced.
Navigation: To be announced.
Helicopters: 1 HAL Dhruv.

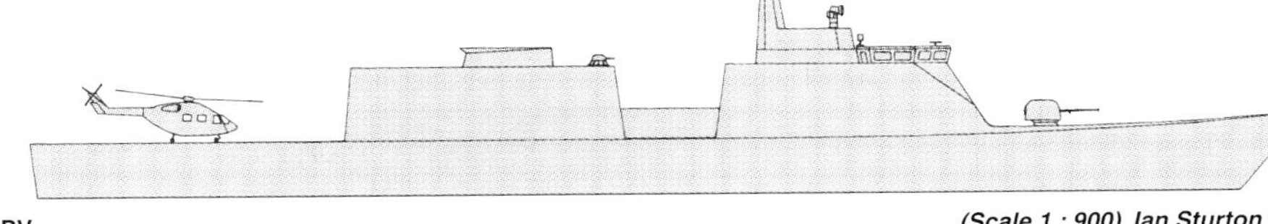

OPV *(Scale 1 : 900), Ian Sturton* / 1164335

Comment: The order for three offshore patrol vessels was announced in 2006 and the order for a fourth was confirmed on 20 April 2007. The ships are to be naval variants of the Coast Guard's Sankalp class under construction at Goa Shipyard.

7 SUPER DVORA MK II CLASS (PBF)

No	*Builders*	*Commissioned*
T 80	IAI, Ramta	14 May 1998
T 81	Goa Shipyard Ltd	29 May 1999
T 82	IAI, Ramta	9 Oct 2003
T 83	Goa Shipyard Ltd	22 Mar 2004
T 84	Goa Shipyard Ltd	19 Apr 2004
T 85	Goa Shipyard Ltd	16 Feb 2005
T 86	Goa Shipyard Ltd	16 Feb 2005

Displacement, tons: 60 full load
Dimensions, feet (metres): 83.3 × 18.4 × 4.9 *(25.4 × 5.6 × 1.5)*
Main machinery: 2 MTU 12V 396TE94 diesels; 4,570 hp(m) *(3.36 MW)*; 2 Arneson ASD 16 surface drives
Speed, knots: 50
Range, n miles: 700 at 42 kt
Complement: 10 (1 officer)
Guns: 2—20 mm.
Weapons control: Elop MSIS optronic director.
Radars: Surface search: Koden; I-band.

Comment: Collaborative programme involving IAI, Ramta, Israel and Goa Shipyard Ltd. T 80 was built at Ramta and T 82 was procured by the Indian Navy from Israel. The other five were assembled at Goa.

SUPER DVORA *2/2001* / 0126188

6 SUKANYA CLASS (PSOH)

Name	*No*	*Builders*	*Launched*	*Commissioned*
SUKANYA	P 50	Korea Tacoma, Masan	1989	31 Aug 1989
SUBHADRA	P 51	Korea Tacoma, Masan	1989	25 Jan 1990
SUVARNA	P 52	Korea Tacoma, Masan	22 Aug 1990	4 Apr 1991
SAVITRI	P 53	Hindustan SY, Vishakapatnam	23 May 1989	27 Nov 1990
SHARADA	P 55	Hindustan SY, Vishakapatnam	22 Aug 1990	27 Oct 1991
SUJATA	P 56	Hindustan SY, Vishakapatnam	25 Oct 1991	3 Nov 1993

Displacement, tons: 1,890 full load
Dimensions, feet (metres): 331.7 oa; 315 wl × 37.7 × 14.4 *(101.1; 96 × 11.5 × 4.4)*
Main machinery: 2 SEMT-Pielstick 16 PA6 V 280 diesels; 12,800 hp(m) *(9.41 MW)* sustained; 2 shafts
Speed, knots: 21
Range, n miles: 5,800 at 15 kt
Complement: 140 (15 officers)

Guns: 3 Bofors: 40 mm/60. 4—12.7 mm MGs.
A/S mortars: 4 RBU 2500 16-tubed trainable launchers; range 2,500 m; warhead 21 kg. Two launchers fitted in forward section.
Radars: Surface search: Racal Decca 2459; I-band.
Navigation: Bharat 1245; I-band.

Helicopters: 1 Chetak.

Programmes: First three ordered in March 1987 from Korea Tacoma to an Ulsan class design. Second four ordered in August 1987. The Korean-built ships commissioned at Masan and then sailed for India where the armament was fitted. Three others of a modified design have been built for the Coast Guard. P 54 transferred to Sri Lanka December 2000.
Structure: Lightly armed and able to 'stage' helicopters, they are fitted out for offshore patrol work only but have the capacity to be much more heavily armed. Fin stabilisers fitted. Firefighting pump on hangar roof aft.

SHARADA (1166553) *3/2007* / 1166553

Operational: These ships are used for harbour defence, protection of offshore installations and patrol of the EEZ. Potential for role change is considerable. *Subhadra* modified in early 2000 to test fire Dhanush (naval version of Prithvi) SRBM from her flight deck. Dhanush was first successfully fired on 20 September 2001. On 7 November 2004, a 350 km range Prithvi 3 solid propellant missile was reportedly fired in the Bay of Bengal. P 50 and P 51 based at Karwar, P 52 at Mumbai, P 53 at Vishakapatnam and the other two at Kochi.
Sales: *Saryu* transferred to Sri Lanka in 2000.

5 SDB MK 3 CLASS (LARGE PATROL CRAFT) (PB)

T 55–59

Displacement, tons: 210 full load
Dimensions, feet (metres): 124 × 24.6 × 6.2 *(37.8 × 7.5 × 1.9)*
Main machinery: 2 MTU 16V 538 TB92 diesels; 6,820 hp(m) *(5 MW)* sustained; 2 shafts
Speed, knots: 30
Complement: 32
Guns: 2 Bofors 40 mm/60; 120 rds/min to 10 km *(5.5 n miles)*; weight of shell 0.89 kg.
Radars: Surface search: Bharat 1245; I-band.

Comment: Built at Garden Reach and Goa and completed 1984–86. Employed as seaward defence forces.

T 56
6/2004, Indian Navy
1042279

6 SDB MK 5 (BANGARAM) CLASS (LARGE PATROL CRAFT) (PBO)

Name	*No*	*Launched*	*Commissioned*
TRINKAT	T 61	28 Sep 2000	24 Aug 2001
TARASA	T 63	2000	24 Aug 2001
BANGARAM	T 65	11 Dec 2004	10 Feb 2006
BITRA	T 66	14 Dec 2004	28 Mar 2006
BATTI MALV	T 67	28 June 2005	31 July 2006
BARATANG	T 68	6 Aug 2005	12 Sep 2006

Displacement, tons: 260 full load
Dimensions, feet (metres): 151.0 × 24.6 × 8.2 *(46.0 × 7.5 × 2.5)*
Main machinery: 2 MTU 16V 538 TB92 diesels; 6,820 hp(m) *(5 MW)* sustained; 2 shafts
Speed, knots: 30
Range, n miles: 2,000 at 12 kt
Complement: 34 (4 officers)
Guns: 1 Medak 30 mm 2A42. 2—7.62 mm MGs.
Radars: Surface search: Bharat 1245; I-band.

Comment: T 61 and T 63 are the two survivors of four commissioned between September 2000 and March 2002. T 62 transferred to the Maldives in 2006 and T 64 to the Seychelles in June 2005. Four (T 65-68) of a modified design have since entered service.

TARASA *3/2007* / 1166555

BANGARAM *3/2007* / 1166554

2 + 5 (3) CAR NICOBAR CLASS (PBO)

Name	*No*	*Builders*	*Launched*	*Commissioned*
CAR NICOBAR	T 69	Garden Reach Shipyard, Kolkatta	23 Nov 2007	16 Feb 2009
CHETLAT	T 70	Garden Reach Shipyard, Kolkatta	27 Nov 2007	16 Feb 2009
CINQUE	T 71	Garden Reach Shipyard, Kolkatta	16 July 2008	Dec 2009
CHERIYAM	T 72	Garden Reach Shipyard, Kolkatta	16 July 2008	Dec 2009
–	–	Rajabagan Shipyard, Kolkatta	2010	2011
–	–	Rajabagan Shipyard, Kolkatta	2010	2011
–	–	Rajabagan Shipyard, Kolkatta	2010	2011

Displacement, tons: 260 full load
Dimensions, feet (metres): 160.4 × 24.6 × 8.5 *(48.9 × 7.5 × 2.6)*
Main machinery: 3 MTU 16V 4000 M90 diesels; 11,238 hp(m) *(8.16 MW)* sustained; 3 Kamewa 71SII waterjets
Speed, knots: 35
Range, n miles: 2,000 at 13 kt

Complement: 35
Guns: 1—30 mm. 2—12.7 mm MGs.
Radars: Surface search: To be announced.

Comment: The design is an improved version of the Bangaram class and other patrol craft built by Garden Reach and may also have drawn on the waterjet propelled Sarojini Naidu class built by Goa Shipyard for the coast guard. Steel hull and aluminium superstructure. The first four ships are under construction at GRSE and three further craft were laid down at Rajabagan Shipyard on 29 July 2008. A class of 10 ships is expected.

AMPHIBIOUS FORCES

Notes: There are plans to acquire further amphibious ships capable of transporting troops and helicopters and of operating in littoral waters. Talks were reported to have taken place with ST Marine Singapore during 2008.

4 + 1 MAGAR CLASS (LSTH)

Name	*No*	*Builders*	*Launched*	*Commissioned*
MAGAR	L 20	Garden Reach	7 Nov 1984	15 July 1987
GHARIAL	L 23	Hindustan/Garden Reach	1 Apr 1991	14 Feb 1997
SHARDUL	L 16	Hindustan/Garden Reach	3 Apr 2004	4 Jan 2007
KESARI	L 15	Garden Reach Shipyard	8 June 2005	5 Apr 2008
AIRAVAT	–	Garden Reach Shipyard	27 Mar 2006	2009

Displacement, tons: 5,655 full load
Dimensions, feet (metres): 409.4 oa; 393.7 wl × 57.4 × 13.1 *(124.8; 120 × 17.5 × 4)*
Main machinery: 2 SEMT-Pielstick 12 PA6 V280 diesels; 8,560 hp(m) *(6.29 MW)* sustained; 2 shafts
Speed, knots: 15
Range, n miles: 3,000 at 14 kt
Complement: 136 (16 officers)
Military lift: 15 tanks plus 8 APC plus 500 troops
Guns: 4 Bofors 40 mm/60. 2—122 mm multibarrel rocket launchers at the bow.
Countermeasures: ESM: Bharat Ajanta; intercept.
Radars: Navigation: Bharat; I-band.
Helicopters: 1 Sea King 42C; platform for 2.

Comment: Based on the *Sir Lancelot* design. *Magar* was built entirely at Garden Reach. *Gharial* ordered in 1985. Built at Hindustan Shipyard but fitted out at Garden Reach. Internal design differs from *Magar*. Carries four LCVPs on davits. Bowdoor. Can beach on gradients 1 in 40 or more. *Magar* refitted in 1995. Both based at Vishakapatnam. *Shardul* and subsequent ships include major design changes. *Magar* and *Gharial* are based at Vishakapatnam and *Shardul* at Karwar.

GHARIAL ***10/2008*, Michael Nitz*** / 1353089

MAGAR ***3/2006, M Mazumdar*** / 1166551

5 POLNOCHNY C (PROJECT 773 I) AND D CLASS (PROJECT 773 IM) (LSM/LSMH)

SHARABH L 17 **CHEETAH** L 18 **MAHISH** L 19 **GULDAR** L 21 **KUMBHIR** L 22

Displacement, tons: 1,150 (C class); 1,190 (D class) full load
Dimensions, feet (metres): 266.7; 275.3 (D class) × 31.8 × 7.9 *(81.3; 83.9 × 9.7 × 2.4)*
Main machinery: 2 Kolomna Type 40-D diesels; 4,400 hp(m) *(3.2 MW)* sustained; 2 shafts
Speed, knots: 16
Range, n miles: 3,000 at 12 kt
Complement: 60 (6 officers)
Military lift: 160 troops; 5 MBT or 5 APC or 5 AA guns or 8 trucks
Guns: 4—30 mm (2 twin) Ak 230. 2—140 mm 18-tubed rocket launchers.
Radars: Navigation: Don 2 or Krivach (SRN 745); I-band
Fire control: Drum Tilt; H/I-band (in D class).
Helicopters: Platform only (in D class).

Comment: A original class of eight built in two batches by Naval Shipyard, Gdynia. The first four (L 14-17) were commissioned in 1975–76. Of these L 14, L 15 and L 16 have been decommissioned. The second batch of four (L 18-22) were commissioned in 1985–86 and are to a modified design with a flight deck forward of the bridge. All are being restricted operationally through lack of spares, but all are seaworthy. Drum Tilt radar removed from some ships. Four Polnochny Ds (L 18-22) form 5th landing Ship Squadron based at Port Blair.

CHEETAH ***3/2007*** / 1166548

8 MK 2/3 LANDING CRAFT (LSM)

L 32–39

Displacement, tons: 500 full load
Dimensions, feet (metres): 188.6 oa; 174.5 pp × 26.9 × 5.2 *(57.5; 53.2 × 8.2 × 1.6)*
Main machinery: 3 Kirloskar-MAN V8V 17.5/22 AMAL diesels; 1,686 hp(m) *(1.24 MW)*; 3 shafts
Speed, knots: 11
Range, n miles: 1,000 at 8 kt
Complement: 167
Military lift: 250 tons; 2 PT 76 or 2 APC. 120 troops
Guns: 2 Bofors 40 mm/60 (aft).
Mines: Can be embarked.
Radars: Navigation: Decca 1229; I-band.

Comment: L 32-35 are Mk 2 craft built 1980–83. L 36-39 are Mk 3 craft built 1986–87. All built by Goa Shipyard. L 36-39 have a considerably modified superstructure and a higher bulwark on the cargo deck. L 32-35 commissioned 1980–83 and L 36-39 1986–87.

L 36 ***2/1999, 92 Wing RAAF*** / 0064719

L 32 ***3/2007*** / 1166547

1 + (1) AUSTIN CLASS (AMPHIBIOUS TRANSPORT DOCK) (LPD)

Name	*No*	*Builders*	*Laid down*	*Launched*	*Commissioned*
JALASHWA (ex-*Trenton*)	L 41 (ex-LPD 14)	Lockheed SB & Construction Co	8 Aug 1966	3 Aug 1968	6 Mar 1971

Displacement, tons: 9,130 light; 16,500–17,244 full load
Dimensions, feet (metres): 570 × 100 (84 hull) × 23 *(173.8 × 30.5; 25.6 × 7)*
Main machinery: 2 Foster-Wheeler boilers; 600 psi *(42.3 kg/cm²)*; 870°F *(467°C)*; 2 De Laval turbines; 24,000 hp *(18 MW)*; 2 shafts
Speed, knots: 21
Range, n miles: 7,700 at 20 kt
Complement: 329 (27 officers)
Military lift: 930 troops; 9 LCM 6s or 4 LCM 8s or 2 LCAC or 20 LVTs. 4 LCPL/LCVP

Guns: 2 General Electric/General Dynamics 20 mm/76 6-barrelled Vulcan Phalanx Mk 15; 3,000 rds/min (4,500 in Block 1) combined to 1.5 km.
2—25 mm Mk 38. 8—12.7 mm MGs.
Countermeasures: Decoys: 4 Loral Hycor SRBOC 6-barrelled Mk 36; IR flares and chaff to 4 km *(2.2 n miles)*.
ESM: SLQ-32(V)1; intercept.
Combat data systems: SATCOM, WSC-3 (UHF), WSC-6 (SHF).
Radars: Air search: Lockheed SPS-40E; B-band.
Surface search: Norden SPS-67; G-band.
Navigation: Raytheon SPS-73(V)12; I-band.
Tacan: URN 25.
IFF: Mk XII UPX-36.

Helicopters: Up to 6 Sea King UH-3H can be carried. Hangar for only 1 light.

Programmes: Ex-LPD 14 authorised in the US Navy's FY65 new construction programme. Transferred as a 'hot transfer' on 17 January 2007 and formally recommissioned on 22 June 2007. The transfer of a second ship (ex-*Nashville*) is no longer considered likely.
Structure: One small telescopic hangar. Flight deck is 168 ft *(51.2 m)* in length. Well-deck 394 × 50 ft (120.1 × 15.2 m).
Operational: Likely to be based at Vishakapatnam.

JALASHWA ***9/2007, Indian Navy*** / 1166556

MINE WARFARE FORCES

Notes: Procurement of up to eight minehunters has been approved. It is anticipated that the ships will be to a foreign design and of GRP construction. Building is expected to take place at Goa Shipyards. The ships are likely to be equipped with a minehunting sonar and with a remote-control mine-disposal system. Following requests for proposals, shortlisted companies are reported to include Intermarine, Sarzana, and Karlskronavarvet. A decision is expected in 2009.

10 PONDICHERRY (NATYA I) CLASS (PROJECT 266M) (MINESWEEPERS—OCEAN) (MSO)

Name	*No*	*Builders*	*Commissioned*
BEDI	M 63	Isora, Leningrad	27 Apr 1979
BHAVNAGAR	M 64	Isora, Leningrad	27 Apr 1979
ALLEPPEY	M 65	Isora, Leningrad	10 June 1980
RATNAGIRI	M 66	Isora, Leningrad	10 June 1980
KARWAR	M 67	Isora, Leningrad	14 July 1986
CANNANORE	M 68	Isora, Leningrad	17 Dec 1987
CUDDALORE	M 69	Isora, Leningrad	29 Oct 1987
KAKINADA	M 70	Isora, Leningrad	23 Dec 1986
KOZHIKODE	M 71	Isora, Leningrad	19 Dec 1988
KONKAN	M 72	Isora, Leningrad	8 Oct 1988

Displacement, tons: 804 full load
Dimensions, feet (metres): 200.1 × 33.5 × 10.8 *(61 × 10.2 × 3)*
Main machinery: 2 Type 504 diesels; 5,000 hp(m) *(3.67 MW)* sustained; 2 shafts; cp props
Speed, knots: 16
Range, n miles: 3,000 at 12 kt
Complement: 82 (10 officers)

Guns: 4—30 mm/65 (2 twin); 500 rds/min to 5 km *(2.7 n miles)*; weight of shell 0.54 kg.
4—25 mm/70 (2 twin); 270 rds/min to 3 km *(1.6 n miles)*.
A/S mortars: 2 RBU 1200 5-tubed fixed; range 1,200 m; warhead 34 kg.
Mines: Can carry 10.
Countermeasures: MCM: 1 GKT-2 contact sweep; 1 AT-2 acoustic sweep; 1 TEM-3 magnetic sweep.
Radars: Navigation: Don 2; I-band
Fire control: Drum Tilt; H/I-band
IFF: 2 Square Head. High Pole B
Sonars: MG 69/79; hull-mounted; active mine detection; high frequency

Programmes: Built for export. Last six were delivered out of pennant number order.
Structure: Steel hulls but do not have stern ramp as in Russian class.
Operational: Some are fitted with two quad SA-N-5 systems. One serves as an AGI. Divided between 19th MCM Squadron based at Mumbai and 21st MCM Squadron based at Vishakapatnam.

KOZHIKODE ***2/2006, M Mazumdar*** / 1164469

SURVEY AND RESEARCH SHIPS

Notes: The National Institute of Oceanography operates several research and survey ships including *Sagar Kanya*, RV *Gaveshini* and *Sagar Shukti*. *Sagar Nidhi*, a 104 m ship built by Fincantieri, Muggiano, entered service in March 2008.

8 SANDHAYAK CLASS (SURVEY SHIPS) (AGSH)

Name	*No*	*Builders*	*Launched*	*Commissioned*
SANDHAYAK	J 18	Garden Reach, Calcutta	6 Apr 1977	1 Mar 1981
NIRDESHAK	J 19	Garden Reach, Calcutta	16 Nov 1978	4 Oct 1982
NIRUPAK	J 14	Garden Reach, Calcutta	10 July 1981	14 Aug 1985
INVESTIGATOR	J 15	Garden Reach, Calcutta	8 Aug 1987	11 Jan 1990
JAMUNA	J 16	Garden Reach, Calcutta	4 Sep 1989	31 Aug 1991
SUTLEJ	J 17	Garden Reach, Calcutta	1 Dec 1991	19 Feb 1993
DARSHAK	J 21	Goa Shipyard	3 Mar 1999	28 Apr 2001
SARVEKSHAK	J 22	Goa Shipyard	24 Nov 1999	14 Jan 2002

Displacement, tons: 1,929 full load
Dimensions, feet (metres): 288 × 42 × 11.1 *(87.8 × 12.8 × 3.4)*
Main machinery: 2 GRSE/MAN 66V 30/45 ATL diesels; 7,720 hp(m) *(5.67 MW)* sustained; 2 shafts; active rudders
Speed, knots: 16. **Range, n miles**: 6,000 at 14 kt; 14,000 at 10 kt
Complement: 178 (18 officers) plus 30 scientists
Guns: 1 or 2 Bofors 40 mm/60.
Countermeasures: ESM: Telegon IV HF D/F.
Radars: Navigation: Racal Decca 1629; I-band.
Helicopters: 1 Chetak.

Comment: Telescopic hangar. Fitted with three echo-sounders, side scan sonar, extensively equipped laboratories, and carries four GRP survey launches on davits amidships. An active rudder with a DC motor gives speeds of up to 5 kt. First three based at Vishakapatnam and have been used as troop transports. *Investigator* is at Mumbai and *Jamuna* and *Sutlej* at Kochi. The last pair were laid down in May and August 1995 and have a secondary role as casualty holding ships.

INVESTIGATOR ***3/2007, Marco Ghiglino*** / 1166546

1 SAGARDHWANI CLASS

Name	*No*	*Builders*	*Commissioned*
SAGARDHWANI	A 74	Garden Reach, Calcutta	30 July 1994

Displacement, tons: 2,050 full load
Dimensions, feet (metres): 279.2 × 42 × 12.1 *(85.1 × 12.8 × 3.7)*
Main machinery: 2 GRSE/MAN 66V 30/45 ATL diesels; 7,720 hp(m) *(5.67 MW)* sustained; 2 shafts; 2 auxiliary thrusters
Speed, knots: 16. **Range, n miles**: 6,000 at 16 kt
Complement: 80 (10 officers) plus 16 scientists
Radars: Navigation: Racal Decca 1629; I-band.
Helicopters: Platform for Alouette III.

Comment: Marine Acoustic Research Ship (MARS) launched in May 1991. The hull and main machinery are very similar to the Sandhayak class survey ships, but there are marked superstructure differences with the bridge positioned amidships and a helicopter platform forward. Aft there are two large cranes and a gantry for deploying and recovering research equipment. The vessel is designed to carry out acoustic and geological research and special attention has been paid to noise reduction. The ship is painted white except for the lift equipment and two boats which are orange. Employed in advanced torpedo trials and missile range support. Based at Kochi.

SAGARDHWANI ***2/2001, Michael Nitz*** / 0534058

1 MAKAR CLASS (SURVEY SHIP) (AGS)

MEEN J 33

Displacement, tons: 210 full load
Dimensions, feet (metres): 123 × 24.6 × 6.2 *(37.5 × 7.5 × 1.9)*
Main machinery: 2 diesels; 1,124 hp(m) *(826 kW)*; 2 shafts
Speed, knots: 12
Range, n miles: 1,500 at 12 kt
Complement: 36 (4 officers)
Guns: 1 Bofors 40 mm/60.
Radars: Navigation: Decca 1629; I-band.

Comment: Built by Goa Shipyard and delivered on 23 June 1984. Similar hull to deleted SDB Mk 2 class but with much smaller engines. Employed as seaward defence craft.

MEEN *4/1992* / 0064723

0 + 6 SURVEY SHIPS (AGS)

Displacement, tons: 260 full load
Dimensions, feet (metres): 163.4 × 52.0 × 7.2 *(49.8 × 15.85 × 2.2)*
Main machinery: 2 (outer) Cummins KTA38-M2 diesels; 2,700 hp *(2 MW)*; 2 (inner) Cummins QSK19M; 1,520 hp *(1.1 MW)*; 2 shafts; cp props
Speed, knots: 18
Range, n miles: 3,000 at 13 kt
Complement: 57 (10 officers)
Guns: 1 — 30 mm. 2 — 12.7 mm MGs.
Radars: Surface search: To be announced.

Comment: Contract for six vessels signed with Alcock Ashdown (Gujarat) Ltd in December 2006 for construction of six survey vessels. Designed by Australian Company Sea Transport, the catamaran hulls are of steel construction with an aluminium superstructure. Delivery of the first vessel is expected in 2009 with further deliveries at six-month intervals. The survey equipment suite includes two Hugin 1000 AUV, the HiPAP subsea positioning equipment, multibeam echosounders and underwater cameras from Kongsberg. There are also two 6.5 m RIB and a 4 wheel-drive vehicle.

TRAINING SHIPS

1 TIR CLASS (TRAINING SHIP) (AXH)

Name	*No*	*Builders*	*Launched*	*Commissioned*
TIR	A 86	Mazagon Dock Ltd, Bombay	15 Apr 1983	21 Feb 1986

Displacement, tons: 3,200 full load
Dimensions, feet (metres): 347.4 × 43.3 × 15.7 *(105.9 × 13.2 × 4.8)*
Main machinery: 2 Crossley-Pielstick 8 PC2V Mk 2 diesels; 7,072 hp(m) *(5.2 MW)* sustained; 2 shafts
Speed, knots: 18. **Range, n miles:** 6,000 at 12 kt
Complement: 239 (35 officers) plus 120 cadets
Guns: 2 Bofors 40 mm/60 (twin) with launchers for illuminants. 4 saluting guns.
Countermeasures: ESM: Telegon IV D/F.
Radars: Navigation: Bharat/Decca 1245; I-band.
Helicopters: Platform for Alouette III.

Comment: Second of class reported ordered May 1986 but was cancelled as an economy measure. Built to commercial standards, Decca collision avoidance plot and SATNAV. Can carry up to 120 cadets and 20 instructors. Based at Kochi.

TIR *2/2001, Michael Nitz* / 0534059

1 LEANDER (BATCH 3A) CLASS (AXH)

Name	*No*	*Builders*	*Commissioned*
KRISHNA (ex-*Andromeda*)	F 46 (ex-F 57)	Portsmouth Dockyard	2 Dec 1968

Displacement, tons: 2,960 full load
Dimensions, feet (metres): 372 × 43 × 18 (screws) *(113.4 × 13.1 × 5.5)*
Main machinery: 2 Babcock & Wilcox boilers; 550 psi *(38.7 kg/cm²)*; 850°F *(454°C)*; 2 White/English Electric turbines; 30,000 hp *(22.4 MW)*; 2 shafts
Speed, knots: 28. **Range, n miles:** 4,000 at 15 kt
Complement: 260 (19 officers)
Guns: 2 Bofors 40 mm/60. 2 Oerlikon 20 mm.
Radars: Air/surface search: Marconi Type 968; D/E-band.
Navigation: Kelvin Hughes Type 1006; I-band.
Helicopters: 1 Chetak.

Comment: Laid down 25 May 1966 and launched 24 May 1967. Acquired from the UK in April 1995 having paid off in June 1993 to a state of extended readiness. Refitted by DML, Devonport, before recommissioning 22 August 1995. The original 114 mm gun turret, Seacat SAM and ASW Limbo mortar were removed in 1979–80 when Exocet SSM, Seawolf SAM, STWS torpedo tubes and facilities for a Lynx helicopter were fitted. Acquired for training purposes to supplement the *Tir*. Armament has been reduced to the minimum required for the training role, and now includes 40 mm guns on either side, aft of the funnel. Based at Kochi.

KRISHNA *8/1995, H M Steele* / 0064724

2 SAIL TRAINING SHIPS (AXS)

VARUNA **TARANGINI** A 75

Displacement, tons: 420 full load
Dimensions, feet (metres): 177.2 × 27.9 × 13.1 *(54 × 8.5 × 4)*
Main machinery: 2 diesels; 640 hp(m) *(470 kW)*; 2 shafts; LIPS props
Speed, knots: 10 (diesels)
Complement: 15 (6 officers) plus 45 cadets

Comment: *Varuna* completed in April 1981 by Alcock-Ashdown, Bhavnagar. Can carry 26 cadets. Details given are for *Tarangini* which is based on a Lord Nelson design by Colin Mudie of Lymington and has been built by Goa Shipyard. Launched on 23 December 1995, and completed in December 1997. Three masted barque, square rigged on forward and main mast and 'fore and aft' rigged on mizzen mast. *Varuna* based at Mumbai and *Tarangini* at Kochi.

TARANGINI *6/2005, Guy Toremans* / 1151260

AUXILIARIES

Notes: (1) There is also a small hospital ship *Lakshadweep* of 865 tons and a crew of 35 including 16 medics.
(2) *Ambika* is a 1,000 ton oiler commissioned in 1995. Built by Hindustan Shipyard, it is based at Vishakhapatnam.
(3) There are two auxiliary cargo ships *Chowra* and *Akabar*.

1 JYOTI CLASS (REPLENISHMENT TANKER) (AORH)

Name	*No*	*Builders*	*Launched*	*Commissioned*
JYOTI	A 58	Admiralty Yard, St Petersburg	8 Dec 1995	20 July 1996

Displacement, tons: 35,900 full load
Dimensions, feet (metres): 587.3 × 72.2 × 26.2 *(179 × 22 × 8)*
Main machinery: 1 Burmeister & Wain diesel; 10,948 hp(m) *(8.05 MW)*; 1 shaft
Speed, knots: 15
Range, n miles: 12,000 at 15 kt
Complement: 92 (16 officers)
Cargo capacity: 25,040 tons diesel
Radars: Navigation: I-band.
Helicopters: Platform for 1 medium.

Comment: This was the third of a class of merchant tankers, modified for naval use for the Indian Navy and acquired in 1995. The ship was laid down in September 1993. Based at Mumbai where she arrived in November 1996. There are two replenishment positions on each side and stern refuelling is an option. Similar ship sold to China and two others are in commercial service.

JYOTI *4/2007, Mitsuhiro Kadota* / 1166545

1 ADITYA CLASS (REPLENISHMENT AND REPAIR SHIP) (AORH/AS)

Name	*No*	*Builders*	*Launched*	*Commissioned*
ADITYA (ex-*Rajaba Gan Palan*)	A 59	Garden Reach, Calcutta	15 Nov 1993	3 Apr 2000

Displacement, tons: 24,600 full load
Measurement, tons: 17,000 dwt
Dimensions, feet (metres): 564.3 × 75.5 × 29.9 *(172 × 23 × 9.1)*
Main machinery: 2 MAN/Burmeister & Wain 16V 40/45 diesels; 23,936 hp(m) *(17.59 MW)* sustained; 1 shaft
Speed, knots: 20
Range, n miles: 10,000 at 16 kt
Complement: 156 (16 officers) + 6 aircrew
Cargo capacity: 14,200 m³ diesel and avcat; 2,250 m³ water; 2,170 m³ ammunition and stores.
Guns: 3 Bofors 40 mm/60.
Helicopters: 1 Chetak.

Comment: Ordered in July 1987 to a Bremer-Vulkan design. Lengthened version of Deepak class but with a multipurpose workshop. Four RAS stations alongside. Fully air conditioned. Building progress was very slow and sea trials were curtailed by propulsion problems during 1999. Ship has the capability to carry a Sea King 42B or KA 28 helicopter. First ship to be based at Karwar with effect from 15 December 2005.

ADITYA *2/2001*, ***Guy Toremans*** / 0121357

1 DIVING SUPPORT SHIP (ASR)

Name	*No*	*Builders*	*Commissioned*
NIREEKSHAK	A 15	Mazagon Dock Ltd, Bombay	8 June 1989

Displacement, tons: 2,160 full load
Dimensions, feet (metres): 231.3 × 57.4 × 16.4 *(70.5 × 17.5 × 5)*
Main machinery: 2 Bergen KRM-8 diesels; 4,410 hp(m) *(3.24 MW)* sustained; 2 shafts; cp props; 2 bow thrusters; 2 stern thrusters; 990 hp(m) *(727 kW)*
Speed, knots: 12
Complement: 63 (15 officers)

Comment: Laid down in August 1982 and launched January 1984. Acquired on lease with an option for purchase which was taken up in March 1995, and the ship was recommissioned on 15 September 1995. The vessel was built for offshore support operations but has been modified for naval requirements. Two DSRV, capable of taking 12 men to 300 m, are carried together with two six-man recompression chambers and one three-man bell. Kongsberg ADP-503 Mk II. Dynamic positioning system. The ship is used for submarine SAR. Based at Mumbai.

NIREEKSHAK ***2/2006, M Mazumdar*** / 1353090

6 SUPPORT TANKERS (AOTL)

POSHAK **PURAN** **PUSHPA** **PRADHAYAK** **PURAK** **PALAN**

Comment: First two built at Mazagon Dock Ltd, Bombay. *Poshak* completed April 1982, and *Puran* in November 1988. *Pushpa* (capacity 650 tons) built at Goa Shipyard and completed in 1990. *Pradhayak, Purak* and *Palan* built at Rajabagan Shipyard, Bombay, the first two in 1977 and *Palan* in May 1986. Cargo capacities vary. Civilian manned.

PURAN ***3/2007, Marco Ghiglino*** / 1166544

3 NICOBAR CLASS (TRANSPORT SHIPS) (APH)

Name	*No*	*Builders*	*Launched*
NICOBAR	–	Szczecin Shipyard, Poland	12 Apr 1990
ANDAMANS (ex-*Nancowry*)	–	Szczecin Shipyard, Poland	5 Oct 1990
SWARAJ DEEP	–	Vishakhapatnam	1997

Displacement, tons: 19,000 full load
Measurement, tons: 14,176 grt
Dimensions, feet (metres): 515.1 × 68.9 × 22 *(157 × 21 × 6.7)*
Main machinery: 2 Cegielski-Burmeister am Wain 6L35MC diesels; 72,000 hp *(5.3 MW)*; 2 shafts; bow thruster
Speed, knots: 16
Complement: 160
Cargo capacity: 1,200 troops
Helicopters: Platform for 1 medium.

Comment: The first two ships designed and built in Poland. *Nicobar* delivered to the Shipping Corporation of India (which operated the ship for the Andaman and Nicobar Islands Administration) on 5 June 1991 and subsequently acquired for use by the Indian Navy in April 1998. *Andamans* delivered to the Shipping Corporation of India on 31 March 1992 and acquired for use by the Indian Navy in April 2000. The ships are used to trans-ship stores and personnel to the Andaman and Nicobar Islands. They have large davits capable of operating LCVPs. *Swaraj Deep* is of a similar design.

NICOBAR ***4/2007*** / 1305303

0 + 1 (1) REPLENISHMENT TANKER (AORH)

Name	*No*	*Builders*	*Laid down*	*Launched*	*Commissioned*
–	–	Fincantieri	2008	2010	2010

Displacement, tons: 27,500 full load
Dimensions, feet (metres): 574.1 × 82.0 × 29.8 *(175.0 × 25.0 × 9.1)*
Main machinery: 2 diesels; 26,800 hp *(20 MW)*; 1 shaft; cp prop
Speed, knots: 20
Range, n miles: 10,000 at 16 kt
Complement: accommodation for 248
Cargo capacity: Liquids: 12,000 tons of fuel, 2,300 tons of AVCAT, 2,000 tons of fresh water, and 1,000 tons of lub oil. Dry cargo: 200 tons ammunition, 150 tons provisions, 20 tons stores, 6–8 containers on the deck

Guns: To be announced.
Countermeasures: To be announced.
Radars: Surface search: To be announced.
Navigation: To be announced.
Helicopters: 1 Sea King.

Programmes: Fincantieri selected in late 2007 for the construction of a new fleet tanker. A contract was expected by the end of the year. The aft part is to be built at Riva Trigoso while the forward part is to be built at Palermo. There is an option for a second unit.
Structure: The design has a RINA classification and satisfies MARPOL and IMO requirements. It incorporates one elevator while internal passageways allow for the passage of fork-lift vehicles. The ship is to be equipped with two beam RAS stations on each side (all capable of transferring fuel, two for transferring 3 ton loads and two for 250 kg loads) and two stern refuelling stations.

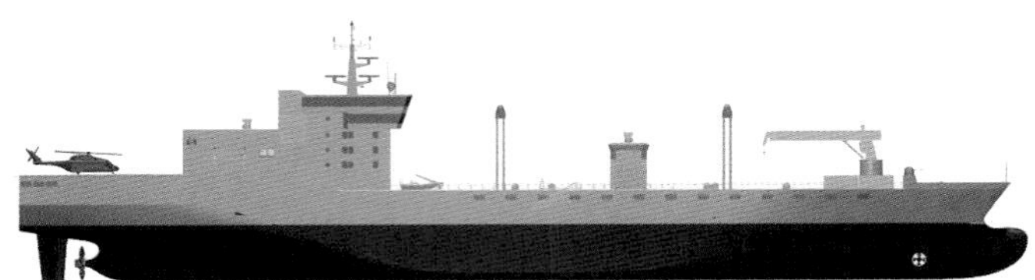
AOR (artist's impression) ***11/2007, Fincantieri*** / 1166542

2 WATER CARRIERS (AWT)

AMBUDA **COCHIN**

Comment: First laid down Rajabagan Shipyard 18 January 1977. Second built at Mazagon Dock Ltd, Bombay. Civilian manned.

AMBUDA ***4/1992*** / 0064729

1 TORPEDO RECOVERY VESSEL (YPT)

A 72

Displacement, tons: 110 full load
Dimensions, feet (metres): 93.5 × 20 × 4.6 *(28.5 × 6.1 × 1.4)*
Main machinery: 2 Kirloskar V12 diesels; 720 hp(m) *(529 kW)*; 2 shafts
Speed, knots: 11
Complement: 13

Comment: Completed in 1981 at Goa Shipyard. Based at Vishakapatnam.

A 72 *2/1989, G Jacobs* / 0506006

3 DIVING TENDERS (YDT)

Displacement, tons: 36 full load
Dimensions, feet (metres): 48.9 × 14.4 × 3.9 *(14.9 × 4.4 × 1.2)*
Main machinery: 2 diesels; 130 hp(m) *(96 kW)*; 2 shafts
Speed, knots: 12

Comment: Built at Cleback Yard. First completed 1979; second and third in 1984.

YDT *9/1996* / 0012531

TUGS

1 TUG (OCEAN) (ATA/ATR)

MATANGA A 53

Displacement, tons: 1,170
Dimensions, feet (metres): 228.5 × 40.4 × 13.6 *(69.64 × 12.3 × 4.1)*
Main machinery: 2 GRSE/MAN G7V diesels; 3,920 hp(m) *(2.88 MW)*; 2 shafts
Speed, knots: 15
Range, n miles: 4,000 at 15 kt
Complement: 78 (8 officers)
Guns: 1 Bofors 40 mm/60.
Radars: Navigation: I-band.

Comment: Built by Garden Reach SY. *Matanga* launched 29 October 1977. Bollard pull of 40 tons and capable of towing a 20,000 ton ship at 8 kt. Carries a divers' decompression chamber and other salvage equipment.

MATANGA *2/2001, Michael Nitz* / 0143309

14 HARBOUR TUGS (YTM/YTL)

SHAMBU SINGH	**MADAN SINGH**	**BHIM**
BC DUTT	**BALRAM**	**AJRAL**
BALSHIL	**ANAND**	**BAHADUR**
TARAFDAAR	**BAJARANG**	**NAKUL**
RAJAJI	**GAJ** A 51	

Measurement, tons: 216 grt
Dimensions, feet (metres): 96.1 × 27.9 × 8.5 *(29.3 × 8.5 × 2.6)*
Main machinery: 2 SEMT-Pielstick 8 PA4 V 200 diesels; 3,200 hp(m) *(2.35 MW)*; 2 shafts
Speed, knots: 11
Complement: 12

Comment: First three built by Mazagon Dock Ltd, Bombay in 1973–74. Five more delivered in 1988–89, and four more in 1991 from Mazagon Dock Ltd, Goa. *Gaj* is a 25 ton bollard pull tug built by Hindustan Shipyard and commissioned on 10 October 2002. Details given are for *Balram* and *Bajrang*; *Rajaji* is of comparable size built in 1982; *Bhim, Balshil* and *Ajral* were built by Tebma Shipyard, Chennai, the others are of varying types.

NAKUL *4/2007* / 1353091

COAST GUARD

Senior Appointments

Director General:
Vice Admiral Anil Chopra, AVSM
Deputy Director General:
Inspector General Achutan Rajasekhar, PTM, TM

Personnel

2009: 6,868 (773 officers)

General

The Coast Guard was constituted as an independent armed force on 19 August 1978. It functions under the Ministry of Defence.
Responsibilities include:

1. Ensuring the safety and protection of artificial islands, offshore terminals, installations and other structures and devices in the Maritime Zones.
2. Measures for the safety of life and property at sea and collection of scientific data as may be prescribed.
3. Measures to preserve and protect the marine environment and control marine pollution.
4. Assisting the Customs and other authorities in anti-smuggling operations.
5. Enforcing the provisions of enactments in force in the Maritime Zones.
6. Protection of fishermen and assistance to them at sea while in distress.

Bases

CG HQ: Delhi
West Region HQ: Mumbai
District 1 HQ: Porbandar
District 2 HQ: Mumbai
District 3 HQ: New Mangalore
District 4 HQ: Kochi
District 11 HQ: Goa
Coast Guard stations: Jakhau, Vadinar, Okha, Beypore, Kavaratti, Vizhinjam
East Region HQ: Chennai
District 5 HQ: Chennai
District 6 HQ: Vishakapatnam
District 7 HQ: Paradip
District 8 HQ: Haldia
Coast Guard stations: Tuticorin, Mandapam, Puducherry, Kakinada
Andaman and Nicobar Region HQ: Port Blair
District 9 HQ: Digupur
District 10 HQ: Campbell Bay

Aviation

Air Squadrons at Daman CGAS 750 (11 Dorniers 228); Kochi CGAS 747 (7 Dorniers 228); Chennai CGAS 744 (7 Dorniers 228); Kolkatta CGAS 700 (2 Dornier 228); Port Blair CGAS 745 (2 Dornier 228); Daman CGAS 841 (4 Chetaks); Mumbai CGAS 842 (3 Chetaks); Goa CGAS 800 (4 Chetaks); Chennai CGAS 848 (3 Chetaks); Vishakapatnam Vajra Flight (Chetaks); Kochi Veera Flight (Chetaks); Port Blair Varad Flight (Chetaks); Porbander Chetak and Dornier Flights; CGEFU Goa (3 ALH).

PATROL FORCES

2 SANKALP CLASS (OFFSHORE PATROL VESSELS) (WPSOH)

Name	*No*	*Builders*	*Laid down*	*Launched*	*Commissioned*
SANKALP	46	Goa Shipyard	17 July 2004	28 Apr 2006	20 May 2008
SAMRAT	47	Goa Shipyard	May 2006	2 July 2007	22 Jan 2009

Displacement, tons: 2,230 full load
Dimensions, feet (metres): 344.5 × 42.3 × 11.8 *(105.0 × 12.9 × 3.6)*
Main machinery: 2 SEMT-Pielstick 20 PA6B stc diesels; 20,900 hp(m) *(15.58 MW)*; 2 shafts; cp props
Speed, knots: 24
Range, n miles: 6,500 at 12 kt
Complement: 106 (12 officers)
Guns: 2 CRN 91—30 mm.
Radars: Surface search: To be announced.
Navigation: To be announced.
Helicopters: 1 HAL Dhruv.

Comment: Designed and built under ABS and IRS classification by Goa Shipyard for patrol and SAR operations, pollution response and firefighting. Three naval variants of the class are also being built.

SANKALP ***5/2008*, Goa Shipyard*** / 1335382

0 + 3 SAMUDRA (UT 517) CLASS (POLLUTION CONTROL VESSELS) (WPSOH)

Name	*No*	*Builders*	*Laid down*	*Launched*	*Commissioned*
SAMUDRA PRAHARI	–	ABG Shipyard, Surat	2004	20 Mar 2007	2009
SAMUDRA PAHAREDAR	–	ABG Shipyard, Surat	2005	2008	2009
SAMUDRA PAVAK	–	ABG Shipyard, Surat	2006	2009	2010

Displacement, tons: 3,300 full load
Dimensions, feet (metres): 308.4 × 50.9 × 14.8 *(94.0 × 15.5 × 4.5)*
Main machinery: 2 Bergen B32 diesels; 8,050 hp *(6.0 MW)*; 2 shafts; cp props. 1 Ulstein Aquamaster bow thruster; 1,185 hp *(883 kW)*
Speed, knots: 20
Range, n miles: 6,000 at 14 kt
Complement: 85 (10 officers)
Guns: 1—30 mm.
Radars: Navigation: To be announced.
Helicopters: Platform for 1 medium.

Comment: Rolls-Royce UT 517 design selected on 25 October 2004 for three environmental protection ships. The ships are to feature a range of Rolls-Royce propulsion, steering and motion control equipment and are similar to those selected for use by the French Navy and Norwegian Coast Guard. The ships are to be capable of deploying a boom system to contain oil spillages while additional tasks are to include surveillance and law enforcement, anti-smuggling and fishery protection, search and rescue, collecting data, and assistance with salvage and fire fighting.

SAMUDRA (UT 517) CLASS (artist's impression) ***10/2004, Rolls-Royce*** / 1042264

0 + 2 (3) COASTAL PATROL VESSELS (PBO)

Name	*No*	*Builders*	*Laid down*	*Launched*	*Commissioned*
–	–	Hindustan Shipyard, Vishakapatnam	26 June 2007	2009	2010
–	–	Hindustan Shipyard, Vishakapatnam	26 June 2007	2009	2010

Displacement, tons: 275 full load
Dimensions, feet (metres): 167.7 × 27.2 × 6.9 *(51.1 × 8.3 × 2.1)*
Main machinery: 3 MTU-F 16V4000 M90 diesels; total of 10,942 hp(m) *(8.2 MW)* sustained; 3 Kamewa 71SII waterjets
Speed, knots: 34
Range, n miles: 1,500 at 14 kt
Complement: 35
Guns: 1—30 mm. 2—12.7 mm MGs.
Radars: Surface search: To be announced.

Comment: The first two of a class of five offshore patrol vessels was laid down in 2007. The vessels are to be modified versions of the Sarojini Naidu class, built at Goa Shipyard, and details are based on these vessels. A fast construction timetable has been set.

4 SAMAR CLASS (OFFSHORE PATROL VESSELS) (WPSOH)

Name	*No*	*Builders*	*Laid down*	*Launched*	*Commissioned*
SAMAR	42	Goa Shipyard	1990	26 Aug 1992	14 Feb 1996
SANGRAM	43	Goa Shipyard	1992	18 Mar 1995	29 Mar 1997
SARANG	44	Goa Shipyard	1993	8 Mar 1997	21 June 1999
SAGAR	45	Goa Shipyard	1999	14 Dec 2001	3 Nov 2003

Displacement, tons: 2,005 full load
Dimensions, feet (metres): 334.6 oa; 315 wl × 37.7 × 11.5 *(102; 96 × 11.5 × 3.5)*
Main machinery: 2 SEMT-Pielstick 16 PA6 V 280 diesels; 12,800 hp(m) *(9.41 MW)* sustained; 2 shafts; LIPS cp props
Speed, knots: 22. **Range, n miles:** 7,000 at 15 kt
Complement: 124 (12 officers)
Guns: 1 OTO Melara 3 in *(76 mm)*/62 Super Rapid; 120 rds/min to 16 km *(8.7 n miles)*; weight of shell 6 kg.
2—12.7 mm MGs.
Weapons control: BEL/Radamec optronic 2400 director.
Radars: Surface search: Decca 2459; F/I-band.
Navigation: BEL 1245; I-band.

Helicopters: 1 Chetak.

Comment: First three ordered in April 1991. Fourth of class ordered 1999. Similar to the Navy's Sukanya class but more heavily armed and carrying a helicopter capable of transporting a Marine contingent. Telescopic hangar.

SAGAR ***5/2007, Hachiro Nakai*** / 1166538

0 + 3 OFFSHORE PATROL VESSELS (WPSOH)

Name	*No*	*Builders*	*Laid down*	*Launched*	*Commissioned*
VISHWAST	30	Goa Shipyard	18 Nov 2006	4 July 2008	2009
–	–	Goa Shipyard	2007	2009	2010
–	–	Goa Shipyard	2007	2009	2011

Displacement, tons: 1,840 full load
Dimensions, feet (metres): 307.4 × 40.0 × 11.8 *(93.7 × 12.2 × 3.6)*
Main machinery: 2 MTU diesels; 24,150 hp(m) *(18.0 MW)*; 2 shafts; cp props
Speed, knots: 26. **Range, n miles:** 4,500 at 16 kt
Complement: 118 (16 officers)
Guns: 1 CRN 91—30 mm.
Radars: Surface search: To be announced.
Navigation: To be announced.
Helicopters: 1 HAL Dhruv.

Comment: Three 90 m offshore patrol craft ordered in 2006. The building programme has not been confirmed.

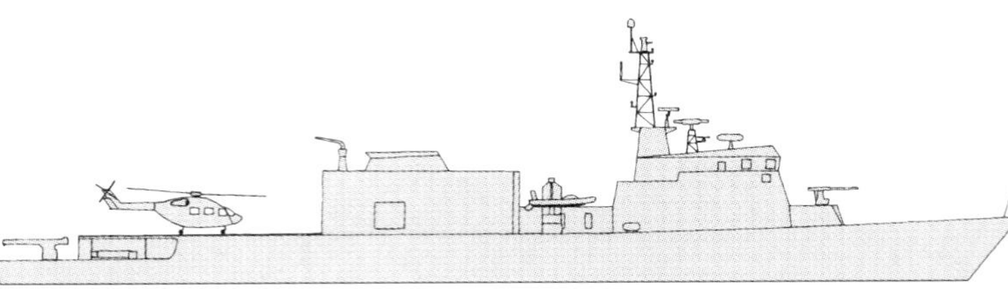

90 m OPV ***(Scale 1 : 900), Ian Sturton*** / 1164336

8 VIKRAM CLASS (OFFSHORE PATROL VESSELS) (WPSOH)

Name	*No*	*Builders*	*Launched*	*Commissioned*
VIKRAM	33	Mazagon Dock, Mumbai	26 Sep 1981	19 Dec 1983
VIJAYA	34	Mazagon Dock, Mumbai	5 June 1982	12 Apr 1985
VEERA	35	Mazagon Dock, Mumbai	30 June 1984	3 May 1986
VARUNA	36	Mazagon Dock, Mumbai	28 Jan 1986	27 Feb 1988
VAJRA	37	Mazagon Dock, Mumbai	3 Jan 1987	22 Dec 1988
VIVEK	38	Mazagon Dock, Mumbai	5 Nov 1987	19 Aug 1989
VIGRAHA	39	Mazagon Dock, Mumbai	27 Sep 1988	12 Apr 1990
VARAD	40	Goa Shipyard	3 Sep 1989	19 July 1990

Displacement, tons: 1,224 full load
Dimensions, feet (metres): 243.1 × 37.4 × 10.5 *(74.1 × 11.4 × 3.2)*
Main machinery: 2 SEMT-Pielstick 16 PA6 V 280 diesels; 12,800 hp(m) *(9.41 MW)* sustained; 2 shafts; cp props
Speed, knots: 22. **Range, n miles:** 4,250 at 12 kt
Complement: 96 (11 officers)
Guns: 1—30 mm.
Weapons control: Lynx optical sights.
Radars: Navigation: 2 Decca 1226; I-band.
Helicopters: 1 HAL (Aerospatiale) Chetak.

Comment: Owes something to a NEVESBU (Netherlands) design, being a stretched version of its 750 ton offshore patrol vessels. Ordered in 1979. Fin stabilisers. Diving equipment. 4.5 ton deck crane. External firefighting pumps. Has one GRP boat and two inflatable craft. This class is considered too small for its required task and hence the need for the larger Samar class. *Varaha* was donated to the Sri Lankan Navy on 25 February 2007.

VIJAYA ***2/2001, Guy Toremans*** / 0121354

8 PRIYADARSHINI CLASS (COASTAL PATROL CRAFT) (WPBO)

Name	*No*	*Builders*	*Commissioned*
PRIYADARSHINI	221	Garden Reach, Calcutta	25 May 1992
RAZIA SULTANA	222	Goa Shipyard	18 Nov 1992
ANNIE BESANT	223	Goa Shipyard	7 Dec 1992
KAMLA DEVI	224	Goa Shipyard	20 May 1992
AMRIT KAUR	225	Goa Shipyard	20 Mar 1993
KANAK LATA BAURA	226	Garden Reach, Calcutta	27 Mar 1997
BHIKAJI CAMA	227	Garden Reach, Calcutta	24 Sep 1997
SUCHETA KRIPALANI	228	Garden Reach, Calcutta	16 Mar 1998

Displacement, tons: 306 full load
Dimensions, feet (metres): 150.9 × 24.6 × 6.2 *(46.0 × 7.5 × 1.9)*
Main machinery: 2 MTU 12V 538 diesels; 4,025 hp(m) *(2.96 MW)* sustained; 2 shafts
Speed, knots: 23. **Range, n miles:** 2,400 at 12 kt
Complement: 34 (7 officers)
Guns: 1—30 mm.
2—7.62 mm MGs.
Radars: Racal Decca 1226 or BEL 1245/6X (221-225); I-band.

Comment: A development of the Tara Bai class. *Razia Sultana* (222), previously thought to have been lost at sea, remains in commission.

KAMLA DEVI *3/2004, Bob Fildes* / 1042270

6 TARA BAI CLASS (COASTAL PATROL CRAFT) (WPBO)

Name	*No*	*Builders*	*Commissioned*
TARA BAI	71	Singapore SBEC	26 June 1987
AHALYA BAI	72	Singapore SBEC	9 Sep 1987
LAKSHMI BAI	73	Garden Reach, Calcutta	20 Mar 1989
AKKA DEVI	74	Garden Reach, Calcutta	9 Aug 1989
NAIKI DEVI	75	Garden Reach, Calcutta	19 Mar 1990
GANGA DEVI	76	Garden Reach, Calcutta	19 Nov 1990

Displacement, tons: 195 full load
Dimensions, feet (metres): 147.3 × 23.0 × 8.5 *(44.9 × 7.0 × 2.6)*
Main machinery: 2 MTU 12V 538 diesels; 4,025 hp(m) *(2.96 MW)* sustained; 2 shafts
Speed, knots: 26. **Range, n miles:** 2,400 at 12 kt
Complement: 34 (7 officers)
Guns: 1 Bofors 40 mm/60.
2—7.6 mm MGs.
Radars: Surface search: Racal Decca 1226 or BEL 1245/6X (221-225); I-band.

Comment: Two ordered in June 1986 with license to build further four in India. These were laid down in 1987.

AKKA DEVI *6/2000, Indian Navy* / 1042263

7 SAROJINI NAIDU CLASS (WPBO)

Name	*No*	*Builders*	*Commissioned*
SAROJINI NAIDU	229	Goa Shipyard	11 Nov 2002
DURGABAI DESHMUKH	230	Goa Shipyard	30 Apr 2003
KASTURBA GANDHI	231	Goa Shipyard	28 Oct 2005
ARUNA ASAF ALI	232	Goa Shipyard	28 Jan 2006
SUBHADRA KUMARI CHAUHAN	233	Goa Shipyard	28 Apr 2006
MEERA BEHAN	234	Goa Shipyard	25 July 2006
SAVITRI BAI PHULE	235	Goa Shipyard	28 Oct 2006

Displacement, tons: 260 full load
Dimensions, feet (metres): 157.8 × 24.6 × 6.6 *(48.1 × 7.5 × 2)*
Main machinery: 3 MTU-F 16V4000 M90 diesels; total of 10,942 hp(m) *(8.2 MW)* sustained; 3 Kamewa 71SII waterjets
Speed, knots: 35
Complement: 35
Guns: 1—30 mm.
2—12.7 mm MGs.
Radars: Surface search: to be announced.

Comment: A new class of patrol ship designed and developed by Goa Shipyard. Following the initial delivery of two vessels, an order for a further five was made in 2004. These have all been commissioned.

SAROJINI NAIDU *11/2002, Indian Coast Guard* / 0530081

7 JIJA BAI MOD 1 CLASS (TYPE 956) (COASTAL PATROL CRAFT) (WPBO)

Name	*No*	*Builders*	*Commissioned*
JIJA BAI	64	Sumidagawa, Tokyo	22 Feb 1984
CHAND BIBI	65	Sumidagawa, Tokyo	22 Feb 1984
KITTUR CHENNAMMA	66	Sumidagawa, Tokyo	21 Oct 1983
RANI JINDAN	67	Sumidagawa, Tokyo	21 Oct 1983
HABBAH KHATUN	68	Garden Reach, Calcutta	27 Apr 1985
RAMADEVI	69	Garden Reach, Calcutta	3 Aug 1985
AVVAIYYAR	70	Garden Reach, Calcutta	19 Oct 1985

Displacement, tons: 181 full load
Dimensions, feet (metres): 144.3 × 24.3 × 7.5 *(44 × 7.4 × 2.3)*
Main machinery: 2 MTU 12V 538 TB82 diesels; 4,025 hp(m) *(2.96 MW)* sustained; 2 shafts
Speed, knots: 25. **Range, n miles:** 2,375 at 14 kt
Complement: 34 (7 officers)
Guns: 1 Bofors 40 mm/60. 2—7.62 mm MGs.
Radars: Surface search: Racal Decca 1226; I-band.

Comment: All were ordered in 1981 and are similar to those in service with the Philippines Coast Guard.

RANI JINDAN *6/1996, Indian Coast Guard* / 0064732

2 SDB MK 2 RAJ CLASS (COASTAL PATROL CRAFT) (WPB)

Name	*No*	*Builders*	*Commissioned*
RAJKIRAN	59	Garden Reach, Calcutta	29 Mar 1984
RAJKAMAL	61	Garden Reach, Calcutta	19 Sep 1986

Displacement, tons: 203 full load
Dimensions, feet (metres): 123 × 24.6 × 5.9 *(37.5 × 7.5 × 1.8)*
Main machinery: 2 MTU 12V 538 diesels; 4,025 hp(m) *(2.96 MW)* sustained; 2 shafts
Speed, knots: 29. **Range, n miles:** 1,400 at 14 kt
Complement: 28 (4 officers)
Guns: 1 Bofors 40/60 mm.
Radars: Surface search: Racal Decca; I-band.

Comment: Earlier vessels of this class belonged to the Navy but have been scrapped.

RAJKAMAL *6/2000, Indian Coast Guard* / 0104591

1 SWALLOW 65 CLASS (WPB)

C 63

Displacement, tons: 32 full load
Dimensions, feet (metres): 65.6 × 15.4 × 5 *(20 × 4.7 × 1.5)*
Main machinery: 2 Detroit 12V-71TA diesels; 840 hp *(627 kW)* sustained; 2 shafts
Speed, knots: 20. **Range, n miles:** 400 at 20 kt
Complement: 9 (1 officer)
Guns: 1—7.62 mm MG.
Radars: Navigation: I-band.

Comment: Built by Swallow Craft Co, Pusan, South Korea in early 1980s. Last remaining craft in service.

C 63 *1982, Swallow Craft* / 0012534

8 INSHORE PATROL CRAFT (WPBF)

C 109–116

Displacement, tons: 5.5 full load
Dimensions, feet (metres): 31.2 × 10.7 × 2.5 *(9.5 × 3.3 × 0.75)*
Main machinery: 2 outboard motors; diesels; 500 hp *(370 kW)*
Speed, knots: 35. **Range, n miles:** 75 at 25 kt
Complement: 2
Guns: 1—7.62 mm MG.

Comment: Built by Bristol Boats Ltd, Kochi. The first craft became operational on 1 December 2004.

9 INSHORE PATROL CRAFT (WPB)

C 131–138 C 140

Displacement, tons: 49 full load
Dimensions, feet (metres): 68.2 × 19 × 5.9 *(20.8 × 5.8 × 1.8)*
Main machinery: 2 Deutz MWM TBD234V12 diesels; 1,646 hp(m) *(1.21 MW)* sustained; 1 Deutz MWM TBD234V8 diesel; 550 hp(m) *(404 kW)* sustained; 3 Hamilton 402 water-jets
Speed, knots: 25. **Range, n miles:** 600 at 15 kt
Complement: 8 (1 officer)
Guns: 1 — 12.7 mm MG.
Radars: Navigation: Furuno; I-band.

Comment: Ordered from Anderson Marine, Goa in September 1990 to a P-2000 design by Amgram, similar to British Archer class. GRP hull. Official description is 'Interceptor Boats'. All built at Goa. Commissioned: *C 131-132* on 16 November 1993, *C 133-134* on 20 May 1994, *C 135-136* on 16 February 1995, *C 137-138* on 4 September 1996, and *C 139* on 16 October 1997. *C 139* was leased to Mauritius in 2001. C 140, was commissioned on 15 November 2003.

C 136 (old number) *2/2001, Sattler/Steele* / 0121360

2 + 11 (5) INSHORE PATROL CRAFT (WPBF)

C 141 C 142

Displacement, tons: 75
Dimensions, feet (metres): 85.3 × 21.6 × 3.9 *(26.0 × 6.6 × 1.18)*
Main machinery: 2 MTU 12V 4000 diesels; 5,470 hp *(4.1 MW)*; 2 Kamewa waterjets
Speed, knots: 45
Complement: To be announced
Guns: To be announced.
Radars: Surface search: To be announced.

Comment: Built by ABG Shipbuilding, Surat and commissioned on 8 February 2002. Aluminium construction. An order for a further 11 craft has been made and these are expected to enter service 2008–10. There is an option for a further five craft.

C 141 *6/2004, Kapil Chandni* / 1042268

6 GRIFFON 8000TD(M) CLASS HOVERCRAFT (UCAC)

H 181–186

Displacement, tons: 18.2; 24.6 full load
Dimensions, feet (metres): 69.5 × 36.1 × 1 *(21.15 × 11 × 0.32)*
Main machinery: 2 MTU 12V 183 TB 32 V12 diesels; 1,600 hp *(1.2 MW)*
Speed, knots: 50. **Range, n miles:** 400 at 45 kt
Complement: 13 (2 officers)
Guns: 1 — 12.7 mm MG.
Radars: Raytheon R-80; I-band.

Comment: Six hovercraft were ordered from GRSE Calcutta in May 1999 for construction in technical collaboration with Griffon UK. The first craft H 181 was commissioned on 18 September 2000, four further in 2001, and the final one on 21 March 2002.

H 185 *6/2004, Kapil Chandni* / 1042269

Indonesia

TENTARA NASIONAL

Country Overview

The Republic of Indonesia gained full independence from the Netherlands in 1949. Straddling the equator, the country comprises more than 13,670 islands, of which some 6,000 are inhabited. The major islands include Sumatra, Java, Sulawesi (Celebes), southern Borneo (Kalimantan) and western New Guinea (Papua). Smaller islands include Madura, western Timor, Lombok, Sumbawa, Flores, and Bali. The Moluccas and Lesser Sunda Islands are the largest island groups. The coastline of 29,550 n miles is with the South China Sea, the Celebes Sea, the Pacific Ocean and the Indian Ocean. The total land area is 741,903 square miles. The capital, largest city and principal port is Jakarta (Java). Further main ports are at Surabaya (Java), Medan (Sumatra) and Ujung Pandang (Sulawesi). An archipelagic state, territorial seas (12 n miles) are claimed. A 200 n mile EEZ has also been claimed but the limits are only partly defined by boundary agreements.

Headquarters Appointments

Chief of the Naval Staff:
Admiral Tedjo Edhy Purdijatno
Vice Chief of the Naval Staff:
Vice Admiral Moeklas Sidik Purnomo
Inspector General of the Navy:
Vice Admiral Moch Sunarto

Fleet Command

Commander-in-Chief Western Fleet (Jakarta):
Rear Admiral Soeparno
Commander-in-Chief Eastern Fleet (Surabaya):
Rear Admiral Slamet Yulistiyono
Commandant of Navy Marine Corps:
Major General Djunaidi Djanri

Personnel

(a) 2009: 57,000 (including 20,000 Marine Commando Corps and 1,000 Naval Air Arm)
(b) Selective national service

Bases

Tanjung Priok (North Jakarta), Ujung (Surabaya), Sabang, Belawan (North Sumatera), Ujung Pandang (South Sulawesi), Balikpapan (East Kalimantan), Jayapura (Irian Jaya), Tanjung Pinang, Bitung (North Sulawesi), Teluk Ratai (South Sumatera), Banjarmasin (South Kalmantan). Naval Air Base at Juanda (Surabaya), Biak (Irian Jaya), Pekan Baru, Sam Ratulangi (North Sulawesi), Sabang, Natuna, P Aru.

Command Structure

Eastern Command (Surabaya)
Western Command (Jakarta)
Training Command
Military Sea Communications Command (Maritime Security Agency)
Military Sealift Command (Logistic Support)
Plans announced in July 2005 include creation of a third naval command based at Sorong, west Irian Jaya and for the Eastern and Western commands to move to Makassar and Tanjung Pinang, Sumatra, respectively. Dates for implementing the changes have not been announced.

Marine Corps

Reorganisation in March 2001 created the 1st Marine Corps Group (1st, 3rd and 5th battalions) based at Surabaya and the Independent Marine Corps Brigade (2nd, 4th and 6th battalions) based in Jakarta. A new formation (7th, 8th and 9th battalions) is to be based at Teluk Ratai, Sumatra. Equipment includes amphibious tanks, field artillery and anti-aircraft missiles and guns. There are plans to expand the Corps to 22,800 by 2009. Further reorganisation is expected to include relocation of the eastern command from Surabaya to Makassar and the central command from Jakarta to Surabaya.

Strength of the Fleet

Type	*Active*	*Building (Projected)*
Patrol Submarines	2	(2)
Frigates	8	–
Corvettes	21	2
Fast Attack Craft-Missile	4	–
Large Patrol Craft	21	–
Patrol craft	17	–
LPD	2	3
LST/LSM	26	–
MCMV	11	–
Survey and Research Ships	8	–
Command Ship	1	–
Replenishment Tankers	2	–
Coastal Tankers	2	–
Support Ships	5	–
Transports	8	–
Sail Training Ships	2	–

Prefix to Ships' Names

KRI (Kapal di Republik Indonesia)

PENNANT LIST

Submarines

401 Cakra
402 Nanggala

Frigates

342 Martadinata
351 Ahmad Yani
352 Slamet Riyadi
353 Yos Sudarso
354 Oswald Siahann
355 Abdul Halim Perdanakusuma
356 Karel Satsuitubun
364 Ki Hajar Dewantara

Corvettes

361 Fatahillah
362 Malahayati
363 Nala
365 Diponegoro
366 Sultan Hasanuddin
367 Sultan Iskandar Muda (bldg)
368 Frans Kaisiepo (bldg)
371 Kapitan Patimura
372 Untung Suropati
373 Nuku
374 Lambung Mangkurat
375 Cut Nyak Dien
376 Sultan Thaha Syaifuddin
377 Sutanto
378 Sutedi Senoputra
379 Wiratno
380 Memet Sastrawiria
381 Tjiptadi
382 Hasan Basri
383 Iman Bonjol
384 Pati Unus
385 Teuku Umar
386 Silas Papare

Patrol Forces

621 Mandau
622 Rencong

PENNANT LIST—*continued*

623 Badik
624 Keris
651 Singa
653 Ajak
801 Pandrong
802 Sura
803 Todak
804 Hiu
805 Layang
806 Lemadang
807 Boa
808 Welang
809 Suluh Pari
810 Katon
811 Kakap
812 Kerapu
813 Tongkol
814 Barakuda
815 Sanca
816 Warakas
817 Panana
818 Kalakae
819 Tedong Naga
820 Viper
821 Piton
822 Weling
823 Matacora
824 Tedung Selar
825 Boiga
826 Kelabang
827 Krait
828 Kala Hitam
829 Tarihu
847 Sibarau
848 Siliman
857 Sigalu
858 Silea
859 Siribua
862 Siada
863 Sikuda
864 Sigurot
866 Cucut
867 Kobra
868 Anakonda
869 Patola
870 Taliwangsa

Amphibious Forces

501 Teluk Langsa
502 Teluk Bayur
503 Teluk Amboina
504 Teluk Kau
508 Teluk Tomini
509 Teluk Ratai
510 Teluk Saleh
511 Teluk Bone
512 Teluk Semangka
513 Teluk Penyu
514 Teluk Mandar
515 Teluk Sampit
516 Teluk Banten
517 Teluk Ende
531 Teluk Gilimanuk
532 Teluk Celukan Bawang
533 Teluk Cendrawasih
534 Teluk Berau
535 Teluk Peleng
536 Teluk Sibolga
537 Teluk Manado
538 Teluk Hading
539 Teluk Parigi
540 Teluk Lampung
541 Teluk Jakarta
542 Teluk Sangkuring
580 Dore
582 Kupang
583 Dili
584 Nusa Utara
590 Makassar
591 Surabaya
971 Tanjung Kambani
972 Dr Soeharso
973 Tanjung Nusanive
974 Tanjung Fataga
981 Karang Pilang
982 Karang Tekok
983 Karang Banteng
984 Karang Galang
985 Karang Unarang

Survey Ships

KAL-IV-02 Baruna Jaya I
KAL-IV-03 Baruna Jaya II
KAL-IV-04 Baruna Jaya III
KAL-IV-05 Baruna Jaya IV
KAL-IV-06 Baruna Jaya VIII
931 Burujulasad
932 Dewa Kembar
933 Jalanidhi

Mine Warfare Forces

711 Pulau Rengat
712 Pulau Rupat
721 Pulau Rote
722 Pulau Raas
723 Pulau Romang
724 Pulau Rimau
726 Pulau Rusa
727 Pulau Rangsang
729 Pulau Rempang

Auxiliaries

543 Teluk Cirebon
544 Teluk Sabang
561 Multatuli
901 Balikpapan
902 Sambu
903 Arun
906 Sungai Gerong
911 Sorong
923 Soputan
924 Leuser
934 Lampo Batang
935 Tambora
936 Bromo
961 Wagio

SUBMARINES

Notes: Two ex-German Type 206 submarines were taken over on 25 September 1997 with plans to refit them, followed by three others. Funds ran out in June 1998 and the whole project was then cancelled. New plans to acquire two submarines from South Korea were announced in October 2003. This probably points to a modified Chang Bogo class. Talks have also, reportedly, taken place with the Russian government.

2 CAKRA TYPE 209/1300 CLASS

Name	*No*	*Builders*	*Laid down*	*Launched*	*Commissioned*
CAKRA	401	Howaldtswerke, Kiel	25 Nov 1977	10 Sep 1980	19 Mar 1981
NANGGALA	402	Howaldtswerke, Kiel	14 Mar 1978	10 Sep 1980	6 July 1981

Displacement, tons: 1,285 surfaced; 1,390 dived
Dimensions, feet (metres): 195.2 × 20.3 × 17.9 *(59.5 × 6.2 × 5.4)*
Main machinery: Diesel-electric; 4 MTU 12V 493 AZ80 GA31L diesels; 2,400 hp(m) *(1.76 MW)* sustained; 4 Siemens alternators; 1.7 MW; 1 Siemens motor; 4,600 hp(m) *(3.38 MW)* sustained; 1 shaft
Speed, knots: 11 surfaced; 21.5 dived
Range, n miles: 8,200 at 8 kt
Complement: 34 (6 officers)

Torpedoes: 8—21 in *(533 mm)* bow tubes. 14 AEG SUT Mod 0; dual purpose; wire-guided; active/passive homing to 12 km *(6.5 n miles)* at 35 kt; 28 km *(15 n miles)* at 23 kt; warhead 250 kg.
Countermeasures: ESM: Thomson-CSF DR 2000U; radar warning.
Weapons control: Signaal Sinbad system.
Radars: Surface search: Thomson-CSF Calypso; I-band.
Sonars: Atlas Elektronik CSU 3-2; active/passive search and attack; medium frequency.
PRS-3/4; (integral with CSU) passive ranging.

Programmes: Ordered on 2 April 1977. Designed by Ingenieurkontor, Lübeck for construction by Howaldtswerke, Kiel and sale by Ferrostaal, Essen-all acting as a consortium.
Modernisation: Major refits at HDW spanning three years from 1986 to 1989. These refits were expensive and lengthy and may have discouraged further orders at that time. *Cakra* refitted again at Surabaya from 1993 completing in April 1997, including replacement batteries and updated Sinbad TFCS. *Nanggala* received a similar refit from October 1997 to mid-1999. *Cakra* began a refit at Daewoo Shipyard, South Korea in 2004 which was completed in 2005. Work is reported to have included new batteries, overhaul of engines and modernisation of the combat system. A similar refit of *Nanggala* was completed in April 2006.
Structure: Have high-capacity batteries with GRP lead-acid cells and battery cooling supplied by Wilhelm Hagen AG. Diving depth, 240 m *(790 ft)*.
Operational: Endurance, 50 days. Operational status of both boats is doubtful.

NANGGALA *8/1999, van Ginderen Collection* / 0080001

FRIGATES

Notes: There were reports in mid-2007 that three Russian Steregushchiy-class frigates were to be procured but these have not been confirmed.

1 SAMADIKUN (CLAUD JONES) CLASS (FF)

Name	*No*	*Builders*	*Laid down*	*Launched*	*Commissioned*
MARTADINATA (ex-*Charles Berry* DE 1035)	342	American SB Co, Toledo, OH	29 Oct 1958	17 Mar 1959	25 Nov 1959

Displacement, tons: 1,720 standard; 1,968 full load
Dimensions, feet (metres): 310 × 38.7 × 18 *(95 × 11.8 × 5.5)*
Main machinery: 2 Fairbanks-Morse 38TD 8-1/8-12 diesels (not in 343); 7,000 hp *(5.2 MW)* sustained; 1 shaft
Speed, knots: 22
Range, n miles: 3,000 at 18 kt
Complement: 171 (12 officers)

Guns: 1 or 2 US 3 in *(76 mm)*/50 Mk 34; 50 rds/min to 12.8 km *(7 n miles)*; weight of shell 6 kg.
2 USSR 37 mm/63 (twin); 160 rds/min to 9 km *(5 n miles)*; weight of shell 0.7 kg.
Torpedoes: 6—324 mm Mk 32 (2 triple) tubes. Honeywell Mk 46; anti-submarine; active/passive homing to 11 km *(5.9 n miles)* at 40 kt; warhead 44 kg.
Depth charges: 2 DC throwers.
Countermeasures: ESM: WLR-1C; radar warning.
Weapons control: Mk 70 Mod 2 for guns.
Radars: Air search: Westinghouse SPS-6E; D-band; range 146 km *(80 n miles)* (for fighter).
Surface search: Raytheon SPS-5D; G/H-band; range 37 km *(20 n miles)*.
Navigation: Racal Decca 1226; I-band
Fire control: Lockheed SPG-52; K-band
Sonars: SQS-45V; hull-mounted; active search and attack; medium/high frequency.

Programmes: Transferred from US 31 January 1974. Refitted at Subic Bay 1979–82.

SAMADIKUN CLASS *10/2001, Chris Sattler* / 0121379

Modernisation: The Hedgehog A/S mortars have been removed, as have the 25 mm guns. Some have a second 76 mm gun vice the 37 mm.
Operational: It was planned that the Van Speijk class would replace these ships. Three have been deleted and the operational status of this last one is doubtful.

6 AHMAD YANI (VAN SPEIJK) CLASS (FFGHM)

Name	*No*	*Builders*	*Laid down*	*Launched*	*Commissioned*
AHMAD YANI (ex-*Tjerk Hiddes*)	351	Nederlandse Dok en Scheepsbouw Mij, Amsterdam	1 June 1964	17 Dec 1965	16 Aug 1967
SLAMET RIYADI (ex-*Van Speijk*)	352	Nederlandse Dok en Scheepsbouw Mij, Amsterdam	1 Oct 1963	5 Mar 1965	14 Feb 1967
YOS SUDARSO (ex-*Van Galen*)	353	Koninklijke Maatschappij de Schelde, Flushing	25 July 1963	19 June 1965	1 Mar 1967
OSWALD SIAHAAN (ex-*Van Nes*)	354	Koninklijke Maatschappij de Schelde, Flushing	25 July 1963	26 Mar 1966	9 Aug 1967
ABDUL HALIM PERDANAKUSUMA (ex-*Evertsen*)	355	Koninklijke Maatschappij de Schelde, Flushing	6 July 1965	18 June 1966	21 Dec 1967
KAREL SATSUITUBUN (ex-*Isaac Sweers*)	356	Nederlandse Dok en Scheepsbouw Mij, Amsterdam	5 May 1965	10 Mar 1967	15 May 1968

Displacement, tons: 2,225 standard; 2,835 full load
Dimensions, feet (metres): 372 × 41 × 13.8 *(113.4 × 12.5 × 4.2)*
Main machinery: 2 Caterpillar 3612 diesels (356); 12,512 hp *(9.2 MW)*; 2 Caterpillar 3616 diesels (351, 351, 353, 355); 14,617 hp *(10.9 MW)*; 2 SEMT Pielstick 12 PA6B (354); 14,000 hp *(10.6 MW)*; 2 shafts
Speed, knots: 28.5
Range, n miles: 4,500 at 12 kt
Complement: 180

Missiles: SSM: 8 McDonnell Douglas Harpoon ❶; active radar homing to 130 km *(70 n miles)* at 0.9 Mach; warhead 227 kg.
SAM: 2 twin Matra Simbad launchers for Mistral; IR homing to 4 km *(2.2 n miles)*; warhead 3 kg.
Guns: 1 OTO Melara 3 in *(76 mm)*/62 compact ❷; 85 rds/min to 16 km *(8.7 n miles)* anti-surface; 12 km *(6.6 n miles)* anti-aircraft; weight of shell 6 kg. 4—12.7 mm MGs.
Torpedoes: 6—324 mm Mk 32 (2 triple) tubes ❸. Honeywell Mk 46; anti-submarine; active/passive homing to 11 km *(5.9 n miles)* at 40 kt; warhead 44 kg.
Countermeasures: Decoys: 2 Knebworth Corvus 8-tubed trainable; radar distraction or centroid chaff to 1 km.
ESM: UA 8/9; UA 13 (355 and 356); radar warning. FH5 D/F.
Combat data systems: SEWACO V action data automation and Daisy data processing.
Weapons control: Signaal LIOD optronic director. Mk 2 fitted in 354, 353 and 356. SWG-1A Harpoon LCS.
Radars: Air search: Signaal LW03 ❹; D-band; range 219 km *(120 n miles)* for 2 m² target.
Air/surface search: Signaal DA05 ❺; E/F-band; range 137 km *(75 n miles)* for 2 m² target.

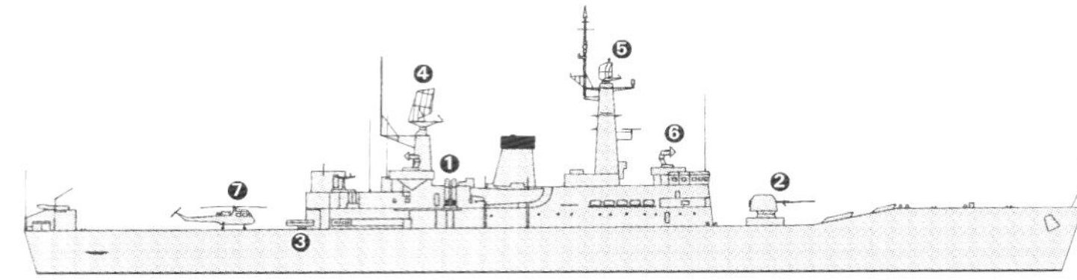

AHMAD YANI *(Scale 1 : 1,200), Ian Sturton* / 1153005

Navigation: Racal Decca 1229; I-band.
Fire control: Signaal M 45 ❻; I/J-band (for 76 mm gun and SSM).
Sonars: Signaal CWE 610; hull-mounted; active search and attack; medium frequency. VDS; medium frequency.

Helicopters: 1 NBO-105C ❼.

Programmes: On 11 February 1986 agreement signed with the Netherlands for transfer of two of this class with an option on two more. Transfer dates: *Tjerk Hiddes*, 31 October 1986; *Van Speijk*, 1 November 1986; *Van Galen*, 2 November 1987; *Van Nes*, 31 October 1988. Contract of sale for the last two of the class signed 13 May 1989. *Evertsen* transferred 1 November 1989 and *Isaac Sweers* 1 November 1990. Ships provided with all spare parts but not towed arrays or helicopters.
Modernisation: This class underwent mid-life modernisation at Rykswerf Den Helder from 1976. This included replacement of 4.5 in turret by 76 mm, A/S mortar by torpedo tubes, new electronics and electrics, updating combat data system, improved communications, extensive automation with reduction in complement, enlarged hangar for Lynx and improved habitability. Harpoon for first two only initially because there was no FMS funding for the others. However the USN then provided sufficient SWG 1A panels for all of the class to be retrofitted with Harpoon missiles. LIOD optronic directors Mk 2 fitted in 354, 353 and 356 in 1996–97. Seacat replaced by Simbad twin launchers. *Ahmad Yani* and *Karel Satsuitubun* appear to have some additional superstructure in place of the Seacat launcher on the hangar roof. All six ships have been re-engined with diesel propulsion. 356 was refitted by Tesco Corp in 2003 and 354 by PT Mulia/PT Pal in 2006. 355 and 351 had been refitted by Tesco in mid-2007 and 352 and 353 are to be completed by Tesco by 2008.
Operational: Operational availability has been drastically reduced by propulsion problems. Harpoon missiles are reported to be time-expired.

KAREL SATSUITUBUN *10/2004, D Pawlenko, RAN* / 1044131

KAREL SATSUITUBUN *11/2004, Chris Gee* / 1047873

CORVETTES

Notes: A programme for the procurement of indigenously built corvettes was launched at PT Pal Shipyard, Surabaya on 8 October 2004. The programme is believed to entail technology transfer from a foreign shipbuilder to enable local construction. Fincantieri was reported to be a strong contender for collaboration but apparent lack of progress with the project suggests that a decision is yet to be made and that another shipbuilder may yet be involved.

3 FATAHILLAH CLASS (FFG/FFGH)

Name	*No*	*Builders*	*Laid down*	*Launched*	*Commissioned*
FATAHILLAH	361	Wilton Fijenoord, Schiedam	31 Jan 1977	22 Dec 1977	16 July 1979
MALAHAYATI	362	Wilton Fijenoord, Schiedam	28 July 1977	19 June 1978	21 Mar 1980
NALA	363	Wilton Fijenoord, Schiedam	27 Jan 1978	11 Jan 1979	4 Aug 1980

Displacement, tons: 1,200 standard; 1,450 full load
Dimensions, feet (metres): 276 × 36.4 × 10.7 *(84 × 11.1 × 3.3)*
Main machinery: CODOG; 1 RR Olympus TM3B gas turbine; 25,440 hp *(19 MW)* sustained; 2 MTU 20V 956 TB92 diesels; 11,070 hp(m) *(8.14 MW)* sustained; 2 shafts; LIPS cp props
Speed, knots: 30. **Range, n miles:** 4,250 at 16 kt
Complement: 89 (11 officers)

Missiles: SSM: 4 Aerospatiale MM 38 Exocet ❶; inertial cruise; active radar homing to 42 km *(23 n miles)* at 0.9 Mach; warhead 165 kg; sea-skimmer.
Guns: 1 Bofors 4.7 in *(120 mm)*/46 ❷; 80 rds/min to 18.5 km *(10 n miles)*; weight of shell 21 kg.
1 or 2 Bofors 40 mm/70 (2 in *Nala*) ❸; 300 rds/min to 12 km *(6.6 n miles)*; weight of shell 0.96 kg.
2 Rheinmetall 20 mm; 1,000 rds/min to 2 km anti-aircraft; weight of shell 0.24 kg.
Torpedoes: 6—324 mm Mk 32 or ILAS 3 (2 triple) tubes (none in *Nala*) ❹. 12 Mk 46 (or A244S); anti-submarine; active/passive homing to 11 km *(5.9 n miles)* at 40 kt; warhead 44 kg.
A/S mortars: 1 Bofors 375 mm twin-barrelled trainable ❺; 54 Erika; range 1,600 m and Nelli; range 3,600 m.

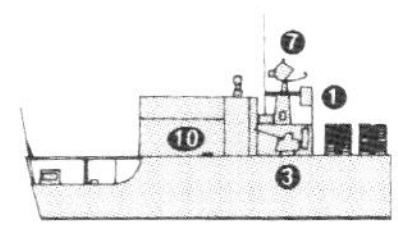
NALA

FATAHILLAH *(Scale 1 : 1,200), Ian Sturton* / 0126692 / 0121374

Countermeasures: Decoys: 2 Knebworth Corvus 8-tubed trainable chaff launchers ❻; radar distraction or centroid modes to 1 km. 1 T-Mk 6; torpedo decoy.
ESM: MEL Susie 1 (UAA-1); radar intercept.
Combat data systems: Signaal SEWACO-RI action data automation.
Weapons control: Signaal LIROD optronic director.
Radars: Air/surface search: Signaal DA05 ❼; E/F-band; range 137 km *(75 n miles)* for 2 m^2 target.
Surface search: Racal Decca AC 1229 ❽; I-band.
Fire control: Signaal WM28 ❾; I/J-band; range 46 km *(25 n miles)*.

Sonars: Signaal PHS-32; hull-mounted; active search and attack; medium frequency.

Helicopters: 1 Westland Wasp (*Nala* only) ❿.

Programmes: Ordered August 1975. Officially rated as Corvettes.
Structure: NEVESBU design. *Nala* is fitted with a folding hangar/landing deck.
Operational: These ships are the busiest of the larger warships. Three successful Exocet (locally modified after life-expiry) firings conducted on 25 August 2002.

NALA *6/2000, van Ginderen Collection* / 0104593

FATAHILLAH *11/2004, Chris Gee* / 1047876

16 KAPITAN PATIMURA (PARCHIM I) CLASS (PROJECT 1331) (FS)

Name	*No*	*Builders*	*Commissioned*	*Recommissioned*
KAPITAN PATIMURA (ex-*Prenzlau*)	371 (ex-231)	Peenewerft, Wolgast	11 May 1983	23 Sep 1993
UNTUNG SUROPATI (ex-*Ribnitz*)	372 (ex-233)	Peenewerft, Wolgast	29 Oct 1983	23 Sep 1993
NUKU (ex-*Waren*)	373 (ex-224)	Peenewerft, Wolgast	23 Nov 1982	15 Dec 1993
LAMBUNG MANGKURAT (ex-*Angermünde*)	374 (ex-214)	Peenewerft, Wolgast	26 July 1985	12 July 1994
CUT NYAK DIEN (ex-*Lübz*)	375 (ex-P 6169, ex-221)	Peenewerft, Wolgast	12 Feb 1982	25 Feb 1994
SULTAN THAHA SYAIFUDDIN (ex-*Bad Doberan*)	376 (ex-222)	Peenewerft, Wolgast	30 June 1982	25 Feb 1995
SUTANTO (ex-*Wismar*)	377 (ex-P 6170, ex-241)	Peenewerft, Wolgast	9 July 1981	10 Mar 1995
SUTEDI SENOPUTRA (ex-*Parchim*)	378 (ex-242)	Peenewerft, Wolgast	9 Apr 1981	19 Sep 1994
WIRATNO (ex-*Perleberg*)	379 (ex-243)	Peenewerft, Wolgast	19 Sep 1981	19 Sep 1994
MEMET SASTRAWIRIA (ex-*Bützow*)	380 (ex-244)	Peenewerft, Wolgast	30 Dec 1981	2 June 1995
TJIPTADI (ex-*Bergen*)	381 (ex-213)	Peenewerft, Wolgast	1 Feb 1985	10 May 1996
HASAN BASRI (ex-*Güstrow*)	382 (ex-223)	Peenewerft, Wolgast	10 Nov 1982	10 May 1996
IMAN BONJOL (ex-*Teterow*)	383 (ex-P 6168, ex-234)	Peenewerft, Wolgast	27 Jan 1984	26 Apr 1994
PATI UNUS (ex-*Ludwiglust*)	384 (ex-232)	Peenewerft, Wolgast	4 July 1983	21 July 1995
TEUKU UMAR (ex-*Grevesmühlen*)	385 (ex-212)	Peenewerft, Wolgast	21 Sep 1984	27 Oct 1996
SILAS PAPARE (ex-*Gadebusch*)	386 (ex-P 6167, ex-211)	Peenewerft, Wolgast	31 Aug 1984	27 Oct 1996

Displacement, tons: 769 standard
Dimensions, feet (metres): 246.7 × 32.2 × 11.5 *(75.2 × 9.8 × 3.5)*
Main machinery: 1 Zvezda M 504A diesel; 4,700 hp *(3.5 MW)* for centreline cp prop
2 Deutz TBD 620 V16 diesels (372, 373, 374, 377, 378, 381); 6,000 hp *(4.5 MW)*
or 2 MTU 16V 4000 M 90 diesels (371, 379, 380, 382, 383 and 386); 7,300 hp *(5.4 MW)*
or 2 CAT 3516B diesels (355, 376, 384, 385); 5,200 hp *(3.9 MW)*; 2 outboard shafts
Speed, knots: 24
Range, n miles: 1,750 at 18 kt
Complement: 64 (9 officers)

Missiles: SAM: SA-N-5/8 launchers fitted in some. May be replaced by twin Simbad launchers.
Guns: 2 USSR 57 mm/75 AK 725 (twin) ❶ automatic; 120 rds/min to 12.7 km *(6.8 n miles)*; weight of shell 2.8 kg.
2—30 mm (twin) ❷; 500 rds/min to 5 km *(2.7 n miles)* anti-aircraft; weight of shell 0.54 kg.
1—20 mm.
Torpedoes: 4—400 mm tubes ❸.
A/S mortars: 2 RBU 6000 12-barrelled trainable launchers ❹; automatic loading; range 6,000 m; warhead 31 kg.
Mines: Mine rails fitted.

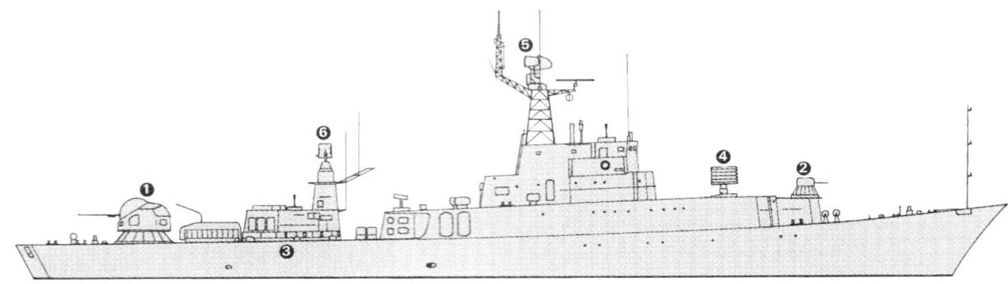

KAPITAN PATIMURA *(Scale 1: 600), Ian Sturton* / 0506007

Countermeasures: Decoys: 2 PK 16 chaff rocket launchers.
ESM: 2 Watch Dog; radar warning.
Radars: Air/surface search: Strut Curve ❺; F-band; range 110 km *(60 n miles)* for 2 m² target.
Navigation: TSR 333; I-band.
Fire control: Muff Cob ❻; G/H-band.
IFF: High Pole B.
Sonars: MG 332T; hull-mounted; active search and attack; high frequency.
Elk Tail; VDS system on starboard side (in some hulls).

Programmes: Ex-GDR ships mostly paid off in 1991. Formally transferred on 4 January 1993 and became Indonesian ships on 25 August 1993. First three arrived Indonesia in November 1993.
Modernisation: All refitted prior to sailing for Indonesia. Range increased and air conditioning added to accommodation. SAM launchers can be carried. A re-engining programme was completed in 2005.

SILAS PAPARE *5/2005, Guy Toremans* / 1153204

PATI UNUS *5/2005, Guy Toremans* / 1153205

4 SIGMA CLASS (CORVETTES) (FS)

Name	*No*	*Builders*	*Laid down*	*Launched*	*Commissioned*
DIPONEGORO	365	Royal Schelde, Vlissengen	24 Mar 2005	16 Sep 2006	2 July 2007
SULTAN HASANUDDIN	366	Royal Schelde, Vlissengen	24 Mar 2005	16 Sep 2006	24 Nov 2007
SULTAN ISKANDAR MUDA	367	Royal Schelde, Vlissengen	8 May 2006	24 Nov 2007	18 Oct 2008
FRANS KAISIEPO	368	Royal Schelde, Vlissengen	8 May 2006	June 2008	7 Mar 2009

Displacement, tons: 1,692 full load
Dimensions, feet (metres): 297.6 × 42.6 × 11.8 *(90.7 × 13.0 × 3.6)*
Main machinery: 2 SEMT Pielstick 20 PA6B diesels; 21,725 hp *(16.2 MW)*; 2 shafts; cp props
Speed, knots: 28
Range, n miles: 4,000 at 18 kt
Complement: 80

Missiles: SAM: 2 quadruple Tetral launchers ❶; MBDA Mistral; IR homing to 4 km *(2.2 n miles)*; warhead 3 kg.
SSM: 4 MBDA mm 40 Exocet Block II ❷; inertial cruise; active radar homing to 70 km *(40 n miles)* at 0.9 Mach; warhead 165 kg; sea-skimmer.
Guns: 1 OTO Melara 3 in *(76 mm)*/62 Super Rapid ❸; 120 rds/min to 16 km *(8.7 n miles)*; weight of shell 6 kg.
2 Giat 20 mm ❹.
Torpedoes: 6—324 mm (2 B 515 triple) tubes ❺. Eurotorp Mu-90; active/passive homing to 25 km *(13.5 n miles)* at 29/50 kt.
Countermeasures: Decoys: 2 Terma SKWS 130 mm launchers.
ESM: Thales DR 3000; intercept.
ECM: Racal Scorpion; jammer.
Combat data systems: Tacticos including Link Y.
Weapons control: LIROD Mk 2 optronic tracker ❻.
Radars: Surface search: Thales MW 08 ❼; G-band.
Navigation: Sperry Marine Bridgemaster E ❽; E/F/I-band.
Sonars: Thales Kingclip; hull-mounted.

Helicopters: Platform only.

Programmes: Contract for the construction of two corvettes, both to be built in the Netherlands, signed on 7 January 2004. The role of the ships is to conduct coastal security operations. Sea trials of *Diponegoro* started in April 2007 and the ship arrived in Indonesia in September 2007. *Hasanuddin* began sea-trials in November 2007. The option to build two further craft was exercised on 18 May 2005. These were also built in the Netherlands and were delivered on 2 December 2008 and early 2009 respectively.
Operational: Exocet is expected to be fitted by 2010.

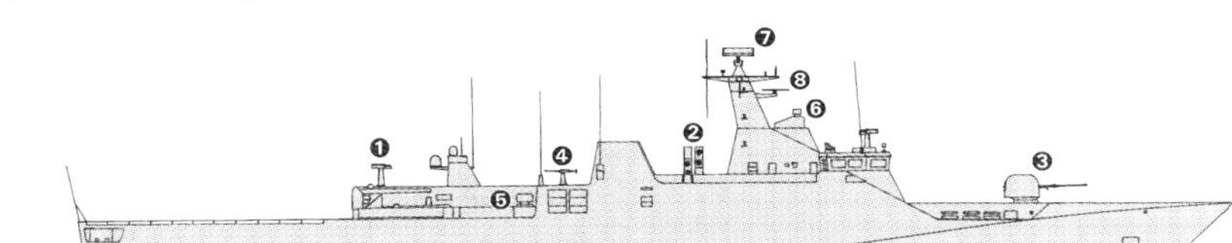

DIPONEGORO *(Scale 1: 900)*, **Ian Sturton** / 1353094

DIPONEGORO *7/2007*, **Michael Nitz** / 1167750

SULTAN ISKANDAR MUDA *10/2008**, **Michael Nitz** / 1353095

SULTAN HASANUDDIN *10/2008**, **Michael Nitz** / 1353096

SHIPBORNE AIRCRAFT

Notes: Six Mi-17 medium lift helicopters for the Indonesian Marine Corps were acquired from Russia in 2008.

Numbers/Type: 6 Dirgantara (MBB) NBO 105CB.
Operational speed: 113 kt *(210 km/h)*.
Service ceiling: 9,845 ft *(3,000 m)*.
Range: 407 n miles *(754 km)*.
Role/Weapon systems: Surveillance/support aircraft. A further three for SAR. Sensors: Thomson-CSF AMASCOS surveillance system; Chlio FLIR. Weapons: Unarmed.

NBO 105C *11/1990* / 0080007

Numbers/Type: 3 Dirgantara (Aerospatiale) NAS-332 Super Puma.
Operational speed: 151 kt *(279 km/h)*.
Service ceiling: 15,090 ft *(4,600 m)*.
Range: 335 n miles *(620 km)*.
Role/Weapon systems: ASW and assault operations with secondary role in utility and SAR; ASVW development possible with Exocet or similar. Sensors: Thomson-CSF Omera radar and Alcatel dipping sonar in some. Weapons: ASW; two Mk 46 torpedoes or depth bombs.

SUPER PUMA (French colours) *6/1994* / 0080008

LAND-BASED MARITIME AIRCRAFT (FRONT LINE)

Numbers/Type: 3 Boeing 737-200 Surveiller.
Operational speed: 462 kt *(856 km/h)*.
Service ceiling: 50,000 ft *(15,240 m)*.
Range: 2,530 n miles *(4,688 km)*.
Role/Weapon systems: Land based for long-range maritime surveillance roles. Air Force manned. Sensors upgraded in 1993–94 to include IFF. Sensors: Motorola APS-135(v) SLAM MR radar, Thomson-CSF Oceanmaster radar. Weapons: Unarmed.

BOEING 737 *9/2003, Boeing* / 0560018

Numbers/Type: 7 PZL Mielec M-28 Bryza.
Operational speed: 181 kt *(335 km/h)*.
Service ceiling: 13,770 ft *(4,200 m)*.
Range: 736 n miles *(1,365 km)*.
Role/Weapon systems: Polish built aircraft based on the USSR Cash light transport. Contract on 18 August 2005 for seven maritime patrol aircraft to be delivered in late 2006. Sensors: PIT ARS-400M radar (SAR/ISAR modes).

Numbers/Type: 25/6 GAF Searchmaster Nomad B/Nomad L.
Operational speed: 168 kt *(311 km/h)*.
Service ceiling: 21,000 ft *(6,400 m)*.
Range: 730 n miles *(1,352 km)*.
Role/Weapon systems: Nomad type built in Australia. Short-range maritime patrol, EEZ protection and anti-smuggler duties. 20 more acquired from Australian Army in August 1997 for use in maritime role. Not all are operational and NC-212 replacements are planned. Sensors: Nose-mounted search radar. Weapons: Unarmed.

Numbers/Type: 8 Northrop F-5E Tiger II.
Operational speed: 940 kt *(1,740 km/h)*.
Service ceiling: 51,800 ft *(15,790 m)*.
Range: 300 n miles *(556 km)*.
Role/Weapon systems: Fleet air defence and strike fighter, formed 'naval co-operation unit'. Planned to be replaced by BAe Hawk 200 in due course. Sensors: AI radar. Weapons: AD; two AIM-9 Sidewinder, two 20 mm cannon. Strike; 3,175 tons of underwing stores.

Numbers/Type: 7 Dirgantara NC 212-200.
Operational speed: 240 kt *(445 km/h)*.
Service ceiling: 26,600 ft *(8,110 m)*.
Range: 669 n miles *(1,240 km)*.
Role/Weapon systems: Surveillance aircraft first delivered in 1996. There are nine further transport aircraft. First aircraft augmented with Thales AMASCOS mission system delivered in mid-2005. Sensors: Thomson-CSF Ocean Master radar. Chlio FLIR. Weapons: ASV; may have Exocet AM 39.

Numbers/Type: 3 Dirgantara CN-235.
Operational speed: 236 kt *(437 km/h)*.
Service ceiling: 25,000 ft *(7,620 m)*.
Range: 1,565 n miles *(2,519 km)*.
Role/Weapon systems: Maritime Patrol aircraft, first of which delivered in 2008. Operated by the Air Force. Sensors: Thales Ocean Master radar, Elettronica ALR 733 RWR, Chlio thermal imager, CAE AN/ASQ-508 MAD.

PATROL FORCES

4 DAGGER CLASS (FAST ATTACK CRAFT—MISSILE) (PTFG)

Name	*No*	*Builders*	*Commissioned*
MANDAU	621	Korea Tacoma, Masan	20 July 1979
RENCONG	622	Korea Tacoma, Masan	20 July 1979
BADIK	623	Korea Tacoma, Masan	Feb 1980
KERIS	624	Korea Tacoma, Masan	Feb 1980

Displacement, tons: 270 full load
Dimensions, feet (metres): 164.7 × 23.9 × 7.5 *(50.2 × 7.3 × 2.3)*
Main machinery: CODOG; 1 GE LM 2500 gas turbine; 23,000 hp *(17.16 MW)* sustained; 2 MTU 12V 331 TC81 diesels; 2,240 hp(m) *(1.65 MW)* sustained; 2 shafts; cp props
Speed, knots: 41 gas; 17 diesel. **Range, n miles**: 2,000 at 17 kt
Complement: 43 (7 officers)
Missiles: SSM: 4 Aerospatiale MM 38 Exocet; inertial cruise; active radar homing to 42 km *(23 n miles)* at 0.9 Mach; warhead 165 kg; sea-skimmer.
Guns: 1 Bofors 57 mm/70 Mk 1; 200 rds/min to 17 km *(9.3 n miles)*; weight of shell 2.4 kg. Launchers for illuminants on each side.
1 Bofors 40 mm/70; 300 rds/min to 12 km *(6.6 n miles)*; weight of shell 0.96 kg.
2 Rheinmetall 20 mm.
Countermeasures: ESM: Thomson-CSF DR 2000S (in 623 and 624); radar intercept.
Weapons control: Selenia NA-18 optronic director.
Radars: Surface search: Racal Decca 1226; I-band.
Fire control: Signaal WM28; I/J-band.

Programmes: PSMM Mk 5 type craft ordered in 1975.
Structure: Shorter in length and smaller displacement than South Korean units. *Mandau* has a different shaped mast with a tripod base.

RENCONG *10/1998* / 0052358

4 TODAK (PB 57) CLASS (NAV V) (LARGE PATROL CRAFT) (PBO)

Name	*No*	*Builders*	*Commissioned*
TODAK	803	PT Pal Surabaya	4 May 2000
HIU	804	PT Pal Surabaya	Sep 2000
LAYANG	805	PT Pal Surabaya	10 July 2002
LEMADANG (ex-*Dorang*)	806	PT Pal Surabaya	Aug 2004

Displacement, tons: 447 full load
Dimensions, feet (metres): 190.6 × 25 × 9.2 *(58.1 × 7.6 × 2.8)*
Main machinery: 2 MTU 16V 956 TB92 diesels; 8,850 hp(m) *(6.5 MW)* sustained; 2 shafts
Speed, knots: 27. **Range, n miles**: 6,100 at 15 kt; 2,200 at 27 kt
Complement: 53

Missiles: SSM: 2 C-802 (YJ-83) (fitted in 804 and 805); mid-course guidance and active radar homing to 150 km *(81 n miles)* at 0.9 Mach; warhead 165 kg.
Guns: 1 Bofors SAK 57 mm/70 Mk 2; 220 rds/min to 14 km *(7.6 n miles)*; weight of shell 2.4 kg.
1 Bofors SAK 40 mm/70; 300 rds/min to 12 km *(6.6 n miles)*; weight of shell 0.96 kg.
2 Rheinmetall 20 mm.
Countermeasures: Decoys: CSEE Dagaie chaff launchers.
ESM: Thomson-CSF DR 3000 S1; intercept.
Combat data systems: TACTICOS type.
Weapons control: Signaal LIOD 73 Ri Mk 2 optronic director.
Radars: Air/surface search: Thales Variant; G-band.
Surface search: Thales Scout; I-band.
Fire control: Signaal LIROD Mk 2; K-band.
Navigation: Kelvin Hughes KH 1007; I-band.

Comment: Ordered in mid-1993 from PT Pal Surabaya. Weapon systems ordered in November 1994. Much improved combat data system is fitted. The after gun was intended to be a second 57 mm but this was changed to a 40 mm. C-802/YJ-83 missiles have been installed in *Layang* and *Hiu*; the other two ships are to be similarly fitted.

LAYANG *6/2007* / 1353097

4 KAKAP (PB 57) CLASS (NAV III AND IV) (LARGE PATROL CRAFT) (PBOH)

Name	No	Builders	Commissioned
KAKAP	811	Lürssen/PT Pal Surabaya	29 June 1988
KERAPU	812	Lürssen/PT Pal Surabaya	5 Apr 1989
TONGKOL	813	PT Pal Surabaya	Dec 1993
BARAKUDA (ex-*Bervang*)	814	PT Pal Surabaya	Aug 1995

Displacement, tons: 423 full load
Dimensions, feet (metres): 190.6 × 25 × 9.2 *(58.1 × 7.6 × 2.8)*
Main machinery: 2 MTU 16V 956 TB92 diesels; 8,850 hp(m) *(6.5 MW)* sustained; 2 shafts
Speed, knots: 28. **Range, n miles:** 6,100 at 15 kt; 2,200 at 27 kt
Complement: 49 plus 8 spare berths
Guns: 1 Bofors 40 mm/70; 240 rds/min to 12.6 km *(6.8 n miles)*; weight of shell 0.96 kg. 2—12.7 mm MGs.
Countermeasures: ESM: Thomson-CSF DR 3000 S1; intercept.
Radars: Surface search: Racal Decca 2459; I-band.
Navigation: KH 1007; I-band.
Helicopters: Platform for 1 NBO-105.

Comment: Ordered in 1982. First pair shipped from West Germany and completed at PT Pal Surabaya. Second pair assembled at Surabaya taking longer than expected to complete. The first three are NAV III SAR and Customs versions and by comparison with NAV I are very lightly armed and have a 13 × 7.1 m helicopter deck in place of the after guns and torpedo tubes. Vosper Thornycroft fin stabilisers are fitted. Can be used for Patrol purposes as well as SAR, and can transport two rifle platoons. There is also a fast seaboat with launching crane at the stern and two water guns for firefighting. The single NAV IV version has some minor variations and is used as Presidential Yacht manned by a special unit.

TONGKOL *2/2001, Sattler/Steele* / 0121380

BARAKUDA (NAV IV) *8/1995, van Ginderen Collection* / 0080012

8 SIBARAU (ATTACK) CLASS (LARGE PATROL CRAFT) (PB)

Name	No	Builders	Commissioned
SIBARAU (ex-*Bandolier*)	847	Walkers, Australia	14 Dec 1968
SILIMAN (ex-*Archer*)	848	Walkers, Australia	15 May 1968
SIGALU (ex-*Barricade*)	857	Walkers, Australia	26 Oct 1968
SILEA (ex-*Acute*)	858	Evans Deakin	24 Apr 1968
SIRIBUA (ex-*Bombard*)	859	Walkers, Australia	5 Nov 1968
SIADA (ex-*Barbette*)	862	Walkers, Australia	16 Aug 1968
SIKUDA (ex-*Attack*)	863	Evans Deakin	17 Nov 1967
SIGUROT (ex-*Assail*)	864	Evans Deakin	12 July 1968

Displacement, tons: 146 full load
Dimensions, feet (metres): 107.5 × 20 × 7.3 *(32.8 × 6.1 × 2.2)*
Main machinery: 2 Paxman 16YJCM diesels; 4,000 hp *(2.98 MW)* sustained; 2 shafts
Speed, knots: 21
Range, n miles: 1,220 at 13 kt
Complement: 19 (3 officers)
Guns: 1 Bofors 40 mm/60. 1—12.5 mm MG.
Countermeasures: ESM: DASA Telegon VIII; intercept.
Radars: Surface search: Decca 916; I-band.

Comment: Transferred from Australia after refit-*Bandolier* 16 November 1973, *Archer* in 1974, *Barricade* March 1982, *Acute* 6 May 1983, *Bombard* September 1983, *Attack* 22 February 1985 (recommissioned 24 May 1985), *Barbette* February 1985, *Assail* February 1986. All carry rocket/flare launchers. Two similar craft with pennant numbers 860 and 861 were built locally in 1982/83 but have not been reported for some years.

SIGALU *4/1999* / 0080013

4 SINGA (PB 57) CLASS (NAV I AND II) (LARGE PATROL CRAFT) (PBO)

Name	No	Builders	Commissioned
SINGA	651	Lürssen/PT Pal Surabaya	Apr 1988
AJAK	653	Lürssen/PT Pal Surabaya	5 Apr 1989
PANDRONG	801	PT Pal Surabaya	1992
SURA	802	PT Pal Surabaya	1993

Displacement, tons: 447 full load (NAV I); 428 full load (NAV II)
Dimensions, feet (metres): 190.6 × 25 × 9.2 *(58.1 × 7.6 × 2.8)*
Main machinery: 2 MTU 16V 956 TB92 diesels; 8,850 hp(m) *(6.5 MW)* sustained; 2 shafts
Speed, knots: 27. **Range, n miles:** 6,100 at 15 kt; 2,200 at 27 kt
Complement: 42 (6 officers)
Guns: 1 Bofors SAK 57 mm/70 Mk 2; 220 rds/min to 14 km *(7.6 n miles)*; weight of shell 2.4 kg.
1 Bofors SAK 40 mm/70; 300 rds/min to 12 km *(6.6 n miles)*; weight of shell 0.96 kg.
2 Rheinmetall 20 mm.
Torpedoes: 2—21 in *(533 mm)* Toro tubes (651 and 653). AEG SUT; anti-submarine; wire-guided; active/passive homing to 12 km *(6.6 n miles)* at 35 kt; 28 km *(15 n miles)* at 23 kt warhead 250 kg.
Countermeasures: Decoys: CSEE Dagaie single trainable launcher; automatic dispenser for IR flares and chaff; H/J-band.
ESM: Thomson-CSF DR 2000 S3 with Dalia analyser; intercept. DASA Telegon VIII D/F.
Weapons control: Thales LIROD 2 (801, 802) optronic director. Signaal WM22 72 Ri WCS (651 and 653).
Radars: Surface search: Racal Decca 2459; I-band; Signaal Scout; H/I-band (801 and 802).
Fire control: Signaal WM22; I/J-band (651 and 653).
Sonars: Signaal PMS 32 (NAV I); active search and attack; medium frequency.

Comment: Class ordered from Lürssen in 1982. First launched and shipped incomplete to PT Pal Surabaya for fitting out in January 1984. Second shipped July 1984. The first two are NAV I ASW versions with torpedo tubes and sonars. The second pair are NAV II AAW versions with an augmented gun armament, an improved surveillance and fire-control radar, but without torpedo tubes and sonars and completed later than expected in 1992–93. Vosper Thornycroft fin stabilisers are fitted.

SINGA (NAV I) *5/1999, G Toremans* / 0080009

AJAK (NAV I) *5/1998, John Mortimer* / 0052359

SURA *5/2000, M Declerck* / 0104597

1 PATROL CRAFT (PB)

Name	*No*	*Builders*	*Launched*	*Commissioned*
CUCUT (ex-*Jupiter*)	866 (ex-A 102)	Singapore SBEC	3 Apr 1990	19 Aug 1991

Displacement, tons: 170 full load
Dimensions, feet (metres): 117.5 × 23.3 × 7.5 *(35.8 × 7.1 × 2.3)*
Main machinery: 2 Deutz MWM TBD234V12 diesels; 1,360 hp(m) *(1 MW)* sustained; 2 shafts; bow thruster
Speed, knots: 14. **Range, n miles:** 200 at 14 kt
Complement: 33 (5 officers)
Guns: 1 Oerlikon 20 mm GAM-BO1. 4—12.7 mm MGs.
Radars: Navigation: Racal Decca; I-band.

Comment: Designed as an underwater search and salvage craft, decommissioned from the Singapore Navy and transferred on 21 March 2002. Deployed as a patrol craft.

CUCUT (Singapore colours) ***6/1994, van Ginderen Collection*** / 0084281

13 KAL-36 PATROL CRAFT (PB)

Name	*No*	*Builders*	*Commissioned*
KOBRA	867	Fasharkan, Mentigi	31 Mar 2003
ANAKONDA	868	Fasharkan, Jakarta	31 Mar 2003
PATOLA	869	PT Pelindo, Tanjung Pinang	Oct 2003
BOA	807	Fasharkan, Mentigi	6 Aug 2004
WELANG	808	Fasharkan, Mentigi	6 Aug 2004
TALIWANGSA	870	Fasharkan, Manokwari	6 Aug 2004
SULUH PARI	809	Fasharkan, Mentigi	20 Jan 2005
KATON	810	Fasharkan, Mentigi	20 Jan 2005
SANCA	815	Fasharkan, Manokwari	20 Jan 2005
WARAKAS	816	Fasharkan, Jakarta	20 Jan 2005
PANANA	817	Fasharkan, Makassar	20 Jan 2005
KALAKAE	818	Fasharkan, Makassar	20 Jan 2005
TEDONG NAGA	819	Fasharkan, Jakarta	20 Jan 2005

Displacement, tons: 90 full load
Dimensions, feet (metres): 118.1 × 23.0 × 4.4 *(36 × 7.0 × 1.35)*
Main machinery: 3 MAN D2842 LE 410 diesels; 3,300 hp *(2.46 MW)*; or 3 Caterpillar 3412E diesels; 3,600 hp *(2.7 MW)*
Speed, knots: 38
Complement: 18
Guns: 1—20 mm. 1—12.7 mm MG.
Radars: Navigation: I-band.

Comment: *Kobra* was the prototype vessel first demonstrated in late 2002. Glass fibre hull. There are some differences in armament and superstructure, some being fitted with a stern ramp for RIB. *Patola* funded by Bali province and others may have been similarly procured. Constructed by variety of shipbuilders and operated by the Indonesian Navy. Further craft are expected.

WARAKAS ***6/2008**** / 1353099

9 KAL-40 CLASS (PATROL CRAFT) (PB)

Name	*No*	*Builders*	*Commissioned*
VIPER	820	Fasharkan, Jakarta	19 Oct 2006
PITON	821	Fasharkan, Mentigi (Riau)	19 Oct 2006
WELING	822	Fasharkan, Mentigi (Riau)	19 Oct 2006
MATACORA	823	Fasharkan, Mentigi (Riau)	14 Mar 2008
TEDUNG SELAR	824	Fasharkan, Jakarta	14 Mar 2008
BOIGA	825	Fasharkan, Manokwari	1 Aug 2007
KRAIT	827	Fasharkan, Mentigi (Riau)	7 Jan 2009
TARIHU	829	Fasharkan, Mentigi (Riau)	7 Jan 2009
ALKURA	830	Fasharkan, Manokwari	2009

Displacement, tons: 100 full load
Dimensions, feet (metres): 131.2 × 23.9 × ? *(40.0 × 7.3 × ?)*
Main machinery: To be announced
Speed, knots: 29
Complement: 25
Guns: 2—25 mm. 2—12.7 mm MGs.

Comment: A successor to the PC-36 class patrol craft and a building programme is in progress. There are variations in design and construction (GRP and aluminium).

KRAIT ***11/2008**** / 1353098

AMPHIBIOUS FORCES

Notes: This section includes some vessels of the Military Sealift Command-Kolinlamil.

3 + 2 MULTIROLE VESSELS (LPD/APCR)

Name	*No*	*Builders*	*Laid down*	*Launched*	*Commissioned*
DR SOEHARSO (ex-*Tanjung Dalpele*)	972	Dae Sun Shipbuilders, Pusan	2002	17 May 2003	Sep 2003
MAKASSAR	590	Dae Sun Shipbuilders, Pusan	2005	7 Dec 2006	29 Apr 2007
SURABAYA	591	Dae Sun Shipbuilders, Pusan	7 Dec 2006	23 Mar 2007	1 Aug 2007
–	–	PT Pal, Surabaya	19 Oct 2006	28 Aug 2008	2009
–	–	PT Pal, Surabaya	19 Oct 2006	2009	2010

Displacement, tons: 7,300 standard; 11,400 full load
Dimensions, feet (metres): 400.00 × 72.2 × 16.1 *(122.0 × 22.0 × 4.9)*
Main machinery: CODAD; 2 B&W 8L28/32A diesels; 5,250 hp *(3.9 MW)*; 2 shafts
Speed, knots: 15
Range, n miles: 8,600 at 12 kt
Complement: 126
Military lift: 13 tanks; 507 troops; 2 LCVPs
Guns: 1—57 mm. 2—40 mm (1 twin).
Radars: Navigation: 2-I-band.
Helicopters: 2 Super Puma.

Programmes: Officially designated a Multipurpose Hospital Ship. Following delivery of the first vessel in mid-2003, a contract for a further four vessels was finalised on 21 December 2004. The first two of these are being built in South Korea and the second two in Indonesia. First steel was cut for the first Indonesian vessel on 19 October 2006.
Structure: Has a docking well, capable of accommodating two LCU-23M, stern and side ramps and hospital facilities.

DR SOEHARSO ***6/2004, Daesun*** / 1047875

MAKASSAR ***3/2007*** / 1166451

2 TROOP TRANSPORT SHIPS (AP)

Name	*No*	*Builders*	*Commissioned*
TANJUNG NUSANIVE (ex-*Kambuna*)	973	Meyer Werft, Papenburg	1984
TANJUNG FATAGAR (ex-*Rinjani*)	974	Meyer Werft, Papenburg	1984

Measurement, tons: 13,954 grt
Dimensions, feet (metres): 472.4 × 76.8 × 19.4 *(144.0 × 23.4 × 5.9)*
Main machinery: 2 MaK diesels; 16,760 hp *(12.5 MW)*; 2 shafts; bow thruster
Speed, knots: 20
Range, n miles: 5,500 at 12 kt
Complement: 119
Guns: To be announced.
Radars: Navigation: I-band.

Comment: Converted passenger ships originally delivered to the Directorate of Sea Communications, Jakarta, in 1984. Capable of transporting 1,600 passengers and used to serve the Indonesian islands in their civilian configuration. Acquired by the Indonesian Navy in early 2005, converted into troop transports and commissioned on 1 September 2005.

5 TROOP TRANSPORT SHIPS (AP)

Name	No	Builders	Commissioned
KARANG PILANG (ex-*Ambulu*)	981	Lürssen Werft, Lemwerder	1998
KARANG TEKOK (ex-*Mahakam*)	982	Lürssen Werft, Lemwerder	1998
KARANG BANTENG (ex-*Serayu*)	983	Lürssen Werft, Lemwerder	1998
KARANG GALANG (ex-*Cisadane*)	984	Lürssen Werft, Lemwerder	1998
KARANG UNARANG (ex-*Barito*)	985	Lürssen Werft, Lemwerder	1998

Displacement, tons: 493 standard
Dimensions, feet (metres): 229.0 × 34.1 × 6.6 *(69.8 × 10.4 × 2.0)*
Main machinery: 4 MTU 16V 595 TE 70L diesels; 20,400 hp *(15.2 MW)*; 2 Kamewa waterjets
Speed, knots: 38. **Range, n miles:** 550 at 35 kt
Guns: 2—20 mm.
Radars: Navigation: I-band.

Comment: Converted passenger ferries of aluminium construction transferred from PT ASDP ferry company. Capable of transporting 600 troops and their equipment. Used to serve the Indonesian islands in their civilian configuration and acquired by the Indonesian Navy between September 2005 and April 2006.

KARANG GALANG *12/2006* / 1164967

7 LST 1-511 AND 512-1152 CLASSES (LST)

Name	No	Builders	Commissioned
TELUK LANGSA (ex-*LST 1128*)	501	Chicago Bridge	9 Mar 1945
TELUK BAYUR (ex-*LST 616*)	502	Chicago Bridge	29 May 1944
TELUK KAU (ex-*LST 652*)	504	Chicago Bridge	1 Jan 1945
TELUK TOMINI (ex-*Inagua Crest*, ex-*Brunei*, ex-*Bledsoe County*, *LST 356*)	508	Charleston, NY	22 Dec 1942
TELUK RATAI (ex-*Teluk Sindoro*, ex-*Inagua Shipper*, ex-*APB 44*, ex-*LST 678*)	509	American Bridge, PA	30 June 1944
TELUK SALEH (ex-*Clark County*, *LST 601*)	510	Chicago Bridge	25 Mar 1944
TELUK BONE (ex-*Iredell County*, *LST 839*)	511	American Bridge, PA	6 Dec 1944

Displacement, tons: 1,653 standard; 4,080 full load
Dimensions, feet (metres): 328 × 50 × 14 *(100 × 15.2 × 4.3)*
Main machinery: 2 GM 12-567A diesels; 1,800 hp *(1.34 MW)*; 2 shafts
Speed, knots: 11.6. **Range, n miles:** 11,000 at 10 kt
Complement: 119 (accommodation for 266)
Military lift: 2,100 tons
Guns: 7—40 mm. 2—20 mm *(Teluk Langsa)*. 8—37 mm (remainder).
Radars: Surface search: SPS-21 *(Teluk Tomini, Teluk Sindoro)*. SPS-53 *(Teluk Saleh, Teluk Bone)*. SO-1 *(Teluk Kau)*. SO-6 *(Teluk Langsa)*.

Comment: *Teluk Saleh* and *Teluk Bone* transferred from USA in June 1961 (and purchased 22 February 1979). *Teluk Kau* and *Teluk Langsa* in July 1970. These ships are used as transports and stores carriers. All are probably in reserve. *Bajur* and *Tomini* serve with the Military Sealift Command.

TELUK RATAI *1/2005, David Boey* / 1154407

1 LST

Name	No	Builders	Commissioned
TELUK AMBOINA	503	Sasebo, Japan	June 1961

Displacement, tons: 2,378 standard; 4,200 full load
Dimensions, feet (metres): 327 × 50 × 15 *(99.7 × 15.3 × 4.6)*
Main machinery: 2 MAN V6V 22/30 diesels; 3,425 hp(m) *(2.52 MW)*; 2 shafts
Speed, knots: 13.1. **Range, n miles:** 4,000 at 13.1 kt
Complement: 88
Military lift: 212 troops; 2,100 tons; 4 LCVP on davits
Guns: 6—37 mm; anti-aircraft.

Comment: Launched on 17 March 1961 and transferred from Japan in June 1961. A faster copy of US LST 511 class with 30 ton crane forward of bridge. Serves with the Military Sealift Command.

TELUK AMBOINA *8/1995, van Ginderen Collection* / 0080018

6 TACOMA TYPE (LSTH)

Name	No	Builders	Commissioned
TELUK SEMANGKA	512	Korea-Tacoma, Masan	20 Jan 1981
TELUK PENYU	513	Korea-Tacoma, Masan	20 Jan 1981
TELUK MANDAR	514	Korea-Tacoma, Masan	July 1981
TELUK SAMPIT	515	Korea-Tacoma, Masan	June 1981
TELUK BANTEN	516	Korea-Tacoma, Masan	May 1982
TELUK ENDE	517	Korea-Tacoma, Masan	2 Sep 1982

Displacement, tons: 3,750 full load
Dimensions, feet (metres): 328 × 47.2 × 13.8 *(100 × 14.4 × 4.2)*
Main machinery: 2 diesels; 12,800 hp(m) *(9.41 MW)* sustained; 2 shafts
Speed, knots: 15
Range, n miles: 7,500 at 13 kt
Complement: 90 (13 officers)
Military lift: 1,800 tons (including 17 MBTs); 2 LCVPs; 200 troops
Guns: 2 or 3 Bofors 40 mm/70. 2 Rheinmetall 20 mm.
Radars: Surface search: Raytheon; E/F-band *(Teluk Banten and Teluk Ende)*.
Navigation: Racal Decca; I-band.
Helicopters: 1 Westland Wasp; 3 NAS-332 Super Pumas can be carried in last pair.

Comment: First four ordered in June 1979, last pair June 1981. No hangar in *Teluk Semangka* and *Teluk Mandar*. Two hangars in *Teluk Ende*. The last pair differ in silhouette having drowned exhausts in place of funnels and having their LCVPs carried forward of the bridge. They also have only two 40 mm guns and an additional radar fitted above the bridge. Battalion of marines can be embarked if no tanks are carried. *Teluk Ende* and *Teluk Banten* act as Command ships, the former also able to serve as a hospital ship.

TELUK BANTEN *1/2005, David Boey* / 1154406

TELUK SAMPIT *1/2005, David Boey* / 1154405

TELUK ENDE *5/2001* / 0126190

54 LANDING CRAFT (LCU)

DORE 580 **KUPANG** 582 **DILI** 583 **NUSA UTARA** 584 **+50**

Displacement, tons: 400 full load
Dimensions, feet (metres): 140.7 × 29.9 × 4.6 *(42.9 × 9.1 × 1.4)*
Main machinery: 4 diesels; 2 shafts
Speed, knots: 12
Range, n miles: 700 at 11 kt
Complement: 17
Military lift: 200 tons

Comment: Details given are for LCUs 582-584 built at Naval Training Centre, Surabaya in 1978–80. Military Sealift Command. LCU 580 is a smaller ship at 275 tons and built in 1968. About 20 LCM 6 type and 30 LCVPs are also in service.

LCVP *8/1995, van Ginderen Collection* / 0080020

12 FROSCH I CLASS (TYPE 108) (LSM)

Name	*No*	*Commissioned*	*Recommissioned*
TELUK GILIMANUK (ex-*Hoyerswerda*)	531 (ex-611)	12 Nov 1976	12 July 1994
TELUK CELUKAN BAWANG (ex-*Hagenow*)	532 (ex-632)	1 Dec 1976	25 Feb 1994
TELUK CENDRAWASIH (ex-*Frankfurt/Oder*)	533 (ex-613)	2 Feb 1977	9 Dec 1994
TELUK BERAU (ex-*Eberswalde-Finow*)	534 (ex-634)	28 May 1977	10 Mar 1995
TELUK PELENG (ex-*Lübben*)	535 (ex-631)	15 Mar 1978	23 Sep 1993
TELUK SIBOLGA (ex-*Schwerin*)	536 (ex-612)	19 Oct 1977	15 Dec 1993
TELUK MANADO (ex-*Neubrandenburg*)	537 (ex-633)	28 Dec 1977	2 June 1995
TELUK HADING (ex-*Cottbus*)	538 (ex-614)	26 May 1978	12 July 1994
TELUK PARIGI (ex-*Anklam*)	539 (ex-635)	14 July 1978	21 July 1995
TELUK LAMPUNG (ex-*Schwedt*)	540 (ex-636)	7 Sep 1979	26 Apr 1994
TELUK JAKARTA (ex-*Eisenhüttenstadt*)	541 (ex-615)	4 Jan 1979	19 Sep 1994
TELUK SANGKURING (ex-*Grimmen*)	542 (ex-616)	4 Jan 1979	9 Dec 1994

Displacement, tons: 1,950 full load
Dimensions, feet (metres): 321.5 × 36.4 × 9.2 *(98 × 11.1 × 2.8)*
Main machinery: 2 diesels; 5,000 hp(m) *(3.68 MW)*; 2 shafts
Speed, knots: 18
Complement: 46
Military lift: 600 tons
Guns: 1 — 40 mm/60. 2 — 37 mm/63 (1 twin). 4 — 25 mm (2 twin).
Mines: Can lay 40 mines through stern doors.
Countermeasures: Decoys: 2 PK 16 chaff launchers.
Radars: Air/surface search: Strut Curve; F-band.
Navigation: TSR 333; I-band.

Comment: All built by Peenewerft, Wolgast. Former GDR ships transferred from Germany on 25 August 1993. Demilitarised with all guns removed, but 37 mm guns have replaced the original 57 mm and 30 mm twin guns. All refitted in Germany prior to sailing. First two arrived Indonesia in late 1993, remainder throughout 1994 and 1995. *Teluk Lampung* damaged by heavy seas during transit in June 1994 but was repaired.

TELUK SANGKURING *1/2005, **David Boey*** / 1154404

TELUK PELENG *1/2005, **David Boey*** / 1164966

1 TRANSPORT SHIP (AP)

Name	*No*	*Builders*	*Commissioned*
TANJUNG KAMBANI (ex-*Dong Yang 6*)	971	Sanuki Shipbuilding, Japan	1982

Displacement, tons: 7,138
Dimensions, feet (metres): 375.6 × 64.9 × 19.7 *(114.5 × 19.8 × 6.0)*
Main machinery: 2 Makita diesels; 8,200 hp *(6.1 MW)*; 2 shafts; cp props
Speed, knots: 18
Complement: To be announced
Military lift: To be announced
Radars: Navigation: 2 I-band.
Helicopters: Platform for 2 medium.

Comment: Former Ro-Ro ferry converted for military use by Daesun Shipbuilders, Pusan, and delivered to the Indonesian Navy on 9 November 2000. Reported to be capable of carrying one battalion which may be disembarked by four LCVPs and/or helicopter.

TANJUNG KAMBANI *6/2007* / 1353100

MINE WARFARE FORCES

9 KONDOR II (TYPE 89) CLASS (MINESWEEPERS — COASTAL) (MSC)

Name	*No*	*Builders*	*Commissioned*
PULAU ROTE (ex-*Wolgast*)	721 (ex-V 811)	Peenewerft, Wolgast	1 June 1971
PULAU RAAS (ex-*Hettstedt*)	722 (ex-353)	Peenewerft, Wolgast	22 Dec 1971
PULAU ROMANG (ex-*Pritzwalk*)	723 (ex-325)	Peenewerft, Wolgast	26 June 1972
PULAU RIMAU (ex-*Bitterfeld*)	724 (ex-332, ex-M 2672)	Peenewerft, Wolgast	7 Aug 1972
KELABANG (ex-*Pulau Rondo*, ex-*Zerbst*)	826 (ex-725, ex-335)	Peenewerft, Wolgast	30 Sep 1972
PULAU RUSA (ex-*Oranienburg*)	726 (ex-341)	Peenewerft, Wolgast	1 Nov 1972
PULAU RANGSANG (ex-*Jüterbog*)	727 (ex-342)	Peenewerft, Wolgast	7 Apr 1973
KALA HITAM (ex-*Pulau Raibu*, ex-*Sömmerda*)	828 (ex-728, ex-311)	Peenewerft, Wolgast	9 Aug 1973
PULAU REMPANG (ex-*Grimma*)	729 (ex-336)	Peenewerft, Wolgast	10 Nov 1973

Displacement, tons: 310 full load
Dimensions, feet (metres): 186 × 24.6 × 7.9 *(56.7 × 7.5 × 2.4)*
Main machinery: 2 Russki Kolomna Type 40-DM diesels; 4,408 hp(m) *(3.24 MW)* sustained; 2 shafts; cp props
Speed, knots: 17
Range, n miles: 2,000 at 14 kt
Complement: 31 (6 officers)
Guns: 6 — 25 mm/80 (3 twin). 1 — 12.7 mm MG.
Mines: 2 rails.
Radars: Navigation: TSR 333; I-band.
Sonars: Bendix AQS 17 VDS; minehunting; active; high frequency (in some).

Comment: Former GDR minesweepers transferred from Germany in Russian dockship *Trans-Shelf* arriving 22 October 1993. Patrol duties take precedence over MCM and ex-*Pulau Rondo* and ex-*Pulau Raibu* formally converted in 2008 when new names and pennant numbers were allocated. There are some variations in armament. *Pulau Rempang, Pulau Rote* and *Pulau Romang* are also used for survey duties. ADI Dyads can be embarked for MCM.

PULAU RIMAU *4/2004, **Chris Sattler*** / 1044128

PULAU RONDO (old number) *4/2004, **John Mortimer*** / 1153200

PALAU RUSA *8/1995, **van Ginderen Collection*** / 0080021

2 PULAU RENGAT (TRIPARTITE) CLASS (MHSC)

Name	*No*	*Builders*	*Launched*	*Commissioned*
PULAU RENGAT	711	van der Giessen-de Noord	23 July 1987	26 Mar 1988
PULAU RUPAT	712	van der Giessen-de Noord	27 Aug 1987	26 Mar 1988

Displacement, tons: 502 standard; 568 full load
Dimensions, feet (metres): 168.9 × 29.2 × 8.2 *(51.5 × 8.9 × 2.5)*
Main machinery: 2 MTU 12V 396 TC82 diesels; 2,610 hp(m) *(1.92 MW)* sustained; 1 shaft; LIPS cp prop; auxiliary propulsion; 3 Turbomeca gas-turbine generators; 2 motors; 2,400 hp(m) *(1.76 MW)*; 2 retractable Schottel propulsors; 2 bow thrusters; 150 hp(m) *(110 kW)*
Speed, knots: 15; 7 auxiliary propulsion
Range, n miles: 3,000 at 12 kt
Complement: 46 plus 4 spare berths

Guns: 2 Rheinmetall 20 mm. Matra Simbad SAM launcher may be added for patrol duties or a third 20 mm gun.
Countermeasures: MCM: OD3 Oropesa mechanical sweep gear; Fiskars F-82 magnetic and SA Marine AS 203 acoustic sweeps; Ibis V minehunting system; 2 PAP 104 Mk 4 mine disposal systems.
Combat data systems: Signaal SEWACO-RI action data automation.
Radars: Navigation: Racal Decca AC 1229C; I-band.
Sonars: Thomson Sintra TSM 2022; active minehunting; high frequency.

Programmes: First ordered on 29 March 1985, laid down 22 July 1985, second ordered 30 August 1985 and laid down 15 December 1985. More were to have been built in Indonesia up to a total of 12 but this programme was cancelled due to lack of funds.
Structure: There are differences in design between these ships and the European Tripartites, apart from their propulsion. Deckhouses and general layout are different as they are required to act as minehunters, minesweepers and patrol ships. Hull construction is GRP shock-proven.
Operational: Endurance, 15 days. Automatic operations, navigation and recording systems, Thomson-CSF Naviplot TSM 2060 tactical display. A 5 ton container can be shipped, stored for varying tasks-research; patrol; extended diving; drone control.

PULAU RUPAT *3/2004, Chris Sattler* / 1044129

SURVEY AND RESEARCH SHIPS

1 RESEARCH SHIP (AGOR)

Name	*No*	*Builders*	*Commissioned*
BARUNA JAYA VIII	KAL-IV-06	Mjellem & Karlsen AS, Bergen	1998

Displacement, tons: 1,476 full load
Dimensions, feet (metres): 174.5 × 41.0 × 14.8 *(53.2 × 12.5 × 4.3)*
Main machinery: 1 Caterpillar 3516BTA diesel; 2,026 bhp *(1.5 MW)*; 1 shaft; cp prop; 1 Schottel SPJ-82TL bow thruster
Speed, knots: 13
Range, n miles: 7,500 at 12 kt
Complement: 42 (11 officers) plus 23 scientific staff
Radars: Navigation: Furuno FAR-2835S; E/F-band.
Furuno FR-2110; I-band.

Comment: Multipurpose survey vessel equipped to conduct fisheries research, geophysics and seabed mapping. Delivered to Indonesia on 28 September 1998. Sensors include Simrad SD570 sonar, EM 1000 multibeam echo sounder and EA 500 single beam echo sounder.

BARUNA JAYA VIII *9/1998, Maritime Photographic* / 0044067

4 RESEARCH SHIPS (AGS/AGOR)

Name	*No*	*Builders*	*Commissioned*
BARUNA JAYA I	KAL-IV-02	CMN, Cherbourg	10 Aug 1989
BARUNA JAYA II	KAL-IV-03	CMN, Cherbourg	25 Sep 1989
BARUNA JAYA III	KAL-IV-04	CMN, Cherbourg	3 Jan 1990
BARUNA JAYA IV	KAL-IV-05	CMN, Cherbourg	2 Nov 1995

Displacement, tons: 1,180 (1,425 IV) full load
Dimensions, feet (metres): 198.2 × 39.7 × 13.8 *(60.4 × 12.1 × 4.2)*
Main machinery: 2 Niigata/SEMT-Pielstick 5 PA5 L 255 diesels; 2,990 hp(m) *(2.2 MW)* sustained; 1 shaft; cp prop; bow thruster
Speed, knots: 14. **Range, n miles:** 7,500 at 12 kt
Complement: 37 (8 officers) plus 26 scientists

Comment: First three ordered from La Manche, Dieppe in February 1985 by the office of Technology, Ministry of Industry and Research. Badly delayed by the closing down of the original shipbuilders (ACM, Dieppe) and construction taken over by CMN at Cherbourg. Fourth of class ordered in 1993 to a slightly enlarged design and with a more enclosed superstructure. *Baruna Jaya 1* is employed on hydrography, the second on oceanography and the third combines both tasks. *Baruna Jaya IV* is operated by the Agency responsible for developing new technology. All are part of the Naval Auxiliary Service.

BARUNA JAYA II *4/1998, John Mortimer* / 0052362

BARUNA JAYA IV *11/1995, van Ginderen Collection* / 0080023

1 HECLA CLASS (SURVEY SHIP) (AGSH)

Name	*No*	*Builders*	*Commissioned*
DEWA KEMBAR (ex-*Hydra*)	932	Yarrow and Co, Blythswood	5 May 1966

Displacement, tons: 1,915 light; 2,733 full load
Dimensions, feet (metres): 260.1 × 49.1 × 15.4 *(79.3 × 15 × 4.7)*
Main machinery: Diesel-electric; 3 Paxman 12YJCZ diesels; 3,780 hp *(2.82 MW)*; 3 generators; 1 motor; 2,000 hp(m) *(1.49 MW)*; 1 shaft; bow thruster
Speed, knots: 14
Range, n miles: 12,000 at 11 kt
Complement: 123 (14 officers)
Guns: 2 — 12.7 mm MGs.
Radars: Navigation: Kelvin Hughes Type 1006; I-band.
Helicopters: 1 Westland Wasp.

Comment: Transferred from UK 18 April 1986 for refit. Commissioned in Indonesian Navy 10 September 1986. SATCOM fitted. Two survey launches on davits.

DEWA KEMBAR *11/1997, van Ginderen Collection* / 0012542

1 RESEARCH SHIP (AGORH)

Name	*No*	*Builders*	*Commissioned*
BURUJULASAD	931	Schlichting, Lübeck-Travemünde	1967

Displacement, tons: 2,165 full load
Dimensions, feet (metres): 269.5 × 37.4 × 11.5 *(82.2 × 11.4 × 3.5)*
Main machinery: 4 MAN V6V 22/30 diesels; 6,850 hp(m) *(5.03 MW)*; 2 shafts
Speed, knots: 19.1. **Range, n miles**: 14,500 at 15 kt
Complement: 108 (15 officers) plus 28 scientists
Guns: 4—12.7 mm (2 twin) MGs.
Radars: Surface search: Decca TM 262; I-band.
Helicopters: 1 Bell 47J.

Comment: *Burujulasad* was launched in August 1965; her equipment includes laboratories for oceanic and meteorological research and a cartographic room. Carries one LCVP and three surveying motor boats. A 37 mm gun was added in 1992 but by 1998 had been removed again.

BURUJULASAD *4/1998, John Mortimer* / 0052361

1 RESEARCH SHIP (AGOR)

Name	*No*	*Builders*	*Commissioned*
JALANIDHI	933	Sasebo Heavy Industries	12 Jan 1963

Displacement, tons: 985 full load
Dimensions, feet (metres): 176.8 × 31.2 × 14.1 *(53.9 × 9.5 × 4.3)*
Main machinery: 1 MAN G6V 30/42 diesel; 1,000 hp(m) *(735 kW)*; 1 shaft
Speed, knots: 11.5. **Range, n miles**: 7,200 at 10 kt
Complement: 87 (13 officers) plus 26 scientists
Radars: Navigation: Nikkon Denko; I-band. Furuno; I-band.

Comment: Launched in 1962. Oceanographic research ship with hydromet facilities and weather balloons. 3 ton boom aft. Operated by the Navy for the Hydrographic Office.

JALANIDHI *8/1995, van Ginderen Collection* / 0080024

TRAINING SHIPS

1 SAIL TRAINING SHIP (AXS)

Name	*No*	*Builders*	*Commissioned*
DEWARUCI	–	HC Stülcken & Sohn, Hamburg	9 July 1953

Displacement, tons: 810 standard; 1,500 full load
Dimensions, feet (metres): 136.2 pp; 191.2 oa × 31.2 × 13.9 *(41.5; 58.3 × 9.5 × 4.2)*
Main machinery: 1 MAN diesel; 600 hp(m) *(441 kW)*; 1 shaft
Speed, knots: 10.5
Complement: 110 (includes 78 midshipmen)

Comment: Barquentine of steel construction. Sail area, 1,305 sq yards *(1,091 sq m)*. Launched on 24 January 1953.

DEWARUCI *6/2005, Martin Mokrus* / 1153201

1 SAIL TRAINING SHIP (AXS)

Name	*Builders*	*Launched*	*Commissioned*
ARUNG SAMUDERA (ex-*Adventurer*)	Hendrik Oosterbroek, Tauranga	July 1991	9 Jan 1996

Measurement, tons: 96 grt
Dimensions, feet (metres): 128 oa; 103.7 wl × 21.3 × 8.5 *(39; 31.6 × 6.5 × 2.6)*
Main machinery: 2 Ford 2725E diesels; 292 hp *(218 kW)*; 2 shafts
Speed, knots: 10 (diesels)
Complement: 20 (includes trainees)

Comment: Three masted schooner acquired from New Zealand. Sail area 433.8 m^2.

ARUNG SAMUDERA *5/2000, A Campanera i Rovira* / 0104601

1 KI HAJAR DEWANTARA CLASS (FFGH/FFT)

Name	*No*	*Builders*	*Laid down*	*Launched*	*Commissioned*
KI HAJAR DEWANTARA	364	Split SY, Yugoslavia	11 May 1979	11 Oct 1980	31 Oct 1981

Displacement, tons: 2,050 full load
Dimensions, feet (metres): 317.3 × 36.7 × 15.7 *(96.7 × 11.2 × 4.8)*
Main machinery: CODOG; 1 RR Olympus TM3B gas turbine; 24,525 hp *(18.3 MW)* sustained; 2 MTU 16V 956TB92 diesels; 11,070 hp(m) *(8.14 MW)* sustained; 2 shafts; cp props
Speed, knots: 26 gas; 20 diesels
Range, n miles: 4,000 at 18 kt; 1,150 at 25 kt
Complement: 76 (11 officers) plus 14 instructors and 100 cadets

Missiles: SSM: 4 Aerospatiale MM 38 Exocet ❶; inertial cruise; active radar homing to 42 km *(23 n miles)* at 0.9 Mach; warhead 165 kg; sea-skimmer.
Guns: 1 Bofors 57 mm/70 ❷; 200 rds/min to 17 km *(9.3 n miles)*; weight of shell 2.4 kg. 2 Rheinmetall 20 mm ❸.
Torpedoes: 2—21 in *(533 mm)* tubes ❹. AEG SUT; dual purpose; wire-guided; active/passive homing to 28 km *(15 n miles)* at 23 kt; 12 km *(6.5 n miles)* at 35 kt; warhead 250 kg.
Depth charges: 1 projector/mortar.
Countermeasures: Decoys: 2—128 mm twin-tubed flare launchers.
ESM: MEL Susie; radar intercept.
Combat data systems: Signaal SEWACO-RI action data automation.
Radars: Surface search: Racal Decca 1229 ❺; I-band.
Fire control: Signaal WM28 ❻; I/J-band.
Sonars: Signaal PHS-32; hull-mounted; active search and attack; medium frequency.

Helicopters: Platform ❼; for 1 NBO-105 helicopter.

Programmes: First ordered 14 March 1978 from Split SY, Yugoslavia where the hull was built and engines fitted. Armament and electronics fitted in the Netherlands and Indonesia.
Structure: For the training role there is a classroom and additional wheelhouse, navigation and radio rooms. Torpedo tubes are fixed in the stern transom. Two LCVP-type ship's boats are carried.
Operational: Used for training and troop transport.

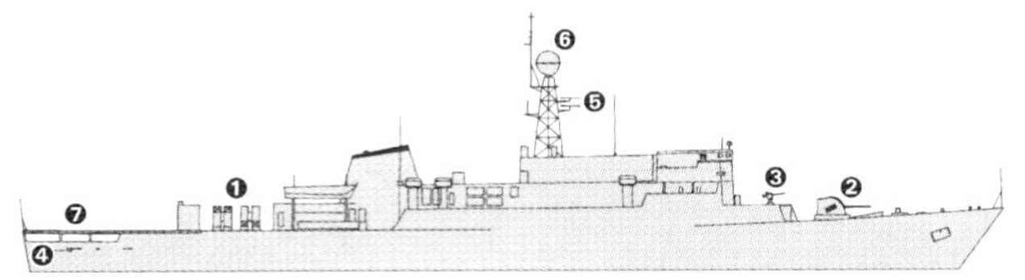

KI HAJAR DEWANTARA *(Scale 1 : 1,200), Ian Sturton* / 0506149

KI HAJAR DEWANTARA *12/1992* / 0080005

AUXILIARIES

Notes: (1) The Don class depot ship *Ratulangi* 400 is in use as a floating workshop at Surabaya naval base, but is not seaworthy.
(2) There is also a small oiler *Sungai Gerong* 906.

1 COMMAND SHIP (AGFH)

Name	*No*	*Builders*	*Launched*	*Commissioned*
MULTATULI	561	Ishikawajima-Harima	15 May 1961	Aug 1961

Displacement, tons: 3,220 standard; 6,741 full load
Dimensions, feet (metres): 365.3 × 52.5 × 23 *(111.4 × 16 × 7)*
Main machinery: 1 Burmeister & Wain diesel; 5,500 hp(m) *(4.04 MW)*; 1 shaft
Speed, knots: 18.5. **Range, n miles:** 6,000 at 16 kt
Complement: 135
Guns: 6 USSR 37 mm/63 (2 twin, 2 single); 160 rds/min to 9 km *(5 n miles)*; weight of shell 0.7 kg.
8—12.7 mm MGs.
Radars: Surface search: Ball End; E/F-band.
Navigation: I-band.
Helicopters: 1 Bell 47J.

Comment: Built as a submarine tender. Original after 76 mm mounting replaced by helicopter deck with a hangar added in 1998. Living and working spaces air conditioned. Capacity for replenishment at sea (fuel oil, fresh water, provisions, ammunition, naval stores and personnel). Medical and hospital facilities. Used as fleet flagship (Eastern Force) and is fitted with ICS-3 communications.

MULTATULI *8/1995, van Ginderen Collection* / 0080025

1 REPLENISHMENT TANKER (AOTL)

Name	*No*	*Builders*	*Commissioned*
SORONG	911	Trogir SY, Yugoslavia	Apr 1965

Displacement, tons: 8,400 full load
Dimensions, feet (metres): 367.4 × 50.5 × 21.6 *(112 × 15.4 × 6.6)*
Main machinery: 1 diesel; 1 shaft
Speed, knots: 15
Complement: 110
Cargo capacity: 4,200 tons fuel; 300 tons water
Guns: 4—12.7 mm (2 twin) MGs.
Radars: Navigation: Don; I-band.

Comment: Has limited underway replenishment facilities on both sides and stern refuelling.

SORONG *8/1995, van Ginderen Collection* / 0080026

1 ROVER CLASS (REPLENISHMENT TANKER) (AORLH)

Name	*No*	*Builders*	*Commissioned*
ARUN (ex-*Green Rover*)	903	Swan Hunter, Tyneside	15 Aug 1969

Displacement, tons: 4,700 light; 11,522 full load
Dimensions, feet (metres): 461 × 63 × 24 *(140.6 × 19.2 × 7.3)*
Main machinery: 2 SEMT-Pielstick 16 PA4 diesels; 15,360 hp(m) *(11.46 MW)*; 1 shaft; Kamewa cp prop; bow thruster
Speed, knots: 19. **Range, n miles:** 15,000 at 15 kt
Complement: 49 (16 officers)
Cargo capacity: 6,600 tons fuel
Guns: 2 Bofors 40 mm/60. 2 Oerlikon 20 mm.
Radars: Navigation: Kelvin Hughes Type 1006; I-band.
Helicopters: Platform for Super Puma.

Comment: Transferred from UK in September 1992 after a refit. Small fleet tanker designed to replenish ships at sea with fuel, fresh water, limited dry cargo and refrigerated stores under all conditions while under way. No hangar but helicopter landing platform is served by a stores lift, to enable stores to be transferred at sea by 'vertical lift'. Capable of HIFR. Used as the Flagship for the Training Commander.

ARUN *10/2004, Chris Gee* / 1047874

2 KHOBI CLASS (COASTAL TANKERS) (AOTL)

BALIKPAPAN 901 **SAMBU** 902

Displacement, tons: 1,525 full load
Dimensions, feet (metres): 206.6 × 33 × 14.8 *(63 × 10.1 × 4.5)*
Main machinery: 2 diesels; 1,600 hp(m) *(1.18 MW)*; 2 shafts
Speed, knots: 13. **Range, n miles:** 2,500 at 12 kt
Complement: 37 (4 officers)
Cargo capacity: 550 tons dieso
Guns: 4—14.5 mm (2 twin) MGs. 2—12.7 mm MGs.
Radars: Navigation: Neptun; I-band.

Comment: *Balikpapan* and *Sambu* are Japanese copies of the Khobi class built in the 1960s.

SAMBU *8/1995, van Ginderen Collection* / 0080028

2 FROSCH II CLASS (TYPE 109) (SUPPORT SHIPS) (AKL/ARL)

Name	*No*	*Builders*	*Commissioned*
TELUK CIREBON (ex-*Nordperd*)	543 (ex-E 171)	Peenewerft, Wolgast	3 Oct 1979
TELUK SABANG (ex-*Südperd*)	544 (ex-E 172)	Peenewerft, Wolgast	26 Feb 1980

Displacement, tons: 1,700 full load
Dimensions, feet (metres): 297.6 × 36.4 × 9.2 *(90.7 × 11.1 × 2.8)*
Main machinery: 2 diesels; 4,408 hp(m) *(3.24 MW)* sustained; 2 shafts
Speed, knots: 18
Cargo capacity: 650 tons
Guns: 4—37 mm/63 (2 twin). 4—25 mm (2 twin).
Countermeasures: Decoys: 2 PK 16 chaff launchers.
Radars: Air/surface search: Strut Curve; F-band.
Navigation: I-band.

Comment: Ex-GDR ships disarmed and transferred from Germany 25 August 1993. 5 ton crane amidships. In GDR service these ships had two twin 57 mm and two twin 25 mm guns plus Muff Cob fire-control radar. Both refitted at Rostock and recommissioned 25 April 1995. 37 mm guns fitted after transfer. Rocket launchers are mounted forward of the bridge.

TELUK SABANG *5/1995, Frank Behling* / 0075856

1 TISZA CLASS (SUPPORT SHIP) (AKL)

WAGIO 961

Displacement, tons: 2,400 full load
Dimensions, feet (metres): 258.4 × 35.4 × 15.1 *(78.8 × 10.8 × 4.6)*
Main machinery: 1 MAN diesel; 1,000 hp(m) *(735 kW)*; 1 shaft
Speed, knots: 12. **Range, n miles:** 3,000 at 11 kt
Complement: 26
Cargo capacity: 875 tons dry; 11 tons liquid
Guns: 4—14.5 mm (2 twin) MGs.
Radars: Navigation: Spin Trough; I-band.

Comment: Built in Hungary. Transferred in 1963–64. Military Sealift Command since 1978.

TISZA CLASS *1/2005, David Boey* / 1154403

TUGS

Notes: Two BIMA VIII class of 423 tons completed in 1991 are not naval. Names *Merapi* and *Merbabu*.

3 HARBOUR TUGS (YTM)

Name	*No*	*Builders*	*Commissioned*
LAMPO BATANG	934	Ishikawajima-Harima	Sep 1961
TAMBORA (Army)	935	Ishikawajima-Harima	June 1961
BROMO	936	Ishikawajima-Harima	Aug 1961

Comment: All of 250 tons displacement. There are a number of other naval tugs in the major ports.

1 NFI CLASS (ATF)

Name	*No*	*Builders*	*Commissioned*
SOPUTAN	923	Dae Sun SB & Eng, Busan	11 Aug 1995

Measurement, tons: 1,279 grt
Dimensions, feet (metres): 217.2 × 39 × 17.1 *(66.2 × 11.9 × 5.2)*
Main machinery: Diesel-electric; 4 SEMT-Pielstick diesel generators; 1 motor; 12,240 hp(m) *(9 MW)*; 1 shaft; bow thruster
Speed, knots: 13.5
Complement: 42
Radars: Navigation: Racal Decca; I-band.

Comment: Ocean Cruiser class NFI. Bollard pull 120 tons.

SOPUTAN *8/1995, van Ginderen Collection* / 0080031

1 FLEET TUG (ATF)

Name	*No*	*Builders*	*Commissioned*
LEUSER	924	PT Dok & Perkapalan Kodja Bahari, Jakarta	2002

Measurement, tons: 1,579 grt
Dimensions, feet (metres): 234.6 × 42.6 × ? *(71.5 × 13.0 × ?)*
Main machinery: 2 Pielstick 16PA5V diesels; 7,700 hp *(5.7 MW)*; 2 shafts
Speed, knots: 15
Complement: To be announced
Radars: Navigation: I-band.

Comment: Fleet tug also employed on hydrographic duties.

CUSTOMS

Notes: Identified by BC (Tax and Customs) preceding the pennant number.

14 COASTAL PATROL CRAFT (WPB)

BC 2001–2007 BC 3001–3007

Displacement, tons: 70.3 full load
Dimensions, feet (metres): 93.5 × 17.7 × 5.5 *(28.5 × 5.4 × 1.7)*
Main machinery: 2 MTU 12V 331TC92 diesels; 2,660 hp(m) *(1.96 MW)* sustained; 2 shafts
Speed, knots: 28-34
Complement: 19
Guns: 1 — 20 mm or 1 — 12.7 mm MG.

Comment: Built CMN Cherbourg. Delivered in 1980 and 1981.

BC 2007 *1/1990, 92 Wing RAAF* / 0506011

10 LÜRSSEN VSV 15 CLASS (WHSIC)

BC 1601–1610

Displacement, tons: 11 full load
Dimensions, feet (metres): 52.5 × 9.2 × 3.3 *(16 × 2.8 × 1)*
Main machinery: 2 MTU diesels; 600 hp(m) *(441 kW)*; 2 shafts
Speed, knots: 50. **Range, n miles:** 750 at 30 kt
Complement: 5 (1 officer)
Guns: 1 — 7.62 mm MG.

Comment: Built in Germany and delivered between November 1998 and June 1999.

BC 1608 *5/1999, Lürssen* / 0080032

36 LÜRSSEN 28 METRE TYPE (WPB)

BC 4001–4006 BC 5001–5006 BC 6001–6006 BC 7001–7006 BC 8001–8006 BC 9001–9006

Displacement, tons: 68 full load
Dimensions, feet (metres): 91.8 × 17.7 × 5.9 *(28 × 5.4 × 1.8)*
Main machinery: 2 Deutz diesels; 2,720 hp(m) *(2 MW)*; or 2 MTU diesels; 2,260 hp(m) *(1.66 MW)*; 2 shafts
Speed, knots: 30. **Range, n miles:** 1,100 at 15 kt; 860 at 28 kt
Complement: 19 (6 officers)
Guns: 1 — 12.7 mm MG.

Comment: Lürssen design, some built by Fulton Marine and Scheepswerven van Langebrugge of Belgium, some by Lürssen Vegesack and some by PT Pal Surabaya (which also assembled most of them). Programme started in 1980. Some of these craft are operated by the Navy, the Police and the Maritime Security Agency.

BC 7001 *5/2000, van Ginderen Collection* / 0104602

5 LÜRSSEN NEW 28 METRE TYPE (WHSIC)

BC 10001–10002 BC 20001–20003

Displacement, tons: 85 full load
Dimensions, feet (metres): 92.5 × 21.7 × 4.6 *(28.2 × 6.6 × 1.4)*
Main machinery: 2 MTU 16V 396 TE94 diesels; 2,955 hp(m) *(2.14 MW)* sustained; 2 shafts
Speed, knots: 40. **Range, n miles:** 1,100 at 30 kt
Complement: 11 (3 officers)
Guns: 2 — 7.62 mm MGs.
Radars: Surface search: Furuno FR 8731; I-band.

Comment: First pair built in Germany and delivered between May 1999 and November 1999. Last three built by PT Pal Surabaya and delivered between September 1999 and November 1999. Aluminium construction.

BC 10001 *5/1999, Lürssen* / 0080034

BC 20001 *9/1999, PT Pal* / 0075857

COAST AND SEAWARD DEFENCE COMMAND

Notes: (1) Established in 1978 as the Maritime Security Agency to control the 200 mile EEZ and to maintain navigational aids. Comes under the Military Sea Communications Agency. Some craft have blue hulls with a diagonal thick white and thin red stripe plus KPLP on the superstructure. In addition to the craft listed there are large numbers of small harbour boats.
(2) There are also a number of civilian manned vessels used for transport and servicing navigational aids.

2 DISASTER RESPONSE SHIPS (WPSO)

ARDA DEDALI **ALUGARA**

Measurement, tons: 530 gross
Dimensions, feet (metres): 196.8 × 26.2 × 10.5 *(60.0 × 8.0 × 3.2)*
Main machinery: 2 MTU 16V4000 M60 diesels; 2 shafts; cp props
Speed, knots: 19.3. **Range, n miles:** 3,000 at 17 kt
Complement: To be announced
Radars: Surface search/navigation: To be announced.

Comment: Built by Niigata Shipbuilding & Repair Inc., a wholly owned subsidiary of Mitsui Engineering & Shipbuilding Co., *Arda Dedali* delivered to the Directorate General of Sea Communication (DGSC) on 27 January 2005. *Alugara* delivered in mid-2005. The ships are designed to undertake disaster relief operations and are equipped to deal with accidents at sea, including rescue and firefighting, and counter-pollution tasks. The ships are likely to be deployed in the Malacca/Singapore Strait region.

ALUGARA *6/2005, Ships of the World* / 1153202

5 KUJANG CLASS (WPB)

KUJANG 201 **PARANG** 202 **CELURIT** 203 **CUNDRIK** 204 **BELATI** 205

Displacement, tons: 162 full load
Dimensions, feet (metres): 125.6 × 19.6 × 6.8 *(38.3 × 6 × 2.1)*
Main machinery: 2 AGO SACM 195 V12 CZSHR diesels; 4,410 hp(m) *(3.24 MW)*; 2 shafts
Speed, knots: 28. **Range, n miles:** 1,500 at 18 kt
Complement: 18
Guns: 1 — 12.7 mm MG.

Comment: Built by SFCN, Villeneuve la Garenne. Completed April 1981 *(Kujang* and *Parang)*, August 1981 *(Celurit)*, October 1981 *(Cundrik)*, December 1981 *(Belati)*. Pennant numbers are preceded by PAT.

CUNDRIK *11/1998, van Ginderen Collection* / 0052366

4 GOLOK CLASS (WSAR)

GOLOK 206 **PANAN** 207 **PEDANG** 208 **KAPAK** 209

Displacement, tons: 190 full load
Dimensions, feet (metres): 123 pp × 23.6 × 6.6 *(37.5 × 7.2 × 2)*
Main machinery: 2 MTU 16V 652 TB91 diesels; 4,610 hp(m) *(3.39 MW)* sustained; 2 shafts
Speed, knots: 25. **Range, n miles:** 1,500 at 18 kt
Complement: 18
Guns: 1 Rheinmetall 20 mm.

Comment: All launched 5 November 1981. First pair completed 12 March 1982. Last pair completed 12 May 1982. Built by Deutsche Industrie Werke, Berlin. Fitted out by Schlichting, Travemünde. Used for SAR and have medical facilities. Pennant numbers preceded by PAT.

KAPAK *11/1998, van Ginderen Collection* / 0052367

15 HARBOUR PATROL CRAFT (WPB)

PAT 01–15

Displacement, tons: 12 full load
Dimensions, feet (metres): 40 × 14.1 × 3.3 *(12.2 × 4.3 × 1)*
Main machinery: 1 Renault diesel; 260 hp(m) *(191 kW)*; 1 shaft
Speed, knots: 14
Complement: 4
Guns: 1 — 7.62 mm MG.

Comment: First six built at Tanjung Priok Shipyard 1978–79. Four more of a similar design built in 1993–94 by Mahalaya Utama Shipyard and delivered from 1995.

HARBOUR PATROL CRAFT TYPE *11/1998, van Ginderen Collection* / 0052368

1 BUOY TENDER (ABU)

Name	*No*	*Builders*	*Commissioned*
JADAYAT	–	Niigata Shipbuilding and Repair	10 Oct 2003

Measurement, tons: 858 grt
Dimensions, feet (metres): 186.7 × 36.0 × 11.5 *(56.9 × 11.0 × 3.5)*
Main machinery: 1 diesel; 985 hp *(735 MW)*; 1 shaft
Speed, knots: 10.5
Complement: 45
Radars: Navigation: I-band.

Comment: Funded by the Nippon Foundation through the Malacca Strait Council.

JADAYAT *7/2004, Ian Edwards* / 1040686

NAVAL AUXILIARY SERVICE

Notes: This is a paramilitary force of non-commissioned craft. They have KAL pennant numbers. About 24 vessels operate in the eastern Fleet and 47 in the western Fleet, and three belong to the Naval Academy. In addition, the Baruna Jaya ships listed under Survey Ships are also part of the NAS.

NAS CRAFT *4/1999* / 0080035

65 KAL KANGEAN CLASS (COASTAL PATROL CRAFT) (WPB)

Displacement, tons: 44.7 full load
Dimensions, feet (metres): 80.4 × 14.1 × 3.3 *(24.5 × 4.3 × 1)*
Main machinery: 2 diesels; 2 shafts
Speed, knots: 18
Guns: 2 USSR 25 mm/80 (twin). 2 USSR 14.5 mm (twin) MGs.

Comment: Ordered from Tanjung Uban Navy Yard in about 1984 and completed between 1987 and 1996. Numbers are uncertain. Have four figure pennant numbers in the 1101 series.

KAL KANGEAN 1112 *10/1998, Trevor Brown* / 0506008

6 CARPENTARIA CLASS (COASTAL PATROL CRAFT) (WPB)

201–206

Displacement, tons: 27 full load
Dimensions, feet (metres): 51.5 × 15.7 × 4.3 *(15.7 × 4.8 × 1.3)*
Main machinery: 2 MTU 8V 331TC92 diesels; 1,770 hp(m) *(1.3 MW)* sustained; 2 shafts
Speed, knots: 29
Range, n miles: 950 at 18 kt
Complement: 10
Guns: 2 — 12.7 mm MGs.
Radars: Surface search: Decca; I-band.

Comment: Built 1976–77 by Hawker de Havilland, Australia. Endurance, four to five days. Transferred from the Navy in the mid-1980s to the Police and now with the Naval Auxiliary Service.

CARPENTARIA 203 *8/1995, van Ginderen Collection* / 0080036

ARMY

Notes: The Army (ADRI) craft have mostly been transferred to the Military Sealift Command (Logistic Support).

27 LANDING CRAFT LOGISTICS (LCL)

ADRI XXXII–LVIII

Displacement, tons: 580 full load
Dimensions, feet (metres): 137.8 × 35.1 × 5.9 *(42 × 10.7 × 1.8)*
Main machinery: 2 Detroit 6-71 diesels; 348 hp(m) *(260 kW)* sustained; 2 shafts
Speed, knots: 10
Range, n miles: 1,500 at 10 kt
Complement: 15
Military lift: 122 tons equipment

Comment: A variety of LCL built in Tanjung Priok Shipyard 1979–82. Details are for *Adri XL*. XXXI sank in February 1993.

ADRI XXXIII *10/1999, David Boey* / 0080037

POLICE

Notes: The police operate about 85 craft of varying sizes including 14 Bango class of 194 tons and 32 Hamilton water-jet craft of 7.9 m, 234 hp giving a speed of 28 kt. Lürssen type (619-623) are identical to Customs craft. Five Polish-built Kutilang class 36 m patrol craft with pennant numbers 638-642 and three Japanese built 27 m patrol craft with pennant numbers 648-650 entered service in 2007.

POLICE 622 *8/1995* / 0080038

POLICE 642 *4/2007, J Ciślak* / 1170185

2 OFFSHORE PATROL CRAFT (PBO)

Name	*No*	*Builders*	*Commissioned*
BISMA	520	Astilleros Gondan, Castropol	May 2003
BALADEWA	521	Astilleros Gondan, Castropol	June 2003

Dimensions, feet (metres): 200.2 × 32.5 × 8.5 *(61.0 × 9.9 × 2.6)*
Main machinery: 2 MTU 12V 595TE 90 diesels; 8,700 hp *(6.5 MW)*
Speed, knots: 22. **Range, n miles:** 3,500 at 12 kt
Helicopters: Platform for one medium.

Comment: Primary role Search and Rescue.

BISMA *5/2003, Astilleros Gondan* / 0569201

Iran

Country Overview

Formerly a constitutional monarchy ruled by a shah, The Islamic Republic of Iran was established in 1979. With an area of 636,296 square miles, it is situated in the Middle East and is bordered to the north by Armenia, Azerbaijan and Turkmenistan, to the west by Iraq and Turkey and to the east by Afghanistan and Pakistan. It has a 1,318 n mile coastline with the Gulf, the Gulf of Oman and the Caspian Sea. The capital and largest city is Tehran. The principal Caspian ports are Bandar-e Anzali and Bandar-e Torkeman while those in the Gulf include the oil-shipping facilities on Kharg Island, Khorramshahr, Bandar-Khomeini and Bandar-Abbas on the strategic Strait of Hormuz. Territorial Seas (12 n miles) are claimed. An EEZ (200 n miles) has been claimed but the limits have not been defined.

Headquarters Appointments

Commander of Navy:
Rear Admiral Habibollah Sayyari
Head of IRCG(N) (Sepah):
Rear Admiral Morteza Saffari

Personnel

2009: 18,000 Navy (including 2,000 Naval Air and Marines), 20,000 IRGCN

Bases

Persian Gulf: Bandar Abbas (MHQ and 1st Naval District), Boushehr (2nd Naval District and also a Dockyard), Kharg Island, Qeshm Island, Bandar Lengeh
Indian Ocean: Chah Bahar (Bandar Beheshti) (3rd Naval District and forward base)
Caspian Sea: Bandar Anzali (4th Naval District)
Pasdaran: Al Farsiyah, Halileh, Sirri, Abu Musa, Larak

Coast Defence

Three Navy and one IRGCN brigades with many fixed installations and command posts. Approximately 100 truck-mounted C 802 and 80 CSSC-3 (Seersucker) Chinese SSMs in at least four sites. The indigenously developed Ra'ad cruise missile and C-701 Kosak may be based at launching bases under construction at Bandar Abbas, Bandar Lengeh, Boushehr and Bandar Khomeini.

Mines

Stocks of up to 3,000 mines are reported including Chinese EM 52 rising mines.

Strength of the Fleet

Type	*Active*	*Building*
Submarines	3	–
Mini Submarines	5	2
Frigates	3	1
Corvettes	2	–
Fast Attack Craft — Missile	22	1
Large Patrol Craft	5	–
Coastal Patrol Craft	120+	–
Landing Ships (Logistic)	7	–
Landing Ships (Tank)	5	–
Landing Craft (Tank)	–	3
Hovercraft	7	–
Replenishment Ship	1	–
Supply Ships	1 (1)	–
Support Ships	7	–
Water Tankers	4	–
Tenders	12	–

Prefix to Ships' Names

IS

PENNANT LIST

Submarines

901	Tareq
902	Noor
903	Yunes

Frigates

71	Alvand
72	Alborz
73	Sabalan

Corvettes

81	Bayandor
82	Naghdi

Patrol Forces

202	Azadi
203	Mehran
211	Parvin
212	Bahram
213	Nahid
P 221	Kaman
P 222	Zoubin
P 223	Khadang
P 224	Peykan
P 225	Joshan
P 226	Falakhon
P 227	Shamshir
P 228	Gorz
P 229	Gardouneh
P 230	Khanjar
P 231	Neyzeh
P 232	Tabarzin
P 313-1	Fath
P 313-2	Nasr
P 313-3	Saf
P 313-4	Ra'd
P 313-5	Fajr
P 313-6	Shams
P 313-7	Me'raj
P 313-8	Falaq
P 313-9	Hadid
P 313-10	Qadr

Mine Warfare Forces

301	Hamzeh

Amphibious Warfare Forces and Auxiliaries

21	Hejaz
22	Karabala
24	Farsi
25	Sardasht
26	Sab Sahel
101	Fouque
411	Kangan
412	Taheri
421	Bandar Abbas
422	Bushehr
424	Daylam
431	Kharg
471	Delvar
472	Sirjan
481	Charak
482	Chiroo
483	Soroo
511	Hengam
512	Larak
513	Tonb
514	Lavan
802	Hamzah

SUBMARINES

Notes: It was announced on 25 August 2008 that a new submarine production line had been initiated. The new Qaaem class is reported to be a coastal submarine capable of carrying torpedoes and mines. According to the Iranian Navy, the boat is to displace of the order of 1,000 tons.

3 KILO CLASS (PROJECT 877 EKM) (SSK)

Name	*No*	*Builders*	*Laid down*	*Launched*	*Commissioned*
TAREQ	901	Admiralty Yard, St Petersburg	1988	1991	21 Nov 1992
NOOR	902	Admiralty Yard, St Petersburg	1989	1992	6 June 1993
YUNES	903	Admiralty Yard, St Petersburg	1990	1993	25 Nov 1996

Displacement, tons: 2,356 surfaced; 3,076 dived
Dimensions, feet (metres): 238.2 × 32.5 × 21.7 *(72.6 × 9.9 × 6.6)*
Main machinery: Diesel-electric; 2 diesels; 3,650 hp(m) *(2.68 MW)*; 2 generators; 1 motor; 5,500 hp(m) *(4.05 MW)*; 1 economic speed motor; 130 hp(m) *(95 kW)*; 1 shaft; 2 auxiliary propulsion motors; 204 hp(m) *(150 kW)*
Speed, knots: 17 dived; 10 surfaced; 9 snorting
Range, n miles: 6,000 at 7 kt snorting; 400 at 3 kt dived
Complement: 53 (12 officers)

Torpedoes: 6—21 in *(533 mm)* tubes; combination of TEST-71/96; wire-guided active/passive homing to 15 km *(8.1 n miles)* at 40 kt; warhead 220 kg and 53-65; passive wake homing to 19 km *(10.3 n miles)* at 45 kt; warhead 350 kg. Total of 18 weapons.
Mines: 24 in lieu of torpedoes.
Countermeasures: ESM: Squid Head; radar warning. Quad Loop D/F.
Weapons control: MVU-119EM Murena TFCS.
Radars: Surface search: Snoop Tray MRP-25; I-band.
Sonars: Sharks Teeth MGK-400; hull-mounted; passive/active search and attack; medium frequency.
Mouse Roar MG-519; active attack; high frequency.

Programmes: Contract signed in 1988 for three of the class. The first submarine to be transferred sailed from the Baltic in October 1992 flying the Russian flag and with a predominantly Russian crew. The second sailed in June 1993. The third completed in 1994 but delivery delayed by funding problems. She arrived in Iran in mid-January 1997.
Modernisation: Chinese YJ-1 or Russian Novator Alfa SSMs may be fitted in due course.
Structure: Diving depth, 240 m *(787 ft)* normal. Has a 9,700 kW/h battery. SA-N-10 SAM system may be fitted, but this is not confirmed.
Operational: Based at Bandar Abbas but planned to move to Chah Bahar (Bandar Beheshti) on the northern shore of the Gulf of Oman. So far a jetty has been extended to facilitate operations. Training is being done with assistance from Russia. Operational effectiveness has been adversely affected by technical difficulties, although previously reported problems with battery cooling and air conditioning were understood to have been overcome using Indian batteries. Following negotiations to upgrade the boats with Rosoboronexport, the Russian arms agency *Tareq* began refit at Bandar Abbas in mid-2005. Refit of *Noor* is expected to follow when *Tareq* is completed in (probably) 2009. *Sevmash* is reported to be providing technical assistance. It is not known whether anti-ship missiles are to be installed but it is not considered likely. A video purporting to show the underwater test-firing of a Thaqeb missile on 27 August 2006 has not been verified.

KILO CLASS ***4/2006*** / 1164704

KILO CLASS ***4/2006*** / 1164703

5 + (1) YONO (IS 120) CLASS (MIDGET SUBMARINES) (SSM)

Displacement, tons: 115 surface; 123 dived
Dimensions, feet (metres): 95.1 × 9.0 × 8.2 *(29.0 × 2.75 × 2.5)*
Main machinery: Diesel-electric
Speed, knots: To be announced
Complement: 32
Torpedoes: 2—21 in *(533 mm)* tubes.
Sonars: To be announced.

Programmes: Little is known about these submarines whose existence was first noted in February 2004. If indigenously built, as has been claimed, this would represent a significant technological development. It is more likely that another country, possibly North Korea, has been involved in the project. The first three submarines are known as *Qadir 1, 2* and *3* and are likely to be employed in shallow areas of the Gulf such as the Strait of Hormuz. A fourth was launched on 28 November 2007 and a fifth on 27 November 2008. A sixth boat is reported to be under consideration.

YONO CLASS *3/2006* / 1164702

1 NAHANG CLASS (MIDGET SUBMARINES) (SSM)

Displacement, tons: To be announced
Dimensions, feet (metres): 82.0 × ? × ? *(25.0 × ? × ?)*
Main machinery: To be announced
Speed, knots: To be announced
Complement: To be announced

Comment: Little is known about this submarine whose existence was noted April 2006. Dimensions are approximate. Whereas it was reported that perhaps two further boats were to be constructed, this is now considered unlikely. It is claimed that the submarine has been indigenously designed and built. The submarine is designed for shallow water operations and potential roles include acting as mothership to swimmer delivery vehicles. Sonars and torpedoes are not fitted.

NAHANG CLASS *4/2006* / 1164701

8 SWIMMER DELIVERY VEHICLES (LDW)

Comment: On 29 August 2000, the first Iranian-built Swimmer Delivery Vehicle (SDV) *Al Sabehat 15* was launched at Bandar Abbas. The 8 m craft can accommodate a two-man crew and has the capability to carry three additional divers. It is well suited to coastal reconnaissance, Special Forces insertion/extraction and mining (it can carry 14 limpet mines) of ports and anchorages but not to open water operations. Four further craft have been reported and three of a different design have also been observed. The Hengam-class LSLs act as motherships.

AL SABEHAT 15 *4/2006* / 1164700

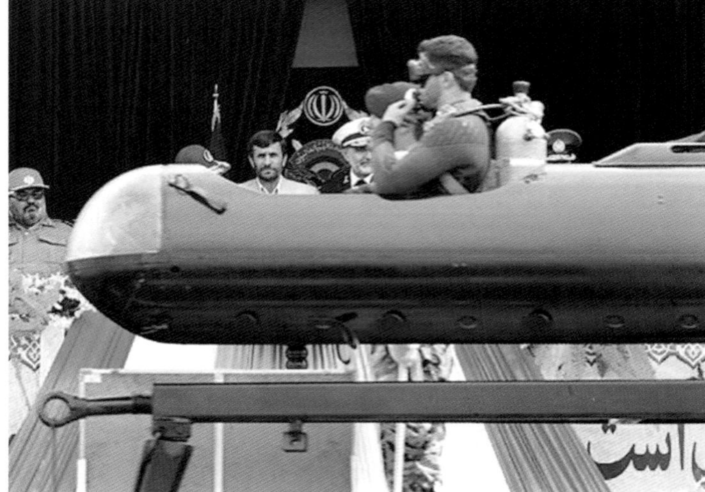

SDV (new type) *4/2006* / 1164699

FRIGATES

3 + 1 ALVAND (VOSPER MK 5) CLASS (FFG)

Name	*No*	*Builders*	*Laid down*	*Launched*	*Commissioned*
ALVAND (ex-*Saam*)	71	Vosper Thornycroft, Woolston	22 May 1967	25 July 1968	20 May 1971
ALBORZ (ex-*Zaal*)	72	Vickers, Barrow	3 Mar 1968	25 July 1969	1 Mar 1971
SABALAN (ex-*Rostam*)	73	Vickers, Newcastle & Barrow	10 Dec 1967	4 Mar 1969	28 Feb 1972
JAMARAN	–	Bandar Abbas		28 Nov 2007	2009

Displacement, tons: 1,350 full load
Dimensions, feet (metres): 310 × 36.4 × 14.1 (screws) *(94.5 × 11.1 × 4.3)*
Main machinery: CODOG (71, 72, 73); 2 RR Olympus TM2A gas turbines; 40,000 hp *(29.8 MW)* sustained; 2 Paxman 16YJCM diesels; 3,800 hp *(2.83 MW)* sustained; 2 shafts; cp props; 2 diesels *(Jamaran)*; 20,000 hp *(14.9 MW)*; 2 shafts
Speed, knots: 39 gas; 18 diesel; 28 *(Jamaran)*
Range, n miles: 3,650 at 18 kt; 550 at 36 kt
Complement: 125 (accommodation for 146)

Missiles: SSM: 4 China C-802 (2 twin) ❶; active radar homing to 120 km *(66 n miles)* at 0.9 Mach; warhead 165 kg; sea-skimmer.
Guns: 1 Vickers 4.5 in *(114 mm)*/55 Mk 8 ❷; 25 rds/min to 22 km *(12 n miles)* anti-surface; 6 km *(3.3 n miles)* anti-aircraft; weight of shell 21 kg.
2 Oerlikon 35 mm/90 (twin) ❸; 550 rds/min to 6 km *(3.3 n miles)*; weight of shell 1.55 kg.
3 Oerlikon GAM-BO1 20 mm ❹. 2—12.7 mm MGs.
Torpedoes: 6—324 mm Mk 32 (2 triple) tubes ❺.
Countermeasures: Decoys: 2 UK Mk 5 rocket flare launchers.
ESM: Decca RDL 2AC; radar warning. Racal FH 5-HF/DF.
Radars: Air/surface search: Plessey AWS 1 ❻; E/F-band; range 110 km *(60 n miles)*.
Surface search: Racal Decca 1226 ❼; I-band.
Navigation: Decca 629; I-band.
Fire control: Contraves Sea Hunter ❽; I/J-band.
IFF: UK Mk 10.

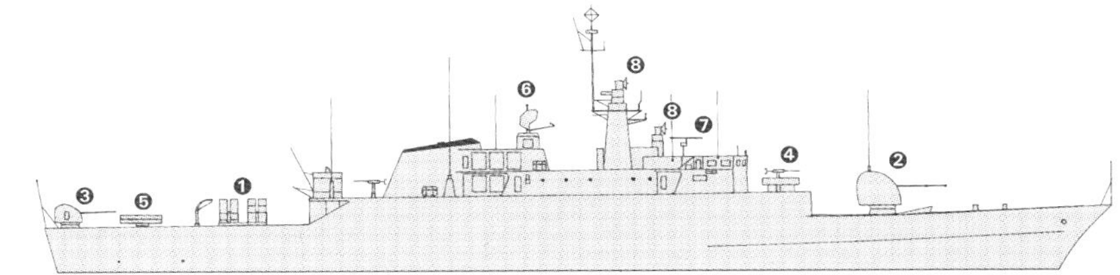

ALVAND *(Scale 1 : 900), Ian Sturton* / 1335484

Sonars: Graseby 174; hull-mounted; active search; medium/high frequency.
Graseby 170; hull-mounted; active attack; high frequency.

Programmes: The first three units were ordered from UK Shipyards on 25 August 1966. A fourth unit, has been under construction at Bandar Abbas, and sea trials are expected to start in 2009. Known as the *Mowj* project, the design is almost certainly very similar to the original Vosper Mk 5 design. The weapons and sensor fit is likely to include a 76 mm gun, four C-802 missiles and, possibly, SM 1 launchers. The ship is to have all diesel propulsion. The design includes a flight deck aft.

Modernisation: Major refits including replacement of 4.5 in Mk 5 gun by Mk 8 completed 1977. Modifications in 1988 included replacing Seacat with a 23 mm gun and boat davits with minor armaments. By mid-1991 the 23 mm and both boats had been replaced by GAM-BO1 20 mm guns and the SSM launcher had effectively become a twin launcher. In 1996/97 two of the class had the Sea Killer SSM replaced by C-802 launchers and a new communications mast fitted between the two fire-control radars. The third has been similarly modified. *Sabalan* appears to be fitted with Rice Screen air/surface search radar. Torpedo tubes which replaced the mortars in *Alvand* were probably taken from decommissioned Babr class.

Structure: Air conditioned throughout. Fitted with Vosper stabilisers.

Operational: *Sahand* sunk by USN on 18 April 1988. *Sabalan* had her back broken by a laser-guided bomb in the same skirmish but was out of dock by the end of 1990 and was operational again in late 1991. ASW mortars probably unserviceable. All are active.

ALVAND *1/2002* / 0569203

SABALAN *2/1998* / 0052371

CORVETTES

2 BAYANDOR (PF 103) CLASS (FS)

Name	*No*	*Builders*	*Laid down*	*Launched*	*Commissioned*
BAYANDOR (ex-US *PF 103*)	81	Levingstone Shipbuilding Co, Orange, TX	20 Aug 1962	7 July 1963	18 May 1964
NAGHDI (ex-US *PF 104*)	82	Levingstone Shipbuilding Co, Orange, TX	12 Sep 1962	10 Oct 1963	22 July 1964

Displacement, tons: 900 standard; 1,135 full load
Dimensions, feet (metres): 275.6 × 33.1 × 10.2 *(84 × 10.1 × 3.1)*
Main machinery: 2 Fairbanks-Morse 38TD8-1/8-9 diesels; 5,250 hp *(3.92 MW)* sustained; 2 shafts
Speed, knots: 20
Range, n miles: 2,400 at 18 kt; 4,800 at 12 kt
Complement: 140

Guns: 2 US 3 in *(76 mm)*/50 Mk 34 ❶; 50 rds/min to 12.8 km *(7 n miles)*; weight of shell 6 kg.
1 Bofors 40 mm/60 (twin) ❷; 120 rds/min to 10 km *(5.5 n miles)*; weight of shell 0.89 kg.
2 Oerlikon GAM-BO1 20 mm ❸. 2—12.7 mm MGs.
Weapons control: Mk 63 for 76 mm gun. Mk 51 Mod 2 for 40 mm guns.
Radars: Air/surface search: Westinghouse SPS-6C ❹; D-band; range 146 km *(80 n miles)* (for fighter).
Surface search: Racal Decca ❺; I-band.
Navigation: Raytheon 1650 ❻; I/J-band.
Fire control: Western Electric Mk 36 ❼; I/J-band.
IFF: UPX-12B.

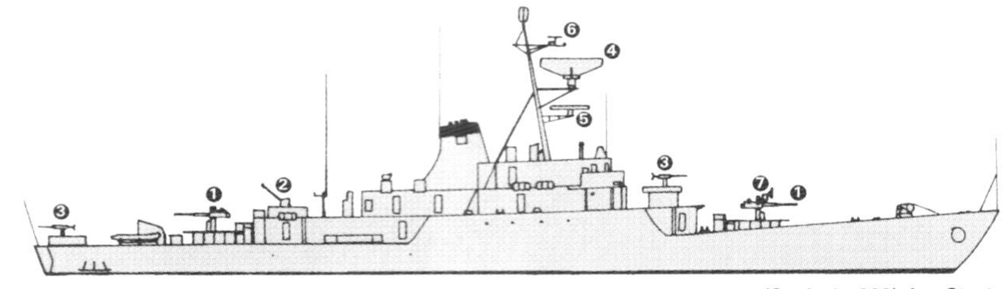
BAYANDOR *(Scale 1 : 900), Ian Sturton* / 0506193

Sonars: EDO SQS-17A; hull-mounted; active attack; high frequency.

Programmes: Transferred from the USA to Iran under the Mutual Assistance programme in 1964.
Modernisation: *Naghdi* change of engines and reconstruction of accommodation completed in mid-1988. 23 mm gun and depth charge racks replaced by 20 mm guns in 1990. *Naghdi* began a substantial modernisation programme in 2007. Upgrades are reported to include the replacement of the 76 mm gun with a modern weapon, installation of four C-802 missile tubes aft of the funnel and of Mk 32 torpedo tubes aft.
Operational: *Milanian* and *Khanamuie* sunk in 1982 during war with Iraq. Both remaining ships are very active. Sonars may have been removed.

BAYANDOR *2/1998* / 0052372

SHIPBORNE AIRCRAFT

Numbers/Type: 9 Agusta AB 204ASW/212.
Operational speed: 104 kt *(193 km/h)*.
Service ceiling: 11,500 ft *(3,505 m)*.
Range: 332 n miles *(615 km)*.
Role/Weapon systems: Mainly engaged in ASV operations in defence of oil installations. Numbers are uncertain. Sensors: APS 705 search radar, dipping sonar (if carried). Weapons: ASW; two China YU-2 torpedoes. ASV; two AS 12 missiles.

AB 212 (Spanish colours) *3/2002, A Campanera i Rovira* / 0529019

Numbers/Type: 9 Agusta-Sikorsky ASH-3D Sea King.
Operational speed: 120 kt *(222 km/h)*.
Service ceiling: 12,200 ft *(3,720 m)*.
Range: 630 n miles *(1,165 km)*.
Role/Weapon systems: Shore-based ASW helicopter to defend major port and oil installations. Six are reported serviceable. Can be embarked in *Kharg*. Sensors: Selenia search radar, dipping sonar. Weapons: ASW; four A244/S torpedoes or depth bombs. ASV; trials of an anti-ship missile 'Fajr-e-Darya' are reported to have taken place. Capabilities not known but could be a development of Sea Killer.

SEA KING *3/1997* / 0012549

LAND-BASED MARITIME AIRCRAFT (FRONT LINE)

Notes: (1) The Air Force also has up to six F-4 Phantoms equipped with C 80IK ASMs for the maritime role.
(2) Two F-27 Fokker Friendship aircraft are used in a utility MPA role.
(3) Two Dornier 228 are also in service but are reported not to be very active.
(4) The Iranian Air Force operates some 14 (plus 18 ex-Iraqi) Su-24 Fencer ground attack, some of which may be 'marinised' for an anti-ship role.
(5) An-140 transport aircraft are under licensed production at Esfahan. The first aircraft flew in January 2001. These are likely to be used as a multipurpose platform including replacement of the ageing P3F fleet.
(6) Approximately seven Harbin Y-12 utility aircraft are used for maritime patrol.

Numbers/Type: 6 Sikorsky RH/MH-53D Sea Stallion.
Operational speed: 125 kt *(232 km/h)*.
Service ceiling: 11,100 ft *(3,385 m)*.
Range: 405 n miles *(750 km)*.
Role/Weapon systems: Surface search helicopter which could be used for mine clearance but so far has only been used for Logistic purposes. Can be carried on Hengam class flight deck. Sensors: Weather radar. Weapons: Unarmed.

Numbers/Type: 5 Lockheed C-130H-MP Hercules.
Operational speed: 325 kt *(602 km/h)*.
Service ceiling: 33,000 ft *(10,060 m)*.
Range: 4,250 n miles *(7,876 km)*.
Role/Weapon systems: Long-range maritime reconnaissance role by Air Force which has a total of 23 of these aircraft. Sensors: Search/weather radar. Weapons: Unarmed.

Numbers/Type: 2 Lockheed P-3F Orion.
Operational speed: 410 kt *(760 km/h)*.
Service ceiling: 28,300 ft *(8,625 m)*.
Range: 4,000 n miles *(7,410 km)*.
Role/Weapon systems: Air Force manned. One of the remaining two aircraft can be used for early warning and control duties for strikes. Replacements are being sought. Sensors: Search radar, sonobuoys. Weapons: ASW; various weapons can be carried. ASV; C-802 SSM.

P3F *12/2001, A Sharma* / 0528307

PATROL FORCES

Notes: (1) There are at least one 13 m (RIB 42SC), one 16.5 m (FB 55), two 12 m (FB 38), two 11 m (RIB 36) and two 16.7 m (RIB 55SC) craft used for maritime enforcement tasks. Designed by FB design of Italy, they are capable of 60-70 kt. Additional units to similar designs have been built in Iran.
(2) The test of a high-speed rocket-torpedo was announced on 2 April 2006. Known as Dalaam, the weapon appears to resemble the Russian Shkval which has a speed of 195 kt and a range of 3.75 n miles. Designed for close-quarter operations, the weapon may be fitted in some patrol craft.

RIB 42 *6/2007, FB design* / 1166564

10 THONDOR (HOUDONG) CLASS
(FAST ATTACK CRAFT—MISSILE) (PTFG)

SHAHID MEHDAVI (ex-*Fath*) P 313-1
SHAHID KORD (ex-*Nasr*) P 313-2
SHAHID SHAFIHI (ex-*Saf*) P 313-3
SHAHID TOWSALI (ex-*Ra'd*) P 313-4
SHAHID HEJAT ZADEH (ex-*Fajr*) P 313-5
SHAHID DARA (ex-*Shams*) P 313-6
SHAHID ABSALAN (ex-*Me'raj*) P 313-7
SHAHID RAHISI RAISI (ex-*Falaq*) P 313-8
SHAHID GOLZAM (ex-*Hadid*) P 313-9
SHAHID SAHRABI (ex-*Qadr*) P 313-10

Displacement, tons: 171 standard; 205 full load
Dimensions, feet (metres): 126.6 × 22.3 × 8.9 *(38.6 × 6.8 × 2.7)*
Main machinery: 3 diesels; 8,025 hp(m) *(7.94 MW)* sustained; 3 shafts
Speed, knots: 35
Range, n miles: 800 at 30 kt
Complement: 28 (3 officers)

Missiles: SSM: 4 China C-802; active radar homing to 120 km *(66 n miles)* at 0.9 Mach; warhead 165 kg; sea-skimmer.
Guns: 2—30 mm/65 (twin) AK 230. 2—23 mm/87 (twin).
Radars: Surface search: China SR-47A; I-band.
Navigation: China RM 1070A; I-band.
Fire control: Rice Lamp Type 341; I/J-band.

Programmes: Negotiations for sale started in 1991 but were held up by arguments over choice of missile. Built at Zhanjiang Shipyard. First five delivered in September 1994 by transporter vessel, second batch in March 1996. Original pennant numbers 301-310. More may be built in Iran under licence.
Structure: The hull is a shortened version of the Chinese Huangfen (Osa 1) class but the superstructure has a lattice mast to support two I-band radars and there is a separate director plinth for the fire-control system. A twin 23 mm gun is fitted aft of the mast.
Operational: Manned by the Pasdaran. Renamed in approximately 2006.

SHAHID GOLZAM *4/2006* / 1164698

SHAHID ABSALAN *4/2006* / 1164697

13 KAMAN (COMBATTANTE II) CLASS
(FAST ATTACK CRAFT—MISSILE) (PGGF)

Name	*No*	*Builders*	*Commissioned*
KAMAN	P 221	CMN, Cherbourg	12 Aug 1977
ZOUBIN	P 222	CMN, Cherbourg	12 Sep 1977
KHADANG	P 223	CMN, Cherbourg	15 Mar 1978
PEYKAN	P 224	Bandar Anzali, Iran	2004
JOSHAN	P 225	Bandar Anzali, Iran	2006
FALAKHON	P 226	CMN, Cherbourg	31 Mar 1978
SHAMSHIR	P 227	CMN, Cherbourg	31 Mar 1978
GORZ	P 228	CMN, Cherbourg	22 Aug 1978
GARDOUNEH	P 229	CMN, Cherbourg	11 Sep 1978
KHANJAR	P 230	CMN, Cherbourg	1 Aug 1981
NEYZEH	P 231	CMN, Cherbourg	1 Aug 1981
TABARZIN	P 232	CMN, Cherbourg	1 Aug 1981
DERAFSH	P 233	Bandar Anzali, Iran	2008

Displacement, tons: 249 standard; 275 full load
Dimensions, feet (metres): 154.2 × 23.3 × 6.2 *(47 × 7.1 × 1.9)*
Main machinery: 4 MTU 16V 538 TB91 diesels; 12,280 hp(m) *(9.03 MW)* sustained; 4 shafts
Speed, knots: 37.5
Range, n miles: 2,000 at 15 kt; 700 at 33.7 kt
Complement: 31

Missiles: SSM: 2 or 4 China C-802 (1 or 2 twin); active radar homing to 120 km *(66 n miles)* at 0.9 Mach; warhead 165 kg; sea-skimmer or 4 McDonnell Douglas Harpoon (2 twin); active radar homing to 40 km *(22 n miles)* at 0.9 Mach; warhead 165 kg; sea-skimmer or Standard SM1-MR box launchers *(Gorz)*.
Guns: 1 OTO Melara 3 in *(76 mm)*/62 compact; 85 rds/min to 16 km *(8.7 n miles)* anti-surface; 12 km *(6.6 n miles)* anti-aircraft; weight of shell 6 kg; 320 rounds.
1 Breda Bofors 40 mm/70; 300 rds/min to 12 km *(6.6 n miles)*; weight of shell 0.96 kg; 900 rounds. Some have a 23 mm or 20 mm gun in place of the 40 mm.
2—12.7 mm MGs.
Countermeasures: ESM: Thomson-CSF TMV 433 Dalia; radar intercept.
ECM: Thomson-CSF Alligator; jammer.
Radars: Surface search/fire control: Signaal WM28; I/J-band.
Navigation: Racal Decca 1226; I-band.
IFF: UPZ-27N/APX-72.

Programmes: Twelve ordered in February 1974. The transfer of the last three craft was delayed by the French Government after the Iranian revolution. On 12 July 1981 France decided to hand them over. This took place on 1 August, on 2 August they sailed and soon after *Tabarzin* was seized by a pro-Royalist group off Cadiz. After the latter surrendered to the French in Toulon further problems were prevented by sending all three to Iran in a merchant ship. Further indigenously built craft have been developed for operations in the Caspian Sea. Known as the SINA 1 programme, the first vessel *(Peykan)* was launched on 29 September 2003, the second *(Joshan)* commissioned in 2006 and a third *(Derafsh)* in 2008. Additional units may be built.
Modernisation: Most of the class fitted with C-802 SSM in 1996–98. *Gorz* has been used for trials, first with Harpoon, and now with SM 1 launchers taken from the deleted Sumner class destroyers.
Structure: Portable SA-7 launchers may be embarked in some.
Operational: The original *Peykan* P 224 was sunk in 1980 by Iraq; *Joshan* P 225 in April 1988 by the US Navy. The new *Peykan* P 224, *Joshan* P 225 and *Derafsh* P 233 are based in the Caspian Sea.

GARDOUNEH (with Harpoon) *11/2001, Royal Australian Navy* / 0528433

SHAMSHIR *4/2006* / 1164696

GORZ (with SM1) *12/2002* / 0569204

3 PARVIN (PGM-71) CLASS (LARGE PATROL CRAFT) (PC)

Name	*No*	*Builders*	*Commissioned*
PARVIN (ex-*PGM 103*)	211	Peterson Builders Inc	1967
BAHRAM (ex-*PGM 112*)	212	Peterson Builders Inc	1969
NAHID (ex-*PGM 122*)	213	Peterson Builders Inc	1970

Displacement, tons: 98 standard; 148 full load
Dimensions, feet (metres): 101 × 21.3 × 8.3 *(30.8 × 6.5 × 2.5)*
Main machinery: 8 GM 6-71 diesels; 2,040 hp *(1.52 MW)* sustained; 2 shafts
Speed, knots: 22
Range, n miles: 1,140 at 17 kt
Complement: 20
Missiles: SSM: 2 launchers.
Guns: 1 Bofors 40 mm/60. 1 GAM-BO1 20 mm. 2—12.7 mm MGs.
Depth charges: 4 racks (8 US Mk 6).
Radars: Surface search: I-band.
Sonars: SQS-17B; hull-mounted active attack; high frequency.

Comment: The heavier 40 mm gun is mounted aft and the 20 mm forward to compensate for the large SQS-17B sonar dome under the bows. Mousetrap A/S mortar removed. Two units have been modified with two missile launchers (of unknown type). Two GAM-BO1 20 mm guns are carried in this variant.

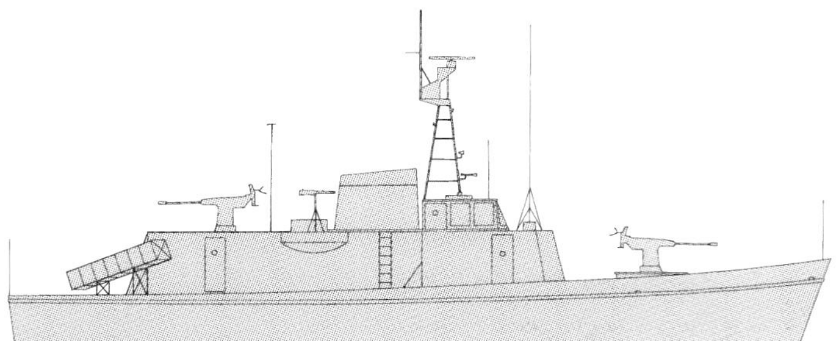

PARVIN CLASS (SSM variant) ***(Scale 1 : 400), Ian Sturton*** / 1166563

PARVIN ***1/2002, A Sharma*** / 0528306

3 KAYVAN (CAPE) CLASS (LARGE PATROL CRAFT) (PB)

KAYVAN 201 (ex-61) **TIRAN** 202 (ex-63) **MAHAN** 204 (ex-64)

Displacement, tons: 98 standard; 148 full load
Dimensions, feet (metres): 95 × 20.2 × 6.6 *(28.9 × 6.2 × 2)*
Main machinery: 24 Cummins NYHMS-1200 diesels; 2,120 hp *(1.58 MW)*; 2 shafts
Speed, knots: 21
Range, n miles: 2,324 at 8 kt
Complement: 15
Guns: 1 Bofors 40 mm/60. 2 USSR 23 mm/80 (twin). 2—12.7 mm MGs.

Comment: Three patrol craft originally built by the US Coast Guard, Curtis Bay, Maryland in the 1950s were withdrawn from Iranian service in approximately 1995. It is reported that they have been refitted and recommissioned. Details are as for the craft in 1994 but it is likely that machinery and armament may now be different.

MAHAN (old number) ***6/1975, Iranian Navy*** / 1293457

10 US MK III CLASS (COASTAL PATROL CRAFT) (PB)

Displacement, tons: 41.6 full load
Dimensions, feet (metres): 65 × 18.1 × 6 *(19.8 × 5.5 × 1.8)*
Main machinery: 3 GM 8V-71TI diesels; 690 hp *(515 kW)* sustained; 3 shafts
Speed, knots: 30
Range, n miles: 500 at 28 kt
Complement: 8
Guns: 1—20 mm GAM-BO1. 1—12.7 mm MG.
Radars: Surface search: RCA LN66; I-band.

Comment: Twenty ordered from Marinette Marine Corporation, Wisconsin, USA; the first delivered in December 1975 and the last in December 1976. A further 50 were ordered in 1976 to be shipped out and completed in Iran. It is not known how many were finally assembled. Six lost in the Gulf War, others have been scrapped. These last 10 are based at Boushehr and Bandar Abbas. Continue to be active.

US Mk III ***5/1999*** / 0080041

10 PASHE (MIG-G-1900) CLASS (COASTAL PATROL CRAFT) (PBF)

Displacement, tons: 30 full load
Dimensions, feet (metres): 64 × 13.8 × 3 *(19.5 × 4.2 × 0.9)*
Main machinery: 2 MWM TBD 234 V12 diesels; 1,646 hp(m) *(1.21 MW)*; 2 shafts
Speed, knots: 36
Complement: 8
Guns: 2—23 mm/80 (twin).
Radars: Surface search: I-band.

Comment: Building in Iran to a modified US Mk II design. Numbers uncertain. Pasdaran craft.

MIG-G-1900 ***1992, Iranian Marine Industries*** / 0080042

20 GHAEM (MIG-S-1800) CLASS (COASTAL PATROL CRAFT) (PB)

Displacement, tons: 60 full load
Dimensions, feet (metres): 61.3 × 18.9 × 3.4 *(18.7 × 5.8 × 1.1)*
Main machinery: 2 MWM TBD 234 V12 diesels; 1,646 hp(m) *(1.21 MW)*; 2 shafts
Speed, knots: 18
Complement: 10
Guns: 1 Oerlikon 20 mm. 2—7.62 mm MGs.
Radars: Surface search: I-band.

Comment: Assembled in Iran as general purpose patrol craft. Numbers uncertain. Pasdaran craft.

GHAEM CLASS ***1996, Joolaee Marine Industries*** / 0506299

15 PEYKAAP I (IPS 16) CLASS (COASTAL PATROL CRAFT) (PTF)

Displacement, tons: 13.75 standard
Dimensions, feet (metres): 53.5 × 12.3 × 2.3 *(16.3 × 3.75 × 0.7)*
Main machinery: 2 diesels; 2,400 hp *(1.79 MW)*; surface piercing propeller
Speed, knots: 52
Complement: 3
Guns: 1—12.7 mm MG.
Torpedoes: 2 lightweight

Comment: Up to 15 of this class in service with the Pasdaran. Built in North Korea, six craft were reported to have been delivered on 8 December 2002 on the Iranian freighter *Iran Meead*. An apparently stealthy craft whose unusual armament of 324 mm lightweight torpedoes suggest a ship-disabling role.

PEYKAAP I CLASS *4/2006* / 1164695

10 TIR (IPS 18) CLASS (COASTAL PATROL CRAFT) (PTF)

Displacement, tons: 28.1 standard
Dimensions, feet (metres): 69.4 × 18.9 × 2.8 *(21.1 × 5.8 × 0.9)*
Main machinery: 3 diesels; 3,600 hp *(2.7 MW)*
Speed, knots: 52
Complement: 6
Guns: 1—12.7 m MG.
Torpedoes: 2—533 mm (unknown type).

Comment: Up to ten of this class in service with the Pasdaran. Built in North Korea, two craft were reported to have been delivered on 8 December 2002 on the Iranian freighter *Iran Meead*. Anti-surface ship role.

TIR and BOGHAMMAR *1/2006, RAAF* / 1167756

3 GAHJAE CLASS (SEMI-SUBMERSIBLE CRAFT) (PTF)

Displacement, tons: 7 approx
Dimensions, feet (metres): 49.2 × 9.8 × 2.3 *(15.0 × 3.0 × 0.7)*
Speed, knots: 50 approx
Torpedoes: 2 lightweight.

Comment: Originally reported as the Taedong-C semi-submersible torpedo boat, three of these craft were reported delivered from North Korea on 8 December 2002 on the Iranian freighter *Iran Meead*. The stealthy design appears to be based on the Peykaap class inshore patrol craft on which the dimensions, which are speculative, are based. The concept of operations is likely to include a high speed surface approach to a target before submerging to a depth of about 3 m to conduct the attack phase using a snort mast.

GAHJAE CLASS (artist's impression) *10/2005* / 1151265

25 PEYKAAP II (IPS 16 MOD) CLASS (COASTAL PATROL CRAFT) (PTG)

Displacement, tons: 13.75 approx
Dimensions, feet (metres): 55.8 × 12.3 × 2.3 *(17.0 × 3.75 × 0.7)*
Main machinery: 2 diesels; 2,400 hp *(1.79 MW)*; surface piercing propeller
Speed, knots: 52 approx
Missiles: 2 FL-10 launchers.

Comment: Slightly larger versions of the torpedo-armed Peykaap I class armed with FL-10 or C-701 (Kosar) or C-704 (Nasr) missiles. Approximately 25 of this class in service with the Pasdaran. Probably built in Iran as a development of the original North Korean design.

PEYKAAP II *6/2008** / 1335384

3 KAJAMI CLASS (SEMI-SUBMERSIBLE CRAFT) (PTF)

Displacement, tons: 30 approx
Dimensions, feet (metres): 68.9 × ? × ? *(21.0 × ? × ?)*
Speed, knots: 50 approx

Comment: Originally reported as the Taedong-B high-speed infiltration craft, two of these craft were reported delivered from North Korea on 8 December 2002 on the Iranian freighter *Iran Meead*. Little is known about the design of the craft except that its concept of operations is likely to include a high speed surface approach to a target before submerging to a depth of about 3 m to conduct the attack phase using a snort mast.

KAJAMI *6/2006* / 1164691

KAJAMI (submerged approach) (artist's impression) *10/2005* / 1151268

15 TARLAN CLASS (INSHORE PATROL CRAFT) (PTF)

Displacement, tons: 8.5 standard
Dimensions, feet (metres): 39.0 × 10.2 × 2.1 *(11.9 × 3.1 × 0.65)*
Main machinery: 2 diesels; 1,320 hp *(985 kW)*; 2 surface piercing propellers
Speed, knots: 50
Complement: 2

Comment: A new class of indigenously built inshore attack craft first reported in 2005. Design features include an aluminium, catamaran hull, probably adapted from a commercial craft, and a 1.5 m high pedestal in the after part of the vessel. This might support a wire/laser guided weapon similar to an Anti-Tank Guided Missile (ATGM). Numbers of craft are uncertain but are likely to increase.

TARLAN CLASS (under construction) *6/2007* / 1166572

6 US MK II CLASS (COASTAL PATROL CRAFT) (PB)

Displacement, tons: 22.9 full load
Dimensions, feet (metres): 49.9 × 15.1 × 4.3 *(15.2 × 4.6 × 1.3)*
Main machinery: 2 GM 8V-71TI diesels; 460 hp *(343 kW)* sustained; 2 shafts
Speed, knots: 28. **Range, n miles:** 750 at 26 kt
Complement: 8
Guns: 2—12.7 mm MGs.
Radars: Surface search: SPS-6; I-band.

Comment: Twenty-six ordered from Peterson, USA in 1976–77. Six were for the Navy and the remainder for the Imperial Gendarmerie. All were built in association with Arvandan Maritime Corporation, Abadan. The six naval units operate in the Caspian Sea. Of the remaining 20, six were delivered complete and the others were only 65 per cent assembled on arrival in Iran. Some were lost when the Iraqi Army captured Koramshahr. Others have been lost at sea. Numbers uncertain.

US Mk II *3/1996* / 0080043

9 C 14 CLASS (PTGF)

611–614 +5

Displacement, tons: 17 standard
Dimensions, feet (metres): 44.8; 45.1 MRL × 15.7 × 2.3 *(13.65; 13.75 × 4.8 × 0.7)*
Main machinery: 2 diesels; 2,300 hp (1.7 MW); 2 surface piercing propellers
Speed, knots: 50
Complement: 5
Missiles: SSM: 4 FL-10 (2 twin) launchers.
Guns: 1—20 mm. 1—12.7 mm MG.
Weapons control: Optronic director.
Radars: Surface search: I-band.

Comment: There are two known variants of this catamaran-hulled class, the prototype of which was reported delivered in late 2000 and commissioned in 2001. Five missile-armed craft are operated by the Pasdaran. The type of missile has not been confirmed but is probably FL-10. Four (611-614) slightly longer (13.75 m) craft are fitted with MRL on the bridge roof and are operated by the navy. Further craft of both variants are likely.

C 14 (missile variant) ***2001, China State Shipbuilding Corporation*** / 0096378

C 14 (MRL variant) ***3/2006*** / 1164690

30 BOGHAMMAR CRAFT (PBF)

Displacement, tons: 6.4 full load
Dimensions, feet (metres): 41.2 × 8.6 × 2.3 *(13 × 2.7 × 0.7)*
Main machinery: 2 Seatek 6-4V-9 diesels; 1,160 hp *(853 kW)*; 2 shafts
Speed, knots: 46. **Range, n miles:** 500 at 40 kt
Complement: 5/6
Guns: 3—12.7 mm MGs. 1 RPG-7 rocket launcher or 106 mm recoilless rifle. 1-12-barrelled 107 mm rocket launcher (MRL).
Radars: Surface search: I-band.

Comment: Ordered in 1983 and completed in 1984–85 for Customs Service. Total of 51 delivered. Used extensively by the Pasdaran. Maximum payload 450 kg. Speed is dependent on load carried. They can be transported by Amphibious Lift Ships and can operate from bases at Farsi, Sirri and Abu Musa Islands with a main base at Bandar Abbas. Re-engined with Seatek diesels from 1991. There are also a further 10-11 m craft with similar characteristics. Known as TORAGH boats and manned by the Pasdaran and the Navy. Numbers approximate.

20 ASHOORA I (MIG-G-0800) CLASS (INSHORE PATROL CRAFT) (PBF)

Displacement, tons: 1.3 full load
Dimensions, feet (metres): 22.3 × 7.4 × 1.2 *(6.7 × 2.3 × 0.4)*
Main machinery: 2 outboards; 240 hp *(179 kW)*
Speed, knots: 40+
Complement: 4
Guns: Various, but can include 1-12-barrelled 107 mm MRL or 1—12.7 mm MG.

Comment: Boston Whaler type craft based on a Watercraft (UK) design. Numerous indigenously constructed GRP hulls. Numbers uncertain. Manned by the Pasdaran and the Navy.

ASHOORA I ***6/1988*** / 0506014

RIVER ROADSTEAD PATROL AND HOVERCRAFT (PBR)

Comment: Numerous craft used by the Revolutionary Guard include:
Type 2: Dimensions, feet (metres): 22.0 × 7.2 *(6.7 × 2.2)*; single outboard engine; 1–12.7 mm MG.
Type 3: Dimensions, feet (metres): 16.4 × 5.2 *(5.0 × 1.6)*; single outboard engine; small arms.
Type 4: Dimensions, feet (metres): 13.1-26.2 × 7.9 *(4-8 × 1.6)*; two outboard engines; small arms.
Type 5: Dimensions, feet (metres): 24.6 × 9.2 *(7.5 × 2.8)*; assault craft.
Type 6: Dimensions, feet (metres): 30.9 × 11.8 *(9.4 × 3.6)*; single outboard engine; 1–12.7 mm MG.
Dhows: Dimensions, feet (metres): 77.1 × 20 *(23.5 × 6.1)*; single diesel engine; mine rails.
Yunus: Dimensions, feet (metres): 27.6 × 9.8 *(8.4 × 3)*; speed 32 kt.
Ashoora II: Dimensions, feet (metres): 26.6 × 7.9 *(8.1 × 2.4)*; two outboards; speed 42 kt; 1–7.62 mm MG.
Kuch: Dimensions, feet (metres): 29.5 × 9.8 *(9.0 × 3.0)*; two outboards; stern dock for jet ski.
Jet Skis: RPGs.

TYPE 4 ***6/2007*** / 1166575

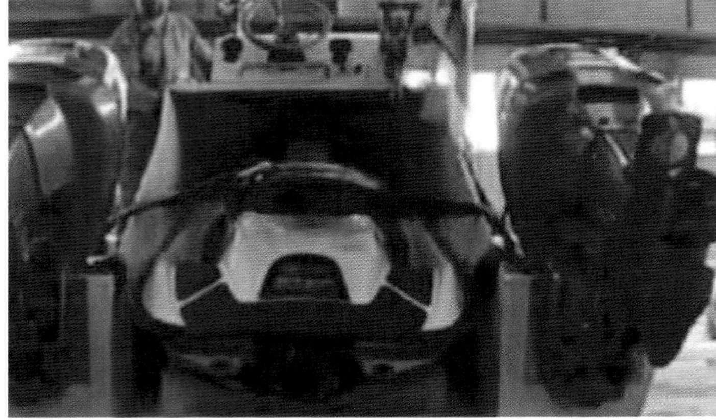

KUCH (with stern dock) ***6/2007*** / 1166576

20 MURCE (MIG-G-0900) CLASS (INSHORE PATROL CRAFT) (PBI)

Displacement, tons: 3.5 full load
Dimensions, feet (metres): 30.2 × 9.2 × 1.5 *(9.2 × 2.8 × 0.45)*
Main machinery: 2 Volvo Penta diesels; 1,260 hp *(940 kW)*
Speed, knots: 30
Complement: 3
Guns: 3—12.7 mm MGs. 1 RPG-7 rocket launcher or 106 mm recoilless rifle. 1-12-barrelled 107 mm rocket launcher (MRL).
Radars: Surface search: I-band.

Comment: Built by MiG, the unarmed variant has been produced in relatively large numbers since the mid-1990s. This approximate number of armed variant is believed to be in Pasdaran or naval service.

MURCE CLASS ***6/2000, MiG*** / 0126375

10 KASHDOM II CLASS (INSHORE PATROL CRAFT) (PBF)

Displacement, tons: 17.5 approx
Dimensions, feet (metres): 52.5 × 9.8 × 3.6 *(16.0 × 3.0 × 1.1)*
Main machinery: 2 diesels; 2,400 hp *(1.8 MW)*; surface piercing propeller
Speed, knots: 50 approx
Complement: 5
Guns: 1—23 mm. 1—12.7 mm MG.

Comment: Probably a development of the C 14 class design, the catamaran-hulled inshore patrol craft. A MRL launcher may also be mounted on the cabin roof. Numbers are approximate.

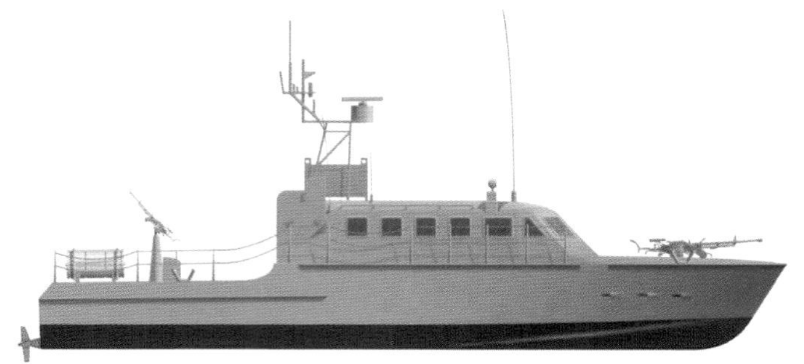

KASHDOM II (artist's impression) ***6/2008**** / 1335383

10 MK 13 PATROL CRAFT (PTGF)

Displacement, tons: To be announced
Dimensions, feet (metres): 45.9 × ? × ? *(14 × ? × ?)*
Speed, knots: To be announced
Missiles: SSM: 2 FL-10 launchers.
Torpedoes: 2—324 mm tubes.

Comment: Approximately four new monohull patrol craft, possibly built in China, delivered in 2006. Armed with both anti-ship missiles and torpedoes.

MK 13 CRAFT *6/2007* / 1166574

3 SEWART CLASS (INSHORE PATROL CRAFT) (PBR)

MAHNAVI-HAMRAZ MAHNAVI-TAHERI MAHNAVI-VAHEDI

Displacement, tons: 9.1 approx
Dimensions, feet (metres): 40.0 × 12.1 × 3.3 *(12.2 × 3.7 × 1.0)*
Main machinery: 2 GM diesels; 348 hp *(260 kW)*; 2 shafts
Speed, knots: 31 approx
Complement: 6
Guns: 1—12.7 mm MG.

Comment: Surviving craft of about nine craft acquired from the US for the then Coast Guard in about 1953. Previously reported as having been decommissioned. Some were transferred to Sudan in 1975. Possibly based in the Caspian Sea.

1 MIL 55 CLASS (INSHORE PATROL CRAFT) (PBF)

Displacement, tons: 15.3
Dimensions, feet (metres): 53.9 × 9.3 × 2.75 *(16.43 × 2.85 × 0.84)*
Main machinery: 2 Isotta Fraschini diesels; 2,400 hp *(1.8 MW)*; surface piercing propeller
Speed, knots: 72 approx
Complement: 5

Comment: Designed by FB design of Italy. Delivered in 2003. Kevlar monohull fast inshore patrol craft for maritime law enforcement tasks.

MIL 55 *4/2006* / 1164694

2 MIL 40 CLASS (INSHORE PATROL CRAFT) (PTF)

Displacement, tons: 6 approx
Dimensions, feet (metres): 42.3 × 8.7 × 2.7 *(12.9 × 2.64 × 0.82)*
Main machinery: 2 Isotta Fraschini diesels; 1,320 hp *(984 kW)*; surface piercing propeller
Speed, knots: 62
Complement: 3

Comment: Designed by FB design of Italy. Delivered in 2002. Kevlar monohull fast inshore patrol craft for maritime law enforcement tasks. The craft can be equipped with a centrally mounted machine-gun forward or with two laterally mounted guns.

MIL 40 *4/2006* / 1164693

AMPHIBIOUS FORCES

Notes: (1) Commercial LSLs have been built at Bandar Abbas. These include two 1,151 grt ships, *Chavoush* launched in December 1995 and *Chalak* in June 1996.
(2) There are an unknown number of small Wing-In-Ground (WIG) vehicles, possibly for operations in the Caspian Sea.
(3) Two indigenously built LCTs were launched on 28 May 2006. Construction is reported to have started in 2005. The 49 × 11.6 m craft are capable of transporting 800 tons of equipment.
(4) The launch of a 50 m landing craft, Liyan 110, was announced in 2008. While described as a commercial craft, the vessel has military applications. In addition, a number of other landing craft are reported to be under consideration.

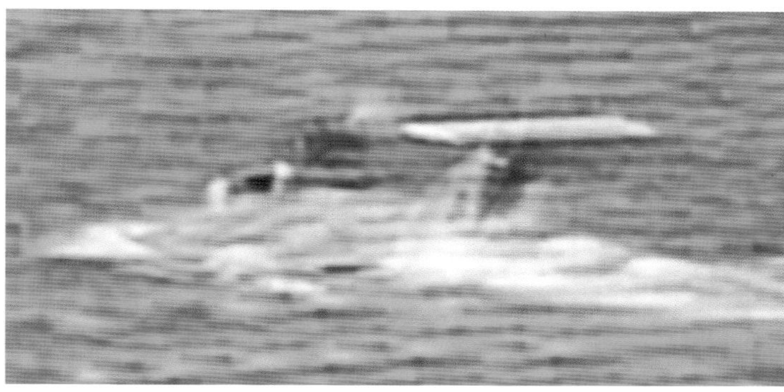

WIG *6/2004* / 1044357

4 HENGAM CLASS (LSLH)

Name	*No*	*Builders*	*Commissioned*
HENGAM	511	Yarrow (Shipbuilders) Ltd, Clyde	12 Aug 1974
LARAK	512	Yarrow (Shipbuilders) Ltd, Clyde	12 Nov 1974
TONB	513	Yarrow (Shipbuilders) Ltd, Clyde	21 Feb 1985
LAVAN	514	Yarrow (Shipbuilders) Ltd, Clyde	16 Jan 1985

Displacement, tons: 2,540 full load
Dimensions, feet (metres): 305 × 49 × 7.3 *(93 × 15 × 2.4)*
Main machinery: 4 Paxman 12YJCM diesels *(Hengam, Larak)*; 3,000 hp *(2.24 MW)* sustained; 2 shafts. 4 MTU 16V 652 TB81 diesels *(Tonb, Lavan)*; 4,600 hp(m) *(3.38 MW)* sustained; 2 shafts
Speed, knots: 14.5
Range, n miles: 4,000+ at 12 kt
Complement: 80
Military lift: Up to 9 tanks depending on size; 600 tons cargo; 227 troops; 10 ton crane

Guns: 4 Bofors 40 mm/60 *(Hengam* and *Larak)*. 8 USSR 23 mm/80 (4 twin) *(Tonb* and *Lavan)*. 2—12.7 mm MGs.
1 BM-21 multiple rocket launcher.
Countermeasures: Decoys: 2 UK Mk 5 rocket flare launchers.
Radars: Navigation: Racal Decca 1229; I-band.
IFF: SSR 1520 *(Hengam* and *Larak)*.
Tacan: URN 25.
Helicopters: Can embark 1 Sikorsky MH-53D.

Programmes: Named after islands in the Gulf. First two ordered 25 July 1972. Four more ordered 20 July 1977. The material for the last two ships of the second order had been ordered by Yarrows when the order was cancelled in early 1979. *Tonb* carried out trials in October 1984 followed by *Lavan* later in the year and both were released by the UK in 1985 as 'Hospital Ships'.
Structure: Smaller than British *Sir Lancelot* design with no through tank deck. Rocket launcher mounted in the bows.
Operational: Two LCVPs and a number of small landing craft can be carried. Can act as Depot Ships for MCMV and small craft and have been used to ferry Pasdaran small craft around the Gulf. The ships may also be used as training platforms for swimmer delivery vehicles.

TONB *6/2004* / 1044354

TONB *10/2004* / 1151273

3 IRAN HORMUZ 24 CLASS (LST)

FARSI 24 **SARDASHT** 25 **SAB SAHEL** 26

Displacement, tons: 2,014 full load
Dimensions, feet (metres): 239.8 × 46.6 × 8.2 *(73.1 × 14.2 × 2.5)*
Main machinery: 2 Daihatsu 6DLM-22 diesels; 2,400 hp(m) *(1.76 MW)*; 2 shafts
Speed, knots: 12
Complement: 30 plus 110 berths
Military lift: 9 tanks, 140 troops

Comment: Built at Inchon, South Korea in 1985–86 and as with the Iran Hormuz 21 class officially classed as Merchant Ships. Have been used to support Pasdaran activities.

IRAN HORMUZ 24 *5/1999* / 0080048

6 KARBALA (MIG-S-3700) CLASS (LSL)

FOUQUE 101 **HORMUZ** 505 – 507
QESHM 504 **FORUR** 506 – 508

Displacement, tons: 276 full load
Dimensions, feet (metres): 121.4 × 26.2 × 4.9 *(37 × 8 × 1.5)*
Main machinery: 2 MWM TBD 234 V8 diesels; 879 hp(m) *(646 kW)*; 2 shafts
Speed, knots: 10
Range, n miles: 400 at 10 kt
Complement: 8
Military lift: 140 tons of vehicles

Comment: *Fouque* assembled in Iran by Martyr Darvishi Marine, Bandar Abbas. Launched in June 1998. Others of the class are in commercial service and more can be taken over by the Navy if required. Two others for the Navy were launched in September 1995 and a further three have also been reported.

KARBALA CLASS *1994, Iranian Marine Industries* / 0080049

2 IRAN HORMUZ 21 CLASS (LST)

HEJAZ 21 **KARABALA** 22

Displacement, tons: 1,280 full load
Measurement, tons: 750 dwt
Dimensions, feet (metres): 213.3 × 39.4 × 8.5 *(65 × 12 × 2.6)*
Main machinery: 2 MAN V12V-12.5/14 or 2 MWM TBD 604 V12 diesels; 1,460 hp(m) *(1.07 MW)*; 2 shafts
Speed, knots: 9
Complement: 12
Military lift: 600 tons

Comment: Officially ordered for 'civilian use' and built by Ravenstein, Netherlands in 1984–85. Both are manned by the Pasdaran. A local version is assembled as the MIG-S-5000 for commercial use. One was launched in mid-1995 at Boushehr and a second in 1997.

6 WELLINGTON (BH.7) CLASS (HOVERCRAFT) (UCAC)

101–106

Displacement, tons: 53.8 full load
Dimensions, feet (metres): 78.3 × 45.6 × 5.6 (skirt) *(23.9 × 13.9 × 1.7)*
Main machinery: 1 RR Proteus 15 M/541 gas turbine; 4,250 hp *(3.17 MW)* sustained
Speed, knots: 70; 30 in Sea State 5 or more
Range, n miles: 620 at 66 kt
Guns: 2 Browning 12.7 mm MGs.
Radars: Surface search: Decca 1226; I-band.

Comment: First pair are British Hovercraft Corporation 7 Mk 4 commissioned in 1970–71 and the next four are Mk 5 craft commissioned in 1974–75. Mk 5 craft fitted for, but not with Standard missiles. Some refitted in UK in 1984. Can embark troops and vehicles or normal support cargoes. The Iranian Aircraft Manufacturing Industries (HESA) is reported to be able to maintain these craft in service.

WELLINGTON MK V *4/2006* / 1164678

1 IRAN CLASS (HOVERCRAFT) (UCAC)

Displacement, tons: 10 full load
Dimensions, feet (metres): 48.4 × 25.3 × 15.9 *(14.8 × 7.7 × 4.8)*
Main machinery: 1 gas turbine
Speed, knots: 60

Comment: The first of a new Iran class was completed in March 2000 and is probably based on the old SRN-6 class on which the approximate dimensions are based. Reports suggest a military lift of 2 tons and 26 troops.

IRAN CLASS *6/2004* / 1044355

AUXILIARIES

Notes: (1) There is also an inshore survey vessel *Abnegar*.
(2) Two 65 ton training vessels of Kialas-C-Qasem class are reported to have commissioned mid-2000. There may be further craft. No other details are known.

4 KANGAN CLASS (WATER TANKERS) (AWT)

KANGAN 411 **TAHERI** 412 **SHAHID MARJANI** **AMIR**

Displacement, tons: 12,000 full load
Measurement, tons: 9,430 dwt
Dimensions, feet (metres): 485.6 × 70.5 × 16.4 *(148 × 21.5 × 5)*
Main machinery: 1 MAN 7L52/55A diesel; 7,385 hp(m) *(5.43 MW)* sustained; 1 shaft
Speed, knots: 15
Complement: 14
Cargo capacity: 9,000 m^3 of water
Guns: 2 USSR 23 mm/80 (twin). 2 — 12.7 mm MGs.
Radars: Navigation: Decca 1229; I-band.

Comment: The first two were built in Mazagon Dock, Bombay in 1978 and 1979. The second pair to a slightly modified design was acquired in 1991–92 but may be civilian manned. Some of the largest water tankers afloat and can be used to supply remote coastal towns and islands. Accommodation is air conditioned. All have a 10 ton boom crane.

TAHERI *5/1989* / 0506013

12 HENDIJAN CLASS (TENDERS) (PBO)

HENDIJAN 1401
SIRIK 1402
KONARAK 1403
GAVATAR 1404
MOOAM 1405
BAHREGAN (ex-*Geno*) 1406
KALAT 1407
GENAVEH 1408
ROSTANI 1409
NAYBAND 1410
MACHAM
KORAMSHAHR

Displacement, tons: 460 full load
Dimensions, feet (metres): 166.7 × 28.1 × 11.5 *(50.8 × 8.6 × 3.5)*
Main machinery: 2 Mitsubishi S16MPTK diesels; 7,600 hp(m) *(5.15 MW)*; 2 shafts
Speed, knots: 25
Complement: 15 plus 90 passengers
Cargo capacity: 40 tons on deck; 95 m³ of liquid/solid cargo space
Guns: 1—20 mm (sometimes fitted in patrol craft). 2—12.7 mm MGs.
Radars: Navigation: Racal Decca or China RM 1070A; I-band.

Comment: First eight built by Damen, Netherlands 1988–91. Remainder built at Bandar Abbas under the MIG-S-4700 programme. Last pair launched on 25 November 1995. Reports of three more being built may be caused by confusion with new corvettes. Variously described in the Iranian press as 'frigates' or 'patrol ships', they are regularly used for coastal surveillance. One is used as a training ship. Pennant numbers in the 1400 series.

NAYBAND *6/2004* / 1044358

2 FLEET SUPPLY SHIPS (AORLH)

Name	*No*	*Builders*	*Commissioned*
BANDAR ABBAS	421	C Lühring Yard, Brake, West Germany	Apr 1974
BUSHEHR	422	C Lühring Yard, Brake, West Germany	Nov 1974

Displacement, tons: 4,673 full load
Measurement, tons: 3,250 dwt; 3,186 gross
Dimensions, feet (metres): 354.2 × 54.4 × 14.8 *(108 × 16.6 × 4.5)*
Main machinery: 2 MAN 6L 52/55 diesels; 12,060 hp(m) *(8.86 MW)* sustained; 2 shafts
Speed, knots: 20. **Range, n miles:** 3,500 at 16 kt
Complement: 59
Guns: 3 GAM-BO1 20 mm can be carried. 2—12.7 mm MGs.
Radars: Navigation: 2 Decca 1226; I-band.
Helicopters: 1 AB 212.

Comment: *Bandar Abbas* launched 11 August 1973, *Boushehr* launched 23 March 1974. Combined tankers and store-ships carrying victualling, armament and general stores. There are no RAS facilities. Telescopic hangar. Both carry 2 SA-7 portable SAM and 20 mm guns have replaced the former armament. *Bandar Abbas* damaged by an explosion in early 1999 but has been repaired.

BANDAR ABBAS *10/2004* / 1151276

1 SUPPORT VESSEL (AGG)

Name	*No*	*Builders*	*Commissioned*
HAMZAH (ex-*Shahsavar*)	802	NV Beele's Scheepwerven, Bolnes, Netherlands	1936

Displacement, tons: 530
Dimensions, feet (metres): 176 × 25.3 × 10.5 *(53.7 × 7.7 × 3.2)*
Main machinery: 2 diesels
Missiles: 4 China C-802; active radar homing to 120 km *(66 n miles)* at 0.9 Mach; warhead 165 kg; sea skimmer.
Guns: 1—20 mm. 1—12.7 mm MG.

Comment: Former Imperial Yacht converted for support duties in the Caspian Sea. Armed with C-802 missiles.

HAMZAH *12/2006* / 1167429

6 DELVAR CLASS (SUPPORT SHIPS) (AEL/AKL/AWT)

DAYLAM (AWT) 424
DELVAR (AEL) 471
SIRJAN (AEL) 472
CHARAK (AKL) 481
CHIROO (AKL) 482
SOROO (AKL) 483

Measurement, tons: 890 gross; 765 dwt
Dimensions, feet (metres): 210 × 34.4 × 10.9 *(64 × 10.5 × 3.3)*
Main machinery: 2 MAN G6V 23.5/33ATL diesels; 1,560 hp(m) *(1.15 MW)*; 2 shafts
Speed, knots: 11
Complement: 20
Guns: 1 GAM-BO1 20 mm. 2—2.7 mm MGs.
Radars: Navigation: Decca 1226; I-band.

Comment: All built by Karachi SY in 1980–82. *Delvar* and *Sirjan* are ammunition ships, *Dayer* and *Dilim* water carriers and the other three are general cargo ships. The water carriers have only one crane (against two on the other types), and have rounded sterns (as opposed to transoms). Re-armed.

DAYLAM *5/2003, A Sharma* / 0569202

CHARAK *10/1997* / 0012563

1 REPLENISHMENT SHIP (AORH)

Name	*No*	*Builders*	*Commissioned*
KHARG	431	Swan Hunter Ltd, Wallsend	5 Oct 1984

Displacement, tons: 11,064 light; 33,014 full load
Measurement, tons: 9,367 dwt; 18,582 gross
Dimensions, feet (metres): 679 × 86.9 × 30 *(207.2 × 26.5 × 9.2)*
Main machinery: 2 Babcock & Wilcox boilers; 2 Westinghouse turbines; 26,870 hp *(19.75 MW)*; 1 shaft
Speed, knots: 21.5
Complement: 248
Guns: 1 OTO Melara 76 mm/62 compact. 4 USSR 23 mm/80 (2 twin). 2—12.7 mm MGs.
Radars: Navigation: Decca 1229; I-band
Tacan: URN 20.
Helicopters: 3 Sea Kings (twin hangar).

Comment: Ordered October 1974. Laid down 27 January 1976. Launched 3 February 1977. Ship handed over to Iranian crew on 25 April 1980 but remained in UK. In 1983 Iranian Government requested this ship's transfer. The UK Government delayed approval until January 1984. On 10 July 1984 began refit at Tyne Ship Repairers. Trials began 4 September 1984 and ship was then delivered without guns which were subsequently fitted. A design incorporating some of the features of the British Ol class but carrying ammunition and dry stores in addition to fuel. Inmarsat fitted.

KHARG *5/1997* / 0052379

KHARG *6/1998* / 0052380

2 FLOATING DOCKS

400 (ex-US *ARD 29*, ex-*FD 4*) **DOLPHIN**

Dimensions, feet (metres): 487 × 80.2 × 32.5 *(149.9 × 24.7 × 10) (400)*
786.9 × 172.1 × 58.4 *(240 × 52.5 × 17.8) (Dolphin)*

Comment: *400* is an ex-US ARD 12 class built by Pacific Bridge, California and transferred in 1977; lift 3,556 tons. *Dolphin* built by MAN-GHH Nordenham, West Germany and completed in November 1985; lift 28,000 tons.

TUGS

17 HARBOUR TUGS (YTB/YTM)

HAAMOON	DEHLORAN	HARI-RUD
ALBAN	KHANDAG	ABAD
ASLAM	MENAB	HANGAM
DARYAVAND II	ATRAK	KARKHEH
HIRMAND	ILAM	ARAS
SEFID-RUD	ARVAND	

Comment: All between 70 and 90 ft in length, built since 1984.

Iraq

Country Overview

The Republic of Iraq was proclaimed in 1958 following a coup d'état. With an area of 168,754 square miles, it is situated in the Middle East and is bordered to the north by Turkey, to the east by Iran (with which it was at war 1980–88), to the west by Jordan and Syria and to the south by Saudi Arabia (with which it jointly administers the Neutral Zone) and Kuwait (which it invaded and occupied 1990–91 until expelled in the Gulf War 1991). It has a 31 n mile coastline with the Gulf. Baghdad is the capital and largest city. There are two ports on the Khawr Abd Allah Channel at Umm Qasr and Khawr al Zubayr. Territorial Seas (12 n miles) are claimed. An EEZ has not been claimed.

In the wake of the US-led occupation in March-April 2003, Iraq remained under coalition control until 30 June 2004 when full authority was handed over to an Iraqi Interim Government. Following elections on 30 January 2005, a new constitution was ratified by public referendum on 15 October 2005. This was followed by a general election on 15 December 2005 to elect a permanent Iraqi National Assembly. All naval coastal defence units, surface ships and aircraft were destroyed or disabled during the war and are unlikely to be resurrected. An oiler *(Agnadeen)* at Alexandria could be reclaimed but this is unlikely to be a high priority. The Iraqi Coastal Defence Force (ICDF), now known as the Iraqi Navy, was formally established at Umm Qasr on 30 September 2004. Key tasks include defence of the Khawr al Amaya (KAAOT) and Al Basra (ABOT) offshore oil terminals.

Headquarters Appointments

Commander Iraqi Navy:
Commodore Muhammed Jawad

Bases

Al Basra (Navy HQ), Khor Az Zubayr, Umm Qasr.

Personnel

2009: 1,166 (176 officers) (including 400 naval infantry)

PATROL FORCES

Notes: (1) The force structure is to be augmented by the procurement of two Offshore Support Vessels (OSVs) and 15 patrol craft (PB). The OSVs, to be built to the ISD Malaysia P 570 design, are to be capable of acting as mother-ships for the PBs operating in the vicinity of offshore oil platforms. The PBs to be built to the ISD P 340 design, are to be capable of remaining at sea for 48 h.
(2) Plans to re-activate the two Assad-class corvettes, under care and maintenance at La Spezia since 1990, have been cancelled and the ships are likely to be sold or scrapped.

5 PREDATOR CLASS (INSHORE PATROL CRAFT) (PB)

P 101–105

Displacement, tons: To be announced
Dimensions, feet (metres): 88.9 × 9.2 × 5.9 *(27.1 × 2.8 × 1.8)*
Main machinery: 2 MTU 12V 396 TE742; 4,025 hp *(3 MW)*
Speed, knots: 32
Complement: 6
Guns: 1 — 7.62 mm MG.

Comment: Built at Wuhan by Nanhua High-Speed Engineering Company and originally acquired in 2002. Maintained in dry-dock at Jebel Ali, UAE, until the first two were commissioned on 4 April 2004. Three further craft followed in May 2004. Acquisition and refit costs funded by the US. The craft were used initially for training of Iraqi personnel but are used increasingly for patrol duties as the navy develops. Based at Umm Qasr.

P 102 *5/2004, US Navy* / 0580527

P 104 *8/2008*, Shaun Jones* / 1335385

2 + 2 DICIOTTI CLASS (OFFSHORE PATROL VESSELS) (PBO)

Displacement, tons: 391
Dimensions, feet (metres): 175.2 × 26.6 × 6.6 *(53.4 × 8.1 × 2.0)*
Main machinery: 2 Isotto Fraschini V1716 T2 MSD diesels; 6,335 hp *(4.7 MW)*; 2 shafts
Speed, knots: 23. **Range, n miles:** 2,100 at 16 kt
Complement: 38 (4 officers)
Guns: 1 OTO Melara 30 mm. 2 — 12.7 mm MGs. 4 — 7.62 mm MGs.
Radars: Surface search: E/F-band.
Navigation: I-band.

Comment: Contract signed with Fincantieri, Muggiano in September 2006 for the construction of four vessels for delivery June 2009-March 2010. Two to be built at Riva Trigoso and two at Muggiano. The steel-hulled design is based on Diciotti (mod Saettia) class vessels in service with the Italian Coast Guard and is generally similar to the ship supplied to Malta in 2005 but with a stern ramp for launching an 11 m RIB. The contract included a training and logistic support package and some additional ex-Italian Coast Guard craft.

DICIOTTI CLASS (Maltese colours) *10/2005, Air Squadron, AFM* / 1133090

2 TYPE 200 (INSHORE PATROL CRAFT) (PBO)

– P 701 (ex-CP 247) – P 702 (ex-CP 250)

Displacement, tons: 22
Dimensions, feet (metres): 49.2 × 14.4 × 5.2 *(15.0 × 4.4 × 1.6)*
Main machinery: 2 Isotta Fraschini ID36-SS-6V diesels; 1,380 hp *(1.0 MW)*; 2 shafts
Speed, knots: 31
Range, n miles: 350 at 31 kt
Complement: 7
Radars: Navigation: I-band.

Comment: Former Italian Coast Guard craft built by Navaltechnica Anzio, 1977–81. Transferred to Iraq in 2006 as part of the contract to procure four Diciotti-class offshore patrol craft.

4 TYPE 2010 (INSHORE CRAFT) (PBR)

– P 203 (ex-CP 2036) – P 204 (ex-CP 2037) – P 205 (ex-CP 2067) – P 206 (ex-CP 2069)

Displacement, tons: 11
Dimensions, feet (metres): 41.0 × 11.8 × 4.3 *(12.5 × 3.6 × 1.3)*
Main machinery: 2 AIFO 8362SRM27 diesels; 550 hp *(398 kW)*; 2 shafts
Speed, knots: 25
Range, n miles: 600 at 12 kt
Complement: 4
Radars: Navigation: I-band.

Comment: Former Italian Coast Guard craft built 1973–85. GRP construction. Transferred to Iraq in 2006 as part of the contract to procure four Diciotti-class offshore patrol craft. Others of the class have been transferred to Albania.

26 DEFENDER CLASS (RESPONSE BOATS) (PBF)

Displacement, tons: 2.7 full load
Dimensions, feet (metres): 25.0 × 8.5 × 8.8 *(7.6 × 2.6 × 2.7)*
Main machinery: 2 Honda outboard motors; 450 hp *(335 kW)*
Speed, knots: 46
Range, n miles: 175 at 35 kt
Complement: 4
Guns: 1 — 12.7 mm MG.
Radars: To be announced.

Comment: High-speed inshore patrol craft of aluminium construction and foam collar built by SAFE Boats International, Port Orchard, Washington. Acquired from the US government and delivered by early 2009. The new patrol craft are to be used for patrol of the Khor Abd Allah waterway.

DEFENDER CLASS (USCG colours) *10/2003, Frank Findler* / 0572753

24 SEASPRAY ASSAULT BOATS (PB)

F 1–F 24

Displacement, tons: To be announced
Dimensions, feet (metres): 31.2 × 11.1 × 1.6 *(9.5 × 3.4 × 0.5)*
Main machinery: 2 Mercury outboards; 500 hp *(375 kW)*
Speed, knots: 50
Range, n miles: 450 at 17 kt
Complement: 5
Radars: Navigation: I-band.

Comment: 24 craft donated by the UAE government in 2005. Designed by Sea Spray Aluminium Boats.

ASSAULT BOAT *9/2008*, Jane's / Tim Fish* / 1294748

Ireland

AN SEIRBHIS CHABHLAIGH

Country Overview

The Republic of Ireland comprises about five sixths of the island of Ireland. Situated west of Great Britain, the country consists of the provinces of Leinster, Munster, Connaught and three counties of the province of Ulster. The remaining six counties of Ulster form Northern Ireland, a constituent part of the United Kingdom. With an area of 27,136 square miles, the country has a 783 n mile coastline with the Atlantic Ocean and Irish Sea. Dublin is the capital, largest city and principal port. There is another major port at Cork. Territorial waters (12 n miles) are claimed. A 200 n mile Fishery zone has also been claimed.

Headquarters Appointments

Flag Officer Commanding Naval Service:
Commodore F Lynch

Bases

Haulbowline Island, Cork Harbour-Naval HQ, Base and Dockyard

Personnel

(a) 2009: 1,144 (189 officers)
(b) Voluntary service
(c) Reserves: 400 (one unit in each of the following cities: Dublin, Waterford, Cork and Limerick)

Fishery Protection

In late 2004 and early 2005, all ships were fitted with the new Lirguard system. This system incorporates the previously separate functions of the database, GIS database display, Vessel Monitoring System (VMS) and legislation browser. This system will be updated several times daily by satellite link from the Fisheries Monitoring Centre (FMC) at Haulbowline. These will provide a near real-time display and analysis tool of fishing activity to allow more intelligent and efficient use of the ships in the Fishery Protection role. Research is also continuing into the incorporation of VMS data with data from Earth Observation (EO) technology.

Prefix to Ships' Names

LÉ (Long Éirennach = Irish Ship)

PATROL FORCES

Notes: The Naval Service Replacement Programme is for the replacement of all eight patrol ships by 2025. The P 21 class is the first to be replaced by 2012. A Request for Proposals (RfP) for one 130-140 m Extended Patrol Vessel (EPV) and two 80-90 m Offshore Patrol Vessels (OPV) was issued on 24 August 2007. The EPV is to have a flight deck and to be capable of carrying troops, vehicles and equipment while the OPVs are required for standard EEZ roles. The RfP contains an option for a second EPV and a third OPV; these may be considered as replacements for *Eithne* and/or for the Peacock class in about 2015. The Roisin class is expected to be replaced in about 2025. A contract for the first three vessels is expected in 2009 with a view to delivery by 2012.

1 EITHNE CLASS (PSOH)

Name	*No*	*Builders*	*Laid down*	*Launched*	*Commissioned*
EITHNE	P 31	Verolme, Cork	15 Dec 1982	19 Dec 1983	7 Dec 1984

Displacement, tons: 1,760 standard; 1,910 full load
Dimensions, feet (metres): 265 × 39.4 × 14.1 *(80.8 × 12 × 4.3)*
Main machinery: 2 Ruston 12RKC diesels; 6,800 hp *(5.07 MW)* sustained; 2 shafts; cp props
Speed, knots: 20+; 19 normal
Range, n miles: 7,000 at 15 kt
Complement: 73 (10 officers)

Guns: 1 Bofors 57 mm/70 Mk 1; 200 rds/min to 17 km *(9.3 n miles)*; weight of shell 2.4 kg.
2 Rheinmetall 20 mm/20. 2 — 7.62 mm MGs.
2 Wallop 57 mm launchers for illuminants.
Weapons control: Signaal LIOD director. 2 Signaal optical sights.
Radars: Air/surface search: Signaal DA05 Mk 4; E/F-band
Surface search: Kelvin Hughes; E/F-band
Navigation: 2 Kelvin Hughes; 6000A; I-band
Tacan: MEL RRB transponder

Helicopters: Not routinely carried.

Programmes: Ordered 23 April 1982 from Verolme, Cork, this was the last ship to be built at this yard.
Structure: Fitted with retractable stabilisers. Closed circuit TV for flight deck operations. Satellite navigation and communications. CTD tactical displays.
Operational: Helicopter no longer operational. Two Delta 7.5 m inboard diesel RIBs fitted in addition to two 5.4 m RIBs in 2003. Long refit (SLEP) in 1998/99.

EITHNE *8/2008*, Maritime Photographic* / 1335792

2 ROISIN CLASS (PSO)

Name	*No*	*Builders*	*Laid down*	*Launched*	*Commissioned*
ROISIN	P 51	Appledore Shipbuilders, Bideford	Dec 1998	12 Aug 1999	15 Dec 1999
NIAMH	P 52	Appledore Shipbuilders, Bideford	June 2000	10 Feb 2001	18 Sep 2001

Displacement, tons: 1,700 full load
Dimensions, feet (metres): 258.7 × 45.9 × 12.8 *(78.9 × 14 × 3.9)*
Main machinery: 2 Wärtsilä 16V26 diesels; 6,800 hp(m) *(5 MW)* sustained; 2 shafts; LIPS cp props; bow thruster; 462 hp(m) *(340 kW)*
Speed, knots: 23
Range, n miles: 6,000 at 15 kt
Complement: 44 (6 officers)
Guns: 1 OTO Melara 3 in *(76 mm)*/62; 85 rds/min to 16 km *(8.6 n miles)*; weight of shell 6 kg.
2—12.7 mm MGs. 4—7.62 mm MGs.
Weapons control: Radamec 1500 optronic director.
Radars: Surface search: Kelvin Hughes; E/F-band
Navigation: Kelvin Hughes; I-band.

Programmes: Contract for first ship signed on 16 December 1997 with 65 per cent of EU funding. Option on a second of class taken up on 6 April 2000.

NIAMH *9/2008*, B Prézelin* / 1335791

Operational: Designated Large Patrol Vessel, the design is a modification of the Mauritius ship *Vigilant* but without the hangar or flight deck. Two Delta 6.5 m and one Avon 5.4 m RIBs are carried. CTD tactical displays.

3 P 21 CLASS (OFFSHORE PATROL VESSELS) (PSO)

Name	*No*	*Builders*	*Launched*	*Commissioned*
EMER	P 21	Verolme, Cork	4 Aug 1977	16 Jan 1978
AOIFE	P 22	Verolme, Cork	12 Apr 1979	29 Nov 1979
AISLING	P 23	Verolme, Cork	3 Oct 1979	21 May 1980

Displacement, tons: 1,019.5
Dimensions, feet (metres): 213.7 × 34.4 × 14 *(65.2 × 10.5 × 4.4)*
Main machinery: 2 SEMT-Pielstick 6 PA6 L 280 diesels; 4,800 hp *(3.53 MW)*; 1 shaft; bow thruster *(Aoife* and *Aisling)*
Speed, knots: 17. **Range, n miles**: 4,000 at 17 kt; 6,750 at 12 kt
Complement: 47 (6 officers)

Guns: 1 Bofors 40 mm/L 70; 300 rds/min to 12 km *(6.5 n miles)*; weight of shell 0.88 kg.
2 GAM-B01 20 mm; 900 rds/min to 2 km.
2—12.7 mm MGs. 2—7.62 mm MGs.
Radars: Surface search: Kelvin Hughes I-band
Navigation: Kelvin Hughes Nucleus 6000A; I-band.

Modernisation: New search radars were fitted in 1994–95. CTD tactical display fitted.
Structure: Stabilisers fitted. *Aoife* and *Aisling* are equipped with a bow thruster. Inmarsat SATCOM fitted.
Operational: *Emer* refitted in 1995, *Aoife* in 1996/97 and *Aisling* in 1997/98. Sonars have been removed.

AISLING *6/2008*, Frank Findler* / 1335790

AISLING *6/2008*, Martin Mokrus* / 1335789

2 P 41 PEACOCK CLASS (COASTAL PATROL VESSELS) (PSO)

Name	*No*	*Builders*	*Commissioned*
ORLA (ex-*Swift*)	P 41	Hall Russell, Aberdeen	3 May 1985
CIARA (ex-*Swallow*)	P 42	Hall Russell, Aberdeen	17 Oct 1984

Displacement, tons: 712 full load
Dimensions, feet (metres): 204.1 × 32.8 × 8.9 *(62.6 × 10 × 2.7)*
Main machinery: 2 Crossley SEMT-Pielstick 18 PA6 V 280 diesels; 14,400 hp(m) *(10.58 MW)* sustained; 2 shafts; auxiliary drive; Schottel prop; 181 hp(m) *(133 kW)*
Speed, knots: 25. **Range, n miles**: 2,500 at 17 kt
Complement: 39 (5 officers)

Guns: 1—3 in (76 mm)/62 OTO Melara compact; 85 rds/min to 16 km *(8.6 n miles)*; weight of shell 6 kg.
2—12.7 mm MGs. 4—7.62 mm MGs.
Weapons control: Radamec 1500 optronic director (for 76 mm).
Radars: Surface search: Kelvin Hughes; I-band
Navigation: Kelvin Hughes Nucleus 5000A /6000A; I-band.

Programmes: *Orla* launched 11 September 1984 and *Ciara* 31 March 1984. Both served in Hong Kong from mid-1985 until early 1988. Acquired from UK and commissioned 21 November 1988. Others of the class acquired by the Philippines in 1997.
Modernisation: New radars fitted in 1993. CTD tactical display fitted.
Structure: Have loiter drive. Displacement increased after building by the addition of more electronic equipment.

CIARA *6/2005, D Jones, Irish Navy* / 1133505

LAND-BASED MARITIME AIRCRAFT

Notes: Five civilian operated Sikorsky S-61 helicopters provide long-range SAR services. They are based at Dublin, Shannon, Waterford and Sligo.

Numbers/Type: 2 Casa CN-235 MP Persuader.
Operational speed: 210 kt *(384 km/h)*.
Service ceiling: 24,000 ft *(7,315 m)*.
Range: 2,000 n miles *(3,218 km)*.
Role/Weapon systems: EEZ surveillance. First one delivered in June 1992 but returned to Spain in 1995. Two more delivered in December 1994. Sensors: Search radar Bendix APS 504(V)5; FLIR. Weapons: Unarmed.

CN-235 MP *7/2003, Paul Jackson* / 0568896

AUXILIARIES

Notes: (1) In addition there are a number of mostly civilian manned auxiliaries including: *Seabhac* a small tug acquired in 1983; *Fainleog, David F* (built in 1962) and *Fiach Dubh* passenger craft, the last two taken over after lease in 1988 and the first in 1983; *Tailte* a Dufour 35 ft sail training yacht bought in 1979 and an elderly training yacht *Creidne*.
(2) *Granuaile* is an 80 m lighthouse tender with a helicopter flight deck forward operated by the Commissioners of Irish Lights. Launched on 14 August 1999 this ship replaced a previous vessel of the same name on 23 March 2000.

GRANUAILE *3/2000, Commissioners of Irish Lights* / 0093593

Israel

HEYL HAYAM

Country Overview

Established in 1948, The State of Israel is situated on the eastern shore of the Mediterranean Sea and has borders to the north with Lebanon, to the north-east with Syria, to the east with Jordan and to the south-west with Egypt. It has coastlines with the Mediterranean (142 n miles) and with the Gulf of Aqaba (5 n miles) in the northern Red Sea. A land area of 8,463 square miles includes East Jerusalem and other territory (including Gaza Strip, the West Bank region of Jordan, the Golan Heights area of south-western Syria) annexed in 1967. Jerusalem is the largest city but, although claimed as the capital, is not so recognised by the United Nations. Many nations maintain embassies at Tel Aviv. Haifa is the principal port. Territorial seas (12 n miles) are claimed but an EEZ is not claimed.

Headquarters Appointments

Commander-in-Chief:
Vice Admiral Eli Marom
Chief of Naval Staff:
Rear Admiral Noam Feig
Head of Naval Operations Command:
Rear Admiral Yochay Ben Yosef

General

Less than 5 per cent of Israeli defence budget is allocated to the Navy.

Personnel

2009:
(a) 9,500 (880 officers) of whom 2,500 are conscripts. Includes a Naval Commando of 300
(b) 3 years' national service for Jews and Druzes

Notes: An additional 5,000 Reserves available on mobilisation.

Bases

Haifa, Ashdod, Eilat
(The repair base at Eilat has a synchrolift)

Coast Defence

There are ten integrated coastal radar and electro-optical surveillance stations. These are to be converted to an unmanned, remote-controlled system employing a wideband communications network.

Prefix to Ships' Names

INS (Israeli Naval Ship)

SUBMARINES

3 + 2 DOLPHIN (TYPE 800) CLASS (SSK)

Name	*No*	*Builders*	*Laid down*	*Launched*	*Commissioned*
DOLPHIN	–	Howaldtswerke/Thyssen Nordseewerke	7 Oct 1994	12 Apr 1996	27 July 1999
LEVIATHAN	–	Howaldtswerke/Thyssen Nordseewerke	13 Apr 1995	25 Apr 1997	15 Nov 1999
TEKUMA	–	Howaldtswerke/Thyssen Nordseewerke	12 Dec 1996	26 June 1998	25 July 2000
–	–	Thyssenkrupp Marine Systems	2007	2009	2012
–	–	Thyssenkrupp Marine Systems	2008	2010	2013

Displacement, tons: 1,640 surfaced; 1,900 dived
Dimensions, feet (metres): 188 × 22.3 × 20.3 *(57.3 × 6.8 × 6.2)*
Main machinery: 3 MTU 16V 396 SE 84 diesels; 4,243 hp(m) *(3.12 MW)* sustained; 3 alternators; 2.91 MW; 1 Siemens motor; 3,875 hp(m) *(2.85 MW)* sustained; 1 shaft
Speed, knots: 20 dived; 11 snorting
Range, n miles: 8,000 at 8 kt surfaced; 420 at 8 kt dived
Complement: 30 (6 officers)

Missiles: SSM: Sub Harpoon; UGM-84C; active radar or GPS homing to 130 km *(70 n miles)* at 0.9 Mach; warhead 227 kg.
SAM: Fitted for Triten anti-helicopter system.
Torpedoes: 4—25.6 in *(650 mm)* and 6—21 in *(533 mm)* bow tubes. STN Atlas DM2A4 Seehecht; wire-guided active homing to 13 km *(7 n miles)* at 35 kt; passive homing to 28 km *(15 n miles)* at 23 kt; warhead 260 kg. Total of 16 torpedoes and 5 SSMs. The four 650 mm tubes may be for SDVs, but could carry torpedoes if liners are fitted.
Mines: In lieu of torpedoes.
Countermeasures: ESM: Elbit Timnex 4CH(V)2; intercept.
Weapons control: STN/Atlas Elektronik ISUS 90-1 TCS.
Radars: Surface search: Elta; I-band.
Sonars: Atlas Elektronik CSU 90; hull-mounted; passive/active search and attack.
Atlas Elektronik PRS-3; passive ranging.
FAS-3; flank array; passive search.

DOLPHIN *6/1999, Michael Nitz* / 0080058

Programmes: In mid-1988 Ingalls Shipbuilding Division of Litton Corporation was chosen as the prime contractor for two IKL-designed Dolphin class submarines to be built in West Germany with FMS funds by HDW in conjunction with Thyssen Nordseewerke. Funds approved in July 1989 with an effective contract date of January 1990 but the project was cancelled in November 1990 due to pressures on defence funds. After the Gulf War in April 1991 the contract was resurrected, this time with German funding for two submarines with an option on a third taken up in July 1994. A contract for the construction of two further modified Dolphin class submarines was signed on 6 July 2006. The new submarines are to be about 10 m longer in order to incorporate air-independent propulsion. The boats are to be built at HDW and TNSW. Israel is to fund two thirds of the budget while the German government is to fund the remaining third. Construction of the first boat is reported to have started in 2007 to meet a delivery date of 2012 but the construction timetable is speculative.
Modernisation: Installation of air-independent propulsion in the first three boats is under consideration.
Structure: Diving depth, 350 m *(1,150 ft)*. Similar to German Type 212 in design but with a 'wet and dry' compartment for underwater swimmers. Two Kollmorgen periscopes. Probably fitted for Triten anti-helicopter SAM system.
Operational: Endurance, 30 days. Used for interdiction, surveillance and special boat operations. Development of a submarine-launched cruise missile would complete the final part of a triad of nuclear deterrents. However, while Israel probably has the expertise and technology to deploy SLCM, little information exists to confirm or deny such a programme. Adaptation of the indigenous Delilah and Popeye groups of missles is a possible option although encapsulation of the missile would pose a significant challenge. Painted blue/green to aid concealment in the eastern Mediterranean. Some other NT 37E torpedoes are embarked until full Seehecht outfits are available. The boats form Flotilla 7 based at Haifa.

LEVIATHAN *4/2006, M Declerck* / 1158549

CORVETTES

Notes: A Request for Information was issued in September 2003 for the acquisition of up to three multimission corvettes. This programme was temporarily superseded in 2004 by a proposal to procure a 13,000 ton amphibious ship, but re-emerged as the priority due to budget realities. Plans for a SAAR 5+ design have been overtaken by ambitions to join the US Navy's Littoral Combat Ship (LCS) programme. A two-year feasibility study to establish whether the LCS seaframe could serve as a basis for future Israeli surface combatants was launched in December 2005. This was followed by a Combat System Configuration phase which was launched in September 2007. This is to examine the compatability of Israeli-made combat systems with the LCS platform. The main focus is the requirement for a multifunction radar to integrate with the combat management system in addition to SM-2 or Barak 8 area missiles and Barak point defence system.

3 EILAT (SAAR 5) CLASS (FSGHM)

Name	*No*	*Builders*	*Laid down*	*Launched*	*Commissioned*
EILAT	501	Ingalls, Pascagoula	24 Feb 1992	9 Feb 1993	24 May 1994
LAHAV	502	Ingalls, Pascagoula	25 Sep 1992	20 Aug 1993	23 Sep 1994
HANIT	503	Ingalls, Pascagoula	5 Apr 1993	4 Mar 1994	7 Feb 1995

Displacement, tons: 1,075 standard; 1,295 full load
Dimensions, feet (metres): 278.9 × 39.0 × 10.5 *(85.0 × 11.9 × 3.2)*
Main machinery: CODOG; 1 GE LM 2500 gas turbine; 30,000 hp *(22.38 MW)* sustained; 2 MTU 12V 1163 TB82 diesels; 6,600 hp(m) *(4.86 MW)* sustained; 2 shafts; Kamewa cp props
Speed, knots: 33 gas; 20 diesels
Range, n miles: 3,500 at 17 kt
Complement: 64 (16 officers) plus 10 (4 officers) aircrew

Missiles: SSM: 8 McDonnell Douglas Harpoon (2 quad) launchers ❶; active radar homing to 130 km *(70 n miles)* at 0.9 Mach; warhead 227 kg.
SAM: 2 Israeli Industries Barak I (vertical launch) ❷; 2 × 32 cells; command line of sight radar or optical guidance to 10 km *(5.5 n miles)* at 2 Mach; warhead 22 kg (see *Operational*).
Guns: OTO Melara 3 in *(76 mm)*/62 compact ❸; 85 rds/min to 16 km *(8.7 n miles)*; weight of shell 6 kg.
The main gun is interchangeable with a Bofors 57 mm gun or Vulcan Phalanx CIWS ❹.
2 Sea Vulcan 20 mm CIWS ❺; range 1 km.
Torpedoes: 6–324 mm Mk 32 (2 triple) tubes ❻. Honeywell Mk 46; anti-submarine; active/passive homing to 11 km *(5.9 n miles)* at 40 kt; warhead 44 kg. Mounted in the superstructure.
Countermeasures: Decoys: 3 Elbit/Deseaver 72-barrelled chaff and IR launchers ❼; Rafael ATC-1 towed torpedo decoy.
ESM: Elisra NS 9003; intercept. Tadiran NATACS.
ECM: 2 Rafael 1010; Elisra NS 9005; jammers.
Combat data systems: Elbit NTCCS using Elta EL/S-9000 computers. Reshet datalink.
Weapons control: 2 Elop MSIS optronic directors ❽.
Radars: Air search: Elta EL/M-2218S ❾; E/F-band.

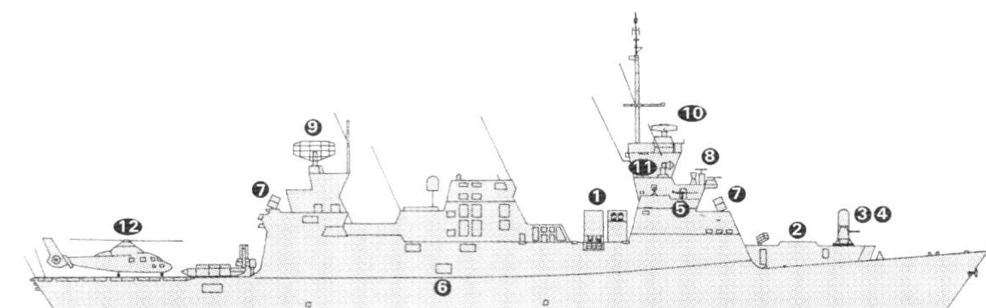

EILAT *(Scale 1 : 900), Ian Sturton* / 1151070

Surface search: Cardion SPS-55 ❿; I-band.
Navigation: I-band.
Fire control: 3 Elta EL/M-2221 GM STGR ⓫; I/K/J-band.
Sonars: EDO Type 796 Mod 1; hull-mounted; search and attack; medium frequency.
Rafael towed array (fitted for).

Helicopters: 1 Dauphin SA 366G ⓬ or Sea Panther can be carried.

Programmes: A design by John J McMullen Associates Inc for Israeli Shipyards, Haifa in conjunction with Ingalls Shipbuilding Division of Litton Corporation which was authorised to act as main contractor using FMS funding. Contract awarded 8 February 1989. All delivered to Israel for combat system installation, first two completed in 1996 and last one in mid-1997. Major refitsof these ships are reported to be under consideration. The option for a fourth SAAR 5 was not taken up and plans to procure a further five new ships (SAAR 5+) under similar FMS funding are now unlikely to be taken forward in view of the requirement for multimission ships.
Structure: Steel hull and aluminium superstructure. Stealth features including resilient mounts for main machinery, funnel exhaust cooling, Radar Absorbent Material (RAM), NBC washdown and Prairie Masker Bubbler system. A secondary operations room is fitted aft. There are some Flag capabilities. Plans to carry Gabriel SSMs have been scrapped because of topweight problems. The planned third MSIS director has not yet been seen on the platform aft of the air search radar.
Operational: Endurance, 20 days. The main role is to counter threats in shipping routes. ICS-2 integrated communications system. The position of the satellite aerial suggests that the SAM after VLS launchers are not used. Barak has still to be installed, because of lack of funds. For the same reason the normal Harpoon load may be reduced to four. *Hanit* damaged by missile attack off Lebanon on 14 July 2006. Repairs were completed on 6 August 2006. All three ships allocated to Flotilla 3.

EILAT *4/2006, M Declerck* / 1158548

HANIT *12/2001, M Declerck* / 0533267

SHIPBORNE AIRCRAFT

Numbers/Type: 7 Eurocopter AS 565SA Sea Panther.
Operational speed: 165 kt *(305 km/h).*
Service ceiling: 16,700 ft *(5,100 m).*
Range: 483 n miles *(895 km).*
Role/Weapon systems: Built by American Eurocopter in Texas. Three delivered by October 1998 with one more in 1999. Roles include reconnaissance, targetting and SAR. Sensors: Telephonics search radar; Elop MSIS for OTHT. Weapons: Unarmed.

AS 565SB *6/2002, Adolfo Ortigueira Gil* / 0567461

LAND-BASED MARITIME AIRCRAFT

Notes: (1) Army helicopters can be used including Cobras and Apaches.
(2) Two C-130 aircraft used for maritime surveillance. There are also two EC-130 Elint aircraft.

Numbers/Type: 3 IAI 1124N Sea Scan.
Operational speed: 471 kt *(873 km/h).*
Service ceiling: 45,000 ft *(13,725 m).*
Range: 2,500 n miles *(4,633 km).*
Role/Weapon systems: Acquired in 1977. Air Force manned. Coastal surveillance tasks with long endurance; used for intelligence gathering. Sensors: Elta EL/M-2022 radar, IFF, MAD, Sonobuoys, and various EW systems of IAI manufacture.

SEA SCAN *6/1994, R A Cooper* / 0503199

PATROL FORCES

Notes: (1) There are about 12 'Firefish' type fast attack boats in service with Special Forces.
(2) A 50 ft *(15.2 m)* shallow draft Stealth craft was built in a Vancouver Shipyard and delivered in late 1998. A second, an Alligator craft, was completed by Oregon Iron Works, Portland in 1999 andpainted dark green. Two diesels giving 35 kt and a Rafael optronic surveillance system are included. Crew of five.

8 + 2 SUPER DVORA MK III CLASS (PTFM)

830–835 +1

Displacement, tons: 72 full load
Dimensions, feet (metres): 89.9 × 18.7 × 3.6 *(27.4 × 5.7 × 1.1)*
Main machinery: 2 MTU 12V 4000 diesels; 2 Arneson ASD16 surface drives (830-835); 2 Rolls Royce Kamewa 63SII waterjets (batch 2)
Speed, knots: 45
Range, n miles: 1,000 at cruising speed
Complement: 5
Guns: 1 Bushmaster 25 mm M242 chain gun. 1—20 mm. 2—7.62 mm MGs.
Weapons control: ELOP optronic director.
Radars: Surface search: I-band.

Comment: An order for six craft was made with IAI-Ramta on 13 January 2002. The first was delivered in July 2004 and entered service in November 2004. The second and third were delivered on 13 July 2005 and a further three on 18 September 2006. An option for another four craft was exercised in 2005. The first of these was delivered in November 2007 and the remainder are to enter service by late 2009.

SUPER DVORA III *4/2006, IAI RAMTA* / 1130539

8 HETZ (SAAR 4.5) CLASS
(FAST ATTACK CRAFT—MISSILE) (PGGM)

Name	*Builders*	*Launched*	*Commissioned*
ROMAT	Israel Shipyards, Haifa	30 Oct 1981	Oct 1981
KESHET	Israel Shipyards, Haifa	Oct 1982	Nov 1982
HETZ (ex-*Nirit*)	Israel Shipyards, Haifa	Oct 1990	Feb 1991
KIDON	Israel Shipyards, Haifa	1993	7 Feb 1994
TARSHISH	Israel Shipyards, Haifa	1995	June 1995
YAFFO	Israel Shipyards, Haifa	1998	1 July 1998
HEREV	Israel Shipyards, Haifa	2002	June 2002
SUFA	Israel Shipyards, Haifa	2002	Aug 2002

Displacement, tons: 488 full load
Dimensions, feet (metres): 202.4; 190.3 (*Romat, Keshet, Hetz*) × 24.9 × 8.2 *(58.0; 61.7 × 7.6 × 2.5)*
Main machinery: 4 MTU 16V 538TB93 or 4 MTU 16V 396TE diesels; 16,600 hp(m) *(12.2 MW)*; 4 shafts
Speed, knots: 31. **Range, n miles:** 3,000 at 17 kt; 1,500 at 30 kt
Complement: 53

Missiles: SSM: 4 McDonnell Douglas Harpoon ❶; active radar homing to 130 km *(70 n miles)* at 0.9 Mach; warhead 227 kg.
6 IAI Gabriel II (removed from some ships) ❷; radar or optical guidance; semi-active radar plus anti-radiation homing to 36 km *(19.4 n miles)* at 0.7 Mach; warhead 75 kg.
SAM: Israeli Industries Barak I (vertical launch) ❸; 32 or 16 cells in 2- or 4-8 pack launchers; command line of sight radar or optical guidance to 10 km *(5.5 n miles)* at 2 Mach; warhead 22 kg. Most fitted for but not with.
Guns: 1 OTO Melara 3 in *(76 mm)*/62 ❹; 85 rds/min to 16 km *(8.7 n miles)*; weight of shell 6 kg.
2 Oerlikon 20 mm; 800 rds/min to 2 km.
1 Rafael Typhoon 25 mm *(Herev).*
1 General Electric/General Dynamics Vulcan Phalanx 6-barrelled 20 mm Mk 15 ❺; 3,000 rds/min combined to 1.5 km anti-missile.
2 or 4—12.7 mm (twin or quad) MGs.
Countermeasures: Decoys: Elbit/Deseaver 72-barrelled launchers for chaff and IR flares ❻.
ESM/ECM: Elisra NS 9003/5; intercept and jammer.
Combat data systems: IAI Reshet datalink.
Weapons control: Galileo OG 20 optical director; Elop MSIS optronic director ❼.
Radars: Air/surface search: Thomson-CSF TH-D 1040 Neptune ❽; G-band.
Fire control: 2 Elta EL/M-2221 GM STGR ❾; I/K/J-band.

Programmes: *Hetz* started construction in 1984 as the fifth of the SAAR 4 class but was not completed, as an economy measure. Taken in hand again in 1989 and fitted out as the trials ship for some of the systems installed in the Eilat class.
Modernisation: *Romat* and *Keshet* were modernised to same standard as *Hetz* in what was called the Nirit programme. The remaining craft were new build and some of these have been given names previously allocated to decommissioned/transferred SAAR 4s.
Structure: The CIWS is mounted in the eyes of the ship replacing the 40 mm gun. The eight pack Barak launchers are fully containerised and require no deck penetration or onboard maintenance. They are fitted aft in place of two of the Gabriel launchers where these are still fitted. The fire-control system for Barak is fitted on the platform aft of the bridge on the port side. Davit scan be installed aft of the Gabriel missiles for special forces boats.

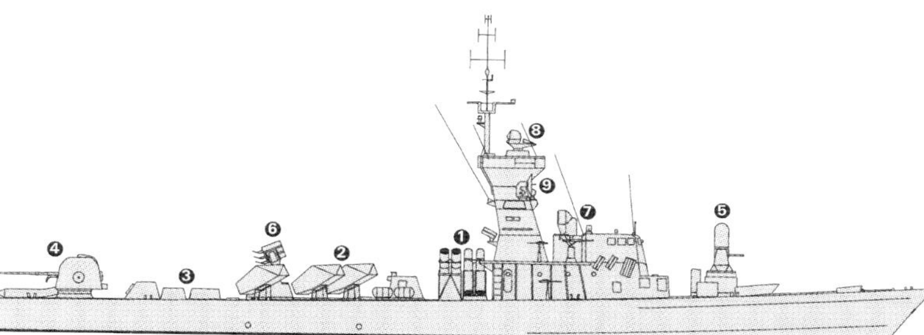

HETZ *(Scale 1 : 600), Ian Sturton* / 0126347

HEREV *4/2006, M Declerck* / 1158547

KESHET *4/2006, M Declerck* / 1158546

15 DABUR CLASS (COASTAL PATROL CRAFT) (PC)

850	**853**	**864**	**868**	**902**	**906**	**910**
851	**860–862**	**865**	**873**	**905**	**909**	

Displacement, tons: 39 full load
Dimensions, feet (metres): 64.9 × 18 × 5.8 *(19.8 × 5.5 × 1.8)*
Main machinery: 2 GM 12V-71TA diesels; 840 hp *(627 kW)* sustained; 2 shafts
About 8 have more powerful GE engines.
Speed, knots: 19; 30 (GE engines). **Range, n miles:** 450 at 13 kt
Complement: 6/9 depending on armament

Guns: 2 Oerlikon 20 mm; 800 rds/min to 2 km.
2—12.7 mm MGs. Carl Gustav 84 mm portable rocket launchers.
Torpedoes: 2—324 mm tubes. Honeywell Mk 46; anti-submarine; active/passive homing to 11 km *(5.9 n miles)* at 40 kt; warhead 44 kg.
Depth charges: 2 racks in some.
Weapons control: Elop optronic director.
Radars: Surface search: Decca Super 101 Mk 3 or HDWS; I-band.
Sonars: Active search and attack; high frequency.

Programmes: Twelve built by Sewart Seacraft USA and remainder by Israel Aircraft Industries (RAMTA) between 1973 and 1977. Final total of 34. Likely to be phased out as new fast attack craft enter service.
Structure: Aluminium hull. Several variations in the armament. Up to eight of the class are fitted with more powerful General Electric engines to increase speed to 30 kt.
Operational: These craft have been designed for overland transport. Good rough weather performance. Portable rocket launchers are carried for anti-terrorist purposes. Not considered fast enough to cope with modern terrorist speedboats and some have been sold as Super Dvoras commissioned. Two based at Eilat, remainder at Ashdod. Incourse of replacement by the Super Dvora III as they enter service and operational numbers are uncertain.
Sales: Four to Argentina in 1978; four to Nicaragua in 1978 and three more in 1996; six to Chile in 1991 and four more in 1995. Five also given to Lebanon Christian Militia in 1976 but these were returned.

DABUR *12/1998* / 0075862

2 RESHEF (SAAR 4) CLASS
(FAST ATTACK CRAFT—MISSILE) (PTG)

Name	*Builders*	*Launched*	*Commissioned*
NITZHON	Israel Shipyards, Haifa	10 July 1978	Sep 1978
ATSMOUT	Israel Shipyards, Haifa	3 Dec 1978	Feb 1979

Displacement, tons: 415 standard; 450 full load
Dimensions, feet (metres): 190.6 × 25 × 8 *(58 × 7.8 × 2.4)*
Main machinery: 4 MTU/Bazán 16V 956TB91 diesels; 15,000 hp(m) *(11.03 MW)* sustained; 4 shafts
Speed, knots: 32. **Range, n miles:** 1,650 at 30 kt; 4,000 at 17.5 kt
Complement: 45

Missiles: SSM: 2-4 McDonnell Douglas Harpoon (twin or quad) launchers; active radar homing to 130 km *(70 n miles)* at 0.9 Mach; warhead 227 kg.
4-6 Gabriel II; radar or TV optical guidance; semi-active radar plus anti-radiation homing to 36 km *(20 n miles)* at 0.7 Mach; warhead 75 kg.
Harpoons fitted with Israeli homing systems. The Gabriel II system carries a TV camera which can transmit a homing picture to the firing ship beyond the radar horizon. The missile fit currently varies in training boats-2 Harpoon, 5 Gabriel II.
Guns: 2 Oerlikon 20 mm; 800 rds/min to 2 km.
1 General Electric/General Dynamics Vulcan Phalanx 6-barrelled 20 mm Mk 15; 3,000 rds/min combined to 1.5 km anti-missile.
2—12.7 mm MGs.
Torpedoes: 6—324 mm (2 triple) tubes.
Countermeasures: Decoys: 1-45-tube, 4- or 6-24-tube, 4 single-tube chaff launchers.
ESM/ECM: Elisra NS 9003/5; intercept and jammer.
Combat data systems: IAI Reshet datalink.
Radars: Air/surface search: Thomson-CSF TH-D 1040 Neptune; G-band; range 33 km *(18 n miles)* for 2 m^2 target.
Fire control: Selenia Orion RTN 10X; I/J-band.
Sonars: EDO 780; VDS; fitted in both ships.

Modernisation: Some of the class modernised to Nirit standards and transferred to the Saar 4.5 class. Gabriel III SSM did not go into production.
Sales: Nine built for South Africa in Haifa and Durban. One transferred to Chile late 1979, one in February 1981, and two more in June 1997. Two transferred to Sri Lanka in 2000.

NITZHON *4/2006, M Declerck* / 1158544

ATSMOUT *4/2006, M Declerck* / 1158545

13 SUPER DVORA MK I AND MK II CLASSES
(FAST ATTACK CRAFT—GUN) (PTFM)

811–819 (Mk I) **820–823 (Mk II)**

Displacement, tons: 54 full load
Dimensions, feet (metres): 71 × 18 × 5.9 screws *(21.6 × 5.5 × 1.8)* (Mk I)
82 × 18.4 × 3.6 *(25 × 5.6 × 1.1)* (Mk II)
Main machinery: 2 Detroit 16V-92TA diesels; 1,380 hp *(1.03 MW)* sustained; 2 shafts (Mk I)
2 MTU 12V 396TE94 diesels; 4,175 hp(m) *(3.07 MW)* sustained; 2 ASD 16 drives (Mk II)
Speed, knots: 36 or 46 (Mk II)
Range, n miles: 1,200 at 17 kt
Complement: 10 (1 officer)

Missiles: SSM Hellfire; range 8 km *(4.3 n miles)*; can be carried.
Guns: 2 Oerlikon 20 mm/80 or 1 Bushmaster 25 mm/87 Mk 96 or 3 Typhoon 12.7 mm (triple) MGs.
2—12.7 or 7.62 mm MGs. 1—84 mm rocket launcher.
Depth charges: 2 racks.
Weapons control: Elop MSIS optronic director.
Radars: Surface search: Raytheon; I-band.

Programmes: An improvement on the Dabur design ordered in March 1987 from Israel Aircraft Industries (RAMTA). First started trials in November 1988, and first two commissioned in June 1989. First 10 are Mk I. From 820 onwards the ships are fitted with more powerful engines for a higher top speed and surface drives which greatly reduce maximum draft. First Mk II commissioned in 1993.
Structure: All gun armament and improved speed and endurance compared with the prototype Dvora. SSM, depth charges, torpedoes or a 130 mm MRL can be fitted if required.
Operational: Two (Mk II) are based at Eilat, the remainder at Haifa. The 25 mm or 12.7 mm Gatling guns can be operated by joystick control from the bridge. Hellfire SSM is sometimes carried.
Sales: Six Mk I sold to Sri Lanka in 1988 and four to Eritrea in 1993. One Mk II to Sri Lanka in 1995 and three more in 1996. One to Slovenia in 1996 and a second in 1997. Two to India in 1997, with more building under licence in India.

SUPER DVORA II 821 *4/2006, M Declerck* / 1158543

SUPER DVORA I 819 *4/2006, M Declerck* / 1158542

SUPER DVORA I 817 *4/2006, M Declerck* / 1158541

3 + 2 SHALDAG CLASS (FAST ATTACK CRAFT—GUN) (PBF)

840 **841** **+1**

Displacement, tons: 58 full load
Dimensions, feet (metres): 81.4 × 19.7 × 3.9 *(24.8 × 6 × 1.2)*
Main machinery: 2 Deutz 620 TB 16V or MTU 396 TE diesels; 5,000 hp(m) *(3.68 MW)*; 2 LIPS or MJP water-jets
Speed, knots: 50
Range, n miles: 700 at 32 kt
Complement: 10
Guns: 1 Rafael Typhoon 25 mm. 1—20 mm.
Weapons control: ELOP compass optronic director. Typhoon GFCS.
Radars: Surface search: MD 3220 Mk II; I-band.

Comment: Order in January 2002 for two craft, with option for two further hulls, made from Israel Shipyards, Haifa. Details reflect those in Sri Lankan service and are thus speculative. Both delivered in late 2003. An option for a further three craft was exercised in 2005. The first of these was delivered in early 2008 and the other two are to enter service by late 2009.

SHALDAG CLASS *8/2005, Jane's* / 0589534

3 STINGRAY INTERCEPTOR CLASS (PBF)

Displacement, tons: 10.5 full load
Dimensions, feet (metres): 39.4 × 14.5 × 2.9 *(12 × 4.4 × 0.9)*
Main machinery: 2 Caterpillar marine diesels; 2 shafts
Speed, knots: 35
Range, n miles: 300 at cruising speed
Complement: 5
Radars: Surface search: I-band.

Comment: Catamaran design of GRP construction built by Stingray Marine of Durbanville, Western Cape and delivered in 1997 and 1998. Based at Eilat.

STINGRAY INTERCEPTOR *2000, Stingray Marine* / 0104866

8 TZIRA (DEFENDER) CLASS (RESPONSE BOATS) (PBF)

Displacement, tons: 2.7 full load
Dimensions, feet (metres): 27.0; 31.0 (Batch 2) × 8.5 × 8.8 *(8.2; 9.5 × 2.6 × 2.7)*
Main machinery: 2 Honda outboard motors; 450 hp *(335 kW)*
Speed, knots: 46
Range, n miles: 175 at 35 kt
Complement: 4
Guns: 1—12.7 mm MG.
Radars: To be announced.

Comment: High-speed inshore patrol craft of aluminium construction and foam collar built by SAFE Boats International, Port Orchard, Washington. Four delivered in September 2005. To be operated by the port-protection unit on border protection and counter-terrorism operations. The craft are two feet longer than those operated by the USCG. A further four Batch 2 craft, built to a lengthened 9.5 m design, were ordered on 9 March 2006.

TZIRA CLASS *4/2006, Richard Scott/NAVYPIX* / 1130534

1 RAFAEL PROTECTOR (UNMANNED SURFACE VEHICLE) (USV)

Displacement, tons: To be announced
Dimensions, feet (metres): 29.5 × ? × ? (9.0 × ? × ?)
Main machinery: 1 diesel; 1 waterjet propulsor
Speed, knots: 30+
Guns: 1 Mini-Typhoon stabilised 12.7 mm MG.
Weapons control: Toplite EO sensor pod.

Comment: Developed jointly by Rafael and Aeronautics Defense Systems, Protector was first revealed in June 2003. It is an unmanned patrol craft based on an 9 m Rigid Inflatable Boat (RIB) with composite-materials superstructure that encloses the sensor pod, navigation radar, GPS antenna and gyrostabilised inertial navigation system. Five video channels are used to transmit the outputs from the Toplite and two deck-mounted cameras back to a remote operator. The vessel also carries microphones and loudspeakers, allowing the operator to hail the crew of a suspicious vessel. With an endurance of about eight hours, it can be controlled by line-of-sight communications from ship or shore for various missions such as force protection, anti-terror surveillance and reconnaissance, mine warfare and electronic warfare. Several systems were earmarked to begin evaluation tests with the Israeli Navy but these were subsequently bought by Singapore in 2004. A series of IN operational evaluations began in 2005.

PROTECTOR *6/2005, Rafael* / 1116232

AUXILIARIES

Notes: (1) Two new construction landing ships are required by the Navy to transport troops. No funds available. A Newport class *Peoria* LST 1183 was authorised for lease from the US but was sunk as a target in 2004.
(2) A Ro-Ro ship *Queshet* is used as a training ship and for research and development. Built in Japan in 1979 and formerly used as a general purpose cargo ship.
(3) Two former merchant ships *Nir* and *Naharya* are used as alongside tenders in Haifa and Eilat respectively.
(4) A 19 m Alligator class semi-submersible craft was reported delivered in 1998. It is likely to be used for special forces operations.

2 STOLLERGRUND CLASS (TYPE 745) (AG)

Name	*No*	*Builders*	*Commissioned*
BAT YAM (ex-*Kalkgrund*)	– (ex-Y 865)	Krögerwerft	23 Nov 1989
BAT GALIM (ex-*Bant*)	– (ex-Y 867)	Krögerwerft	28 May 1990

Displacement, tons: 450 full load
Dimensions, feet (metres): 126.6 × 30.2 × 10.5 *(38.6 × 9.2 × 3.2)*
Main machinery: 1 Deutz-MWM BV6M628 diesel; 1,690 hp(m) *(1.24 MW)* sustained; 1 shaft; bow thruster
Speed, knots: 12. **Range, n miles:** 1,000 at 12 kt
Complement: 7 plus 6 trials personnel

Comment: Ex-German Navy trials and support vessels transferred to the Israeli Navy in December 2005. Both ships are fitted with I-band radars and an intercept sonar. Likely to be based at Haifa.

BAT GALIM *12/2005, Michael Nitz* / 1153206

1 ASHDOD CLASS (LCT)

Name	*No*	*Builders*	*Commissioned*
ASHDOD	61	Israel Shipyards, Haifa	1966

Displacement, tons: 400 standard; 730 full load
Dimensions, feet (metres): 205.5 × 32.8 × 5.8 *(62.7 × 10 × 1.8)*
Main machinery: 3 MWM diesels; 1,900 hp(m) *(1.4 MW)*; 3 shafts
Speed, knots: 10.5
Complement: 20
Guns: 2 Oerlikon 20 mm.

Comment: Used as a trials ship for Barak VLS. Based at Ashdod but refitted at Eilat in 1999. Operational status doubtful.

ASHDOD *3/1989* / 0080070

Italy

MARINA MILITARE

Country Overview

Italy is situated in southern Europe and comprises, in addition to the Italian mainland, the islands of Sardinia, Sicily, Elba and many smaller islands. Enclaves within mainland Italy are the independent countries of San Marino and Vatican City. With an area of 116,341 square miles, it is bordered to the north by France, Switzerland, Austria and Slovenia. It has a 2,700 n mile coastline with the Mediterranean, Ionian, Adriatic, Tyrrhenian Sea and Ligurian Seas. The capital and largest city is Rome while the principal ports are Genoa, Naples, Trieste, Taranto, Palermo and Venice. Territorial waters (12 n miles) are claimed but an EEZ has not been claimed.

Headquarters Appointments

Chief of Naval Staff:
Admiral Paulo la Rosa
Vice Chief of Naval Staff:
Rear Admiral Luigi Binelli-Mantelli
Chief of Joint Military Intelligence:
Rear Admiral Bruno Branciforte
Chief of Procurement:
Engineer Vice Admiral Dino Nascetti
Chief of Technical Support:
Engineer Vice Admiral Alberto Gauzolino
Chief of Naval Personnel:
Vice Admiral Claudio de Polo

Flag Officers

Commander, Allied Naval Forces, Southern Europe (Naples):
Vice Admiral Maurizio Gemignani
Commander-in-Chief of Fleet (Rome):
Vice Admiral Giuseppe Lertora
Commander, Tyrrhenian Sea (La Spezia):
Vice Admiral Franco Paoli
Commander, Ionian Sea (Taranto):
Vice Admiral Gianmaria Faggioni
Commander, Adriatic Sea (Ancona):
Rear Admiral Mario Fumagalli
Commander, Sicily (Augusta):
Rear Admiral Andrea Toscano
Commander, Sardinia (Cagliari):
Commodore Ermengildo Ugazzi
Commander, High Seas Fleet (COMFORAL):
Rear Admiral Rinaldo Veri
Commander, Naval Group (COMGRUPNAVIT) (Taranto):
Commodore Ruggero di Biase
Commander (1st Frigate Squadron) (Taranto):
Sandro Fabiani Latini
Commander, Naval Group (2nd Frigate Squadron) (La Spezia):
Captain Carlo Dardengo
Commander, MCM Forces (COMFORDRAG) (La Spezia):
Captain Guido Rando
Commander, Amphibious Force (COMFORSBARC) (Brindisi):
Commodore Claudio Confessore
Commander, Training Command (MARICENTADD) (Taranto):
Commodore Michele Saponaro
Commander, Coastal and Patrol Forces (COMFORPAT) (Augusta):
Commodore Roberto Camerini
Commander, Naval Air Arm (COMFORAER) (Rome):
Commodore Paolo Treu
Commander Submarine Force (COMFORSUB) (Taranto):
Captain Giovanni Ferini

Flag Officers—*continued*

Commander, Naval Special Forces (COMSUBIN) (La Spezia):
Commodore Guiseppe Cavo Dragone
Commander Coast Guard:
Vice Admiral Luciano Dassatti

Diplomatic Representation

Naval Attaché in Bonn:
Captain Fabio Ricciardelli
Naval Attaché in Peking:
Captain Roberto Gargiulo
Naval Attaché in London:
Commodore Francesco di Biase
Naval Attaché in Moscow:
Captain Giampero Bernadis
Naval Attaché in Paris:
Captain Roberto Ive
Naval Attaché in Washington:
Captain Maurizio Ertreo
Defence Attaché in Tokyo:
Commodore Giuseppe Piro

Bases

Regional Commands: La Spezia (Tyrrhenian Sea), Taranto (Ionian Sea), Ancona (Adriatic Sea), Augusta (Sicily), Cagliari (Sardinia).
Main bases (Major Arsenals/Navy Shipyards): Taranto, La Spezia.
Secondary base (Minor Arsenal/Navy Shipyard): Augusta.
Minor bases: Brindisi.

Organisation

CINCNAV is responsible for all operational activities. There are six subordinate commands:
High-Sea Forces Command (COMFORAL) including all Major and Amphibious Ships. Based in Taranto with subordinated command COMGRUPNAVIT.
Patrol Forces Command (COMFORPAT) Corvettes and OPVs. Based in Augusta.
Naval Air Command. Based at Santa Rosa, Rome.
Submarine Force Command. Based at Taranto.
Mine Countermeasures Command. Based at La Spezia.
COMFORSBARC with San Marco Regiment, Carlotto (logistic) regiment and one assault boat group. Based at Brindisi.
Special Forces Command (COMSUBIN) Commandos and support craft. Based near La Spezia. Controlled directly by Chief of Naval Staff.

Prefix to Ships' Names

ITS (Italian Ship)

Strength of the Fleet

Type	*Active*	*Building (Planned)*
Submarines	6	2 (1)
Aircraft Carriers	2	–
Destroyers	3	1
Frigates	12	6 (4)
Corvettes	8	6
Offshore Patrol Vessels	10	–
Coastal Patrol Craft	4	–
LPD/LHD	3	2
Minehunters/sweepers	12	4
Survey/Research Ships	7	–
Replenishment Tankers	3	2
Coastal Tankers	11	–
Coastal Transports	6	–
Sail Training Ships	8	–
Training Ships	3	–
Lighthouse Tenders	5	–
Salvage Ships	1	1

Personnel

2009: 34,000 (4,150 officers) including 1,550 naval air and 2,100 naval infantry (amphib). National service has been terminated.

Naval Air Arm

Catania (Fontanarossa): AB-212 (2nd), SH-3D (3rd)
Catania (Sigonella): Atlantic (41st)
La Spezia (Luni): AB-212 (1st), SH-3D (5th), EH-101 (5th), EH-101 (OEU)
Taranto (Grottaglie): AV-8B/TAV-8B (7th), AB-212 (4th), AB-212 (Amphib), SH-3 (Amphib)

Naval Infantry and Army Amphibious Units

A Landing Force Command was established in 1998 including a collaborative Spanish/Italian amphibious brigade (SIAF). Landing Force Command is based at Brindisi and comprises the San Marco assault regiment (two assault battalions), the Carlotto support regiment (one logistic and one training battalion) and a Landing Craft Group. The Amphibious assault air squadron has eight modified SH-3D and seven modified AB-212 helicopters.

The Italian Army operates an amphibious regiment named 'Serenissima' which is based at Venice. It is equipped with four LCM, six LCVP and 47 rigid raider and assault craft.

The 'National Projection Force' was established in June 2006. It consists of Navy assets, the Army 'Serenissima' amphibious regiment and selected (earmarked) Army combat support units (two armoured cavalry squadrons, two combat engineering companies, two AA artillery batteries and a squadron of six A 129 attack helicopters). The first commitment of the force was in the Lebanon in 2006.

DELETIONS

Submarines

2007 *Leonardo da Vinci*

PENNANT LIST

Submarines

S 522 Salvatore Pelosi
S 523 Giuliano Prini
S 524 Primo Longobardo
S 525 Gianfranco Gazzana Priaroggia
S 526 Salvatore Todaro
S 527 Scire

Light Aircraft Carriers

C 550 Cavour
C 551 Giuseppe Garibaldi

Destroyers

D 553 Andrea Doria
D 554 Caio Duilio
D 560 Luigi Durand de la Penne
D 561 Francesco Mimbelli

Frigates

F 570 Maestrale
F 571 Grecale
F 572 Libeccio
F 573 Scirocco
F 574 Aliseo
F 575 Euro
F 576 Espero
F 577 Zeffiro
F 582 Artigliere
F 583 Aviere
F 584 Bersagliere
F 585 Granatiere

Corvettes

F 551 Minerva
F 552 Urania
F 553 Danaide
F 554 Sfinge
F 555 Driade
F 556 Chimera
F 557 Fenice
F 558 Sibilla

Patrol Forces

P 401 Cassiopea
P 402 Libra
P 403 Spica
P 404 Vega
P 405 Esploratore
P 406 Sentinella
P 407 Vedetta
P 408 Staffetta
P 409 Sirio
P 410 Orione
P 490 Comandante Cigala Fulgosi
P 491 Comandante Borsini
P 492 Comandante Bettica
P 493 Comandante Foscari

Minehunters

M 5550 Lerici
M 5551 Sapri
M 5552 Milazzo
M 5553 Vieste
M 5554 Gaeta
M 5555 Termoli
M 5556 Alghero
M 5557 Numana
M 5558 Crotone
M 5559 Viareggio
M 5560 Chioggia
M 5561 Rimini

Amphibious Forces

L 9892 San Giorgio
L 9893 San Marco
L 9894 San Giusto

Survey and Research Ships

A 5303 Ammiraglio Magnaghi
A 5304 Aretusa
A 5308 Galatea
A 5315 Raffaele Rossetti
A 5320 Vincenzo Martellotta
A 5340 Elettra

Auxiliaries

A 5302 Caroly
A 5309 Anteo
A 5311 Palinuro
A 5312 Amerigo Vespucci
A 5313 Stella Polare
A 5316 Corsaro II
A 5318 Prometeo
A 5319 Ciclope
A 5322 Capricia
A 5323 Orsa Maggiore
A 5324 Titano
A 5325 Polifemo
A 5326 Etna
A 5327 Stromboli
A 5328 Gigante
A 5329 Vesuvio
A 5330 Saturno
A 5347 Gorgona
A 5348 Tremiti
A 5349 Caprera
A 5351 Pantelleria
A 5352 Lipari
A 5353 Capri
A 5359 Bormida
A 5364 Ponza
A 5365 Tenace
A 5366 Levanzo
A 5367 Tavolara
A 5368 Palmaria
A 5370 Panarea
A 5371 Linosa
A 5372 Favignana
A 5373 Salina
A 5376 Ticino
A 5377 Tirso
A 5379 Astice
A 5380 Mitilo
A 5382 Porpora
A 5383 Procida
Y 413 Porto Fossone
Y 416 Porto Torres
Y 417 Porto Corsini
Y 421 Porto Empedocle
Y 422 Porto Pisano
Y 423 Porto Conte
Y 425 Porto Ferraio
Y 426 Porto Venere
Y 428 Porto Salvo
Y 498 Mario Marino
Y 499 Alcide Pedretti

SUBMARINES

2 + 2 (1) TODARO (TYPE 212A) CLASS (SSK)

Name	*No*	*Builders*	*Laid down*	*Launched*	*Commissioned*
SALVATORE TODARO	S 526	Fincantieri, Muggiano	Jan 2001	6 Nov 2003	29 Mar 2006
SCIRÈ	S 527	Fincantieri, Muggiano	Apr 2002	18 Dec 2004	19 Feb 2007
–	–	Fincantieri, Muggiano	2010	2013	2015
–	–	Fincantieri, Muggiano	2011	2014	2016

Displacement, tons: 1,490 surfaced; 1,700 dived
Dimensions, feet (metres): 187.0 × 23 × 19.7 *(57.0 × 7 × 6)*
Main machinery: Diesel-electric; 1 MTU 16V 396 diesel; 4,243 hp(m) *(3.12 MW)*; 1 alternator; 1 Siemens PEM motor; 3,875 hp(m) *(2.85 MW)*; 1 shaft; Siemens/HDW PEM 9 fuel cell (AIP) modules; 306 kW
Speed, knots: 20 dived; 12 surfaced
Range, n miles: 8,000 at 8 kt surfaced
Complement: 27 (8 officers)

Torpedoes: 6–21 in *(533 mm)* bow tubes; water ram discharge; WASS Black Shark; wire (fibre-optic cable) guided; active/passive homing to 50 km *(27 n miles)* at 50 kt; warhead 250 kg. A 184 Mod 3 also carried. Total 12 weapons.
Mines: In lieu of torpedoes.

Countermeasures: Decoys: Fitted for CIRCE Torpedo countermeasures.
ESM: EADS FL 1800U; intercept.
Weapons control: Kongsberg MSI-90U TFCS.
Radars: Navigation: KH 1007; I-band.
Sonars: STN Atlas Elektronik DBQS-40; passive ranging and intercept; FAS-3 Flank and passive towed array.
STN Atlas Moa 3070, mine detection, active, high frequency.

Programmes: German design phase first completed in 1992 by ARGE 212 (HDW/TNSW) in conjunction with IKL. MoU signed with Germany 22 April 1996 for a common design. First pair ordered from Fincantieri in August 1997. First steel cut for first of class 19 July 1999, and for second in July 2000. Government approval to procure second pair was given on 21 April 2008 and a contract is expected in 2009. Delivery of both boats is to be made by 2016. A fifth boat, to enter service in 2025, is projected.
Structure: Equipped with a hybrid fuel cell/battery propulsion based on the Siemens PEM fuel cell technology. The submarine is designed with a partial double hull which has a larger diameter forward. This is joined to the after end by a short conical section which houses the fuel cell plant. Two LOX tanks and hydrogen stored in metal cylinders are carried around the circumference of the smaller hull section. Italian requirements included a greater diving depth, improved external communications, and better submerged escape facilities. The final design is identical to the German submarines. Fitted with Zeiss search and attack periscopes.
Operational: Dived speeds up to 8 kt are projected, without use of main battery.

SALVATORE TODARO *4/2006, Giorgio Ghiglione* / 1159972

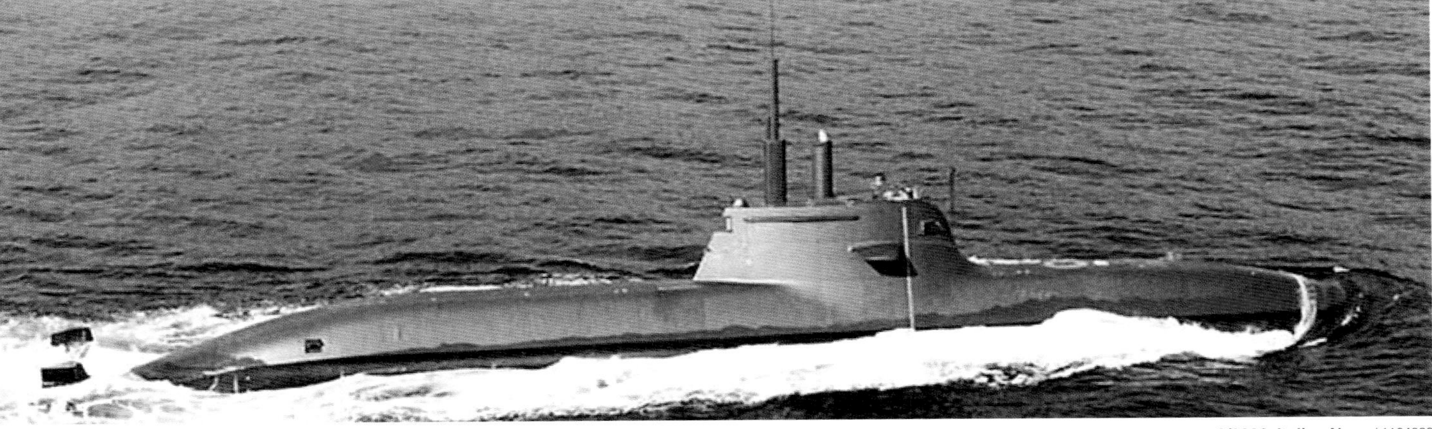

SALVATORE TODARO *9/2006, Italian Navy* / 1164688

SALVATORE TODARO *6/2007, Ships of the World* / 1166594

4 IMPROVED SAURO CLASS (SSK)

Name	*No*	*Builders*	*Laid down*	*Launched*	*Commissioned*
SALVATORE PELOSI	S 522	Fincantieri, Monfalcone	24 May 1984	29 Dec 1986	14 July 1988
GIULIANO PRINI	S 523	Fincantieri, Monfalcone	30 May 1985	12 Dec 1987	11 Nov 1989
PRIMO LONGOBARDO	S 524	Fincantieri, Monfalcone	19 Dec 1991	20 June 1992	20 May 1994
GIANFRANCO GAZZANA PRIAROGGIA	S 525	Fincantieri, Monfalcone	12 Nov 1992	26 June 1993	12 Apr 1995

Displacement, tons: 1,476 (1,653, S 524-5) surfaced; 1,662 (1,862, S 524-5) dived
Dimensions, feet (metres): 211.2 (217.8 S 524-5) × 22.3 × 18.4 *(64.4 (66.4) × 6.8 × 5.6)*
Main machinery: Diesel-electric; 3 Fincantieri GMT 210.16 SM diesels; 3,672 hp(m) *(2.7 MW)* sustained; 3 generators; 2.16 MW; 1 motor; 3,128 hp(m) *(2.3 MW)*; 1 shaft
Speed, knots: 11 surfaced; 19 dived; 12 snorting
Range, n miles: 11,000 at 11 kt surfaced; 250 at 4 kt dived
Complement: 51 (7 officers)

Torpedoes: 6—21 in *(533 mm)* bow tubes. 12 Whitehead A184 Mod 3; dual purpose; wire-guided; active/passive homing to 25 km *(13.7 n miles)* at 24 kt; 17 km *(9.2 n miles)* at 38 kt; warhead 250 kg. Swim-out discharge.
Countermeasures: ESM: Elettronica BLD-727; radar warning; 2 aerials-1 on a mast, second in search periscope.
Weapons control: STN Atlas ISUS 90-20.
Radars: Search/navigation: SMA BPS 704; I-band; also periscope radar for attack ranging.
Sonars: Selenia Elsag IPD 70/S; linear passive array; 200 Hz-7.5 kHz; active and UWT transducers in bow (15 kHz).

Programmes: The first two were ordered in March 1983 and the second pair in July 1988.
Modernisation: An upgrade programme included replacement of acoustic sensors, weapons control system (STN Atlas ISUS 90-20) and communications. Work on all four boats was completed in late 2004.
Structure: Pressure hull of HY 80 steel with a central bulkhead for escape purposes. Diving depth, 300 m *(985 ft)* (test) and 600 m *(1,970 ft)* (crushing). The second pair has a slightly longer hull to give space for SSMs.
Periscopes: Kollmorgen; S 76 Mod 322 with laser range finder attack; S 76 Mod 323 with ESM-search. Wave contour snort head has a very low radar profile. All boats have anechoic tiles.
Operational: Two Lital Mk 39 inertial navigation; Sepa autopilot. Endurance, 45 days. Service lives: 2016 (S 522 and S 523); 2020 (S 524 and S 525).

GIULIANO PRINI — ***6/2005, John Brodie*** / 1153247

GIULIANO PRINI — ***6/2005, John Mortimer*** / 1153233

PRIMO LONGOBARDO — ***6/2004, Diego Quevedo*** / 1044360

AIRCRAFT CARRIERS

0 + 1 CAVOUR CLASS (CV)

Name	*No*	*Builders*	*Laid down*	*Launched*	*Commissioned*
CAVOUR (ex-*Andrea Doria*)	C 550	Fincantieri Muggiano/Riva Trigoso	17 July 2001	20 July 2004	Apr 2009

Displacement, tons: 27,100 full load
Dimensions, feet (metres): 772.9 oa; 707.3 wl × 128 oa; 96.8 wl × 24.6 *(235.6; 215.6 × 39; 29.5 × 7.5)*
Flight deck, feet (metres): 721.8 × 111.5 *(220 × 34)*
Main machinery: COGAG: 4 GE/Fiat LM 2500 gas turbines; 118,000 hp(m) *(88 MW)* sustained; 2 shafts; cp props; bow and stern thrusters; 6 Wärtsilä 2.2 MW diesel generators and 2 Ansaldo Sistemi Industriali shaft generators
Speed, knots: 28. **Range, n miles**: 7,000 at 16 kt
Complement: 528 ship plus 168 air group plus 145 staff (CJTF or CATF/CLF) plus 325 marines (90 additional marines for short period). Total accommodation for 1,205
Military lift: (garage only): 100 wheeled vehicles or 60 armoured vehicles or 24 MBTs (Ariete) or mixture

Missiles: SAM: 32 (4-8 cell Sylver VLS) Aster 15; inertial mid-course guidance; active radar homing to 30 km *(16 n miles)* at 3 Mach; warhead 15 kg.
Guns: 2 OTO Melara 3 in *(76 mm)*/62 Super Rapid. 120 rds/min to 16 km *(8.7 n miles)*; weight of shell 6 kg. 3 OTO Melara KBA 25/80 mm.
Countermeasures: Decoys: 2 Breda SCLAR-H 20-barrel trainable chaff/decoy launchers.
TCM: 2 SLAT TCM launchers.
ESM: Thales Radar and Comms intercept ❶.
ECM: Thales Nettuno.
Combat data systems: 'Horizon' derivative flag and command support system. Links 11 and 16; provision for Link 22. Satcom ❷.
Weapons control: Galileo Avionica SASS optronic director. 2 Alenia NA25XP.
Radars: Long-range air search: SPS 798 (RAN-40L); D-band ❸.
Air search and missile guidance: Alenia Marconi EMPAR; G-band ❹.
CCA: SPN-41; J-band.
Surface search: SPS-791 (RAN-30X/I) ❺; I-band.
Fire control: 2 Alenia Marconi NA 25XP; I-band.
Navigation: SPN-753G(V) ❻; I-band.
CCA: Finnemeccanica SPN 720(V)5; I-band.
Tacan: SRN-15A.
Sonars: WASS SNA-2000 mine avoidance sonar (bow dome).

Fixed-wing aircraft: 8 AV-8B Harrier II or JSF.
Helicopters: 12 EH 101 (fitted also for AB 212, NH90 and SH-3D).

Programmes: Following a study phase which included significant changes to the initial configuration of the Nuova Unita Maggiore (NUM) design, the Italian government placed a contract with Fincantieri for the construction of a ship to replace *Vittorio Veneto* in 2007. Capabilities include afloat command, air and amphibious operations. The bow section of the ship was constructed at Muggiano and the centre and stern sections at Riva Trigoso. The ship is to be joined, outfitted and tested at Muggiano. A second contract, for the development and supply of the combat system was signed with an AMS-led industrial group in October 2002.
Structure: The flight deck features six helicopter take-off spots, one spot for SAR, eight parking spots and a 12° ski jump. A notional air group includes 12 EH-101 helicopters and 8 AV-8B Harrier IIs. There is provision in the design to operate JSF and UAVs. The hangar/garage can accommodate various combinations of aircraft and vehicles (including MBT and trucks). There are two 30 ton lifts, one forward of the island and the other starboard side aft. Two Ro-Ro ramps are positioned aft and starboard side. Two 15 ton and one 7 ton lifts are fitted for ordnance and logistic needs respectively. The VLS silos for Aster are located on the port quarter and starboard bow. There is a 430 m³ hospital facility.
Operational: Sea trials started in 2006. The first year of operation, known as the Warranty Period, began in March 2008. This is to be followed by a four-month maintenance period and by combat system integration and certification during 2009.

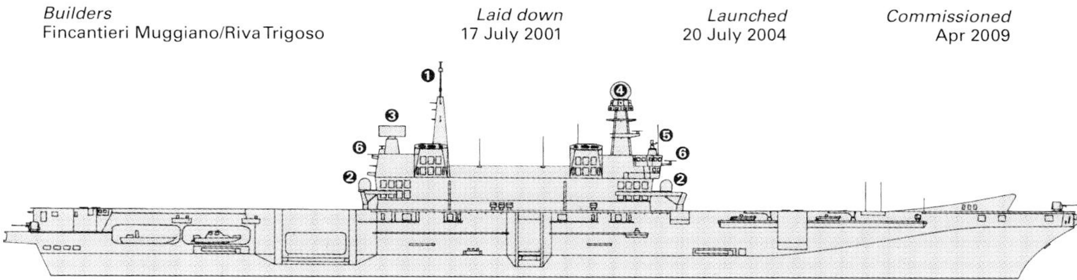

CAVOUR ***(Scale 1 : 1,800), Ian Sturton*** / 1167425

CAVOUR ***12/2006, Giorgio Ghiglione*** / 1167417

CAVOUR ***4/2008*, Ships of the World*** / 1335465

CAVOUR ***12/2007, Italian Navy*** / 1170078

1 GARIBALDI CLASS (CVGM)

Name	*No*	*Builders*	*Laid down*	*Launched*	*Commissioned*
GIUSEPPE GARIBALDI	C 551	Italcantieri, Monfalcone	26 Mar 1981	4 June 1983	30 Sep 1985

Displacement, tons: 10,100 standard; 13,850 full load
Dimensions, feet (metres): 591 × 110.2 × 22 *(180 × 33.4 × 6.7)*
Flight deck, feet (metres): 570.2 × 99.7 *(173.8 × 30.4)*
Main machinery: COGAG; 4 Fiat/GE LM 2500 gas turbines; 81,000 hp *(60 MW)* sustained; 2 shafts
Speed, knots: 30
Range, n miles: 7,000 at 20 kt
Complement: 582 ship plus 230 air group (accommodation for 825 including Flag and staff)

Missiles: SAM: 2 Selenia Elsag Albatros octuple launchers ❶; 48 Aspide; semi-active radar homing to 13 km *(7 n miles)* at 2.5 Mach; height envelope 15-5,000 m *(49.2-16,405 ft)*; warhead 30 kg.
Guns: 6 Breda 40 mm/70 (3 twin) MB ❷; 300 rds/min to 12.5 km *(6.8 n miles)* anti-surface; 4 km *(2.2 n miles)* anti-aircraft; weight of shell 0.96 kg.
Torpedoes: 6–324 mm B-515 (2 triple) tubes ❸. Honeywell Mk 46; anti-submarine; active/passive homing to 11 km *(5.9 n miles)* at 40 kt; warhead 44 kg. Being replaced by new MU 90.
Countermeasures: Decoys: SLQ-25 Nixie; noisemaker.
2 Breda SCLAR 105 mm 20-barrelled launchers; trains and elevates; chaff to 5 km *(2.7 n miles)*; illuminants to 12 km *(6.6 n miles)*. SLAT in 2002.
ESM/ECM: Elettronica Nettuno SLQ-732; integrated intercept and jamming system.
Combat data systems: IPN 20 (SADOC 2) action data automation including Links 11 and 14. SATCOM ❹.
Weapons control: 3 Alenia NA 30E electro-optical back-up for SAM. 3 Dardo NA21 for guns.

Radars: Long-range air search Hughes SPS-52C ❺; 3D; E/F-band; range 440 km *(240 n miles)*.
Air search: Selenia SPS-768 (RAN 3L) ❻; D-band; range 220 km *(120 n miles)*.
Air/surface search: Selenia SPS-774 (RAN 10S) ❼; E/F-band.
Surface search/target indication: SMA SPS-702 UPX; 718 beacon; I-band.
Navigation: ARPA SPN-753 G(V); I-band.
Fire control: 3 Selenia SPG-75 (RTN 30X) ❽; I/J-band; range 15 km *(8 n miles)* (for Albatros).
3 Selenia SPG-74 (RTN 20X) ❾; I/J-band; range 13 km *(7 n miles)* (for Dardo).
CCA: Selenia SPN-728(V)1; I-band.
IFF: Mk XII. Tacan: SRN-15A.
Sonars: Raytheon DE 1160 LF; bow-mounted; active search; medium frequency.

Fixed-wing aircraft: 15 AV-8B Harrier II.
Helicopters: 18 SH-3D Sea King or EH 101 Merlin helicopters (12 in hangar, 6 on deck). The total capacity is either 15 Harriers or 18 helicopters, but this leaves no space for movement. In practice a combination is embarked (see *Operational*).

Programmes: Contract awarded 21 November 1977. The design work completed February 1980. Started sea trials 3 December 1984.
Modernisation: A major C[4]I upgrade programme, completed in September 2003, has given the ship a Maritime Component Commander (MCC) capability. Improvements to the combat data system include a MCC data system and Link 16. SATCOM domes have replaced the TESEO launchers which have been removed. SHF SATCOM has been installed in the old positions of the chaff launchers while SCLAR-D chaff launchers have been installed on new sponsons aft and below the flight deck. Other work includes modernisation of the ESM/ECM equipment, replacement of the DE 1150F sonar with DMSS 2000 and the fitting of an electro-optic tracking device on the bridge roof in lieu of SPN-728 radar which has been removed. A major refit is planned 2013–15 although the scope of this is to be decided. *Garibaldi* has also been equipped to control RQ-1B Predator UAV and to exploit its imagery.
Structure: Six decks with 13 vertical watertight bulkheads. Fitted with 6.5° ski-jump and VSTOL operating equipment. Two 15 ton lifts 18 × 10 m *(59 × 32.8 ft)*. Hangar size 110 × 15 × 6 m *(361 × 49.2 × 19.7 ft)*. Hangar capacity is for 10 Harriers or 12 Sea Kings. Has a slightly narrower flight deck than UK Invincible class. Two MEN class fast personnel launches (capacity 250) can be embarked for amphibious operations or disaster relief.
Operational: Fleet Flagship. Equipped for Joint Task Force command and control. The long-standing dispute between the Navy and the Air Force concerning the former's operation of fixed-wing aircraft (dating back to pre-Second World War legislation) was finally resolved by legislation passed on 29 January 1989. Embarked aircraft are operated by the Navy with the Air Force providing evaluation and maintenance. The carrier has operated in the assault role with seven SH-3D, four AB 212 and Army helicopters including six AB 205, three A 129 and two CH-47. First operational Harriers embarked for permanent duty in December 1994.

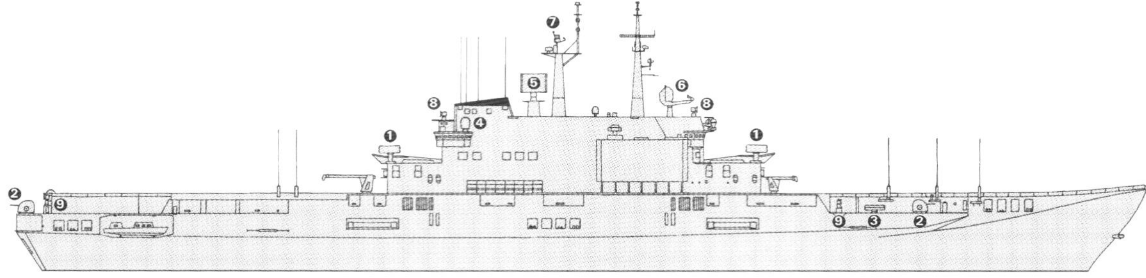

GIUSEPPE GARIBALDI ***(Scale 1 : 1,200), Ian Sturton*** / 1043173

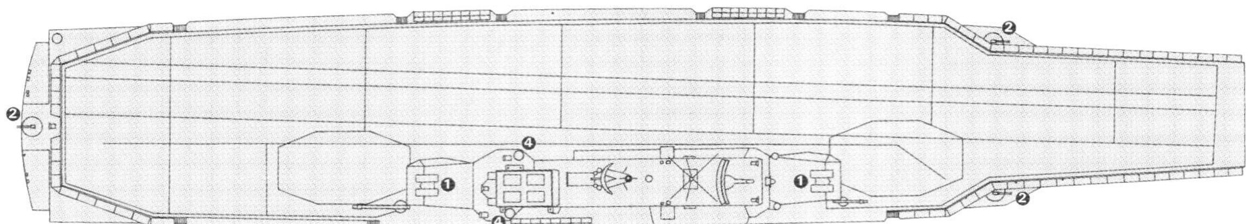

GIUSEPPE GARIBALDI ***(Scale 1 : 1,200), Ian Sturton*** / 1043172

GIUSEPPE GARIBALDI ***8/2004, Guy Toremans*** / 1044368

GIUSEPPE GARIBALDI

7/2004, United States Navy / 1043185

GIUSEPPE GARIBALDI

6/2005, Marco Ghiglino / 1153230

DESTROYERS

1 + 1 ANDREA DORIA (HORIZON) CLASS (DDGHM)

Name	*No*	*Builders*	*Laid down*	*Launched*	*Commissioned*
ANDREA DORIA (ex-*Carlo Bergamini*)	D 553	Fincantieri, Riva Trigoso/Muggiano	19 July 2002	14 Oct 2005	2009
CAIO DUILIO	D 554	Fincantieri, Riva Trigoso/Muggiano	19 Sep 2003	23 Oct 2007	2010

Displacement, tons: 6,635 full load
Dimensions, feet (metres): 501.6 oa; 464.9 wl × 66.6 × 26.2 *(152.9; 141.7 × 20.3 × 8.0)*
Main machinery: CODOG: 2 GE LM 2500 gas turbines; 55,750 hp(m) *(41 MW)*; 2 SEMT Pielstick 12 PA6B STC diesels; 11,700 hp(m) *(8.6 MW)*; 2 shafts; cp props
Speed, knots: 29
Range, n miles: 7,000 at 18 kt
Complement: 200 (35 officers)

Missiles: SSM: 8 (2 quad) OTO Melara Teseo Mk 2A ❶; mid-course guidance; active radar homing to 160 km *(86 n miles)* at 0.9 Mach; warhead 210 kg.
SAM: DCN Sylver VLS ❷ PAAMS (principal anti-air missile system); 48 cells for Aster 15 and Aster 30 weapons; range (Aster 30) 120 km *(65 n miles)*.
Guns: 3 Otobreda 76 mm/62 Super Rapid ❸.
2 Breda Oerlikon 25 mm/80 ❹.
Torpedoes: 2 fixed launchers ❺. Eurotorp Mu 90 Impact torpedoes.
Countermeasures: Decoys: 2 Otobreda SCLAR-H chaff/IR flare launchers ❻. SLAT torpedo defence system.
ESM/ECM: Elettronica JANEWS ❼.
Combat data systems: DCN/Alenia CMS; Link 16. Link 14 SATCOM ❽.
Weapons control: Sagem Vampir optronic director ❾.
Radars: Air/surface search: S 1850M ❿; D-band.
Surveillance/fire control: Alenia EMPAR ⓫; G-band; multifunction.
Surface search: Alenia RASS ⓬; E/F-band.
Fire control: 2 Alenia Marconi NA 25XP ⓭.
Navigation: Alenia SPN 753(V)4 ⓮; I-band.
Sonars: Thomson Marconi 4110CL; hull-mounted; active search and attack; medium frequency.

Helicopters: 1 Augusta/Westland EH 101 Merlin ⓯ or NH-90.

Programmes: Three-nation project for a new air defence ship with Italy, France and UK. Joint project office established in 1993. Memorandum of Understanding for joint development signed 11 July 1994. After UK withdrew in April 1999, an agreement was signed on 7 September 1999 between France and Italy to continue. Following a preliminary agreement on 2 August 2000, a Memorandum of Understanding was signed by the French and Italian Defence Ministries on 22 September 2000 for the joint development of the 'Horizon' destroyer. A Horizon Joint Venture Company was created by DCN/Thomson-CSF and Fincantieri/Finmeccanica on 16 October 2000. The first batch of two vessels for each country was ordered on 27 October 2000. Plans for a second batch of two ships have been cancelled.
Operational: *Andrea Doria* started sea trials in October 2006 and is to become fully operational in 2009. *Caio Duilio* is expected to be commissioned in 2010.

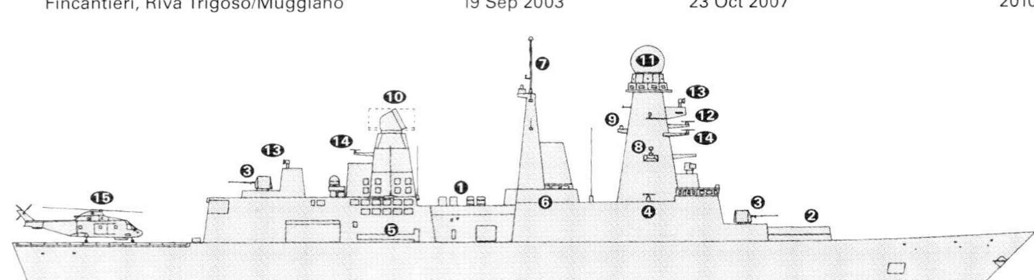

ANDREA DORIA ***(Scale 1 : 1,200), Ian Sturton*** / 1167423

ANDREA DORIA ***9/2006, Giorgio Ghiglione*** / 1159975

ANDREA DORIA
3/2008*, Giorgio Ghiglione
1335476

CAIO DUILIO ***4/2008*, Giorgio Ghiglione*** / 1335477

2 DE LA PENNE (EX-ANIMOSO) CLASS (DDGHM)

Name	*No*	*Builders*	*Laid down*	*Launched*	*Commissioned*
LUIGI DURAND DE LA PENNE (ex-*Animoso*)	D 560	Fincantieri, Riva Trigoso/Muggiano	20 Jan 1988	29 Oct 1989	18 Mar 1993
FRANCESCO MIMBELLI (ex-*Ardimentoso*)	D 561	Fincantieri, Riva Trigoso/Muggiano	15 Nov 1989	13 Apr 1991	19 Oct 1993

Displacement, tons: 4,330 standard; 5,400 full load
Dimensions, feet (metres): 487.4 × 52.8 × 28.2 (sonar) *(147.7 × 16.1 × 8.6)*
Flight deck, feet (metres): 78.7 × 42.7 *(24 × 13)*
Main machinery: CODOG; 2 Fiat/GE LM 2500 gas turbines; 54,000 hp *(40.3 MW)* sustained; 2 GMT BL 230.20 DVM diesels; 12,600 hp(m) *(9.3 MW)* sustained; 2 shafts; cp props
Speed, knots: 31 (21 on diesels)
Range, n miles: 7,000 at 18 kt
Complement: 331 (25 officers)

Missiles: SSM: 4 or 8 OTO Melara/Matra Teseo Mk 2 (TG 2) (2 or 4 twin) ❶; mid-course guidance; active radar homing to 160 km *(86.4 n miles)* at 0.9 Mach; warhead 210 kg; sea-skimmer.
Mk 3 with radar/IR homing to 300 km *(162 n miles)*; warhead 160 kg in due course.
A/S: OTO Melara/Matra Milas launcher; inertial guidance with command update to 55 km (29.8 n miles) at 0.9 Mach; payload Mk 46 Mod 5 or Mu 90 torpedo; 4 weapons (see Modernisation).
SAM: 40 Raytheon Standard SM-1MR Block VI; Mk 13 Mod 4 launcher ❷; command guidance; semi-active radar homing to 38 km (20.5 n miles) at 2 Mach.
Selenia Albatros Mk 2 octuple launcher for Aspide ❸; semi-active radar homing to 13 km *(7 n miles)* at 2.5 Mach; 16 missiles. Automatic reloading.
Guns: 1 OTO Melara 5 in *(127 mm)*/54 ❹; 45 rds/min to 23 km *(12.42 n miles)*; weight of shell 32 kg.
3 OTO Melara 3 in *(76 mm)*/62 Super Rapid ❺; 120 rds/min to 16 km *(8.7 n miles)*; weight of shell 6 kg. 2—20 mm.
Torpedoes: 6—324 mm B-515 (2 triple) tubes ❻. Honeywell Mk 46; anti-submarine; active/passive homing to 11 km *(5.9 n miles)* at 40 kt; warhead 44 kg. May be replaced by Whitehead Mu 90 in due course.
Countermeasures: Decoys: 2 CSEE Sagaie chaff launchers ❼. 1 SLQ-25 Nixie anti-torpedo system.
ESM/ECM: Elettronica SLQ-732 Nettuno ❽; integrated intercept and jamming system. SLC 705.
Combat data systems: Selenia Elsag IPN 20 (SADOC 2); Links 11 and 14. SATCOM.
Weapons control: 4 Dardo-E systems (3 channels for Aspide). Milas TFCS.
Radars: Long-range air search: Hughes SPS-52C; 3D ❾; E/F-band.
Air search: Selenia SPS-768 (RAN 3L) ❿; D-band.
Air/surface search: Selenia SPS-774 (RAN 10S) ⓫; E/F-band.
Surface search: SMA SPS-702 ⓬; I-band.
Fire control: 4 Selenia SPG-76 (RTN 30X) ⓭; I/J-band (for Dardo).
2 Raytheon SPG-51D ⓮; G/I-band (for SAM).
Navigation: SMA SPN-748; I-band.
IFF: Mk X/XII. Tacan: SRN-15A.
Sonars: Raytheon DE 1164 LF-VDS; integrated bow and VDS; active search and attack; medium frequency (3.75 kHz (hull); 7.5 kHz (VDS)).

Helicopters: 2 AB 212ASW ⓯; SH-3D Sea King and EH 101 Merlin capable.

Programmes: Order placed 9 March 1986 with Riva Trigoso. All ships built at Riva Trigoso are completed at Muggiano after launching. Names changed on 10 June 1992 to honour former naval heroes. Acceptance dates were delayed by reduction gear radiated noise problems which have been resolved.
Modernisation: Milas ASW launchers fitted by late 2004. New sonar dome fitted in D 560 in 2000 increased draft by 1.5 m. A major 2-year upgrade is being undertaken in D 561 to be completed late 2009 and D 560 (starting in 2009). SPS-52C is to be removed. SPS-768 is to be replaced by AMS RAN-40L (SPS-798) (also fitted in *Cavour*); SPS-774 to be replaced by AMS RAN-21S (SPS-794); SPS-702 to be replaced by SPN-753 ARPA; Dardo-E to be replaced by four new fire-control systems (Dardo-F with RTN-30X); Sagem IRST and new combat data system to be installed. Link 16 is also to be added while Teseo Mk 2 is to be upgraded to Mk 2/A configuration.
Structure: Kevlar armour fitted. Steel alloys used in superstructure. Prairie Masker noise suppression system. The 127 mm guns are ex-Audace class B turrets. Fully stabilised. Hangar is 18.5 m in length.
Operational: It is likely that both ships will be reclassified as frigates once the SM-1 missile system is phased out in about 2015. The ships are expected to remain in service until about 2025.

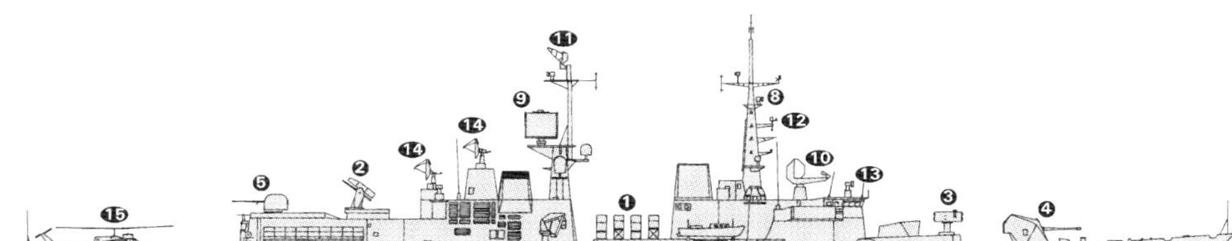

FRANCESCO MIMBELLI *(Scale 1 : 1,200), Ian Sturton* / 0569913

LUIGI DURAND DE LA PENNE *6/2004, John Brodie* / 1044362

LUIGI DURAND DE LA PENNE *5/2004, B Sullivan* / 1044363

FRANCESCO MIMBELLI *5/2003, A Sharma* / 0570684

FRIGATES

8 MAESTRALE CLASS (FFGHM)

Name	No	Builders	Laid down	Launched	Commissioned
MAESTRALE	F 570	Fincantieri, Riva Trigoso	8 Mar 1978	2 Feb 1981	6 Mar 1982
GRECALE	F 571	Fincantieri, Muggiano	21 Mar 1979	12 Sep 1981	5 Feb 1983
LIBECCIO	F 572	Fincantieri, Riva Trigoso	1 Aug 1979	7 Sep 1981	5 Feb 1983
SCIROCCO	F 573	Fincantieri, Riva Trigoso	26 Feb 1980	17 Apr 1982	20 Sep 1983
ALISEO	F 574	Fincantieri, Riva Trigoso	10 Aug 1980	29 Oct 1982	7 Sep 1983
EURO	F 575	Fincantieri, Riva Trigoso	15 Apr 1981	25 Apr 1983	24 Jan 1984
ESPERO	F 576	Fincantieri, Riva Trigoso	29 July 1982	19 Nov 1983	4 May 1984
ZEFFIRO	F 577	Fincantieri, Riva Trigoso	15 Mar 1983	19 May 1984	4 May 1985

Displacement, tons: 2,500 standard; 3,200 full load
Dimensions, feet (metres): 405 × 42.5 × 15.1 *(122.7 × 12.9 × 4.6)*
Flight deck, feet (metres): 89 × 39 *(27 × 12)*
Main machinery: CODOG; 2 Fiat/GE LM 2500 gas turbines; 50,000 hp *(37.3 MW)* sustained; 2 GMT B 230.20 DVM diesels; 11,000 hp(m) *(8.1 MW)* sustained; 2 shafts; LIPS cp props
Speed, knots: 32 gas; 21 diesels
Range, n miles: 6,000 at 16 kt
Complement: 205 (16 officers)

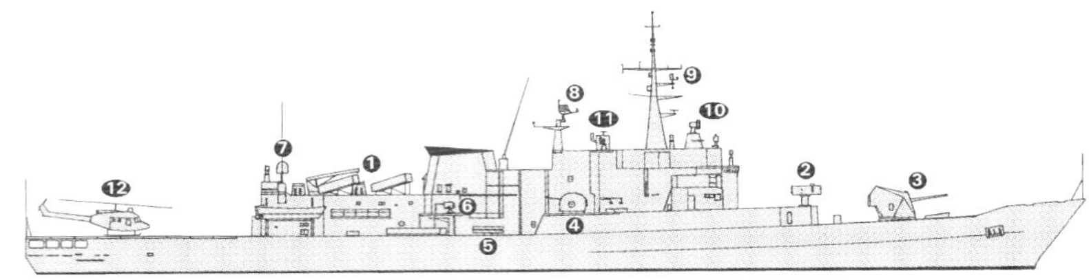

MAESTRALE *(Scale 1 : 1,200), Ian Sturton* / 0569915

Missiles: SSM: 4 OTO Melara Teseo Mk 2 (TG 2) ❶; mid-course guidance; active radar homing to 160 km *(86.4 n miles)*; warhead 210 kg; sea-skimmer. Mk 3 with radar/IR homing to 300 km *(162 n miles)*; warhead 160 kg in due course.
SAM: Selenia Albatros octuple launcher; 16 Aspide ❷; semi-active homing to 13 km *(7 n miles)* at 2.5 Mach; height envelope 15-5,000 m *(49.2-16,405 ft)*; warhead 30 kg.
Guns: 1 OTO Melara 5 in *(127 mm)*/54 automatic ❸; 45 rds/min to 23 km *(12.42 n miles)* anti-surface; 7 km *(3.8 n miles)* anti-aircraft; weight of shell 32 kg; fires chaff and illuminants.
4 Breda 40 mm/70 (2 twin) compact ❹; 300 rds/min to 12.5 km *(6.8 n miles)* anti-surface; 4 km *(2.2 n miles)* anti-aircraft; weight of shell 0.96 kg.
2 Oerlikon 20 mm fitted for Gulf deployments in 1990–91. 2 Breda Oerlikon 25 mm/90 (twin) tested in *Espero*.
Torpedoes: 6—324 mm US Mk 32 (2 triple) tubes ❺. Honeywell Mk 46; anti-submarine; active/passive homing to 11 km *(5.9 n miles)* at 40 kt; warhead 44 kg.
Countermeasures: Decoys: 2 Breda 105 mm SCLAR 20-tubed trainable chaff rocket launchers ❻; chaff to 5 km *(2.7 n miles)*; illuminants to 12 km *(6.6 n miles)*. 2 Dagaie chaff launchers.
SLQ-25; towed torpedo decoy. Prairie Masker; noise suppression system.
ESM: Elettronica SLR-4; intercept.
ECM: 2 SLQ-D; jammers.
Combat data systems: IPN 20 (SADOC 2) action data automation; Link 11. SATCOM ❼.
Weapons control: NA 30 for Albatros and 5 in guns. 2 Dardo (Dardo-F in F 572, F 573, F 577) for 40 mm guns. Galileo Avionica SASS IRST (F 572, F 573, F 577).
Radars: Air/surface search: Selenia SPS-774 SPS-794 (F 572, F 573, F 577) (RAN 10S (RAN 21S)) ❽; E/F-band.
Surface search: SMA SPS-702 ❾; I-band.
Navigation: SMA SPN-703 (SPN-753 (F 572, F 573, F 577)); I-band.
Fire control: Selenia SPG-75 (RTN 30X) ❿; I/J-band (for Albatros and 12.7 mm gun).
2 Selenia SPG-74 (RTN 20X) ⓫; I/J-band; range 15 km *(8 n miles)* (for Dardo).
IFF: Mk XII.
Sonars: Raytheon DE 1164; hull-mounted; VDS; active/passive attack; medium frequency. VDS can be towed at up to 28 kt. Maximum depth 300 m. Modified to include mine detection active high frequency.

Helicopters: 2 AB 212ASW ⓬.

Programmes: First six ordered December 1976 and last pair in October 1980. All Riva Trigoso ships completed at Muggiano after launch.
Modernisation: Hull and VDS sonars modified from 1994 to give better shallow water performance and a mine detection capability. A major upgrade is in progress. F 573 was completed in late 2006 and F 577 was completed in 2007 and F 572 in November 2008. F 571 is to follow. SPS-774 to be replaced by AMS RAN-21S (SPS-794), SPN-703 to be replaced by SPN-753 ARPA, Dardo to be replaced by two new fire-control systems (Dardo-F with RTN-30X), Galileo Avionica SASS IRST and new combat data system to be installed.
Structure: There has been a notable increase of 34 ft in length and 5 ft in beam over the Lupo class to provide for the fixed hangar and VDS, the result providing more comfortable accommodation but a small loss of top speed. Fitted with stabilisers.
Operational: A towed passive LF array may be attached to the VDS body. Aft A 184 torpedo tubes have been removed. F 571, F 572, F 573 and F 577 to remain in service until 2015–2018. F 570, F 574, F 575 and F 576 are to be decommissioned 2012–2015.

ALISEO *4/2006, M Declerck* / 1164685

MAESTRALE *1/2008*, Giorgio Ghiglione* / 1335478

4 ARTIGLIERE (LUPO) CLASS (FFGHM)

Name	*No*	*Builders*	*Laid down*	*Launched*	*Commissioned*
ARTIGLIERE (ex-*Hittin*)	F 582 (ex-F 14)	Fincantieri, Ancona	31 Mar 1982	27 July 1983	28 Oct 1994
AVIERE (ex-*Thi Qar*)	F 583 (ex-F 15)	Fincantieri, Ancona	3 Sep 1982	19 Dec 1984	4 Jan 1995
BERSAGLIERE (ex-*Al Yarmouk*)	F 584 (ex-F 17)	Fincantieri, Riva Trigoso	12 Mar 1984	18 Apr 1985	8 Nov 1995
GRANATIERE (ex-*Al Qadisiya*)	F 585 (ex-F 16)	Fincantieri, Ancona	1 Dec 1983	1 June 1985	20 Mar 1996

Displacement, tons: 2,208 standard; 2,525 full load
Dimensions, feet (metres): 371.3 × 37.1 × 12.1 *(113.2 × 11.3 × 3.7)*
Main machinery: CODOG; 2 Fiat/GE LM 2500 gas turbines; 50,000 hp *(37.3 MW)* sustained; 2 GMT BL 230.20 M diesels; 7,800 hp(m) *(5.7 MW)* sustained; 2 shafts; LIPS cp props
Speed, knots: 35 turbines; 21 diesels
Range, n miles: 5,000 at 15 kt on diesels
Complement: 177 (13 officers)

Missiles: SSM: 8 OTO Melara Teseo Mk 2 (TG 2) ❶; mid-course guidance; active radar homing to 160 km *(86.4 n miles)* at 0.9 Mach; warhead 210 kg; sea-skimmer.
SAM: Selenia Elsag Aspide octuple launcher ❷; semi-active radar homing to 14.6 km *(8 n miles)* at 2.5 Mach; warhead 39 kg. 8 reloads.
Guns: 1 OTO Melara 5 in *(127 mm)*/54 ❸; 45 rds/min to 23 km *(12.42 n miles)* anti-surface; 7 km *(3.8 n miles)* anti-aircraft; weight of shell 32 kg.
4 Breda 40 mm/70 (2 twin) compact ❹; 300 rds/min to 12.5 km *(6.8 n miles)* anti-surface; 4 km *(2.2 n miles)* anti-aircraft; weight of shell 0.96 kg.
2 Oerlikon 20 mm can be fitted.
Countermeasures: Decoys: 2 Breda 105 mm SCLAR 20-tubed trainable ❺; chaff to 5 km *(2.7 n miles)*; illuminants to 12 km *(6.6 n miles)*.
ESM/ECM: Selenia SLQ-747 (INS-3M); intercept and jammer.
Combat data systems: IPN 10 mini SADOC action data automation; Link 11. SATCOM.
Weapons control: 2 Elsag Mk 10 Argo with NA 21 directors for missiles and 5 in gun. 2 Dardo for 40 mm guns.
Radars: Air search: Selenia SPS-774 (RAN 10S) ❻; E/F-band.
Surface search: Selenia SPQ-712 (RAN 12 L/X) ❼; I-band.
Navigation: SMA SPN-703; I-band.
Fire control: 2 Selenia SPG-70 (RTN 10X) ❽; I/J-band; range 40 km *(22 n miles)* (for Argo).
2 Selenia SPG-74 (RTN 20X) ❾; I/J-band; range 15 km *(8 n miles)* (for Dardo).
IFF: Mk XII.

Helicopters: 1 AB 212 ❿.

Programmes: On 20 January 1992 it was decided to transfer the four ships built for Iraq to the Italian Navy. The original sale to Iraq was first delayed by payment problems and then cancelled in 1990 when UN embargoes were placed on military sales to Iraq. After several attempts by the Italian Defence Committee to cancel the project, finance was finally authorised in July 1993.
Modernisation: The details given are for the ships as modernised for Italian service. All ASW equipment removed, new combat and communications systems to Italian standards and a major upgrading of damage control and accommodation facilities. F 584 is unlikely to become the test platform for the 127/64 LW gun and Vulcano long-range guided munitions.
Operational: The first two commissioned with only machinery, damage control and accommodation upgraded. The weapon systems' changes were made during 1995. The last pair entered service fully modified. Official designation is Fleet Patrol Ships. *Granatiere* expected to be used as an interim Mine Command and Support Ship. F 582 and F 583 (expected to be decommissioned 2012–14) based at Taranto; F 584 and F 585 based at La Spezia.

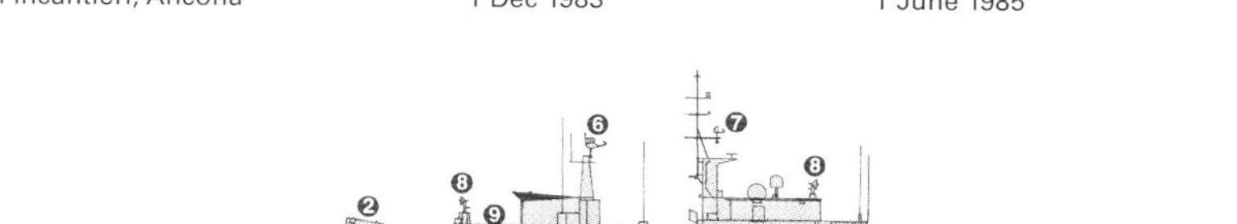
ARTIGLIERE ***(Scale 1 : 1,200), Ian Sturton*** / 0506300

ARTIGLIERE ***2/2002, Giorgio Ghiglione*** / 0528350

BERSAGLIERI ***1/2005, Camil Busquets i Vilanova*** / 1153225

0 + 6 (4) BERGAMINI CLASS (MULTIMISSION FRIGATES) (FFGH)

Name	*No*	*Builders*	*Laid down*	*Launched*	*Commissioned*
CARLO BERGAMINI	–	Fincantieri, Riva Trigoso	4 Feb 2008	2010	2012
CARLO MARGOTTINI	–	Fincantieri, Riva, Trigoso	2009	2011	2013

Displacement, tons: 4,500 standard; 5,950 full load
Dimensions, feet (metres): 466.5 oa; 449.8 wl × 64.6 × 17.7 *(142.2; 137.1 × 19.7 × 5.4)*
Main machinery: CODLOG/CODLAG; 1 General Electric LM 2500 gas turbine; 40,230 hp *(30 MW)*; 4 diesels; 11,270 hp *(8.4 MW)*; 2 motors; 5,900 hp *(4.4 MW)*; 2 shafts; cp props
Speed, knots: 27
Range, n miles: 6,000 at 15 kt
Complement: 145 (accommodation for 165)

Missiles: SLCM: to be decided.
SAM: 16 Sylver A50 cell VLS for Aster 15/30 ❶.
SSM: 4 (8 in GP variant): Teseo Mk 2/A ❷.
Guns: 1 OTO 127 mm/64ER ❸ (GP). 2 (ASW) (1 GP) OTO 76 mm SR ❹. 2—25 mm.
Torpedoes: 4 (2 twin) tubes; MU-90 ❺.
A/S mortars: 4 MILAS (ASW variant).
Countermeasures: Decoys: 2 Breda SCLAR-H 20-barrel trainable chaff/decoy launchers.
TCM: SLAT launchers.
ESM: Radar and Comms intercept.
ECM: jammer.
Combat data systems: Cavour derivative system.
Weapons control: Galileo Avionica SASS IRST optronic director ❻.
Radars: Air search: Alenia EMPAR; G-band ❼.
Surface search: SPS 791 (RAN-30X/I) ❽; I-band.
Navigation: 1 SPN-753 ❾; I-band.
SPN-741 ❿; I-band.
Fire control: Alenia Marconi NA-25XP ⓫; J-band.
Sonars: Thales TUS 4110CL; hull-mounted (bow dome).
Thales TUS 4249 active/passive towed array.
Mine avoidance sonar.

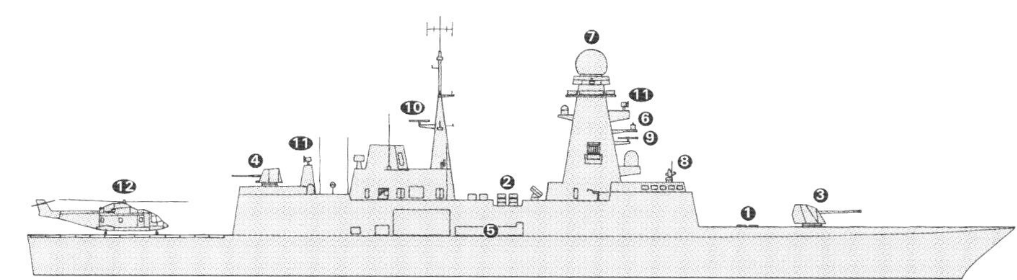
BERGAMINI (GP variant) ***(Scale 1 : 1,200), Ian Sturton*** / 1153004

Helicopters: 2 NH 90 or 1 NH 90 ⓬ plus 1 EH 101.

Programmes: Agreement reached on 7 November 2002 for a 27 ship collaborative programme with France. The original Italian requirement was for 10 frigates with common hull and machinery in two variants. Four ASW and six GP (general purpose/land-attack) ships were to replace the Lupo and Maestrale classes. Contract for the first phase awarded on 16 November 2005 to Orizzonte Sistemi Navali (Fincantieri/Finmeccanica joint venture) for the construction of a first batch of two (1 GP, 1 ASW) ships. Plans to procure a second batch of four ships (1 GP, 3 ASW) were confirmed by the Italian government in 2008 but, following curtailment of the French programme, it is possible that plans for a third batch of four GP variants will be abandoned. Provisional names for Batch 2 are: *Virginio Fasan*; *Luigi Rizzo*; *Alpino*; *Carabiniere*. There are no plans to acquire an AAW variant as Aster 15 and 30 can be fired from the A50 launcher.
Structure: The class has a conventional hull design. The main engine room contains the gas turbine and two diesel generators while the aft machinery space contains the motors. The Italian variants have a higher foredeck (an extra deck) than their French counterparts. Particular attention has been paid to signature reduction. The radar signature is expected to be comparable to that of the French La Fayette class while exhaust cooling measures are expected to achieve a comparatively low IR signature. Acoustic quietening is to be achieved by the rafting of engines and motors and the use of electric propulsion. The Italian variants are to be fitted with controllable pitch propellers.

CORVETTES

Notes: The future corvette programme is for six new ships to enter service 2018–2022. Outline requirements are for vessels of 2,000-2,500 tons displacement, 105-115 m length, 14-16 m beam, a speed of 30 kt and complement of 80 (accommodation for 120). A flight deck and hangar to operate NH-90 or EH-101 helicopters is to be included. Main armament is to be a 76 mm Super-Rapid gun while the ships are also to have the capability to operate one 11 m and one 7 m RHIB. Propulsion is likely to be all-diesel in a CODAD arrangement. Other design features are to include a reconfigurable deck, below the flight deck, for manned and unmanned craft, MCM vehicles, containerised mine laying and so on. Radar cross-section reduction measures are to be incorporated in a steel hull and composite superstructure.

8 MINERVA CLASS (FSM)

Name	*No*	*Builders*	*Laid down*	*Launched*	*Commissioned*
MINERVA	F 551	Fincantieri, Riva Trigoso	11 Mar 1985	3 Apr 1986	10 June 1987
URANIA	F 552	Fincantieri, Riva Trigoso	4 Apr 1985	21 June 1986	1 June 1987
DANAIDE	F 553	Fincantieri, Muggiano	26 June 1985	18 Oct 1986	9 Sep 1987
SFINGE	F 554	Fincantieri, Muggiano	2 Sep 1986	16 May 1987	13 Feb 1988
DRIADE	F 555	Fincantieri, Riva Trigoso	18 Mar 1988	11 Mar 1989	19 Apr 1990
CHIMERA	F 556	Fincantieri, Riva Trigoso	21 Dec 1988	7 Apr 1990	15 Jan 1991
FENICE	F 557	Fincantieri, Riva Trigoso	6 Sep 1988	9 Sep 1989	11 Sep 1990
SIBILLA	F 558	Fincantieri, Muggiano	16 Oct 1989	15 Sep 1990	16 May 1991

Displacement, tons: 1,029 light; 1,285 full load
Dimensions, feet (metres): 284.1 × 34.5 × 10.5 *(86.6 × 10.5 × 3.2)*
Main machinery: 2 Fincantieri GMT BM 230.20 DVM diesels; 11,000 hp(m) *(8.1 MW)* sustained; 2 shafts; cp props
Speed, knots: 24. **Range, n miles**: 3,500 at 18 kt
Complement: 106 (8 officers)

Missiles: SAM: Selenia Elsag Albatros octuple launcher (F 555-558) ❶; 8 Aspide; semi-active radar homing to 13 km *(7 n miles)* at 2.5 Mach; height envelope 15-5,000 m *(49.2-16,405 ft)*; warhead 30 kg. Capacity for larger magazine.
Guns: 1 OTO Melara 3 in *(76 mm)*/62 Compact ❷; 85 rds/min to 16 km *(8.7 n miles)* anti-surface; 12 km *(6.6 n miles)* anti-aircraft; weight of shell 6 kg.
Torpedoes: 6—324 mm Whitehead B 515 (2 triple) tubes (F 555-558) ❸. Honeywell Mk 46; active/passive homing to 11 km *(5.9 n miles)* at 40 kt; warhead 44 kg. Being replaced by Whitehead Mu 90.
Countermeasures: Decoys: 2 Wallop Barricade double layer launchers for chaff and IR flares. SLQ-25 Nixie; towed torpedo decoy.
ESM/ECM: Selenia SLQ-747 intercept and jammer.
Combat data systems: Selenia IPN 10 Mini SADOC action data automation; Link 11. SATCOM.

DRIADE — *(Scale 1 : 900), Ian Sturton* / 0506019

Weapons control: 1 Elsag Dardo E system. Selenia/Elsag NA 18L Pegaso optronic director ❹. Elmer TLC system.
Radars: Air/surface search: Selenia SPS-774 (RAN 10S) ❺; E/F-band.
Navigation: SMA SPN-728(V)2 ❻; I-band.
Fire control: Selenia SPG-76 (RTN 30X) ❼; I/J-band (for Albatros and gun).
Sonars: Raytheon/Elsag DE 1167; hull-mounted; active search and attack; 7.5-12 kHz.

Programmes: First four ordered in November 1982, second four in January 1987. A third four were planned, but this plan was overtaken by the acquisition of the Artigliere class.
Structure: The funnels remodelled to reduce turbulence and IR signature. Two fin stabilisers. The ships are not fitted for or with SSM.
Operational: Omega transit fitted. Intended for a number of roles including EEZ patrol, fishery protection and Commanding Officers' training. SAM launchers and torpedo tubes removed from first four units which are likely to be dedicated to a training role. All based at Augusta, Sicily. The first four units are to be decommissioned in 2014–15 and the remainder by 2020.

DRIADE — *4/2002, Schaeffer/Marsan* / 0528348

SFINGE — *9/2003, Giorgio Ghiglione* / 0570674

SHIPBORNE AIRCRAFT

Notes: It is planned to procure up to 26 STOVL variants (F-35B) of the Joint Strike Fighter to enter service from about 2015.

Numbers/Type: 15/2 McDonnell Douglas AV-8B/TAV-8B Harrier II Plus.
Operational speed: 562 kt *(1,041 km/h).*
Service ceiling: 50,000 ft *(15,240 m).*
Range: 800 n miles *(1,480 km).*
Role/Weapon systems: Two trainers delivered in July 1991 plus 15 front-line aircraft from 1994 to December 1997. Sensors: Radar derived from Hughes APG-65, FLIR, ALQ-164 ESM. Weapons: Maverick ASM; AMRAAM AIM-120B AAM; JDAM bombs and 25 mm cannon.

HARRIER PLUS *6/2005*, ***Paul Jackson*** / 1153222

Numbers/Type: 22 Agusta/Westland EH 101 Merlin.
Operational speed: 160 kt *(296 km/h).*
Service ceiling: 15,000 ft *(4,572 m).*
Range: 550 n miles *(1,019 km).*
Role/Weapon systems: Primary anti-submarine role with secondary anti-surface and troop carrying capabilities. 16 ordered in October 1995 and approved in July 1997. Six delivered by mid-2002 and further 10 by June 2004. Total of eight for ASW/ASV, four for AEW and four amphibious support (ASH). Four further special operations aircraft ordered in 2002 for delivery 2005–06. Two additional ASV variants ordered in 2005. Sensors: APS-784 (ASW/ASV version), APS-717(ASH version); Eliradar HEW-784 (AEW version) radar, L-3 HELRAS dipping sonar, Star Safire FLIR, ALR 735 ESM, ELT 156X ESM, Marconi RALM 1 decoys, Link 11, sonobuoy acoustic processor. Weapons: ASW; four Mk 46 or Mu 90 torpedoes. ASV; four Marte Mk 2/S ASM capability for guidance of ship-launched SSM.

EH 101 *3/2008**, ***Michael Nitz*** / 1335389

Numbers/Type: 1 NH Industries NH 90 NFH.
Operational speed: 157 kt *(291 km/h).*
Service ceiling: 13,940 ft *(4,250 m).*
Range: 621 n miles *(1,150 km).*
Role/Weapon systems: Two variants to replace the AB-212: 35 combat helicopters for ASW/ASV; 10 TTH utility/assault helicopters. First aircraft to be delivered in 2009. Sensors (ASW variant): Galileo Avionica ENR radar, Sagem OLOSP FLIR, L3 HELRAS dipping sonar, OTS-90 acoustic system processor. Weapons: Mu-90 torpedoes, Marte Mk 2/S ASM. TTH variant has no radar but is fitted with FLIR-111 navigation aid.

NH 90 *3/2004*, ***NHI*** / 0062373

Numbers/Type: 36 Agusta-Bell 212.
Operational speed: 106 kt *(196 km/h).*
Service ceiling: 17,000 ft *(5,180 m).*
Range: 360 n miles *(667 km).*
Role/Weapon systems: ASW/ECM/Assault helicopter; mainly deployed to escorts, but also shore-based for ASW support duties and nine used for assault. Five are for EW. To be replaced by NFH-90. Sensors: Selenia APS 705 (APS 707 in five Artigliere class aircraft) search/attack radar, Safire II EO turret (in some), AQS-13B dipping sonar or GUFO (not in Artigliere aircraft) ESM/ECM. Weapons: ASW; two Mk 46 torpedoes. Assault aircraft have an armoured cabin, no sensors and are armed with two 7.62 mm MGs and two 70 mm MRLs.

AB-212 *6/2001*, ***Adolfo Ortigueira Gil*** / 0528387

Numbers/Type: 24 Agusta-Sikorsky SH-3D/H Sea King.
Operational speed: 120 kt *(222 km/h).*
Service ceiling: 12,200 ft *(3,720 m).*
Range: 630 n miles *(1,165 km).*
Role/Weapon systems: ASW helicopter; embarked in larger ASW ships, including CVL; also shore-based for medium ASV-ASW in Mediterranean Sea; eight are fitted for ASV, 10 with ASW and EW equipment, six transport/assault. To be replaced by EH-101. Sensors: Selenia APS 705 search radar, AQS-13B dipping sonar, sonobuoys. ESM/ECM. Weapons: ASW; four Mk 46 torpedoes. ASV; two Marte 2 missiles. Assault aircraft have armoured cabins, no sensors, and are armed with two 7.62 mm MGs.

SEA KING *6/2003*, ***Adolfo Ortigueira Gil*** / 0570676

LAND-BASED MARITIME AIRCRAFT

Notes: (1) It is planned to procure up to eight Boeing P-8A Poseidon maritime patrol aircraft for entry into service in about 2015.
(2) It is planned to procure three Boeing 737 AEW Wedgetail aircraft (with option for one further) to be operated by a joint Navy/Air Force Squadron.
(3) One Agusta A 109 transport helicopter procured in 2002 for liaison duties.
(4) Five RQ-1B Predator are owned and maintained by the Italian Air Force. These can be controlled from the carrier *Giuseppe Garibaldi.*

Numbers/Type: 18 Bréguet Atlantic 1.
Operational speed: 355 kt *(658 km/h).*
Service ceiling: 22,800 ft *(10,000 m).*
Range: 4,855 n miles *(8,995 km).*
Role/Weapon systems: Air Force shore-based for long-range MR and shipping surveillance; wartime role includes ASW support to helicopters. Sensors: Thomson-CSF Iguane radar, ECM/ESM, MAD, sonobuoys; Marconi ASQ-902 acoustic system. Weapons: ASW; nine torpedoes (including Mk 46 torpedoes) or depth bombs or mines.

ATLANTIC *6/2005*, ***Paul Jackson*** / 1153221

Numbers/Type: 15 Panavia Tornado IDS.
Operational speed: 2.2 Mach.
Service ceiling: 80,000 ft *(24,385 m).*
Range: 1,500 n miles *(2,780 km).*
Role/Weapon systems: Air Force swing wing strike and recce; part of a force of a total of 100 aircraft of which 15 are used for maritime operations based at Gioia de Colle. Sensors: Texas Instruments nav/attack systems. Weapons: ASV; four Kormoran missiles; two 27 mm cannon. AD; four AIM-9L Sidewinder.

TORNADO IDS *8/2001*, ***C Hoyle/Jane's*** / 0034970

Numbers/Type: 3 Piaggio P-180 Avanti Maritime.
Operational speed: 260 kt *(482 km/h).*
Service ceiling: 39,000 ft *(11,885 m).*
Range: 1,195 n miles *(2,213 km).*
Role/Weapon systems: Maritime version of business aircraft. Two aircraft procured in 2002 for liaison duties since retrofitted with FLIR to conduct surveillance. Third aircraft ordered in 2005. Sensors: FLIR.

P-180 MARITIME *7/2005, Massimo Annati* / 1127625

Numbers/Type: 4 EADS ATR-42.
Operational speed: 300 kt *(556 km/h).*
Service ceiling: 18,000 ft *(5,485 m).*
Range: 1,600 n miles *(2,963 km).*
Role/Weapon systems: Four aircraft ordered in 2005 for operation by the Navy in surveillance and SAR roles. Sensors: Airborne Tactical Observation and Surveillance System (ATOS), with two tactical consoles and one communication console; SV-2022 radar, Galileo EOST-23 FLIR, Elettronica ALR-733 ESM. Link-11 datalink, defensive suite with chaffs/flare launchers. Weapons: pod-mounted MG.

ATR-42 *6/2005, Paul Jackson* / 1127626

PATROL FORCES

6 COMANDANTE CLASS PATROL VESSELS (PSOH)

Name	*No*	*Builders*	*Launched*	*Commissioned*
COMANDANTE CIGALA FULGOSI	P 490	Fincantieri, Riva Trigoso	7 Oct 2000	31 July 2001
COMANDANTE BORSINI	P 491	Fincantieri, Riva Trigoso	17 Feb 2001	4 Dec 2001
COMANDANTE BETTICA	P 492	Fincantieri, Riva Trigoso	23 June 2001	4 Apr 2002
COMANDANTE FOSCARI	P 493	Fincantieri, Riva Trigoso	24 Nov 2001	1 Aug 2002
SIRIO	P 409	Fincantieri, Riva Trigoso	11 May 2002	31 May 2003
ORIONE	P 410	Fincantieri, Riva Trigoso	24 July 2002	1 Aug 2003

Displacement, tons: 1,520 full load
Dimensions, feet (metres): 290.0 × 40 × 15.1 (screws) *(88.4 × 12.2 × 4.6)*
Main machinery: 2 GM Trieste-Wärtsilä W18-V 26 XIV diesels; 17,600 hp(m) *(13.2 MW)*; 2 shafts; cp props; bow thruster
2 Wärtsilä 12V26X diesels (P 409-410); 11,585 hp *(8.64 MW)*; 2 shafts; cp props; bow thruster
Speed, knots: 26 (22 kt for P 409-410)
Range, n miles: 3,500 at 14 kt
Complement: 60 (5 officers)

Guns: 1 Otobreda 3 in *(76 mm)*/62 compact (P 490–492 and P 409–410 (planned)) ❶.
1 Otobreda 3 in *(76 mm)*/62 Super Rapid (P 493).
2 Otobreda 25 mm/90 ❷.
Countermeasures: Decoys: Chaff launcher.
ESM/ECM: Selenia SLQ-747; intercept and jammer.
Combat data systems: AMS IPNS.
Weapons control: 1 optronic director ❸.
Radars: Surface search: SPS 791 (RAN-30X/I) ❹; I-band.
Fire control: SPG 76 (RTN 25X) ❺; I/J-band.
Navigation: SPS 753 ❻; I-band.

Helicopters: 1 AB 212 ❼; or NH90 in due course.

Programmes: Four (P 490-493) for the Navy, and two funded by the Ministry of Transport, manned by the Navy, but equipped with more simple command data systems for anti-pollution and SAR tasks.
Modernisation: A mid-life upgrade for P 490-493 is planned 2014–18. This is likely to include Davide 76 mm guided munitions.
Structure: Stealth features in naval vessels include IR suppression and reduced radar cross-section. P 493 has a superstructure of composite material. P 409-410 appear to be less stealthy, have less powerful engines, no hangar and no countermeasures.
Operational: All based at Augusta, Sicily.

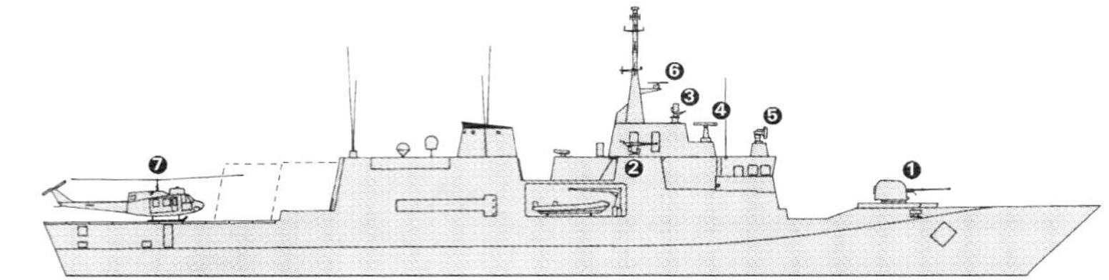

COMANDANTE FOSCARI *(Scale 1 : 900), Ian Sturton* / 0589003

COMANDANTE BORSINI *3/2008*, Guy Toremans* / 1335390

SIRIO *6/2007, Ships of the World* / 1166593

4 CASSIOPEA CLASS (OFFSHORE PATROL VESSELS) (PSOH)

Name	*No*	*Builders*	*Laid down*	*Launched*	*Commissioned*
CASSIOPEA	P 401	Fincantieri, Muggiano	16 Dec 1987	20 July 1988	6 July 1989
LIBRA	P 402	Fincantieri, Muggiano	17 Dec 1987	27 July 1988	28 Nov 1989
SPICA	P 403	Fincantieri, Muggiano	5 Sep 1988	27 May 1989	3 May 1990
VEGA	P 404	Fincantieri, Muggiano	20 June 1989	24 Feb 1990	25 Oct 1990

Displacement, tons: 1,002 standard; 1,475 full load
Dimensions, feet (metres): 261.8 × 38.7 × 11.5 *(79.8 × 11.8 × 3.5)*
Flight deck, feet (metres): 72.2 × 26.2 *(22 × 8)*
Main machinery: 2 Fincantieri/GMT BL 230.16 M diesels; 7,940 hp(m) *(5.84 MW)* sustained; 2 shafts; LIPS cp props
Speed, knots: 20. **Range, n miles:** 3,300 at 17 kt
Complement: 65 (5 officers)

Guns: 1 OTO Melara 3 in *(76 mm)*/62; 60 rds/min to 16 km *(8.7 n miles)*; weight of shell 6 kg. Breda Oerlikon 25 mm/90. 2—12.7 mm MGs.
Weapons control: Argo NA 10.
Radars: Surface search: SMA SPS-702(V)2; I-band.
Navigation: SMA SPN-748(V)2; I-band.
Fire control: Selenia SPG-70 (RTN 10X); I/J-band.

Helicopters: 1 AB 212ASW.

Programmes: Ordered in December 1986 for operations in EEZ. Officially 'pattugliatori marittimi'. Funded by the Ministry of Transport but all operated by the Navy.
Structure: Fitted for firefighting, rescue and supply tasks. Telescopic hangar. The 20 mm guns were old stock taken from deleted Bergamini class and have been replaced by 25 mm guns. There is a 500 m³ tank for storing oil polluted water.
Operational: All based at Augusta. To remain in service until 2020.

VEGA *3/2001, Giorgio Ghiglione* / 0130329

4 ESPLORATORE CLASS (PB)

Name	*No*	*Builders*	*Launched*	*Commissioned*
ESPLORATORE	P 405	Coinaval, La Spezia	4 Nov 1996	26 June 1997
SENTINELLA	P 406	Coinaval, La Spezia	13 Nov 1997	10 July 1998
VEDETTA	P 407	Coinaval, La Spezia	11 Jan 1997	29 July 1999
STAFFETTA	P 408	Coinaval, La Spezia/Oromare	Nov 2002	6 July 2005

Displacement, tons: 165 full load
Dimensions, feet (metres): 122 × 23.3 × 6.2 *(37.2 × 7.1 × 1.9)*
Main machinery: 2 Isotta Fraschini M1712T2 diesels; 3,810 hp(m) *(2.8 MW)*; 2 shafts
Speed, knots: 20. **Range, n miles:** 1,200 at 20 kt
Complement: 14 (2 officers)
Guns: 1 Oerlikon 20 mm/70. 2—7.62 mm MGs.
Weapons control: AESN Medusa optronic director to be fitted.
Radars: Surface search: 2 SPS-753B/C; F/I-band.

Comment: Ordered from Ortona Shipyard in December 1993 but the contract was then transferred to Coinaval Yards, La Spezia in 1994 which caused inevitable delays and construction did not start until 1995. An option on a fourth of class, was taken up in February 1998 but shipbuilding programme delayed launch until January 2001 when it was transferred to Oromare shipyard for completion which was further delayed by financial problems. Based in Red Sea for Multinational Force Observer (MFO) operations. To return to Adriatic on completion.

ESPLORATORE *3/2008*, Giorgio Ghiglione* / 1335467

AMPHIBIOUS FORCES

Notes: (1) Following the establishment of the National Projection Force in 2006, two Amphibious Battle Groups are to become operational in late 2008. Further improvement to power projection capabilities forces, an enhancement to amphibious lift, is under consideration. The first step is the procurement of two 170 m LHDs of 16-18,000 tons to replace/supplement the present force. To enter service in 2017 and 2022, broad capabilities are to include accommodation for 450 troops, 1,000-1,200 lane-metres for vehicles, five landing spots on the flight deck, a stern well-dock for four LCM and davits for three LCVPs.
(2) A Ro-Ro ship MV *Major* built in 1984 is on long term charter to the Army Mobility and Transport Command. 6,830 tons displacement with 1,240 m of vehicle lanes. Can carry 3,955 tons of cargo.
(3) There are also 54 Rigid Raider Craft in service with Amphibious Forces.

2 PEDRETTI CLASS (SPECIAL OPERATIONS SUPPORT CRAFT) (YDT)

Name	*No*	*Builders*	*Commissioned*
ALCIDE PEDRETTI	Y 499 (ex-MEN 213)	Crestitalia-Ameglia	23 Oct 1984
MARIO MARINO	Y 498 (ex-MEN 214)	Crestitalia-Ameglia	21 Dec 1984

Displacement, tons: 75.4 *(Alcide Pedretti)*, 69.5 *(Mario Marino)* full load
Dimensions, feet (metres): 86.6 × 22.6 × 3.3 *(26.4 × 6.9 × 1)*
Main machinery: 2 Isotta Fraschini ID 36 SS 12V diesels; 2,640 hp(m) *(1.94 MW)* sustained; 2 shafts
Speed, knots: 25. **Range, n miles:** 450 *(Alcide Pedretti)*, 250 *(Mario Marino)* at 23 kt
Complement: 8 (1 officer)
Radars: Navigation: I-band.

Comment: Both laid down 8 September 1983. For use by assault swimmers of COMSUBIN. Both have decompression chambers. *Alcide Pedretti* has a floodable dock aft and is used for combat swimmers and special operations, while *Mario Marino* is fitted for underwater work and rescue missions. Based at Varignano, La Spezia. A similar but more heavily equipped vessel serves with the UAE Navy.

ALCIDE PEDRETTI *10/1999, Giorgio Ghiglione* / 0080088

9 MTM 217 CLASS (LCM)

MEN 217–222 **MEN 227–228** **MEN 551**

Displacement, tons: 64.6 full load
Dimensions, feet (metres): 60.7 × 16.7 × 3 *(18.5 × 5.1 × 0.9)*
Main machinery: 2 Fiat diesels; 560 hp(m) *(412 kW)*; 2 shafts
Speed, knots: 9
Range, n miles: 300 at 9 kt
Complement: 3
Military lift: 30 tons

Comment: First six built at Muggiano, La Spezia by Fincantieri. Three completed 9 October 1987 for *San Giorgio*, three completed 8 March 1988 for *San Marco*. Three more ordered in March 1991 from Balzamo Shipyard and completed in 1993 for *San Giusto*. Others of this class are also in service with the Army.

MEN 219 and 220 *2000, M Annati* / 0104881

3 SAN GIORGIO CLASS (LPD)

Name	*No*	*Builders*	*Laid down*	*Launched*	*Commissioned*
SAN GIORGIO	L 9892	Fincantieri, Riva Trigoso	27 June 1985	25 Feb 1987	9 Oct 1987
SAN MARCO	L 9893	Fincantieri, Riva Trigoso	28 June 1986	21 Oct 1987	18 Mar 1988
SAN GIUSTO	L 9894	Fincantieri, Riva Trigoso	30 Nov 1992	2 Dec 1993	9 Apr 1994

Displacement, tons: 6,687 standard; 7,960 (8,000 *San Giusto*) full load
Dimensions, feet (metres): 449.5 (*San Giusto*); 437.2 × 67.3 × 17.4 *(137; 133.3 × 20.5 × 5.3)*
Flight deck, feet (metres): 328.1 × 67.3 *(100 × 20.5)*
Main machinery: 2 Fincantieri GMT A 420.12 diesels; 16,800 hp(m) *(12.35 MW)* sustained; 2 shafts; LIPS cp props; bow thruster
Speed, knots: 21. **Range, n miles**: 7,500 at 16 kt; 4,500 at 20 kt
Complement: 168 (12 officers); 167 (15 officers) *(San Giusto)*
Military lift: Battalion of 400 plus 30-36 APCs or 30 medium tanks. 2 LCMs in stern docking well. 3 *(San Giusto)* or 2 (*San Giorgio* and *San Marco*) LCVPs on sponsons. 1 LCPL

Guns: 1 OTO Melara 3 in *(76 mm)*/62 (Compact in *San Giusto*); 60 rds/min to 16 km *(8.7 n miles)*; weight of shell 6 kg.
2 Breda Oerlikon 25 mm/90. 2—12.7 mm MGs.
Countermeasures: ESM: SLR 730; intercept.
ESM/ECM: SLQ-747 *(San Giusto)*.
Combat data systems: Selenia IPN 20 *(San Giusto)*. Marisat. SATCOM.
Weapons control: Elsag NA 10.
Radars: Surface search: SMA SPS-702; I-band
Navigation: SMA SPN-748; I-band
Fire control: Selenia SPG-70 (RTN 10X); I/J-band

Helicopters: 3 SH-3D Sea King or EH 101 Merlin or 5 AB 212.

Programmes: *San Giorgio* ordered 26 November 1983, *San Marco* on 5 March 1984 and *San Giusto* 1 March 1991. Launching dates of the first two are slightly later than the 'official' launching ceremony because of poor weather and for the third because of industrial problems.
Modernisation: 25 mm guns replaced 20 mm from 1999. Modifications to *San Giorgio* include removal of the 76 mm gun, movement of LCVPs from davits to a new sponson, and lengthening and enlargement of the flight deck to allow two Merlin and two AB 212 to operate simultaneously on deck. Work completed in early 2003. Similar work on *San Marco* completed in March 2004. *San Giusto* has been fitted with an MCC data system to enable her to act as CJTF. *San Giusto* is to undergo a mid-life modernisation programme 2012–13.
Structure: Aircraft carrier type flight deck with island to starboard. Following modernisation, *San Giorgio* and *San Marco* have four landing spots, a stern docking well (20.5 × 7 m), 2 LCVPs on a port side sponson, a 30 ton lift and two 40 ton travelling cranes for LCMs. *San Giusto* is of similar design, but was 300 tons heavier on build to include extra accommodation, 3 LCVP sponsons and a slightly longer island. Bow doors and beaching capability removed from *San Marco* and *San Giorgio* in refit.
Operational: *San Marco* was paid for by the Ministry of Civil Protection, is specially fitted for disaster relief but is run by the Navy. All are based at Brindisi and assigned to COMFORAL. One of the three ships carries out the annual Summer cruise for officer and petty officer cadets. *San Giorgio* and *San Marco* are expected to decommission in 2017 and 2022 respectively when replaced by new LHDs.

SAN GIORGIO **8/2003, C D Yaylali** / 0570661

SAN MARCO **6/2007, *Ships of the World*** / 1166592

SAN GIUSTO **9/2004, John Brodie** / 1044369

0 + 4 MODIFIED MTM 217 CLASS (LCM)

Displacement, tons: 34 standard; 65 full load
Dimensions, feet (metres): 64.0 × 16.7 × 3.0 *(19.5 × 5.1 × 0.9)*
Main machinery: 2 diesels; 2 shafts
Speed, knots: 9. **Range, n miles**: 300 at 9 kt
Complement: 3

Comment: Four new LCM under construction at Vittoria Shipyard, Adria. Slightly larger versions than MTM 217 class to accommodate latest army armoured vehicles. Ballistic protection fitted. Delivery expected from mid-2009.

17 MTP 96 CLASS (LCVP)

MDN 94–104 **MDN 108–109** **MDN 114–117**

Displacement, tons: 14.3 full load
Dimensions, feet (metres): 44.9 × 12.5 × 2.3 *(13.7 × 3.8 × 0.7)*
Main machinery: 2 diesels; 700 hp(m) *(515 kW)*; 2 shafts or 2 water-jets
Speed, knots: 29 or 22. **Range, n miles**: 100 at 12 kt
Complement: 3

Comment: Built by Technomatic Ancona in 1985 (two), Technomatic Bari in 1987–88 (six) and Technoplast Venezia 1991–94 (nine). Can carry 45 men or 4.5 tons of cargo. These craft have Kevlar armour. The most recent versions have water-jet propulsion which gives a top speed of 29 kt (22 kt fully laden). This is being backfitted to all GRP LCVPs.

MDN 101 **10/2001, Chris Sattler** / 0130326

MINE WARFARE FORCES

Notes: Following a feasibility study completed by Intermarine in 2003, four new larger MCM vessels are planned to enter service in about 2020. The new vessels are to be faster than traditional MCM units, have a better signature reduction (acoustic, magnetic, IR and radar), longer range, and superior armament and countermeasures. The new MCMV is to be capable of operating as a platform for remotely controlled autonomous unmanned vehicles, capable of both minehunting and minesweeping. These are likely to be based on four types: Remus, Pluto Gigas, RHIB-based USV, Mi-Ki (Plutino) one-shot mine-destructors.

12 LERICI/GAETA CLASS (MINEHUNTERS/SWEEPERS) (MHSC)

Name	*No*	*Builders*	*Launched*	*Commissioned*
LERICI	M 5550	Intermarine, Sarzana	3 Sep 1982	22 Mar 1985
SAPRI	M 5551	Intermarine, Sarzana	5 Apr 1984	4 June 1985
MILAZZO	M 5552	Intermarine, Sarzana	4 Jan 1985	6 Aug 1985
VIESTE	M 5553	Intermarine, Sarzana	18 Apr 1985	2 Dec 1985
GAETA	M 5554	Intermarine, Sarzana	28 July 1990	3 July 1992
TERMOLI	M 5555	Intermarine, Sarzana	15 Dec 1990	13 Nov 1992
ALGHERO	M 5556	Intermarine, Sarzana	11 May 1991	31 Mar 1993
NUMANA	M 5557	Intermarine, Sarzana	26 Oct 1991	30 July 1993
CROTONE	M 5558	Intermarine, Sarzana	11 Apr 1992	19 Jan 1994
VIAREGGIO	M 5559	Intermarine, Sarzana	3 Oct 1992	1 July 1994
CHIOGGIA	M 5560	Intermarine, Sarzana	9 May 1994	19 May 1996
RIMINI	M 5561	Intermarine, Sarzana	17 Sep 1994	26 Nov 1996

Displacement, tons: 620 (697, *Gaeta* onwards) full load
Dimensions, feet (metres): 164 (172.1 *Gaeta*) × 32.5 × 8.6 *(50 (52.5) × 9.9 × 2.6)*
Main machinery: 1 Fincantieri GMT BL 230.8 M diesel (passage); 1,985 hp(m) *(1.46 MW)* sustained; 1 shaft; LIPS cp prop; 3 Isotta Fraschini ID 36 SS 6V diesels (hunting); 1,481 hp(m) *(1.1 MW)* sustained; 3 hydraulic 360° rotating thrust props; 506 hp(m) *(372 kW)* (1 fwd, 2 aft)
Speed, knots: 14; 6 hunting. **Range, n miles:** 1,500 at 14 kt
Complement: 44 (4 officers) including 7 divers

Guns: 1 Oerlikon 20 mm/70.
Countermeasures: Minehunting: 1 Plutogigas and 1 Pluto standard RoV; 1 SMIN Mk 2 and 1 Pluto Plus (*Gaeta* onwards); diving equipment and Galeazzi recompression chamber; Galeazzi Z1 two-man recompression chamber (*Gaeta* onwards).
Minesweeping: Oropesa Mk 4 wire sweep.
Combat data systems: Motorola MRS III/GPS Eagle precision navigation system with Datamat SMA SSN-714V(3) automatic plotting and radar indicator IP-7113. Datamat SMA SSN-714 V(2) (*Gaeta* onwards).
Radars: Navigation: SMA SPN-728V(3); I-band.
Sonars: FIAR SQQ-14(IT) VDS (lowered from keel forward of bridge); classification and route survey; high frequency.

Programmes: First four (Lerici class) ordered 7 January 1978 under Legge Navale. Next six (Gaeta class) ordered from Intermarine 30 April 1988 and two more in 1991. The Gaeta-class ships are 2 m longer and are of an improved design. Construction of Gaetas started in 1988. The last pair delayed by budget cuts but re-ordered on 17 September 1992.
Modernisation: Improvements to Gaeta class include a better minehunting sonar system which was backfitted to the Lerici class in 1991. Other Gaeta upgrades include a third hydraulic system, improved electrical generators, Pluto Gigas ROV, a new type of recompression chamber, and a reduced magnetic signature. Modernisation of the eight Gaeta class is to be implemented 2010–2013. Upgrades are planned to include: replacement of SQQ-14 sonar with Thales 2093; a new combat data system Datamat 712(V)3; replacement of the SMIN Mk 2 ROVs with Plutogigas and provision of Plutino. Miki expendable mine neutralisation system. Some alterations to the superstructure will be required.
Structure: Of heavy GRP throughout hull, decks and bulkheads, with frames eliminated. All machinery is mounted on vibration dampers and main engines made of a magnetic material. Fitted with crane for launching RoVs and for diving operations.
Operational: Endurance, 12 days. For long passages passive roll-stabilising tanks can be used for extra fuel increasing range to 4,000 miles at 12 kt.
Two Lerici class are likely to decommission in 2015 and the other two in 2020.
Sales: Four to Malaysia, two to Nigeria, two to Thailand and three to Finland. 12 of a modified design built by the US and six by Australia.

LERICI *1/2008*, Giorgio Ghiglione* / 1335468

RIMINI *1/2008*, Giorgio Ghiglione* / 1335469

SURVEY AND RESEARCH SHIPS

1 SURVEY SHIP (AGORH/AGE/AGI)

Name	*No*	*Builders*	*Commissioned*
ELETTRA	A 5340	Fincantieri, Muggiano	2 Apr 2003

Displacement, tons: 3,180 full load
Dimensions, feet (metres): 305.1 × 49.9 × 17.1 *(93 × 15.2 × 5.2)*
Main machinery: Diesel electric; 2 Wartsila CW 12V 200 diesel generators; 5,750 kVA. 2 ABB motors; 4,023 hp *(3 MW)*; 2 shafts; bow thruster
Speed, knots: 17. **Range, n miles:** 8,000 at 12 kt
Complement: 94 (12 officers)
Radars: Navigation: I-band.
Helicopters: Platform for one medium.

Comment: Ordered on 1 December 1999; construction started in March 2000 and launch on 24 July 2002. The design is derived from that of the NATO *Alliance* but is equipped as an intelligence collector. The propulsion system, based on two multi permanent magnet electric motors, is the first of its type to be fitted in a surface vessel.

ELETTRA *9/2008*, Giorgio Ghiglione* / 1335470

1 SURVEY SHIP (AGSH)

Name	*No*	*Builders*	*Commissioned*
AMMIRAGLIO MAGNAGHI	A 5303	Fincantieri, Riva Trigoso	2 May 1975

Displacement, tons: 1,700 full load
Dimensions, feet (metres): 271.3 × 44.9 × 11.5 *(82.7 × 13.7 × 3.5)*
Main machinery: 2 GMT B 306 SS diesels; 3,000 hp(m) *(2.2 MW)*; 1 shaft; cp prop; auxiliary motor; 240 hp(m) *(176 kW)*; bow thruster
Speed, knots: 16. **Range, n miles:** 6,000 at 12 kt (1 diesel); 4,200 at 16 kt (2 diesels)
Complement: 148 (14 officers, 15 scientists)
Guns: 1 Breda 40 mm/70 (not fitted).
Radars: Navigation: SMA 3 RM 20; I-band.
Helicopters: Platform only.

Comment: Ordered under 1972 programme. Laid down 13 June 1973. Launched 11 October 1974. Full air conditioning, bridge engine controls, flume-type stabilisers. Equipped for oceanographical studies including laboratories and underwater TV. Two Qubit Trac V integrated navigation and logging systems and a Chart V data processing system installed in 1992 to augment the existing Trac 100-based HODAPS. Carries four surveying motor boats and up to two RHIBs. To be decommissioned 2012–13.

AMMIRAGLIO MAGNAGHI *7/2008*, Giorgio Ghiglione* / 1335479

2 SURVEY SHIPS (AGS)

Name	*No*	*Builders*	*Commissioned*
ARETUSA	A 5304	Intermarine	10 Jan 2002
GALATEA	A 5308	Intermarine	10 Jan 2002

Displacement, tons: 415 full load
Dimensions, feet (metres): 128.6 × 41.3 × 8.2 *(39.2 × 12.6 × 2.5)*
Main machinery: Diesel electric; 2 Isotta Fraschini V170812 ME diesels; 2 ABB generators 1,904 hp(m) *(1.4 MW)*; 2 shafts; Schottel props; 2 bow thrusters
Speed, knots: 13. **Range, n miles:** 1,700 at 13 kt
Complement: 29 (4 officers)
Guns: 2—7.62 mm MGs.
Radars: 2 Navigation; I-band.

Comment: GRP catamaran design. Ordered in January 1998. *Aretusa* launched 8 May 2000 and *Galatea* 7 June 2000. Fitted with Kongsberg EA 500 single-beam echo sounder, towed sidescan sonar and dynamic positioning system.

GALATEA *1/2004, Giorgio Ghiglione* / 1044371

1 RESEARCH SHIP (AG/AGOR)

Name	*No*	*Builders*	*Launched*	*Commissioned*
RAFFAELE ROSSETTI	A 5315	Picchiotti, Viareggio	12 July 1986	20 Dec 1986

Displacement, tons: 320 full load
Dimensions, feet (metres): 146.3 × 25.9 × 6.9 *(44.6 × 7.9 × 2.1)*
Main machinery: 2 Fincantieri Isotta Fraschini ID 36 N 6V diesels; 3,520 hp(m) *(2.55 kW)* sustained; 2 shafts; cp props; bow thruster
Speed, knots: 17.5
Range, n miles: 700 at 15 kt
Complement: 17 (2 officers)

Comment: Five different design torpedo tubes fitted for above and underwater testing and trials. Other equipment for research into communications, surface and air search as well as underwater weapons. There is a stern doorway which is partially submerged and the ship has a set of 96 batteries to allow 'silent' propulsion. Operated by the Permanent Commission for Experiments of War Materials at La Spezia.

RAFFAELE ROSSETTI *4/2005, Giorgio Ghiglione* / 1153242

1 RESEARCH SHIP (AG/AGE)

Name	*No*	*Builders*	*Commissioned*
VINCENZO MARTELLOTTA	A 5320	Picchiotti, Viareggio	22 Dec 1990

Displacement, tons: 340 full load
Dimensions, feet (metres): 146.3 × 25.9 × 7.5 *(44.6 × 7.9 × 2.3)*
Main machinery: 2 Fincantieri Isotta Fraschini ID 36 SS 16V diesels; 3,520 hp(m) *(2.59 MW)* sustained; 2 shafts; cp props; bow thruster
Speed, knots: 17. **Range, n miles:** 700 at 15 kt
Complement: 19 (2 officers)

Comment: Launched on 28 May 1988. Has one 21 in *(533 mm)* and three 12.75 in *(324 mm)* torpedo tubes and acoustic equipment to operate a 3-D tracking range for torpedoes or underwater vehicles. Like *Rossetti* she is operated by the Commission for Experiments at La Spezia.

VINCENZO MARTELLOTTA *9/2008*, Giorgio Ghiglione* / 1335471

TRAINING SHIPS

Notes: (1) In addition to the ships listed the LPDs are used in a training role.
(2) There is a requirement for new training ships to replace the Aragosta class but the programme is not funded.

1 SAIL TRAINING SHIP (AXS)

Name	*No*	*Builders*	*Commissioned*
AMERIGO VESPUCCI	A 5312	Castellammare	15 May 1931

Displacement, tons: 3,543 standard; 4,146 full load
Dimensions, feet (metres): 229.5 pp; 270 oa hull; 330 oa bowsprit × 51 × 22 *(70; 82.4; 100 × 15.5 × 7)*
Main machinery: Diesel-electric; 2 Fiat B 306 ESS diesel generators; 2 Marelli motors; 2,000 hp(m) *(1.47 MW)*; 1 shaft
Speed, knots: 10. **Range, n miles:** 5,450 at 6.5 kt
Complement: 243 (13 officers)
Radars: Navigation: 2 SMA SPN-748; I-band.

Comment: Launched on 22 March 1930. Hull, masts and yards are of steel. Sail area, 22,604 sq ft. Extensively refitted at La Spezia Naval Dockyard in 1973 and again in 1984. Used for Naval Academy Summer cruise with up to 150 trainees.

AMERIGO VESPUCCI *7/2004, Ships of the World* / 1044364

1 SAIL TRAINING SHIP (AXS)

Name	*No*	*Builders*	*Commissioned*
PALINURO (ex-*Commandant Louis Richard*)	A 5311	Ch Dubigeon, Nantes	1934

Displacement, tons: 1,042 standard; 1,450 full load
Measurement, tons: 858 gross
Dimensions, feet (metres): 193.5 × 32.8 × 15.7 *(59 × 10 × 4.8)*
Main machinery: 1 GMT A 230.6N diesel; 600 hp *(447 kW)*; 1 shaft
Speed, knots: 7.5
Range, n miles: 5,390 at 7.5 kt
Complement: 69 (6 officers)
Radars: Navigation: SPN-748; I-band.

Comment: Barquentine launched in 1934. Purchased in 1951. Rebuilt in 1954–55 and commissioned in Italian Navy on 1 July 1955. Sail area, 1,152 sq ft. She was one of the last two French Grand Bank cod-fishing barquentines. Owned by the Armement Glâtre she was based at St Malo until bought by Italy. Used for seamanship basic training.

PALINURO *10/2008*, Giorgio Ghiglione* / 1335480

3 ARAGOSTA (HAM) CLASS (AXL)

ASTICE A 5379 **MITILO** A 5380 **PORPORA** A 5382

Displacement, tons: 188 full load
Dimensions, feet (metres): 106 × 21 × 6 *(32.5 × 6.4 × 1.8)*
Main machinery: 2 Fiat-MTU 12V 493 TY7 diesels; 2,200 hp(m) *(1.62 MW)* sustained; 2 shafts
Speed, knots: 14
Range, n miles: 2,000 at 9 kt
Complement: 13 (2 officers)
Radars: Navigation: BX 732; I-band.

Comment: Builders: CRDA, Monfalcone: *Astice*. Picchiotti, Viareggio: *Mitilo*. Costaguta, Voltri: *Porpora*. Similar to the late UK Ham class. All constructed to the order of NATO in 1955–57. Designed armament of one 20 mm gun not mounted. Originally class of 20. Remaining three converted for training 1986. *Porpora* used by the Naval Academy. *Astice* has a modified bridge structure. To be decommissioned in 2012.

ASTICE *1/2008*, Giorgio Ghiglione* / 1335472

5 SAIL TRAINING YACHTS (AXS)

Name	*No*	*Builders*	*Commissioned*
CAROLY	A 5302	Baglietto, Varazze	1948
STELLA POLARE	A 5313	Sangermani, Chiavari	8 Oct 1965
CORSARO II	A 5316	Costaguta, Voltri	5 Jan 1961
CAPRICIA	A 5322	Bengt-Plym	1963
ORSA MAGGIORE	A 5323	Tencara, Venezia	1994

Comment: The first three are sail training yachts between 40 and 60 tons with a crew including trainees of about 16. *Capricia* is a yawl of 55 tons and was donated by the Agnelli foundation as replacement for *Cristoforo Colombo II* which was not completed when the shipyard building her went bankrupt. *Capricia* commissioned in the Navy 23 May 1993. *Orsa Maggiore* is a ketch of 70 tons.

STELLA POLARE *7/2007, Giorgio Ghiglione* / 1166587

1 SAIL TRAINING SHIP (AXS)

ITALIA

Displacement, tons: 32 full load
Dimensions, feet (metres): 61.0 × 9.2 × ? *(200.0 × 30.2 × ?)*
Main machinery: 1 diesel; 480 hp *(358 kW)*
Complement: 10 plus 100 passengers

Comment: The world's largest brigantine donated by the Italian Yacht Club to the Italian Navy in 2008. The vessel has 1,300 m² of sails.

ITALIA *6/2008*, Annati Collection* / 1335388

RESCUE VEHICLES

1 RESCUE SUBMERSIBLE

SRV 300

Displacement, tons: 27
Dimensions, feet (metres): 27.7 × 10.2 × 10.4 *(8.46 × 3.13 × 3.17)*
Main machinery: 1 electric motor; 27 hp *(20 kW)*; 2 transverse/vertical thrusters; 27 hp *(20 kW)*
Speed, knots: 2.5. **Range, n miles**: 15 at 2 kt
Complement: 2

Comment: Free-swimming Submarine Rescue Vehicle (SRV) built by Drass Galeazzi Srl which entered service in 2005. The SRV can be launched and recovered in up to Sea State 3 from *Anteo* or a suitably equipped commercial or military 'mothership' equipped with a portable launch-and-recovery system. SRV 300 can mate at up to angles of 45° and is capable of rescuing groups of up to 12 at a time. Capable of reaching depths down to 300 m, the vehicle is equipped with an external manipulator and underwater television cameras.

SRV 300 *6/2008*, Italian Navy* / 1305307

AUXILIARIES

Notes: (1) It is planned to replace *Stromboli* and *Vesuvio* with two new Logistic Support ships. The broad requirement is for double-hulled ships, to comply with MARPOL regulations, of about 18,000 tons displacement and capable of 20 kt. Equipped with two RAS fuel stations per side, one stern fuel station and one RAS solid station per side, the ships are to carry of the order of 6,400 cum F76 diesel, 1,500 cum F44 aviation fuel, 1,000 cum fresh water, 300 tons of aviation and naval ordnance, 120 tons of provisions and spares and space for 12 TEU containers. There is to be a hangar for one EH-101 and a 20-bed hospital to provide role 2 medical support. The complement is to be approximately 165 with accommodation for over 200. An order is expected in 2012.
(2) Replacement of the submarine-rescue and deep-diving support capability by an Underwater Support Ship is under consideration. The preferred solution to replace *Anteo* and the decommissioned *Proteo* is likely to be the lease of a purpose-built platform capable of acting as mother-ship for a submarine rescue system as well as support for deepwater divers and MCM. A contract is expected in 2009.

1 ETNA CLASS (REPLENISHMENT TANKER) (AORH)

Name	*No*	*Builders*	*Laid down*	*Launched*	*Commissioned*
ETNA	A 5326	Fincantieri, Riva Trigoso	4 July 1995	12 July 1997	29 Aug 1998

Displacement, tons: 13,400 full load
Dimensions, feet (metres): 480.6 × 68.9 × 24.3 *(146.5 × 21 × 7.4)*
Flight deck, feet (metres): 91.9 × 68. 9 *(28 × 21)*
Main machinery: 2 Sulzer 12 ZAV 40S diesels; 22,400 hp(m) *(16.46 MW)* sustained; 2 shafts; bow thruster
Speed, knots: 21
Range, n miles: 7,600 at 18 kt
Complement: 162 (14 officers) plus 81 spare
Cargo capacity: 6,350 tons gas oil; 1,200 tons JP5; 2,100 m^3 ammunition and stores
Guns: 1 OTO Melara 76 mm/62. 2 Breda Oerlikon 25 mm/93.
Radars: Surface search: SMA SPS-702(V)3; I-band.
Navigation: GEM SPN-753; I-band.
Helicopters: 1 EH 101 Merlin or SH-3D or 2 AB 212.

Comment: Details revised in 1992 for an order 29 July 1994. Construction authorised on 3 January 1995. The main gun is not fitted, and the specification includes a CIWS on the hangar roof. Two RAS stations on each side. A similar ship has been built for Greece. A major upgrade to C^{4}I capability has given the ship a Maritime Component Commander capability. A mid-life update is planned 2014–15.

ETNA *3/2008*, Michael Nitz* / 1335387

2 STROMBOLI CLASS (REPLENISHMENT TANKERS) (AORH)

Name	*No*	*Builders*	*Launched*	*Commissioned*
STROMBOLI	A 5327	Fincantieri, Riva Trigoso	20 Feb 1975	20 Nov 1975
VESUVIO	A 5329	Fincantieri, Muggiano	4 June 1977	18 Nov 1978

Displacement, tons: 3,556 light; 8,706 full load
Dimensions, feet (metres): 423.1 × 59 × 21.3 *(129 × 18 × 6.5)*
Main machinery: 2 GMT C428 SS diesels; 9,600 hp(m) *(7.06 MW)*; 1 shaft; LIPS cp prop
Speed, knots: 18.5. **Range, n miles**: 5,080 at 18 kt
Complement: 131 (10 officers)
Cargo capacity: 3,000 tons FFO; 1,000 tons dieso; 400 tons JP5; 300 tons other stores
Guns: 1 OTO Melara 3 in *(76 mm)*/62.
1—40 mm. 2—25 mm.
Weapons control: Argo NA 10 system.
Radars: Surface search: SMA SPQ-2; I-band.
Navigation: SMA SPN-748; I-band.
Fire control: Selenia SPG-70 (RTN 10X); I/J-band.
Helicopters: Platform for 1 medium.

Comment: *Vesuvio* was the first large ship to be built at Muggiano (near La Spezia) since the Second World War and the first with funds under Legge Navale 1975. Beam and stern refuelling stations for fuel and stores. Also Vertrep. The two ships have different midships crane arrangements. Similar ship built for Iraq and laid up in Alexandria since 1986. 20 mm guns replaced by 25 mm from 2002. To remain in service until replaced by Logistic Support Ships from about 2014.

VESUVIO *10/2007, Giorgio Ghiglione* / 1166588

4 MCC 1101 CLASS (WATER TANKERS) (AWT)

PANAREA (ex-*MCC 1101*) A 5370
LINOSA (ex-*MCC 1102*) A 5371
FAVIGNANA (ex-*MCC 1103*) A 5372
SALINA (ex-*MCC 1104*) A 5373

Displacement, tons: 898 full load
Dimensions, feet (metres): 155.2 × 32.8 × 10.8 *(47.3 × 10 × 3.3)*
Main machinery: 2 Fincantieri Isotta Fraschini ID 36 SS 6V diesels; 1,320 hp(m) *(970 kW)* sustained; 2 shafts
Speed, knots: 13
Range, n miles: 1,500 at 12 kt
Complement: 12 (2 officers)
Cargo capacity: 550 tons
Radars: Navigation: SPN-753; I-band.

Comment: Built by Ferrari, La Spezia and completed one in 1986, two in May 1987, one in May 1988.

FAVIGNANA *7/2003, Giorgio Ghiglione* / 0570663

1 BORMIDA CLASS (WATER TANKER) (AWT)

BORMIDA (ex-*GGS 1011*) A 5359

Displacement, tons: 736 full load
Dimensions, feet (metres): 131.9 × 23.6 × 10.5 *(40.2 × 7.2 × 3.2)*
Main machinery: 1 diesel; 130 hp(m) *(95.6 kW)*; 1 shaft
Speed, knots: 7
Complement: 11 (1 officer)
Cargo capacity: 260 tons

Comment: Converted at La Spezia in 1974.

BORMIDA *9/2002, Giorgio Ghiglione* / 0528367

2 SIMETO CLASS (WATER TANKERS) (AWT)

Name	*No*	*Builders*	*Commissioned*
TICINO	A 5376	Poli Shipyard, Pellestrina	10 June 1994
TIRSO	A 5377	Poli Shipyard, Pellestrina	12 Mar 1994

Displacement, tons: 1,858 full load; 1,968 *(Ticino* and *Tirso)* full load
Dimensions, feet (metres): 229 × 33.1 × 14.4 *(69.8 × 10.1 × 4.1)*
Main machinery: 2 GMT B 230.6 BL diesels; 2,530 hp(m) *(1.86 MW)* sustained; 2 shafts; cp props; bow thruster; 300 hp(m) *(220 kW)*
Speed, knots: 13. **Range, n miles**: 1,800 at 12 kt
Complement: 36 (3 officers)
Cargo capacity: 1,130 tons; 1,200 tons *(Ticino* and *Tirso)*
Guns: 1—20 mm/70. 2—7.62 mm MGs can be carried.
Radars: Navigation: 2 SPN-753B(V); I-band.

Comment: Guns are not normally carried. *Simeto* transferred to Tunisia on 30 June 2003.

TICINO *2/2006, Maritime Photographic* / 1154402

5 PONZA CLASS (LIGHTHOUSE TENDERS) (ABU)

Name	*No*	*Builders*	*Commissioned*
PONZA	A 5364	Morini Yard, Ancona	9 Dec 1988
LEVANZO	A 5366	Morini Yard, Ancona	24 Jan 1989
TAVOLARA	A 5367	Morini Yard, Ancona	12 Apr 1989
PALMARIA	A 5368	Morini Yard, Ancona	12 May 1989
PROCIDA	A 5383	Morini Yard, Ancona	14 Nov 1990

Displacement, tons: 608 full load
Dimensions, feet (metres): 186 × 35.4 × 8.2 *(56.7 × 10.8 × 2.5)*
Main machinery: 2 Fincantieri Isotta Fraschini ID 36 SS 8V diesels; 1,760 hp(m) *(1.29 MW)* sustained; 2 shafts; cp props; bow thruster; 120 hp(m) *(88 kW)*
Speed, knots: 14.5
Range, n miles: 1,500 at 14 kt
Complement: 34 (2 officers)
Guns: 2—7.62 mm MGs.
Radars: Navigation: SPN-732; I-band.

Comment: MTF 1304-1308. Similar to MTC 1011 class.

PALMARIA *6/2004, Giorgio Ghiglione* / 1044375

6 MTC 1011 CLASS (RAMPED TRANSPORTS) (AKL)

Name	*No*	*Builders*	*Commissioned*
GORGONA (1011)	A 5347	CN Mario Marini	23 Dec 1986
TREMITI (1012)	A 5348	CN Mario Marini	2 Mar 1987
CAPRERA (1013)	A 5349	CN Mario Marini	10 Apr 1987
PANTELLERIA (1014)	A 5351	CN Mario Marini	26 May 1987
LIPARI (1015)	A 5352	CN Mario Marini	10 July 1987
CAPRI (1016)	A 5353	CN Mario Marini	16 Sep 1987

Displacement, tons: 631 full load
Dimensions, feet (metres): 186 × 32.8 × 8.2 *(56.7 × 10 × 2.5)*
Main machinery: 2 CRM 12D/SS diesels; 1,760 hp(m) *(1.29 MW)*; 2 shafts
Speed, knots: 14.5. **Range, n miles**: 1,500 at 14 kt
Complement: 32 (4 officers)
Guns: 1 Oerlikon 20 mm (fitted for). 2—7.62 mm MGs.
Radars: Navigation: SMA SPN-748; I-band.

Comment: As well as transporting stores, oil or water they can act as support ships for Light Forces, salvage ships or minelayers. Stern ramp fitted. 1011 based at La Spezia, 1012 at Ancona, 1013 at La Maddalena and 1014 at Taranto. To be decommissioned 2012–13.

CAPRI *4/2008*, Giorgio Ghiglione* / 1335473

1 SALVAGE SHIP (ARSH)

Name	*No*	*Builders*	*Launched*	*Commissioned*
ANTEO	A 5309	C N Breda-Mestre	11 Nov 1978	31 July 1980

Displacement, tons: 3,200 full load
Dimensions, feet (metres): 322.8 × 51.8 × 16.7 *(98.4 × 15.8 × 5.1)*
Main machinery: 2 GMT A 230.12 diesels; 5,000 hp(m) *(3.68 MW)*; 2 motors; 6,000 hp(m) *(4.41 MW)*; 1 shaft; 2 bow thrusters; 1,000 hp(m) *(735 kW)*
Speed, knots: 20. **Range, n miles**: 4,000 at 14 kt
Complement: 121 (including salvage staff)
Guns: 2 Oerlikon 20 mm/70 fitted during deployments.
Radars: Surface search: SMA SPN-751; I-band.
Navigation: SMA SPN-748; I-band.
Helicopters: 1 AB 212.

Comment: Ordered mid-1977. Comprehensively fitted with flight deck and hangar, extensive salvage gear, including rescue bell and recompression chambers. Carries four lifeboats of various types. Three firefighting systems. Full towing equipment. Carries midget submarine, *Usel*, of 13.2 tons dived with dimensions 26.2 × 6.2 × 8.9 ft *(8 × 1.9 × 2.7 m)*. Carries SRV 300 rescue vehicle, launched and recovered from the stern, and a McCann diving bell. An atmospheric diving suit or 'newtsuit' can also be deployed. To be replaced by Underwater Support Ship in about 2012.

ANTEO *7/2007, Marco Ghiglino* / 1170077

7 DEPOLI CLASS TANKERS (AOTL/AWT)

GGS 1012–1014 **GRS/G 1010–1012** **GRS/J 1013**

Dimensions, feet (metres): 128.3 × 27.9 × 10.2 *(39.1 × 8.5 × 3.1)*
Main machinery: 2 diesels; 748 hp(m) *(550 kW)*; 2 shafts
Speed, knots: 11
Complement: 12
Cargo capacity: 500 m³ liquids
Radars: Navigation: I-band.

Comment: Built by DePoli and delivered between February 1990 and February 1991. The GGS series is for water, GRS/G for fuel and GRS/J for JP5.

GGS 1012 *5/2005, Giorgio Ghiglione* / 1153240

1 MEN 212 CLASS (YPT)

MEN 212

Displacement, tons: 32 full load
Dimensions, feet (metres): 58.4 × 16.7 × 3.3 *(17.8 × 5.1 × 1)*
Main machinery: 2 HP diesels; 1,380 hp(m) *(1.01 MW)*; 2 shafts
Speed, knots: 22. **Range, n miles:** 250 at 20 kt
Complement: 4
Radars: Navigation: SPN-732; I-band.

Comment: Torpedo Recovery Vessel completed in October 1983 by Crestitalia. GRP construction with a stern ramp. Capacity for up to three torpedoes.

MEN 212 *8/2003, P Marsan* / 0570664

2 MEN 215 CLASS (YFU/YFB)

MEN 215 **MEN 216**

Displacement, tons: 82 full load
Dimensions, feet (metres): 89.6 × 23 × 3.6 *(27.3 × 7 × 1.1)*
Main machinery: 2 Isotta Fraschini ID 36 SS 12V diesels; 2,640 hp(m) *(1.94 MW)* sustained; 2 shafts
Speed, knots: 28. **Range, n miles:** 250 at 14 kt
Complement: 4
Radars: Navigation: SPN-732; I-band.

Comment: Fast personnel launches completed in June 1986 by Crestitalia. Can also be used for amphibious operations or disaster relief. One is based at La Spezia and one in Taranto, where they are used as local ferries.

MEN 216 *3/1998, Giorgio Ghiglione* / 0052424

HARBOUR CRAFT

Comment: There are large numbers of naval manned harbour craft with MDN, MCN, MBN and MEN numbers. *Argo* (ex-MEN 209) is being used as a Presidential yacht. There is also a ferry *Cheradi* Y 402 at Taranto. Craft with VF numbers are non-naval.

MCN 1634 *5/2001, L-G Nilsson* / 0130349

ARGO *5/2000, Giorgio Ghiglione* / 0104891

19 FLOATING DOCKS

Number	*Date*	*Capacity-tons*
GO 1	1942	1,000
GO 5	1893	100
GO 8	1904	3,800
GO 10	1900	2,000
GO 11	1920	2,700
GO 17	1917	500
GO 18A	1920	800
GO 18B	1920	600
GO 20	1935	1,600
GO 22–23	1935	1,000
GO 51	1971	2,000
GO 52–54	1988–93	6,000
GO 55–57	1995–96	850
GO 58	1995	2,000

Comment: Stationed at La Spezia *(GO 52)*, Augusta *(GO 53)* and Taranto *(GO 54)*.

TUGS

7 OCEAN TUGS (ATR)

PROMETEO A 5318
CICLOPE A 5319
TITANO A 5324
POLIFEMO A 5325
GIGANTE A 5328
SATURNO A 5330
TENACE A 5365

Displacement, tons: 658 full load
Dimensions, feet (metres): 127.6 × 32.5 × 12.1 *(38.9 × 9.9 × 3.7)*
Main machinery: 2 GMT B 230.8 M diesels; 3,970 hp(m) *(2.02 MW)* sustained; 2 shafts; LIPS cp props
Speed, knots: 14.5
Range, n miles: 3,000 at 14 kt
Complement: 12
Radars: Navigation: SPN-748; I-band.

Comment: Details given are for all except A 5318. Built by CN Ferrari, La Spezia. Completed *Ciclope*, 5 September 1985; *Titano*, 7 December 1985; *Polifemo*, 21 April 1986; *Gigante*, 18 July 1986; *Saturno* 5 April 1988 and *Tenace* 9 July 1988. All fitted with firefighting equipment and two portable submersible pumps. Bollard pull 45 tons. *Prometeo* was completed 14 August 1975 and is slightly larger at 746 tons and has single engine propulsion.

TITANO *3/2008*, Giorgio Ghiglione* / 1335474

POLIFEMO *9/2002, Martin Mokrus* / 0528363

9 COASTAL TUGS (YTB)

PORTO FOSSONE Y 413	**PORTO EMPEDOCLE** Y 421	**PORTO FERRAIO** Y 425
PORTO TORRES Y 416	**PORTO PISANO** Y 422	**PORTO VENERE** Y 426
PORTO CORSINI Y 417	**PORTO CONTE** Y 423	**PORTO SALVO** Y 428

Displacement, tons: 412 full load
Measurement, tons: 122 dwt
Dimensions, feet (metres): 106.3 × 27.9 × 12.8 *(32.4 × 8.5 × 3.9)*
Main machinery: 1 GMT B 230.8 M diesels; 1,600 hp(m) *(1.18 MW)* sustained; 1 shaft; cp prop
Speed, knots: 12.7. **Range, n miles:** 4,000 at 12 kt
Complement: 13
Radars: Navigation: GEM BX 132; I-band.

Comment: Details given are for all except Y 436 and 443. Six ordered from CN De Poli (Pellestrina) and further three from Ferbex (Naples) in 1986.
Delivery dates *Porto Salvo* (13 September 1985), *Porto Pisano* (22 October 1985), *Porto Ferraio* (20 July 1985), *Porto Conte* (21 November 1985), *Porto Empedocle* (19 March 1986), *Porto Venere* (16 May 1989), *Porto Fossone* (24 September 1990), *Porto Torres* (16 January 1991) and *Porto Corsini* (4 March 1991).
Fitted for firefighting and anti-pollution. Carry a 1 ton telescopic crane. Based at Taranto, La Spezia, Augusta and La Maddalena. *Porto d'Ischia* transferred to Tunisia in 2002 and *Riva Trigoso* decommissioned.

PORTO TORRES *9/2008*, Giorgio Ghiglione* / 1335475

32 HARBOUR TUGS (YTM)

RP 101 Y 403W (1972)	**RP 113** Y 463 (1978)	**RP 125** Y 478 (1983)
RP 102 Y 404 (1972)	**RP 114** Y 464 (1980)	**RP 126** Y 479 (1983)
RP 103 Y 406 (1974)	**RP 115** Y 465 (1980)	**RP 127** Y 480 (1984)
RP 104 Y 407 (1974)	**RP 116** Y 466 (1980)	**RP 128** Y 481 (1984)
RP 105 Y 408 (1974)	**RP 118** Y 468 (1980)	**RP 129** Y 482 (1984)
RP 106 Y 410 (1974)	**RP 119** Y 470 (1980)	**RP 130** Y 483 (1985)
RP 108 Y 452 (1975)	**RP 120** Y 471 (1980)	**RP 131** Y 484 (1985)
RP 109 Y 456 (1975)	**RP 121** Y 472 (1984)	**RP 132** Y 485 (1985)
RP 110 Y 458 (1975)	**RP 122** Y 473 (1981)	**RP 133** Y 486 (1985)
RP 111 Y 460 (1975)	**RP 123** Y 467 (1981)	**RP 134** Y 487 (1985)
RP 112 Y 462 (1975)	**RP 124** Y 477 (1981)	

Displacement, tons: 120 full load
Dimensions, feet (metres): 64.9 × 17.1 × 6.9 *(19.8 × 5.2 × 2.1)*
Main machinery: 1 Fiat diesel; 368 hp *(270 kW)*; 1 shaft
Speed, knots: 9.5

Comment: *RP 101-124* built by Visitini, Dorada 1972–81. *RP 125-134* are larger tugs as shown in details.

RP 129 *11/2004, Declerck/Cracco* / 1043182

RP 124 *9/2008*, Giorgio Ghiglione* / 1335481

ARMY

Notes: The following units are operated by the 'Serenissima Amphibious Regiment' in the Venice Lagoons area. EIG means Italian Army Craft and is part of the hull number. Four LCM (EIG 28-31), 60 tons; two LCVP (EIG 26, 27), 13 tons; four recce craft (EIG 32, 33, 48, 49), 5 tons; two command craft (EIG 208, 210), 21.5 tons; one rescue tug (EIG 209), 45 tons; one inshore tanker (EIG 44), 95 tons; one ambulance and rescue craft (EIG 142) and about 70 minor craft (ferries, barges, river boats, rigid inflatable raiders).

ARMY CRAFT *7/1993, van Ginderen Collection* / 0075865

GOVERNMENT MARITIME FORCES

Notes: Consideration has been given to combine all these forces into one Coast Guard.

CUSTOMS (SERVIZIO NAVALE GUARDIA DI FINANZA)

Notes: (1) The force is operated by the Ministry of Finance but in time of war would come under the command of the Marina Militare. The force is organised into five air-naval task groups based at La Spezia, Cagliari, Taranto, Messina and Trapani. Each is composed of one command craft (Zara or Mazzei classes), six to nine FPB (Bigliani or Corrubia classes), three to four AB-412HP helicopters and up to two NH-500 helicopters. All the fixed-wing aircraft (12 P-166 (being upgraded to DP1 configuration) and three ATR-42) are based at Pratica di Mare within the Air Scouting Squadron. Other components include a technical-logistic support centre at Nisida and the Nautical Training Centre at Gaeta. There are a further 14 minor bases.
(2) In addition to the classes detailed, there is a large number of smaller (under 15 m) craft. These include: 30 V 5500 class (12.5 m); 18 V 5800 class (12.6 m); 26 VAI 200 class (9.9 m).

ATR-42 *8/2006, Frank Findler* / 1166590

V 5538 *4/2006, M Declerck* / 1158722

1 TRAINING SHIP (AX)

GIORGIO CINI

Displacement, tons: 800 full load
Dimensions, feet (metres): 172.2 × 32.8 × 9.5 *(54.0 × 10.0 × 2.9)*
Main machinery: 1 Fiat B306-SS diesel; 1,500 hp *(1.1 MW)*; 1 shaft
Speed, knots: 14
Range, n miles: 800 at 14 kt
Radars: Navigation: 2 BX-732; I-band.

Comment: Former merchant navy training ship acquired in 1981 for training role.

GIORGIO CINI *10/2008*, Giorgio Ghiglione* / 1335482

1 ANTONIO ZARA CLASS (PB)

Name	*No*	*Builders*	*Commissioned*
GIOVANNI DENARO	P 03	Fincantieri, Muggiano	20 Mar 1998

Displacement, tons: 340 full load
Dimensions, feet (metres): 167 × 24.6 × 6.2 *(51 × 7.5 × 1.9)*
Main machinery: 2 GMT BL 230.12 M diesels; 5,956 hp(m) *(4.38 MW)* sustained; 2 shafts
4 MTU 16V 396TB94 diesels; 13,029 hp(m) *(9.58 MW)* sustained; 2 shafts (P 03)
Speed, knots: 27; 35 (P 03)
Range, n miles: 3,800 at 15 kt
Complement: 33 (3 officers)
Guns: 1 or 2 Breda 30 mm/70 (single or twin). 2—7.62 mm MGs.
Weapons control: Selenia Pegaso or AESN Medusa (P 03) optronic director.
Radars: Surface search: Gemant 2 ARPA and SPN 749; I-band.

Comment: Similar to the Ratcharit class built for Thailand in 1976–79. First pair ordered in August 1987. Third ordered in October 1995 with more powerful engines and with a modified armament of a single 30 mm gun with a Medusa optronic director. All are fitted with an infra-red search and surveillance sensor (AMS SVIR). The first pair were decommissioned in 2007.

GIOVANNI DENARO *6/2006, Guardia di Finanza* / 1158732

9 MAZZEI CLASS (PB/YXT)

Name	*No*	*Builders*	*Commissioned*
MAZZEI	G 01	Intermarine, Sarzana	Apr 1998
VACCARO	G 02	Intermarine, Sarzana	May 1998
DI BARTOLO	G 03	Intermarine, Sarzana	Oct 2003
AVALLONE	G 04	Intermarine, Sarzana	Dec 2003
OLTRAMONTI	G 05	Intermarine, Sarzana	Apr 2004
BARBARISO	G 06	Intermarine, Sarzana	Jan 2007
PAOLINI	G 07	Intermarine, Sarzana	Apr 2007
GRECO	G 08	Intermarine, Sarzana	Feb 2008
CINULI	G 09	Intermarine, Sarzana	Apr 2008

Displacement, tons: 138 full load
Dimensions, feet (metres): 116.5; 119.7 (G 08, G 09) × 24.8 × 3.6 *(35.5; 36.5 × 7.6 × 1.1)*
Main machinery: 2 MTU 16V 396TB94 (MTU 16V 4000 M 90 G 08, G 09) diesels; 5,800 hp(m) *(4.26 MW)* sustained; 2 shafts
Speed, knots: 35. **Range, n miles:** 700 at 18 kt
Complement: 19 + 18 trainees (G 01 and G 02)
Guns: 1 Breda Mauser 30 mm/70. 2—7.62 mm MGs.
Weapons control: Elsag Medusa optronic director.
Radars: GEM 3072A ARPA; I-band.
Navigation: GEM 1410; I-band.

Comment: Based on the Bigliani class but with an extended hull. G 01 and G 02 used as training ships. All are being fitted with an infra-red search and surveillance sensor (AMS SVIR). G 03-09 are used as command units for air-naval task group.

DI BARTOLO *8/2007, Marco Ghiglino* / 1170074

22 + 5 BIGLIANI CLASS (PB)

OTTONELLI G 78
BARLETTA G 79
BIGLIANI G 80
CAVAGLIA G 81
GALIANO G 82
MACCHI G 83
SMALTO G 84
FORTUNA G 85
BUONOCORE G 86
SQUITIERI G 87
LA MALFA G 88
ROSATI G 89
LAGANÀ G 116
SANNA G 117
INZUCCHI G 118
VITALI G 119
CALABRESE G 120
URSO G 121
LA SPINA G 122
SALONE G 123
CAVATORTO G 124
FUSCO G 125
DE ROSA G 126
ZACCOLA G 127
STANISCI G 128
SOTTILE G 129
DE FALCO G 130

Displacement, tons: 87 (98 G 126-130) full load
Dimensions, feet (metres): 86.6; 94.5 (G 126-130) × 23 × 3.6 *(26.4; 28.8 × 7 × 1.1)*
Main machinery: 2 MTU 16V 396TB94 diesels; 6,850 hp(m) *(5.12 MW)* sustained; 2 shafts
Speed, knots: 42. **Range, n miles:** 770 at 18 kt
Complement: 12
Guns: 1 Breda Mauser 30 mm/80. 2—7.62 mm MGs. 1 Breda 12.7 mm.
Combat data systems: AMS IPNS.
Weapons control: Elsag Medusa Mk 4 optronic director.
Radars: Surface search: GEM 3072A ARPA; I-band.
Navigation: GEM 1410; I-band.

Comment: First eight built by Crestitalia and delivered from October 1987 to September 1992. Three more were ordered from Crestitalia/Intermarine in October 1994 and were delivered from December 1996 to April 1997. A fourth was delivered in late 1999. There are minor structural differences between Series I (G 80-81), Series II (G 82-87) and Series III (G 78-79, G88-89). Ten series IV (G 116-125) craft ordered from Intermarine, Sarzana, for delivery in 2004–06. These include Kevlar armour and are fitted with a remote-control Breda 12.7 mm gun and 40 mm grenade launcher. All are being fitted with an infra-red search and surveillance sensor (AMS SVIR). A further five craft (G 126-130) are under construction. These are stretched versions to be delivered in 2009.

LAGANA *6/2007, Marco Ghiglino* / 1170073

24 CORRUBIA CLASS (PBF)

ALBERTI G 92
ANGELINI G 93
CAPPELLETTI G 94
CIORLIERI G 95
D'AMATO G 96
FAIS G 97
FELICIANI G 98
GARZONI G 99
LIPPI G 100
LOMBARDI G 101
MICCOLI G 102
TREZZA G 103
APRUZZI G 104
BALLALI G 105
BOVIENZO G 106
CARRECA G 107
CONVERSANO G 108
INZERILLI G 109
LETIZIA G 110
MAZZARELLA G 111
NIOI G 112
PARTIPILO G 113
PULEO G 114
ZANNOTTI G 115

Displacement, tons: 92 full load
Dimensions, feet (metres): 87.9 × 24.9 × 3.9 *(26.8 × 7.6 × 1.2)*
Main machinery: 2 Isotta Fraschini ID 36 SS 16V diesels; 6,400 hp(m) *(4.7 MW)*; 2 shafts (G 90-91)
2 MTU 16V 396TB94; 5,800 hp(m) *(4.26 MW)* sustained; 2 shafts (G 92-103)
Speed, knots: 43. **Range, n miles:** 700 at 20 kt
Complement: 12 (1 officer)
Guns: 1 Breda Mauser 30 mm/70 (G 90-103). 1 Astra 20 mm (G 104-115). 2—7.62 mm MGs.
Weapons control: Elsag Medusa optronic director.
Radars: Surface search: GEM 3072A ARPA; I-band.
Navigation: GEM 1210; I-band.

Comment: First two built by Cantieri del Golfo, Gaeta, delivered in 1990 and decommissioned in 2007. Others built by Cantieri del Golfo (G 92-100),and Crestitalia (G 101-103), and Intermarine from 1995 onwards. G 115 completed in 1999. There are minor structural differences between the second series (G 92-103) and the third batch (G 104-115). All are being fitted with an infra-red search and surveillance sensor (AMS SVIR).

CONVERSANO *6/2005, Marco Ghiglino* / 1153210

16 MEATINI CLASS

G 26
G 40
G 44
G 46–47
G 49
G 50–52
G 56–58
G 60–61
G 64–65

Displacement, tons: 40 full load
Dimensions, feet (metres): 65.9 × 17.1 × 3.3 *(20.1 × 5.2 × 1)*
Main machinery: 2 CRM 18D/52 diesels; 2,500 hp(m) *(1.84 MW)*; 2 shafts
Speed, knots: 34. **Range, n miles:** 550 at 20 kt
Complement: 11 (1 officer)
Guns: 1—12.7 mm MG.
Radars: Surface search: 1 GEM 1210; I-band.

Comment: Fifty-six of the class built from 1970 to 1978. Replacement by new craft is in progress.

DARIDA *4/2004, Giorgio Ghiglione* / 1044378

5 + 18 BURATTI CLASS (PB)

BURATTI G 200
DE IANNI G 201
SALERNO G 202
ROSSI G 203
GARULLI G 204
SANGES G 205
CORRIAS G 206
CORTILE G 207
CASOTTI G 208
PRATA G 209
MARRA G 210
GOTTARDI G 211
LA PICCIRELLA G 212
PERISSINOTTO G 213
ROCCA G 214
BERTOLDI G 215
VERDECCHIA G 216
DE SANTIS G 217
PICCINNI LEOPARDI G 218
BIANCO G 219
STARACE G 220
CULTRONA G 221
BENVENUTI G 222

Displacement, tons: 55 full load
Dimensions, feet (metres): 72.2 × 17.7 × 6.6 *(22.0 × 5.4 × 2.0)*
Main machinery: 2 MTU 12V2000-M93 diesels; 3,595 hp(m) *(2.68 MW)* sustained; 2 shafts
Speed, knots: 33. **Range, n miles:** 850 at 25 kt
Complement: 8
Radars: Surface search: To be announced.

Comment: A total of 23 of a new class of craft to replace the Meatini class ordered from Intermarine in September 2006. The first two craft commissioned in March 2008.

BURATTI *6/2008*, Annati Collection* / 1335386

32 V 5000/6000 CLASS (FAST PATROL CRAFT) (HSIC)

V 5000–5020 **V 5100** **V 6003–6012**

Displacement, tons: 16 (V 6000), 27 (V 5000) full load
Dimensions, feet (metres): 53.8 × 9.2 × 2.6 *(16.4 × 2.8 × 0.8)*
Main machinery: 4 Seatek 6-4V-10D diesels; 2,856 hp(m) *(2.13 MW)* sustained; 4 surface-piercing propellers
2 MTU 8V 396TE94 diesels (V 5000)
Speed, knots: 70 (V 6000); 52 (V 5000)
Complement: 4
Radars: Surface search: I-band.

Comment: V 6003-6012 were delivered in 2002–03.

V 6006 *6/2005, Marco Ghiglino* / 1153209

V 5006 *6/2001, Guardia di Finanzia* / 0130143

34 + 36 V 2000 CLASS (FAST PATROL CRAFT) (PBF)

V 2000–2033

Displacement, tons: 11 full load
Dimensions, feet (metres): 43.3 × 11.2 × 2.9 *(13.2 × 3.4 × 0.9)*
Main machinery: 2 Seatek 600 diesels; 1,240 hp(m) *(925 kW)* sustained; 2 Kamewa waterjets
Speed, knots: 45. **Range, n miles:** 380 at 33 kt
Complement: 4
Radars: Surface search: GEM SC412; I-band.

Comment: Constructed by Cantieri Navali, Vittoria. Twenty-eight delivered by 2007. A total of 70 craft to be built.

V 2012 *7/2007, Giorgio Ghiglione* / 1166589

35 V 600 FALCO CLASS (FAST PATROL CRAFT) (PCF)

V 601–635

Displacement, tons: 4 full load
Dimensions, feet (metres): 33.5 × 9.2 × 2.6 *(10.2 × 2.8 × 0.8)*
Main machinery: 2 VM MD 706 diesels
Speed, knots: 54. **Range, n miles:** 200 at 33 kt
Complement: 4
Radars: Surface search: I-band.

Comment: FB design RIB designed for high-speed interception work. First prototype delivered in 2001.

V 612 *6/2007, Marco Ghiglino* / 1166568

COAST GUARD (GUARDIA COSTIERA—CAPITANERIE DI PORTO)

Notes: This is a force which is affiliated with the Marina Militare under whose command it would be placed in an emergency. The Coast Guard denomination was given after the Sea Protection Law in 1988. The force is responsible for the Italian Maritime Rescue Co-ordination Centre (MRCC) in Rome and 13 sub-centres (MRSC). The SAR network consists of 109 stations, three air stations and one helicopter station. All vessels havea red diagonal stripe painted on the white hull and many are armed with 7.62 mm MGs. There are some 10,500 naval personnel including 1,200 officers of which about half are doing national service. Ranks are the same as the Navy. In addition to the Saettia class (detailed separately), the following craft are in service. All have the prefix CP (Capitaneria di Porto):

1. SAR craft: *Giulio Ingianni* CP 409 (205 tons); *Francesco Mazzinghi* CP 405, *Antonio Scialoja* CP 406, *Michele Lolini* CP 407, *Mario Grabar* CP 408 (136 tons), *Oreste Cavallari* CP 401, *Renato Pennetti* CP 402, *Walter Fachin* CP 403, *Gaetano Magliano* CP 404 (100 tons); CP 314-318 (45 tons).
2. Fast Patrol craft: CP 265-292 (54 tons), CP 261-264 (30 tons), CP 245-260 (22 tons), CP 454-456 (19.4 tons).
3. Inshore Patrol Craft: five craft CP 2201-CP 2205 (15 tons); 51 craft CP 2001-CP 2083 (9-15 tons); 20 craft CP 2084-CP 2103 (11.7 tons); 65 craft CP 506-CP 571 (7.5 tons); 8 craft CP 6002-CP 6021 (3.7 tons); 13 craft CP 801-CP 813 (9.1 tons); 25 craft CP 814-CP 824, CP 863-CP 871, CP 882-CP 883, CP 890-CP 892 (12.5 tons); 6 craft CP 829-CP 831, CP 836-CP 838 (12 tons);48 craft CP 825-CP 828, CP 832-CP 835, CP 839-CP 862, CP 872-CP 881, CP 884-CP 889 (12 tons); 60 RHIB CG 20 class.
4. Aircraft include 14 Piaggio P 166 DL3-SEM and two ATR 42MP maritime patrol, 12 Griffon AB-412-CP helicopters and two AW 139 helicopters.
5. CP 451 is a 1,278 ton training ship (ex-US ATF *Bannock*); *Barbara* CP 452 (190 tons) is a former naval Range Safety patrol craft which recommissioned in late 1999.
6. CP 210 and CP 211 are airboats used for SAR in the Venice Lagoon area.

ANTONIO SCIALOJA *8/2004, Paolo Marsan* / 1044379

CP 288 *5/2007, Marco Ghiglino* / 1166569

P 166 *6/2006, Guardia Costiera* / 1158730

6 SAETTIA CLASS (SAR)

Name	*No*	*Builders*	*Commissioned*
SAETTIA	CP 901	Fincantieri, Muggiano	Dec 1985
UBALDO DICIOTTI	CP 902	Fincantieri, Muggiano	20 July 2002
LUIGI DATTILO	CP 903	Fincantieri, Muggiano	28 Nov 2002
MICHELE FIORILLO	CP 904	Fincantieri, Muggiano	7 Apr 2003
ANTONIO PELUSO	CP 905	Fincantieri, Muggiano	2 July 2003
ORAZIO CORSI	CP 906	Fincantieri, Muggiano	7 Feb 2004

Displacement, tons: 427 full load
Dimensions, feet (metres): 173.3 × 26.6 × 6.6 *(52.8 × 8.1 × 2.0)*
Main machinery: 4 Isotta Fraschini V1716T2MSD diesels; 12,660 hp *(9.44 MW)*; 4 cp props; bow thruster
Speed, knots: 29. **Range, n miles:** 1,800 at 18 kt
Complement: 30 (2 officers)
Guns: 1 Oerliken 20 mm/70.
Weapons control: Eurocontrol optronic sensor.
Radars: Surface search: SPN 753; I-band.

Comment: Details are for CP 902-906 which were ordered on 29 June 2000. CP 901 was built as an attack missile craft demonstrator by Fincantieri in 1984 and was later taken over by the Coast Guard on 20 July 1999. 30 tons lighter and with some structural differences, she is powered by 4 MTU 16V538TB93 engines providing 17,598 hp and a top speed of 40 kt. She is armed with an Otobreda 25 mm gun. All the vessels form a 'Squadrilla' based at Messina, Sicily, whose role is fishery protection and immigration control.

ANTONIO PELUSO *10/2008*, Giorgio Ghiglione* / 1335483

POLICE (SERVIZIO NAVALE CARABINIERI)

Notes: (1) The Carabinieri established its maritime force in 1969 and has some 600 personnel. There are 172 craft in service or building which operate in coastal waters within the 3 mile limit and in inshore waters. Craft currently in service include: 23-800 class of 28 tons; 6-700 class of 15 tons; 22-600 class of 12 tons; 25 N 500 class of 6 tons; 3 S 500 class of 18 tons; 72-200 class of 2 tons, 28 minor craft and 30 RHIBs.
Most are capable of 20 to 25 kt except the 800 class at 35 kt.
(2) The 700 class programme was cancelled after delivery of the first craft in 2006.
(3) There is also a Sea Police Force of the State. All craft have POLIZIA written on the side. Vessels include 37 Squalo class of 14 tons, 4 Nelson class of 11 tons, 7 Intermarine class of 8.4 tons, 37 Crestitalia class of 6 tons and 25 Aquamaster/Drago classes of 3 tons. Speeds vary between 23 and 45 kt.

809 *11/2007, Marco Ghiglino* / 1170072

Jamaica

Country Overview

Jamaica gained independence in 1962; the British monarch, represented by a governor-general, is head of state. The island country (area 4,244 square miles), third-largest of the Greater Antilles, is situated south of Cuba and has a 552 n mile coastline with the Caribbean Sea. Kingston is the capital, largest town and principal port. An archipelagic state, territorial seas (12 n miles) are claimed. A 200 n mile Exclusive Economic Zone (EEZ) has been claimed but the limits are not fully defined.

Headquarters Appointments

Commanding Officer Coast Guard:
Commander Kenneth A Douglas

Personnel

(a) 2009: 241 (17 officers) Regulars
(b) 32 (8 officers) Reserve Forces

Aviation

Seven helicopters (three Bell 412 and four Bell 407) are used for SAR and land operations. One Cessna 210M is used for liaison duties. Two Diamond DA 40 fixed-wing aircraft and one Bell 406B are used for training at the Flight Training School.

Bases

Headquarters: HMJS *Cagway*, Port Royal.
Bases: Discovery Bay, Pedro Cays, Port Antonio, Port Morant, Montego Bay and Black River.

COAST GUARD

3 COUNTY (DAMEN STAN PATROL 4207) CLASS (PB)

Name	*No*	*Builders*	*Commissioned*
CORNWALL	421	Damen Shipyard, Gorinchem	27 Oct 2005
MIDDLESEX	422	Damen Shipyard, Gorinchem	7 Apr 2006
SURREY	423	Damen Shipyard, Gorinchem	26 June 2007

Displacement, tons: 205
Dimensions, feet (metres): 140.4 × 23.3 × 8.3 *(42.8 × 7.11 × 2.52)*
Main machinery: 2 Caterpillar 3516B DI-TA; 5,600 hp *(4.17 MW)*; 2 cp props
Speed, knots: 26
Complement: 18 (4 officers)
Guns: 2 — 12.7 mm MGs.

Comment: Contract signed on 21 April 2004 with Damen Shipyard Gorinchem for construction of three Damen 4207 offshore patrol craft. Details are based on those in UK Customs service.

SURREY (on trials) *11/2006, Martyn Westers* / 1164414

3 FAST COASTAL INTERCEPTORS (PBF)

CG 131–133

Displacement, tons: 11 full load
Dimensions, feet (metres): 44 × 10.5 × 3 *(13.4 × 3.2 × 0.92)*
Main machinery: 2 Caterpillar 3196 diesels; 1,140 hp *(850 kW)*; two twin disc waterjets
Speed, knots: 37
Range, n miles: 400 at 20 kt
Complement: 6
Guns: 1 — 7.62 mm M60 MG.
Radars: Surface search: Raytheon Pathfinder; I-band.

Comment: Aluminium construction. Built by Silver Ships, Mobile, Alabama. Funded by the US State Department, Narcotics Affairs Section. Delivered in March 2003.

CG 131 *6/2003, JDFCG* / 0568335

1 HERO CLASS (PB)

Name	*No*	*Builders*	*Commissioned*
PAUL BOGLE	P 8	Lantana Boatyard Inc, FL	17 Sep 1985

Displacement, tons: 93 full load
Dimensions, feet (metres): 105 × 20.6 × 7 *(32 × 6.3 × 2.1)*
Main machinery: 3 MTU 8V 396TB93 diesels; 3,270 hp(m) *(2.4 MW)* sustained; 3 shafts
Speed, knots: 32
Complement: 20 (4 officers)
Guns: 1 Oerlikon 20 mm. 2—12.7 mm MGs.
Radars: Surface search: Furuno 2400; I-band.
Navigation: Sperry 4016; I-band.

Comment: Of all-aluminium construction, launched in 1984. *Paul Bogle* was originally intended for Honduras as the third of the Guardian class. Similar to patrol craft in Honduras and Grenada navies. Refitted in March 1998 at Network Marine, Louisiana and further refitted in 2004-05 by Damen Shipyards, Gorinchem.

PAUL BOGLE *6/1999, **JDFCG*** / 0080126

4 DAUNTLESS CLASS (INSHORE PATROL CRAFT) (PB)

CG 121–124

Displacement, tons: 11 full load
Dimensions, feet (metres): 40 × 14 × 4.3 *(12.2 × 4.3 × 1.3)*
Main machinery: 2 Caterpillar 3208TA diesels; 870 hp *(650 kW)*; 2 shafts
Speed, knots: 27
Range, n miles: 600 at 18 kt
Complement: 5
Guns: 1—7.62 mm MG (can be carried).
Radars: Surface search: Raytheon 40X; I-band.

Comment: Delivered in September and November 1992, January 1993 and May 1994. Built by SeaArk Marine, Monticello. Aluminium construction. Craft of this class have been distributed throughout the Caribbean under FMS funding. Two craft were refitted during 2006.

CG 121 ***10/2000*** / 0121383

4 FAST COASTAL INTERCEPTORS (PBF)

CG 134–137

Displacement, tons: 7.5 full load
Dimensions, feet (metres): 44.0 × 9.0 × 3.0 *(13.4 × 2.75 × 0.9)*
Main machinery: 3 Yanmar diesels; 945 hp *(704 kW)*; Bravo X drives
Speed, knots: 45
Range, n miles: 600 at 25 kt
Complement: 4

Comment: Manufactured by Nor-Tech, Fort Myers, Florida. Composite and glass-fibre hull with V-bottomed hull. The first two donated by the US Southern Command in February 2008 and the second two in October 2008. Employed on counter drugs duties.

CG 134 ***6/2008*, Jamaica Coast Guard*** / 1335391

Japan

MARITIME SELF-DEFENCE FORCE (MSDF) KAIJOU JIEI-TAI

Country Overview

Japan is a constitutional monarchy in East Asia that comprises four main islands: Hokkaido, Honshu, Shikoku and Kyushu. It also includes the Ryukyu Islands to the southwest and more than 1,000 lesser islands. The sovereignty of the South Kuril Islands (Etorofu, Kunashiri, Shikotan and the Habomai Group) is disputed with Russia. With an overall area of 145,850 square miles it has a coastline of 16,065 n miles, with the Pacific Ocean, Sea of Japan, the La Perouse Strait (which separates it from Sakhalin Island), Sea of Okhotsk, East China Sea and the Korea Strait (which separates it from South Korea). The capital and largest city is Tokyo while the principal ports are Yokohama, Osaka and Kobe. Territorial seas of 12 n miles (3 n miles in Korea Strait) are claimed. A 200 n mile EEZ has also been claimed but the limits have not been defined.

Headquarters Appointments

Chief of Staff, Maritime Self-Defence Force:
Admiral Keiji Akaboshi
Commander-in-Chief, Self-Defence Fleet:
Vice Admiral Tooru Izumi

Senior Appointments

Commander Fleet Escort Force:
Vice Admiral Katsutoshi Kawano
Commander Fleet Air Force:
Vice Admiral Sadayoshi Matsuoka
Commander Fleet Submarine Force:
Vice Admiral Masao Kobayashi

Diplomatic Representation

Defence (Naval) Attaché in London:
Captain Hiroyuki Terada

Personnel

2009: 45,716 (including Naval Air) plus 3,418 civilians

Organisation of the Major Surface Units of Japan (MSDF)

The Fleet Escort and Air Forces were reorganised on 26 March 2008. There are also two Submarine Flotillas (Kure and Yokosuka), one Minesweeper Flotilla (Yokosuka), one Transport Command (Kure), one Sea Supply Command (Yokosuka) and five District Flotillas (Yokosuka, Kure, Sasebo, Maizuru and Oominato). The District Flotillas are composed of an AMS and a number of MSC and patrol craft. The Fleet Training Group is based at Kure.

Fleet Escort Force (Yokosuka)
Sawakasi (DDG 170) Flagship

Escort Flotilla 1 (Yokosuka)
Escort Division 1 (Y)
Shirane (DDH 143)
Shimakaze (DDG 172)
Murasame (DD 101)
Akebono (DD 108)
Escort Division 5 (Y)
Kongou (DDG 173)
Ikazuchi (DD 107)
Suzunami (DD 114)
Sawagiri (DD 157)

Escort Flotilla 2 (Sasebo)
Escort Division 2 (S)
Kurama (DDH 144)
Ashigara (DDG 178)
Yuugiri (DD 153)
Amagiri (DD 154)
Escort Division 6 (S)
Choukai (DDG 176) (S)
Harusame (DD 102) (Y)
Takanami (DD 110) (Y)
Oonami (DD 111) (Y)

Escort Flotilla 3 (Maizuru)
Escort Division 3 (M)
Haruna (DDH 141)
Atago (DDG 177)
Makinami (DD 112)
Setogiri (DD 156)
Escort Division 7 (M)
Myoukou (DDG 175) (M)
Yuudachi (DD 103)
Kirisame (DD 104) (S)
Ariake (DD 109) (S)

Escort Flotilla 4 (Kure)
Escort Division 4 (O)
Hiei (DDH 142) (K)
Hatakaze (DDG 171) (Y)
Hamagiri (DD 155) (O)
Umigiri (DD 158) (K)
Escort Division 8 (K)
Kirishima (DDG 174) (K)
Inazuma (DD 105) (K)
Samidare (DD 106) (K)
Sazanami (DD 113) (K)
Escort Division 11 (Y)
Hatsuyuki (DD 122)
Shirayuki (DD 123)
Sawayuki (DD 125)
Escort Division 12 (K)
Yamayuki (DD 129)
Matsuyuki (DD 130)
Setoyuki (DD 131)
Escort Division 13 (S)
Isoyuki (DD 127)
Harayuki (DD 128)
Asayuki (DD 132)
Escort Division 14 (M)
Mineyuki (DD 124)
Hamayuki (DD 126)
Abukama (DE 129)
Escort Division 15 (O)
Yuubari (DE 127)
Yuubetsu (DE 228)
Jintsu (DE 230)
Chikuma (DE 233)
Escort Division 16 (S)
Ooyodo (DE 231)
Sendai (DE 232)
Tone (DE 234)

Strength of the Fleet (31 March 2009)

Type	*Active (Auxiliary)*	*Building (Projected)*
Submarines	16 (2)	4
Helicopter carriers	1	1
Destroyers	43	2 (2)
Frigates	8	–
Patrol Forces	7	–
LSTs	3	–
LCUs	4	–
LCACs	6	–
Landing Craft (LCM)	12	–
MCM Tenders/Controllers	4	–
Minesweepers—Ocean	3	–
Minesweepers—Coastal	24	2 (1)
Major Auxiliaries	35	1 (1)

Bases

Naval-Yokosuka, Kure, Sasebo, Maizuru, Ohminato
NavalAir-Atsugi, Hachinohe, Iwakuni, Kanoya, Komatsujima, Naha, Ozuki, Oominato, Ohmura, Shimofusa, Tateyama, Tokushima, Ioujima, Maizuru

Coast Defence

The Army controls 100 SSM-1 truck-mounted sextuple launchers.

New Construction Programme (Warships)

2007 1—5,000 ton DD, 1—2,900 ton SS, 1—3,200 ton AGS.
2008 1—5,000 ton DD, 1—2,900 ton SS, 1—570 ton MSC.
2009 2—5,500 ton DD, 1—570 ton MSC, 1—4,900 ton ARC.

Naval Air Force

10 Air Patrol Sqns: P-3C, EP-3, OP-3C, SH-60J/K
Five Air Training Sqns: P-3C, YS-11, TC-90, T-5, OH-6D, SH-60J
One Air Training Support Squadron: U-36A, UP-3D, LC-90
One Transport Sqn: YS-11, LC-90
One MCM Sqn: MH-53E, MCH-101
Fleet Air Force (Atsugi)
Air Training Command (Shimofusa)
Air Wings at Kanoya (Wing 1), Hachinohe (Wing 2), Atsugi (Wing 4), Naha (Wing 5), Tateyama (Wing 21), Ohmura (Wing 22), Iwakuni (Wing 31)

DELETIONS AND CONVERSIONS

Submarines

2006 *Sachisio, Hamashio*
2008 *Hayashio* (converted), *Yukishio*

Destroyers

2007 *Tachikaze*
2008 *Asakaze*
2009 *Haruna*

Frigates

2007 *Ishikari*

Patrol Forces

2008 PG 01, PG 02

Mine Warfare Forces

2006 *Hahajima, Ogishima* (converted)
2007 *Yurishima*
2008 *Hikoshima*
2009 *Kamishima*

Auxiliaries

2008 *Shirase*

PENNANT LIST

Submarines-Patrol

SS 501	Souryu
SS 502	Unryu (bldg)
SS 503	– (bldg)
SS 504	– (bldg)
SS 505	– (bldg)
SS 583	Harushio
SS 584	Natsushio
SS 586	Arashio
SS 587	Wakashio
SS 588	Fuyushio
SS 590	Oyashio
SS 591	Michishio
SS 592	Uzushio
SS 593	Makishio
SS 594	Isoshio
SS 595	Narushio
SS 596	Kuroshio
SS 597	Takashio
SS 598	Yaeshio
SS 599	Setoshio
SS 600	Mochishio

Submarines-Auxiliary

TSS 3601	Asashio
TSS 3606	Hayashio

Helicopter Carriers

DDH 181	Hyuga
DDH 182	– (bldg)

Destroyers

DD 101	Murasame
DD 102	Harusame
DD 103	Yuudachi
DD 104	Kirisame
DD 105	Inazuma
DD 106	Samidare
DD 107	Ikazuchi
DD 108	Akebono
DD 109	Ariake
DD 110	Takanami
DD 111	Oonami
DD 112	Makinami
DD 113	Sazanami
DD 114	Suzunami
DD 122	Hatsuyuki
DD 123	Shirayuki
DD 124	Mineyuki
DD 125	Sawayuki
DD 126	Hamayuki
DD 127	Isoyuki
DD 128	Haruyuki
DD 129	Yamayuki
DD 130	Matsuyuki
DD 131	Setoyuki
DD 132	Asayuki
DDH 142	Hiei
DDH 143	Shirane
DDH 144	Kurama
DD 153	Yuugiri
DD 154	Amagiri
DD 155	Hamagiri
DD 156	Setogiri
DD 157	Sawagiri
DD 158	Umigiri
DDG 170	Sawakaze
DDG 171	Hatakaze
DDG 172	Shimakaze
DDG 173	Kongou
DDG 174	Kirishima
DDG 175	Myoukou
DDG 176	Choukai
DDG 177	Atago
DDG 178	Ashigara

Frigates

DE 227	Yuubari
DE 228	Yuubetsu
DE 229	Abukuma
DE 230	Jintsu
DE 231	Ooyodo
DE 232	Sendai
DE 233	Chikuma
DE 234	Tone

Patrol Forces

PG 823	PG 03
PG 824	Hayabusa
PG 825	Wakataka
PG 826	Ootaka
PG 827	Kumataka
PG 828	Umitaka
PG 829	Shirataka

Minehunters/Sweepers-Ocean

MSO 301	Yaeyama
MSO 302	Tsushima
MSO 303	Hachijyo

Minesweepers-Coastal

MSC 601	Hirashima
MSC 602	Yakushima
MSC 603	Takashima (bldg)
MSC 670	Awashima
MSC 672	Uwajima
MSC 673	Ieshima
MSC 674	Tsukishima
MSC 675	Maejima
MSC 676	Kumejima
MSC 677	Makishima
MSC 678	Tobishima
MSC 679	Yugeshima
MSC 680	Nagashima
MSC 681	Sugashima
MSC 682	Notojima
MSC 683	Tsunoshima
MSC 684	Naoshima
MSC 685	Toyoshima
MSC 686	Ukushima
MSC 687	Izushima
MSC 688	Aishima
MSC 689	Aoshima
MSC 690	Miyajima
MSC 691	Shishijima
MSC 692	Kuroshima

MCM Tenders/Control Ships

MCL 726	Ogishima
MCL 727	Sakushima
MST 463	Uraga
MST 464	Bungo

Amphibious Forces

LCU 2001	Yusotei-Ichi-Go
LCU 2002	Yusotei-Ni-Go
LST 4001	Oosumi
LST 4002	Shimokita
LST 4003	Kunisaki
LSU 4171	Yura
LSU 4172	Noto

Submarine Depot/Rescue Ships

AS 405	Chiyoda
ASR 403	Chihaya

Fleet Support Ships

AOE 422	Towada
AOE 423	Tokiwa
AOE 424	Hamana
AOE 425	Mashuu
AOE 426	Oumi

Training Ships

TV 3508	Kashima
TV 3513	Shimayuki
TV 3515	Yamagiri
TV 3516	Asagiri

Training Support Ships

ATS 4202	Kurobe
ATS 4203	Tenryu
AMS 4301	Hiuchi
AMS 4302	Suou
AMS 4303	Amakusa
AMS 4304	Genkai
AMS 4305	Enshuu

Cable Repair Ship

ARC 482	Muroto

Icebreakers

AGB 5003	Shirase

Survey and Research Ships

AGS 5102	Futami
AGS 5103	Suma
AGS 5104	Wakasa
AGS 5105	Nichinan
AGS 5106	– (bldg)
ASE 6101	Kurihama
ASE 6102	Asuka

Ocean Surveillance Ships

AOS 5201	Hibiki
AOS 5202	Harima

Tenders

ASY 91	Hashidate
YDT 01-06	–

SUBMARINES

1 + 4 SOURYU CLASS (SSK)

Name	*No*	*Builders*	*Laid down*	*Launched*	*Commissioned*
SOURYU	SS 501	Mitsubishi, Kobe	31 Mar 2005	5 Dec 2007	30 Mar 2009
UNRYU	SS 502	Kawasaki Kobe	31 Mar 2006	15 Oct 2008	Mar 2010
–	SS 503	Mitsubishi, Kobe	6 Feb 2007	Oct 2009	Mar 2011
–	SS 504	Kawasaki, Kobe	31 Mar 2008	Oct 2010	Mar 2012
–	SS 505	Mitsubishi, Kobe	2009	2011	2013

Displacement, tons: 2,900 standard; 4,200 dived
Dimensions, feet (metres): 275.6 × 29.9 × 33.8 *(84.0 × 9.1 × 10.5)*
Main machinery: Diesel-stirling-electric; 2 diesels; 4 Kockums Stirling AIP; 1 motor; 8,000 hp *(5.96 MW)*; 1 shaft
Speed, knots: 20 dived; 12 surfaced
Range, n miles: To be announced
Complement: 70

Missiles: SSM: McDonnell Douglas Sub-Harpoon; active radar homing to 130 km *(70 n miles)* at 0.9 Mach; warhead 227 kg.
Torpedoes: 6–21 in *(533 mm)* bow tubes. Japanese Type 89; wire-guided (option); active/passive homing to 50 km *(27 n miles)* at 40/55 kt; warhead 267 kg. Type 80 ASW. SSM and torpedoes (total unknown).
Countermeasures: To be announced.
Weapons control: To be announced.
Radars: Surface search: JRC ZPS-6F; I-band.
Sonars: Hughes/OKI ZQQ 7; hull and flank arrays; active/passive search and attack; medium/low frequency. Towed array.

SOURYU *10/2008*, Hachiro Nakai* / 1353105

Programmes: First of new class authorised in FY04 budget, second in FY05 budget, third in FY06 budget, fourth in FY07 budget and fifth in FY08 budget.

Structure: The hull design is based on the Oyashio class and incorporates the Swedish Stirling air-independent propulsion system. Components of this system are provided by Kockums for assembly by KHI.

11 OYASHIO CLASS (SSK)

Name	*No*	*Builders*	*Laid down*	*Launched*	*Commissioned*
OYASHIO	SS 590	Kawasaki, Kobe	26 Jan 1994	15 Oct 1996	16 Mar 1998
MICHISHIO	SS 591	Mitsubishi, Kobe	16 Feb 1995	18 Sep 1997	10 Mar 1999
UZUSHIO	SS 592	Kawasaki, Kobe	6 Mar 1996	26 Nov 1998	9 Mar 2000
MAKISHIO	SS 593	Mitsubishi, Kobe	26 Mar 1997	22 Sep 1999	29 Mar 2001
ISOSHIO	SS 594	Kawasaki, Kobe	9 Mar 1998	27 Nov 2000	14 Mar 2002
NARUSHIO	SS 595	Mitsubishi, Kobe	2 Apr 1999	4 Oct 2001	3 Mar 2003
KUROSHIO	SS 596	Kawasaki, Kobe	27 Mar 2000	23 Oct 2002	8 Mar 2004
TAKASHIO	SS 597	Mitsubishi, Kobe	30 Jan 2001	1 Oct 2003	9 Mar 2005
YAESHIO	SS 598	Kawasaki, Kobe	15 Jan 2002	4 Nov 2004	9 Mar 2006
SETOSHIO	SS 599	Mitsubishi, Kobe	23 Jan 2003	5 Oct 2005	28 Feb 2007
MOCHISHIO	SS 600	Kawasaki, Kobe	23 Feb 2004	6 Nov 2006	6 Mar 2008

Displacement, tons: 2,750 standard; 3,500 dived
Dimensions, feet (metres): 268 × 29.2 × 24.3 *(81.7 × 8.9 × 7.4)*
Main machinery: Diesel-electric; 2 Kawasaki 12V25S diesels; 5,520 hp(m) *(4.1 MW)*; 2 Kawasaki alternators; 3.7 MW; 2 Toshiba motors; 7,750 hp(m) *(5.7 MW)*; 1 shaft
Speed, knots: 12 surfaced; 20 dived
Complement: 70 (10 officers)

Missiles: SSM: McDonnell Douglas Sub-Harpoon; active radar homing to 130 km *(70 n miles)* at 0.9 Mach; warhead 227 kg.
Torpedoes: 6–21 in *(533 mm)* tubes; Type 89; wire-guided; active/passive homing to 50 km *(27 n miles)*/38 km *(21 n miles)* at 40/55 kt; warhead 267 kg and Type 80 ASW. Total of 20 SSM and torpedoes.
Countermeasures: ESM: NZLR-1B; radar warning.
Weapons control: SMCS type TFCS.
Radars: Surface search: JRC ZPS 6D; I-band.
Sonars: Hughes/Oki ZQQ 6; hull and flank arrays; active/passive search and attack; medium/low frequency.
Towed array; passive search; very low frequency.

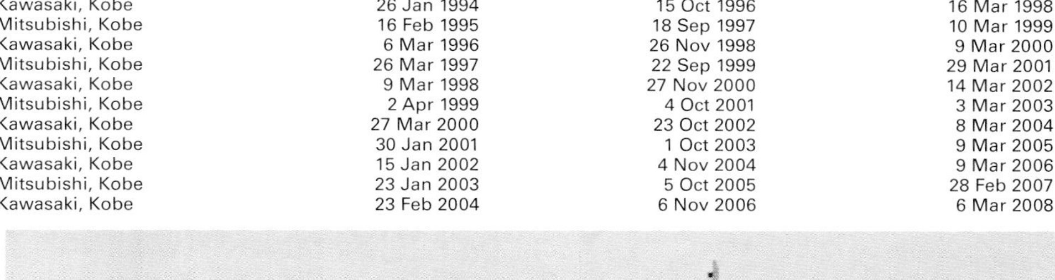
SETOSHIO *9/2007, Hachiro Nakai* / 1305087

Programmes: First of a new class approved in the 1993 budget and then one a year up to FY03.
Structure: Fitted with large flank sonar arrays which are reported as the reason for the increase in displacement over the Harushio class. Double hull sections forward and aft and anechoic tiles on the fin. A new type of deck casing and faired fin are other distinguishing features. Diving depth 650 m *(2,130 ft)*.

MOCHISHIO *3/2008*, Hachiro Nakai* / 1353106

KUROSHIO *7/2008*, Hachiro Nakai* / 1353107

7 HARUSHIO CLASS (SSK)

Name	*No*	*Builders*	*Laid down*	*Launched*	*Commissioned*
HARUSHIO	SS 583	Mitsubishi, Kobe	21 Apr 1987	26 July 1989	30 Nov 1990
NATSUSHIO	SS 584	Kawasaki, Kobe	8 Apr 1988	20 Mar 1990	20 Mar 1991
HAYASHIO	TSS 3606 (ex-SS 585)	Mitsubishi, Kobe	9 Dec 1988	17 Jan 1991	25 Mar 1992
ARASHIO	SS 586	Kawasaki, Kobe	8 Jan 1990	17 Mar 1992	17 Mar 1993
WAKASHIO	SS 587	Mitsubishi, Kobe	12 Dec 1990	22 Jan 1993	1 Mar 1994
FUYUSHIO	SS 588	Kawasaki, Kobe	12 Dec 1991	16 Feb 1994	7 Mar 1995
ASASHIO	TSS 3601 (ex-SS 589)	Mitsubishi, Kobe	24 Dec 1992	12 July 1995	12 Mar 1997

Displacement, tons: 2,450 (2,900, TSS 3601) standard; 3,200 (3,700, TSS 3601) dived
Dimensions, feet (metres): 252.6; 285.5 (TSS 3601) × 32.8 × 25.3 *(77; 87 × 10 × 7.7)*
Main machinery: Diesel-electric; 2 Kawasaki 12V25/25S diesels; 5,520 hp(m) *(4.1 MW)*; 2 Kawasaki alternators; 3.7 MW; 2 Fuji motors; 7,200 hp(m) *(5.3 MW)*; 1 shaft
4 Stirling engines (TSS 3601) Kockums V4-275R Mk 2; 348 hp *(260 kW)*
Speed, knots: 12 surfaced; 20 dived
Complement: 75 (10 officers); 70 (10 officers) (TS 3601)

Missiles: SSM: McDonnell Douglas Sub-Harpoon; active radar homing to 130 km *(70 n miles)* at 0.9 Mach; warhead 227 kg.

Torpedoes: 6—21 in *(533 mm)* tubes. Japanese Type 89; wire-guided (option); active/passive homing to 50 km *(27 n miles)*/38 km *(21 n miles)* at 40/55 kt; warhead 267 kg; depth to 900 m, and Type 80 ASW. Total of 20 SSM and torpedoes.
Countermeasures: ESM: NZLR-1; radar warning.
Radars: Surface search: JRC ZPS 6; I-band.
Sonars: Hughes/Oki ZQQ 5B; hull-mounted; active/passive search and attack; medium/low frequency.
ZQR 1 towed array similar to BQR 15; passive search; very low frequency.

Programmes: First approved in 1986 estimates and then one per year until 1992.

Structure: The slight growth in all dimensions is a natural evolution from the Yuushio class and includes more noise reduction, towed sonar and wireless aerials, as well as anechoic coating. Double hull construction. *Asashio* had a slightly larger displacement on build and a small cutback in the crew as a result of greater systems automation for machinery and snorting control. The hull was extended in 2001 to accommodate an AIP module (Stirling engine) which was fitted by Mitsubishi, Kobe. Diving depth 550 m *(1,800 ft)*.
Operational: A remote periscope viewer is fitted in *Asashio*. *Asashio* is an experimental submarine which has been used for testing of AIP propulsion.

NATSUSHIO *10/2006, Guy Toremans* / 1167174

ARASHIO *8/2008*, Hachiro Nakai* / 1353108

WAKASHIO *10/2006, Michael Nitz* / 1167173

HELICOPTER CARRIERS

1 + 1 HYUGA CLASS (CVHG)

Name	*No*	*Builders*	*Laid down*	*Launched*	*Commissioned*
HYUGA	DDH 181	IHI Marine United, Yokohama	11 May 2006	23 Aug 2007	18 Mar 2009
–	DDH 182	IHI Marine United, Yokohama	30 May 2008	Aug 2009	Mar 2011

Displacement, tons: 13,500 standard; 18,000 full load
Dimensions, feet (metres): 646.3 × 108.3 × 31.8 *(197.0 × 33.0 × 9.7)*
Main machinery: COGAG; 4 LM 2500 gas turbines; 2 shafts
Speed, knots: 30
Range, n miles: 6,000 at 20 kt
Complement: 322 (+25 HQ staff)

Missiles: SAM: Raytheon Sea Sparrow RIM-162 ESSM; Lockheed Martin Marietta Mk 41 Mod 5 sixteen cell vertical launcher ❶; semi-active radar homing to 18.0 km *(9.7 n miles)* at 3.6 Mach; warhead 38 kg. 64 missiles.
A/S: Vertical launch ASROC.

Guns: 2 GE 20 mm/76 Sea Vulcan 20 ❷; 3 barrels per mounting; 1,500 rds/min.
2—12.7 mm MGs.
Torpedoes: 6—324 mm (2 triple) HOS-303 tubes ❸.
Countermeasures: Decoys: 4 Hycor Mk 137 sextuple RBOC chaff launchers.
ESM/ECM: NOLQ-3C.
Combat data systems: Link 16.
Radars: Air search/Fire control: Melco FCS-3; G/H/I-band.
Navigation: JRC OPS-20C; I-band.
Sonars: Bow-mounted sonar. OQQ 21.

Helicopters: 3 SH-60K plus 7 SH-60K or 7 MCH-101.

Programmes: Two new aviation capable ships to replace the Haruna class authorised in the FY01-05 and FY05-09 programmes. The first authorised in the FY04 budget and the second in the FY06 budget.
Structure: Broadly similar to the Spanish light carrier *Príncipe de Asturias* although not fitted with a ski jump and VSTOL capability. The flight deck has two lifts and four helicopter spots. The Mk 41 VLS launcher is situated on the starboard quarter.
Operational: To be capable of acting as Command Vessels.

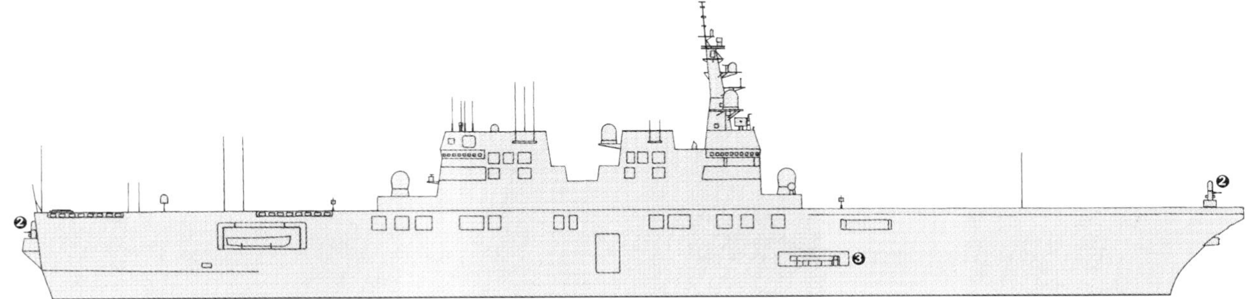

HYUGA *(Scale 1 : 1,200), Ian Sturton* / 1153013

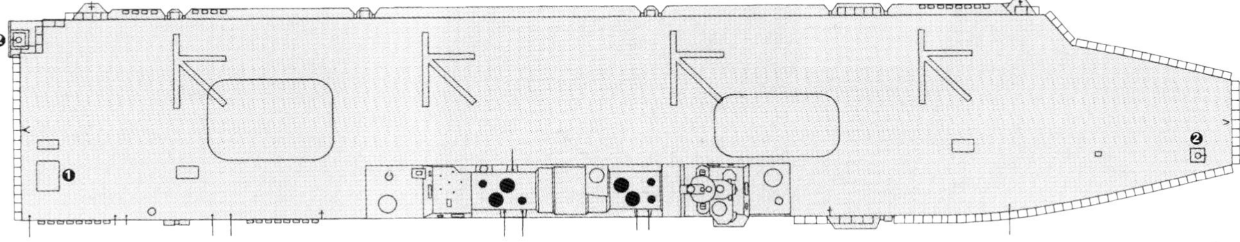

HYUGA *(Scale 1 : 1,200), Ian Sturton* / 1153012

HYUGA *7/2008*, Hachiro Nakai* / 1353109

HYUGA *7/2008*, Ships of the World* / 1353184

DESTROYERS

2 ATAGO CLASS (DDGHM)

Name	*No*	*Builders*	*Laid down*	*Launched*	*Commissioned*
ATAGO	DDG 177	Mitsubishi, Nagasaki	5 Apr 2004	24 Aug 2005	15 Mar 2007
ASHIGARA	DDG 178	Mitsubishi, Nagasaki	6 Apr 2005	30 Aug 2006	13 Mar 2008

Displacement, tons: 7,700 standard; 10,000 full load
Dimensions, feet (metres): 540.1 × 68.9 × 20.3 *(164.9 × 21.0 × 6.2)*
Main machinery: COGAG; 4 GE LM 2500 gas turbines; 102,160 hp *(76.21 MW)* sustained; 2 shafts; cp props
Speed, knots: 30
Range, n miles: 4,500 at 20 kt
Complement: 309 (27 officers)

Missiles: SSM: 8 Mitsubishi Type 90 SSM-1B (2 quad) ❶; active radar homing to 200 km *(108 n miles)* at 0.9 Mach; warhead 270 kg.
SAM: Raytheon Standard SM-2MR Block IIIB. FMC Mk 41 VLS; 64 cells forward ❷ 32 cells aft ❸; command/inertial guidance; semi-active radar homing to 167 km *(90 n miles)* at 2.5 Mach.
A/S: Vertical launch ASROC; inertial guidance to 1.6-10 km *(1-5.4 n miles)*; payload Mk 46 Mod 5 Neartip.
Guns: 1 United States Mk 45 Mod 4 5 in *(127 mm)*/62 ❹; 20 rds/min to 23 km *(12.6 n miles)*; weight of shell 32 kg. 2 GE/GD 20 mm/76 Mk 15 Vulcan Phalanx Block IB ❺; 4,500 rds/min combined to 1.5 km.
Torpedoes: 6—324 mm (2 triple) HOS 302 tubes ❻. Honeywell Mk 46 Mod 5 Neartip; anti-submarine; active/passive homing to 11 km *(5.9 n miles)* at 40 kt; warhead 44 kg.
Countermeasures: Decoys: 4 Mk 36 SRBOC ❼ 6-barrelled Mk 36 chaff launchers; Type 4 towed torpedo decoy.
ESM/ECM: NOLQ-2B ❽.

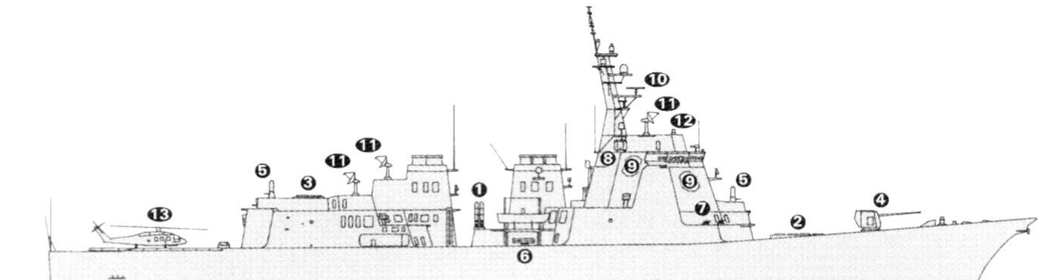

ATAGO *(Scale 1 : 1,500)*, ***Ian Sturton*** / 1167684

Combat data systems: Aegis NTDS with Link 11. AN/USC-42 SATCOM.
Radars: Air search: RCA SPY 1D(V) ❾; 3D; F-band.
Surface search: JRC OPS-28E ❿; G-band.
Navigation: JRC OPS-20; I-band.
Fire control: 3 SPG-62 ⓫; 1 Mk 2/21 ⓬; I/J-band. 2 AN/UPS-2; J-band.
Sonars: SQS-53C bow sonar.

Helicopters: 1 Mitsubishi/Sikorsky SH-60J/K ⓭.

Programmes: Two ships authorised in the FY01-05 programme. The first authorised in the FY02 budget and the second in FY03 budget.
Structure: The upgrade from the Kongou class includes one hangar for embarked helicopters. The arrangement of vertical launchers is different to that of the Kongou class: there are 64 cells forward (rather than 29) and 32 aft (61).
Operational: *Atago* sailed for sea trials on 17 May 2006.

ASHIGARA ***3/2008*, Hachiro Nakai*** / 1353110

ATAGO ***6/2007, Ships of the World*** / 1305058

4 KONGOU CLASS (DDGHM)

Name	No	Builders	Laid down	Launched	Commissioned
KONGOU	DDG 173	Mitsubishi, Nagasaki	8 May 1990	26 Sep 1991	25 Mar 1993
KIRISHIMA	DDG 174	Mitsubishi, Nagasaki	7 Apr 1992	19 Aug 1993	16 Mar 1995
MYOUKOU	DDG 175	Mitsubishi, Nagasaki	8 Apr 1993	5 Oct 1994	14 Mar 1996
CHOUKAI	DDG 176	Ishikawajima Harima, Tokyo	29 May 1995	27 Aug 1996	20 Mar 1998

Displacement, tons: 7,250 standard; 9,485 full load
Dimensions, feet (metres): 528.2 × 68.9 × 20.3; 32.7 (sonar) *(161 × 21 × 6.2; 10)*
Main machinery: COGAG; 4 GE LM 2500 gas turbines; 102,160 hp *(76.21 MW)* sustained; 2 shafts; cp props
Speed, knots: 30
Range, n miles: 4,500 at 20 kt
Complement: 300 (27 officers)

Missiles: SSM: 8 McDonnell Douglas Harpoon Block 1B (2 quad) ❶ launchers; active radar homing to 92 km *(50 n miles)* at 0.9 Mach; warhead 227 kg.
SAM: Raytheon Standard SM-2MR Block IIIA. FMC Mk 41 VLS (29 cells) forward ❷. Martin Marietta Mk 41 VLS (61 cells) aft ❸; command/inertial guidance; semi-active radar homing to 167 km *(90 n miles)* at 2.5 Mach. Standard SM-3 Block 1A (DDG 173, 175, 176); command/inertial/GPS guidance and IR homing to 650 n miles *(1,200 km)* at 3 Mach. Total of 90 Standard and ASROC weapons.
A/S: Vertical launch ASROC; inertial guidance to 1.6-10 km *(1-5.4 n miles)*; payload Mk 46 Mod 5 Neartip.
Guns: 1 OTO Melara 5 in *(127 mm)*/54 Compatto ❹; 45 rds/min to 23 km *(12.42 n miles)*; weight of shell 32 kg.
2 GE/GD 20 mm/76 Mk 15 Vulcan Phalanx Block IB ❺. 6 barrels per mounting; 3,000 rds/min combined to 1.5 km.
Torpedoes: 6—324 mm (2 triple) HOS 302 tubes ❻. Honeywell Mk 46 Mod 5 Neartip; anti-submarine; active/passive homing to 11 km *(5.9 n miles)* at 40 kt; warhead 44 kg.
Countermeasures: Decoys: 4 Mk 36 SRBOC ❼ 6-barrelled Mk 36 chaff launchers; Type 4 towed torpedo decoy.
ESM/ECM: Melco NOLQ 2; intercept/jammer.
Combat data systems: Aegis NTDS with Link 11. SATCOM WSC-3/OE-82C ❽. ORQ-1 helicopter datalink ❾.

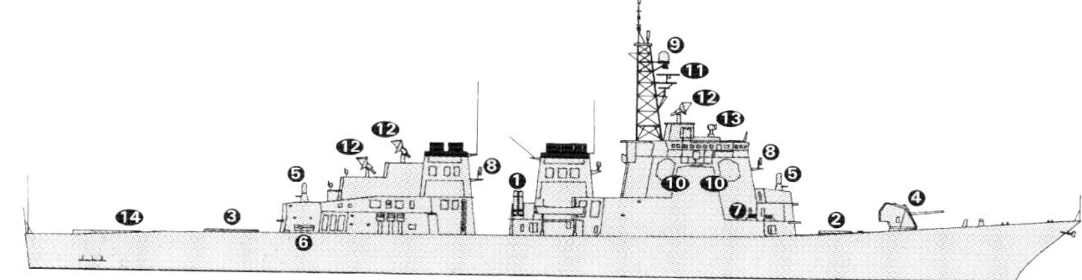

KONGOU

(Scale 1 : 1,500), Ian Sturton / 0130387

Weapons control: 3 Mk 99 Mod 1 MFCS. Type 2-21 GFCS. Mk 116 Hitachi OYQ 102 (Mod 7 for ASW).
Radars: Air search: RCA SPY 1D ❿; 3D; F-band.
Surface search: JRC OPS-28D ⓫; G-band.
Navigation: JRC OPS-20; I-band.
Fire control: 3 SPG-62 ⓬; 1 Type 2-21 ⓭; I/J-band.
IFF: UPX 29.
Sonars: Nec OQS 102 (SQS-53B/C) bow-mounted; active search and attack.
Oki OQR 2 (SQR-19A (V)) TACTASS; towed array; passive; very low frequency.

Helicopters: Platform ⓮ and fuelling facilities for SH-60J.

Programmes: Proposed in the FY87 programme; first one accepted in FY88 estimates, second in FY90, third in FY91, fourth in FY93. Designated as destroyers but these ships are of cruiser size. The combination of cost and US Congressional reluctance to release Aegis technology slowed the programme down. The ships' names were last used by battleships and cruisers of the Second World War era.
Modernisation: These ships are undergoing an upgrade programme to include Aegis Baseline 3.6.1 and Standard SM-3Block 1A missiles. *Kongou* was completed in 2007 and a successful SM-3 test-firing was conducted on 17 December 2007. *Choukai* completed upgrade in 2008 and *Myoukou* and *Kirishima* are to be completed in 2009 and 2011 respectively.
Structure: This is an enlarged and improved version of the USN *Arleigh Burke* with a lightweight version of the Aegis system. There are two missile magazines. OQS 102 plus OQR 2 towed array is the equivalent of SQQ-89. Prairie-Masker acoustic suppression system.
Operational: As well as air defence of the Fleet, these ships contribute to the air defences of mainland Japan.

CHOUKAI

7/2008, Hachiro Nakai* / 1353112

MYOUKOU

4/2008, Hachiro Nakai* / 1353111

0 + 2 (2) 19DD CLASS (DESTROYER) (DDHM)

Name	*No*	*Builders*	*Laid down*	*Launched*	*Commissioned*
–	–	Mitsubishi, Nagasaki	July 2009	Sep 2010	Mar 2012
–	–	Mitsubishi, Nagasaki	2010	2011	Mar 2013

Displacement, tons: 5,000 standard
Dimensions, feet (metres): 492.1 × 57.7 × ?; 32.8 (sonar) *(150.0 × 17.6 × ?; 10.0)*
Main machinery: COGAG: 4 gas turbines; 2 shafts
Speed, knots: 30. **Range, n miles**: To be announced
Complement: To be announced

Missiles: SSM: 8 Mitsubishi Type 90 (2 quad) ❶.
SAM: Lockheed Martin Mk 41 vertical launcher (32 cells forward) ❷; Raytheon RIM-162 ESSM.
Guns: 1—5 in *(127 mm)*/62 Mk 45 Mod 4 ❸.
2 Raytheon 20 mm/76 Vulcan Phalanx ❹.
Torpedoes: 6—324 mm (2 triple) tubes.
Countermeasures: To be announced.
Combat data systems: To be announced.
Weapons control: To be announced.
Radars: Air search: Melco FCS-3 ❺; G/H/I-band.
Surface search: To be announced.
Fire control: Melco FCS-3; G/H/I-band.
Navigation: To be announced.
Sonars: Bow-mounted sonar.

Helicopters: 2 Mitsubishi/Sikorsky SH-60J/K ❻ or 1 MCH-101.

19DD CLASS ***(Scale 1 : 1,200), Ian Sturton*** / 1353185

Programmes: First authorised in FY07 and second in FY08 budget. Two more authorised in FY09 budget. The ships are to replace the Hatsuyuki class in the current inventory.

Structure: Measures to reduce the radar cross-section include a new design mast.

2 HATAKAZE CLASS (DDGHM)

Name	*No*	*Builders*	*Laid down*	*Launched*	*Commissioned*
HATAKAZE	DDG 171	Mitsubishi, Nagasaki	20 May 1983	9 Nov 1984	27 Mar 1986
SHIMAKAZE	DDG 172	Mitsubishi, Nagasaki	30 Jan 1985	30 Jan 1987	23 Mar 1988

Displacement, tons: 4,600 (4,650, DDG 172) standard; 5,900 full load
Dimensions, feet (metres): 492 × 53.8 × 15.7 *(150 × 16.4 × 4.8)*
Main machinery: COGAG; 2 RR Olympus TM3B gas turbines; 49,400 hp *(36.8 MW)* sustained; 2 RR Spey SM1A gas turbines; 26,650 hp *(19.9 MW)* sustained; 2 shafts; Kamewa cp props
Speed, knots: 30
Complement: 260 (23 officers)

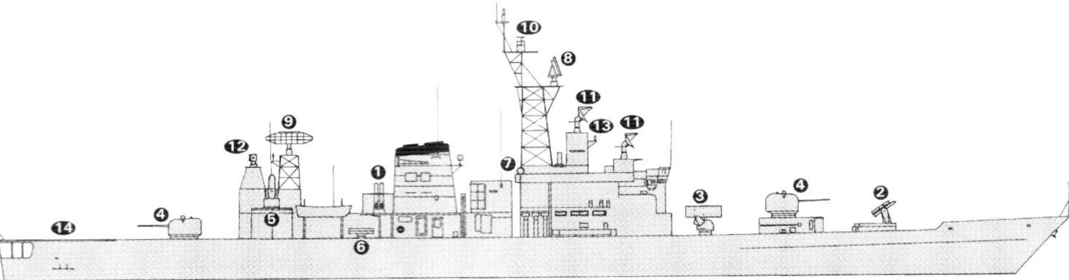

HATAKAZE ***(Scale 1 : 1,200), Ian Sturton*** / 0506023

Missiles: SSM: 8 McDonnell Douglas Harpoon Block 1B ❶; active radar homing to 92 km *(50 n miles)* at 0.9 Mach; warhead 227 kg.
SAM: 40 Raytheon Standard SM-1MR Block VIA; Mk 13 Mod 4 launcher ❷; command guidance; semi-active radar homing to 38 km *(20.5 n miles)* at 2 Mach; height envelope 45-18,288 m *(150-60,000 ft)*.
A/S: Honeywell ASROC Mk 112 octuple launcher ❸; inertial guidance to 1.6-10 km *(1-5.4 n miles)* at 0.9 Mach; payload Mk 46 Mod 5 Neartip. Reload capability.
Guns: 2 FMC 5 in *(127 mm)*/54 Mk 42 automatic ❹; 20-40 rds/min to 24 km *(13 n miles)* anti-surface; 14 km *(7.6 n miles)* anti-aircraft; weight of shell 32 kg.
2 General Electric/General Dynamics 20 mm Phalanx Mk 15 CIWS ❺; 6 barrels per mounting; 3,000 rds/min combined to 1.5 km.
Torpedoes: 6—324 mm Type 68 or HOS 301 (2 triple) tubes ❻. Honeywell Mk 46 Mod 5 Neartip; anti-submarine; active/passive homing to 11 km *(5.9 n miles)* at 40 kt; warhead 44 kg.
Countermeasures: Decoys: 2 Loral Hycor SRBOC 6-barrelled Mk 36 chaff launchers; range 4 km *(2.2 n miles)*.
ESM/ECM: Melco NOLQ-1; intercept/jammer. Fujitsu OLR 9B; intercept.
Combat data systems: OYQ-4 Mod 1 action data automation; Link 11. SATCOM ❼.
Weapons control: Type 2-21C for 127 mm guns. General Electric Mk 74 Mod 13 for Standard.
Radars: Air search: Hughes SPS-52C ❽; 3D; E/F-band.
Melco OPS-11C ❾; B-band.
Surface search: JRC OPS-28B ❿; G/H-band.
Navigation: JRC OPS-20; I-band.
Fire control: 2 Raytheon SPG-51C ⓫; G-band.
Melco 2-21 ⓬; I/J-band. Type 2-12 ⓭; I-band.
Sonars: Nec OQS 4 Mod 1; bow-mounted; active search and attack; medium frequency.

Helicopters: Platform for 1 SH-60J Seahawk ⓮.

Programmes: DDG 171 provided for in 1981 programme. DDG 172 provided for in 1983 programme, ordered 29 March 1984.

SHIMAKAZE ***7/2008*, Hachiro Nakai*** / 1353113

5 TAKANAMI CLASS (DDGHM)

Name	*No*	*Builders*	*Laid down*	*Launched*	*Commissioned*
TAKANAMI	DD 110	IHI Marine United, Yokosuka (Uraga)	25 Apr 2000	26 July 2001	12 Mar 2003
OONAMI	DD 111	Mitsubishi, Nagasaki	17 May 2000	20 Sep 2001	13 Mar 2003
MAKINAMI	DD 112	IHI Marine United, Yokohama	7 July 2001	8 Aug 2002	18 Mar 2004
SAZANAMI	DD 113	Mitsubishi, Nagasaki	4 Apr 2002	29 Aug 2003	16 Feb 2005
SUZUNAMI	DD 114	IHI Marine United, Yokohama	24 Sep 2003	26 Aug 2004	16 Feb 2006

Displacement, tons: 4,650 standard; 6,300 full load
Dimensions, feet (metres): 495.4 × 57.1 × 17.4 *(151 × 17.4 × 5.3)*
Main machinery: COGAG; 2 RR Spey SM1C gas turbines; 26,600 hp *(19.9 MW)* sustained; 2 GE LM 2500 gas turbines; 32,500 hp *(24.3 MW)* sustained; 2 shafts
Speed, knots: 30
Complement: 176

Missiles: SSM: 8 Mitsubishi Type 90 SSM-1B (2 quad) ❶; active radar homing to 150 km *(81 n miles)* at 0.9 Mach; warhead 225 kg.
SAM: Mk 41 VLS 32 cells ❷ Sea Sparrow RIM 162 ESSM (PIP); semi-active radar homing to 18 km *(9.7 n miles)* at 3.6 Mach; warhead 38 kg and VL ASROC; internal guidance to 1.6-10 km *(1-5.4 n miles)*; payload Mk 46 Mod 5 Neartip.
Guns: 1 Otobreda 5 in *(127 mm)*/54 ❸; 45 rds/min to 24 km *(12.42 n miles)*; weight of shell 32 kg.
2 General Electric/General Dynamics 20 mm Phalanx Mk 15 CIWS ❹; 6 barrels per mounting; 3,000 rds/min combined to 1.5 km.
Torpedoes: 6—324 mm HOS-302 (2 triple) tubes ❺ Mk 46 Mod 5; anti-submarine; active/passive homing to 11 km *(5.9 n miles)* at 40 kt; warhead 44 kg.
Countermeasures: Decoys: 4 Mk 36 SRBOC chaff launchers ❻. SLQ-25 Nixie towed torpedo decoy.
ESM/ECM: Nec NOLQ 3; intercept and jammer.

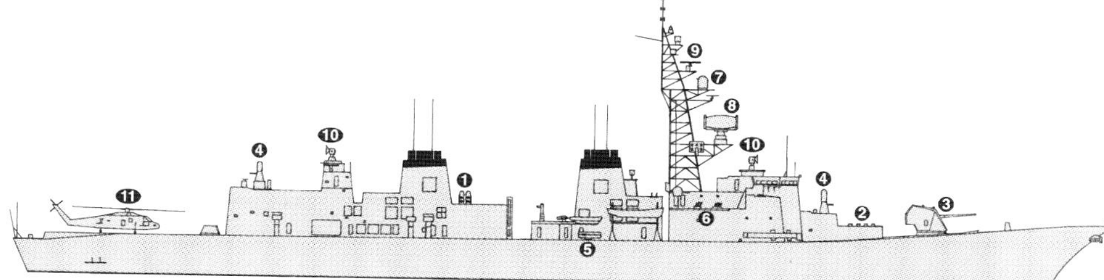

TAKANAMI CLASS *(Scale 1 : 1,200), Ian Sturton* / 0080138

Combat data systems: OYQ-9 with Link 11. ORQ-1B helicopter datalink ❼.
Weapons control: Hitachi OYQ-103 ASW control system.
Radars: Air search: Melco OPS-24B ❽; 3D; D-band.
Surface search: JRC OPS-28D ❾; G-band.
Fire control: Two FCS 2-31B ❿.
Navigation: OPS-20; I-band.
Sonars: OQS-5; Bow-mounted; active search and attack; low frequency.
OQR-2; towed array; passive search; very low frequency.

Helicopters: 1 Mitsubishi/Sikorsky SH-60J/K ⓫.

Programmes: First two approved in FY98, then one a year up to FY01.
Structure: Murasame class modified to fit a Mk 41 VLS, improved missile fire control and new sonar.

MAKINAMI *6/2007, Hachiro Nakai* / 1305079

SUZUNAMI *10/2008*, Michael Nitz* / 1353180

9 MURASAME CLASS (DDGHM)

Name	*No*	*Builders*	*Laid down*	*Launched*	*Commissioned*
MURASAME	DD 101	Ishikawajima Harima, Tokyo	18 Aug 1993	23 Aug 1994	12 Mar 1996
HARUSAME	DD 102	Mitsui, Tamano	11 Aug 1994	16 Oct 1995	24 Mar 1997
YUUDACHI	DD 103	Marine United (Sumitomo, Uraga)	18 Mar 1996	19 Aug 1997	4 Mar 1999
KIRISAME	DD 104	Mitsubishi, Nagasaki	3 Apr 1996	21 Aug 1997	18 Mar 1999
INAZUMA	DD 105	Mitsubishi, Nagasaki	8 May 1997	9 Sep 1998	15 Mar 2000
SAMIDARE	DD 106	Marine United (Ishikawajima Harima, Tokyo)	11 Sep 1997	24 Sep 1998	21 Mar 2000
IKAZUCHI	DD 107	Hitachi, Maizuru	25 Feb 1998	24 June 1999	14 Mar 2001
AKEBONO	DD 108	Marine United (Ishikawajima Harima, Tokyo)	29 Oct 1999	25 Sep 2000	19 Mar 2002
ARIAKE	DD 109	Mitsubishi, Nagasaki	18 May 1999	16 Oct 2000	6 Mar 2002

Displacement, tons: 4,550 standard; 6,200 full load
Dimensions, feet (metres): 495.4 × 57.1 × 17.1 *(151 × 17.4 × 5.2)*
Main machinery: COGAG; 2 RR Spey SM1C gas turbines; 26,600 hp *(19.9 MW)* sustained; 2 GE LM 2500 gas turbines; 32,500 hp *(24.3 MW)* sustained; 2 shafts
Speed, knots: 30
Complement: 165

Missiles: SSM: 8 Type 90 SSM-1B ❶ (Harpoon); active radar homing to 130 km *(70 n miles)* at 0.9 Mach; warhead 227 kg.
SAM: Raytheon Mk 48 VLS 16 cells ❷ Sea Sparrow RIM-7P; semi-active radar homing to 16 km *(8.5 n miles)* at 2.5 Mach; warhead 38 kg.
A/S: Mk 41 VL ASROC 16 cells ❸. Total of 29 missiles can be carried.
Guns: 1 Otobreda 3 in *(76 mm)*/62 compact ❹; 85 rds/min to 16 km *(8.6 n miles)* anti-surface; 12 km *(6.5 n miles)* anti-aircraft; weight of shell 6 kg.
2 General Electric/General Dynamics 20 mm Phalanx Mk 15 CIWS ❺; 6 barrels per mounting; 3,000 rds/min combined to 1.5 km.
Torpedoes: 6—324 mm HOS 302 (2 triple) tubes ❻ Mk 46 Mod 5; anti-submarine; active/passive homing to 11 km *(5.9 n miles)* at 40 kt; warhead 44 kg.
Countermeasures: Decoys: 4 Mk 36 SRBOC chaff launchers ❼. Type 4 towed torpedo decoy.
ESM/ECM: Nec NOLQ 3; intercept and jammer.
Combat data systems: OYQ-9B with Link 11. ORQ-1 helicopter datalink ❽.
Weapons control: Hitachi OYQ-103 ASW control system.
Radars: Air search: Melco OPS-24B ❾; 3D; D-band.
Surface search: JRC OPS-28D ❿; G-band.
Fire control: 2 Type 2-31 ⓫.
Navigation: OPS-20; I-band.
Sonars: Mitsubishi OQS-5; hull-mounted; active search and attack; low frequency.
OQR-1 towed array; passive search; very low frequency.

Helicopters: 1 SH-60J Seahawk ⓬.

Programmes: First one approved in FY91 as an addition to the third Aegis-type destroyer. Second approved in FY92. Two more approved in FY94, two in FY95, one in FY96 and two in FY97. The programme was given added priority as the Kongou class was reduced to four ships because of the cost of Aegis.
Modernisation: DD 103, 108 and 109 converted to fire ESSM 2007–08. One further ship to be converted in 2009.
Structure: More like a mini-Kongou than an enlarged Asagiri class, with VLS and a much reduced complement. Stealth features are evident in sloping sides and rounded superstructure. Indal RAST helicopter hauldown.
Operational: ASROC missiles are not carried. *Kirisame* deployed to Indian Ocean in November 2001 to provide non-combatant support to US forces.

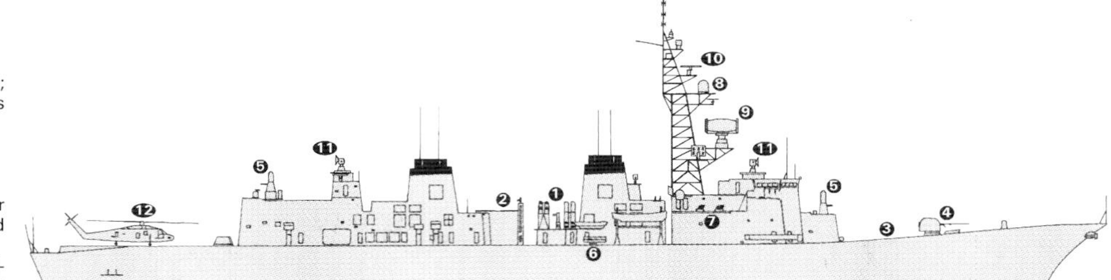

MURASAME ***(Scale 1 : 1,200), Ian Sturton*** / 0506235

INAZUMA ***7/2008*, Hirotoshi Yamamoto*** / 1353166

AKEBONO ***4/2008*, Hachiro Nakai*** / 1353165

ARIAKE ***10/2008*, Hachiro Nakai*** / 1353164

6 ASAGIRI CLASS (DDGHM)

Name	*No*	*Builders*	*Laid down*	*Launched*	*Commissioned*
YUUGIRI	DD 153	Sumitomo, Uraga	25 Feb 1986	21 Sep 1987	28 Feb 1989
AMAGIRI	DD 154	Ishikawajima Harima, Tokyo	3 Mar 1986	9 Sep 1987	17 Mar 1989
HAMAGIRI	DD 155	Hitachi, Maizuru	20 Jan 1987	4 June 1988	31 Jan 1990
SETOGIRI	DD 156	Sumitomo, Uraga	9 Mar 1987	12 Sep 1988	14 Feb 1990
SAWAGIRI	DD 157	Mitsubishi, Nagasaki	14 Jan 1987	25 Nov 1988	6 Mar 1990
UMIGIRI	DD 158	Ishikawajima Harima, Tokyo	31 Oct 1988	9 Nov 1989	12 Mar 1991

Displacement, tons: 3,500 (DD 153-154), (3,550, DD 155-158) standard; 4,900 (DD 153-154) (4,950 DD 155-158) full load
Dimensions, feet (metres): 449.4 × 48 × 14.6 *(137 × 14.6 × 4.5)*
Main machinery: COGAG; 4 RR Spey SM1A gas turbines; 53,300 hp *(39.8 MW)* sustained; 2 shafts; cp props
Speed, knots: 30+
Complement: 220

Missiles: SSM: 8 McDonnell Douglas Harpoon (2 quad) launchers ❶; active radar homing to 130 km *(70 n miles)* at 0.9 Mach; warhead 227 kg.
SAM: Raytheon Sea Sparrow RIM-7M Mk 29 (Type 3/3A) octuple launcher ❷; semi-active radar homing to 16 km *(8.5 n miles)* at 2.5 Mach; warhead 38 kg; 20 missiles.
A/S: Honeywell ASROC Mk 112 octuple launcher ❸; inertial guidance to 1.6-10 km *(1-5.4 n miles)* at 0.9 Mach; payload Mk 46 Mod 5 Neartip. Reload capability.
Guns: 1 Otobreda 3 in *(76 mm)*/62 compact ❹; 85 rds/min to 16 km *(8.6 n miles)* anti-surface; 12 km *(6.5 n miles)* anti-aircraft; weight of shell 6 kg.
2 General Electric/General Dynamics 20 mm Phalanx Mk 15 CIWS ❺; 6 barrels per mounting; 3,000 rds/min combined to 1.5 km.
Torpedoes: 6—324 mm Type 68 (2 triple) HOS 301 tubes ❻. Honeywell Mk 46 Mod 5 Neartip; anti-submarine; active/passive homing to 11 km *(5.9 n miles)* at 40 kt; warhead 44 kg.
Countermeasures: Decoys: 2 Loral Hycor SRBOC 6-barrelled Mk 36 chaff launchers ❼; range 4 km *(2.2 n miles)*.
1 SLQ-25 Nixie or Type 4; towed torpedo decoy.
ESM: Nec NOLR 6C or NOLR 8 (DD 152) ❽; intercept.
ECM: Fujitsu OLT-3; jammer.

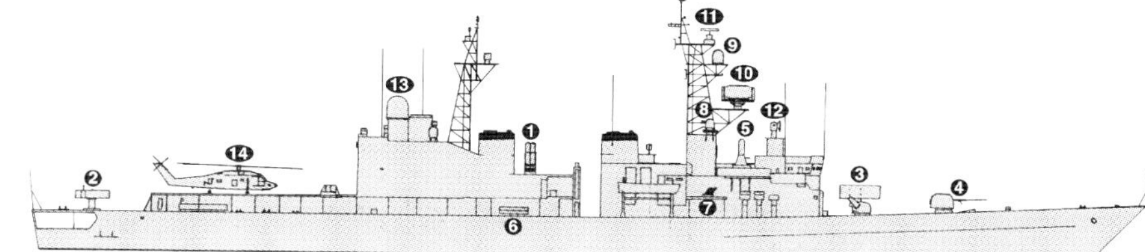

UMIGIRI *(Scale 1 : 1,200), Ian Sturton* / 0012635

Combat data systems: OYQ-7B data automation; Link 11/14. SATCOM. ORQ-1 helicopter datalink ❾ for SH-60J.
Radars: Air search: Melco OPS-14C (DD 151-154); D-band.
Melco OPS-24 (DD 155-158) ❿; 3D; D-band.
Surface search: JRC OPS-28C ⓫; G-band (DD 151, 152, 155-158).
JRC OPS-28C-Y; G-band (DD 153-154).
Navigation: JRC OPS-20; I-band.
Fire control: Type 2-22 (for guns) ⓬. Type 2-12E (for SAM) (DD 151-154); Type 2-12G (for SAM) ⓭ (DD 155-158).
Tacan: ORN-6D (URN 25).
Sonars: Mitsubishi OQS 4A (II); hull-mounted; active search and attack; low frequency.
OQR-1; towed array; passive search; very low frequency.

Helicopters: 1 SH-60J Seahawk ⓮.

Programmes: DD 153-154 in 1984 estimates, DD 155-157 in 1985 and DD 158 in 1986.

Modernisation: The last four were fitted on build with improved air search radar, updated fire-control radars and a helicopter datalink. Plans to fit the first four may have been postponed. *Umigiri* also commissioned with a sonar towed array which has been fitted to the rest of the class.
Structure: Because of the enhanced IR signature and damage to electronic systems on the mainmast caused by after funnel gases there were modifications to the original design to help contain the problem. The mainmast is now slightly higher and has been offset to port. The forward funnel is also offset slightly to port and the after funnel to the starboard side of the superstructure. The hangar structure is asymmetrical extending to the after funnel on the starboard side but only to the mainmast to port. SATCOM is fitted at the after end of the hangar roof.
Operational: Beartrap helicopter hauldown system. *Yamagiri* (D 152) converted to training ship on 18 March 2004 and *Asagiri* (D 151) on 16 February 2005.

HAMAGIRI *4/2008*, Hachiro Nakai* / 1353167

SAWAGIRI *4/2008*, Hachiro Nakai* / 1353168

11 HATSUYUKI CLASS (DDGHM)

Name	*No*	*Builders*	*Laid down*	*Launched*	*Commissioned*
HATSUYUKI	DD 122	Sumitomo, Uraga	14 Mar 1979	7 Nov 1980	23 Mar 1982
SHIRAYUKI	DD 123	Hitachi, Maizuru	3 Dec 1979	4 Aug 1981	8 Feb 1983
MINEYUKI	DD 124	Mitsubishi, Nagasaki	7 May 1981	19 Oct 1982	26 Jan 1984
SAWAYUKI	DD 125	Ishikawajima Harima, Tokyo	22 Apr 1981	21 June 1982	15 Feb 1984
HAMAYUKI	DD 126	Mitsui, Tamano	4 Feb 1981	27 May 1982	18 Nov 1983
ISOYUKI	DD 127	Ishikawajima Harima, Tokyo	20 Apr 1982	19 Sep 1983	23 Jan 1985
HARUYUKI	DD 128	Sumitomo, Uraga	11 Mar 1982	6 Sep 1983	14 Mar 1985
YAMAYUKI	DD 129	Hitachi, Maizuru	25 Feb 1983	10 July 1984	3 Dec 1985
MATSUYUKI	DD 130	Ishikawajima Harima, Tokyo	7 Apr 1983	25 Oct 1984	19 Mar 1986
SETOYUKI	DD 131	Mitsui, Tamano	26 Jan 1984	3 July 1985	11 Dec 1986
ASAYUKI	DD 132	Sumitomo, Uraga	22 Dec 1983	16 Oct 1985	20 Feb 1987

Displacement, tons: 2,950 (3,050 from DD 129 onwards) standard; 4,000 (4,200) full load
Dimensions, feet (metres): 426.4 × 44.6 × 13.8 (14.4 from 129 onwards) *(130 × 13.6 × 4.2) (4.4)*
Main machinery: COGOG; 2 Kawasaki-RR Olympus TM3B gas turbines; 49,400 hp *(36.8 MW)* sustained; 2 RR Type RM1C gas turbines; 9,900 hp *(7.4 MW)* sustained; 2 shafts; cp props
Speed, knots: 30; 19 cruise
Complement: 195 (200, DD 124 onwards)

Missiles: SSM: 8 McDonnell Douglas Harpoon (2 quad) launchers ❶; active radar homing to 130 km *(70 n miles)* at 0.9 Mach; warhead 227 kg.
SAM: Raytheon Sea Sparrow RIM-7M Mk 29 Type 3A launcher ❷; semi-active radar homing to 16 km *(8.5 n miles)* at 2.5 Mach; warhead 38 kg; 12 missiles.
A/S: Honeywell ASROC Mk 112 octuple launcher ❸; inertial guidance to 1.6-10 km *(1-5.4 n miles)* at 0.9 Mach; payload Mk 46 Mod 5 Neartip.
Guns: 1 Otobreda 3 in *(76 mm)*/62 compact ❹; 85 rds/min to 16 km *(8.6 n miles)* anti-surface; 12 km *(6.5 n miles)* anti-aircraft; weight of shell 6 kg.
2 General Electric/General Dynamics 20 mm Phalanx Mk 15 CIWS ❺; 6 barrels per mounting; 3,000 rds/min combined to 1.5 km.
Torpedoes: 6—324 mm Type 68 or HOS 301 (2 triple) tubes ❻. Honeywell Mk 46 Mod 5 Neartip; anti-submarine; active/passive homing to 11 km *(5.9 n miles)* at 40 kt; warhead 44 kg.

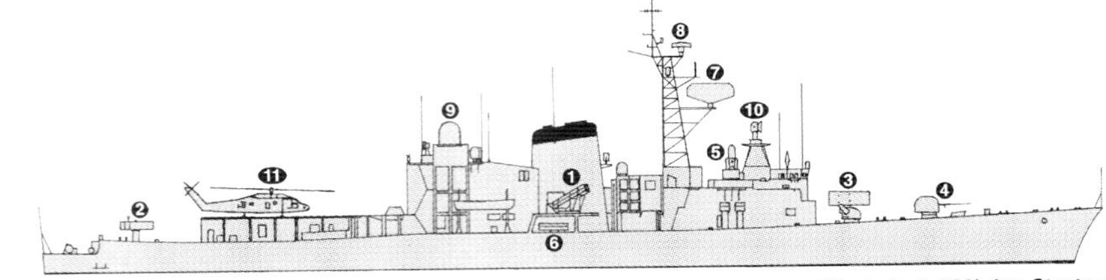
HATSUYUKI *(Scale 1 : 1,200), Ian Sturton* / 0506301

Countermeasures: Decoys: 2 Loral Hycor SRBOC 6-barrelled Mk 36 chaff launchers; range 4 km *(2.2 n miles)*.
ESM: Nec NOLR 6C; intercept.
ECM: Fujitsu OLT 3; jammer.
Combat data systems: OYQ-5B action data automation. SATCOM.
Radars: Air search: Melco OPS-14B ❼; D-band.
Surface search: JRC OPS-18C ❽; G-band.
Navigation: JRC OPS-20; I-band.
Fire control: Type 2-12 A ❾; I/J-band (for SAM).
2 Type 2-21/21A ❿; I/J-band (for guns).
Tacan: ORN-6C-Y (DD 122, 125 and 132); ORN-6C (remainder).
Sonars: Nec OQS 4A (II) (SQS-23 type); bow-mounted; active search and attack; low frequency.
OQR 1 TACTASS (in some); passive; low frequency.

Helicopters: 1 SH-60J Seahawk ⓫.

Modernisation: *Shirayuki* retrofitted with Phalanx in early 1992, and the rest of the class by 1996. *Matsuyuki* first to get sonar towed array in 1990 and *Hatsuyuki* in 1994; the others are being fitted. All of the class converted to carry Seahawk helicopters.
Structure: Fitted with fin stabilisers. Steel in place of aluminium alloy for bridge etc after DD 129 which increased displacement.
Operational: Canadian Beartrap helicopter landing aid. Improved ECM equipment in the last two of the class. Last of class *Shimayuki* converted to a training ship 18 March 1999.

SHIRAYUKI *4/2008*, Hachiro Nakai* / 1353169

SETOYUKI *7/2008*, Hachiro Nakai* / 1353170

1 TACHIKAZE CLASS (DDGM)

Name	*No*	*Builders*	*Laid down*	*Launched*	*Commissioned*
SAWAKAZE	DDG 170	Mitsubishi, Nagasaki	14 Sep 1979	4 June 1981	30 Mar 1983

Displacement, tons: 3,950 standard; 5,200 full load
Dimensions, feet (metres): 469 × 47 × 15.1 *(143 × 14.3 × 4.6)*
Main machinery: 2 Mitsubishi boilers; 600 psi *(40 kg/cm²)*; 850°F *(454°C)*; 2 Mitsubishi turbines; 60,000 hp(m); *(44.7 MW)*; 2 shafts
Speed, knots: 32
Complement: 250

Missiles: SSM: 8 McDonnell Douglas Harpoon Block 1B; active radar homing to 92 km *(50 n miles)* at 0.9 Mach; warhead 227 kg HE.
SAM: Raytheon Standard SM-1MR Block VIA; Mk 13 Mod 4 launcher ❶; command guidance; semi-active radar homing to 38 km *(20.5 n miles)* at 2 Mach; height envelope 45-18,288 m *(150-60,000 ft)*; 40 missiles (SSM and SAM combined).
A/S: Honeywell ASROC Mk 112 octuple launcher ❷; inertial guidance to 1.6-10 km *(1-5.4 n miles)* at 0.9 Mach; payload Mk 46 Mod 5 Neartip.
Guns: 1 or 2 FMC 5 in *(127 mm)*/54 Mk 42 automatic ❸; 20-40 rds/min to 24 km *(13 n miles)* anti-surface; 14 km *(7.6 n miles)* anti-aircraft; weight of shell 32 kg.
2 General Electric/General Dynamics 20 mm Phalanx CIWS Mk 15 ❹; 6 barrels per mounting; 3,000 rds/min combined to 1.5 km.
Torpedoes: 6—324 mm Type 68 or HOS 301 (2 triple) tubes ❺. Honeywell Mk 46 Mod 5 Neartip; anti-submarine; active/passive homing to 11 km *(5.9 n miles)* at 40 kt; warhead 44 kg.
Countermeasures: Decoys: 4 Loral Hycor SRBOC Mk 36 multibarrelled chaff launchers. SLQ-25 towed torpedo decoy.
ESM: Nec NOLQ 1; intercept.
ECM: Fujitsu OLT 3; jammer.
Combat data systems: OYQ-4 action data automation; Links 11 and 14. SATCOM.
Weapons control: 2 Mk 74 Mod 13 missile control directors. US Mk 114 ASW control. GFCS-2-21 for gun.
Radars: Air search: Melco OPS-11C ❻; B-band.
Hughes SPS-52C ❼; 3D; E/F-band.
Surface search: JRC OPS-28 ❽; G-band.
Navigation: JRC OPS-20; I-band.
Fire control: 2 Raytheon SPG-51 ❾; G/I-band.
Type 2 FCS ❿; I/J-band.
IFF: NYPX-2.
Sonars: Nec OQS-3A (Type 66); bow-mounted; active search and attack; low frequency.

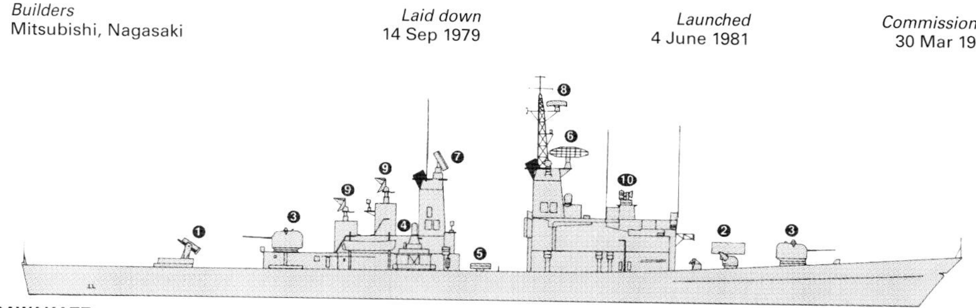

SAWAKAZE *(Scale 1 : 1,200), Ian Sturton* / 0506024

SAWAKAZE *8/2008*, Hachiro Nakai* / 1353171

Modernisation: CIWS added in 1987.
Operational: *Tachikaze* decommissioned on 15 January 2007 and *Asakaze* on 12 March 2008.

2 SHIRANE CLASS (DDHM)

Name	*No*	*Builders*	*Laid down*	*Launched*	*Commissioned*
SHIRANE	DDH 143	Ishikawajima Harima, Tokyo	25 Feb 1977	18 Sep 1978	17 Mar 1980
KURAMA	DDH 144	Ishikawajima Harima, Tokyo	17 Feb 1978	20 Sep 1979	27 Mar 1981

Displacement, tons: 5,200 standard; 7,200 full load
Dimensions, feet (metres): 521.5 × 57.5 × 17.5 *(159 × 17.5 × 5.3)*
Main machinery: 2 IHI boilers; 850 psi *(60 kg/cm²)*; 900°F *(480°C)*; 2 IHI turbines; 70,000 hp(m) *(51.5 MW)*; 2 shafts
Speed, knots: 31 (144); 32 (143)
Complement: 350; 360 (DDH 144) plus 20 staff

Missiles: SAM: Raytheon Sea Sparrow RIM-7M; Type 3 launcher ❶; semi-active radar homing to 16 km *(8.5 n miles)* at 2.5 Mach; warhead 38 kg; 24 missiles.
A/S: Honeywell ASROC Mk 112 octuple launcher ❷; inertial guidance to 10 km *(5.4 n miles)* at 0.9 Mach; payload Mk 46 Mod 5 Neartip.
Guns: 2 FMC 5 in *(127 mm)*/54 Mk 42 automatic ❸; 20-40 rds/min to 24 km *(13 n miles)* anti-surface; 14 km *(7.6 n miles)* anti-aircraft; weight of shell 32 kg.
2 General Electric/General Dynamics 20 mm Phalanx Mk 15 CIWS ❹; 6 barrels per mounting; 3,000 rds/min combined to 1.5 km.
Torpedoes: 6—324 mm HOS 301 (2 triple) tubes ❺. Honeywell Mk 46 Mod 5 Neartip; anti-submarine; active/passive homing to 11 km *(5.9 n miles)* at 40 kt; warhead 44 kg.
Countermeasures: Decoys: 4 Mk 36 SRBOC chaff launchers. Prairie Masker; blade rate suppression system.
ESM/ECM: Melco NOLQ 1; intercept/jammer. Fujitsu OLR 9B; intercept.
Combat data systems: OYQ-3B; Links 11 and 14. SATCOM ❻.

Weapons control: Singer Mk 114 for ASROC and TFCS; Type 72-1A GFCS.
Radars: Air search: Nec OPS-12 ❼; 3D; D-band.
Surface search: JRC OPS-28 ❽; G-band.
Navigation: JRC OPS-20; I-band.
Fire control: Type 2-12 ❾; I/J-band.
2 Type 72-1A FCS ❿; I/J-band.
Tacan: ORN-6C/6C-Y.
Sonars: EDO/Nec SQS-35(J); VDS; active/passive search; medium frequency.
Nec OQS 101; bow-mounted; low frequency.
EDO/Nec SQR-18A; towed array; passive; very low frequency.

Helicopters: 3 SH-60J Seahawk ⓫.

SHIRANE *(Scale 1 : 1,500), Ian Sturton* / 1153010

Programmes: One each in 1975 and 1976 programmes.
Modernisation: DDH 143 refit in 1989–90. Both fitted with CIWS and towed array sonars by mid-1990. DDH 144 upgraded with Type 3 launcher to fire RIM-7M during 2003–04 refit at Mitsubishi, Nagasaki. DDH 143 similarly upgraded at IHI Yokohama in 2004.
Structure: Fitted with Vosper Thornycroft fin stabilisers. The after funnel is set to starboard and the forward one to port. The crane is on the starboard after corner of the hangar. Bear Trap helicopter hauldown gear.
Operational: *Shirane* badly damaged by a fire in December 2007 and repair plans are under consideration.

KURAMA *10/2006, Hachiro Nakai* / 1040629

1 HARUNA CLASS (DDHM)

Name	*No*	*Builders*	*Laid down*	*Launched*	*Commissioned*
HIEI	DDH 142	Ishikawajima Harima, Tokyo	8 Mar 1972	13 Aug 1973	27 Nov 1974

Displacement, tons: 4,950 (5,050, DDH 142) standard; 6,900 full load
Dimensions, feet (metres): 502 × 57.4 × 17.1 *(153 × 17.5 × 5.2)*
Main machinery: 2 Mitsubishi (DDH 141) or IHI (DDH 142) boilers; 850 psi *(60 kg/cm²)*; 900°F *(480°C)*; 2 Mitsubishi (DDH 141) or IHI (DDH 142) turbines; 70,000 hp *(51.5 MW)*; 2 shafts
Speed, knots: 31
Complement: 370 (360, DDH 141) (36 officers)

Missiles: SAM: Raytheon Sea Sparrow RIM-7M Mk 29 (Type 3A) octuple launcher ❶; semi-active radar homing to 16 km *(8.5 n miles)* at 2.5 Mach; warhead 38 kg; 24 missiles.
A/S: Honeywell ASROC Mk 112 octuple launcher ❷; inertial guidance to 1.6-10 km *(1-5.4 n miles)* at 0.9 Mach; payload Mk 46 Mod 5 Neartip.
Guns: 2 FMC 5 in *(127 mm)*/54 Mk 42 automatic ❸; 20–40 rds/min to 24 km *(13 n miles)* anti-surface; 14 km *(7.6 n miles)* anti-aircraft; weight of shell 32 kg.
2 General Electric/General Dynamics 20 mm Phalanx Mk 15 CIWS ❹; 6 barrels per mounting; 3,000 rds/min combined to 1.5 km.
Torpedoes: 6—324 mm HOS 301 (2 triple) tubes ❺. Honeywell Mk 46 Mod 5 Neartip; anti-submarine; active/passive homing to 11 km *(5.9 n miles)* at 40 kt; warhead 44 kg.

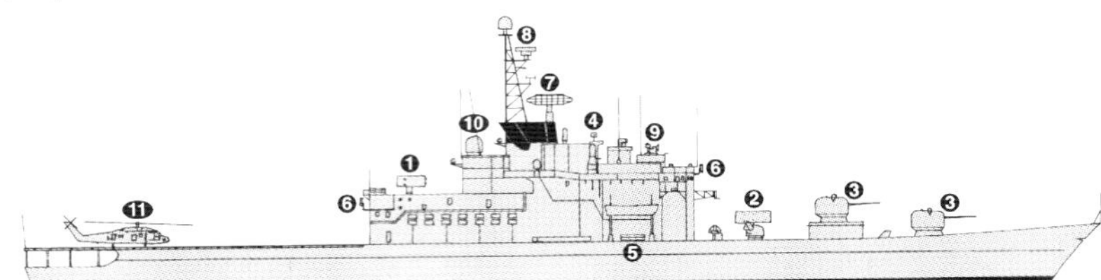

HARUNA *(Scale 1 : 1,500), Ian Sturton* / 0012641

Countermeasures: Decoys: 4 Loral Hycor SRBOC Mk 36 multibarrelled chaff launchers.
ESM/ECM: Melco NOLQ 1; intercept/jammer. Fujitsu OLR 9; intercept.
Combat data systems: OYQ-7B action data automation; Links 11 and 14; US SATCOM ❻.
Weapons control: 2 Type 2-12 FCS (1 for guns, 1 for SAM).
Radars: Air search: Melco OPS-11C ❼; B-band.
Surface search: JRC OPS-28C/28C-Y ❽; G-band.
Fire control: 1 Type 1A ❾; I/J-band (guns).
1 Type 2-12 ❿; I/J-band (SAM).
Navigation: JRC OPS-20; I-band.
IFF: YPA-2. YPX-3.
Tacan: Nec ORN-6D/6C.

Sonars: Sangamo/Mitsubishi OQS 3; bow-mounted; active search and attack; low frequency with bottom bounce.

Helicopters: 3 SH-60J Seahawk ⓫.

Programmes: Ordered under the third five-year defence programme (from 1967–71).
Modernisation: DDH 142 received FRAM from 31 August 1987 to 30 March 1989 at IHI, Tokyo; included Sea Sparrow, two CIWS and chaff launchers.
Structure: The funnel is offset slightly to port. Fitted with fin stabilisers. A heavy crane has been fitted on the top of the hangar, starboard side.
Operational: Fitted with Canadian Beartrap hauldown gear.

HIEI *4/2008*, Hachiro Nakai* / 1353172

FRIGATES

Notes: The MSDF classifies these ships as Destroyer Escorts.

6 ABUKUMA CLASS (FFGM/DE)

Name	*No*	*Builders*	*Laid down*	*Launched*	*Commissioned*
ABUKUMA	DE 229	Mitsui, Tamano	17 Mar 1988	21 Dec 1988	12 Dec 1989
JINTSU	DE 230	Hitachi, Maizuru	14 Apr 1988	31 Jan 1989	28 Feb 1990
OOYODO	DE 231	Mitsui, Tamano	8 Mar 1989	19 Dec 1989	23 Jan 1991
SENDAI	DE 232	Sumitomo, Uraga	14 Apr 1989	26 Jan 1990	15 Mar 1991
CHIKUMA	DE 233	Hitachi, Maizuru	14 Feb 1991	22 Jan 1992	24 Feb 1993
TONE	DE 234	Sumitomo, Uraga	8 Feb 1991	6 Dec 1991	8 Feb 1993

Displacement, tons: 2,000 standard; 2,550 full load
Dimensions, feet (metres): 357.6 × 44 × 12.5 *(109 × 13.4 × 3.8)*
Main machinery: CODOG; 2 RR Spey SM1A gas turbines; 26,650 hp *(19.9 MW)* sustained; 2 Mitsubishi S12U-MTK diesels; 6,000 hp(m) *(4.4 MW)*; 2 shafts
Speed, knots: 27
Complement: 120

Missiles: SSM: 8 McDonnell Douglas Harpoon (2 quad) launchers ❶; active radar homing to 130 km *(70 n miles)* at 0.9 Mach; warhead 227 kg.
A/S: Honeywell ASROC Mk 112 octuple launcher ❷; inertial guidance to 1.6-10 km *(1-5.4 n miles)* at 0.9 Mach; payload Mk 46 Mod 5 Neartip.
Guns: 1 Otobreda 3 in *(76 mm)*/62 compact ❸; 85 rds/min to 16 km *(8.6 n miles)* anti-surface; 12 km *(6.5 n miles)* anti-aircraft; weight of shell 6 kg.
1 General Electric/General Dynamics 20 mm Phalanx CIWS Mk 15 ❹; 6 barrels per mounting; 3,000 rds/min combined to 1.5 km.
Torpedoes: 6—324 mm HOS 301 (2 triple) tubes ❺. Honeywell Mk 46 Mod 5 Neartip; anti-submarine; active/passive homing to 11 km *(5.9 n miles)* at 40 kt; warhead 44 kg.
Countermeasures: Decoys: 2 Loral Hycor SRBOC 6-barrelled Mk 36 chaff launchers.
ESM: Nec NOLR-8; intercept.
Combat data systems: OYQ-6. SATCOM.
Weapons control: Type 2-21; GFCS.
Radars: Air search: Melco OPS-14C ❻; D-band.
Surface search: JRC OPS-28D (DE 233-234); JRS OPC-28C (remainder) ❼; G-band.
Fire control: Type 2-21 ❽.
Sonars: Hitachi OQS-8; hull-mounted; active search and attack; medium frequency.
SQR-19A towed passive array in due course.

Programmes: First pair of this class approved in 1986 estimates, ordered March 1987; second pair in 1987 estimates, ordered February 1988; last two in 1989 estimates, ordered 24 January 1989. The name of the first of class commemorates that of a light cruiser which was sunk in the battle of Leyte Gulf in October 1944.

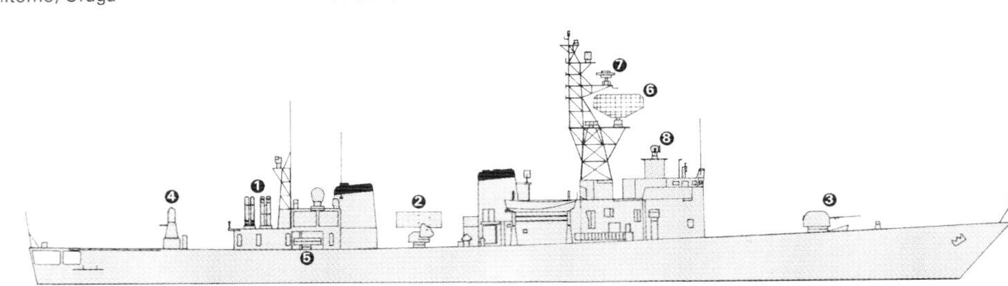

ABUKUMA *(Scale 1 : 900), Ian Sturton* / 0506197

JINTSU *4/2008*, Hachiro Nakai* / 1353173

Structure: Stealth features include non-vertical and rounded surfaces. German RAM PDMS may be fitted later, although this now seems unlikely, and space has been left for a towed sonar array. SATCOM fitted aft of the after funnel.

2 ISHIKARI/YUUBARI CLASS (FFG/DE)

Name	*No*	*Builders*	*Laid down*	*Launched*	*Commissioned*
YUUBARI	DE 227	Sumitomo, Uraga	9 Feb 1981	22 Feb 1982	18 Mar 1983
YUUBETSU	DE 228	Hitachi, Maizuru	14 Jan 1982	25 Jan 1983	14 Feb 1984

Displacement, tons: 1,470 standard; 1,690 full load
Dimensions, feet (metres): 298.5 × 35.4 × 11.8 *(91.0 × 10.8 × 3.6)*
Main machinery: CODOG; 1 Kawasaki/RR Olympus TM3B gas turbine; 24,700 hp *(18.4 MW)* sustained; 1 Mitsubishi/MAN 6DRV diesel; 4,700 hp(m) *(3.45 MW)*; 2 shafts; cp props
Speed, knots: 25
Complement: 95

Missiles: SSM: 8 McDonnell Douglas Harpoon (2 quad) launchers ❶; active radar homing to 130 km *(70 n miles)* at 0.9 Mach; warhead 227 kg.
Guns: 1 Otobreda 3 in *(76 mm)*/62 compact ❷; 85 rds/min to 16 km *(8.6 n miles)* anti-surface; 12 km *(6.5 n miles)* anti-aircraft; weight of shell 6 kg. 1 General Electric/General Dynamics 20 mm Phalanx (unlikely to be fitted) ❸.
Torpedoes: 6 — 324 mm Type 68 (2 triple) tubes ❹. Honeywell Mk 46 Mod 5 Neartip; anti-submarine; active/passive homing to 11 km *(5.9 n miles)* at 40 kt; warhead 44 kg.
A/S mortars: 1 — 375 mm Bofors Type 71 4 to 6-barrelled trainable rocket launcher ❺; automatic loading; range 1.6 km.

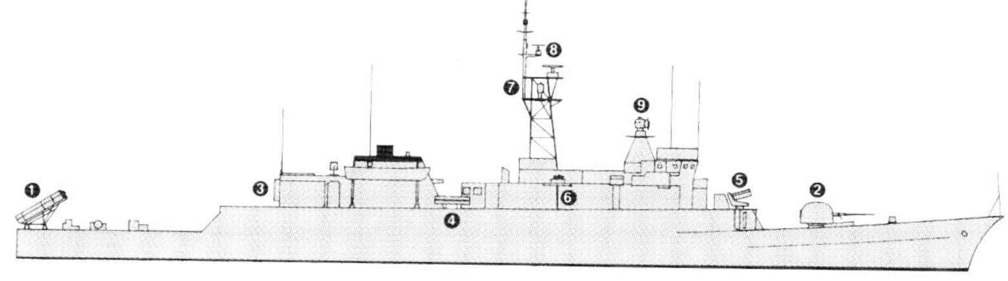

YUUBARI *(Scale 1 : 900), Ian Sturton* / 0506026

Countermeasures: Decoys: 2 Loral Hycor SRBOC 6-barrelled Mk 36 chaff launchers ❻; range 4 km *(2.2 n miles)*.
ESM: Nec NOLR 6B ❼; intercept.
Combat data systems: OYQ-5.
Weapons control: Type 2-21 system for 76 mm gun.
Radars: Surface search: JRC OPS-28B/28-1 ❽; G-band.
Navigation: Fujitsu OPS-19B; I-band.

Fire control: Type 2-21 ❾; I/J-band.
Sonars: Nec SQS-36J; hull-mounted; active/passive; medium frequency.

Programmes: The name *Yuubari* commemorates that of a light cruiser sunk in the Second World War.
Structure: *Yuubari* and *Yuubetsu* were slightly larger versions of *Ishikari* which was decommissioned in 2007.

YUUBARI *10/2006, Hachiro Nakai* / 1040640

SHIPBORNE AIRCRAFT

Numbers/Type: 83/15 Sikorsky/Mitsubishi SH-60J/SH-60K (Seahawk).
Operational speed: 139 kt *(257 km/h)*.
Service ceiling: 13,500 ft *(4,090 m)*
Range: 600 n miles *(1,110 km)*.
Role/Weapon systems: ASW helicopter; started replacing HSS-2B in July 1991; built in Japan; prototypes fitted by Mitsubishi with Japanese avionics and mission equipment. Overall requirement for 103 aircraft. SH-60K are upgraded aircraft with an improved tactical data processing system. Sensors: Texas Instruments APS 124 search radar; sonobuoys plus datalink; Bendix AQS 18/Nippon HQS 103 dipping sonar, ECM, HLR 108 ESM. Weapons: ASW; two Mk 46 torpedoes or depth bombs. 2 HellfireASM (SH-60K).

SH-60K *10/2006, Hachiro Nakai* / 1040641

Numbers/Type: 2/1 Agusta Westland/Kawasaki MCH-101/CH-101.
Operational speed: 150 kt *(278 km/h)*.
Service ceiling: 15,000 ft *(4,575 m)*.
Range: 610 n miles *(1,129 km)*.
Role/Weapon systems: Based on the Agusta Westland EH-101. There are to be 11 MCH-101 AMCM and cargo carrying aircraft to replace the MH-53E. Three CH-101 are to replace the S-61A support aircraft deployed in the ice-patrol ship.

MCH-101 *11/2006, Japanese Navy* / 1167169

LAND-BASED MARITIME AIRCRAFT

Notes: Aircraft type names are not used by the MSDF.

Numbers/Type: 10 NAMC YS-11.
Operational speed: 248 kt *(459 km/h)*.
Service ceiling: 21,500 ft *(6,580 m)*.
Range: 1,960 n miles *(3,629 km)*.
Role/Weapon systems: First flew in 1962. Of 182 aircraft constructed, 10 remain in service. Of these, two YS-11EA are EW trainers while there are believed to be four YS-11B configured for Sigint operations. These are equipped with dorsal and ventral blade antennas and with radomes. These aircraft may be designated YS-11EL. Other variants include two YS-11FC flight checkers, a YS-11NT navigational trainer and YS-11C transport aircraft.

YS-11 *9/2008*, Hachiro Nakai* / 1353175

CH-101 *9/2008*, Hachiro Nakai* / 1353174

Numbers/Type: 95/5/1/3/5 Lockheed/Kawasaki P-3C/EP-3/UP-3C/UP-3D/OP-3C.
Operational speed: 395 kt *(732 km/h)*.
Service ceiling: 28,300 ft *(8,625 m)*.
Range: 3,300 n miles *(6,100 km)*.
Role/Weapon systems: Long-range MR/ASW and surface surveillance and attack. Most maritime surveillance is done by these aircraft. Sensors: APS-115 radar, ASQ-81 MAD, AQA 7 processor, Unisys CP 2044 computer, IFF, ECM, ALQ 78, ESM, ALR 66, sonobuoys. Weapons: ASW; eight Mk 46 torpedoes, depth bombs or mines, four underwing stations for Harpoon and ASM-1.

P-3C *9/2008*, Hachiro Nakai* / 1353176

EP-3 *9/2008*, Hachiro Nakai* / 1353177

Numbers/Type: 6 Shinmeiwa US-1A Rescue.
Operational speed: 265 kt *(491 km/h)*.
Service ceiling: 28,400 ft *(8,655 m)*.
Range: 2,300 n miles *(4,260 km)*.
Role/Weapon systems: Turboprop amphibian designed for maritime patrol and SAR missions. Crew of 12. Accommodation for 16 survivors or 12 stretchers.

US-1A *7/2008*, Hachiro Nakai* / 1353115

Numbers/Type: 10 Sikorsky/Mitsubishi S-80M-1 (Sea Dragon) (MH53E).
Operational speed: 170 kt *(315 km/h)*.
Service ceiling: 18,500 ft *(5,640 m)*.
Range: 1,120 n miles *(2,000 km)*.
Role/Weapon systems: Three-engined AMCM helicopter tows Mk 103, 104, 105 and 106 MCM sweep equipment; self-deployed. Weapons: Two 12.7 mm guns for mine disposal.

MH-53E *9/2008*, Hachiro Nakai* / 1353104

Numbers/Type: 2 Kawasaki XP-1.
Operational speed: 448 kt *(830 km/h)*.
Service ceiling: 36,100 ft *(11,000 m)*.
Range: 4,320 n miles *(8,000 km)*.
Role/Weapon systems: The first test version of the XP-1 future maritime patrol aircraft was rolled out on 4 July 2007. The aircraft has been under full development since 2001 and is to replace the P-3C inventory in due course. The aircraft incorporates the world's first Fly-By-Light (FBL) system. The aircraft is to be equipped with new acoustic and radar systems. Following flight testing, the aircraft is to be delivered to the Ministry of Defence by the end of 2008. Up to 70 aircraft may be acquired.

XP-1 *10/2008*, Ships of the World* / 1353183

Numbers/Type: 3 Shinmeiwa US-2.
Operational speed: 300 kt *(556 km/h)*.
Service ceiling: 28,400 ft *(8,655 m)*.
Range: 2,500 n miles *(4,630 km)*.
Role/Weapon systems: Following trials, two former experimental aircraft entered service in 2007. A further aircraft was authorised in the FY07 budget. The US-2 is an upgraded version of the US-1A and is designed for maritime patrol and SAR missions. Sensors: Thales Ocean Master radar.

US-2 *12/2008*, Hachiro Nakai* / 1353114

PATROL FORCES

6 HAYABUSA CLASS (PGGF)

Name	*No*	*Builders*	*Launched*	*Commissioned*
HAYABUSA	824	Mitsubishi, Shimonoseki	13 June 2001	25 Mar 2002
WAKATAKA	825	Mitsubishi, Shimonoseki	13 Sep 2001	25 Mar 2002
OOTAKA	826	Mitsubishi, Shimonoseki	13 May 2002	24 Mar 2003
KUMATAKA	827	Mitsubishi, Shimonoseki	2 Aug 2002	24 Mar 2003
UMITAKA	828	Mitsubishi, Shimonoseki	21 May 2003	24 Mar 2004
SHIRATAKA	829	Mitsubishi, Shimonoseki	8 Aug 2003	24 Mar 2004

Displacement, tons: 200 standard; 240 full load
Dimensions, feet (metres): 164.4 × 27.6 × 13.8 *(50.1 × 8.4 × 4.2)*
Main machinery: 3 LM 500-G07 gas turbines 16,200 hp *(12.08 MW)*; 3 water jets
Speed, knots: 44
Complement: 18 (+3 staff)
Missiles: 4 Mitsubishi Type 90 SSM-1B; active radar homing to 130 km *(70 n miles)* at 0.9 Mach; warhead 227 kg.
Guns: 1 OTO Melara 3 in *(76 mm)*/62 compact; 85 rds/min to 16 km *(8.7 n miles)* anti-surface; 12 km *(6.6 n miles)* anti-aircraft; weight of shell 6 kg.
2—12.7 mm MGs.
Countermeasures: Decoys: Chaff launchers.
ESM/ECM: NOLR-9B.
Radars: Surface search: OPS-18-3; G-band.
Fire control: Type 2-31C.
Navigation: OPS-20; I-band.

Comment: First pair authorised in FY99 budget, second pair in FY00 and third pair in FY01. Single hull.

OOTAKA *10/2008*, Hachiro Nakai* / 1353116

1 PG 01 (SPARVIERO) CLASS (FAST ATTACK HYDROFOILS—MISSILE) (PTGK)

Name	*No*	*Builders*	*Launched*	*Commissioned*
MISAIRUTEI-SAN-GOU	823	Sumitomo, Uraga	15 June 1994	13 Mar 1995

Displacement, tons: 50 standard; 60 full load
Dimensions, feet (metres): 71.5 × 22.9 × 4.6 *(21.8 × 7 × 1.4)* (hull)
80.7 × 23.1 × 14.4 *(24.6 × 7 × 4.4)* (foilborne)
Main machinery: 1 GE/IHI LM 500 gas turbine; 5,000 hp *(3.72 MW)* sustained; 1 pumpjet (foilborne); 1 diesel; 1 retractable prop (hullborne)
Speed, knots: 46; 8 (diesel). **Range, n miles:** 400 at 40 kt; 1,000 at 8 kt
Complement: 11 (3 officers)
Missiles: SSM: 4 Mitsubishi Type 90 SSM-1B (derivative of land-based system); range 150 km *(81 n miles)*.
Guns: 1 GE 20 mm/76 Sea Vulcan; 3 barrels per mounting; 1,500 rds/min combined to 4 km *(2.2 n miles)*.
Countermeasures: Decoys: 2 Loral Hycor Mk 36 SRBOC chaff launchers.
ESM/ECM: NOLR-9B.
Combat data systems: Link 11.
Radars: Surface search: JRC OPS-28-2; G-band.
Navigation: JRC OPS-20; I-band.

Comment: Classified as Guided Missile Patrol Boats. First two approved in FY90 and one more approved in FY92. The first two were decommissioned in 2008.

PG 01 CLASS *7/2006, Hachiro Nakai* / 1040645

AMPHIBIOUS FORCES

3 OOSUMI CLASS (LPD/LSTH)

Name	*No*	*Builders*	*Laid down*	*Launched*	*Commissioned*
OOSUMI	LST 4001	Mitsui, Tamano	6 Dec 1995	18 Nov 1996	11 Mar 1998
SHIMOKITA	LST 4002	Mitsui, Tamano	30 Nov 1999	29 Nov 2000	12 Mar 2002
KUNISAKI	LST 4003	Universal, Maizuru	7 Sep 2000	13 Dec 2001	26 Feb 2003

Displacement, tons: 8,900 standard; 14,000 full load
Dimensions, feet (metres): 584 × 84.6 × 19.7 *(178 × 25.8 × 6)*
Flight deck, feet (metres): 426.5 × 75.5 *(130 × 23)*
Main machinery: 2 Mitsui 16V42MA diesels; 26,000 hp(m) *(19.4 MW)*; 2 shafts; 2 bow thrusters
Speed, knots: 22
Complement: 135
Military lift: 330 troops; 2 LCAC; 10 Type 90 tanks or 1,400 tons cargo

Guns: 2 GE/GD 20 mm Vulcan Phalanx Mk 15 ❶. 6 barrels per mounting; 3,000 rds/min combined to 1.5 km.
Countermeasures: ESM/ECM.
Radars: Air search: Mitsubishi OPS-14C ❷; C-band.
Surface search: JRC OPS-28D ❸; G-band.
Navigation: JRC OPS-20; I-band.

Helicopters: Platform for 2 CH-47J.

Programmes: A 5,500 ton LST was requested and not approved in the 1989 or 1990 estimates. The published design resembled the Italian San Giorgio with a large flight deck and a stern dock. No further action was taken for two years but the FY93 request included a larger ship showing the design of a USN LPH, although smaller in size. This vessel, with some modifications, was authorised in the 1993 estimates. A second of class approved in FY98 and third in FY99.

Structure: Through deck, flight deck and stern docking well make this more like a mini LHA than an LST, except that the ship is described as providing only 'platform and refuelling facilities for helicopters'.

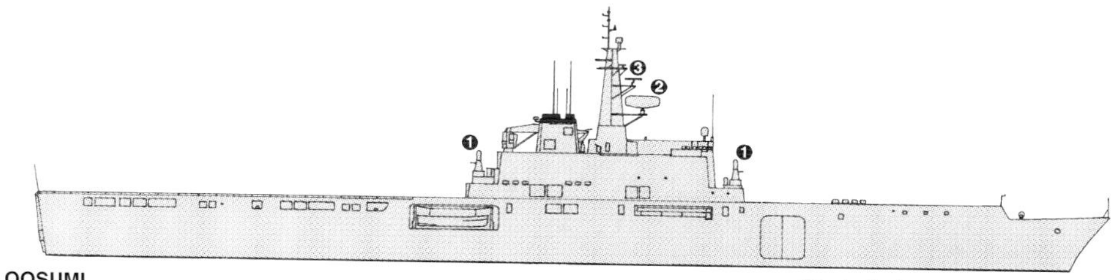

OOSUMI ***(Scale 1 : 1,500), Ian Sturton*** / 0012652

OOSUMI ***5/2008*, Hachiro Nakai*** / 1353117

SHIMOKITA ***4/2008*, Hachiro Nakai*** / 1353118

2 YURA CLASS (LSU/LCU)

Name	No	Builders	Commissioned
YURA	LSU 4171	Sasebo Heavy Industries	27 Mar 1981
NOTO	LSU 4172	Sasebo Heavy Industries	27 Mar 1981

Displacement, tons: 590 standard
Dimensions, feet (metres): 190.2 × 31.2 × 5.6 *(58 × 9.5 × 1.7)*
Main machinery: 2 Fuji 6L27.5XF diesels; 3,250 hp(m) *(2.39 MW)*; 2 shafts; cp props
Speed, knots: 12
Complement: 31
Military lift: 70 troops
Guns: 1 GE 20 mm/76 Sea Vulcan 20; 3 barrels per mounting; 1,500 rds/min combined to 4 km *(2.2 n miles)*.
Radars: Navigation: Fujitsu OPS-9B; I-band.

Comment: Both laid down 23 April 1980. 4171 launched 15 October 1980 and 4172 on 12 November 1980.

YURA *8/2007, Hachiro Nakai* / 1305066

2 YUSOUTEI CLASS (LCU)

Name	No	Builders	Commissioned
YUSOUTEI-ICHI-GOU	LCU 2001	Sasebo Heavy Industries	17 Mar 1988
YUSOUTEI-NI-GOU	LCU 2002	Sasebo Heavy Industries	11 Mar 1992

Displacement, tons: 420 standard; 540 full load
Dimensions, feet (metres): 170.6 × 28.5 × 5.2 *(52 × 8.7 × 1.6)*
Main machinery: 2 Mitsubishi S6U-MTK diesels; 3,000 hp(m) *(2.23 MW)*; 2 shafts
Speed, knots: 12
Complement: 28
Guns: 1 GE 20 mm/76 Sea Vulcan; 3 barrels per mounting; 1,500 rds/min combined to 4 km *(2.2 n miles)*.
Radars: Navigation: OPS-9B/26; I-band.

Comment: First approved in 1986 estimates, laid down 11 May 1987, launched 9 October 1987. Second approved in FY90 estimates, laid down 15 May 1991, launched 7 October 1991; plans for a third have been scrapped. Official names are LCU 01 and LCU 02.

YUSOUTEI-ICHI-GOU *10/2008*, Hachiro Nakai* / 1353119

6 LANDING CRAFT AIR CUSHION (LCAC)

AIR CUSHION-TEI (1–6) GOU LCAC 2101–2106

Displacement, tons: 100 standard; 180 full load
Dimensions, feet (metres): 88 oa (on cushion) (81 between hard structures) × 47 beam (on cushion) (43 beam hard structure) × 2.9 draught (off cushion) *(26.8 (24.7) × 14.3 (13.1) × 0.9)*
Main machinery: 4 Avco-Lycoming TF-40B gas turbines; 2 for propulsion and 2 for lift; 16,000 hp *(12 MW)* sustained; 2 shrouded reversible-pitch airscrews (propulsion); 4 double entry fans, centrifugal or mixed flow (lift)
Speed, knots: 40 (loaded)
Range, n miles: 300 at 35 kt; 200 at 40 kt
Complement: 5
Military lift: 24 troops; 1 MBT or 60-75 tons
Radars: Navigation: LN-66; I-band.

Comment: Built by Textron Marine, New Orleans for embarkation in LPDs. Approval for sale given by US on 8 April 1994. First two commissioned in March 1998, second two in March 2002 and third in February 2003. Cargo space capacity is 1,809 sq ft.

LCAC 2103 *7/2008*, Hachiro Nakai* / 1353120

10 LCM TYPE (LCM)

YF 2121 YF 2124–25 YF 2127–29 YF 2132 YF 2135 YF 2138 YF 2141

Displacement, tons: 25 standard
Dimensions, feet (metres): 55.8 × 14 × 2.3 *(17.0 × 4.3 × 0.7)*
Main machinery: 2 Isuzu E120-MF6R diesels; 480 hp(m) *(353 kW)*; 2 shafts
Speed, knots: 10
Range, n miles: 130 at 9 kt
Complement: 3
Military lift: 34 tons or 80 troops

Comment: Built in Japan. *YF 2127-29* commissioned in March 1992, *2132* in March 1993, *2135* in March 1995, *2138* in March 1996 and *2141* in March 1997. *YF 2150-51* are 50 ton vessels built by Yokohama Yacht and completed in March 2003. With a military lift of 100 tons they are capable of 16 kt.

YF 2135 *10/2007, Hachiro Nakai* / 1305095

2 YF 2150 CLASS LCM (LCM)

YF 2150–51

Displacement, tons: 50 standard
Dimensions, feet (metres): 121.4 × 22.0 × 11.2 *(19.8 × 5.4 × 2.3)*
Main machinery: 2 Mitsubishi S12R-MTK diesels; 3,000 hp *(2.24 MW)*; 2 waterjets
Speed, knots: 16
Complement: 4
Military lift: 100 troops or 1 vehicle

Comment: Built in Japan by Universal, Keihin and commissioned on 19 March 2003.

YF 2150 *10/2007, Hachiro Nakai* / 1305096

MINE WARFARE FORCES

2 URAGA CLASS (MINESWEEPER TENDERS) (MSTH/ML)

Name	No	Builders	Launched	Commissioned
URAGA	MST 463	Hitachi, Maizuru	22 May 1996	19 Mar 1997
BUNGO	MST 464	Mitsui, Tamano	24 Apr 1997	23 Mar 1998

Displacement, tons: 5,650 standard; 6,850 full load
Dimensions, feet (metres): 462.6 × 72.2 × 17.7 *(141 × 22 × 5.4)*
Main machinery: 2 Mitsui 16V42MA diesels; 19,500 hp(m) *(14.33 MW)*; 2 shafts
Speed, knots: 22
Complement: 160
Guns: 1 OTO Melara 3 in *(76 mm)*/62 compact (MST 464); 85 rds/min to 16 km *(8.6 n miles)*; weight of shell 6 kg.
Mines: Laying capability; 4 rails (Type 3). 200 mines.
Radars: Air search: OPS-14C; C-band.
Fire control: Type 2-23; I/J-band.
Navigation: JRC OPS-39C; I-band.
Helicopters: Platform for 1 MH-53E.

Comment: First one authorised 15 February 1994 and laid down 19 May 1995; second authorised in FY95 and laid down 4 July 1996. Capable of laying mines, from four internal rails. Phalanx is planned to be fitted forward of the bridge and on the superstructure aft of the funnel.

URAGA *2/2008*, Hachiro Nakai* / 1353121

3 YAEYAMA CLASS (MINESWEEPERS—OCEAN) (MSO)

Name	*No*	*Builders*	*Launched*	*Commissioned*
YAEYAMA	MSO 301	Hitachi Zosen, Kanagawa	29 Aug 1991	16 Mar 1993
TSUSHIMA	MSO 302	Nippon Koukan, Tsurumi	20 Sep 1991	23 Mar 1993
HACHIJYO	MSO 303	Nippon Koukan, Tsurumi	15 Dec 1992	24 Mar 1994

Displacement, tons: 1,000 standard; 1,200 full load
Dimensions, feet (metres): 219.8 × 38.7 × 10.2 *(67 × 11.8 × 3.1)*
Main machinery: 2 Mitsubishi 6NMU-TA1 diesels; 2,400 hp(m) *(1.76 MW)*; 2 shafts; 1 hydrojet bow thruster; 350 hp(m) *(257 kW)*
Speed, knots: 14
Complement: 60
Guns: 1 JM-61 20 mm/76 Sea Vulcan; 3 barrels per mounting; 1,500 rds/min combined to 4 km *(2.2 n miles)*.
Radars: Surface search: Fujitsu OPS-39B; I-band.
Sonars: Raytheon SQQ-32 VDS; high frequency; active.

Comment: First two approved in 1989 estimates, third in 1990. First laid down 30 August 1990, second 20 July 1990 and third 17 May 1991. Wooden hulls. Fitted with S 7 deep sea minehunting system, S 8 (SLQ-48) deep sea moored minesweeping equipment and ADI Dyad sweeps. Appears to be a derivative of the USN Avenger class. An integrated tactical system is fitted. Termination of the programme at three of the class suggests similar problems to US ships of the same class.

TSUSHIMA *7/2006, Hachiro Nakai* / 1040651

2 NIIJIMA CLASS (DRONE CONTROL SHIPS) (MCSD)

Name	*No*	*Builders*	*Commissioned*
OGISHIMA	MCL 726 (ex-MSC 666)	Hitachi, Kanagawa	19 Dec 1987
SAKUSHIMA	MCL 727 (ex-MSC 671)	Nippon Koukan, Tsurumi	19 Dec 1989

Displacement, tons: 440 standard; 510 full load
Dimensions, feet (metres): 180.4 × 30.8 × 8.2 *(55 × 9.4 × 2.5)*
Main machinery: 2 Mitsubishi 12ZC diesels; 1,440 hp(m) *(1.06 MW)*; 2 shafts
Speed, knots: 14
Complement: 28
Guns: 1 GE 20 mm/76 Sea Vulcan 20; 3 barrels per mounting; 1,500 rds/min combined to 4 km *(2.2 n miles)*.
Radars: Surface search: Fujitsu OPS-9B; I-band.

Comment: Both converted to act as Minesweeper Control Ship (MCLs) and equipped to operate SAM remote controlled drones. All minesweeping gear removed. *Ogishima* converted as MCL on 8 February 2006.

NIIJIMA CLASS (with SAM 02) *2/2008*, Hachiro Nakai* / 1353133

6 SAM CLASS (MSD)

SAM 01–06

Displacement, tons: 20 full load
Dimensions, feet (metres): 59.1 × 20 × 5.2 *(18 × 6.1 × 1.6)*
Main machinery: 1 Volvo Penta TAMD 70D diesel; 210 hp(m) *(154 kW)*; 1 Schottel prop
Speed, knots: 8. **Range, n miles:** 330 at 8 kt

Comment: First pair acquired from Karlskronavarvet, Sweden in February 1998 followed by two more in December 1998 and two more in 2000. Remote controlled magnetic and acoustic catamaran sweepers operated by *Kamishima* and *Ogishima*.

SAM 02 *2/2008*, Hachiro Nakai* / 1353124

12 SUGASHIMA CLASS (MINEHUNTER (COASTAL)) (MHC)

Name	*No*	*Builders*	*Launched*	*Commissioned*
SUGASHIMA	MSC 681	NKK, Tsurumi	25 Aug 1997	16 Mar 1999
NOTOJIMA	MSC 682	Hitachi, Kanagawa	3 Sep 1997	16 Mar 1999
TSUNOSHIMA	MSC 683	Hitachi, Kanagawa	22 Oct 1998	13 Mar 2000
NAOSHIMA	MSC 684	NKK, Tsurumi	7 Oct 1999	16 Mar 2001
TOYOSHIMA	MSC 685	Hitachi, Kanagawa	13 Sep 2000	4 Mar 2002
UKUSHIMA	MSC 686	Universal, Keihin (Tsurumi)	17 Sep 2001	18 Mar 2003
IZUSHIMA	MSC 687	Universal, Keihin (Kanawaga)	31 Oct 2001	18 Mar 2003
AISHIMA	MSC 688	Universal, Keihin (Tsurumi)	8 Oct 2002	16 Feb 2004
AOSHIMA	MSC 689	Universal, Keihin (Kanawaga)	16 Sep 2003	9 Feb 2005
MIYAJIMA	MSC 690	Universal, Keihin (Tsurumi)	10 Oct 2003	9 Feb 2005
SHISHIJIMA	MSC 691	Universal, Keihin (Tsurumi)	29 Sep 2004	8 Feb 2006
KUROSHIMA	MSC 692	Universal, Keihin (Tsurumi)	31 Aug 2005	23 Feb 2007

Displacement, tons: 510 standard; 590 full load
Dimensions, feet (metres): 177.2 × 30.8 × 9.8 *(54.0 × 9.4 × 3.0)*
Main machinery: 2 Mitsubishi 6 NMU-TAI diesels; 1,800 hp(m) *(1.33 MW)*; 2 shafts; bow thrusters
Speed, knots: 14. **Range, n miles:** 2,500 at 10 kt
Complement: 45
Guns: 1 JM-61 20 mm/76 Sea Vulcan; 3 barrels for mounting; 1,500 rds/min combined to 4 km *(2 n miles)*.
Combat data systems: AMS/NEC Nautis-M type MCM control system.
Radars: Surface search: Fujitsu OPS-39B; I-band.
Sonars: THALES Hitachi GEC Type 2093 VDS; high frequency; active.

Comment: First pair authorised in FY95, third in FY96, fourth in FY97, fifth in FY98, sixth and seventh in FY99, eighth in FY00, ninth and tenth in FY01, eleventh in FY02 and twelfth in FY03. Hull is similar to *Uwajima* but the upper deck is extended aft to provide more stowage for mine disposal gear, and there are twin funnels. PAP 104 Mk 5 ROVs are carried and ADI Dyad minesweeping gear fitted.

NAOSHIMA *2/2008*, Hachiro Nakai* / 1353122

2 + 1 HIRASHIMA CLASS (MINESWEEPERS/MINEHUNTERS—COASTAL) (MHSC)

Name	*No*	*Builders*	*Launched*	*Commissioned*
HIRASHIMA	MSC 601	Universal, Keihin (Tsurumi)	27 Sep 2006	11 Mar 2008
YAKUSHIMA	MSC 602	Universal, Keihin (Tsurumi)	26 Sep 2007	6 Mar 2009
TAKASHIMA	MSC 603	Universal, Keihin (Tsurumi)	25 Sep 2008	Mar 2010

Displacement, tons: 570 standard; 650 full load
Dimensions, feet (metres): 187 × 32.1 × 14.4 *(57.0 × 9.8 × 4.4)*
Main machinery: 2 Mitsubishi 6 NMU diesels; 2,200 hp *(1.64 MW)*; 2 shafts; bow thrusters
Speed, knots: 14
Complement: 45
Guns: 1—20 mm Sea Vulcan.
Sonars: Hitachi ZQS 4; hull-mounted; high frequency.

Comment: First authorised in FY04 budget, second in FY05 budget and third in FY06 budget. Wooden hull. Equipped with S-10 minesweeping and disposal system.

HIRASHIMA *3/2008*, Hachiro Nakai* / 1353123

0 + 2 IMPROVED HIRASHIMA CLASS (MINESWEEPERS—COASTAL) (MSC)

Name	*No*	*Builders*	*Laid down*	*Launched*	*Commissioned*
–	–	–	2009	2010	2012

Displacement, tons: 570 standard
Dimensions, feet (metres): 206.7 × 32.1 × 14.4 *(63.0 × 9.8 × 4.4)*
Main machinery: 2 diesels; 2 shafts
Speed, knots: 14
Complement: To be announced
Guns: 1—30 mm (remote controlled).

Comment: A larger, improved version of the Hirashima class. FRP construction. First authorised in FY08 budget and second in FY09 budget.

10 HATSUSHIMA/UWAJIMA CLASS (MINEHUNTERS/SWEEPERS—COASTAL) (MHSC)

Name	No	Builders	Commissioned
AWASHIMA	MSC 670	Hitachi, Kanagawa	13 Dec 1989
UWAJIMA	MSC 672	Nippon Koukan, Tsurumi	19 Dec 1990
IESHIMA	MSC 673	Hitachi, Kanagawa	19 Dec 1990
TSUKISHIMA	MSC 674	Hitachi, Kanagawa	17 Mar 1993
MAEJIMA	MSC 675	Hitachi, Kanagawa	15 Dec 1993
KUMEJIMA	MSC 676	Nippon Koukan, Tsurumi	12 Dec 1994
MAKISHIMA	MSC 677	Hitachi, Kanagawa	12 Dec 1994
TOBISHIMA	MSC 678	Nippon Koukan, Tsurumi	10 Mar 1995
YUGESHIMA	MSC 679	Hitachi, Kanagawa	11 Dec 1996
NAGASHIMA	MSC 680	Nippon Koukan, Tsurumi	25 Dec 1996

Displacement, tons: 440 (490, MSC 672-680) standard; 520 (550 MSC 670-671) (570 MSC 672-680) full load
Dimensions, feet (metres): 180.4 (190.3, MSC 670 onwards) × 30.8 × 8.2 (9.5) *(55 (58.0) × 9.4 × 2.5 (2.9))*
Main machinery: 2 Mitsubishi 6NMU-TAI diesels; 1,800 hp(m) *(1.3 MW)*; 2 shafts
Speed, knots: 14
Range, n miles: 2,500 at 10 kt
Complement: 45

Guns: 1 JM-61 20 mm/76 Sea Vulcan 20; 3 barrels per mounting; 1,500 rds/min combined to 4 km *(2.2 n miles)*.
Radars: Surface search: Fujitsu OPS-9 or OPS-39 (MSC 674 onwards); I-band.
Sonars: Nec/Hitachi ZQS 2B or ZQS 3 (MSC 672 onwards); hull-mounted; minehunting; high frequency.

Programmes: First ordered in 1976. Last two authorised in FY94. Because of the new sonar and mine detonating equipment vessels from MSC 672 onwards are known as the Uwajima class.
Structure: From MSC 670 onwards the hull is lengthened by 2.7 m in order to improve the sleeping accommodation from three tier to two tier bunks. Hulls are made of wood. The last pair has more powerful engines developing 1,800 hp(m) *(1.32 MW)*.
Operational: Fitted with S 4 (S 7 from MSC 672 onwards) mine detonating equipment, a remote-controlled counter-mine charge. Four clearance divers are carried. Earlier vessels of the class converted to drone control or paid off at a rate of one or two a year.

MAKISHIMA *7/2008*, Hachiro Nakai* / 1353125

SURVEY AND RESEARCH SHIPS

Notes: Survey ships are also included in the Coast Guard section.

2 HIBIKI CLASS (OCEAN SURVEILLANCE SHIPS) (AGOSH)

Name	No	Builders	Launched	Commissioned
HIBIKI	AOS 5201	Mitsui, Tamano	27 July 1990	30 Jan 1991
HARIMA	AOS 5202	Mitsui, Tamano	11 Sep 1991	10 Mar 1992

Displacement, tons: 2,850 standard; 3,000 full load
Dimensions, feet (metres): 219.8 × 98.1 × 24.6 *(67 × 29.9 × 7.5)*
Main machinery: Diesel-electric; 4 Mitsubishi Stu diesels; 3,000 hp(m) *(2.2 MW)*; 4 generators; 2 motors; 3,000 hp(m) *(2.2 MW)*; 2 shafts
Speed, knots: 11 (3 towing)
Range, n miles: 3,800 at 10 kt
Complement: 40
Radars: Surface search: JRC OPS-16; G-band.
Navigation: Koden OPS-9; I-band.
Sonars: UQQ 2 SURTASS; passive surveillance.
Helicopters: Platform only.

Comment: First authorised 24 January 1989, laid down 28 November, second approved in FY90, laid down 26 December 1990. Auxiliary Ocean Surveillance (AOS) ships to a SWATH design similar to USN TAGOS-19 class. A data collection station is based at Yokosuka Bay using WSC-6 satellite data relay to the AOS.

HARIMA *4/2007, Hachiro Nakai* / 1305102

0 + 1 SURVEY SHIP (AGS)

Name	No	Builders	Laid down	Launched	Commissioned
–	AGS 5106	Mitsui, Tamano	Dec 2008	June 2009	Mar 2010

Displacement, tons: 3,200 standard
Dimensions, feet (metres): 337.9 × 53.8 × 14.8 *(103.0 × 16.4 × 4.5)*
Main machinery: Diesel-electric; 2 shafts
Speed, knots: 16
Range, n miles: To be announced
Complement: 80
Radars: Navigation: I-band.

Comment: New survey ship authorised in FY07 budget.

1 NICHINAN CLASS (SURVEY SHIP) (AGS)

Name	No	Builders	Launched	Commissioned
NICHINAN	AGS 5105	Mitsubishi, Shimonoseki	11 June 1998	24 Mar 1999

Displacement, tons: 3,300 standard; 4,500 full load
Dimensions, feet (metres): 364.2 × 55.8 × 14.8 *(111 × 17 × 4.5)*
Main machinery: Diesel-electric; 2 Mitsubishi S16U diesel generators; 3 motors; 3,600 hp(m) *(2.7 MW)*; 2 shafts; bow and stern thrusters
Speed, knots: 18
Complement: 90

Comment: Authorisation approved in FY96. Combination cable repair and hydrographic survey ship. Equipped with one ROV.

NICHINAN *8/2007, Hachiro Nakai* / 1305104

1 SUMA CLASS (AGS)

Name	No	Builders	Launched	Commissioned
SUMA	AGS 5103	Hitachi, Maizuru	1 Sep 1981	30 Mar 1982

Displacement, tons: 1,180 standard; 1,700 full load
Dimensions, feet (metres): 236.2 × 42 × 11.1 *(72 × 12.8 × 3.4)*
Main machinery: 2 Fuji 6L27.5XF diesels; 3,000 hp(m) *(2.24 MW)*; 2 shafts; cp props; bow thruster
Speed, knots: 15
Complement: 64 plus 5 scientists
Countermeasures: ESM: NOLR-6.
Radars: Navigation: OPS-20; I-band.

Comment: Laid down 24 September 1980. Carries an 11 m launch for surveying work.

SUMA *2/1999, Hachiro Nakai* / 0080180

2 FUTAMI CLASS (AGS)

Name	No	Builders	Launched	Commissioned
FUTAMI	AGS 5102	Mitsubishi, Shimonoseki	9 Aug 1978	27 Feb 1979
WAKASA	AGS 5104	Hitachi, Maizuru	21 May 1985	25 Feb 1986

Displacement, tons: 2,050 standard; 3,175 full load
Dimensions, feet (metres): 318.2 × 49.2 × 13.8 *(97 × 15 × 4.2)*
Main machinery: 2 Kawasaki-MAN V8V22/30ATL diesels; 4,000 hp(m) *(2.94 MW)* (AGS 5102); 2 Fuji 8L27.5XF diesels; 3,250 hp(m) *(2.39 MW)* (AGS 5104); 2 shafts; cp props; bow thruster
Speed, knots: 16
Complement: 105 (95 AG 5104)
Radars: Navigation: JRC OPS-18-3; G-band.

Comment: AGS 5102 laid down 20 January 1978, AGS 5104 21 August 1984. Built to merchant marine design. Carry an RCV-225 remote-controlled rescue/underwater survey submarine. *Wakasa* has a slightly taller funnel.

FUTAMI *8/2008*, Hachiro Nakai* / 1353126

1 KURIHAMA CLASS (ASE/AGE)

Name	*No*	*Builders*	*Launched*	*Commissioned*
KURIHAMA	ASE 6101	Sasebo Heavy Industries	20 Sep 1979	8 Apr 1980

Displacement, tons: 950 standard; 1,100 full load
Dimensions, feet (metres): 223 × 37.9 × 9.8 (screws) *(68 × 11.6 × 3)*
Main machinery: 2 Fuji 6S30B diesels; 2,600 hp(m) *(1.94 MW)*; 2 shafts; 2 cp props; 2 auxiliary electric props; bow thruster
Speed, knots: 15
Complement: 40 plus 12 scientists
Radars: Navigation: Fujitsu OPS-9B; I-band.

Comment: Experimental ship built for the Technical Research and Development Institute and used for testing underwater weapons and sensors.

KURIHAMA *5/2006, **Hachiro Nakai*** / 1040618

1 ASUKA CLASS (AGEH)

Name	*No*	*Builders*	*Launched*	*Commissioned*
ASUKA	ASE 6102	Sumitomo, Uraga	21 June 1994	22 Mar 1995

Displacement, tons: 4,250 standard; 6,200 full load
Dimensions, feet (metres): 495.4 × 56.8 × 16.4 *(151 × 17.3 × 5)*
Main machinery: COGLAG; 2 IHI/GE LM 2500 gas turbines; 43,000 hp *(31.6 MW)*; 2 shafts; cp props
Speed, knots: 27
Complement: 70 plus 100 scientists
Missiles: SAM: 8 cell VLS.
Weapons control: Type 3 FCS.
Radars: Air search: SPY-1D type; E/F-band.
Air/surface search: Melco OPS-14C; D-band.
Surface search: JRC OPS-18-1; G-band.
Fire control: Type 3; I/J-band.
Sonars: Bow-mounted; active search; medium frequency.
Towed passive/active array in due course.
Helicopters: 1 SH-60J Seahawk.

Comment: Included in the FY92 programme and laid down 21 April 1993. For experimental and weapon systems testing which started with the FCS 3 in 1996. The bow sonar dome extends aft to the bridge. The VLS system is on the forecastle. Surveillance and countermeasures systems are also evaluated.

ASUKA *8/2008*, **Hachiro Nakai*** / 1353127

RESCUE VEHICLES

2 RESCUE SUBMARINES (DSRV)

Displacement, tons: 40
Dimensions, feet (metres): 40.7 × 10.5 × 14.1 *(12.4 × 3.2 × 4.6)*
Main machinery: Electric; 30 hp *(22 kW)*; single shaft
Speed, knots: 4
Complement: 2

Comment: Rescue submersibles built by Kawasaki Heavy Industries, Kobe and delivered on 27 August 1999. Space for 12 people. Sonars are fitted on the bow, upper and lower casings for depth sounding and obstacle avoidance. Can be deployed in the submarine rescue ships *Chiyoda* (AS 405) and *Chihaya* (ASR 403).

DSRV *7/2005, **Hachiro Nakai*** / 1153295

TRAINING SHIPS

1 SHIMAYUKI CLASS (TRAINING SHIP) (AXGHM/TV)

Name	*No*	*Builders*	*Commissioned*
SHIMAYUKI	TV 3513 (ex-DD 133)	Mitsubishi, Nagasaki	17 Feb 1987

Displacement, tons: 3,050 standard; 4,200 full load
Dimensions, feet (metres): 426.4 × 44.6 × 14.4 *(130 × 13.6 × 4.4)*
Main machinery: COGOG; 2 Kawasaki-RR Olympus TM3B gas turbines; 45,000 hp *(33.5 MW)* sustained; 2 RR Type RM1C gas turbines; 9,900 hp *(7.4 MW)* sustained; 2 shafts; cp props
Speed, knots: 30; 19 cruise
Complement: 200

Missiles: SSM: 8 McDonnell Douglas Harpoon (2 quad) launchers; active radar homing to 130 km *(70 n miles)* at 0.9 Mach; warhead 227 kg.
SAM: Raytheon Sea Sparrow RIM-7M Mk 29 Type 3A launcher; semi-active radar homing to 16 km *(8.5 n miles)* at 2.5 Mach; warhead 38 kg; 12 missiles.
A/S: Honeywell ASROC Mk 112 octuple launcher; inertial guidance to 1.6-10 km *(1-5.4 n miles)* at 0.9 Mach; payload Mk 46 Mod 5 Neartip.
Guns: 1 OTO Melara 3 in *(76 mm)*/62 compact; 85 rds/min to 16 km *(8.6 n miles)* anti-surface; 12 km *(6.5 n miles)* anti-aircraft; weight of shell 6 kg.
2 General Electric/General Dynamics 20 mm Phalanx Mk 15 CIWS; 6 barrels per mounting; 3,000 rds/min combined to 1.5 km.
Torpedoes: 6—324 mm Type 68 (2 triple) tubes. Honeywell Mk 46 Mod 5 Neartip; anti-submarine; active/passive homing to 11 km *(5.9 n miles)* at 40 kt; warhead 44 kg.
Countermeasures: Decoys: 2 Loral Hycor SRBOC 6-barrelled Mk 36 chaff launchers; range 4 km *(2.2 n miles)*.
ESM: NOLR 6C; intercept.
ECM: Fujitsu OLT 3; jammer.
Combat data systems: OYQ-5 action data automation; Link 14 (receive only). SATCOM.
Radars: Air search: Melco OPS-14B; D-band.
Surface search: JRC OPS-18-1; G-band.
Fire control: Type 2-12 A; I/J-band (for SAM).
2 Type 2-21/21A; I/J-band (for guns).
Tacan: ORN-6C.
Sonars: Nec OQS 4A (II) (SQS-23 type); bow-mounted; active search and attack; low frequency.
Helicopters: Platform for 1 SH-60J Seahawk.

Comment: Converted to training ship in March 1999. Helicopter hangar converted to lecture rooms.

SHIMAYUKI *8/2007, **Mick Prendergast*** / 1305107

1 KASHIMA CLASS (TRAINING SHIP) (AXH/TV)

Name	*No*	*Builders*	*Launched*	*Commissioned*
KASHIMA	TV 3508	Hitachi, Maizuru	23 Feb 1994	26 Jan 1995

Displacement, tons: 4,050 standard; 5,400 full load
Dimensions, feet (metres): 469.2 × 59.1 × 15.1 *(143 × 18 × 4.6)*
Main machinery: CODOG; 2 RR Spey SM1C gas-turbines; 27,000 hp *(20.1 MW)* sustained; 2 Mitsubishi S16U-MTK diesels; 8,000 hp(m) *(5.88 MW)*; 2 shafts
Speed, knots: 25
Range, n miles: 7,000 at 18 kt
Complement: 360 (includes 125 midshipmen)
Guns: 1 OTO Melara 76 mm/62. 2—40 mm saluting guns.
Torpedoes: 6—324 mm (2 triple) tubes.
Radars: Air/surface search: Melco OPS-14C; D-band.
Surface search: JRC OPS-18-1; D-band.
Navigation: Fujitsu OPS-20; I-band.
Fire control: Type 2-23; I/J-band.
Sonars: Hull-mounted; active search and attack; medium frequency. OQS-4.
Helicopters: Platform for 1 medium.

Comment: Approved in FY91 as a dedicated training ship but the project postponed to FY92 as a budget saving measure. Laid down 20 April 1993.

KASHIMA *4/2008*, **Kazumasa Watanabe*** / 1353103

2 ASAGIRI CLASS (TRAINING SHIPS) (AX/TV)

Name	*No*	*Builders*	*Laid down*	*Launched*	*Commissioned*
YAMAGIRI	TV 3515 (ex-DD 152)	Mitsui, Tamano	5 Feb 1986	8 Oct 1987	25 Jan 1989
ASAGIRI	TV 3516 (ex-DD 151)	Ishikawajima Harima, Tokyo	13 Feb 1985	19 Sep 1986	17 Mar 1988

Displacement, tons: 3,500 standard; 4,900 full load
Dimensions, feet (metres): 449.4 × 48 × 14.6 *(137 × 14.6 × 4.5)*
Main machinery: COGAG; 4 RR Spey SM1A gas turbines; 53,300 hp *(39.8 MW)* sustained; 2 shafts; cp props
Speed, knots: 30+
Complement: 220

Missiles: SSM: 8 McDonnell Douglas Harpoon (2 quad) launchers; active radar homing to 130 km *(70 n miles)* at 0.9 Mach; warhead 227 kg.
SAM: Raytheon Sea Sparrow Mk 29 (Type 3/3A) octuple launcher; semi-active radar homing to 14.6 km *(8 n miles)* at 2.5 Mach; warhead 39 kg; 20 missiles.
A/S: Honeywell ASROC Mk 112 octuple launcher; inertial guidance to 1.6-10 km *(1-5.4 n miles)* at 0.9 Mach; payload Mk 46 Mod 5 Neartip. Reload capability.
Guns: 1 Otobreda 3 in *(76 mm)*/62 compact; 85 rds/min to 16 km *(8.6 n miles)* anti-surface; 12 km *(6.5 n miles)* anti-aircraft; weight of shell 6 kg.
2 General Electric/General Dynamics 20 mm Phalanx Mk 15 CIWS; 6 barrels per mounting; 3,000 rds/min combined to 1.5 km.
Torpedoes: 6—324 mm Type 68 (2 triple) HOS 301 tubes. Honeywell Mk 46 Mod 5 Neartip; anti-submarine; active/passive homing to 11 km *(5.9 n miles)* at 40 kt; warhead 44 kg.
Countermeasures: Decoys: 2 Loral Hycor SRBOC 6-barrelled Mk 36 chaff launchers; range 4 km *(2.2 n miles)*.
1 SLQ-25 Nixie or Type 4; towed torpedo decoy.
ESM: Nec NOLR 6C or NOLR 8 (DD 152); intercept.
ECM: Fujitsu OLT-3; jammer.
Combat data systems: OYQ-7B data automation; Link 11/14. SATCOM. ORQ-1 helicopter datalink for SH-60J.
Radars: Air search: Melco OPS-14C; D-band.
Surface search: JRC OPS-28C; G-band.
Fire control: Type 2-22 (for guns). Type 2-12E (for SAM).
Tacan: ORN-6D (URN 25).
Sonars: Mitsubishi OQS 4A (II); hull-mounted; active search and attack; low frequency.
OQR-1; towed array; passive search; very low frequency.

Helicopters: Platform for 1 SH-60J Seahawk.

Comment: TV 3515 converted to training ship on 18 March 2004 and TV 3516 on 16 February 2005. Hangars converted to lecture rooms.

ASAGIRI *7/2008*, A A de Kruijf* / 1353181

1 TENRYU CLASS (TRAINING SUPPORT SHIP) (AVHM/TV)

Name	*No*	*Builders*	*Launched*	*Commissioned*
TENRYU	ATS 4203	Sumitomo, Uraga	14 Apr 1999	17 Mar 2000

Displacement, tons: 2,450 standard; 2,750 full load
Dimensions, feet (metres): 347.8 × 54.1 × 13.5 *(106 × 16.5 × 4.1)*
Main machinery: 4 Niigata 8MG28H diesels; 12,800 hp(m) *(9.5 MW)* sustained; 2 shafts
Speed, knots: 22
Complement: 140
Guns: 1 OTO Melara 3 in *(76 mm)*/62 compact; 85 rds/min to 16 km *(8.6 n miles)*; weight of shell 6 kg.
Radars: Air/surface search: Melco OPS-14; D-band.
Surface search: OPS-28D; G/H-band.
Fire control: Type 2-22; I/J-band.
Helicopters: 1 medium.

Comment: Authorised in 1997 budget as a replacement for *Azuma* and laid down 19 June 1998. Carries four BQM-34J drones and four Northrop Chukar III drones used for evaluating performance of ships SAM systems. Improved 'Kurobe' design.

TENRYU *4/2008*, Hachiro Nakai* / 1353102

1 KUROBE CLASS (TRAINING SUPPORT SHIP) (AVM/TV)

Name	*No*	*Builders*	*Commissioned*
KUROBE	ATS 4202	Nippon Koukan, Tsurumi	23 Mar 1989

Displacement, tons: 2,200 standard; 2,750 full load
Dimensions, feet (metres): 331.4 × 54.1 × 13.1 *(101 × 16.5 × 4)*
Main machinery: 4 Fuji 8L27.5XF diesels; 9,160 hp(m) *(6.8 MW)*; 2 shafts; cp props
Speed, knots: 20
Complement: 155 (17 officers)
Guns: 1 FMC/OTO Melara 3 in *(76 mm)*/62 Mk 75; 85 rds/min to 16 km *(8.6 n miles)* anti-surface; 12 km *(6.5 n miles)* anti-aircraft; weight of shell 6 kg.
Radars: Air search: Melco OPS-14C; D-band.
Surface search: JRC OPS-18-1; G-band.
Fire control: Type 2-22; I/J-band.

Comment: Approved under 1986 estimates, laid down 31 July 1987, launched 23 May 1988. Carries four BQM-34AJ high-speed drones and four Northrop Chukar II drones with two stern launchers. Used for training crews in anti-aircraft operations and evaluating the effectiveness and capability of ships' anti-aircraft missile systems.

KUROBE *7/2008*, Hachiro Nakai* / 1353101

1 TRAINING TENDER (YXT)

YTE 13

Displacement, tons: 179 standard
Dimensions, feet (metres): 115.0 × 24.2 × 5.6 *(35.3 × 7.4 × 1.72)*
Main machinery: 2 Yanmar 12 LAK ST2 diesels; 2,200 hp(m) *(1.16 MW)*; 2 shafts
Speed, knots: 16

Comment: Approved in FY00 budget and commissioned in 2002. Assigned to 1st Maritime Service School for cadet training.

YTE 13 *6/2005, Hachiro Nakai* / 1153301

AUXILIARIES

2 MASHUU CLASS (FAST COMBAT SUPPORT SHIPS) (AOE/AORH)

Name	*No*	*Builders*	*Laid down*	*Launched*	*Commissioned*
MASHUU	AOE 425	Mitsui, Tamano	21 Jan 2002	5 Feb 2003	15 Mar 2004
OUMI	AOE 426	Universal, Maizuru	7 Feb 2003	19 Feb 2004	3 Mar 2005

Displacement, tons: 13,500 standard; 25,000 full load
Dimensions, feet (metres): 725 × 88.6 × 27,2 *(221 × 27 × 8.3)*
Main machinery: 2 Kawasaki RR Spey SM1C gas turbines; 40,000 hp *(29.8 MW)*; 2 shafts
Speed, knots: 24
Complement: 145
Guns: 2—20 mm CIWS (to be fitted).
Countermeasures: Decoys: 4 SRBOC Mk 36 chaff and IR launchers.
Radars: Navigation: I-band.
Helicopters: 2 medium.

Comment: First ship approved in FY00 and second in FY01. Capacity for 30 containers. Cranes capable of lifting 15 tons. Three replenishment at sea positions on each side.

MASHUU *10/2008*, Michael Nitz* / 1353182

6 300 TON CLASS (EOD TENDERS) (YDT)

YDT 01–06

Displacement, tons: 300 standard
Dimensions, feet (metres): 150.9 × 28.2 × 7.2 *(46 × 8.6 × 2.2)*
Main machinery: 2 Niigata 6NSDL diesels; 1,500 hp(m) *(1.1 MW)*; 2 shafts
Speed, knots: 15
Complement: 15 plus 15 divers
Radars: Navigation: I-band.

Comment: Built by Maehata Zousen. First pair approved in FY98, third in FY99, fourth in FY00 and fifth and sixth in FY01. First two commissioned 24 March 2000, third on 21 March 2001, fourth in December 2001 and last two on 14 March 2003. Used as diving tenders.

YDT 05 *4/2008*, Hachiro Nakai* / 1353128

1 CHIYODA CLASS
(SUBMARINE TENDER DEPOT AND RESCUE SHIP) (AS/ASRH)

Name	*No*	*Builders*	*Launched*	*Commissioned*
CHIYODA	AS 405	Mitsui, Tamano	7 Dec 1983	27 Mar 1985

Displacement, tons: 3,650 standard; 5,400 full load
Dimensions, feet (metres): 370.6 × 57.7 × 15.1 *(113 × 17.6 × 4.6)*
Main machinery: 2 Mitsui 8L42M diesels; 11,500 hp(m) *(8.6 MW)*; 2 shafts; cp props; bow and stern thrusters
Speed, knots: 17
Complement: 120 plus 80 submarine crew rest facility
Radars: Navigation: JRC OPS-16; G-band.
Sonars: SQS-36D.
Helicopters: Platform for up to MH-53 size.

Comment: Laid down 19 January 1983. Carries a 40 ton Deep Submergence Rescue Vehicle (DSRV), which is lowered and recovered through a centreline moonpool. The DSRV can mate to a decompression chamber. A personnel transfer capsule can also be deployed. Flagship Second Submarine Flotilla based at Yokosuka.

CHIYODA *1/2007, Hachiro Nakai* / 1305114

1 CHIHAYA CLASS (SUBMARINE RESCUE SHIP) (ASRH)

Name	*No*	*Builders*	*Launched*	*Commissioned*
CHIHAYA	ASR 403	Mitsui, Tamano	8 Oct 1998	23 Mar 2000

Displacement, tons: 5,450 standard; 6,900 full load
Dimensions, feet (metres): 419.9 × 65.6 × 16.7 *(128 × 20 × 5.1)*
Main machinery: 2 Mitsui 12V 42M-A diesels; 19,500 hp(m) *(14.33 MW)*; 2 shafts; 2 bow and 2 stern thrusters
Speed, knots: 21
Complement: 125
Radars: Navigation: OPS-20; I-band.
Helicopters: Platform for up to MH-53 size.

Comment: Authorisation approved in the 1996 budget as a replacement for *Fushimi*. Laid down 13 October 1997. Fitted with a search sonar and carries a 40 ton DSRV. Also used as a hospital ship.

CHIHAYA *7/2008*, Hachiro Nakai* / 1353129

3 TOWADA CLASS
(FAST COMBAT SUPPORT SHIPS) (AOE/AORH)

Name	*No*	*Builders*	*Launched*	*Commissioned*
TOWADA	AOE 422	Hitachi, Maizuru	25 Mar 1986	24 Mar 1987
TOKIWA	AOE 423	Ishikawajima Harima, Tokyo	23 Mar 1989	12 Mar 1990
HAMANA	AOE 424	Hitachi, Maizuru	18 May 1989	29 Mar 1990

Displacement, tons: 8,150 standard; 15,850 full load
Dimensions, feet (metres): 547.8 × 72.2 × 26.9 *(167 × 22 × 8.2)*
Main machinery: 2 Mitsui 16V42MA diesels; 26,000 hp(m) *(19.4 MW)*; 2 shafts
Speed, knots: 22. **Range, n miles:** 10,500 at 20 kt
Complement: 140
Cargo capacity: 5,700 tons
Countermeasures: Decoys: 2 chaff launchers can be fitted.
Radars: Surface search: JRC OPS-18-1/28C; G-band.
Helicopters: Platform for MH-53 size.

Comment: First approved under 1984 estimates, laid down 17 April 1985. Second and third of class in 1987 estimates. AOE 423 laid down 12 May 1988, and AOE 424 8 July 1988. Three replenishment at sea positions on each side (two fuel only, one stores).

TOWADA *7/2006, Hachiro Nakai* / 1040592

34 HARBOUR TANKERS (YO/YW/YG)

Comment: There are: 18 of 490 tons (YO 14, 21-27, 29-31, 33-39); eight of 310 tons (YW 17-24); one of 290 tons (YO 13); seven of 270 tons (YG 202-206, YO 28, YO 32).

YO 21 *2/2008*, Hachiro Nakai* / 1353130

2 FIREFIGHTING TENDERS (YTR)

YR 01–02

Displacement, tons: 60 standard
Dimensions, feet (metres): 82.0 × 18.0 × 3.6 *(25.0 × 5.5 × 1.1)*
Main machinery: 1 Isuzu Marine UM6WGITCG diesels; 750 hp *(560 kW)*; 2 Isuzu Marine UM6RB diesels; 1,040 hp *(775 kW)*; 3 shafts
Speed, knots: 19
Complement: 10

Comment: Built in Japan by Ishikawajima-Harima Heavy Industries. *YR 01* approved in FY99 budget and commissioned in 2001. *YR 02* approved in FY00 budget and commissioned in 2002. Fitted with three waterjets forward and a crane aft.

YR 01 *9/2002, Takatoshi Okano* / 0570888

1 MUROTO CLASS (CABLE REPAIR SHIP) (ARC)

Name	*No*	*Builders*	*Launched*	*Commissioned*
MUROTO	ARC 482	Mitsubishi, Shimonoseki	25 July 1979	27 Mar 1980

Displacement, tons: 4,500 standard; 6,000 full load
Dimensions, feet (metres): 436.2 × 57.1 × 18.7 *(133 × 17.4 × 5.7)*
Main machinery: 4 Kawasaki-MAN V8V22/30ATL diesels; 8,800 hp(m) *(6.6 MW)*; 2 shafts; bow thruster
Speed, knots: 18
Complement: 135
Radars: Navigation: Fujitsu OPS-9B; I-band.

Comment: Ocean survey capability. Laid down 28 November 1978. Similar vessels in civilian use.

MUROTO *7/2006, Hachiro Nakai* / 1040593

1 HASHIDATE CLASS (ASY/YAC)

Name	*No*	*Builders*	*Launched*	*Commissioned*
HASHIDATE	ASY 91	Hitachi, Kanagawa	26 July 1999	30 Nov 1999

Displacement, tons: 400 standard; 490 full load
Dimensions, feet (metres): 203.4 × 30.8 × 6.6 *(62 × 9.4 × 2.0)*
Main machinery: 2 Niigata 16V 16FX diesels; 5,500 hp(m) *(4.04 MW)*; 2 shafts
Speed, knots: 20
Range, n miles: 1,000 at 12 kt
Complement: 29 plus 130 passengers

Comment: Authorised in FY97 budget. Laid down 28 October 1998. Has replaced *Hiyodori* as a ceremonial yacht. Has facilities for disaster relief. Based at Yokosuka.

HASHIDATE *9/2007, Hachiro Nakai* / 1305113

5 HIUCHI CLASS (MULTIPURPOSE SUPPORT SHIPS) (YTT)

Name	*No*	*Builders*	*Launched*	*Commissioned*
HIUCHI	AMS 4301	NKK, Tsurumi	4 Sep 2001	27 Mar 2002
SUOU	AMS 4302	Universal, Keihin (Tsurumi)	25 Apr 2003	16 Mar 2004
AMAKUSA	AMS 4303	Universal, Keihin (Tsurumi)	6 Aug 2003	16 Mar 2004
GENKAI	AMS 4304	Universal, Keihin (Tsurumi)	24 May 2007	20 Feb 2008
ENSHUU	AMS 4305	Universal, Keihin (Tsurumi)	9 Aug 2007	20 Feb 2008

Displacement, tons: 980 standard
Dimensions, feet (metres): 213.3 × 39.4 × 11.5 *(65 × 12 × 3.5)*
Main machinery: 2 Daihatsu 6 DKM-28 (L) diesels; 5,000 hp(m) *(3.67 MW)*; 2 shafts
Speed, knots: 15
Complement: 40
Radars: Navigation: OPS-26B; I-band.

Comment: First authorised in FY99, two more in FY01 and two further in FY05 budget. Equipped for torpedo launch and recovery. Replaced ASU 81 class. Used as an ocean tug.

AMAKUSA *4/2008*, Hachiro Nakai* / 1353131

7 LANDING CRAFT (LIGHTER) (YL)

YL 9–15

Displacement, tons: 120 full load
Dimensions, feet (metres): 88.6 × 23.0 × 3.4 *(27.0 × 7.0 × 1.04)*
Main machinery: 2 Isuzu diesels; 560 hp *(410 kW)*; 2 shafts
Speed, knots: 10
Complement: 5

Comment: Cargo lighters constructed by Ishihara, Takasogo. First entered service in 1980 and latest in 1998. Equipped with a bow ramp and two 2 ton cranes.

YL 10 *4/2007, Hachiro Nakai* / 1305117

ICEBREAKERS

0 + 1 FUTURE ICEBREAKER (AGBH)

Name	*No*	*Builders*	*Laid down*	*Launched*	*Commissioned*
SHIRASE	AGB 5003	Universal, Maizuru	15 Mar 2007	16 Apr 2008	May 2009

Displacement, tons: 12,500 standard; 20,000 full load
Dimensions, feet (metres): 452.7 × 91.9 × 30.2 *(138.0 × 28.0 × 9.2)*
Main machinery: Diesel-electric; 4 Mitsui 16V42M-B diesels; 4 generators; 4 motors; 30,000 hp *(22 MW)*; 2 shafts
Speed, knots: 19.5. **Range, n miles**: 30,000 at 15 kt
Complement: 179 (34 officers) plus 80 scientists
Cargo capacity: 1,100 tons
Radars: Surface search: JRC OPS-18-3; G/H-band.
Navigation: Fujitsu OPS-39D; I-band.
Tacan: ORN-6E.
Helicopters: 2 CH-101.

Comment: New Antarctic expedition ship planned to replace the decommissioned *Shirase*.

SHIRASE *4/2008*, Hachiro Nakai* / 1305319

TUGS

22 OCEAN TUGS (ATA/YT)

YT 58 YT 63–74 YT 78–79 YT 81 YT 84 YT 86 YT 89–90 YT 92 YT 94

Displacement, tons: 260 standard
Dimensions, feet (metres): 93 × 28 × 8.2 *(28.4 × 8.6 × 2.5)*
Main machinery: 2 Niigata 6L25B diesels; 1,800 hp(m) *(1.32 MW)*; 2 shafts
Speed, knots: 11
Complement: 10

Comment: *YT 58* entered service on 31 October 1978, *YT 63* on 27 September 1982, *YT 64* on 30 September 1983, *YT 65* on 20 September 1984, *YT 66* on 20 September 1985, *YT 67* on 4 September 1986, *YT 68* on 9 September 1987, *YT 69* on 16 September 1987, *YT 70* on 2 September 1988, *YT 71* on 28 July 1989, *YT 72* on 28 July 1990, *YT 73* on 31 July 1991, *YT 74* on 30 September 1991, *YT 78* in July 1994, *YT 79* on 29 September 1994, *YT 81* on 8 July 1996, *YT 84* on 30 September 1998, *YT 86* on 21 March 2000, *YT 89* and *90* on 16 March 2001, YT 92 on 17 March 2006 and YT 94 in March 2007. All built by Yokohama Yacht.

YT 78 *7/2008*, Hachiro Nakai* / 1353132

21 COASTAL AND HARBOUR TUGS (YTM/YTB)

YT 53–57 YT 59–62 YT 75–77 YT 80 YT 82–83 YT 85 YT 87–88 YT 91 YT 93

Displacement, tons: 53 standard
Dimensions, feet (metres): 55.8 × 15.8 × 7.8 *(17.0 × 4.8 × 2.4)*
Main machinery: 2 Isuzu UM6SD1TCB diesels; 500 hp (373 kW); 2 shafts
Speed, knots: 8
Complement: 4

Comment: Details given are for 50 ton class (YT 75-77, YT 80, YT 85, YT 87-88, YT 91 and YT 93). There are also four of 190 tons (YT 53, YT 55-57), two of 35 tons (YT 60-61), one of 30 tons (YT 62) and two of 29 tons (YT 54, YT 59).

YT 83 *1/2007, Hachiro Nakai* / 1305110

COAST GUARD

KAIJYOU HOANCHOU

Headquarters Appointments

Commandant of the Coast Guard:
Teiji Iwasaki

Establishment

The Japan Coast Guard (Maritime Safety Agency before 1 April 2000) was established on 1 May 1948. Its five missions are Maintenance of Maritime Order, Maritime Search and Rescue, Maritime Environmental Protection and Enforcement, Maritime Traffic Safety and Co-operation with other national and international agencies. The HQ is at Tokyo, the Coast Guard Academy is at Kure and the Coast Guard School is at Maizuru.

The main operational branches are the Guard and Rescue, the Hydrographic and the Maritime Traffic Departments. Regional offices control the 11 districts with their location as follows (airbases in brackets): RMS 1-Otaru (Chitose, Hakodate, Kushiro); 2-Shiogama (Sendai); 3-Yokohama (Haneda); 4-Nagoya (Ise); 5-Kobe; 6-Hiroshima (Hiroshima); 7-Ube (Fukuoka); 8-Maizuru (Miho); 9-Niigata (Niigata); 10-Kagoshima (Kagoshima); 11-Naha (Naha, Ishigaki). This organisation includes, as well as the JCG HQ, 67 CG offices, 63 CG stations, 13 CG air stations, seven district communication centres, seven traffic advisory service centres, two hydrographic observatories, two aids to navigation offices, one Special Rescue station, one Special Security station, one National Strike Team station and one Transnational Organised Crime Strike Force station.

Personnel

2009: 12,258 (2,630 officers)

Strength of the Fleet

Type	*Active*	*Building*
GUARD AND RESCUE SERVICE		
Patrol Vessels:		
Large with helicopter (PLH)	13	–
Large (PL)	40	4
Medium (PM)	42	7
Small (PS)	29	–
Firefighting Vessels (FL)	5	–
Patrol Craft:		
Patrol Craft (PC)	63	3
Patrol Craft (CL)	178	8
Firefighting Craft (FM)	4	–
Special Service Craft:		
Monitoring Craft (MS)	3	–
Guard Boats (GS)	2	–
Surveillance Craft (SS)	42	–
Oil Recovery Craft (OR)	5	–
Oil Skimming Craft (OS)	3	–
Oil Boom Craft (OX)	19	–

Strength of the Fleet — *continued*

Type	*Active*	*Building*
HYDROGRAPHIC SERVICE		
Surveying Vessels:		
Large (HL)	5	–
Small (HS)	8	–
AIDS TO NAVIGATION SERVICE		
Aids to Navigation Research Vessel (LL)	1	–
Buoy Tenders:		
Large (LL)	2	–
Aids to Navigation Tenders:		
Medium (LM)	8	–
Small (LS)	13	–

DELETIONS

2006 *Iwaki, Rishiri, Choukai, Nojima, Kuma, Tone, Hayagumo, Miyazuki*, LS 161, LS 164-167, LS 189, LS 212
2007 CL 206-209, 231, 237, 240, 255, LM 201, LS 168, 188-193, 213-215, OR 01-05, OS 01-03.
2008 *Esan, Rebun, Amagi, Hateruma, Bihoro, Kuzuryu, Ooyodo, Akigumo, Yaegumo, Natsugumo, Kaiou*, CL 211, CL 213, CL 215, CL 226, CL 228, CL 232, CL 234, CL 252, CL 258, CL 260, OX 03, OX 05-07, OX 09-19, CL 262-263
2009 *Matsushima, Tosa, Kikuchi, Natori, Akagi, Tsukuba, Natsuzuki, Tatsugumo*

LARGE PATROL VESSELS

1 SHIKISHIMA CLASS (PLH/PSOH)

Name	*No*	*Builders*	*Laid down*	*Launched*	*Commissioned*
SHIKISHIMA	PLH 31	Ishikawajima Harima, Tokyo	24 Aug 1990	27 June 1991	8 Apr 1992

Displacement, tons: 6,500 standard; 9,350 full load
Dimensions, feet (metres): 492.1 × 54.1 × 29.5 *(150 × 16.5 × 9.0)*
Main machinery: 2 SEMT-Pielstick 16 PC2.5 V 400; 20,800 hp(m) *(15.29 MW)*; 2 shafts; bow thruster
Speed, knots: 25
Range, n miles: 20,000 at 18 kt
Complement: 110 plus 30 aircrew
Guns: 4 Oerlikon 35 mm/90 Type GDM-C (2 twin); 1,100 rds/min to 6 km *(3.2 n miles)*; weight of shell 1.55 kg.
2 JM-61 MB 20 mm Gatling.
Radars: Air/surface search: Melco Ops 14; D-band.
Surface search: JMA 1576; I-band.
Navigation: JMA 1596; I-band.
Helo control: JMA 3000; I-band.
Tacan: ORN-6 (URN 25).
Helicopters: 2 Aerospatiale A 332 L1.

Comment: Authorised in the FY89 programme in place of the third Mizuho class. Used to escort the plutonium transport ship. SATCOM fitted.

SHIKISHIMA *5/2008*, Kazumasa Watanabe* / 1353134

2 MIZUHO CLASS (PLH/PSOH)

Name	*No*	*Builders*	*Launched*	*Commissioned*
MIZUHO	PLH 21	Mitsubishi, Nagasaki	5 June 1985	19 Mar 1986
YASHIMA	PLH 22	Nippon Koukan, Tsurumi	20 Jan 1988	1 Dec 1988

Displacement, tons: 4,900 standard; 5,204 full load
Dimensions, feet (metres): 426.5 × 50.9 × 17.7 *(130 × 15.5 × 5.4)*
Main machinery: 2 SEMT-Pielstick 14 PC2.5 V 400 diesels; 18,200 hp(m) *(13.38 MW)* sustained; 2 shafts; cp props; bow thruster
Speed, knots: 23
Range, n miles: 8,500 at 22 kt
Complement: 100 plus 30 aircrew
Guns: 1 Oerlikon 35 mm/90; 550 rds/min to 6 km *(3.2 n miles)* anti-surface; 5 km *(2.7 n miles)* anti-aircraft; weight of shell 1.55 kg.
1 JM-61 MB 20 mm Gatling.
Radars: Surface search: JMA 8303; I-band.
Navigation/helo control: 2 JMA 3000; I-band.
Helicopters: 2 Fuji-Bell 212.

Comment: PLH 21 ordered under the FY83 programme laid down 27 August 1984. PLH 22 in 1986 estimates, laid down 3 October 1987. Two sets of fixed electric fin stabilisers that have a lift of 26 tons ×2 and reduce rolling by 90 per cent at 18 kt. Employed in search and rescue outside the 200 mile economic zone.

MIZUHO *5/2005, Hachiro Nakai* / 1153305

1 IZU CLASS (PL/PSOH)

Name	*No*	*Builders*	*Launched*	*Commissioned*
IZU	PL 31	Kawasaki, Sakaide	7 Feb 1997	25 Sep 1997

Displacement, tons: 3,500 normal
Dimensions, feet (metres): 360.9 × 49.2 × 17.4 *(110 × 15 × 5.3)*
Main machinery: 2 diesels; 12,000 hp(m) *(8.82 MW)*; 2 shafts; bow thruster
Speed, knots: 20
Complement: 40 plus 70 spare
Guns: 1 Oerlikon 35 mm. 1 JM-61 MB 20 mm Gatling.
Radars: Surface search: I-band.
Navigation: I-band.
Helicopters: Platform for 1 Fuji-Bell 212.

Comment: Authorised in the FY95 programme. Laid down 22 March 1996. Replaced the former *Izu* in 1998, taking the same name and pennant number. Carries two launches.

IZU *6/2004, Japan Coast Guard* / 1153306

10 SOYA CLASS (PLH/PSOH)

Name	*No*	*Builders*	*Commissioned*
SOYA	PLH 01	Nippon Kokan, Tsurumi	22 Nov 1978
TSUGARU	PLH 02	IHI, Tokyo	17 Apr 1979
OOSUMI	PLH 03	Mitsui Tamano	18 Oct 1979
HAYATO (ex-*Uraga*)	PLH 04	Hitachi, Maizuru	5 Mar 1980
ZAO	PLH 05	Mitsubishi, Nagasaki	19 Mar 1982
CHIKUZEN	PLH 06	Kawasaki, Kobe	28 Sep 1983
SETTSU	PLH 07	Sumitomo, Oppama	27 Sep 1984
ECHIGO	PLH 08	Mitsui Tamano	28 Feb 1990
RYUKYU	PLH 09	Mitsubishi, Nagasaki	31 Mar 2000
DAISEN	PLH 10	Nippon Kokan, Tsurumi	1 Oct 2001

Displacement, tons: 3,200 normal; 4,037 full load
Dimensions, feet (metres): 323.4 × 51.2 × 17.1 *(98.6 × 15.6 × 5.2)* (PLH 01)
345.8 × 47.9 × 15.7 *(105.4 × 14.6 × 4.8)*
Main machinery: 2 SEMT-Pielstick 12 PC2.5 V 400 diesels; 15,604 hp(m) *(11.47 MW)* sustained; 2 shafts; cp props; bow thruster
Speed, knots: 21 (PLH 01); 22 (others)
Range, n miles: 5,700 at 18 kt
Complement: 71 (PLH 01-04); 69 (others)
Guns: 1 Bofors 40 mm or Oerlikon 35 mm. 1 Oerlikon 20 mm (PLH 01, 02, 05-07) or 1—20 mm JM61MB Gatling gun.
Radars: Surface search: JMA 1576; I-band.
Navigation: JMA 1596; I-band.
Helo control: JMA 1596; I-band.
Helicopters: 1 Fuji-Bell 212.

Comment: PLH 01 has an icebreaking capability while the other ships are only ice strengthened. Fitted with both fin stabilisers and anti-rolling tanks of 70 tons capacity. The fixed electric hydraulic fins have a lift of 26 tons ×2 at 18 kt which reduces rolling by 90 per cent at that speed. At slow speed the reduction is 50 per cent, using the tanks. PLH 04 name changed on 27 March 1997. PLH 10 laid down 8 March 1999.

SOYA *5/2008*, Kazumasa Watanabe* / 1353135

1 MIURA CLASS (PL/PSOH)

Name	*No*	*Builders*	*Launched*	*Commissioned*
MIURA	PL 22	Sumitomo, Uraga	11 Mar 1998	28 Oct 1998

Displacement, tons: 3,000 normal
Dimensions, feet (metres): 377.3 × 45.9 × 15.7 *(115 × 14 × 4.8)*
Main machinery: 2 diesels; 8,000 hp(m) *(5.88 MW)*; 2 shafts; cp props
Speed, knots: 18
Complement: 40 plus 10 spare
Guns: 1 Oerlikon 35 mm. 1—20 mm JM 61-B Gatling.

Comment: Authorised in FY96 programme. Laid down in October 1996. Has replaced ship of the same name.

MIURA *3/2007, Hachiro Nakai* / 1305135

1 KOJIMA CLASS (PL/PSOH)

Name	*No*	*Builders*	*Commissioned*
KOJIMA	PL 21	Hitachi, Maizuru	11 Mar 1993

Displacement, tons: 2,650 normal; 2,950 full load
Dimensions, feet (metres): 377.3 × 45.9 × 23.9 *(115 × 14 × 7.3)*
Main machinery: 2 diesels; 8,000 hp(m) *(5.9 MW)*; 2 shafts; cp props
Speed, knots: 18
Range, n miles: 7,000 at 15 kt
Complement: 118
Guns: 1 Oerlikon 35 mm/90. 1—20 mm JM-61B Gatling. 1—12.7 mm MG.
Radars: Navigation: Two JMA 1596; I-band.
Helicopters: Platform for 1 medium.

Comment: Authorised in the FY90 programme and ordered in March 1991. Laid down 7 November 1991, launched 10 September 1992. Training ship which has replaced the old ship of the same name and pennant number. SATCOM fitted.

KOJIMA *5/2008*, Kazumasa Watanabe* / 1353136

1 NOJIMA CLASS (PL/PSOH)

Name	*No*	*Builders*	*Commissioned*
OKI (ex-*Nojima*)	PL 01	Ishikawajima Harima, Tokyo	21 Sep 1989

Displacement, tons: 1,500 normal
Dimensions, feet (metres): 285.4 × 34.4 × 11.5 *(87 × 10.5 × 3.5)*
Main machinery: 2 Fuji 8S40B diesels; 8,120 hp(m) *(5.97 MW)*; 2 shafts
Speed, knots: 19
Complement: 34
Guns: 1 Oerlikon 35 mm/90. 1—20 mm JM-61B Gatling.
Radars: Navigation: 2 JMA 1596; I-band.
Helicopters: Platform for 1 Bell 212.

Comment: Laid down 16 August 1988 and launched 30 May 1989. Equipped as surveillance and rescue command ship. SATCOM fitted. Name changed on 30 November 1997.

OKI *7/2005, Hachiro Nakai* / 1153307

3 HIDA CLASS (PL/PSO)

Name	*No*	*Builders*	*Launched*	*Commissioned*
HIDA	PL 51	Mitsubishi, Shimonoseki	9 Aug 2005	18 Apr 2006
AKAISHI	PL 52	Mitsubishi, Shimonoseki	21 Oct 2005	18 Apr 2006
KISO	PL 53	IHI Marine United, Yokohama	17 Aug 2007	11 Mar 2008

Displacement, tons: 1,800 standard
Dimensions, feet (metres): 362.6 × 42.7 × 19.7 *(95.0 × 13.0 × 6.0)*
Main machinery: 4 diesels; waterjet propulsion
Speed, knots: 30
Guns: 1—40 mm Bofors Mk 3. 1—20 mm JM61 Gatling.
Helicopters: Platform for one medium.

Programmes: Two ships authorised in FY03 budget and a third in FY04 budget.

AKAISHI *5/2007, Hachiro Nakai* / 1305063

7 OJIKA CLASS (PL/PSOH)

Name	*No*	*Builders*	*Launched*	*Commissioned*
ERIMO (ex-*Ojika*)	PL 02	Mitsui, Tamano	23 Apr 1991	31 Oct 1991
KUDAKA	PL 03	Hakodate Dock	10 May 1994	25 Oct 1994
YAHIKO (ex-*Satsuma*)	PL 04	Sumitomo, Uraga	3 June 1995	26 Oct 1995
DEJIMA (ex-*Hakata*)	PL 05	Ishikawajima, Tokyo	6 July 1998	26 Nov 1998
KURIKOMA (ex-*Dejima*)	PL 06	Mitsui, Tamano	28 June 1999	29 Oct 1999
SATAUMA	PL 07	Kawasaki, Kobe	3 June 1999	29 Oct 1999
TOSA (ex-*Motobu*)	PL 08	Sasebo Heavy Industries	5 June 2000	31 Oct 2000

Displacement, tons: 1,883 normal
Dimensions, feet (metres): 299.9 × 36.1 × 11.5 *(91.4 × 11 × 3.5)*
Main machinery: 2 Fuji 8S40B diesels; 7,000 hp(m) *(5.15 MW)*; 2 shafts; cp props; 2 bow thrusters
Speed, knots: 18
Range, n miles: 4,400 at 15 kt
Complement: 38
Guns: 1 Oerlikon 35 mm/90. 1—20 mm JM-61B Gatling.
Radars: Navigation: JMA 1596; I-band.
Helicopters: Platform for 1 Bell 212 or Super Puma.

Comment: Equipped as SAR command ships. SATCOM fitted. 30 ton bollard pull. Stern dock for RIB. PL 04 name changed 28 September 1999. PL 02 name changed 1 October 2000. PL 06 name changed 4 January 2005. PL 05 changed name on 26 December 2008 and PL 08 on 29 January 2009.

KURIKOMA *5/2008*, Hachiro Nakai* / 1353138

16 SHIRETOKO CLASS (PL/PSO)

Name	*No*	*Builders*	*Commissioned*
SHIRETOKO	PL 101	Mitsui Tamano	8 Nov 1978
WAKASA	PL 103	Kawasaki, Kobe	29 Nov 1978
KII (ex-*Shimanto*, ex-*Yahiko*)	PL 104	Mitsubishi, Shimonoseki	16 Nov 1978
SHIKINE	PL 109	Usuki	20 Sep 1979
SURUGA	PL 110	Kurushima	28 Sep 1979
NOTO	PL 115	Miho	30 Nov 1979
REBUN (ex-*Iwami*, ex-*Kudaka*, ex-*Daisetsu*, ex-*Kurikoma*)	PL 117	Hakodate	31 Jan 1980
SHIMOKITA	PL 118	Ishikawajima, Kakoki	12 Mar 1980
SUZUKA	PL 119	Kanazashi	7 Mar 1980
KUNISAKI	PL 120	Kouyo	29 Feb 1980
IWAMI (ex-*Goto*)	PL 122	Onomichi	29 Feb 1980
KOSHIKI	PL 123	Kasado	25 Jan 1980
KATORI	PL 125	Tohoku	21 Oct 1980
KUNIGAMI	PL 126	Kanda	17 Oct 1980
ETOMO	PL 127	Naikai	17 Mar 1982
ESAN (ex-*Yonakuni*, ex-*Amagi*, ex-*Mashu*)	PL 128	Shiikoku	12 Mar 1982

Displacement, tons: 974 normal; 1,360 full load
Dimensions, feet (metres): 255.8 × 31.5 × 10.5 *(78 × 9.6 × 3.2)*
Main machinery: 2 Fuji 8S40B; 8,120 hp(m) *(5.97 MW)*; or 2 Niigata 8MA40 diesels; 2 shafts; cp props
Speed, knots: 20
Range, n miles: 4,400 at 17 kt
Complement: 41
Guns: 1 Bofors 40 mm or 1 Oerlikon 35 mm or 1 JM-61 20 mm Gatling (PL 101). 1 Oerlikon 20 mm (PL 101-105, 127 and 128).
Radars: Surface search: JMA 1576; I-band.
Navigation: JMA 1596; I-band.

Comment: Average time from launch to commissioning was about four to five months. Designed for EEZ patrol duties. PL 117 changed her name on 1 April 1988, on 1 August 1994, on 1 October 2000 and on 12 December 2008. PL 122 changed named on 19 December 2008. PL 128 changed 1 April 1997, on 12 February 2005 and on 19 December 2008. PL 104 changed name on 28 September 1999 and again on 1 October 2004. PL 105 paid off on 20 October 2000 after being involved in a collision. PL 116 paid off on 12 February 2005, PL 108 and 112 on 12 March 2006 and PL 106 and 113 on 18 March 2006. PL 121 paid off on 5 February 2008, PL 124 on 27 February 2008, PL 102 and PL 111 on 12 December 2008. PL 107 paid off on 7 February 2009 and PL 114 on 29 January 2009.

KOSHIKI *5/2008*, Hachiro Nakai* / 1353137

3 ASO CLASS (PL/PSO)

Name	*No*	*Builders*	*Laid down*	*Launched*	*Commissioned*
ASO	PL 41	Mitsubishi, Shimonseki	18 Dec 2003	28 Oct 2004	15 Mar 2005
DEWA	PL 42	Universal, Keihin	5 Apr 2004	9 May 2005	12 Apr 2006
HAKUSAN	PL 43	Universal, Keihin	5 Apr 2004	5 Oct 2005	12 Apr 2006

Displacement, tons: 770 standard
Dimensions, feet (metres): 259.2 × 32.8 × 19.7 *(79.0 × 10.0 × 6.0)*
Main machinery: 4 diesels, waterjet propulsion
Speed, knots: 30
Guns: 1—40 mm.

Comment: PL 41 authorised in FY02 budget and PL 42-43 in FY03 budget.

HAKUSAN *5/2007, Hachiro Nakai* / 1305132

5 + 4 HATERUMA CLASS (PL/PSO)

Name	*No*	*Builders*	*Laid down*	*Launched*	*Commissioned*
HATERUMA	PL 61	Mitsui, Tamano	7 Feb 2007	10 Aug 2007	31 Mar 2008
HAKATA	PL 62	Mitsui, Tamano	20 Nov 2007	19 June 2008	2 Feb 2009
YONAKUNI	PL 63	Mitsui, Tamano	20 Nov 2007	19 June 2008	2 Feb 2009
MOTOBU	PL 64	Mitsui, Tamano	1 Mar 2008	30 Sep 2008	Mar 2009
KUNIGAMI	PL 65	Mitsui, Tamano	1 Mar 2008	30 Sep 2008	Mar 2009
–	PL 66	Mitsui, Tamano	–	–	Mar 2010
–	PL 67	Mitsui, Tamano	–	–	Mar 2010
–	PL 68	Mitsui, Tamano	–	–	Mar 2010
–	PL 69	Mitsui, Tamano	–	–	Mar 2010

Displacement, tons: 1,300 standard
Dimensions, feet (metres): 292.0 × 36.1 × 16.4 *(89.0 × 11.0 × 5.0)*
Main machinery: 4 diesels; waterjet propulsion
Speed, knots: 30
Guns: 1—30 mm.
Helicopters: Platform for 1 medium.

Comment: One authorised in FY05 budget, four in FY06 budget and four in FY07 budget.

HATERUMA *3/2008*, Hirotoshi Yamamoto* / 1353139

SHIPBORNE AIRCRAFT

Numbers/Type: 21/8 Bell 212/412.
Operational speed: 103 kt *(191 km/h)*.
Service ceiling: 10,000 ft *(3,048 m)*.
Range: 412 n miles *(763 km)*.
Role/Weapon systems: Liaison, medium-range support and SAR. Sensors: Search radar. Weapons: Unarmed.

BELL 212 *5/2008*, Hachiro Nakai* / 1353141

BELL 412 *5/2005, Mitsuhiro Kadota* / 1153338

Numbers/Type: 4 Aerospatiale AS 332L1 Super Puma.
Operational speed: 125 kt *(231 km/h)*.
Service ceiling: 15,090 ft *(4,600 m)*.
Range: 500 n miles *(926 km)*.
Role/Weapon systems: Medium lift, support and SAR. Sensors: Search radar. Weapons: Unarmed.

AS 332L1 *5/2008*, Hachiro Nakai* / 1353140

Numbers/Type: 4 Sikorsky S-76C.
Operational speed: 135 kt *(250 km/h)*.
Service ceiling: 11,800 ft *(3,505 m)*.
Range: 607 n miles *(1,125 km)*.
Role/Weapon systems: Utility aircraft acquired in 1994–98. One aircraft lost on 10 January 2005. Up to 20 required to replace Bell 212s. Sensors: Search radar. Weapons: Unarmed.

S-76C *5/2007, Hachiro Nakai* / 1305137

Numbers/Type: 4 Bell 206B Jet Ranger.
Operational speed: 115 kt *(213 km/h)*.
Service ceiling: 13,500 ft *(4,115 m)*.
Range: 368 n miles *(682 km)*.
Role/Weapon systems: Support helicopter for reconnaissance and SAR.

Bell 206B *6/2005, Japan Coast Guard* / 1154399

Numbers/Type: 2 Eurocopter EC 225.
Operational speed: 149 kt *(276 km/h)*.
Service ceiling: 13,120 ft *(4,000 m)*.
Range: 500 n miles *(926 km)*.
Role/Weapon systems: SAR and coastal surveillance helicopter ordered on 5 December 2005 and delivered in September 2007. To replace the AS 332 Super Puma in due course.

EC 225 *9/2008*, Hachiro Nakai* / 1353142

Numbers/Type: 3 AgustaWestland AW 139.
Operational speed: 167 kt *(309 km/h)*.
Service ceiling: 19,460 ft *(5,931 m)*.
Range: 307 n miles *(568 km)*.
Role/Weapon systems: Medium-range support and SAR helicopter selected in late 2006 as the replacement for the Bell fleet. A total of 24 aircraft is expected.

AW 139 *5/2008*, Hachiro Nakai* / 1353143

LAND-BASED MARITIME AIRCRAFT (FRONT LINE)

Notes: There is also a Cessna U 206G.

Numbers/Type: 3/10 Beech Super King Air 200T/Super King Air 350.
Operational speed: 200 kt *(370 km/h)*.
Service ceiling: 35,000 ft *(10,670 m)*.
Range: 1,460 n miles *(2,703 km)*.
Role/Weapon systems: Visual reconnaissance in support of EEZ. Two are trainers. Sensors: Weather/search radar. Weapons: Unarmed.

BEECH 350 *5/2005, Mitsuhiro Kadota* / 1153337

Numbers/Type: 5 NAMCYS-11A.
Operational speed: 230 kt *(425 km/h)*.
Service ceiling: 21,600 ft *(6,580 m)*.
Range: 1,960 n miles *(3,629 km)*.
Role/Weapon systems: Maritime surveillance and associated tasks. Sensors: Weather/search radar. Weapons: Unarmed.

YS-11A *5/2005, Mitsuhiro Kadota* / 1153336

Numbers/Type: 2 Gulfstream Aerospace G-V.
Operational speed: 510 kt *(945 km/h)*.
Service ceiling: 41,000 ft *(12,500 m)*.
Range: 6,500 n miles *(12,040 km)*.
Role/Weapon systems: Reconnaissance version of long-range business jet ordered on 14 November 2001 and delivered in 2004. Sensors: Ocean Master radar, FLIR, AMASCOS mission system. Can also drop liferafts.

GULFSTREAM G-V *5/2005, Hachiro Nakai* / 1153311

Numbers/Type: 2 Dassault Falcon 900.
Operational speed: 428 kt *(792 km/h)*.
Service ceiling: 51,000 ft *(15,544 m)*.
Range: 4,170 n miles *(7,722 km)*.
Role/Weapon systems: Maritime surveillance. Sensors: Weather/search radar. Weapons: Unarmed.

FALCON 900 *5/2008*, Hachiro Nakai* / 1353144

Numbers/Type: 4 SAAB 340B.
Operational speed: 250 kt *(463 km/h)*.
Service ceiling: 25,000 ft *(7,620 m)*.
Range: 570 n miles *(1,056 km)*.
Role/Weapon systems: Patrol aircraft procured in 1997. Two SAR variants were delivered in 2007.

SAAB 340B *10/2008*, Hachiro Nakai* / 1353145

Numbers/Type: 3 Bombardier DHC-8-315.
Operational speed: 265 kt *(491 km/h)*.
Service ceiling: 14,775 ft *(4,503 m)*.
Range: 1,630 n miles *(3,020 km)*.
Role/Weapon systems: Maritime surveillance variant of the Dash-8 Q300 regional airliner selected by the Japanese Coast Guard in December 2006 and delivered in 2008. Sensors: not confirmed but likely to include surveillance radar and FLIR.

MEDIUM PATROL VESSELS

14 TESHIO CLASS (PM/PSO)

Name	No	Builders	Commissioned
NATSUI (ex-*Teshio*)	PM 01	Shikoku	30 Sep 1980
KITAKAMI (ex-*Oirose*)	PM 02	Naikai	29 Aug 1980
BIHORO (ex-*Echizen*)	PM 03	Usuki	30 Sep 1980
TOKACHI	PM 04	Narazaki	24 Mar 1981
HITACHI	PM 05	Tohoku	19 Mar 1981
OKITSU	PM 06	Usuki	17 Mar 1981
ISAZU	PM 07	Naikai	18 Feb 1982
CHITOSE	PM 08	Shikoku	15 Mar 1983
KUWANO	PM 09	Naikai	10 Mar 1983
SORACHI	PM 10	Tohoku	30 Aug 1984
YUBARI	PM 11	Usuki	28 Nov 1985
MOTOURA	PM 12	Shikoku	21 Nov 1986
KANO	PM 13	Naikai	13 Nov 1986
SENDAI	PM 14	Shikoku	1 June 1988

Displacement, tons: 630 normal; 670 full load
Dimensions, feet (metres): 222.4 × 25.9 × 6.6 *(67.8 × 7.9 × 2.7)*
Main machinery: 2 Fuji 6S32F or Arakata 6M31E diesels; 3,650 hp(m) *(2.69 MW)*; 2 shafts
Speed, knots: 18
Range, n miles: 3,200 at 16 kt
Complement: 33
Guns: 1 JN-61B 20 mm Gatling.
Radars: Navigation: 2 JMA 159B; I-band.

Comment: First three built under FY79 programme and second three under FY80, seventh under FY81, PM 08-09 under FY82, PM 10 under FY83, PM 11 under FY84, PM 12-13 under FY85, PM 14 under FY87. *Isazu* has an additional structure aft of the mainmast which is used as a classroom. PM 03 changed name on 30 March 2008.

KUWANO *5/2005, Mitsuhiro Kadota* / 1153333

10 BIHORO CLASS (350-M4 TYPE) (PM/PSO)

Name	No	Builders	Commissioned
ISHIKARI	PM 78	Tohoku	13 Mar 1976
ABUKUMA	PM 79	Tohoku	30 Jan 1976
ISUZU	PM 80	Naikai	10 Mar 1976
HOROBETSU	PM 83	Tohoku	27 Jan 1977
SHIRAKAMI	PM 84	Tohoku	24 Mar 1977
MATSUURA (ex-*Sagami*)	PM 85	Naikai	30 Nov 1976
MISASA (ex-*Yoshino*)	PM 87	Usuki	28 Jan 1977
CHIKUGO	PM 90	Naikai	27 Jan 1978
YAMAKUNI	PM 91	Usuki	26 Jan 1978
KATSURA	PM 92	Shikoku	15 Feb 1978

Displacement, tons: 615 normal; 636 full load
Dimensions, feet (metres): 208 × 25.6 × 8.3 *(63.4 × 7.8 × 2.5)*
Main machinery: 2 Niigata 6M31EX diesels; 3,000 hp(m) *(2.21 MW)*; 2 shafts; cp props
Speed, knots: 18
Range, n miles: 3,200 at 16 kt
Complement: 34
Guns: 1 USN 20 mm/80 Mk 10.
Radars: Navigation: JMA 1596 and JMA 1576; I-band.

Comment: PM 85 and 87 changed names 3 April 2000, PM 93 on 1 April 2001 and PM 88 on 12 March 2006. PM 73 paid off on 30 March 2008, PM 82 on 5 February 2008, PM 93 on 30 March 2008, PM 81 on 23 January 2009 and PM 88 on 22 February 2009.

CHIKUGO *6/2007, Hachiro Nakai* / 1305120

2 TAKATORI CLASS (PM/PBO)

Name	No	Builders	Commissioned
TAKATORI	PM 89	Naikai	24 Mar 1978
KUMANO	PM 94	Namura	23 Feb 1979

Displacement, tons: 634 normal
Dimensions, feet (metres): 152.5 × 30.2 × 9.3 *(46.5 × 9.2 × 2.9)*
Main machinery: 2 Niigata 6M31EX diesels; 3,000 hp(m) *(2.21 MW)*; 2 shafts; cp props
Speed, knots: 15. **Range, n miles:** 700 at 14 kt
Complement: 34
Radars: Navigation: JMA 1596 and JMA 1576; I-band.

Comment: SAR vessels equipped for salvage and firefighting.

TAKATORI *5/2008*, Michael Nitz* / 1353146

4 AMAMI CLASS (PM/PBO)

Name	No	Builders	Commissioned
AMAMI	PM 95	Hitachi, Kanagawa	28 Sep 1992
KUROKAMI (ex-*Matsuura*)	PM 96	Hitachi, Kanagawa	24 Nov 1995
KUNASHIRI	PM 97	Mitsubishi, Shimonoseki	26 Aug 1998
MINABE	PM 98	Mitsubishi, Shimonoseki	26 Aug 1998

Displacement, tons: 230 normal
Dimensions, feet (metres): 183.7 × 24.6 × 6.6 *(56 × 7.5 × 2)*
Main machinery: 2 Fuji 8S40B diesels; 8,120 hp(m) *(5.97 MW)*; 2 shafts; cp props
Speed, knots: 25
Guns: 1—20 mm JM-61B Gatling.
Radars: Navigation: I-band.

Comment: First one authorised in the FY91 programme; laid down 22 October 1991. Second authorised in FY93 programme; laid down 7 October 1994. Last pair authorised in FY96 programme and both laid down 30 September 1997. Stern ramp for launching RIB. PM 96 changed name 3 April 2000. PM 95 damaged in incident with possible North Korean intelligence collection ship on 22 December 2001.

AMAMI *6/2007, Hachiro Nakai* / 1305121

1 TESHIO CLASS (ICEBREAKER) (PM/AGOB)

Name	No	Builders	Commissioned
TESHIO	PM 15	Nippon Koukan, Tsurumi	19 Oct 1995

Displacement, tons: 550 normal
Dimensions, feet (metres): 180.4 × 34.8 × 12.8 *(55 × 10.6 × 3.9)*
Main machinery: 2 diesels; 3,600 hp(m) *(2.65 MW)*; 2 shafts; bow thruster
Speed, knots: 14.5
Complement: 35
Guns: 1—20 mm JM-61B Gatling.
Radars: Navigation: 2 sets; I-band.

Comment: Authorised in FY93; laid down 7 October 1994, launched 20 April 1995. Has an icebreaker bow.

TESHIO *6/2002, Japan Coast Guard* / 0570891

9 + 7 TOKARA CLASS (PM/PBO)

Name	*No*	*Builders*	*Commissioned*
TOKARA	PM 21	Universal, Keihin (Tsurumi)	12 Mar 2003
FUKUE	PM 22	Mitsubishi, Shimonoseki	12 Mar 2003
OIRASE	PM 23	Universal, Keihin (Tsurumi)	18 Mar 2004
FUJI	PM 24	Universal, Keihin (Tsurumi)	30 Apr 2008
ECHIZEN	PM 25	Universal, Keihin (Tsurumi)	30 Apr 2008
KIKUCHI	PM 26	Universal, Keihin (Tsurumi)	7 Feb 2009
YOSHINO	PM 27	Universal, Keihin (Tsurumi)	Mar 2009
ISUZU	PM 28	Universal, Keihin (Tsurumi)	Mar 2009
YAMAKUNI	PM 29	Universal, Keihin (Tsurumi)	June 2009
–	PM 30	Universal, Keihin (Tsurumi)	Mar 2010
–	PM 31	Universal, Keihin (Tsurumi)	Mar 2010
–	PM 32	Universal, Keihin (Tsurumi)	Mar 2010
–	PM 33	–	Mar 2011
–	PM 34	–	Mar 2011
–	PM 35	–	July 2011
–	PM 36	–	July 2011

Displacement, tons: 335 standard
Dimensions, feet (metres): 183.8 × 32.4 × 14.4 *(56.0 × 8.5 × 4.4)*
Main machinery: 3 diesels; 3 waterjets
Speed, knots: 30+
Guns: 1 — 20 mm Gatling gun. 1 — 12.7 mm MG

Comment: First two authorised in FY01, third in FY02, six further in FY06, three in FY07 and four in FY08.

FUJI *5/2008*, Hachiro Nakai* / 1353147

SMALL PATROL VESSELS

12 + (2) MIHASHI AND RAIZAN CLASS (PS/PBF)

Name	*No*	*Builders*	*Commissioned*
SHINZAN (ex-*Akiyoshi*, ex-*Mihashi*)	PS 01	Mitsubishi, Shimonoseki	9 Sep 1988
SAROMA	PS 02	Hitachi, Kanagawa	24 Nov 1989
INASA	PS 03	Mitsubishi, Shimonoseki	31 Jan 1990
KIRISHIMA	PS 04	Hitachi, Kanagawa	22 Mar 1991
KAMUI	PS 05	Mitsubishi, Shimonoseki	31 Jan 1994
RAIZAN (ex-*Banna*, ex-*Bizan*)	PS 06	Hitachi, Kanagawa	31 Jan 1994
ASHITAKI	PS 07	Mitsui, Tamano	30 Sep 1994
KARIBA (ex-*Kurama*)	PS 08	Mitsubishi, Shimonoseki	29 Aug 1995
ARASE	PS 09	Mitsubishi, Shimonoseki	29 Jan 1997
SANBE	PS 10	Hitachi, Kanagawa	29 Jan 1997
MIZUKI	PS 11	Mitsui, Tamano	9 June 2000
KOUYA	PS 12	Universal, Keihin	18 Mar 2004
TSUKUBA	PS 13	Mitsubishi, Shimonoseki	2009
AKAGI	PS 14	Mitsubishi, Shimonoseki	2009

Displacement, tons: 195 normal
Dimensions, feet (metres): 141.1 × 24.6 × 5.6 *(43 × 7.5 × 1.7)*
Main machinery: 2 SEMT-Pielstick 16 PA4 V 200 VGA diesels; 7,072 hp(m) *(5.2 MW)*; 2 shafts
1 SEMT-Pielstick 12 PA4 V 200 VGA diesel; 2,720 hp(m) *(2 MW)*; Kamewa 80 water-jet
Speed, knots: 35. **Range, n miles:** 650 at 34 kt
Complement: 34
Guns: 1 — 12.7 mm MG or 1 — 20 mm JM 61 Gatling (being progressively fitted).
Radars: Navigation: Furuno; I-band.

Comment: Capable of 15 kt on the water-jet alone. PS 01 name changed 28 January 1997 and again on 24 January 2001, PS 06 on 17 April 1999 and again on 1 August 2008. PS 08 on 29 March 2004. PS 11 authorised in FY98 programme and PS 12 in FY02 programme. PS 13-14 authorised in FY07 budget.

KAMUI *5/2008*, Hachiro Nakai* / 1353148

2 TAKATSUKI CLASS (PS/PBF)

Name	*No*	*Builders*	*Commissioned*
TAKATSUKI	PS 108	Mitsubishi, Shimonoseki	23 Mar 1992
NOBARU	PS 109	Hitachi, Kanagawa	22 Mar 1993

Displacement, tons: 115 normal; 180 full load
Dimensions, feet (metres): 114.8 × 22 × 4.3 *(35 × 6.7 × 1.3)*
Main machinery: 2 MTU 16V 396TB94 diesels; 5,200 hp(m) *(3.82 MW)*; 2 Kamewa 71 water-jets
Speed, knots: 35
Complement: 13
Guns: 1 — 12.7 mm MG.
Radars: Navigation: I-band.

Comment: First authorised in the FY91 programme, second in FY92. Aluminium hulls.

TAKATSUKI *5/2005, Mitsuhiro Kadota* / 1153329

5 AKAGI CLASS (PS/PB)

Name	*No*	*Builders*	*Commissioned*
KONGOU	PS 103	Ishihara	16 Mar 1987
KATSURAGI	PS 104	Ishihara	24 Mar 1988
BIZAN (ex-*Hiromine*)	PS 105	Yokohama Yacht Co	24 Mar 1988
SHIZUKI	PS 106	Sumidagawa	24 Mar 1988
TAKACHIHO	PS 107	Sumidagawa	24 Mar 1988

Displacement, tons: 115 full load
Dimensions, feet (metres): 114.8 × 20.7 × 4.3 *(35 × 6.3 × 1.3)*
Main machinery: 2 Pielstick 16 PA4 V 185 diesels; 5,344 hp(m) *(3.93 MW)* sustained; 2 shafts
Speed, knots: 28
Range, n miles: 500 at 20 kt
Complement: 22
Guns: 1 Browning 12.7 mm MG.
Radars: Navigation: 1 set; I-band.

Comment: Carry a 25-man inflatable rescue craft. The last four were ordered on 31 August 1987 and commissioned less than seven months later. PS 105 name changed on 1 October 2004. PS 101 and 102 paid off on 6 February 2009.

BIZAN *7/2006, Hachiro Nakai* / 1040608

6 TSURUUGI CLASS (PS/PBOF)

Name	*No*	*Builders*	*Commissioned*
TSURUUGI	PS 201	Hitachi, Kanagawa	15 Feb 2001
HOTAKA	PS 202	Mitsubishi, Shimonoseki	16 Mar 2001
NORIKURA	PS 203	Mitsui, Tamano	16 Mar 2001
KAIMON	PS 204	Mitsui, Tamano	21 Apr 2004
ASAMA	PS 205	Mitsui, Tamano	21 Apr 2004
HOUOU	PS 206	Mitsui, Tamano	27 Jan 2005

Displacement, tons: 220 standard
Dimensions, feet (metres): 164.1 × 26.2 × 13.1 *(50.0 × 8.0 × 4.0)*
Main machinery: 3 diesels; 3 waterjets
Speed, knots: 35
Guns: 1 — 20 mm JM-61 RFS Gatling.

Comment: First three authorised in FY99 budget, fourth and fifth in FY02 budget and sixth in FY03 budget.

ASAMA *5/2007, Hachiro Nakai* / 1305123

COASTAL PATROL CRAFT

4 YODO CLASS (PC/YTR)

Name	*No*	*Builders*	*Launched*	*Commissioned*
YODO	PC 51	Sumidagawa	2 Oct 2001	29 Mar 2002
KOTOBIKI	PC 52	Sumidagawa	23 Oct 2002	27 Mar 2003
NACHI	PC 53	Ishihara	29 Jan 2003	27 Mar 2003
NUNOBIKI	PC 54	Sumidagawa	4 Dec 2002	27 Mar 2003

Displacement, tons: 125 standard
Dimensions, feet (metres): 121.4 × 22.0 × 11.2 *(37.0 × 6.7 × 3.4)*
Main machinery: 2 diesels; 2 waterjets
Speed, knots: 25

Comment: The first authorised in FY00 budget, three more in FY01 budget. Also equipped for firefighting and replaced firefighting vessel of the same name.

YODO *5/2008*, Hachiro Nakai* / 1353149

13 MURAKUMO CLASS (PC/PB)

Name	*No*	*Builders*	*Commissioned*
KITAGUMO	PC 202	Hitachi, Kanagawa	17 Mar 1978
YUKIGUMO	PC 203	Hitachi, Kanagawa	27 Sep 1978
KAWAGIRI	PC 210	Hitachi, Kanagawa	27 July 1979
TOSAGIRI (ex-*Bizan*, ex-*Teruzuki*)	PC 211	Mitsubishi, Shimonoseki	26 June 1979
NIJIGUMO	PC 214	Mitsubishi, Shimonoseki	29 Jan 1981
ISEYUKI (ex-*Hamayuki*)	PC 216	Hitachi, Kanagawa	27 Feb 1981
ISONAMI	PC 217	Mitsubishi, Shimonoseki	19 Mar 1981
NAGOZUKI	PC 218	Hitachi, Kanagawa	29 Jan 1981
YAEZUKI	PC 219	Hitachi, Kanagawa	19 Mar 1981
HAMAYUKI (ex-*Yamayuki*)	PC 220	Hitachi, Kanagawa	16 Feb 1982
KOMAYUKI	PC 221	Mitsubishi, Shimonoseki	10 Feb 1982
UMIGIRI	PC 222	Hitachi, Kanagawa	17 Feb 1983
ASAGIRI	PC 223	Mitsubishi, Shimonoseki	23 Feb 1983

Displacement, tons: 85 normal
Dimensions, feet (metres): 98.4 × 20.7 × 7.2 *(30 × 6.3 × 2.2)*
Main machinery: 2 Ikegai MTU MB 16V 652 SB70 diesels; 4,400 hp(m) *(3.23 MW)* sustained; 2 shafts
Speed, knots: 30
Range, n miles: 350 at 28 kt
Complement: 13
Guns: 1 — 12.7 mm MG.
Radars: Navigation: I-band.

Comment: PC 211 name changed on 17 April 1999 and again on 1 October 2004. P 216 changed name on 22 February 2001 and PC 220 on 18 March 2006. PC 206 paid off on 21 February 2008, PC 207-208 on 15 February 2008, PC 212 and PC 215 on 20 February 2009.

KAWAGIRI *5/2004, Mitsuhiro Kadota* / 1044450

MURAKUMO CLASS *5/2008*, Hachiro Nakai* / 1353150

12 HAYAGUMO CLASS (PC/PBF)

Name	*No*	*Builders*	*Commissioned*
HAYAGUMO (ex-*Hamayuki*, ex-*Kagayuki*)	PC 105	Mitsubishi, Shimonoseki	24 Dec 1999
MURAKUMO	PC 106	Hitachi, Kanagawa	19 Aug 2002
IZUNAMI	PC 107	Mitsui, Tamano	18 Mar 2003
YAMAGUMO	PC 108	Sumidagawa	4 Mar 2008
NATSUGUMO	PC 109	Sumidagawa	4 Mar 2008
AKIGUMO	PC 110	Sumidagawa	10 Mar 2008
TATSUGUMO	PC 111	Sumidagawa	Mar 2009
IKIGUMO	PC 112	Sumidagawa	Mar 2009
NATSUZUKI	PC 113	Sumidagawa	Mar 2009
–	PC 114	Sumidagawa	July 2009
–	PC 115	Sumidagawa	July 2009
–	PC 116	Sumidagawa	July 2009

Displacement, tons: 100 standard
Dimensions, feet (metres): 105.0 × 21.3 × 10.8 *(32.0 × 6.5 × 3.3)*
Main machinery: 2 diesels; 5,200 hp(m) *(3.82 MW)*; 2 waterjets
Speed, knots: 36
Complement: 10
Guns: 1 — 12.7 mm MG.

Comment: Larger version of Asogiri class with waterjet propulsion and higher top speed. PC 105 changed name on 22 February 2001 and again on 18 March 2006. PC 106 authorised in FY01 budget and PC 107 in FY01 extra budget. PC 108-110 authorised in FY06 budget and PC 111-116 in FY07 budget.

HAYAGUMO *7/2008*, Hachiro Nakai* / 1353151

9 AKIZUKI CLASS (PC/SAR)

Name	*No*	*Builders*	*Commissioned*
URAYUKI	PC 72	Mitsubishi, Shimonoseki	31 May 1975
HATAGUMO	PC 75	Mitsubishi, Shimonoseki	21 Feb 1976
MAKIGUMO	PC 76	Mitsubishi, Shimonoseki	19 Mar 1976
HAMAZUKI	PC 77	Mitsubishi, Shimonoseki	29 Nov 1976
ISOZUKI	PC 78	Mitsubishi, Shimonoseki	18 Mar 1977
SHIMANAMI	PC 79	Mitsubishi, Shimonoseki	23 Dec 1977
YUZUKI	PC 80	Mitsubishi, Shimonoseki	22 Mar 1979
TAMANAMI (ex-*Hanayuki*)	PC 81	Mitsubishi, Shimonoseki	27 Mar 1981
AWAGIRI	PC 82	Mitsubishi, Shimonoseki	24 Mar 1983

Displacement, tons: 77 normal
Dimensions, feet (metres): 85.3 × 20.7 × 6.9 *(26 × 6.3 × 2.1)*
Main machinery: 3 Mitsubishi 12DM20MTK diesels; 3,000 hp(m) *(2.21 MW)*; 3 shafts
Speed, knots: 22. **Range, n miles:** 220 at 21.5 kt
Complement: 10
Radars: Navigation: FRA 10 Mk 2; I-band.

Comment: Aluminium hulls. Used mostly for SAR. Being paid off.

AWAGIRI *9/2008*, Hachiro Nakai* / 1353152

1 MATSUNAMI CLASS (PC/PB)

Name	*No*	*Builders*	*Commissioned*
MATSUNAMI	PC 01	Mitsubishi, Shimonoseki	22 Feb 1995

Displacement, tons: 165 normal
Dimensions, feet (metres): 114.8 × 26.2 × 10.8 *(35 × 8 × 3.3)*
Main machinery: 2 diesels; 5,200 hp(m) *(3.82 MW)*; 2 water-jets
Speed, knots: 25
Complement: 30
Radars: Navigation: I-band.

Comment: Has replaced old craft of the same name. Laid down 10 May 1994. Used for patrol and for VIPs.

MATSUNAMI *5/2007, Hachiro Nakai* / 1305126

3 SHIMAGIRI CLASS (PC/PB)

Name	*No*	*Builders*	*Commissioned*
SHIMAGIRI	PC 83	Hitachi, Kanagawa	7 Feb 1985
OKINAMI (ex-*Setogiri*)	PC 84	Hitachi, Kanagawa	22 Mar 1985
HAYAGIRI	PC 85	Mitsubishi, Shimonoseki	22 Feb 1985

Displacement, tons: 51 normal
Dimensions, feet (metres): 75.5 × 17.4 × 6.2 *(23 × 5.3 × 1.9)*
Main machinery: 2 Ikegai 12V 175 RTC diesels; 3,000 hp(m) *(2.21 MW)*; 2 shafts
Speed, knots: 30
Complement: 10
Guns: 1 — 12.7 mm MG (not in all).
Radars: Navigation: FRA 10 Mk 2; I-band.

Comment: Aluminium hulls. PC 84 name changed 1 October 2000.

HAYAGIRI *4/2003*, **Bob Fildes** / 0570885

1 SHIKINAMI CLASS (PC/PB)

Name	*No*	*Builders*	*Commissioned*
ASOYUKI	PC 74	Hitachi, Kanagawa	16 June 1975

Displacement, tons: 46 normal
Dimensions, feet (metres): 69 × 17.4 × 3.3 *(21 × 5.3 × 1)*
Main machinery: 2 MTU MB 12V 493 TY7 diesels; 2,200 hp(m) *(1.62 MW)* sustained; 2 shafts
Speed, knots: 26
Range, n miles: 230 at 23.8 kt
Complement: 10
Radars: Navigation: MD 806; I-band.

Comment: Built completely of light alloy. PC 69 paid off 8 December 1999 and PC 70 on 19 October 2000.

ASOYUKI *9/2008**, **Hirotoshi Yamamoto** / 1353153

2 NATSUGIRI CLASS (PC/PB)

Name	*No*	*Builders*	*Commissioned*
NATSUGIRI	PC 86	Sumidagawa	29 Jan 1990
SUGANAMI	PC 87	Sumidagawa	29 Jan 1990

Displacement, tons: 68 normal
Dimensions, feet (metres): 88.6 × 18.4 × 3.9 *(27 × 5.6 × 1.2)*
Main machinery: 2 diesels; 3,000 hp(m) *(2.21 MW)*; 2 shafts
Speed, knots: 27
Complement: 10
Radars: Navigation: I-band.

Comment: Built under FY88 programme. Steel hulls.

SUGANAMI *5/2008**, **Hachiro Nakai** / 1353154

15 HAYANAMI CLASS (PC/PB/YTR)

Name	*No*	*Builders*	*Commissioned*
HAYANAMI	PC 11	Sumidagawa	25 Mar 1993
SETOGIRI (ex-*Shikinami*)	PC 12	Sumidagawa	24 Mar 1994
MIZUNAMI	PC 13	Ishihara	24 Mar 1994
IYONAMI	PC 14	Sumidagawa	30 June 1994
KURINAMI	PC 15	Sumidagawa	30 Jan 1995
HAMANAMI	PC 16	Sumidagawa	28 Mar 1996
SHINONOME	PC 17	Ishihara	29 Feb 1996
HARUNAMI	PC 18	Ishihara	28 Mar 1996
KIYOZUKI	PC 19	Sumidagawa	23 Feb 1996
AYANAMI	PC 20	Yokohama Yacht	28 Mar 1996
TOKINAMI	PC 21	Yokohama Yacht	28 Mar 1996
HAMAGUMO	PC 22	Sumidagawa	27 Aug 1999
AWANAMI	PC 23	Sumidagawa	27 Aug 1999
URANAMI	PC 24	Sumidagawa	24 Jan 2000
SHIKINAMI	PC 25	Ishihara	24 Oct 2000

Displacement, tons: 110 normal; 190 full load
Dimensions, feet (metres): 114.8 × 20.7 × 7.5 *(35 × 6.3 × 2.3)*
Main machinery: 2 diesels; 4,000 hp(m) *(2.94 MW)*; 2 shafts
Speed, knots: 25
Complement: 13
Guns: 1 — 12.7 mm MG.
Radars: Navigation: I-band.

Comment: One more authorised in FY99 budget. From PC 22 onwards these craft are equipped for firefighting. PC 12 changed name 1 October 2000.

AWANAMI *5/2008**, **Hachiro Nakai** / 1353155

206 + 8 COASTAL PATROL AND RESCUE CRAFT (CL/PB)

CL 01–09	**CL 233**	**CL 244–249**	**CL 256–257**	**CL 264**
CL 11–158	**CL 238–239**	**CL 251**	**CL 259**	**GS 01–02**
CL 214	**CL 241–242**	**CL 253–254**	**CL 261**	**SS 51–77**

Comment: Some have firefighting capability. Built by Shigi, Ishihara, Sumidagawa, Yokohama Yacht Co and Yamaha. For coastal patrol and rescue duties. Built of high tensile steel. Fourteen CL 11 class authorised in FY01 budget, eight in FY05 extra budget, eight in FY06 extra budget and eight in FY07 extra budget. CL 05-09 (ex-LS 231-235) were converted in 2008.

CL 138 *5/2008**, **Hachiro Nakai** / 1353156

SS 59 *5/2008**, **Hachiro Nakai** / 1353157

4 ASOGIRI CLASS (PC/PB)

Name	*No*	*Builders*	*Commissioned*
ASOGIRI	PC 101	Yokohama Yacht	19 Dec 1994
MUROZUKI	PC 102	Ishihara	27 July 1995
WAKAGUMO	PC 103	Ishihara	17 July 1996
KAGAYUKI (ex-*Naozuki*)	PC 104	Sumidagawa	23 Jan 1997

Displacement, tons: 88 normal
Dimensions, feet (metres): 108.3 × 20.7 × 4.6 *(33 × 6.3 × 1.4)*
Main machinery: 2 diesels; 5,200 hp(m) *(3.82 MW)*; 2 shafts
Speed, knots: 30
Complement: 10
Guns: 1 — 12.7 mm MG.

Comment: First pair authorised in FY93 programme, third and fourth in FY95. PC 104 changed names on 1 April 2006.

MUROZUKI *8/2001, Hachiro Nakai* / 0130250

FIREFIGHTING VESSELS AND CRAFT

1 MODIFIED HIRYU CLASS (FL/YTR)

Name	*No*	*Builders*	*Launched*	*Commissioned*
HIRYU	FL 01	NKK, Tsurumi	5 Sep 1997	24 Dec 1997

Displacement, tons: 280 normal
Dimensions, feet (metres): 114.8 × 40 × 8.9 *(35 × 12.2 × 2.7)*
Main machinery: 2 diesels; 4,000 hp(m) *(2.94 MW)*; 2 shafts
Speed, knots: 14
Complement: 15

Comment: Authorised in FY96 programme. Catamaran design. Replaced ship of the same name and pennant number.

HIRYU *5/2007, Hachiro Nakai* / 1305130

4 HIRYU CLASS (FL/YTR)

Name	*No*	*Builders*	*Commissioned*
SHORYU	FL 02	Nippon Kokan, Tsurumi	4 Mar 1970
NANRYU	FL 03	Nippon Kokan, Tsurumi	4 Mar 1971
KAIRYU	FL 04	Nippon Kokan, Tsurumi	18 Mar 1977
SUIRYU	FL 05	Yokohama Yacht Co	24 Mar 1978

Displacement, tons: 215 normal
Dimensions, feet (metres): 90.2 × 34.1 × 7.2 *(27.5 × 10.4 × 2.2)*
Main machinery: 2 Ikegai MTU MB 12V 493 TY7 diesels; 2,200 hp(m) *(1.62 MW)* sustained; 2 shafts
Speed, knots: 13.2
Range, n miles: 300 at 13 kt
Complement: 14

Comment: Catamaran type fire boats designed and built for firefighting services to large tankers.

KAIRYU *9/2008*, Hachiro Nakai* / 1353158

4 NUNOBIKI CLASS (FM/YTR)

Name	*No*	*Builders*	*Commissioned*
SHIRAITO	FM 04	Yokohama Yacht Co	25 Feb 1975
MINOO	FM 08	Sumidagawa	27 Jan 1978
RYUSEI	FM 09	Yokohama Yacht Co	24 Mar 1980
KIYOTAKI	FM 10	Sumidagawa	25 Mar 1981

Displacement, tons: 89 normal
Dimensions, feet (metres): 75.4 × 19.7 × 5.2 *(23 × 6 × 1.6)*
Main machinery: 1 MTU MB 12V 493 TY7 diesel; 1,100 hp(m) *(810 kW)* sustained; 1 shaft
2 Nissan diesels; 500 hp(m) *(515 kW)*; 3 shafts
Speed, knots: 14
Range, n miles: 180 at 13.5 kt
Complement: 12
Radars: Navigation: FRA 10; I-band.

Comment: Equipped for chemical firefighting. FM 01 paid off 31 October 2000 and FM 02 in 2002. FM 05, FM 06 and FM 07 paid off on 11 March 2003.

KIYOTAKI *10/2003, Hachiro Nakai* / 0570706

SURVEY SHIPS

1 SHOYO CLASS (AGS)

Name	*No*	*Builders*	*Launched*	*Commissioned*
SHOYO	HL 01	Mitsui, Tamano	23 June 1997	20 Mar 1998

Displacement, tons: 3,000 normal
Dimensions, feet (metres): 321.5 × 49.9 × 11.8 *(98 × 15.2 × 3.6)*
Main machinery: Diesel-electric; 2 diesels; 8,100 hp(m) *(5.95 MW)*; 2 motors; 5,712 hp(m) *(4.2 MW)*; 2 shafts; cp props
Speed, knots: 17
Complement: 60

Comment: Authorised in FY95 programme. Laid down 4 October 1996. Has replaced former *Shoyo*.

SHOYO *5/2008*, Hachiro Nakai* / 1353159

1 TENYO CLASS (AGS)

Name	*No*	*Builders*	*Commissioned*
TENYO	HL 04	Sumitomo, Oppama	27 Nov 1986

Displacement, tons: 770 normal
Dimensions, feet (metres): 183.7 × 32.2 × 9.5 *(56 × 9.8 × 2.9)*
Main machinery: 2 Akasaka diesels; 1,300 hp(m) *(955 kW)*; 2 shafts
Speed, knots: 13
Range, n miles: 5,400 at 12 kt
Complement: 43 (18 officers)
Radars: Navigation: 2 JMA 1596; I-band

Comment: Laid down 11 April 1986, launched 5 August 1986. Based at Tokyo.

TENYO *6/2006, Okano Takatoshi* / 1040613

1 TAKUYO CLASS (AGS)

Name	*No*	*Builders*	*Commissioned*
TAKUYO	HL 02	Nippon Kokan, Tsurumi	31 Aug 1983

Displacement, tons: 3,000 normal
Dimensions, feet (metres): 314.9 × 46.6 × 15.1 *(96 × 14.2 × 4.6)*
Main machinery: 2 Fuji 6S40B diesels; 6,090 hp(m) *(4.47 MW)*; 2 shafts; cp props
Speed, knots: 17
Range, n miles: 12,000 at 16 kt
Complement: 60 (24 officers)
Radars: Navigation: 2 sets; I-band.

Comment: Laid down on 14 April 1982, launched on 24 March 1983. Based at Tokyo. Side scan sonar fitted. Two survey launches.

TAKUYO *5/2008*, Hachiro Nakai* / 1353160

2 MEIYO CLASS (AGS)

Name	*No*	*Builders*	*Commissioned*
MEIYO	HL 03	Kawasaki, Kobe	24 Oct 1990
KAIYO	HL 05	Mitsubishi, Shimonoseki	7 Oct 1993

Displacement, tons: 550 normal
Dimensions, feet (metres): 196.9 × 34.4 × 10.2 *(60 × 10.5 × 3.1)*
Main machinery: 2 Daihatsu 6 DLM-24 diesels; 3,000 hp(m) *(2.2 MW)*; 2 shafts; bow thruster
Speed, knots: 15
Range, n miles: 5,280 at 11 kt
Complement: 25 + 13 scientists
Radars: Navigation: 2 sets; I-band.

Comment: *Meiyo* laid down 24 July 1989 and launched 29 June 1990; *Kaiyo* laid down 7 July 1992 and launched 26 April 1993. Have anti-roll tanks and resiliently mounted main machinery. Has a 12 kHz bottom contour sonar. A large survey launch is carried on the port side.

KAIYO *6/2007, Hachiro Nakai* / 1305061

7 HAMASHIO CLASS (YGS)

Name	*No*	*Builders*	*Commissioned*
HAMASHIO	HS 21	Yokohama Yacht	25 Mar 1991
ISOSHI	HS 22	Yokohama Yacht	25 Mar 1993
UZUSHIO	HS 23	Yokohama Yacht	22 Dec 1995
OKISHIO	HS 24	Ishihara	4 Mar 1999
ISESHIO	HS 25	Ishihara	10 Mar 1999
HAYASHIO	HS 26	Ishihara	10 Mar 1999
KURUSHIMA	HS 27	Nissui Marine	26 Mar 2003

Displacement, tons: 42 normal
Dimensions, feet (metres): 66.6 × 14.8 × 3.9 *(20.3 × 4.5 × 1.2)*
Main machinery: 3 diesels; 1,015 hp(m) *(746 kW)*; 3 shafts
Speed, knots: 15
Complement: 10
Radars: Navigation: I-band.

Comment: Survey launches. HS 27 authorised in FY01 extra budget.

HAMASHIO *5/2008*, Hachiro Nakai* / 1353161

AIDS TO NAVIGATION SERVICE

1 SUPPLY SHIP (AKSL)

Name	*No*	*Builders*	*Commissioned*
TSUSHIMA	LL 01	Mitsui, Tamano	9 Sep 1977

Displacement, tons: 1,950 normal
Dimensions, feet (metres): 246 × 41 × 13.8 *(75 × 12.5 × 4.2)*
Main machinery: 1 Fuji-Sulzer 8S40C diesel; 4,200 hp(m) *(3.09 MW)*; 1 shaft; cp prop; bow thruster
Speed, knots: 15.5
Range, n miles: 10,000 at 15 kt
Complement: 54

Comment: Lighthouse Supply Ship launched 7 April 1977. Fitted with tank stabilisers. Equipped with modern electronic instruments for carrying out research on electronic aids to navigation.

TSUSHIMA *5/2008*, Hachiro Nakai* / 1353162

2 HOKUTO CLASS (ABU)

Name	*No*	*Builders*	*Commissioned*
HOKUTO	LL 11	Sasebo	29 June 1979
GINGA	LL 13	Kawasaki, Kobe	18 Mar 1980

Displacement, tons: 700 normal
Dimensions, feet (metres): 180.4 × 34.8 × 8.7 *(55 × 10.6 × 2.7)*
Main machinery: 2 Asakasa MH23R diesels; 1,030 hp(m) *(757 kW)*; 2 shafts
Speed, knots: 12
Range, n miles: 3,900 at 12 kt
Complement: 31 (9 officers)

Comment: Used as buoy tenders. LL 12 paid off on 31 March 2008.

HOKUTO *5/2004, Hachiro Nakai* / 1044459

1 SUPPLY SHIP (AKSL)

Name	*No*	*Builders*	*Commissioned*
ZUIUN	LM 101	Usuki	27 July 1983

Displacement, tons: 370 normal
Dimensions, feet (metres): 146.3 × 24.6 × 7.2 *(44.6 × 7.5 × 2.2)*
Main machinery: 2 Mitsubishi-Asakasa MH23R diesels; 1,030 hp(m) *(757 kW)*; 2 shafts
Speed, knots: 13.5
Range, n miles: 1,000 at 13 kt
Complement: 20

Comment: Classed as a medium tender and used to service lighthouses. Can carry 85 tons of stores.

ZUIUN *6/2003, Japan Coast Guard* / 0570701

7 SUPPLY CRAFT (AKSL)

Name	*No*	*Builders*	*Commissioned*
SEIUN	LM 202	Sumidagawa	22 Feb 1989
SEKIUN	LM 203	Ishihara	12 Mar 1991
HOUUN	LM 204	Ishihara	22 Feb 1991
REIUN	LM 205	Ishihara	28 Feb 1992
GENUN	LM 206	Wakamatsu	19 Mar 1996
AYABANE	LM 207	Ishihara	9 Mar 2000
KOUN	LM 208	Sumidagawa	16 Mar 2001

Displacement, tons: 58 full load
Dimensions, feet (metres): 75.5 × 19.7 × 3.3 *(23 × 6 × 1)*
Main machinery: 2 GM 12V-71TA diesels; 840 hp *(627 kW)* sustained; 2 shafts
Speed, knots: 14
Range, n miles: 250 at 14 kt
Complement: 9
Radars: Navigation: FRA 10 Mk III; I-band.

Comment: LM 114 decommissioned on 31 March 2006 and LM 201 on 31 March 2007.

KOUN *5/2008*, Hachiro Nakai* / 1353163

13 SMALL TENDERS (YAG)

LS 169–170 **LS 194–195** **LS 201** **LS 216–223**

Displacement, tons: 27 full load
Dimensions, feet (metres): 65 × 14.7 × 7.5 *(20 × 4.5 × 2.3)*
Main machinery: 2 diesels; 1,820 hp(m) *(1.34 MW)*; 2 shafts
Speed, knots: 25
Complement: 8

Comment: Details given are for *LS 231-233*. Others with varying characteristics. LS 161, LS 164-167 and LS 212 decommissioned on 31 March 2006, LS 189 on 8 December 2006, LS 188-193. LS 213-215 converted to coastal patrol craft on 31 March 2007.

LS 232 *7/2006, Hachiro Nakai* / 1040611

ENVIRONMENT MONITORING CRAFT

3 SERVICE CRAFT (YPC)

Name	*No*	*Builders*	*Commissioned*
KINUGASA	MS 01	Ishihara, Takasago	31 Jan 1992
SAIKAI	MS 02	Ishihara, Takasago	4 Feb 1994
KATSUREN	MS 03	Sumidagawa	18 Dec 1997

Displacement, tons: 39 normal
Dimensions, feet (metres): 59.1 × 29.5 × 4.3 *(18 × 9 × 1.3)*
Main machinery: 2 diesels; 1,000 hp(m) *(735 kW)*; 2 shafts
Speed, knots: 15
Complement: 8

Comment: Details given are for *Kinugasa* which has a catamaran hull. *Saikai* and *Katsuren* are monohulls of 26 tons. Used for monitoring pollution.

KINUGASA *10/2007, Mick Prendergast* / 1305060

SAIKAI *8/2006, Hachiro Nakai* / 1040583

Jordan

Country Overview

The Hashemite Kingdom of Jordan is situated in the Middle East. With an area of 34,492 square miles, it has borders to the north with Syria, to the east with Iraq, to the west with Israel and the West Bank and to the east and south with Saudi Arabia. It has a 14 n mile coastline with the Gulf of Aqaba (in the northern Red Sea) on which Aqaba, the only seaport, is situated. Amman is the capital and largest city. Territorial seas (3 n miles) are claimed but an Exclusive Economic Zone (EEZ) is not claimed.

Headquarters Appointments

Commander Naval Forces:
Major General Dari Al Zaben
Deputy Commander:
Colonel Abdelkareem Fdoul

Organisation

The Royal Jordanian Naval Force comes under the Director of Operations at General Headquarters.

Bases

Aqaba

Personnel

(a) 2009: 500 officers and men
(b) Voluntary service

PATROL FORCES

Notes: In addition to the craft listed, there are also four 17 ft launches and four 14 ft GRP boats used by the Underwater Swimmer unit.

3 AL HUSSEIN (HAWK) CLASS (FAST ATTACK CRAFT—GUN) (PB)

AL HUSSEIN 101 **AL HASSAN** 102 **KING ABDULLAH** 103

Displacement, tons: 124 full load
Dimensions, feet (metres): 100 × 22.5 × 4.9 *(30.5 × 6.9 × 1.5)*
Main machinery: 2 MTU 16V 396TB94 diesels; 5,800 hp(m) *(4.26 MW)* sustained; 2 shafts
Speed, knots: 32
Range, n miles: 750 at 15 kt; 1,500 at 11 kt
Complement: 16 (3 officers)
Guns: 1 Oerlikon GCM-A03 30 mm. 1 Oerlikon GAM-BO1 20 mm. 2—12.5 mm MGs.
Countermeasures: Decoys: 2 Wallop Stockade chaff launchers.
Combat data systems: Racal Cane 100.
Weapons control: Radamec Series 2000 optronic director for 30 mm gun.
Radars: Surface search: Kelvin Hughes 1007; I-band.

Comment: Ordered from Vosper Thornycroft in December 1987. GRP structure. First one on trials in May 1989 and completed December 1989. Second completed in March 1990 and the third in early 1991. All transported to Aqaba in September 1991.

AL HUSSEIN *4/2006, M Declerck* / 1164802

4 FAYSAL CLASS (INSHORE PATROL CRAFT) (PB)

FAYSAL **HUSSEIN** (ex-*Han*) **HASSAN** (ex-*Hasayu*) **MUHAMMED**

Displacement, tons: 8 full load
Dimensions, feet (metres): 38 × 13.1 × 1.6 *(11.6 × 4 × 0.5)*
Main machinery: 2 6M 8V715 diesels; 600 hp *(441 kW)*; 2 shafts
Speed, knots: 22
Range, n miles: 240 at 20 kt
Complement: 8
Guns: 1—12.7 mm MG. 1—7.62 mm MG.
Radars: Surface search: Decca; I-band.

Comment: Acquired from Bertram, Miami in 1974. GRP construction. Still operational and no replacements are planned yet.

MUHAMMED *3/2004, Bob Fildes* / 0587768

2 HASHIM (ROTORK) CLASS (PB)

HASHIM **FAISAL**

Displacement, tons: 9 full load
Dimensions, feet (metres): 41.7 × 10.5 × 3 *(12.7 × 3.2 × 0.9)*
Main machinery: 2 Deutz diesels; 240 hp *(179 kW)*; 2 shafts
Speed, knots: 28
Complement: 5
Military lift: 30 troops
Guns: 1—12.7 mm MG. 1—7.62 mm MG.
Radars: Surface search: Furuno; I-band.

Comment: Delivered in late 1990 for patrolling the Dead Sea. Due to the annual decrease of water depth, the original three craft were moved to Aqaba in 2000. *Hamza* scrapped in 2006.

HASHIM CLASS *3/2004, Bob Fildes* / 0587769

4 ABDULLAH (DAUNTLESS) CLASS (PATROL CRAFT) (PB)

68171–68174

Displacement, tons: 14.5 full load
Dimensions, feet (metres): 43.3 × 13.8 × 4.4 *(13.2 × 4.2 × 1.35)*
Main machinery: 2 Cummins QSM-11 diesels; 1,160 hp *(865 kW)*; 2 shafts
Speed, knots: 35
Complement: 4
Guns: 2—12.5 mm MGs. 2—7.62 mm MGs.
Radars: Navigation: Raymarine RL70C; I-band.

Comment: Sea Ark Dauntless design acquired in 2006.

ABDULLAH 68174 *4/2006, M Declerck* / 1164801

4 FAISAL (COMMANDER) CLASS (PATROL CRAFT) (PB)

FAISAL 1–4

Displacement, tons: 3.4 full load
Dimensions, feet (metres): 26.6 × 10.2 × 1.5 *(8.1 × 3.1 × 0.45)*
Main machinery: 2 Evinrude outboard motors; 500 hp *(375 kW)*
Speed, knots: 46
Complement: 3
Guns: 2—12.5 mm MGs.
Radars: Navigation: Raymarine RL70C; I-band.

Comment: Sea Ark Commander design acquired in 2006.

FAISAL CLASS *6/2006, Jordanian Navy* / 1164800

Kazakhstan

Country Overview

Formerly part of the USSR, the Republic of Kazakhstan declared its independence in 1991. Situated in Central Asia, it has an area of 1,049,155 square miles and is bordered to the north and west with Russia, to the east with China and to the south with Kyrgyzstan, Uzbekistan, and Turkmenistan. It has a 755 n mile coastline with the Caspian Sea on which Aktau, the principal port, is situated. Astana became the capital city in 1995 while Almaty, the former capital, is the largest city. Maritime claims in the Caspian Sea are not clear. The naval Flotilla was inaugurated by President Nazarbayev in June 1998. The plan was to absorb about 30 per cent of the former USSR Caspian Flotilla, but many of these craft are derelict.

Headquarters Appointments

Commander, Navy:
Rear Admiral Ratmir Komratov

Bases

Aktau (Caspian) (HQ)
Aralsk (Aral Sea), Bautino (Caspian)

Personnel

2009: 3,000

PATROL FORCES

Notes: (1) Plans to expand the Navy were announced by the commander of the navy in July 2003. This was re-affirmed by the Kazakh Ministry of Defence in March 2007 and a Directorate for naval forces was established in January 2008.
(2) There is also an ex-trawler *Tyulen II* of 39 m with a single diesel of 578 hp(m) *(425 kW)* capable of 10 kt. Acquired in 1997.
(3) Six Customs cutters acquired from the UAE in 1998. At least one sunk in transit.
(4) Five Guardian class Boston Whalers delivered in November 1995 are reported operational.
(5) Plans to transfer three Yevgenya class from Russia appear to have been abandoned.
(6) Three 14 m Sunkar-M class patrol craft were reported in service in 2006. They are capable of 40 kt.
(7) There is an undisclosed number of SAFE Boats Archangel class 13 m response craft.

2 TURK (AB 25) CLASS (PB)

Name	*No*	*Builders*	*Commissioned*
– (ex-AB 32)	– (ex-P 132)	Haliç Shipyard	6 June 1969
– (ex-AB 26)	– (ex-P 126)	Haliç Shipyard	6 Feb 1970

Displacement, tons: 170 full load
Dimensions, feet (metres): 132 × 21 × 5.5 *(40.2 × 6.4 × 1.7)*
Main machinery: 4 SACM-AGO V16 CSHR diesels; 9,600 hp(m) *(7.06 MW)*; 2 cruise diesels; 300 hp(m) *(220 kW)*; 2 shafts
Speed, knots: 22
Complement: 31
Guns: 1 Bofors 40 mm/70. 1 Oerlikon 20 mm.
Radars: Surface search: Racal Decca; I-band.

Comment: Presented by the Turkish Navy on 3 July 1999 (AB 32) and 25 July 2001 (AB 26) at Geljuk. May have retained active sonar and ASW rocket launcher but this is unlikely.

TURK CLASS (Turkish colours) *10/2000, Selim San* / 0106636

4 KW 15 (TYPE 369) CLASS (PB)

ALMATY (ex-*KW 15*) 2013 (ex-201)
AKTAU (ex-*KW 16*) 2023 (ex-202)
ATYRAU (ex-*KW 17*) 2033 (ex-203)
SCHAMBYL (ex-*KW 20*) 2043 (ex-204)

Displacement, tons: 70 full load
Dimensions, feet (metres): 93.5 × 15.4 × 4.9 *(28.9 × 4.7 × 1.5)*
Main machinery: 2 Mercedes-Benz diesels; 2,000 hp(m) *(1.47 MW)*; 2 shafts
Speed, knots: 25
Complement: 17
Guns: 2—20 mm can be fitted.
Radars: Surface search: Kelvin Hughes 14/9; I-band.

Comment: Transferred from Germany at Wilhelmshaven on 23 August 1996. Built in Germany 1952–53 and paid off in 1994, having been used for river patrols and later as range safety craft. Disarmed on transfer. Reported as being non-operational.

ALMATY (old number) *8/1996, Michael Nitz* / 0080219

1 ZHUK (PROJECT 1400) CLASS (PB)

BERKUT

Displacement, tons: 39 full load
Dimensions, feet (metres): 78.7 × 16.4 × 3.9 *(24 × 5 × 1.2)*
Main machinery: 2 Type M401B diesels; 2,200 hp(m) *(1.6 MW)* sustained; 2 shafts
Speed, knots: 30. **Range, n miles:** 1,100 at 15 kt
Complement: 11
Guns: 2—14.5 mm (twin); 1—12.7 mm MG.
Radars: Surface search: Spin Trough; I-band.

Comment: Built at the Zenith Shipyard, Uralsk, and commissioned 15 July 1998. Reports of a second craft have not been confirmed.

ZHUK (Russian colours) *11/1996, MoD Bonn* / 0019041

1 DAUNTLESS CLASS (PB)

ABAY

Displacement, tons: 11 full load
Dimensions, feet (metres): 42 × 14 × 4.3 *(12.8 × 4.3 × 1.3)*
Main machinery: 2 Detroit 8V-92TA diesels; 1,270 hp *(935 kW)*; 2 shafts
Speed, knots: 35
Range, n miles: 600 at 18 kt
Complement: 5
Guns: 1—12.7 mm MG. 2—7.62 mm MGs.
Radars: Surface search: Furuno; I-band.

Comment: Ordered under US funding in November 1995. Built by SeaArk, Monticello. Used to interdict the smuggling of nuclear materials across the Caspian Sea.

DAUNTLESS CLASS *7/1996, SeaArk Marine* / 0080220

2 SAYGAK (PROJECT 1408) CLASS (PB)

Displacement, tons: 13 full load
Dimensions, feet (metres): 46.3 × 11.5 × 3 *(14.1 × 3.5 × 0.9)*
Main machinery: 1 diesel; 980 hp(m) *(720 kW)*; 1 water-jet
Speed, knots: 35
Range, n miles: 135 at 35 kt
Complement: 6
Guns: 2—7.62 mm MGs.
Radars: Surface search: I-band.

Comment: Russian-built small craft primarily found on the Amur river. Built in 1995 and acquired in early 1996.

SAYGAK (Russian colours) *7/1996, Hartmut Ehlers* / 0052520

Kenya

Country Overview

A former British colony, The Republic of Kenya gained independence in 1963. Located astride the Equator, the country has an area of 224,082 square miles and has borders to the north with Somalia and Ethiopia and to the south with Tanzania. It has a 292 n mile coastline with the Indian Ocean. The country includes almost all of Lake Turkana (Lake Rudolf) and a small portion of Lake Victoria. The capital and largest city is Nairobi and the main seaport is Mombasa. Kisumu isa port on Lake Victoria. Perhaps the first proponent of the Exclusive Economic Zone (EEZ) concept, Kenya claims a 200 n mile EEZ whose limits have been partly defined. Territorial seas (12 n miles) are claimed.

Headquarters Appointments

Commander, Navy:
Major General Samson J Mwathethe

Personnel

(a) 2009: 1,370 plus 120 marines
(b) Voluntary service

Bases

Mombasa (Mtongwe port), Manda, Malindi, Lamu, Kisumu (Lake Victoria)

Coast Defence

There are nine Masura coastal radar stations spread along the coast. Each station has 30 ft fast boats to investigate contacts.

Customs/Police

There are some 14 Customs and Police patrol craft of between 12 and 14 m. Mostly built by Cheverton, Performance Workboats and Fassmer in the 1980s. One Cheverton 18 m craft acquired in early 1997.

PATROL FORCES

Notes: There are also five Spanish built inshore patrol craft of 16 m armed with 12.7 mm MGs and driven by twin 538 hp diesels for a speed of 16 kt. Acquired in 1995, they have pennant numbers P 943-947.

2 NYAYO CLASS (FAST ATTACK CRAFT—MISSILE) (PGGF)

Name	*No*	*Builders*	*Launched*	*Commissioned*
NYAYO	P 3126	Vosper Thornycroft	20 Aug 1986	23 July 1987
UMOJA	P 3127	Vosper Thornycroft	5 Mar 1987	16 Sep 1987

Displacement, tons: 310 light; 430 full load
Dimensions, feet (metres): 186 × 26.9 × 7.9 *(56.7 × 8.2 × 2.4)*
Main machinery: 4 Paxman Valenta 18CM diesels; 15,000 hp *(11.19 MW)* sustained; 4 shafts; 2 motors (slow speed patrol); 100 hp *(74.6 kW)*
Speed, knots: 40
Range, n miles: 2,000 at 18 kt
Complement: 40

Missiles: SSM: 4 OTO Melara/Matra Otomat Mk 2 (2 twin); active radar homing to 160 km *(86.4 n miles)* at 0.9 Mach; warhead 210 kg; sea-skimmer for last 4 km *(2.2 n miles)*.
Guns: 1 OTO Melara 3 in *(76 mm)*/62; 85 rds/min to 16 km *(8.7 n miles)* anti-surface; 12 km *(6.5 n miles)* anti-aircraft; weight of shell 6 kg.
2 Oerlikon/BMARC 30 mm GCM-AO2 (twin); 650 rds/min to 10 km *(5.4 n miles)* anti-surface; 3 km *(1.6 n miles)* anti-aircraft; weight of shell 0.36 kg.
2 Oerlikon/BMARC 20 mm A41A; 800 rds/min to 2 km; weight of shell 0.24 kg.
Countermeasures: Decoys: 2 Wallop Barricade 18-barrelled launchers; Stockade and Palisade rockets.
ESM: Racal Cutlass; radar warning.
ECM: Racal Cygnus; jammer.
Weapons control: CAAIS 450.
Radars: Surface search: Plessey AWS 4; E/F-band; range 101 km *(55 n miles)*.
Navigation: Decca AC 1226; I-band.
Fire control: Marconi ST802; I-band.

Programmes: Ordered in September 1984. Sailed in company from the UK, arriving at Mombasa 30 August 1988. Similar to Omani Province class.
Operational: First live Otomat firing in February 1989. RIB carried right aft. Form Squadron 86. Both ships awaiting refit.

NYAYO *2/2001, Sattler/Steele* / 0114357

1 MAMBA CLASS (LARGE PATROL CRAFT) (PB)

Name	*No*	*Builders*	*Commissioned*
MAMBA	P 3100	Brooke Marine, Lowestoft	7 Feb 1974

Displacement, tons: 125 standard; 160 full load
Dimensions, feet (metres): 123 × 22.5 × 5.2 *(37.5 × 6.9 × 1.6)*
Main machinery: 2 Paxman 16YJCM diesels; 4,000 hp *(2.98 MW)* sustained; 2 shafts
Speed, knots: 25
Range, n miles: 3,300 at 13 kt
Complement: 25 (3 officers)

Missiles: SSM: 4 IAI Gabriel II.
Guns: 2 Oerlikon/BMARC 30 mm GCM-A02 (twin); 650 rds/min to 10 km *(5.4 n miles)* anti-surface; 3 km *(1.6 n miles)* anti-aircraft; weight of shell 0.36 kg.
Radars: Navigation: Decca AC 1226; I-band.
Fire control: Selenia RTN 10X; I/J-band; range 40 km *(22 n miles)*.

Programmes: Laid down 17 February 1972, launched 6 November 1973.
Modernisation: New missiles, gunnery equipment and optronic director fitted in 1982.
Operational: Refitted at Vosper Thornycroft 1989–90. Although still seagoing, operational capability is limited. Gabriel system non-operational.

MAMBA *6/2002* / 0533319

2 SHUPAVU CLASS (LARGE PATROL CRAFT) (PBO)

SHUJAA P 3130 **SHUPAVU** P 3131

Displacement, tons: 480 full load
Dimensions, feet (metres): 190.3 × 26.9 × 9.2 *(58 × 8.2 × 2.8)*
Main machinery: 2 diesels; 2 shafts
Speed, knots: 22
Complement: 24
Guns: 1 OTO Melara 3 in *(76 mm)*/62; 85 rds/min to 16 km *(8.7 n miles)* anti-surface; 12 km *(6.5 n miles)* anti-aircraft; weight of shell 6 kg. 1 Mauser 30 mm.
Weapons control: Breda optronic director.
Radars: Surface search: I-band.

Comment: Built to civilian standards at Astilleros Gondan, Castropol and delivered in 1997 when they were taken over by the Navy. Armament fitted in Kenya.

SHUJAA *2/2001, Michael Nitz* / 0137788

1 ARCHANGEL CLASS (RESPONSE BOAT) (PBF)

Displacement, tons: 12.6 full load
Dimensions, feet (metres): 42.5 × 13.3 × 7.2 *(12.9 × 4.1 × 2.3)*
Main machinery: 2 Caterpillar C9 diesels; 550 hp *(409 kW)*; 2 Hamilton 322 waterjets
Speed, knots: 36
Range, n miles: 300 at 25 kt
Complement: 6
Guns: 2—7.62 mm MGs.
Radars: Navigation: Furuno; I-band.

Comment: High-speed inshore patrol craft of aluminium construction and foam collar built by SAFE Boats International, Port Orchard, Washington. Donated by the US government on 9 October 2006. The new patrol craft is to be used for monitoring the coastline and deterrence of criminal activity including illegal arms and drug running.

ARCHANGEL CLASS *6/2006, SAFE Boats* / 1164947

5 DEFENDER CLASS (RESPONSE BOATS) (PBF)

PB 211–215

Displacement, tons: 2.7 full load
Dimensions, feet (metres): 25.0 × 8.5 × 3.6 *(7.6 × 2.6 × 1.1)*
Main machinery: 2 Honda outboard motors; 450 hp *(335 kW)*
Speed, knots: 46
Range, n miles: 175 at 35 kt
Complement: 4
Guns: 1—12.7 mm MG.
Radars: To be announced.

Comment: High-speed inshore patrol craft of aluminium construction and foam collar built by SAFE Boats International, Port Orchard, Washington. Donated by the US government on 9 October 2006. The new patrol craft are to be used for monitoring the coastline and deterrence of criminal activity including illegal arms and drug running.

PB 212 *6/2006, SAFE Boats* / 1335394

AUXILIARIES

2 GALANA CLASS (LCM)

Name	*No*	*Builders*	*Commissioned*
GALANA	L 38	Astilleros Gondan, Spain	Feb 1994
TANA	L 39	Astilleros Gondan, Spain	Feb 1994

Displacement, tons: 1,400 full load
Dimensions, feet (metres): 208.3 × 43.6 × 7.9 *(63.5 × 13.3 × 2.4)*
Main machinery: 2 MTU/Bazán diesels; 2,700 hp(m) *(1.98 MW)* sustained; 2 shafts; bow thruster
Speed, knots: 12.5
Complement: 30
Radars: Navigation: Racal Decca; I-band.

Comment: Acquired by Galway Ltd for civilian use and taken over by the Navy for logistic support. The 4 m wide ramp is capable of taking 70 ton loads. Guns may be fitted in due course.

TANA *2/1999* / 0052523

2 TENDER (LCM)

Dimensions, feet (metres): 60 × 15.7 × 4.9 *(18.3 × 4.8 × 1.5)*
Main machinery: 2 Caterpillar 3306B-DIT diesels; 880 hp(m) *(647 kW)*; 2 shafts
Speed, knots: 10
Range, n miles: 200 at 10 kt
Complement: 2 plus 136 passengers

Comment: Built by Souters, Cowes and delivered in 1998. Personnel tenders.

SURVEY AND RESEARCH SHIPS

0 + 1 SURVEY SHIP (AGS)

JASIRI

Displacement, tons: 1,052 full load
Dimensions, feet (metres): 278.9 × 42.6 × 9.8 *(85.0 × 13.0 × 3.0)*
Main machinery: 2 MTU 20V 1163 diesels; 7,180 hp *(5.35 MW)*; 2 shafts
Speed, knots: 28
Range, n miles: 5,500 at 12 kt
Complement: 50 (accommodation for 81)
Guns: 1—30 mm. 2—25 mm. 2—12.7 mm MGs.
Weapons control: Optronic director.
Radars: Air/surface search: E/F-band.
Surface search: E/F-band.
Navigation: I-band.

Comment: Contract for the procurement of a new ship signed between the government of Kenya and Euromarine on 15 July 2003. Subsequently, Astilleros Gondan was subcontracted to undertake construction of the vessel. The ship was launched in January 2005. However, following the return of the standby crew to Kenya in July 2005, the future of the ship became uncertain. Although outstanding problems were reportedly resolved on 3 May 2007 the ship had not been delivered by early 2009.

JASIRI *5/2007* / 1335393

Kiribati

Country Overview

The Republic of Kiribati, formerly the Gilbert Islands, is a south Pacific island group which gained independence in 1979 after the other part of the former British colony, the Ellice Islands, became independent as Tuvalu the previous year. Straddling the equator some 1,385 n miles southwest of Hawaii, it comprises from west to east Banaba (Ocean Island) and three detached island groups: the 16 Gilbert Islands, including Tarawa, on which the capital, Bairiki, is located, nine Phoenix Islands and eight of the 11 Line Islands. About 20 of the 34 islands are permanently inhabited. An archipelagic state, territorial seas (12 n miles) are claimed. An Exclusive Economic Zone (EEZ) (200 n miles) is also claimed but limits have not been fully defined by boundary agreements.

Headquarters Appointments

Head of Police Maritime Unit:
Assistant Superintendent John Mote

Bases

Tarawa

PATROL FORCES

1 PACIFIC CLASS (LARGE PATROL CRAFT) (PB)

Name	*No*	*Builders*	*Commissioned*
TEANOAI	301	Transfield Shipbuilding	22 Jan 1994

Displacement, tons: 165 full load
Dimensions, feet (metres): 103.3 × 26.6 × 6.9 *(31.5 × 8.1 × 2.1)*
Main machinery: 2 Caterpillar 3516TA diesels; 4,400 hp *(3.28 MW)* sustained; 2 shafts
Speed, knots: 18
Range, n miles: 2,500 at 12 kt
Complement: 18 (3 officers)
Guns: Can carry 1—12.7 mm MG but is unarmed.
Radars: Navigation: Furuno 1011; I-band.

Comment: The Pacific Patrol Boat programme was started by Australia in 1987. *Teanoai*, the 16th of the class, was handed over to Kiribati in 1994. The Australian government has announced that the programme will be extended so that all 22 boats will be able to operate for 30 years. *Teanoai* completed a half-life refit at Gladstone in 2001 and a life extension refit in 2008.

TEANOAI *9/2008** *Kiribati Marine Police* 1335214

Korea, North
PEOPLE'S DEMOCRATIC REPUBLIC

Country Overview

The Democratic People's Republic of Korea (DPRK) was proclaimed in 1948 and occupies the northern part of the Korean peninsula. Located in north-eastern Asia and with an area of 46,540 square miles, it is bordered to the north by China and Russia and to the south by South Korea. It has a 1,350 n mile coastline with the Sea of Japan and the Yellow Sea. The capital and largest city is Pyóngyang while the principal ports are Nampo and Haeju on the west coast and Chojin and Wónsan on the east coast. Territorial seas (12 n miles) are claimed. A 200 n mile EEZ has also been claimed but the limits have not been defined. A source of tension at sea is the dispute concerning the status of the *Northern Limit Line* and a number of South Korean islands off the south-west coast of DPRK.

The North Korean Navy is principally a coastal force and is the lowest priority military service. Ships are allocated to East or West Fleet Command. The Navy is manpower intensive and most equipment is technologically outdated and incapable of bluewater operations. Nevertheless, considerable emphasis has been placed on high speed infiltration and assault craft and the ability to conduct special forces operations. Fishing vessels are likely to be converted and/or commandeered for military use while ocean-going merchant vessels are likely to have military roles including arms transfers and intelligence gathering.

Headquarters Appointments

Commander of the Navy:
Admiral Kim Yun-Sim
Commander West Sea Fleet:
Rear Admiral Jyung Myung-Do
Commander East Sea Fleet:
Rear Admiral Park Won-Shik

Bases

Naval Headquarters: Pyongyang.
East Fleet Command (HQ T'oejo-dong (Nagwon-up)).
East coast: T'oejo-dong, Ch'aho (submarines), Munch'on-up, Mayang-do (submarines), Najin.
Minor bases: Chakto-dong (Chakto-ri), Hodo-ri, Kosong-up (Changjon-ni), Mugye-ri, Ohang-ni, Puam-dong, Sinch'ang-nodongjagu, Chongjin, Songjin (Kimch'aek), Songjon-pardo, Wonsan, Yoho-ri, Yongam-ni and Yukt'aedong-ni.
West Fleet Command: (HQ Namp'o).
West coast: Namp'o (Chinnamp'o), Pipa-got (submarines) and Sagon-ni (Sa-got).
Minor bases: Cho-do, Haeju, Kwangyang-ni, Sunwi-do, Yongdok and Yongamp'o.

Personnel

(a) 2009: 46,000 officers and other ranks
(b) 5 years' national service

Maritime Security Battalions

In addition to the Navy there is a Coastal and Port Security Police Force which would be subordinate to the Navy in war. It is reported that the strength of this force is 10-15 Chong-Jin patrol craft and 130 patrol boats of various types.

Naval Aviation

There is believed to be a battalion-sized naval support/ASW air unit containing ASW, helicopter and transport elements. The ASW element consists of 10-20 Mi-14PL Haze-A ASW helicopters acquired during the late 1980s and early 1990s. The majority are thought to be subordinated to the East Sea Fleet although there are no details as to how they are organised and deployed. In addition, there are reported to be a small number of Ka-32S Helix although their role is unclear.

Coastal Defence

Considerable emphasis is given to coastal defence. There are believed to be two missile regiments (one in each fleet), a large number of surveillance radar companies and numerous artillery batteries. Missile sites are reported to be located at An-gol, Chakto-dong, Mayang-do, Sinsang-ni, and Unami-ni on the East Sea coast; and Chungsan, Hwajin-ni, Pip'a-got and Tungsan-got on the West Sea coast. Target acquisitionis provided by organic target acquisition radar and ESM. There are numerous other soft sites available for redeployment and truck-mounted mobility is a key feature of the system. Major ports and naval bases are likely to be heavily defended.

Strength of the Fleet

Type	*Active*
Submarines—Patrol	23
Submarines—Coastal	32
Submarines—Midgets	23
Frigates	3
Corvettes	4
Patrol Forces	400+
Amphibious Craft	129
Hovercraft (LCPA)	135
Minesweepers	24
Depot Ships for Midget Submarines	8
Survey Vessels	4

DELETIONS

Notes: The order of battle and fleet dispositions represent the best estimates that can be made based on incomplete information.

SUBMARINES

Notes: (1) There are four obsolete ex-Soviet Whiskey class based at Mayang-do used for training. Probably restricted to periscope depth when dived.
(2) Reports of a sea-based ballistic missile capability have not been substantiated. A surface-ship based system is considered more likely than a submarine-launched missile which would present considerable technical challenges.
(3) It is likely that there are further midget submarines, possibly similar to the Iranian Yono class. Numbers have not been confirmed.

23 (+10 RESERVE) YUGO AND P-4 CLASS (MIDGET SUBMARINES) (SSW)

Displacement, tons: 90 surfaced; 110 dived
Dimensions, feet (metres): 65.6 × 10.2 × 15.1 *(20 × 3.1 × 4.6)*
Main machinery: 2 diesels; 320 hp(m) *(236 kW)*; 1 shaft
Speed, knots: 12 surfaced; 8 dived
Range, n miles: 550 at 10 kt surfaced; 50 at 4 kt dived
Complement: 4 plus 6-7 divers
Torpedoes: 2—406 mm tubes.
Radars: Navigation: I-band.

Comment: Built at Yukdaeso-ri shipyard since early 1960s. More than one design. Details given are for the latest type, at least one of which has been exported to Iran, and have been building since 1987 to a Yugoslavian design. Some have two short external torpedo tubes and some have a snort mast. The conning tower acts as a wet and dry compartment for divers. There is a second and smaller propeller for slow speed manoeuvring while dived. Twelve of the class are designated P-4s and belong to the KWP. This type has two internal torpedo tubes. Operate from eight merchant mother ships (see *Auxiliaries*). Some have been lost in operations against South Korea, the most recent in June 1998. Two exported to Vietnam in June 1997. There are also about 50 two-man submersibles of Italian design 4.9 × 1.4 m. Overall numbers are approximate due to scrapping of older units.

YUGO P-4 *6/1998, Ships of the World* / 0052525

23 ROMEO (PROJECT 033) CLASS (SS)

Displacement, tons: 1,475 surfaced; 1,830 dived
Dimensions, feet (metres): 251.3 × 22 × 17.1 *(76.6 × 6.7 × 5.2)*
Main machinery: Diesel-electric; 2 Type 37-D diesels; 4,000 hp(m) *(2.94 MW)*; 2 motors; 2,700 hp(m) *(1.98 MW)*; 2 creep motors; 2 shafts
Speed, knots: 15 surfaced; 13 dived
Range, n miles: 9,000 at 9 kt surfaced
Complement: 54 (10 officers)

Torpedoes: 8—21 in *(533 mm)* tubes (6 bow, 2 stern). 14 probably SAET-60; passive homing up to 15 km *(8.1 n miles)* at 40 kt; warhead 400 kg. Also some 53-56 may be carried.
Mines: 28 in lieu of torpedoes.
Countermeasures: ESM: China Type 921A Golf Ball (Stop Light); radar warning.
Radars: Surface search: Snoop Plate/Tray; I-band.
Sonars: Pike Jaw; hull-mounted; active.
Feniks; hull-mounted; passive.

Programmes: Two transferred from China 1973, two in 1974 and three in 1975. First three of class built at Sinpo and Mayang-do shipyards in 1976. Programme ran at about one every 14 months until 1995 when it stopped in favour of the Sang-O class. One reported sunk in February 1985.
Operational: Seventeen are stationed on east coast and have occasionally operated in Sea of Japan. The remainder, including four ex-Chinese units, are based on the west coast. By modern standards these are basic attack submarines with virtually no anti-submarine performance or potential and their operational status is doubtful.

ROMEO (China colours) *3/1995, van Ginderen Collection* / 0080222

32 SANG-O CLASS (SSC)

Displacement, tons: 256 surfaced; 277 dived
Dimensions, feet (metres): 116.5 × 12.5 × 12.1 *(35.5 × 3.8 × 3.7)*
Main machinery: 1 Russian diesel generator; 1 North Korean motor; 1 shaft; shrouded prop
Speed, knots: 7.6 surfaced; 7.2 snorting; 8.8 dived
Range, n miles: 2,700 at 7 kt
Complement: 19 (2 officers) plus 6 swimmers

Torpedoes: 2 or 4—21 in *(533 mm)* tubes (in some). Probably Russian Type 53-56.
Mines: 16 can be carried (in some).
Radars: Surface search: Furuno; I-band.
Sonars: Russian hull-mounted; passive/active search and attack.

Programmes: Started building in 1995 at Sinpo accelerating up to about four to six a year by 1996. Reported to have been building at about three a year from 1997. One reported delivered in 2002 and one in 2003 and overall numbers reflect an estimated building rate of almost two per year.
Structure: A variation of a reverse engineered Yugoslav design. There are at least two types, one with torpedo tubes and one capable of carrying up to 16 externally-fitted bottom mines. There is a single periscope and a VLF radio receiver in the fin. Rocket launchers and a 12.7 mm MG can be carried. Diving depth 180 m *(590 ft)*. A longer (39 m) variant submarine may replace older boats.
Operational: Used extensively for infiltration operations. The submarine can bottom, and swimmer disembarkation is reported as being normally exercised from periscope depth. One of the class grounded and was captured by South Korea on 18 September 1996. Some crew members may be replaced by special forces for short operations. 17 stationed on east coast.

SANG-O CLASS *9/1996* 0080223

FRIGATES

Notes: The hull of what is probably an ex-Russian Krivak III frigate is at Nampo naval shipyard. All weapons and sensors have been removed from the ship and the future of the vessel is unclear. If the ship were to be re-armed and activated, it would represent a significant increase in the capabilities of the surface fleet.

1 SOHO CLASS (FFGH)

Name	*No*	*Builders*	*Laid down*	*Launched*	*Commissioned*
–	823	Najin Shipyard	June 1980	Nov 1981	May 1982

Displacement, tons: 1,640 full load
Dimensions, feet (metres): 242.1 × 50.9 × 12.5 *(73.8 × 15.5 × 3.8)*
Main machinery: 2 diesels; 15,000 hp(m) *(11.03 MW)*; 2 shafts
Speed, knots: 23
Complement: 189 (17 officers)

Missiles: SSM: 4 CSS-N-2 ❶; active radar or IR homing to 46 km *(25 n miles)* at 0.9 Mach; warhead 513 kg.
Guns: 1—3.9 in *(100 mm)*/56 ❷; 40° elevation; 15 rds/min to 16 km *(8.6 n miles)*; weight of shell 15.6 kg.
4—37 mm/63 (2 twin) ❸.
4—30 mm/65 (2 twin) ❹. 4—25 mm/60 (2 twin) ❺.
A/S mortars: 2 RBU 1200 5-tubed fixed launchers ❻; range 1,200 m; warhead 34 kg.
Countermeasures: ESM: China RW-23 Jug Pair (Watch Dog); intercept.
Radars: Surface search: Square Tie ❼; I-band.
Fire control: Drum Tilt ❽; H/I-band.
Navigation: I-band.
Sonars: Stag Horn; hull-mounted; active search and attack; high frequency.

Helicopters: Platform for 1 medium.

SOHO *(Scale 1 : 600), Ian Sturton* / 0506237

Programmes: Planned class of six but only one was ordered.
Structure: One of the largest warships built anywhere with a twin hull design and a helicopter deck aft. Has a large central superstructure to carry the heavy gun armament.
Operational: Probably very weather limited like many catamaran designs. Base and operational status not known.

2 NAJIN CLASS (FFG)

531 591

Displacement, tons: 1,500 full load
Dimensions, feet (metres): 334.6 × 32.8 × 8.9 *(102 × 10 × 2.7)*
Main machinery: 3 SEMT-Pielstick Type 16 PA6 280 diesels; 18,000 hp(m) *(13.2 MW)*; 3 shafts
Speed, knots: 24
Range, n miles: 4,000 at 13 kt
Complement: 180 (16 officers)

Missiles: SSM: 2 CSS-N-1 ❶; active radar or IR homing to 46 km *(25 n miles)* at 0.9 Mach; warhead 513 kg HE. Replaced torpedo tubes on both ships.
Guns: 2—3.9 in *(100 mm)*/56 ❷; 40° elevation; 15 rds/min to 16 km *(8.6 n miles)*; weight of shell 15.6 kg.
4—57 mm/80 (2 twin) ❸; 120 rds/min to 6 km *(3.2 n miles)*; weight of shell 2.8 kg.
12 or 4—30 mm/60 (6 or 2 twin) ❹ (see *Structure*).
12—25 mm (6 twin) ❺.
A/S mortars: 2 RBU 1200 5-tubed fixed launchers ❻; range 1,200 m; warhead 34 kg (not in *531*).
Depth charges: 2 projectors; 2 racks. 30 weapons.

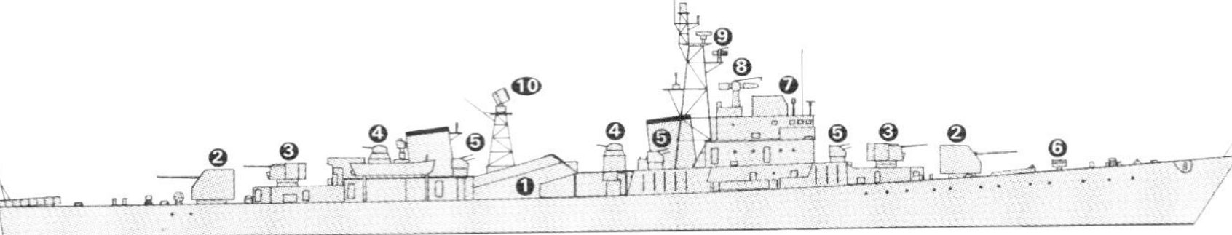

NAJIN

(Scale 1 : 900), Ian Sturton / 0506153

Mines: 30 (estimated).
Countermeasures: Decoys: 6 chaff launchers.
ESM: China RW-23 Jug Pair (Watch Dog); intercept.
Weapons control: Optical director ❼.
Radars: Air search: Square Tie ❽; I-band.
Surface search: Pot Head ❾; I-band.
Navigation: Pot Drum; H/I-band.
Fire control: Drum Tilt ❿; H/I-band.
IFF: High Pole. Square Head.
Sonars: Stag Horn; hull-mounted; active search; high frequency.

Programmes: Built at Najin and Nampo shipyards. First completed 1973, second 1975.
Structure: There is some resemblance to the ex-Soviet Kola class, now deleted. The original torpedo tubes were replaced by CSS-N-1 missile launchers in the mid-1980s and the RBU 1200 mortars have been removed in at least one of the class. Gun armaments differ, one having six twin 30 mm while the other only has one twin 30 mm and six twin 25 mm.
Operational: One based on each coast but seldom seen at sea.

NAJIN 531

5/1993, JMSDF / 0080224

CORVETTES

1 TRAL CLASS (FS)

671

Displacement, tons: 580 full load
Dimensions, feet (metres): 203.7 × 23.9 × 7.8 *(62.1 × 7.3 × 2.4)*
Main machinery: 2 diesels; 3,000 hp(m) *(2.21 MW)*; 2 shafts
Speed, knots: 16
Range, n miles: 2,700 at 16 kt
Complement: 60 (7 officers)

Guns: 1—85 mm/52 tank turret ❶.
2—37 mm/6 (single) ❷.
16—14.5 mm ❸; 4 quad.
Depth charges: 2 rails.
Mines: 30.
Radars: Surface search: Pot Head or Don 2 ❹; I-band.
Navigation: Model 351; I-band.
IFF: Ski Pole.

TRAL 671

(Scale 1 : 600), Ian Sturton / 0506198

Programmes: Two Tral class fleet minesweepers of 1930s vintage were transferred from the USSR in the mid-1950s, were paid off in the early 1980s but one returned to service in the early 1990s.

Structure: Minelaying rails are visible along the whole of upper deck aft of the bridge superstructure.
Operational: Based on the east coast (Najin or Kosong-up).

TRAL 671

5/1993, JMSDF / 0080225

4 SARIWON CLASS (FS)

611–614

Displacement, tons: 650 full load
Dimensions, feet (metres): 203.7 × 23.9 × 7.8 *(62.1 × 7.3 × 2.4)*
Main machinery: 2 diesels; 3,000 hp(m) *(2.21 MW)*; 2 shafts
Speed, knots: 16
Range, n miles: 2,700 at 16 kt
Complement: 60 (7 officers)

Guns: 4—57 mm/80 (2 twin). 4—37 mm/6 (2 twin). 16—14.5 mm (4 quad).
A/S mortars: 2 RBU 1200 5-tubed fixed launchers.
Depth charges: 2 rails.
Mines: 30
Radars: Surface search: Pot Head or Don 2; I-band.
Navigation: Model 351; I-band.
IFF: Ski Pole.
Sonars: Stag Horn; hull-mounted; active; high frequency.

Programmes: Four Sariwon class built in North Korea in the mid-1960s.
Structure: Sariwon design based on the original USSR fleet minelayer Tral or Fugas class which entered service in the 1930s. One Sariwon is reported as having sonar and ASW armament. Minelaying rails are visible along the upper deck aft of the superstructure.
Operational: Based on the east coast at Najin or Kosong-up.

PATROL FORCES

Notes: There is reported to be a new class of hovercraft or Surface Effect Ship (SES) designed for patrol duties. The 38 × 12 m craft have a displacement of 170 tons and are reported to have a speed of 48 kt. They are armed with a 57 mm gun forward and a 39 mm gun aft.

12 OSA CLASS (PROJECT 205) (FAST ATTACK CRAFT—MISSILE) (PTFG)

Displacement, tons: 171 standard; 210 full load
Dimensions, feet (metres): 126.6 × 24.9 × 8.9 *(38.6 × 7.6 × 2.7)*
Main machinery: 3 Type M 503A diesels; 8,025 hp(m) *(5.9 MW)* sustained; 3 shafts
Speed, knots: 35
Range, n miles: 800 at 30 kt
Complement: 30
Missiles: SSM: 4 SS-N-2A Styx; active radar or IR homing to 46 km *(25 n miles)* at 0.9 Mach; warhead 513 kg.
Guns: 4—30 mm/65 (2 twin) AK 230; 500 rds/min to 5 km *(2.7 n miles)*; weight of shell 0.54 kg.
Countermeasures: ESM: China BM/HZ 8610; intercept (Huangfen class).
Radars: Surface search: Square Tie; I-band.
Fire control: Drum Tilt; H/I-band (Osa I).
IFF: High Pole B. Square Head.

Programmes: There are eight Osa I class remaining of 12 transferred from the USSR in 1968 and four more in 1972–83. Four are based on each coast. In addition, there are four Huangfen class acquired from China in 1980 and based on the west coast.

OSA I 0506031

10 SOJU CLASS (FAST ATTACK CRAFT—MISSILE) (PTG)

Displacement, tons: 265 full load
Dimensions, feet (metres): 139.4 × 24.6 × 5.6 *(42.5 × 7.5 × 1.7)*
Main machinery: 3 Type M 503A diesels; 8,025 hp(m) *(5.9 MW)* sustained; 3 shafts
Speed, knots: 34
Range, n miles: 600 at 30 kt
Complement: 32 (4 officers)
Missiles: SSM: 4 SS-N-2 Styx; active radar or IR homing to 46 km *(25 n miles)* at 0.9 Mach; warhead 513 kg.
Guns: 4—30 mm/65 (2 twin) AK 230; 500 rds/min to 5 km *(2.7 n miles)*; weight of shell 0.54 kg.
Countermeasures: ESM: China BM/HZ 8610; intercept.
Radars: Surface search: Square Tie; I-band.
Fire Control: Drum Tilt; H/I-band.

Comment: North Korean built and enlarged version of Osa class. First completed in 1981; built at about one per year at Nampo, Najin and Yongampo shipyards, but the programme terminated in 1996. Six based on the east coast and four on the west.

12 KOMAR CLASS (PROJECT 183) (FAST ATTACK CRAFT—MISSILE) (PTFG)

Displacement, tons: 75 standard; 85 full load
Dimensions, feet (metres): 84 × 24 × 5.9 *(25.6 × 7.3 × 1.8)*
Main machinery: 4 Type M 50 diesels; 4,400 hp(m) *(3.3 MW)* sustained; 4 shafts
Speed, knots: 40
Range, n miles: 400 at 30 kt
Complement: 19
Missiles: SSM: 2 SS-N-2A Styx or CSS-N-1; active radar or IR homing to 46 km *(25 n miles)* at 0.9 Mach; warhead 513 kg.
Guns: 2—25 mm/80 (twin); 270 rds/min to 3 km *(1.6 n miles)*; weight of shell 0.34 kg. 2—14.5 mm (twin) MGs.
Radars: Surface search: Square Tie; I-band.
IFF: Square Head.

Programmes: There are six Komar class remaining of 10 transferred from the USSR. Wooden hulls have been replaced by steel. There are also six Sohung class, North Korean copies of the Komar class, first built in 1980–81 and no longer in production. The 'Komars' and four 'Sohung' are based on the east coast.

KOMAR 0506032

6 HAINAN CLASS (LARGE PATROL CRAFT) (PC)

201–204 292–293

Displacement, tons: 375 standard; 392 full load
Dimensions, feet (metres): 192.8 × 23.6 × 6.6 *(58.8 × 7.2 × 2)*
Main machinery: 4 Kolomna/PCR Type 9-D-8 diesels; 4,000 hp(m) *(2.94 MW)*; 4 shafts
Speed, knots: 30.5
Range, n miles: 1,300 at 15 kt
Complement: 69
Guns: 4—57 mm/70 (2 twin); 120 rds/min to 8 km *(4.4 n miles)*; weight of shell 2.8 kg. 4—25 mm/80 (2 twin); 270 rds/min to 3 km *(1.6 n miles)*; weight of shell 0.34 kg.
A/S mortars: 4 RBU 1200 5-tubed launchers; range 1,200 m; warhead 34 kg.
Depth charges: 2 projectors; 2 racks for 30 DCs.
Mines: Laying capability for 12.
Countermeasures: Decoys: 2 PK 16 chaff launchers.
ESM: China BM/HZ 8610; intercept.
Radars: Surface search: Pot Head (Model 351); I-band.
Sonars: Stag Ear; hull-mounted; active search and attack; high frequency.

Comment: Transferred from China in 1975 (two), 1976 (two), 1978 (two). All based on the west coast.

HAINAN (China colours) *4/1998* / 0080226

19 SO 1 CLASS (LARGE PATROL CRAFT) (PC)

Displacement, tons: 170 light; 215 normal
Dimensions, feet (metres): 137.8 × 19.7 × 5.9 *(42 × 6 × 1.8)*
Main machinery: 3 Kolomna Type 40-D diesels; 6,600 hp(m) *(4.85 MW)* sustained; 3 shafts
Speed, knots: 28
Range, n miles: 1,100 at 13 kt
Complement: 31
Guns: 1—85 mm/52; 18 rds/min to 15 km *(8 n miles)*; weight of shell 9.5 kg. 2—37 mm/63 (twin); 160 rds/min to 9 km *(4.9 n miles)*; weight of shell 0.7 kg. 4 or 6—25 mm/60 (2 or 3 twin); 270 rds/min to 3 km *(1.6 n miles)*; weight of shell 0.34 kg. 4—14.5 mm/93 MGs.
A/S mortars: 4 RBU 1200 5-tubed launchers; range 1,200 m; warhead 34 kg.
Radars: Surface search: Pot Head (Model 351); I-band.
Navigation: Don 2; I-band.
IFF: Ski Pole or Dead Duck.
Sonars: Stag Ear; hull-mounted; active.

Comment: Eight transferred by the USSR in early 1960s, with RBU 1200 ASW rocket launchers and depth charges instead of the 85 mm and 37 mm guns. Remainder built in North Korea to modified design. Twelve are fitted out for ASW with sonar and depth charges; the other seven are used as gunboats. The majority are based on the east coast.

SO 1 (USSR colours) *1988* / 0506030

13 SHANGHAI II CLASS (FAST ATTACK CRAFT—GUN) (PBT)

381–388 391–395

Displacement, tons: 113 standard; 131 full load
Dimensions, feet (metres): 126.3 × 17.7 × 5.6 *(38.5 × 5.4 × 1.7)*
Main machinery: 2 Type L12-180 diesels; 2,400 hp(m) *(1.76 MW)* (forward) 2 Type 12-D-6 diesels; 1,820 hp(m) *(1.34 MW)* (aft); 4 shafts
Speed, knots: 30
Range, n miles: 700 at 16.5 kt
Complement: 34
Guns: 4—37 mm/63 (2 twin); 160 rds/min to 9 km *(4.9 n miles)*; weight of shell 0.7 kg. 4—25 mm/60 (2 twin); 270 rds/min to 3 km *(1.6 n miles)*; weight of shell 0.34 kg. 2—3 in *(76 mm)* recoilless rifles.
Depth charges: 8.
Mines: Rails can be fitted for 10 mines.
Countermeasures: ESM: China BM/HZ 8610; intercept.
Radars: Surface search: Pot Head (Model 351) or Skin Head; I-band.

Comment: Acquired from China since 1967. Based in the west fleet.

SHANGHAI II *1994* / 0080227

12 TAECHONG CLASS (LARGE PATROL CRAFT) (PC)

Displacement, tons: 385 standard; 410 full load (I); 425 full load (II)
Dimensions, feet (metres): 196.3 (I); 199.5 (II) × 23.6 × 6.6 *(59.8; 60.8 × 7.2 × 2)*
Main machinery: 4 Kolomna Type 40-D diesels; 8,800 hp(m) *(6.4 MW)* sustained; 4 shafts
Speed, knots: 25
Range, n miles: 2,000 at 12 kt
Complement: 80
Guns: 1–3.9 in *(100 mm)*/56 (Taechong II); 15 rds/min to 16 km *(8.6 n miles)*; weight of shell 15.6 kg or 1–85 mm/52.
2–57 mm/70 (twin); 120 rds/min to 8 km *(4.4 n miles)*; weight of shell 2.8 kg.
4–30 mm/65 (2 twin) (Taechong II). 2–25 mm/60 (twin) (Taechong I).
16 or 4–14.5 mm MGs (4 quad (Taechong II); 2 twin (Taechong I)).
A/S mortars: 2 RBU 1200 5-tubed fixed launchers; range 1,200 m; warhead 34 kg.
Depth charges: 2 racks.
Radars: Surface search: Pot Head (Model 351); I-band.
Fire control: Drum Tilt; H/I-band.
IFF: High Pole A. Square Head.
Sonars: Stag Ear; hull-mounted; active attack; high frequency.

Comment: North Korean class of mid-1970s design, slightly larger than the Hainan class. There are seven Taechong I class and five Taechong II. The latter, built at Najin shipyard up to 1995, are slightly longer and more heavily armed. Based in both fleets.

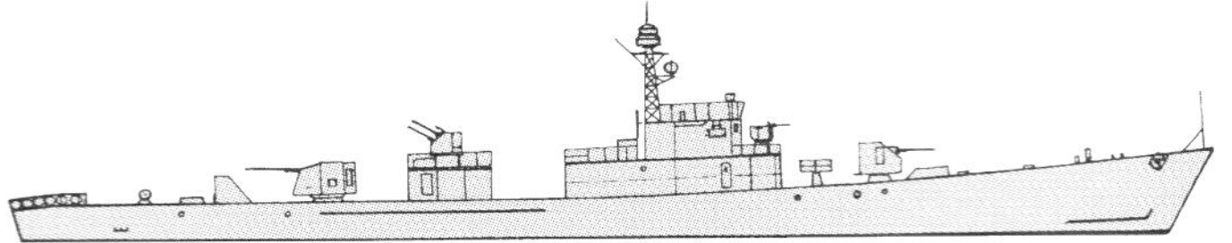

TAECHONG ***(not to scale)*** / 0506033

TAECHONG II (with *Najin*) ***1998*** / 0506034

6 CHONG-JU CLASS (LARGE PATROL CRAFT) (PC)

Displacement, tons: 205 full load
Dimensions, feet (metres): 138.8 × 23.6 × 6.9 *(42.3 × 7.2 × 2.1)*
Main machinery: 4 diesels; 4,406 hp(m) *(3.24 MW)*; 4 shafts
Speed, knots: 20
Range, n miles: 1,350 at 12 kt
Complement: 48 (7 officers)
Missiles: SSM: 4 CSS-N-1; active radar or IR homing to 46 km *(25 n miles)* at 0.9 Mach; warhead 513 kg. In three of the class.
Guns: 1–85 mm/52; 18 rds/min to 15 km *(8 n miles)*; weight of shell 9.5 kg.
4–37 mm/63 (2 twin). 4–25 mm/60 (2 twin).
4–14.5 mm/93 (2 twin) MGs.
A/S mortars: 2 RBU 1200; 5-tubed launchers; range 1,200 m; warhead 34 kg.
Radars: Surface search: Pot Head (Model 351); I-band.
Sonars: Stag Ear; hull-mounted; active attack; high frequency.

Comment: Built between 1975 and 1989. At least one has been converted to fire torpedoes and three others have CSS-N-1 missiles and resemble the Soju class. Based in both fleets.

59 CHAHO CLASS (FAST ATTACK CRAFT—GUN) (PTF)

Displacement, tons: 82 full load
Dimensions, feet (metres): 85.3 × 19 × 6.6 *(26 × 5.8 × 2)*
Main machinery: 4 Type M 50 diesels; 4,400 hp(m) *(3.2 MW)* sustained; 4 shafts
Speed, knots: 37
Range, n miles: 1,300 at 18 kt
Complement: 16 (2 officers)
Guns: 1 BM 21 multiple rocket launcher. 2 USSR 23 mm/87 (twin). 2–14.5 mm (twin) MGs.
Radars: Surface search: Pot Head (Model 351); I-band.

Comment: Building in North Korea since 1974. Based on P 6 hull. Three transferred to Iran in April 1987. Still building and new hulls are replacing the old ones. 35 based in the east and 24 in the west.

CHAHO (Iranian colours) ***4/1998*** / 0506035

54 CHONG-JIN CLASS (FAST ATTACK CRAFT—GUN) (PTF/PTK)

Displacement, tons: 80 full load
Dimensions, feet (metres): 85.3 × 19 × 5.9 *(26 × 5.8 × 1.8)*
Main machinery: 4 Type M 50 diesels; 4,400 hp(m) *(3.2 MW)* sustained; 4 shafts
Speed, knots: 36. **Range, n miles:** 450 at 30 kt
Complement: 17 (3 officers)
Guns: 1–85 mm/52; 18 rds/min to 15 km *(8 n miles)*; weight of shell 9.5 kg.
4 or 8–14.5 mm (2 or 4 twin) MGs.
Radars: Surface search: Skin Head; I-band.
IFF: High Pole B; Square Head.

Comment: Particulars similar to Chaho class of which this is an improved version. Building began about 1975. About one third reported to be a hydrofoil development. Up to 15 are operated by the Coastal Security Force. Based in both fleets.

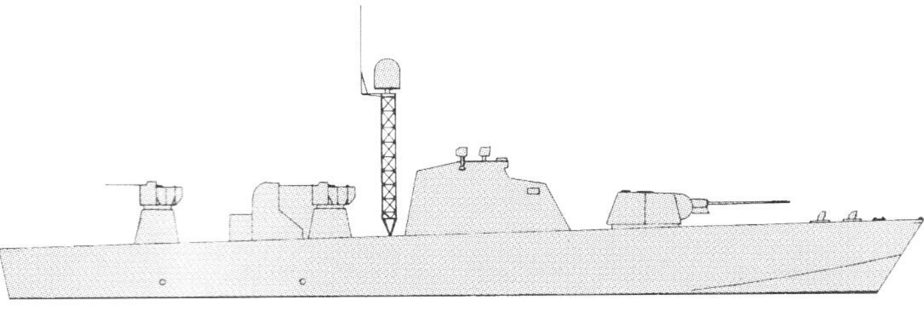

CHONG-JIN ***(not to scale), Ian Sturton*** / 0506036

33 SINPO CLASS (FAST ATTACK CRAFT—TORPEDO) (PTF/PTK)

Displacement, tons: 64 standard; 73 full load
Dimensions, feet (metres): 85.3 × 20 × 4.9 *(26 × 6.1 × 1.5)*
Main machinery: 4 Type M 50 diesels; 4,400 hp(m) *(3.2 MW)* sustained; 4 shafts
Speed, knots: 45. **Range, n miles:** 450 at 30 kt; 600 at 15 kt
Complement: 15
Guns: 4–25 mm/80 (2 twin) (original). 2–37 mm (others). 6–14.5 mm MGs (Sinpo class).
Torpedoes: 2–21 in *(533 mm)* tubes (in some). Sinpo class has no tubes.
Depth charges: 8 in some.
Radars: Surface search: Skin Head; I-band (some have Furuno).
IFF: Dead Duck. High Pole.

Comment: Thirteen craft remain of the 27 P 6 class transferred from the USSR and 15 Shantou class transferred from China. Some of the P 6s have hydrofoils and one sank in June 1999. The Sinpo (or Sinnam) class are locally built versions of these craft of which 20 now remain. Based in both fleets.

P 6 0506037

SINPO 471 0506038

142 KU SONG, SIN HUNG AND MOD SIN HUNG CLASSES (FAST ATTACK CRAFT—TORPEDO) (PTF/PTK)

Displacement, tons: 42 full load
Dimensions, feet (metres): 75.4 × 16.1 × 5.5 *(23 × 4.9 × 1.7)*
Main machinery: 2 Type M 50 diesels; 2,200 hp(m) *(1.6 MW)* sustained; 2 shafts
Speed, knots: 40; 50 (Mod Sin Hung)
Range, n miles: 500 at 20 kt
Complement: 20 (3 officers)
Guns: 4–14.5 mm (2 twin) MGs.
Torpedoes: 2–18 in *(457 mm)* or 2–21 in *(533 mm)* tubes (not fitted in all).
Radars: Surface search: Skin Head; I-band.
IFF: Dead Duck.

Comment: Ku Song and Sin Hung built in North Korea between mid-1950s and 1970s. Frequently operated on South Korean border. A modified version of Sin Hung with hydrofoils built from 1981–85. Fifty craft, previously thought to have been scrapped, are in various states of repair. Based in both fleets.

SIN HUNG (no torpedo tubes) ***1991*** / 0506039

MODIFIED FISHING VESSELS
(COASTAL PATROL CRAFT) (PB/AGI)

Comment: Approximately 15 fishing vessels have been converted for naval use. Some act as patrol craft, others as AGIs. The vessel sunk by the Japanese Coast Guard on 22 December 2001 carried a 14.5 mm machine-gun, two anti-air missile launchers and numerous small arms. The stern was fitted with outward opening doors.

MFV 801 *7/1991, G Jacobs* / 0506040

Fishing Vessel (being salvaged) *9/2002, P A News* / 0522267

HIGH-SPEED AND SEMI-SUBMERSIBLE INFILTRATION CRAFT
(HSIC/PBF)

Displacement, tons: 5 full load
Dimensions, feet (metres): 30.5 × 8.2 × 3.1 *(9.3 × 2.5 × 1)*
Main machinery: 1 diesel; 260 hp(m) *(191 kW)*; 1 shaft
Speed, knots: 35
Complement: 2
Guns: 1 — 7.62 mm MG.
Radars: Navigation: Furuno 701; I-band.

Comment: Up to a hundred built for Agent infiltration and covert operations. These craft have a very low radar cross-section and 'squat' at high speeds. High rate of attrition. A newer version was reported in 1998. This is 12.8 m in length and has a top speed of about 45 kt. It is reported to travel on the surface until submerging to a depth of 3 m using a snort mast. It has a dived speed of 4 kt.

HSIC *1991, J Bermudez* / 0506041

15 TB 11PA AND 10 TB 40A CLASSES
(INSHORE PATROL CRAFT) (PBF)

Displacement, tons: 8 full load
Dimensions, feet (metres): 36.7 × 8.6 × 3.3 *(11.2 × 2.7 × 1)*
Main machinery: 2 diesels; 520 hp(m) *(382 kW)*; 2 shafts
Speed, knots: 35. **Range, n miles:** 200 at 15 kt
Complement: 4
Guns: 1 — 7.62 mm MG.
Radars: Surface search: Furuno; I-band.

Comment: High-speed patrol boats. Reinforced fibreglass hull. Design closely resembles a number of UK/Western European commercial craft. Larger hull design, known as 'TB 40A' also built. Both classes being operated by the Coastal Security Force.

AMPHIBIOUS FORCES

18 HUNGNAM CLASS (LCM)

Displacement, tons: 70 full load
Dimensions, feet (metres): 55.8 × 14.4 × 3.9 *(17 × 4.4 × 1.2)*
Main machinery: 2 diesels; 2 shafts
Speed, knots: 6
Guns: 2 — 14.5 mm (twin).

Comment: 1980s vintage. Based in both fleets.

10 HANTAE CLASS (LSM)

Displacement, tons: 350 full load
Dimensions, feet (metres): 157.5 × 21.3 × 6.6 *(48 × 6.5 × 2)*
Main machinery: 2 diesels; 4,352 hp(m) *(3.2 MW)*; 2 shafts
Speed, knots: 18. **Range, n miles:** 2,000 at 12 kt
Complement: 36 (4 officers)
Military lift: 350 troops plus 3 MBTs
Guns: 8 — 25 mm/80 (4 twin).

Comment: Built in the early 1980s. Most are based on the east coast.

96 NAMPO CLASS (LLP)

Displacement, tons: 75 full load
Dimensions, feet (metres): 85.3 × 19 × 5.6 *(26 × 5.8 × 1.7)*
Main machinery: 4 Type M 50 diesels; 4,400 hp(m) *(3.2 MW)* sustained; 4 shafts
Speed, knots: 36. **Range, n miles:** 450 at 30 kt
Complement: 19
Military lift: 35 troops
Guns: 4 — 14.5 mm (2 twin) MGs.
Radars: Surface search: Skin Head; I-band.

Comment: A class of assault landing craft. Similar to the Chong-Jin class but with a smaller forward gun mounting and with retractable ramp in bows. Building began about 1975. Several have been deleted due to damage. There are 18 of the original class and 73 of a modified version which have a covered-in deck. Most have bow doors welded shut. Four sold to Madagascar in 1979 but now deleted. The Nampo D is the latest version with a multihull design. The first of these entered service in 1997 and four further craft have followed. Based in both fleets.

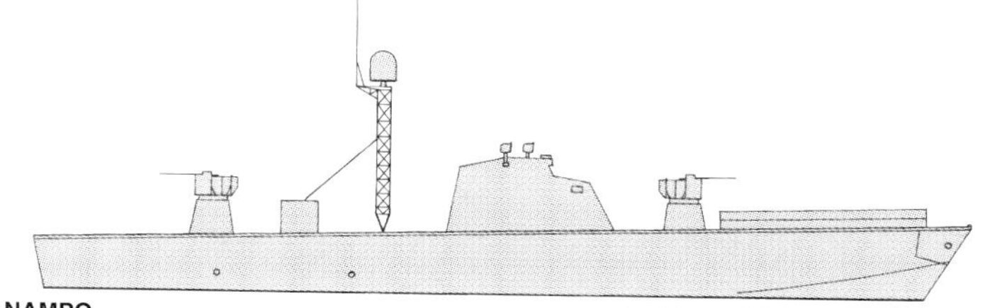

NAMPO *(not to scale), Ian Sturton* / 0506042

7 HANCHON CLASS (LCM)

Displacement, tons: 145 full load
Dimensions, feet (metres): 117.1 × 25.9 × 3.9 *(35.7 × 7.9 × 1.2)*
Main machinery: 2 Type 3-D-12 diesels; 600 hp(m) *(443 kW)* sustained; 2 shafts
Speed, knots: 10. **Range, n miles:** 600 at 6 kt
Complement: 15 (1 officer)
Military lift: 2 tanks or 300 troops
Guns: 2 — 14.5 mm/93 (twin) MG.
Radars: Surface search: Skin Head; I-band.

Comment: Built in the 1980s. Based in both fleets.

136 KONGBANG CLASS (HOVERCRAFT) (LCPA)

Comment: Three types: one Type I, 57 Type II and 78 are Type III. Length 25 m (I), 21 m (II) and 18 m (III). A series of high-speed air cushion landing craft first reported in 1987 and building continued until 1996 and then stopped. Use of air cushion technology is an adoption of commercial technology based on the SRN-6. Kongbang II has twin propellers and can carry up to 50 commandos at 50 kt. Kongbang III has a single propeller and can take about 40 troops at 40 kt. All are radar fitted. Some have Styx SSM missiles. Older craft are being replaced continuously in a high priority programme. Divided between both fleets.

MINE WARFARE FORCES

24 YUKTO CLASS (COASTAL MINESWEEPERS) (MSC)

Displacement, tons: 60 full load (I); 52 full load (II)
Dimensions, feet (metres): 78.7 × 13.1 × 5.6 *(24 × 4 × 1.7)* (Yukto I)
68.9 × 13.1 × 5.6 *(21 × 4 × 1.7)* (Yukto II)
Main machinery: 2 diesels; 2 shafts
Speed, knots: 18
Complement: 22 (4 officers)
Guns: 1 — 37 mm/63 or 2 — 25 mm/80 (twin). 2 — 14.5 mm/93 (twin) MGs.
Mines: 2 rails for 4.
Radars: Surface search: Skin Head; I-band.

Comment: North Korean design built in the 1980s. There are 19 Yukto I and five Yukto II. The Yukto II have no after gun. Wooden construction. Based in both fleets.

SURVEY SHIPS

Notes: The Hydrographic Department has four survey ships but also uses a number of converted fishing vessels.

AUXILIARIES

Notes: (1) Trawlers operate as AGIs on the South Korean border where several have been sunk over the years. In addition many ocean-going commercial vessels are used for carrying weapons and ammunition worldwide in support of international terrorism. (2)There are also eight ocean cargo ships adapted as mother ships for midget submarines. Their names are *Soo Gun-Ho, Dong Geon Ae Gook-Ho, Dong Hae-Ho, Choong Seong-Ho Number One, Choong Seong-Ho Number Two, Choong Seong-Ho Number Three, Hae Gum Gang-Ho* and the *Song Rim-Ho* .

1 KOWAN CLASS (ASR)

Displacement, tons: 2,010 full load
Dimensions, feet (metres): 275.6 × 46.9 × 12.8 *(84 × 14.3 × 3.9)*
Main machinery: 4 diesels; 8,160 hp(m) *(6 MW)*; 2 shafts
Speed, knots: 16
Complement: 150
Guns: 12 — 14.5 mm (6 twin) MGs.
Radars: Navigation: Furuno; I-band.

Comment: Used as a submarine rescue ship. Probable catamaran construction. Based at Ch'aho.

Korea, South

REPUBLIC

Country Overview

The Republic of Korea was proclaimed in 1948 and occupies the southern part of the Korean peninsula. Located in northeastern Asia and with an area of 38,375 square miles, it is bordered to the north by North Korea. It has a 1,300 n miles coastline with the Sea of Japan, the Yellow Sea and the Korea Strait, which separates it from Japan. There are numerous offshore islands in the south and west, the largest of which is Cheju. A source of tension at sea is the dispute concerning the status of the *Northern Limit Line* and a number of South Korean islands off the southwest coast of DPRK. The capital and largest city is Seoul. The principal port is Pusan while others include Inchon, the major port on the Yellow Sea, Mokp'o and Kunsan. Territorial seas (12 n miles) are claimed. A 200 n mile EEZ has also been claimed but the limits have not been defined.

Headquarters Appointments

Chief of Naval Operations:
Admiral Jung Ok-Keun
Commandant Marine Corps:
Vice Admiral Lee Sang-Ro
Vice Chief of Naval Operations:
Vice Admiral Seo Yang-Won

Operational Commands

Commander-in-Chief Fleet:
Vice Admiral Yoon Yeong
Commander First Fleet:
Rear Admiral Chung Ok-Geun
Commander Second Fleet:
Rear Admiral Jang Seung-Hak

Operational Commands — *continued*

Commander Third Fleet:
Rear Admiral Lee Hong-Hee

Personnel

(a) 2009: Regulars: 35,000 (Navy) and 25,000 (Marines) Conscripts: 19,000 (Navy and Marines)
(b) 2¼ years' national service for conscripts
(c) Reserves: 9,000

Bases

Major: Chinhae (Fleet HQ), Donghae (1st Fleet), Pyongtaek (2nd Fleet), Pusan (3rd Fleet)
Minor: Cheju, Mokpo, Mukho, Pohang
Aviation: Pohang (MPA base), Chinhae, Cheju
Marines: Pohang, Kimpo, Pengyongdo

A new base is under construction at Hwasun-ni on the south coast of Cheju Island. Completion is expected in 2014.

Organisation

In 1986 the Navy was reorganised into three Fleets, each commanded by a Rear Admiral, whereas the Marines retained two Divisions and one brigade plus smaller and support units. From October 1973 the RoK Marine Force was placed directly under the RoK Navy command with a Vice Chief of Naval Operations for Marine Affairs replacing the Commandant of Marine Corps. The Marine Corps was re-established as an independent service on 1 November 1987.

1st Fleet (East coast): No 11, 12, 13 DD/FF Sqn; No 101, 102 Coastal Defence Sqn; 181, 191, 111, 121 Coastal Defence Units; 121st Minesweeper Sqn.

2nd Fleet (West coast): No 21, 22, 23 DD/FF Sqn; No 201, 202 Coastal Defence Sqn; 211, 212 Coastal Defence Units; 522nd Minesweeper Sqn.

3rd Fleet (Southern peninsular): 301, 302, 303 DD/FF Sqn; 304, 406th Coastal Defence Units.

Coast Defence

Three batteries of Marines with truck-mounted quadruple Harpoon SSM launchers.

Pennant Numbers

Numbers ending in 4 are not used as they are considered unlucky.

Strength of the Fleet

Type	*Active (Reserve)*	*Building (Proposed)*
Submarines (Patrol)	11	7 (9)
Submarines (Midget)	11	–
Destroyers	10	2
Frigates	9	1 (23)
Corvettes	28	–
Fast Attack Craft—Missile	1	8 (11)
Fast Attack Craft—Patrol	81	–
Minehunters	6	–
Minesweepers	3	–
Minelayers	1	–
LPD	1	(2)
LSTs	6	–
LCU/LCM/LCF	10	–
Logistic Support Ships	3	–
Salvage/Rescue Ships	3	–

PENNANT LIST

Submarines

061	Chang Bogo
062	Yi Chon
063	Choi Muson
065	Park Wi
066	Lee Jongmu
067	Jung Woon
068	Lee Sunsin
069	Na Daeyong
071	Lee Eokgi
072	Sohn Won-il
073	Jeongji
075	Ahn Jung-Geun (bldg)

Destroyers

971	Kwanggaeto Daewang
972	Euljimundok
973	Yangmanchun
975	Chungmugong Yi Sun-Shin
976	Moonmu Daewang
977	Daejoyoung
978	Wang Geon
979	Gang Gam Chan
981	Choi Young
991	Sejong Daewang
992	Yi i

Frigates

951	Ulsan
952	Seoul
953	Chung Nam
955	Masan
956	Kyong Buk
957	Chon Nam
958	Che Ju
959	Pusan
961	Chung Ju

Corvettes

751	Dong Hae
752	Su Won
753	Kang Reung
755	An Yang
756	Po Hang
757	Kun San
758	Kyong Ju
759	Mok Po
761	Kim Chon
762	Chung Ju
763	Jin Ju
765	Yo Su
766	Jin Hae
767	Sun Chon
768	Yee Ree
769	Won Ju
771	An Dong
772	Chon An
773	Song Nam
775	Bu Chon
776	Jae Chon
777	Dae Chon
778	Sok Cho
779	Yong Ju
781	Nam Won
782	Kwan Myong
783	Sin Hung
785	Kong Ju

Patrol Forces

711	Yoon Young-Ha

Mine Warfare Forces

560	Won San
561	Kang Kyeong
562	Kang Jin
563	Ko Ryeong
565	Kim Po
566	Ko Chang
567	Kum Wha
571	Yang Yang
572	Ongjin

Amphibious Forces

6111	Dokdo
677	Su Yong
678	Buk Han
681	Kojoon Bong
682	Biro Bong
683	Hyangro Bong
685	Seongin Bong

Auxiliaries

21	Cheong Hae Jin
27	Pyong Taek
28	Kwang Yang
57	Chun Jee
58	Dae Chung
59	Hwa Chun
AGS 11	Sunjin

SUBMARINES

Notes: (1) The Type 214 programme is to be followed by the KSS-3 programme on which design work began in 2007. Construction of the first hull is expected to start in 2010 or 2011 to meet an in-service date of 2017. Up to nine submarines are planned, probably in batches of three. The new submarines are to be of about 3,000 tons.
(2) Reports of a nuclear submarine programme (SSX) have been officially denied.

11 MIDGET SUBMARINES (SSW)

052 (Dolgorae) **053** (Dolgorae)W

Displacement, tons: 150 surfaced; 175 dived (Dolgorae); 70 surfaced; 83 dived (Cosmos)
Dimensions, feet (metres): 82 × 6.9 *(25 × 2.1)* (Cosmos)
Main machinery: Diesel-electric; 1 diesel generator; 1 motor; 1 shaft
Speed, knots: 9 surfaced; 6 dived
Complement: 6 + 8 swimmers
Torpedoes: 2—406 mm tubes (Dolgorae). 2—533 mm tubes (Cosmos).
Sonars: Atlas Elektronik; hull-mounted; passive search; high frequency.

Comment: Two KSS-1 Dolgorae class which entered service in 1983. Nine Cosmos class type used by Marines. Limited endurance, for use only in coastal waters. Fitted with Pilkington Optronics periscopes (CK 37 in Dolgorae and CK 41 in Cosmos). Numbers of each type confirmed but the Dolgorae class are being replaced by more Cosmos. All are based at Cheju Island.

DOLGORAE
11/1985, G Jacobs
0506044

9 CHANG BOGO (TYPE 209/1200) CLASS (SSK)

Name	*No*	*Builders*	*Laid down*	*Launched*	*Commissioned*
CHANG BOGO	061	HDW, Kiel	1989	18 June 1992	2 June 1993
YI CHON	062	Daewoo, Okpo	1990	14 Oct 1992	30 Apr 1994
CHOI MUSON	063	Daewoo, Okpo	1991	25 Aug 1993	27 Feb 1995
PARK WI	065	Daewoo, Okpo	1992	20 May 1994	3 Feb 1996
LEE JONGMU	066	Daewoo, Okpo	1993	17 Apr 1995	29 Aug 1996
JUNG WOON	067	Daewoo, Okpo	1994	7 May 1996	29 Aug 1997
LEE SUNSIN	068	Daewoo, Okpo	1995	21 May 1998	15 June 1999
NA DAEYONG	069	Daewoo, Okpo	1996	15 June 1999	Nov 2000
LEE EOKGI	071	Daewoo, Okpo	1997	26 May 2000	30 Nov 2001

Displacement, tons: 1,100 surfaced; 1,285 dived
Dimensions, feet (metres): 185.0 × 20.3 × 18 *(56.4 × 6.2 × 5.5)*
Main machinery: Diesel-electric; 4 MTU 12V 396 SE diesels; 3,800 hp(m) *(2.8 MW)* sustained; 4 alternators; 1 motor; 4,600 hp(m) *(3.38 MW)* sustained; 1 shaft
Speed, knots: 11 surfaced/snorting; 22 dived
Range, n miles: 7,500 at 8 kt surfaced
Complement: 33 (6 officers)

Missiles: SSM: McDonnell Douglas UGM-84B Sub Harpoon; active radar homing to 130 km *(70 n miles)* at 0.9 Mach; warhead 227 kg (fitted to at least three boats).

Torpedoes: 8—21 in *(533 mm)* bow tubes. 14 System Technik Nord (STN) SUT Mod 2; wire-guided; active/passive homing to 12 km *(6.6 n miles)* at 35 kt or 28 km *(15.1 n miles)* at 23 kt; warhead 260 kg. Swim-out discharge.
Mines: 28 in lieu of torpedoes.
Countermeasures: ESM: Argo; radar warning.
Weapons control: Atlas Elektronik ISUS 83 TFCS.
Radars: Navigation: I-band.
Sonars: Atlas Elektronik CSU 83; hull-mounted; passive search and attack; medium frequency.

Programmes: First three ordered in late 1987, one built at Kiel by HDW, and two assembled at Okpo by Daewoo from material packages transported from Germany. Second three ordered in October 1989 and a further batch of three in January 1994.
Modernisation: Mid-life upgrade of all nine boats is under consideration. It is envisaged that AIP propulsion and Sub-Harpoon SSM may be fitted in stretched hulls.
Structure: Type 1200 similar to those built for the Turkish Navy with a heavy dependence on Atlas Elektronik sensors and STN torpedoes. Diving depth 250 m *(820 ft)*. A passive towed array may be fitted in due course.
Operational: An indigenous torpedo based on the Honeywell NP 37 may be available in due course. The class is split between the three Fleets. Operations conducted off Hawaii from 1997 to improve operating standards.

PARK WI *10/2008**, ***Guy Toremans*** / 1353189

CHOI MUSON *10/2008**, ***Michael Nitz*** / 1353190

CHOI MUSON *10/2008**, ***Michael Nitz*** / 1353191

2 + 7 KSS-2 (TYPE 214) CLASS (SSK)

Name	*No*	*Builders*	*Laid down*	*Launched*	*Commissioned*
SOHN WON-IL	072	Hyundai, Ulsan	2003	9 June 2006	26 Dec 2007
JEONGJI	073	Hyundai, Ulsan	2004	13 June 2007	2 Dec 2008
AHN JUNG-GEUN	075	Hyundai, Ulsan	2005	4 June 2008	Nov 2009
–	076	Daewoo, Okpo	2010	2013	2014

Displacement, tons: 1,700 surfaced; 1,860 dived
Dimensions, feet (metres): 213.3 × 20.7 × 19.7 *(65 × 6.3 × 6)*
Main machinery: 1 MTU 16V 396 diesel; 4,243 hp *(3.12 MW)*; 1 Siemens Permasyn motor; 3,875 hp(m) *(2.85 MW)*; 1 shaft; 2 HDW PEM fuel cells; 240 kW; sodium sulphide high-energy batteries
Speed, knots: 20 dived; 12 surfaced
Complement: 27 (5 officers)
Torpedoes: 8—21 in *(533 mm)* bow tubes.
Countermeasures: Decoys: ESM.
Weapons control: STN Atlas.
Radars: Surface search: I-band.
Sonars: Bow, flank and towed arrays.

Programmes: Decision taken in November 2000 to order three HDW designed Air Independent Propulsion (AIP) submarines. The boats are being built by Hyundai Heavy Industries with the German Submarine Corporation, led by HDW, providing construction plans, materials and other equipment. First steel cut for the first of class in November 2002. A contract for the supply of six further material packages was signed with HDW in December 2008. Construction of this second batch is expected to start in 2010. The first boat is to be constructed by Daewoo and successor boats are likely to be built at the rate of one per year.
Structure: The Type 214 is a synthesis of the proven Type 209 design with AIP from the Type 212. South Korea is the second customer for the Type 214 after Greece. Details given are mainly for the Type 214 as advertised by HDW but changes may have been made. Diving depth 400 m.

SOHN WON-IL ***10/2008*, Guy Toremans*** / 1353187

SOHN WON-IL ***10/2008*, Michael Nitz*** / 1353188

DESTROYERS

6 KDX-2 CLASS (DDGHM)

Name	*No*	*Builders*	*Laid down*	*Launched*	*Commissioned*
CHUNGMUGONG YI SUN-SHIN	975	Daewoo, Okpo	2001	20 May 2002	2 Dec 2003
MOONMU DAEWANG	976	Hyundai, Ulsan	2002	11 Apr 2003	30 Sep 2004
DAEJOYOUNG	977	Daewoo, Okpo	2002	12 Nov 2003	30 June 2005
WANG GEON	978	Hyundai, Ulsan	2003	4 May 2005	2 Oct 2007
GANG GAM CHAN	979	Daewoo, Okpo	2004	16 Mar 2006	10 Nov 2006
CHOI YOUNG	981	Hyundai, Ulsan	2005	20 Oct 2006	5 Sep 2008

Displacement, tons: 4,500 standard; 5,500 full load
Dimensions, feet (metres): 506.6 × 55.5 × 14.1 *(154.4 × 16.9 × 4.3)*
Main machinery: CODOG; 2 GE LM 2500 gas turbines; 58,200 hp *(43.42 MW)* sustained; 2 MTU 20V 956 TB92 diesels; 8,000 hp(m) *(5.88 MW)*; 2 shafts
Speed, knots: 29. **Range, n miles:** 4,000 at 18 kt
Complement: 200 (18 officers)

Missiles: SSM: 8 Harpoon Block 1C (2 quad) ❶; active radar homing to 124 km (67 n miles) at 0.9 Mach; warhead 227 kg
SAM: Mk 41 Mod 2 VLS ❷ 32 cells for Raytheon SM-2MR (Block IIIA); command/inertial guidance; semi-active radar homing to 167 km *(90 n miles)* at 2.5 Mach.
1 Raytheon RAM M 49 launcher RIM 116 ❸; 21 rounds per launcher; passive IR/anti-radiation homing to 9.6 km *(5.2 n miles)* at 2.5 Mach; warhead 9.1 kg.
A/S: ASROC VLS; inertial guidance 1.6-10 km *(1-5.4 n miles)* at 0.9 Mach; payload Mk 48.
Guns: 1 United Defense 5 in *(127 mm)*/62 Mk 45 Mod 4 ❹; 20 rds/min to 23 km *(12.6 n miles)*; weight of shell 32 kg.
1 Signaal Goalkeeper 30 mm ❺; 7 barrels per mounting; 4,200 rds/min to 1.5 km.
Torpedoes: 6—324 mm Mk 32 (2 triple) tubes ❻; Alliant techsystems Mk 46 Mod 5; anti-submarine; active/passive homing to 11 km *(5.9 n miles)* at 40 kt; warhead 44 kg.
Countermeasures: 4 chaff launchers. ESM/ECM.
Combat data systems: BAeSema/Samsung KD COM-2; Link 11.
Weapons control: Marconi Mk 14 weapons direction system.
Radars: Air search: Raytheon SPS-49(V)5 ❼; C/D-band.
Surface search: Signaal MW08 ❽; G-band.
Navigation: I-band ❾.
Fire control: 2 Signaal STIR 240 ❿; I/J/K-band.
Sonars: DSQS-23; hull-mounted; active search; medium frequency. Daewoo Telecom towed array; passive low frequency.

Helicopters: 1 Westland Super Lynx Mk 99 ⓫.

CHUNGMUGONG YI SUN-SHIN *(Scale 1 : 1,200)*, *Ian Sturton* / 1153009

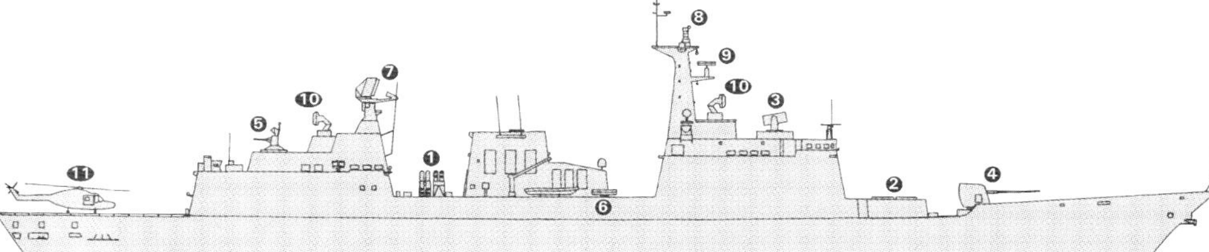

GANG GAM CHAN *10/2008**, *Michael Nitz* / 1353192

Programmes: Approval for first three given in late 1996 but the final decision was not taken until 1998. Contract to design and build the first of class won by Daewoo in November 1999. The first of a second batch of three was launched at Hyundai in May 2005 and the second at Daewoo in March 2006. Work on the sixth ship is underway at Hyundai.
Operational: Successful SM-2 firings conducted on the Pacific Missile Range Facility, off Hawaii, in mid-2004.

CHOI YOUNG *10/2008**, *Guy Toremans* / 1353193

MOONMU DAEWANG *10/2008**, *Guy Toremans* / 1353194

1 + 2 SEJONG DAEWANG (KDX-3) CLASS (DDGHM)

Name	*No*	*Builders*	*Laid down*	*Launched*	*Commissioned*
SEJONG DAEWANG	991	Hyundai, Ulsan	12 Nov 2004	25 May 2007	22 Dec 2008
YI I	992	Daewoo, Okpo	25 July 2007	14 Nov 2008	2010
–	993	Hyundai, Ulsan	2009	2011	2012

Displacement, tons: 7,650 standard; 10,290 full load
Dimensions, feet (metres): 544.3 × 68.9 × 34.4 *(165.9 × 21.0 × 10.5)*
Main machinery: COGAG; 4 GE LM 2500 gas turbines; 105,000 hp *(78.33 MW)* sustained; 2 shafts; cp props
Speed, knots: 30
Range, n miles: 5,000 at 14 kt

Missiles: SLCM: 32 Cheon Ryong land-attack missiles ❶; inertial/GPS guidance to 1,500 km *(810 n miles)* at 0.7 Mach; warhead 500 kg.
SSM: 8 McDonnell Douglas Harpoon Block 1C ❷; active homing to 124 km *(67 n miles)* at 0.9 Mach; warhead 227 kg.
SAM: Mk 41 VLS; 80 cells for Standard SM-2 MR Block IIIB ❸; command/inertial guidance; semi-active radar homing to 167 km *(90 n miles)* at 2.5 Mach; 2 magazines; 48 missile tubes forward, 32 aft.
1 GMLS Mk 49 RAM RIM-116 ❹; 21 rounds; passive IR/anti-radiation homing to 9.6 km *(5.2 n miles)* at 2 Mach; warhead 9.1 kg.
A/S: 16 Loral ASROC VLA ❶; inertial guidance 1.6-16.6 km *(1-9 n miles)*.
Guns: 1 United Defence 5 in *(127 mm)*/54 Mk 45 Mod 4 ❺; 20 rds/min to 23 km *(12.6 n miles)*; anti-surface; weight of shell 32 kg.
1 Signaal/General Electric 30 mm 7-barrelled Goalkeeper ❻; 4,200 rds/min to 1.5 km.
Torpedoes: 6—324 mm (2 triple) Mk 32 tubes ❼; K745 LW (Blue Shark); anti-submarine; active/passive homing to 11 km *(5.9 n miles)* at 40 kt; warhead 44 kg.

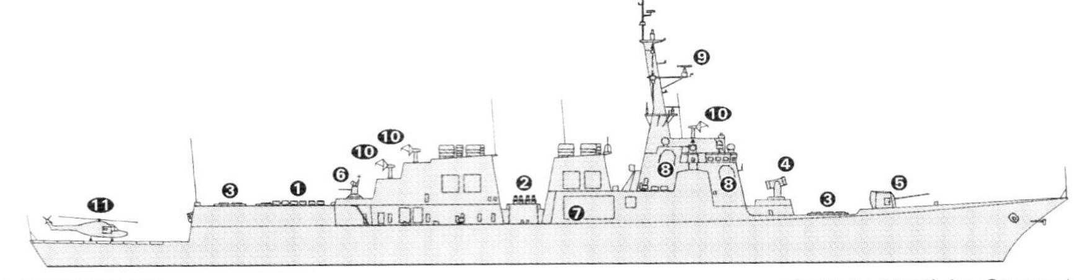

SEJONG DAEWANG *(Scale 1 : 1,500), Ian Sturton* / 1167965

Combat data systems: Aegis Baseline 7.1.
Weapons control: To be announced.
Radars: Air search/fire control: SPY 1D(V) phased arrays ❽; 3D; F-band.
Surface search: Norden/DRS SPS-67(V) ❾; G-band.
Fire control: 3 Raytheon SPG-62 ❿; I/J-band.
Navigation: To be announced.
Sonars: Lockheed Martin SQQ-89(V); underwater combat system with SQS-53C bow mounted; active search and attack.

Helicopters: 2 Westland Super Lynx Mk 99 ⓫.

Programmes: The KDX-3 programme is the third phase of a surface ship modernisation programme that began with the KDX-1 programme in the early 1990s. The current programme consists of three ships but a class of six vessels is expected. Lockheed Martin was selected on 24 July 2002 to supply the combat data system and multifunction radar and South Korea is the fifth nation to operate the AEGIS system. The details of the Cheon Ryong cruise missile are speculative.
Structure: A development of the Arleigh Burke class, the South Korean variant also incorporates the AN/SPY-1D AEGIS system but the design has been enlarged to accommodate additional weapon systems. The ships have three magazines: the forward Mk 41 VLS launcher consists of 48 cells for SM-2 missiles which may also be launched from a 32-cell Mk 41 VLS aft. A separate, indigenous 48-cell VLS launcher aft contains 32 Hyunmoo land attack cruise missiles and 16 ASROC anti-submarine missiles. There are hangar facilities for two helicopters.

SEJONG DAEWANG *10/2008*, Michael Nitz* / 1353198

SEJONG DAEWANG *10/2008*, Michael Nitz* / 1353199

3 KWANGGAETO DAEWANG (KDX-1) CLASS (DDGHM)

Name	*No*	*Builders*	*Laid down*	*Launched*	*Commissioned*
KWANGGAETO DAEWANG	971	Daewoo, Okpo	June 1995	28 Oct 1996	24 July 1998
EULJIMUNDOK	972	Daewoo, Okpo	Jan 1996	16 Oct 1997	20 June 1999
YANGMANCHUN	973	Daewoo, Okpo	Aug 1997	19 Oct 1998	29 June 2000

Displacement, tons: 3,855 full load
Dimensions, feet (metres): 444.2 × 46.6 × 13.8 (135.4 × 14.2 × 4.2)
Main machinery: CODOG; 2 GE LM 2500 gas turbines; 58,200 hp *(43.42 MW)* sustained; 2 MTU 20V 956 TB92 diesels; 8,000 hp(m) *(5.88 MW)*; 2 shafts
Speed, knots: 30
Range, n miles: 4,000 at 18 kt
Complement: 170 (15 officers)

Missiles: SSM: 8 McDonnell Douglas Harpoon Block 1C (2 quad) launchers ❶; active radar homing to 130 km *(70 n miles)* at 0.9 Mach; warhead 227 kg.
SAM: Raytheon Sea Sparrow; Mk 48 Mod 2 VLS launcher ❷ for 16 cells RIM-7P; semi-active radar homing to 16 km *(8.5 n miles)* at 2.5 Mach; warhead 38 kg.
Guns: 1 Otobreda 5 in *(127 mm)*/54 ❸; 45 rds/min to 23 km *(12.4 n miles)*; weight of shell 32 kg.
2 Signaal 30 mm Goalkeeper ❹; 7 barrels per mounting; 4,200 rds/min combined to 2 km.
Torpedoes: 6—324 mm (2 triple) Mk 32 tubes ❺; Alliant Techsystems Mk 46 Mod 5; anti-submarine; active/passive homing to 11 km *(5.9 n miles)* at 40 kt; warhead 44 kg.
Countermeasures: Decoys: 4 CSEE Dagaie Mk 2 chaff launchers ❻. SLQ-25 Nixie towed torpedo decoy.

KWANGGAETO DAEWANG

(Scale 1 : 1,200), Ian Sturton / 0572485

ESM/ECM: Argo AR 700/APECS II ❼; intercept and jammer.
Combat data systems: BAeSEMA/Samsung SSCS Mk 7; Litton NTDS (Link 11). SATCOM ❽.
Radars: Air search: Raytheon SPS-49V5 ❾; C/D-band.
Surface search: Signaal MW08 ❿; G-band.
Fire control: 2 Signaal STIR 180 ⓫; I/J/K-band.
Navigation: Daewoo DTR 92 (SPS 55M) ⓬; I-band,
IFF: UPX-27.
Sonars: Atlas Elektronik DSQS-21BZ; hull-mounted active search; medium frequency.
Daewoo Telecom towed array; passive low frequency.

Helicopters: 1 Westland Super Lynx ⓭.

Programmes: Project KDX-1. A much delayed programme. The first keel was to have been laid down at Daewoo in late 1992 for completion in 1996, but definition studies extended to late 1993, when contracts started to be signed for the weapon systems. First steel cut at Daewoo Okpo in April 1994.
Structure: Emphasis is on air defence but the design took so long to reach fulfilment that it was overtaken by the KDX-2. McTaggart Scott Trigon 5 helo handling system.
Operational: The Goalkeepers are also used against close-in surface threats using FAPDS (Frangible Armour Penetrating Discarding Sabot).

KWANGGAETO DAEWANG

10/2008*, Michael Nitz / 1353196

KWANGGAETO DAEWANG

10/2008*, Guy Toremans / 1353195

YANGMANCHUN

10/2008*, Michael Nitz / 1353197

FRIGATES

9 ULSAN CLASS (FFG)

Name	*No*	*Builders*	*Laid down*	*Launched*	*Commissioned*
ULSAN	951	Hyundai, Ulsan	1979	8 Apr 1980	1 Jan 1981
SEOUL	952	Hyundai, Ulsan	1982	24 Apr 1984	30 June 1985
CHUNG NAM	953	Korean SEC, Pusan	1984	26 Oct 1984	1 June 1986
MASAN	955	Korea Tacoma	1983	26 Oct 1984	20 July 1985
KYONG BUK	956	Daewoo, Okpo	1984	15 Jan 1986	30 May 1986
CHON NAM	957	Hyundai, Ulsan	1986	19 Apr 1988	17 June 1989
CHE JU	958	Daewoo, Okpo	1986	3 May 1988	1 Jan 1990
PUSAN	959	Hyundai, Ulsan	1990	20 Feb 1992	1 Jan 1993
CHUNG JU	961	Daewoo, Okpo	1990	20 Mar 1992	1 June 1993

Displacement, tons: 1,496 light; 2,180 full load (2,300 for FF 957-961)
Dimensions, feet (metres): 334.6 × 37.7 × 11.5 *(102 × 11.5 × 3.5)*
Main machinery: CODOG; 2 GE LM 2500 gas turbines; 53,640 hp *(40 MW)* sustained; 2 MTU 16V 538 TB82 diesels; 5,940 hp(m) *(4.37 MW)* sustained; 2 shafts; cp props
Speed, knots: 34; 18 on diesels
Range, n miles: 4,000 at 15 kt
Complement: 150 (16 officers)

Missiles: SSM: 8 McDonnell Douglas Harpoon (4 twin) launchers ❶; active radar homing to 130 km *(70 n miles)* at 0.9 Mach; warhead 227 kg.
Guns: 2—3 in *(76 mm)*/62 OTO Melara compact ❷; 85 rds/min to 16 km *(8.6 n miles)* anti-surface; 12 km *(6.5 n miles)* anti-aircraft; weight of shell 6 kg.
8 Emerson Electric 30 mm (4 twin) (FF 951-955) ❸; 6 Breda 40 mm/70 (3 twin) (FF 956-961) ❹.
Torpedoes: 6—324 mm Mk 32 (2 triple) tubes ❺. Honeywell Mk 46 Mod 1; anti-submarine; active/passive homing to 11 km *(5.9 n miles)* at 40 kt; warhead 44 kg.
Depth charges: 12.
Countermeasures: Decoys: 4 Loral Hycor SRBOC 6-barrelled Mk 36 launchers ❻; range 4 km *(2.2 n miles)*.
SLQ-25 Nixie; towed torpedo decoy.
ESM: ULQ-11K; intercept.
Combat data systems: Samsung/Ferranti WSA 423 action data automation (FF 957-961). Litton systems retrofitted to others. Link 11 in three of the class. WSC-3 SATCOM (F 957).
Weapons control: 1 Signaal Liod optronic director (FF 951-956) ❼; 1 Radamec System 2400 optronic director (FF 957-961) ❽.
Radars: Air/surface search: Signaal DA05 ❾; E/F-band.
Surface search: Signaal ZW06 (FF 951-956) ❿; Marconi S 1810 (FF 957-961) ⓫; I-band.
Fire control: Signaal WM28 (FF 951-956) ⓬; Marconi ST 1802 (FF 957-961) ⓭; I/J-band.
Navigation: Raytheon SPS-10C (FF 957-961) ⓮; I-band.
Tacan: SRN 15.

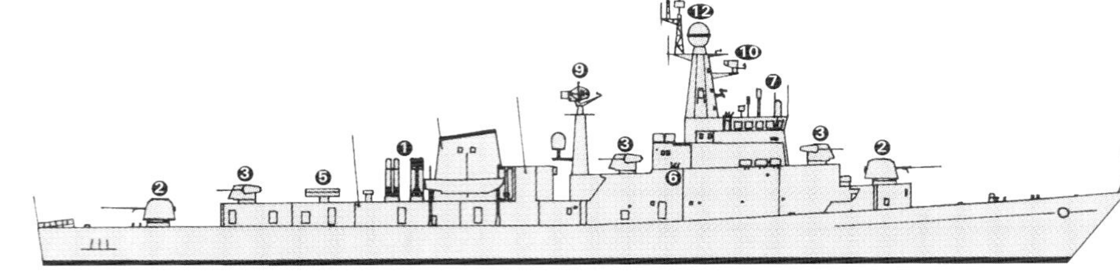

ULSAN *(Scale 1 : 900), Ian Sturton* / 0506154

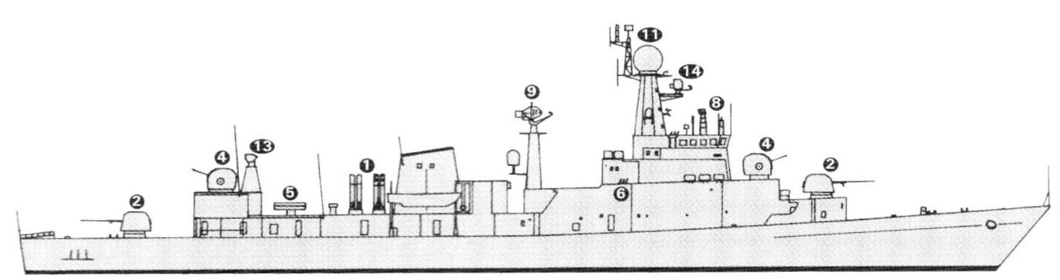

CHE JU *(Scale 1 : 900), Ian Sturton* / 0506155

Sonars: Raytheon DE 1167; hull-mounted; active search and attack; medium frequency.

Modernisation: New sonars fitted. WSC-3 SATCOM fitted in *Chon Nam*.
Structure: Steel hull with aluminium alloy superstructure. There are three versions. The first five ships are the same but *Kyong Buk* has the four Emerson Electric twin 30 mm guns replaced by three Breda twin 40 mm, and the last four of the class have a built-up gun platform aft and a different combination of surface search, target indication and navigation radars. Weapon systems integration caused earlier concern and a Ferranti combat data system has been installed in the last five; Litton Systems Link 11 fitted in three of the class.
Operational: *Che Ju* and *Chung Nam* conducted the first ever deployment of South Korean warships to Europe during a four month tour from September 1991 to January 1992. Trainees were embarked. Three of the class have a shore datalink and act as local area commanders to control attack craft carrying out coastal protection patrols.

CHE JU *10/2002, Guy Toremans* / 0528915

ULSAN *8/2000, van Ginderen Collection* / 0104996

CHUNG JU

2/2001, Ships of the World / 0130106

CHUNG NAM

10/2008, Michael Nitz* / 1353201

CHON NAM

10/2008, Michael Nitz* / 1353200

0 + 1 FUTURE FRIGATES (FFX) (FFGHM)

Name	No	Builders	Laid down	Launched	Commissioned
–	–	Hyundai, Ulsan	20 Jan 2009	2010	2011

Displacement, tons: 2,300 standard; 3,200 full load
Dimensions, feet (metres): To be announced
Main machinery: CODAG to be announced
Speed, knots: 32
Range, n miles: 4,500 at 13 kt
Complement: 170

Missiles: SSM: To be announced.
SAM: 1 Mk 49 RAM RIM-116; 21 rounds; passive IR/anti-radiation homing to 9.6 km *(5.2 n miles)* at 2 Mach, warhead 9.1 kg.
Guns: 1—127 mm. 1—30 mm 7-barrelled Goalkeeper; 4,200 rds/min to 1.5 km.
Torpedoes: 6—324 mm (2 triple) tubes.
Combat data systems: To be announced.
Weapons control: To be announced.
Radars: Air search/fire control: To be announced (3D).
Surface search: To be announced.
Navigation: To be announced.
Sonars: Hull-mounted and towed-array.

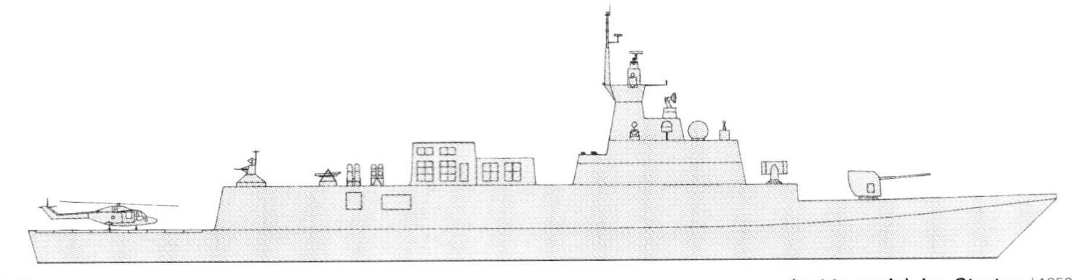

FFX *(not to scale)*, **Ian Sturton** / 1353186

Helicopters: 1 Westland Super Lynx Mk 99.

Programmes: Hyundai Heavy Industries awarded the contract in early 2009 for the construction of the lead ship of a new FFX class of frigates. The first six of the class are to replace the Ulsan class by 2015. A further 18 ships are projected to enter service by 2020 to replace the Po Hang and Dong Hae classes.

CORVETTES

24 PO HANG CLASS (FS/FSG)

Name	No	Builders	Commissioned
PO HANG	756	Korea SEC, Pusan	Dec 1984
KUN SAN	757	Korea Tacoma	Dec 1984
KYONG JU	758	Hyundai, Ulsan	Nov 1986
MOK PO	759	Daewoo, Okpo	Aug 1986
KIM CHON	761	Korea SEC, Pusan	May 1985
CHUNG JU	762	Korea Tacoma	May 1985
JIN JU	763	Hyundai, Ulsan	June 1988
YO SU	765	Daewoo, Okpo	Nov 1988
JIN HAE	766	Korea SEC, Pusan	Feb 1989
SUN CHON	767	Korea Tacoma	June 1989
YEE REE	768	Hyundai, Ulsan	June 1989
WON JU	769	Daewoo, Okpo	Aug 1989
AN DONG	771	Korea SEC, Pusan	Nov 1989
CHON AN	772	Korea Tacoma	Nov 1989
SONG NAM	773	Daewoo, Okpo	May 1989
BU CHON	775	Hyundai, Ulsan	Apr 1989
JAE CHON	776	Korea SEC, Pusan	May 1989
DAE CHON	777	Korea Tacoma	Apr 1989
SOK CHO	778	Korea SEC, Pusan	Feb 1990
YONG JU	779	Hyundai, Ulsan	Mar 1990
NAM WON	781	Daewoo, Okpo	Apr 1990
KWAN MYONG	782	Korea Tacoma	July 1990
SIN HUNG	783	Korea SEC, Pusan	Mar 1993
KONG JU	785	Korea Tacoma	July 1993

Displacement, tons: 1,220 full load
Dimensions, feet (metres): 289.7 × 32.8 × 9.5 *(88.3 × 10 × 2.9)*
Main machinery: CODOG; 1 GE LM 2500 gas turbine; 26,820 hp *(20 MW)* sustained; 2 MTU 12V 956 TB82 diesels; 6,260 hp(m) *(4.6 MW)* sustained; 2 shafts; Kamewa cp props
Speed, knots: 32
Range, n miles: 4,000 at 15 kt (diesel)
Complement: 95 (10 officers)

Missiles: SSM: 2 Aerospatiale MM 38 Exocet (756-759) ❶; inertial cruise; active radar homing to 42 km *(23 n miles)* at 0.9 Mach; warhead 165 kg; sea-skimmer.
4 McDonnell Douglas Harpoon (762, 769, 777, 779) (2 twin) launchers ❷; active radar homing to 130 km *(70 n miles)* at 0.9 Mach; warhead 227 kg.
Guns: 1 or 2 OTO Melara 3 in *(76 mm)*/62 compact ❸; 85 rds/min to 16 km *(8.6 n miles)* anti-surface; 12 km *(6.5 n miles)* anti-aircraft; weight of shell 6 kg.
4 Emerson Electric 30 mm (2 twin) (756-759) ❹; 4 Breda 40 mm/70 (2 twin) (761 onwards) ❺.
Torpedoes: 6—324 mm Mk 32 (2 triple) tubes ❻. Honeywell Mk 46; anti-submarine; active/passive homing to 11 km *(5.9 n miles)* at 40 kt; warhead 44 kg.
Depth charges: 12 (761 onwards).
Countermeasures: Decoys: 4 MEL Protean fixed launchers; 36 grenades.
2 Loral Hycor SRBOC 6-barrelled Mk 36 launchers (in some); range 4 km *(2.2 n miles)*.
ESM/ECM: THORN EMI or NobelTech; intercept/jammer.
Combat data systems: Signaal Sewaco ZK (756-759); Ferranti WSA 423 (761 onwards).
Weapons control: Signaal Liod or Radamec 2400 (766 onwards) optronic director ❼.
Radars: Surface search: Marconi 1810 ❽ and/or Raytheon SPS-64 ❾; I-band.
Fire control: Signaal WM28 ❿; I/J-band; or Marconi 1802 ⓫; I/J-band.
Sonars: Signaal PHS-32; hull-mounted; active search and attack; medium frequency.

Programmes: First laid down early 1983. The programme terminated in 1993.
Structure: The first four are Exocet fitted and have a different weapon systems arrangement. The remainder have an improved combat data system with Ferranti/Radamec/Marconi fire-control systems and radars as in the later versions of the Ulsan class.

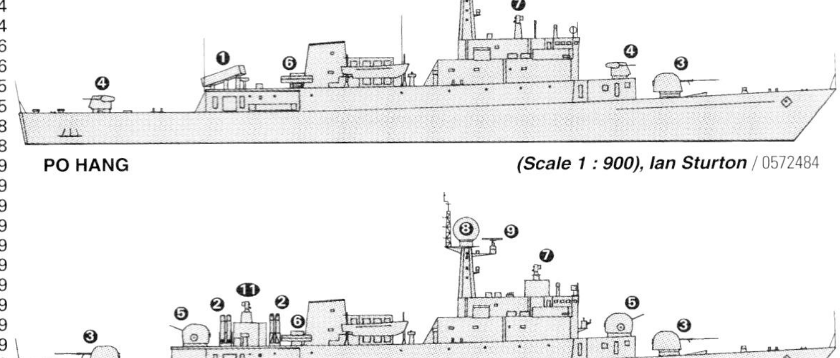

PO HANG *(Scale 1 : 900)*, **Ian Sturton** / 0572484

WON JU *(Scale 1 : 900)*, **Ian Sturton** / 0569920

CHUNG JU *10/2008**, **Michael Nitz** / 1353203

KUN SAN *10/2008**, **Guy Toremans** / 1353202

YO SU *10/2008**, **Michael Nitz** / 1353204

4 DONG HAE CLASS (FS)

Name	*No*	*Builders*	*Commissioned*
DONG HAE	751	Korea SEC, Pusan	Aug 1982
SU WON	752	Korea Tacoma	Oct 1983
KANG REUNG	753	Hyundai, Ulsan	Nov 1983
AN YANG	755	Daewoo, Okpo	Dec 1983

Displacement, tons: 1,076 full load
Dimensions, feet (metres): 256.2 × 31.5 × 8.5 *(78.1 × 9.6 × 2.6)*
Main machinery: CODOG; 1 GE LM 2500 gas turbine; 26,820 hp *(20 MW)* sustained; 2 MTU 12V 956 TB82 diesels; 6,260 hp(m) *(4.6 MW)* sustained; 2 shafts; Kamewa cp props
Speed, knots: 31. **Range, n miles:** 4,000 at 15 kt (diesel)
Complement: 95 (10 officers)

Guns: 1 OTO Melara 3 in *(76 mm)*/62 compact ❶; 85 rds/min to 16 km *(8.6 n miles)*; weight of shell 6 kg.
4 Emerson Electric 30 mm (2 twin) ❷. 2 Bofors 40 mm/60 (twin) ❸.
Torpedoes: 6—324 mm Mk 32 (2 triple) tubes ❹. Honeywell Mk 46; anti-submarine; active/passive homing to 11 km *(5.9 n miles)* at 40 kt; warhead 44 kg.
Depth charges: 12.
Countermeasures: Decoys: 4 MEL Protean chaff launchers.
ESM/ECM: THORN EMI or NobelTech; intercept and jammer.
Combat data systems: Signaal Sewaco ZK.
Weapons control: Signaal Liod optronic director ❺.
Radars: Surface search: Raytheon SPS-64 ❻; I-band.
Fire control: Signaal WM28 ❼; I/J-band.
Sonars: Signaal PHS-32; hull-mounted; active search and attack; medium frequency.

Programmes: This was the first version of the corvette series, with four being ordered in 1980, one each from the four major warship building yards.
Structure: The design was too small for the variety of different weapons which were intended to be fitted for different types of warfare and was therefore discontinued in favour of the Po Hang class.

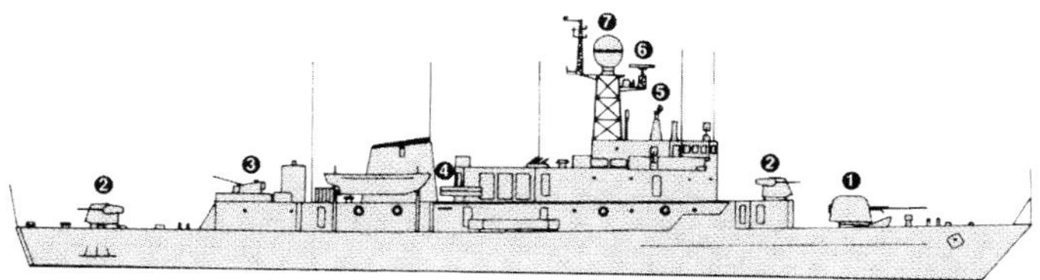

DONG HAE *(Scale 1 : 900), Ian Sturton* / 0506046

KANG REUNG *10/2008*, Chris Sattler* / 1353205

SHIPBORNE AIRCRAFT

Notes: A Request for Proposals for eight mine-hunting helicopters is expected in 2009.

Numbers/Type: 12/13 Westland Lynx Mk 99/Mk 99A.
Operational speed: 125 kt *(231 km/h)*.
Service ceiling: 12,000 ft *(3,660 m)*.
Range: 320 n miles *(593 km)*.
Role/Weapon systems: 12 Mk 99 helicopters delivered by 1991; 13 Mk 99A ordered in June 1997 and delivered in 1999/2000. Sensors: Ferranti Sea Spray Mk 3 radar and Racal ESM. Bendix AQS 18(V) dipping sonar and ASQ 504(V) MAD in ASW versions. Weapons: 4 BAe Sea Skua missiles. Mk 46 (Mod 5) torpedo (in ASW version). Sea Skua may be replaced in due course.

LYNX MK 99A *10/2008*, Michael Nitz* / 1353206

Numbers/Type: 5 Aerospatiale SA 316B/SA 319B Alouette III.
Operational speed: 113 kt *(210 km/h)*.
Service ceiling: 10,500 ft *(3,200 m)*.
Range: 290 n miles *(540 km)*.
Role/Weapon systems: Marine support helicopter; operated by RoK Marine Corps. Sensors: None. Weapons: Unarmed.

ALOUETTE III *6/2008*, Annati Collection* / 1353207

Numbers/Type: 19 Sikorsky UH-60P Blackhawk.
Operational speed: 145 kt *(268 km/h)*.
Service ceiling: 18,700 ft *(5,070 m)*.
Range: 315 n miles *(583 km)*.
Role/Weapon systems: Korean built variant of Sikorsky UH-60L. Naval version used for SAR and operations from *Dokdo*.

UH-60P *10/2008*, Michael Nitz* / 1353208

LAND-BASED MARITIME AIRCRAFT (FRONT LINE)

Notes: (1) F-16 fighters are capable of firing Harpoon ASV missiles.
(2) There are also 5 UH-1 utility helicopters.
(3) Eight Lockheed P-3B Orion are to be reactivated and upgraded. KAI and L-3 Communications selected in December 2004 to undertake the work. The contract is to be completed by 2010.
(4) Additional assault helicopters may be required to augment the UH-60P already in service.

Numbers/Type: 8 Lockheed P-3C Orion Update III.
Operational speed: 411 kt *(761 km/h)*.
Service ceiling: 28,300 ft *(8,625 m)*.
Range: 4,000 n miles *(7,410 km)*.
Role/Weapon systems: Maritime patrol aircraft ordered in December 1990. First pair delivered April 1995, remainder April 1996. To be replaced by eight upgraded P-3B by 2010. The Update III version is fitted with ASQ-212 tactical computer. Sensors: APS-134 or 137(V)6 search radar; AAS-36 IR. Weapons: four Harpoon ASM.

P-3C *8/2008*, Michael Nitz* / 1353210

Numbers/Type: 5 Rheims-Cessna F 406 Caravan II.
Operational speed: 229 kt *(424 km/h)*.
Service ceiling: 30,000 ft *(9,145 m)*.
Range: 1,153 m *(2,135 km)*.
Role/Weapon systems: Maritime surveillance version ordered in 1997 with first one delivered in mid-1999. Sensors: APS 134 radar; Litton FLIR. Weapons: none.

F 406 *6/2008*, Annati Collection* / 1353209

PATROL FORCES

1 + 8 (11) GUMDOKSURI CLASS (FAST ATTACK CRAFT) (PGGF)

Name	*No*	*Builders*	*Laid down*	*Launched*	*Commissioned*
YOON YOUNG-HA	711	Hanjin Heavy Industries, Pusan	2005	28 June 2007	17 Dec 2008

Displacement, tons: 440 standard; 570 full load
Dimensions, feet (metres): 206.7 × 29.5 × 16.4 *(63.0 × 9.0 × 5.0)*
Main machinery: CODAG; 2 GE LM 500 gas turbines; 10,900 hp *(8.1 MW)*; 2 MTU 16V 1163 diesels; 15,880 hp *(11.8 MW)*
Speed, knots: 41. **Range, n miles:** 2,000 at 15 kt
Complement: 40
Missiles: SSM: 4 Harpoon (2 twin).
Guns: 1—3 in *(76 mm)*. 1—40 mm.
Radars: Air/surface search: Thales MW 08; G-band.
Fire control: Saab Ceros 200; J-band.
Navigation: I-band.

Comment: A new class of patrol craft to replace Sea Dolphin class. Following construction of the first of class by Hanjin, hulls 2-5 are to be built by STX Shipbuilding, Jinhae, and hulls 6-9 by Hanjin. A class of 20 is projected.

YOON YOUNG-HA *10/2008*, Michael Nitz* / 1353214

81 SEA DOLPHIN/WILDCAT CLASS (FAST ATTACK CRAFT—PATROL) (PBF/PTF)

PKM 212–375 series

Displacement, tons: 148 full load
Dimensions, feet (metres): 121.4 × 22.6 × 5.6 *(37 × 6.9 × 1.7)*
Main machinery: 2 MTU MD 16V 538 TB90 diesels; 6,000 hp(m) *(4.41 MW)* sustained; 2 shafts
Speed, knots: 37
Range, n miles: 600 at 20 kt
Complement: 31 (5 officers)
Guns: 2 Emerson Electric 30 mm (twin) or USN 3 in *(76 mm)*/50 or Bofors 40 mm/60. 2 GE/GD 20 mm Sea Vulcan Gatlings (in most).
2—12.7 mm MGs. Rocket launchers in lieu of after Gatling in some.
Weapons control: Optical director.
Radars: Surface search: Raytheon 1645; I-band.

Comment: Fifty-four Sea Dolphins built by Korea SEC, and 47 Wildcats by Korea Tacoma. First laid down 1978. The class has some gun armament variations and some minor superstructure changes in later ships. These craft form the basis of the coastal patrol effort against incursions by North Korean amphibious units. Five sold to the Philippines in 1995, two transferred to Bangladesh in 2000 and a further two in 2004. Some deleted so far, others are in reserve.

SEA DOLPHIN 281 *10/2008*, Guy Toremans* / 1353212

SEA DOLPHIN 296 *10/2008*, Guy Toremans* / 1353211

SEA DOLPHIN 362 *10/2008*, Michael Nitz* / 1353213

AMPHIBIOUS FORCES

Notes: The LST-2 programme is for four 4,500 ton LSTs to replace the ageing 512-1152 class ships and to augment the Alligator class.

10 LCM 8 CLASS (LCM)

Displacement, tons: 115 full load
Dimensions, feet (metres): 74.5 × 21 × 4.6 *(22.7 × 6.4 × 1.4)*
Main machinery: 4 GM 6-71 diesels; 696 hp *(519 kW)* sustained; 2 shafts
Speed, knots: 11
Complement: 11
Military lift: 55 tons

Comment: Previously US Army craft. Transferred in September 1978.

LCM 87 *10/2008*, Michael Nitz* / 1353219

4 ALLIGATOR CLASS (LSTH)

Name	*No*	*Builders*	*Launched*	*Commissioned*
KOJOON BONG	681	Korea Tacoma, Masan	Sep 1992	June 1993
BIRO BONG	682	Korea Tacoma, Masan	Dec 1996	Nov 1997
HYANGRO BONG	683	Korea Tacoma, Masan	Oct 1998	Aug 1999
SEONGIN BONG	685	Korea Tacoma, Masan	Feb 1999	Nov 1999

Displacement, tons: 1,900 standard; 4,278 full load
Dimensions, feet (metres): 369.1 × 50.2 × 9.8 *(112.5 × 15.3 × 3)*
Main machinery: 2 SEMT-Pielstick 16 PA6 V 280; 12,800 hp(m) *(9.41 MW)* sustained; 2 shafts; cp props
Speed, knots: 16
Range, n miles: 4,500 at 12 kt
Complement: 169
Military lift: 200 troops; 15 MBT; 6—3 ton vehicles; 4 LCVPs.
Guns: 2 Breda 40 mm/70 (LST 683, 685). 2—30 mm (1 twin) (LST 681). 2 Vulcan 20 mm Gatlings.
Countermeasures: Decoys: 1 RBOC chaff launcher.
ESM: radar intercept.
Weapons control: Selenia NA 18. Optronic director. Daeyoung WCS-86.
Radars: Surface search: Raytheon SPS 64; E/F-band.
Navigation: Raytheon SPS 64; I-band.
Tacan: SRN 15.
Helicopters: Platform for 1 UH-60A.

Comment: First one ordered in June 1990 from Korea Tacoma, Masan but delayed by financial problems. Korea Tacoma became Hanjin Heavy Industries. Design improvements include stern ramp for underway launching of LVTs, helicopter deck, and a lengthened bow ramp. There are unlikely to be further orders.

KOJOON BONG *10/2008*, Michael Nitz* / 1353217

HYANGRO BONG *10/2008*, Michael Nitz* / 1353218

2 LST 512-1152 CLASS (LST)

Name	*No*	*Builders*	*Commissioned*
SU YONG (ex-*Kane County* LST 853)	677	Chicago Bridge	11 Dec 1945
BUK HAN (ex-*Lynn County* LST 900)	678	Dravo, Pittsburg	28 Dec 1944

Displacement, tons: 1,653 standard; 2,366 beaching; 4,080 full load
Dimensions, feet (metres): 328 × 50 × 14 (screws) *(100 × 15.2 × 4.3)*
Main machinery: 2 GM 12-567A diesels; 1,800 hp *(1.34 MW)*; 2 shafts
Speed, knots: 10
Complement: 80
Military lift: 2,100 tons including 20 tanks and 2 LCVPs
Guns: 8 Bofors 40 mm (2 twin, 4 single). 2 Oerlikon 20 mm.

Comment: Former US Navy tank landing ships. Transferred to South Korea between 1955 and 1959. All purchased 15 November 1974. Planned to be replaced by the Alligator class but two reported as still in service.

BUK HAN *10/1997* / 0081165

1 + (2) AMPHIBIOUS TRANSPORT DOCK (LPD)

Name	*No*	*Builders*	*Laid down*	*Launched*	*Commissioned*
DOKDO	6111	Hanjin Heavy Industries, Pusan	2003	12 July 2005	3 July 2007

Displacement, tons: 13,000 standard; 19,000 full load
Dimensions, feet (metres): 656.3 × 105.0 × 21.33 *(200.0 × 32.0 × 6.5)*
Main machinery: CODAD: 4 SEMT Pielstick 16PC 2.5 STC diesels; 41,615 hp(m) *(30.6 MW)* sustained; 2 shafts
Speed, knots: 22
Complement: 400 ship plus 700
Military lift: 700 troops, 10 tanks and two air-cushion landing craft
Missiles: 1 Raytheon Mk 49 launcher RAM 116 ❶; 21 rds; passive IR/anti-radiation homing to 9.6 km *(5.2 n miles)* at 2.5 Mach; warhead 9.1 kg.
Guns: 2 TNNL Goalkeeper ❷ 30 mm; 4,200 rds/min to 1.5 km.
Combat data systems: Based on Tacticos.

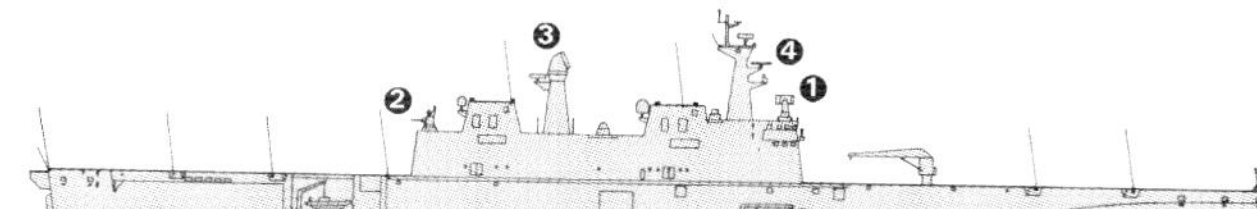
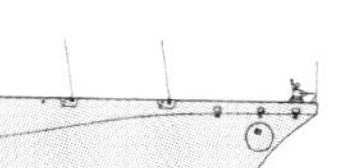
DOKDO

(Scale 1 : 2,400), Ian Sturton / 1166667

Radars: Air search: Thales SMART L ❸; 3D; D-band.
Surface search: Signaal MW 08 ❹; G-band.
Navigation: To be announced.
CCA: Galileo Avionica SPN-720; I-band.

Helicopters: 10 UH-60.

Programmes: The contract for an amphibious assault ship was placed with Hanjin Heavy Industries on 28 October 2002. An order for a second ship, possibly to be called *Marado*, is expected in 2008 and a third ship is also under consideration.
Structure: The design includes a well dock.

DOKDO

10/2008, Michael Nitz* / 1353215

DOKDO

12/2007, Michael Nitz / 1170070

DOKDO

10/2008, Michael Nitz* / 1353216

3 TSAPLYA (MURENA E) (PROJECT 12061) CLASS (ACV)

621–623

Displacement, tons: 108 standard; 150 full load
Dimensions, feet (metres): 102.7 × 48.5 × 4.9 *(31.3 × 14.8× 1.5)*
Main machinery: 2 PR-77 gas turbines for lift and propulsion; 8,000 hp *(5.88 MW)*
Speed, knots: 50
Range, n miles: 500 at 50 kt
Complement: 11 (3 officers) + 100 troops
Guns: 2—30 mm AK 306M. 2—30 mm grenade launchers. 2—12.7 mm MGs.

Comment: Ordered on 5 August 2002. Designed by Almaz, all built at Khabarovsk. First laid down on 26 April 2004 and delivered to Inchon on 11 November 2005. The second and third delivered in November and December 2006 respectively. Capable of carrying one medium tank or 130 troops.

TSAPLYA 621 *6/2006* / 1164765

MISCELLANEOUS LANDING CRAFT

Comment: A considerable number of US LCVP type built of GRP in South Korea. In addition there were plans to build up to 20 small hovercraft for special forces; first two reported building in 1994, and one seen on sea trials in May 1995. Also 56 combat support boats of 8 m were ordered from FBM Marine for assembly by Hanjin Heavy Industries.

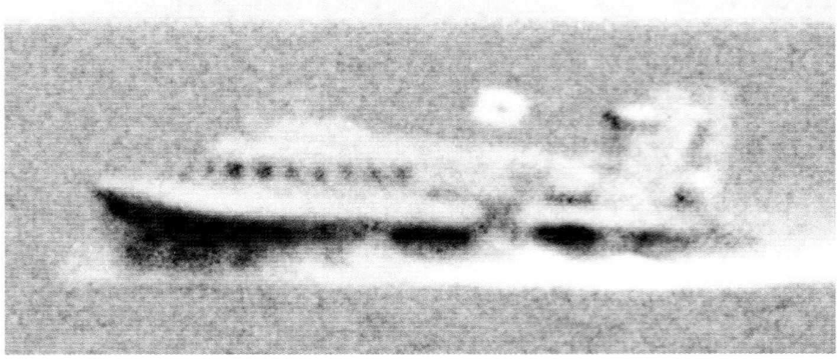

HOVERCRAFT *5/1995, David Jordan* / 0081167

2 LSF-II LANDING CRAFT AIR CUSHION (LCAC)

631–632

Displacement, tons: 100 standard; 155 full load
Dimensions, feet (metres): 88.0 (on cushion) × 47.0 (on cushion) *(26.8 × 14.3)*
Main machinery: 4 Vericor Power Systems ETF40B gas turbines for propulsion and lift; 15,800 hp *(11.8 MW)*; 2 shrouded reversible-pitch airscrews (propulsion); 4 double-entry centrifugal fans (lift)
Speed, knots: 40
Range, n miles: 300 at 35 kt
Complement: 5
Military lift: 23 troops; 1 main battle tank or 55 tons
Guns: 1—20 mm.
Radars: To be announced.

Comment: LSF II is a high-speed air-cushion craft of aluminium construction developed and manufactured by Hanjin Heavy Industries for operations in conjunction with the LPD *Dokdo*. The design appears to be based on the US Navy's LCAC design. Both delivered in mid-2007.

LCAC 632 *10/2008*, Michael Nitz* / 1353220

MINE WARFARE FORCES

6 SWALLOW CLASS (MINEHUNTERS) (MHSC)

Name	*No*	*Builders*	*Commissioned*
KANG KYEONG	561	Kangnam Corporation	Dec 1986
KANG JIN	562	Kangnam Corporation	May 1991
KO RYEONG	563	Kangnam Corporation	Nov 1991
KIM PO	565	Kangnam Corporation	Apr 1993
KO CHANG	566	Kangnam Corporation	Oct 1993
KUM WHA	567	Kangnam Corporation	Apr 1994

Displacement, tons: 470 standard; 520 full load
Dimensions, feet (metres): 164 × 27.2 × 8.6 *(50 × 8.3 × 2.6)*
Main machinery: 2 MTU diesels; 2,040 hp(m) *(1.5 MW)* sustained; 2 Voith-Schneider props; bow thruster; 102 hp(m) *(75 kW)*
Speed, knots: 15
Range, n miles: 2,000 at 10 kt
Complement: 44 (5 officers) plus 4 divers
Guns: 1 Oerlikon 20 mm. 2—7.62 mm MGs.
Countermeasures: MCM: 2 Gaymarine Pluto remote-control submersibles (possibly to be replaced by Double Eagle).
Combat data systems: Racal MAINS 500.
Radars: Navigation: Raytheon SPS 64; I-band.
Sonars: GEC-Marconi 193M Mod 1 or Mod 3; minehunting; high frequency.

Comment: Built to a design developed independently by Kangnam Corporation but similar to the Italian Lerici class. GRP hull. Single sweep gear deployed at 8 kt. Decca/Racal plotting system. First delivered at the end of 1986 for trials. Two more with some modifications ordered in 1988, three more in 1990.

KANG KYEONG *10/2008*, Michael Nitz* / 1353221

1 WON SAN CLASS (MINELAYER) (MLH)

Name	*No*	*Builders*	*Launched*	*Commissioned*
WON SAN	560	Hyundai, Ulsan	Sep 1996	Sep 1997

Displacement, tons: 3,300 full load
Dimensions, feet (metres): 340.6 × 49.2 × 11.2 *(103.8 × 15 × 3.4)*
Main machinery: CODAD; 4 SEMT-Pielstick 12 PA6 diesels; 17,200 hp(m) *(12.64 MW)*; 2 shafts
Speed, knots: 22
Range, n miles: 4,500 at 15 kt
Complement: 160
Guns: 1 OTO Melara 3 in *(76 mm)*/62; 85 rds/min to 16 km *(8.6 n miles)*; weight of shell 6 kg. 2 Breda 40 mm/70.
Torpedoes: 6—324 mm Mk 32 (2 triple) launchers.
Mines: 2 stern launchers. Up to 300.
Countermeasures: Decoys: 2 chaff launchers. ESM/ECM.
Weapons control: Radamec optronic director.
Radars: Air/surface search: E/F-band.
Fire control: Marconi 1802; I/J-band.
Navigation: I-band.
Sonars: Bow-mounted; active search and attack; medium frequency.
Helicopters: Platform only.

Comment: Project design contract ordered October 1991 and completed July 1993 by Hyundai. Order to build given in October 1994.

WON SAN *3/2004, Chris Sattler* / 1042336

3 YANG YANG CLASS (MSC/MHC)

Name	*No*	*Builders*	*Commissioned*
YANG YANG	571	Kangnam Corporation	Dec 1999
ONGJIN	572	Kangnam Corporation	Feb 2004
HAE NAM	573	Kangnam Corporation	Mar 2005

Displacement, tons: 880 full load
Dimensions, feet (metres): 195 × 34.4 × 9.8 *(59.4 × 10.5 × 3.0)*
Main machinery: 2 MTU diesels; 4,000 hp(m) *(2.98 MW)* sustained; 2 Voith-Schneider props; bow thruster; 134 hp(m) *(100 kW)*
Speed, knots: 15
Range, n miles: 3,000 at 12 kt
Complement: 56 (7 officers) plus 5 divers

Guns: 1—20 mm Sea Vulcan Gatling. 2—7.62 mm MGs.
Countermeasures: MCM: BAE Systems deep mechanical and combined influence sweep system. 2 Gayrobot Pluto GIGAS ROVs.
Combat data systems: Thomson Marconi TSM 2061 Mk 3.
Radars: Navigation: Raytheon; I-band.
Sonars: Thomson Marconi Type 2093 VDS; minehunting; active multifrequency.

Comment: The first one ordered in late 1995 and a second pair delivered by 2005. Further orders are possible. A large version of the Swallow class built to a design developed by Kangnam Corporation. GRP hull. The integrated navigation and dynamic positioning system developed by Kongsberg Simrad.

ONGJIN *10/2008*, Michael Nitz* / 1353222

SURVEY SHIPS

18 SURVEY SHIPS (AGOR)

PUSAN 801	**PUSAN** 806	**201–204**
PUSAN 802	**PUSAN** 810	**208–209**
PUSAN 803	**CH'UNGNAM** 821	**215–217**
PUSAN 805	**KANGWON** 831	**220**

Comment: All ships are painted white with a distinctive yellow coloured crest on the funnel. Most were commissioned in the 1980s. The Hydrographic Service is responsible to the Ministry of Transport.

201 *10/2008*, Guy Toremans* / 1353224

202 *4/2000, M Declerck* / 0105000

217 *10/2008*, Guy Toremans* / 1353223

RESCUE VEHICLES

1 RESCUE SUBMERSIBLE

DSRV II

Displacement, tons: 25
Dimensions, feet (metres): 31.5 × 8.9 × 12.5 *(9.6 × 2.7 × 3.8)*
Main machinery: 2 electric motors; 26.8 hp *(20 kW)*; 4 tiltable side thrusters; 16 hp *(12 kW)*
Speed, knots: 3
Complement: 2 pilots and 1 rescue chamber operator

Comment: James Fisher Defence Limited announced on 13 December 2006 that it had been awarded a contract to deliver a new Submarine Rescue Vehicle (SRV) to the Republic of Korea Navy. It was delivered in November 2008. The new submarine rescue vehicle, DSAR-5, is based on the LR5/DSAR-1, in-service with the Royal Navy until replaced in 2008. Lithium based battery technology enables the underwater endurance to be increased significantly over conventional lead-acid based systems. DSAR-5 has two compartments. The forward compartment houses the pilot and co-pilot while the aft compartment carries the RCO and up to 16 rescuees. Capable of operating at a depth of 500 m in currents of up to 3 kt, rescuees may be transferred under pressure to the medical and decompression facilities onboard the submarine rescue mothership *Cheong-Hae-Jin*.

AUXILIARIES

Notes: The South Korean Navy also operates nine small harbour tugs (designated YTLs). These include one ex-US Navy craft and five ex-US Army craft. There are also approximately 35 small service craft in addition to the YO-type tankers listed and the harbour tugs. These craft include open lighters, floating cranes, diving tenders, dredgers, ferries, non self-propelled fuel barges, pontoon barges, and sludge removal barges; most are former US Navy craft.

1 CHEONG HAE JIN CLASS (ARS)

Name	*No*	*Builders*	*Launched*	*Commissioned*
CHEONG HAE JIN	21	Daewoo, Okpo	Oct 1995	30 Nov 1996

Displacement, tons: 4,300 full load
Dimensions, feet (metres): 337.3 × 53.8 × 15.1 *(102.8 × 16.4 × 4.6)*
Main machinery: Diesel-electric; 4 MAN Burmeister & Wain 16V 28/32 diesels; 11,800 hp(m) *(8.67 MW)*; 2 motors; 5,440 hp(m) *(4 MW)*; 2 shafts; cp props; 3 bow and 2 stern thrusters
Speed, knots: 18
Range, n miles: 9,500 at 15 kt
Complement: 130
Guns: 1 GE/GD 20 mm Vulcan Gatling (can be fitted). 6—12.7 mm MGs.
Radars: Navigation: I-band.
Sonars: Hull-mounted; active search; high frequency.
Helicopters: Platform for 1 light.

Comment: Ordered in 1992. Laid down December 1994. A multipurpose salvage and submarine rescue ship which can carry DSRV II as well as two LCVPs on davits plus a diving bell for nine men and a decompression chamber. Two large hydraulic cranes fore and aft and one towing winch. There are also two salvage ships which belong to the Coast Guard.

CHEONG HAE JIN *9/2003, Hartmut Ehlers* / 0570936

2 EDENTON CLASS (SALVAGE SHIPS) (ATS)

Name	*No*	*Builders*	*Commissioned*
PYONG TAEK (ex-*Beaufort*)	27	Brooke Marine, Lowestoft	22 Jan 1972
KWANG YANG (ex-*Brunswick*)	28	Brooke Marine, Lowestoft	19 Dec 1972

Displacement, tons: 2,929 full load
Dimensions, feet (metres): 282.6 × 50 × 15.1 *(86.1 × 15.2 × 4.6)*
Main machinery: 4 Paxman 12YJCM diesels; 6,000 hp *(4.48 MW)* sustained; 2 shafts; cp props; bow thruster
Speed, knots: 16. **Range, n miles:** 10,000 at 13 kt
Complement: 129 (7 officers)
Guns: 2 Oerlikon 20 mm Mk 68.
Radars: Navigation: Sperry SPS-53; I/J-band.

Comment: Transferred from USA on 29 August 1996. Capable of (1) ocean towing, (2) supporting diver operations to depths of 850 ft, (3) lifting submerged objects weighing as much as 600,000 lb from a depth of 120 ft by static tidal lift or 30,000 lb by dynamic lift, (4) fighting ship fires. Fitted with 10 ton capacity crane forward and 20 ton capacity crane aft. Both recommissioned 28 February 1997.

PYONG TAEK (US colours) *12/1995, Giorgio Arra* / 0506303

3 CHUN JEE CLASS (LOGISTIC SUPPORT SHIPS) (AORH)

Name	*No*	*Builders*	*Launched*	*Commissioned*
CHUN JEE	57	Hyundai, Ulsan	May 1990	Dec 1990
DAE CHUNG	58	Hyundai, Ulsan	Jan 1997	1 Dec 1997
HWA CHUN	59	Hyundai, Ulsan	July 1997	Mar 1998

Displacement, tons: 4,180 standard; 9,180 full load
Dimensions, feet (metres): 426.5 × 58.4 × 21.3 *(130 × 17.8 × 6.5)*
Main machinery: 2 SEMT-Pielstick 16 PA6 V 280 (AO 57) or 12 PC2.5 diesels; 12,800 hp(m) *(9.4 MW)* sustained; 2 shafts
Speed, knots: 20. **Range, n miles:** 4,500 at 15 kt
Cargo capacity: 4,200 tons liquids; 450 tons solids
Guns: 4 Emerlec 30 mm (2 twin) or 2 Breda 40 mm/70. 2 GE/GD 20 mm Vulcan Gatlings.
Radars: Navigation: 2 Racal Decca; I-band.
Helicopters: Platform for 1 medium.

Comment: *Chun Jee* laid down September 1989. Underway replenishment stations on both sides. Helicopter for Vertrep but no hangar. There are three 6 ton lifts. Possibly based on Italian Stromboli class. Second of class was to have followed on but was eventually ordered together with the third in May 1995, to a slightly different design. More may be built when funds are available.

DAE CHUNG *10/2008*, Guy Toremans* / 1353225

HWA CHUN *10/2007, Adolfo Ortigueira Gil* / 1166666

1 TRIALS SUPPORT SHIP (AGE)

Name	*No*	*Builders*	*Launched*	*Commissioned*
SUNJIN	AGS 11	Hyundai, Ulsan	Nov 1992	Apr 1993

Displacement, tons: 320 full load
Dimensions, feet (metres): 113.2 × 49.2 × 12.1 *(34.5 × 15 × 3.7)*
Main machinery: 1 MTU 16V 396 TE74L diesel; 2,680 hp(m) *(2 MW)*; 1 shaft; cp prop; 2 bow thrusters
Speed, knots: 21. **Range, n miles:** 600 at 16 kt
Complement: 5 plus 20 scientists
Guns: 1 — 20 mm Gatling.
Radars: Navigation: I-band.

Comment: Experimental design built by Hyundai. Ordered June 1991, laid down June 1992. Aluminium SWATH hull with dynamic positioning system. Fitted with various trials equipment including an integrated navigation system and torpedo tracking pinger system. VDS and towed arrays. Used by the Defence Development Agency and civilian operated.

SUNJIN *1993, Hyundai* / 0081169

TUGS

Notes: In addition to the Edenton class ATS there are a further 10 harbour tugs and numerous port service auxiliaries.

HARBOUR TUG *10/2008*, Guy Toremans* / 1353226

COAST GUARD

Notes: (1) The Republic of Korea Coast Guard was originally established as the Maritime Safety Division on 12 December 1953. After becoming the Maritime Police Unit in 1962, it separated from the national police in 1996 and changed its name to the Coast Guard in December 2000. It is responsible for Maritime Security (including maritime counter-terrorism), Search and Rescue, Marine Environmental Protection, Marine Pollution Response and Maritime Safety. With its Headquarters at Songo, Incheon, it has four regional headquarters at Incheon, Mokpo, Busan and Donghae. There are 13 coast guard stations at Sogcho, Donghae, Pohang, Ulsan, Busan, Tongyeong, Yeosu, Wando, Cheju, Mokpo, Gunsan, Taean and Incheon. Patrol ships and craft are painted with blue hulls and white superstructure; the word "Police" is painted on the side of the superstructure. Larger salvage ships are painted white with the word "Police" and a red-yellow-blue diagonal stripe on the side of the hull. The Police Coast Guard academy was established in 2004.
(2) Aviation assets include a Bombardier Challenger 604 maritime surveillance aircraft, Kamov Ka-27 Helix and Bell 412 SAR helicopters, and AS 565 MB helicopters.

3 MAZINGER CLASS (PSO)

PC 1001–1003

Displacement, tons: 1,200 full load
Dimensions, feet (metres): 264.1 × 32.2 × 11.5 *(80.5 × 9.8 × 3.2)*
Main machinery: 2 SEMT-Pielstick 12 PA6 V 280 diesels; 9,600 hp(m) *(7.08 MW)* sustained; 2 shafts
Speed, knots: 22
Range, n miles: 7,000 at 18 kt
Complement: 69 (11 officers)
Guns: 1 Bofors 40 mm/70. 4 Oerlikon 20 mm (2 twin).
Radars: Surface search: Raytheon; I-band.

Comment: Ordered 7 November 1980 from Korea Tacoma and Hyundai. *PC 1001* delivered 29 November 1981. *PC 1002* 31 August 1982 and *PC 1003* on 31 August 1983. All-welded mild steel construction. Used for offshore surveillance and general coast guard duties. *PC 1001* is the Coast Guard Command ship. Only three of this class were completed.

MAZINGER (old colours) *1987, Korea Tacoma* / 0506048

1 HAN KANG CLASS (PG)

HAN KANG PC 1005

Displacement, tons: 1,180 full load
Dimensions, feet (metres): 289.7 × 32.8 × 9.5 *(88.3 × 10 × 2.9)*
Main machinery: CODOG; 1 GE LM 2500 gas turbine; 26,820 hp *(20 MW)* sustained; 2 MTU 12V 956 TB82 diesels; 6,260 hp(m) *(4.6 MW)* sustained; 3 shafts
Speed, knots: 32
Range, n miles: 4,000 at 15 kt
Complement: 72 (11 officers)
Guns: 1 OTO Melara 76/62 compact. 1 Bofors 40 mm/70. 2 GE/GD 20 mm Vulcan Gatlings.
Weapons control: Signaal LIOD optronic director.
Radars: Surface search: Raytheon SPS-64(V); I-band.
Fire control: Signaal WM28; I/J-band.

Comment: Built between May 1984 and December 1985 by Daewoo. Same hull as Po Hang class but much more lightly armed. Only one of the class was completed.

HAN KANG *9/2000* / 0097740

6 430 TON CLASS (PBO)

300–303 402–403

Displacement, tons: 430 full load
Dimensions, feet (metres): 176.2 × 24.3 × 7.9 *(53.7 × 7.4 × 2.4)*
Main machinery: 2 MTU 16V 396 TB83 diesels; 1,990 hp(m) *(1.49 MW)*; 2 shafts; cp props
Speed, knots: 19
Range, n miles: 2,100 at 17 kt
Complement: 14
Guns: 1 or 2 GD/GE 20 mm Vulcan Gatlings. 4—12.7 mm MGs.
Radars: Surface search: Raytheon; I-band.

Comment: All built between 1990 and 1995 by Hyundai except 301 which was built by Daewoo. Multipurpose patrol ships.

300 *3/1996, D Swetnam* / 0081172

301 *8/2000, van Ginderen Collection* / 0097741

23 SEA WOLF/SHARK CLASS (PBO)

207	**255–259**	**265–269**	**275–277**
251–253	**261–263**	**271–273**	

Displacement, tons: 310 full load
Dimensions, feet (metres): 158.1 × 23.3 × 8.2 *(48.2 × 7.1 × 2.5)*
Main machinery: 2 diesels; 7,320 hp(m) *(5.38 MW)*; 2 shafts
Speed, knots: 25. **Range, n miles:** 2,400 at 15 kt
Complement: 35 (3 officers)
Guns: 4 Oerlikon 20 mm (2 twin or 1 twin, 2 single). Some have a twin Bofors 40 mm/70 vice the twin Oerlikon. 2 Browning 12.7 mm MGs.
Radars: Surface search: I-band.

Comment: First four ordered in 1979–80 from Korea SEC (Sea Shark), Hyundai and Korea Tacoma (Sea Wolf). Programme terminated in 1988. Pennant numbers in 200 series up to 277.

SEA WOLF 207 *5/1997, van Ginderen Collection* / 0012711

4 BUKHANSAN CLASS (PBO)

BUKHANSAN 278 **CHULMASAN** 279 **P 281** **P 282**

Displacement, tons: 380 full load
Dimensions, feet (metres): 174.2 × 24 × 7.2 *(53.1 × 7.3 × 2.2)*
Main machinery: 2 MTU diesels; 8,300 hp(m) *(6.1 MW)* sustained; 2 shafts
Speed, knots: 28. **Range, n miles:** 2,500 at 15 kt
Complement: 35 (3 officers)
Guns: 1 Breda 40 mm/70. 1 GE/GD 20 mm Vulcan Gatling. 2—12.7 mm MGs.
Weapons control: Radamec optronic director.
Radars: Surface search: I-band.

Comment: Follow on to Sea Wolf class developed by Hyundai in 1987. Ordered in 1988 from Hyundai and Daewoo respectively. First pair in service in 1989, and second pair in 1990.

CHULMASAN (old colours) *1989, Daewoo* / 0506049

5 HYUNDAI TYPE (PB)

105 **113** **118** **121** **125**

Displacement, tons: 110 full load
Dimensions, feet (metres): 105.6 × 19.7 × 4.6 *(32.2 × 6 × 1.4)*
Main machinery: 2 diesels; 2 shafts
Speed, knots: 25
Complement: 19
Guns: 1 Rheinmetall 20 mm. 2—12.7 mm MGs.
Radars: Surface search: Furuno; I-band.

Comment: Ordered in 1996 and delivered from June 1997.

HYUNDAI 125 *6/2008*, Harald Carstens* / 1353227

1 SALVAGE SHIP (ARSH)

Name	*No*	*Builders*	*Launched*	*Commissioned*
TAE PUNG YANG I	3001	Hyundai, Ulsan	Oct 1991	18 Feb 1993

Displacement, tons: 3,200 standard; 4,300 full load
Dimensions, feet (metres): 343.5 × 49.2 × 17 *(104.7 × 15 × 5.2)*
Main machinery: 4 Ssangyong MAN Burmeister & Wain 16V 28/32 diesels; 4,800 hp(m) *(3.53 MW)*; 2 shafts; cp props; bow and stern thrusters
Speed, knots: 21
Range, n miles: 8,500 at 15 kt
Complement: 121
Guns: 1 GD/GE 20 mm Vulcan Gatling. 6—12.7 mm MGs.
Radars: Navigation: I-band.
Helicopters: 1 light.

Comment: Laid down February 1991. Has a helicopter deck and hangar, an ROV capable of diving to 300 m and a firefighting capability. Dynamic positioning system. Can be used for cable laying. Operates for the Marine Police.

TAE PUNG YANG 1 *10/2008*, Guy Toremans* / 1353228

1 SALVAGE SHIP (ARSH)

Name	*No*	*Builders*	*Commissioned*
JAEMIN I	1501	Daewoo, Okpo	28 Dec 1992

Displacement, tons: 2,072 full load
Dimensions, feet (metres): 254.6 × 44.3 × 13.8 *(77.6 × 13.5 × 4.2)*
Main machinery: 2 MTU diesels; 8,000 hp(m) *(5.88 MW)*; 2 shafts; cp props
Speed, knots: 18
Range, n miles: 4,500 at 12 kt
Complement: 92
Guns: 1 GD/GE 20 mm Vulcan Gatling.
Radars: Navigation: I-band.

Comment: Ordered in 1990. Fitted with diving equipment and has a four point mooring system. Carries two LCVPs.

JAEMIN I *8/2000* / 0097745

1 SALVAGE SHIP (ARS)

Name	*No*	*Builders*	*Launched*	*Commissioned*
JAEMIN II	1502	Hyundai, Ulsan	15 July 1995	Apr 1996

Displacement, tons: 2,500 full load
Dimensions, feet (metres): 288.7 × 47.6 × 15.1 *(88 × 14.5 × 4.6)*
Main machinery: 2 MTU diesels; 12,662 hp(m) *(9.31 MW)*; 2 shafts; Kamewa cp props; bow and stern thrusters
Speed, knots: 20
Range, n miles: 4,500 at 15 kt
Complement: 81
Guns: 1 GE/GD 20 mm Vulcan Gatling.
Radars: Navigation: I-band.

Comment: Ordered in December 1993 for Maritime Police. A general purpose salvage ship capable of towing, firefighting, supply or patrol duties.

JAEMIN II *8/1999,* ***Ships of the World*** / 0081176

1 SALVAGE SHIP (ARSH)

Name	*No*	*Builders*	*Commissioned*
JAEMIN III	1503	Hyundai, Ulsan	Nov 1998

Displacement, tons: 4,200 full load
Dimensions, feet (metres): 362.6 × 50.5 × 16 *(110.5 × 15.4 × 4.9)*
Main machinery: 2 diesels; 2 shafts
Speed, knots: 18
Complement: 120
Guns: 2 GE 20 mm Vulcan Gatlings. 6—12.7 mm MGs.
Radars: Navigation: I-band.

Comment: Ordered in 1996, from Hyundai, Ulsan. Large helicopter deck but no hangar.

JAEMIN III *10/2008*,* ***Guy Toremans*** / 1353229

1 DAEWOO TYPE (PSO)

SUMJINKANG PC 1006

Displacement, tons: 1,650 full load
Dimensions, feet (metres): 275.6 × 34.1 × 11.8 *(84 × 10.4 × 3.6)*
Main machinery: 2 Wärtsilä Nohab 16V25 diesels; 10,000 hp(m) *(7.35 MW)* sustained; 2 shafts
Speed, knots: 21
Range, n miles: 4,500 at 18 kt
Complement: 57 (7 officers)
Guns: 1—20 mm Sea Vulcan Gatling. 4—12.7 mm MGs.
Radars: Surface search: I-band.

Comment: Ordered in 1997 from Daewoo. Described as a multipurpose patrol ship. Launched 22 January 1999, and delivered 20 June 1999.

SUMJINKANG *6/2006,* ***Korea Coast Guard*** / 1159985

6 SEA DRAGON/WHALE CLASS (PBO)

PC 501–503 **PC 505–507**

Displacement, tons: 640 full load
Dimensions, feet (metres): 199.5 × 26.2 × 8.9 *(60.8 × 8 × 2.7)*
Main machinery: 2 SEMT-Pielstick 12 PA6 V 280 diesels; 9,600 hp(m) *(7.08 MW)* sustained; 2 shafts
Speed, knots: 24
Range, n miles: 6,000 at 15 kt
Complement: 40 (7 officers)
Guns: 1 Bofors 40 mm/60. 2 Oerlikon 20 mm. 2 Browning 12.7 mm MGs.
Radars: Navigation: Two sets.

Comment: Delivered 1978–1982 by Hyundai, Korea and Korea Tacoma. Fitted with SATNAV. Welded steel hull. Armament varies between ships, one 76 mm gun can be mounted on the forecastle. Variant of this class built for Bangladesh and delivered in October 1997.

SEA DRAGON 502 *6/2006,* ***Korea Coast Guard*** / 1159982

INSHORE PATROL CRAFT (PBR)

Displacement, tons: 47 full load
Dimensions, feet (metres): 69.9 × 17.7 × 4.6 *(21.3 × 5.4 × 1.4)*
Main machinery: 2 diesels; 1,800 hp(m) *(1.32 MW)*; 2 shafts
Speed, knots: 22
Range, n miles: 400 at 12 kt
Complement: 11
Guns: 1 Rheinmetall 20 mm. 3—12.7 mm MGs.
Radars: Surface search: Furuno; I-band.

Comment: Details are for the largest design of patrol craft. There are numbers of this type of vessel used for inshore patrol work. All Police craft have P pennant numbers. Armaments vary.

P 01 *10/2008*,* ***Michael Nitz*** / 1353230

P 135 *10/2008*,* ***Guy Toremans*** / 1353231

1 + (1) SAMBONGHO CLASS (PATROL SHIP) (PSO)

Name	*No*	*Builders*	*Commissioned*
SAMBONGHO	5001	Hyundai, Ulsan	23 Apr 2002

Displacement, tons: 5,000 (approx) full load
Dimensions, feet (metres): To be announced
Main machinery: To be announced
Speed, knots: To be announced
Guns: 2—20 mm.
Radars: Navigation: I-band.
Helicopters: 1 large.

Comment: The largest ship in the Coast Guard. A second ship may be under construction.

SAMBONGHO *6/2006,* ***Korea Coast Guard*** / 1159986

1 SALVAGE SHIP (ARSH)

Name	*No*	*Builders*	*Commissioned*
TAE PUNG YANG II	3002	Hyundai, Ulsan	31 Oct 1988

Displacement, tons: 3,900 standard
Dimensions, feet (metres): 362.5 × 50.5 × 16.1 *(110.5 × 15.4 × 4.9)*
Main machinery: 2 diesels; 2 shafts
Speed, knots: 18
Complement: 120
Guns: 2—20 mm Vulcan Gatlings. 6—12.7 mm MGs.
Radars: Surface search: I-band.
Helicopters: Platform for 1 large.

Comment: Ordered from Hyundai in mid-1996. Also used for SAR operations.

TAE PUNG YANG II *6/2006, Korea Coast Guard* / 1159984

3 SALVAGE SHIPS (ARSH)

Name	*No*	*Builders*	*Commissioned*
TAE PUNG YANG VI	3006		
TAE PUNG YANG VII	3007	Hanjin Heavy Industries, Pusan	28 Aug 2006
TAE PUNG YANG VIII	3008		

Displacement, tons: 4,000 (approx) full load
Dimensions, feet (metres): 362.5 × 50.5 × 16.1 *(110.5 × 15.4 × 4.9)*
Main machinery: 2 SEMT Pielstick 12PA6B STC diesels; 2 shafts
Speed, knots: 21
Range, n miles: 4,500 at 15 kt
Complement: 120
Guns: 1—20 mm. 2—12.7 mm MGs.
Radars: Navigation: I-band.
Helicopters: Platform for 1 large.

Comment: Three new multipurpose EEZ patrol and salvage ships believed to be of the same class. Details are based on those of *Tae Pung Yang II* and may be different.

TAE PUNG YANG VI *10/2008*, Guy Toremans* / 1353232

2 SALVAGE SHIPS (ARSH)

Name	*No*	*Builders*	*Commissioned*
JAEMIN VII	1507	Hanjin Heavy Industries, Pusan	
JAEMIN VIII	1508	Hyundai, Ulsan	20 Oct 2005

Displacement, tons: 2,728 full load
Dimensions, feet (metres): 320.5 × 45.9 × 14.1 *(97.7 × 14.0 × 4.3)*
Main machinery: 2 diesels; 2 shafts
Speed, knots: To be announced
Range, n miles: 4,500 at 15 kt
Guns: 1—20 mm. 2—12.7 mm MGs.
Radars: Navigation: I-band.

Comment: Two new salvage ships reported to be of the same class. Details are those published for *Jaemin VII*.

JAEMIN VII *6/2006, Korea Coast Guard* / 1159983

Kuwait

Country Overview

Formerly a British protectorate, the Kingdom of Kuwait gained independence in 1961. Situated on the northwestern coast of the Gulf, it is bordered to the north by Iraq and to the south by Saudi Arabia. The country's total area, including the islands of Bubiyan, Warbah, and Faylakah, is 6,880 square miles. It has a 269 n mile coastline with the Gulf. The capital, largest city and principal port is Kuwait City. The country was annexed by Iraq from August 1990 to February 1991when the country was liberated. Territorial seas (12 n miles) are claimed. An EEZ has not been claimed.

Headquarters Appointments

Commander of the Navy:
Major General Ahmed Yousuf Al Mulla
Deputy Commander of the Navy:
Brigadier Marzouk Hassan al Bader

Personnel

2009: 2,700 (including 500 Coast Guard)

Aviation

The Air Force operates five Eurocopter AS 532C Cougar helicopters armed with Exocet AM 39 ASMs and 40 F/A-18C/D Hornets.

Bases

Navy: Ras Al Qalayah
Coast Guard: Shuwaikh, Umm Al-Hainan, Al-Bida

PATROL FORCES

Notes: There is a requirement for two Fast Missile Strike Craft. This programme has superseded plans to acquire offshore patrol vessels armed with SSMs. The outline requirement calls for craft of 57-72 m.

1 TNC 45 TYPE (FAST ATTACK CRAFT—MISSILE) (PGGF)

Name	*No*	*Builders*	*Commissioned*
AL SANBOUK	P 4505	Lürssen, Vegesack	26 Apr 1984

Displacement, tons: 255 full load
Dimensions, feet (metres): 147.3 × 23 × 7.5 *(44.9 × 7 × 2.3)*
Main machinery: 4 MTU 16V 538TB92 diesels; 13,640 hp(m) *(10 MW)* sustained; 4 shafts
Speed, knots: 41. **Range, n miles:** 1,800 at 16 kt
Complement: 35 (5 officers)

Missiles: SSM: 4 Aerospatiale MM 40 Exocet; inertial cruise; active radar homing to 70 km *(40 n miles)* at 0.9 Mach; warhead 165 kg; sea-skimmer.
Guns: 1 OTO Melara 3 in *(76 mm)*/62 compact; 85 rds/min to 16 km *(8.6 n miles)* anti-surface; 12 km *(6.5 n miles)* anti-aircraft; weight of shell 6 kg.
2 Breda 40 mm/70 (twin); 300 rds/min to 12.5 km *(6.6 n miles)*; weight of shell 0.96 kg.
Countermeasures: Decoys: CSEE Dagaie; IR flares and chaff; H/J-band.
ESM: Racal Cutlass; intercept.
Weapons control: PEAB 9LV 228 system; Link Y; CSEE Lynx optical sight.
Radars: Air/surface search: Ericsson Sea Giraffe 50HC; G/H-band.
Fire control: Philips 9LV 200; J-band.
Navigation: Decca TM 1226C; I-band.

AL SANBOUK *3/2003, A Sharma* / 0568872

Programmes: Six ordered from Lürssen in 1980 and delivered in 1983-84.
Operational: *Al Sanbouk* escaped to Bahrain when the Iraqis invaded in August 1990, but the rest of this class was taken over by the Iraqi Navy, and either sunk or severely damaged by Allied forces in February 1991. The ship was refitted by Lürssen in 1995 and again in 2004.

8 UM ALMARADIM (COMBATTANTE I) CLASS (PBM)

Name	*No*	*Builders*	*Launched*	*Commissioned*
UM ALMARADIM	P 3711	CMN, Cherbourg	27 Feb 1997	31 July 1998
OUHA	P 3713	CMN, Cherbourg	29 May 1997	31 July 1998
FAILAKA	P 3715	CMN, Cherbourg	29 Aug 1997	19 Dec 1998
MASKAN	P 3717	CMN, Cherbourg	6 Jan 1998	19 Dec 1998
AL-AHMADI	P 3719	CMN, Cherbourg	2 Apr 1998	1 July 1999
ALFAHAHEEL	P 3721	CMN, Cherbourg	16 June 1998	1 July 1999
AL-YARMOUK	P 3723	CMN, Cherbourg	3 Mar 1999	7 June 2000
GAROH	P 3725	CMN, Cherbourg	June 1999	7 June 2000

Displacement, tons: 245 full load
Dimensions, feet (metres): 137.8 oa; 121.4 wl × 26.9 × 6.2 *(42; 37 × 8.2 × 1.9)*
Main machinery: 2 MTU 16V 538 TB93 diesels; 4,000 hp(m) *(2.94 MW)*; 2 Kamewa waterjets
Speed, knots: 30. **Range, n miles**: 1,350 at 14 kt
Complement: 29 (5 officers)

Missiles: SSM: 4 BAe Sea Skua (2 twin). Semi-active radar homing to 15 km *(8.1 n miles)* at 0.9 Mach.
SAM: Sadral sextuple launcher fitted for only.
Guns: 1 Otobreda 40 mm/70; 120 rds/min to 12.5 km *(6.8 n miles)*; weight of shell 0.96 kg. 1 Giat 20 mm M 621. 2 — 12.7 mm MGs.
Countermeasures: Decoys: 2 Dagaie Mk 2 chaff launchers fitted for only.
ESM: Thomson-CSF DR 3000 S1; intercept.
Combat data systems: Thomson-CSF TAVITAC NT; Link Y.
Weapons control: CS Defence Najir Mk 2 optronic director.
Radars: Air/surface search: Thomson-CSF MRR; 3D; G-band.
Fire control: BAe Seaspray Mk 3; I/J-band (for SSM).
Navigation: Litton Marine 20V90; I-band.

Programmes: Contract signed with CMN Cherbourg on 27 March 1995. First steel cut 9 June 1995. Names are taken from former Kuwaiti patrol craft.
Structure: Late decisions were made on the missile system which has been fitted in the last pair on build and to the remainder from 2000. Provision is also made for Simbad SAM and Dagaie decoy launchers, which may be fitted later. Positions of smaller guns are uncertain.
Operational: Training done in France. The aim is to have 10 crews capable of manning the eight ships. First four arrived in the Gulf in mid-August 1999, second four arrived in mid-2000.

AL-AHMADI *3/2007, Edward McDonnell* / 1170189

OUHA *3/2003, A Sharma* / 1133078

1 FPB 57 TYPE (FAST ATTACK CRAFT — MISSILE) (PGGF)

Name	*No*	*Builders*	*Commissioned*
ISTIQLAL	P 5702	Lürssen, Vegesack	9 Aug 1983

Displacement, tons: 410 full load
Dimensions, feet (metres): 190.6 × 24.9 × 8.9 *(58.1 × 7.6 × 2.7)*
Main machinery: 4 MTU 16V 956 TB91 diesels; 15,000 hp(m) *(11 MW)* sustained; 4 shafts
Speed, knots: 36
Range, n miles: 1,300 at 30 kt
Complement: 40 (5 officers)

Missiles: SSM: 4 Aerospatiale MM 40 Exocet; inertial cruise; active radar homing to 70 km *(40 n miles)* at 0.9 Mach; warhead 165 kg; sea-skimmer.
Guns: 1 OTO Melara 3 in *(76 mm)*/62 compact; 85 rds/min to 16 km *(8.6 n miles)* anti-surface; 12 km *(6.5 n miles)* anti-aircraft; weight of shell 6 kg.
2 Breda 40 mm/70 (twin); 300 rds/min to 12.5 km *(6.6 n miles)*; weight of shell 0.96 kg.
Mines: Fitted for minelaying.
Countermeasures: Decoys: CSEE Dagaie trainable mounting; automatic dispenser; IR flares and chaff; H/J-band.
ESM: Racal Cutlass; radar intercept.
ECM: Racal Cygnus; jammer.
Weapons control: PEAB 9LV 228 system; Link Y; CSEE Lynx optical sight.
Radars: Surface search: Marconi S 810 (after radome); I-band; range 43 km *(25 n miles)*.
Navigation: Decca TM 1226C; I-band.
Fire control: Philips 9LV 200; J-band.

Programmes: Two ordered from Lürssen in 1980.
Operational: *Istiqlal* escaped to Bahrain when the Iraqis invaded in August 1990. The second of this class was captured and sunk in February 1991. Having been laid up since 1997 *Istiqlal* was refitted at Lürssen 2003–2005. In addition to operational roles, it is also used as a training ship.

ISTIQLAL *4/2005, Michael Nitz* / 1121416

0 + (10) MK V CLASS (INTERCEPTION CRAFT) (PBF)

Displacement, tons: 54 full load
Dimensions, feet (metres): 90.0 × 18.0 × 4.75 *(27.4 × 5.5 × 1.5)*
Main machinery: 2 MTU 12V 396 TE94 diesels; 4,500 hp *(3.36 MW)*; 2 Kamewa waterjets
Speed, knots: 45
Range, n miles: 600 at 35 kt
Complement: 5 plus 16 troops
Guns: 1 Rheinmetall MLG 27 mm (remotely operated).
Countermeasures: ESM: To be announced.
Radars: Navigation: I-band.

Comment: The US Congress was advised on 17 December 2005 of the possible sale of 12 (later reduced to 10) interception craft. With a higher superstructure, the craft are to be a modified version of the US Mk V Pegasus class and are to be built by US Marine Inc, Gulfport, Mississippi. The keel of the first of class is expected to be laid in 2009.

MK V (US colours) *4/2003, A Sharma* / 0572743

AUXILIARIES

1 SAWAHIL CLASS (SUPPORT SHIP)

AL DORRAR (ex-*Qaruh*, ex-*Sawahil 35*) S 5509

Measurement, tons: 545 dwt
Dimensions, feet (metres): 181.8 × 65.6 × 6.6 *(55.4 × 20 × 2)*
Main machinery: 2 diesels; 2,400 hp(m) *(1.76 MW)*; 2 shafts
Speed, knots: 9
Complement: 40
Guns: 2 — 12.7 mm MGs.
Radars: Navigation: Racal Decca; I-band.

Comment: This is a Sawahil class oil rig replenishment and accommodation ship which was built in South Korea in 1986. She escaped to Bahrain during the Iraqi invasion, and is back in service. High-level helicopter platform aft. Used as a utility transport. Refitted in 1996/97.

AL DORRAR *3/2007, Edward McDonnell* / 1170188

COAST GUARD

PATROL FORCES

Headquarters Appointments

Director of Coast Guard:
Brigadier Jassim al Failakia

16 VICTORY TEAM P 46 CLASS (PATROL CRAFT) (PBF)

Displacement, tons: 8.5
Dimensions, feet (metres): 45.9 × 10.6 × 2.6 *(14.0 × 3.23 × 0.8)*
Main machinery: 2 Yanmar 6CX diesels; 930 hp *(690 kW)*; 2 Arneson ASD 8 surface drives
Speed, knots: 52. **Range, n miles:** 200 at 50 kt
Complement: 4
Guns: 2—12.7 mm MGs.
Radars: Navigation.

Comment: Contract for 16 craft signed in April 2004 with delivery of the final vessel expected by mid-2006. The Victory Team of Dubai design is a twin-stepped deep-'vee' monohull developed from its offshore power boats. The hull, deck and internal assembly are built from a sandwich composite comprising a glass fibre, kevlar and carbon mix to provide structural integrity at a minimum weight. The cockpit is protected by 17 mm Dyneema Ballistic panelling.

P 46 *3/2005, Victory Team* / 1127034

4 INTTISAR (OPV 310) CLASS (PB)

Name	*No*	*Builders*	*Commissioned*
INTTISAR	P 301	Australian Shipbuilding Industries	20 Jan 1993
AMAN	P 302	Australian Shipbuilding Industries	20 Jan 1993
MAIMON	P 303	Australian Shipbuilding Industries	7 Aug 1993
MOBARK	P 304	Australian Shipbuilding Industries	7 Aug 1993

Displacement, tons: 150 full load
Dimensions, feet (metres): 103.3 oa; 88.9 wl × 21.3 × 6.6 *(31.5; 27.1 × 6.5 × 2)*
Main machinery: 2 MTU 16V 396TB94 diesels; 5,800 hp(m) *(4.26 MW)* sustained; 2 shafts; 1 MTU 8V 183TE62 diesel; 750 hp(m) *(550 kW)* maximum; 1 Hamilton 422 water-jet
Speed, knots: 28. **Range, n miles:** 300 at 28 kt
Complement: 11 (3 officers)
Guns: 1 Oerlikon 20 mm. 1—12.7 mm MG.
Radars: Surface search: 2 Racal Decca; I-band.

Comment: First two ordered from Australian Shipbuilding Industries in 1991. Second pair ordered in July 1992. Steel hulls, aluminium superstructure. The third engine drives a small waterjet to provide a loiter capability. Carries an RIB. Used by the Coast Guard.

AMAN *1992, Australian Shipbuilding Industries* / 0081178

10 SUBAHI CLASS (PB)

Name	*No*	*Builders*	*Commissioned*
RAYYAN	P 300	OCEA, St Nazaire	23 Aug 2005
SUBAHI	P 308	OCEA, St Nazaire	6 Aug 2003
JABERI	P 309	OCEA, St Nazaire	Dec 2003
SAAD	P 310	OCEA, St Nazaire	Feb 2004
AHMADI	P 311	OCEA, St Nazaire	Mar 2004
NAIF	P 312	OCEA, St Nazaire	May 2004
THAFIR	P 313	OCEA, St Nazaire	July 2004
MARZOUG	P 314	OCEA, St Nazaire	Sep 2004
MASH'NOOR	P 315	OCEA, St Nazaire	Jan 2005
WADAH	P 316	OCEA, St Nazaire	May 2005

Displacement, tons: 116 full load
Dimensions, feet (metres): 115.5 × 22.3 × 4.0 *(35.2 × 6.8 × 1.2)*
Main machinery: 2 MTU 12V 4000 M70 diesels; 4,600 hp *(3.43 MW)*; 2 Kamewa waterjets
Speed, knots: 32
Range, n miles: 300 at 28 kt
Complement: 11 (3 officers)
Guns: 1 Oerlikon 20 mm. 2—12.7 mm MGs.
Radars: Sperry Bridgemaster E; I-band.

Comment: Built by OCEA, France based on Al Shaheed class design. Aluminium construction. Operated by the Coast Guard. P 300 is a VIP variant equipped with three cabins.

MARZOUG *8/2004, B Prézelin* / 1133080

RAYYAN *7/2006, B Prézelin* / 1040681

3 INSHORE PATROL CRAFT (PBR)

KASSIR T 205 **DASTOOR** T 210 **MAHROOS** T 215

Displacement, tons: to be announced
Dimensions, feet (metres): 70.9 × 19.5 × 4.9 *(21.6 × 5.96 × 1.5)*
Main machinery: 2 MTU 12V 183TE92 diesels; 1,800 hp *(1.45 MW)*; 2 shafts
Speed, knots: 25. **Range, n miles:** 325 at 25 kt
Complement: 3 + 41 passengers
Radars: Navigation: to be announced.

Comment: Order for three craft for the Coast Guard announced on 7 January 2003. Based on the 22 m craft in service with the New South Wales Police, the vessels were constructed by Austal Ships subsidiary, Image Marine and delivered in June 2004. Aluminium hull.

DASTOOR *6/2004, Austal Ships* / 0587772

3 AL SHAHEED CLASS (PB)

Name	*No*	*Builders*	*Commissioned*
AL SHAHEED	P 305	OCEA, Les Sables d'Olonne	July 1997
BAYAN	P 306	OCEA, Les Sables d'Olonne	Apr 1999
DASMAN	P 307	OCEA, Les Sables d'Olonne	2001

Displacement, tons: 104 full load
Dimensions, feet (metres): 109.3 × 23 × 4 *(33.3 × 7 × 1.2)*
Main machinery: 2 MTU 12V 396TE94; 4,352 hp(m) *(3.2 MW)* sustained; 2 shafts
Speed, knots: 30. **Range, n miles:** 360 at 25 kt
Complement: 11 (3 officers)
Guns: 1 Oerlikon 20 mm. 2—12.7 mm MGs.
Radars: Surface search: Racal Decca 20V 90TA; E/F-band.
Navigation: Racal Decca Bridgemaster ARPA; I-band.

Comment: Built by OCEA, France to FPB 100K design. Operated by the Coast Guard.

AL SHAHEED *10/1997, Ships of the World* / 0012718

33 AL-SHAALI TYPE (INSHORE PATROL CRAFT) (PBF)

Comment: Ten 10 m and 23 8.5 m patrol craft built by Al-Shaali Marine, Dubai, and delivered in June 1992. Also used by UAE Coast Guard. More Rapid Intervention patrol craft are to be acquired in due course.

12 MANTA CLASS (INSHORE PATROL CRAFT) (PBF)

1B 1501–1523 series

Displacement, tons: 10 full load
Dimensions, feet (metres): 45.9 × 12.5 × 2.3 *(14 × 3.8 × 0.7)*
Main machinery: 2 Caterpillar 3208 diesels; 810 hp(m) *(595 kW)* sustained; 2 shafts
Speed, knots: 40. **Range, n miles**: 180 at 35 kt
Complement: 4
Guns: 3 Herstal M2HB 12.7 mm MGs.
Radars: Surface search: Furuno; I-band.

Comment: Original craft ordered in September 1992 from Simonneau Marine and delivered in 1993. Aluminium construction. This version has two inboard engines. Pennant numbers are in odd number sequence. All the class reported to be inoperable due to technical problems. An underlying cause may be that the boats were fitted with inboard engines although designed for outboards.

MANTA 1501 *11/1996* / 0012719

6 COUGAR ENFORCER 40 CLASS (INSHORE PATROL CRAFT) (PBF)

Displacement, tons: 5.7 full load
Dimensions, feet (metres): 40 × 9 × 2.1 *(12.2 × 2.8 × 0.80)*
Main machinery: 2 Sabre 380 S diesels; 760 hp(m) *(559 kW)*; 2 Arneson ASD 8 surface drives; 2 shafts
Speed, knots: 45
Range, n miles: 250 at 35 kt
Complement: 4
Guns: 1 — 12.7 mm MG.
Radars: Surface search: Koden; I-band.

Comment: First one completed in July 1996 for the Coastguard by Cougar Marine, Warsash. The craft has a V monohull design.

ENFORCER 40 *7/1996, Cougar Marine* / 0081179

17 COUGAR TYPE (INSHORE PATROL CRAFT) (PBF)

Comment: Three Cat 900 (32 ft) three Predator 1100 (35 ft) and three Predator 1000 (33 ft) all powered by two Yamaha outboards (400 hp(m) *(294 kW)*). Four Type 1200 (38 ft) and four Type1300 (41 ft) all powered by two Sabre diesels (760 hp(m) *(559 kW)*). All based on the high-performance planing hull developed for racing, and acquired in 1991–92. Most have a 7.62 mm MG and a Kroden I-band radar. Used by the Coast Guard.

COUGAR 1200 *1991, Cougar Marine* / 0081180

AUXILIARIES

Notes: (1) A 95 m ship of about 2,000 tons is required to act as a support ship for patrol vessels. It would also be equipped to undertake a training role. Revised bids were submitted in June 2001 but there have been no further developments.
(2) There is a logistic craft P 140.
(3) There is an ex-oilrig supply vessel *Abdul Jaal* with pennant number B 45.

P 140 *10/2002* / 0587770

1 LOADMASTER MK 2 (LOGISTIC SUPPORT CRAFT) (LCU)

SAFFAR (ex-*Jalbout*) L 403

Displacement, tons: 420 full load
Dimensions, feet (metres): 108.3 × 33.5 × 5.7 *(33.0 × 10.2 × 1.75)*
Main machinery: 2 Caterpillar V12 diesels; 1,000 hp *(745 kW)*; 2 props
Speed, knots: 10
Complement: 7 (1 officer)
Radars: Navigation: I-band.

Comment: Built by Fairey Marine Cowes, UK and entered service in 1985. Captured by Iraqi forces in 1990 and subsequently recovered and reactivated in 1992.

SAFFAR *5/2001* / 0525907

2 AL TAHADDY CLASS (LCU)

Name	*No*	*Builders*	*Commissioned*
AL SOUMOOD	L 401	Singapore SBEC	July 1994
AL TAHADDY	L 402	Singapore SBEC	July 1994

Displacement, tons: 215 full load
Dimensions, feet (metres): 141.1 × 32.8 × 6.2 *(43 × 10 × 1.9)*
Main machinery: 2 MTU diesels; 2 shafts
Speed, knots: 13
Complement: 12
Military lift: 80 tons
Radars: Navigation: Racal Decca; I-band.

Comment: Ordered in 1993 and launched on 15 April 1994. Multipurpose supply ships with cargo tanks for fuel, fresh water, refrigerated stores and containers on the main deck. Has 3 ton crane. Capable of beaching. Used by the Coast Guard.

AL TAHADDY *1/1999, Maritime Photographic* / 0053294

1 LANDING SUPPLY CRAFT (LCU)

L 404

Measurement, tons: 300 dwt
Dimensions, feet (metres): 160.8 × ? × ? *(49.0 × ? × ?)*
Main machinery: 2 diesels; 2 shafts
Speed, knots: 12
Complement: 12
Radars: Navigation: I-band.

Comment: Contract for the design and build of a landing craft signed with Singapore Technologies Marine Ltd (ST Marine) on 8 October 2004. The multipurpose vessel is to be used for transport and supply operations as well as law enforcement duties in the Arabian Gulf. In addition to carrying roll-on roll-off goods on the main deck, the vessel is also designed to transport liquid, refrigeration and general cargoes. Delivery of the ship was made in late 2005.

1 SAWAHIL CLASS (AGH)

SAWAHIL (ex-*Sawahil 50*) B 50

Measurement, tons: 545 dwt
Dimensions, feet (metres): 181.8 × 31.5 × 6.6 *(55.4 × 9.6 × 2)*
Main machinery: 2 diesels; 2,400 hp(m) *(1.76 MW)*; 2 shafts
Speed, knots: 9
Complement: 40
Guns: 2—12.7 mm MGs.
Radars: Navigation: Racal Decca; I-band.

Comment: This is a Sawahil class oil rig replenishment and accommodation ship which was built in South Korea in 1986 and taken on by the Coast Guard in 1990. She escaped to Bahrain during the Iraqi invasion, and is back in service. High-level helicopter platform aft. Used as a utility transport. Refitted in 1996/97. A similar vessel, *Al Dorrar*, is operated by the navy.

SAWAHIL CLASS *11/1997, Kuwait Navy* / 0012721

Latvia

LATVIJAS JURAS SPEKI

Country Overview

The Republic of Latvia regained independence in 1991 after 51 years as a Soviet republic. Situated in northeastern Europe, the country has an area of 24,938 square miles and borders to the north with Estonia, east with Russia and to the south with Belarus and Lithuania. It has a 286 n mile coastline with the Baltic Sea. Riga is the capital, largest city and principal port. Territoral seas (12 n miles) are claimed but while it has claimed a 200 n mile Exclusive Economic Zone (EEZ), its limits have not been fully defined by boundary agreements.

Headquarters Appointments

Commander of the Navy:
Commander Aleksandrs Pavlovičs

Bases

Liepaja, Ventspils, Riga

Personnel

2009: 600 Navy (including Coast Guard)

Coastal Surveillance

Work began in 2002 on a maritime sea surveillance system which includes Swedish PS2-39 radars at Jurmalciens, Liepaja, Pavilosta, Ventspils, Ovisi, Mikeltornis, Kolka and Riga. The system is to become operational in 2010. The Latvian AIS (Automatic Indentification System) was commissioned in 2005 and is part of the HELCOM network that links other Baltic and Scandinavian navies. The Maritime Search and Rescue Coordination Centre (MRCC) is based at Riga.

Coast Guard

These ships have a diagonal thick white and thin white line on the hull, and have KA numbers. They operate as part of the Navy.

PATROL FORCES

4 STORM CLASS (PB)

Name	*No*	*Builders*	*Commissioned*
ZIBENS (ex-*Djerv*)	P 01 (ex-P 966)	Westermoen, Mandal	1966
LODE (ex-*Hvass*)	P 02 (ex-P 972)	Westermoen, Mandal	1966
LINGA (ex-*Gnist*)	P 03 (ex-P 979)	Bergens Mek Verksteder	1967
BULTA (ex-*Traust*)	P 04 (ex-P 973)	Bergens Mek Verksteder	1967

Displacement, tons: 135 full load
Dimensions, feet (metres): 120 × 20 × 5 *(36.5 × 6.1 × 1.5)*
Main machinery: 2 MTU MB 872A diesels; 7,200 hp(m) *(5.3 MW)* sustained; 2 shafts
Speed, knots: 32
Complement: 20 (4 officers)
Guns: 1 Bofors 40 mm/60 (P 04). 1 TAK Bofors 76 mm; 1 Bofors 40 mm/70 (P 01, P 02 and P 03).
Radars: Surface search: Racal Decca TM 1226; I-band.

Comment: P 04 disarmed and acquired from Norway on 13 December 1994 as a gun patrol craft. Recommissioned 1 February 1995 at Liepaja. 40 mm gun fitted aft in 1998. P 01, P 02 and P 03 transferred from Norway and recommissioned 11 June 2001. Service lives extended to 2010. Other craft given to Lithuania and Estonia.

ZIBENS *7/2007, Michael Nitz* / 1166754

LINGA *6/2006, E & M Laursen* / 1166811

0 + 5 SWATH PATROL SHIPS (PB)

Displacement, tons: 125 full load
Dimensions, feet (metres): 84.1 × 46.8 × 8.9 *(25.65 × 14.26 × 2.7)*
Main machinery: Diesel-electric: 2 MAN diesels; 2 motors; 2 shafts
Speed, knots: 20
Complement: To be announced
Guns: To be announced.
Radars: To be announced.

Comment: Contract signed with Abeking & Rasmussen, Lemwerder, on 23 June 2008 for the construction of five SWATH patrol vessels. The ships are to be constructed at Lemwerder and delivered in co-operation with Riga Shipyard. The vessels are derived from the design of SWATH pilot boats, on which indicative details are based, which have been in operation since 1999. The roles of the ships are to be patrol and surveillance of territorial waters and EEZ and feature a modular mission bay in the forward section. Delivery of the first-of-class is planned in December 2010.

SWATH PATROL VESSEL *4/2007, Guy Toremans* / 1335256

MINE WARFARE FORCES

5 ALKMAAR (TRIPARTITE) CLASS (MINEHUNTERS) (MHC)

Name	*No*	*Laid down*	*Launched*	*Commissioned*
IMANTA (ex-*Harlingen*)	M 04 (ex-M 854)	30 Nov 1981	9 July 1983	12 Apr 1984
VIESTURS (ex-*Scheveningen*)	M 05 (ex-M 855)	24 May 1982	2 Dec 1983	18 July 1984
TALIVALDIS (ex-*Dordrecht*)	M 06 (ex-M 852)	5 Jan 1981	26 Feb 1983	16 Nov 1983
VISVALDIS (ex-*Alkmaar*)	M 07 (ex-M 850)	30 Jan 1979	18 May 1982	28 May 1983
RŪSIŅŠ (ex-*Delfzyl*)	M 08 (ex-M 851)	29 May 1980	29 Oct 1982	17 Aug 1983

Displacement, tons: 562 standard; 595 full load
Dimensions, feet (metres): 168.9 × 29.2 × 8.5 *(51.5 × 8.9 × 2.6)*
Main machinery: 1 Stork Wärtsilä A-RUB 215X-12 diesel; 1,860 hp(m) *(1.35 MW)* sustained; 1 shaft; LIPS cp props; 2 active rudders; 2 motors; 240 hp(m) *(179 kW)*; 2 bow thrusters
Speed, knots: 12 diesel; 7 electric
Range, n miles: 3,000 at 12 kt
Complement: 29-42 depending on task

Guns: 1 Giat 20 mm. 2—12.7 mm MGs.
Countermeasures: MCM: 2 PAP 104 remote-controlled submersibles.
Combat data systems: Signaal Sewaco IX. SATCOM.
Radars: Navigation: Racal Decca TM 1229C or Consilium Selesmar MM 950; I-band.
Sonars: Thomson Sintra DUBM 21A; hull-mounted; minehunting; 100 kHz (±10 kHz).

Programmes: Originally procured for the Royal Netherlands Navy, these ships were part of the Netherlands commitment to a tripartite co-operative plan between Netherlands, Belgium and France for GRP hulled minehunters. All five ships built by van der Giessen-de Noord. Ex-*Alkmaar*, *Delfzyl* and *Dordrecht* were withdrawn from RNLN service in 2000 and *Harlingen* and *Scheveningen* in 2003. *Imanta* was handed over on 6 March 2007, *Viesturs* on 5 September 2007 and *Talivaldis* in January 2008, *Visvaldis* in October 2008 and *Rūsiņš* in June 2009.
Modernisation: The ships are to be overhauled before entering Latvian service and a mid-life upgrade may also be considered.
Structure: A 5 ton container can be shipped, stored for varying tasks-research; patrol; extended diving; drone control.
Operational: Endurance, 15 days. Automatic radar navigation system. Automatic data processing and display. EVEC 20. Decca Hi-fix positioning system. Alcatel dynamic positioning system.

IMANTA *2/2007, Michael Nitz* / 1190986

TALIVALDIS *5/2008*, Frank Findler* / 1335255

AUXILIARIES

1 VIDAR CLASS (MCCS/AG)

Name	*No*	*Builders*	*Launched*	*Commissioned*
VIRSAITIS (ex-*Vale*)	A 53 (ex-N 53)	Mjellem and Karlsen, Bergen	5 Aug 1977	10 Feb 1978

Displacement, tons: 1,500 standard; 1,673 full load
Dimensions, feet (metres): 212.6 × 39.4 × 13.1 *(64.8 × 12 × 4)*
Main machinery: 2 Wichmann 7AX diesels; 4,200 hp(m) *(3.1 MW)*; 2 shafts; auxiliary motor; 425 hp(m) *(312 kW)*; bow thruster
Speed, knots: 14
Complement: 50
Guns: 1 Bofors 40 mm/70; 300 rds/min to 12 km *(6.6 n miles)*; weight of shell 0.96 kg.
Weapons control: TVT optronic director.
Radars: Surface search: 2 Racal Decca TM 1226; I-band.
Sonars: Simrad; hull-mounted; search and attack; medium/high frequency.

Programmes: Decommissioned from Norwegian Navy in 2001 and transferred to Latvia on 27 January 2003.
Operational: Former minelayer modified to undertake mine countermeasures command and support roles. Additional tasks are likely to include training and support of diving operations.

VIRSAITIS *9/2007, Maritime Photographic* / 1167976

1 GOLIAT CLASS (PROJECT 667R) (ATA)

PERKONS A 18 (ex-H 18)

Displacement, tons: 150 full load
Dimensions, feet (metres): 70.2 × 20 × 8.5 *(21.4 × 6.1 × 2.6)*
Main machinery: 1 Buckau-Wolf 8NVD diesel; 300 hp(m) *(221 kW)*; 1 shaft
Speed, knots: 9
Complement: 8 (2 officers)

Comment: Built at Gdynia in the 1960s and transferred from Poland 16 November 1993 at Liepaja.

PERKONS *4/1995, Hartmut Ehlers* / 0506239

1 LOGISTICS VESSEL (AKS/AXL)

Name	*No*	*Builders*	*Commissioned*
VARONIS (ex-*Buyskes*)	A 90 (ex-A 904)	Boele's Scheepswerven	9 Mar 1973

Displacement, tons: 967 standard; 1,033 full load
Dimensions, feet (metres): 196.6 × 36.4 × 12 *(60 × 11.1 × 3.7)*
Main machinery: Diesel-electric; 3 Paxman 12 RPH diesel generators; 2,100 hp *(1.57 MW)*; 1 motor; 1,400 hp(m) *(1.03 MW)*; 1 shaft
Speed, knots: 13.5. **Range, n miles:** 3,000 at 11.5 kt
Complement: 43 (6 officers)
Radars: Navigation: Racal Decca 1229; I-band.
Sonars: Side scanning and wreck search.

Comment: Originally designed and operated as a hydrographic vessel by the Royal Netherlands Navy from which she was decommissioned in 2003. Donated to Latvia on 8 November 2004 for use as a logistic and training vessel. Hydrographic launches were not transferred and the ship is fitted with an inflatable boat.

VARONIS *7/2007, Freddy Phillips* / 1335254

COAST GUARD

1 LOKKI CLASS (PB)

TIIRA

Displacement, tons: 76 full load
Dimensions, feet (metres): 87.9 × 18 × 6.2 *(26.8 × 5.5 × 1.9)*
Main machinery: 2 MTU 8V 396TB82 diesels; 1,740 hp(m) *(1.28 MW)* sustained 2 MTU 8V 396TB84 diesels; 2,100 hp(m) *(1.54 MW)* sustained; 2 shafts
Speed, knots: 25
Complement: 6

Comment: Donated by Finland in 2001. Armament and sonar removed. Operated by the State Border Security Service.

LOKKI class (Finnish colours) *6/2001, Finnish Navy* / 0114723

5 KBV 236 CLASS (WPB)

KRISTAPS KA 01 (ex-KBV 244) **AUSMA** KA 07 (ex-KBV 260) **KLINTS** KA 09 (ex-KBV 250)
GAISMA KA 06 (ex-KBV 249) **SAULE** KA 08 (ex-KBV 256)

Displacement, tons: 17 full load
Dimensions, feet (metres): 63 × 13.1 × 4.3 *(19.2 × 4 × 1.3)*
Main machinery: 2 Volvo Penta TMD 100C diesels; 526 hp(m) *(387 kW)*; 2 shafts
Speed, knots: 20
Complement: 3 (1 officer)
Radars: Navigation: Raytheon or Furuno; I-band.

Comment: Former Swedish Coast Guard vessel built in 1964. First one recommissioned 5 March 1993, second pair 9 November 1993 and last pair 27 April 1994. KA 01, 06 and 09 are based at Bolderaja, 07 at Liepaja and 08 at Ventspils. Not all are identical. All belong to Coast Guard.

GAISMA *8/2004, Guy Toremans* / 0587773

SAULE *6/2006, Latvian Navy* / 1164481

1 PATROL CRAFT (WPB)

ASTRA KA 14

Displacement, tons: 22 full load
Dimensions, feet (metres): 74.8 × 18.4 × 9.2 *(22.8 × 5.6 × 2.8)*
Main machinery: 3 Scania D91 1467M diesels; 1,850 hp *(1.38 MW)*
Speed, knots: 25
Range, n miles: 575 at 25 kt
Complement: 4 (1 officer)
Radars: Navigation: Furuno; I-band.

Comment: Built in Finland in 1996. Commissioned on 12 March 2001.

ASTRA *4/2007, E & M Laursen* / 1166813

2 HARBOUR PATROL CRAFT (WPB)

KA 10 **KA 11**

Displacement, tons: 9.6 full load *(KA 10-11)*; 5.4 full load *(KA 12)*
Dimensions, feet (metres): 41.3 × 10.5 × 2 *(12.6 × 3.2 × 0.6)*
Main machinery: 1 3D6C diesel; 150 hp(m) *(110 kW)*; 1 shaft
Speed, knots: 13
Complement: 2
Radars: Navigation: Furuno; I-band.

Comment: Former USSR craft acquired in 1993-94. *KA 10* and *11* were Sverdlov class cruiser boats.

KA 11 *9/1996, Hartmut Ehlers* / 0506304

1 VALPAS CLASS (OFFSHORE PATROL VESSEL) (WPBO)

VALPAS

Displacement, tons: 545 full load
Dimensions, feet (metres): 159.1 × 27.9 × 12.5 *(48.5 × 8.5 × 3.8)*
Main machinery: 1 Werkspoor diesel; 2,000 hp(m) *(1.47 MW)*; 1 shaft; cp prop
Speed, knots: 15
Complement: 18
Guns: 1 Oerlikon 20 mm.
Sonars: Simrad SS105; active scanning; 14 kHz.

Comment: An improvement on the *Silmä* design. Built by Laivateollisuus, Turku, and commissioned 21 July 1971. Ice strengthened. Donated by Finland on 25 September 2002 and operated by State Border Security Service.

VALPAS *5/2003, J Ciślak* / 0568321

LAND-BASED MARITIME AIRCRAFT

Numbers/Type: 2 Mi-8 MTV1 Hip H.
Operational speed: 124 kt *(230 km/h)*.
Service ceiling: 16,400 ft *(5,000 m)*.
Range: 324 n miles *(600 km)*.
Role/Weapon systems: SAR aircraft acquired in 1999. Operated by the Air Force.

Mi-8 *4/2007, Freddy Philips* / 1166812

Lebanon

Country Overview

The Lebanese Republic gained independence from France in 1946 but was devastated by civil war between 1975–1991. Situated on the eastern shore of the Mediterranean Sea, it has an area of 4,015 square miles and is bordered to the north and east by Syria and to the south by Israel. It has a 121 n mile coastline with the Mediterranean Sea.

The capital, largest city and principal port is Beirut. Other important ports include Tripoli and Sidon. Territorial seas (12 n miles) are claimed but an EEZ is not claimed.

Headquarters Appointments

Navy Commander:
Rear Admiral Ali El Moallem

Personnel

2009: 1,100 (395 officers)

Bases

Beirut (HQ), Jounieh

PATROL FORCES

Notes: (1) There is a patrol craft of unknown type with pennant number 501.
(2) Ten interceptor craft were donated by the UAE in 2008. There are four 14.5 m diesel-engined craft and six 12.5 m petrol-engined craft.

501 — *5/2006, Marco Ghiglino* / 1164962

7 TRACKER MK 2 CLASS (COASTAL PATROL CRAFT) (PB)

TRIPOLI (ex-*Attacker*) 301
JOUNIEH (ex-*Fencer*) 302
BATROUN (ex-*Safeguard*) 303
BYBLOS (ex-*Chaser*) 304
BEIRUT (ex-*HunterII*) 305
SIDON (ex-*Striker*) 306
SARAFAND (ex-*Swift*) 307

Displacement, tons: 38 full load
Dimensions, feet (metres): 65.6 × 17 × 4.9 *(20 × 5.2 × 1.5)*
Main machinery: 2 Detroit 12V-71TA diesels; 840 hp *(616 kW)* sustained; 2 shafts
Speed, knots: 21. **Range, n miles:** 650 at 14 kt
Complement: 13 (1 officer)
Guns: 3—12.7 mm MGs.
Radars: Surface search: Racal Decca 1216; I-band.

Comment: All built at Cowes and Southampton. GRP construction. The ex-Royal Naval Units were originally commissioned in March 1983. Three transferred from UK on 17 July 1992 after serving as patrol craft for British bases in Cyprus. The other two were acquired in 1993. The two ex-UK Customs Craft (*Batroun* and *Sarafand*) were originally commissioned in 1979 and acquired in late 1993.

JOUNIEH — *7/2006, Marco Ghiglino* / 1164961

25 INSHORE PATROL CRAFT (PBR)

401 **403–418** **420–427**

Displacement, tons: 6 full load
Dimensions, feet (metres): 26.9 × 8.2 × 2 *(8.2 × 2.5 × 0.6)*
Main machinery: 2 Sabre 212 diesels; 212 hp(m) *(156 kW)*; 2 waterjets
Speed, knots: 22
Range, n miles: 154 at 22 kt
Complement: 4
Guns: 3—5.56 mm MGs.

Comment: M-boot type used by the US Army on German rivers and 27 were transferred in January 1994. Called Combat Support Boats, there are 20 operational and five laid up. Two were decommissioned in 2002.

403 — *7/2006, Marco Ghiglino* / 1164960

1 PATROL SHIP (PB)

AAMCHIT (ex-*Bremen 2*)

Measurement, tons: To be announced
Dimensions, feet (metres): 111.5 × 17.1 × 5.9 *(34.0 × 5.2 × 1.8)*
Main machinery: 2 diesels; 3,900 hp *(2.9 MW)*; 2 shafts
Speed, knots: 28
Range, n miles: To be announced
Complement: To be announced

Comment: Former City of Bremen Maritime Police vessel built by Schiffswerft Ernst Menzer, Hamburg-Bergedorf in 1974 and transferred to Lebanon on 7 June 2007. The contract includes a training package.

AAMCHIT (German police colours) — *8/2006, Frank Findler* / 1167959

1 PATROL SHIP (PB)

NAQUORA (ex-*Bremen 9*)

Displacement, tons: 32 full load
Dimensions, feet (metres): 65.6 × 18.4 × 4.8 *(20.0 × 5.6 × 1.45)*
Main machinery: 2 MTU 12V 183TE92 diesels; 1,970 hp *(1.5 MW)*; 2 shafts
Speed, knots: 32
Range, n miles: 300 at 25 kt
Complement: 6

Comment: Former City of Bremen Maritime Police vessel built by Fassmer Werft in 1992 and transferred to Lebanon on 7 June 2007. Aluminium construction. The contract includes a training package. The design includes space for a 3 m interceptor craft.

NAQUORA (outboard ship) — *4/2007, Frank Findler* / 1167958

1 PATROL SHIP (PB)

Name	*No*	*Builders*	*Commissioned*
TABARJA (ex-*Bergen*)	– (ex-Y 838)	Lürssen, Vegesack	19 May 1994

Displacement, tons: 126 full load
Dimensions, feet (metres): 91.2 × 19.7 × 4.6 *(27.8 × 6.0 × 1.4)*
Main machinery: 2 KHD TBD 234 diesels; 2,054 hp *(1.51 MW)*; 2 shafts
Speed, knots: 16
Complement: 15

Comment: Former German Range Safety Craft donated by the German Navy on 17 June 2008.

TABARJA (German colours) *6/2007, Michael Nitz* / 1166744

AMPHIBIOUS FORCES

2 FRENCH EDIC CLASS (LCT)

Name	*No*	*Builders*	*Commissioned*
SOUR	21	SFCN, Villeneuve la Garonne	28 Mar 1985
DAMOUR	22	SFCN, Villeneuve la Garonne	28 Mar 1985

Displacement, tons: 670 full load
Dimensions, feet (metres): 193.5 × 39.2 × 4.2 *(59 × 12 × 1.3)*
Main machinery: 2 SACM MGO 175 V12 M1 diesels; 1,200 hp(m) *(882 kW)*; 2 shafts
Speed, knots: 10. **Range, n miles:** 1,800 at 9 kt
Complement: 20 (2 officers)
Military lift: 96 troops; 11 trucks or 8 APCs
Guns: 2 Oerlikon 20 mm. 1—81 mm mortar. 2—12.7 mm MGs. 1—7.62 mm MG.
Radars: Navigation: Decca; I-band.

Comment: Both were damaged in early 1990 but repaired in 1991 and are fully operational. Used by the Marine Regiment formed in 1997.

DAMOUR *5/2006, Marco Ghiglino* / 1164964

Libya

Country Overview

The Socialist People's Libyan Arab Jamahiriyah is situated in north Africa. With an area of 679,362 square miles, it has a 956 n mile coastline with the Mediterranean Sea and is bordered to the east by Egypt, to the south by Sudan, Chad and Niger and to the west by Algeria and Tunisia. The capital and largest city is Tripoli which, with Benghazi, is a principal port. Territorial seas (12 n miles) are claimed. An EEZ has not been claimed. The status of the Gulf of Sirte, which Libya claims as internal waters, is disputed by numerous states including USA, United Kingdom, France, Italy and Greece.

Headquarters Appointments

Chief of Staff Navy:
Rear Admiral Muhammad al Shaybani Ahmad al Suwaihili

Headquarters Appointments—*continued*

Deputy Chief of Staff Navy:
Captain al-Din Mufti

Personnel

(a) 2009: 8,000 officers and ratings, including Coast Guard
(b) Voluntary service

Bases

Naval HQ at Al Khums.
Operating Ports at Tripoli, Darnah (Derna) and Benghazi.
Naval bases at Al Khums and Tobruq.
Submarine base at Ras Hilal.
Naval air station at Al Girdabiyah.
Naval infantry battalion at Sidi Bilal.

Coast Defence

Batteries of truck-mounted SS-C-3 Styx missiles.

General

Specialist teams in unconventional warfare are a threat and most Libyan vessels can lay mines, but overall operational effectiveness is very low, not least because of poor maintenance and stores support. Sanctions imposed by the UN in April 1992 were reported as 'destroying' the Fleet. The situation improved in late 1995 when mostly Ukrainian technicians were hired on maintenance contracts. Further progress was reported in 1998 and the situation could improve following the lifting of UN sanctions on 12 September 2003. The EU arms embargo was lifted on 11 October 2004 although export licences are still required.

SUBMARINES

Notes: Acquisition of up to two Type 636 diesel submarines from Russia is reported to be under consideration.

2 FOXTROT CLASS (PROJECT 641) (SS)

AL KHYBER 315 **AL HUNAIN** 316

Displacement, tons: 1,950 surfaced; 2,475 dived
Dimensions, feet (metres): 299.5 × 24.6 × 19.7 *(91.3 × 7.5 × 6)*
Main machinery: Diesel-electric; 3 Type 37-D diesels (1 × 2,700 and 2 × 1,350); 6,000 hp(m) *(4.4 MW)*; 3 motors; 5,400 hp(m) *(3.97 MW)*; 3 shafts; 1 auxiliary motor; 140 hp(m) *(103 kW)*
Speed, knots: 16 surfaced; 15 dived
Range, n miles: 20,000 at 8 kt surfaced; 380 at 2 kt dived
Complement: 75 (8 officers)

Torpedoes: 10—21 in *(533 mm)* (6 bow, 4 stern) tubes. SAET-60; passive homing to 15 km *(8.1 n miles)* at 40 kt; warhead 400 kg, and SET-65E; active/passive homing to 15 km *(8.1 n miles)* at 40 kt; warhead 205 kg or Type 53-56. Total of 22 torpedoes.
Mines: 44 in place of torpedoes.
Countermeasures: ESM: Stop Light; radar warning.
Radars: Surface search: Snoop Tray; I-band.
Sonars: Herkules; hull-mounted; active; medium frequency. Feniks; hull-mounted; passive.

Programmes: Six of the class originally transferred from USSR; this last one in April 1982.
Operational: Libyan crews trained in the USSR and much of the maintenance was done by Russian personnel. No routine patrols have been seen since 1984 although both boats have been reported to conduct surface patrols. One submarine was reported to be in dry dock at Tripoli during 2003 and *Al Khyber* reportedto be sea-going. However a return to full operational capability remains highly unlikely.

FOXTROT *6/1992, van Ginderen Collection* / 0081190

FRIGATES

Notes: (1) The *Dat Assawari* F 211 is a training hulk alongside in Tripoli.
(2) Two decommissioned Koni-class frigates may be acquired from Montenegro, possibly as spares.

2 KONI (PROJECT 1159) CLASS (FFGM)

AL HANI PF 212 **AL QIRDABIYAH** PF 213

Displacement, tons: 1,440 standard; 1,900 full load
Dimensions, feet (metres): 316.3 × 41.3 × 11.5 *(96.4 × 12.6 × 3.5)*
Main machinery: CODAG; 1 SGW, Nikolayev, M8B gas turbine (centre shaft); 18,000 hp(m) *(13.25 MW)* sustained; 2 Russki B-68 diesels; 15,820 hp(m) *(11.63 MW)* sustained; 3 shafts
Speed, knots: 27 on gas; 22 on diesel
Range, n miles: 1,800 at 14 kt
Complement: 120

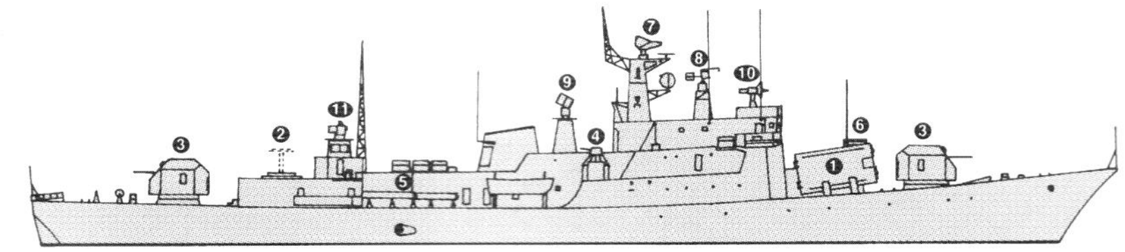

AL HANI *(Scale 1 : 900), Ian Sturton* / 0506050

Missiles: SSM: 4 Soviet SS-N-2C Styx (2 twin) launchers ❶; active radar/IR homing to 83 km *(45 n miles)* at 0.9 Mach; warhead 513 kg; sea-skimmer at end of run.
SAM: SA-N-4 Gecko twin launcher ❷; semi-active radar homing to 15 km *(8 n miles)* at 2.5 Mach; altitude 9.1-3,048 m *(29.5-10,000 ft)*; warhead 50 kg; 20 missiles.
Guns: 4 USSR 3 in *(76 mm)*/59 AK 726 (2 twin) ❸; 90 rds/min to 16 km *(8.5 n miles)* anti-surface; weight of shell 5.9 kg.
4 USSR 30 mm/65 (2 twin) automatic ❹; 500 rds/min to 2 km *(1.1 n miles)*; weight of shell 0.54 kg.
Torpedoes: 4 — 406 mm (2 twin) tubes amidships ❺. USET-95; active/passive homing to 10 km *(5.5 n miles)* at 30 kt; warhead 100 kg.
A/S mortars: 1 RBU 6000 12-tubed trainable launcher ❻; automatic loading; range 6,000 m; warhead 31 kg.
Depth charges: 2 racks.
Mines: Capacity for 20.
Countermeasures: Decoys: 2 — 16-barrelled chaff launchers. Towed torpedo decoys.
ESM: 2 Watch Dog; radar warning.
Radars: Air search: Strut Curve ❼; F-band; range 110 km *(60 n miles)* for 2 m² target.
Surface search: Plank Shave ❽; E/F-band.
Navigation: Don 2; I-band.
Fire control: Drum Tilt ❾; H/I-band (for 30 mm).
Hawk Screech ❿; I-band; range 27 km *(15 n miles)* (for 76 mm).
Pop Group ⓫; F/H/I-band (for SAM).
IFF: High Pole B. Square Head.
Sonars: Hercules (MG 322); hull-mounted; active search and attack; medium frequency.

Programmes: Type III Konis built at Zelenodolsk and transferred from the Black Sea. 212 commissioned 28 June 1986 and 213 on 24 October 1987.
Structure: SSMs mounted either side of small deckhouse on forecastle behind gun. A deckhouse amidships contains air conditioning machinery. Changes to the standard Koni include SSM, four torpedo tubes, only one RBU 6000 and Plank Shave surface search and target indication radar. Camouflage paint applied in 1991.
Operational: One of the class fired an exercise Styx missile in September 1999. 213 has been reported active but the operational status of 212 is doubtful.

AL HANI *7/1999, van Ginderen Collection* / 0081191

CORVETTES

1 NANUCHKA II (PROJECT 1234) CLASS (MISSILE CORVETTE) (FSGM)

TARIQ IBN ZIYAD (ex-*Ean Mara*) 416

Displacement, tons: 660 full load
Dimensions, feet (metres): 194.5 × 38.7 × 8.5 *(59.3 × 11.8 × 2.6)*
Main machinery: 6 M 504 diesels; 26,112 hp(m) *(19.2 MW)*; 3 shafts
Speed, knots: 33. **Range, n miles:** 2,500 at 12 kt; 900 at 31 kt
Complement: 42 (7 officers)

Missiles: SSM: 4 Soviet SS-N-2C Styx launchers; auto-pilot; active radar/IR homing to 83 km *(45 n miles)* at 0.9 Mach; warhead 513 kg HE; sea-skimmer at end of run.
SAM: SA-N-4 Gecko twin launcher; semi-active radar homing to 15 km *(8 n miles)* at 2.5 Mach; altitude 9.1-3,048 m *(29.5-10,000 ft)*; warhead 50 kg HE; 20 missiles.
Guns: 2 USSR 57 mm/75 AK 725 (twin) automatic; 120 rds/min to 12.7 km *(6.8 n miles)*; weight of shell 2.8 kg.
Countermeasures: Decoys: 2 chaff 16-barrelled launchers.
ESM: Bell Tap; radar warning.
Radars: Surface search: Square Tie; I-band (Bandstand radome).
Navigation: Don 2; I-band.
Fire control: Muff Cob; G/H-band.
Pop Group; F/H/I-band (for SAM).

Programmes: First transferred from USSR in October 1981; second in February 1983; third in February 1984; fourth in September 1985.
Structure: Camouflage paint applied in 1991 but have been reported as having blue hulls since 1993.
Operational: *Ean Zaquit* (419) sunk on 24 March 1986. *Ean Mara* (416) severely damaged on 25 March 1986 by forces of the US Sixth Fleet; repaired in Leningrad and returned to Libya in early 1991 as the *Tariq Ibn Ziyad*. *Ean Al Gazala* (417) probably in reserve as a source of spares and *Ean Zarrah* (418) reported non-operational. Reports of refit plans are doubtful.

TARIQ IBN ZIYAD *7/1991, van Ginderen Collection* / 0081192

LAND-BASED MARITIME AIRCRAFT

Numbers/Type: 2/5 Aerospatiale SA 321 Frelon/SA 324 Super Frelon.
Operational speed: 134 kt *(248 km/h)*.
Service ceiling: 10,000 ft *(3,050 m)*.
Range: 440 n miles *(815 km)*.
Role/Weapon systems: Obsolescent helicopter; Air Force manned but used for naval support tasks. Most are non-operational due to lack of spares. Sensors: None. Weapons: Fitted for Exocet AM 39.

Numbers/Type: 5 Aerospatiale SA 316B Alouette III.
Operational speed: 113 kt *(210 km/h)*.
Service ceiling: 10,500 ft *(3,200 m)*.
Range: 290 n miles *(540 km)*.
Role/Weapon systems: Support helicopter. Probably non-operational. Another six are used by the Police. Sensors: None. Weapons: Unarmed.

PATROL FORCES

Notes: (1) More than 50 remote-control explosive craft acquired from Cyprus. Based on Q-Boats with Q-26 GRP hulls and speed of about 30 kt. Also reported that 15 31 ft craft delivered by Storebro, and 60 more built locally are similarly adapted. No reports of recent activity.
(2) There is also a Hamelin 37 m patrol craft *Al Kifah* 206 based at Tripoli.
(3) Six 30 m patrol craft had been acquired for the Libyan Coast Guard by late 2007. The PV30 craft were constructed by Adria-Mar Shipbuilding, Croatia. The vessels are capable of 33 kt.

4 OSA II (PROJECT 205) CLASS (FAST ATTACK CRAFT—MISSILE) (PTFG)

AL ZUARA 513 **AL RUHA** 515 **AL FIKAH** 523 **AL MATHUR** 525

Displacement, tons: 245 full load
Dimensions, feet (metres): 126.6 × 24.9 × 8.8 *(38.6 × 7.6 × 2.7)*
Main machinery: 3 Type M 504 diesels; 10,800 hp(m) *(7.94 MW)* sustained; 3 shafts
Speed, knots: 37
Range, n miles: 800 at 30 kt; 500 at 35 kt
Complement: 30

Missiles: SSM: 4 Soviet SS-N-2C Styx; active radar or IR homing to 83 km *(45 n miles)* at 0.9 Mach; warhead 513 kg HE; sea-skimmer at end of run.
Guns: 4 USSR 30 mm/65 (2 twin) automatic; 500 rds/min to 5 km *(2.7 n miles)*; weight of shell 0.54 kg.
Radars: Surface search: Square Tie; I-band; range 73 km *(45 n miles)*.
Fire control: Drum tilt; H/I-band.
IFF: 2 Square Head. High Pole.

Programmes: The first craft arrived from USSR in October 1976, four more in August–October 1977, a sixth in July 1978, three in September-October 1979, one in April 1980, one in May 1980 (521) and one in July 1980 (529).
Structure: Some painted with camouflage stripes in 1991 and some were given blue hulls in 1993.
Operational: There have been few sightings of these ships at sea in recent years. One fired an exercise Styx missile in September 1999. The following eight craft are reported non-operational: *Al Katum* 511, *Al Baida* 517, *Al Nabha* 519, *Al Safhra* 521, *Al Mosha* 527, *Al Sakab* 529, *Al Bitar* 531 and *Al Sadad* 533. Based at Tobruk.

AL MATHUR ***1993*** / 0506157

7 COMBATTANTE II G CLASS (FAST ATTACK CRAFT—MISSILE) (PGGF)

SHEHAB (ex-*Beir Gtifa*) 522
WAHAG (ex-*Beir Gzir*) 524
SHOUAIAI (ex-*Beir Algandula*) 528
SHOULA (ex-*Beir Ktitat*) 532
SHAFAK (ex-*Beir Alkrarim*) 534
RAD (ex-*Beir Alkur*) 538
LAHEEB (ex-*Beir Alkuefat*) 542

Displacement, tons: 311 full load
Dimensions, feet (metres): 160.7 × 23.3 × 6.6 *(49 × 7.1 × 2)*
Main machinery: 4 MTU 20V 538 TB91 diesels; 15,360 hp(m) *(11.29 MW)* sustained; 4 shafts
Speed, knots: 39. **Range, n miles:** 1,600 at 15 kt
Complement: 27

Missiles: SSM: 4 OTO Melara/Matra Otomat Mk 2 (TG1); active radar homing to 80 km *(43.2 n miles)* at 0.9 Mach; warhead 210 kg.
Guns: 1 OTO Melara 3 in *(76 mm)*/62 compact; 85 rds/min to 16 km *(8.6 n miles)* anti-surface; 12 km *(6.8 n miles)* anti-aircraft; weight of shell 6 kg.
2 Breda 40 mm/70 (twin); 300 or 450 rds/min to 12.5 km *(6.8 n miles)* anti-surface; 4 km *(2.2 n miles)* anti-aircraft; weight of shell 0.96 kg.
Weapons control: CSEE Panda director. Thomson-CSF Vega II system.
Radars: Surface search: Thomson-CSF Triton; G-band; range 33 km *(18 n miles)* for 2 m^2 target.
Fire control: Thomson-CSF Castor IIB; I-band; range 15 km *(8 n miles)* (associated with Vega fire-control system).

Programmes: Ordered from CMN Cherbourg in May 1977. 518 completed February 1982; 522 3 April 1982; 524 29 May 1982; 528 5 September 1982; 532 29 October 1982; 534 17 December 1982; 542 29 July 1983.
Structure: Steel hull with alloy superstructure.
Operational: *Waheed* (526) sunk on 24 March 1986 and one other severely damaged on 25 March 1986 by forces of the US Sixth Fleet. 524, 534 and 542 visited Malta in late 2001. The following are reported non-operational: *Sharara* 518 and *Bark* 536. *Rad* 538 is reported in poor condition. *Laheeb* refitted by Adria-Mar Shipbuilding, Croatia, in 2008. Further craft expected to follow.

SHAFAK ***1993*** / 0506156

AMPHIBIOUS FORCES

Notes: (1) Three Polochny D class landing craft (*Ibn Al Hadrami* 112, *Ibn Umayaa* 116 and *Ibn Al Farat* 118) are in reserve and are unlikely to be restored to operational status.
(2) Three Turkish Ç 107 class LCTs (*Ibn Al Idrisi* 130, *Ibn Marwan* 131 and *El Kobayat* 132) are non-operational.

2 PS 700 CLASS (LSTH)

Name	*No*	*Builders*	*Commissioned*
IBN OUF	132	CNI de la Mediterranée	11 Mar 1977
IBN HARITHA	134	CNI de la Mediterranée	10 Mar 1978

Displacement, tons: 2,800 full load
Dimensions, feet (metres): 326.4 × 51.2 × 7.9 *(99.5 × 15.6 × 2.4)*
Main machinery: 2 SEMT-Pielstick 16 PA4 V 185 diesels; 5,344 hp(m) *(3.93 MW)* sustained; 2 shafts; cp props
Speed, knots: 15.4
Range, n miles: 4,000 at 14 kt
Complement: 35
Military lift: 240 troops; 11 tanks
Weapons control: CSEE Panda director.
Radars: Air search: Thomson-CSF Triton; D-band.
Surface search: Decca 1226; I-band.
Helicopters: 1 Aerospatiale SA 316B Alouette III.

Comment: 132 laid down 1 April 1976 and 134 laid down 18 April 1977, launched 18 October 1977. Both ships refitted in Croatia in 2008.

IBN HARITHA ***5/2004, Italian Navy*** / 1153376

2 SLINGSBY SAH 2200 (HOVERCRAFT) (UCAC)

Displacement, tons: 5.5 full load
Dimensions, feet (metres): 34.8 × 13.8 *(10.6 × 4.2)*
Main machinery: 1 diesel; 300 hp(m) *(224 kW)*
Speed, knots: 40
Range, n miles: 400 at 30 kt
Complement: 2
Military lift: 2.2 tons
Guns: 1—12.7 mm MG.
Radars: Surface search: I-band.

Comment: Ordered in September 1999 for delivery to Greece in mid-2000 and subsequently to Libya in 2001.

MINE WARFARE FORCES

4 NATYA (PROJECT 266ME) CLASS (OCEAN MINESWEEPERS) (MSO)

RAS AL FULAIJAH 117 **RAS AL QULA** 119 **RAS AL MASSAD** 123 **RAS AL HANI** 125

Displacement, tons: 804 full load
Dimensions, feet (metres): 200.1 × 33.5 × 10.8 *(61 × 10.2 × 3)*
Main machinery: 2 Type M 504 diesels; 5,000 hp(m) *(3.67 MW)* sustained; 2 shafts; cp props
Speed, knots: 16. **Range, n miles:** 3,000 at 12 kt
Complement: 67
Guns: 4 USSR 30 mm/65 (2 twin) automatic; 500 rds/min to 5 km *(2.7 n miles)*; weight of shell 0.54 kg.
4 USSR 25 mm/60 (2 twin); 270 rds/min to 3 km *(1.6 n miles)*; weight of shell 0.34 kg.
A/S mortars: 2 RBU 1200 5-tubed fixed launchers; elevating; range 1,200 m; warhead 34 kg.
Mines: 10.
Countermeasures: MCM: 1 GKT-2 contact sweep; 1 AT-2 acoustic sweep; 1 TEM-3 magnetic sweep.
Radars: Surface search: Don 2; I-band.
Fire control: Drum Tilt; H/I-band.
IFF: 2 Square Head. 1 High Pole B.
Sonars: Hull-mounted; active search; high frequency.

Comment: Transferred from USSR between 1981 and 1986. At least one of the class painted in green striped camouflage in 1991. Others may have blue hulls. Capable of magnetic, acoustic and mechanical sweeping. Mostly used for coastal patrols and never observed minesweeping. *Ras Al Massad* has been used for training cruises. The following are non-operational: *Al Tiyar* 111, *Al Isar* 113, *Ras Al Hamman* 115 and *Ras Al Madwar* 121.

NATYA ***2/1988*** / 0506051

AUXILIARIES

Notes: (1) *Zeltin* 711 is used as an alongside tender for patrol forces but is no longer capable of going to sea.
(2) The Vosper class *Tobruk* is used for alongside training.
(3) There are about eight 60 m trawlers employed on intelligence collection tasks. They include: *Al Nasim, Al Rabat, Al Sahfq, Al Yakada* and *Zarqa al Yammana.*

10 TRANSPORTS (AG/ML)

GARYOUNIS (ex-*Mashu*)	**GARNATA** (ex-*Monte Granada*)	**HANNA**
EL TEMSAH	**TOLETELA** (ex-*Monte Toledo*)	**GHARDIA**
DERNA	**RAHMA** (ex-*Krol*)	
GHAT	**LA GRAZIETTA**	

Measurement, tons: 2,412 gross
Dimensions, feet (metres): 546.3 × 80.1 × 21.3 *(166.5 × 24.4 × 6.5)*
Main machinery: 2 SEMT-Pielstick diesels; 20,800 hp(m) *(15.29 MW)*; 2 shafts; bow thruster
Speed, knots: 20

Comment: Details are for *Garyounis*, a converted Ro-Ro passenger/car ferry used as a training vessel in 1989. In addition the 117 m *El Temsah* was refitted and another four of these vessels are of Ro-Ro design. All are in regular civilian service and *Garyounis* is also used by the military. All have minelaying potential.

GARNATA *8/2004, Martin Mokrus* / 1153372

2 FLOATING DOCKS

Comment: One of 5,000 tons capacity at Tripoli. One of 3,200 tons capacity acquired in April 1985.

1 SPASILAC CLASS (SALVAGE SHIP) (ARS)

AL MUNJED (ex-*Zlatica*) 722

Displacement, tons: 1,590 full load
Dimensions, feet (metres): 182 × 39.4 × 14.1 *(55.5 × 12 × 4.3)*
Main machinery: 2 diesels; 4,340 hp(m) *(3.19 MW)*; 2 shafts; cp props; bow thruster
Speed, knots: 13
Range, n miles: 4,000 at 12 kt
Complement: 50
Guns: 4—12.7 mm MGs. Can also be fitted with 8—20 mm (2 quad) and 2—20 mm.
Radars: Surface search: Racal Decca; I-band.

Comment: Transferred from Yugoslavia in 1982. Fitted for firefighting, towing and submarine rescue-carries recompression chamber. Built at Tito SY, Belgrade. Used as the lead vessel for the 1998 training cruise. Refitted in Croatia in 2008.

SPASILAC (Iraqi colours) *1988, Peter Jones* / 0506054

1 YELVA (PROJECT 535M) CLASS (DIVING TENDER) (YDT)

AL MANOUD PVM 917

Displacement, tons: 300 full load
Dimensions, feet (metres): 134.2 × 26.2 × 6.6 *(40.9 × 8 × 2)*
Main machinery: 2 Type 3-D-12A diesels; 630 hp(m) *(463 kW)* sustained; 2 shafts
Speed, knots: 12.5
Complement: 30
Radars: Navigation: Spin trough; I-band.
IFF: High Pole.

Comment: Built in early 1970s. Transferred from USSR December 1977. Carries two 1.5 ton cranes and has a portable decompression chamber. Based at Tripoli but its operational status is unknown.

YELVA (Russian colours) *7/1996, Hartmut Ehlers* / 0506306

TUGS

6 COASTAL TUGS (YTB)

RAS EL HILAL A 31	**AL KERIAT**	– **A 33**	– **A 35**
AL AHWEIRIF A 32	**AL TABKAH**	– **A 34**	

Comment: Three 34.8 m built in Portugal in 1976–78. The other three are 26.6 m built in the Netherlands in 1979–80. All are in service.

Lithuania

KARINES JURU PAJEGOS

Country Overview

The Republic of Lithuania regained independence in 1991 after 51 years as a Soviet republic. Situated in northeastern Europe, the country has an area of 25,175 square miles and borders to the north with Latvia, to the east and south with Belarus, to the southwest with Poland and the Russian exclave of Kaliningrad. It has a 58 n mile coastline with the Baltic Sea. Vilnius is the capital and largest city while Klaipeda is the principal port. Territorial seas (12 n miles) are claimed but while it has claimed a 200 n mile Exclusive Economic Zone (EEZ), its limits have not been fully defined by boundary agreements.

Headquarters Appointments

Commander of the Navy:
Commander Arūras Stank
Chief of Staff:
Commander Eduard Karlonas

Personnel

2009: 643

Bases

Klaipeda

State Border Police (Pakrančių Apsauga)

Coast Guard Force formed in late 1992. Name changed in 1996 to Border Police. Vessels have one thick and one thin diagonal yellow stripe on the hull.

FRIGATES

1 GRISHA III (ALBATROS) CLASS (PROJECT 1124M) (FFLM)

Name	*No*	*Builders*	*Commissioned*	*Recommissioned*
AUKŠTAITIS	F 12 (ex-MPK 44)	Kiev Shipyard	15 Aug 1980	6 Nov 1992

Displacement, tons: 950 standard; 1,200 full load
Dimensions, feet (metres): 233.6 × 32.2 × 12.1 *(71.2 × 9.8 × 3.7)*
Main machinery: CODAG; 1 gas-turbine; 15,000 hp(m) *(11 MW)*; 2 diesels; 16,000 hp(m) *(11.8 MW)*; 3 shafts
Speed, knots: 30
Range, n miles: 2,500 at 14 kt diesels; 950 at 27 kt
Complement: 67 (9 officers)

Missiles: SAM: SA-N-4 Gecko twin launcher ❶; semi-active radar homing to 15 km *(8 n miles)* at 2.5 Mach; warhead 50 kg; altitude 9.1-3,048 m *(30-10,000 ft)*; 20 missiles.
Guns: 2—57 mm/75 AK 725 (twin) ❷; 120 rds/min to 12.7 km *(6.8 n miles)*; weight of shell 2.8 kg.
1—30 mm/65 ❸; 6 barrels; 3,000 rds/min combined to 2 km.
2—12.7 mm MGs.
A/S mortars: 2 RBU 6000 12-tubed trainable ❹; range 6,000 m; warhead 31 kg.
Depth charges: 2 racks (12).
Mines: Capacity for 18 in lieu of depth charges.
Countermeasures: Decoys: 1 PK-16 (F 11) chaff launcher.
ESM: 2 Watch Dog.

AUKŠTAITIS *(Scale 1 : 600), Ian Sturton* / 0587562

Radars: Air/surface search: Strut Curve ❺; F-band.
Navigation: Terma Scanter; I-band.
Fire control: Pop Group ❻; F/H/I-band (for SA-N-4). Bass Tilt ❼; H/I-band (for guns).
Sonars: Bull Nose; hull-mounted; active search and attack; high/medium frequency.

Programmes: Transferred from the Russian Baltic Fleet in 1993.
Modernisation: Torpedo tubes removed from F 12 in 1996 and from F 11 in 1997.
Operational: *Žemaitis* was decommissioned in 2008. *Aukštaitis* is to be decommissioned in 2009.

GRISHA III CLASS *6/2005, Frank Findler* / 1133087

GRISHA III CLASS *6/2004, Harald Carstens* / 0589759

PATROL FORCES

2 STORM CLASS (PB)

Name	*No*	*Builders*	*Commissioned*
SELIS (ex-*Skudd*)	P 32 (ex-P 967)	Bergens Mek Verksteder	1966
SKALVIS (ex-*Steil*)	P 33 (ex-P 969)	Westermoen, Mandal	1967

Displacement, tons: 138 full load
Dimensions, feet (metres): 120 × 20.3 × 5.9 *(36.5 × 6.2 × 1.8)*
Main machinery: 2 MTU MB 16V 538 TB90 diesels; 6,000 hp(m) *(4.41 MW)* sustained; 2 shafts
Speed, knots: 32
Range, n miles: 550 at 32 kt
Complement: 23 (4 officers)
Guns: 1 Bofors 3 in *(76 mm)*/50; 30° elevation; 30 rds/min to 13 km *(7 n miles)*. Surface fire only; weight of shell 5.9 kg.
1 Bofors 40 mm/70; 90° elevation; 300 rds/min to 12 km *(6.6 n miles)*; weight of shell 0.96 kg.
Weapons control: TVT 300 optronic tracker.
Radars: Furuno; I-band.

Comment: P 32 and P 33 transferred from Norway in June 2001. P 31 decommissioned in 2007. Others of the class given to Latvia and Estonia.

SKALVIS *4/2002, Guy Toremans* / 0524995

2 + 1 FLYVEFISKEN CLASS (PBO)

Name	*No*	*Builders*	*Commissioned*
ŽEMAITIS (ex-*Flyvefisken*)	P 11 (ex-P 550)	Danyard A/S, Aalborg	19 Dec 1989
DJUKAS (ex-*Hajen*)	P 12 (ex-P 551)	Danyard A/S, Aalborg	19 July 1990
– (ex-*Lommen*)	– (ex-P 559)	Danyard A/S, Aalborg	21 Jan 1994

Displacement, tons: 480 full load
Dimensions, feet (metres): 177.2 × 29.5 × 8.2 *(54 × 9 × 2.5)*
Main machinery: 2 diesels; 5,800 hp(m) *(4.26 MW)* sustained; 2 shafts; cp props; bow thruster
Speed, knots: 20
Range, n miles: 2,400 at 18 kt
Complement: 29

Guns: 1 OTO Melara 3 in *(76 mm)*/62 Super Rapid; dual purpose; 120 rds/min to 16 km *(8.7 n miles)*.
2—12.7 mm MGs.
Countermeasures: To be announced.
Combat data systems: To be announced.
Weapons control: To be announced.
Radars: Surface search: Terma Scanter Mil; I-band.
Navigation: Furuno; I-band.
Fire control: To be announced.

Programmes: Standard Flex 300 ships built for the Danish Navy to meet requirement for re-role by the interchange of mission-specific containers. Three ships decommissioned in 2005. Following an agreement in March 2007, ex-*Flyvefisken* and ex-*Hajen* were handed over on 30 May 2008 and 28 January 2009 respectively. Ex-*Lommen* is to be transferred in 2009. Of the four container positions, one crane module is to be installed in an aft position while the 76 mm gun is to occupy the forward position. The other two positions are to be covered. The original CODAG propulsion system is to be replaced by two diesel engines powering two of the three shafts.
Operational: Likely to be employed on offshore patrol duties.

DJUKAS *12/2008*, Per Körnefeldt* / 1335794

1 COASTAL PATROL CRAFT (PB/YFS)

HK 21 (ex-*Vilnele*)

Displacement, tons: 88 full load
Dimensions, feet (metres): 75.8 × 19 × 5.9 *(23.1 × 5.8 × 1.8)*
Main machinery: 2 diesels; 600 hp(m) *(441 kW)*; 2 shafts
Speed, knots: 12
Complement: 5
Guns: 1—12.7 mm MG.

Comment: Acquired in 1992. Used as a hydrographic vessel.

HK 21 *6/2004, Lithuanian Navy* / 0589761

MINE WARFARE FORCES

2 LINDAU (TYPE 331) CLASS (MINEHUNTERS) (MHC)

Name	*No*	*Builders*	*Commissioned*
SŪDUVIS (ex-*Koblenz*)	M 52 (ex-M 1071)	Burmester, Bremen	8 July 1958
KURŠIS (ex-*Marburg*)	M 51 (ex-M 1080)	Burmester, Bremen	11 June 1959

Displacement, tons: 463 full load
Dimensions, feet (metres): 154.5 × 27.2 × 9.8 (9.2 Troika) *(47.1 × 8.3 × 3) (2.8)*
Main machinery: 2 MTU MD diesels; 4,000 hp(m) *(2.94 MW)*; 2 shafts
Speed, knots: 16.5. **Range, n miles:** 850 at 16.5 kt
Complement: 42 (5 officers)
Guns: 1 Bofors 40 mm/70. 2—12.7 mm MGs.
Radars: Navigation: Raytheon Mariner Pathfinder; I-band.
Sonars: Plessey 193 m; minehunting; high frequency (100/300 kHz).
EdgeTech DF-1000 sidescan (M 51); high frequency (100/400 kHz).

Comment: M 52 acquired from Germany in June 1999 and recommissioned 2 December 1999. M 51 transferred in November 2000. Converted to minehunters in 1978. Hulls of wooden construction. Full minehunting equipment including PAP 104 ROVs transferred with the vessels.

SŪDUVIS *9/2007, Maritime Photographic* / 1335793

0 + 2 HUNT CLASS (MINEHUNTERS—COASTAL) (MHC)

Name	*No*	*Builders*	*Launched*	*Commissioned*
– (ex-*Cottesmore*)	– (ex-M 32)	Yarrow Shipbuilders, Glasgow	9 Feb 1982	24 June 1983
– (ex-*Dulverton*)	– (ex-M 35)	Vosper Thornycroft, Woolston	3 Nov 1982	4 Nov 1983

Displacement, tons: 615 standard; 750 full load
Dimensions, feet (metres): 187.0 wl; 197.0 oa × 32.8 × 11.2 *(57.0; 60.0 × 10.0 × 3.4)*
Main machinery: To be announced.
Speed, knots: To be announced. **Range, n miles:** To be announced.
Complement: To be announced
Guns: To be announced.
Countermeasures: MCM: Expendable mine-disposal system.
Combat data systems: To be announced.
Radars: To be announced.
Sonars: Thales 2193; hull-mounted; minehunting; 100/300 kHz.

Comment: The contract to refit, upgrade and transfer two former Royal Navy mine-countermeasures vessels was announced on 27 November 2008. All minehunting and minesweeping equipment was removed from both ships during conversion in 1997 to undertake patrol duties during their latter days in RN service. Both ships subsequently decommissioned in 2005. Thales UK is to act as prime contractor for the upgrade which is likely to involve a substantial package including a new command system (possibly NAUTIS III as fitted in RN Hunt class), minehunting sonar, propulsion machinery, expendable mine disposal equipment (possibly based on Seafox C) and radars. The re-activation is to be undertaken in a UK shipyard and both ships are expected to enter Lithuanian service in late 2010.

HUNT CLASS *4/2007, Derek Fox* / 1305229

AUXILIARIES

Notes: *Victoria* 245 is an ex-Swedish Coast Guard vessel now owned by the Fishery Inspection Service.

1 HARBOURTUG (YTL)

H 22 (ex-A 330)

Displacement, tons: 35
Dimensions, feet (metres): 48 × 14.8 × 8.2 *(14.65 × 4.5 × 2.5)*
Main machinery: 1 Scania-Vabis DSI 11R82A diesel; 230 hp *(171 kW)*
Speed, knots: 9
Complement: 4
Radars: Navigation: Racal Decca; I-band.

Comment: Ex-Swedish *Atlas* transferred in 2000.

H 22 *6/2003, Hartmut Ehlers* / 0561507

1 KUTTER CLASS (PB)

LOKYS (ex-*Apollo*) H 23

Displacement, tons: 35 full load
Dimensions, feet (metres): 60.4 × 17.1 × 10.5 *(18.4 × 5.2 × 3.2)*
Main machinery: 1 diesel; 165 hp(m) *(121 kW)*; 1 shaft
Speed, knots: 9
Complement: 5
Radars: Surface search: Raytheon RM 1290S; I-band.

Comment: Built in the 1930s and served with the Danish Naval Home Guard. Transferred in July 1997. Manned by naval personnel.

LOKYS *6/2005, Lithuanian Navy* / 1129992

1 VIDAR CLASS (MCCS/AG)

Name	*No*	*Builders*	*Launched*	*Commissioned*
JOTVINGIS (ex-*Vidar*)	N 42 (ex-N 52)	Mjellem and Karlsen, Bergen	18 Mar 1977	21 Oct 1977

Displacement, tons: 1,500 standard; 1,673 full load
Dimensions, feet (metres): 212.6 × 39.4 × 13.1 *(64.8 × 12 × 4)*
Main machinery: 2 Wichmann 7AX diesels; 4,200 hp(m) *(3.1 MW)*; 2 shafts; auxiliary motor; 425 hp(m) *(312 kW)*; bow thruster
Speed, knots: 15
Complement: 50

Guns: 2 Bofors 40 mm/70; 300 rds/min to 12 km *(6.6 n miles)*; weight of shell 0.96 kg.
Mines: 300-400 (depending on type) on three decks
Weapons control: TVT optronic director.
Radars: Surface search: 2 Racal Decca TM 1226; I-band.
Sonars: Simrad; hull-mounted; search and attack; medium/high frequency.

Programmes: Decommissioned from Norwegian Navy in 2005 and transferred to Lithuania on 27 June 2006.
Operational: Former minelayer modified to undertake mine countermeasures command and support roles. Additional tasks include logistic support.

VIDAR CLASS *Per Körnefeldt* / 1133083

STATE BORDER SECURITY SERVICE

1 LOKKI CLASS (PB)

KIHU 102 (ex-003)

Displacement, tons: 76 full load
Dimensions, feet (metres): 87.9 × 17 × 6.2 *(26.8 × 5.2 × 1.9)*
Main machinery: 2 MTU 8V 396 TB84 diesels; 2,120 hp(m) *(1.58 MW)* sustained; 2 shafts
Speed, knots: 25
Complement: 6
Radars: Navigation: Furuno FR 2010 and FCR 1411; I-band.

Comment: Armament and sonar removed on transfer. Donated by Finland in 1998.

KIHU *6/2003, Hartmut Ehlers* / 0561506

1 KBV 041 CLASS (PB)

MADELEINE 042 (ex-KBV 041)

Displacement, tons: 69 full load
Dimensions, feet (metres): 73.5 × 17.72 × 5.6 *(22.4 × 5.4 × 1.7)*
Main machinery: 2 diesels; 450 hp(m) *(331 kW)*; 2 shafts
Speed, knots: 10
Complement: 4
Radars: Navigation: Furuno FRS 1000C and FR 1510; I-band.

Comment: Class B sea truck transferred from the Swedish Coast Guard in April 1995. Used for pollution control in Swedish service but now used as patrol craft.

MADELEINE *6/2003, Hartmut Ehlers* / 0561504

1 KBV 101 CLASS (PB)

LILIAN 101 (ex-KBV 101)

Displacement, tons: 69 full load
Dimensions, feet (metres): 82 × 16.4 × 6.5 *(25 × 5 × 2)*
Main machinery: 2 Cummins KTA38-M diesels; 2,120 hp(m) *(1.56 MW)*; 2 shafts
Speed, knots: 18
Range, n miles: 1,000 at 15 kt
Complement: 5
Radars: Navigation: Furuno FR 2010 and FCR 1411; I-band.

Comment: Built in Sweden in 1969. Transferred from Swedish Coast Guard on 24 June 1996. Used in Swedish service as a salvage diving vessel and had a high frequency active hull-mounted sonar.

LILIAN *6/2003, Hartmut Ehlers* / 0561503

1 CHRISTINA (GRIFFON 2000 TD) CLASS HOVERCRAFT (UCAC)

CHRISTINA

Displacement, tons: 5 full load
Dimensions, feet (metres): 41.35 × 20 *(12.6 × 6.1)*
Main machinery: 1 Deutz BF8L diesel; 355 hp *(265 kW)*
Speed, knots: 35
Complement: 3
Radars: Furuno 1000C; I-band.

Comment: Built by Griffon UK and delivered in 2000. Similar to crafts supplied to Estonia and Finland.

CHRISTINA
6/2001, Lithuanian Navy
0114364

Macedonia, Former Yugoslav Republic of

Country Overview

The Former Yugoslav Republic of Macedonia declared its independence in 1991. A land-locked country with an area of 9,928 square miles, it is situated in south-eastern Europe and is bordered to the north by Serbia, to the east by Bulgaria, to the south by Greece and to the west by Albania. Parts of the borders with Albania and Greece pass through the two principal lakes, Ohrid and Prespa. The capital and largest city is Skopje.

PATROL FORCES

Notes: The Macedonian Lake Service (Ezerska sluzba - EZ) consists of about 400 soldiers and is nominally an independent arm of the Army although in practice it is almost integrated with Land Forces. In addition up to five ex-Yugoslavian Army patrol boats on Lake Ohrid, there are two further small craft on Lake Prespa although their operational status is doubtful.

5 BOTICA CLASS (TYPE 16) (RIVER PATROL CRAFT) (PBR)

303–305 +2

Displacement, tons: 23 full load
Dimensions, feet (metres): 55.8 × 11.8 × 2.8 *(17.0 × 3.6 × 0.8)*
Main machinery: 2 diesels; 464 hp *(340 kW)*; 2 shafts
Speed, knots: 15. **Range, n miles:** 340 at 14 kt
Complement: 7
Military lift: 3 tons or 30 troops
Guns: 1 Oerlikon 20 mm. 2—7.62 mm MGs.
Radars: Decca 110; I-band.

Comment: Former Yugoslavian craft which entered service in the 1970s. Two are reported operational. There is a similar craft in Serbian Navy service.

BOTICA 304 *6/2007, Freivogel Collection* / 1167944

Madagascar

MALAGASY REPUBLIC MARINE

Country Overview

Formerly a French Protectorate, the Malagasy Republic became self-governing in 1958 and fully independent in 1960. It adopted the name Democratic Republic of Madagascar in 1975. Situated in the Indian Ocean and separated from the southeastern coast of Africa by the Mozambique Channel, it comprises Madagascar Island, the fourth largest island in the world, and several small islands. The country's total area is 226,658 square miles and it has a coastline of 2,608 n miles. Antananarivo is the capital while Toamasina is the principal commercial port. There are further ports at Antsiranana, Mahajanga and Toliara. Territorial seas (12 n miles) are claimed. An Exclusive Economic Zone (EEZ) has been claimed but boundaries have not been agreed.

Headquarters Appointments

Head of Navy:
Rear Admiral Ratsimitsetra

Personnel

2009: 430 officers and men (including Marine Company of 120 men)

Bases

Antsiranana (main), Toamasina, Mahajanga, Toliara, Nosy Bé, Tolanoro, Manakara.

PATROL FORCES

1 CHAMOIS CLASS (SUPPLY TENDER) (AG/PB)

MATSILO (ex-*Chamois*) (ex-A 767)

Displacement, tons: 495 full load
Dimensions, feet (metres): 136.1 × 24.6 × 10.5 *(41.5 × 7.5 × 3.2)*
Main machinery: 2 SACM AGO 175 V16 diesels; 2,700 hp(m) *(1.98 MW)*; 2 shafts; cp props; bow thruster
Speed, knots: 14
Range, n miles: 6,000 at 12 kt
Complement: 13 plus 7 spare
Cargo capacity: 100 tons cargo; 165 tons of fuel or water
Radars: Navigation: Racal Decca 1226; I-band.

Comment: Built by La Perrière, Lorient and commissioned in the French Navy 24 September 1976. Paid off in 1995 and transferred from France in May 1996. Can act as a tug (bollard pull 25 tons) or for SAR and supply tasks but is mostly used as a patrol craft. There are two 30 ton winches and up to 100 tons of stores can be carried on deck.

MATSILO
6/1999, Madagascar Navy
0081203

6 PATROL CRAFT (PB)

Displacement, tons: 17.7 full load
Dimensions, feet (metres): 44.0 × 12.5 × 3.9 *(13.4 × 3.8 × 1.2)*
Main machinery: 2 General Motors Detroit 6V53 diesels; 2 shafts
Speed, knots: 13.
Range, n miles: 200 at 11 kt
Complement: 3
Radars: Furuno; I-band.

Comment: Former US Coast Guard lifeboats (MLB) constructed in the 1960s. Formally donated on 12 February 2003 for use as coastal surveillance and SAR vessels. All six craft refitted at Galveston, Texas, before transfer and a further unit was transferred as spares.

MLBs (Seychelles colours) *9/2003, Seychelles Coast Guard* / 0568334

AMPHIBIOUS FORCES

1 EDIC CLASS

AINA VAO VAO (ex-*L9082*)

Displacement, tons: 250 standard; 670 full load
Dimensions, feet (metres): 193.5 × 39.2 × 4.5 *(59 × 12 × 1.3)*
Main machinery: 2 SACM MGO diesels; 1,000 hp(m) *(753 kW)*; 2 shafts
Speed, knots: 8. **Range, n miles:** 1,800 at 8 kt
Complement: 32 (3 officers)
Military lift: 250 tons
Guns: 2 Giat 20 mm.

Comment: Built in 1964 by Chantier Naval Franco-Belge. Transferred from France 28 September 1985 having been paid off by the French Navy in 1981. Repaired by the French Navy in 1996 and now back in service.

AINA VAO VAO *6/1999, Madagascar Navy* / 0081202

AUXILIARIES

Notes: (1) There are three Aigrette class harbour tugs, *Tourterelle*, was acquired from France in 1975 and *Engoulevent* and *Martin-Pêcheur* May 1996.
(2) There is also a 400 ton coastal tug *Trozona*.
(3) A former trawler, *Daikannon Maru*, is employed on fishery protection duties.

Malawi

Country Overview

Formerly the British Protectorate of Nyasaland, the Republic of Malawi gained independence in 1964. A landlocked country situated in east Central Africa, it is bordered to the north by Tanzania, to the west by Zambia and to the south and east by Mozambique. The country's total area is 45,747 square miles, nearly a quarter of which is water. The principal lake is Lake Malawi (formerly Lake Nyasa), with which there is a shoreline of some 475 n miles. The largest city is Blantyre and the capital, since 1975, is Lilongwe. The naval base at Monkey Bay is situated on a peninsula at the south of the lake.

Headquarters Appointments

Commander of the Malawi Army Marine Unit:
Colonel G A Ziyabu

Bases

Monkey Bay, Lake Malawi

Personnel

2009: 225

PATROL FORCES

Notes: One survey craft built in France in 1988 is operated on Lake Malawi by Department of Surveys.

1 ANTARES CLASS (PB)

KASUNGU (ex-*Chikala*) P 703

Displacement, tons: 41 full load
Dimensions, feet (metres): 68.9 × 16.1 × 4.9 *(21 × 4.9 × 1.5)*
Main machinery: 2 Poyaud 520 V12 M2 diesels; 1,300 hp(m) *(956 kW)*; 2 shafts
Speed, knots: 22. **Range, n miles:** 650 at 15 kt
Complement: 16
Guns: 1 MG 21 20 mm. 2—7.62 mm MGs.
Radars: Surface search: Decca; I-band.

Comment: Built in prefabricated sections by SFCN Villeneuve-la-Garenne and shipped to Malawi for assembly on 17 December 1984. Commissioned May 1985. Operational status doubtful.

KASUNGU *6/1996, Malawi Navy* / 0012737

2 NAMACURRA CLASS (PB)

KANING'A (ex-*Y 1520*) P 704 +1

Displacement, tons: 5 full load
Dimensions, feet (metres): 29.5 × 9 × 2.8 *(9 × 2.7 × 0.8)*
Main machinery: 2 BMW 3.3 outboards; 380 hp(m) *(279 kW)*)
Speed, knots: 32. **Range, n miles:** 180 at 20 kt
Complement: 4
Guns: 1—12.7 mm MG. 2—7.62 mm MGs.
Radars: Surface search: Decca; I-band.

Comment: First craft donated by South Africa on 29 October 1988. A second was donated in February 2008.

KANING'A *6/1997, Malawi Navy* / 0012736

1 ROTORK CLASS (LCU)

CHIKOKO I L 702

Displacement, tons: 9 full load
Dimensions, feet (metres): 41.5 × 10.5 × 1.5 *(12.7 × 3.2 × 0.5)*
Main machinery: 2 Volvo diesels; 260 hp(m) *(191 kW)*; 2 shafts
Speed, knots: 24
Range, n miles: 3,000 at 15 kt
Complement: 8
Guns: 3—7.62 mm MGs.

Comment: Built by Rotork Marine. Needs a refit but no funds are available.

CHIKOKO I *6/1996, Malawi Navy* / 0012738

Malaysia

TENTERA LAUT DIRAJA

Country Overview

The Federation of Malaysia was formed in 1963. Situated in south-east Asia, its two regions are separated by some 350 n miles of the South China Sea. Peninsular Malaysia (formerly West Malaysia) is bordered to the north by Thailand and to the south by Singapore (which left the federation in 1965) and includes 11 states occupying the southern half of the Malay Peninsula. To the east, the states (former British colonies) of Sabah and Sarawak (which surrounds the sultanate of Brunei) occupy the northern third of the island of Borneo, the remainder of which forms the Indonesian province of Kalimantan. With an overall land area of 127,320 square miles, Malaysia has a coastline of 2,527 n miles with the Strait of Malacca, the South China Sea, the Sulu and Celebes Seas. Kuala Lumpur is the capital and largest city while the principal ports are Penang, Port Klang, Tanjung Pelepas, Kuantan, Kota Kinabalu and Kuching. Territorial seas (12 n miles) are claimed. An EEZ (200 n miles) is claimed but the limits have not been fully defined.

Headquarters Appointments

Chief of Navy:
Admiral Datuk Abdul Aziz bin Haji Jaafar
Deputy Chief of Navy:
Vice Admiral Dato' Hj Mohammed Noordin bin Ali
Fleet Commander:
Vice Admiral Dato' Ahmad Kamarulzaman bin Hj Ahmad Badaruddin
Commander Naval Area I (Kuantan):
Captain Abdul Aziz bin Hj Mohd Dom

Headquarters Appointments — *continued*

Commander Naval Area II (Sabah and Sarawak):
Commodore Syed Zahiruddin Putra
Commander Naval Area III (Langkawi):
Commodore Abdul Ghani bin Othman

Personnel

(a) 2009: 19,561 (2,385 officers)
(b) Voluntary service: Royal Malaysian Navy Voluntary Reserve (RMNVR): Total, 3,202 (872 officers)

Coastal Defence

Procurement of a coastal surveillance system is under consideration.

Bases

(a) Lumut Naval Base comprises HQ Fleet Operations, HQ Fleet System, HQ Support, HQ Air, Mine Warfare and Diving Centre (KD *Duyong*) and HQ Special Forces *(Paskal)*
(b) Naval Area 1 HQ - Kuantan (West of longitude 109E)
(c) Naval Area 2 HQ - Kota Kinabalu (East of longitude 109E). Comprises HQ Submarine Force, Kota Kinabalu Naval Base, Sandakan Naval Base (KD *Sri Sandakan*), Semporna Naval Base (KD *Sri Semporna*) and KD *Sri Tawau*
(d) Naval Area 3 HQ - Langkawi Island
(e) Naval Area 4 HQ (Designated) - Kuching, Sarawak
(f) Others – Naval Education Training Command, Kuala Lumpur (ex-KD *Sri Klang*), National Hydrographic Centre, Kuala Lumpur, and Tanjung Pengelih, Johor (KD *Sultan Ismail*).
(g) Bases for regular reserve forces situated in Penang, Perak, Selangor, Kuala Lumpur, Labuan Federal Territory, Pahang, Johor, Terengganu, Sabah and Sarawak.

Prefix to Ships' Names

The names of Malaysian warships are prefixed by KD (Kapal DiRaja meaning His Majesty's Ship).

Maritime Patrol Craft

There are large numbers of armed patrol craft belonging to the Police, Customs and Fisheries Departments. Details at the end of the section.

Strength of the Fleet

Type	*Active*	*Building (Planned)*
Submarines	–	2
Frigates	2	(2)
Corvettes	7	5
Logistic Support Vessels	2	–
Fast Attack Craft—Missile	8	–
Fast Attack Craft—Gun	6	–
Patrol Craft	18	–
Minehunters	4	–
Survey Ships	2	1
LSTs	1	–
Training Ships	2	–

PENNANT LIST

Frigates

29	Jebat
30	Lekiu

Corvettes

25	Kasturi
26	Lekir
134	Laksamana Hang Nadim
135	Laksamana Tun Abdul Jamil
136	Laksamana Muhammad Amin
137	Laksamana Tan Pusmah
171	Kedah
172	Pahang
173	Perak
174	Terengganu (bldg)
175	Kelantan (bldg)
176	Selangor (bldg)

Patrol Forces

47	Sri Perlis
49	Sri Johor
3501	Perdana
3502	Serang
3503	Ganas
3504	Ganyang
3505	Jerong
3506	Todak
3507	Paus
3508	Yu
3509	Baung
3510	Pari
3511	Handalan
3512	Perkasa
3513	Pendekar
3514	Gempita

Mine Warfare Forces

11	Mahamiru
12	Jerai
13	Ledang
14	Kinabalu

Amphibious Forces

331	Sri Gaya
322	Sri Tiga
1503	Sri Indera Sakti
1504	Mahawangsa
1505	Sri Inderapura

Training Ships

76	Hang Tuah
A 13	Tunas Samudera

Survey Ships

151	Perantau
255	Mutiara

Auxiliaries

4	Penyu

SUBMARINES

Notes: (1) There are no plans to procure mini-submarines as has been previously reported.
(2) The French Agosta class submarine *Ouessant* is on loan to Malaysia to provide initial training which started in early 2005. The boat continues to belong to the French Navy and is based at Brest. The submarine may go to Malaysia on completion of training in 2009.
(3) The full details of the future submarine rescue capability are yet to be announced. The capability is likely to be based around the ships *Mahsuri* and *Setia Sekal*.

1 + 1 SCORPENE CLASS (SSK)

Name	*No*	*Builders*	*Laid down*	*Launched*	*Commissioned*
TUNKU ABDUL RAHMAN	–	DCN, Cherbourg	25 Apr 2004	23 Oct 2007	28 Jan 2009
TUN RAZAK	–	Navantia, Cartagena	25 Apr 2005	8 Oct 2008	Oct 2009

Displacement, tons: 1,559 surfaced; 1,758 dived
Dimensions, feet (metres): 221.6 × 20.3 × 17.7 *(67.56 × 6.2 × 5.4)*
Main machinery: Diesel electric; 2 SEMT-Pielstick 12 PA4 200 SM DS diesels; 1 Jeumont Industrie motor; 4,290 hp *(3.2 MW)*; 1 shaft
Speed, knots: 20.5 dived; 12 surfaced
Range, n miles: 360 at 4 kt dived; 6,000 at 8 kt surfaced
Complement: 31 (7 officers)

Missiles: SSM: Aerospatiale SM39 Exocet; launched from 21 in *(533 mm)* torpedo tubes; inertial cruise; active radar homing to 50 km *(27 n miles)* at 0.9 Mach; warhead 165 kg.
Torpedoes: 6—21 in *(533 mm)* tubes. WASS Black Shark torpedoes; wire (fibre-optic cable) guided; active and passive homing to 50 km *(27 n miles)* at 50 kt, warhead 250 kg. Total of 18 weapons.
Countermeasures: ESM: Thales DR 3000; intercept.
Weapons control: UDS International SUBTICS.
Radars: Navigation: I-band.
Sonars: Hull mounted; active/passive search and attack, medium frequency.

Programmes: Contract for the construction of two submarines awarded to Armaris and IZAR on 5 June 2002. A four-year training programme aboard an Agosta-70 (ex-*Ouessant*) is included in the package. First steel cut for first of class 2 December 2003. The two forward modules were constructed by DCN and the two aft modules by Navantia.
Structure: Similar in design to the Chilean boats. Diving depth more than 300 m *(984 ft)*. Option to retrofit AIP at a later date.
Operational: Following sea trials, the first boat is to arrive in Malaysia in August 2009 and the second in 2010. To be based in Naval Area 2 at Sepanggar Naval Base, Sabah.

TUNKU ABDUL RAHMAN ***3/2008*, B Prézelin*** / 1305321

TUNKU ABDUL RAHMAN

5/2008, B Prézelin* / 1335485

TUNKU ABDUL RAHMAN

5/2008, B Prézelin* / 1335486

FRIGATES

Notes: The decision to build two new frigates was announced on 17 July 2006. The sections of the ships are to be built at BAE Systems' facilities at Govan and Scotstoun and final assembly is to take place at Labuan Shipyard. The 112 m ships are likely to be a development of the Lekiu class. An order is not expected until 2010.

2 LEKIU CLASS

Name	*No*	*Builders*	*Laid down*	*Launched*	*Commissioned*
JEBAT	29	Yarrow (Shipbuilders), Glasgow	Nov 1994	27 May 1995	20 Nov 1999
LEKIU	30	Yarrow (Shipbuilders), Glasgow	Mar 1994	3 Dec 1994	9 Oct 1999

Displacement, tons: 1,845 standard; 2,390 full load
Dimensions, feet (metres): 346 oa; 319.9 wl × 42 × 11.8 *(105.5; 97.5 × 12.8 × 3.6)*
Main machinery: CODAD; 4 MTU 20V 1163 TB93 diesels; 33,300 hp(m) *(24.5 MW)* sustained; 2 shafts; Kamewa cp props
Speed, knots: 28
Range, n miles: 5,000 at 14 kt
Complement: 146 (18 officers)

LEKIU — **(Scale 1 : 900), Ian Sturton** / 0081204

Missiles: SSM: 8 Aerospatiale MM 40 Exocet Block II ❶; inertial cruise; active radar homing to 70 km *(40 n miles)* at 0.9 Mach; warhead 165 kg; sea-skimmer.
SAM: British Aerospace VLS Seawolf; 16 launchers ❷; command line of sight (CLOS) radar/TV tracking to 6 km *(3.3 n miles)* at 2.5 Mach; warhead 14 kg.
Guns: 1 Bofors 57 mm/70 SAK Mk 2 ❸; 220 rds/min to 17 km *(9.3 n miles)*; weight of shell 2.4 kg.
2 MSI 30 mm/75 DS 30B ❹; 650 rds/min to 10 km *(5.4 n miles)*; weight of shell 0.36 kg.
Torpedoes: 6 Whitehead B 515 324 mm (2 triple) tubes ❺; anti-submarine; Marconi Stingray; active/passive homing to 11 km *(5.9 n miles)* at 45 kt; warhead 35 kg (shaped charge).

Countermeasures: Decoys: 2 Super Barricade 12-barrelled launchers for chaff ❻; Graseby Sea Siren torpedo decoy.
ESM: AEG Telefunken/Marconi Mentor; intercept.
Combat data systems: GEC-Marconi Nautis-F; Signaal Link Y Mk 2.
Electro-optic systems: Radamec 2400 Optronic director ❼. Thomson-CSF ITL 70 (for Exocet); GEC-Marconi Type V 3901 thermal imager.
Radars: Air search: Signaal DA08 ❽; E/F-band.
Surface search: Ericsson Sea Giraffe 150HC ❾; G/H-band.
Navigation: Racal Decca; I-band.
Fire control: 2 Marconi 1802 ❿; I/J-band.

Sonars: Thomson Sintra Spherion; hull-mounted active search and attack; medium frequency.

Helicopters: 1 Westland Super Lynx ⓫.

Programmes: GEC Naval Systems Frigate 2000 design with a modern combat data system and automated machinery control.
Operational: Delivery dates were delayed by weapon system integration problems but both arrived in Malaysia in early 2000. Form 23rd Frigate Squadron.

LEKIU — **6/2007, Royal Malaysian Navy** / 1167989

JEBAT — **7/2008*, John Mortimer** / 1335395

CORVETTES

2 KASTURI (TYPE FS 1500) CLASS (FSGH)

Name	*No*	*Builders*	*Laid down*	*Launched*	*Commissioned*
KASTURI	25	Howaldtswerke, Kiel	3 Jan 1983	14 May 1983	15 Aug 1984
LEKIR	26	Howaldtswerke, Kiel	3 Jan 1983	14 May 1983	15 Aug 1984

Displacement, tons: 1,500 standard; 1,850 full load
Dimensions, feet (metres): 319.1 × 37.1 × 11.5 *(97.3 × 11.3 × 3.5)*
Main machinery: 4 MTU 20V 1163 TB92 diesels; 23,400 hp(m) *(17.2 MW)* sustained; 2 shafts
Speed, knots: 28; 18 on 2 diesels
Range, n miles: 3,000 at 18 kt; 5,000 at 14 kt
Complement: 124 (13 officers)

Missiles: SSM: 8 Aerospatiale MM 40 Exocet Block II ❶; inertial cruise; active radar homing to 70 km *(40 n miles)* at 0.9 Mach; warhead 165 kg; sea-skimmer.
Guns: 1 Creusot-Loire 3.9 in *(100 mm)*/55 Mk 2 compact ❷; 20/45/90 rds/min to 17 km *(9.2 n miles)* anti-surface; 6 km *(3.2 n miles)* anti-aircraft; weight of shell 13.5 kg.
1 Bofors 57 mm/70 ❸; 200 rds/min to 17 km *(9.2 n miles)*; weight of shell 2.4 kg. Launchers for illuminants.
4 Emerson Electric 30 mm (2 twin) ❹; 1,200 rds/min combined to 6 km *(3.2 n miles)*; weight of shell 0.35 kg.
A/S mortars: 1 Bofors 375 mm twin trainable launcher ❺; automatic loading; range 3,600 m.
Countermeasures: Decoys: 2 CSEE Dagaie trainable systems; replaceable containers for IR or chaff.
ESM: Rapids.
ECM: MEL Scimitar; jammer.
Combat data systems: Signaal Sewaco-MA. Link Y Mk 2.
Electro-optic systems: 2 Signaal LIOD optronic directors.
Radars: Air/surface search: Signaal DA08 ❻; F-band.

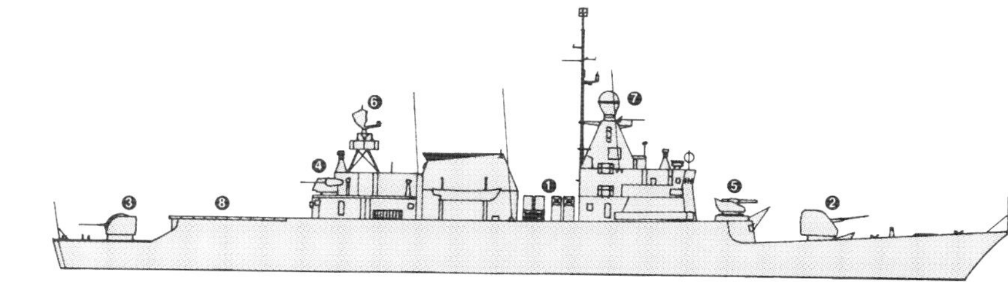

KASTURI

(Scale 1 : 900), Ian Sturton / 0506055

Navigation: Kelvin Hughes 1007; I-band.
Fire control: Signaal WM22 ❼; I/J-band.
IFF: US Mk 10.
Sonars: Atlas Elektronik DSQS-21C; hull-mounted; active search and attack; medium frequency.

Helicopters: Platform for 1 medium ❽.

Programmes: First two ordered in February 1981. Fabrication began early 1982.
Modernisation: An extensive Ship Life Extension Programme (SLEP) for both ships started in 2007. The upgrade includes a new Combat Data System (Tacticos), IFF, Target Designation Sight (TDS), Mirador optronic director, and underwater telephone. Bofors 375 A/S launchers are to be replaced by 324 mm torpedo tubes with A244S torpedoes while the 30 mm armament is to be replaced by new 30 mm MSI DS30B REMSIG guns. The 100 mm gun forward is to be replaced by a Bofors 57 mm gun while the aft 57 mm gun is to be removed to facilitate extension of the flight deck. Super Barricade is to replace the Dagaie chaff system while the MEL Scimitar jammer is to be removed. The refits are to be completed by 2009 and 2010 respectively.
Structure: Near sisters to the Colombian ships with differing armament.
Operational: Form 22nd Corvette Squadron.

LEKIR

12/2007, Michael Nitz / 1170224

KASTURI

12/2005, Chris Sattler / 1153383

KASTURI

12/2005, Hartmut Ehlers / 1154644

3 + 3 KEDAH (MEKO 100 RMN) CLASS (FSGHM)

Name	*No*	*Builders*	*Laid down*	*Launched*	*Commissioned*
KEDAH	171	Blohm + Voss/Penang Shipbuilding	13 Nov 2001	21 Mar 2003	5 June 2006
PAHANG	172	Blohm + Voss/Penang Shipbuilding	21 Dec 2001	2 Oct 2003	3 Aug 2006
PERAK	173	Boustead Naval Shipyard, Lumut	2 Jan 2003	12 Nov 2007	Mar 2009
TERENGGANU	174	Boustead Naval Shipyard, Lumut	Aug 2004	6 Dec 2007	July 2009
KELANTAN	175	Boustead Naval Shipyard, Lumut	July 2005	24 Nov 2008	Nov 2009
SELANGOR	176	Boustead Naval Shipyard, Lumut	July 2006	2009	Mar 2010

Displacement, tons: 1,650 full load
Dimensions, feet (metres): 298.9 × 42.2 × 11.1 *(91.1 × 12.85 × 3.4)*
Main machinery: 2 Caterpillar 3616 diesels; 14,617 hp(m) *(10.9 MW)* sustained; 2 shafts; cp propellors
Speed, knots: 22
Range, n miles: 6,050 at 12 kt
Complement: 68 (11 officers)

Missiles: Fitted for SSM (MM40) ❶ and SAM (RAM CIWS) ❷.
Guns: 1 Otobreda 3 in *(76 mm)*/62 ❸; Super Rapid; 120 rds/min to 16 km *(8.7 n miles)*; weight of shell 6 kg.
1—30 mm Otobreda/Mauser ❹. 2—12.7 mm MGs.
Countermeasures: Decoys: RBOC chaff launcher.
Combat data systems: STN Atlas Cosys 110M1.
Electro-optic systems: Contraves TMEO optronic director ❺.
Radars: Air/surface search: EADS TRS-3D/16ES ❻; G-band.
Navigation: Atlas Electronik 9600 ARPA; I-band.
Sonars: Fitted for.
Helicopters: Platform for medium helicopter.

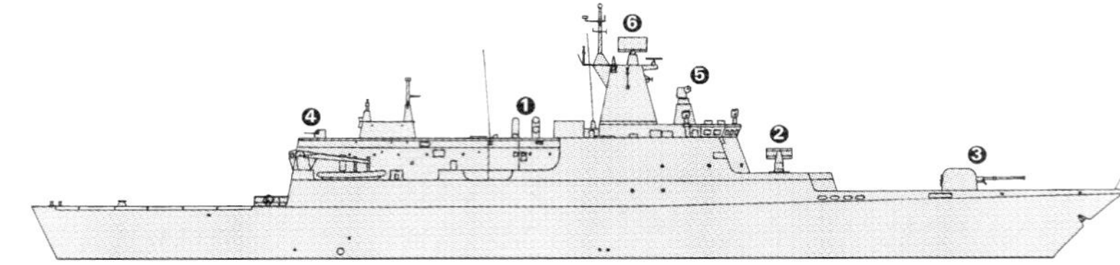

KEDAH *(Scale 1 : 900), Ian Sturton* / 1044256

Programmes: An agreement between the Malaysian government, the Penang Shipbuilding Corporation (PSC) and German Naval Group consortium (led by Blohm + Voss) was reached in November 2000 for the supply of an initial batch of six vessels. The first two OPVs were built in Germany for shipment to Malaysia and assembly and fitting out at Lumut. The other four ships are under construction in Malaysia. Following technical problems and construction delays PSC reverted to state control as Boustead Naval Shipyard which took over the programme in September 2005.
Structure: Design based on Blohm + Voss MEKO 100 including measures to reduce the radar and IR signatures. Space has been included for future enhancements which may include SSM, SAM, sonar and an EW suite.
Operational: Principal tasks are expected to be maritime surveillance and patrol duties in the Malaysian EEZ. The first two are to be based at Sepanggar.

PAHANG *6/2007, Royal Malaysian Navy* / 1167988

KEDAH *12/2007, Michael Nitz* / 1170225

4 LAKSAMANA (ASSAD) CLASS (FSGM)

Name	No	Builders	Laid down	Launched	Commissioned
LAKSAMANA HANG NADIM (ex-*Khalid Ibn Al Walid*)	F 134 (ex-F 216)	Fincantieri, Breda, Mestre	3 June 1982	5 July 1983	28 July 1997
LAKSAMANA TUN ABDUL JAMIL (ex-*Saad Ibn Abi Waccade*)	F 135 (ex-F 218)	Fincantieri, Breda, Marghera	17 Sep 1982	2 Dec 1983	28 July 1997
LAKSAMANA MUHAMMAD AMIN (ex-*Abdulla Ben Abi Sarh*)	F 136 (ex-F 214)	Fincantieri, Breda, Mestre	22 Mar 1982	5 July 1983	31 July 1999
LAKSAMANA TAN PUSMAH (ex-*Salahi Ad Deen Alayoori*)	F 137 (ex-F 220)	Fincantieri, Breda, Marghera	17 Sep 1982	30 Mar 1984	31 July 1999

Displacement, tons: 705 full load
Dimensions, feet (metres): 204.4 × 30.5 × 8 *(62.3 × 9.3 × 2.5)*
Main machinery: 4 MTU 20V 956 TB92 diesels; 20,120 hp(m) *(14.8 MW)* sustained; 4 shafts
Speed, knots: 36. **Range, n miles**: 2,300 at 18 kt
Complement: 47

Missiles: SSM: 6 OTO Melara/Matra Otomat Teseo Mk 2 (TG 2) (3 twin) ❶; command guidance; active radar homing to 180 km *(98.4 n miles)* at 0.9 Mach; warhead 210 kg; sea-skimmer.
SAM: 1 Selenia/Elsag Albatros launcher ❷ (4 cell-2 reloads); Aspide; semi-active radar homing to 13 km *(7 n miles)* at 2.5 Mach; height envelope 15-5,000 m *(49.2-16,405 ft)*; warhead 30 kg.
Guns: 1 OTO Melara 3 in *(76 mm)*/62 Super Rapid ❸; 120 rds/min to 16 km *(8.7 n miles)* anti-surface; 12 km *(6.6 n miles)* anti-aircraft; weight of shell 6 kg.
2 Breda 40 mm/70 (twin) ❹; 300 rds/min to 12.5 km *(6.8 n miles)*; weight of shell 0.96 kg.
Torpedoes: 6—324 mm ILAS 3 (2 triple) tubes ❺. Whitehead A244S; anti-submarine; active/passive homing to 7 km *(3.8 n miles)*; warhead 34 kg (shaped charge).
Countermeasures: Decoys: 2 Breda 105 mm 6-tubed multipurpose launchers; chaff to 5 km *(2.7 n miles)*; illuminants to 12 km *(6.6 n miles)*.
ESM: Selenia INS-3; intercept.
ECM: Selenia TQN-2; jammer.
Combat data systems: Selenia IPN 10 (136, 137); Alenia IPN-S (134, 135); Signaal/AESN Link Y Mk 2.
Weapons control: 2 Selenia NA 21; Dardo.

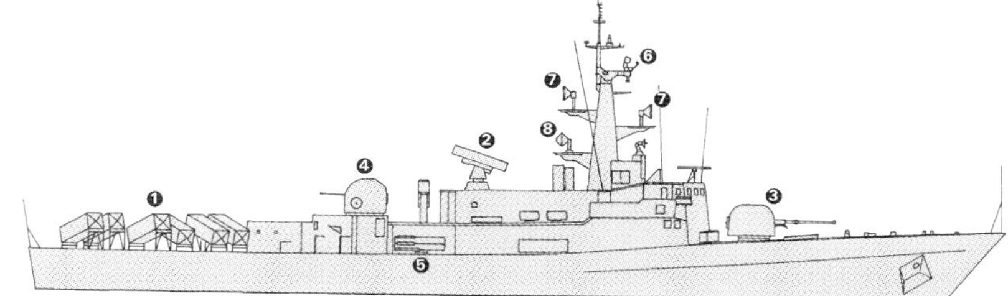

LAKSAMANA HANG NADIM *(Scale 1 : 600), Ian Sturton* / 0126348

Radars: Air/surface search: Selenia RAN 12L/X ❻; D/I-band; range 82 km *(45 n miles)*.
Navigation: Kelvin Hughes 1007; I-band.
Fire control: 2 Selenia RTN 10X ❼; I/J-band; 1 Selenia RTN 20X ❽; I/J-band.
Sonars: Atlas Elektronik ASO 84-41; hull-mounted; active search and attack.

Programmes: Ordered in February 1981 for the Iraqi Navy and fell foul of UN sanctions before they could either be paid for or delivered. Subsequently completed in 1988 and maintained by Fincantieri. Two near sister ships were paid for by Iraq and remain laid up at La Spezia. Contract signed on 26 October 1995, and confirmed on 26 July 1996, to transfer two of the class to the Malaysian Navy after refit at Muggiano and three months training in Italy. Contract for two more signed on 20 February 1997 for conversion and delivery.
Modernisation: Super Rapid 76 mm gun, datalink, new navigation radar and GPS fitted in 1996. Bridge wings are extended to the after gun deck. Contract signed with Alenia Marconi on 11 April 2002 to upgrade command systems of F 134 and F 135 to IPN-S.
Structure: NBC citadel and full air conditioning fitted.
Operational: First pair arrived in Malaysia in September 1997. Second pair delayed by payment problems but arrived in September 1999. Constitute 24th Corvette Squadron.
Opinion: This was an unusual purchase because of the lack of equipment commonality with the rest of the Fleet.

LAKSAMANA MUHAMMAD AMIN *12/2007, Michael Nitz* / 1170223

LAKSAMANA TAN PUSMAH *10/2003, Hartmut Ehlers* / 0567894

SHIPBORNE AIRCRAFT

Notes: (1) Sikorsky S-61A Nuri Army support helicopter can be embarked in the two Logistic Support Ships.
(2) The procurement of six anti-submarine helicopters is under consideration. Contenders include the AgustaWestland AW 101, NH Industries NH 90 and Sikorsky MH-60R Seahawk.

NURI *6/1997* / 0081211

Numbers/Type: 6 GKN Westland Super Lynx.
Operational speed: 132 kt *(244 km/h).*
Service ceiling: 10,000 ft *(3,048 m).*
Range: 320 n miles *(593 km).*
Role/Weapon systems: Ordered on 3 September 1999. All delivered in 2003. ASW, ASuW and surveillance roles. Sensors: Seaspray radar; Sky Guardian 2500 ESM; MST-S FLIR. Weapons: ASW; two A244S torpedoes. ASV; three Sea Skua ASM; 2—12.7 mm MG.

SUPER LYNX *6/2007, Royal Malaysian Navy* / 1167987

LAND-BASED MARITIME AIRCRAFT

Notes: The Air Force has eight F/A-18D fighter-bombers with Harpoon ASM, and 15 Hawk fighters with Sea Eagle ASM.

Numbers/Type: 6 Aerospatiale AS 555 Fennec.
Operational speed: 120 kt *(222 km/h).*
Service ceiling: 10,000 ft *(3,050 m).*
Range: 389 n miles *(722 km).*
Role/Weapon systems: Unarmed aircraft ordered late 2001 for delivery in June 2004. Utility, SAR and training roles. Sensors: Bendix RDR 1500B radar; EWR 99 Fruit RWR; ARGOS 410-A5 FLIR. Weapons: 7.62 mm MG.

FENNEC *6/2007, Royal Malaysian Navy* / 1167986

Numbers/Type: 4 Beechcraft B 200T Super King.
Operational speed: 282 kt *(523 km/h).*
Service ceiling: 35,000 ft *(10,670 m).*
Range: 2,030 n miles *(3,756 km).*
Role/Weapon systems: Used for maritime surveillance. Acquired in 1994. Air Force operated. Sensors: Search radar. Weapons: Unarmed.

SUPER KING *6/1993* / 0084007

PATROL FORCES

17 COMBATBOAT 90H (PBF)

TEMPUR 1
TEMPUR 11–14
TEMPUR 21–24
TEMPUR 31–34
TEMPUR 41–44

Displacement, tons: 19 full load
Dimensions, feet (metres): 52.2 × 12.5 × 2.6 *(15.9 × 3.8 × 0.8)*
Main machinery: 2 Volvo Penta TAMD 163P diesels; 1,500 hp(m) *(1.1 MW)*; 2 waterjets
Speed, knots: 45. **Range, n miles:** 240 at 30 kt
Complement: 3
Guns: 1—7.62 mm MG.
Radars: Surface search: I-band.

Comment: Ordered from Dockstavarvet in Sweden in April 1997. Have more powerful engines than the boats in Swedish service. Primary role is maritime law enforcement particularly on east coast of Sabah. Three Combatboat 90E are operated by the Customs service.

TEMPUR 31 *6/2007, Royal Malaysian Navy* / 1167984

4 HANDALAN (SPICA-M) CLASS (FAST ATTACK CRAFT—MISSILE) (PTFG)

Name	*No*	*Builders*	*Commissioned*
HANDALAN	3511	Karlskrona, Sweden	26 Oct 1979
PERKASA	3512	Karlskrona, Sweden	26 Oct 1979
PENDEKAR	3513	Karlskrona, Sweden	26 Oct 1979
GEMPITA	3514	Karlskrona, Sweden	26 Oct 1979

Displacement, tons: 240 full load
Dimensions, feet (metres): 142.6 × 23.3 × 7.4 (screws) *(43.6 × 7.1 × 2.4)*
Main machinery: 3 MTU 16V 538 TB91 diesels; 9,180 hp(m) *(6.75 MW)* sustained; 3 shafts
Speed, knots: 34.5. **Range, n miles:** 1,850 at 14 kt
Complement: 40 (6 officers)

Missiles: SSM: 4 Aerospatiale MM 38 Exocet; inertial cruise; active radar homing to 42 km *(23 n miles)* at 0.9 Mach; warhead 165 kg; sea-skimmer.
Guns: 1 Bofors 57 mm/70 Mk 1; 200 rds/min to 17 km *(9.2 n miles)*; weight of shell 2.4 kg. Illuminant launchers.
1 Bofors 40 mm/70; 300 rds/min to 12 km *(6.5 n miles)* anti-surface; 4 km *(2.2 n miles)* anti-aircraft; weight of shell 0.96 kg.
Countermeasures: ESM: Thales DR 3000; intercept.
Weapons control: 1 PEAB 9LV212 Mk 2 weapon control system with TV tracking. LME anti-aircraft laser and TV rangefinder.
Radars: Surface search: Philips 9GR 600; I-band (agile frequency).
Navigation: Kelvin Hughes 1007; I-band.
Fire control: Philips 9LV 212; J-band.

Programmes: Ordered 15 October 1976. All named in one ceremony on 11 November 1978, arriving in Port Klang on 26 October 1979.
Modernisation: There are plans to replace the MM 38 with MM 40 or Teseo missiles and to update radar and EW.
Operational: Form 2nd Fast Attack Craft Squadron and based in Area 1.

GEMPITA *12/2007, Chris Sattler* / 1170003

4 PERDANA (LA COMBATTANTE II) CLASS (FAST ATTACK CRAFT—MISSILE) (PTFG)

Name	*No*	*Builders*	*Launched*	*Commissioned*
PERDANA	3501	CMN, Cherbourg	31 May 1972	21 Dec 1972
SERANG	3502	CMN, Cherbourg	22 Dec 1971	31 Jan 1973
GANAS	3503	CMN, Cherbourg	26 Oct 1972	28 Feb 1973
GANYANG	3504	CMN, Cherbourg	16 Mar 1972	20 Mar 1973

Displacement, tons: 234 standard; 265 full load
Dimensions, feet (metres): 154.2 × 23.1 × 12.8 *(47 × 7 × 3.9)*
Main machinery: 4 MTU MB 870 diesels; 14,000 hp(m) *(10.3 MW)*; 4 shafts
Speed, knots: 36.5. **Range, n miles:** 800 at 25 kt; 1,800 at 15 kt
Complement: 30 (4 officers)

Missiles: SSM: 2 Aerospatiale MM 38 Exocet; inertial cruise; active radar homing to 42 km *(23 n miles)* at 0.9 Mach; warhead 165 kg; sea-skimmer. Not always carried.
Guns: 1 Bofors 57 mm/70; 200 rds/min to 17 km *(9.2 n miles)*; weight of shell 2.4 kg.
1 Bofors 40 mm/70; 300 rds/min to 12 km *(6.5 n miles)* anti-surface; 4 km *(2.2 n miles)* anti-aircraft; weight of shell 0.96 kg.
Countermeasures: Decoys: 4—57 mm chaff/flare launchers.
ESM: Thomson-CSF DR 3000; intercept.
Weapons control: Thomson-CSF Vega optical for guns.
Radars: Air/surface search: Thomson-CSF TH-D 1040 Triton; G-band; range 33 km *(18 n miles)* for 2 m² target.
Navigation: Kelvin Hughes 1007; I-band.
Fire control: Thomson-CSF Pollux; I/J-band; range 31 km *(17 n miles)* for 2 m² target.

Programmes: Left Cherbourg for Malaysia 2 May 1973.
Modernisation: There are plans to replace MM 38 with MM 40 or Teseo SSMs and to update radar and EW.
Structure: All of basic La Combattante II design with steel hulls and aluminium superstructure.
Operational: Form 1st Fast Attack Craft Squadron and based in Area 1.

GANYANG ***12/2005, Chris Sattler*** / 1153393

6 JERONG CLASS (FAST ATTACK CRAFT—GUN) (PB)

Name	*No*	*Builders*	*Commissioned*
JERONG	3505	Hong Leong-Lürssen, Butterworth	27 Mar 1976
TODAK	3506	Hong Leong-Lürssen, Butterworth	16 June 1976
PAUS	3507	Hong Leong-Lürssen, Butterworth	16 Aug 1976
YU	3508	Hong Leong-Lürssen, Butterworth	15 Nov 1976
BAUNG	3509	Hong Leong-Lürssen, Butterworth	11 Jan 1977
PARI	3510	Hong Leong-Lürssen, Butterworth	23 Mar 1977

Displacement, tons: 244 full load
Dimensions, feet (metres): 147.3 × 23 × 8.3 *(44.9 × 7 × 2.5)*
Main machinery: 3 MTU MB 16V 538 TB90 diesels; 9,000 hp(m) *(6.6 MW)* sustained; 3 shafts
Speed, knots: 32. **Range, n miles:** 2,000 at 14 kt
Complement: 36 (4 officers)
Guns: 1 Bofors 57 mm/70 Mk 1. 200 rds/min to 17 km *(9.2 n miles)*; weight of shell 2.4 kg.
1 Bofors 40 mm/70.
Countermeasures: ESM: Thales DR 3000; intercept.
Radars: Surface search: Kelvin Hughes 1007; I-band.

Comment: Lürssen 45 type. Illuminant launchers on both gun mountings. Design of hull modification is reported to have been contracted. Form 6th Fast Attack Squadron based at Labuan.

TODAK ***6/2007, Royal Malaysian Navy*** / 1167985

2 31 METRE PATROL CRAFT (PB)

Name	*No*	*Builders*	*Commissioned*
SRI PERLIS	47	Vosper Ltd, Portsmouth	24 Jan 1968
SRI JOHOR	49	Vosper Ltd, Portsmouth	14 Feb 1968

Displacement, tons: 96 standard; 109 full load
Dimensions, feet (metres): 103 × 19.8 × 5.5 *(31.4 × 6 × 1.7)*
Main machinery: 2 MTU MD 655/18 diesels; 3,500 hp(m) *(2.57 MW)*; 2 shafts
Speed, knots: 27
Range, n miles: 1,400 at 14 kt
Complement: 22 (3 officers)
Guns: 2 Bofors 40 mm/70. 2—7.62 mm MGs.
Radars: Surface search: Racal Decca Bridgemaster ARPA; I-band.

Comment: Two boats of the Kris class ordered in 1965 for delivery between 1966 and 1968. Prefabricated steel construction and fitted with air conditioning and Vosper roll damping equipment. These two craft form the 12th Patrol Boat Squadron based at Lumut. The remaining craft of the 13th and 14th Squadrons have been transferred to the Maritime Enforcement Agency (MMEA).

31 METRE CLASS ***11/2001, Maritime Photographic*** / 0130744

AMPHIBIOUS FORCES

Notes: There is a requirement for up to three multirole support ships. The ships are to be capable of transporting up to 700 troops in addition to vehicles, guns and helicopters and will also have hospital facilities.

1 NEWPORT CLASS (LSTH)

Name	*No*	*Builders*	*Laid down*	*Launched*	*Commissioned*
SRI INDERAPURA (ex-*Spartanburg County*)	1505 (ex-1192)	National Steel, San Diego	7 Feb 1970	11 Nov 1970	1 Sep 1971

Displacement, tons: 4,975 light; 8,450 full load
Dimensions, feet (metres): 522.3 (hull) × 69.5 × 17.5 (aft) *(159.2 × 21.2 × 5.3)*
Main machinery: 6 ALCO 16-251 diesels; 16,500 hp *(12.3 MW)* sustained; 2 shafts; cp props; bow thruster
Speed, knots: 20. **Range, n miles:** 14,250 at 14 kt
Complement: 257 (13 officers)
Military lift: 400 troops (20 officers); 500 tons vehicles; 3 LCVPs and 1 LCPL on davits

Guns: 1 General Electric/General Dynamics 20 mm Vulcan Phalanx Mk 15.
Radars: Surface search: Raytheon SPS-67; G-band.
Navigation: Marconi LN66; I/J-band.
Kelvin Hughes 1007; I-band.

Helicopters: Platform only.

SRI INDERAPURA ***7/2007, Robert Pabst*** / 1166814

Programmes: Transferred by sale from the USN 16 December 1994, arriving in Malaysia in June 1995. Second authorised for transfer by lease in 1998 but this was not confirmed.
Structure: The hull form required to achieve 20 kt would not permit bow doors, thus these ships unload by a 112 ft ramp over their bow. The ramp is supported by twin derrick arms. A ramp just forward of the superstructure connects the lower tank deck with the main deck and a vehicle passage through the superstructure provides access to the parking area amidships. A stern gate to the tank deck permits unloading of amphibious tractors into the water, or unloading of other vehicles into an LCU or onto a pier. Vehicle stowage covers 19,000 sq ft. Length over derrick arms is 562 ft *(171.3 m)*; full load draught is 11.5 ft forward and 17.5 ft aft.
Operational: 3 in guns removed before transfer. Repeated refits in Johore shipyard between late 1995 and 1998. Damaged by fire on 15 December 2002 at Lumut but subsequently repaired. Forms 32 Sealift Squadron.

5 LCP

RCP 2 **RCP 3** **RCP 6** **RCP 8** **RCP 9**

Displacement, tons: 30 full load
Main machinery: 2 diesels; 330 hp *(246 kW)*; 2 shafts
Speed, knots: 17
Military lift: 35 troops

Comment: Malaysian built and in service 1974–84. Transferred to the Army in 1993.

130 DAMEN ASSAULT CRAFT 540

Dimensions, feet (metres): 17.7 × 5.9 × 2 *(5.4 × 1.8 × 0.6)*
Main machinery: 1 outboard; 40 hp(m) *(29.4 kW)*
Speed, knots: 12
Military lift: 10 troops

Comment: First 65 built by Damen Gorinchem, Netherlands in 1986. Remainder built by Limbungan Timor SY. Army assault craft. Manportable and similar to Singapore craft. Used by the Army. Some have been deleted.

2 FAST TROOP VESSELS (AP)

SRI GAYA 331 **SRI TIGA** 332

Displacement, tons: 116.5 full load
Dimensions, feet (metres): 123.1 × 23.0 × 3.6 *(37.5 × 7.0 × 1.1)*
Main machinery: 4 MAN D2842 LE 408 diesels; 2,080 hp *(1.55 MW)*; 4 water-jets
Speed, knots: 25
Range, n miles: 540
Complement: 8
Military lift: 32 troops + stores
Radars: Navigation: Furuno; I-band.

Comment: Design based on Australian Wave Master fast-ferry monohull. Procured to transport troops and stores particularly in Sabah and Sarawak waters. Built by Naval Dockyard, Lumut and commissioned on 29 May 2001. Based at Kota Kinabalu.

SRI GAYA *12/2005, Chris Sattler* / 1153396

2 LOGISTIC SUPPORT SHIPS (AOR/AE/AXH)

Name	*No*	*Builders*	*Commissioned*
SRI INDERA SAKTI	1503	Bremer Vulkan	24 Oct 1980
MAHAWANGSA	1504	Korea Tacoma	16 May 1983

Displacement, tons: 4,300 (1503); 4,900 (1504) full load
Dimensions, feet (metres): 328; 337.9 (1504) × 49.2 × 15.7 *(100; 103 × 15 × 4.8)*
Main machinery: 2 Deutz KHD SBV6M540 diesels; 5,865 hp(m) *(4.31 MW)*; 2 shafts; cp props; bow thruster
Speed, knots: 16.5
Range, n miles: 4,000 at 14 kt
Complement: 136 (14 officers) plus 65 spare
Military lift: 17 tanks; 600 troops
Cargo capacity: 1,300 tons dieso; 200 tons fresh water (plus 48 tons/day distillers)

Guns: 2 Bofors 57 mm Mk 1 (1 only fwd in 1503). 2 Oerlikon 20 mm.
Countermeasures: ESM: Thales DR 3000; intercept.
Radars: Navigation: Kelvin Hughes 1007; I-band.

Helicopters: 1 Sikorsky S-61A Nuri (army support) can be carried (1504 only).

Programmes: Ordered in October 1979 and 1981 respectively.
Structure: Fitted with stabilising system, vehicle deck, embarkation ramps port and starboard, recompression chamber and a stern anchor. Large operations room and a conference room are provided. Transfer stations on either beam and aft, light jackstay on both sides and a 15 ton crane for replenishment at sea. 1504 has additional capacity to transport ammunition and the funnel has been removed to enlarge the flight deck which is also higher in the superstructure.
Operational: Used as training ships for cadets in addition to main roles of long-range support of Patrol Forces and MCM vessels, command and communications and troop or ammunition transport. Form 31 Squadron.

SRI INDERA SAKTI *6/2007, Royal Malaysian Navy* / 1170005

MAHAWANGSA *12/2007, Chris Sattler* / 1170002

MINE WARFARE FORCES

4 MAHAMIRU (LERICI) CLASS (MINEHUNTERS) (MHC)

Name	*No*	*Builders*	*Launched*	*Commissioned*
MAHAMIRU	11	Intermarine, Italy	23 Feb 1984	11 Dec 1985
JERAI	12	Intermarine, Italy	5 Jan 1984	11 Dec 1985
LEDANG	13	Intermarine, Italy	14 July 1983	11 Dec 1985
KINABALU	14	Intermarine, Italy	19 Mar 1983	11 Dec 1985

Displacement, tons: 610 full load
Dimensions, feet (metres): 167.3 × 32.5 × 9.2 *(51 × 9.9 × 2.8)*
Main machinery: 2 MTU 12V 396TC82 diesels (passage); 2,605 hp(m) *(1.91 MW)* sustained; 2 shafts; Kamewa cp props; 3 Fincantieri Isotta Fraschini ID 36 SS 6V diesels; 1,481 hp(m) *(1.09 MW)* sustained; 2 Riva Calzoni hydraulic thrust jets
Speed, knots: 16 diesels; 7 thrust jet
Range, n miles: 2,000 at 12 kt
Complement: 42 (5 officers)
Guns: 1 Bofors 40 mm/70; 300 rds/min to 12.5 km *(6.8 n miles)*; weight of shell 0.96 kg.
Countermeasures: Thomson-CSF IBIS II minehunting system; 2 improved PAP 104 ROVs. Oropesa 'O' MIS-4 mechanical sweep.
Radars: Navigation: Kelvin Hughes 1007; Thomson-CSF Tripartite III; I-band.
Sonars: Thomson Sintra TSM 2022 Mk III with Display 2060; minehunting; high frequency.

Comment: Ordered on 20 February 1981. All arrived in Malaysia on 26 March 1986. Heavy GRP construction without frames. Snach active tank stabilisers. Draeger Duocom decompression chamber. Slightly longer than Italian sisters. Endurance, 14 days. Upgrade of tactical data system completed in 2001; Minehunting Tactical Display System (MTDS) installed by Altech Defence System, South Africa. A SLEP for *Mahamiru* and *Ledang* was completed in 2007. Upgrades included TSM Mk III sonar, MTDS adaptation and Kongsberg navigation echo-sounder. The other two ships are to be similarly modified. Form the 26th Mine Countermeasures Squadron.

MAHAMIRU *12/2007, Chris Sattler* / 1170001

SURVEY SHIPS

1 SURVEY VESSEL (AGSH)

Name	*No*	*Builders*	*Commissioned*
MUTIARA	255 (ex-152)	Hong Leong-Lürssen, Butterworth	12 Jan 1978

Displacement, tons: 1,905 full load
Dimensions, feet (metres): 232.9 × 42.6 × 13.1 *(71 × 13 × 4)*
Main machinery: 2 Deutz SBA12M528 diesels; 4,000 hp(m) *(2.94 MW)*; 2 shafts
Speed, knots: 16
Range, n miles: 4,500 at 16 kt
Complement: 155 (14 officers)
Guns: 4 Oerlikon 20 mm (2 twin).
Radars: Navigation: 2 Racal Decca 1226/1229; I-band.
Helicopters: Platform only.

Comment: Ordered in early 1975. Carries satellite navigation, auto-data system and computerised fixing system. Davits for six survey launches. Forms part of 36 Squadron.

MUTIARA *12/2005, Chris Sattler* / 1153397

1 SURVEY VESSEL (AGS)

Name	*No*	*Builders*	*Commissioned*
PERANTAU	151	Hong Leong-Lürssen, Butterworth	12 Oct 1998

Displacement, tons: 1,996 full load
Dimensions, feet (metres): 222.4 × 43.6 × 13.1 *(67.8 × 13.3 × 4)*
Main machinery: 2 Deutz/MWM SBV8 M628 diesels; 4,787 hp(m) *(3.52 MW)*; 2 shafts; Berg cp props; Schottel bow thruster
Speed, knots: 16. **Range, n miles:** 6,000 at 10 kt
Complement: 94 (17 officers)
Guns: 4 Oerlikon 20 mm (2 twin).
Radars: Navigation: STN Atlas; I-band.

Comment: Ordered from Krogerwerft in 1996. The ship is equipped with two survey launches and four multipurpose boats and has three winches and two cranes, including a hoist for a STN Atlas side scan sonar. Full range of hydrographic and mapping equipment embarked. Forms part of 36 Squadron.

PERANTAU *6/2007, **Royal Malaysian Navy*** / 1167982

TRAINING SHIPS

1 HANG TUAH (TYPE 41/61) CLASS (FFH/AX)

Name	*No*	*Builders*	*Commissioned*
HANG TUAH (ex-*Mermaid*)	76	Yarrow (Shipbuilders), Glasgow	16 May 1973

Displacement, tons: 2,300 standard; 2,520 full load
Dimensions, feet (metres): 339.3 × 40 × 16 (screws) *(103.5 × 12.2 × 4.9)*
Main machinery: 2 Stork Wärtsilä 12SW28 diesels; 9,928 hp(m) *(7.3 MW)* sustained; 2 shafts; cp props
Speed, knots: 24. **Range, n miles:** 4,800 at 15 kt
Complement: 210
Guns: 1 Bofors 57 mm/70 Mk 1; 200 rds/min to 17 km *(9.2 n miles)*; weight of shell 2.4 kg. 2 Bofors 40 mm/70; 300 rds/min to 12 km *(6.5 n miles)* anti-surface; 4 km *(2.2 n miles)* anti-aircraft; weight of shell 0.96 kg.
Radars: Navigation: Kelvin Hughes 1007; I-band.
Helicopters: Platform for 1 medium.

Comment: Originally built for Ghana as a display ship for ex-President Nkrumah but put up for sale after his departure. She was launched without ceremony on 29 December 1966 and completed in 1968. Commissioned in Royal Navy 16 May 1973 and transferred to Royal Malaysian Navy May 1977. Refitted in 1991–92 to become a training ship. Main gun and main engines replaced in 1995–96.Sonars and Limbo ASW mortars removed. There are no plans for further modifications. Forms 21st Frigate Squadron.

HANG TUAH *12/2007, **Chris Sattler*** / 1168000

1 SAIL TRAINING SHIP (AXS)

Name	*No*	*Builders*	*Commissioned*
TUNAS SAMUDERA	A 13	Brooke Yacht, Lowestoft	16 Oct 1989

Displacement, tons: 239 full load
Dimensions, feet (metres): 114.8 × 25.6 × 13.1 *(35 × 7.8 × 4)*
Main machinery: 2 Perkins diesels; 370 hp *(272 kW)*; 2 shafts
Speed, knots: 9
Complement: 10 plus 26 trainees
Radars: Navigation: Racal Decca; I-band.

Comment: Laid down 1 December 1988 and launched 4 August 1989. Two-masted brig manned by the Navy but used for training all sea services.

TUNAS SAMUDERA *7/2007, **B Prézelin*** / 1166815

1 NAVAL TRAINING SHIP (AX)

FAJAR SAMUDERA (ex-*Yufu*, ex-*Ferry Sunrise*)

Measurement, tons: 4,476 gross
Dimensions, feet (metres): 295.6 × 51.2 × 14.8 *(90.1 × 15.6 × 4.5)*
Main machinery: 2 Daihatsu diesels; 7,200 hp *(5.4 MW)*; 2 shafts
Speed, knots: 19
Complement: 25 plus 350 trainees
Radars: Navigation: I-band.

Comment: Former passenger/Ro-Ro ship constructed by Kanda Shipbuilding Company, Japan in 1989. Leased as a training ship by the Royal Malaysian Navy.

FAJAR SAMUDERA *6/2007, **Royal Malaysian Navy*** / 1170009

1 SAIL TRAINING SHIP (AXS)

PUTERI MAHSURI (ex-*Kanrin Maru*)

Measurement, tons: 794 gross
Dimensions, feet (metres): 215.9 oa; 158.1 wl × 34.4 × 14.8 *(65.8; 48.2 × 10.5 × 4.5)*
Main machinery: 2 Mitsubishi diesels; 938 hp *(700 kW)*; 1 shaft; cp prop
Speed, knots: 7
Complement: 40
Radars: Furuno FR-1510; I-band.

Comment: Three-masted sailing barque constructed by De Merwede shipyard Netherlands, in 1991. Leased as a training vessel by the Royal Malaysian Navy.

PUTERI MAHSURI *6/2007, **Royal Malaysian Navy*** / 1170008

AUXILIARIES

Notes: (1) There are six miscellaneous personnel launches: *Kempong, Kuramah, Mangkasa, Patak, Selar* and *Tepuruk*.
(2) An ex-tug, *Penyu* (465 tons) is used as a diving tender. Commissioned in 1979, it has a complement of 26.

PENYU *10/2003, **Hartmut Ehlers*** / 0567883

4 COASTAL SUPPLY SHIPS AND TANKERS (AOTL/AKSL)

LANG TIRAM **LANG SIPUT** **MELEBAN** **JERNIH**

Comment: Various auxiliaries mostly acquired in the early 1980s. There are also Sabah supply ships identified by M numbers.

1 DIVING SUPPORT/SALVAGE VESSEL (ARS)

MAHSURI (ex-*Bremen*)

Measurement, tons: 4,112 gross
Dimensions, feet (metres): 301.8 × 62.3 × 24.3 *(92.0 × 19.0 × 7.4)*
Main machinery: 2 MAK diesels; 4,800 hp *(3.53 MW)*; 1 shaft; 1 Ulstein bow thruster
Speed, knots: 14
Complement: 80
Radars: Atlas 9600; E/F/I-band.

Comment: Former research ship constructed by Schichau-Unterwester, Bremerhaven, in 1972. Extensively refitted in 2001. Leased as a multirole vessel by the Royal Malaysian Navy. Capabilities include hydrographic survey, diving support, submarine rescue and accommodation vessel. It is also used for training.

MAHSURI *12/2007, Chris Sattler* / 1167999

1 DIVING SUPPORT/SALVAGE SHIP (ARS)

SETIA SEKAL (ex-*Orient Explorer*, ex-*Lady Gay*)

Measurement, tons: 994 gross
Dimensions, feet (metres): 189.9 × 43.3 × 14.8 *(57.9 × 13.2 × 4.5)*
Main machinery: 4 Daihatsu diesels; 4,200 hp *(3.1 MW)*; 2 shafts; 2 kort nozzles; 1 Kamewa bow thruster; 300 hp *(225 kW)*
Speed, knots: 12
Complement: 40
Radars: 2 Furuno; I-band.

Comment: Ex-anchor handling tug constructed by Carrington Slipway, Newcastle, NSW in 1974. Refitted by Pan United Shipyard in 1996. Leased as a diving support and salvage vessel by the Royal Malaysian Navy. Equipped with a four-point mooring system, hydra-lift 10-ton crane and a two-unit diving chamber for a total of six men. Also fitted with hospital facilities and a workshop. There is a Launch And Recovery System (LARS) for a wet-bell system capable of mixed-gas diving to 90 m.

SETIA SEKAL *6/2007, Royal Malaysian Navy* / 1170007

TUGS

10 HARBOUR TUGS (YTM/YTL)

TUNDA SATU 1	**TERITUP** A 10	**SOTONG** A 6
TUNDA SATU 2	**SIPUT** A 9	**KUPANG** A 7
TUNDA SATU 3	**BELANKAS** A 11	**KEPAH** A 8
KETAM A 5		

TUNDA SATU 1 *6/2007, Royal Malaysian Navy* / 1170006

COAST GUARD (MARITIME ENFORCEMENT AGENCY)

Headquarters Appointments

Director General:
Admiral Datuk Mohd Amdan bin Kurish

Establishment

The Malaysian Maritime Enforcement Agency (MMEA) (or Agensi Penguatkuasaan Maritim Malaysia (APMM)) commenced operations on 30 November 2005. Under the provisions of ACT 633, which came into force on 15 February 2005, the MMEA shall be under the general command and control of the Armed Forces of Malaysia during any period of emergency, special crisis or war.

The MMEA is established through an amalgamation of resources of existing Maritime agencies that include the Royal Malaysian Navy, Royal Malaysian Police, Customs, Fisheries, Marine and Immigration Department. The MMEA has a force of approximately 100 over vessels comprising ships and craft. There are plans to purchase helicopters and fixed-wing aircraft.

Principal Missions

Enforcement of law and order under Malaysian Federal Law
Maritime search and rescue
Air and coastal surveillance
Maintenance of maritime safety and security
Control and prevention of maritime pollution
Prevention and suppression of piracy and illicit traffic in narcotic drugs

Personnel

2009: 2,000 approx
There are plans to build up to a force of about 4,025 personnel.

Organisation

The Malaysian Maritime Zone is divided into five maritime regions which consist of 18 maritime districts.

Bases

MMEA HQ: Putrajaya
Northern Peninsula: Regional HQ: Langkawi (HQ)
District: Langkawi, Pulau Pinang, Lumut
Southern Peninsula: Regional HQ: Johore Bahru
District: Johore Baharu, Port Klang, Kuala Linggi, Tanjung Sedili
Eastern Peninsula: Regional HQ: Kuantan
District: Kuantan, Kuala Tregganu, Tok Bali
Sarawak: Regional HQ: Kuching
District: Kuching, Bintulu, Miru
Sabah: Regional HQ: Kota Kinabalu
District: Kota Kinabalu, Labuan, Kudat, Sandakan, Tawau

PATROL FORCES

Notes: (1) There are 38 RHIB craft with pennant numbers 711-738.
(2) There is one 9 m patrol craft *Pengaman 1* (ex-*Mastura*) with pennant number 901.
(3) There are five craft *Pelindung 1* (ex-PL 27), *Pelindung 2* (ex-PL 48), *Pelindung 3* (ex-PL 50), *Pelindung 4* (ex-PL 59), *Pelindung 5* (ex-PL 60) with pennant numbers 701-705.

PELINDUNG 4 (police colours) *12/2007, Chris Sattler* / 1167994

2 LANGKAWI CLASS (OFFSHORE PATROL VESSELS) (PSOH)

Name	No	Builders	Launched	Commissioned
LANGKAWI (ex-*Musytari*)	7501 (ex-160)	Korea Shipbuilders, Pusan	20 July 1984	19 Dec 1985
BANGGI (ex-*Marikh*)	7502 (ex-161)	Malaysia SB and E Co, Johore	21 Jan 1985	9 Apr 1987

Displacement, tons: 1,300 full load
Dimensions, feet (metres): 246 × 35.4 × 12.1 *(75 × 10.8 × 3.7)*
Main machinery: 2 SEMT-Pielstick diesels; 12,720 hp(m) *(9.35 MW)*; 2 shafts
Speed, knots: 22
Range, n miles: 5,000 at 15 kt
Complement: 76 (10 officers)
Guns: 1 – 57 mm.
2 Emerson Electric 30 mm (twin); 1,200 rds/min combined to 6 km *(3.2 n miles)*; weight of shell 0.35 kg.
Countermeasures: ESM: Thales DR 3000; intercept.
Weapons control: PEAB 9LV 230 optronic system.
Radars: Air/surface search: Signaal DA05; E/F-band; range 137 km *(75 n miles)* for 2 m^2 target.
Navigation: Kelvin Hughes 1007; I-band.
Fire control: Philips 9LV; J-band.
Helicopters: Platform for 1 medium.

Programmes: Ordered in June 1983.
Structure: Flight deck suitable for Sikorsky S-61A Nuri army support helicopter.
Operational: These ships were transferred from the Malaysian Navy on 23 June 2006 and became operational in 2007. Based in the Eastern Peninsula region.

BANGGI (old number) *12/2005, Chris Sattler* / 1153391

LANGKAWI *12/2007, Michael Nitz* / 1167980

15 SIPADAN CLASS (PB)

Name	No	Builders	Commissioned
SIPADAN (ex-*Sri Sarawak*)	3131 (ex-3145)	Vosper Ltd, Portsmouth	30 Sep 1964
LANG (ex-*Kris*)	3132 (ex-34)	Vosper Ltd, Portsmouth	1 Jan 1966
SEGANTANG (ex-*Sundang*)	3133 (ex-36)	Vosper Ltd, Portsmouth	29 Nov 1966
JARAK (ex-*Badek*)	3134 (ex-37)	Vosper Ltd, Portsmouth	15 Dec 1966
KUKUP (ex-*Panah*)	3135 (ex-42)	Vosper Ltd, Portsmouth	27 July 1967
SEMPADI (ex-*Kelewang*)	3136 (ex-45)	Vosper Ltd, Portsmouth	4 Oct 1967
LABAS (ex-*Sri Sabah*)	3137 (ex-3144)	Vosper Ltd, Portsmouth	2 Sep 1964
NYIREH (ex-*Sri Negri Sembilan*)	3138 (ex-3146)	Vosper Ltd, Portsmouth	28 Sep 1964
KURAMAN (ex-*Renchong*)	3139 (ex-38)	Vosper Ltd, Portsmouth	17 Jan 1967
SIAMIL (ex-*Tombak*)	3140 (ex-39)	Vosper Ltd, Portsmouth	2 Mar 1967
PEMANGGIL (ex-*Kerambit*)	3141 (ex-43)	Vosper Ltd, Portsmouth	28 July 1967
BIDONG (ex-*Beladau*)	3142 (ex-44)	Vosper Ltd, Portsmouth	12 Sep 1967
SATANG (ex-*Rentaka*)	3143 (ex-46)	Vosper Ltd, Portsmouth	22 Sep 1967
RUMBIA (ex-*Sri Melaka*)	3144 (ex-3147)	Vosper Ltd, Portsmouth	2 Nov 1964
LIGITAN (ex-*Lembing*)	3145 (ex-40)	Vosper Ltd, Portsmouth	12 Apr 1967

Displacement, tons: 96 standard; 109 full load
Dimensions, feet (metres): 103 × 19.8 × 5.5 *(31.4 × 6 × 1.7)*
Main machinery: 2 Bristol Siddeley or MTU MD 655/18 diesels; 3,500 hp(m) *(2.57 MW)*; 2 shafts
Speed, knots: 27
Range, n miles: 1,400 (1,660 Sabah class) at 14 kt
Complement: 22 (3 officers)

Guns: 2 Bofors 40 mm/70. 2 – 7.62 mm MGs.
Radars: Surface search: Racal Decca Bridgemaster ARPA; I-band.

Comment: The four ex-Sabah class were ordered in 1963 for delivery in 1964. The boats of the ex-Kris class were ordered in 1965 for delivery between 1966 and 1968. All are of prefabricated steel construction and are fitted with air conditioning and Vosper roll damping equipment. The differences between the classes are minor, the later ones having improved radar, communications, evaporators and engines of MTU, as opposed to Bristol Siddeley construction. All have been refitted to extend their operational lives and transferred from the Malaysian Navy to MMEA by June 2006. Similar craft in service in Panama.

KUKUP *12/2005, Chris Sattler* / 1153401

15 GAGAH CLASS (PBF)

GAGAH (ex-*Lang Malam*) 3901 (ex-PZ 2)
TABAH (ex-*Lang Lebah*) 3902 (ex-PZ 3)
CEKAL (ex-*Lang Kuik*) 3903 (ex-PZ 4)
BERANI (ex-*Kurita*) 3904 (ex-PZ 7)
SETIA (ex-*Serangan Batu*) 3905 (ex-PZ 8)
AMANAH (ex-*Harimau Bintang*) 3906 (ex-PZ 9)
JUJUR (ex-*Harimau Kimbang*) 3907 (ex-PZ 10)
IKHLAS (ex-*Harimau Akar*) 3908 (ex-PZ 12)
BUDIMAN (ex-*Mersuji*) 3909 (ex-PZ 14)
TEGAS (ex-*Lang Hitam*) 3910 (ex-PZ 1)
MULIA (ex-*Balong*) 3911 (ex-PZ 5)
BIJAK (ex-*Belian*) 3912 (ex-PZ 6)
ADIL (ex-*Harimau Belang*) 3913 (ex-PZ 11)
PINTAR (ex-*Perangan*) 3914 (ex-PZ 13)
BISTARI (ex-*Alu-Alu*) 3915 (ex-PZ 15)

Displacement, tons: 230 full load
Dimensions, feet (metres): 126.3 × 22.9 × 5.9 *(38.5 × 7 × 1.8)*
Main machinery: 2 MTU 20V 538TB92 diesels; 8,360 hp(m) *(6.14 MW)* sustained; 2 shafts
Speed, knots: 35
Range, n miles: 1,200 at 15 kt
Complement: 38 (4 officers)
Guns: 1 Bofors 40 mm/70 (in a distinctive plastic turret).
1 Oerlikon 20 mm. 2 FN 7.62 mm MGs.
Radars: Navigation: Kelvin Hughes; I-band.

Comment: Ordered from Hong Leong-Lürssen, Butterworth, Malaysia in 1979. First delivered August 1980, last in April 1983. All transferred from the Marine Police to the Maritime Enforcement Agency and became operational in November 2005.

TEGAS *12/2007, Chris Sattler* / 1167998

5 RAMUNIA (BAHTERA) CLASS (PATROL CRAFT) (PB)

RAMUNIA (ex-*Bahtera Kinabalu*) 3221 (ex-K ?)
MARUDU (ex-*Bahtera Bayu*) 3222 (ex-K 37)
DANGA (ex-*Bahtera Hijau*) 3223 (ex-K 38)
SIANGIN (ex-*Bahtera Jerai*) 3224 (ex-K 40)
KIMANIS (ex-*Bahtera Juang*) 3225 (ex-K 33)

Displacement, tons: 143 full load
Dimensions, feet (metres): 106.2 × 23.6 × 5.9 *(32.4 × 7.2 × 1.8)*
Main machinery: 2 Paxman Valenta 16CM diesels; 6,650 hp *(5 MW)* sustained; 2 shafts
1 Cummins diesel; 575 hp *(423 kW)*; 1 shaft
Speed, knots: 27; 8 on cruise diesel
Range, n miles: 2,000 at 8 kt
Complement: 26
Guns: 1 Oerlikon 20 mm. 2—7.62 mm MGs.
Radars: Surface search: Kelvin Hughes; I-band.

Comment: Vosper 32 m craft ordered February 1981 from Malaysia Shipyard and Engineering Company with technical support from Vosper Thornycroft (Private) Ltd, Singapore. Two completed 1982, the remainder in 1983–84. Five transferred from the Customs Service to the MMEA in June 2005.

SIANGIN *12/2007, Michael Nitz* / 1167979

2 RHU CLASS (PB)

RHU 2601 (ex-P 202) **STAPA** 2602 (ex-P 204)

Displacement, tons: 99 full load
Dimensions, feet (metres): 88.2 × 19.0 × ? *(26.9 × 5.8 × ?)*
Main machinery: 2 Deutz 16M 816CR diesels; 2 shafts
Speed, knots: 20
Complement: 15
Radars: Navigation: I-band.

Comment: Former Fisheries Department craft built in 1990 and transferred in 2006.

STAPA (Fisheries colours) *12/1999, Sattler/Steele* / 0081228

4 MALAWALI CLASS (PATROL CRAFT) (PB)

MALAWALI (ex-*Bintang Utara*) 2551
SERASAN (ex-*Bintang Timur*) 2552
MANJUNG (ex-*Bintang Manjung*) 2553
TEBRAU (ex-*Bintang Baru*) 2554

Displacement, tons: 63.5 full load
Dimensions, feet (metres): 82.0 × 19.7 × ? *(25.0 × 6.0 × ?)*
Main machinery: 2 Deutz 16M 816CR diesels; 2 shafts
Speed, knots: 25
Complement: 12
Radars: Navigation: I-band.

Comment: Built in 1999 and transferred from the Marine Department to the MMEA in April 2006.

2 NUSA CLASS (PATROL CRAFT) (PB)

NUSA (ex-*Rajawali 11*) 2201 **RENTAP** (ex-*Rajawali 111*) 2202

Displacement, tons: 53 full load
Dimensions, feet (metres): 72.2 × 19.7 × ? *(22.0 × 6.0 × ?)*
Main machinery: 2 Deutz 16M 816CR diesels; 2 shafts
Speed, knots: 25
Complement: 14
Radars: Navigation: I-band.

Comment: Built in 1993 and transferred from the Marine Department to the MMEA in April 2006.

4 SEMBILANG CLASS (PATROL CRAFT) (PB)

SEMBILANG 2161 (ex-P 101)
ALU-ALU 2162 (ex-P 102)
MERSUJI 2163 (ex-P 103)
SIAKAP 2164 (ex-P 104)

Displacement, tons: 77 full load
Dimensions, feet (metres): 68.9 × 18.0 × ? *(21.0 × 5.5 × ?)*
Main machinery: 2 Deutz SBA 12M 816SR diesels; 2 shafts
Speed, knots: 25
Complement: 12
Radars: Navigation: I-band.

Comment: Former Fisheries Department craft. Built in 1986 and transferred in 2006.

1 PENINJAU CLASS (PATROL CRAFT) (PB)

PENINJAU 1701 (ex-P 301)

Displacement, tons: To be announced
Dimensions, feet (metres): 55.8 × ? × ? *(17.0 × ? × ?)*
Main machinery: To be announced
Speed, knots: To be announced
Complement: To be announced
Guns: To be announced.
Radars: Navigation: I-band.

Comment: Former Fisheries Department craft transferred in 2006.

2 PENGGALANG CLASS (PATROL CRAFT) (PB)

PENGGALANG 1 1801 **PENGGALANG 2** 1802

Displacement, tons: 10.8
Dimensions, feet (metres): 59.0 × 14.6 × ? *(18.0 × 4.45 × ?)*
Main machinery: 2 CAT C18 diesels; 2 shafts
Speed, knots: 45
Complement: 10
Guns: 2—7.62 mm MGs.
Radars: Navigation: I-band.

Comment: Transferred from the Marine Department to the MMEA in 2006.

PENGGALANG 1 *12/2007, Chris Sattler* / 1167997

4 PENYELAMAT CLASS (PATROL CRAFT) (PB)

PENYELAMAT 1 (ex-*Chendering*) 1571
PENYELAMAT 2 (ex-*Rhu*) 1572
PENYELAMAT 3 (ex-*Murau*) 1573
PENYELAMAT 4 (ex-*Lanngun*) 1574

Displacement, tons: 15.0
Dimensions, feet (metres): 49.2 × ? × ? *(15.0 × ? × ?)*
Main machinery: To be announced
Speed, knots: To be announced
Complement: To be announced
Guns: To be announced.
Radars: Navigation: I-band.

Comment: Transferred from the Marine Department to the MMEA in 2006.

8 PENGAWAL CLASS (PATROL CRAFT) (PB)

PENGAWAL 1 (ex-*Labian*) 1411
PENGAWAL 2 (ex-*Bidadari*) 1412
PENGAWAL 3 (ex-*Kubung*) 1413
PENGAWAL 4 (ex-*Serapi*) 1414
PENGAWAL 5 (ex-*Memerang Laut*) 1415
PENGAWAL 6 (ex-*Subis*) 1416
PENGAWAL 7 (ex-*Niah*) 1417
PENGAWAL 8 (ex-*Murud*) 1418

Displacement, tons: To be announced
Dimensions, feet (metres): 45.9 × ? × ? *(14.0 × ? × ?)*
Main machinery: To be announced
Speed, knots: To be announced
Complement: To be announced
Guns: To be announced.
Radars: Navigation: I-band.

Comment: Transferred from the Marine Department to the MMEA in 2006.

2 13 m PATROL CRAFT (PB)

PENGAWAL 11 (ex-*Matang*) 1311
PENGAWAL 12 (ex-*Nyabau*) 1312

Displacement, tons: To be announced
Dimensions, feet (metres): 42.6 × ? × ? *(13.0 × ? × ?)*
Main machinery: To be announced
Speed, knots: To be announced
Complement: To be announced
Guns: To be announced.
Radars: Navigation: I-band.

Comment: Transferred from the Marine Department to the MMEA in 2006.

TRAINING SHIPS

1 MARLIN CLASS (TRAINING VESSEL) (AX)

MARLIN 4001

Displacement, tons: 270
Dimensions, feet (metres): 131.2 × 23.6 × ? (40.0 × 7.2 × ?)
Main machinery: To be announced
Speed, knots: To be announced
Complement: 29
Radars: Navigation: I-band.

Comment: A new training ship built and donated by The Nippon Foundation. The ship was handed over at Port Klang on 1 June 2006. Based at Lumut.

MARLIN *12/2007, Michael Nitz* / 1167978

GOVERNMENT MARITIME FORCES

Notes: The Fire and Rescue Department operates at least eight 10 m rescue craft. Helicopters include Mi-17 and Agusta Westland A 109.

POLICE

6 BROOKE MARINE 29 METRE CLASS (PBF)

SANGITAN PX 28
SABAHAN PX 29
DUNGUN PX 30
TIOMAN PX 31
TUMPAT PX 32
SEGAMA PX 33

Displacement, tons: 114 full load
Dimensions, feet (metres): 95.1 × 19.7 × 5.6 *(29 × 6 × 1.7)*
Main machinery: 2 Paxman Valenta 6CM diesels; 2,250 hp *(1.68 MW)* sustained; 2 shafts
Speed, knots: 36
Range, n miles: 1,200 at 24 kt
Complement: 18 (4 officers)
Guns: 1 Oerlikon 20 mm. 2—7.62 mm MGs.

Comment: Ordered 1979 from Penang Shipbuilding Co. First delivery June 1981, last pair completed June 1982. Brooke Marine provided lead yard services.

SANGITAN *1991, RM Police* / 0506056

120 INSHORE/RIVER PATROL CRAFT (PBI/PBR)

Comment: Built in several batches and designs since 1964. Some are armed with 7.62 mm MGs. All have PX/PA/PC/PSC/PGR numbers. Included are 23 Simonneau SM 465 type (PC 6-28) built between January 1992 and mid-1993, six Vosper craft (PX 19-24) constructed in 1972–3, Camar class (PA series), and ten Penyengat class (PSC series).

PC 6 (SIMONNEAU) *4/1997, Maritime Photographic* / 0012763

PA 30 *12/2007, Chris Sattler* / 1167996

PSC 19 *12/2007, Chris Sattler* / 1167995

6 STAN PATROL 1500 CLASS (PBF)

Dimensions, feet (metres): 48.6 × 8.9 × 2.6 *(14.8 × 2.7 × 0.8)*
Main machinery: 4 diesels; 4,500 hp(m) *(33.1 MW)*; 4 shafts; LIPS props
Speed, knots: 55
Complement: 8
Guns: 2—12.7 mm MGs.

Comment: Built in Malaysia and completed in 1998/99. Details are not confirmed.

CUSTOMS

Notes: In addition there are about 25 interceptor craft of 9 m, and 30 of 13.7 m and some inflatable chase boats.

HELANG LAUT 4 *12/2005, Chris Sattler* / 1153406

KB 82 *12/2005, Chris Sattler* / 1153407

10 PERANTAS FAST INTERCEPT CRAFT (PBF)

KB 59 **KB 71** **+8**

Displacement, tons: 16.2 full load
Dimensions, feet (metres): 54.1 × 12.8 × ? *(16.5 × 3.9 × ?)*
Main machinery: 2 MTU 12V183TE94 diesels; 2,600 hp *(1.94 MW)*; 2 Kamewa waterjets
Speed, knots: 45
Range, n miles: 400 at 40 kt
Complement: 8

Comment: Built by Destination Marine Services, Port Klang. GRP hulls.

KB 59 *12/2007, Chris Sattler* / 1167993

4 PEMBANTERAS CLASS (PB)

Displacement, tons: 58 full load
Dimensions, feet (metres): 94.5 × 19.4 × 6.6 *(28.8 × 5.9 × 2)*
Main machinery: 2 Deutz SBA16M816C diesels; 3,140 hp(m) *(2.31 MW)*; 2 shafts
Speed, knots: 20
Complement: 8

Comment: Built at Limbungan Timor shipyard, Terengganu and completed in 1993.

KA 45 *9/2003, Hartmut Ehlers* / 0567886

9 VOSPER 32 METRE (BAHTERA CLASS) PATROL CRAFT (PB)

JUANG K 33	– K 35	**BAYU** K 37	– K 39	– K 42
PULAI K 34	**PERAK** K 36	**HIJAU** K 38	– K 41	

Displacement, tons: 143 full load
Dimensions, feet (metres): 106.2 × 23.6 × 5.9 *(32.4 × 7.2 × 1.8)*
Main machinery: 2 Paxman Valenta 16CM diesels; 6,650 hp *(5 MW)* sustained; 2 shafts
1 Cummins diesel; 575 hp *(423 kW)*; 1 shaft
Speed, knots: 27; 8 on cruise diesel
Range, n miles: 2,000 at 8 kt
Complement: 26
Guns: 1 Oerlikon 20 mm. 2—7.62 mm MGs.
Radars: Surface search: Kelvin Hughes; I-band.

Comment: Ordered February 1981 from Malaysia Shipyard and Engineering Company with technical support from Vosper Thornycroft (Private) Ltd, Singapore. Two completed 1982, the remainder in 1983–84. Names are preceded by 'Bahtera'. Five vessels have been transferred to the new Maritime Enforcement Agency.

BAHTERA PERAK *12/2007, Chris Sattler* / 1167992

FISHERIES DEPARTMENT

Notes: Patrol craft have distinctive thick blue and thin red diagonal bands on the hull and have been mistaken for a Coast Guard. All have P numbers. There is also a research vessel *K K Senangin II*. There have been 12 craft transferred to the new Maritime Enforcement Agency.

PL 101 *12/2007, Chris Sattler* / 1167991

K K SENANGIN II *9/2003, Hartmut Ehlers* / 0567880

Maldives

Country Overview

Formerly a British Protectorate, The Maldives gained independence in 1965 and a republic was established in 1968. Situated in the northern Indian Ocean, southwest of the southern tip of India, the country comprises a 468 n mile long chain of nearly 2,000 small coral islands that are grouped together into clusters of atolls. The capital and principal commercial centre is Malé and other populous atolls include Suvadiva and Tiladummati. An archipelagic state, territorial waters (12 n miles) are claimed. A 200 n mile Exclusive Economic Zone (EEZ) has been claimed although the limits have only been partly defined by boundary agreements.

Headquarters Appointments

Director General of Coast Guard:
Colonel Zakariyya Mansoor

Bases

Malé, Kaadeddhoo

Personnel

2009: 400

COAST GUARD

Notes: (1) All pennant numbers add up to seven.
(2) The ex-UK patrol craft *Kingfisher* was acquired by a civilian company in early 1997. It is painted white and is used as a survey ship.
(3) There are also four RIBs in service.

1 SDB MK 5 CLASS (LARGE PATROL CRAFT) (PBO)

HURAWEE (ex-*Tillanchang*) – (ex-T 62)

Displacement, tons: 260 full load
Dimensions, feet (metres): 151.0 × 24.6 × 8.2 *(46.0 × 7.5 × 2.5)*
Main machinery: 2 MTU 16V 538TB92 diesels; 6,820 hp(m) *(5 MW)* sustained; 2 shafts
Speed, knots: 30. **Range, n miles:** 2,000 at 12 kt
Complement: 34 (4 officers)
Guns: 1 Medak 30 mm 2A42.
Radars: Surface search: Bharat 1245; I-band.

Comment: Built at Garden Reach and first commissioned in 2002. Transferred from the Indian Navy and recommissioned on 16 April 2006.

SDB MK 5 CLASS (Indian colours) *5/2002* / 0534083

2 GHAZEE CLASS (PB)

ISKANDHAR 223 **GHAZEE** 214

Displacement, tons: 58 full load
Dimensions, feet (metres): 80.1 × 19.0 × 4.1 *(24.4 × 5.8 × 1.3)*
Main machinery: 2 Paxman diesels; 8,506 hp(m) *(6.26 MW)*; 2 Kamewa waterjets
Speed, knots: 37
Range, n miles: 600 at 25 kt
Complement: 18
Guns: 1 – 20 mm MG. 2 – 7.62 mm MGs.
Radars: Surface search/navigation: JRC-JMA 2254; I-band.

Comment: Ordered from Colombo Dockyard in 1997. *Ghazee* commissioned on 20 January 1998 and *Iskandhar* on 7 December 1998. Employed on security, fishery protection and SAR tasks.

GHAZEE *6/2005, Maldives Coast Guard* / 1133514

3 TRACKER II CLASS (PB)

KAANI 133 (ex-11) **MIDHILI** 151 (ex-13) **NIROLHU** 106 (ex-14)

Displacement, tons: 39 full load
Dimensions, feet (metres): 66.3 × 17.1 × 4.9 *(20.2 × 5.2 × 1.5)*
Main machinery: 2 Detroit 12V-71TA diesels; 840 hp *(627 kW)* sustained; 2 shafts
Speed, knots: 25. **Range, n miles:** 450 at 20 kt
Complement: 10
Guns: 1 – 12.7 mm MG. 1 – 7.62 mm MG.
Radars: Surface search: JRC-JMA; I-band.

Comment: First one ordered June 1985 from Fairey Marine, UK and commissioned in April 1987. Three more acquired July 1987 ex-UK Customs craft. GRP hulls. Used for fishery protection and security patrols. *Kuredhi* decommissioned in 2002.

NIROLHU *6/2005, Maldives Coast Guard* / 1133513

1 CHEVERTON CLASS (PB)

BUREVI 115 (ex-7)

Displacement, tons: 26 full load
Dimensions, feet (metres): 56.7 × 14.4 × 4.3 *(17.3 × 4.4 × 1.3)*
Main machinery: 2 MAN B&W diesels; 850 hp *(634 kW)* sustained; 2 shafts
Speed, knots: 23. **Range, n miles:** 590 at 18 kt
Complement: 10
Guns: 1 – 12.7 mm MG. 1 – 7.62 mm MG.
Radars: Surface search: JRC; I-band.

Comment: GRP hull and aluminium superstructure. Originally built by Fairey Marine, UK, for Kiribati and subsequently sold to Maldives and commissioned on 11 September 1981. Used for security and SAR operations.

BUREVI *6/2005, Maldives Coast Guard* / 1133512

3 HARBOUR PATROL CRAFT (PB)

HP 1 **HP 2** **HP 4**

Displacement, tons: 6 full load
Dimensions, feet (metres): 36.1 × 7.5 × 1.6 *(11.0 × 2.3 × 0.5)*
Main machinery: 2 Yamaha outboard engines; 500 hp *(375 kW)*
Speed, knots: 30
Range, n miles: 90 at 25 kt
Complement: 8
Guns: 1 – 7.62 mm MG.

Comment: Built by Gulf Craft Service based in the Maldives. GRP hull. First craft commissioned 12 December 1999. Used for harbour patrol and SAR duties.

HARBOUR PATROL CRAFT *6/2005, Maldives Coast Guard* / 1133510

1 LANDING CRAFT (LCM)

LC 1

Displacement, tons: 38.4
Dimensions, feet (metres): 68.6 × 16.4 × 2.3 *(20.9 × 5.0 × 0.7)*
Main machinery: 2 MAN B&W D 2842 LE 401 diesels; 2 Hamilton waterjets
Speed, knots: 20
Range, n miles: 500 at 18 kt
Complement: 7
Guns: 2 – 7.62 mm MGs.
Radars: Surface search/Navigation: JRC; I-band.

Comment: Built by Colombo Dockyard and commissioned on 12 December 1999. Aluminium hull and superstructure. Used for carrying troops and supplies.

LC 1 *6/2005, Maldives Coast Guard* / 1133511

Malta

Country Overview

Formerly a British colony, the Republic of Malta gained independence in 1964. Situated 45 n miles south of Sicily, the country comprises the islands of Malta (95 square miles), Gozo (26 square miles), Comino, Kemmunett, and Filfla. It has a 76 n mile coastline with the Mediterranean Sea. The capital, largest town and principal port is Valletta. Territorial seas (12 n miles) are claimed. A fishery management and conservation zone of 25 n miles is also claimed.

Headquarters Appointments

Officer Commanding Maritime Squadron:
Major Wallace Camilleri

General

The Maritime Squadron of the Armed Forces of Malta was established in November 1970. An independent unit of the Armed Forces of Malta, it is employed primarily as a Coast Guard.

Personnel

2009: 242 (14 officers)

PATROL FORCES

2 MARINE PROTECTOR CLASS (PB)

P 51 **P 52**

Displacement, tons: 91 full load
Dimensions, feet (metres): 86.9 × 19 × 5.2 *(26.5 × 5.8 × 1.6)*
Main machinery: 2 MTU 8V 396 TE94 diesels; 2,680 hp(m) *(1.97 MW)* sustained; 2 shafts
Speed, knots: 25. **Range, n miles:** 900 at 8 kt
Complement: 10 (1 officer)
Radars: Navigation: I-band.

Comment: Built by Bollinger Shipyards to US Coast Guard specifications. The vessels are based on the hull of the Damen Stan Patrol 2600 in service with the Hong Kong police. Steel hull with GRP superstructure. A stern ramp is used for launching a 5.5 m RIB. P 51 was commissioned 18 November 2002 and P 52 was commissioned 7 July 2004.

P 51 ***11/2007, Marco Ghiglino*** / 1170193

1 DICIOTTI CLASS (OFFSHORE PATROL VESSEL) (PBO)

P 61

Displacement, tons: 393 full load
Dimensions, feet (metres): 175.2 × 26.6 × 17.7 *(53.4 × 8.1 × 5.4)*
Main machinery: 2 Isotto Fraschini V1716T2 MSD diesels; 6,335 hp *(4.7 MW)*; 2 shafts
Speed, knots: 23. **Range, n miles:** 2,100 at 16 kt
Complement: 25 (4 officers)
Guns: 1 Otobreda 25 mm. 2—12.7 mm MGs.
Radars: Surface search: E/F-band.
Navigation: I-band.
Helicopters: Platform for 1 medium.

Comment: Financed from the 5th Italo-Maltese Protocol, contract signed on 12 March 2004 with Fincantieri, Muggiano, Italy for the construction of one vessel. The ship was commissioned on 3 November 2005. The contract included a training and logistic support package. Design based on Diciotti (modified Saettia) class vessels in service with the Italian Coast Guard. Steel hull with helicopter deck and stern ramp for launching a 6.5 m RIB.

P 61 ***10/2005, Air Squadron, AFM*** / 1133090

2 BREMSE CLASS (INSHORE PATROL CRAFT) (PBI)

P 32 (ex-G 33/GS 20) **P 33** (ex-G 22/GS 22)

Displacement, tons: 42 full load
Dimensions, feet (metres): 74.1 × 15.4 × 3.6 *(22.6 × 4.7 × 1.1)*
Main machinery: 2 Iveco (P 32) diesels; 1,000 hp(m) *(745 kW)*; 2 shafts
Speed, knots: 17
Complement: 9
Guns: 1—12.7 mm MG.
Radars: Surface search: Racal 1290A; I-band.

Comment: Built in 1971–72 for the ex-GDR GBK. Transferred from Germany in mid-1992. Others of the class acquired by Tunisia. *P 32* completed mid-life upgrade in 2005. *P 33* is in reserve but it is unlikely to be upgraded.

P 32 ***11/2007, Marco Ghiglino*** / 1170192

2 SWIFT CLASS (HARBOUR PATROL CRAFT) (YP)

P 23 (ex-*C 6823*) **P 24** (ex-*C 6824*)

Displacement, tons: 22.5 full load
Dimensions, feet (metres): 50 × 13 × 4.9 *(15.6 × 4 × 1.5)*
Main machinery: 2 GM 12V-71 diesels; 680 hp *(507 kW)* sustained; 2 shafts
Speed, knots: 25
Range, n miles: 400 at 18 kt
Complement: 6
Guns: 1—12.7 mm MG.
Radars: Surface search: Furuno 1040; I-band.

Comment: Built by Sewart Seacraft Ltd in 1967. Transferred from US in February 1971. Have an operational endurance of about 24 hours. Modernised in Malta in 1998/99.

P 24 ***11/2007, Marco Ghiglino*** / 1170191

2 SUPERVITTORIA 800 CLASS (SAR)

MELITA I **MELITA II**

Displacement, tons: 12.5 full load
Dimensions, feet (metres): 37.7 × 16.1 × 2.6 *(11.5 × 4.9 × 0.8)*
Main machinery: 2 Cummins 6CTA 8.3 DIAMONS; 840 hp(m) *(618 kW)*; 2 Kamewa FF310 waterjets
Speed, knots: 34
Range, n miles: 160 at 34 kt
Complement: 4
Radars: Surface search: Raytheon Pathfinder SL 70; I-band.

Comment: Built in 1998 by Vittoria Naval Shipyard, Italy, for the Civil Protection Department of Malta. Transferred to the Armed Forces of Malta (AFM) in May 1999 for search and rescue duties. Although still the property of the Civil Protection Department, the Melita I and II are operated and maintained by the Maritime Squadron of the AFM.

MELITA I ***11/2007, Marco Ghiglino*** / 1170190

1 HIGH-SPEED INTERCEPTION CRAFT (HSIC)

P 01

Displacement, tons: 3.4 full load
Dimensions, feet (metres): 34.0 × 8.8 × 2.6 *(10.37 × 2.67 × 0.8)*
Main machinery: 2 VM diesels; 600 hp *(450 kW)*; 2 shafts
Speed, knots: 50+. **Range, n miles:** 200 at 35 kt
Complement: 2 plus 8
Guns: 1 – 7.62 mm MG.
Radars: Navigation: Furuno; I-band.

Comment: Co-financed by the EU. RIB 33SC designed and built by FB Design, Italy, and commissioned in February 2006. The high-speed interception craft is to provide support to maritime law enforcement agencies and special forces.

P 01 — *6/2006, Lawrence Dalli* / 1159416

BN ISLANDER — *2001, Douglas-John Falzon* / 0114534

LAND-BASED MARITIME AIRCRAFT

Notes: The Armed Forces of Malta operate two Britten-Norman BN-2B maritime patrol aircraft, five BAe Bulldog T. Mk 1 observation aircraft, two Nardi-MD NH 500HM, five SA.316B/D Alouette III and two AB-47G-2 helicopters.

ALOUETTE III — *4/2006, Frank Findler* / 1305138

NH 500 — *4/2002, Adolfo Ortigueira Gil* / 0568875

Marshall Islands

Country Overview

The Republic of the Marshall Islands was a US-administered UN Trust territory from 1947 before becoming a self-governing republic in 1979. In 1986, a Compact of Free Association, delegating to the US the responsibility for defence and foreign affairs, came into effect. The country consists of some 1,200 atolls and reefs in the central Pacific. There are two main island groups: the Ratak and Ralik chains. Majuro is the capital island. Kwajalein is the largest atoll and is leased as a US missile test range. Bikini and Enewetak are former US nuclear test sites. An archipelagic state, territorial seas (12 n miles) are claimed. An Exclusive Economic Zone (EEZ) (200 n miles) is also claimed but limits have not been fully defined.

Headquarters Appointments

Chief of Surveillance:
Major Thomas Heine

Personnel

2009: 30

Bases

Majuro

PATROL FORCES

1 PACIFIC CLASS (LARGE PATROL CRAFT) (PB)

Name	*No*	*Builders*	*Commissioned*
LOMOR	03	Australian Shipbuilding Industries	29 June 1991

Displacement, tons: 162 full load
Dimensions, feet (metres): 103.3 × 26.6 × 6.9 *(31.5 × 8.1 × 2.1)*
Main machinery: 2 Caterpillar 3516TA diesels; 4,400 hp *(3.3 MW)* sustained; 2 shafts
Speed, knots: 20
Range, n miles: 2,500 at 12 kt
Complement: 17 (3 officers)
Guns: 1 – 12.7 mm MG.
Radars: Surface search: Furuno 8111; I-band.

Comment: The 14th craft to be built in this series for a number of Pacific Island coast guards. Ordered in 1989. Following the decision by the Australian government to extend the Pacific Patrol Boat project to a 30-year life for each boat, *Lomor* completed a half-life refit in 1999 and a life-extension refit in December 2008.

LOMOR — *12/2008*, Chris Sattler* / 1335795

Mauritania

MARINE MAURITANIENNE

Country Overview

A former French colony, The Islamic Republic of Mauritania gained full independence in 1960. With an area of 397,955 square miles, it is situated in northwestern Africa and has borders to the north with western Sahara and Algeria, to the east with Mali and to the south with Senegal. It has a 405 n mile coastline with the Atlantic Ocean. The capital and largest city is Nouakchott while Nouadhibou is the principal port. Territorial seas (12 n miles) are claimed but while it has claimed a 200 n mile Exclusive Economic Zone (EEZ), its limits have not been defined by boundary agreements.

Headquarters Appointments

Commander of Navy:
Captain Isselkou Ould Cheikh El-Weli

Personnel

(a) 2009: 500 (40 officers) plus 200 marines
(b) Voluntary service

Bases

Port Etienne, Nouadhibou (new quay began construction in 2007)
Port Friendship, Nouakchott

PATROL FORCES

Notes: Two 16 m Rodman 55M (ex-M 02 and M 05) and two 12 m Saeta 12 (ex-L 01 and L 03) were transferred from the Spanish Guardia Civil in 2006.

1 OPV 54 CLASS (PBO)

Name	*No*	*Builders*	*Launched*	*Commissioned*
ABOUBEKR BEN AMER	P 541	Leroux & Lotz, Lorient	17 Dec 1993	7 Apr 1994

Displacement, tons: 374 full load
Dimensions, feet (metres): 177.2 × 32.8 × 9.2 *(54 × 10 × 2.8)*
Main machinery: 2 MTU 16V 396 TE94 diesels; 5,712 hp(m) *(4.2 MW)* sustained; 2 auxiliary motors; 250 hp(m) *(184 kW)*; 2 shafts; cp props
Speed, knots: 23 (8 on motors)
Range, n miles: 4,500 at 12 kt
Complement: 21 (3 officers)
Guns: 2 – 12.7 mm MGs.
Radars: Surface search: Racal Decca Bridgemaster 250; I-band.

Comment: Ordered in September 1992. This is the prototype to a Serter design of three similar craft built for the French Navy. Stern ramp for a 30 kt RIB. Option on a second of class not taken up. Refitted at Lorient 2001.

ABOUBEKR BEN AMER *7/2001, Peron/Marsan* / 0137787

1 PATRA CLASS (LARGE PATROL CRAFT) (PB)

Name	*No*	*Builders*	*Commissioned*
EL NASR (ex-*Le Dix Juillet*, ex-*Rapière*)	P 411	Auroux, Arcachon	14 May 1982

Displacement, tons: 147.5 full load
Dimensions, feet (metres): 132.5 × 19.4 × 5.2 *(40.4 × 5.9 × 1.6)*
Main machinery: 2 Wärtsilä UD 33 V12 diesels; 4,340 hp(m) *(3.2 MW)* sustained; 2 shafts
Speed, knots: 26.3
Range, n miles: 1,750 at 10 kt
Complement: 20 (2 officers)
Guns: 1 Bofors 40 mm/60. 1 Oerlikon 20 mm. 2 – 12.7 mm MGs.
Radars: Surface search: Racal/Decca 1226; I-band.

Comment: Originally built as a private venture by Auroux. Carried out trials with French crew as *Rapière*. Laid down 15 February 1980, launched 3 June 1981, commissioned for trials 1 November 1981. Transferred to Mauritania in 1982. Re-engined in 1993–94.

EL NASR *4/1998* / 0052598

1 LARGE PATROL CRAFT (PBO)

Name	*No*	*Builders*	*Commissioned*
VOUM-LEGLEITA (ex-*Poseidon*)	B 551 (ex-A 12)	Bazán	8 Aug 1964

Displacement, tons: 1,069 full load
Dimensions, feet (metres): 183.5 × 32.8 × 13.1 *(55.9 × 10 × 4)*
Main machinery: 2 Sulzer diesels; 3,200 hp *(2.53 MW)*; 1 shaft; cp prop
Speed, knots: 15
Range, n miles: 4,640 at 14 kt
Complement: 60
Guns: 2 Oerlikon 20 mm.
Radars: Navigation: 2 Decca TM 626; I-band.

Comment: Ocean going tug transferred from Spain in January 2000, about a year later than planned. Used primarily as an OPV and for fishery protection.

VOUM-LEGLEITA *1/2000, Diego Quevedo* / 0081240

1 HUANGPU CLASS (PB)

LIMAM EL HADRAMI P 601

Displacement, tons: 430 full load
Dimensions, feet (metres): 196.8 × 26.9 × 14.8 *(60.0 × 8.2 × 4.5)*
Main machinery: 3 MTU 12V 4000 diesels; 3 shafts
Speed, knots: 20
Guns: 4 – 37 mm (2 twin). 4 – 14.5 mm (2 twin).
Radars: Navigation: I-band.
Fire control: Type 347G; I-band.

Comment: Delivered from China on 20 April 2002.

LIMAN EL HADRAMI *12/2006, Adolfo Ortigueira Gil* / 1164957

1 ARGUIN CLASS (PBO)

Name	*Builders*	*Commissioned*
ARGUIN	Fassmer Werft, Berne/Motzen, Germany	17 July 2000

Measurement, tons: 1,000 dwt
Dimensions, feet (metres): 178.8 × 35.8 × 14.8 *(54.5 × 10.9 × 4.5)*
Main machinery: 2 MaK 6M20 diesels; 2,735 hp *(2.04 MW)*; 1 shaft; cp prop
Speed, knots: 16.5. **Range, n miles**: 15,000 at 12 kt
Complement: 13

Comment: Ordered in 1998. Hull construction at Yantar, Kaliningrad. Steel hull and superstructure. Equipped with interception craft on centreline ramp in mother-daughter configuration.

ARGUIN *7/2000, Fassmer Werft* / 1044268

4 MANDOVI CLASS (INSHORE PATROL CRAFT) (PB)

Displacement, tons: 15 full load
Dimensions, feet (metres): 49.2 × 11.8 × 2.6 *(15 × 3.6 × 0.8)*
Main machinery: 2 Deutz MWM TBD232V12 Marine diesels; 750 hp(m) *(551 kW)*; 2 Hamilton water-jets
Speed, knots: 24. **Range, n miles**: 250 at 14 kt
Complement: 8
Guns: 1 – 7.62 mm MG.
Radars: Navigation: Furuno FR 8030; I-band.

Comment: Built by Garden Reach, Calcutta and delivered from India in 1990. Some may not be operational.

2 CONJERA CLASS (PB)

Name	*No*	*Builders*	*Commissioned*
– (ex-*Dragonera*)	– (ex-P 32)	Bazán, Ferrol	31 Dec 1981
– (ex-*Alcanada*)	– (ex-P 34)	Bazán, Ferrol	10 May 1982

Displacement, tons: 85 full load
Dimensions, feet (metres): 106.6 × 17.4 × 4.6 *(32.2 × 5.3 × 1.4)*
Main machinery: 2 MTU-Bazán MA 16V 362 SB80 diesels; 2,450 hp *(1.8 MW)*; 2 shafts
Speed, knots: 13. **Range, n miles**: 1,200 at 13 kt
Complement: 12
Guns: 1 Oerlikon 20 mm/120 Mk 10. 1 – 12.7 mm MG.
Radars: Surface search: Furuno; I-band.

Comment: Former Spanish coastal patrol craft transferred in 2007. The details are as for the vessels in Spanish service and may differ.

CONJERA CLASS *9/2006, Adolfo Ortigueira Gil* / 1040693

1 RAIDCO RPB 18 CLASS (PATROL CRAFT) (PB)

YACOUB OULD RAJEL

Displacement, tons: To be announced
Dimensions, feet (metres): 58.3 × 15.1 × 4.1 *(17.8 × 4.6 × 1.25)*
Main machinery: 2 MAN V12 diesels; 1,500 hp *(1.1 MW)*; 2 shafts
Speed, knots: 23.
Radars: Navigation: I-band.

Comment: Donated by the European Union, the vessel was built by Raidco Marine and delivered in 2000. Steel hull and aluminium superstructure. Used for fishery protection. A similar craft, *Dah Ould Bah*, is operated by the Customs Service.

LAND-BASED MARITIME AIRCRAFT

Numbers/Type: 2 Piper Cheyenne II.
Operational speed: 283 kt *(524 km/h)*.
Service ceiling: 31,600 ft *(9,630 m)*.
Range: 1,510 n miles *(2,796 km)*.
Role/Weapon systems: Coastal surveillance and EEZ protection acquired 1981. Sensors: Bendix 1400 weather radar; cameras. Weapons: Unarmed.

Mauritius

Country Overview

A former British colony, the Republic of Mauritius gained independence in 1968 and became a republic in 1992. Situated in the western Indian Ocean, east of Madagascar, it comprises the islands of Mauritius (720 square miles), Rodrigues (42 square miles), the Agalega islands to the north and the St Brandon Group (also known as the Cargados Carajos Shoals) to the northeast. The capital, largest town and principal port is Port Louis. Territorial seas (12 n miles) are claimedbut, while it has declared a 200 n mile Exclusive Economic Zone (EEZ), the claim is complicated by disputes over the sovereignty of Tromelin Island (France) and Diego Garcia (UK).

A maritime security force was established in 1974 with the donation of MNS *Amar* by India. The National Coast Guard, a specialised wing of the Mauritius Police Force, was formed in 1987.

Headquarters Appointments

Commandant National Coast Guard:
Commander Mahendra V S Negi

Bases

Port Louis (plus 24 manned CG stations)

Personnel

2009: 750 (including officers on deputation)

Maritime Aircraft

2 Dornier 228 (MPCG 1 and 3).
1 Britten-Norman BN-2-T Defender (MPCG 2).

COAST GUARD

Notes: There are approximately 60 inshore craft (RHIBs, glass fibre boats and so on) in addition to those listed.

1 VIGILANT CLASS (PSOH)

Name	*No*	*Builders*	*Launched*	*Commissioned*
VIGILANT	21	Talcahuano Yard, Chile	6 Dec 1995	27 June 1996

Displacement, tons: 1,650 full load
Dimensions, feet (metres): 246.1 × 45.9 × 12.8 *(75 × 14 × 3.9)*
Main machinery: 4 Caterpillar 3516 diesels; 11,530 hp *(8.6 MW)*; 2 shafts; cp props; bow thruster; 671 hp *(500 kW)*
Speed, knots: 22
Range, n miles: 6,500 at 19 kt
Complement: 57 (11 officers) plus 20 spare
Guns: 2 Bofors 40 mm/56 (1 twin). 2—12.7 mm MGs.
Radars: Surface search: Kelvin Hughes; I-band.
Helicopters: 1 light.

Comment: Contract signed with the Western Canada Marine Group in March 1994. Keel was laid in April 1994. All-steel construction. The ship can be operated by a crew of 18. Full helicopter facilities are included in the design which is based on a Canadian Fisheries vessel *Leonard J Cowley*. The ship was refitted in India 2003–04.

VIGILANT *2/2001, Sattler/Steele / 0114366*

1 SDB MK 3 CLASS (PB)

GUARDIAN

Displacement, tons: 210 full load
Dimensions, feet (metres): 124 × 24.6 × 6.2 *(37.8 × 7.5 × 1.9)*
Main machinery: 2 MTU 16V 538 TB92 diesels; 6,820 hp(m) *(5 MW)* sustained; 2 shafts
Speed, knots: 21
Complement: 32
Guns: 1 Bofors 40 mm/60; 120 rds/min to 10 km *(5.5 n miles)*; weight of shell 0.89 kg.
Radars: Surface search: Furuno FK 1505 DA; I-band.

Comment: Transferred from Indian Navy in 1993. Built by Garden Reach, Calcutta in 1984. Underwent mid-life upgrade at Mumbai 2005–06.

GUARDIAN *7/2003, Arjun Sarup / 0568319*

2 ZHUK (TYPE 1400M) CLASS (PB)

RESCUER **RETRIEVER**

Displacement, tons: 39 full load
Dimensions, feet (metres): 78.7 × 16.4 × 3.9 *(24 × 5 × 1.2)*
Main machinery: 2 M 401B diesels; 2,200 hp(m) *(1.6 MW)* sustained; 2 shafts
Speed, knots: 30
Range, n miles: 1,100 at 15 kt
Complement: 14 (2 officers)
Guns: 4—12.7 mm (2 twin) MGs.
Radars: Surface search: Spin Trough; I-band.

Comment: Acquired from the USSR on 3 December 1989. *Rescuer* machinery systems upgraded in 2004. Similar refit planned for *Retriever*.

RETRIEVER *7/2003, Arjun Sarup / 0568318*

1 P-2000 CLASS (PB)

OBSERVER *(ex-C 39)*

Displacement, tons: 40 full load
Dimensions, feet (metres): 68.2 × 19 × 5.9 *(20.8 × 5.8 × 1.8)*
Main machinery: 2 Deutz MWM TBD234 V12 diesels; 1,646 hp(m) *(1.21 MW)* sustained; 1 Deutz MWM TBD234 V8 diesel; 550 hp(m) *(404 kW)* sustained; 3 Hamilton 402 waterjets
Speed, knots: 25. **Range, n miles:** 600 at 15 kt
Complement: 8 (1 officer)
Guns: 1—7.62 mm MG.
Radars: Navigation: Furuno; I-band.

Comment: Leased from the Indian Coast Guard in 2001. Originally commissioned in 1997, one of ten ordered from Anderson Marine, Goa in September 1990 to a P-2000 design by Amgram, similar to Archer class. GRP hull. Built at Goa.

OBSERVER *6/2005, Mauritius Coast Guard / 1133238*

4 HEAVY DUTY BOATS (PBI)

HDB 01–04

Displacement, tons: 5
Dimensions, feet (metres): 29.25 × 11.5 × 1.5 *(8.9 × 3.5 × 0.45)*
Main machinery: 2 Johnson outboard motors; 400 hp
Speed, knots: 45. **Range, n miles:** 300 at 35 kt
Complement: 4 (plus 14 passengers)

Comment: An initial order of four boats supplied by M/S Praga Marine, India in 2000. Option for six additional boats.

HEAVY DUTY BOAT *2000, Mauritius Coast Guard* / 0105127

8 KAY MARINE HEAVY DUTY BOATS (PBI)

HDB 5–12

Displacement, tons: 6
Dimensions, feet (metres): 29.0 × 10.5 × 1.5 *(8.85 × 3.21 × 0.45)*
Main machinery: 2 Suzuki (1 twin) outboard motors; 450 hp
Speed, knots: 40
Complement: 18 including passengers

Comment: Acquired from Kay Marine Malaysia in November 2002. Deep Vee monohull of aluminium construction.

KAY MARINE HDB 05 *8/2003, Arjun Sarup* / 0568316

4 HALMATIC HEAVY DUTY BOATS (PBI)

HDB 13–16

Displacement, tons: 6
Dimensions, feet (metres): 30.2 × 10.2 × 3.3 *(9.2 × 3.1 × 1.0)*
Main machinery: 2 Yamaha V6 outboard motors; 450 hp
Speed, knots: 35
Complement: 18 including passengers

Comment: Acquired from Halmatic Ltd UK in June 2003.

HALMATIC HDB 16 *7/2003, Arjun Sarup* / 0568315

6 TORNADO VIKING 580 RHIB (PBI)

Displacement, tons: 2
Dimensions, feet (metres): 18.7 × 8.5 × 2.5 *(5.7 × 2.6 × 0.75)*
Main machinery: 1 Yamaha outboard motor; 90 hp
Speed, knots: 35
Complement: 10 including passengers

Comment: Acquired in 2004.

VIKING 580 *6/2004, Mauritius Coast Guard* / 0589763

Mexico

MARINA NACIONAL

Country Overview

The United Mexican States is a federal republic in North America. A total land area of 756,066 square miles includes a number of offshore islands. Bordered to the north by the United States and to the south by Belize and Guatemala, it has a 1,382 n mile coastline with the Caribbean and Gulf of Mexico and 3,656 n mile coastline with the Pacific Ocean. The capital and largest city is Mexico City while the principal ports are Acapulco (Pacific) and Veracruz (Gulf of Mexico). Territorial seas (12 n miles) are claimed. A 200 n mile EEZ has also been claimed but the limits have not been fully defined by boundary agreements.

Headquarters Appointments

Secretary of the Navy:
Admiral Marco Mariano Francisco Saynez Mendoza
Under-Secretary of the Navy:
Admiral Raúl Santos Galán Villanueva
Commander of the Navy:
Admiral Moses Gomez Cabrera
Inspector General of the Navy:
Admiral Sergio Enrique Henaro Galán
Chief of the Naval Staff:
Admiral Jorge Humberto Pastor Gómez

Flag Officers

Commander in Chief, Gulf and Caribbean:
Admiral Joseph Mars Camarena
Commander in Chief, Pacific:
Admiral Nestor Amador Evencio Yee

Personnel

(a) 2009: 46,972 officers and men (including 946 Naval Air Force and 11,385 Marines)
(b) Military service

Naval Bases and Commands

The Naval Command is split between the Pacific and Gulf areas each with a Commander-in-Chief with HQs at Manzanillo and Tuxpan respectively. Each area has three naval Regions which are further subdivided into Zones (9), Sectors (11) and Subsectors (7). There is a Central Naval Region that has an HQ in Mexico City.

Gulf Area
First Naval Region (HQ Tuxpan, Veracruz).
I Naval Zone (HQ Ciudad Madero, Tamaulipas).
Naval Sector (Matamoros, Tamaulipas).
Naval Sector (La Pesca, Tamaulipas).
III Naval Zone (HQ Veracruz, Veracruz).
Naval Sector (HQ Coatzacoalcos, Veracruz).
Third Naval Region (HQ Ciudad del Carmen, Campeche).
V Naval Zone (HQ Frontera Tabasco, Campeche).
VII Naval Zone (HQ Lerma, Campeche).
Naval Sector (HQ Champotón, Campeche).
Fifth Naval Region (HQ Isla Mujeres, Quintana Roo).
IX Naval Zone (HQ Yukalpeten, Yucatán).
XI Naval Zone (HQ Chetumal, Quintana Roo).
Naval Subsector (HQ Isla Cozumel, Quintana Roo).

Pacific Area
Second Naval Region (HQ Ensenada, Baja California).
Naval Sector (HQ Puerto Cortez, Baja California).
Fourth Naval Region (HQ Guaymas, Sonora).
Naval Sector (HQ San Felipe, Baja California).
Naval Sector (HQ Puerto Peñasco, Baja California).
II Naval Zone (HQ La Paz, Baja California Sur).
Naval Sector (HQ Santa Rosaliá, Baja California Sur).
Naval Sector (HQ Los Cabos, Baja California Sur).
IV Naval Zone (HQ Mazatlán, Sinaloa).
Naval Sector (HQ Topolobampo, Sinaloa).
Sixth Naval Region (HQ Manzanillo, Colima).
Naval Sector (HQ Isla Socorro, Colima).
VI Naval Zone (HQ San Blas, Nyarit).
VIII Naval Zone (HQ Puerto Vallarta Jalisco).
X Naval Zone (HQ Lázaro Cárdenas, Michoacán).
Eighth Naval Region (HQ Acapulco, Guerrero).
Naval Sector (HQ Ixtapa Zihuatanejo, Guerrero).
XII Naval Zone (HQ Salina Cruz, Oaxaca)
Naval Sector (HQ Huatulco, Oaxaca).
XIV Naval Zone (HQ Puerto Chiapas, Chiapas).

Naval Air Force

Six naval air bases at Mexico City, Veracruz, Campeche, Chetumal, Tapachula and La Paz; there are two Naval Air Stations at Guaymas and Tampico.

Marine Forces

There are two Amphibious Reaction Forces, based at Manzanillo and Tuxpan; one Parachute Battalion, 30 Infantry Battalions and one Presidential Guards Battalion based in Mexico City.

Strength of the Fleet

Type	*Active*	*Building*
Destroyers	1	–
Frigates	7	–
Gunships	19	2
Large Patrol Craft	26	–
Coast Guard	11	–
Coastal and River Patrol Craft	60	12
Survey Ships	7	–
Support Ships	7	–
Tankers	2	–
Sail Training Ship	1	–

Names and Pennant Numbers

Many of the ship names and pennant numbers were changed in early 1994 and again in 2001. Destroyers and frigates are named after Aztec emperors and forerunners of the Independence War (1810–1825). Gunboats are named after naval and military heroes.

DELETIONS

Patrol Forces

2007 *Manuel Crescencio Rejon*

PENNANT LIST

Destroyers

D 102	Netzahualcoyotl

Frigates

F 201	Nicolas Bravo
F 202	Hermengildo Galeana
F 211	Ignacio Allende
F 212	Mariano Abasolo
F 213	Guadaloupe Victoria
F 214	Francisco Javier Mina

Patrol Forces

A 301	Huracán
A 302	Tormenta
PC 202	Cordova
PC 206	Ignacio López Rayón
PC 208	Juan Antomio de la Fuente
PC 209	Leon Guzman
PC 210	Ignacio Ramirez
PC 211	Ignacio Mariscal
PC 212	Heriberto Jara Corona
PC 214	Colima
PC 215	José Joaquin Fernandez de Lizardi
PC 216	Francisco J Mugica
PC 218	José Maria del Castillo Velazco
PC 220	José Natividad Macias
PC 223	Tamaulipas
PC 224	Yucatan
PC 225	Tabasco
PC 226	Cochimie
PC 228	Puebla
PC 230	Leon Vicario
PC 231	Josefa Ortiz de Dominguez
PC 241	Démocrata
PC 271	Cabo Corrientes
PC 272	Cabo Corzo
PC 273	Cabo Catoche
PC 281	Punta Morro
PC 282	Punta Mastun
PI 1101	Polaris
PI 1102	Sirius
PI 1103	Capella
PI 1104	Canopus
PI 1105	Vega
PI 1106	Achernar
PI 1107	Rigel
PI 1108	Arcturus
PI 1109	Alpheratz
PI 1110	Procyon
PI 1111	Avior
PI 1112	Deneb
PI 1113	Formalhaut
PI 1114	Pollux
PI 1115	Regulus
PI 1116	Acrux
PI 1117	Spica
PI 1118	Hadar
PI 1119	Shaula
PI 1120	Mirfak
PI 1121	Ankaa
PI 1122	Bellatrix
PI 1123	Elnath
PI 1124	Alnilam
PI 1125	Peacock
PI 1126	Betelgeuse
PI 1127	Adhara
PI 1128	Alioth
PI 1129	Rasalhague
PI 1130	Nunki
PI 1131	Hamal
PI 1132	Suhail
PI 1133	Dubhe
PI 1134	Denebola
PI 1135	Alkaid
PI 1136	Alphecca
PI 1137	Eltanin
PI 1138	Kochab
PI 1139	Enif
PI 1140	Schedar
PI 1141	Markab
PI 1142	Megrez
PI 1143	Mizar
PI 1144	Phekda
PI 1145	Acamar
PI 1146	Diphda
PI 1147	Menkar
PI 1148	Sabik
PI 1201	Isla Coronado
PI 1202	Isla Lobos
PI 1203	Isla Guadalupe
PI 1204	Isla Cozumel
PI 1301	Acuario
PI 1302	Aguila
PI 1303	Aries
PI 1304	Auriga
PI 1305	Cancer
PI 1306	Capricorno
PI 1307	Centauro
PI 1308	Geminis
PI 1401	Miaplacidus
PI 1402	Algol
PI 1403	Castor
PI 1404	Merak
PI 1405	Caph
PI 1406	Mirach
PO 102	Juan de la Barrera
PO 103	Mariano Escobedo
PO 104	Manuel Doblado
PO 106	Santos Degollado
PO 108	Juan Alvares
PO 109	Manuel Gutierrez Zamora
PO 110	Valentin Gomez Farias
PO 113	Ignacio Vallarta
PO 114	Jesus Gonzalez Ortega
PO 117	Mariano Matamoros
PO 121	Cadete Virgilio Uribe
PO 122	Teniente José Azueta
PO 123	Capitán de Fragata Pedro Sáinz de Baranda
PO 124	Comodoro Carlos Castillo Bretón
PO 125	Vicealmirante Othón P Blanco
PO 126	Contralmirante Angel Ortiz Monasterio
PO 131	Capitán de Navio Sebastian José Holzinger
PO 132	Capitán de Navio Blas Godinez
PO 133	Brigadier José Mariá de la Vega
PO 134	General Felipe B Berriozábal
PO 141	Justo Sierra Mendez
PO 143	Guillermo Prieto
PO 144	Matias Romero
PO 151	Durango
PO 152	Sonora
PO 153	Guanajuato
PO 154	Veracruz
PO 161	Oaxaca
PO 162	Baja California

Amphibious Forces

A 402	Manzanillo
A 411	Rio Papaloapan
A 412	Usumacinta

Survey and Research Ships

BI 01	Alejandro de Humboldt
BI 02	Onjuku
BI 03	Altair
BI 04	Antares
BI 05	Rio Suchiate
BI 06	Rio Ondo
BI 08	Arrecife Alacrán
BI 09	Arrecife Rizo
BI 10	Arrecife Cabezo
BI 11	Arrecife Anegada de Adentro
BI 12	Rio Tuxpan

Auxiliaries

AMP 01	Huasteco
AMP 02	Zapoteco
ARE 01	Otomi
ARE 02	Yaqui
ARE 03	Seri
ARE 04	Cora
ARE 05	Iztaccihuatl
ARE 06	Popocateptl
ARE 07	Citlaltepl
ARE 08	Xinantecatl
ARE 09	Matlalcueye
ARE 10	Tlaloc
ATQ 01	Aguascalientes
ATQ 02	Tlaxcala
ATR 01	Maya
ATR 03	Tarasco

Training Ships

D 111	Comodoro Manual Azueta
BE 01	Cuauhtemoc
BI 07	Moctezuma II

DESTROYERS

1 QUETZALCOATL (GEARING FRAM I) CLASS (DDH)

Name	*No*	*Builders*	*Laid down*	*Launched*	*Commissioned*
NETZAHUALCOYOTL (ex-*Steinaker* DD 863)	D 102 (ex-E 11, ex-E 04)	Bethlehem, Staten Island	1 Sep 1944	13 Feb 1945	26 May 1945

Displacement, tons: 3,030 standard; 3,690 full load
Dimensions, feet (metres): 390.2 × 41.9 × 15 *(118.7 × 12.5 × 4.6)*
Main machinery: 4 Babcock & Wilcox boilers; 600 psi *(43.3 kg/cm²)*; 850°F *(454°C)*; 2 GE turbines; 60,000 hp *(45 MW)*; 2 shafts
Speed, knots: 15
Range, n miles: 5,800 at 15 kt
Complement: 250

Guns: 4 USN 5 in *(127 mm)*/38 (2 twin) Mk 38 ❶; 15 rds/min to 17 km *(9.3 n miles)* anti-surface; 11 km *(5.9 n miles)* anti-aircraft; weight of shell 25 kg.
Countermeasures: ESM: WLR-1; radar warning.
Weapons control: Mk 37 GFCS. Mk 112 TFCS.
Radars: Air search: Lockheed SPS-40; B-band (E 10). Westinghouse SPS-29 ❷; B/C-band (E 11).
Surface search: Kelvin Hughes 17/9 ❸; I-band.
Navigation: Marconi LN66; I-band.
Fire control: Western Electric Mk 12/22 ❹; I/J-band.

NETZAHUALCOYOTL *(Scale 1 : 1,200), Ian Sturton* / 1170227

Helicopters: 1 MBB BO 105 CB ❺.

Programmes: Transferred from US by sale 24 February 1982.
Modernisation: A Bofors 57 mm gun was mounted between the torpedo tubes in B gun position in 1993 but removed in 2002. Flight deck slightly extended in 1996. New topmast and search radar also fitted in 1996. ASROC launchers, torpedo tubes and sonar reported removed in 1996.
Structure: The devices on top of the funnel are to reduce IR signature.
Operational: Top speed much reduced from the original 32 kt. Helicopter seldom carried. Pennant number changed in 2001. Based at Manzanillo.

NETZAHUALCOYOTL *6/1995, Mexican Navy* / 1133543

FRIGATES

4 ALLENDE (KNOX) CLASS (FFHM)

Name	*No*	*Builders*	*Laid down*	*Launched*	*Commissioned*
IGNACIO ALLENDE (ex-*Stein*)	F 211 (ex-E 50, ex-FF 1065)	Lockheed	1 June 1970	19 Dec 1970	8 Jan 1972
MARIANO ABASOLO (ex-*Marvin Shields*)	F 212 (ex-E 51, ex-FF 1066)	Todd Shipyards	12 Apr 1968	23 Oct 1969	10 Apr 1971
GUADALOUPE VICTORIA (ex-*Pharris*)	F 213 (ex-E 52, ex-FF 1094)	Avondale Shipyards	11 Feb 1972	16 Dec 1972	26 Jan 1974
FRANCISCO JAVIER MINA (ex-*Whipple*)	F 214 (ex-FF 1062)	Todd Shipyards	24 Apr 1967	12 Apr 1968	22 Aug 1970

Displacement, tons: 3,011 standard; 4,260 full load
Dimensions, feet (metres): 439.6 × 46.8 × 15; 24.8 (sonar) *(134 × 14.3 × 4.6; 7.8)*
Main machinery: 2 Combustion Engineering/Babcock & Wilcox boilers; 1,200 psi *(84.4 kg/cm²)*; 950°F *(510°C)*; 1 Westinghouse turbine; 35,000 hp *(26 MW)*; 1 shaft
Speed, knots: 27
Range, n miles: 4,000 at 22 kt on 1 boiler
Complement: 288 (20 officers)

Missiles: SAM: 1 octuple Mk 25 launcher for Sea Sparrow RIM-7P (in F 211) ❶ (see *Structure*); semi-active radar homing to 16 km *(8.5 n miles)* at 2.5 Mach; warhead 38 kg. SA-N-10; IR homing to 5 km *(2.7 n miles)* at 1.7 Mach; warhead 1.5 kg.
A/S: Honeywell ASROC Mk 16 octuple launcher with reload system (has 2 cells modified to fire Harpoon) ❷; inertial guidance to 1.6–10 km *(1-5.4 n miles)*; payload Mk 46.
Guns: 1 FMC 5 in *(127 mm)*/54 Mk 42 Mod 9 ❸; 20–40 rds/min to 24 km *(13 n miles)* anti-surface; 14 km *(7.7 n miles)* anti-aircraft; weight of shell 32 kg.
Torpedoes: 4—324 mm Mk 32 (2 twin) fixed tubes ❹. 22 Honeywell Mk 46; anti-submarine; active/passive homing to 11 km *(5.9 n miles)* at 40 kt; warhead 44 kg.
Countermeasures: Decoys: 2 Loral Hycor SRBOC 6-barrelled fixed Mk 36 ❺; IR flares and chaff to 4 km *(2.2 n miles)*. T Mk-6 Fanfare/SLQ-25 Nixie; torpedo decoy. Prairie Masker hull and blade rate noise suppression.
ESM: SLQ-32(V)2 ❻; intercept.

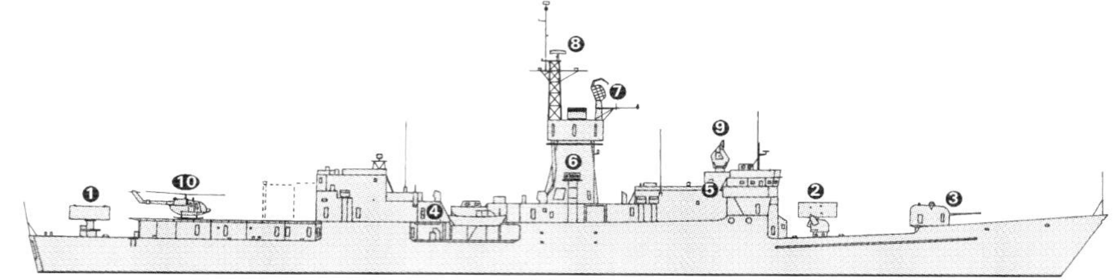

IGNACIO ALLENDE *(Scale 1 : 1,200), Ian Sturton* / 0114668

Weapons control: Mk 68 Mod 3 GFCS. Mk 114 Mod 6 ASW FCS. Mk 1 target designation system. MMS target acquisition sight (for mines, small craft and low flying aircraft).
Radars: Air search: Lockheed SPS-40B ❼; B-band.
Surface search: Raytheon SPS-10 or Norden SPS-67 ❽; G-band.
Navigation: Marconi LN66; I-band.
Fire control: Western Electric SPG-53D/F ❾; I/J-band.
Tacan: SRN 15.
Sonars: EDO/General Electric SQS-26CX; bow-mounted; active search and attack; medium frequency.

Helicopters: 1 BO 105 CB ❿.

Programmes: First pair decommissioned from USN in 1992/93. Both transferred on 29 January 1997 and arrived in Mexico 16 August 1997. Both then underwent extensive refits, entering service on 23 November 1998. Third of class *(ex-Pharris)* transferred 2 February 2000 and recommissioned on 16 March 2000. The fourth ship *(ex-Whipple)* transferred in August 2001 and recommissioned on 1 November 2002.
Modernisation: To be fitted with SSM (Harpoon or Gabriel II).
Structure: Four Mk 32 torpedo tubes are fixed in the midships structure, two to a side, angled out at 45°. The original Knox class SAM launcher has been put back aft, in F 211 only.
Operational: In US service these ships had Harpoon SSM, but it is reported that these weapons are not carried. Pennant numbers changed in 2001. All based at Tuxpan.

IGNACIO ALLENDE (old number) ***11/1998, Mexican Navy*** / 0017679

IGNACIO ALLENDE ***6/2005, Mexican Navy*** / 1153500

2 BRAVO (BRONSTEIN) CLASS (FFH)

Name	*No*	*Builders*	*Laid down*	*Launched*	*Commissioned*
NICOLAS BRAVO (ex-*McCloy*)	F 201 (ex-E 40, ex-FF 1038)	Avondale Shipyards	15 Sep 1961	9 June 1962	21 Oct 1963
HERMENEGILDO GALEANA (ex-*Bronstein*)	F 202 (ex-E 42, ex-FF 1037)	Avondale Shipyards	16 May 1961	31 Mar 1962	16 June 1963

Displacement, tons: 2,360 standard; 2,650 full load
Dimensions, feet (metres): 371.5 × 40.5 × 13.5; 23 (sonar) *(113.2 × 12.3 × 4.1; 7)*
Main machinery: 2 Foster-Wheeler boilers; 1 De Laval geared turbine; 20,000 hp *(14.92 MW)*; 1 shaft
Speed, knots: 23.5. **Range, n miles:** 3,924 at 15 kt
Complement: 207 (17 officers)

Missiles: A/S: Honeywell ASROC Mk 112 octuple launcher ❶.
Guns: 2 USN 3 in *(76 mm)*/50 (twin) Mk 33 ❷; 50 rds/min to 12.8 km *(7 n miles)*; weight of shell 6 kg, or 1 Bofors 57 mm/70 Mk 2; 220 rds/min to 17 km *(9.3 n miles)*; weight of shell 2.4 kg.
Torpedoes: 6—324 mm US Mk 32 Mod 7 (2 triple) tubes ❸. 14 Honeywell Mk 46; anti-submarine; active/passive homing to 11 km *(5.9 n miles)* at 40 kt; warhead 44 kg.
Countermeasures: Decoys: 2 Loral Hycor 6-barrelled fixed Mk 33; IR flares and chaff to 4 km *(2.2 n miles)*.
T-Mk 6 Fanfare; torpedo decoy system.
Weapons control: Mk 56 GFCS. Mk 114 ASW FCS. Mk 1 target designation system. Elsag NA 18 optronic director may be fitted.
Radars: Air search: Lockheed SPS-40D ❹; B-band; range 320 km *(175 n miles)*.
Surface search: Raytheon SPS-10F ❺; G-band.

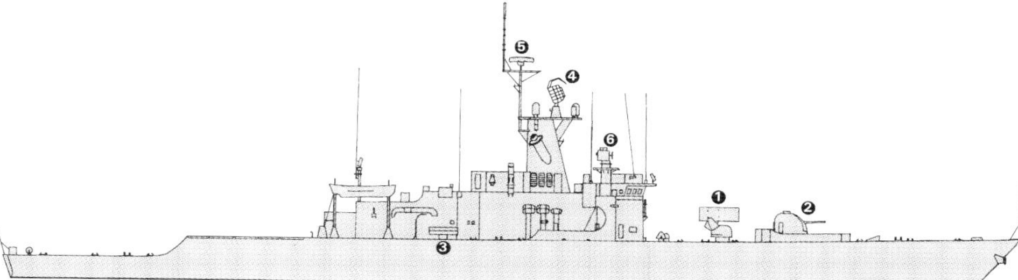

NICOLAS BRAVO

(Scale 1 : 900), Ian Sturton / 0506240

Navigation: Marconi LN66; I-band.
Fire control: General Electric Mk 35 ❻; I/J-band.
Sonars: EDO/General Electric SQS-26 AXR; bow-mounted; active search and attack; medium frequency.

Helicopters: Platform and some facilities but no hangar.

Programmes: Transferred from the US to Mexico by sale 12 November 1993 having paid off in December 1990.

Modernisation: Bofors 57 mm SAK may be fitted to replace the Mk 33 gun, possibly with an Elsag NA 18 optronic director.
Structure: Position of stem anchor and portside anchor (just forward of gun mount) necessitated by large bow sonar dome. As built, a single 3 in (Mk 34) open mount was aft of the helicopter deck; removed for installation of towed sonar which has since been taken out.
Operational: ASROC is non-operational. Pennant numbers changed in 2001. Both based at Manzanillo.

HERMENEGILDO GALEANA

6/2004, Mexican Navy / 0589778

HERMENEGILDO GALEANA

6/2004, Mexican Navy / 0589777

SHIPBORNE AIRCRAFT

Numbers/Type: 6 MD 902 Explorer.
Operational speed: 113 kt *(210 km/h)*.
Service ceiling: 9,845 ft *(3,000 m)*.
Range: 407 n miles *(754 km)*.
Role/Weapon systems: Coastal patrol helicopter acquired 1999–2000 for patrol, fisheries protection and EEZ protection duties; SAR as secondary role. Sensors: Bendix search radar. Weapons: MGs or rocket pods.

BO 105CB *9/1994*, **Mexican Navy** / 0052606

Numbers/Type: 11 Bolkow BO 105.
Operational speed: 100 kt *(185 km/h)*.
Service ceiling: 17,000 ft *(5,180 m)*.
Range: 160 n miles *(296 km)*.
Role/Weapon systems: Coastal patrol helicopter acquired 1982–86 for patrol, fisheries protection and EEZ protection duties; SAR as secondary role. A modernisation programme was announced in October 2003; the first upgraded aircraft was delivered in 2004 and the programme was completed by late 2006. Sensors: Bendix search radar. Weapons: MGs or rocket pods.

BO 105 *6/2004*, **Mexican Navy** / 1133542

Numbers/Type: 2 Eurocopter AS 555 AF Fennec.
Operational speed: 121 kt *(225 km/h)*.
Service ceiling: 13,120 ft *(4,000 m)*.
Range: 389 n miles *(722 km)*.
Role/Weapon systems: Patrol helicopter for EEZ protection and SAR. Operated from Oaxaca class patrol ships. More may be acquired when funds are available. Sensors: Bendix 1500 search radar. Weapons: Can carry up to two torpedoes, rocket pods or an MG.

AS 555 AF *6/2005*, **Mexican Navy** / 1133541

Numbers/Type: 4 Eurocopter AS 565ME Panther.
Operational speed: 165 kt *(305 km/h)*.
Service ceiling: 15,223 ft *(4,640 m)*.
Range: 200 n miles *(370 km)*.
Role/Weapon systems: Transport and reconnaissance helicopter procured in June 2005. Four further aircraft are to be acquired. Capable of carrying eight passengers or 1,000 kg load.

AS 565 ME *6/2005*, **Mexican Navy** / 1133540

LAND-BASED MARITIME AIRCRAFT (FRONT LINE)

Notes: (1) Transport aircraft used include two Rockwell 306 Sabreliners, three Learjets, one Dash 8-200, 28 Mil Mi-17, four Mil Mi-2 Hoplite and four MD 500E.
(2) Training aircraft include eight Aeromacchi M-290TP Redigos, 14 Maule MX-7-180, nine Zlin Z242L, three Beech B55 Baron, one Cessna 402C, four Lancair and five Schweizer 300C.
(3) Two Cessna C-208 Grand Caravan Elint aircraft are to be transferred from the US. To be equipped with radar and FLIR.

Mi-2 *6/2005*, **Mexican Navy** / 1133539

Mi-17 *6/2005*, **Mexican Navy** / 1133537

SABRELINER *6/2005*, **Mexican Navy** / 1133538

Numbers/Type: 3 Grumman E-2C Hawkeye.
Operational speed: 323 kt *(598 km/h)*.
Service ceiling: 37,000 ft *(11,278 m)*.
Range: 1,540 n miles *(2,852 km)*.
Role/Weapon systems: Acquired from Israel in 2004 after refurbishment by Israel Aircraft Industries' (IAI's) Bedek Aviation Group. Equipment details are speculative. Sensors: ESM: ALR-73 PDS; Airborne tactical data system with Links 4A and 11; AN/APS-125 radar; Mk XII IFF. Weapons: Unarmed.

E-2C *6/2004*, **Mexican Navy** / 0589773

Numbers/Type: 7 CASA C-212 Aviocar.
Operational speed: 190 kt *(353 km/h)*.
Service ceiling: 24,000 ft *(7,315 m)*.
Range: 1,650 n miles *(3,055 km)*.
Role/Weapon systems: Acquired from 1987 and used for Maritime Surveillance. Two aircraft upgraded in Spain with EADS/CASA Integrated Tactical System (FITS) in 2003. The remainder upgraded in Mexico by late 2006. One aircraft lost in November 2006. Sensors: Search radar; APS 504. Weapons: Unarmed.

C-212 *6/2005*, **Mexican Navy** / 1133536

Numbers/Type: 4 Rockwell Turbo Commander.
Operational speed: 250 kt *(463 km/h)*.
Service ceiling: 31,000 ft *(9,450 m)*.
Range: 480 n miles *(890 km)*.
Role/Weapon systems: Acquired in 1992. Used for reconnaissance and transport.

TURBO COMMANDER *6/2004, Mexican Navy* / 1133544

Numbers/Type: 6 Antonov AN-32B.
Operational speed: 250 kt *(463 km/h)*.
Service ceiling: 26,000 ft *(7,925 m)*.
Range: 750 n miles *(1,390 km)*.
Role/Weapon systems: Acquired 1997–99. Used for transport and reconnaissance. Two aircraft fitted with FLIR.

An-32B *6/2004, Mexican Navy* / 0589775

Numbers/Type: 2 Casa CN-235 MP Persuader.
Operational speed: 210 kt *(384 km/h)*.
Service ceiling: 24,000 ft *(7,315 m)*.
Range: 2,000 n miles *(3,218 km)*.
Role/Weapon systems: EEZ surveillance. Two ordered in September 2008 with plans for a further four. Sensors and weapons to be announced.

CN-235 MP (Irish colours) *7/2003, Paul Jackson* / 0568896

PATROL FORCES

Notes: The Caribe project was initiated in about 1998 and involves the construction of 31 m patrol craft of 110 tons. One is under construction at ASTIMAR 3 and was reported 30 per cent completed in September 2006.

2 HURACAN (SAAR 4.5) CLASS (FAST ATTACK CRAFT—MISSILE) (PTG)

Name	*No*	*Builders*	*Launched*	*Commissioned*
HURACAN (ex-*Aliya*)	301	Israel Shipyards, Haifa	11 July 1980	11 July 1980
TORMENTA (ex-*Geoula*)	302	Israel Shipyards, Haifa	Oct 1980	31 Dec 1980

Displacement, tons: 498 full load
Dimensions, feet (metres): 202.4 × 24.9 × 9.2 *(61.7 × 7.6 × 2.8)*
Main machinery: 4 MTU/Bazán 16V 956 TB91 diesels; 15,000 hp(m) *(11.03 MW)* sustained; 4 shafts
Speed, knots: 31
Range, n miles: 3,000 at 17 kt; 1,500 at 30 kt
Complement: 53

Missiles: SSM: 4 IAI Gabriel II; radar or optical guidance; semi-active radar plus anti-radiation homing to 36 km *(19.4 n miles)* at 0.7 Mach; warhead 75 kg or 4 McDonnell Douglas Harpoon; active radar homing to 130 km *(70 n miles)* at 0.9 Mach; warhead 227 kg.
Guns: 2 Oerlikon 20 mm; 800 rds/min to 2 km.
1 General Electric/General Dynamics Vulcan Phalanx 6-barrelled 20 mm Mk 15; 3,000 rds/min combined to 1.5 km anti-missile.
4—12.7 mm (twin or quad) MGs.
Countermeasures: Decoys: 1—45-tube, 4—24-tube, 4 single-tube chaff launchers.
ESM/ECM: Elisra NS 9003/5; intercept and jammer.
Combat data systems: IAI Reshet datalink.
Radars: Air/surface search: Thomson-CSF TH-D 1040 Neptune; G-band.
Fire control: Selenia Orion RTN-10X; I/J-band.

Programmes: First two of the original class of five Saar 4.5s, before conversions from Saar 4s were started. Transferred to Mexico on 1 June 2004.
Modernisation: Harpoon may have replaced Gabriel in one or both ships.

HURACAN *7/2004, Diego Quevedo* / 0583999

Structure: The CIWS mounted in the eyes of the ship replaced a 40 mm gun.

Operational: Test-firing of a Gabriel missile took place in June 2005. Both based at Coatzacoalcos.

TORMENTA *7/2004, Diego Quevedo* / 0584000

4 HOLZINGER (ÁGUILA) CLASS (GUNSHIPS) (PSOH)

Name	*No*	*Builders*	*Laid down*	*Launched*	*Commissioned*
CAPITÁN DE NAVIO SEBASTIAN JOSÉ HOLZINGER (ex-*Uxmal*)	PO 131 (ex-C 01, ex-GA 01)	ASTIMAR 20, Salina Cruz, Oaxaco	1 June 1985	1 June 1988	1 May 1991
CAPITÁN DE NAVIO BLAS GODINEZ (ex-*Mitla*)	PO 132 (ex-C 02, ex-GA 02)	ASTIMAR 1, Tampico, Tamaulipas	1 July 1985	22 Mar 1988	1 Nov 1991
BRIGADIER JOSÉ MARIÁ DE LA VEGA (ex-*Peten*)	PO 133 (ex-C 03, ex-GA 03)	ASTIMAR 20, Salina Cruz, Oaxaco	22 Sep 1986	1 June 1988	16 Mar 1994
GENERAL FELIPE B BERRIOZÁBAL (ex-*Anahuac*)	PO 134 (ex-C 04, ex-GA 04)	ASTIMAR 1, Tampico, Tamaulipas	9 Mar 1988	21 Apr 1991	18 Mar 1994

Displacement, tons: 1,290 full load
Dimensions, feet (metres): 244.1 × 34.4 × 11.1 *(74.4 × 10.5 × 3.4)*
Main machinery: 2 MTU 20V 956 TB92 diesels; 11,700 hp(m) *(8.6 MW)* sustained; 2 shafts
Speed, knots: 22
Range, n miles: 3,820 at 16 kt
Complement: 75 (11 officers)

Guns: 1 Bofors 57 mm/70 Mk 2 (PO 133, PO 134); 220 rds/min to 17 km *(9.3 n miles)*; weight of shell 2.4 kg or 2 Bofors 40 mm/60 (1 twin) (PO 131, PO 132).
Combat data systems: Elsag 2 CSDA-10.
Weapons control: Elsag NA 18 optronic director (PO 133, PO 134).
Radars: Surface search: Raytheon SPS-64(V)6A; I-band.
Navigation: Kelvin Hughes Nucleus; I-band.

Helicopters: 1 MBB BO 105 CB.

Programmes: Originally four were ordered from Tampico and Veracruz. First laid down November 1983, second in 1984 but then there were delays caused by financial problems. Named after military heroes.
Structure: An improved variant of the Bazán Halcon (Uribe) class with a flight deck extended to the stern.
Operational: Pennant numbers changed in 2001. All based at Lazaro.

GENERAL FELIPE B BERRIOZÁBAL *6/2005, Mexican Navy* / 1133533

3 SIERRA CLASS (GUNSHIPS) (PSOH)

Name	*No*	*Builders*	*Laid down*	*Launched*	*Commissioned*
JUSTO SIERRA MENDEZ	PO 141 (ex-C 2001)	ASTIMAR 1, Tampico, Tamaulipas	19 Jan 1998	1 June 1998	1 June 1998
GUILLERMO PRIETO	PO 143 (ex-C 2003)	ASTIMAR 1, Tampico, Tamaulipas	1 June 1998	18 Sep 1999	18 Sep 1999
MATIAS ROMERO	PO 144 (ex-C 2004)	ASTIMAR 20, Salina Cruz, Oaxaco	23 July 1998	17 Sep 1999	17 Sep 1999

Displacement, tons: 1,344 full load
Dimensions, feet (metres): 231.0 × 34.4 × 9.2 *(70.4 × 10.5 × 2.8)*
Main machinery: 2 Caterpillar 3616 V16 diesels; 6,197 hp(m) *(4.55 MW)*; 2 shafts
Speed, knots: 18
Complement: 76 (10 officers)

Missiles: SA-N-10 (PO 144); IR homing to 5 km *(2.7 n miles)* at 1.7 Mach; warhead 1.5 kg.
Guns: 1 Bofors 57 mm/70 Mk 3; 220 rds/min to 17 km *(9.3 n miles)*; weight of shell 2.4 kg.
Combat data systems: Alenia 2.
Weapons control: Saab EOS 450 optronic director.
Radars: Air/surface search: E/F-band.
Surface search: I-band.

Helicopters: 1 MD 902 Explorer.

Programmes: Follow on to the Holzinger class. Ordered in 1997.
Structure: Derived from the Holzinger class but with a markedly different superstructure. All ships carry 11 m interceptor craft capable of 50 kt.
Operational: All based at Acapulco. PO 142 *Benito Juarez* badly damaged by fire in October 2003 and subsequently decommissioned. The ship was sunk as a target in July 2007.

JUSTO SIERRA MENDEZ *6/2005, Mexican Navy* / 1133535

JUSTO SIERRA MENDEZ *6/2004, Mexican Navy* / 0589771

4 DURANGO CLASS (GUNSHIPS) (PSOH)

Name	*No*	*Builders*	*Laid down*	*Launched*	*Commissioned*
DURANGO	PO 151	ASTIMAR 1, Tampico, Tamaulipas	18 Dec 1999	11 Sep 2000	11 Sep 2000
SONORA	PO 152	ASTIMAR 20, Salina Cruz, Oaxaco	14 Dec 1999	4 Sep 2000	4 Sep 2000
GUANAJUATO	PO 153	ASTIMAR 1, Tampico, Tamaulipas	2000	13 Dec 2001	13 Dec 2001
VERACRUZ	PO 154	ASTIMAR 20, Salina Cruz, Oaxaco	4 Sep 2000	17 Dec 2001	17 Dec 2003

Displacement, tons: 1,470 full load
Dimensions, feet (metres): 268.4 × 34.4 × 9.2 *(81.8 × 10.5 × 2.8)*
Main machinery: 2 Caterpillar 3616 V16 diesels; 6,197 hp(m) *(4.55 MW)*; 2 shafts
Speed, knots: 18
Complement: 76 (10 officers)

Guns: 1 Bofors 57 mm/70 Mk 3; 220 rds/min to 17 km *(9.3 n miles)*; weight of shell 2.4 kg.
Combat data systems: Alenia 2.
Weapons control: Saab EOS 450 optronic director.
Radars: Air/surface search: E/F-band.
Surface search: I-band.

Helicopters: 1 MD 902 Explorer.

Programmes: Follow on to the Sierra class. Ordered on 1 June 1998.
Structure: Derived from the Holzinger class but with a markedly different superstructure. Durango class slightly larger than the Sierra class. All ships carry 11 m interceptor craft capable of 50 kt.
Operational: PO 151 and PO 152 based at Guaymas and PO 153 and PO 154 at Coatzacoalcos.

DURANGO *6/2004, Mexican Navy / 0589770*

2 + 2 (2) OAXACA CLASS (GUNSHIPS) (PSOH)

Name	*No*	*Builders*	*Laid down*	*Launched*	*Commissioned*
OAXACA	PO 161	ASTIMAR 20, Salina Cruz, Oaxaco	17 Dec 2001	11 Apr 2003	Feb 2005
BAJA CALIFORNIA	PO 162	ASTIMAR 1, Tampico, Tamaulipas	13 Dec 2001	21 May 2003	Apr 2007
BICENTENARIO	PO 163	ASTIMAR 20, Salina Cruz, Oaxaco	11 Apr 2003	2009	2010
INDEPENDENCIA	PO 164	ASTIMAR 1, Tampico, Tamaulipas	21 May 2003	2009	2010

Displacement, tons: 1,680
Dimensions, feet (metres): 282.2 × 34.4 × 9.3 *(86.0 × 10.5 × 3.6)*
Main machinery: 2 Caterpillar 3916 V16 diesels; 2 shafts
Speed, knots: 20
Complement: 77
Guns: 1 Oto Melara 3 in *(76 mm)*/62 Compact; 85 rds/min to 16 km *(8.7 n miles)*; weight of shell 6 kg. 1 Oto Melara 25 mm. 2—12.7 mm MGs.

Combat data systems: Alenia.
Radars: Surface search/navigation: Terma Scanter 2001; I-band.
Fire control: Alenia NA-25; I-band.
Helicopters: Eurocopter AS 565 Panther.

Programmes: The programme was originally for six ships. Construction of PO 163 and PO 164 was suspended for about two years but was resumed in 2007. Delivery of both ships is now expected in 2010. A further two ships are expected to be laid down in 2009.
Structure: A further derivation of the basic Holzinger class and a slightly longer version of the Durango class. Capable of operating a helicopter and equipped with a fast 11 m interception boat capable of 50 kt.
Operational: PO 161 and PO 162 based at Coatzacoalcos.

OAXACA *9/2007, Mario R V Carneiro / 1353233*

6 URIBE CLASS (GUNSHIPS) (PSOH)

Name	*No*	*Builders*	*Laid down*	*Launched*	*Commissioned*
CADETE VIRGILIO URIBE	PO 121 (ex-C 11, ex-GH 01)	Bazán, San Fernando	1 July 1981	12 Nov 1981	1 Aug 1982
TENIENTE JOSÉ AZUETA	PO 122 (ex-C 12, ex-GH 02)	Bazán, San Fernando	7 Sep 1981	12 Dec 1981	23 Sep 1982
CAPITÁN de FRAGATA PEDRO SÁINZ de BARANDA	PO 123 (ex-C 13, ex-GH 03)	Bazán, San Fernando	22 Oct 1981	29 Jan 1982	1 May 1983
COMODORO CARLOS CASTILLO BRETÓN	PO 124 (ex-C 14, ex-GH 04)	Bazán, San Fernando	11 Nov 1981	26 Feb 1982	24 Feb 1983
VICEALMIRANTE OTHÓN P BLANCO	PO 125 (ex-C 15, ex-GH 05)	Bazán, San Fernando	18 Dec 1981	26 Mar 1982	24 Feb 1983
CONTRALMIRANTE ANGEL ORTIZ MONASTERIO	PO 126 (ex-C 16, ex-GH 06)	Bazán, San Fernando	30 Dec 1981	4 May 1982	24 Feb 1983

Displacement, tons: 988 full load
Dimensions, feet (metres): 219.9 × 34.4 × 11.5 *(67 × 10.5 × 3.5)*
Main machinery: 2 MTU-Bazán 16V 958TB92 diesels; 7,500 hp(m) *(5.52 MW)* sustained; 2 shafts
Speed, knots: 22. **Range, n miles:** 5,000 at 13 kt
Complement: 46 (7 officers)

Guns: 1 Bofors 40 mm/70; 300 rds/min to 12.5 km *(6.7 n miles)*; weight of shell 0.96 kg.
Weapons control: Naja optronic director.
Radars: Surface search: Decca AC 1226; I-band.
Navigation: I-band.
Tacan: SRN 15.

Helicopters: 1 MBB BO 105 CB.

Programmes: Ordered in 1980 to a Halcon class design. Contracts for a further eight of the class have been shelved. Pennant numbers changed in 1992. Named after naval heroes.
Modernisation: An upgrade programme for all six ships was in progress in 2006.
Structure: Flight deck extends to the stern. Similar ships built for Argentina.
Operational: Used for EEZ patrol. Pennant numbers changed in 2001. Basing: Lázaro (PO 121, 122); Manzanillo (PO 123); Ensenada (PO 124, 125, 126).

COMODORO CARLOS CASTILLO BRETÓN *9/2008*, Julio Montes* / 1353234

10 VALLE (AUK) CLASS (COAST GUARD) (PG/PGH)

JUAN DE LA BARRERA (ex-*Guillermo Prieto*, ex-*Symbol* MSF 123) PO 102 (ex-C 71, ex-G-02)
MARIANO ESCOBEDO (ex-*Champion* MSF 314) PO 103 (ex-C 72, ex-G-03)
MANUEL DOBLADO (ex-*Defense* MSF 317) PO 104 (ex-C 73, ex-G-05)
SANTOS DEGOLLADO (ex-*Gladiator* MSF 319) PO 106 (ex-C 75, ex-G-07)
JUAN N ALVARES (ex-*Ardent* MSF 340) PO 108 (ex-C 77, ex-G-09)
MANUEL GUTIERREZ ZAMORA (ex-*Roselle* MSF 379) PO 109 (ex-C 78, ex-G-10)
VALENTIN GOMEZ FARIAS (ex-*Starling* MSF 64) PO 110 (ex-C 79, ex-G-11)
IGNACIO L VALLARTA (ex-*Velocity* MSF 128) PO 113 (ex-C 82, ex-G-14)
JESUS GONZALEZ ORTEGA (ex-*Chief* MSF 315) PO 114 (ex-C 83, ex-G-15)
MARIANO MATAMOROS (ex-*Hermenegildo Galeana*, ex-*Sage* MSF 111) PO 117 (ex-C 86, ex-G-19)

Displacement, tons: 1,065 standard; 1,250 full load
Dimensions, feet (metres): 221.2 × 32.2 × 9.2 *(67.5 × 9.8 × 2.8)*
Main machinery: Diesel-electric; 2 Caterpillar diesels; 2 shafts
Speed, knots: 18
Range, n miles: 6,900 at 10 kt
Complement: 73 (9 officers)
Guns: 1 USN 3 in *(76 mm)*/50. 4 Bofors 40 mm/60 (2 twin). 4—12.7 mm (2 twin) MGs (in some on quarterdeck).
Radars: Surface search: Kelvin Hughes 14/9 (in most); I-band.
Helicopters: Platform for 1 BO 105 (PO 103, 104 and 110).

Comment: Transferred from US, six in February 1973, four in April 1973, nine in September 1973. Eight have since been deleted. Employed on Coast Guard duties. All built during Second World War. Variations are visible in the mid-ships section where some have a bulwark running from the break of the forecastle to the quarterdeck. Minesweeping gear removed. All ships re-engined1999–2002. Some carry a Pirana 26 kt motor launch armed with 40 mm grenade launchers and 7.62 mm MGs. P 103, P 104 and P 110 have had helicopter flight decks installed aft. Plans to fit flight decks in the others have been shelved. PO 102, 103, 104, 106, 108 and 113 based at Lazaro; PO 109 and 114 based at Tampico; PO 110 and 117 based at Ensenada.

SANTOS DEGOLLADO *6/2005, Mexican Navy* / 1133532

48 POLARIS CLASS (COMBATBOAT 90 HMN) (PBF)

POLARIS PI 1101	**FOMALHAUT** PI 1113	**PEACOCK** PI 1125	**ELTANIN** PI 1137
SIRIUS PI 1102	**POLLUX** PI 1114	**BETELGEUSE** PI 1126	**KOCHAB** PI 1138
CAPELLA PI 1103	**RÉGULUS** PI 1115	**ADHARA** PI 1127	**ENIF** PI 1139
CANOPUS PI 1104	**ACRUX** PI 1116	**ALIOTH** PI 1128	**SCHEDAR** PI 1140
VEGA PI 1105	**SPICA** PI 1117	**RASALHAGUE** PI 1129	**MARKAB** PI 1141
ACHERNAR PI 1106	**HADAR** PI 1118	**NUNKI** PI 1130	**MEGREZ** PI 1142
RIGEL PI 1107	**SHAULA** PI 1119	**HAMAL** PI 1131	**MIZAR** PI 1143
ARCTURUS PI 1108	**MIRFAK** PI 1120	**SUHAIL** PI 1132	**PHEKDA** PI 1144
ALPHERATZ PI 1109	**ANKAA** PI 1121	**DUBHE** PI 1133	**ACAMAR** PI 1145
PROCYÓN PI 1110	**BELLATRIX** PI 1122	**DENEBOLA** PI 1134	**DIPHDA** PI 1146
AVIOR PI 1111	**ELNATH** PI 1123	**ALKAID** PI 1135	**MENKAR** PI 1147
DENEB PI 1112	**ALNILÁN** PI 1124	**ALPHECCA** PI 1136	**SABIK** PI 1148

Displacement, tons: 19 full load
Dimensions, feet (metres): 52.8 × 12.5 × 2.9 *(16.1 × 3.8 × 0.9)*
Main machinery: 2 CAT 3406E diesels; 1,605 hp(m) *(1.18 MW)*; 2 waterjets
Speed, knots: 47
Range, n miles: 240 at 30 kt
Complement: 4
Guns: 1 Oto Melara 12.7 mm MG (PL 1141-1148). 1—12.7 mm MG (others).
Radars: Surface search: Litton Decca Bridgemaster E; I-band.

Comment: All named after stars. First 12 ordered from Dockstavarvet, Sweden, on 15 April 1999, second batch of eight on 29 July 1999 and last batch of 20 on 1 February 2000. All delivered by 2001. A further batch of eight constructed at ASTIMAR 3, Coatzacoalcos, and delivered 2004–05. These craft are in service with the Swedish and Norwegian navies and with paramilitary forces in Malaysia and China. Based at Lerma (1103, 1104); Cozumel (1143, 1144); Yucalpeten (1107, 1108); Isla Mujeres (1109, 1110); Tuxpan (1113, 1114, 1105, 1106); Chetumel (1101, 1102, 1128, 1129); Veracruz (1131, 1132); Ensenada (1111, 1112, 1123); Manzanillo (1115, 1116);Topolobampo (1118); Mazatlan (1121, 1122); Puerto Cortes (1141); Puerto Vallarta (1124, 1136); Acapulco (1126, 1127); Guaymas (1130, 1139); Puerto Penasco (1138); Isla Socorro (1135); Frontera (1142); Puerto Chiapas (1117, 1120); Los Cabos (1119, 1147); Huatulco (1133, 1134); Isla Maria Nay (1137); San Blas Nay (1145, 1146); La Paz (1148); Lazaro (1125, 1140).

RÉGULUS *6/2005, Mexican Navy* / 1133526

1 + 1 (4) DÉMOCRATA CLASS (PBO)

Name	No	Builders	Launched	Commissioned
DÉMOCRATA	PC 241 (ex-C 101)	ASTIMAR 6, Varadero, Guaymas	16 Oct 1997	9 Jan 1998
FRANCISCO I MADERO	–	ASTIMAR 3, Coatzacoalcos, Veracruz	8 June 2007	–

Displacement, tons: 450 full load
Dimensions, feet (metres): 172.2 × 29.5 × 8.8 *(52.5 × 9 × 2.7)*
Main machinery: 2 MTU 20V 956 TB92 diesels; 6,119 hp(m) *(4.5 MW)*; 2 shafts
Speed, knots: 30
Complement: 36 (13 officers)
Guns: 2 Bofors 40 mm/60 (twin).
Radars: Surface search: Racal Decca; E/F-band.

Comment: Based at Yukalpeten. A second slightly longer (58 m) unit is under construction and was launched in 2007. Further units may be built subject to funding. A 50 kt Boston Whaler launch is carried at the stern.

DÉMOCRATA *6/2004, Mexican Navy* / 0589769

3 CAPE (PGM 71) CLASS (LARGE PATROL CRAFT) (PB)

Name	No	Builders	Recommissioned
CABO CORRIENTES (ex-*Jalisco*, ex-*Cape Carter*)	PC 271 (ex-P 42)	CG Yard, Curtis Bay	16 Mar 1990
CABO CORZO (ex-*Nayarit*, ex-*Cape Hedge*)	PC 272 (ex-P 43)	CG Yard, Curtis Bay	21 Apr 1990
CABO CATOCHE (ex-*Cape Hattaras*)	PC 273 (ex-P 44)	CG Yard, Curtis Bay	18 Mar 1991

Displacement, tons: 98 standard; 148 full load
Dimensions, feet (metres): 95 × 20.2 × 6.1 *(28.9 × 6.2 × 1.85)*
Main machinery: 2 GM 16V-149TI diesels; 2,322 hp *(1.73 MW)* sustained; 2 shafts
Speed, knots: 20. **Range, n miles:** 2,500 at 10 kt
Complement: 14 (1 officer)
Guns: 1—20 mm. 2—12.7 mm MGs.
Radars: Navigation: Raytheon SPS-64; I-band.

Comment: All built in 1953; have been re-engined and extensively modernised. Transferred under the FMS programme, having paid off from the US Coast Guard. Pennant numbers changed in 2001. PC 271 and PC 272 based at Puerto Vallarta and PC 273 at Isla Cozumel.

CABO CORZO *6/2005, Mexican Navy* / 1133531

2 POINT CLASS (LARGE PATROL CRAFT) (PB)

Name	No	Builders	Recommissioned
PUNTA MORRO (ex-*Point Verde*)	PC 281 (ex-P 60, ex-P 45)	CG Yard, Curtis Bay	19 July 1991
PUNTA MASTUN (ex-*Point Herron*)	PC 282 (ex-P 61, ex-P 46)	CG Yard, Curtis Bay	19 July 1991

Displacement, tons: 67 full load
Dimensions, feet (metres): 83 × 17.2 × 5.8 *(25.3 × 5.2 × 1.8)*
Main machinery: 2 Caterpillar diesels; 1,600 hp *(1.19 MW)*; 2 shafts
Speed, knots: 12. **Range, n miles:** 1,500 at 8 kt
Complement: 10
Guns: 2—12.7 mm MGs (can be carried).
Radars: Surface search: Raytheon SPS-64; I-band.

Comment: Ex-US Coast Guard craft built in 1961. Steel hulls and aluminium superstructures. Speed much reduced from original 23 kt. Pennant numbers changed in 2001. Both based at Lerma.

PUNTA MASTUN *6/2005, Mexican Navy* / 1133529

19 AZTECA CLASS (LARGE PATROL CRAFT) (PB)

Name	No	Builders	Commissioned
MATIAS DE CORDOVA (ex-*Guaycura*)	PC 202 (ex-P 02)	Scott & Sons, Bowling	6 Jan 1974
IGNACIO LÓPEZ RAYÓN (ex-*Tarahumara*)	PC 206 (ex-P 06)	Ailsa Shipbuilding Co Ltd	18 Apr 1975
JUAN ANTONIO DE LA FUENTE (ex-*Mexica*)	PC 208 (ex-P 08)	Ailsa Shipbuilding Co Ltd	28 Dec 1975
LEON GUZMAN (ex-*Zapoteca*)	PC 209 (ex-P 09)	Scott & Sons, Bowling	1 June 1975
IGNACIO RAMIREZ (ex-*Huastela*)	PC 210 (ex-P 10)	Ailsa Shipbuilding Co Ltd	1 June 1975
IGNACIO MARISCAL (ex-*Mazahua*)	PC 211 (ex-P 11)	Ailsa Shipbuilding Co Ltd	25 Dec 1975
HERIBERTO JARA CORONA (ex-*Huichol*)	PC 212 (ex-P 12)	Ailsa Shipbuilding Co Ltd	17 Nov 1975
COLIMA (ex-*Yacqui*)	PC 214 (ex-P 14)	Scott & Sons, Bowling	1 July 1975
JOSE JOAQUIN FERNANDEZ DE LIZARDI (ex-*Tlapaneco*)	PC 215 (ex-P 15)	Ailsa Shipbuilding Co Ltd	1 July 1976
FRANCISCO J MUGICA (ex-*Tarasco*)	PC 216 (ex-P 16)	Ailsa Shipbuilding Co Ltd	1 June 1976
JOSE MARIA DEL CASTILLO VELAZCO (ex-*Otomi*)	PC 218 (ex-P 18)	Lamont & Co Ltd	1 Nov 1976
JOSE NATIVIDAD MACIAS (ex-*Pimas*)	PC 220 (ex-P 20)	Lamont & Co Ltd	29 Dec 1976
TAMAULIPAS (ex-*Mazateco*)	PC 223 (ex-P 23)	ASTIMAR 3, Coatzacoalcos	18 May 1977
YUCATAN (ex-*Tolteca*)	PC 224 (ex-P 24)	ASTIMAR 3, Coatzacoalcos	18 May 1977
TABASCO (ex-*Maya*)	PC 225 (ex-P 25)	ASTIMAR 3, Coatzacoalcos	1 Dec 1978
COCHIMIE (ex-*Veracruz*)	PC 226 (ex-P 26)	ASTIMAR 3, Coatzacoalcos	1 Dec 1978
PUEBLA (ex-*Totonaca*)	PC 228 (ex-P 28)	ASTIMAR 3, Coatzacoalcos	1 Aug 1982
LEONA VICARIO (ex-*Olmeca*)	PC 230 (ex-P 30)	ASTIMAR 20, Salina Cruz, Oaxaco	1 May 1977
JOSEFA ORTIZ DE DOMINGUEZ (ex-*Tlahuica*)	PC 231 (ex-P 31)	ASTIMAR 20, Salina Cruz, Oaxaco	1 June 1977

Displacement, tons: 148 full load
Dimensions, feet (metres): 112.7 × 28.3 × 7.2 *(34.4 × 8.7 × 2.2)*
Main machinery: 2 Paxman 12YJCM diesels; 3,000 hp *(2.24 MW)* sustained; 2 shafts
Speed, knots: 24
Range, n miles: 1,537 at 14 kt
Complement: 24 (2 officers)
Guns: 1 Bofors 40 mm/60; 300 rds/min to 12 km *(6.5 n miles)* anti-surface; 4 km *(2.2 n miles)* anti-aircraft; weight of shell 2.4 kg.
1 Oerlikon 20 mm or 1—7.62 mm MG.
Radars: Surface search: Kelvin Hughes; I-band.

Comment: Ordered by Mexico on 27 March 1973 from Associated British Machine Tool Makers Ltd to a design by TT Boat Designs, Bembridge, Isle of Wight. The first 21 were modernised in 1987 in Mexico with spare parts and equipment supplied by ABMTM Marine Division who supervised the work which included engine refurbishment and the fitting of air conditioning. Names and pennant numbers changed in 2001. Based at: Veracruz (PC 223, 228); Yukaltepen (PC 224, 225, 226); Salina Cruz (PC 206, 209); Puerto Chiapas (PC 218, 220); Guaymas (PC 210, 214); Mazatlan (PC 211, 230, 231); Acapulco (PC 212, 215); La Paz (PC 208, 216); Ciudad Madero (PC 202).

JOSE NATIVIDAD MACIAS *6/2005, Mexican Navy* / 1133528

4 ISLA CLASS (FAST ATTACK CRAFT) (PBF)

Name	No	Builders	Commissioned
ISLA CORONADO	PI 1201 (ex-P 51)	Equitable Shipyards	1 Sep 1993
ISLA LOBOS	PI 1202 (ex-P 52)	Equitable Shipyards	1 Nov 1993
ISLA GUADALUPE	PI 1203 (ex-P 53)	Equitable Shipyards	1 Feb 1994
ISLA COZUMEL	PI 1204 (ex-P 54)	Equitable Shipyards	1 Apr 1994

Displacement, tons: 52 full load
Dimensions, feet (metres): 82 × 17.7 × 3.9 *(25 × 5.4 × 1.2)*
Main machinery: 3 Detroit diesels; 16,200 hp *(12.9 MW)*; 3 Arneson surface drives
Speed, knots: 50
Range, n miles: 1,200 at 30 kt
Complement: 9 (3 officers)
Guns: 1—12.7 mm MG. 2—7.62 mm MGs.
Radars: Surface search: Raytheon SPS 69; I-band.
Fire control: Thomson-CSF Agrion; J-band.

Comment: Built by the Trinity Marine Group to an XFPB (extra fast patrol boat) design. Deep Vee hulls with FRP/Kevlar construction. Similar craft built for US Navy. May be fitted with MM 15 SSMs in due course and armed with 40 mm or 20 mm guns. Pennant numbers changed 2001. Based at Topolobampo (PI 1201, 1202) and Guaymas (PI 1203, 1204).

ISLA CORONADO *6/2005, Mexican Navy* / 1133527

8 ACUARIO CLASS (COMBATBOAT 90HMN) (PBF)

ACUARIO PI 1301	**ARIES** PI 1303	**CANCER** PI 1305	**CENTAURO** PI 1307
AGUILA PI 1302	**AURIGA** PI 1304	**CAPRICORNO** PI 1306	**GEMINIS** PI 1308

Displacement, tons: 19 full load
Dimensions, feet (metres): 52.8 × 12.5 × 2.9 *(16.1 × 3.8 × 0.9)*
Main machinery: 2 CAT 3406E diesels; 1,605 hp(m) *(1.18 MW)*; 2 waterjets
Speed, knots: 47. **Range, n miles**: 240 at 30 kt
Complement: 4
Guns: 1 Oto Melara 12.7 mm MG.
Radars: Surface search: Litton Decca Bridgemaster E; I-band.

Comment: A further development of the Polaris class which are based on the Swedish Combatboat 90 and built by ASTIMAR 3, Coatzacoalcos. 1301 and 1302 commissioned on 1 June 2004 and 1303-1306 on 1 September 2004. P 1307-1308 commissioned on 1 September 2004 and known as Acuario B class. Based at Puerto Peñasco (1301); El Mezquital (1302, 1303); Frontera (1304); Ciudad Madero (1305, 1306); Ensenada (1307); Manzanillo (1308). All named after stars.

AGUILA *6/2005, Mexican Navy* / 1133523

6 + 5 POLARIS II CLASS (COMBATBOAT 90 HMN) (PBF)

MIAPLACIDUS PI 1401	**BEAVER** PI 1403	**CAPH** PI 1405
ALGOL PI 1402	**MERAK** PI 1404	**MIRACH** PI 1406

Displacement, tons: 19 full load
Dimensions, feet (metres): 52.5 × 11.2 × 2.9 *(16.0 × 3.4 × 0.9)*
Main machinery: 2 MAN diesels; 2,200 hp(m) *(1.62 MW)*; 2 waterjets
Speed, knots: 50. **Range, n miles**: 240 at 30 kt
Complement: 4
Guns: 1 Oto Melara 12.7 mm MG.
Radars: Surface search: Litton Decca Bridgemaster E; I-band.

Comment: A further development of the Polaris and Acuario classes. The first of class was delivered by Dockstavarvet, Sweden, on 10 August 2005 and three further craft were completed at ASTIMAR 3 by 2007. Two further craft delivered in January 2008. Based at Isla Cozumel (1401, 1402) and Ciudad del Carmen (1403, 1404). A class of 11 is expected.

MIAPLACIDUS *6/2005, Mexican Navy* / 1133524

0 + 6 (24) DEFENDER CLASS (RESPONSE BOATS) (PBF)

Displacement, tons: 2.7 full load
Dimensions, feet (metres): 10.1 × ? × ? *(33.3 × ? × ?)*
Main machinery: 3 outboard motors; 825 hp *(615 kW)*
Speed, knots: 50
Complement: 4
Guns: 2—12.7 mm MGs.
Radars: To be announced.

Comment: High-speed inshore patrol craft of aluminium construction and foam collar built by SAFE Boats International, Port Orchard, Washington. An initial order for six craft was made in December 2007 for delivery in 2009. A further 24 craft are expected by 2012.

61 FAST PATROL CRAFT (PBF)

G 01-36 +25

Dimensions, feet (metres): 22.3 × 7.5 × 1 *(6.8 × 2.3 × 0.3)*
Main machinery: 2 Johnson outboards; 280 hp *(209 kW)*
Speed, knots: 40
Range, n miles: 190 at 40 kt
Complement: 2
Guns: 1 or 2—7.62 mm MGs.

Comment: Details are for the 36 G 01-36 Piraña class. Acquired in 1993/94. An 11.6 m 50 kt Interceptor class launch is carried in *Démocrata* and modified 10.5 m versions are embarked in the Sierra, Durango and Oaxaca classes. Ten are in service and more may be acquired. There are also ten 29 ft Mako Marine craft, with twin Mercury outboards acquired in 1995. Five Sea Force 730 RIBs with Hamilton water-jets, also acquired in 1995–96.

INTERCEPTOR (old number) *7/1998, Mexican Navy* / 0052610

PIRAÑA CLASS *9/2002, Julio Montes* / 0533285

INTERCEPTOR (mod) *6/2004, Mexican Navy* / 0589767

AMPHIBIOUS FORCES

1 PANUCO CLASS (AP)

Name	*No*	*Builders*	*Commissioned*
MANZANILLO (ex-*Clearwater County*)	A 402 (ex-A 02)	Chicago Bridge & Iron Co	31 Mar 1944

Displacement, tons: 4,080 full load
Dimensions, feet (metres): 328 × 50 × 14 *(100 × 15.3 × 4.3)*
Main machinery: 2 GM 12-567A diesels; 1,800 hp *(1.34 MW)*; 2 shafts
Speed, knots: 11
Range, n miles: 6,000 at 11 kt
Complement: 250
Guns: 8 Bofors 40 mm (2 twin, 4 single).

Comment: Ex-US LST 452 class transferred and recommissioned on 1 July 1972. Deployed also as SAR and disaster relief ship. Based at Manzanillo.

TRANSPORT SHIP
7/1991, Harald Carstens
0081259

2 NEWPORT CLASS (LSTH)

Name	*No*	*Builders*	*Laid down*	*Launched*	*Commissioned*	*Recommissioned*
RIO PAPALOAPAN (ex-*Sonora*, ex-*Newport*)	A 411 (ex-A-04, ex-LST-1179)	Philadelphia Naval Shipyard	1 Nov 1966	3 Feb 1968	7 June 1969	5 June 2001
USUMACINTA (ex-*Frederick*)	A 412 (ex-LST-1184)	National Steel & Shipbuilding Co	13 Apr 1968	8 Mar 1969	11 Apr 1970	1 Dec 2002

Displacement, tons: 4,975 light; 8,450 full load
Dimensions, feet (metres): 522.3 (hull) × 69.5 × 17.5 (aft) *(159.2 × 21.2 × 5.3)*
Main machinery: 6 General Motors 16-645-E5 diesels; 16,500 hp *(12.3 MW)* sustained; 2 shafts; cp props; bow thruster
Speed, knots: 20
Range, n miles: 14,250 at 14 kt
Complement: 257 (13 officers)
Military lift: 400 troops; 500 tons vehicles; 3 LCVPs and 1 LCPL on davits.
Guns: 4 USN 3 in *(76 mm)*/50 (A 411).
Radars: Surface search: Raytheon SPS-10F; G-band.
Navigation: Raytheon SPS-64; I-band.

Helicopters: Platform only.

Programmes: A-411 sold to Mexico by the US Navy on 18 January 2001. A-412 sold on 9 December 2002. Both ships employed in amphibious role rather than as transport ships as previously reported. A 411 based at Tampico and A 412 at Manzanillo.
Modernisation: A new surface search radar reported installed in both ships by 2008.

PAPALOAPAN *8/2008*, A A de Kruijf* / 1353236

PAPALOAPAN *8/2008*, Michael Nitz* 1353235

SURVEY AND RESEARCH SHIPS

1 SUPPORT SHIP (AKS)

Name	*No*	*Builders*	*Commissioned*
RIO SUCHIATE (ex-*Monob 1*)	BI 05 (ex-A 27, ex-YAG 61, ex-YW 87)	Zenith Dredge Co	11 Nov 1943

Displacement, tons: 1,390 full load
Dimensions, feet (metres): 193.6 × 32.5 × 9.5 *(59.9 × 9.9 × 2.9)*
Main machinery: 1 Caterpillar D 398 diesel; 850 hp *(634 kW)*; 1 shaft
Speed, knots: 9
Range, n miles: 2,500 at 9 kt
Complement: 21

Comment: Acquired from US on 1 August 1996. The ship was converted from a water carrier to an acoustic research role in 1969, and had four laboratories in US service. Adapted to act also in support ship role in 1997. New pennant number in 2001. Based at Guaymas.

RIO SUCHIATE *6/2005, Mexican Navy* / 1170196

2 ROBERT D CONRAD CLASS (RESEARCH SHIPS) (AGOR)

Name	*No*	*Builders*	*Commissioned*
ALTAIR (ex-*James M Gilliss*)	BI 03 (ex-H 05, ex-AGOR 4)	Christy Corp, WI	5 Nov 1962
ANTARES (ex-*S P Lee*)	BI 04 (ex-H 06, ex-AG 192)	Defoe, Bay City	2 Dec 1962

Displacement, tons: 1,370 full load
Dimensions, feet (metres): 208.9 × 40 × 15.4 *(63.7 × 12.2 × 4.7)*
Main machinery: Diesel-electric; 2 Caterpillar diesel generators; 1,200 hp *(895 kW)*; 2 motors; 1,000 hp *(746 kW)*; 1 shaft; bow thruster
Speed, knots: 13.5
Range, n miles: 10,500 at 10 kt
Complement: 41 (12 officers) plus 15 scientists
Radars: Navigation: Raytheon 1025; Raytheon R4iY; I-band.

Comment: *Altair* leased from US 14 June 1983. Refitted and modernised in Mexico. Recommissioned 23 November 1984. Primarily used for oceanography. *Antares* served as an AGI with the USN until February 1974 when she transferred on loan to the Geological Survey. Acquired by sale and recommissioned on 1 December 1992. New pennant numbers in 2001. Based at Manzanillo (BI 03) and Tampico (BI 04).

ALTAIR *6/2005, Mexican Navy* / 1133519

4 ARRECIFE (EX-OLMECA II) CLASS (SURVEY CRAFT) (YGS)

ALACRAN BI 08 (ex-PR 301)
RIZO BI 09 (ex-PR 310)
CABEZO BI 10 (ex-PR 304)
ANEGAGADA DE ADENTRO BI 11 (ex-PR 309)

Displacement, tons: 18 full load
Dimensions, feet (metres): 54.8 × 14.4 × 3.9 *(16.7 × 4.4 × 1.2)*
Main machinery: 2 Detroit 8V-92TA diesels; 700 hp *(562 kW)* sustained; 2 shafts
Speed, knots: 20. **Range, n miles**: 460 at 10 kt
Complement: 15 (2 officers)
Guns: 1 — 12.7 mm MG.
Radars: Navigation: Raytheon 1900; I-band.

Comment: Built at Acapulco and completed between 1982 and 1989. GRP hulls. Converted for inshore hydrographic duties in 2003. All have *Arrecife* in front of the names. Based at Manzanillo (BI 08, 09) and Veracruz (BI 10, 11).

ALACRAN *6/2005, Mexican Navy* / 1133518

1 SURVEY SHIP (AGS)

Name	*No*	*Builders*	*Commissioned*
RIO HONDO (ex-*Deer Island*)	BI 06 (ex-H 08, ex-A 26, ex-YAG 62)	Halter Marine	May 1962

Displacement, tons: 400 full load
Dimensions, feet (metres): 120.1 × 27.9 × 6.9 *(36.6 × 8.5 × 2.1)*
Main machinery: 2 General Motors 7122-700 diesels; 2 shafts
Speed, knots: 10
Range, n miles: 6,000 at 10 kt
Complement: 20

Comment: Acquired from US on 1 August 1996 and adapted for a support ship role in 1997. Converted to Survey Ship in 1999. Used in US service from 1983 as an acoustic research ship to test noise reduction equipment. Started life as an oil rig supply tug. New pennant number in 2001. Based at Coatzacoalcos.

RIO HONDO (old number) *4/1999, M Declerck* / 0081258

1 HUMBOLDT CLASS (RESEARCH SHIP) (AGOR)

Name	*No*	*Builders*	*Recommissioned*
ALEJANDRO DE HUMBOLDT	BI 01 (ex-H 03)	JG Hitzler, Elbe	22 June 1987

Displacement, tons: 585 standard; 700 full load
Dimensions, feet (metres): 140.7 × 32 × 13.5 *(42.3 × 9.6 × 4.1)*
Main machinery: 1 MAN R8V 22/30 diesel; 2 shafts
Speed, knots: 14
Complement: 20 (4 officers)
Radars: Navigation: Kelvin Hughes; I-band.

Comment: Former trawler built in Germany and launched in January 1970. Converted in 1982 to become a hydrographical and acoustic survey ship. Based at Manzanillo. New pennant number in 2001.

ALEJANDRO DE HUMBOLDT (old number) *6/2001, Mexican Navy* / 0114671

1 SURVEY SHIP (AGS)

Name	*No*	*Builders*	*Commissioned*
RIO TUXPAN (ex-*Whiting*)	BI 12	Marietta Manufacturing Company, Mt Pleasant, West Virginia	July 1963

Displacement, tons: 907
Dimensions, feet (metres): 163.0 × 33.0 × 12.2 *(49.7 × 10.1 × 3.7)*
Main machinery: 2 General Motors diesels; 1,600 hp *(1.2 MW)*; 2 cp props
Speed, knots: 12
Range, n miles: 5,700 at 11 kt
Complement: 30 (7 officers)
Radars: Surface search: E/F-band.
Navigation: I-band.

Comment: Ex-US NOAA ship designed for hydrographic and bathymetric survey work. Decommissioned in May 2003 and transferred to the Mexican Navy in April 2005. Equipped (in NOAA service) with Intermediate Depth Swath Survey System (IDSSS) (36 kHz), Deep Water Echo Sounder (12 kHz), Shallow Water Echo Sounder (100 kHz), Hydrographic Survey Sounder (24 and 100 kHz), EG&G 270 Side Scan Sonar and Klein T-5000 High Speed/High Resolution Side Scan Sonar. Based at Tuxpan.

RIO TUXPAN *4/2005, NOAA* / 1133517

1 ONJUKU CLASS (SURVEY SHIP) (AGS)

Name	*No*	*Builders*	*Commissioned*
ONJUKU	BI 02 (ex-H 04)	Uchida Shipyard	10 Jan 1980

Displacement, tons: 494 full load
Dimensions, feet (metres): 121 × 26.2 × 11.5 *(36.9 × 8 × 3.5)*
Main machinery: 1 Yanmar 6UA-UT diesel; 700 hp(m) *(515 kW)*; 1 shaft
Speed, knots: 10
Range, n miles: 5,645 at 10.5 kt
Complement: 20 (4 officers)
Radars: Navigation: Furuno; I-band.
Sonars: Furuno; hull-mounted; high frequency active.

Comment: Launched 9 December 1977 in Japan. Sonar is a fish-finder type. New pennant number in 2001. Based at Veracruz.

ONJUKU *6/2005, Mexican Navy* / 1133520

TRAINING SHIPS

1 TRAINING SHIP (AGSC)

MOCTEZUMA II BI 07 (ex-A-09)

Displacement, tons: 150 full load
Dimensions, feet (metres): 78.7 × 20.3 × 13.1 *(24.0 × 6.2 × 4.0)*
Main machinery: 1 Detroit diesel; 192 hp *(143 kW)*; 1 shaft
Speed, knots: 17 (sail); 3 (diesel)
Complement: 18 (5 officers)

Comment: Two-masted sailing vessel built in 1972 and taken over by the Navy on 6 December 1985. Also used for oceanographic research. Based at Acapulco.

MOCTEZUMA II *6/2007, Mexican Navy* / 1170194

1 SAIL TRAINING SHIP (AXS)

Name	*No*	*Builders*	*Launched*	*Commissioned*
CUAUHTÉMOC	BE 01 (ex-A 07)	Astilleros Talleres Calaya SA, Bilbao	9 Jan 1982	23 Sep 1982

Displacement, tons: 1,662 full load
Dimensions, feet (metres): 296.9 (bowsprit); 220.5 wl × 39.4 × 17.7 *(90.5; 67.2 × 12 × 5.4)*
Main machinery: 1 Detroit 12V-149T diesel; 1,125 hp *(839 kW)*; 1 shaft
Speed, knots: 17 sail; 7 diesel
Complement: 268 (20 officers, 90 midshipmen)
Guns: 2—65 mm Schneider Model 1902 saluting guns.

Comment: Has 2,368 m^2 of sail. Similar ships in Ecuador, Colombia and Venezuela. Based at Acapulco.

CUAUHTÉMOC *7/2006, Chris Sattler* / 1164736

1 MANUEL AZUETA (EDSALL) CLASS (FF/AX)

Name	*No*	*Builders*	*Laid down*	*Launched*	*Commissioned*
COMODORO MANUEL AZUETA (ex-*Hurst* DE 250)	D 111 (ex-E 30, ex-A 06)	Brown SB Co, Houston, TX	27 Jan 1943	14 Apr 1943	30 Aug 1943

Displacement, tons: 1,400 standard; 1,850 full load
Dimensions, feet (metres): 302.7 × 36.6 × 13 *(92.3 × 11.3 × 4)*
Main machinery: 4 Fairbanks-Morse 38D8-1/8-10 diesels; 7,080 hp *(5.3 MW)* sustained; 2 shafts
Speed, knots: 12
Range, n miles: 13,000 at 12 kt
Complement: 216 (15 officers)

Guns: 2 USN 3 in *(76 mm)*/50; 20 rds/min to 12 km *(6.6 n miles)*; weight of shell 6 kg.
8 Bofors 40 mm/60 (1 quad, 2 twin) Mk 2 and Mk 1; 120 rds/min to 10 km *(5.5 n miles)*; weight of shell 0.89 kg.
2 Oerlikon 20 mm. 2—37 mm saluting guns.
Weapons control: Mk 52 (for 3 in); Mk 51 Mod 2 (for 40 mm).
Radars: Surface search: Kelvin Hughes Type 17; I-band.
Navigation: Kelvin Hughes Type 14; I-band.

Programmes: Transferred from US 1 October 1973.
Modernisation: OTO Melara 76 mm gun fitted in 1995 but subsequently removed and US 3 in gun restored.
Operational: Employed as training ship and based at Tuxpan. A/S weapons and sensors removed. Speed much reduced. Pennant number changed in 2001.

COMODORO MANUEL AZUETA *6/2005, Mexican Navy* / 1133545

AUXILIARIES

Notes: (1) Procurement of up to two Hospital Ships is reported to be under consideration. (2) Procurement of up to two logistic support vessels, capable of carrying 120 marines and of operating helicopters, is reported to be under consideration.

1 LOGISTIC SUPPORT SHIP (AKS)

Name	*No*	*Builders*	*Recommissioned*
MAYA (ex-*Rio Nautla*)	ATR 01 (ex-A 20, ex-A 23)	Isla Gran Cayman, Ru	1 June 1988

Displacement, tons: 924 full load
Dimensions, feet (metres): 160.1 × 38.1 × 11.5 *(48.8 × 11.6 × 3.5)*
Main machinery: 1 MAN diesel; 1 shaft
Speed, knots: 12
Complement: 15 (8 officers)

Comment: First launched in 1962 and acquired for the Navy in 1988. Unarmed. New name and pennant number in 2001. Based at Mazatlan.

MAYA *6/2004, Mexican Navy* / 0589766

1 LOGISTIC SUPPORT SHIP (AK)

Name	*No*	*Builders*	*Recommissioned*
TARASCO (ex-*Rio Lerma*, ex-*Sea Point*, ex-*Tricon*, ex-*Marika*, ex-*Arneb*)	ATR 03 (ex-A 22, A 25)	Solvesborg, Sweden	1 Mar 1990

Displacement, tons: 1,970 full load
Dimensions, feet (metres): 315.0 × 40.7 × 15.8 *(96.0 × 12.4 × 4.8)*
Main machinery: 1 Deutz RBV8M 358 diesel; 2,100 hp(m) *(1.54 MW)*; 1 shaft
Speed, knots: 14
Complement: 35
Cargo capacity: 778 tons

Comment: Built in 1962 as a commercial ship and taken into the Navy in 1990. New name and pennant number in 2001. Based at Tampico.

TARASCO *6/2005, Mexican Navy* / 1133516

17 DREDGERS (YM)

BANDERAS ADR 01 (ex-D 01)
MAGDALENA ADR 02 (ex-D 02)
KINO ADR 03 (ex-D 03)
YAVAROS ADR 04 (ex-D 04)
CHAMELA ADR 05 (ex-D 05)
TEPOCA ADR 06 (ex-D 06)
TODO SANTOS ADR 07 (ex-D 21)
ASUNCION ADR 08 (ex-D 22)
ALMEJAS ADR 09 (ex-D 23)
CHACAGUA ADR 10 (ex-D 24)
COYUCA ADR 11 (ex-D 25)
FARRALLON ADR 12 (ex-D 26)
CHAIREL ADR 13 (ex-D 27)
SAN ANDRES ADR 14 (ex-D 28)
SAN IGNACIO ADR 15 (ex-D 29)
TERMINOS ADR 16 (ex-D 30)
TECULAPA ADR 17 (ex-D 31)

Comment: Ships vary in size from 113 m *Kino* to 8 m *Terminos*. Most were taken over by the navy from the Transport Ministry in 1994.

2 HUASTECO CLASS (APH/AK/AH)

Name	*No*	*Builders*	*Commissioned*
HUASTECO (ex-*Rio Usumacinta*)	AMP 01 (ex-A 10, ex-A 21)	Tampico, Tampa	21 May 1986
ZAPOTECO (ex-*Rio Coatzacoalcos*)	AMP 02 (ex-A 11, ex-A 22)	Salina Cruz	1 Sep 1986

Displacement, tons: 1,854 standard; 2,650 full load
Dimensions, feet (metres): 227 × 42 × 15.5 *(69.2 × 12.8 × 4.73)*
Main machinery: 1 GM-EMD diesel; 3,600 hp(m) *(2.65 MW)*; 1 shaft
Speed, knots: 14.5
Range, n miles: 5,500 at 14 kt
Complement: 85 plus 300 passengers
Guns: 1 Bofors 40/60 Mk 3.
Radars: Navigation: I-band.
Helicopters: Platform for 1 MBB BO 105C.

Comment: Used in a training role but can also serve as troop transports, supply or hospital ships. New names and pennant numbers in 2001. AMP 01 based at Tampico and AMP 02 at Manzanillo.

HUASTECO *7/2004, Diego Quevedo* / 0589765

2 AGUASCALIENTES CLASS (YOG/YO)

Name	*No*	*Builders*	*Recommissioned*
AGUASCALIENTES (ex-*Las Choapas*)	ATQ 01 (ex-A 45, ex-A 03)	Geo H Mathis Co Ltd	26 Nov 1964
TLAXCALA (ex-*Amatlan*)	ATQ 02 (ex-A 46, ex-A 04)	Geo Lawley & Son, Neponset, MA	26 Nov 1964

Displacement, tons: 895 standard; 1,480 full load
Dimensions, feet (metres): 173.9 × 32.8 × 10.2 *(53.0 × 10.0 × 3.1)*
Main machinery: 1 Fairbanks-Morse diesel; 500 hp *(373 kW)*; 1 shaft
Speed, knots: 6
Complement: 26 (5 officers)
Cargo capacity: 6,570 barrels
Guns: 1 Oerlikon 20 mm.

Comment: Former US self-propelled fuel oil barges built in 1943. Purchased in August 1964. New names and pennant numbers in 2001. ATQ 01 based at Puerto Cortes and ATQ 02 at Coatzacoalcos.

TLAXCALA *6/2005, Mexican Navy* / 1133515

5 FLOATING DOCKS (YOG/YO)

ADI 01 (ex-US ARD 2)
ADI 02 (ex-US ARD 15)
ADI 03 (ex-US AFDL 28)
ADI 04 (ex-US ARD 11)
– (ex-US ARD 31)

Comment: ARD 2 (150 × 24.7 m) transferred 1963 and ARD 11 (same size) 1974 by sale. Lift 3,550 tons. Two 10 ton cranes and one 100 kW generator. ARD 15 has the same capacity and facilities-transferred 1971 by lease. AFDL 28 built in 1944, transferred 1973. Lift, 1,000 tons. ARD 30 transferred on 20 March 2001 and ARD 31 in 2004.

TUGS

6 HARBOUR TUGS (YTL)

IZTACCIHUATL ARE 05 (ex-R-60)
POPOCATEPTL ARE 06 (ex-R-61)
CITLALTEPL ARE 07 (ex-R-62)
XINANTECATL ARE 08 (ex-R-63)
MATLALCUEYE ARE 09 (ex-R-64)
TLALOC ARE 10 (ex-R-65)

Displacement, tons: 140 full load
Dimensions, feet (metres): 73.8 × 22.3 × 9.8 *(22.5 × 6.8 × 3.0)*
Complement: 12

Comment: Details are for ARE 05 built by Seadrec, Ltd, and taken over by the Navy on 1 November 1994. Based at: Tuxpan (ARE 05); Manzanillo (ARE 06); Mazatlán (ARE 07); Ciudad Madero (ARE 08); Salina Cruz (ARE 09); Coatzacoalcos (ARE 10).

4 ABNAKI CLASS (ATF)

Name	*No*	*Builders*	*Commissioned*
OTOMI (ex-*Kukulkan*, ex-*Molala* ATF 106)	ARE 01 (ex-A 52, ex-A 17)	United Eng Co, Alameda, CA	29 Sep 1943
YAQUI (ex-*Ehacatl*, ex-*Abnaki* ATF 96)	ARE 02 (ex-A 53, ex-A 18)	Charleston SB and DD Co	15 Nov 1943
SERI (ex-*Tonatiuh*, ex-*Cocopa* ATF 101)	ARE 03 (ex-A 54, ex-A 19)	Charleston SB and DD Co	25 Mar 1944
CORA (ex-*Chac*, ex-*Hitchiti* ATF 103)	ARE 04 (ex-A 55, ex-A 20)	Charleston SB and DD Co	27 May 1944

Displacement, tons: 1,640 full load
Dimensions, feet (metres): 205 × 38.5 × 17 *(62.5 × 11.7 × 5.2)*
Main machinery: Diesel-electric; 4 Busch-Sulzer BS-539 diesels; 6,000 hp *(4.48 MW)*; 4 generators; 1 motor; 3,000 hp(m) *(2.24 MW)*; 1 shaft
Speed, knots: 10
Range, n miles: 6,500 at 10 kt
Complement: 75
Guns: 1 US 3 in *(76 mm)*/50 Mk 22.
Radars: Navigation: Marconi LN66; I-band.

Comment: *Otomi* transferred from US 27 September 1978, remainder 1 October 1978. All by sale. Speed reduced. Based at Tampico (ARE 01, ARE 03) and Manzanillo (ARE 02, ARE 04).

SERI *6/2003, Mexican Navy* / 0567905

Federated States of Micronesia

Country Overview

The Federated States of Micronesia was a US-administered UN Trust territory from 1947 before becoming a self-governing republic in 1979. In 1986, a Compact of Free Association, delegating to the US the responsibility for defence and foreign affairs, came into effect. Composed of the states of Pohnpei (location of capital, Palikir), Kosrae, Chuuk, and Yap, the country consists of 607 islands in the western Pacific Ocean which extend 1,566 n miles across the Caroline Islands archipelago. Moen Island in Chuuk, is the largest community. Territorial seas (12 n miles) are claimed. An Exclusive Economic Zone (EEZ) (200n miles) is also claimed but limits have not been fully defined.

Headquarters Appointments

Maritime Wing Commander:
Commander Robert Maluweirang

Personnel

2009: 120

Bases

Kolonia (main base), Kosral, Moen, Takatik.

PATROL FORCES

3 PACIFIC CLASS (LARGE PATROL CRAFT) (PB)

Name	*No*	*Builders*	*Commissioned*
PALIKIR	FSM 01	Australian Shipbuilding Industries	28 Apr 1990
MICRONESIA	FSM 02	Australian Shipbuilding Industries	3 Nov 1990
INDEPENDENCE	FSM 05	Transfield	22 May 1997

Displacement, tons: 162 full load
Dimensions, feet (metres): 103.3 × 26.6 × 6.9 *(31.5 × 8.1 × 2.1)*
Main machinery: 2 Caterpillar 3516TA diesels; 4,400 hp *(3.28 MW)* sustained; 2 shafts
Speed, knots: 20
Range, n miles: 2,500 at 12 kt
Complement: 17 (3 officers)
Radars: Surface search: Furuno 1011; I-band.

Comment: First pair ordered in June 1989 from Australian Shipbuilding Industries. Training and support provided by Australia at Port Kolonia. Third of class negotiated with Transfield (former ASI) in 1997. Following the decision by the Australian government to extend the Pacific Patrol Boat programme to enable 30-year boat lives, *Palikir, Micronesia* and *Independence*, underwent half-life refits in 1998, 1999 and 2003. A life-extension refit for *Palikir* was completed in 2007 and is due for *Micronesia* in 2009 and *Independence* in 2011.

MICRONESIA
11/1990, Royal Australian Navy
0506060

Montenegro

Country Overview

The Republic of Montenegro was formed following a referendum on 21 May 2006 in which the people voted for independence and for the dissolution of the Federal Republic of Serbia and Montenegro which itself was the rump of the former Yugoslavia. A formal declaration of independence was made by the Montenegro Assembly on 3 June 2006. With an area of 5,333 square miles, it is located in south-eastern Europe in the Balkan Peninsula and is bordered to the north-west by Bosnia, to the east by Serbia, to the south by Albania and to the west by Croatia. It has a 158 n mile coastline with the Adriatic Sea on which Bar and Tivat are the principal ports. The capital and largest city is Podgorica. Territorial waters (12 n miles) are claimed but an EEZ has not been claimed.

The provisions of the Union Constitution were that, in the event of dissolution, the armed forces of Serbia and Montenegro would be split in such a way that each state keeps the assets in its territory. Therefore, all of the former navy of Serbia and Montenegro transferred to Montenegro in June 2006, except for the former Danuble Flotilla, which transferred to Serbian land forces. While the future size and shape of the Montenegrin Navy is yet to be decided, it is expected that the force will drawn down into a small Coast Guard force and that most former units will be sold or scrapped.

Headquarters Appointments

Commander-in-Chief:
Rear Admiral Dragan Samardzić

Personnel

2009: 1,100

Bases

Headquarters and Base: Bar

Organisation

Montenegrin naval forces are to be re-organised into five detachments: Patrol forces; search and rescue; coastal reconnaissance; coast guard; training. All naval facilities have been concentrated at Bar and the naval repair and maintenance yard at Tivat has been sold. All special forces have been consolidated under the command of the army. Former coastal defence missile systems have reportedly been sold to Egypt.

SUBMARINES

Notes: All former patrol submarines have been decommissioned or scrapped. The Sava-class boats *Sava* and *Drava* are to be sold. The Heroj-class boats *Heroj, Junak* and *Uskuk* are all likely to be scrapped while all five Una class midget submarines have been laid-up or scrapped.

2 R-2 MALA CLASS (TWO-MAN SWIMMER DELIVERY VEHICLES) (LDW)

Displacement, tons: 1.4
Dimensions, feet (metres): 16.1 × 4.6 × 4.3 *(4.9 × 1.4 × 1.3)*
Main machinery: 1 motor; 4.7 hp(m) *(3.5 kW)*; 1 shaft
Speed, knots: 4.4
Range, n miles: 18 at 4.4 kt; 23 at 3.7 kt
Complement: 2
Mines: 250 kg of limpet mines.

Comment: Free-flood craft with the main motor, battery, navigation pod and electronic equipment housed in separate watertight cylinders. Instrumentation includes aircraft type gyrocompass, magnetic compass, depth gauge (with 0-100 m scale), echo-sounder, sonar and two searchlights. Constructed of light aluminium and plexiglass, it is fitted with fore and after-hydroplanes, the tail being a conventional cruciform with a single rudder abaft the screw. Large perspex windows give a good all-round view. Operating depth 60 m *(196.9 ft)* maximum. Two operated by Croatia. Two reported sold to Syria and one to Sweden.

Notes: There are also reported to be four R-1 craft. Transportable in submarine torpedo tubes and crewed by one man, they are 3.7 m craft, powered by a 1 kW electric motor and 24V silver-zinc batteries. Capable of 2.8 kt, they can dive to 60 m. They have a range of 4 n miles. Of a total twelve reported to have been manufactured. A further six units have probably been deleted, one unit is in Croatia and one was exported to Sweden.

R-2
6/2003, Serbia and Montenegro Navy
0572433

FRIGATES

Notes: The two decommissioned Koni-class frigates, *Beograd* and *Podgorica*, may be sold.

1 KOTOR CLASS (FFGM)

Name	*No*	*Builders*	*Launched*	*Commissioned*
NOVI SAD (ex-*Pula*)	34	Tito Shipyard, Kraljevica	18 Dec 1986	Nov 1988

Displacement, tons: 1,870 full load
Dimensions, feet (metres): 317.3 × 42 × 13.7 *(96.7 × 12.8 × 4.2)*
Main machinery: CODAG; 1 SGW Nikolayev gas turbine; 18,000 hp(m) *(13.2 MW)*; 2 SEMT-Pielstick 12 PA6 V 280 diesels; 9,600 hp(m) *(7.1 MW)* sustained; 3 shafts
Speed, knots: 27 gas; 22 diesel. **Range, n miles:** 1,800 at 14 kt
Complement: 110

Missiles: SSM: 4 SS-N-2C Styx ❶; active radar or IR homing to 83 km *(45 n miles)* at 0.9 Mach; warhead 513 kg; sea-skimmer at end of run.
SAM: SA-N-4 Gecko twin launcher ❷; semi-active radar homing to 15 km *(8 n miles)* at 2.5 Mach; height envelope 9-3,048 m *(29.5-10,000 ft)*; warhead 50 kg.
Guns: 4 USSR 3 in *(76 mm)*/59 AK 726 (2 twin) (1 mounting only in 33 and 34) ❸; 90 rds/min to 16 km *(8.5 n miles)*; weight of shell 6.8 kg.
4 USSR 30 mm/65 (2 twin) ❹; 500 rds/min to 5 km *(2.7 n miles)*; weight of shell 5.9 kg.
A/S mortars: 2 RBU 6000 12-barrelled trainable ❺; range 6,000 m; warhead 31 kg.
Mines: Can lay mines.
Countermeasures: Decoys: 2 Wallop Barricade double layer chaff launchers.

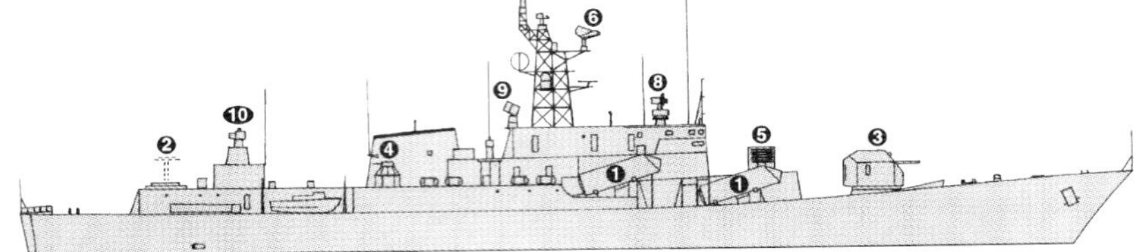

KOTOR CLASS *(Scale 1 : 900)*, **Ian Sturton** / 0506341

Radars: Air/surface search: Strut Curve ❻; F-band.
Navigation: Palm Frond; I-band.
Fire control: PEAB 9LV200 ❽; I-band (for 76 mm and SSM).
Drum Tilt ❾; H/I-band (for 30 mm).
Pop Group ❿; F/H/I-band (for SAM).
IFF: High Pole; 2 Square Head.
Sonars: Bull Nose; hull-mounted; active search and attack; medium frequency.

Programmes: Built under licence. Type name, VPB (Veliki Patrolni Brod).

Modernisation: Combat data system fitted in 2000. SS-N-2C missiles, SA-N-4 missiles and RBU 6000 rocket launchers are to be removed. Following a refit, which may include installation of a flight deck aft, *Novi Sad* is to be employed as an offshore patrol vessel.
Structure: The hull is similar to the Russian Koni class but are to a Yugoslavian design.
Operational: VPB 33 *Kotor* has been decommissioned but may be re-activated subject to funding. Based at Bar.

KOTOR CLASS *6/1998*, **Yugoslav Navy** / 0050746

PATROL FORCES

Notes: Acquisition of two Minerva-class corvettes from Italy was reported in 2007 to be under consideration but there have been no indications of progress.

2 KONČAR CLASS (TYPE 240) (PTFG)

Name	*No*	*Builders*	*Launched*	*Commissioned*
JORDAN NIKOLOV ORCE	405	Tito Shipyard, Kraljevica	26 Apr 1979	Aug 1979
ANTE BANINA	406	Tito Shipyard, Kraljevica	23 Nov 1979	Nov 1980

Displacement, tons: 271 full load
Dimensions, feet (metres): 147.6 × 27.6 × 8.5 *(45 × 8.4 × 2.6)*
Main machinery: CODAG; 2 RR Proteus gas turbines; 7,100 hp *(5.29 MW)* sustained; 2 MTU 16V 538TB91 diesels; 6,000 hp(m) *(4.41 MW)* sustained; 4 shafts; cp props
Speed, knots: 38
Range, n miles: 490 at 38 kt; 870 at 23 kt (diesels)
Complement: 30 (5 officers)
Missiles: SSM: 2 SS-N-2B Styx; active radar or IR homing to 46 km *(25 n miles)* at 0.9 Mach; warhead 513 kg.
Guns: 2 Bofors 57 mm/70; 200 rds/min to 17 km *(9.3 n miles)*; weight of shell 2.4 kg.
2—128 mm rocket launchers for illuminants.
2—30 mm/65 (twin) or 1—30 mm/65 AK 630 may be fitted in place of the after 57 mm.
Countermeasures: 2 Wallop Barricade double layer chaff launchers.
Weapons control: PEAB 9LV 202 GFCS.
Radars: Surface search: Decca 1226; I-band.
Fire control: Philips TAB; I/J-band.

Programmes: Type name, Raketna Topovnjaca.
Structure: Aluminium superstructure. Designed by the Naval Shipping Institute in Zagreb based on Swedish Spica class with bridge amidships like Malaysian boats. The after 57 mm gun is replaced by a twin 30 mm mounting in at least one of the class.
Operational: 402 was taken by Croatia in 1991. 401 and 404 have been decommissioned but may be re-activated subject to funding, 403 has been decommissioned. 405 and 406 are to remain in service but the SS-N-2B missile system is likely to be removed.

JORDAN NIKOLOV ORCE *9/2006*, **Freivogel Collection** / 1164682

ANTE BANINA *9/2006*, **Freivogel Collection** / 1164681

AMPHIBIOUS FORCES

1 SILBA CLASS (LCT/ML)

Name	*No*	*Builders*	*Commissioned*
– (ex-*Silba*)	DBM 241	Brodosplit Shipyard, Split	1990

Displacement, tons: 880 full load
Dimensions, feet (metres): 163.1 oa; 144 wl × 33.5 × 8.5 *(49.7; 43.9 × 10.2 × 2.6)*
Main machinery: 2 Burmeister & Wain Alpha 10V23L-VO diesels; 3,100 hp(m) *(2.28 MW)* sustained; 2 shafts; cp props
Speed, knots: 12
Range, n miles: 1,200 at 12 kt
Complement: 33 (3 officers)
Military lift: 460 tons or 6 medium tanks or 7 APCs or 4—130 mm guns plus towing vehicles or 300 troops with equipment
Missiles: 1 SA-N-5 Grail quad mounting.
Guns: 4—30 mm/65 (2 twin) AK 230.
4—20 mm M75 (quad). 2—128 mm illuminant launchers.
Mines: 94 Type SAG-1.
Radars: Surface search: Racal Decca; I-band.

Comment: Ro-ro design with bow and stern ramps. Can be used for minelaying, transporting weapons or equipment and troops. Two further craft, launched in 1992 and 1994, are in the Croatian Navy and this final craft is to be sold, possibly to Egypt.

KRK *6/1998, MoD Bonn* / 0050751

7 TYPE 22 (LCU)

DJC 627 **DJC 628** **DJC 411** (ex-DJC 632) **DJC 412** (ex-DJC 625) **DJC 413** (ex-DJC 630) **DJC 414** (ex-DJC 621) **DJC 415** (ex-DJC 631)

Displacement, tons: 48 full load
Dimensions, feet (metres): 73.2 × 15.7 × 3.3 *(22.3 × 4.8 × 1)*
Main engines: 2 MTU diesels; 1,740 hp(m) *(1.28 MW)*; 2 water-jets
Speed, knots: 30. **Range, n miles:** 320 at 22 kt
Complement: 8
Military lift: 40 troops or 15 tons cargo
Guns: 2—20 mm M71. 1—30 mm grenade launcher.
Radars: Navigation: Decca 101; I-band.

Comment: Built of polyester and glass fibre. Last one completed in 1987. Based in Danube Flotilla. All are likely to be sold.

DJC 411 *6/2008*, Freivogel Collection* / 1335396

3 TYPE 21 (LCU)

DJC 614 **DJC 616** **DJC 618**

Displacement, tons: 32 full load
Dimensions, feet (metres): 69.9 × 15.7 × 5.2 *(21.3 × 4.8 × 1.6)*
Main machinery: 1 diesel; 1,450 hp(m) *(1.07 MW)*; 1 shaft
Speed, knots: 23
Range, n miles: 320 at 22 kt
Complement: 6
Military lift: 6 tons
Guns: 1—20 mm M71.

Comment: The survivors of a class of 20 built between 1976 and 1979. Four held by Croatia in 1991 of which three have paid off. Others sunk or scrapped. Some of these may be laid up and all are likely to be offered for sale.

DJC 616 and 618 *4/2007, Marco Ghiglino* / 1167915

AUXILIARIES

Notes: (1) Two 22 m inshore survey vessels BH 12 and CH 1 are operated by the Naval Hydrological Institute. BH 11 has been donated to a civilian institute.
(2) There are seven tenders BM 58, BM 65, BM 66, BM 67, BM 70 and BS 22. Most of these are reported to have been sold.
(3) There are five diving tenders BRM 81, BRM 84, BRM 85, BRM 87 and BRM 88.
(4) *Alga* PV 17 is a 44 m water tanker which is laid-up.

1 SAIL TRAINING SHIP (AXS)

JADRAN

Displacement, tons: 737 full load
Dimensions, feet (metres): 196.9 × 29.2 × 13.3 *(60.0 × 8.9 × 4.05)*
Main machinery: 1 Burmeister Alpha diesel; 353 hp *(263 kW)*
Speed, knots: 10.4
Radars: 1 FR 2120 and 1 FR 7061; I-band.

Comment: The contract for a barquentine sail training ship was signed on 4 September 1930 with the German shipbuilding company H C Stülcken & Son of Hamburg. She was launched on 25 June 1931 and arrived in Tivat on 16 July 1933. During the Second World War, she was used by the Italian Navy under the name of *Marco Polo* before being allowed to fall into disrepair. She returned to Yugoslavia in 1946 and was reconstructed in her original form at Tivat.

JADRAN *6/2005, John Mortimer* / 1151388

1 LUBIN CLASS (TRANSPORT SHIP) (AKR)

LUBIN PO 91

Displacement, tons: 860 full load
Dimensions, feet (metres): 190.9 × 36.1 × 9.2 *(58.2 × 11.0 × 2.8)*
Main machinery: 2 diesels; 3,500 hp(m) *(2.57 MW)*; 2 shafts; cp props
Speed, knots: 16
Range, n miles: 1,500 at 16 kt
Complement: 43
Military lift: 150 troops; 6 tanks
Guns: 1 Bofors 40 mm/70. 4—20 mm M75. 128 mm rocket launcher for illuminants.

Comment: Fitted with bow doors and two upper-deck cranes. Ro-Ro cargo ship built in Split in the 1980s and used as an ammunition transport. Based at Bar. This ship had been assessed decommissioned in the early 1990s but has been officially reported as being in good condition and operational. The ship is likely to be sold.

LUBIN *5/2004, Sieche Collection* / 1044503

1 DRINA CLASS (AOTL)

SIPA PN 27

Displacement, tons: 430 full load
Dimensions, feet (metres): 151 × 23.6 × 10.2 *(46 × 7.2 × 3.1)*
Main machinery: 1 diesel; 300 hp(m) *(220 kW)*; 1 shaft
Speed, knots: 7
Complement: 12
Missiles: SAM: 1 SA-N-5.
Guns: 6 Hispano 20 mm (1 quad, 2 single).

Comment: Built at Kraljevica in mid-1950s. Based at Bar. The ship is likely to be sold.

SIPA *6/2003, Serbia and Montenegro Navy* / 1044504

TUGS

Notes: There are three coastal tugs PR 37, PR 38 and PR 41 (armed with a 20 mm gun) and seven harbour tugs LR 23, LR 72, LR 74, LR 75, LR 77 and LR 80.

PR 41 *6/2007, Freivogel Collection* / 1167938

POLICE

2 MIRNA CLASS (TYPE 140) (PB)

BAR (ex-*Učka*) P 01 (ex-174)
HERCEG NOVI (ex-*Kosmaj*) P 03 (ex-178)

Displacement, tons: 142 full load
Dimensions, feet (metres): 104.9 × 22 × 7.5 *(32 × 6.7 × 2.3)*
Main machinery: 2 SEMT-Pielstick 12 PA4 200 VGDS diesels; 5,292 hp(m) *(3.89 MW)* sustained; 2 shafts
Speed, knots: 28
Range, n miles: 400 at 20 kt
Complement: 19 (3 officers)
Guns: 1 Bofors 40 mm/70. 4—20 mm (quad). 2—128 mm illuminant launchers.
Depth charges: 8 DCs.
Radars: Surface search: Racal Decca 1216C; I-band.
Sonars: Simrad SQS-3D/3F; active; high frequency.

Comment: Builders, Kraljevica Yard. Launched between June 1981 and December 1983. An unusual feature of this design is the fitting of an electric outboard motor giving a speed of up to 6 kt. One sunk possibly by a limpet mine in November 1991. Four held by Croatia, five have been sold to civilian use and two transferred from the Montenegrin Navy to the Police in 2006.

HERCEG NOVI *4/2007, Marco Ghiglino* / 1167914

Morocco

MARINE ROYALE MAROCAINE

Country Overview

Formerly divided into French and Spanish protectorates, the Kingdom of Morocco gained independence in 1956. Situated in north-western Africa, it has an area of 172,414 square miles and is bordered to the east by Algeria; it occupies 80 per cent of Western Sahara (formerly Spanish Sahara), the country to the south. Two Spanish exclaves, Ceuta and Melilla, are located on the Mediterranean coast. It has coastlines with Atlantic Ocean (756 n miles) and Mediterranean Sea (238 n miles). The capital is Rabat while Casablanca is the largest city and principal port. Other ports are at Tangier, Agadir, Kenitra, Mohammedia, and Safi. Territorial seas (12 n miles) are claimed. An EEZ (200 n mile) has also been claimed but its limits have not been fully defined.

Headquarters Appointments

Inspector of the Navy:
Rear Admiral Mohamed Berrada Kouzi

Personnel

(a) 2009: 7,800 officers and ratings (including 1,500 Marines)
(b) 18 months' national service

Bases

Casablanca (HQ), Safi, Agadir, Kenitra, Tangier, Dakhla, Al Hoceima

Aviation

The Ministry of Fisheries operates 11 Pilatus Britten-Norman Defender maritime surveillance aircraft.

FRIGATES

2 FLOREAL CLASS (FFGHM)

Name	*No*	*Builders*	*Laid down*	*Launched*	*Commissioned*
MOHAMMED V	611	Chantiers de L'Atlantique, St Nazaire	June 1999	9 Mar 2001	12 Mar 2002
HASSAN II	612	Chantiers de L'Atlantique, St Nazaire	Dec 1999	11 Feb 2002	20 Dec 2002

Displacement, tons: 2,950 full load
Dimensions, feet (metres): 306.8 × 45.9 × 14.1 *(93.5 × 14 × 4.3)*
Main machinery: CODAD; 4 SEMT-Pielstick 6 PA6 L 280 diesels; 9,600 hp(m) *(7.06 MW)* sustained; 2 shafts; LIPS cp props; bow thruster; 340 hp(m) *(250 kW)*
Speed, knots: 20
Range, n miles: 10,000 at 15 kt
Complement: 89 (11 officers)

Missiles: SSM: 2 Aerospatiale MM 38 Exocet ❶.
SAM: 2 Matra Simbad twin launchers ❷ can replace 20 mm guns or Dagaie launcher.
Guns: 1 Otobreda 76 mm/62 ❸.
2 Giat 20 F2 20 mm ❹ (fitted for but not with).
Countermeasures: Decoys: 2 CSEE Dagaie Mk II ❺; 10-barrelled trainable launchers; chaff and IR flares.
ESM: Thomson-CSF ARBR 17 ❻; radar intercept.
Weapons control: CSEE Najir 2000 optronic director ❼.
Radars: Surface search/Fire control: Thales WM28 ❽; I/J-band.

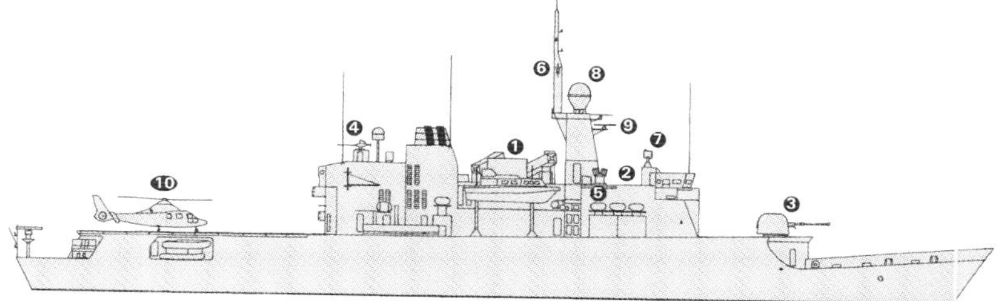

MOHAMMED V *(Scale 1 : 900), Ian Sturton* / 1151071

Navigation: 2 Decca Bridgemaster E ❾; I-band (1 for helicopter control).

Helicopters: 1 Aerospatiale AS 565MA Panther ❿.

Programmes: Contract signed with Alstom on 12 July 1999. 611 delivered on 12 March 2002 and 612 on 20 December 2002.
Structure: Constructed to DNV standards. Very similar to ships in French service with 76 mm in place of 100 mm gun.

HASSAN II *3/2006, M Declerck* / 1164956

HASSAN II *7/2008*, M Declerck* / 1353239

1 MODIFIED DESCUBIERTA CLASS (FFGM)

Name	*No*	*Builders*	*Laid down*	*Launched*	*Commissioned*
LIEUTENANT COLONEL ERRHAMANI	501	Bazán, Cartagena	20 Mar 1979	26 Feb 1982	28 Mar 1983

Displacement, tons: 1,233 standard; 1,479 full load
Dimensions, feet (metres): 291.3 × 34 × 12.5 *(88.8 × 10.4 × 3.8)*
Main machinery: 4 MTU-Bazán 16V 956 TB91 diesels; 15,000 hp(m) *(11 MW)* sustained; 2 shafts; cp props
Speed, knots: 25.5
Range, n miles: 4,000 at 18 kt (1 engine)
Complement: 100

Missiles: SSM: 4 Aerospatiale MM 38 Exocet ❶; inertial cruise; active radar homing to 42 km *(23 n miles)* at 0.9 Mach; warhead 165 kg; sea-skimmer. Frequently not embarked.
SAM: Selenia/Elsag Albatros octuple launcher ❷; 24 Aspide; semi-active radar homing to 13 km *(8 n miles)* at 2.5 Mach; height envelope 15-5,000 m *(49.2-16,405 ft)*; warhead 30 kg.
Guns: 1 OTO Melara 3 in *(76 mm)*/62 compact ❸; 85 rds/min to 16 km *(8.6 n miles)* anti-surface; 12 km *(6.5 n miles)* anti-aircraft; weight of shell 6 kg.
2 Breda Bofors 40 mm/70 ❹; 300 rds/min to 12.5 km *(6.7 n miles)*; weight of shell 0.96 kg.
Torpedoes: 6—324 mm Mk 32 (2 triple) tubes ❺. Honeywell Mk 46 Mod 1; anti-submarine; active/passive homing to 11 km *(5.9 n miles)* at 40 kt; warhead 44 kg.
A/S mortars: 1 Bofors SR 375 mm twin trainable launcher ❻; range 3.6 km *(1.9 n miles)*; 24 rockets.

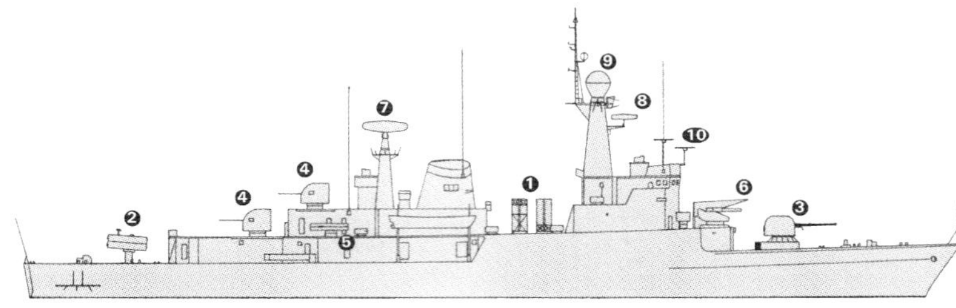

LIEUTENANT COLONEL ERRHAMANI ***(Scale 1 : 900), Ian Sturton*** / 1151072

Countermeasures: Decoys: 2 CSEE Dagaie double trainable mounting; IR flares and chaff; H/J-band.
ESM/ECM: Elettronica ELT 715; intercept and jammer.
Combat data systems: Signaal SEWACO-MR action data automation. SATCOM.
Radars: Air/surface search: Signaal DA05 ❼; E/F-band (see *Operational*).
Surface search: Signaal ZW06 ❽; I-band.
Fire control: Signaal WM25/41 ❾; I/J-band; range 46 km *(25 n miles)*.
Navigation: 2 Decca ❿; I-band.

Sonars: Raytheon DE 1160 B; hull-mounted; active/passive; medium range; medium frequency.

Programmes: Ordered 7 June 1977.
Modernisation: New 40 mm guns fitted in 1995. Refit in Spain in 1996.
Operational: The ship is fitted to carry Exocet but the missiles are seldom embarked. The air search radar was removed in 1998 but reinstated in 1999.

LIEUTENANT COLONEL ERRHAMANI ***6/2006, B Prézelin*** / 1040673

LIEUTENANT COLONEL ERRHAMANI ***6/2006, B Prézelin*** / 1040674

0 + 1 FREMM CLASS (FSG)

Name	*No*	*Builders*	*Laid down*	*Launched*	*Commissioned*
–	–	DCNS, Lorient	2009	2011	2013

Displacement, tons: 4,500 standard; 6,000 full load
Dimensions, feet (metres): 449.5 oa; 419.9 wl × 62.3 × 16.4 *(137.0; 128.0 × 19.0 × 5.0)*
Main machinery: CODLOG; 1 Fiat/GE LM 2500+ G4 gas turbine; 47,370 hp(m) *(34.8 MW)*; 2 Jeumont motors; 2 shafts
Speed, knots: 28
Range, n miles: 6,000 at 15 kt
Complement: 108 (22 officers) (accommodation for 145)

Missiles: SAM: 16 (2 octuple) cell Sylver A43 VLS for MBDA Aster 15; inertial guidance, mid-course update and final active homing to 30 km *(16.2 n miles)* at 3 Mach.
SSM: 8 MBDA MM 40 Exocet Block III; inertial cruise; active radar homing to 180 km *(100 n miles)* at 0.9 Mach; warhead 165 kg; sea-skimmer.
Guns: 1 OTO Melara 3 in (76 mm)/62 Super Rapid; 120 rds/min to 16 km *(8.7 n miles)*; weight of shell 6 kg. 2—12.7 mm MGs.
Torpedoes: 6—324 mm (2 B 515 triple) tubes; Eurotorp Mu-90; active/passive homing to 25 km *(13.5 n miles)* at 29/50 kt.
Countermeasures: Decoys: 2 EADS NGDS 12-barrelled chaff, IR and anti-torpedo decoy launchers.
ESM: ARBR 21; intercept.
ECM: To be announced.
Combat data systems: DCN/Thales SETIS CMS.
Weapons control: 1 optronic FCS.
Radars: Air/Surface search: Thales Herakles 3-D multifunction; E/F-band.

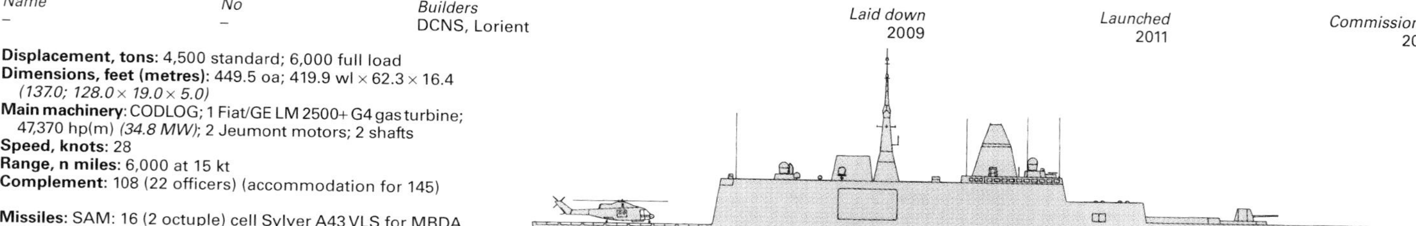

FREMM *(Scale 1 : 1,200), Ian Sturton* / 1304075

Navigation: To be announced.
Fire control: Alenia Marconi NA-25XP; J-band.
Sonars: Thales TUS 4110CL; hull mounted (bow dome); active search and attack.
Thales Captas UMS-4249 active/passive towed array (to be confirmed).

Helicopters: To be announced.

Programmes: The order for one FREMM frigate was first announced on 22 October 2007 and later confirmed by French Prime Minister François Fillon on 18 April 2008. The ship, to be delivered by 2013, is the first export order for the 27-ship Franco-Italian joint programme. The ship is required to extend the patrol capabilities of the Moroccan Navy and to enable joint operations with NATO and other navies. Details are based on the ships being procured for the French Navy and may be different.
Structure: FREMM has a conventional hull design. The main engine room contains the gas turbine and two diesel generators while the aft machinery space contains the motors. Particular attention has been paid to signature reduction. The radar signature is expected to be comparable to that of the La Fayette class while exhaust cooling measures are expected to achieve a comparatively low IR signature. Acoustic quietening is to be achieved by the rafting of engines and motors and the use of electric propulsion. The Herakles radar is housed in the foremast and communications and IFF in the after mast.

CORVETTES

0 + 3 SIGMA CLASS (FSG)

Name	*No*	*Builders*	*Laid down*	*Launched*	*Commissioned*
–	–	Schelde Shipbuilding, Vlissengen	15 Apr 2008	2009	2010
–	–	Schelde Shipbuilding, Vlissengen	2009	2011	2011
–	–	Schelde Shipbuilding, Vlissengen	2008	2010	2012

Displacement, tons: 2,100 (2,300 Sigma 10513) full load
Dimensions, feet (metres): 321.2 (344.8) × 42.7 × 13.1 *(97.9; 105.1 Sigma 10513 × 13.0 × 4.0)*
Main machinery: 2 Pielstick 20PA6B STC diesels; 22,030 hp *(16.2 MW)*; 2 shafts; cp props
Speed, knots: 28. **Range, n miles:** 4,000 at 18 kt
Complement: 91 (101 Sigma 10513)

Missiles: SAM: 12 (2 sextuple) MBDA VL MICA; command/inertial guidance; radar/IR homing to 20 km *(10.8 n miles)*; warhead 12 kg.
SSM: 4 MBDA MM40 Exocet Block II; inertial cruise; active radar homing to 70 km *(40 n miles)* at 0.9 Mach; warhead 165 kg; sea-skimmer.
Guns: 1 OTO Melara 3 in (76 mm)/62 Super Rapid; 120 rds/min to 16 km *(8.7 n miles)*; weight of shell 6 kg. 2 Giat 20 mm.
Torpedoes: 6—324 mm (2 B 515 triple) tubes; Eurotorp Mu-90; active/passive homing to 25 km *(13.5 n miles)* at 29/50 kt.
Countermeasures: Decoys: To be announced.
ESM: Thales Vigile.

SIGMA 10513 *(Scale 1 : 900), Ian Sturton* / 1353237

ECM: Thales Scorpion.
Torpedo defence: To be announced.
Combat data systems: Thales Tacticos.
Weapons control: Thales LIROD Mk 2 optronic tracker.
Radars: Air/Surface search: Thales SMART-S; 3D; E/F-band.
Navigation: To be announced.
Sonars: Thales Kingklip.

Helicopters: To be announced.

Programmes: Contract for the construction of three corvettes, all to be built in the Netherlands, announced on 6 February 2008. Two ships are 98 m Sigma 9813 and one is a lengthened 105 m Sigma 10513. First steel was cut for the lead (105 m) ship on 27 February 2008. The ships, which are to have common systems, are required to extend the patrol capabilities of the Moroccan Navy and to enable joint operations with NATO and other navies.

SHIPBORNE AIRCRAFT

Numbers/Type: 3 Eurocopter AS 565MB Panther.
Operational speed: 165 kt *(305 km/h)*.
Service ceiling: 16,700 ft *(5,100 m)*
Range: 483 n miles *(895 km)*.
Role/Weapon systems: Procured from France for operation from Floréal class. Sensors: Thomson-CSF Varan radar. FLIR. Weapons: 7.62 mm MG.

PANTHER (French colours) *9/1998, M Declerck* / 0052167

PATROL FORCES

Notes: There are two patrol craft, pennant numbers 105-106, of unknown type.

106 *3/2006, M Declerck* / 1164949

2 OKBA (PR 72) CLASS (LARGE PATROL CRAFT) (PG)

Name	*No*	*Builders*	*Commissioned*
OKBA	302	SFCN, Villeneuve la Garenne	16 Dec 1976
TRIKI	303	SFCN, Villeneuve la Garenne	12 July 1977

Displacement, tons: 375 standard; 445 full load
Dimensions, feet (metres): 188.8 × 25 × 7.1 *(57.5 × 7.6 × 2.1)*
Main machinery: 2 SACM AGO V16 ASHR diesels; 5,520 hp(m) *(4.1 MW)*; 2 shafts
Speed, knots: 20
Range, n miles: 2,500 at 16 kt
Complement: 53 (5 officers)
Guns: 1 OTO Melara 3 in *(76 mm)*/62 compact; 85 rds/min to 16 km *(8.6 n miles)* anti-surface; 12 km *(6.5 n miles)* anti-aircraft; weight of shell 6 kg.
1 Bofors 40 mm/70; 300 rds/min to 12.5 km *(6.7 n miles)*; weight of shell 0.96 kg.
Weapons control: 2 CSEE Panda optical directors.
Radars: Surface search: Racal Decca 1226; I-band.

Comment: Ordered June 1973. *Okba* launched 10 October 1975, *Triki* 1 February 1976. Can be Exocet fitted (with Vega control system). *Triki* refitted at Lorient 2002–03. Modifications included installation of a funnel and removal of two diesels and two shafts. Speed reduced to 20 kt. Similar refit for *Okba* completed in early 2005.

TRIKI *6/2003, B Prézelin* / 0589787

4 LAZAGA CLASS (FAST ATTACK CRAFT—MISSILE) (PGG)

Name	*No*	*Builders*	*Commissioned*
COMMANDANT EL KHATTABI	304	Bazán, San Fernando	26 July 1981
COMMANDANT BOUTOUBA	305	Bazán, San Fernando	2 Aug 1982
COMMANDANT EL HARTY	306	Bazán, San Fernando	20 Nov 1981
COMMANDANT AZOUGGARH	307	Bazán, San Fernando	25 Feb 1982

Displacement, tons: 425 full load
Dimensions, feet (metres): 190.6 × 24.9 × 8.9 *(58.1 × 7.6 × 2.7)*
Main machinery: 2 MTU-Bazán 16V 956 TB91 diesels; 7,500 hp(m) *(5.51 MW)* sustained; 2 shafts
Speed, knots: 30
Range, n miles: 3,000 at 15 kt
Complement: 41
Missiles: SSM: 4 Aerospatiale MM 38 Exocet; inertial cruise; active radar homing to 42 km *(23 n miles)* at 0.9 Mach; warhead 165 kg; sea-skimmer.
Guns: 1 OTO Melara 3 in *(76 mm)*/62 compact; 85 rds/min to 16 km *(8.6 n miles)* anti-surface; 12 km *(6.5 n miles)* anti-aircraft; weight of shell 6 kg.
1 Breda Bofors 40 mm/70; 300 rds/min to 12.5 km *(6.7 n miles)*; weight of shell 0.96 kg.
2 Oerlikon 20 mm/90 GAM-BO1; 800 rds/min to 2 km.
Weapons control: CSEE Panda optical director.
Radars: Surface search: Signaal ZW06; I-band; range 26 km *(14 n miles)*.
Fire control: Signaal WM25; I/J-band; range 46 km *(25 n miles)*.
Navigation: Furuno; I-band.

Comment: Ordered from Bazán, San Fernando (Cadiz), Spain 14 June 1977. New Bofors guns fitted aft in 1996/97. 76 mm gun removed from 305 in 1998. *El Harty* and *Azouggarh* refitted by Navantia, Cartagena, 2008–09.

COMMANDANT BOUTOUBA ***9/2008*, Diego Quevedo*** / 1353240

COMMANDANT AZOUGGARH ***2/2005, Marco Ghiglino*** / 1133095

4 OSPREY MK II CLASS (LARGE PATROL CRAFT) (PBO)

Name	*No*	*Builders*	*Commissioned*
EL HAHIQ	308	Danyard A/S, Frederikshavn	11 Nov 1987
EL TAWFIQ	309	Danyard A/S, Frederikshavn	31 Jan 1988
EL HAMISS	316	Danyard A/S, Frederikshavn	9 Aug 1990
EL KARIB	317	Danyard A/S, Frederikshavn	23 Sep 1990

Displacement, tons: 475 full load
Dimensions, feet (metres): 179.8 × 34 × 8.5 *(54.8 × 10.5 × 2.6)*
Main machinery: 2 MAN Burmeister & Wain Alpha 12V23/30-DVO diesels; 4,440 hp(m) *(3.23 MW)* sustained; 2 water-jets
Speed, knots: 22
Range, n miles: 4,500 at 16 kt
Complement: 15 plus 20 spare berths
Guns: 1 Bofors 40 mm/60. 2 Oerlikon 20 mm.
Radars: Surface search: Racal Decca; I-band.
Navigation: Racal Decca; I-band.

Comment: First two ordered in September 1986; two more on 30 January 1989. There is a stern ramp with a hinged cover for launching the inspection boat. Used for Fishery Protection duties.

EL HAMISS ***3/2006, M Declerck*** / 1164955

6 CORMORAN CLASS (LARGE PATROL CRAFT) (PBO)

Name	*No*	*Builders*	*Launched*	*Commissioned*
L V RABHI	310	Bázan, San Fernando	23 Sep 1987	16 Sep 1988
ERRACHIQ	311	Bázan, San Fernando	23 Sep 1987	16 Dec 1988
EL AKID	312	Bázan, San Fernando	29 Mar 1988	4 Apr 1989
EL MAHER	313	Bázan, San Fernando	29 Mar 1988	20 June 1989
EL MAJID	314	Bázan, San Fernando	21 Oct 1988	26 Sep 1989
EL BACHIR	315	Bázan, San Fernando	21 Oct 1988	19 Dec 1989

Displacement, tons: 425 full load
Dimensions, feet (metres): 190.6 × 24.9 × 8.9 *(58.1 × 7.6 × 2.7)*
Main machinery: 2 MTU-Bazán 16V 956 TB82 diesels; 8,340 hp(m) *(6.13 MW)* sustained; 2 shafts
Speed, knots: 22. **Range, n miles**: 6,100 at 12 kt
Complement: 36 (4 officers) plus 15 spare
Guns: 1 Bofors 40 mm/70. 2 Giat 20 mm.
Weapons control: CSEE Lynx optronic director.
Radars: Surface search: Racal Decca; I-band.

Comment: Three ordered from Bazán, Cadiz in October 1985 as a follow on to the Lazaga class of which these are a slower patrol version with a 10 day endurance. Option on three more taken up. Used for fishery protection. Armament removed from some. *El Akid*, *El Majid* and *El Bachir* refitted by Raidco Marine 2007–08.

EL AKID ***6/2006, B Prézelin*** / 1040669

5 RAÏS BARGACH CLASS (TYPE OPV 64) (PSO)

Name	*No*	*Builders*	*Launched*	*Commissioned*
RAÏS BARGACH	318	Leroux & Lotz, Lorient	9 Oct 1995	14 Dec 1995
RAÏS BRITEL	319	Leroux & Lotz, Lorient	19 Mar 1996	14 May 1996
RAÏS CHARKAOUI	320	Leroux & Lotz, Lorient	25 Sep 1996	10 Dec 1996
RAÏS MAANINOU	321	Leroux & Lotz, Lorient	7 Mar 1997	21 May 1997
RAÏS AL MOUNASTIRI	322	Leroux & Lotz, Lorient	15 Oct 1997	17 Dec 1997

Displacement, tons: 580 full load
Dimensions, feet (metres): 210 × 37.4 × 9.8 *(64 × 11.4 × 3)*
Main machinery: 2 Wärtsilä Nohab 25 V16 diesels; 10,000 hp(m) *(7.36 MW)* sustained; 2 Leroy auxiliary motors; 326 hp(m) *(240 kW)*; 2 shafts; cp props
Speed, knots: 24; 7 (on motors)
Range, n miles: 4,000 at 12 kt
Complement: 24 (3 officers) + 30 spare
Guns: 1 Bofors 40 mm/60. 1 Oerlikon 20 mm. 4—14.5 mm MGs (2 twin).
Radars: Surface search: Racal Decca Bridgemaster; I-band.

Comment: First pair ordered to a Serter design from Leroux & Lotz, Lorient in December 1993, second pair in October 1994. Option on fifth taken up in 1996. There is a stern door for launching a 7 m RIB, a water gun for firefighting and two passive stabilisation tanks. This version of the OPV 64 does not have a helicopter deck and the armament is fitted after delivery. Manned by the Navy for the Fisheries Department. Based at Agadir.

RAÏS BRITEL ***4/2007, Rafael Carrera Gonzalez*** / 1170199

RAÏS AL MOUNASTIRI ***9/2005, S Dominguez Llosá*** / 1040670

6 EL WACIL (P 32) CLASS (COASTAL PATROL CRAFT) (PB)

Name	*No*	*Builders*	*Launched*	*Commissioned*
EL WACIL	203	CMN, Cherbourg	12 June 1975	9 Oct 1975
EL JAIL	204	CMN, Cherbourg	10 Oct 1975	3 Dec 1975
EL MIKDAM	205	CMN, Cherbourg	1 Dec 1975	30 Jan 1976
EL KHAFIR	206	CMN, Cherbourg	21 Jan 1976	16 Apr 1976
EL HARIS	207	CMN, Cherbourg	31 Mar 1976	30 June 1976
EL ESSAHIR	208	CMN, Cherbourg	2 June 1976	16 July 1976

Displacement, tons: 74 light; 89 full load
Dimensions, feet (metres): 105 × 17.7 × 4.6 *(32 × 5.4 × 1.4)*
Main machinery: 2 SACM MGO 12V BZSHR diesels; 2,700 hp(m) *(1.98 MW)*; 2 shafts
Speed, knots: 28
Range, n miles: 1,500 at 15 kt
Complement: 17
Guns: 1 Oerlikon 20 mm.
Radars: Surface search: Decca; I-band.

Comment: Ordered in February 1974. In July 1985 a further four of this class were ordered from the same builders but for the Customs Service. Wooden hull sheathed in plastic.

EL JAIL *9/2004, S D Llosá* / 1044135

10 VCSM CLASS (PATROL CRAFT) (PB)

P 107–116

Displacement, tons: 40 full load
Dimensions, feet (metres): 65.6 × 16.4 × 4.9 *(20.0 × 5.0 × 1.5)*
Main machinery: 2 MAN V12 diesels; 2,000 hp *(1.47 MW)*; 2 shafts
Speed, knots: 25
Range, n miles: 530 at 15 kt
Complement: 5
Guns: 1 — 7.62 mm MG.
Radars: Navigation: Furuno; I-band.

Comment: Coastal Surveillance craft ordered from Raidco Marine in 2005 (4) and 2006 (6), built at l'Herbaudière and delivered in 2006–08. Raidco RPB 20 design. GRP hull and superstructure. A 4.9 m RIB can be embarked on an inclined ramp at the stern. There are 24 similar 'Vedettes' craft in service with the French Navy.

P 107 *6/2006, B Prézelin* / 1040671

1 PATROL VESSEL (PBO)

Name	*No*	*Builders*	*Commissioned*
– (ex-*Cygnet*)	323 (ex-P 261)	R Dunston Ltd, Hessle	8 July 1976

Displacement, tons: 194 full load
Dimensions, feet (metres): 120 × 23.6 × 6.5 *(36.6 × 7.2 × 2.0)*
Main machinery: 2 Paxman 16YJCM diesels; 4,200 hp *(3.1 MW)*; 2 shafts
Speed, knots: 21
Range, n miles: 2,000 at 14 kt
Complement: 21 (4 officers)
Guns: 1 — 12.7 mm MG.
Radars: Navigation: I-band.

Comment: Former Royal Navy Bird class patrol craft sold to a private buyer and delivered to Agadir on 11 April 1997. The ship was later implicated in a counter-drugs operation and the vessel was confiscated by the Moroccan authorities. It has since been operated by the Moroccan Navy.

323 *3/2006, M Declerck* / 1164950

0 + 4 OFFSHORE PATROL VESSELS (PSO)

Displacement, tons: To be announced
Dimensions, feet (metres): 229.7 × 37.1 × ? *(70.0 × 11.3 × ?)*
Main machinery: 2 Wärtsilä diesels; 2 shafts
Speed, knots: 22
Range, n miles: To be announced.
Complement: 64
Guns: 1 — 76 mm. 1 — 40 mm.
Radars: Surface search: To be announced.
Navigation: I-band.

Comment: The order for four patrol vessels was announced on 30 May 2008. Designed by Raidco Marine, the ships are to be built by Aker Yards, Lanester. Delivery of the first vessel is to be made in 2010 and the remainder at one-year intervals.

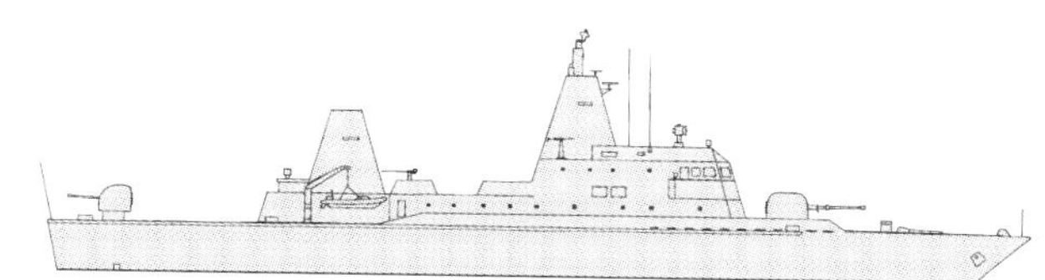

RAIDCO OPV *(Scale 1 : 900), Ian Sturton* / 1353238

AMPHIBIOUS FORCES

1 NEWPORT CLASS (LSTH)

Name	*No*	*Builders*	*Commissioned*
SIDI MOHAMMED BEN ABDALLAH (ex-*Bristol County*)	407 (ex-1198)	National Steel, San Diego	5 Aug 1972

Displacement, tons: 4,975 light; 8,450 full load
Dimensions, feet (metres): 522.3 (hull) × 69.5 × 17.5 (aft) *(159.2 × 21.2 × 5.3)*
Main machinery: 6 ALCO 16-251 diesels; 16,500 hp *(12.3 MW)* sustained; 2 shafts; cp props; bow thruster
Speed, knots: 20
Range, n miles: 14,250 at 14 kt
Complement: 257 (13 officers)
Military lift: 400 troops (20 officers); 500 tons vehicles; 3 LCVPs and 1 LCPL on davits
Guns: 1 GE/GD 20 mm 6-barrelled Vulcan Phalanx Mk 15.
Radars: Surface search: Raytheon SPS-67; G-band.
Navigation: Marconi LN66; I/J-band.
Helicopters: Platform only.

Comment: Received from the US by grant transfer on 16 August 1994. Has replaced *Arrafiq*. The ship was non-operational by late 1995 and although back in service, has so far proved to be a poor bargain. The bow ramp is supported by twin derrick arms. A ramp just forward of the superstructure connects the lower tank deck with the main deck anda vehicle passage through the superstructure provides access to the parking area amidships. A stern gate to the tank deck permits unloading of amphibious tractors into the water, or unloading of other vehicles into an LCU or on to a pier. Vehicle stowage covers 19,000 sq ft. Length over derrick arms is 562 ft *(171.3 m)*; full load draught is 11.5 ft forward and 17.5 ft aft. Based at Casablanca.

SIDI MOHAMMED BEN ABDALLAH *7/2007, Shaun Jones* / 1170198

3 BATRAL CLASS (LSMH)

Name	*No*	*Builders*	*Commissioned*
DAOUD BEN AICHA	402	Dubigeon, Normandie	28 May 1977
AHMED ES SAKALI	403	Dubigeon, Normandie	Sep 1977
ABOU ABDALLAH EL AYACHI	404	Dubigeon, Normandie	Mar 1978

Displacement, tons: 750 standard; 1,409 full load
Dimensions, feet (metres): 262.4 × 42.6 × 7.9 *(80 × 13 × 2.4)*
Main machinery: 2 SACM Type 195 V12 CSHR diesels; 3,600 hp(m) *(2.65 MW)* sustained; 2 shafts
Speed, knots: 16
Range, n miles: 4,500 at 13 kt
Complement: 47 (3 officers)
Military lift: 140 troops; 12 vehicles or 300 tons
Guns: 2 Bofors 40 mm/70. 2—81 mm mortars. 2—12.7 mm MGs.
Radars: Surface search: Thomson-CSF DRBN 32 (Racal Decca 1226); I-band.
Helicopters: Platform only.

Comment: Two ordered on 12 March 1975. Third ordered 19 August 1975. Of same type as the French *Champlain*. Vehicle-stowage above and below decks. *Daoud Ben Aicha* was refitted in Lorient by Leroux & Lotz in 1995 and *Abou Abdallah el Ayachi* in 1997.

DAOUD BEN AICHA *10/2004, Carlos Pardo Gonzalez* / 1133132

1 CTM (LCM)

Displacement, tons: 59 standard; 150 full load
Dimensions, feet (metres): 78.0 × 21.0 × 4.2 *(23.8 × 6.4 × 1.3)*
Main machinery: 2 Poyaud V8520NS diesels; 450 hp *(331 kW)*; 2 shafts
Speed, knots: 9.5
Range, n miles: 380 at 8 kt
Complement: 4 plus 200 passengers
Military lift: 90 tons (maximum); 48 tons normal
Guns: 1—12.7 mm MG.
Radars: Navigation: I-band.

Comment: Ex-CTM-5 transferred from France in August 2000.

LCM *6/2006, S Dominguez Llosá* / 1040668

SURVEY AND RESEARCH SHIPS

1 ROBERT D CONRAD CLASS (AGOR)

Name	*No*	*Builders*	*Commissioned*
ABU AL BARAKAT AL BARBARI (ex-*Bartlett*)	802 (ex-702, ex-T-AGOR 13)	Northwest Marine Iron Works, Portland, OR	31 Mar 1969

Displacement, tons: 1,200 light; 1,370 full load
Dimensions, feet (metres): 208.9 × 40 × 15.3 *(63.7 × 12.2 × 4.7)*
Main machinery: Diesel-electric; 2 Caterpillar D 378 diesel generators; 1 motor; 1,000 hp *(746 kW)*; 1 shaft; bow thruster
Speed, knots: 13.5
Range, n miles: 12,000 at 12 kt
Complement: 41 (9 officers, 15 scientists)
Radars: Navigation: TM 1660/12S; I-band.

Comment: Leased from the USA on 26 July 1993. Fitted with instrumentation and laboratories to measure gravity and magnetism, water temperature, sound transmission in water, and the profile of the ocean floor. Special features include 10 ton capacity boom and winches for handling over-the-side equipment; bow thruster; 620 hp gas turbine (housed in funnel structure) for providing 'quiet' power when conducting experiments; can propel the ship at 6.5 kt.
Ships of this class are in service with Brazil, Mexico, Chile, Tunisia and Portugal.

ABU EL BARAKAT AL BARBARI *11/2004, Marco Ghiglino* / 1133094

AUXILIARIES

Notes: (1) There is also a yacht, *Essaouira*, 60 tons, from Italy in 1967, used as a training vessel for watchkeepers.
(2) Bazán delivered a harbour pusher tug, similar to Spanish Y 171 class, in December 1993.
(3) There are two sail training craft *Al Massira* and *Boujdour*.
(4) There is a stern trawler used as a utility and diver support vessel (803 (ex-YFU 14)).

803 *9/2004, S D Llosá* / 1044141

1 LOGISTIC SUPPORT SHIP (AKS)

EL AIGH (ex-*Merc Nordia*) 405

Measurement, tons: 1,500 grt
Dimensions, feet (metres): 252.6 × 40 × 15.4 *(77 × 12.2 × 4.7)*
Main machinery: 1 Burmeister & Wain diesel; 1,250 hp(m) *(919 kW)*; 1 shaft
Speed, knots: 11
Complement: 25
Guns: 2—14.5 mm MGs.

Comment: Logistic support vessel with four 5 ton cranes. Former cargo ship with ice-strengthened bow built by Fredrickshavn Vaerft in 1973 and acquired in 1981.

EL AIGH *5/1994, M Declerck* / 0506199

1 DAKHLA CLASS (LOGISTIC SUPPORT SHIP) (AKS)

Name	*No*	*Builders*	*Launched*	*Commissioned*
DAKHLA	408	Leroux & Lotz, Lorient	5 June 1997	1 Aug 1997

Displacement, tons: 2,160 full load
Dimensions, feet (metres): 226.4 × 37.7 × 13.8 *(69 × 11.5 × 4.2)*
Main machinery: 1 Wärtsilä Nohab 8V25 diesel; 2,300 hp(m) *(1.69 MW)* sustained; 1 shaft; cp prop
Speed, knots: 12
Range, n miles: 4,300 at 12 kt
Complement: 24 plus 22 spare
Cargo capacity: 800 tons
Guns: 2—12.7 mm MGs.
Radars: Navigation: 2 Racal Decca Bridgemaster ARPA; I-band.

Comment: Ordered from Leroux & Lotz, Nantes in 1995. Side entry for vehicles. One 15 ton crane. Based at Agadir.

DAKHLA *8/1997, Leroux & Lotz* / 0012789

CUSTOMS/COAST GUARD/POLICE

Notes: (1) The Coast Guard was created by Royal Decree on 9 September 1997. Responsibility for Search and Rescue conferred on the Ministère des Pêches Maritimes (MPM). Operational control is exercised from the National Rescue Service HQ at Rabat in co-ordination with the Merchant Marine HQ at Casablanca.
(2) There is a 17 m SAR craft *Al Fida* delivered in August 2002.
(3) There are four SAR craft: *Rif, Loukouss, Souss* and *Dghira.*

AL FIDA ***7/2004, S D Llosá*** / 1044137

SOUSS ***7/1995, Zamacona*** / 1044138

2 SAR CRAFT (SAR)

AL AMANE 2344 **AIT BAÂMRANE** 2345

Displacement, tons: 68 full load
Dimensions, feet (metres): 51.7 × 14.7 × 3.4 *(15.75 × 4.48 × 1.05)*
Main machinery: 2 Volvo D12; 1,300 hp *(970 kW)*; Hamilton waterjets
Speed, knots: 34
Complement: 4

Comment: Constructed by Auxnaval Shipbuilders, Spain and delivered in March 2003. Aluminium hull.

AL AMANE ***7/2003, Auxnaval*** / 1044136

2 SAR CRAFT (SAR)

AL WHADA 12-64 **SEBOU** 12-65

Displacement, tons: 70 full load
Dimensions, feet (metres): 68.0 × 19.2 × 5.9 *(20.7 × 5.8 × 1.8)*
Main machinery: 2 MAN D2842 LE401 diesels; 2,000 hp *(1.49 MW)*; 2 shafts
Speed, knots: 20
Complement: 4

Comment: Constructed by Auxnaval, Asturias, Spain and delivered in 2004.

AL WHADA ***7/2004, Auxnaval*** / 1044139

4 ERRAID (P 32) CLASS (COASTAL PATROL CRAFT) (WPB)

Name	*No*	*Builders*	*Launched*	*Commissioned*
ERRAID	209	CMN, Cherbourg	20 Dec 1987	18 Mar 1988
ERRACED	210	CMN, Cherbourg	21 Jan 1988	15 Apr 1988
EL KACED	211	CMN, Cherbourg	10 Mar 1988	17 May 1988
ESSAID	212	CMN, Cherbourg	19 May 1988	4 July 1988

Displacement, tons: 89 full load
Dimensions, feet (metres): 105 × 17.7 × 4.6 *(32 × 5.4 × 1.4)*
Main machinery: 2 SACM MGO 12V BZSHR diesels; 2,700 hp(m) *(1.98 MW)*; 2 shafts
Speed, knots: 28
Range, n miles: 1,500 at 15 kt
Complement: 17
Guns: 1 Oerlikon 20 mm.
Radars: Navigation: Decca; I-band.

Comment: Similar to the El Wacil class listed under Patrol Forces. Ordered in July 1985.

EL KACED ***6/1999*** / 0081279

18 ARCOR 46 CLASS (COASTAL PATROL CRAFT) (WPB)

Displacement, tons: 15 full load
Dimensions, feet (metres): 47.6 × 13.8 × 4.3 *(14.5 × 4.2 × 1.3)*
Main machinery: 2 SACM UD18V8 M5D diesels; 1,010 hp(m) *(742 kW)* sustained; 2 shafts
Speed, knots: 32
Range, n miles: 300 at 20 kt
Complement: 6
Guns: 2 Browning 12.7 mm MGs.
Radars: Surface search: Furuno 701; I-band.

Comment: Ordered from Arcor, La Teste in June 1985. GRP hulls. Delivered in groups of three from April to September 1987. Used for patrolling the Mediterranean coastline.

ARCOR 46 CLASS ***9/2004, S D Llosá*** / 1044140

3 SAR CRAFT (SAR)

HAOUZ **ASSA** **TARIK**

Displacement, tons: 40 full load
Dimensions, feet (metres): 63.6 × 15.7 × 4.3 *(19.4 × 4.8 × 1.3)*
Main machinery: 2 diesels; 1,400 hp(m) *(1.03 MW)*; 2 shafts
Speed, knots: 20
Complement: 6

Comment: Rescue craft built by Schweers, Bardenfleth and delivered in 1991.

15 ARCOR 53 CLASS (COASTAL PATROL CRAFT) (WPBF)

Displacement, tons: 17 full load
Dimensions, feet (metres): 52.5 × 13 × 3.9 *(16 × 4 × 1.2)*
Main machinery: 2 Saab DSI-14 diesels; 1,250 hp(m) *(919 kW)*; 2 shafts
Speed, knots: 35. **Range, n miles:** 300 at 20 kt
Complement: 6
Guns: 1 – 12.7 mm MG.
Radars: Surface search: Furuno; I-band.

Comment: Ordered from Arcor, La Teste in 1990 for the Police Force. Delivered at one a month from October 1992.

ARCOR 53 CLASS *3/2006, M Declerck* / 1164948

Mozambique

MARINHA MOÇAMBIQUE

Country Overview

The Republic of Mozambique gained independence from Portugal in 1975. Situated in south-eastern Africa, it has an area of 308,642 square miles and is bordered to the north by Tanzania, to the south by South Africa and Swaziland and to the west by Zimbabwe, Zambia, and Malawi. It has a 1,334 n mile coastline with the Mozambique Channel of the Indian Ocean. Maputo (formerly Lourenço Marques) is the capital, largest city and principal port. There is another major port at Beira. Territorial Seas (12 n miles) are claimed. A 200 n mile EEZ has also been claimed but the limits are not fully defined by boundary agreements.

All the Russian built Zhuks and Yevgenyas have sunk alongside or been sold. There are some motorboats operational on Lake Malawi.

Headquarters Appointments

Commander of the Navy:
Rear Admiral Patricio Jotamo

Personnel

2009: 200

Bases

Maputo (Naval HQ); Nacala; Beira; Pemba (Porto Amelia); Metangula (Lake Malawi); Tete (River Zambesi); Inhambane.

PATROL FORCES

Notes: A total of eight patrol craft have been reported donated by the US. Probably the widely exported Defender class, three were delivered on 21 December 2006, three on 19 March 2007 and the remaining two in late 2007.

2 NAMACURRA CLASS (INSHORE PATROL CRAFT) (PB)

Y 07 (ex-Y 1507) **Y 30** (ex-Y 1530)

Displacement, tons: 5 full load
Dimensions, feet (metres): 29.5 × 9 × 2.8 *(9 × 2.7 × 0.8)*
Main machinery: 2 Yamaha outboards; 380 hp(m) *(2.79 kW)*
Speed, knots: 32
Range, n miles: 180 at 20 kt
Complement: 4
Guns: 1 – 12.7 mm MG. 2 – 7.62 mm MGs.
Depth charges: 1 rack.
Radars: Surface search: Furuno; I-band.

Comment: Built in South Africa in 1980–81. Can be transported by road. Donated by South Africa in 2004.

NAMACURRA (South African colours) *8/2001, van Ginderen Collection* / 0132783

Myanmar

TATMADAW YAY

Country Overview

The Union of Myanmar, also known as the Republic of Burma, gained independence in 1948. Situated in South East Asia, it has an area of 261,218 square miles, is bordered to the north-east by China, to the north-west by India and Bangladesh and to the south-east by Laos and Thailand. It has a 1,042 n mile coastline with the Andaman Sea and the Bay of Bengal. The administrative capital became Pyinmana on 6 November 2005. Rangoon (Yangon) is the commercial capital, largest city and principal port. Some 6,900 n miles of navigable inland waterways are important transport arteries. Territorial waters (12 n miles) are claimed. A 200 n mile EEZ has been claimed although the limits have only been partly defined by boundary agreements.

Headquarters Appointments

Commander in Chief:
Rear Admiral Nyan Tun

Personnel

(a) 2009: 13,000 (this may include 800 naval infantry)
(b) Voluntary service

Bases

There are five regional commands with principal bases as indicated:
Ayeyarwady (Irawaddy): Monkey Point (Navy HQ), Yangon (Rangoon), Thilawa (dockyard), Great Coco Island
Taninthayi (Tenasserim): Myeik (Mergui) (Regional HQ), Zadetgyi Island (Base 58, St Matthew's Island), Kathekyun (Ketthayin), Pale Island, Thetkatan (Kadan Island)
Danyawady: Hainggyi Island (Regional HQ), Pathein
Mawrawady: Mawlamyine (Moulmein) (Regional HQ), Kyaikkami, Dawei (Tavoy)
Panmawady: Kyaukpyu (Regional HQ), Akyab (Base 18, Sittwe), Thandwe
The Headquarters of Training Command is at Thilawa in Rangoon. The main training depot is currently at Syriam (Thanlyin), but is to be transferred to Seikkyi, near the mouth of the Hlaing (Rangoon) River.
The Pathein base will reportedly be moved to Pyadatgyi Island, where an expanded airfield will permit the basing of air force equipment and personnel as well as navy.
The Great Coco Island base has also been expanded through the construction of a large landing jetty to replace the existing small pier. It is also the site of a Chinese surveillance installation.

Organisations

Naval units are usually commanded directly from Rangoon, but operational control is occasionally delegated to regional commands.

Naval Infantry

The existence of 800 naval infantry has been previously reported but not confirmed.

FRIGATES

Notes: A programme for the procurement of a 110 m frigate of about 3,000 tons has reportedly been initiated. While further details are not known and it is unclear whether construction has started, the project is likely to have received Chinese assistance. This is reported to have included supply of diesel engines in 2007.

CORVETTES

3 ANAWRAHTA CLASS (CORVETTES) (FSG)

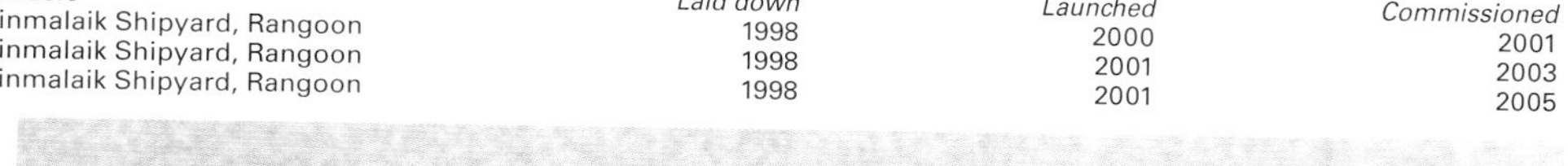

Name	*No*	*Builders*	*Laid down*	*Launched*	*Commissioned*
ANAWRAHTA	771	Sinmalaik Shipyard, Rangoon	1998	2000	2001
BAYINTNAUNG	772	Sinmalaik Shipyard, Rangoon	1998	2001	2003
–	–	Sinmalaik Shipyard, Rangoon	1998	2001	2005

Displacement, tons: 1,088 full load
Dimensions, feet (metres): 252.6 × ? × ?
(77.0 × ? × ?)
Main machinery: To be announced
Speed, knots: To be announced
Complement: 101 (15 officers)

Missiles: SSM: 4 C-802; mid-course guidance and active radar homing to 150 km *(81 n miles)* at 0.9 Mach; warhead 165 kg.
Guns: 1 OTO Breda 3 in *(76 mm)*/62 compact; 85 rds/min to 16 km *(8.7 n miles)* anti-surface; 12 km *(6.5 n miles)* anti-aircraft; weight of shell 6 kg.
2 Breda 40 mm/70 (twin); 300 rds/min to 12.5 km *(6.8 n miles)*; weight of shell 0.96 kg.
Countermeasures: To be announced.
Radars: Surface search: To be announced.
Navigation: To be announced
Fire control: To be announced
Sonars: To be announced

Helicopters: Platform for 1 medium.

Programmes: The programme to acquire ships to replace the now decommissioned PCE-827 and Admirable class corvettes was probably instituted in the 1990s. As frigates initially proved to be too expensive, three Chinese hulls are believed to have been acquired in about 1998 for fitting out at Sinmalaik Shipyard. There have been reports that Israeli electronic systems (radars and sonar) have been fitted. The details of the programme are speculative.

ANAWRAHTA *12/2004* / 0581402

Operational: There has been speculation that these vessels were to be armed with four C-801 anti-ship missiles but is unclear as to whether they have been fitted. The first ship conducted sea trials in 2001 when the second ship was reportedly nearing completion. Three ships were reported in commission by 2004 although there have been no known sightings of the second twoships. *Anawrahta* visited Port Blair in January 2006 and *Bayintnaung* participated in Exercise Milan 2008.

ANAWRAHTA ***1/2006, Indian Navy*** / 1158724

PATROL FORCES

Notes: There is a new class of river patrol craft known as the Ngaman class. These 8 m craft are of a Boston Whaler type and are armed with a 12.5 mm gun in the bow and a twin 7.62 mm aft. Locally built, the craft have probably replaced the PBR Mk II class which have been decommissioned.

6 HOUXIN (TYPE 037/1G) CLASS (FAST ATTACK CRAFT—GUN) (PTG)

MAGA 471 **SAITTRA** 472 **DUWA** 473 **ZEYDA** 474 **475** **476**

Displacement, tons: 478 full load
Dimensions, feet (metres): 206 × 23.6 × 7.9 *(62.8 × 7.2 × 2.4)*
Main machinery: 4 PR 230ZC diesels; 4,000 hp(m) *(2.94 MW)*; 4 shafts
Speed, knots: 28. **Range, n miles:** 1,300 at 15 kt
Complement: 71

Missiles: SSM: 4 YJ-1 (C-801) (2 twin); active radar homing to 40 km *(22 n miles)* at 0.9 Mach; warhead 165 kg; sea skimmer. C-802 may be fitted in due course.
Guns: 4—37 mm/63 Type 76A (2 twin); 180 rds/min to 8.5 km *(4.6 n miles)*; weight of shell 1.42 kg.
4—14.5 mm Type 69 (2 twin).
Countermeasures: ESM/ECM: intercept and jammer.
Radars: Surface search: Square Tie; I-band.
Fire control: Rice Lamp; I-band.

Programmes: First pair arrived from China in December 1995, second pair in mid-1996 and last two in late 1997. The first four were wrongly reported as Hainan class.
Structure: Details given are for this class in Chinese service.
Operational: *475* damaged in a collision during sea trials in August 1996. All based at Rangoon.

ZEYDA ***6/2001*** / 0130747

2 OSPREY CLASS (OFFSHORE PATROL VESSELS) (PBO)

Name	*No*	*Builders*	*Commissioned*
INDAW	FV 55	Frederikshavn Dockyard	30 May 1980
INYA	FV 57	Frederikshavn Dockyard	25 Mar 1982

Displacement, tons: 385 standard; 505 full load
Dimensions, feet (metres): 164 × 34.5 × 9 *(50 × 10.5 × 2.8)*
Main machinery: 2 Burmeister and Wain Alpha diesels; 4,640 hp(m) *(3.4 MW)*; 2 shafts; cp props
Speed, knots: 20. **Range, n miles:** 4,500 at 16 kt
Complement: 20 (5 officers)
Guns: 1 Bofors 40 mm/60. 2 Oerlikon 20 mm.

Comment: Operated by Burmese Navy for the People's Pearl and Fishery Department. Helicopter deck with hangar in *Indaw*. Carry David Still craft or RIBs capable of 25 kt. *Inya* reported to be in poor condition. Both based at Rangoon. A third of class, *Inma*, reported to have sunkin 1987. A similar ship is in service in Namibia.

INYA ***1980*** / 0056642

9 MYANMAR CLASS (COASTAL PATROL CRAFT) (PGG)

551–558 560

Displacement, tons: 213 full load
Dimensions, feet (metres): 147.3 × 23 × 8.2 *(45 × 7 × 2.5)*
Main machinery: 2 Mercedes-Benz diesels; 2 shafts
Speed, knots: 30+
Complement: 34 (7 officers)
Missiles: 4 YJ-1 (Eagle Strike) (C-801) (2 twin) launchers; active radar homing to 40 km *(22 n miles)* at 0.9 Mach; warhead 165 kg.
Guns: 2—37 mm (twin), 4—23 mm (2 twin) (gun-armed variant).
4—30 mm AK 230 (2 twin), 4—14.5 mm (1 quad) (missile-armed variant).
Radars: Surface search: I-band.
Fire control: Rice Lamp; I-band.

Comment: First ship under construction at the Naval Engineering Depot, Rangoon in 1991. *551* launched on 2 January 1996 and *552* on 4 January 1996. Four further vessels reported in service by 2004, a further two in 2005 and a further one by 2007. There appear to be three variants of the class. Possibly four (*556-558* and *560*) have missile launchers believed to house C-801. These have a higher mainmast and an additional radar. The remainder (*551-552* and *553-555*) are gun-armed but with differences in superstructure.

MYANMAR CLASS 556 ***6/2007*** / 1170200

MYANMAR CLASS 553 ***6/2001*** / 0130746

MYANMAR CLASS 556-558 ***11/2005*** / 1151121

3 PB 90 CLASS (COASTAL PATROL CRAFT) (PB)

424–426

Displacement, tons: 92 full load
Dimensions, feet (metres): 89.9 × 21.5 × 7.2 *(27.4 × 6.6 × 2.2)*
Main machinery: 3 diesels; 4,290 hp(m) *(3.15 MW)*; 3 shafts
Speed, knots: 32
Range, n miles: 400 at 25 kt
Complement: 17
Guns: 8—20 mm M75 (two quad). 2—128 mm launchers for illuminants.
Radars: Surface search: Decca 1226; I-band.

Comment: Built by Brodotechnika, Yugoslavia for an African country and completed in 1986–87. Laid up when the sale did not go through and shipped to Burma arriving in October 1990. All are active. Based at Rangoon.

PB 90 (Yugoslav colours) ***1990, Yugoslav FDSP*** / 0056643

9 HAINAN (TYPE 037) CLASS (COASTAL PATROL CRAFT) (PC)

YAN YE AUNG 445	**YAN NYEIN AUNG** 443
YAN WIN AUNG 448	**YAN PAING AUNG** 447
YAN MYAT AUNG 442	**YAN ZWE AUNG** 450
YAN MIN AUNG 446	**YAN KHWIN AUNG** 444
YAN AYE AUNG 449	

Displacement, tons: 375 standard; 392 full load
Dimensions, feet (metres): 192.8 × 23.6 × 7.2 *(58.8 × 7.2 × 2.2)*
Main machinery: 4 PCR/Kolomna Type 9-D-8 diesels; 4,000 hp(m) *(2.94 MW)* sustained; 4 shafts
Speed, knots: 30.5
Range, n miles: 1,300 at 15 kt
Complement: 69
Guns: 4 China 57 mm/70 (2 twin); 120 rds/min to 12 km *(6.5 n miles)*; weight of shell 6.31 kg.
4 USSR 25 mm/60 (2 twin); 270 rds/min to 3 km *(1.6 n miles)* anti-aircraft; weight of shell 0.34 kg.
A/S mortars: 4 RBU 1200 5-tubed fixed launchers; range 1,200 m; warhead 34 kg.
Depth charges: 2 BMB-2 projectors; 2 racks.
Mines: Rails fitted.
Countermeasures: ESM: Intercept.
Radars: Surface search: Pot Head; I-band.
Navigation: Raytheon Pathfinder; I-band.
IFF: High Pole.
Sonars: Stag Ear; hull-mounted; active search and attack; high frequency.

Comment: First six delivered from China in January 1991, four more in mid-1993. The first six originally had double figure pennant numbers which have been changed to three figures. These ships are the later variant of this class with tripod masts. Based at Rangoon. *Yan Sit Aung* (441) reported sunk during cyclone Nargis (May 2008).

YAN WIN AUNG *9/1993* / 0056641

YAN KHWIN AUNG *3/2008** / 1353241

4 RIVER GUNBOATS (EX-TRANSPORTS) (PBR)

SAGU **SEINDA** **SHWETHIDA** **SINMIN**

Displacement, tons: 98 full load
Dimensions, feet (metres): 94.5 × 22 × 4.5 *(28.8 × 6.7 × 1.4)*
Main machinery: 1 Crossley ERL 6-cyl diesel; 160 hp *(119 kW)*; 1 shaft
Speed, knots: 12
Complement: 32
Guns: 1—40 mm/60 *(Sagu)*. 1—20 mm (3 in *Sagu*).

Comment: Built in mid-1950s. *Sinmin, Seinda* and *Shwethida* have a roofed-in upper deck with a 20 mm gun forward of the funnel. *Sagu* has an open upper deck aft of the funnel but with a 40 mm gun forward and mountings for 20 mm aft on the upper deck and midships either side on the lower deck. Based at Moulmein and at least two are operational. Four other ships of the same type are unarmed and are listed under *Auxiliaries*.

SEINDA *8/1994* / 0056649

6 BURMA PGM TYPE (COASTAL PATROL CRAFT) (PB)

PGM 412–415 **THIHAYARZAR I** **THIHAYARZAR II**

Displacement, tons: 168 full load
Dimensions, feet (metres): 110 × 22 × 6.5 *(33.5 × 6.7 × 2)*
Main machinery: 2 Deutz SBA16MB816 LLKR diesels; 2,720 hp(m) *(2 MW)*; 2 shafts
Speed, knots: 16. **Range, n miles:** 1,400 at 14 kt
Complement: 17
Guns: 2 Bofors 40 mm/60.

Comment: Built by Burma Naval Dockyard modelled on the US PGM 43 type. First two completed 1983. Two more craft with different superstructure but with identical dimensions and named *Thihayarzar I* and *II* were delivered by Myanma Shipyard to the Customs on 27 June 1993. Both craft may be lightly armed.

PGM 415 *4/1993* / 0056644

THIHAYARZAR CLASS *11/2005* / 1151118

1 IMPROVED Y 301 CLASS (RIVER GUNBOAT) (PBR)

Y 311

Displacement, tons: 250 full load
Dimensions, feet (metres): 121.4 × 24 × 3.9 *(37 × 7.3 × 1.2)*
Main machinery: 2 MTU MB diesels; 1,000 hp(m) *(735 kW)*; 2 shafts
Speed, knots: 12
Complement: 37
Guns: 2 Bofors 40 mm/60. 4 Oerlikon 20 mm.
Radars: Surface search: Raytheon; I-band.

Comment: Built at Simmilak in 1969 and based on similar Yugoslav craft which have been scrapped. Y 312 sunk during cyclone Nargis (May 2008). Based at Sittwe.

Y 311 *11/2005* / 1151120

6 CARPENTARIA CLASS (RIVER PATROL CRAFT) (PBR)

112–117

Displacement, tons: 26 full load
Dimensions, feet (metres): 51.5 × 15.7 × 4.3 *(15.7 × 4.8 × 1.3)*
Main machinery: 2 MTU 8V 331TC92 diesels; 1,770 hp(m) *(1.3 MW)* sustained; 2 shafts
Speed, knots: 29. **Range, n miles:** 950 at 18 kt
Complement: 10
Guns: 1 Oerlikon 20 mm. 1—12.7 mm MG.

Comment: Built by De Havilland Marine, Sydney. First two delivered 1979, remainder in 1980. Similar to craft built for Indonesia. Based at Rangoon.

CARPENTARIA 113 *1991* / 0056651

25 MICHAO CLASS (PBR)

001–025

Comment: Small craft, 52 ft *(15.8 m)* long, acquired from Yugoslavia in 1965. Also used to ferry troops and two are used as VIP launches. 1 to 7 based at Rangoon; 8 to 16 at Moulmein and 17 to 25 at Sittwe.

MICHAO CLASS *5/1995* / 0056650

2 CGC TYPE (RIVER GUNBOATS) (PBR)

MGB 102 **MGB 110**

Displacement, tons: 49 standard; 66 full load
Dimensions, feet (metres): 83 × 16 × 5.5 *(25.3 × 4.9 × 1.7)*
Main machinery: 4 GM diesels; 800 hp *(596 kW)*; 2 shafts
Speed, knots: 11
Complement: 16
Guns: 1 Bofors 40 mm/60. 1 Oerlikon 20 mm.

Comment: Ex-USCG type cutters with new hulls built in Burma. Completed in 1960. Based at Rangoon but have not been seen recently.

MGB 110 0505966

10 Y 301 CLASS (RIVER GUNBOATS) (PBR)

Y 301–310

Displacement, tons: 120 full load
Dimensions, feet (metres): 104.8 × 24 × 3 *(32 × 7.3 × 0.9)*
Main machinery: 2 MTU MB diesels; 1,000 hp(m) *(735 kW)*; 2 shafts
Speed, knots: 13
Complement: 29
Guns: 2 Bofors 40 mm/60 or 1 Bofors 40 mm/60 and 1 Vickers 2-pdr.

Comment: All of these boats were completed in 1958 at the Uljanik Shipyard, Pula, Yugoslavia. Y 301, 303 and 307 based at Moulmein. The remainder at Rangoon.

Y 306 *3/2008** / 1353242

3 SWIFT TYPE PGM (COASTAL PATROL CRAFT) (PB)

PGM 421–423

Displacement, tons: 128 full load
Dimensions, feet (metres): 103.3 × 23.8 × 6.9 *(31.5 × 7.2 × 3.1)*
Main machinery: 2 MTU 12V 331TC81 diesels; 2,450 hp(m) *(1.8 MW)* sustained; 2 shafts
Speed, knots: 27
Range, n miles: 1,800 at 18 kt
Complement: 25
Guns: 2 Bofors 40 mm/60. 2 Oerlikon 20 mm. 2—12.7 mm MGs.
Radars: Surface search: Raytheon 1500; I-band.

Comment: Swiftships construction completed between March and September 1979. Acquired 1980 through Vosper, Singapore. *PGM 421* previously reported sunk in 1990s but reported to have been repaired. Based at Rangoon.

PGM *6/1991* / 0056645

6 PGM 43 TYPE (COASTAL PATROL CRAFT) (PB)

PGM 401–406

Displacement, tons: 141 full load
Dimensions, feet (metres): 101 × 21.1 × 7.5 *(30.8 × 6.4 × 2.3)*
Main machinery: 8 GM 6-71 diesels; 1,392 hp *(1.04 MW)* sustained; 2 shafts
Speed, knots: 17
Range, n miles: 1,000 at 15 kt
Complement: 17
Guns: 1 Bofors 40 mm/60. 2 Oerlikon 20 mm (twin). 2—12.7 mm MGs.
Radars: Surface search: Raytheon 1500 (PGM 405-406).
EDO 320 (PGM 401-404); I/J-band.

Comment: First four built by Marinette Marine in 1959; last pair by Peterson Shipbuilders in 1961. PGM 401-403 based at Moulmein and 404-405 at Rangoon. PGM 406 at Sittwe.

PGM 406 *3/1992* / 0056646

9 RIVER PATROL CRAFT (PBR)

RPC 11–19

Displacement, tons: 37 full load
Dimensions, feet (metres): 50 × 14 × 3.5 *(15.2 × 4.3 × 1.1)*
Main machinery: 2 Thornycroft RZ 6 diesels; 250 hp *(186 kW)*; 2 shafts
Speed, knots: 10
Range, n miles: 400 at 8 kt
Complement: 8
Guns: 1 Oerlikon 20 mm or 2—12.7 mm MGs (twin). 1—12.7 mm MG.

Comment: Built by the Naval Engineering Depot, Rangoon. First five in mid-1980s; second batch of a modified design in 1990–91. Sometimes used by the Naval Infantry and can carry up to 35 troops. Based at Rangoon.

AMPHIBIOUS FORCES

1 LCU

AIYAR LULIN 603

Displacement, tons: 360 full load
Dimensions, feet (metres): 119 × 34 × 6 *(36.3 × 10.4 × 1.8)*
Main machinery: 4 GM diesels; 600 hp *(448 kW)*; 2 shafts
Speed, knots: 10
Range, n miles: 1,200 at 8 kt
Complement: 14
Military lift: 168 tons
Guns: 1—12.7 mm MG.

Comment: Completed in Rangoon in 1966 to the US 1610 design. Based at Rangoon.

AIYAR LULIN *1990* / 0056654

10 LCM 3 TYPE

LCM 701–710

Displacement, tons: 52 full load
Dimensions, feet (metres): 50 × 14 × 4 *(15.2 × 4.3 × 1.2)*
Main machinery: 2 Gray Marine 64 HN9 diesels; 330 hp *(246 kW)*; 2 shafts
Speed, knots: 9
Complement: 5

Comment: US-built LCM type landing craft. Used as local transports for stores and personnel. Cargo capacity, 30 tons. Guns have been removed. Based at Sittwe.

LCM 704 *5/1994* / 0056655

4 ABAMIN CLASS (LCU)

AIYAR MAI 604 **AIYAR MAUNG** 605 **AIYAR MINTHAMEE** 606 **AIYAR MINTHAR** 607

Displacement, tons: 250 full load
Dimensions, feet (metres): 125.6 × 29.8 × 4.6 *(38.3 × 9.1 × 1.4)*
Main machinery: 2 Kubota diesels; 600 hp(m) *(441 kW)*; 2 shafts
Speed, knots: 10
Complement: 10
Military lift: 100 tons
Guns: 1 — 12.7 mm MG.

Comment: All built by Yokohama Yacht in 1969. Based at Rangoon.

AIYAR MAUNG *1991* / 0056653

3 LCU

001–003

Comment: Operated by the Army. Dimensions not known.

LANDING CRAFT 003 *7/1992* / 0056652

MINE WARFARE FORCES

Notes: Up to two Chinese-built minesweepers are expected to be acquired when funds are available.

SURVEY SHIPS

Notes: Thu Tay Thi means 'survey vessel'.

1 SURVEY CRAFT (AGSC)

Name	*No*	*Builders*	*Commissioned*
YAY BO	807	Damen, Netherlands	1958

Displacement, tons: 108 full load
Dimensions, feet (metres): 98.4 × 22.3 × 4.9 *(30 × 6.8 × 1.5)*
Main machinery: 2 diesels; 2 shafts
Speed, knots: 10
Complement: 34 (2 officers)
Guns: 1 — 12.7 mm MG.

Comment: Used for river surveys. Based at Rangoon.

YAY BO *1990* / 0056656

AUXILIARIES

Notes: As well as the ships listed below there is a small coastal oil tanker, a harbour tug and several harbour launches and personnel carriers.

1 TRANSPORT VESSEL (AK)

AYIDAWAYA

Displacement, tons: 805 full load
Dimensions, feet (metres): 163.4 × 27.6 × 12.1 *(49.8 × 8.4 × 3.7)*
Main machinery: 1 diesel; 600 hp(m) *(441 kW)*; 1 shaft
Speed, knots: 12
Complement: 30

Comment: Built in Norway in 1975. Acquired in 1991 and used as transport for stores and personnel.

AYIDAWAYA *12/1991* / 0056658

1 BUOY TENDER (ABU)

HSAD DAN

Displacement, tons: 706 full load
Dimensions, feet (metres): 130.6 × 37.1 × 8.9 *(39.8 × 11.3 × 2.7)*
Main machinery: 2 Deutz BA8M816 diesels; 1,341 hp(m) *(986 kW)*; 2 shafts
Speed, knots: 10
Complement: 23

Comment: Built by Italthai in 1986. Operated by the Rangoon Port Authority but manned by the Navy.

HSAD DAN *5/1992* / 0056662

8 MFVS

511 **520–523** **901** **905–906**

Comment: Armed vessels of approximately 200 tons *(901)*, 80 tons *(905, 906)* and 50 tons (remainder) with a 12.7 mm or 6.72 mm MG mounted above the bridge in some. All have navigational radars. Based at Rangoon.

MFV *8/1990* / 0104255

4 TRANSPORT VESSELS (AKL)

SABAN **SETHYA** **SHWEPAZUN** **SETYAHAT**

Displacement, tons: 98 full load
Dimensions, feet (metres): 94.5 × 22 × 4.5 *(28.8 × 6.7 × 1.4)*
Main machinery: 1 Crossley ERL 6-cyl diesel; 160 hp *(119 kW)*; 1 shaft
Speed, knots: 12
Complement: 30

Comment: These are sister ships to the armed gunboats shown under *Patrol Forces*. It is possible that a 20 mm gun may be mounted on some occasions. Based at Rangoon.

SHWEPAZUN *1991* / 0056661

1 TRANSPORT VESSEL (AKL)

PYI DAW AYE

Displacement, tons: 850 full load
Dimensions, feet (metres): 163 × 27 × 11.5 *(49.7 × 8.3 × 3.5)*
Main machinery: 2 diesels; 600 hp *(447 kW)*; 2 shafts
Speed, knots: 11
Complement: 12

Comment: Completed in about 1975. Dimensions are approximate. Naval manned.

PYI DAW AYE *1991* / 0056663

PRESIDENTIAL YACHT

1 TRANSPORT SHIP (YAC)

YADANABON

Comment: Built in Burma and used for VIP cruises on the Irrawaddy river and in coastal waters. Armed with 2-7.62 mm MGs and manned by the Navy.

PRESIDENT'S YACHT *1990* / 0056665

Namibia

Country Overview

Formerly South West Africa and governed by South Africa, Namibia gained independence in 1990 although South Africa continued to administer an enclave containing the principal seaport, Walvis Bay, until 1994. With an area of 318,252 square miles, it has borders to the north with Angola and to the south with South Africa. It has an 848 n mile coastline with the south Atlantic Ocean. The capital and largest city is Windhoek and there is another port at Lüderitz. Territorial seas (12 n miles) are claimed. It also claims a 200 n mile Exclusive Economic Zone (EEZ) but its limits have not been fully defined by boundary agreements.

The Maritime Wing became the Navy on 7 October 2004.

Headquarters Appointments

Head of Navy:
Captain Peter Vilho

Bases

Walvis Bay

Personnel

2009: 350

Aviation

Five ex-US Air Force Cessna O-2A observation aircraft operate in a maritime surveillance role.

PATROL FORCES

1 IMPERIAL MARINHEIRO CLASS (COASTAL PATROL SHIP) (PB)

Name	*No*	*Builders*	*Commissioned*
LIEUTENANT GENERAL DIMO HAMAAMBO (ex-*Purus*)	C 11 (ex-V 23)	Smit, Kinderdijk, Netherlands	17 Apr 1955

Displacement, tons: 911 standard; 1,025 full load
Dimensions, feet (metres): 184 × 30.5 × 11.7 *(56 × 9.3 × 3.6)*
Main machinery: 2 Sulzer 6TD36 diesels; 2,160 hp(m) *(1.59 MW)*; 2 shafts
Speed, knots: 16
Complement: 64 (6 officers)
Guns: 1—3 in *(76 mm)*/50 Mk 33; 50 rds/min to 12.8 km *(6.9 n miles)*; weight of shell 6 kg. 2 or 4 Oerlikon 20 mm.
Radars: Surface search: Racal Decca; I-band.

Comment: Built for Brazilian Navy as fleet tug but subsequently classified as a corvette. Withdrawn from Brazilian service in 2002 and recommissioned into the Namibian Navy on 27 August 2004.

LIEUTENANT GENERAL DIMO HAMAAMBO *2/2006, W Clements* / 1040664

1 GRAJAÚ CLASS (LARGE PATROL CRAFT) (PBO)

Name	*No*	*Builders*	*Laid down*	*Launched*	*Commissioned*
BRENDAN SIMBWAYE	P 48	Inace, Fortalesa	25 Feb 2005	1 May 2008	Dec 2008

Displacement, tons: 263 full load
Dimensions, feet (metres): 152.6 × 24.6 × 7.5 *(46.5 × 7.5 × 2.3)*
Main machinery: 2 MTU 16V 396 TB94 diesels; 5,800 hp(m) *(4.26 MW)* sustained; 2 shafts
Speed, knots: 26
Range, n miles: 2,200 at 12 kt
Complement: 29 (4 officers)
Guns: 1 Bofors 40 mm/70. 2 Oerlikon 20 mm.
Radars: Surface search: Racal Decca 1290A; I-band.

Comment: Following an agreement between the governments of Namibia and Brazil in November 2003, the project for a new patrol ship is being conducted by EMGEPRON which contracted Inace for the construction of the vessel. The ship is to be similar to *Guanabara* built for the Brazilian Navy in 1999, and on which details are based.

GRAJAÚ CLASS (Brazilian colours) *2/2001, Mario R V Carneiro* / 0130468

0 + 4 TRACKER II CLASS (COASTAL PATROL CRAFT) (PB)

Displacement, tons: 31 standard; 45 full load
Dimensions, feet (metres): 68.6 × 17 × 4.8 *(20.9 × 5.2 × 1.5)*
Main machinery: 2 MTU 8V 396 TB83 diesels; 2,100 hp(m) *(1.54 MW)* sustained; 2 shafts
Speed, knots: 25. **Range, n miles:** 600 at 15 kt
Complement: 8 (2 officers)
Guns: 2 — 12.7 mm MGs.
Radars: Surface search: Racal Decca RM 1070A; I-band.

Comment: Construction of four new craft is to begin once the patrol ship *Brendan Simbwaye* is completed in late 2008. The first two are to be delivered in 2009 and the second pair in 2010.

TRACKER II CLASS (Brazilian colours) *10/2003, Gomel/Marsan* / 0569150

1 PATROL SHIP (PBO)

Name	*No*	*Builders*	*Commissioned*
ORYX (ex-*S to S*)	P 01	Burmeister/Abeking & Rasmussen	May 1975

Displacement, tons: 406 full load
Dimensions, feet (metres): 149.9 × 28.9 × 7.9 *(45.7 × 8.8 × 2.4)*
Main machinery: 2 Deutz RSBA 16M diesels; 2,000 hp(m) *(1.47 MW)*; 1 shaft; cp prop; bow thruster
Speed, knots: 14. **Range, n miles:** 4,100 at 11 kt
Complement: 20 (6 officers)
Guns: 1 — 12.7 mm MG.
Radars: Surface search: Furuno ARPA FR 1525; I-band.
Navigation: Furuno FR 805D; I-band.

Comment: Built for the Nautical Investment Company, Panama and used as a yacht by the Managing Director of Fiat. Acquired in 1993 by Namibia. Replaced by *Nathanael Maxwilili* in fishery protection role and transferred to the navy as a patrol ship in 2002.

ORYX *6/1997* / 0081282

2 NAMACURRA CLASS (INSHORE PATROL CRAFT) (PB)

– (ex-Y 1501) – (ex-Y 1510)

Displacement, tons: 5 full load
Dimensions, feet (metres): 29.5 × 9 × 2.8 *(9 × 2.7 × 0.8)*
Main machinery: 2 Yamaha outboards; 380 hp(m) *(2.79 kW)*
Speed, knots: 32. **Range, n miles:** 180 at 20 kt
Complement: 4
Guns: 1 — 12.7 mm MG. 2 — 7.62 mm MGs.
Depth charges: 1 rack.
Radars: Surface search: Furuno; I-band.

Comment: Built in South Africa in 1980–81. Can be transported by road. Donated by South Africa on 29 November 2002.

NAMACURRA *8/2001, van Ginderen Collection* / 0132783

GOVERNMENT MARITIME FORCES

Notes: There are also four research ships: *Benguela, Welwitschia, Nautilus II* and *Kuiseb*.

1 OSPREY FV 710 CLASS (PBOH)

Name	*No*	*Builders*	*Commissioned*
TOBIAS HAINYEKO (ex-*Havørnen*)	–	Frederikshavn Vaerft	July 1979

Displacement, tons: 505 full load
Dimensions, feet (metres): 164 × 34.5 × 9 *(50 × 10.5 × 2.8)*
Main machinery: 2 Burmeister & Wain Alpha 16V23L diesels; 4,640 hp(m) *(3.41 MW)*; 2 shafts; cp props
Speed, knots: 20. **Range, n miles:** 4,000 at 15 kt
Complement: 15 plus 20 spare
Radars: Surface search: Furuno ARPA FR 1525; I-band.
Navigation: Furuno FRM 64; I-band.

Comment: Donated by Denmark in late 1993, retaining some Danish crew. Recommissioned 15 December 1994. The helicopter deck can handle up to Lynx size aircraft and there is a slipway on the stern for launching an RIB. Similar ships in service in Greece, Morocco and Myanmar.

TOBIAS HAINYEKO *6/2008** / 1335397

2 PATROL SHIPS (PBOH)

Name	*Builders*	*Commissioned*
NATHANAEL MAXWILILI	Moen Slip AS, Kolvereid, Norway	14 May 2002
ANNA KAKURUKAZE MUNGUNDA	Freire Shipyards, Vigo	10 Feb 2004

Displacement, tons: 1,500
Dimensions, feet (metres): 189.0 × 41.0 × 13.8 *(57.6 × 12.5 × 4.2)*
Main machinery: 2 Deutz SBV8M diesel; 4,063 hp *(3.03 MW)*; 2 shafts; Kamewa Ulstein bow thruster; 385 hp *(285 kW)*
Speed, knots: 17. **Range, n miles:** 8,200 at 16 kt
Radars: Furuno FR-2125; I-band.
Helicopters: Platform only.

Comment: *Nathanael Maxwilili* ordered in 1999. Financed by NORAD (Norwegian Agency for Development Co-Operation). *Anna Kakurukaze Mungunda* was financed by the Spanish government. Equipped with inspection craft for fishery protection role.

NATHANAEL MAXWILILI *2/2006, W Clements* / 1040666

ANNA KAKURUKAZE MUNGUNDA *3/2005, W Clements* / 1040667

NATO

Overview

The North Atlantic Treaty Organisation (NATO) was formed under Article 9 of the North Atlantic Treaty signed on 4 April 1949. Now comprising 26 members, the original signatories were Belgium, Canada, Denmark, France, Iceland, Italy, Luxembourg, Netherlands, Norway, Portugal, UK and US. Greece and Turkey were admitted to the alliance in 1952, West Germany in 1955, and Spain in 1982. In 1990 the newly unified Germany replaced West Germany. Three former members of the Warsaw Pact, Czech Republic, Hungary and Poland were admitted in 1999. Seven further countries: Bulgaria, Estonia, Latvia, Lithuania, Romania, Slovakia and Slovenia, became members on 29 March 2004. A new NATO-Russia council was inaugurated on 28 May 2002.

RESEARCH SHIPS

1 RESEARCH SHIP (AGOR)

Name	*No*	*Builders*	*Launched*	*Commissioned*
ALLIANCE	A 1456	Fincantieri, Muggiano	9 July 1986	6 May 1988

Displacement, tons: 2,466 standard; 3,180 full load
Dimensions, feet (metres): 305.1 × 49.9 × 17.1 *(93 × 15.2 × 5.2)*
Main machinery: Diesel-electric; 2 Fincantieri GMT B 230.12 M diesels; 6,079 hp(m) *(4.47 MW)* sustained; 2 AEG CC 3127 generators; 2 AEG motors; 4,039 hp(m) *(2.97 MW)* sustained; 2 shafts; bow thruster
Speed, knots: 16. **Range, n miles:** 7,200 at 11 kt
Complement: 24 (10 officers) plus 23 scientists
Radars: Navigation: 2 Kelvin Hughes ARPA; E/F- and I-bands.
Sonars: TVDS towed active VDS 200 Hz-4 kHz; medium and low frequency passive towed line arrays.

Comment: Built at La Spezia. NATO's first wholly owned ship is a Public Service vessel of the German Navy with a German, British and Italian crew. Designed for oceanography and acoustic research. Based at La Spezia and operated by NATO Undersea Research Centre. Facilities include extensive laboratories, position location systems, silent propulsion, and overside deployment equipment. Can tow a 20 ton load at 12 kt. A Kongsberg gas turbine on 02 deck provides silent propulsion power at 1,945 hp *(1.43 MW)* up to speeds of 12 kt. Atlas hydrosweep side scan echo-sounder fitted in 1993. Qubit KH TRAC integrated navigational system fitted in 1995. Carries two Watercraft R6 RIBs. Similar ships in Taiwan and Italian navies.

ALLIANCE *4/2008*, Michael Nitz* / 1335796

1 COASTAL RESEARCH VESSEL (AGOR(C))

Name	*No*	*Builders*	*Commissioned*
LEONARDO	A 5390	McTay Marine Ltd	6 Sep 2002

Displacement: tons: 393 full load
Dimensions, feet (metres): 93.8 × 29.5 × 8.2 *(28.6 × 9.0 × 2.5)*
Main machinery: Diesel-electric; 1,570 hp *(1,170 kW)*; 2 azimuth thrusters; 1—360° bow thruster
Speed, knots: 11. **Range, n miles:** 1,500 at 11 kt
Complement: 5 + 7 scientific staff
Radars: Navigation: 2 sets; I-band.
Sonars: Kongsberg Simrad multibeam echo-sounders.

Comment: The order for a coastal underwater research vessel was placed by NATO Undersea Research Centre in December 2000. Designed by Corlett and Partners, construction of the hull was undertaken by Remontowa in Poland while the superstructure and final assembly was undertaken by the prime contractor, McTay Marine Ltd. The ship is equipped with a moon pool, oceanographic winches, two cranes and Kongsberg navigation/research suite. A 20 ft container can be embarked to augment the main scientific laboratory. Based at La Spezia, the vessel is the first Italian Public Service vessel.

LEONARDO *1/2004, Giorgio Ghiglione* / 1133136

Netherlands

Country Overview

The Kingdom of the Netherlands is situated in north-western Europe. With an area of 16,033 square miles, it is bordered to the east by Germany and to the south by Belgium. It has a 244 n mile coastline with the North Sea. The country also includes the self-governing Caribbean territories of Netherlands Antilles and Aruba. The seat of government is at The Hague while Amsterdam is the official capital, largest city and a major port. Rotterdam is one of the world's leading seaports. Both ports are linked both to the North Sea and to a comprehensive system of inland waterways whose total length is some 2,725 n miles. Territorial seas (12 n miles) are claimed. An EEZ and a Fishery Zone (200 n miles) have also been declared.

Headquarters Appointments

Commander, Royal Netherlands Navy:
Lieutenant General R L Zuiderwijk
Deputy Commander:
Rear Admiral W Nagtegaal
Director, Planning and Control:
Commodore F J Schipper
Director, Operations:
Brigadier R Verkerk
Director, Operational Support:
Commodore J Snoeks
Director, Personnel:
Commodore H I Heine

Commands

Commander Netherlands Maritime Force:
Commodore P J Bindt
Flag Officer Netherlands Forces Caribbean:
Commodore P W Lenselink

Diplomatic Representation

Defence Attaché in Washington:
Commodore M B Hijmans
Naval Attaché in Beijing:
Captain W Klaas

Diplomatic Representation — *continued*

Naval Attaché in London and Lisbon:
Captain M C Wouters
Naval Attaché in Madrid:
Lieutenant Colonel F G T Mugie
Naval Attaché in Ankara:
Commander A J Wesselingh
Naval Attaché in Washington:
Captain V C Windt
Naval Attaché in Oslo, Stockholm and Copenhagen:
Captain G F T van der Putten
Naval Attaché in the Gulf:
Commander R J C M van de Rijdt
Naval Attaché in Caracas, Georgetown and Paramaribo:
Commander A Brokke
Naval Attaché in Riga, Talinn, Vilnius and Helsinki:
Commander B J Gerrits
Naval Attaché in Berlin:
Commander M F L Walther
Naval Attaché in Bucharest and Sofia:
Lieutenant Colonel J Korteweg
Naval Attaché in Kigali, Kinshasa, Kampala and Bujumbura:
Lieutenant Colonel P R van Staalduinen

Personnel

(a) 2009: 6,750 naval and 2,900 Marines
(b) Voluntary service

Bases

Naval HQ: Den Helder
Main Base: Den Helder
Minor Bases: Flushing, Amsterdam and Curaçao
MAS De Kooy (helicopters)
R Neth Marines: Rotterdam, Doorn and Texel

Naval Air Arm

All military helicopter operations were combined in the Netherlands Defence Helicopter Command on 4 July 2008. All maritime helicopter operations are conducted from Maritime Air Station De Kooy.

Squadron	*Aircraft*	*Task*
7	Lynx (SH-14D)	Utility and Transport/SAR
860	Lynx (SH-14D)	Embarked

Royal Netherlands Marine Corps

Five Marine battalions; two manoeuvre, one combat support battalion, one combat service support and one amphibious support battalion. Two infantry companies in the Netherlands Antilles and Aruba.

Prefix to Ships' Names

Hr Ms

Strength of the Fleet

Type	*Active*	*Building (Projected)*
Submarines	4	–
Frigates	6	–
Offshore Patrol Vessels	–	4
Mine Hunters	10	–
Submarine Support Ship	1	–
Amphibious Transport Ship (LPD)	2	–
Landing Craft	17	12
Survey Ships	2	–
Combat Support Ships	3	(1)
Training Ships	2	–

Fleet Disposition

Operational Control of Belgium and Netherlands surface forces is under Admiral Benelux Command at Den Helder.

DELETIONS

Frigates

2006	*Witte de With, Tjerk Hiddes* (both to Chile)
2007	*Karel Doorman* (Belgium)
2008	*Willem Van Der Zaan* (Belgium), *Van Nes* (Portugal), *Van Galen* (Portugal)
2009	*Van Galen* (Portugal)

PENNANT LIST

Submarines

S 802	Walrus
S 803	Zeeleeuw
S 808	Dolfijn
S 810	Bruinvis

Frigates

F 802	De Zeven Provincien
F 803	Tromp
F 804	De Ruyter
F 805	Evertsen
F 828	Van Speijk
F 831	Van Amstel

Patrol Forces

P 810	Jaguar (CG)
P 811	Panter (CG)
P 812	Poema (CG)

Mine Warfare Vessels

M 853	Haarlem
M 856	Maassluis
M 857	Makkum
M 858	Middelburg
M 859	Hellevoetsluis
M 860	Schiedam
M 861	Urk
M 862	Zierikzee
M 863	Vlaardingen
M 864	Willemstad

Amphibious Forces

L 800	Rotterdam
L 801	Johan De Witt

Auxiliaries

A 802	Snellius
A 803	Luymes
A 804	Pelikaan
A 832	Zuiderkruis
A 836	Amsterdam
A 851	Cerberus
A 852	Argus
A 853	Nautilus
A 854	Hydra
A 874	Linge
A 875	Regge
A 876	Hunze
A 877	Rotte
A 878	Gouwe
A 900	Mercuur
A 902	Van Kinsbergen
Y 8005	Nieuwediep
Y 8018	Breezand
Y 8019	Balgzand
Y 8050	Urania
Y 8055	Schelde
Y 8056	Wierbalg
Y 8057	Malzwin
Y 8058	Zuidwal
Y 8059	Westwal
Y 8760	Patria

SUBMARINES

Notes: Operational analysis to establish the requirements for a future submarine capability, to enter service from about 2025, has been initiated.

4 WALRUS CLASS (SSK)

Name	*No*	*Builders*	*Laid down*	*Launched*	*Commissioned*
WALRUS	S 802	Rotterdamse Droogdok Mij, Rotterdam	11 Oct 1979	26 Oct 1985 (13 Sep 1989)	25 Mar 1992
ZEELEEUW	S 803	Rotterdamse Droogdok Mij, Rotterdam	24 Sep 1981	20 June 1987	25 Apr 1990
DOLFIJN	S 808	Rotterdamse Droogdok Mij, Rotterdam	12 June 1986	25 Apr 1990	29 Jan 1993
BRUINVIS	S 810	Rotterdamse Droogdok Mij, Rotterdam	14 Apr 1988	25 Apr 1992	5 July 1994

Displacement, tons: 2,465 surfaced; 2,800 dived
Dimensions, feet (metres): 223.1 × 27.6 × 23 *(67.7 × 8.4 × 7)*
Main machinery: Diesel-electric; 3 SEMT-Pielstick 12 PA4 200 VG diesels; 6,300 hp(m) *(4.63 MW)*; 3 alternators; 2.88 MW; 1 Holec motor; 6,910 hp(m) *(5.1 MW)*; 1 shaft
Speed, knots: 12 surfaced; 20 dived
Range, n miles: 10,000 at 9 kt snorting
Complement: 52 (7 officers)

Missiles: SSM: McDonnell Douglas Sub Harpoon; active radar homing to 130 km *(70 n miles)* at 0.9 Mach; warhead 227 kg.
Torpedoes: 4—21 in *(533 mm)* tubes. Honeywell Mk 48 Mod 4; wire-guided; active/passive homing to 38 km *(20.5 n miles)* active at 55 kt; 50 km *(27 n miles)* passive at 40 kt; warhead 267 kg; 20 torpedoes or missiles carried. Mk 19 Turbine ejection pump. Mk 67 water-ram discharge.
Mines: 40 in lieu of torpedoes.
Countermeasures: ESM: L3 DR 3000; radar warning.
Weapons control: Signaal SEWACO VIII action data automation. Signaal Gipsy data system. GTHW integrated Harpoon and Torpedo FCS.
Radars: Surface search: Signaal/Racal: ZW07; I-band.
Sonars: Thomson Sintra TSM 2272 Eledone Octopus; hull-mounted; passive/active search and attack; medium frequency.
GEC Avionics Type 2026; towed array; passive search; very low frequency.
Thomson Sintra DUUX 5; passive ranging and intercept.

Programmes: Contract for the building of the first was signed 16 June 1979, the second was on 17 December 1979. In 1981 various changes to the design were made which resulted in a delay of one to two years. *Dolfijn* and *Bruinvis* ordered 16 August 1985; prefabrication started late 1985. Completion of *Walrus* delayed by serious fire 14 August 1986; hull undamaged but cabling and computers destroyed. *Walrus* relaunched 13 September 1989.
Modernisation: A snort exhaust diffuser was fitted to *Zeeleeuw* in 1996. The rest of the class have been similarly modified. A life-extension programme for all four boats is planned to start in 2011 and to be completed in 2018. Upgrades are likely to include platform (including pressure hull) preservation measures, replacement of the combat management system, installation of an optronic mast (to replace one periscope) and upgrade of the sonar.
Structure: These are improved Zwaardvis class with similar dimensions and silhouettes except for X stern. Use of H T steel increases the diving depth by some 50 per cent. Diving depth, 300 m *(984 ft)*. Pilkington Optronics CK 24 search and CH 74 attack periscopes.
Operational: Weapon systems evaluations completed 1990–93. Sub Harpoon is not carried.

BRUINVIS *9/2006, J Brodie* / 1166675

DOLFIJN *6/2008*, Maritime Photographic* / 1335285

BRUINVIS *7/2007, Michael Nitz* / 1166635

WALRUS *4/2008*, Van Zaalen* / 1335286

FRIGATES

4 DE ZEVEN PROVINCIEN CLASS (FFGHM)

Name	*No*	*Builders*	*Laid down*	*Launched*	*Commissioned*
DE ZEVEN PROVINCIEN	F 802	Royal Schelde, Vlissingen	1 Sep 1998	8 Apr 2000	26 Apr 2002
TROMP	F 803	Royal Schelde, Vlissingen	3 Sep 1999	7 Apr 2001	14 Mar 2003
DE RUYTER	F 804	Royal Schelde, Vlissingen	1 Sep 2000	13 Apr 2002	22 Apr 2004
EVERTSEN	F 805	Royal Schelde, Vlissingen	6 Sep 2001	19 Apr 2003	10 June 2005

Displacement, tons: 6,048 full load
Dimensions, feet (metres): 473.1 oa; 428.8 wl × 61.7 × 17.1 *(144.2; 130.7 × 18.8 × 5.2)*
Flight deck, feet (metres): 88.6 × 61.7 *(27 × 18.8)*
Main machinery: CODOG; 2 RR SM1C Spey; 52,300 hp *(39 MW)* sustained; 2 Stork-Wärtsilä 16V 26 ST diesels; 13,600 hp(m) *(10 MW)*; 2 shafts; LIPS; cp props
Speed, knots: 28. **Range, n miles:** 5,000 at 18 kt
Complement: 204 (32 officers) including staff

Missiles: SSM: 8 McDonnell Douglas Harpoon Block 1D; active radar homing to 240 km *(130 n miles)* at 0.9 Mach; warhead 227 kg ❶.
SAM: Mk 41 VLS (40 cells) ❷; 32 Raytheon Standard SM2-MR (Block IIIA); command/inertial guidance; semi-active radar homing to 167 km *(90 n miles)* at 2.5 Mach.
32 Evolved Sea Sparrow RIM 162B (quad pack); semi-active radar homing to 18 km *(9.7 n miles)* at 3.6 Mach; warhead 38 kg.
Guns: 1 Otobreda 5 in *(127 mm)*/54 ❸; 45 rds/min to 23 km *(12.42 n miles)* anti-surface; weight of shell 32 kg.
2 Thales Goalkeeper 30 mm ❹; 4,200 rds/min to 1.5 km.
2 Browning 12.7 mm MGs ❺.
Torpedoes: 4—323 mm (2 twin) Mk 32 Mod 9 fixed launchers ❻. Mk 46 Mod 5 torpedoes.
Countermeasures: 4 SRBOC Mk 36 chaff launchers; Nixie torpedo decoy.
ESM/ECM: Racal Sabre ❼; intercept/jammer.
Combat data systems: CAMS Force Vision SEWACO XI; Link 11/16; SATCOMS ❽.
Weapons control: Thales Sirius IRST optronic director ❾. Thales Mirador Trainable Electro-Optical Observation System (TEOOS) ❿.

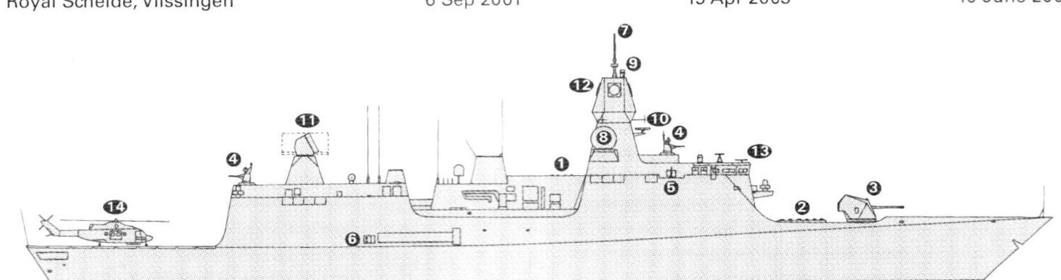

DE ZEVEN PROVINCIEN *(Scale 1 : 1,200), Ian Sturton* / 0569256

Radars: Air search: Thales SMART L ⓫; 3D; D-band.
Air/surface search/fire control: Thales APAR ⓬; I/J-band.
Surface search: Thales Scout ⓭; I-band.
IFF: Mk XII.
Sonars: STN Atlas DSQS 24C; bow-mounted; active search and attack; medium frequency.

Helicopters: 1 NH90 NFH/Lynx ⓮.

Programmes: Project definition awarded to Royal Schelde on 15 December 1993 with a contract for first two ships and detailed design following on 30 June 1995. Second pair ordered 5 February 1997. Shipyards in Germany (ARGE for Type 124) collaborated to achieve some commonality of design and equipment.
Modernisation: Plans to install an additional 8-cell Mk 41 VLS launcher for Tactical Tomahawk IV were cancelled on 14 May 2007. Other improvements to achieve a TBMD capability remain under consideration. TBMD trials were conducted by *Tromp* at the Pacific Missile Test Range Facility, Hawaii, in November-December 2006. A test version of an Extended Long-Range (ELR) mode of SMART L was assessed. A long-range guided munitions capability is also under consideration.
Structure: As well as the listed equipment the ship is to have an electro-optic surveillance system and a navigation radar. The Scout radar is a Low Probability Intercept (LPI) set. High standards of stealth and NBC protection are part of the design. DCN Samahé helicopter handling system. Space exists to retrofit an additional 8-cell Mk 41 launcher alongside the four already fitted.
Operational: All ships fitted with command facilities. NFH 90 helicopter planned for 2009.

DE ZEVEN PROVINCIEN *7/2008*, B Sullivan* / 1335284

EVERTSEN *7/2008*, Camil Busquets i Vilanova* / 1335283

DE RUYTER *3/2007, M Declerck* / 1166633

TROMP *9/2006, Harald Carstens* / 1164988

DE ZEVEN PROVINCIEN *6/2008*, J Brodie* / 1335257

2 KAREL DOORMAN CLASS (FFGHM)

Name	*No*	*Builders*	*Laid down*	*Launched*	*Commissioned*
VAN AMSTEL	F 831	Koninklijke Maatschappij De Schelde, Flushing	3 May 1988	19 May 1990	27 May 1993
VAN SPEIJK	F 828	Koninklijke Maatschappij De Schelde, Flushing	1 Oct 1991	26 Mar 1994	7 Sep 1995

Displacement, tons: 3,320 full load
Dimensions, feet (metres): 401.2 oa; 374.7 wl × 47.2 × 14.1 *(122.3; 114.2 × 14.4 × 4.3)*
Flight deck, feet (metres): 72.2 × 47.2 *(22 × 14.4)*
Main machinery: CODOG; 2 RR Spey SM1C; 33,800 hp *(25.2 MW)* sustained; 2 Stork-Wärtsilä 12SW280 diesels; 9,790 hp(m) *(7.2 MW)* sustained; 2 shafts; LIPS cp props
Speed, knots: 30 (Speys); 21 (diesels)
Range, n miles: 5,000 at 18 kt
Complement: 156 (16 officers) (accommodation for 163)

Missiles: SSM: 8 McDonnell Douglas Harpoon Block 1C (2 quad) launchers ❶; active radar homing to 124 km *(67 n miles)* at 0.9 Mach; warhead 227 kg.
SAM: Raytheon Sea Sparrow RIM 7P Mk 48 vertical launchers ❷; semi-active radar homing to 16 km *(8.5 n miles)* at 2.5 Mach; warhead 38 kg; 16 missiles. Canisters mounted on port side of hangar.
Guns: 1—3 in *(76 mm)*/62 OTO Melara compact Mk 100 ❸; 100 rds/min to 16 km *(8.6 n miles)* anti-surface; 12 km *(6.5 n miles)* anti-aircraft; weight of shell 6 kg. This is the version with an improved rate of fire.
1 Signaal SGE-30 Goalkeeper with General Electric 30 mm 7-barrelled ❹; 4,200 rds/min combined to 2 km.
2 Oerlikon 20 mm; 800 rds/min to 2 km.
Torpedoes: 4—324 mm US Mk 32 Mod 9 (2 twin) tubes (mounted inside the after superstructure) ❺. Honeywell Mk 46 Mod 5; anti-submarine; active/passive homing to 11 km *(5.9 n miles)* at 40 kt; warhead 44 kg.
Countermeasures: Decoys: 2 Loral Hycor SRBOC 6-tubed fixed Mk 36 quad launchers; IR flares and chaff to 4 km *(2.2 n miles)*.
SLQ-25 Nixie towed torpedo decoy.
ESM/ECM: Argo APECS II (includes AR 700 ESM) ❻; intercept and jammers.
Combat data systems: Signaal SEWACO VIIB action data automation; Link 11. SATCOM ❼. WSC-6 twin aerials.

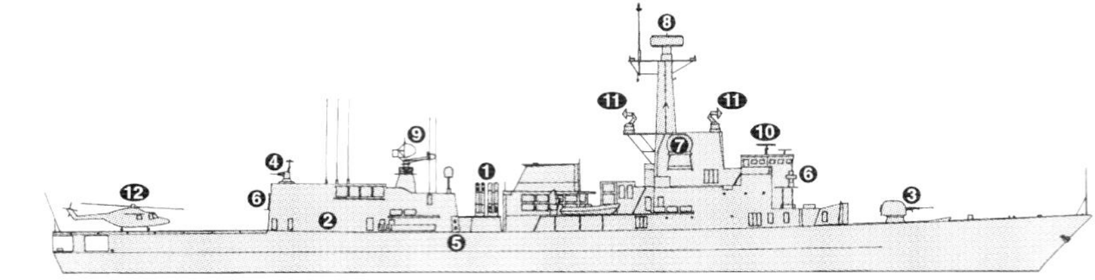

VAN SPEIJK *(Scale 1 : 1,200), Ian Sturton* / 0012800

Weapons control: Signaal IRSCAN infra-red detector (fitted in F 829 for trials and may be retrofitted in all in due course). Signaal VESTA helo transponder.
Radars: Air/surface search: Signaal SMART ❽; 3D; F-band.
Air search: Signaal LW08 ❾; D-band.
Surface search: Signaal Scout ❿; I-band.
Navigation: Racal Decca 1226; I-band.
Fire control: 2 Signaal STIR ⓫; I/J/K-band; range 140 km *(76 n miles)* for 1 m^2 target.
Sonars: Signaal PHS-36; hull-mounted; active search and attack; medium frequency.
Thomson Sintra Anaconda DSBV 61; towed array; passive low frequency. LFAS may be fitted in due course.

Helicopters: 1 Westland SH-14 Lynx ⓬.

Programmes: Declaration of intent signed on 29 February 1984 although the contract was not signed until 29 June 1985 by which time the design had been completed. A further four ordered 10 April 1986. Names were shuffled to make the new *Van Speijk* the last of the class but she retained her allocated pennant number.
Modernisation: SEWACO VII(A) operational from January 1992 and VII(B) from mid-1994. By 1994 all fitted with APECS II EW system and DSBV 61 towed array. SHF SATCOM based on the USN WSC-6, with twin aerials providing a 360° coverage even at high latitudes. Scout radar fitted on bridge roof in 1997. A mid-life modernisation is planned for F 831 and F 828 2010–12. Upgrades are to include modifications to operate the NH-90 helicopter, replacement of the combat data system by Guardian MFF, addition of a Thales Seastar radar, installation of a low-frequency active sonar and replacement of SATCOM systems. Platform systems are also to be upgraded.
Structure: The VLS SAM is similar to Canadian Halifax and Greek MEKO classes. The ship is designed to reduce radar and IR signatures and has extensive NBCD arrangements. Full automation and roll stabilisation fitted. The APECS jammers are mounted starboard forward of the bridge and port aft corner of the hangar. The SAM launchers have been given added protection and better stealth features with a flat screen in some of the class.
Operational: F 832 and F 830 sold to Chile and transferred in November 2005 and mid-2006 respectively. F 827 and F 829 transferred to Belgium in March 2007 and March 2008 respectively and F 833 to Portugal in December 2008. F 834 is to transfer to Portugal in November 2009.

VAN SPEYK *7/2008*, Linda de Kruijf* / 1335282

VAN AMSTEL *7/2008*, Frank Findler* / 1335258

SHIPBORNE AIRCRAFT

Numbers/Type: 12/8 NH Industries NH 90 NFH/NH 90 MTTH.
Operational speed: 157 kt *(291 km/h)*.
Service ceiling: 13,940 ft *(4,250 m)*.
Range: 621 n miles *(1,150 km)*.
Role/Weapon systems: Twelve NH 90 NFH to enter service from 2009 and eight troop-carrying TTH from 2013. NFH variant equipped for ASW/ASuW duties and for SAR. Sensors: Thales Oceanmaster radar, Elac Nautic HELRAS dipping sonar, FLIR and ESM. Weapons: 2 Mk 46 torpedoes.

NH 90 *4/2008*, RNLN* / 1335281

Numbers/Type: 21 Westland Lynx Mks 25B/27A/81A.
Operational speed: 125 kt *(232 km/h)*.
Service ceiling: 12,500 ft *(3,810 m)*.
Range: 320 n miles *(590 km)*.
Role/Weapon systems: ASW, SAR and utility helicopter series all converted to SH-14D type. Mk 25B, Mk 27A and Mk 81A can all be embarked for ASW duties in escorts. To be replaced by NH 90 NFH from 2009. Sensors: Ferranti Sea Spray radar, Alcatel DUAV-4 dipping sonar, FLIR Model 2000; Ferranti AWARE-3 ESM. Weapons: Two Mk 46 torpedoes or depth bombs.

LYNX *7/2008*, Frank Findler* / 1335259

PATROL FORCES

0 + 4 HOLLAND CLASS (OFFSHORE PATROL VESSELS) (PSO)

Name	*No*	*Builders*	*Laid down*	*Launched*	*Commissioned*
HOLLAND	P 840	Schelde, Vlissingen	2008	2009	2011
ZEELAND	P 841	Schelde, Vlissingen	2008	2010	2011
FRIESLAND	P 842	Damen Shipyard, Galatz	2009	2011	2012
GRONINGEN	P 843	Damen Shipyard, Galatz	2010	2012	2013

Displacement, tons: 3,750 full load
Dimensions, feet (metres): 355.6 oa; 336.9 wl × 50.0 × 14.9 *(108.4; 102.7 × 15.24 × 4.55)*
Main machinery: Diesel-hybrid: 2 MAN 12V 28/33D diesels; 14,480 hp *(10.8 MW)*; 3 Caterpillar 3508B generators; 3,895 hp *(2.9 MW)*; 2 motors; 1,070 hp *(800 kW)*; 2 shafts; cp props; 1 bow thruster; 536 hp *(400 kW)*
Speed, knots: 22
Range, n miles: 5,000 at 16 kt
Complement: 50 plus 40 non-permanent
Guns: 1 OTO Melara 3 in *(76 mm)*/62 compact; 85 rds/min to 16 km *(8.7 n miles)*; weight of shell 6 kg. 1 OTO Melara 30 mm/70 (remotely operated); 200 rds/min; 2 OTO Melara Hitrole (remotely operated) 12.7 mm MGs; 6—7.62 mm MGs.
Combat data systems: SEWACO CMS. Link 11/16 SATCOM.
Electro-optic systems: Thales Gatekeeper; IR and TV.
Radars: Thales SMILE; E/F-band.
Surface search: Thales SEASTAR; I-band.
Navigation: 2 (to be announced); I-band.
Helicopters: 1 NH-90.

Comment: Contract for the design and build of four patrol ships awarded to Schelde Naval shipbuilding on 20 December 2007. The role of the ships is to conduct low-intensity military operations including maritime interdiction, counter-terrorism and humanitarian assistance. The ships are to be fitted with two water guns. Design features include an integrated mast for sensors and communications and provision to accommodate additional payloads, including stowage for two 20 ft containers or pallets in a multifunction space beneath the flight deck. A 10 tonne crane is fitted on the starboard side for cargo handling. Two 12 m RHIBs can be embarked: one may be launched and recovered via a stern slipway, the other from a boat davit on the port side.

HOLLAND CLASS *12/2007, Thales* / 1170067

AMPHIBIOUS FORCES

5 LCU MK IX (LCU)

L 9525–L 9529

Displacement, tons: 260 full load
Dimensions, feet (metres): 118.4 × 22.4 × 4.3 *(36.1 × 6.8 × 1.3)*
Main machinery: Diesel-electric; 2 Caterpillar 3412C diesel generators; 1,496 hp(m) *(1.1 MW)*; 2 Alconza D400 motors; 2 Schottel pumpjets; 2 pump jets
Speed, knots: 9. **Range, n miles**: 400 at 8 kt
Complement: 5 plus 2 spare
Military lift: 130 troops or 2 Warriors or 1 BARV or up to 3 trucks
Guns: 1—12.7 mm MG; 1—7.62 mm MG.
Radars: Navigation: I-band.

Comment: Ordered from Visser Dockyard, Den Helder on 19 July 1996. Steel vessels of which the first commissioned 7 April 1998. The others have been fabricated in Romania and fitted out by Visser in 1999/2000. Embarked in *Rotterdam*. L 9526 lengthened by 8.8 m at Visser dockyard in 2004 and the remainder in 2005–06.

L 9528 *7/2008*, A A de Kruijf* / 1335279

6 LCVP MK III (LCVP)

L 9536–L 9541

Displacement, tons: 30 full load
Dimensions, feet (metres): 55.4 × 15.7 × 3.6 *(16.9 × 4.8 × 1.1)*
Main machinery: 2 diesels; 750 hp(m) *(551 kW)*; 2 shafts
Speed, knots: 14 (full load); 16.5 (light)
Range, n miles: 200 at 12 kt
Complement: 3
Military lift: 34 troops or 7 tons or 2 Land Rovers or 1 Snowcat
Guns: 1—7.62 mm MG.
Radars: Navigation: Racal Decca 110; I-band.

Comment: Ordered from van der Giessen-de Noord 10 December 1988. First one laid down 10 August 1989, commissioned 16 October 1990. Last one commissioned 19 October 1992.

L 9539 *7/2008*, Frank Findler* / 1335262

1 ROTTERDAM CLASS (LPD)

Name	*No*	*Builders*	*Laid down*	*Launched*	*Commissioned*
ROTTERDAM	L 800	Royal Schelde, Vlissingen	25 Jan 1996	22 Feb 1997	18 Apr 1998

Displacement, tons: 12,750 full load
Dimensions, feet (metres): 544.6 × 82 × 19.3 *(166 × 25 × 5.9)*
Flight deck, feet (metres): 183.7 × 82 *(56 × 25)*
Main machinery: Diesel-electric; 4 Stork Wärtsilä 12SW28 diesel generators; 14.6 MW sustained; 2 Holec motors; 16,320 hp(m) *(12 MW)*; 2 shafts; bow thruster
Speed, knots: 19
Range, n miles: 6,000 at 12 kt
Complement: 113 (13 officers) + 611 (41 officers) Marines
Military lift: 611 troops; 170 APCs or 33 MBTs. 6 LCVP Mk 3 or 4 LCU Mk 9 or 4 LCM 8

Guns: 2 Signaal Goalkeeper 30 mm ❶. 8—12.7 mm MGs.
Countermeasures: Decoys: 4 SRBOC chaff launchers ❷; Nixie torpedo decoy system.
ESM/ECM: Intercept and jammer.
Combat data systems: SATCOM ❸; Link 11. MCCIS.
Weapons control: Signaal IRSCAN infra-red director.
Radars: Air/surface search: Signaal DA08 ❹; E/F-band.
Surface search: Signaal Scout/Kelvin Hughes ARPA ❺; I-band.
Navigation and CCA: 2 sets; I-band.

Helicopters: 6 NH90 ❻ or 4 Merlin/Sea King.

Programmes: Project definition for a joint design with Spain completed in December 1993. Contract signed with Royal Schelde 25 April 1994.
Structure: Facilities to transport a fully equipped Marine battalion with docking facilities for landing craft and a two spot helicopter flight deck with hangar space for six NH 90. 25 ton crane for disembarkation. Full hospital facilities. Built to commercial standards with military command and control and NBCD facilities. Can carry up to 30 torpedoes and 300 sonobuoys.
Operational: Alternative employment as an SAR ship for environmental and disaster relief tasks.

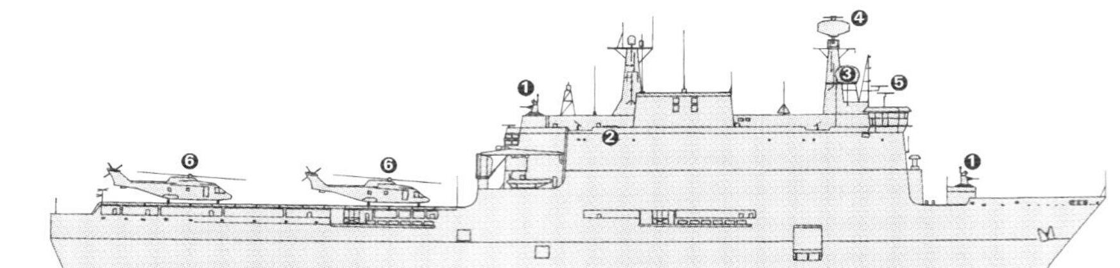

ROTTERDAM *(Scale 1 : 1,500), Ian Sturton* / 0534086

ROTTERDAM *7/2007, M Declerck* / 1166627

ROTTERDAM *5/2007, J Brodie* / 1166680

ROTTERDAM *6/2008*, Richard Scott* / 1335280

1 JOHAN DE WITT CLASS (LPD)

Name	*No*	*Builders*	*Laid down*	*Launched*	*Commissioned*
JOHAN DE WITT	L 801	Royal Schelde, Vlissingen	18 June 2003	13 May 2006	30 Nov 2007

Displacement, tons: 16,680 full load
Dimensions, feet (metres): 578.7 × 95.8 × 18.0 *(176.4 × 29.2 × 5.5)*
Flight deck, feet (metres): 190.3 × 82.0 *(58 × 25)*
Main machinery: Diesel-electric; 4 Wärtsilä 12V26A diesel generators; 19,310 hp *(14.4 MW)* sustained; 2 Schottel SEP 5 podded propulsors; 14,750 hp *(11 MW)*; 2 Schottel bow thrusters; 2,400 hp *(1.8 MW)*
Speed, knots: 19
Range, n miles: 10,000 at 12 kt
Complement: 146 (17 officers) + 555 Marines or 402 CJTF
Military lift: 555 troops; 170 APCs or 33 MBTs. 4 LCVP and 2 LCU or 2 LCM

Guns: 2 Signaal Goalkeeper 30 mm ❶. 4—12.7 mm MGs.
Countermeasures: Decoys: 4 SRBOC chaff/IR launchers ❷; Nixie torpedo decoy system.
ESM: ARGO Systems AR-900; intercept.
Combat data systems: 1 CAMS/Force Vision CMS; 2 Raytheon SHF SATCOM ❸; 2 Surcom UHF SATCOM; 1 AEHF SATCOM; Link 11 (16 and 22 planned); MCCIS.
Radars: Air/surface search: Thales VARIANT 2 ❹; G/I-band.
Surface search: Thales/Kelvin Hughes ARPA ❺; I-band.
Navigation: 1 Consilium Selesmar; I-band. 2 Consilium Selesmar ❻; E/F-band.

Helicopters: 6 NH 90 ❼ or 4 Merlin.

Programmes: Contract signed with Royal Schelde 3 May 2002. The hull was constructed at the Damen-owned Galati yard in Romania and arrived at the Schelde yard on 3 December 2004 for completion. To be fitted with command and control facilities for an afloat CJTF-HQ.
Structure: Facilities to transport a fully equipped Marine battalion with docking facilities for landing craft and a two spot helicopter flight deck with hangar space for six NH90. 25 ton crane for disembarkation. Full hospital facilities. Built to commercial standards with military command and control and NBCD facilities. Can carry up to 30 torpedoes and 300 sonobuoys. Based on the L 800 design but larger and wider. The flight deck is also stronger.
Operational: Alternative employment as an SAR ship for environmental and disaster relief tasks.

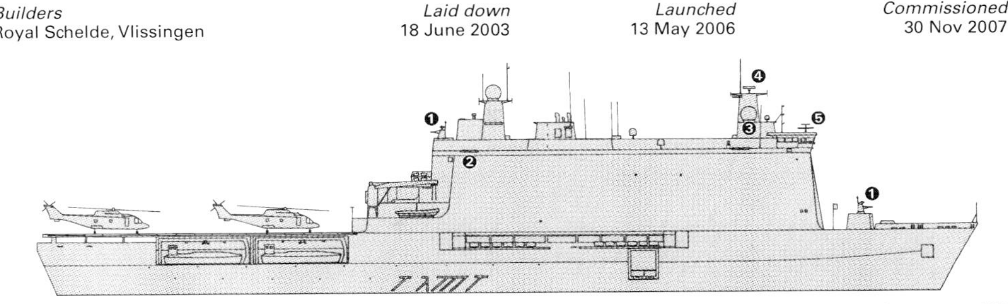

JOHAN DE WITT *(Scale 1 : 1,500), Ian Sturton* / 1170084

JOHAN DE WITT *11/2007, J Brodie* / 1335260

JOHAN DE WITT *7/2007, Michael Nitz* / 1166628

JOHAN DE WITT *7/2007, Michael Nitz* / 1166629

6 LCVP MK 2 (LANDING CRAFT) (LCVP)

L 9530–L 9535

Displacement, tons: 13.6 full load
Dimensions, feet (metres): 52.5 × 14.4 × 4.3 *(16.0 × 4.4 × 1.3)*
Main machinery: 1 DAF diesel; 260 hp *(194 kW)*; 1 Schottel swivelling prop
Complement: 3 plus 25 troops
Guns: 1 — 7.62 mm MG.
Radars: Furuno; I-band.

Comment: Built at the Naval Shipyard Den Helder and entered service 1984–86. GRP construction.

L 9534 *7/2008*, Frank Findler* / 1335261

4 + 8 LCVP MK V (LANDING CRAFT) (LCVP)

L 9565–L 9576

Displacement, tons: 23.7 full load
Dimensions, feet (metres): 50.8 × 14.0 × 5.25 *(15.5 × 4.27 × 1.6)*
Main machinery: 2 Volvo D9 575 diesels; 2 Ultrajet 410 waterjets
Speed, knots: 17. **Range, n miles:** 200 at 15 kt
Complement: 3
Military lift: 35 troops or 8.2 tons of vehicles and stores
Guns: 2 — 7.62 mm MGs.
Radars: Raymarine; I-band.

Comment: Contract signed on 13 December 2006 with Damen Shipyards Gorinchem for the construction and delivery of 12 Landing Craft Vehicle Personnel (LCVP). The craft are being built by Scheepswerf Visser in Den Helder. The first four are to be delivered by 2009 and the remaining eight by 2011.

L 9565 *8/2008*, RNLN* / 1335270

MINE WARFARE FORCES

10 ALKMAAR (TRIPARTITE) CLASS (MINEHUNTERS) (MHC)

Name	*No*	*Laid down*	*Launched*	*Commissioned*
HAARLEM	M 853	16 June 1981	6 May 1983	12 Jan 1984
MAASSLUIS	M 856	7 Nov 1982	5 May 1984	12 Dec 1984
MAKKUM	M 857	25 Feb 1983	27 Sep 1984	13 May 1985
MIDDELBURG	M 858	11 July 1983	23 Feb 1985	10 Dec 1986
HELLEVOETSLUIS	M 859	12 Dec 1983	18 July 1985	20 Feb 1987
SCHIEDAM	M 860	6 May 1984	20 Dec 1985	9 July 1986
URK	M 861	1 Oct 1984	2 May 1986	10 Dec 1986
ZIERIKZEE	M 862	25 Feb 1985	4 Oct 1986	7 May 1987
VLAARDINGEN	M 863	6 May 1986	4 Aug 1988	15 Mar 1989
WILLEMSTAD	M 864	3 Oct 1986	27 Jan 1989	20 Sep 1989

Displacement, tons: 620 standard; 650 full load
Dimensions, feet (metres): 168.9 × 29.2 × 8.5 *(51.5 × 8.9 × 2.6)*
Main machinery: 1 Stork Wärtsilä A-RUB 215X-12 diesel; 1,860 hp(m) *(1.35 MW)* sustained; 1 shaft; LIPS cp prop; 2 active rudders; 2 motors; 240 hp(m) *(179 kW)*; 2 bow thrusters
Speed, knots: 15 diesel; 7 electric
Range, n miles: 3,000 at 12 kt
Complement: 29-42 depending on task

Guns: 3 — 12.7 mm MGs.
Countermeasures: MCM: Atlas Seafox MIDS.
Combat data systems: Atlas Elektronic IMCMS. SATCOM.
Radars: Navigation: Consilium Selesmar MM 950; I-band.
Sonars: Thales TSM 2022 Mk III; hull-mounted; minehunting; 100, 200 and 400 kHz and Double Eagle Mk III Mod 1 variable depth sonar.

Programmes: The two Indonesian ships ordered in 1985 took the place of M 863 and 864 whose laying down was delayed as a result. This class is the Netherlands' part of a tripartite co-operative plan with Belgium and France for GRP hulled minehunters. The whole class built by van der Giessen-de Noord. Ships were launched virtually ready for trials.
Modernisation: An extensive modernisation programme is underway at Den Helder between mid-2003 and 2010 to extend service life to 2020. Upgrades include a MCM command and control system, an Integrated Mine Countermeasures System (comprising hull-mounted and self-propelled variable-depth sonar (installed in Double Eagle Mk III Mod 1 RoV)) and a Mine-Identification and Disposal System (MIDS) based on the Atlas Seafox. Linked to the ship by a 3,000 m fibre optic tether, one variant (Seafox-C) is used for mine disposal and the other (Seafox-I) is used for identification. Modernisation of eight ships had been completed by late 2008. M 864 and M 857 are to be completed by 2010.
Structure: A 5 ton container can be shipped, stored for varying tasks-research; patrol; extended diving; drone control.
Operational: Endurance, 15 days. MHCs are sometimes assigned to coast guard operations.
Sales: Two of a modified design to Indonesia, completed March 1988. M 850-852 decommissioned in 2000. M 854 and M 855 decommissioned in 2003. All five have been sold to Latvia and transfer is to be completed by 2009.

WILLEMSTAD *6/2008*, Michael Winter* / 1335263

MAASSLUIS *6/2008*, Michael Nitz* / 1335278

SURVEY SHIPS

2 SNELLIUS CLASS (SURVEY SHIPS) (AGSH)

Name	*No*	*Builders*	*Launched*	*Commissioned*
SNELLIUS	A 802	Royal Schelde, Vlissingen	30 Apr 2003	11 Dec 2003
LUYMES	A 803	Royal Schelde, Vlissingen	22 Aug 2003	3 June 2004

Displacement, tons: 1,875 full load
Dimensions, feet (metres): 246.1 × 43.0 × 13.1 *(75 × 13.1 × 4)*
Main machinery: Diesel electric; 3 diesel generators; 2,652 hp(m) *(1.95 MW)*; 1 motor; 1,360 hp(m) *(1 MW)*; 1 shaft; cp prop
Speed, knots: 12. **Range, n miles:** 4,300 at 12 kt
Complement: 13 plus 5 scientists plus 24 spare
Radars: Navigation: E/F- and I-band.
Sonars: Multi and single beam; high frequency; active

Comment: Designed for military and civil hydrographic surveys. Both laid down on 25 June 2002.

SNELLIUS *7/2007, Michael Nitz* / 1166642

LUYMES *7/2007, M Declerck* / 1166643

TRAINING SHIPS

Notes: Two Dokkum class minesweepers are used by Sea Cadets.

1 TRAINING SHIP (AXL)

Name	*No*	*Builders*	*Commissioned*
VAN KINSBERGEN	A 902	Damen Shipyards	2 Nov 1999

Displacement, tons: 630 full load
Dimensions, feet (metres): 136.2 × 30.2 × 10.8 *(41.5 × 9.2 × 3.3)*
Main machinery: 2 Caterpillar 3508 BI-TA; 1,572 hp(m) *(1.16 MW)* sustained; 2 shafts; bow thruster; 272 hp(m) *(200 kW)*
Speed, knots: 13
Complement: 5 plus 3 instructors and 16 students
Radars: Navigation: Consilium Selesmar; I-band.

Comment: Launched 30 August 1999. Has replaced *Zeefakkel* as the local training ship at Den Helder. Carries a 25 kt RIB.

VAN KINSBERGEN *6/2008*, Michael Nitz* / 1335277

1 SAIL TRAINING SHIP (AXS)

Name	*No*	*Builders*	*Commissioned*
URANIA (ex-*Tromp*)	Y 8050	Haarlem	23 Apr 1938

Displacement, tons: 75 full load
Dimensions, feet (metres): 87.9 × 19.8 × 8.5 *(26.8 × 6.05 × 2.6)*
Main machinery: 1 Caterpillar diesel; 235 hp(m) *(186 kW)*; 1 shaft
Speed, knots: 10 diesel; 12 sail
Complement: 3 + 14 trainees

Comment: Schooner used for training in seamanship. Refit 2001–04 included a new hull and aluminium masts.

URANIA *5/2008*, A A de Kruijf* / 1335276

AUXILIARIES

Notes: (1) In addition to the vessels listed there are large numbers of non self-propelled craft with Y pennant numbers, and six harbour launches Y 8200–8203 and 9001-9002.
(2) An Accommodation Ship *Thetis* (A 887) is based at Den Helder and provides harbour training for divers and underwater swimmers.

1 AMSTERDAM CLASS (FAST COMBAT SUPPORT SHIP) (AORH)

Name	*No*	*Builders*	*Laid down*	*Launched*	*Commissioned*
AMSTERDAM	A 836	Merwede, Hardinxveld, and Royal Schelde, Vlissingen	25 May 1992	11 Sep 1993	2 Sep 1995

Displacement, tons: 17,040 full load
Dimensions, feet (metres): 544.6 × 72.2 × 26.2 *(166 × 22 × 8)*
Main machinery: 2 Bazán/Burmeister & Wain 16V 40/45 diesels; 24,000 hp(m) *(17.6 MW)* sustained; 1 shaft; LIPS cp prop
Speed, knots: 20
Range, n miles: 13,440 at 20 kt
Complement: 160 (23 officers) including 24 aircrew plus 20 spare

Cargo capacity: 6,815 tons dieso; 1,660 tons aviation fuel; 290 tons solids
Guns: 2 Oerlikon 20 mm. 1 Signaal Goalkeeper 30 mm CIWS.
Countermeasures: Decoys: 4 SRBOC Mk 36 chaff launchers. Nixie towed torpedo decoy.
ESM: Ferranti AWARE-4; radar warning
Weapons control: Signaal IRSCAN infrared director.
Radars: Surface search and helo control: 2 Kelvin Hughes; F-band.

Helicopters: 3 Lynx or 3 SH-3D or 3 NH90 or 2 EH 101.

Programmes: NP/SP AOR 90 replacement for *Poolster* ordered 14 October 1991. Hull built by Merwede, with fitting out by Royal Schelde from October 1993. A similar ship has been built for the Spanish Navy.
Structure: Close co-operation between Dutch Nevesbu and Spanish Bazán led to this design which has maintenance workshops as well as four abeam and one stern RAS/FAS station, and one Vertrep supply station. Built to merchant ship standards but with military NBC damage control.

AMSTERDAM *11/2007, Derek Fox* / 1335265

1 SUBMARINE SUPPORT SHIP AND TORPEDO TENDER (ASL/YTT)

Name	*No*	*Builders*	*Commissioned*
MERCUUR	A 900	Koninklijke Maatschappij de Schelde	21 Aug 1987

Displacement, tons: 1,400 full load
Dimensions, feet (metres): 212.6 × 39.4 × 14.1 *(64.8 × 12 × 4.3)*
Main machinery: 2 Brons 61-20/27 diesels; 1,100 hp(m) *(808 kW)*; 2 shafts; bow thruster
Speed, knots: 14
Complement: 39 (6 officers)
Torpedoes: 3—324 mm (triple) tubes. 1—21 in *(533 mm)* underwater tube.
Mines: Can lay mines.
Radars: Navigation: Racal Decca 1229; I-band.
Sonars: SQR-01; hull-mounted; passive search.

Comment: Replacement for previous ship of same name. Ordered 13 June 1984. Laid down 6 November 1985. Floated out 25 October 1986. Can launch training and research torpedoes above and below the waterline. Services, maintains and recovers torpedoes.

MERCUUR *6/2008*, Martin Mokrus* / 1335266

1 MODIFIED POOLSTER CLASS (FAST COMBAT SUPPORT SHIP) (AORH)

Name	*No*	*Builders*	*Laid down*	*Launched*	*Commissioned*
ZUIDERKRUIS	A 832	Verolme Shipyards, Alblasserdam	16 July 1973	15 Oct 1974	27 June 1975

Displacement, tons: 16,900 full load
Measurement, tons: 10,000 dwt
Dimensions, feet (metres): 556 × 66.6 × 27.6 *(169.6 × 20.3 × 8.4)*
Main machinery: 2 Stork-Werkspoor TM410 diesels; 21,000 hp(m) *(15.4 MW)*; 1 shaft; LIPS cp props
Speed, knots: 21
Complement: 266 (17 officers)
Cargo capacity: 10,300 tons including 8-9,000 tons oil fuel
Guns: 1 Signaal Goalkeeper 30 mm CIWS. 5 Oerlikon 20 mm.
Countermeasures: Decoys: 2 Loral Hycor SRBOC Mk 36 fixed 6-barrelled launchers; IR flares and chaff.
ESM: Ferranti AWARE-4; radar warning
Weapons control: Signaal IRSCAN.
Radars: Air/surface search: Racal Decca 2459; F/I-band.
Navigation: 2 Racal Decca TM 1226C; Signaal SCOUT; I-band
Helicopters: 1 Westland UH-14A Lynx.

Structure: Helicopter deck aft. Funnel heightened by 4.5 m *(14.8 ft)*. 20 mm guns, containerised Goalkeeper CIWS and SATCOM, fitted for operational deployments.
Operational: Capacity for five helicopters with A/S weapons. Two fuelling stations each side for underway replenishment. Planned to remain in commission until replaced by the Joint Support Ship in about 2014.
Sales: *Poolster* sold to Pakistan in June 1994.

ZUIDERKRUIS *9/2006, M Declerck* / 1164979

0 + 1 JOINT LOGISTIC SUPPORT SHIP (AFSH)

Name	*No*	*Laid down*	*Launched*	*Commissioned*
–	–	2010	2013	2015

Displacement, tons: 27,000 full load
Dimensions, feet (metres): 672.5 × 98.4 × 21.3 *(205.0 × 30.0 × 6.5)*
Main machinery: Diesel-electric; 2 shafts; 2 bow thrusters; 1 stern thruster
Speed, knots: 20
Complement: 175 plus 300 embarked force
Guns: 2 Thales Goalkeeper 30 mm. 2—300 mm. 4—12.7 mm MGs.
Countermeasures: Decoys: To be announced.
Combat data systems: Link 11. Provision for Link 16/22. SATCOM.
Electro-optic systems: Thales Gatekeeper; IR and TV.
Radars: Air/Surface search/navigation: Thales SMILE; E/F-band.
Surface search: Thales SEASTAR; I-band.
Navigation: I-band.
Helicopters: 6 NH 90 or 2 Chinooks.

Comment: A contract is expected in 2009 for the construction of a multipurpose ship capable of maritime logistic support, strategic sealift and support of land-based forces. Secondary tasks are to be disaster relief, humanitarian aid and civil operations. There are to be three replenishment (fuel, water, solids) stations (two abeam and one astern). The ship will have 2,000 lane metres of space for vehicles/containers, weapons for an infantry company and or 9,000 m³ of fuel and 125 m³/day water. Fitted with two 40 ton cranes and a number of cargo lifts, the ship is also to be capable of embarking two LCVPs. There are to be two vehicle ramps, one on the starboard side and one on the quarter. A medical support facility, workshops and a logistics support centre are also to be included. The flight deck has two spots for Chinook-sized helicopters.

JOINT SUPPORT SHIP (artist's impression) *6/2007, Royal Netherlands Navy* / 1166650

1 TANKER (AOTL)

Name	*No*	*Builders*	*Commissioned*
PATRIA	Y 8760	De Hoop, Schiedam	9 June 1998

Displacement, tons: 681 full load
Dimensions, feet (metres): 145.3 × 22.4 × 8.9 *(44.4 × 6.9 × 2.8)*
Main machinery: 1 Volvo Penta TADM 122A; 381 hp(m) *(280 kW)*; 1 shaft
Speed, knots: 9.5
Complement: 2
Radars: Navigation: Furuno RHRS-2002R; I-band.

PATRIA *7/2005, A A de Kruijf* / 1151128

1 LOGISTIC SUPPORT VESSEL (AP)

Name	*No*	*Builders*	*Laid down*	*Launched*	*Commissioned*
PELIKAAN	A 804	Damen Shipyard	25 Aug 2005	7 Feb 2006	12 June 2006

Displacement, tons: 1,700 full load
Dimensions, feet (metres): 214.6 × 43.5 × 9.8 *(65.4 × 13.25 × 3.0)*
Main machinery: 2 Caterpillar 3516B TA diesels; 4,000 hp *(3 MW)*; 2 shafts
Speed, knots: 14.5
Complement: 14 (2 officers) plus 15 extra plus 45 temporary
Guns: 4—12.7 mm MGs.
Radars: Navigation: I-band.

Comment: In January 2005 a contract was signed between the Royal Netherlands Navy and Damen Shipyards for the design and construction of a Logistic Support Vessel (LSV) to provide sealift for the RNLMC in the Caribbean. The ship has replaced the old vessel of the same name. Following construction of the hull at the Damen-owned Galatz shipyard in Romania, the ship was completed at Gorinchem. A large cargo area is located at main deck level and can accommodate six rigid raiding craft, four trucks and a range of support equipment. Loading and unloading is facilitated by a deck crane.

PELIKAAN *6/2006, I J Plokker* / 1040762

1 SUPPORT CRAFT (YFL)

Name	*No*	*Builders*	*Commissioned*
NIEUWEDIEP	Y 8005	Akerboom, Leiden	Feb 1972

Displacement, tons: 27 full load
Dimensions, feet (metres): 58.4 × 14.1 × 4.9 *(17.8 × 4.3 × 1.5)*
Main machinery: 2 Volvo Penta diesels; 600 hp(m) *(441 kW)*; 2 shafts
Speed, knots: 10
Complement: 4

Comment: Acquired by the Navy in February 1992 as a passenger craft.

NIEUWEDIEP *7/2008*, Frank Findler* / 1335264

4 CERBERUS CLASS (DIVING TENDERS) (YDT)

Name	*No*	*Builders*	*Commissioned*
CERBERUS	A 851	Visser, Den Helder	28 Feb 1992
ARGUS	A 852	Visser, Den Helder	2 June 1992
NAUTILUS	A 853	Visser, Den Helder	18 Sep 1992
HYDRA	A 854	Visser, Den Helder	20 Nov 1992

Displacement, tons: 223 full load
Dimensions, feet (metres): 89.9 × 27.9 × 4.9 *(27.4 × 8.5 × 1.5)*
Main machinery: 2 Volvo Penta TAMD122A diesels; 760 hp(m) *(560 kW)*; 2 shafts
Speed, knots: 12. **Range, n miles:** 750 at 12 kt
Complement: 8 (2 officers)
Radars: Navigation: Racal Decca; I-band.

Comment: Ordered 29 November 1990. Capable of maintaining 10 kt in Sea State 3. Can handle a 2 ton load at 4 m from the ship's side. *Hydra* lengthened by 10.5 m to provide more accommodation and recommissioned on 13 March 1998.

NAUTILUS *10/2007, A A de Kruijf* / 1166651

HYDRA *6/2008*, A A de Kruijf* / 1335275

TUGS

7 HARBOUR TUGS (YTL)

BREEZAND Y 8018 **SCHELDE** Y 8055 **MALZWIN** Y 8057 **WESTWAL** Y 8059
BALGZAND Y 8019 **WIERBALG** Y 8056 **ZUIDWAL** Y 8058

Comment: *Breezand* completed December 1989, *Balgzand* January 1990. The others are smaller pusher tugs and were completed December 1986 to February 1987. All built by Delta Shipyard.

MALZWIN *7/2008*, Frank Findler* / 1335268

5 COASTAL TUGS (YTM)

Name	*No*	*Builders*	*Commissioned*
LINGE	A 874	Delta SY, Sliedrecht	20 Feb 1987
REGGE	A 875	Delta SY, Sliedrecht	6 May 1987
HUNZE	A 876	Delta SY, Sliedrecht	20 Oct 1987
ROTTE	A 877	Delta SY, Sliedrecht	20 Oct 1987
GOUWE	A 878	Delta SY, Sliedrecht	21 Feb 1997

Displacement, tons: 380 full load
Dimensions, feet (metres): 90.2 × 27.2 × 8.9 *(27.5 × 8.3 × 2.7)*
Main machinery: 2 Stork-Werkspoor or 2 Caterpillar (A 878) diesels; 1,600 hp(m) *(1.18 MW)*; 2 Kort nozzle props
Speed, knots: 11
Complement: 7
Radars: Racal Decca; I-band.

Comment: Order for first four placed in 1986. Based at Den Helder. A fifth of class was ordered in June 1996 to replace *Westgat*.

ROTTE *7/2008*, Frank Findler* / 1335269

ARMY

Notes: Six craft are operated by the Corps of Military Police: RV 160, RV 161, RV 162, RV 168, RV 169 and RV 180.

RV 162 *7/2008*, Michael Winter* / 1335267

1 DIVING VESSEL (YDT)

RV 50

Dimensions, feet (metres): 137.3 × 31.2 × 4.9 *(41.8 × 9.5 × 1.5)*
Main machinery: 2 diesels; 476 hp(m) *(350 kW)*; 2 shafts; 1 bow thruster
Speed, knots: 8
Complement: 21
Radars: Navigation: JRC JMA 606; I-band.

Comment: Built by Vervako as a diving training ship and commissioned 3 November 1989. There is a moonpool aft with a 50 m diving bell, and a decompression chamber.

RV 50 *10/2004, Bram Plokker* / 1047865

COAST GUARD (KUSTWACHT)

Notes: (1) On 26 February 1987, many of the maritime services were merged to form a Coast Guard with its own distinctive colours. Included were assorted craft of the Ministries that signed the Coast Guard Agreement. From 1 June 1995 the operational command of the Coast Guard became the responsibility of the Royal Netherlands Navy. On 1 January 2007 the Coast Guard became an independent civil organisation under the Ministry of Defence.
(2) The following ships, craft and aircraft are permanently available for Coast Guard duties: *Waker, Visarend, Zeearend, Barend Biesheuvel* and two Dornier-228 surveillance.
(3) In addition, the Coast Guard can call upon the following ships and craft:

- Ministry of Transport and Public Works: *Frans Naerebout, Rotterdam, Terschelling, Nieuwediep, Schuitegat, Vliestroom, Waddenzee, Zirfaea, Jan van Gent, Stormmeeuw.*
- Ministry of Defence: Minehunters of the Alkmaar class and military police vessel R-180.
- Ministry of Home Affairs: P 41, P 42, P 44, P 48, P 49.
- Royal Netherlands Sea-Rescue organisation: 65 lifeboats in 42 stations.

WAKER *6/2008*, MOD Netherlands* / 1335274

VISAREND (Finance) *7/2006, A A de Kruijf* / 1164974

BAREND BIESHEUVEL (Agriculture) *6/2002, Imtech Marine and Offshore* / 0534130

Do 228 *6/2008*, MOD Netherlands* / 1335273

COAST GUARD (ANTILLES AND ARUBA)

Notes: (1) Netherlands Antilles and Aruba Coast Guard (NAACG) formed 23 January 1996. Headquarters is co-located with the RNLN at Parera, Curaçao. There are three sub-stations at Curaçao, Aruba and St Maarten.
(2) Twelve 12 m Super RHIB, capable of 40 kt, have been procured for counter-drug operations. In 2004, two were stationed at Aruba, two at Curacao and one at St Maarten. Four followed in 2005 and the final three in 2006.
(3) Maritime patrol duties in the Caribbean are undertaken by two de Havilland DASH 8 aircraft and one Eurocopter AS 355 helicopter.

SUPER RHIB *6/2008*, RNLN* / 1335272

DASH 8 *9/2008*, Larry Every* / 1335271

3 STAN PATROL 4100 CUTTERS (PB)

Name	*No*	*Builders*	*Commissioned*
JAGUAR	P 810	Damen Shipyards	2 Nov 1998
PANTER	P 811	Damen Shipyards	18 Jan 1999
POEMA	P 812	Damen Shipyards	19 Mar 1999

Displacement, tons: 205 full load
Dimensions, feet (metres): 140.4 × 22.3 × 8.2 *(42.8 × 6.8 × 2.5)*
Main machinery: 2 Caterpillar 3516B diesels; 5,685 hp(m) *(4.18 MW)*; 2 shafts; LIPS cp props; bow thruster
Speed, knots: 26
Range, n miles: 2,000 at 12 kt
Complement: 11 plus 6 police
Guns: 1 — 12.7 mm MG.
Radars: Surface search: Signaal Scout; I-band.
Navigation: Kelvin Hughes; I-band

Comment: Ordered from Damen shipyards in March 1997 for delivery in late 1998. Equipped with surveillance passive sensors. The cutters have a gas citadel. A 30 kt RIB is launched through a transom door. Based at Willemstad, Curaçao.

JAGUAR *6/2006, M Declerck* / 1164973

New Zealand

Country Overview

New Zealand is an independent island country situated in the south Pacific Ocean with which it has a 8,170 n mile coastline. The British monarch, represented by a governor-general, is head of state. Situated about 865 n miles south-east of Australia, it comprises two main islands, North and South islands, which are separated by the Cook Strait. In addition there are numerous smaller islands including Stewart Island and the Auckland Islands. The overall area is 104,454 square miles. Overseas territories include Ross Dependency (Antarctica) and Tokelau (north of Samoa). In addition, the Cook Islands and Niue are self-governing territories in free association. The capital is Wellington and largest city is Auckland; both are ports located on North Island. Other principal ports are Tauranga, Lyttelton (near Christchurch), and Port Chalmers (Dunedin). Territorial seas (12 n miles) are claimed. An EEZ (200 n mile) is also claimed.

Headquarters Appointments

Chief of Navy:
Rear Admiral D I Ledson, ONZM
Deputy Chief of Navy:
Commodore B Pepperell, MBE

Headquarters Appointments — *continued*

Commander Joint Forces:
Major General R R Jones
Maritime Component Commander:
Commodore A J Parr, MVO

Diplomatic Representation

Defence Adviser, Washington:
Commodore P J Williams
Naval Adviser, London:
Commander C J Hoey
Naval Adviser, Canberra:
Commander K A Robb
Naval Adviser, Washington:
Commander M R Worsfold

Personnel

2009: 2,014 regulars and 308 reserves

Bases

Headquarters Joint Forces New Zealand (established 1 July 2001)
Naval Staff: HMNZS Wakefield (Wellington)
HMNZS Philomel (Auckland)

RNZNVR Divisions

Auckland: HMNZS *Ngapona*
Wellington: HMNZS *Olphert*
Christchurch: HMNZS *Pegasus*
Dunedin: HMNZS *Toroa*

Prefix to Ships' Names

HMNZS

DELETIONS

Patrol Forces

2007 *Moa, Kiwi, Wakakura, Hinau*

FRIGATES

2 ANZAC (MEKO 200) CLASS (FFHM)

Name	*No*	*Builders*	*Laid down*	*Launched*	*Commissioned*
TE KAHA	F 77	Transfield Defence Systems, Williamstown	19 Sep 1994	22 July 1995	22 July 1997
TE MANA	F 111	Tenix Defence Systems, Williamstown	28 June 1996	10 May 1997	10 Dec 1999

Displacement, tons: 3,600 full load
Dimensions, feet (metres): 387.1 oa; 357.6 wl × 48.6 × 14.3 *(118; 109 × 14.8 × 4.4)*
Main machinery: CODOG; 1 GE LM 2500 gas turbine; 30,172 hp *(22.5 MW)* sustained; 2 MTU 12V 1163 TB83 diesels; 8,840 hp(m) *(6.5 MW)* sustained; 2 shafts; cp props
Speed, knots: 27. **Range, n miles:** 6,000 at 18 kt
Complement: 163

Missiles: SAM: Raytheon Sea Sparrow RIM-7P; Lockheed Martin Marietta Mk 41 Mod 5 octuple cell vertical launcher ❶; semi-active radar homing to 16 km *(8.5 n miles)* at 2.5 Mach; warhead 38 kg. ESSM in due course.
Guns: 1 FMC 5 in *(127 mm)*/54 Mk 45 Mod 2 ❷; 20 rds/min to 23 km *(12.6 n miles)*; weight of shell 32 kg.
1 GE/GD 20 mm Vulcan Phalanx 6 barrelled Mk 15 Block 1 Baseline 2B ❸; 4,500 rds/min combined to 1.5 km.
2 Rafael Mini-Typhoon 12.7 mm remote-controlled guns.
Torpedoes: 6—324 mm US Mk 32 Mod 5 (2 triple) tubes ❹; Mk 46 Mod 2; anti-submarine; active/passive homing to 11 km *(5.9 n miles)* at 40 kt; warhead 44 kg.
Countermeasures: Decoys: 2 Loral Hycor Mk 36 Mod 1 chaff launchers ❺. SLQ-25A torpedo decoy system.
ESM: DASA Maigret; Racal Thorn Sceptre A; intercept (to be replaced by Racal Centaur in 2005).
Combat data systems: CelsiusTech 9LV 453 Mk 3. Link 11; GCCS-M.
Weapons control: CelsiusTech 9LV 453 optronic director ❻. Raytheon CWI Mk 73 Mod 1 (for SAM).
Radars: Air search: Raytheon SPS-49(V)8 ❼; C/D-band.
Air/surface search: CelsiusTech 9LV 453 TIR (Ericsson Tx/Rx) ❽; G-band.
Navigation: Atlas Elektronik 9600 ARPA; I-band.
Fire control: CelsiusTech 9LV 453 ❾; G-band.
IFF: Cossor Mk XII.
Sonars: Thomson Sintra Spherion B Mod 5; hull-mounted; active search and attack; medium frequency.

Helicopters: 1 SH-2G (NZ) Super Seasprite ❿.

Programmes: Contract signed with Amecon consortium on 19 November 1989 to build eight Blohm + Voss designed MEKO 200 ANZ frigates for Australia and two for New Zealand. Options on a third of class were turned down in November 1998. Modules constructed at Newcastle, Australia and Whangarei, New Zealand, and shipped to Melbourne for final assembly. The two New Zealand ships are the second and fourth of the class. First steel cut on *Te Kaha* on 11 February 1993. *Te Kaha* means Prowess. *Te Mana* means Power.
Modernisation: The ANZAC Ship will undergo a series of modifications during the period 2009–2014. In Phase I, the CIWS is being upgraded to Block 1B status. Concurrently, the diesel engines are to be replaced with an updated version and a new integrated propulsion management system is to be fitted. Other platform modifications are being undertaken to enhance services and stability margins. Phase II is to be an upgrade of weapon systems and sensors. The combat data system is to be replaced and the point-defence missile is to be upgraded. There are also to be improvements to ISR systems and measures to improve interoperability.
Structure: The ships include space and weight provision for considerable enhancement including canister-launched SSM, an additional fire-control channel and ECM. Signature suppression features are incorporated in the design. All-steel construction. Fin stabilisers. McTaggert Scott Trigon 3 helicopter traversing system. Two RHIBs are carried.

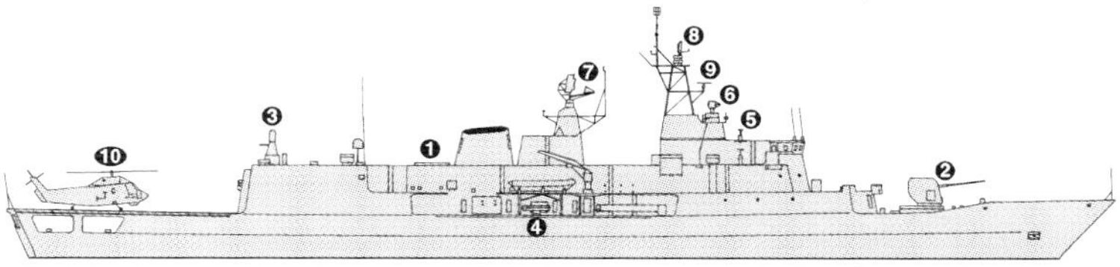

TE KAHA *(Scale 1 : 1,200), Ian Sturton* / 0081317

TE MANA *4/2005, Chris Sattler* / 1133137

TE KAHA *9/2006, Ships of the World* / 1158744

SHIPBORNE AIRCRAFT

Numbers/Type: 5 Kaman SH-2G (NZ) Super Seasprite.
Operational speed: 130 kt *(241 km/h)*.
Service ceiling: 22,500 ft *(6,860 m)*.
Range: 400 n miles *(740 km)*.
Role/Weapon systems: Last of five delivered in February 2003. Sensors: Litton ASN 150 C2; Telephonics APS 143 radar; AAQ 32 Safire IRDS; ALR 100 ESM; ALE 47 ECM. Weapons: ASW; 2 Mk 46 torpedoes or Mk 11 depth bomb; ASV; 2 Hughes Maverick AGM 65D (NZ); 1 — 7.62 mm M60 MG.

SUPER SEASPRITE — *5/2003, A Sharma* / 0567466

Numbers/Type: 8 NH Industries NH 90.
Operational speed: 165 kt *(305 km/h)*.
Service ceiling: 9,720 ft *(2,960 m)*.
Range: 430 n miles *(796 km)*.
Role/Weapon systems: Eight helicopters, similar to the MH 90s ordered by Australia, planned to enter service between 2010 and 2013. Four will be able to embark in *Canterbury*. Sensors: Likely to include NR-90 radar, FLIR. Flash dipping sonar. Weapons: Mu 90 torpedoes and possible ASM.

NH 90 — *4/2006, NH Industries* / 0062373

LAND-BASED MARITIME AIRCRAFT

Numbers/Type: 6 Lockheed P-3K2 Orion.
Operational speed: 405 kt *(750 km/h)*.
Service ceiling: 30,000 ft *(9,146 m)*.
Range: 4,000 n miles *(7,410 km)*.
Role/Weapon systems: Purchased in 1966. Long-range surveillance and reconnaissance patrol; updated 1984. Modernisation of airframes (Project Kestrel) undertaken 1995–2001 for 20 year extension. Upgrade project in progress to modernise mission avionics, sensors and communication/navigation systems. The upgrade is to include an Elta EL/M-2022(V)3 radar and Wescam MX-20 FLIR. Contract signed with L-3 communications on 4 October 2004. The first upgraded aircraft is to be delivered in 2008 and programme is to be completed by 2010. Operated by RNZAF. Sensors: APS-134 radar, ASQ-10 MAD, acoustic processor, AYK 14 computers, IFF, ESM, SSQ 53/62 sonobuoys. Weapons: ASW; eight Mk 46 torpedoes, Mk 80 series depth bombs.

P-3K2 — *7/2004, Paul Jackson* / 0589788

PATROL FORCES

1 + 1 PROTECTOR CLASS (OFFSHORE PATROL VESSELS) (PBO)

Name	*No*	*Builders*	*Laid down*	*Launched*	*Commissioned*
OTAGO	P 148	Tenix Defence Systems, Williamstown	16 Dec 2005	18 Nov 2006	2009
WELLINGTON	P 55	Tenix Defence Systems, Williamstown	2 June 2007	27 Oct 2007	2009

Displacement, tons: 1,600
Dimensions, feet (metres): 278.9 × 45.9 × 11.8 *(85.0 × 14.0 × 3.6)*
Main machinery: 2 MAN Burmeister & Wain 12 RK 280 diesels; 2 shafts; cp props
Speed, knots: 22
Range, n miles: 6,000 at 15 kt
Complement: 35 plus 44 spare
Guns: 1 MSI DS 25M Autsig 25 mm. 2 — 12.7 mm MGs.
Radars: Navigation: I-band.
Helicopters: 1 SH-2G Super Seasprite.

Programmes: Following selection as 'Project Protector' prime contractor in April 2004, Tenix Defence awarded contract for final design and construction on 28 July 2004. The ships are to meet patrol and surveillance requirements in support of civil agencies in New Zealand's EEZ and the Southern Ocean and to assist South Pacific states to patrol their EEZs. Manufacturing of modules started at Tenix's Whangerai Shipyard in New Zealand in February 2005. Final assembly is being undertaken at Williamstown, Victoria.
Structure: The design is a lengthened, helicopter-capable variant of a Kvaerner Masa Marine design in service in Ireland and Mauritius. They are to be ice-strengthened.

OTAGO — *6/2008*, RNZN* / 1335399

2 + 2 LAKE CLASS (INSHORE PATROL VESSELS) (PBO)

Name	*No*	*Builders*	*Laid down*	*Launched*	*Commissioned*
ROTOITI	P 3569	Tenix Defence Systems, Williamstown	3 Mar 2006	4 Aug 2007	2009
HAWEA	P 3571	Tenix Defence Systems, Williamstown	13 Dec 2006	15 Dec 2007	2009
PUKAKI	P 3568	Tenix Defence Systems, Williamstown	21 June 2007	10 May 2008	2009
TAUPO	P 3570	Tenix Defence Systems, Williamstown	14 Dec 2007	23 Aug 2008	2009

Displacement, tons: 340
Dimensions, feet (metres): 180.4 × 29.5 × 9.5 *(55.0 × 9.0 × 2.9)*
Main machinery: 2 MAN Burmeister & Wain 12VP 185 diesels; 2 shafts; cp props
Speed knots: 25
Range, n miles: 3,000 at 15 kt
Complement: 20 plus 16 spare
Guns: 3 — 12.7 mm MGs.
Radars: Navigation: I-band.

Programmes: Following selection as 'Project Protector' prime contractor in April 2004, Tenix Defence awarded contract for final design and construction on 29 July 2004. The ships are to operate in support of civil agencies to meet patrol and surveillance requirements in New Zealand's inshore zone (out to 24 n miles), particularly around North Island, Marlborough Sounds and Tasman Bay. Manufacturing started at Tenix's Whangerai Shipyard in New Zealand in early 2005.
Structure: The Tenix design is based on the 56 m San Juan class built for the Philippines Coast Guard. Capable of operating in up to Sea State 5, they will be able to launch and recover rigid hull inflatable boats in up to Sea State 4.

HAWEA — *5/2008*, RNZN* / 1335398

SURVEY AND RESEARCH SHIPS

1 STALWART CLASS (AGS)

Name	*No*	*Builders*	*Commissioned*
RESOLUTION (ex-*Tenacious*)	A 14 (ex-TAGOS 17)	Halter Marine, Moss Point	29 Sep 1989

Displacement, tons: 2,262 full load
Dimensions, feet (metres): 224 × 43 × 18.7 *(68.3 × 13.1 × 5.7)*
Main machinery: Diesel-electric; 4 Caterpillar D 398B diesel generators; 3,200 hp *(2.39 MW)*; 2 motors; 1,600 hp *(1.2 MW)*; 2 shafts; bow thruster; 550 hp *(410 kW)*
Speed, knots: 11. **Range, n miles:** 19,000 at 11 kt
Complement: 49
Radars: Navigation: 2 Raytheon; I-band.

Comment: Laid up by USN in 1995 and acquired in September 1996. Reactivated in October 1996 and commissioned into RNZN 13 February 1997 for passage to New Zealand. Conversion commenced mid-1997 to suit the ship for hydrography with secondary role of acoustic research for about three months per year, replacing both *Tui* and *Monowai*. Second stage of conversion to fit Atlas Elektronik MD 2/30 multibeam echo-sounder, completed in January 1999. A fixed dome increased the ship's draught. A DGPS and a towed array fitted for acoustic research. A new survey boat with Atlas Elektronik MD20 multibeam echo sounder was embarked in 2001. The ship has been repainted grey.

RESOLUTION ***3/2006, Chris Sattler*** / 1158701

1 SURVEY MOTOR BOAT (YGS)

ADVENTURE A 05

Displacement, tons: 9
Dimensions, feet (metres): 31.8 × 11.5 × 2.3 *(9.7 × 3.5 × 0.7)*
Main machinery: 2 Volvo-Penta AD31P/DP diesels; 300 hp *(223 kW)*
Speed, knots: 25. **Range, n miles:** 1,000 at 10 kt
Complement: 3
Radars: Navigation: I-band.

Comment: Aluminium catamaran craft built in Kumeu, North Auckland, in 1998. While usually operated as a tender from *Resolution*, she is capable of independent inshore hydrographic operations and short coastal passages. She is fitted with an echo sounder whose data can be integrated with the multibeam system fitted in *Resolution*.

ADVENTURE ***4/2008, Chris Sattler*** / 1305309

AUXILIARIES

Notes: (1) Options for the replacement of *Endeavour* are under consideration. The successor ship is likely to be a joint-support vessel with a broader range of capabilities. Commonality with *Canterbury* is likely to be a key factor.
(2) In addition to vessels listed below there are three 12 m sail training craft used for seamanship training: *Paea II, Mako II, Manga II* (sail nos 6911-6913).

PAEA ***2002, RNZN*** / 0525919

2 LANDING CRAFT (LCM)

LC 01 **LC 02**

Displacement, tons: 55 standard; 100 full load
Dimensions, feet (metres): 75.5 × 21.0 × ? *(23.0 × 6.4 × ?)*
Main machinery: 2 Scania D19 44M diesels; 630 hp *(470 kW)*; 2 Veth Z-drive azimuth thrusters
Speed, knots: 9
Range, n miles: 250 at 9 kt
Complement: 3
Military lift: 2 armoured fighting vehicles (NZLAV)

Comment: Designed by Iv-Nevesbu b.v. (Papendrecht, Netherlands) and constructed by Zwijnenburg, Rotterdam, the craft are to be carried in *Canterbury*. Operable in Sea State 3, onload and offload can be achieved (empty) using *Canterbury's* 60 tonne crane or alternatively via the stern ramp. The LCMs are designed for beach landings and are fitted with a ballasting system to allow the safe onload and offload of cargo. They are also fitted with a kedge anchor. The stern ramp of *Canterbury* has 'marriage blocks' to facilitate correct alignment on the ramp.

LC 02 ***6/2007, RNZN*** / 1170065

1 REPLENISHMENT TANKER (AORH)

Name	*No*	*Builders*	*Launched*	*Commissioned*
ENDEAVOUR	A 11	Hyundai, South Korea	14 Aug 1987	6 Apr 1988

Displacement, tons: 12,390 full load
Dimensions, feet (metres): 453.1 × 60 × 23 *(138.1 × 18.4 × 7.3)*
Main machinery: 1 MAN-Burmeister & Wain 12V32/36 diesel; 5,780 hp(m) *(4.25 MW)* sustained; 1 shaft; LIPS cp prop
Speed, knots: 13.5
Range, n miles: 8,000 at 13.5 kt
Complement: 49 (10 officers)
Cargo capacity: 5,500 tons dieso; 100 tons Avcat; 20 containers
Radars: Navigation: Racal Decca 1290A/9; ARPA 1690S; I-band.
Helicopters: Platform only.

Comment: Ordered July 1986. Laid down 10 April 1987. Completion delayed by engine problems but arrived in New Zealand in May 1988. Two abeam RAS rigs (one QRC, one Probe). Fitted with Inmarsat. Standard merchant design modified on building to provide a relatively inexpensive replenishment tanker. Modifications are to be undertaken in 2009 to convert the ship's tanks to meet double-skinning requirements demanded by MARPOL regulations. This will extend the ship's life to 2013.

ENDEAVOUR ***7/2007, Chris Sattler*** / 1166623

1 MOA CLASS (TRAINING SHIP) (AXL)

Name	*No*	*Builders*	*Commissioned*
KAHU (ex-*Manawanui*)	A 04 (ex-A 09)	Whangarei Engineering and Construction Co Ltd	28 May 1979

Displacement, tons: 91.5 standard; 105 full load
Dimensions, feet (metres): 88 × 20 × 7.2 *(26.8 × 6.1 × 2.2)*
Main machinery: 2 Cummins KT-1150M diesels; 710 hp *(530 kW)*; 2 shafts
Speed, knots: 12
Range, n miles: 1,000 at 11 kt
Complement: 16
Radars: Navigation: Racal Decca Bridgemaster 2000; I-band.

Comment: Same hull design as former Patrol Craft. Now used for navigation and seamanship training and as a standby diving tender.

KAHU ***3/2006, Chris Sattler*** / 1158699

1 DIVING TENDER (YDT)

Name	*No*	*Builders*	*Commissioned*
MANAWANUI (ex-*Star Perseus*)	A 09	Cochrane, Selby	May 1979

Displacement, tons: 911 full load
Dimensions, feet (metres): 143 × 31.2 × 10.5 *(43.6 × 9.5 × 3.2)*
Main machinery: 2 Caterpillar D 379TA diesels; 1,130 hp *(843 kW)*; 2 shafts; cp props; bow thruster
Speed, knots: 10.7. **Range, n miles**: 5,000 at 10 kt
Complement: 24 (2 officers)
Radars: Surface search: Racal Decca Bridgemaster 2000; I-band.
Sonars: Klein 595 Tracpoint; side scan; active high frequency.

Comment: North Sea Oil Rig Diving support vessel commissioned into the RNZN on 5 April 1988. Completed conversion in December 1988 and has replaced the previous ship of the same name which proved to be too small for the role. Equipment includes two Phantom HDX remote-controlled submersibles, a decompression chamber (to 250 ft), wet diving bell and 13 ton crane. Fitted with Inmarsat. MCAIS data system, side scan sonar and GPS fitted in 1995. More modifications are planned to enable the ship to do some of the work previously undertaken by *Tui*. This includes a stern gantry and general purpose winches for research including MCM. Used to support RAN submarine trials in 1996/97.

MANAWANUI *10/2006, **Chris Sattler*** / 1158734

1 CANTERBURY CLASS (MULTIROLE VESSEL) (AKRH/AX)

Name	*No*	*Builders*	*Laid down*	*Launched*	*Commissioned*
CANTERBURY	L 421	Merwede Shipyard, Netherlands	6 Sep 2005	11 Feb 2006	12 June 2007

Displacement, tons: 8,870
Dimensions, feet (metres): 430.4 × 76.8 × 18.4 *(131.2 × 23.4 × 5.6)*
Main machinery: CODAGE; 2 Wärtsilä 9L32 diesels; 12,000 hp *(9 MW)*; 2 shafts; cp props
Speed, knots: 19
Range, miles: 6,000 at 15 kt
Complement: 53 + accommodation for 250 troops and 47 additional
Guns: 1 MSI DS 25M Autsig 25 mm. 2 — 12.7 mm MGs.
Military lift: 1 infantry company including Light Armoured Vehicles and equipment. 2 LCM.
Radars: Navigation: 2 I-band.
Helicopters: 2 SH-2G Super Seasprites.

Programmes: Following selection as 'Project Protector' prime contractor in April 2004, Tenix Defence awarded contract for final design and construction on 29 July 2004. The ship was constructed in the Netherlands and fitted out by Tenix at Williamstown, Victoria.
Structure: With a design based on a commercial roll-on/roll-off vessel, the ship is built to comply with Lloyds Register of Shipping rules. The ship is ice-strengthened for operations in the Southern Ocean and the Ross Sea. Staff facilities are incorporated. Following an independent review to investigate problems arising during the introduction of the ship into service, remedial work is required to improve safety and stability in high sea states.

CANTERBURY *9/2007, **Chris Sattler*** / 1166624

Operational: The ship provides a limited tactical sealift capacity for disaster relief, humanitarian relief operations, peace support operations, military support activities and development assistance support. The ship is also used as the principal sea training platform for the RNZN.

CANTERBURY *9/2007, **Chris Sattler*** / 1166639

Nicaragua

FUERZA NAVAL-EJERCITO DE NICARAGUA

Country Overview

The Republic of Nicaragua is the largest Central American republic. After many years of civil war, a 1989 peace plan introduced a more stable period of democratic government. With an area of 50,893 square miles, it is situated between Honduras to the north and Costa Rica to the south. It has a 381 n mile coastline with the Caribbean and a 225 n mile coastline with the Pacific Ocean. Lake Nicaragua (Cocibolca), the largest lake in central America, and Lake Managua (Xolotlán) are connected by the river Tipitapa. The capital and largest city is Managua while Corinto, on the Pacific coast, is the principal port. Nicaragua has not claimed an EEZ but is one of a few coastal states which claims a 200 n mile territorial sea.

Headquarters Appointments

Head of Navy:
Rear Admiral Juan Santiago Estrada García

Personnel

2009: 910 officers and men

Bases

Pacific: Corinto (HQ), San Juan del Sur, Puerto Sandino y Potosi
Atlantic: Bluefields (HQ), El Bluff, Puerto Cabezas, Corn Island, San Juan del Norte

PATROL FORCES

Notes: There are reported plans to procure four Damen Stan Patrol 2606 patrol craft.

3 DABUR CLASS (PB)

GC 201 **GC 202** **GC 205**

Displacement, tons: 39 full load
Dimensions, feet (metres): 64.9 × 18 × 5.8 *(19.8 × 5.5 × 1.8)*
Main machinery: 2 Caterpillar 3406 diesels; 1,500 hp *(1.1 MW)* sustained; 2 shafts
Speed, knots: 20
Range, n miles: 450 at 13 kt
Complement: 12
Guns: 2 — 12.7 mm MGs.
Radars: Surface search: Furuno 2115; I-band.

Comment: *GC 201*, *203* and *205* were acquired from Israel in May 1996. All three craft re-engined: *GC 205* in 2004, *GC 202* in 2006 and *GC 201* in 2008. All are operational on the Atlantic coast.

GC 201 ***4/2008*, Nicaraguan Navy*** / 1335288

4 RODMAN 101 CLASS (PB)

GP 401–404

Displacement, tons: 63 full load
Dimensions, feet (metres): 98.4 × 19.4 × 4.3 *(30.0 × 5.9 × 1.3)*
Main machinery: 2 Caterpillar 3412C diesels; 2,800 hp *(2.06 MW)*; 2 Hamilton waterjets
Speed, knots: 30
Range, n miles: 800 at 12 kt
Complement: 12
Radars: Navigation: Furuno FR 2115; I-band.

Comment: GRP hull. Built by Rodman, Vigo and donated by the Spanish government in 2007. Employed on fishery protection duties and operated by the navy. Based on both coasts.

GP 404 ***6/2008*, Nicaraguan Navy*** / 1335289

4 INTERCEPTOR CRAFT (PBF)

Displacement, tons: To be announced
Dimensions, feet (metres): 44.0 × 9.0 × 3.0 *(13.4 × 2.75 × 0.9)*
Main machinery: 3 Yanmar diesels; 945 hp *(704 kW)*; Bravo X drives
Speed, knots: 60
Range, n miles: 600 at 25 kt
Complement: 6

Comment: Manufactured by Nor-Tech, Fort Myers, FL. Composite and glass-fibre hull with V-bottomed hull. Donated by the US Southern Command in 2007. Employed on counter drugs, arms trafficking and illegal immigration duties.

INTERCEPTOR CRAFT ***6/2007, US Southern Command*** / 1167968

19 ASSAULT AND RIVER CRAFT (PBF)

Comment: There are approximately 21 Colombian-built Eduardoño class 10 to 13 m assault craft, capable of 50 kt and 12 m 'Cigarette' craft capable of 45 kt. These are divided between the Atlantic and Pacific.
Sixteen Zodiac RIBs with 40 hp engines were donated by the US in mid-2006.

EDUARDOÑO CLASS ***6/2008*, Nicaraguan Navy*** / 1335287

CIGARETTE CLASS ***6/2008*, Nicaraguan Navy*** / 1335290

EDUARDOÑO CLASS ***6/2008*, Nicaraguan Navy*** / 1335291

Nigeria

Country Overview

Formerly a British protectorate, the Federal Republic of Nigeria gained full independence in 1960. With an area of 356,669 square miles, it is situated in western Africa and is bordered to the north by Niger, to the east by Chad and Cameroon and to the west by Benin. It has a 459 n mile coastline with the Gulf of Guinea. Abuja is the capital while Lagos (the capital until 1991) is the largest city, commercial centre and one of its principal ports. There are other ports at Port Harcourt, Warri, Calabar, Bonny, and Burutu. Territorial Seas (12 n miles) are claimed. An EEZ (200 n miles) has been claimed but the limits have not been defined.

The Navy has suffered from chronic lack of investment over the last ten years but there are signs that a refit programme is attempting to restore a core seagoing capability for operations within the Nigerian EEZ. However, the operational status of weapon systems and sensors remains doubtful.

Headquarters Appointments

Chief of the Naval Staff:
Vice Admiral Iko Ibrahim

Headquarters Appointments — *continued*

Flag Officer Western Command:
Rear Admiral Ola Sahad Ibrahim
Flag Officer Eastern Command:
Rear Admiral Igwe Ben Acholonu

Personnel

a) 2009: 8,000 (650 officers) including Coast Guard
b) Voluntary service

Bases

Apapa-Lagos: Western Naval Command; Naval Base Lagos (NNS *Onaku*), Naval College (NNS *Olokun*) and Naval Training (NNS *Quorra*).
Calabar: Eastern Naval Command; Naval Base Calabar (NNS *Anansu*), Naval Base Warri (NNS *Umalokun*) and Naval Base Port Harcourt (NNS *Okemini*). There is a forward operating base NNS *Pathfinder* at Bonny Island, Rivers State and plans for further bases at Egwuama, Bayelsa State and Forcados in Delta State. This is in addition to those already established at Ibaka, Akwa-Ibom State and Igbokada in Ondo State.

Naval Aviation

The official list includes two Lynx Mk 89, 12 MBB BO 105C, three Fokker F27 and 14 Dornier Do 128-6MPA. These aircraft are believed not to be operational. Four Agusta A 109E were procured from Italy in September 2004 for patrol duties, one of which was lost in April 2007.

Prefix to Ships' Names

NNS

Port Security Police

A separate force of 1,600 officers and men in Lagos.

Coastal Defence

There are plans to build a national coastal defence system although the status of the programme is unclear.

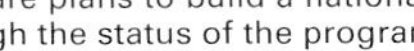

FRIGATES

1 MEKO TYPE 360 H1 (FFGHM)

Name	No	Builders	Laid down	Launched	Commissioned
ARADU (ex-*Republic*)	F 89	Blohm & Voss, Hamburg	1 Dec 1978	25 Jan 1980	20 Feb 1982

Displacement, tons: 3,360 full load
Dimensions, feet (metres): 412 × 49.2 × 19 (screws) (125.6 × 15 × 5.8)
Main machinery: CODOG; 2 RR Olympus TM3B gas turbines; 50,880 hp *(37.9 MW)* sustained; 2 MTU 20V 956 TB92 diesels; 10,420 hp(m) *(7.71 MW)* sustained; 2 shafts; 2 Kamewa cp props
Speed, knots: 30.5
Range, n miles: 6,500 at 15 kt
Complement: 195 (26 officers)

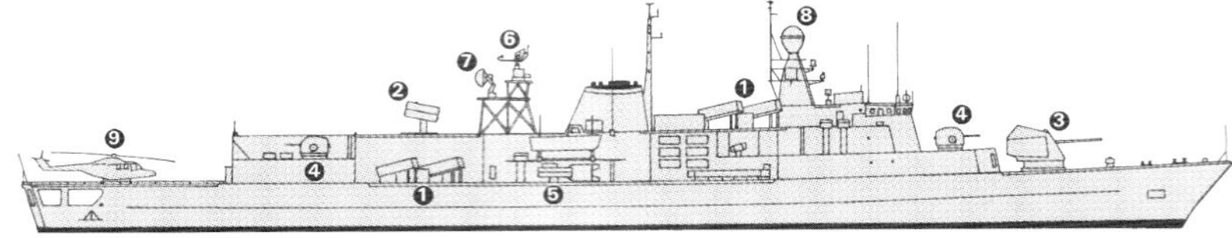

ARADU

(Scale 1 : 1,200), Ian Sturton / 0081331

Missiles: SSM: 8 OTO Melara/Matra Otomat Mk 1 ❶; active radar homing to 80 km *(43.2 n miles)* at 0.9 Mach; warhead 210 kg. SAM: Selenia Elsag Albatros octuple launcher ❷; 24 Aspide; semi-active radar homing to 13 km *(7 n miles)* at 2.5 Mach; warhead 30 kg.
Guns: 1 OTO Melara 5 in *(127 mm)*/54 ❸; 45 rds/min to 23 km *(12.4 n miles)*; weight of shell 32 kg.
8 Breda Bofors 40 mm/70 (4 twin) ❹; 300 rds/min to 12.5 km *(6.8 n miles)* anti-surface; weight of shell 0.96 kg.
Torpedoes: 6—324 mm Plessey STWS-1B (2 triple) tubes ❺. 18 Whitehead A244S; anti-submarine; active/passive homing to 7 km *(3.8 n miles)* at 33 kt; warhead 34 kg (shaped charge).
Depth charges: 1 rack.

Countermeasures: Decoys: 2 Breda 105 mm SCLAR 20-tubed trainable; chaff to 5 km *(2.7 n miles)*; illuminants to 12 km *(6.6 n miles)*. ESM: Decca RDL-2; intercept. ECM: RCM-2; jammer.
Combat data systems: Sewaco-BV action data automation.
Weapons control: M20 series GFCS. Signaal Vesta ASW.
Radars: Air/surface search: Plessey AWS 5 ❻; E/F-band.
Navigation: Racal Decca 1226; I-band.
Fire control: Signaal STIR ❼; I/J/K-band. Signaal WM 25 ❽; I/J-band.
Sonars: Atlas Elektronik EA80; hull-mounted; active search and attack; medium frequency.

Helicopters: 1 Lynx Mk 89 ❾.

Modernisation: Refit started at Wilmot Point, Lagos with Blohm & Voss assistance in 1991 and completed in February 1994.
Operational: Had two groundings and a major collision in 1987 and ran aground again during post refit trials in early 1994. Assessed as beyond economical repair in 1995 but managed to go to sea in early 1996, and again in 1997 when she broke down for several months in Monrovia. Back in Lagos on one engine in 1998 for further repairs. SSM system reported being refitted in 1999. Followinga refit at Lagos, attended Fleet Review at Portsmouth, UK, in June 2005 and participated in fleet exercises in January 2007.

ARADU

9/2007, Mario R V Carneiro / 1353243

CORVETTES

1 MK 9 VOSPER THORNYCROFT TYPE (FSM)

Name	No	Builders	Commissioned
ENYMIRI	F 84	Vosper Thornycroft	2 May 1980

Displacement, tons: 680 standard; 780 full load
Dimensions, feet (metres): 226 × 31.5 × 9.8 *(69 × 9.6 × 3)*
Main machinery: 4 MTU 20V 956 TB92 diesels; 22,140 hp(m) *(16.27 MW)* sustained; 2 shafts; 2 Kamewa cp props
Speed, knots: 27. **Range, n miles:** 2,200 at 14 kt
Complement: 90 (including Flag Officer)

Missiles: SAM: Short Brothers Seacat triple launcher.
Guns: 1 OTO Melara 3 in *(76 mm)*/62 Mod 6 compact; 85 rds/min to 16 km *(8.7 n miles)*; weight of shell 6 kg.
1 Breda Bofors 40 mm/70 Type 350; 300 rds/min to 12.5 km *(6.8 n miles)*; weight of shell 0.96 kg.
2 Oerlikon 20 mm.
A/S mortars: 1 Bofors 375 mm twin launcher; range 1,600 or 3,600 m.
Countermeasures: ESM: Decca Cutlass; radar warning.
Weapons control: Signaal WM20 series.
Radars: Air/surface search: Plessey AWS 2; E/F-band.
Navigation: Racal Decca TM 1226; I-band.
Fire control: Signaal WM24; I/J-band; range 46 km *(25 n miles)*.
Sonars: Plessey PMS 26; lightweight; hull-mounted; active search and attack; 10 kHz.

Programmes: Ordered from Vosper Thornycroft 22 April 1975.
Operational: *Enymiri* was damaged by fire in 2005 but had returned to service by early 2007 when it took part in fleet exercises. Sister ship *Erinomi* assessed as beyond economical repair in 1996.

ENYMIRI

5/1999 / 0081333

PATROL FORCES

Notes: (1) All the Coastal Patrol Craft belong to the Coast Guard. Some 38 craft were acquired in the mid-1980s from various shipbuilders including Simonneau, Damen, Swiftships, Intermarine, Watercraft, Van Mill and Rotork. Few of these vessels have been reported at sea in recent years although some are visible, laid up ashore, and are still serviceable.
(2) A Damen 2600 Mk II patrol craft was acquired from South Africa in 2001.
(3) Four 8 m Night Cat 27, capable of 70 kt, were delivered by Intercept Boats in 2003–04.
(4) Several 20 m VCSM craft were acquired from Raidco Marine in 2008.

P 236 (Simonneau)

5/2002 / 0528302

VCSM craft

8/2008, B Prézelin* / 1353244

3 EKPE (LÜRSSEN 57) CLASS (LARGE PATROL CRAFT) (PGF)

Name	*No*	*Builders*	*Commissioned*
EKPE	P 178	Lürssen, Vegesack	Aug 1980
DAMISA	P 179	Lürssen, Vegesack	Apr 1981
AGU	P 180	Lürssen, Vegesack	Apr 1981

Displacement, tons: 444 full load
Dimensions, feet (metres): 190.6 × 24.9 × 10.2 *(58.1 × 7.6 × 3.1)*
Main machinery: 4 MTU 16V 956TB92 diesels; 17,700 hp(m) *(13 MW)* sustained; 2 shafts
Speed, knots: 42
Range, n miles: 2,000 at 10 kt
Complement: 40
Guns: 1 OTO Melara 3 in *(76 mm)*/62; 60 rds/min to 16 km *(8.7 n miles)*; weight of shell 6 kg.
2 Breda 40 mm/70 (twin); 4 Emerson Electric 30 mm (2 twin).
Radars: Surface search: Racal Decca TM 1226; I-band.
Fire control: Signaal WM28; I/J-band.

Programmes: Ordered in 1977. Major refit in 1984 at Vegesack.
Operational: P 178 refitted at Lagos in 1995 but broke down en route to Sierra Leone in 1997. P 179 believed to be operational but the operational status of the other two is doubtful.

EKPE *3/1998* / 0052656

4 BALSAM CLASS (PBO)

Name	*No*	*Builders*	*Commissioned*
KYANWA (ex-*Sedge*)	A 501 (ex-WLB 402)	Marine Iron and Shipbuilding Corp, Duluth, Minnesota	5 July 1944
OLOGBO (ex-*Cowslip*)	A 502 (ex-WLB 277)	Marine Iron and Shipbuilding Corp, Duluth, Minnesota	17 Oct 1942
NWAMBA (ex-*Firebush*)	A 503 (ex-WLB 393)	Marine Iron and Shipbuilding Corp, Duluth, Minnesota	20 July 1944
OBULA (ex-*Sassafras*)	A 504 (ex-WLB 401)	Marine Iron and Shipbuilding Corp, Duluth, Minnesota	23 May 1944

Displacement, tons: 1,034 full load
Dimensions, feet (metres): 180 × 37 × 12 *(54.9 × 11.3 × 3.8)*
Main machinery: Diesel electric; 2 diesels; 1,402 hp *(1.06 MW)*; 1 motor; 1,200 hp *(895 kW)*; 1 shaft; bow thruster
Speed, knots: 13
Range, n miles: 8,000 at 12 kt
Complement: 53
Guns: 2 — 12.7 mm MGs.
Radars: Navigation: Raytheon SPS-64(V)1.

Comment: First ship transferred from the US Coast Guard on 30 September 2002, second on 30 December 2002, third on 30 June 2003 and fourth on 30 October 2003. Transfer of a fifth vessel is unlikely.

NWAMBA *6/2008** / 1353245

15 DEFENDER CLASS (RESPONSE BOATS) (PBF)

P 313–327

Displacement, tons: 2.7 full load
Dimensions, feet (metres): 25.0 × 8.5 × 8.8 *(7.6 × 2.6 × 2.7)*
Main machinery: 2 Honda outboard motors; 450 hp *(335 kW)*
Speed, knots: 46
Range, n miles: 175 at 35 kt
Complement: 4
Guns: 1 — 12.7 mm MG.
Radars: To be announced.

Comment: High-speed inshore patrol craft of aluminium construction and foam collar built by SAFE Boats International, Port Orchard, Washington. An initial order for ten craft, with an option for five further craft, placed in August 2004 through USCG Foreign Military Sales programme. First four delivered on 13 December 2004 and second batch of four on 9 February 2005. Two were delivered in May 2005 and the final five on 5 July 2005.

DEFENDER CLASS *2/2005, SAFE Boats International* / 0590666

3 COMBATTANTE IIIB CLASS (FAST ATTACK CRAFT — MISSILE) (PGGF)

Name	*No*	*Builders*	*Commissioned*
SIRI	P 181	CMN, Cherbourg	19 Feb 1981
AYAM	P 182	CMN, Cherbourg	11 June 1981
EKUN	P 183	CMN, Cherbourg	18 Sep 1981

Displacement, tons: 385 standard; 430 full load
Dimensions, feet (metres): 184 × 24.9 × 7 *(56.2 × 7.6 × 2.1)*
Main machinery: 4 MTU 16V 956TB92 diesels; 17,700 hp(m) *(13 MW)* sustained; 2 shafts
Speed, knots: 38
Range, n miles: 2,000 at 15 kt
Complement: 42

Missiles: SSM: 4 Aerospatiale MM 38 Exocet; inertial cruise; active radar homing to 42 km *(23 n miles)* at 0.9 Mach; warhead 165 kg; sea-skimmer.
Guns: 1 OTO Melara 3 in *(76 mm)*/62; 60 rds/min to 16 km *(8.7 n miles)*; weight of shell 6 kg.
2 Breda 40 mm/70 (twin); 300 rds/min to 12.5 km *(6.8 n miles)*; weight of shell 0.96 kg.
4 Emerson Electric 30 mm (2 twin); 1,200 rds/min combined to 6 km *(3.3 n miles)*; weight of shell 0.35 kg.
Countermeasures: ESM: Decca RDL; radar intercept.
Weapons control: Thomson-CSF Vega system. 2 CSEE Panda optical directors.
Radars: Air/surface search: Thomson-CSF Triton (TRS 3033); G-band.
Navigation: Racal Decca TM 1226; I-band. Fire control: Thomson-CSF Castor II (TRS 3203); I/J-band.

Programmes: Ordered in late 1977. Finally handed over in February 1982 after delays caused by financial problems.
Modernisation: Major refit and repairs carried out at Cherbourg from March to December 1991 but the ships were delayed by financial problems.
Operational: *Ayam* believed to be operational and sister ships *Siri* and *Ekun* are reported to be seagoing.

AYAM (outboard DAMISA) *5/2002* / 0528300

AMPHIBIOUS FORCES

1 FDR TYPE RO-RO 1300 (LST)

Name	*No*	*Builders*	*Commissioned*
AMBE	LST 1312	Howaldtswerke, Hamburg	11 May 1979

Displacement, tons: 1,470 standard; 1,860 full load
Dimensions, feet (metres): 285.4 × 45.9 × 7.5 *(87 × 14 × 2.3)*
Main machinery: 2 MTU 16V 956TB92 diesels; 8,850 hp(m) *(6.5 MW)* sustained; 2 shafts
Speed, knots: 17
Range, n miles: 5,000 at 10 kt
Complement: 56 (6 officers)
Military lift: 460 tons and 220 troops long haul; 540 troops or 1,000 troops seated short haul; can carry 5 — 40 ton tanks
Guns: 1 Breda 40 mm/70. 2 Oerlikon 20 mm.
Radars: Navigation: Racal Decca 1226; I-band.

Comment: Ordered September 1976. Built to a design prepared for the FGN. Has 19 m bow ramps and a 4 m stern ramp. Reported that bow ramps are welded shut. Second of class, *Offiom*, beyond repair but *Ambe* reported active in 2007.

AMBE *7/1997* / 0012836

MINE WARFARE FORCES

2 LERICI CLASS (MINEHUNTERS/SWEEPERS) (MHSC)

Name	*No*	*Builders*	*Commissioned*
OHUE	M 371	Intermarine SY, Italy	28 May 1987
BARAMA	M 372	Intermarine SY, Italy	25 Feb 1988

Displacement, tons: 540 full load
Dimensions, feet (metres): 167.3 × 32.5 × 9.2 *(51 × 9.9 × 2.8)*
Main machinery: 2 MTU 12V 396 TB83 diesels; 3,120 hp(m) *(2.3 MW)* sustained; 2 waterjets
Speed, knots: 15.5
Range, n miles: 2,500 at 12 kt
Complement: 50 (5 officers)
Guns: 2 Emerson Electric 30 mm (twin); 1,200 rds/min combined to 6 km *(3.3 n miles)*; weight of shell 0.35 kg.
2 Oerlikon 20 mm GAM-BO1.
Countermeasures: MCM: Fitted with 2 Pluto remote-controlled submersibles, Oropesa 'O' Mis 4 and Ibis V control system.
Radars: Navigation: Racal Decca 1226; I-band.
Sonars: Thomson Sintra TSM 2022; hull-mounted; mine detection; high frequency.

Comment: *Ohue* ordered in April 1983 and *Barama* in January 1986. *Ohue* laid down 23 July 1984 and launched 22 November 1985, *Barama* laid down 11 March 1985, launched 6 June 1986. GRP hulls but, unlike Italian and Malaysian versions they do not have separate hydraulic minehunting propulsion. Carry Galeazzi two-man decompression chambers. Both were refitted in 1999, after operations off Liberia. *Barama* reported refitted in late 2004 but the operational effectiveness of both ships in their MCM role is doubtful.

OHUE *7/1987, Marina Fraccaroli* / 0506063

SURVEY SHIPS

1 SURVEY SHIP (AGS)

Name	*No*	*Builders*	*Launched*	*Commissioned*
LANA	A 498	Brooke Marine, Lowestoft	4 Mar 1976	18 July 1976

Displacement, tons: 1,088 full load
Dimensions, feet (metres): 189 × 37.5 × 12 *(57.8 × 11.4 × 3.7)*
Main machinery: 2 Lister Blackstone diesels; 2,640 hp *(1.97 MW)*; 2 shafts
Speed, knots: 16
Range, n miles: 4,500 at 12 kt
Complement: 52 (12 officers)
Radars: Navigation: Decca; I-band.

Comment: Similar to UK Bulldog class. Ordered in 1973. Rarely goes to sea.

LANA *5/1999* / 0081334

TUGS

3 COASTAL TUGS (YTB/YTL)

COMMANDER APAYI JOE A 499 **DOLPHIN MIRA** **DOLPHIN RIMA**

Comment: A 499 is of 310 tons and was built in 1983. The two Dolphin tugs are under repair.

COMMANDER APAYI JOE *11/1983, Hartmut Ehlers* / 0506064

Norway

Country Overview

The Kingdom of Norway is a constitutional monarchy occupying the northwest part of the Scandinavian Peninsula. With an area of 125,016 square miles, it is bordered to the east by Sweden and to the northeast by Finland and Russia. The coastline of 11,842 n miles with the Atlantic Ocean (Norwegian Sea), Arctic Ocean (Barents Sea), North Sea and Skagerrak Strait contains numerous fjords and offshore islands. External territories in the Arctic Ocean include the Svalbard archipelago and Jan Mayen Island while the uninhabited Bouvet Island lies in the south Atlantic. Territorial claims in Antarctica include the territory known as Queen Maud Land and Peter I Island. The capital, largest city and principal port is Oslo. Other ports include Bergen, Trondheim and Stavanger. Territorial seas (12 n miles) and an EEZ (200 n miles) are claimed.

Headquarters Appointments

Chief of Naval Staff:
Rear Admiral H Bruun-Hanssen
Deputy Chief of Naval Staff:
Commodore Commodore Lars Johan Fleisje
Commander Coast Guard:
Commodore A I Skram
Commander Norwegian Fleet:
Commodore H Tronstad

Diplomatic Representation

Defence Attaché in Ankara:
Captain Helge Moen

Diplomatic Representation — *continued*

Defence Attaché in Helsinki:
Captain Ernst Egelid
Defence Attaché in London:
Colonel K H Hamre
Defence Attaché in Madrid:
Captain Jan Krohn-Hansen
Defence Attaché in Moscow:
Commodore Geir A M Osen
Defence Attaché in Paris:
Captain Per Norvald Svartefoss
Defence Attaché in Stockholm:
Colonel K O Drivenes
Defence Attaché in Washington:
Major General T H Knutsen
Defence Attaché in Warsaw:
Lieutenant Colonel T Larsen Bergheim
Defence Attaché in Berlin:
Colonel Iver Tokstad
Defence Attaché in Riga:
Colonel Svein Ruderaas
Defence Attaché in Rome:
Captain G Myrseth
Defence Attaché in Kiev:
Colonel Tommy Johansen
Defence Attaché in Bucharest:
Colonel T Lysentøen
Defence Attaché in The Hague:
Commander T Andersson
Defence Attaché in Belgrade:
Lieutenant Colonel T Haaverstad

Personnel

(a) 2009: 3,200 officers and ratings
(b) 9 to 12 months' national service (up to 40 per cent of ships complement)

Coast Artillery

The fixed defence system of nine coastal forts and controlled minefields is in long-term storage. As a result, the Coastal Ranger Command was established in 2001 with a headquarters at Trondenes.

Coast Guard

Founded April 1977 with operational command held by Norwegian Defence Command. Main bases at Sortland (North) and Haakonsvern (South). Tasks include fishery protection, customs, police, SAR and environmental duties at sea.

Bases

Reitan (Bodø): National Operational HQ (from 8/2009)
Haakonsvern (Bergen): Main Naval Base
Laksevaag (Bergen): Submarine Repair
Ramsund: Supply, repair and maintenance
Sortland: Coast Guard Base.

Air Force Squadrons (see *Shipborne* and *Land-based Aircraft*)

Aircraft (Squadron)	*Location*	*Duties*
Sea King Mk 43 (330)	Bodø, Banak, Sola, Ørland	SAR
Orion P-3N/C (333)	Andøya	MPA
Lynx (337)	Coast Guard vessels/ Bardufoss	MP
Bell 412 (719, 339 & 720)	Bodø, Rygge, Bardufoss	Army Transport

Prefix to Ships' Names

KNM (Naval)
K/V (Coast Guard)

Strength of the Fleet

Type	*Active*	*Building (Projected)*
Submarines—Coastal	6	–
Frigates	3	2
Patrol craft	23	5
Minesweepers/Hunters	6	–
Auxiliaries	1	–
Naval District Auxiliaries	8	–
Coast Guard Vessels	13	2 (5)
Survey Vessels	6	–

DELETIONS

Frigates

2006 *Trondheim*
2007 *Narvik*

Patrol Forces

2007 *Hauk, Ørn, Skarv, Teist, Lom, Falk, Gribb, Erle*
2008 *Terne, Tjeld, Jo, Stegg, Ravn, Geir*

Auxiliaries

2008 *Horten*

PENNANT LIST

Notes: Naval District Auxiliaries are listed on page 573.

Submarines

S 300 Ula
S 301 Utsira
S 302 Utstein
S 303 Utvaer
S 304 Uthaug
S 305 Uredd

Frigates

F 310 Fridtjof Nansen
F 311 Roald Amundsen
F 312 Otto Sverdrup
F 313 Helge Ingstad (bldg)
F 314 Thor Heyerdahl (bldg)

Minesweepers/Hunters

M 341 Karmøy
M 342 Måløy
M 343 Hinnøy
M 350 Alta
M 351 Otra
M 352 Rauma

Minelayers

N 50 Tyr

Patrol Forces

P 358 Hessa
P 359 Vigra
P 960 Skjold
P 961 Storm
P 962 Skudd
P 963 Steil
P 964 Glimt
P 965 Gnist

Auxiliaries

A 533 Norge
A 535 Valkyrien

Coast Guard

W 303 Svalbard
W 312 Ålesund
W 314 Stålbas
W 318 Harstad
W 319 Leikven
W 320 Nordkapp
W 321 Senja
W 322 Andenes
W 330 Nornen
W 331 Farm
W 332 Heimdal
W 333 Njord
W 334 Tor
W 340 Barentshav
W 341 Sortland
W 342 Bergen

SUBMARINES

Notes: Norway withdrew from the 'Viking' submarine project on 13 June 2003 at the end of the Project Definition Phase Step 1. Studies into the replacement of the current submarine capability from about 2020 were launched in late 2007. Following initial conceptual work, a more detailed project definition study is expected to start in 2009.

6 ULA CLASS (SSK)

Name	*No*	*Builders*	*Laid down*	*Launched*	*Commissioned*
ULA	S 300	Thyssen Nordseewerke, Emden	29 Jan 1987	28 July 1988	27 Apr 1989
UREDD	S 305	Thyssen Nordseewerke, Emden	23 June 1988	22 Sep 1989	3 May 1990
UTVAER	S 303	Thyssen Nordseewerke, Emden	8 Dec 1988	19 Apr 1990	8 Nov 1990
UTHAUG	S 304	Thyssen Nordseewerke, Emden	15 June 1989	18 Oct 1990	7 May 1991
UTSTEIN	S 302	Thyssen Nordseewerke, Emden	6 Dec 1989	25 Apr 1991	14 Nov 1991
UTSIRA	S 301	Thyssen Nordseewerke, Emden	15 June 1990	21 Nov 1991	30 Apr 1992

Displacement, tons: 1,040 surfaced; 1,150 dived
Dimensions, feet (metres): 193.6 × 17.7 × 15.1 *(59 × 5.4 × 4.6)*
Main machinery: Diesel-electric; 2 MTU 16V 396 SB83 diesels; 2,700 hp(m) *(1.98 MW)* sustained; 1 Siemens motor; 6,000 hp(m) *(4.41 MW)*; 1 shaft
Speed, knots: 11 surfaced; 23 dived
Range, n miles: 5,000 at 8 kt
Complement: 21 (5 officers)

Torpedoes: 8—21 in *(533 mm)* bow tubes. 14 AEG DM 2A3 Sehecht; dual purpose; wire-guided; active/passive homing to 28 km *(15 n miles)* at 23 kt; 13 km *(7 n miles)* at 35 kt; warhead 260 kg; depth to 460 m.
Countermeasures: ESM: Argo S 5; radar warning.
Weapons control: Kongsberg MSI-90(U) TFCS.
Radars: Surface search: Kelvin Hughes 1007; I-band.
Sonars: Atlas Elektronik CSU 83; active/passive intercept search and attack; medium frequency.
Thomson Sintra; flank array; passive; low frequency.

Programmes: Contract signed on 30 September 1982. This was a joint West German/Norwegian effort known as Project 210 in Germany. Although final assembly was at Thyssen a number of pressure hull sections were provided by Norway.
Modernisation: MSI-90U being upgraded 2000–2005. A mid-life upgrade of all six boats is in progress 2007–15. The programme includes updates to the sonar and communications systems and a number of platform improvements.
Structure: Diving depth, 250 m *(820 ft)*. The basic command and weapon control systems are Norwegian, the attack sonar is German but the flank array, based on piezoelectric polymer antenna technology, was developed in France and substantially reduces flow noise. Calzoni Trident modular system of non-penetrating masts has been installed. Zeiss periscopes.

UTHAUG *5/2007, Harald Carstens* / 1166610

UTHAUG *5/2007, Jurg Kürsener* / 1166611

FRIGATES

3 + 2 FRIDTJOF NANSEN CLASS (FFGHM)

Name	*No*	*Builders*	*Laid down*	*Launched*	*Commissioned*
FRIDTJOF NANSEN	F 310	Navantia, Ferrol	9 Apr 2003	3 June 2004	5 Apr 2006
ROALD AMUNDSEN	F 311	Navantia, Ferrol	3 June 2004	25 May 2005	21 May 2007
OTTO SVERDRUP	F 312	Navantia, Ferrol	25 May 2005	28 Apr 2006	30 Apr 2008
HELGE INGSTAD	F 313	Navantia, Ferrol	28 Apr 2006	23 Nov 2007	2009
THOR HEYERDAHL	F 314	Navantia, Ferrol	23 Nov 2007	11 Feb 2009	2010

Displacement, tons: 5,290 full load
Dimensions, feet (metres): 437.0 × 55.1 × 16.1 *(133.2 × 16.8 × 4.9)*
Main machinery: CODAG; 1 GE LM 2500 gas turbine; 26,112 hp *(19.2 MW)*; 2 Bazán Bravo 12V diesels; 12,240 hp(m) *(9 MW)*; 2 shafts; cp props; bow thruster; 1,360 hp(m) *(1 MW)*
Speed, knots: 26
Range, n miles: 4,500 at 16 kt
Complement: 120 (50 officers) plus 26 spare

Missiles: SSM: 8 Kongsberg NSM ❶; inertial, GPS and terrain mapping guidance and passive IR homing to 185 km *(100 n miles)* at 0.95 Mach; warhead 120 kg.
SAM: Mk 41 VLS (8 cells) ❷; 32 Evolved Sea Sparrow RIM 162B; semi-active radar homing to 18 km *(9.7 n miles)* at 3.6 Mach; warhead 38 kg.
Guns: 1 Oto Melara 76 mm/62 Super Rapid ❸. 120 rds/min to 15.75 km *(8.5 n miles)* anti-surface; 12 km *(6.5 n miles)* anti-aircraft; weight of shell 6 kg.
4—12.7 mm MGs. Fitted for 1—40 mm/70.
Torpedoes: 4—324 mm (2 double) tubes ❹. Marconi Stingray; active/passive homing to 11 km *(5.9 n miles)* at 45 kt; warhead 35 kg shaped charge.
Countermeasures: Decoys: Terma SKWS chaff, IR. LOKI 130 mm acoustic decoy.
ESM: Condor CS-3701; intercept ❺.
Combat data systems: AEGIS with ASW and ASuW segments from Kongsberg; Link 11 (fitted for Link 16/22).

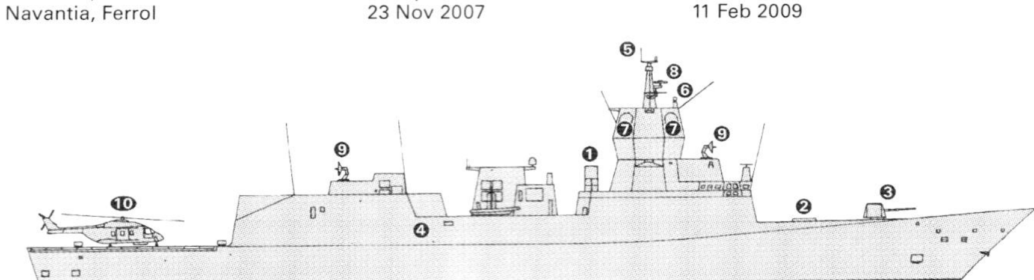

FRIDTJOF NANSEN *(Scale 1 : 1,200), Ian Sturton* / 1190985

Weapons control: Sagem VIGY 20 optronic director ❻.
Radars: Air search: Lockheed Martin SPY-1F ❼; E/F-band.
Surface search: Litton; E/I-band ❽.
Fire control: 2 Mk 82 (SPG-62); I/J-band ❾.
Navigation: 2 Litton; I-band. IFF: Mk XII.
Sonars: Thomson Marconi Spherion MRS 2000 and Mk 2 CAPTAS; combined active/passive towed array.

Helicopters: 1 NH 90 ❿.

Programmes: Design Definition for a new class of frigates started in March 1997. Izar and Lockheed Martin selected in March 2000 and contract signed 23 June 2000. Most of the construction is being undertaken by Navantia (formerly Izar). Two Norwegian shipyards, Bergen Makaniske Verksted and Aker Yards, Florø,are collaborating to build modules for each ship. These are shipped to Ferrol where final assembly takes place. The building programme has been delayed by disputes over quality control and contractual arrangements. Planned commissioning dates could be affected.
Modernisation: Stingray torpedoes are to be upgraded or replaced in due course.
Structure: The design is based on the Alvaro de Bazan class. Damage control is automated through the Integrated Platform Management System.
Operational: *Fridtjof Nansen* successfully conducted Combat Systems Ship Qualification Trials with the US Navy in mid-2007.

ROALD AMUNDSEN *5/2008*, Michael Nitz* / 1335809

FRIDTJOF NANSEN *4/2008*, Derek Fox* / 1335797

FRIDTJOF NANSEN *4/2006, Ships of the World* / 1159236

FRIDTJOF NANSEN *6/2008*, Royal Norwegian Navy* / 1335802

SHIPBORNE AIRCRAFT

Numbers/Type: 14 NH Industries NH 90 NFH.
Operational speed: 157 kt *(291 km/h).*
Service ceiling: 13,940 ft *(4,250 m).*
Range: 621 n miles *(1,150 km).*
Role/Weapon systems: Delivery of 14 aircraft, reconfigurable for ASW and Coast Guard missions, is to begin in 2010. Flight of the first aircraft took place on 20 December 2006. Option for further ten SAR aircraft. Sensors: Thales ENR surveillance radar, TUS FLASH dipping sonar. Weapons: NSM missiles, Stingray (to be upgraded or replaced) torpedoes.

NH 90 *6/2008*, Norwegian Navy* / 1335801

Numbers/Type: 6 Westland Lynx Mk 86.
Operational speed: 125 kt *(232 km/h).*
Service ceiling: 12,500 ft *(3,810 m).*
Range: 320 n miles *(590 km).*
Role/Weapon systems: Operated by Air Force on behalf of the Coast Guard for fishery protection, offshore oil protection and SAR; embarked in CG vessels and shore-based. To be replaced by NH 90 from 2010. Sensors: Search radar, FLIR may be fitted, ESM. Weapons: Generally unarmed.

LYNX *6/2002, Royal Norwegian Navy* / 0572608

LAND-BASED MARITIME AIRCRAFT

Notes: The Air Force has a total of 56 F-16 Falcons armed with Penguin 3 ASMs.

Numbers/Type: 4 Lockheed P-3C Orion.
Operational speed: 410 kt *(760 km/h).*
Service ceiling: 28,300 ft *(8,625 m).*
Range: 4,000 n miles *(7,410 km).*
Role/Weapon systems: Long-range MR and oceanic surveillance duties in peacetime, with ASW added as a war role. Updated in 1998–99 with new radars and new tactical computers. P-3Ns used by Coast Guard paid off in 1999. Sensors: APS-137(V)5 radar, ASQ-81 MAD, AQS-212 processor and computer, IFF, AAR-36 IR detection; AAR-47 ESM; ALE 47 countermeasures; sonobuoys. Weapons: ASW; 8 MUSL Stingray (to be upgraded or replaced) torpedoes, depth bombs or mines. ASV; Penguin NFT Mk 3 ASM.

P-3C *6/2001, A Sharma* / 0130100

Numbers/Type: 12 Westland Sea King Mk 43B.
Operational speed: 125 kt *(232 km/h).*
Service ceiling: 10,500 ft *(3,200 m).*
Range: 630 n miles *(1,165 km).*
Role/Weapon systems: SAR, surface search and surveillance helicopter; supplemented by civil helicopters in wartime. Two 43B delivered in May 1996; remainder updated to 43B standard. Sensors: FLIR 2000 and dual Bendix radars RDR 1500 and RDR 1300. Weapons: Generally unarmed.

SEA KING 43B *2001, GKN Westland* / 0051448

PATROL FORCES

Notes: There is an inshore patrol craft *Kaholmen* SHV 121 delivered in about 2005.

1 + 5 SKJOLD CLASS (PTGMF)

Name	*No*	*Builders*	*Launched*	*Commissioned*
SKJOLD	P 960	Kvaerner Mandal	22 Sep 1998	17 Apr 1999
STORM	P 961	Umoe Mandal	30 Oct 2006	2009
SKUDD	P 962	Umoe Mandal	30 Apr 2007	2009
STEIL	P 963	Umoe Mandal	15 Jan 2008	2009
GLIMT	P 964	Umoe Mandal	2008	2010
GNIST	P 965	Umoe Mandal	2008	2010

Displacement, tons: 273 full load
Dimensions, feet (metres): 155.8 × 44.3 × 7.5; 2.6 on cushion *(47.5 × 13.5 × 2.3; 0.8)*
Main machinery: CODAG: 2 Pratt & Whitney gas turbines; 16,100 hp *(12 MW)*
2 MTU 12V 183TE92 diesels (lift); 990 hp *(740 kW)*; 2 Kamewa waterjets
Speed, knots: 60; 40 in Sea State 3
Range, n miles: 800 at 40 kt
Complement: 20
Missiles: 8 SSM; 8 Kongsberg NSM inertial, GPS and terrain matching guidance and passive IR homing to 185 km *(100 n miles)* at 0.95 Mach; warhead 120 kg.
SAM: Mistral; IR homing to 4 km *(2.2 n miles)* at 2.5 Mach; warhead 3 kg.
Guns: 1 Oto Melara 76 mm/62. Super Rapid; 120 rds/min to 16 km *(8.7 n miles)*; weight of shell 6 kg. 2—12.7 mm MGs.
Countermeasures: 1 Rheinmetall MASS-1L.
ESM: EDO CS 370; intercept.
Combat data systems: DCN Senit 2000; Link 11/16.
Weapons control: Sagem VIGX-20 optronic director.
Radars: Air/surface search: Thales MRR; 3D-NG; G-band.
Navigation: I-band.
Fire control: CelsiusTech Ceros 200; J-band.

Programmes: Project SMP 6081. A preproduction version (P 960) ordered 30 August 1996. This was tested by the Norwegian Navy from 1999–2001 and was evaluated by the USN and USCG in 2001–02. The Norwegian parliament decided on 23 October 2003 that five additional vessels were to be built. Contract with Skjold Prime Consortium, comprising Umoe Mandal, Armaris and Kongsberg Defence & Aerospace, was signed 28 November 2003. Ships are being built at Umoe Mandal shipyard for delivery by 2009. P 960 is to be used for crew training and is to be upgraded to production standard after the other five vessels have been delivered.
Structure: SES hull with advanced stealth technology including anechoic coatings. Building on experience in US trials, a more raked bow has been adopted to improve performance into sea. The foredeck structure is also to be strengthened around the gun mounting. Two quadruple SSM launchers are to be recessed aft of the bridge. These will elevate to fire and then retract.

STORM *6/2008*, Royal Norwegian Navy* / 1335800

STORM *6/2008*, Royal Norwegian Navy* / 1335799

20 COMBATBOAT 90N (LCP)

TRONDENES L 4510 (ex-KA 1)
HYSNES L 4511 (ex-KA 2)
HELLEN L 4512 (ex-KA 3)
TORÅS L 4513 (ex-KA 4)
MØVIK L 4514 (ex-KA 5)
SKROLSVIK L 4520 (ex-KA 11)
KRÅKENES L 4521 (ex-KA 12)
STANGNES L 4522 (ex-KA 13)
KJØKØY L 4523 (ex-KA 14)
MØRVIKA L 4524 (ex-KA 15)
KOPÅS L 4525 (ex-KA 16)
TANGEN L 4526 (ex-KA 17)
ODDANE L 4527 (ex-KA 18)
MALMØYA L 4528 (ex-KA 19)
BRETTINGEN L 4529 (ex-KA 21)
LØKHAUG L 4530 (ex-KA 22)
SØVIKNES L 4531 (ex-KA 23)
OSTERNES L 4532 (ex-KA 31)
FJELL L 4533 (ex-KA 32)
LERØY L 4534 (ex-KA 33)

Displacement, tons: 19 full load
Dimensions, feet (metres): 52.2 × 12.5 × 2.6 *(15.9 × 3.8 × 0.8)*
Main machinery: 2 SAAB Scania DSI 14 diesels; 1,104 hp(m) *(812 kW)* or 1,251 hp(m) *(920 kW)* (KA 21-43) sustained; 2 FF 450 water-jets or 2 Kamewa FF 410 (KA 21-43)
Speed, knots: 35 or 40; 20 in Sea State 3
Range, n miles: 240 at 20 kt
Complement: 3
Military lift: 2.8 tons or 20 troops
Guns: 1 — 12.7 mm MG.
Radars: Navigation: I-band.

Comment: Ordered from Dockstavarvet, Sweden. Four Batch 1 units delivered for trials in July and October 1996. Three more of the class delivered in 1997, 13 in 1998. Used to carry mobile light missile units and prime method of transportation for new Coastal Ranger Commando. Similar in most details to the Swedish Coastal Artillery craft. Names are mostly taken from Coastal Fortresses. Evaluation of these craft as a launch platform for the Hellfire missile took place on *Mørvika* in May 2004. Pennant numbers were changed in 2004.

KJØKØY *6/2008*, Royal Norwegian Navy* / 1335798

7 ALUSAFE 1290 CLASS (INSHORE PATROL CRAFT) (PB)

L 4540–L 4546

Displacement, tons: 7.6
Dimensions, feet (metres): 43.2 × 11.5 × 2.5 *(12.9 × 3.5 × 0.75)*
Main machinery: 2 Volvo Penta TAMD 74 EDC diesels; 900 hp *(670 kW)*; 2 Kamewa K28 waterjets
Speed, knots: 42
Complement: 2 (plus 13 troops)
Guns: 2 — 12.7 mm MGs.

Comment: Aluminium hull. Built by Maritime Partner, Ålesund and delivered in 2002. Designed for used by the Norwegian Naval Home Guard as multifunction assault and patrol vessels by the coastal rangers. The craft are also available as tactical logistics craft and to support police, customs, environmental and fishery authorities.

L 4540 *6/2008*, Richard Scott* / 1335808

4 HÅREK (ALUSAFE 1300) CLASS (INSHORE PATROL CRAFT) (PB)

HÅREK SHV 101
KVITSØY SHV 104
SLOTTERØY SHV 105
HALTEN SHV 106

Displacement, tons: 10
Dimensions, feet (metres): 43.6 × 12.0 × 2.5 *(13.3 × 3.65 × 0.75)*
Main machinery: 2 Volvo Penta TAMD 74EDC diesels; 900 hp *(670 kW)*; 2 Kamewa K28 waterjets
Speed, knots: 40
Complement: 2 (plus 13 troops)
Guns: 2 — 12.7 mm MGs.

Comment: Aluminium hull. Built by Maritime Partner, Ålesund and delivered in 2003. Based at Stavanger, Bergen and Trondheim. Designed for use by the Norwegian Naval Home Guard as multifunction patrol vessels. The craft are also available to support police, customs, environmental and fishery authorities.

KVITSØY *6/2008*, Richard Scott* / 1335807

2 GYDA CLASS (INSHORE PATROL CRAFT) (PB)

HVASSER SHV 102
HEKKINGEN SHV 103

Displacement, tons: 14 full load
Dimensions, feet (metres): 44.8 × 13.4 × 2.9 *(13.65 × 4.1 × 0.9)*
Main machinery: 2 Volvo Penta TAMD 74 EDC diesels; 1,750 hp *(1.3 MW)*; 2 Kamewa K32 waterjets
Speed, knots: 42
Complement: 2 (plus 13 troops)
Guns: 2 — 12.7 mm MGs.

Comment: Aluminium hull. Built by Henriksen Mekaniske Verksted, Tøsnsberg and delivered in 2003. Designed for use by the Norwegian Naval Home Guard as patrol vessels.

HVASSER *6/2006, E & M Laursen* / 1040662

MINE WARFARE FORCES

6 OKSØY/ALTA CLASS (MINEHUNTERS/SWEEPERS) (MHCM/MSCM)

Name	*No*	*Builders*	*Commissioned*
Hunters			
KARMØY	M 341	Kvaerner Mandal	24 Oct 1994
MÅLØY	M 342	Kvaerner Mandal	24 Mar 1995
HINNØY	M 343	Kvaerner Mandal	8 Sep 1995
Sweepers			
ALTA	M 350	Kvaerner Mandal	12 Jan 1996
OTRA	M 351	Kvaerner Mandal	8 Nov 1996
RAUMA	M 352	Kvaerner Mandal	2 Dec 1996

Displacement, tons: 375 full load
Dimensions, feet (metres): 181.1 × 44.6 × 8.2 (2.76 cushion) *(55.2 × 13.6 × 2.5; 0.84)*
Main machinery: 2 MTU 12V 396 TE84 diesels; 3,700 hp(m) *(2.72 MW)* sustained; 2 Kvaerner Eureka water-jets; 2 MTU 8V 396TE54 diesels; 1,740 hp(m) *(1.28 MW/60 Hz)* sustained; lift engines
Speed, knots: 23
Range, n miles: 1,500 at 20 kt
Complement: 40 (14 officers) (minehunters); 32 (10 officers) (minesweepers)

Missiles: SAM: Matra Sadral twin launcher; Mistral; IR homing to 4 km *(2.2 n miles)*; warhead 3 kg.
Guns: 1 or 2 Rheinmetall 20 mm. 3—12.7 mm MGs.
Countermeasures: MCMV: 2 Pluto submersibles (minehunter); mechanical, AGATE (air gun and transducer equipment) acoustic and Elma magnetic sweep (minesweepers). Minesweeper mini torpedoes can be carried.
Radars: Navigation: 2 Racal Decca; I-band.
Sonars: Thales TSM 2022 Mk 3; hull mounted; high frequency.

Programmes: Order placed with Kvaerner on 9 November 1989.
Modernisation: Both minehunters and minesweepers are being upgraded with new sonars (TSM 2022), new tactical C2 system and new dynamic positioning system. The Kongsberg Simrad Hugin 1000 AUV is to be installed in all ships. The AUV is to be used for mine reconnaissance and rapid environmental assessment.
Structure: Design developed by the Navy in Bergen with the Defence Research Institute and Norsk Veritas and uses an air cushion created by the surface effect between two hulls. The hull is built of Fibre Reinforced Plastics (FRP) in sandwich configuration. The ROVs are carried in a large hangar and are launched by two hydraulic cranes. The minesweeper has an A frame aft for the sweep gear. SAM launcher mounted forward of the bridge.
Operational: Simrad Albatross tactical system including mapping; Cast/Del Norte mobile positioning system with GPS. The catamaran design is claimed to give higher transit speeds with lesser installed power than a traditional hull design. Other advantages are lower magnetic and acoustic signatures, clearer water for sonar operations and less susceptibility to shock. *Orkla* M 353 was lost after a catastrophic fire on 19 November 2002. M 354 was decommissioned in 2004 and M 340 in 2005.

HINNØY *3/2007, M Declerck* / 1166614

KARMØY *11/2004, Michael Nitz* / 1043497

OTRA *5/2006, Frank Findler* / 1040663

SURVEY AND RESEARCH SHIPS

1 RESEARCH SHIP (AGEH)

Name	*Builders*	*Launched*	*Commissioned*
MARJATA	Tangern Verft A/S	18 Dec 1992	July 1994

Displacement, tons: 7,560 full load
Dimensions, feet (metres): 267.4 × 130.9 × 19.7 *(81.5 × 39.9 × 6)*
Main machinery: Diesel-electric; 2 MTU Siemens 16V 396 TE diesels; 7,072 hp(m) *(5.2 MW)*; 2 Dresser Rand/Siemens gas-turbine generators; 9,792 hp(m) *(7.2 MW)*; 2 Siemens motors; 8,160 hp(m) *(6 MW)*; 2 Schottel 3030 thrusters. 1 Siemens motor; 2,720 hp(m); *(2 MW)*; 1 Schottel thruster (forward)
Speed, knots: 15
Complement: 14 plus 31 scientists
Helicopters: Platform for one medium

Comment: Ordered in February 1992 from Langsten Slip og Batbyggeri to replace the old ship of the same name. Called Project Minerva. Design developed by Ariel A/S, Horten. The three main superstructure-mounted cupolas contain ELINT and SIGINT equipment. Hull-reinforced to allow operations in fringe ice. Equipment includes Sperry radars, Elac sonars, Siemens TV surveillance, and a fully equipped helicopter flight deck. The unconventional hull which gives the ship an extraordinary length to beam ratio of 2:1 is said to give great stability and dynamic qualities.

MARJATA *6/2000, Royal Norwegian Navy* / 0105173

5 SURVEY SHIPS (AGS)

Name	*Displacement tons*	*Launched*	*Officers*	*Crew*
OLJEVERN 01	200	1978	2	6
OLJEVERN 02	200	1978	2	6
OLJEVERN 03	200	1978	2	6
OLJEVERN 04	200	1978	2	6
GEOFJORD	364	1958	2	6

Comment: Under control of Ministry of Environment based at Stavanger. *Oljevern 01* and *03* have red hulls and work for the Pollution Control Authority.

GEOFJORD *5/2002, L-G Nilsson* / 0528972

TRAINING SHIPS

2 TRAINING SHIPS (AXL)

Name	*No*	*Builders*	*Commissioned*
HESSA (ex-*Hitra*, ex-*Marsteinen*)	P 358	Fjellstrand, Omastrand	Jan 1978
VIGRA (ex-*Kvarven*)	P 359	Fjellstrand, Omastrand	July 1978

Displacement, tons: 39 full load
Dimensions, feet (metres): 77 × 16.4 × 3.5 *(23.5 × 5 × 1.1)*
Main machinery: 2 GM 12V-71 diesels; 1,800 hp *(1.34 MW)*; 2 shafts
Speed, knots: 20
Complement: 5 plus 13 trainees
Guns: 1—12.7 mm Browning MG.
Radars: Navigation: Racal Decca; I-band.

Comment: The vessels are designed for training students at the Royal Norwegian Naval Academy in navigation, manoeuvring and seamanship. All-welded aluminium hulls. Also equipped with an open bridge and a blind pilotage position below deck. 18 berths.

VIGRA *4/2002, P Froud* / 0529133

AUXILIARIES

Notes: A concept study to explore options for afloat replenishment and logistic support is in progress. Potential conclusions include a multirole Ro-Ro ship and an AOR to support the new frigates. An acquisition programme, is as yet unfunded.

1 SUPPLY AND RESCUE VESSEL

Name	*No*	*Builders*	*Commissioned*
VALKYRIEN	A 535	Ulstein Hatlo	1981

Displacement, tons: 3,000 full load
Dimensions, feet (metres): 223.1 × 47.6 × 16.4 *(68 × 14.5 × 5)*
Main machinery: Diesel-electric; 4 diesels; 10,560 hp(m) *(7.76 MW)* sustained; 2 motors; 3.14 MW; 2 shafts; 2 bow thrusters; 1,600 hp(m) *(1.18 MW)*; 1 stern thruster; 800 hp(m) *(588 kW)*
Speed, knots: 16
Complement: 13
Missiles: SAM: Mistral; IR homing to 4 km *(2.2 n miles)* at 2.5 Mach; warhead 3 kg.
Guns: 3—12.7 mm MGs.
Radars: Navigation: 2 Furuno; H/I-band.

Comment: Tug/supply ship acquired in 1994 for supply and SAR duties. Bollard pull 128 tons. Can carry a 700 ton deck load. Oil recovery equipment is also carried.

VALKYRIEN ***6/2008*, Maritime Photographic*** / 1335806

7 COASTAL VESSELS (YPT/YDT)

Notes: Due to re-organisation of the coastal vessels, the naval districts no longer operate many of the vessels previously assigned. The following remain in service and are prefaced by two letters as follows: HT (torpedo recovery), HM (multirole), HS (tugs), HD (diving), HP (personnel), HR (rescue). *Hitra* (HP 15) is also used for training cruises. All are less than 300 tons displacement.

Name	*No*	*Speed, knots*	*Commissioned*	*Role*
VIKEN	HD 2	12	1984	Cargo (4 tons)/Passengers (40) Diving vessel
TORPEN	HM 3	12	1977	Cargo (100 tons)/Passengers (15)
KJEØY	HM 7	10	1993	Training ship/Passengers (30)
HITRA	HP 15	–	–	Passengers (30)
KARLSØY	HT 3	10	1978	Torpedo fishing vessel
SLEIPNER	HS 4	11	2002	Tug/Cargo (10 tons)
MJØLNER	HS 5	11	2002	Tug/Cargo (10 tons)

SLEIPNER ***5/2008*, Marco Ghiglino*** / 1335805

VIKEN ***7/2003, Declerck/Steeghers*** / 1043508

1 SUPPORT SHIP (AGDS)

Name	*No*	*Builders*	*Commissioned*
TYR (ex-*Standby Master*)	N 50	Alesund Mekaniske Verksted	1981

Displacement, tons: 495 full load
Dimensions, feet (metres): 138.8 × 33.1 × 11.5 *(42.3 × 10.1 × 3.5)*
Main machinery: 2 Deutz SBA12M816 diesels; 1,300 hp(m) *(956 kW)*; 1 shaft; cp prop; 1 MWM diesel; 150 hp(m) *(110 kW)*; bow and stern thrusters
Speed, knots: 12
Complement: 22 (7 officers)
Mines: 2 rails.
Radars: Navigation: Furuno 711 and Furuno 1011; I-band.

Comment: Former oil rig pollution control ship. Acquired in December 1993 and converted by Mjellum & Karlsen, Bergen. Recommissioned 7 March 1995 as a minelayer, and for the maintenance of controlled minefields but principal current task is to support underwater operations. Carries a ROV.

TYR ***6/2008*, Maritime Photographic*** / 1335804

ROYAL YACHTS

1 ROYAL YACHT (YAC)

Name	*No*	*Builders*	*Commissioned*
NORGE (ex-*Philante*)	A 533	Camper & Nicholson's Ltd, Southampton	1937

Displacement, tons: 1,786 full load
Dimensions, feet (metres): 263 × 38 × 15.2 *(80.2 × 11.6 × 4.6)*
Main machinery: 2 Bergen KRMB-8 diesels; 4,850 hp(m) *(3.6 MW)* sustained; 2 shafts; bow thruster
Speed, knots: 17
Complement: 50 (18 officers)
Radars: Navigation: 2 Decca; I-band.

Comment: Built to the order of the late T O M Sopwith as an escort and store vessel for the yachts *Endeavour I* and *Endeavour II* Launched on 17 February 1937. Served in the Royal Navy as an anti-submarine escort during the Second World War, after which she was purchased by the Norwegian people for King Haakon and reconditioned as a Royal Yacht at Southampton. Can accommodate about 50 people in addition to crew. Repaired after serious fire on 7 March 1985 when the ship was fitted with a bow-thruster.

NORGE ***6/2005, E & M Laursen*** / 1151137

COAST GUARD (KYSTVAKT)

3 CHARTERED SHIPS (WPBO)

Name	*No*	*Tonnage*	*Completion*
ÅLESUND	W 312	1,357	1996
STÅLBAS	W 314	850	1955
LEIKVIN	W 319	1,300	1969

Comment: All armed with one 40 mm/60 gun. Some ships are operated with two crews, changing over every three weeks. *Leikvin* and *Stålbas* are to be replaced by Barentshav class when they enter service from 2009.

1 ARCTIC CLASS (WPSOH)

Name	*No*	*Builders*	*Commissioned*
SVALBARD	W 303	Tangen Verft, Krager	5 Jan 2002

Displacement, tons: 6,300 full load
Dimensions, feet (metres): 340.3 × 62.7 × 21.3 *(103.7 × 19.1 × 6.5)*
Main machinery: Diesel electric; 4 Rolls Royce diesel generators; 10 MW; 2 azimuth pods; 1 bow thruster
Speed, knots: 17
Range, n miles: 10,000 at 13 kt
Complement: 50
Guns: 1 Bofors 57 mm/70.
Radars: Air/Surface search: EADS TRS-3D; G-band.
Surface search/navigation: Kongsberg Bridgeline 10; I-band.
Helicopters: Platform for 1 NH 90 or Lynx.

Comment: Project definition completed in 1997 for an ice-reinforced vessel equipped with a helicopter. Built to Det Norske Veritas standards. Contract placed 15 December 1999 with Langsten Slip and Båtbyggeri A/S, Tomrefjord. Ship launched February 2001. Fitted for firefighting and counter-pollution work. There are two motor cutters and a sea-raider type dinghy. The ship underwent refit at Fiskerstrand Verft in 2006.

SVALBARD *7/2003, Freddie Philips* / 0572601

1 ULSTEIN UT 512 (SALVAGE AND RESCUE TUG) (ARS)

Name	*No*	*Builders*	*Commissioned*
HARSTAD	W 318	Aker Søviknes	28 Jan 2005

Displacement, tons: 3,130 full load
Dimensions, feet (metres): 272.3 × 50.8 × 19.7 *(83.0 × 15.5 × 6.0)*
Main machinery: 2 Bergen B 32: 40L diesels; 10,730 hp *(8 MW)*; 2 Kamewa Ulstein cp props; two bow thrusters; 1 Kamewa Ulstein 736 kW tunnel thruster; 1 Ulstein Aquamaster swing-up 883 kW azimuth thruster
Speed, knots: 19
Complement: 26
Guns: 1 – 57 mm.

Comment: Contract awarded in November 2003 for vessel designed by Rolls-Royce for a variety of coastguard and EEZ management roles. These include offshore standby and rescue, firefighting, salvage, pollution prevention, general law enforcement operations and fishery control. The ship is to be capable of operating the NATO Submarine Rescue System. Built by Aker's Søviknes yard based on steelwork from Aker Tulcea in Romania. The ship is owned by Remøy Shipping, who operates the ship on long term charter.

HARSTAD *6/2008*, Richard Scott* / 1335803

1 + 2 BARENTSHAV (VS 794) CLASS (SALVAGE AND RESCUE TUGS) (ARS)

Name	*No*	*Builders*	*Commissioned*
BARENTSHAV	W 340	Myklebust Verft AS	2009
BERGEN	W 341	Myklebust Verft AS	2009
SORTLAND	W 342	Myklebust Verft AS	2010

Displacement, tons: 4,000 full load
Dimensions, feet (metres): 305.8 × 54.5 × 19.0 *(93.2 × 16.6 × 5.8)*
Main machinery: LNG/diesel-electric; 1 Bergen B32 diesel; 5,364 hp *(4 MW)*; 3 Mitsubishi GS 16R generators; 3,480 hp *(2.6 MW)*; 1 Mitsubishi GS 12R generator; 860 hp *(642 kW)*; 1 motor; 1 shaft
Speed, knots: 20
Complement: 16
Guns: 1 – 40 mm/70.
Radars: Air/Surface search: To be announced.
Surface search/Navigation: To be announced.

Comment: Contract signed on 21 October 2005 with designer Vik-Sandvik AS and owner Remøy Management for the delivery of three coast guard vessels. The ships are to be operated by the Coast Guard on long term charter. The vessels are to be equipped with the same kind of rescue and environmental protection equipment as that in the UT 512 design *Harstad*. The vessels are of particular interest in that they are some of the world's first naval vessels to use a hybrid propulsion system based on diesel and liquid natural gas (LNG). The hulls are under construction in Romania and are to be fitted out in Norway from 2009.

BARENTSHAV (artist's impression) *1/2006, Myklebust Verft* / 1159233

3 NORDKAPP CLASS (WPSOH)

Name	*No*	*Builders*	*Launched*	*Commissioned*
NORDKAPP	W 320	Bergens Mek Verksteder	2 Apr 1980	25 Apr 1981
SENJA	W 321	Horten Verft	16 Mar 1980	6 Mar 1981
ANDENES	W 322	Haugesund Mek Verksted	21 Mar 1981	30 Jan 1982

Displacement, tons: 3,300 full load
Dimensions, feet (metres): 346 × 47.9 × 16.1 *(105.5 × 14.6 × 4.9)*
Main machinery: 4 Wichmann 9AXAG diesels; 16,163 hp(m) *(11.9 MW)*; 2 shafts
Speed, knots: 21. **Range, n miles:** 7,500 at 15 kt
Complement: 52 (6 aircrew)
Missiles: SSM: Fitted for 6 Kongsberg Penguin II but not embarked.
SAM: Fitted for MBDA Simbad.
Guns: 1 Bofors 57 mm/70; 200 rds/min to 17 km *(9.3 n miles)*; weight of shell 2.4 kg.
4 Rheinmetall 20 mm/20; 1,000 rds/min to 2 km.
Torpedoes: 6 – 324 mm US Mk 32 (2 triple) tubes. Honeywell Mk 46; anti-submarine; active/passive homing to 11 km *(5.9 n miles)* at 40 kt; warhead 44 kg. Mountings only in peacetime.
Depth charges: 1 rack.
Countermeasures: Decoys: 2 chaff launchers.
Combat data systems: Navkis or EDO (after modernisation). SATCOM can be carried.
Weapons control: Sagem Vigy 20 optronic director.
Radars: Air/surface search: EADS TRS-3D; G-band.
Navigation: Atlas; I-band.
Sonars: Simrad SP 270; hull-mounted; 24-30 kHz.

Helicopters: 1 Westland Lynx Mk 86.

Programmes: In November 1977 the Coast Guard budget was cut resulting in a reduction of the building programme from seven to three ships.
Modernisation: A modernisation programme was conducted 2001–03. Upgrades included an optronic director, new hull-mounted sonar, new air search radar and combat data system. A further refit programme for all three ships was conducted by Fiskerstrand Verft in 2006.
Structure: Ice strengthened. Fitted for firefighting, anti-pollution work, all with two motor cutters and a Gemini-type dinghy. SATCOM fitted for Gulf deployment.
Operational: Bunks for 109. War complement increases to 76.

ANDENES *6/2005, E & M Laursen* / 1151136

4 FISHERY PROTECTION SHIPS (WPSOH)

Name	*No*	*Tonnage*	*Completion*
TITRAN	KV 1	96	1992
GARSØY	KV 6	95	1988
ÅHAV	KV 7	50	1981
THORSTEINSON	KV 26	272	1960

Comment: An Inshore Patrol Force was established in January 1997. This comprises mostly chartered ships with KV pennant numbers. KV 1-7 are coastal cutters. Five new ships are to replace older ships from 2006.

GARSØY *6/2005, Globke Collection* / 1151135

5 + (5) NORNEN CLASS (PATROL VESSELS) (PBO)

Name	*No*	*Builders*	*Commissioned*
NORNEN	W 330	Gryfia Shipyard, Szczecin	2006
FARM	W 331	Gryfia Shipyard, Szczecin	2006
HEIMDAL	W 332	Gryfia Shipyard, Szczecin	2008
NJORD	W 333	Gryfia Shipyard, Szczecin	2008
TOR	W 334	Gryfia Shipyard, Szczecin	2008

Displacement, tons: 743 full load
Dimensions, feet (metres): 154.8 × 33.8 × 10.8 *(47.2 × 10.3 × 3.3)*
Main machinery: Diesel-electric; 2 azimuth thrusters
Speed, knots: 16
Complement: 20

Comment: Contract awarded in February 2005 to Remøy Management and Remøy Shipping for the construction of five new vessels with an option for a further five. The original plan was for the ships to be owned and managed by the shipping companies and chartered to the Coast Guard. However, this was overtaken by the decision in July 2008 to purchase all five ships. The design, developed by Skipsteknisk AS, is called ST-610. The ships are employed out to 24 n miles from the coast and are equipped to conduct towing, counter-pollution operations, fire-fighting and general patrol duties. Two fast rescue craft are carried and there is space for 100 m³ of cargo space on deck and 90 m³ in the hold.

HEIMDAL *4/2007, L-G Nilsson* / 1166620

Oman

Country Overview

The Sultanate of Oman is an independent Middle-East state extending along the south-east coast of the Arabian Peninsula. It is bordered to the south-west by the Republic of Yemen, to the west by Saudi Arabia and to the north-west by the United Arab Emirates which separates a small exclave on the Musandam peninsula, on the south side of the Strait of Hormuz, from the rest of the country. Masirah island and the Khuriya Muriya Islands lie off the south-east coast. With an area of 82,030 square miles, it has a 1,129 n mile coastline with the Indian Ocean and Gulf of Oman. The capital, largest city and principal port is Muscat while there is a further port at Salalah. Territorial seas (12 n miles) are claimed. An EEZ (200 n miles) has also been claimed but its limits have only been partly defined by boundary agreements.

Headquarters Appointments

Commander Royal Navy of Oman:
Rear Admiral (Liwaa Rukn Bahry) Salim bin Abdullah bin Rashid al Alawi
Principal Staff Officer:
Commodore (Ameed) Abdullah Khamis Abdullah Al-Raisi
Director General Operations and Plans:
Commodore (Ameed) Abdullah Khamis Abdullah Al-Raisi
Commander Coast Guard:
Captain (Aqeed Bahry) Hamdan bin Marhoon Al Mamary
Commander Royal Yacht Squadron:
Commodore (Ameed) J M Knapp

Bases

Said bin Sultan, Widam A'Sahil (main base, dockyard and shiplift)
Ras Musandam
Muaskar al Murtafa'a (headquarters)

Personnel

(a) 2009: 4,200 officers and men
(b) Voluntary service

CORVETTES

1 PATROL SHIP (FSH/AXL/AGS)

Name	*No*	*Builders*	*Commissioned*
AL MABRUKAH (ex-*Al Said*)	Q 30 (ex-A 1)	Brooke Marine, Lowestoft	1971

Displacement, tons: 900 full load
Dimensions, feet (metres): 203.4 × 35.1 × 9.8 *(62 × 10.7 × 3)*
Main machinery: 2 Paxman Valenta 12CM diesels; 5,000 hp *(3.73 MW)* sustained; 2 shafts
Speed, knots: 12
Complement: 39 (7 officers) plus 32 trainees

Guns: 1 Bofors 40 mm/70. 2 Oerlikon 20 mm A41A.
Countermeasures: Decoys: Wallop Barricade 18-barrelled chaff launcher.
ESM: Racal Cutlass; radar warning.
Radars: Surface search: Racal Decca TM 1226; I-band.

Helicopters: Platform only.

Comment: Built by Brooke Marine, Lowestoft. Launched 7 April 1970 as a yacht for the Sultan of Oman. Carried on board is one Rotork landing craft. Converted to training/patrol ship in 1983 with enlarged helicopter deck, additional accommodation and armament. Re-classified as a corvette and pennant number changed in 1997. Fitted with survey equipment in 2000, as an additional role.

AL MABRUKAH *6/2003, Royal Navy of Oman* / 0589799

2 QAHIR CLASS (FSGMH)

Name	*No*	*Builders*	*Laid down*	*Launched*	*Commissioned*
QAHIR AL AMWAJ	C 31	Vosper Thornycroft, Woolston	21 May 1993	21 Sep 1994	3 Sep 1996
AL MUA'ZZAR	C 32	Vosper Thornycroft, Woolston	4 Apr 1994	26 Sep 1995	13 Apr 1997

Displacement, tons: 1,450 full load
Dimensions, feet (metres): 274.6 oa; 249.3 wl × 37.7 × 11.8 *(83.7; 76 × 11.5 × 3.6)*
Main machinery: CODAD; 4 Crossley SEMT-Pielstick 16 PA6 V 280 STC; 28,160 hp(m) *(20.7 MW)* sustained; 2 shafts; Kamewa cp props
Speed, knots: 28
Range, n miles: 4,000 at 10 kt
Complement: 76 (14 officers) plus 3 spare

Missiles: SSM: 8 Aerospatiale MM 40 Block 2 Exocet ❶; inertial cruise; active radar homing to 70 km *(40 n miles)* at 0.9 Mach; warhead 165 kg; sea-skimmer.
SAM: Thomson-CSF Crotale NG octuple launcher ❷; 16 VT1; command line of sight guidance; radar/IR homing to 13 km *(7 n miles)* at 2.4 Mach; warhead 14 kg.
Guns: 1 OTO Melara 3 in *(76 mm)*/62 Super Rapid ❸; 120 rds/min to 16 km *(8.7 n miles)*; weight of shell 6 kg.
2 Oerlikon/Royal Ordnance 20 mm GAM-BO1 ❹.
2—7.62 mm MGs.
Torpedoes: 6—324 mm (2 triple) tubes may be fitted in due course.
Countermeasures: Decoys: 2 Barricade 12-barrelled chaff and IR launchers ❺.
ESM: Thomson-CSF DR 3000 ❻; intercept.
Combat data systems: Signaal/Thomson-CSF TACTICOS; Link Y; SATCOM.
Weapons control: Signaal STING optronic and radar tracker ❼; 2 Signaal optical directors.
Radars: Air/surface search: Signaal MW08 ❽; G-band.
Fire control: Signaal STING ❼; I/J-band. Thomson-CSF DRBV 51C ❾; J-band (for Crotale).
Navigation: Kelvin Hughes 1007; I-band.
Sonars: Thomson Sintra/BAeSEMA ATAS; towed array; active search; 3 kHz (may be fitted).

Helicopters: Platform for 1 Super Lynx ❿.

Programmes: Vosper Thornycroft signed the Muheet Project contract on 5 April 1992. First steel cut 23 September 1992. C 31 accepted on 27 March 1996, and C 32 on 26 November 1996. Commissioned after operational work up in the UK, and on return to Oman. Names mean Conqueror of the Waves, and The Supported.
Structure: The ship is based on the Vigilance class design with enhanced stealth features. It is possible lightweight torpedo tubes may be fitted. The towed array, if fitted, adds another 8 tons on the stern but does not affect the helicopter deck. RAM (Radar Absorbent Material) is widely used on the superstructure.
Operational: The helicopter platform can support a Super Puma sized aircraft.

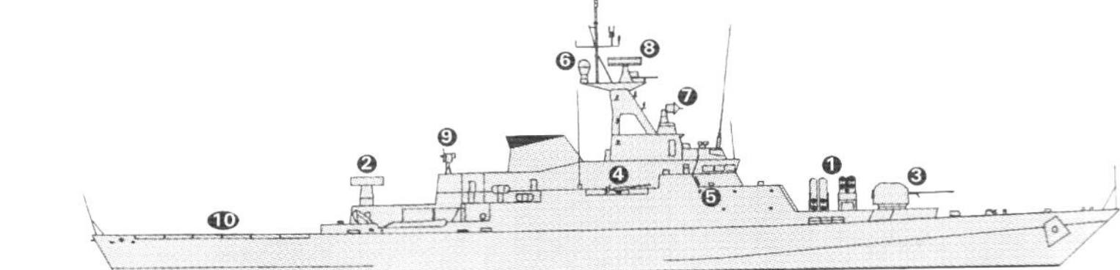

QAHIR AL AMWAJ *(Scale 1 : 900), Ian Sturton* / 0506243

AL MUA'ZZAR *6/2005, E & M Laursen* / 1151140

QAHIR AL AMWAJ *3/2008*, Michael Nitz* / 1353247

0 + 3 PROJECT KHAREEF (CORVETTES) (FSGHM)

Name	*No*	*Builders*	*Laid down*	*Launched*	*Commissioned*
–	–	VT Shipbuilding, Portsmouth	2007	2009	2010
–	–	VT Shipbuilding, Portsmouth	2007	2009	2010
–	–	VT Shipbuilding, Portsmouth	2008	2010	2011

Displacement, tons: 2,500 standard
Dimensions, feet (metres): 323.1 × 47.9 × 13.4 *(98.5 × 14.6 × 4.1)*
Main machinery: 2 diesels; 2 shafts
Speed, knots: 25
Complement: To be announced

Missiles: SSM: 8 MBDA MM 40 Exocet Block 3 ❶.
SAM: 12 (2 sextuple) MBDA VL MICA; command/inertial guidance ❷; radar/IR homing to 20 km *(10.8 n miles)*; warhead 12 kg.
Guns: 1 OTO Melara 3 in *(76 mm)*/62 Super Rapid ❸. 2 MSI-Defence DS 30M 30 mm ❹.
Countermeasures: Decoys: 2 Rheinmetall MASS-2L launchers ❺.
ESM: Thales Vigile 400 ❻.
Combat data systems: Thales Tacticos. Link Y Mk 2.
Weapons control: Thales STING Mk 2 optronic and radar tracker ❼.
Radars: Air/surface search: Thales SMART-S ❽; E/F-band.
Navigation: To be announced ❾.
Fire control: Thales STING ❼; I/J-band.

Helicopters: 1 Super Lynx ❿.

Programmes: The contract for the design and build of three Project Khareef patrol ships with an initial logistics support package, was signed with VT Shipbuilding on 15 January 2007. All three vessels are to be built at Portsmouth with the handover of the lead ship scheduled for early 2010. The others are to follow at six-month intervals.
Structure: The design is derived from VT Multipurpose Ocean Patrol vessel family.

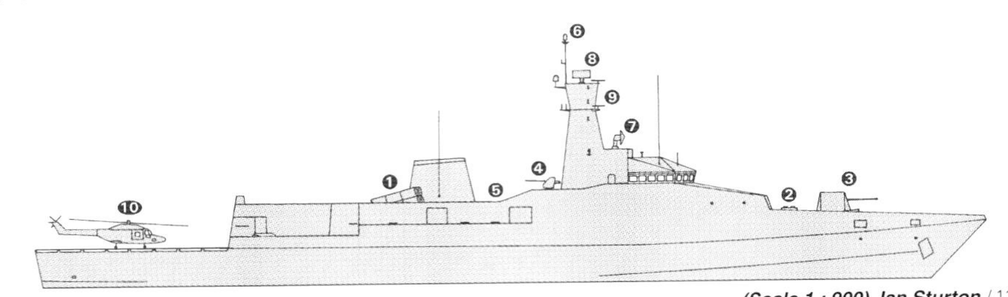

PROJECT KHAREEF *(Scale 1 : 900), Ian Sturton* / 1170226

PROJECT KHAREEF CORVETTE
1/2007, VT Group
1190513

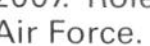

SHIPBORNE AIRCRAFT

Numbers/Type: 16 GKN Westland Super Lynx 300.
Operational speed: 120 kt *(222 km/h)*.
Service ceiling: 10,000 ft *(3,048 m)*.
Range: 320 n miles *(593 km)*.
Role/Weapon systems: Contract signed 19 January 2002. Ten had been delivered by early 2007. Roles include maritime surveillance, armed escort and SAR. Operated by the Air Force.

SUPER LYNX *5/2006* / 1167504

PATROL FORCES

Notes: Replacement of the Dhofar class is under consideration.

4 DHOFAR (PROVINCE) CLASS (FAST ATTACK CRAFT—MISSILE) (PGGF)

Name	*No*	*Builders*	*Launched*	*Commissioned*
DHOFAR	Z 10	Vosper Thornycroft	14 Oct 1981	7 Aug 1982
AL SHARQIYAH	Z 11	Vosper Thornycroft	2 Dec 1982	5 Dec 1983
AL BAT'NAH	Z 12	Vosper Thornycroft	4 Nov 1982	18 Jan 1984
MUSSANDAM	Z 14	Vosper Thornycroft	19 Mar 1988	31 Mar 1989

Displacement, tons: 311 light; 394 full load
Dimensions, feet (metres): 186 × 26.9 × 7.9 *(56.7 × 8.2 × 2.4)*
Main machinery: 4 Paxman Valenta 18CM diesels; 15,000 hp *(11.2 MW)* sustained; 4 shafts; auxiliary propulsion; 2 motors; 200 hp *(149 kW)*
Speed, knots: 38. **Range, n miles:** 2,000 at 18 kt
Complement: 45 (5 officers) plus 14 trainees
Missiles: SSM: 8 (6 in Z 10) Aerospatiale MM 40 Exocet; inertial cruise; active radar homing to 70 km *(40 n miles)* at 0.9 Mach; warhead 165 kg; sea-skimmer.
Guns: 1 OTO Melara 3 in *(76 mm)*/62 compact; 85 rds/min to 16 km *(8.7 n miles)*; weight of shell 6 kg.
2 Breda 40 mm/70 (twin); 300 rds/min to 12.5 km *(6.8 n miles)*; weight of shell 0.96 kg.
2—20 mm.
Countermeasures: Decoys: 2 Wallop Barricade fixed triple barrels; for chaff and IR flares.
ESM: Racal Cutlass; radar warning.
ECM: Scorpion; jammer.
Weapons control: Sperry Sea Archer (B 10). Philips 9LV 307 (remainder).
Radars: Air/surface search: Plessey AWS 4 or AWS 6; E/F-band.
Fire control: Philips 9LV 307; I/J-band.
Navigation: KH 1007 ARPA; I-band.

Programmes: First ordered in 1980, two more in January 1981 and fourth in January 1986.
Structure: Similar to Kenyan Nyayo class. Mast structures are different dependent on radars fitted.
Operational: Pennant numbers have been changed from B to Z.

AL SHARQIYAH *6/2003, Royal Navy of Oman* / 1167443

DHOFAR *6/2003, Royal Navy of Oman* / 0567467

3 AL BUSHRA CLASS (PBO)

Name	*No*	*Builders*	*Laid down*	*Launched*	*Commissioned*
AL BUSHRA	Z 1	CMN, Cherbourg/Wudam Dockyard	10 Nov 1993	3 May 1995	15 June 1995
AL MANSOOR	Z 2	CMN, Cherbourg/Wudam Dockyard	12 Apr 1994	3 May 1995	10 Aug 1995
AL NAJAH	Z 3	CMN, Cherbourg/Wudam Dockyard	27 June 1994	5 Mar 1996	15 Apr 1996

Displacement, tons: 475 full load
Dimensions, feet (metres): 178.6 × 26.2 × 8.9 *(54.5 × 8 × 2.7)*
Main machinery: 2 MTU 16V 538 TB93 diesels; 8,000 hp(m) *(5.88 MW)* sustained; 2 shafts
Speed, knots: 24. **Range, n miles:** 2,400 at 15 kt
Complement: 43 (8 officers)

Guns: 1 OTO Melara 76 mm/62 Compact; 85 rds/min to 16 km *(8.7 n miles)*; weight of shell 6 kg.
2 Oerlikon/Royal Ordnance 20 mm GAM-BO1.
2—12.7 mm MGs.
Countermeasures: Decoys: Plessey Barricade chaff launcher.
ESM: Thomson-CSF DR 3000; intercept.
Weapons control: CelsiusTech 9LV 207 Mk 3 command system and optronic director.
Radars: Surface search: Kelvin Hughes 1007 ARPA; I-band.

Programmes: Project Mawj order for three, with an option on five more, on 1 September 1993. The ships have had additional weapon systems fitted in Wudam dockyard.
Structure: Same hull design as the French P 400 class. 20 mm guns, and countermeasures were not fitted at Cherbourg and are planned to be installed in due course. 76 mm guns were fitted from 1998 from deleted Al Waafi class. The plan to fit torpedoes and sonars has been shelved.
Operational: First pair arrived in Oman on 28 September 1995, last one on 29 June 1996. Pennant numbers have been changed from B to Z.

AL MANSOOR *6/2003, Royal Navy of Oman* / 0589798

4 SEEB (VOSPER 25) CLASS (COASTAL PATROL CRAFT) (PB)

Name	*No*	*Builders*	*Commissioned*
SEEB	Z 20	Vosper Private, Singapore	15 Mar 1981
SHINAS	Z 21	Vosper Private, Singapore	15 Mar 1981
SADH	Z 22	Vosper Private, Singapore	15 Mar 1981
KHASSAB	Z 23	Vosper Private, Singapore	15 Mar 1981

Displacement, tons: 74 full load
Dimensions, feet (metres): 82.8 × 19 × 5.2 *(25 × 5.8 × 1.6)*
Main machinery: 2 MTU 12V 331 TC92 diesels; 2,660 hp(m) *(1.96 MW)* sustained; 2 shafts
1 Cummins N-855M diesel for slow cruising; 189 hp *(141 kW)* sustained; 1 shaft
Speed, knots: 25; 8 (Cummins diesel)
Range, n miles: 750 at 14 kt
Complement: 13
Guns: 1 Oerlikon 20 mm GAM-BO1. 2—7.62 mm MGs.
Radars: Surface search: Racal Decca 1226; I-band.

Comment: Arrived in Oman on 19 May 1981 having been ordered one month earlier. The craft were built on speculation and completed in 1980. Pennant numbers have been changed from B to Z.

SADH *10/2004* / 1151306

AMPHIBIOUS FORCES

Notes: There are also some French-built Havas Mk 8 two-man SDVs in service.

1 LANDING SHIP-LOGISTIC (LSTH)

Name	*No*	*Builders*	*Commissioned*
NASR AL BAHR	A 2	Brooke Marine, Lowestoft	6 Feb 1985

Displacement, tons: 2,500 full load
Dimensions, feet (metres): 305 × 50.8 × 8.5 *(93 × 15.5 × 2.6)*
Main machinery: 2 Paxman Valenta 18 CM diesels; 7,500 hp *(5.6 MW)* sustained; 2 shafts; cp props
Speed, knots: 12
Range, n miles: 5,500 at 15 kt
Complement: 104 (13 officers)
Military lift: 7 MBT or 400 tons cargo; 190 troops; 2 LCVPs
Guns: 2 Breda 40 mm/70 (1 twin). 2 Oerlikon 20 mm GAM-BO1. 2—12.7 mm MGs.
Countermeasures: Decoys: Wallop Barricade double layer chaff launchers.
Weapons control: PEAB 9LV 107 GFCS and CSEE Lynx optical sight.
Radars: Surface search/navigation: 2 Racal Decca 1226; I-band.
Helicopters: Platform for Super Puma.

Comment: Ordered 18 May 1982. Launched 16 May 1984. Similar to Algerian LSLs. Carries one 16 ton crane. Bow and stern ramps. Full naval command facilities. The forward ramp is of two sections measuring length 59 ft (when extended) × 16.5 ft breadth *(18 × 5 m)*, and the single section stern ramp measures 14 × 16.5 ft *(4.3 × 5 m)*. Both hatches can support a 60 ton tank. The tank deck side bulkheads extend 7.5 ft *(2.25 m)* above the upper deck between the forecastle and the forward end of the superstructure, and provides two hatch openings to the tank deck below. Positioned between the hatches is a 2 ton crane with athwartship travel. New engine exhaust system and funnel fitted in 1997. Aft Oerlikon gun removed. Ship is also used as a ratings' training vessel. Pennant number has been changed from L to A.

NASR AL BAHR *2/2002, A Sharma* / 0533304

1 LANDING CRAFT (LCT)

AL MUNASSIR A 1

Displacement, tons: 850 approx
Dimensions, feet (metres): 210 × 39.4 × 8.7 *(64.0 × 12.0 × 2.7)*
Main machinery: 2 Caterpillar 3508 diesels; 3,620 hp *(2.7 MW)*; 2 shafts
Speed, knots: 11
Complement: 19 (plus 56 troops)
Military lift: Military vehicles

Comment: The Project Mahmal contract was placed with Abu Dhabi Ship Building on 13 March 2005. The vessel is likely to be similar to those delivered to the UAE in 2004. Details are speculative. The ship was launched on 17 May 2006 and sea trials had started by the end of 2006.

3 LCMs (LSTH)

Name	*No*	*Builders*	*Commissioned*
SABA AL BAHR	A 8 (ex-L 8)	Vosper Private, Singapore	17 Sep 1981
AL DOGHAS	A 9 (ex-L 9)	Vosper Private, Singapore	10 Jan 1983
AL TEMSAH	A 10 (ex-L 10)	Vosper Private, Singapore	12 Feb 1983

Displacement, tons: 230 full load
Dimensions, feet (metres): 108.2 (83.6, C 8) × 24.3 × 4.3 *(33 (25.5) × 7.4 × 1.3)*
Main machinery: 2 Caterpillar 3408TA diesels; 1,880 hp *(1.4 MW)* sustained; 2 shafts
Speed, knots: 8
Range, n miles: 1,400 at 8 kt
Complement: 11
Military lift: 100 tons
Radars: Navigation: Furuno 701; I-band.

Comment: First one launched 30 June 1981. Second pair of similar but not identical ships, launched 12 November and 15 December 1982. Pennant numbers have been changed from L to A.

AL TEMSAH *6/2003, Royal Navy of Oman* / 0567468

1 LCU (LSTH)

Name	*No*	*Builders*	*Commissioned*
AL NEEMRAN	A 7 (ex-L 7)	Lewis Offshore, Stornoway	1979

Measurement, tons: 85 dwt
Dimensions, feet (metres): 84 × 24 × 6 *(25.5 × 7.4 × 1.8)*
Main machinery: 2 diesels; 300 hp *(220 kW)*; 2 shafts
Speed, knots: 7/8
Complement: 6
Radars: Navigation: Furuno; I-band.

Comment: Second of class deleted in 1993. Pennant number has been changed from L to A.

TRAINING SHIPS

1 SAIL TRAINING SHIP (AXS)

Name	*No*	*Builders*	*Recommissioned*
SHABAB OMAN (ex-*Captain Scott*)	S 1	Herd and Mackenzie, Buckie, Scotland	1979

Displacement, tons: 386 full load
Dimensions, feet (metres): 144.3 × 27.9 × 15.1 *(44 × 8.5 × 4.6)*
Main machinery: 2 Gardner diesels; 460 hp *(343 kW)*; 2 shafts
Speed, knots: 10 (diesels)
Complement: 20 (5 officers) plus 3 officers and 24 trainees

Comment: Topsail schooner built in 1971 and taken over from Dulverton Trust in 1977 used for sail training. Name means Omani Youth.

SHABAB OMAN *8/2008*, Frank Findler* / 1353246

AUXILIARIES

Notes: (1) In addition to the listed vessels there are four 12 m Cheverton Work boats (W 41-44) and eight 8 m Work boats (W 4-11).
(2) The contract for five 52 m catamaran vessels was signed with Rodriguez Cantieri Navali on 8 April 2006. Three are to be used for transport and two for rescue. Delivery is expected to be completed in 2009.

1 SUPPLY SHIP (AKS)

Name	*No*	*Builders*	*Launched*	*Commissioned*
AL SULTANA	T 1 (ex-A 2, ex-S 2)	Conoship, Groningen	18 May 1975	4 June 1975

Measurement, tons: 1,380 dwt
Dimensions, feet (metres): 215.6 × 35 × 13.5 *(65.7 × 10.7 × 4.2)*
Main machinery: 1 Mirrlees Blackstone diesel; 1,120 hp(m) *(835 kW)*; 1 shaft
Speed, knots: 11
Complement: 20
Radars: Navigation: Racal Decca TM 1226; I-band.

Comment: Major refit in 1992. Has a 1 ton crane. Pennant number changed in 1997 and again in 2002.

AL SULTANA *4/2002, Schaeffer/Marsan* / 0533305

2 FAST TRANSPORT SHIPS (AP)

SHINAS HORMUZ

Measurement, tons: 146 dwt
Dimensions, feet (metres): 212.6 × 54.1 × 6.9 *(64.8 × 16.5 × 2.1)*
Main machinery: 4 MTU 20V 1163 TB73L diesels; 34,865 hp *(26 MW)*; 4 Kamewa 90 waterjets
Speed, knots: 50. **Range, n miles:** 450 at 40 kt
Complement: 12
Military lift: 203 passengers and 56 vehicles including 54 lane-metres of trucks
Radars: Navigation.
Helicopters: Platform for one medium.

Comment: Contract signed with Austal Ships on 15 May 2006 for the construction of two multipurpose passenger/vehicle ferries. They are of a twin-hull catamaran design and of aluminium construction. The vessels act as intra-theatre sealift ships in an emergency and, at other times, they are used commercially as passenger ferries. The first vessel was launched on 27 September 2007; the second was delivered in July 2008. They are based around the Musandam Peninsula.

SHINAS *10/2007, Austal Ships* / 1293474

ROYAL YACHTS

Notes: The Royal Yacht Squadron of Oman is a distinct service that is not part of the Royal Navy of Oman. Based at Muscat, the squadron consists of three major units and a number of smaller craft.

1 ROYAL YACHT (YAC)

Name	*No*	*Builders*	*Commissioned*
AL SAID	–	Picchiotti SpA, Viareggio	July 1982

Displacement, tons: 3,800 full load
Dimensions, feet (metres): 340.5 × 62.4 × 15.4 *(103.8 × 19.0 × 4.7)*
Main machinery: 2 GMT A 420.6 H diesels; 8,400 hp(m) *(6.17 MW)* sustained; 2 shafts; cp props; bow thruster
Speed, knots: 18
Complement: 156 (16 officers)
Radars: Navigation: Decca TM 1226C; ACS 1230C; I-band.

Comment: Fitted with helicopter deck and fin stabilisers. Carries three Puma C service launches and one Rotork beach landing craft. A variety of small arms carried.

AL SAID *12/2005, Hartmut Ehlers* / 1167444

1 SUPPORT SHIP (AKSH)

Name	*No*	*Builders*	*Launched*	*Commissioned*
FULK AL SALAMAH (ex-*Ghubat Al Salamah*)	–	Bremer-Vulkan	29 Aug 1986	3 Apr 1987

Measurement, tons: 10,797 grt; 3,239 net
Dimensions, feet (metres): 447.5 × 68.9 × 19.7 *(136.4 × 21 × 6)*
Main machinery: 4 Fincantieri GMT A 420.6 H diesels; 16,800 hp(m) *(12.35 MW)* sustained; 2 shafts; cp props
Speed, knots: 19.5
Military lift: 240 troops
Radars: Navigation: 2 Racal Decca; I-band.
Helicopters: Up to 2 AS 332C Super Pumas.

Comment: Primary role is to support the Royal Yacht on deployments. Secondary roles include government, environmental and training duties. Reported to be fitted with Javelin air-defence missile system.

FULK AL SALAMAH *12/2005, Hartmut Ehlers* / 1167445

1 ROYAL DHOW (YAC)

Name	*No*	*Builders*	*Commissioned*
ZINAT AL BIHAAR	–	–	1988

Displacement, tons: 510 light
Dimensions, feet (metres): 200.2 × 32.2 × 12.8 *(61 × 9.8 × 3.9)*
Main machinery: 2 Siemens motors; 965 hp *(720 kW)*; 2 shafts
Speed, knots: 11.5

Comment: Three-masted wooden sailing vessel built in Oman on traditional lines.

ZINAT AL BIHAAR *4/2004, Derek Fox* / 0589797

POLICE

Notes: (1) In addition to the vessels listed below there are several harbour craft including a Cheverton 8 m work boat *Zahra 24, Zahra 16* and a fireboat pennant number *10*. There are also two Pilatus aircraft for SAR.
(2) 15 FPBs between 11 and 30 m may be ordered in due course. These could be for the Navy if it takes over Fishery Protection duties from the Police.

ZAHRA 16 *6/2003, Hartmut Ehlers* / 0567471

3 CG 29 TYPE (COASTAL PATROL CRAFT) (PB)

HARAS 7 H 7 **HARAS 9** H 9 **HARAS 10** H 10

Displacement, tons: 84 full load
Dimensions, feet (metres): 94.8 × 17.7 × 4.3 *(28.9 × 5.4 × 1.3)*
Main machinery: 2 MTU 12V 331 TC92 diesels; 2,660 hp(m) *(1.96 MW)* sustained; 2 shafts
Speed, knots: 25
Range, n miles: 600 at 15 kt
Complement: 13
Guns: 2 Oerlikon 20 mm GAM-BO1.
Radars: Navigation: Racal Decca 1226; I-band.

Comment: Built by Karlskrona Varvet. Commissioned in 1981–82. GRP Sandwich hulls.

HARAS 9 *12/2000* / 0114776

1 + 2 FAST PATROL CRAFT (PBF)

Displacement, tons: 54 full load
Dimensions, feet (metres): 90.0 × 18.0 × 4.75 *(27.4 × 5.5 × 1.5)*
Main machinery: 2 MTU 12V 4000M 90 diesels; 5,470 hp *(4.1 MW)*; 2 Kamewa 56SII waterjets
Speed, knots: 45
Range, n miles: 1,200 at 30 kt
Complement: 12 (2 officers)
Guns: 1 – 12.7 mm MG. 2 – 7.62 mm MGs.
Radars: Navigation: I-band.

Comment: Order placed on 9 June 2005 with United States Marine, Gulfport, Mississippi, for three interception craft under the Foreign Military Sales programme. With a higher superstructure, the craft are a modified version of the US Mk V Pegasus class. The first boat was delivered in January 2008 and the contract includes a training and support package. Roles include anti-smuggling and anti-narcotics.

1 P 1903 TYPE (COASTAL PATROL CRAFT) (PB)

HARAS 8 H 8

Displacement, tons: 32 full load
Dimensions, feet (metres): 63 × 15.7 × 5.2 *(19.2 × 4.8 × 1.6)*
Main machinery: 2 MTU 8V 331 TC92 diesels; 1,770 hp(m) *(1.3 MW)*; 2 shafts
Speed, knots: 30
Range, n miles: 1,650 at 17 kt
Complement: 10
Guns: 2 – 12.7 mm MGs.
Radars: Navigation: Racal Decca 1226; I-band.

Comment: Built by Le Comte, Netherlands. Commissioned August 1981. Type 1903 Mk III.

HARAS 8 *10/1992, Hartmut Ehlers* / 0506067

1 CG 27 TYPE (COASTAL PATROL CRAFT) (PB)

HARAS 6 H 6

Displacement, tons: 53 full load
Dimensions, feet (metres): 78.7 × 18 × 6.2 *(24 × 5.5 × 1.9)*
Main machinery: 2 MTU 12V 331 TC92 diesels; 2,660 hp(m) *(1.96 MW)* sustained; 2 shafts
Speed, knots: 25
Complement: 11
Guns: 1 Oerlikon 20 mm GAM-BO1.
Radars: Navigation: Furuno 701; I-band.

Comment: Completed in 1980 by Karlskrona Varvet. GRP hull.

HARAS 6 *10/1992, Hartmut Ehlers* / 0506068

14 RODMAN 58 CLASS (PB)

HARAS 21–34

Displacement, tons: 19 full load
Dimensions, feet (metres): 59.0 × 16.0 × 3.9 *(18.0 × 4.9 × 1.2)*
Main machinery: 2 diesels; 2,000 hp *(1.49 MW)*; 2 waterjets
Speed, knots: 34. **Range, n miles:** 450 at 17 kt
Complement: 5
Radars: Navigation: I-band.

Comment: GRP hull. Built in 2002–03 by Rodman, Vigo.

HARAS 25 *3/2007, Marco Ghiglino* / 1170202

1 P 2000 TYPE (COASTAL PATROL CRAFT) (PB)

DHEEB AL BAHAR 1 Z 1

Displacement, tons: 80 full load
Dimensions, feet (metres): 68.2 × 19 × 5 *(20.8 × 5.8 × 1.5)*
Main machinery: 2 MTU 12V 396 TB93 diesels; 3,260 hp(m) *(2.4 MW)* sustained; 2 shafts
Speed, knots: 40
Range, n miles: 423 at 36 kt; 700 at 18 kt
Guns: 1 – 12.7 mm MG.
Radars: Surface search: Furuno 701; I-band.

Comment: Delivered January 1985 by Watercraft Ltd, Shoreham, UK. GRP hull. Similar to UK Archer class. Carries SATNAV.

DHEEB AL BAHAR 1 *6/2003, Hartmut Ehlers* / 0589794

2 D 59116 TYPE (COASTAL PATROL CRAFT) (PB)

DHEEB AL BAHAR 2 Z 2 **DHEEB AL BAHAR 3** Z 3

Displacement, tons: 65 full load
Dimensions, feet (metres): 75.5 × 17.1 × 3.9 *(23 × 5.2 × 1.2)*
Main machinery: 2 MTU 12V 396 TB93 diesels; 3,260 hp(m) *(2.4 MW)* sustained; 2 shafts
Speed, knots: 36
Range, n miles: 420 at 30 kt
Complement: 11
Guns: 1 – 12.7 mm MG.
Radars: Surface search: Furuno 711-2; Furuno 2400; I-band.

Comment: Built by Yokohama Yacht Co, Japan. Commissioned in 1988.

DHEEB AL BAHAR 3 *6/2003, Hartmut Ehlers* / 0567470

5 INSHORE PATROL CRAFT (PBI)

ZAHRA 14 Z 14 **ZAHRA 15** Z 15 **ZAHRA 17** Z 17 **ZAHRA 18** Z 18 **ZAHRA 21** Z 21

Displacement, tons: 16; 18 (*Zahra 18* and *21*) full load
Dimensions, feet (metres): 45.6 × 14.1 × 4.6 *(13.9 × 4.3 × 1.4)*
52.5 × 13.8 × 7.5 *(16 × 4.2 × 2.3)* (*Zahra 18* and *21*)
Main machinery: 2 Cummins VTA-903M diesels; 643 hp *(480 kW)*; 2 shafts
Speed, knots: 36
Range, n miles: 510 at 22 kt
Complement: 5-6
Guns: 1 or 2 – 7.62 mm MGs.
Radars: Navigation: Decca 101; I-band.

Comment: *Zahra 14, 15* and *17* built by Watercraft, Shoreham, UK and completed in 1981. *Zahra 21* completed by Emsworth SB in 1987 to a slightly different design. *Zahra 18* built by Lecomte in 1987.

ZAHRA 17 (alongside Zahra 14) *6/2003, Hartmut Ehlers* / 0567472

12 SEASPRAY ASSAULT BOATS (PB)

Displacement, tons: To be announced
Dimensions, feet (metres): 31.2 × 10.2 × 1.6 *(9.5 × 3.1 × 0.5)*
Main machinery: 2 outboards; 500 hp *(375 kW)*
Speed, knots: 50
Range, n miles: 450 at 17 kt
Complement: 5
Radars: Navigation: I-band.

Comment: Abu Dhabi Ship Building awarded contract in January 2004. Designed by SeaSpray Aluminium Boats. To be employed in policing, patrol and interception roles by the navy and police.

1 DIVING CRAFT (YDT)

SABHUR 7 (ex-*Zahra 27*)

Displacement, tons: 13 full load
Dimensions, feet (metres): 59 × 12.4 × 3.6 *(18 × 3.8 × 1.1)*
Main machinery: 2 Volvo Penta AQD70D diesels; 430 hp(m) *(316 kW)* sustained; 2 shafts
Speed, knots: 20
Complement: 4
Guns: 2 – 7.62 mm MGs.

Comment: Rotork Type, the last of several logistic support craft, delivered in 1981 and now used as a diving boat. Similar craft used by the Navy.

SABHUR 7 *12/2005, Hartmut Ehlers* / 1167446

5 VOSPER 75 ft TYPE (COASTAL PATROL CRAFT) (PB)

HARAS 1-5 H 1 **HARAS 2** H 2 **HARAS 3** H 3 **HARAS 4** H 4 **HARAS 5** H 5

Displacement, tons: 50 full load
Dimensions, feet (metres): 75 × 20 × 5.9 *(22.9 × 6.1 × 1.8)*
Main machinery: 2 Caterpillar D 348 diesels; 1,450 hp *(1.08 MW)* sustained; 2 shafts
Speed, knots: 24.5
Range, n miles: 1,000 at 11 kt
Complement: 11
Guns: 1 Oerlikon 20 mm GAM-BO1.
Radars: Navigation: Decca 101; I-band.

Comment: First four completed 22 December 1975 by Vosper Thornycroft. GRP hulls. *Haras 5* commissioned November 1978.

HARAS 3 *3/2004, Bob Fildes* / 0589795

20 HALMATIC COUGAR ENFORCER 33 (FAST PATROL CRAFT) (PBF)

Displacement, tons: 5.4 full load
Dimensions, feet (metres): 35.7 × 9.3 × 2.5 *(10.88 × 2.84 × 0.75)*
Main machinery: 2 Yanmar diesels; 2 Hamilton waterjets
Speed, knots: 45
Range, n miles: 120 at 45 kt

Comment: Based on Cougar 33 deep Vee hull form, first batch of five craft supplied by Halmatic in March 2003 with further 15 delivered by late 2003. Deployed in coastal patrol and interception role.

ENFORCER 33 *3/2007, Marco Ghiglino* / 1170201

Pakistan

Country Overview

The Islamic Republic of Pakistan gained independence in 1947. Situated in south Asia, it has an area of 307,293 square miles and is bordered to the west by Iran, to the north by Afghanistan and to the south by India. It has a 567 n mile coastline with the Arabian Sea. The former province of East Pakistan seceded in 1971 and assumed the name Bangladesh. The status of Jammu and Kashmir is disputed with India. The capital is Islamabad while Karachi is the largest city and principal port. There is a further port at Muhammad bin Qasim. Territorial waters (12 n miles) are claimed. A 200 n mile EEZ has been claimed but the limits have not been defined.

Headquarters Appointments

Chief of the Naval Staff:
Admiral Noman Bashir, HI (M)
Vice Chief of Naval Staff:
Vice Admiral Asaf Humayun, HI (M)
Deputy Chief of Naval Staff (Operations):
Rear Admiral Tanveer Faiz, SI (M)

Senior Appointments

Commander Pakistan Fleet:
Rear Admiral Mohammad Asif Sandila, SI (M)
Commander Karachi:
Vice Admiral Saleem Ahmad Meenai, HI (M)
Commander Coastal Area:
Rear Admiral Muhammad Shafi, SI (M)
Commander Logistics:
Rear Admiral Bakhtiar Mohsin, HI (M)
Commander North Navy:
Commodore Syed Hassan Mustafa, SI (M)
Director General Maritime Security Agency:
Rear Admiral Azher Shamim Anwar, SI (M)

Diplomatic Representation

Naval Adviser in London:
Commodore Asif Saleem
Naval Attaché in Qatar:
Commodore Kalim Shaukat
Naval Attaché in Kuala Lumpur:
Commodore Ayaz Ahmed Nasir
Naval Attaché in Paris:
Captain Asif Khaliq
Naval Attaché in Tehran:
Captain Moazzam Ilyas
Naval Attaché in New Delhi:
Captain Javid Iqbal
Naval Attaché in Washington:
Captain Muhammad Fayyaz Gilani
Naval Adviser in New Delhi:
Captain Javaid Iqbal
Naval Attaché in Bonn:
Captain Muhammad Shafiq
Naval Attaché in Beijing:
Captain Mirza Foad Amin Baig
Defence Attaché in Muscat:
Captain Shahid Sohail Rao

Personnel

(a) 2009: 25,100 (2,980 officers) including 1,200 Marines and 1,000 (36 officers) seconded to the MSA
(b) Voluntary service
(c) Reserves 5,000

Bases

PNS *Haider* (Naval HQ); PNS *Akram* (Gwadar Naval Base); PNS *Iqbal* (Commando Base); PNS *Mehran* (Karachi Naval Air Station); PNS *Qasim* (Marines HQ/Base), Jinnah Naval Base (Port Ormara)

Prefix to Ships' Names

PNS

Maritime Security Agency

Set up in 1986. Main purpose is to patrol the EEZ in co-operation with the Navy and the Army-manned Coast Guard.

Marines

A Marine Commando Unit was formed at PNS *Iqbal*, Karachi in 1991.

Strength of the Fleet

Type	*Active*	*Building*
Submarines—Patrol	5	(3)
Submarines—Midget	3	–
Destroyers/Frigates	7	3
Fast Attack Craft—Missile	4	–
Large Patrol Craft	2	–
Hovercraft	4	–
Minehunters	3	–
Survey Ship	1	–
Tankers	5	–
Maritime Security Agency		
Destroyers	1	–
Large Patrol Craft	4	2
Fast Attack Craft—Gun	2	–

DELETIONS

Frigates

2006 *Zulfiquar*

PENNANT LIST

Submarines

S 135	Hashmat
S 136	Hurmat
S 137	Khalid
S 138	Saad
S 139	Hamza

Destroyers/Frigates

D 181	Tariq
D 182	Babur
D 183	Khaibar
D 184	Badr
D 185	Tippu Sultan
D 186	Shahjahan
251	Zulfiquar
252	Shamsheer (bldg)
253	Saif (bldg)

Mine Warfare Forces

M 163	Muhafiz
M 164	Mujahid
M 166	Munsif

Patrol Forces

P 140	Rajshahi
P 157	Larkana
P 1023	Jurrat
P 1028	Quwwat
P 1029	Jalalat
P 1030	Shujaat

Maritime Security Agency

D 156	Nazim
1060	Barkat
1061	Rehmat
1062	Nusrat
1063	Vehdat
1066	Subqat
1068	Rafaqat

Auxiliaries

A 20	Moawin
A 21	Kalmat
A 40	Attock
A 44	Bholu
A 45	Gama
A 47	Nasr
A 49	Gwadar
–	Janbaz
SV 48	Behr Paima

SUBMARINES

Notes: A competition for the acquisition of three new diesel-electric sumarines was launched in 2006. Air-independent propulsion is a requirement and principal contenders are reported to include the French (DCN) Scorpene class and Germany's (HDW) Type 214. The submarines are expected to be built in Pakistan.

2 HASHMAT (AGOSTA 70) CLASS (SSK)

Name	*No*	*Builders*	*Laid down*	*Launched*	*Commissioned*
HASHMAT (ex-*Astrant*)	S 135	Dubigeon Normandie, Nantes	15 Sep 1976	14 Dec 1977	17 Feb 1979
HURMAT (ex-*Adventurous*)	S 136	Dubigeon Normandie, Nantes	18 Sep 1977	1 Dec 1978	18 Feb 1980

Displacement, tons: 1,490 surfaced; 1,740 dived
Dimensions, feet (metres): 221.7 × 22.3 × 17.7 (*67.6 × 6.8 × 5.4*)
Main machinery: Diesel-electric; 2 SEMT-Pielstick 16 PA4 V 185 VG diesels; 3,600 hp(m) (*2.65 MW*); 2 Jeumont Schneider alternators; 1.7 MW; 1 motor; 4,600 hp(m) (*3.4 MW*); 1 cruising motor; 32 hp(m) (*23 kW*); 1 shaft
Speed, knots: 12 surfaced; 20 dived
Range, n miles: 8,500 at 9 kt snorting; 350 at 3.5 kt dived
Complement: 59 (8 officers)

Missiles: SSM: McDonnell Douglas Sub Harpoon; active radar homing to 130 km (*70 n miles*) at 0.9 Mach; warhead 227 kg.
Torpedoes: 4—21 in (*533 mm*) bow tubes. ECAN F17P; wire-guided; active/passive homing to 20 km (*10.8 n miles*) at 40 kt; warhead 250 kg; water ram discharge gear. E14, E15 and L3 torpedoes are also available. Total of 20 torpedoes and missiles.
Mines: Stonefish.
Countermeasures: ESM: DR-3000; intercept and warning.
Radars: Surface search: Thomson-CSF DRUA 33; I-band.
Sonars: Thomson Sintra TSM 2233D; passive search; medium frequency.
Thomson Sintra DUUA 2B; active/passive search and attack; 8 kHz active.
Thomson Sintra TSM 2933D towed array; passive; very low frequency.

Programmes: Purchased from France in mid-1978 after United Nations' ban on arms sales to South Africa. *Hashmat* arrived Karachi 31 October 1979, *Hurmat* arrived 11 August 1980.
Structure: Diving depth, 300 m (*985 ft*). Both were modified to fire Harpoon in 1985 but may have had to acquire the missiles through a third party.
Operational: Assigned to 5th Submarine Squadron.

HURMAT *3/2000*, **Michael Nitz** / 1305311

3 KHALID (AGOSTA 90B) CLASS (SSK)

Name	*No*	*Builders*	*Laid down*	*Launched*	*Commissioned*
KHALID	S 137	DCN, Cherbourg	15 July 1995	18 Dec 1998	6 Sep 1999
SAAD	S 138	DCN, Cherbourg/PN Dockyard, Karachi	2 Dec 1999	24 Aug 2002	12 Dec 2003
HAMZA	S 139	Karachi Shipyard and Engineering Works	2000	10 Aug 2006	26 Sep 2008

Displacement, tons: 1,510 surfaced; 1,760 dived (1,980 with MESMA)
Dimensions, feet (metres): 221.7; 250.0 (S 139) × 22.3 × 17.7 *(67.6; 76.2 (S 139) × 6.8 × 5.4)*
Main machinery: Diesel-electric; 2 SEMT-Pielstick 16 PA4 V 185 VG diesels; 3,600 hp(m) *(2.65 MW)*; 2 Jeumont Schneider alternators; 1.7 MW; 1 Jeumont motor; 2,992 hp(m) *(2.2 MW)*; 1 cruising motor; 32 hp(m) *(23 kW)*; 1 shaft
Speed, knots: 12 surfaced; 20 dived
Range, n miles: 8,500 at 9 kt snorting; 350 at 3.5 kt dived
Complement: 36 (7 officers)

Missiles: SSM: 4 Aerospatiale Exocet SM 39; inertial cruise; active radar homing to 50 km *(27 n miles)* at 0.9 Mach; warhead 165 kg.
Torpedoes: 4—21 in *(533 mm)* bow tubes. 16 ECAN F17P Mod 2; wire-guided; active/passive homing to 20 km *(10.8 n miles)* at 40 kt; warhead 250 kg. Total of 20 weapons.
Mines: Stonefish.
Countermeasures: ESM: Thomson-CSF DR-3000U; intercept.
Weapons control: Thomson Sintra SUBTICS Mk 2.
Radars: Surface search: KH 1007; I-band.
Sonars: Thomson Sintra TSM 2233 suite; bow cylindrical, passive ranging and intercept, and clip-on towed arrays.

SAAD *9/2003*, **DCN** / 0562934

Programmes: A provisional order for a second batch of three more Agostas was reported in September 1992 and this was confirmed on 21 September 1994. First one built in France. Parts for S 138 sent to Pakistan in April 1998 and for S 139 in September 1998.
Structure: The last of the class has a 200 kW MESMA liquid oxygen AIP system, thereby extending the hull by 8.6 m. The MESMA AIP system has a power output of 200 kW which quadruples dived performance at 4 kt. The MESMA system is to be retrofitted in S 137 and S 138 during their next major refits from about 2012. Hulls also have much improved acoustic quietening and a full integrated sonar suite including flank, intercept and towed arrays. SOPOLEM J 95 search and STS 95 attack periscopes. Sagem integrated navigation system. HLES 80 steel. Diving depth of 320 m *(1,050 ft)*.
Operational: *Khalid* completed 29 April 1999 and sailed for Pakistan in November 1999. Assigned to 5th Submarine Squadron.

HAMZA *8/2006*, **DCN** / 1164868

3 MIDGET SUBMARINES (SSW)

X 01–X 03

Displacement, tons: 118 dived
Dimensions, feet (metres): 91.2 × 18.4 *(27.8 × 5.6)*
Speed, knots: 7 dived
Range, n miles: 2,200 surfaced; 60 dived
Complement: 8 + 8 swimmers
Torpedoes: 2—21 in *(533 mm)* tubes; 2 ALCATEL E 14/E 15; active homing to 12 km *(6.5 n miles)* at 25 kt; passive homing to 28 km *(15 n miles)* at 23 kt; warhead 300 kg plus either two short range active/passive homing torpedoes or two SDVs.
Mines: 12 Mk 414 Limpet type.
Sonars: Hull mounted; active/passive; high frequency.

Comment: MG 110 type built in Pakistan under supervision by Cosmos. These are enlarged SX 756 of Italian Cosmos design. Diving depth of 150 m and can carry eight swimmers with 2 tons of explosives as well as two CF2 FX 60 SDVs (swimmer delivery vehicles). Pilkington Optronics CK 39 periscopes. Reported as having a range of 1,000 n miles and an endurance of 20 days. All have been upgraded since 1995 with improved sensors and weapons. However, reports that *X 01* has been equipped with Harpoon are not considered likely. All are active.

X 03 *5/2003* / 0569226

FRIGATES

Notes: Procurement of second-hand frigates is under consideration.

6 TARIQ (AMAZON) CLASS (TYPE 21) (FFHM/FFGH)

Name	*No*	*Builders*	*Laid down*	*Launched*	*Commissioned*	*Recommissioned*
TARIQ (ex-*Ambuscade*)	D 181 (ex-F 172)	Yarrow Shipbuilders, Glasgow	1 Sep 1971	18 Jan 1973	5 Sep 1975	28 July 1993
BABUR (ex-*Amazon*)	D 182 (ex-F 169)	Vosper Thornycroft, Woolston	6 Nov 1969	26 Apr 1971	11 May 1974	30 Sep 1993
KHAIBAR (ex-*Arrow*)	D 183 (ex-F 173)	Yarrow Shipbuilders, Glasgow	28 Sep 1972	5 Feb 1974	29 July 1976	1 Mar 1994
BADR (ex-*Alacrity*)	D 184 (ex-F 174)	Yarrow Shipbuilders, Glasgow	5 Mar 1973	18 Sep 1974	2 July 1977	1 Mar 1994
TIPPU SULTAN (ex-*Avenger*)	D 185 (ex-F 185)	Yarrow Shipbuilders, Glasgow	30 Oct 1974	20 Nov 1975	19 July 1978	23 Sep 1994
SHAHJAHAN (ex-*Active*)	D 186 (ex-F 171)	Vosper Thornycroft, Woolston	23 July 1971	23 Nov 1972	17 June 1977	23 Sep 1994

Displacement, tons: 3,100 standard; 3,700 full load
Dimensions, feet (metres): 384 oa; 360 wl × 41.7 × 19.5 (screws) *(117; 109.7 × 12.7 × 5.9)*
Main machinery: COGOG; 2 RR Olympus TM3B gas turbines; 50,000 hp *(37.3 MW)* sustained; 2 RR Tyne RM1C gas turbines (cruising); 9,900 hp *(7.4 MW)* sustained; 2 shafts; cp props
Speed, knots: 30; 18 on Tynes
Range, n miles: 4,000 at 17 kt; 1,200 at 30 kt
Complement: 221 (23 officers) (accommodation for 192)

Missiles: SSM: 4 McDonnell Douglas Harpoon 1C (1) fitted in D 186, D 184 and D 182.
SAM: China LY 60N sextuple launchers (2) semi-active radar homing to 13 km *(7 n miles)* at 2.5 Mach; warhead 33 kg (D 185, D 181 and D 183).
Guns: 1 Vickers 4.5 in *(114 mm)*/55 Mk 8 (3); 25 rds/min to 22 km *(11.9 n miles)* anti-surface; 6 km *(3.3 n miles)* anti-aircraft; weight of shell 21 kg.
Hughes 20 mm Vulcan Phalanx Mk 15 (4); 3,000 rds/min to 1.5 km (D 181, D 183, D 184 and D 186).
2 MSI DS 30B 30 mm/75 (6) (D 182, D 185 and D 186).
4—12.7 mm MGs.
Torpedoes: 6—324 mm Plessey STWS Mk 2 (2 triple) tubes (7) (D 184 and D 186); others fitted with 2 Bofors Type 43X2 single launchers for Swedish Type 45 torpedoes.
Countermeasures: Decoys: Graseby Type 182; towed torpedo decoy.
2 Rheinmetall MASS launchers (D 181-186) (8) Mk 36 SRBOC (9) (D 181 and D 182).
ESM: Thomson-CSF DR 3000S; intercept.
Combat data systems: CAAIS combat data system with Ferranti FM 1600B computers (D 186 and D 184). CelsiusTech 9LV Mk 3 including Link Y (in remainder).
Weapons control: Ferranti WSA-4 digital fire-control system. CSEE Najir Mk 2 optronic director (10) (D 182, D 185 and D 186).
Radars: Air/surface search: Marconi Type 992R (11); E/F-band (D 182, D 184 and D 186). Signaal DA08 (12); F-band (D 181, D 183 and D 185).
Surface search: Kelvin Hughes Type 1007 (13) or Type 1006 (D 184 and D 186); I-band.
Fire control: 1 Selenia Type 912 (RTN 10X) (14); I/J-band (D 182, D 184 and D 186).
1 China LL-1 (15) (for LY 60N); I/J-band (D 185, D 181 and D 183).

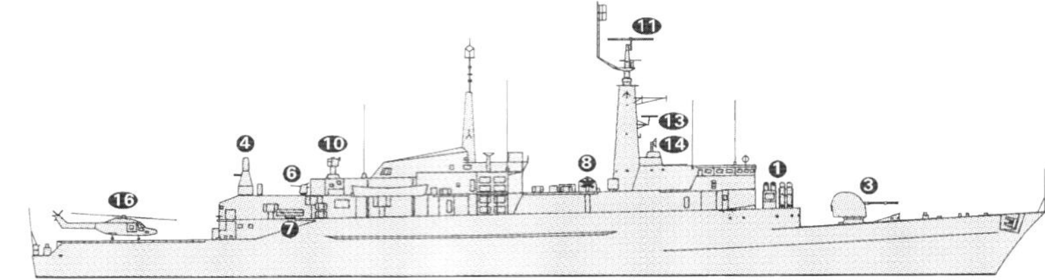

SHAHJAHAN *(Scale 1 : 1,200)*, *Ian Sturton* / 0114784

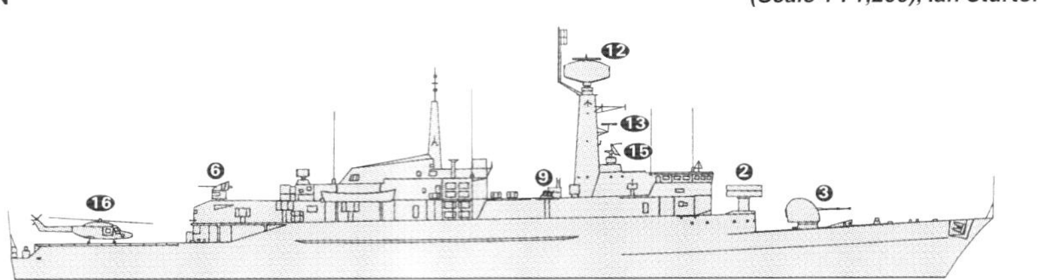

TIPPU SULTAN *(Scale 1 : 1,200)*, *Ian Sturton* / 1133556

Sonars: Graseby Type 184P; hull-mounted; active search and attack; medium frequency.
Kelvin Hughes Type 162M; hull-mounted; bottom classification; 50 kHz.
Helicopters: 1 Alouette III (16).

Programmes: Acquired from the UK in 1993–94. *Tariq* arrived in Karachi 1 November 1993 and the last pair in January 1995. These ships replaced the Garcia and Brooke classes and have been classified as destroyers.
Modernisation: Exocet, torpedo tubes and Lynx helicopter facilities were all added in RN service, but torpedo tubes were subsequently removed in all but *Badr* and *Shahjahan* and all retrofitted by Pakistan using Swedish equipment. Exocet was not transferred and the obsolete Seacat SAM system was replaced by Phalanx taken from the Gearings. Chinese LY 60N, which is a copy of Aspide, has been fitted in three of the class, Harpoon in three others. New EW equipment has been installed. There are still plans to update the hull sonars but there is no evidence that ATAS sonar has been fitted in D 183 and D 185 as previously reported. Other equipment upgrades include a DA08 search radar in three of the class, an optronic director, new 30 mm and 20 mm guns, SRBOC chaff launchers. An improved combat data system with a datalink to shore HQ is also fitted in four of the class.
Structure: Due to cracking in the upper deck structure large strengthening pieces have been fixed to the ships' side at the top of the steel hull as shown in the illustration. The addition of permanent ballast to improve stability has increased displacement by about 350 tons. Further hull modifications to reduce noise and vibration started in 1988 and completed in all of the class by 1992.
Operational: Form 25th Destroyer Squadron.

SHAHJAHAN *12/2007, Chris Sattler* / 1170021

BADR *6/2000, Pakistan Navy* / 0105184

BABUR *7/2008*, John Mortimer* / 1353249

TARIQ *6/2000, Pakistan Navy* / 0105185

KHAIBAR *6/2000, Pakistan Navy* / 0105186

1 + 3 SWORD (F-22P) CLASS (FFGH)

Name	*No*	*Builders*	*Laid down*	*Launched*	*Commissioned*
ZULFIQUAR	251	Hudong-Zhonghua Shipyard, Shanghai	12 Oct 2006	7 Apr 2008	31 Oct 2008
SHAMSHEER	252	Hudong-Zhonghua Shipyard, Shanghai	13 July 2007	31 Oct 2008	2010
SAIF	253	Hudong-Zhonghua Shipyard, Shanghai	4 Nov 2008	2009	2010
–	–	Karachi Shipyard and Engineering Works	2009	2011	2013

Displacement, tons: 2,250 full load
Dimensions, feet (metres): 403.5 × 45.9 × ?
(123.0 × 14.0 × ?)
Main machinery: 2 diesels; 2 shafts
Speed, knots: 27
Range, n miles: 4,000 at 18 kt
Complement: 170

Missiles: SSM: 8 C-802 (YJ-83/CSS-N-8 Saccade) ❶; mid-course guidance and active radar homing to 150 km *(81 n miles)* at 0.9 Mach; warhead 165 kg; sea skimmer.
SAM: 1 HQ-7 (Crotale) octuple launcher CSA-N-4 ❷; line of sight guidance to 13 km *(7 n miles)* at 2.4 Mach; warhead 14 kg.
Guns: 1—3 in (76 mm) AK 176M ❸.
2—30 mm Type 730 ❹; 7 barrels per mounting; 4,200 rds/min combined to 1.5 km.
Torpedoes: 6—324 mm (2 triple) tubes.
Countermeasures: Decoys/ESM/ECM: To be announced.
Combat data systems: To be announced.
Weapons control: Optronic director to be announced.
Radars: Air search: Type 517 Knife Rest ❺; A-band.
Air/surface search: Type 363 Seagull S ❻; E/F-band.
Fire control: Type 343G ❼; I-band (for SSM and 76 mm gun).
Type 347G(2) ❽; I-band for Type 730.
Type 345 (MR 35) ❾; I/J-band (for SAM).
Navigation: To be announced.
Sonars: Atlas Electronik DSQS-23BZ; hull-mounted; active search and attack; medium frequency.

Helicopters: 1 Harbin Zhi-9C Haitun ❿.

Programmes: A contract to procure four frigates from China was signed on 4 April 2005. The ships, three of which are to be built in Shanghai and the fourth at Karachi, look to be based on the Type 054 Jiangkai class in service in the PLA(N). Technology transfer is a key element of the deal and the contract includes the upgrade of KSEW Shipyard, training and technical assistance. Steel was first cut for the first of class on 12 October 2006. Details of weapons and sensors are indicative and are based on the Jiangwei II class in PLA(N) service. A second batch of ships may be ordered.

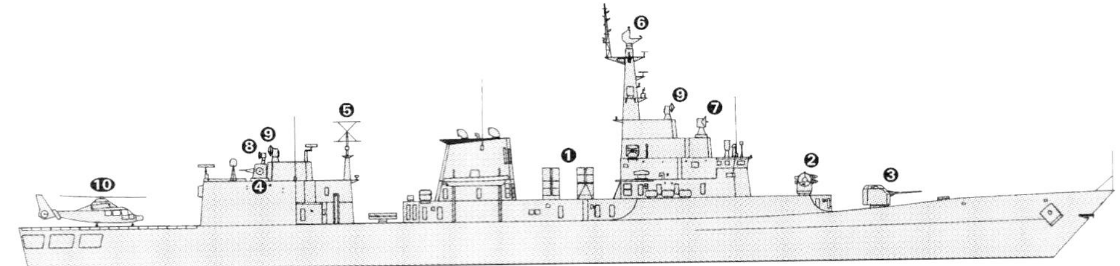

ZULFIQUAR *(Scale 1 : 900), Ian Sturton* / 1353248

ZULFIQUAR *12/2008** / 1353250

SHIPBORNE AIRCRAFT

Numbers/Type: 6 Westland Sea King Mk 45/45A.
Operational speed: 125 kt *(232 km/h)*.
Service ceiling: 10,500 ft *(3,200 m)*.
Range: 630 n miles *(1,165 km)*.
Role/Weapon systems: Sensors: ARI 5955 search radar, Marconi Type 2069 dipping sonar, Star SAFIRE FLIR. AQS-928G acoustic processors. Weapons: ASW; two Mk 46 torpedoes; Mk 11 depth charges. ASV; one AM 39 Exocet missile.

SEA KING *6/2007, Hachiro Nakai* / 1166819

Numbers/Type: 4/10 Aerospatiale SA 316 Alouette III/SA 319B Alouette III.
Operational speed: 113 kt *(210 km/h)*.
Service ceiling: 10,660 ft *(3,250 m)*.
Range: 270 n miles *(500 km)*.
Role/Weapon systems: Reconnaissance helicopter. Two SA 319B procured in mid-1970s and fitted with radar and MAD. Eight further SA 319B (eight ex-French Air Force) purchased in 2005 for delivery in 2008 after refurbishment. Four SA 316 acquired in 1994. Sensors: Weather/search radar and MAD (in two SA 319B). Weapons: ASW: Mk 11 depth charges, and MG1 A3 gun.

ALOUETTE III *6/2003, Pakistan Navy* / 0569234

Numbers/Type: 6 Hai Z-9EC.
Operational speed: 140 kt *(260 km/h)*.
Service ceiling: 15,000 ft *(4,572 m)*.
Range: 200 n miles *(370 km)*.
Role/Weapon systems: ASW helicopter procured in conjunction with Zulfiquar class frigate programme. Chinese design based on Dauphin 2. Sensors: KLC-1 radar; ESM, DSE Sonar. Weapons: up to four ET-52C torpedoes.

LAND-BASED MARITIME AIRCRAFT

Notes: The Maritime Security Agency operates three Britten-Norman Maritime Defenders. with Bendix RDR 1400C radars.

DEFENDER *8/1996, MSA* / 0081375

Numbers/Type: 10 Lockheed P-3C Orion (Update II).
Operational speed: 410 kt *(760 km/h)*.
Service ceiling: 28,300 ft *(8,625 m)*.
Range: 4,000 n miles *(7,410 km)*.
Role/Weapon systems: Order of first two completed in 1991 but held up by the Pressler amendment, until delivery in December 1996. May be used for Elint. Eight further aircraft donated by the United States in September 2005. The first two, delivered in early 2007, are to have an avionics upgrade at a later date. The remaining six are to be upgraded before delivery. Sensors: APS-115 search radar; up to 100 sonobuoys; ASQ 81 MAD; ESM. Weapons: four Whitehead A 244 torpedoes or Mk 11 depth charges for ASW; Harpoon.

P-3C *6/2001, Pakistan Navy* / 0114783

Numbers/Type: 6 Fokker F27-200.
Operational speed: 250 kt *(463 km/h)*.
Service ceiling: 29,500 ft *(8,990 m)*.
Range: 2,700 n miles *(5,000 km)*.
Role/Weapon systems: Acquired in 1994–96 for maritime surveillance and limited ASW. One further aircraft acquired in 2007. Sensors: OM 100 radar, Thomson-CSF DR 3000A ESM. Star SAFIRE FLIR. Weapons: Mk II depth charge.

FOKKER F27-200 *6/2001*, ***Pakistan Navy*** / 0114780

Numbers/Type: 2 Breguet Atlantic 1.
Operational speed: 355 kt *(658 km/h)*.
Service ceiling: 32,800 ft *(10,000 m)*.
Range: 4,855 n miles *(8,995 km)*.
Role/Weapon systems: Long-range MR/ASW cover for Arabian Sea; ex-French and Dutch stock. Upgraded in 1992–93. Three more acquired in 1994 for spares. Sensors: Thomson-CSF Ocean Master radar, Thomson-CSF DR 3000A ESM, MAD, sonobuoys, Sadang 1C sonobuoy signal processor. Weapons: ASW; nine Mk 46 torpedoes, Mk 11 depth bombs, mines. ASV; AM 39 Exocet missiles.

ATLANTIC 1 *6/2001*, ***Pakistan Navy*** / 0114781

Numbers/Type: 12 AMD-BA Mirage III.
Operational speed: 750 kt *(1,390 km/h)*.
Service ceiling: 59,055 ft *(18,000 m)*.
Range: 740 n miles *(1,370 km)*.
Role/Weapon systems: Operated by the Air Force, and all can be used for maritime strike. Sensors: Thomson-CSF radar. Weapons: ASV; two AM 39 Exocet or Harpoon; two 30 mm DEFA.

MIRAGE III *6/2004*, ***Pakistan Navy*** / 1044171

Numbers/Type: 5 Saab 2000 AEW.
Operational speed: 250 kt *(463 km/h)*.
Service ceiling: 25,000 ft *(7,620 m)*.
Range: 570 n miles *(1,056 km)*.
Role/Weapon systems: Air Force operated early warning aircraft. Modified version of Saab 340B special mission aircraft derived from regional transport aircraft. Dorsal-mounted main radar. First aircraft rolled out in mid-June 2008 for delivery in 2009. Sensors: Ericsson Erieye radar, ESM, ECM.

SAAB 2000 AEW *5/2008**, ***Saab*** / 1330714

PATROL FORCES

Notes: Eight Mekat type catamarans ordered in late 1997. These may be operated by the Customs.

2 JALALAT CLASS (FAST ATTACK CRAFT—MISSILE) (PTG)

Name	*No*	*Builders*	*Launched*	*Commissioned*
JALALAT	1029 (ex-1022)	PN Dockyard, Karachi	16 Nov 1996	14 Aug 1997
SHUJAAT	1030	PN Dockyard, Karachi	26 Mar 1999	30 Sep 1999

Displacement, tons: 185 full load
Dimensions, feet (metres): 128 × 22 × 5.4 *(39 × 6.7 × 1.64)*
Main machinery: 2 MTU diesels; 5,984 hp(m) *(4.4 MW)* sustained; 2 shafts
Speed, knots: 23. **Range, n miles**: 2,000 at 17 kt
Complement: 31 (3 officers)
Missiles: SSM: 4 China C 802 Saccade (2 twin); active radar homing to 120 km *(66 n miles)* at 0.9 Mach; warhead 165 kg; sea skimmer.
Guns: 2—37 mm/63 (twin); 180 rds/min to 8.5 km *(4.6 n miles)*; weight of shell 1.42 kg.
Countermeasures: Decoys: chaff launcher.
ESM: Thales DR 3000.
Radars: Surface search: Kelvin Hughes Type 756; I-band.
Fire control: Type 47G (for gun); Type TR 47G A/R (for SSM); I-band.

Comment: Designed with Chinese assistance to replace deleted Hegu class. Same hull as *Larkana*.

JALALAT *3/2007* / 1170017

2 JURRAT CLASS (FAST ATTACK CRAFT—MISSILE) (PTG)

Name	*No*	*Builders*	*Launched*	*Commissioned*
JURRAT	1023	Karachi Shipyards and Engineering Works	9 Sep 2004	24 Feb 2006
QUWWAT	1028	Karachi Shipyards and Engineering Works	13 Sep 2004	24 Feb 2006

Displacement, tons: 225 standard; 250 full load
Dimensions, feet (metres): 127.4 × 26.2 × 4.9 *(38.85 × 8.0 × 1.85)*
Main machinery: 3 MTU 16V 4000 M70; 3 shafts; ducted propellers
Speed, knots: 32. **Range, n miles**: 1,700 at 15 kt
Complement: 35 (3 officers)
Missiles: SSM: 4 China C 802 Saccade (2 twin); active radar homing to 120 km *(66 n miles)* at 0.9 Mach; warhead 165 kg; sea skimmer.
Guns: 2—25 mm (twin).
Countermeasures: Decoys: chaff launcher.
ESM: RW-28 CB; warning receiver.
Radars: Surface search: Type SR 47A; I-band.
Fire control: Type 47G (for gun); Type TR 47G A/R (for SSM); I-band.

Comment: Both ordered in September 2002 and laid down 4 April 2003. Built at KSEW, reportedly in co-operation with Thai company Marsun. Steel hull and aluminium superstructure.

JURRAT *3/2008**, ***Michael Nitz*** / 1305312

1 TOWN CLASS (LARGE PATROL CRAFT) (PB)

Name	*No*	*Builders*	*Commissioned*
RAJSHAHI	P 140	Brooke Marine	1965

Displacement, tons: 115 standard; 143 full load
Dimensions, feet (metres): 107 × 20 × 6.9 *(32.6 × 6.1 × 2.1)*
Main machinery: 2 MTU 12V 538 diesels; 3,400 hp(m) *(2.5 MW)*; 2 shafts
Speed, knots: 24
Complement: 19
Guns: 2 Bofors 40 mm/60. 2—12.7 mm MGs.
Radars: Surface search: Pot Head; I-band.

Comment: The last survivor in Pakistan of a class of four built by Brooke Marine in 1965. Steel hull and aluminium superstructure. Assigned to 10th Patrol Squadron.

RAJSHAHI *6/2003*, ***Pakistan Navy*** / 0569233

1 LARKANA CLASS (LARGE PATROL CRAFT) (PB)

Name	*No*	*Builders*	*Commissioned*
LARKANA	P 157	PN Dockyard, Karachi	6 June 1994

Displacement, tons: 180 full load
Dimensions, feet (metres): 128 × 22 × 5.4 *(39 × 6.7 × 1.7)*
Main machinery: 2 MTU diesels; 5,984 hp(m) *(4.4 MW)* sustained; 2 shafts
Speed, knots: 23. **Range, n miles:** 2,000 at 17 kt
Complement: 25 (3 officers)
Guns: 2 Type 76A 37 mm/63 (twin). 4—25 mm/60 (2 twin).
Depth charges: 2 Mk 64 launchers.
Radars: Surface search: Kelvin Hughes Type 756; I-band.

Comment: Ordered in 1991 and started building in October 1992. Has replaced the last of the Hainan class. The missile version on the same hull has taken priority but more may be built. Assigned to 10th Patrol Squadron.

LARKANA *9/2004* / 1133552

4 GRIFFON 2000 TDX(M) (HOVERCRAFT) (UCAC)

Displacement, tons: 7.5 full load
Dimensions, feet (metres): 39.0 × 20.0 *(11.9 × 6.1)*
Main machinery: 1 Deutz BF8L513 diesel; 355 hp *(265 kW)* sustained
Speed, knots: 35. **Range, n miles:** 300 at 25 kt
Complement: 2
Military lift: 25 troops or 2 tons
Guns: 2—12.7 mm MGs.
Radars: Navigation: I-band.

Comment: Acquired from Griffon, UK. First craft delivered in April 2004 and the last in July 2005. The first two are of a modular design to enable rapid role-change. The second two have fixed roofs.

GRIFFON 2000 *6/2005, Griffon Hovercraft* / 1153502

2 KAAN 15 (FAST INTERVENTION CRAFT) (PBF)

P 01 **P 02**

Displacement, tons: 19 full load
Dimensions, feet (metres): 54.8 × 13.2 × 3.9 *(16.7 × 4.04 × 1.2)*
Main machinery: 2 MTU 12V 183TE93 diesels; 2,300 hp(m) *(1.69 MW)*; 2 Arneson ASD 12 B1L surface drives
Speed, knots: 54. **Range, n miles:** 350 at 35 kt
Complement: 4 plus 8 mission crew
Guns: 2—12.7 mm MGs.

Comment: Built by Yonca Shipyard, Turkey. Advanced composites structure. The first delivered on 17 August 2004 and the second on 14 October 2004. To be operated by Special Services Group based at PNS Iqbar. Details based on those in Turkish Coast Guard service.

P 01 *7/2004, Selçuk Emre* / 1044173

2 KAAN 33 (FAST ATTACK CRAFT) (PGGF)

ZARRAR P 03 **KARRAR** P 04

Displacement, tons: 120 full load
Dimensions, feet (metres): 116.8 × 22.0 × 4.7 *(35.6 × 6.7 × 1.4)*
Main machinery: CODAG: 1 Honeywell TF50 gas turbine; 2 MTU 12V 4000 M90 diesels; 7,396 hp(m) *(5.44 MW)*; 3 MJP 650/750 waterjets
Speed, knots: 65 (28 on diesels). **Range, n miles:** 970 at 15 kt
Complement: 18 (2 officers)
Missiles: SSM: 4 McDonnell Douglas Harpoon Block 2; active radar homing to 130 km *(70 n miles)* at 0.9 Mach; warhead 227 kg.
Guns: 1—30 mm. 2—12.7 mm MGs.

Comment: Following a tendering process, two MRTP 33 fast attack craft ordered from Yonca-Onuk Shipyard, Turkey on 8 June 2006. Construction began in February 2007 and delivery of the first of class was made on 26 November 2007. The second followed in April 2008. With advanced composites structure, the craft are improved versions of those in service in the Turkish Coast Guard. The craft are to be used for patrol of littoral waters, maritime interdiction and special forces operations.

ZARRAR *6/2007, Yonca-Onuk* / 1353251

4 MILITARY ASSAULT CRAFT (LCP)

114 **+3**

Displacement, tons: To be announced
Dimensions, feet (metres): To be announced
Main machinery: To be announced
Speed, knots: 30
Complement: 4 plus 14 troops
Guns: 2—12.7 mm MGs.

Comment: Built by Marsun Shipyard, Thailand. The first was delivered on 11 December 2004. Appearance is similar to SEAL assault craft in service with the Thai Navy.

MILITARY ASSAULT CRAFT 114 *3/2007* / 1170019

MINE WARFARE FORCES

3 MUNSIF (ÉRIDAN) CLASS (MINEHUNTERS) (MHSC)

Name	*No*	*Builders*	*Launched*	*Commissioned*
MUNSIF (ex-*Sagittaire*)	M 166	Lorient Dockyard	9 Nov 1988	27 July 1989
MUHAFIZ	M 163	Lorient Dockyard	8 July 1995	15 May 1996
MUJAHID	M 164	Lorient/PN Dockyard, Karachi	28 Jan 1997	9 July 1998

Displacement, tons: 562 standard; 595 full load
Dimensions, feet (metres): 168.9 × 29.2 × 9.5 *(51.5 × 8.9 × 2.9)*
Main machinery: 1 Stork Wärtsilä A-RUB 215X-12 diesel; 1,860 hp(m) *(1.37 MW)* sustained; 1 shaft; LIPS cp prop; auxiliary propulsion; 2 motors; 240 hp(m) *(179 kW)*; 2 active rudders; 2 bow thrusters
Speed, knots: 15; 7 on auxiliary propulsion
Range, n miles: 3,000 at 12 kt
Complement: 46 (5 officers)
Guns: 1 GIAT 20F2 20 mm; 1—12.7 mm MG.
Countermeasures: MCM; 2 PAP 104 Mk 5 systems; mechanical sweep gear. Elesco MKR 400 acoustic sweep; MRK 960 magnetic sweep.
Combat data systems: Thomson-CSF TSM 2061 Mk 2 tactical system in the last pair.
Radars: Navigation: Racal Decca 1229 (M 166) or Kelvin Hughes 1007; I-band.
Sonars: Thomson Sintra DUBM 21B or 21D (163 and 164); hull-mounted; active; high frequency; 100 kHz (±10 kHz).
Thomson Sintra TSM 2054 MCM towed array may be included.

Comment: Contract signed with France 17 January 1992. The first recommissioned into the Pakistan Navy on 24 September 1992 after active service in the Gulf with the French Navy in 1991. Sailed for Pakistan in November 1992. The second was delivered in April 1996. The last one was transferred to Karachi by transporter ship in April 1995 with a final package following in November 1995. Form 21st Mine Countermeasures Squadron.

MUHAFIZ *3/2008*, Guy Toremans* / 1305314

SURVEY SHIPS

Notes: Acquisition of a new oceanographic research vessel was reported in November 2002 to have received Presidential approval. It is not clear whether this is to be a specialist or a multipurpose vessel.

1 SURVEY SHIP (AGS/AGOR)

Name	*No*	*Builders*	*Laid down*	*Launched*	*Commissioned*
BEHR PAIMA	SV 48	Ishikawajima, Japan	16 Feb 1982	7 July 1982	27 Dec 1982

Measurement, tons: 1,183 gross
Dimensions, feet (metres): 200.1 × 38.7 × 12.1 *(61 × 11.8 × 3.7)*
Main machinery: 2 Daihatsu 6DSM-22 diesels; 2,000 hp(m) *(1.47 MW)*; 2 shafts; cp props; bow thruster
Speed, knots: 13.7
Range, n miles: 5,400 at 12 kt
Complement: 84 (16 officers)

Comment: Ordered in November 1981. Hydrographic and oceanographic research vessel. Equipped with multibeam echo-sounder, deep echo sounder and carries two survey motor boats for inshore operations.

BEHR PAIMA *6/2003, **Pakistan Navy*** / 0569231

AUXILIARIES

Notes: An order for two unspecified 1,600-ton auxiliary ships was placed with Karachi Shipyard and Engineering Works (KSEW) in May 2007. The first was laid down on 27 February 2008. The ships are required for logistic support, SAR, mine-laying and torpedo-recovery tasks.

1 FUQING CLASS (AORH)

Name	*No*	*Builders*	*Commissioned*
NASR (ex-*X-350*)	A 47	Dalian Shipyard	27 Aug 1987

Displacement, tons: 7,500 standard; 21,750 full load
Dimensions, feet (metres): 561 × 71.5 × 30.8 *(171 × 21.8 × 9.4)*
Main machinery: 1 Sulzer 8RLB66 diesel; 13,000 hp(m) *(9.56 MW)*; 1 shaft
Speed, knots: 18
Range, n miles: 18,000 at 14 kt
Complement: 130 (during visit to Australia in October 1988 carried 373 (23 officers) including 100 cadets)
Cargo capacity: 10,550 tons fuel; 1,000 tons dieso; 200 tons feed water; 200 tons drinking water
Guns: 1 GE/GD Vulcan Phalanx CIWS. 4—37 mm (2 twin). 2—12.7 mm MGs.
Countermeasures: Decoys: SRBOC Mk 36 chaff launcher. 2 Rheinmetall MASS launchers.
ESM: Thales DR 3000.
Radars: Navigation: 1 Kelvin Hughes 1007; 1 SPS 66; I-band.
Helicopters: 1 SA 319B Alouette III.

Comment: Similar to Chinese ships of the same class. Two replenishment at sea positions on each side for liquids and one for solids. Phalanx fitted on the hangar roof in 1995. Assigned to 42nd Auxiliary Squadron.

NASR *7/2008*, **John Mortimer*** / 1353252

2 COASTAL TANKERS (AOTL)

Name	*No*	*Builders*	*Commissioned*
GWADAR	A 49	Karachi Shipyard	1984
KALMAT	A 21	Karachi Shipyard	29 Aug 1992

Measurement, tons: 831 grt
Dimensions, feet (metres): 206 × 37.1 × 9.8 *(62.8 × 11.3 × 3)*
Main machinery: 1 Sulzer diesel; 550 hp(m) *(404 kW)*; 1 shaft
Speed, knots: 10
Complement: 25
Cargo capacity: 340 m³ fuel or water
Guns: 2—7.62 mm MGs.

Comment: Assigned to 42nd Auxiliary Squadron.

GWADAR *3/2008*, **Guy Toremans*** / 1305313

1 POOLSTER CLASS (AORH)

Name	*No*	*Builders*	*Commissioned*	*Recommissioned*
MOAWIN (ex-*Poolster*)	A 20 (ex-A 835)	Rotterdamse Droogdok Mij	10 Sep 1964	28 July 1994

Displacement, tons: 16,800 full load
Measurement, tons: 10,000 dwt
Dimensions, feet (metres): 552.2 × 66.6 × 26.9 *(168.3 × 20.3 × 8.2)*
Main machinery: 2 boilers; 2 turbines; 22,000 hp(m) *(16.2 MW)*; 1 shaft
Speed, knots: 21
Complement: 200 (17 officers)
Cargo capacity: 10,300 tons including 8-9,000 tons oil fuel
Guns: 4—20 mm Oerlikon (2 twin). 2—12.7 mm MGs.
Countermeasures: Decoys: SRBOC Mk 36 chaff launcher.
ESM: SLQ-32.
Radars: Air/surface search: Racal Decca 2459; F/I-band.
Navigation: Racal Decca TM 1229C; I-band.
Sonars: Signaal CWE 10; hull-mounted; active search; medium frequency.
Helicopters: 1 Sea King.

Comment: Acquired from the Netherlands Navy. Helicopter deck aft. Funnel heightened by 4.5 m *(14.8 ft)*. Capacity for five Lynx sized helicopters. Two fuelling stations each side for underway replenishment. Phalanx to be fitted in due course. Assigned to 42nd Auxiliary Squadron.

MOAWIN *6/2007, **Hachiro Nakai*** / 1166816

1 TANKER (AOTL)

ATTOCK A 40

Displacement, tons: 1,200 full load
Dimensions, feet (metres): 177.2 × 32.3 × 15.1 *(54 × 9.8 × 4.6)*
Main machinery: 2 diesels; 800 hp(m) *(276 kW)*; 2 shafts
Speed, knots: 8
Complement: 18
Cargo capacity: 550 tons fuel
Guns: 2 Oerlikon 20 mm.

Comment: Built in Italy in 1957. Assigned to 42nd Auxiliary Squadron.

ATTOCK *6/2004, **Pakistan Navy*** / 1044169

TUGS

Notes: *Jandar* and *Jafakash* are two pusher tugs (10 ton bollard pull) built by Karachi Shipyard and commissioned in 2000.

JANDAR and JAFAKASH *6/2003, Pakistan Navy* / 1044170

5 COASTAL TUGS (YTB)

Name	*No*	*Builders*	*Commissioned*
BHOLU	A 44	Giessendam Shipyard, Netherlands	Apr 1991
GAMA	A 45	Giessendam Shipyard, Netherlands	Apr 1991
JANBAZ	–	Karachi Shipyard	Sep 1990
JOSHILA	–	Karachi Shipyard	Sep 2000
DELAIR	–	Karachi Shipyard	Sep 2000

Displacement, tons: 265 full load
Dimensions, feet (metres): 85.3 × 22.3 × 9.5 *(26 × 6.8 × 2.9)*
Main machinery: 2 Cummins KTA38-M diesels; 1,836 hp *(1.26 MW)* sustained; 2 shafts
Speed, knots: 12
Complement: 6

Comment: Details are for *Bholu* and *Gama*, built by Damen Shipyards and which entered service in 1991. *Janbaz* and *Joshila* were built by Karachi Shipyard and delivered in 1990 and 2000 respectively.

JOSHILA *5/2003* / 0569222

MARITIME SECURITY AGENCY

Notes: (1) All ships are painted white with a distinctive diagonal blue and red band and MSA on each side.
(2) One Britten-Norman Maritime Defender acquired in 1993, a second in 1994 and a third on 8 August 2004. Based near Karachi with 93 Squadron.
(3) Plans for new aircraft are under consideration.

2 SHANGHAI II CLASS (FAST ATTACK CRAFT—GUN) (PB)

SUBQAT P 1066 **RAFAQAT** P 1068

Displacement, tons: 131 full load
Dimensions, feet (metres): 127.3 × 17.7 × 5.6 *(38.8 × 5.4 × 1.7)*
Main machinery: 2 Type L12-180 diesels; 2,400 hp(m) *(1.76 MW)* (forward); 2 Type 12-D-6 diesels; 1,820 hp(m) *(1.34 MW)* (aft); 4 shafts
Speed, knots: 30. **Range, n miles**: 700 at 16.5 kt
Complement: 34
Guns: 4—37 mm/63 (2 twin). 2—25 mm/80 (twin).
Depth charges: 2 projectors; 8 weapons.
Mines: Fitted with mine rails for approx 10 mines.
Radars: Surface search: Anritsu ARC-32A; I-band.

Comment: Four of the class were transferred from the Navy in 1986 and two more in 1998. The last pair were then replaced by naval craft. All were originally acquired from China 1972–1976.

SUBQAT *5/2003* / 0569223

1 GEARING (FRAM 1) CLASS (DD)

Name	*No*	*Builders*	*Commissioned*
NAZIM (ex-*Tughril*)	D 156 (ex-D 167)	Todd Pacific	4 Aug 1945

Displacement, tons: 2,425 standard; 3,500 full load
Dimensions, feet (metres): 390.5 × 41.2 × 19 *(119 × 12.6 × 5.8)*
Main machinery: 4 Babcock & Wilcox boilers; 600 psi *(43.3 kg/cm²)*; 850°F *(454°C)*; 2 GE turbines; 60,000 hp *(45 MW)*; 2 shafts
Speed, knots: 32. **Range, n miles**: 4,500 at 16 kt
Complement: 180 (15 officers)
Guns: 2 US 5 in *(127 mm)*/38 Mk 38 (twin); 15 rds/min to 17 km *(9.3 n miles)* anti-surface; 11 km *(5.9 n miles)*; anti-aircraft; weight of shell 25 kg.
4—25 mm (2 twin).
Torpedoes: 6—324 mm Mk 32 (2 triple) tubes.
Countermeasures: Decoys: 2 Plessey Shield 6-barrelled fixed launchers; chaff and IR flares in distraction, decoy or centroid modes.
Weapons control: Mk 37 for 5 in guns. OE 2 SATCOM.
Radars: Surface search: Raytheon/Sylvania; SPS-10; G-band.
Navigation: KH 1007; I-band.
Fire control: Western Electric Mk 25; I/J-band.

Comment: Transferred from the US on 30 September 1980 to the Navy. Passed on to the MSA in 1998 and renamed. This is the third Gearing to be renamed *Nazim*, the previous pair having been sunk as targets. All weapon systems removed except the torpedo tubes and main gun. Serves as the MSA Flagship.

NAZIM *3/2007, Paul Daly* / 1170020

4 BARKAT CLASS (PBO)

Name	*No*	*Builders*	*Commissioned*
BARKAT	1060 (ex-P 60)	China Shipbuilding Corp	29 Dec 1989
REHMAT	1061 (ex-P 61)	China Shipbuilding Corp	29 Dec 1989
NUSRAT	1062 (ex-P 62)	China Shipbuilding Corp	13 June 1990
VEHDAT	1063 (ex-P 63)	China Shipbuilding Corp	13 June 1990

Displacement, tons: 435 full load
Dimensions, feet (metres): 190.3 × 24.9 × 7.5 *(58 × 7.6 × 2.3)*
Main machinery: 4 MTU 16V 396TB93 diesels; 8,720 hp(m) *(6.4 MW)* sustained; 4 shafts
Speed, knots: 27. **Range, n miles**: 1,500 at 12 kt
Complement: 50 (5 officers)
Guns: 2—37 mm/63 (1 twin). 2—14.5 mm/60 (twin).
Radars: Surface search: 2 Anritsu ARC-32A; I-band.

Comment: Type P58A patrol craft built in China for the MSA. First two arrived in Karachi at the end of January 1990, second pair in August 1990. Some of this type of ship are in service with Chinese paramilitary forces.

VEHDAT *6/1994, Maritime Security Agency* / 0081380

1 HUANGFEN CLASS (PATROL BOAT) (PB)

SADAQAT (ex-*Dehshat*) P 1069 (ex-P 1026)

Displacement, tons: 171 standard; 205 full load
Dimensions, feet (metres): 126.6 × 24.9 × 8.9 *(38.6 × 7.6 × 2.7)*
Main machinery: 3 Type 42-160 diesels; 12,000 hp(m) *(8.8 MW)* sustained; 3 shafts
Speed, knots: 28. **Range, n miles**: 800 at 22 kt
Complement: 28
Guns: 4 Norinco 25 mm/80 (2 twin); 270 rds/min to 3 km *(1.6 n miles)*; weight of shell 0.34 kg.
Radars: Surface search: Square Tie; I-band.

Comment: Originally transferred to the Pakistan Navy in April 1984. The then missile-armed craft were Chinese versions of the Soviet Osa II class. This craft was transferred to the MSA on 25 June 2005.

SADAQAT *6/2005, Maritime Security Agency* / 1164330

3 GUNS CLASS (PATROL BOATS) (PB)

GUNS MS 111 **SUR** MS 112 **MALAN** MS 113

Displacement, tons: 15 full load
Dimensions, feet (metres): 42.6 × 12.0 × 3.3 *(13.0 × 3.65 × 1.0)*
Main machinery: 2 Yamaha ME 730TIL diesels; 636 hp *(475 kW)*; 2 shafts
Speed, knots: 21
Complement: 6
Guns: 1 — 7.62 mm MG.
Radars: Navigation: JRC 1500; I-band.

Comment: Manufactured by Karachi Shipyard and Engineering Works and commissioned in 2006. GRP construction.

MALAN ***6/2006, Maritime Security Agency*** / 1164331

COAST GUARD

Notes: (1) Unlike the Maritime Security Agency which comes under the Defence Ministry, the official Coast Guard was set up in 1985 and is manned by the Army and answerable to the Ministry of the Interior.
(2) The Customs Service is manned by naval personnel. It operates approximately 18 craft.

1 SWALLOW CLASS (PB)

SAIF

Displacement, tons: 52 full load
Dimensions, feet (metres): 65.6 × 15.4 × 4.3 *(20.0 × 4.7 × 1.3)*
Main machinery: 2 GM Detroit 12V71T1 diesels; 2,120 hp *(1.58 MW)*; 2 shafts
Speed, knots: 25
Range, n miles: 500 at 20 kt
Complement: 8
Guns: 2 — 12.7 mm MGs

Comment: Built by Swallowcraft/Kangnam and delivered in 1986.

4 CRESTITALIA MV 55 CLASS (PBF)

SADD P 551 **SHABHAZ** P 552 **VAQAR** P 553 **BURQ** P 554

Displacement, tons: 23 full load
Dimensions, feet (metres): 54.1 × 17.1 × 2.95 *(16.5 × 5.2 × 0.9)*
Main machinery: 2 MTU diesels; 2,200 hp *(1.64 MW)*; 2 shafts
Speed, knots: 35
Range, n miles: 425 at 25 kt
Complement: 5

Comment: Delivered in 1987.

SHABHAZ ***5/2003*** / 0569228

Palau

Country Overview

The Republic of Palau was a US-administered UN Trust territory from 1947 before becoming independent in 1994 when a Compact of Free Association, delegating to the US the responsibility for defence and foreign affairs, came into effect. Situated in the western Pacific Ocean, the country comprises about 200 of the Caroline Islands archipelago spread in a chain about 350 n miles long. These include Koror (the administrative centre), Babelthuap (the largest island), Arakabesan, Malakal and Peleliu. The capital is currently on Koror, but a new capital is being built in eastern Babelthuap. Territorial seas (3 n miles) are claimed. An extended fisheries zone (200 n miles) is also claimed but limits have not been fully defined.

Headquarters Appointments

Chief of Division of Marine Law Enforcement:
Captain Ellender Ngirameketii

PATROL FORCES

1 PACIFIC CLASS (LARGE PATROL CRAFT) (PB)

Name	*No*	*Builders*	*Commissioned*
PRESIDENT H I REMELIIK	001	Transfield Shipbuilding	May 1996

Displacement, tons: 162 full load
Dimensions, feet (metres): 103.3 × 26.6 × 6.9 *(31.5 × 8.1 × 2.1)*
Main machinery: 2 Caterpillar 3516TA diesels; 4,400 hp *(3.28 MW)* sustained; 2 shafts
Speed, knots: 20
Range, n miles: 2,500 at 12 kt
Complement: 17 (3 officers)
Guns: 2 — 7.62 mm MGs.
Radars: Surface search: Furuno 1011; I-band.

Comment: Ordered in 1995. This was the 21st hull in the Pacific class programme. Following the decision by the Australian government to extend the Pacific Patrol Boat project, the ship underwent a half-life refit at Gladstone in 2003. A life-extension refit will be required in 2010/11.

PRESIDENT H I REMELIIK
6/2004, Division of Marine Law Enforcement, Palau
1044175

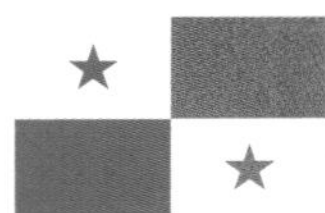

Panama

SERVICIO MARITIMO NACIONAL

Country Overview

The Republic of Panama is an independent state situated on the isthmus linking South America with Central and North America. Bordered to the west by Costa Rica and to the east by Colombia, it has an area of 29,157 square miles and a 664 n mile coastline with the north Pacific Ocean and of 370 n miles with the Caribbean. The country is bisected by the Panama Canal. A new treaty in 1977 ended US operation, maintenance and defence of the canal in 1999. The capital is Panama City while the main ports are Balboa, Cristóbal, Coco Solo, Bahía Las Minas, Vacamonte, Almirante and Puerto Armuelles. Territorial seas (12 n miles) are claimed. An Exclusive Economic Zone (EEZ) (200 n miles) has been defined by boundary agreements. Reform of the security apparatus led to the creation of the Panamanian Public Forces, which includes the National Maritime Service, in 1994.

Headquarters Appointments

Director General National Maritime Service:
Rodrigo Cigarruista Tobias

Personnel

(a) 2009: 620
(b) Voluntary service

Bases

Isla Flamenco (HQ) (Punta Brujas - HQ designate), Quebrada de Piedra, Largo Remo (under construction), Punta Cocos (air), Kuna Yala (air) (under construction)

PATROL FORCES

Notes: (1) A patrol craft *Cocle* P 814 has been reported.
(2) Four interceptor craft, capable of 35 kt, donated by the United States in July 2007.
(3) A patrol craft *Carlos Jacome* has been reported.

1 BALSAM CLASS (PBO)

Name	*No*	*Builders*	*Commissioned*
INDEPENDENCIA (ex-*Sweetgum*)	A 401 (ex-WLB 309)	Marine Iron and Shipbuilding Corp, Duluth, Minnesota	20 Nov 1943

Displacement, tons: 1,034 full load
Dimensions, feet (metres): 180 × 37 × 12 *(54.9 × 11.3 × 3.8)*
Main machinery: Diesel electric; 2 diesels; 1,402 hp *(1.06 MW)*; 1 motor; 1,200 hp *(895 kW)*; 1 shaft; bow thruster
Speed, knots: 13
Range, n miles: 8,000 at 12 kt
Complement: 53
Guns: 2 — 12.7 mm MGs.
Radars: Navigation: Raytheon SPS-64(V)1.

Comment: Transferred from US Coast Guard on 15 February 2002. Operates as an offshore patrol ship.

INDEPENDENCIA ***1/2004*** / 0587788

2 VOSPER TYPE (COASTAL PATROL CRAFT) (PB)

Name	*No*	*Builders*	*Commissioned*
PANQUIACO	P 301 (ex-GC 10)	Vospers, Portsmouth	July 1971
LIGIA ELENA	P 302 (ex-GC 11)	Vospers, Portsmouth	July 1971

Displacement, tons: 96 standard; 145 full load
Dimensions, feet (metres): 103 × 18.9 × 5.8 *(31.4 × 5.8 × 1.8)*
Main machinery: 2 Detroit diesels; 5,000 hp *(3.73 MW)*; 2 shafts
Speed, knots: 18
Range, n miles: 1,500 at 14 kt
Complement: 17 (3 officers)
Guns: 2 — 7.62 mm MGs.
Radars: Surface search: Raytheon R-81; I-band.

Comment: *Panquiaco* launched on 22 July 1970, *Ligia Elena* on 25 August 1970. Hull of welded mild steel and upperworks of welded or buck-bolted aluminium alloy. Vosper fin stabiliser equipment. P 302 was sunk in December 1989, but subsequently recovered. Both vessels had major repairs in the Coco Solo shipyard from September 1992. This included new engines, a new radar and replacement guns. Pacific Flotilla. Similar craft in service in Malaysia.

LIGIA ELENA ***6/2003, Panama Maritime Service*** / 0568905

1 COASTAL PATROL CRAFT (PB)

Name	*No*	*Builders*	*Commissioned*
NAOS (ex-*Erline*)	P 303 (ex-RV 821)	Equitable, NO	Dec 1964

Displacement, tons: 120 full load
Dimensions, feet (metres): 105 × 24.9 × 6.9 *(32 × 7.6 × 2.1)*
Main machinery: 2 Caterpillar diesels; 2 shafts
Speed, knots: 10. **Range, n miles:** 550 at 8 kt
Complement: 11 (2 officers)
Guns: 2 — 7.62 mm MGs.
Radars: Surface search: Raymarx 2600; I-band.

Comment: Served as a support/research craft at the US Underwater Systems establishment at Bermuda. Transferred from US in July 1992 and recommissioned in December 1992. Refitted in 1997 with new engines. Pacific Flotilla.

NAOS ***6/2002, Panama Maritime Service*** / 0525006

1 COASTAL PATROL CRAFT (PB)

ESCUDO DE VERAGUAS (ex-*Aun Sin Nombre*, ex-*Kathyuska Kelly*) P 305 (ex-P 206)

Displacement, tons: 158 full load
Dimensions, feet (metres): 90.5 × 24.1 × 6.1 *(27.6 × 7.3 × 1.9)*
Main machinery: 2 Detroit 12V-71 diesels; 840 hp *(627 kW)* sustained; 2 shafts
Speed, knots: 10
Complement: 10 (2 officers)
Guns: 1 — 12.7 mm MG.
Radars: Surface search: Raytheon; I-band

Comment: Confiscated drug runner craft taken into service in 1996. Also used for transport duties. Caribbean Flotilla.

ESCUDO DE VERAGUAS ***11/1998, Panama Maritime Service*** / 0052687

1 COASTAL PATROL CRAFT (PB)

TABOGA P 306

Comment: Details not confirmed. Possibly a confiscated vessel.

TABOGA ***6/2003, Panama Maritime Service*** / 0568904

1 NEGRITA CLASS (COASTAL PATROL CRAFT) (PB)

CACIQUE NOME (ex-*Negrita*) P 203

Displacement, tons: 68 full load
Dimensions, feet (metres): 80 × 15 × 6 *(24.4 × 4.6 × 1.8)*
Main machinery: 2 Detroit 12V-71 diesels; 840 hp *(627 kW)*; 2 shafts
Speed, knots: 13. **Range, n miles:** 250 at 10 kt
Complement: 8 (2 officers)
Guns: 2—7.62 mm MGs.
Radars: Surface search: Raytheon 71; I-band.

Comment: Former oilfield crew boat completely rebuilt in the Coco Solo shipyard and recommissioned 5 May 1993. Pacific Flotilla.

CACIQUE NOME ***8/1998, Panama Maritime Service*** / 0052688

5 POINT CLASS (COASTAL PATROL CRAFT) (PB)

Name	*No*	*Builders*	*Commissioned*
3 DE NOVIEMBRE (ex-*Point Barrow*)	P 204 (ex-82348)	CG Yard, MD	4 Oct 1964
10 DE NOVIEMBRE (ex-*Point Huron*)	P 206 (ex-82357)	CG Yard, MD	17 Feb 1967
28 DE NOVIEMBRE (ex-*Point Frances*)	P 207 (ex-82356)	CG Yard, MD	3 Feb 1967
4 DE NOVIEMBRE (ex-*Point Winslow*)	P 208 (ex-82360)	J M Martinac, Tacoma	3 Mar 1967
5 DE NOVIEMBRE (ex-*Point Hannon*)	P 209 (ex-82355)	J M Martinac, Tacoma	23 Jan 1967

Displacement, tons: 69 full load
Dimensions, feet (metres): 83 × 17.2 × 5.8 *(25.3 × 5.2 × 1.8)*
Main machinery: 2 Cummins V-12-900M diesels; 1,600 hp *(1.18 MW)*; 2 shafts
Speed, knots: 18. **Range, n miles:** 1,500 at 8 kt
Complement: 10 (2 officers)
Guns: 2—7.62 mm MGs.
Radars: Surface search: Raytheon Pathfinder; I-band.

Comment: P 204 transferred from US Coast Guard 7 June 1991 and recommissioned 10 July 1991. P 206 and P 207 transferred 22 April 1999. P 208 transferred 20 September 2000 and P209 on 11 January 2001. Carry a RIB with a 40 hp engine. Caribbean Flotilla.

28 DE NOVIEMBRE ***6/2003, Panama Maritime Service*** / 0568902

3 COASTAL PATROL CRAFT (PB)

CHIRIQUI P 841 **VERAGUAS** P 842 **BOCAS DEL TORO** P 843

Displacement, tons: 46 full load
Dimensions, feet (metres): 73.8 × 17.3 × 2.9 *(22.5 × 5.3 × 0.9)*
Main machinery: 3 Detroit 12V 71 diesels; 1,260 hp *(940 kW)* sustained; 3 shafts
Speed, knots: 20
Complement: 7 (1 officer)
Guns: 2—7.62 mm MGs.
Radars: Surface search: Furuno 1411; I-band.

Comment: Ex-US Sea Spectre PB Mk IV Class transferred as Grant-Aid from the US in March 1998. Used for drug prevention patrols in both Flotillas.

BOCAS DEL TORO ***6/2003*** / 0568903

2 HARBOUR PATROL CRAFT (PB)

PANAMA P 101 **CALAMAR** P 102 (ex-PC 3602)

Displacement, tons: 11 full load
Dimensions, feet (metres): 36 × 13 × 3 *(11 × 4 × 0.9)*
Main machinery: 1 Detroit 6-71T diesel; 300 hp *(224 kW)*; 1 shaft
Speed, knots: 15
Range, n miles: 160 at 12 kt
Complement: 5
Guns: 1—7.62 mm MG.

Comment: Ex-US personnel landing craft. P 102 in service from December 1992, P 101 from February 1998. GRP construction. Pacific flotilla.

CALAMAR ***8/1996, Panama Maritime Service*** / 0506310

6 FAST PATROL BOATS (PBF)

BPC 2201 **BPC 2203** **BPC 2206–2209**

Dimensions, feet (metres): 22.3 × 7.5 × 2 *(6.8 × 2.3 × 0.6)*
Main machinery: 2 Johnson outboards; 280 hp *(209 kW)*
Speed, knots: 35
Complement: 4
Guns: 1—7.62 mm MG.

Comment: *BPC 2201-2205* are Boston Whaler Piraña class acquired between June 1991 and October 1992.

BPC 2203 ***11/1998, Panama Maritime Service*** / 0052690

11 FAST PATROL BOATS (PBF)

BPC 3201 **BPC 3202** **BPC 3207** **BPC 3208** **BPC 3209** **BPC 3214** **BPC 3215** **BPC 3220** **BPC 3222** **BPC 3223** **BPC 3225**

Dimensions, feet (metres): 33.5 × 7.5 × 2 *(10.2 × 2.3 × 0.6)*
Main machinery: 2 Yamaha outboards; 400 hp(m) *(294 kW)*
Speed, knots: 35
Complement: 4
Guns: 1—7.62 mm MG.

Comment: Eduardoño class acquired between June 1995 and October 1998.

BPC 3202 ***6/2003, Panama Maritime Service*** / 0587789

4 INTERCEPTOR CRAFT (PBF)

Displacement, tons: To be announced
Dimensions, feet (metres): 44.0 × 9.0 × 3.0 *(13.4 × 2.75 × 0.9)*
Main machinery: 3 Yanmar diesels; 945 hp *(704 kW)*; Bravo X drives
Speed, knots: 60
Range, n miles: 600 at 25 kt
Complement: 6

Comment: Manufactured by Nor-Tech, Fort Myers, FL. Composite and glass-fibre hull with V-bottomed hull. Donated by the US Southern Command in 2007. Employed on counter drugs, arms trafficking and illegal immigration duties.

INTERCEPT CRAFT *6/2007, US Southern Command* / 1167968

LAND-BASED MARITIME AIRCRAFT

Numbers/Type: 3 CASA C-212 Aviocar.
Operational speed: 190 kt *(353 km/h)*.
Service ceiling: 24,000 ft *(7,315 m)*.
Range: 1,650 n miles *(3,055 km)*.
Role/Weapon systems: Air Force operated coastal patrol aircraft for EEZ protection and anti-smuggling duties. Sensors: APS-128 radar, limited ESM. Weapons: ASW; two Mk 44/46 torpedoes. ASV; two rocket or machine gun pods.

C-212 *6/2003, Adolfo Ortigueira Gil* / 0587787

Numbers/Type: 1 Pilatus Britten-Norman Islander.
Operational speed: 150 kt *(280 km/h)*.
Service ceiling: 18,900 ft *(5,760 m)*.
Range: 1,500 n miles *(2,775 km)*.
Role/Weapon systems: Air Force operated coastal surveillance duties. Sensors: Search radar. Weapons: Unarmed.

AUXILIARIES

Notes: (1) There are two auxiliary craft *Frailes del Norte* T 06 (ex-US LCM 8 class) and *Frailes del Sur* T 07.
(2) *General Esteban Huertas* (ex-YFU 81) has been reported with pennant number A 402 and may have replaced *Flamenco* in July 2004.

FRAILES DEL NORTE *6/2003, Panama Maritime Service* / 0568901

1 LOGISTIC CRAFT (YAG)

ISLA PARIDAS (ex-*Endeavour*) L 21

Displacement, tons: 120 full load
Dimensions, feet (metres): 75 × 14 × 7 *(22.9 × 4.3 × 2.1)*
Main machinery: 1 Caterpillar diesel; 365 hp *(270 kW)*; 1 shaft
Speed, knots: 12
Complement: 7 (1 officer)
Radars: Navigation: Furuno; I-band.

Comment: Acquired in September 1991. Pacific flotilla.

1 COASTAL PATROL CRAFT (YO)

FLAMENCO (ex-*Scheherazade*) A 402 (ex-P 304, ex-WB 831)

Displacement, tons: 220 full load
Dimensions, feet (metres): 105 × 25 × 6.9 *(32 × 7.6 × 2.1)*
Main machinery: 2 Caterpillar diesels; 2 shafts
Speed, knots: 10
Complement: 11 (2 officers)
Guns: 2—7.62 mm MGs.
Radars: Surface search: Furuno FCR 1411; I-band.

Comment: Built in 1963. Transferred from US 22 July 1992 and commissioned in December 1992. Former US wooden hulled COOP craft. Refitted in Panama in 1994. Now used as a refuelling auxiliary. May have been replaced by ex-YFU 81.

FLAMENCO (old number) *12/1998, Panama Maritime Service* / 0052686

1 MSB 5 CLASS (YAG)

NOMBRE DE DIOS (ex-*MSB 25*) L 16

Displacement, tons: 44 full load
Dimensions, feet (metres): 57.2 × 15.5 × 4 *(17.4 × 4.7 × 1.2)*
Main machinery: 2 Detroit diesels; 600 hp *(448 kW)*; 2 shafts
Speed, knots: 12
Complement: 6 (1 officer)
Guns: 1—7.62 mm MG.
Radars: Navigation: Raytheon Raystar; I-band.

Comment: Built between 1952 and 1956. Former US minesweeping boat. Served in the canal area until 1992 and transferred from US to Panama in December 1992 after refit. Wooden hull, new engine. Used as logistic craft. Pacific flotilla.

NOMBRE DE DIOS *6/2003* / 0568899

6 SUPPORT CRAFT (YAG)

DORADO I BA 055	**DORADO III** –	**PORTOBELO** BA 058
DORADO II BA 056	**AGUACERO** BA 057	**FANTASMA AZUL** BA 059

Comment: *Dorado I* and *II* acquired in February 1998 and are used as 40 kt supply craft. *Aguacero* is a confiscated 50 kt power boat taken into service in November 1998.

DORADO I *12/1998, Panama Maritime Service* / 0052692

Papua New Guinea

Country Overview

Papua New Guinea lies north of Australia in the eastern half of New Guinea which it shares with the Indonesian province of Irian Jaya. An Australian-administered UN Trust territory from 1949, it became independent in 1975. Its head of state is the British sovereign, who is represented by a Governor-General. Its many island groups include the Bismarck and Louisiade Archipelagos, the Trobriand Islands, the D'Entrecasteaux Islands and Woodlark Island. Amongst other islands are Bougainville (a nine-year separatist conflict ended in 1997) and Buka. It has a 2,781 n mile coastline. The capital, principal city and port is Port Moresby. An archipelagic state, territorial seas (12 n miles) are claimed. A 200 n mile Exclusive Economic Zone (EEZ) has also been claimed but the limits have not been fully defined by boundary agreements.

Headquarters Appointments

Commander Defence Forces:
Commodore Peter Ilau, CBE
Director Maritime Operations:
Commander Murphy Kila

Bases

Port Moresby (HQ PNGDF and PNGDF Landing Craft Base); Lombrum (Manus)

Prefix to Ships' Names

HMPNGS

PATROL FORCES

4 PACIFIC CLASS (LARGE PATROL CRAFT) (PB)

Name	*No*	*Builders*	*Commissioned*
RABAUL (ex-*Tarangau*)	01	Australian Shipbuilding Industries	16 May 1987
DREGER	02	Australian Shipbuilding Industries	31 Oct 1987
SEEADLER	03	Australian Shipbuilding Industries	29 Oct 1988
MORESBY (ex-*Basilisk*)	04	Australian Shipbuilding Industries	1 July 1989

Displacement, tons: 162 full load
Dimensions, feet (metres): 103.3 × 26.6 × 6.9 *(31.5 × 8.1 × 2.1)*
Main machinery: 2 Caterpillar 3516TA diesels; 4,400 hp *(3.3 MW)* sustained; 2 shafts
Speed, knots: 20. **Range, n miles:** 2,500 at 12 kt
Complement: 17 (3 officers)
Guns: 1 Oerlikon GAM-BO1 20 mm. 2—7.62 mm MGs.
Radars: Surface search: Furuno 1011; I-band.

Comment: Contract awarded in 1985 to Australian Shipbuilding Industries (Hamilton Hill, West Australia) under Australian Defence co-operation. These are the first, third, sixth and seventh of the class and some of the few to be armed. All upgraded, during half-life refits in Australia with new radars and navigation support systems in 1997/98. Following the decision by the Australian government to extend the Pacific Patrol Boat project, *Rabaul* underwent a life-extension refit at Gladstone in 2003 and *Dreger* at Townsville in 2004. Similar refits conducted for *Seeadler* and *Moresby* atTownsville in 2006 and 2007 respectively.

MORESBY *7/2008*, John Mortimer* / 1335213

AUXILIARIES

2 LANDING CRAFT (LSM)

Name	*No*	*Builders*	*Commissioned*
SALAMAUA	31	Walkers Ltd, Maryborough	19 Oct 1973
BUNA	32	Walkers Ltd, Maryborough	7 Dec 1973

Displacement, tons: 310 light; 503 full load
Dimensions, feet (metres): 146 × 33 × 6.5 *(44.5 × 10.1 × 1.9)*
Main machinery: 2 GM diesels; 2 shafts
Speed, knots: 10
Range, n miles: 3,000 at 10 kt
Complement: 15 (2 officers)
Military lift: 160 tons
Guns: 2—12.7 mm MGs.
Radars: Navigation: Racal Decca RM 916; I-band.

Comment: Transferred from Australia in 1975. Underwent extensive refits 1985–86. Both vessels reported operational in 2008.

SALAMAUA *12/1990, James Goldrick* / 0081510

Paraguay

ARMADA NACIONAL

Country Overview

The Republic of Paraguay is one of two landlocked countries in South America; Bolivia is the other. With an area of 157,048 square miles, it has borders to the north with Bolivia, to the east with Brazil and to the south with Argentina. There are some 1,800 n miles of internal waterways including the principal rivers, the Pilcomayo, Paraguay and Alto Paraná. Navigable by large ships for much of their length, they link the capital, largest city and principal port, Asunción, with the Rio de la Plata estuary on the Atlantic Ocean. Other ports include Ciudad del Este, Encarnación and Concepción.

Headquarters Appointments

Commander-in-Chief of the Navy:
Rear Admiral Cibar Benitez Caceres

Personnel

2009: 3,600 including 300 Coast Guard, 800 marines and 100 naval air

Bases

Main Base: Puerto Sajonia, Asunción
Minor Bases: Base Naval de Bahia Negra (BNBN) (on upper Paraguay river)
Base Naval de Salto del Guaira (BNSG) (on upper Paraná river)
Base Naval de Ciudad del Este (BNCE) (on Paraná river)
Base Naval de Encarnacion (BNE) (on Paraná river)
Base Naval de Ita-Pirú (BNIP) (on Paraná river)

Training

Specialist training is done with Argentina (Exercise Sirena), Brazil (Exercise Ninfa) and US (Exercise Unitas).

Marine Corps

BIM 1: Puerto Rosario
BIM 2: Puerto Vallemi
BIM 3: Asunción
BIM 5: Bahia Negra
Detachments at Pozo Hondo and Ita-Pirú
BIM 8: Saltos del Guairá
Detachments at Ciudad del Este and Encarnación

Naval Aviation

Fixed Wing: Asunción International Airport
Helicopters: Puerto Sajonia

Coast Guard

Prefectura General Naval

PATROL FORCES

Notes: An unnamed 10 m patrol craft is based at Asuncion. Twelve 5 to 6 m patrol craft (LP 30-41) of four different types were commissioned in 2007; six further were ordered in 2008.

1 RIVER DEFENCE VESSEL (PGR)

Name	*No*	*Builders*	*Commissioned*
PARAGUAY	C 1	Odero, Genoa	May 1931

Displacement, tons: 636 standard; 865 full load
Dimensions, feet (metres): 231 × 35 × 5.3 *(70 × 10.7 × 1.7)*
Main machinery: 2 boilers; 2 Parsons turbines; 3,800 hp *(2.83 MW)*; 2 shafts
Speed, knots: 17
Range, n miles: 1,700 at 16 kt
Complement: 86
Guns: 4—4.7 in *(120 mm)* (2 twin). 3—3 in *(76 mm)*. 2—40 mm.
Mines: 6.
Radars: Navigation *(Paraguay)*; I-band.

Comment: Refitted in 1975. Has 0.5 in side armour plating and 0.3 in on deck. Still in restricted operational service with boiler problems. Plans to re-engine with diesels have not yet been implemented and the ship is probably non-operational. Based at Asunción. Gun tubs on either side of bridge can be fitted with single 20 mm guns.

PARAGUAY and TENIENTE FARINA *4/2003, Hartmut Ehlers* / 0587791

PARAGUAY *5/2000, Hartmut Ehlers* / 0105192

1 ITAIPÚ CLASS (RIVER DEFENCE VESSEL) (PBR)

Name	*No*	*Builders*	*Commissioned*
ITAIPÚ	P 05 (ex-P 2)	Arsenal de Marinha, Rio de Janeiro	2 Apr 1985

Displacement, tons: 365 full load
Dimensions, feet (metres): 151.9 × 27.9 × 4.6 *(46.3 × 8.5 × 1.4)*
Main machinery: 2 MAN V6V16/18TL diesels; 1,920 hp(m) *(1.41 MW)*; 2 shafts
Speed, knots: 14
Range, n miles: 6,000 at 12 kt
Complement: 40 (9 officers) plus 30 marines
Guns: 1 Bofors 40 mm/60. 2—81 mm mortars. 4—12.7 mm MGs.
Radars: Navigation: I-band.
Helicopters: Platform for 1 HB 350B or equivalent.

Comment: Ordered late 1982. Launched 16 March 1984. Same as Brazilian Roraima class. Has some hospital facilities. Based at Asunción.

ITAIPÚ *4/2003, Hartmut Ehlers* / 0567473

2 BOUCHARD CLASS (PATROL SHIPS) (PBR)

Name	*No*	*Builders*	*Commissioned*
NANAWA (ex-*Bouchard* M 7)	P 02 (ex-M 1)	Rio Santiago Naval Yard	27 Jan 1937
TENIENTE FARINA (ex-*Py* M 10)	P 04 (ex-M 3)	Rio Santiago Naval Yard	1 July 1939

Displacement, tons: 450 standard; 620 normal; 650 full load
Dimensions, feet (metres): 197 × 24 × 8.5 *(60 × 7.3 × 2.6)*
Main machinery: 2 sets MAN 2-stroke diesels; 2,000 hp(m) *(1.47 MW)*; 2 shafts
Speed, knots: 16
Range, n miles: 6,000 at 12 kt
Complement: 70
Guns: 4 Bofors 40 mm/60 (2 twin). 2—12.7 mm MGs.
Mines: 1 rail.
Radars: Navigation: I-band.

Comment: Former Argentinian minesweepers of the Bouchard class. Launched on 20 March 1936 and 31 March 1938 respectively. Transferred from the Argentine Navy to the Paraguayan Navy; *Nanawa* recommissioned 14 March 1964; *Teniente Farina* 6 May 1968. Based at Asunción. A third ship, *Capitán Meza*, was scrapped between 1995–97.

NANAWA *6/1990, Paraguay Navy* / 0081514

NANAWA *5/2000, Hartmut Ehlers* / 0105194

1 RIVER PATROL CRAFT (PBR)

Name	*No*	*Builders*	*Commissioned*
CAPITÁN CABRAL (ex-*Triunfo*)	P 01 (ex-P 1, ex-A 1)	Werf-Conrad, Haarlem	1908

Displacement, tons: 180 standard; 206 full load
Dimensions, feet (metres): 107.2 × 23.5 × 6.7 *(32.7 × 7.2 × 2.0)*
Main machinery: 1 Caterpillar 3408 diesel; 360 hp *(269 kW)*; 1 shaft
Speed, knots: 9
Complement: 25
Guns: 1 Bofors 40 mm/60. 2 Oerlikon 20 mm. 2—12.7 mm MGs.
Radars: Navigation: I-band.

Comment: Former tug. Launched in 1907. Still in excellent condition. Vickers guns were replaced and a diesel engine fitted by Arsenal de Marina in 1984. Based at Asunción.

CAPITÁN CABRAL *4/2003, Hartmut Ehlers* / 0567474

2 MODIFIED HAI OU CLASS (PBF)

CAPITÁN ORTIZ P 06 **TENIENTE ROBLES** P 07

Displacement, tons: 47 full load
Dimensions, feet (metres): 70.8 × 18 × 3.3 *(21.6 × 5.5 × 1)*
Main machinery: 2 MTU 12V 331TC82 diesels; 2,605 hp(m) *(1.92 MW)* sustained; 2 shafts
Speed, knots: 36
Range, n miles: 700 at 32 kt
Complement: 10
Guns: 1—20 mm Type 75. 3—12.7 mm MGs.
Radars: Surface search: I-band.

Comment: Developed by Taiwan from Dvora class hulls and presented as a gift in 1996. It is possible that these craft are the two original Dvora hulls acquired by Taiwan.

CAPITÁN ORTIZ *4/2003, Hartmut Ehlers* / 0567475

2 RIVER PATROL CRAFT (PBR)

YHAGUY P 08 **TEBICUARY** P 09

Displacement, tons: 25
Dimensions, feet (metres): 52.8 × 14.8 × 2.6 *(16.1 × 4.5 × 0.8)*
Main machinery: Caterpillar diesel; 800 hp *(596 kW)*
Speed, knots: 40
Guns: 3—7.62 mm MGs (fitted for).
Radars: Surface search: Furuno; I-band.

Comment: Two former Taiwan coast guard patrol boats transferred 23 June 1999. Capable of 40 kt and armed with two 7.26 mm MGs. Two sister craft transferred to Gambia in 1999.

TEBICUARY *4/2003, Hartmut Ehlers* / 0567476

5 RIVER PATROL CRAFT (PBR)

LP 07 (ex-P 07) **P 107** (ex-P 08) **LP 09** (ex-P 09) **LP 10** (ex-P 10) **LP 11** (ex-P 11)

Displacement, tons: 18 full load
Dimensions, feet (metres): 48.2 × 10.2 × 2.6 *(14.7 × 3.1 × 0.8)*
Main machinery: 2 GM 6-71 diesels; 340 hp *(254 kW)*; 2 shafts
Speed, knots: 12. **Range, n miles:** 240 at 12 kt
Complement: 4
Guns: 2—12.7 mm MGs.

Comment: Built by Arsenal de Marina, Paraguay. *LP 07* launched March 1989, *P 107* and *LP09* in February 1990 and *LP 10-11* in October 1991. The programme was then aborted. Bases: *LP 07* (Isla Margarita); *LP 107* (Lake Itaipu); *LP 09* (Bahia Negra); *LP 10* (Asuncion); *LP 11* (Encarnacion).

LP 10 *4/2003, Hartmut Ehlers* / 0567477

6 TYPE 701 CLASS (PBR)

– LP 01 (ex-P 105) – LP 102 (P 102) – LP 104 (ex-P 104)
– LP 101 (ex-P 101) **MIGUEL SOTOA** P 103 **MANUEL TRUJILLO** P 106

Displacement, tons: 15 full load
Dimensions, feet (metres): 42.5 × 12.8 × 3 *(13 × 3.9 × 0.9)*
Main machinery: 2 diesels; 500 hp *(373 kW)*; 2 shafts
Speed, knots: 20
Complement: 7
Guns: 2—12.7 mm MGs.

Comment: Built by Sewart in 1970. Delivered 1967–71. *LP 105* is in reserve. Bases: LP 01 (Asuncion); LP 101 (Ayolas); LP 102 (Asuncion); P 103 (Lake Itaipu); LP 104 (Fuerte Olimpo); P 106 (Lake Itaipu).

LP 104 *4/2003, Hartmut Ehlers* / 0567478

LAND-BASED MARITIME AIRCRAFT

Notes: The Naval Aviation inventory includes four fixed wing aircraft (two Cessna 150, two Cessna 310K and one Cessna 401A) in addition to the two Helibras Esquilo. Four further Robinson R44 helicopters have not been ordered, as previously reported.

Numbers/Type: 2 Helibras HB 350B Esquilo.
Operational speed: 125 kt *(232 km/h)*.
Service ceiling: 10,000 ft *(3,050 m)*.
Range: 390 n miles *(720 km)*.
Role/Weapon systems: Support helicopter for riverine patrol craft. Delivered in July 1985.

ESQUILO *5/2000, Hartmut Ehlers* / 0105198

AUXILIARIES

Notes: In addition to the craft listed, there are three LCVPs (EDVP 1-3), two service craft (Arsenal 1 and 2) one utility launch *(Teniente Cabrera)*, one suction dredger *(Teniente Oscar Carreras Saguier)*, one floating crane *(Grua Flotante)* and one floating dry dock (*Dique Flotante* (ex-AFDL 26)).

EDVP-03 *4/2003, Hartmut Ehlers* / 0587790

1 HYDROGRAPHIC LAUNCH (YGS)

SUBOFICIAL ROGELIO LESME LPH 01 (ex-LH 1)

Displacement, tons: 16 full load
Dimensions, feet (metres): 65.5 × 10.2 × 2.6 *(14.7 × 3.1 × 0.8)*
Main machinery: 1 Mercedes-Benz diesel; 100 hp *(74 kW)*; 1 shaft
Speed, knots: 13
Complement: 5

Comment: Built in 1958.

1 TRAINING SHIP/TRANSPORT (AK/AX)

Name	*No*	*Builders*	*Commissioned*
GUARANI (ex-*Cerro Cora*)	–	Tomas Ruiz de Velasco, Bilbao	Feb 1968

Measurement, tons: 714 gross; 1,047 dwt
Dimensions, feet (metres): 240.3 × 36.3 × 11.9 *(73.6 × 11.1 × 3.7)*
Main machinery: 1 MWM diesel; 1,300 hp(m) *(956 kW)*; 1 shaft
Speed, knots: 13
Complement: 21
Cargo capacity: 1,000 tons

Comment: Refitted in 1975 after a serious fire in the previous year off the coast of France. Used to spend most of her time acting as a freighter on the Asunción-Europe run, commercially operated for the Paraguayan Navy. Since 1991 she has only been used for river service and for training cruises Asunción-Montevideo. Reported laid up and probably not operational.

GUARANI *4/2003, Hartmut Ehlers* / 0567480

1 RIVER TRANSPORT (AKL)

TENIENTE HERREROS (ex-*Presidente Stroessner*) T 1

Displacement, tons: 420 full load
Dimensions, feet (metres): 124 × 29.5 × 7.2 *(37.8 × 9 × 2.2)*
Main machinery: 2 MWM diesels; 330 hp(m) *(243 kW)*
Speed, knots: 10
Complement: 10
Cargo capacity: 120 tons

Comment: Built by Arsenal de Marina in 1964 from an old hull.

TENIENTE HERREROS *5/1991, Paraguay Navy* / 0081518

1 PRESIDENTIAL YACHT (MYAC)

3 de FEBRERO (ex-*26 de Febrero*)

Displacement, tons: 98.5 full load
Dimensions, feet (metres): 92.2 × 19.7 × 5.2 *(28.1 × 6.0 × 1.6)*
Main machinery: 2 Rolls Royce; 517 hp *(386 kW)*; 2 shafts
Speed, knots: 11
Range, n miles: 1,350 at 11 kt
Complement: 6 + 8 guests

Comment: Built by Naval Arsenal Asunción and launched in 1972. Entered service in 1982.

3 de FEBRERO *4/2003, Hartmut Ehlers* / 0567479

TUGS

3 TUGS (YTM/YTL)

TRIUNFO R 4 (ex-YTL 567) **ANGOSTURA** R 5 (ex-YTL 211) **ESPERANZA** R 7

Displacement, tons: 70 full load
Dimensions, feet (metres): 65 × 16.4 × 7.5 *(19.8 × 5 × 2.3)*
Main machinery: 1 Caterpillar 3408 diesel; 360 hp *(269 kW)*; 1 shaft
Speed, knots: 9
Complement: 5

Comment: Harbour tugs transferred under MAP. YTL 211 leased in March 1965; YTL 567 loaned in April 1974. Both sold on 11 February 1977. R 5 rebuilt by Arsenal de Marinha in 1992 and equipped with Caterpillar engine. Details given are for R 4 and R 5. R 7 is a smaller 15 m vessel.

TRIUNFO *4/2003, Hartmut Ehlers* / 0567481

Peru

ARMADA PERUANA

Country Overview

The Republic of Peru is situated in western South America. With an area of 496,225 square miles it has borders to the north with Ecuador and Colombia, to the east with Brazil and Bolivia and to the south with Chile. It has a coastline of 1,850 n miles with the Pacific Ocean. Lima is capital and largest city and is served by the port of Callao. There are further ports at Paita, Salaverry, Chimbote, Pisco, San Juan, Matarani and Ilo. Inland, Iquitos and Pucallpa are linked to the Atlantic Ocean by the Amazon River. Lake Titicaca is also an important waterway. Peru has not claimed an EEZ but is one of a few coastal states which claims a 200 n mile territorial sea.

Headquarters Appointments

Commander of the Navy:
Admiral Carlos Gamarra Eliás
Chief of the Naval Staff:
Vice Admiral Rolando Navarrete Salomón
Inspector General:
Vice Admiral Jorge de la Puente Ribeyro
Commander Pacific Operations Command (Callao):
Vice Admiral Alberto Lozada Frías

Headquarters Appointments — *continued*

Commander Amazon Operations Command (Iquitos):
Vice Admiral José Cueto Aservi
Director General, Coast Guard:
Rear Admiral Fergán Herrera Cuntti
Commander, Surface Forces:
Rear Admiral Raúl Vásquez Alvarado
Commander, Submarines:
Rear Admiral Jaime Navach Gamio
Commander, Special Operations Force:
Rear Admiral Erick Giovannini Freire
Commander, Naval Aviation:
Rear Admiral José Paredes Lora
Commander, Naval Infantry Force:
Captain Carlos Tello Aliaga

Personnel

(a) 2009: 23,715 (2,000 officers)
(b) 2 years' voluntary military service

Organisation and Bases

2 Operational Commands: Pacific (Callao) and Amazon (Iquitos).
5 Naval Zones: 1st (Piura), 2nd (Callao), 3rd (Arequipa), 4th (Pucallpa) and 5th (Iquitos).
Coast Guard General Directorate (Callao).
Callao: Main Naval Base, dockyard with shipbuilding capacity, one dry dock, three floating docks, one floating crane; training schools, Submarine Naval Station. Main Naval Air Base near Jorge Chavez International Airport.
San Lorenzo: Naval Station.
Iquitos: River base for Amazon Flotilla; small building yard, repair, facilities, floating dock.
Pucallpa: River base with logistic facilities.
San Juan de Marcona: Naval Aviation Training School and airfield.
Paita: Naval Station with logistic facilities.
Chimbote: Naval Base, dockyard for small vessels, logistic facilities.
Puerto Maldonado: River Base.
Puno: Lake Titicaca Lake Station.
La Punta (Naval Academy).
Naval Stations with logistic facilities at El Salto (Tumbes), Mollendo (Arequipa), El Estrecho and Gueppi (Amazon).

Marines

The Peruvian Marines comprise 3,500 men whose Headquarters is at Ancón. The force includes a Marine Brigade, the Amphibious Support Group and Recon Forces. The Marine Brigade has three battalions: First Battalion - Guarnición de Marina; Second Battalion - Guardia Chalaca; Third Battalion (including Fire Support Group armed with 122 mm howitzer and 120 mm mortar and Engineer Support company) - Vencedores de Punta Melpelo. The Amphibious Support Group is composed of the Vehicles and Motor Transport battalions. Recon Forces include a Commando and anti-terrorist companies. Additionally, the Peruvian Marines have jungle battalions at Iquitos and Pucallpa (BIMSE 1 and BIMSE 2).

Special Operations

The Special Operations Command is responsible for the organisation, equipment, training and control of the operations of its subordinate Units; these Units are: the North, Central, South and Northwest Special Operations Groups, the Diving and Salvage Group, the Explosives Ordnance Unit, The Special Operations Station and the Special Operations School.

Prefix to Ships' Names

BAP (Buque Armada Peruana).

Coast Guard

A separate service set up in 1975 with a number of light forces transferred from the Navy.

PENNANT LIST

Submarines

SS 31	Angamos
SS 32	Antofagasta
SS 33	Pisagua
SS 34	Chipana
SS 35	Islay
SS 36	Arica

Cruisers

CLM 81	Almirante Grau

Frigates

FM 51	Carvajal
FM 52	Villavisencio
FM 53	Montero
FM 54	Mariategui
FM 55	Aguirre
FM 56	Palacios
FM 57	Bolognesi
FM 58	Quiñones

Patrol Forces

CF 11	Amazonas
CF 12	Loreto
CF 13	Marañón
CF 14	Ucayali
CF 16	Manuel Clavero (bldg)
CF 17	Putumayo (bldg)
CM 21	Velarde
CM 22	Santillana
CM 23	De los Heros
CM 24	Herrera
CM 25	Larrea
CM 26	Sanchez Carrión

Amphibious Forces

DT 141	Paita
DT 142	Pisco
DT 143	Callao
DT 144	Eten

Survey Ships

AH 171	Carrasco
AH 172	Stiglich
AH 175	Carrillo
AH 176	Melo
AEH 174	Macha

Auxiliaries

ABH 302	Morona
ABH 306	Puno
ACA 111	Caloyeras
ACP 118	Noguera
ACP 119	Gauden
AMB 160	Unanue
ALY 313	Marte
ARB 120	Mejia
ARB 121	Huertas
ARB 123	Guardian Rios
ARB 126	Dueñas
ARB 128	Olaya
ARB 129	Selendon
ATC 131	Mollendo
ATP 154	Bayovar
ATP 155	Zorritos
ART 322	San Lorenzo

SUBMARINES

Notes: Replacement of the current submarine flotilla is under consideration.

6 ANGAMOS/ISLAY (TYPE 209/1200) CLASS (SSK)

Name	*No*	*Builders*	*Laid down*	*Launched*	*Commissioned*
ANGAMOS (ex-*Casma*)	SS 31	Howaldtswerke, Kiel	15 July 1977	31 Aug 1979	19 Dec 1980
ANTOFAGASTA	SS 32	Howaldtswerke, Kiel	3 Oct 1977	19 Dec 1979	20 Feb 1981
PISAGUA	SS 33	Howaldtswerke, Kiel	15 Aug 1978	19 Oct 1980	12 July 1983
CHIPANA	SS 34	Howaldtswerke, Kiel	1 Nov 1978	19 May 1981	20 Sep 1982
ISLAY	SS 35	Howaldtswerke, Kiel	15 Mar 1971	11 Oct 1973	29 Aug 1974
ARICA	SS 36	Howaldtswerke, Kiel	1 Nov 1971	5 Apr 1974	21 Jan 1975

Displacement, tons: 1,185 surfaced; 1,290 dived
Dimensions, feet (metres): 183.7 × 20.3 × 17.9 *(56 × 6.2 × 5.5)*
Main machinery: Diesel-electric; 4 MTU 12V 493 AZ80 GA31L diesels; 2,400 hp(m) *(1.76 MW)* sustained; 4 Siemens alternators; 1.7 MW; 1 Siemens motor; 4,600 hp(m) *(3.38 MW)* sustained; 1 shaft
Speed, knots: 11 surfaced/snorting; 21.5 dived
Range, n miles: 240 at 8 kt
Complement: 35 (5 officers) (*Islay* and *Arica*); 31 (others)

Torpedoes: 8—21 in *(533 mm)* tubes. 14 AEG SST4; wire-guided; active/passive homing to 12/28 km *(6.5/15 n miles)* at 35/23 kt; warhead 260 kg. Swim-out discharge.
Countermeasures: ESM: Radar warning.
Weapons control: Sepa Mk 3 or Signaal Sinbad M8/24 (*Angamos* and *Antofagasta*).
Radars: Surface search: Thomson-CSF Calypso; I-band.
Sonars: Atlas Elektronik CSU 3; active/passive search and attack; medium/high frequency.
Thomson Sintra DUUX 2C or Atlas Elektronik PRS 3; passive ranging.

Programmes: Two Type 209 (SS 35-36) ordered 1969. Two further Type 209 boats (SS 31-32) ordered 12 August 1976. Two Type 1200 (SS 33-34) ordered 21 March 1977. Designed by Ingenieurkontor, Lübeck for construction by Howaldtswerke, Kiel and sale by Ferrostaal, Essen all acting as a consortium.
Modernisation: Sepa Mk 3 fire control fitted progressively from 1986. *Angamos* modernised with new batteries, sonar and EW suite. Torpedoes are to be replaced by Atlas Elektronik SUT Mod 3. An update programme for all six boats is in progress. Work on *Islay* and *Arica* is to be of more limited scope than the other four boats.
Structure: A single-hull design with two ballast tanks and forward and after trim tanks. Fitted with snort and remote machinery control. The single screw is slow revving, very high-capacity batteries with GRP lead-acid cells and battery cooling-by Wilh Hagen and VARTA. Fitted with two periscopes and Omega receiver. Foreplanes retract. Diving depth, 250 m *(820 ft)*.
Operational: Endurance, 50 days. Four are in service, two in refit or reserve at any one time. *Angamos* took part in multinational exercises in mid-2004 during which she achieved 156 days at sea.

PISAGUA *6/2004*, **Peruvian Navy** / 1127035

ISLAY *6/2004*, **Peruvian Navy** / 1121516

CRUISERS

1 DE RUYTER CLASS (CG/CLM)

Name	*No*	*Builders*	*Laid down*	*Launched*	*Commissioned*
ALMIRANTE GRAU (ex-*De Ruyter*)	CLM 81	Wilton-Fijenoord, Schiedam	5 Sep 1939	24 Dec 1944	18 Nov 1953

Displacement, tons: 12,165 full load
Dimensions, feet (metres): 624.5 × 56.7 × 22 *(190.3 × 17.3 × 6.7)*
Main machinery: 4 Werkspoor-Yarrow boilers; 2 De Schelde-Parsons turbines; 85,000 hp *(62.5 MW)*; 2 shafts
Speed, knots: 32
Range, n miles: 7,000 at 12 kt
Complement: 953 (49 officers)

Missiles: SSM: 8 OTO Melara/Matra Otomat Mk 2 (TG 1) ❶; active radar homing to 80 km *(43.2 n miles)* at 0.9 Mach; warhead 210 kg; sea-skimmer for last 4 km *(2.2 n miles)*.
Guns: 8 Bofors 6 in *(152 mm)*/53 (4 twin) ❷; 15 rds/min to 26 km *(14 n miles)*; weight of shell 46 kg.
4 Otobreda 40 mm/70 (2 twin) ❸; 120 rds/min to 12.5 km *(6.8 n miles)*; weight of shell 0.96 kg.
4 Bofors 40 mm/70 ❹; 300 rds/min to 12 km *(6.6 n miles)*; weight of shell 0.96 kg.
Countermeasures: Decoys: 2 Dagaie and 1 Sagaie chaff launchers.
Combat data systems: Signaal Sewaco PE SATCOM ❺.
Weapons control: 2 Lirod 8 optronic directors ❻.
Radars: Air search: AN/SPS-6 ❼; D-band.
Surface search/target indication: Signaal DA08 ❽; E/F-band.
Navigation: Racal Decca 1226; I-band.
Fire control: Signaal WM25 ❾; I/J-band (for 6 in guns); range 46 km *(25 n miles)*.
Signaal STIR ❿; I/J/K-band; range 140 km *(76 n miles)* for 1 m² target.

Programmes: Transferred by purchase from Netherlands 7 March 1973 and commissioned in Peruvian Navy 23 May 1973.
Modernisation: Taken in hand for a two and a half year modernisation at Amsterdam Dry Dock Co in March 1985. This was to include reconditioning of mechanical and electrical engineering systems, fitting of SSM and SAM, replacement of electronics and fitting of one CSEE Sagaie and two Dagaie launchers. In 1986 financial constraints limited the work but much had been done to update sensors and fire-control equipment. Sailed for Peru 23 January 1988 without her secondary gun armament, which was completed at Sima Yard, Callao. Sonar has been removed. SATCOM fitted aft.
Operational: Expected to be decommissioned in 2010.

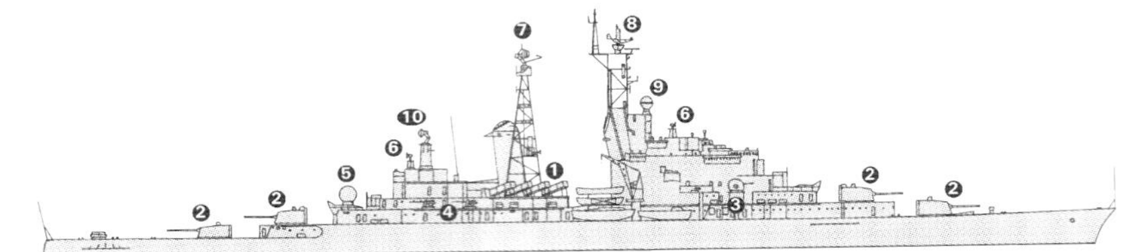

ALMIRANTE GRAU *(Scale 1 : 1,800), Ian Sturton* / 0126352

ALMIRANTE GRAU *11/2004, Globke Collection* / 1127047

FRIGATES

4 AGUIRRE (LUPO) CLASS (FFGHM)

Name	*No*	*Builders*	*Laid down*	*Launched*	*Commissioned*
AGUIRRE (ex-*Orsa*)	FM 55 (ex-F 567)	Fincantieri, Muggiano	1 Aug 1977	1 Mar 1979	1 Mar 1980
PALACIOS (ex-*Lupo*)	FM 56 (ex-F 564)	Fincantieri, Riva Trigoso	11 Oct 1974	29 July 1976	12 Sep 1977
BOLOGNESI (ex-*Perseo*)	FM 57 (ex-F 566)	Fincantieri, Riva Trigoso	24 Feb 1977	12 July 1978	1 Mar 1980
QUIÑONES (ex-*Sagittario*)	FM 58 (ex-F 565)	Fincantieri, Riva Trigoso	4 Feb 1976	22 June 1977	18 Nov 1978

Displacement, tons: 2,208 standard; 2,500 full load
Dimensions, feet (metres): 371.3 × 37.1 × 12.1 *(113.2 × 11.3 × 3.7)*
Main machinery: CODOG; 2 GE/Fiat LM 2500 gas turbines; 50,000 hp *(37.3 MW)* sustained; 2 GMT BL 230. 20M diesels; 10,000 hp(m) *(7.3 MW)* sustained; 2 shafts; LIPS cp props
Speed, knots: 35 (21 on diesels)
Range, n miles: 4,350 at 16 kt
Complement: 185 (20 officers)

Missiles: SSM: 8 OTO Melara/TESEO Mk 2 (TG 2) ❶; active radar homing to 180 km *(91.2 n miles)* at 0.9 Mach; warhead 210 kg; sea-skimmer.
SAM: Raytheon NATO Sea Sparrow RIM-7M Mk 29 octuple launcher ❷; semi-active radar homing to 14.6 km *(8 n miles)* at 2.5 Mach; warhead 39 kg.
Guns: 1 OTO Melara 5 in *(127 mm)*/54 ❸; 45 rds/min to 16 km *(8.7 n miles)*; weight of shell 32 kg.
4 Breda 40 mm/70 (2 twin) ❹; 300 rds/min to 12.5 km *(6.8 n miles)*; weight of shell 0.96 kg.
2 Oerlikon 20 mm may be fitted.
Torpedoes: 6—324 mm Mk 32 (2 triple) tubes ❺. Mk 44; anti-submarine; active homing to 5 km *(2.7 n miles)* at 30 kt; warhead 34 kg (shaped charge).
Countermeasures: Decoys: 2 Breda 105 mm SCLAR 20-barrelled trainable launchers ❻; multipurpose; chaff to 5 km *(2.7 n miles)*; illuminants to 12 km *(6.6 n miles)*; HE bombardment.
ESM: SLR-4; intercept.
ECM: 2 SLQ-D; jammer.
Torpedo decoy: SLQ-25 Nixie.
Combat data systems: Selenia IPN 20 (SADOC 2) action data automation. Link 11 (SATCOM).
Weapons control: 2 Elsag Mk 10 Argo with NA-21 directors. Dardo system for 40 mm.
Radars: Air search: Selenia SPS-774 (RAN 10S) ❼; E/F-band.
Surface search: SMA SPS 702 ❽; I-band.
SMA SPQ-2F ❾; I-band.
Navigation: SMA SPN-748; I-band.
Fire control: Selenia SPG-70 (RTN 10X) ❿ I/J-band.
2 Selenia SPG-74 (RTN 20X) ⓫; I/J-band.
1 US Mk 95 Mod 1 ⓬; I-band.
Sonars: Raytheon DE 1160B; hull-mounted; active search and attack; medium frequency.

Helicopters: 1 Agusta AB 212ASW ⓭.

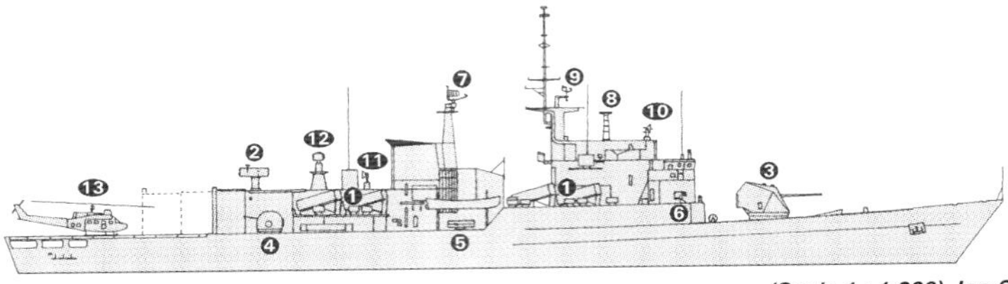

BOLOGNESI *(Scale 1 : 1,200), Ian Sturton* / 1159992

PALACIOS *6/2006, Peruvian Navy* / 1164741

Programmes: *Palacios* and *Aguirre* formally transferred from the Italian Navy on 3 November 2004, without ammunition, torpedoes, SSM and helicopters. Following eight-month refits at Fincantieri, Muggiano they both arrived at Callao in mid-2005. A contract for the refit and transfer of two further decommissioned ships, *Sagittario* and *Perseo* was signed on 28 October 2005. Both ships were commissioned on 23 January 2006. *Bolognesi* arrived at Callao on 18 August 2006 and *Quiñones* on 20 January 2007.

4 CARVAJAL (MODIFIED LUPO) CLASS (FFGHM)

Name	*No*	*Builders*	*Laid down*	*Launched*	*Commissioned*
CARVAJAL	FM 51	Fincantieri, Riva Trigoso	8 Aug 1974	17 Nov 1976	5 Feb 1979
VILLAVISENCIO	FM 52	Fincantieri, Riva Trigoso	6 Oct 1976	7 Feb 1978	25 June 1979
MONTERO	FM 53	SIMA, Callao	Oct 1978	8 Oct 1982	25 July 1984
MARIATEGUI	FM 54	SIMA, Callao	1979	8 Oct 1984	10 Oct 1987

Displacement, tons: 2,208 standard; 2,500 full load
Dimensions, feet (metres): 371.3 × 37.1 × 12.1 *(113.2 × 11.3 × 3.7)*
Main machinery: CODOG; 2 GE/Fiat LM 2500 gas turbines; 50,000 hp *(37.3 MW)* sustained; 2 GMT A 230.20 M diesels; 8,000 hp(m) *(5.88 MW)* sustained; 2 shafts; LIPS cp props
Speed, knots: 35
Range, n miles: 3,450 at 20.5 kt
Complement: 185 (20 officers)

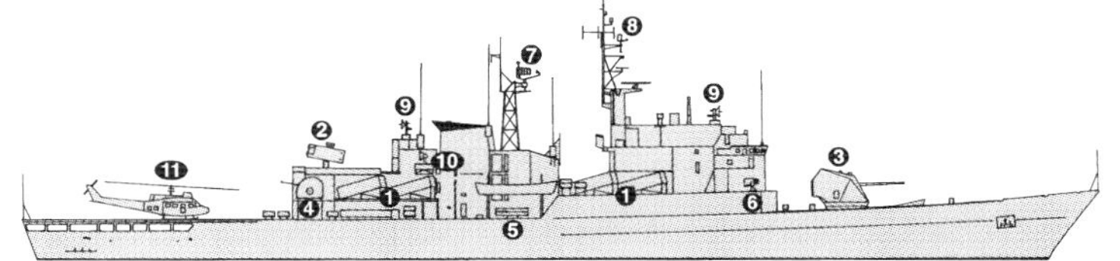

MARIATEGUI ***(Scale 1 : 1,200), Ian Sturton*** / 0105275

Missiles: SSM: 8 OTO Melara/Matra Otomat Mk 2 (TG 1) ❶; active radar homing to 80 km *(43.2 n miles)* at 0.9 Mach; warhead 210 kg; sea-skimmer for last 4 km *(2.2 n miles)*.
SAM: Selenia Elsag Albatros octuple launcher ❷; 8 Aspide; semi-active radar homing to 13 km *(7 n miles)* at 2.5 Mach; height envelope 15–5,000 m *(49.2–16,405 ft)*; warhead 30 kg.
An SA-N-10 launcher (MPG-86) may be fitted on the stern.
Guns: 1 OTO Melara 5 in *(127 mm)*/54 ❸; 45 rds/min to 16 km *(8.7 n miles)*; weight of shell 32 kg.
4 Breda 40 mm/70 (2 twin) ❹; 300 rds/min to 12.5 km *(6.8 n miles)*; weight of shell 0.96 kg.
Torpedoes: 6—324 mm ILAS (2 triple) tubes ❺; Mk 44; anti-submarine; active homing to 5 km *(2.7 n miles)* at 30 kt; warhead 34 kg (shaped charge).
Countermeasures: Decoys: 2 Breda 105 mm SCLAR 20-barrelled trainable launchers ❻; multipurpose; chaff to 5 km *(2.7 n miles)*; illuminants to 12 km *(6.6 n miles)*; HE bombardment.
ESM: Elettronica Lambda; intercept.

Combat data systems: Selenia IPN-10 action data automation.
Weapons control: 2 Elsag Mk 10 Argo with NA-21 directors. Dardo system for 40 mm.
Radars: Air search: Selenia RAN 10S (FM 52-54) ❼; E/F-band. Signaal LW 08 (FM 51); D-band.
Surface search: Selenia RAN 11LX ❽; D/I-band.
Navigation: SMA 3 RM 20R; I-band.
Fire control: 2 RTN 10X ❾; I/J-band.
2 RTN 20X ❿; I/J-band (for Dardo).
Sonars: EDO 610E; hull-mounted; active search and attack; medium frequency.

Helicopters: 1 Agusta AB 212ASW ⓫. 1 Agusta ASH-3D Sea King (deck only) (FM 51 and 54).

Programmes: *Montero* and *Mariategui* were the first major warships to be built on the Pacific Coast of South America, although some equipment was provided by Fincantieri.

Modernisation: FM 51 and FM 54 have had flight deck extensions in order to operate Sea Kings from the deck although they cannot be stowed in the hangar. Similar extensions to FM 52 and 53 were made in 2007. SA-N-10 (MPG-86) may be fitted on the sterns of two ships. LW 08 (ex-*Almirante Grau*) replaced RAN 10S in FM 51 in 2003. A mid-life refit of FM 51-54, to include propulsion systems and the modernisation of Aspide, is reported to be under consideration.
Structure: FM 51-54 differ from those built for Italian service by having a fixed hangar and higher 40 mm mounts. The SAM system is also different. The ships were commissioned with a step-down from the flight deck to the stern although this has been modified in FM 51 and 54.
Operational: Helicopter provides an over-the-horizon targeting capability for SSM. HIFR facilities fitted to FM 52 and 53 in 1989 to allow refuelling of Sea King helicopters.

MARIATEGUI ***8/2006, Michael Nitz*** / 1335412

CARVAJAL ***6/2008*, Annati Collection*** / 1335411

SHIPBORNE AIRCRAFT

Numbers/Type: 5 Agusta AB 212ASW.
Operational speed: 106 kt *(196 km/h)*.
Service ceiling: 14,200 ft *(4,330 m)*.
Range: 230 n miles *(425 km)*.
Role/Weapon systems: ASW and surface search helicopter for smaller escorts. Sensors: Selenia search radar, Bendix ASQ-18 dipping sonar, ECM. Weapons: ASW; two Mk 44, Mk 46 or 244/S torpedoes or depth bombs.

AB 212 *8/2006, Michael Nitz* / 1335400

Numbers/Type: 3 Agusta-Sikorsky ASH-3D Sea King.
Operational speed: 120 kt *(222 km/h)*.
Service ceiling: 12,200 ft *(3,720 m)*.
Range: 630 n miles *(1,165 km)*.
Role/Weapon systems: ASW helicopter; can be operated from two FFGs. Sensors: Selenia search radar, Bendix ASQ-18 dipping sonar, sonobuoys. Weapons: ASW; four Mk 44, Mk 46 or 244/S torpedoes or depth bombs or mines. ASV; two AM 39 Exocet missiles.

ASH-3D *6/2004, Peruvian Navy* / 1127039

LAND-BASED MARITIME AIRCRAFT (FRONT LINE)

Notes: (1) There are also three Mi-8T transport helicopters.
(2) There are three Fokker: one F-27 200, one F-27 600 and one F-27 500.
(3) There are two Antonov AN-32B transport aircraft.
(4) Five Beech T-34C are used for training.
(5) There is one Cessna 206 and two Cessna 150.
(6) There are three Bell 206B training helicopters.
(7) Six Enstrom F-28F training helicopters were ordered in January 2008.

Mi-8T *6/2000, Peruvian Navy* / 0105208

ENSTROM F-28F *6/2008*, Peruvian Navy* / 1335410

Numbers/Type: 5 Beechcraft Super King Air 200T.
Operational speed: 282 kt *(523 km/h)*.
Service ceiling: 35,000 ft *(10,670 m)*.
Range: 2,030 n miles *(3,756 km)*.
Role/Weapon systems: Coastal surveillance and EEZ patrol duties. Sensors: Search radar, cameras. Weapons: Unarmed.

PATROL FORCES

Notes: (1) Procurement of 10 hovercraft for river policing is under consideration.
(2) Eight 7.4 m river patrol craft, similar to the Pirañas class, operate on the River Amazon.

6 VERLARDE (PR-72P) CLASS (FAST ATTACK CRAFT—MISSILE) (CM/PGGFM)

Name	*No*	*Builders*	*Launched*	*Commissioned*
VELARDE	CM 21	SFCN, France	16 Sep 1978	25 July 1980
SANTILLANA	CM 22	SFCN, France	11 Sep 1978	25 July 1980
DE LOS HEROS	CM 23	SFCN, France	20 May 1979	17 Nov 1980
HERRERA	CM 24	SFCN, France	16 Feb 1979	26 Feb 1981
LARREA	CM 25	SFCN, France	12 May 1979	16 June 1981
SANCHEZ CARRIÓN	CM 26	SFCN, France	28 June 1979	18 Sep 1981

Displacement, tons: 470 standard; 560 full load
Dimensions, feet (metres): 210 × 27.4 × 5.2 *(64 × 8.4 × 2.6)*
Main machinery: 4 SACM AGO 240 V16 M7 (CM 21, 23, 25) or 4 MTU 12V 595 (CM 22, 24, 26) diesels; 22,200 hp(m) *(16.32 MW)* sustained; 4 shafts
Speed, knots: 37
Range, n miles: 2,500 at 16 kt
Complement: 36 plus 10 spare

Missiles: SSM: 4 Aerospatiale MM 38 Exocet; inertial cruise; active radar homing to 42 km *(23 n miles)* at 0.9 Mach; warhead 165 kg; sea-skimmer.
SAM: An SA-N-10 launcher (MPG-86) may be fitted on the stern.
Guns: 1 OTO Melara 3 in *(76 mm)*/62; 85 rds/min to 16 km *(8.7 n miles)*; weight of shell 6 kg.
2 Breda 40 mm/70 (twin); 300 rds/min to 12.5 km *(6.8 n miles)*; weight of shell 0.96 kg.
Countermeasures: ESM: Thomson-CSF DR 2000; intercept.
Weapons control: CSEE Panda director. Vega system.
Radars: Surface search: Thomson-CSF Triton; G-band; range 33 km *(18 n miles)* for 2 m² target.
Navigation: Racal Decca 1226; I-band.
Fire control: Thomson-CSF/Castor II; I/J-band; range 15 km *(8 n miles)* for 1 m² target.

Programmes: Ordered late 1976. Hulls of *Velarde, De los Heros, Larrea* subcontracted to Lorient Naval Yard, the others being built at Villeneuve-la-Garenne. Classified as corvettes.
Modernisation: CM 22, 24 and 26 re-engined in 2000. The other three craft are to be similarly modernised.

VELARDE *11/2004, Globke Collection* / 1047863

2 MARAÑON CLASS (RIVER GUNBOATS) (CF/PGR)

Name	*No*	*Builders*	*Commissioned*
MARAÑON	CF 13 (ex-CF 401)	John I Thornycroft & Co Ltd	July 1951
UCAYALI	CF 14 (ex-CF 402)	John I Thornycroft & Co Ltd	June 1951

Displacement, tons: 365 full load
Dimensions, feet (metres): 154.8 wl × 32 × 4 *(47.2 × 9.7 × 1.2)*
Main machinery: 2 MTU 485 diesels; 800 hp *(597 kW)*; 2 shafts
Speed, knots: 12
Range, n miles: 6,000 at 10 kt
Complement: 40 (2 officers)
Guns: 2—3 in *(76 mm)*/50. 3 Bofors 40 mm/60. 2 Oerlikon 20 mm.

Comment: Ordered early in 1950 and launched 7 March and 23 April 1951 respectively. Employed on police duties in Upper Amazon. Superstructure of aluminium alloy. Based at Iquitos.

MARAÑÓN *6/2006, Peruvian Navy* / 1164740

2 LORETO CLASS (RIVER GUNBOATS) (CF/PGR)

Name	*No*	*Builders*	*Commissioned*
AMAZONAS	CF 11 (ex-CF 403)	Electric Boat Co, Groton	1935
LORETO	CF 12 (ex-CF 404)	Electric Boat Co, Groton	1935

Displacement, tons: 250 standard
Dimensions, feet (metres): 145 × 22 × 4 *(44.2 × 6.7 × 1.2)*
Main machinery: 2 diesels; 750 hp(m) *(551 kW)*; 2 shafts
Speed, knots: 12
Range, n miles: 4,000 at 10 kt
Complement: 35 (2 officers)
Guns: 1—3 in *(76 mm)*. 3 Bofors 40 mm/60. 2 Oerlikon 20 mm.

Comment: Launched in 1934. In Upper Amazon Flotilla, based at Iquitos. The after 3 in gun has been replaced by a third 40 mm. Likely to be replaced by the Manuel Clavero class.

LORETO ***6/2008*, Peruvian Navy*** / 1335409

1 + 1 (2) MANUEL CLAVERO CLASS (RIVER GUNBOATS) (CF/PGR)

Name	*No*	*Builders*	*Launched*	*Commissioned*
MANUEL CLAVERO	CF 16	Sima Iquitos	10 June 2008	2009
PUTUMAYO	CF 17	Sima Iquitos	2008	2009

Displacement, tons: 344 full load
Dimensions, feet (metres): 149.9 × 34.8 × 7.5 *(45.7 × 10.6 × 2.3)*
Main machinery: 3 CAT diesels; 1,365 hp *(1 MW)*; 3 shafts
Speed, knots: 14
Range, n miles: 6,580 at 10 kt
Complement: 28 (3 officers) + 20 marines
Guns: 2—40 mm AGLs. 5—12.7 mm MGs. 2—7.62 mm MGs.
Radars: Navigation: Furuno; I-band.

Comment: Construction of the first of class began on 6 May 2006. The second is expected in early 2009 and both are to replace the Loreto class. Two further vessels may be ordered. Two 5.8 m fast interception craft are carried.

MANUEL CLAVERO ***6/2008*, Peruvian Navy*** / 1335408

AMPHIBIOUS FORCES

Notes: (1) There are plans for up to three 300 ft LSLs to be locally built when funds are available.
(2) Two Newport class LSTs (possibly *Freno* and *Racine*) may be acquired from the US Navy in 2009.

4 PAITA (TERREBONNE PARISH) CLASS (LSTH)

Name	*No*	*Builders*	*Commissioned*
PAITÁ (ex-*Walworth County* LST 1164)	DT 141	Ingalls SB	26 Oct 1953
PISCO (ex-*Waldo County* LST 1163)	DT 142	Ingalls SB	17 Sep 1953
CALLAO (ex-*Washoe County* LST 1165)	DT 143	Ingalls SB	30 Nov 1953
ETEN (ex-*Traverse County* LST 1160)	DT 144	Bath Iron Works	19 Dec 1953

Displacement, tons: 2,590 standard; 5,800 full load
Dimensions, feet (metres): 384 × 55 × 17 *(117.1 × 16.8 × 5.2)*
Main machinery: 4 GM 16-278A diesels; 6,000 hp *(4.48 MW)*; 2 shafts
Speed, knots: 15
Range, n miles: 15,000 at 9 kt
Complement: 116
Military lift: 2,000 tons; 395 troops
Guns: 5 Bofors 40 mm/60 (2 twin, 1 single).
Radars: Navigation: I-band.

Comment: Four transferred from USA on loan 7 August 1984, recommissioned 4 March 1985. Have small helicopter platform. Original 3 in guns replaced by 40 mm. Lease extended by grant aid in August 1989, again in August 1994, and again in April 1999. All are active.

PAITÁ ***11/2004, Globke Collection*** / 1047862

3 PUNTA MALPELO CLASS (RIVER ASSAULT CRAFT) (DLS/PBF)

Name	*No*	*Builders*	*Commissioned*
PUNTA MALPELO	DLS 381	Construcciones Náuticas, Peru	1996
PUNTA MERO	DLS 382	Construcciones Náuticas, Peru	1996
PUNTA SAL	DLS 383	Construcciones Náuticas, Peru	1996

Displacement, tons: To be announced
Dimensions, feet (metres): 42.0 × 11.0 × 3.0 *(12.8 × 3.36 × 0.91)*
Main machinery: 2 Diesel Volvo Penta TAMD/B; 286 hp(m) *(200 kW)*; 2 Hamilton waterjets
Speed, knots: 32
Range, n miles: 500 at 27 kt
Complement: 7
Guns: 1—40 mm AGL. 1—12.7 mm MG. 2—7.62 mm MGs.

Comment: Acquired in 1996.

SURVEY AND RESEARCH SHIPS

Notes: AH 177 is a 5 ton fast survey craft.

1 INSHORE SURVEY CRAFT (AGSC/EH)

Name	*No*	*Builders*	*Commissioned*
MACHA	AEH 174	SIMA, Chimbote	Apr 1982

Displacement, tons: 49 standard; 53 full load
Dimensions, feet (metres): 64.9 × 17.1 × 3 *(19.8 × 5.2 × 0.9)*
Main machinery: 2 Caterpillar 3406-TA diesels; 543 hp *(400 kW)*; 2 shafts
Speed, knots: 13
Complement: 8 (2 officers)

Comment: Side scan sonar for plotting bottom contours. EH (Embarcacion Hidrográfica).

MACHA ***6/2000, Peruvian Navy*** / 0105213

1 DOKKUM CLASS (AGSC/EH)

Name	*No*	*Builders*	*Commissioned*
CARRASCO (ex-*Abcoude*)	AH 171 (ex-M 810)	Smulders, Schiedam	18 May 1956

Displacement, tons: 373 standard; 453 full load
Dimensions, feet (metres): 152.9 × 28.9 × 7.5 *(46.6 × 8.8 × 2.3)*
Main machinery: 2 Fijenoord MAN V64 diesels; 2,500 hp(m) *(1.84 MW)*; 2 shafts
Speed, knots: 16
Range, n miles: 2,500 at 10 kt
Complement: 27-36
Guns: 2 Oerlikon 20 mm/70.
Radars: Navigation: Racal Decca TM 1229C; I-band.

Comment: Service with the Netherlands Navy as a minesweeper included modernisation in the mid-1970s and a life prolonging refit in the late 1980s. *Carrasco* placed in reserve in 1993 and transferred to Peru 16 July 1994. The ship has been acquired for hydrographic duties. Two more were planned to follow in mid-1996 but the transfer was cancelled.

CARRASCO *6/2004, Peruvian Navy* / 1127040

2 VAN STRAELEN CLASS (AGSC/EH)

Name	*No*	*Builders*	*Commissioned*
CARRILLO (ex-*van Hamel*)	AH 175	De Vries, Amsterdam	14 Oct 1960
MELO (ex-*van der Wel*)	AH 176	De Vries, Amsterdam	6 Oct 1961

Displacement, tons: 169 full load
Dimensions, feet (metres): 108.6 × 18.2 × 5.2 *(33.1 × 5.6 × 1.6)*
Main machinery: 2 GM diesels; 1,100 hp(m) *(808 kW)* sustained; 2 shafts
Speed, knots: 13
Complement: 17 (2 officers)
Guns: 1—20 mm

Comment: Both built as inshore minesweepers. Acquired 23 February 1985 for conversion with new engines and survey equipment.

MELO *2000, Peruvian Navy* / 0105212

1 RIVER SURVEY CRAFT (AGSC/AH)

Name	*No*	*Builders*	*Commissioned*
STIGLICH	AH 172	Sima, Iquitos	1981

Displacement, tons: 230 standard; 250 full load
Dimensions, feet (metres): 112.2 × 25.9 × 5.6 *(34.2 × 7.9 × 1.7)*
Main machinery: 2 Caterpillar 3304 diesels; 500 hp *(367 kW)*; 2 shafts
Speed, knots: 9
Complement: 22 (2 officers)

Comment: *Stiglich* is based at Iquitos for survey work on the Upper Amazon.

STIGLICH *6/1999, Peruvian Navy* / 0081533

AUXILIARIES

Notes: (1) All auxiliaries may be used for commercial purposes if not required for naval use.
(2) There are three small river hospital craft: *Corrientes* (ABH 303), *Curaray* (ABH 304) and *Pastaza* (ABH 305).
(3) There are four Rio Comaina class 30 m fuel barges (ABP 336-339); *Rio Comaina*, *Rio Huazaga*, *Rio Chinganaza*, *Rio Cenepa*
(4) There are two 15 m river cargo barges (ABC 360-361).

1 MOLLENDO CLASS (TRANSPORT) (AOR)

Name	*No*	*Builders*	*Commissioned*
MOLLENDO (ex-*Ilo*)	ATC 131	SIMA, Callao	15 Dec 1971

Displacement, tons: 18,400 full load
Measurement, tons: 13,000 dwt
Dimensions, feet (metres): 507.7 × 67.3 × 27.2 *(154.8 × 20.5 × 8.3)*
Main machinery: 1 Burmeister & Wain 6K47 diesel; 11,600 hp(m) *(8.53 MW)*; 1 shaft
Speed, knots: 15.6
Complement: 60
Cargo capacity: 13,000 tons

Comment: Sister ship *Rimac* has been scrapped.

MOLLENDO *3/2008*, Hachiro Nakai* / 1335487

3 HARBOUR TANKERS (FUEL/WATER) (YW/YO)

CALOYERAS ACA 111 (ex-*YW 128*) **NOGUERA** ACP 118 (ex-*YO 221*)
GAUDEN ACP 119 (ex-*YO 171*)

Displacement, tons: 1,390 full load
Dimensions, feet (metres): 174 × 32 × 13.3 *(52.3 × 9.8 × 4.1)*
Main machinery: 1 GM diesel; 560 hp *(418 kW)*; 1 shaft
Speed, knots: 8
Complement: 23
Cargo capacity: 200,000 gallons
Radars: Navigation: Raytheon; I-band.

Comment: *YO 221* (fuel) transferred from US to Peru January 1975; *YO 171* (fuel) 20 January 1981; *YW 128* (water) 26 January 1985.

GAUDEN *6/2006, Peruvian Navy* / 1164739

1 TORPEDO RECOVERY VESSEL (YPT)

Name	*No*	*Builders*	*Commissioned*
SAN LORENZO	ART 322	Lürssen/Burmeister	1 Dec 1981

Displacement, tons: 58 standard; 65 full load
Dimensions, feet (metres): 82.7 × 18.4 × 5.6 *(25.2 × 5.6 × 1.7)*
Main machinery: 2 MTU 8V 396 TC82 diesels; 1,740 hp(m) *(1.28 MW)* sustained; 2 shafts
Speed, knots: 19. **Range, n miles:** 500 at 15 kt
Complement: 9

Comment: Can carry four long or eight short torpedoes.

SAN LORENZO *6/2006, Peruvian Navy* / 1164737

1 MORONA CLASS (RIVER HOSPITAL CRAFT) (ABH)

Name	*No*	*Builders*	*Commissioned*
MORONA	ABH 302	Sima, Iquitos	13 May 1976

Displacement, tons: 150 full load
Dimensions, feet (metres): 98.4 × 19.7 × 2.0 *(30.0 × 6.0 × 0.6)*
Main machinery: 2 Caterpillar 3304 diesels; 150 hp *(112 kW)* sustained; 2 shafts
Speed, knots: 12
Complement: 22 (2 officers)

Comment: *Morona* is used as a hospital craft and has a red cross on her superstructure.

MORONA *6/2008*, Peruvian Navy* / 1335406

1 LAKE HOSPITAL CRAFT (AH)

Name	*No*	*Builders*	*Commissioned*
PUNO (ex-*Yapura*)	ABH 306	J Watt Co, Thames Iron Works	18 May 1872

Displacement, tons: 500 full load
Dimensions, feet (metres): 125.1 × 19.7 × 13.1 *(38.13 × 6.0 × 4.0)*
Main machinery: 1 diesel; 1 shaft
Speed, knots: 14
Complement: 24 (1 officer)

Comment: Stationed on Lake Titicaca. 500 grt and has a diesel engine. The second of the class was finally paid off in 1990.

PUNO *8/1999, A Campanera i Rovira* / 0081535

1 MARTE CLASS (SAIL TRAINING CRAFT) (AXS)

Name	*No*	*Builders*	*Commissioned*
MARTE (ex-*Neptuno*, ex-*Noah's Ark*)	ALY 313	James O Rasborough, Halifax, Canada	1974

Displacement, tons: 49 standard; 55 full load
Dimensions, feet (metres): 66.6 × 17.0 × 6.4 *(20.30 × 5.18 × 1.95)*
Main machinery: Two Perkins 130C diesels; 260 hp *(194 kW)*; 2 props
Speed, knots: 8
Complement: 26
Radars: Surface search: Furuno; I-band.

Comment: Used for cadet instruction at the Naval Academy.

MARTE *6/2004, Peruvian Navy* / 1127042

3 FLOATING DOCKS (AH)

ADF 104 **ADF 106** **ADF 107**

Displacement, tons: 4,500 *(104)*; 1,900 *(106)*; 5,200 *(107)*

Comment: *106* (ex-US *AFDL 33*) transferred 1959; *107* (ex-US *ARD 8*) transferred 1961; *104* built at SIMA, Callao in 1991.

2 BAYÓVAR CLASS (TANKERS) (AOT)

Name	*No*	*Builders*	*Commissioned*
BAYÓVAR (ex-*Petr Shmidt*)	ATP 154	Kherson Shipyard	1987
ZORRITOS (ex-*Grigoriy Nesterenko*)	ATP 155	Kherson Shipyard	1986

Displacement, tons: 38,290 full load
Measurement, tons: 18,625 grt
Dimensions, feet (metres): 587.3 × 83.0 × 36.1 *(179.0 × 25.3 × 11.0)*
Main machinery: 1 B&W 6L67GFCA diesel; 11,900 hp *(8.9 MW)*; 1 shaft
Speed, knots: 15
Complement: To be announced

Comment: Russian-built tankers acquired on 22 December 2006 and commissioned into the Peruvian Navy at Callao on 15 April 2007. They have replaced *Talara* and *Lobitos*.

BAYÓVAR *6/2008*, Peruvian Navy* / 1335407

TUGS

Notes: (1) There are three river tugs *Rio Tapuina* AER 180, *Rio Gaudin* AER 186 and *Rio Zambrano* AER 187.
(2) There are also five small harbour tugs *Mejia* ARB 120, *Huertas* ARB 121, *Dueñas* ARB 126, *Olaya* ARB 128 and *Selendón* ARB 129.
(3) There is a 43 m salvage tug *Unanue* (AMB 160), first commissioned in 1944, transferred from the US in 1961.

1 CHEROKEE CLASS (SALVAGE TUG) (ATS)

Name	*No*	*Builders*	*Commissioned*
GUARDIAN RIOS (ex-*Pinto* ATF 90)	ARB 123	Cramp, Philadelphia, PA	1 Apr 1943

Displacement, tons: 1,640 full load
Dimensions, feet (metres): 205 × 38.5 × 17 *(62.5 × 11.7 × 5.2)*
Main machinery: Diesel-electric; 4 GM 12-278 diesels; 4,400 hp *(3.28 MW)*; 4 generators; 1 motor; 3,000 hp *(2.24 MW)*; 1 shaft
Speed, knots: 16.5
Range, n miles: 6,500 at 16 kt
Complement: 99
Guns: 2—20 mm.

Comment: Transferred from USA on loan in 1960, sold 17 May 1974. Fitted with powerful pumps and other salvage equipment.

GUARDIAN RIOS *6/2006, Peruvian Navy* / 1164738

COAST GUARD

5 RIO NEPEÑA CLASS (LARGE PATROL CRAFT) (WPB)

Name	*No*	*Builders*	*Commissioned*
RIO NEPEÑA	PC 243	SIMA, Chimbote	1 Dec 1981
RIO TAMBO	PC 244	SIMA, Chimbote	10 Mar 1982
RIO OCOÑA	PC 245	SIMA, Chimbote	14 July 1983
RIO HUARMEY	PC 246	SIMA, Chimbote	8 Oct 1984
RIO ZAÑA	PC 247	SIMA, Chimbote	12 Feb 1985

Displacement, tons: 253 standard; 296 full load
Dimensions, feet (metres): 167 × 24.8 × 5.6 *(50.9 × 7.4 × 1.7)*
Main machinery: 4 Bazán MAN V8V diesels; 5,640 hp(m) *(4.15 MW)*; 2 shafts
Speed, knots: 23
Range, n miles: 3,050 at 17 kt
Complement: 39 (4 officers)
Guns: 1 Oerlikon 20 mm. 2—12.7 mm MGs.
Radars: Surface search: Decca 1226; I-band.

Comment: Have aluminium alloy superstructures. The prototype craft was scrapped in 1990. *Rio Ocoña* completed refit in July 1996 and the rest of the class were refitted at one per year.

RIO OCOÑA *11/2004, Globke Collection* / 1047861

6 CHICAMA (DAUNTLESS) CLASS (PBR)

CHICAMA PC 216
HUANCHACO PC 217
CHORRILLOS PC 218
CHANCAY PC 219
CAMANA PC 220
CHALA PC 221

Displacement, tons: 14 full load
Dimensions, feet (metres): 40 × 14 × 4.4 *(12.2 × 4.3 × 1.3)*
Main machinery: 2 Caterpillar 3208TA diesels; 870 hp *(650 kW)*; 2 shafts
Speed, knots: 27. **Range, n miles:** 600 at 18 kt
Complement: 5 (1 officer)
Guns: 1—12.7 mm MG. 1—7.62 mm MG.
Radars: Surface search: Furuno 821; I-band.

Comment: Ordered in February 2000 under FMS funding. Built by SeaArk Marine, Arkansas. First pair delivered in August 2000 remainder in November 2000. Formerly river patrol craft, now operational on Pacific Coast.

CHANCAY *6/2004, Peruvian Coast Guard* / 1127045

1 RIVER PATROL CRAFT (PBR)

Name	*No*	*Builders*	*Commissioned*
RIO PIURA	PC 242 (ex-P 252)	Viareggio, Italy	5 Sep 1960

Displacement, tons: 44 standard; 55 full load
Dimensions, feet (metres): 65.7 × 17 × 3.2 *(20 × 5.2 × 1)*
Main machinery: 2 GM 8V-71 diesels; 460 hp *(344 kW)* sustained; 2 shafts
Speed, knots: 15
Range, n miles: 1,000 at 16 kt
Complement: 9 (2 officers)
Guns: 2—12.7 mm MGs. 1 Oerlikon 20 mm.
Radars: Navigation: Raytheon; I-band.

Comment: Ordered in 1959. Armament changed in 1992. Refitted in 1996.

RIO PIURA *6/2004, Peruvian Coast Guard* / 1127043

1 PGM 71 CLASS (LARGE PATROL CRAFT) (PB)

Name	*No*	*Builders*	*Commissioned*
RIO CHIRA	PM 223 (ex-PGM 111)	SIMA, Callao	29 May 1972

Displacement, tons: 136 standard; 147 full load
Dimensions, feet (metres): 118.2 × 21 × 6 *(36.0 × 6.4 × 1.8)*
Main machinery: 2 Detroit GN-71 diesels; 1,450 hp *(1.08 MW)*; 2 shafts
Speed, knots: 15
Range, n miles: 1,500 at 10 kt
Complement: 16 (3 officers)
Guns: 1—12.7 mm MG.
Radars: Surface search: Raytheon; I-band.

Comment: Acquired from the Navy in 1975. Paid off in 1994 but back in service again in 1997, with refurbished engines.

RIO CHIRA *2000, Peruvian Coast Guard* / 0105218

10 ZORRITOS CLASS (RIVER PATROL CRAFT) (PBR)

Name	*No*	*Builders*	*Commissioned*
ZORRITOS	PC 222	SIMA, Callao	23 Sep 2003
PUNTA ARENAS	PC 224	SIMA, Callao	23 Sep 2003
SANTA ROSA	PC 225	SIMA, Callao	23 Sep 2003
PACASMAYO	PC 226	SIMA, Callao	23 Sep 2003
BARRANCA	PC 227	SIMA, Callao	23 Sep 2003
COISHCO	PC 228	SIMA, Callao	Oct 2004
INDEPENDENCIA	PC 229	SIMA, Callao	Oct 2004
SAN NICOLAS	PC 230	SIMA, Callao	Oct 2004
MATARANI	PC 234	SIMA, Callao	Oct 2004
SAMA	PC 238	SIMA, Callao	Oct 2004

Displacement, tons: 12 full load
Dimensions, feet (metres): 40.0 × 13.8 × 2.3 *(12.2 × 4.2 × 0.7)*
Main machinery: 2 Caterpillar 3126 diesels; 550 hp *(411 kW)*; 2 shafts
Speed, knots: 24
Complement: 5 (1 officer)
Guns: 1—12.7 mm MG.
Radars: Surface search: Furuno; I-band.

SAN NICOLAS *11/2004, Globke Collection* / 1133139

9 LA CRUZ CLASS (HARBOUR PATROL CRAFT) (PBR)

Name	*No*	*Builders*	*Commissioned*
LA CRUZ	DCB 350	Cougar Marine, Miami	1992
CABO BLANCO	DCB 351	Cougar Marine, Miami	1992
COLÁN	DCB 352	Cougar Marine, Miami	1992
SAMANCO	DCB 353	Cougar Marine, Miami	1992
BESIQUE	DCB 354	Cougar Marine, Miami	1992
SALINAS	DCB 355	Cougar Marine, Miami	1993
ANCÓN	DCB 356	Cougar Marine, Miami	1993
PARACAS	DCB 357	Cougar Marine, Miami	1993
LA PUNTA	DCB 358	Cougar Marine, Miami	1993

Displacement, tons: 2.0
Dimensions, feet (metres): 21.6 × 7.2 × 0.6 *(6.6 × 2.2 × 0.2)*
Main machinery: 1 Evinrude outboard diesel; 200 hp *(150 kW)*
Speed, knots: 30. **Range, n miles:** 240 at 15 kt
Complement: 4

1 RÍO CAÑETE CLASS (COASTAL PATROL CRAFT) (PBR)

Name	*No*	*Builders*	*Commissioned*
RÍO CAÑETE	PC 231	Astillero España	1985

Displacement, tons: 4
Dimensions, feet (metres): 33 × 12 × 6 *(10.0 × 3.7 × 1.8)*
Main machinery: 2 diesels; 230 hp *(170 kW)*; 2 shafts
Speed, knots: 18
Complement: 6

Comment: Built in Spain in 1985. Classified as coast patrol.

RÍO CAÑETE *6/2008*, Peruvian Navy* / 1335405

2 RÍO SANTA CLASS (COASTAL PATROL CRAFT) (PBR)

Name	*No*	*Builders*	*Commissioned*
RÍO SANTA	PC 232	Cía Nauticas – Callao	1981
RÍO MAJES	PC 233	Cía Nauticas – Callao	1982

Displacement, tons: 14 standard; 15 full load
Dimensions, feet (metres): 34.5 × 10.5 × 6.2 *(10.5 × 3.1 × 1.9)*
Main machinery: 2 Evinrude BE200CXCM outboard; 400 hp *(300 kW)*
Speed, knots: 20. **Range, n miles:** 86 at 20 kt
Complement: 6
Radars: Surface search: Furuno.

Comment: Built in 1981–82.

RÍO SANTA *6/2008*, Peruvian Navy* / 1335404

2 RÍO VIRU CLASS (COASTAL PATROL CRAFT) (PBR)

Name	*No*	*Builders*	*Commissioned*
RÍO VIRU	PC 235	Camcraft Inc, Louisiana	1981
RÍO LURIN	PC 236	Camcraft Inc, Louisiana	1982

Displacement, tons: 13 standard; 14 full load
Dimensions, feet (metres): 43.0 × 13 × 6 *(13.1 × 4 × 1.8)*
Main machinery: 2 General Motors Detroit Diesel 6-71 diesels; 500 hp *(373 kW)*; 2 shafts
Speed, knots: 15. **Range, n miles:** 210 at 11 kt
Complement: 6
Guns: 1 — 12.7 mm MG.
Radars: Surface search: Raytheon 2800; I-band.

Comment: Aluminium hulls.

RÍO VIRU *6/2008*, Peruvian Navy* / 1335403

3 MÁNCORA CLASS (HARBOUR PATROL BOATS) (PBR)

Name	*No*	*Builders*	*Commissioned*
MÁNCORA	DCB 212	Cougar Marine, Florida	1993
HUAURA	DCB 213	Cougar Marine, Florida	1993
QUILCA	DCB 214	Cougar Marine, Florida	1993

Displacement, tons: 3.5
Dimensions, feet (metres): 25 × 7.6 × 3 *(7.62 × 2.33 × 0.91)*
Main machinery: 1 Volvo Penta AD 41B diesel; 200 hp *(150 kW)*; 1 shaft
Speed, knots: 32
Range, n miles: 180 at 35 kt
Complement: 3

MÁNCORA *6/2008*, Peruvian Navy* / 1335402

25 RIVER AND LAKE PATROL CRAFT (PBR)

PUCUSANA PC 215
CONTAMANA PF 250
NUEVA REQENA PF 251
ATALAYA PF 252
ZORRILLOS PF 253
POYENI PF 254
AGUAYTIA PF 255
PUERTO INCA PF 256
SAN ALEJANDRO PF 257
RÍO HUALLAGA PF 260
RÍO SANTIAGO PF 261
RÍO PUTUMAYO PF 262
RÍO NANAY PF 263
RIO NAPO LIF 264
RIO YAVARI LIF 265
RIO MATADOR LIF 266
RIO ITAYA LIF 270
RIO PATAYACU LIF 271
RIO ZAPOTE LIF 272
RIO CHAMBIRA LIF 273
RIO TAMBOPATA PF 274
RIO RAMIS PL 290
RIO ILAVE PL 291
JULI PL 293
MOHO PL 294

Comment: PC 215 is a 9 m craft constructed at Callao in 1997. PF 250-257 are aluminium craft built by Sima, Iquitos. PF 260-263 are 10 m craft built by Sima, Iquitos 1994–95. LIF 264-266 are 8 m craft built by Sima, Iquitos 1998–99. They are employed on the Amazon River. LIF 270-273 are 6 m craft built by Sima, Iquitos 1998–99. Deployed on the Amazon River. PF 274 is an aluminium-hulled 8 m craft, originally commissioned into the Peruvian Navy in 1977. PL 290-291 are 10 m craft built by American Shipbuilding, Florida in 1982. They are based on Lake Titicaca. PL 293-294 are 12 m craft, similar to the Zorritos class, and are based on Lake Titicaca.

RIO HUALLAGA *6/2008*, Peruvian Navy* / 1335401

RIO NAPO *6/2000, Peruvian Navy* / 0105221

Philippines

Country Overview

The Republic of the Philippines was formally proclaimed in 1946. Situated between Taiwan to the north and Indonesia and Malaysia to the south, the country comprises about 7,100 islands with a total coastline of 19,597 n miles with the South China, Philippine and Celebes Seas. Eleven islands, Bohol, Cebu, Leyte, Luzon, Masbate, Mindanao, Mindoro, Negros, Palawan, Panay, and Samar, contain the majority of the population. Most remaining islands are less than 1 square mile in area. The capital, principal city and port is Manila. Other important ports include Davao, Cebu and Zamboanga. An archipelagic state, territorial seas (12 n miles) are claimed. A 200 n mile EEZ has also been claimed but the limits have not been defined.

Headquarters Appointments

Flag Officer-in-Command:
Rear Admiral Ferdinand S Golez
Commander Fleet:
Rear Admiral George T Uy
Commandant Coast Guard:
Vice Admiral Wilfredo D Tamayo
Commandant Marines:
Major General Mohammad Ben Dolorfino

Personnel

(a) 2009: 22,000 Navy; 8,700 Marines; 3,500 Coast Guard
(b) Reserves: 17,000

Organisation

The Naval Headquarters is at Manila. The fleet is divided into functional units including the Ready Force, Patrol Force, Service Force, Assault Craft Force, Naval Air Group and Naval Special Warfare Group. There are six operational areas of responsibility: Southern Luzon; Northern Luzon; Central; West; Western Mindanao and Eastern Mindanao. The Coast Guard was transferred to the Department of Transport and Communication in 1998. There are eight Coast Guard Districts, 47 stations and 154 Coast Guard Detachment units.

Marine Corps

Marines comprise three tactical brigades composed of 10 tactical battalions, one support regiment, a service group, a guard battalion and a reconnaissance battalion. Headquarters at Ternate, Manila Bay. Deployed in Mindanao and Palawan.

Bases

Main: Cavite.
Operational: San Vicente, Mactan, Ternate.
Stations: Cebu, Davao, Legaspi, Bonifacio, Tacloban, San Miguel, Ulugan, Balabne, Puerto Princesa, Pagasa.

Prefix to Ships' Names

BRP: Barko Republika Pilipinas

Strength of the Fleet

Type	*Active*	*Building*
Frigates	(1)	–
Corvettes	13	–
Fast Attack Craft	6	–
Large Patrol Craft	5	1 (3)
Coastal Patrol Craft	37	2
LST/LSV Transports	8	–
LCM/LCU/RUC/LCVP	44	–
Repair Ship	1	–
Tankers	4	–

Coast Guard

Tenders	4	–
Patrol Craft	58	1

PENNANT LIST

Frigates

PF 11 Rajah Humabon

Corvettes

PS 19 Miguel Malvar
PS 20 Magat Salamat
PS 22 Sultan Kudarat
PS 23 Datu Marikudo
PS 28 Cebu
PS 29 Negros Occidental
PS 31 Pangasinan
PS 32 Iloilo
PS 35 Emilio Jacinto
PS 36 Apolinario Mabini
PS 37 Artemio Ricarte
PS 38 General Mariano Alvares
PS 70 Quezon
PS 74 Rizal

Patrol Forces

PG 101 Kagitingan
PG 102 Bagong Lakas
PG 104 Bagong Silang
PG 110 Tomas Batilo
PG 111 Bonny Serrano
PG 112 Bienvenido Salting
PG 114 Salvador Abcede
PG 115 Ramon Aguirre
PG 116 Nicolas Mahusay
PG 140 Emilo Aguinaldo
PG 141 Antonio Luna
PG 370 José Andrada
PG 371 Enrique Jurado
PG 372 Alfredo Peckson
PG 374 Simeon Castro
PG 375 Carlos Albert
PG 376 Heracleo Alano
PG 377 Liberato Picar
PG 378 Hilario Ruiz
PG 379 Rafael Pargas
PG 380 Nestor Reinoso
PG 381 Dioscoro Papa
PG 383 Ismael Lomibao
PG 384 Leovigildo Gantioque
PG 385 Federico Martir
PG 386 Filipino Flojo
PG 387 Anastacio Cacayorin
PG 388 Manuel Gomez
PG 389 Testimo Figuracion
PG 390 José Loor SR
PG 392 Juan Magluyan
PG 393 Florenca Nuno
PG 394 Alberto Navaret
PG 395 Felix Apolinario
PG 396 Brigadier Abraham Campo
PG 840 Conrado Yap
PG 842 Tedorico Dominado Jr
PG 843 Cosme Acosta
PG 844 José Artiaga Jr
PG 846 Nicanor Jimenez
PG 847 Leopoldo Regis
PG 848 Leon Tadina
PG 849 Loreto Danipog
PG 851 Apollo Tiano
PG 853 Sulpicio Hernandez

Auxiliaries

LT 86 Zamboanga Del Sur
LT 87 South Cotabato
LT 501 Laguna
LT 504 Lanao Del Norte
LT 516 Kalinga Apayao
LC 550 Bacolod City
LC 551 Dagupan City
AT 25 Ang Pangulo
AW 33 Lake Bulusan
AW 34 Lake Paoay
AF 72 Lake Taal
AF 78 Lake Buhi
AC 90 Mactan
AD 617 Yakal

Coast Guard

AE 46 Cape Bojeador
PG 61 Agusan
PG 62 Catanduanes
PG 63 Romblon
PG 64 Palawan
AT 71 Mangyan
AU 75 Bessang Pass
AE 79 Limasawa
AG 89 Kalinga
AU 100 Tirad Pass
001 San Juan
002 Esda II

FRIGATES

Notes: *Rajah Lakandula*, paid off in 1988, is still afloat as an alongside HQ and depot ship.

1 CANNON CLASS (FF)

Name	*No*	*Builders*	*Laid down*	*Launched*	*Commissioned*
RAJAH HUMABON (ex-*Hatsuhi* DE 263, ex-*Atherton* DE 169)	PF 11 (ex-PF 78)	Norfolk Navy Yard, Portsmouth, VA	14 Jan 1943	27 May 1943	29 Aug 1943

Displacement, tons: 1,390 standard; 1,750 full load
Dimensions, feet (metres): 306 × 36.6 × 14 *(93.3 × 11.2 × 4.3)*
Main machinery: Diesel-electric; 2 GM EMD 16V-645E7 diesels; 5,800 hp *(4.32 MW)*; 4 generators; 2 motors; 2 shafts
Speed, knots: 18
Range, n miles: 6,000 at 14 kt
Complement: 165

Guns: 3 US 3 in *(76 mm)*/50 Mk 22; 20 rds/min to 12 km *(6.6 n miles)*; weight of shell 6 kg.
6 US/Bofors 40 mm/56 (3 twin). 4 Oerlikon 20 mm/70; 4—12.7 mm MGs.
Weapons control: Mk 52 GFCS with Mk 41 rangefinder for 3 in guns. 3 Mk 51 Mod 2 GFCS for 40 mm.
Radars: Surface search: Raytheon SPS-5; G/H-band.
Navigation: RCA/GE Mk 26; I-band.
Sonars: SQS-17B; hull-mounted; active search and attack; medium/high frequency.

Programmes: *Hatsuhi* originally transferred by the US to Japan 14 June 1955 and paid off June 1975 reverting to US Navy. Transferred to Philippines 23 December 1978. Towed to South Korea 1979 for overhaul and modernisation. Recommissioned 27 February 1980. A sister ship *Datu Kalantiaw* lost during Typhoon Clara 20 September 1981.
Modernisation: Upgrade plans have been suspended.
Operational: Hedgehog A/S mortars have been reported.

RAJAH HUMABON ***10/2001, Chris Sattler*** / 0126280

CORVETTES

3 JACINTO (PEACOCK) CLASS (FS)

Name	*No*	*Builders*	*Launched*	*Commissioned*	*Recommissioned*
EMILIO JACINTO (ex-*Peacock*)	PS 35 (ex-P 239)	Hall Russell, Aberdeen	1 Dec 1982	14 July 1984	4 Aug 1997
APOLINARIO MABINI (ex-*Plover*)	PS 36 (ex-P 240)	Hall Russell, Aberdeen	12 Apr 1983	20 July 1984	4 Aug 1997
ARTEMIO RICARTE (ex-*Starling*)	PS 37 (ex-P 241)	Hall Russell, Aberdeen	11 Sep 1983	10 Aug 1984	4 Aug 1997

Displacement, tons: 763 full load
Dimensions, feet (metres): 204.1 × 32.8 × 8.9 *(62.6 × 10 × 2.7)*
Main machinery: 2 Crossley Pielstick 18 PA6 V 280 diesels; 14,000 hp(m) *(10.6 MW)* sustained; 2 shafts; 1 retractable Schottel prop; 181 hp *(135 kW)*
Speed, knots: 25
Range, n miles: 2,500 at 17 kt
Complement: 31 (6 officers) plus 7 spare berths

Guns: 1 — 3 in *(76 mm)*/62 OTO Melara compact; 85 rds/min to 16 km *(8.6 n miles)* anti-surface; 12 km *(6.5 n miles)* anti-aircraft; weight of shell 6 kg.
1 MSI Defence Systems 25 mm.
4 FN 7.62 mm MGs.
Weapons control: Radamec 1500 optronic director.
Radars: Sperry Marine Bridgemaster E; E/F/I-bands.

Programmes: Letter of Intention to purchase from the UK signed in November 1996. Transferred 1 August 1997 after sailing from Hong Kong on 1 July 1997. Others of the class in service with the navy of the Irish Republic.
Modernisation: An upgrade programme was agreed in 2002 and a contract was signed on 6 December 2004 for phase one of the work which included overhaul of the 76 mm gun, installation of a MSI Defense Systems 25 mm mounting on the stern, replacement of Sea Archer fire-control system with a Radamec 1500 optronic director, replacement of the navigation radar with Sperry Marine Bridgemaster E and new navigation systems. Phase one was completed in September 2006. Phases two and three are to involve new propulsion and safety systems.
Structure: Fitted with telescopic cranes, loiter drive and replenishment at sea equipment. In UK service, two fast pursuit craft were carried.
Operational: These ships are the workhorses of the fleet. Based at Cavite.

ARTEMIO RICARTE *6/2008*, Ships of the World* / 1353255

1 CYCLONE CLASS (COASTAL PATROL SHIP) (PB)

Name	*No*	*Builders*	*Commissioned*
GENERAL MARIANO ALVARES (ex-*Cyclone*)	PS 38 (ex-PC 1)	Bollinger, Lockport	7 Aug 1993

Displacement, tons: 386 full load
Dimensions, feet (metres): 179 × 25.9 × 7.9 *(54.6 × 7.9 × 2.4)*
Main machinery: 4 Paxman Valenta 16RP200CM diesels; 13,400 hp *(10 MW)* sustained; 4 shafts
Speed, knots: 35
Range, n miles: 2,500 at 12 kt
Complement: 28 (4 officers) plus 8
Countermeasures: Decoys: 2 Mk 52 sextuple and/or Wallop Super Barricade Mk 3 chaff launchers.
ESM: Privateer APR-39; radar warning.
Weapons control: Marconi VISTAR IM 405 IR system.
Radars: Surface search: 2 Sperry RASCAR; E/F/I/J-band.
Sonars: Wesmar; hull-mounted; active; high frequency.

Programmes: Transferred from the USN to the Philippines in February 2004 following refit at Bollinger. Recommissioned on 8 March 2004.
Modernisation: All armament was removed before transfer from the USN. New armament is likely to include two 25 mm guns and 12.7 mm machine guns.
Structure: Design based on Vosper Thornycroft Ramadan class modified for USN requirements including 1 in armour on superstructure. The craft has a slow speed loiter capability and has been modified to incorporate a semi-dry well, boat ramp and stern gate to facilitate deployment and recovery of a fully loaded RIB while the ship is making way.

GENERAL MARIANO ALVARES
3/2004, US Embassy, Manila
0563762

2 AUK CLASS (FS)

Name	*No*	*Builders*	*Laid down*	*Launched*	*Commissioned*
RIZAL (ex-*Murrelet* MSF 372)	PS 74 (ex-PS 69)	Savannah Machine & Foundry Co, GA	24 Aug 1944	29 Dec 1944	21 Aug 1945
QUEZON (ex-*Vigilance* MSF 324)	PS 70	Associated Shipbuilders, Seattle, WA	28 Nov 1942	5 Apr 1943	28 Feb 1944

Displacement, tons: 1,090 standard; 1,250 full load
Dimensions, feet (metres): 221.2 × 32.2 × 10.8 *(67.4 × 9.8 × 3.3)*
Main machinery: Diesel-electric; 2 GM EMD 16V-645E6 diesels; 5,800 hp *(4.32 MW)*; 2 generators; 2 motors; 2 shafts
Speed, knots: 18
Range, n miles: 5,000 at 14 kt

Complement: 80 (5 officers)
Guns: 2 US 3 in *(76 mm)*/50 Mk 26; 20 rds/min to 12 km *(6.6 n miles)*; weight of shell 6 kg.
4 US/Bofors 40 mm/56 (2 twin); 160 rds/min to 11 km *(5.9 n miles)*; weight of shell 0.9 kg.
2 Oerlikon 20 mm (twin). 2—12.7 mm MGs.
Radars: Surface search: Raytheon SPS-5C; G/H-band.
Navigation: DAS 3; I-band.

Programmes: *Rizal* transferred from the US to the Philippines on 18 June 1965 and *Quezon* on 19 August 1967.
Modernisation: Upgrade plans have been suspended.
Structure: Upon transfer the minesweeping gear was removed and a second 3 in gun fitted aft.
Operational: Both ships were to have been deleted in 1994 but have been retained until new class of OPVs is built. Sonar equipment and depth charges have been removed.

RIZAL *10/2001, Chris Sattler / 0534068*

8 PCE 827 CLASS (FS)

Name	*No*	*Builders*	*Commissioned*
MIGUEL MALVAR (ex-*Ngoc Hoi*, ex-*Brattleboro* PCER 852)	PS 19	Pullman Standard Car Co, Chicago	26 May 1944
MAGAT SALAMAT (ex-*Chi Lang II*, ex-*Gayety* MSF 239)	PS 20	Winslow Marine Co, Seattle, WA	14 June 1944
SULTAN KUDARAT (ex-*Dong Da II*, ex-*Crestview* PCER 895)	PS 22	Willamette Iron & Steel Corporation, Portland, OR	30 Oct 1943
DATU MARIKUDO (ex-*Van Kiep II*, ex-*Amherst* PCER 853)	PS 23	Pullman Standard Car Co, Chicago	16 June 1944
CEBU (ex-*PCE 881*)	PS 28	Albina E and M Works, Portland, OR	31 July 1944
NEGROS OCCIDENTAL (ex-*PCE 884*)	PS 29	Albina E and M Works, Portland, OR	30 Mar 1944
PANGASINAN (ex-*PCE 891*)	PS 31	Willamette Iron & Steel Corp, Portland, OR	15 June 1944
ILOILO (ex-*PCE 897*)	PS 32	Willamette Iron & Steel Corp, Portland, OR	6 Jan 1945

Displacement, tons: 640 standard; 914 full load
Dimensions, feet (metres): 184.5 × 33.1 × 9.5 *(56.3 × 10.1 × 2.9)*
Main machinery: 2 GM 12-278A diesels; 2,200 hp *(1.64 MW)*; 2 shafts
Speed, knots: 15
Range, n miles: 6,600 at 11 kt
Complement: 85 (8 officers)
Guns: 1 US 3 in *(76 mm)*/50; 20 rds/min to 12 km *(6.6 n miles)*; weight of shell 6 kg.
2 to 6 US/Bofors 40 mm/56 (single or 1—3 twin); 160 rds/min to 11 km *(5.9 n miles)*; weight of shell 0.9 kg.
2 Oerlikon 20 mm/70; 800 rds/min to 2 km.
Radars: Surface search: SPS-50 (PS 23). SPS-21D (PS 19, 28). CRM-NIA-75 (PS 29, 31, 32). SPS-53A (PS 20).
Navigation: RCA SPN-18; I/J-band.

Programmes: Five transferred from the US to the Philippines in July 1948 (PS 28-32); PS 22 to South Vietnam from US Navy on 29 November 1961, PS 20 in April 1962, PS 19 on 11 July 1966, and PS 23 in June 1970. PS 19, 20 and 22 to Philippines November 1975 and PS 23 5 April 1976.
Modernisation: PS 19, 22, 31 and 32 refurbished in 1990–91, PS 23 and 28 in 1992 and the last pair in 1996/97.
Structure: First three were originally fitted as rescue ships (PCER). A/S equipment has been removed or is inoperable. PS 20 has some minor structural differences having been built as an Admirable class MSF.
Operational: PS 29 is probably not operational.

CEBU *5/2000, M Declerck / 0105225*

LAND-BASED MARITIME AIRCRAFT

Notes: There are two Cessna 177 Cardinal transport aircraft.

Numbers/Type: 7 PADC (Pilatus Britten-Norman) Islander F27MP.
Operational speed: 150 kt *(280 km/h)*.
Service ceiling: 18,900 ft *(5,760 m)*.
Range: 1,500 n miles *(2,775 km)*.
Role/Weapon systems: Short-range MR and SAR aircraft. First purchased in 1989. Three transferred from the Air Force. An upgrade programme, including engines, avionics and communications systems has been completed on five aircraft. The remaining two aircraft are to be similarly modernised. Sensors: Search radar, cameras. Weapons: Unarmed.

Numbers/Type: 5 PADC (MBB) BO 105C.
Operational speed: 145 kt *(270 km/h)*.
Service ceiling: 17,000 ft *(5,180 m)*.
Range: 355 n miles *(657 km)*.
Role/Weapon systems: Sole shipborne helicopter; some shore-based for SAR; some commando support capability. Purchased at the rate of one per year from 1986 to 1992. Upgrade of avionics and communications is planned. Sensors: Some fitted with search radar. Weapons: Unarmed.

F-27MP *10/2001, Adolfo Ortigueira Gil / 0567482*

PATROL FORCES

Notes: Plans to procure three offshore patrol craft have been suspended although they remain a long-term aspiration.

2 AGUINALDO CLASS (LARGE PATROL CRAFT) (PBO)

Name	*No*	*Builders*	*Commissioned*
EMILIO AGUINALDO	PG 140	Cavite, Sangley Point	21 Nov 1990
ANTONIO LUNA	PG 141	Cavite, Sangley Point	27 May 1999

Displacement, tons: 236 full load
Dimensions, feet (metres): 144.4 × 24.3 × 5.2 *(44 × 7.4 × 1.6)*
Main machinery: 2 MTU 16V-396TB94 diesels; 3,480 hp *(2.59 MW)* sustained; 2 shafts
Speed, knots: 28. **Range, n miles:** 1,100 at 18 kt
Complement: 58 (6 officers)
Guns: 2 Bofors 40 mm/60. 2 Oerlikon 20 mm. 4—12.7 mm MGs.
Radars: Surface search: Raytheon; I-band.

Comment: Steel hulls of similar design to *Tirad Pass*. First of class launched 23 June 1984 but only completed in 1990. Second laid down 2 December 1990 and launched 23 June 1992. A third ship was laid down on 14 February 1994 and launched in April 2000. While the superstructure is 70 per cent completed, outfitting was not completed due to budget constraints.

EMILIO AGUINALDO *6/1993* / 0081540

2 POINT CLASS (PB)

Name	*No*	*Builders*	*Commissioned*
ALBERTO NAVARET (ex-*Point Evans*)	PG 394 (ex-82354)	CG Yard, Maryland	10 Jan 1967
BRIGADIER ABRAHAM CAMPO (ex-*Point Doran*)	PG 396 (ex-82375)	CG Yard, Maryland	1 June 1970

Displacement, tons: 67 full load
Dimensions, feet (metres): 83 × 17.2 × 5.8 *(25.3 × 5.2 × 1.8)*
Main machinery: 2 Caterpillar 3412 diesels; 1,600 hp *(1.19 MW)*; 2 shafts
Speed, knots: 23. **Range, n miles:** 1,500 at 8 kt
Complement: 10
Guns: 2—12.7 mm MGs.
Radars: Surface search: Furuno; I-band.

Comment: PG 394 transferred from US Coast Guard 16 November 1999. Second transferred 22 March 2001. This class is in service with many other navies.

POINT CLASS (US colours) *4/1992, van Ginderen Collection* / 0081549

3 KAGITINGAN CLASS (LARGE PATROL CRAFT) (PB)

Name	*No*	*Builders*	*Commissioned*
KAGITINGAN	P 101	Hamelin SY, Germany	9 Feb 1979
BAGONG LAKAS	PG 102 (ex-P 102)	Hamelin SY, Germany	9 Feb 1979
BAGONG SILANG	PG 104 (ex-P 104)	Hamelin SY, Germany	July 1979

Displacement, tons: 150 full load
Dimensions, feet (metres): 121.4 × 20.3 × 5.6 *(37 × 6.2 × 1.7)*
Main machinery: 2 MTU MB 16V-538TB91 diesels; 2,500 hp(m) *(1.86 MW)* sustained; 2 shafts
Speed, knots: 21
Complement: 30 (4 officers)
Guns: 2—30 mm (twin). 4—12.7 mm MGs. 2—7.62 mm MGs.
Radars: Surface search: I-band.

Comment: Based at Cavite. P 103 paid off and used for spares. All still in service.

BAGONG LAKAS *1993, Philippine Navy* / 0506161

8 TOMAS BATILO (SEA DOLPHIN) CLASS (FAST ATTACK CRAFT) (PBF)

TOMAS BATILO PG 110
BONNY SERRANO PG 111
BIENVENIDO SALTING PG 112
SALVADOR ABCEDE PG 114
RAMON AGUIRRE PG 115
NICOLAS MAHUSAY PG 116
+2

Displacement, tons: 150 full load
Dimensions, feet (metres): 121.4 × 22.6 × 5.6 *(37 × 6.9 × 1.7)*
Main machinery: 2 MTU 20V-538TB91 diesels; 9,000 hp(m) *(6.71 MW)* sustained; 2 shafts
Speed, knots: 38
Range, n miles: 600 at 20 kt
Complement: 31 (5 officers)
Guns: 2 Emerson Electric 30 mm (twin); 1,200 rds/min combined to 6 km *(3.2 n miles)*; weight of shell 0.35 kg.
1 Bofors 40 mm/60. 2 Oerlikon 20 mm.
Weapons control: Optical director.
Radars: Surface search: Raytheon 1645; I-band.

Comment: Six transferred from South Korea on 15 June 1995. Part of the PKM 200 series. Different armament to South Korean ships of the same class. A further two were transferred on 7 December 2006. Refit of two other vessels is under consideration.

BIENVENIDO SALTING *6/1996, Philippine Navy* / 0506311

22 JOSÉ ANDRADA CLASS (COASTAL PATROL CRAFT) (PB)

JOSÉ ANDRADA PG 370
ENRIQUE JURADO PG 371
ALFREDO PECKSON PG 372
SIMEON CASTRO PG 374
CARLOS ALBERT PG 375
HERACLEO ALANO PG 376
LIBERATO PICAR PG 377
HILARIO RUIZ PG 378
RAFAEL PARGAS PG 379
NESTOR REINOSO PG 380
DIOSCORO PAPA PG 381
ISMAEL LOMIBAO PG 383
LEOVIGILDO GANTIOQUE PG 384
FEDERICO MARTIR PG 385
FILIPINO FLOJO PG 386
ANASTACIO CACAYORIN PG 387
MANUEL GOMEZ PG 388
TESTIMO FIGURACION PG 389
JOSÉ LOOR SR PG 390
JUAN MAGLUYAN PG 392
FLORENCA NUNO PG 393
FELIX APOLINARIO PG 395

Displacement, tons: 56 full load
Dimensions, feet (metres): 78 × 20 × 5.8 *(23.8 × 6.1 × 1.8)*
Main machinery: 2 Detroit 16V-92TA diesels; 1,380 hp *(1.03 MW)* sustained; 2 shafts
Speed, knots: 28
Range, n miles: 1,200 at 12 kt
Complement: 8—12 (1 officer)
Guns: 1 Bushmaster 25 mm or Bofors 40 mm/60.
4—12.7 mm Mk 26 MGs. 2—7.62 mm M60 MGs.
Radars: Surface search: Raytheon SPS-64(V)2; I-band.

Comment: There are four batches of this class. Batch I (PCF 370-378), Batch II (PCF 379-390), Batch III (PCF 392-393) and Batch IV (PCF 395). The main difference between batches include weapons, electronics and accommodation. First four ordered from Halter Marine in August 1989 under FMS and built at Equitable Shipyards, New Orleans, as were a further four ordered in 1990. Eight more ordered in March 1993 with co-production between Halter Marine and AG&P Shipyard, Batangas. An additional three were ordered in 1995. Built to US Coast Guard standards with an aluminium hull and superstructure. The main gun may be fitted in all after some minor modifications. PG 392 delivered in March 1998, PG 393 in July 1998 and PG 395 on 10 October 2000.

TESTIMO FIGURACION *5/2000, M Declerck* / 0105226

JUAN MAGLUYAN *6/2008*, Ships of the World* / 1353253

4 PCF 65 (SWIFT MK 3) CLASS (COASTAL PATROL CRAFT) (PB)

PC 351–354

Displacement, tons: 29 standard; 37 full load
Dimensions, feet (metres): 65 × 16 × 3.4 *(19.8 × 4.9 × 1)*
Main machinery: 3 GM 12V-71TI diesels; 840 hp *(616 kW)* sustained; 3 shafts
Speed, knots: 25
Complement: 8
Guns: 2 — 12.7 mm MGs.
Radars: Surface search: Koden; I-band.

Comment: Improved Swift type inshore patrol boats built by Peterson and delivered 1975–76. Aluminium construction. Some that were laid up have been returned to service. New radars fitted.

PC 354 — *5/1998, John Mortimer* / 0081551

10 CONRADO YAP (SEA HAWK/KILLER) CLASS (COASTAL PATROL CRAFT) (PBF)

CONRADO YAP PG 840
TEDORICO DOMINADO JR PG 842
COSME ACOSTA PG 843
JOSÉ ARTIAGA JR PG 844
NICANOR JIMENEZ PG 846
LEOPOLDO REGIS PG 847
LEON TADINA PG 848
LORETO DANIPOG PG 849
APOLLO TIANO PG 851
SULPICIO FERNANDEZ PG 853

Displacement, tons: 74.5 full load
Dimensions, feet (metres): 83.7 × 17.7 × 6.2 *(25.5 × 5.4 × 1.9)*
Main machinery: 2 MTU 16V-538TB91 diesels; 5,000 hp(m) *(3.72 MW)*; 2 shafts
Speed, knots: 38
Range, n miles: 290 at 20 kt
Complement: 15 (3 officers)
Guns: 1 Bofors 40 mm/60. 2 Oerlikon 20 mm (twin) Mk 16.
Radars: Surface search: Raytheon 1645; I-band.

Comment: Type PK 181 built by Korea Tacoma and Hyundai 1975–78. Twelve craft transferred from South Korea 19 June 1993. Eight were commissioned 23 June 1993 and a further four on 23 June 1994. However PC 845 and PC 852 have not been reactivated and are probably used as spares.

CONRADO YAP CLASS — *1993, Philippine Navy* / 0506162

SURVEY AND RESEARCH SHIPS

Notes: (1) Survey ships are operated by Coast and Geodetic Survey of Ministry of National Defence and are not naval. These include: *Atyimba, Alunya, Arinya, Bantay Kalikasan* and *Explorer*.
(2) Two research ships *Fort San Antonio* (AM 700) and *Fort Abad* (AM 701) were acquired in 1993.

AUXILIARIES

Notes: (1) All LSTs, LSVs, LCMs and LCUs are classified as Transports.
(2) Procurement of a multirole vessel, capable of transporting 500 troops, is under consideration. The broad requirement is for a 150 m vessel capable of 20 kt.

2 BACOLOD CITY (FRANK S BESSON) CLASS (LSVH)

Name	*No*	*Builders*	*Commissioned*
BACOLOD CITY	LC 550	Moss Point Marine	1 Dec 1993
DAGUPAN CITY (ex-*Cagayan De Oro City*)	LC 551	Moss Point Marine	5 Apr 1994

Displacement, tons: 4,265 full load
Dimensions, feet (metres): 272.8 × 60 × 12 *(83.1 × 18.3 × 3.7)*
Main machinery: 2 GM EMD 16V-645E6 diesels; 5,800 hp *(4.32 MW)* sustained; 2 shafts; bow thruster; 250 hp *(187 kW)*
Speed, knots: 11.6
Range, n miles: 6,000 at 11 kt
Complement: 30 (6 officers)
Military lift: 2,280 tons (900 for amphibious operations) of vehicles, containers or cargo, plus 150 troops; 2 LCVPs on davits
Radars: Navigation: Raytheon SPS-64(V)2; I-band.
Helicopters: Platform for 1 BO 105C.

Comment: Contract announced by Trinity Marine 3 April 1992 for two ships with an option on a third which was not taken up. Ro-ro design with 10,500 sq ft of deck space for cargo. Capable of beaching with 4 ft over the ramp on a 1 : 30 offshore gradient with a 900 ton cargo. Similar to US Army vessels but with only a bow ramp. The stern ramp space is used for accommodation for 150 troops and a helicopter platform is fitted over the stern.

BACOLOD CITY — *6/2008*, Ships of the World* / 1353254

DAGUPAN CITY — *12/1999, Sattler/Steele* / 0081544

5 LST 512-1152 CLASS (TRANSPORT SHIPS) (LST)

Name	*No*	*Builders*	*Commissioned*
ZAMBOANGA DEL SUR (ex-*Cam Ranh*, ex-*Marion County* LST 975)	LT 86	Bethlehem Steel, Hingham, Mass	3 Feb 1945
SOUTH COTABATO (ex-*Cayuga County* LST 529)	LT 87	Bethlehem Steel, Hingham, Mass	28 Feb 1944
LAGUNA (ex-*T-LST 230*)	LT 501	American Bridge, Ambridge, PA	3 Nov 1943
LANAO DEL NORTE (ex-*T-LST 566*)	LT 504	Missouri Valley Bridge and Iron Co, Evansville, Ind	29 May 1944
KALINGA APAYAO (ex-*Can Tho*, ex-*Garrett County* AGP 786, ex-LST 786)	LT 516 (ex-AE 516)	Dravo Corp., Pittsburgh, PA	28 Aug 1944

Displacement, tons: 1,620 standard; 2,472 beaching; 4,080 full load
Dimensions, feet (metres): 328 × 50 × 14 *(100 × 15.2 × 4.3)*
Main machinery: 2 GM 12-567A diesels; 1,800 hp *(1.34 MW)*; 2 shafts
Speed, knots: 10
Complement: Varies-approx 60-110 (depending upon employment)
Military lift: 2,100 tons. 16 tanks or 10 tanks plus 200 troops
Guns: 6 US/Bofors 40 mm (2 twin, 2 single) or 4 Oerlikon 20 mm (in refitted ships).
Radars: Navigation: Raytheon SPS-64(V)2; I-band.

Programmes: Transferred from US Navy in 1976 with exception of LT 87 and LT 516 which were used as light craft repair ships in South Vietnam and have retained amphibious capability (transferred to Vietnam 1970 and to Philippines 1976, acquired by purchase 5 April 1976). LT 86 transferred (grant aid) 17 November 1975. LT 501 and 504 commissioned in Philippine Navy 8 August 1978 and LT 507 on 18 October 1978.
Modernisation: Several have had major refits including replacement of frames and plating as well as engines and electrics and provision for four 20 mm guns to replace the 40 mm guns.
Structure: Some of the later ships have tripod masts, others have pole masts.
Operational: All are used for general cargo work in Philippine service. Fourteen were deleted in 1989 and one sank in 1991. Two paid off in 1992 and one in 1993. *South Cotabato* was also paid off in 1993 but brought back in to service in 1994. *Benguet* broke down in the South China Sea in April 1995 and had to betaken in tow. *Benguet* again grounded in the Spratly Islands on 3 November 1999 and after a month on the rocks is probably beyond economical repair. One further ship, *Sierra Madre* is reported to be used as an observation post in the Spratly Islands. Replacements are needed but have not been given priority.

LANAO DEL NORTE — *1993, Philippine Navy* / 0506163

1 ACHELOUS CLASS (REPAIR SHIP) (ARL)

Name	*No*	*Builders*	*Commissioned*
YAKAL (ex-*Satyr* ARL 23, ex-LST 852)	AD 617 (ex-AR 517)	Chicago Bridge & Iron	20 Nov 1944

Displacement, tons: 4,342 full load
Dimensions, feet (metres): 328 × 50 × 14 *(100 × 15.2 × 4.3)*
Main machinery: 2 GM 12-567A diesels; 1,800 hp *(1.34 MW)*; 2 shafts
Speed, knots: 11.6
Complement: 220 approx
Guns: 4 US/Bofors 40 mm (quad). 10 Oerlikon 20 mm (5 twin).

Comment: Transferred from the US to the Philippines on 24 January 1977 by sale. (Originally to South Vietnam 30 September 1971). Converted during construction. Extensive machine shop, spare parts stowage, and logistic support.

YAKAL *1994, Philippine Navy / 0081545*

42 LCM/LCU

Comment: Ex-US minor landing craft mostly transferred in the mid-1970s. 11 LCM 6, five LCM 8, eight LCU, 14 RUC and two LCVP. Used as transport vessels.

LCU 286 *5/1998, van Ginderen Collection / 0052706*

1 ALAMOSA CLASS (SUPPLY SHIP) (AK)

Name	*No*	*Builders*	*Commissioned*
MACTAN (ex-*Kukui*, ex-*Colquith*)	AC 90 (ex-TK 90)	Froemming, Milwaukee	22 Sep 1944

Displacement, tons: 2,500 light; 7,570 full load
Dimensions, feet (metres): 338.5 × 50 × 18 *(103.2 × 15.2 × 5.5)*
Main machinery: 1 Nordberg diesel; 1,700 hp *(1.27 MW)*; 1 shaft
Speed, knots: 11
Complement: 85
Guns: 2—12.7 mm MGs.

Comment: Transferred from the US Coast Guard on 1 March 1972. Used to supply military posts and lighthouses in the Philippine archipelago. Was to have been paid off in 1994 but has been kept in service.

MACTAN *4/1996, Philippine Navy / 0506312*

1 TRANSPORT VESSEL (AP)

Name	*No*	*Builders*	*Commissioned*
ANG PANGULO (ex-*The President*, ex-*Roxas*, ex-*Lapu-Lapu*)	AT 25 (ex-TP 777)	Ishikawajima, Japan	1959

Displacement, tons: 2,239 standard; 2,727 full load
Dimensions, feet (metres): 257.6 × 42.6 × 21 *(78.5 × 13 × 6.4)*
Main machinery: 2 Mitsui DE642/VBF diesels; 5,000 hp(m) *(3.68 MW)*; 2 shafts
Speed, knots: 18. **Range, n miles:** 6,900 at 15 kt
Complement: 81 (8 officers)
Guns: 3 Oerlikon 20 mm/70 Mk 4. 8—7.62 mm MGs.
Radars: Navigation RCA CRMN-1A-75; I-band.

Comment: Built as war reparation; launched in 1958. Was used as presidential yacht and command ship with accommodation for 50 passengers. Originally named *Lapu-Lapu* after the chief who killed Magellan; renamed *Roxas* on 9 October 1962 after the late Manuel Roxas, the first President of the Philippines Republic. Renamed *The President* in 1967 and *Ang Pangulo* in 1975. In early 1987 was earmarked to transport President Marcos to Hong Kong and exile. The ship is now used as an attack transport, and still as a Presidential Yacht.

ANG PANGULO *5/1998, John Mortimer / 0081546*

2 YW TYPE (WATER TANKERS) (AWT)

Name	*No*	*Builders*	*Commissioned*
LAKE BULUSAN	AW 33 (ex-YW 111)	Marine Iron, Duluth	1 Aug 1945
LAKE PAOAY	AW 34 (ex-YW 130)	Leathem D Smith, Sturgeon Bay	28 Aug 1945

Displacement, tons: 1,237 full load
Dimensions, feet (metres): 174 × 32.7 × 13.2 *(53 × 10 × 4)*
Main machinery: 2 GM 8-278A diesels; 1,500 hp *(1.12 MW)*; 2 shafts
Speed, knots: 7.5
Complement: 29
Cargo capacity: 200,000 gallons
Guns: 1 Bofors 40/60. 1 Oerlikon 20 mm.

Comment: Basically similar to YOG type but adapted to carry fresh water. Transferred from the US to the Philippines on 16 July 1975.

LAKE PAOAY *5/1998, van Ginderen Collection / 0052708*

2 YOG TYPE (TANKERS) (YO)

Name	*No*	*Builders*	*Commissioned*
LAKE BUHI (ex-*YOG 73*)	AF 78 (ex-YO 78)	Puget Sound, Bremerton	28 Nov 1944
LAKE TAAL (ex-*YOG*)	AF 72 (ex-YO 72)	Puget Sound, Bremerton	14 Apr 1945

Displacement, tons: 447 standard; 1,400 full load
Dimensions, feet (metres): 174 × 32.7 × 13.2 *(53 × 10 × 4)*
Main machinery: 2 GM 8-278A diesels; 1,500 hp *(1.12 MW)*; 2 shafts
Speed, knots: 8
Complement: 28
Cargo capacity: 6,570 barrels dieso and gasoline
Guns: 2 Oerlikon 20 mm/70 Mk 4.

Comment: Former US Navy gasoline tankers. Transferred in July 1967 on loan and by purchase 5 March 1980.

LAKE BUHI *1993, Philippine Navy / 0506164*

4 FLOATING DOCKS (YFD)

YD 200 (ex-*AFDL 24*) **YD 204** (ex-*AFDL 20*) **YD 205** (ex-*AFDL 44*) – (ex-*AFDL 40*)

Comment: Floating steel dry docks built in the USA; all are former US Navy units with *YD 200* transferred in July 1948, *YD 204* in October 1961 (sale 1 August 1980), *YD 205* in September 1969 and *AFDL 40* in 1994.
Capacities: *YD 205*, 2,800 tons; *YD 200* and *YD 204*, 1,000 tons. In addition there are two floating cranes, *YU 206* and *YU 207*, built in US in 1944 and capable of lifting 30 tons.

TUGS

Notes: A number of harbour tugs have been acquired from the US. The latest type is ex-Army of 390 tons, a speed of 12 kt and a bollard pull of 12 tons.

HARBOUR TUG *5/1998*, ***John Mortimer*** / 0052709

COAST GUARD

Notes: (1) Some of the PCF craft listed are manned by the Navy as is the buoy tender *Mangyan*.
(2) The Coast Guard also operates one LCM 6 (BM 270), one LCVP (BV 182) and a River Utility Craft VU 463.
(3) Ten Rodman 101 and four Rodman 38 were ordered for delivery to the Police by 2005.

4 SAN JUAN CLASS (WPBO)

Name	*No*	*Builders*	*Commissioned*
SAN JUAN	001	Tenix Defence Systems	19 June 2000
EDSA II (ex-*Don Emilio*)	002 (ex-419)	Tenix Defence Systems	14 Dec 2000
PAMPANGA	003	Tenix Defence Systems	30 Jan 2003
BATANGAS	004	Tenix Defence Systems	8 Aug 2003

Displacement, tons: 500 full load
Dimensions, feet (metres): 183.7 × 34.5 × 9.8 *(56 × 10.5 × 3)*
Main machinery: 2 Caterpillar 3612 diesels; 4,800 hp(m) *(3.53 MW)* sustained; 2 shafts; cp props
Speed, knots: 24.5
Range, n miles: 3,000 at 15 kt
Complement: 38
Radars: Navigation: I-band
Helicopters: Platform for one light.

Comment: First reported ordered in mid-1997. Construction of first of class started in February 1999. Steel hull and aluminium superstructure. Primarily used for SAR with facilities for 300 survivors. Fire-fighting and pollution control equipment included. A contract for a further two vessels was finalised in December 2001.

SAN JUAN *6/2000*, ***Tenix Shipbuilding*** / 0105228

4 ILOCOS NORTE CLASS (PATROL CRAFT) (PB)

Name	*No*	*Builders*	*Commissioned*
ILOCOS NORTE	3501	Tenix Defence Systems	9 May 2003
NUEVA VIZCAYA	3502	Tenix Defence Systems	8 Aug 2003
ROMBLON	3503	Tenix Defence Systems	20 Oct 2003
DAVAO DEL NORTE	3504	Tenix Defence Systems	16 Jan 2004

Displacement, tons: 115
Dimensions, feet (metres): 114.9 × 24.0 × 7.5 *(35.0 × 7.3 × 2.3)*
Main machinery: 2 diesels; 2 shafts. 1 loiter waterjet
Speed, knots: 23
Range, n miles: 2,000 at 12 kt
Complement: 11
Guns: 2—30 mm (1 twin). 2—12.7 mm MGs.
Radars: Navigation: I-band

Comment: Contract on 9 December 2001 for the construction of four search and rescue vessels. An option for a further ten craft is unlikely to be taken. Based on Bay class design with steel hull and aluminium superstructure.

NUEVA VIZCAYA *8/2003*, ***Tenix*** / 0569803

1 BALSAM CLASS (TENDER) (AKLH)

Name	*No*	*Builders*	*Commissioned*
KALINGA (ex-*Redbud, WAGL 398*, ex-*Redbud, T-AKL 398*)	AG 89	Marine Iron, Duluth	2 May 1944

Displacement, tons: 950 standard; 1,041 full load
Dimensions, feet (metres): 180 × 37 × 13 *(54.8 × 11.3 × 4)*
Main machinery: Diesel-electric; 2 diesels; 1,710 hp *(1.28 MW)*; 2 generators; 1 motor; 1,200 hp *(895 kW)*; 1 shaft
Speed, knots: 12
Range, n miles: 3,500 at 7 kt
Complement: 53
Guns: 2—12.7 mm MGs.
Radars: Navigation: Sperry SPS-53; I/J-band.
Helicopters: Platform for 1 light.

Comment: Originally US Coast Guard buoy tender (WAGL 398). Transferred to US Navy on 25 March 1949 as AG 398 and then to the Philippine Navy 1 March 1972. One 20 ton derrick. New engines fitted.

KALINGA *1994*, ***Philippine Navy*** / 0506201

3 BUOY TENDERS (ABU)

CAPE BOJEADOR (ex-*FS 203*) AE 46 (ex-TK 46)
LIMASAWA (ex-*Nettle* WAK 129, ex-*FS 169*) AE 79 (ex-TK 79)
MANGYAN (ex-*Nasami*, ex-*FS 408*) AT 71 (ex-AE 71, ex-AS 71)

Displacement, tons: 470 standard; 950 full load
Dimensions, feet (metres): 180 × 32 × 10 *(54.9 × 9.8 × 3)*
Main machinery: 2 GM 6-278A diesels; 1,120 hp *(836 kW)*; 2 shafts
Speed, knots: 10
Range, n miles: 4,150 at 10 kt
Complement: 50
Cargo capacity: 400 tons
Guns: 1—12.7 mm MG can be carried.
Radars: Navigation: RCA CRMN 1A 75; I-band.

Comment: Former US Army FS 381 and FS 330 type freight and supply ships built in 1943–44. First two are employed as tenders for buoys and lighthouses. *Mangyan* transferred 24 September 1976 by sale. *Limasawa* acquired by sale 31 August 1978. One 5 ton derrick. *Cape Bojeador* paid off in 1988 but was back in service in 1991 after a major overhaul. *Mangyan* reclassified AT in 1993 and belongs to the Navy. Masts and superstructures have minor variations.

CAPE BOJEADOR *1993*, ***Philippine Navy*** / 0506165

2 LARGE PATROL CRAFT (PB)

Name	*No*	*Builders*	*Commissioned*
TIRAD PASS	AU 100 (ex-SAR 100)	Sumidagawa, Japan	1974
BESSANG PASS	AU 75 (ex-SAR 99)	Sumidagawa, Japan	1974

Displacement, tons: 279 full load
Dimensions, feet (metres): 144.3 × 24.3 × 4.9 *(44 × 7.4 × 1.5)*
Main machinery: 2 MTU 12V 538 TB82 diesels; 4,050 hp(m) *(2.98 MW)*; 2 shafts
Speed, knots: 27.5
Range, n miles: 2,300 at 14 kt
Complement: 32
Guns: 4—12.7 mm (2 twin) MGs.

Comment: Paid for under Japanese war reparations. Similar type as *Emilio Aguinaldo*. *Bessang Pass* grounded in 1983 but was recovered.

TIRAD PASS *1992, Philippine Navy* / 0081548

4 PGM-39 CLASS (LARGE PATROL CRAFT) (PB)

Name	*No*	*Builders*	*Commissioned*
AGUSAN (ex-*PGM 39*)	PG 61	Tacoma, WA	Mar 1960
CATANDUANES (ex-*PGM 40*)	PG 62	Tacoma, WA	Mar 1960
ROMBLON (ex-*PGM 41*)	PG 63	Peterson Builders, WI	June 1960
PALAWAN (ex-*PGM 42*)	PG 64	Tacoma, WA	June 1960

Displacement, tons: 124 full load
Dimensions, feet (metres): 100.3 × 18.6 × 6.9 *(30.6 × 5.7 × 2.1)*
Main machinery: 2 MTU MB 12V 493 TY57 diesels; 2,200 hp(m) *(1.6 MW)* sustained; 2 shafts
Speed, knots: 17
Range, n miles: 1,400 at 11 kt
Complement: 26-30
Guns: 2 Oerlikon 20 mm. 2—12.7 mm MGs. 1—81 mm mortar.
Radars: Surface search: Alpelco DFR-12; I/J-band.

Comment: Steel-hulled craft built under US military assistance programmes. Assigned US PGM-series numbers while under construction. Transferred upon completion. These craft are lengthened versions of the US Coast Guard 95 ft Cape class patrol boat design. Operational status is doubtful.

AGUSAN *1994, Philippine Navy* / 0081550

10 PCF 46 CLASS (COASTAL PATROL CRAFT) (PB)

DB 411	**DB 417**	**DB 422**	**DB 429**	**DB 435**
DB 413	**DB 419**	**DB 426**	**DB 431–432**	

Displacement, tons: 21 full load
Dimensions, feet (metres): 45.9 × 14.5 × 3.3 *(14 × 4.4 × 1)*
Main machinery: 2 Cummins diesels; 740 hp *(552 kW)*; 2 shafts
Speed, knots: 25
Range, n miles: 1,000 at 15 kt
Complement: 8
Guns: 2—12.7 mm (twin) MGs. 1—7.62 mm M60 MG.
Radars: Surface search: Kelvin Hughes 17; I-band.

Comment: Built by Marcelo Yard, Manila and were to have been delivered 1976–78 at the rate of two per month. By the end of 1976, 25 had been completed but a serious fire in the shipyard destroyed 12 new hulls and halted production. Some deleted.

DB 435 *1993, Philippine Navy* / 0506166

12 PCF 50 (SWIFT MK 1 AND MK 2) CLASS (COASTAL PATROL CRAFT) (PB)

DF 300–303 **DF 305** **DF 307–313**

Displacement, tons: 22.5 full load
Dimensions, feet (metres): 50 × 13.6 × 4 *(15.2 × 4.1 × 1.2)* (Mk 1) 51.3 × 13.6 × 4 *(15.6 × 4.1 × 1.2)* (Mk 2)
Main machinery: 2 GM 12-71 diesels; 680 hp *(504 kW)* sustained; 2 shafts
Speed, knots: 28
Range, n miles: 685 at 16 kt
Complement: 6
Guns: 2—12.7 mm (twin) MGs. 2 M—79 40 mm grenade launchers.
Radars: Surface search: Decca 202; I-band.

Comment: Most built in the USA. Built for US military assistance programmes and transferred in the late 1960s. Some built in 1970 in the Philippines (ferro-concrete) with enlarged superstructure. *DF 300-303* are Swift Mk 1. *DF 305* and *DF 307-313* are Swift Mk 2.

DF 308 *5/1998, van Ginderen Collection* / 0081552

10 PCF 65 (SWIFT MK 3) CLASS (COASTAL PATROL CRAFT) (PB)

DF 325–332 **DF 334** **DF 347**

Displacement, tons: 29 standard; 37 full load
Dimensions, feet (metres): 65 × 16 × 3.4 *(19.8 × 4.9 × 1)*
Main machinery: 3 GM 12V-71TI diesels; 840 hp *(616 kW)* sustained; 3 shafts
Speed, knots: 25
Complement: 8
Guns: 2—12.7 mm MGs.
Radars: Surface search: Koden; I-band.

Comment: Improved Swift type inshore patrol boats built by Peterson and delivered 1975–76. Alumnium construction. Some that were laid up have been returned to service. New radars fitted.

DF 347 *5/1998, Sattler & Steele* / 0052711

3 DE HAVILLAND CLASS (PB)

DF 321–323

Displacement, tons: 25 full load
Dimensions, feet (metres): 54.8 × 16.4 × 4.3 *(16.7 × 5 × 1.3)*
Main machinery: 2 diesels; 740 hp *(552 kW)*; 2 shafts
Speed, knots: 25
Range, n miles: 450 at 14 kt
Complement: 8
Guns: 2—12.7 mm MGs.

Comment: Locally built in the mid-1980s. Others of this type have been paid off and numbers are uncertain.

DF 321 — *5/1998, van Ginderen Collection* / 0052713

1 CORREGIDOR CLASS (BUOY TENDER) (ABU)

Name	*No*	*Builders*	*Commissioned*
CORREGIDOR	AG 891	Niigata Engineering, Japan	2 Mar 1998

Displacement, tons: 1,130 full load
Dimensions, feet (metres): 186.7 × 26.1 × 12.5 *(56.9 × 11.0 × 3.8)*
Main machinery: 2 Niigata diesels; 2 shafts
Speed, knots: 13
Range, n miles: 4,000 at 11 kt
Complement: 37
Radars: Navigation: I-band.

Comment: Lighthouse and buoy tender. Similar to *Jadayat* in service in Indonesia.

11 CUTTERS (PBR)

CGC 103 CGC 110 CGC 115 CGC 128–130 CGC 132–136

Displacement, tons: 13 full load
Dimensions, feet (metres): 40 × 13.6 × 3 *(12.2 × 4.1 × 0.9)*
Main machinery: 2 Detroit diesels; 560 hp *(418 kW)*; 2 shafts
Speed, knots: 28
Complement: 5
Guns: 1—12.7 mm MG. 1—7.62 mm MG.

Comment: Built at Cavite Yard from 1984. One deleted in 1994. Used for harbour patrols. There are also some small unarmed Police craft.

CGC 130 — *1994, Philippine Navy* / 0081553

Poland

MARYNARKA WOJENNA

Country Overview

The modern democratic era of the Republic of Poland began in 1989 after forty-two years of communist rule. Situated in central Europe, the country has an area of 120,725 square miles and is bordered to the north by Russia (Kaliningrad), to the east by Lithuania, Belarus, and Ukraine, to the south by the Czech Republic and Slovakia and to the west by Germany. It has a 265 n mile coastline with the Baltic Sea. Warsaw is the capital and largest city while Gdansk, Szczecin and Gdynia are the principal ports. Territorial seas (12 n miles) are claimed but while it has claimed a 200 n mile EEZ, its limits have not been fully defined by boundary agreements.

Headquarters Appointments

Commander-in-Chief:
Vice Admiral Andrzej Karweta
Deputy Commander-in-Chief:
Rear Admiral Waldemar Gluszko
Chief of Naval Training:
Vice Admiral Maciej Węglewski
Commander Maritime Operations Centre:
Rear Admiral Jerzy Patz
Commander 3rd Flotilla:
Rear Admiral Marek Kurzyk
Commander 8th Flotilla:
Rear Admiral Jerzy Lenda

Diplomatic Representation

Defence and Naval Attaché in London:
Colonel K Szymanski

Personnel

(a) 2009: 14,100
(b) 12 months' national service

Prefix to Ships' Names

ORP, standing for *Okret Rzeczypospolitej Polskiej*

Strength of the Fleet

Type	*Active*	*Building*
Submarines—Patrol	5	–
Frigates	2	2 (5)
Corvettes	4	–
Fast Attack Craft—Missile	2	–
Coastal Patrol Craft	4	–
Minehunters—Coastal	20	(14)
LSTs	5	–
LCUs	3	–
Survey and Research Ships	2	–
AGIs	2	–
Training Ships	2	–
Salvage Ships	6	–
Tankers	4	–
Logistic Support Ship	1	–

Sea Department of the Border Guard (MOSG)

A para-naval force, subordinate to the Minister of the Interior.

Bases

Gdynia (3rd Naval Flotilla), Swinoujscie (8th Coastal Defence Flotilla), Kolobrzeg, Gdansk (Frontier Guard)

Naval Aviation

HQ at Gdynia-Babie Doly
28th Naval Squadron (Gdynia) (An-28, W-3, SH-2G, Mi-17, Mi-2)
29th Naval Squadron (Darlowo) (W-3, Mi-14)
30th Naval Squadron (Siemirowice) (An-28)

Coast Defence

Two divisions with 24-57 mm guns.

DELETIONS

Corvettes

2008 *Metalowiec, Rolnik*

Patrol Forces

2006 *Świnoujście, Wladyslawowo*, KP 167, KP 168, KP 171, KP 174

Auxiliaries

2006 *Semko, Slimak*
2007 *Krab, Gniewko*, H 3, M 37, B 9, B 12

PENNANT LIST

Submarines

291	Orzeł
294	Sókol
295	Sęp
296	Bielik
297	Kondor

Frigates

272	Generał Kazimierz Pułaski
273	Generał Tadeusz Kościuszko

Corvettes

240	Kaszub
421	Orkan
422	Piorun
423	Grom

Mine Warfare Forces

621	Flaming
623	Mewa
624	Czajka
630	Goplo
631	Gardno
632	Bukowo
633	Dabie
634	Jamno
635	Mielno
636	Wicko
637	Resko
638	Sarbsko
639	Necko
640	Naklo
641	Druzno
642	Hancza
643	Mamry
644	Wigry
645	Sniardwy
646	Wdzydze

Amphibious Forces

821	Lublin
822	Gniezno
823	Krakow
824	Poznan
825	Torun
851	KD 11
852	KD 12
853	KD 13

Survey Ships and AGIs

262	Nawigator
263	Hydrograf
265	Heweliusz
266	Arctowski

Auxiliaries

251	Wodnik
253	Iskra
281	Piast
282	Lech
511	Kontradmiral X Czernicki
R 11	Gniewko
R 14	Zbyszko
R 15	Macko
SD 11	Wrona
SD 13	–
Z 1	Baltyk
Z 3	Krab
Z 8	Meduza

Maritime Frontier Guard

SG 311	Kaper I
SG 312	Kaper II
SG 323	Zefir
SG 325	Tecza

SUBMARINES

4 SOKÓL (KOBBEN) (TYPE 207) CLASS (SSK)

Name	*No*	*Builders*	*Laid down*	*Launched*	*Commissioned*	*Recommissioned*
SOKÓL (ex-*Stord*)	294 (ex-S 308)	Rheinstahl – Nordseewerke, Emden	1 Apr 1966	2 Sep 1966	14 Feb 1967	4 June 2002
SĘP (ex-*Skolpen*)	295 (ex-S 306)	Rheinstahl – Nordseewerke, Emden	1 Nov 1965	24 Mar 1966	17 Aug 1966	16 Aug 2002
BIELIK (ex-*Svenner*)	296 (ex-S 309)	Rheinstahl – Nordseewerke, Emden	8 Sep 1966	27 Jan 1967	12 Jun 1967	8 Sep 2003
KONDOR (ex-*Kunna*)	297 (ex-S 319)	Rheinstahl – Nordseewerke, Emden	3 Mar 1964	16 Jul 1964	29 Oct 1964	20 Oct 2004

Displacement, tons: 459 standard; 524 dived
Dimensions, feet (metres): 155.5 × 15 × 14 *(47.4 × 4.6 × 4.3)*
Main machinery: Diesel-electric; 2 MTU 12V 493 AZ80 GA31L diesels; 1,200 hp(m) *(880 kW)* sustained; 1 motor; 1,800 hp(m) *(1.32 MW)* sustained; 1 shaft
Speed, knots: 12 surfaced; 18 dived
Range, n miles: 5,000 at 8 kt (snorting)
Complement: 21 (5 officers)

Torpedoes: 8—21 in *(533 mm)* bow tubes.
Countermeasures: ESM: Argo radar warning.
Weapons control: Kongsberg MSI-70U TFCS.
Radars: Surface search: Kelvin Hughes 1007; I-band.
Sonars: Atlas Elektronik CSU 83; passive search and attack; medium/high frequency.

Programmes: Commissioned into the Norwegian Navy from 1964, the original building cost was shared between the Norwegian and US governments. Decommissioned from the Norwegian Navy in 2001. Following announcement on 18 January 2002, four submarines transferred to the Polish Navy. A fifth, ex-*Kobben*, was transferred for spares and as a floating training base. The contract also includes provision of in-service support. These submarines are understood to be a stop-gap measure to maintain a submarine capability until about 2012 when these may be replaced.
Modernisation: All modernised at Urivale Shipyard, Bergen between 1989–1992.
Structure: A development of the German Type 205 class, they have a diving depth of 650 ft *(200 m)*. Pilkington optronics CK 30 search periscope.
Operational: Based at Gdynia.

SOKÓL *8/2007,* ***Maritime Photographic*** / 1166689

KONDOR ***11/2007, Ian Harris*** / 1166690

1 KILO CLASS (PROJECT 877EM) (SSK)

Name	*No*	*Builders*	*Commissioned*
ORZEŁ	291	Sudomekh, Leningrad	29 Apr 1986

Displacement, tons: 2,457 surfaced; 3,180 dived
Dimensions, feet (metres): 238.2 × 32.5 × 21.3 *(72.6 × 9.9 × 6.5)*
Main machinery: Diesel-electric; 2 DL 42M diesels; 3,650 hp(m) *(2.68 MW)*; 2 generators; 6 MW; 1 PG 141 motor; 5,900 hp(m) *(4.34 MW)*; 1 shaft; 2 auxiliary motors; 204 hp(m) *(150 kW)*; 1 economic speed motor; 130 hp *(95 kW)*
Speed, knots: 10 surfaced; 17 dived; 9 snorting
Range, n miles: 6,000 at 7 kt snorting; 400 at 3 kt dived
Complement: 60 (16 officers)

Missiles: SAM: 8 SA-N-5 (Strela 2M).
Torpedoes: 6–21 in *(533 mm)* tubes. Combination of 53-65; anti-surface; passive/wake homing to 19 km *(10.3 n miles)* at 45 kt; warhead 300 kg and TEST-71; anti-submarine; active/passive homing to 15 km *(8.1 n miles)* at 40 kt; warhead 205 kg. 53-56 WA and SET 53 M can also be carried. Total of 18 torpedoes.
Mines: 24 in lieu of torpedoes.
Countermeasures: ESM: Brick Group (MRP-25); radar warning; Quad Loop HF D/F.
Weapons control: Murena MWU 110 TFCS.
Radars: Surface search: Racal Decca Bridgemaster; I-band.
Sonars: Shark Teeth (MGK-400); hull-mounted; passive search and attack (some active capability); low/medium frequency.
Mouse Roar (MG 519); active mine detection; high frequency.

Programmes: This was the second transfer of this class, the first being to India and others have since gone to Romania, Algeria, Iran and China. It was expected that more than one would be acquired as part of an exchange deal with the USSR for Polish-built amphibious ships, but this class is considered too large for Baltic operations and subsequent transfers were of the Foxtrot class.
Structure: Diving depth, 240 m *(787 ft)*. Has two torpedo tubes modified for wire guided anti-submarine torpedoes.
Operational: Based at Gdynia.

ORZEL — *5/2007, J Ciślak* / 1166688

FRIGATES

0 + 2 (5) PROJECT 621 GAWRON II (MEKO A 100) CLASS (FSGHM)

Name	*No*	*Builders*	*Laid down*	*Launched*	*Commissioned*
–	–	Naval Shipyard, Gdynia	28 Oct 2001	2009	2011
–	–	Naval Shipyard, Gdynia	2003	2009	2012

Displacement, tons: 2,035 full load
Dimensions, feet (metres): 312.3 × 43.6 × 11.8 *(95.2 × 13.13 × 3.6)*
Main machinery: CODAG; 1 General Electric LM 2500 gas turbine; 2 diesels; 2 shafts
Speed, knots: 30
Range, n miles: 4,000 at 15 kt
Complement: 74

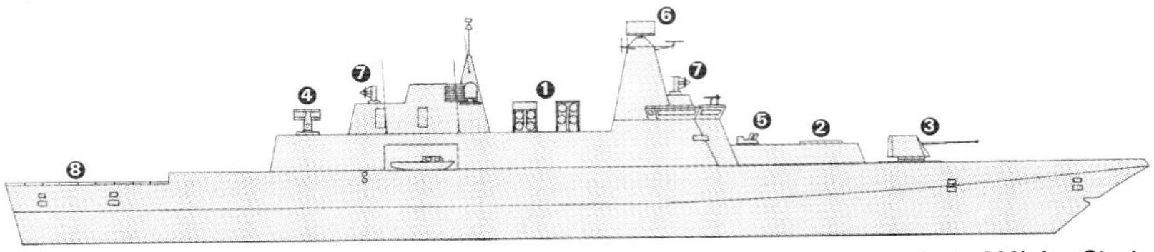

Missiles: SSM: 8 Saab RBS-15 Mk 3 ❶.
SAM: Raytheon RIM-162 Evolved Sea Sparrow; VLS ❷.
Guns: 1–3 in *(76 mm)*/62 ❸. 2–35 mm. RAM ❹.
A/S mortars: 2 ASW 601 ❺.
Countermeasures: Decoys: 1-10 barrelled Jastrzab 122 mm; chaff and IR flares.
ESM: Radar warning.
TCM: C310 torpedo decoy system.
Combat data systems: Signaal TACTICOS or Saab Tech 9LV.

PROJECT 621 — *(Scale 1 : 900), Ian Sturton* / 0526837

Radars: Air/surface search ❻; fire control ❼; navigation.
Sonars: Hull mounted; active; medium frequency.
Helicopters: Platform for 1 medium ❽.

Programmes: Design definition by German Corvette Consortium (Blohm + Voss, Lürssen, Thyssen and HDW) which is to act as subcontractor to the shipbuilder. There are options for a further five vessels. Details of the design and of the building programme have not been released but, given continuing funding problems, it is unlikely that the first of class will enter service before 2011.
Structure: The design is based on the MEKO A 100.

PROJECT 621 — *2001, Polish Navy* / 0114788

2 OLIVER HAZARD PERRY CLASS (FFGHM)

Name	*No*	*Builders*	*Laid down*	*Launched*	*Commissioned*	*Recommissioned*
GENERAŁ KAZIMIERZ PUŁASKI (ex-*Clark*)	272 (ex-FFG 11)	Bath Iron Works	17 July 1978	24 Mar 1979	9 May 1980	15 Mar 2000
GENERAŁ TADEUSZ KOŚCIUSZKO (ex-*Wadsworth*)	273 (ex-FFG 9)	Todd Shipyards, San Pedro	13 July 1977	29 July 1978	28 Feb 1980	28 June 2002

Displacement, tons: 2,750 light; 3,638 full load
Dimensions, feet (metres): 445 × 45 × 14.8; 24.5 (sonar) *(135.6 × 13.7 × 4.5; 7.5)*
Main machinery: 2 GE LM 2500 gas turbines; 41,000 hp *(30.59 MW)* sustained; 1 shaft; cp prop
2 auxiliary retractable props; 650 hp *(484 kW)*
Speed, knots: 29
Range, n miles: 4,500 at 20 kt
Complement: 200 (15 officers) including 19 aircrew

Missiles: SSM: 4 McDonnell Douglas Harpoon Block 1G; active radar homing to 95 km *(51 n miles)* at 0.9 Mach; warhead 227 kg.
SAM: 36 Raytheon SM-1MR Block VI; command guidance; semi-active radar homing to 38 km *(20.5 n miles)* at 2 Mach.
1 Mk 13 Mod 4 launcher for both SSM and SAM missiles ❶.
Guns: 1 OTO Melara 3 in *(76 mm)*/62 Mk 75 ❷; 85 rds/min to 16 km *(8.7 n miles)* anti-surface; 12 km *(6.6 n miles)* anti-aircraft; weight of shell 6 kg.
1 General Electric/General Dynamics 20 mm/76 6-barrelled Mk 15 Vulcan Phalanx ❸; 3,000 rds/min combined to 1.5 km.
4—12.7 mm MGs.
Torpedoes: 6—324 mm Mk 32 (2 triple) tubes ❹. 24 Whitehead A244 Mod 3. To be replaced by Mu-90 Impact from 2002.
Countermeasures: Decoys: 2 Loral Hycor SRBOC 6-barrelled fixed Mk 36 ❺; IR flares and chaff to 4 km *(2.2 n miles)*.
T-Mk 6 Fanfare/SLQ-25 Nixie; torpedo decoy.

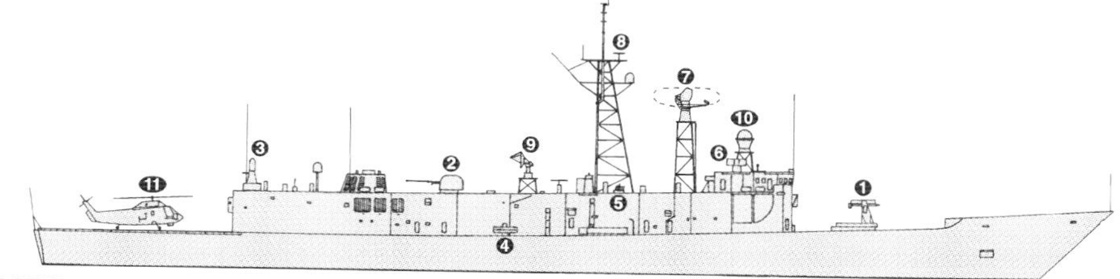

PUŁASKI

(Scale 1 : 1,200), Ian Sturton / 0105229

ESM/ECM: SLQ-32(V)2 ❻; radar warning. Sidekick modification adds jammer and deception system.
Combat data systems: NTDS with Link 11 and 14. SATCOM SRR-1, WSC-3 (UHF).
Weapons control: SWG-1 Harpoon LCS. Mk 92 (Mod 2), WCS with CAS (Combined Antenna System). The Mk 92 is the US version of the Signaal WM28 system. Mk 13 weapon direction system. 2 Mk 24 optical directors.
Radars: Air search: Raytheon SPS-49(V)4 ❼; C/D-band.
Surface search: ISC Cardion SPS-55 ❽; I-band.
Fire control: Lockheed STIR (modified SPG-60) ❾; I/J-band.
Sperry Mk 92 (Signaal WM28) ❿; I/J-band.
Navigation: Furuno; I-band.
Tacan: URN 25. IFF Mk XII AIMS UPX-29.

Sonars: SQQ 89(V)2 (Raytheon SQS 56 and Gould SQR 19); hull-mounted active search and attack; medium frequency and passive towed array; very low frequency.

Helicopters: 2 Kaman SH-2G Seasprite ⓫.

Programmes: *Pułaski* approved for transfer from US by grant in 1999.
Modernisation: Harpoon missiles are to be replaced by RBS 15 Mk 2 missiles from about 2009.
Structure: Details given are for the ship in service with the US Navy.
Operational: Based at Gdynia.

PUŁASKI

10/2007, Michael Nitz / 1166687

PUŁASKI

3/2008*, B Sullivan / 1353257

KOŚCIUSZKO

10/2007, J Cislak / 1166686

CORVETTES

1 KASZUB CLASS (PROJECT 620) (FSM)

Name	*No*	*Builders*	*Laid down*	*Launched*	*Commissioned*
KASZUB	240	Northern Shipyard, Gdansk	9 June 1984	11 May 1986	15 Mar 1987

Displacement, tons: 1,051 standard; 1,183 full load
Dimensions, feet (metres): 270 × 32.8 × 10.2; 16.1 (sonar) *(82.3 × 10 × 3.1; 4.9)*
Main machinery: CODAD; 4 Cegielski-Sulzer AS 16V 25/30 diesels; 16,900 hp(m) *(12.42 MW)*; 2 shafts; cp props
Speed, knots: 27. **Range, n miles:** 3,500 at 14 kt; 350 at 26 kt
Complement: 82 (10 officers)

Missiles: SAM: 2 SA-N-5 quad launchers ❶; IR homing to 10 km *(5.5 n miles)* at 1.5 Mach. VLS system to replace after 23 mm gun.
Guns: 1 USSR 3 in *(76 mm)*/59 AK 176 ❷; 120 rds/min to 16 km *(8.5 n miles)*; weight of shell 5.9 kg.
6 ZU-23-2M Wrobel 23 mm/87 (3 twin) ❸; 400 rds/min combined to 2 km.
Torpedoes: 4—21 in *(533 mm)* (2 twin) tubes ❹. SET-53M; passive homing to 15 km *(8.1 n miles)* at 29 kt; warhead 100 kg.
A/S mortars: 2 RBU 6000 12-tubed trainable ❺; range 6,000 m; warhead 31 kg; 120 rockets.
Depth charges: 2 rails. 12 charges.
Countermeasures: Decoys: 1-10 barrelled 122 mm Jastrzab launcher ❻ for chaff.
ESM: Intercept.
Weapons control: Drakon TFCS.
Radars: Air/surface search: Strut Curve (MR 302) ❼; F-band.
Surface search: Racal Bridgemaster C-252 ❽; I-band.
Navigation: Racal Bridgemaster C-341; I-band.
IFF: RAWAR SA-10M2.
Sonars: MG 322T; hull-mounted; active search; medium frequency.
MG 329M; stern-mounted dipping type mounted on the transom; active; high frequency.

Programmes: Second of class cancelled in 1989 and a class of up to ten more ships based on the Kaszub hull and specialised for anti-submarine warfare has been shelved.
Structure: Design based on Grisha class but with many alterations. The 76 mm gun was fitted in late 1991. New decoy system fitted in 1999. There is space for a fire-control director on the bridge roof.
Operational: Based at Gdynia.

KASZUB *(Scale 1 : 900), Ian Sturton* / 0081558

KASZUB 5/2008*, J Ciślak / 1353258

KASZUB 7/2006, A A de Kruijf / 1164451

3 ORKAN (SASSNITZ) CLASS (PROJECT 660 (ex-151)) (FSGM)

Name	*No*	*Builders*	*Launched*	*Commissioned*
ORKAN	421	Peenewerft/Northern Shipyard, Gdansk	29 Sep 1990	18 Sep 1992
PIORUN	422	Peenewerft/Northern Shipyard, Gdansk	19 Oct 1990	11 Mar 1994
GROM (ex-*Huragan*)	423	Peenewerft/Northern Shipyard, Gdansk	11 Dec 1990	28 Mar 1995

Displacement, tons: 331 standard; 326 full load
Dimensions, feet (metres): 163.4 oa; 147.6 wl × 28.5 × 7.2 *(49.8; 45 × 8.7 × 2.2)*
Main machinery: 3 Type M 520T diesels; 16,000 hp(m) *(11.93 MW)* sustained; 3 shafts
Speed, knots: 38. **Range, n miles:** 1,600 at 14 kt
Complement: 36 (4 officers)

Missiles: SSM: 8 (2 quad) launchers; Saab RBS-15 Mk 3; active radar homing to 200 km *(108 n miles)* at 0.8 Mach; warhead 150 kg.
SAM: SA-N-5 Grail quad launcher; manual aiming; IR homing to 6 km *(3.2 n miles)* at 1.5 Mach; warhead 1.5 kg.
Guns: 1 USSR 3 in *(76 mm)*/59 AK 176; 120 rds/min to 16 km *(8.5 n miles)*; weight of shell 5.9 kg.
1—30 mm/65 AK 630; 6 barrels; 3,000 rds/min combined to 2 km.
Countermeasures: Decoys: 8-9 barrelled Jastrzab 81 mm and 1-10 barrelled Jastrzab 122 mm chaff and IR launchers.
ESM: PIT intercept.
Combat data systems: Signaal TACTICOS.
Weapons control: Thales STING optronic director.
Radars: Surface search: AMB Sea Giraffe; G-band.
Fire control: Bass Tilt MR-123; H/I-band.
Navigation: PIT; I-band.
IFF: Square Head; Salt Pot.

Programmes: Originally six of this former GDR Sassnitz class were to be built at Peenewerft for Poland. Three units were acquired and completed at Gdansk.
Modernisation: Contract with Thales Naval Nederland (TNNL) as prime contractor for upgrade of all three ships signed 29 June 2001. New equipment includes RBS-15 Mk 3 missiles, TACTICOS combat data system, STING optronic director, AMB Sea Giraffe surveillance radar, PIT navigational radar and ESM equipment, improved communications and Link 11. Refit of *Piorun* was completed by 2003 and the other two ships in 2006. RBS 15 Mk 3 missiles are to replace Mk 2 missiles from 2009.
Structure: Unlike the German Coast Guard vessels of the same class, these ships have retained three engines.
Operational: Based at Gdynia.

PIORUN 5/2008*, J Ciślak / 1353259

SHIPBORNE AIRCRAFT

Numbers/Type: 4 Kaman SH-2G (P) Seasprite.
Operational speed: 130 kt *(241 km/h)*.
Service ceiling: 22,500 ft *(6,860 m)*.
Range: 367 n miles *(697 km)*.
Role/Weapon systems: First two delivered in 2002. Second pair in August 2003. Sensors: LN66/HP radar; ALR-66 ESM, ALE-39 ECM, AQS-81(V)2 MAD, AAQ-16 FLIR, ARR 57/84 sonobuoy receivers. Weapons: ASW: two A244S torpedoes (Mu 90 from 2002). ASV: one 7.62 mm MG.

SH-2G *7/2006, J Ciślak* / 1164448

LAND-BASED MARITIME AIRCRAFT (FRONT LINE)

Notes: In addition there are 6 TS training aircraft.

Numbers/Type: 10/2/1/2 PZL Mielec M-28 B1R/M-28E/M-28RF/M-28TD Bryza.
Operational speed: 181 kt *(335 km/h)*.
Service ceiling: 13,770 ft *(4,200 m)*.
Range: 736 n miles *(1,365 km)*.
Role/Weapon systems: Based on the USSR Cash light transport and used for maritime patrol and SAR. First one delivered in January 1995. B1R upgrade programme includes MSC-400 mission system, ARS-400 radar (with SAR/ISAR modes), torpedoes, sonobuoys, MAD, direction finder and Link 11. Sensors: Search radar ARS 400; ESM. Weapons: 2 SAB 100 bombs.

M-28 B1R *5/2008*, J Ciślak* / 1353260

Numbers/Type: 10/3 Mil Mi-14PL Haze A/Mi-14PS Haze C.
Operational speed: 120 kt *(222 km/h)*.
Service ceiling: 16,000 ft *(4,670 m)*.
Range: 500 n miles *(1,100 km)*.
Role/Weapon systems: PL for ASW, PS for SAR. PL operates in co-operation with surface units. Adapted for landing and taking off from water. Sensors: I-2ME search radar; APM-60, MAD, sonobuoys, MGM 329M VDS. Weapons: ASW; Whitehead A 244 torpedoes, depth bombs and mines. Arming with Penguin ASM is also under consideration.

Mi-14PL *8/2008*, J Ciślak* / 1353261

Numbers/Type: 2/7 PZL Świdnik W-3 Sokol/W-3RM Anakonda.
Operational speed: 119 kt *(220 km/h)*.
Service ceiling: 19,672 ft *(6,000 m)*.
Range: 335 n miles *(620 km)*.
Role/Weapon systems: W-3 for transport, W-3RM for SAR. Operates in co-operation with surface units. Adapted for landing and taking off from water. Sensors: RDS-82 VP Meteo, FLIR.

W-3RM *5/2008*, J Ciślak* / 1353262

Numbers/Type: 3/1 Mil Mi-2RM Hoplite/Mi-2D.
Operational speed: 100 *(180 km/h)*.
Service ceiling: 13,200 ft *(4,000 m)*.
Range: 300 n miles *(550 km)*.
Role/Weapon systems: Mi-2D is for transport aircraft and Mi-2RM is for SAR.

Mi-2RM *7/2000, J Ciślak* / 0105237

Numbers/Type: 2 Mi-17 Hip.
Operational speed: 124 kt *(230 km/h)*.
Service ceiling: 16,400 ft *(5,000 m)*.
Range: 324 n miles *(600 km)*.
Role/Weapon systems: Transport aircraft. First one delivered in 2001.

Mi-17 *7/2006, J Ciślak* / 1164445

AMPHIBIOUS FORCES

5 LUBLIN CLASS (PROJECT 767) (LST/MINELAYERS) (LST/ML)

Name	*No*	*Builders*	*Launched*	*Commissioned*
LUBLIN	821	Northern Shipyard, Gdansk	12 July 1988	12 Oct 1989
GNIEZNO	822	Northern Shipyard, Gdansk	7 Dec 1988	23 Feb 1990
KRAKOW	823	Northern Shipyard, Gdansk	7 Mar 1989	27 June 1990
POZNAN	824	Northern Shipyard, Gdansk	5 Jan 1990	8 Mar 1991
TORUN	825	Northern Shipyard, Gdansk	8 June 1990	24 May 1991

Displacement, tons: 1,350 standard; 1,745 full load
Dimensions, feet (metres): 313 × 35.4 × 6.6 *(95.4 × 10.8 × 2)*
Main machinery: 3 Cegielski 6ATL25D diesels; 5,390 hp(m) *(3.96 MW)* sustained; 3 shafts
Speed, knots: 16
Range, n miles: 1,400 at 16 kt
Complement: 50 (5 officers)
Military lift: 9 Type T-72 tanks or 9 APC or 17 medium or light trucks. 80 troops plus equipment (821-823); 125 troops plus equipment (824); 135 troops and equipment (825).
Missiles: SAM/Guns: 8 ZU-23-2MR 23 mm Wrobel II (4 twin); combination of 2 SA-N-5 missiles; IR homing to 6 km *(3.2 n miles)* at 1.5 Mach; warhead 1.5 kg and guns; 400 rds/min combined.
Depth charges: 9 throwers for counter-mining.
Mines: 50-134.
Countermeasures: Decoys: 2 12-barrelled 70 mm Derkacz chaff launchers (821 and 825). 2 12-barrelled Jastrzab chaff launchers (822-824).
Radars: Navigation: SRN 7453 and SRN 443XTA; I-band.

Comment: Designed with a through deck from bow to stern and can be used as minelayers as well as for amphibious landings. Folding bow and stern ramps and a stern anchor are fitted. The ship has a pressurised citadel for NBC defence and an upper deck washdown system. Mining capabilities upgraded in 1997/98. Based at Swinoujscie.

GNIEZNO *9/2008*, J Ciślak* / 1353263

3 DEBA CLASS (PROJECT 716) (LCU)

Name	*No*	*Builders*	*Launched*	*Commissioned*
KD 11	851	Naval Shipyard, Gdynia	13 Nov 1987	7 Aug 1988
KD 12	852	Naval Shipyard, Gdynia	2 July 1990	2 Jan 1991
KD 13	853	Naval Shipyard, Gdynia	26 Oct 1990	3 May 1991

Displacement, tons: 176 full load
Dimensions, feet (metres): 122 × 23.3 × 5.6 *(37.2 × 7.1 × 1.7)*
Main machinery: 3 Type M 401A diesels; 3,000 hp(m) *(2.2 MW)*; 3 shafts
Speed, knots: 20
Range, n miles: 430 at 16 kt
Complement: 12
Military lift: 1 tank or 2 vehicles up to 20 tons and 50 troops
Guns: 2 ZU-23-2M 23 mm (twin).
Radars: Surface search: SRN 207A; I-band.

Comment: The plan was to build 12 but the programme was suspended at three through lack of funds. A similar design has been assembled in Iran. Can carry up to six launchers for strung-out charges. Based at Swinoujscie.

KD 11 *9/2003, J Ciślak* / 0567514

MINE WARFARE FORCES

Notes: The next-generation Mine Countermeasures programme (Kormoran II) is under consideration.

3 KROGULEC CLASS (PROJECT 206FM) (MHCM)

Name	*No*	*Builders*	*Commissioned*
FLAMING	621	Gdynia Shipyard	11 Oct 1966
MEWA	623	Gdynia Shipyard	21 May 1967
CZAJKA	624	Gdynia Shipyard	23 June 1967

Displacement, tons: 550 full load
Dimensions, feet (metres): 190.9 × 25.3 × 6.9 *(58.2 × 7.7 × 2.1)*
Main machinery: 2 Sulzer/Cegielski 6AL 25/30 diesels; 2,203 hp(m) *(1.62 MW)*; 2 shafts; LIPS cp props
Speed, knots: 17
Range, n miles: 2,000 at 12 kt
Complement: 52 (6 officers)

Missiles: SAM: 2 Fasta-4M quad launchers. SA-N-5. 2 SA-N-10 (Grom) to be fitted in due course.
Guns: SAM/guns: 2 Wrobel ZU-23-2MR 23 mm (twin) with 2 SA-N-5 missiles.
Depth charges: 2 racks.
Mines: 6—12 depending on type.
Countermeasures: Decoys: 6—9 barrelled Jastrzab 2 launchers for chaff.
ECM: PIT Bren system being fitted.
MCM: 2 Bofors MT2W mechanical, 1 TEM-PE-2MA magnetic and 1 MTA-2 acoustic sweeps. CTM Ukwial ROV with sonar, TV and charges. 10 ZHH 230 sonobuoys.
Combat data systems: CTM Pstrokosz command support system.
Radars: Navigation: Racal Decca Bridgemaster; I-band.
IFF: RAWAR SC-10D2
Sonars: CTM SHL-100MA hull mounted; active minehunting; high frequency; Politechnica Gdansk SHL-200 VDS.

Comment: All taken out of service in 1997. New armament and minehunting equipment installed. Divers recompression chamber carried. *Mewa* returned to service in May 1999, *Czajka* in May 2000 and *Flaming* in 2001. Life extended by 10 years. Based at Swinoujscie.

CZAJKA *5/2008*, J Ciślak* / 1353264

13 GOPLO (NOTEC) CLASS (PROJECT 207P/207DM) (MINESWEEPERS/HUNTERS—COASTAL) (MHC)

Name	*No*	*Builders*	*Launched*	*Commissioned*
GOPLO	630	Naval Shipyard, Gdynia	16 Apr 1981	13 Mar 1982
GARDNO	631	Naval Shipyard, Gdynia	23 June 1993	31 Mar 1984
BUKOWO	632	Naval Shipyard, Gdynia	28 July 1984	23 June 1985
DABIE	633	Naval Shipyard, Gdynia	21 June 1985	11 May 1986
JAMNO	634	Naval Shipyard, Gdynia	11 Feb 1986	11 Oct 1986
MIELNO	635	Naval Shipyard, Gdynia	27 June 1986	9 May 1987
WICKO	636	Naval Shipyard, Gdynia	20 Mar 1987	12 Oct 1987
RESKO	637	Naval Shipyard, Gdynia	1 Oct 1987	26 Mar 1988
SARBSKO	638	Naval Shipyard, Gdynia	10 May 1988	12 Oct 1988
NECKO	639	Naval Shipyard, Gdynia	21 Nov 1988	9 May 1989
NAKLO	640	Naval Shipyard, Gdynia	29 May 1989	2 Mar 1990
DRUZNO	641	Naval Shipyard, Gdynia	29 Nov 1989	21 Sep 1990
HANCZA	642	Naval Shipyard, Gdynia	9 July 1990	1 Mar 1991

Displacement, tons: 216 full load
Dimensions, feet (metres): 126.3 × 24.3 × 5.9 *(38.5 × 7.4 × 1.8)*
Main machinery: 2 M 401A1 diesels; 1,874 hp(m) *(1.38 MW)* sustained; 2 shafts
Speed, knots: 14
Range, n miles: 1,100 at 9 kt
Complement: 29 (6 officers)
Guns: 2 ZU-23-2MR 23 mm (twin); 400 rds/min combined to 2 km.
Depth charges: 24
Mines: 6-24
Countermeasures: MCM: MMTK1 mechanical; MTA 1 acoustic and TEM-PE 1 magnetic sweeps.
Radars: Navigation: Bridgemaster; I-band.
Sonars: MG 89 or MG 79; active minehunting; high frequency.

Comment: *Goplo* is an experimental prototype numbered 207D. The 23 mm guns have replaced the original 25 mm. GRP hulls. All are to be upgraded to 207DM for minehunting, and to carry divers. Named after lakes. *Goplo* based at Gdynia, the remainder at Swinoujscie.

GOPLO *5/2008*, J Ciślak* / 1353265

4 MAMRY (NOTEC II) CLASS (PROJECT 207M) (MINESWEEPERS/HUNTERS—COASTAL) (MHSCM)

Name	*No*	*Builders*	*Launched*	*Commissioned*
MAMRY	643	Naval Shipyard, Gdynia	20 Sep 1991	25 Sep 1992
WIGRY	644	Naval Shipyard, Gdynia	28 Nov 1992	14 May 1993
SNIARDWY	645	Naval Shipyard, Gdynia	20 June 1993	28 Jan 1994
WDZYDZE	646	Naval Shipyard, Gdynia	24 June 1994	2 Dec 1994

Displacement, tons: 216 full load
Dimensions, feet (metres): 126.3 × 24.3 × 5.9 *(38.5 × 7.4 × 1.8)*
Main machinery: 2 M 401A diesels; 1,874 hp(m) *(1.38 MW)*; 2 shafts
2 auxiliary motors; 816 hp(m) *(60 kW)*
Speed, knots: 14
Range, n miles: 865 at 14 kt
Complement: 27 (5 officers)
Missiles: SAM/Guns: 2 ZU-23-2MR 23 mm Wrobel II (twin); combination of 2 SA-N-5 missiles; IR homing to 6 km *(3.2 n miles)* at 1.5 Mach; warhead 1.5 kg and guns; 400 rds/min combined to 2 km.
Mines: 6-24 depending on type.
Countermeasures: MCM: MMTK 1m mechanical, MTA 2 acoustic and TEM-PE 1m magnetic sweeps.
Radars: Navigation: SRN 401XTA; I-band.
Sonars: SHL 100/200; hull mounted/VDS; active minehunting; high frequency.

Comment: Modified version of the 207P and equipped to carry divers. Identical hull to the 207P. All based at Gdynia. An enlarged design, the Type 207 MCMV with a length of 43.5 m, is a longer term project.

SNIARDWY ***6/2007, Frank Findler*** / 1166673

SURVEY AND RESEARCH SHIPS

2 MODIFIED FINIK 2 CLASS (PROJECT 874) (AGS)

Name	*No*	*Builders*	*Launched*	*Commissioned*
HEWELIUSZ	265	Northern Shipyard, Gdansk	11 Sep 1981	27 Nov 1982
ARCTOWSKI	266	Northern Shipyard, Gdansk	20 Nov 1981	27 Nov 1982

Displacement, tons: 1,135 standard; 1,218 full load
Dimensions, feet (metres): 202.1 × 35.4 × 10.8 *(61.6 × 10.8 × 3.3)*
Main machinery: 2 Cegielski-Sulzer 6AL25/30 diesels; 1,920 hp(m) *(1.4 MW)*; 2 auxiliary motors; 204 hp(m) *(150 kW)*; 2 shafts; cp props; bow thruster
Speed, knots: 13
Range, n miles: 5,900 at 11 kt
Complement: 49 (10 officers)
Radars: Navigation: SRN 7453 Nogat; SRN 743X; I-band.

Comment: Sister ships to Russian class which were built in Poland, except that *Heweliusz* and *Arctowski* have been modified and have no buoy handling equipment. Equipment includes Atlas Deso, Atlas Ralog and Atlas Dolog survey. Both ships are based at Gdynia. One sister ship, *Planeta*, is civilian operated and the other, *Zodiak*, was decommissioned in 2003.

ARCTOWSKI ***5/2007, J Ciślak*** / 1166597

HEWELIUSZ ***5/2008*, J Ciślak*** / 1353266

2 SURVEY CRAFT (PROJECT 4234) (AGSC)

Name	*Builders*	*Commissioned*
K 10	Wisla, Gdansk	6 Feb 1989
K 4	Wisla, Gdansk	25 Sep 1989

Displacement, tons: 45 full load
Dimensions, feet (metres): 62 × 14.4 × 4.9 *(18.9 × 4.4 × 1.5)*
Main machinery: 1 Wola DM 150 diesel; 160 hp(m) *(117 kW)* sustained; 1 shaft
Speed, knots: 9
Complement: 10
Radars: Navigation: SRN 207A; I-band.

Comment: Coastal survey craft based at Gdynia. There are a number of survey launches and buoy tenders listed under *Auxiliaries*.

K 10 ***5/2000, J Ciślak*** / 0105248

4 SURVEY CRAFT (PROJECT III/C) (AGSC)

M 35 **M 38–40**

Displacement, tons: 10 full load
Dimensions, feet (metres): 36.1 × 10.5 × 2.3 *(11 × 3.2 × 0.7)*
Main machinery: 1 Puck Rekin SW 400/MZ diesel; 95 hp(m) *(70 kW)*; 1 shaft
Speed, knots: 8
Range, n miles: 184 at 8 kt
Complement: 5
Radars: Navigation: SRN 207A; I-band.

Comment: Based at Gdynia and Swinoujscie (M 35).

M 40 ***3/2003, J Ciślak*** / 0567515

INTELLIGENCE VESSELS

2 MODIFIED MOMA CLASS (PROJECT 863) (AGI)

Name	*No*	*Builders*	*Commissioned*
NAWIGATOR	262	Northern Shipyard, Gdansk	17 Feb 1975
HYDROGRAF	263	Northern Shipyard, Gdansk	8 May 1976

Displacement, tons: 1,677 full load
Dimensions, feet (metres): 240.5 × 35.4 × 12.8 *(73.3 × 10.8 × 3.9)*
Main machinery: 2 Zgoda-Sulzer 6TD48 diesels; 3,300 hp(m) *(2.43 MW)* sustained; 2 shafts
Speed, knots: 17
Range, n miles: 7,200 at 12 kt
Complement: 87 (10 officers)
Missiles: 2 Fasta-4M quad launchers. SA-N-5.
Guns: 4—25 mm (2 twin) (262).
Countermeasures: ESM/ECM: intercept and jammer.
Radars: Navigation: 2 SRN 7453 Nogat; I-band.

Comment: Much altered in the upperworks and unrecognisable as Momas. The forecastle in *Hydrograf* is longer than in *Nawigator* and one deck higher. *Hydrograf* fitted for but not with two twin 25 mm gun mountings. Forward radome replaced by a cylindrical type in *Nawigator* and after ones removed on both ships. Based at Gdynia.

NAWIGATOR *5/2007, M Declerck* / 1166598

HYDROGRAF *7/2008*, A Sheldon-Duplaix* / 1353267

TRAINING SHIPS

Notes: The three masted sailing ship *Dar Mlodziezy* is civilian owned and operated but also takes naval personnel for training.

1 WODNIK CLASS (PROJECT 888) (AXTH)

Name	*No*	*Builders*	*Launched*	*Commissioned*
WODNIK	251	Northern Shipyard, Gdansk	19 Nov 1975	28 May 1976

Displacement, tons: 1,697 standard; 1,745 full load
Dimensions, feet (metres): 234.3 × 38.1 × 14.8 *(72.2 × 11.9 × 4.1)*
Main machinery: 2 Zgoda-Sulzer 6TD48 diesels; 2,650 hp(m) *(1.95 MW)* sustained; 2 shafts; cp props
Speed, knots: 16
Range, n miles: 7,200 at 11 kt
Complement: 56 (24 officers) plus 101 midshipmen
Guns: 4 ZU-23-2MR Wrobel 23 mm (2 twin). 2—30 mm AK 230 (1 twin).
Radars: Navigation: 2 SRN 7453 Nogat; I-band.
Helicopters: Platform for 1 light.

Comment: Sister to former GDR *Wilhelm Pieck* and two Russian ships. Converted to a hospital ship (150 beds) in 1990 for deployment to the Gulf. Armament removed as part of the conversion but partially restored in 1992. Based at Gdynia. Second of class in reserve from 1999.

WODNIK *7/2008*, B Prézelin* / 1353256

1 ISKRA CLASS (PROJECT B79) (SAIL TRAINING SHIP) (AXS)

Name	*No*	*Builders*	*Launched*	*Commissioned*
ISKRA	253	Gdansk Shipyard	6 Mar 1982	11 Aug 1982

Displacement, tons: 498 full load
Dimensions, feet (metres): 160.8 × 26.6 × 13.1 *(49 × 8.1 × 4.0)*
Main machinery: 1 Wola 75H12 diesel; 310 hp(m) *(228 kW)*; 1 auxiliary shaft; cp prop
Speed, knots: 9 (diesel)
Complement: 14 (6 officers) plus 50 cadets
Radars: Navigation: SRN 206; I-band.

Comment: Barquentine with 1,040 m² of sail. Used by the Naval Academy for training with a secondary survey role. Based at Gdynia.

ISKRA *6/2005, Michael Nitz* / 1151322

AUXILIARIES

Note: Procurement of up to four Strategic Support Ships is under development. The broad requirement is for ships of approximately 10,000 tons with the capability of transporting about 500 troops plus some 20 vehicles and up to six helicopters.

1 PROJECT 890 CLASS (LOGISTICS SUPPORT VESSEL) (AKHM/APHM/AGI)

Name	*No*	*Builders*	*Commissioned*
KONTRADMIRAL X CZERNICKI	511	Northern Shipyard, Gdansk	1 Sep 2001

Displacement, tons: 2,250 full load
Dimensions, feet (metres): 242.1 × 45.3 × 14.1 *(73.8 × 13.8 × 4.3)*
Main machinery: 2 Cegielski-Sulzer AL25D diesels; 2,934 hp(m) *(2.16 MW)* sustained; 2 shafts
Speed, knots: 14.1
Range, n miles: 7,000 at 12 kt
Complement: 38
Military lift: 140 troops with full individual armament or ten 20 ft containers or four 20 ft containers and six STAR 266 army trucks
Missiles: SAM/Guns: 1 ZU 23-2MR Wrobel I/II mounts: combination of 2 Strela 2M (Grail) missiles and 2—23 mm guns.
Countermeasures: Decoys: 4 WNP81/9 9 barrelled 81 mm Jastrzab chaff launchers.
ESM: PIT intercept.
Radars: Surface search: SRN; E/F-band.
Navigation: SRN; I-band.
Helicopters: Platform for 1 helicopter (up to 10 ton).

Comment: Conversion from a Project 130 Degaussing Vessel to Logistic Support Ship in Northern Shipyard, Gdansk, included new upper and forward hull sections, provision of a helicopter deck and NBC protection. The ship has a 16 ton hydraulic crane and after ramp. The multirole ship is capable of sealift, acting as a forward maintenance unit and maritime surveillance and reconnaissance (using containerised ESM sensors) and replenishment at sea. Based at Swinoujscie.

KONTRADMIRAL X CZERNICKI *3/2006, Frank Findler* / 1164318

1 BALTYK CLASS (PROJECT ZP 1200) (TANKER) (AORL)

Name	*No*	*Builders*	*Commissioned*
BALTYK	Z 1	Naval Shipyard, Gdynia	11 Mar 1991

Displacement, tons: 2,937 standard; 3,049 full load
Dimensions, feet (metres): 278.2 × 43 × 15.4 *(84.8 × 13.1 × 4.7)*
Main machinery: 2 Cegielski 8 ASL 25 diesels; 4,025 hp(m) *(2.96 MW)*; 2 shafts; cp props
Speed, knots: 15
Range, n miles: 4,250 at 12 kt
Complement: 34 (4 officers)
Cargo capacity: 1,184 tons fuel, 92.7 tons lub oil
Guns: 4 ZU-23-2M Wrobel 23 mm (2 twin).
Radars: Navigation: SRN 7453 and SRN 207A; I-band.

Comment: Beam replenishment stations, one each side. First of a projected class of four, of which the others were cancelled. Based at Gdynia.

BALTYK *1/2008*, J Ciślak* / 1353268

1 MOSKIT CLASS (PROJECT B 199) (TANKER) (AOTL)

Name	*No*	*Builders*	*Launched*	*Commissioned*
MEDUZA	Z 8	Rzeczna, Wroclaw Shipyard	14 Sep 1969	21 July 1970

Displacement, tons: 1,225 full load
Dimensions, feet (metres): 190.3 × 30.5 × 10.8 *(58 × 9.3 × 3.3)*
Main machinery: 1 Magdeburg diesel; 965 hp(m) *(720 kW)*; 1 shaft
Speed, knots: 10
Range, n miles: 1,200 at 10 kt
Complement: 21 (3 officers)
Cargo capacity: 656.5 tons
Guns: 4 ZU-23-2M 23 mm (2 twin).
Radars: Navigation: TRN 823; I-band.

Comment: Z 3 decommissioned in 2007. Based at Swinoujscie.

MEDUZA *7/2004, J Ciślak* / 1044484

1 KORMORAN CLASS (YPT)

No	*Builders*	*Launched*	*Commissioned*
K 8	Naval Shipyard, Gdynia	26 Aug 1970	3 July 1971

Displacement, tons: 150 full load
Dimensions, feet (metres): 114.8 × 19.7 × 5.2 *(35 × 6 × 1.6)*
Main machinery: 2 Type M 50F5 diesels; 2,200 hp(m) *(1.6 MW)*; 2 shafts
Speed, knots: 19
Range, n miles: 550 at 15 kt
Complement: 24
Guns: 2 ZU-23-2M Wrobel 23 mm (twin).
Radars: Navigation: SRN 206/301; I-band.

Comment: Armament updated in 1993. Both based at Gdynia.

K 8 *6/2008*, J Ciślak* / 1353272

2 MROWKA CLASS (PROJECT B 208) (DEGAUSSING VESSELS) (YDG)

Name	*No*	*Builders*	*Commissioned*
WRONA	SD 11	Naval Shipyard, Gdynia	10 Oct 1971
–	SD 13	Naval Shipyard, Gdynia	16 Dec 1972

Displacement, tons: 660 full load
Dimensions, feet (metres): 144.4 × 26.6 × 9.5 *(44 × 8.1 × 2.9)*
Main machinery: 1 6NV D36 diesel; 957 hp(m) *(704 kW)*; 1 shaft
Speed, knots: 9.5. **Range, n miles**: 2,230 at 9.5 kt
Complement: 37
Guns: 2—25 mm (twin) (SD 11 and 13); 2 ZU-23-2M Wrobel 23 mm (twin) (SD 12).
Radars: Navigation: SRN 206; I-band.

Comment: SD 12 decommissioned in 2005. SD 11 based at Swinoujscie and SD 13 based at Gdynia.

SD 13 *5/2008*, J Ciślak* / 1353269

2 PIAST CLASS (PROJECT 570M) (SALVAGE SHIPS) (ARS)

Name	*No*	*Builders*	*Commissioned*
PIAST	281	Northern Shipyard, Gdansk	26 Jan 1974
LECH	282	Northern Shipyard, Gdansk	30 Nov 1974

Displacement, tons: 1,887 full load
Dimensions, feet (metres): 238.5 × 39.0 × 13.4 *(72.7 × 11.9 × 4.1)*
Main machinery: 2 Zgoda-Sulzer 6TD48 diesels; 3,300 hp(m) *(2.43 MW)* sustained; 2 shafts; cp props
Speed, knots: 15. **Range, n miles**: 3,000 at 12 kt
Complement: 56 (8 officers) plus 12 spare
Missiles: SAM: 2 Fasta 4M twin launchers for SA-N-5.
Guns: 4—25 mm (2 twin).
Radars: Navigation: 2 SRN 7453 Nogat; I-band.

Comment: Basically a Moma class hull with towing and firefighting capabilities. Ice-strengthened hulls. Wartime role as hospital ships. Carry three-man diving bells capable of 100 m depth and a decompression chamber. ROV added and other salvage improvements made in 1997/98. Based at Gdynia. Guns may not be carried.

PIAST *6/2008*, J Ciślak* / 1353270

2 ZBYSZKO CLASS (PROJECT B 823) (SALVAGE SHIPS) (ARS)

Name	*No*	*Builders*	*Commissioned*
ZBYSZKO	R 14	Ustka Shipyard	8 Nov 1991
MACKO	R 15	Ustka Shipyard	20 Mar 1992

Displacement, tons: 380 full load
Dimensions, feet (metres): 114.8 × 26.2 × 9.8 *(35 × 8 × 3)*
Main machinery: 1 Sulzer 6AL20/24D; 750 hp(m) *(551 kW)*; 1 shaft
Speed, knots: 11. **Range, n miles**: 3,000 at 10 kt
Complement: 15
Radars: Navigation: SRN 402X; I-band.

Comment: Type B-823 ordered 30 May 1988. Carries a decompression chamber and two divers. Mobile gantry crane on the stern. Based at Gdynia.

MACKO *5/2008*, J Ciślak* / 1353271

1 TRANSPORT CRAFT (PROJECT MS-3600) (YFB)

M 1

Displacement, tons: 74 full load
Dimensions, feet (metres): 94.2 × 19 × 4.3 *(28.7 × 5.8 × 1.3)*
Main machinery: 3 M50F5 diesels; 3,600 hp(m) *(2.65 MW)*; 3 shafts
Speed, knots: 27
Complement: 7 plus 30
Radars: Navigation: SRN 207A; I-band.

Comment: Can be used as emergency patrol craft. Based at Gdynia as an Admirals' launch.

M1 — *5/2007, J Ciślak* / 1166603

6 MISCELLANEOUS HARBOUR CRAFT (YFB)

B 3 **B 7** **B 11** **M 12** **M 21** **M 22**

Comment: M numbers are patrol launches; B numbers are freighters and oil lighters.

M 22 — *6/2008*, J Ciślak* / 1353273

B 7 — *6/2008*, J Ciślak* / 1353274

TUGS

2 H 960 CLASS (ATA)

H 6 **H 8**

Displacement, tons: 340 full load
Dimensions, feet (metres): 91.2 × 26.2 × 12.1 *(27.8 × 8 × 3.7)*
Main machinery: 1 Sulzer GATL 25 D diesels; 1,306 hp(m) *(960 kW)*; 1 shaft
Speed, knots: 12. **Range, n miles:** 1,150 at 12 kt
Complement: 17 (1 officer)
Radars: Navigation: SRN 401 XTA; I-band.

Comment: Built at Nauta Ship Repair Yard, Gdynia and commissioned 25 September 1992 and 19 March 1993 respectively. Based at Swinoujscie *(H 6)* and Gdynia *(H 8)*.

H 8 — *6/2008*, J Ciślak* / 1353275

5 HARBOUR TUGS (PROJECTS H 900, H 800, H 820) (YTB/YTM)

H 4 (Project 900) **H 5** (Project 900) **H 7** (Project 900) **H 9** (Project 820) **H 10** (Project 820)

Displacement, tons: 218 full load
Dimensions, feet (metres): 84 × 22.3 × 11.5 *(25.6 × 6.8 × 3.5)*
Main machinery: 1 Cegielski-Sulzer 6AL20/24H diesel; 935 hp(m) *(687 kW)*; 1 shaft
Speed, knots: 11. **Range, n miles:** 1,500 at 10 kt
Complement: 17
Radars: Navigation: SRN 206; I-band.

Comment: Details given are for *H 4, 5* and *7*. Completed 1979–81. Have firefighting capability except *H 9-10* . *H 9-10* completed in 1993.

H 5 — *10/2007, J Ciślak* / 1166606

SEA DETACHMENT OF THE BORDER GUARD (MOSG)

Headquarters Appointments

Commandant MOSG:
Captain Piotr Stocki
Deputy Commandant:
Commander Wojciech Heninborch
Deputy Commandant:
Commander Roman Słowiński

Bases

Gdansk (HQ and Kaszubski Division)
Swinoujscie (Pomorski Division)

General

MOSG (Morski Oddzial Strazy Granicznej) formed on 1 August 1991. Vessels have blue hulls with red and yellow striped insignia. Superstructures are painted white. The use of ships' names was discontinued in 2004. MOSG also operates one PZL M 20 Mewa, one W-3 AM Anakonda helicopter and one M-28 Skytruck.

PATROL FORCES

2 KAPER CLASS (PROJECT SKS-40) (LARGE PATROL CRAFT) (WPB)

No	*Builders*	*Commissioned*
SG-311	Wisla Yard, Gdansk	21 Jan 1991
SG-312	Wisla Yard, Gdansk	3 Apr 1992

Displacement, tons: 470 full load
Dimensions, feet (metres): 139.4 × 27.6 × 9.2 *(42.5 × 8.4 × 2.8)*
Main machinery: 2 Sulzer 8ATL25/30 diesels; 4,720 hp(m) *(3.47 MW)*; 2 shafts; cp props
Speed, knots: 17. **Range, n miles:** 2,800 at 14 kt
Complement: 15
Guns: 2 – 7.62 mm MGs.
Radars: SRN 207; I-band.
Navigation: Racal Decca; I-band.

Comment: *Kaper I* completed at Wisla Yard, Gdansk in January 1991, *Kaper II* on 1 October 1994. Have Simrad fish-finding sonars fitted. Used for Fishery Protection. 311 based at Gdansk and 312 at Kolobrzeg.

SG-311 — *5/2004, J Ciślak* / 1044493

6 WISLOKA CLASS (PROJECT 90) (COASTAL PATROL CRAFT) (WPB)

SG-142 SG-144–146 SG-150 SG-152

Displacement, tons: 45 full load
Dimensions, feet (metres): 69.6 × 14.8 × 5.2 *(21.2 × 4.5 × 1.6)*
Main machinery: 2 Wola 31 ANM28 H12A diesels; 1,000 hp(m) *(735 kW)*; 2 shafts
Speed, knots: 18
Range, n miles: 300 at 18 kt
Complement: 6
Guns: 2 — 12.7 mm MGs (twin).
Radars: Surface search: SRN 207; I-band.

Comment: Built at Wisla Shipyard, Gdansk and completed between October 1973 and August 1977. Three are based at Gdansk and three at Swinoujscie.

SG-152 *4/2004, Hartmut Ehlers* / 1044494

1 PATROL LAUNCH (PROJECT M-35) (WYFL)

SG 036

Displacement, tons: 41 full load
Dimensions, feet (metres): 35.3 × 14.4 × 5.2 *(10.7 × 4.4 × 1.6)*
Main machinery: 1 Wola DM 150 diesel; 150 hp *(112 kW)*
Speed, knots: 8
Complement: 4

Comment: Built in 1985. Similar to those in Polish naval service.

SG 036 *3/2006, J Ciślak* / 1164431

6 SPORTIS CLASS (PROJECT 7500) (FAST INTERCEPT CRAFT) (WPBF)

SG-002–007

Displacement, tons: 2
Dimensions, feet (metres): 24.6 × 9.2 × 1.3 *(7.5 × 2.8 × 0.4)*
Main machinery: Volvo Penta 230 hp (170 kW)
Speed, knots: 42
Complement: 3

Comment: Built in Bojano in 1996. Four craft are to be replaced by 9.5 m fast intercept craft in late 2009.

SG-007 *3/2006, J Ciślak* / 1164430

1 PATROL CRAFT (PROJECT MI-6) (WPB)

SG-008

Displacement, tons: 16
Dimensions, feet (metres): 42.7 × 12.14 × 3.6 *(13.0 × 3.7 × 1.1)*
Main machinery: 1 Wola; 200 hp *(147 kW)*; 1 shaft
Speed, knots: 11
Complement: 4

Comment: Harbour craft built at Wisla Shipyard, Gdansk, 1989.

SG-008 *3/2006, J Ciślak* / 1164429

4 IC 16 M III (PBF)

SG 213–216

Displacement, tons: 19 full load
Dimensions, feet (metres): 52.2 × 13.0 × 2.95 *(15.9 × 3.96 × 0.9)*
Main machinery: 2 Scania diesels; 1,580 hp(m) *(1.18 MW)*; 2 Rolls-Royce FF 410 waterjets
Speed, knots: 42. **Range, n miles:** 330 at 32 kt
Complement: 4
Radars: Surface search: Furuno M 1934C; I-band.

Comment: Four ordered from Dockstavarvet, Sweden and entered into service October-November 2007.

SG-213 *6/2008*, J Ciślak* / 1353276

SG-215 *10/2007, J Ciślak* / 1166609

2 STRAZNIK CLASS (PROJECT SAR-1500) (WPBF)

No	*Builders*	*Commissioned*
SG-211	Damen Yard, Gdynia	29 Apr 2000
SG-212	Damen Yard, Gdynia	7 July 2000

Displacement, tons: 26
Dimensions, feet (metres): 49.9 × 17.7 × 2.95 *(15.2 × 5.39 × 0.90)*
Main machinery: 2 MAN D2848 diesels; 1,360 hp *(1,000 kW)*; water jet system
Speed, knots: 35. **Range, n miles:** 200 at 30 kt
Complement: 4 (1 officer)
Guns: 1 — 7.62 mm MG.
Radars: Surface search: SIMRAD; I-band.

Comment: Contract between MOSG and Damen Shipyard signed 5 October 1999. Based on Dutch SAR 1500 lifeboat. Hull and superstructure of aluminium alloy.

SG-211 *10/2007, J Ciślak* / 1166607

6 MODIFIED SPORTIS CLASS (PROJECT S-6100) (FAST INTERCEPT CRAFT) (WPBF)

SG 061–066

Displacement, tons: 1.9
Dimensions, feet (metres): 20.0 × 7.5 × 1.3 *(6.1 × 2.3 × 0.4)*
Main machinery: 2 Johnson outboard motors; 120 hp *(89.6 kW)*
Speed, knots: 35
Complement: 2

Comment: Built at Bojano in 2001. Located at Border units along the coast.

SG 063 *6/2003, MOSG* / 0567506

2 GRIFFON 2000 TDX CLASS (HOVERCRAFT) (UCAC)

SG 411–412

Displacement, tons: 3.5 full load
Dimensions, feet (metres): 39.0 × 15.7 *(11.9 × 4.8)*
Main machinery: 1 Deutz BF 6M 1015 CP diesel; 442 hp *(330 kW)*
Speed, knots: 30
Range, n miles: 450 at 35 kt
Complement: 3
Radars: Navigation: SIMRAD RA 83P; I-band.

Comment: Built by Griffon Hovercraft, Southampton and delivered in 2006. Aluminium hull. Employed as patrol craft in shallow waters and rivers.

SG 411 *6/2008*, J Ciślak* / 1353277

Portugal

MARINHA PORTUGUESA

Country Overview

The Republic of Portugal is situated in south-western Europe in the western portion of the Iberian Peninsula. It is bordered to the north and east by Spain and has a 967 n mile coastline with the Atlantic Ocean. The Azores and Madeira Islands in the Atlantic are integral parts of the republic, the total area of which is 35,553 square miles. Lisbon is the capital, largest city and principal port. There are further ports at Leixões (near Oporto), Setúbal, and Funchal (Madeira). Territorial seas (12 n miles) and an EEZ (200 n miles) are claimed.

Headquarters Appointments

Chief of Naval Staff:
Admiral Fernando José Ribeiro de Melo Gomes
Deputy Chief of Naval Staff:
Vice Admiral Rui Cardoso de Telles Palhinha
Naval Commander:
Vice Admiral José Carlos Torrado Saldanha Lopes
Azores Maritime Zone Commander:
Rear Admiral Agostinho Ramos da Silva
Madeira Maritime Zone Commander:
Captain António Manuel de Carvalho Coelho Cândido
Marine Corps Commander:
Rear Admiral Luís Miguel de Matos Cortes Picciochi

Diplomatic Representation

Defence and Naval Attaché in Dublin and The Hague:
Lieutenant Colonel Jorge Manuel da Costa Ramos
Defence Attaché in Washington and Ottawa:
Captain Carlos Nelson Lopes da Costa
Defence Attaché in Luanda, Kinshasa, Brazzaville and Windhoek:
Colonel Jorge Dias Teixeira
Defence Attaché in Maputo, Lillongwe, Harare and Dar-Es-Salam:
Colonel Joaquim Humberto Arriaga da Câmara Stone
Defence Attaché in Madrid, Cairo and Athens:
Captain António Manuel Henriques Gomes
Defence Attaché in S. Tomé and Libreville:
Captain João Francisco Franco Facada

Diplomatic Representation — *continued*

Defence Attaché in Bissau, Conakry and Dakar:
Colonel Francisco António Coelho Nogueira
Defence Attaché in Brasilia:
Colonel Jorges Esteves Pereira Nunes dos Santos
Defence Attaché in Berlin, Prague, Copenhagen, Stockholm and Oslo:
Lieutenant Colonel José Fernando Alves Gaspar
Defence Attaché in Warsaw, Budapest, Kiev, Bucharest and Bratislava:
Colonel José Carlos de Almeida Marques
Defence Attaché in Canberra, Dili and Jakarta:
Colonel Cipriano Fernando Mendes Figueiredo
Defence Attaché in Paris, Luxembourg and Brussels:
Colonel Paulo José Reis Mateus
Defence Attaché in Rabat and Tunis:
Colonel João Guilherme Machado Vieira
Defence Attaché in Praia:
Colonel José António Sardinha Teles Alface
Defence Attaché in Moscow and Sofia:
Colonel Cláudio Martins Lopes
Defence Attaché in Rome, Tel-Aviv and Ankara:
Lieutenant Colonel Eduardo Jorge Pontes de Albuquerque Faria

Personnel

2009: 10,100 (1,570 officers) including 1,350 marines

Marine Corps

2 battalions, 1 special operations detachment, 1 naval police unit

Bases

Main Base: Lisbon-Alfeite
Dockyard: Arsenal do Alfeite
Fleet Support: Porto, Portimão, Funchal, Ponta Delgada, Tróia
Air Base: Montijo (Lisbon)

Naval Air

The helicopter squadron was formally activated on 23 September 1993 at Montijo air force base, Lisbon. Operational and logistic procedures are similar to the air force.

Prefix to Ships' Names

NRP (Navio da República Portuguesa)

Strength of the Fleet

Type	*Active (Reserve)*	*Building (Projected)*
Submarines (Patrol)	1	2
Frigates	4	1
Corvettes	7	–
Patrol Craft	4	8
Coastal/River Patrol Craft	12	8
LPD	–	1
LCTs/LST	1	–
Survey Ships and Craft	7	–
Sail Training Ships	5	–
Replenishment Tanker	1	(1)
Buoy Tenders	2	2

DELETIONS

Submarines

2005 *Delfim*

Frigates

2007 *Comandante Sacadura Cabral*
2008 *Comandante João Belo*

PENNANT LIST

Submarines

S 164 Barracuda

Frigates

F 330 Vasco da Gama
F 331 Alvares Cabral
F 332 Corte Real
F 333 Bartolomeu Dias
F 334 D Francisco da Almeida

Corvettes

F 471 Antonio Enes
F 475 João Coutinho
F 476 Jacinto Candido
F 477 Gen Pereira d'Eça
F 486 Baptista de Andrade
F 487 João Roby
F 488 Afonso Cerqueira

Patrol Forces

P 370 Rio Minho
P 1140 Cacine
P 1144 Quanza
P 1146 Zaire
P 1150 Argos
P 1151 Dragão
P 1152 Escorpião
P 1153 Cassiopeia
P 1154 Hidra
P 1155 Centauro
P 1156 Orion
P 1157 Pégaso
P 1158 Sagitario
P 1161 Save
P 1165 Aguia
P 1167 Cisne

Amphibious Forces

LDG 203 Bacamarte

Service Forces

A 520 Sagres
A 521 Schultz Xavier
A 522 D. Carlos I
A 523 Almirante Gago Coutinho
A 5203 Andromeda
A 5204 Polar
A 5205 Auriga
A 5210 Bérrio
UAM 201 Creoula
UAM 813 Bellatrix
UAM 814 Canopus

SUBMARINES

1 ALBACORA (DAPHNÉ) CLASS (SSK)

Name	*No*	*Builders*	*Laid down*	*Launched*	*Commissioned*
BARRACUDA	S 164	Dubigeon-Normandie, Nantes	19 Oct 1965	24 Apr 1967	4 May 1968

Displacement, tons: 869 surfaced; 1,043 dived
Dimensions, feet (metres): 189.6 × 22.3 × 17.1 *(57.8 × 6.8 × 5.2)*
Main machinery: Diesel-electric; 2 SEMT-Pielstick 12 PA4 V 185 diesels; 2,450 hp(m) *(1.8 MW)*; 2 Jeumont Schneider alternators; 1.7 MW; 2 motors; 2,600 hp(m) *(1.9 MW)*; 2 shafts
Speed, knots: 13.5 surfaced; 16 dived
Range, n miles: 2,710 at 12.5 kt surfaced; 2,130 at 10 kt snorting
Complement: 54 (7 officers)

Torpedoes: 12—21.7 in *(550 mm)* (8 bow, 4 stern) tubes. ECAN E14; anti-surface; passive homing to 12 km *(6.6 n miles)* at 25 kt; warhead 300 kg or ECAN L3; anti-submarine; active homing to 5.5 km *(3 n miles)* at 25 kt; warhead 200 kg. No reloads
Countermeasures: ESM: ARUR; radar warning.
Weapons control: DLT D3 torpedo control.
Radars: Surface search: Kelvin Hughes KH 1007; I-band.
Sonars: Thomson Sintra DSUV 2; passive search and attack; medium frequency.
DUUA 2; active search and attack; 8.4 kHz.
L-3 ELAK NAUTIK LOPAS 8300; passive search.

Modernisation: New radar fitted in 1993–94.
Structure: Diving depth, 300 m *(984 ft)*.
Operational: *Albacora* paid off mid-2000 and cannibalised for spares. *Delfim* decommissioned in 2005 and is to become a museum ship at Viana do Castelo. *Barracuda* expected to remain in service until December 2009.

BARRACUDA *9/2005*, ***B Prézelin*** / 1153408

BARRACUDA *9/2005*, ***B Prézelin*** / 1153409

0 + 2 TYPE 209PN CLASS (SSK)

Name	*No*	*Builders*	*Laid down*	*Launched*	*Commissioned*
TRIDENTE	S 170	Howaldtswerke, Kiel	7 Mar 2005	15 July 2008	2010
ARPÃO	S 171	Howaldtswerke, Kiel	5 July 2006	2009	2011

Displacement, tons: 1,700 (surfaced); 1,970 (dived)
Dimensions, feet (metres): 222.8 × 20.7 × 21.6 *(67.9 × 6.3 × 6.6)*
Main machinery: 2 MTU 16V 396 diesels; 5,600 hp(m) *(4.17 MW)*; 1 Siemens Permasyn motor; 1 shaft; 2 HDW PEM fuel cells; 240 kW
Speed, knots: 20 dived; 12 surfaced
Complement: 32 (5 officers)

Torpedoes: 8—21 in *(533 mm)* bow tubes. WASS Black Shark; wire (fibre optic cable)-guided; active/passive homing to 50 km *(27 n miles)* at 50 kt; warhead 250 kg. 16 weapons including torpedoes and SSM.
Countermeasures: To be announced.
Weapons control: Atlas Elektronik ISUS 90/50.
Radars: To be announced.
Sonars: Cylindrical array with intercept passive array, passive range sonar, flank array and mine-avoidance sonar.

Programmes: Contract signed on 21 April 2004 with German Submarine Consortium (GSC) for construction and delivery of two boats with option for a third. The consortium consists of Howaldtswerke-Deutsche Werft, Kiel, Nordseewerke, Emden (NSWE) and Ferrostaal, Essen.
Structure: Very similar to the Type 214 Air-Independent Propulsion (AIP) submarines under construction for Greece. Diving depth likely to be about 400 m *(1,300 ft)*.
Operational: To form 5 Squadron on commissioning.

TRIDENTE
7/2008*, Michael Nitz
1336040

FRIGATES

1 + 1 KAREL DOORMAN CLASS (FFGHM)

Name	*No*	*Builders*	*Laid down*	*Launched*	*Commissioned*
BARTOLOMEU DIAS (ex-*Van Nes*)	F 333 (ex-F 833)	Koninklijke Maatschappij De Schelde, Flushing	10 Jan 1990	16 May 1992	2 June 1994
D. FRANCISCO DA ALMEIDA (ex-*Van Galen*)	F 334 (ex-F 834)	Koninklijke Maatschappij De Schelde, Flushing	7 June 1990	21 Nov 1992	1 Dec 1994

Displacement, tons: 3,320 full load
Dimensions, feet (metres): 401.2 oa; 374.7 wl × 47.2 × 14.1 *(122.3; 114.2 × 14.4 × 4.3)*
Flight deck, feet (metres): 72.2 × 47.2 *(22 × 14.4)*
Main machinery: CODOG; 2 RR Spey SM1C; 33,800 hp *(25.2 MW)* sustained; 2 Stork-Wärtsilä 12SW280 diesels; 9,790 hp(m) *(7.2 MW)* sustained; 2 shafts; LIPS cp props
Speed, knots: 30 (Speys); 21 (diesels)
Range, n miles: 5,000 at 18 kt
Complement: 156 (16 officers) (accommodation for 163)

Missiles: SSM: 8 McDonnell Douglas Harpoon Block 1C (2 quad) launchers ❶; active radar homing to 130 km *(70 n miles)* at 0.9 Mach; warhead 227 kg.
SAM: Raytheon Sea Sparrow Mk 48 vertical launchers ❷; semi-active radar homing to 14.6 km *(8 n miles)* at 2.5 Mach; warhead 39 kg; 16 missiles. Canisters mounted on port side of hangar.
Guns: 1—3 in *(76 mm)*/62 OTO Melara compact Mk 100 ❸; 100 rds/min to 16 km *(8.6 n miles)* anti-surface; 12 km *(6.5 n miles)* anti-aircraft; weight of shell 6 kg. 1 Signaal SGE-30 Goalkeeper with General Electric 30 mm 7-barrelled ❹; 4,200 rds/min combined to 2 km. 2 Oerlikon 20 mm; 800 rds/min to 2 km.
Torpedoes: 4—324 mm US Mk 32 Mod 9 (2 twin) tubes (mounted inside the after superstructure) ❺. Honeywell Mk 46 Mod 5; anti-submarine; active/passive homing to 11 km *(5.9 n miles)* at 40 kt; warhead 44 kg.
Countermeasures: Decoys: 2 Loral Hycor SRBOC 6-tubed fixed Mk 36 quad launchers; IR flares and chaff to 4 km *(2.2 n miles)*.
SLQ-25 Nixie towed torpedo decoy.
ESM/ECM: Argo APECS II (includes AR 700) ESM) ❻; intercept and jammers.
Combat data systems: Signaal SEWACO VIIB action data automation; Link 11. SATCOM ❼. WSC-6 twin aerials.
Weapons control: Signaal IRSCAN infra-red detector. Signaal VESTA helo transponder.
Radars: Air/surface search: Signaal SMART ❽; 3D; F-band.
Air search: Signaal LW08 ❾; D-band.
Surface search: Signaal Scout ❿; I-band.
Navigation: Racal Decca 1226; I-band.
Fire control: 2 Signaal STIR ⓫; I/J/K-band; range 140 km *(76 n miles)* for 1 m² target.
Sonars: Signaal PHS-36; hull-mounted; active search and attack; medium frequency.
Thomson Sintra Anaconda DSBV 61; towed array; passive low frequency.

Helicopters: 1 Super Sea Lynx Mk 95 ⓬.

Programmes: The Declaration of Intent to purchase two ex-Netherlands frigates was announced on 1st November 2006. The ships are to replace the João Belo-class frigates. This is to be followed by a contract for the supply of the two ships, a support package, weapons transfer, joint upgrades and crew training. Ex-*Van Nes* transferred in late 2008 and ex-*Van Galen* is to transfer on 1 November 2009.

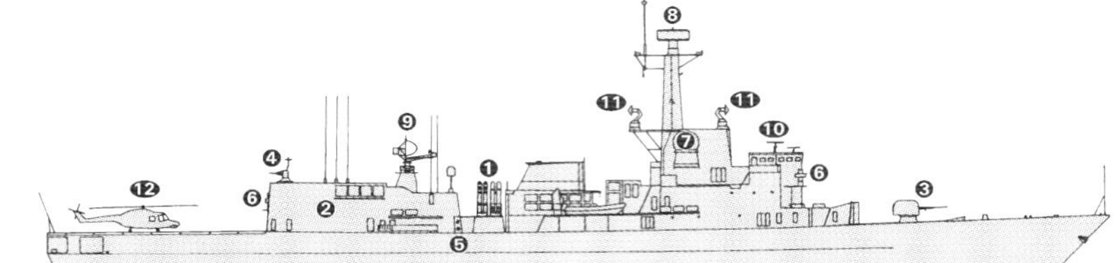

BARTOLOMEU DIAS ***(Scale 1 : 1,200), Ian Sturton*** / 1164924

BARTOLOMEU DIAS ***7/2008*, A A de Kruijf*** / 1336039

Modernisation: A modernisation package is expected to be implemented before transfer.
Structure: The VLS SAM is similar to Canadian Halifax and Greek MEKO classes. The ship is designed to reduce radar and IR signatures and has extensive NBCD arrangements. Full automation and roll stabilisation fitted. The APECS jammers are mounted starboard forward of the bridge and port aft corner of the hangar.

3 VASCO DA GAMA (MEKO 200 PN) CLASS (FFGH)

Name	*No*	*Builders*	*Laid down*	*Launched*	*Commissioned*
VASCO DA GAMA	F 330	Blohm + Voss, Hamburg	1 Feb 1989	26 June 1989	18 Jan 1991
ALVARES CABRAL	F 331	Howaldtswerke, Kiel	2 June 1989	6 June 1990	24 May 1991
CORTE REAL	F 332	Howaldtswerke, Kiel	24 Nov 1989	6 June 1990	22 Nov 1991

Displacement, tons: 2,700 standard; 3,300 full load
Dimensions, feet (metres): 380.3 oa; 357.6 pp × 48.7 × 20 *(115.9; 109 × 14.8 × 6.1)*
Main machinery: CODOG; 2 GE LM 2500 gas turbines; 53,000 hp *(39.5 MW)* sustained; 2 MTU 12V 1163 TB83 diesels; 8,840 hp(m) *(6.5 MW)*; 2 shafts; cp props
Speed, knots: 32 gas; 20 diesel
Range, n miles: 4,900 at 18 kt; 9,600 at 12 kt
Complement: 182 (23 officers) (including aircrew of 16 (4 officers)) plus 16 Flag Staff

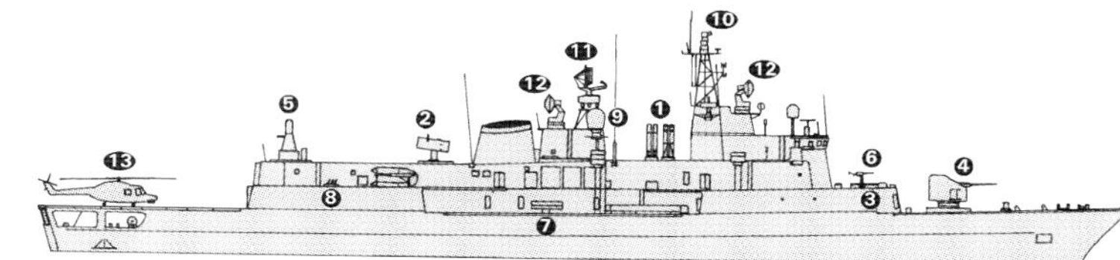

VASCO DA GAMA

(Scale 1 : 1,200), Ian Sturton / 0567520

Missiles: SSM: 8 McDonnell Douglas Harpoon (2 quad) launchers ❶; active radar homing to 130 km *(70 n miles)* at 0.9 Mach; warhead 227 kg.
SAM: Raytheon Sea Sparrow Mk 29 Mod 1 octuple launcher ❷; RIM-7M/P; semi-active radar homing to 16 km *(8.5 n miles)* at 2.5 Mach; warhead 38 kg. Space left for VLS Sea Sparrow ❸.
Guns: 1 Creusot-Loire 3.9 in *(100 mm)*/55 Mod 68 CADAM ❹; 60 rds/min to 17 km *(9 n miles)* anti-surface; 8 km *(4.4 n miles)* anti-aircraft; weight of shell 13.5 kg.
1 General Electric/General Dynamics Vulcan Phalanx 20 mm Block 1B ❺; 6 barrels per mounting; 3,000 rds/min combined to 1.5 km.
2 Oerlikon 20 mm (on VLS deck) ❻ can be carried.
Torpedoes: 6—324 mm US Mk 32 (2 triple) tubes ❼. Honeywell Mk 46 Mod 5; anti-submarine; active/passive homing to 11 km *(5.9 n miles)* at 40 kt; warhead 44 kg.
Countermeasures: Decoys: 2 Loral Hycor Mk 36 SRBOC 6-barrelled chaff launchers ❽. Sea Gnat.
SLQ-25 Nixie; towed torpedo decoy.
ESM/ECM: APECS II; intercept and jammer.

Combat data systems: Signaal SEWACO action data automation with STACOS tactical command; Link 11 and 14. Matra Marconi SCOT 3 SATCOM ❾ (1 set between 3 ships).
Weapons control: SWG 1A(V) for SSM. Vesta Helo transponder with datalink for OTHT.
Radars: Air search: Signaal MW08 (derived from Smart 3D) ❿; 3D; G-band.
Air/surface search: Signaal DA08 ⓫; F-band.
Navigation: Kelvin Hughes Type 1007; I-band.
Fire control: 2 Signaal STIR ⓬; I/J/K-band; range 140 km *(76 n miles)* for 1 m² target.
IFF Mk 12 Mod 4.
Sonars: Computing Devices (Canada) SQS-510(V); hull-mounted; active search and attack; medium frequency.

Helicopters: 2 Super Sea Lynx Mk 95 ⓭.

Programmes: The contract for all three was signed on 25 July 1986. These are Meko 200 type ordered from a consortium of builders. As well as Portugal, which provided 40 per cent of the cost, assistance was given by NATO with some missile, CIWS and torpedo systems being provided by the US.
Modernisation: Full mid-life refits are planned 2011–2017. Upgrades are likely to include improvements to the combat data system, increased force protection capabilities and measures to counter asymmetric threats.
Structure: All-steel construction. Stabilisers fitted. Full RAS facilities. Space has been left for a sonar towed array and for VLS Sea Sparrow.
Operational: Designed primarily as ASW ships. SCOT SATCOM rotated between the three ships. 20 mm guns can be mounted on the VLS deck. Three year running cycles include 18 months at full readiness, three months training and six months refit.

VASCO DA GAMA

6/2008, M Declerck* / 1335419

VASCO DA GAMA

5/2008, Harald Carstens* / 1335418

ALVARES CABRAL

9/2008, J Brodie* / 1335488

CORVETTES

3 BAPTISTA DE ANDRADE CLASS (FSH)

Name	*No*	*Builders*	*Laid down*	*Launched*	*Commissioned*
BAPTISTA DE ANDRADE	F 486	Empresa Nacional Bazán, Cartagena	1 Sep 1972	13 Mar 1973	19 Nov 1974
JOÃO ROBY	F 487	Empresa Nacional Bazán, Cartagena	1 Dec 1972	3 June 1973	18 Mar 1975
AFONSO CERQUEIRA	F 488	Empresa Nacional Bazán, Cartagena	10 Mar 1973	6 Oct 1973	26 June 1975

Displacement, tons: 1,203 standard; 1,380 full load
Dimensions, feet (metres): 277.5 × 33.8 × 10.2 *(84.6 × 10.3 × 3.1)*
Main machinery: 2 OEW Pielstick 12 PC2.2 V 400 diesels; 12,000 hp(m) *(8.82 MW)* sustained; 2 shafts
Speed, knots: 22
Range, n miles: 5,900 at 18 kt
Complement: 71 (7 officers)

Guns: 1 Creusot-Loire 3.9 in *(100 mm)*/55 Mod 1968; 80 rds/min to 17 km *(9 n miles)* anti-surface; 8 km *(4.4 n miles)* anti-aircraft; weight of shell 13.5 kg.
2 Bofors 40 mm/70; 300 rds/min to 12 km *(6.6 n miles)*; weight of shell 0.96 kg.
Radars: Navigation: 1 Racal Decca RM 316P and 1 KH 5000 Nucleos 2; I-band.

Helicopters: Platform only.

Programmes: Reclassified as corvettes.
Modernisation: Communications equipment updated 1988–91. Previous modernisation programme was abandoned in 1998. Between 1999 and 2001 ASW and weapons control systems removed.
Operational: Class is used for Maritime Law Enforcement/SAR/Fishery Protection and for Humanitarian Operations. To be replaced by Viana do Castelo class by 2019. To be decommissioned 2009–18.

ALFONSO CERQUEIRA *7/2007, A A de Kruijf* / 1166696

JOÃO ROBY *7/2007, Michael Nitz* / 1166695

4 JOÃO COUTINHO CLASS (FSH)

Name	*No*	*Builders*	*Laid down*	*Launched*	*Commissioned*
ANTONIO ENES	F 471	Empresa Nacional Bazán, Cartagena	10 Apr 1968	16 Aug 1969	18 June 1971
JOÃO COUTINHO	F 475	Blohm + Voss, Hamburg	24 Dec 1968	2 May 1969	28 Feb 1970
JACINTO CANDIDO	F 476	Blohm + Voss, Hamburg	10 Feb 1969	16 June 1969	29 May 1970
GENERAL PEREIRA D'EÇA	F 477	Blohm + Voss, Hamburg	21 Apr 1969	26 July 1969	10 Oct 1970

Displacement, tons: 1,203 standard; 1,380 full load
Dimensions, feet (metres): 277.5 × 33.8 × 10.8 *(84.6 × 10.3 × 3.3)*
Main machinery: 2 OEW Pielstick 12 PC2.2 V 400 diesels; 12,000 hp(m) *(8.82 MW)* sustained; 2 shafts
Speed, knots: 22. **Range, n miles:** 5,900 at 18 kt
Complement: 70 (7 officers)
Guns: 2 US 3 in *(76 mm)*/50 (twin) Mk 33; 50 rds/min to 12.8 km *(7 n miles)*; weight of shell 6 kg.
2 Bofors 40 mm/60 (twin); 300 rds/min to 12 km *(6.6 n miles)*; weight of shell 0.89 kg.
Weapons control: Mk 51 GFCS for 40 mm.
Radars: Air/surface search: Kelvin Hughes 1007; I-band.
Navigation: Racal Decca RM 1226C; I-band.

Helicopters: Platform only.

Programmes: Reclassified as corvettes.

Modernisation: A programme for this class to include SSM and PDMS has been shelved. In 1989–91 the main radar was updated and SATCOM (INMARSAT) installed. Also fitted with SIFICAP which is a Fishery Protection data exchange system by satellite to the main database ashore.
Operational: A/S equipment no longer operational and laid apart on shore. Crew reduced as a result. To be replaced by Viana do Castelo class by 2019. To be decommissioned 2009–18.

ANTONIO ENES *12/2007, Diego Quevedo* / 1335417

SHIPBORNE AIRCRAFT

Notes: Procurement of three further Lynx helicopters is under consideration. Options include Mk 95 aircraft, Super Lynx 300 (including upgrade of current aircraft) or second-hand aircaft.

Numbers/Type: 5 Westland Super Navy Lynx Mk 95.
Operational speed: 125 kt *(231 km/h).*
Service ceiling: 12,000 ft *(3,660 m).*
Range: 320 n miles *(593 km).*
Role/Weapon systems: Ordered 2 November 1990 for MEKO 200 frigates; two are updated HAS 3 and three were new aircraft, all delivered in August and November 1993. Sensors: Bendix 1500B radar; Bendix AQS-18V dipping sonar; Racal RNS 252 datalink. Weapons: Mk 46 torpedoes. 1—12.7 mm MG.

SUPER LYNX *9/2002, H M Steele* / 0534127

LAND-BASED MARITIME AIRCRAFT

Notes: All Air Force manned.

Numbers/Type: 5/2 CASA C-212-200 Aviocar/C-212-300 Aviocar.
Operational speed: 190 kt *(353 km/h).*
Service ceiling: 24,000 ft *(7,315 m).*
Range: 1,650 n miles *(3,055 km).*
Role/Weapon systems: The first five are for short-range SAR support and transport operations. The last pair were ordered in February 1993 for maritime patrol and fisheries surveillance off the Azores and Madeira. Sensors: Search radar and MAD. FLIR and datalink (last pair). Weapons: Unarmed.

CASA 212 *6/2001, Adolfo Ortigueira Gil* / 0529552

Numbers/Type: 5 Lockheed P3 CUP Orion.
Operational speed: 410 kt *(760 km/h).*
Service ceiling: 28,300 ft *(8,625 m).*
Range: 4,000 n miles *(7,410 km).*
Role/Weapon systems: Five P-3P long-range surveillance aircraft acquired from Australia and modernised to 3P standard in 1987. These aircraft have been replaced by five P-3 CUP aircraft acquired from the Netherlands in 2005. Contract signed with Lockheed Martin on 3 January 2008 for upgrade work on all five aircraft. This is to include upgrade of the mission system and provision of improved ESM, acoustic processing, communications and sensor systems. First upgraded aircraft to be delivered late 2009 and programme to be completed by late 2012. Sensors: APS-134/137 radar, ASQ-81 MAD, AQS-901 sonobuoy processor, AQS-114 computer, IFF, ALR-66 ECM/ESM. Weapons: ASW; eight Mk 46 torpedoes, depth bombs or mines; ASV; 10 underwing stations for Harpoon.

P-3 CUP *2/2006, Portuguese Airforce* / 1130518

Numbers/Type: 6/2/4 AgustaWestland EH 101 Mk 514/Mk 515/Mk 516.
Operational speed: 160 *(296 km/h).*
Service ceiling: 15,000 ft *(4,572 m).*
Range: 550 n miles *(1,019 km).*
Role/Weapon systems: Contract in 2001 for a total of 12 utility variants of the EH 101. Six Mk 514 are configured for SAR duties, two Mk 515 for fishery protection and four Mk 516 for Combat SAR. The aircraft are designed for rapid role-change. Military lift is 28 troops and up to four tonnes underslung. Sensors: Galileo search radar, FLIR and defensive aids suite. Weapons: unarmed.

EH 101 *6/2007, Portuguese Navy* / 1166694

PATROL FORCES

2 + 2 (6) VIANA DO CASTELO (NPO 2000) CLASS (PSOH)

Name	*No*	*Builders*	*Commissioned*
VIANA DO CASTELO	P 360	Viana do Castelo Shipyards	Mar 2009
FIGUEIRA DA FOZ	P 361	Viana do Castelo Shipyards	June 2009
PONTA DELGADA	P 362	Viano do Castelo Shipyards	2011
SINES	P 363	Viano do Castelo Shipyards	2012

Displacement, tons: 1,716 full load
Dimensions, feet (metres): 272.6 × 42.5 × 12.1 *(83.1 × 12.95 × 3.69)*
Main machinery: 2 Wärtsilä 12V 26 diesels; 10,460 hp *(7.8 MW)*; 2 shafts
Speed, knots: 20
Range, n miles: 5,000 at 15 kt
Complement: 38 (5 officers)
Guns: 1 Bofors 40 mm/60. 2—12.7 mm MGs.
Weapons control: Sagem optronic director.
Radars: Surface search/navigation: 2 Kelvin Hughes; E/F/I-band.
Helicopters: Platform for one Lynx Mk 95.

Comment: Designed for EEZ patrol duties. Contract on 15 October 2002 with Viana do Castelo Shipyards for two Offshore Patrol vessels. Construction started in 2003 and the first two ships were floated out on 1 October 2005; a further sixare planned to be delivered by 2019 to replace the corvettes. Two further modified vessels, a Buoy Tender and a Pollution Control Ship, were ordered in May 2004 and are to be delivered in 2011 and 2012.

FIGUEIRA DA FOZ *6/2007, Massimo Annati* / 1166693

4 CACINE CLASS (LARGE PATROL CRAFT) (PBO)

Name	*No*	*Builders*	*Commissioned*
CACINE	P 1140	Arsenal do Alfeite	May 1969
QUANZA	P 1144	Estaleiros Navais do Mondego	May 1969
ZAIRE	P 1146	Estaleiros Navais do Mondego	Nov 1970
SAVE	P 1161	Arsenal do Alfeite	May 1973

Displacement, tons: 292.5 standard; 310 full load
Dimensions, feet (metres): 144 × 25.2 × 7.1 *(44 × 7.7 × 2.2)*
Main machinery: 2 MTU 12V 538TB80 diesels; 3,750 hp(m) *(2.76 MW)* sustained; 2 shafts
Speed, knots: 20. **Range, n miles:** 4,400 at 12 kt
Complement: 33 (3 officers)
Guns: 1 Bofors 40 mm/60. 1 Oerlikon 20 mm/65.
Radars: Surface search: Kelvin Hughes Type 1007; I/J-band.

Comment: Originally mounted a second Bofors aft but most have been removed as has the 37 mm rocket launcher. Have SIFICAP satellite data handling system for Fishery Protection duties. An RIB is carried. Two of the class are based at Madeira on a two month rotational basis. Re-engined in 1992–94. To be decommissioned 2009–12 and replaced by LFC 2005 vessels from 2011.

CACINE *12/2003, Martin Mokrus* / 1044180

ZAIRE *5/2006, A A de Kruijf* / 1040764

4 CENTAURO CLASS (RIVER PATROL CRAFT) (PBR)

Name	*No*	*Builders*	*Commissioned*
CENTAURO	P 1155	Arsenal do Alfeite	20 Mar 2000
ORION	P 1156	Arsenal do Alfeite	27 Mar 2001
PÉGASO	P 1157	Estaleiros Navals do Mondego	27 Mar 2001
SAGITARIO	P 1158	Estaleiros Navals do Mondego	27 Mar 2001

Displacement, tons: 89 full load
Dimensions, feet (metres): 93.2 × 19.5 × 4.6 *(28.4 × 5.95 × 1.4)*
Main machinery: 2 Cummins KTA-50-M2 diesels; 3,600 hp(m) *(2.64 MW)*; 2 shafts
Speed, knots: 26. **Range, n miles:** 640 at 20 kt
Complement: 8 (1 officer)
Guns: 1 Oerlikon 20 mm/65.
Radars: 1 Furuno FCR-1411 MK3.

Comment: Similar to Argos class but of aluminium hull. Capable of full speed operation up to Sea State 3. Carries a semi-rigid boat with a 50 hp outboard engine. The boat is recoverable via a stern well at up to 10 kt. To be refitted 2012–13.

SAGITARIO *10/2006, Adolfo Ortigueira Gil* / 1040677

2 ALBATROZ CLASS (RIVER PATROL CRAFT) (PBR)

Name	*No*	*Builders*	*Commissioned*
AGUIA	P 1165	Arsenal do Alfeite	28 Feb 1975
CISNE	P 1167	Arsenal do Alfeite	31 Mar 1976

Displacement, tons: 45 full load
Dimensions, feet (metres): 77.4 × 18.4 × 5.2 *(23.6 × 5.6 × 1.6)*
Main machinery: 2 Cummins diesels; 1,100 hp *(820 kW)*; 2 shafts
Speed, knots: 20. **Range, n miles:** 2,500 at 12 kt
Complement: 8 (1 officer)
Guns: 1 Oerlikon 20 mm/65. 2 — 12.7 mm MGs
Radars: Surface search: Decca RM 316P; I-band

Comment: One other is used for harbour patrol duties. Two transferred to East Timor in 2001. Expected to be decommissioned 2012–13.

AGUIA *10/2006, Adolfo Ortigueira Gil* / 1335420

5 ARGOS CLASS (RIVER PATROL CRAFT) (PBR)

Name	*No*	*Builders*	*Commissioned*
ARGOS	P 1150	Arsenal do Alfeite	2 July 1991
DRAGÃO	P 1151	Arsenal do Alfeite	18 Oct 1991
ESCORPIÃO	P 1152	Arsenal do Alfeite	26 Nov 1991
CASSIOPEIA	P 1153	Conafi	11 Nov 1991
HIDRA	P 1154	Conafi	18 Dec 1991

Displacement, tons: 94 full load
Dimensions, feet (metres): 89.2 × 19.4 × 4.6 *(27.2 × 5.9 × 1.4)*
Main machinery: 2 MTU 12V 396 TE84 diesels; 3,700 hp(m) *(2.73 MW)* sustained; 2 shafts
Speed, knots: 26. **Range, n miles:** 1,350 at 15 kt
Complement: 12 (1 officer)
Guns: 2 — 12.7 mm MGs (1150-1154).
Radars: Navigation: Furuno 1505 DA or Furuno FR 1411; I-band.

Comment: First five ordered in 1989 and 50 per cent funded by the EC. Of GRP construction, capable of full speed operation up to Sea State 3. Carries a RIB with a 37 hp outboard engine. The boat is recoverable via a stern well at up to 10 kt.

HIDRA *9/2007, Marco Ghiglino* / 1170064

0 + 8 COASTAL (LFC 2005) PATROL CRAFT (PBO)

Displacement, tons: 660 full load
Dimensions, feet (metres): 196.5 × 32.4 × 8.8 *(59.9 × 9.9 × 2.7)*
Main machinery: 4 diesels; 12,100 hp *(9 MW)*; 2 shafts
Speed, knots: 25. **Range, n miles:** To be announced
Complement: 20 (3 officers)
Guns: 1 Bofors 40 mm/60. 1 — 12.7 mm MG.
Weapons control: Optronic director.
Radars: To be announced.

Comment: Preliminary contract with Viana do Castelo Shipyard for the construction of eight patrol vessels was let on 19 December 2005. Designed for EEZ patrol and fishery protection, the ships are to replace the Cacine class and are to enter service 2011–14.

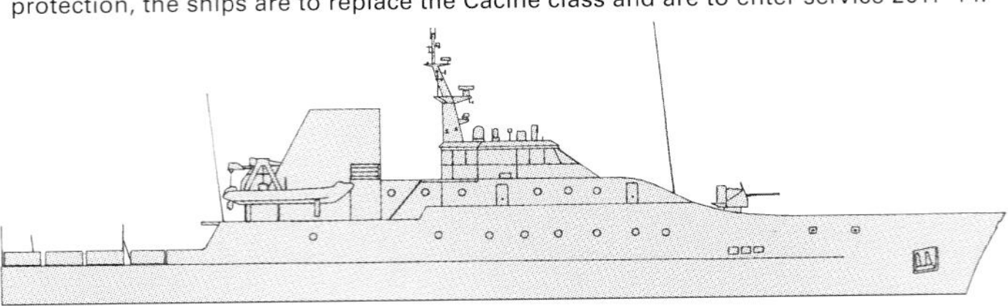

LFC *(not to scale), Ian Sturton* / 1154415

1 RIO MINHO CLASS (RIVER PATROL CRAFT) (PBR)

Name	*No*	*Builders*	*Commissioned*
RIO MINHO	P 370	Arsenal do Alfeite	1 Aug 1991

Displacement, tons: 72 full load
Dimensions, feet (metres): 73.5 × 19.7 × 2.6 *(22.4 × 6 × 0.8)*
Main machinery: 2 KHD-Deutz diesels; 664 hp(m) *(488 kW)*; 2 Schottel pumpjets
Speed, knots: 9.5. **Range, n miles:** 420 at 7 kt
Complement: 8 (1 officer)
Guns: 1 — 7.62 mm MG.
Radars: Navigation: Furuno FR 1505DA; I-band.

RIO MINHO *6/2008*, Portuguese Navy* / 1335421

AMPHIBIOUS FORCES

Notes: Four new LCMs are to be constructed as part of the LPD (NAVPOL) contract.

0 + 1 AMPHIBIOUS TRANSPORT SHIP (LPD)

Name	*No*	*Builders*	*Laid down*	*Launched*	*Commissioned*
ALFONSO DE ALBUQUERQUE	–	Viana do Castelo Shipyard	2012	2013	2014

Displacement, tons: 10,500 full load
Dimensions, feet (metres): 531.5 × 82.0 × 17.1 *(162.0 × 25.0 × 5.2)*
Flight deck, feet (metres): To be announced
Main machinery: Diesel-electric; 4 diesels; 18,775 hp *(14 MW)*; 2 shafts
Speed, knots: 19. **Range, n miles:** 6,000 at 14 kt
Complement: 150
Military lift: 650 troops; 4 LCM, 76 vehicles (including 40 light armoured vehicles), 53 light inflatable boats, 3,000 m^3 of storage space

Missiles: SAM: 2 RAM 21-cell Mk 49 launchers.
Guns: Medium calibre and CIWS.
Countermeasures: To be announced.
Combat data systems: To be announced.
Weapons control: To be announced.
Radars: Air/surface search: 3D radar to be announced.
Surface search: To be announced.
Navigation: To be announced.

Helicopters: Landing spots for 4 EH-101 or 6 Lynx.

Programmes: The Portuguese Ministry of Defence signed a Declaration of Intentions on 16 February 2005 with ENVC Shipyard for the design and construction of a Landing Platform Dock (LPD). The contract is understood to be part of an offset agreement arising from the contract with the German Submarine Consortium for two Type 209PN submarines. The project is known as Navio Polivalente Logístico (NAVPOL). Construction of LCMs is understood to be included in the contract.
Structure: The design is very similar to the Schelde Enforcer 1300 and is to include a dock, flight deck, hangar, vehicle garage and hospital.
Operational: Following endorsement of the Portuguese National Defence Strategic Concept (NDSC) in 2003, the new LPD is to be the centrepiece of the future Portuguese Navy and is to be designed to support worldwide joint operations of national and allied armed forces, including humanitarian aid and/or disaster relief. The ship is to be capable of projecting and supporting a battalion of troops.

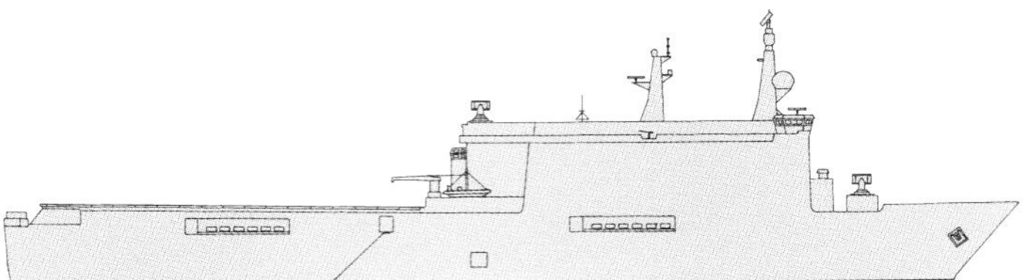

NAVPOL *(Scale 1 : 1,500), Ian Sturton* / 1153002

1 BOMBARDA CLASS (LCU)

Name	*No*	*Builders*	*Commissioned*
BACAMARTE	LDG 203	Arsenal do Alfeite	Dec 1985

Displacement, tons: 652 full load
Dimensions, feet (metres): 184.3 × 38.7 × 6.2 *(56.2 × 11.8 × 1.9)*
Main machinery: 2 MTU MB diesels; 910 hp(m) *(669 kW)*; 2 shafts
Speed, knots: 9.5. **Range, n miles:** 2,600 at 9 kt
Complement: 21 (3 officers)
Military lift: 350 tons
Guns: 2 Oerlikon 20 mm.
Radars: Navigation: Decca RM 316P; I-band.

Comment: Similar to French EDIC. To be decommissioned in 2015.

BACAMARTE *10/2006, Adolfo Ortigueira Gil* / 1040678

SURVEY SHIPS

2 STALWART CLASS (AGS)

Name	*No*	*Builders*	*Commissioned*
D. CARLOS I (ex-*Audacious*, ex-*Dauntless*)	A 522 (ex-T-AGOS 11)	Tacoma Boat	18 June 1989
ALMIRANTE GAGO COUTINHO (ex-*Assurance*)	A 523 (ex-T-AGOS 5)	Tacoma Boat	1 May 1985

Displacement, tons: 2,285 full load
Dimensions, feet (metres): 224 × 43 × 15.9 *(68.3 × 13.1 × 4.6)*
Main machinery: Diesel-electric; 4 Caterpillar D 398B diesel generators; 3,200 hp *(2.39 MW)*; 2 GE motors; 1,600 hp *(1.2 MW)*; 2 shafts; bow thruster; 550 hp *(410 kW)*
Speed, knots: 11. **Range, n miles:** 4,000 at 11 kt; 6,450 at 3 kt
Complement: 31 (6 officers) plus 15 scientists
Radars: Navigation: 2 Raytheon; I-band.

Comment: Paid off from USN in November 1995. First one acquired 21 July 1996. Refitted to serve as a hydrographic ship, operating predominantly off the west coast of Africa. Recommissioned 9 December 1996. A second of class acquired by gift 30 September 1999, has been similarly refitted and recommissioned 26 January 2000.

D. CARLOS I *11/2006, Marco Ghiglino* / 1164952

2 ANDROMEDA CLASS (AGSC)

Name	*No*	*Builders*	*Commissioned*
ANDROMEDA	A 5203	Arsenal do Alfeite	1 Feb 1987
AURIGA	A 5205	Arsenal do Alfeite	1 July 1987

Displacement, tons: 245 full load
Dimensions, feet (metres): 103.3 × 25.4 × 8.2 *(31.5 × 7.7 × 2.5)*
Main machinery: 1 MTU 12V 396 TC62 diesel; 1,200 hp(m) *(880 kW)* sustained; 1 shaft
Speed, knots: 12
Range, n miles: 1,980 at 10 kt
Complement: 17 (3 officers)
Radars: Navigation: Koden; I-band.

Comment: Both ordered in January 1984. *Auriga* has a research submarine ROV Phantom S2 and a Klein side scan sonar. Mostly used for oceanography.

ANDROMEDA *8/1997, van Ginderen Collection* / 0012932

3 SURVEY CRAFT (YGS)

CORAL UAM 801 **ATLANTA** (ex-*Hidra*) UAM 802 **FISALIA** UAM 805

Comment: Craft are of 36 tons launched in 1980.

FISALIA *3/1992, van Ginderen Collection* / 0081611

TRAINING SHIPS

1 SAIL TRAINING SHIP (AXS)

Name	*No*	*Builders*	*Commissioned*
SAGRES (ex-*Guanabara*, ex-*Albert Leo Schlageter*)	A 520	Blohm + Voss, Hamburg	10 Feb 1938

Displacement, tons: 1,725 standard; 1,940 full load
Dimensions, feet (metres): 231 wl; 295.2 oa × 39.4 × 17 *(70.4; 90 × 12 × 5.2)*
Main machinery: 2 MTU 12V 183 TE92 auxiliary diesels; 1 shaft
Speed, knots: 10.5
Range, n miles: 5,450 at 7.5 kt on diesel
Complement: 162 (12 officers)
Radars: Navigation: 1 Racal Decca and 1 KH 1500 Nucleos 2; I-band.

Comment: Former German sail training ship launched 30 October 1937. Sister of US Coast Guard training ship *Eagle* (ex-German *Horst Wessel*) and Soviet *Tovarisch* (ex-German *Gorch Fock*). Taken by the USA as a reparation after the Second World War in 1945 and sold to Brazil in 1948. Purchased from Brazil and commissioned in the Portuguese Navy on 2 February 1962 at Rio de Janeiro and renamed *Sagres*. Sail area, 20,793 sq ft. Height of main mast, 142 ft. Phased refits 1987–88 and again in 1991–92 which included new engines, improved accommodation, hydraulic crane and updated navigation equipment. A further refit is planned 2011–13.

SAGRES *7/2006, B Prézelin* / 1040679

1 SAIL TRAINING SHIP (AXS)

Name	*No*	*Builders*	*Commissioned*
CREOULA	UAM 201	Lisbon Shipyard	1937

Displacement, tons: 818 standard; 1,055 full load
Dimensions, feet (metres): 221.1 × 32.5 × 13.8 *(67.4 × 9.9 × 4.2)*
Main machinery: 1 MTU 8V 183 TE92 auxiliary diesel; 665 hp(m) *(490 kW)*; 1 shaft

Comment: Ex-deep sea sail fishing ship used off the coast of Newfoundland for 36 years. Bought by Fishing Department in 1976 to turn into a museum ship but because she was still seaworthy it was decided to convert her to a training ship. Recommissioned in the Navy in 1987. Refit completed in 1992 including a new engine and improved accommodation. A life-extension refit is under consideration.

CREOULA *6/2005, Portuguese Navy* / 1153417

1 SAIL TRAINING YACHTS (AXS)

POLAR (ex-*Anne Linde*) A 5204

Displacement, tons: 70
Dimensions, feet (metres): 75 × 16 × 8.2 *(22.9 × 4.9 × 2.5)*
Radars: Navigation: Raytheon; I-band.

Comment: Sail number P-551 is displayed.

POLAR *6/2007, **Portuguese Navy*** / 1166692

2 SAIL TRAINING YACHTS (AXS)

BELLATRIX UAM 813 **CANOPUS** UAM 814

Displacement, tons: 12 *(Bellatrix)*; 10 *(Canopus)*
Dimensions, feet (metres): 47.4 × 14.4 × 8.9 *(14.45 × 4.4 × 2.7) (Bellatrix)*
47.6 × 13.9 × 6.9 *(14.52 × 4.23 × 2.1) (Canopus)*
Complement: 8
Radars: Furuno; I-band.

Comment: Both attached to the naval school at Lisbon.

BELLATRIX *6/2007, **Portuguese Navy*** / 1166691

AUXILIARIES

Notes: (1) Two craft are employed on Pollution Control tasks. *Vazante* (UAM 687) is 14 tons and *Enchente* (UAM 688) is 65 tons. *Barrocas* (UAM 854) is an accommodation barge. *Marateca* (UAM 304) and *Meuro* (UAM 305) are fuel lighters.
(2) Studies for the procurement of a new AOR, to enter service in about 2016, are in progress.

1 BUOY TENDER (ABU)

Name	*No*	*Builders*	*Commissioned*
GUIA	UAM 676	S Jacinto, Aveiro	30 Jan 1985

Displacement, tons: 70 full load
Dimensions, feet (metres): 72.2 × 25.9 × 7.2 *(22 × 7.9 × 2.2)*
Main machinery: 1 Deutz MWM SBA6M816 diesel; 465 hp(m) *(342 kW)* sustained; 1 Schottel Navigator prop
Speed, knots: 8.5 (3.5 on auxiliary engine)
Complement: 6

Comment: Belongs to the Lighthouse Service.

GUIA *6/2005, **Portuguese Navy*** / 1153416

1 ROVER CLASS (REPLENISHMENT TANKER) (AORLH)

Name	*No*	*Builders*	*Launched*	*Commissioned*
BÉRRIO (ex-*Blue Rover*)	A 5210 (ex-A 270)	Swan Hunter	11 Nov 1969	15 July 1970

Displacement, tons: 4,700 light; 11,522 full load
Dimensions, feet (metres): 461 × 63 × 24 *(140.6 × 19.2 × 7.3)*
Main machinery: 2 SEMT-Pielstick 16 PA4 185 diesels; 15,360 hp(m) *(11.46 MW)*; 1 shaft; Kamewa cp prop; bow thruster
Speed, knots: 19
Range, n miles: 15,000 at 15 kt
Complement: 54 (7 officers)
Cargo capacity: 6,600 tons fuel
Guns: 2 Oerlikon 20 mm.
Countermeasures: Decoys: 2 Vickers Corvus launchers. 2 Plessey Shield launchers. 1 Graseby Type 182; towed torpedo decoy.
Radars: Navigation: Kelvin Hughes Type 1006; I-band.
Helicopters: Platform for 1 medium.

Comment: Transferred from UK and recommissioned 31 March 1993. Small fleet tanker designed to replenish oil and aviation fuel, fresh water, limited dry cargo and refrigerated stores under all conditions while under way. Full refit in 1990–91 gave a service life expectancy until 2005 and a further refit is to be undertaken to prolong life until about 2015. No hangar but helicopter landing platform is served by a stores lift, to enable stores to be transferred at sea by 'vertical lift'. Capable of HIFR. Can pump fuel at 600 m³/h. Others of the class in service in Indonesia and the UK.

BÉRRIO *4/2000, **Maritime Photographic*** / 0105268

1 BUOY TENDER (ABU)

Name	*No*	*Builders*	*Commissioned*
SCHULTZ XAVIER	A 521	Alfeite Naval Yard	14 July 1972

Displacement, tons: 900 full load
Dimensions, feet (metres): 184 × 33 × 12.5 *(56 × 10 × 3.8)*
Main machinery: 2 diesels; 2,400 hp(m) *(1.76 MW)*; 2 shafts
Speed, knots: 14.5
Range, n miles: 3,000 at 12.5 kt
Complement: 54 (4 officers)

Comment: Used for servicing navigational aids and as an occasional tug. Expected to be decommissioned in 2013 and replaced by Viano do Castelo class.

SCHULTZ XAVIER *12/2006, **Marco Ghiglino*** / 1164951

8 CALMARIA CLASS (HARBOUR PATROL CRAFT) (YP)

CALMARIA UAM 642
CIRRO UAM 643
VENDAVAL UAM 644
MONCÃO UAM 645
SUÃO UAM 646
MACAREU UAM 647
PREIA-MAR UAM 648
BAIXA-MAR UAM 649

Displacement, tons: 12 full load
Dimensions, feet (metres): 39 × 12.5 × 2.3 *(11.9 × 3.8 × 0.7)*
Main machinery: 2 Bazán MAN 2866 LXE diesels; 881 hp(m) *(648 kW)*; 2 water-jets
Speed, knots: 32
Range, n miles: 275 at 20 kt
Complement: 3
Guns: 1 — 7.62 mm MG.
Radars: Surface search: Furuno 1830; I-band.

Comment: Harbour patrol craft similar to Spanish Guardia Civil del Mar Saetta II craft. Ordered from Bazán, Cadiz on 8 January 1993. First pair completed 30 November 1993, third one on 18 January 1994. Remainder delivered between August and December 1994. GRP hulls.

BAIXA-MAR *5/2008*, Marco Ghiglino* / 1335414

55 MISCELLANEOUS SERVICE CRAFT (YAG)

UAM 101–102	**UAM 612**	**UAM 636**	**UAM 669**	**UAM 852**
UAM 122	**UAM 618–619**	**UAM 639**	**UAM 673**	**UAM 901**
UAM 203	**UAM 623–624**	**UAM 640–641**	**UAM 675**	**UAM 907–908**
UAM 304	**UAM 626**	**UAM 650–651**	**UAM 684–696**	**UAM 913**
UAM 601–602	**UAM 629**	**UAM 659**	**UAM 810–812**	**UAM 918**
UAM 605	**UAM 631**	**UAM 662**	**UAM 830**	
UAM 610	**UAM 634**	**UAM 667**	**UAM 840**	

Displacement, tons: 18 full load
Dimensions, feet (metres): 47.6 × 14.1 × 2.6 *(14.5 × 4.3 × 0.8)*
Main machinery: 2 diesels; 640 hp *(478 kW)*; 2 waterjets
Speed, knots: 27
Range, n miles: 150 at 15 kt

Comment: Details are for UAM 601-602 commissioned in 2007. The remaining craft are personnel and other service craft.

UAM 696 *4/2008*, Marco Ghiglino* / 1335413

UAM 852 *3/2002, Diego Quevedo* / 0534049

GOVERNMENT MARITIME FORCES

POLICE (GUARDIA NACIONAL REPUBLICANA)

12 CONAFI 55 CLASS

Displacement, tons: 18 full load
Dimensions, feet (metres): 55.8 × 12.5 × 2.9 *(17.0 × 3.8 × 0.9)*
Main machinery: 2 MTU 12V 183TE93 diesels; 2,400 hp(m) *(1.8 MW)*; 2 waterjets
Speed, knots: 48
Range, n miles: 400 at 18 kt
Complement: 5

Comment: Built at Conafi Shipyards with collaboration with Rodman and delivered between 2000 and 2002.

CONAFI 55 *10/2006, Adolfo Ortigueira Gil* / 1040675

4 RODMAN 38 CLASS (PB)

Displacement, tons: 10 full load
Dimensions, feet (metres): 36.1 × 12.8 × 2.3 *(11.0 × 3.9 × 0.7)*
Main machinery: 2 diesels; 400 hp *(300 kW)*; 2 waterjets
Speed, knots: 28
Range, n miles: 300 at 15 kt
Complement: 4

Comment: GRP hull. Built by Rodman, Vigo in 1985–87.

RODMAN 38 *10/2006, Adolfo Ortigueira Gil* / 1040676

Qatar

Country Overview

Formerly a British protectorate from 1916, the State of Qatar gained its independence in 1971. Situated on the eastern side of the Arabian Peninsula, it occupies the Qatar Peninsula which has a 304 n mile coastline with the Gulf. With an area of 4,416 square miles, it is bordered to the south by Saudi Arabia and the United Arab Emirates. The dispute with Bahrain over sovereignty of the Hawar islands was settled on 16 March 2001. The capital, largest city and principal port is Doha. Territorial seas (12 n miles) are claimed. An EEZ (200 n miles) has been claimed but the limits are not defined.

Headquarters Appointments

Commander Naval Force:
Commodore Mohammed Nasir Al-Muhannadi
Commander Coast Guard:
Colonel Ali al-Mannai

Personnel

2009: 1,800 officers and men (including Marine Police)

Bases

Doha (main); Halul Island (secondary)

Coast Defence

Two truck-mounted batteries of Exocet MM 40 quad launchers.

Prefix to Ships' Names

QENS (Qatar Emiri Navy)

PATROL FORCES

Notes: A programme for the replacement of some or all of the attack craft inventory was launched in October 2007.

4 BARZAN (VITA) CLASS (PGGFM)

Name	*No*	*Builders*	*Laid down*	*Launched*	*Commissioned*
BARZAN	Q04	Vosper Thornycroft	Feb 1994	1 Apr 1995	9 May 1996
HUWAR	Q05	Vosper Thornycroft	Aug 1994	15 July 1995	10 June 1996
AL UDEID	Q06	Vosper Thornycroft	Mar 1995	21 Mar 1996	16 Dec 1996
AL DEEBEL	Q07	Vosper Thornycroft	Aug 1995	31 Aug 1996	3 July 1997

Displacement, tons: 376 full load
Dimensions, feet (metres): 185.7 × 29.5 × 8.2 *(56.3 × 9 × 2.5)*
Main machinery: 4 MTU 20V 538 TB93 diesels; 18,740 hp(m) *(13.8 MW)* sustained; 4 shafts
Speed, knots: 35
Range, n miles: 1,800 at 12 kt
Complement: 35 (7 officers)

Missiles: SSM: 8 Aerospatiale MM 40 Exocet (Block II) ❶; inertial cruise; active radar homing to 70 km *(40 n miles)* at 0.9 Mach; warhead 165 kg; sea-skimmer.
SAM: Matra Sadral sextuple launcher for Mistral ❷; IR homing to 4 km *(2.2 n miles)*; warhead 3 kg.
Guns: 1 OTO Melara 76 mm/62 Super Rapid ❸; 120 rds/min to 16 km *(8.7 n miles)*; weight of shell 6 kg.
1 Signaal Goalkeeper 30 mm ❹; 7 barrels; 4,200 rds/min combined to 2 km. 2—12.7 mm MGs.
Countermeasures: Decoys: CSEE Dagaie Mk 2 ❺ for chaff and IR flares.
ESM: Thomson-CSF DR 3000S ❻; intercept.
ECM: Dassault Salamandre ARBB 33 ❼; jammer.
Combat data systems: Signaal SEWACO FD with Thomson-CSF TACTICOS; Link Y.
Weapons control: Signaal STING optronic director. Signaal IRSCAN electro-optical tracker ❽.
Radars: Air/surface search: Thomson-CSF MRR ❾; G-band.
Navigation: Kelvin Hughes 1007 ❿; I-band.
Fire control: Signaal STING ⓫; I/J-band.

Programmes: Order announced on 4 June 1992 by Vosper Thornycroft. First steel cut 20 July 1993.
Structure: Vita design derivative based on the hull used for Oman and Kenya in the 1980s. Steel hull and aluminium superstructure. CSEE Sidewind EW management system is installed and a Racal Thorn data distribution system is used. Baffles have been added around the ECM aerials to prevent mutual interference with other sensors. An advanced machinery control and surveillance system allows one-man operation of main propulsion, electrical generation and auxiliary systems from the bridge. The bridge staff are also able to monitor the state of all compartments for damage control purposes.
Operational: First pair arrived in the Gulf in August 1997, second pair in May 1998. All of the class carry 40 kt RIBs with twin 60 hp outboards.

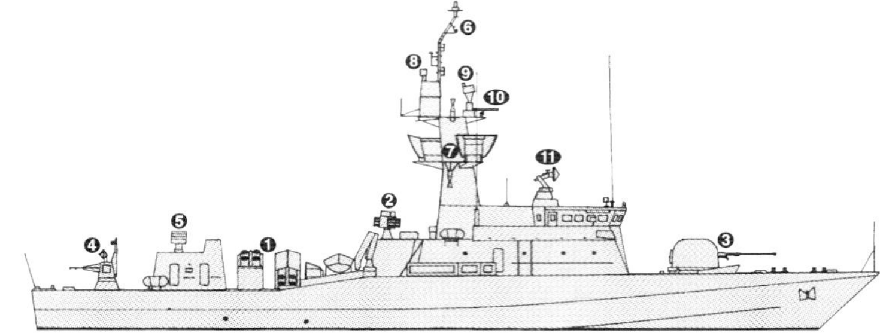

BARZAN *(Scale 1 : 600), Ian Sturton* / 0012934

AL DEEBEL *7/2001, Ships of the World* / 0121395

AL DEEBEL *10/2000* / 0121394

3 DAMSAH (COMBATTANTE III M) CLASS (FAST ATTACK CRAFT—MISSILE) (PGGF)

Name	*No*	*Builders*	*Launched*	*Commissioned*
DAMSAH	Q 01	CMN, Cherbourg	17 June 1982	10 Nov 1982
AL GHARIYAH	Q 02	CMN, Cherbourg	23 Sep 1982	10 Feb 1983
RBIGAH	Q 03	CMN, Cherbourg	22 Dec 1982	11 May 1983

Displacement, tons: 345 standard; 395 full load
Dimensions, feet (metres): 183.7 × 26.9 × 7.2 *(56 × 8.2 × 2.2)*
Main machinery: 4 MTU 20V 538 TB93 diesels; 18,740 hp(m) *(13.8 MW)* sustained; 4 shafts
Speed, knots: 38.5. **Range, n miles:** 2,000 at 15 kt
Complement: 41 (6 officers)

Missiles: SSM: 8 Aerospatiale MM 40 Exocet; inertial cruise; active radar homing to 70 km *(40 n miles)* at 0.9 Mach; warhead 165 kg; sea-skimmer.
Guns: 1 OTO Melara 3 in *(76 mm)*/62; 60 rds/min to 16 km *(8.7 n miles)*; weight of shell 6 kg.
2 Breda 40 mm/70 (twin); 300 rds/min to 12.5 km *(6.8 n miles)*; weight of shell 0.96 kg.
4 Oerlikon 30 mm/75 (2 twin); 650 rds/min to 10 km *(5.5 n miles)*.
Countermeasures: Decoys: CSEE Dagaie trainable single launcher; 6 containers; IR flares and chaff; H/J-band.
ESM/ECM: Racal Cutlass/Cygnus.
Weapons control: Vega system. 2 CSEE Naja optical directors.
Radars: Surface search: Thomson-CSF Triton; G-band.
Navigation: Racal Decca 1226; I-band.
Fire control: Thomson-CSF Castor II; I/J-band; range 15 km *(8 n miles)* for 1 m² target.

Programmes: Ordered in 1980. All arrived at Doha July 1983. All refitted in 1996/98.

AL GHARIYAH ***10/2001*** / 0121393

RBIGAH ***7/2001, Ships of the World*** / 0121396

3 DAMEN POLYCAT 1450 CLASS (COASTAL PATROL CRAFT) (PB)

Q 31–36 series

Displacement, tons: 18 full load
Dimensions, feet (metres): 47.6 × 15.4 × 4.9 *(14.5 × 4.7 × 2.1)*
Main machinery: 2 Detroit 12V-71TA diesels; 840 hp *(627 kW)* sustained; 2 shafts
Speed, knots: 26
Complement: 11
Guns: 1 Oerlikon 20 mm
Radars: Navigation: Racal Decca; I-band

Comment: Three remain of six delivered February-May 1980.

Q 33 ***3/1980, Damen SY*** / 0081617

AUXILIARIES

Notes: There are a number of amphibious craft including an LCT *Rabha* of 160 ft *(48.8 m)* with a capacity for three tanks and 110 troops, acquired in 1986–87. Also four Rotork craft and 30 Sea Jeeps in 1985. It is not clear how many of the smaller craft are for civilian use.

POLICE

Notes: (1) Requirements have been reported for patrol craft, two of 24 m, two of 22 m and 19 of 12 m. Also for two hovercraft.
(2) Two Halmatic 18 m pilot boats (based on Arun class lifeboat hull) delivered in 2000.

4 CRESTITALIA MV-45 CLASS (PB)

RG 91–94

Displacement, tons: 17 full load
Dimensions, feet (metres): 47.6 × 12.5 × 2.6 *(14.5 × 3.8 × 0.8)*
Main machinery: 2 diesels; 1,270 hp(m) *(933 kW)*; 2 shafts
Speed, knots: 32
Range, n miles: 275 at 29 kt
Complement: 6
Guns: 1 Oerlikon 20 mm. 2—7.62 mm MGs.
Radars: Surface search: I-band.

Comment: Built by Crestitalia and delivered in mid-1989. GRP construction.

4 DV 15 FAST INTERCEPT CRAFT (HSIC)

Displacement, tons: 12 full load
Dimensions, feet (metres): 50.9 × 9.8 × 2.6 *(15.5 × 3.0 × 0.8)*
Main machinery: 2 diesels; 2 surface drives
Speed, knots: 55
Range, n miles: 400 at 30 kt
Complement: 4
Guns: 1 — 12.7 mm MG.
Radars: Surface search: I-band.

Comment: Built by CMN Cherbourg and delivered in 2006 to replace P 1200 class. The option for a further two craft has not been taken up. Composite hull construction similar to those in Yemeni service. Roles include coastal protection and security of offshore oil and gas installations.

DV 15 class *2/2003, CMN* / 0531701

3 HALMATIC M 160 CLASS (PB)

Displacement, tons: 20 full load
Dimensions, feet (metres): 52.5 × 15.4 × 4.6 *(16 × 4.7 × 1.4)*
Main machinery: 2 MTU diesels; 520 hp(m) *(388 kW)* sustained; 2 shafts
Speed, knots: 27
Range, n miles: 500 at 17 kt
Complement: 6
Guns: 1 — 7.62 mm MG.
Radars: Surface search: Racal Decca; I-band.

Comment: Order confirmed on 11 October 1995. Delivered to Police in November 1996. Similar to Police craft obtained by Caribbean countries.

HALMATIC 739 *3/2008*, Michael Nitz* / 1353278

Romania

Country Overview

Situated in south-eastern Europe, the Republic of Romania has an area of 91,700 square miles and is bordered to the north by Ukraine and Moldova, to the west by Hungary and Serbia, and to the south by Bulgaria. The River Danube forms much of the southern border. Romania has a coastline of 121 n miles with the Black Sea on which Constanta, linked to the Danube port of Cernavodà by canal, is the principal seaport. Prominent river ports include Galati and Bràila on the lower Danube, and Giurgiu, which has pipeline connections to the Ploiesti oil fields. The capital and largest city is Bucharest. Territorial waters (12 n miles) are claimed. An EEZ (299 n miles) is claimed but the limits have not been defined.

Headquarters Appointments

Commander-in-Chief of the Navy:
Rear Admiral Dorin Dănilă

Personnel

a) 2009: 8,215 Navy
b) Reserves: 500

Organisation

The Navy is composed of the Naval Forces Staff (Bucharest), the Naval Operational Command, Fleet Command, Naval Academy, Hydrographic Directorate, Naval Academy, Diving Centre, Electronic Warfare Unit, Logistic Base and one Naval Infantry Battalion.

Bases

Black Sea-Mangalia (Training); Constanta (Naval Operational Command and Naval Logistic Base)
Danube-Brăila, Tulcea

Border Guard

Responsible for land and sea borders and has four brigades, two of which have sea forces based at Orsova and Constanta.

Strength of the Fleet

Type	*Active (Reserve)*
Frigates	3
Corvettes	4
Patrol craft	24
Minelayer/MCM Support	1
Minesweepers (Coastal and River)	4
Training Ships	2
Survey Ships	2

PENNANT LIST

Frigates

111	Marasesti
221	Regele Ferdinand
222	Regina Maria

Corvettes

260	Admiral Petre Barbuneanu
263	Vice Admiral Eugeniu Rosca
264	Contre Admiral Eustatiu Sebastian
265	Admiral Horia Macelariu

Patrol Forces

45	Mikhail Kogalniceanu
46	I C Bratianu
47	Lascar Catargiu
176	Rahova
177	Opanez
178	Smardan
179	Posada
180	Rovine
188	Zborul
189	Pescarusul
190	Lastunul

Mine Warfare Forces

24	Lieutenant Remus Lepri
25	Lieutenant Lupu Dunescu
29	Lieutenant Dimitrie Nicolescu
30	Sub Lieutenant Alexandru Axente
274	Vice Admiral Constantin Balescu

Survey Ships

75	Grigore Antipa
115	Emil Racovita

Training Ships

288	Mircea
521	Delfinul

Auxiliaries

281	Constanta
283	Midia
296	Electronica
298	Magnetica
500	Grozavu
501	Hercules
532	Tulcea

SUBMARINES

Notes: The Kilo-class submarine *Delfinul* 521 has not been to sea in recent years and there are no plans to refit her.

FRIGATES

2 BROADSWORD CLASS (TYPE 22) (FFHM)

Name	*No*	*Builders*	*Laid down*	*Launched*	*Commissioned*	*Recommissioned*
REGINA MARIA (ex-*London*)	222 (ex-F 95)	Yarrow Shipbuilders, Glasgow	7 Feb 1983	27 Oct 1984	5 June 1987	21 Apr 2005
REGELE FERDINAND (ex-*Coventry*)	221 (ex-F 98)	Swan Hunter Shipbuilders, Wallsend-on-Tyne	29 Mar 1984	8 Apr 1986	14 Oct 1988	9 Sep 2004

Displacement, tons: 4,100 standard; 4,800 full load
Dimensions, feet (metres): 480.5 × 48.5 × 21 (*146.5 × 14.8 × 6.4*)
Main machinery: CODOG: 2 RR Olympus TM3B gas turbines; 50,000 hp (*37.3 MW*) sustained; 2 RR Tyne RM1C gas turbines; 9,900 hp (*7.4 MW*); 2 shafts; cp props
Speed, knots: 30; 18 on Tynes
Complement: 203

Guns: 1 OTO Melara 3 in (*76 mm*)/62 Super Rapid ❶; 120 rds/min to 16 km (*8.7 n miles*); weight of shell 6 kg.
Torpedoes: 6–324 mm Plessey STWS Mk 2 (2 triple) tubes.
Countermeasures: Decoys: 2 Terma 130 mm DL-12 12-barrelled chaff launchers ❷.
Combat data systems: Ferranti CACS 1.
Weapons control: Radamec 2500 optronic director ❸. Nautis 3 fire-control system.
Radars: Air/surface search: Marconi Type 967 ❹; D/E-band.
Navigation: Kelvin-Hughes Type 1007 ❺; I-band.
Sonars: Ferranti/Thomson Sintra Type 2050; hull-mounted search and attack.

Helicopters: Platform for 1 medium.

Programmes: Originally successors to the UK Leander class, these ships entered RN service in 1987 but were withdrawn, half-way through their ships' lives, as a result of the 1998 UK Defence Review. Sale agreement signed on 14 January 2003 included platform overhaul, installation of reconditioned engines and combat system modernisation. Training is also included in the package. Following trials and sea training, *Regele Ferdinand* arrived in Romania on 10 December 2004 and *Regina Maria* in 2005. A 15-year through-life support contract with BAE Systems was signed in October 2005.
Modernisation: BAE Systems was prime contractor and FSL sub-contractor for reactivation and modernisation. The CACS command system was upgraded and 76 mm gun installed. A second-phase upgrade is to be undertaken in Romania although a firm timetable is yet to be announced. This is expected to include a towed-array sonar, air-defence and anti-ship weapons, an improved EW suite and small calibre guns.
Structure: Broadsword Batch 2 ships were stretched versions of Batch 1. The flight decks are capable of embarking medium helicopters.
Operational: Trials with a Puma helicopter were conducted in May 2008.

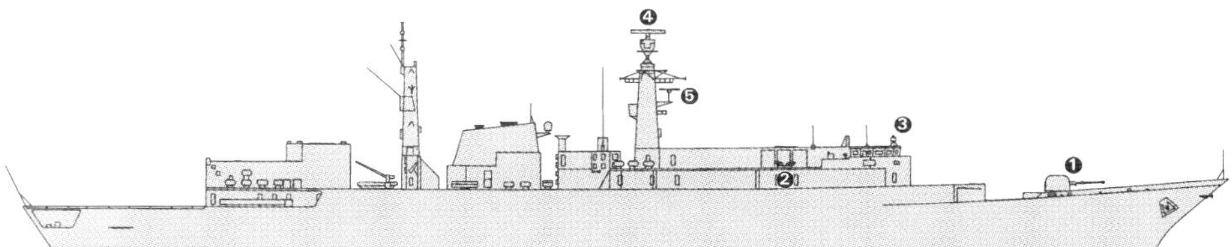

REGELE FERDINAND *(Scale 1 : 1,200), Ian Sturton* / 1044184

REGELE FERDINAND *11/2004, John Brodie* / 1133559

REGINA MARIA *6/2005, Maritime Photographic* / 1133562

REGELE FERDINAND *11/2004, B Sullivan* / 1133560

1 MARASESTI CLASS (FFGH)

Name	*No*	*Builders*	*Laid down*	*Launched*	*Commissioned*
MARASESTI (ex-*Muntenia*)	111	Mangalia Shipyard	7 Aug 1979	4 June 1981	3 June 1985

Displacement, tons: 5,790 full load
Dimensions, feet (metres): 474.4 × 48.6 × 23 *(144.6 × 14.8 × 7)*
Main machinery: 4 diesels; 32,000 hp(m) *(23.5 MW)*; 4 shafts
Speed, knots: 27
Complement: 270 (25 officers)

Missiles: SSM: 8 SS-N-2C Styx ❶; active radar or IR homing to 83 km *(45 n miles)* at 0.9 Mach; warhead 513 kg.
Guns: 4 USSR 3 in *(76 mm)*/59 AK 726 (2 twin) ❷; 90 rds/min to 16 km *(8.5 n miles)*; weight of shell 5.9 kg.
4—30 mm/65 ❸; 6 barrels per mounting; 3,000 rds/min to 2 km.
Torpedoes: 6—21 in *(533 mm)* (2 triple) tubes ❹. Russian 53—65; passive/wake homing to 25 km *(13.5 n miles)* at 50 kt; warhead 300 kg.
A/S mortars: 2 RBU 6000 ❺; 12-tubed trainable; range 6,000 m; warhead 31 kg.
Countermeasures: Decoys: 2 PK 16 chaff launchers.
ESM/ECM: 2 Watch Dog; intercept. Bell Clout and Bell Slam.
Radars: Air/surface search: Strut Curve ❻; F-band.
Surface search: Plank Shave ❼; E-band.
Fire control: Two Drum Tilt ❽; H/I-band.
Hawk Screech ❾; I-band.
Navigation: Nayada (MR 212); Racal Decca; I-band.
IFF: High Pole B.
Sonars: Hull-mounted; active search and attack; medium frequency.
Helicopters: 2 IAR-316 Alouette III ❿.

Modernisation: Attempts have been made to modernise some of the electronic equipment. Also topweight problems have been addressed by reducing the height of the mast structures and lowering the Styx missile launchers by one deck. Two RBU 6000s have replaced the RBU 1200. Communications have been upgraded to enable NATO interoperability but there are no further modernisation plans.
Structure: A distinctive Romanian design. Originally thought to be powered by gas turbines but a diesel configuration including four shafts is now confirmed.

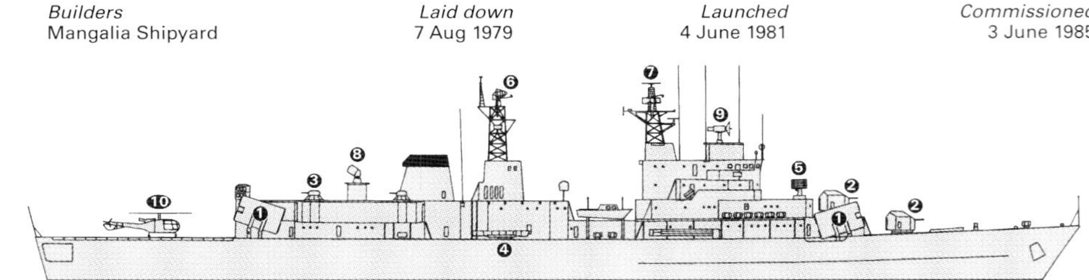

MARASESTI *(Scale 1 : 1,200), Ian Sturton* / 1044186

MARASESTI *1/2001, van Ginderen Collection* / 0106855

Operational: Deactivated in June 1988 due to manpower and fuel shortages but modernisation work was done from 1990 to 1992 and sea trials started in mid-1992. Carried out a major naval exercise in September 1993, which included firing the Styx missile. Deployed to the Mediterranean in September 1994 for a short cruise, in 1995 on two occasions and again in March 1998. Reclassified as frigate in 2001. Based at Constanta.

MARASESTI *6/2004, C D Yaylali* / 0589801

MARASESTI *7/1995, Diego Quevedo* / 0052762

CORVETTES

Notes: The multifunction corvette programme is for a class of four corvettes to replace the Tetal and Improved Tetal classes. The broad requirement is for a 2,000-ton ship that is fully compatible with NATO requirements. The ships, to be built in Romania, are likely to have ASW, ASuW and crisis-stabilisation roles. The procurement process is expected to start in 2009.

2 TETAL CLASS (FS)

Name	*No*	*Builders*	*Launched*	*Commissioned*
ADMIRAL PETRE BARBUNEANU	260	Mangalia Shipyard	23 May 1981	4 Feb 1983
VICE ADMIRAL EUGENIU ROSCA	263	Mangalia Shipyard	11 July 1985	23 Apr 1987

Displacement, tons: 1,440 full load
Dimensions, feet (metres): 303.1 × 38.4 × 9.8 *(92.4 × 11.7 × 3)*
Main machinery: 4 diesels; 13,000 hp(m) *(9.6 MW)*; 4 shafts
Speed, knots: 24
Complement: 98

Guns: 4 USSR 3 in *(76 mm)*/59 AK 726 (2 twin) ❶; 90 rds/min to 16 km *(8.5 n miles)*; weight of shell 5.9 kg.
4 USSR 30 mm/65 (2 twin) ❷; 500 rds/min to 4 km *(2.2 n miles)*; weight of shell 0.54 kg.
2—14.5 mm MGs ❸.
Torpedoes: 4—21 in *(533 mm)* (2 twin) tubes ❹. Russian 53-65; passive/wake homing to 25 km *(13.5 n miles)* at 50 kt; warhead 300 kg
A/S mortars: 2 RBU 2500 16-tubed trainable ❺; range 2,500 m; warhead 21 kg.
Countermeasures: Decoys: 2 PK 16 chaff launchers ❻.
ESM: 2 Watch Dog; intercept.

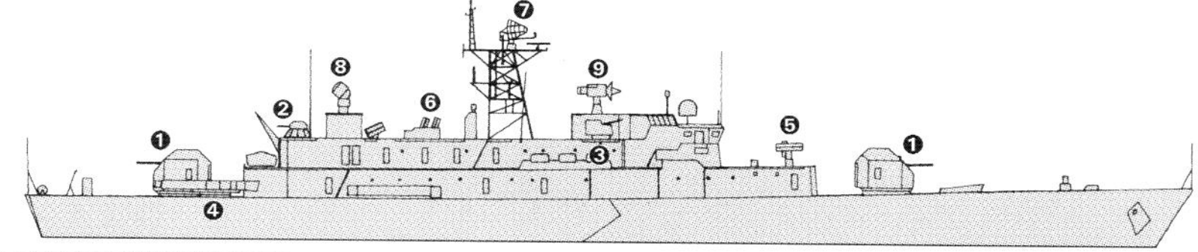

ADMIRAL PETRE BARBUNEANU

(Scale 1 : 900), *Ian Sturton* / 1167440

Radars: Air/surface search: Strut Curve ❼; F-band.
Fire control: Drum Tilt ❽; H/I-band. Hawk Screech ❾; I-band.
Navigation: Nayada; I-band.
IFF: High Pole.
Sonars: Hercules (MG 322); Hull-mounted; active search and attack; medium frequency.

Programmes: Building terminated in 1987 in favour of the improved design with a helicopter platform.
Structure: A modified Soviet Koni design.
Operational: Both based at Constanta. Two decommissioned in 2004.

ADMIRAL PETRE BARBUNEANU

5/2008, C D Yaylali* / 1353282

2 IMPROVED TETAL CLASS (FSH)

Name	*No*	*Builders*	*Launched*	*Commissioned*
CONTRE ADMIRAL EUSTATIU SEBASTIAN	264	Mangalia Shipyard	12 Apr 1988	30 Dec 1989
ADMIRAL HORIA MACELARIU	265	Mangalia Shipyard	15 May 1994	29 Sep 1997

Displacement, tons: 1,500 full load
Dimensions, feet (metres): 303.1 × 38.4 × 10 *(92.4 × 11.7 × 3.1)*
Main machinery: 4 diesels; 13,000 hp(m) *(9.6 MW)*; 4 shafts
Speed, knots: 24
Complement: 95

Guns: 1 USSR 3 in *(76 mm)*/59 AK 176 ❶; 120 rds/min to 15 km *(8 n miles)*; weight of shell 5.9 kg.
2—30 mm/65 AK 630 ❷; 6 barrels per mounting; 3,000 rds/min to 2 km.
2—30 mm/65 AK 306 ❸; 6 barrels per mounting; 3,000 rds/min to 2 km.
Torpedoes: 4—21 in *(533 mm)* (2 twin) tubes ❹. Russian 53-65; passive/wake homing to 25 km *(13.5 n miles)* at 50 kt; warhead 300 kg.
A/S mortars: 2 RBU 6000 ❺; 12-tubed trainable; range 6,000 m; warhead 31 kg.
Countermeasures: Decoys: 2 PK 16 chaff launchers ❻.
ESM: 2 Watch Dog; intercept.
Radars: Air/surface search: Strut Curve ❼; F-band.
Fire control: Drum Tilt ❽; H/I-band.
Navigation: Nayada; I-band.
IFF: High Pole.
Sonars: Hull-mounted; active search and attack; medium frequency.
Helicopters: 1 IAR-316 Aloutte III ❾.

Programmes: Follow on to Tetal class. Second of class was delayed when work stopped for a time in 1993–94.
Structure: As well as improved armament and a helicopter deck, there are superstructure changes from the original Tetals, but the hull and propulsion machinery are the same.
Operational: Both based at Mangalia.

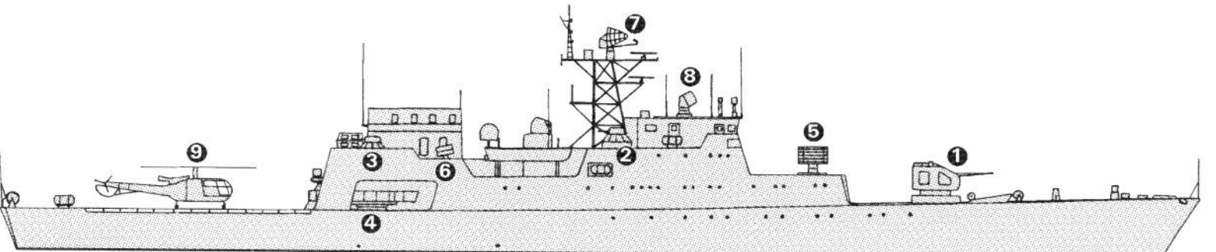

ADMIRAL HORIA MACELARIU

(Scale 1 : 900), *Ian Sturton* / 1044187

CONTRE ADMIRAL EUSTATIU SEBASTIAN

4/2007, C D Yaylali / 1167803

ADMIRAL HORIA MACELARIU

11/2007, Selim San / 1353283

SHIPBORNE AIRCRAFT

Numbers/Type: 5 IAR-316B Alouette III.
Operational speed: 113 kt *(210 km/h).*
Service ceiling: 10,500 ft *(3,200 m).*
Range: 290 n miles *(540 km).*
Role/Weapon systems: ASW helicopter. Sensors: Nose-mounted search radar. Weapons: ASW; two lightweight torpedoes.

Numbers/Type: 3 IAR Brasov 330 Puma.
Operational speed: 139 kt *(257 km/h).*
Service ceiling: 15,750 ft *(4,800 m).*
Range: 297 n miles *(550 km).*
Role/Weapon systems: Eurocopter Puma built under license in Romania. Three aircraft procured by Romanian Navy in 2008. All upgraded to SOCAT configuration undertaken by IAR Brasov and Elbit Systems, Israel. The upgrade includes improved avionics. The helicopters are used in utility and SAR roles but could be upgraded with sensors and weapons in parallel with the Type 22 frigate modernisation programme.

IAR 330 *9/2005*, ***MOD Romania*** / 1169422

LAND-BASED MARITIME AIRCRAFT

Numbers/Type: 5 Mil Mi-14PL Haze A.
Operational speed: 124 kt *(230 km/h).*
Service ceiling: 15,000 ft *(4,570 m).*
Range: 432 n miles *(800 km).*
Role/Weapon systems: Medium-range ASW helicopter. Sensors: Short Horn search radar, dipping sonar, MAD, sonobuoys. Weapons: ASW; internally stored torpedoes, depth mines and bombs.

HAZE PL (Polish colours) ***6/2000*** / 0105235

PATROL FORCES

Notes: There is a total of about 20 river patrol boats. These include three 27 ft Boston Whalers presented by the US in March 1993 for Customs/Police patrols on the Danube in support of UN sanctions operations. There is also a hovercraft built at Mangalia in 1998.

5 BRUTAR II CLASS (RIVER MONITORS) (PGR)

Name	*No*	*Builders*	*Commissioned*
RAHOVA	176	Mangalia Shipyard	14 Apr 1988
OPANEZ	177	Mangalia Shipyard	24 July 1990
SMARDAN	178	Mangalia Shipyard	24 July 1990
POSADA	179	Mangalia Shipyard	14 May 1992
ROVINE	180	Mangalia Shipyard	30 June 1993

Displacement, tons: 410 full load
Dimensions, feet (metres): 150 × 26.4 × 4.9 *(45.7 × 8 × 1.5)*
Main machinery: 2 diesels; 2,700 hp(m) *(2 MW)*; 2 shafts
Speed, knots: 16
Guns: 1—100 mm (tank turret). 2—30 mm (twin). 10—14.5 mm (2 quad, 2 single) MGs. 2—122 mm BM-21 rocket launchers; 40-tubed trainable.
Radars: Navigation: I-band.

Comment: Operational as patrol craft on the Danube. The first is a Brutar I. The next pair are Brutar IIs based at Tulcea and the last two are Brutar IIs based at Mangalia.

OPANEZ *10/2003*, ***Freddy Philips*** / 0589804

ROVINE *6/2008**, ***Lemachko Collection*** / 1353281

12 VD 141 CLASS (RIVER PATROL CRAFT) (PBR)

141–165 series

Displacement, tons: 97 full load
Dimensions, feet (metres): 109 × 15.7 × 2.8 *(33.3 × 4.8 × 0.9)*
Main machinery: 2 diesels; 870 hp(m) *(640 kW)*; 2 shafts
Speed, knots: 13
Guns: 4—14.5 mm (2 twin) MGs.
Mines: 6.
Radars: Navigation: Nayada; I-band.

Comment: Built in Romania at Dobreta Severin Shipyard 1976–84. Ex river minesweepers now employed as patrol craft on the Danube.

VD 159 *6/2008**, ***Lemachko Collection*** / 1353279

3 KOGALNICEANU CLASS (RIVER MONITORS) (PGR)

Name	*No*	*Builders*	*Recommissioned*
MIKHAIL KOGALNICEANU	45	Drobeta Santierul, Turnu Severin	19 Dec 1993
I C BRATIANU	46	Drobeta Santierul, Turnu Severin	28 Dec 1994
LASCAR CATARGIU	47	Drobeta Santierul, Turnu Severin	22 Nov 1996

Displacement, tons: 575 full load
Dimensions, feet (metres): 170.6 × 29.5 × 5.6 *(52 × 9 × 1.7)*
Main machinery: 2 24-H-165 RINS diesels; 4,400 hp(m) *(3.3 MW)*; 2 shafts
Speed, knots: 18
Guns: 2—100 mm (tank turrets). 4—30 mm (2 twin). 4—14.5 mm (2 twin). 2—122 mm BM-21 rocket launchers.
Radars: Navigation: I-band.

Comment: Based at Braila.

I C BRATIANU *6/1999*, ***Romanian Navy*** / 0081622

1 NEUSTADT CLASS (PB)

GENERAL PARASCHIV VASILESCU (ex-*Bayreuth*) 10 (ex-BG 17)

Displacement, tons: 218 full load
Dimensions, feet (metres): 127.1 × 23 × 5 *(38.5 × 7 × 2.2)*
Main machinery: 2 MTU MD diesels; 6,000 hp(m) *(4.41 MW)*; 1 MWM diesel; 685 hp(m) *(500 kW)*; 3 shafts
Speed, knots: 30
Range, n miles: 450 at 27 kt
Complement: 17
Guns: 2—7.62 mm MGs.
Radars: Surface search: Selenia ARP 1645; I-band.
Navigation: Racal Decca Bridgemaster MA 180/4; I-band.

Comment: Built in 1970 by Lürssen, Vegesack. Transferred from German Border Guard on 10 January 2004. Operated by the Romanian Border Guard and based in Constanta.

3 ZBORUL (TARANTUL I) CLASS (PROJECT 1241 RE) (FSG)

Name	*No*	*Builders*	*Commissioned*
ZBORUL	188	Petrovsky Shipyard	Dec 1990
PESCARUSUL	189	Petrovsky Shipyard	Feb 1992
LASTUNUL	190	Petrovsky Shipyard	Feb 1992

Displacement, tons: 385 standard; 455 full load
Dimensions, feet (metres): 184.1 × 37.7 × 8.2 *(56.1 × 11.5 × 2.5)*
Main machinery: COGAG; 2 Type DR 77 gas turbines; 16,016 hp(m) *(11.77 MW)* sustained; 2 Nikolayev Type DR 76 gas turbines with reversible gearboxes; 4,993 hp(m) *(3.67 MW)* sustained; 2 shafts
Speed, knots: 36
Range, n miles: 2,000 at 20 kt; 400 at 36 kt
Complement: 41 (5 officers)

Missiles: 4 SS-N-2C Styx (2 twin); active radar or IR homing to 83 km *(45 n miles)* at 0.9 Mach; warhead 513 kg.
Guns: 1 USSR 3 in *(76 mm)*/59 AK 176; 120 rds/min to 15 km *(8 n miles)*; weight of shell 5.9 kg.
2—30 mm/65 AK 630; 6 barrels per mounting; 3,000 rds/min to 2 km.
Countermeasures: 2 PK 16 chaff launchers.
ESM: 2 Watch Dog; intercept.
Weapons control: Hood Wink optronic director.
Radars: Air/surface search: Plank Shave; E-band.
Fire control: Bass Tilt; H/I-band.
Navigation: Spin Trough; I-band.
IFF: Square Head. High Pole.

Comment: Built in 1985 and later transferred from the USSR. Export version similar to those built for Poland, India and Yemen. Based at Mangalia. *Pescarusul* carried out SS-N-2C firing on 28 May 2006.

LASTUNUL *6/1998, Valentino Cluru / 0052766*

MINE WARFARE FORCES

Notes: The MCMV programme is for a class of four ships to replace the Corsar and Musca classes. The broad requirement is for a minehunter equipped with mine-detection sonar, unmanned vehicles for mine-detection and destruction and a decompression chamber for EOD teams. The procurement process is expected to start in 2009.

1 CORSAR CLASS (MINELAYER/MCM SUPPORT SHIP) (ML/MCS)

Name	*No*	*Builders*	*Commissioned*
VICE ADMIRAL CONSTANTIN BALESCU	274	Mangalia Shipyard	16 Nov 1981

Displacement, tons: 1,450 full load
Dimensions, feet (metres): 259.1 × 34.8 × 11.8 *(79 × 10.6 × 3.6)*
Main machinery: 2 diesels; 6,400 hp(m) *(4.7 MW)*; 2 shafts
Speed, knots: 19
Complement: 75
Guns: 1—57 mm/70. 4—30 mm/65 (2 twin) AK 230. 8—14.5 mm (2 quad) MGs.
A/S mortars: 2 RBU 1200 5-tubed fixed; range 1,200 m; warhead 34 kg.
Mines: 200.
Countermeasures: ESM: Watch Dog; intercept.
Radars: Air/surface search: Strut Curve; F-band.
Navigation: Don 2; I-band.
Fire control: Muff Cob; G/H-band. Drum Tilt; H/I-band.
Sonars: Tamir II; hull-mounted; active search; high frequency.

Comment: Has a large crane on the after deck. Similar to survey ship *Grigore Antipa*. Based at Constanta.

VICE ADMIRAL CONSTANTIN BALESCU *6/1999, Romanian Navy / 0081627*

4 MUSCA CLASS (MINESWEEPERS—COASTAL) (MSC)

Name	*No*	*Builders*	*Commissioned*
LIEUTENANT REMUS LEPRI	24	Mangalia Shipyard	23 Apr 1987
LIEUTENANT LUPU DUNESCU	25	Mangalia Shipyard	6 Jan 1989
LIEUTENANT DIMITRIE NICOLESCU	29	Mangalia Shipyard	7 Dec 1989
SUB LIEUTENANT ALEXANDRU AXENTE	30	Mangalia Shipyard	7 Dec 1989

Displacement, tons: 790 full load
Dimensions, feet (metres): 194.2 × 31.1 × 9.2 *(59.2 × 9.5 × 2.8)*
Main machinery: 2 diesels; 4,800 hp(m) *(3.5 MW)*; 2 shafts
Speed, knots: 17
Complement: 60
Missiles: SAM: 2 quad SA-N-5 launchers.
Guns: 4—30 mm/65 (2 twin) AK 230.
A/S mortars: 2 RBU 1200 5-tubed fixed; range 1,200 m; warhead 34 kg.
Radars: Surface search: Krivach; I-band.
Fire control: Drum Tilt; H/I-band.
Navigation: Nayada; I-band.
Sonars: Hull-mounted; active search; high frequency.

Comment: Reported as having a secondary mining capability but this is not confirmed. Based at Mangalia.

SUB LIEUTENANT ALEXANDRU AXENTE *8/2004 / 1133557*

SURVEY AND RESEARCH SHIPS

1 CORSAR CLASS (RESEARCH SHIP) (AGOR)

Name	*No*	*Builders*	*Commissioned*
GRIGORE ANTIPA	75	Mangalia Shipyard	25 May 1980

Displacement, tons: 1,450 full load
Dimensions, feet (metres): 259.1 × 34.8 × 11.8 *(79 × 10.6 × 3.6)*
Main machinery: 2 diesels; 6,400 hp(m) *(4.7 MW)*; 2 shafts
Speed, knots: 19
Complement: 75
Radars: Navigation: Nayada; I-band.

Comment: Large davits aft for launching manned submersible. Same hull as Corsar class. Used as a research ship and for diving support. Based at Constanta.

GRIGORE ANTIPA *5/1998, Diego Quevedo / 0052770*

1 RESEARCH SHIP (AGS)

Name	*No*	*Builders*	*Commissioned*
EMIL RACOVITA	115	Drobeta Severin Shipyard	30 Oct 1977

Displacement, tons: 1,900 full load
Dimensions, feet (metres): 229.9 × 32.8 × 12.7 *(70.1 × 10 × 3.9)*
Main machinery: 1 diesel; 3,285 hp(m) *(2.4 MW)*; 1 shaft
Speed, knots: 11
Complement: 80

Comment: Modernised in the mid-1980s. Similar design to *Grigore Antipa*. Used as a hydrographic ship.

EMIL RACOVITA *2001, Romanian Navy / 0114548*

TRAINING SHIPS

Notes: *Neptun* belongs to the Merchant Navy.

1 SAIL TRAINING SHIP (AXS)

Name	*No*	*Builders*	*Launched*	*Commissioned*
MIRCEA	288	Blohm + Voss, Hamburg	29 Sep 1938	29 Mar 1939

Displacement, tons: 1,604 full load
Dimensions, feet (metres): 206; 266.4 (with bowsprit) × 39.3 × 16.5 *(62.8; 81.2 × 12 × 5.2)*
Main machinery: 1 MaK 6M 451 auxiliary diesel; 1,000 hp(m) *(735 kW)*; 1 shaft
Speed, knots: 8
Range, n miles: 5,000 at 8 kt
Complement: 83 (5 officers) plus 140 midshipmen
Radars: Navigation: Decca 202; I-band.

Comment: Refitted at Hamburg in 1966. Sail area, 5,739 m² *(18,830 sq ft)*. A smaller version of US Coast Guard cutter *Eagle*, German *Gorch Fock* and Portuguese *Sagres*. Based at Constanta.

MIRCEA *7/2007, Giorgio Ghiglione* / 1353280

AUXILIARIES

2 CROITOR CLASS (LOGISTIC SUPPORT SHIPS) (AETLMH)

Name	*No*	*Builders*	*Commissioned*
CONSTANTA	281	Braila Shipyard	15 Sep 1980
MIDIA	283	Braila Shipyard	26 Feb 1982

Displacement, tons: 2,850 standard; 3,500 full load
Dimensions, feet (metres): 354.3 × 44.3 × 12.5 *(108 × 13.5 × 3.8)*
Main machinery: 2 diesels; 6,500 hp(m) *(4.8 MW)*; 2 shafts
Speed, knots: 16
Missiles: SAM: 2 SA-N-5 Grail quad launchers; manual aiming; IR homing to 6 km *(3.2 n miles)* at 1.5 Mach; warhead 1.5 kg.
Guns: 2—57 mm/70 (twin). 4—30 mm/65 (2 twin). 8—14.5 mm (2 quad) MGs.
A/S mortars: 2 RBU 1200 5-tubed fixed; range 1,200 m; warhead 34 kg.
Countermeasures: ESM: 2 Watch Dog; intercept.
Radars: Air/surface search: Strut Curve; F-band.
Navigation: Krivach; I-band.
Fire control: Muff Cob; G/H-band. Drum Tilt; H/I-band.
Sonars: Tamir II; hull-mounted; active attack; high frequency.
Helicopters: 1 IAR-316 Alouette III type.

Comment: These ships are a scaled down version of Soviet Don class. Forward crane for ammunition replenishment. Some ASW escort capability. Can carry Styx missiles and torpedoes. Based at Constanta.

CONSTANTA *6/2001, Schaeffer/Marsan* / 0533268

1 FLAG OFFICERS BARGE (AOTL)

RINDUNICA

Displacement, tons: 40 full load
Dimensions, feet (metres): 78.7 × 16.4 × 3.6 *(24 × 5 × 1.1)*
Main machinery: 2 diesels; 2,200 hp(m) *(1.6 MW)*; 2 shafts
Speed, knots: 28
Complement: 6

Comment: Used as a barge by the Commander-in-Chief.

RINDUNICA *1/1995* / 0081637

2 DEGAUSSING SHIPS (ADG/AGI)

Name	*No*	*Builders*	*Commissioned*
ELECTRONICA	296	Braila Shipyard	6 Aug 1973
MAGNETICA	298	Mangalia Shipyard	18 Dec 1989

Displacement, tons: 299 full load
Dimensions, feet (metres): 134 × 21.6 × 10.7 *(40.8 × 6.6 × 3.2)*
Main machinery: Diesel-electric; 1 diesel generator; 600 kW; 1 shaft
Speed, knots: 12.5
Complement: 18
Guns: 2—14.5 mm (twin) MGs. 2—12.7 mm MGs.

Comment: Built for degaussing ships up to 3,000 tons displacement. Electronica is used as an AGI. Based at Tulcea.

MAGNETICA *6/1999, Romanian Navy* / 0081632

2 COASTAL TANKERS (AOTL)

530–531

Displacement, tons: 1,042 full load
Dimensions, feet (metres): 181.2 × 30.9 × 13.4 *(55.2 × 9.4 × 4.1)*
Main machinery: 2 diesels; 1,800 hp(m) *(1.3 MW)*; 2 shafts
Speed, knots: 12.5
Cargo capacity: 500 tons oil
Guns: 1—37 mm. 2—12.7 mm MGs.

Comment: Built by Braila Shipyard and both commissioned 15 June 1971. Based at Constanta.

531 *6/1999, Romanian Navy* / 0081636

1 TANKER (AOT)

TULCEA 532

Displacement, tons: 2,170 full load
Dimensions, feet (metres): 250.4 × 41 × 16.4 *(76.3 × 12.5 × 5)*
Main machinery: 2 diesels; 4,800 hp(m) *(3.5 MW)*; 2 shafts
Speed, knots: 16
Cargo capacity: 1,200 tons oil
Guns: 2—30 mm/65 (twin). 4—14.5 mm (2 twin) MGs.

Comment: First one built by Tulcea Shipyard and commissioned 24 December 1992. Second of class reported in 1997 but not confirmed. Based at Constanta.

TULCEA *2001, Romanian Navy* / 0114542

TUGS

Notes: There are also a number of harbour and river tugs, some of which are armed. These include two Roslavl (101 and 116) at Mangalia.

HARBOUR TUG 570 *12/1994* / 0081638

2 OCEAN TUGS (ATA)

GROZAVU 500 **HERCULES** 501

Displacement, tons: 3,600 full load
Dimensions, feet (metres): 212.6 × 47.9 × 18 *(64.8 × 14.6 × 5.5)*
Main machinery: 2 diesels; 5,000 hp(m) *(3.7 MW)*; 2 shafts
Speed, knots: 12
Guns: 2—30 mm (twin). 8—14.5 mm (2 quad) MGs.

Comment: First one built at Oltenitza Shipyard and commissioned 29 June 1993. Second of class completed in 1995. Based at Constanta.

GROZAVU
2001, Romanian Navy
0114543

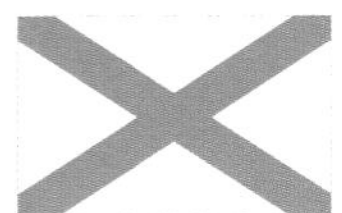

Russian Federation

ROSIYSKIY VOENNOMORSKY FLOT

Country Overview

Formerly a constituent republic of the Soviet Union, the Russian Federation was established as an independent state in 1991. The largest country in the world with an area of 6,592,850 square miles, it is bordered to the south by North Korea, China, Mongolia, Kazakhstan, Azerbaijan and Georgia and to the west by Norway, Finland, Latvia, Estonia, Ukraine and Belarus, which with Lithuania separates the Kaliningrad oblast (formerly Königsberg) from the rest of Russia. It has a 20,331 n mile coastline with the Arctic and Pacific Oceans and the Caspian, Baltic and Black Seas. These three seas are inter-connected by an extensive inland waterway system whose main components are the Volga and Don rivers, the Volga-Don canal and the Volga-Baltic Waterway. A canal also links the system to the capital and largest city, Moscow. The Amur River is the most important navigable river in the far east region. Offshore, principal islands in the Arctic Ocean include the Franz Josef Land and Severnaya Zemlya archipelagos, Novaya Zemlya, Vaygach Island, the New Siberian Islands and Wrangel Island. In the Pacific lie the Kuril Islands, which extend from the Kamchatka Peninsula, and Sakhalin Island. Principal seaports include Novorossiysk (Black Sea), St Petersburg and Kaliningrad (Baltic), Nakhodka, Vostochnyy, Vladivostok, and Vanino (Pacific) and Murmansk and Archangel (Arctic). Major river ports include Rybinsk, Nizhniy Novgorod, Samara, Volgograd, Astrakhan and Rostov-on-Don. Territorial waters (12 n miles) are claimed. An EEZ (200 n miles), is also claimed and the limits have been partly defined by boundary agreements.

Headquarters Appointments

Commander-in-Chief:
Admiral Vladimir Vysotskiy
Chief of Naval Staff:
Admiral Mikhail Abramov
Deputy Commander-in-Chief:
Admiral Alexander Tatarinov

Senior Appointments

Commander, Northern Fleet:
Vice Admiral Nikolai Maksimov
Commander, Pacific Fleet:
Vice Admiral Konstantin Sidenko
Commander, Black Sea Fleet:
Vice Admiral Alexander Kletskov
Commander, Baltic Fleet:
Vice Admiral Viktor Mardusin
Commander, Caspian Flotilla:
Rear Admiral Viktor Kravchuk

Personnel

(a) 2009: 161,000 not including naval aviation and naval infantry. The approximate division is 50,000 in the North, 41,000 in the Pacific, 36,000 in the Baltic, 23,000 in the Black Sea and 11,000 in the Caspian.
(b) Approximately 30 per cent volunteers (officers and senior ratings) – remainder two years' national service (or three years if volunteered)

Associated Navies

The Soviet Union was dissolved in December 1991. In 1992 a Commonwealth of Independent States was formed from the Republics of the former Union, but without the Baltic States. In the Baltic the Russian flotilla had withdrawn from the former East German and Polish ports by 1993 and from the Baltic Republics by the end of 1994. The Caspian flotilla divided with some units going to Azerbaijan, Kazakhstan and Turkmenistan. In the Black Sea the division of the Fleet between Russia and Ukraine was finally implemented in 1997. Facilities are shared in some Crimean ports.

Main Bases

North: Severomorsk (HQ), Polyarny, Gremika, Zapadnaya Litsa, Gadzhievo, Vidyayevo
Baltic: Kaliningrad (HQ), St Petersburg, Kronshtadt, Baltiysk
Black Sea: Sevastopol (HQ) (Crimea), Tuapse, Novorssiysk, Feodosiya
Caspian: Astrakhan (HQ), Makhachkala
Pacific: Vladivostok (HQ), Sovetskaya Gavan, Magadan, Petropavlovsk, Komsomolsk, Rybachiy, Pavlosk, Razboynik, Strelok, Rakushka Bay. A new submarine base is to be built at Vilyuchinsk, near Petropavlovsk.

Operational

From 1991 a shortage of funds to pay for dockyard repairs, spare parts and fuel meant that many major surface warships were rarely at sea, and few operated away from their local exercise areas. Activity levels temporarily rose from 1996 but many ships, although technically in commission, remained in harbour. Activity reached a low point in 2002 but, in recent years, improvements in the budgetary situation and the publication of a new naval doctrine have led to a higher operational tempo. A busier pattern of exercises and operations was initiated in 2003 and activity levels were maintained during 2007.

Coast Defence

The Command of Naval Infantry and Coastal Artillery and Missiles includes a Division of Coastal Artillery and three Mechanised Infantry (Coastal Defence Troops) Brigades, an Artillery Self-Propelled Brigade, plus the units of Naval Infantry (five Brigades and one Division) and a number of minor units. The force of Coastal Artillery includes 19 Missile Batallions (SSC-1 Sepal SS-C-3 Styx) and 11 Gun Batallions (130 mm and 152 mm). Many of these units are in reserve. The Naval Infantry were deployed in Chechnya in 2000.

Pennant Numbers

There have been no major changes to pennant numbers since 1993 except when ships transfer fleets.

Class and Weapon Systems Names

Most Russian ship class names differ from those allocated by NATO. In such cases the Russian name is placed in brackets after the NATO name. Project numbers are also placed in brackets. Weapon systems retain their NATO names with the Russian name, when known, placed in brackets. Some equipment now has three names – NATO, Russian Navy and Russian export.

Civilian Support Ships

Previously, civilian manned research ships and some icebreakers were effectively under naval control and were therefore included in the former Soviet/Russian section. These ships have been removed as all are now employed solely for commercial purposes.

Strength of the Fleet

Type	*Active*	*Building*
Submarines (SSBN)	15	2 (5)
Submarines (SSGN/SSN)	26	1
Submarines (SSK)	20	2
Auxiliary Submarines (SSA(N))	7	–
Aircraft Carriers (CV)	1	–
Battle Cruisers (CGN)	1	–
Cruisers (CG)	4	–
Destroyers (DDG)	17	–
Frigates (FFG)	7	8 (19)
Frigates (FF and FFL)	24	–
Corvettes	48	–
Patrol Forces	6	2 (2)
Minesweepers–Ocean	13	–
Minesweepers–Coastal	33	–
LSTs	18	1
Hovercraft (Amphib)	10	–
Replenishment Tankers	20	–
Hospital Ships	3	–

Notes:
There are large numbers of most classes 'in reserve', and flying an ensign so that skeleton crews may still be paid. The list above reflects only those units assessed as having some realistic operational capability or some prospect of returning to service after refit.

Fleet Disposition (1 January 2009)

Type	*Northern*	*Baltic*	*Black Sea*	*Pacific*	*Caspian*
SSBN	10	–	–	5	–
SSGN/SSN	16	–	–	9	–
SSK	7	3	1	9	–
SSA(N)	8	–	–	–	–
CV	1	–	–	–	–
CGN	1	–	–	–	–
CG	1	–	2	1	–
DDG	7	2	1	7	–
FFG	–	4	2	–	1
FF and FFL	9	–	6	9	–
Corvettes	4	19	9	14	2
LST	4	4	6	4	–
MCMV	12	10	9	8	3
AOR	7	4	3	7	–

Notes: MCMV are divided evenly between the four main Fleets plus a few in the Caspian Sea.

DELETIONS

Submarines

2006 1 Victor III *(Perm)*
2008 1 Delta III *(Borisoglebsk)*

Destroyers

2007 1 Udaloy *(Marshall Vasilevsky)*, 1 Sovremenny *(Rastoropny)*

Frigates

2006 1 Krivak I *(Letuchy)*
2007 1 Krivak *(Zadorny)*

Corvettes

2006 1 Nanuchka *(Meteor)*
2008 2 Parchim *(Bashkortostan*, MPK 67*)*

Amphibious Forces

2008 *Mitrofan Moskalenko*

PENNANT LIST

Submarines
Ballistic Missile Submarines

Borey class
– Yuri Dolgoruky
– Alexander Nevsky (bldg)
– Vladimir Monomach (bldg)

Typhoon class
806 Severstal (TK 20)
824 Dmitry Donskoy (TK 208)
828 Arkhangelsk (TK 17)

Delta IV class
805 Tula (K 114)
807 Ekaterinburg (K 84)
820 Briansk (K 117)
827 Verchoture (K 51)
839 Karelia (K 18)
849 Novomoskvosk (K 407)

Delta III class
862 Ryazan (K 44)
912 Zelenograd (K 506)
915 Podolsk (K 223)
938 Petropavlosk-Kamchatsky (K 211)
993 Syvatoy Giorgiy Pobedonosets (K 433)

Attack Submarines

Oscar II class
812 Voronezh (K 119)
816 Smolensk (K 410)
847 Orel (K 266)
902 Tomsk (K 150)
904 Cheliabinsk (K 442)
919 Krasnoyarsk (K 173)
920 Vilyachinsk (K 456)
947 Omsk (K 186)

Yasen class
– Severodvisnk (K 329) (bldg)

Akula I and II classes
– Nerpa (K 152)
835 Gepard (K 335)
853 Tigr (K 154)
867 Volk (K 461)
872 Leopard (K 328)
878 Pantera (K317)
890 Vepr (K 157)
951 Kuzbass (K 419)
970 Samara (K 295)
985 Kashalot (K 322)
997 Magadan (K 331)

Sierra I and II classes
602 Nizhny Novgorod (K 534)
648 Kostroma (K 276)
663 Pskov (K 336)

Victor III class
618 Obninsk (B 128)
654 Snezhnogorsk (B 388)
661 Tambov (B 448)
684 Danil Moskovskiy (B 414)

Auxiliary Submarines

656 Orienburg (BS 136)
AS 13 –
AS 15 –
AS 21 –
AS 23 –
AS 33 –
AS 35 –

Patrol Submarines

– Kronshtadt (bldg)
– Sevastopol (bldg)
– B 394
– B 445
405 Vologda (B 402)
409 Magneto-Gorsk (B 471)
425 Jaroslavl (B 808)
429 Lipetsk (B 177)
431 Vladikavkaz (B 459)
440 Novosibirsk (B 401)
468 Kaluga (B 800)
469 Vyborg (B 227)
477 Saint Petersburg
487 B 806
504 Chita (B 260)
507 Mogochey (B 345)
521 Krasnokamensk (B 190)
529 B 187
545 B 439
547 Ust-Kamshatsk (B 464)
549 Ust-Bolsheretsk (B 494)
554 Alrosa (B 871)

Aircraft Carriers

063 Admiral Kuznetsov

Battle Cruisers

099 Pyotr Velikiy

Cruisers

011 Varyag
055 Marshal Ustinov
121 Moskva
707 Ochakov
713 Kerch

Destroyers

400 Vitse Admiral Kulakov
406 Gremyashchiy
434 Admiral Ushakov
543 Marshal Shaposhnikov
548 Admiral Panteleyev
564 Admiral Tributs
572 Admiral Vinogradov
605 Admiral Levchenko
610 Nastoychivy
619 Severomorsk
620 Bespokoiny
650 Admiral Chabanenko
678 Admiral Kharlamov
715 Bystry
754 Bezboyaznennyy
778 Burny
810 Smetlivy

Frigates

– Admiral Gorshkov (bldg)
– Soobrazitelny (bldg)
– Boiky (bldg)
– Sovershenny (bldg)
– Stoiky (bldg)
– Dagestan (bldg)
053 Povorino
054 Eisk
055 Kasimov
059 Akelsandrovets
060 Anadyr (BG)
064 Muromets
071 Suzdalets
079 Predanyy (BG)
103 Kedrov (BG)
106 MPK 197
113 Menzhinsky (BG)
113 Yunga
129 MPK 139
138 Naryan-Mar
156 Orel (BG)
158 Dzerzhinksky (BG)
160 Vorovsky (BG)
164 Onega
170 Zorkiy (BG)
171 MPK 113
175 Pskov (BG)
178 Smelyy (BG)
190 Monchegorsk
196 Sneznogorsk
199 Brest
323 Metel
332 MPK 107
350 Sovetskaya Gavani
354 Stelyak
362 MPK 17
369 MPK 191
375 MPK 82
390 Korets
392 MPK 178
530 Steregushchiy (bldg)
691 Tatarstan
702 Pylky
712 Neustrashimy
727 Yaroslav Mudryy (bldg)
731 Neukrotimy
801 Ladny
808 Pytlivy

Training Ships

200 Perekop
210 Smolny

Corvettes

218 Aleksin
232 Kalmykia
243 MPK 227
245 MPK 105
304 MPK 192
308 Zelenodolsk
311 Kazanets
409 Moroz
418 Inej
423 Smerch
450 Razliv

Corvettes—*continued*

520 Rassvet
526 Nakat
535 Aysberg
540 Priboy
551 Liven
555 Geyzer
560 Zyb
570 Passat
615 Bora
616 Samum
617 Mirazh
620 Shtyl
705 Stupinets
825 Dmitrovgrad
874 Morshansk
954 Ivanovets

Mine Warfare Forces

402 Polyarny
418 Buevlyanin
425 Kolomna
426 Mineralny Vodi
438 Leytenant Ilin
443 Kotelnich
454 Yelnya
466 Avangard
469 Yadryn
500 Yusup Akaev
501 German Ugryumov
505 Aleksey Lebedev
522 Sergei Kolbassev
564 Magamed Gadgiev
718 MT 265
738 MT 264
770 Valentin Pikul
806 Motorist
811 V Gumavenko
831 Kommendor
855 Kontradmiral Vlasov
901 A Zheleznyakov
908 Vitse Admiral Zakharin
909 Vitse Admiral Zhukov
911 Ivan Golubets
912 Turbinist
913 Kovrovets

Amphibious Forces

012 Olenegorskiy Gorniak
016 Georgiy Pobedonosets
027 Kondopoga
031 Alexander Otrakovskiy
055 BDK-98
066 Oslyabya
077 Peresvet
081 Nikolay Vilkov
102 Kaliningrad
110 Alexander Shabalin
127 Minsk
130 Korolev
148 Orsk
150 Saratov
151 Azov
152 Nikolay Filchenkov
156 Yamal
158 Tsesar Kunikov
770 Yevgeniy Kocheshkov
782 Mordoviya

Auxiliaries

204 Apsheron
506 Dauriya
600 Zvezdochka
MB 52 Sputnik
MB 165 Serdity
MB 169 Pochetnyy
MB 171 Loksa
MB 178 Saturn
SB 3 Ayanka
SB 6 Moshchny
SB 131 Nicolay Chiker
SB 135 Fotiy Krylov
SB 921 Paradoks
SB 922 Shakhter
SFP 177 Akademik Isanin
SFP 183 Akademir Seminikhin

Intelligence Collection Ships

– Yuri Ivanov
GS 19 Zhigulevsk
GS 31 Tchusovoy
GS 39 Syzran
SSV 080 Pribaltika
SSV 169 Tavriya
SSV 175 Viktor Leonov
SSV 201 Priazove
SSV 208 Kurily
SSV 231 Vassily Tatischev
SSV 418 Ekvator
SSV 512 Kildin
SSV 520 Feodor Golovin
SSV 571 Belomore
SSV 824 Liman

SUBMARINES

Strategic Missile Submarines (SSBN)

3 TYPHOON (AKULA) CLASS (PROJECT 941/941U) (SSBN)

Name	*No*	*Builders*	*Laid down*	*Launched*	*Commissioned*
DMITRIY DONSKOY (TK 208)	824	Severodvinsk Shipyard	30 June 1976	23 Sep 1979	12 Dec 1981
ARKHANGELSK (TK 17)	828	Severodvinsk Shipyard	24 Feb 1985	Aug 1986	6 Nov 1987
SEVERSTAL (TK 20)	806	Severodvinsk Shipyard	6 Jan 1986	July 1988	4 Sep 1989

Displacement, tons: 18,500 surfaced; 26,500 dived
Dimensions, feet (metres): 562.7 oa; 541.3 wl × 80.7 × 42.7 *(171.5; 165 × 24.6 × 13)*
Main machinery: Nuclear; 2 VM-5 PWR; 380 MW; 2 GT3A turbines; 81,600 hp(m) *(60 MW)*; 2 emergency motors; 517 hp(m) *(380 kW)*; 2 shafts; shrouded props; 2 thrusters (bow and stern); 2,860 hp(m) *(1.5 MW)*
Speed, knots: 25 dived; 12 surfaced
Complement: 175 (55 officers)

Missiles: SLBM: 20 Makeyev SS-N-20 (RSM 52/3M20) Sturgeon; three-stage solid fuel rocket; stellar inertial guidance to 8,300 km *(4,500 n miles)*; warhead nuclear 10 MIRV each of 200 kT; CEP 500 m. 2 missiles can be fired in 15 seconds.
SAM: SA-N-8 SAM capability when surfaced.
A/S: Novator SS-N-15 Starfish; inertial flight to 45 km *(24.3 n miles)*; warhead nuclear 200 kT or Type 40 torpedo.
Torpedoes: 6—21 in *(533 mm)* tubes. Combination of torpedoes. The weapon load includes a total of 22 torpedoes and A/S missiles.
Mines: Could be carried in lieu of torpedoes.
Countermeasures: Decoys: MG 34/44 tube launched decoys.
ESM: Rim Hat (Nakat M); radar warning. Park Lamp D/F.

Weapons control: 3R65 data control system.
Radars: Surface search: Snoop Pair (Albatros); I/J-band.
Sonars: Shark Gill; hull-mounted; passive/active search and attack; low/medium frequency.
Shark Rib flank array; passive; low frequency.
Mouse Roar; hull-mounted; active attack; high frequency.
Pelamida towed array; passive search; very low frequency.

Modernisation: First of class TK 208 started refit at Severodvinsk in 1994, was relaunched on 26 June 2002 and started sea trials in August 2004. It conducted the first submerged test launch of the Bulava missile on 21 December 2005 and is expected to remain in service as an operational unit, although it is unclear whether some or all missile tubes have been converted for Bulava firing. TK 20 may be converted to accommodate the Bulava missile in order to remain in service beyond 2010 but the future of TK 17 is unclear.
Structure: This is the largest type of submarine ever built. Two separate 7.2 m diameter hulls covered by a single outer free-flood hull with anechoic Cluster Guard tiles plus separate 6 m diameter pressure-tight compartments in the fin and fore-ends. There is a 1.2 m separation between the outer and inner hulls along the sides. The unique features of Typhoon areher enormous size and the fact that the missile tubes are mounted forward of the fin. The positioning of the launch tubes mean a fully integrated weapons area in the bow section leaving space abaft the fin for the provision of two nuclear reactors, one in each hull. The fin configuration indicates a designed capability to break through ice cover up to 3 m thick; the retractable forward hydroplanes, the rounded hull and the shape of the fin are all related to under-ice operations. Diving depth, 1,000 ft *(300 m)*.
Operational: Strategic targets are within range from anywhere in the world. Two VLF/ELF communication buoys are fitted. VLF navigation system for under-ice operations. Pert Spring SATCOM mast, Cod Eye radiometric sextant and Kremmny 2 IFF. All based in the Northern Fleet at Zapadnaya Litsa. Of six boats completed, the second and third, TK 202 and TK 12 have been formally decommissioned while the fourth of class TK 13 is expected to follow. TK 17 was damaged by fire during a missile loading accident in 1991 but was subsequently repaired. Old hulls are being disposed of under the Co-operative Threat Reduction Programme.

SEVERSTAL ***1/1997*** / 0081639

6 DELTA IV (DELFIN) CLASS (PROJECT 667BDRM) (SSBN)

Name	*No*	*Builders*	*Laid down*	*Launched*	*Commissioned*
VERCHOTURE (K 51)	827	Severodvinsk Shipyard	23 Feb 1981	Jan 1984	29 Dec 1984
EKATERINBURG (K 84)	807	Severodvinsk Shipyard	Nov 1983	Dec 1984	Feb 1985
TULA (K 114)	805	Severodvinsk Shipyard	Dec 1985	Sep 1986	Jan 1987
BRIANSK (K 117)	820	Severodvinsk Shipyard	Sep 1986	Sep 1987	Mar 1988
KARELIA (K 18)	839	Severodvinsk Shipyard	Sep 1987	Nov 1988	Sep 1989
NOVOMOSKOVSK (K 407)	849	Severodvinsk Shipyard	Nov 1988	Oct 1989	1991

Displacement, tons: 10,800 surfaced; 13,500 dived
Dimensions, feet (metres): 544.6 oa; 518.4 wl × 39.4 × 28.5 *(166; 158 × 12 × 8.7)*
Main machinery: Nuclear; 2 VM-4 PWR; 180 MW; 2 GT3A-365 turbines; 37,400 hp(m) *(27.5 MW)*; 2 emergency motors; 612 hp(m) *(450 kW)*; 2 shafts
Speed, knots: 24 dived; 14 surfaced
Complement: 130 (40 officers)

Missiles: SLBM: 16 Makeyev SS-N-23 (R 29RM Sineva); 3-stage liquid fuel rocket; stellar inertial guidance to 8,300 km *(4,500 n miles)*; warhead nuclear 4-10 MIRV each of 100 kT; CEP 500 m. Same diameter as SS-N-18 but longer.
A/S: Novator SS-N-15 Starfish; inertial flight to 45 km *(24.3 n miles)*; warhead nuclear 200 kT or Type 40 torpedo.
Torpedoes: 4—21 in *(533 mm)* tubes. Combination of 53 cm torpedoes. Total of 18 weapons.
Countermeasures: ESM: Brick Pulp/Group; radar warning. Park Lamp D/F.

Radars: Surface search: Snoop Tray; I-band.
Sonars: Shark Gill; hull-mounted; passive/active search and attack; low/medium frequency.
Shark Hide flank array; passive; low frequency.
Mouse Roar; hull-mounted; active attack; high frequency.
Pelamida towed array; passive search; very low frequency.

Programmes: Construction first ordered 10 December 1975. This programme completed in late 1990 and included seven boats.
Modernisation: The Sineva missile is being progressively fitted throughout the class. A successful test firing from K 114 was conducted on 11 October 2008.
Structure: A slim fitting is sited on the after fin which is reminiscent of a similar tube in one of the November class in the early 1980s. This is a dispenser for a sonar thin line towed array. The other distinguishing feature, apart from the size being greater than Delta III, is the pressure-tight fitting on the after end of the missile tube housing, which may be a TV camera to monitor communications buoy and wire retrieval operations. This is not fitted in all of the class. Brick Spit optronic mast. Diving depth, 1,300 ft *(400 m)*. The outer casing has a continuous acoustic coating and fewer free flood holes than the Delta III.
Operational: Two VLF/ELF communication buoys. Navigation systems include SATNAV, SINS, Cod Eye. Pert Spring SATCOM. Missile launch is conducted at keel depth 55 m and at a speed of 6 kt.
All operational units are part of the 12th Squadron based in the Northern Fleet at Saida Guba. Long refits have been completed as follows: K 51 (1999); K 84 (2002); K 114 (2005); K 117 (2007). The refit of K 18 was reported to have started in 2007 and was completed on 23 November 2008 when the boat was floated out. The refit of K 407 will complete the refit cycle. The class is likely to remain in service until about 2020. K 64 has been paid off, but there are reports that she may be undergoing conversion to an auxiliary submarine role.

DELTA IV *6/2003, Lemachko Collection* / 1042306

KARELIA and VERCHOTURE *9/2000, Lemachko Collection* / 0126226

5 DELTA III (KALMAR) CLASS (PROJECT 667BDR) (SSBN)

Name	*No*	*Builders*	*Laid down*	*Launched*	*Commissioned*
RYAZAN (K 44)	862	Severodvinsk Shipyard	May 1978	Sep 1978	Aug 1979
ZELENOGRAD (K 506)	912	Severodvinsk Shipyard	Sep 1978	Mar 1979	Nov 1979
PETROPAVLOSK KAMCHATSKY (K 211)	938	Severodvinsk Shipyard	Apr 1979	Dec 1979	Aug 1980
PODOLSK (K 223)	915	Severodvinsk Shipyard	Nov 1979	Apr 1980	25 Dec 1980
SYVATOY GIORGIY POBEDONOSETS (K 433)	993	Severodvinsk Shipyard	Apr 1980	Nov 1980	Aug 1981

Displacement, tons: 10,550 surfaced; 13,250 dived
Dimensions, feet (metres): 524.9 oa; 498.7 wl × 39.4 × 28.5 *(160; 152 × 12 × 8.7)*
Main machinery: Nuclear; 2 VM-4 PWR; 180 MW; 2 GT3A-635 turbines; 37,400 hp(m) *(27.5 MW)*; 2 emergency motors; 612 hp(m) *(450 kW)*; 2 shafts
Speed, knots: 24 dived; 14 surfaced
Complement: 130 (20 officers)

Missiles: SLBM: 16 Makeyev SS-N-18 (RSM 50) Stingray (Volna); 2-stage liquid fuel rocket with post boost vehicle (PBV); stellar inertial guidance; 3 variants:
Mod 1; range 6,500 km *(3,500 n miles)*; warhead nuclear 3 MIRV each of 200 kT; CEP 900 m.
Mod 2; range 8,000 km *(4,320 n miles)*; warhead nuclear 450 kT; CEP 900 m.
Mod 3; range 6,500 km *(3,500 n miles)*; warhead nuclear 7 MIRV 100 kT; CEP 900 m.
Mods 1 and 3 were the first MIRV SLBMs in Soviet service.
Torpedoes: 4—21 in *(533 mm)* and 2—400 mm tubes. Combination of torpedoes. Total of 16 weapons.
Countermeasures: ESM: Brick Pulp/Group; radar warning. Park Lamp D/F.
Radars: Surface search: Snoop Tray; I-band.
Sonars: Shark Teeth; hull-mounted; passive/active search and attack; low/medium frequency.
Shark Hide flank array; passive; low frequency.
Mouse Roar; hull-mounted; active attack; high frequency.
Pelamida towed array; passive search; very low frequency.

Modernisation: The dispenser tube on the after fin has been fitted to most of the class. It was planned to retrofit SS-N-23 but this was shelved.
Structure: The missile casing is higher than in the decommissioned Delta I class to accommodate SS-N-18 missiles. The outer casing has a continuous 'acoustic' coating but is less streamlined and has more free flood holes than the Delta IV. Brick Spit optronic mast. Diving depth, 1,050 ft *(320 m)*.
Operational: ELF/VLF communications with floating aerial and buoy; UHF and SHF aerials. Navigation equipment includes Cod Eye radiometric sextant, SATNAV, SINS and Omega. Pert Spring SATCOM. Kremmny 2 IFF. Of the 14 hulls completed, the first of class (K 441) paid of in 1996, three more in 1997 and another two by 1999. Four of these (K 449, K 455, K 487 and K 490) are laid up in fleet bases. The operational state of the remaining six has been variously reported but it must be assumed that they can still fire missiles. K 44 test-fired an SS-N-18 on 1 August 2008 and thereafter conducted an Arctic transit to join the Pacific Fleet in September 2008. It became part of the 16th squadron based in Rybachiy (Kamchatka) in the Pacific. The remaining Northern Fleet unit, K 804, was decommissioned in 2008. The last hull of the class K 129 converted to a DSRV carrier with missile tubes removed. It is expected that the whole class is to have been decommissioned by about 2013.

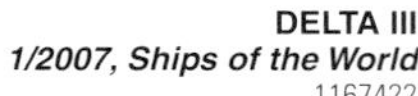
DELTA III
1/2007, Ships of the World
1167422

DELTA III ***12/2005, Ships of the World*** / 1151151

DELTA III ***1/2007, Ships of the World*** / 1167421

1 + 2 (5) BOREY CLASS (PROJECT 955/955A) (SSBN)

Name	*No*	*Builders*	*Laid down*	*Launched*	*Commissioned*
YURI DOLGORUKY	–	Sevmashpredpriyatiye, Severodvinsk	2 Nov 1996	15 Apr 2007	2009
ALEXANDER NEVSKY	–	Sevmashpredpriyatiye, Severodvinsk	19 Mar 2004	2009	2010
VLADIMIR MONOMACH	–	Sevmashpredpriyatiye, Severodvinsk	19 Mar 2006	2010	2011

Displacement, tons: 14,720 surfaced; 19,400 dived
Dimensions, feet (metres): 557.7 × 22.3 × 29.5 *(170.0 × 13.5 × 9.0)*
Main machinery: Nuclear; 2 VM-5 PWR; 380 MW; 2 GT3A turbines; 60,000 hp(m) *(44.8 MW)*; 2 emergency motors; 517 hp(m) *(380 kW)*; 1 shaft; pump jet propulsor
Speed, knots: 25 dived; 15 surfaced
Complement: 107

Missiles: SLBM: 16 Bulava 30 (R-30); three-stage solid fuel rocket; inertial guidance with stellar and Glonass update to 8,300 km *(4,500 n miles)*; warhead nuclear 6-10 MIRV each of 150 kT; CEP 250 m.
A/S: SAM: To be announced.
SSM: Possible Klub-S (a possible cruise missile capability has also been reported).
Torpedoes: 6—21 in *(533 mm)* tubes. Combination of torpedoes, A/S missiles and surface-to-surface missiles.
Mines: Could be carried in lieu of torpedoes.
Countermeasures: To be announced.
Weapons control: To be announced.
Radars: Surface search: To be announced.
Sonars: Integrated sonar suite likely to include flank array, towed array, conformal bow array and mine avoidance.

Programmes: The programme was initiated in 1982, but has been frustrated both by funding difficulties and by missile development problems. A first of class was laid down in November 1996, at which stage the plan was to field a new strategic missile SS-NX-28. This missile programme was cancelled in 1998 and construction of the boat was subsequently halted while development of a new missile, a navalised version of the SS-27 Topol-M (known as Bulava 30), was undertaken. A class of eight boats is expected.
Structure: In order to accommodate the smaller Bulava missile, the new submarine class incorporates significant modifications of the original *Yuri Dolgoruky*. Reportedly, the first of class includes the bow and stern pressure sections and propulsion train of Akula II K 337 *Cougar* whose construction was halted. Similarly, the second of class *Alexander Nevsky* (Project 955A) is said to include sections of Akula I K 333 *Rhys*. These are the first Russian nuclear submarines to be equipped with a pump-jet propulsor. Diving depth 450 m.
Operational: A full test launch of the 'Bulava' missile was conducted on 27 September 2005 from the Typhoon class SSBN, *Dmitriy Donskoy* and the first submerged launch on 21 December 2005. Unsuccessful tests followed on 7 September, 25 October and 24 December 2006. A further successful test was achieved on 28 June 2007. Tests in 2008 were conducted on 18 September (partial success), 28 November (success) and 23 December (failure). *Yuri Dolgorukiy* is expected to begin sea trials by mid-2009 and is to be based in the Northern Fleet.

YURI DOLGORUKY *4/2007* / 1167779

YURI DOLGORUKY *4/2007* / 1170213

Attack Submarines (SSN/SSGN)

Notes: Attack submarines are coated with Cluster Guard anechoic tiles. All submarines are capable of laying mines from their torpedo tubes. All SSNs are fitted with non-acoustic environmental sensors for measuring discontinuities caused by the passage of a submarine in deep water.

0 + 1 YASEN CLASS (PROJECT 885) (SSN/SSGN)

Name	*No*	*Builders*	*Laid down*	*Launched*	*Commissioned*
SEVERODVINSK (K 329)	–	Severodvinsk Shipyard	21 Dec 1993	2009	2010

Displacement, tons: 5,900 surfaced; 8,600 dived
Dimensions, feet (metres): 364.2 × 39.4 × 27.6 *(111 × 12 × 8.4)*
Main machinery: Nuclear; 1 PWR; 195 MW; 2 GT3A turbines; 43,000 hp(m) *(31.6 MW)*; 1 shaft; pump-jet propulsor; 2 spinners
Speed, knots: 28 dived; 17 surfaced
Complement: 80 (30 officers)

Missiles: SLCM/SSM: Novator Alfa SS-N-27.
8 VLS launchers in after casing. Total of 24 missiles.
A/S: SS-N-15. Fired from torpedo tubes.
Torpedoes: 8—21 in *(533 mm)* tubes. Inclined outwards. Total of about 30 weapons.
Countermeasures: ESM: Radar warning.
Radars: Surface search: I-band.
Sonars: Irtysh Amfora system includes bow-mounted spherical array; passive/active search and attack; low frequency.
Flank and towed arrays; passive; very low frequency.

Programmes: Malakhit design. Confirmed building in 1993. Reported plans were for seven of the class to replace the Victor III class. While it was initially reported that these were to be multipurpose SSNs derived from the Akula II class, delays in the the programme suggest that there has been considerable scope for re-design and/or technical upgrade. The building of a second ofclass has been reported but not confirmed.
Structure: Some of the details given are speculative. VLS launchers for SSMs, canted torpedo tubes and spherical bow sonars are all new to Russian designs.

SEVERODVINSK *6/2006, A Sheldon-Duplaix* / 1158520

8 OSCAR II (ANTYEY) (PROJECT 949B) (SSGN)

Name	*No*	*Builders*	*Laid down*	*Launched*	*Commissioned*
KRASNOYARSK (K 173)	919	Severodvinsk Shipyard	4 Aug 1983	Mar 1986	24 Feb 1987
VORONEZH (K 119)	812	Severodvinsk Shipyard	1984	1986	1988
SMOLENSK (K 410)	816	Severodvinsk Shipyard	1986	1988	1990
CHELIABINSK (K 442)	904	Severodvinsk Shipyard	1987	1989	29 Dec 1990
VILYACHINSK (K 456)	920	Severodvinsk Shipyard	1988	1990	1991
OREL (K 266) (ex-*Severodvinsk*)	847	Severodvinsk Shipyard	1989	22 May 1992	Dec 1992
OMSK (K 186)	947	Severodvinsk Shipyard	1990	8 May 1993	15 Dec 1993
TOMSK (K 150)	902	Severodvinsk Shipyard	1993	18 July 1996	28 Feb 1997

Displacement, tons: 13,900 surfaced; 18,300 dived
Dimensions, feet (metres): 505.2 × 59.7 × 29.5 *(154 × 18.2 × 9)*
Main machinery: Nuclear; 2 VM-5 PWR; 380 MW; 2 GT3A turbines; 98,000 hp(m) *(72 MW)*; 2 shafts; 2 spinners
Speed, knots: 28 dived; 15 surfaced
Complement: 107 (48 officers)

Missiles: SSM: 24 Chelomey SS-N-19 Shipwreck (Granit); inertial with command update guidance; active radar homing to 20-550 km *(10.8-300 n miles)* at 2.5 Mach; warhead 750 kg HE or 500 kT nuclear. Novator Alfa SS-N-27 may be carried in due course.
A/S: Novator SS-N-15 Starfish (Tsakra) fired from 53 cm tubes; inertial flight to 45 km *(24.3 n miles)*; warhead nuclear 200 kT or Type 40 torpedo.
Novator SS-N-16 Stallion fired from 65 cm tubes; inertial flight to 100 km *(54 n miles)*; payload nuclear 200 kT (Vodopad) or Type 40 torpedo (Veder).
Torpedoes: 4—21 in *(533 mm)* and 2—26 in *(650 mm)* tubes. Combination of 65 and 53 cm torpedoes. Total of 28 weapons including tube-launched A/S missiles.

Mines: 32 can be carried.
Countermeasures: ESM: Rim Hat; intercept.
Weapons control: Punch Bowl for third party targeting.
Radars: Surface search: Snoop Pair or Snoop Half; I-band.
Sonars: Shark Gill; hull-mounted; passive/active search and attack; low/medium frequency.
Shark Rib flank array; passive; low frequency.
Mouse Roar; hull-mounted; active attack; high frequency.
Pelamida towed array; passive search; very low frequency.

Programmes: Building of a class of 14 began in 1978. Two Oscar Is and 11 Oscar IIs were completed. Work on the 12th Oscar II (K 139, *Belgorod*) was thought to have stopped but it was announced by the Defence Minister on 16 July 2004 that the boat would be completed. Although a further announcement on 20 July 2006 said that no further funding would be made available there were reports that work had continued in 2007 but no further reports in 2008.
Modernisation: Replacement of the SS-N-19 missiles is reported to be under consideration.

Structure: SSM missile tubes are in banks of 12 either side and external to the 8.5 m diameter pressure hull; they are inclined at 40° with one hatch covering each pair, the whole resulting in the very large beam. The position of the missile tubes provides a large gap of some 4 m between the outer and inner hulls. Diving depth, 1,000 ft *(300 m)* although 2,000 ft *(600 m)* is claimed. There are 10 watertight compartments.
Operational: ELF/VLF communications buoy. All have a tube on the rudder fin as in Delta IV which is used for dispensing a thin line towed sonar array. Pert Spring SATCOM. K 119, K 410 and K 266 are based at Litsa South in the Northern Fleet and K 442, K 186, K 150, K 173 and K 456 at Tarya Bay in the Pacific. In 1999 one Northern Fleet unit deployed for the first Russian SSGN patrol in the Mediterranean for 10 years. At the same time a Pacific Fleet unit sailed to the western seaboard of the United States. The two Oscar Is (K 206 and K 525) have been scrapped. K 148 and K 132 are laid up awaiting disposal and K 141 *(Kursk)* sunk as the result of an internal weapon explosion on 12 August 2000. The submarine was raised in late 2001 and broken up ashore.

OSCAR II *11/2001, **Ships of the World*** / 0528392

OREL *6/2005, **Lemachko Collection*** / 1159844

TOMSK

6/2005, Lemachko Collection / 1159843

OSCAR II

11/2006, Ships of the World / 1159978

OREL

9/2001, Ships of the World / 0126366

11 AKULA (SCHUKA-B) CLASS (PROJECT 971/971U/09710) (SSN)

Name	*No*	*Builders*	*Laid down*	*Launched*	*Commissioned*
KASHALOT (K 322)	985	Komsomolsk Shipyard	1983	1985	1986
MAGADAN (K 331) (ex-*Narwhal*)	997	Komsomolsk Shipyard	1984	1986	1990
PANTERA (K 317)	878	Severodvinsk Shipyard	Nov 1986	May 1990	30 Dec 1990
VOLK (K 461)	867	Severodvinsk Shipyard	1986	11 June 1991	30 Dec 1991
KUZBASS (K 419) (ex-*Morzh*)	951	Komsomolsk Shipyard	1984	1989	1991
LEOPARD (K 328)	872	Severodvinsk Shipyard	Oct 1988	28 July 1992	Dec 1992
TIGR (K 154)	853	Severodvinsk Shipyard	1989	10 June 1993	Dec 1993
SAMARA (K 295) (ex-*Drakon*)	970	Komsomolsk Shipyard	1985	15 July 1994	29 July 1995
NERPA (K 152)	–	Komsomolsk Shipyard	1986	24 June 2006	2007
VEPR (II) (K 157)	890	Severodvinsk Shipyard	1991	10 Dec 1994	Dec 1995
GEPARD (II) (K 335)	835	Severodvinsk Shipyard	1991	18 Aug 1999	29 July 2001

Displacement, tons: 7,500 surfaced; 9,100 (9,500 Akula II) dived
Dimensions, feet (metres): 360.1 oa; 337.9 wl × 45.9 × 34.1 *(110; 103 × 14 × 10.4)*
Main machinery: Nuclear; 1 VM-5 PWR; 190 MW; 2 GT3A turbines; 47,600 hp(m) *(35 MW)*; 2 emergency propulsion motors; 750 hp(m) *(552 kW)*; 1 shaft; 2 spinners; 1,006 hp(m) *(740 kW)*
Speed, knots: 28 dived; 10 surfaced
Complement: 62 (31 officers)

Missiles: SLCM/SSM: Reduga SS-N-21 Sampson (Granat) fired from 21 in *(533 mm)* tubes; land-attack; inertial/terrain-following to 3,000 km *(1,620 n miles)* at 0.7 Mach; warhead nuclear 200 kT. CEP 150 m. Flies at a height of about 200 m.
Novator Alfa SS-N-27 subsonic flight with supersonic boost for terminal flight; 180 km *(97 mm)*; warhead 200 kg. May be fitted in due course.
SAM: SA-N-5/8 Strela portable launcher. 18 missiles.
A/S: Novator SS-N-15 Starfish (Tsakra) fired from 53 cm tubes; inertial flight to 45 km *(24.3 n miles)*; warhead nuclear 200 kT or Type 40 torpedo.
Novator SS-N-16 Stallion fired from 650 mm tubes; inertial flight to 100 km *(54 n miles)*; payload nuclear 200 kT (Vodopad) or Type 40 torpedo (Veder).
Torpedoes: 4—21 in *(533 mm)* and 4—25.6 in *(650 mm)* tubes. Combination of 53 and 65 cm torpedoes. Tube liners can be used to reduce the larger diameter tubes to 533 mm. Total of 40 weapons. In addition the Improved Akulas and Akula IIs have six additional 533 mm external tubes in the upper bow area.
Countermeasures: ESM: Rim Hat; intercept.
Radars: Surface search: Snoop Pair or Snoop Half with back-to-back aerials on same mast as ESM.
Sonars: Shark Gill (Skat MGK 503); hull-mounted; passive/active search and attack; low/medium frequency.
Mouse Roar; hull-mounted; active attack; high frequency.
Skat 3 towed array; passive; very low frequency.

Programmes: Malakhit design. From K 461 onwards, the Akula Is were 'improved'. K 157 was the first Akula II to complete and she was followed by K 835. The fate of a third Akula II (K 337 Cougar) has not been confirmed but it is believed that the bow and stern pressure sections have been incorporated in the new SSBN *Yuri Dolgoruky*. Akula I K 152 had been building for nearly 20 years at Komsomolsk before being launched in 2006. The submarine is to be leased for 10 years by the Indian Navy from 2009 following certification by the Russian Navy.
Structure: The very long fin is particularly notable. Has the same broad hull as Sierra and has reduced radiated noise levels by comparison with Victor III of which she is the traditional follow-on design. A number of prominent non-acoustic sensors appear on the fin leading-edge and on the forward casing in the later Akulas. The engineering standards around the bridge and casing are noticeably to a higher quality than other classes. The design has been incrementally improved with reduced noise levels, boundary layer suppression and active noise cancellation reported in the later units. The Improved hulls have an additional six external torpedo tubes and the two Akula IIs have been lengthened by 3.7 m to incorporate further noise reduction developments. There are six watertight compartments. Operational diving depth, 1,476 ft *(450 m)*.
Operational: Pert Spring SATCOM. K 461, K 328, K 154, K 335, K 157 and K 317 are based in the Northern Fleet at Saida Guba. K 331, K 419, K 295 and K 985 are based in the Pacific Fleet at Tarya Bay. These submarines are the core units of the Russian SSN force. *Vepr* visited Brest in September 2004, the first visit by a Russian nuclear submarine to a foreign port. K 317 *Pantera* had a serious fire in November 2006. K 152 began sea trials in October 2008. In an accident on 8 November 2008, 20 people were killed by the accidental activation of a fire-extinguishing system.

KUZBASS ***6/2007, Ships of the World*** / 1305156

VEPR (Akula II) ***9/2004, B Prézelin*** / 1042291

VEPR ***9/2004, B Prézelin*** / 1042292

KUZBASS

6/2007, Ships of the World / 1305155

1 SIERRA I (BARRACUDA) CLASS (PROJECT 945) (SSN)

Name	*No*	*Builders*	*Laid down*	*Launched*	*Commissioned*
KOSTROMA (K 276) (ex-*Krab*)	648	Nizhny Novgorod/Severodvinsk Shipyard	8 May 1982	29 June 1983	21 Sep 1984

Displacement, tons: 7,200 surfaced; 8,100 dived
Dimensions, feet (metres): 351 × 41 × 28.9 *(107 × 12.5 × 8.8)*
Main machinery: Nuclear; 1 VM-5 PWR; 190 MW; 1 GT3A turbine; 47,500 hp(m) *(70 MW)*; 2 emergency motors; 2,004 hp(m) *(1.5 MW)*; 1 shaft; 2 spinners; 1,006 hp(m) *(740 kW)*
Speed, knots: 34 dived; 10 surfaced
Complement: 61 (31 officers)

Missiles: SLCM: Raduga SS-N-21 Sampson (Granat) fired from 21 in *(533 mm)* tubes; land-attack; inertial/terrain-following to 3,000 km *(1,620 n miles)* at 0.7 Mach; warhead nuclear 200 kT. CEP 150 m. Probably flies at a height of about 200 m.
A/S: Novator SS-N-15 Starfish (Tsakra) fired from 53 cm tubes; inertial flight to 45 km *(24.3 n miles)*; warhead nuclear 200 kT or Type 40 torpedo.
Novator SS-N-16 Stallion fired from 65 cm tubes; inertial flight to 100 km *(54 n miles)*; payload nuclear 200 kT (Vodopad) or Type 40 torpedo (Veder).
Torpedoes: 4—25.6 in *(650 mm)* and 4—21 in *(533 mm)* tubes. Combination of 65 and 53 cm torpedoes. Total of 40 weapons.
Mines: 42 in lieu of torpedoes.
Countermeasures: ESM: Rim Hat/Bald Head; intercept. Park Lamp D/F.
Radars: Surface search: Snoop Pair with back-to-back ESM aerial.
Sonars: Shark Gill; hull-mounted; passive/active search and attack; low/medium frequency.
Shark Rib flank array; passive; low frequency.
Mouse Roar; hull-mounted; active attack; high frequency.
Skat 3 towed array; passive; very low frequency.

Programmes: Launched at Gorky (Nizhny Novgorod) and transferred by river/canal to be fitted out at Severodvsinsk.
Structure: Based on design experience gained with deleted Alfa class, pressure hull constructed of titanium alloy, providing deep diving capability. Magnetic signature also reduced. Distance between hulls increases survivability and reduces radiated noise. There are six watertight compartments. The pod on the after fin is larger than that in 'Victor III'. Bulbous casing at the after end of the fin is for a towed communications buoy. Diving depth 2,460 ft *(750 m)*.
Operational: Pert Spring SATCOM. Based in the Northern Fleet at Ara Guba. It is believed that K 276 was in a collision with USS *Baton Rouge* on 11 February 1992. A second of class K 239 *Karp* is laid up.

KOSTROMA

6/2002, Lemachko Collection / 0547070

2 SIERRA II (KONDOR) CLASS (PROJECT 945B) (SSN)

Name	*No*	*Builders*	*Laid down*	*Launched*	*Commissioned*
PSKOV (K 336) (ex-*Okun*)	663	Nizhny Novgorod	May 1990	June 1992	12 Aug 1993
NIZHNY NOVGOROD (K 534) (ex-*Zubatka*)	602	Nizhny Novgorod	June 1986	June 1988	28 Dec 1990

Displacement, tons: 7,600 surfaced; 9,100 dived
Dimensions, feet (metres): 364.2 × 46.6 × 28.9 *(111 × 14.2 × 8.8)*
Main machinery: Nuclear; 1 VM-5 PWR; 190 MW; 1 GT3A turbine; 47,500 hp(m) *(70 MW)*; 2 emergency motors; 2,004 hp(m) *(1.5 MW)*; 1 shaft; 2 spinners; 1,006 hp(m) *(740 kW)*
Speed, knots: 32 dived; 10 surfaced
Complement: 61 (31 officers)

Missiles: SLCM: Raduga SS-N-21 Sampson (Granat) fired from 21 in *(533 mm)* tubes; land-attack; inertial/terrain-following to 3,000 km *(1,620 n miles)* at 0.7 Mach; warhead nuclear 200 kT. CEP 150 m. Flies at a height of about 200 m.
SAM: SA-N-5/8 Strela portable launcher; 12 missiles.
A/S: Novator SS-N-15 Starfish (Tsakra) fired from 53 cm tubes; inertial flight to 45 km *(24.3 n miles)*; warhead nuclear 200 kT or Type 40 torpedo.
Novator SS-N-16 Stallion fired from 65 cm tubes; inertial flight to 100 km *(54 n miles)*; payload nuclear 200 kT (Vodopad) or Type 40 torpedo (Veder).
Torpedoes: 4—25.6 in *(650 mm)* and 4—21 in *(533 mm)* tubes. Combination of 65 and 53 cm torpedoes. Total of 40 weapons.
Mines: 42 in lieu of torpedoes.
Countermeasures: ESM: Rim Hat; intercept. Park Lamp D/F.
Radars: Surface search: Snoop Pair with back-to-back ESM aerial.
Sonars: Shark Gill; hull-mounted; passive/active search and attack; low/medium frequency.
Shark Rib flank array; passive; low frequency.
Mouse Roar; hull-mounted; active attack; high frequency.
Skat 3 towed array; passive; very low frequency.

Programmes: A third of class K 536 *Mars*, was scrapped before completion in July 1992.
Structure: Titanium hull. The towed communications buoy has been recessed. A 10 point environmental sensor is fitted at the front end of the fin. The standoff distance between hulls is considerable and has obvious advantages for radiated noise reduction and damage resistance. Diving depth, 2,460 ft *(750 m)*. Numbers and sizes of torpedo tubes are uncertain with different figures given by Russian sources. There are seven watertight compartments.
Operational: Based in the Northern Fleet, at Ara Guba. K 534 completed a refit/refuel in May 2008.

SIERRA II *8/1998* / 0050009

SIERRA II *6/1997* / 0019009

PSKOV (with KOSTROMA (Sierra I)) *6/2002, Lemachko Collection* / 0570928

4 VICTOR III (SCHUKA) CLASS (PROJECT 671 RTMK) (SSN)

Name	*No*	*Builders*	*Laid down*	*Launched*	*Commissioned*
SNEZHNOGORSK (B 388) (ex-*Petrozavodsk*)	654	Admiralty, Leningrad	8 Sep 1987	3 June 1988	30 Nov 1988
OBNINSK (B 138)	618	Admiralty, Leningrad	7 Dec 1988	5 Aug 1989	10 May 1990
DANIL MOSKOVSKIY (B 414)	684	Admiralty, Leningrad	1 Dec 1988	31 Aug 1990	30 Dec 1990
TAMBOV (B 448)	661	Admiralty, Leningrad	31 Jan 1991	17 Oct 1991	24 Sep 1992

Displacement, tons: 4,850 surfaced; 6,300 dived
Dimensions, feet (metres): 351.1 × 34.8 × 24.3 *(107 × 10.6 × 7.4)*
Main machinery: Nuclear; 2 VM-4 PWR; 150 MW; 2 turbines; 31,000 hp(m) *(22.7 MW)*; 1 shaft; 2 spinners; 1,020 hp(m) *(750 kW)*
Speed, knots: 30 dived; 10 surfaced
Complement: 98 (17 officers)

Missiles: SLCM: Raduga SS-N-21 Sampson (Granat) fired from 21 in *(533 mm)* tubes; land-attack; inertial/terrain-following to 3,000 km *(1,620 n miles)* at 0.7 Mach. CEP 150 m or Novator Alfa SS-N-27; to 180 km *(97 n miles)*; warhead 200 kg.
A/S: Novator SS-N-15 Starfish (Tsakra) fired from 53 cm tubes; inertial flight to 45 km *(24.3 n miles)*; Type 40 torpedo.
Novator SS-N-16 Stallion fired from 65 cm tubes; inertial flight to 100 km *(54 n miles)*; payload nuclear 200 kT (Vodopad) or Type 40 torpedo (Veder).

Torpedoes: 4—21 in *(533 mm)* and 2—25.6 in *(650 mm)* tubes. Combination of 53 and 65 cm torpedoes. Can carry up to 24 weapons. Liners can be used to reduce 650 mm tubes to 533 mm.
Mines: Can carry 36 in lieu of torpedoes.
Countermeasures: ESM: Brick Group (Brick Spit and Brick Pulp); intercept. Park Lamp D/F.
Radars: Surface search: Snoop Tray 2; I-band.
Sonars: Shark Gill; hull-mounted; passive/active search and attack; low/medium frequency.
Shark Rib flank array; passive; low frequency.
Mouse Roar; hull-mounted; active attack; high frequency.
Scat 3 towed array; passive; very low frequency.

Programmes: The first of class was completed at Komsomolsk in 1978. With construction also being carried out at Admiralty Yard, Leningrad, there was a very rapid building programme up to the end of 1984. Construction then continued only at Leningrad and at a rate of about one per year which terminated in 1991. The last of the class of 26 boats completed sea trials in October 1992. Of these, the first 21 hulls were designated Type 671RTM. The final five hulls were designated Type 671RTMK to reflect modifications to fire cruise missiles. The last four of these are in service.
Structure: The streamlined pod on the stern fin is a towed sonar array dispenser. Water environment sensors are mounted at the front of the fin and on the forward casing as in the Akula and Sierra classes. Diving depth, 1,300 ft *(400 m)*.
Operational: VLF communications buoy. VHF/UHF aerials. Navigation equipment includes SINS and SATNAV. Pert Spring SATCOM. Kremmny 2 IFF. Much improved acoustic quietening puts the radiated noise levels at the upper limits of the USN Los Angeles class. All remaining operational units are based in the Northern Fleet at Litsa South or Ara Guba although they rarely go to sea. Twenty two have paid off so far although up to nine of these are in reserve and laid up at anchorages in both Fleets.

VICTOR III *2000, Lemachko Collection* / 0126230

DANIL MOSKOVSKY *7/2004* / 1042331

Patrol Submarines (SSK)

Notes: (1) One remaining target submarine of the Bravo class (379) is used for alongside training and one remaining modified Romeo class submarine is used for trials. Both are based in the Black Sea.
(2) Tango class B 380, previously reported as undergoing reactivation, has been decommissioned.

1 + 2 LADA CLASS (PROJECT 677) (SSK)

Name	*No*	*Builders*	*Laid down*	*Launched*	*Commissioned*
SAINT PETERSBURG	477	Admiralty, St Petersburg	26 Dec 1997	28 Oct 2004	2009
KRONSHTADT	–	Admiralty, St Petersburg	28 July 2005	2009	2010
SEVASTOPOL	–	Admiralty, St Petersburg	10 Nov 2006	2010	2011

Displacement, tons: 1,765 surfaced; 2,650 dived
Dimensions, feet (metres): 219.2 × 23.6 × 14.4 *(66.8 × 7.2 × 4.4)*
Main machinery: Diesel-electric; 2 diesel generators; 3,400 hp(m) *(2.5 MW)*; 1 motor; 5,576 hp(m) *(4.1 MW)*; 1 shaft
Speed, knots: 21 dived; 10 surfaced
Range, n miles: 6,000 at 7 kt snorting
Complement: 37

Missiles: SLCM: Novator Alfa Klub SS-N-27 (3M-54 anti-ship missiles); active radar homing to 180 km *(97.2 n miles)* at 0.7 Mach (cruise) and 2.5 Mach (attack); warhead 450 kg. Novator Klub SS-N-30 (3M14) land-attack guidance to 300 km *(162 n miles)* at 0.7 Mach; warhead 450 kg.
Torpedoes: 6—21 in *(533 mm)* tubes. 18 weapons.
Mines: In lieu of torpedoes.
Countermeasures: ESM: Intercept.
Radars: Surface search: I-band.
Sonars: Conformal bow and flank arrays; active/passive; medium frequency. Towed array (low frequency).

SAINT PETERSBURG *6/2005, A Sheldon-Duplaix* / 1127919

Programmes: The national variant of this submarine is known as the Lada class. Work began on the first of class in 1996 and construction started in St Petersburg in 1987. A second and third of class are also under construction. The export version of the submarine is known as the Amur class of which there are six designs based on different surface displacements (550, 750, 950, 1450, 1650 and 1850). The 'Amur 1650' probably has the most export potential and it was possibly in anticipation of an order from India and China that work began on such a submarine in 1997 at the same time as the similar Lada class. Work was temporarily suspended in 1998, and the hull may have been subsumed in the Lada construction programme.

Structure: The first Russian single-hulled submarine, built to a Rubin design based on the 'Amur 1650'. A fuel cell plug (for AIP) of about 12 m can be inserted to allow installation of AIP although this is unlikely in the near future. Diving depth: 820 ft *(250 m)*. A non-hull penetrating optronic periscope supplied by Elektropribor, is fitted.

Operational: Sea trials of the first of class started on 29 November 2005 and a second round of trials in August 2006. Apparent delays in achieving operational status suggest there may be technical problems.

SAINT PETERSBURG *6/2005, A Sheldon-Duplaix* / 1127920

SAINT PETERSBURG *6/2005, A Sheldon-Duplaix* / 1127918

19 KILO CLASS (PROJECT 877K/877M/636) (SSK)

Name	*No*	*Builders*	*Laid down*	*Launched*	*Commissioned*
CHITA (B 260)	504	Komsomolsk Shipyard	Sep 1980	19 Aug 1981	Dec 1981
VYBORG (B 227)	469	Komsomolsk Shipyard	Sep 1981	Sep 1982	Dec 1982
VOLOGDA (B 402)	405	Nizhny Novgorod	Feb 1983	1984	27 Dec 1984
B 806	487	Nizhny Novgorod	–	–	1986
B 439	545	Komsomolsk Shipyard	1985	1985	1986
B 445	–	Komsomolsk Shipyard	1986	1987	Dec 1987
JAROSLAVL (B 808)	425	Nizhny Novogorod	–	–	1988
B 394	–	Komsomolsk Shipyard	–	–	Dec 1988
KALUGA (B 800)	468	Nizhny Novgorod	–	–	1989
UST-KAMSHATS (B 464)	547	Komsomolsk Shipyard	1988	1988	1989
NOVOSIBIRSK (B 401)	440*	Nizhny Novgorod	June 1988	Aug 1989	4 Jan 1990
MAGNETO-GORSK (B 471)	409	Nizhny Novgorod	–	–	1990
UST-BOLSHERETSK (B 494)	549	Komsomolsk Shipyard	1989	1990	1990
VLADIKAVKAZ (B 459, ex-B 434)	431	Nizhny Novgorod	–	–	1990
ALROSA (B 871)	554	Nizhny Novgorod	May 1998	Aug 1989	Dec 1990
LIPETSK (B 177)	429	Nizhny Novgorod	–	–	1991
B 187	529*	Komsomolsk Shipyard	1990	1990	1991
KRASNOKAMENSK (B 190)	521*	Komsomolsk Shipyard	8 May 1992	1993	1993
MOGOCHEY (B 345)	507	Komsomolsk Shipyard	22 Apr 1993	1993	22 Jan 1994

*indicates Project 636

Displacement, tons: 2,325 surfaced; 3,076 dived
Dimensions, feet (metres): 238.2; 242.1 (Project 636) × 32.5 × 21.7 *(72.6; 73.8 × 9.9 × 6.6)*
Main machinery: Diesel-electric; Type 4-2DL-42M 2 diesels (Type 4-2AA-42M in Project 636); 3,650 hp(m) *(2.68 MW)*; 2 generators; 1 motor; 5,900 hp(m) *(4.34 MW)*; 1 shaft; 2 auxiliary MT-168 motors; 204 hp(m) *(150 kW)*; 1 economic speed motor; 130 hp(m) *(95 kW)*
Speed, knots: 17 dived; 10 surfaced; 9 snorting
Range, n miles: 6,000 at 7 kt snorting; 400 at 3 kt dived
Complement: 52 (13 officers)

Missiles: SSM: Novator Alfa SS-N-27 may be fitted in due course.
SAM: 6-8 SA-N-5/8; IR homing from 600 to 6,000 m at 1.65 Mach; warhead 2 kg; portable launcher stowed in a well in the fin between snort and W/T masts.
Torpedoes: 6–21 in *(533 mm)* tubes. 18 combinations of 53 cm torpedoes. USET-80 is wire-guided in the 4B version (from 2 tubes).
Mines: 24 in lieu of torpedoes.
Countermeasures: ESM: Squid Head or Brick Pulp; radar warning. Quad Loop D/F.
Weapons control: MVU-110EM or MVU-119EM Murena torpedo fire-control system.
Radars: Surface search: Snoop Tray (MRP-25); I-band.
Sonars: Shark Teeth/Shark Fin (MGK-400); hull-mounted; passive/active search and attack; medium frequency. Mouse Roar; hull-mounted; active attack; high frequency.

Programmes: Also known as the Vashavyanka class, first launched in 1979 at Komsomolsk and commissioned 12 September 1980. Subsequent construction also at Nizhny Novgorod. A total of 24 were built for Russia of which six were of the improved Project 636 variant.
Structure: Had a better hull form than the Tango class but was nevertheless considered fairly basic by comparison with contemporary western designs. Diving depth 790 ft *(240 m)* normal. Battery has a 9,700 kW/h capacity. The basic 'Kilo' was the Project 877; 877K has an improved fire-control system and 877M includes wire-guided torpedoes from two tubes. Project 636 is an improved design with uprated diesels, a propulsion motor rotating at half the speed (250 rpm), higher standards of noise reduction and an automated combat information system capable of providing simultaneous fire-control data on five targets. Pressure hull length is 170 ft *(51.8 m)* or 174 ft *(53 m)* for Project 636. Foreplanes on the hull are just forward of the fin. Project 636 can be identified by a vertical cut off to the after casing. B 871 has been fitted with a pump jet propulsor.
Operational: With a reserve of buoyancy of 32 per cent and a heavily compartmented pressure hull, this class is capable of being holed and still surviving. B 401, B 402, B 808, B 459, B 471, B 800 and B 177 are based in the Northern Fleet, B 260, B 445, B 494, B 190, B 345, B 187, B 464, B 439 and B 394 are based in the Pacific, B 806 and B 227 in the Baltic and B 871 in the Black Sea. Russian made batteries have been a source of problems in warm water operations.
Sales: Exports of Project 877 have been to Poland (one), Romania (one), India (ten), Algeria (two), Iran (three) and China (two). The only exports of Project 636 have been to China (two). A further eight were ordered by China in 2002. Export versions have the letter E after the project number.

ALROSA *4/2006, Lemachko Collection* / 1159847

B 345 *10/2006, Hachiro Nakai* / 1159885

TUR *8/2004, E & M Laursen* / 1042296

Auxiliary Submarines (SSA(N))

Notes: (1) There are a number of Swimmer Delivery Vessels (SDV) in service including Siren (three-man) and Triton, Sever and Elbrus types.
(2) A new auxiliary submarine (SSAN) was launched at Severodvinsk Shipyard on 6 August 2003. Nicknamed 'Losharik', she is likely to be used for scientific research and is reported to be similar to but not the same as the Uniform class. It is known both as Project 210 and as Project 10831. It has a pennant number of AS 12 and is reported to have become operational in 2007.
(3) The Delta IV class K 64, which was decommissioned in about 2002, may be undergoing conversion to an auxiliary submarine role.

1 PROJECT 20120 EXPERIMENTAL SUBMARINE (SSA)

Name	*No*	*Builders*	*Laid down*	*Launched*	*Commissioned*
SAROV (B-90)	–	Nizhny Novgorod Shipyard/ Severodvinsk Shipyard	–	17 Dec 2007	7 Aug 2008

Displacement, tons: 4,000 approx
Dimensions, feet (metres): To be announced
Main machinery: Diesel-electric + nuclear
Speed, knots: To be announced
Complement: 52
Torpedoes: To be announced.
Mines: To be announced.
Countermeasures: ESM: To be announced.
Radars: Surface search: To be announced.
Sonars: To be announced.

Comment: It is reported that the design of the submarine was developed by Rubin in about 1989, that construction was initiated at Nizhny Novgorod and that, following transfer in about 2003, the boat was completed at the Sevmash Shipyard at Severodvinsk. It is thought to be equipped with a hybrid propulsion system which combines a diesel-electric plant with a small nuclear reactor. The function of the reactor is to keep a charge on the battery and thereby achieve an air-independent system with almost unlimited underwater endurance on relatively quiet electric propulsion. While details of the submarine have not been confirmed, its length appears to be of the order of 100 m and there is evidence both of a raised area on the upper casing aft of the fin and also of bulges on the side of the forward casing. It is believed that the principal role of the submarine is to act as test bed for the development and testing of unmanned submersibles, weapons and underwater equipment. Operational experience of an auxiliary nuclear power plant was gained in the modified Juliett class (Project 651E) K-68 in the 1980s.

SAROV *6/2008** / 1353320

3 PALTUS/X-RAY (PROJECT 1851) CLASS (SSAN/SSA)

AS 23 (X-Ray) **AS 35** **AS 21**

Displacement, tons: 730 dived
Dimensions, feet (metres): 173.9 × 12.5 × 13.8 *(53 × 3.8 × 4.2)*
Main machinery: Nuclear; 1 reactor; 10 MW; 1 shaft; ducted thrusters
Speed, knots: 6 dived
Complement: 14

Comment: Details given are for the two Paltus (Nelhma) class (A 21, AS 35). The first was launched at Sudomekh, St Petersburg in April 1991, a second of class in September 1994 and a third was started but not completed. This is a follow-on to the single 44 m 520 ton X-Ray (AS 23) class which was first seen in 1984 and after a long spell out of service was back in operation in 1999. Paltus probably owes much to the USN NR 1. Paltus is associated with the Delta III Stretch SSAN which acts as a mother ship for special operations. Titanium hulled and very deep diving to 1,000 m *(3,280 ft)*. Paltus based in the Northern Fleet at Olenya Guba, X-Ray at Yagri Island.

PALTUS (artist's impression) *1994* / 0506318

3 UNIFORM (KACHALOT) CLASS (PROJECT 1910) (SSAN)

No	*Builders*	*Laid down*	*Launched*	*Commissioned*
AS 13	Sudomekh, Leningrad	20 Oct 1977	25 Nov 1982	31 Dec 1986
AS 15	Sudomekh, Leningrad	23 Feb 1983	29 Apr 1988	30 Dec 1991
AS 33	Sudomekh, St Petersburg	16 July 1990	26 Aug 1995	Feb 1998

Displacement, tons: 1,340 surfaced; 1,580 dived
Dimensions, feet (metres): 226.4 × 23.0 × 17.0 *(69.0 × 7.0 × 5.2)*
Main machinery: Nuclear; 1 PWR; 15 MW; 2 turbines; 10,000 hp(m) *(7.35 MW)*; 1 shaft; 2 thrusters
Speed, knots: 10 surfaced; 28 dived
Complement: 36
Radars: Navigation: Snoop Slab; I-band.

Comment: Research and development nuclear-powered submarines. Have single hulls and 'wheel' arches either side of the fin which house side thrusters. These are titanium hulled and very deep diving submarines (possibly down to 700 m *(2,300 ft)*), based in the Northern Fleet at Olenya Guba, and are used mainly for ocean bed operations. Plans to build more of the class were thought to have been shelved. It is not clear whether an auxiliary submarine (AS 12) launched on 6 August 2003 is a fourth 'Uniform' or a different design.

UNIFORM *6/2004, Lemachko Collection* / 1159848

1 DELTA III STRETCH (PROJECT 667 BDR) (SSAN)

Name	*No*	*Builders*	*Laid down*	*Launched*	*Commissioned*
ORIENBURG (BS 136 (ex-K 129))	656	Severodvinsk Shipyard	Feb 1979	Mar 1981	5 Nov 1981

Dimensions, feet (metres): 534.9 × 39.4 × 28.5 *(163 × 12 × 8.7)*
Main machinery: Nuclear: 2 VM-4 PWR; 180 MW; 2 GT 3A-635 turbines; 37,400 hp(m) *(27.5 MW)*; 2 emergency motors; 612 hp(m) *(450 kW)*; 2 shafts
Speed, knots: 24 dived; 14 surfaced
Complement: 130 (40 officers)

Torpedoes: 4—21 in *(533 mm)* and 2—400 mm tubes.
Countermeasures: ESM: Brick Pulp/Group; radar warning.
Radars: Surface search: Snoop Tray; I-band.
Sonars: Shark Teeth; hull mounted; active/passive search; low/medium frequency.
Shark Hide; flank array; passive low frequency.
Mouse Roar; hull mounted; active high frequency.

Comment: Originally launched in 1981, this former SSBN has been converted by replacing the central section with a 43 m plug, extending the overall hull length by 3 m. The submarine was reported to have returned to service in 2003 and has replaced the Yankee Stretch as the Paltus mother-ship. Based in the Northern Fleet.

ORIENBURG *3/2006, Lemachko Collection* / 1167505

AIRCRAFT CARRIERS

Note: (1) Of the former aircraft carriers of the Kiev class, *Kiev* was sold to China for scrap in 2000; *Minsk* and *Novorossiysk* were sold to a South Korean Corporation in 1994. *Minsk* later became a tourist attraction in Shenzen, China, while *Novorossiysk* was scrapped in India. *Admiral Gorshkov* (ex-*Baku*) has been sold to the Indian Navy and is undergoing refit and reactivation.
(2) The requirement for a new class of four aircraft carriers was announced in mid-2005. This was re-stated by the Commander-in-Chief in 2008. While work has almost certainly begun on the project, funding could prove to be an obstacle.

1 KUZNETSOV (OREL) CLASS (PROJECT 1143.5/6) (CVGM)

Name	*No*	*Builders*	*Laid down*	*Launched*	*Commissioned*
ADMIRAL KUZNETSOV (ex-*Tbilisi*, ex-*Leonid Brezhnev*)	063	Nikolayev South, Ukraine	1 Apr 1982	16 Dec 1985	25 Dec 1990

Displacement, tons: 45,900 standard; 58,500 full load
Dimensions, feet (metres): 999 oa; 918.6 wl × 229.7 oa; 121.4 wl × 34.4 *(304.5; 280 × 70; 37 × 10.5)*
Flight deck, feet (metres): 999 × 229.7 *(304.5 × 70)*
Main machinery: 8 boilers; 4 turbines; 200,000 hp(m) *(147 MW)*; 4 shafts
Speed, knots: 30. **Range, n miles:** 3,850 at 29 kt; 8,500 at 18 kt
Complement: 1,960 (200 officers) plus 626 aircrew plus 40 Flag staff

Missiles: SSM: 12 Chelomey SS-N-19 Shipwreck (3M-45) launchers (flush mounted) ❶; inertial guidance with command update; active radar homing to 20-550 km *(10.8-300 n miles)* at 2.5 Mach; warhead 500 kT nuclear or 750 kg HE.
SAM: 4 Altair SA-N-9 Gauntlet (Klinok) sextuple vertical launchers (192 missiles) ❷; command guidance and active radar homing to 12 km *(6.5 n miles)* at 2 Mach; warhead 15 kg. 24 magazines; 192 missiles; 4 channels of fire.
SAM/Guns: 8 Altair CADS-N-1 (Kortik/Kashtan) ❸; each has a twin 30 mm Gatling combined with 8 SA-N-11 (Grisson) and Hot Flash/Hot Spot fire-control radar/optronic director. Laser beam-riding guidance for missiles to 8 km *(4.4 n miles)*; warhead 9 kg; 9,000 rds/min combined to 2 km (for guns).
Guns: 6—30 mm/65 ❹ AK 630; 6 barrels per mounting; 3,000 rds/min combined to 2 km. Probably controlled by Hot Flash/Hot Spot on CADS-N-1.
A/S mortars: 2 RBU 12,000 ❺; range 12,000 m; warhead 80 kg. UDAV-1M; torpedo countermeasure.
Countermeasures: Decoys: 10 PK 10 and 4 PK 2 chaff launchers.
ESM/ECM: 8 Foot Ball. 4 Wine Flask (intercept). 4 Flat Track. 10 Ball Shield A and B.
Weapons control: 3 Tin Man optronic trackers. 2 Punch Bowl SATCOM datalink ❻. 2 Low Ball SATNAV ❼. 2 Bell Crown and 2 Bell Push datalinks.
Radars: Air search: Sky Watch; four Planar phased arrays ❽; 3D.
Air/surface search: Top Plate B ❾; D/E-band.
Surface search: 2 Strut Pair ❿; F-band.
Navigation: 3 Palm Frond; I-band.
Fire control: 4 Cross Sword (for SAM) ⓫; K-band. 8 Hot Flash; J-band.
Aircraft control: 2 Fly Trap B; G/H-band.
Tacan: Cake Stand ⓬.
IFF: 4 Watch Guard.
Sonars: Bull Horn and Horse Jaw; hull-mounted; active search and attack; medium/low frequency.

Fixed-wing aircraft: 18 Su-33 Flanker D; 4 Su-25 UTG Frogfoot.
Helicopters: 15 Ka-27 Helix. 2 Ka-31 RLD Helix AEW.

ADMIRAL KUZNETSOV ***10/2004, Ships of the World*** / 1042330

Programmes: This was a logical continuation of the deleted Kiev class. The full name of *Kuznetsov* is *Admiral Flota Sovietskogo Sojuza Kuznetsov*. The second of class, *Varyag*, was between 70 and 80 per cent complete by early 1993 at Nikolayev in the Ukraine. Building was then terminated after an unsuccessful attempt by the Navy to fund completion. Subsequently the ship was bought by Chinese interests and, having arrived at Dalian in March 2002 now appears to be undergoing re-activation by the PLA(N).
Structure: The hangar is 183 × 29.4 × 7.5 m and can hold up to 18 Flanker aircraft. There are two starboard side lifts, a ski jump of 14° and an angled deck of 7°. There are four arrester wires. The SSM system is in the centre of the flight deck forward with flush deck covers. The ship has some 16.5 m of freeboard. There is no Bass Tilt radar and the ADG guns are controlled by Kashtan fire-control system. The ship suffers from severe water distillation problems.

Operational: AEW, ASW and reconnaissance tasks undertaken by Helix helicopters. The aircraft complement listed is based on the number which might be embarked for normal operations but the Russians claim a top limit of 60. *Kuznetsov* conducted extensive flight operations throughout the second half of both 1993 and 1994, and was at sea again by September 1995 after a seven month refit. Deployed to the Mediterranean for 80 days in early 1996 before returning to the Northern Fleet. Refitted from mid-1996 to mid-1998. Sailed for a VIP demonstration in August 1998 and then continued trials and training in-area. There were limited local exercises in 2000 but no activity in 2001 and 2002. The ship left the jetty for Navy Days in 2003. The ship participated in Northern Fleet exercises in the North Atlantic in August-September 2005 and again in October 2006. A three-month Atlantic/Mediterranean deployment began in December 2007 and was repeated in 2008/09.

ADMIRAL KUZNETSOV
1/2008*, Ships of the World
1305317

ADMIRAL KUZNETSOV ***1/2008*, Ships of the World*** / 1305318

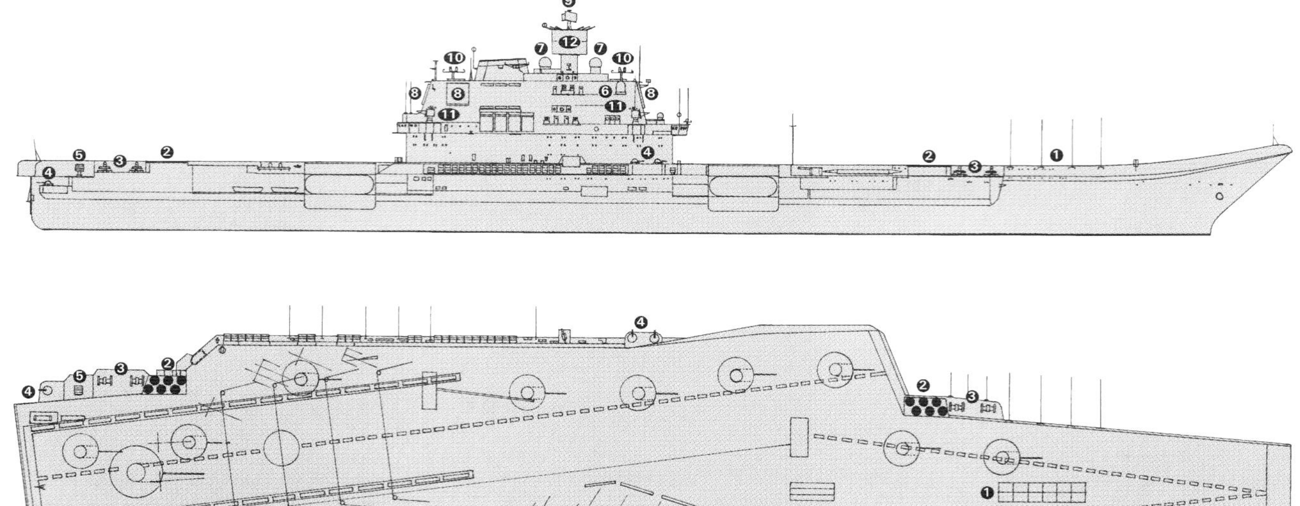

ADMIRAL KUZNETSOV ***(Scale 1 : 1,800), Ian Sturton*** / 0506078

BATTLE CRUISERS

1 KIROV (ORLAN) CLASS (PROJECT 1144.1/1144.2) (CGHMN)

Name	*No*	*Builders*	*Laid down*	*Launched*	*Commissioned*
PYOTR VELIKIY (ex-*Yuri Andropov*)	099 (ex-183)	Baltic Yard 189, St Petersburg	11 Mar 1986	29 Apr 1989	9 Apr 1998

Displacement, tons: 19,000 standard; 24,300 full load
Dimensions, feet (metres): 826.8; 754.6 wl × 93.5 × 29.5 *(252; 230 × 28.5 × 9.1)*
Main machinery: CONAS; 2 KN-3 PWR; 300 MW; 2 oil-fired boilers; 2 GT3A-688 turbines; 140,000 hp(m) *(102.9 MW)*; 2 shafts
Speed, knots: 30
Range, n miles: 14,000 at 30 kt
Complement: 726 (82 officers) plus 18 aircrew

Missiles: SSM: 20 Chelomey SS-N-19 Shipwreck (3M 45) (P-700 Granit) (improved SS-N-12 with lower flight profile) ❶; inertial guidance with command update; active radar homing to 20-450 km *(10.8-243 n miles)* at 1.6 Mach; warhead 350 kT nuclear or 750 kg HE; no reloads.
SAM: 12 SA-N-6/SA-N-20 Grumble (Fort/Fort M) vertical launchers ❷; 8 rounds per launcher; command guidance; semi-active radar homing to 100 km *(54 n miles)*; warhead 90 kg (or nuclear?); 96 missiles.
2 SA-N-4 Gecko twin launchers ❸; semi-active radar homing to 15 km *(8 n miles)* at 2.5 Mach; warhead 50 kg; altitude 9.1-3,048 m *(30-10,000 ft)*; 40 missiles.
2 SA-N-9 Gauntlet (Kinzhal) octuple vertical launchers ❹; command guidance; active radar homing to 12 km *(6.5 n miles)* at 2 Mach; warhead 15 kg; altitude 3.4-12,192 m *(10-40,000 ft)*; 128 missiles; 4 channels of fire.
SAM/Guns: 6 CADS-N-1 (Kortik/Kashtan) ❺; each has a twin 30 mm Gatling combined with 8 SA-N-11 (Grisson) and Hot Flash/Hot Spot fire-control radar/optronic director. Laser beam-riding guidance for missiles to 8 km *(4.4 n miles)*; warhead 9 kg; 9,000 rds/min combined to 2 km (for guns).
A/S: Novator SS-N-15 (Starfish); inertial flight to 45 km *(24.3 n miles)*; payload Type 40 torpedo or nuclear warhead; fired from fixed torpedo tubes behind shutters in the superstructure.

Guns: 2 — 130 mm/54 (twin) AK 130 ❻; 70 rds/min to 22 km *(12 n miles)*; weight of shell 33.4 kg.
Torpedoes: 10 — 21 in *(533 mm)* (2 quin) tubes. Combination of 53 cm torpedoes. Mounted in the hull adjacent the RBU 1000s on both quarters. Fixed tubes behind shutters can fire either SS-N-15 or Type 40 torpedoes.
A/S mortars: 1 RBU 12,000 ❼; 10 tubes per launcher; range 12,000 m; warhead 80 kg.
2 RBU 1000 6-tubed aft ❽; range 1,000 m; warhead 55 kg.
UDAV-1M; torpedo countermeasures.
Countermeasures: Decoys: 2 twin PK 2 150 mm chaff launchers. Towed torpedo decoy.
ESM/ECM: 8 Foot Ball. 4 Wine Flask (intercept). 8 Bell Bash. 4 Bell Nip. Half Cup (laser intercept).
Combat data systems: Lesorub-44.
Weapons control: 4 Tin Man optronic trackers ❾. 2 Punch Bowl C SATCOM ❿. 4 Low Ball SATNAV. 2 Bell Crown and 2 Bell Push datalinks.
Radars: Air search: Top Pair (Top Sail + Big Net) ⓫; 3D; C/D-band; range 366 km *(200 n miles)* for bomber, 183 km *(100 n miles)* for 2 m² target.
Air/surface search: Top Plate ⓬; 3D; D/E-band.
Navigation: 3 Palm Frond; I-band.
Fire control: Cross Sword ⓭; K-band (for SA-N-9). Top Dome for SA-N-6 ⓮; Tomb Stone J-band (for Fort M) ⓯. 2 Pop Group, F/H/I-band (for SA-N-4) ⓰. Kite Screech ⓱; H/I/K-band (for main guns). 6 Hot Flash for CADS-N-1; I/J-band.
Aircraft control: Flyscreen B; I-band.
IFF: Salt Pot A and B.
Tacan: 2 Round House B ⓲.
Sonars: Horse Jaw (Polinom); hull-mounted; active search and attack; low/medium frequency.
Horse Tail; VDS; active search; medium frequency. Depth to 150–200 m *(492.1–656.2 ft)* depending on speed.

Helicopters: 3 Ka-27 Helix ⓳.

Programmes: Design work started in 1968. Type name is *atomny raketny kreyser* meaning nuclear-powered missile cruiser. A fifth of class was scrapped before being launched in 1989.
Structure: The Kirov class were the first Russian surface warships with nuclear propulsion. In addition to the nuclear plant a unique maritime combination with an auxiliary oil-fuelled system has been installed. This provides a superheat capability, boosting the normal steam output by some 50 per cent. The SS-N-19 tubes are set at an angle of about 45°. CADS-N-1 with a central fire-control radar on six mountings, each of which has two cannon and eight missile launchers. Two are mounted either side of the SS-N-19 forward and four on the after superstructure. Same A/S system as the frigate *Neustrashimy* with fixed torpedo tubes in ports behind shutters in the superstructure for firing SS-N-15 or Type 45 torpedoes. There are reported to be about 500 SAM of different types. *Velikiy*, the only operational ship, has a Tomb Stone fire-control radar instead of a forward Top Dome for SA-N-20 which is a maritime variant of SA-10C.
Operational: Based in the Northern Fleet. Over-the-horizon targeting for SS-N-19 provided by Punch Bowl SATCOM or helicopter. The first ship of the class of four, *Admiral Ushakov*, was formally decommissioned in 2004 and is to be scrapped. The second ship, *Admiral Lazarev* has also been decommissioned. And is also likely to be scrapped. Plans to refit the third ship, *Admiral Nakhimov*, laid up since 1999, appear to have been revived but funding continues to be problematical. The scope of the work is substantial and includes nuclear refuelling and replacement of the SS-N-19 missile system. The refit is likely to take up to four years to complete. *Pyotr Velikiy* conducted an extensive deployment in 2008–09. Visits were undertaken in the Mediterranean, Caribbean and South Africa. Exercises included INDRA-2009 with the Indian Navy.

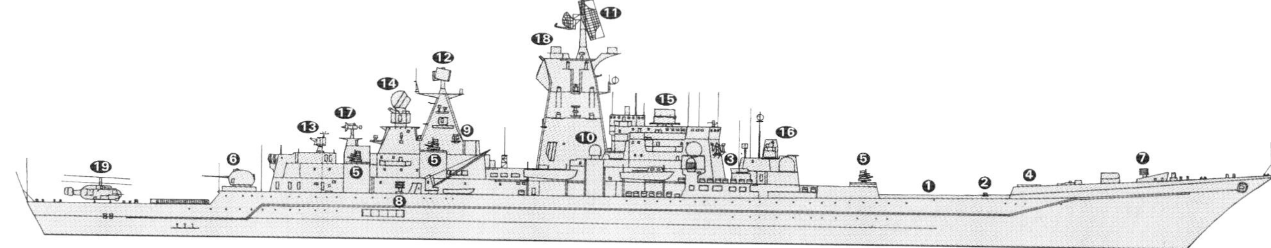

PYOTR VELIKIY
(Scale 1 : 1,500), Ian Sturton / 0528401

PYOTR VELIKIY
11/2008*, A Sheldon-Duplaix / 1353321

PYOTR VELIKIY
11/2008*, A Sheldon-Duplaix / 1353322

CRUISERS

3 SLAVA (ATLANT) CLASS (PROJECT 1164) (CGHM)

Name	*No*	*Builders*	*Laid down*	*Launched*	*Commissioned*
MOSKVA (ex-*Slava*)	121	Nikolayev North (61 Kommuna), Ukraine	5 Nov 1976	27 July 1979	30 Dec 1982
MARSHAL USTINOV	055	Nikolayev North (61 Kommuna), Ukraine	5 Oct 1978	25 Feb 1982	15 Sep 1986
VARYAG (ex-*Chervona Ukraina*)	011	Nikolayev North (61 Kommuna), Ukraine	31 July 1979	28 Aug 1983	25 Dec 1989

Displacement, tons: 9,380 standard; 11,490 full load
Dimensions, feet (metres): 611.5 × 68.2 × 27.6 *(186.4 × 20.8 × 8.4)*
Main machinery: COGAG; 4 gas-turbines; 88,000 hp(m) *(64.68 MW)*; 2 M-70 gas-turbines; 20,000 hp(m) *(14.7 MW)*; 2 shafts
Speed, knots: 32
Range, n miles: 2,200 at 30 kt; 7,500 at 15 kt
Complement: 476 (62 officers)

Missiles: SSM: 16 Chelomey SS-N-12 (8 twin) Sandbox (Bazalt) launchers ❶; inertial guidance with command update; active radar homing to 550 km *(300 n miles)* at 1.7 Mach; warhead nuclear 350 kT or HE 1,000 kg.
SAM: 8 SA-N-6 Grumble (Fort) vertical launchers ❷; 8 rounds per launcher; command guidance; semi-active radar homing to 100 km *(54 n miles)*; warhead 90 kg (or nuclear?); altitude 27,432 m *(90,000 ft)*. 64 missiles.
2 SA-N-4 Gecko twin retractable launchers ❸; semi-active radar homing to 15 km *(8 n miles)* at 2.5 Mach; warhead 50 kg; altitude 9.1-3,048 m *(30-10,000 ft)*; 40 missiles.
Guns: 2—130 mm/54 (twin) AK 130 ❹; 70 rds/min to 22 km *(12 n miles)*; weight of shell 33.4 kg.
6—30 mm/65 AK 650; ❺ 6 barrels per mounting; 3,000 rds/min to 2 km.
Torpedoes: 10—21 in *(533 mm)* (2 quin) tubes ❻. Combination of 53 cm torpedoes.
A/S mortars: 2 RBU 6000 12-tubed trainable ❼; range 6,000 m; warhead 31 kg.
Countermeasures: Decoys: 2 PK 2 chaff launchers.
ESM/ECM: 8 Side Globe (jammers). 4 Rum Tub (intercept).
Weapons control: 2 Tee Plinth and 3 Tilt Pot optronic directors. 2 Punch Bowl satellite data receiving/targeting systems. 2 Bell Crown and 2 Bell Push datalinks.
Radars: Air search: Top Pair (Top Sail + Big Net) ❽; 3D; C/D-band; range 366 km *(200 n miles)* for bomber, 183 km *(100 n miles)* for 2 m^2 target.
Air/surface search: Top Steer ❾ or Top Plate *(Varyag)*; 3D; D/E-band.
Navigation: 3 Palm Frond; I-band.
Fire control: Front Door ❿; F-band (for SS-N-12). Top Dome ⓫; J-band (for SA-N-6). 2 Pop Group ⓬; F/H/I-band (for SA-N-4). 3 Bass Tilt ⓭; H/I-band (for Gatlings). Kite Screech ⓮; H/I/K-band (for 130 mm).
IFF: Salt Pot A and B. 2 Long Head.
Sonars: Bull Horn and Steer Hide (Platina); hull-mounted; active search and attack; low/medium frequency.

Helicopters: 1 Ka-27 Helix ⓯.

VARYAG *10/2008*, **Mick Prendergast*** / 1353324

Programmes: Built at the same yard as the Kara class. This is a smaller edition of the dual-purpose surface warfare/ASW *Kirov*, designed as a conventionally powered back-up for that class. The fourth of class, originally being completed for Ukraine, was transferred to Russia in July 1995 but returned to Ukraine in February 1999 for completion. However, work was not finished due to lack of funds. Re-sale back to Russia is unlikely. A fifth of class was started but cancelled in October 1990.
Structure: The notable gap abaft the twin funnels (SA-N-6 area) is traversed by a large crane which stows between the funnels. The hangar is recessed below the flight deck with an inclined ramp. The torpedo tubes are behind shutters in the hull below the Top Dome radar director aft. Air conditioned citadels for NBCD. There is a bridge periscope.
Operational: The SA-N-6 system effectiveness is diminished by having only one radar director. Over-the-horizon targeting for SS-N-12 provided by helicopter or Punch Bowl SATCOM. *Moskva* is based in the Black Sea Fleet at Sevastopol and conducted an Indian Ocean deployment in 2003. Her nine-year refit was beset by payment problems. Some funds were provided by the city of Moscow. *Marshal Ustinov* deployed to the Northern Fleet in March 1987 and completed refit at St Petersburg in May 1995 where she remained until January 1998, when she transferred back to the Northern Fleet and is based at Severomorsk and is active. *Varyag* transferred to Petropavlovsk in the Pacific in October 1990.

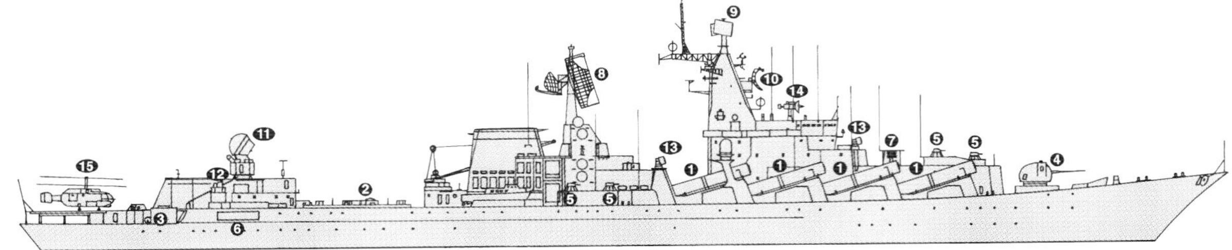
VARYAG *(Scale 1 : 1,200), **Ian Sturton*** / 0050017

VARYAG *12/2005, **Ships of the World*** / 1151150

MOSKVA *10/2008*, **Laursen/Jarnasen*** / 1353323

1 KARA (BERKOT-B) CLASS (PROJECT 1134B) (CGHM)

Name	*No*	*Builders*	*Laid down*	*Launched*	*Commissioned*
KERCH	713 (ex-711)	Nikolayev North (61 Kommuna), Ukraine	30 Apr 1971	21 July 1972	25 Dec 1974

Displacement, tons: 7,650 standard; 9,900 full load
Dimensions, feet (metres): 568 × 61 × 22 *(173.2 × 18.6 × 6.7)*
Main machinery: COGAG; 4 gas turbines; 108,800 hp(m) *(80 MW)*; 2 gas turbines; 13,600 hp(m) *(10 MW)*; 2 shafts
Speed, knots: 32
Range, n miles: 9,000 at 15 kt cruising turbines; 3,000 at 32 kt
Complement: 390 (49 officers)

Missiles: SAM: 2 SA-N-3 Goblet twin launchers ❶; semi-active radar homing to 55 km *(30 n miles)* at 2.5 Mach; warhead 80 kg; altitude 91.4-22,860 m *(300-75,000 ft)*; 72 missiles.
2 SA-N-4 Gecko twin launchers (twin either side of mast) ❷; semi-active radar homing to 15 km *(8 n miles)* at 2.5 Mach; warhead 50 kg; altitude 9.1-3,048 m *(30-10,000 ft)*; 40 missiles.
A/S: 2 Raduga SS-N-14 Silex (Rastrub) quad launchers ❸; command guidance to 55 km *(30 n miles)* at 0.95 Mach; payload nuclear 5 kT or Type 40 torpedo or E53-72 torpedo. SSM version; range 35 km *(19 n miles)*; warhead 500 kg.
Guns: 4—3 in *(76 mm)*/59 AK 726 (2 twin) ❹; 90 rds/min to 16 km *(8.5 n miles)*; weight of shell 5.9 kg.
4—30 mm/65 ❺; 6 barrels per mounting; 3,000 rds/min combined to 2 km.
Torpedoes: 10—21 in *(533 mm)* (2 quin) tubes ❻. Combination of 53 cm torpedoes.
A/S mortars: 2 RBU 6000 12-tubed trainable ❼; range 6,000 m; warhead 31 kg.
2 RBU 1000 6-tubed (aft) ❽; range 1,000 m; warhead 55 kg; torpedo countermeasures.
Countermeasures: Decoys: 2 PK 2 chaff launchers. 1 BAT-1 torpedo decoy.
ESM/ECM: 8 Side Globe (jammers). 2 Bell Slam. 2 Bell Clout, 4 Rum Tub (intercept) (fitted on mainmast).
Weapons control: 4 Tilt Pot optronic directors. Bell Crown, Bike Pump and Hat Box datalinks.
Radars: Air search: Flat Screen (may have been removed) ❾; E/F-band.
Air/surface search: Head Net C ❿; 3D; E-band; range 128 km *(70 n miles)*.
Navigation: 2 Don Kay; I-band. Don 2 or Palm Frond; I-band.
Fire control: 2 Head Light B/C ⓫; F/G/H-band (for SA-N-3 and SS-N-14). 2 Pop Group ⓬; F/H/I-band (for SA-N-4). 2 Owl Screech ⓭; G-band (for 76 mm). 2 Bass Tilt ⓮; H/I-band (for 30 mm).
Tacan: Fly Screen A or Fly Spike.
IFF: High Pole A. High Pole B.

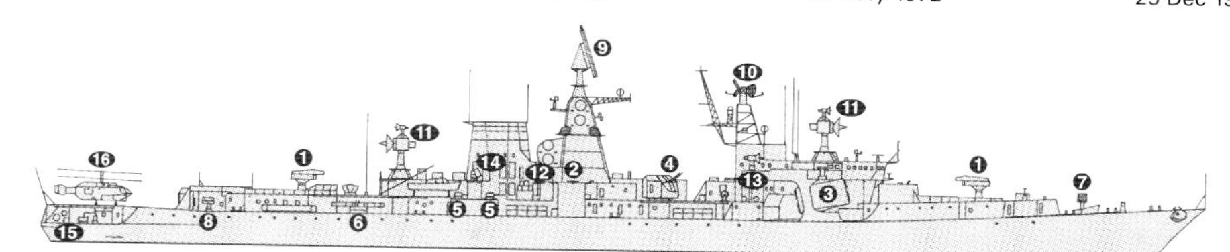

KERCH
(Scale 1 : 1,500), **Ian Sturton** / 0081651

KERCH
*10/2008**, **Laursen/Jarnasen** / 1353325

Sonars: Bull Nose (Titan 2-MG 332); hull-mounted; active search and attack; low/medium frequency.
Mare Tail; VDS (Vega-M 325) ⓯; active search; medium frequency.

Helicopters: 1 Ka-27 Helix ⓰.

Programmes: Type name is *bolshoy protivolodochny korabl*, meaning large anti-submarine ship.
Modernisation: The Flat Screen air search radar, replaced Top Sail.
Structure: The helicopter is raised to flight deck level by a lift. In addition to the 8 tubes for the SS-N-14 A/S system and the pair of twin launchers for SA-N-3 system with Goblet missiles, Kara class mounts the SA-N-4 system in 2 silos, either side of the mast. The SA-N-3 system has only 2 loading doors per launcher and a larger launching arm.
Operational: Two of the class started refits in July 1987 and have been scrapped by the Ukraine. One more was scrapped in the Pacific in 1996. *Petropavlovsk* is laid up in the Pacific and is unlikely to go to sea again. In the Black Sea, there have been several reports of work being done on *Ochakov*, but these have not been confirmed. Formally, she remains in service. *Azov* was cannibalised for spares in 1998. *Kerch* is based in the Black Sea at Sevastopol and completed a refit in 2005.

DESTROYERS

Notes: There have been reports of a programme to replace the ageing Udaloy and Sovremenny class inventories. Project 21956 is reportedly for a 9,000-ton ship but the status of the project has not been confirmed.

1 KASHIN (PROJECT 61) CLASS (DDGM)

Name	*No*	*Builders*	*Laid down*	*Launched*	*Commissioned*
SMETLIVY	810	Nikolayev North, Ukraine	15 July 1966	26 Aug 1967	25 Sep 1969

Displacement, tons: 4,010 standard; 4,750 full load
Dimensions, feet (metres): 472.4 × 51.8 × 15.4 *(144 × 15.8 × 4.7)*
Main machinery: COGAG; 4 DE 59 gas turbines; 72,000 hp(m) *(52.9 MW)*; 2 shafts
Speed, knots: 32. **Range, n miles:** 4,000 at 18 kt; 1,520 at 32 kt
Complement: 280 (25 officers)

Missiles: SSM: 8 Zvezda SS-N-25 (KH 35 Uran) (2 quad) ❶.
SAM: 2 SA-N-1 Goa twin launchers ❷; command guidance to 31.5 km *(17 n miles)* at 2 Mach; warhead 72 kg; altitude 91.4-22,860 m *(300-75,000 ft)*; 32 missiles.
Guns: 2—3 in *(76 mm)*/59 AK 726 (1 or 2 twin) ❸; 90 rds/min to 16 km *(8.5 n miles)*; weight of shell 5.9 kg.
Torpedoes: 5—21 in *(533 mm)* (quin) tubes ❹. Combination of 53 cm torpedoes.
A/S mortars: 2 RBU 6000 12-tubed trainable ❺; range 6,000 m; warhead 31 kg; 120 rockets.
Countermeasures: Decoys: PK 16 chaff launchers (modified). 2 towed torpedo decoys.
ESM/ECM: 2 Bell Shroud. 2 Watch Dog.
Weapons control: 3 Tee Plinth and 4 Tilt Pot optronic directors.
Radars: Air/surface search: Head Net C ❻; 3D; E-band.
Big Net ❼; C-band.

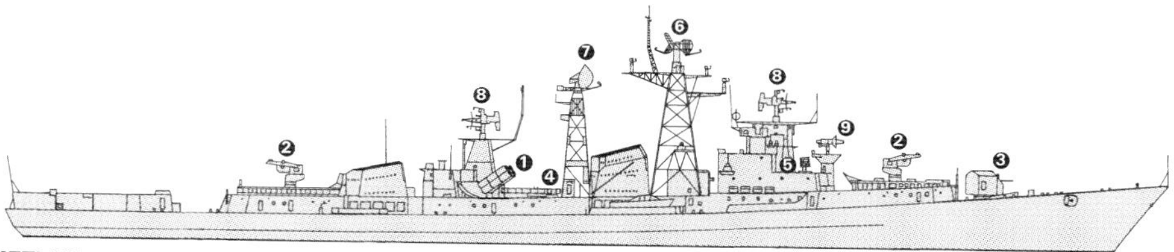

SMETLIVY
(Scale 1 : 1,200), **Ian Sturton** / 0126351

Navigation: 2 Don 2/Don Kay/Palm Frond; I-band.
Fire control: 2 Peel Group ❽; H/I-band (for SA-N-1). 1 Owl Screech ❾; G-band (for guns).
IFF: High Pole B.
Sonars: Bull Nose (MGK 336) or Wolf Paw; hull-mounted; active search and attack; medium frequency.
Vega; VDS; active search; medium frequency.

Programmes: The first class of warships in the world to rely entirely on gas-turbine propulsion. Type name is *bolshoy protivolodochny korabl*, meaning large anti-submarine ship.

Modernisation: Modernised with a VDS aft, vice the after gun, and fitted for SS-N-25 in place of the RBU 1000 launchers.
Operational: Based in the Black Sea. Refitted from 1990 to 1996 but back in service in 1997. Deployed to the Indian Ocean in 2003 and remains active.
Sales: Additional ships of a modified design built for India. First transferred September 1980, the second in June 1982, the third in 1983, the fourth in August 1986 and the fifth and last in January 1988.

SMETLIVY
*10/2008**, **Laursen/Jarnasen** / 1353327

1 UDALOY II (FREGAT) CLASS (PROJECT 1155.1) (DDGHM)

Name	*No*	*Builders*	*Laid down*	*Launched*	*Commissioned*
ADMIRAL CHABANENKO	650 (ex-437)	Yantar, Kaliningrad 820	15 Sep 1988	14 Dec 1992	20 Feb 1999

Displacement, tons: 7,700 standard; 8,900 full load
Dimensions, feet (metres): 536.4 × 63.3 × 24.6 *(163.5 × 19.3 × 7.5)*
Main machinery: COGAG; 2 gas turbines; 48,600 hp(m) *(35.72 MW)*; 2 gas turbines; 24,200 hp(m) *(17.79 MW)*; 2 shafts
Speed, knots: 28
Range, n miles: 4,000 at 18 kt
Complement: 249 (29 officers)

Missiles: SSM: 8 Raduga SS-N-22 Sunburn (3M-82 Moskit) (2 quad) ❶; active/passive radar homing to 160 km *(87 n miles)* at 2.5 Mach (4.5 for attack); warhead nuclear or HE 300 kg; sea-skimmer.
SAM: 8 SA-N-9 Gauntlet (Klinok) vertical launchers ❷; command guidance; active radar homing to 12 km *(6.5 n miles)* at 2 Mach; warhead 15 kg. 64 missiles; 4 channels of fire.
SAM/Guns: 2 CADS-N-1 (Kashtan) ❸; each with twin 30 mm Gatling; combined with 8 SA-N-11 (Grisson) and Hot Flash/Hot Spot fire-control radar/optronic director. Laser beam guidance for missiles to 8 km *(4.4 n miles)*; warhead 9 kg; 9,000 rds/min combined to 1.5 km for guns.
A/S: Novator SS-N-15 (Starfish); inertial flight to 45 km *(24.3 n miles)*; payload Type 40 torpedo or nuclear, fired from torpedo tubes.
Guns: 2—130 mm/54 (twin) AK 130 ❹; 70 rds/min to 22 km *(12 n miles)*; weight of shell 33.4 kg.
Torpedoes: 8—21 in *(533 mm)* (2 quad tubes) ❺. Combination of 53 cm torpedoes. The tubes are protected by flaps in the superstructure.
A/S mortars: 2 RBU 6000 ❻. 12-tubed trainable; range 6,000 m; warhead 31 kg.
Countermeasures: 8 PK 10 and 2 PK 2 chaff launchers ❼.
ESM/ECM: 2 Wine Glass (intercept). 2 Bell Shroud. 2 Bell Squat. 4 Half Cup laser warner. 2 Shot Dome.
Weapons control: M 145 radar and optronic system. 2 Bell Crown datalink. Band Stand ❽ datalink for SS-N-22; 2 Light Bulb, 2 Round House and 1 Bell Nest datalinks.
Radars: Air search: Strut Pair II ❾; F-band.
Top Plate ❿; 3D; D/E-band.
Surface search: 3 Palm Frond ⓫; I-band.
Fire control: 2 Cross Swords ⓬; K-band (for SA-N-9). Kite Screech ⓭; H/I/K-band (for 100 mm gun).
Band Stand (Mineral ME) ❽; D-band (for SS-N-22).
CCA: Fly Screen B ⓮.
IFF: Salt Pot B and C.

Sonars: Horse Jaw (Polinom); hull-mounted; active search and attack; medium/low frequency.
Horse Tail; VDS; active search; medium frequency.

Helicopters: 2 Ka-27 Helix A ⓯.

Programmes: A single ship follow-on class from the Udaloys. NATO designator Balcom 12. At least two more were projected with names *Admiral Basisty* and *Admiral Kucherov*; *Basisty* was scrapped in March 1994, and *Kucherov* was never started.
Structure: Similar size to the Udaloy and has the same propulsion machinery. Improved combination of weapon systems owing something to both the Sovremenny and the Neustrashimy classes. The distribution of SA-N-9 launchers may be the same as Udaloy class. The torpedo tubes are protected by a hinged flap in the superstructure.
Operational: Sea trials started on 14 September 1995 from Baltiysk. Deployed to the Northern Fleet in March 1999 when the pennant number changed. Based at Severomorsk. Deployed with *Pyotr Velikiy* in 2008–09.

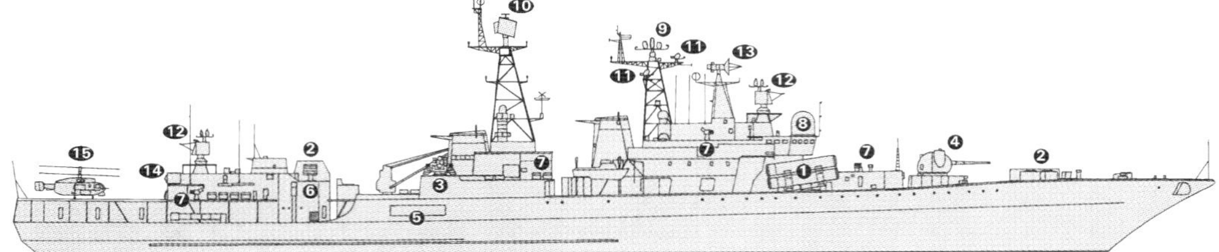

ADMIRAL CHABANENKO *(Scale 1 : 1,200), Ian Sturton* / 0569929

ADMIRAL CHABANENKO *9/2006, B Sullivan* / 1164812

ADMIRAL CHABANENKO *8/2002* / 0528328

8 UDALOY (FREGAT) CLASS (PROJECT 1155) (DDGHM)

Name	*No*	*Builders*	*Laid down*	*Launched*	*Commissioned*
VITSE ADMIRAL KULAKOV	400	Zhdanov Yard, Leningrad 190	4 Nov 1977	16 May 1980	10 Jan 1982
ADMIRAL TRIBUTS	564	Zhdanov Yard, Leningrad 190	19 Apr 1980	26 Mar 1983	30 Dec 1985
MARSHAL SHAPOSHNIKOV	543	Yantar, Kaliningrad 820	25 May 1983	27 Dec 1984	30 Dec 1985
SEVEROMORSK (ex-*Simferopol*, ex-*Marshal Budienny*)	619	Yantar, Kaliningrad 820	12 June 1984	24 Dec 1985	30 Dec 1987
ADMIRAL LEVCHENKO (ex-*Kharbarovsk*)	605	Zhdanov Yard, Leningrad 190	27 Jan 1982	21 Feb 1985	30 Sep 1988
ADMIRAL VINOGRADOV	572	Yantar, Kaliningrad 820	5 Feb 1986	4 June 1987	30 Dec 1988
ADMIRAL KHARLAMOV	678	Yantar, Kaliningrad 820	7 Aug 1986	29 June 1988	30 Dec 1989
ADMIRAL PANTELEYEV	548	Yantar, Kaliningrad 820	28 Jan 1988	7 Feb 1990	19 Dec 1991

Displacement, tons: 6,700 standard; 8,500 full load
Dimensions, feet (metres): 536.4 × 63.3 × 24.6 *(163.5 × 19.3 × 7.5)*
Flight deck, feet (metres): 65.6 × 59 *(20 × 18)*
Main machinery: COGAG; 2 gas turbines; 55,500 hp(m) *(40.8 MW)*; 2 gas turbines; 13,600 hp(m) *(10 MW)*; 2 shafts
Speed, knots: 29
Range, n miles: 2,600 at 30 kt; 7,700 at 18 kt
Complement: 249 (29 officers)

Missiles: SAM: 8 SA-N-9 Gauntlet (Klinok) vertical launchers ❶; command guidance; active radar homing to 12 km *(6.5 n miles)* at 2 Mach; warhead 15 kg; altitude 3.4-12,192 m *(10-40,000 ft)*; 64 missiles; four channels of fire.
The launchers are set into the ships' structures with 6 ft diameter cover plates-4 on the forecastle, 2 between the torpedo tubes and 2 at the forward end of the after deckhouse between the RBUs.
A/S: 2 Raduga SS-N-14 Silex (Rastrub) quad launchers ❷; command guidance to 55 km *(30 n miles)* at 0.95 Mach; payload nuclear 5 kT or Type 40 torpedo or Type E53-72 torpedo. SSM version; range 35 km *(19 n miles)*; warhead 500 kg.
Guns: 2—3.9 in *(100 mm)*/70 ❸; 60 rds/min to 21.5 km *(11.5 n miles)*; weight of shell 15.6 kg.
4—30 mm/65 AK 630 ❹; 6 barrels per mounting; 3,000 rds/min combined to 2 km.
Torpedoes: 8—21 in *(533 mm)* (2 quad) tubes ❺. Combination of 53 cm torpedoes.
A/S mortars: 2 RBU 6000 12-tubed trainable ❻; range 6,000 m; warhead 31 kg.
Mines: Rails for 26 mines.
Countermeasures: Decoys: 2 PK-2 and 8 PK-10 chaff launchers. US Masker type noise reduction.
ESM/ECM: 2 Foot Ball B (*Levchenko* onwards); 2 Wine Glass (intercept). 6 Half Cup laser warner (*Levchenko* onwards); 2 Bell Squat (jammers).

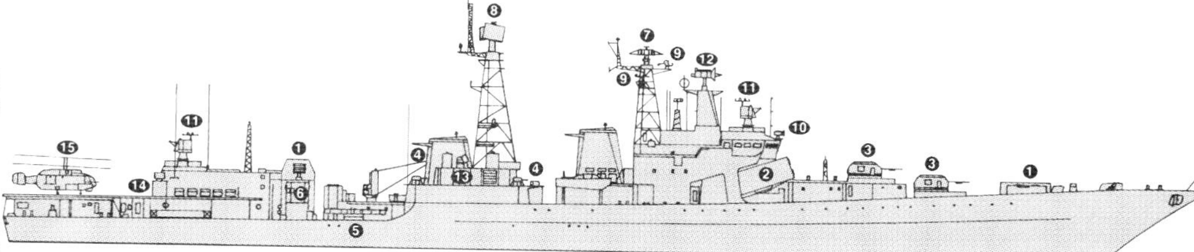

SEVEROMORSK *(Scale 1 : 1,200), Ian Sturton* / 0506079

Weapons control: MP 145 radar and optronic system. 2 Bell Crown and Round House C datalink.
Radars: Air search: Strut Pair ❼; F-band.
Top Plate ❽; 3D; D/E-band.
Surface search: 3 Palm Frond ❾; I-band.
Fire control: 2 Eye Bowl ❿; F-band (for SS-N-14). 2 Cross Sword ⓫; K-band (for SA-N-9). Kite Screech ⓬; H/I/K-band (for 100 mm guns). 2 Bass Tilt ⓭; H/I/K-band (for 30 mm guns).
IFF: Salt Pot A and B. Box Bar A and B.
Tacan: 2 Round House.
CCA: Fly Screen B (by starboard hangar) ⓮. 2 Fly Spike B.
Sonars: Horse Jaw (Polinom); hull-mounted; active search and attack; low/medium frequency.
Mouse Tail; VDS; active search; medium frequency.

Helicopters: 2 Ka-27 Helix A ⓯.

Programmes: Design approved in October 1972. Successor to Kresta II class but based on Krivak class. Type name is *bolshoy protivolodochny korabl* meaning large anti-submarine ship. Programme stopped at 12 in favour of Udaloy II class (Type 1155.1).

Structure: The two hangars are set side by side with inclined elevating ramps to the flight deck. Has pre-wetting NBCD equipment and replenishment at sea gear. Active stabilisers are fitted. The chaff launchers are on both sides of the foremast and inboard of the torpedo tubes. Cage Flask aerials are mounted on the mainmast spur and on the mast on top of the hangar. There are indications of a nuclear release mechanism, or interlock, on the lower tubes of the SS-N-14 launchers.
Operational: These general purpose ships have good sea-keeping and endurance and are the backbone of the fleet. Based as follows: Northern Fleet- *Severomorsk, Kulakov, Kharlamov* and *Levchenko*; Pacific Fleet- *Shaposhnikov, Panteleyev, Vinogradov* and *Tributs*. *Vinogradov* was in collision in April 2000 but was quickly repaired. *Severomorsk* deployed to St Petersburg for refit in June 1998 completing in late 2000, and *Levchenko* followed in November 1999 completing in 2001. The fourth of class, *Zakharov* was scrapped after a fire in March 1992. *Tributs* was in reserve in 1994 and had a machinery space fire in September 1995, was back in service in mid-1999. *Udaloy* and *Spiridonov* have been laid up or scrapped. *Kulakov* is expected to return to service in 2009 following a refit. *Vasilevsky* was decommissioned in 2007.

MARSHAL SHAPOSHNIKOV *6/2006, Ships of the World* / 1159991

ADMIRAL LEVCHENKO *6/2005, Jurg Kürsener* / 1151345

ADMIRAL PANTELEYEV *10/2008*, Guy Toremans* / 1353328

7 SOVREMENNY (SARYCH) CLASS (PROJECT 956/956A) (DDGHM)

Name	*No*	*Builders*	*Laid down*	*Launched*	*Commissioned*
BURNY	778	Zhdanov Yard, Leningrad (190)	4 Nov 1983	30 Dec 1986	30 Sep 1988
GREMYASHCHIY (ex-*Bezuderzhny*)	406	Zhdanov Yard, Leningrad (190)	23 Nov 1984	30 May 1987	30 Dec 1988
BYSTRY	715	Zhdanov Yard, Leningrad (190)	29 Oct 1985	28 Nov 1987	30 Sep 1989
BEZBOYAZNENNYY	754	Zhdanov Yard, Leningrad (190)	8 Jan 1987	18 Feb 1989	28 Nov 1990
BESPOKOINY	620	Zhdanov Yard, Leningrad (190)	18 Apr 1987	22 Feb 1992	29 Dec 1993
NASTOYCHIVY (ex-*Moskowski Komsomolets*)	610	Zhdanov Yard, Leningrad (190)	7 Apr 1988	15 Feb 1992	27 Mar 1993
ADMIRAL USHAKOV (ex-*Besstrashny*)	434	Zhdanov Yard, Leningrad (190)	16 Apr 1988	31 Dec 1992	17 Apr 1994

Displacement, tons: 6,500 standard; 7,940 full load
Dimensions, feet (metres): 511.8 × 56.8 × 21.3 (*156 × 17.3 × 6.5*)
Main machinery: 4 KVN boilers; 2 GTZA-674 turbines; 99,500 hp(m) (*73.13 MW*) sustained; 2 shafts; bow thruster
Speed, knots: 32
Range, n miles: 2,400 at 32 kt; 6,500 at 20 kt; 4,000 at 14 kt
Complement: 296 (25 officers) plus 60 spare

Missiles: SSM: 8 Raduga SS-N-22 Sunburn (3M-80 Zubr) (2 quad) launchers ❶; active/passive radar homing to 110 km (*60 n miles*) at 2.5 (4.5 for attack) Mach; warhead nuclear 200 kT or HE 300 kg; sea-skimmer. From *Bespokoiny* onwards the launchers are longer and fire a modified missile (3M-82 Moskit) with a range of 160 km (*87 n miles*).
SAM: 2 SA-N-7 Gadfly 3S 90 (Uragan) ❷; command/semi-active radar and IR homing to 25 km (*13.5 n miles*) at 3 Mach; warhead 70 kg; altitude 15-14,020 m (*50-46,000 ft*); 44 missiles. Multiple channels of fire. From *Bespokoiny* onwards the same launcher is used for the SA-N-7b Grizzly.
Guns: 4—130 mm/54 (2 twin) AK 130 ❸; 70 rds/min to 22 km (*12 n miles*); weight of shell 33.4 kg.
4—30 mm/65 AK 630 ❹; 6 barrels per mounting; 3,000 rds/min combined to 2 km.
Torpedoes: 4—21 in (*533 mm*) (2 twin) tubes ❺. Combination of 53 cm torpedoes.
A/S mortars: 2 RBU 1000 (Smerch 3) 6-barrelled ❻; range 1,000 m; warhead 100 kg; 120 rockets carried. Torpedo countermeasure.
Mines: Mine rails for up to 22.
Countermeasures: Decoys: 8 PK 10 and 2 PK 2 chaff launchers.
ESM/ECM: 4 Foot Ball (some variations including 2 Bell Shroud and 2 Bell Squat). 6 Half Cup laser warner.
Combat data systems: Sapfir-U.
Weapons control: 1 Squeeze Box optronic director and laser rangefinder ❼. Band Stand ❽ datalink for SS-N-22. Bell Nest, 2 Light Bulb and 2 Tee Pump datalinks.

NASTOYCHIVY *7/2008*, Per Körnefeldt* / 1353329

Radars: Air search: Top Plate (MR-750 Fregat) ❾; 3D; D/E-band.
Surface search: 3 Palm Frond (MR 212/201) ❿; I-band.
Fire control: 6 Front Dome ⓫; G-band (for SA-N-7/17). Kite Screech (MR-184) ⓬; H/I/K-band (for 130 mm guns). 2 Bass Tilt ⓭; H/I-band (for 30 mm guns).
Band Stand (Mineral ME) ❽; D-band (for SS-N-22).
IFF: Salt Pot A and B. High Pole A and B. Long Head.
Tacan: 2 Light Bulb.
Sonars: Bull Horn (MGK-335 Platina) and Whale Tongue; hull-mounted; active search and attack; medium frequency.

Helicopters: 1 Kamov Ka-27 Helix ⓮.

Programmes: Type name is *eskadrenny minonosets* meaning destroyer. From *Bespokoiny* onwards the class is known as 956A. Total of 17 built for Russia, two (hulls 18 and 19) for China, and one more (*Bulny*) which is unlikely to be completed unless for export.
Structure: Telescopic hangar. The fully automatic 130 mm gun was first seen in 1976. Chaff launchers are fitted on both sides of the foremast and either side of the after SAM launcher. A longer range version of SS-N-22 has been introduced in the Type 956A. This has slightly longer launch tubes. Also the SAM system has been improved to take the SA-N-17. There are also some variations in the EW fit.
Operational: A specialist surface warfare ship complementing the ASW-capable Udaloy class. Based as follows: Northern Fleet—*Admiral Ushakov, Gremyashchiy*. Pacific Fleet—*Burny, Bezboyaznennyy* and *Bystry*. Baltic Fleet—*Nastoychivy* and *Bespokoiny*. So far 11 others have paid off or are non-operational. *Bystry* completed refit in 2002 and *Bezboyaznennyy* in 2004. 434 renamed *Admiral Ushakov* in 2004. Steam-plant reliability has been a class problem.
Sales: Hulls 18 and 19 which were near completion in 1996, were sold to China and sailed in December 1999 and December 2000 respectively, from the Baltic to the South China Sea. A contract for the procurement of two new ships was signed by the Chinese government on 3 January 2002.

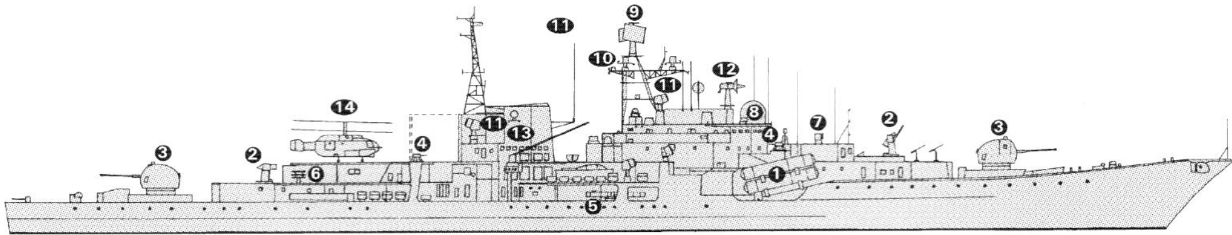

BYSTRY *(Scale 1 : 1,200), Ian Sturton* / 1151086

BURNY *10/2005, Ships of the World* / 1151154

FRIGATES

0 + 1 GROM CLASS (PROJECT 1244.1) (FFG)

Name	*No*	*Builders*	*Laid down*	*Launched*	*Commissioned*
BORODINO (ex-*Novik*)	–	Yantar, Kaliningrad	26 July 1997	2001	2009

Displacement, tons: 3,600 full load
Dimensions, feet (metres): 400.3 × 49.2 × 31.2 (sonar) (*122.0 × 15.0 × 9.5*)
Main machinery: CODAG; 2 gas turbines; 2 diesels; 2 shafts
Speed, knots: 30

Missiles: SSM: Space for eight or 16 Zvezda SS-N-25 (KH 35 Uran) ❶ (2 quad); active radar homing to 130 km (*70.2 n miles*) at 0.9 Mach; warhead 145 kg; sea skimmer.
SAM: Space for VLS system ❷.
Guns: 1—3 in (*76 mm*)/59 AK 176 ❸.
2—30 mm AK 630 ❹.
Radars: Air/surface search: Top Plate (Fregate M) ❺; 3D; D/E-band.
Surface search: Cross Dome; E/F-band ❻.
Fire control: Bass Tilt; H/I-band ❼.
Sonars: Hull mounted and VDS.

Helicopters: 1 Ka-29 Helix.

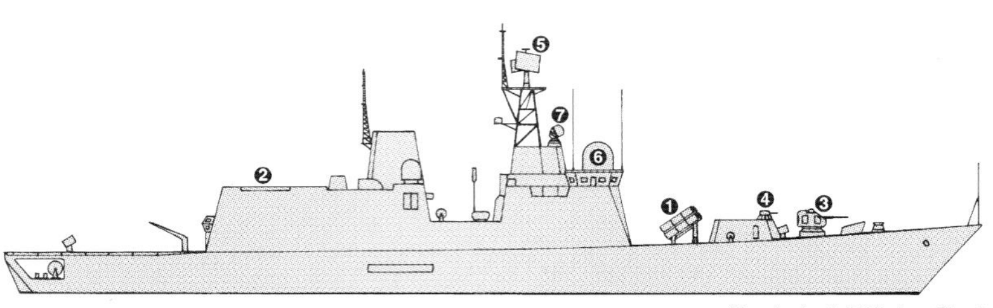

NOVIK *(Scale 1 : 1,200), Ian Sturton* / 0019031

Programmes: Designed by Almaz. Considerable publicity when keel laid down in 1997 but the project stalled due to budget cuts. However, building was reported to have been restarted in 2003 and it is speculated that the ship was being modified to act as an unarmed training ship in 2004. Building progress is very slow.
Structure: Most details are speculative and are based on the original published export design.
Operational: Likely to be based in the Baltic Fleet.

4 KRIVAK (PROJECT 1135/1135M/1135MP) CLASS (FFM)

Name	*No*	*Type*	*Builders*	*Laid down*	*Launched*	*Commissioned*
NEUKROTIMY	731	II	Yantar, Kaliningrad	22 Jan 1976	27 June 1977	30 Dec 1977
PYLKY	702	I Mod	Zhdanov, Leningrad	16 May 1977	20 Aug 1978	28 Dec 1978
LADNY	801	I	Kamish-Burun, Kerch	25 May 1979	7 May 1980	29 Dec 1980
PYTLIVY	808	II	Yantar, Kaliningrad	27 June 1979	16 Apr 1981	30 Nov 1981

Displacement, tons: 3,100 standard; 3,650 full load
Dimensions, feet (metres): 405.2 × 46.9 × 24 (sonar) *(123.5 × 14.3 × 7.3)*
Main machinery: COGAG; 2 M8K gas-turbines; 55,500 hp(m) *(40.8 MW)*; 2 M 62 gas-turbines; 13,600 hp(m) *(10 MW)*; 2 shafts
Speed, knots: 32. **Range, n miles:** 4,000 at 14 kt; 1,600 at 30 kt
Complement: 194 (18 officers)

Missiles: SSM: 8 Zvezda SS-N-25 (KH 35 Uran) (2 quad) ❶; (Krivak I after modernisation); fitted for but not with.
SAM: 2 SA-N-4 Gecko (Zif 122) twin launchers ❷; Osa-M semi-active radar homing to 15 km *(8 n miles)* at 2.5 Mach; warhead 50 kg; altitude 9.1-3,048 m *(30-10,000 ft)*; 40 missiles.
A/S: Raduga SS-N-14 Silex quad launcher ❸; command guidance to 55 km *(30 n miles)* at 0.95 Mach; payload nuclear 5 kT or Type 40 torpedo or Type E53-72 torpedo. SSM version; range 35 km *(19 n miles)*; warhead 500 kg.
Guns: 4—3 in *(76 mm)*/59 AK 726 (2 twin) (Krivak I) ❹; 90 rds/min to 16 km *(8.5 n miles)*; weight of shell 5.9 kg.
2—3.9 in *(100 mm)*/70 AK 100 (Krivak II) ❺; 60 rds/min to 21.5 km *(11.5 n miles)*; weight of shell 15.6 kg.
Torpedoes: 8—21 in *(533 mm)* (2 quad) tubes ❻. Combination of 53 cm torpedoes.
A/S mortars: 2 RBU 6000 12-tubed trainable ❼; (not in modernised Krivak I); range 6,000 m; warhead 31 kg.
Mines: Capacity for 16.
Countermeasures: Decoys: 4 PK 16 or 10 PK 10 chaff launchers. Towed torpedo decoy.
ESM/ECM: 2 Bell Shroud. 2 Bell Squat. Half Cup laser warning (in some).
Radars: Air search: Head Net C ❽; 3D; E-band; or Half Plate (Krivak I mod) ❾.
Surface search: Don Kay or Palm Frond or Don 2 or Spin Trough ❿; I-band.

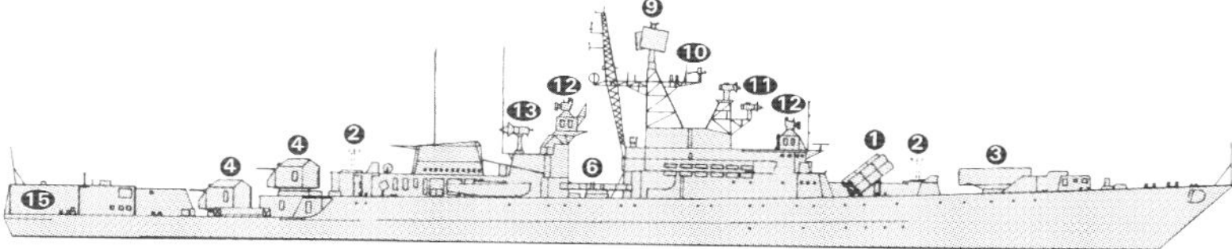

KRIVAK I (mod)

(Scale 1 : 1,200), Ian Sturton / 0506083

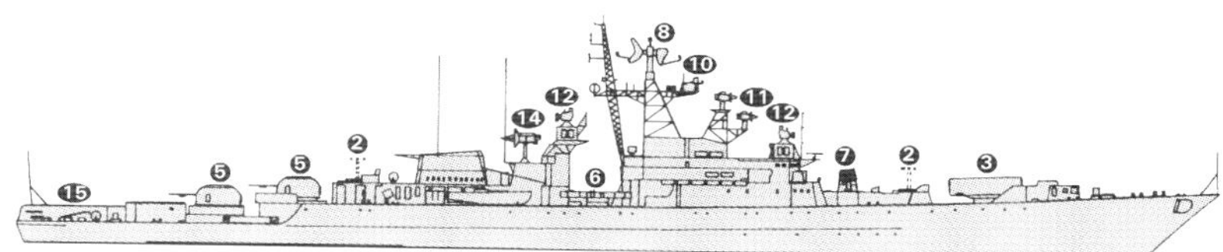

KRIVAK II

(Scale 1 : 1,200), Ian Sturton / 0506084

Fire control: 2 Eye Bowl ⓫; F-band (for SS-N-14). 2 Pop Group ⓬; F/H/I-band (for SA-N-4). Owl Screech (Krivak I) ⓭; G-band. Kite Screech (Krivak II) ⓮; H/I/K-band. Plank Shave (Harpun B) (for SS-N-25) not fitted.
IFF: High Pole B.
Sonars: Bull Nose (MGK-335S or MG-332); hull-mounted; active search and attack; medium frequency.
Mare Tail (MGK-345) or Steer Hide (some Krivak Is after modernisation); VDS (MG 325) ⓯; active search; medium frequency.

Programmes: Type name was originally *bolshoy protivolodochny korabl*, meaning large anti-submarine ship. Changed in 1977–78 to *storozhevoy korabl* meaning escort ship. The naval Krivaks I and II are known as the Burevestnik class and the border guard ships Krivak III (listed separately) as Nerey class.
Modernisation: Top Plate radar has replaced Head Net in some and a more modern VDS is also fitted. SS-N-25 launchers are fitted in *Pylky*. This programme has stopped and missiles are not embarked. The launchers replaced the RBU mountings.
Structure: The modified Krivak I class has a larger bow. Krivak II class has Y-gun mounted higher than in Krivak I and the break to the quarterdeck further aft apart from other variations noted above.
Operational: Black Sea: *Ladny, Pytlivy*. Baltic: *Pylky, Neukrotimy*.

PYTLIVY (II)

6/2006, Marco Ghiglino / 1164810

LADNY (I)

7/2000, Hartmut Ehlers / 0105545

LADNY (I)

10/2007, Rafael Cabrera / 1170210

2 NEUSTRASHIMY (JASTREB) CLASS (PROJECT 1154) (FFHM)

Name	*No*	*Builders*	*Laid down*	*Launched*	*Commissioned*
NEUSTRASHIMY	712	Yantar, Kaliningrad	27 Mar 1987	25 May 1988	24 Jan 1993
YAROSLAV MUDRYY	727	Yantar, Kaliningrad	27 May 1988	1991	2009

Displacement, tons: 3,450 standard; 4,250 full load
Dimensions, feet (metres): 425.3 oa; 403.5 wl × 50.9 × 15.7 *(129.6; 123 × 15.5 × 4.8)*
Main machinery: COGAG; 2 gas turbines; 48,600 hp(m) *(35.72 MW)*; 2 gas turbines; 24,200 hp(m) *(17.79 MW)*; 2 shafts
Speed, knots: 30. **Range, n miles**: 4,500 at 16 kt
Complement: 210 (35 officers)

Missiles: SSM: Fitted for but not with 16 SS-N-25 (4 quad). SS-CX-5 Sapless (possibly a version of SS-N-22 (Moskit M)) may be carried (see *Torpedoes*).
SAM: 4 SA-N-9 Gauntlet (Klinok) octuple vertical launchers ❶; command guidance; active radar homing to 12 km *(6.5 n miles)* at 2 Mach; warhead 15 kg. 32 missiles.
SAM/Guns: 2 CADS-N-1 (Kortik/Kashtan) (3M87) ❷; each has a twin 30 mm Gatling combined with 8 SA-N-11 (Grisson) and Hot Flash/Hot Spot fire-control radar/optronic director. Laser beam guidance for missiles to 8 km *(4.4 n miles)*; warhead 9 kg; 9,000 rds/min (combined) to 1.5 km (for guns).
A/S: SS-N-15/16; inertial flight to 120 km *(65 n miles)*; payload Type 40 torpedo or nuclear warhead; fired from torpedo tubes.
Guns: 1—3.9 in *(100 mm)*/59 A 190E ❸; 80 rds/min to 21.5 km *(11.5 n miles)*; weight of shell 15.6 kg.
Torpedoes: 6—21 in *(533 mm)* tubes combined with A/S launcher ❹; can fire SS-N-15/16 missiles with Type 40 anti-submarine torpedoes or 53 cm torpedoes.
A/S mortars: 1 RBU 12,000 ❺; 10-tubed trainable; range 12,000 m; warhead 80 kg.
Mines: 2 rails.
Countermeasures: Decoys: 8 PK 10 and 2 PK 16 chaff launchers.

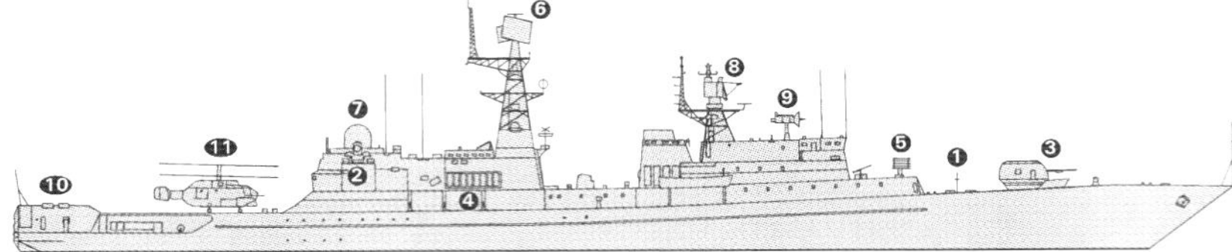

NEUSTRASHIMY *(Scale 1 : 1,200), Ian Sturton* / 0569927

ESM/ECM: Intercept and jammers. 2 Foot Ball; 2 Half Hat; 4 Half Cup laser intercept.
Weapons control: 2 Bell Crown datalink.
Radars: Air search: Top Plate ❻; 3D; D/E-band.
Air/surface search: Cross Dome ❼; E/F-band.
Navigation: 2 Palm Frond; I-band.
Fire control: Cross Sword ❽ (for SAM); K-band. Kite Screech B ❾ (for SSM and guns); I-band.
IFF: 2 Salt Pot; 4 Box Bar.
Sonars: Ox Yoke and Whale Tongue; hull-mounted; active search and attack; medium frequency.
Ox Tail; VDS ❿ or towed sonar array.

Helicopters: 1 Ka-27 Helix ⓫.

Programmes: At least four of the class were planned. The first of the class started sea trials in the Baltic in December 1990. Second of class *(Yaroslav Mudryy)* was launched in May 1991, but in October 1988 the shipyard stated that the hull would be sold for scrap. However, after several years' inaction, work recommenced in 2002 and it was confirmed in 2005 that the ship is to be completed. Sea trials began on 26 February 2009. The export version of the ship is known as 'Korsar'. The third ship *(Tuman)* was launched in July 1993 with only the hull completed and work stopped in December 1997 without any work being done. She is unlikely to be completed.
Structure: Slightly larger than the Krivak and has a helicopter which is a standard part of the armament of modern Western frigates. There are two horizontal launchers at main deck level on each side of the ship, angled at 18° from forward. These double up for A/S missiles of the SS-N-15/16 type using a 'plunge-fly-plunge' launch and flight and normal torpedoes. Similar launchers are behind shutters in the last three of the Kirov class. The helicopter deck extends across the full width of the ship. The after funnel is unusually flush decked but both funnels have been slightly extended after initial sea trials. Attempts have been made to incorporate stealth features. Main propulsion is the same as the Udaloy II class. Reported as having a basic computerised combat data system.
Operational: Based in the Baltic at Baltiysk.

NEUSTRASHIMY *6/2008*, Michael Nitz* / 1353330

NEUSTRASHIMY *11/2008*, US Navy* / 1353331

YAROSLAV MUDRYY *2/2009** / 1353675

1 + 1 GEPARD (PROJECT 11661) CLASS (FFGM)

Name	*No*	*Builders*	*Laid down*	*Launched*	*Commissioned*
TATARSTAN (ex-*Albatros*)	691	Zelenodolsk, Kazan, Tartarstan	15 Sep 1992	July 1993	12 July 2002
DAGESTAN (ex-*Burevestnik*)	–	Zelenodolsk, Kazan, Tartarstan	1994	2009	2010

Displacement, tons: 1,560 standard; 1,930 full load
Dimensions, feet (metres): 335.3 × 43.0 × 17.4 *(102.2 × 13.1 × 5.3)*
Main machinery: CODOG; 2 gas turbines; 30,850 hp(m) *(23.0 MW)*; 1 Type 61D diesel; 7,375 hp(m) *(5.5 MW)*; 2 shafts; cp props
Speed, knots: 26 (18 on diesels)
Range, n miles: 5,000 at 10 kt
Complement: 103 (accommodation for 131)

Missiles: SSM: 8 Zvezda SS-N-25 (KH 35 Uran) (2 quad) ❶; IR or radar homing to 130 km *(70.2 n miles)* at 0.9 Mach; warhead 145 kg; sea-skimmer.
SAM: 1 SA-N-4 Gecko twin launcher ❷; semi-active radar homing to 15 km *(8 n miles)* at 2.5 Mach; warhead 50 kg. 20 weapons.
Guns: 1—3 in *(76 mm)*/59 AK-176 ❸; 120 rds/min to 15 km *(8 n miles)*; weight of shell 5.9 kg.
2—30 mm/65 AK-630 ❹; 6 barrels per mounting; 3,000 rds/min combined to 2 km.
Torpedoes: 4—21 in *(533 mm)* (2 twin) tubes ❺ (probably not fitted).
A/S mortars: 1 RBU 6000 12-tubed trainable ❻ (probably not fitted).
Mines: 2 rails. 48 mines.
Countermeasures: Decoys: 4 PK 16 chaff launchers.
ESM/ECM: 2 Bell Shroud. 2 Bell Squat. Intercept and jammers.
Weapons control: 2 Light Bulb datalink. Hood Wink and Odd Box optronic systems. Band Stand ❼ datalink.
Radars: Air/surface search: Cross Dome ❽; E/F-band.
Fire control: Bass Tilt ❾; H/I-band (for guns). Pop Group ❿; F/H/I-band (for SAM). Garpun-B (for SSM); I/J-band. Band Stand (Mineral ME) ❼; D-band (for SS-N-25).
Navigation: Nayada; I-band.
IFF: 2 Square Head. 1 Salt Pot B.
Sonars: Ox Yoke; hull-mounted; active search and attack; medium frequency (probably not fitted).
Ox Tail (probably not fitted); VDS; active search and attack; medium frequency.

TATARSTAN *(Scale 1 : 900), Ian Sturton* / 1042094

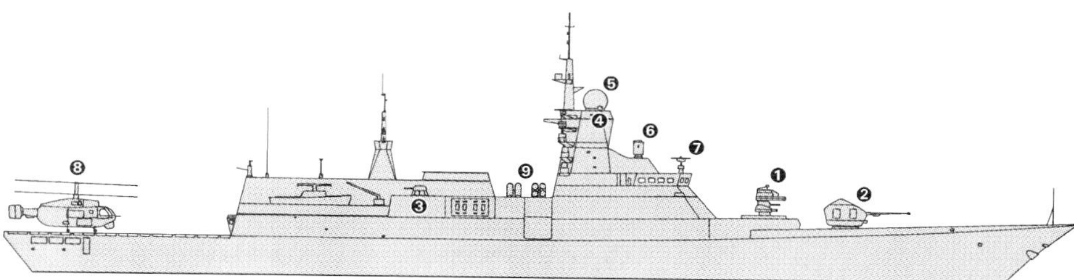

TATARSTAN *6/2005, Lemachko Collection* / 1154646

Programmes: Intended as a successor to the Koni class, the Gepard family of ships, of which there were some five variants, was developed with export in mind. The first of class *Yastreb* was laid down in 1988 but was later broken up in 1992. The second and third of class were to have been exported abroad but, following the completion of *Tatarstan* for the Russian Navy, a second ship *Dagestan* (ex-*Burevestnik*) is expected to follow in 2010.
Operational: Flagship of the Caspian Flotilla, the newly commissioned *Tatarstan* took part in the large Caspian naval exercise in August 2002.

1 + 4 (2) STEREGUSHCHIY CLASS (PROJECT 20380) (FFGHM)

Name	*No*	*Builders*	*Laid down*	*Launched*	*Commissioned*
STEREGUSHCHIY	530	Severnaya, St Petersburg	21 Dec 2001	16 May 2006	14 Nov 2007
SOOBRAZITELNY	–	Severnaya, St Petersburg	20 May 2003	2008	2010
BOIKY	–	Severnaya, St Petersburg	27 July 2005	2009	2010
SOVERSHENNY	–	Komsomolsk Shipyard	30 June 2006	2010	2011
STOIKY	–	Severnaya, St Petersburg	10 Nov 2006	2010	2011

Displacement, tons: 2,200 full load
Dimensions, feet (metres): 342.8 × 36.4 × 12.1 *(104.5 × 11.1 × 3.7)*
Main machinery: CODAD; 4 16 D 49 diesels; 24,000 hp *(17.9 MW)*; 2 shafts
Speed, knots: 26
Range, n miles: 3,500 at 14 kt
Complement: 100

Missiles: 1 CADS-N-1 (Kashtan) ❶; twin 30 mm Gatling combined with 8 SA-N-11 (Grisson) (9M311) and Hot Flash/Hot Spot fire-control radar/optronic director. Laser beam guidance for missiles to 8 km *(4.4 n miles)*; warhead 9 kg; 9,000 rds/min combined to 1.5 km for guns.
SA-N-10 (Igla).
Guns: 1—100 mm A-190 ❷; 80 rds/min to 21.5 km *(11.6 n miles)* weight of shell 15.6 kg. 2—30 mm/65 AK 630 ❸; 6 barrels per mounting; 3,000 rds/min to 2 km. 2—14.5 mm MGs.
Torpedoes: 8 Paket 324 mm (2 quad) tubes. MTT anti-torpedo; active/passive homing to 5 km *(2.7 n miles)*; warhead 70 kg.
Countermeasures: Decoys: 4 PK 10 launchers.
ESM/ECM: Pribor TK-25.
Combat data systems: MARS Sigma.
Weapons control: 2 MTK-201 optronic directors ❹.
Radars: Air/surface search: Furke-E; 3D ❺; E/F-band.
Surface search: Granit Monument; I-band.
Fire control: Ratep 5P-10E Puma ❻; I-band (for 100 mm gun).
Navigation: I-band ❼.
Sonars: Zarya; bow-mounted. Vinyetka low frequency active/passive towed array.

Helicopters: 1 Ka-27 Helix ❾.

Programmes: Multipurpose frigate designed to replace the Grisha class. The first batch being built at St Petersburg consists of four ships. A second building line has been started at Komsomolsk where orders for at least a further two ships are expected. There is an export version known as Project 20382 Tigr.
Structure: Steel hull. Composite superstructure. Bulbous bow. Nine watertight sub-divisions. Combined bridge and command centre. Space and weight provision for eight SS-N-25 missiles ❽.
Operational: *Steregushchiy* started sea trials in November 2006.

STEREGUSHCHIY *(Scale 1 : 900), Ian Sturton* / 1170229

STEREGUSHCHIY *6/2007, Ships of the World* / 1305154

STEREGUSHCHIY *5/2007, Ships of the World* 1167743

24 GRISHA (ALBATROS) (PROJECT 1124/1124M/1124K/1124EM) CLASS (FFLM)

North
ONEGA (ex-*MPK 7*) 164
MONCHEGORSK (ex-*MPK 14*) 190
SNEZNOGORSK (ex-*MPK 59*) 196
MPK 113 171
NARYAN-MAR (ex-*MPK 130*) 138
MPK 139 129
BREST (ex-*MPK 194*) 199
MPK 197 106
YUNGA (ex-*MPK 203*) 113

Pacific
MPK 17 362
METEL (ex-*MPK 64*) 323
MPK 82 375
MPK 107 332
SOVETSKAYA GAVANI (ex-*Leninskaya Kuznitsa*, ex-*MPK 125*) 350
MPK 178 (III) 392
MPK 191 (III) 369
STELYAK (ex-MPK 221) 354
KORETS (ex-*MPK 222*) 390

Black Sea
ALEKSANDROVETS (ex-*MPK 49 (III)*) 059
SUZDALETS (ex-*MPK 118*) 071
MUROMETS (ex-*MPK 134*) 064
KASIMOV (ex-*MPK 199*) 055
POVORINO (ex-*MPK 207*) 053
EISK (ex-*MPK 217*) 054

Displacement, tons: 950 standard; 1,200 full load
Dimensions, feet (metres): 233.6 × 32.2 × 12.1 (*71.2 × 9.8 × 3.7*)
Main machinery: CODAG; 1 gas-turbine; 15,000 hp(m) (*11 MW*); 2 diesels; 16,000 hp(m) (*11.8 MW*); 3 shafts
Speed, knots: 30
Range, n miles: 2,500 at 14 kt; 1,750 at 20 kt diesels; 950 at 27 kt
Complement: 70 (5 officers) (Grisha III); 60 (Grisha I)

Missiles: SAM: SA-N-4 Gecko twin launcher ❶; semi-active radar homing to 15 km (*8 n miles*) at 2.5 Mach; warhead 50 kg; altitude 9.1-3,048 m (*30-10,000 ft*); 20 missiles (see *Structure* for SA-N-9).
Guns: 2—57 mm/80 (twin) ❷; 120 rds/min to 6 km (*3.3 n miles*); weight of shell 2.8 kg.
1—3 in (*76 mm*)/59 AK 176 (Grisha V) ❸; 120 rds/min to 15 km (*8 n miles*); weight of shell 5.9 kg.
1—30 mm/65 (Grisha III and V classes) ❹; 6 barrels; 3,000 rds/min combined to 2 km.
Torpedoes: 4—21 in (*533 mm*) (2 twin) tubes ❺. Combination of 53 cm torpedoes.
A/S mortars: 2 RBU 6000 12-tubed trainable ❻; range 6,000 m; warhead 31 kg. (Only 1 in Grisha Vs.).
Depth charges: 2 racks (12).
Mines: Capacity for 18 in lieu of depth charges.
Countermeasures: Decoys: 4 PK 10 or 2 PK 16 chaff launchers.
ESM: 2 Watch Dog.
Radars: Air/surface search: Strut Curve (Strut Pair in early Grisha Vs) ❼; F-band; range 110 km (*60 n miles*) for 2 m^2 target.
Half Plate Bravo (in later Grisha Vs); E/F-band.
Navigation: Don 2; I-band.

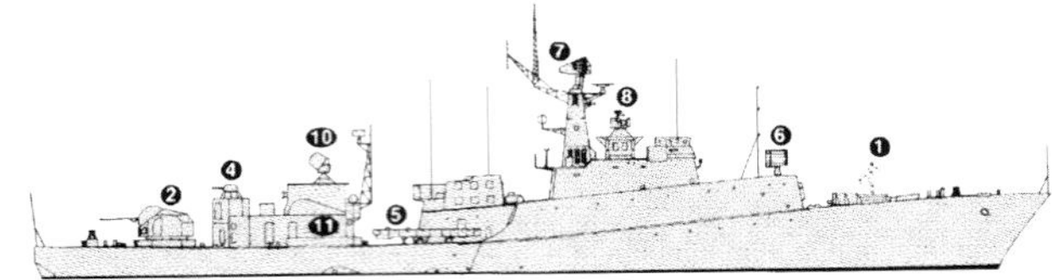

GRISHA III *(Scale 1 : 900), Ian Sturton* / 0506081

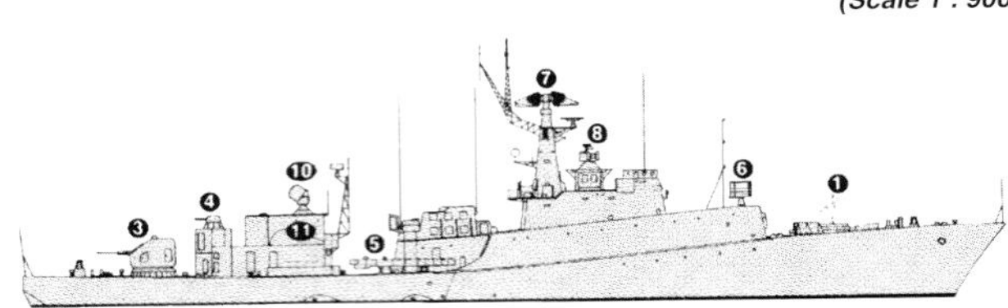

GRISHA V *(Scale 1 : 900), Ian Sturton* / 0506082

Fire control: Pop Group ❽; F/H/I-band (for SA-N-4). Bass Tilt (Grisha III and V) ❿; H/I-band (for 57/76 mm and 30 mm).
IFF: High Pole A or B. Square Head. Salt Pot.
Sonars: Bull Nose; hull-mounted; active search and attack; high/medium frequency.
Elk Tail; VDS ⓫; active search; high frequency. Similar to Hormone helicopter dipping sonar.

Programmes: Grisha III 1973–85 (three remaining); Grisha V 1982–1996 onwards (22 remaining). All were built at Kiev, Kharbarovsk and Zelenodolsk. Type name is *maly protivolodochny korabl* meaning small anti-submarine ship.

Structure: Grisha III class has Muff Cob radar removed, Bass Tilt and 30 mm ADG (fitted aft), and Rad-haz screen removed from abaft funnel as a result of removal of Muff Cob. Grisha V is similar to Grisha III with the after twin 57 mm mounting replaced by a single Tarantul type 76 mm gun.
Operational: Nine Grisha Vs are stationed in the Northern Fleet, two Grisha III and seven Vs in the Pacific and one III and five Vs in the Black Sea. The modified Grisha III, known as Grisha IV, has been decommissioned.
Sales: Two Grisha III to Lithuania in November 1992. One Grisha V in 1994 and four Grisha II in 1996 to Ukraine.

MPK 191 (III) *12/2005, Ships of the World* / 1151147

KASIMOV *5/2008*, C D Yaylali* / 1353332

SUZDALETS *5/2006, Lemachko Collection* / 1159860

0 + 1 (19) ADMIRAL GORSHKOV (PROJECT 22350) CLASS (FFGH)

Name	*No*	*Builders*	*Laid down*	*Launched*	*Commissioned*
ADMIRAL GORSHKOV	–	Severnaya Verf, St Petersburg	1 Feb 2006	2011	2013

Displacement, tons: 4,500
Dimensions, feet (metres): 433 × 52.5 × ?
(132 × 16 × ?)
Main machinery: To be announced
Speed, knots: To be announced
Range, n miles: To be announced
Complement: To be announced

Missiles: SSM: 8 SS-N-26 (Oniks) (3M55): inertial guidance and active/passive radar homing to 300 km *(162 n miles)* at 2.6 Mach; sea skimmer in terminal phase; warhead 250 kg; VLS silo.
SAM: SA-N-7 Gadfly (Uragan); command/semi-active radar and IR homing to 25 km *(13.5 n miles)* at 3 Mach; warhead 70 kg; VLS silo.
1 CADS-N-1 (Kashtan); has 30 mm Gatling combined with 8 SA-N-11 (Grisson) and Hot Flash/Hot Spot radar/optronic director; laser beam for guidance for missiles to 8 km *(4.4 n miles)*; warhead 9 kg; 9,000 rds/min to 1.5 km for guns.
A/S: Medvedka 2 (SS-N-29); inertial flight to 25 km *(13.5 n miles)*; payload Type 40 torpedo.
Guns: 1 — 130 mm A-192.
Torpedoes: To be announced.
Countermeasures: To be announced.

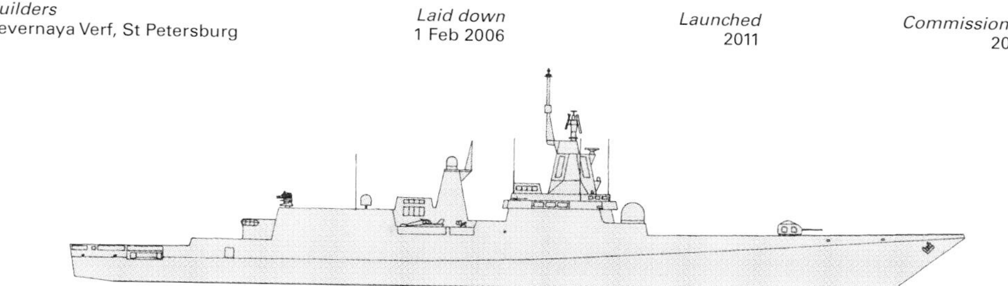

ADMIRAL GORSHKOV *(Scale 1 : 1,200), Ian Sturton* / 1159411

Combat data systems: To be announced.
Weapons control: To be announced.
Radars: Air search: To be announced.
Surface search: To be announced.
Fire control: To be announced.
Navigation: To be announced.
Sonars: To be announced.

Helicopters: 1 Ka-32.

Programmes: Severnaya Verf shipyard contracted on 21 October 2005 to build the lead Project 22350 frigate. Up to 20 ships of the class may be procured. Designed by the Severnoye Design Bureau, it is the first new class of major surface combatants to be procured in 15 years. The ship may be equipped with Brahmos rather than SS-N-26 missiles.
Structure: Slightly longer and wider than the Talwar class from which the design is reported to be developed.
Operational: The first ship is likely to be based in the Baltic.

CORVETTES

7 PARCHIM II CLASS (PROJECT 1331) (FFLM)

ZELENODOLSK (ex-MPK 99) 308
MPK 105 245
MPK 192 304
KAZANETS (ex-MPK 205) 311
ALEKSIN (ex-MPK 224) 218
MPK 227 243
KALMYKIA (ex-MPK 229) 232

Displacement, tons: 769 standard; 960 full load
Dimensions, feet (metres): 246.7 × 32.2 × 14.4
(75.2 × 9.8 × 4.4)
Main machinery: 3 Type M 504A diesels; 10,812 hp(m) *(7.95 MW)* sustained; 3 shafts
Speed, knots: 26. **Range, n miles:** 2,500 at 12 kt
Complement: 70 (8 officers)

Missiles: SAM: 2 SA-N-5 Grail quad launchers ❶; manual aiming; IR homing to 6 km *(3.2 n miles)* at 1.5 Mach; altitude to 2,500 m *(8,000 ft)*; warhead 1.5 kg.
Guns: 1 — 3 in *(76 mm)*/59 AK 176 ❷; 120 rds/min to 15 km *(8 n miles)*; weight of shell 5.9 kg.
1 — 30 mm/65 AK 630 ❸; 6 barrels; 3,000 rds/min combined to 2 km.
Torpedoes: 4 — 21 in *(533 mm)* (2 twin) tubes ❹. Combination of 53 cm torpedoes.
A/S mortars: 2 RBU 6000 12-tubed trainable ❺; range 6,000 m; warhead 31 kg. 96 weapons.
Depth charges: 2 racks.
Mines: Rails fitted.
Countermeasures: Decoys: 2 PK 16 chaff launchers.
ESM: 2 Watch Dog; intercept.
Weapons control: Hood Wink and Odd Box optronic systems.
Radars: Air/surface search: Cross Dome ❻; E/F-band.
Navigation: TSR 333 or Nayala or Kivach III; I-band.

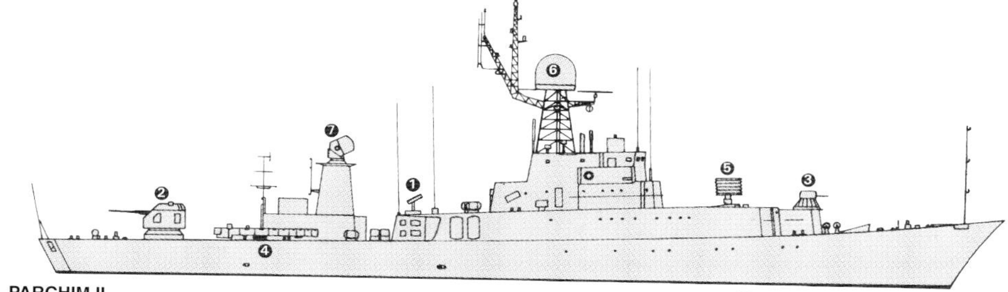

PARCHIM II *(Scale 1 : 600), Ian Sturton* / 0506204

Fire control: Bass Tilt ❼; H/I-band.
IFF: High Pole A.
Sonars: Bull Horn; hull-mounted; active search and attack; medium frequency.
Lamb Tail; helicopter type VDS; high frequency.

Programmes: Built in the GDR at Peenewerft, Wolgast for the USSR. First one commissioned 19 December 1986 and the last on 6 April 1990.

Structure: Similar design to the ex-GDR Parchim I class now serving with the Indonesian Navy but some armament differences.
Operational: All operate in the Baltic and are based at Baltiysk or Kronshtadt. All of the class refitted at Rostock in 1994–95. *Bashkortostan* (MPK 228) damaged by fire in 1999 and again in 2008. She is unlikely to be repaired.

ALEKSIN *7/2008*, Hartmut Ehlers* / 1353298

2 DERGACH (SIVUCH) (PROJECT 1239) CLASS (PGGJM)

Name	*No*	*Builders*	*Launched*	*Commissioned*
BORA (ex-*MRK 27*)	615	Zelenodolsk, Kazan	1987	20 May 1997
SAMUM (ex-*MRK 17*)	616 (ex-575, ex-890)	Zelenodolsk, Kazan	1992	31 Dec 1995

Displacement, tons: 1,050 full load
Dimensions, feet (metres): 211.6 × 55.8 × 12.5 *(64.5 × 17 × 3.8)*
Main machinery: CODOG; 2 gas turbines; 55,216 hp(m) *(40.6 MW)*; 2 diesels; 10,064 hp(m) *(7.4 MW)*; 2 hydroprops; 2 auxiliary diesels; 2 props on retractable pods
Speed, knots: 53 foil; 12 hullborne
Range, n miles: 600 at 50 kt; 2,500 at 12 kt
Complement: 67 (8 officers)

Missiles: SSM: 8 SS-N-22 (2 quad) Sunburn (3M-82 Moskit) launchers ❶; active radar homing to 160 km *(87 n miles)* at 2.5 Mach; warhead nuclear or 200 kT or HE 300 kg; sea-skimmer.
SAM: SA-N-4 Gecko twin launcher ❷; semi-active radar homing to 15 km *(8 n miles)* at 2.5 Mach; warhead 50 kg; 20 missiles.
Guns: 1—3 in *(76 mm)*/59 AK 176 ❸; 120 rds/min to 15 km *(8 n miles)*; weight of shell 5.9 kg.
2—30 mm/65 AK 630 ❹; 6 barrels per mounting; 3,000 rds/min combined to 2 km.
Countermeasures: Decoys: 2 PK 16 and 2 PK 10 chaff launchers.
ESM/ECM: 2 Foot Ball A. 2 Half Hats.
Weapons control: 2 Light Bulb datalink ❺. Band Stand ❻ datalink for SS-N-22; Bell Nest.
Radars: Air/surface search: Cross Dome ❼; E/F-band.
Fire control: Bass Tilt ❽; H/I-band (for guns).
Pop Group ❾; F/H/I-band (for SAM).
Band Stand (Mineral ME) ❻; D-band (for SS-N-22).
Navigation: SRN-207; I-band.
IFF: Square Head. Salt Pot.

Programmes: Almaz design approved 24 December 1980. Classified as a PGGA (Guided Missile Patrol Air Cushion Vessels). Both did trials from 1989 (Bora) and 1993 *(Samum)* before being accepted into service.
Structure: Twin-hulled surface effect design. The auxiliary diesels are for slow speed operations.
Operational: The design was unreliable but efforts were made in 1996/97 to restore both to an operational state. SS-N-22 missiles were test-fired in April 2003. Both ships have camouflaged hulls and are based at Sevastopol.

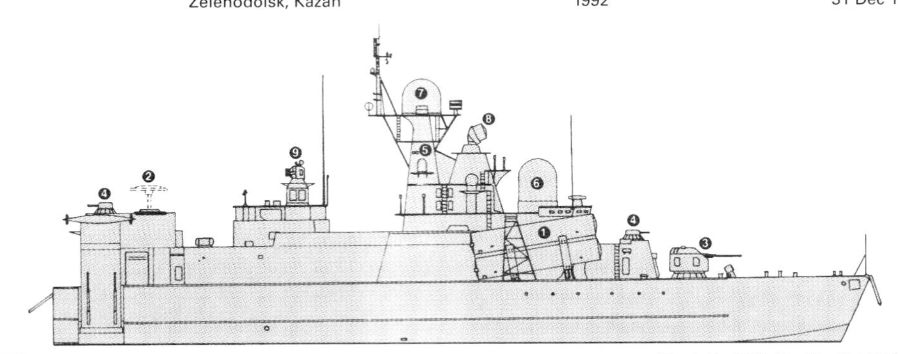

BORA *(Scale 1 : 600), Ian Sturton* / 0506086

BORA *10/2008*, Laursen/Jarnasen* 1353333

SAMUM *6/2003, Lemachko Collection* / 0580532

25 TARANTUL (MOLNYA) (PROJECT 1241.1/1241.1M/1241.1MP/1242.1) CLASS (FSGM)

Baltic
R 47 819
DIMITROVGRAD (ex-R 291) 825
R 125 (II) 833
R 257 852
R 187 855
R 2 870
MORSHANSK (ex-R 293) 874
R 5 992

Pacific
R 29 (II) 916
R 20 921
R 14 924
R 18 937
R 11 940
R 24 946
R 297 954
R 298 971
R 19 978
R 79 (II) 995

Black Sea
R 109 952
R 239 953
IVANOVETS (ex-R 334) 954
R 60 955
R 71 (II) 962

Caspian
MAK 160 (II) (ex-R 160) 054
STUPINETS (II) (ex-R 101) 705

Displacement, tons: 385 standard; 455 full load
Dimensions, feet (metres): 184.1 × 37.7 × 8.2 *(56.1 × 11.5 × 2.5)*
Main machinery: COGAG; 2 Nikolayev Type DR 77 gas turbines; 16,016 hp(m) *(11.77 MW)* sustained; 2 Nikolayev Type DR 76 gas turbines with reversible gearboxes; 4,993 hp(m) *(3.67 MW)* sustained; 2 shafts or CODOG with 2 CM 504 diesels; 8,000 hp(m) *(5.88 MW)*, replacing second pair of gas-turbines in Tarantul IIIs
Speed, knots: 36. **Range, n miles:** 400 at 36 kt; 1,650 at 14 kt
Complement: 34 (5 officers)

Missiles: SSM: 4 Raduga SS-N-2D Styx (2 twin) launchers (Tarantul II); active radar or IR homing to 83 km *(45 n miles)* at 0.9 Mach; warhead 513 kg; sea-skimmer at end of run.
4 Raduga SS-N-22 Sunburn (3M-82 Moskit) (2 twin) launchers (Tarantul III); active radar homing to 160 km *(87 n miles)* at 2.5 Mach; warhead nuclear 200 kT or HE 300 kg; sea-skimmer. Modified version in Type 1242.1.
SAM: SA-N-5 Grail quad launcher; manual aiming; IR homing to 6 km *(3.2 n miles)* at 1.5 Mach; altitude to 2,500 m *(8,000 ft)*; warhead 1.5 kg.
Guns: 1—3 in *(76 mm)*/59 AK 176; 120 rds/min to 15 km *(8 n miles)*; weight of shell 5.9 kg.
2—30 mm/65; 6 barrels per mounting; 3,000 rds/min to 2 km.
Countermeasures: Decoys: 2 PK 16 or 4 PK 10 (Tarantul III) chaff launchers.
ESM: 2 Foot Ball, 2 Half Hat (in some).
Weapons control: Hood Wink optronic director. Light Bulb datalink. Band Stand; datalink for SSM; Bell Nest.
Radars: Air/surface search: Plank Shave or Positiv E (Tarantul 874); I-band.
Navigation: Kivach III; I-band.
Fire control: Bass Tilt; H/I-band.
Band Stand (Mineral ME); D-band (for SS-N-22).
IFF: Square Head. High Pole B.
Sonars: Foal Tail; VDS; active search; high frequency.

Programmes: Tarantul II were built at Kolpino, Petrovsky, Leningrad and in the Pacific in 1980–86. Production of Taruntul IIIs then continued until 1995. One more was launched in September 1997 at Rybinsk, and a Tarantul III at Kolpino completed in December 1999 for the Baltic Fleet. Type name is *raketny kater* meaning missile cutter.
Modernisation: Tarantul III 874 served as a trials platform for a modified version of SS-N-22 with a longer range; the missile is distinguished by end caps on the launcher doors. Tarantul II 962 served as a trials platform for the CADS-N-1 point defence system in the Black Sea.

MORSHANSK *7/2008*, Per Körnefeldt* / 1353334

IVANOVETS *10/2008*, Laursen/Jarnasen* / 1353335

Structure: Basically same hull as Pauk class, without extension for sonar. The single Type 1242.1 has a Positiv E radar.
Sales: Tarantul I class-one to Poland 28 December 1983, second in April 1984, third in March 1988 and fourth in January 1989. One to India in April 1987, second in January 1988, third in December 1988, fourth in November 1989 and fifth in January 1990. Two to Yemen in November 1990 and January 1991. One to Romania in December 1990, two more in February 1992. One Tarantul II to Bulgaria in March 1990. Two Tarantul Is to Vietnam in 1996 and two more in 1999.

R 71 *6/2005, Lemachko Collection* / 1159875

14 NANUCHKA CLASS (PROJECT 1234.1/1234.7) (FSG)

North	Baltic	Pacific	Black Sea
RASSVET 520	**LIVEN** 551	**MOROZ** 409	**SHTYL** 620
PRIBOY 540	**GEYZER** 555	**RAZLIV** 450	**MIRAZH** 617
AYSBERG 535	**ZYB** 560	**SMERCH** 423	
NAKAT (IV) 526	**PASSAT** 570	**INEJ** 418	

Displacement, tons: 660 full load
Dimensions, feet (metres): 194.5 × 38.7 × 8.5 *(59.3 × 11.8 × 2.6)*
Main machinery: 6 M 504 diesels; 26,112 hp(m) *(19.2 MW)*; 3 shafts
Speed, knots: 33
Range, n miles: 2,500 at 12 kt; 900 at 31 kt
Complement: 42 (7 officers)

Missiles: SSM: 6 Chelomey SS-N-9 Siren (Malakhit) (2 triple) launchers ❶; command guidance and IR and active radar homing to 110 km *(60 n miles)* at 0.9 Mach; warhead nuclear 250 kT or HE 500 kg. Nanuchka IV has 2 sextuple launchers for trials of SS-NX-26; radar homing to 300 km *(161.9 n miles)* at Mach 2–3.5.
SAM: SA-N-4 Gecko twin launcher ❷; semi-active radar homing to 15 km *(8 n miles)* at 2.5 Mach; warhead 50 kg; altitude 9.1-3,048 m *(30-10,000 ft)*; 20 missiles. Some anti-surface capability.
Guns: 1—3 in *(76 mm)*/59 AK 176 ❸; 120 rds/min to 15 km *(8 n miles)*; weight of shell 5.9 kg.
1—30 mm/65 ❹; 6 barrels; 3,000 rds/min combined to 2 km.
Countermeasures: Decoys: 4 PK 10 chaff launchers ❺.
ESM: Foot Ball and Half Hat A and B. 4 Half Cup laser warners.

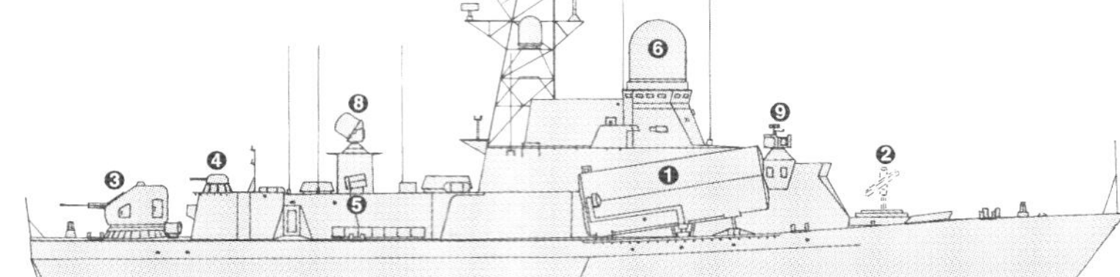

NANUCHKA III ***(Scale 1 : 600), Ian Sturton*** / 0105552

Weapons control: 2 Bell Nest or Light Bulb (datalinks). Band Stand ❻ datalink for SS-N-9.
Radars: Air/surface search: Peel Pair ❼; I-band or Plank Shave; E/F-band.
Fire control: Bass Tilt ❽; H/I-band. Pop Group ❾; F/H/I-band (for SA-N-4).
Band Stand (Mineral ME) ❻; D-band (for SS-N-9).
Navigation: Nayada; I-band.
IFF: High Pole. Square Head. Spar Stump. Salt Pot A and B.

Programmes: Built from 1969 onwards at Petrovsky, Leningrad and in the Pacific. The Nanuchka III were first seen in 1978. The Nanuchka IV *(Nakat)* was completed in 1987 as a trials ship. Type name is *maly raketny korabl* meaning small missile ship.
Structure: The Nanuchka IV is similar in detail to Nanuchka III except that she is the trials vehicle for SS-NX-26.
Operational: Intended for deployment in coastal waters although formerly deployed in the Mediterranean (in groups of two or three), North Sea and Pacific.

PASSAT ***6/2008*, Frank Findler*** / 1353297

SHTYL ***10/2008*, Laursen/Jarnasen*** / 1353336

SHIPBORNE AIRCRAFT

Notes: (1) A smaller variant of the Kamov Ka-60 is reported to have been offered to the Russian Navy. The Ka-40 anti-submarine helicopter has been under development as a potential replacement for the Ka-27 since 1990. There have been no recent developments.
(2) Haze B helicopters have all been placed in reserve as have all Ka-25 Hormones. A few of the latter remain active and probably have a training role.

Numbers/Type: 17/2 Sukhoi Su-33 Flanker D/Su-33 UB.
Operational speed: 1,345 kt *(2,500 km/h).*
Service ceiling: 59,000 ft *(18,000 m).*
Range: 2,160 + n miles *(4,000 km).*
Role/Weapon systems: Fleet air defence fighter. 20 production aircraft delivered of which 2 have been lost. 10 are believed to be operational. All based in the Northern Fleet. Most training is done from a simulated flight deck ashore. Sensors: Track-while-scan pulse Doppler radar, IR scanner. Weapons: One 30 mm cannon, 10 AAMs (AA-12, AA-11, AA-8).

FLANKER *2/1996* / 0506323

Numbers/Type: 5 Sukhoi Su-25UT Frogfoot UTG.
Operational speed: 526 kt *(975 km/h).*
Service ceiling: 22,965 ft *(7,000 m).*
Range: 675 n miles *(1,250 km).*
Role/Weapon systems: The UTG version is the two seater ground attack aircraft used for deck training in the carrier *Kuznetsov* . About 40 more of these aircraft are Air Force. Sensors: Laser rangefinder, ESM, ECM. Weapons: One 30 mm cannon, AAMs (AA-8), rockets, bombs.

FROGFOOT *2/1996* / 0506324

Numbers/Type: 2 Kamov Ka-31 Helix RLD.
Operational speed: 119 kt *(220 km/h).*
Service ceiling: 11,480 ft *(3,500 m).*
Range: 162 n miles *(300 km).*
Role/Weapon systems: AEW conversions with a solid-state radar under the fuselage. Eight sold to India. Sensors: Oko E-801 Surveillance radar, datalinks. Weapons: Unarmed.

HELIX RLD *9/1995* / 0506325

Numbers/Type: 56/28/5 Kamov Ka-27PI Helix A/Ka-29 Helix B/Ka-32 Helix D.
Operational speed: 135 kt *(250 km/h).*
Service ceiling: 19,685 ft *(6,000 m).*
Range: 432 n miles *(800 km).*
Role/Weapon systems: ASW helicopter; three main versions—'A' for ASW, 'B' for assault and D for SAR; deployed to surface ships and some shore stations. Sensors: Osminog Splash Drop search radar, VGS-3 dipping sonar, sonobuoys, MAD, ESM. Weapons: ASW; three APR-2 torpedoes, nuclear or conventional S3V depth bombs or mines. Assault type: Two UV-57 rocket pods (2 × 32).

HELIX *6/2008*, Ships of the World* / 1353315

LAND-BASED MARITIME AIRCRAFT (FRONT LINE)

Notes: (1) The MiG-29 Fulcrum D has been abandoned by the Navy and the Ka-34 Hokum is not in production. Yak-41 Freestyle is not being developed but the prototype is for sale. Fitter C/D, Badgers and Bear D aircraft were out of service by 1995, Blinders and Bear G by 1997, and Mail and Haze A/C by 1999 (except for three still active in the Black Sea Fleet).
(2) Tu-204P has been proposed as an ASW/reconnaissance aircraft to replace the 'May'. It would be a development of the commercial transport aircraft.
(3) Two Ilyushin Il-20 Coot A Elint aircraft are probably non-operational.

Numbers/Type: 30 Ilyushin Il-38 May.
Operational speed: 347 kt *(645 km/h).*
Service ceiling: 32,800 ft *(10,000 m).*
Range: 3,887 n miles *(7,200 km).*
Role/Weapon systems: Long-range MR and ASW. 14 in the North, 16 in the Pacific. Test flights of an upgraded version started in 2002 and continued in 2003. Sensors: Wet Eye search/weather radar, MAD, sonobuoys. Weapons: ASW; internal storage for 6 tons weapons.

MAY *6/2004, Paul Tompkins* / 0001128

Numbers/Type: 48 Tupolev Tu-22 M Backfire C.
Operational speed: 2.0 Mach.
Service ceiling: 60,000 ft *(18,300 m).*
Range: 2,500 n miles *(4,630 km).*
Role/Weapon systems: Medium-range nuclear/conventional strike and reconnaissance. About 20 are operational. Sensors: Down Beat search/Fan Tail attack radars, EW. Weapons: ASV; 12 tons of 'iron' bombs or standoff missiles AS-4 Kitchen (Kh 22N(A)) and AS-6 Kickback (Kh 15P). Self-defence; two 23 mm cannon.

BACKFIRE *6/2003, Paul Jackson* / 0547316

Numbers/Type: 23/10 Tupolev Tu-142 Bear F/Tu-142 Bear J.
Operational speed: 500 kt *(925 km/h).*
Service ceiling: 60,000 ft *(18,300 m).*
Range: 6,775 n miles *(12,550 km).*
Role/Weapon systems: Multimission long-range aircraft (ASW and communications variants). 36 in the North, remainder Pacific. Sensors: Wet Eye search radar, ESM; search radar, sonobuoys, EW, MAD (F), ELINT systems (J). The Bear J is reported to be equipped with VLF communications for SSBN connectivity. Weapons: ASW; various torpedoes, depth bombs and/or mines (F). Self-defence; some have two 23 mm or more cannon.

BEAR F *6/2008*, Ships of the World* / 1353316

Numbers/Type: 9 Antonov An-12 Cub ('Cub B/C/D') ('Cub C/D' ECM/ASW).
Operational speed: 419 kt *(777 km/h)*.
Service ceiling: 33,500 ft *(10,200 m)*.
Range: 3,075 n miles *(5,700 km)*.
Role/Weapon systems: Used either for intelligence gathering (B) or electronic warfare (C, D); is versatile with long range. Sensors: Search/weather radar, three EW blisters (B), tail-mounted EW/Elint equipment in addition (C/D). Weapons: Self-defence; two 23 mm cannon (B and D only).

Numbers/Type: 51 Sukhoi Su-24 Fencer D/E.
Operational speed: 1.15 Mach.
Service ceiling: 57,400 ft *(17,500 m)*.
Range: 950 n miles *(1,755 km)*.
Role/Weapon systems: Fitted for maritime reconnaissance (47) and strike (4). Sensors: Radar and EW. Weapons: 30 mm Gatling gun; various ASM missiles and bombs; some have 23 mm cannon.

FENCER E *6/1999, Jane's* / 0048910

PATROL FORCES

1 + 2 (2) BUYAN (PROJECT 21630) CLASS (PG)

ASTRAKHAN 012 (ex-101) **VOLGODONSK** (ex-*Kaspiysk*) **MAKHACHKALA**

Displacement, tons: 520 full load
Dimensions, feet (metres): 203.4 × 31.5 × 6.7 *(62.0 × 9.6 × 2.1)*
Main machinery: 2 Zvezda M520 diesels; 9,900 hp *(7.35 MW)*; 2 waterjets
Speed, knots: 26
Range, n miles: 1,500 at 15 kt
Complement: To be announced

Missiles: SAM: SA-16 Gubka (Strelets); IR homing to 5 km *(2.7 n miles)* at 2.6 Mach; warhead 1.3 kg.
Guns: 1 — 3.9 in *(100 mm)* A 190; 80 rds/min to 20 km *(10.8 n miles)*; weight of shell 16 kg.
2 — 30 mm/65 AK 306; 6 barrels per mounting; 3,000 rds/min to 2 km.
2 — 14.5 mm MGs. 3–7.62 mm MGs.
1 — 122 mm UMS-73 Grad-M multibarrelled rocket launcher.
Countermeasures: Decoys: 2 KT 216 launchers.
Radars: Air/surface search: Cross Dome (Positiv-E); E/F-band.
Fire control: Bass Tilt (MR-123); I/J-band.
Navigation: I-band.

Comment: Designed by Zelenodolsk Design Bureau and built by Almaz, St Petersburg. *Astrakhan* laid down on 30 January 2004 and launched on 7 October 2005. *Volgodonsk* laid down on 25 February 2005 and *Makhachkala* on 24 March 2006. Heavily armed gunboat designed for littoral operations. The design includes radar and IR signature reduction measures including below water-line exhaust. The first became operational in the Caspian Sea in mid-2007 but the second pair appear to be delayed. At least two further units are expected.

ASTRAKHAN (old number) *6/2006, Lemachko Collection* / 1159863

4 MATKA (VEKHR) CLASS (PROJECT 206MP) (FAST ATTACK CRAFT — MISSILE HYDROFOIL) (PGGK)

BOROVSK (ex-R 25) 706
KARACHEJEVO-CHERKESSIA 701
VOLGOCHERENSK (ex-R 44) 966
BUDENOVSK 702

Displacement, tons: 225 standard; 260 full load
Dimensions, feet (metres): 129.9 × 24.9 (41 over foils) × 6.9 (13.1 over foils) *(39.6 × 7.6; 12.5 × 2.1; 4)*
Main machinery: 3 Type M 504 diesels; 10,800 hp(m) *(7.94 MW)* sustained; 3 shafts
Speed, knots: 40. **Range, n miles:** 600 at 35 kt foilborne; 1,500 at 14 kt hullborne
Complement: 33

Missiles: SSM: 2 SS-N-2C/D Styx; active radar or IR homing to 83 km *(45 n miles)* at 0.9 Mach; warhead 513 kg; sea-skimmer at end of run.
8 SS-N-25 (in *966*); radar homing to 130 km *(70.2 n miles)* at 0.9 Mach; warhead 145 kg; sea-skimmer.
Guns: 1 — 3 in *(76 mm)*/59 AK 176; 120 rds/min to 15 km *(8 n miles)*; weight of shell 5.9 kg.
1 — 30 mm/65 AK 630; 6 barrels per mounting; 3,000 rds/min to 2 km.
Countermeasures: Decoys: 2 PK 16 chaff launchers.
ESM: Clay Brick; intercept.
Weapons control: Hood Wink optronic directors.
Radars: Air/surface search: Plank Shave; E-band.
Navigation: SRN-207; I-band.
Fire control: Bass Tilt; H/I-band.
IFF: High Pole B or Salt Pot B and Square Head.

Programmes: In early 1978 the first of class was seen. Built at Kolpino Yard, Leningrad. Production stopped in 1983 being superseded by Tarantul class. Type name is *raketny kater* meaning missile cutter.
Structure: Similar hull to the deleted Osa class with similar single hydrofoil system to Turya class. The combination has produced a better sea-boat than the Osa class. *Volgocherensk* in the Black Sea was the trials craft for the SS-N-25.
Operational: *Volgocherensk* is based in the Black Sea and the other three are based in the Caspian. Five units transferred to Ukraine in 1996.

R 44 *6/2003, Lemachko Collection* / 0570912

1 MUKHA (SOKOL) (PROJECT 1145) CLASS (FAST ATTACK CRAFT — PATROL HYDROFOIL) (PGK)

VLADIMIRETS (ex-*MPK 220*) 060

Displacement, tons: 400 full load
Dimensions, feet (metres): 164 × 27.9 (33.5 over foils) × 13.1 (19.4 foils) *(50 × 8.5; 10.2 × 4; 5.9)*
Main machinery: CODOG; 2 Type NK-12M gas turbines; 23,046 hp(m) *(16.95 MW)* sustained; 2 diesels; 2,400 hp(m) *(1.76 MW)*; 2 shafts
Speed, knots: 40; 12 hullborne
Complement: 45

Guns: 1 — 3 in *(76 mm)*/59 AK 176; 120 rds/min to 15 km *(8 n miles)*; weight of shell 5.9 kg.
2 — 30 mm/65 AK 630; 6 barrels per mounting; 3,000 rds/min combined to 2 km
Torpedoes: 8 — 16 in *(406 mm)* (2 quad) tubes. SAET-40; anti-submarine; active/passive homing to 10 km *(5.4 n miles)* at 30 kt; warhead 100 kg
Countermeasures: Decoys: 2 PK 16 chaff launchers
ESM: Radar warning
Radars: Surface search: Peel Cone; E-band
Navigation: SRN 206; I-band
Fire control: Bass Tilt; H/I-band
Sonars: Foal Tail; VDS; active search; high frequency

Comment: Built in 1986 at Feodosuja. Features include a hydrofoil arrangement with a single fixed foil forward, large gas-turbine exhausts aft, and trainable torpedo mountings. The only ship of the class, which was used as a trials platform for the Medveka ASW guided weapon, is based in the Black Sea. The vessel was badly damaged in a storm on 11 November 2007 and its future is unclear.

VLADIMIRETS *10/2008*, Laursen/Jarnasen* / 1353337

AMPHIBIOUS FORCES

Notes: (1) It was announced in mid-2005 that a new large landing ship displacing 8,000-9,000 tons was to be laid down by late 2005. Further details have not been announced.
(2) A new LCU, known as the Project 21820 Dyugon class, was laid down in 2006. A larger version of the Serna class, it is under construction at Volga Shipyard.

0 + 1 (5) MODIFIED ALLIGATOR (PROJECT 11711E) CLASS (LSTHM)

Name	*No*	*Builders*	*Laid down*	*Launched*	*Commissioned*
IVAN GREN	–	Yantar, Kaliningrad	23 Dec 2004	2009	2010

Displacement, tons: 5,000 full load
Dimensions, feet (metres): 419.9 × 54.1 × 11.8 *(128.0 × 16.5 × 3.6)*
Main machinery: 2 diesels; 10,000 hp(m) *(7.5 MW)*; 2 shafts
Speed, knots: 18. **Range, n miles:** 3,500 at 16 kt
Complement: 100
Military lift: 300 troops; 13-60 ton tanks or 36 armoured personnel carriers

Missiles: 2-140 mm multilaunch rocket system.
Guns: 1 — 3 in *(76 mm)*/60; AK-176; 120 rds/min to 15 km *(8 n miles)*; weight of shell 7 kg.
2 — 30 mm/65 AK-630; 6 barrels per mounting; 3,000 rds/min to 2 km.
Radars: To be announced.
Helicopters: 1 Ka-29 Helix B.

Comment: First of a new class of amphibious ship which, based on the Project number, is likely to be a modified version of the Alligator class landing ships which were built between 1966–76. Progress is slow but up to six ships, to replace the Alligator class, are expected.

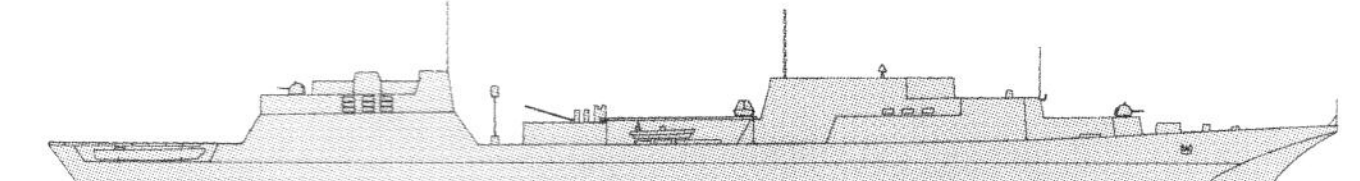

IVAN GREN *(Scale 1 : 1,500), Ian Sturton* / 1353317

14 ROPUCHA (PROJECT 775/775M) CLASS (LSTM)

North:	**OLENEGORSKIY GORNIAK** 012	**GEORGIY POBEDONOSETS** 016	**KONDOPOGA** 027	**ALEXANDER OTRAKOVSKIY** 031
Baltic:	**KALININGRAD** 102	**ALEXANDER SHABALIN** 110	**MINSK** 127	**KOROLEV** 130 (II)
Black:	**AZOV** 151 (II)	**YAMAL** 156	**TSESAR KUNIKOV** 158	
Pacific:	**BDK-98** 055	**OSLYABYA** (ex-*Mukhtar Avezov*) 066	**PERESVET** (ex-*Nicolay Korsakov*) 077 (II)	

Displacement, tons: 4,400 full load
Dimensions, feet (metres): 369.1 × 49.2 × 12.1 *(112.5 × 15 × 3.7)*
Main machinery: 2 Zgoda-Sulzer 16ZVB40/48 diesels; 19,230 hp(m) *(14.14 MW)* sustained; 2 shafts
Speed, knots: 17.5
Range, n miles: 3,500 at 16 kt; 6,000 at 12 kt
Complement: 95 (7 officers)
Military lift: 10 MBT plus 190 troops or 24 AFVs plus 170 troops or mines

Missiles: SAM: 4 SA-N-5 Grail quad launchers (in at least two ships); manual aiming; IR homing to 6 km *(3.2 n miles)* at 1.5 Mach; altitude to 2,500 m *(8,000 ft)*; warhead 1.5 kg; 32 missiles.
Guns: 4—57 mm/75 AK 725 (2 twin) ❶ (Ropucha I); 120 rds/min to 12.7 km *(6.8 n miles)*; weight of shell 2.8 kg.
1—76 mm/59 AK 176 (Ropucha II); 120 rds/min to 15 km *(8 n miles)*; weight of shell 5.9 kg.
2—30 mm/65 AK 630 (Ropucha II).
2—122 mm UMS-73 Grad-M (in some) ❷. 2—40-barrelled rocket launchers; range 9 km *(5 n miles)*.
Mines: 92 contact type.
Weapons control: 2 Squeeze Box optronic directors ❸. Hood Wink and Odd Box.
Radars: Air/surface search: Strut Curve ❹ (Ropucha I) or Cross Dome (Ropucha II); F-band.
Navigation: Don 2 or Nayada; I-band.
Fire control: Muff Cob ❺ (Ropucha I); G/H-band.
Bass Tilt (Ropucha II): H/I-band.
IFF: 2 High Pole A or Salt Pot A.
Sonars: Mouse Tail VDS can be carried.

Programmes: Ropucha Is completed at Northern Shipyard, Gdansk, Poland in two spells from 1974–78 (12 ships) and 1980–88. Ropucha IIs started building in 1987 with the first one commissioning in May 1990. The third and last of the class completed in January 1992. Type name is *bolshoy desantny korabl* (BDK) meaning large landing ship.
Structure: A Ro-Ro design with a tank deck running the whole length of the ship. All have very minor differences in appearance. These ships have a higher troop-to-vehicle ratio than the Alligator class. At least five of the class have rocket launchers at the after end of the forecastle. The second type have a 76 mm gun forward in place of one twin 57 mm and an ADG aft instead of the second. Radar and EW suites are also different. The after mast has been replaced by a solid extension to the superstructure.
Operational: Eleven more have been deleted so far.
Sales: One to South Yemen in 1979, returned to Russia in late 1991 for refit and was back in Aden in 1993. One to Ukraine in 1996.

ROPUCHA I *(Scale 1 : 1,200), Ian Sturton* / 0506247

TSESAR KUNIKOV *8/2007, Marco Ghiglino* / 1353338

AZOV (ROPUCHA II) *2/2006, C D Yaylali* / 1159878

4 ALLIGATOR (TAPIR) (PROJECT 1171) CLASS (LSTM)

SARATOV (ex-*Voronezhsky Konsomolets*) 50
NIKOLAY FILCHENKOV 152
NIKOLAY VILKOV 081 (IV)
ORSK (ex-*Nicolay Obyenko*) 148

Displacement, tons: 3,400 standard; 4,700 full load
Dimensions, feet (metres): 370.7 × 50.8 × 14.7 *(113 × 15.5 × 4.5)*
Main machinery: 2 diesels; 9,000 hp(m) *(6.6 MW)*; 2 shafts
Speed, knots: 18. **Range, n miles:** 10,000 at 15 kt
Complement: 100
Military lift: 300 troops; 1,750 tons including about 20 tanks and various trucks; 40 AFVs

Missiles: SAM: 2 or 3 SA-N-5 Grail twin launchers; manual aiming; IR homing to 6 km *(3.2 n miles)* at 1.5 Mach; altitude to 2,500 m *(8,000 ft)*; warhead 1.5 kg; 16 missiles.
Guns: 2—57 mm/75 AK 725 (twin); 120 rds/min to 12 km *(6.8 n miles)*; weight of shell 2.8 kg.
4—25 mm/80 (2 twin) (Type 4); 270 rds/min to 3 km *(1.6 n miles)*; weight of shell 0.34 kg.
1—122 mm UMS-72 Grad-M; 2-40-barrelled rocket launchers (in Types 3 and 4); range 9 km *(5 n miles)*.
Weapons control: 1 Squeeze Box optronic director (Types 3 and 4).
Radars: Surface search: 2 Don 2; I-band.

Programmes: First ship commissioned in 1966 at Kaliningrad. Last of class in service completed in 1976. Type name is *bolshoy desantny korabl* meaning large landing ship. One more Type 3 in service with Ukraine.
Structure: These ships have ramps on the bow and stern. In Type 3 the bridge structure has been raised and a forward deck house has been added to accommodate shore bombardment rocket launchers. Type 4 is similar to Type 3 with the addition of two twin 25 mm gun mountings on centreline abaft the bridge superstructure. As well as a tank deck 300 ft long stretching right across the hull there are two smaller deck areas and a hold.
Operational: In the 1980s the class operated regularly off West Africa, in the Mediterranean and in the Indian Ocean, usually with Naval Infantry units embarked. Half the class have been scrapped or laid up. Of the remainder, *Vilkov* is in the Pacific and the others in the Black Sea.
Sales: One to Ukraine in 1995.

SARATOV *10/2008*, Laursen/Jarnasen* / 1353339

2 POMORNIK (ZUBR) (PROJECT 1232.2) CLASS (ACVM/LCUJM)

YEVGENIY KOCHESHKOV (ex-*MDK-118*) 770
MORDOVIYA (ex-*MDK-94*) 782

Displacement, tons: 550 full load
Dimensions, feet (metres): 189 × 84 *(57.6 × 25.6)*
Main machinery: 5 Type NK-12MV gas-turbines; 2 for lift, 23,672 hp(m) *(17.4 MW)* nominal; 3 for drive, 35,508 hp(m) *(26.1 MW)* nominal
Speed, knots: 63
Range, n miles: 300 at 55 kt
Complement: 31 (4 officers)
Military lift: 3 MBT or 10 APC plus 230 troops (total 130 tons)

Missiles: SAM: 2 SA-N-5 Grail quad launchers; manual aiming; IR homing to 6 km *(3.2 n miles)* at 1.5 Mach; altitude to 2,500 m *(8,000 ft)*; warhead 1.5 kg.
Guns: 2—30 mm/65 AK 630; 6 barrels per mounting; 3,000 rds/min combined to 2 km.
2—140 mm A-22 Ogon 22-barrelled rocket launchers.
Mines: 2 rails can be carried for 80.
Countermeasures: Decoys: MS227 chaff launcher.
ESM: Tool Box; intercept.
Weapons control: Quad Look (DWU-3) (modified Squeeze Box) optronic director.
Radars: Surface search: Curl Stone; I-band.
Fire control: Bass Tilt; H/I-band.
IFF: Salt Pot A/B. Square Head.

Comment: First of class delivered 1986, commissioned in 1988. Last of class launched December 1994. Produced at St Petersburg and at Feodosiya. Bow and stern ramps for ro-ro working. Last survivors are based at Baltiysk and one is still operated by Ukraine. One (plus one from Ukraine) transferred and two new build for Greece by 2005. These are the first Former Soviet Union (FSU) naval platform sales to a NATO country.

MORDOVIYA *7/2008*, Hartmut Ehlers* / 1353296

1 POLNOCHNY B CLASS (PROJECT 771) (LSM)

VTR 140

Displacement, tons: 760 standard; 834 full load
Dimensions, feet (metres): 246.1 × 31.5 × 7.5 *(75 × 9.6 × 2.3)*
Main machinery: 2 Kolomna Type 40-D diesels; 4,400 hp(m) *(3.2 MW)* sustained; 2 shafts
Speed, knots: 19
Range, n miles: 1,000 at 18 kt
Complement: 40-42
Military lift: 180 troops; 350 tons including 6 tanks
Missiles: SAM: 4 SA-N-5 Grail quad launchers.
Guns: 2 or 4—30 mm (1 or 2 twin).
2—140 mm WM-18 rocket launchers; 18 barrels.
Weapons control: PED-1 system.
Radars: Surface search: Spin Trough; I-band.
Fire control: Drum Tilt; H/I-band (for 30 mm guns).
IFF: High Pole A. Square Head.

Comment: Built at Northern Shipyard, Gdansk, Poland in 1970. VTR 140 serves in the Northern Fleet as a logistic support ship. Others of the class are in reserve.

VTR 140 *7/2006, Lemachko Collection* / 1159870

6 ONDATRA (AKULA) (PROJECT 1176) CLASS (LCMS)

DKA 70 677	**DKA 164** –	**DKA 464** –
DKA 148 –	**DKA 325** 799	**DKA 704** 640

Displacement, tons: 145 full load
Dimensions, feet (metres): 78.7 × 16.4 × 4.9 *(24 × 5 × 1.5)*
Main machinery: 2 diesels; 300 hp(m) *(220 kW)*; 2 shafts
Speed, knots: 10
Range, n miles: 500 at 5 kt
Complement: 5
Military lift: 1 MBT

Comment: First completed in 1979 and associated with *Ivan Rogov*. 33 deleted so far. Tank deck of 45 × 13 ft. Two to Yemen in 1983. Two of unknown pennant number are based in the Caspian. The remainder are in the Baltic.

DKA 70 *6/2008** / 1353340

4 SERNA CLASS (LCU)

DKA 67 747 – 645 **DKA 144** 575 +1

Displacement, tons: 105 full load
Dimensions, feet (metres): 86.3 × 19 × 5.2 *(26.3 × 5.8 × 1.6)*
Main machinery: 2 M 503A3 diesels; 5,522 hp(m) *(4.06 MW)*; 2 shafts
Speed, knots: 30
Range, n miles: 100 at 30 kt; 600 at 22 kt
Complement: 6
Military lift: 45 tons or 100 troops

Comment: High-speed utility landing craft capable of beaching and in service in May 1995. Have an 'air-lubricated' hull. Designed for both military and civilian use by the R Alexeyev Central Design Bureau and built at Nizhny Novgorod. Can be armed. DKA-67 is operational in the Baltic Fleet and two are reported to be in the Caspian. Three others have been sold commercially.

SERNA CLASS *8/2007, Lemachko Collection* / 1353295

2 AIST (DZHEYRAN) (PROJECT 1232.1) CLASS (ACV/LCUJ)

MDK 18 608 **MDK 88** 609

Displacement, tons: 298 full load
Dimensions, feet (metres): 155.2 × 58.4 *(47.3 × 17.8)*
Main machinery: 2 Type NK-12M gas turbines driving 4 axial lift fans and 4 propeller units for propulsion; 19,200 hp(m) *(14.1 MW)* nominal
Speed, knots: 70
Range, n miles: 120 at 50 kt
Complement: 15 (3 officers)
Military lift: 80 tons or 4 light tanks plus 50 troops or 2 medium tanks plus 200 troops or 3 APCs plus 100 troops
Guns: 4—30 mm/65 (2 twin) AK 630; 6 barrels per mounting; 3,000 rds/min combined to 2 km
Countermeasures: Decoys: 2 PK 16 chaff launchers
Radars: Surface search: Kivach; I-band
Fire control: Drum Tilt; H/I-band
IFF: High Pole B. Square Head

Comment: First produced at Leningrad in 1970, subsequent production at rate of about six every four years. The first large hovercraft for naval use. Similar to UK SR. N4. Type name is *maly desantny korabl na vozdushnoy podushke* meaning small ACV. Modifications have been made to the original engines and some units have been reported as carrying two SA-N-5 quadruple SAM systems and chaff launchers. Based in the Caspian.

AIST CLASS *9/2000, J Ciślak* / 0105561

3 LEBED (KALMAR) (PROJECT 1206) CLASS (ACV/LCUJ)

639 **640** **641**

Displacement, tons: 87 full load
Dimensions, feet (metres): 80.1 × 36.7 *(24.4 × 11.2)*
Main machinery: 2 Ivchenko AI-20K gas turbines for lift and propulsion; 8,000 hp(m) *(5.88 MW)*
Speed, knots: 50
Range, n miles: 100 at 50 kt
Complement: 6 (2 officers)
Military lift: 2 light tanks or 40 tons cargo or 120 troops
Guns: 2—30 mm/65 AK 630; 6 barrels per mounting; 3,000 rds/min combined to 2 km
Radars: Navigation Kivach; I-band

Comment: First entered service 1975. Can be carried in Ivan Rogov class. Has a bow ramp with gun on starboard side and the bridge to port. All based in the Caspian. *639* and *640* took part in the Caspian Sea exercise in July 2002.

LEBED 641 *6/2005, Lemachko Collection* / 1159874

3 GUS (SKAT) (PROJECT 1205) CLASS (ACV/LCMJ)

631 **615** **650**

Displacement, tons: 17 light; 27 full load
Dimensions, feet (metres): 69.9 × 27.5 × 0.6 *(21.3 × 8.4 × 0.2)*
Main machinery: 3 TVD 10 gas turbines for lift and propulsion
Speed, knots: 49
Range, miles: 200 at 49 kt
Complement: 7 + 24 troops

Comment: Last survivors of an original class of 32 which entered service 1969–76. Based in the Caspian.

GUS *6/1992, Lemachko Collection* / 0583302

MINE WARFARE FORCES

Notes: (1) All remaining Yevgenya (Korond) class MHCs were laid up by 2001, except for two in the Caspian Sea which may still be used as patrol craft. These include RT 236 (259).
(2) Some 40 to 50 craft of various dimensions, some with cable reels, some self-propelled and unmanned, some towed and unmanned are reported including the 8 m Kater and Volga unmanned mine clearance craft.

RT 236 *7/2006, Lemachko Collection* / 1305146

11 NATYA I (AKVAMAREN) (PROJECT 266M) CLASS (MINESWEEPERS—OCEAN) (MSOM)

North	Pacific	Black
MOTORIST 806	**MT 265** 718	**VALENTIN PIKUL** 770
KOMENDOR 831	**MT 264** 738	**VITSEADMIRAL ZHUKOV** 909
KONTRADMIRAL VLASOV (ex-*Machinist*) 855		**IVAN GOLUBETS** (ex-*Radist*) 911
		TURBINIST 912
		KOVROVETS 913
		VITSE-ADMIRAL ZAKHARIN 908 (ex-611)

Displacement, tons: 804 full load
Dimensions, feet (metres): 200.1 (219.8 Natya III) × 33.5 × 9.8 *(61; 67 × 10.2 × 3)*
Main machinery: 2 Type M 504 diesels; 5,000 hp(m) *(3.67 MW)* sustained; 2 shafts; cp props
Speed, knots: 16
Range, n miles: 3,000 at 12 kt
Complement: 67 (8 officers)

Missiles: SAM: 2 SA-N-5/8 Grail quad launchers (in some); manual aiming; IR homing to 6 km *(3.2 n miles)* at 1.5 Mach; altitude to 2,500 m *(8,000 ft)*; warhead 1.5 kg; 18 missiles.
Guns: 4—30 mm/65 (2 twin) AK 230; 500 rds/min to 6.5 km *(3.5 n miles)*; weight of shell 0.54 kg or 2—30 mm/65 AK 306; 6 barrels per mounting; 3,000 rds/min combined to 2 km.
4—25 mm/80 (2 twin); 270 rds/min to 3 km *(1.6 n miles)*; weight of shell 0.34 kg.
A/S mortars: 2 RBU 1200 5-tubed fixed; range 1,200 m; warhead 34 kg.
Depth charges: 62.
Mines: 10.
Countermeasures: MCM: 1 or 2 GKT-2 contact sweeps; 1 AT-2 acoustic sweep; 1 TEM-3 magnetic sweep.
Radars: Surface search: Don 2 or Long Trough; I-band.
Fire control: Drum Tilt; H/I-band (not in all).
IFF: 2 Square Head. High Pole B.
Sonars: MG 79/89; hull-mounted; active minehunting; high frequency.

Programmes: First reported in 1970. Built at Kolpino and Khabarovsk. Type name is *morskoy tralshchik* meaning seagoing minesweeper. MT 264 and MT 265 were a new variant commissioned in 1989 in which AK 306 mounts replaced the twin AK 230 mounts. One further unit, known as Naty aIII started construction in 1994. *Valentin Pikul*, left St Petersburg for the Black Sea in July 2002. A further development of the class (known as the Agat class), *Vitseadmiral Zacharin*, was launched at the Kolpino Yard on 26 May 2006.
Structure: Some have hydraulic gantries aft. Have aluminium/steel alloy hulls. Some have Gatling 30 mm guns and a different radar configuration without Drum Tilt. The Natya IIIs are 6 m longer than earlier ships.
Operational: Usually operate in home waters but have deployed to the Mediterranean, Indian Ocean and West Africa. Sweep speed is 14 kt.
Sales: India (two in 1978, two in 1979, two in 1980, one in August 1986, two in 1987, three in 1988). Libya (two in 1981, two in February 1983, one in August 1983, one in January 1984, one in January 1985, one in October 1986). Syria (one in 1985). Yemen (one in 1991). Ethiopia (one in 1991). Some have been deleted.

IVAN GOLUBETS *10/2008*, Laursen/Jarnasen* / 1353341

KONTRADMIRAL VLASOV *6/2006, Lemachko Collection* / 1305151

VALENTIN PIKUL *5/2006, C D Yaylali* 1159881

2 GORYA (TYPE 12660) CLASS (MINEHUNTERS—OCEAN) (MHOM)

Name	*No*	*Builders*	*Laid down*	*Launched*	*Commissioned*
A ZHELEZNYAKOV	901 (ex-811)	Kolpino Yard, Leningrad	28 Feb 1985	17 July 1986	30 Dec 1988
V GUMANENKO	811(ex-812, ex-762)	Kolpino Yard, Leningrad	15 Sep 1985	4 Mar 1991	9 Jan 1994

Displacement, tons: 1,130 full load
Dimensions, feet (metres): 216.5 × 36.1 × 10.8 *(66.0 × 11.0 × 3.3)*
Main machinery: 2 M 503 diesels; 5,000 hp(m) *(3.7 MW)*; 2 shafts
Speed, knots: 15
Range, n miles: 3,000 at 12 kt
Complement: 65 (7 officers)

Missiles: 2 SA-N-5 Grail quad launchers; IR homing to 6 km *(3.2 n miles)* at 1.5 Mach.
Guns: 1—3 in *(76 mm)*/60 AK 176; 120 rds/min to 12 km *(6.4 n miles)*; weight of shell 7 kg.
1—30 mm/65 AK 630; 6 barrels; 3,000 rds/min to 2 km.
Countermeasures: Decoys: 2 PK 16 chaff launchers.
ESM: Cross Loop; Long Fold.
Radars: Surface search: Palm Frond; I-band.
Navigation: Nayada; I-band.
Fire control: Bass Tilt; H/I-band.
IFF: Salt Pot C. 2 Square Head.
Sonars: Hull-mounted; active search; high frequency.

Programmes: A third of class was started but has been scrapped.
Structure: Appears to carry mechanical, magnetic and acoustic sweep gear and may have accurate positional fixing equipment. A remote-controlled submersible is housed behind the sliding doors in the superstructure below the AK 630 mounting. Two 406 mm torpedo tubes are reported as used for mine countermeasures.
Operational: 811 is based in the Black Sea. 812 transferred from the Baltic to the Northern Fleet in 2000.

V GUMANENKO (old number) *6/2005, Lemachko Collection* / 1159871

24 SONYA (YAKHONT) (PROJECT 12650/1265M) CLASS (MINESWEEPERS—HUNTERS/COASTAL) (MHSC/MHSCM)

North	Pacific	Baltic	Caspian	Black
POLYARNY (ex-BT 97) 402	**BT 232** 525	**ALEKSEY LEBEDEV** 505	**BT 48** 513	**LEYTENANT ILIN** (ex-BT 40) 438
KOLOMNA 425	**BT 256** 560	**BT 230** 510	**BT 44** 563	**MINERALNY VODI** (ex-BT 241) 426
BUEVLYANIN 418	**BT 215** 593	**SERGEI KOLBASSEV** (ex-BT 213) 522	**MAGAMED GADGIEV** 564	
KOTELNICH 443	**BT 114** 542		**GERMAN UGRYUMOV** 501	
YELNYA (ex-BT 50) 454	**BT 115** 561		**YUSUP AKAEV** 107	
AVANGARD 466	**BT 100** 565			
YADRYN 469				

Displacement, tons: 450 full load
Dimensions, feet (metres): 157.4 × 28.9 × 6.6 *(48 × 8.8 × 2)*
Main machinery: 2 Kolomna Type 9-D-8 diesels; 2,000 hp(m) *(1.47 MW)* sustained; 2 shafts
Speed, knots: 15
Range, n miles: 3,000 at 10 kt
Complement: 43 (5 officers)
Missiles: SAM: 2 quad SA-N-5 launchers (in some).
Guns: 2—30 mm/65 AK 630 or 2—30 mm/65 (twin) and 2—25 mm/80 (twin).
Mines: 8.
Radars: Surface search: Don 2 or Kivach or Nayada; I-band.
IFF: 2 Square Head. High Pole B.
Sonars: MG 69/79; hull-mounted; active minehunting; high frequency.

Comment: Wooden hull with GRP sheath. Built at about two a year at Petrozavodsk and at Ulis, Vladivostok (Pacific). First reported 1973 and the last one commissioned in January 1995. Type name is *bazovy tralshchik* meaning base minesweeper. Some have two twin 30 mm Gatling guns, others one 30 mm/65 (twin) plus one 25 mm (twin). In addition there area further 50 in reserve. At least one of the Caspian Sea units has been transferred to the Federal Border Guard.
Transfers: Bulgaria, four in 1981–85. Cuba, four in 1980–85. Syria, one in 1986. Vietnam, one in February 1987, one in February 1988, one in July 1989 and one in February 1990. Ethiopia, one in February 1991. Ukraine, two in 1996.

SERGEI KOLBASSEV *7/2008*, Hartmut Ehlers* / 1353286

YUSUP AKAEV *4/2006, Lemachko Collection* / 1305143

9 LIDA (SAPFIR) (PROJECT 10750) CLASS (MINEHUNTERS—COASTAL) (MHC)

RT 249 206	**RT 231** 219	**RT 341** 331
RT 273 210	**RT 252** 239	**RT 210** 340
RT 233 215	**RT 57** 316	**RT 248** 348

Displacement, tons: 135 full load
Dimensions, feet (metres): 103.3 × 21.3 × 5.2 *(31.5 × 6.5 × 1.6)*
Main machinery: 3 D12MM diesels; 900 hp(m) *(690 kW)*; 3 shafts
Speed, knots: 12
Range, n miles: 650 at 10 kt
Complement: 14 (1 officer)
Guns: 1—30 mm/65 AK 630; 6 barrels; 3,000 rds/min to 2 km.
Countermeasures: MCM: AT-6 acoustic, SEMT-1 magnetic and GKT-3M wire sweeps.
Radars: Surface search: Pechora; MR241; I-band.
Sonars: Kabarga I; minehunting; high frequency.

Comment: Type name *Reydnyy Tralshchik* meaning roadstead minesweeper. A follow-on to the Yevgenya class started construction in 1989 at Kolpino Yard, St Petersburg. Similar in appearance to Yevgenya. Building rate was about three a year to 1992 and then slowed to one a year until 1995. Some are painted a blue/grey colour. All are in the Baltic except *RT 233* which is in the Caspian.

RT 273 *7/2008*, Hartmut Ehlers* / 1353285

3 OLYA (MALAKHIT) (PROJECT 1259) CLASS (MINEHUNTERS—INSHORE) (MSB)

202 **230** **235**

Displacement, tons: 64 full load
Dimensions, feet (metres): 84.6 × 14.9 × 3.3 *(25.8 × 4.5 × 1.0)*
Main machinery: 2 Type 3D 6S11/235 diesels; 471 hp(m) *(364 kW)*; 2 shafts
Speed, knots: 12
Range, n miles: 500 at 12 kt
Complement: 15
Guns: 2—25 mm/80 (twin).
Radars: Surface search/navigation: Don 2; I-band.

Comment: Built in 1973–75 and, although believed to have been deleted in 2001, were reported in 2008 to have been reactivated.

OLYA 202 *7/2008*, Hartmut Ehlers* / 1353284

3 TOLYA (PROJECT 696) CLASS (MINEHUNTERS—COASTAL) (MSI)

229 **+2**

Displacement, tons: 95 full load
Dimensions, feet (metres): 78.7 × 17.7 × 7.2 *(24.0 × 5.4 × 2.2)*
Main machinery: 2 diesels; 500 hp(m) *(367 kW)*; 2 shafts
Speed, knots: 12
Range, n miles: 300 at 10 kt
Complement: 15
Guns: 2—12.7 mm MGs.
Radars: Navigation: Spin Trough; I-band.

Comment: The first ship commissioned in 1992 and the second pair in early 1993. Capable of drone control. Based in the Baltic. Although believed to have been deleted in 2001, were reported in 2008 to have been reactivated.

TOLYA 229 *7/2008*, Hartmut Ehlers* / 1353293

SURVEY AND RESEARCH SHIPS

Notes: (1) Civilian research ships are now all used for commercial purposes only or are laid up, and are no longer naval associated, although some can still be leased for short operations. The former section has therefore been deleted since 1998.
(2) A new Project 19920 hydrographic ship, *Victor Faleev* (BGK 797) was laid down by Vostochnaya Shipyard, Vladivostok on 17 October 2006 and launched on 22 July 2008. The vessel is approximately 1,000 tons displacement and is to be based in the Pacific Fleet.

VICTOR FALEEV *7/2008*, Lemachko Collection* / 1353676

2 SIBIRIYAKOV (PROJECT 865) CLASS (AGOR)

SIBIRIYAKOV **ROMZUALD MUKLEVITCH**

Displacement, tons: 3,422 full load
Dimensions, feet (metres): 281.2 × 49.2 × 16.4 *(85.7 × 15 × 5)*
Main machinery: Diesel-electric; 2 Cegielski-Sulzer 12AS25 diesels; 6,480 hp(m) *(4.44 MW)* sustained; 2 motors; 2 shafts; cp props; bow and stern thrusters
Speed, knots: 14. **Range, n miles:** 11,000 at 14 kt
Complement: 58 plus 12 scientists
Guns: 1—30 mm AK 630 can be carried.
Radars: Navigation: 2 Nayada; I-band.

Comment: Built in Northern Shipyard, Gdansk 1990–92. Has a pressurised citadel for NBC defence, and a degaussing installation. Six separate laboratories for hydrographic and geophysical research. Two submersibles can be embarked. Both ships are very active, *Sibiriyakov* in the Baltic at Kronstadt, and *Muklevitch* in the North.

SIBIRIYAKOV *5/2000* / 0105564

2 AKADEMIK KRYLOV (PROJECT 852/856) CLASS (AGORH)

LEONID DEMIN **ADMIRAL VLADIMIRSKIY**

Displacement, tons: 9,100 full load
Dimensions, feet (metres): 482.3 × 60.7 × 20.3 *(147 × 18.5 × 6.2)*
Main machinery: 4 Sulzer diesels; 14,500 hp(m) *(10.7 MW)*; 2 shafts; bow and stern thrusters
Speed, knots: 20. **Range, n miles:** 36,000 at 15 kt
Complement: 120
Radars: Navigation: Nayada, Palm Frond and Don 2; I-band
Helicopters: 1 Hormone

Comment: Built in Szczecin 1974–79. Carry two survey launches and have 26 laboratories. Based in the Baltic at Kronstadt. *Akademik Krylov* sold to a Greek company in 1993 and now flies the Cyprus flag. *Admiral Vladimirskiy*, previously inactive at Kronstadt, has been reactivated in the Baltic.

LEONID DEMIN *5/1994* / 0081696

7 MOMA (PROJECT 861) CLASS (AGS)

ANTARES
SEVER (AGE)
ANTARKTYDA
MARS
KRILON
ANDROMEDA
CHELEKEN

Displacement, tons: 1,550 full load
Dimensions, feet (metres): 240.5 × 36.8 × 12.8 *(73.3 × 11.2 × 3.9)*
Main machinery: 2 Zgoda-Sulzer 6TD48 diesels; 3,300 hp(m) *(2.43 MW)* sustained; 2 shafts; cp props
Speed, knots: 17. **Range, n miles:** 9,000 at 11 kt
Complement: 55
Radars: Navigation: Nayada and Don 2; I-band.
IFF: High Pole A.

Comment: Built at Northern Shipyard, Gdansk 1967–72. Some of the class are particularly active in ASW research associated operations. Four laboratories. One survey launch and a 7 ton crane. The AGE is fitted with bow probes. Two (*Krilon* and *Mars*) in the Northern Fleet, two *(Antarktyda* and *Antares)* in the Pacific, two (*Cheleken* and *Sever*) in the Black and one *(Andromeda)* in the Baltic. One transferred to Ukraine.

CHELEKEN *10/2008*, Laursen/Jarnasen* / 1353342

14 YUG (PROJECT 862) CLASS (AGS/AGI/AGE)

North	Pacific	Baltic	Black
PLUTON	**V ADM VORONTSOV** (ex-*Briz*)	**PERSEY**	**DONUZLAV**
STRELETS	**PEGAS**	**NIKOLAY MATUSEVICH**	**STVOR**
GORIZONT	**MARSHAL GELOVANI**		
GIDROLOG			
VIZIR			
SENEZH			
TEMRYUK (ex-*Mangyshlak*)			
SSV 700			

Displacement, tons: 2,500 full load
Dimensions, feet (metres): 270.6 × 44.3 × 13.1 *(82.5 × 13.5 × 4)*
Main machinery: 2 Zgoda-Sulzer Type 6TD48 diesels; 3,300 hp(m) *(2.43 MW)* sustained; 2 auxiliary motors; 272 hp(m) *(200 kW)*; 2 shafts; cp props; bow thruster; 300 hp *(220 kW)*
Speed, knots: 15
Range, n miles: 9,000 at 12 kt
Complement: 46 (8 officers) plus 20 scientists
Guns: 6—25 mm/80 (3 twin) (fitted for but not with).
Radars: Navigation: Palm Frond or Nayada; I-band.

Comment: Built at Northern Shipyard, Gdansk 1977–83. Have 4 ton davits at the stern and two survey craft. Others have minor variations around the stern area. *Pluton* 028 and *Strelets* 025 have been taken over by the Arctic Border Guard. SSV 700 is to a modified design and is classified as AGE.

DONUZLAV *10/2008*, Laursen/Jarnasen* / 1353343

TEMRYUK *10/2006, Lemachko Collection* / 1167419

1 SAMARA (PROJECT 860) CLASS (AGS)

GIGROMETER

Displacement, tons: 1,050 standard; 1,270 full load
Dimensions, feet (metres): 193.5 × 34.4 × 12.5 *(59.0 × 10.5 × 3.8)*
Main machinery: 2 Zgoda-Sulzer Type 6TD48 diesels; 3,300 hp(m) *(2.43 MW)* sustained; 2 shafts; cp props
Speed, knots: 15. **Range, n miles:** 6,200 at 10 kt
Complement: 45
Radars: Navigation: Don 2; I-band.

Comment: The last survivor of eight built at Northern Shipyard Gdansk 1962–65 for hydrographic surveying and research. Has laboratories, one survey launch and a 5 ton crane. Based in the Baltic.

SAMARA CLASS *4/1992, van Ginderen Collection* / 0506090

25 FINIK (PROJECT 872) CLASS (AGS/AGE/AE)

North:	**GS 87**	**GS 260**	**GS 271**	**GS 278**	**GS 297**	**GS 392**	**GS 405**	
Pacific:	**GS 44**	**GS 47**	**GS 84**	**GS 200**	**GS 272**	**GS 296**	**GS 397**	**GS 404**
Black:	**GS 78**	**GS 86**	**GS 402**	**PETR GRADOV** (ex-VTR 75)				
Baltic:	**GS 270**	**GS 399**	**GS 400**	**GS 403**				
Caspian:	**GS 202**	**GS 301**						

Displacement, tons: 1,200 full load
Dimensions, feet (metres): 201.1 × 35.4 × 10.8 *(61.3 × 10.8 × 3.3)*
Main machinery: 2 Cegielski-Sulzer 6AL25/30 diesels; 1,920 hp(m) *(1.4 MW)*; auxiliary propulsion; 2 motors; 204 hp(m) *(150 kW)*; 2 shafts; cp props; bow thruster
Speed, knots: 13
Range, n miles: 3,000 at 13 kt
Complement: 26 (5 officers) plus 9 scientists
Radars: Navigation: Kivach B; I-band.

Comment: Improved Biya class. Built at Northern Shipyard, Gdansk 1978–83. Fitted with 7 ton crane for buoy handling. Can carry two self-propelled pontoons and a boat on well-deck. Some have been used commercially. Ships of same class serve in the Polish Navy. Three transferred to Ukraine in 1997. Some may be laid up. VTR 75, originally built as a survey ship, was converted for use as an ammunition carrier in 2000.

GS 403 *10/2002, Lemachko Collection* / 0570911

PETR GRADOV *10/2008*, Laursen/Jarnasen* / 1353344

60 GPB-480 (PROJECT 1896) CLASS (INSHORE SURVEY CRAFT) (YGS)

BGK series

Displacement, tons: 116 full load
Dimensions, feet (metres): 93.8 × 17.1 × 5.6 *(28.6 × 5.2 × 1.7)*
Main machinery: 1 diesel; 300 hp(m) *(223 kW)*; 1 shaft
Speed, knots: 12

Comment: Entered service from 1955. Numbers approximate. Inshore survey craft equipped with two 1.5 ton derricks.

BGK 889 *10/2008*, Laursen/Jarnasen* / 1353345

8 BIYA (PROJECT 870/871) CLASS (AGS)

North	Pacific	Baltic	Caspian
GS 193	**GS 198**	**GS 204**	**GS 202**
	GS 200	**GS 208**	
	GS 210	**GS 214**	
	GS 269		

Displacement, tons: 766 full load
Dimensions, feet (metres): 180.4 × 32.1 × 8.5 *(55 × 9.8 × 2.6)*
Main machinery: 2 diesels; 1,200 hp(m) *(882 kW)*; 2 shafts; cp props
Speed, knots: 13
Range, n miles: 4,700 at 11 kt
Complement: 25
Radars: Navigation: Don 2; I-band.

Comment: Built at Northern Shipyard, Gdansk 1972–76. With laboratory and one survey launch and a 5 ton crane. Two transferred to Ukraine in 1997.

GS 269 *9/2007, Lemachko Collection* / 1353287

6 KAMENKA (PROJECT 870/871) CLASS (AGS)

GS 66 **GS 113** **GS 118** **GS 199** **GS 207** **GS 211**

Displacement, tons: 760 full load
Dimensions, feet (metres): 175.5 × 29.8 × 8.5 *(53.5 × 9.1 × 2.6)*
Main machinery: 2 Sulzer diesels; 1,800 hp(m) *(1.32 MW)*; 2 shafts; cp props
Speed, knots: 14. **Range, n miles**: 4,000 at 10 kt
Complement: 25
Radars: Navigation: Don 2; I-band.
IFF: High Pole.

Comment: Built at Northern Shipyard, Gdansk 1968–69. A 5 ton crane forward. They do not carry a survey launch but have facilities for handling and stowing buoys. Two in the Baltic and four in the Pacific. One transferred to Vietnam in 1979, one to Estonia in 1996 and one to Ukraine in 1997.

GS 118 *6/2003, Lemachko Collection* / 0570901

9 ONEGA (PROJECT 1806) CLASS (AGS)

VICTOR SUBBOTIN	**SFP 173**	**SFP 295**
AKADEMIK SEMINIKHIN SFP 183	**SFP 240**	**SFP 542**
AKADEMIK ISANIN SFP 586	**SFP 286**	**SFP 562**

Displacement, tons: 2,150 full load
Dimensions, feet (metres): 265.7 × 36 × 13.7 *(81 × 11 × 4.2)*
Main machinery: 2 gas turbines; 8,000 hp(m) *(5.88 MW)*; 1 shaft
Speed, knots: 20
Complement: 45
Radars: Navigation: Nayada; I-band.

Comment: Built at Zelenodolsk and first seen in September 1973. Helicopter platform but no hangar in earlier ships of the class but in later hulls the space is taken up with more laboratory accommodation. Used as hydroacoustic monitoring ships. *Akademik Seminikhin* was completed in October 1992 and *Victor Subbotin* in 2006. One to Ukraine in 1997. *Victor Subbotin* based in the Baltic. *Akademik Seminikhin* in the Black Sea, *Akademik Isanin*, SFP 240, SFP 286, and SFP 562 in the Northern Fleet and SFP 173, SFP 295 and SFP 542 in the Pacific.

AKADEMIK SEMINIKHIN *10/2008*, Laursen/Jarnasen* / 1353346

SFP 286 *7/2006, Lemachko Collection* / 1305145

2 VINOGRAD CLASS (AGOR)

GS 525–526

Displacement, tons: 498 full load
Dimensions, feet (metres): 108.3 × 34.1 × 9.1 *(33 × 10.4 × 2.8)*
Main machinery: Diesel-electric; 2 diesels; 2 motors; 1,200 hp(m) *(882 kW)*; 2 trainable props
Speed, knots: 9
Range, n miles: 1,000 at 6 kt
Complement: 19

Comment: Built by Rauma-Repola, Finland, 1985–87 as hydrographic research ships. *GS 525* commissioned 12 November 1985 and *GS 526* on 17 December 1985. *525* is in the Baltic and *526* in the North. Both have side scan sonars. A similar ship has been reported operating with the Northern Fleet.

GS 525 ***6/1998, Hartmut Ehlers*** / 0050054

1 MARSHAL NEDELIN (PROJECT 1914) CLASS (MISSILE RANGE SHIP) (AGMH)

MARSHAL KRYLOV

Displacement, tons: 24,500 full load
Dimensions, feet (metres): 695.5 × 88.9 × 25.3 *(212 × 27.1 × 7.7)*
Main machinery: 2 gas turbines; 54,000 hp(m) *(40 MW)*; 2 shafts
Speed, knots: 20. **Range, n miles:** 22,000 at 16 kt
Complement: 450
Radars: Air search: Top Plate.
Navigation: 3 Palm Frond; I-band.
Helo control: Fly Screen B; I-band.
Space trackers: End Tray (balloons). Quad Leaf. 3 Quad Wedge. 4 smaller aerials.
Tacan: 2 Round House.
Helicopters: 2-4 Ka-32 Helix C.

Comment: Completed at Admiralty Yard, Leningrad 23 February 1990. Fitted with a variety of space and missile associated electronic systems. Fitted for but not with six twin 30 mm/65 ADG guns and three Bass Tilt fire-control radars. Naval subordinated, the task is monitoring missile tests with a wartime role of command ship. The Ship Globe radome is for SATCOM. Based in the Pacific and active. Second of class deleted.

MARSHAL KRYLOV ***10/1995, van Ginderen Collection*** / 0506249

1 PROJECT 19910 CLASS (AGS)

VAYGACH

Displacement, tons: To be announced
Dimensions, feet (metres): 185.0 × 38.4 × 9.6 *(56.4 × 11.7 × 2.94)*
Main machinery: Diesel-electric; 2 diesel generators; 2 motors; 1,475 hp *(1.1 MW)*; 2 shafts
Speed, knots: 12
Complement: 20
Radars: To be announced.

Comment: New class of hydrographic ship built by Vympel Shipyard, Rybinsk, and launched on 28 August 2006. Completed in 2007, she is based in the Baltic. Further ships are expected.

VAYGACH ***9/2007, Lemachko Collection*** / 1305148

1 MOD SORUM (PROJECT 1454) CLASS (RESEARCH SHIP) (AGE)

TCHUSOVOY GS 31 (ex-OS 572)

Displacement, tons: 1,250 standard; 1,695 full load
Dimensions, feet (metres): 193.9 × 41.3 × 15.1 *(59.1 × 12.6 × 4.6)*
Main machinery: Diesel electric; 2 Type 5-2 DW2 diesel generators; 2,900 hp(m) *(2.13 MW)*; 1 motor; 2,000 hp(m) *(1.47 MW)*; 1 shaft
Speed, knots: 14
Range, n miles: 3,500 at 13 kt
Complement: 60
Radars: Navigation: 2 Don 2 or Nayada; I-band.

Comment: A variant of the Sorum class ocean tug design completed at Yaroslavl in 1987. The ship was originally built as a towed-array trials platform; the array and towing winch are contained in the aft superstructure. Based in the Northern Fleet, the ship is deployed on general research duties.

TCHUSOVOY ***7/2008**** / 1336045

1 ZVEZDOCHKA (PROJECT 20180) CLASS (AGE/ASR)

Name	*No*	*Builders*	*Laid down*	*Launched*	*Commissioned*
ZVEZDOCHKA	600	Zvezdochka Shipyard, Severodvinsk	3 Sep 2004	26 Dec 2007	2008

Displacement, tons: 5,000
Dimensions, feet (metres): 314.9 × ? × ? *(96.0 × ? × ?)*
Main machinery: Diesel electric
Speed, knots: To be announced
Range, n miles: To be announced
Complement: To be announced
Radars: To be announced.

Comment: Multipurpose ship capable of conducting and supporting salvage operations, underwater research and transport of ammunition. The ship is capable of operating small submersibles and is equipped with a 150 ton crane and a forward helicopter deck.

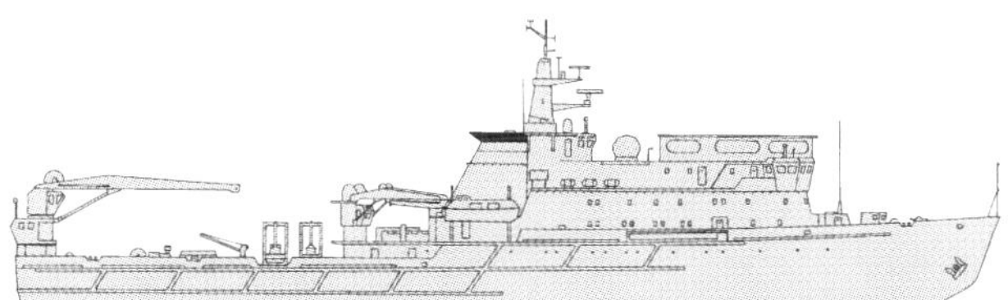

ZVEZDOCHKA ***(Scale 1 : 1,200), Ian Sturton*** / 1353318

ZVEZDOCHKA ***12/2007, Lemachko Collection*** / 1353294

INTELLIGENCE VESSELS

Notes: (1) About half the AGIs are fitted with SA-N-5/8 SAM launchers.
(2) SSV in pennant numbers of some AGIs is a contraction of *sudno svyazy* meaning communications vessel.
(3) GS in pennant numbers of some AGIs is a contraction of *gidrograficheskoye sudno* meaning survey ship.
(4) Activity reported in all Fleet areas, as well as in the Mediterranean, in 2008.

0 + 2 PROJECT 18280 CLASS (AGI)

Name	*Builders*	*Laid down*	*Launched*	*Commissioned*
ADMIRAL YURI IVANOV	Severnaya, St Petersburg	28 Dec 2004	2009	2010

Displacement, tons: 4,000
Dimensions, feet (metres): 311.7 × 52.5 × 13.1 *(95.0 × 16.0 × 4.0)*
Main machinery: To be announced
Speed, knots: To be announced
Range, n miles: To be announced
Complement: 120
Radars: To be announced.

Comment: A new class of AGI. The first is to be based in the Pacific Fleet and the second in the Northern Fleet.

6 VISHNYA (PROJECT 864) CLASS (AGIM)

Name	*No*	*Builders*	*Commissioned*
TAVRIYA	SSV 169	Northern Shipyard, Gdansk	Dec 1987
VIKTOR LEONOV	SSV 175	Northern Shipyard, Gdansk	July 1988
PRIAZOVE	SSV 201	Northern Shipyard, Gdansk	Jan 1987
KURILY	SSV 208	Northern Shipyard, Gdansk	Apr 1987
VASSILY TATISCHEV (ex-*Pelengator*)	SSV 231	Northern Shipyard, Gdansk	Apr 1989
FEODOR GOLOVIN (ex-*Meridian*)	SSV 520	Northern Shipyard, Gdansk	July 1986

Displacement, tons: 3,470 full load
Dimensions, feet (metres): 309.7 × 47.9 × 14.8 *(94.4 × 14.6 × 4.5)*
Main machinery: 2 Zgoda 12AV25/30 diesels; 4,406 hp(m) *(3.24 MW)* sustained; 2 auxiliary electric motors; 286 hp(m) *(210 kW)*; 2 shafts; cp props
Speed, knots: 16
Range, n miles: 7,000 at 14 kt
Complement: 146
Missiles: SAM: 2 SA-N-5 Grail quad launchers; manual aiming; IR homing to 6 km *(3.2 n miles)* at 1.5 Mach; altitude to 2,500 m *(8,000 ft)*; warhead 1.5 kg.
Guns: 2—30 mm/65 AK 630; 6 barrels per mounting. 2—72 mm 4-tubed rocket launchers.
Radars: Surface search: 2 Nayada; I-band.
Sonars: Lamb Tail VDS can be carried.

Comment: SSV 231 and 520 based in the Baltic, SSV 201 in the Black Sea, SSV 169 and SSV 175 in the Northern Fleet and SSV 208 in the Pacific. All have a full EW fit plus optronic systems and datalinks. Punch Bowl is fitted in SSV 231 and possibly in others. Some superstructure differences in all of the class. SSV 231 reported with modified mainmast in 2006. NBC pressurised citadels. Ice-strengthened hulls. All are comparatively active.

FEODOR GOLOVIN *6/2005, **Lemachko Collection*** / 1159861

PRIAZOVE *9/2000, **Lemachko Collection*** / 0126220

VASSILY TATISCHEV *5/2007, **M Declerck*** / 1170205

2 BALZAM (ASIA) (PROJECT 1826) CLASS (AGIM)

Name	*No*	*Builders*	*Commissioned*
PRIBALTIKA	SSV 080	Yantar, Kaliningrad	July 1984
BELOMORE	SSV 571	Yantar, Kaliningrad	Dec 1987

Displacement, tons: 4,500 full load
Dimensions, feet (metres): 344.5 × 50.9 × 16.4 *(105 × 15.5 × 5)*
Main machinery: 2 diesels; 18,000 hp(m) *(13.2 MW)*; 2 shafts
Speed, knots: 20
Range, n miles: 7,000 at 16 kt
Complement: 200
Missiles: SAM: 2 SA-N-5 Grail quad launchers; manual aiming; IR homing to 6 km *(3.2 n miles)* at 1.5 Mach; altitude to 2,500 m *(8,000 ft)*; warhead 1.5 kg; 16 missiles.
Guns: 1—30 mm/65 AK 630; 6 barrels per mounting.
Radars: Surface search: Palm Frond and Don Kay; I-band.
Sonars: Lamb Tail/Mouse Tail VDS can be fitted.

Comment: Notable for twin radomes. Full EW and optronic fits. The first class of AGI to be armed. SSV 571 based in the Northern fleet and SSV 080 is based in the Pacific. Capable of underway replenishment.

PRIBALTIKA *6/2006, **Ships of the World*** / 1159979

3 MOMA (PROJECT 861M) CLASS (AGI/AGIM)

EKVATOR SSV 418 **LIMAN** SSV 824 **KILDIN** (mod) SSV 512

Displacement, tons: 1,240 standard; 1,600 full load
Dimensions, feet (metres): 240.5 × 36.8 × 12.8 *(73.3 × 11.2 × 3.9)*
Main machinery: 2 Zgoda-Sulzer 6TD48 diesels; 3,300 hp(m) *(2.43 MW)* sustained; 2 shafts; cp props
Speed, knots: 17
Range, n miles: 9,000 at 11 kt
Complement: 66 plus 19 scientists
Missiles: SAM: 2 SA-N-5 Grail quad launchers in some.
Radars: Surface search: 2 Don 2; I-band.

Comment: Modernised ships have a foremast in the fore well-deck and a low superstructure before the bridge. Non-modernised ships retain their cranes in the forward well-deck. Similar class operates as survey ships. Built at Gdansk, Poland between 1968–72. All based in the Black Sea. One to Ukraine in 1996.

EKVATOR AND KILDIN *10/2008*, **Laursen/Jarnasen*** / 1353347

2 ALPINIST (PROJECT 503M/R) CLASS (AGIM)

ZHIGULEVSK GS 19 **SYZRAN** GS 39

Displacement, tons: 1,260 full load
Dimensions, feet (metres): 177.1 × 34.4 × 13.1 *(54 × 10.5 × 4)*
Main machinery: 1 SKL 8 NVD 48 A2U diesel; 1,320 hp(m) *(970 kW)* sustained; 1 shaft; bow thruster
Speed, knots: 13
Range, n miles: 7,000 at 13 kt
Complement: 50
Missiles: SAM: 1 SA-N-5 Grail quad launcher (GS 39).
Countermeasures: ESM: 2 Watch Dog; intercept.
Radars: Surface search: Nayada and Kivach; I-band.
Sonars: Paltus; active; high frequency.

Comment: Similar to Alpinist stern-trawlers which were built at about 10 a year at the Leninskaya Kuznitsa yard at Kiev and at the Volvograd shipyard. These AGIs were built at Kiev. In 1987 and 1988 forecastle was extended further aft and the electronics fit upgraded. Both based in the Baltic. *GS 7* probably non-operational in the Pacific. A fourth of class converted for ASW training was laid up in 1997.

ZHIGULEVSK *8/2007, **Lemachko Collection*** / 1305144

DEEP SUBMERGENCE VEHICLES

1 BESTER CLASS RESCUE SUBMERSIBLES (PROJECT 18270) (DSRV)

AS 36

Displacement, tons: 50 dived
Dimensions, feet (metres): 57.4 × 12.8 × 16.7 *(17.5 × 3.9 × 5.1)*
Main machinery: Battery-powered; 1 propeller; 2 vertical thrusters; 2 horizontal thrusters
Speed, knots: 4. **Range, n miles:** 11.5 at 2.5 kt
Complement: 3 + 18 passengers

Comment: Designed by the Lazurit Central Design Bureau and built at the Krasnoye Sormovo Shipyard, Nizhny Novgorod in 1994. Can mate with hulls at angles of 45° to horizontal. Endurance 4 hours. Can be carried onboard rescue ship *Alagez* or the salvage *Mikhail Rudnitsky*. Reported diving depth of over 750 m. Has an underwater manipulation system and four viewing ports. AS 36 based in Northern Fleet.

BESTER *6/2004, S Breyer* / 1127289

5 PRIZ (PROJECT 1855) CLASS (SALVAGE SUBMERSIBLES) (DSRV)

AS 22 **AS 26** **AS 28** **AS 30** **AS 34**

Displacement, tons: 58 dived
Dimensions, feet (metres): 44.3 × 12.5 × 12.8 *(13.5 × 3.8 × 3.9)*
Speed, knots: 3.3. **Range, n miles:** 21 at 2.3 kt
Complement: 4 + 20 passengers

Comment: Designed by the Lazurit Central Design Bureau and built in Nizhny Novgorod 1986–89. Can be carried onboard rescue ship *Alagez* or from the salvage ship *Mikhail Rudnitsky*. Has titanium hull and reported diving depth of over 1,000 m. Endurance 2-3 hours submerged. Has an underwater manipulation system. One (possibly AS 32) was involved in the *Kursk* rescue attempt. AS 28 became trapped on the sea-bottom off the Kamchatka peninsula on 5 August 2005. It was later rescued with the help of the British submarine rescue system. AS 34 based in Northern Fleet. AS 28 in Pacific Fleet.

AS 34 *6/2008*, Richard Scott* / 1336057

3 UNDERWATER WORKING VEHICLES (PROJECT 1839)

AS 25 **+2**

Displacement, tons: 47 dived
Dimensions, feet (metres): 44.6 × 11.5 × 9.5 *(13.6 × 3.5 × 2.9)*
Speed, knots: 3.5
Complement: 3

Comment: Entered naval service from 1984. Designed to perform underwater technical work and to assist in submarine rescue operations in depths up to 500 m. Double-hulled.

AS 25 *6/2008*, Richard Scott* / 1336054

4 SALVAGE SUBMERSIBLES (PROJECT 1837) (DSRV)

Displacement, tons: 45 dived
Dimensions, feet (metres): 41.7 × 11.5 × 10.7 *(12.7 × 3.5 × 3.25)*
Speed, knots: 3.6. **Range, n miles:** 16 at 2 kt
Complement: 3 + 11 passengers

Comment: Designed and built by Sudomekh, St Petersburg. Can be carried onboard Kashtan class SS 750 rescue ship and Elbrus class *Alagez*. Has double hull and diving depth of 500 m. Equipped with an underwater manipulation system. Twelve reported to have been built of which some were reported to have been decommissioned in the 1990s. Operational numbers are approximate.

1 RUS (PROJECT 16810) CLASS (RESEARCH SUBMERSIBLE)

AS 37

Displacement, tons: 25 dived
Dimensions, feet (metres): 26.2 × 12.8 × 12.6 *(8.0 × 3.9 × 3.85)*
Speed, knots: 3
Complement: 3

Comment: Entered naval service in 2000. Designed to perform research and technical underwater work at up to 6,000 m. Titanium spherical hull. Three horizontal propulsion motors, two vertical propulsion motors and one thruster. Based in Baltic fleet.

2 POISK-2 (PROJECT 1832) CLASS (RESEARCH SUBMERSIBLES)

Displacement, tons: 65 dived
Dimensions, feet (metres): 53.5 × 8.2 × 10.8 *(16.3 × 2.5 × 3.3)*
Speed, knots: 3
Complement: 3

Comment: Entered naval service in 1988 and 1989. Designed to perform research and technical underwater work at up to 2,000 m.

TRAINING SHIPS

Notes: The Mir class sail training ships have no military connections.

2 SMOLNY (PROJECT 887) CLASS

PEREKOP 200 **SMOLNY** 210

Displacement, tons: 9,150 full load
Dimensions, feet (metres): 452.8 × 53.1 × 21.3 *(138 × 16.2 × 6.5)*
Main machinery: 2 Zgoda Sulzer 12ZV 40/48 diesels; 15,000 hp(m) *(11 MW)*; 2 shafts
Speed, knots: 20. **Range, n miles:** 9,000 at 15 kt
Complement: 137 (12 officers) plus 330 cadets
Guns: 4—3 in *(76 mm)*/60 (2 twin). 4—30 mm/65 (2 twin)
A/S mortars: 2 RBU 2500
Countermeasures: ESM: 2 Watch Dog; radar warning
Radars: Air/surface search: Head Net C; 3D; E-band; range 128 km *(70 n miles)*.
Navigation: 4 Don 2; I-band. Don Kay *(Perekop)*; I-band.
Fire control: Owl Screech; G-band. Drum Tilt; H/I-band.
IFF: 2 High Pole A. Square Head.
Sonars: Mouse Tail VDS; active; high frequency.

Comment: Built at Szczecin, Poland. *Smolny* completed in 1976, *Perekop* in 1977. Have considerable combatant potential. Both are active in the Baltic.

PEREKOP *6/2007, Selim San* / 1170204

10 PETRUSHKA (UK-3) CLASS (AXL)

MK 391	**MK 1277**	**MK 1407–1411**
MK 405	**MK 1303**	**MK 1556**

Displacement, tons: 335 full load
Dimensions, feet (metres): 129.3 × 27.6 × 7.2 *(39.4 × 8.4 × 2.2)*
Main machinery: 2 Wola H12 diesels; 756 hp(m) *(556 kW)*; 2 shafts
Speed, knots: 11. **Range, n miles:** 1,000 at 11 kt
Complement: 13 plus 30 cadets

Comment: Training vessels built at Wisla Shipyard, Poland; first one commissioned in 1989. Very similar to the SK 620 class used as ambulance craft. Used for seamanship and navigation training and may be commercially owned.

PETRUSHKA CLASS *6/2003, E & M Laursen* / 0570909

AUXILIARIES

Notes: Two Belyanka-class tankers *Amur* and *Pinega* are used for stowing low level radioactive waste.

2 AMGA (PROJECT 1791) CLASS (MISSILE SUPPORT SHIPS) (AEM)

VETLUGA **DAUGAVA**

Displacement, tons: 6,100 *(Vetluga)*, 6,350 *(Daugava)* full load
Dimensions, feet (metres): 354.3 × 59 × 14.8 *(108 × 18 × 4.5) (Vetluga)*
Main machinery: 2 diesels; 9,000 hp(m) *(6.6 MW)*; 2 shafts
Speed, knots: 16
Range, n miles: 4,500 at 14 kt
Complement: 210
Guns: 4—25 mm/80 (2 twin)
Radars: Surface search: Strut Curve; F-band.
Navigation: Don 2; I-band.
IFF: High Pole B.

Comment: Built at Gorkiy. Ships with similar duties to the Lama class. Fitted with a large 55 ton crane forward and thus capable of handling much larger missiles than their predecessors. Each ship has a different length and type of crane to handle later types of missiles. Designed for servicing submarines. *Vetluga* completed in 1976 and *Daugava* (5m longer than *Vetluga*) in 1981. Both are in the Pacific Fleet. A third of class is laid up in the North.

DAUGAVA *3/2003, Lemachko Collection* / 0573518

13 AMUR (PROJECT 304/304M) CLASS (REPAIR SHIPS) (AR)

AMUR I
PM 10 **PM 15** **PM 30** **PM 56** **PM 64** **PM 82** **PM 138** **PM 140** **PM 156**
AMUR II
PM 59 **PM 69** **PM 86** **PM 97**

Displacement, tons: 5,500 full load
Dimensions, feet (metres): 400.3 × 55.8 × 16.7 *(122 × 17 × 5.1)*
Main machinery: 1 Zgoda 8 TAD-48 diesel; 3,000 hp(m) *(2.2 MW)*; 1 shaft
Speed, knots: 12
Range, n miles: 13,000 at 8 kt
Complement: 145
Radars: Navigation: Kivach or Palm Frond or Nayada; I-band.

Comment: Amur I class general purpose depot and repair ships completed 1968–83 in Szczecin, Poland. Successors to the Oskol class. Carry two 5 ton cranes and have accommodation for 200 from ships alongside. Amur II class has extra deckhouse forward of the funnel. Built at Szczecin 1983–85. Three Amur IIs are based in the Pacific and one in the North. Three are laid up in the Baltic. PM 9 transferred to Ukraine.

AMUR II PM 86 *9/2000, J Cislak* / 0105571

AMUR I PM 138 *9/2002, Globke Collection* / 0528330

1 MALINA (PROJECT 2020) CLASS (NUCLEAR SUBMARINE SUPPORT SHIP) (AS)

PM 63

Displacement, tons: 10,500 full load
Dimensions, feet (metres): 449.5 × 68.9 × 18.4 *(137 × 21 × 5.6)*
Main machinery: 4 gas turbines; 60,000 hp(m) *(44 MW)*; 2 shafts
Speed, knots: 17
Complement: 260
Radars: Navigation: 2 Palm Frond or 2 Nayada; I-band.

Comment: Built at Nikolayev. First deployed to Pacific in 1986. PM is an abbreviation of Plavuchaya Masterskaya (Floating workshop). A fourth of class *(PM 16)* launched early in 1992, was not completed. Designed to support nuclear-powered submarines and surface ships. Carry two 15 ton cranes. Based in the Northern Fleet. PM 12 and PM 74 are inactive.

PM 74 *7/1996* / 0081704

2 VYTEGRALES II (PROJECT 596P) CLASS (SUPPLY SHIPS) (AKH/AGF)

APSHERON (ex-*Vagales*) 204 **DAURIYA** (ex-*Vyborgles*) 506

Displacement, tons: 6,150 full load
Dimensions, feet (metres): 400.3 × 55.1 × 22.3 *(122.1 × 16.8 × 6.8)*
Main machinery: 1 Burmeister & Wain 950VTBF diesel; 5,200 hp(m) *(3.82 MW)*; 1 shaft
Speed, knots: 15
Complement: 46
Radars: Navigation: Nayada or Palm Frond or Spin Trough; I-band.
CCA: Fly Screen.
Helicopters: 1 Ka-25 Hormone C.

Comment: Standard timber carriers of a class of 27. These ships were modified for naval use in 1966–68 with helicopter flight deck. Built at Zhdanov Yard, Leningrad between 1963 and 1966. *Dauriya* has a deckhouse over the aft hold. The first of class, completed in 1962, was originally *Vytegrales*, but this was later changed to *Kosmonaut Pavel Belyayev* and, with three other ships of this class, converted to Space Support Ships. The civilian-manned ships together with these naval ships are often incorrectly called Vostok or Baskunchak class. *Apsheron* and *Dauriya* are in the Black Sea, *Sevan* and *Yamal* have been decommissioned. Two others transferred to Ukraine in 1996.

DAURIYA *7/2000, Hartmut Ehlers* / 0105572

30 BOLVA (PROJECT 688/688A) CLASS (BARRACKS SHIPS) (YPB)

Displacement, tons: 6,500
Dimensions, feet (metres): 560.9 × 45.9 × 9.8 *(171 × 14 × 3)*
Cargo capacity: 350-400 tons

Comment: A total of 59 built by Valmet Oy, Helsinki between 1960 and 1984. Of the remaining 30 ships, six are Bolva 1, 16 are Bolva 2 and eight are Bolva 3. Used for accommodation of ships' companies during refit and so on. The Bolva 2 and 3 have a helicopter pad. Have accommodation facilities for about 400 people. No means of propulsion but can be steered. In addition there are several other types of Barracks Ships including five ex-Atrek class depot ships as well as converted merchant ships and large barges. At least 18 have been scrapped.

IMATRA (at Sevastopol) *3/2002, Hartmut Ehlers* / 0529803

5 BORIS CHILIKIN (PROJECT 1559V) CLASS (REPLENISHMENT SHIPS) (AOR)

BORIS BUTOMA **IVAN BUBNOV** **SEGEI OSIPOV** (ex-*Dnestr*) **VLADIMIR KOLECHITSKY** **GENRICH GASANOV**

Displacement, tons: 23,450 full load
Dimensions, feet (metres): 531.5 × 70.2 × 33.8 *(162.1 × 21.4 × 10.3)*
Main machinery: 1 diesel; 9,600 hp(m) *(7 MW)*; 1 shaft
Speed, knots: 17
Range, n miles: 10,000 at 16 kt
Complement: 75 (without armament)
Cargo capacity: 13,000 tons oil fuel and dieso; 400 tons ammunition; 400 tons spares; 400 tons victualling stores; 500 tons fresh water

Guns: 4—57 mm/80 (2 twin). Most are fitted for but not with the guns.
Radars: Air/surface search/fire control: Strut Curve (fitted for but not with). Muff Cob (fitted for but not with).
Navigation: 2 Nayada or Palm Frond (plus Don 2 in *V Kolechitsky*); I-band.
IFF: High Pole B.

Programmes: Based on the Veliky Oktyabr merchant ship tanker design. Built at the Baltic Yard, Leningrad; *Vladimir Kolechitsky* completed in 1972, *Osipov* in 1973, *Ivan Bubnov* in 1975, *Genrich Gasanov* in 1977. Last of class *Boris Butoma* completed in 1978.
Structure: This is the only class of purpose-built underway fleet replenishment ships for the supply of both liquids and solids. Although most operate in merchant navy paint schemes, all wear naval ensigns.
Operational: Earlier ships can supply solids on both sides forward. Later ships supply solids to starboard, liquids to port forward. All can supply liquids either side aft and astern. *Osipov* and *Gasanov* are based in the North, *Bubnov* in the Black Sea, *Butoma* and *Kolechitsky* in the Pacific. Most are used for commercial purposes. *Boris Chilikin* transferred to Ukraine in 1997.

SERGEI OSIPOV *1/2008*, B Prézelin* / 1353288

VLADIMIR KOLECHITSKY *3/2001, Ships of the World* / 0126357

2 DUBNA CLASS (REPLENISHMENT TANKERS) (AOL/AOT)

DUBNA **PECHENGA**

Displacement, tons: 11,500 full load
Dimensions, feet (metres): 426.4 × 65.6 × 23.6 *(130 × 20 × 7.2)*
Main machinery: 1 Russkiy 8DRPH23/230 diesel; 6,000 hp(m) *(4.4 MW)*; 1 shaft
Speed, knots: 16
Range, n miles: 7,000 at 16 kt
Complement: 70
Cargo capacity: 7,000 tons fuel; 300 tons fresh water; 1,500 tons stores
Radars: Navigation: 2 Nayada; I-band.

Programmes: Completed 1974 at Rauma-Repola, Finland.
Structure: *Dubna* has 1 ton replenishment stations forward. Normally painted in merchant navy colours.
Operational: *Dubna* can refuel on either beam and astern. *Pechenga* has had RAS gear removed. Based in North. One of the class transferred to Ukraine in 1997. *Irkut* is believed to have been sold commercially in 1999.

DUBNA *7/1996, van Ginderen Collection* / 0019061

PECHENGA *6/2006, Ships of the World* / 1159988

6 MOD ALTAY CLASS (PROJECT 160) (REPLENISHMENT TANKERS) (AOL)

PRUT **KOLA** **YELNYA** **IZHORA** **ILIM** **YEGORLIK**

Displacement, tons: 7,250 full load
Dimensions, feet (metres): 348 × 51 × 22 *(106.2 × 15.5 × 6.7)*
Main machinery: 1 Burmeister & Wain BM550VTBN110 diesel; 3,200 hp(m) *(2.35 MW)*; 1 shaft
Speed, knots: 14. **Range, n miles:** 8,600 at 12 kt
Complement: 60
Cargo capacity: 4,400 tons oil fuel; 200 m³ solids
Radars: Navigation: 2 Don 2 or 2 Spin Trough; I-band.

Comment: Built from 1967–72 by Rauma-Repola, Finland. Modified for alongside replenishment. This class is part of 38 ships, being the third group of Rauma types built in Finland in 1967. *Ilim* and *Yegorlik* transferred to civilian companies in 1996/97 and operate in the Pacific with *Izhora*. *Prut* in the North, *Yelnya* and *Kola* in the Baltic.

KOLA *1/1997, van Ginderen Collection* / 0019062

2 OLEKMA CLASS (PROJECT 92) (REPLENISHMENT TANKERS) (AORL)

OLEKMA **IMAN**

Displacement, tons: 7,300 full load
Dimensions, feet (metres): 344.5 × 47.9 × 22 *(105.1 × 14.6 × 6.7)*
Main machinery: 1 Burmeister & Wain diesel; 2,900 hp(m) *(2.13 MW)*; 1 shaft
Speed, knots: 14. **Range, n miles:** 8,000 at 14 kt
Complement: 40
Cargo capacity: 4,500 tons oil fuel; 180 m³ solids
Radars: Navigation: Don 2 or Nayada and Spin Trough; I-band.

Comment: Built by Rauma-Repola, Finland in 1966. Modified for replenishment with refuelling rig abaft the bridge as well as astern refuelling. *Olekma* based in the Baltic and *Iman* in the Black Sea.

IMAN *6/2006* / 1164807

5 UDA CLASS (PROJECT 577D) (REPLENISHMENT TANKERS) (AOL)

LENA **TEREK** **VISHERA** **KOYDA** **DUNAY**

Displacement, tons: 5,500 standard; 7,126 full load
Dimensions, feet (metres): 400.3 × 51.8 × 20.3 *(122.1 × 15.8 × 6.2)*
Main machinery: 2 diesels; 9,000 hp(m) *(6.6 MW)*; 2 shafts
Speed, knots: 17
Range, n miles: 4,000 at 15 kt
Complement: 85
Cargo capacity: 2,900 tons oil fuel; 100 m³ solids
Radars: Navigation: 2 Don 2 or Nayada/Palm Frond; I-band.
IFF: High Pole A.

Comment: Built between 1962 and 1967 at Vyborg Shipyard. All have a beam replenishment capability. Guns removed. *Vishera* and *Dunay* in the Pacific, *Terek* in the Northern Fleet, *Koyda* in the Black Sea and *Lena* in the Baltic.

LENA *8/2004* / 1042325

2 MANYCH (PROJECT 1549) CLASS (WATER TANKERS) (AWT)

MANYCH **TAGIL**

Displacement, tons: 7,700 full load
Dimensions, feet (metres): 380.5 × 51.5 × 23.0 *(116.0 × 15.7 × 7.0)*
Main machinery: 2 diesels; 9,000 hp(m) *(6.6 MW)*; 2 shafts
Speed, knots: 18
Range, n miles: 7,500 at 16 kt
Complement: 90
Cargo capacity: 4,400 tons
Radars: Air/surface search: Strut Curve; E/F-band.
Navigation: Don Kay; I-band.

Comment: Distilled water carrier built at Vyborg and completed in 1972. Decommissioned and disarmed in 1996 but returned to service in 1998 after refit in Bulgaria. *Manych* based in the Black Sea.

MANYCH *10/2008*, Laursen/Jarnasen* / 1353349

1 KALININGRADNEFT CLASS (SUPPORT TANKER) (AORL)

VYAZMA (ex-*Katun*)

Displacement, tons: 8,600 full load
Dimensions, feet (metres): 380.5 × 56 × 21 *(116 × 17 × 6.5)*
Main machinery: 1 Russkiy Burmeister & Wain 5DKRP50/110-2 diesel; 3,850 hp(m) *(2.83 MW)*; 1 shaft
Speed, knots: 14
Range, n miles: 5,000 at 14 kt
Complement: 32
Cargo capacity: 5,400 tons oil fuel and other liquids
Radars: Navigation: Okean; I-band.

Comment: Built by Rauma-Repola, Finland in 1982. Can refuel astern. At least an additional 20 of this class operate with the fishing fleets. Operational in the Northern Fleet.

KALININGRADNEFT CLASS *11/1991, G Jacobs* / 0506092

30 TOPLIVO CLASS (PROJECT 1844/1844D) CLASS (YO)

VTN series

Displacement, tons: 1,180 full load
Dimensions, feet (metres): 178.1 × 24.3 × 10.5 *(54.3 × 7.4 × 3.2)*
Main machinery: 1 diesel; 600 hp *(450 kW)*; 1 shaft
Speed, knots: 10
Range, n miles: 1,500 at 10 kt
Complement: 20
Radars: Navigation: Don-2; I-band.

Comment: Details given are for the Toplivo-2 class, some of which were built in Egypt but the majority in the USSR. The Toplivo-3 class, built in the USSR, are slightly larger at 1,300 tons full load. Numbers remaining in service are approximate. All the original Toplivo-1 class are believed to have been decommissioned.

VTN 30 *7/2008*, Hartmut Ehlers* / 1353290

5 KHOBI CLASS (PROJECT 437M) CLASS (YO)

LOVAT **SISOLA** **SOSHA** **ORSHA** **INDIGA** (ex-*Seyma*)

Displacement, tons: 1,520 full load
Dimensions, feet (metres): 221.1 × 33.1 × 11.8 *(67.4 × 10.1 × 3.6)*
Main machinery: 1 diesel; 1,600 hp *(1.2 MW)*; 2 shafts
Speed, knots: 13
Range, n miles: 2,000 at 10 kt
Complement: 30
Radars: Navigation: Don-2; I-band.

Comment: *Sisola* based in the North, *Sosha*, *Lovat* and *Orsha* in the Baltic and *Indiga* in the Black Sea. Used for the transport of all forms of liquids.

LOVAT *7/2008*, Hartmut Ehlers* / 1353289

3 OB (PROJECT 320) CLASS (HOSPITAL SHIPS) (AHH)

YENISEI **SVIR** **IRTYSH**

Displacement, tons: 11,570 full load
Dimensions, feet (metres): 499.7 × 63.6 × 20.5 *(152.3 × 19.4 × 6.3)*
Main machinery: 2 Zgoda-Sulzer 12ZV40/48; 15,600 hp(m) *(11.47 MW)* sustained; 2 shafts; cp props
Speed, knots: 19
Range, n miles: 10,000 at 18 kt
Complement: 124 plus 83 medical staff
Radars: Navigation: 3 Don 2 or 3 Nayada; I-band.
IFF: High Pole A.
Helicopters: 1 Ka-25 Hormone C.

Comment: Built at Szczecin, Poland. *Yenisei* completed 1981 and is based in the Black Sea. *Svir* completed in early 1989 and transferred to the Northern Fleet in September 1989. *Irtysh* completed in June 1990, was stationed in the Gulf in 1990–91 and is now based in the Pacific. A fourth of class is derelict and a fifth was cancelled. Have 100 beds and seven operating theatres. The first purpose-built hospital ships in the Navy, a programme which may have been prompted by the use of several merchant ships off Angola for Cuban casualties in the 'war of liberation.' NBC pressurised citadel. Ship stabilisation system. Decompression chamber. All are in use, mostly as alongside medical facilities.

YENISEI *10/2008*, Laursen/Jarnasen* / 1353351

3 KLASMA (PROJECT 1274) CLASS (CABLE SHIPS) (ARC)

DONETS **INGURI** **YANA**

Displacement, tons: 6,000 standard; 6,900 full load
Measurement, tons: 3,400 dwt; 5,786 gross
Dimensions, feet (metres): 427.8 × 52.5 × 19 *(130.5 × 16 × 5.8)*
Main machinery: Diesel-electric; 5 Wärtsilä Sulzer 624TS diesel generators (4 in *Ingul* and *Yana*); 5,000 hp(m) *(3.68 MW)*; 2 motors; 2,150 hp(m) *(1.58 MW)*; 2 shafts
Speed, knots: 14
Range, n miles: 12,000 at 14 kt
Complement: 118
Radars: Navigation: Spin Trough and Nayada; I-band.

Comment: *Yana* built by Wärtsilä, Helsingforsvarvet, Finland in 1962; *Donets* at the Wärtsilä, Åbovarvet in 1968–69. *Donets* is of a slightly modified design. *Inguri* completed in 1978. All are ice strengthened and can carry 1,650 miles of cable. *Yana* is distinguished by gantry right aft. *Donets* is in the Baltic, and the other two are in the North. All are active and can be leased for commercial use. One to Ukraine in 1997.

KLASMA *3/1992* / 0081709

4 EMBA (PROJECT 1172/1175) CLASS (CABLE SHIPS) (ARC)

SETUN (I) **NEPRYADAVA** (I) **KEM** (II) **BIRIUSA** (II)

Displacement, tons: 2,050 full load (Group I); 2,400 (Group II)
Dimensions, feet (metres): 249 × 41.3 × 9.8 *(75.9 × 12.6 × 3)* (Group I)
282.4 × 41.3 × 9.9 *(86.1 × 12.6 × 3)* (Group II)
Main machinery: Diesel-electric; 2 Wärtsilä Vasa 6R22 diesel alternators; 2,350 kVA 60 Hz; 2 motors; 1,360 hp(m) *(1 MW)*; 2 shafts (Group I)
2 Wärtsilä Vasa 8R22 diesel alternators; 3,090 kVA 60 Hz; 2 motors; 2,180 hp(m) *(1.6 MW)*; 2 shafts (Group II)
The 2 turnable propulsion units can be inclined to the ship's path giving, with a bow thruster, improved turning movement
Speed, knots: 11
Complement: 40
Radars: Navigation: Kivach and Don 2; I-band.

Comment: Both Emba Is built in 1981. Designed for shallow water cable-laying. Carry 380 tons of cable. Order placed with Wärtsilä in January 1985 for two larger (Group II) ships; *Kem* completed on 23 October 1986. Can lay about 600 tons of cable. Designed for use off Vladivostok but also capable of operations in inland waterways. *Setun* is based in the Black Sea, *Nepryadava* in the Baltic, and *Kem* and *Biriusa* are in the Pacific. Both of the latter two were active in 2005.

SETUN *6/2003, Lemachko Collection* / 0573515

4 MIKHAIL RUDNITSKY (PROJECT 05360/1) CLASS (SALVAGE AND MOORING VESSELS) (ARS)

MIKHAIL RUDNITSKY **GEORGY KOZMIN** **GEORGY TITOV** **SAYANY**

Displacement, tons: 10,700 full load
Dimensions, feet (metres): 427.4 × 56.7 × 23.9 *(130.3 × 17.3 × 7.3)*
Main machinery: 1 S5DKRN62/140-3 diesel; 6,100 hp(m) *(4.48 MW)*; 1 shaft
Speed, knots: 16
Range, n miles: 12,000 at 15.5 kt
Complement: 72 (10 officers)
Radars: Navigation: Palm Frond; Nayada; I-band.
Sonars: MG 89 *(Sayany)*.

Comment: Built at Vyborg, based on Moskva Pionier class merchant ship hull. First completed 1979, second in 1980, third in 1983 and fourth in 1984. Fly flag of Salvage and Rescue Service. Have two 40 ton and one 20 ton lift with cable fairleads forward and aft. This lift capability is adequate for handling small submersibles, such as Project 1855 Priz, one of which is carried in the centre hold. *Sayany* is also described as a research ship and has a high-frequency sonar. *Rudnitsky* and Project 1837 submersible took part in the *Kursk* rescue attempts in August 2000. *Rudnitsky* and *Titov* in the Northern Fleet and the other two in the Pacific.

GEORGY TITOV *6/2008*, Richard Scott* / 1353352

8 KASHTAN (PROJECT 141) CLASS (BUOY TENDERS) (ABU/AGL/ARS)

ALEXANDR PUSHKIN (ex-KIL 926) **KIL 143** **KIL 164** **KIL 498** **KIL 927** **KIL 158** **SS 750** (ex-KIL 140) **KIL 168**

Displacement, tons: 4,600 full load
Dimensions, feet (metres): 313.3 × 56.4 × 16.4 *(95.5 × 17.2 × 5)*
Main machinery: 4 Wärtsilä diesels; 29,000 hp(m) *(2.31 MW)*; 2 shafts
Speed, knots: 13.5
Complement: 51 plus 20 spare berths
Radars: Navigation: 2 Nayada; I-band.

Comment: Enlarged Sura class built at the Neptun Shipyard, Rostock. Ordered 29 August 1986; *Alexandr Pushkin* handed over in June 1988 and is classified as an AGL in the Baltic; *927* to the Pacific in July 1989; *143* to the North in July 1989; *158* to the Black Sea in November 1989; *164* to the North in January 1990; *498* to the Pacific in November 1990 and *168* to the Pacific in mid-1991. Lifting capacity: one 130 ton lifting frame, one 100 ton derrick, one 12.5 ton crane and one 10 ton derrick. All are civilian operated except *SS 750* in the Baltic which is used to support Project 1837 submersibles AS 22 and AS 26. *158* deployed to Tartous for several months in late 2002.

KIL 158 *10/2008*, Laursen/Jarnasen* / 1353353

KIL 168 *6/2007, Ships of the World* / 1305157

4 SURA (PROJECT 145) CLASS (BUOY TENDERS) (ABU)

KIL 22 **KIL 27** **KIL 29** **KIL 31**

Displacement, tons: 2,370 standard; 3,150 full load
Dimensions, feet (metres): 285.4 × 48.6 × 16.4 *(87 × 14.8 × 5)*
Main machinery: Diesel-electric; 4 diesel generators; 2 motors; 2,240 hp(m) *(1.65 MW)*; 2 shafts
Speed, knots: 12. **Range, n miles:** 2,000 at 11 kt
Complement: 40
Cargo capacity: 900 tons cargo; 300 tons fuel for transfer
Radars: Navigation: 2 Don 2; I-band.

Comment: Heavy lift ships built as mooring and buoy tenders at Rostock in East Germany between 1965 and 1976. Lifting capacity: one 65 ton derrick and one 65 ton stern cage. Have been seen to carry 12 m DSRVs. *KIL 27* is in the Pacific, *KIL 29* in the Baltic and *KIL 22* and *KIL 31* in the North. Four others are laid up. One to Ukraine in 1997.

KIL 31 *4/1996, van Ginderen Collection* / 0506326

1 ELBRUS (OSIMOL) (PROJECT 537) CLASS (SUBMARINE RESCUE SHIP) (ASRH)

ALAGEZ

Displacement, tons: 19,000 standard; 22,500 full load
Dimensions, feet (metres): 575.8 × 80.4 × 27.9 *(175.5 × 24.5 × 8.5)*
Main machinery: Diesel-electric; 4 diesel generators; 2 motors; 20,000 hp(m) *(14.7 MW)*; 2 shafts
Speed, knots: 17. **Range, n miles:** 14,500 at 15 kt
Complement: 420
Radars: Navigation: 2 Nayada and 2 Palm Frond; I-band.
Helicopters: 1 Ka-25 Hormone C.

Comment: Very large submarine rescue and salvage ship with icebreaking capability, possibly in view of under-ice capability of some SSBNs. Built at Nikolayev, and completed in 1982. Can carry two submersibles in store abaft the funnel which are launched from telescopic gantries. Based in the Pacific. Probably disarmed.

ALAGEZ *6/2004, Ships of the World* / 0583298

24 SHELON I/II (PROJECT 1388/1388M) CLASS (YPT/YAG)

TL and KRKH series

Displacement, tons: 270 full load
Dimensions, feet (metres): 150.9 × 19.7 × 6.6 *(46 × 6 × 2)*
Main machinery: 2 diesels; 8,976 hp(m) *(6.6 MW)*; 2 shafts
Speed, knots: 26
Range, n miles: 1,500 at 10 kt
Complement: 14
Radars: Navigation: Spin Trough or Kivach; I-band.

Comment: Type I built 1978–84. Built-in weapon recovery ramp aft. Type II built 1985–87. Type IIs can be used as environmental monitoring ships. One is an Admirals' yacht in the Baltic, and others are used as personnel transports.

KRKH 1668 *9/2008*, Frank Findler* / 1353308

TL 1603 *7/2008*, Hartmut Ehlers* / 1353291

48 FLAMINGO (TANYA) (PROJECT 1415) CLASS (TENDERS) (YDT)

Displacement, tons: 42 full load
Dimensions, feet (metres): 72.8 × 12.8 × 4.6 *(22.2 × 3.9 × 1.4)*
Main machinery: 1 Type 3-D-12 diesel; 300 hp(m) *(220 kW)* sustained; 1 shaft
Speed, knots: 12
Complement: 8

Comment: Successor to Nyryat II. There are some 28 with RVK numbers (diving tenders). There are also about 20 (PSKA numbers) assigned to the Border Guard for harbour patrol duties. These are known as the Kulik class. Other craft have BSK, RK (workboats) PRDKA (counterswimmer cutter) and BGK (inshore survey) numbers.

RVK 1579 *7/2008*, Hartmut Ehlers* / 1353307

35 POLUCHAT I, II AND III CLASSES (PROJECT 364) (YPT)

TL series

Displacement, tons: 70 standard; 100 full load
Dimensions, feet (metres): 97.1 × 19 × 4.8 *(29.6 × 5.8 × 1.5)*
Main machinery: 2 M 50 diesels; 2,200 hp(m) *(1.6 MW)* sustained; 2 shafts
Speed, knots: 20
Range, n miles: 1,500 at 10 kt
Complement: 15
Guns: 2—14.5 mm (twin) MGs (in some).
Radars: Spin Trough; I-band.

Comment: Employed as specialised or dual-purpose torpedo recovery vessels and/or patrol boats. They have a stern slipway. Several exported as patrol craft. Some used by the Border Guard.
Transfers: Algeria, Angola, Congo (three), Ethiopia (one), Guinea-Bissau, India, Indonesia (three), Iraq (two), Mozambique, Somalia (six), Syria, Tanzania, Vietnam (five), North Yemen (two), South Yemen.

POLUCHAT I *11/1991, MoD Bonn* / 0081713

20 NYRYAT 2 (PROJECT 522) CLASS (DIVING TENDERS) (YDT)

RVK Series

Displacement, tons: 56 full load
Dimensions, feet (metres): 70.5 × 11.5 × 3.3 *(21.5 × 3.5 × 1)*
Main machinery: 1 Type 3-D-12 diesel; 300 hp(m) *(220 kW)* sustained; 1 shaft
Speed, knots: 12
Complement: 8
Guns: Some carry 1—12.7 mm MG on the forecastle.

Comment: Nyryat 2 are the diving tender variants of the 1950s PO 2 class workboat design widely used for both military and civilian use.
Transfers: Albania, Bulgaria, Cuba, Guinea, Iraq. Many deleted.

RVK 860 *7/2006, Lemachko Collection* / 1159850

30 NYRYAT I (PROJECT 1896) CLASS (TENDERS) (YDT)

Displacement, tons: 120 full load
Dimensions, feet (metres): 93 × 18 × 5.5 *(28.4 × 5.5 × 1.7)*
Main machinery: 1 diesel; 450 hp(m) *(331 kW)*; 1 shaft
Speed, knots: 12.5. **Range, n miles**: 1,500 at 10 kt
Complement: 15
Guns: 1—12.7 mm MG (in some).

Comment: Built from 1955. Can operate as patrol craft or diving tenders with recompression chamber. Similar hull and propulsion used for inshore survey craft. Some have BGK, VM or GBP (survey craft) numbers.
Transfers: Albania, Algeria, Cuba, Egypt, Iraq, North Yemen. Many deleted.

NYRYAT I *10/2008*, Laursen/Jarnasen* / 1353354

15 SK 620 CLASS (DRAKON) (TENDERS) (YH/YFL)

MK 391	**MK 1407–1409**	**PSK 405**	**PSK 1411**	**SN 109**	**SN 128**	**SN 1318**
MK 1303	**PSK 382**	**PSK 673**	**PSK 1518**	**SN 126**	**SN 401**	**SN 1520**

Displacement, tons: 236 full load
Dimensions, feet (metres): 108.3 × 24.3 × 6.9 *(33 × 7.4 × 2.1)*
Main machinery: 2 56ANM30-H12 diesels; 620 hp(m) *(456 kW)* sustained; 2 shafts
Speed, knots: 12. **Range, n miles**: 1,000 at 12 kt
Complement: 14 plus 3 spare

Comment: Built at Wisla Shipyard, Poland as a smaller version of the Petrushka class training ship. PSK series serve as harbour ferries. Mostly used as hospital tenders capable of carrying 15 patients.

PSK 405 *7/2001, J Cislak* / 0528310

28 YELVA (KRAB) (PROJECT 535M) CLASS (DIVING TENDERS) (YDT)

VM 20	**VM 263**	**VM 420**	**VM 907–910**
VM 72	**VM 268**	**VM 425**	**VM 915**
VM 146	**VM 270**	**VM 429**	**VM 916**
VM 153	**VM 277**	**VM 725**	**VM 919**
VM 154	**VM 409**	**VM 807**	
VM 250	**VM 413–416**	**VM 809**	

Displacement, tons: 295 full load
Dimensions, feet (metres): 134.2 × 26.2 × 6.6 *(40.9 × 8 × 2)*
Main machinery: 2 Type 3-D-12A diesels; 630 hp(m) *(463 kW)* sustained; 2 shafts
Speed, knots: 12.5. **Range, n miles:** 1,870 at 12 kt
Complement: 30
Radars: Navigation: Spin Trough; I-band.

Comment: Diving tenders built 1971–83. Carry a 1 ton crane and diving bell. Some have submersible recompression chamber. Ice strengthened. One to Cuba 1973, one to Libya 1977. Some have probably been decommissioned.

VM 909 *7/2008*, Hartmut Ehlers* / 1353306

3 PROJECT 11980 (DIVING TENDERS) (YDT)

VM 596 **+2**

Displacement, tons: 330 full load
Dimensions, feet (metres): 121.7 × 25.3 × 8.2 *(37.1 × 7.7 × 2.5)*
Main machinery: 2 diesels; 525 hp *(385 kW)*; 2 shafts
Speed, knots: 12.5
Complement: 29

Comment: A new class of diving vessel designed by Almaz Central Design Bureau and built at Vympel Shipyard, Rybinsk. Construction started in the early 1990s but the building programme was suspended until new funds were assigned in 2002. The ship is designed to support diving and salvage operations down to a depth of 60 m and is equipped with the Falkon remote-controlled underwater equipment, which can work at depths up to 300 m. It also carries hydrological instruments and welding equipment for deep-sea work, a satellite television system and a barochamber. The lead vessel was commissioned in the Northern Fleet on 28 November 2004 and is based at Severomorsk. Two further units may also have been built.

VM 596 *7/2008** / 1336044

1 SALVAGE LIFTING SHIP (YS)

Name	*Builders*	*Launched*	*Commissioned*
KOMMUNA (ex-*Volkhov*)	De Schelde, Vlissingen	30 Nov 1913	27 July 1915

Displacement, tons: 2,450 full load
Dimensions, feet (metres): 315.0 × 66.9 × 15.4 *(96.0 × 20.4 × 4.7)*
Main machinery: 2 diesels; 2 shafts
Speed, knots: 10. **Range, n miles:** 1,700 at 6 kt
Complement: 250
Radars: Navigation: I-band.

Comment: Catamaran-hulled vessel fitted with four lifting rigs to enable sunken submarines to be lifted between the hulls. Laid down in 1912, the vessel was thought to have been decommissioned in 1978 but returned to service after a refit from 1980–84. Now based at Sevastopol to support the operation of submersibles.

KOMMUNA *10/2008*, Laursen/Jarnasen* / 1353355

27 POZHARNY I (PROJECT 364) CLASS (FIREFIGHTING CRAFT) (YTR)

PZHK 3	**PZHK 36–37**	**PZHK 59**	**PZHK 79**
PZHK 5	**PZHK 41–47**	**PZHK 64**	**PZHK 82**
PZHK 17	**PZHK 49**	**PZHK 66**	**PZHK 84**
PZHK 30–32	**PZHK 53–55**	**PZHK 68**	**PZHK 86**

Displacement, tons: 180 full load
Dimensions, feet (metres): 114.5 × 20 × 6 *(34.9 × 6.1 × 1.8)*
Main machinery: 2 Type M 50 diesels; 2,200 hp(m) *(1.6 MW)* sustained; 2 shafts
Speed, knots: 12. **Range:** 250 at 12 kt
Complement: 26
Guns: 4—12.7 mm (2 twin) MGs (in some).

Comment: Total of 84 built from mid-1950s to mid-1960s. Harbour fire boats but can be used for patrol duties. One transferred to Iraq (now deleted) and two to Ukraine.

POZHARNY I *8/2000, Lemachko Collection* / 0126224

15 MORKOV (PROJECT 1461.3) CLASS (YTR)

PZHK 415	**PZHK 1296**	**PZHK 1544–1547**	**PZHK 1859**
PZHK 417	**PZHK 1378**	**PZHK 1560**	**PZHK 2055**
PZHK 900	**PZHK 1514–1515**	**PZHK 1680**	

Displacement, tons: 320 full load
Dimensions, feet (metres): 119.8 × 25.6 × 7.2 *(36.5 × 7.8 × 2.2)*
Main machinery: 2 diesels; 1,040 hp(m) *(764 kW)*; 2 shafts
Speed, knots: 12.5. **Range:** 250 at 12 kt
Complement: 20

Comment: Carry four water monitors. Completed in 1984–86 at Rybinsk. Can be used for patrol/towage. Some are under civilian control.

PZHK 1680 *7/2008*, Hartmut Ehlers* / 1353305

13 PELYM (PROJECT 1799) CLASS (DEGAUSSING SHIPS) (YDG)

SR 26	**SR 188**	**SR 267**	**SR 370**
SR 111	**SR 203**	**SR 280**	**SR 455**
SR 179–180	**SR 233**	**SR 334**	**AKADEMIK VLADIMIR KOTELNIKOV**

Displacement, tons: 1,370 full load
Dimensions, feet (metres): 214.8 × 38 × 11.2 *(65.5 × 11.6 × 3.4)*
Main machinery: 1 diesel; 1,536 hp(m) *(1.13 MW)*; 1 shaft
Speed, knots: 14
Range, n miles: 1,000 at 13 kt
Complement: 70
Radars: Navigation: Don 2; I-band

Comment: Built from 1970 to 1987 at Khabarovsk and Gorokhovets. Earlier ships have stump mast on funnel, later ships a tripod main mast and a platform deck extending to the stern. *Kotelnikov* was laid down in 1991 and commissioned into the Northern Fleet in 2007. Type name is *sudno razmagnichivanya* meaning degaussing ship. One to Cuba 1982. Several in reserve.

SR 26 *10/2008*, Laursen/Jarnasen* / 1353356

HARBOUR CRAFT (YFL/YFU)

Comment: There are numerous types of officers' yachts, harbour work-boats, training cutters and trials vessels in all of the major Fleet bases. Class names include P 02 (Project 376) *Bryza* (Project 772), *Nazhimovets* (Project 286), *Admiralets* (Project 371), *Slavyanka* (Project 20150), *Albatros* (Project 183), Project 14670, Project 360 and Project 1733.

KSV 11 (ALBATROS CLASS) *7/2008*, Hartmut Ehlers* / 1353304

15 BEREZA (PROJECT 130) CLASS (DEGAUSSING SHIPS) (YDG)

North	Baltic	Black
SR 74	SR 28	SR 137
SR 216	SR 120	SR 541
SR 478	SR 245	SR 939
SR 548	SR 479	
SR 569	SR 570	
SR 938	SR 936	

Displacement, tons: 1,850 standard; 2,051 full load
Dimensions, feet (metres): 228 × 45.3 × 13.1 *(69.5 × 13.8 × 4)*
Main machinery: 2 Zgoda-Sulzer 8AL25/30 diesels; 2,938 hp(m) *(2.16 MW)* sustained; 2 shafts; cp props
Speed, knots: 13. **Range, n miles**: 1,000 at 13 kt
Complement: 48
Radars: Navigation: Kivach; I-band.

Comment: First completed at Northern Shipyard, Gdansk 1984–1991. One transferred to Bulgaria in 1988. Have NBC citadels and three laboratories. Several in reserve. One to Ukraine in 1997. SR 938 converted to a logistic ship for service in the Polish Navy.

SR 541 *10/2008*, Laursen/Jarnasen* / 1353357

0 + 1 (1) IGOR BELOUSOV (PROJECT 23100) CLASS (SUBMARINE RESCUE SHIP) (ASRH)

Name	*Builders*	*Launched*	*Commissioned*
IGOR BELOUSOV	Admiralty Shipyard, St Petersburg	24 Dec 2005	2009

Displacement, tons: 5,300
Dimensions, feet (metres): 351.7 × 56.4 × 26.6 *(107.2 × 17.2 × 8.1)*
Main machinery: To be announced
Speed, knots: 15. **Range, n miles**: 3,000 at 12 kt
Complement: To be announced
Guns: To be announced.
Radars: To be announced.
Helicopters: To be announced.

Comment: Developed by the Almaz Central Marine Design Bureau. Initially, it is expected that two ships are to be built, one each for the Northern and Pacific fleets. The first of class is named after a former minister of shipbuilding of the USSR. A further two ships may be built in order to equip all four fleets. In addition to its principal submarine rescue role, it is likely to have a secondary role as a research ship. Equipment is likely to include a submergence vehicle capable of operation at a depth of down to 700 m, special-purpose deep diver equipment, and a helicopter. In addition, the ship is to be capable of deploying the British Seaeye Panther Plus Remotely Operated Vehicle (ROV). The ROV is to be fitted with sonar, an acoustic tracking system, a suite of cameras to provide rescue planners with underwater pictures of the submarine on the seabed and various cutters and manipulators. The ROV is also capable of inserting emergency life support stores into a distressed submarine and of connecting hoses and lines to a submarine's salvage connections.

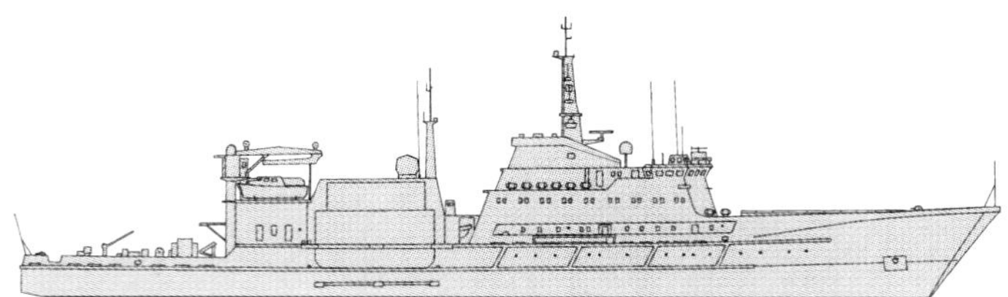

IGOR BELOUSOV *(Scale 1 : 1,200), Ian Sturton* / 1353319

1 NEPA (PROJECT 530) CLASS (SUBMARINE RESCUE SHIP) (ASR)

KARPATY

Displacement, tons: 9,800 full load
Dimensions, feet (metres): 424.9 × 63.0 × 21.0 *(129.5 × 19.2 × 6.4)*
Main machinery: Diesel-electric; 4 diesel generators; 2 motors; 8,000 hp(m) *(5.88 MW)*; 2 shafts
Speed, knots: 16
Range, n miles: 8,000 at 14 kt
Complement: 270
Radars: Navigation: I-band.

Comment: Built at Nikolayev Shipyard and originally commissioned on 29 March 1967. Submarine rescue and salvage ship with a high stern which extends over the water to facilitate rescue operations. Equipped with two 750-ton lifts which can work in tandem. Also fitted with a 100-ton lift, one 60-ton derrick and two 10-ton derricks. Can carry rescue bells, two submersibles and decompression chambers. Based in the Baltic at Kronshadt and although previously reported decommissioned, appeared to be undergoing a refit during 2007.

1 LAMA (TYPE 323/323B) CLASS (MISSILE SUPPORT SHIP) (AEM)

GENERAL RYABIKOV

Displacement, tons: 4,600 full load
Dimensions, feet (metres): 370 × 49.2 × 14.4 *(112.8 × 15 × 4.4)*
Main machinery: 2 diesels; 4,800 hp(m) *(3 MW)*; 2 shafts
Speed, knots: 14
Range, n miles: 6,000 at 10 kt
Complement: 200
Missiles: SAM: 4 SA-N-5 Grail quad launchers.
Guns: 4—25 mm/80.
Radars: Surface search: Strut Curve; F-band.
Navigation: Don 2; I-band.
IFF: 2 Square Head. High Pole A.

Comment: Built 1968 at Nikolayev. The engines are sited aft to allow for a very large and high hangar or hold amidships for carrying missiles or weapons' spares for submarines, surface ships and missile craft. This is about 12 ft high above the main deck. There are doors at the forward end with rails leading in and a raised turntable gantry or 20 ton travelling cranes for armament supply. The well-deck is about 40 ft long, enough for most missiles to fit horizontally before being lifted for loading. Type name is *plavuchaya masterskaya* meaning floating workshop. Based in the Black Sea and used as a troop-ship during Black Sea operations in 2008. *Voronezh* has been renamed VTR 33 and is an alongside civilian-manned support ship.

GENERAL RYABIKOV *10/2008*, Laursen/Jarnasen* / 1353348

1 MUNA (TYPE 1823) CLASS (AEL)

VTR 94

Displacement, tons: 690 full load
Dimensions, feet (metres): 165 × 26.9 × 9.5 *(50.3 × 8.2 × 2.9)*
Main machinery: 1 diesel; 300 hp(m) *(220 kW)*; 1 shaft
Speed, knots: 10
Range, n miles: 3,000 at 10 kt
Complement: 40
Radars: Navigation: Kivach; I-band.

Comment: Built in the 1970s and converted at Nikolayev in 1990. Used as ammunition transport ship in the Black Sea.

VTR 94 *10/2008*, Laursen/Jarnasen* / 1353350

ICEBREAKERS

Notes: Only military icebreakers are shown in this section. Other icebreakers come under civilian management and are now used predominantly for commercial purposes. Civilian ships include the nuclear powered *Taymyr, Vaygach, Arktika, Rossiya, S Soyuz, Yamal,* all of which are operated by the Murmansk Shipping Company. Diesel powered ships include: 20,000 tons: *Ermak, Admiral Makarov, Krasin*; 15,400 tons: *Moskva, St Petersburg*; 14,600 tons: *Kapitan Sorokin, Kapitan Dranitsyn, Kapitan Nikolayev, Kapitan Khlebnikov*; 7,700 tons: *Mudyug*; 6,200 tons: *Magadan, Dikson*; 2,900 tons: *Afanasy Nikitin, Fedor Litke, Georgiy Sedov, Ivan Kruzenshtern, Ivan Moskvitin, Petr Pakhtsuvov, Semen Chelyushkin, Semen Dezhnev, Vasily Poyarkov, Vladimir Rusanov, Yuriy Lisyansky*; 2,240 tons: *Kapitan Bukayev, Kapitan Chadayev, Kapitan Chechkin, Kapitan Krutov, Kapitan Plakhin, Kapitan Zarubin*; 2,200 tons: *Kapitan Babichev, Kapitan Borodkin, Kapitan Chudinov, Kapitan Demidov, Kapitan Evdokimov, Kapitan Metsayk, Kapitan Moshkin, Kapitan Yevdokimov, Avraamiy Zavenyagin*; 2,100 tons: *Kapitan A Radzhabov, Kapitan Kosolabov, Kapitan M Izmaylov*. The growing demand for oil tanker shipments in the Arctic region means that there is a potential shortage of icebreakers. This may be met by completing *50 Let Pobeda*, a 25,000 ton nuclear-powered vessel which has been at Baltic Shipyard, St Petersburg since 1989. Following post-refit sea trials, she returned to service in 2007. *Arktika, Rossiya* and *Taymyr* are due life-extension refits.

50 LET POBEDA ***6/2005*** / 1164805

4 DOBRYNYA NIKITICH (PROJECT 97) CLASS (AGB)

BURAN **PERESVET** **SADKO** **ILYA MUROMETS**

Displacement, tons: 2,995 full load
Measurement, tons: 2,254 gross; 1,118 dwt; 50 net
Dimensions, feet (metres): 222.1 × 59.4 × 20 *(67.7 × 18.1 × 6.1)*
Main machinery: Diesel-electric; 3 Type 13-D-100 or 3 Wärtsilä 6L 26 *(Kruzenshtern)* diesel generators; 3 motors; 5,400 hp(m) *(4 MW)*; 3 shafts (1 fwd, 2 aft)
Speed, knots: 14.5. **Range, n miles:** 5,500 at 12 kt
Complement: 45
Guns: 2—57 mm/70 (twin). 2—37 mm/63.
Radars: Navigation: 2 Don 2; I-band.

Comment: Built at Admiralty Yard, Leningrad between 1960 and 1971. *Kavraysky* is in the Northern Fleet and *Buran* in the Baltic. Of the 18 others originally built, some have been decommissioned and others (about eight) transferred to civilian service.

BURAN ***6/2004, Marco Ghiglino*** / 1151373

TUGS

Notes: SB means *Spasatelny Buksir* or Salvage Tug. MB means *Morskoy Buksir* or Seagoing Tug.

2 BAKLAZHAN (PROJECT 5757) CLASS (SALVAGE TUGS) (ATS)

NICOLAY CHIKER SB 131 **FOTIY KRYLOV** SB 135

Displacement, tons: 7,300 standard; 8,000 full load
Dimensions, feet (metres): 324.8 × 64.0 × 23.3 *(99.0 × 19.5 × 7.1)*
Main machinery: 4 Wärtsilä diesels; 24,120 hp(m) *(18.0 MW)*; 2 shafts
Speed, knots: 18
Range, n miles: 11,000 at 16 kt
Radars: Navigation: I-band.

Comment: Both ships constructed by Hollming, Rauma, Finland. Laid down in 1987 and entered service with the Soviet Navy in 1989. Under ownership of Russian company Sovfracht, operated by Greek company Tsavliris during the 1990s before returning to Russian naval service in about 2006. Both tugs are probably still available for commercial use. Equipped with three water cannons.

2 NEFTEGAZ (PROJECT B-92) CLASS (ATA)

ILGA **KALAR**

Displacement, tons: 4,013 full load
Dimensions, feet (metres): 264.8 × 53.5 × 16.4 *(80.3 × 16.3 × 5.0)*
Main machinery: 2 Sulzer diesels; 7,200 hp *(5.3 MW)*; 2 shafts; cp props
Speed, knots: 15. **Range, n miles:** 5,000 at 12 kt
Complement: 23
Radars: Navigation: I-band.

Comment: Large oilfield support tugs built by A Warski SY, Szczecin, Poland. Taken over for naval service; some 40 others are in civilian service. Now employed as ocean-going rescue tugs with heavy towing and firefighting capabilities. *Kalar* also operates in the salvage role. Capacity of 600 tons cargo on deck and 1,000 m³ of liquid cargo. Entered naval service in 1983 *(Ilga)* and 1990 *(Kalar)*. *Ilga* based in the Northern Fleet and *Kalar* in the Pacific.

KALAR ***12/2005, Ships of the World*** / 1151145

1 PRUT (PROJECT 527M) CLASS (RESCUE TUG) (ATS)

EPRON

Displacement, tons: 2,120 standard; 2,800 full load
Dimensions, feet (metres): 295.9 × 46.9 × 18.0 *(90.2 × 14.3 × 5.5)*
Main machinery: Diesel-electric; 4 diesel generators; 2 motors; 10,000 hp(m) *(7.35 MW)*; 2 shafts
Speed, knots: 20. **Range, n miles:** 9,000 at 16 kt
Complement: 140
Radars: Navigation: Don-2; I-band.

Comment: Large rescue tug built at Nikolayev, Ukraine and completed in 1968. Carries two heavy-duty derricks, submersible recompression chambers, rescue chambers and bells. Last survivor of the class which is based in the Black Sea.

EPRON ***9/2004, Hartmut Ehlers*** / 1042286

3 INGUL (PROJECT 1453) CLASS (SALVAGE TUGS) (ATS)

PAMIR **MASHUK** **ALTAY** (ex-*Karabakh*)

Displacement, tons: 4,050 full load
Dimensions, feet (metres): 304.4 × 50.5 × 19 *(92.8 × 15.4 × 5.8)*
Main machinery: 2 Type 58-D-4R diesels; 6,000 hp(m) *(4.4 MW)*; 2 shafts; cp props
Speed, knots: 19. **Range, n miles:** 9,000 at 19 kt
Complement: 71 plus salvage party of 18
Radars: Navigation: 2 Palm Frond; I-band.
IFF: High Pole. Square Head.

Comment: Built at Admiralty Yard, Leningrad in 1975–84. NATO class name the same as one of the Klasma class cable-ships. Naval-manned arctic salvage and rescue tugs. Two more, *Yaguar* (Murmansk) and *Bars* (Vladivostok), operate with the merchant fleet. Carry salvage pumps, diving and firefighting gear as well as a high-line for transfer of personnel. Fitted for guns but these are not carried. *Pamir* and *Altay* in the North, *Mashuk* in the Pacific.

PAMIR ***7/2008**** / 1353358

3 SLIVA (PROJECT 712) CLASS (SALVAGE TUGS) (ATS)

SB 406 **PARADOKS** SB 921 **SHAKHTER** SB 922

Displacement, tons: 3,050 full load
Dimensions, feet (metres): 227 × 50.5 × 16.7 *(69.2 × 15.4 × 5.1)*
Main machinery: 2 Russkiy SEMT-Pielstick 6 PC2.5 L 400 diesels; 7,020 hp(m) *(5.2 MW)* sustained; 2 shafts; cp props; bow thruster
Speed, knots: 16.
Range: 6,000 at 16 kt
Complement: 43 plus 10 salvage party
Radars: Navigation: 2 Nayada; I-band.

Comment: Built at Rauma-Repola, Finland. Based on Goryn design. *SB 406* completed 20 February 1984. Second pair ordered 1984 *SB 921* completed 5 July 1985 and *SB 922* on 20 December 1985. *SB 922* named *Shakhter* in 1989. A fourth of class, *Iva* SB 408, was sold illegally to a Greek company in March 1993 and now flies the flag of Cyprus but is operated as a 'joint venture' with the Russian Navy. Diving facilities to 60 m. Bollard pull 60 tons. *SB 406* based in the Northern Fleet, *SB 921* in the Baltic and *SB 922* in the Black Sea.

SB 921 *7/2008*, Hartmut Ehlers* / 1353302

5 KATUN CLASS (PROJECT 1893/1993) (SALVAGE TUGS) (ATS)

Katun I: **PZHS 64, 96, 98, 123, 273, 282, 309, 551**
Katun II: **PZHS 64, 92**

Displacement, tons: 1,005 (Katun I); 1,220 (Katun II) full load
Dimensions, feet (metres): 205.3 × 33.1 × 11.5 *(62 × 10.1 × 3.5)* (Katun I)
Main machinery: 2 diesels; 5,000 hp(m) *(3.68 MW)*; 2 shafts
Speed, knots: 17. **Range, n miles:** 2,000 at 17 kt
Complement: 32
Radars: Navigation: Spin Trough or Kivach (Katun II); I-band.
IFF: High Pole A.

Comment: Eight Katun I built at Kolpino 1970–78. Equipped for firefighting and rescue. Two remaining Katun II *PZHS 92* and *95* have an extra bridge level and lattice masts. *273* based in the Caspian; *95* and *209* in the Pacific; *64, 92* and *98* in the North, *282* and *551* in the Baltic and *123* in the Black Sea.

PZHS 282 (Katun I) *8/2004* / 1042310

10 GORYN (PROJECT 714) CLASS (ARS/ATA)

MB 15	**MB 38**	**MB 119**	**SB 521–523**
EVGENY KHOROV MB 35	**MB 105**	**SB 36**	**SB 931**

Displacement, tons: 2,240 standard; 2,600 full load
Dimensions, feet (metres): 208.3 × 46.9 × 16.7 *(63.5 × 14.3 × 5.1)*
Main machinery: 2 Russkiy SEMT-Pielstick 6 PC2.5 L 400 diesels; 7,020 hp(m) *(5.2 MW)* sustained; 2 shafts; cp props; bow thruster
Speed, knots: 15
Complement: 43 plus 16 spare berths
Radars: Navigation: 2 Don 2 or Nayada or Kivach; I-band.

Comment: Built by Rauma-Repola 1977–83. Have sick-bay. First ships have goalpost mast with 10 and 5 ton derricks and bollard pull of 35 tons. Remainder have an A-frame mast with a 15 ton crane and bollard pull of 45 tons. SB number indicates a 'rescue' tug. Three in the North, four in the Pacific, two in the Baltic and one in the Black Sea. One transferred to Ukraine in 1997.

SB 522 *10/2008*, Guy Toremans* / 1353359

13 SORUM (PROJECT 745) CLASS (ATA)

MB 4	**MB 28**	**MB 56**	**MB 61**	**MB 99**	**MB 110**	**MB 304**
MB 19	**MB 37**	**MB 58**	**MB 76**	**MB 100**	**MB 148**	

Displacement, tons: 1,660 full load
Dimensions, feet (metres): 190.2 × 41.3 × 15.1 *(58 × 12.6 × 4.6)*
Main machinery: Diesel-electric; 2 Type 5-2-DW2 diesel generators; 2,900 hp(m) *(2.13 MW)*; 1 motor; 2,000 hp(m) *(1.47 MW)*; 1 shaft
Speed, knots: 14
Range, n miles: 3,500 at 13 kt
Complement: 35
Guns: 4—30 mm/65 (2 twin) (all fitted for, but only Border Guard ships carry them).
Radars: Navigation: 2 Don 2 or Nayada; I-band.
IFF: High Pole B.

Comment: A class of ocean tugs with firefighting and diving capability. Built in Yaroslavl and Oktyabskoye from 1973 to 1989, design used for Ministry of Fisheries rescue tugs.

MB 100 *7/2008** / 1353360

14 OKHTENSKY (PROJECT 733/733S) CLASS (ARS/ATA)

AYANKA SB 3	**SPUTNIK** MB 52	**LOKSA** MB 171
MOSHCHNY SB 6	**MB 162**	**MB 172**
SB 5	**SERDITY** MB 165	**MB 174**
MB 21	**MB 166**	**SATURN** MB 178
MB 23	**POCHETNYY** MB 169	

Displacement, tons: 948 full load
Dimensions, feet (metres): 156.1 × 34 × 13.4 *(47.6 × 10.4 × 4.1)*
Main machinery: Diesel-electric; 2 BM diesel generators; 1 motor; 1,500 hp(m) *(1.1 MW)*; 1 shaft
Speed, knots: 13
Range, n miles: 8,000 at 7 kt; 6,000 at 13 kt
Complement: 40
Guns: 2—57 mm/70 (twin) or 2—25 mm/80 (twin) (Border Guard only).
Radars: Navigation: 1 or 2 Don 2 or Spin Trough; I-band.
IFF: High Pole B.

Comment: Ocean-going salvage (MB) and rescue tugs (SB). First of a total of 62 completed 1958. Fitted with powerful pumps and other apparatus for salvage. A number of named ships are operated by the Border Guard and are armed. Two to Ukraine in 1997. Many have been scrapped.

MB 23 *10/2008*, Laursen/Jarnasen* / 1353361

18 PROMETEY (PROJECT 498/04983/04985) CLASS (TUGS) (YTB)

RB 1	**RB 98**	**RB 179**	**RB 239**	**RB 296**	**RB 360**
RB 7	**RB 158**	**RB 201–202**	**RB 262**	**RB 314**	**RB 362**
RB 57	**RB 173**	**RB 217**	**RB 265**	**RB 327**	

Displacement, tons: 360 full load
Dimensions, feet (metres): 96.1 × 27.2 × 10.5 *(29.3 × 8.3 × 3.2)*
Main machinery: 2 diesels; 1,200 hp(m) *(895 kW)*; 2 shafts
Speed, knots: 11

Comment: Entered service 1973–83. Bollard pull 14 tons. Later versions have more powerful engines. Based in the Northern, Pacific, Baltic and Black Sea Fleets.

RB 201 *8/2008*, Hartmut Ehlers* / 1353300

11 STIVIDOR (PROJECT 192) CLASS (TUGS) (YTB)

RB 22	**RB 108–109**	**RB 167**	**RB 247**	**RB 325–326**
RB 40	**RB 136**	**RB 244**	**RB 280**	

Displacement, tons: 575 full load
Dimensions, feet (metres): 117.1 × 31.1 × 15.1 *(35.7 × 9.5 × 4.6)*
Main machinery: 2 diesels; 2,400 hp(m) *(1.78 MW)*; 2 shafts; bow-thruster
Speed, knots: 12

Comment: Entered service 1980–90. Bollard pull 35 tons. Equipped with three water cannons. Based in the Northern, Pacific and Black Sea Fleets.

RB 325 *6/2007, Lemachko Collection* / 1305147

37 SIDEHOLE I AND II (PROJECT 737 K/M) CLASS (TUGS) (YTB)

BUK 600	**RB 29**	**RB 192**	**RB 233**	**RB 250**
RB 2	**RB 43**	**RB 193**	**RB 237**	**RB 255**
RB 5	**RB 44**	**RB 194**	**RB 240**	**RB 256**
RB 17	**RB 46**	**RB 197**	**RB 244**	**RB 310**
RB 20	**RB 49**	**RB 198**	**RB 246**	**RB 311**
RB 23	**RB 51**	**RB 199**	**RB 247**	
RB 25	**RB 52**	**RB 212**	**RB 248**	
RB 26	**RB 168**	**RB 232**	**RB 249**	

Displacement, tons: 206 full load
Dimensions, feet (metres): 79.4 × 23.0 × 11.1 *(24.2 × 7.0 × 3.4)*
Main machinery: 2 diesels; 900 hp(m) *(670 kW)*; 2 shafts
Speed, knots: 10

Comment: Entered service 1973–83. Bollard pull 10 tons. Based in all fleets.

RB 249 (Sidehole II) *7/2008*, Hartmut Ehlers* / 1353303

RUSSIAN FEDERAL BORDER GUARD SERVICE (EX MARITIME BORDER GUARD)

General

(1) The Border Guard would be integrated with naval operations in a crisis. Formerly run by the KGB, the force came under the Ministry of Defence in October 1991 and was then given to the Ministry of Interior in December 1993. It merged with the Federal Security Service on 11 March 2003.
(2) From 1993 the Border Guard started to fly its own ensign which is the St Andrews Cross with a white border on a green background. Diagonal stripes are painted on the hull which from 2004 have been painted blue.
(3) Roles include Law Enforcement, Port Security, Counter Intelligence, Counter Terrorism and Fishery Protection.

Personnel

2009: 10,000 approx

FRIGATES

5 GRISHA (ALBATROS) (PROJECT 1124P/1124M/1124MP/1124MU) CLASS (FFLM)

NADEZHNYY (II) – **SMELYY** (III) 178 **DOZORNYY** (II) 113 **ZORKIY** (III) 170 **PREDANYY** (II) 079

Displacement, tons: 860 standard; 990 full load
Dimensions, feet (metres): 233.6 × 32.2 × 21.1 *(71.2 × 9.8 × 3.7)*
Main machinery: CODAG; 1 gas turbine; 15,000 hp(m) *(11 MW)*; 2 diesels; 16,000 hp(m) *(11.8 MW)*; 3 shafts
Speed, knots: 30. **Range, n miles:** 2,500 at 14 kt
Complement: 83 (5 officers) (Grisha III); 79 (Grisha II)

Missiles: SAM: SA-N-4 Gecko twin launcher; semi-active radar homing to 15 km *(8 n miles)* at 2.5 Mach; warhead 50 kg; 20 missiles.
Guns: 2 (4)—57 mm/80 (twin/2 twin) (Grisha III/II); 120 rds/min to 6 km *(3.3 n miles)*; weight of shell 2.8 kg.
1—3 in *(76 mm)*/60 (Grisha V); 120 rds/min to 15 km *(8 n miles)*; weight of shell 5.9 kg.
1—30 mm/65 (Grisha III and V classes) AK 630; 6 barrels; 3,000 rds/min combined to 2 km.
Torpedoes: 4—21 in *(533 mm)* (2 twin) tubes. Combination of 53 cm torpedoes.
A/S mortars: 2 RBU 6000 12-tubed trainable; range 6,000 m; warhead 31 kg. (Only 1 in Grisha V).
Depth charges: 2 racks (12).
Mines: Capacity for 18 in lieu of depth charges.
Countermeasures: Decoys: 4 PK 10 or 2 PK 16 chaff launchers.
ESM: 2 Watch Dog.
Radars: Air/surface search: Strut Curve (Strut Pair in Grisha V); F-band.
Navigation: Don 2; I-band.
Fire control: Pop Group; F/H/I-band (for SA-N-4). Bass Tilt (Grisha III and V); H/I-band (for 57/76 mm and 30 mm).
IFF: High Pole A or B. Square Head. Salt Pot.
Sonars: Bull Nose; hull-mounted; active search and attack; high/medium frequency.
Elk Tail; VDS, active search; high frequency. Similar to Hormone helicopter dipping sonar.

Programmes: Surviving ships of Grisha class variants built for the Border Guard. Some ships, previously reported to have been decommissioned, have been reported operational although the overal status of the class remains unclear. Grisha II (1973–74), Grisha III (1981–85) and Grisha V (1985 onwards). All were built at Kharbarovsk and Zelenodolsk.
Structure: Grisha III class has Muff Cob radar removed, Bass Tilt and 30 mm ADG (fitted aft), and Rad-haz screen removed from abaft funnel as a result of removal of Muff Cob. Grisha V is similar to Grisha III with the after twin 57 mm mounting replaced by a single 76 mm gun.
Operational: Divided between the Northern and Pacific Fleets.

7 KRIVAK III (NEREY) (PROJECT 1135MP) CLASS (FFHM)

Name	*No*	*Builders*	*Laid down*	*Launched*	*Commissioned*
MENZHINSKY	113	Kamish-Burun, Kerch	14 Aug 1981	31 Dec 1982	29 Dec 1983
DZERZHINSKY	158 (ex-097)	Kamish-Burun, Kerch	11 Jan 1984	2 Mar 1984	29 Dec 1984
OREL (ex-*Imeni XXVII Sezda KPSS*)	156	Kamish-Burun, Kerch	26 Sep 1983	2 Nov 1985	30 Sep 1986
PSKOV (ex-*Imeni LXX Letiya VCHK-KGB*)	175 (ex-104)	Kamish-Burun, Kerch	–	1987	30 Dec 1987
ANADYR (ex-*Imeni LXX Letiya Pogranvoysk*)	060	Kamish-Burun, Kerch	22 Oct 1987	28 Mar 1988	16 Aug 1989
KEDROV	103	Kamish-Burun, Kerch	5 Nov 1988	30 Apr 1989	20 Nov 1990
VOROVSKY	160 (ex-052)	Kamish-Burun, Kerch	20 Feb 1990	28 July 1990	29 Dec 1990

Displacement, tons: 3,100 standard; 3,650 full load
Dimensions, feet (metres): 405.2 × 46.9 × 24 (sonar) *(123.5 × 14.3 × 7.3)*
Main machinery: COGAG; 2 M8K gas-turbines; 55,500 hp(m) *(40.8 MW)*; 2 M 62 gas-turbines; 13,600 hp(m) *(10 MW)*; 2 shafts
Speed, knots: 32
Range, n miles: 4,000 at 14 kt; 1,600 at 30 kt
Complement: 194 (18 officers)

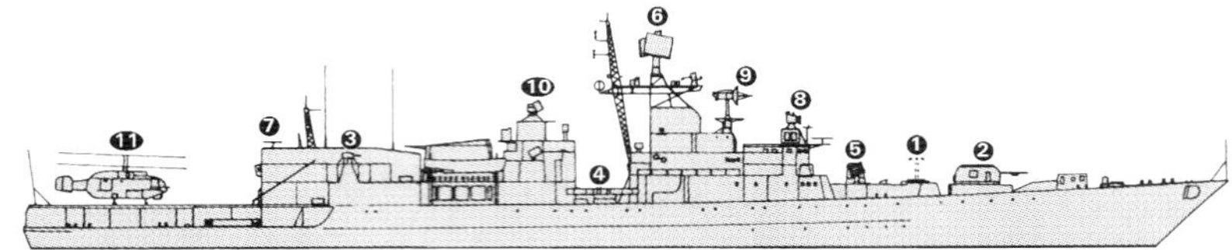
KRIVAK III ***(Scale 1 : 1,200), Ian Sturton*** / 0506085

Missiles: SAM: 1 SA-N-4 Gecko (Zif 122) twin launchers ❶; Osa-M semi-active radar homing to 15 km *(8 n miles)* at 2.5 Mach; warhead 50 kg; altitude 9.1-3,048 m *(30-10,000 ft)*; 20 missiles.
Guns: 1—3.9 in *(100 mm)*/70 AK 100 ❷; 60 rds/min to 21.5 km *(11.5 n miles)*; weight of shell 15.6 kg.
2—30 mm/65 ❸; 6 barrels per mounting; 3,000 rds/min combined to 2 km.
Torpedoes: 8—21 in *(533 mm)* (2 quad) tubes ❹. Combination of 53 cm torpedoes (see table at front of section).
A/S mortars: 2 RBU 6000 12-tubed trainable ❺; range 6,000 m; warhead 31 kg. MRG-7 55 mm grenade launcher.
Mines: Capacity for 16.

Countermeasures: Decoys: 4 PK 16 or 10 PK 10 chaff launchers. Towed torpedo decoy.
ESM/ECM: 2 Bell Shroud. 2 Bell Squat. Half Cup laser warning (in some).
Radars: Air search: Top Plate ❻; 3D; D/E-band.
Surface search: Peel Cone ❼; I-band.
Fire control: Pop Group ❽; F/H/I-band (for SA-N-4). Kite Screech ❾; H/I/K-band. Bass Tilt ❿; H/I-band.
IFF: High Pole B. Salt Pot.
Sonars: Bull Nose (MGK-335S or MG-332); hull-mounted; active search and attack; medium frequency.

Helicopters: 1 Ka-27 Helix ⓫.

Programmes: Type name was originally *bolshoy protivolodochny korabl*, meaning large anti-submarine ship. Changed in 1977–78 to *storozhevoy korabl* meaning escort ship. The naval Krivaks are known as the Burevestnik class.
Structure: Krivak III class built for the former KGB but now under Border Guard Control. The removal of SS-N-14 and one SA-N-4 mounting compensates for the addition of a hangar and flight deck.
Sales: The Talwar class is an improved version of the Krivak III built for India. Three of the Krivak III class transferred to Ukraine in July 1997.

VOROVSKY ***11/2007, Lemachko Collection*** / 1353301

PSKOV ***6/2005, Lemachko Collection*** / 1159852

PATROL FORCES

Notes: In addition to the patrol forces listed, *Pluton* 028 and *Strelets* 025, two Yug class former research vessels, are operated as patrol craft in Arctic waters.

8 ALPINIST (PROJECT 503) CLASS (PBO)

ANTIAS ARGAL BARS DIANA PALIYA PARELLA KURS GRINDA

Displacement, tons: 1,150 full load
Dimensions, feet (metres): 176.2 × 34.4 × 13.4 *(53.7 × 10.5 × 4.1)*
Main machinery: 1 diesel; 1 shaft; cp prop
Speed, knots: 12. **Range, n miles:** 7,000 at 12 kt
Complement: 44

Comment: Trawler design adapted for use as fishery protection role. The named ships were built at Volgograd and at Khabarovsk between 1997 and 2000 while the latest two (unnamed) ships were built at Yarslavl and entered service in late 2001.

ALPINIST *9/2006, Globke Collection* / 1159884

4 KOMANDOR CLASS (PSO)

KOMANDOR SHKIPER GYEK HERLUF BIDSTRUP MANCHZHUR

Displacement, tons: 2,435 full load
Dimensions, feet (metres): 289.7 × 44.6 × 15.4 *(88.3 × 13.6 × 4.7)*
Main machinery: 2 Russkiy SEMT-Pielstick 6 PC2.5 L400 diesels; 7,020 hp(m) *(5.2 MW)*; 1 shaft; cp prop; bow thruster
Speed, knots: 20
Range, n miles: 7,000 at 19 kt
Complement: 42
Radars: Navigation: Furuno; I-band.
Helicopters: 2 Ka-32 Helix D for SAR.

Comment: Specialist offshore patrol vessels ordered in December 1987 from Danyard, Frederikshaven, Denmark and delivered 1989–1990. The hangar is below the helicopter deck. Transferred from the Ministry of Fisheries to the Federal Border Guard and based in the Pacific.

MANCHZHUR *6/2003, Lemachko Collection* / 0580538

5 IVAN SUSANIN (PROJECT 97P) CLASS (PATROL SHIPS) (PGH)

AISBERG 161 **MURMANSK** (ex-*Dunay*) 018 **NEVA** 170 **ANADYR** 173 **VOLGA** 183

Displacement, tons: 3,567 full load
Dimensions, feet (metres): 229.7 × 59.4 × 21 *(70 × 18.1 × 6.4)*
Main machinery: Diesel-electric; 3 Type 13-D-150 diesel generators; 3 motors; 5,400 hp(m) *(4 MW)*; 3 shafts (1 fwd, 2 aft)
Speed, knots: 14.5
Range, n miles: 5,500 at 12.5 kt
Complement: 45
Guns: 2—3 in *(76 mm)*/59 AK 726 (twin); 90 rds/min to 16 km *(8.5 n miles)*; weight of shell 5.9 kg. 2—30 mm/65 AK 630 (not in all).
Radars: Surface search: Strut Curve; F-band.
Navigation: 2 Don Kay or Palm Frond; I-band.
Fire control: Hawk Screech; I-band.
Helicopters: Platform only.

Comment: Built at Admiralty Yard, Leningrad between 1974 and 1981. Generally similar to Dobrynya Nikitich class though larger with a tripod mast and different superstructure. Former icebreakers operated primarily as patrol ships. Two in the Pacific and three in the Northern Fleet. Two deleted so far.

VOLGA *11/2007, Lemachko Collection* / 1353309

18 SORUM (PROJECT 745P) CLASS (PBO)

AMUR 043	**KAMCHATKA** 198	**ZABAYKALYE** 196
MAGADNETS 044	**GENERAL MATROSOV** 101	**TVER** 022
AMUR 010	**SAKHALIN** 185	**PRIMORYE** 172
BREST 106	**URAL** 016	**LADOGA** 058
CHUKOTKA 011	**BAYKAL** (ex-*Yan Berzin*) 105	**VICTOR KINGISEPP** (ex-*Vyatka*) 035
KARELIA 103	**ZAPOLARYE** 038	**BUG** 142

Displacement, tons: 1,660 full load
Dimensions, feet (metres): 190.2 × 41.3 × 15.1 *(58 × 12.6 × 4.6)*
Main machinery: Diesel-electric; 2 Type 5-2-DW2 diesel generators; 2,900 hp(m) *(2.13 MW)*; 1 motor; 2,000 hp(m) *(1.47 MW)*; 1 shaft
Speed, knots: 14
Range, n miles: 3,500 at 13 kt
Complement: 35
Guns: 4—30 mm/65 (2 twin) (all fitted for, but only Border Guard ships carry them).
Radars: Navigation: 2 Don 2 or Nayada; I-band.
IFF: High Pole B.

Comment: A class of ocean tugs armed for use as patrol vessels in the North, Pacific, Baltic and Caspian. Built in Yaroslavl and Oktyabskoye from 1973 to 1989, design used for Ministry of Fisheries rescue tugs.

CHUKOTKA *5/2008*, Hachiro Nakai* / 1353292

1 + (9) SPRUT (PROJECT 6457S) CLASS (PSO)

Name	*No*	*Builders*	*Laid down*	*Launched*	*Commissioned*
SPRUT	–	Yantar Shipyard, Kaliningrad	27 May 2002	12 Oct 2007	2008

Displacement, tons: 900 standard
Dimensions, feet (metres): 216.2 × 34.8 × 11.5 *(65.9 × 10.6 × 3.5)*
Main machinery: 1 MTU 16V 1163 diesel; 7,000 hp(m) *(5.2 MW)*; 1 shaft; fixed propeller
Speed, knots: 21.5
Range, n miles: 12,000 at 12 kt
Complement: 15 + 10 in temporary accommodation
Radars: Surface search: I-band.
Navigation: I-band.
Helicopters: Platform for 1 light.

Comment: Specialist Fishery Protection vessel based on German Coast Guard Bad Bramstedt design. Steel hull with aluminium superstructure. Equipped with a high speed RHIB for interception. A class of ten is planned.

SPRUT *9/2008*, Frank Findler* / 1353310

17 PAUK I (MOLNYA) (PROJECT 12412) CLASS (FAST ATTACK CRAFT—PATROL) (PCM)

TOLYATTI (ex-*PSKR-804*) 021
NAKHODKA (ex-*PSKR-818*) 023
KALININGRAD (ex-*PSKR-802*) 024
YAROSLAVL (ex-*PSKR-810*) 031
YASTREB (ex-*PSKR-816*) 037
SARYCH (ex-*PSKR-811*) 040
GRIF (ex-*PSKR-808*) 041
ORLAN (ex-*PSKR-814*) 042
CHEBOKSARY (ex-*PSKR-817*) 052
SOKOL (ex-*PSKR-812*) 063
MINSK (ex-*PSKR-806*) 065
NIKOLAY KAPLUNOV (ex-*PSKR-815*) 077
KOBCHIK (ex-*PSKR-807*) 078
KRECHET (ex-*PSKR-809*) 099
BERKUT (ex-*PSKR-800*) 152
KORSHUN (ex-*PSKR-805*) 161
VORON (ex-*PSKR-801*) 163

Displacement, tons: 440 full load
Dimensions, feet (metres): 189 × 33.5 × 10.8 *(57.6 × 10.2 × 3.3)*
Main machinery: 2 Type M 521 diesels; 16,184 hp(m) *(11.9 MW)* sustained; 2 shafts
Speed, knots: 32
Range, n miles: 2,400 at 14 kt
Complement: 38

Missiles: SAM: SA-N-5 Grail quad launcher; manual aiming; IR homing to 6 km *(3.2 n miles)* at 1.5 Mach; altitude to 2,500 m *(8,000 ft)*; warhead 1.5 kg; 8 missiles.
Guns: 1—3 in *(76 mm)*/59 AK 176; 120 rds/min to 15 km *(8 n miles)*; weight of shell 5.9 kg. 1—30 mm/65 AK 630; 6 barrels; 3,000 rds/min combined to 2 km.
Torpedoes: 4—16 in *(406 mm)* tubes. For torpedo details see table at front of section.
A/S mortars: 2 RBU 1200 5-tubed fixed; range 1,200 m; warhead 34 kg.
Depth charges: 2 racks (12).
Countermeasures: Decoys: 2 PK 16 or 4 PK 10 chaff launchers.
ESM: 3 Brick Plug and 2 Half Hat; radar warning.
Weapons control: Hood Wink optronic director.
Radars: Air/surface search: Peel Cone; E/F-band.
Surface search: Kivach or Pechora or SRN 207; I-band.
Fire control: Bass Tilt; H/I-band.
Sonars: Foal Tail; VDS (mounted on transom); active attack; high frequency.

Programmes: First laid down in 1977 and completed in 1979. In series production at Yaroslavl in the Black Sea and at Vladivostok until 1988 when the Svetlyak class took over. Type name is *maly protivolodochny korabl* meaning small anti-submarine ship. An improved version building at Kharbarovsk in 1995 was not completed.
Structure: An ASW version of the Tarantul class having the same hull form with a 1.8 m extension for dipping sonar. *Berkut, Voron* and *Kaliningrad* have a lower bridge than others. A modified version (Pauk II) with a longer superstructure, two twin 533 mm torpedo tubes and a radome similar to the Parchim class built for export.
Operational: Five in the Baltic, two in the Black Sea and the remainder in the Pacific. In addition five naval craft are laid up in the Baltic and one in the Black Sea.
Sales: One to Bulgaria in September 1989 and a second in December 1990. Two to Ukraine in 1996. A variant design built for Vietnam.

KRECHET *8/2008*, E & M Laursen* / 1353362

3 TERRIER (PROJECT 14170) CLASS (PB)

001–003

Displacement, tons: 8.3 full load
Dimensions, feet (metres): 38.4 × 10.2 × 1.6 *(11.7 × 3.1 × 0.5)*
Main machinery: 2 diesels; 2 waterjets
Speed, knots: 32
Range, n miles: 120 at 30 kt
Complement: 6

Comment: Built at Zelenodolsk in 2000.

TERRIER 001 *5/2006, Lemachko Collection* / 1159853

2 PAUK II (PROJECT 1241 PE) CLASS (PCM)

NOVOROSSIYSK 043 **KUBAN** 149

Displacement, tons: 495 full load
Dimensions, feet (metres): 191.9 × 33.5 × 11.2 *(58.5 × 10.2 × 3.4)*
Main machinery: 2 Type M 521 diesels; 16,184 hp(m) *(11.9 MW)* sustained; 2 shafts
Speed, knots: 32
Range, n miles: 2,400 at 14 kt
Complement: 32

Missiles: SAM: SA-N-5 quad launcher; manual aiming, IR homing to 10 km *(5.4 n miles)* at 1.5 Mach; warhead 1.1 kg.
Guns: 1 USSR 76 mm/50 AK 176; 120 rds/min to 15 km *(8 n miles)*; weight of shell 5.9 kg. 1—30 mm/65 AK 630; 6 barrels; 3,000 rds/min combined to 2 km.
Torpedoes: 4—21 in *(533 mm)* (2 twin) fixed tubes.
A/S mortars: 2 RBU 1200 5-tubed fixed; range 1,200 m; warhead 34 kg.
Radars: Air/surface search: Cross Dome (Positiv E); E/F-band.
Navigation: Pechora; I-band.
Fire control: Bass Tilt; H/I-band.
Sonars: Rat Tail; VDS (on transom); attack; high frequency.

Comment: Built at Yaroslav Shipyard and entered service in 1997–98 when they were transferred to the Border Guard. Originally intended for Iraq, export Pauk II variant of the type sold to India and Cuba. Has a longer superstructure than the Pauk I with a radome similar to the Parchim II class. The torpedo tubes must be trained out to launch. Both operate in the Black Sea.

3 MURAVEY (ANTARES) (PROJECT 133) CLASS (PCK)

DELFIN **RYBA** **TUAPSE**

Displacement, tons: 212 full load
Dimensions, feet (metres): 126.6 × 24.9 × 6.2; 14.4 (foils) *(38.6 × 7.6 × 1.9; 4.4)*
Main machinery: 2 gas turbines; 22,600 hp(m) *(16.6 MW)*; 2 shafts
Speed, knots: 60
Range, n miles: 410 at 12 kt
Complement: 30 (5 officers)

Guns: 1—3 in *(76 mm)*/60; 120 rds/min to 15 km *(8 n miles)*; weight of shell 7 kg. 1—30 mm/65 AK 630; 6 barrels; 3,000 rds/min combined to 2 km.
Weapons control: Hood Wink optronic director.
Radars: Surface search: Peel Cone; E-band.
Fire control: Bass Tilt; H/I-band.
Sonars: Rat Tail; VDS; active attack; high frequency; dipping sonar.

Comment: Thirteen hydrofoil craft built at Feodosiya in the mid-1980s for the USSR Border Guard. Three transferred to Ukraine and the remainder decommissioned. Two are reported to be operational.

MURAVEY CLASS *3/1998, Ukraine Coast Guard* / 0050319

1 MUSTANG (PROJECT 18623) CLASS (PBF)

817

Displacement, tons: 35.5 full load
Dimensions, feet (metres): 65.6 × 14.8 × 3.6 *(20.0 × 4.5 × 1.1)*
Main machinery: 2 Zvezda M-470 diesels; 2,950 hp *(2.2 MW)*; 2 Kamewa waterjets
Speed, knots: 45
Range, n miles: 350 at 40 kt
Complement: 6

Comment: Designed by Redan Bureau, St Petersburg and built at Yaroslavl in 2000.

MUSTANG *6/2005, A Sheldon-Duplaix* / 1127917

12 + 1 (3) SOBOL (PROJECT 12200) CLASS (PBF)

BSK 1–12

Displacement, tons: 54 full load
Dimensions, feet (metres): 90.9 × 18.4 × 3.6 *(27.7 × 5.6 × 1.1)*
Main machinery: 2 diesels; 3,600 hp *(2.6 MW)*; 2 shafts
Speed, knots: 47
Range, n miles: 700 at 40 kt
Complement: 6
Missiles: SAM: SA-N-10 (Igla).
Guns: 1—30 mm AK-306. 1—14.5 mm MG.

Comment: Built at Almaz St Petersburg and at Soznovka Zavod, Rybinsk and delivered 2000–03. One further craft reported under construction and a further three are expected.

SOBOL CLASS (artist's impression) ***6/2004, S Breyer*** / 1042412

22 SVETLYAK (PROJECT 1041Z) CLASS (FAST ATTACK CRAFT—PATROL) (PGM)

PODOLSK (ex-*PSKR-920*) 017
NEVELSK (ex-*PSKR-915*) 023
YUZHNO-SAKHALINSK (ex-*PSKR-918*) 026
SOCHI (ex-*PSKR-906*) 028
SIKTIVKAR (ex-*PSKR-911*) 099
SOKOL 063
BRIZ (ex-*PSKR-908*) 065
STOROCHEVIK 076
NEPTUN 077
CHOLMSK (ex-*PSKR-903*) 088
PTER. ALMAZ 027
STAVROPOL (ex-*PSKR-902*) 100
KIZLJAR (ex-*PSKR-913*) 139
DERBENT (ex-*PSKR-912*) 102
KORSAKOV (ex-*PSKR-914*) 118
– (ex-*PSKR 923*) 126
– (ex-*PSKR 910*) 132
ANATOLY KOROLEV (ex-*PSKR 916*) 137
VYBORG (ex-*PSKR-909*) 141
ALMAZ (ex-*PSKR-913*) 143
– (ex-*PSKR 907*) 104
– (ex-*PSKR 901*) 174

Displacement, tons: 375 full load
Dimensions, feet (metres): 159.1 × 30.2 × 11.5 *(48.5 × 9.2 × 3.5)*
Main machinery: 3 diesels; 14,400 hp(m) *(10.58 MW)*; 3 shafts
Speed, knots: 31
Range, n miles: 2,200 at 13 kt
Complement: 36 (4 officers)

Missiles: SAM: SA-N-5 Grail quad launcher; manual aiming; IR homing to 6 km *(3.2 n miles)* at 1.5 Mach; warhead 1.5 kg.
Guns: 1—3 in *(76 mm)*/59 AK 176; 120 rds/min to 15 km *(8 n miles)*; weight of shell 5.9 kg. 1 or 2—30 mm/65 AK 630; 6 barrels; 3,000 rds/min combined to 2 km; 12 missiles.
Torpedoes: 2—16 in *(406 mm)* tubes; SAET-40; anti-submarine; active/passive homing to 10 km *(5.4 n miles)* at 30 kt; warhead 100 kg.
Depth charges: 2 racks; 12 charges.
Countermeasures: Decoys: 2 PK 16 chaff launchers.
Weapons control: Hood Wink optronic director.
Radars: Air/surface search: Peel Cone; E-band.
Fire control: Bass Tilt (MP 123); H/I-band.
Navigation: Palm Frond B; I-band.
IFF: High Pole B. Square Head.
Sonars: Rat Tail; VDS; active search; high frequency.

Comment: A class of attack craft for the Border Guard built at Vladivostok, St Petersburg and Yaroslavl. Series production after first of class trials in 1989. Although deliveries have been very slow in recent years, the class may still be building with the most recent launch in May 2000. A further two craft were delivered in 2007. One has a second AK 630 gun vice the 76 mm and no Bass Tilt radars. Six in the Northern Fleet, three in the Baltic, seven in the Pacific, two in the Caspian and two in the Black Sea are all known to be active. Two have been built for Vietnam. Three additional craft operated by the Navy.

PODOLSK ***7/2008*, Hartmut Ehlers*** / 1353311

15 STENKA (TARANTUL) (PROJECT 205P) CLASS (FAST ATTACK CRAFT—PATROL) (PTF)

PSKR-714 014	**PSKR-717** 078	**PSKR-641** 133
PSKR-660 044	**PSKR-712** 132	**PSKR-725** 134
PSKR-700 047	**PSKR-665** 113	**PSKR-631** 137
PSKR-715 048	**PSKR-657** 126	**PSKR-659** 139
PSKR-718 053	**PSKR-690** 129	**PSKR-723** 143

Displacement, tons: 211 standard; 253 full load
Dimensions, feet (metres): 129.3 × 25.9 × 8.2 *(39.4 × 7.9 × 2.5)*
Main machinery: 3 Type M 517 or M 583 diesels; 14,100 hp(m) *(10.36 MW)*; 3 shafts
Speed, knots: 37
Range, n miles: 800 at 24 kt; 500 at 35 kt; 2,300 at 14 kt
Complement: 25 (5 officers)
Guns: 4—30 mm/65 (2 twin) AK 230.
Torpedoes: 4—16 in *(406 mm)* tubes.
Depth charges: 2 racks.
Radars: Surface search: Pot Drum or Peel Cone; H/I- or E-band.
Fire control: Drum Tilt; H/I-band.
Navigation: Palm Frond; I-band.
IFF: High Pole. 2 Square Head.
Sonars: Stag Ear or Foal Tail; VDS; high frequency; Hormone type dipping sonar.

Comment: Based on the hull design of the Osa class. Construction started in 1967 and continued at a rate of about five a year at Petrovsky, Leningrad and Vladivostok for the Border Guard. Programme terminated in 1989 at a total of 133 hulls. Type name is *pogranichny storozhevoy korabl* meaning border patrol ship. Four based in the Baltic, five in the Black Sea, one in the Pacific, and five in the Caspian Sea.
Transfers include: Cuba, two in February 1985 and one in August 1985. Four to Cambodia in October 1985 and November 1987. Five transferred to Azerbaijan control in November 1992 and 10 more to Ukraine.

STENKA ***6/2000*** / 0126309

1 + (3) SOKZHOI CLASS (PROJECT 14230) (PBF)

ALBATROS

Displacement, tons: 97.7 full load
Dimensions, feet (metres): 114.8 × 25.7 × 6.6 *(35.0 × 7.85 × 2.0)*
Main machinery: 2 Zvezda M535 diesels; 9,923 hp(m) *(7.4 MW)* sustained; 2 shafts
Speed, knots: 50
Range, n miles: 800
Complement: 16
Guns: 2—30 mm AK-306. 1—14.5 mm MG.

Comment: First of a new class of patrol craft launched at Volga Yard, Nizhny Novgorod on 23 June 2000. A feature of the design is that an air-cushion is generated below the hull to produce a planing effect to reduce drag. The machine-gun is mounted in a barbette in the forward part of the craft. Project 14232 is a family of high-speed air-cavern vessels based on a unified platform design developed by the Alekseyev Hydrofoil Design Bureau, Nizhny Novgorod. Other variants of the design have different superstructure configuration, armament and equipment. These include two unarmed vessels of the sister Project 14232 Mercury class *(Petr Matveyev* (TS-100) and *Pavel Vereshchagin* (TS-101)*)* built for the customs service at Yaroslavl between 1996–2000. Two more of this type ship are to be completed in Yaroslavl and Khabarovsk.

SOKZHOI CLASS ***4/2006, Lemachko Collection*** / 1159854

PAVEL VERESHCHAGIN (Customs) ***6/2003, E & M Laursen*** / 0570902

9 + (11) MIRAZH (PROJECT 14310) CLASS (PBF)

117 401 402 +6

Displacement, tons: 126 full load
Dimensions, feet (metres): 114.2 × 21.7 × 6.1 *(34.8 × 6.6 × 1.85)*
Main machinery: 2 Zvezda M-521 diesels; 16,184 hp(m) *(11.9 MW)*; 2 shafts
Speed, knots: 48
Range, n miles: 1,500 at 8 kt
Complement: 12 (2 officers)
Guns: 1 — 30 mm AK 306.
2 — 7.62 mm MGs.
Radars: Surface search: I-band.

Comment: Designed by Almaz and built by Vympel Shipbuilding, Rybinsk. Aluminium-magnesium alloy construction. Three vessels authorised for construction in 1993 but only first of class was completed in 1998. It entered service with the Border Guard in 2001 and has been based in the Caspian Sea. Nine craft are believed to be in service and a class of 20 craft is reported to be required.

MIRAZH *6/2008** / 1353313

12 ZHUK (GRIF) (PROJECT 1400/1400M) CLASS (COASTAL PATROL CRAFT) (PB)

PSKA series

Displacement, tons: 39 full load
Dimensions, feet (metres): 78.7 × 16.4 × 3.9 *(24 × 5 × 1.2)*
Main machinery: 2 Type M 401B diesels; 2,200 hp(m) *(1.6 MW)* sustained; 2 shafts
Speed, knots: 30
Range, n miles: 1,100 at 15 kt
Complement: 11 (3 officers)
Guns: 2 — 14.5 mm (twin, fwd) MGs. 1 — 12.7 mm (aft) MG.
Radars: Surface search: Spin Trough; I-band.

Comment: Under construction from 1976. Manned by the Border Guard. Export versions have twin (over/under) 14.5 mm aft. Some have twin guns forward and aft. Ukraine Border Guard and has received 12 from the Russians. Eight are in the Baltic and four in the Black Sea. These are the last operational units.
Transfers: Algeria (one in 1981), Angola (one in 1977), Benin (four in 1978–80), Bulgaria (five in 1977), Cape Verde (one in 1980), Congo (three in 1982), Cuba (40 in 1971–88), Equatorial Guinea (three in 1974–75), Ethiopia (two in October 1982 and two in June 1990), Guinea (two in July 1987), Iraq (five in 1974–75), Cambodia (three in 1985–87), Mauritius (two in January 1990), Mozambique (five in 1978–80), Nicaragua (eight in 1982–86), Seychelles (one in 1981, one in October 1982), Somalia (one in 1974), Syria (six in 1981–84), Vietnam (nine in 1978–88 (at least one passed on to Cambodia), five in 1990 and two in 1995), North Yemen (five in 1978–87), South Yemen (two in 1975). Many have been deleted.

ZHUK 616 *7/2008*, Hartmut Ehlers* / 1353312

6 MANGUST (PROJECT 12150) CLASS (PBF)

VASILY ILYASHENKO ANDREY ROZHKOV SVYATAYA KSENIYA +3

Displacement, tons: 28.7 standard
Dimensions, feet (metres): 64.0 × 15.1 × 3.8 *(19.5 × 4.6 × 1.15)*
Main machinery: 2 Zvezda M-470 diesels; 2 Arneson dive props
Speed, knots: 53
Range, n miles: 410 at 35 kt
Complement: 6
Guns: 2 — 14.5 mm MGs.
Radars: Navigation: I-band.

Comment: Prototype TS 300 built by Vympel, Rybinsk for the Customs service and completed in 1998. GRP construction. First Border Guard unit entered service in 2001. Further orders are expected.

MANGUST 601 *6/2005, A Sheldon-Duplaix* / 1164804

1 A-125 CLASS (PBF)

VALENTIN CHUJKIN

Displacement, tons: 26.0 full load
Dimensions, feet (metres): 57.7 × 13.8 × 3.3 *(17.6 × 4.2 × 1.0)*
Main machinery: 2 MTU 8V2000M90 diesels; 1,830 hp *(1.34 MW)*; 2 waterjets
Speed, knots: 45
Complement: To be announced

Comment: Designed and built by Almaz, St Petersburg and delivered in 2004.

A-125 *6/2005, A Sheldon-Duplaix* / 1164803

27 TYPE 1496 CLASS (PBO)

Displacement, tons: 107 full load
Dimensions, feet (metres): 76.8 × 19.3 × 6.1 *(23.4 × 5.9 × 1.9)*
Main machinery: 1 diesel; 315 hp *(230 kW)*; 1 shaft; fixed propeller
Speed, knots: 10
Range, n miles: 450 at 10 kt
Guns: 1 — 14.5 mm MG.
Radars: Surface search/navigation: I-band.

Comment: Former tugs employed as patrol craft. Likely to be armed.

TYPE 1496 *8/2006, Lemachko Collection* / 1159858

0 + 1 PROJECT 22460 CLASS (PATROL SHIP) (PSO)

Displacement, tons: 630 full load
Dimensions, feet (metres): 205.0 × ? × ? *(62.5 × ? × ?)*
Main machinery: To be announced
Speed, knots: 30
Range, n miles: 3,500 at 12 kt
Complement: 44
Helicopters: Platform for 1 medium.

Comment: First vessel of a new class of helicopter-capable patrol ships laid down at Almaz, St Petersburg on 3 September 2007.

17 KULIK (PROJECT 1415PV) CLASS (PB)

Displacement, tons: 54 full load
Dimensions, feet (metres): 69.5 × 12.8 × 4.6 *(21.2 × 3.9 × 1.4)*
Main machinery: 1 diesel; 300 hp *(225 kW)*; 1 shaft
Speed, knots: 12
Range, n miles: 200 at 11 kt
Complement: 4
Radars: Navigation: I-band.

Comment: Harbour patrol craft built in the 1970/80s. Similar craft, known as the Flamingo class, built for the Navy.

KULIK CLASS *6/2006, Lemachko Collection* / 1305142

2 ENFORCER II CLASS (PATROL CRAFT) (PB)

Displacement, tons: 8.3 full load
Dimensions, feet (metres): 37.3 × 9.6 × 2.9 *(11.36 × 2.94 × 0.9)*
Main machinery: 2 Volvo Penta D9 diesels; 1,000 hp *(736 kW)*; 2 Rolls Royce FF310 waterjets
Speed, knots: 42
Range, n miles: 200 at 30 kt
Complement: 2

Comment: Built by Dockstavarvet, Sweden, the craft are derived from the Combatboat 90 concept and are known as the HSPC 11.3M design. The aluminium construction craft are to be used for patrols on Russian inland waterways. Both delivered in June 2008.

ENFORCER II *6/2008*, Lemachko Collection* / 1305320

RIVER PATROL FORCES

Notes: Attached to Black Sea and Pacific Fleets for operations on the Danube, Amur and Usuri Rivers, and to the Caspian Flotilla.

2 YAZ (SLEPEN) (PROJECT 1208) CLASS (PGR)

BLAGOVESHCHENSK 066 **SHKVAL** 106

Displacement, tons: 440 full load
Dimensions, feet (metres): 180.4 × 29.5 × 4.9 *(55 × 9 × 1.5)*
Main machinery: 3 diesels; 11,400 hp(m) *(8.39 MW)*; 3 shafts
Speed, knots: 24
Range, n miles: 1,000 at 10 kt
Complement: 32 (4 officers)
Guns: 2—115 mm tank guns (TB 62) or 100 mm/56.
2—30 mm/65 AK 630; 6 barrels per mounting.
4—12.7 mm MGs (2 twin).
2—40 mm mortars on after deckhouse.
Radars: Surface search: Spin Trough; I-band.
Fire control: Bass Tilt; H/I-band.
IFF: High Pole B. Square Head.

Comment: First entered service in Amur Flotilla 1978. Built at Khabarovsk until 1987. All but these last two have been placed in reserve.

BLAGOVESHCHENSK *6/1995, Lemachko Collection* / 0570903

8 PIYAVKA (PROJECT 1249) CLASS (PBR)

PSKR 52 117	**PSKR 54** 146	**PSKR 56** 093	**PSKR 58** 123
PSKR 53 065	**PSKR 55** 013	**PSKR 57** 058	**PSKR 59** 189

Displacement, tons: 229 full load
Dimensions, feet (metres): 136.5 × 20.7 × 2.9 *(41.6 × 6.3 × 0.9)*
Main machinery: 3 diesels; 3,300 hp(m) *(2.42 MW)*; 2 shafts
Speed, knots: 17
Complement: 30 (4 officers)
Guns: 1—30 mm/65 AK 630; 6 barrels. 2—14.5 mm (twin) MGs.
Radars: Surface search: Spin Trough; I-band.

Comment: Built at Khabarovsk 1979–84. Based in Amur Flotilla mostly for logistic support.

PSKR 58 *6/2003, Lemachko Collection* / 0580529

3 OGONEK (PROJECT 12130) CLASS (PBR)

Displacement, tons: 98 full load
Dimensions, feet (metres): 109.6 × 13.8 × 2.6 *(33.4 × 4.2 × 0.8)*
Main machinery: 2 diesels; 2 shafts
Speed, knots: 25
Complement: 17 (2 officers)
Guns: 2—30 mm AK 630.

Comment: A smaller version of the Piyavka class built at Khabarovsk from 1999. Numbers in service are uncertain.

OGONEK *4/2006, Lemachko Collection* / 1159869

15 SHMEL (PROJECT 1204) CLASS (PGR)

PSKR series

Displacement, tons: 77 full load
Dimensions, feet (metres): 90.9 × 14.1 × 3.9 *(27.7 × 4.3 × 1.2)*
Main machinery: 2 Type M 50 diesels; 2,200 hp(m) *(1.6 MW)* sustained; 2 shafts
Speed, knots: 25
Range, n miles: 600 at 12 kt
Complement: 12 (4 officers)
Guns: 1—3 in *(76 mm)*/48 (tank turret). 1—25 mm/70 (later ships). 2—14.5 mm (twin) MGs (earlier ships). 5—7.62 mm MGs. 1 BP 6 rocket launcher; 18 barrels.
Mines: Can lay 9.
Radars: Surface search: Spin Trough; I-band.

Comment: Completed at Kerch and Nikolayev North (61 Kommuna) 1967–74. Some of the later ships also mount one or two multibarrelled rocket launchers amidships. The 7.62 mm guns fire through embrasures in the superstructure with one mounted on the 76 mm. Can be carried on land transport. Type name is *artillerisky kater* meaning artillery cutter. About 70 have been scrapped or laid up so far including the last naval units. These last survivors are based on the Amur River and belong to the Border Guard. Transfers: Four to Cambodia (1984–85) (since decommissioned). Some have been taken over by Belorussian forces, and others allocated to Ukraine.

SHMEL *6/2000, Lemachko Collection* / 0106875

4 VOSH (MOSKIT) (PROJECT 1248) CLASS (PGR)

STORM 146 **GROZA** 057 **KHABAROVSK** 137 **SHKVAL** 138

Displacement, tons: 229 full load
Dimensions, feet (metres): 140.1 × 20.7 × 3.3 *(42 × 6.3 × 1)*
Main machinery: 3 diesels; 3,300 hp(m) *(2.42 MW)*; 3 shafts
Speed, knots: 17
Complement: 34 (3 officers)
Guns: 1 — 3 in *(76 mm)*/48 (tank turret). 1 — 30 mm/65 AK 630. 2 — 12.7 mm (twin) MGs.
Countermeasures: 1 twin barrel decoy launcher.
Radars: Surface search: Spin Trough; I-band.

Comment: Built at Sretensk on the Shilka river 1980–84. Based on Amur River. Same hull as Piyavka.

KHABAROVSK *3/2006, Lemachko Collection* / 1159857

15 SAYGAK (PROJECT 14081/14081M) CLASS (PBF)

Displacement, tons: 11.5 full load
Dimensions, feet (metres): 45.9 × 11.5 × 2.1 *(14.0 × 3.5 × 0.65)*
Main machinery: 1 Zvezda M-401B diesel; 1,000 hp *(746 kW)*; 1 waterjet
Speed, knots: 38
Range, n miles: 135 at 35 kt
Complement: 2 plus 8
Radars: Navigation: I-band.

Comment: Built by Kama Zavod, Perm and entered service 1986–2000. Used for riverine and lake patrol. Others are used by the Customs service.

SAYGAK 069 *7/2006, Lemachko Collection* / 1159868

AUXILIARIES

10 NEON ANTONOV (PROJECT 1595) CLASS (TRANSPORTS) (AK)

VASILIY SUNTZOV 154 **VYACHESLAV DENISOV** 176 **IVAN YEVTEYEV** 105 **IVAN LEDNEV** 115 **MIKHAIL KONOVALOV** 184 **SERGEY SUDETSKY** 143 **NIKOLAY SIPYAGIN** 063 **NIKOLAY STARSHINOV** 119 **DVINA** 199 **NEON ANTONOV** 124

Displacement, tons: 6,400 full load
Dimensions, feet (metres): 311.7 × 48.2 × 21.3 *(95 × 14.7 × 6.5)*
Main machinery: 2 diesels; 7,000 hp(m) *(5.15 MW)*; 2 shafts
Speed, knots: 17
Range, n miles: 8,500 at 13 kt
Complement: 45
Cargo capacity: 2,500 tons
Missiles: SAM: 2 SA-N-5 Grail twin launchers; manual aiming; IR homing to 6 km *(3.2 n miles)* at 1.5 Mach; altitude to 2,500 m *(8,000 ft)*; warhead 1.5 kg.
Guns: 2 — 30 mm/65 (twin). 4 — 14.5 mm (2 twin) MGs. 4 — 12.7 mm MGs.
Radars: Navigation: Don Kay; Spin Trough or Palm Frond; I-band.

Comment: Ten of the class built at Nikolayev from 1975 to early 1980s. All in the Pacific except *Dvina* and *Irbit* which are operated by the Russian Navy. Have two small landing craft aft. Armament is not normally mounted.

MIKHAIL KONOVALOV *5/2006, Lemachko Collection* / 1159872

6 KANIN CLASS (PROJECT 16900A) (AKL)

CHANTIJ-MANSISK **JURGA** **ARCHANGELSK** **KANIN** **URENGOY** **ANATOLY SHILINSKY**

Displacement, tons: 920 full load
Dimensions, feet (metres): 149.6 × 28.9 × 8.2 *(45.6 × 8.8 × 2.5)*
Main machinery: 2 diesels; 800 hp(m) *(558 kW)*; 2 shafts
Speed, knots: 9
Range, n miles: 3,500 at 9 kt
Complement: 22

Comment: Built in the Pacific since 1996 for the Border Guard. Others may be building for commercial service. Ice reinforced bows for Arctic service. *Chantij-Mansisk* based in the Black Sea.

CHANTIJ-MANSISK *7/2007, Lemachko Collection* / 1353314

1 BASKUNCHAK CLASS (PROJECT 1545) (AO)

SOVETSKIY POGRANICHNIK 102

Displacement, tons: 1,260 standard; 2,940 full load
Dimensions, feet (metres): 274.3 × 39.4 × 16.1 *(83.6 × 12.0 × 4.9)*
Main machinery: 1 diesel; 2,000 hp *(1.49 MW)*; 1 shaft
Speed, knots: 13
Range, n miles: 5,000 at 12 kt
Complement: 30
Radars: Navigation: 1 Don-2; I-band.

Comment: Built at Zaliv Shipyard, Kerch, and completed in about 1968. Has ice-reinforced bow and is based in the Pacific.

SOVETSKIY POGRANICHNIK *6/2005, Lemachko Collection* / 1159248

AMPHIBIOUS FORCES

4 CZILIM (PROJECT 20910) CLASS (ACV/UCAC)

Displacement, tons: 8.6 full load
Dimensions, feet (metres): 39.4 × 19 *(12 × 5.8)*
Main machinery: 2 Deutz BF 6M 1013 diesels; 435 hp(m) *(320 kW)* sustained; for lift and propulsion
Speed, knots: 40
Range, n miles: 300 n miles at 30 kt
Complement: 2 + 6 Border Guard
Guns: 1 — 7.62 mm MG. 1 — 40 mm RPG.
Radars: Navigation: I-band.

Comment: Ordered from Jaroslawski Sudostroiteinyj Zawod to an Almaz design for Special Forces of the Border Guard. First one laid down 24 February 1998 and in service in early 2001. Further vessels are expected.

CZILIM *6/2001, S Breyer* / 0126219

7 TSAPLYA (MURENA) (PROJECT 12061) CLASS (ACV)

DK-143 659 **DK-453** 668 **DK-285** 680 **DK-447** 699
DK-259 665 **DK-323** 670 **DK-458** 688

Displacement, tons: 149 full load
Dimensions, feet (metres): 103.7 × 47.6 × 5.2 *(31.6 × 14.5 × 1.6)*
Main machinery: 2 MT-70M gas turbines for lift and propulsion; 8,000 hp *(5.88 MW)*
Speed, knots: 50
Range, n miles: 500 at 50 kt
Complement: 11 (3 officers) + 100 troops
Guns: 2 — 300 mm AK 306M. 2 — 30 mm grenade launchers. 2 — 12.7 mm MGs.

Comment: Larger version of the Lebed class designed for river patrol. Built at Khabarovsk between 1987 and 1992. Operated on Amur river system.

TSAPLYA
6/2003, Lemachko Collection
0580542

St Kitts and Nevis

Country Overview

The Federation of St Kitts and Nevis gained independence in 1983; the British monarch, represented by a governor-general, is the head of state. Located at the northern end of the Leeward Islands in the Lesser Antilles chain, the country comprises St Kitts (formerly Saint Christopher) (68 square miles) and, 2 n miles to the southeast, Nevis (36 square miles). The constitution allows for the secession of Nevis from the federation. The capital of St Kitts and of the federation is Basseterre; Charlestown is the capital and largest town on Nevis. Territorial seas (12 n miles) are claimed. A 200 n mile Exclusive Economic Zone (EEZ) has been claimed but the limits are not defined. The Coast Guard was part of the Police Force until 1997 when it transferred to the Regular Corps of the Defence Force.

Headquarters Appointments

Commanding Officer Coast Guard:
Lieutenant Colonel Patrick Wallace

Bases

Basseterre

Personnel

2009: 45

COAST GUARD

Notes: (1) There is a 40 kt RIB number *C 420*.
(2) A 920 Zodiac RHIB was donated by the US government in 2003.

1 SWIFTSHIPS 110 ft CLASS (PB)

STALWART C 253

Displacement, tons: 100 normal
Dimensions, feet (metres): 116.5 × 25 × 7 *(35.5 × 7.6 × 2.1)*
Main machinery: 4 Detroit 12V-71TA diesels; 1,680 hp *(1.25 MW)* sustained; 4 shafts
Speed, knots: 21
Range, n miles: 1,800 at 15 kt
Complement: 14
Guns: 2 — 12.7 mm MGs. 2 — 7.62 mm MGs.
Radars: Surface search: Raytheon; I-band.
Navigation: Furuno; I-band.

Comment: Built by Swiftships, Morgan City, and delivered August 1985. Aluminium alloy hull and superstructure.

STALWART ***3/1998*** / 0050088

1 DAUNTLESS CLASS (PB)

ARDENT C 421

Displacement, tons: 11 full load
Dimensions, feet (metres): 40 × 14 × 4.3 *(12.2 × 4.3 × 1.3)*
Main machinery: 2 Caterpillar 3208TA diesels; 870 hp *(650 kW)*; 2 shafts
Speed, knots: 27
Range, n miles: 600 at 18 kt
Complement: 4
Guns: 1 — 7.62 mm MG.
Radars: Surface search: Raytheon; I-band.

Comment: Built by SeaArk Marine under FMS funding and commissioned 8 August 1995. Aluminium construction.

ARDENT ***8/1996, St Kitts-Nevis Police*** / 0081725

1 FAIREY MARINE SPEAR CLASS (PB)

RANGER I

Displacement, tons: 4.3 full load
Dimensions, feet (metres): 29.8 × 9.5 × 2.8 *(9.1 × 2.8 × 0.9)*
Main machinery: 2 Ford Mermaid diesels; 360 hp *(268 kW)*; 2 shafts
Speed, knots: 20
Complement: 2
Guns: Mountings for 2 — 7.62 mm MGs.

Comment: Ordered for the police in June 1974 and delivered 10 September 1974. Refitted 1986. Considerably slower than when new but still in service.

RANGER I ***1992, St Kitts-Nevis Police*** / 0081726

2 BOSTON WHALERS (PBF)

ROVER I C 087 **ROVER II** C 088

Displacement, tons: 3 full load
Dimensions, feet (metres): 22 × 7.5 × 2 *(6.7 × 2.3 × 0.6)*
Main machinery: 1 Johnson outboard; 223 hp *(166 kW)*
Speed, knots: 35
Range, n miles: 70 at 35 kt
Complement: 2

Comment: Delivered in May 1988.

ROVER I
1990, St Kitts-Nevis Police
0081727

St Lucia

Country Overview

St Lucia gained independence in 1979; the British monarch, represented by a governor-general, is the head of state. The island (238 square miles) is one of the Windward Islands of the Lesser Antilles chain and is located between Martinique to the north and St Vincent to the south. The capital, main town and principal port is Castries, on the northwestern coast. Territorial seas (12 n miles) are claimed. Exclusive Economic Zone (EEZ) limits will not be fully defined until outstanding boundary disagreements have been resolved.

Headquarters Appointments

Coast Guard Commander:
Assistant Superintendent Winston Mitille

Bases

Castries, Vieux-Fort

Personnel

2009: 47

COAST GUARD

1 POINT CLASS (PB)

ALPHONSE REYNOLDS (ex-*Point Turner*) P 01 (ex-WPB 82365)

Displacement, tons: 66 full load
Dimensions, feet (metres): 83 × 17.2 × 5.8 *(25.3 × 5.2 × 1.8)*
Main machinery: 2 Caterpillar 3412 diesels; 1,600 hp *(1.19 MW)*; 2 shafts
Speed, knots: 23
Range, n miles: 1,500 at 8 kt
Complement: 10
Guns: 2—12.7 mm MGs.
Radars: Surface search: Raytheon SPS-64(V)1; I-band.

Comment: Ex-US Coast Guard ship transferred on 3 April 1998. Originally built at Curtis Bay and first commissioned 14 April 1967.

ALPHONSE REYNOLDS ***12/2004, Margaret Organ*** / 1042343

1 SWIFT 65 ft CLASS (PB)

DEFENDER P 02

Displacement, tons: 42 full load
Dimensions, feet (metres): 64.9 × 18.4 × 6.6 *(19.8 × 5.6 × 2)*
Main machinery: 2 Detroit 12V-71 diesels; 680 hp *(507 kW)* sustained; 2 shafts
Speed, knots: 22
Range, n miles: 1,500 at 18 kt
Complement: 7
Radars: Surface search: Furuno; I-band.

Comment: Ordered from Swiftships, Morgan City in November 1983. Commissioned 3 May 1984. Similar to craft supplied to Antigua and Dominica. Painted grey instead of original blue and white.

DEFENDER ***10/1999, St Lucia CG*** / 0081729

1 DAUNTLESS CLASS (PB)

PROTECTOR P 04

Displacement, tons: 11 full load
Dimensions, feet (metres): 40 × 14 × 4.3 *(12.2 × 4.3 × 1.3)*
Main machinery: 2 Caterpillar 3208TA diesels; 870 hp *(650 kW)*; 2 shafts
Speed, knots: 27
Range, n miles: 600 at 18 kt
Complement: 4
Radars: Surface search: Raytheon; I-band.

Comment: Ordered October 1994. Built by SeaArk Marine under FMS funding and commissioned 9 October 1995.

PROTECTOR ***6/2008*, St Lucia CG*** / 1335425

4 HARBOUR CRAFT (PB)

P 03 **P 05** **P 06** **P 07**

Comment: *P 03* is a 9 m Zodiac 920 RHIB donated by the United States in 2004. *P 05* is a 35 kt Hurricane RIB acquired in June 1993 and *P 06* and *P 07* are 45 kt Mako craft acquired in November 1995.

P 05 ***6/2008*, St Lucia CG*** / 1335424

St Vincent and the Grenadines

Country Overview

St Vincent and the Grenadines gained independence in 1979; the British monarch, represented by a governor-general, is the head of state. Lying between St Lucia to the north and Grenada to the south, they form part of the Windward Islands in the Lesser Antilles chain and comprise the island of St Vincent (133 square miles) and the 32 northernmost islands and cays of the Grenadines group including (north to south): Bequia, Mustique, Canouan, Mayreau, Union Island, Palm (formerly Prune) Island, and Petit St Vincent. The capital, largest town, and principal port is Kingstown, St Vincent. An archipelagic state, territorial seas (12 n miles) are claimed. A 200 n mile Exclusive Economic Zone (EEZ) has been claimed but the limits are not defined.

Headquarters Appointments

Coast Guard Commander:
Brenton Cain

Bases

Calliaqua, Bequia, Union Island

Personnel

2009: 84

COAST GUARD

1 SWIFTSHIPS 120 ft CLASS (PB)

CAPTAIN MULZAC SVG 01

Displacement, tons: 101
Dimensions, feet (metres): 120 × 25 × 7 *(36.6 × 7.6 × 2.1)*
Main machinery: 4 Detroit 12V-71TA diesels; 1,360 hp *(1.01 MW)* sustained; 4 shafts
Speed, knots: 21
Range, n miles: 1,800 at 15 kt
Complement: 14 (4 officers)
Guns: 2—12.7 mm MGs. 2—7.62 mm MGs.
Radars: Surface search: Furuno 1411 Mk II; I/J-band.

Comment: Ordered in August 1986. Built by Swiftships, Morgan City and delivered 13 June 1987. Aluminium construction. Carries a RIB with a 40 hp outboard.

CAPTAIN MULZAC *6/1994, St Vincent Coast Guard* / 0081730

1 DAUNTLESS CLASS (PB)

HAIROUN SVG 04

Displacement, tons: 11 full load
Dimensions, feet (metres): 40 × 14 × 4.3 *(12.2 × 4.3 × 1.3)*
Main machinery: 2 Caterpillar 3208TA diesels; 870 hp *(650 kW)*; 2 shafts
Speed, knots: 27
Range, n miles: 600 at 18 kt
Complement: 4
Guns: 1—7.62 mm MG.
Radars: Surface search: Raytheon; I-band.

Comment: Ordered October 1984. Built by SeaArk Marine under FMS funding and commissioned 8 June 1995. Aluminium construction. The craft was refitted in late 2008.

HAIROUN *7/1997* / 0019082

4 HARBOUR CRAFT (PB)

SVG 03 **SVG 06** **SVG 07** **H K TANNIS** SVG 10

Comment: *SVG 03* is a 30 kt Zodiac RIB. *SVG 06*, acquired in 2008, is a 7.5 m RHIB. *SVG 07*, acquired in 2003, is a 9 m RHIB. *H K Tannis* is a 13.5 m RHIB with waterjet propulsion. It was acquired in 2005.

SVG 07 *6/2008*, St Vincent Coast Guard* / 1335426

H K TANNIS *6/2008*, St Vincent Coast Guard* / 1335427

Samoa

Country Overview

Samoa was a New Zealand-administered UN Trust territory until it became independent in 1962. At the same time a Treaty of Friendship delegated responsibility to New Zealand for foreign affairs. An island nation, it lies in the south Pacific Ocean, approximately midway between Hawaii and New Zealand, in the western portion of the Samoan archipelago. There are two main islands, Savai'i and Upolu, and several smaller islands, of which only two, Apolima and Manono, are inhabited. The capital and chief port is Apia on Upolu. An archipelagic state, territorial seas (12 n miles) are claimed. An Exclusive Economic Zone (EEZ) (200 n miles) is also claimed but limits have not been fully defined by boundary agreements.

Headquarters Appointments

Head of Police Maritime Division:
Commissioner Papali'i Lorenese Neru

Headquarters Appointments — *continued*

Maritime Surveillance Adviser:
Commander A R Powell, RAN

Bases

Apia

PATROL FORCES

1 PACIFIC CLASS (LARGE PATROL CRAFT) (PB)

Name	*No*	*Builders*	*Commissioned*
NAFANUA	–	Australian Shipbuilding Industries	5 Mar 1988

Displacement, tons: 165 full load
Dimensions, feet (metres): 103.3 × 26.6 × 6.9 *(31.5 × 8.1 × 2.1)*
Main machinery: 2 Caterpillar 3516TA diesels; 4,400 hp *(3.28 MW)* sustained; 2 shafts
Speed, knots: 20
Range, n miles: 2,500 at 12 kt
Complement: 17 (3 officers)
Guns: 2—7.62 mm MGs.
Radars: Surface search: Furuno FR-1510; I-band.

Comment: Under the Defence Co-operation Programme Australia has provided 22 Pacific class patrol craft to Pacific islands. Training, operational and technical assistance is provided by the Royal Australian Navy. *Nafanua* ordered 3 October 1985. Refitted in 1996. Following the decision by the Australian government to extend the Pacific Patrol Boat programme, a life-extension refit was undertaken at Townsville in 2005.

NAFANUA *6/2005, Samoa Police* / 1127921

Saudi Arabia

Country Overview

The Kingdom of Saudi Arabia occupies most of the Arabian Peninsula and is bordered to the north by Jordan, Iraq, and Kuwait, to the south by Oman and the Republic of Yemen and to the east by Qatar and the United Arab Emirates. With an area of 864, 869 square miles, it has coastlines with the Red Sea (972 n miles) and the Gulf (454 n miles). The capital and largest city is Riyadh while the principal ports are Jiddah and Yanbu al Bahr on the Red Sea, and the major oil-exporting ports of Al Jabayl, Ad Dammam, and Ras Tanura on the Gulf. Territorial seas (12 n miles) are claimed. An EEZ has not been claimed.

Headquarters Appointments

Chief of Naval Staff:
H H Vice Admiral Prince Fahad Bin Abdullah Bin Mohammed Al Saud
Commander Eastern Fleet:
Rear Admiral Mohammad Abdul Khalij Al Asseri
Commander Western Fleet:
Rear Admiral Dakheel Allah Ahmed Al-Wakdani
Director Frontier Force (Coast Guard):
Lieutenant General Mujib bin Muhammad Al-Qahtani

Personnel

(a) 2009: 15,500 officers and men (including 3,000 marines)
(b) Voluntary service

Bases

Naval HQ: Riyadh
Main bases: Jiddah (HQ Western Fleet), Al Jubail (HQ Eastern Fleet), Aziziah (Coast Guard). Jizan (Red Sea)
Minor bases (Naval and Coast Guard): Ras Tanura, Al Dammam, Yanbou Al Bahr, Ras al-Mishab, Al Wajh, Al Qatif, Haqi, Al Sharmah, Qizan, Duba

General

Funding for the Navy has the lowest defence service priority. New programmes are slow to come forward, and the operational status of existing ships is variable.

Command and Control

The USA provided an update of command and control capabilities during the period 1991–95, including a commercial datalink to improve interoperability.

Coast Defence

Truck-mounted Otomat batteries.

Coast Guard

Part of the Frontier Force under the Minister for Defence and Aviation. 5,500 officers and men. It is not always clear which ships belong to the Navy and which to the Coast Guard.

Strength of the Fleet

Type	*Active*	*Building*
Frigates	7	–
Corvettes—Missile	4	–
Fast Attack Craft—Missile	9	–
Patrol Craft	56	–
Minehunters	3	–
Minesweepers—Coastal	4	–
Replenishment Tankers	2	–

SUBMARINES

Notes: (1) Orders for patrol submarines are a low priority although training has been done in France and Pakistan.
(2) Interest has been shown in the acquisition of Midget Submarines.

FRIGATES

Notes: The programme to replace the Madina-class frigates is expected to make progress in 2009. A requirement for up to six ships is reported. Principal contenders are likely to be French FREMM class and one of the US Littoral Combat Ship variants.

3 AL RIYADH (MODIFIED LA FAYETTE) CLASS (TYPE F-3000S) (FFGHM)

Name	*No*	*Builders*	*Laid down*	*Launched*	*Commissioned*
AL RIYADH	812	DCN, Lorient	29 Sep 1999	1 Aug 2000	26 July 2002
MAKKAH	814	DCN, Lorient	25 Aug 2000	20 July 2001	3 Apr 2004
AL DAMMAM	816	DCN, Lorient	26 Aug 2001	7 Sep 2002	23 Oct 2004

Displacement, tons: 4,650 full load
Dimensions, feet (metres): 438.43 × 56.4 × 13.5 (133.6 × 17.2 × 4.1)
Main machinery: CODAD; 4 SEMT-Pielstick 16 PA6 STC diesels; 28,000 hp(m) *(20.58 MW)* sustained; 2 shafts; LIPS cp props; bow thruster
Speed, knots: 25. **Range, n miles:** 7,000 at 15 kt
Complement: 181 (25 officers); accommodation for 190

Missiles: SSM: 8 Aerospatiale MM 40 Block II Exocet ❶; inertial cruise; active radar homing to 70 km *(40 n miles)* at 0.9 Mach; warhead 165 kg; sea-skimmer.
SAM: Eurosam SAAM ❷; 2 octuple Sylver A43 VLS for Aster 15; command guidance active radar homing to 15 km *(8.1 n miles)* anti-missile, at 30 km *(16.2 n miles)* anti-aircraft. 16 missiles.
Guns: 1 OTO Melara 3 in *(76 mm)*/62 Super Rapid ❸; 120 rds/min to 16 km *(8.7 n miles)*; weight of shell 6 kg.
2 Giat 15B 20 mm ❹; 800 rds/min to 3 km; weight of shell 0.1 kg.
2—12.7 mm MGs.
Torpedoes: 4—21 in *(533 mm)* tubes; ECAN F17P; anti-submarine; wire-guided active/passive homing to 20 km *(10.8 n miles)* at 40 kt; warhead 250 kg.
Countermeasures: Decoys: 2 Matra Dagaie Mk 2 ❺; 10-barrelled trainable launchers; chaff and IR flares. SLAT anti-wake homing torpedoes system (when available).
RESM: Thomson-CSF (DR 3000-S2) ❻; intercept. Sagem Telegon 10.
CESM: Thales Altesse; intercept.
ECM: 2 Thales Salamandre; jammers.
Combat data systems: Thales Senit 7.
Weapons control: Thales Castor IIJ radar/EO tracker.
Radars: Air search: Thales DRBV 26C Jupiter II ❼; D-band.
Surveillance/Fire control: Thomson-CSF Arabel 3D ❽; I/J-band.

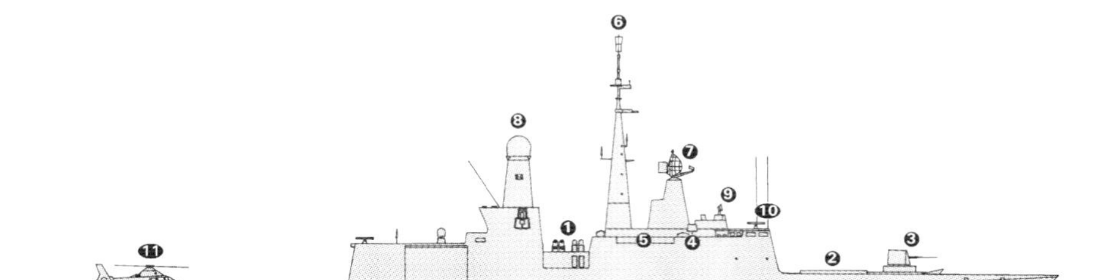

AL RIYADH *(Scale 1 : 1,200), Ian Sturton* / 1044496

Fire control: Thomson-CSF Castor II UJ ❾; J-band; range 15 km *(8 n miles)* for 1 m^2 target.
Navigation: 2 Racal Decca 1226 ❿; I-band. A second set fitted for helicopter control.
Sonars: Thomson Marconi CAPTAS 20; active low frequency; towed array.

Helicopters: 1 Dauphin 2 ⓫.

Programmes: A provisional order was made on 11 June 1989, but this was not finally confirmed until 19 November 1994 when a contract for two ships was authorised under the Sawari II programme. Thomson-CSF was the prime contractor. On 25 May 1997 an order for a third ship was placed together with a substantial enhancement of the weapon systems in all three. First steel cut 13 December 1997. Following handover, 812 started an eight month training programme which concluded in March 2003. 814 started sea trials on 9 September 2002 and 816 in mid-2003. SAM successfully tested in 816 in April 2004.
Structure: The design is a development of the French La Fayette class. Some 10 m longer, space and weight included for two more octuple SAM launchers or A50 launcher for Aster 30. Provision is made for a larger NH 90 type helicopter in the future, DCN Samahé helo handling system. STAF stabilisers. Originally planned to be fitted with a 100 mm gun, the contract was amended to incorporate a 76 mm mounting instead.
Operational: OTHT link for helicopters and Air Force F-15s. *Makkah* seriously damaged in a grounding incident 80 miles north of Jiddah in December 2004. The ship was refloated by the Tsavliris Salvage Group in early 2005 and was towed to Jiddah. However, in view of the severity of damage, the ship is unlikely to be repaired.

MAKKAH *3/2004, B Prézelin* / 1044497

AL DAMMAM *6/2004, B Prézelin* / 1044498

AL RIYADH *3/2006* / 1167506

4 MADINA (TYPE F 2000S) CLASS (FFGHM)

Name	*No*	*Builders*	*Laid down*	*Launched*	*Commissioned*
MADINA	702	Lorient (DTCN)	15 Oct 1981	23 Apr 1983	4 Jan 1985
HOFOUF	704	CNIM, Seyne-sur-Mer	14 June 1982	24 June 1983	31 Oct 1985
ABHA	706	CNIM, Seyne-sur-Mer	7 Dec 1982	23 Dec 1983	4 Apr 1986
TAIF	708	CNIM, Seyne-sur-Mer	1 Mar 1983	25 May 1984	29 Aug 1986

Displacement, tons: 2,000 standard; 2,870 full load
Dimensions, feet (metres): 377.3 × 41 × 16 (sonar) *(115 × 12.5 × 4.9)*
Main machinery: CODAD; 4 SEMT-Pielstick 16 PA6 280V BTC diesels; 38,400 hp(m) *(28 MW)* sustained; 2 shafts
Speed, knots: 30
Range, n miles: 8,000 at 15 kt; 6,500 at 18 kt
Complement: 179 (15 officers)
Missiles: SSM: 8 OTO Melara/Matra Otomat Mk 2 (2 quad) ❶; active radar homing to 160 km *(86.4 n miles)* at 0.9 Mach; warhead 210 kg; sea-skimmer for last 4 km *(2.2 n miles)*. ERATO system allows mid-course guidance by ship's helicopter.
SAM: Thomson-CSF Crotale Naval octuple launcher ❷; command line of sight guidance; radar/IR homing to 13 km *(7 n miles)* at 2.4 Mach; warhead 14 kg; 26 missiles.
Guns: 1 Creusot-Loire 3.9 in *(100 mm)*/55 compact Mk 2 ❸; 20/45/90 rds/min to 17 km *(9.3 n miles)* weight of shell 13.5 kg.
4 Breda 40 mm/70 (2 twin) ❹; 300 rds/min to 12.5 km *(6.8 n miles)*; weight of shell 0.96 kg.
Torpedoes: 4—21 in *(533 mm)* tubes ❺. ECAN F17P; anti-submarine; wire-guided; active/passive homing to 20 km *(10.8 n miles)* at 40 kt; warhead 250 kg.
Countermeasures: Decoys: CSEE Dagaie double trainable mounting ❻; IR flares and chaff; H/J-band.
ESM: Thomson-CSF DR 4000; intercept; HF/DF.
ECM: Thomson-CSF Janet; jammer.

MADINA *(Scale 1 : 1,200), Ian Sturton* / 0506097

Combat data systems: Thomson-CSF TAVITAC action data automation; capability for Link W.
Weapons control: Vega system. 3 CSEE Naja optronic directors. Alcatel DLT for torpedoes.
Radars: Air/surface search/IFF: Thomson-CSF Sea Tiger (DRBV 15) ❼; E/F-band; range 110 km *(60 n miles)* for 2 m² target.
Navigation: 2 Racal Decca TM 1226; I-band.
Fire control: Thomson-CSF Castor IIB/C ❽; I/J-band; range 15 km *(8 n miles)* for 1 m² target.
Thomson-CSF DRBC 32 ❾; I/J-band (for SAM).
Sonars: Thomson Sintra Diodon TSM 2630; hull-mounted; active search and attack with integrated Sorel VDS ❿; 11, 12 or 13 kHz.

Helicopters: 1 SA 365F Dauphin 2 ⓫.

Programmes: Ordered in 1980, the major part of the Sawari I contract. Agreement for France to provide supplies and technical help.
Modernisation: The class have been upgraded by DCN Toulon, *Madina* completed in April 1997. *Hofouf* in mid-1998. *Abha* in late 1999, and *Taif* in March 2000. Improvements included updating TAVITAC, Otomat missiles, both sonars and fittinga Samahé 110 helo handling system.
Structure: Fitted with Snach/Saphir folding fin stabilisers.
Operational: Navigation: CSEE Sylosat. Helicopter can provide mid-course guidance for SSM. All based at Jiddah. Only a few weeks a year are spent at sea.

TAIF ***6/2002*** / 0526835

HOFOUF ***3/2006*** / 1167507

CORVETTES

4 BADR CLASS

Name	*No*	*Builders*	*Laid down*	*Launched*	*Commissioned*
BADR	612	Tacoma Boatbuilding Co, Tacoma	6 Oct 1979	26 Jan 1980	30 Nov 1980
AL YARMOOK	614	Tacoma Boatbuilding Co, Tacoma	3 Jan 1980	13 May 1980	18 May 1981
HITTEEN	616	Tacoma Boatbuilding Co, Tacoma	19 May 1980	5 Sep 1980	3 Oct 1981
TABUK	618	Tacoma Boatbuilding Co, Tacoma	22 Sep 1980	18 June 1981	10 Jan 1983

Displacement, tons: 870 standard; 1,038 full load
Dimensions, feet (metres): 245 × 31.5 × 8.9 *(74.7 × 9.6 × 2.7)*
Main machinery: CODOG; 1 GE LM 2500 gas turbine; 23,000 hp *(17.2 MW)* sustained; 2 MTU 12V 652 TB91 diesels; 3,470 hp(m) *(2.55 MW)* sustained; 2 shafts; cp props
Speed, knots: 30 gas; 20 diesels
Range, n miles: 4,000 at 20 kt
Complement: 58 (7 officers)

Missiles: SSM: 8 McDonnell Douglas Harpoon (2 quad) launchers ❶; active radar homing to 130 km *(70 n miles)* at 0.9 Mach; warhead 227 kg.
Guns: 1 FMC/OTO Melara 3 in *(76 mm)*/62 Mk 75 Mod 0 ❷; 85 rds/min to 16 km *(8.7 n miles)*; weight of shell 6 kg.
1 General Electric/General Dynamics 20 mm 6-barrelled Vulcan Phalanx ❸; 3,000 rds/min combined to 2 km.
2 Oerlikon 20 mm/80 ❹.
1—81 mm mortar. 2—40 mm Mk 19 grenade launchers.
Torpedoes: 6—324 mm US Mk 32 (2 triple) tubes ❺. Honeywell Mk 46; anti-submarine; active/passive homing to 11 km *(5.9 n miles)* at 40 kt; warhead 44 kg.
Countermeasures: Decoys: 2 Loral Hycor SRBOC 6-barrelled fixed Mk 36 ❻; IR flares and chaff to 4 km *(2.2 n miles)*.
ESM: SLQ-32(V)1 ❼; intercept.

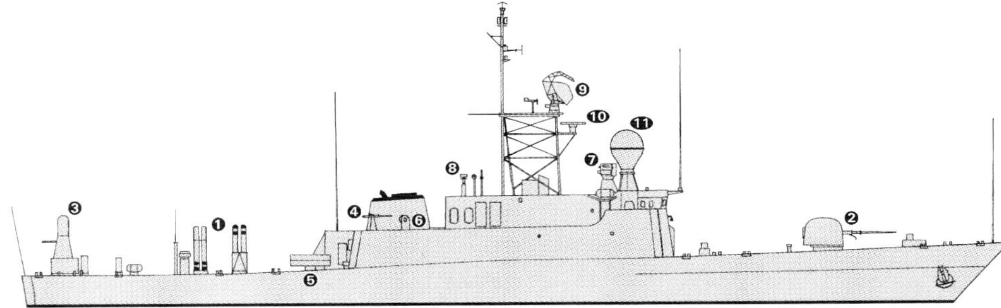

BADR *(Scale 1 : 600), Ian Sturton* / 0506250

Weapons control: Mk 24 optical director ❽. Mk 309 for torpedoes. Mk 92 Mod 5 GFCS. FSI Safire FLIR.
Radars: Air search: Lockheed SPS-40B ❾; B-band; range 320 km *(175 n miles)*.
Surface search: ISC Cardion SPS-55 ❿; I/J-band.
Fire control: Sperry Mk 92 ⓫; I/J-band.

Sonars: Raytheon SQS-56 (DE 1164); hull-mounted; active search and attack; medium frequency.

Modernisation: Refitting done in Saudi Arabia with US assistance. FLIR being fitted from 1998.
Structure: Fitted with fin stabilisers.
Operational: All based at Al Jubail on the east coast and spend little time at sea.

AL YARMOOK *2/1997, van Ginderen Collection* / 0019085

SHIPBORNE AIRCRAFT

Notes: Procurement of a new shipborne helicopter is under consideration. Up to 10 are required for deployment to the Al Riyadh class frigates and for other tasks.

Numbers/Type: 15/6 Aerospatiale AS 565SA 2/365N Dauphin 2.
Operational speed: 140 kt *(260 km/h)*.
Service ceiling: 15,000 ft *(4,575 m)*.
Range: 410 n miles *(758 km)*.
Role/Weapon systems: AS 565SA is the ASV/ASW helicopter; procured for embarked naval aviation force; surface search/attack is the primary role. Sensors: Thomson-CSF Agrion 15 radar; Crouzet MAD. Weapons: ASV; four AS/15TT missiles. ASW; 2 Mk 46 torpedoes. AS 365N is for SAR and is operated by the Armed Forces Medical Services. Sensors: Omera DRB 32 search radar. Weapons: Unarmed.

DAUPHIN 2 *4/2002, Aerospatiale* / 0093192

LAND-BASED MARITIME AIRCRAFT

Notes: (1) Six P-3C Orion or CASA CN-235 patrol aircraft may be acquired in due course.
(2) Five Boeing E3-A AEW aircraft in service with Air Force.

Numbers/Type: 12 Aerospatiale AS 532SC Cougar.
Operational speed: 150 kt *(280 km/h)*.
Service ceiling: 15,090 ft *(4,600 m)*.
Range: 335 n miles *(620 km)*.
Role/Weapon systems: First pair delivered in August 1989. Total of 12 by the end of 1990. Shared with the Coast Guard. Sensors: Omera search radar Safire AAQ-22 FLIR from 1998. Weapons: ASV; Giat 20 mm cannon; AM39 Exocet or Sea Eagle ASM.

AS 532 Cougar *6/1990, Paul Jackson* / 0062140

PATROL FORCES

9 AL SIDDIQ CLASS (PGGF)

Name	*No*	*Builders*	*Launched*	*Commissioned*
AL SIDDIQ	511	Peterson, WI	22 Sep 1979	15 Dec 1980
AL FAROUQ	513	Peterson, WI	17 May 1980	22 June 1981
ABDUL AZIZ	515	Peterson, WI	23 Aug 1980	3 Sep 1981
FAISAL	517	Peterson, WI	15 Nov 1980	23 Nov 1981
KHALID	519	Peterson, WI	23 Mar 1981	11 Jan 1982
AMYR	521	Peterson, WI	13 June 1981	21 June 1982
TARIQ	523	Peterson, WI	23 Sep 1981	11 Aug 1982
OQBAH	525	Peterson, WI	12 Dec 1981	18 Oct 1982
ABU OBAIDAH	527	Peterson, WI	3 Apr 1982	6 Dec 1982

Displacement, tons: 495 full load
Dimensions, feet (metres): 190.5 × 26.5 × 6.6 *(58.1 × 8.1 × 2)*
Main machinery: CODOG; 1 GE LM 2500 gas turbine; 23,000 hp *(17.2 MW)* sustained; 2 MTU 12V 652TB91 diesels; 3,470 hp(m) *(2.55 MW)* sustained; 2 shafts; cp props
Speed, knots: 38 gas; 25 diesel
Range, n miles: 2,900 at 14 kt
Complement: 38 (5 officers)

Missiles: SSM: 4 McDonnell Douglas Harpoon (2 twin) launchers; active radar homing to 130 km *(70 n miles)* at 0.9 Mach; warhead 227 kg.
Guns: 1 FMC/OTO Melara 3 in *(76 mm)*/62 Mk 75 Mod 0; 85 rds/min to 16 km *(8.7 n miles)*; weight of shell 6 kg.
1 General Electric/General Dynamics 20 mm 6-barrelled Vulcan Phalanx; 3,000 rds/min combined to 2 km.
2 Oerlikon 20 mm/80; 800 rds/min to 2 km anti-aircraft.
2—81 mm mortars. 2—40 mm Mk 19 grenade launchers.
Countermeasures: Decoys: 2 Loral Hycor SRBOC 6-barrelled fixed Mk 36; IR flares and chaff to 4 km *(2.2 n miles)*.
ESM: SLQ-32(V)1; intercept.
Weapons control: Mk 92 mod 5 GFCS. FSI Safire FLIR. Link W.
Radars: Surface search: ISC Cardion SPS-55; I/J-band.
Fire control: Sperry Mk 92; I/J-band.

Modernisation: Safire FLIR and Link W being fitted.
Operational: *Amyr* and *Tariq* operate from Jiddah, the remainder are based at Al Jubail. *Faisal* damaged in the Gulf War in 1991 but was operational again in 1994.

ABU OBAIDAH *6/2001, Ships of the World* / 0126360

17 HALTER TYPE (COASTAL PATROL CRAFT) (PB)

52–68

Displacement, tons: 56 full load
Dimensions, feet (metres): 78 × 20 × 5.8 *(23.8 × 6.1 × 1.8)*
Main machinery: 2 Detroit 16V-92TA diesels; 1,380 hp *(1.03 MW)* sustained; 2 shafts
Speed, knots: 28. **Range, n miles:** 1,200 at 12 kt
Complement: 8 (2 officers)
Guns: 2—25 mm Mk 38. 2—7.62 mm MGs.
Radars: Surface search: Raytheon SPS-64; I-band.

Comment: Ordered from Halter Marine 17th February 1991. Aluminium construction. Last delivered in January 1993. Same type for Philippines.

HALTER TYPE *8/1990, Trinity Marine* / 0080563

39 SIMONNEAU 51 TYPE (INSHORE PATROL CRAFT) (PBI)

Displacement, tons: 22 full load
Dimensions, feet (metres): 51.8 × 15.7 × 5.9 *(15.8 × 4.8 × 1.8)*
Main machinery: 4 outboards; 2,400 hp(m) *(1.76 MW)*
Speed, knots: 33
Range, n miles: 375 at 25 kt
Guns: 1—12.7 mm MG. 2—7.62 mm MGs.
Radars: Surface search: Furuno; I-band.

Comment: First 20 ordered from France in June 1988 and delivered in 1989–90. A second batch of 20 ordered in 1991. Aluminium construction. Used by naval commandos. These craft were also reported as Panhards. One deleted so far.

SIMONNEAU TYPE *1989, Simonneau Marine* / 0506098

MINE WARFARE FORCES

4 ADDRIYAH (MSC 322) CLASS (MINESWEEPERS/HUNTERS—COASTAL) (MHSC)

Name	*No*	*Builders*	*Launched*	*Commissioned*
ADDRIYAH	MSC 412	Peterson, WI	20 Dec 1976	6 July 1978
AL QUYSUMAH	MSC 414	Peterson, WI	26 May 1977	15 Aug 1978
AL WADEEAH	MSC 416	Peterson, WI	6 Sep 1977	7 Sep 1979
SAFWA	MSC 418	Peterson, WI	7 Dec 1977	2 Oct 1979

Displacement, tons: 320 standard; 407 full load
Dimensions, feet (metres): 153 × 26.9 × 8.2 *(46.6 × 8.2 × 2.5)*
Main machinery: 2 Waukesha L1616 diesels; 1,200 hp *(895 kW)*; 2 shafts
Speed, knots: 13
Complement: 39 (4 officers)
Guns: 1 Oerlikon 20 mm.
Radars: Surface search: ISC Cardion SPS-55; I/J-band.
Sonars: GE SQQ-14; VDS; active minehunting; high frequency.

Comment: Ordered on 30 September 1975 under the International Logistics Programme. Wooden structure. Fitted with fin stabilisers, wire and magnetic sweeps and also for minehunting. *Addriyah* based at Jiddah, the remainder at Al Jubail. Expected to be replaced by arrival of Sandowns but all are still in service mostly as patrol craft.

AL QUYSUMAH ***6/1996, van Ginderen Collection*** / 0019090

3 AL JAWF (SANDOWN) CLASS (MINEHUNTERS—COASTAL) (MHC)

Name	*No*	*Builders*	*Launched*	*Commissioned*
AL JAWF	420	Vosper Thornycroft	2 Aug 1989	12 Dec 1991
SHAQRA	422	Vosper Thornycroft	15 May 1991	7 Feb 1993
AL KHARJ	424	Vosper Thornycroft	8 Feb 1993	7 Aug 1997

Displacement, tons: 450 standard; 480 full load
Dimensions, feet (metres): 172.9 × 34.4 × 6.9 *(52.7 × 10.5 × 2.1)*
Main machinery: 2 Paxman 6RP200E diesels; 1,500 hp *(1.12 MW)* sustained; Voith-Schneider propulsion; 2 shafts; 2 Schöttel bow thrusters
Speed, knots: 13 diesels; 6 electric drive
Range, n miles: 3,000 at 12 kt
Complement: 34 (7 officers) plus 6 spare berths
Guns: 2 Electronics & Space Emerlec 30 mm (twin); 1,200 rds/min combined to 6 km *(3.3 n miles)*; weight of shell 0.35 kg.
Countermeasures: Decoys: 2 Loral Hycor SRBOC Mk 36 Mod 1 6-barrelled chaff launchers.
ESM: Thomson-CSF Shiploc; intercept.
MCM: ECA mine disposal system; 2 PAP 104 Mk 5.
Combat data systems: Plessey Nautis M action data automation.
Weapons control: Contraves TMEO optronic director (Seahawk Mk 2).
Radars: Navigation: Kelvin Hughes Type 1007; I-band.
Sonars: Plessey/MUSL Type 2093; VDS; high frequency.

Comment: Three ordered 2 November 1988 from Vosper Thornycroft. Option for three more appears to have been abandoned. GRP hulls. Combines vectored thrust units with bow thrusters and Remote Controlled Mine Disposal System (RCMDS). *Al Jawf* sailed for Saudi Arabia in November 1995, *Shaqra* in November 1996, and *Al Kharj* in August 1997. All based at Al Jubail.

SHAQRA ***3/2008*, Guy Toremans*** / 1353363

AUXILIARIES

2 BORAIDA (MOD DURANCE) CLASS (REPLENISHMENT SHIPS) (AORH)

Name	*No*	*Builders*	*Launched*	*Commissioned*
BORAIDA	902	La Ciotat, Marseilles	22 Jan 1983	29 Feb 1984
YUNBOU	904	La Ciotat, Marseilles	20 Oct 1984	29 Aug 1985

Displacement, tons: 11,200 full load
Dimensions, feet (metres): 442.9 × 61.3 × 22.9 *(135 × 18.7 × 7)*
Main machinery: 2 SEMT-Pielstick 14 PC2.5 V 400 diesels; 18,200 hp(m) *(13.4 MW)* sustained; 2 shafts; LIPS cp props
Speed, knots: 20.5
Range, n miles: 7,000 at 15 kt
Complement: 129 plus 11 trainees
Cargo capacity: 4,350 tons diesel; 350 tons AVCAT; 140 tons fresh water; 100 tons victuals; 100 tons ammunition; 70 tons spares
Guns: 4 Breda Bofors 40 mm/70 (2 twin); 300 rds/min to 12.5 km *(6.8 n miles)*; weight of shell 0.96 kg.
Weapons control: 2 CSEE Naja optronic directors. 2 CSEE Lynx optical sights.
Radars: Navigation: 2 Decca; I-band.
Helicopters: 2 SA 365F Dauphin or 1 AS 332SC Super Puma.

Comment: Contract signed October 1980 as part of Sawari I programme. Both upgraded by DCN at Toulon; *Boraida* in 1996/97, followed by *Yunbou*, in 1997/98. Refuelling positions: Two alongside, one astern. Also serve as training ships and as depot and maintenance ships. Helicopters can have ASM or ASW armament. Both based at Jiddah.

YUNBOU ***1/1998*** / 0016635

BORAIDA ***9/2003, Hartmut Ehlers*** / 0567897

4 LCU 1610 CLASS (TRANSPORTS) (YFU)

AL QIAQ (ex-*SA 310*) 212
AL SULAYEL (ex-*SA 311*) 214
AL ULA (ex-*SA 312*) 216
AFIF (ex-*SA 313*) 218

Displacement, tons: 375 full load
Dimensions, feet (metres): 134.9 × 29 × 6.1 *(41.1 × 8.8 × 1.9)*
Main machinery: 4 GM diesels; 1,000 hp *(746 kW)*; 2 Kort nozzles
Speed, knots: 11
Range, n miles: 1,200 at 8 kt
Complement: 14 (2 officers)
Military lift: 170 tons; 20 troops
Guns: 2—12.7 mm MGs.
Radars: Navigation: Marconi LN66; I-band.

Comment: Built by Newport Shipyard, Rhode Island. Transferred from US June/July 1976. Based at Al Jubail.

LCU 1610 (US colours) ***9/1997, Hachiro Nakai*** / 0016483

4 LCM 6 CLASS (TRANSPORTS) (YFU)

DHEBA 220 **UMLUS** 222 **AL LEETH** 224 **AL QUONFETHA** 226

Displacement, tons: 62 full load
Dimensions, feet (metres): 56.2 × 14 × 3.9 *(17.1 × 4.3 × 1.2)*
Main machinery: 2 GM diesels; 450 hp *(336 kW)*; 2 shafts
Speed, knots: 9. **Range, n miles:** 130 at 9 kt
Complement: 5
Military lift: 34 tons or 80 troops
Guns: 2—40 mm Mk 19 grenade launchers.

Comment: Four transferred July 1977 and four in July 1980. The first four have been cannibalised for spares. Based at Jiddah.

ROYAL YACHTS

1 ROYAL YACHT (YACH)

Name	*No*	*Builders*	*Commissioned*
AL YAMAMA	–	Elsinore, Denmark	Feb 1981

Displacement, tons: 1,660 full load
Dimensions, feet (metres): 269 × 42.7 × 10.8 *(82 × 13 × 3.3)*
Main machinery: 2 MTU 12V 1163 TB82 diesels; 6,000 hp(m) *(4.41 MW)*; 2 shafts; cp props; bow thruster; 300 hp(m) *(221 kW)*
Speed, knots: 19
Complement: 42 plus 56 spare
Helicopters: Platform for 1 medium.

Comment: Ordered by Iraq but not delivered because of the war with Iran. Given to Saudi Arabia by Iraq in 1988. Based at Dammam.

1 PEGASUS CLASS (HYDROFOIL) (YAGJ)

AL AZIZIAH

Displacement, tons: 115 full load
Dimensions, feet (metres): 89.9 × 29.9 × 6.2 *(27.4 × 9.1 × 1.9)*
Main machinery: 2 Allison 501-KF20A gas turbines; 8,660 hp *(6.46 MW)* sustained; 2 waterjets (foilborne); 2 Detroit 8V92 diesels; 606 hp *(452 kW)* sustained; 2 shafts (hullborne)
Speed, knots: 46. **Range, n miles:** 890 at 42 kt
Guns: 2 General Electric 20 mm Sea Vulcan.
Weapons control: Kollmorgen GFCS; Mk 35 optronic director.

Comment: Ordered in 1984 from Lockheed and subcontracted to Boeing, Seattle; delivered in August 1985. Mostly used as a tender to the Royal Yacht.

1 ROYAL YACHT (YACH)

Name	*No*	*Builders*	*Commissioned*
ABDUL AZIZ	–	Halsingør Waerft, Denmark	12 June 1984

Displacement, tons: 5,200 full load
Measurement, tons: 1,450 dwt
Dimensions, feet (metres): 482.2 × 59.2 × 16.1 *(147 × 18 × 4.9)*
Main machinery: 2 Lindholmen-Pielstick 12 PC2.5 V diesels; 15,600 hp(m) *(11.47 MW)* sustained; 2 shafts
Speed, knots: 22
Complement: 65 plus 4 Royal berths and 60 spare
Helicopters: 1 Bell 206B JetRanger type.

Comment: Completed March 1983 for subsequent fitting out at Vosper's Ship Repairers, Southampton. Helicopter hangar set in hull forward of bridge-covers extend laterally to form pad. Swimming pool. Stern ramp leading to garage. Based at Jiddah. Operated by the Coast Guard.

ABDUL AZIZ *7/2008*, Selim San* / 1353364

TUGS

13 COASTAL TUGS (YTB/YTM)

RADHWA 1–6, 14–15 **TUWAIG 113** **DAREEN 111**
RADHWA 12 **RADHWA 16** **RADHWA 17**

Comment: *Radhwa 12, 16* and *17* are 43 m YTMs built in 1982–83. *Tuwaig* and *Dareen* are ex-US YTB transferred in October 1975. These two are used to tow targets for weapons firing exercises and are based at Al Jubail and Damman respectively. The remainder are all of about 35 m built in Singapore and the Netherlands between 1981 and 1983.

YTB TYPE (US colours) *9/1992, Jürg Kürsener* / 0080564

COAST GUARD

Notes: Three 32 m fireboats *Jubail I*, *Jubail 2* and *Jubail 3*, entered service in 1982.

2 SEA GUARD CLASS (WPBF)

AL RIYADH 304 **ZULURAB** 305

Displacement, tons: 56 full load
Dimensions, feet (metres): 73.8 × 18.4 × 5.6 *(22.5 × 5.6 × 1.7)*
Main machinery: 2 MTU 12V 331 TC92 diesels; 2,920 hp(m) *(21.46 MW)*; 2 shafts
Speed, knots: 35
Complement: 10
Guns: 2 Giat 20 mm (twin). 2—7.62 mm MGs.
Radars: Surface search: Racal Decca; I-band.
Fire control: Thomson-CSF Agrion; J-band.

Comment: Built by Simonneau Marine and delivered by SOFREMA in April 1992. Aluminium construction. Both based at Jiddah. The SSM launcher shown in the picture is not fitted.

ZULURAB *1992, Simonneau Marine* / 0080565

4 STAN PATROL 2606 CRAFT (COASTAL PATROL CRAFT) (WPB)

ASSIR 317 **ALDHAHRAN** 318 **ALKAHRJ** 319 **ARAR** 320

Displacement, tons: 55 (approx) full load
Dimensions, feet (metres): 87.0 × 20.3 × 6.1 *(26.5 × 6.2 × 1.8)*
Main machinery: 2 MTU 12V 396 TE94 diesels; 4,429 hp *(3.3 MW)*; 2 shafts
Speed, knots: 28

Comment: Built by Damen Shipyards, Gorinchem and delivered 2002–03.

ARAR *7/2002, A A de Kruijf* / 0533301

4 AL JOUF CLASS (WPBF)

AL JOUF 351 **TURAIF** 352 **HAIL** 353 **NAJRAN** 354

Displacement, tons: 210 full load
Dimensions, feet (metres): 126.6 × 26.2 × 6.2 *(38.6 × 8 × 1.9)*
Main machinery: 3 MTU 16 V 538 TB93 diesels; 11,265 hp(m) *(8.28 MW)* sustained; 3 shafts
Speed, knots: 38. **Range, n miles:** 1,700 at 15 kt
Complement: 20 (4 officers)
Guns: 2 Oerlikon GAM-BO1 20 mm. 2—12.7 mm MGs.
Radars: Surface search: Racal S 1690 ARPA; I-band.
Navigation: Racal Decca RM 1290A; I-band.

Comment: Ordered on 18 October 1987 from Blohm + Voss. First two completed 15 June 1989; second pair 20 August 1989. Steel hulls with aluminium superstructure. *Hail* and *Najran* based at Jiddah in the Red Sea and the others at Aziziah.

AL JOUF *6/1989, Blohm + Voss* / 0080566

2 AL JUBATEL CLASS (WPB)

AL JUBATEL **SALWA**

Displacement, tons: 95 full load
Dimensions, feet (metres): 86 × 19 × 6.9 *(26.2 × 5.8 × 2.1)*
Main machinery: 2 MTU 16V 396 TB94 diesels; 5,800 hp(m) *(4.26 MW)* sustained; 2 shafts
Speed, knots: 34
Range, n miles: 1,100 at 25 kt
Complement: 12 (4 officers)
Guns: 1 Oerlikon/GAM-BO1 20 mm. 2—12.7 mm MGs.
Radars: Surface search: Racal Decca AC 1290; I-band.

Comment: Built by Abeking & Rasmussen, completed in April 1987. Smaller version of Turkish SAR 33 Type. Steel construction. One based at Jizan and one at Al Wajh.

AL JUBATEL ***1987, Abeking & Rasmussen*** / 0080567

3 SLINGSBY SAH 2200 HOVERCRAFT (UCAC)

Dimensions, feet (metres): 34.8 × 13.8 *(10.6 × 4.2)*
Main machinery: 1 Deutz BF6L913C diesel; 192 hp(m) *(141 kW)* sustained; lift and propulsion
Speed, knots: 40
Range, n miles: 500 at 40 kt
Complement: 2
Military lift: 2.2 tons or 16 troops
Guns: 1—7.62 mm MG.

Comment: Supplied by Slingsby Amphibious Hovercraft, York in December 1990. Have Kevlar armour. These craft have replaced the SRN type.

SAH 2200 ***1990, Slingsby*** / 0080568

1 TRAINING SHIP (AXL)

TABBOUK

Displacement, tons: 585 full load
Dimensions, feet (metres): 196.8 × 32.8 × 5.8 *(60 × 10 × 1.8)*
Main machinery: 2 MTU MD 16V 538 TB80 diesels; 5,000 hp(m) *(3.68 MW)* sustained; 2 shafts
Speed, knots: 20
Range, n miles: 3,500 at 12 kt
Complement: 26 (6 officers) plus 70 trainees
Guns: 1 Oerlikon GAM-BO1 20 mm.
Radars: Surface search: Racal Decca TM 1226; I-band.
Navigation: Racal Decca 2690BT; I-band.

Comment: Built by Bayerische, Germany and commissioned 1 December 1977. Based at Jiddah.

5 GRIFFON 8000 TD(M) CLASS (HOVERCRAFT) (LCAC)

Displacement, tons: 18.2; 24.6 full load
Dimensions, feet (metres): 69.5 × 36.1 × 1 *(21.15 × 11 × 0.32)*
Main machinery: 2 MTU 12V 183 TB32 V12 diesels; 1,600 hp *(1.2 MW)*
Speed, knots: 50
Range, n miles: 400 at 45 kt
Complement: 4 (2 officers) (accommodation for further 16)
Guns: 1—12.7 mm MG.
Radars: Raytheon R-80; I-band.

Comment: Five hovercraft ordered from Griffon in 2000 for delivery in 2001. Payload of about 8 tonnes. Similar to those supplied to Indian Coast Guard but with different superstructure. Three based on west coast and two on east coast.

GRIFFON 8000 (Indian colours) ***9/2000, Indian Coast Guard*** / 0104592

INSHORE PATROL CRAFT (PBI)

Numbers	*Type*	*Date*	*Speed*
12	Rapier 15.2 m	1976	28
2	Enforcer, USA, 9.4 m	1980s	30
30	Simonneau SM 331, 9.3 m	1992	40
40	Simonneau Naja 12	1990	50
60	Boston Whalers, 8.3 m	1980s	30

Comment: About 150 mostly Task Force Boats. Many are based at Jiddah with the rest spread around the other bases. Most are armed with MGs and the larger craft have I-band radars.

SIMONNEAU SM 331 ***6/1992, Simonneau Marine*** / 0080569

3 SMALL TANKERS (YO)

AL FORAT **DAJLAH** **AL NIL**

Displacement, tons: 233 full load
Dimensions, feet (metres): 94.2 × 21.3 × 6.9 *(28.7 × 6.5 × 2.1)*
Main machinery: 2 Caterpillar D343 diesels; 2 shafts
Speed, knots: 12
Range, n miles: 500 at 12 kt
Radars: Navigation: Decca 110; I-band.

Comment: *Al Nil* based at Aziziah, the others at Jiddah.

Senegal

MARINE SÉNÉGALAISE

Country Overview

The Republic of Senegal was a French colony until 1960 when it gained independence. Situated in western Africa, it has an area of 75,750 square miles and is bordered to the north by Mauritania and to the south by Guinea and Guinea-Bissau. Its 286 n mile coastline with the Atlantic Ocean is divided in two by the coast of Gambia with which the country was united to form the confederation of Senegambia between 1981–89. The capital, largest city and principal port is Dakar. Territorial seas (12 n miles) are claimed. A 200 n mile Exclusive Economic Zone (EEZ) has been declared but its limits have only been partially defined by boundary agreements.

Headquarters Appointments

Head of Navy: Captain Ousmane Oumar Baila Kane

Personnel

(a) 2009: 900 officers and men
(b) 2 years' conscript service

Bases

Dakar, Elinkine (Casamance)

PATROL FORCES

Notes: Four RAIDCO 12 m RIBs (*Ibra Faye* P 16, *Ousmane Diop Coumba Pathe* P 17, *El Hadji Mbor Diagne* P 18, *Alieu Codou N'Doye* P 19) with waterjet propulsion, are operated by the Fishery Protection Directorate. They were procured in 2005.

1 IMPROVED OSPREY 55 CLASS (LARGE PATROL CRAFT) (PBO)

Name	*No*	*Builders*	*Commissioned*
FOUTA	–	Danyard A/S, Fredrikshavn	1 June 1987

Displacement, tons: 470 full load
Dimensions, feet (metres): 180.5 × 33.8 × 8.5 *(55 × 10.3 × 2.6)*
Main machinery: 2 MAN Burmeister & Wain Alpha 12V23/30-DVO diesels; 4,400 hp(m) *(3.23 MW)* sustained; 2 shafts; cp props
Speed, knots: 20. **Range, n miles**: 4,000 at 16 kt
Complement: 38 (4 officers) plus 8 spare
Guns: 1 Hispano Suiza 30 mm. 1 Giat 20 mm.
Radars: Surface search: Furuno FR 1411; I-band.
Navigation: Furuno FR 1221; I-band.

Comment: Ordered in 1985. Intended for patrolling the EEZ rather than as a warship, hence the modest armament. A 25 kt rigid inflatable boat can be launched from a stern ramp which has a protective hinged door. Similar vessels built for Morocco.

FOUTA ***5/2008*, B Prézelin*** / 1335293

1 PR 72M CLASS (PBO)

Name	*No*	*Builders*	*Commissioned*
NJAMBUUR	P 773	SFCN, Villeneuve-la-Garenne	Feb 1983

Displacement, tons: 451 full load
Dimensions, feet (metres): 191.0 × 26.9 × 7.2 *(58.2 × 8.2 × 2.2)*
Main machinery: 2 UD 33V16M6D diesels; 5,470 hp *(4.08 MW)* sustained; 2 shafts
Speed, knots: 16. **Range, n miles**: 2,160 at 15 kt
Complement: 46
Guns: 2 OTO Melara 3 in *(76 mm)*/62 compact; 85 rds/min to 16 km *(8.7 n miles)*; weight of shell 6 kg.
2—20 mm Oerlikon. 2—12.7 mm MGs.
Weapons control: 2 CSEE Naja optical directors.
Radars: Surface search: FR 7112 and FR 2105; I-band.

Comment: Ordered in 1979 and launched 23 December 1980. Completed September 1981 for shipping of armament at Lorient. Underwent overhaul at Lorient 2001–2002.

NJAMBUUR ***5/2008*, B Prézelin*** / 1335296

2 PR 48 CLASS (LARGE PATROL CRAFT) (PBO)

Name	*No*	*Builders*	*Launched*	*Commissioned*
POPONGUINE	–	SFCN, Villeneuve-la-Garenne	22 Mar 1974	10 Aug 1974
PODOR	–	SFCN, Villeneuve-la-Garenne	20 July 1976	13 July 1977

Displacement, tons: 250 full load
Dimensions, feet (metres): 156 × 23.3 × 8.1 *(47.5 × 7.1 × 2.5)*
Main machinery: 2 SACM AGO V12 CZSHR diesels; 4,340 hp(m) *(3.2 MW)*; 2 shafts
Speed, knots: 23. **Range, n miles**: 2,000 at 16 kt
Complement: 33 (3 officers)
Guns: 2 Bofors 40 mm/70. 2—7.62 mm MGs.
Radars: Surface search: Furuno; I-band.

Comment: Ordered in 1973 and 1975. *Saint-Louis* decommissioned in 2003 and the operational status of the remaining two is doubtful.

PODOR ***5/2008*, B Prézelin*** / 1335294

1 INTERCEPTOR CLASS (COASTAL PATROL CRAFT) (PB)

Name	*No*	*Builders*	*Commissioned*
SÉNÉGAL II	–	Les Bateaux Turbec Ltd, Sainte Catherine, Canada	Feb 1979

Displacement, tons: 62 full load
Dimensions, feet (metres): 86.9 × 19.3 × 5.2 *(26.5 × 5.8 × 1.6)*
Main machinery: 2 diesels; 2,700 hp *(2.01 MW)*; 2 shafts
Speed, knots: 32.5
Guns: 1—20 mm Giat.
Radars: Surface search: Furuno; I-band.

Comment: Used for EEZ patrol. *Sine-Saloum II* and *Casamance II* were decommissioned in 2004.

SÉNÉGAL II ***5/2008*, B Prézelin*** / 1335295

2 PETERSON MK 4 CLASS (PB)

Name	*No*	*Builders*	*Commissioned*
MATELOT ALIOUNE SAMB	–	Peterson Builders Inc	28 Oct 1993
MATELOT OUMAR NDOYE	–	Peterson Builders Inc	4 Nov 1993

Displacement, tons: 22 full load
Dimensions, feet (metres): 51.3 × 14.8 × 4.3 *(15.6 × 4.5 × 1.3)*
Main machinery: 2 Detroit 6V-92TA diesels; 520 hp *(388 kW)*; 2 shafts
Speed, knots: 24
Range, n miles: 500 at 20 kt
Complement: 6
Guns: 2—12.7 mm (twin) MGs. 2—7.62 mm (twin) MGs.
Radars: Surface search: Furuno; I-band.

Comment: Ordered in September 1992. Same type delivered to Cape Verde, Gambia and Guinea-Bissau (since deleted) under FMS. Carries an RIB on the stern.

OUMAR NDOYE ***5/2008*, B Prézelin*** / 1335301

2 VCSM CLASS (PB)

ALPHONSE FAYE **BAYE SOGUI**

Displacement, tons: 42
Dimensions, feet (metres): 65.6 × 17.1 × 4.9 *(20.0 × 5.2 × 1.5)*
Main machinery: 2 MAN V12 diesels; 2,000 hp *(1.47 MW)*; 2 shafts
Speed, knots: 25. **Range, n miles**: 530 at 15 kt
Complement: 5
Guns: 1—7.62 mm MG.
Radars: Navigation: Furuno; I-band.

Comment: Two Raidco Marine RPB 20 class were procured in July 2004 and May 2005 respectively. Similar to French VCSM class. Operated by the Fishery Protection Directorate. Two others are operated by the Customs service.

BAYE SOGUI ***6/2008*, Senegal Navy*** / 1335302

LAND-BASED MARITIME AIRCRAFT

Numbers/Type: 1 De Havilland Canada DHC-6 Twin Otter.
Operational speed: 168 kt *(311 km/h)*.
Service ceiling: 23,200 ft *(7,070 m)*.
Range: 1,460 n miles *(2,705 km)*.
Role/Weapon systems: Procured in 1982. Used for coastal surveillance but effectiveness limited. Backed up by a French Navy Breguet Atlantique based at Dakar. Sensors: Search radar. Weapons: Unarmed.

AMPHIBIOUS FORCES

1 CTM (LCM)

CTM (ex-*CTM 2*, ex-*CTM 5*)

Displacement, tons: 150 full load
Dimensions, feet (metres): 78 × 21 × 4.2 *(23.8 × 6.4 × 1.3)*
Main machinery: 2 Poyaud 520 V8 diesels; 225 hp(m) *(165 kW)*; 2 shafts
Speed, knots: 9.5
Range, n miles: 350 at 8 kt
Complement: 6
Military lift: 90 tons

Comment: Transferred from French Navy in September 1999. Has a bow ramp.

CTM *12/2001* / 0525011

1 EDIC CLASS (LCT)

FALEMÉ II (ex-*Javeline* L 9070)

Displacement, tons: 710 full load
Dimensions, feet (metres): 194.9 × 39 × 5.9 *(59.4 × 11.9 × 1.8)*
Main machinery: 2 SACM Uni Diesel UD 30 VIZ M1 diesels; 1,200 hp(m) *(882 kW)* sustained; 2 shafts
Speed, knots: 10.5
Range, n miles: 1,000 at 10 kt
Complement: 12
Military lift: 336 tons
Guns: Fitted for 2 Giat 20F2 20 mm.
Radars: Navigation: Racal Decca 1229; I-band.

Comment: Ex-*Javeline* was the first of the second series of EDICs. Originally commissioned in 1967, it was loaned to Senegal on 16 October 1995 and was formally transferred on 12 January 2000. The craft replaced a first series EDIC.

FALEMÉ II *5/2008*, B Prézelin* / 1335299

1 EDIC 700 CLASS (LCT)

Name	*No*	*Builders*	*Launched*	*Commissioned*
KARABANE	841	SFCN, Villeneuve-la-Garenne	6 Mar 1986	30 Jan 1987

Displacement, tons: 736 full load
Dimensions, feet (metres): 193.5 × 39 × 5.6 *(59 × 11.9 × 1.7)*
Main machinery: 2 SACM MGO 175 V12 ASH diesels; 1,200 hp(m) *(882 kW)* sustained; 2 shafts
Speed, knots: 12
Range, n miles: 1,800 at 10 kt
Complement: 18 (33 spare billets)
Military lift: 12 trucks; 340 tons equipment
Guns: Fitted for 2 Giat 20 mm.
Radars: Navigation: Racal Decca 1226; I-band.

Comment: Ordered May 1985, delivered 23 June 1986 from France. Second of class from France in 1995 and returned again in 1996.

KARABANE *5/2008*, B Prézelin* / 1335300

AUXILIARIES

Notes: There is also a 44 m buoy tender *Samba Laobe Fall*. Built by Océa des Sables d'Olonne in 2007, it is civilian operated.

1 HARBOUR TUG (YTM)

CHEIKH OUMAR FALL (ex-*Olivier*)

Displacement, tons: 105
Dimensions, feet (metres): 68.9 × 22.6 × 10.5 *(21.0 × 6.9 × 3.2)*
Main machinery: 1 SACM-Wärtsilä UD 30 V12 diesel; 700 hp *(515 kW)*; 1 shaft
Speed, knots: 10
Complement: 6
Radars: Navigation: Raytheon; I-band.

Comment: Former French navy tug, completed at St Nazaire in 1965, donated in 1999.

CHEIKH OUMAR FALL *5/2008*, B Prézelin* / 1335298

1 FISHERIES RESEARCH VESSEL (AG)

ITAF DEME

Displacement, tons: 318
Dimensions, feet (metres): 124.7 × 26.2 × 11.2 *(38.0 × 8.0 × 3.4)*
Main machinery: 1 Yanmar diesel; 1,000 hp *(810 kW)*; 1 shaft
Speed, knots: 12
Complement: 18
Radars: Navigation: Furuno; I-band.

Comment: Modified purse-seiner converted to a fishery research role. Operated by the navy.

ITAF DEME *5/2008*, B Prézelin* / 1335297

Serbia

Country Overview

The Republic of Serbia was formed following a referendum on 21 May 2006 in which the people of Montenegro voted for independence and for the dissolution of the Federal Republic of Serbia and Montenegro; this itself was the rump of the former Yugoslavia. On 5 June 2006 the Serbian National Assembly decreed Serbia to be the continuing international personality of Serbia and Montenegro. With an area of 34,116 square miles, it is located in south-eastern Europe in the Balkan Peninsula and is bordered to the west by Montenegro, Bosnia and Croatia, to the north by Hungary, to the east by Romania and Bulgaria and to the south by Albania and Macedonia. A land-locked country, the principal river is the Danube which enters the country from the north and after passing through the capital Belgrade goes on to form part of the eastern border. Other rivers include the Sova and Tisza.

The provisions of the Union Constitution were that, in the event of dissolution, the armed forces of Serbia and Montenegro would be split in such a way that each state keeps the assets in its territory. The former navy of Serbia and Montenegro transferred to Montenegro in June 2006, except for the former Danube Flotilla, which is now subordinate to the Serbian land forces as the River Detachment. While the future of the detachment is unclear, it is likely to be reduced and reshaped to undertake civil authority missions, the responsibility for which may be transferred to the police.

Headquarters Appointments

Commander, Riverine Flotilla:
Captain Nebojša Joksimović

Bases

Novi Sad and Pancevo.

PATROL FORCES

6 TYPE 20 BISCAYA CLASS (RIVER PATROL CRAFT) (PBR)

PC 211–216

Displacement, tons: 55 standard
Dimensions, feet (metres): 71.5 × 17 × 3.9 *(21.8 × 5.3 × 1.2)*
Main machinery: 2 diesels; 1,156 hp(m) *(850 kW)*; 2 shafts
Speed, knots: 16. **Range, n miles:** 200 at 15 kt
Complement: 10
Guns: 2 Oerlikon 20 mm.
Radars: Surface search: Decca 110; I-band.

Comment: Completed in the late 1980s. Steel hull with GRP superstructure. All active with the Riverine Flotilla.

PC 215 — *1988, Yugoslav Navy* / 0084261

1 RIVER PATROL BOAT (PBR)

PC 111

Displacement, tons: 29 full load
Dimensions, feet (metres): 79.1 × 13.5 × 2.9 *(24.1 × 4.1 × 0.9)*
Main machinery: 2 diesels; 652 hp(m) *(486 kW)*; 2 shafts
Speed, knots: 17. **Range, n miles:** 720 at 17 kt
Complement: 6
Guns: 2—20 mm.

Comment: Built for US Navy's Rhine River patrol and transferred in the 1950s.

PC 111 — *6/2008*, Freivogel Collection* / 1335423

1 BOTICA CLASS (TYPE 16) (RIVER PATROL CRAFT) (PBR)

PC 302

Displacement, tons: 23 full load
Dimensions, feet (metres): 55.8 × 11.8 × 2.8 *(17.0 × 3.6 × 0.8)*
Main machinery: 2 diesels; 464 hp(m) *(340 kW)*; 2 shafts
Speed, knots: 15. **Range, n miles:** 340 at 14 kt
Complement: 7
Guns: 1 Oerlikon 20 mm (fitted for). 2—7.62 mm MGs.

Comment: Built in about 1970 and reactivated having been decommissioned in the 1990s. Used for riverine patrols. Can carry up to 30 troops.

PC 302 — *5/2004, Sieche Collection* / 0583300

MINE WARFARE FORCES

4 NESTIN CLASS (RIVER MINESWEEPERS) (MSR)

Name	*No*	*Builders*	*Commissioned*
MOTAJICA	M 332	Brodotehnika, Belgrade	18 Dec 1976
VUČEDOL	M 335	Brodotehnika, Belgrade	1979
DJERDAP	M 336	Brodotehnika, Belgrade	1980
NOVI SAD	M 341	Brodotehnika, Belgrade	8 June 1996

Displacement, tons: 65 full load
Dimensions, feet (metres): 88.6 × 21.7 × 5.2 *(27 × 6.3 × 1.6)*
Main machinery: 2 diesels; 520 hp(m) *(382 kW)*; 2 shafts
Speed, knots: 15
Range, n miles: 860 at 11 kt
Complement: 17
Guns: 6 Hispano 20 mm (quad fwd, 2 single aft). Some may still have a 40 mm gun forward.
8—20 mm (quad fwd and aft) (M 341).
Mines: 24 can be carried.
Countermeasures: MCMV: Magnetic, acoustic and explosive sweeping gear.
Radars: Surface search: Racal Decca 1226; I-band.

Comment: Some transferred to Hungary and Iraq. One more completed in 1996. The class is based at Novi Sad as part of the Riverine Flotilla. One deleted in 1997 and a further three in 2007. M 341, which replaced the previously deleted M 337, is to a modified design which includes different armament.

DJERDAP — *6/2008*, Freivogel Collection* / 1335444

AUXILIARIES

1 KOZARA CLASS (HEADQUARTERS SHIP) (PBR)

KOZARA (ex-*Oregon*, ex-*Kriemhild*) RPB 30

Displacement, tons: 695 full load
Dimensions, feet (metres): 219.8 × 31.2 × 4.6 *(67 × 9.5 × 1.4)*
Main machinery: 2 Deutz RV6M545 diesels; 800 hp(m) *(588 kW)*; 2 shafts
Speed, knots: 12
Guns: 9 Hispano Suiza 20 mm (3 triple).

Comment: Former Presidential Yacht on Danube. Built in Austria in 1940. Acts as Flagship of the Riverine Flotilla. A similar ship served in the Russian Black Sea Fleet before being transferred to Ukraine. Although previously believed to have been decommissioned, continues to be used to accommodate Riverine Flotilla Staff.

KOZARA — *6/2003, Serbian Navy* / 0572439

1 SABAC CLASS (DEGAUSSING VESSEL) (YDG)

SABAC RSRB 36

Displacement, tons: 110 standard
Dimensions, feet (metres): 105.6 × 23.3 × 3.9 *(32.2 × 7.1 × 1.2)*
Main machinery: 1 diesel; 528 hp(m) *(388 kW)*; 1 shaft
Speed, knots: 10
Range, n miles: 660 at 10 kt
Complement: 20
Guns: 2—20 mm M71.
Radars: Navigation: Decca 101; I-band.

Comment: Built in 1985. Used to degauss River vessels up to a length of 50 m.

SABAC *6/2008*, Freivogel Collection* / 1335422

Seychelles

Country Overview

A former British colony, the Republic of the Seychelles became independent in 1976. Situated in the western Indian Ocean, northeast of Madagascar, the archipelago consists of some 90 islands, disposed over 13,000 square miles in two groups. The 40 islands of the northern group include the principal islands: Mahé (the largest), Praslin, Silhouette and La Digue. The 50 or so low-lying coral islands in the south are mostly uninhabited. Victoria (Mahé) is the capital, largest town and principal port. Territorial seas (12 n miles) are claimed. A 200 n mile Exclusive Economic Zone (EEZ) has been declared but the limits have not been fully defined by boundary agreements.

Headquarters Appointments

Commander of the Coast Guard:
Lieutenant Colonel D Gertrude

Bases

Port Victoria, Mahé

Personnel

2009: 300 including 80 air wing and 100 marines

LAND-BASED MARITIME AIRCRAFT

Numbers/Type: 1 Britten-Norman BN-2A21 Maritime Defender.
Operational speed: 150 kt *(280 km/h)*.
Service ceiling: 18,900 ft *(5,760 m)*.
Range: 1,500 n miles *(2,775 km)*.
Role/Weapon systems: Coastal surveillance and surface search aircraft delivered in 1980. Sensors: Search radar. Weapons: Provision for rockets or guns.

BN2T-4S (Irish Police colours) *8/1997* / 0016662

COAST GUARD

1 ZHUK (PROJECT 1400M) CLASS (COASTAL PATROL CRAFT) (PB)

Name	*No*	*Builders*	*Commissioned*
FORTUNE	604	USSR	6 Nov 1982

Displacement, tons: 39 full load
Dimensions, feet (metres): 78.7 × 16.4 × 3.9 *(24 × 5 × 1.2)*
Main machinery: 2 Type M 401B diesels; 2,200 hp *(1.6 MW)* sustained; 2 shafts
Speed, knots: 30
Range, n miles: 1,100 at 15 kt
Complement: 12 (3 officers)
Guns: 4—14.5 mm (2 twin) MGs.
Radars: Surface search: Furuno; I-band.

Comment: Two transferred from USSR. Second of class paid off in 1996 and used for spares.

FORTUNE *6/1998, Seychelles Coast Guard* / 0050097

1 COASTAL PATROL CRAFT (PB)

JUNON 602

Displacement, tons: 40 full load
Dimensions, feet (metres): 60.0 × 16.7 × 5.9 *(18.3 × 5.1 × 1.8)*
Speed, knots: 20
Complement: 5
Radars: Surface search: Furuno; I-band.

Comment: Former Port and Marine Services patrol boat reintegrated into the Coast Guard in 2003.

JUNON *9/2003, Seychelles Coast Guard* / 0568333

5 PATROL CRAFT (PB)

ARIES VIRGO LIBRA TAURUS PISCES

Displacement, tons: 17.7 full load
Dimensions, feet (metres): 44.0 × 12.5 × 3.9 *(13.4 × 3.8 × 1.2)*
Main machinery: 2 General Motors Detroit 6V53 diesels; 2 shafts
Speed, knots: 13. **Range, n miles:** 200 at 11 kt
Complement: 3
Radars: Surface search: Furuno; I-band.

Comment: Former US Coast Guard lifeboats (MLB) constructed in the 1960s. Three were transported to the Seychelles onboard USS *Anchorage* in October 2000 and a further two onboard USS *Tarawa* in December 2000.

MLBs *9/2003, Seychelles Coast Guard* / 0568334

1 TYPE FPB 42 (LARGE PATROL CRAFT) (PB)

Name	*No*	*Builders*	*Commissioned*
ANDROMACHE	605	Picchiotti, Viareggio	10 Jan 1983

Displacement, tons: 268 full load
Dimensions, feet (metres): 137.8 × 26 × 8.2 *(41.8 × 8 × 2.5)*
Main machinery: 2 Paxman Valenta 16 CM diesels; 6,650 hp *(5 MW)* sustained; 2 shafts
Speed, knots: 26
Range, n miles: 3,000 at 16 kt
Complement: 22 (3 officers)
Guns: 1 Oerlikon 25 mm. 2—7.62 mm MGs.
Radars: Surface search: 2 Furuno; I-band.

Comment: Ordered from Inma, La Spezia in November 1981. A second of class reported ordered in 1991 but the order was not confirmed.

ANDROMACHE
3/1997
0019096

1 SDB MK 5 CLASS (LARGE PATROL CRAFT) (PBO)

TOPAZ (ex-*Tarmugli*) 606 (ex-T 64)

Displacement, tons: 260 full load
Dimensions, feet (metres): 151.0 × 24.6 × 8.2 *(46.0 × 7.5 × 2.5)*
Main machinery: 2 MTU 16V 538 TB92 diesels; 6,820 hp(m) *(5 MW)* sustained; 2 shafts
Speed, knots: 30
Range, n miles: 2,000 at 12 kt
Complement: 34 (4 officers)
Guns: 1 Medak 30 mm 2A42.
Radars: Surface search: Bharat 1245; I-band.

Comment: Built at Garden Reach and first commissioned in 2002. Transferred from the Indian Navy and recommissioned on 23 February 2005.

SDB MK 5 CLASS *5/2002* / 0534083

Sierra Leone

Country Overview

A former British colony, Sierra Leone became independent in 1961. Located in west Africa, the country has an area of 27,699 square miles, a 217 n mile coastline with the Atlantic Ocean and is bordered to the north by Guinea and to the south by Liberia. The capital, largest city and principal port is Freetown. Territorial seas (12 n miles) and an EEZ (200 n miles) are claimed.

Headquarters Appointments

Commander Maritime Wing:
Captain Daniel Mansaray

Personnel

(a) 2009: 270 (38 officers)
(b) Voluntary service

Bases

Freetown (Murray Town) HQ and Training Base.
Freetown (Government wharf) Main Base.
Forward operating bases at Yeliboya, Tombo, Bonthe (Sherbo Is) and Sulima.

PATROL FORCES

Notes: (1) Five small inshore patrol craft have been acquired to operate from Murray Town and the forward operating bases.
(2) Acquisition of a surveillance aircraft and of further patrol craft is under consideration.

1 SHANGHAI III (TYPE 062/1) CLASS (PB)

SIR MILTON PB 105

Displacement, tons: 170 full load
Dimensions, feet (metres): 134.5 × 17.4 × 5.9 *(41.0 × 5.3 × 1.8)*
Main machinery: 4 Chinese L12-180A diesels; 4,400 hp(m) *(3.22 MW)* sustained; 4 shafts
Speed, knots: 25
Range, n miles: 750 at 17 kt
Complement: 43
Guns: 4 China 37 mm/63 (2 twin); 180 rds/min to 8.5 km *(4.6 n miles)*; weight of shell 1.42 kg.
4 China 25 mm (2 twin).
Radars: Surface search: Pot Head or Anritsu 726; I-band.

Comment: Transferred from China on 10 March 2006 to replace *Alimany Rassin*. Fully operational.

SIR MILTON *6/2006, RSLAF (MW)* / 1164270

3 SEA ARK 32 ft CUTTERS (PB)

01–03

Displacement, tons: 5.5 full load
Dimensions, feet (metres): 32.0 × 12.0 × 3.2 *(9.8 × 3.6 × 1.0)*
Main machinery: 2 Yanmar 6LYAM-STP diesels; 740 hp (550 kW); 2 Konrad drives
Speed, knots: 34
Complement: 4
Radars: Navigation: Furuno; I-band.

Comment: Sea Ark Dauntless RAM design donated by the US on 26 May 2006. Although not permanently fitted with weapons, always patrol with light weapons. Fully operational.

SEA ARK 01 *6/2006, RSLAF (MW)* / 1164269

Singapore

Country Overview

Formerly under British rule, the Republic of Singapore became self-governing in 1959. It joined Malaysia in 1963, but separated from the Federation in 1965 to become a sovereign state. With an area of 247 square miles and a coastline of 104 n miles, the main island is separated from the southern tip of Malaysia by the narrow Johore Strait. There are 59 small adjacent islets. To the south the Singapore Strait, an important shipping channel linking the Indian Ocean with the South China Sea, separates the island from the Riau archipelago of Indonesia. Territorial seas (3 n miles) are claimed. An EEZ is not claimed.

Headquarters Appointments

Chief of the Navy:
Rear Admiral Chew Men Leong
Chief of Staff:
Rear Admiral Tan Kai Hoe
Fleet Commander:
Rear Admiral Ng Chee Peng
Commander Police Coast Guard:
Deputy Assistant Commissioner Teo Kian Teck

Personnel

(a) 2009: 4,500 officers and men including 1,800 conscripts
(b) National Service: two and a half years for Corporals and above; two years for the remainder
(c) 5,000 reservists (operationally trained)

Bases

Tuas (Jurong), Changi, Sembawang

Organisation

Five Commands: Fleet, Naval Diving Unit, Coastal, Naval Logistics and Training.
Fleet: First Flotilla (six Victory, six Sea Wolf).
Third Flotilla (four LSTs, Fast Craft at Civil Squadron).
Coastal Command: (11 Fearless, four Bedok, 12 PBs)
Coastal Command operates five unmanned Giraffe 100 air/surface surveillance radar sites at Changi, Pedra Branca, St John's Island, Sultan Shoal Lighthouse and Raffles Lighthouse. Air and surface track data is passed to HQ RSN.

Prefix to Ships' Names

RSS

Special Forces

Singapore's special forces include the Naval Diving Unit, Singapore Army Special Operations Force and Singapore Police Special Tactics and Rescue unit.

Police Coast Guard

The Police Coast Guard is a unit of the Singapore Police Force and was first established in 1924. Its role is to maintain coastal security within Singapore territorial waters and to support the Singapore Armed Forces in emergencies. Its four regional commands are Brani (SE sector), Gul (SW sector), Seletar (NE sector) and Lim Chu Kang (NW sector). The PCG HQ moved to a new site at Brani (near Sentosa) on 20 March 2006. The Coastal Patrol Squadron and Special Task Squadron operate under central control. All vessels have Police Coast Guard on the superstructure and a white-red-white diagonal stripe on the hull except for Interceptor craft which have dark blue hulls with grey superstructures. Personnel numbers are about 1,000.

Strength of the Fleet

Type	*Active*	*Building (Projected)*
Submarines	4	2
Frigates	6	–
Missile Corvettes	6	–
Offshore Patrol Vessels	11	–
Inshore Patrol Craft	12	–
Minehunters	4	–
LSL/LPD	4	–
LCMs	4	–

SUBMARINES

0 + 2 VÄSTERGÖTLAND (A 17) CLASS (SSK)

Name	*No*	*Builders*	*Laid down*	*Launched*	*Commissioned*
– (ex-*Västergötland*)	–	Kockums, Malmö	10 Jan 1983	17 Sep 1986	27 Nov 1987
– (ex-*Hälsingland*)	–	Kockums, Malmö	1 Jan 1984	31 Aug 1987	20 Oct 1988

Displacement, tons: 1,500 surfaced; 1,600 dived
Dimensions, feet (metres): 198.5 × 20 × 18.4 *(60.5 × 6.1 × 5.6)*
Main machinery: Diesel-Stirling-electric; 2 Hedemora V12A/15 diesels; 2,200 hp(m) *(1.62 MW)*; 2 Kockums Stirling Mk III AIP; 204 hp *(150 kW)*; 1 Jeumont Schneider motor; 1,800 hp(m) *(1.32 MW)*; 1 shaft; LIPS prop
Speed, knots: 10 surfaced; 20 dived
Complement: 27 (5 officers)

Torpedoes: 6—21 in *(533 mm)* tubes. 12 WASS Black Shark; wire (fibre-optic cable) guided; active/passive homing to 50 km *(27 n miles)* at 50 kt; warhead 250 kg; swim-out discharge.
3—15.75 in *(400 mm)* tubes. 6 FFV Type 431/451; anti-submarine; wire-guided; active/passive homing to 20 km *(10.8 n miles)* at 25 kt; warhead 45 kg shaped charge or a small charge anti-intruder version is available
Mines: 12 Type 47 swim-out mines in lieu of torpedoes.
Countermeasures: ESM: Argo AR-700-S5; or Condor CS 3701; intercept.
Weapons control: Ericsson IPS-17 (Sesub 900A) TFCS.
Radars: Navigation: Terma; I-band.
Sonars: Atlas Elektronik CSU 83; hull-mounted; passive search and attack; medium frequency.
Flank array; passive search; low frequency.

Programmes: Original design contract awarded by the Swedish Navy to Kockums, Malmö on 17 April 1978. Contract for construction signed 8 December 1981. Following discussions between the governments of Sweden and Singapore in 2005, both submarines are to be transferred to the Singapore Navy as part of a package that includes modernisation refits to incorporate Air-Independent Propulsion (AIP) systems prior to delivery. On entry into Singapore service in about 2010, the boats are likely to replace two of the Challenger class, also procured from Sweden, that entered service from 2000.
Modernisation: The modernisation package is expected to be similar to those given to the Södermanland class. This included the installation of Air Independent Propulsion (Stirling Mk 3 AIP) by the insertion of a 12 m plug in the pressure hull. Other work included the installation of a pressurised diver's lock-out in the base of the sail to facilitate special forces operations and a new climate control system. The Thales Optronics CK 038 periscope was upgraded with a thermal imaging camera and an improved image intensifier. A new active sonar suite, Subac, may also be installed.
Structure: Single hulled with an X-type rudder/after hydroplace design. Diving depth 300 m *(984 ft)*. Anechoic coating.
Operational: Sea trials of the first boat are likely to start in 2009.
Opinion: The A 14 submarines transferred to Singapore in the mid-1990s under projects Riken I and Riken II gave the Singapore Navy its first experience of submarine operations. The procurement of *Västergötland* and *Hälsingland* will offer a significant improvement in capability but may again serve as a stepping-stone towards procuring a class of next-generation submarines. In this respect, further collaboration with Sweden in its A 26 submarine programme is a possibility.

VÄSTERGÖTLAND CLASS *3/2004*, ***John Brodie*** / 1043520

CONQUEROR *3/2000*, ***Per Körnefeldt*** / 0084434

4 CHALLENGER (SJÖORMEN) CLASS (SSK)

Name	*Builders*	*Laid down*	*Launched*	*Commissioned*
CHALLENGER (ex-*Sjöbjörnen*)	Karlskronavarvet	1967	6 Aug 1968	28 Feb 1969
CENTURION (ex-*Sjöörmen*)	Kockums	1965	25 Jan 1967	31 July 1968
CONQUEROR (ex-*Sjölejonet*)	Kockums	1966	29 June 1967	16 Dec 1968
CHIEFTAIN (ex-*Sjohunden*)	Kockums	1966	21 Mar 1968	25 June 1969

Displacement, tons: 1,130 surfaced; 1,210 dived
Dimensions, feet (metres): 167.3 × 20 × 19 *(51 × 6.1 × 5.8)*
Main machinery: Diesel-electric; 2 Hedemora-Pielstick V12A/A2/15 diesels; 2,200 hp(m) *(1.62 MW)*; 1 ASEA motor; 1,500 hp(m) *(1.1 MW)*; 1 shaft
Speed, knots: 12 surfaced; 20 dived
Complement: 23 (7 officers)

Torpedoes: 4—21 in *(533 mm)* bow tubes. 10 FFV Type 613; anti-surface; wire-guided; passive homing to 15 km *(8.2 n miles)* at 45 kt; warhead 250 kg.
2—16 in *(400 mm)* tubes: 4 FFV Type 431; anti-submarine; wire-guided; active/passive homing to 20 km *(10.8 n miles)* at 25 kt; warhead 45 kg shaped charge.
Mines: Minelaying capability.
Weapons control: UDS SUBTICS.
Radars: Navigation: Terma; I-band.
Sonars: Plessey Hydra; hull-mounted; passive search and attack; medium frequency.

Programmes: It was announced on 23 September 1995 that a submarine would be acquired from Sweden for training purposes only. Three more of the same class acquired in July 1997 for conversion plus one more for spares.
Modernisation: A contract for new periscope systems was awarded to Kollmorgen Electro Optical in January 2005. Options include Model 76 and Model 90.
Structure: Albacore hull. Twin-decked. Diving depth, 150 m *(492 ft)*. Air conditioning added for tropical service, together with battery cooling.
Operational: *Challenger* re-launched on 26 September 1997, *Conqueror* and *Centurion* on 28 May 1999 and *Chieftain* on 22 May 2001. *Conqueror* was recommissioned in Singapore on 24 July 2000 and *Chieftain* on 24 August 2002. *Challenger* and *Centurion* remained in Sweden to support training until January 2004 when they were transported to Singapore. Ex-*Sjohasten* was also shipped as a source of spares. *Centurion* was recommissioned on 26 June 2004. The four submarines form 171 squadron. Based at Changi.

CONQUEROR *9/2000, Sattler/Steele* / 0105592

CONQUEROR *8/2006, Jürg Kürsener* / 1164545

FRIGATES

6 FORMIDABLE (PROJECT DELTA) CLASS (FFGHM)

Name	*No*	*Builders*	*Laid down*	*Launched*	*Commissioned*
FORMIDABLE	68	DCN, Lorient	14 Nov 2002	7 Jan 2004	5 May 2007
INTREPID	69	Singapore SB and Marine	8 Mar 2003	3 July 2004	5 Feb 2008
STEADFAST	70	Singapore SB and Marine	15 Nov 2003	28 Jan 2005	5 Feb 2008
TENACIOUS	71	Singapore SB and Marine	22 May 2004	15 July 2005	5 Feb 2008
STALWART	72	Singapore SB and Marine	12 Nov 2005	9 Dec 2005	16 Jan 2009
SUPREME	73	Singapore SB and Marine	17 May 2005	9 May 2006	16 Jan 2009

Displacement, tons: 3,200 full load
Dimensions, feet (metres): 374.0 × 52.5 × 16.4 *(114 × 16.0 × 5.0)*
Main machinery: CODAD; 4 MTU 20V 8000 M90 diesels; 48,276 hp *(36 kW)*; 2 shafts; cp props; bow thruster
Speed, knots: 27. **Range, n miles:** 4,000 at 15 kt
Complement: 71 + 15 aircrew

Missiles: SSM: 8 Boeing Harpoon ❶; active radar homing to 130 km *(70 n miles)* at 0.9 Mach; warhead 227 kg.
SAM: Eurosam SAAAM; 2 octuple Sylver A 43 VLS; 2 octuple Sylver A 50 VLS ❷ for MBDA Aster 15; command guidance active radar homing to 15 km *(8.1 n miles)* anti-missile and to 30 km *(16.2n miles)* anti-aircraft. 32 missiles.
Guns: 1 OTO Melara 3 in *(76 mm)*/62 Super rapid ❸; 120 rds/min to 16 km *(8.7 n miles)*; weight of shell 6 kg.
2—20 mm. 2—12.7 mm MGs.
Torpedoes: 6—324 mm (2 triple (recessed)) ❹ tubes. Eurotorp A 244/S Mod 3; anti-submarine; active/passive homing to 7 km *(3.8 n miles)* at 33 kt; warhead 34 kg (shaped charge).
Countermeasures: Decoys: 3 EADS NGDS 8-barrelled chaff ❺, IR and anti-torpedo decoy launchers.
ESM: RAFAEL C-PEARL-M; intercept.
Combat data systems: DSTA/ST Electronics system.
Weapons Control: 2 EADS Nagir 2000 optronic directors ❻.
Radars: Air/search: Thales Herakles 3-D radar multifunction ❼; E/F-band.
Surface search/Navigation: 2 Terma Scanter 2001 ❽; I-band.
Sonars: EDO 980 ALOFTS VDS; low frequency (2 kHz).
Helicopters: 1 S-70B Seahawk ❾.

Programmes: Ordered from DCN International on 6 March 2000. First steel cut for hulls two and three on 2 October 2002. Prime Contractor is Singapore's Defence Science and Technology Agency (DSTA) who are also leading combat system integration in partnership with ST Electronics.

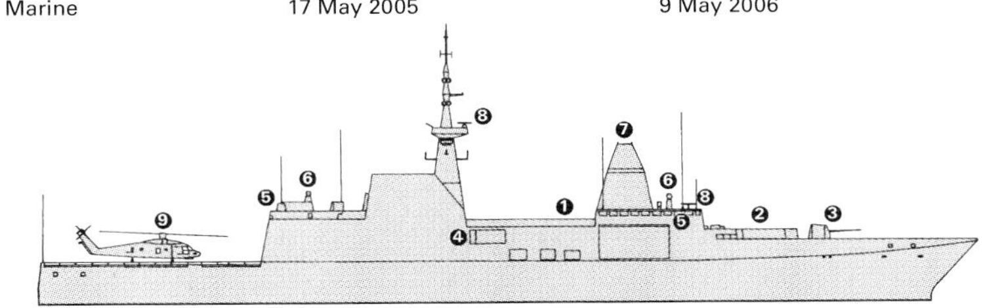

FORMIDABLE *(Scale 1 : 1,200), Ian Sturton* / 1153492

FORMIDABLE *5/2005, B Prézelin* / 1133566

Structure: Derived from La Fayette class but there are notable differences to accommodate the weapon and sensor fit. Two of the four VLS modules are reported to be Sylver A 50, capable of launching the longer Aster 30 area-defence missile. Aster 15 successfully launched from *Intrepid* on 3 April 2008.
Operational: The ships form 185 Squadron based at Changi.

STEADFAST *8/2008*, Michael Nitz* / 1353365

FORMIDABLE *10/2004, B Prézelin* / 1044523

CORVETTES

6 VICTORY CLASS (FSGM)

Name	*No*	*Builders*	*Launched*	*Commissioned*
VICTORY	P 88	Lürssen Werft, Bremen	8 June 1988	18 Aug 1990
VALOUR	P 89	Singapore SB and Marine	10 Dec 1988	18 Aug 1990
VIGILANCE	P 90	Singapore SB and Marine	27 Apr 1989	18 Aug 1990
VALIANT	P 91	Singapore SB and Marine	22 July 1989	25 May 1991
VIGOUR	P 92	Singapore SB and Marine	1 Dec 1989	25 May 1991
VENGEANCE	P 93	Singapore SB and Marine	23 Feb 1990	25 May 1991

Displacement, tons: 595 full load
Dimensions, feet (metres): 204.7 oa; 190.3 wl × 27.9 × 10.2 *(62.4; 58 × 8.5 × 3.1)*
Main machinery: 4 MTU 16V 538 TB93 diesels; 15,020 hp(m) *(11 MW)* sustained; 4 shafts
Speed, knots: 35
Range, n miles: 2,000 at 22 kt
Complement: 49 (8 officers)

Missiles: SSM: 8 McDonnell Douglas Harpoon (1); active radar homing to 130 km *(70 n miles)* at 0.9 Mach; warhead 227 kg.
SAM: 2 Octuple IAI/Rafael Barak I (2) radar or optical guidance to 10 km *(5.5 m)* at 2 Mach; warhead 22 kg.
Guns: 1 OTO Melara 3 in *(76 mm)*/62 Super Rapid (3); 120 rds/min to 16 km *(8.7 n miles)*; weight of shell 6 kg.
4 CIS 50 12.7 mm MGs.
Torpedoes: 6—324 mm Whitehead B 515 (2 triple) tubes (4). Whitehead A 244S; anti-submarine; active/passive homing to 7 km *(3.8 n miles)* at 33 kt; warhead 34 kg (shaped charge).
Countermeasures: Decoys: 2 Plessey Shield 9-barrelled chaff launchers (5). 4 Rafael (2 twin) long-range chaff launchers to be fitted below the bridge wings.
ESM: Elisra SEWS (6); intercept.
ECM: Rafael RAN 1101; (7) jammer.
Combat data systems: Elbit command system. SATCOM (8).
Weapons control: Elbit MSIS optronic director (9).

VICTORY *(Scale 1 : 600), Ian Sturton* / 0114802

Radars: Surface search: Ericsson/Radamec Sea Giraffe 150HC (10); G/H-band.
Navigation: Kelvin Hughes 1007; I-band.
Fire control: 2 Elta EL/M-2221(X) (11); I/J/K-band.
Sonars: Thomson Sintra TSM 2064; VDS (12); active search and attack.

Programmes: Ordered in June 1986 to a Lürssen MGB 62 design similar to Bahrain and UAE vessels.

Modernisation: Barak launchers fitted on either side of the VDS, together with a second fire-control radar on the platform aft of the mast and an optronic director on the bridge roof. Rudder roll stabilisation retrofitted to improve sea-keeping qualities. Unidentified EW antennae have been installed below RAN 1101.
Operational: Form 188 Squadron, part of the First Flotilla. Designated Missile Corvettes (MCV). First live Barak firing in September 1997.

VENGEANCE *5/2004, David Boey* / 1044508

VENGEANCE *7/2008*, John Mortimer* / 1353366

SHIPBORNE AIRCRAFT

Numbers/Type: 6 Sikorsky S-70B Seahawk.
Operational speed: 135 kt *(250 km/h)*.
Service ceiling: 10,000 ft *(3,050 m)*.
Range: 600 n miles *(1,110 km)*.
Role/Weapon systems: Contract placed 21 January 2005 for six new helicopters for operation from Formidable class frigates. Delivery by 2010. Roles ASW, ASV and surveillance. Weapons and sensors to be announced.

LAND-BASED MARITIME AIRCRAFT

Notes: (1) The Air Force also has 40 F-16D Block 52+, 28 F-5 S/T Tiger II and 20 F-16C.
(2) There are also six CH-47D used for maritime tasks and 20 AH-64D Apache Longbow.
(3) Plans to replace E-2C Hawkeye aircraft with four Gulfstream 550 (G 550) AEW aircraft were announced in May 2007.

Numbers/Type: 4 Northrop Grumman E-2C Hawkeye.
Operational speed: 323 kt *(598 km/h)*.
Service ceiling: 30,800 ft *(9,390 m)*.
Range: 1,000 n miles *(1,850 km)*.
Role/Weapon systems: Delivered in 1987 for air control and surveillance of shipping in sea areas around Singapore. Form 111 Squadron. Sensors: APS-138 radar; datalink for SSM targeting. Weapons: Unarmed.

HAWKEYE *9/2003, **David Boey*** / 0567531

Numbers/Type: 5 Fokker F50 Mk 2S Enforcer.
Operational speed: 220 kt *(463 km/h)*.
Service ceiling: 29,500 ft *(8,990 m)*.
Range: 2,700 n miles *(5,000 km)*.
Role/Weapon systems: In service from September 1995. Part of Air Force 121 Squadron but with mixed crews and under naval op con. One possibly modified for Sigint. Sensors: Texas Instruments APS-134(V)7 radar; GEC FLIR; Elta ESM. Jammer fitted under wing-tip. Weapons: Harpoon ASM; mines; A-244S torpedoes.

FOKKER F 50 *9/2003, **David Boey*** / 0567532

PATROL FORCES

2 RAFAEL PROTECTOR UNMANNED SURFACE VEHICLES (USV)

Displacement, tons: To be announced
Dimensions, feet (metres): 29.5 × ? × ? *(9.0 × ? × ?)*
Main machinery: 1 diesel; 1 waterjet propulsor
Speed, knots: 30+
Guns: 1 Mini-Typhoon stabilised 12.7 mm MG.
Weapons control: Toplite EO sensor pod.

Comment: Developed jointly by Rafael and Aeronautics Defense Systems, Protector was first revealed in June 2003. It is an unmanned patrol craft based on an 9 m Rigid Inflatable Boat (RIB) with composite-materials superstructure that encloses the sensor pod, navigation radar, GPS antenna and gyrostabilised inertial navigation system. Five video channels are used to transmit the outputs from the Toplite and two deck-mounted cameras back to a remote operator. The vessel also carries microphones and loudspeakers, allowing the operator to hail the crew of a suspicious vessel. With an endurance of about eight hours, it can be controlled by line-of-sight communications from ship or shore for various missions such as force protection, anti-terror surveillance and reconnaissance, mine warfare and electronic warfare. An unconfirmed number procured by the Singapore Navy in 2004 to support maritime security and interdiction operations in the Northern Arabian Gulf. They were operated by *RSS Resolution* during a deployment that ended in March 2005. The Singapore Navy also participates in the US Navy's Spartan technology demonstrator programme.

PROTECTOR *5/2005, **Guy Toremans*** / 1127050

11 FEARLESS CLASS (PCM/PGM)

Name	No	Builders	Launched	Commissioned
FEARLESS	94	Singapore STEC	18 Feb 1995	5 Oct 1996
BRAVE	95	Singapore STEC	9 Sep 1995	5 Oct 1996
GALLANT	97	Singapore STEC	27 Apr 1996	3 May 1997
DARING	98	Singapore STEC	27 Apr 1996	3 May 1997
DAUNTLESS	99	Singapore STEC	23 Nov 1996	3 May 1997
RESILIENCE	82	Singapore STEC	23 Nov 1996	7 Feb 1998
UNITY	83	Singapore STEC	19 July 1997	7 Feb 1998
SOVEREIGNTY	84	Singapore STEC	19 July 1997	7 Feb 1998
JUSTICE	85	Singapore STEC	18 Oct 1997	7 Feb 1998
FREEDOM	86	Singapore STEC	18 Oct 1997	22 Aug 1998
INDEPENDENCE	87	Singapore STEC	18 Apr 1998	22 Aug 1998

Displacement, tons: 500 full load
Dimensions, feet (metres): 180.4 × 28.2 × 8.9 *(55 × 8.6 × 2.7)*
Main machinery: 2 MTU 12V 595 TE90 diesels; 8,554 hp(m) *(6.29 MW)* sustained; 2 Kamewa water-jets
Speed, knots: 20
Range, n miles: 1,800 at 15 kt
Complement: 32 (5 officers)

Missiles: SAM: Matra Simbad twin launcher; Mistral; IR homing to 4 km *(2.2 n miles)*; warhead 3 kg.
Guns: 1 OTO Melara 3 in *(76 mm)*/62 Super Rapid; 120 rds/min to 16 km *(8.7 n miles)*; weight of shell 6 kg. 4 CIS 50 12.7 mm MGs.
1—25 mm Bushmaster (82).
Torpedoes: 6—324 mm Whitehead B515 (triple) tubes; (94-99) Whitehead A244S; active/passive homing to 7 km *(3.8 m)* at 33 kt; warhead 34 kg (shaped charge).
Countermeasures: Decoys: 2 GEC Marine Shield III 102 mm sextuple fixed chaff launchers.
ESM: Elisra NS-9010C; intercept.
Weapons control: ST 3100 WCS. Elbit MSIS optronic director.
Radars: Surface search and fire control: Elta EL/M-2228(X); I-band.
Navigation: Kelvin Hughes 1007; I-band.
Sonars: Thomson Sintra TSM 2362 Gudgeon; hull-mounted; active attack; medium frequency (94-99 only).
Towed array fitted in *Brave*.

Programmes: Contract awarded on 27 February 1993 for 12 patrol vessels to Singapore Shipbuilding and Engineering.
Structure: First six are ASW specialist ships. All have water-jet propulsion. Second batch were to have been fitted with Gabriel II SSMs but this plan has been shelved. MSIS director being fitted. *Fearless* modified with new EW radome on mainmast. Simbad SAM in *Brave* replaced by towed array and in *Resilience* by 25 mm Bushmaster. *Sovereignty* has deck crane to facilitate special forces operations.
Operational: All serve with Coastal Command. The first five form 189 Squadron and the second six 182 Squadron. *Unity* is to be used as a test bed for new technologies including an Indep 21 combat system. *Courageous* badly damaged in collision on 3 January 2003 and unlikely to be repaired.

SOVEREIGNTY *5/2004, **David Boey*** / 1044510

BRAVE (with VDS) *3/2004, **Bob Fildes*** / 1044509

RESILIENCE *8/2007, **Bob Fildes*** / 1353367

12 INSHORE PATROL CRAFT (PB)

FB 31–42

Displacement, tons: 20 full load
Dimensions, feet (metres): 47.6 × 13.8 × 3.6 *(14.5 × 4.2 × 1.1)*
Main machinery: 2 MAN D2848 LE 401 diesels; 1,341 hp(m) *(1 MW)*; 2 Hamilton 362 water-jets
Speed, knots: 30
Complement: 5
Guns: 1 — 40 mm grenade launcher. 1 — 12.7 mm MG. 2 — 7.62 mm MGs.
Radars: Surface search: Racal Decca; I-band.

Comment: Built by Singapore SBEC and delivered in 1990–91. Based at Tuas. Designated Fast Boats (FB). Some are kept in storage at Tuas. Similar to Police PT 1-19 class.

FB 35 *5/2007, Guy Toremans* / 1167801

AMPHIBIOUS FORCES

Notes: (1) The Tiger 40 hovercraft acquired in 1997 is beyond repair but the design may be used again for a repeat order.
(2) Trials of at least one hovercraft ACVI were reported in early 2005.

ACVI *5/2005, Guy Toremans* / 1127051

10 DIVING SUPPORT CRAFT (YTB)

Comment: Boston Whalers used by the Naval Diving Unit. Armed with 7.62 mm MGs and 40 mm grenade launchers.

BOSTON WHALER *8/2000, David Boey* / 0105601

100 LANDING CRAFT (LCVP/FCEP)

Displacement, tons: 4 full load
Dimensions, feet (metres): 44.6 × 12.1 × 2 *(13.6 × 3.7 × 0.6)*
Main machinery: 2 MAN D2866 LE diesels; 816 hp(m) *(600 kW)*; sustained; 2 Hamilton 362 water-jets
Speed, knots: 20. **Range, n miles**: 100 at 20 kt
Complement: 3
Military lift: 4 tons or 30 troops

Comment: Fast Craft, Equipment and Personnel (FCEP), built by Singapore SBEC from 1989 and are used to transport troops around the Singapore archipelago. They have a single bow ramp and can carry a rifle platoon. More than 25 are in service and the rest in storage. Have numbers in the 500 and 800 series except for those carried in LSTs.

LCVPs *8/2003, David Boey* / 0567534

4 RPL TYPE (LCU)

RPL 60–63

Displacement, tons: 151 standard
Dimensions, feet (metres): 120.4 × 28 × 5.9 *(36.7 × 8.5 × 1.8)*
Main machinery: 2 MAN D2540MLE diesels; 860 hp(m) *(632 kW)*; 2 Schottel props
Speed, knots: 10.7
Complement: 6
Military lift: 2 tanks or 450 troops or 110 tons cargo (fuel or stores)

Comment: First pair built at North Shipyard Point, second pair by Singapore SBEC. First two launched August 1985, next two in October 1985. Cargo deck 86.9 × 21.6 ft *(26.5 × 6.6 m)*. Bow ramp suitable for beaching.

RPL 60 *6/2001, John Mortimer* / 0126301

6 FAST INTERCEPT CRAFT (HSIC)

Displacement, tons: 12.5 full load
Dimensions, feet (metres): 47.6 × 9.4 × 4.4 *(14.5 × 2.85 × 1.35)*
Main machinery: Triple Seatek diesels coupled to Trimax drives
Speed, knots: 55+
Guns: 2 CIS 40 mm AGL.
2 CIS 50 12.7 mm MGs.
1 — 7.62 mm GPMG.
Radars: Raytheon SL 72.

Comment: Details are of craft used by Naval Diving Unit. The multistep planing hull design is similar to that in UK service. At least five other planing and wave-piercing craft are reported to be in service with special forces units.

FIC 145 *9/2002, David Boey* / 0554729

450 ASSAULT CRAFT (LCA)

Dimensions, feet (metres): 17.7 × 5.9 × 2.3 *(5.4 × 1.8 × 0.7)*
Main machinery: 1 outboard; 50 hp(m) *(37 kW)*
Speed, knots: 12
Military lift: 12 troops
Guns: 1—7.62 mm MG or 40 mm grenade launcher.

Comment: Built by Singapore SBEC. Man-portable craft which can carry a section of troops in the rivers and creeks surrounding Singapore island. Numbers are approximate.

ASSAULT CRAFT *9/1995, David Boey* / 0080588

30 LANDING CRAFT UTILITY (LCU)

300 series

Dimensions, feet (metres): 75.4 × 19.7 × 2.6 *(23 × 6 × 0.8)*
Main machinery: 2 MAN 2842 LZE diesels; 4,400 hp(m) *(3.23 MW)*; 2 Kamewa water-jets
Speed, knots: 20. **Range, n miles:** 180 at 15 kt
Complement: 4
Military lift: 18 tons
Guns: 2—12.7 mm MGs or 40 mm grenade launchers.

Comment: This is a larger and much faster version of the LCVPs. Construction started in 1993. Designated Fast Craft Utility (FCU).

LCU 394 *12/2007, Chris Sattler* / 1353370

4 ENDURANCE CLASS (LPDM)

Name	*No*	*Builders*	*Laid down*	*Launched*	*Commissioned*
ENDURANCE	207	Singapore Technologies Marine, Banoi	26 Mar 1997	14 Mar 1998	18 Mar 2000
RESOLUTION	208	Singapore Technologies Marine, Banoi	22 Oct 1997	1 Aug 1998	18 Mar 2000
PERSISTENCE	209	Singapore Technologies Marine, Banoi	3 Apr 1998	13 Mar 1999	7 Apr 2001
ENDEAVOUR	210	Singapore Technologies Marine, Banoi	15 Oct 1998	12 Feb 2000	7 Apr 2001

Displacement, tons: 8,500 full load
Dimensions, feet (metres): 462.6 pp × 68.9 × 16.4 *(141 × 21 × 5)*
Main machinery: 2 Ruston 16RK 270 diesels; 12,000 hp(m) *(8.82 MW)*; 2 shafts; Kamewa cp props; bow thruster
Speed, knots: 15
Range, n miles: 10,400 at 12 kt
Complement: 65 (8 officers)
Military lift: 350 troops; 18 tanks; 20 vehicles; 4 LCVP

Missiles: SAM: 2 Matra Simbad twin launchers for Mistral ❶; IR homing to 4 km *(2.2 n miles)*; warhead 3 kg. 2 Barak octuple launchers may be fitted in due course.
Guns: 1 Otobreda 76 mm/62 Super Rapid ❷; 120 rds/min to 16 km *(8.7 n miles)*; weight of shell 6 kg.
1—25 mm Bushmaster (can be fitted).
5—12.7 mm MGs.
Weapons control: CS Defense NAJIR 2000 optronic director ❸.
Radars: Air/surface search: Elta EL/M-2238 ❹; E/F-band.
Navigation: Kelvin Hughes Type 1007; I-band.
Helicopters: 2 Super Pumas.

Programmes: Ordered in September 1994 and confirmed in mid-1996.
Structure: US drive through design with bow and stern ramps. Single intermediate deck with three hydraulic ramps. Helicopter platform aft. Indal ASIST helo handling system. Dockwell for four LCUs and davits for four LCVPs. Two 25 ton cranes. Four 36 m self-propelled pontoons can be secured to winching points on the ships' sides. Protector unmanned surface vehicles were operated from *Resolution* in 2005.
Operational: *Endurance* completed the RSN's first round-the-world deployment in late 2000. *Resolution* deployed in November 2004 as part of coalition forces in northern Gulf. Based at Changi. Form 191 Squadron.

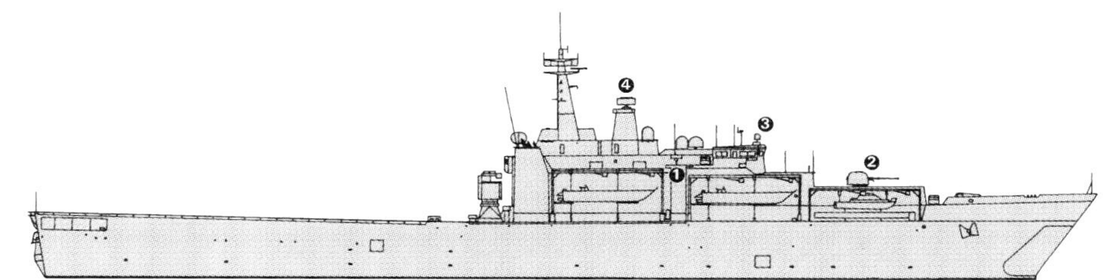

RESOLUTION *(Scale 1 : 1,200), Ian Sturton* / 1153491

RESOLUTION *12/2007, Chris Sattler* / 1353368

PERSISTENCE *10/2008*, Michael Nitz* / 1353369

MINE WARFARE FORCES

4 BEDOK (LANDSORT) CLASS (MINEHUNTERS) (MHC)

Name	*No*	*Builders*	*Launched*	*Commissioned*
BEDOK	M 105	Kockums/Karlskrona	24 June 1993	7 Oct 1995
KALLANG	M 106	Singapore Shipbuilding	29 Jan 1994	7 Oct 1995
KATONG	M 107	Singapore Shipbuilding	8 Apr 1994	7 Oct 1995
PUNGGOL	M 108	Singapore Shipbuilding	16 July 1994	7 Oct 1995

Displacement, tons: 360 full load
Dimensions, feet (metres): 155.8 × 31.5 × 7.5 *(47.5 × 9.6 × 2.3)*
Main machinery: 4 Saab Scania diesels; 1,592 hp(m) *(1.17 MW)*; coupled in pairs to 2 Voith Schneider props
Speed, knots: 15
Range, n miles: 2,000 at 10 kt
Complement: 31 (5 officers)

Guns: 1 Bofors 40 mm/70. 4—12.7 mm MGs.
Mines: 2 rails.
Weapons control: Thomson-CSF TSM 2061 Mk II minehunting and mine disposal system. Signaal WM20 director.
Radars: Navigation: Norcontrol DB 2000; I-band.
Sonars: Thomson-CSF TSM 2022; hull-mounted; minehunting; high frequency.

Programmes: Kockums/Karlskrona design ordered in February 1991. *Bedok* started trials in Sweden in December 1993, and was shipped to Singapore in early 1994 to complete. Prefabrication work done for the other three in Sweden with assembly and fitting out in Singapore at Benoi Basin.
Structure: GRP hulls. Two PAP 104 Mk V ROVs embarked. Racal Precision Navigation system. Two sets of Swedish SAM minesweeping system. Magnavox GPS.
Operational: Form 194 Squadron, based at Tuas.

PUNGGOL *4/2004, John Mortimer* / 1133564

BEDOK *2/2005, Chris Sattler* / 1133563

AUXILIARIES

Notes: (1) There is one Floating Dock with a lift of 600 tons. *FD 2* at Changi.
(2) A 2,700 ton oil rig supply ship MV *Kendrick*, built in Poland in 1985, is chartered to support submarine rescue operations. Additional roles include acting as a target ship for submarine torpedo firings and torpedo recovery.
(3) MV *Avatar*, a Ro-Ro vessel, is leased to support submarine rescue operations.
(4) It was announced on 14 March 2007 that ST Marine had been awarded a contract to provide a new Submarine Support and Rescue Vessel (SSRV) to replace *Kendrick* and *Avatar* in mid-2009. The new ship is to act as mothership for a DSAR-5 submarine rescue vehicle.

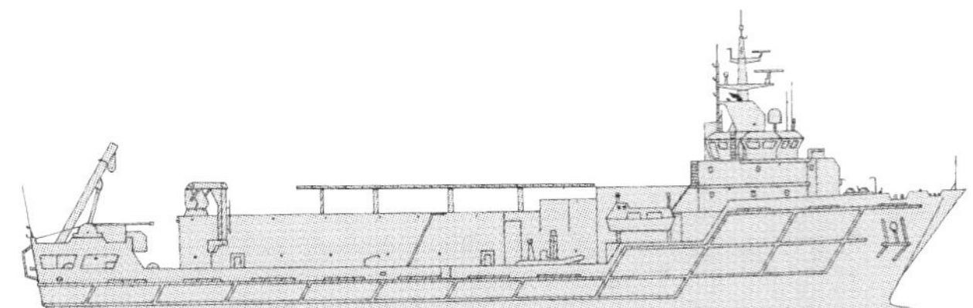

SSRV (indicative design) *(Scale 1 : 1,200), Ian Sturton* / 1166671

KENDRICK *8/2005, David Boey* / 1164538

AVATAR *3/2005, David Boey* / 1164537

POLICE COAST GUARD

12 SHARK CLASS (WPB)

HAMMERHEAD SHARK (ex-*Swift Archer*) PH 50 (ex-P 16)
MAKO SHARK (ex-*Swift Lancer*) PH 51 (ex-P 12)
WHITE SHARK (ex-*Swift Swordsman*) PH 52 (ex-P 14)
BLUE SHARK (ex-*Swift Combatant*) PH 53 (ex-P 18)
TIGER SHARK (ex-*Swift Knight*) PH 54 (ex-P 11)
BASKING SHARK (ex-*Swift Warrior*) PH 55 (ex-P 15)
SANDBAR SHARK (ex-*Swift Chieftain*) PH 56 (ex-P 23)
THRESHER SHARK (ex-*Swift Conqueror*) PH 57 (ex-P 21)
WHITETIP SHARK (ex-*Swift Warlord*) PH 58 (ex-P 17)
BLACKTIP SHARK (ex-*Swift Challenger*) PH 59 (ex-P 19)
GOBLIN SHARK (ex-*Swift Cavalier*) PH 60 (ex-P 20)
SCHOOL SHARK (ex-*Swift Centurion*) PH 61 (ex-P 22)

Displacement, tons: 45.7 full load
Dimensions, feet (metres): 74.5 × 20.3 × 5.2 *(22.7 × 6.2 × 1.6)*
Main machinery: 2 Deutz BA16M816 diesels; 2,680 hp(m) *(1.96 MW)* sustained; 2 shafts
Speed, knots: 32
Range, n miles: 550 at 20 kt; 900 at 10 kt
Complement: 15
Guns: 1 Oerlikon 20 mm GAM-BO1. 2 CIS 90 12.7 mm MGs.
Radars: Surface search: Decca 1226; I-band.

Comment: Built by Singapore SBEC and all completed 20 October 1981 for the Navy. First four transferred from the Navy on 15 February 1993, second four on 8 April 1994, last four on 7 November 1996. All to be fitted with ARPA radar in due course. Employed on territorial waters patrol.

HAMMERHEAD SHARK *4/2004, Bob Fildes* / 1044518

2 COMMAND CRAFT (WPB)

MANTA RAY PT 20 **EAGLE RAY** PT 30

Dimensions, feet (metres): 65.6 × 19.7 × 3.3 *(20.0 × 6.0 × 1.0)*
Main machinery: 2 MTU 16V 2000 M90 diesels; 2 Hamilton 521 water-jets
Speed, knots: 30
Complement: 5
Guns: 2—7.62 mm MGs.

Comment: Built by Asia-Pacific Geraldton, Singapore to a Geraldton, Australia design. These command craft are larger versions of the 18 m patrol craft.

MANTA RAY *4/2002, David Boey* / 0554731

25 PATROL CRAFT (WPB)

PT 21–29 PT 31–39 PT 61–67

Dimensions, feet (metres): 59.1 × 17.7 × 3 *(18 × 5.4 × 0.9)*
Main machinery: 2 MTU 16V 2000M 90 diesels; 2 Hamilton 521 waterjets
Speed, knots: 40
Complement: 5
Guns: 2—7.62 mm MGs.

Comment: 18 patrol craft built by Geraldton Boats, Australia in 1999. A further seven patrol craft delivered late 2000.

PT 34 *8/2007, Bob Fildes* / 1353371

19 PATROL CRAFT (WPB)

PT 1–19

Displacement, tons: 20 full load
Dimensions, feet (metres): 47.6 × 13.8 × 3.9 *(14.5 × 4.2 × 1.2)*
Main machinery: 2 MAN D2542MLE diesels; 1,076 hp(m) *(791 kW)*; or MTU 12V 183TC91 diesels; 1,200 hp(m) *(882 kW)* maximum; 2 shafts
Speed, knots: 30. **Range, n miles:** 310 at 22 kt
Complement: 4 plus 8 spare berths
Guns: 1—7.62 mm MG.
Radars: Surface search: Furuno or Racal Decca Bridgemaster; I-band.

Comment: First 13 completed by Singapore SBEC between January and August 1984, two more completed February 1987 and eight more (including two Command Boats) in 1989. Of aluminium construction. Four are operated by Customs and Excise. There are differences in the deckhouses between earlier and later vessels. Employed on patrol duties in southern territorial waters.

PT 12 *7/2007, Bob Fildes* / 1353372

11 INTERCEPTOR CRAFT (PBF)

SAILFISH PK 10
SPEARFISH PK 20
WHITE MARLIN PK 21
SILVER MARLIN PK 22
STRIPED MARLIN PK 23
BLACK MARLIN PK 24
BLUE MARLIN PK 25
JUMPING MARLIN PK 26
BILLFISH PK 30
SWORDFISH PK 40
SPIKEFISH PK 50

Dimensions, feet (metres): 42 × 10.5 × 1.6 *(12.8 × 3.2 × 0.5)*
Main machinery: 3 Mercruiser 502 Magnum diesels; 3 shafts
Speed, knots: 50
Complement: 5
Guns: 1—7.62 mm MG.

Comment: First five built locally and delivered in 1995. Colours have been changed to dark blue hulls and grey superstructures, to make the craft less visible at sea. Six more ordered from Pro Marine/North Shipyard in 1999 to a slightly different design, with twin outboard motors.

SWORDFISH *4/2002, David Boey* / 0554733

WHITE MARLIN *1/2000, David Boey* / 0105606

HARBOUR CRAFT

Comment: There are large numbers of harbour craft, many of them armed, with PC numbers. These include four RHIBs with Yamaha 200 hp outboards capable of 43 kt, and with pennant numbers PJ 1-4.

RHIB *9/2002, David Boey* / 1044506

0 + 10 DAMEN STAN PATROL 3507 (PATROL CRAFT) (WPB)

Displacement, tons: 140 full load
Dimensions, feet (metres): 114.8 × 24.3 × 5.7 *(35.0 × 7.4 × 1.75)*
Main machinery: 3 MTU 16V 4000 M71 diesels; 3 Hamilton waterjets
Speed, knots: 38
Range, n miles: 900 at 15 kt
Complement: 14 (plus 20 passengers)
Guns: 1—25 mm. 2—12.7 mm MGs.

Comment: Following initiation of the bid process in December 2004, five bids had been received by 18 April 2005. Contract for ten new craft, to replace the Shark class, awarded to Damen Shipyards, Singapore, on 20 June 2006. The craft are of aluminium monohull construction. The contract includes the provision of training, spares and other services. The first of class is to enter service in 2009 with the completion of the programme by 2011. The craft are to be equipped with night-vision equipment.

DAMEN 3507 *6/2006, Damen Shipyards* / 1164497

32 FAST RESPONSE CRAFT (PBF)

PC 201–232

Dimensions, feet (metres): 37.7 × 10.8 × 1.6 *(11.5 × 3.3 × 0.5)*
Main machinery: 3 Mercury outboard motors; 750 hp *(560 kW)*
Speed, knots: 40

Comment: Order placed August 2000 with Asia Pac Geraldton for 20 craft delivered in 2002. A further twelve craft were later added.

PC 209 *4/2002, David Boey* / 0554734

CUSTOMS

Notes: Customs Craft include CE 1-4 and CE 5-8, the latter being sisters to PT 1 Police Craft.

CE 8 *10/2002, Mick Prendergast* / 0533877

Slovenia

Country Overview

Formerly a constituent republic of Yugoslavia, the Republic of Slovenia proclaimed its independence in 1991. Situated in south-eastern Europe, it is bordered to the north by Austria and Hungary, to the south by Croatia and to the west by Italy. With an area of 7,820 square miles, it has a short 25 n mile coastline with the Adriatic Sea on which the port of Koper is located. The capital and largest city is Ljubljana. Territorial waters (12 n miles) are claimed.

Headquarters Appointments

Chief of General Staff:
Lieutenant General Albin Gutman

Headquarters Appointments—*continued*

Chief of Navy Detachment:
Commander Ivan Žnidar

General

Navy formed in January 1993.

Personnel

2009: 56

Bases

Koper

PATROL FORCES

1 SUPER DVORA MK II (PBF)

Name	*No*	*Builders*	*Commissioned*
ANKARAN	HPL 21	IAI Ramta	Aug 1996

Displacement, tons: 58 full load
Dimensions, feet (metres): 82 × 18.4 × 3.6 *(25 × 5.6 × 1.1)*
Main machinery: 2 MTU 12V 396TE94 diesels; 4,570 hp(m) *(3.36 MW)*; 2 ASD 15 surface drives
Speed, knots: 45. **Range, n miles:** 700 at 30 kt
Complement: 10 (5 officers)
Guns: 2 Oerlikon 20 mm; 2—7.62 mm MGs.
Weapons control: Elop MSIS optronic director.
Radars: Surface search: Raytheon; I-band.

Comment: Delivered in August 1996 at Isola base. Plans for a second craft have been cancelled.

ANKARAN *6/1999, Slovenian Navy* / 0080597

0 + 1 SVETLYAK (PROJECT 1041Z) CLASS (PATROL SHIP) (PBO)

Displacement, tons: 375 full load
Dimensions, feet (metres): 159.1 × 30.2 × 11.5 *(48.5 × 9.2 × 3.5)*
Main machinery: 3 diesels; 14,400 hp(m) *(10.58 MW)*; 3 shafts
Speed, knots: 31. **Range, n miles:** 2,200 at 13 kt
Complement: 36 (4 officers)
Missiles: SAM: SA-N-10 Igla quad launcher; manual aiming; IR homing to 6 km *(3.2 n miles)* at 1.5 Mach; warhead 1.5 kg.
Guns: 1—30 mm/65 AK 306; 6 barrels; 3,000 rds/min combined to 2 km; 12 missiles. 2—14.5 mm.
Radars: Surface search: To be announced.
Navigation: To be announced.

Comment: It was announced on 18 July 2008 that one Svetlyak patrol ship is to be acquired from Russia, reportedly as part of a deal to recover Yugoslav era debt. The ships are based on those in service in the Russian Border Guard. Similar craft have been exported Vietnam.

POLICE

Notes: In addition there is a 40 kt cabin cruiser *Sinji Galeb* (P 101) and two RIBs.

1 HARBOUR PATROL CRAFT (PBF)

Name	*No*	*Builders*	*Commissioned*
LADSE	P 111	Aviotechnica	21 June 1995

Displacement, tons: 44 full load
Dimensions, feet (metres): 65.3 × 16.4 × 3 *(19.9 × 5 × 0.9)*
Main machinery: 2 MTU 8V 396TE84 diesels; 2,400 hp(m) *(1.76 MW)*; 2 shafts
Speed, knots: 40
Range, n miles: 270 at 38 kt
Complement: 10
Guns: 1—7.62 mm MG.
Radars: Surface search: I-band.

Comment: Acquired from Italy in 1995.

LADSE *10/1997* / 0080598

Solomon Islands

Country Overview

Formerly a British protectorate, the Solomon Islands gained independence in 1978. Its head of state is the British sovereign, who is represented by a Governor-General. Situated in the southwest Pacific Ocean, east of New Guinea, the country comprises more than 35 islands and numerous atolls which extend some 650 n miles from east to west and includes most of the Solomon Islands group. The six main islands are: Guadalcanal, Malaita, New Georgia, San Cristobal (now Makira), Santa Isabel and Choiseul. Vella Lavella, Ontong Java, Rennell, Bellona and the Santa Cruz islands are also part of the group, together with the Florida, Russell, Reef and Duff island groups. Honiara, on Guadalcanal, is the capital and principal port. An archipelagic state, territorial seas (12 n miles) are claimed. An Exclusive Economic Zone (EEZ) (200 n miles) is also claimed but limits have not been fully defined by boundary agreements. Patrol boats are operated by the National Surveillance and Reconnaissance Force (NSRF).

Headquarters Appointments

Director of Maritime forces:
Chief Superintendent Eddie Tokuru

Bases

Honiara (HQ NSRF)

Personnel

2009: 60 (14 officers)

Prefix to Ships' Names

RSIPV

POLICE

2 PACIFIC CLASS (LARGE PATROL CRAFT) (PB)

Name	*No*	*Builders*	*Commissioned*
LATA	03	Australian Shipbuilding Industries	3 Sep 1988
AUKI	04	Australian Shipbuilding Industries	2 Nov 1991

Displacement, tons: 162 full load
Dimensions, feet (metres): 103.3 × 26.6 × 7.5 *(31.5 × 8.1 × 2.3)*
Main machinery: 2 Caterpillar 3516TA diesels; 4,400 hp *(3.28 MW)* sustained; 2 shafts
Speed, knots: 20
Range, n miles: 2,230 at 12 kt
Complement: 14 (1 officer)
Guns: 3—12.7 mm MGs.
Radars: Surface search: Furuno 8100-D; I-band.

Comment: Built under the Australian Defence Co-operation Programme. Training, operational and technical assistance provided by the Royal Australian Navy. Aluminium construction. Nominal endurance of 10 days. The Australian government has extended the Pacific Patrol Boat programme but, following suspension of most of support of the Solomon Islands' craft in 2001, an overdue half-life refit was not completed for *Auki* until 2002. Life-extension refit for *Lata* completed at Townsville in 2005. *Auki* is due for a similar refit in 2010.

AUKI *6/2006, Chris Sattler* / 1164971

LATA *6/2006, Chris Sattler* / 1164970

1 INSHORE PATROL CRAFT (PBR)

JACKPOT

Comment: Details are not known.

JACKPOT *4/2007, Chris Sattler* / 1335212

South Africa

Country Overview

The Republic of South Africa is bordered to the north by Namibia, Botswana, Zimbabwe, Mozambique and Swaziland. With an area of 472,731 square miles, it has a 1,512 n mile coastline with the south Atlantic and Indian Oceans. South Africa also has sovereignty over the Prince Edward Islands which lie some 950 n miles south-east of Port Elizabeth. The independent country of Lesotho forms an enclave in the eastern part of the country. The administrative capital of South Africa is Pretoria and the judicial capital is Bloemfontein. Cape Town is the legislative capital and a prominent port. There are further ports at Mossel Bay, Port Elizabeth, East London, Durban, Saldanha, and Richards Bay. Territorial seas (12 n miles) are claimed. It also claims a 200 n mile EEZ but its limits have not been fully defined.

Headquarters Appointments

Chief of the Navy:
Vice Admiral J Mudimu
Chief of Naval Staff:
Rear Admiral M Magalefa
Flag Officer Fleet:
Rear Admiral R W Higgs

Personnel

(a) 2009: 4,728 naval
(b) 2,266 (Public Service Act Personnel)

Prefix to Ships' Names

SAS (South African Ship)

Bases

Simon's Town (main); Durban (naval station); Port Elizabeth (naval station).
Saldanha Bay (ratings' training), Gordon's Bay (officer training).

DELETIONS

Patrol Forces

2007 *Makhanda*

SUBMARINES

3 TYPE 209/1400 MOD (SA) CLASS (SSK)

Name	*No*	*Builders*	*Laid down*	*Launched*	*Commissioned*
MANTHATISI	S 101	Howaldswerke, Kiel	22 May 2001	15 June 2004	3 Nov 2005
CHARLOTTE MAXEKE	S 102	Thyssen Nordseewerke, Emden	12 Nov 2003	4 May 2005	14 Mar 2007
QUEEN MODJADJI I	S 103	Thyssen Nordseewerke, Emden	Nov 2004	14 Mar 2007	30 Jan 2008

Displacement, tons: 1,454 surfaced; 1,594 dived
Dimensions, feet (metres): 201.5 × 24.7 × 18.8 *(62 × 7.6 × 5.8)*
Main machinery: Diesel electric: 4 MTU 12V 396 diesels; 3,800 hp(m) *(2.8 MW)*; 4 alternators; 1 Siemens motor; 5,032 hp(m) *(3.7 MW)*; 1 shaft
Speed, knots: 10 surfaced; 21.5 dived

Complement: 30
Torpedoes: 8—21 in *(533 mm)* bow tubes. 14 torpedoes.
Countermeasures: ESM: Grintek Avitronics; intercept.
Weapons control: STN Atlas ISUS 90 TFCS.
Radars: Surface search: I-band.
Sonars: STN Atlas CSU-90; hull mounted and flank arrays.

Programmes: Being acquired from the German Submarine Consortium. Final approval given on 15 September 1999. Contract signed on 7 July 2000. *Manthatisi* arrived at Simon's Town on 7 April 2006, *Charlotte Maxeke* on 26 April 2007 and *Queen Modjadji I* on 22 May 2008.
Structure: Diving depth 250 m *(820 ft)*. Zeiss optronic mast.

QUEEN MODJADJI I — *4/2008*, Michael Nitz* / 1335825

CHARLOTTE MAXEKE — *3/2008*, M Declerck* / 1335824

MANTHATISI — *2/2006, Michael Nitz* / 1158714

FRIGATES

4 VALOUR CLASS (MEKO A-200 SAN) (FFGHM)

Name	No	Builders	Laid down	Launched	Commissioned
AMATOLA	F 145	Blohm + Voss, Hamburg	2 Aug 2001	6 June 2002	16 Feb 2006
ISANDLWANA	F 146	Howaldswerke, Kiel	26 Oct 2001	5 Dec 2002	27 July 2006
SPIOENKOP	F 147	Blohm + Voss, Hamburg	28 Feb 2002	6 June 2003	16 Feb 2007
MENDI	F 148	Howaldswerke, Kiel	28 June 2002	15 June 2004	20 Mar 2007

Displacement, tons: 3,590 full load
Dimensions, feet (metres): 397 × 53.8 × 20.3 (121 × 16.4 × 6.2)
Main machinery: CODAG; 1 GE LM 2500 gas turbine 26,820 hp(m) *(20 MW)*; 2 MTU 16V 1163 TB93 diesels 16,102 hp(m) *(11.84 MW)*; 2 shafts; LIPS cp props; 1 LIPS LJ210E waterjet (centreline)
Speed, knots: 28
Range, n miles: 7,700 at 15 kt
Complement: 100 plus 20 spare

Missiles: SSM: 8 MBDA Exocet MM 40 Block 2 ❶; inertial cruise; active radar homing to 70 km *(40 n miles)* at 0.9 Mach; warhead 165 kg.
SAM: Denel Umkhonto 16 cell VLS ❷ inertial guidance with mid-course guidance and IR homing to 12 km *(6.5 n miles)* at 2.4 Mach; warhead 23 kg.
Guns: 1 Otobreda 76 mm/62 compact ❸.
2 LIW DPG 35 mm (twin) ❹. 2 Oerlikon 20 mm Mk 1. 2 Reutech 12.7 mm MGs.
Countermeasures: Decoys: 2 Super Barricade chaff launchers ❺.
CESM: Grintek EWASION.
RESM: Avitronics/Sysdel.
Combat data systems: ADS CMS.
Weapons control: 2 Reutech RTS 6400 optronic trackers.
Radars: Air/surface search: Thales MRR ❻ 3D; G-band.
Fire control: 2 Reutech RTS 6400 ❼; I/J-band.
Navigation/helo control: 2 Racal Bridgemaster E ❽; I-band.
Sonars: Thomson Marconi 4132 Kingklip; hull mounted, active search; medium frequency.

Helicopters: 1 Super Lynx ❾ from 2007.

Programmes: Contract for four ships, with option for one further, signed on 3 December 1999 with ESACC which includes Blohm + Voss, HDW, TRT, African Defence Systems and Thomson-CSF. Contract effective 28 April 2000. *Amatola* arrived at Simon's Town on 4 November 2003 for weapon systems integration by African Defence Systems. The fourth ship, *Mendi*, was commissioned in early 2007. An option for a fifth ship is unlikely to be exercised.
Structure: The design includes radar and IR signature reduction measures. Exhaust gases are expelled just above the waterline.
Modernisation: Exocet MM 40 Block 2 to be replaced by Block 3 missiles. Installation of a bow-thruster to improve low-speed manoeuvring is under consideration. The 76 mm gun may be replaced by a 127 mm or navalised 155 mm gun.

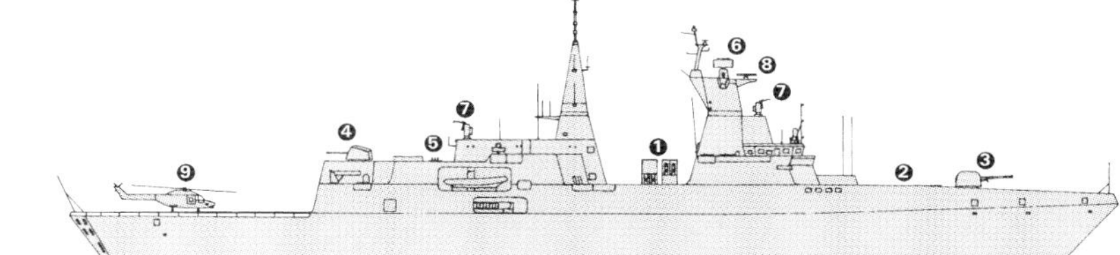

AMATOLA *(Scale 1 : 1,200), Ian Sturton* / 1159221

ISANDLWANA *5/2008*, Guy Toremans* / 1335823

AMATOLA *5/2008*, M Declerck* / 1335822

SPIOENKOP *9/2009*, Michael Nitz* / 1335821

SHIPBORNE AIRCRAFT

Numbers/Type: 4 Agusta-Westland Super Lynx 300.
Operational speed: 120 kt *(222 km/h)*.
Service ceiling: 10,000 ft *(3,048 m)*.
Range: 320 n miles *(593 km)*.
Role/Weapon systems: Ordered on 14 August 2003 for delivery in 2007. Surveillance. Sensors: Telephonics APS-143 B(V)3 radar; ESM: Sea Raven 118; Cumulus Leo Mk II FLIR. Weapons: Unarmed (torpedoes and ASM may be fitted in future upgrades).

SUPER LYNX *3/2008*, Guy Toremans* / 1335820

Numbers/Type: 8 Aerospatiale SA 330E/H/J Oryx.
Operational speed: 139 kt *(258 km/h)*.
Service ceiling: 15,750 ft *(4,800 m)*.
Range: 297 n miles *(550 km)*.
Role/Weapon systems: Support helicopter; allocated by SAAF for naval duties and can be embarked in *Drakensberg*. Sensors: Doppler navigation with search radar. Weapons: Unarmed but can mount Armscor 30 mm Rattler.

ORYX *9/2008*, Michael Nitz* / 1335819

LAND-BASED MARITIME AIRCRAFT

Notes: Alouette utility helicopters have been replaced by Agusta A-109.

Numbers/Type: 5 Douglas Turbodaks.
Operational speed: 161 kt *(298 km/h)*.
Service ceiling: 24,000 ft *(7,315 m)*.
Range: 1,390 n miles *(2,575 km)*.
Role/Weapon systems: A number of Dakotas has been converted for MR/SAR and other tasks. Additional fuel tanks extend the range to 2,620 n miles *(4,800 km)*. Sensors: Elta M-2022 search radar and FLIR; Sysdel ESM; sonobuoy acoustic processor. Weapons: Unarmed.

DOUGLAS DC-3 *6/2003, South African Navy* / 0568890

PATROL FORCES

Notes: (1) It is planned to acquire an initial batch of six 80-95 m offshore patrol vessels to replace the Warrior and River classes. The ships are to be built between 2011–16 in a South African shipyard. To be armed with a 76 mm gun, and possibly a short-range air-defence system, the ships are to be capable of operating helicopters.
(2) As a result of experience in peacekeeping operations, an Operational Boat Squadron has been established to support the Army in peacekeeping, in other operations on lakes and rivers and in coastal security operations. Fifteen new 10 m craft are to be acquired to replace or supplement the current inventory of Namacurra craft.

2 WARRIOR (EX-MINISTER) CLASS (PATROL SHIP) (PG)

Name	*No*	*Builders*	*Commissioned*
ISAAC DYOBHA (ex-*Frans Erasmus*)	P 1565	Sandock Austral, Durban	27 July 1979
GALESHEWE (ex-*Hendrik Mentz*)	P 1567	Sandock Austral, Durban	11 Feb 1983

Displacement, tons: 430 full load
Dimensions, feet (metres): 204 × 25 × 8 *(62.2 × 7.8 × 2.4)*
Main machinery: 4 Maybach MTU 16V 965 TB91 diesels; 15,000 hp(m) *(11 MW)* sustained; 4 shafts
Speed, knots: 32
Range, n miles: 1,500 at 30 kt; 3,600+ at economical speed
Complement: 52 (7 officers)

Guns: 2 OTO Melara 3 in *(76 mm)*/62 compact; 85 rds/min to 16 km *(8.7 n miles)*; weight of shell 6 kg; 500 rounds per gun.
2 LIW Mk 1 20 mm. 2—12.7 mm MGs.

Countermeasures: Decoys: 4 ACDS launchers for chaff.
ESM: Delcon (ADS/Sysdel) EW system.
ECM: Elta Rattler; jammer.
Combat data systems: Air/surface search: ADS Diamant (after upgrade). Mini action data automation with Link.
Radars: Elta EL/M 2208; E/F-band.
Fire control: Selenia RTN 10X; I/J-band.

Programmes: Contract signed with Israel in late 1974 for this class, similar to Saar 4 class. Three built in Haifa and reached South Africa in July 1978. The ninth craft launched late March 1986. Three more improved vessels of this class were ordered but subsequently cancelled. The last of the class was finally christened in March 1992. Pennant numbers restored to the ships side and stern in 1994.
Modernisation: Ship life extension programme included a new communications refit, improvements to EW sensors, a third-generation target designation assembly, a computer-assisted action information system served by datalinks, improvements to fire control, and a new engine room monitoring system. P 1565 completed upgrade in April 1999, P 1567 in March 2000 and P 1569 in mid-2000.
Operational: All are based at Simon's Town. Likely to be decommissioned in 2009. Skerpioen missiles have been removed.

GALESHEWE *9/2008*, Michael Nitz* / 1335818

3 T CRAFT CLASS (PB)

Name	*No*	*Builders*	*Commissioned*
TOBIE	P 1552	T Craft International, Cape Town	18 July 2003
TERN	P 1553	T Craft International, Cape Town	18 July 2003
TEKWANE	P 1554	T Craft International, Cape Town	22 July 2003

Displacement, tons: 36 full load
Dimensions, feet (metres): 72.2 × 23 × 3 *(22 × 7 × 0.9)*
Main machinery: 2 ADE 444TI 12V diesels; 2,000 hp *(1.5 MW)*; 2 Hamilton waterjets
Speed, knots: 32. **Range, n miles**: 530 at 22 kt
Complement: 16 (1 officer)
Guns: 1—12.7 mm MG.
Weapons control: Hesis optical director.
Radars: Surface search: Racal Decca; I-band.

Comment: Twin hulled catamarans of GRP sandwich construction. Capable of carrying up to 15 people. Originally ordered in mid-1991 but not fully commissioned until 2003. Carries an RIB in the stern well. Three of this type built for Israel in 1997. *Tekwane* based at Durban, and the other two at Simon's Town.

TOBIE ***9/2008*, Michael Nitz*** / 1335817

21 NAMACURRA CLASS (INSHORE PATROL CRAFT) (PB)

Y 1500 series

Displacement, tons: 5 full load
Dimensions, feet (metres): 29.5 × 9 × 2.8 *(9 × 2.7 × 0.8)*
Main machinery: 2 Yamaha outboards; 380 hp(m) *(279 kW)*
Speed, knots: 32. **Range, n miles**: 180 at 20 kt
Complement: 4
Guns: 1—12.7 mm MG. 2—7.62 mm MGs.
Depth charges: 1 rack.
Radars: Surface search: Furuno; I-band.

Comment: Built in South Africa in 1980–81. Can be transported by road. Two transferred to Malawi in 1988 and 2008 and Y 1506 has sunk at sea. Y 1501 and Y 1510 donated to Namibia on 29 November 2002 and Y 1507 and Y 1530 donated to Mozambique in 2004. Two further craft donated to the Angolan Navy in 2006. Based at Simon's Town, Durban, Cape Town, Saldanha Bay, Gordon's Bay, Port Elizabeth and East London. Three are operated on Lake Tanganyika as part of a peace-keeping force in Burundi.

NAMACURRA ***2/2008*, Guy Toremans*** / 1335816

MINE WARFARE FORCES

Notes: Mine countermeasures capability is likely to be replaced by autonomous underwater vehicles rather than by specialist ships.

3 RIVER CLASS (COASTAL MINEHUNTERS) (MHC)

Name	*No*	*Builders*	*Commissioned*
UMKOMAAS (ex-*Navors I*)	M 1499	Abeking & Rasmussen/Sandock Austral	13 Jan 1981
UMZIMKULU (ex-*Navors III*)	M 1142	Sandock Austral	30 Oct 1981
UMHLOTI (ex-*Navors IV*)	M 1212	Sandock Austral	15 Dec 1981

Displacement, tons: 380 full load
Dimensions, feet (metres): 157.5 × 27.9 × 8.2 *(48 × 8.5 × 2.5)*
Main machinery: 2 MTU 12V 652 TB81 diesels; 4,515 hp(m) *(3.32 MW)*; 2 Voith Schneider props
Speed, knots: 16. **Range, n miles**: 2,000 at 13 kt
Complement: 40 (7 officers)
Guns: 1 Oerlikon 20 mm GAM-BO1. 2—12.7 mm MGs. 2—7.62 mm MGs.
Countermeasures: MCM: 2 PAP 104 remote-controlled submersibles.
Radars: Navigation: Decca; I-band.
Sonars: Klein VDS; side scan; high frequency.

Comment: Ordered in 1978 as Research Vessels to be operated by the Navy for the Department of Transport. The lead ship *Navors I* was shipped to Durban from Germany in the heavy lift ship *Uhenfels* in June 1980 for fitting out, shortly followed by the second. The last pair were built in Durban. The vessels were painted blue with white upperworks and formed the First Research Squadron. Painted grey and renamed in 1982 but continued to fly the national flag and not the naval ensign. The prefix RV was only changed to SAS on 3 February 1988 when they were formally accepted as naval ships. Minehunting capability could be enhanced by substituting the diving container on the after deck with lightweight mechanical and acoustic sweeping gear. Carry an RIB and a decompression chamber. M1499 refitted in 2002. M 1213 placed in reserve in 2005 and unlikely to be re-activated. The remaining three are to continue in service until 2010.

UMKOMAAS ***9/2008*, Michael Nitz*** / 1335815

SURVEY AND RESEARCH SHIPS

Notes: It is planned to acquire a new hydrographic survey ship to replace *Protea*. The ship is likely to be built in South Africa, in parallel with but distinct from the offshore patrol ship project, and is planned to enter service in about 2015.

1 HECLA CLASS (AGSH)

Name	*No*	*Builders*	*Commissioned*
PROTEA	A 324	Yarrow (Shipbuilders) Ltd	23 May 1972

Displacement, tons: 2,733 full load
Dimensions, feet (metres): 260.1 × 49.1 × 15.6 *(79.3 × 15 × 4.7)*
Main machinery: Diesel-electric; 3 MTU diesels; 3,840 hp *(2.68 MW)* sustained; 3 generators; 1 motor; 2,000 hp *(1.49 MW)*; 1 shaft; cp prop; bow thruster
Speed, knots: 14
Range, n miles: 12,000 at 11 kt
Complement: 124 (10 officers)
Guns: 2—12.7 mm MGs.
Radars: Navigation: Racal Decca; I-band.
Helicopters: 1 Alouette III.

Comment: Laid down 20 July 1970. Launched 14 July 1971. Equipped for hydrographic survey with limited facilities for the collection of oceanographical data and for this purpose fitted with special communications equipment, Polaris survey system, survey launches *Malgas* and *Seemeeu* and facilities for helicopter operations. Hull strengthened for navigation in ice and fitted with a passive roll stabilisation system. New engines and full overhaul in 1995–96. Carries EGNG sidescan sonar and two survey boats. Fitted for two 20 mm guns.

PROTEA ***3/2008*, Frank Findler*** / 1335810

1 ANTARCTIC SURVEY AND SUPPLY VESSEL (AGOBH)

Name	*Builders*	*Launched*	*Commissioned*
S A AGULHAS	Mitsubishi, Shimonoseki	30 Sep 1977	31 Jan 1978

Measurement, tons: 5,353 gross
Dimensions, feet (metres): 358.3 × 59 × 19 *(109.2 × 18 × 5.8)*
Main machinery: 2 Mirrlees-Blackstone K6 major diesels; 6,600 hp *(4.49 MW)*; 1 shaft; bow and stern thrusters
Speed, knots: 14
Range, n miles: 8,200 at 14 kt
Complement: 40 plus 92 spare berths
Radars: Navigation: Racal Decca; I-band.
Helicopters: 2 SA 330J Puma.

Comment: Red hull and white superstructure. A Department of Environmental Affairs vessel, civilian manned and operated by Smit Pentow Marine. Major refit March to October 1992; 25 ton crane moved forward, transverse thrusters and roll damping fitted, improved navigation and communications equipment. A hinged hatch has been fitted at the stern to recover towed equipment.

AGULHAS ***5/2008*, M Declerck*** / 1335814

AUXILIARIES

Notes: It is planned to acquire two Strategic Support Ships to enter service from about 2014. The primary function is to transport, land and support some 1,500 troops with up to 350 vehicles either by sealift or by a combination of helicopters and landing craft. An LHD design is likely to be required to fulfil this and wider missions of disaster relief and logistic support. A third ship, configured as a replenishment ship, is planned to replace *Drakensberg* in about 2017.

1 FLEET REPLENISHMENT SHIP (AORH)

Name	*No*	*Builders*	*Launched*	*Commissioned*
DRAKENSBERG	A 301	Sandock Austral, Durban	24 Apr 1986	11 Nov 1987

Displacement, tons: 6,000 light; 12,500 full load
Dimensions, feet (metres): 482.3 × 64 × 25.9 *(147 × 19.5 × 7.9)*
Main machinery: 2 diesels; 16,320 hp(m) *(12 MW)*; 1 shaft; cp prop; bow thruster
Speed, knots: 20+
Range, n miles: 8,000 at 15 kt
Complement: 96 (10 officers) plus 10 aircrew plus 22 spare
Cargo capacity: 5,500 tons fuel; 750 tons ammunition and dry stores; 2 Lima LCUs
Guns: 4 Oerlikon 20 mm GAM-BO1. 8—12.7 mm MGs.
Helicopters: 2 SA 330H/J Oryx.

Comment: The largest ship built in South Africa and the first naval vessel to be completely designed in that country. In addition to her replenishment role she is employed on SAR, patrol and surveillance with a considerable potential for disaster relief. There are two 10-ton cranes to lower/recover LCUs or Namacurra craft. Two abeam positions and astern fuelling, jackstay and vertrep. Two helicopter landing spots, one forward and one astern. Main secondary role is the transport of consumables, but can also be used to support small craft and transport a limited number of troops.

DRAKENSBERG *5/2008*, M Declerck* / 1335813

6 LIMA CLASS (LCU)

Displacement, tons: 7.3 full load
Dimensions, feet (metres): 29.8 × 11.6 × 2.3 *(9.1 × 3.55 × 0.7)*
Main machinery: 2 outboards; 400 hp *(298 kW)*
Speed, knots: 38
Range, n miles: 120 at 26 kt
Complement: 3

Comment: Built in 2003 by Stingray Marine, Cape Town. GRP construction. Capable of carrying 24 troops or 2.5 tons of cargo. Two craft can be carried in *Drakensberg*.

L 27 *8/2003, Helmoed-Römer Heitman* / 0530510

TUGS

Notes: There is also a harbour tug *De Neys*.

1 COASTAL TUG (YTB)

DE MIST

Displacement, tons: 275 full load
Dimensions, feet (metres): 112.5 × 25.6 × 11.1 *(34.3 × 7.8 × 3.4)*
Main machinery: 2 Mirlees-Blackstone diesels; 2,440 hp *(1.82 MW)*; 2 Voith-Schneider props
Speed, knots: 12
Complement: 11

Comment: Completed by Dorbyl Long, Durban on 23 December 1978.

DE MIST *7/2006, Robert Pabst* / 1305213

1 COASTAL TUG (YTB)

UMALUSI (ex-*Golden Energy*)

Displacement, tons: 315 full load
Dimensions, feet (metres): 98.5 × 32.8 × 17.1 *(30 × 10 × 5.2)*
Main machinery: 2 Caterpillar V6 diesels
Speed, knots: 10
Complement: 10

Comment: Completed in 1995 by Jaya Holding Ltd. Acquired from Taikong Trading Company in January 1997.

UMALUSI *3/2008*, M Declerck* / 1335812

2 HARBOUR TUGS (YAG/YTB)

INDLOVU **TSHUKUDU**

Displacement, tons: 110 full load
Dimensions, feet (metres): 67.3 × 19.8 × 8.9 *(20.5 × 6.04 × 2.7)*
Main machinery: 2 Cummins KTA19M4 diesels; 1,400 hp *(1.05 MW)*; fixed props with Kort nozzles
Speed, knots: 11
Complement: 6

Comment: Built by Farocean Marine, Cape Town and delivered in April 2006. Principal role to assist submarine berthing but also employed as multirole tenders.

INDLOVU *5/2008*, Guy Toremans* / 1335811

GOVERNMENT MARITIME FORCES

Notes: (1) The Department of Environmental Affairs has three research vessels: *Ellen Khuzwayo* (600 grt, delivered in September 2007), *Africana* of 2,471 grt and *Algoa* of 760 grt. There are also three fishery protection vessels: *Patella, Pelagus* and *Jasus.* A contract was signed in 2003 with Damen Shipyards, Gorinchem for the construction of one offshore and three inshore Fishery and Environmental Protection vessels. *Sarah Baartman* is an 83 m offshore patrol vessel whose design is based on the Dutch fishery patrol vessel *Barend Biesheuve.* Built at Damen Shipyards, Okean (Ukraine) and outfitted at Royal Schelde Yard, Vlissingen, delivery was made in June 2004. *Lilian Ngoyi, Ruth First* and *Victoria Mxenge* are three 47 m inshore patrol vessels whose design is based on the Damen Stan Patrol 4207 in service with UK Customs and the Jamaican Coast Guard. Built by Farocean Marine, Cape Town, deliveries were made in November 2004, February 2005 and May 2005 respectively. There is also a 14 m interception craft *Florence Mkhize.*
(2) A 50 m trawler, *Eagle Star,* is used as a training ship for the Department of Environmental Affairs.

RUTH FIRST *3/2008*, M Declerck* / 1335826

ELLEN KHUZWAYO *8/2007, Robert Pabst* / 1305212

Spain

ARMADA ESPAÑOLA

Country Overview

The Kingdom of Spain is a constitutional monarchy that occupies the greater part of the Iberian Peninsula in southwest Europe. It is bordered to the north by France and Andorra and to the west by Portugal. It has a 2,678 n mile coastline with the Atlantic Ocean and Mediterranean Sea. With a total area of 194,897 square miles, the country comprises the mainland, the Balearic Islands in the Mediterranean and the Canary Islands in the Atlantic Ocean. There are also two small exclaves in Morocco, Ceuta and Melilla and three island groups near the Moroccan coast, Peñón de Vélez de la Gomera, the Alhucemas and the Chafarinas. The British dependency of Gibraltar is situated at the southern extremity of Spain. Madrid is the capital and largest city while Barcelona, Algeciras, Valencia and Bilbao are the principal ports. Territorial seas (12 n miles) and an EEZ (200 n miles) are claimed.

Headquarters Appointments

Chief of the Naval Staff:
Admiral Sebastián Zaragoza Soto
Second Chief of the Naval Staff:
Vice Admiral Manuel Rebollo García
Chief of Fleet Support:
Admiral Miguel Ángel Beltrán Bengoechea
Chief of Naval Personnel:
Admiral Emilio José Nieto Manso

Commands

Commander-in-Chief of the Fleet (ALFLOT):
Admiral Fernando Armada Vadillo
Commander-in-Chief, Maritime Action (ALMART):
Admiral Juan Carlos Muñoz Delgado Díaz del Río
Commander, Spanish Maritime Forces (SPMARFOR):
Vice Admiral José Francisco Palomino Ulla
Commander, Logistic Support (Cartagena):
Vice Admiral Manuel Otero Penelas
Commander, Logistic Support (Cadiz):
Vice Admiral Juan Francisco Serón Martínez
Commander, Logistic Support (Ferrol):
Vice Admiral Francisco Cañete Muñoz
Commander-in-Chief, Canary Islands Zone (ALCANAR):
Vice Admiral Juan Tortosa Saavedra
Marines General Commander (COMGEIM):
Major General Juan Antonio Chicharro Ortega
Commander, Fleet Task Group (COMGRUFLOT):
Rear Admiral Santiago Bolibar Piñeiro
Commander, Northern Forces (AMARFER):
Rear Admiral Gonzalo Sirvent Zaragoza
Commander, Straits Forces (AMARDIZ):
Rear Admiral Fernando Hernándex Moreno

Diplomatic Representation

Naval Attaché in Brasilia:
Captain Francisco Avilés Beriguistain
Naval Attaché in Lisbon:
Captain Juan Pablo Estrada Madariaga
Naval Attaché in London and Dublin:
Captain José Joaquín Crespo Páramo
Naval Attaché in Paris:
Commander Luis Fernando Serrano Huici
Naval Attaché in Rabat:
Commander Manuel Caridad Villaverde
Naval Attaché in Rome:
Commander Antonio González Llanos López
Naval Attaché in Santiago, Lima and La Paz:
Captain Antonio Manuel Pérez Fernández

Diplomatic Representation — *continued*

Naval Attaché in Washington:
Captain Juan Carlos San Martin Naya
Naval Attaché in Oslo, Stockholm and Helsinki:
Captain Ricardo Galán Moreno
Naval Attaché in Bangkok, Manila and Singapore:
Captain José Manuel Verdugo Páez
Naval Attaché in Pretoria:
Colonel (Marines) Juan Ángel López Díaz
Naval Attaché in Athens:
Captain Angel Cabrera Juega
Naval Attaché in Kuala Lumpur:
Captain Felipe Juste Pérez

Personnel

2009: Navy: 14,093 (2,594 officers)
Marines: 5,098 (497 officers)

Bases

Naval Zones are being re-organised into a single Area. Headquarters are to be in Cartagena with subordinate commands in Ferrol, Cádiz and Las Palmas.
Ferrol: Cantabrian Zone HQ-Ferrol arsenal, support centre at La Graña, naval school at Marín, Pontevedra.
Cádiz: Straits Zone HQ-La Carraca arsenal, fleet command HQ and naval air base at Rota, amphibious base at Puntales. Marines Brigade (TEAR) HQ at San Fernando, Cádiz.
Cartagena: Maritime Action, HQ-Cartagena arsenal, underwater weapons and divers school at La Algameca; support base at Mahón, Minorca and at Soller and Porto Pi, Majorca, submarine weapons schools at La Algameca and Porto Pi base, Majorca. Naval Infantry school at Cartagena.
Las Palmas: Canaries Zone HQ-Las Palmas arsenal.

Naval Air Service

The Naval Air Arm Flotilla is based at Rota.

Type	*Escuadrilla*
AB 212	3
Cessna Citation II	4
Sikorsky SH-3D/G Sea King	5
Sikorsky SH-3E Sea King (AEW)	
Hughes 500M (Training)	6
EAV-8B Harrier II/Harrier Plus	9
Sikorsky SH-60B Seahawk	10

Guardia Civil del Mar

Started operations in 1992. For details, see end of section.

Fleet Deployment

(1) Fleet (under Commander-in-Chief, Fleet)
  (a) *Principe de Asturias* (based at Rota)
  (b) Escuadrillas de Escoltas:
    31st Squadron; 1 Baleares class plus 4 Álvaro de Bazan class (based at Ferrol)
    41st Squadron; 6 Santa María class (based at Rota)
  (c) Amphibious Forces: (1 LST and 2 LPD at Rota, small units at Puntales, Cádiz).
    Naval infantry at San Fernando.
  (d) Fuerza de Medidas contra Minas: (based at Cartagena)
    6 MSCs, 1 MCCS

Fleet Deployment — *continued*

  (e) Flotilla de Submarinos: (based at Cartagena)
    All submarines
(2) Flotilla de Aeronaves: (based at Rota)
  (a) Maritime Action units (under Commander-in-Chief, Maritime Action)
  (b) Cantabrian Zone:
    1 Ocean Tug, 8 Tugs, 4 Patrol Ships, 5 Large Patrol Craft, 7 Coastal Patrol Craft, 1 Logistics Support Ship, 4 Sail Training Ships, 5 Training Craft
  (c) Straits Zone:
    1 oiler, 6 Oceanographic Ships, 1 Sail Training Ship, 4 Fast Attack Craft, 1 Transport, 1 Ocean Tug, 7 Tugs, 1 Water-boat
  (d) Mediterranean Zone:
    4 Fast Attack Craft, 4 Patrol Ships, 1 Water-boat, 7 Tugs, 1 Frogman Support Ship
  (e) Canaries Zone:
    4 Patrol Ships, 2 Tugs
  (f) Minor auxiliaries. Identified by 'Y' pennant numbers and form Tren Naval.

Prefix to Ships' Names

SPS (Spanish Ship)

Strength of the Fleet

Type	*Active*	*Building (Planned)*
Submarines—Patrol	4	4 (4)
Aircraft Carriers	1	–
Frigates	10	1 (1)
Offshore Patrol Vessels	13	4 (6)
Coastal Patrol Craft	20	–
Inshore Patrol Craft	3	–
LHD	–	1
LPDs	2	–
LSTs	2	–
Minehunters	6	–
MCM support ship	1	–
Survey and Research Ships	7	–
Replenishment Tankers	2	1
Tankers	8	–
Transport Ships	4	–
Training Ships	15	–
Ocean Tugs	2	–
Submarine Rescue	1	(1)

DELETIONS

Submarines

2006 *Marsopa*

Frigates

2006 *Andalucia, Extremadura*
2009 *Asturias*

Amphibious Warfare Forces

2006 L 072

PENNANT LIST

Submarines

S 71	Galerna
S 72	Siroco
S 73	Mistral
S 74	Tramontana

Aircraft Carriers

R 11	Príncipe de Asturias

Frigates

F 81	Santa María
F 82	Victoria
F 83	Numancia
F 84	Reina Sofía
F 85	Navarra
F 86	Canarias
F 101	Alvaro de Bazán
F 102	Almirante Don Juan de Borbón
F 103	Blas de Lezo
F 104	Mendez Nuñez
F 105	Roger de Lauria (bldg)

Patrol Forces

P 11	Barceló
P 12	Laya
P 14	Ordóñez
P 15	Acevedo
P 16	Cándido Pérez
P 21	Anaga
P 22	Tagomago
P 23	Marola
P 24	Mouro
P 25	Grosa
P 26	Medas
P 27	Izaro
P 28	Tabarca
P 30	Bergantín
P 31	Conejera
P 32	Dragonera
P 33	Espalmador
P 34	Alcanada
P 41	Meteoro (bldg)
P 42	Rayo (bldg)
P 43	Relámpago (bldg)
P 44	Torna (bldg)
P 61	Chilreu
P 62	Alboran
P 63	Arnomendi
P 64	Tarifa
P 71	Serviola
P 72	Centinela
P 73	Vigía
P 74	Atalaya
P 75	Descubierta
P 76	Infanta Elena
P 77	Infanta Cristina
P 78	Cazadora
P 79	Vencedora
P 81	Toralla
P 82	Formentor
P 201	Cabo Fradera

Amphibious Forces

L 41	Hernán Cortés
L 42	Pizarro
L 51	Galicia
L 52	Castilla
L 61	Rey Juan Carlos I (bldg)

Mine Warfare Forces

M 11	Diana
M 31	Segura
M 32	Sella
M 33	Tambre
M 34	Turia
M 35	Duero
M 36	Tajo

Survey Ships

A 23	Antares
A 24	Rigel
A 31	Malaspina
A 32	Tofiño
A 33	Hespérides
A 52	Las Palmas
A 91	Astrolabio
A 92	Escandallo
A 111	Alerta

Auxiliaries

A 01	Contramaestre Casado
A 04	Martín Posadillo
A 05	El Camino Español
A 11	Marqués de la Ensenada
A 14	Patiño
A 15	Cantabria (bldg)
A 20	Neptuno
A 51	Mahón
A 53	La Graña
A 65	Marinero Jarano
A 66	Condestable Zaragoza
A 71	Juan Sebastián de Elcano
A 72	Arosa
A 74	La Graciosa
A 75	Sisargas
A 76	Giralda
A 77	Sálvora
A 78	Peregrina
A 82	Contramaestre Navarrete
A 83	Contramaestre Sánchez Fernández
A 84	Contramaestre Antero
A 85	Contramaestre Lamadrid
A 101	Mar Caribe
A 121	Guardiamarina Barrutia
A 122	Guardiamarina Chereguini
A 123	Guardiamarina Rull
A 124	Guardiamarina Salas

SUBMARINES

0 + 4 (4) S 80A CLASS (SSK)

Name	*No*	*Builders*	*Laid down*	*Launched*	*Commissioned*
–	S 81	Navantia, Cartagena	13 Dec 2007	2011	2013
–	S 82	Navantia, Cartagena	2008	2012	2014
–	S 83	Navantia, Cartagena	2009	2013	2014
–	S 84	Navantia, Cartagena	2010	2014	2015

Displacement, tons: 2,198 surfaced; 2,426 dived
Dimensions, feet (metres): 233.0 × 23.9 × 20.3 *(71.0 × 7.3 × 6.2)*
Main machinery: Diesel electric; 3 MTU 16V 396 SE 84L diesels; 4,825 hp *(3.6 MW)*; 1 motor; 3,500 hp *(2.6 MW)*; 1 shaft; AIP (UTC ethanol reformer fuel cell) system; 300 kW
Speed, knots: 12 surfaced; 20 dived
Complement: 32 plus 8

Missiles: SLCM: Raytheon Tomahawk Block IV; land attack.
SSM: Boeing Sub Harpoon.
Torpedoes: 6—21 in *(533 mm)* bow tubes. Atlas Elektronik DM2A4 torpedoes.
Countermeasures: ESM: To be announced.
Decoys: 20 ejectors.
Weapons control: Lockheed Martin/Navantia system.
Radars: Indra Aries-S; I-band.
Sonars: SAES Solarsub towed passive array. Lockheed-Martin integrated sonar suite including cylindrical, passive ranging, flank, acoustic intercept and mine-detection arrays.

Programmes: Approval for the procurement of four submarines was given by the Spanish Cabinet on 5 September 2003. Contract awarded on 25 March 2004. Navantia (55 per cent) and Lockheed Martin contracted to develop core combat system in July 2005. This includes the sonar suite and command and control module. A second batch of four boats may follow. Steel for the first-of-class cut in June 2006 and for the second on 13 December 2006.
Structure: The design includes Air-Independent Propulsion (AIP) accommodated in a 7.9 m section. Single hull construction. There is an attack periscope (with thermal imager) and a surveillance periscope (comprising HDTV, colour camera, thermal imager and laser rangefinder). There is a lock-in/lock-out hatch for special forces.
Operational: Endurance of 15 days at 4 kt on AIP propulsion is required.

S 80 (artist's impression) *12/2007, Navantia* / 1294252

4 GALERNA (AGOSTA) (S 70) CLASS (SSK)

Name	*No*	*Builders*	*Laid down*	*Launched*	*Commissioned*
GALERNA	S 71	Bazán, Cartagena	5 Sep 1977	5 Dec 1981	22 Jan 1983
SIROCO	S 72	Bazán, Cartagena	27 Nov 1978	13 Nov 1982	5 Dec 1983
MISTRAL	S 73	Bazán, Cartagena	30 May 1980	14 Nov 1983	5 June 1985
TRAMONTANA	S 74	Bazán, Cartagena	10 Dec 1981	30 Nov 1984	27 Jan 1986

Displacement, tons: 1,490 surfaced; 1,740 dived
Dimensions, feet (metres): 221.7 × 22.3 × 17.7 *(67.6 × 6.8 × 5.4)*
Main machinery: Diesel-electric; 2 SEMT-Pielstick 16 PA4 V 185 VG diesels; 3,600 hp(m) *(2.7 MW)*; 2 Jeumont Schneider alternators; 1.7 MW; 1 motor; 4,600 hp(m) *(3.4 MW)*; 1 cruising motor; 32 hp(m) *(23 kW)*; 1 shaft
Speed, knots: 12 surfaced; 20 dived; 17.5 sustained
Range, n miles: 8,500 snorting at 9 kt; 350 dived on cruising motor at 3.5 kt
Complement: 54 (6 officers)

Torpedoes: 4—21 in *(533 mm)* tubes. 20 combination of (a) ECAN L5 Mod 3/4; dual purpose; active/passive homing to 9.5 km *(5.1 n miles)* at 35 kt; warhead 150 kg; depth to 550 m *(1,800 ft)*.
(b) ECAN F17 Mod 2; wire-guided; active/passive homing to 20 km *(10.8 n miles)* at 40 kt; warhead 250 kg; depth 600 m *(1,970 ft)*.
Mines: 19 can be carried if torpedo load is reduced to 9.
Countermeasures: ESM: THORN EMI/Inisel Manta E; radar warning.
Weapons control: DLA-2A TFCS.
Radars: Surface search: Thomson-CSF DRUA 33C; I-band.
Sonars: Thomson Sintra DSUV 22; passive search and attack; medium frequency.
Thomson Sintra DUUA 2A/2B; active search and attack; 8 or 8.4 kHz active.
DUUX 2A/5; passive; rangefinding. Eledone; intercept.
SAES Solarsub towed passive array; low frequency.

Programmes: First two ordered 9 May 1975 and second pair 29 June 1977. Built with some French advice. About 67 per cent of equipment and structure from Spanish sources.
Modernisation: Modernised with improved torpedo fire control, new ESM and IR enhanced periscopes. New main batteries installed with central control monitoring. *Galerna* started in April 1993 and completed in late 1994, *Siroco* in mid-1995, *Tramontana* in early 1997, and *Mistral* in 2000. The plan to fit SSM has been shelved. Solarsub towed arrays are being fitted to all of the class during overhauls. At least one submarine capable of being fitted with Dry Dock Shelter.
Structure: Diving depth, 300 m *(984 ft)*.
Operational: Endurance, 45 days. Based at Cartagena.

MISTRAL ***4/2008*, B Prézelin*** / 1335827

GALERNA ***8/2004, E & M Laursen*** / 1044546

AIRCRAFT CARRIERS

1 PRINCIPE DE ASTURIAS CLASS (CV)

Name	*No*	*Builders*	*Laid down*	*Launched*	*Commissioned*
PRÍNCIPE DE ASTURIAS (ex-*Almirante Carrero Blanco*)	R 11	Bazán, Ferrol	8 Oct 1979	22 May 1982	30 May 1988

Displacement, tons: 17,188 full load
Dimensions, feet (metres): 642.7 oa; 615.2 pp × 79.7 × 30.8 *(195.9; 187.5 × 24.3 × 9.4)*
Flight deck, feet (metres): 575.1 × 95.1 *(175.3 × 29)*
Main machinery: 2 GE LM 2500 gas turbines; 46,400 hp *(34.61 MW)* sustained; 1 shaft; LIPS cp prop; 2 motors; 1,600 hp(m) *(1.18 MW)*; retractable prop
Speed, knots: 25 (4.5 on motors)
Range, n miles: 6,500 at 20 kt
Complement: 555 (90 officers) plus 208 (Flag Staff (7 officers) and Air Group)

Guns: 4 Bazán Meroka Mod 2A/2B 12-barrelled 20 mm/120 ❶; 3,600 rds/min combined to 2 km.
2 Rheinmetall 37 mm saluting guns.
Countermeasures: Decoys: 4 Loral Hycor SRBOC 6-barrelled fixed Mk 36; IR flares and chaff to 4 km *(2.2 n miles)*.
SLQ-25 Nixie; towed torpedo decoy.
US Prairie/Masker; hull noise/blade rate suppression.
ESM/ECM: Elettronica Nettunel; intercept and jammers.

Combat data systems: Tritan Digital Command and Control System NTDS; Links 11 and 14. Marconi Matra SCOT 3 Secomsat ❷. SSR-1, WSC-3 (UHF).
Weapons control: 4 Selenia directors (for Meroka). Radamec 2000 series.
Radars: Air search: Hughes SPS-52C/D ❸; 3D; E/F-band; range 439 km *(240 n miles)*.
Surface search: ISC Cardion SPS-55 ❹; I/J-band.
Aircraft control: ITT SPN-35A ❺; J-band.
Fire control: 4 Sperry/Lockheed VPS 2 ❻; I-band (for Meroka).
RTN 11L/X; I/J-band; missile warning.
Selenia RAN 12L (target designation); I/J-band.
Tacan: URN 25.

Fixed-wing aircraft: 6-12 AV-8B Harrier II/Harrier Plus.
Helicopters: 6-10 SH-3 Sea Kings; 2-4 AB 212EW.

Programmes: Ordered on 29 June 1977. Associated US firms were Gibbs and Cox, Dixencast, Bath Iron Works and Sperry SM. Commissioning delays caused by changes to command and control systems and the addition of a Flag Bridge.
Modernisation: After two years' service some modifications were made to the port after side of the island, to improve briefing rooms and provide sheltered parking space for FD vehicles. Also improved accommodation has been added on for six officers and 50 specialist ratings. A mid-life refit is expected when the Strategic Projection ship enters service.
Structure: Based on US Navy Sea Control Ship design. 12° ski-jump of 46.5 m. Two flight deck lifts, one right aft. Two LCVPs carried. Two pairs of fin stabilisers. The hangar is 24,748 sq ft *(2,300 m²)*. The Battle Group Commander occupies the lower bridge. Two saluting guns have been mounted on the port quarter.
Operational: Three Sea Kings have Searchwater AEW radar. Aircraft complement could be increased to 37 (parking on deck) in an emergency but maximum operational number is 29 (17 in hangar, 12 on deck). A typical air wing includes eight/ten AV-8B/AV-8B Plus, five SH-3 (including two AEW) and three/four AB-212. Based at Rota.
Sales: Modified design built for Thailand.

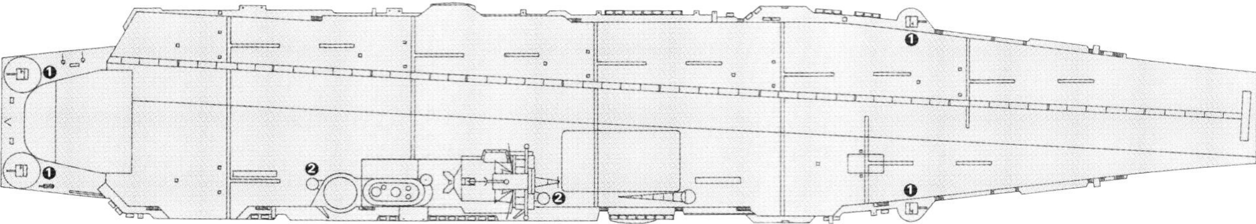

PRÍNCIPE DE ASTURIAS *(Scale 1 : 1,200), Ian Sturton* / 0130391

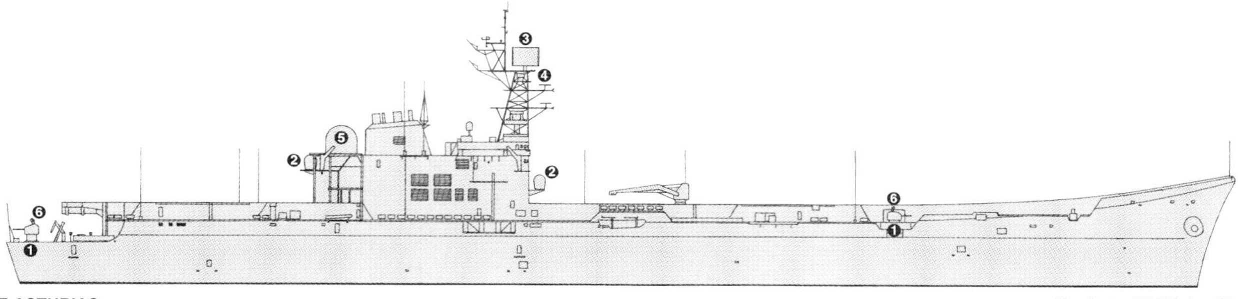

PRÍNCIPE DE ASTURIAS *(Scale 1 : 1,200), Ian Sturton* / 0506330

PRÍNCIPE DE ASTURIAS *6/2006, B Prézelin* / 1040726

PRÍNCIPE DE ASTURIAS *6/2005, Per Körnefeldt* / 1153450

PRÍNCIPE DE ASTURIAS *6/2003, Spanish Navy* / 0570978

FRIGATES

Notes: Studies for a new frigate class, to replace the Santa María class from about 2020, are in progress.

4 + 1 (1) ALVARO DE BAZÁN CLASS (FFGHM)

Name	*No*	*Builders*	*Laid down*	*Launched*	*Commissioned*
ALVARO DE BAZÁN	F 101	Navantia, Ferrol	14 June 1999	31 Oct 2000	19 Sep 2002
ALMIRANTE DON JUAN DE BORBÓN	F 102	Navantia, Ferrol	27 Oct 2000	28 Feb 2002	3 Dec 2003
BLAS DE LEZO	F 103	Navantia, Ferrol	28 Feb 2002	16 May 2003	16 Dec 2004
MENDEZ NUÑEZ	F 104	Navantia, Ferrol	16 May 2003	12 Nov 2004	21 Mar 2006
ROGER DE LAURIA	F 105	Navantia, Ferrol	Feb 2009	Nov 2010	July 2012

Displacement, tons: 5,853 full load
Dimensions, feet (metres): 480.3 oa; 437 pp × 61 × 23.6 *(146.4; 133.2 × 18.6 × 7.2)*
Flight deck, feet (metres): 86.6 × 56 *(26.4 × 17)*
Main machinery: CODOG; 2 GE LM 2500 gas turbines; 47,328 hp(m) *(34.8 MW)* sustained; 2 Bazán/Caterpillar diesels; 12,240 hp(m) *(9 MW)* sustained; 2 shafts; LIPS cp props
Speed, knots: 28
Range, n miles: 4,500 at 18 kt
Complement: 200 (35 officers)

Missiles: SSM: 8 Boeing Harpoon Block 2 ❶; active radar homing to 124 km *(67 n miles)* at 0.9 Mach; warhead 227 kg.
SAM: Mk 41 VLS (48 cells) ❷ 32 Raytheon SM-2MR (Block IIIA/IIIB); command/inertial guidance; semi-active radar homing to 167 km *(90 n miles)* at 2.5 Mach. 64 Evolved Sea Sparrow RIM 162 B (in quadpacks); semi-active radar homing to 18 km *(9.7 n miles)* at 3.6 Mach; warhead 39 kg.
Guns: 1 FMC 5 in *(127 mm)*/54 Mk 45 Mod 2 ❸ (ex-US); 20 rds/min to 23 km (*12.6 n miles*); weight of shell 32 kg. 1 Bazán 20 mm/120 Meroka 2B ❹; 3,600 rds/min to 2 km (fitted for but not with) 2 Oerlikon 20 mm.
Torpedoes: 4—323 mm (2 twin) Mk 32 Mod 9 fixed launchers ❺. Honeywell Mk 46 Mod 5; anti-submarine; active/passive homing to 11 km *(5.9 n miles)* at 40 kt; warhead 44 kg.
A/S mortars: 2 ABCAS/SSTDS launchers.
Countermeasures: Decoys: 4 SRBOC Mk 36 Mod 2 chaff launchers ❻. SLQ-25A Nixie torpedo decoy.
ESM: Regulus Mk-9500; ❼ intercept.
ECM: Ceselsa Aldebaran ❽; jammer.
Combat data systems: Lockheed Aegis Baseline 5 Phase III (DANCS); Link 11/16. SCOT 3, SATURN 3S.
Weapons control: Sirius optronic director ❾; FABA Dorna GFCS. Sainsel DLT 309TFCS. SQR-4 helo datalink.
Radars: Air/surface search: Aegis SPY-1D ❿. E/F-band.
Surface search: DRS SPS-67 (RAN 12S) ⓫. G-band.

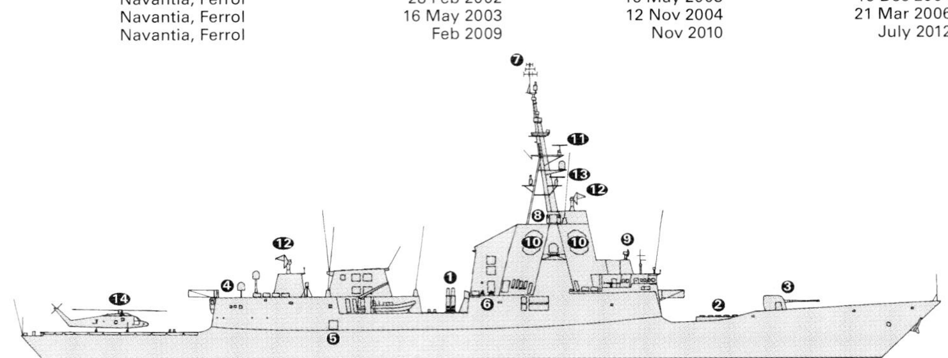

BLAS DE LEZO (*Scale 1 : 1,200*), *Ian Sturton* / 1153003

Fire control: 2 Raytheon SPG-62 Mk 99 (for SAM) ⓬. I/J-band.
Navigation: 1 Raytheon SPS-73(v) ⓭; I-band.
Sonars: Raytheon DE 1160 LF; hull-mounted; active search and attack; medium frequency. Possible ATAS active towed sonar.

Helicopters: 1 SH-60B Seahawk Lamps III ⓮.

Programmes: Project definition from September 1992 to July 1995, and then extended to July 1996 to incorporate Aegis. Design collaboration with German and Netherlands shipyards started 27 January 1994. Spain withdrew from the APAR air defence radar project in June 1995 and decided to incorporate Aegis SPY-1D into the design. Production order for four Flight I ships agreed on 21 October 1996 and building approved 24 January 1997. FSC in November 1997. The acquisition of a fifth ship was authorised by the Spanish government on 27 May 2005 and a contract was signed in July 2006. A sixth ship may be procured. These modified ships are likely to be fitted with SPY-1D(V) radar and are to be known as Flight II.
Modernisation: Flight I ships are to be upgraded to Baseline S-2 Standard in 2008–09. This may include a ballistic missile detect and track capability and possibly Tomahawk land-attack missiles. SM-2 Block IIIA missiles are likely to be replaced by Block IIIB.
Structure: The inclusion of SPY-1D radar increased the original size of the ship and caused major changes to the shape of the superstructure. Stealth technology incorporated. Indal RAST helicopter system. Hangar for one helicopter. 127 mm gun for gunfire support to land forces, taken from USN *Tarawa* class. RAM may be fitted vice Meroka.
Operational: All based at Ferrol as the 31st Squadron. F 101 operated as part of USS *Roosevelt* carrier strike group in 2005 and completed round the world deployment in 2007.

ALMIRANTE DON JUAN DE BORBÓN *5/2008*, B Prézelin* / 1335828

BLAS DE LEZO *5/2008*, Michael Nitz* / 1335866

6 SANTA MARÍA CLASS (FFGHM)

Name	*No*	*Builders*	*Laid down*	*Launched*	*Commissioned*
SANTA MARÍA	F 81	Bazán, Ferrol	23 May 1982	24 Nov 1984	12 Oct 1986
VICTORIA	F 82	Bazán, Ferrol	16 Aug 1983	23 July 1986	11 Nov 1987
NUMANCIA	F 83	Bazán, Ferrol	8 Jan 1986	30 Jan 1987	8 Nov 1988
REINA SOFÍA (ex-*América*)	F 84	Bazán, Ferrol	12 Dec 1987	19 July 1989	18 Oct 1990
NAVARRA	F 85	Bazán, Ferrol	15 Apr 1991	23 Oct 1992	30 May 1994
CANARIAS	F 86	Bazán, Ferrol	15 Apr 1992	21 June 1993	14 Dec 1994

Displacement, tons: 3,610 standard; 3,969 full load
Dimensions, feet (metres): 451.2 × 46.9 × 24.6
(137.7 × 14.3 × 7.5)
Main machinery: 2 GE LM 2500 gas turbines; 41,000 hp *(30.59 MW)* sustained; 1 shaft; cp prop
2 auxiliary retractable props; 650 hp *(484 kW)*
Speed, knots: 29. **Range, n miles:** 4,500 at 20 kt
Complement: 223 (13 officers)

Missiles: SSM: 8 McDonnell Douglas Harpoon Block 1B; active radar homing to 92 km *(50 n miles)* at 0.9 Mach; warhead 227 kg.
SAM: 32 Raytheon SM-1MR Block VI; Mk 13 Mod 4 launcher ❶; command guidance; semi-active radar homing to 38 km *(20.5 n miles)* at 2 Mach.
Both missile systems share a common magazine.
Guns: 1 OTO Melara 3 in *(76 mm)*/62 ❷; 85 rds/min to 16 km *(8.7 n miles)*; weight of shell 6 kg.
1 Bazán 20 mm/120 12-barrelled Meroka Mod 2A or 2B ❸; 3,600 rds/min combined to 2 km. 2—12.7 mm MGs.
Torpedoes: 6—324 mm US Mk 32 (2 triple) tubes ❹. Honeywell/Alliant Mk 46 Mod 5; anti-submarine; active/passive homing to 11 km *(5.9 n miles)* at 40 kt; warhead 44 kg.
Countermeasures: Decoys: 4 Loral Hycor SRBOC 6-barrelled fixed Mk 37 Mod 1/2 ❺; IR flares and chaff to 4 km *(2.2 n miles)*.
Prairie/Masker: hull noise/blade rate suppression.
SLQ-25 Nixie; torpedo decoy.
ESM/ECM: Rigel or MK 3600/3700; intercept and jammer.
Combat data systems: IPN 10 action data automation; Link 11. SQQ 28 LAMPS III helo datalink. Saturn and SCOT 3 Secomsat ❻ fitted.
Weapons control: Loral Mk 92 Mod 2 (Mod 6 with CORT in F 85 and 86). Enosa optronic tracker for Meroka 2B.
Radars: Air search: Raytheon SPS-49(V)4/6 ❼; C/D-band; range 457 km *(250 n miles)*.
Surface search: Raytheon SPS-55 ❽; I-band.
Navigation: Raytheon 1650/9 ❾; I/J-band.
Fire control: RCA Mk 92 Mod 4/6 ❿; I/J-band.
Raytheon STIR ⓫; I/J-band.
Selenia RAN 12L ⓬; D-band (for Meroka).
Sperry/Lockheed VPS 2 ⓭; I-band (for Meroka).
Tacan: URN 25.
Sonars: Raytheon SQS-56 (DE 1160); hull-mounted; active search and attack; medium frequency.
Gould SQR-19(V)2 (F 85-86); tactical towed array (TACTAS); passive; very low frequency.

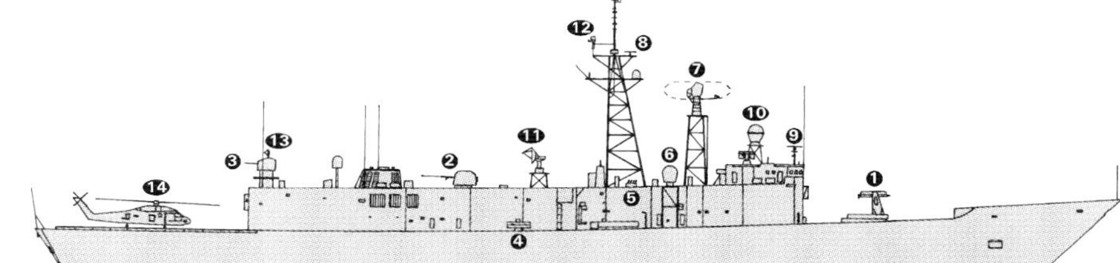
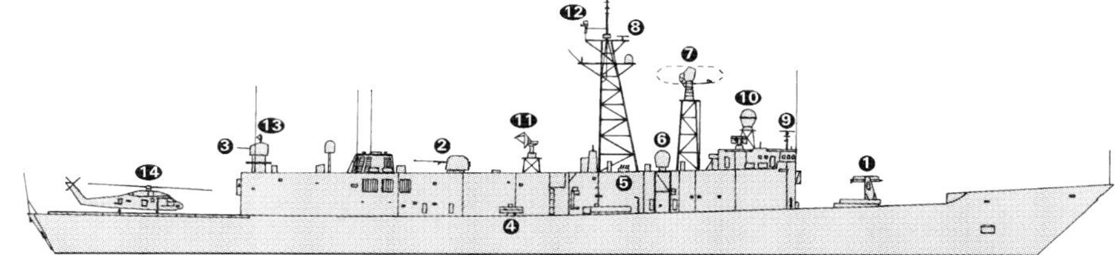

REINA SOFÍA ***(Scale 1 : 1,200), Ian Sturton*** / 0130395

CANARIAS ***1/2005, Camil Busquets i Vilanova*** / 1153476

Helicopters: 2 Sikorsky SH-60B ⓮ (only one normally embarked).

Programmes: Three ordered 29 June 1977. The execution of this programme was delayed due to the emphasis placed on the carrier construction. The fourth ship was ordered on 19 June 1986, and numbers five and six on 26 December 1989.
Modernisation: F 85 and F 86 are fitted with the improved Mod 2B Meroka CIWS which includes an Enosa optronic tracker. SCOT SATCOM fitted in F 85 and F 84. Others may be similarly fitted. All modernised with RAN 12L target designator for Meroka but VPS 2 fire-control radar is yet to be replaced by RAN 30X radar. A modernisation programme was initiated in 2005. The programme includes improvements to habitability, hull systems upgrades (to extend ships' lives) and enhancements to sensors and displays. This includes a new sonar suite and new EW equipment (Rigel or Mk 3600/3700). Upgrades to F 81-84 have been completed and are to be followed by F 85-86.
Structure: Based on the US FFG 7 Oliver Perry class although broader in the beam and therefore able to carry more topweight. Fin stabilisers fitted. RAST helicopter handling system. *Navarra* and *Canarias* have an indigenous combat data system thereby increasing national inputs to 75 per cent.
Operational: All based at Rota as the 41st Squadron.

REINA SOFIA ***6/2007, John Brodie*** / 1166820

VICTORIA ***11/2007, Adolfo Ortigueira Gil*** / 1170034

SHIPBORNE AIRCRAFT

Notes: An initial purchase of 11 NH90 helicopters, to replace the SH-3 and AB-212 fleets, was announced on 20 May 2005. This is likely to include a mixture of naval tactical, AEW and transport versions. Entry into service is expected in 2015.

Numbers/Type: 4/12/1 BAe/McDonnell Douglas EAV-8B (Harrier II)/EAV-8B (Harrier Plus)/ TAV-8B.
Operational speed: 562 kt *(1,041 km/h).*
Service ceiling: Not available.
Range: 480 n miles *(889 km).*
Role/Weapon systems: First batch of nine delivered in 1987–88 and a further eight in 1996–97. Four Harrier II to be upgraded to AV-8B with APG-65 radar plus FLIR by 2004. A further TAV-8B twin seat delivered in September 2000. Sensors: ECM; ALQ 164. Weapons: Strike; two 25 mm GAU-12/U cannon, two or four AIM-9L Sidewinders, two or four AGM-65E Mavericks; up to 16 GP bombs. AMRAAM AIM-120 in updated aircraft.

HARRIER PLUS *2/2004, Guy Toremans* / 1044542

Numbers/Type: 8 Sikorsky SH-3D/G/H Sea King.
Operational speed: 118 kt *(219 km/h).*
Service ceiling: 14,700 ft *(4,480 m).*
Range: 542 n miles *(1,005 km).*
Role/Weapon systems: Former ASW helicopters converted to tactical transport and special forces role. ASW equipment fitted for but not with. Can be replaced in 48 hours. Converted to 3H standard in 1996–97. Sensors: APN-217 Doppler radar and IFF.

SH-3D *5/2008*, M Declerck* / 1335865

Numbers/Type: 3 Sikorsky SH-3D Sea King AEW.
Operational speed: 110 kt *(204 km/h).*
Service ceiling: 14,700 ft *(4,480 m).*
Range: 542 n miles *(1,005 km).*
Role/Weapon systems: Three Sea King helicopters were taken in hand in 1986 for conversion to AEW role to provide organic cover; first entered service August 1987. Sensors: THORN EMI Searchwater (to be replaced by Racal 2000) radar, ESM. Weapons: Unarmed.

SEA KING AEW *10/2008*, Adolfo Ortigueira Gil* / 1335864

Numbers/Type: 8 Agusta AB 212.
Operational speed: 106 kt *(196 km/h).*
Service ceiling: 14,200 ft *(4,330 m).*
Range: 230 n miles *(426 km).*
Role/Weapon systems: Surface search. All ASW equipment removed. Weapons: 1—12.7 mm MG and 70 mm rocket launchers.

AB 212 *10/2007, Adolfo Ortigueira Gil* / 1170032

Numbers/Type: 11 Sikorsky SH-60B Seahawk (LAMPS III).
Operational speed: 135 kt *(249 km/h).*
Service ceiling: 10,000 ft *(3,050 m).*
Range: 600 n miles *(1,110 km).*
Role/Weapon systems: ASW helicopter. First six delivered in 1988–89 for FFG 7 frigates. Six more Block 1 acquired in 2002 for F 100 class. First six aircraft being upgraded to Block 1 with first three aircraft completed by 2005. The other three are to follow. Sensors: Search radar, FLIR (Block I), sonobuoys, ECM/ESM. Weapons: ASW; two Mk 46 torpedoes or depth bombs. ASV; AGM-119B Penguin and AGM-114B/K Hellfire.

SH-60B *10/2008*, Adolfo Ortigueira Gil* / 1335863

Numbers/Type: 9 Hughes 500MD.
Operational speed: 110 kt *(204 km/h).*
Service ceiling: 10,000 ft *(3,050 m).*
Range: 203 n miles *(376 km).*
Role/Weapon systems: Used for training; secondary role is SAR and surface search. ASW role removed.

500 MD *10/2007, Adolfo Ortigueira Gil* / 1170031

LAND-BASED MARITIME AIRCRAFT (FRONT LINE)

Notes: (1) The Air Force F/A-18 Hornet (C.15) and EurofighterTyphoon (C.16) can be armed with Harpoon ASM. Air Force CN-235 are not used for maritime role.
(2) Three CASA C-212/400 are operated by the Fishery Department and are based at Torrejón (Madrid), Jerez and Alicante. Two Agusta A-109C and two Dauphin N3 helicopters are based at Alicante, Jerez and Santander and Canary Islands.

Numbers/Type: 3 Cessna Citation II (C-550).
Operational speed: 275 kt *(509 km/h).*
Service ceiling: 27,750 ft *(8,458 m).*
Range: 2,000 n miles *(3,704 km).*
Role/Weapon systems: Used for transport, training and reconnaissance.

CESSNA CITATION *6/2004, Adolfo Ortigueira Gil* / 1044550

Numbers/Type: 14 CASA C-212 Aviocar.
Operational speed: 190 kt *(353 km/h).*
Service ceiling: 24,000 ft *(7,315 m).*
Range: 1,650 n miles *(3,055 km).*
Role/Weapon systems: Operated by Air Force. Primary role SAR, secondary role surveillance. Based at Mallorca, Las Palmas and Madrid. Six are leased by Customs. Sensors: APS-128 radar, MAD, sonobuoys and ESM. Weapons (not SAR role): ASW; Mk 46 torpedoes or depth bombs. ASV; two rockets or machine gun pods.

C-212 *5/2002, Adolfo Ortigueira Gil* / 0528933

Numbers/Type: 3 Fokker F27 Maritime.
Operational speed: 250 kt *(463 km/h)*.
Service ceiling: 29,500 ft *(8,990 m)*.
Range: 2,700 n miles *(5,000 km)*.
Role/Weapon systems: Canaries and offshore patrol by Air Force. Are to be replaced by CN-235 in due course. Sensors: APS-504 search radar, cameras. Weapons: none.

F-27 *6/2004, Adolfo Ortigueira Gil* / 1044552

Numbers/Type: 2/5 Lockheed P-3A Plus Orion/P-3B Plus Orion.
Operational speed: 410 kt *(760 km/h)*.
Service ceiling: 28,300 ft *(8,625 m)*.
Range: 4,000 n miles *(7,410 km)*.
Role/Weapon systems: Air Force operation for long-range MR/ASW. Original P-3A aircraft supplemented in 1988 by P-3B Orions from Norway after Lockheed modernisation. P-3A aircraft upgraded to P-3A plus in 1995–97. The five P-3Bs are undergoing modernisation programme with improved acoustic signal processor, ALR-66 ESM, FLIR and new radar and communications. Sensors: APS-134 (Searchwater 2000 in due course); FLIR; search radar, AQS-81MAD, ALR 66 V(3) ECM/ESM, 87 sonobuoys. Weapons: ASW; eight torpedoes or depth bombs internally; 10 underwing stations. ASV; four Harpoon or 127 mm rockets.

P-3B *7/2002, Adolfo Ortigueira Gil* / 0528935

Numbers/Type: 10 Eurocopter AS 332 Super Puma.
Operational speed: 130 kt *(240 km/h)*.
Service ceiling: 15,090 ft *(4,600 m)*.
Range: 672 n miles *(1,245 km)*.
Role/Weapon systems: Air Force operated for SAR/CSAR. Based at Mallorca, Las Palmas and Madrid.

AS 332 *7/2001, Adolfo Ortigueira Gil* / 0528932

PATROL FORCES

6 DESCUBIERTA CLASS (PSOH/MCS/FSGM)

Name	*No*	*Builders*	*Laid down*	*Launched*	*Commissioned*
DESCUBIERTA	P 75 (ex-F 31)	Bazán, Cartagena	16 Nov 1974	8 July 1975	18 Nov 1978
DIANA	M 11 (ex-F 32)	Bazán, Cartagena	8 July 1975	26 Jan 1976	30 June 1979
INFANTA ELENA	P 76 (ex-F 33)	Bazán, Cartagena	26 Jan 1976	14 Sep 1976	12 Apr 1980
INFANTA CRISTINA	P 77 (ex-F 34)	Bazán, Cartagena	11 Sep 1976	25 Apr 1977	24 Nov 1980
CAZADORA	P 78 (ex-F 35)	Bazán, Ferrol	14 Dec 1977	17 Oct 1978	20 July 1982
VENCEDORA	P 79 (ex-F 36)	Bazán, Ferrol	1 June 1978	27 Apr 1979	18 Mar 1983

Displacement, tons: 1,233 standard; 1,666 full load
Dimensions, feet (metres): 291.3 × 34 × 12.5 *(88.8 × 10.4 × 3.8)*
Main machinery: 4 MTU-Bazán 16V 956 TB91 diesels; 15,000 hp(m) *(11 MW)* sustained; 2 shafts; cp props
Speed, knots: 25
Range, n miles: 4,000 at 18 kt; 7,500 at 12 kt
Complement: 118 (10 officers) plus 30 marines

Guns: 1 OTO Melara 3 in *(76 mm)*/62 compact; 85 rds/min to 16 km *(8.7 n miles)*; weight of shell 6 kg.
2 Oerlikon 20 mm/120.
Countermeasures: ESM: Elsag Mk 1000 (part of Deneb system); or Mk 1600; intercept.
ECM: Ceselsa Canopus; or Mk 1900; jammer.
Combat data systems: Tritan IV. Saturn SATCOM.
Weapons control: Signaal WM25; GM 101.
Radars: Air/surface search: Signaal DA05/2 (not M 11); E/F-band; range 137 km *(75 n miles)* for 2 m^2 target.
Radars: Surface search: Signaal ZW06 (not M 11); I-band.
Navigation: 2 Furuno; I-band.
Fire control: Signaal WM22/41 or WM25 system (not M 11); I/J-band; range 46 km *(25 n miles)*.

Programmes: Officially rated as Corvettes. *Diana* (tenth of the name) originates with the galley *Diana* of 1570. *Infanta Elena* and *Infanta Cristina* are named after the daughters of King Juan Carlos. Approval for second four ships given on 21 May 1976. First four ordered 7 December 1973 (83 per cent Spanish ship construction components) and two more from Bazán, Ferrol on 25 May 1976.
Structure: Original Portuguese 'João Coutinho' design by Comodoro de Oliveira PN developed by Blohm + Voss and considerably modified by Bazán including use of Y-shaped funnel. Noise reduction measures include Masker fitted to shafts, auxiliary gas-turbine generator fitted on upper deck, all main and auxiliary diesels sound-mounted. Fully stabilised. Automatic computerised engine and alternator control; two independent engine rooms; normal running on two diesels.
Operational: P 75 completed conversion to an OPV, with capability to act as helicopter platform, in 2000. Most major weapon systems removed. M 11 completed conversion to MCMV support role in 2000 and based at Cartagena. P 79 converted to OPV role in 2003, P 77 and P 78 in 2004 and P 76 in 2005. P 75, P 76 and P 77 based at Cartagena and P 78 and P 79 at Las Palmas.
Sales: F 37 and F 38 sold to Egypt prior to completion. One to Morocco in 1983.

INFANTA ELENA *11/2008*, M Declerck* / 1335860

DESCUBIERTA *11/2007, Adolfo Ortigueira Gil* / 1335861

4 SERVIOLA CLASS (OFFSHORE PATROL VESSELS) (PSOH)

Name	*No*	*Builders*	*Laid down*	*Launched*	*Commissioned*
SERVIOLA	P 71	Bazán, Ferrol	17 Oct 1989	10 May 1990	22 Mar 1991
CENTINELA	P 72	Bazán, Ferrol	12 Dec 1989	30 Mar 1990	24 Sep 1991
VIGÍA	P 73	Bazán, Ferrol	30 Oct 1990	12 Apr 1991	24 Mar 1992
ATALAYA	P 74	Bazán, Ferrol	14 Dec 1990	22 Nov 1991	29 June 1992

Displacement, tons: 1,147 full load
Dimensions, feet (metres): 225.4; 206.7 pp × 34 × 11 *(68.7; 63 × 10.4 × 3.4)*
Main machinery: 2 MTU-Bazán 16V 956 TB91 diesels; 7,500 hp(m) *(5.5 MW)* sustained; 2 shafts; LIPS cp props
Speed, knots: 19
Range, n miles: 8,000 at 12 kt
Complement: 42 (8 officers) plus 6 spare berths

Guns: 1 US 3 in *(76 mm)*/50 Mk 27; 20 rds/min to 12 km *(6.6 n miles)*; weight of shell 6 kg.
2—12.7 mm MGs.
Countermeasures: ESM: ULQ-13 (in P 71).
Weapons control: Bazán Alcor or MSP 4000 (P 73) optronic director. Hispano mini combat system. SATCOM.
Radars: Surface search: Racal Decca 2459; I-band.
Navigation: Racal Decca ARPA 2690 BT; I-band.

Helicopters: Platform for 1 AB 212.

Programmes: Project B215 ordered from Bazán, Ferrol in late 1988. The larger Milano design was rejected as being too expensive.
Modernisation: The guns are old stock refurbished but could be replaced by an OTO Melara 76 mm/62 or a Bofors 40 mm/70 Model 600 if funds can be found. Other equipment fits could include four Harpoon SSM, Meroka CIWS, Sea Sparrow SAM or a Bofors 375 mm ASW rocket launcher. No plans to carry out any of these improvements so far. EW equipment fitted in Serviola for training.
Structure: A modified Halcón class design similar to ships produced for Argentina and Mexico. Helicopter facilities enabling operation in up to Sea State 4 using non-retractable stabilisers. Three firefighting pumps.
Operational: For EEZ patrol. *Vigía* based at Cádiz, *Serviola* and *Atalaya* at Ferrol and *Centinela* at Las Palmas.

VIGIA ***11/2008*, Adolfo Ortigueira Gil*** / 1335859

ATALAYA ***6/2004, Adolfo Ortigueira Gil*** / 1044551

1 PESCALONSO CLASS (OFFSHORE PATROL CRAFT) (PSO)

Name	*No*	*Builders*	*Commissioned*
CHILREU (ex-*Pescalonso 2*)	P 61	Gijon, Asturias	30 Mar 1992

Displacement, tons: 2,101 full load
Dimensions, feet (metres): 222.4 × 36.1 × 15.4 *(67.8 × 11 × 4.7)*
Main machinery: 1 MaK 6M-453K diesel; 2,460 hp(m) *(1.81 MW)* sustained; 1 shaft; cp prop
Speed, knots: 12. **Range, n miles:** 1,500 at 12 kt
Complement: 35 (7 officers)
Guns: 1 — 12.7 mm MG.
Radars: Surface search: 2 Consilium Selesmar; E/F/I-band.

Comment: Launched 2 May 1988 and purchased by the Fisheries Department for the Navy to use as a Fishery Protection vessel based at Ferrol. Former stern ramp trawler. Inmarsat fitted.

CHILREU ***11/2007, B Prézelin*** / 1166822

3 ALBORAN CLASS (OFFSHORE PATROL CRAFT) (PSOH)

Name	*No*	*Builders*	*Commissioned*
ALBORAN	P 62	Freire, Vigo	8 Jan 1997
ARNOMENDI	P 63	Freire, Vigo	13 Dec 2000
TARIFA	P 64	Freire, Vigo	14 June 2004

Displacement, tons: 1,963 full load
Dimensions, feet (metres): 218.2 × 36.1 × 14.4 *(66.5 × 11 × 4.4)*
Main machinery: 1 Krupp MaK 6 M 453C diesel; 2,400 hp(m) *(1.76 MW)* sustained (P 62); 1 Krupp MaK 8M25 diesel; 3,250 hp(m) *(2.39 MW)* sustained (P 63); 1 diesel generator and motor for emergency propulsion; 462 hp(m) *(340 kW)*; 1 shaft; bow thruster; 350 hp(m) *(257 kW)*
Speed, knots: 13 (P 62); 15.8 (P 63) (3.5 on emergency motor)
Range, n miles: 20,000 at 13 kt
Complement: 37 (7 officers) plus 9 spare
Guns: 2 — 12.7 mm MGs.
Radars: Surface search: Furuno FAR-2825; I-band.
Navigation: Furuno FR-2130S; I-band.
Helicopters: Platform for 1 light.

Comment: *Alboran* launched in 1991 and purchased by the Fisheries Department to use as a Fishery Protection vessel based at Cartagena. *Arnomendi*, with a slightly larger bridge and more powerful engine, based at Las Palmas, Canary Islands. *Tarifa* is fitted with anti-pollution equipment and is based at Cartagena.

ALBORAN ***10/2008*, Adolfo Ortigueira Gil*** / 1335858

5 BARCELÓ CLASS (LARGE PATROL CRAFT) (PB)

Name	*No*	*Builders*	*Commissioned*
BARCELÓ	P 11	Lürssen, Vegesack	20 Mar 1976
LAYA	P 12	Bazán, La Carraca	23 Dec 1976
ORDÓÑEZ	P 14	Bazán, La Carraca	7 June 1977
ACEVEDO	P 15	Bazán, La Carraca	14 July 1977
CÁNDIDO PÉREZ	P 16	Bazán, La Carraca	25 Nov 1977

Displacement, tons: 145 full load
Dimensions, feet (metres): 118.7 × 19 × 6.2 *(36.2 × 5.8 × 1.9)*
Main machinery: 2 MTU-Bazán MD 16V 538 TB90 diesels; 6,000 hp(m) *(4.41 MW)* sustained; 2 shafts
Speed, knots: 22. **Range, n miles:** 1,200 at 17 kt
Complement: 19 (3 officers)
Guns: 1 Breda 40 mm/70. 1 Oerlikon 20 mm/85. 2 — 12.7 mm MGs.
Torpedoes: Fitted for 2 — 21 in *(533 mm)* tubes.
Weapons control: CSEE optical director.
Radars: Surface search: Raytheon 1220/6XB; I/J-band.

Comment: Ordered 5 December 1973. All manned by the Navy although building cost was borne by the Ministry of Commerce. Of LürssenTNC 36 design. Reported as able to take two or four surface-to-surface missiles instead of 20 mm gun and torpedo tubes. 40 mm gun removed from *Barceló*. Plans to transfer to the Guardia Civil del Mar have been shelved. *Javier Quiroga* decommissioned in 2005. Speed much reduced from original 36 kt.

CÁNDIDO PÉREZ ***8/2007, Marco Ghiglino*** / 1170221

4 CONEJERA CLASS (COASTAL PATROL CRAFT) (PB)

Name	*No*	*Builders*	*Commissioned*
CONEJERA	P 31	Bazán, Ferrol	31 Dec 1981
DRAGONERA	P 32	Bazán, Ferrol	31 Dec 1981
ESPALMADOR	P 33	Bazán, Ferrol	10 May 1982
ALCANADA	P 34	Bazán, Ferrol	10 May 1982

Displacement, tons: 85 full load
Dimensions, feet (metres): 106.6 × 17.4 × 4.6 *(32.2 × 5.3 × 1.4)*
Main machinery: 2 MTU-Bazán MA 16V 362 SB80 diesels; 2,450 hp(m) *(1.8 MW)*; 2 shafts
Speed, knots: 13
Range, n miles: 1,200 at 13 kt
Complement: 12
Guns: 1 Oerlikon 20 mm/120 Mk 10. 1 — 12.7 mm MG.
Radars: Surface search: Furuno; I-band.

Comment: Ordered in 1978, funded jointly by the Navy and the Ministry of Commerce. Naval manned. Speed reduced from original 25 kt. Basing: P 31 Málaga; P 32 Huelva; P 33/34 Barcelona.

CONEJERA ***8/2007, Marco Ghiglino*** / 1170222

2 TORALLA CLASS (COASTAL PATROL CRAFT) (PB)

Name	*No*	*Builders*	*Commissioned*
TORALLA	P 81	Viudes, Barcelona	29 Apr 1987
FORMENTOR	P 82	Viudes, Barcelona	23 June 1988

Displacement, tons: 102 full load
Dimensions, feet (metres): 93.5 × 21.3 × 5.9 *(28.5 × 6.5 × 1.8)*
Main machinery: 2 MTU-Bazán 8V 396 TB93 diesels; 2,100 hp(m) *(1.54 MW)* sustained; 2 shafts
Speed, knots: 19
Range, n miles: 1,000 at 12 kt
Complement: 13
Guns: 1 Browning 12.7 mm MG.
Radars: Surface search: Racal Decca RM 1070; I-band.
Navigation: Racal Decca RM 270; I-band.

Comment: Wooden hull with GRP sheath. Very similar to Customs Alcaravan class. *Formentor* refitted in 1996–97. Based at Cartagena.

TORALLA ***10/2008*, Adolfo Ortigueira Gil*** / 1335856

2 P 101 CLASS (PBR)

P 114 **P 111**

Displacement, tons: 18.5 standard; 20.8 full load
Dimensions, feet (metres): 44.9 × 14.4 × 4.3 *(13.7 × 4.4 × 1.3)*
Main machinery: 2 Baudouin-Interdiesel DNP-350; 768 hp(m) *(564 kW)*; 2 shafts
Speed, knots: 23.3
Range, n miles: 430 at 18 kt
Complement: 6
Guns: 1 — 12.7 mm MG.
Radars: Surface search: Decca 110; I-band.

Comment: Ordered under the programme agreed 13 May 1977, funded jointly by the Navy and the Ministry of Commerce. Built to the Aresa LVC 160 design by Aresa, Arenys de Mar, Barcelona. GRP hull. Eight of the class conduct harbour auxiliary duties with Y numbers, the remainder paid off in 1993. P 111 transferred back again to patrol duties in 1996 and is based at Ayamonte (Huelva). P 114 is also used for patrol duties and is based at Ceuta.

P 101 class ***6/2000, Adolfo Ortigueira Gil*** / 0087858

9 ANAGA CLASS (LARGE PATROL CRAFT) (PB)

Name	*No*	*Builders*	*Commissioned*
ANAGA	P 21	Bazán, La Carraca	14 Oct 1980
TAGOMAGO	P 22	Bazán, La Carraca	30 Jan 1981
MAROLA	P 23	Bazán, La Carraca	4 June 1981
MOURO	P 24	Bazán, La Carraca	14 July 1981
GROSA	P 25	Bazán, La Carraca	15 Sep 1981
MEDAS	P 26	Bazán, La Carraca	16 Oct 1981
IZARO	P 27	Bazán, La Carraca	9 Dec 1981
TABARCA	P 28	Bazán, La Carraca	30 Dec 1981
BERGANTÍN	P 30	Bazán, La Carraca	28 July 1982

Displacement, tons: 319 full load
Dimensions, feet (metres): 145.6 × 21.6 × 8.2 *(44.4 × 6.6 × 2.5)*
Main machinery: 1 MTU-Bazán 16V 956 SB90 diesel; 4,000 hp(m) *(2.94 MW)* sustained; 1 shaft; cp prop
Speed, knots: 16. **Range, n miles:** 4,000 at 13 kt
Complement: 25 (3 officers)
Guns: 1 FMC 3 in *(76 mm)*/50 Mk 22. 1 Oerlikon 20 mm Mk 10. 2—7.62 mm MGs.
Radars: Surface search: 1 Racal Decca 1226; I-band.
Navigation: Consilium Selesmar SRL MM 950; F/I-band.

Comment: Ordered from Bazán, Cádiz on 22 July 1978. For fishery and EEZ patrol duties. Rescue and firefighting capability. Speed reduced from original 20 kt.

TABARCA ***10/2008*, Adolfo Ortigueira Gil*** / 1335857

1 INSHORE/RIVER PATROL LAUNCH (PBR)

Name	*No*	*Builders*	*Commissioned*
CABO FRADERA	P 201	Bazán, La Carraca	11 Jan 1963

Displacement, tons: 21 full load
Dimensions, feet (metres): 58.3 × 13.8 × 3 *(17.8 × 4.2 × 0.9)*
Main machinery: 2 diesels; 280 hp(m) *(206 kW)*; 2 shafts
Speed, knots: 11
Complement: 9
Guns: 1—7.62 mm MG.
Radars: Surface search: Furuno; I-band.

Comment: Based at Tuy on River Miño for border patrol with Portugal.

CABO FRADERA ***4/2003, Camil Busquets i Vilanova*** / 0570981

0 + 4 (4) OFFSHORE PATROL SHIPS (PSO)

Name	*No*	*Builders*	*Laid down*	*Launched*	*Commissioned*
METEORO	P 41	Navantia, Puerto Real	2007	2009	July 2010
RAYO	P 42	Navantia, Puerto Real	2008	2009	Dec 2010
RELÁMPAGO	P 43	Navantia, Puerto Real	2008	2009	Apr 2011
TORNA	P 44	Navantia, Puerto Real	2009	2010	Aug 2011

Displacement, tons: 2,490 full load
Dimensions, feet (metres): 308.1 × 46.6 × 14.1 *(93.9 × 14.2 × 4.3)*
Main machinery: CODAE; 2 diesels; 12,000 hp *(9 MW)*; 2 motors; 2,000 hp *(1.5 MW)*; 2 cp props; bow thruster
Speed, knots: 20.5. **Range, n miles:** 8,000 at 12 kt
Complement: 35 (5 officers)
Guns: 1 Oto Melara 3 in *(76 mm)*/62. 2—20 mm (to be confirmed).
Combat data systems: SCOMBA. Link 11 and 22. Inmarsat. Secomsat.
Countermeasures: Decoys: To be announced.
ESM/ECM: Rigel.
RESM: To be announced.
Weapons control: Dorna optronic director.
Radars: Surface search: Indra Aries; I-band.
Fire control: Dorna; K-band.
Helicopters: Platform for 1 NH90.

Comment: A programme for the procurement of a new class of up to eight multirole offshore patrol vessels known as Buques de Accion Maritima (BAM) was initiated in 2004. The modular design allows other variants of the BAM design to be capable of conducting intelligence, hydrographic and diving support tasks. Authorisation for the first batch of four patrol ships was made by the Spanish government on 20 May 2005 and a contract for their construction was signed with Navantia on 31 July 2006. The ships are to be capable of operating a helicopter and are to be equipped with two RIBs for boarding/interception operations.

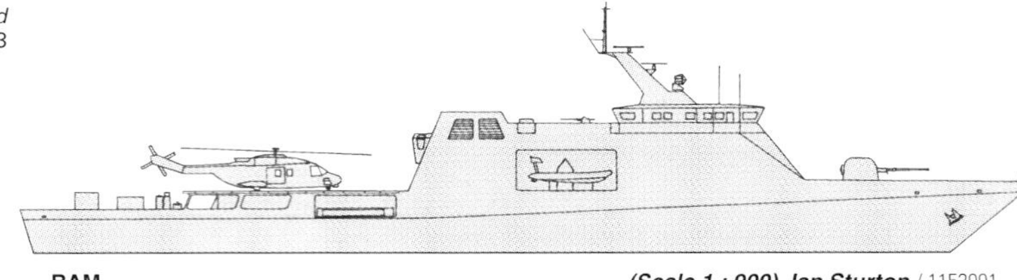

BAM ***(Scale 1 : 900), Ian Sturton*** / 1153001

AMPHIBIOUS FORCES

2 NEWPORT CLASS (LSTH)

Name	*No*	*Builders*	*Laid down*	*Launched*	*Commissioned*
HERNÁN CORTÉS (ex-*Barnstable County*)	L 41 (ex-L 1197)	National Steel, San Diego	19 Dec 1970	2 Oct 1971	27 May 1972
PIZARRO (ex-*Harlan County*)	L 42 (ex-L 1196)	National Steel, San Diego	7 Nov 1970	24 July 1971	8 Apr 1972

Displacement, tons: 4,975 light; 8,550 full load
Dimensions, feet (metres): 522.3 (hull) × 69.5 × 18.2 (aft) *(159.2 × 21.2 × 5.5)*
Main machinery: 6 Alco 16-251 diesels; 16,500 hp *(12.3 MW)* sustained; 2 shafts; cp props; bow thruster
Speed, knots: 20
Range, n miles: 14,250 at 14 kt
Complement: 255 (15 officers)
Military lift: 374 troops; (20 officers) 500 tons vehicles; 2 LCVPs and 2 LCPLs on davits

Guns: 1 General Electric/General Dynamics 20 mm Vulcan Phalanx Mk 15. 2 Oerlikon 20 mm/85. 4—12.7 mm MGs.
Countermeasures: ESM: Celesa Deneb.
Radars: Surface search: Raytheon SPS-10F/67; G-band.
Navigation: Marconi LN66; I-band.

Helicopters: Platform only for 3 AB 212.

Programmes: Transferred from the US on 26 August 1994 and 14 April 1995.
Structure: The 3 in guns removed on transfer. The ramp is supported by twin derrick arms. A ramp just forward of the superstructure connects the lower tank deck with the main deck and a vehicle passage through the superstructure provides access to the parking area amidships. A stern gate to the tank deck permits unloading of amphibious tractors into the water, or unloading of other vehicles into an LCU or on to a pier. Vehicle stowage covers 19,000 sq ft. Length over derrick arms is 562 ft *(171.3 m)*; full load draught is 11.5 ft forward and 17.5 ft aft. Bow thruster fitted to hold position offshore while unloading amphibious tractors. SCOT 3 SATCOM fitted in 1995–96. Can carry four Mexeflotes, two of them powered.
Operational: Based at Rota. *Hernán Cortés* reported to have been decommissioned in 2006 but to remain in service until 2009. *Pizarro* to follow as the Strategic Projection Ship enters service.

PIZARRO ***5/2004, Marco Ghiglino*** / 1153478

2 GALICIA CLASS (LPD)

Name	*No*	*Builders*	*Laid down*	*Launched*	*Commissioned*
GALICIA	L 51	Bazán, Ferrol	31 May 1996	21 July 1997	30 Apr 1998
CASTILLA	L 52	Bazán, Ferrol	11 Dec 1997	14 June 1999	26 June 2000

Displacement, tons: 13,815 full load
Dimensions, feet (metres): 524.9 oa; 465.9 pp × 82 × 19.3 *(160; 142 × 25 × 5.9)*
Flight deck, feet (metres): 196.9 × 82 *(60 × 25)*
Main machinery: 2 Bazán/Caterpillar 3612 diesels; 12,512 hp(m) *(9.2 MW)*; 2 shafts; LIPS cp props; bow thruster 680 hp(m) *(500 kW)*
Speed, knots: 20
Range, n miles: 6,000 at 12 kt
Complement: 115 plus 12 spare; 189 (L 52)
Military lift: 543 or 404 (L 52) fully equipped troops and 72 (staff and aircrew)
6 LCVP or 4 LCM or 1 LCU and 1 LCVP. 130 APCs or 33 MBTs.

Guns: 1 Bazán 20 mm/120 12-barrelled Meroka (fitted for) ❶; 3,600 rds/min combined to 2 km. 2 Oerlikon GAM-B01 20 mm.
Countermeasures: Decoys: 4 SRBOC chaff launchers.
ESM: Intercept.
Combat data systems: SICOA (L 52); SATCOM; Link 11.
Radars: Surface search: TRS 3D/16 (L 52) ❷; G-band.
Surface search: Kelvin Hughes ARPA ❸; I-band.
Navigation/helo control: I-band.

Helicopters: 6 AB 212 or 4 SH-3D Sea King ❹ or 4 Eurocopter Tiger.

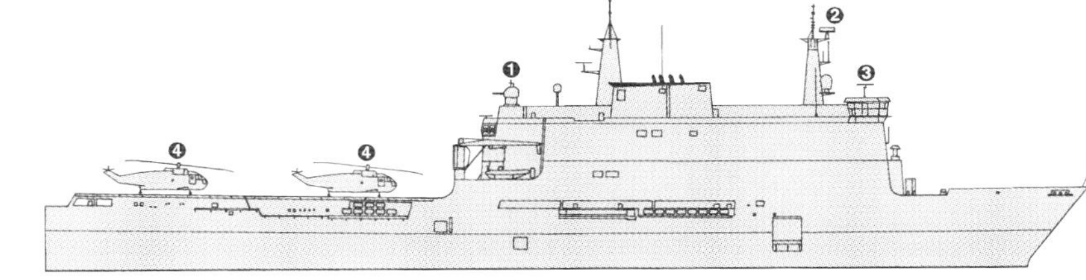

CASTILLA *(Scale 1 : 1,500), Ian Sturton* / 0106549

Programmes: Originally started as a national project by the Netherlands. In 1990 the ATS was seen as a possible solution to fulfil the requirements for a new LPD. Joint project definition study announced in July 1991 and completed in December 1993 and the first ship was authorised on 29 July 1994. The second of class ordered 9 May 1997.
Modernisation: L 52 C^2 capabilities upgraded in 2002–03 to support Flagship requirements. L 52 embarked the HQ of the Spanish High Readiness Force (Maritime) in November 2003 as part of the NATO Response Force. Both ships are to be fitted with RAM CIWS.

Structure: Able to transport a fully equipped battalion of marines providing a built-in dock for landing craft and a helicopter flight deck for debarkation in offshore conditions. Docking well is 885 m^2; vehicle area 1,010 m^2. Access hatch on the starboard side. Hospital facilities. Built to commercial standards with military command and control and NBCD facilities. *Castilla* has improved command and control facilities with two operations centres, one for amphibious and one for a combat group.
Operational: Alternatively can also be used for a general logistic support for both military and civil operations, including environmental and disaster relief tasks. Based at Rota.

GALICIA *6/2007, John Brodie* / 1166821

GALICIA *6/2007, H M Steele* / 1170041

0 + 1 STRATEGIC PROJECTION SHIP (LHD)

Name	*No*	*Builders*	*Laid down*	*Launched*	*Commissioned*
REY JUAN CARLOS I	L 61	Navantia, Ferrol	20 May 2005	10 Mar 2008	Dec 2009

Displacement, tons: 27,079 full load
Dimensions, feet (metres): 757.2 × 105.0 × 23.0 *(230.8 × 32.0 × 7.0)*
Flight deck, feet (metres): 663.9 × 105.0 *(202.3 × 32)*
Main machinery: CODAGE; 1 GE LM 2500 gas turbine; 26,550 hp *(19.8 MW)*; 2 MAN 324016V; 21,080 hp *(15.7 MW)*; 2 Siemens-Schottel podded propulsors; 29,500 hp *(22 MW)*
Speed, knots: 21. **Range, n miles**: 9,000 at 15 kt
Complement: 243 (plus 1,220 including flag staff, air group and 900 landing force)
Guns: 4—20 mm. 2—12.7 mm MGs.
Countermeasures: Decoys: Chaff launchers. SLQ-25a Nixie torpedo decoy.
Combat data systems: Link 11, 16. SATCOM.
Radars: Air search: Indra Lanza; D-band.
Surface search/navigation: 3 Indra Aries; I-band.
Helicopters: 6 landing spots for helicopter or AV-8 operations.

Programmes: Approval for the procurement of a Strategic Projection Ship was given by the Spanish Cabinet on 5 September 2003. Contract for design and construction was awarded in March 2004.
Structure: The hangar is 1,000 m². There are two 27-tonne aircraft elevators to the flight deck. Below the hangar there is a 2,000 m² garage. Typical transport configurations include: 46 tanks and 42 Leopard; 70 containers of 20 tons; 32 NH-90 or 19 AV-8 or 12 CH-47 or 12 NH 90 and 11 AV-8. The landing dock (69.3 × 16 m) is to be capable of operating four LCM (1E) landing craft or at least one landing craft air cushion. Medical facilities will include operating rooms, intensive care unit and sick bay. There is space and weight reserved for a point-defence system.
Operational: The principal roles are amphibious, strategic projection of land forces and disaster relief. The ship will also be capable of operating the fixed-wing aircraft of *Principe de Asturias*.
Sales: Two similar ships are to be built for the Australian Navy.

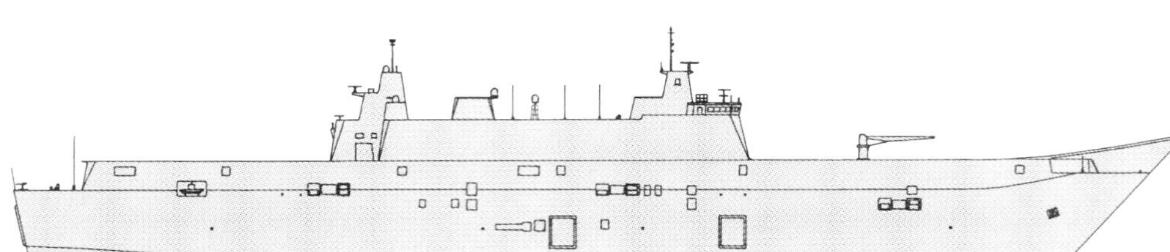

REY JUAN CARLOS I *(Scale 1 : 2,400), Ian Sturton* / 1164922

REY JUAN CARLOS I *7/2008*, Navantia* / 1335855

REY JUAN CARLOS I *3/2008*, Ships of the World* / 1335830

14 LCM (1E)

L 601–614

Displacement, tons: 108 full load
Dimensions, feet (metres): 76.5 × 21 × 3.4 *(23.3 × 6.4 × 1.1)*
Main machinery: 2 MAN-D 2842-LE 402 diesels; 2,200 hp(m) *(1.62 MW)*; 2 MJP-650 DD waterjets
Speed, knots: 14
Range, n miles: 160 at 12 kt
Complement: 3
Military lift: 100 tons or one main battle tank

Comment: L 601-602 built by IZAR, San Fernando, for LPDs and delivered in early 2001. Bow and stern ramps. Steel construction with wheelhouse of composites. Maximum speed in ballast is 22 kt. Based at Puntales. An order for a further 12 craft made in November 2004. First three laid down in 2005 and completed by 2007. A further nine builtby Navantia, San Fernando. All delivered by early 2008.

L 603 *6/2007, Camil Busquets i Vilanova* / 1170024

40 LANDING CRAFT

Comment: Apart from those used for divers there are 14 LCM 6 *(L 161-167, L 261-267)*, 16 LCVP and 8 LCPL. All of the LCM 6, eight of the LCVPs and most of the LCPs were built in Spanish Shipyards 1986–88. There are also two tug pontoons (mexeflotes) *(L 91-L 92)* completed in 1995. Most of these craft are laid up.

LCM L 162 *10/1993, Diego Quevedo* / 0506170

MINE WARFARE FORCES

6 SEGURA CLASS (MINEHUNTERS) (MHC)

Name	*No*	*Builders*	*Launched*	*Commissioned*
SEGURA	M 31	Bazán, Cartagena	25 July 1997	27 Apr 1999
SELLA	M 32	Bazán, Cartagena	6 July 1998	28 May 1999
TAMBRE	M 33	Bazán, Cartagena	5 Mar 1999	18 Feb 2000
TURIA	M 34	Bazán, Cartagena	22 Nov 1999	16 Oct 2000
DUERO	M 35	Izar, Cartagena	28 April 2003	5 July 2004
TAJO	M 36	Izar, Cartagena	10 June 2004	10 Jan 2005

Displacement, tons: 530 full load
Dimensions, feet (metres): 177.2 oa; 167.3 wl × 35.1 × 7.2 *(54; 51 × 10.7 × 2.2)*
Main machinery: 2 MTU-Bazán 6V 396 TB83 diesels; 1,523 hp(m) *(1.12 MW)*; 2 motors (for hunting); 200 kW; 2 Voith Schneider props; 2 side thrusters; 150 hp(m) *(110 kW)*
Speed, knots: 14; 7 (hunting)
Range, n miles: 2,000 at 12 kt
Complement: 41 (7 officers)
Guns: 1 Bazán/Oerlikon 20 mm GAM-BO1.
Countermeasures: MCM: FABA/Inisel system. 2 Gayrobot Pluto Plus ROVs.
Combat data systems: FABA/SMYC Nautis.
Radars: Navigation: Kelvin-Hughes 1007; I-band.
Sonars: Raytheon/ENOSA SQQ-32 multifunction VDS mine detection; high frequency.

Comment: On 4 July 1989 a technology transfer contract was signed with Vosper Thornycroft to allow Bazán to design a new MCM vessel based on the Sandown class. The order for four of the class was authorised on 7 May 1993, and an agreement signed on 26 November 1993 between DCN and Bazán provided for training in GRP technology. The first of class laid down 30 May 1995. Two more ordered on 26 January 2001. An option for two further ships is unlikely to be exercised. Sonar includes side scanning, and a towed body tracking and positioning system. M 35 and M 36 are to be fitted with the Minesniper mine disposal system. M 31-34 are to be retrofitted in due course. Form 1st MCM Squadron based at Cartagena.

SEGURA *11/2008*, Adolfo Ortigueira Gil* / 1335854

SURVEY AND RESEARCH SHIPS

1 DARSS CLASS (RESEARCH SHIP) (AGI/AGOR)

Name	*No*	*Builders*	*Commissioned*
ALERTA (ex-*Jasmund*)	A 111	Peenewerft, Wolgast	6 Dec 1992

Displacement, tons: 2,292 full load
Dimensions, feet (metres): 250.3 × 39.7 × 13.8 *(76.3 × 12.1 × 4.2)*
Main machinery: 1 Kolomna Type 40-DM diesel; 2,200 hp(m) *(1.6 MW)* sustained; 1 shaft; cp prop
Speed, knots: 11
Range, n miles: 1,000 at 11 kt
Complement: 60
Guns: Fitted for 3 twin 25 mm/70. 2—12.7 mm MGs.
Radars: Navigation: Racal Decca; I-band.

Comment: Former GDR depot ship launched on 27 February 1982 and converted to an AGI, with additional accommodation replacing much of the storage capacity. Was to have transferred to Ecuador in 1991 but the sale was cancelled. Commissioned in the Spanish Navy and sailed from Wilhelmshaven for a refit at Las Palmas prior to being based at Cartagena and used as an AGI and equipment trials ship. Saturn 35 SATCOM.

ALERTA *10/2008*, Adolfo Ortigueira Gil* / 1335853

2 CASTOR CLASS (SURVEY SHIPS) (AGS)

Name	*No*	*Builders*	*Commissioned*
ANTARES	A 23	Bazán, La Carraca	21 Nov 1974
RIGEL	A 24	Bazán, La Carraca	21 Nov 1974

Displacement, tons: 363 full load
Dimensions, feet (metres): 125.9 × 24.9 × 10.2 *(38.4 × 7.6 × 3.1)*
Main machinery: 1 Sulzer 4TD36 diesel; 720 hp(m) *(530 kW)*; 1 shaft
Speed, knots: 11.5
Range, n miles: 3,620 at 8 kt
Complement: 36 (4 officers)
Radars: Navigation: Raytheon 1620; I/J-band.

Comment: Fitted with Raydist, Omega and digital presentation of data. Likely to be decommissioned in the near future. Based at Cadiz.

ANTARES *10/2008*, Adolfo Ortigueira Gil* / 1335852

1 RESEARCH SHIP (AGOBH)

Name	*No*	*Builders*	*Commissioned*
HESPÉRIDES (ex-*Mar Antártico*)	A 33	Bazán, Cartagena	16 May 1991

Displacement, tons: 2,738 full load
Dimensions, feet (metres): 270.7 oa; 255.2 wl × 46.9 × 14.8 *(82.5; 77.8 × 14.3 × 4.5)*
Main machinery: Diesel-electric; 4 MAN-Bazán 14V20/27 diesels; 6,860 hp(m) *(5 MW)* sustained; 4 generators; 2 AEG motors; 3,800 hp(m) *(2.8 MW)*; 1 shaft; bow and stern thrusters; 350 hp(m) *(257 kW)* each
Speed, knots: 15. **Range, n miles:** 12,000 at 13 kt
Complement: 39 (9 officers) plus 30 scientists
Radars: Surface search: Racal/Hispano ARPA 2690; I-band.
Navigation: Racal 2690 ACS; F-band.
Helicopters: 1 AB 212

Comment: Ordered in July 1988 from Bazán, Cartagena, by the Ministry of Education and Science. Laid down in 1989, launched 12 March 1990. Has 330 sq m of laboratories, Simbad ice sonar. Dome in keel houses several sensors. Ice-strengthened hull capable of breaking first year ice up to 45 cm at 5 kt. Based at Cartagena, the main task is to support the Spanish base at Livingston Island, Antarctica. Manned and operated by the Navy. Has a telescopic hangar. Modifications made to superstructure in 2004 to increase accommodation for scientific staff.

HESPÉRIDES *5/2006, Adolfo Ortigueira Gil* / 1040691

1 RESEARCH SHIP (AGOB)

Name	*No*	*Builders*	*Commissioned*
LAS PALMAS (ex-*Somiedo*)	A 52	Astilleros Atlántico, Santander	1978

Displacement, tons: 1,450 full load
Dimensions, feet (metres): 134.5 × 38.1 × 18 *(41 × 11.6 × 5.5)*
Main machinery: 2 AESA/Sulzer 16ASV25/30 diesels; 7,744 hp(m) *(5.69 MW)*; 2 shafts
Speed, knots: 13. **Range, n miles:** 27,000 at 12 kt
Complement: 33 (8 officers) plus 45 scientists
Guns: 2—12.7 mm MGs.
Radars: Navigation: 2 Racal Decca; I-band.

Comment: Built as a tug for Compania Hispano Americana de Offshore SA. Commissioned in the Navy 30 July 1981. Converted in 1988 for Polar Research Ship duties in Antarctica with an ice strengthened bow, an enlarged bridge and two containers aft for laboratories. Based at Cartagena.

LAS PALMAS *10/2008*, Adolfo Ortigueira Gil* / 1335851

2 MALASPINA CLASS (SURVEY SHIPS) (AGS)

Name	*No*	*Builders*	*Commissioned*
MALASPINA	A 31	Bazán, La Carraca	21 Feb 1975
TOFIÑO	A 32	Bazán, La Carraca	23 Apr 1975

Displacement, tons: 820 standard; 1,090 full load
Dimensions, feet (metres): 188.9 × 38.4 × 12.8 *(57.6 × 11.7 × 3.9)*
Main machinery: 2 San Carlos MWM TbRHS-345-61 diesels; 3,600 hp(m) *(2.64 MW)*; 2 shafts; LIPS cp props
Speed, knots: 15
Range, n miles: 4,000 at 12 kt; 3,140 at 14.5 kt
Complement: 63 (9 officers)
Guns: 2 Oerlikon 20 mm.
Radars: Navigation: Raytheon 1220/6XB; I/J-band.

Comment: Ordered mid-1972. Both named after their immediate predecessors. Developed from British Bulldog class. Fitted with two Atlas DESO-10 AN 1021 (280-1,400 m) echo-sounders, retractable Burnett 538-2 sonar for deep sounding, Egg Mark B side scan sonar, Raydist DR-S navigation system, Hewlett Packard 2100A computer inserted into Magnavox Transit satellite navigation system, active rudder with fixed pitch auxiliary propeller. *Malaspina* used for a NATO evaluation of a Ship's Laser Inertial Navigation System (SLINS) produced by British Aerospace. Based at Cadiz.

MALASPINA *11/2008*, Adolfo Ortigueira Gil* / 1335850

2 LHT-130 CLASS (SURVEY MOTOR BOATS) (YGS)

Name	*No*	*Builders*	*Commissioned*
ASTROLABIO	A 91	Rodman, Vigo	30 Nov 2001
ESCANDALLO	A 92	Rodman, Vigo	27 Feb 2004

Displacement, tons: 8 full load
Dimensions, feet (metres): 41.3 × 13.8 × 1.6 *(12.6 × 4.2 × 0.5)*
Main machinery: 2 diesels; 700 hp *(522 kW)*; 2 shafts
Speed, knots: 30

Comment: Support craft of the Hydrographic Flotilla. Based at Puntales and transportable by road, rail, ship or aircraft.

ESCANDALLO *10/2008*, Adolfo Ortigueira Gil* / 1335849

TRAINING SHIPS

7 SAIL TRAINING SHIPS (AXS)

Name	*No*	*Builders*	*Commissioned*
JUAN SEBASTIÁN DE ELCANO	A 71	Echevarrieta, Cádiz	17 Aug 1928
AROSA	A 72	Inglaterra	1 Apr 1981
LA GRACIOSA (ex-*Dejá Vu*)	A 74	Inglaterra	30 June 1988
GIRALDA (ex-*Southern Cross*)	A 76	Morris & Mortimer, Argyll	26 Aug 1993
SISARGAS	A 75	Novo Glass, Polinya	18 May 1995
SÁLVORA	A 77	–	29 May 2001
PEREGRINA	A 78	–	22 Feb 2007

Displacement, tons: 3,420 standard; 3,656 full load
Dimensions, feet (metres): 308.5 oa × 43.3 × 24.6 *(94.1 × 13.15 × 7.46)*
Main machinery: 1 Deutz MWM KHD 6M diesel; 1,950 hp(m) *(1.43 MW)*; 1 shaft
Speed, knots: 9
Range, n miles: 10,000 at 9 kt
Complement: 347 (students 120)
Guns: 2—37/80 mm Bazán saluting guns.
Radars: Navigation: 2 Racal Decca; I-band.

Comment: Details are for A 71 (based at La Carraca) which is a four masted top-sail schooner-near sister of Chilean *Esmeralda*. Named after the first circumnavigator of the world (1519-22) who succeeded to the command of the expedition led by Magellan after the latter's death. Laid down 24 November 1925. Launched on 5 March 1927. Carries 230 tons oil fuel. Engine replaced in 1992. Six further are based at the Naval School, Marín. A ketch (A 72) (52 tons and 22.84 m in length), a schooner (A 74) (16.8 m in length), a 90 tons ketch (A 75) launched in 1958 and formerly owned by the father of King Juan Carlos I and presented to the Naval School in 1993, an ex-yacht (A 76) and a yacht (A 77).

JUAN SEBASTIAN DE ELCANO *6/2005, Frank Findler* / 1040692

4 TRAINING CRAFT (AXL)

Name	*No*	*Builders*	*Commissioned*
CONTRAMAESTRE NAVARRETE (ex-*Guardiamarina Salas*)	A 82	Cartagena	10 May 1983
CONTRAMAESTRE SÁNCHEZ FERNÁNDEZ (ex-*Guardiamarina Godinez*)	A 83	Cartagena	4 July 1984
CONTRAMAESTRE ANTERO (ex-*Guardiamarina Rull*)	A 84	Cartagena	11 June 1984
CONTRAMAESTRE LAMADRID (ex-*Guardiamarina Chereguini*)	A 85	Cartagena	11 June 1984

Displacement, tons: 56 full load
Dimensions, feet (metres): 62 × 16.7 × 5.2 *(18.9 × 5.1 × 1.6)*
Main machinery: 2 MAN diesels; 2 shafts
Speed, knots: 13
Complement: 15; 22 (A 81)
Radars: Navigation: Halcon 948; I-band.

Comment: Former tenders to Naval School transferred to Naval Specialist School, Ferrol, in 2007. The craft have been assigned new names.

CONTRAMAESTRE LAMADRID *6/2007, Roberto Marin* / 1170044

4 RODMAN 66 CLASS (AXT)

Name	*No*	*Builders*	*Commissioned*
GUARDIAMARINA BARRUTIA	A 121	Rodman, Vigo	2007
GUARDIAMARINA CHEREGUINI	A 122	Rodman, Vigo	2007
GUARDIAMARINA RULL	A 123	Rodman, Vigo	2007
GUARDIAMARINA SALAS	A 124	Rodman, Vigo	2008

Displacement, tons: 36
Dimensions, feet (metres): 67.2 × 16.0 × 3.1 *(20.5 × 4.9 × 0.96)*
Main machinery: 2 Caterpillar diesels; 1,500 hp *(1.1 MW)*; 2 shafts
Speed, knots: 20
Range, n miles: 500 at 15 kt
Complement: 16
Radars: Navigation: Furuno; I-band.

Comment: GRP hull. New craft which replaced Naval School tenders in 2007/08.

GUARDIAMARINA CHEREGUINI *12/2006, Adolfo Ortigueira Gil* / 1167149

AUXILIARIES

Notes: There are plans to acquire a new submarine rescue ship to replace *Neptuno*.

0 + 1 FLEET REPLENISHMENT SHIP (AORH)

Name	*No*	*Builders*	*Laid down*	*Launched*	*Commissioned*
CANTABRIA	A 15	Navantia, San Fernando	18 July 2007	21 July 2008	Sep 2009

Displacement, tons: 19,500 full load
Dimensions, feet (metres): 570.5 × 75.5 × 26.2 *(173.9 × 23.0 × 8.0)*
Main machinery: 2 diesels; 29,200 hp *(21.8 MW)*; 1 shaft
Speed, knots: 21
Range, n miles: 6,000 at 13 kt
Complement: 112
Cargo capacity: 6,400 tons dieso; 1,600 tons aviation fuel
Guns: To be announced.
Countermeasures: To be announced.
Combat data systems: To be announced.
Radars: To be announced.
Helicopters: 2 SH-3D Sea King or 3 AB 212.

Comment: Similar in design to Patiño class with improved capabilities including double-hull, container cargo capacity, enhanced sensors and a combat data system. Two RAS stations on each side and one stern refuelling station. There is to be a small hospital with 10 beds. Contract for construction of the ship signed on 30 December 2004.

CANTABRIA *10/2008*, Navantia* / 1335829

1 PATIÑO CLASS (FLEET LOGISTIC TANKER) (AORH)

Name	*No*	*Builders*	*Launched*	*Commissioned*
PATIÑO	A 14	Bazán, Ferrol	22 June 1994	16 June 1995

Displacement, tons: 5,762 light; 17,045 full load
Dimensions, feet (metres): 544.6 × 72.2 × 26.2 *(166 × 22 × 8)*
Main machinery: 2 Bazán/Burmeister & Wain 16V40/45 diesels; 24,000 hp(m) *(17.6 MW)* sustained; 1 shaft; LIPS cp prop
Speed, knots: 20
Range, n miles: 13,440 at 20 kt
Complement: 146 plus 19 aircrew plus 20 spare
Cargo capacity: 6,815 tons dieso; 1,660 tons aviation fuel; 500 tons solids
Guns: 2 Bazán 20 mm/120 Meroka CIWS (fitted for). 2 Oerlikon 20 mm/90.
Countermeasures: Decoys: 4 SRBOC chaff launchers. Nixie torpedo decoy.
ESM/ECM: Aldebaran intercept and jammer.
Radars: 3 navigation/helo control; I-band.
Helicopters: 2 SH-3D Sea King or 3 AB 212.

Comment: The Bazán design AP 21 was rejected in favour of this joint Netherlands/Spain design. Ordered on 26 December 1991. Laid down 1 July 1993. Two supply stations each side for both liquids and solids. Stern refuelling. One Vertrep supply station, and workshops for aircraft maintenance. Medical facilities. Built to merchant ship standards with military NBC. Accommodation for up to 50 female crew members. SCOT 3 SATCOM to be fitted. Based at Ferrol.

PATIÑO *6/2007, Maritime Photographic* / 1170043

1 TRANSPORT SHIP (AKRH)

Name	*No*	*Builders*	*Commissioned*
MARTÍN POSADILLO (ex-*Rivanervión*, ex-*Cala Portals*)	A 04 (ex-ET-02)	Duro Felguera, Gijon	1973

Displacement, tons: 1,920 full load
Dimensions, feet (metres): 246.1 × 42.7 × 14.1 *(75 × 13 × 4.3)*
Main machinery: 1 BMW diesel; 2,400 hp(m) *(1.77 MW)*; 1 shaft
Speed, knots: 10
Complement: 18
Military lift: 42 trucks plus 25 jeeps
Helicopters: Platform for 1 Chinook.

Comment: Ro-Ro ship taken on by the Army in 1990 and transferred to the Navy on 14 February 2000. Based at Cartagena.

MARTÍN POSADILLO *4/2008*, Adolfo Ortigueira Gil* / 1335848

1 TRANSPORT SHIP (APH)

Name	*No*	*Builders*	*Recommissioned*
CONTRAMAESTRE CASADO (ex-*Thanasis-K*, ex-*Fortuna Reefer*, ex-*Bonzo*, ex-*Bajamar*, ex-*Leeward Islands*)	A 01	Eriksberg-Göteborg, Sweden	15 Dec 1982

Displacement, tons: 4,965 full load
Dimensions, feet (metres): 343.4 × 46.9 × 29.2 *(104.7 × 14.3 × 8.9)*
Main machinery: 1 Burmeister & Wain diesel; 3,600 hp(m) *(2.65 MW)*; 1 shaft
Speed, knots: 14. **Range, n miles:** 8,000 at 14 kt
Complement: 72
Guns: 2 Oerlikon 20 mm.
Radars: Navigation: Racal Decca 1226 and 626; I-band.

Comment: Built in 1953. Impounded as smuggler. Delivered after conversion 6 December 1983. Has a helicopter deck. Since 2001, based at La Carraca (Cadiz).

CONTRAMAESTRE CASADO *10/2008*, Adolfo Ortigueira Gil* / 1335846

6 HARBOUR TANKERS (YO)

No	*Displacement, tons*	*Dimensions, metres*	*Cargo, tons fuel*	*Commissioned*
Y 231	524	37.9 × 7.0 × 3.1	300	1981
Y 251	830	46.7 × 8.4 × 3.1	500	1981
Y 252	337	34.3 × 6.2 × 2.5	193	1965
Y 253	337	34.3 × 6.2 × 2.5	193	1965
Y 254	214.7	27.2 × 6.2 × 2.2	100	1981
Y 255	524	37.6 × 7 × 2.9	300	1981

Comment: All built by Bazán at Cádiz and Ferrol.

Y 251 *11/2003, Diego Quevedo* / 0570953

1 TRANSPORT SHIP (AKR)

Name	*No*	*Builders*	*Commissioned*
EL CAMINO ESPAÑOL (ex-*Araguary*, ex-*Cyndia*)	A 05 (ex-ET 03)	Maua, Rio de Janeiro	Oct 1984

Displacement, tons: 5,804 full load
Dimensions, feet (metres): 313.6 × 59.8 × 15.2 *(95.5 × 18.3 × 4.6)*
Main machinery: 2 Sulzer diesels; 6,482 hp(m) *(4.76 MW)*; 2 shafts
Speed, knots: 12
Complement: 24 (3 officers) plus 40 Army
Military lift: 24 tanks plus 15 trucks and 102 jeeps
Radars: Navigation: I-band.

Comment: Acquired by the Army in early 1999 but commissioned into the Navy on 21 September 1999. Ro-Ro design converted for military use by Bazán in Cartagena. Used for logistic support of armed forces. Has two 25 ton cranes. Based at Cartagena.

EL CAMINO ESPAÑOL *10/2008*, Adolfo Ortigueira Gil* / 1335845

1 FLEET TANKER (AORLH)

Name	*No*	*Builders*	*Launched*	*Commissioned*
MARQUÉS DE LA ENSENADA (ex-*Mar del Norte*)	A 11	Bazán, Ferrol	5 Oct 1990	3 June 1991

Displacement, tons: 13,592 full load
Dimensions, feet (metres): 403.9 oa; 377.3 wl × 64 × 25.9 *(123.1; 115 × 19.5 × 7.9)*
Main machinery: 1 MAN-Bazán 18V40/50A; 11,247 hp(m) *(8.27 MW)* sustained; 1 shaft
Speed, knots: 16
Range, n miles: 10,000 at 15 kt
Complement: 80 (11 officers)
Cargo capacity: 7,498 tons dieso; 1,746 tons JP-5; 120 tons deck cargo
Guns: 2—12.7 mm MGs.
Radars: Surface search: Racal Decca 2459; I/F-band.
Navigation: Racal Decca ARPA 2690/9; I-band.
Helicopters: 1 AB 212 or similar.

Comment: Ordered 30 December 1988; laid down 16 November 1989. The deletion of the *Teide* left a serious deficiency in the Fleet's at sea replenishment capability which has been restored by the *Patiño*. In addition, and as a stop gap, this tanker was built at one third of the cost of the larger support ship. Two Vertrep stations and a platform for a Sea King size helicopter. Replenishment stations on both sides and one astern. Provision for Meroka CIWS four chaff launchers as well as ESM. Has a small hospital. Based at Rota.

MARQUÉS DE LA ENSENADA *3/2008*, Michael Winter* / 1335831

2 LOGISTIC SUPPORT SHIPS (ATF/AGDS)

Name	*No*	*Builders*	*Commissioned*
MAR CARIBE (ex-*Amatista*)	A 101	Duro Felguera, Gijon	24 Mar 1975
NEPTUNO (ex-*Mar Rojo*, ex-*Amapola*)	A 20 (ex-A 102)	Duro Felguera, Gijon	24 Mar 1975

Displacement, tons: 1,860 full load
Dimensions, feet (metres): 176.4 × 38.8 × 14.8 *(53.8 × 11.8 × 4.5)*
Main machinery: 2 Echevarria-Burmeister & Wain 18V23HU diesels; 4,860 hp(m) *(3.57 MW)*; 2 shafts; bow thruster
Speed, knots: 12
Range, n miles: 6,000 at 10 kt
Complement: 44

Comment: Two offshore oil rig support tugs were acquired and commissioned into the Navy 14 December 1988. Bollard pull, 80 tons. *Neptuno* converted as a diver support vessel and submarine rescue ship. She has a dynamic positioning system and carries a side scan mine detection high-frequency sonar as well as a semi-autonomous remote-controlled DSRV. The control cable restricts operations to within 75 m of an auxiliary diving unit. The DSRV is launched and recovered by a hydraulic arm. *Mar Caribe* works with Amphibious Forces and is based at Cadiz. *Neptuno* based at Cartagena.

MAR CARIBE *10/2008*, Adolfo Ortigueira Gil* / 1335847

NEPTUNO *11/2002, A Campanera i Rovira* / 0570952

1 WATER TANKER (AWT)

Name	*No*	*Builders*	*Commissioned*
MARINERO JARANO	A 65 (ex-AA 31)	Bazán, Cádiz	16 Mar 1981

Displacement, tons: 549 full load
Dimensions, feet (metres): 123 × 23 × 9.8 *(37.5 × 7 × 3)*
Main machinery: 1 diesel; 600 hp(m) *(441 kW)*; 1 shaft
Speed, knots: 10
Complement: 13
Cargo capacity: 300 tons

Comment: Similar to Y 231 and Y 255 (harbour tankers). Based at Cartagena.

MARINERO JARANO *9/2003, Diego Quevedo* / 0570951

1 WATER TANKER (AWT)

Name	*No*	*Builders*	*Commissioned*
CONDESTABLE ZARAGOZA	A 66 (ex-AA 41)	Bazán, Cádiz	16 Oct 1981

Displacement, tons: 895 full load
Dimensions, feet (metres): 152.2 × 27.6 × 11.2 *(46.4 × 8.4 × 3.4)*
Main machinery: 1 diesel; 700 hp(m) *(515 kW)*; 1 shaft
Speed, knots: 10
Complement: 16
Cargo capacity: 600 tons

Comment: Based at Puntales (Cadiz).

CONDESTABLE ZARAGOZA *2/1995, Diego Quevedo* / 0080637

42 HARBOUR LAUNCHES (YDT/YFL)

Y 502–511	**Y 534–535**	**Y 545**	**Y 554–558**	**Y 584**
Y 521–531	**Y 539–540**	**Y 548–549**	**Y 579–582**	**Y 586–589**

Comment: Some used as diving tenders, others as harbour ferries. Some are former patrol craft of the P 101 and P 202 class. *Y 540* is an Admirals' Yacht.

Y 558 *10/2008*, Adolfo Ortigueira Gil* / 1335844

Y 549 *10/2007, Adolfo Ortigueira Gil* / 1170036

47 BARGES (YO/YE)

Comment: Have Y numbers. Four in 200 series carry fuel, Five in 300 for ammunition and general stores, eight in 400 for anti-pollution. Some floating pontoons have L numbers.

Y 221 *10/2005, Adolfo Ortigueira Gil* / 1153458

TUGS

1 OCEAN TUG (ATA)

Name	*No*	*Builders*	*Commissioned*
MAHÓN (ex-*Circos*)	A 51	Astilleros Atlántico, Santander	1978

Displacement, tons: 1,450 full load
Dimensions, feet (metres): 134.5 × 38.1 × 18 *(41 × 11.6 × 5.5)*
Main machinery: 2 AESA/Sulzer 16ASV25/30 diesels; 7,744 hp(m) *(5.69 MW)*; 2 shafts
Speed, knots: 13
Range, n miles: 27,000 at 12 kt (A 52)
Complement: 33 (8 officers) plus 45 scientists
Guns: 2—12.7 mm MGs.
Radars: Navigation: 2 Racal Decca; I-band.

Comment: Built for Compania Hispano Americana de Offshore SA. Commissioned in the Navy 30 July 1981. Based at Ferrol.

MAHÓN *7/2000, Adolfo Ortigueira Gil* / 0105651

1 OCEAN TUG (ATA)

Name	*No*	*Builders*	*Commissioned*
LA GRAÑA (ex-*Punta Amer*)	A 53 (ex-Y 119)	Astilleros Luzuriaga, San Sebastian	1982

Displacement, tons: 664 full load
Dimensions, feet (metres): 102.4 × 27.6 × 10.5 *(31.2 × 8.4 × 3.2)*
Main machinery: 1 diesel; 3,240 hp(m) *(2.38 MW)*; 1 Voith Schneider prop
Speed, knots: 13
Range, n miles: 1,750 at 12 kt
Complement: 28

Comment: Former civilian tug acquired by Navy on 20 October 1987. Now designated as ocean-going. Based at Cadiz.

LA GRAÑA *6/2006, Adolfo Ortigueira Gil* / 1170035

31 COASTAL AND HARBOUR TUGS (YTB/YTM/YTL)

No	*Displacement tons (full load)*	*HP/speed*	*Commissioned*
Y 116	422	1,620/12	1981
Y 118	236	1,750/12	1989–91
Y 121	236	1,750/12	1989–91
Y 122	236	1,500/12	1999–02
Y 123	236	1,500/12	1999–02
Y 124	236	1,500/12	1999–02
Y 125	236	1,500/12	1999–02
Y 126	236	1,500/12	1999–02
Y 120 (ex-*Punta Roca*)	260	1,750/12	1988
Y 137	80	200/8	1965
Y 138	80	200/8	1965
Y 139	80	200/8	1965
Y 140	70	200/8	1965–67
Y 141	229	800/11	1981
Y 142	229	800/11	1981
Y 144	195	2,030/11	1983
Y 145	195	2,030/11	1983
Y 147	87	400/10	1987/1999
Y 148	87	400/10	1987/1999
Y 172	10	440/11	1982/1985
Y 173	10	440/11	1982/1985
Y 174	10	440/11	1982/1985
Y 175	10	440/11	1982/1985
Y 176	10	440/11	1982/1985
Y 177	10	440/11	1982/1985
Y 178	10	440/11	1982/1985
Y 179	10	440/11	1982/1985
Y 180	10	540/9	2005
Y 181	10	540/9	2005
Y 182	10	540/9	2005
Y 183	10	540/9	2005

Comment: *Y 143* has a troop carrying capability. *Y 171-176* are pusher tugs for submarines. *Y 118, Y 121-126* have Voith Schneider propulsion.

Y 124 *10/2008*, Adolfo Ortigueira Gil* / 1335843

GOVERNMENT MARITIME FORCES

POLICE (GUARDIA CIVIL—MARITIME SERVICE)

Notes: Created by Royal decree on 22 February 1991 and owned by the Ministry of Interior. Bases at Algeciras, Alicante, Almeria, Barcelona, Bilbao, Cadiz, Cartagena, Castellon, Ceuta, Corralejo, Gijón, Huelva, La Coruña, Lanzarote, Las Palmas, Malaga, Main, Motril, Palma, Pontevedra, Santander, Tarragona, Valencia and Vizcaya. Personnel strength 1,000 (35 officers). The force has taken over the anti-terrorist role and some general patrol duties as a peacetime paramilitary organisation coming under the Ministry of Defence in war. In addition to the craft listed there are some 42 smaller craft (under 9 m). All vessels are armed. 18 BO 105, 8 BK-117 and 31 Eurocopter EC-135 helicopters are used for coastal patrols and are based at Tenerife, Seville, Valencia, Mallorca, Huesca, Logroño, Leon and La Coruña. Two EADS/CASA 235 maritime patrol aircraft are to enter service in 2009.

EC-135 *6/2004, Oris* / 1044563

BK 117 *10/2005, Adolfo Ortigueira Gil* / 1153462

1 IZAR IVP-22 CLASS (WPB)

SALEMA A 01

Displacement, tons: 52 full load
Dimensions, feet (metres): 80.4 × 19.6 × 5.9 *(24.5 × 5.96 × 1.8)*
Main machinery: 2 MAN diesels; 1,100 hp *(820 kW)*
Speed, knots: 20
Range, n miles: 400 at 12 kt
Complement: 8
Guns: 1 — 12.7 mm MG.
Radars: Navigation: I-band.

Comment: Built by Bazán, San Fernando. Steel hull. Commissioned on 24 June 1999 having been procured by Agriculture and Fisheries Ministry for operation by Guardia Civil. Hull lengthened in 2003 to facilitate operation of RIB. Based at Algeciras.

SALEMA *10/2005, Adolfo Ortigueira Gil* / 1153463

3 RODMAN 82 CLASS (WPB)

RIO GUADIARO (ex-*Seriola*) A 02 **RIO PISUERGA** A 03 **RIO NALON** A 04

Displacement, tons: 93 full load
Dimensions, feet (metres): 85.3 × 19.4 × 4.3 *(26.0 × 5.9 × 1.3)*
Main machinery: 2 diesels; 1,400 hp *(1.04 MW)*; 2 waterjets
Speed, knots: 30
Range, n miles: 720 at 17 kt
Complement: 9
Guns: 1 LAG 40 mm grenade launcher.
Radars: Navigation: I-band.

Comment: Built in 2001 by Rodman, Vigo. A 02 based at Alicante, A 03 at Algeciras and A 04 at Asturias. A 02 purchased by Fisheries department.

RIO NALON *6/2007, Camil Busquets i Vilanova* / 1170025

13 RODMAN 101 CLASS (WPB)

RIO PALMA A 05
RIO ANDARAX A 06
RIO GUADALOPE A 07
RIO ALMANZORA A 08
RIO NERVION A 09
RIO GUADALAVIAR A 10
RIO CABRIEL A 11
RIO CERVANTES A 12
RIO ARA A 13
RIO ADAJA A 14
RIO DUERO A 15
RIO GUADIANA A 16
RIO FRANCOLI A 17

Displacement, tons: 109 full load
Dimensions, feet (metres): 98.4 × 19.4 × 4.3 *(30.0 × 5.9 × 1.3)*
Main machinery: 2 Caterpillar 3412C diesels; 2,800 hp *(2.06 MW)*; 2 Hamilton waterjets
Speed, knots: 30. **Range, n miles:** 800 at 12 kt
Complement: 9
Guns: 1 LAG 40 mm grenade launcher.
Radars: Navigation: I-band.

Comment: GRP hull. Built by Rodman, Vigo and delivered in 2002 (A 05), 2003 (A 06-08), 2004 (A 09-13), 2005 (A 14) and 2006 (A 15-17). A 05 A 06, A 08 and A 16 purchased by Agriculture and Fisheries Ministry. All operated by Guardia Civil.

RIO FRANCOLI *11/2008*, Adolfo Ortigueira Gil* / 1335840

9 RODMAN 55M CLASS (WPBF)

M 02–M 14 series

Displacement, tons: 15.7 full load
Dimensions, feet (metres): 54.1 × 12.5 × 2.3 *(16.5 × 3.8 × 0.7)*
Main machinery: 2 MAN D2848-LXE diesels; 1,360 hp(m) *(1 MW)* sustained; 2 Hamilton water-jets
Speed, knots: 35
Range, n miles: 500 at 25 kt
Complement: 7
Guns: 1 — 12.7 mm MG.
Radars: Surface search: Ericsson; I-band.

Comment: GRP hulls built by Rodman, Vigo. First five in service in 1992, three in 1993, six more in 1995–96. M 01 sunk in 2002. Known as Baltic class. Two transferred to Mauritania in 2006 and two to Gambia in 2007.

M 10 *6/2008*, M Declerck* / 1335837

2 RODMAN 55 CANARIAS CLASS (WPBF)

TINEYCHEIDE M 15 **ALMIRANTE DIAZ PIMIENTA** M 16

Displacement, tons: 18.5
Dimensions, feet (metres): 57.1 × 12.5 × 2.6 *(17.4 × 3.8 × 0.8)*
Main machinery: 2 MAN D2848 LXE406 diesels; 2,300 hp *(1.71 MW)*; 2 Hamilton waterjets
Speed, knots: 48
Range, n miles: 400 at 25 kt
Complement: 5
Guns: 1 — 12.7 mm MG.
Radars: Navigation: I-band.

Comment: GRP hull built by Rodman, Vigo. Purchased in 1999 by Canary Islands Agriculture and Fishery Department. Based at Lanzarote. Same class sold to Cyprus.

ALMIRANTE DIAZ PIMIENTA *2/2008*, Adolfo Ortigueira Gil* / 1335842

14 RODMAN 55HJ CLASS (PB)

RIO ARBA M 17
RIO CAUDAL M 18
RIO BERNESGA M 19
RIO MARTIN M 20
RIO GUADALOBON M 21
RIO CEDENTA M 22
RIO LADRA M 23
RIO CERVERA M 24
RIO JUCAR M 25
RIO GALLO M 26
RIO JILOCA M 27
RIO ALFAMBRA M 28
RIO SANTA EULALIA M 29
RIO ULLA M 30

Displacement, tons: 20 full load
Dimensions, feet (metres): 55.8 × 12.5 × 2.9 *(17.0 × 3.8 × 0.9)*
Main machinery: 2 MAN D2848 LXE406 diesels; 2,300 hp *(1.71 MW)*; 2 Hamilton waterjets
Speed, knots: 52
Range, n miles: 400 at 25 kt
Complement: 5
Radars: Navigation: I-band.

Comment: GRP hull built by Rodman, Vigo. Similar to Colimbo class of Spanish Customs. M 17-24 delivered in 2004 and M 25-30 in 2005.

RIO CERVERA *9/2008*, Diego Quevedo* / 1335838

1 RODMAN 58 CLASS (PB)

CORVO MARINO M 31

Displacement, tons: 20.0 full load
Dimensions, feet (metres): 59.1 × 16.1 × 3.9 *(18.0 × 4.9 × 1.2)*
Main machinery: 2 diesels; 2,000 hp *(1.5 MW)*; 2 Hamilton waterjets
Speed, knots: 34
Range, n miles: 450 at 25 kt
Complement: 5
Guns: 1 – 7.62 mm MG.
Radars: Navigation: Furuno; I-band.

Comment: GRP hull built by Rodman, Vigo. Purchased in 2006 for patrol duties around Cies Islands off Vigo. Based at Naval School, Marin.

CORVO MARINO *6/2007, L M Rodriguez Garcia* / 1170039

9 SAETA-12 CLASS (WPBF)

L 02 **L 04–11**

Displacement, tons: 14 full load
Dimensions, feet (metres): 39 × 12.5 × 2.3 *(11.9 × 3.8 × 0.7)*
Main machinery: 2 MAN D2848-LXE diesels; 1,360 hp(m) *(1 MW)* sustained; 2 Hamilton water-jets
Speed, knots: 38
Range, n miles: 300 at 25 kt
Complement: 4
Guns: 1 – 7.62 mm MG.
Radars: Surface search: Ericsson; I-band.

Comment: GRP hulls built by Bazán and delivered in 1993–97. Known as Aegean class. L 03 deleted in 2004 following an accident. Two (possibly including L 12) transferred to Mauritania in 2006.

L 11 *11/2008*, Adolfo Ortigueira Gil* / 1335839

1 PATROL SHIP (PBO)

RIO MIÑO (ex-*Hoyo Maru*, ex-*Amazonas Reefer I*)

Measurement, tons: 349 gross
Dimensions, feet (metres): 169.9 × 28.2 × 10.8 *(51.8 × 8.6 × 3.3)*
Main machinery: 1 diesel; 1,000 hp *(736 kW)*; 1 shaft
Speed, knots: 12
Complement: 30
Radars: Navigation: I-band.

Comment: Former fishing boat constructed by Narosaki Zosen Shipyard, Japan, in 1984. Steel construction with bulbous bow. Converted to patrol boat in 2007 and recommissioned on 2 September 2007. Based at Las Palmas, Canary Islands for patrol duties between the islands and the African coastline.

RIO MIÑO *9/2007, Joaquin Ojedo* / 1170042

6 RODMAN 66 CLASS (PB)

CANAL BOCAYNA M 34
PICO DEL TEIDE M 35
RIO GUADALQUIVIR M 36
RIO TORDERA M 37
RIO PAS M 38
RIO GUADALENTIN M 39

Displacement, tons: 36 full load
Dimensions, feet (metres): 67.2 × 16.1 × 3.1 *(20.5 × 4.9 × 0.96)*
Main machinery: 2 MAN D2848 diesels; 2,200 hp *(1.64 MW)*; 2 Hamilton HM 461 waterjets
Speed, knots: 30
Range, n miles: 450 at 22 kt
Complement: 6
Radars: Navigation: Furuno; I-band.

Comment: Built by Rodman to replace the Saeta class which are to be withdrawn from service. *Canal Bocayna* (Fuerteventura) delivered on 28 January 2008, *Pico del Tiede* (Tenerife) on 11 February 2008, *Rio Guadalquivir* (Cadiz) on 16 May 2008, *Rio Tordera* (Almeria) in June 2008, *Rio Pas* (Santander) on 11 June 2008 and *Rio Guadalentin* (Cartagena) in July 2008.

RIO TORDERA *11/2008*, Adolfo Ortigueira Gil* / 1335841

RESEARCH SHIPS

Notes: Nine civilian research ships are owned by the Government Science and Technology Ministry and by the Agriculture Fishery and Food Ministry. Those operated by the Instítuto Español de Oceanografía (IEO) are *Vizconde de Eza* (1,400 tons), *Cornide de Saavedra* (1,113 tons), *F P Navarro* (178 tons), *Odón de Buen* (64 tons), *Lura* (34 tons), *José Rioja* (32 tons), *J M Navaz* (30 tons), *Emma Bardán* (209 tons) and *Miguel Oliver* (1,200 tons). Those operated by CSIC are *Garcia del Cid* (539 tons), *Mytilus* (170 tons) and *Sarmiento de Gamboa* (2,980 tons). The ships operate in co-operation with the Spanish Navy ship *Hespérides* and the French research ship *Thalassa*. A new ship is to be delivered to CSIC in 2006.

VIZCONDE DE EZA *6/2005, Adolfo Ortigueira Gil* / 1153454

SARMIENTO DE GAMBOA *5/2008*, Adolfo Ortigueira Gil* / 1335834

CUSTOMS

Notes: Customs service is the responsibility of the Ministry of Treasure. All carry ADUANAS on ships' sides. Some of the larger vessels are armed with machine guns. Ships are based at 17 ports including Ceuta and Melilla in north Africa. There are also three MBB-105, one MBB-117 and two AS 365 Dauphin helicopters. Six CASA C-212 patrol aircraft were transferred to the Air Force in 1997 and are operated by the 37th Air Wing.

CASA C-212 *3/2003, Adolfo Ortigueira Gil* / 0570963

46 PATROL CRAFT (PB)

Name	*Displacement, tons (full load)*	*HP/speed*	*Commissioned*
ÁGUILA	80	2,700/29	1974
ALBATROS II and ALBATROS III	85	2,700/29	1964–69
ALCA I and ALCA III	24	2,000/45	1987–88
ALCAUDON II/ALCOTÁN/FENIX	18.5	1,200/55	1997–99
ALCAVARÁN I/ALCAVARÁN II/ ALCAVARÁNIII/ALCAVARÁN IV/ ALCAVARÁN V	85	3,920/28	1984–87
COLIMBO II	17	2,400/50	1999–03
CORMORÁN/HJ 1/COLIMBO III/ COLIMBO IV	17	2,400/52	1986–03
FULMAR	623	5,400/21	2006
GAVILÁN II/GAVILÁN III/GAVILÁN IV	65	3,200/26	1983–87
ARAO/GERIFALTE I/DÉCIMO ANIVERSARIO/ABANTO/PAIÑO/ SACRE/ALBATROS	46	2,366/35	2001/2003/2006
HJA	12	2,200/55	1994
HJ III/HJ IV/HJ V/HJ VI/HJ VII/ HJ VIII/HJ IX/HJ X	20	2,300/50	1986–89
HALCÓN II/HALCÓN III	68	3,200/28	1980–83
IMP I/IMP II	5	600/40	1989
IPP I and IPP III	2	200/50	1989
MILANO II	15	2,000/50	1999
PETREL I	1,600	1,200/12	1994
VA II/VA III/VA IV/VA V	23	1,400/27	1985

Comment: These craft are also listed as auxiliary ships of the Navy. Flagship is *Petrel I* for which replacement is under construction at Astilleros Gondan for delivery in 2006.

PETREL I *11/2003, Javier Somavilla* / 0570950

GERIFALTE I *11/2005, Adolfo Ortigueira Gil* / 1153455

HJ-VI *9/2008*, Adolfo Ortigueira Gil* / 1335836

FULMAR *5/2006, Gondán* / 1335835

MARITIME RESCUE, SAFETY AND LOGISTIC SUPPORT

Notes: These roles are discharged by two services: SASEMAR (Sociedad Estatal de Salvamento y Seguridad Maritima) is under the direction of the Merchant Marine but may come under a Coast Guard service in due course. It operates 11 salvage tugs (*Don India, Clara Campoamor, Punta Mayor, Alfonso de Chaves, Ria de Vigo, Punta Salinas, Off Valencia, L'Albufera, Golfo de Vizcaya, Catalunya* and *Remolcanosa Cinco*), five anti-pollution ships and 55 fast rescue craft. Aircraft assets include three EADS/CASA C-235 and 10 helicopters (AW-139 and Sikorsky S-61). All ships are painted red with a white stripe on the hull. ISM (Instituto Social de la Marina) operates one specialised medical and logistic ship for support of fishing vessels. *Esperenza del Mar* (5,000 tons) is based at Las Palmas (Canary Islands) Naval Base and *Juan de la Cosa* is based at Santander.

SALVAMAR ALBORAN *1/2005, Adolfo Ortigueira Gil* / 1153456

ESPERANZA DEL MAR *9/2001, Adolfo Ortigueira Gil* / 0130140

CLARA CAMPOAMOR *11/2007* / 1335833

S 61 *10/2008*, Adolfo Ortigueira Gil* / 1335832

Sri Lanka

Country Overview

Formerly known as Ceylon, the Democratic Socialist Republic of Sri Lanka gained independence in 1948. Situated off the southeast coast of India, from which it is separated by the Palk Strait and Gulf of Mannar, it has an area of 25,326 square miles and a coastline of 723 n miles with the Indian Ocean. The capital of Sri Lanka is Sri Jayavardhanapura (Kotte) while Colombo is the largest city and principal port. There are further ports at Trincomalee, Kankasanthurai and Galle. Territorial waters (12 n miles) are claimed. A 200 n mile EEZ has been claimed although the limits have only been partly defined by boundary agreements.

Headquarters Appointments

Commander of the Navy:
Vice Admiral W K J Karannagoda, RSP, VSV, USP
Chief of Staff:
Rear Admiral M R U Siriwardana, USP
Director General, Operations:
Rear Admiral D W A S Dissanayake, WV, RSP, VSV, USP

Area Commanders

Commander Western Naval Area:
Rear Admiral W M K N Weerakoon, USP

Area Commanders — *continued*

Commander North Central Naval Area:
Rear Admiral W M L T B Illangakoon, RSP, USP
Commander Northern Naval Area:
Rear Admiral T S G Samarasinghe, RSP, VSV, USP
Commander Eastern Naval Area:
Rear Admiral S M B Weerasekara, RSP, USP
Commander Southern Naval Area:
Commodore R C Wijegunarathne, WV, RSP, USP

Personnel

(a) 2009: 35,148 (1,720 officers) regulars
(b) SLVNF: 7,351 (333 officers)
(c) Reserve force (regular): 730 (7 officers)
(d) Reserve force (volunteer): 143 (8)

Bases

Navy HQ: Colombo.
Western Command HQ: Colombo port (other bases at Welisara and Kalpitiya Training Centre at Thalathoya).
Eastern Command HQ: Trincomalee port (other bases at Nilaweli, Pulmudai, Sampoor, Thavulwewa and Thiriyaya, Naval Academy at Trincomalee).
Southern Command HQ: Galle port (other bases at Tangalle, Boossa training centre and Kirinda harbour).
Northern Command HQ: Kankasanthurai port (other bases at Madagal, Karainagar, Velerni Island, Mandathive Island, Nagadeepa Island and Pungudathive Island).
North Central Command HQ: Medawachchiya (other bases at Punewa training centre, Silavathurai, Mullikulam, Mannar Town, Thalaimannar and Mannar Island).

Pennant Numbers

Pennant numbers were reviewed in 1996 and 2002.

Prefix To Ships Names

SLNS.

DELETIONS

Patrol Forces

2006 P 418 (sunk in action), P 476 (sunk in action)
2008 P 438 (sunk in action)

Auxiliaries

2008 A 520

PATROL FORCES

Notes: It is planned to acquire six fast attack craft and four 41 m patrol craft in 2009.

1 SUKANYA CLASS (OFFSHORE PATROL VESSEL) (PSOH)

Name	*No*	*Builders*	*Launched*	*Commissioned*
SAYURA (ex-*Saryu*)	P 620 (ex-54)	Hindustan SY, Vishakapatnam	16 Oct 1989	8 Oct 1991

Displacement, tons: 1,890 full load
Dimensions, feet (metres): 331.7 oa; 315 wl × 37.7 × 14.4 *(101.1; 96 × 11.5 × 4.4)*
Main machinery: 2 SEMT-Pielstick 16 PA6 V 280 diesels; 12,800 hp(m) *(9.41 MW)* sustained; 2 shafts
Speed, knots: 21
Range, n miles: 5,800 at 15 kt
Complement: 140 (15 officers)
Guns: 1 Bofors 40 mm/60. 4 China 14.5 mm (twin). 4—12.7 mm MGs.
Radars: Surface search: Racal Decca 2459; I-band.
Navigation: Bharat1245; I-band.

Comment: Transferred from India and recommissioned on 9 December 2000.

SAYURA *12/2007, **Chris Sattler*** / 1170045

1 RELIANCE CLASS (PSOH)

Name	*No*	*Builders*	*Commissioned*
SAMUDURA (ex-*Courageous*)	P 621 (ex-WMEC 622)	Coast Guard Yard, Baltimore	8 Dec 1967

Displacement, tons: 1,129 full load
Dimensions, feet (metres): 210.5 × 34 × 10.5 *(64.2 × 10.4 × 3.2)*
Main machinery: 2 Alco 16V-251 diesels; 6,480 hp *(4.83 MW)* sustained; 2 shafts; LIPS cp props
Speed, knots: 18. **Range, n miles:** 6,100 at 14 kt; 2,700 at 18 kt
Complement: 75 (12 officers)
Guns: 1 Boeing 25 mm/87 Mk 38 Bushmaster; 200 rds/min to 6.8 km *(3.4 n miles)*. 2—12.7 mm MGs.
Radars: Surface search: Hughes/Furuno SPS-73; I-band.
Helicopters: Platform for one medium.

Comment: Transferred from USCG to Sri Lanka on 24 June 2004. During 34 years in USCG service, underwent Major Maintenance Availability (MMA) in 1989. The exhausts for main engines, ship service generators and boilers were run in a vertical funnel which reduced flight deck size. Capable of towing ships up to 10,000 tons.

SAMUDURA *6/2007, **Sri Lanka Navy*** / 1167812

1 JAYASAGARA CLASS (OFFSHORE PATROL VESSEL) (PB)

Name	*No*	*Builders*	*Launched*	*Commissioned*
JAYASAGARA	P 601	Colombo Dockyard	26 May 1983	9 Dec 1983

Displacement, tons: 330 full load
Dimensions, feet (metres): 130.5 × 23 × 7 *(39.8 × 7 × 2.1)*
Main machinery: 2 MAN 8L20/27 diesels; 2,180 hp(m) *(1.6 MW)* sustained; 2 shafts
Speed, knots: 15
Range, n miles: 3,000 at 11 kt
Complement: 52 (4 officers)
Guns: 2 China 25 mm/80 (twin). 2 China 14.5 mm (twin) MGs. 2—12.7 mm MGs. 2—40 mm AGL. 2—7.62 mm MGs.
Radars: Surface search: Anritsu RA 723; I-band.

Comment: Ordered from Colombo Dockyard on 31 December 1981. Second of class sunk by Tamil forces in September 1994.

JAYASAGARA *6/2004, **Sri Lanka Navy*** / 1044193

2 SAAR 4 CLASS (FAST ATTACK CRAFT—MISSILE) (PGG)

Name	*No*	*Builders*	*Launched*	*Commissioned*
NANDIMITHRA (ex-*Moledt*)	P 701	Israel Shipyard, Haifa	22 Mar 1979	May 1979
SURANIMALA (ex-*Komemiut*)	P 702	Israel Shipyard, Haifa	19 July 1978	Aug 1980

Displacement, tons: 415 standard; 450 full load
Dimensions, feet (metres): 190.6 × 25 × 8 *(58 × 7.8 × 2.4)*
Main machinery: 4 MTU/Bazán 16V 956TB91 diesels; 15,000 hp(m) *(11.03 MW)* sustained; 4 shafts
Speed, knots: 32
Range, n miles: 1,650 at 30 kt; 4,000 at 17.5 kt
Complement: 75

Missiles: 3 Gabriel II; radar or TV optical guidance; semi-active radar plus anti-radiation homing to 36 km *(20 n miles)* at 0.7 Mach; warhead 75 kg.
Guns: 1 OTO Melara 3 in *(76 mm)*/62 compact; 85 rds/min to 16 km *(8.7 n miles)*; weight of shell 6 kg. Adapated for shore bombardment.
1—40 mm.
2 Rafael Typhoon 20 mm. 2—20 mm. 2—12.7 mm MGs. 2—40 mm AGL.
Radars: Air/surface search: Thomson-CSF TH-D 1040 Neptune; G-band; range 33 km *(18 n miles)* for 2 m² target.
Fire control: Selenia Orion RTN 10X; I-band.

Comment: Transferred from Israel and recommissioned on 9 December 2000.

NANDIMITHRA *10/2003, **Hartmut Ehlers*** / 0570991

5 SHANGHAI II (TYPE 062) CLASS (FAST ATTACK CRAFT—GUN) (PB)

WEERAYA P 311 (ex-P 3141)
JAGATHA P 315 (ex-P 3146)
ABEETHA II P 316
EDITHARA II P 317
WICKRAMA II P 318

Displacement, tons: 139 full load
Dimensions, feet (metres): 127.3 × 17.7 × 5.2 *(38.8 × 5.4 × 1.6)*
Main machinery: 4 Type L12-180 diesels; 4,800 hp(m) *(3.53 MW)*; 4 shafts
Speed, knots: 28. **Range, n miles:** 750 at 16 kt
Complement: 44
Guns: 4 (2 in P 311, P 315) Royal Ordnance GCM-AO3 30 mm (2 (1 in P 311, P 315) twin).
4—37 mm 2 (twin) (P 311, P 315).
4 China 14.5 mm (2 twin) MG.
2—7.62 mm MGs.
2—40 mm AGL (P 311, P 315).
Radars: Surface search: Koden MD 3220 Mk 2; I-band.
Navigation: Furuno 825 D; I-band.

Comment: Five transferred by China in 1971 of which four since decommissioned and *Weeraya* remains in service. Two further craft transferred in 1980 of which *Jagatha* remains in service. Three further craft (*Abeetha II*, *Edithara II* and *Wickrama II*) are modified craft with improved habitability but similar specifications. These were built at Qinxin Shipyard and commissioned on 11 June 2000.

WEERAYA *6/2001, Sri Lanka Navy* / 0130146

EDITHARA II *6/2003, Sri Lanka Navy* / 0570992

1 MOD SHANGHAI II CLASS (FAST ATTACK CRAFT—GUN) (PB)

Name	*No*	*Builders*	*Commissioned*
RANARISI	P 322	Guijiang Shipyard	14 July 1992

Displacement, tons: 150 full load
Dimensions, feet (metres): 134.5 × 17.7 × 5.2 *(41 × 5.4 × 1.6)*
Main machinery: 4 diesels; 4,800 hp(m) *(3.53 MW)*; 4 shafts
Speed, knots: 29
Range, n miles: 750 at 16 kt
Complement: 44 (4 officers)
Guns: 2 Royal Ordnance GCM-AO3 30 mm (1 twin). 2—25 mm.
4 China 14.5 mm (twin) Type 69. 2—12.7 mm MGs. 2—40 mm AGL.
Radars: Surface search: Racal Decca; I-band.

Comment: Acquired from China in September 1991. Automatic guns and improved habitability. *Ranaviru* and *Ranasuvu* destroyed by Tamil guerrillas.

RANARISI *6/2003, Sri Lanka Navy* / 0570988

3 HAIZHUI (TYPE 062/1G) CLASS (PB)

Name	*No*	*Builders*	*Commissioned*
RANAJAYA	P 330	Guijiang Shipyard	22 May 1996
RANADEERA	P 331	Guijiang Shipyard	22 May 1996
RANAWICKRAMA	P 332	Guijiang Shipyard	22 May 1996

Displacement, tons: 170 full load
Dimensions, feet (metres): 134.5 × 17.4 × 5.9 *(41 × 5.3 × 1.8)*
Main machinery: 4 Type L12-180A diesels; 4,400 hp(m) *(3.22 MW)* sustained; 4 shafts
Speed, knots: 21
Complement: 44
Guns: 2 China 37 mm/63 (1 twin). 1—30 mm GCM-A03. 4 China 25 mm/60 (2 twin). 2—12.7 mm MGs. 2—40 mm AGL.
Radars: Surface search: Anritsu 726UA; I-band.

Comment: Transferred from China by lift ship after delivery in 1995.

RANAWICKRAMA *6/2008*, Sri Lanka Navy* / 1335871

2 MOD HAIZHUI (LUSHUN) (TYPE 062/1G) CLASS (FAST ATTACK CRAFT—GUN) (PB)

PRATHPA P 340
UDARA P 341

Displacement, tons: 212 full load
Dimensions, feet (metres): 149 × 21 × 5.6 *(45.5 × 6.4 × 1.7)*
Main machinery: 4 Type Z12V 190 BCJ diesels; 4,800 hp(m) *(3.53 MW)*; 4 shafts
Speed, knots: 28
Range, n miles: 750 at 16 kt
Complement: 44 (3 officers)
Guns: 4 China 37 mm/63 (2 twin) Type 76.
2 China 14.5 mm (1 twin) Type 82 MGs.
2—12.7 mm MGs.
2—40 mm AGL.
Radars: Surface search: Racal Decca RM 1070A; I-band.

Comment: Built at Lushun Dockyard, Darlin. Commissioned on 2 March 1998. Larger version of Haizhui class.

UDARA *6/2005, Sri Lanka Navy* / 1153483

28 COLOMBO MK I/II/III/IV CLASS (FAST ATTACK CRAFT—GUN) (PBF)

P 410–415, P 417, P 419–424, P 430, P 432–437, P 439, P 450–451, P 490–492, P 494, P 497

Displacement, tons: 56 full load
Dimensions, feet (metres): 79.7 × 18.6 × 3.9 *(24.3 × 5.7 × 1.2)*
Main machinery: 2 MTU 12V 396 TE94 diesels (Mk I/II) or 2 Deutz TBD 620 16V (Mk III/IV); 4,570 hp(m) *(3.36 MW)*; ASD 16 surface drives
Speed, knots: 45. **Range, n miles:** 850 at 16 kt
Complement: 20
Guns: 1 Rafael Typhoon 23 mm. 1 Oerlikon 20 mm. 4—12.7 mm MGs. 8—7.62 mm MGs. 2—40 mm AGL.
Weapons control: Elop MSIS optronic director; Typhoon GFCS.
Radars: Surface search: Furuno FR 8250 or Corden Mk 2; I-band.

Comment: Built by Colombo Dockyard to the Israeli Shaldag design. Deliveries of Mk I (P 450-451) began in 1996 and of Mk II (P 490-492, P 494, P 497) began in 1997. P 493 and P 496 sunk in action in 2000. Deliveries of Mk III (P 410-415, P 417, P 419-424) began in 2000 and of Mk IV (P 430, 432-439) in 2005. P 418 sunk in action in May 2006 and P 438 in March 2008.

COLOMBO MK II *6/2006, Sri Lanka Navy* / 1164412

COLOMBO MK III *6/2006, Sri Lanka Navy* / 1164411

6 SHALDAG CLASS (FAST ATTACK CRAFT—GUN) (PBF)

P 470 (ex-P 491) **P 471** (ex-P 492) **P 472** **P 473** **P 474** **P 475**

Displacement, tons: 58 full load
Dimensions, feet (metres): 81.4 × 19.7 × 3.9 *(24.8 × 6 × 1.2)*
Main machinery: 2 Deutz 620 TB 16V diesels; 5,000 hp(m) *(3.68 MW)*; 2 LIPS or MJP water-jets
Speed, knots: 50
Range, n miles: 700 at 32 kt
Complement: 20
Guns: 1 Rafael Typhoon 23 mm. 1—20 mm. 2—12.7 mm MGs. 6—7.62 mm MGs. 2—40 mm AGL.
Weapons control: ELOP compass optronic director. Typhoon GFCS.
Radars: Surface search: MD 3220 Mk II; I-band.

Comment: Originally launched in December 1989, first one acquired from the Israeli Shipyards, Haifa on 24 January 1996, second 20 July 1996 and third on 16 February 2000. Four more followed. Same hull used for the Colombo class. Also in service in Cyprus. P 476 sunk on 7 January 2006.

SHALDAG CLASS ***6/2003, Sri Lanka Navy*** / 0570989

4 SUPER DVORA MK I CLASS (FAST ATTACK CRAFT—GUN) (PBF)

P 440 (ex-P 465) **P 441** (ex-P 466) **P 442** (ex-P 467) **P 443** (ex-P 468)

Displacement, tons: 54 full load
Dimensions, feet (metres): 73.5 × 18 × 5.8 *(22.4 × 5.5 × 1.8)*
Main machinery: 2 MTU 12V 396TB93 diesels; 3,260 hp(m) *(2.4 MW)* sustained; 2 shafts
Speed, knots: 46
Range, n miles: 1,200 at 17 kt
Complement: 20 (1 officer)
Guns: 2 Oerlikon 20 mm. 2—12.7 mm MGs. 4—40 mm AGL.
Radars: Surface search: Decca 926; I-band.

Comment: Ordered from Israel Aircraft Industries in October 1986 and delivered in 1987–88. A more powerful version of the Dvora class. *P 464* was destroyed by Tamil guerrillas on 29 August 1993 and *P 463* on 29 August 1995. These craft have a deeper draft than the Mk II version with surface drives.

P 443 (ex-P 468) ***1995, Sri Lanka Navy*** / 0130147

4 SUPER DVORA MK II CLASS (FAST ATTACK CRAFT—GUN) (PBF)

P 460 (ex-P 441) **P 462** (ex-P 497) **P 464** **P 465**

Displacement, tons: 64 full load
Dimensions, feet (metres): 82 × 18.4 × 3.6 *(25 × 5.6 × 1.1)*
Main machinery: 2 MTU 12V 396 TE94 diesels; 4,570 hp(m) *(3.36 MW)*; ASD16 surface drives
Speed, knots: 50
Range, n miles: 700 at 30 kt
Complement: 20 (1 officer)
Guns: 1 Rafael Typhoon 23 mm.
4—12.7 mm MGs. 6—7.62 mm MGs. 2—40 mm AGL.
Weapons control: Elop MSIS optronic director; Typhoon GFCS.
Radars: Surface search: Koden MD 3220; I-band.

Comment: First four ordered from Israel Aircraft Industries Ramta in early 1995. A slightly larger version of the Mk 1. First one delivered 5 November 1995, second 30 April 1996, third 22 June 1996 and fourth in December 1996. Two more were acquired on 9 June 1999 and 15 September 1999 respectively. The engines are an improved version of those fitted in the Israeli Navy craft. P 463 sunk in action in 2000. P 461 reported lost in action.

SUPER DVORA Mk II ***11/1999*** / 0080697

3 DVORA CLASS (FAST ATTACK CRAFT—GUN) (PBF)

P 401–403 (ex-*P 420* (ex-*P 453*)–*P 422* (ex-*P 456*))

Displacement, tons: 47 full load
Dimensions, feet (metres): 70.8 × 18 × 5.8 *(21.6 × 5.5 × 1.8)*
Main machinery: 2 MTU 12V 331TC81 diesels; 2,605 hp(m) *(1.91 MW)* sustained; 2 shafts
Speed, knots: 36
Range, n miles: 1,200 at 17 kt
Complement: 18
Guns: 2 Oerlikon 20 mm. 2—12.7 mm MGs. 6—7.62 mm MGs. 2—40 mm AGL.
Radars: Surface search: Anritsu 721UA; I-band.

Comment: 'Dvora' class, first pair of which transferred from Israel early 1984, next four in October 1986. Built by Israel Aircraft Industries. One sunk by Tamil forces on 29 August 1995 and second on 30 March 1996. One more deleted in late 1996. Not downgraded to patrol craft as previously reported but speed may have been reduced.

DVORA CLASS ***6/2003, A Sharma*** / 0570995

3 SOUTH KOREAN KILLER CLASS (FAST ATTACK CRAFT—GUN) (PBF)

P 404 (ex-*P 430* (ex-*P 473*)) **P 405** (ex-*P 431* (ex-*P 474*)) **P 406** (ex-*P 432* (ex-*P 475*))

Displacement, tons: 56 full load
Dimensions, feet (metres): 75.5 × 17.7 × 5.9 *(23 × 5.4 × 1.8)*
Main machinery: 2 MTU 396TB93 diesels; 3,260 hp(m) *(2.4 MW)* sustained; 2 shafts
Speed, knots: 40
Complement: 18
Guns: 2 Oerlikon 20 mm. 2—12.7 mm MGs. 6—7.62 mm MGs.
Radars: Surface search: Racal Decca 926; I-band.

Comment: 'South Korean Killer' class, built by Korea SB and Eng, Buson. All commissioned February 1988. Not downgraded to patrol craft as previously reported but speed may have been reduced.

KILLER CLASS ***6/2003, A Sharma*** / 0570994

5 TRINITY MARINE CLASS (FAST ATTACK CRAFT—GUN) (PBF)

P 480–481 **P 483–485**

Displacement, tons: 68 full load
Dimensions, feet (metres): 81.7 × 17.7 × 4.9 *(24.9 × 5.4 × 1.5)*
Main machinery: 2 MTU 12V 396TE94 diesels; 4,570 hp(m) *(3.36 MW)* sustained; 2 water-jets
Speed, knots: 47. **Range, n miles:** 600 at 17 kt
Complement: 20
Guns: 2 Oerlikon 20 mm. 2—12.7 mm MGs. 2—7.62 mm MGs. 1 Grenade launcher.
Radars: Surface search: Raytheon R 1210; I-band.

Comment: All built at Equitable Shipyard, New Orleans. First three delivered in January 1997; second three in September 1997. All aluminium construction. P 482 sunk in action in 2000.

P 480 *1/1997, Sri Lanka Navy* / 0080701

3 COASTAL PATROL CRAFT (PB)

P 201 **P 211** **P 215**

Displacement, tons: 21 full load
Dimensions, feet (metres): 46.6 × 12.8 × 3.3 *(14.2 × 3.9 × 1)*
Main machinery: 2 Detroit 8V-71TA diesels; 460 hp *(343 kW)*; 2 shafts
Speed, knots: 20. **Range, n miles:** 450 at 14 kt
Complement: 15 (1 officer)
Guns: 2—12.7 mm MGs.
Radars: Surface search: Furuno FR 2010; I-band.

Comment: Built by Colombo DY and commissioned in 1982 *(P 201)*, June 1986 *(P 211)* and 1993 *(P 215)*. P 241 and P 243 decommissioned in 2001 and *P 214* and *P 233* no longer in service.

P 201 *6/2003, Sri Lanka Navy* / 0570987

4 CHEVERTON CLASS COASTAL PATROL CRAFT (PB)

P 221 (ex-*P 421*) **P 222** (ex-*P 422*) **P 223** (ex-*P 423*) **P 224** (ex-*P 424*)

Displacement, tons: 22 full load
Dimensions, feet (metres): 55.9 × 14.8 × 3.9 *(17 × 4.5 × 1.2)*
Main machinery: 2 Detroit 8V-71TA diesels; 460 hp *(343 kW)*; 2 shafts
Speed, knots: 23. **Range, n miles:** 1,000 at 12 kt
Complement: 15
Guns: 1—12.7 mm MG.
Radars: Surface search: Racal Decca 110; I-band.

Comment: Used for general patrol duties. Built by Cheverton Workboats, UK and commissioned in 1977. One paid off in 1996.

P 222 *6/2004, Sri Lanka Navy* / 1044192

3 SIMONNEAU CLASS (PBF)

P 250 (ex-*P 410*, ex-*P 483*) **P 252** (ex-*P 412*, ex-*P 485*) **P 253** (ex-*P 413*, ex-*P 486*)

Displacement, tons: 28 full load
Dimensions, feet (metres): 56.8 × 16.1 × 4.6 *(17.3 × 4.9 × 1.4)*
Main machinery: 2 MTU 12V 183 TE93 diesels; 2,300 hp(m) *(1.69 MW)*; 2 Hamilton water-jets
Speed, knots: 42. **Range, n miles:** 500 at 35 kt
Complement: 15
Guns: 1 DCN 20 mm. 2—12.7 mm MGs. 2—7.62 mm MGs.
Radars: Surface search: Racal Decca; I-band.

Comment: Simonneau Marine Type 508 craft. First pair completed in December 1993 and shipped to Colombo in 1994. Second pair built in Colombo and completed in 1995. The plan to build more was shelved. Downgraded to patrol craft on 1 August 2000. Speed likely to have been reduced. *P 251* sunk in 2001.

SIMONNEAU CLASS *6/2004, Sri Lanka Navy* / 1044191

42 INSHORE PATROL CRAFT (PBR)

P 106–107 (ex-P 151–152)
P 115–118 (ex-P 163–166)
P 119 (ex-P 169)
P 120–122 (ex-P 171–173)
P 123 (ex-P 175)
P 124 (ex-P 180)
P 126 (ex-P 182)
P 127–132 (ex-P 184–189)
P 133–136 (ex-P 191–194)
P 137–138 (ex-P 196–197)
P 140–145 (ex-P 120–125)
P 146–150 (ex-P 127–131)
P 151–156 (ex-P 133–138)

Displacement, tons: 10 full load
Dimensions, feet (metres): 44.3 × 9.8 × 1.6 *(13.5 × 3 × 0.5)*
Main machinery: 2 Cummins 6BTA5.9-M2; 584 hp *(436 kW)* sustained; 2 water-jets
Speed, knots: 33. **Range, n miles:** 330 at 25 kt
Complement: 5
Guns: 2—12.7 mm MGs. 2—7.62 mm MGs.
Radars: Surface search: Furuno 1941; I-band.

Comment: First pair (P 106, 107) built by TAOS Yacht Company, Colombo, and delivered in 1991. Next 23 (P115-124, P 126-138) built by Blue Star Marine, Colombo and delivered between 1994 and 1998. There are minor superstructure differences between the first pair and the rest. P 140-156 built by SLN, IPCCP Welisara. P 162, P 168, P 174 and P 182 sunk in action. P 101 and P 104 decommissioned.

INSHORE PATROL CRAFT *6/2006, Sri Lanka Navy* / 1164410

4 INSHORE PATROL CRAFT (TYPE BSM) (PBR)

P 145–147 **P 149**

Displacement, tons: 3.5 full load
Dimensions, feet (metres): 42 × 8 × 1.6 *(12.8 × 2.4 × 0.5)*
Main machinery: 2 outboard motors; 280 hp *(209 kW)*
Speed, knots: 30
Complement: 9
Guns: 1—12.7 mm MG.

Comment: Acquired in 1988 from Blue Star Marine. Similar to *P 111* but with outboard engines. *P 143* (ex-P 150) was mined and sunk in August 1991 and again sunk in 1995.

INSHORE PATROL CRAFT *6/2004, Sri Lanka Navy* / 1044190

4 INSHORE PATROL CRAFT (TYPE CME) (PBR)

P 110 **P 111** **P 112** **P 113**

Displacement, tons: 5 full load
Dimensions, feet (metres): 44 × 9.8 × 1.6 *(13.4 × 3 × 0.5)*
Main machinery: 2 Yamaha D 343 diesels; 730 hp(m) *(544 kW)* sustained; 2 shafts
Speed, knots: 26
Complement: 5
Guns: 1—12.7 mm MG. 1—7.62 mm MG.
Radars: Surface search: Furuno FR 1941; I-band.

Comment: Built by Consolidated Marine Engineers, Sri Lanka. First nine delivered in 1988; four more in 1992 and two more in 1994. Most of these craft have been destroyed.

P 111 *6/2003, Sri Lanka Navy* / 0570986

1 VIKRAM CLASS (OFFSHORE PATROL VESSEL) (PSOH)

Name	*No*	*Builders*	*Launched*	*Commissioned*
SAGARA (ex-*Varaha*)	P 622 (ex-41)	Goa Shipyard	5 Nov 1990	11 Mar 1992

Displacement, tons: 1,224 full load
Dimensions, feet (metres): 243.1 × 37.4 × 10.5 *(74.1 × 11.4 × 3.2)*
Main machinery: 2 SEMT-Pielstick 16 PA6V280 diesels; 12,800 hp *(9.41 MW)* sustained; 2 shafts; cp props
Speed, knots: 22
Range, n miles: 4,250 at 12 kt
Complement: 96 (11 officers)
Guns: 1—30 mm. 1—23 mm.
Radars: Surface search/navigation: Furuno 2127; I-band.
Helicopters: Platform for 1 light.

Comment: Former Indian Coast Guard ship donated and recommissioned on 25 February 2007.

SAGARA *6/2008*, Sri Lanka Navy* / 1335872

12 MK III INSHORE PATROL CRAFT (PBF)

P 010–021

Displacement, tons: 8 full load
Dimensions, feet (metres): 46.6 × ? × ? *(14.2 × ? × ?)*
Main machinery: 2 Yanmar 6LY2A STP diesels; 737 hp(m) *(550 kW)*; 2 shafts
Speed, knots: 38
Complement: 8
Guns: 1—23 mm; 1—14.5 mm.
Radars: Surface search: Furuno; I-band.

Comment: Built by Sri Lanka Navy.

P 012 *6/2008*, Sri Lanka Navy* / 1335870

103 INSHORE PATROL CRAFT (PBF)

Z 101–203

Displacement, tons: 2.6 full load
Dimensions, feet (metres): 23.0 × ? × ? *(7.0 × ? × ?)*
Main machinery: 2 outboard motors; 400 hp(m) *(298 kW)*
Speed, knots: 40
Complement: 8
Guns: 1—23 mm or 1—14.5 mm. 4—7.62 mm MGs.

Comment: Built by Sri Lanka Navy.

Z 101 *6/2008*, Sri Lanka Navy* / 1335869

AMPHIBIOUS FORCES

1 YUHAI (WUHU-A) (TYPE 074) CLASS (LSM)

Name	*No*	*Builders*	*Commissioned*
SHAKTHI	L 880	China	22 May 1996

Displacement, tons: 799 full load
Dimensions, feet (metres): 191.6 × 34.1 × 8.9 *(58.4 × 10.4 × 2.7)*
Main machinery: 2 MAN 8 L 20/27 diesels; 4,900 hp(m) *(3.6 MW)*; 2 shafts
Speed, knots: 14
Range, n miles: 1,000 at 12 kt
Complement: 60
Military lift: 150 tons
Guns: 10—14.5 mm/93 (5 twin) MGs. 6—12.7 mm MGs.
Radars: Navigation: Racal Decca; I-band.

Comment: Transferred by lift ship from China arriving 13 December 1995. A planned second of class was built but not acquired.

SHAKTHI *5/1996, Sri Lanka Navy* / 0080710

2 LANDING CRAFT (LCM)

Name	*No*	*Builders*	*Commissioned*
RANAGAJA	L 839	Colombo Dockyard	15 Nov 1991
RANAVIJAYA	L 836	Colombo Dockyard	21 July 1994

Displacement, tons: 268 full load
Dimensions, feet (metres): 108.3 × 26 × 4.9 *(33 × 8 × 1.5)*
Main machinery: 2 Caterpillar diesels; 1,524 hp *(1.14 MW)*; 2 shafts
Speed, knots: 8
Range, n miles: 1,800 at 8 kt
Complement: 28 (2 officers)
Guns: 4 China 14.5 mm (2 twin). 2—12.7 mm MGs.
Radars: Navigation: Furuno FCR 1421; I-band.

Comment: Two built in 1983 and acquired in October 1985. Third of the class taken over by the Navy in September 1991 and a fourth in March 1992. *Kandula* sank in October 1992 and the hulk was salvaged in mid-December. *Pabbatha* sank in action in February 1998.

RANAVIJAYA *6/2008*, Sri Lanka Navy* / 1335867

2 YUNNAN CLASS (TYPE 067)

L 820 **L 821**

Displacement, tons: 135 full load
Dimensions, feet (metres): 93.8 × 17.7 × 4.9 *(28.6 × 5.4 × 1.5)*
Main machinery: 2 diesels; 600 hp(m) *(441 kW)*; 2 shafts
Speed, knots: 12
Range, n miles: 500 at 10 kt
Complement: 22 (2 officers)
Military lift: 46 tons
Guns: 4—14.5 mm (2 twin) MGs. 2—7.62 mm MGs
Radars: Surface search: Fuji; I-band.

Comment: First one acquired from China in May 1991, second in May 1995.

L 821 *6/2008*, Sri Lanka Navy* / 1335868

1 M 10 CLASS HOVERCRAFT (UCAC)

A 530

Displacement, tons: 18 full load
Dimensions, feet (metres): 67.6 × 28.9 *(20.6 × 8.8)*
Main machinery: 2 Deutz diesels; 1,050 hp(m) *(772 kW)*
Speed, knots: 40; 7 with cushion deflated
Range, n miles: 600 at 30 kt
Complement: 10
Military lift: 56 troops or 20 troops plus 2 vehicles
Guns: 1—12.7 mm MG.
Radars: Navigation: Furuno; I-band.

Comment: Acquired from ABS Hovercraft/Vosper Thornycroft in April 1998 and designated a Utility Craft Air Cushion (UCAC). Has a Kevlar superstructure. More may be ordered in due course.

A 530 *6/2006, Sri Lanka Navy* / 1164409

3 FAST PERSONNEL CARRIERS (LCP)

Name	*No*	*Builders*	*Commissioned*
HANSAYA (ex-*Offshore Pioneer*)	A 540	Sing Koon Seng, Singapore	20 Dec 1987
– (ex-*Lanka Rani*)	A 542	Kvaerner Fielistrand Ltd, Singapore	2000
– (ex-*Lanka Devi*)	A 543	Kvaerner Fielistrand Ltd, Singapore	2000

Displacement, tons: 444 full load
Dimensions, feet (metres): 131.2 × 33.1 × 5.9 *(40.0 × 10.1 × 1.8)*
Main machinery: 2 MTU 16V 396 TE 74L; 1,800 hp(m) *(1.32 MW)*; 2 shafts
Speed, knots: 30
Range, n miles: 650 at 20 kt
Complement: 30 (4 officers)
Military lift: 60 tons; 120 troops
Guns: 1 Oerlikon 20 mm. 2—12.7 mm MGs.
Radars: Navigation: Furuno FR 1012; I-band.

Comment: A 540 acquired in January 1986 from Aluminium Shipbuilders. Catamaran hull built as oil rig tender. Now used as fast transport. A 541 decommissioned in 2002. Details are as for A 543 which was acquired from Ceylon Shipping Corporation.

A 543 *6/2006, Sri Lanka Navy* / 1164408

AUXILIARIES

1 SUPPORT/TRAINING SHIP (AA/AX)

Name	*No*	*Builders*	*Commissioned*
– (ex-*Simon Keghian*)	A 521	BPKSKP, Gdynia, Poland	1972

Displacement, tons: 592 full load
Dimensions, feet (metres): 177.2 × 36.1 × 20.1 *(54.0 × 11.0 × 6.3)*
Main machinery: 1 DUVANT CREPELLE 8R26L diesel; 1,320 hp(m) *(970 kW)* sustained; 1 shaft
Speed, knots: 10
Range, n miles: 5,500 at 9 kt
Complement: 57 (7 officers)
Guns: 6—12.7 mm MGs. 2—40 mm AGLs.
Radars: Surface search/navigation: Furuno FR 2125; I-band.

Comment: Former deep-sea fishing trawler donated by the Lorient-Matara Friendship Foundation of France and commissioned into the Sri Lanka Navy on 26 April 2005. The ship was donated on humanitarian grounds, following the tsunami of 26 December 2004, and it is understood that the vessel is used by the navy in support of fishing activities and as a training vessel.

A 521 *6/2007, Sri Lanka Navy* / 1167813

1 TRANSPORT SHIP (AP)

Name	*No*	*Builders*	*Commissioned*
– (ex-*Djursland*)	A 545	Mjellem & Karlsen	1971

Displacement, tons: 1,746 full load
Measurement, tons: 8,531 grt
Dimensions, feet (metres): 311.7 × 57.1 × 12.1 *(95.0 × 17.4 × 3.7)*
Main machinery: 4 MTU 20V 1163TB73 diesels; 2 shafts
Speed, knots: 24
Range, n miles: 1,800 at 18 kt
Complement: 107 (7 officers)
Guns: 6—12.7 mm MGs. 2—40 mm AGLs.
Radars: Surface search/navigation: Kelvin Hughes; E/F/I-band.

Comment: Ro-Ro ferry on bare boat charter from Indonesia from 2006.

A 545 *6/2006, Sri Lanka Navy* / 1164405

Sudan

Country Overview

The Republic of Sudan is situated in north-eastern Africa. The largest country in Africa, it has an area of 967,500 square miles and is bordered to the north by Egypt, to the east by Eritrea and Ethiopia, to the south by Kenya, Uganda and the Democratic Republic of the Congo and to the west by the Central African Republic, Chad, and Libya. It has a 459 n mile coastline with the Red Sea. Khartoum is the capital and largest city and Port Sudan is the principal port. There are about 2,867 n miles of navigable waterways. Territorial waters (12 n miles) are claimed. An EEZ has not been claimed.

The country has been ravaged by civil war in recent years but a Comprehensive Peace Agreement was finally concluded on 9 January 2005. This allows for the south to become a self-administering region until 2011 by when its future status will be decided by referendum.

Naval Forces are part of the Army and have low budgetary priority.

Headquarters Appointments

Commander, Naval Forces:
Lieutenant General Al-Zain Hamad Balla

Personnel

(a) 2009: 1,300 officers and men
(b) Voluntary service

Establishment

The Navy was established in 1962 to operate on the Red Sea coast and on the River Nile.

Bases

Port Sudan (HQ). Flamingo Bay (Red Sea), Khartoum (Nile), Kosti (Nile).

PATROL FORCES

4 KURMUK (TYPE 15) CLASS (INSHORE PATROL CRAFT) (PBR)

KURMUK 502 **QAYSAN** 503 **RUMBEK** 504 **MAYOM** 505

Displacement, tons: 19.5 full load
Dimensions, feet (metres): 55.4 × 12.8 × 2.3 *(16.9 × 3.9 × 0.7)*
Main machinery: 2 diesels; 330 hp(m) *(243 kW)*; 2 shafts
Speed, knots: 16
Range, n miles: 160 at 12 kt
Complement: 6
Guns: 1 Oerlikon 20 mm; 2—7.62 mm MGs.

Comment: Delivered by Yugoslavia on 18 May 1989 for operations on the White Nile. All based at Flamingo Bay.

KURMUK *1989, G Jacobs* / 0506101

4 SEWART CLASS (INSHORE PATROL CRAFT) (PBR)

MAROUB 1161 **FIJAB** 1162 **SALAK** 1163 **HALOTE** 1164

Displacement, tons: 9.1 full load
Dimensions, feet (metres): 40 × 12.1 × 3.3 *(12.2 × 3.7 × 1)*
Main machinery: 2 GM diesels; 348 hp *(260 kW)*; 2 shafts
Speed, knots: 31
Complement: 6
Guns: 1—12.7 mm MG.

Comment: Transferred by Iranian Coast Guard in 1975. All are based at Flamingo Bay but operational status is doubtful.

7 ASHOORA I CLASS (INSHORE PATROL CRAFT) (PBR)

Displacement, tons: 3 full load
Dimensions, feet (metres): 26.6 × 8 × 1.6 *(8.1 × 2.4 × 0.5)*
Main machinery: 2 Yamaha outboards; 400 hp(m) *(294 kW)*
Speed, knots: 42
Complement: 2
Guns: 1—7.62 mm MG.

Comment: Acquired from Iran in 1992–94. Four based at Flamingo Bay and three at Khartoum but operational status is doubtful.

ASHOORA I *1992, IRI Marine Industries* / 0080715

AUXILIARIES

Notes: (1) In addition there are two small miscellaneous support ships. *Baraka* 21 a water boat, and a Rotork 512 craft. Both restored with Iranian assistance.
(2) Five Type II LCVPs were delivered from Yugoslavia in 1991 and are based at Kosti.

2 SUPPLY SHIPS (AFL)

SOBAT 221 **DINDER** 222

Displacement, tons: 410 full load
Dimensions, feet (metres): 155.1 × 21 × 7.5 *(47.3 × 6.4 × 2.3)*
Main machinery: 3 Gray Marine diesels; 495 hp *(369 kW)*; 3 shafts
Speed, knots: 9
Complement: 15
Guns: 1 Oerlikon 20 mm. 2—12.7 mm MGs.
Comment: Two Yugoslav MFPD class LCTs transferred in 1969. Used for transporting ammunition, petrol and general supplies.

Suriname

Country Overview

Formerly known as Dutch Guiana, the Republic of Suriname gained full independence in 1975. With an area of 63,037 square miles it has borders to the east with French Guiana, to the west with Guyana and to the south with Brazil; its 208 n mile coastline is on the Atlantic Ocean. The capital, largest city and chief port is Paramaribo. Territorial seas (12 n miles) and a fisheries zone (200 n miles) are claimed. There are further ports at Nieuw-Nickerie, Moengo, Paranam and Smalkalden. Territorial waters (12 n miles) are claimed. A 200 n mile Exclusive Economic Zone (EEZ) has also been claimed but the limits are not defined.

Headquarters Appointments

Commander Marine Section:
Lieutenant Colonel Henk Mohamatsaid

Personnel

2009: 240 (25 officers)

Bases

Kruktu Tere, Paramaribo

Aircraft

Two CASA C-212-400 Aviocar aircraft acquired for maritime patrol in 1998/99.

PATROL FORCES

3 RODMAN 101 CLASS (PB)

JARABAKKA P 01 **SPARI** P 02 **GRAMORGU** P 03

Displacement, tons: 72 full load
Dimensions, feet (metres): 98.4 × 19.4 × 4.3 *(30.0 × 5.9 × 1.3)*
Main machinery: 2 MTU 12V 2000 diesels; 2,900 hp *(2.16 MW)* sustained; 2 Hamilton 571 water-jets
Speed, knots: 26
Range, n miles: 800 at 12 kt
Complement: 9
Guns: 1—40 mm grenade launcher.
Radars: Surface search: 2 Furuno; I-band.

Comment: Ordered in December 1997, from Rodman, Vigo. First one delivered in February 1999, second and third on 3 July 1999. Carry a RIB with twin outboards. Operational status doubtful.

SPARI *3/2001, Adolfo Ortigueira Gil* / 1305139

5 RODMAN 55M CLASS (PBR)

P 04–08

Displacement, tons: 16 full load
Dimensions, feet (metres): 57.1 × 12.8 × 2.3 *(17.4 × 3.9 × 0.7)*
Main machinery: 2 MAN D2848-LXE diesels; 1,360 hp(m) *(1 MW)* sustained; 2 Hamilton water-jets
Speed, knots: 35
Range, n miles: 500 at 25 kt
Complement: 7
Guns: 1 — 12.7 mm MG.
Radars: Surface search: Furuno; I-band.

Comment: Ordered in December 1997 from Rodman, Vigo. First one delivered in October 1998, remainder in April 1999. Carry a RIB with a single outboard engine. Operational status doubtful.

P 06 *4/1999, **Rodman Group*** / 1305140

Sweden
SVENSKA MARINEN

Country Overview

The Kingdom of Sweden is a constitutional monarchy occupying the eastern part of the Scandinavian Peninsula. With an area of 173,730 square miles, it is bordered to the north and west by Norway and to the north-east by Finland. It has a 1,740 n mile coastline with the Gulf of Bothnia, the Baltic Sea, the Öresund, Kattegatt, and Skagerrak. The country comprises the mainland and the islands of Gotland and Öland in the Baltic Sea. The capital and largest city is Stockholm which is also a leading port. Others include Göteborg, Malmö and Norrköping. Territorial seas (12 n miles) and an EEZ (200 n miles) are claimed.

Headquarters Appointments

Chief of Naval Staff:
Rear Admiral Anders Grenstad

Diplomatic Representation

Defence Attaché in Washington:
Major General Jan Andersson
Defence Attaché in Tokyo:
Colonel Sven-Åke Asklander
Defence Attaché in Tel Aviv:
Colonel Stephan Tyrling
Defence Attaché in Beijing:
Colonel Hans Norman
Defence Attaché in Copenhagen:
Captain Lennart Bengtsson
Defence Attaché in Bern:
Lieutenant Colonel Olle Hultgren
Defence Attaché in Talinn and Riga:
Lieutenant Colonel Hans Hansson

Diplomatic Representation — *continued*

Defence Attaché in Oslo:
Colonel PIngemar Gustafsson
Defence Attaché in The Hague:
Lieutenant Colonel Anders Waldén
Defence Attaché in Kuala Lumpur:
Lieutenant Colonel Lars Enlund
Defence Attaché in Warsaw and Vilnius:
Lieutenant Colonel Tapani Mattus
Defence Attaché in Addis Ababa:
Lieutenant Colonel Percy Hansson
Defence Attaché in Ottawa:
Lieutenant Colonel Håkan Sjöberg
Defence Attaché in London and Dublin:
Captain Bo Rask
Naval Attaché in Moscow, Minsk and Tblisi:
Captain Christian Allerman
Naval Attaché in Washington:
Colonel Lars-Olof Corneliusson
Defence Attaché in Paris and Madrid:
Colonel Bertil Dahlrot
Defence Attaché in Singapore and Bangkok:
Captain Karl Henriksson
Defence Attaché in Berlin:
Colonel Mals Andersson
Defence Attaché in Sarajevo:
Colonel Christer Svensson
Defence Attaché in Helsinki:
Colonel Bengt Nylander
Defence Attaché in Athens:
Lieutenant Colonel Anders Andersson
Defence Attaché in Rome:
Colonel Thomas Bergqvist
Defence Attaché in Pretoria:
Colonel Carl Wärnberg
Defence Attaché in Ankara:
Colonel Anders Stenström
Defence Attaché in Vienna:
Lieutenant Colonel Leif Küller

Diplomatic Representation — *continued*

Defence Attaché in Brasilia:
Lieutenant Colonel Christer Ohlsson
Defence Attaché in Canberra:
Captain Johin Hahn
Defence Attaché in Budapest, Zagreb and Sofia:
Lieutenant Colonel Jerker Fredholm
Defence Attaché in Kiev:
Colonel Christer Holm
Defence Attaché in Islamabad:
Lieutenant Colonel Clas Göran Jonsson
Defence Attaché in New Delhi:
Colonel Krister Edvardson
Defence Attaché in Cairo and Amman:
Colonel Lars Norberg

Organisation

The Navy consists of the Fleet and the Amphibious Battalion (ex-Coastal Artillery). The Navy is organised into one submarine flotilla, two naval warfare flotillas, one amphibious regiment, one main naval base and one naval warfare centre.

Personnel

(a) 2009: 6,070 including 1,600 officers, 370 civilians, 2,400 reserve officers and 1,700 national servicemen
(b) 11 months' national service

Bases

Karlskrona, Berga (Stockholm).

Strength of the Fleet

Type	*Active*	*Building (Planned)*
Submarines—Patrol	4	–
Missile Corvettes	9	–
Inshore Patrol Craft	13	–
Minesweepers/ Hunters—Coastal	7	–
Minesweepers—Inshore	4	–
LCMs	9	–
Electronic Surveillance Ship	1	–
Transport Ships	1	–
Repair and Support Ships	11	–

DELETIONS

Corvettes

2006 *Göteborg, Kalmar*

Mine Warfare Forces

2006 *Arkösund,* M 505

Amphibious Forces

2006 LCU 208, 215, 223, 230-232, 234, 235, 237, 241, 244, 247, 248, 252, 258, 261-264, 267-269, 281, 283

Auxiliaries

2006 *Achilles, Hermes, Pingvinen*

Training Ships

2006 *Viksten,* M 21, M 22

PENNANT LIST

Corvettes

K 11	Stockholm
K 12	Malmö
K 22	Gävle
K 24	Sundsvall
K 31	Visby
K 32	Helsingborg
K 33	Härnösand
K 34	Nyköping
K 35	Karlstad

Patrol Forces

77	Huvudskär
81	Tapper
82	Djärv
83	Dristig
84	Händig
85	Trygg
86	Modig
87	Hurtig
88	Rapp
89	Stolt
90	Ärlig
91	Munter
92	Orädd

Mine Warfare Forces

M 11	Styrsö
M 12	Spårö
M 13	Skaftö
M 14	Sturkö
M 71	Landsort
M 72	Arholma
M 73	Koster
M 74	Kullen
M 75	Vinga
M 76	Ven
M 77	Ulvön
MRF 01	Sökaren

Auxiliaries

15	Grundsund
18	Fårösund
20	Furusund
A 201	Orion
A 212	Ägir
A 214	Belos III
A 247	Pelikanen
A 264	Trossö
A 265	Visborg
A 322	Heros
A 324	Hera
A 343	Sleipner
A 344	Loke
M 04	Carlskrona

Training ships

S 01	Gladan
S 02	Falken

SUBMARINES

Notes: (1) The Swedish requirement for two new submarines is being taken forward via the Next Generation Submarine (NGS) (formerly Viking) project. This had been a bilateral programme with Denmark, following the withdrawal of Norway at the end of Project Definition Phase (PDP) Step 1 on 13 June 2003, but in wake of approval of the 2005–09 Defence Plan by the Danish parliament on 10 June 2004, Denmark also decided to end participation. The contract for PDP Step 2, was signed on 6 October 2003, but future progress is likely to be driven by two main factors: the requirement for the boats to enter service in about 2015–18 and the aspiration to find a partner country to take the project forward.
(2) A prototype Swimmer Delivery Vehicle (SDV) began trials in late 2008; the 10.3 m carbon-fibre craft is capable of carrying six divers and 300 kg of equipment. There are three modes of operation: surface, semi-submerged (skimmer) and submerged. A 235 kW MTU diesel driving a waterjet provides propulsive power in surfaced and skimmer modes while four Tecnadyne thrusters powered by 24 Optima batteries provides underwater propulsion. Buoyancy is adjusted using inflatable pontoons on the sides of the craft. Subject to successful completion of the trials and the incorporation of modifications, orders for the craft are expected in 2009 with delivery of the first in 2010.

1 MIDGET SUBMARINE (SSW)

SPIGGEN II

Displacement, tons: 17 dived
Dimensions, feet (metres): 34.8 × 5.6 × 4.6 *(10.6 × 1.7 × 1.4)*
Main machinery: 1 Volvo Penta diesel; 1 shaft
Speed, knots: 5 dived; 6 surfaced
Complement: 4

Comment: Built by Försvarets Materielverk and commissioned on 19 June 1990. Has an endurance of 14 days and a diving depth of 100 m *(330 ft)*, and is used as a target for ASW training. Refitted by Kockums and back in service in December 1996.

SPIGGEN II
*8/1998, **Per Körnefeldt***
0050201

2 SÖDERMANLAND (A 17) CLASS (SSK)

Name	*No*	*Builders*	*Laid down*	*Launched*	*Commissioned*
SÖDERMANLAND	–	Kockums, Malmö	2 Feb 1985	12 Apr 1988	21 Apr 1989
ÖSTERGÖTLAND	–	Kockums, Malmö	15 Oct 1985	9 Dec 1988	10 Jan 1990

Displacement, tons: 1,500 surfaced; 1,600 dived
Dimensions, feet (metres): 198.5 × 20 × 18.4 *(60.5 × 6.1 × 5.6)*
Main machinery: Diesel-Stirling-electric; 2 Hedemora V12A/15 diesels; 2,200 hp(m) *(1.62 MW)*; 2 Kockums Stirling Mk III AIP; 204 hp *(150 kW)*; 1 Jeumont Schneider motor; 1,800 hp(m) *(1.32 MW)*; 1 shaft; LIPS prop
Speed, knots: 10 surfaced; 20 dived
Complement: 27 (5 officers)

Torpedoes: 6—21 in *(533 mm)* tubes. 12 FFV Type 613; anti-surface; wire-guided; passive homing to 20 km *(10.8 n miles)* at 45 kt; warhead 240 kg. swim-out discharge.
3—15.75 in *(400 mm)* tubes. 6 FFV Type 431/451; anti-submarine; wire-guided; active/passive homing to 20 km *(10.8 n miles)* at 25 kt; warhead 45 kg shaped charge or a small charge anti-intruder version is available.
Mines: 12 Type 47 swim-out mines in lieu of torpedoes.
Countermeasures: ESM: Argo AR-700-S5; or Condor CS 3701; intercept.
Weapons control: Ericsson IPS-17 (Sesub 900A) TFCS.
Radars: Navigation: Terma; I-band.
Sonars: Atlas Elektronik CSU 83; hull-mounted; passive search and attack; medium frequency.
Reson Subac; active search (from 2008).
Flank array; passive search; low frequency.

Programmes: Design contract awarded to Kockums, Malmö on 17 April 1978. Contract for construction of these boats signed 8 December 1981. Kockums built midship section and carried out final assembly while Karlskrona built bow and stern sections.
Modernisation: Modernised variants of the Västergötland class. Mid-life refit of both boats began with *Södermanland* at Kockums in late 2000. The principal upgrade was the installation of Air Independent Propulsion (Stirling Mk 3 AIP) by the insertion of a 12 m plug in the pressure hull. Other work included the installation of a pressurised diver's lock-out in the base of the sail to facilitate special forces operations. The refit also included a new climate control system. Thales Optronics CK 038 periscope has been upgraded with a thermal imaging camera and an improved image intensifier. A new command and control system is to be installed in *Södermanland* during a further refit which began in late 2008. Plans for a new active sonar suite, Subac, have been postponed.
Structure: Single hulled with an X type rudder/after hydroplane design. Diving depth 300 m *(984 ft)*. Anechoic coating.
Operational: *Södermanland* relaunched on 8 September 2003 and, after six-months sea trials, returned to service in mid-2004, *Östergötland* was relaunched on 3 September 2004 and returned to service in 2005.

SÖDERMANLAND *5/2006, Michael Nitz* / 1164723

SÖDERMANLAND *5/2006, Frank Findler* / 1159909

SÖDERMANLAND *6/2006, John Brodie* / 1159976

3 GOTLAND (A 19) CLASS (SSK)

Name	*No*	*Builders*	*Laid down*	*Launched*	*Commissioned*
GOTLAND	–	Kockums, Malmö	20 Nov 1992	2 Feb 1995	2 Sep 1996
UPPLAND	–	Kockums, Malmö	14 Jan 1994	9 Feb 1996	1 May 1997
HALLAND	–	Kockums, Malmö	21 Oct 1994	27 Sep 1996	1 Oct 1997

Displacement, tons: 1,494 surfaced; 1,599 dived
Dimensions, feet (metres): 198.2 × 20.3 × 18.4 *(60.4 × 6.2 × 5.6)*
Main machinery: Diesel-stirling-electric; 2 MTU diesels; 2 Kockums V4-275R Stirling AIP; 204 hp(m) *(150 kW)*; 1 Jeumont Schneider motor; 1 shaft; LIPS prop
Speed, knots: 10 surfaced; 20 dived
Complement: 27 (5 officers)

Torpedoes: 4—21 in *(533 mm)* bow tubes; 12 FFV Type 613/62; anti-surface; wire-guided; passive homing to 20 km *(10.8 n miles)* at 45 kt; warhead 240 kg or Bofors Type 62 (2000); wire-guided; active/passive homing to 50 km *(27 n miles)* at 20-50 kt; warhead 250 kg. swim-out discharge.
2—15.75 in *(400 mm)* bow tubes; 6 Swedish Ordnance Type 432/451; anti-submarine; wire-guided; active/passive homing to 20 km *(10.8 n miles)* at 25 kt; warhead 45 kg. Shaped charge or a small charge anti-intruder version.
Mines: 12 Type 47 swim-out mines in lieu of torpedoes.
Countermeasures: ESM: Racal THORN Manta S; radar warning.
Weapons control: CelsiusTech IPS-19 (Sesub 940A); TFCS.
Radars: Navigation: Terma Scanter; I-band.
Sonars: STN/Atlas Elektronik CSU 90-2; hull-mounted; bow, flank and intercept arrays; passive search and attack.
Reson Subac; active search (from 2008).

Programmes: In October 1986 a research contract was awarded to Kockums for a design to replace the Sjöormen class. Ordered on 28 March 1990.
Modernisation: A mid-life update for all three boats is planned. Upgrades are likely to include a new combat management system. Work is likely to start in 2010.

Structure: The design has been developed on the basis of the Type A 17 series but this class is the first to be built with Air Independent Propulsion as part of the design. This type of AIP runs on liquid oxygen and diesel in a helium environment. Space has been reserved to fit two more V4-275R engines in due course. Single electro-optic periscope. The periscope is the only hull penetrating mast. Anechoic coatings are being applied. The four 21 in torpedo tubes are mounted over the smaller 15.75 in tubes. The smaller tubes can be tandem-loaded with two torpedoes per tube.
Operational: Reported as being able to patrol at 5 kt for several weeks without snort charging. The Type 47 mine swims out to a predetermined position before laying itself on the bottom. *Gotland* participated in exercises with the USN on the west coast of the US 2005–07.

UPPLAND *7/2004, E & M Laursen* / 1043523

UPPLAND *6/2003, L-G Nilsson* / 0572636

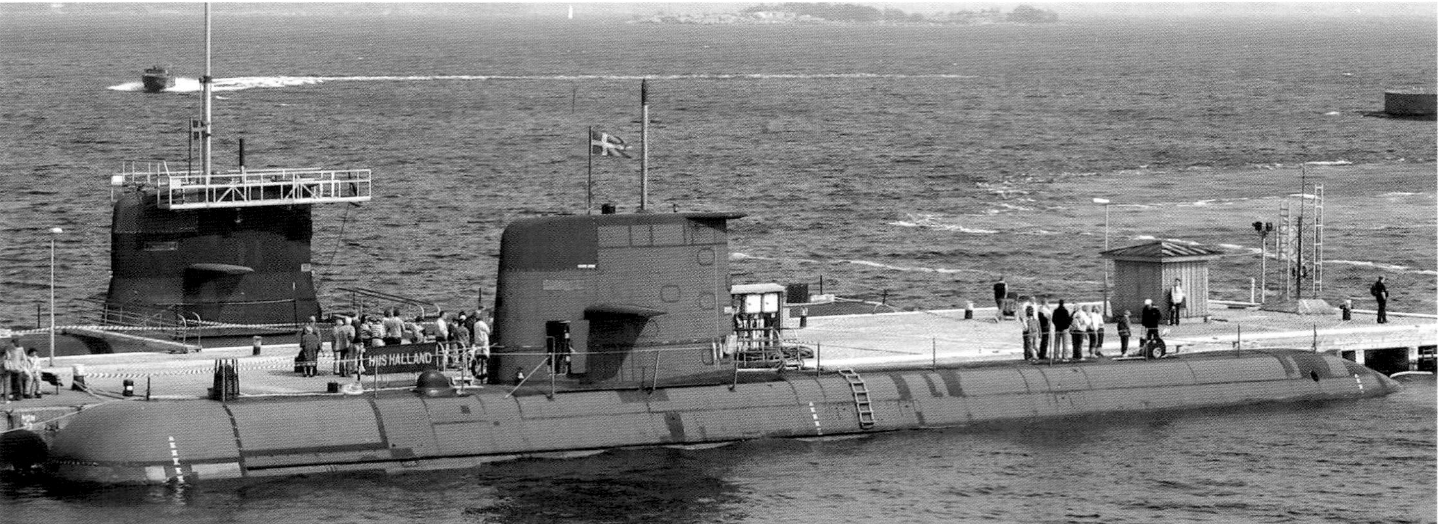

HALLAND *5/2006, L-G Nilsson* / 1164725

CORVETTES

4 + 1 VISBY CLASS (FSGH)

Name	*No*	*Builders*	*Laid down*	*Launched*	*Commissioned*
VISBY	K 31	Karlskronavarvet	17 Dec 1996	8 June 2000	12 June 2006
HELSINGBORG	K 32	Karlskronavarvet	June 1997	27 June 2003	24 Apr 2006
HÄRNÖSAND	K 33	Karlskronavarvet	Dec 1997	16 Dec 2004	12 June 2006
NYKÖPING	K 34	Karlskronavarvet	June 1998	18 Aug 2005	24 Aug 2006
KARLSTAD	K 35	Karlskronavarvet	Dec 1999	24 Aug 2006	2008

Displacement, tons: 620 full load
Dimensions, feet (metres): 239.5 × 34.1 × 7.9 *(73.0 × 10.4 × 2.4)*
Main machinery: CODOG; 4 AlliedSignal TF 50A gas turbines; 21,760 hp(m) *(16 MW)*; 2 MTU 16V N90 diesels; 3,536 hp(m) *(2.6 MW)*; 2 Kamewa 125 water-jets; bow thruster
Speed, knots: 35; 15 (diesels)
Complement: 43 (10 officers)

Missiles: SSM: 8 RBS 15 Mk II (Batch 2) inertial guidance; active radar homing to 110 km *(54 n miles)* at 0.8 Mach; warhead 150 kg.
Guns: 1 Bofors 57 mm/70 SAK Mk 3 ❶. 220 rds/min to 17 km *(9.3 n miles)*; weight of shell 2.4 kg. 2—12.7 mm MGs.
Torpedoes: 4 fixed 400 mm tubes ❷. Type 45 anti-submarine/surface; wire guided active homing to 20 km *(10.8 n miles)* at 25 kt; warhead 45 kg shaped charge.
Mines: Can be carried.
Countermeasures: Decoys: Rheinmetal MASS-HIDD ❸.
MCMV: STN Atlas Seafox Combat (C) sonar/TV sensor; range 500 m at 6 kt; shaped charge. Saab Underwater Systems Double Eagle Mk III ROV fitted with Reson triple frequency sonar.
ESM: Condor Systems CS 3701; intercept and jammer.
Combat data systems: CelsiusTech 9LV Mk 3E CETRIS with Link.
Weapons control: Optronic director.
Radars: Air/surface search: Ericsson Sea Giraffe AMB 3D; G-band.
Surface search: Terma Scanter 2001 ❹; E/F/I-band.
Fire control: CEROS 200 Mk 3 ❺; I/J-band.

VISBY CLASS *(Scale 1 : 600), Ian Sturton* / 1166652

Sonars: General Dynamics Canada Hydra Suite; bow mounted active high frequency (86 kHz) plus passive towed array and VDS (26 kHz) active.

Helicopters: Platform for 1 Agusta A 109M ❻.

Programmes: Order for first two with an option for two more on 17 October 1995. Second pair ordered 17 December 1996 and third pair in mid-1999. However, due to cost overruns, order reduced on 9 October 2001 to five ships.
Structure: Stealth features developed from the trials vessel *Smyge* but without the twin hull design for which this ship was considered too large. A hangar for the helicopter is not to be included. The hull is of Carbon Fibre Reinforced Plastic used in a sandwich construction and the superstructure is covered with RAM. A Double Eagle Mk III ROV-Swith active sonar is carried in the MCM role as well as expendable mini torpedoes for mine countermeasures. There is provision for a SAM system to be installed at a later date.
Operational: The first of class, was launched at Karlskrona shipyard on 8 June 2000 but delays in outfitting schedule led to 10-month slippage of contractor's sea trials until 7 December 2001. The combat system was installed in *Visby* late 2002 followed by trials from late 2003. Other ships were fitted on build. The test and evaluation period has been exhaustive and there has been an overall 5-year slippage in the programme. A 10-month work-package, known as a Special Period (SP) has been defined to address signature, sensor integration, weapon integration, and safety issues. The first ship is to start SP in 2009 and is to become operational in 2010. The other ships are to follow at six-month intervals; the final vessel is to be completed in 2012.

HELSINGBORG *8/2006, Frank Findler* / 1166654

NYKÖPING *9/2007, Michael Nitz* / 1166709

2 GÖTEBORG CLASS (FSG)

Name	*No*	*Builders*	*Laid down*	*Launched*	*Commissioned*
GÄVLE	K 22	Karlskronavarvet	21 Mar 1988	23 Mar 1990	1 Feb 1991
SUNDSVALL	K 24	Karlskronavarvet	20 Nov 1989	29 Nov 1991	7 July 1993

Displacement, tons: 300 standard; 399 full load
Dimensions, feet (metres): 187 × 26.2 × 6.6 *(57 × 8 × 2)*
Main machinery: 3 MTU 16V 396TB94 diesels; 8,700 hp(m) *(6.4 MW)* sustained; Kamewa 80562-6 water-jets; bow thrusters
Speed, knots: 30
Complement: 36 (7 officers) plus 4 spare berths

Missiles: SSM: 8 Saab RBS 15 Mark II (4 twin) launchers ❶; inertial guidance; active radar homing to 110 km *(59.4 n miles)* at 0.8 Mach; warhead 150 kg.
Guns: 1 Bofors 57 mm/70 Mk 2 ❷; 220 rds/min to 17 km *(9.3 n miles)*; weight of shell 2.4 kg.
1 Bofors 40 mm/70 (stealth dome) ❸; 330 rds/min to 12.5 km *(6.8 n miles)*; weight of shell 0.96 kg.
Torpedoes: 4—15.75 in *(400 mm)* tubes can be fitted ❹. Swedish Ordnance Type 43/45; anti-submarine.
A/S mortars: 4 Saab 601 ❺ 9-tubed launchers; range 1,200 m; shaped charge.
Depth charges: On mine rails.
Mines: Minelaying capability.
Countermeasures: Decoys: Rheinmetal MASS-1L decoy system.
ESM: Condor CS 3701; intercept.
ECM: Rafael Shark/RAN-1101; jammer.
Combat data systems: CelsiusTech 9LV Mk 3 SESYM. Link 11.

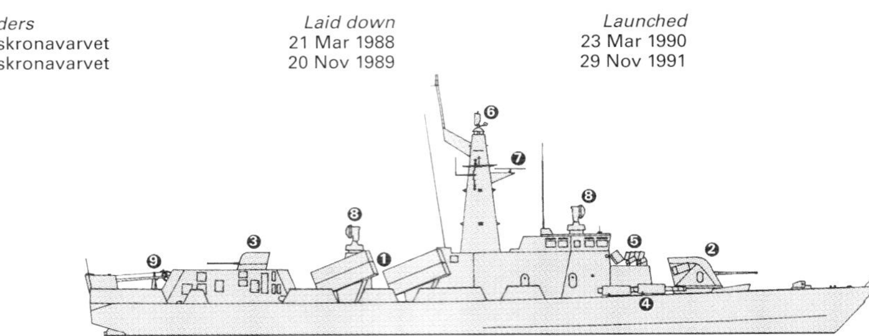

GÄVLE **(Scale 1 : 600), Ian Sturton** / 1153882

Weapons control: 2 Bofors Electronics 9LV 200 Mk 3 Sea Viking (K 22) or Signaal IRST (K 24) optronic directors. Bofors Electronics 9LV 450 GFCS. RC1-400 MFCS. 9AU-300 ASW control system with AQS 928G/SM sonobuoy processor. Bofors 9EW 400 EW control.
Radars: Air/surface search: Ericsson Sea Giraffe 150 HC ❻; G-band.
Navigation: Terma PN 612 ❼; I-band.
Fire control: 2 Bofors Electronics 9GR 400 ❽; I/J-band.
Sonars: Hydra multisonar system (K 22) ❾; bow-mounted active high-frequency plus passive towed array and active VDS.
Simrad SA 950 (K 24); hull-mounted; active attack.
STN Atlas passive towed array; low frequency. Thomson-Sintra TSM 2643 VDS.

Programmes: Ordered 1 December 1985 as replacements for Spica I class.
Modernisation: *Gävle* refitted to accommodate Hydra towed array, jammer and 40 mm gun with stealth dome. Bridge wings removed and topmast modified. *Sundsvall* may be similarly refitted. Both ships are to receive a mid-life upgrade starting in 2010.
Structure: Efforts have been made to reduce radar and IR signatures.

SUNDSVALL **8/2007, B Prézelin** / 1166670

GÄVLE **4/2007, Michael Nitz** / 1166710

2 STOCKHOLM CLASS (FSG)

Name	*No*	*Builders*	*Laid down*	*Launched*	*Commissioned*
STOCKHOLM	K 11	Karlskronavarvet	1 Aug 1982	24 Aug 1984	22 Feb 1985
MALMÖ	K 12	Karlskronavarvet	14 Mar 1983	22 Mar 1985	10 May 1985

Displacement, tons: 350 standard; 372 full load
Dimensions, feet (metres): 164 × 24.6 × 10.8 *(50 × 7.5 × 3.3)*
Main machinery: CODAG; 1 Allied Signal TF50A gas turbine; 5,440 hp(m) *(4.0 MW)* sustained; 2 MTU 16V 396 TB94 diesels; 5,277 hp(m) *(3.9 MW)* sustained; 3 shafts; Kamewa props
Speed, knots: 32 gas; 20 diesel
Complement: 33 (7 officers)

Missiles: SSM: 8 Saab RBS 15 Mk II (4 twin) launchers ❶; inertial guidance; active radar homing to 110 km *(54 n miles)* at 0.8 Mach; warhead 150 kg.
Guns: 1 Bofors 57 mm/70 Mk 2 ❷; 220 rds/min to 13.5 km *(7.3 n miles)*; weight of shell 2.4 kg.
Torpedoes: 4 – 15.75 in *(400 mm)* tubes; Swedish Ordnance Type 45; anti-submarine/surface; wire guided active homing to 20 km *(10.8 n miles)* at 25 kt; warhead 45 kg shaped charge.
A/S mortars: 4 Saab 601 ❸ 9-tubed launchers; range 1,200 m; shaped charge.
Mines: Minelaying capability.
Countermeasures: Decoys: Rheinmetal MASS-1L decoy system ❹.
ESM: Condor CS 3701; intercept and warning.
Combat data systems: SAAB Tech 9LV Mk 3E Cetris; datalink.
Weapons control: Philips 9LV 300 GFCS including a 9LV 100 optronic director and laser range-finder.

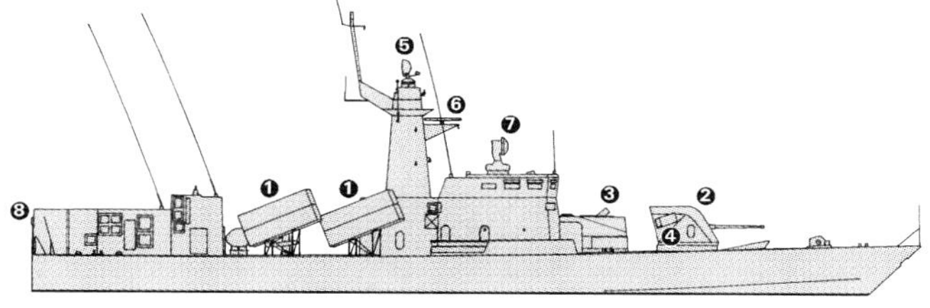

MALMÖ *(Scale 1 : 600), Ian Sturton* / 1153880

Radars: Air/surface search: Ericsson Sea Giraffe 50HC ❺; G-band.
Navigation: Terma Scanter ❻; I-band.
Fire control: Philips 9LV 200 Mk 3 ❼; J-band.
Sonars: Simrad SA 950; hull-mounted; active attack.
Thomson Sintra TSM 2642 Salmon ❽; VDS; search; medium frequency.

Programmes: Orders placed in September 1981. Developed from Spica II class.
Modernisation: RBS 15 missile upgraded to Mk II from 1994. Improved A/S mortar fitted in 1998–99. Extensive mid-life upgrade carried out 1999–2002. Modernisation included removal of the 21 in torpedo tubes and the aft 40 mm mounting and modification of the superstructure to reduce radar and IR signatures. The bridge wings have been removed and a pylon mast has replaced a lattice structure. Upgrades include a new propulsion system, combat data system and EW systems. The decoys are situated on either side of the gun turret. Both ships are to be fitted with CDC Hydra sonar.
Operational: Both ships are expected to remain in service beyond 2015. *Malmö* ran aground on 10 October 2006 but has since returned to service.

MALMÖ *10/2007, Michael Nitz* / 1166712

STOCKHOLM *6/2007, H M Steele* / 1166711

SHIPBORNE AIRCRAFT

Numbers/Type: 20 Agusta A 109M (Hkp-15).
Operational speed: 152 kt *(280 km/h)*.
Service ceiling: 16,500 ft *(5,029 m)*.
Range: 447 n miles *(827 km)*.
Role/Weapon systems: Military version of A 109E with Turbomeca Arrius 2K2 engine. Swedish Armed Forces ordered 20 on 20 June 2001. Of these, eight are to be 'navalised' for operation from Visby class and from shore bases. First delivered on 3 Feb 2006 and the remainder by 2009. ASW and ASV roles.

Hkp-15 *6/2006, Royal Swedish Navy* / 1164715

LAND-BASED MARITIME AIRCRAFT (FRONT LINE)

Notes: In addition 11 AS 332 Super Puma helicopters are used for SAR.

Numbers/Type: 18 NH Industries NH 90.
Operational speed: 157 kt *(291 km/h)*.
Service ceiling: 13,940 ft *(4,250 m)*.
Range: 621 n miles *(1,150 km)*.
Role/Weapon systems: Eighteen aircraft to be procured for tactical troop transport and ASW role. Modular construction is to enable rapid re-roling. There are to be 5 sets of ASW sensors for delivery between 2007 and 2010. Sensors: Telephonics APS-143B(V) ocean eye radar, Galileo Avionica FLIR, Thales FLASH-S dipping sonar. Weapons: To be announced.

NH 90 *6/2006, Royal Swedish Navy* / 1164714

PATROL FORCES

1 TYPE 72 INSHORE PATROL CRAFT (PBR)

HUVUDSKÄR 77

Displacement, tons: 30 full load
Dimensions, feet (metres): 69.2 × 15 × 4.3 *(21.1 × 4.6 × 1.3)*
Main machinery: 3 diesels; 3 shafts
Speed, knots: 22
Guns: 1 — 20 mm.
Depth charges: Carried in all of the class.
Radars: Surface search: Decca RM 914; I-band.
Sonars: Simrad; hull-mounted; active search; high frequency.

Comment: Last remaining vessel of a class built in 1966-67. Modernised in the 1980s with a tripod mast and radar mounted over the bridge.

TYPE 72 *6/1994, Curt Borgenstam* / 0080731

12 TAPPER CLASS (PBR)

TAPPER 81	**DRISTIG** 83	**TRYGG** 85	**HURTIG** 87	**STOLT** 89	**MUNTER** 91
DJÄRV 82	**HÄNDIG** 84	**MODIG** 86	**RAPP** 88	**ÄRLIG** 90	**ORÄDD** 92

Displacement, tons: 57 full load
Dimensions, feet (metres): 71.9 × 17.7 × 4.9 *(21.9 × 5.4 × 1.5)*
Main machinery: 2 MWM TBD234V16 diesels; 1,812 hp(m) *(1.33 MW)* sustained; 2 shafts
Speed, knots: 25
Complement: 9
Guns: 2 — 12.7 mm MGs.
A/S mortars: 4 Elma/Saab grenade launchers; range 300 m; warhead 4.2 kg shaped charge.
Depth charges: 18.
Mines: 2 rails (in four of the class).
Radars: Surface search: 2 Racal Decca; I-band.
Sonars: Simrad; hull-mounted; active search; high frequency.

Comment: Seven Type 80 ordered from Djupviksvarvet in early 1992, and delivered between February 1993 and December 1995. Five more ordered in 1995 for delivery at six month intervals between December 1996 and January 1999. A Phantom HD-2 ROV is carried. This is equipped with a Tritech ST 525 imaging sonar.

TRYGG *5/2006, L-G Nilsson* / 1164713

TAPPER *3/2006, Per Körnefeldt* / 1159924

1 COASTAL PATROL CRAFT (PB)

Name	*No*	*Builders*	*Commissioned*
ÖSTHAMMAR	SVK 11 (ex-V 11)	Djupviks Varvet	1 Mar 1985

Displacement, tons: 50 full load
Dimensions, feet (metres): 76.8 × 16.7 × 3.6 *(23.4 × 5.1 × 1.1)*
Main machinery: 2 MTU 8V396 TB83 diesels; 2,100 hp *(1.6 MW)*; 2 shafts
Speed, knots: 30
Complement: 7 (3 officers)
Radars: Navigation: I-band.

Comment: Former patrol craft originally commissioned in 1985 and later decommissioned in 2002. Reactivated in 2008 as patrol craft in Sjövärnskåren (SVK).

ÖSTHAMMAR *7/2008*, A Sheldon-Duplaix* / 1336051

1 JÄGAREN CLASS (COASTAL PATROL CRAFT) (PC)

Name	*No*	*Builders*	*Commissioned*
JÄGAREN	V 150	Bergens MV, Norway	24 Nov 1972

Displacement, tons: 120 standard; 150 full load
Dimensions, feet (metres): 120 × 20.7 × 5.6 *(36.6 × 6.3 × 1.7)*
Main machinery: 2 Cummins KTA50-M; 2,500 hp *(1.87 MW)* sustained; 2 shafts
Speed, knots: 20. **Range, n miles:** 550 at 20 kt
Complement: 15 (3 officers)
Guns: 1 Bofors 40 mm/70.
Mines: 2 rails.
Radars: Surface search/navigation: To be announced.

Comment: Originally constructed as a prototype for the deleted Hugin class, the vessel was converted for patrol duties in 1988. Decommissioned in 2002, she was reactivated as a patrol and general duties craft in 2008 following a four month refit. The ship is reported to have been fitted with a new surface search radar and the aft of the ship to have been modified to provide stowage space for oil recovery equipment.

JÄGAREN *8/1997, Frank Behling* / 0019191

AMPHIBIOUS FORCES

145 COMBATBOAT 90H/90HS (STRIDSBÅT) (LCPFM)

803–946 BLÅTUNGA 947

Displacement, tons: 19 full load
Dimensions, feet (metres): 52.2 × 12.5 × 2.6 *(15.9 × 3.8 × 0.8)*
Main machinery: 2 Saab Scania DSI 14 diesels; 1,250 hp(m) *(935 kW)* (1,350 hp(m) in 90HS *(1,000 kW)*); 2 Kamewa water-jets
Speed, knots: 35-50; 20 (Sea State 3). **Range, n miles:** 240 at 30 kt
Complement: 3
Military lift: 20 troops plus equipment or 2.8 tons
Missiles: SSM: Rockwell RBS 17 Hellfire; semi-active laser guidance to 5 km *(3 n miles)* at 1.0 Mach; warhead 8 kg.
Guns: 3 — 12.7 mm MGs.
Mines: 4 (or 6 depth charges).
Radars: Navigation: Racal Decca; RD 360 or Furuno 8050; I-band.

Comment: The first two prototypes (801-802) ordered in January 1988 are no longer in service. Twelve more (803-814) built in 1991–92. There were 63 (815-877) ordered from Dockstavarvet and Gotlands Varv in mid-January 1992, with an option for 30 more (878-907) which was taken up in 1994. The building period for these completed in mid-1997. A further 40 (908-947) were ordered in August 1996 and delivery was completed in October 2003. Of these, the last 27 (90HS) units were all modified to undertake international peacekeeping operations by the inclusion of armoured protection, an NBC citadel and air conditioning. All have a 20° deadrise and all carry four six-man inflatable rafts. 947 is equipped as VIP craft. It is planned to upgrade a further 60-70 craft to the 90HS standard. There were 22 (90N) of the class delivered to Norway 1999, 40 (90 HEX) to Mexico, 17 (90H) to Malaysia and three (90 HEX) to the Hellenic Coast Guard.

COMBATBOAT 821 *6/2006, Per Körnefeldt* / 1159925

COMBATBOAT 825 *5/2007, Per Körnefeldt* / 1166708

5 COMBATBOAT 90E (STRIDSBÅT) (YH)

101 series

Displacement, tons: 9 full load
Dimensions, feet (metres): 39 × 9.5 × 2.3 *(11.9 × 2.9 × 0.7)*
Main machinery: 1 Scania AB DSI 14 diesel; 398 hp(m) *(293 kW)* sustained; FFJet 410 water-jet
Speed, knots: 40; 37 (laden)
Complement: 2
Military lift: 2 tons or 6-10 troops
Radars: Navigation: Furuno 8050; I-band.

Comment: Ambulance boats that may also be used for stores. First batch ordered from Storebro Royal Cruiser AB in 1995 for delivery from August 1995–98. Second batch ordered in 1997 for delivery in 1998–99. Of 54 that entered service, 49 have been decommissioned and sold or donated.

COMBATBOAT 90E *8/2002, E & M Laursen* / 0529915

9 LCMs (TROSSBÅT)

603–606 **608–610** **653** **657**

Displacement, tons: 55 full load
Dimensions, feet (metres): 68.9 × 19.7 × 4.9 *(21 × 6 × 1.5)*
Main machinery: 2 Scania DSI 11/40 M2 diesels; 340 hp(m) *(250 kW)*; 2 Schottel props
Speed, knots: 10
Military lift: 30 tons
Radars: Navigation: Racal Decca 914C; I-band.

Comment: Completed from 1980–88. Classified as Trossbåt (support boat). Built by Djupviksvarvet. Eight have been deleted.

LCM 609 *5/2004, E & M Laursen* / 1043535

0 + 1 (4) COMBATBOAT 2010M (PBF)

Displacement, tons: 56 full load
Dimensions, feet (metres): 79.1 × 17.2 × 3.8 *(24.1 × 5.24 × 1.17)*
Main machinery: 2 diesels; 2 waterjets
Speed, knots: 37
Guns: 1 Patria Hägglunds 120 mm advanced mortar system.

Comment: Following trials in a converted Combatboat 90H, a prototype of a mortar-armed fast support craft has been ordered. The vessel is to be larger than the existing CB 90 series. A test and evaluation period was planned to start in the second half of 2008 and an initial production run of four vessels is projected to start in 2011.

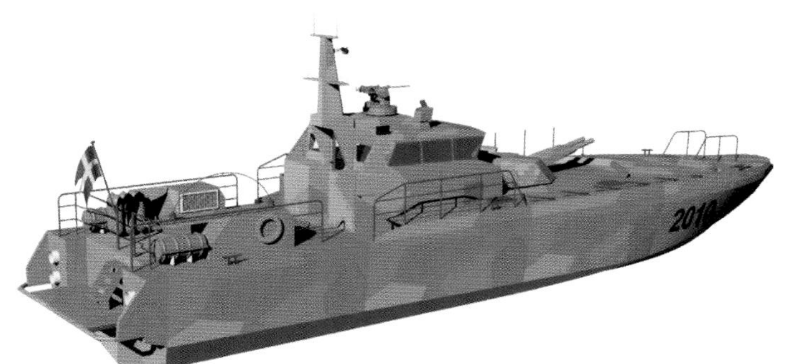

COMBATBOAT 2010M (artist's impression) *5/2007, Dockstavarvet* / 1184950

2 TRANSPORTBÅT 2000 (AGF/YFLB)

451 **452**

Displacement, tons: 43 full load
Dimensions, feet (metres): 77.1 × 16.7 × 3.3 *(23.5 × 5.1 × 1)*
Main machinery: 3 Saab Scania DSI 14 diesels or 3 Volvo Penta 163 diesels; 1,194 hp(m) *(878 kW)* sustained; 3 FFJet 450 or 3 Kamewa K40 waterjets
Speed, knots: 25
Complement: 3
Military lift: 45 troops or 10 tons
Guns: 2 — 12.7 mm MGs.
Radars: Navigation: Terma; I-band.

Comment: Two similar prototypes ordered from Djupviks Shipyard in 1997. Both configured as command boats.

TRANSPORTBÅT 452 *6/2000, Michael Nitz* / 0106583

3 GRIFFON 8100TD (TYPE 392) CLASS HOVERCRAFT (UCAC)

302–304

Displacement, tons: 18.2; 24.6 full load
Dimensions, feet (metres): 73.8 × 36.1 × 1 *(22.5 × 11.0 × 0.32)*
Main machinery: 2 Iveco diesels; 2,000 hp *(1.5 MW)*
Speed, knots: 42
Range, n miles: 400 at 45 kt
Complement: 13 (2 officers)
Guns: 1 — 12.7 mm MG.
Radars: Raytheon; I-band.

Comment: Three hovercraft ordered in July 2005. The first delivered in October 2006 and the second two in 2007. The aluminium-hulled craft are stretched versions of the Griffon 8000TD. Capable of carrying an 11 ton payload, the craft are to be fitted with ballistic protection and nbc protection.

GRIFFON 8100TD *9/2007, Richard Scott/NAVYPIX* / 1169099

82 RAIDING CRAFT (GRUPPBÅT) (LCP)

Displacement, tons: 3 full load
Dimensions, feet (metres): 26.2 × 6.9 × 1 *(8 × 2.1 × 0.3)*
Main machinery: 1 Volvo Penta TAMD 42WJ diesel; 230 hp(m) *(169 kW)*; 1 Kamewa 240 waterjet
Speed, knots: 30
Complement: 2
Military lift: 1 ton

Comment: Small raiding craft are used throughout the Archipelago. Some have been decommissioned.

GRUPPBÅT *5/2006, E & M Laursen* / 1159938

MINE WARFARE FORCES

Notes: A transportable COOP system was ordered in 1991. The unit can be shifted from one ship to another and comprises a container, processing module and tactical display, an underwater positioning system, sonar, Sea Eagle ROV and mine disposal charge. Optimised for shallow water surveillance and can be used in conjunction with other MCM systems. The primary role is route survey.

5 SAM CLASS (MCM DRONES) (MSD)

SAM 01–02 **SAM 04** **SAM 06–07**

Displacement, tons: 20 full load
Dimensions, feet (metres): 59.1 × 20 × 5.2 *(18 × 6.1 × 1.6)*
Main machinery: 1 Volvo Penta TAMD70D diesel; 210 hp(m) *(154 kW)*; 1 Schottel prop
Speed, knots: 8
Range, n miles: 330 at 8 kt

Comment: Built by Karlskronavarvet in 1983. *SAM 03* and *05* sold to the USA for Gulf operation in March 1991 and replaced in 1992/93. Remote-controlled catamaran magnetic and acoustic sweepers operated by the Landsort, Koster, Visby and Styrsö classes. Six sold to Japan.

SAM 07 *4/2003, Per Körnefeldt* / 0572624

2 LANDSORT CLASS (MINEHUNTERS) (MHSCDM)

Name	*No*	*Builders*	*Launched*	*Commissioned*
LANDSORT	M 71	Karlskronavarvet	2 Nov 1982	19 Apr 1984
ARHOLMA	M 72	Karlskronavarvet	2 Aug 1984	23 Nov 1984

Displacement, tons: 270 standard; 360 full load
Dimensions, feet (metres): 155.8 × 31.5 × 7.3 *(47.5 × 9.6 × 2.2)*
Main machinery: 4 Saab-Scania DSI 14 diesels; 1,592 hp(m) *(1.17 MW)* sustained; coupled in pairs to 2 Voith Schneider props
Speed, knots: 15
Range, n miles: 2,000 at 12 kt
Complement: 29 (12 officers) plus 4 spare

Guns: 1 Bofors 40 mm/70 Mod 48; 240 rds/min to 12.5 km *(6.8 n miles)*; weight of shell 0.96 kg. Bofors Sea Trinity CIWS trial carried out in *Vinga* (fitted in place of 40 mm/70). 2 — 7.62 mm MGs.
Countermeasures: Decoys: 2 Philips Philax fixed launchers can be carried with 4 magazines each holding 36 grenades; IR/chaff.
MCM: This class is fitted for mechanical sweeps for moored mines as well as magnetic and acoustic sweeps. In addition it is possible to operate two SAM drones (see separate entry). Fitted with 2 Sutec Sea Eagle or Double Eagle remote-controlled units with 600 m tether and capable of 350 m depth.
Weapons control: Philips 9LV 100 optronic director. Philips 9 MJ 400 minehunting system.
Radars: Navigation: Thomson-CSF Terma; I-band.
Sonars: Thomson-CSF TSM-2022; Racal Decca 'Mains' control system; hull-mounted; minehunting; high frequency.

Programmes: These first two of this class ordered in early 1981.
Modernisation: The other five ships of the class, now known as the Koster class, are being modernised. These two ships are not to be upgraded.
Structure: The GRP mould for the hull has also been used for the Coast Guard former KBV 171 class.
Operational: The integrated navigation and action data automation system developed by Philips and Racal Decca. Both ships likely to be decommissioned in 2012.
Sales: Four built for Singapore.

ARHOLMA *10/2007, Michael Nitz* / 1166707

5 KOSTER CLASS

Name	No	Builders	Launched	Commissioned
KOSTER	M 73	Karlskronavarvet	16 Jan 1986	30 May 1986
KULLEN	M 74	Karlskronavarvet	15 Aug 1986	28 Nov 1986
VINGA	M 75	Karlskronavarvet	14 Aug 1987	27 Nov 1987
VEN	M 76	Karlskronavarvet	10 Aug 1988	12 Dec 1988
ULVÖN	M 77	Karlskronavarvet	4 Mar 1992	9 Oct 1992

Displacement, tons: 270 standard; 360 full load
Dimensions, feet (metres): 155.8 × 31.5 × 7.3 *(47.5 × 9.6 × 2.2)*
Main machinery: 4 Saab-Scania DSI 14 diesels; 1,592 hp(m) *(1.17 MW)* sustained; coupled in pairs to 2 Voith Schneider props
Speed, knots: 15
Range, n miles: 2,000 at 12 kt
Complement: 29 (12 officers) plus 4 spare

Guns: 1 Bofors 40 mm/70 Mod 48; 240 rds/min to 12.5 km *(6.8 n miles)*; weight of shell 0.96 kg. Bofors Sea Trinity CIWS trial carried out in *Vinga* (fitted in place of 40 mm/70). 2—7.62 mm MGs.
Countermeasures: Decoys: 2 Philips Philax fixed launchers can be carried with 4 magazines each holding 36 grenades; IR/chaff.
MCM: This class is fitted for mechanical sweeps for moored mines as well as magnetic and acoustic sweeps. In addition it is possible to operate two SAM drones (see separate entry). Fitted with Double Eagle Mk III ROV with variable depth sonar and Sea Fox C expendable mine disposal system.
Combat data systems: Atlas Elektronik Integrated Mine Countermeasures System.
Weapons control: Saab Philips 9LV 200 Mk II radar and optronic director.
Radars: Navigation: Litton Marine Bridgemaster; I-band.
Fire control: Saab Philips 9LV 200 Mk II; I-band.
Sonars: Atlas Elektronik HMS-12M triple frequency high resolution. Kongsberg HIPAP 500 positioning system.

Programmes: The first four ordered in 1984 and the fifth in 1989.
Modernisation: All five ships of the former Landsort class are undergoing a two-stage upgrade at Kockums, Karlskrona. The first phase, to enable participation in international operations, was undertaken in *Kullen* and *Ven* in 2003 and *Koster*, *Vinga* and *Ulvön* in 2005. A second more extensive mid-life modernisation includes installation of a new command system, an integrated mine countermeasures system (comprising hull-mounted sonar and VDS installed in Double Eagle ROV), and a mine-identification and disposal system based on the Atlas SeaFox. Delivery schedule: *Koster* (November 2008); *Vinga* (February 2009); *Ulvön* (July 2009); *Kullen* (January 2010); *Ven* (August 2010).

VEN ***10/2007, Michael Nitz*** / 1166706

4 STYRSÖ CLASS (MINESWEEPERS/HUNTERS—INSHORE) (MHSDI/YDT)

Name	No	Builders	Launched	Commissioned
STYRSÖ	M 11	Karlskronavarvet	8 Mar 1996	20 Sep 1996
SPÅRÖ	M 12	Karlskronavarvet	30 Aug 1996	21 Feb 1997
SKAFTÖ	M 13	Karlskronavarvet	20 Jan 1997	13 June 1997
STURKÖ	M 14	Karlskronavarvet	27 June 1997	19 Dec 1997

Displacement, tons: 205 full load
Dimensions, feet (metres): 118.1 × 25.9 × 7.2 *(36 × 7.9 × 2.2)*
Main machinery: 2 Saab Scania DSI 14 diesels; 1,104 hp(m) *(812 kW)*; 2 shafts; bow thruster
Speed, knots: 13
Complement: 17 (9 officers)
Guns: 2—12.7 mm MGs.
Countermeasures: MCM: AK-90 acoustic, EL-90 magnetic, and mechanical sweeps.
2 Sutec Sea Eagle/Double Eagle ROVs equipped with Tritech SE 500 sonar and mine disposal charges.
Combat data systems: Ericsson tactical data system with datalink.
Radars: Navigation: Racal Bridgemaster: I-band.
Sonars: Reson Sea Bat 8100; mine avoidance; active; high frequency.
EG & G side scan; active for route survey; high frequency.

Comment: Contract awarded to KKV and Erisoft AB on 11 February 1994. Capable of operating two SAM drones. *Spårö* and *Sturkö* have been modified to act as diving support ships.

SKAFTÖ ***10/2007, Harald Carstens*** / 1166705

1 MSF MK 1 CLASS (MSD)

SÖKAREN MRF 01

Displacement, tons: 128 full load
Dimensions, feet (metres): 86.9 × 23 × 6.9 *(26.5 × 7 × 2.1)*
Main machinery: 2 Scania DSI 14 diesels; 1,000 hp(m) *(736 kW)*; 2 Schottel azimuth thrusters
Speed, knots: 12
Complement: 6
Radars: Navigation: Bridgewater E; I-band.
Sonars: STS 2054 side scan active; high frequency.

Comment: MCMV drone with GRP hull transferred from Denmark in 2001 for evaluation following cancellation of SAM II drone project.

SÖKAREN ***5/2004, E & M Laursen*** / 1043531

INTELLIGENCE VESSELS

1 ELECTRONIC SURVEILLANCE SHIP (AGIH)

Name	No	Builders	Launched	Commissioned
ORION	A 201	Karlskronavarvet	30 Nov 1983	7 June 1984

Displacement, tons: 1,400 full load
Dimensions, feet (metres): 201.1 × 32.8 × 9.8 *(61.3 × 10 × 3)*
Main machinery: 2 Hedemora V8A diesels; 1,800 hp(m) *(1.32 MW)* sustained; 2 shafts; cp props
Speed, knots: 15
Complement: 35
Radars: Navigation: Terma Scanter 009; I-band.
Helicopters: Platform for 1 light.

Comment: Ordered 23 April 1982. Laid down 28 June 1982. The communications aerials are inside the elongated dome.

ORION ***9/2006, Frank Findler*** / 1159910

RESCUE VEHICLES

1 RESCUE SUBMERSIBLE (DSRV)

URF

Displacement, tons: 52
Dimensions, feet (metres): 45.6 × 10.5 × 9.2 *(13.9 × 3.2 × 2.8)*
Main machinery: Electric/hydraulic: single shaft
Speed, knots: 3
Complement: 4

Comment: Rescue submersible URF (*Ubåts Räddnings Farkost*) was launched by Kockums on 17 April 1978 and commissioned in 1979. The double-hulled vehicle is capable of operating down to 460 m with an endurance of 85 hours. The URF can mate with the hull of a submarine at angles up to 45° and is equipped with a lockout chamber that can support two divers to 300 m. It has a rescue capacity of 35 per dive and submariners can be transferred directly from the pressurised hull of the submarine to a compression chamber on board the support ship *Belos*. The vehicle is normally based at the Naval Diving Centre at Berga but can be transported by road using a specially designed trailer to a site suitable for loading on to the support ship. URF is to be modernised in 2009 (plans to replace her with S-SRV have been shelved).

URF ***8/2004, E & M Laursen*** / 1043538

TRAINING SHIPS

2 SAIL TRAINING SHIPS (AXS)

Name	*No*	*Builders*	*Commissioned*
GLADAN	S 01	Naval Dockyard, Stockholm	1947
FALKEN	S 02	Naval Dockyard, Stockholm	1947

Displacement, tons: 225 standard
Dimensions, feet (metres): 112.8 × 23.6 × 13.8 *(34.4 × 7.2 × 4.2)*
Main machinery: 1 diesel; 120 hp(m) *(88 kW)*; 1 shaft

Comment: Sail training ships. Two masted schooners. Sail area, 512 sq m. Both had major overhauls in 1986–88 in which all technical systems were replaced.

FALKEN *5/2007, **Derek Fox*** / 1166653

5 ALTAIR CLASS (TRAINING VESSELS) (YXT)

ALTAIR A 501 **ANTARES** A 502 **ARCTURUS** A 503 **ARGO** A 504 **ASTREA** A 505

Displacement, tons: 85 full load
Dimensions, feet (metres): 85.0 × 19.7 × 5.6 *(25.9 × 6.0 × 1.7)*
Main machinery: 2 MTU 12V 2000 M90 diesels; 2,500 hp *(1.86 MW)*; 2 shafts
Speed, knots: 24. **Range, n miles:** 530 at 11 kt
Complement: 4 plus 6 cadets

Comment: Contract placed with Swede Ship Marine AB on 12 May 2006 for five training vessels of aluminium construction; the ships are to be built by Djupviks Varv. The vessels are to be used for cadets' seamanship and navigation training and are to replace the M 15 class minesweepers. The ships are to have a secondary SAR role. The first vessel was delivered in May 2008 and the remainder are to follow by May 2009.

ALTAIR *6/2008*, **Swedish Navy*** / 1335876

AUXILIARIES

Notes: The Combat Support Ship (L 10) project is for two ships capable of conducting replenishment at sea, amphibious support, repair and maintenance, medical support and transport of about 170 troops. Conceptual work suggests that the requirement might be met by a modified Ro-Ro ferry design. The ships would be of about 145 m length, include bow doors and stern ramps, a vehicle deck of about 400 lane-metres, a hangar for two NH90 and a flight deck. There would be space on the upper deck for the stowage of 10 Combatboat 90H and two Combatboat 2010. Subject to approval of the project, a competitive tendering process is planned to lead to a construction contract in 2010 and delivery of the first ship in 2013.

1 TRANSPORT (AKR)

Name	*No*	*Builders*	*Commissioned*
SLEIPNER (ex-*Ardal*)	A 343	Bergen	1980

Displacement, tons: 1,049 full load
Dimensions, feet (metres): 163.1 × 36.1 × 11.5 *(49.7 × 11 × 3.5)*
Main machinery: 1 Normo diesel; 1,300 hp(m) *(956 kW)*; 1 shaft
Speed, knots: 12
Complement: 12
Cargo capacity: 260 tons

Comment: Former Ro-Ro vessel acquired in 1992 from a Norwegian Shipping Company. There is a stern ramp and side door.

SLEIPNER *7/2003, **E & M Laursen*** / 0572629

1 TROSSÖ CLASS (SUPPORT SHIP) (AGP)

Name	*No*	*Builders*	*Commissioned*
TROSSÖ (ex-*Arnold Viemer*, ex-*Livonia*)	A 264	Valmet, Finland	1 Jan 1984

Displacement, tons: 2,140 full load
Dimensions, feet (metres): 234.9 × 42 × 14.8 *(71.6 × 12.8 × 4.5)*
Main machinery: 2 Russkiy G74 36/45 diesels; 3,084 hp(m) *(2.27 MW)*; 2 shafts
Speed, knots: 14
Complement: 64

Comment: Built as a survey ship for the USSR and used in the Baltic as an AGOR. Taken on by the Estonian Marine Institute and then transferred to Sweden on 23 September 1996. Converted as a depot ship for corvettes and patrol craft and back in service in 1997. Can act as a Headquarters Ship. A second vessel, *Ornö*, was purchased in 2001 but rebuilding of the ship was abandoned in November 2001 due to its poor material state.

TROSSÖ *10/2007, **Michael Nitz*** / 1166703

1 CARLSKRONA CLASS (SUPPORT SHIP) (AG)

Name	*No*	*Builders*	*Launched*	*Commissioned*
CARLSKRONA	M 04	Karlskronavarvet	28 June 1980	11 Jan 1982

Displacement, tons: 3,600 full load
Dimensions, feet (metres): 346.7 × 49.9 × 13.1 *(105.7 × 15.2 × 4)*
Main machinery: 4 Nohab F212 D825 diesels; 10,560 hp(m) *(7.76 MW)*; 2 shafts; cp props
Speed, knots: 20
Complement: 50 plus 136 trainees. Requires 118 as operational minelayer
Guns: 2 Bofors 57 mm/70. 2 Bofors 40 mm/70.
Mines: Can lay 105.
Countermeasures: 2 Philips Philax chaff/IR launchers.
ESM: Argo AR 700; intercept.
Radars: Air/surface search: Ericsson Sea Giraffe 50HC; G/H/I-band.
Surface search: Raytheon; E/F-band.
Fire control: 2 Philips 9LV 200 Mk 2; I/J-band.
Navigation :Terma Scanter 009; I-band.
Helicopters: Platform only.

Comment: Ordered 25 November 1977, laid down in sections late 1979 and launched at the same time as Karlskrona celebrated its tercentenary. Former minelayer now employed on miscellaneous support and training tasks.

CARLSKRONA *7/2008** / 1335875

1 ÄLVSBORG CLASS (SUPPORT SHIP) (AKH)

Name	*No*	*Builders*	*Launched*	*Commissioned*
VISBORG	A 265	Karlskronavarvet	25 Jan 1975	6 Feb 1976

Displacement, tons: 2,400 standard; 2,650 full load
Dimensions, feet (metres): 303.1 × 48.2 × 13.2 *(92.4 × 14.7 × 4)*
Main machinery: 2 Nohab-Polar diesels; 4,200 hp(m) *(3.1 MW)*; 1 shaft; cp prop; bow thruster; 350 hp(m) *(257 kW)*
Speed, knots: 16
Complement: 95
Guns: 3 Bofors 40 mm/70 SAK 48.
ESM: Argo 700; intercept.
Radars: Surface search: Raytheon; E/F-band.
Fire control: Philips 9LV 200 Mk 2; I/J-band.
Navigation: Terma Scanter 009; I-band.
Helicopters: Platform only.

Comment: Laid down on 16 October 1973. Formerly a minelayer, now supply ship for second surface flotilla. Sister ship transferred to Chile in 1996.

VISBORG *9/2007, **Maritime Photographic*** / 1166704

1 FURUSUND CLASS
(SALVAGE AND DIVING SUPPORT SHIP) (ARS)

Name	*No*	*Builders*	*Launched*	*Commissioned*
FURUSUND	20	ASI Verken	16 Dec 1982	10 Oct 1983

Displacement, tons: 225 full load
Dimensions, feet (metres): 106.9 × 26.9 × 7.5 *(32.6 × 8.2 × 2.3)*
Main machinery: Diesel-electric; 2 Scania GAS 1 diesel generators; 2 motors; 416 hp(m) *(306 kW)*; 2 shafts
Speed, knots: 11.5
Complement: 24
Guns: 1 — 12.7 mm MG.
Mines: 22 tons.
Radars: Navigation: Racal Decca 1226; I-band.

Comment: Former minelayer built for the Coastal Artillery. Now employed as a salvage and diving support ship.

FURUSUND *5/2001, Per Körnefeldt* / 0131140

2 ARKÖSUND CLASS (SERVICE SHIPS) (YAG)

GRUNDSUND 15 **FÅRÖSUND** (ex-*Öresund*) 18

Displacement, tons: 200 standard; 245 full load
Dimensions, feet (metres): 102.3 × 24.3 × 10.2 *(31.2 × 7.4 × 3.1)*
Main machinery: Diesel-electric; 2 Nohab/Scania diesel generators; 2 motors; 460 hp(m) *(338 kW)*; 2 shafts
Speed, knots: 12
Complement: 24
Guns: 4 — 7.62 mm MGs.
Mines: 2 rails; 26 tons.
Radars: Navigation: Racal Decca 1226; I-band.

Comment: All completed by 1954–1957. Former Coastal Artillery craft for laying and maintaining minefields. One deleted in 1992, one in 1996, *Skramsösund* in 1998, *Kalmarsund* and *Barösund* in 2004 and *Arkösund* in 2006. 40 mm guns removed. Employed as general service craft.

FÅRÖSUND *10/2007, Michael Nitz* / 1166702

1 DIVER SUPPORT SHIP (YDT/AGF)

ÄGIR (ex-*Bloom Syrveyor*) A 212

Displacement, tons: 117 full load
Dimensions, feet (metres): 82 × 24.9 × 6.6 *(25 × 7.6 × 2)*
Main machinery: 2 GM diesels; 2 shafts
Speed, knots: 11
Complement: 15
Radars: Navigation: Terma; I-band.

Comment: Built in Norway in 1984. Acquired in 1989.

ÄGIR *5/2006, Per Körnefeldt* / 1159921

1 SALVAGE SHIP (ARSH)

Name	*No*	*Builders*	*Recommissioned*
BELOS III (ex-*Energy Supporter*)	A 214	De Hoop, Netherlands	Nov 1992

Measurement, tons: 5,096 grt
Dimensions, feet (metres): 344.2 × 59.1 × 16.7 *(104.9 × 18 × 5.1)*
Main machinery: 5 MAN 9ASL 25/30 diesel alternators; 8.15 MW; 2 motors; 5,110 hp(m) *(3.76 MW)*; 2 azimuth thrusters and 3 bow thrusters
Speed, knots: 14
Complement: 50 (22 officers)

Comment: Bought from Midland and Scottish Resources in mid-1992 and arrived in Sweden in November 1992. Replaced the previous ship of the same name which paid off in April 1993. Ice-strengthened hull and fitted with a helicopter platform. Acts as the support ship for the rescue submersible URF. Equipped with Dynamic Positioning System MOSHIP. Life-extension refit completed in December 2005.

BELOS III *8/2004, E & M Laursen* / 1043539

1 TORPEDO AND MISSILE RECOVERY VESSEL (YPT)

Name	*No*	*Builders*	*Commissioned*
PELIKANEN	A 247	Djupviksvarvet	26 Sep 1963

Displacement, tons: 144 full load
Dimensions, feet (metres): 108.2 × 19 × 7.2 *(33 × 5.8 × 2.2)*
Main machinery: 2 MTU MB diesels; 1,040 hp(m) *(764 kW)*; 2 shafts
Speed, knots: 14
Complement: 14
Radars: Navigation: Terma; I-band.

Comment: Torpedo recovery and rocket trials vessel.

PELIKANEN *5/2005, E & M Laursen* / 1153897

16 SUPPORT VESSEL (TROSSBÅT) (YAG)

662–677

Displacement, tons: 60 full load
Dimensions, feet (metres): 80.1 × 17.7 × 4.6 *(24.4 × 5.4 × 1.4)*
Main machinery: 3 Saab Scania DSI 14 diesels; 1,194 hp(m) *(878 kW)* sustained; 3 FFJet 450 water-jets
Speed, knots: 25; 13 (laden)
Complement: 3
Military lift: 22 tons
Guns: 1 — 12.7 mm MG.
Radars: Navigation: Terma; I-band.

Comment: Prototype Trossbåt-built at Holms Shipyard in 1991 and capable of carrying 15 tons of deck cargo and 9 tons internal cargo or 17 troops plus mines. Aluminium hull with a bow ramp. Some ice capability. A second prototype delivered in late 1993, and the first production vessel in 1996. Eight vessels have been modified to undertake international peacekeeping operations by the inclusion of armoured protection, an NBC citadel and air conditioning.

TROSSBÅT 668 *8/2002, E & M Laursen* / 0529906

1 SUPPORT SHIP (AKL)

Name	*No*	*Builders*	*Commissioned*
LOKE	A 344	Oskarsham Shipyard	Sep 1994

Displacement, tons: 455 full load
Dimensions, feet (metres): 117.8 × 29.5 × 8.6 *(35.9 × 9 × 2.7)*
Main machinery: 2 Scania diesels; 2 shafts
Speed, knots: 12
Complement: 8
Cargo capacity: 50 tons or 50 passengers
Radars: Navigation: Terma; I-band.

Comment: General support craft which can be used as a ferry. Landing craft bow.

LOKE ***4/2004, E & M Laursen*** / 1043540

TUGS

2 COASTAL TUGS (YTM)

HEROS A 322 **HERA** A 324

Displacement, tons: 185 standard; 215 full load
Dimensions, feet (metres): 80.5 × 22.6 × 13.1 *(24.5 × 6.9 × 4)*
Main machinery: 1 diesel; 600 hp(m) *(441 kW)*; 1 shaft
Speed, knots: 11
Complement: 8

Comment: Details given for A 322 launched in 1957. Second is smaller at 127 tons and was launched in 1969–71. Both are icebreaking tugs.

HERA ***6/2000, E & M Laursen*** / 0106591

9 COASTAL TUGS (YTL)

A 702–705 **A 751** **A 753–756**

Displacement, tons: 42 full load
Dimensions, feet (metres): 50.9 × 16.4 × 8.9 *(15.5 × 5 × 2.7)*
Main machinery: 1 diesel; 1 shaft
Speed, knots: 9.5
Complement: 6

Comment: Can carry 40 people. Icebreaking tugs. *702-703* used by Amphibious Corps. All can carry mines.

A 702 ***5/2005, Per Körnefeldt*** / 1153899

COAST GUARD (KUSTBEVAKNING)

Establishment: Established in 1638, and for 350 years was a part of the Swedish Customs administration. From 1 July 1988 the Coast Guard became an independent civilian authority with a Board supervised by the Ministry of Defence. Organised in four regions with a central Headquarters.

Duties: Responsible for civilian surveillance of Swedish waters, fishery zone and continental shelf. Supervises and enforces fishing regulations, customs, dumping and pollution regulations, environmental protection and traffic regulations. Also concerned with prevention of drug running and forms part of the Swedish search and rescue organisation.

Headquarters Appointments

Director General:
Christina Salomonson

Bases

HQ: Karlskrona
Regional HQs: Karlskrona, Härnösand, Stockholm, Gothenburg
There are 26 Coast Guard stations.

Personnel

2009: 748

Aircraft: Two Bombardier Dash 8Q which were ordered in 2005.

Ships: Pennant numbers prefixed by KBV but the KBV is not displayed. Vessels are not normally armed.

2 + 1 KBV 001 CLASS (MULTIPURPOSE VESSELS) (WPSO)

No	*Builders*	*Launched*	*Commissioned*
KBV 001	Damen Shipyard, Galati	20 Feb 2008	2009
KBV 002	Damen Shipyard, Galati	14 Aug 2008	2009
KBV 003	Damen Shipyard, Galati	2009	2009

Displacement, tons: 5,756 full load
Dimensions, feet (metres): 266.4 × 52.5 × 18.1 *(81.2 × 16.0 × 5.5)*
Main machinery: Diesel-electric; 3 Caterpillar 3516 diesel generators; 7,800 hp *(5.82 MW)*; 2 Caterpillar 3512 diesel generators; 3,650 hp *(2.72 MW)*; 2 Rolls Royce Aquamaster US 355 FP azimuth thrusters; 2 retractable bow thrusters (850 kW and 415 kW).
Speed, knots: 16
Complement: 15
Radars: Navigation: Sperry Bridgemaster; E/F/I-band.

Comment: Contract signed on 20 December 2005 with Damen Shipyards for the construction of two multipurpose vessels to be capable of towing, fire-fighting, oil recovery, environmental-control, fishery control, control of territorial waters, rescue operations and diving support. A third vessel was ordered on 19 April 2007. The ships are designed by Schelde Naval Shipbuilding and are being built and outfitted at Damen Shipyard, Galati, Romania. KBV 001 is to be based at Gothenburg and KBV 002 at Slite, Gotland.

KBV 001 (artist's impression) ***12/2005, Damen Shipyards*** / 1041661

3 KBV 101 CLASS (MEDIUM ENDURANCE CUTTERS) (WMEC/PB)

KBV 103–105

Displacement, tons: 65 full load
Dimensions, feet (metres): 87.6 × 16.4 × 7.2 *(26.7 × 5 × 2.2)*
Main machinery: 2 Cummins KTA38-M diesels; 2,120 hp *(1.56 MW)*; 2 shafts
Speed, knots: 21. **Range, n miles:** 1,000 at 15 kt
Complement: 5 plus 2 spare
Sonars: Hull-mounted; active search; high frequency.

Comment: Built 1969–73 at Djupviksvarvet. Class A cutters. All-welded aluminium hull and upperworks. Equipped for salvage divers. Modernisation with new diesels, a new bridge and new electronics completed in 1988. *KBV 101* transferred to Lithuania in 1996.

KBV 103 ***5/2007, E & M Laursen*** / 1170080

1 KBV 181 CLASS (HIGH ENDURANCE CUTTER) (WHEC/PBO)

KBV 181

Displacement, tons: 991 full load
Dimensions, feet (metres): 183.7 oa; 167.3 wl × 33.5 × 15.1 *(56; 51 × 10.2 × 4.6)*
Main machinery: 2 Wärtsilä Vasa 8R22 diesels; 3,755 hp(m) *(2.76 MW)* sustained; 1 shaft; Kamewa cp prop; bow thruster
Speed, knots: 16. **Range, n miles:** 2,800 at 15 kt
Complement: 11
Guns: 1 Oerlikon 20 mm (if required).
Radars: Navigation: Furuno FAR 2830; I-band.
Sonars: Simrad Subsea; active search; high frequency.

Comment: Ordered from Rauma Shipyards in August 1989 and built at Uusikaupunki. Commissioned 30 November 1990. Unarmed in peacetime. Equipped as a Command vessel for SAR and anti-pollution operations. All-steel construction similar to Finnish *Tursas*.

KBV 181 *6/2007*, ***Swedish Coast Guard*** / 1170063

2 KBV 201 CLASS (HIGH ENDURANCE CUTTERS) (WHEC/PBO)

KBV 201–202

Displacement, tons: 476 full load
Dimensions, feet (metres): 170.6 × 28.2 × 7.9 *(52 × 8.6 × 2.4)*
Main machinery: 2 MWM 610 diesels; 5,440 hp(m) *(4 MW)*; 2 MWM 616 diesels; 1,904 hp(m) *(1.4 MW)*; 2 shafts; Kamewa cp props; 2 bow thruster 424 hp(m) *(312 kW)*
Speed, knots: 21. **Range, n miles:** 1,340 at 16 kt
Complement: 9
Radars: Navigation: E/F- and I-band.

Comment: Ordered from Kockums in January 1999 and built at Karlskrona. First one delivered in March 2001 and second in September 2001. Steel hulls. Multirole vessels for surveillance and environmental protection. Stern ramp for launching a RIB.

KBV 201 *11/2007*, ***Swedish Coast Guard*** / 1170062

3 KBV 288 CLASS (MEDIUM ENDURANCE CUTTERS) (WMEC/PBO)

KBV 288–290

Displacement, tons: 53 full load
Dimensions, feet (metres): 71.5 × 17.7 × 5.9 *(21.8 × 5.4 × 1.8)*
Main machinery: 2 Cummins KTA38-M or MWM diesels; 2,120 hp *(1.56 MW)*; 2 shafts
Speed, knots: 24
Complement: 5
Radars: Navigation: Furuno; I-band.

Comment: An improved design of the KBV 281 class which entered service 1990–93.

KBV 290 *7/2008** / 1335874

6 KBV 281 CLASS (MEDIUM ENDURANCE CUTTERS) (WMEC/PB)

KBV 281–283 **KBV 285–287**

Displacement, tons: 45 full load
Dimensions, feet (metres): 71.5 × 16.4 × 6.2 *(21.8 × 5 × 1.9)*
Main machinery: 2 Cummins KTA38-M or MWM diesels; 2,120 hp *(1.56 MW)*; 2 shafts
Speed, knots: 27
Complement: 4
Radars: Navigation: Furuno; I-band.

Comment: Built by Djupviksvarvet and delivered at one a year from 1979. Last one commissioned in 1990. Aluminium hulls. Some of the class have an upper bridge.

KBV 287 *5/2004*, ***P Marsan*** / 1043544

11 KBV 301 CLASS (MEDIUM ENDURANCE CUTTERS) (WMEC/PB)

KBV 301–311

Displacement, tons: 35 full load
Dimensions, feet (metres): 65.6 × 15.1 × 3.6 *(20 × 4.6 × 1.1)*
Main machinery: 2 MTU 183 TE92 diesels; 1,830 hp(m) *(1.35 MW)* sustained; 2 MTP 7500S or Kamewa water-jets
Speed, knots: 34
Range, n miles: 500 at 25 kt
Complement: 4
Radars: Navigation: 2 Kelvin Hughes 6000; I-band.

Comment: Built at Karlskronavarvet. First one delivered in May 1993 and the remainder ordered in December 1993. Three delivered in 1995, four in 1996 and the last three in 1997. Five deleted in 2006.

KBV 307 *5/2007*, ***E & M Laursen*** / 1170081

3 KBV 591 (GRIFFON 2000TDX) CLASS (HOVERCRAFT) (UCAC)

KBV 591–593

Displacement, tons: 3.5 full load
Dimensions, feet (metres): 38.4 × 19.4 *(11.7 × 5.9)*
Main machinery: 1 Deutz BF8L diesel; 350 hp(m) *(235 kW)*
Speed, knots: 50
Range, n miles: 450 at 35 kt
Complement: 3
Radars: Navigation: Furuno 7010 D; I-band.

Comment: Built by Griffon Hovercraft, Southampton and delivered in 1992–93. Aluminium hulls. Based at Stockholm, Lutea and Umea.

KBV 591 *6/2003*, ***Swedish Coast Guard*** / 0572610

60 COAST GUARD PATROL CRAFT (SMALL) (PB)

KBV 401–408 +52

Displacement, tons: 2.2 full load
Dimensions, feet (metres): 29.7 × 8.5 × 2.9 *(9.05 × 2.6 × 0.9)*
Main machinery: 2 Yamaha outboard engines; 500 hp *(372 kW)*
Speed, knots: 55
Range, n miles: 100 at 35 kt
Complement: 3

Comment: Details are for *KBV 401-408* built in 1994–95. There is a total of some 60 speed boats with Raytheon radars.

KBV 454 *7/2008** / 1335873

POLLUTION CONTROL CRAFT (YPC)

Number	*Displacement (tons)*	*Comment*
KBV 004	450	Built by Lunde in 1978. Has helipad and carries salvage divers
KBV 005	990	Ice Class 1A built in 1980 and acquired in 1993
KBV 010	400	Built by Lunde in 1985. Oil spill clean-up craft
KBV 020	60	Catamaran design built by Djupviks in 1982
KBV 044	100	Class B Sea Trucks built by Djupviks in 1976. Oil spill clean-up craft
KBV 045	230	Pollution control craft built by Lunde 1980–83. Have bow ramp
KBV 046	230	Pollution control craft built by Lunde 1980–83. Have bow ramp
KBV 047	230	Pollution control craft built by Lunde 1980–83. Have bow ramp
KBV 048	230	Pollution control craft built by Lunde 1980–83. Have bow ramp
KBV 049	230	Pollution control craft built by Lunde 1980–83. Have bow ramp
KBV 050	340	Enlarged version of KBV 045 class with bow ramp. Built by Lunde in 1983
KBV 051	340	Enlarged version of KBV 045 class with bow ramp. Built by Lunde in 1983

Comment: The KBV 031 Project is for a class of four 50 m multipurpose environmental protection craft to replace older oil-recovery vessels. Built by Peene Werft, Wolgart, the first is to be delivered in April 2011.

KBV 048 *5/2006, E & M Laursen* / 1159940

KBV 051 *5/2007, Per Körnefeldt* / 1166697

GOVERNMENT MARITIME FORCES

CIVILIAN SURVEY AND RESEARCH SHIPS

Notes: (1) Owned and manned (since 1 January 2002) by the National Maritime Administration.
(2) There is a research ship *Argos*. Civilian manned and owned by the National Board of Fisheries. A second civilian ship *Ocean Surveyor* belongs to the Geological Investigation but has been leased as a Support Ship on occasions.
(3) The Board of Navigation owns two buoy tenders *Scandica* and *Baltica* built in 1982 and two lighthouse tenders *Fyrbyggaren* and *Fyrbjörn*.

SCANDICA *6/2000, Curt Borgenstam* / 0106585

1 SURVEY SHIP (AGS)

JACOB HÄGG

Displacement, tons: 192 standard
Dimensions, feet (metres): 119.8 × 24.6 × 5.6 *(36.5 × 7.5 × 1.7)*
Main machinery: 4 Saab Scania DSI 14 diesels; 1,592 hp(m) *(1.17 MW)* sustained; 2 shafts
Speed, knots: 16
Complement: 13 (5 officers)

Comment: Laid down April 1982 at Djupviks Shipyard. Launched 12 March 1983. Completed 16 May 1983. Aluminium hull.

JACOB HÄGG *5/1998, J Cislak* / 0050199

1 SURVEY SHIP (AGS)

NILS STRÖMCRONA

Displacement, tons: 210 full load
Dimensions, feet (metres): 98.4 × 32.8 × 5.9 *(30 × 10 × 1.8)*
Main machinery: 4 Saab Scania DSI 14 diesels; 1,592 hp(m) *(1.17 MW)* sustained; 2 shafts; bow and stern thrusters
Speed, knots: 12
Complement: 14 (5 officers)

Comment: Completed 28 June 1985. Of catamaran construction-each hull of 3.9 m made of aluminium.

NILS STRÖMCRONA *9/2001, Per Körnefeldt* / 0131143

Switzerland

Country Overview

A landlocked western European country, the Swiss Confederation has an area of 15,940 square miles and is bordered by France, Germany, Austria, Liechtenstein and Italy. The largest city is Zurich and the capital is Bern. The principal lakes are Lake Geneva in the southwest and Lake Constance in the northeast. Others not wholly within Swiss borders are Lake Lugano and Lake Maggiore. The river Rhine, whose source is in the Swiss Alps, is navigable northwards and downstream from the port of Basel. One company of patrol boats, part of the Swiss Army, is available for operations on lakes Constance, Geneva and Maggiore.

Diplomatic Representation

Defence Attaché in London:
Colonel D P Bader

ARMY

Notes: (1) There are also large numbers of flat bottomed raiding craft powered by single 40 hp outboard engines.
(2) There are a number of 6 m rescue craft equipped with a hydraulic ramp.

11 AQUARIUS CLASS (PATROUILLENBOOT 80) (PBR)

ANTARES	**SATURN**	**PERSEUS**	**MARS**
AQUARIUS	**URANUS**	**SIRIUS**	**POLLUX**
ORION	**CASTOR**	**VENUS**	

Displacement, tons: 7 full load
Dimensions, feet (metres): 35.1 × 10.8 × 3.6 *(10.7 × 3.3 × 1.1)*
Main machinery: 2 Volvo KAD 3 diesels; 460 hp(m) *(338 kW)*; 2 shafts
Speed, knots: 35
Complement: 7
Guns: 2—12.7 mm MGs.
Radars: Surface search: JFS Electronic 364; I-band.

Comment: Builders Müller AG, Spiez. GRP hulls, wooden superstructure. *Aquarius* commissioned in 1978, *Pollux* in 1984, the remainder in 1981. Re-engined with diesels which have replaced the former petrol engines.

AQUARIUS ***10/1997, Swiss Army*** / 0019223

Syria

Country Overview

The Syrian Arab Republic was proclaimed in 1961 following brief federation with Egypt as the United Arab Republic from 1958. Situated in the Middle East, the country has an area of 71,498 square miles and is bordered to the north by Turkey, to the east by Iraq, to the south by Jordan and Israel and to the west by Lebanon. It has a 104 n mile coastline with the Mediterranean Sea. The capital and largest city is Damascus while the principal ports are Latakia and Tartus. It is the only country to claim 35 n mile Territorial seas. An EEZ is not claimed.

Headquarters Appointments

Commander-in-Chief Navy:
Major General Wael Nasser

Organisation

Naval Forces come under the command of the Chief of General Staff, Commander of Land Forces.

Personnel

(a) 2009: 3,200 officers and men (2,500 reserves)
(b) 18 months' national service

Bases

Latakia, Tartous, Al-Mina-al-Bayda, Baniyas

Coast Defence

Coastal defence has been under naval control since 1984. A missile brigade is equipped with SS-C-1 Sepal and SS-C-3 Styx with sites at Tartous (2), Baniyas and Latakia. Two artillery battalions have a total of 36-130 mm guns and 12-100 mm guns. Coastal observation sites are manned by an Observation Battalion. There are two infantry brigades each of which is assigned to a coastal zone.

FRIGATES

2 PETYA III (PROJECT 159A) CLASS (FFL)

1-508 (ex-12) **AL HIRASA** 2-508 (ex-14)

Displacement, tons: 950 standard; 1,180 full load
Dimensions, feet (metres): 268.3 × 29.9 × 9.5 *(81.8 × 9.1 × 2.9)*
Main machinery: CODAG; 2 gas turbines; 30,000 hp(m) *(22 MW)*; 1 Type 61V-3 diesel; 5,400 hp(m) *(3.97 MW)* sustained (centre shaft); 3 shafts
Speed, knots: 32
Range, n miles: 4,870 at 10 kt; 450 at 29 kt
Complement: 98 (8 officers)

Guns: 4—3 in *(76 mm)*/59 AK 726 (2 twin) ❶; 90 rds/min to 16 km *(8.5 n miles)*; weight of shell 5.9 kg.
Torpedoes: 3—21 in *(533 mm)* (triple) tubes ❷. SAET-60; active/passive homing to 15 km *(8.1 n miles)* at 40 kt; warhead 100 kg.
A/S mortars: 4 RBU 2500 16-tubed trainable ❸; range 2,500 m; warhead 21 kg.

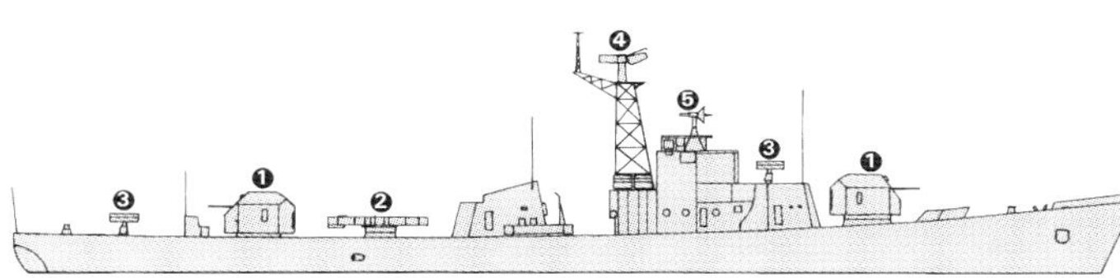

PETYA 1-508 ***(Scale 1 : 900), Ian Sturton*** / 0506171

Depth charges: 2 racks.
Mines: Can carry 22.
Radars: Surface search: Slim Net ❹; E/F-band.
Navigation: Don 2; I-band.
Fire control: Hawk Screech ❺; I-band.
IFF: High Pole B. 2 Square Head.
Sonars: Herkules; hull-mounted; active search and attack; high frequency.

Programmes: Transferred by the USSR in July 1975 and March 1975.
Operational: Based at Tartous. *2-508* in dock in mid-1998 to 2000 and reported to be sea-going. *1-508* reported non-operational in 2008.

AL HIRASA ***6/2001*** / 0121400

LAND-BASED MARITIME AIRCRAFT

Numbers/Type: 11/2 Mil Mi-14P Haze A/Mi-14P Haze C.
Operational speed: 124 kt *(230 km/h).*
Service ceiling: 15,000 ft *(4,570 m).*
Range: 432 n miles *(800 km).*
Role/Weapon systems: Medium-range ASW helicopter. Sensors: Short Horn search radar, dipping sonar, MAD, sonobuoys. Weapons: ASW; internally stored torpedoes, depth mines and bombs.

Numbers/Type: 2 Kamov Ka-28 Helix.
Operational speed: 135 kt *(250 km/h).*
Service ceiling: 19,685 ft *(6,000 m).*
Range: 432 n miles *(800 km).*
Role/Weapon systems: ASW helicopter. Delivered in February 1990. Sensors: Splash Drop search radar, dipping sonar, sonobuoys, MAD, ECM. Weapons: ASW; 3 torpedoes, depth bombs, mines.

PATROL FORCES

Notes: (1) Five Szkwal 12 m patrol launches are reported to be in service. Previously in service with the Polish Coast Guard, they were transferred in 1995.
(2) There is an unarmed 18 m diving tender *Palmyra* built by Ocea de Saint-Nazaire in 2005.

16 OSA (PROJECT 205) CLASS (FAST ATTACK CRAFT—MISSILE) (PTFG)

21–26 (Osa I) **31–40** (Osa II)

Displacement, tons: 245 full load
Dimensions, feet (metres): 126.6 × 24.9 × 8.8 *(38.6 × 7.6 × 2.7)*
Main machinery: 3 Type M 504 (Osa II)/M 503 (Osa I) diesels; 8,025/10,800 hp(m) *(6.0/8.1 MW)* sustained; 3 shafts
Speed, knots: 35 (Osa I), 37 (Osa II). **Range, n miles:** 500 at 35 kt
Complement: 25 (3 officers)
Missiles: SSM: 4 SS-N-2C; active radar or IR homing to 83 km *(43 n miles)* at 0.9 Mach; warhead 513 kg; sea-skimmer at end of run.
Guns: 4—30 mm/65 (2 twin); 500 rds/min to 5 km *(2.7 n miles)*; weight of shell 0.54 kg.
Countermeasures: Decoys: PK 16 chaff launcher.
Radars: Surface search: Square Tie; I-band.
Fire control: Drum Tilt; H/I-band.
IFF: 2 Square Head. High Pole A or B.

Programmes: Delivered: October 1979 (two), November 1979 (two), August 1982 (one), September 1982 (one) and May 1984 (two). Further craft acquired.
Structure: Two are modified (Nos 39 and 40).
Operational: Osa I are based at Tartous and Osa II based at Latakia. All are still fully operational and active. The Osa Is are fitted with SSN 2A/B.

OSA II 38 ***6/1998*** / 0050214

6 TIR II (IPS 18) CLASS (INSHORE PATROL CRAFT) (PTFG)

Displacement, tons: 28.1 standard
Dimensions, feet (metres): 69.4 × 18.9 × 2.8 *(21.1 × 5.8 × 0.9)*
Speed, knots: 52
Complement: 6
Missiles: SSM: 2 Noor (C-802); active radar homing to 120 km *(66 n miles)* at 0.9 Mach; warhead 165 kg.

Comment: The first three craft with missile racks, but without missiles, were delivered in mid-2006. Probably built in Iran and based on those supplied in December 2002 by North Korea.

TIR II (artist's impression) ***6/2007*** / 1167967

8 ZHUK (GRIF) (PROJECT 1400M) CLASS (COASTAL PATROL CRAFT) (PB)

1-8 2-8 3-8 4-8 5-8 6-8 7-8 8-8

Displacement, tons: 39 full load
Dimensions, feet (metres): 78.7 × 16.4 × 3.9 *(24 × 5 × 1.2)*
Main machinery: 2 Type M 401B diesels; 2,200 hp(m) *(1.6 MW)* sustained; 2 shafts
Speed, knots: 30. **Range, n miles:** 1,100 at 15 kt
Complement: 11 (3 officers)
Guns: 4—14.5 mm (2 twin) MGs.
Radars: Surface search: Spin Trough; I-band.

Comment: Three transferred from USSR in August 1981, three on 25 December 1984 and two more in the late 1980s. Based at Tartous and Latakia. About half the craft are operational.

ZHUK 5-8 ***6/1998*** / 0050215

AMPHIBIOUS FORCES

3 POLNOCHNY B CLASS (PROJECT 771) (LSM)

1-114 2-114 3-114

Displacement, tons: 760 standard; 834 full load
Dimensions, feet (metres): 246.1 × 31.5 × 7.5 *(75 × 9.6 × 2.3)*
Main machinery: 2 Kolomna Type 40-D diesels; 4,400 hp(m) *(3.2 MW)* sustained; 2 shafts
Speed, knots: 19
Range, n miles: 1,500 at 15 kt
Complement: 40
Military lift: 180 troops; 350 tons cargo
Guns: 4—30 mm/65 (2 twin); 500 rds/min to 5 km *(2.7 n miles)*; weight of shell 0.54 kg.
2—140 mm rocket launchers; 18 barrels per launcher; range 9 km *(5 n miles).*
Radars: Surface search: Spin Trough; I-band.
Fire control: Drum Tilt; H/I-band.

Comment: Built at Northern Shipyard, Gdansk. First transferred from USSR January 1984, two in February 1985 from Black Sea. All based at Tartous and still active.

POLNOCHNY B (Russian colours) ***1988*** / 0506104

MINE WARFARE FORCES

1 SONYA (YAKHONT) (PROJECT 12650) CLASS (COASTAL MINEHUNTER) (MHC)

532

Displacement, tons: 450 full load
Dimensions, feet (metres): 157.4 × 28.9 × 6.6 *(48 × 8.8 × 2)*
Main machinery: 2 Kolomna Type 9-D-8 diesels; 2,000 hp(m) *(1.47 MW)* sustained; 2 shafts
Speed, knots: 15
Range, n miles: 3,000 at 10 kt
Complement: 43 (5 officers)
Missiles: SAM: 2 quad SA-N-5 launchers.
Guns: 2—30 mm/65 AK 630 or 2—30 mm/65 (twin) and 2—25 mm/80 (twin).
Mines: 8.
Radars: Surface search: Don 2 or Kivach or Nayada; I-band.
IFF: 2 Square Head. High Pole B.
Sonars: MG 69/79; hull-mounted; active minehunting; high frequency.

Comment: Wooden hull with GRP sheath. Transferred to Syria in 1986. Reported decommissioned in 2004 but apparently operational again in 2006.

SONYA CLASS (Russian colours) ***6/2003, Guy Toremans*** / 0570933

1 NATYA (PROJECT 266M) CLASS (MSC/AGORM)

642

Displacement, tons: 804 full load
Dimensions, feet (metres): 200.1 × 33.5 × 10.8 *(61 × 10.2 × 3)*
Main machinery: 2 Type 504 diesels; 5,000 hp(m) *(3.67 MW)* sustained; 2 shafts
Speed, knots: 16
Range, n miles: 3,000 at 12 kt
Complement: 65
Missiles: SAM: 2 SA-N-5 Grail quad launchers; manual aiming; IR homing to 6 km *(3.2 n miles)* at 1.5 Mach; altitude to 2,500 m *(8,000 ft)*; warhead 1.5 kg; 16 missiles.
Guns: 4—30 mm/65 (2 twin) can be fitted.
Radars: Surface search: Don 2; I-band.
Fire control: Drum Tilt; H/I-band.

Comment: Arrived in Tartous from USSR in January 1985. Has had sweeping gear and guns removed and converted to serve as an AGOR. Painted white. Based at Latakia in reasonable condition. Reported active.

NATYA 642 ***6/1996*** / 0080764

5 YEVGENYA (PROJECT 1258) CLASS (MINESWEEPERS—INSHORE) (MSI/PC)

4-507 5-507 6-507 7-507 8-507

Displacement, tons: 77 standard; 90 full load
Dimensions, feet (metres): 80.7 × 18 × 4.9 *(24.6 × 5.5 × 1.5)*
Main machinery: 2 Type 3-D-12 diesels; 600 hp(m) *(444 kW)*; 2 shafts
Speed, knots: 11
Range, n miles: 300 at 10 kt
Complement: 10
Guns: 2—14.5 mm (twin) MGs (first pair). 2—25 mm/80 (twin) (second pair).
Radars: Surface search: Spin Trough; I-band.
IFF: High Pole.
Sonars: MG-7; stern-mounted VDS; active; high frequency.

Comment: First transferred from USSR 1978, two in 1985 and two in 1986. Second pair by Ro-flow from Baltic in February 1985 being new construction with tripod mast. Based at Tartous, at least two are operational. Both *4-507* and *5-507*, thought to have been deleted, were reported operational in 2006.

YEVGENYA (Ukraine colours) ***6/2003, Ships of the World*** / 0572652

TRAINING SHIPS

1 TRAINING SHIP (AX/AKR)

AL ASSAD

Displacement, tons: 3,500 full load
Dimensions, feet (metres): 344.5 × 56.4 × 13.1 *(105 × 17.2 × 4)*
Main machinery: 2 Zgoda-Sulzer 6ZL40/48 diesels; 8,700 hp(m) *(6.4 MW)*; 2 shafts; bow thruster
Speed, knots: 16
Range, n miles: 4,500 at 15 kt
Complement: 56 plus 140 cadets
Radars: Navigation: Decca Seamaster; E/F- and I-band.

Comment: Built in Polnochny Shipyard, Gdansk and launched 18 February 1987. Delivered in late 1988. Ro-ro design used as a naval training ship. Unarmed but has minelaying potential. Based at Latakia and occasionally deploys on cruises.

AL ASSAD ***7/2003, B Prézelin*** / 0570997

AL ASSAD
6/2007, Camil Busquets i Vilanova
1167859

Taiwan

REPUBLIC OF CHINA

Country Overview

The Republic of China was established in 1949 when the Nationalist government of China withdrew to Taiwan (Formosa) and established its headquarters. Though in practice an autonomous state, Taiwan is still formally a province of China and, as such, is claimed by the People's Republic of China. The country comprises the island of Taiwan (area 13,900 square miles), the Pescadores, or P'eng-hu Islands, the Quemoy Islands off the mainland city of Amoy (Xiamen), and the Matsu group off Fuzhou (Foochow). It has a 783 n mile coastline with East China Sea, Pacific Ocean and South China Sea. The capital and largest city of Taiwan is Taipei while Chi-lung (Keelung), Hualien, Kao-hsiung and T'ai-chung are the principal ports. Territorial seas (12 n miles) are claimed. A 200 n mile EEZ and Fishery Zone have also been claimed.

Headquarters Appointments

Commander-in-Chief:
Admiral Wang Li-Sheng
Commandant of Marine Corps:
Lieutenant General Yu Shang-Wen

Senior Flag Officers

Fleet Commander:
Vice Admiral Hu Chai-Kwei

Senior Flag Officers—*continued*

Director of Logistics:
Vice Admiral Gan Ke-Chiang
Commander East Command:
Vice Admiral Chang Hai-Ping

Personnel

(a) 2009: 46,500 in Navy, 15,000 in Marine Corps
(b) 1 year 4 months conscript service

Bases

Tsoying: HQ First Naval District (Southern Taiwan, Pratas and Spratly). Main Base, HQ of Fleet Command, Naval Aviation Group and Marine Corps. Base of southern patrol and transport squadrons. Officers and ratings training, Naval Academy, Naval shipyard.
Kaohsiung; Naval shipyard.
Makung (Pescadores): HQ Second Naval District (Pescadores, Quemoy and Wu Ch'iu). Base for attack squadrons. Naval shipyard and training facilities.
Keelung: HQ Third Naval District (Northern Taiwan and Matsu group). Base of northern patrol and transport squadrons. Naval shipyard.
Hualien: Naval Aviation Command.
Suao: East Coast Command, submarine depot and shipyard.
Minor bases at Hualien, Tamshui, Hsinchu, Wuchi and Anping.
Building: Taitung.

Organisation

1. Fleet Command:
124th Attack squadron, based at Tsoying
142nd Support squadron, based at Kaohsiung
146th Attack squadron, based at Pescadores
151st Amphibious squadron, based at Tsoying
168th Patrol squadron, based at Suao
192nd Mine Warfare squadron, based at Tsoying
256th Submarine Unit, based at Tsoying.
2. Naval Aviation Command: There are two Groups. The fixed-wing Group based at Pingtung-North consists of two squadrons (133 and 134). The helicopter Group consists of three squadrons 501 squadron is based at Tsoying, 701 squadron at Hualien and 702 squadron at Tsoying.

Coast Defence

The land-based SSM command has six squadrons equipped with Hsiung-Feng II SSM at Tonying Island of the Matsu Group, Siyu Island of the Pescadores, Shiao Liuchiu off Kaohsiung, north of Keelung harbour, Tsoying naval base and Hualien. The ROCMC deploy eight SAM Platoons, equipped with Chaparral SAM quad-launchers, to the offshore island of Wuchiu, and Pratas islets in the South China Sea. There are also a number of 127 mm guns.

Marine Corps

Increased to three brigades in 2002 supported by one amphibious regiment and one logistics regiment. Equipped with M-116, M-733, LARC-5, LVTP5 (to be replaced by AAV-7A-IRAM/RS) personnel carriers and LVTH6 armour tractors. Based at Tsoying and in southern Taiwan. Spratly detachment provided by the Coast Guard from 1 January 2000 and Marine Corps detachment withdrawn from Pratas Islands at the same time.

Coast Guard

Formerly the Maritime Security Police but name changed on 1 January 2000. Comes under the Minister of the Interior but its numerous patrol boats are integrated with the Navy for operational purposes.

Strength of the Fleet

Type	*Active (Reserve)*	*Building/ Transfer (Planned)*
Submarines	4	(8)
Destroyers	4	–
Frigates	22	–
Corvettes	–	(10)
Fast Attack Craft (Missile)	50	2 (27)
Large Patrol Craft	20	–
Ocean Minesweepers	4	–
Coastal Minesweepers/Hunters	8	(2)
LSD	2	(1)
Landing Ships (LST and LSM)	14	–
LCUs	18	–
Survey Ships	1	–
Combat Support Ships	1	–
Transports	3	–
Salvage Ships	1	–
Coast Guard	18	–

PENNANT LIST

Submarines

791	Hai Shih
792	Hai Bao
793	Hai Lung
794	Hai Hu

Destroyers

1801	Kee Lung
1802	Suao
1803	Tsoying
1805	Makung

Frigates

932	Chin Yang
933	Fong Yang
934	Feng Yang
935	Lan Yang
936	Hae Yang
937	Hwai Yang
938	Ning Yang
939	Yi Yang
1101	Cheng Kung
1103	Cheng Ho
1105	Chi Kuang
1106	Yueh Fei
1107	Tzu-I
1108	Pan Chao
1109	Chang Chien
1110	Tien Tan (bldg)
1202	Kang Ding
1203	Si Ning
1205	Kun Ming
1206	Di Hua
1207	Wu Chang
1208	Chen Te

Patrol Forces

PCL 1	Ning Hai
PCL 2	An Hai
601	Lung Chiang
602	Sui Chang
603	Jin Chiang
605	Tan Chiang
606	Hsin Chiang
607	Feng Chiang
608	Tseng Chiang
609	Kao Chiang
610	Jing Chiang
611	Hsian Chiang
612	Tsi Chiang
614	Po Chiang
615	Chan Chiang
617	Chu Chiang

Amphibious Forces

191	Chung Cheng
193	Shiu Hai
201	Chung Hai
205	Chung Chien
208	Chung Shun
216	Chung Kuang
217	Chung Chao
218	Chung Chi
221	Chung Chuan
226	Chung Chih
227	Chung Ming
230	Chung Pang
231	Chung Yeh
232	Chung Ho
233	Chung Ping
401	Ho Chi
402	Ho Huei
403	Ho Yao
406	Ho Chao
481	Ho Shun
484	Ho Chung
488	Ho Shan
489	Ho Chuan
490	Ho Seng
491	Ho Meng
492	Ho Mou
493	Ho Shou
494	Ho Chun
495	Ho Yung
LCC1	Kao Hsiung
SB 1	Ho Chie
SB 2	Ho Ten

Mine Warfare Forces

158	Yung Chuan
162	Yung Fu
167	Yung Ren
168	Yung Sui
1301	Yung Feng
1302	Yung Chia
1303	Yung Ting
1305	Yung Shun
1306	Yung Yang
1307	Yung Tzu
1308	Yung Ku
1309	Yung Teh

Auxiliaries and Survey Ships

524	Yuen Feng
525	Wu Kang
526	Hsin Kang
530	Wu Yi
552	Ta Hu
1601	Ta Kuan

Tugs

ATF 551	Ta Wan
ATF 553	Ta Han
ATF 554	Ta Kang
ATF 555	Ta Fung
ATF 563	Ta Tai

SUBMARINES

Notes: (1) Project Kwang Hua 8: Following the announcement in 2001 by the US government that it will support the acquisition of eight diesel submarines, debate has centred on how these will be procured. Northrop Grumman has reportedly offered a modernised version of the Barbel class, which dates from the 1950s. The licence of a design from a third country has proved to be problematic in view of the re-affirmation of earlier decisions by the governments of the Netherlands (1992) and Germany (1993) not to grant export licences for Taiwan. Efforts to sell the Agosta class were similarly discouraged by the French government while Australia has rejected expressions of interest in the Collins class. An indigenous build programme remains a possibility although this would present significant technical and financial challenges. By early 2009, a US-built submarine still seemed to be the only potential, albeit increasingly unlikely, solution.
(2) The procurement of up to 12 swimmer delivery vehicles from the United Arab Emirates is under consideration.

2 HAI LUNG CLASS (SSK)

Name	*No*	*Builders*	*Laid down*	*Launched*	*Commissioned*
HAI LUNG	793	Wilton Fijenoord, Netherlands	Dec 1982	6 Oct 1986	9 Oct 1987
HAI HU	794	Wilton Fijenoord, Netherlands	Dec 1982	20 Dec 1986	9 Apr 1988

Displacement, tons: 2,376 surfaced; 2,660 dived
Dimensions, feet (metres): 219.6 × 27.6 × 22 *(66.9 × 8.4 × 6.7)*
Main machinery: Diesel-electric; 3 Bronswerk D-RUB 215-12 diesels; 4,050 hp(m) *(3 MW)*; 3 alternators; 2.7 MW; 1 Holec motor; 5,100 hp(m) *(3.74 MW)*; 1 shaft
Speed, knots: 12 surfaced; 20 dived
Range, n miles: 10,000 at 9 kt surfaced
Complement: 67 (8 officers)

Missiles: SSM: McDonnell Douglas UGM-84L Block II; active radar homing to 124 km *(67 n miles)* at 0.9 Mach; warhead 227 kg (to be fitted).
Torpedoes: 6—21 in *(533 mm)* bow tubes. 20 AEG SUT; dual purpose; wire-guided; active/passive homing to 12 km *(6.6 n miles)* at 35 kt; warhead 250 kg.
Countermeasures: ESM: Argo AR 700SF and Elbit Timnex 4CH(V)2; intercept.
Weapons control: Sinbads M TFCS.
Radars: Surface search: Signaal ZW06; I-band.
Sonars: Signaal SIASS-Z; hull-mounted; passive/active intercept search and attack; low/medium frequency. Fitted for but not with towed passive array.

Programmes: Order signed with Wilton Fijenoord in September 1981 for these submarines with variations from the standard Netherlands Zwaardvis design. Construction was delayed by the financial difficulties of the builders but was resumed in 1983. Sea trials of *Hai Lung* in March 1987 and *Hai Hu* in January 1988 and both submarines were shipped out on board a heavy dock vessel. The names mean *Sea Dragon* and *Sea Tiger*.
Modernisation: Plans to fit both submarines with McDonnell Douglas UGM-84L Block II Sub Harpoon were first announced in September 2005 and later confirmed on 3 October 2008. Harpoon is likely to be a stand-alone system rather than being integrated with the fire-control system.
Structure: The four horns on the forward casing are Signaal sonar intercept transducers. Torpedoes manufactured under licence in Indonesia.
Operational: Hsiung Feng II submerged launch SSMs are planned to be part of the weapons load and a torpedo tube launched version is being developed, although no recent progress has been reported. Belong to 256th Submarine Unit based at Tsoying.

HAI HU and HAI LUNG — *11/2004, Ships of the World* / 1044575

2 GUPPY II CLASS (SS)

Name	*No*	*Builders*	*Laid down*	*Launched*	*Commissioned*
HAI SHIH (ex-*Cutlass* SS 478)	791 (ex-SS 91)	Portsmouth Navy Yard	22 July 1944	5 Nov 1944	17 Mar 1945
HAI BAO (ex-*Tusk* SS 426)	792 (ex-SS 92)	Federal SB & DD Co, Kearney, New Jersey	23 Aug 1943	8 July 1945	11 Apr 1946

Displacement, tons: 1,870 standard; 2,420 dived
Dimensions, feet (metres): 307.5 × 27.2 × 18 *(93.7 × 8.3 × 5.5)*
Main machinery: Diesel-electric; 3 Fairbanks-Morse diesels; 4,500 hp *(3.3 MW)*; 2 Elliott motors; 5,400 hp *(4 MW)*; 2 shafts
Speed, knots: 18 surfaced; 15 dived
Range, n miles: 8,000 at 12 kt surfaced
Complement: 75 (7 officers)

Torpedoes: 10—21 in *(533 mm)* (6 fwd, 4 aft) tubes. AEG SUT; active/passive homing to 12 km *(6.5 n miles)* at 35 kt; 28 km *(15 n miles)* at 23 kt; warhead 250 kg.
Countermeasures: ESM: WLR-1/3; radar warning.
Radars: Surface search: US SS 2; I-band.
Sonars: EDO BQR 2B; hull-mounted; passive search and attack; medium frequency.
Raytheon/EDO BQS 4C; adds active capability to BQR 2B.
Thomson Sintra DUUG 1B; passive ranging.

Programmes: Originally fleet-type submarines of the US Navy's Tench class; extensively modernised under the Guppy II programme. *Hai Shih* transferred in April 1973 and *Hai Bao* in October the same year.
Structure: After 56 years in service diving depth is very limited.
Operational: Kept in service because of difficulty in buying replacements, but operational status doubtful. Likely to have an alongside training role only. Belong to the 256th Submarine Unit based at Tsoying.

HAI BAO *11/2004, Ships of the World* / 1044574

DESTROYERS

Notes: Acquisition of the Aegis Combat System remains a firm aspiration but, following the decision to procure the Kidd class DDGs as an interim measure, this is unlikely before 2012.

4 KEELUNG (KIDD) CLASS (DDGHM)

Name	*No*	*Builders*	*Laid down*	*Launched*	*Commissioned*
KEELUNG (ex-*Chi Teh*, ex-*Scott*)	1801 (ex-DD 995)	Ingalls Shipbuilding	12 Feb 1979	1 Mar 1980	24 Oct 1981
SUAO (ex-*Wu Teh*, ex-*Callaghan*)	1802 (ex-DD 994)	Ingalls Shipbuilding	23 Oct 1978	1 Dec 1979	29 Aug 1981
TSOYING (ex-*Ming Teh*, ex-*Kidd*)	1803 (ex-DD 993)	Ingalls Shipbuilding	26 June 1978	11 Aug 1979	27 June 1981
MAKUNG (ex-*Tong-Teh*, ex-*Chandler*)	1805 (ex-DD 996)	Ingalls Shipbuilding	7 May 1979	24 May 1980	13 Mar 1982

Displacement, tons: 6,950 light; 9,574 full load
Dimensions, feet (metres): 563.3 × 55 × 20 *(171.7 × 16.8 × 6.2)*
Main machinery: 4 GE LM 2500 gas turbines; 86,000 hp *(64.16 MW)* sustained; 2 shafts
Speed, knots: 33. **Range, n miles:** 6,000 at 20 kt
Complement: 363 (31 officers)

Missiles: SSM: 4 McDonnell Douglas RGM 84L Block 2 Harpoon (1 quad) launchers ❶; active radar homing to 124 km *(67 n miles)* at 0.9 Mach; warhead 227 kg.
SAM: 37 Raytheon Standard SM-2 MR Block IIIA; command/inertial guidance; semi-active radar homing to 167 km *(90 n miles)* at 2.5 Mach. 2 twin Mk 26 launchers ❷.
Guns: 2 FMC 5 in *(127 mm)*/54 Mk 45 Mod 0 ❸; 20 rds/min to 23 km *(12.6 n miles)*; weight of shell 32 kg.
2 General Electric/General Dynamics 20 mm Vulcan Phalanx 6-barrelled Mk 15 ❹; 3,000 rds/min (4,500 in Block 1).
4—12.7 mm MGs.
Torpedoes: 6—324 mm Mk 32 (2 triple) tubes ❺. Honeywell Mk 46 Mod 5; anti-submarine; active/passive homing to 11 km *(5.9 n miles)* at 40 kt; warhead 44 kg. Torpedoes fired from inside the hull under the hangar.
Countermeasures: Decoys: 4 Loral Hycor SRBOC 6-barrelled fixed Mk 36; IR flares and chaff to 4 km *(2.2 n miles)*. SLQ-25 Nixie; torpedo decoy.
Combat data systems: ACDS Block 1 Level 1 with datalinks.
Weapons control: SWG-1A Harpoon LCS. 2 Mk 74 MFCS. Mk 86 Mod 5 GFCS. Mk 116 FCS for ASW. Mk 14 WDS. SYS 2(V)2 IADT. 4 SYR 3393 for SAM mid-course guidance.
Radars: Air search: ITT SPS-48E ❻; 3D; E/F-band.
Raytheon SPS-49(V)5 ❼; C/D-band.
Air/surface search: ISC Cardion SPS-55 ❽; I/J-band.
Navigation: Raytheon SPS-64; I/J-band.
Fire control: 2 Raytheon SPG-51D ❾, 1 Lockheed SPG-60 ❿, 1 Lockheed SPQ-9A ⓫.
Sonars: General Electric/Hughes SQS-53D; bow-mounted; search and attack; medium frequency.
Gould SQR-19 (TACTAS); passive towed array (may be fitted).

Helicopters: 1 Sikorsky S-70C(M) ⓬.

KEELUNG *(Scale 1 : 1,500), Ian Sturton* / 1167441

KEELUNG *6/2006, Defence International* / 1167511

Programmes: Originally ordered by the Iranian government in 1974, the contracts were taken over by the US Navy on 25 July 1979. All paid off from USN service in 1998–99. Offered to the Taiwan government, intention to buy confirmed on 2 October 2001.
Modernisation: All received major modernisation from 1988–90. Further package completed prior to transfer. ASROC has been removed.

Structure: Optimised for general warfare, mainmast and radar aerials are in different configuration than Spruance class.
Operational: *Keelung* and *Suao* arrived in Taiwan on 8 December 2005 and were recommissioned on 17 December 2005. *Tsoying* and *Makung* arrived in October 2006. All four ships are to be based initially at Suao while a deepwater jetty at Tsoying is completed.

FRIGATES

Notes: The Kuang Hua 7 programme has superseded the former Kuang Hua 5 programme for the procurement of a new class of frigates/corvettes to replace the Knox class frigates. It is understood that there is a requirement for up to eight new ships of above 2,000 tons with a main armament of Hsiung Feng-II missiles. It is not clear whether the ships are to be procured abroad (ex-US Spruance class are a possibility) or built locally.

8 CHENG KUNG CLASS (KWANG HUA 1 PROJECT) (FFGHM)

Name	*No*	*Builders*	*Laid down*	*Launched*	*Commissioned*
CHENG KUNG	1101	China SB Corporation, Kaohsiung	7 Jan 1990	5 Oct 1991	7 May 1993
CHENG HO	1103	China SB Corporation, Kaohsiung	21 Dec 1990	15 Oct 1992	28 Mar 1994
CHI KUANG	1105	China SB Corporation, Kaohsiung	4 Oct 1991	27 Sep 1993	4 Mar 1995
YUEH FEI	1106	China SB Corporation, Kaohsiung	5 Sep 1992	26 Aug 1994	7 Feb 1996
TZU-I	1107	China SB Corporation, Kaohsiung	7 Aug 1994	13 July 1995	9 Jan 1997
PAN CHAO	1108	China SB Corporation, Kaohsiung	25 July 1995	4 July 1996	16 Dec 1997
CHANG CHIEN	1109	China SB Corporation, Kaohsiung	4 Dec 1995	14 May 1997	1 Dec 1998
TIEN TAN	1110	China SB Corporation, Kaohsiung	21 Feb 2001	15 Oct 2002	11 Mar 2004

Displacement, tons: 2,750 light; 4,105 full load
Dimensions, feet (metres): 453 × 45 × 14.8; 24.5 (sonar) *(138.1 × 13.7 × 4.5; 7.5)*
Main machinery: 2 GE LM 2500 gas turbines; 41,000 hp *(30.59 MW)* sustained; 1 shaft; cp prop
2 auxiliary retractable props; 650 hp *(484 kW)*
Speed, knots: 29. **Range, n miles:** 4,500 at 20 kt
Complement: 234 (15 officers) including 19 aircrew

Missiles: SSM: 8 Hsiung Feng II/III ❶ (2 quad); inertial guidance; active radar/IR homing to 80 (200 Hsiung Feng III) km *(43.2 (108) n miles)* at 0.85 Mach (2 Mach); warhead 190 kg.
SAM: 40 Raytheon Standard SM1-MR Block VIA; Mk 13 launcher ❷; command guidance; semi-active radar homing to 38 km *(20.5 n miles)* at 2 Mach.
Guns: 1 OTO Melara 76 mm/62 Mk 75 ❸; 85 rds/min to 16 km *(8.7 n miles)*; weight of shell 6 kg.
2 Bofors 40 mm/70 ❹. 3—20 mm Type 75 (on hangar roof when fitted).
1 GE/GD 20 mm/76 Vulcan Phalanx 6-barrelled Mk 15 ❺; 3,000 rds/min combined to 1.5 km.
Torpedoes: 6—324 mm Mk 32 (2 triple) tubes ❻. Honeywell/ Alliant Mk 46 Mod 5; anti-submarine; active/passive homing to 11 km *(5.9 n miles)* at 40 kt; warhead 44 kg.
Countermeasures: Decoys: 4 Kung Fen 6 chaff launchers or locally produced version of RBOC (114 mm). SLQ-25A Nixie; torpedo decoy.
ESM/ECM: Chang Feng IV (locally produced version of SLQ-32(V)2 with Sidekick); combined radar warning and jammers.
Combat data systems: Norden SYS-2(V)2 action data automation with UYK 43 computer. Ta Chen link (from *Chi Kuang* onwards and being backfitted).

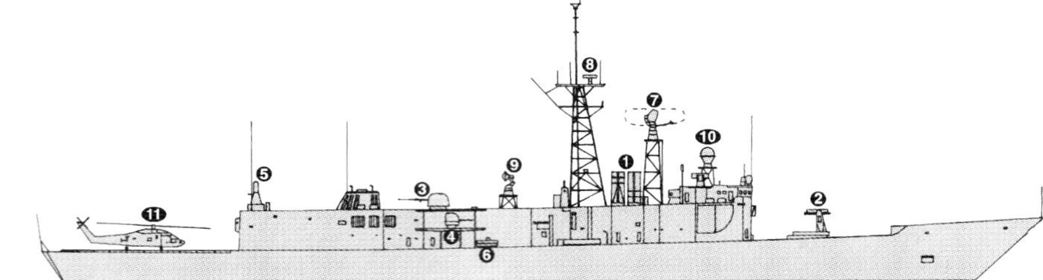

CHENG KUNG *(Scale 1 : 1,200), Ian Sturton* / 0019226

Weapons control: Loral Mk 92 Mod 6. Mk 13 Mod 4 weapon direction system. Mk 114 ASW. 2 Mk 24 optical directors. Mk 309 TFCS.
Radars: Air search: Raytheon SPS-49(V)5 or SPS-49A (1108-9) ❼; C/D-band.
Surface search: ISC Cardion SPS-55 ❽ or Raytheon Chang Bai; I/J-band.
Fire control: USN UD 417 STIR ❾; I/J-band.
Unisys Mk 92 Mod 6 ❿; I/J-band.
Sonars: Raytheon SQS-56/DE 1160P; hull-mounted; active search and attack; medium frequency.
SQR-18A(V)2; passive towed array or BAe/Thomson Sintra ATAS active towed array (from *Chi Kuang* onwards).

Helicopters: 2 Sikorsky S-70C(M) ⓫ (only 1 embarked).

Programmes: First two ordered 8 May 1989. Named after Chinese generals and warriors. An eighth of class was ordered in late July 1999. Originally this ship was planned to be the first of a Flight II design, which was scrapped.
Modernisation: Hsiung Feng III supersonic missiles have been installed in some ships including *Cheng Kung*. All eight ships are to be fitted. A mid-life upgrade for the class is likely to include the installation of RAM PDMS and the replacement of Standard SM-1 with SM-2. The Mk 96 direction system is also likely to be upgraded to Mod 12.
Structure: Similar to the USS *Ingraham*. RAST helicopter hauldown. The area between the masts had to be strengthened to take the Hsiung Feng II missiles. Prairie Masker hull acoustic suppression system fitted.
Operational: Form the 146th Squadron based at Makung (Pescadores).

CHENG HO *10/2001, Chris Sattler* / 0534104

TIEN TAN *4/2007, Chris Sattler* / 1170238

6 KANG DING (LA FAYETTE) CLASS (KWANG HUA 2 PROJECT) (FFGHM)

Name	*No*	*Builders*	*Laid down*	*Launched*	*Commissioned*
KANG DING	1202	Lorient Dockyard/Kaohsiung Shipyard	26 Aug 1993	12 Mar 1994	24 May 1996
SI NING	1203	Lorient Dockyard/Kaohsiung Shipyard	27 Apr 1994	5 Nov 1994	15 Sep 1996
KUN MING	1205	Lorient Dockyard/Kaohsiung Shipyard	7 Nov 1994	13 May 1995	26 Feb 1997
DI HUA	1206	Lorient Dockyard/Kaohsiung Shipyard	1 July 1995	27 Nov 1995	14 Aug 1997
WU CHANG	1207	Lorient Dockyard/Kaohsiung Shipyard	1 July 1995	27 Nov 1995	16 Dec 1997
CHEN TE	1208	Lorient Dockyard/Kaohsiung Shipyard	27 Dec 1995	2 Aug 1996	16 Jan 1998

Displacement, tons: 3,800 full load
Dimensions, feet (metres): 407.5 × 50.5 × 18 (screws) *(124.2 × 15.4 × 5.5)*
Main machinery: CODAD; 4 SEMT-Pielstick 12 PA6 V 280 STC diesels; 23,228 hp(m) *(17.08 MW)*; 2 shafts; LIPS cp props
Speed, knots: 25
Range, n miles: 7,000 at 15 kt
Complement: 134 (15 officers) plus 25 spare

Missiles: SSM: 8 Hsiung Feng II (2 quad) ❶; inertial guidance; active radar/IR homing to 80 km *(43.2 n miles)* at 0.85 Mach; warhead 190 kg.
SAM: 1 Sea Chaparral quad launcher ❷; IR homing to 3 km *(1.6 n miles)* supersonic; warhead 5 kg.
Guns: 1 OTO Melara 76 mm/62 Mk 75 ❸; 85 rds/min to 16 km *(8.7 n miles)*; weight of shell 6 kg.
1 Hughes 20 mm/76 Vulcan Phalanx Mk 15 Mod 2 ❹.
2 Bofors 40 mm/70 ❺. 2 CS 20 mm Type 75.
Torpedoes: 6—324 mm Mk 32 (2 triple) tubes ❻; Alliant Mk 46 Mod 5; active/passive homing to 11 km *(5.9 n miles)* at 40 kt; warhead 44 kg.
Countermeasures: Decoys: 2 CSEE Dagaie chaff launchers ❼.
ESM/ECM: Thomson-CSF DR 3000S; intercept and jammer. Chang Feng IV (1206); intercept and jammer.
Combat data systems: Thomson-CSF TACTICOS. Link W (Ta Chen).
Weapons control: CSEE Najir Mk 2 optronic director ❽.

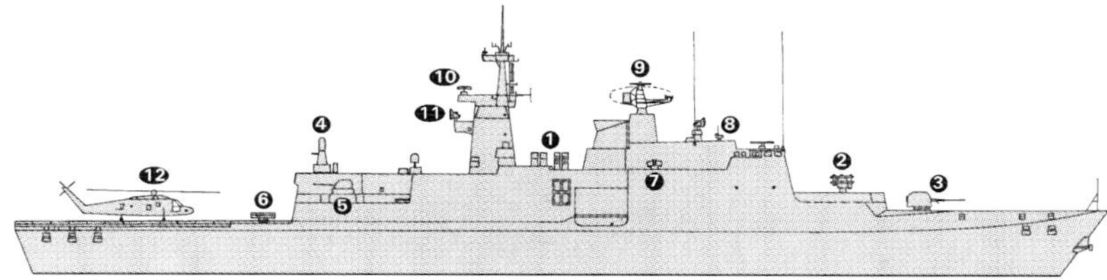

KANG DING ***(Scale 1 : 1,200), Ian Sturton*** / 0121405

Radars: Air/surface search: Thomson-CSF DRBV-26D Jupiter II (with LW08 aerial) ❾; D-band.
Surface search: Thomson-CSF Triton G ❿; G-band.
Fire control: 2 Thomson-CSF Castor IIC ⓫; I/J-band.
Navigation/helo control: 2 Racal Decca 20V90; I-band.
Sonars: BAe/Thomson Sintra ATAS (V)2; active towed array.
Thomson Sintra Spherion B; bow-mounted; active search; medium frequency.

Helicopters: 1 Sikorsky S-70C(M)1 ⓬ Thunderhawk.

Programmes: Sale of up to 16 of the class authorised by the French government in August 1991. Contract for six signed with Thomson-CSF in early 1992, manufactured in France with some weapon assembly by China SB Corporation at Kaohsiung in Taiwan. First one to Taiwan in March 1996 and the last in January 1998. Names are those of Chinese cities. Second batch of 10 to be built by China SB Corporation was planned but this now seems unlikely.
Modernisation: There are plans to move Phalanx to the bridge roof and fit two 10-round RAM launchers on the hangar.
Structure: There are considerable differences with the French 'La Fayette' design in both superstructure and weapon systems. A comprehensive ASW fit has been added as well as additional gun armament. There is also no stern hatch for launching RIBs. Some of the weapons were fitted after arrival in Taiwan. DCN Samahé helicopter landing gear installed.
Operational: Form 124 Squadron based at Tsoying.

DI HUA ***4/2006, Chris Sattler*** / 1170237

KANG DING ***4/2007, Chris Sattler*** / 1170236

8 KNOX CLASS (FFGH)

Name	No	Builders	Laid down	Launched	Commissioned	Recommissioned
CHIN YANG (ex-*Robert E Peary*)	932 (ex-FF 1073)	Lockheed Shipbuilding	20 Dec 1970	23 June 1971	23 Sep 1972	6 Oct 1993
FONG YANG (ex-*Brewton*)	933 (ex-FF 1086)	Avondale Shipyards	2 Oct 1970	24 July 1971	8 July 1972	6 Oct 1993
FENG YANG (ex-*Kirk*)	934 (ex-FF 1087)	Avondale Shipyards	4 Dec 1970	25 Sep 1971	9 Sep 1972	6 Oct 1993
LAN YANG (ex-*Joseph Hewes*)	935 (ex-FF 1078)	Avondale Shipyards	15 May 1969	7 Mar 1970	22 Apr 1971	4 Aug 1995
HAE YANG (ex-*Cook*)	936 (ex-FF 1083)	Avondale Shipyards	20 Mar 1970	23 Jan 1971	18 Dec 1971	4 Aug 1995
HWAI YANG (ex-*Barbey*)	937 (ex-FF 1088)	Avondale Shipyards	5 Feb 1971	4 Dec 1971	11 Nov 1972	4 Aug 1995
NING YANG (ex-*Aylwin*)	938 (ex-FF 1081)	Avondale Shipyards	13 Nov 1969	29 Aug 1970	18 Sep 1971	18 Oct 1999
YI YANG (ex-*Valdez*)	939 (ex-FF 1096)	Avondale Shipyards	30 June 1972	24 Mar 1973	27 July 1974	18 Oct 1999

Displacement, tons: 3,011 standard; 3,877 (932, 935), 4,260 (933, 934) full load
Dimensions, feet (metres): 439.6 × 46.8 × 15; 24.8 (sonar) *(134 × 14.3 × 4.6; 7.8)*
Main machinery: 2 Combustion Engineering/Babcock & Wilcox boilers; 1,200 psi *(84.4 kg/cm²)*; 950°F *(510°C)*; 1 turbine; 35,000 hp *(26 MW)*; 1 shaft
Speed, knots: 27. **Range, n miles:** 4,000 at 22 kt on 1 boiler
Complement: 288 (17 officers) including aircrew

Missiles: SSM: 8 McDonnell Douglas Harpoon ❶; active radar homing to 130 km *(70 n miles)* at 0.9 Mach; warhead 227 kg.
SAM: 10 General Dynamics SM1-MR (2 triple, 2 twin) ❷; command guidance; semi-active radar homing to 46 km (25 n miles) at 2 Mach (fitted in all but 932 and 937).
A/S: Honeywell ASROC Mk 16 octuple launcher with reload system (has 2 cells modified to fire Harpoon) ❸; inertial guidance from 1.6-10 km *(1-5.4 n miles)*; payload Mk 46 Mod 5 Neartip.
Guns: 1 FMC 5 in *(127 mm)*/54 Mk 42 Mod 9 ❸; 20-40 rds/min to 24 km *(13 n miles)* anti-surface; 14 km *(7.7 n miles)* anti-aircraft; weight of shell 32 kg to be replaced by 1 OTO Melara 3 in *(76 mm)*/62 Mk 75; 85 rds/min to 16 km *(8.7 n miles)*; weight of shell 6 kg.
1 General Electric/General Dynamics 20 mm/76 6-barrelled Mk 15 Vulcan Phalanx ❹; 3,000 rds/min combined to 1.5 km.
4 Type 75 20 mm.
Countermeasures: Decoys: 2 Loral Hycor SRBOC 6-barrelled fixed Mk 36 ❺; IR flares and chaff to 4 km *(2.2 n miles)*.
T Mk 6 Fanfare/SLQ-25 Nixie; torpedo decoy. Prairie Masker hull and blade rate noise suppression.
ESM/ECM: SLQ-32(V)2 ❻; radar warning. Sidekick modification adds jammer and deception system.
Combat data systems: Link 14 receive only. Link W may be fitted. FFISTS (Frigate Integrated Shipboard Tactical System). RADDS (Radar Displays and Distribution System).
Weapons control: SWG-1A Harpoon LCS. Mk 68 GFCS. Mk 114 ASW FCS. Mk 1 target designation system. SRQ-4 for LAMPS I.
Radars: Air search: Lockheed SPS-40B (fitted in 932, 937) ❼; B-band or Signaal DA 08; E/F-band.
Surface search: Raytheon SPS-10 or Norden SPS-67 ❽; G-band.
Navigation: Marconi LN66; I-band.
Fire control: Western Electric SPG-53A/D/F (fitted in 932, 937) ❾; or Signaal STIR; I/J-band.
Tacan: SRN 15. IFF: UPX-12.
Sonars: EDO/General Electric SQS-26CX; bow-mounted; active search and attack; medium frequency.
EDO SQR-18A(V)1; passive towed array.

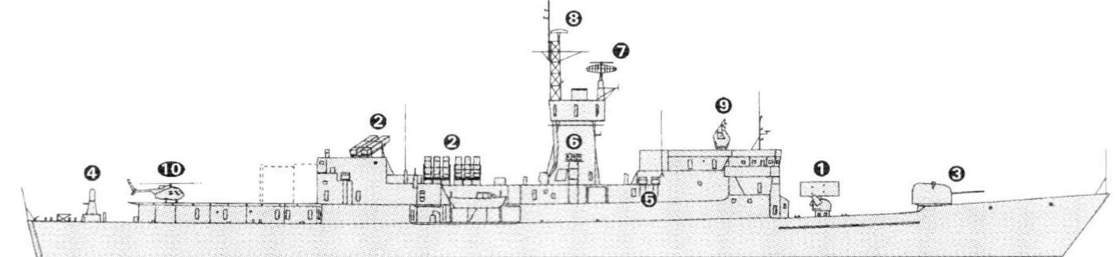

FONG YANG *(Scale 1 : 1,200), Ian Sturton* / 1293480

FONG YANG *12/2005, Ships of the World* / 1151164

Helicopters: 1 MD 500 ❿.

Programmes: *Fong Yang* leased from the US on 23 July 1992, *Chin Yang* 7 August 1992 and *Feng Yang* 6 August 1993. *Hae Yang* leased 31 May 1994; *Hwai Yang* 21 June 1994 and *Lan Yang* 30 June 1994. The second batch of three were overhauled and upgraded by Long Beach Shipyard, California. *Ning Yang* and *Yi Yang* transferred by sale on 29 April 1998, and refitted at Denton Shipyard, South Carolina. The transfer of a third (ex-*Pharris* 1094) was declined as were further offers of ex-*Whipple* (1062) and ex-*Downes* (1070) for use as spares.
Modernisation: A programme to equip all eight ships with a limited air-defence capability has been initiated. SPS-40 radar is being replaced by DA-08; SPG-53A is being replaced by STIR; 10 standard SM-1 MR (ex-Gearing class) are being installed on top of the hangar. The 127 mm gun is being replaced by the OTO Melara 76 mm/62.
Structure: ASROC-torpedo reloading capability (note slanting face of bridge structure immediately behind ASROC). Four Mk 32 torpedo tubes are fixed in the midships structure, two to a side, angled out at 45°. The arrangement provides improved loading capability over exposed triple Mk 32 torpedo tubes. A 4,000 lb lightweight anchor is fitted on the port side and an 8,000 lb anchor fits into the after section of the sonar.
Operational: Seasprite helicopters were planned to be embarked but this now seems unlikely. All of the class are assigned to 168 Patrol Squadron at Suao. *Lan Yang* is the Flagship.

SHIPBORNE AIRCRAFT

Notes: Negotiations to acquire SH-2F Seasprite helicopters for the Knox class, conducted for several years, have not been satisfactorily concluded.

Numbers/Type: 21 Sikorsky S-70C(M)1 Thunderhawks.
Operational speed: 145 kt *(269 km/h)*.
Service ceiling: 19,000 ft *(5,790 m)*.
Range: 324 n miles *(600 km)*.
Role/Weapon systems: First delivered in 1991. This is a variant of the SH-60B and became seaborne with the first Cheng Kung and Kang Ding class frigates. 701 and 702 Squadrons. Two modified for EW and Sigint role. Another 14 S-70B/C SAR and assault aircraft belong to the Air Force. Sensors: APS 128 search radar; Litton ALR 606(V)2 ESM; ARR 84 sonobuoy receiver with Litton ASN 150 datalink; Allied AQS 18(V)3 dipping sonar; ASQ 504 MAD. Ta Chen datalink to be fitted. Weapons: ASW; two Hughes Mk 46 Mod 5 torpedoes or two Mk 64 depth bombs. ASV; could carry ASM.

THUNDERHAWK *1/2000, C Chung* / 0106599

Numbers/Type: 9 Hughes MD 500/ASW.
Operational speed: 110 kt *(204 km/h)*.
Service ceiling: 16,000 ft *(4,880 m)*.
Range: 203 n miles *(376 km)*.
Role/Weapon systems: Short-range ASW helicopter with limited surface search capability. 501 ASW Squadron. Sensors: Search radar, Texas Instruments ASQ 81(V)2 MAD. Weapons: ASW; one Mk 46 Mod 5 torpedo or two depth bombs. ASV; could carry machine gun pods.

MD 500 *1/1995, L J Lamb* / 0080778

LAND-BASED MARITIME AIRCRAFT

Notes: (1) Four Grumman E-2T Hawkeye AEW aircraft were acquired by the Air Force in February 1995. These are to be upgraded to the Hawkeye 2000 configuration.
(2) Plans, under the 2001 US arms package, to acquire 12 P-3C maritime patrol aircraft were confirmed on 16 February 2008. Eight of the aircraft are to be manufactured in Taiwan. To be delivered from 2011.
(3) Plans to acquire 12 MH-53E Sea Dragon minehunting helicopters were also agreed in the 2001 agreement but continue to be delayed.

Numbers/Type: 3/21 Grumman S-2E/S-2T (Turbo) Trackers.
Operational speed: 130 kt *(241 km/h)*.
Service ceiling: 25,000 ft *(7,620 m)*.
Range: 1,350 n miles *(2,500 km)*.
Role/Weapon systems: Patrol and ASW tasks transferred to the Navy in July 1998; 21 aircraft updated with turboprop engines and new sensors. Based at Pintung. To be replaced by P-3C when they enter service. Sensors: APS 504 search radar, ESM, MAD, AAS 40 FLIR, SSQ-41B, SSQ-47B sonobuoys; AQS 902F sonobuoy processor; ASN 150 datalink. Weapons: ASW; four Mk 44 torpedoes, Mk 54 depth charges or Mk 64 depth bombs or mines. ASV; Hsiung Feng II ASM; six 127 mm rockets.

TRACKER *6/2002, Adolfo Ortigueira Gil* / 0569245

PATROL FORCES

Notes: All coastal patrol craft were transferred to the Maritime Police on 8 December 1992. The Maritime Police became the Coast Guard 1 February 2000.

12 + (12) JIN CHIANG CLASS (LARGE PATROL CRAFT) (PCG)

Name	*No*	*Builders*	*Launched*	*Commissioned*
JIN CHIANG	603	Lien-Ho, Kaohsiung	1 May 1994	1 Dec 1994
TAN CHIANG	605	China SB, Kaohsiung	18 June 1998	7 Sep 1999
HSIN CHIANG	606	China SB, Kaohsiung	14 Aug 1998	7 Sep 1999
FENG CHIANG	607	China SB, Kaohsiung	22 Oct 1998	29 Oct 1999
TSENG CHIANG	608	China SB, Kaohsiung	16 Nov 1998	29 Oct 1999
KAO CHIANG	609	China SB, Kaohsiung	15 Dec 1998	29 Oct 1999
JING CHIANG	610	China SB, Kaohsiung	13 May 1999	15 Feb 2000
HSIAN CHIANG	611	China SB, Kaohsiung	16 July 1999	15 Feb 2000
TSI CHIANG	612	China SB, Kaohsiung	22 Dec 1999	15 Feb 2000
PO CHIANG	614	China SB, Kaohsiung	22 Dec 1999	21 July 2000
CHAN CHIANG	615	China SB, Kaohsiung	21 Jan 2000	21 July 2000
CHU CHIANG	617	China SB, Kaohsiung	25 Feb 2000	21 July 2000

Displacement, tons: 680 full load
Dimensions, feet (metres): 201.4 × 31.2 × 9.5 *(61.4 × 9.5 × 2.9)*
Main machinery: 2 MTU 20V 1163TB93 diesels; 20,128 hp(m) *(14.79 MW)*; 2 shafts
Speed, knots: 25
Range, n miles: 4,150 at 15 kt
Complement: 50 (7 officers)

Missiles: SSM: 4 Hsiung Feng I; radar or optical guidance to 36 km *(19.4 n miles)* at 0.7 Mach; warhead 75 kg or 4 Hsiung Feng II (606, 607); inertial guidance; active radar/IR homing to 80 km *(43.2 n miles)* at 0.85 Mach; warhead 190 kg.
4 Hsiung Feng II (in some); inertial guidance; active radar/IR homing to 80 km *(43.2 n miles)* at 0.85 kg Mach; warhead 190 kg.
Guns: 1 Bofors 40 mm/70. 1 CS 20 mm Type 75. 2—12.7 mm MGs.
Depth charges: 2 racks.
Mines: 2 rails for Mk 6.
Weapons control: Honeywell H 930 Mod 2 MFCS. Contraves WCS.
Rafael Sea Eye FLIR; range out to 3 km.
Radars: Air/surface search: Marconi LN66; I-band.
Fire control: Hughes HR-76C5; I/J-band.
Navigation: Racal Decca Bridgemaster; I-band.
Sonars: Simrad; search and attack; high frequency.

Programmes: Kwang Hua Project 3 design by United Ship Design Centre. First one laid down 25 June 1993. Eleven more ordered 26 June 1997. A further 12 were to have been delivered by 2010 but there have been no reports of progress.
Modernisation: *Hsin Chiang* and *Feng Chiang* have been upgraded with an Oto 76 mm gun and four Hsiung Feng II missiles. A mast to carry the datalink radome has also been added. All ships may be similarly modified in due course and it is likely that Hsiung Feng II missiles will be replace with Hsiung Feng III.

PO CHIANG *12/2005, Ships of the World* / 1151163

HSIN CHIANG *6/2006* / 1167508

2 LUNG CHIANG CLASS (FAST ATTACK CRAFT—MISSILE) (PGGF)

Name	*No*	*Builders*	*Commissioned*
LUNG CHIANG	601 (ex-PGG 581)	Tacoma Boatbuilding, WA	15 May 1978
SUI CHIANG	602 (ex-PGG 582)	China SB Corporation, Kaohsiung	31 Dec 1981

Displacement, tons: 270 full load
Dimensions, feet (metres): 164.5 × 23.1 × 9.5 *(50.2 × 7.3 × 2.9)*
Main machinery: CODAG; 3 Avco Lycoming TF-40A gas turbines; 12,000 hp *(8.95 MW)* sustained; 3 Detroit 12V-149TI diesels; 2,736 hp *(2.04 MW)* sustained; 3 shafts; cp props
Speed, knots: 20 kt diesels; 38 kt gas
Range, n miles: 3,100 at 12 kt on 1 diesel; 800 at 36 kt
Complement: 38 (5 officers)

Missiles: SSM: 4 Hsiung Feng I; radar or optical guidance to 36 km *(19.4 n miles)* at 0.7 Mach; warhead 75 kg.
Guns: 1 OTO Melara 3 in *(76 mm)*/62; 60 rds/min to 16 km *(8.7 n miles)*; weight of shell 6 kg.
1 Bofors 40 mm/70. 2—12.7 mm MGs.
Countermeasures: Decoys: 4 Israeli AV2 (601) or SMOC-4 (602) chaff launchers.
ESM: WD-2A; intercept.
Combat data systems: IPN 10 action data automation.
Weapons control: NA 10 Mod 0 GFCS. Honeywell H 930 Mod 2 MFCS (602).
Radars: Surface/air search: Selenia RAN 11 L/X; D/I-band.
Fire control: RCA HR 76; I/J-band (for SSM) (602).
Selenia RAN IIL/X; I/J-band for SSM (601).
Navigation: SPS-58(A); I-band.

Programmes: Similar to the US Patrol Ship Multi-Mission Mk 5 (PSMM Mk 5). Second of class was built to an improved design. A much larger number of this class was intended, all to be armed with Harpoon. However at that time the US ban on export of Harpoon to Taiwan coupled with the high cost and doubts about seaworthiness caused the cancellation of this programme.
Structure: Fin stabilisers were fitted to help correct the poor sea-keeping qualities of the design. Both have had engine room fires caused by overheating in GT gearboxes.
Operational: *Lung Chiang* may be non-operational.

SUI CHIANG *4/1997, Ships of the World* / 0019231

47 HAI OU CLASS (FAST ATTACK CRAFT—MISSILE) (PTG)

FABG 7–12	**FABG 23–30**	**FABG 41–45**	**FABG 59**
FABG 14–21	**FABG 32–39**	**FABG 47–57**	

Displacement, tons: 47 full load
Dimensions, feet (metres): 70.8 × 18 × 3.3 *(21.6 × 5.5 × 1)*
Main machinery: 2 MTU 12V 331TC82 diesels; 2,605 hp(m) *(1.92 MW)* sustained; 2 shafts
Speed, knots: 30
Range, n miles: 700 at 32 kt
Complement: 10 (2 officers)

Missiles: SSM: 2 Hsiung Feng I; radar or optical guidance to 36 km *(19.4 n miles)* at 0.7 Mach; warhead 75 kg.
Guns: 1 CS 20 mm Type 75. 2—12.7 mm MGs.
Countermeasures: Decoys: 4 Israeli AV2 chaff launchers.
ESM: WD-2A; intercept.
Weapons control: Kollmorgen Mk 35 optical director.
Radars: Surface search: Marconi LN66; I-band.
Fire control: RCA R76 C5; I-band.

Programmes: This design was developed by Sun Yat Sen Scientific Research Institute from the basic Israeli Dvora plans. Built by China SB Corporation (Tsoying SY), Kaohsiung except for the first pair (FABG 5-6) which were the original Dvora class hulls and were commissioned on 31 December 1977.
Structure: Aluminium alloy hulls. The first series had a solid mast and the missiles were nearer the stern. Second series changed to a lattice mast and moved the missiles further forward allowing room for two 12.7 mm MGs right aft. One 20 mm has been added on the stern.
Operational: The prototype reached 45 kt on trials but top speeds are now reported as being much reduced. These craft often carry shoulder-launched SAMs. One task is to provide exercise high-speed targets in shallow waters. From 1997 organised in five divisions based at Makung, Tamsui, Tsoying, Suao and Keelung. Not all are operational and the class is likely to be paid off as the Kwang Hua 6 class enter service.
Sales: Two similar craft to Paraguay in 1996.

FABG 50 *12/2005, Ships of the World* / 1151162

1 + 2 (27) KWANG HUA 6 CLASS (PTG)

FACG 60

Displacement, tons: 180 standard
Dimensions, feet (metres): 112.2 × 24.9 × 6.2 *(34.2 × 7.6 × 1.9)*
Main machinery: 3 MTU 16V 4000 diesels; 9,600 hp *(7.2 MW)*; 3 shafts
Speed, knots: 33. **Range, n miles:** 1,150 at 22 kt
Complement: 14
Missiles: SSM: 4 Hsiung Feng II; inertial guidance; active radar/IR homing to 80 km *(43.2 n miles)* at 0.85 Mach; warhead 190 kg.
Guns: 2 CS 20 mm Type 75.
Countermeasures: Decoys: Chaff launchers. ESM.
Weapons control: Optronic director.
Radars: Surface search: Fire control.

Comment: Funds allocated for the budget period July 1998 to June 2003 to build these craft in Taiwan to replace the Hai Ou class. First of class laid down in early 2001 and launched on 26 September 2002. Commissioned in October 2003 but subsequently damaged by typhoon in September 2008. Construction of remaining craft was delayed into 2007 when work on two boats was reportedly initiated.

FACG 60 *12/2005, Ships of the World* / 1151161

8 NING HAI CLASS (LARGE PATROL CRAFT) (PCF)

NING HAI PCL 1 **AN HAI** PCL 2 **PCL 3** **PCL 5–9**

Displacement, tons: 143 full load
Dimensions, feet (metres): 105 × 29.5 × 5.9 *(32 × 9 × 1.8)*
Main machinery: 3 MTU 12V 396TB93 diesels; 4,890 hp(m) *(3.6 MW)* sustained; 3 shafts
Speed, knots: 40
Complement: 18 (2 officers)
Guns: 1 Bofors 40 mm/60. 1 CS 20 mm Type 75.
Depth charges: 2 racks.
Radars: Surface search: Decca; I-band.
Sonars: Hull-mounted; active search and attack; high frequency.

Comment: Built to Vosper QAF design by China SB Corporation, Kaohsiung in 1987–90. Previously reported numbers had been exaggerated. They are used mainly for harbour defence against midget submarines and frogmen and also for Fishery protection tasks.

PCL 5 *6/2002, Ships of the World* / 0569243

AMPHIBIOUS FORCES

1 CABILDO CLASS (LSDM)

Name	*No*	*Builders*	*Commissioned*
CHUNG CHENG (ex-*Comstock*)	191 (ex-LSD 19)	Newport News, Virginia	2 July 1945

Displacement, tons: 4,790 standard; 9,375 full load
Dimensions, feet (metres): 475 × 76.2 × 18 *(144.8 × 23.2 × 5.5)*
Main machinery: 2 boilers; 435 psi *(30.6 kg/cm²)*; 740°F *(393°C)*; 2 turbines; 7,000 hp *(5.22 MW)*; 2 shafts
Speed, knots: 15.4. **Range, n miles:** 8,000 at 15 kt
Complement: 316
Military lift: 3 LCUs or 18 LCMs or 32 LVTs in docking well
Missiles: SAM: 1 Sea Chaparral quadruple launcher.
Guns: 12 Bofors 40 mm/56 (2 quad, 2 twin).
Weapons control: US Mk 26 Mod 4.
Radars: Surface search: Raytheon SPS-5; G/H-band.
Navigation: Marconi LN66; I-band.

Comment: Launched 28 April 1945 and transferred to Taiwan on 1 October 1985 having been bought from a ship breaker. SAM system fitted in 1992. Collision with merchant ship on 28 June 2001 resulted in five months repair work. Second of class scrapped in mid-1999.

CHUNG CHENG *6/2000, Ships of the World* / 1190409

1 ANCHORAGE CLASS (LSDH)

Name	*No*	*Builders*	*Commissioned*
SHIU HAI (ex-*Pensacola*)	LSD 193 (ex-LSD 38)	General Dynamics, Quincy	27 Mar 1971

Displacement, tons: 8,600 light; 13,700 full load
Dimensions, feet (metres): 553.3 × 84 × 20 *(168.6 × 25.6 × 6)*
Main machinery: 2 Foster-Wheeler boilers; 600 psi *(42.3 kg/cm²)*; 870°F *(467°C)*; 2 De Laval turbines; 24,000 hp *(18 MW)*; 2 shafts
Speed, knots: 22
Range, n miles: 14,800 at 12 kt
Complement: 374 (24 officers)
Military lift: 366 troops (18 officers); 2 LCU or 18 LCM 6 or 9 LCM 8 or 50 LVT; 1 LCM 6 on deck; 2 LCPL and 1 LCVP on davits. Aviation fuel, 90 tons
Guns: 2 General Electric/General Dynamics 20 mm/76 6-barrelled Vulcan Phalanx Mk 15; 3,000 rds/min combined to 1.5 km.
2—25 mm Mk 38. 6—12.7 mm MGs.
Countermeasures: Decoys: 4 Loral Hycor SRBOC 6-barrelled Mk 36; IR flares and chaff to 4 km *(2.2 n miles)*.
ESM: SLQ-32(V)1; intercept.
Radars: Air search: Lockheed SPS-40B; B-band.
Surface search: Raytheon SPS-10F; G-band.
Navigation: Marconi LN66; I-band.
Helicopters: Platform only.

Comment: First one acquired from US Navy 30 September 1999 and arrived in Taiwan on 2 June 2000. Transfer of ex-*Anchorage* (LSD 36) did not take place as expected in 2004 although procurement of a further amphibious ship remains a requirement. Has a docking well 131.1 × 15.2 m and two 50 ton cranes. Based at Tsoying.

SHIU HAI *6/2000, Ships of the World* / 1167449

2 NEWPORT CLASS (LSTH)

Name	*No*	*Builders*	*Commissioned*
CHUNG HO (ex-*Manitowic*)	232 (ex-LST 1180)	Philadelphia Shipyard	24 Jan 1970
CHUNG PING (ex-*Sumter*)	233 (ex-LST 1181)	Philadelphia Shipyard	20 June 1970

Displacement, tons: 4,975 light; 8,450 full load
Dimensions, feet (metres): 522.3 × 69.5 × 17.5 *(159.2 × 21.2 × 5.3)*
Main machinery: 6 ALCO 16-251 diesels; 16,500 hp *(12.3 MW)* sustained; 2 shafts; cp props; bow thruster
Speed, knots: 20
Range, n miles: 14,250 at 14 kt
Complement: 257 (13 officers)
Military lift: 400 troops; 500 tons vehicles; 3 LCVPs and 1 LCPL on davits
Guns: 1 General Electric/General Dynamics 20 mm Vulcan Phalanx Mk 15.
4—40 mm/60 (2 twin).
Countermeasures: ESM: WD-2A (233); intercept.
ESM/ECM: Chang Feng III (232); intercept and jammer.
Radars: Surface search: Raytheon SPS-67; G-band.
Navigation: Marconi LN66; I-band.
Helicopters: Platform only.

Comment: First pair transferred from USA by lease confirmed for both ships on 1 July 1995. Refitted at Newport News and recommissioned 8 May 1997, sailing for Taiwan after a short operational work-up. Purchased outright on 29 September 2000. Transfer of further ships is unlikely. These ships unload by a 112 ft ramp over their bow. The ramp is supported by twin derrick arms. A ramp just forward of the superstructure connects the lower tank deck with the main deck and a vehicle passage through the superstructure provides access to the parking area amidships. A stern gate to the tank deck permits unloading of amphibious tractors into the water, or unloading of other vehicles into an LCU or on to a pier. Vehicle stowage covers 19,000 sq ft. Length over derrick arms is 562 ft *(171.3 m)*; full load draught is 11.5 ft forward and 17.5 ft aft. Bow thruster fitted to hold position offshore while unloading amphibious tractors.

CHUNG HO *6/2000, Sattler/Steele* / 0106602

11 LST 1-510 AND 512-1152 CLASSES (LST)

CHUNG HAI (ex-*LST 755*) 201 (ex-697)
CHUNG CHIEN (ex-*LST 716*) 205 (ex-679)
CHUNG SHUN (ex-*LST 732*) 208 (ex-624)
CHUNG KUANG (ex-*LST 503*) 216 (ex-646)
CHUNG SUO (ex-*Bradley County* LST 400) 217 (ex-667)
CHUNG CHI (ex-*LST 279*) 218
CHUNG CHUAN (ex-*LST 1030*) 221 (ex-651)
CHUNG CHIH (ex-*Sagadahoc County* LST 1091) 226 (ex-655)
CHUNG MING (ex-*Sweetwater County* LST 1152) 227 (ex-681)
CHUNG PANG (ex-*LST 578*) 230 (ex-629)
CHUNG YEH (ex-*Sublette County* LST 1144) 231 (ex-699)

Displacement, tons: 1,653 standard; 4,080 (3,640, 1-510 class) full load
Dimensions, feet (metres): 328 × 50 × 14 *(100 × 15.2 × 4.3)*
Main machinery: 2 GM 12-567A diesels; 1,800 hp *(1.34 MW)*; 2 shafts
Speed, knots: 11.6. **Range, n miles:** 15,000 at 10 kt
Complement: Varies-100-125 in most ships
Guns: Varies-up to 10 Bofors 40 mm/56 (2 twin, 6 single) with some modernised ships rearmed with 2 USN 3 in *(76 mm)*/50 and 6—40 mm (3 twin).
Several Oerlikon 20 mm (twin or single).
Radars: Navigation: US SO 1, 2 or 8; I-band.

Comment: Constructed between 1943 and 1945. These ships have been rebuilt in Taiwan. Six transferred from US in 1946; two in 1947; one in 1948; eight in 1958; one in 1959; two in 1960; and one in 1961. Some have davits forward and aft. Pennant numbers have reverted to those used in the 1960s. One deleted in 1990, six more in 1993, one more in 1995 after going aground, and two more in1997. The midships deck is occasionally used as a helicopter platform. These last 11 may be retained due to the cancellation of the programme for more locally built AKs.

CHUNG SUO *6/2000, DTM* / 0126196

1 LST 512-1152 CLASS (FLAGSHIP) (AGF)

Name	*No*	*Builders*	*Commissioned*
KAO HSIUNG (ex-*Chung Hai*, ex-*Dukes County* LST 735)	LCC 1 (ex-219, ex-663)	Dravo Corporation, Neville Island, Penn	26 Apr 1944

Displacement, tons: 1,653 standard; 3,675 full load
Dimensions, feet (metres): 328 × 50 × 14 *(100 × 15.2 × 4.3)*
Main machinery: 2 GM 12-567A diesels; 1,800 hp *(1.34 MW)*; 2 shafts
Speed, knots: 11.6. **Range, n miles:** 11,200 at 10 kt
Complement: 195
Guns: 8 Bofors 40 mm/56 (3 twin, 2 single).
Radars: Air search: Raytheon SPS 58; D-band.
Surface search: Raytheon SPS-10; G-band.

Comment: Launched on 11 March 1944. Transferred from US in May 1957 for service as an LST. Converted to a flagship for amphibious operations and renamed and redesignated (AGC) in 1964. Purchased November 1974. Note lattice mast above bridge structure, modified bridge levels, and antenna mountings on main deck. Redesignated as Command and Control Ship LCC 1.

KAO HSIUNG *6/1999* / 0080783

170 LCM 6 CLASS (LCM)

Displacement, tons: 57 full load
Dimensions, feet (metres): 56.4 × 13.8 × 3.9 *(17.2 × 4.2 × 1.2)*
Main machinery: 2 diesels; 450 hp *(336 kW)*; 2 shafts
Speed, knots: 9
Military lift: 34 tons
Guns: 1—12.7 mm MG.

Comment: Some built in the US, some in Taiwan. 20 were exchanged for torpedoes with Indonesia. Some 55 have been deleted in the last four years. Form part of 151 Squadron.

LCM 6 *7/2000, C Chung* / 0106603

10 LCU 501 CLASS (LCU)

HO CHI (ex-*LCU 1212*) 401
HO HUEI (ex-*LCU 1218*) 402
HO YAO (ex-*LCU 1244*) 403
HO CHAO (ex-*LCU 1429*) 406
HO SHUN (ex-*LCU 1225*) 481
HO CHUNG (ex-*LCU 849*) 484
HO CHUN (ex-*LCU 892*) 494
HO YUNG (ex-*LCU 1271*) 495
HO CHIE (ex-*LCU 700*) SB 1
HO TEN (ex-*LCU 1367*) SB 2

Displacement, tons: 158 light; 309 full load
Dimensions, feet (metres): 119 × 32.7 × 5 *(36.3 × 10 × 1.5)*
Main machinery: 3 GM 6-71 diesels; 522 hp *(390 kW)* sustained; 3 shafts
Speed, knots: 10
Complement: 10-25
Guns: 2 Oerlikon 20 mm. Some also may have 2—12.7 mm MGs.

Comment: Built in US in the 1940s and transferred in 1959. *SB 1* and *SB 2* are used as auxiliaries. *Ho Feng* 405 converted for ferry duties in 1998 and serves Matzu island.

HO SHUN *6/2000, DTM* / 0569238

6 LCU 1466 CLASS (LCU)

HO SHAN (ex-*LCU 1596*) 488
HO CHUAN (ex-*LCU 1597*) 489
HO SENG (ex-*LCU 1598*) 490
HO MENG (ex-*LCU 1599*) 491
HO MOU (ex-*LCU 1600*) 492
HO SHOU (ex-*LCU 1601*) 493

Displacement, tons: 180 light; 360 full load
Dimensions, feet (metres): 119 × 34 × 6 *(36.3 × 10.4 × 1.8)*
Main machinery: 3 Gray Marine 64 YTL diesels; 675 hp *(504 kW)*; 3 shafts
Speed, knots: 10
Range, n miles: 800 at 11 kt
Complement: 15-25
Military lift: 167 tons or 300 troops
Guns: 3 Oerlikon 20 mm. Some may also have 2—12.7 mm MGs.

Comment: Built by Ishikawajima Heavy Industries Co, Tokyo, Japan, for transfer to Taiwan; completed in March 1955. All originally numbered in 200 series; subsequently changed to 400 series.

HO CHUAN *1991* / 0506105

2 TAIWAN TYPE LCU (LCU)

HO FONG LCU 497 **HO HU** LCU 498

Displacement, tons: 190 light; 439 full load
Dimensions, feet (metres): 135.5 × 29.9 × 6.9 *(41.3 × 9.1 × 2.1)*
Main machinery: 4 Detroit diesels; 1,200 hp *(895 kW)*; 2 Kort nozzle props
Speed, knots: 11
Range, n miles: 1,200 at 10 kt
Complement: 16
Military lift: 180 tons or 350 troops
Guns: 2—12.7 mm MGs.

Comment: Locally built versions of US types. Ramps at both ends.

HO FONG *6/2000, DTM* / 0569237

100 LCVPS AND ASSAULT CRAFT

Comment: Some ex-US, and some built in Taiwan. Most are armed with one or two 7.62 mm MGs. Two transferred to Indonesia in 1988. About 20 deleted in the last three years and 30 transferred to Honduras in 1996 for River operations. There are also a number of amphibious reconnaissance boats in the ARP 1000, 2000 and 3000 series. Form part of 151 Squadron.

TYPE 272 *1989, (DTM (Raymond Cheung))* / 0506106

MINE WARFARE FORCES

Notes: There are plans to acquire eight GRP minehunters to replace the inventory of ageing wooden-hull minesweepers. The first two ships are to be two Osprey class, transferred from the US Navy, while a further six, probably based on the Lerici class, are to be built in Taiwan.

4 AGGRESSIVE CLASS (MINESWEEPERS) (MSO)

Name	*No*	*Builders*	*Commissioned*
YUNG YANG (ex-*Implicit*)	1306 (ex-455)	Wilmington Boat	10 Mar 1954
YUNG TZU (ex-*Conquest*)	1307 (ex-488)	Martenac, Tacoma	20 July 1955
YUNG KU (ex-*Gallant*)	1308 (ex-489)	Martenac, Tacoma	14 Sep 1955
YUNG TEH (ex-*Pledge*)	1309 (ex-492)	Martenac, Tacoma	20 Apr 1956

Displacement, tons: 720 standard; 780 full load
Dimensions, feet (metres): 172.5 × 35.1 × 14.1 *(52.6 × 10.7 × 4.3)*
Main machinery: 4 Packard ID-1700 or Waukesha diesels; 2,280 hp *(1.7 MW)*; 2 shafts; cp props
Speed, knots: 14. **Range, n miles**: 3,000 at 10 kt
Complement: 86 (7 officers)
Guns: 2 — 12.7 mm MGs.
Radars: Navigation: Sperry SPS-53L; I-band.
Sonars: General Electric SQQ-14; VDS; active minehunting; high frequency.

Comment: Transferred by sale to Taiwan from the USN 3 August and 30 September 1994. Delivery was delayed into 1995 while replanking work was carried out in the US. All recommissioned 1 March 1995. Second batch of three planned to transfer but were subsequently scrapped after cannibalisation for spares. All are fitted with SLQ-37 mechanical acoustic and magnetic sweeps and can carry an ROV. Plans to update the class with a Unisys SYQ-12 minehunting system and Pluto ROVs have probably been overtaken by the new MCMV programme.

YUNG KU *6/2000, DTM* / 0569242

4 ADJUTANT AND MSC 268 CLASSES (MINESWEEPERS — COASTAL) (MSC)

YUNG CHUAN (ex-*MSC 278*) 158
YUNG FU (ex-*Macaw*, ex-*MSC 77*) 162
YUNG REN (ex-*St Nicholas*, ex-*MSC 64*) 167
YUNG SUI (ex-*Disksmude*, ex-*MSC 65*) 168

Displacement, tons: 375 full load
Dimensions, feet (metres): 144 × 27.9 × 8 *(43.9 × 8.5 × 2.4)*
Main machinery: 2 GM 8-268A diesels; 880 hp *(656 kW)*; 2 shafts
Speed, knots: 13. **Range, n miles**: 2,500 at 12 kt
Complement: 35
Guns: 1 Oerlikon 20 mm.
Radars: Navigation: Decca 707; I-band.
Sonars: Simrad 950; hull-mounted; minehunting; high frequency.

Comment: Non-magnetic, wood-hulled minesweepers built in the US in the 1950s specifically for transfer to allied navies. All refitted 1984–86. All are in very poor condition. Several deleted so far. Two put back in service in 1996 and one in 1997 to replace three others paid off.

YUNG CHUAN *6/2000, DTM* / 0569241

4 YUNG FENG (MWV 50) CLASS (MINEHUNTERS — COASTAL) (MHC)

YUNG FENG 1301 **YUNG CHIA** 1302 **YUNG TING** 1303 **YUNG SHUN** 1305

Displacement, tons: 500 full load
Dimensions, feet (metres): 163.1 × 28.5 × 10.2 *(49.7 × 8.7 × 3.1)*
Main machinery: 2 MTU 8V 396 TB93 diesels; 2,180 hp(m) *(1.6 MW)* sustained; 2 shafts
Speed, knots: 14. **Range, n miles**: 3,500 at 14 kt
Complement: 45 (5 officers)
Guns: 1 — 20 mm. 2 — 12.7 mm MGs.
Radars: Navigation: I-band.
Sonars: TSM-2022; hull-mounted; active minehunting; high frequency.

Comment: Built for the Chinese Petroleum Corporation by Abeking & Rasmussen at Lemwerder, Germany. First four delivered in 1991 as offshore oil rig support ships and then converted for minehunting in Taiwan. Thomson Sintra IBIS V minehunting system is fitted and two STN Pinguin B3 ROVs are carried.

YUNG FENG *6/2000, DTM* / 0569240

0 + 2 OSPREY CLASS (MINEHUNTERS — COASTAL) (MHC)

Name	*No*	*Builders*	*Launched*	*Commissioned*
– (ex-*Oriole*)	– (ex-MHC 55)	Intermarine, Savannah	22 May 1993	16 Sep 1995
– (ex-*Falcon*)	– (ex-MHC 59)	Intermarine, Savannah	3 June 1995	26 Oct 1997

Displacement, tons: 930 full load
Dimensions, feet (metres): 187.8 × 35.9 × 9.5 *(57.2 × 11 × 2.9)*
Main machinery: 2 Isotta Fraschini ID 36 SS 8V AM diesels; 1,600 hp(m) *(1.18 MW)* sustained; 2 Voith-Schneider props; 3 Isotta Fraschini ID 36 diesel generators; 984 kW
Speed, knots: 10. **Range, n miles**: 1,500 at 10 kt
Complement: 51 (5 officers)
Guns: 2 — 12.7 mm MGs.
Countermeasures: MCM: Alliant SLQ-48 mine neutralisation system ROV (with 1,070 m cable). Degaussing DGM-4.
Combat data systems: Unisys SYQ 13 and SYQ 109; integrated combat and machinery control system. USQ-119E(V), UHF Dama, and OTCIXS provide GCCS connectivity.
Radars: Surface search: Raytheon SPS-64(V)9; I-band.
Navigation: R41XX; I-band.
Sonars: Raytheon/Thomson Sintra SQQ-32(V)3; VDS; active minehunting; high frequency.

Programmes: Original design contract for Lerici-class minehunters was awarded in August 1986 to Intermarine USA which built eight of the 12 ships of the class for the US Navy. Authority to transfer both vessels to Taiwan was sought in 2007 and both are likely to be delivered in 2009.
Structure: Construction is of monocoque GRP throughout hull, with frames eliminated. Main machinery is mounted on GRP cradles and provided with acoustic enclosures. SQQ-32 is deployed from a central well forward. Fitted with Voith cycloidal propellers which eliminate need for forward thrusters during station keeping.

SURVEY AND RESEARCH SHIPS

1 ALLIANCE CLASS (AGOR)

Name	*No*	*Builders*	*Launched*	*Commissioned*
TA KUAN	1601	Fincantieri, Muggiano	17 Dec 1994	27 Sep 1995

Displacement, tons: 2,466 standard; 3,180 full load
Dimensions, feet (metres): 305.1 × 49.9 × 16.7 *(93 × 15.2 × 5.1)*
Main machinery: Diesel-electric; 3 MTU/AEG diesel generators; 5,712 hp(m) *(4.2 MW)*; 2 AEG motors; 5,100 hp(m) *(3.75 MW)*; 2 shafts; bow thruster; stern trainable and retractable thruster
Speed, knots: 15. **Range, n miles**: 12,000 at 12 kt
Complement: 82
Guns: 2 — 12.7 mm MGs.
Radars: Navigation: H/I-band.

Comment: Ordered in June 1993 and laid down 8 April 1994. Almost identical to the NATO vessel. Designed for oceanography and hydrographic research. Facilities include laboratories, position location systems, and overside deployment equipment. Equipment includes a Simrad side scan sonar EM 1200, deep and shallow echo-sounders, two radars, Navsat and Satcom, an ROV for remote inspection, and a dynamic positioning system with bow thruster and stern positioning propeller.

TA KUAN *8/1997, C Chung* / 0019239

AUXILIARIES

1 COMBAT SUPPORT SHIP (AOEHM)

Name	*No*	*Builders*	*Launched*	*Commissioned*
WU YI	530	China SB Corporation, Keelung	4 Mar 1989	23 June 1990

Displacement, tons: 7,700 light; 17,000 full load
Dimensions, feet (metres): 531.8 × 72.2 × 28 *(162.1 × 22 × 8.6)*
Main machinery: 2 MAN 14-cyl diesels; 25,000 hp(m) *(18.37 MW)*; 2 shafts
Speed, knots: 21. **Range, n miles:** 9,200 at 10 kt
Cargo capacity: 9,300 tons
Missiles: SAM: 1 Sea Chaparral quad launcher.
Guns: 2 Bofors 40 mm/70. 2 Oerlikon 20 mm GAM-BO1. 4—12.7 mm MGs.
Countermeasures: Decoys: 2 chaff launchers.
ESM: Radar warning.
Radars: 2 navigation; I-band.
Helicopters: Platform for CH-47 or S-70C(M)1.

Comment: Largest unit built so far for the Taiwanese Navy. Design assisted by the United Shipping Design Center in the US. Beam replenishment rigs on both sides. SAM system on forecastle, 40 mm guns aft of the funnels.

WU YI *3/2004*, ***Chris Sattler*** / 1044573

3 WU KANG CLASS (ATTACK TRANSPORTS) (AKM)

Name	*No*	*Builders*	*Commissioned*
YUEN FENG	524	China SB Corporation, Keelung	10 Sep 1982
WU KANG	525	China SB Corporation, Keelung	9 Oct 1984
HSIN KANG	526	China SB Corporation, Keelung	30 Nov 1988

Displacement, tons: 2,804 standard; 4,845 full load
Dimensions, feet (metres): 334 × 59.1 × 16.4 *(101.8 × 18 × 5)*
Main machinery: 2 diesels; 2 shafts; bow thruster
Speed, knots: 20. **Range, n miles:** 6,500 at 12 kt
Complement: 61 (11 officers)
Military lift: 1,400 troops
Missiles: SAM: 1 Sea Chaparral quad launcher.
Guns: 2 Bofors 40 mm/60. 2 or 4—12.7 mm MGs.
Countermeasures: ESM: WD-2A (524 only); intercept.

Comment: First three were built and then the programme stopped. Restarted with the fourth of class laid down in July 1994. The plan was to build at about one a year to a final total of seven, but the programme has been cancelled without the fourth ship being completed. With a helicopter platform, stern docking facility and davits for four LCVP, the design resembles an LPD. Used mostly for supplying garrisons in offshore islands, and on the Spratley and Pratas islands in the South China Sea. SAM launcher is mounted aft of the foremast. Accommodation is air conditioned. *Hsin Kang* was badly damaged in harbour in collision with a merchant ship in March 1996, but was back in service by mid-1999.

HSIN KANG *6/2002*, ***Ships of the World*** / 0569239

1 SALVAGE SHIP (ARS)

Name	*No*	*Builders*	*Commissioned*
TA HU (ex-*Grapple*)	552 (ex-ARS 7)	Basalt Rock, USA	16 Dec 1943

Displacement, tons: 1,557 standard; 1,745 full load
Dimensions, feet (metres): 213.5 × 39 × 15 *(65.1 × 11.9 × 4.6)*
Main machinery: Diesel-electric; 4 Cooper Bessemer GSB-8 diesels; 3,420 hp *(2.55 MW)*; 2 generators; 2 motors; 2 shafts
Speed, knots: 14. **Range, n miles:** 8,500 at 13 kt
Complement: 85
Guns: 2 Oerlikon 20 mm.
Radars: Navigation: SPS-53; I-band.

Comment: Fitted for salvage, towing and compressed-air diving. *Ta Hu* transferred from US 1 December 1977 by sale. The reported transfer from the US of ex-*Conserver* did not take place.

TA HU *6/2005*, ***C Chung*** / 1151389

6 FLOATING DOCKS (YFD)

HAY TAN (ex-*AFDL 36*) AFDL 1
KIM MEN (ex-*AFDL 5*) AFDL 2
HAN JIH (ex-*AFDL 34*) AFDL 3
FO WU 5 (ex-*ARD 9*) ARD 5
FO WU 6 (ex-*Windsor* ARD 22) ARD 6
FO WU 7 (ex-*AFDM 6*)

Comment: Former US Navy floating dry docks. *Hay Tan* transferred in March 1947, *Kim Men* in January 1948, *Han Jih* in July 1959, *Fo Wu 5* in June 1971, *Fo Wu 6* in June 1971. *Fo Wu 6* by sale 19 May 1976 and *Fo Wu 5* on 12 January 1977. *Fo Wu 7* transferred by sale in 1999.

TUGS

5 CHEROKEE CLASS (ATF/ARS)

TA WAN (ex-*Apache*) ATF 551
TA HAN (ex-*Tawakoni*) ATF 553
TA KANG (ex-*Achomawi*) ATF 554
TA FUNG (ex-*Narragansett*) ATF 555
TA TAI (ex-*Shakori*) ATF 563

Displacement, tons: 1,235 standard; 1,731 full load
Dimensions, feet (metres): 205 × 38.5 × 17 *(62.5 × 11.7 × 5.2)*
Main machinery: Diesel-electric; 4 GM 12-278 diesels; 4,400 hp *(3.28 MW)*; 4 generators; 1 motor; 3,000 hp *(2.24 MW)*; 1 shaft
Speed, knots: 15
Range, n miles: 6,000 at 14 kt
Complement: 85
Guns: 1 Bofors 40 mm/60. Several 12.7 mm MGs.

Comment: All built between 1943 and 1945. *Ta Wan* transferred from US in June 1974; *Ta Han* in June 1978; and the last three in June 1991 together with two more which were cannibalised for spares.

TA HAN ***4/1995*** / 0080790

11 HARBOUR TUGS (YTL)

YTL 16–17 **YTL 27–30** **YTL 32–36**

Comment: Replacements for the old US Army type which were scrapped in 1990/91. Some are used for fire fighting.

YTL 36 *5/1997*, ***van Ginderen Collection*** / 0019242

19 LARGE HARBOUR TUGS (YTB)

YTB 37–39 **YTL 41–43** **YTB 45–49** **YTB 150–157**

Comment: Various types of about 30 m length.

YTL 45 *10/2006*, ***Bob Fildes*** / 1170235

COAST GUARD

Headquarters Appointments

Director General of Maritime Patrol Directorate (Maritime Patrol):
Lin Fu-An
Director General of Coastal Patrol Directorate (Coastal Patrol):
Heh Shiang Tai

Notes: The Taiwan Coast Guard was established on 1 February 2000 by merging the former agencies of Maritime Police, Customs and Coastal Defense Command. It is responsible for the safety and security of Taiwan's coastline and waters. The missions are: coastal and harbour security, maritime law enforcement, anti-smuggling, anti-terrorism, SAR, fishery protection and pollution control. It consists of two major wings. The Maritime Patrol wing has 3,000 personnel in 21 patrol detachments around the coast. The Coastal Patrol wing has 14,701 personnel in four local coastal patrol offices: Northern, Central, Southern and Eastern.

Bases

HQ: Wunshan District, Taipei

2 HO HSING CLASS (OFFSHORE PATROL CRAFT) (WPSO)

HO HSING 101 **WEI HSUNG** 102

Displacement, tons: 1,823 full load
Dimensions, feet (metres): 270 × 38.1 × 13.5 *(82.3 × 11.6 × 4.1)*
Main machinery: 2 MTU 16V 1163 TB93 diesels; 15,470 hp(m) *(11.5 MW)* sustained; 2 shafts; cp props; bow thruster
Speed, knots: 22
Range, n miles: 6,000 at 16 kt
Complement: 80 (18 officers)
Guns: 1—20 mm. 2—12.7 mm MGs.
Radars: Surface search/navigation: Furuno; E/F/I-bands.

Comment: Built by the China SB Corporation, Keelung, to a Tacoma design and both delivered 26 December 1991. Four high-speed interceptor boats are carried on individual davits. This is a variant of the US Coast Guard Bear class.

HO HSING *6/2008*, Taiwan Coast Guard* / 1353377

1 OFFSHORE PATROL VESSEL (WPSO)

SHUN HU 1

Displacement, tons: 1,126 full load
Dimensions, feet (metres): 193.2 × 31.5 × 12.8 *(58.9 × 9.6 × 3.9)*
Main machinery: 2 Yanmar T 260-ET diesels; 3,000 hp(m) *(2.2 MW)*; 2 shafts
Speed, knots: 16
Range, n miles: 1,500 at 12 kt
Complement: 25
Radars: To be announced.

Comment: Commissioned in 1992.

SHUN HU 1 *6/2008*, Taiwan Coast Guard* / 1353374

2 OFFSHORE PATROL CRAFT (WPSO)

MOU HSING 105 **FU HSING** 106

Displacement, tons: 866 full load
Dimensions, feet (metres): 223.1 × 31.5 × 10.5 *(68.0 × 9.6 × 3.2)*
Main machinery: 2 MTU 16V 1163 TB93 diesels; 15,470 hp(m) *(11.5 MW)* sustained; 2 shafts
Speed, knots: 28
Range, n miles: 4,500 at 12 kt
Complement: 50
Guns: 2—12.7 mm MGs.
Radars: Surface search/navigation: Furuno; E/F/I-bands.

Comment: Ordered from Wilton Fijenoord in September 1986, and commissioned 14 June 1988.

FU HSING *9/2002, C Chung* / 0534122

2 OFFSHORE PATROL VESSELS (WPBO)

SHUN HU 2 **SHUN HU 3**

Displacement, tons: 839 full load
Dimensions, feet (metres): 169.0 × 27.5 × 12.1 *(51.5 × 8.4 × 3.7)*
Main machinery: 1 DAIHASU 6DLM-32F diesel; 2,500 hp(m) *(1.8 MW)*; 1 shaft
Speed, knots: 16. **Range, n miles:** 10,000 at 12 kt
Complement: 22
Radars: To be announced.

Comment: Commissioned in 1992.

SHUN HU 2 *9/2008*, Naruhito Saro* / 1353373

2 PAO HSING CLASS (OFFSHORE PATROL CRAFT) (WPSO)

CHIN HSING 108 **TEH HSING** 109

Displacement, tons: 591 full load
Dimensions, feet (metres): 199.5 × 25.6 × 11.5 *(60.8 × 7.8 × 3.5)*
Main machinery: 2 MAN 12V25/30 diesels; 6,480 hp(m) *(4.8 MW)* sustained; 2 shafts
Speed, knots: 20. **Range, n miles:** 2,000 at 14 kt
Complement: 50
Guns: 2—12.7 mm MGs.
Radars: Surface search: JRC; I-band.

Comment: Delivered 23 May 1985. Built by Keelung yard of China SB Corporation.

CHIN HSING *6/2008*, Taiwan Coast Guard* / 1353378

2 OFFSHORE PATROL CRAFT (WPSO)

KINMEN 123 **LIENCHIANG** 125

Displacement, tons: 688 full load
Dimensions, feet (metres): 213.5 × 38.4 × 10.1 *(65.1 × 11.7 × 3.1)*
Main machinery: 4 MTU 16V 4000 M90 diesels; 13,080 hp(m) *(9.7 MW)*; 4 waterjets
Speed, knots: 30. **Range, n miles:** 4,600 at 12 kt
Complement: 38
Guns: 1—20 mm.
Radars: Surface search/navigation: Furuno; E/F/I-bands.

Comment: Built by Jong Shyn Ship Building Corporation. Both launched in May 2007 and commissioned on 28 January 2008.

LIENCHIANG *6/2008*, Taiwan Coast Guard* / 1353381

4 OFFSHORE PATROL CRAFT (WPSO)

TAICHUNG 117 **KEELUNG** 118 **HUALIEN** 119 **PENHU** 120

Displacement, tons: 620 full load
Dimensions, feet (metres): 208.3 × 30.4 × 12.5 *(63.5 × 9.28 × 3.8)*
Main machinery: 2 MTU 1163 TB93 diesels; 15,470 hp(m) *(11.5 MW)* sustained; 2 shafts
Speed, knots: 30
Range, n miles: 4,500 at 22 kt
Complement: 40
Guns: 1 – 20 mm T 75. 2 – 12.7 mm MGs.
Radars: Surface search/navigation: Furuno; E/F/I-bands.

Comment: Built by Ching-Fu SB Corporation in Kaohsiung, to Lürssen Asia design. Delivered 28 June 2001. Two high-speed interceptor boats are carried on individual davits.

KEELUNG *6/2008*, **Taiwan Coast Guard*** / 1353379

1 COASTAL PATROL VESSEL (WPB)

SHUN HU 6

Displacement, tons: 204 full load
Dimensions, feet (metres): 125.0 × 23.0 × 8.5 *(38.1 × 7.0 × 2.6)*
Main machinery: 2 MTU 396TE84 diesels; 3,640 hp(m) *(2.7 MW)*; 2 shafts
Speed, knots: 20
Range, n miles: 4,000 at 15 kt
Complement: 15
Radars: To be announced.

Comment: Commissioned in 1992.

SHUN HU 6 *6/2008*, **Taiwan Coast Guard*** / 1353376

1 COASTAL PATROL VESSEL (WPB)

SHUN HU 5

Displacement, tons: 139 full load
Dimensions, feet (metres): 103.3 × 19.7 × 4.1 *(31.5 × 6.0 × 1.25)*
Main machinery: 2 MTU 331TC92 diesels; 2,920 hp(m) *(2.2 MW)*; 2 shafts
Speed, knots: 20
Range, n miles: 2,000 at 15 kt
Complement: 15
Radars: To be announced.

Comment: Commissioned in 1992.

SHUN HU 5 *6/2008*, **Taiwan Coast Guard*** / 1353375

2 OFFSHORE PATROL VESSEL (WPSO)

TAIPEI 116 **NANTOU** 122

Displacement, tons: 700 full load
Dimensions, feet (metres): 201.4 × 31.2 × 11.8 *(61.4 × 9.5 × 3.6)*
Main machinery: 2 MTU 20V 1163 TB93 diesels; 15,470 hp(m) *(11.5 MW)*; 2 shafts
Speed, knots: 30. **Range, n miles:** 4,600 at 22 kt
Complement: 33
Guns: 2 – 20 mm T75. 2 – 12.7 mm MGs.
Radars: Surface search/navigation: Furuno; E/F/I-bands.

Comment: Based on the naval Jin Chiang class, ship built by Chung-Hsin Ship Building Corporation. *Taipei* launched in November 1999 and commissioned on 20 March 2000. *Nantou* commissioned on 29 April 2005.

NANTOU *6/2008*, **Taiwan Coast Guard*** / 1353380

5 COASTAL PATROL CRAFT (WPB)

PP 10025–10029

Displacement, tons: 118 full load
Dimensions, feet (metres): 112.5 × 23.0 × 4.9 *(34.3 × 7.0 × 1.5)*
Main machinery: 2 MTU 16V 4000 M70 diesels; 6,220 hp *(4.6 MW)*; 2 waterjets
Speed, knots: 34. **Range, n miles:** 1,400 at 20 kt
Guns: 2 – 12.7 mm MGs.
Radars: Surface search/navigation: Furuno; E/F/I-bands.

Comment: Larger variants of the PP 10001 class.

PP 10028 *6/2008*, **Taiwan Coast Guard*** / 1353382

15 COASTAL PATROL CRAFT (WPB)

PP 10001 **PP 10003** **10005–10009** **10013** **10017–10019**

Displacement, tons: 103 full load
Dimensions, feet (metres): 100.0 × 22.3 × 9.8 *(30.5 × 6.8 × 3.0)*
Main machinery: 2 MTU 396 diesels; 6,000 hp(m) *(4.4 MW)*; 2 shafts
Speed, knots: 30. **Range, n miles:** 800 at 22 kt
Guns: 2 – 12.7 mm MGs (aft).
Radars: Surface search/navigation: Furuno; E/F/I-bands.

Comment: The first pair were former naval craft transferred 8 December 1992. Two more completed in October 1994, three more by February 1995.

PP 10017 *10/2001, **C Chung*** / 0126205

13 COASTAL PATROL CRAFT (WPBF)

PP 6001–6003 6005–6007 6009–6012 6014–6016

Displacement, tons: 68 full load
Dimensions, feet (metres): 91.9 × 20.3 × 7.9 *(28 × 6.2 × 2.4)*
Main machinery: 2 Paxman 12V P185 diesels; 6,645 hp(m) *(4.89 MW)* sustained; 2 shafts; cp props
Speed, knots: 40. **Range, n miles:** 600 at 25 kt
Complement: 13
Guns: 1 — 12.7 mm MG.
Radars: Surface search: 2 Furuno; I-band.

Comment: Built by Lung Teh Shipyard, Taiwan from March 1996. First six delivered in 1997 and following seven in 2001. GRP hulls with some Kevlar protection. Can carry a 6.5 m RIB.

PP 6006 *6/2008*, Taiwan Coast Guard* / 1353383

16 COASTAL PATROL CRAFT (WPB)

PP 3516–3522 PP 3525 PP 3527 PP 3530–3531 PP 3535–3539

Displacement, tons: 56 full load
Dimensions, feet (metres): 68.9 × 16.4 × 4.9 *(21.0 × 5.0 × 1.5)*
Main machinery: 2 MAN 12V183 diesels; 2,300 hp(m) *(1.7 MW)*; 2 shafts
Speed, knots: 302. **Range, n miles:** 400 at 22 kt
Complement: 8
Guns: 1 — 12.7 mm MG.
Radars: To be announced.

PP 3537 *6/2008*, Taiwan Coast Guard* / 1353385

9 COASTAL PATROL CRAFT (WPB)

PP 5033 PP 5035 PP 5037–5039 PP 5050–5053

Displacement, tons: 52 full load
Dimensions, feet (metres): 86.6 × 20.3 × 3.6 *(26.4 × 6.2 × 1.1)*
Main machinery: 2 MAN 2842LE 410 diesels; 4,400 hp(m) *(3.3 MW)*; 4 waterjets
Speed, knots: 37
Range, n miles: 600 at 22 kt
Complement: 17
Guns: 1 — 12.7 mm MG.
Radars: To be announced.

PP 5050 *6/2008*, Taiwan Coast Guard* / 1353384

3 COASTAL RESCUE CRAFT (AVR)

RB 01–03

Displacement, tons: 43 full load
Dimensions, feet (metres): 62.3 × 18.4 × 3.9 *(19.0 × 5.6 × 1.2)*
Main machinery: 2 MAN D2482 LE406 diesels; 1,400 hp(m) *(1.0 MW)*; 2 shafts
Speed, knots: 25
Range, n miles: 260 at 18 kt
Complement: 6
Radars: Surface search/navigation: 2 Furuno; I-band.

Comment: Self-righting built by Lung Teh Shipyard, Taiwan and delivered in 2002. Equipped with fire-fighting and towing capabilities.

RB 01 *6/2008*, Taiwan Coast Guard* / 1353388

14 COASTAL PATROL CRAFT

PP 3002–3003 PP 3005–3009 PP 3011–3012 PP 3015–3019

Displacement, tons: 29 full load
Dimensions, feet (metres): 65.6 × 15.7 × 6.5 *(20.0 × 4.8 × 2.0)*
Main machinery: 3 MAN 2842LE 402 diesels; 3,300 hp(m) *(2.5 MW)*; 3 shafts
Speed, knots: 45. **Range, n miles:** 600 at 33 kt
Complement: 8
Guns: 1 — 12.7 mm MG.
Radars: To be announced.

PP 3007 *6/2008*, Taiwan Coast Guard* / 1353386

47 INSHORE PATROL CRAFT (WPBR)

PP 2001 PP 2005–2010 PP 2021–2023 PP 2035–2038 PP 2055–2056 PP 2065–2067
PP 2003 PP 2012–2019 PP 2025–2033 PP 2050–2053 PP 2058–2063

Displacement, tons: 21 full load
Dimensions, feet (metres): 48.4 × 12.5 × 6.5 *(14.7 × 3.8 × 2.0)*
Main machinery: 2 MAN 2840LE401 diesels; 1,640 hp(m) *(1.2 MW)*; 2 shafts
Speed, knots: 35. **Range, n miles:** 250 at 26 kt
Complement: 6
Guns: 1 — 12.7 mm MG.
Radars: To be announced.

PP 2029 *6/2008*, Taiwan Coast Guard* / 1353387

CUSTOMS

4 HAI CHENG CLASS (COASTAL PATROL CRAFT) (WPB)

HAI CHENG HAI EN HAI LIANG HAI CHING

Displacement, tons: 147 full load
Dimensions, feet (metres): 100 × 22.3 × 11.6 *(30.5 × 6.8 × 3.6)*
Main machinery: 2 MTU diesels; 6,000 hp(m) *(4.4 MW)*; 2 shafts
Speed, knots: 30
Complement: 8
Guns: 2 — 9 mm T75.
Radars: Surface search: Decca; I-band.

Comment: Transferred to Customs on 26 December 2000.

HAI CHENG CLASS *12/2000, Taiwan Customs* / 0114556

1 YUN HSING CLASS (COASTAL PATROL CRAFT) (ABU)

YUN HSING

Displacement, tons: 964 full load
Dimensions, feet (metres): 213.3 × 32.8 × 9.5 *(65 × 10 × 2.9)*
Main machinery: 2 MAN 12V 25/30 diesels; 7,183 hp(m) *(5.28 MW)*; 2 shafts
Speed, knots: 18
Complement: 67
Guns: 2—12.7 mm MGs.
Radars: Surface search: JRC; I-band.

Comment: Built by China SB Corporation and delivered 28 December 1987. Operated by Customs as a light-house tender.

YUN HSING *1/2000, C Chung* / 0106606

4 HAI YING CLASS (COASTAL PATROL CRAFT) (WPB)

HAI YING **HAI TUNG** **HAI KO** **HAI TA**

Displacement, tons: 99.43 full load
Dimensions, feet (metres): 82.8 × 19.0 × 10.7 *(25.25 × 5.8 × 3.3)*
Main machinery: 2 Deutz MWM TBD 620 V12 diesels; 4,314 bhp *(2,646 kW)*; 2 shafts
Speed, knots: 32.6
Complement: 7
Guns: 2—9 mm T75.
Radars: Surface search: Furuno; I-band.

Comment: Transferred to Customs on 28 December 2000.

HAI YING CLASS *12/2000, Taiwan Customs* / 0114555

Tanzania

Country Overview

The United Republic of Tanzania was formed by the federation of the former British protectorates of Tanganyika and Zanzibar in 1964. It also includes Pemba, Mafia and other offshore islands. Situated in south-eastern Africa, it has a total area of 364,900 square miles and is bordered to the north by Uganda and Kenya, to the west by Rwanda, Burundi, Democratic Republic of Congo and Zambia and to the south by Mozambique and Malawi. It has a 767 n mile coastline with the Indian Ocean. The country also includes parts of Lake Tanganyika, Lake Victoria and Lake Malawi. Dodoma is the capital while the former capital, Dar es Salaam, is the largest city and principal port. Territorial seas (12 n miles) are claimed. A 200 n mile EEZ has also been claimed but the limits are not fully defined by boundary agreements.

Headquarters Appointments

Chief of Naval Operations:
Brigadier General Said Omar

General

The Tanzanian People's Defence Force includes the Army, Air Defence Command and a naval wing.
There is a small Coastguard Service (KMKM), based on Zanzibar, which uses small boats for anti-smuggling patrols.

Personnel

(a) 2009: 1,050 (including Zanzibar)
(b) Voluntary service

Coast Defence

85 mm mobile gun battery.

Bases

Dar Es Salaam, Zanzibar, Mtwara. Kigoma (Lake Tanganyika) and Mwanza (Lake Victoria).

PATROL FORCES

Notes: The Police have four Yulin class patrol boats which are probably non-operational.

2 SHANGHAI II CLASS (FAST ATTACK CRAFT—GUN) (PB)

MZIZI P 67 **MZIA** P 68

Displacement, tons: 134 full load
Dimensions, feet (metres): 127.3 × 17.7 × 5.6 *(38.8 × 5.4 × 1.7)*
Main machinery: 2 Type L12-180 diesels; 2,400 hp(m) *(1.76 MW)* (forward); 2 Type 12-D-6 diesels; 1,820 hp(m) *(1.34 MW)* (aft); 4 shafts
Speed, knots: 30. **Range, n miles:** 700 at 16.5 kt
Complement: 38
Guns: 4—37 mm/63 (2 twin). 4—25 mm/80 (2 twin).
Radars: Surface search: Skin Head; E/F-band.

Comment: Two transferred from China in June 1992. Based at Dar Es Salaam.

MZIZI *11/2005, Rob Cabo* / 1151073

2 HUCHUAN CLASS (FAST ATTACK CRAFT—TORPEDO) (PTK)

P 43–44

Displacement, tons: 39 standard; 45.8 full load
Dimensions, feet (metres): 71.5 × 20.7 oa × 11.8 (hullborne) *(21.8 × 6.3 × 3.6)*
Main machinery: 3 Type M 50 diesels; 3,300 hp(m) *(2.4 MW)* sustained; 3 shafts
Speed, knots: 50. **Range, n miles:** 500 at 30 kt
Complement: 16
Guns: 4—14.5 mm (2 twin) MGs.
Torpedoes: 2—21 in *(533 mm)* tubes.
Radars: Surface search: Skin Head; E/F-band.

Comment: Four transferred from the People's Republic of China 1975. After a major effort in 1992, were all operational and reported to be in good condition but by 1998 two had been laid up. Present operational status is unclear but one at least appears to have had torpedo tubes removed. Based at Dar Es Salaam.

HUCHUAN *6/2003* / 0587794

2 PROTECTOR CLASS (PATROL CRAFT) (PB)

NGUNGURI (ex-*Vincent*) P 19 **MAMBA** (ex-*Vigilant*) P 20

Displacement, tons: 100 full load
Dimensions, feet (metres): 84.3 × 20.3 × 5.6 *(25.7 × 6.2 × 1.7)*
Main machinery: 2 Paxman diesels; 2,880 hp *(2.15 MW)*; 2 shafts. 1 Perkins diesel; 200 hp *(150 kW)*; 1 waterjet
Speed, knots: 25
Complement: 4
Radars: Navigation: 2 Decca; I-band.

Comment: Both built for UK Customs by FBM Marine in 1998 (ex-*Vigilant*) and 1993 (ex-*Vincent*). Subsequently sold to Damen Shipyards, Netherlands, in September 2004. Following refit, entered Tanzanian service in 2005. Based at Dar Es Salaam.

NGUNGURI *11/2005, Rob Cabo* / 1151081

2 VOSPER THORNYCROFT 75 ft TYPE (COASTAL PATROL CRAFT) (PB)

Displacement, tons: 70 full load
Dimensions, feet (metres): 75 × 19.5 × 8 *(22.9 × 6 × 2.4)*
Main machinery: 2 Caterpillar D 348 diesels; 1,450 hp *(1.08 MW)* sustained; 2 shafts
Speed, knots: 24.5. **Range, n miles:** 800 at 20 kt
Complement: 11
Guns: 2 Oerlikon 20 mm GAM-BO1.
Radars: Surface search: Furuno; I-band.

Comment: First pair delivered 6 July 1973, second pair 1974. Used for anti-smuggling patrols off Zanzibar. Two still operational.

VOSPER 75 ft (Omani colours) *1984, N Overington* / 0506066

AUXILIARIES

2 YUCH'IN (TYPE 069) CLASS (LCU)

PONO L 08 **KIBUA** L 09

Displacement, tons: 85 full load
Dimensions, feet (metres): 81.2 × 17.1 × 4.3 *(24.8 × 5.2 × 1.3)*
Main machinery: 2 diesels; 600 hp(m) *(441 kW)*; 2 shafts
Speed, knots: 12. **Range, n miles:** 450 at 11.5 kt
Complement: 12
Military lift: 46 tons
Guns: 4 — 14.5 mm (2 twin) MGs.
Radars: Navigation: Fuji; I-band.

Comment: Transferred from China in 1995 probably to replace the Police Yuchai transport craft. Based at Dar-es-Salaam. *Pono* reported to be operational.

PONO *1/2001* / 0109946

Thailand

Country Overview

The Kingdom of Thailand (formerly Siam) is a constitutional monarchy in South East Asia. With an area of 198,114 square miles, it is bordered to the west by Burma, to the east by Laos and Cambodia and to the south by Malaysia. It has a 1,739 n mile coastline with the Gulf of Thailand and with the Andaman Sea. The capital, largest city and principal port (which also serves neighbouring Laos) is Bangkok. Territorial seas (12 n miles). An EEZ (200 n miles) is claimed and the limits have been partly defined by boundary agreements.

Headquarters Appointments

Commander-in-Chief of the Navy:
Admiral Khamthorn Pumhiran
Deputy Commander-in-Chief:
Admiral Somded Tongpiam
Assistant Commander-in-Chief:
Admiral Nibhon Chaksudul
Chief of Staff:
Admiral Rapol Khamklai
Deputy Chiefs of Staff:
Vice Admiral Yuttana Phagpolngam
Vice Admiral Weerapol Kitsombat

Senior Appointments

Commander-in-Chief, Fleet:
Admiral Suppakorn Burana-Dilok
Deputy Commanders-in-Chief, Fleet:
Vice Admiral Sommart Wimuktanont
Vice Admiral Piti Uttamot
Chief of Staff, Fleet:
Vice Admiral Sirichai Kanistkul

Diplomatic Representation

Naval Attaché in London:
Captain Chorchat Gra-tes
Naval Attaché in Washington:
Captain Bhichate Tanasate
Naval Attaché in Paris:
Captain Chaiyanan Nuntawit
Naval Attaché in Canberra:
Captain Adoong Pan-lam
Naval Attaché in Madrid:
Captain Thanee Phudpad

Diplomatic Representation *— continued*

Naval Attaché in New Delhi:
Captain Duesdee Sangkhapreecha
Naval Attaché in Singapore:
Captain Suteepong Kaewtab
Naval Attaché in Kuala Lumpur:
Captain Aran Namphol
Naval Attaché in Beijing:
Captain Bhanu Boonyaviroj
Naval Attaché in Rome:
Captain Phongthep Nuethep
Naval Attaché in Manila:
Captain Wilers Smabut
Naval Attaché in Tokyo:
Captain Sambhand Sundra-Krud
Naval Attaché in Yangon:
Captain Choomsak Nakwijit
Naval Attaché in Hanoi:
Captain Wipaks Noichinda
Naval Attaché in Phnom Penh:
Captain Nopphorn Vudhironarit

Personnel

(a) 2009: Navy, 74,000 (including 2,000 Naval Air Arm, 11,000 Marines and Coastal Defense Command)
(b) 2 years' national service (28,000 conscripts)

Organisation

First naval area command (Upper Thai Gulf)
Second naval command (Lower Thai Gulf)
Third naval command (Andaman Sea)

Bases

Bangkok, Sattahip, Songkhla, Phang-Nga (west coast)

Naval Aviation

First air wing (U-Tapao)
Second air wing (Songkhla)
101 Sqdn MPA/ASW
102 Sqdn MPA/ASuW
103 Sqdn Utility
104 Sqdn Maritime Strike
105 Sqdn Matador
201 Sqdn Central Patrol
202 Bell Helos
203 Sikorsky Helos

Prefix to Ships' Names

HTMS

Strength of the Fleet

Type	*Active*	*Building (Projected)*
Aircraft Carrier	1	–
Frigates	8	–
Corvettes	7	–
Fast Attack Craft (Missile)	6	–
Fast Attack Craft (Gun)	3	–
Offshore Patrol Craft	9	2
Coastal Patrol Craft	52	–
MCM Support Ship	1	–
Minehunters	4	–
Coastal Minesweepers	2	–
MSBs	12	–
LPDs	–	1
LSTs	6	–
Hovercraft	3	–
Survey Vessels	5	–
Replenishment Ship	1	–
MCMV Depot Ship	1	–
Tankers/Transports	8	–
Training Ships	3	(1)

Coast Defence

Coastal Defence Command was rapidly expanded to the 1992 two Division level after the government charged the RTN with the responsibility of defending the entire Eastern Seaboard. Ships and aircraft are rotated monthly from the Navy. Equipment includes 10 batteries of truck-mounted Exocet MM 40, 155 and 130 mm guns for coastal defence, 76, 40, 37, 20 mm guns and PL-9B SAM for air defence.

Marine Police

Acts as a Coast Guard in inshore waters with some 60 armed patrol craft and another 65 equipped with small arms only.

PENNANT LIST

Aircraft Carriers

911 Chakri Naruebet

Frigates

421 Naresuan
422 Taksin
433 Makut Rajakumarn
455 Chao Phraya
456 Bangpakong
457 Kraburi
458 Saiburi
461 Phuttha Yotfa Chulalok
462 Phuttha Loetla Naphalai

Corvettes

431 Tapi
432 Khirirat
441 Rattanakosin
442 Sukothai
511 Pattani
512 Narathiwat
531 Khamronsin
532 Thayanchon
533 Longlom

Patrol Forces

311 Prabparapak
312 Hanhak Sattru
313 Suphairin
321 Ratcharit
322 Witthayakhom
323 Udomdet
331 Chon Buri
332 Songkhla
333 Phuket
521 Sattahip
522 Klongyai
523 Takbai
524 Kantang
525 Thepha
526 Taimuang
541 Hua Hin
542 Klaeng
543 Si Racha

Mine Warfare Forces

612 Bangkeo
613 Donchedi
621 Thalang
631 Bang Rachan
632 Nongsarai
633 Lat Ya
634 Tha Din Daeng

Amphibious Forces

712 Chang
713 Pangan
714 Lanta
715 Prathong
721 Sichang
722 Surin
741 Prab
742 Satakut
761 Mataphon
762 Rawi
763 Adang
764 Phetra
765 Kolam
766 Talibong
771 Thong Kaeo
772 Thong Lang
773 Wang Nok
774 Wang Nai
781 Man Nok
782 Man Klang
783 Man Nai

Training Ships

413 Pin Klao
611 Phosamton

Survey and Research Ships

811 Chanthara
812 Suk

Auxiliaries

821 Suriya
831 Chula
832 Samui
833 Prong
834 Proet
835 Samed
841 Chuang
842 Chik
851 Klueng Badaan
852 Marn Vichai
853 Rin
854 Rang
855 Samaesan
856 Raet
861 Kled Keo
871 Similan

SUBMARINES

Notes: Acquisition of a submarine force remains a high priority but funding difficulties continue to frustrate plans.

AIRCRAFT CARRIERS

1 CHAKRI NARUEBET CLASS (CVM)

Name	*No*	*Builders*	*Laid down*	*Launched*	*Commissioned*
CHAKRI NARUEBET	911	Bazán, Ferrol	12 July 1994	20 Jan 1996	27 Mar 1997

Displacement, tons: 11,485 full load
Dimensions, feet (metres): 599.1 oa; 538.4 wl × 100.1 oa; 73.8 wl × 20.3 *(182.6; 164.1 × 30.5; 22.5 × 6.2)*
Flight deck, feet (metres): 572.8 × 90.2 *(174.6 × 27.5)*
Main machinery: CODOG; 2 GE LM 2500 gas turbines; 44,250 hp *(33 MW)* sustained; 2 MTU 16V 1163 TB83 diesels; 11,780 hp(m) *(8.67 MW)*; 2 shafts; LIPS cp props
Speed, knots: 26; 16 (diesels). **Range, n miles**: 10,000 at 12 kt
Complement: 455 (62 officers) plus 146 aircrew plus 4 (Royal family)

Missiles: SAM: 1 Mk 41 LCHR 8 cell VLS launcher (fitted for but not with) ❶.
3 Matra Sadral sextuple launchers for Mistral ❷; IR homing to 4 km *(2.2 n miles)*; warhead 3 kg.
Guns: 2—30 mm. To be fitted.
Combat data systems: Tritan derivative with Unisys UYK-3 and 20 computers.
Radars: Air search: Hughes SPS-52C ❸; E/F-band.
Surface search: SPS-64 ❹; I-band. To be fitted.
Fire control: to be fitted.
Navigation: Kelvin Hughes; I-band.
Aircraft control: Kelvin Hughes; E/F-band.
Tacan: URN 25.

Fixed-wing aircraft: 6 AV-8S Matador (Harrier).
Helicopters: 6 S-70B-7 Seahawk; Chinook capable.

Programmes: An initial contract for a 7,800 ton vessel with Bremer Vulcan was cancelled on 22 July 1991 and replaced on 27 March 1992 with a government to government contract for a larger ship to be built by Bazán. Fabrication started in October 1993. Sea trials conducted from November 1996 to January 1997 followed by an aviation work-up at Rota from April 1997. The ship arrived in Thailand on 10 August 1997.
Structure: Similar to Spanish *Príncipe de Asturias*. 12° ski jump and two 20 ton aircraft lifts. Provision made to fit a Mk 41 VLS launcher, a surface search radar, EW systems, a hull mounted sonar and CIWS. Matra Sadral fitted in 2001. Hangar can take up 10 Sea Harrier or Seahawk aircraft.
Operational: Main tasks are SAR co-ordination and EEZ surveillance. Secondary role is air support for all maritime operations. Due to funding shortages, the ship rarely goes to sea and fixed-wing flying has been conducted from shore bases.

CHAKRI NARUEBET *(Scale 1 : 1,500), Ian Sturton* / 0080799

CHAKRI NARUEBET *1/2004, Thai Navy League* / 0589816

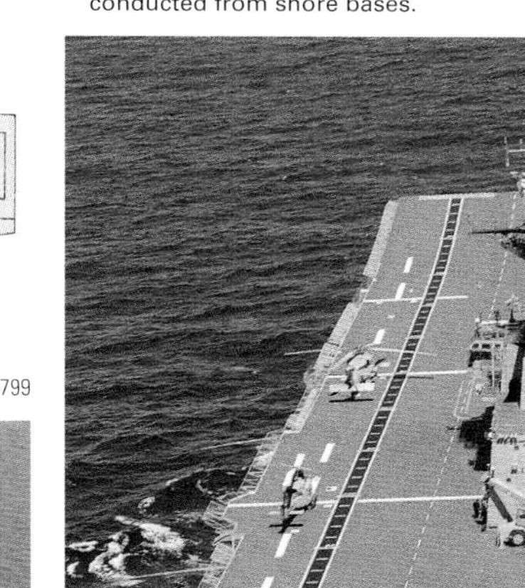

CHAKRI NARUEBET *5/1997, S G Gaya* / 0019250

CHAKRI NARUEBET *1/2004, Thai Navy League* / 0589817

FRIGATES

Notes: It was announced on 22 July 2003 that two frigates were to be procured from the UK. These were likely to be based on the design of those acquired by the Royal Malaysian Navy. This programme is likely to have been superseded by plans to acquire offshore patrol vessels for which UK shipbuilder BVT Surface Fleet is reported to be a leading, but not the only, contender.

2 NARESUAN CLASS (TYPE 25T) (FFGHM)

Name	*No*	*Builders*	*Laid down*	*Launched*	*Commissioned*
NARESUAN	421 (ex-621)	Zhonghua SY, Shanghai	Feb 1992	24 July 1993	15 Dec 1994
TAKSIN	422 (ex-622)	Zhonghua SY, Shanghai	Nov 1992	14 May 1994	28 Sep 1995

Displacement, tons: 2,500 standard; 2,980 full load
Dimensions, feet (metres): 393.7 × 42.7 × 12.5 *(120 × 13 × 3.8)*
Main machinery: CODOG; 2 GE LM 2500 gas turbines; 44,250 hp *(33 MW)* sustained; 2 MTU 20 V 1163 TB83 diesels; 11,780 hp(m) *(8.67 MW)* sustained; 2 shafts; LIPS cp props
Speed, knots: 32
Range, n miles: 4,000 at 18 kt
Complement: 150

Missiles: SSM: 8 McDonnell Douglas Harpoon (2 quad) launchers ❶; active radar homing to 130 km *(70 n miles)* at 0.9 Mach; warhead 227 kg.
SAM: Mk 41 LCHR 8 cell VLS launcher ❷ Sea Sparrow RIM-7M; semi-active radar homing to 16 km *(8.5 n miles)* at 2.5 Mach; warhead 38 kg (fitted for but not with).
Guns: 1 FMC 5 in *(127 mm)*/54 Mk 45 Mod 2 ❸; 20 rds/min to 23 km *(12.6 n miles)*; weight of shell 32 kg.
4 China 37 mm/76 (2 twin) H/PJ 76 A ❹; 180 rds/min to 8.5 km *(4.6 n miles)* anti-aircraft; weight of shell 1.42 kg.
Torpedoes: 6—324 mm Mk 32 Mod 5 (2 triple) tubes ❺. Honeywell Mk 46; active/passive homing to 11 km *(5.9 n miles)* at 40 kt; warhead 44 kg.
Countermeasures: Decoys: 4 China Type 945 GPJ 26-barrelled launchers ❻; chaff and IR.
ESM/ECM: Elettronica Newton Beta EW System; intercept and jammer.
Weapons control: 1 JM-83H Optical Director ❼.
Radars: Air search: Signaal LW08 ❽; D-band.
Surface search: China Type 360 ❾; E/F-band.
Navigation: 2 Raytheon SPS-64(V)5; I-band.
Fire control: 2 Signaal STIR ❿; I/J/K-band (for SSM and 127 mm). After one to be fitted.
China 374 G ⓫ (for 37 mm).
Sonars: China SJD-7; hull-mounted; active search and attack; medium frequency.

Helicopters: 1 Super Lynx ⓬ in due course or 1 Sikorsky S-70B-7 Seahawk.

Programmes: Contract signed 21 September 1989 for construction of two ships by the China State SB Corporation (CSSC) with delivery in 1994. US and European weapon systems were fitted as funds became available. The first ship sailed for Bangkok without most weapon systems in January 1995 with the second following in October 1995.
Structure: Jointly designed by the Royal Thai Navy and China State Shipbuilding Corporation (CSSC). This is a design incorporating much Western machinery and equipment and provides enhanced capabilities by comparison with the four Type 053 class. The anti-aircraft guns are Breda 40 mm types with 37 mm ammunition and they are controlled by a Chinese RTN-20 Dardo tracker.
Operational: *Naresuan* acted as one of the escorts for the aircraft carrier during her aviation work-up in Spanish waters in 1997.

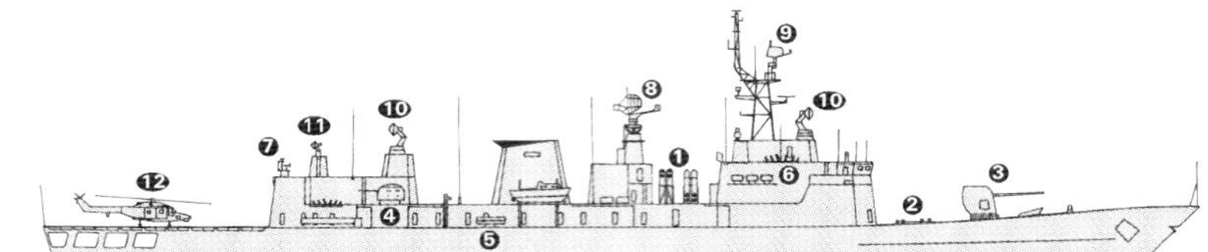

NARESUAN ***(Scale 1 : 1,200), Ian Sturton*** / 0543398

TAKSIN ***8/2005, Chris Sattler*** / 1153917

TAKSIN ***8/2005, Chris Sattler*** / 1153916

NARESUAN ***10/2008*, Michael Nitz*** / 1353391

4 CHAO PHRAYA CLASS (TYPES 053 HT AND 053 HT (H)) (FFG/FFGH)

Name	*No*	*Builders*	*Laid down*	*Launched*	*Commissioned*
CHAO PHRAYA	455	Hudong SY, Shanghai	1989	24 June 1990	5 Apr 1991
BANGPAKONG	456	Hudong SY, Shanghai	1989	25 July 1990	20 July 1991
KRABURI	457	Hudong SY, Shanghai	1990	28 Dec 1990	16 Jan 1992
SAIBURI	458	Hudong SY, Shanghai	1990	27 Aug 1991	4 Aug 1992

Displacement, tons: 1,676 standard; 1,924 full load
Dimensions, feet (metres): 338.5 × 37.1 × 10.2 *(103.2 × 11.3 × 3.1)*
Main machinery: 4 MTU 20V 1163 TB83 diesels; 29,440 hp(m) *(21.6 MW)* sustained; 2 shafts; LIPS cp props
Speed, knots: 30
Range, n miles: 3,500 at 18 kt
Complement: 168 (22 officers)

Missiles: SSM: 8 Ying Ji (Eagle Strike) (C-801) ❶; active radar/IR homing to 85 km *(45.9 n miles)* at 0.9 Mach; warhead 165 kg; sea-skimmer. This is the extended range version.
SAM: 1 HQ-61 launcher for PL-9 or Matra Sadral for Mistral to be fitted.
Guns: 2 (457 and 458) or 4 China 100 mm/56 (1 or 2 twin) ❷; 25 rds/min to 22 km *(12 n miles)*; weight of shell 15.9 kg.
8 China 37 mm/76 (4 twin) H/PJ 76 A ❸; 180 rds/min to 8.5 km *(4.6 n miles)* anti-aircraft; weight of shell 1.42 kg.
A/S mortars: 2 RBU 1200 (China Type 86) 5-tubed fixed launchers ❹; range 1,200 m.
Depth charges: 2 BMB racks.
Countermeasures: Decoys: 2 China Type 945 GPJ 26-barrelled chaff launchers.
ESM: China Type 923(1); intercept.
ECM: China Type 981(3); jammer.
Combat data systems: China Type ZKJ-3 or STN Atlas mini COSYS action data automation being fitted.
Radars: Air/surface search: China Type 354 Eye Shield ❺; G-band.
Surface search/fire control: China Type 352C Square Tie ❻; I-band (for SSM).
Fire control: China Type 343 Sun Visor ❼; I-band (for 100 mm).
China Type 341 Rice Lamp ❽; I-band (for 37 mm).
Navigation: Racal Decca 1290 A/D ARPA and Anritsu RA 71CA ❾; I-band.
IFF: Type 651.
Sonars: China Type SJD-5A; hull-mounted; active search and attack; medium frequency.

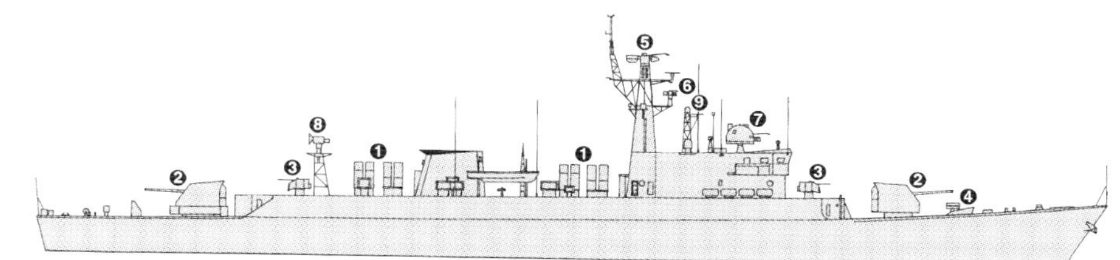

CHAO PHRAYA *(Scale 1 : 900), Ian Sturton* / 0080802

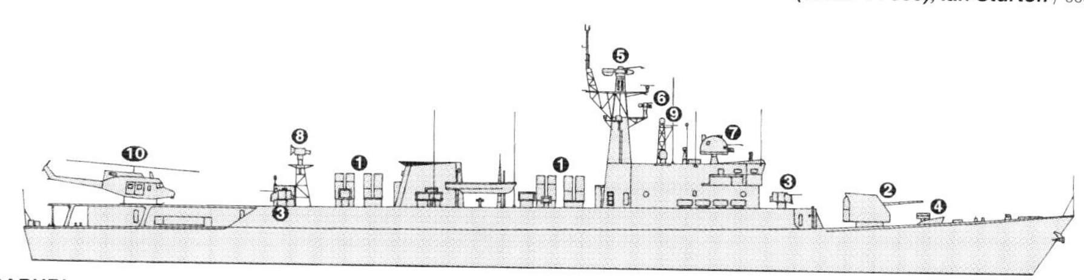

KRABURI *(Scale 1 : 900), Ian Sturton* / 0080803

Helicopters: Platform for 1 Bell 212 (457 and 458) ❿.

Programmes: Contract signed 18 July 1988 for four modified Jianghu class ships to be built by the China State SB Corporation (CSSC).
Modernisation: A mini COSYS system was acquired for two of the class in 1999.
Structure: Thailand would have preferred only the hulls but China insisted on full armament. The first two ships are the Type III variant with 100 mm guns, fore and aft, and the second two are a variation with a helicopter platform replacing the after 100 mm gun. German communication equipment fitted. The EW fit is Italian designed.
Operational: On arrival in Thailand each ship was docked to make good poor shipbuilding standards and improve damage control capabilities. The ships are mostly used for rotating monthly to the Coast Guard, and for training, although *Kraburi* was part of the escort force for the aircraft carrier in Spanish waters in 1997. *Kraburi* damaged by the tsunami on 26 December 2004 but had been restored to operational service by February 2005.

BANGPAKONG *10/2002, John Mortimer* / 0529998

SAIBURI *6/2008*, Ships of the World* / 1353389

2 KNOX CLASS (FFGHM)

Name	*No*	*Builders*	*Laid down*	*Launched*	*Commissioned*
PHUTTHA YOTFA CHULALOK (ex-*Truett*)	461 (ex-FF 1095)	Avondale Shipyards	27 Apr 1972	3 Feb 1973	1 June 1974
PHUTTHA LOETLA NAPHALAI (ex-*Ouellet*)	462 (ex-FF 1077)	Avondale Shipyards	15 Jan 1969	17 Jan 1970	12 Dec 1970

Displacement, tons: 3,011 standard; 4,260 full load
Dimensions, feet (metres): 439.6 × 46.8 × 15; 24.8 (sonar) *(134 × 14.3 × 4.6; 7.8)*
Main machinery: 2 Combustion Engineering/Babcock & Wilcox boilers; 1,200 psi *(84.4 kg/cm²)*; 950°F *(510°C)*; 1 turbine; 35,000 hp *(26 MW)*; 1 shaft
Speed, knots: 27. **Range, n miles:** 4,000 at 22 kt on 1 boiler
Complement: 288 (17 officers)

Missiles: SSM: 8 McDonnell Douglas Harpoon; active radar homing to 130 km *(70 n miles)* at 0.9 Mach; warhead 227 kg.
A/S: Honeywell ASROC Mk 16 octuple launcher with reload system (has 2 starboard cells modified to fire Harpoon) ❶; inertial guidance to 1.6-10 km *(1-5.4 n miles)*; payload Mk 46.
Guns: 1 FMC 5 in *(127 mm)*/54 Mk 42 Mod 9 ❷; 20–40 rds/min to 24 km *(13 n miles)* anti-surface; 14 km *(7.7 n miles)* anti-aircraft; weight of shell 32 kg.
1 General Electric/General Dynamics 20 mm/76 6-barrelled Mk 15 Vulcan Phalanx ❸; 3,000 rds/min combined to 1.5 km.
Torpedoes: 4—324 mm Mk 32 (2 twin) fixed tubes ❹. 22 Honeywell Mk 46; anti-submarine; active/passive homing to 11 km *(5.9 n miles)* at 40 kt; warhead 44 kg.
Countermeasures: Decoys: 2 Loral Hycor SRBOC 6-barrelled fixed Mk 36 ❺; IR flares and chaff to 4 km *(2.2 n miles)*. T Mk-6 Fanfare/SLQ-25 Nixie; torpedo decoy. Prairie Masker hull and blade rate noise suppression.
ESM/ECM: SLQ-32(V)2 ❻; radar warning. Sidekick modification adds jammer and deception system.
Combat data systems: Link 14 receive only.
Weapons control: SWG-1A Harpoon LCS. Mk 68 GFCS. Mk 114 ASW FCS. Mk 1 target designation system. MMS target acquisition sight (for mines, small craft and low-flying aircraft).
Radars: Air search: Lockheed SPS-40B ❼; B-band; range 320 km *(175 n miles)*.
Surface search: Raytheon SPS-10 or Norden SPS-67 ❽; G-band.
Navigation: Marconi LN66; I-band.
Fire control: Western Electric SPG-53A/D/F ❾; I/J-band.
Tacan: SRN 15. IFF: UPX-12.
Sonars: EDO/General Electric SQS-26CX; bow-mounted; active search and attack; medium frequency.
EDO SQR-18(V) TACTASS; passive; low frequency.

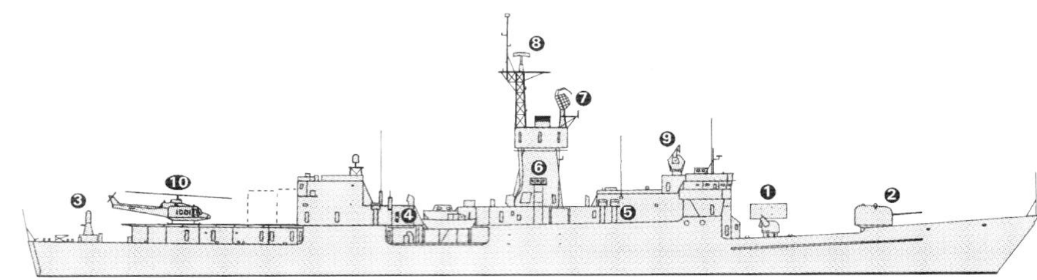

PHUTTHA YOTFA CHULALOK — ***(Scale 1 : 1,200), Ian Sturton*** / 0543397

PHUTTHA LOETLA NAPHALAI — ***1/2001, Thai Navy League*** / 0105841

Helicopters: 1 Bell 212 ❿.

Programmes: The first ship transferred on five year lease from the USA on 30 July 1994. This was renewed by grant in 1999. The second transferred on lease 27 November 1996 and arrived in Thailand in November 1998.

Structure: Four Mk 32 torpedo tubes are fixed in the midships structure, two to a side, angled out at 45°. The arrangement provides improved loading capability over exposed triple Mk 32 torpedo tubes. A 4,000 lb lightweight anchor is fitted on the port side and an 8,000 lb anchor fits into the after section of the sonar dome.

1 YARROW TYPE (FFH)

Name	*No*	*Builders*	*Laid down*	*Launched*	*Commissioned*
MAKUT RAJAKUMARN	433 (ex-7)	Yarrow Shipbuilders	11 Jan 1970	18 Nov 1971	7 May 1973

Displacement, tons: 1,650 standard; 1,900 full load
Dimensions, feet (metres): 320 × 36 × 18.1 *(97.6 × 11 × 5.5)*
Main machinery: CODOG; 1 RR Olympus TM3B gas turbine; 22,500 hp *(16.8 MW)* sustained; 1 Crossley-SEMT-Pielstick 12 PC2.2 V 400 diesel; 6,000 hp(m) *(4.4 MW)* sustained; 2 shafts
Speed, knots: 26 gas; 18 diesel
Range, n miles: 5,000 at 18 kt; 1,200 at 26 kt
Complement: 140 (16 officers)

Guns: 2 Vickers 4.5 in *(114 mm)*/55 Mk 8 ❶; 25 rds/min to 22 km *(12 n miles)* anti-surface; 6 km *(3.3 n miles)* anti-aircraft; weight of shell 21 kg.
2 Breda 40 mm/70 (twin) ❷; 300 rds/min to 12.5 km *(6.8 n miles)*; weight of shell 0.96 kg.
2 Oerlikon 20 mm.
Torpedoes: 6 Plessey PMW 49A tubes ❸ Mk 46; active/passive homing to 11 km *(5.9 n miles)* at 40 kt; warhead 44 kg.
Depth charges: 1 rack.
Countermeasures: Decoys: 2 Loral Mk 135 chaff launchers
ESM/ECM: Elettronica Newton ❹; intercept and jammer. WLR-1; radar warning.
Combat data systems: Signaal Sewaco TH.
Radars: Air/surface search: Signaal DA05 ❺; E/F-band; range 137 km *(75 n miles)* for 2 m² target.
Surface search: Signaal ZW06 ❻; I-band.

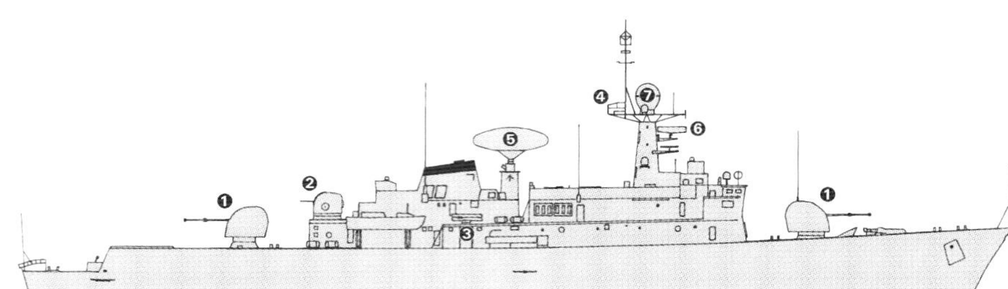

MAKUT RAJAKUMARN — ***(Scale 1 : 900), Ian Sturton*** / 1167964

Fire control: Signaal WM22/61 ❼; I/J-band; range 46 km *(25 n miles)*.
Navigation: Racal Decca; I-band.
Sonars: Atlas Elektronik DSQS-21C; hull-mounted; active search and attack; medium frequency.

Helicopters: A small helicopter can land when the Mortar Mk 10 well is closed.

Programmes: Ordered on 21 August 1969.
Modernisation: A severe fire in February 1984 resulted in extensive work including replacement of the Olympus gas turbine, a new ER control room and central electric switchboard. Further modifications included the removal of Seacat SAM system and the installation of new EW equipment in 1993. In 1997 two Bofors 40 mm were fitted on the old Seacat mounting, and torpedo tubes replaced the old Bofors abreast the funnel. The Limbo mortar mountings have been removed.
Operational: The ship is largely automated with a consequent saving in complement, and has been most successful in service. Has lost its Flagship role to one of the Chinese-built frigates and is employed on general duties rather than as a training ship as previously reported.

MAKUT RAJAKUMARN — ***2/2004, Bob Fildes*** / 0589813

CORVETTES

2 + (2) PATTANI CLASS (OFFSHORE PATROL VESSELS) (PBOH)

Name	*No*	*Builders*	*Laid down*	*Launched*	*Commissioned*
PATTANI	511	Hudong Shipyard, Shanghai	2003	19 Sep 2004	16 Dec 2005
NARATHIWAT	512	Hudong Shipyard, Shanghai	2004	Mar 2005	16 Apr 2006

Displacement, tons: 1,300; 1,440 full load
Dimensions, feet (metres): 313.3 × 38.0 × 10.2 *(95.5 × 11.6 × 3.1)*
Main machinery: 2 Ruston diesels; 15,660 hp *(11.7 MW)*; 2 shafts; cp props
Speed, knots: 25
Range, n miles: 3,500 at 15 kt
Complement: 78 (18 officers)

Guns: 1 OTO Melara 3 in *(76 mm)*/62 ❶; 85 rds/min to 16 km *(8.6 n miles)*. 2—20 mm.
Combat data systems: COSYS.
Weapons control: Optronic director combined with TMX.
Radars: Air/surface search: Alenia Marconi SPS 791 (RAN-30X/I) ❷; I-band.
Surface search ❸: To be announced.
Fire control: Oerlikon/Contraves TMX ❹; I/J-band.
Navigation: I-band.

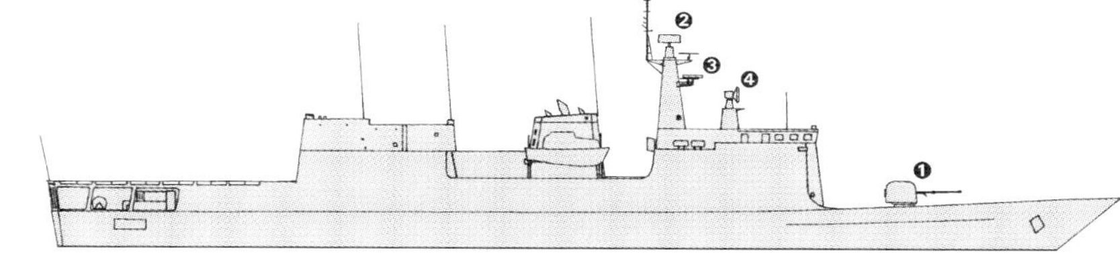

PATTANI ***(Scale 1 : 900), Ian Sturton*** / 1353390

Helicopters: Platform for one medium.

Programmes: The contract for two Offshore Patrol Vessels was signed with China Shipbuilding Trading Company on 20 December 2002. A further two vessels are projected.

Structure: Space and weight provision for the addition of eight SSM, CIWS (probably Matra Sadral) and ASW capabilities at a later date.
Operational: *Pattani* arrived at Sattahip on 16 December 2005. *Narathiwat* followed on 4 May 2006.

PATTANI ***10/2008*, Michael Nitz*** / 1353392

NARATHIWAT ***3/2007, Thai Navy League*** / 1353393

2 RATTANAKOSIN CLASS (FSGM)

Name	*No*	*Builders*	*Laid down*	*Launched*	*Commissioned*
RATTANAKOSIN	441 (ex-1)	Tacoma Boatbuilders, WA	6 Feb 1984	11 Mar 1986	26 Sep 1986
SUKHOTHAI	442 (ex-2)	Tacoma Boatbuilders, WA	26 Mar 1984	20 July 1986	10 June 1987

Displacement, tons: 960 full load
Dimensions, feet (metres): 252 × 31.5 × 8 *(76.8 × 9.6 × 2.4)*
Main machinery: 2 MTU 20V 1163TB83 diesels; 14,730 hp(m) *(10.83 MW)* sustained; 2 shafts; Kamewa cp props
Speed, knots: 26. **Range, n miles:** 3,000 at 16 kt
Complement: 87 (15 officers) plus Flag Staff

Missiles: SSM: 8 McDonnell Douglas Harpoon (2 quad) launchers ❶; active radar homing to 130 km *(70 n miles)* at 0.9 Mach; warhead 227 kg (84A) or 258 kg (84B/C).
SAM: Selenia Elsag Albatros octuple launcher ❷; 24 Aspide; semi-active radar homing to 13 km *(7 n miles)* at 2.5 Mach; height envelope 15-5,000 m *(49.2-16,405 ft)*; warhead 30 kg.
Guns: 1 OTO Melara 3 in *(76 mm)*/62 ❸; 60 rds/min to 16 km *(8.7 n miles)*; weight of shell 6 kg.
2 Breda 40 mm/70 (twin) ❹; 300 rds/min to 12.5 km *(6.8 n miles)*; weight of shell 0.96 kg.
2 Rheinmetall 20 mm ❺.
Torpedoes: 6—324 mm US Mk 32 (2 triple) tubes ❻. MUSL Stingray; active/passive homing to 11 km *(5.9 n miles)* at 45 kt; warhead 35 kg (shaped charge); depth to 750 m *(2,460 ft)*.
Countermeasures: Decoys: CSEE Dagaie 6- or 10-tubed trainable; IR flares and chaff; H- to J-band.
ESM: Elettronica; intercept.
Weapons control: Signaal Sewaco TH action data automation. Lirod 8 optronic director ❼.

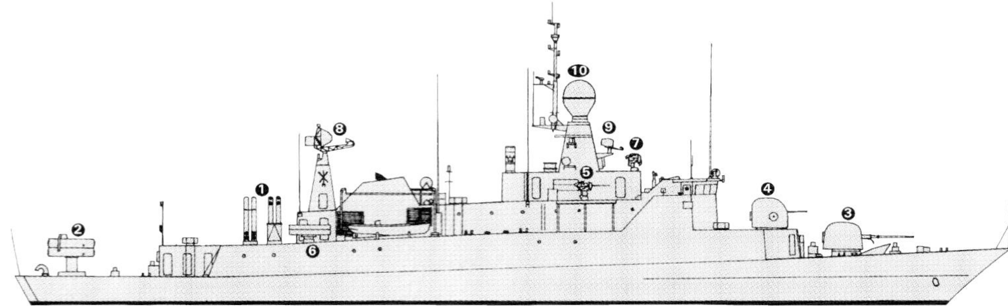

RATTANAKOSIN ***(Scale 1 : 600), Ian Sturton*** / 0506173

Radars: Air/surface search: Signaal DA05 ❽; E/F-band; range 137 km *(75 n miles)* for 2 m² target.
Surface search: Signaal ZW06 ❾; I-band.
Navigation: Decca 1226; I-band.
Fire control: Signaal WM25/41 ❿; I/J-band; range 46 km *(25 n miles)*.
Sonars: Atlas Elektronik DSQS-21C; hull-mounted; active search and attack; medium frequency.

Programmes: Contract signed with Tacoma on 9 May 1983. Intentions to build a third were overtaken by the Vosper corvettes.
Structure: There are some similarities with the missile corvettes built for Saudi Arabia five years earlier. Space for Phalanx aft of the Harpoon launchers, but there are no plans to fit.

SUKHOTHAI ***7/2008*, John Mortimer*** / 1353394

3 KHAMRONSIN CLASS (FS)

Name	*No*	*Builders*	*Laid down*	*Launched*	*Commissioned*
KHAMRONSIN	531 (ex-1)	Ital Thai Marine, Bangkok	15 Mar 1988	15 Aug 1989	29 July 1992
THAYANCHON	532 (ex-2)	Ital Thai Marine, Bangkok	20 Apr 1988	7 Dec 1989	5 Sep 1992
LONGLOM	533 (ex-3)	Bangkok Naval Dockyard	15 Mar 1988	8 Aug 1989	2 Oct 1992

Displacement, tons: 630 full load
Dimensions, feet (metres): 203.4 oa; 186 wl × 26.9 × 8.2 *(62; 56.7 × 8.2 × 2.5)*
Main machinery: 2 MTU 12V 1163 TB93; 9,980 hp(m) *(7.34 MW)* sustained; 2 Kamewa cp props
Speed, knots: 25. **Range, n miles:** 2,500 at 15 kt
Complement: 57 (6 officers)

Guns: 1 OTO Melara 76 mm/62 Mod 7 ❶; 60 rds/min to 16 km *(8.7 n miles)*; weight of shell 6 kg.
2 Breda 30 mm/70 (twin) ❷; 800 rds/min to 12.5 km *(6.8 n miles)*; weight of shell 0.37 kg.
2—12.7 mm MGs.
Torpedoes: 6 Plessey PMW 49A (2 triple) launchers ❸; MUSL Stingray; active/passive homing to 11 km *(5.9 n miles)* at 45 kt; warhead 35 kg shaped charge.
Combat data systems: Plessey Nautis P action data automation.
Weapons control: British Aerospace Sea Archer 1A Mod 2 optronic GFCS ❹
Radars: Air/surface search: Plessey AWS 4 ❺; E/F-band.
Navigation: Racal Decca 1226; I-band.

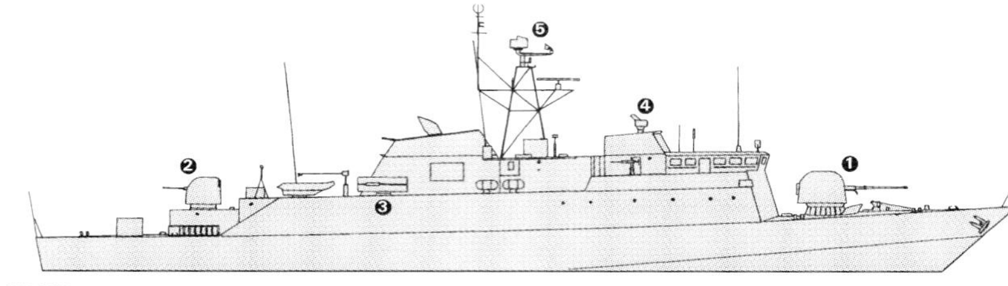

KHAMRONSIN ***(Scale 1 : 600), Ian Sturton*** / 0572649

Sonars: Atlas Elektronik DSQS-21C; hull-mounted; active search and attack; medium frequency.

Programmes: Contract signed on 29 September 1987 with Ital Thai Marine of Bangkok for the construction of two ASW corvettes and for technical assistance with a third to be built in Bangkok Naval Dockyard. A fourth of the class with a different superstructure and less armament was ordered by the Police in September 1989.
Structure: The vessels are based on a Vosper Thornycroft Province class 56 m design stretched by increasing the frame spacing along the whole length of the hull. Depth charge racks and mine rails may be added.

THAYANCHON ***12/2007, Michael Nitz*** / 1353395

2 TAPI (PF 103) CLASS (FS)

Name	*No*	*Builders*	*Laid down*	*Launched*	*Commissioned*
TAPI	431 (ex-5)	American SB Co, Toledo, OH	1 July 1970	17 Oct 1970	19 Nov 1971
KHIRIRAT	432 (ex-6)	Norfolk SB & DD Co	18 Feb 1972	2 June 1973	10 Aug 1974

Displacement, tons: 885 standard; 1,172 full load
Dimensions, feet (metres): 275 × 33 × 10; 14.1 (sonar) *(83.8 × 10 × 3; 4.3)*
Main machinery: 2 Fairbanks-Morse 38TD8-1/8-9 diesels; 5,250 hp *(3.9 MW)* sustained; 2 shafts
Speed, knots: 20
Range, n miles: 2,400 at 18 kt
Complement: 135 (15 officers)

Guns: 1 OTO Melara 3 in *(76 mm)*/62 compact ❶; 85 rds/min to 16 km *(8.7 n miles)* anti-surface; 12 km *(6.6 n miles)* anti-aircraft; weight of shell 6 kg.
1 Bofors 40 mm/70 ❷; 300 rds/min to 12.5 km *(6.8 n miles)*; weight of shell 0.96 kg.
2 Oerlikon 20 mm ❸. 2—12.7 mm MGs.
Torpedoes: 6—324 mm US Mk 32 (2 triple) tubes ❹. Honeywell Mk 46; anti-submarine; active/passive homing to 11 km *(5.9 n miles)* at 40 kt; warhead 44 kg.
Depth charges: 1 rack.
Combat data systems: Signaal Sewaco TH.
Radars: Air/surface search: Signaal LW04 ❺; D-band; range 137 km *(75 n miles)* for 2 m² target.
Surface search: Raytheon SPS-53E ❻; I-band.

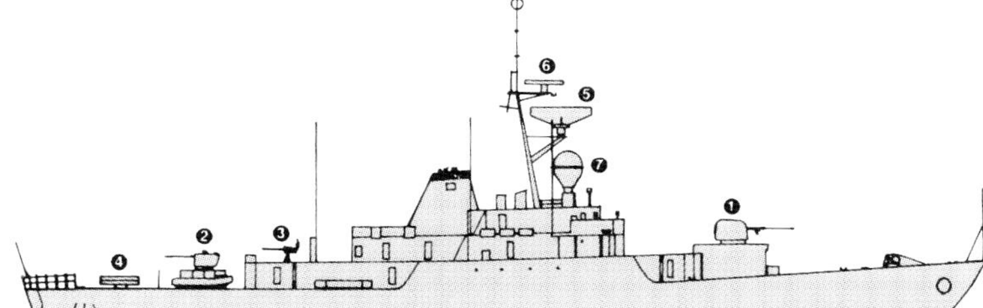

TAPI *(Scale 1 : 900), Ian Sturton* / 0506109

Fire control: Signaal WM22-61 ❼; I/J-band; range 46 km *(25 n miles)*.
IFF: UPX-23.
Sonars: Atlas Elektronik DSQS-21C; hull-mounted; active search and attack; medium frequency.

Programmes: *Tapi* was ordered on 27 June 1969. *Khirirat* was ordered on 25 June 1971.

Modernisation: *Tapi* completed 1983 and *Khirirat* in 1987. This included new gunnery and radars and a slight heightening of the funnel. Further modernisation in 1988–89 mainly to external and internal communications.
Structure: Of similar design to the Iranian ships of the Bayandor class.
Operational: Used for EEZ patrols.

TAPI *6/2001, Royal Thai Navy* / 0130171

SHIPBORNE AIRCRAFT

Numbers/Type: 4 Bell 214 ST.
Operational speed: 120 kt *(228 km/h)*.
Service ceiling: 13,200 ft *(4,025 m)*.
Range: 400 n miles *(740 km)*.
Role/Weapon systems: Procured in 1987 for maritime surveillance and utility roles.

BELL 214 *6/2004, Royal Thai Navy* / 1044195

Numbers/Type: 7/2 BAe/McDonnell Douglas AV-8A (Harrier)/TAV-8A (Harrier).
Operational speed: 640 kt *(1,186 km/h)*.
Service ceiling: 51,200 ft *(15,600 m)*.
Range: 800 n miles *(1,480 km)*.
Role/Weapon systems: AV-8S supplied via USA to Spain and transferred in 1996. Sensors: None. Weapons: Strike; two 30 mm Aden cannon, two AIM-9 Sidewinder or 20 mm/127 mm rockets and 'iron' bombs.

HARRIER *1/2001, Thai Navy League* / 0130153

Numbers/Type: 2 AgustaWestland Super Lynx 300.
Operational speed: 125 kt *(231 km/h)*.
Service ceiling: 12,000 ft *(3,660 m)*.
Range: 340 n miles *(630 km)*.
Role/Weapon systems: Two helicopters ordered 7 August 2001 for ASW, ASV and surveillance roles. Delivered in 2005.

SUPER LYNX *9/2004, AgustaWestland* / 0566704

Numbers/Type: 6 Sikorsky S-70B7 Seahawk.
Operational speed: 135 kt *(250 km/h)*.
Service ceiling: 10,000 ft *(3,050 m)*.
Range: 600 n miles *(1,110 km)*.
Role/Weapon systems: Multimission helicopters delivered by June 1997. Plans to acquire ASW equipment have been abandoned. Sensors: Telephonics APS-143(V)3 radar; ASN 150 databus; provision for sonobuoys and dipping sonar; ALR 606(V)2 ESM. Weapons: Provision for ASM and MUSL Stingray torpedoes.

SEAHAWK *7/2005, Thai Navy League* / 1153913

Numbers/Type: 4 Bell 212.
Operational speed: 100 kt *(185 km/h)*.
Service ceiling: 13,200 ft *(4,025 m)*.
Range: 200 n miles *(370 km)*.
Role/Weapon systems: Commando assault and general support. At least two transferred from Army. May be sold to help pay for new shipborne helicopter. Mostly based ashore but operate from Normed class and frigates. Weapons: Pintle-mounted M60 machine guns.

BELL 212 *6/2000, Thai Navy League* / 0105842

LAND-BASED MARITIME AIRCRAFT (FRONT LINE)

Notes: There are also five Cessna Bird Dog light reconnaissance aircraft, 9 Cessna Skywagon and two UH-1H helicopters.

Numbers/Type: 4 Sikorsky S-76B.
Operational speed: 145 kt *(269 km/h)*.
Service ceiling: 6,500 ft *(1,980 m)*.
Range: 357 n miles *(661 km)*.
Role/Weapon systems: Six originally acquired in 1996 for maritime surveillance and utility purposes. Sensors: Weather radar. Weapons: Unarmed.

S-76 *8/1996, Royal Thai Navy* / 0050241

Numbers/Type: 2/1 Lockheed P-3T Orion/UP-3T Orion.
Operational speed: 411 kt *(761 km/h)*.
Service ceiling: 28,300 ft *(8,625 m)*.
Range: 4,000 n miles *(7,410 km)*.
Role/Weapon systems: Delivered in 1996. Two for ASW and one utility. Two more are required. Sensors: APS-115 radar, ECM/ESM. Weapons: ASW; Mk 46 or Stingray torpedoes. ASV; four Harpoon.

ORION *8/1997, Royal Thai Navy* / 0019261

Numbers/Type: 13/4 Vought A-7E Corsair II/TA-7E Corsair II.
Operational speed: 600 kt *(1,112 km/h)*.
Service ceiling: 50,000 ft *(15,240 m)*.
Range: 2,000 n miles *(3,705 km)*.
Role/Weapon systems: Delivered in 1996–97 from the US. Reconditioning programme in progress 2004. Weapons: AIM-9L Sidewinder; 1—20 mm cannon.

CORSAIR II *8/1996, Royal Thai Navy* / 0053451

Numbers/Type: 3/2 Fokker F27 Maritime 200ME/F27 Maritime 400M.
Operational speed: 250 kt *(463 km/h)*.
Service ceiling: 25,000 ft *(7,620 m)*.
Range: 2,700 n miles *(5,000 km)*.
Role/Weapon systems: Increased coastal surveillance and response is provided, including ASW and ASV action by 200ME. 400M is for transport. Sensors: APS-504 search radar, Bendix weather radar, ESM and MAD equipment. Weapons: ASW; four Mk 46 or Stingray torpedoes or depth bombs or mines. ASV; two Harpoon ASM.

FOKKER 400 *1994, Royal Thai Navy* / 0053452

Numbers/Type: 5 GAF N24A Searchmaster B (Nomad).
Operational speed: 168 kt *(311 km/h)*.
Service ceiling: 21,000 ft *(6,400 m)*.
Range: 730 n miles *(1,352 km)*.
Role/Weapon systems: Short-range MR for EEZ protection and anti-smuggling operations. Sensors: Search radar, cameras. Weapons: Unarmed.

NOMAD (US colours) *2/2004, ASTA* / 0010107

Numbers/Type: 6 Dornier 228.
Operational speed: 200 kt *(370 km/h)*.
Service ceiling: 28,000 ft *(8,535 m)*.
Range: 940 n miles *(1,740 km)*.
Role/Weapon systems: Coastal surveillance and EEZ protection. Three acquired in 1991, three more in 1996. Sensors: APS-128/504 search radar.

DORNIER 228 *6/1996, Royal Thai Navy* / 0019262

Numbers/Type: 2 Canadair CL-215.
Operational speed: 206 kt *(382 km/h)*.
Service ceiling: 10,000 ft *(3,050 m)*.
Range: 1,125 n miles *(2,085 km)*.
Role/Weapon systems: Used for general purpose transport, SAR and fire-fighting.

CL-215 *1993, Royal Thai Navy* / 0053453

Numbers/Type: 7/2 Summit T-337SP/T-337G.
Operational speed: 200 kt *(364 km/h)*.
Service ceiling: 20,000 ft *(6,100 m)*.
Range: 900 n miles *(1,650 km)*.
Role/Weapon systems: Maritime surveillance and targeting. Weapons: LAU-32 and 59A rocket launchers, CBU-14 bomblets and 12.7 mm MG.

PATROL FORCES

3 HUA HIN CLASS (PSO)

Name	*No*	*Builders*	*Laid down*	*Launched*	*Commissioned*
HUA HIN	541	Asimar, Samut Prakarn	Mar 1997	3 Mar 1999	25 Mar 2000
KLAENG	542	Asimar, Samut Prakarn	May 1997	19 Apr 1999	17 Jan 2001
SI RACHA	543	Bangkok Naval Dockyard	Dec 1997	6 Sep 1999	17 Jan 2001

Displacement, tons: 645 full load
Dimensions, feet (metres): 203.4 × 29.2 × 8.9 *(62 × 8.9 × 2.7)*
Main machinery: 3 Paxman 12VP 185 diesels; 10,372 hp(m) *(7.63 MW)* sustained; 3 shafts; 1 LIPS cp prop (centreline)
Speed, knots: 25. **Range, n miles:** 2,500 at 15 kt
Complement: 45 (11 officers)

Guns: 1—3 in *(76 mm)*/50 Mk 22 ❶; 50 rds/min to 12 km *(6.5 n miles)*; weight of shell 6 kg.
1 Bofors 40 mm/60 ❷; 2 Oerlikon 20 mm GAM-BO1 ❸.
2—12.7 mm MGs.
Weapons control: Optronic director ❹.
Radars: Surface search: Sperry Rascar ❺; E/F-band.
Navigation: Sperry Apar; I-band.

Programmes: Ordered in September 1996 from Asian Marine. Delayed and reported cancelled by the Thai Navy in late 1997 but, despite being beset by building delays, all three ships had entered service by 2001.
Modernisation: Due to budgetary constraints, older weapon systems have been installed as a temporary measure. A new 76 mm/62 gun and 40 mm/70 are planned to be fitted.
Structure: Derived from the Khamronsin design.

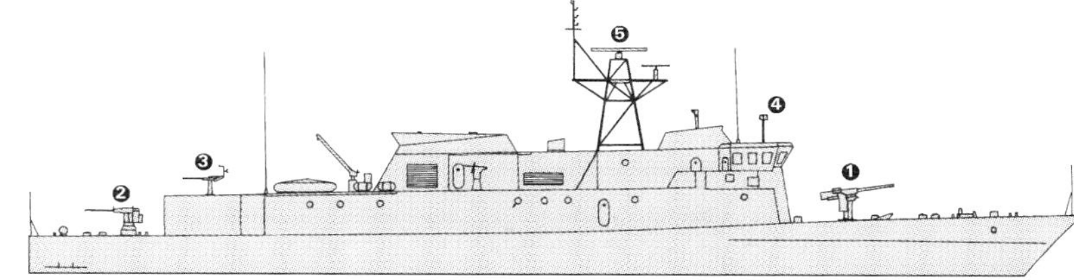

HUA HIN *(Scale 1 : 600), Ian Sturton* / 0587563

KLAENG *6/2001, Royal Thai Navy* / 0130174

3 RATCHARIT CLASS (FAST ATTACK CRAFT—MISSILE) (PGGF)

Name	*No*	*Builders*	*Commissioned*
RATCHARIT	321 (ex-4)	CN Breda (Venezia)	10 Aug 1979
WITTHAYAKHOM	322 (ex-5)	CN Breda (Venezia)	12 Nov 1979
UDOMDET	323 (ex-6)	CN Breda (Venezia)	21 Feb 1980

Displacement, tons: 235 standard; 270 full load
Dimensions, feet (metres): 163.4 × 24.6 × 7.5 *(49.8 × 7.5 × 2.3)*
Main machinery: 3 MTU MD 20V 538 TB91 diesels; 11,520 hp(m) *(8.47 MW)* sustained; 3 shafts; Kamewa cp props
Speed, knots: 37
Range, n miles: 2,000 at 15 kt
Complement: 45 (7 officers)

Missiles: SSM: 4 Aerospatiale MM 38 Exocet; inertial cruise; active radar homing to 42 km *(23 n miles)* at 0.9 Mach; warhead 165 kg; sea-skimmer.
Guns: 1 OTO Melara 3 in *(76 mm)*/62 compact; 85 rds/min to 16 km *(8.7 n miles)* anti-surface; 12 km *(6.6 n miles)* anti-aircraft; weight of shell 6 kg.
1 Bofors 40 mm/70; 300 rds/min to 12.5 km *(6.8 n miles)*; weight of shell 0.96 kg.
2—12.7 mm MGs.
Countermeasures: ESM: Racal RDL-2; intercept.
Radars: Surface search: Decca; I-band.
Fire control: Signaal WM25; I/J-band; range 46 km *(25 n miles)*.

Programmes: Ordered June 1976. *Ratcharit* launched 30 July 1978, *Witthayakhom* 2 September 1978 and *Udomdet* 28 September 1978.
Structure: Standard Breda BMB 230 design.

WITTHAYAKHOM *6/2007, Thai Navy League* / 1167912

3 PRABPARAPAK CLASS (FAST ATTACK CRAFT—MISSILE) (PTFG)

Name	*No*	*Builders*	*Commissioned*
PRABPARAPAK	311 (ex-1)	Singapore SBEC	28 July 1976
HANHAK SATTRU	312 (ex-2)	Singapore SBEC	6 Nov 1976
SUPHAIRIN	313 (ex-3)	Singapore SBEC	1 Feb 1977

Displacement, tons: 224 standard; 268 full load
Dimensions, feet (metres): 149 × 24.3 × 7.5 *(45.4 × 7.4 × 2.3)*
Main machinery: 4 MTU 16V 538TB92 diesels; 13,640 hp(m) *(10 MW)* sustained; 4 shafts
Speed, knots: 40
Range, n miles: 2,000 at 15 kt; 750 at 37 kt
Complement: 41 (5 officers)

Missiles: SSM: 5 IAI Gabriel I (1 triple, 2 single) launchers; radar or optical guidance; semi-active radar homing to 20 km *(10.8 n miles)* at 0.7 Mach; warhead 75 kg.
Guns: 1 Bofors 57 mm/70; 200 rds/min to 17 km *(9.3 n miles)*; weight of shell 2.4 kg. 8 rocket illuminant launchers on either side of 57 mm gun.
1 Bofors 40 mm/70; 300 rds/min to 12 km *(6.6 n miles)*; weight of shell 0.96 kg.
Countermeasures: ESM: Racal RDL-2; intercept.
Radars: Surface search: Kelvin Hughes Type 17; I-band.
Fire control: Signaal WM28/5 series; I/J-band.

Programmes: Ordered June 1973. Built under licence from Lürssen. Launch dates- *Prabparapak* 29 July 1975, *Hanhak Sattru* 28 October 1975, *Suphairin* 20 February 1976.
Modernisation: There are plans to replace Gabriel possibly by RBS 15.
Structure: Same design as Lürssen standard 45 m class built for Singapore. Normally only three Gabriel SSM are carried.

PRABPARAPAK *6/2001, Royal Thai Navy* / 0130172

3 CHON BURI CLASS (FAST ATTACK CRAFT—GUN) (PG)

Name	*No*	*Builders*	*Commissioned*
CHON BURI	331 (ex-1)	CN Breda (Venezia) Mestre	22 Feb 1983
SONGKHLA	332 (ex-2)	CN Breda (Venezia) Mestre	15 July 1983
PHUKET	333 (ex-3)	CN Breda (Venezia) Mestre	13 Jan 1984

Displacement, tons: 450 full load
Dimensions, feet (metres): 198 × 29 × 15 *(60.4 × 8.8 × 4.5)*
Main machinery: 3 MTU 20V 538TB92 diesels; 12,795 hp(m) *(9.4 MW)* sustained; 3 shafts; cp props
Speed, knots: 30
Range, n miles: 2,500 at 18 kt; 900 at 30 kt
Complement: 41 (6 officers)
Guns: 2 OTO Melara 3 in *(76 mm)*/62; 85 rds/min to 16 km *(8.7 n miles)*; weight of shell 6 kg. 2 Breda 40 mm/70 (twin).
Countermeasures: Decoys: 4 Hycor Mk 135 chaff launchers.
ESM: Elettronica Newton; intercept.
Weapons control: Signaal Lirod 8 optronic director.
Radars: Surface search: Signaal ZW06; I-band.
Fire control: Signaal WM22/61; I/J-band; range 46 km *(25 n miles)*.

Comment: Ordered in 1979 (first pair) and 1981. Laid down – *Chon Buri* 15 August 1981 (launched 29 November 1982), *Songkhla* 15 September 1981 (launched 6 September 1982), *Phuket* 15 December 1981 (launched 3 February 1983). Steel hulls, alloy superstructure. Can be adapted to carry SSMs.

PHUKET *10/2001, **Chris Sattler*** / 0130157

CHON BURI ***9/2003, Hartmut Ehlers*** / 0572642

6 SATTAHIP (PSMM MK 5) CLASS (LARGE PATROL CRAFT) (PG)

Name	*No*	*Builders*	*Commissioned*
SATTAHIP	521 (ex-4)	Ital Thai (Samutprakarn) Ltd	16 Sep 1983
KLONGYAI	522 (ex-5)	Ital Thai (Samutprakarn) Ltd	7 May 1984
TAKBAI	523 (ex-6)	Ital Thai (Samutprakarn) Ltd	18 July 1984
KANTANG	524 (ex-7)	Ital Thai (Samutprakarn) Ltd	14 Oct 1985
THEPHA	525 (ex-8)	Ital Thai (Samutprakarn) Ltd	17 Apr 1986
TAIMUANG	526 (ex-9)	Ital Thai (Samutprakarn) Ltd	17 Apr 1986

Displacement, tons: 270 standard; 300 full load
Dimensions, feet (metres): 164.5 × 23.9 × 5.9 *(50.1 × 7.3 × 1.8)*
Main machinery: 2 MTU 16V 538TB92 diesels; 6,820 hp(m) *(5 MW)* sustained; 2 shafts
Speed, knots: 22
Range, n miles: 2,500 at 15 kt
Complement: 56
Guns: 1 OTO Melara 3 in *(76 mm)*/62 (in 521-523). 1 USN 3 in *(76 mm)*/50 Mk 26 (in 524-526). 1 Bofors 40 mm/70 or 40 mm/60. 2 Oerlikon 20 mm GAM-BO1. 2—12.7 mm MGs.
Weapons control: NA 18 optronic director (in 521-523).
Radars: Surface search: Decca; I-band.

Comment: First four ordered 9 September 1981, *Thepha* on 27 December 1983 and *Taimuang* on 31 August 1984.

TAKBAI ***10/1999, Royal Thai Navy*** / 0080815

3 T 81 CLASS (COASTAL PATROL CRAFT) (PB)

T 81–83

Displacement, tons: 120 full load
Dimensions, feet (metres): 98.8 × 20.7 × 5.6 *(30.1 × 6.3 × 1.7)*
Main machinery: 2 MTU 16V 2000TE90 diesels; 3,600 hp(m) *(2.56 MW)*; 2 shafts
Speed, knots: 25. **Range, n miles:** 1,300 at 15 kt
Complement: 28 (3 officers)
Guns: 1 Bofors 40 mm/70. 1 Oerlikon 20 mm. 2—12.7 mm MGs.
Radars: Surface search: Sperry SM 5000; I-band.

Comment: Ordered in October 1996 from ASC Silkline in Pranburi. First one commissioned 5 August 1999, second 9 December 1999 and the third in 2000. Plans for seven more have been shelved.

T 83 ***3/2004, Bob Fildes*** / 0589810

10 PGM 71 CLASS (COASTAL PATROL CRAFT) (PB)

T 11–19 T 110

Displacement, tons: 130 standard; 147 full load
Dimensions, feet (metres): 101 × 21 × 6 *(30.8 × 6.4 × 1.9)*
Main machinery: 2 GM diesels; 1,800 hp *(1.34 MW)*; 2 shafts
Speed, knots: 18.5. **Range, n miles:** 1,500 at 10 kt
Complement: 30
Guns: 1 Bofors 40 mm/60. 1 Oerlikon 20 mm. 2—12.7 mm MGs.
In some craft the 20 mm gun has been replaced by an 81 mm mortar/12.7 mm combined mounting aft.
Radars: Surface search: Decca 303 *(T 11* and *12)* or Decca 202 (remainder); I-band.

Comment: Built by Peterson Inc between 1966 and 1970. Transferred from US. Likely to be decommissioned as modified T 91 class enter service.

T 16 ***10/1999, Royal Thai Navy*** / 0080816

9 T 91 CLASS (COASTAL PATROL CRAFT) (PB)

T 91–99

Displacement, tons: 87.5 *(T 91-92)*, 117 (remainder) standard
Dimensions, feet (metres): 103.4 × 17.6 × 4.9 *(31.5 × 5.4 × 1.5)* *(T 91-92)*
111.6 × 18.7 × 4.9 *(34.0 × 5.7 × 1.5)* (remainder)
Main machinery: 2 MTU 12V 538 TB81/82 diesels; 3,300 hp(m) *(2.43 MW)*/4,430 hp(m) *(3.26 MW)* sustained; 2 shafts
Speed, knots: 25. **Range, n miles:** 700 at 21 kt
Complement: 21 *(T 91-92)*; 25 (remainder)
Guns: 2 or 1 Bofors 40 mm/60 *(T 91* and *T 99)*. 1 Oerlikon 20 mm GAM-BO1 *(T 91* and *T 99)*. 2—12.7 mm MGs *(T 93-99)*.
Weapons control: Sea Archer 1A optronic director *(T 99* only).
Radars: Surface search: Raytheon SPS-35 (1500B); I-band.

Comment: Built by Royal Thai Naval Dockyard, Bangkok. *T 91* commissioned in 1965; *T 92-93* in 1973; *T 94-98* between 1981 and 1984; *T 99* in 1987. *T 91* has an extended upperworks and a 20 mm gun in place of the after 40 mm. *T 99* has a single Bofors 40/70, one Oerlikon 20 mm and two MGs. Major refits from 1983–86 for earlier vessels of the class.

T 96 ***10/2001, Chris Sattler*** / 0130457

3 + (6) T 991 CLASS (COASTAL PATROL CRAFT) (PB)

No	Builders	Launched	Commissioned
T 991	Bangkok Naval Dockyard	2006	30 Apr 2007
T 992	Marsun Shipyard	6 Sep 2007	Dec 2007
T 993	Marsun Shipyard	6 Sep 2007	Dec 2007

Displacement, tons: 186 full load
Dimensions, feet (metres): 127.0 × 21.2 × 5.9 *(38.7 × 6.45 × 1.8)*
Main machinery: 2 MTU 16V 4000 M 90 diesels; 7,400 hp *(5.5 MW)*; 2 shafts
Speed, knots: 27
Complement: 30
Guns: 2 MSI DS-30M 30 mm. 2—12.7 mm MGs.
Weapons control: Thales Mirador optronic director.
Radars: Surface search/navigation: To be announced.

Comment: Modified versions of the T 91 class. First vessel laid down at Naval Dockyard on 9 September 2005. Two further craft delivered by December 2007. A further six craft are planned.

T 991 *12/2007, M Mazumdar* / 1353396

9 SWIFT CLASS (COASTAL PATROL CRAFT) (PB)

T 21–29

Displacement, tons: 22 full load
Dimensions, feet (metres): 50 × 13 × 3.5 *(15.2 × 4 × 1.1)*
Main machinery: 2 Detroit diesels; 480 hp *(358 kW)*; 2 shafts
Speed, knots: 25
Range, n miles: 400 at 25 kt
Complement: 8 (1 officer)
Guns: 1—81 mm mortar. 2—12.7 mm MGs.
Radars: Surface search: Raytheon Pathfinder; I-band.

Comment: Transferred from US Navy from 1967–75.

T 21 *7/2008*, Thai Navy League* / 1353397

13 T 213 CLASS (COASTAL PATROL CRAFT) (PB)

T 213–214 T 216–226

Displacement, tons: 35 standard
Dimensions, feet (metres): 64 × 17.5 × 5 *(19.5 × 5.3 × 1.5)*
Main machinery: 2 MTU diesels; 715 hp(m) *(526 kW)*; 2 shafts
Speed, knots: 25
Complement: 8 (1 officer)
Guns: 1 Oerlikon 20 mm. 1—81 mm mortar with 12.7 mm MG.
Radars: Surface search: Racal Decca 110; I-band.

Comment: Built by ItalThai Marine Ltd. Commissioned-*T 213-214*, 29 August 1980; *T 216-218*, 26 March 1981; *T 219-223*, 16 September 1981; *T 224*, 19 November 1982; *T 225* and *T 226*, 28 March 1984. Construction of *T 227-230* is not to have been completed. Of alloy construction. Used for fishery patrol and coastal control duties. *T 215* damaged beyond repair by tsunami on 26 December 2004 and replaced by *T 227*.

T 219 *9/2003, Hartmut Ehlers* / 0572643

1 T 227 CLASS (COASTAL PATROL CRAFT) (PB)

Displacement, tons: 42 full load
Dimensions, feet (metres): 70.0 × 17.4 × 4.9 *(21.3 × 5.3 × 1.5)*.
Main machinery: 2 MTU diesels; 1,200 hp *(895 kW)*; 2 shafts
Speed, knots: 28
Complement: 8 (1 officer)
Guns: 1—20 mm. 2—12.7 mm MGs.
Radars: Surface search/navigation: I-band.

Comment: Larger variant of the T 213 class built by Marsun and launched on 1 September 2006 to replace T 215 which was lost in the tsunami of 26 December 2004.

T 227 *12/2006, Marsun* / 1190410

3 SEAL ASSAULT CRAFT (LCP)

Comment: Locally built for special forces operations. Details are not known but reported to be larger and faster than PBR Mk II craft. Equipped with stern ramp.

T 242 (SEAL) *5/1997, A Sharma* / 0050242

13 PBR MK II (RIVER PATROL CRAFT) (PBR)

Displacement, tons: 8 full load
Dimensions, feet (metres): 32.1 × 11.5 × 2.3 *(9.8 × 3.5 × 0.7)*
Main machinery: 2 Detroit diesels; 430 hp *(321 kW)*; 2 Jacuzzi water-jets
Speed, knots: 25
Range, n miles: 150 at 23 kt
Complement: 4
Guns: 2—7.62 mm MGs. 1—60 mm mortar.
Radars: Raytheon SPS-66; I-band.

Comment: Transferred from US from 1967–73. Employed on Mekong River. Reported to be getting old, numbers are reducing and maximum speed has been virtually halved. All belong to the Riverine and SEAL Squadron.

PBR MK II *6/2002, Thai Navy League* / 0543390

3 SEA SPECTRE MK III CLASS (PB)

T 210–212

Displacement, tons: 28; 37 full load
Dimensions, feet (metres): 65.0 × 18.0 × 5.9 *(19.8 × 5.5 × 1.8)*
Main machinery: 3 Detroit diesels; 1,800 hp *(1.34 MW)*; 3 shafts
Speed, knots: 30
Range, n miles: 450 at 20 kt
Complement: 9 (1 officer)
Guns: 2 Oerlikon 20 mm. 1—12.7 MG.
Radars: Surface search: Raytheon; I-band.

Comment: Aluminium hulled craft built by Peterson. Transferred from the US in 1975.

90 ASSAULT BOATS (LCP)

Displacement, tons: 0.4 full load
Dimensions, feet (metres): 16.4 × 6.2 × 1.3 *(5 × 1.9 × 0.4)*
Main machinery: 1 outboard; 150 hp *(110 kW)*
Speed, knots: 24
Complement: 2
Guns: 1—7.62 mm MG.

Comment: Part of the Riverine Squadron with the PBRs and two PCFs. Can carry six people. Numbers uncertain.

ASSAULT BOAT *6/2002, Thai Navy League* / 0530060

AMPHIBIOUS FORCES

Note: There are approximately 24 landing craft of about 100 tons operated by the Army.

2 NORMED CLASS (LSTH)

Name	*No*	*Builders*	*Launched*	*Commissioned*
SICHANG	721 (ex-LST 6)	Ital Thai	14 Apr 1987	9 Oct 1987
SURIN	722 (ex-LST 7)	Bangkok Dock Co Ltd	12 Apr 1988	16 Dec 1988

Displacement, tons: 3,540 standard; 4,235 full load
Dimensions, feet (metres): 337.8; 357.6 (722) × 51.5 × 11.5 *(103; 109 × 15.7 × 3.5)*
Main machinery: 2 MTU 20V 1163 TB82 diesels; 11,000 hp(m) *(8.1 MW)* sustained; 2 shafts; cp props
Speed, knots: 16. **Range, n miles:** 7,000 at 12 kt
Complement: 53
Military lift: 348 troops; 14 tanks or 12 APCs or 850 tons cargo; 3 LCVP; 1 LCPL
Guns: 2 Bofors 40 mm/70. 2 Oerlikon GAM-CO1 20 mm. 2—12.7 mm MGs. 1—81 mm mortar.
Weapons control: 2 BAe Sea Archer Mk 1A optronic directors.
Radars: Navigation: Racal Decca 1226; I-band.
Helicopters: Platform for 2 Bell 212.

Comment: First ordered 31 August 1984 to a Chantier du Nord (Normed) design. Second ordered to a modified design and lengthened to accommodate a battalion. The largest naval ships yet built in Thailand. Have bow doors and a 17 m ramp.

SURIN *11/2001, Maritime Photographic* / 0130163

SICHANG *2/2004, Bob Fildes* / 0589812

2 LSIL 351 CLASS

PRAB 741 (ex-LSIL 1) **SATAKUT** 742 (ex-LSIL 2)

Displacement, tons: 230 standard; 399 full load
Dimensions, feet (metres): 157 × 23 × 6 *(47.9 × 7 × 1.8)*
Main machinery: 4 GM diesels; 2,320 bhp *(1.73 MW)*; 2 shafts
Speed, knots: 15. **Range, n miles:** 5,600 at 12.5 kt
Complement: 49 (7 officers)
Military lift: 101 tons or 76 troops
Guns: 1 US 3 in *(76 mm)*/50. 1 Bofors 40 mm/60. 2 Oerlikon 20 mm/70.
Radars: Surface search: Raytheon SPS-35 (1500B); I-band.

Comment: *Prab* transferred to Thailand in October 1946. *Satakut* was refitted in the mid-1990s.

PRAB *6/2005, Thai Navy League* / 1153910

4 LST 512-1152 CLASS (LST)

Name	*No*	*Builders*	*Commissioned*
CHANG (ex-*Lincoln County* LST 898)	712 (ex-LST 2)	Dravo Corporation	29 Dec 1944
PANGAN (ex-*Stark County* LST 1134)	713 (ex-LST 3)	Chicago Bridge and Iron Co, ILL	7 Apr 1945
LANTA (ex-*Stone County* LST 1141)	714 (ex-LST 4)	Chicago Bridge and Iron Co, ILL	9 May 1945
PRATHONG (ex-*Dodge County* LST 722)	715 (ex-LST 5)	Jefferson B & M Co, Ind	13 Sep 1944

Displacement, tons: 1,650 standard; 3,640/4,145 full load
Dimensions, feet (metres): 328 × 50 × 14 *(100 × 15.2 × 4.4)*
Main machinery: 2 GM 12-567A diesels; 1,800 hp *(1.34 MW)*; 2 shafts
Speed, knots: 11.5. **Range, n miles:** 9,500 at 9 kt
Complement: 80; 157 (war)
Military lift: 1,230 tons max; 815 tons beaching
Guns: 1—3 in (76 mm).
8 Bofors 40 mm/60 (2 twin, 4 single) (can be carried).
2—12.7 mm MGs *(Chang)*. 2 Oerlikon 20 mm (others).
Weapons control: 2 Mk 51 GFCS. 2 optical systems.
Radars: Navigation: Racal Decca 1229; I/J-band.

Comment: *Chang* transferred from USA in August 1962. *Pangan* 16 May 1966, *Lanta* on 15 August 1973 (by sale 1 March 1979) and *Prathong* on 17 December 1975. *Chang* has a reinforced bow and waterline. *Lanta, Prathong* and *Chang* have mobile crane on the well-deck. All have tripod mast.

LANTA *5/2002, Mick Prendergast* / 0530001

3 MAN NOK CLASS (LCU)

Name	*No*	*Builders*	*Launched*	*Commissioned*
MAN NOK	781	Sahai Sant, Pratum Thani	1 May 2001	6 Dec 2001
MAN KLANG	782	Sahai Sant, Pratum Thani	1 May 2001	14 Nov 2001
MAN NAI	783	Sahai Sant, Pratum Thani	1 May 2001	6 Dec 2001

Displacement, tons: 170 light; 550 full load
Dimensions, feet (metres): 172 × 36.7 × 5.9 *(52.4 × 11.2 × 1.8)*
Main machinery: 2 Caterpillar 3432 DITA diesels; 700 hp(m) *(515 kW)*; 2 shafts
Speed, knots: 12. **Range, n miles:** 1,500 at 10 kt
Complement: 30 (3 officers)
Military lift: 2 M60 tanks or 25 tons vehicles
Guns: 2 Oerlikon 20 mm.
Radars: Navigation: I-band.

Comment: Ordered from Silkline ASC in 1997. All three craft launched 1 May 2000.

MAN NAI *5/2002, Mick Prendergast* / 0530000

0 + 1 ENDURANCE CLASS (LPD)

Displacement, tons: 8,500 full load
Dimensions, feet (metres): 462.6 pp × 68.9 × 16.4 *(141 × 21 × 5)*
Main machinery: 2 diesels; 12,000 hp(m) *(8.82 MW)*; 2 shafts; Kamewa cp props; bow thruster
Speed, knots: 15. **Range, n miles:** 10,400 at 12 kt
Complement: 65 (8 officers)
Military lift: 350 troops; 18 tanks; 20 vehicles; 4 LCVP

Missiles: SAM: To be announced.
Guns: To be announced.
Radars: Air/surface search: To be announced.
Navigation: To be announced.
Helicopters: Platform for 2.

Programmes: It was announced in November 2008 that ST Marine (Singapore) had been awarded the contract for the design and manufacture of an LPD that is reported to be similar to the Endurance class in service with the Singapore Navy. Construction is expected to start in 2009 with delivery planned for 2012.
Structure: The Endurance class is a US drive-through design with bow and stern ramps. Single intermediate deck with three hydraulic ramps. Helicopter platform aft. Indal ASIST helo handling system. Dockwell for four LCUs and davits for four LCVPs. Two 25 ton cranes. Four 36 m self-propelled pontoons can be secured to winching points on the ships' sides.

4 THONG KAEO CLASS (LCU)

Name	*No*	*Builders*	*Commissioned*
THONG KAEO	771 (ex-7)	Bangkok Dock Co Ltd	23 Dec 1982
THONG LANG	772 (ex-8)	Bangkok Dock Co Ltd	19 Apr 1983
WANG NOK	773 (ex-9)	Bangkok Dock Co Ltd	16 Sep 1983
WANG NAI	774 (ex-10)	Bangkok Dock Co Ltd	11 Nov 1983

Displacement, tons: 193 standard; 396 full load
Dimensions, feet (metres): 134.5 × 29.5 × 6.9 *(41 × 9 × 2.1)*
Main machinery: 2 GM 16V-71 diesels; 1,400 hp *(1.04 MW)*; 2 shafts
Speed, knots: 10
Range, n miles: 1,200 at 10 kt
Complement: 31 (3 officers)
Military lift: 3 lorries; 150 tons equipment
Guns: 2 Oerlikon 20 mm. 2—7.62 mm MGs.

Comment: Ordered in 1980.

WANG NAI *5/1997, Maritime Photographic* / 0019276

6 MATAPHON CLASS (LCM/LCVP/LCP)

MATAPHON 761 (ex-LCU 1260) **ADANG** 763 (ex-LCU 861) **KOLAM** 765 (ex-LCU 904)
RAWI 762 (ex-LCU 800) **PHETRA** 764 (ex-LCU 1089) **TALIBONG** 766 (ex-LCU 753)

Displacement, tons: 145 standard; 330 full load
Dimensions, feet (metres): 120.4 × 32 × 4 *(36.7 × 9.8 × 1.2)*
Main machinery: 3 Gray Marine 65 diesels; 675 hp *(503 kW)*; 3 shafts
Speed, knots: 10
Range, n miles: 650 at 8 kt
Complement: 13
Military lift: 150 tons or 3-4 tanks or 250 troops
Guns: 4 Oerlikon 20 mm (2 twin).
Radars: Navigation: Raytheon Pathfinder; I-band.

Comment: Transferred from US 1946–47. Employed as transport ferries.

TALIBONG *11/2001, Maritime Photographic* / 0130160

40 LANDING CRAFT (LCM/LCVP/LCA)

Displacement, tons: 56 full load
Dimensions, feet (metres): 56.1 × 14.1 × 3.9 *(17.1 × 4.3 × 1.2)*
Main machinery: 2 Gray Marine 64 HN9 diesels; 330 hp *(264 kW)*; 2 shafts
Speed, knots: 9. **Range, n miles:** 135 at 9 kt
Complement: 5
Military lift: 34 tons

Comment: Details given are for the 24 ex-US LCMs delivered in 1965–69. The 12 ex-US LCVPs can lift 40 troops and are of 1960s vintage. The four LCAs can lift 35 troops and were built in 1984 in Bangkok.

LCM 208 *11/1998, Thai Navy League* / 0050247

3 GRIFFON 1000 TD HOVERCRAFT (UCAC)

401–403

Dimensions, feet (metres): 27.6 × 12.5 *(8.4 × 3.8)*
Main machinery: 1 Deutz BF6L913C diesel; 190 hp(m) *(140 kW)*
Speed, knots: 33. **Range, n miles:** 200 at 27 kt
Complement: 2
Cargo capacity: 1,000 kg plus 9 troops
Radars: Navigation: Raytheon; I-band.

Comment: Acquired in mid-1990 from Griffon Hovercraft. Although having an obvious amphibious capability they are also used for rescue and flood control.

GRIFFON 401 *6/1999, Royal Thai Navy* / 0084413

0 + 2 LANDING CRAFT UTILITY (LCU)

Dimensions, feet (metres): 75.4 × 19.7 × 2.6 *(23 × 6 × 0.8)*
Main machinery: 2 MAN 2842 LZE diesels; 4,400 hp(m) *(3.23 MW)*; 2 Kamewa waterjets
Speed, knots: 20. **Range, n miles:** 180 at 15 kt
Complement: 4
Military lift: 18 tons
Guns: 2—12.7 mm MGs or 40 mm grenade launchers.

Comment: It was announced in November 2008 that ST Marine (Sinagpore) had been awarded the contract for the design and construction of two 23 m landing craft to be operated from the LPD, also under construction. The details of the craft are assumed to be similar to those in service in Singapore.

LCU (Singapore colours) *12/2005, Chris Sattler* / 1164539

0 + 2 LANDING CRAFT (LCVP)

Displacement, tons: 4 full load
Dimensions, feet (metres): 44.6 × 12.1 × 2 *(13.6 × 3.7 × 0.6)*
Main machinery: 2 MAN D2866 LE diesels; 815 hp(m) *(600 kW)* sustained; 2 Hamilton 362 waterjets
Speed, knots: 20. **Range, n miles:** 100 at 20 kt
Complement: 3
Military lift: 4 tons or 30 troops

Comment: It was announced in November 2008 that ST Marine (Singapore) had been awarded the contract for the design and construction of two 13 m landing craft to be operated from the LPD, also under construction. The details of the craft are assumed to be similar to those in service in Singapore. With a single bow ramp, they can carry a rifle platoon.

LCVPs *8/2003, David Boey* / 0567534

MINE WARFARE FORCES

1 MCM SUPPORT SHIP (MCS)

Name	*No*	*Builders*	*Commissioned*
THALANG	621 (ex-1)	Bangkok Dock Co Ltd	4 Aug 1980

Displacement, tons: 1,000 standard
Dimensions, feet (metres): 185.5 × 33 × 10 *(55.7 × 10 × 3.1)*
Main machinery: 2 MTU diesels; 1,310 hp(m) *(963 kW)*; 2 shafts
Speed, knots: 12
Complement: 77
Guns: 1 Bofors 40 mm/60. 2 Oerlikon 20 mm. 2—12.7 mm MGs.
Radars: Surface search: Racal Decca 1226; I-band.

Comment: Has minesweeping capability. Two 3 ton cranes provided for change of minesweeping gear in MSCs-four sets carried. Design by Ferrostaal, Essen. Has dormant minelaying capability.

THALANG *11/2001, Maritime Photographic* / 0130165

2 LAT YA (GAETA) CLASS (MINEHUNTERS/SWEEPERS) (MHSC)

Name	*No*	*Builders*	*Launched*	*Commissioned*
LAT YA	633	Intermarine, Sarzana	30 Mar 1998	18 June 1999
THA DIN DAENG	634	Intermarine, Sarzana	31 Oct 1998	18 Dec 1999

Displacement, tons: 680 full load
Dimensions, feet (metres): 172.1 × 32.4 × 9.4 *(52.5 × 9.9 × 2.9)*
Main machinery: 2 MTU 8V 396 TE74K diesels; 1,600 hp(m) *(1.18 MW)* sustained; 2 Voith Schneider props; auxiliary propulsion; 2 hydraulic motors
Speed, knots: 14. **Range, n miles**: 2,000 at 12 kt
Complement: 50 (8 officers)
Guns: 1 MSI 30 mm.
Countermeasures: MCM: Atlas MWS 80-6 minehunting system. Magnetic, acoustic and mechanical sweeps; ADI Mini Dyad, Noise Maker, Bofors MS 106, 2 Pluto Plus ROVs.
Radars: Navigation: Atlas Elektronik 9600M (ARPA); I-band.
Sonars: Atlas Elektronik DSQS-11M; hull-mounted; active; high frequency.

Comment: Invitations to tender lodged by 3 April 1996. Ordered 19 September 1996. Specifications include hunting at up to 6 kt and sweeping at 10 kt. No further ships are planned.

THA DIN DAENG — *4/2004, John Mortimer* / 1153909

2 BANG RACHAN CLASS (MINEHUNTERS/SWEEPERS) (MHSC)

Name	*No*	*Builders*	*Commissioned*
BANG RACHAN	631 (ex-2)	Lürssen Vegesack	29 Apr 1987
NONGSARAI	632 (ex-3)	Lürssen Vegesack	17 Nov 1987

Displacement, tons: 444 full load
Dimensions, feet (metres): 161.1 × 30.5 × 8.2 *(49.1 × 9.3 × 2.5)*
Main machinery: 2 MTU 12V 396 TB83 diesels; 3,120 hp(m) *(2.3 MW)* sustained; 2 shafts; Kamewa cp props; auxiliary propulsion; 1 motor
Speed, knots: 17; 7 (electric motor). **Range, n miles**: 3,100 at 12 kt
Complement: 33 (7 officers)
Guns: 3 Oerlikon GAM-BO1 20 mm.
Countermeasures: MCM: MWS 80R minehunting system. Acoustic, magnetic and mechanical sweeps. 2 Gaymarine Pluto 15 remote-controlled submersibles.
Radars: Navigation: 2 Atlas Elektronik 8600 ARPA; I-band.
Sonars: Atlas Elektronik DSQS-11H; hull-mounted; minehunting; high frequency.

Comment: First ordered from Lürssen late 1984, arrived Bangkok 22 October 1987. Second ordered 5 August 1985 and arrived in Bangkok May 1988. Amagnetic steel frames and deckhouses, wooden hull. Motorola Miniranger MRS III precise navigation system. Draeger decompression chamber.

NONGSARAI — *2/2005, Chris Sattler* / 1153911

12 MSBS (MSR)

MLM 6–10 MSB 11–17

Displacement, tons: 25 full load
Dimensions, feet (metres): 50.2 × 13.1 × 3 *(15.3 × 4 × 0.9)*
Main machinery: 1 Gray Marine 64 HN9 diesel; 165 hp *(123 kW)*; 1 shaft
Speed, knots: 8
Complement: 10
Guns: 2—7.62 mm MGs.

Comment: Three transferred from USA in October 1963 and two in 1964. More were built locally from 1994. Wooden hulled, converted from small motor launches. Operated on Chao Phraya river.

MLM 11 — *10/1995, Royal Thai Navy* / 0080822

2 BLUEBIRD CLASS (MINESWEEPERS—COASTAL) (MSC)

Name	*No*	*Builders*	*Commissioned*
BANGKEO (ex-*MSC 303*)	612 (ex-6)	Dorchester SB Corporation, Camden	9 July 1965
DONCHEDI (ex-*MSC 313*)	613 (ex-8)	Peterson Builders Inc, Sturgeon Bay, WI	17 Sep 1965

Displacement, tons: 317 standard; 384 full load
Dimensions, feet (metres): 145.3 × 27 × 8.5 *(44.3 × 8.2 × 2.6)*
Main machinery: 2 GM 8-268 diesels; 880 hp *(656 kW)*; 2 shafts
Speed, knots: 13
Range, n miles: 2,750 at 12 kt
Complement: 43 (7 officers)
Guns: 2 Oerlikon 20 mm/80 (twin).
Countermeasures: MCM: US Mk 4 (V). Mk 6. US Type Q2 magnetic.
Radars: Navigation: Decca TM 707; I-band.
Sonars: UQS-1; hull-mounted; minehunting; high frequency.

Comment: Constructed for Thailand. One paid off in 1992 and one in 1995. The last two are in limited operational service and at least one is to be retained for training duties.

DONCHEDI — *11/2001, Maritime Photographic* / 0130164

SURVEY AND RESEARCH SHIPS

Notes: There is also a civilian research vessel *Chulab Horn* which completed in 1986.

1 SURVEY SHIP (AGSH)

Name	*No*	*Builders*	*Laid down*	*Launched*	*Commissioned*
PHARUEHATSABODI	813	Unithai Shipyard and Engineering, Laem Chambang	25 Aug 2006	14 Feb 2008	19 Aug 2008

Displacement, tons: To be announced
Dimensions, feet (metres): 217.5 × 50.2 × 10.2 *(66.3 × 13.2 × 3.1)*
Main machinery: Diesel-electric; 3 diesel generators; 2,652 hp(m) *(1.95 MW)*; 1 motor; 1,073 hp(m) *(800 kW)*; 2 azimuth thrusters; 1 bow thruster
Speed, knots: 12. **Range, n miles**: 3,000 at 12 kt
Complement: 13 (accommodation for 71)
Radars: Navigation: E/F- and I-band.
Sonars: Multi- and single-beam; high frequency; active.

Comment: Multipurpose hydrographic and oceanographic survey, training and mine countermeasures vessel ordered 22 December 2005 from a consortium comprising Schelde Naval Shipbuilding, Flushing, and Unithai Shipyard and Engineering, Thailand. The ship is a derivative of the Snellius class vessels built for the RNLN. The ship was built in Thailand. Hydrographic equipment includes an exploration computer system; multibeam echosounder; single-beam echosounder; side-scan sonar; Ultra-Short BaseLine (USBL); Motion and Reference Unit (MRU); draught indication system; tidal measurement system; seawater collection system; seawater measurement system; expendable bathythermograph/sound velocity meter; current flow measurement system; current meter system; sediment collection system; and oceanography equipment.

PHARUEHATSABODI — *2/2008*, Thai Navy League* / 1353399

1 OCEANOGRAPHIC SHIP (AGOR)

Name	*No*	*Builders*	*Commissioned*
SUK	812	Bangkok Dock Co Ltd	3 Mar 1982

Displacement, tons: 1,450 standard; 1,526 full load
Dimensions, feet (metres): 206.3 × 36.1 × 13.4 *(62.9 × 11 × 4.1)*
Main machinery: 2 MTU diesels; 2,400 hp(m) *(1.76 MW)*; 2 shafts
Speed, knots: 15
Complement: 86 (20 officers)
Guns: 2 Oerlikon 20 mm. 2—7.62 mm MGs.
Radars: Navigation: Racal Decca 1226; I-band.

Comment: Laid down 27 August 1979, launched 8 September 1981. Designed for oceanographic and survey duties.

SUK ***5/1999, van Ginderen Collection*** / 0080828

1 SURVEY SHIP (AGS)

Name	*No*	*Builders*	*Commissioned*
CHANTHARA	811 (ex-AGS 11)	Lürssen Werft	30 May 1961

Displacement, tons: 870 standard; 996 full load
Dimensions, feet (metres): 229.2 × 34.5 × 10 *(69.9 × 10.5 × 3)*
Main machinery: 2 KHD diesels; 1,090 hp(m) *(801 kW)*; 2 shafts
Speed, knots: 13.25
Range, n miles: 10,000 at 10 kt
Complement: 68 (8 officers)
Guns: 2 Bofors 40 mm/60.

Comment: Laid down on 27 September 1960. Launched on 17 December 1960. Has served as a Royal Yacht.

CHANTHARA ***7/2008*, Thai Navy League*** / 1353398

TRAINING SHIPS

1 ALGERINE CLASS (AXL)

Name	*No*	*Builders*	*Commissioned*
PHOSAMTON (ex-*Minstrel*)	*611 (ex-415*, ex-MSF 1)	Redfern Construction Co	9 June 1945

Displacement, tons: 1,040 standard; 1,335 full load
Dimensions, feet (metres): 225 × 35.5 × 11.5 *(68.6 × 10.8 × 3.5)*
Main machinery: 2 boilers; 2 reciprocating engines; 2,000 ihp *(1.49 MW)*; 2 shafts
Speed, knots: 16
Range, n miles: 4,000 at 10 kt
Complement: 103
Guns: 1 USN 3 in *(76 mm)*/50. 1 Bofors 40 mm/60. 4 Oerlikon 20 mm.
Radars: Navigation: Raytheon Pathfinder; I-band.

Comment: Transferred from UK in April 1947. Received engineering overhaul in 1984. Minesweeping gear replaced by a deckhouse to increase training space. Vickers 4 in gun replaced.

PHOSAMTON ***8/2002, John Mortimer*** / 0529999

1 CANNON CLASS (FFT)

Name	*No*	*Builders*	*Laid down*	*Launched*	*Commissioned*
PIN KLAO (ex-*Hemminger* DE 746)	413 (ex-3, ex-1)	Western Pipe & Steel Co	1943	12 Sep 1943	30 May 1944

Displacement, tons: 1,240 standard; 1,930 full load
Dimensions, feet (metres): 306 × 36.7 × 14 *(93.3 × 11.2 × 4.3)*
Main machinery: Diesel-electric; 4 GM 16-278A diesels; 6,000 hp *(4.5 MW)*; 4 generators; 2 motors; 2 shafts
Speed, knots: 20
Range, n miles: 10,800 at 12 kt; 6,700 at 19 kt
Complement: 192 (14 officers)

Guns: 3 USN 3 in *(76 mm)*/50 Mk 22; 20 rds/min to 12 km *(6.6 n miles)*; weight of shell 6 kg.
6 Bofors 40 mm/60 (3 twin); 120 rds/min to 10 km *(5.5 n miles)*; weight of shell 0.89 kg.
Torpedoes: 6—324 mm US Mk 32 (2 triple) tubes; anti-submarine.
A/S mortars: 1 Hedgehog Mk 10 multibarrelled fixed; range 250 m; warhead 13.6 kg; 24 rockets.
Depth charges: 8 projectors; 2 racks.
Countermeasures: ESM: WLR-1; radar warning.
Weapons control: Mk 52 radar GFCS for 3 in guns. Mk 63 radar GFCS for aft gun only. 2 Mk 51 optical GFCS for 40 mm.
Radars: Air/surface search: Raytheon SPS-5; G/H-band
Navigation: Raytheon SPS-21; G/H-band
Fire control: Western Electric Mk 34; I/J-band
RCA/General Electric Mk 26; I/J-band
IFF: SLR 1.
Sonars: SQS-11; hull-mounted; active attack; high frequency.

Programmes: Transferred from US Navy at New York Navy Shipyard in July 1959 under MDAP and by sale 6 June 1975.
Modernisation: The three 21 in torpedo tubes were removed and the 20 mm guns were replaced by 40 mm. The six A/S torpedo tubes were fitted in 1966.
Operational: Used mostly as a training ship.

PIN KLAO ***6/1997, Royal Thai Navy*** / 0019254

AUXILIARIES

1 SIMILAN (HUDONG) CLASS (TYPE R22T) (REPLENISHMENT SHIP) (AORH)

Name	*No*	*Builders*	*Launched*	*Commissioned*
SIMILAN	871	Hudong Shipyard, Shanghai	9 Nov 1995	12 Sep 1996

Displacement, tons: 23,000 full load
Dimensions, feet (metres): 562.3 × 80.7 × 29.5 *(171.4 × 24.6 × 9)*
Main machinery: 2 HD-SEMT-Pielstick 16 PC2 6V400; 24,000 hp(m) *(17.64 MW)*; 2 shafts; Kamewa cp props
Speed, knots: 19
Range, n miles: 10,000 at 15 kt
Complement: 157 (19 officers) plus 26
Cargo capacity: 9,000 tons fuel, water, ammunition and stores
Radars: Air/surface search: Eye Shield (Type 354); E/F-band.
Navigation: Racal Decca 1290 ARPA; I-band.
Helicopters: 1 Seahawk type.

Comment: Contract signed with China State Shipbuilding Corporation on 29 September 1993. Fabrication started in December 1994. Two replenishment at sea positions each side and facilities for Vertrep. This ship complements the carrier and the new frigates to give the Navy a full deployment capability. Four twin 37 mm guns (Type 354) and associated Rice Lamp FC radar were not fitted.

SIMILAN ***10/1998, Thai Navy League*** / 0050248

1 REPLENISHMENT TANKER (AORL)

Name	*No*	*Builders*	*Launched*
CHULA	831 (ex-2)	Singapore SEC	24 Sep 1980

Displacement, tons: 2,000 full load
Measurement, tons: 960 dwt
Dimensions, feet (metres): 219.8 × 31.2 × 14.4 *(67 × 9.5 × 4.4)*
Main machinery: 2 MTU 12V 396 TC62 diesels; 2,400 hp(m) *(1.76 MW)* sustained; 2 shafts
Speed, knots: 14
Complement: 39 (7 officers)
Cargo capacity: 800 tons oil fuel
Guns: 2 Oerlikon 20 mm.
Radars: Navigation: Racal Decca 1226; I-band.

Comment: Replenishment is done by a hose handling crane boom.

CHULA *6/1998, Royal Thai Navy* / 0050249

4 HARBOUR TANKERS (YO)

PRONG 833 (ex-YO 5)
PROET 834 (ex-YO 9)
SAMED 835 (ex-YO 10)
CHIK 842 (ex-YO 11)

Displacement, tons: 360 standard; 485 full load
Dimensions, feet (metres): 122.7 × 19.7 × 8.7 *(37.4 × 6 × 2.7)*
Main machinery: 1 GM 8-268A diesel; 500 hp(m) *(368 kW)*; 1 shaft
Speed, knots: 9
Cargo capacity: 210 tons

Comment: Details are for 834, 835 and 842. Built by Bangkok Naval Dockyard. 834 commissioned 27 January 1967, remainder the same year. Details of 833 not known but reported to be approximately 180 tons.

SAMED *5/1999* / 0080829

1 HARBOUR TANKER (YO)

SAMUI 832 (ex-YOG 60, ex-YO 4)

Displacement, tons: 1,420 full load
Dimensions, feet (metres): 174.5 × 32 × 15 *(53.2 × 9.7 × 4.6)*
Main machinery: 1 Union diesel; 600 hp *(448 kW)*; 1 shaft
Speed, knots: 8
Complement: 29
Cargo capacity: 985 tons fuel
Guns: 2 Oerlikon 20 mm can be carried.
Radars: Navigation: Raytheon Pathfinder; I-band

SAMUI *12/1995* / 0506255

1 WATER TANKER (YW)

Name	*No*	*Builders*	*Commissioned*
CHUANG	841 (ex-YW 5)	Royal Thai Naval Dockyard, Bangkok	1965

Displacement, tons: 305 standard; 485 full load
Dimensions, feet (metres): 136 × 24.6 × 10 *(42 × 7.5 × 3.1)*
Main machinery: 1 GM diesel; 500 hp *(373 kW)*; 1 shaft
Speed, knots: 11
Complement: 29
Guns: 1 Oerlikon 20 mm.

Comment: Launched on 14 January 1965.

CHUANG (alongside Proet) *5/1997, Maritime Photographic* / 0019284

1 TRANSPORT SHIP (AKS)

Name	*No*	*Builders*	*Commissioned*
KLED KEO	861 (ex-AF-7)	Norfjord, Norway	1948

Displacement, tons: 450 full load
Dimensions, feet (metres): 150.1 × 24.9 × 14 *(46 × 7.6 × 4.3)*
Main machinery: 1 CAT diesel; 900 hp(m) *(662 kW)*; 1 shaft
Speed, knots: 12
Complement: 54 (7 officers)
Guns: 3 Oerlikon 20 mm.

Comment: Former Norwegian transport acquired in 1956. Paid off in 1990 but back in service in 1997. Operates with the patrol boat squadron.

KLED KEO *6/1998, Royal Thai Navy* / 0050250

1 BUOY TENDER (ABU)

Name	*No*	*Builders*	*Commissioned*
SURIYA	821	Bangkok Dock Co Ltd	15 Mar 1979

Displacement, tons: 690 full load
Dimensions, feet (metres): 177.8 × 33.5 × 10.2 *(54.2 × 10.2 × 3.1)*
Main machinery: 2 MTU diesels; 1,310 hp(m) *(963 kW)*; 2 shafts; bow thruster; 135 hp(m) *(99 kW)*
Speed, knots: 12
Complement: 60 (12 officers)
Radars: Navigation: Racal Decca; I-band.

Comment: Can carry 20 mm guns.

SURIYA *11/2001, Maritime Photographic* / 0130167

TUGS

2 COASTAL TUGS (YTB)

RIN 853 (ex-ATA 5) **RANG** 854 (ex-ATA 6)

Displacement, tons: 350 standard
Dimensions, feet (metres): 106 × 29.7 × 15.2 *(32.3 × 9 × 4.6)*
Main machinery: 1 MWM TBD441V/12K diesel; 2,100 hp(m) *(1.54 MW)*; 1 shaft
Speed, knots: 12. **Range, n miles:** 1,000 at 10 kt
Complement: 19

Comment: Launched 12 and 14 June 1980 at Singapore Marine Shipyard. Both commissioned 5 March 1981. Bollard pull 22 tons.

RANG *1992, Royal Thai Navy* / 0080830

2 SAMAESAN CLASS (COASTAL TUGS) (YTR)

SAMAESAN 855 **RAET** 856

Displacement, tons: 300 standard
Dimensions, feet (metres): 82 × 27.9 × 7.9 *(25 × 8.5 × 2.4)*
Main machinery: 2 Caterpillar 3512TA diesels; 2,350 hp(m) *(1.75 MW)* sustained; 2 Aquamaster US 901 props
Speed, knots: 10
Complement: 6

Comment: Contract signed 23 September 1992 for local construction at Thonburi Naval dockyard. Completed in December 1993. Equipped for firefighting.

RAET *5/1997, A Sharma* / 0050251

2 YTL 422 CLASS (YTL)

KLUENG BADAAN 851 (ex-YTL 2) **MARN VICHAI** 852 (ex-YTL 3)

Displacement, tons: 63 standard
Dimensions, feet (metres): 64.7 × 16.5 × 6 *(19.7 × 5 × 1.8)*
Main machinery: 1 diesel; 240 hp *(179 kW)*; 1 shaft
Speed, knots: 8

Comment: Built by Central Bridge Co, Trenton and bought from Canada 1953.

KLUENG BADAAN *11/2001, Maritime Photographic* / 0130166

POLICE

Notes: (1) There is also a Customs service, subordinate to the Marine Police, which operates unarmed patrol craft with CUSTOMS on the hull, and a Fishery Patrol Service also unarmed but vessels are painted blue with broad white and narrow gold diagonal stripes on the hull. Two Hydrofoil craft are on loan from the Police to the Customs service.
(2) There are large numbers of RIBs in service.

1 VOSPER THORNYCROFT TYPE (LARGE PATROL CRAFT) (PSO)

SRINAKARIN 1804

Displacement, tons: 630 full load
Dimensions, feet (metres): 203.4 × 26.9 × 8.2 *(62 × 8.2 × 2.5)*
Main machinery: 2 Deutz MWM BV16M628 diesels; 9,524 hp(m) *(7 MW)* sustained; 2 shafts; Kamewa cp props
Speed, knots: 25
Range, n miles: 2,500 at 15 kt
Complement: 45
Guns: 4—30 mm (2 twin).
Radars: Surface search: Racal Decca 1226; I-band.

Comment: Ordered in September 1989 from Ital Thai Marine. Same hull as the Khamronsin class corvettes for the Navy but much more lightly armed. Delivered in April 1992.

SRINAKARIN *6/2003, Royal Thai Navy* / 0572648

2 HAMELN TYPE (LARGE PATROL CRAFT) (PBO)

DAMRONG RACHANUPHAP 1802 **LOPBURI RAMES** 1803

Displacement, tons: 430 full load
Dimensions, feet (metres): 186 × 26.6 × 8 *(56.7 × 8.1 × 2.4)*
Main machinery: 4 MTU diesels; 4,400 hp(m) *(3.23 MW)*; 2 shafts
Speed, knots: 23
Complement: 45
Guns: 2 Oerlikon 30 mm/75 (twin). 2 Oerlikon 20 mm.
Radars: Surface search: Racal Decca 1226; I-band.

Comment: Delivered by Schiffwerft Hameln, Germany, on 3 January 1969 and 10 December 1972 respectively.

LOPBURI RAMES *6/2003, Royal Thai Navy* / 0572647

2 SUMIDAGAWA TYPE (COASTAL PATROL CRAFT) (PB)

CHASANYABADEE 1101 **PHROMYOTHEE** 1103

Displacement, tons: 130 full load
Dimensions, feet (metres): 111.5 × 19 × 9.1 *(34 × 5.8 × 2.8)*
Main machinery: 3 Ikegai diesels; 4,050 hp(m) *(2.98 MW)*; 3 shafts
Speed, knots: 32
Complement: 23
Guns: 2—12.7 mm MGs.
Radars: Surface search: Racal Decca; I-band.

Comment: Commissioned in August 1972 and May 1973 respectively.

PHROMYOTHEE *1990, Marine Police* / 0080833

1 YOKOHAMA TYPE (COASTAL PATROL CRAFT) (PB)

CHAWENGSAK SONGKRAM 1102

Displacement, tons: 190 full load
Dimensions, feet (metres): 116.5 × 23 × 11.5 *(35.5 × 7 × 3.5)*
Main machinery: 4 Ikegai diesels; 5,400 hp(m) *(3.79 MW)*; 2 shafts
Speed, knots: 32
Complement: 18
Guns: 2 Oerlikon 20 mm.

Comment: Commissioned 13 April 1973. A second of class operates for the Customs with the number 1201.

CHAWENGSAK SONGKRAM *1990, Marine Police* / 0080834

1 ITALTHAI MARINE TYPE (COASTAL PATROL CRAFT) (PB)

SRIYANONT 901

Displacement, tons: 52 full load
Dimensions, feet (metres): 90 × 16 × 6.5 *(27.4 × 4.9 × 2)*
Main machinery: 2 Deutz BA16M816 diesels; 2,680 hp(m) *(1.97 MW)* sustained; 2 shafts
Speed, knots: 23
Complement: 14
Guns: 1 Oerlikon 20 mm. 2—7.62 mm MGs.
Radars: Surface search: Racal Decca; I-band.

Comment: Commissioned 12 June 1986.

SRIYANONT *12/2001, Thai Navy League* / 0130155

1 BURESPADOONGKIT CLASS (COASTAL PATROL CRAFT) (PB)

BURESPADOONGKIT 813

Displacement, tons: 65 full load
Dimensions, feet (metres): 80.5 × 19.4 × 6 *(24.5 × 5.9 × 1.8)*
Main machinery: 2 SACM UD 23 V12 M5D diesels; 2,534 hp(m) *(1.86 MW)* sustained; 2 shafts
Speed, knots: 28
Range, n miles: 650 at 20 kt
Complement: 14
Guns: 1 Oerlikon GAM-CO1 20 mm; 2—7.62 mm MGs.

Comment: Built by Matsun, Thailand and commissioned 9 August 1995. Badly damaged in the Tsunami of 26 December 2004.

BURESPADOONGKIT *6/1999, Marine Police* / 0080835

3 CUTLASS CLASS (COASTAL PATROL CRAFT) (PB)

PHRAONGKAMROP 807 **PICHARNPHOLAKIT** 808 **RAMINTHRA** 809

Displacement, tons: 34 full load
Dimensions, feet (metres): 65 × 17 × 8.3 *(19.8 × 5.2 × 2.5)*
Main machinery: 3 Detroit 12V-71TA diesels; 1,020 hp(m) *(761 kW)* sustained; 3 shafts
Speed, knots: 25
Complement: 14
Guns: 1 Oerlikon 20 mm. 2—7.62 mm MGs.

Comment: Delivered by Halter Marine, New Orleans, and all commissioned on 9 March 1969. Aluminium hulls.

PICHARNPHOLAKIT *6/1999* / 0080836

3 TECHNAUTIC TYPE (COASTAL PATROL CRAFT) (PB)

810–812

Displacement, tons: 50 full load
Dimensions, feet (metres): 88.6 × 19.4 × 6.2 *(27 × 5.9 × 1.9)*
Main machinery: 3 Isotta Fraschini diesels; 2,500 hp(m) *(1.84 MW)*; 3 Castoldi hydrojets
Speed, knots: 27
Complement: 14
Guns: 1 Oerlikon 20 mm GAM-BO1. 2—7.62 mm MGs.

Comment: Delivered by Technautic, Bangkok in 1984.

812 *1990, Marine Police* / 0080837

5 ITALTHAI MARINE TYPE (COASTAL PATROL CRAFT) (PB)

625–629

Displacement, tons: 42 full load
Dimensions, feet (metres): 64 × 17.5 × 5 *(19.5 × 5.3 × 1.5)*
Main machinery: 2 MAN D2842LE diesels; 1,350 hp(m) *(992 kW)* sustained; 2 shafts
Speed, knots: 27
Complement: 14
Guns: 1—12.7 mm MG.

Comment: Built in Bangkok 1987–90. Aluminium hulls. More of the class operated by the Fishery Patrol Service.

ITAL THAI 626 *3/2004, Bob Fildes* / 0589814

8 MARSUN TYPE (COASTAL PATROL CRAFT) (PB)

630–637

Displacement, tons: 38 full load
Dimensions, feet (metres): 65.6 × 18.2 × 5 *(20 × 5.6 × 1.5)*
Main machinery: 2 MAN D2840LXE diesels; 1,640 hp(m) *(1.2 MW)* sustained; 2 shafts
Speed, knots: 25
Complement: 11
Guns: 1 — 12.7 mm MG.

Comment: Built by Marsun, Thailand and commissioned from 2 August 1994.

MARSUN 634 *3/2004, Bob Fildes* / 0589815

17 TECHNAUTIC TYPE (COASTAL PATROL CRAFT) (PB)

608–624

Displacement, tons: 30 full load
Dimensions, feet (metres): 60 × 16 × 2.9 *(18.3 × 4.9 × 0.9)*
Main machinery: 2 Isotta Fraschini ID 36 SS 8V diesels; 1,760 hp(m) *(1.29 MW)* sustained; 2 Castoldi hydrojets
Speed, knots: 27
Complement: 11
Guns: 1 — 12.7 mm MG.

Comment: Built from 1983–87 in Bangkok. Operational status of some of these craft doubtful.

TECHNAUTIC 609 *11/2001, Maritime Photographic* / 0130168

2 MARSUN TYPE (PB)

539–540

Displacement, tons: 30 full load
Dimensions, feet (metres): 57 × 16 × 3 *(17.4 × 4.9 × 0.9)*
Main machinery: 2 Detroit 12V-71TA diesels; 840 hp *(627 kW)* sustained; 2 shafts
Speed, knots: 25
Complement: 8
Guns: 1 — 12.7 mm MG.

Comment: Built in Thailand. Both commissioned 26 March 1986.

MARSUN 539 *11/2001, Maritime Photographic* / 0130169

38 RIVER PATROL BOATS (PBR)

301–338

Displacement, tons: 5 full load
Dimensions, feet (metres): 37.1 × 11.1 × 2.3 *(11.3 × 3.4 × 0.7)*
Main machinery: 2 diesels; 2 shafts
Speed, knots: 25

26 SUMIDAGAWA TYPE (RIVER PATROL CRAFT) (PBR)

513–538

Displacement, tons: 18 full load
Dimensions, feet (metres): 54.1 × 12.5 × 2.3 *(16.5 × 3.8 × 0.7)*
Main machinery: 2 Cummins diesels; 800 hp *(597 kW)*; 2 shafts
Speed, knots: 23
Complement: 6
Guns: 1 — 12.7 mm MG.

Comment: First 21 built by Sumidagawa, last five by Captain Co, Thailand 1978–79.

SUMIDAGAWA 529 *6/1999, Marine Police* / 0080841

SUMIDAGAWA 526 *6/2003, Royal Thai Navy* / 0572646

20 CAMCRAFT TYPE (RIVER PATROL CRAFT) (PBR)

415–440 series

Displacement, tons: 13 full load
Dimensions, feet (metres): 40 × 12 × 3.2 *(12.2 × 3.7 × 1)*
Main machinery: 2 Detroit diesels; 540 hp *(403 kW)*; 2 shafts
Speed, knots: 25
Complement: 6

Comment: Delivered by Camcraft, Louisiana. Aluminium hulls. Numbers uncertain.

CAMCRAFT 435 *6/1999, Marine Police* / 0080842

1 RIVER PATROL CRAFT (PBR)

339

Displacement, tons: 5 full load
Dimensions, feet (metres): 37 × 11 × 6 *(11.3 × 3.4 × 1.8)*
Main machinery: 2 diesels; 2 shafts
Speed, knots: 25
Complement: 4

Comment: Built in 1990.

RIVER PATROL CRAFT 339 (alongside Technautic 609) *7/2000* / 0106613

Togo

Country Overview

Formerly French Togoland, the Togolese Republic gained full independence in 1960 having rejected proposals to be united with Ghana. Situated in west Africa, it has an area of 21,925 square miles and borders to the east with Benin and to the west with Ghana. Togo has a short coastline of 30 n miles with the Gulf of Guinea. Lomé is the capital, largest town and principal port. Togo is the only coastal state to claim territorial seas of 30 n miles. A 200 n mile Exclusive Economic Zone (EEZ) is also claimed but this has not been defined by boundary agreements.

Headquarters Appointments

Commanding Officer, Navy:
Captain Attiogbe Ametipe

Personnel

2009:
(a) 250
(b) Conscription (2 years)

Bases

Lomé

PATROL FORCES

2 COASTAL PATROL CRAFT (PB)

Name	*No*	*Builders*	*Launched*
KARA	P 761	Chantiers Navals de l'Esterel, Cannes	18 May 1976
MONO	P 762	Chantiers Navals de l'Esterel, Cannes	16 June 1976

Displacement, tons: 80 full load
Dimensions, feet (metres): 105 × 19 × 5.3 *(32 × 5.8 × 1.6)*
Main machinery: 2 MTU MB 12V 493 TY60 diesels; 2,000 hp(m) *(1.47 MW)* sustained; 2 shafts
Speed, knots: 30. **Range, n miles:** 1,500 at 15 kt
Complement: 17 (1 officer)
Missiles: SSM: Aerospatiale SS 12M; wire-guided to 5 km *(3 n miles)* subsonic; warhead 30 kg.
Guns: 1 Bofors 40 mm/70. 1 Oerlikon 20 mm.
Radars: Surface search: Decca 916; I-band.

Comment: Both craft seagoing but missile system probably not operational.

MONO *6/1998* / 0050252

Tonga

Country Overview

A former British protectorate, the Kingdom of Tonga became a sovereign state in 1970. Situated in the southwestern Pacific Ocean some 1,080 n miles northeast of New Zealand, the country consists of more than 170 islands and islets running generally north-south. There are three main groups, Tongatapu, Ha'apai and Vava'u, and several outlying islands. Nuku'alofa, on Tongatapu Island, is the capital, largest town and principal port. Territorial seas (12 n miles) are claimed. An Exclusive Economic Zone (EEZ) (200 n miles) is claimed but limits have not been fully defined by boundary agreements.

Headquarters Appointments

Commanding Officer, Navy:
Commander Sione Fifita

Personnel

2009: 125

Bases

Touliki Base, Nuku'alofa (HMNB *Masefield*)

Prefix to Ships' Names

VOEA (Vaka O Ene Afio)

PATROL FORCES

Notes: A Beech 18 aircraft was acquired in May 1995 for maritime surveillance.

3 PACIFIC CLASS (LARGE PATROL CRAFT) (PB)

Name	*No*	*Builders*	*Commissioned*
NEIAFU	P 201	Australian Shipbuilding Industries	28 Oct 1989
PANGAI	P 202	Australian Shipbuilding Industries	30 June 1990
SAVEA	P 203	Australian Shipbuilding Industries	23 Mar 1991

Displacement, tons: 162 full load
Dimensions, feet (metres): 103.3 × 26.6 × 6.9 *(31.5 × 8.1 × 2.1)*
Main machinery: 2 Caterpillar 3516TA diesels; 2,820 hp *(2.1 MW)* sustained; 2 shafts
Speed, knots: 20
Range, n miles: 2,500 at 12 kt
Complement: 17 (3 officers)
Guns: 2 — 12.7 mm MGs.
Radars: Surface search: Furuno 1101; I-band.

Comment: Part of the Pacific Forum Australia Defence co-operation. First laid down 30 January 1989, second 2 October 1989, third February 1990. *Savea* has a hydrographic survey capability. Following half-life refits 1998–99 and the decision of the Australian government to extend the Pacific Patrol Boat programme, *Neiafu, Pangai* and *Savea* are due life-extension refits in 2008, 2009 and 2010 respectively.

PANGAI *2/2003, Chris Sattler* / 0558665

AUXILIARIES

1 LCM

Name	*No*	*Builders*	*Commissioned*
LATE (ex-*1057*)	C 315	North Queensland, Cairns	1 Sep 1982

Displacement, tons: 116 full load
Dimensions, feet (metres): 73.5 × 21 × 3.3 *(22.4 × 6.4 × 1)*
Main machinery: 2 Detroit 12V-71 diesels; 680 hp *(507 kW)* sustained; 2 shafts
Speed, knots: 10
Range, n miles: 480 at 10 kt
Complement: 5
Cargo capacity: 54 tons
Guns: 1 — 7.62 mm MG can be carried.
Radars: Surface search: Koden MD 305; I-band.

Comment: Acquired from the Australian Army for inter-island transport. Reported in a poor state of repair and operational status is doubtful.

LATE *6/1999, Tongan Navy* / 0084414

Trinidad and Tobago

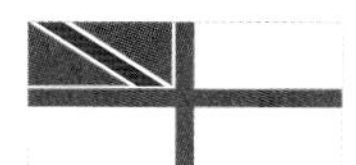

Country Overview

Trinidad and Tobago gained independence in 1962 and became a republic in 1976. The country lies at the southern end of the Lesser Antilles chain and comprises the main islands of Trinidad (1,864 square miles), Tobago (116 square miles) and 21 minor islands and rocks. Trinidad is close to the northeastern coast of Venezuela and the mouth of the Orinoco River. The capital, largest town, and principal port is Port-of-Spain, Trinidad. An archipelagic state, territorial seas (12 n miles) are claimed. While a 200 n mile Exclusive Economic Zone (EEZ) has been claimed, the limits have only been partly defined by boundary agreements.

Headquarters Appointments

Commanding Officer, Coast Guard:
Captain Jewah Ramoutar

Aircraft

The Coast Guard operates three Cessna (Types 172, 402B and 310R) for surveillance and two C26B acquired in 1999. These aircraft can be backed by Air Division Gazelle and Sikorsky S-76 helicopters when necessary.

Personnel

(a) 2009: 1,381 (50 officers)
(b) Voluntary service

Bases

Staubles Bay (HQ)
Hart's Cut, Tobago, Point Fortin
Piarco (Air station), Cedros
Galeota

Coast Defence

There are plans to install a coastal radar system.

Prefix to Ships' Names

TTS

COAST GUARD

Notes: It is planned to procure six interceptor craft and four helicopters.

1 ISLAND CLASS (PBO)

Name	*No*	*Builders*	*Commissioned*
NELSON (ex-*Orkney*)	CG 20 (ex-P 299)	Hall Russell	25 Feb 1977

Displacement, tons: 925 standard; 1,260 full load
Dimensions, feet (metres): 176 wl; 195.3 oa × 36 × 15 *(53.7; 59.5 × 11 × 4.5)*
Main machinery: 2 Ruston 12RKC diesels; 5,640 hp *(4.21 MW)* sustained; 1 shaft; cp prop
Speed, knots: 16.5
Range, n miles: 7,000 at 12 kt
Complement: 35 (5 officers)
Guns: 2 — 7.62 mm MGs can be carried.
Radars: Navigation: Kelvin Hughes Type 1006; I-band.

Comment: Transferred from the UK Navy on 18 December 2000 and recommissioned on 22 February 2001. Based at Port of Spain.

NELSON ***1/2001, H M Steele*** / 0106616

1 TYPE CG 40 (LARGE PATROL CRAFT) (PB)

Name	*No*	*Builders*	*Commissioned*
CASCADURA	CG 6	Karlskronavarvet	15 June 1980

Displacement, tons: 210 full load
Dimensions, feet (metres): 133.2 × 21.9 × 5.2 *(40.6 × 6.7 × 1.6)*
Main machinery: 2 Paxman Valenta 16CM diesels; 6,700 hp *(5 MW)* sustained; 2 shafts
Speed, knots: 30
Range, n miles: 3,000 at 15 kt
Complement: 25
Guns: 1 Bofors 40 mm/70. 1 Oerlikon 20 mm.
Weapons control: Optronic GFCS.
Radars: Surface search: Racal Decca 1226; I-band.

Comment: Ordered in Sweden mid-1978. Laid down early 1979. Fitted with foam-cannon oil pollution equipment and for oceanographic and hydrographic work. Nine spare berths. The hull is similar to Swedish Spica class but with the bridge amidships. Refitted in 1989 and 1998/99. *Barracuda* decommissioned in 2005.

CASCADURA ***1/1994, Maritime Photographic*** / 0506207

4 POINT CLASS (COASTAL PATROL CRAFT) (PB)

Name	*No*	*Builders*	*Commissioned*
COROZAL POINT (ex-*Point Heyer*)	CG 7 (ex-82369)	J Martinac, Tacoma	3 Aug 1967
CROWN POINT (ex-*Point Bennett*)	CG 8 (ex-82351)	Coast Guard Yard, Curtis Bay	19 Dec 1966
GALERA POINT (ex-*Point Bonita*)	CG 9 (ex-82347)	J Martinac, Tacoma	12 Sep 1966
BARCOLET POINT (ex-*Point Highland*)	CG 10 (ex-82333)	Coast Guard Yard, Curtis Bay	27 June 1962

Displacement, tons: 66 full load
Dimensions, feet (metres): 83 × 17.2 × 5.8 *(25.3 × 5.2 × 1.8)*
Main machinery: 2 Caterpillar 3412 diesels; 1,600 hp *(1.19 MW)*; 2 shafts
Speed, knots: 23. **Range, n miles:** 1,500 at 8 kt
Complement: 10
Guns: 2 — 7.62 mm MGs.
Radars: Surface search: Raytheon SPS-64(V)I and Raytheon SPS 69AN; I-band.

Comment: CG 7 and CG 8 transferred from US Coast Guard 12 February 1999 and CG 9 on 14 November 2000. CG 10 transferred on 24 July 2001.

GALERNA POINT ***6/2007, Trinidad and Tobago Coast Guard*** / 1170216

4 SOUTER WASP 17 METRE CLASS (COASTAL PATROL CRAFT) (PB)

Name	*No*	*Builders*	*Commissioned*
PLYMOUTH	CG 27	WA Souter, Cowes	27 Aug 1982
CARONI	CG 28	WA Souter, Cowes	27 Aug 1982
GALEOTA	CG 29	WA Souter, Cowes	27 Aug 1982
MORUGA	CG 30	WA Souter, Cowes	27 Aug 1982

Displacement, tons: 20 full load
Dimensions, feet (metres): 55.1 × 13.8 × 4.6 *(16.8 × 4.2 × 1.4)*
Main machinery: 2 MANN 8V diesels; 1,470 hp *(1.1 MW)*; 2 shafts
Speed, knots: 32
Range, n miles: 500 at 18 kt
Complement: 7 (2 officers)
Guns: 1 — 7.62 mm MG.
Radars: Surface search: Raytheon SPS 69AN; I-band.

Comment: GRP hulls. All refitted from September 1997 with new engines.

PLYMOUTH ***6/2007, Trinidad and Tobago Coast Guard*** / 1335303

2 WASP 20 METRE CLASS (COASTAL PATROL CRAFT) (PB)

Name	*No*	*Builders*	*Commissioned*
KAIRI (ex-*Sea Bird*)	CG 31	WA Souter, Cowes	Dec 1982
MORIAH (ex-*Sea Dog*)	CG 32	WA Souter, Cowes	Dec 1982

Displacement, tons: 32 full load
Dimensions, feet (metres): 65.8 × 16.5 × 5 *(20.1 × 5 × 1.5)*
Main machinery: 2 MANN 12V diesels; 2,400 hp *(1.79 MW)*; 2 shafts
Speed, knots: 30. **Range, n miles:** 450 at 30 kt
Complement: 6 (2 officers)
Guns: 2—7.62 mm MGs.
Radars: Surface search: Decca 150; I-band.

Comment: Ordered 30 September 1981. Aluminium alloy hull. Transferred from the Police in June 1989. New engines in 1999.

KAIRI *7/2001, Margaret Organ* / 0114370

1 SWORD CLASS (COASTAL PATROL CRAFT) (PB)

Name	*No*	*Builders*	*Commissioned*
MATELOT (ex-*Sea Skorpion*)	CG 33	SeaArk Marine	May 1979

Displacement, tons: 15.5 full load
Dimensions, feet (metres): 44.9 × 13.4 × 4.3 *(13.7 × 4.1 × 1.3)*
Main machinery: 2 GM diesels; 850 hp *(634 kW)*; 2 shafts
Speed, knots: 28. **Range, n miles:** 500 at 20 kt
Complement: 6
Guns: 1—7.62 mm MG.
Radars: Surface search: Decca 150; I-band.

Comment: Two transferred from the Police 30 June 1989, one scrapped in 1990. Refitted in 1998.

MATELOT *1/1994, Maritime Photographic* / 0506174

0 + 3 OFFSHORE PATROL VESSELS (PSO)

CG 55–57

Displacement, tons: 2,250 full load
Dimensions, feet (metres): 296.9 × 44.3 × 11.5 *(90.5 × 13.5 × 3.5)*
Main machinery: 2 MAN 16RK 280 diesels; 2 shafts
Speed, knots: 25. **Range, n miles:** 5,500 at 12 kt
Complement: 34 plus 5 trainees plus 50 embarked force
Guns: 1 MSI DS 30M 30 mm. 2 MSI DS 25M 25 mm. 2—12.7 mm MGs.
Weapons control: Ultra Osiris optronic director.
Radars: Air/surface search: Terma 4100; E/F-band.
Navigation: I-band.
Helicopters: Platform for one medium.

Comment: Contract for the design and construction of three offshore patrol vessels signed with VT Shipbuilding on 5 April 2007. First steel was cut on 23 January 2008. The ships are to be used for EEZ management, special operations and maritime law enforcement tasks. An improved River class design, the ships are to be equipped with a 16 tonne crane, space for ISO containers (for disaster relief or military stores) and a 39 kt Pacific 24 RIB. The first two ships are to be launched in 2009 and the third in 2010.

CG 55 (artist's impression) *4/2007, VT Group* / 1165760

12 INTERCEPTION CRAFT (PBF)

CG 001–002 **CG 004–006** **CG 012–018**

Comment: CG 001-002 are 31 ft Bowen craft acquired in May 1991. They are capable of 40 kt. CG 004-006 are 25 ft RHIBs with Johnson outboards acquired from the US in 1993. They are capable of 45 kt. CG 012-013 are Midnight Express craft. CG 014-015 are 40 ft Formula 111 craft acquired from the US in 2005. They are capable of 60 kt. CG 016-018 are 40 ft Phantom Enforcer craft manufactured in Trinidad. They are capable of 60 kt.

CG 002 *6/2007, Trinidad and Tobago Coast Guard* / 1170215

CG 012 *6/2007, Trinidad and Tobago Coast Guard* / 1170214

2 OFFSHORE PATROL VESSEL (PBO)

GASPER GRANDE CG 21 **CHACACHACARE** CG 22

Displacement, tons: 200 full load
Dimensions, feet (metres): 151.9 × 29.8 × 7.9 *(46.3 × 9.1 × 2.4)*
Main machinery: 4 Cummins K38 diesels; 2 shafts
Speed, knots: 20
Range, n miles: 3,300 at 12 kt
Complement: 19
Guns: 2—30 mm. 2—12.7 mm MGs.
Radars: Surface search: E/F-band.
Navigation: I-band.

Comment: As part of the contract, signed with VT Shipbuilding on 5 April 2007, to build three new 90 m offshore patrol vessels, an interim patrol capability is being provided at least until the new vessels start entering service from 2009. Both vessels were commissioned on 23 April 2008. The interim vessels are former US oil-rig crew ships modified to undertake patrol tasks. The ships are equipped with a 39 kt Halmatic Pacific 24 RIB.

CHACACHACARE *1/2008*, Trinidad and Tobago Coast Guard* / 1170217

0 + 6 PATROL CRAFT (PB)

GC 231–236

Measurement, tons: 16 dwt
Dimensions, feet (metres): 98.4 × 21.0 × 4.9 *(30.0 × 6.4 × 1.5)*
Main machinery: 2 MTU 16V 2000 M92 diesels; 4,370 hp *(3.26 MW)*; 2 Kamewa waterjets
Speed, knots: 40. **Range, n miles:** 1,000 at 10 kt
Complement: 12
Guns: 1—20 mm. 3—12.7 mm MGs.
Radars: Surface search/Navigation: To be announced.

Comment: The contract with Austal Shipbuilding for the construction of six patrol craft was announced on 18 March 2008. The monohull craft, of aluminium construction, are to be used for safety of shipping, environmental protection, counter-drugs and SAR duties. The contract includes a five-year support programme and training package. All six craft are to be delivered by early 2010.

PATROL CRAFT (artist's impression) *3/2008*, Austal* / 1294460

1 AUXILIARY VESSEL

REFORM A 04

Comment: Used for Port Services and other support functions.

CUSTOMS

Notes: Among other craft, the Customs service operate a High Speed Interception craft *Kenneth Mohammed.*

KENNETH MOHAMMED *2/2001, van Ginderen Collection* / 0114369

Tunisia

Country Overview

Formerly a French protectorate, the Tunisian Republic gained independence in 1956 and became a republic in 1957. Situated in northern Africa, it has an area of 63,170 square miles and is bordered to the west by Algeria and to the south by Libya. It has a 619 n mile coastline with the Mediterranean Sea. The capital and largest city is the seaport of Tunis. There are further ports at Bizerta, Sousse, Sfax and Gabès while as-Sukhayrah, specialises in petroleum bunkering. Territorial seas (12 n miles) are claimed. An EEZ has not been claimed.

Headquarters Appointments

Naval Chief of Staff:
Rear Admiral Tarek Faouzi El Arbi

Personnel

(a) 2009: 4,800 officers and men (including 800 conscripts)
(b) 1 year's national service

Bases

Bizerte, Sfax, La Goulette, Kelibia

PATROL FORCES

3 COMBATTANTE III M CLASS (FAST ATTACK CRAFT—MISSILE) (PGGF)

Name	*No*	*Builders*	*Launched*	*Commissioned*
LA GALITÉ	501	CMN, Cherbourg	16 June 1983	27 Feb 1985
TUNIS	502	CMN, Cherbourg	27 Oct 1983	27 Mar 1985
CARTHAGE	503	CMN, Cherbourg	24 Jan 1984	29 Apr 1985

Displacement, tons: 345 standard; 425 full load
Dimensions, feet (metres): 183.7 × 26.9 × 7.2 *(56 × 8.2 × 2.2)*
Main machinery: 4 MTU 20V 538 TB93 diesels; 18,740 hp(m) *(13.8 MW)* sustained; 4 shafts
Speed, knots: 38.5
Range, n miles: 700 at 33 kt; 2,800 at 10 kt
Complement: 35
Missiles: SSM: 8 Aerospatiale MM 40 Exocet (2 quad) launchers; inertial cruise; active radar homing to 70 km *(40 n miles)* at 0.9 Mach; warhead 165 kg; sea-skimmer.
Guns: 1 OTO Melara 3 in *(76 mm)*/62; 55-65 rds/min to 16 km *(8.7 n miles)*; weight of shell 6 kg. 2 Breda 40 mm/70 (twin); 300 rds/min to 12.5 km *(6.8 n miles)*; weight of shell 0.96 kg. 4 Oerlikon 30 mm/75 (2 twin); 650 rds/min to 10 km *(5.5 n miles)*; weight of shell 1 kg or 0.36 kg.
Countermeasures: Decoys: 1 CSEE Dagaie trainable launcher; IR flares and chaff.
ESM: Thomson-CSF; DR 2000; intercept.
Combat data systems: Tavitac action data automation.
Weapons control: 2 CSEE Naja optronic directors for 30 mm. Thomson-CSF Vega II for SSM, 76 mm and 40 mm.
Radars: Air/surface search: Thomson-CSF Triton S; G-band; range 33 km *(18 n miles)* for 2 m² target.
Fire control: Thomson-CSF Castor II; I/J-band; range 31 km *(17 n miles)* for 2 m² target.

Programmes: Ordered 27 June 1981.
Operational: CSEE Sylosat navigation system. All three ships operating but reported in need of refits.

CARTHAGE *8/2004, Schaeffer/Marsan* / 1044197

CARTHAGE *8/2004, B Prézelin* / 1044198

3 MODIFIED HAIZHUI CLASS (LARGE PATROL CRAFT) (PB)

UTIQUE P 207 **JERBA** P 208 **KURIAT** P 209

Displacement, tons: 120 full load
Dimensions, feet (metres): 114.8 × 17.7 × 5.9 *(35 × 5.4 × 1.8)*
Main machinery: 4 MWM TB 604 BV12 diesels; 4,400 hp(m) *(3.22 MW)* sustained; 4 shafts
Speed, knots: 28
Range, n miles: 750 at 17 kt
Complement: 39
Guns: 4 China 25 mm/80 (2 twin).
Radars: Surface search: Pot Head; I-band.

Comment: Delivered from China in March 1994. These craft resemble a smaller version of the Haizhui class in service with the Chinese Navy but with a different armament and some superstructure changes. Built to Tunisian specifications.

KURIAT *4/1995* / 0080852

3 BIZERTE CLASS (TYPE PR 48) (LARGE PATROL CRAFT) (PBOM)

Name	*No*	*Builders*	*Commissioned*
BIZERTE	P 301	SFCN, Villeneuve-la-Garenne	10 July 1970
HORRIA (ex-*Liberté*)	P 302	SFCN, Villeneuve-la-Garenne	Oct 1970
MONASTIR	P 304	SFCN, Villeneuve-la-Garenne	25 Mar 1975

Displacement, tons: 250 full load
Dimensions, feet (metres): 157.5 × 23.3 × 7.5 *(48 × 7.1 × 2.3)*
Main machinery: 2 MTU 16V 652TB81 diesels; 4,600 hp(m) *(3.4 MW)* sustained; 2 shafts
Speed, knots: 20. **Range, n miles:** 2,000 at 16 kt
Complement: 34 (4 officers)
Missiles: SSM: 8 Aerospatiale SS 12M; wire-guided to 5.5 km *(3 n miles)* subsonic; warhead 30 kg.
Guns: 4—37 mm/63 (2 twin). 2—14.5 mm MGs.
Radars: Surface search: Thomson-CSF DRBN 31; I-band.

Comment: First pair ordered in 1968, third in August 1973. Guns changed in 1994. All are active.

BIZERTE *3/2002, van Ginderen Collection* / 0141859

HORRIA *10/2001* / 0533311

6 ALBATROS CLASS (TYPE 143B) (PG)

Name	*No*	*Builders*	*Commissioned*
HAMILCAR (ex-*Sperber*)	505 (ex-P 6115)	Kroger, Rendsburg	27 Sep 1976
HANNON (ex-*Greif*)	506 (ex-P 6116)	Lurssen, Vegesack	25 Nov 1976
HIMILCON (ex-*Geier*)	507 (ex-P 6113)	Lurssen, Vegesack	2 June 1976
HANNIBAL (ex-*Seeadler*)	508 (ex-P 6118)	Lurssen, Vegesack	28 Mar 1977
HASDRUBAL (ex-*Habicht*)	509 (ex-P 6119)	Kroger, Rendsburg	23 Dec 1977
GISCON (ex-*Kormoran*)	510 (ex-P 6120)	Lurssen, Vegesack	29 July 1977

Displacement, tons: 398 full load
Dimensions, feet (metres): 189 × 25.6 × 8.5 *(57.6 × 7.8 × 2.6)*
Main machinery: 4 MTU 16V 956TB91 diesels; 17,700 hp(m) *(13 MW)* sustained; 4 shafts
Speed, knots: 40. **Range, n miles:** 1,300 at 30 kt
Complement: 40 (4 officers)

Guns: 2 OTO Melara 3 in *(76 mm)*/62 compact; 85 rds/min to 16 km *(8.6 n miles)* anti-surface; 12 km *(6.5 n miles)* anti-aircraft; weight of shell 6 kg.
2—12.7 mm MGs (may be fitted).
Torpedoes: 2—21 in *(533 mm)* aft tubes. AEG Seeal; wire-guided; active homing to 13 km *(7 n miles)* at 35 kt; passive homing to 28 km *(15 n miles)* at 23 kt; warhead 260 kg.
Countermeasures: Decoys: Buck-Wegmann Hot Dog/Silver Dog; IR/chaff dispenser.
ESM/ECM: Racal Octopus (Cutlass intercept, Scorpion jammer).
Combat data systems: AEG/Signaal command and fire-control system; Link 11.
Weapons control: ORG7/3 optronics GFCS. STN Atlas WBA optronic sensor to be fitted.
Radars: Surface search/fire control: Signaal WM27; I/J-band.
Navigation: SMA 3 RM 20; I-band.

Programmes: Sold to Tunisia on being decommissioned from the German Navy in 2005.
Structure: Wooden hulled craft.
Operational: 505 and 506 transferred on 4 July 2005, 507 and 508 in September 2005 and 509 and 510 on 13 December 2005. Exocet missiles were not transferred although the containers remain on board.

HASDRUBAL *12/2005, Martin Mokrus* / 1167949

HAMILCAR *7/2005, B Prézelin* / 1133152

4 COASTAL PATROL CRAFT (PB)

Name	*No*	*Builders*	*Commissioned*
ISTIKLAL (ex-*VC 11, P 761*)	P 201	Ch Navals de l'Esterel	Apr 1957
JOUMHOURIA	P 202	Ch Navals de l'Esterel	Jan 1961
AL JALA	P 203	Ch Navals de l'Esterel	Nov 1963
REMADA	P 204	Ch Navals de l'Esterel	July 1967

Displacement, tons: 60 standard; 80 full load
Dimensions, feet (metres): 104 × 19 × 5.3 *(31.5 × 5.8 × 1.6)*
Main machinery: 2 MTU MB 12V 493 TY70 diesels; 2,200 hp(m) *(1.62 MW)* sustained; 2 shafts
Speed, knots: 30
Range, n miles: 1,500 at 15 kt
Complement: 17 (3 officers)
Guns: 2 Oerlikon 20 mm.
Radars: Surface search: Racal Decca 1226; I-band.

Comment: *Istiklal* transferred from France March 1959. Wooden hulls. At least one may belong to the Coast Guard.

JOUMHOURIA *3/2006, M Declerck* / 1167533

6 COASTAL PATROL CRAFT (PB)

V 101–106

Displacement, tons: 38 full load
Dimensions, feet (metres): 83 × 15.6 × 4.2 *(25 × 4.8 × 1.3)*
Main machinery: 2 Detroit 12V-71TA diesels; 840 hp *(627 kW)* sustained; 2 shafts; LIPS cp props
Speed, knots: 23
Range, n miles: 900 at 15 kt
Complement: 11
Guns: 1 Oerlikon 20 mm.
Radars: Surface search: Racal Decca 1226; I-band.

Comment: Built by Chantiers Navals de l'Esterel and commissioned in 1961–63. Two further craft of the same design *(Sabaq el Bahr* T 2 and *Jaouel el Bahr* T 1) but unarmed were transferred to the Fisheries Administration in 1971-same builders. Refitted in 1997/98. *V 102* is Coast Guard.

V 105 *3/2006, M Declerck* / 1167532

TRAINING/SURVEY SHIPS

Notes: *Degga* A 707 and *El Jem* A 708 are converted fishing vessels used for divers' training.

EL JEM *7/2002, Schaeffer/Marsan* / 0533312

1 WILKES CLASS (AGS)

Name	*No*	*Builders*	*Launched*	*Commissioned*
KHAIREDDINE (ex-*Wilkes*)	A 700 (ex-T-AGS 33)	Defoe SB Co, Bay City, MI	31 July 1969	28 June 1971

Displacement, tons: 2,843 full load
Dimensions, feet (metres): 285.3 × 48 × 15.1 *(87 × 14.6 × 4.6)*
Main machinery: Diesel-electric; 2 Alco diesel generators; 1 Westinghouse/GE motor; 3,600 hp *(2.69 MW)*; 1 shaft; bow thruster; 350 hp *(261 kW)*
Speed, knots: 15
Range, n miles: 8,000 at 13 kt
Complement: 37
Radars: Navigation: RM 1650/9X; I-band.

Comment: Decommissioned on 29 August 1995 and transferred from the USA by grant aid on 29 September 1995. Designed specifically for surveying operations. Bow propulsion unit for precise manoeuvrability and station keeping. Second of class planned for transfer but not confirmed.

KHAIREDDINE ***7/2007, Bob Fildes*** / 1167858

1 ROBERT D CONRAD CLASS (AGOR/AX)

Name	*No*	*Builders*	*Launched*	*Commissioned*
N N O SALAMMBO (ex-*De Steiguer*)	A 701 (ex-T-AGOR 12)	Northwest Iron Works	13 June 1966	28 Feb 1969

Displacement, tons: 1,370 full load
Dimensions, feet (metres): 208.9 × 40 × 15.3 *(63.7 × 12.2 × 4.7)*
Main machinery: Diesel-electric; 2 Cummins diesel generators; 1 motor; 1,000 hp *(746 kW)*; 1 shaft; bow thruster; 350 hp *(257 kW)*
Speed, knots: 13
Range, n miles: 12,000 at 12 kt
Complement: 40
Radars: Navigation: Raytheon 1650/6X; I-band.

Comment: Transferred from USA on 2 November 1992 and recommissioned on 11 February 1993. Built as an oceanographic research ship. Special features include a 10 ton boom, and a gas turbine for quiet propulsion up to 6 kt. Used primarily for training having replaced the frigate *Inkadh*, which is now an accommodation hulk.

N N O SALAMMBO ***7/1997, Camil Busquets i Vilanova*** / 0019296

AUXILIARIES

1 SIMETO CLASS (WATER TANKER) (AWT)

AIN ZAGHOUAN (ex-*Simeto*) – (ex-A 5375)

Displacement, tons: 1,858 full load
Dimensions, feet (metres): 229 × 33.1 × 14.4 *(69.8 × 10.1 × 4.1)*
Main machinery: 2 GMT B 230.6 BL diesels; 2,530 hp(m) *(1.86 MW)* sustained; 2 shafts; cp props; bow thruster; 300 hp(m) *(220 kW)*
Speed, knots: 13. **Range, n miles:** 1,800 at 12 kt
Complement: 36 (3 officers)
Cargo capacity: 1,130 tons
Guns: 1—20 mm/70. 2—7.62 mm MGs can be carried.
Radars: Navigation: 2 SPN-753B(V); I-band.

Comment: Built by Cinet, Molfetta and originally commissioned on 9 July 1988. Transferred from Italy on 30 June 2003.

SIMETO CLASS (Italian colours) ***2/2000, van Ginderen Collection*** / 0104888

2 WHITE SUMAC CLASS (BUOY TENDERS) (ABU)

Name	*No*	*Launched*	*Recommissioned*
TABARKA (ex-*White Heath*)	A 804 (ex-WLM 545)	21 July 1943	31 Mar 1998
TAGUERMESS (ex-*White Lupine*)	A 805 (ex-WLM 546)	28 July 1943	31 Mar 1998

Displacement, tons: 485 full load
Dimensions, feet (metres): 133 × 31 × 9 *(40.5 × 9.5 × 2.7)*
Main machinery: 2 Caterpillar diesels; 600 hp *(448 kW)*; 2 shafts
Speed, knots: 9
Complement: 24
Radars: Navigation: Raytheon; I-band.

Comment: Former US Coast Guard vessels transferred by gift on 10 June 1998. Arrived in Tunisia one month later.

TAGUERMESS (US colours) ***9/1997, Harald Carstens*** / 0012986

1 COASTAL TUG (YTB)

SIDI DAOUD (ex-*Porto D'Ischia*) – (ex-Y436)

Displacement, tons: 412 full load
Measurement, tons: 122 dwt
Dimensions, feet (metres): 106.3 × 27.9 × 12.8 *(32.4 × 8.5 × 3.9)*
Main machinery: 1 GMT B 230.8 M diesels; 1,600 hp(m) *(1.18 MW)* sustained; 1 shaft; cp prop
Speed, knots: 12.7
Range, n miles: 4,000 at 12 kt
Complement: 13
Radars: Navigation: GEM BX 132; I-band.

Comment: Built in 1970. Transferred from Italy in November 2002.

COASTAL TUG (Italian colours) ***5/2001, Giorgio Ghiglione*** / 0130337

1 BUOY TENDER (ABU)

SIDI BOU SAID A 802

Displacement, tons: To be announced
Dimensions, feet (metres): 127.3 × 33.6 × 5.9 *(38.8 × 10.2 × 1.8)*
Main machinery: 2 Caterpillar 3406 CTA/B diesels; 810 hp(m) *(600 kW)*; 2 shafts
Speed, knots: 10
Complement: To be announced
Radars: Navigation: I-band.

Comment: Built by and procured from Damen, Gorinchem, in 1998. Painted white.

NATIONAL GUARD

Notes: (1) *Tazarke* P 205 and *Menzel Bourguiba* P 206 may have transferred from the Navy to the National Guard but this is not confirmed.
(2) There are at least 12 further patrol craft; *GN 1602, GN 1701, GN 1704, GN 1705, GN 1105, GN 1401, GN 1402, GN 1403, GN 1407, GN 2004, GN 2005* and *GN 907*.

GN 1407 *3/2006, M Declerck* / 1167535

GN 1701 *6/2004, Marco Ghiglino* / 1133146

6 KONDOR I CLASS (PBO)

RAS EL BLAIS (ex-*Demmin*) 601
RAS AJDIR (ex-*Malchin*) 602
RAS EL EDRAK (ex-*Altentreptow*) 603
RAS EL MANOURA (ex-*Templin*) 604
RAS ENGHELA (ex-*Ahrenshoop*) 605
RAS IFRIKIA (ex-*Warnemunde*) 606

Displacement, tons: 377 full load
Dimensions, feet (metres): 170.3 × 23.3 × 7.2 *(51.9 × 7.1 × 2.2)*
Main machinery: 2 Russki/Kolomna 40-DM; 4,408 hp(m) *(3.24 MW)* sustained; 2 shafts; cp props
Speed, knots: 20. **Range, n miles**: 1,800 at 15 kt
Complement: 24
Guns: 2 — 25 mm (twin) can be carried.
Radars: Navigation: TSR 333 or Racal Decca 360; I-band.

Comment: Former GDR minesweepers built at Peenewerft, Wolgast in 1969. First four transferred in May 1992, one in August 1997 and the last one in May 2000. In German service they were fitted with a twin 25 mm gun and a hull-mounted sonar. *Ras Ifrikia* which was used as a fishery protection and research vessel in East German and, later, German service has a more extensive superstructure. These ships may belong to the Navy. Ships of the same class acquired by Cape Verde. Reported operational.

RAS ENGHELA *8/1997, Diego Quevedo* / 0050258

RAS IFRIKIA *5/2000, Kristian Lundgren* / 0567538

4 GABES CLASS (PB)

GABES **JERBA** **KELIBIA** **TABARK**

Displacement, tons: 18 full load
Dimensions, feet (metres): 42.3 × 12.5 × 3 *(12.9 × 3.8 × 0.9)*
Main machinery: 2 diesels; 800 hp(m) *(588 kW)*; 2 shafts
Speed, knots: 38. **Range, n miles**: 250 at 15 kt
Complement: 6
Guns: 2 — 12.7 mm MGs.

Comment: Built by SBCN, Loctudy in 1988-89.

GABES *1/1995* / 0080857

5 BREMSE CLASS (PB)

SBEITLA (ex-*G 32*)
BULLARIJIA (ex-*G 36*)
UTIQUE GN 2301 (ex-*G 37*)
UERKOUANE (ex-*G 38*)
SELEUTA (ex-*G 39*)

Displacement, tons: 42 full load
Dimensions, feet (metres): 74.1 × 15.4 × 3.6 *(22.6 × 4.7 × 1.1)*
Main machinery: 2 SKL 6VD 18/5 AL-1 diesels; 944 hp(m) *(694 kW)* sustained; 2 shafts
Speed, knots: 14
Complement: 6
Guns: 2 — 14.5 mm (twin) MGs can be carried.
Radars: Navigation: TSR 333; I-band.

Comment: Built in 1971-72 for the ex-GDR GBK. Transferred from Germany in May 1992. Others of the class sold to Malta and Cyprus.

UTIQUE *3/2006, M Declerck* / 1167534

2 SOCOMENA (PATROL CRAFT) (PB)

ASSAD BIN FOURAT **MOHAMMED BRAHIM REJEB**

Displacement, tons: 32 full load
Dimensions, feet (metres): 67.3 × 15.4 × 4.3 *(20.5 × 4.7 × 1.3)*
Main machinery: 2 diesels; 1,000 hp(m) *(735 kW)*; 2 shafts
Speed, knots: 28. **Range, n miles**: 500 at 20 kt
Complement: 8
Guns: 1 — 12.7 mm MG.

Comment: Built by Socomena Bizerte, with assistance from South Korea, and completed 2 March 1986.

SOCOMENA CRAFT (inboard) *3/2002, van Ginderen Collection* / 0141833

4 RODMAN 38 CLASS (PB)

Displacement, tons: 11.2 full load
Dimensions, feet (metres): 38.7 × 12.8 × 2.82 *(11.6 × 3.9 × 0.86)*
Main machinery: 2 diesels; 2 shafts
Speed, knots: 28. **Range, n miles**: 300 at 28 kt
Complement: 4
Radars: Navigation: I-band.

Comment: GRP hull. Two supplied in 2000 and two in 2002. Built by Rodman, Vigo for Customs Service.

RODMAN 38 *6/2004* / 1133149

Turkey

TÜRK DENIZ KUVVETLERI

Country Overview

The modern Republic of Turkey was founded in 1923. Situated in south-east Europe and south-west Asia, the country has an area of 300,948 square miles and is bordered to the north-west by Bulgaria and Greece, to the north-east by Georgia and Armenia, to the east by Iran and to the south with Iraq and Syria. It has a 739 n mile coastline with the Black Sea and 3,149 n mile coastline with the Aegean and Mediterranean Seas. The capital is Ankara, while the leading ports are Istanbul (largest city) and Izmir. In addition, Black Sea ports include Trabzon, Giresun, Samsun, and Zonguldak while Iskenderun and Mersin lie on the Mediterranean. Territorial waters for Black Sea and Mediterranean (12 n miles) are claimed and for Aegean (6 n miles). An EEZ (200 n miles) is claimed in the Black Sea only.

Headquarters Appointments

Commander-in-Chief, Turkish Naval Forces:
Admiral M Metin Ataç
Chief of Naval Staff:
Vice Admiral E Murat Bilgel
Chief of Coast Guard:
Rear Admiral A Can Erenoğlu

Flag Officers

Comturfleet (Gölcük):
Admiral E Uğur Yiğit
Comtursarnorth (Istanbul):
Vice Admiral A Feyyaz Öğütcü
Comtursarsouth (Izmir):
Vice Admiral S Erdal Bucak
Comturnavtrain (Istanbul):
Rear Admiral Kadir Sağdiç
Comturampgroup (Foça):
Rear Admiral Baha Eren
Comtursuracgroup (Gölcük):
Rear Admiral Bülent Bostanoğlu
Comturfastgroup (Gölcük):
Rear Admiral Hasan Uşaklioğlu
Comturminegroup (Erdek):
Rear Admiral Yalçin Kavukçuoğlu
Comtursubgroup (Gölcük):
Rear Admiral Serdar Dülger
Comturespatgroup (Izmir):
Rear Admiral Kemalettin Gür
Comiststrait (Istanbul):
Rear Admiral Ibrahim Akin
Comcanstrait (Çanakkale):
Rear Admiral Erhan Akporay
Comturageanzone (Izmir):
Rear Admiral S Tayfun Atilir

Flag Officers — *continued*

Comturmedzone (Mersin):
Rear Admiral Soner Polat
Comtursouthtskgrp (Aksaz):
Rear Admiral Fikret Güneş
Comturnavgolbase (Gölcük):
Rear Admiral Doğan Denizmen
Comturnavaksbase (Aksaz):
Rear Admiral Celal Parlakoğlu
Comturmairbase (Topel):
Rear Admiral Deniz Dağlilar
Comturblackzone (Ereğli):
Rear Admiral Türker Ertürk
Comturmarbde (Foça):
Rear Admiral Ufuk Aslan
Comturampships (Foça):
Rear Admiral Cem Gürdeniz
Comturnaviskbase (Iskenerun):
Rear Admiral Ismail Taylan

Personnel

(a) 2009: 55,000 (5,500 officers) including 31,000 conscripts, 3,000 Marines and 900 Air Arm (reserves 70,000)
(b) 15 months' national service

Organisation

Fleet HQ (Ankara), Fleet Command (Gölcük), Northern Area Command (Black Sea and Marmara), Southern Area Command (Aegean and Mediterranean), Naval Training Command (Istanbul).

Bases

Headquarters: Ankara
Black Sea: Ereğli, Bartin, Samsun, Trabzon
Marmara: Istanbul, Erdek, Çanakkale, Gölcük
Mediterranean: Izmir, Foça, Antalya, Mersin, Iskenderun, Aksaz
Dockyards: Gölcük, Pendik (Istanbul), Izmir

Prefix to Ships' Names

TCG (Turkish Republic Ship)
TCSG (Turkish Republic Coast Guard)

Strength of the Fleet (including Coast Guard)

Type	*Active*	*Building (Planned)*
Submarines—Patrol	14	(6)
Frigates	17	–
Corvettes	6	1 (11)
Fast Attack Craft—Missile	25	2
Large Patrol Craft	18	16
Minesweepers/Hunters—Coastal	14	2
Minesweepers—Inshore	4	–
LSTs/Minelayers	5	–
LCTs	24	–
Survey Vessels	3	–
Training Ships	10	–
Fleet Support Ships	2	–
Tankers	4	–
Transports—Large and small	13	–
Salvage Ships	3	(3)
Boom Defence Vessels	2	–

Pennant Numbers

From mid-1997 all pennant numbers have been repainted in non-reflective paint.

Marines

Total: 3,000
One brigade of HQ company, three infantry battalions, one artillery battalion, support units.

Coast Guard (Sahil Güvenlik)

Formed in July 1982 from the naval wing of the Jandarma. Prefix J replaced by SG and paint scheme is very light grey with a diagonal stripe forward. About 1,700 officers and men. Plans to establish a coastal surveillance system were announced in June 2008. The coastline is to be broken down into some 31 sectors in which radar and other sensors would be established. Requests for Proposals were issued to a large number of international and national companies.

DELETIONS

Frigates

2006 *Karadeniz*
2007 *Muavenet*

Auxiliaries

2006 *Eceabat*

PENNANT LIST

Submarines

S 347	Atilay
S 348	Saldiray
S 349	Batiray
S 350	Yildiray
S 351	Doğanay
S 352	Dolunay
S 353	Preveze
S 354	Sakarya
S 355	18 Mart
S 356	Anafartalar
S 357	Gür
S 358	Çanakkale
S 359	Burakreis
S 360	1. Inönü

Frigates

F 240	Yavuz
F 241	Turgutreis
F 242	Fatih
F 243	Yildirim
F 244	Barbaros
F 245	Orucreis
F 246	Salihreis
F 247	Kemalreis
F 253	Zafer
F 490	Gaziantep
F 491	Giresun
F 492	Gemlik
F 493	Gelibolu
F 494	Gökçeada
F 495	Gediz
F 496	Gökova
F 497	Göksu

Corvettes

F 500	Bozcaada
F 501	Bodrum
F 502	Bandirma
F 503	Beykoz
F 504	Bartin
F 505	Bafra
F 511	Heybeliada (bldg)

Mine Warfare Forces (Sweepers/Hunters)

M 260	Edincik
M 261	Edremit
M 262	Enez
M 263	Erdek
M 264	Erdemli
M 265	Alanya
M 266	Amasra
M 267	Ayvalik
M 268	Akçakoca (bldg)
M 269	Anamur (bldg)
M 270	Akçay (bldg)
M 500	Foça
M 501	Fethiye
M 502	Fatsa
M 503	Finike
M 514	Silifke
M 515	Saros
M 516	Sigacik
M 517	Sapanca
M 518	Sariyer
P 313-314	MTB 3-4
P 316-319	MTB 6-9

Amphibious Forces

L 401	Ertuğrul
L 402	Serdar
NL 123	Sarucabey
NL 124	Karamürselbey
NL 125	Osman Gazi

Patrol Forces

P 114	Akhisar
P 121	AB 21
P 122	AB 22
P 123	AB 23
P 124	AB 24
P 127	AB 27
P 128	AB 28
P 129	AB 29
P 131	AB 31
P 135	AB 35
P 136	AB 36
P 301	Kozlu
P 302	Kuşadasi
P 307	Karamürsel
P 308	Kerempe
P 309	Kilimli
P 321	Denizkuşu
P 322	Atmaca
P 323	Şahin
P 324	Kartal
P 326	Pelikan
P 327	Albatros
P 328	Şimşek
P 329	Kasirga
P 330	Kiliç
P 331	Kalkan
P 332	Mizrak
P 333	Tufan
P 334	Meltem
P 335	Imbat
P 336	Zipkin (bldg)
P 337	Atak (bldg)
P 338	Bora (bldg)
P 340	Doğan
P 341	Marti
P 342	Tayfun
P 343	Volkan
P 344	Rüzgar
P 345	Poyraz
P 346	Gurbet
P 347	Firtina
P 348	Yildiz
P 349	Karayel
P 531	Terme

Auxiliaries

P 305	AG 5
P 306	AG 6
A 570	Taşkizak
A 571	Albay Hakki Burak
A 572	Yuzbasi Ihsan Tolunay
A 573	Binbaşi Sadettin Gürcan
A 576	Değirmendere
A 577	Sokullu Mehmet Paşa
A 578	Darica
A 579	Cezayirli Gazi Hasan Paşa
A 580	Akar
A 581	Çinar
A 582	Kemer
A 585	Akin
A 586	Akbas
A 587	Gazal
A 588	Çandarli
A 589	Işin
A 590	Inebolu
A 592	Karadeniz Ereğli
A 594	Çubuklu
A 595	Yarbay Kudret Güngör
A 596	Ulubat
A 597	Van
A 598	Söğüt
A 599	Çeşme
A 600	Kavak
A 1531	E 1
A 1532	E 2
A 1533	E 3
A 1534	E 4
A 1535	E 5
A 1536	E 6
A 1537	E 7
A 1538	E 8
A 1542	Söndüren 2
A 1543	Söndüren 3
A 1544	Söndüren 4
A 1600	Iskenderun
Y 50	Gölcük
Y 51	Söndüren 1
Y 52	Doğanarslan
Y 53	Kuvvet
Y 55	Atil
Y 56	Pendik
Y 57	Aksaz
Y 64	Ersev Bayrak
Y 90	Deney
Y 95	Torpido Tenderi
Y 98	Takip 1
Y 99	Takip 2
Y 112	Pinar 2
Y 113	Pinar 3
Y 114	Pinar 4
Y 116	Pinar 6
Y 139	Yakit
Y 140	H 500
Y 141	H 501
Y 142	H 502
Y 160	Önder
Y 161	Öncü
Y 162	Özgen
Y 163	Öden
Y 164	Özgür

SUBMARINES

8 PREVEZE (TYPE 209/1400) CLASS (SSK)

Name	*No*	*Builders*	*Laid down*	*Launched*	*Commissioned*
PREVEZE	S 353	Gölcük, Kocaeli	12 Sep 1989	22 Oct 1993	22 Mar 1994
SAKARYA	S 354	Gölcük, Kocaeli	1 Feb 1990	28 July 1994	6 Jan 1995
18 MART	S 355	Gölcük, Kocaeli	28 July 1994	25 Aug 1997	27 Aug 1997
ANAFARTALAR	S 356	Gölcük, Kocaeli	1 Aug 1995	1 Sep 1998	12 Oct 1998
GÜR	S 357	Gölcük, Kocaeli	21 Feb 2000	24 Feb 2003	24 July 2003
ÇANAKKALE	S 358	Gölcük, Kocaeli	19 Dec 2000	23 June 2004	26 July 2005
BURAKREIS	S 359	Gölcük, Kocaeli	19 Dec 2001	5 Sep 2005	15 Feb 2006
1. INÖNÜ	S 360	Gölcük, Kocaeli	2 Jan 2003	24 May 2007	22 July 2007

Displacement, tons: 1,454 surfaced; 1,586 dived
Dimensions, feet (metres): 203.4 × 20.3 × 18 *(62 × 6.2 × 5.5)*
Main machinery: Diesel-electric; 4 MTU 12V 396 SB83 diesels; 3,800 hp(m) *(2.8 MW)* sustained; 4 alternators; 1 Siemens motor; 4,000 hp(m) *(3.38 MW)* sustained; 1 shaft
Speed, knots: 10 surfaced/snorting; 21.5 dived
Range, n miles: 8,200 at 8 kt surfaced; 400 at 4 kt dived
Complement: 30 (8 officers)

Missiles: McDonnell Douglas Sub Harpoon; active radar homing to 130 km *(70 n miles)* at 0.9 Mach; warhead 227 kg.
Torpedoes: 8—21 in *(533 mm)* bow tubes. GEC-Marconi Tigerfish Mk 24 Mod 2; wire-guided; active/passive homing to 13 km *(7 n miles)* at 35 kt active; 29 km *(15.7 n miles)* at 24 kt passive; warhead 134 kg or STN Atlas DM 2A4 (S 357 onwards). Total of 14 torpedoes and missiles.
Mines: In lieu of torpedoes.
Countermeasures: ESM: Racal Porpoise or Racal Sealion (UAP) (S 357 onwards); intercept.
Weapons control: Atlas Elektronik ISUS 83-2 TFCS. Link 11 receive only.
Radars: Surface search: I-band.
Sonars: Atlas Elektronik CSU 83; passive/active search and attack; medium/high frequency.
Atlas Elektronik TAS-3; towed array; passive low frequency.
STN Atlas flank array; passive low frequency.

Programmes: Order for first two signed in Ankara on 17 November 1987 with option on two more taken up in 1993. Four more ordered 22 July 1998. All built with HDW prefabrication and assembly at Gölcük. The last four are called the Gür class.
Structure: Single hull design. Diving depth, 280 m *(820 ft)*. Kollmorgen masts. Four torpedo tubes can be used for SSM. STN Atlas flank arrays fitted in 1998/99 to the first four.
Operational: Endurance, 50 days.

ÇANAKKALE *9/2005, Selçuk Emre* / 1133567

18 MART *7/2000, Michael Nitz* 0106618

PREVEZE *10/2003, C D Yaylali* / 0567543

ANAFARTALAR *4/2001, Selçuk Emre* / 0132789

6 ATILAY (209) CLASS (TYPE 1200) (SSK)

Name	*No*	*Builders*	*Laid down*	*Launched*	*Commissioned*
ATILAY	S 347	Howaldtswerke, Kiel	1 Dec 1972	23 Oct 1974	12 Mar 1976
SALDIRAY	S 348	Howaldtswerke, Kiel	2 Jan 1973	14 Feb 1975	15 Jan 1977
BATIRAY	S 349	Howaldtswerke, Kiel	1 June 1975	24 Oct 1977	7 Nov 1978
YILDIRAY	S 350	Gölcük, Izmit	1 May 1976	20 July 1979	20 July 1981
DOĞANAY	S 351	Gölcük, Izmit	21 Mar 1980	16 Nov 1983	16 Nov 1984
DOLUNAY	S 352	Gölcük, Izmit	9 Mar 1981	22 July 1988	29 June 1990

Displacement, tons: 980 surfaced; 1,185 dived
Dimensions, feet (metres): 200.8 × 20.3 × 17.9 *(61.2 × 6.2 × 5.5)*
Main machinery: Diesel-electric; 4 MTU 12V 493 TY60 diesels; 2,400 hp(m) *(1.76 MW)* sustained; 4 alternators; 1.7 MW; 1 Siemens motor; 4,600 hp(m) *(3.38 MW)* sustained; 1 shaft
Speed, knots: 11 surfaced; 22 dived
Range, n miles: 7,500 at 8 kt surfaced
Complement: 38 (9 officers)

Torpedoes: 8—21 in *(533 mm)* tubes. 14 AEG SST 4; wire-guided; active/passive homing to 28 km *(15.3 n miles)* at 23 kt; 12 km *(6.6 n miles)* at 35 kt; warhead 260 kg. Swim-out discharge.
Countermeasures: ESM: Thomson-CSF DR 2000 or Racal Sealion (UAP) or Racal Porpoise; intercept
Weapons control: Signaal M8 (S 347-348). Signaal Sinbads (remainder). Link 11 receive.
Radars: Surface search: S 63B; I-band.
Sonars: Atlas Elektronik CSU 3; hull-mounted; passive/active search and attack; medium/high frequency.

Programmes: Designed by Ingenieurkontor, Lübeck for construction by Howaldtswerke, Kiel and sale by Ferrostaal, Essen, all acting as a consortium. Last three built in Turkey with assistance given by HDW.
Modernisation: Mid-life upgrades are planned, for the last four boats. The programme, which may include command system and weapon system upgrades was planned to have started in 2006 although details have not been confirmed.
Structure: A single-hull design with two ballast tanks and forward and after trim tanks. Fitted with snort and remote machinery control. The single screw is slow revving. Very high-capacity batteries with GRP lead-acid cells and battery cooling-by Wilh Hagen. Active and passive sonar, sonar detection equipment, sound ranging gear and underwater telephone. Fitted with two periscopes, radar and Omega receiver. Fore-planes retract. Diving depth, 250 m *(820 ft)*.
Operational: Endurance, 50 days. Some US Mk 37 torpedoes may also be carried.

DOĞANAY *10/2006, B Prézelin* / 1164271

YILDIRAY *1/2002, M Declerck* / 0132790

0 + (6) TYPE 214 CLASS (SSK)

Displacement, tons: 1,700 surfaced; 1,860 dived
Dimensions, feet (metres): 213.3 × 20.7 × 19.7 *(65 × 6.3 × 6)*
Main machinery: 1 MTU 16V 396 diesel; 4,243 hp *(3.12 MW)*; 1 Siemens Permasyn motor; 3,875 hp(m) *(2.85 MW)*; 1 shaft; 2 HDW PEM fuel cells; 240 kW; sodium sulphide high-energy batteries
Speed, knots: 20 dived; 12 surfaced
Complement: 27 (5 officers)

Torpedoes: 8—21 in *(533 mm)* bow tubes.
Countermeasures: Decoys: ESM.
Weapons control: STN Atlas.
Radars: Surface search: I-band.
Sonars: Bow, flank and towed arrays.

Programmes: It was announced on 22 July 2008 that negotiations to procure six Type 214 submarines, equipped with Air Independent Propulsion (AIP), were to be opened with HDW. The boats are to be built at Gölcük Shipyard and delivery of the first boat is planned in 2015.
Structure: The Type 214 is a synthesis of the proven Type 209 design with AIP from the Type 212. Turkey is the third customer for the Type 214. Details are based on those in South Korean service and may be different.

TYPE 214 CLASS *10/2008*, Michael Nitz* / 1353402

FRIGATES

Notes: The Turkish Frigate 2000 (TF 2000) project for a class of four ships is unlikely to be taken forward until further progress has been made with the MILGEM project.

4 BARBAROS CLASS (MEKO 200TN II-A/B) (FFGHM)

Name	*No*	*Builders*	*Laid down*	*Launched*	*Commissioned*
BARBAROS	F 244	Blohm + Voss, Hamburg	18 Mar 1993	29 Sep 1993	16 Mar 1995
ORUCREIS	F 245	Gölcük, Kocaeli	15 Sep 1993	28 July 1994	10 May 1996
SALIHREIS	F 246	Blohm + Voss, Hamburg	24 July 1995	26 Sep 1997	17 Dec 1998
KEMALREIS	F 247	Gölcük, Kocaeli	4 Apr 1997	24 July 1998	8 June 2000

Displacement, tons: 3,380 full load
Dimensions, feet (metres): 387.1 × 48.6 × 14.1; 21 (sonar) *(118 × 14.8 × 4.3; 6.4)*
Main machinery: CODOG; 2 GE LM 2500 gas turbines; 60,000 hp *(44.76 MW)* sustained; 2 MTU 16V 1163 TB83 diesels; 11,780 hp(m) *(8.67 MW)* sustained; 2 shafts; Escher Wyss; cp props
Speed, knots: 32
Range, n miles: 4,100 at 18 kt
Complement: 187 (22 officers) plus 9 aircrew plus 8 spare

Missiles: SSM: 8 McDonnell Douglas Harpoon (2 quad) launchers ❶; active radar homing to 130 km *(70 n miles)* at 0.9 Mach; warhead 227 kg.
SAM: Raytheon Sea Sparrow RIM-7M Mk 29 Mod 1 octuple launcher ❷ (F 244 and F 245) and VLS Mk 41 Mod 8 ❸ (F 246 and F 247); semi-active radar homing to 16 km *(8.5 n miles)* at 2.5 Mach; warhead 38 kg. RIM-162 Evolved Sea Sparrow (ESSM) in due course.
Guns: 1 FMC 5 in *(127 mm)*/54 Mk 45 Mod 1/2 ❹; 20 rds/min to 23 km *(12.6 n miles)* anti-surface; 15 km *(8.2 n miles)* anti-aircraft; weight of shell 32 kg.
3 Oerlikon-Contraves 25 mm Sea Zenith ❺; 4 barrels per mounting; 3,400 rds/min combined to 2 km.
Torpedoes: 6—324 mm Mk 32 Mod 5 (2 triple) tubes ❻. Honeywell Mk 46 Mod 5; anti-submarine; active/passive homing to 11 km *(5.9 n miles)* at 40 kt; warhead 44 kg.
Countermeasures: Decoys: 2 Loral Hycor 6-tubed fixed Mk 36 Mod 1 SRBOC ❼; IR flares and chaff to 4 km *(2.2 n miles)*.
Nixie SLQ-25; towed torpedo decoy.
ESM/ECM: Racal Cutlass/Scorpion; intercept and jammer.
Combat data systems: Thomson-CSF/Signaal STACOS Mod 3; Link 11. WSC 3V(7) SATCOMs. Marisat.
Weapons control: 2 Siemens Albis optronic directors ❽. SWG-1A for Harpoon.
Radars: Air search: Siemens/Plessey AWS 9 (Type 996) ❾; 3D; E/F-band.
Air/surface search: Plessey/BAe AWS 6 Dolphin ❿; G-band.
Fire control: 1 or 2 (F 246-247) Signaal STIR ⓫; I/J/K-band (for SAM); range 140 km *(76 n miles)* for 1 m² target.
Contraves TMKu (F 244-245) ⓬; I/J-band (for SSM and 127 mm).
2 Contraves Seaguard ⓭; I/J-band (for 25 mm).
Navigation: Racal Decca 2690 BT ARPA; I-band.
Tacan: URN 25. IFF Mk XII Mod 4.
Sonars: Raytheon SQS-56 (DE 1160); hull-mounted; active search and attack; medium frequency.

Helicopters: 1 AB 212ASW ⓮ or S-70B Seahawk.

Programmes: First pair ordered 19 January 1990, second pair authorised 14 December 1992. Programme started 5 November 1991 with construction commencing in June 1992 in Germany. Completion of the last one delayed by the Gölcük earthquake in 1999.
Structure: An improvement on the Yavuz class. Mk 29 Sea Sparrow launchers fitted in the first two, while the second pair have Mk 41 VLS aft of the funnel, which are to be retrofitted in the first two. The ships have CODOG propulsion for a higher top speed. Other differences with *Yavuz* include a full command system, improved radars and a citadel for NBCD protection. A bow bulwark has been added in the second pair.
Operational: The AB 212 helicopter has Sea Skua anti-ship missiles. All can be used as Flagships.

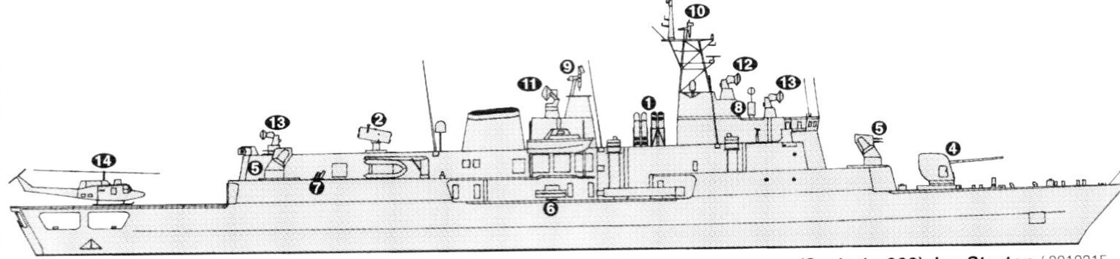

BARBAROS *(Scale 1 : 900), Ian Sturton* / 0019315

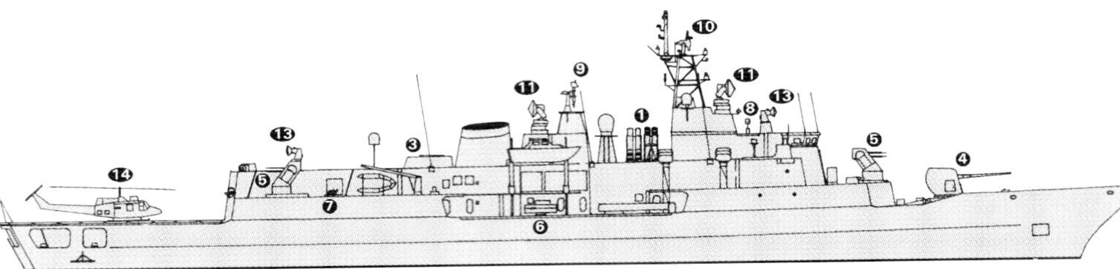

SALIHREIS *(Scale 1 : 900), Ian Sturton* / 1153494

ORUCREIS *8/2008*, C D Yaylali* / 1353403

SALIHREIS *6/2008*, Giorgio Ghiglione* / 1353400

KEMALREIS *11/2007, Selim San* / 1353404

4 YAVUZ CLASS (MEKO 200 TN) (FFGHM)

Name	*No*	*Builders*	*Laid down*	*Launched*	*Commissioned*
YAVUZ	F 240	Blohm + Voss, Hamburg	30 May 1985	7 Nov 1985	17 July 1987
TURGUTREIS (ex-*Turgut*)	F 241	Howaldtswerke, Kiel	20 May 1985	30 May 1986	4 Feb 1988
FATIH	F 242	Gölcük, Izmit	1 Jan 1986	24 Apr 1987	28 Aug 1988
YILDIRIM	F 243	Gölcük, Izmit	24 Apr 1987	22 July 1988	17 Nov 1989

Displacement, tons: 2,414 standard; 2,919 full load
Dimensions, feet (metres): 378.9 × 46.6 × 13.5 *(115.5 × 14.2 × 4.1)*
Main machinery: CODAD; 4 MTU 20V 1163 TB93 diesels; 29,940 hp(m) *(22 MW)* sustained; 2 shafts; cp props
Speed, knots: 27
Range, n miles: 4,100 at 18 kt
Complement: 180 (24 officers)

Missiles: SSM: 8 McDonnell Douglas Harpoon (2 quad) launchers ❶; active radar homing to 130 km *(70 n miles)* at 0.9 Mach; warhead 227 kg.
SAM: Raytheon Sea Sparrow RIM-7M Mk 29 Mod 1 octuple launcher ❷; semi-active radar homing to 16 km *(8.5 n miles)* at 2.5 Mach; warhead 38 kg.
Guns: 1 FMC 5 in *(127 mm)*/54 Mk 45 Mod 1 ❸; 20 rds/min to 23 km *(12.6 n miles)* anti-surface; 15 km *(8.2 n miles)* anti-aircraft; weight of shell 32 kg.
3 Oerlikon-Contraves 25 mm Sea Zenith ❹; 4 barrels per mounting; 3,400 rds/min combined to 2 km.
Torpedoes: 6—324 mm Mk 32 (2 triple) tubes ❺. Honeywell Mk 46 Mod 5; anti-submarine; active/passive homing to 11 km *(5.9 n miles)* at 40 kt; warhead 44 kg.
Countermeasures: Decoys: 2 Loral Hycor 6-tubed fixed Mk 36 Mod 1 SRBOC ❻; IR flares and chaff to 4 km *(2.2 n miles)*.
Nixie SLQ-25; towed torpedo decoy.
ESM/ECM: Signaal Rapids/Ramses; intercept and jammer.
Combat data systems: Signaal STACOS-TU; action data automation; Link 11. WSC 3V(7) SATCOMs. Marisat.
Weapons control: 2 Siemens Albis optronic directors (for Sea Zenith). SWG-1A for Harpoon.
Radars: Air search: Signaal DA08 ❼; F-band.
Air/surface search: Plessey AWS 6 Dolphin ❽; G-band.
Fire control: Signaal STIR ❾; I/J/K-band (for SAM); range 140 km *(76 n miles)* for 1 m² target.
Signaal WM25 ❿; I/J-band (for SSM and 127 mm).
2 Contraves Seaguard ⓫; I/J-band (for 25 mm).
Navigation: Racal Decca TM 1226; I-band.
Tacan: URN 25. IFF Mk XII.

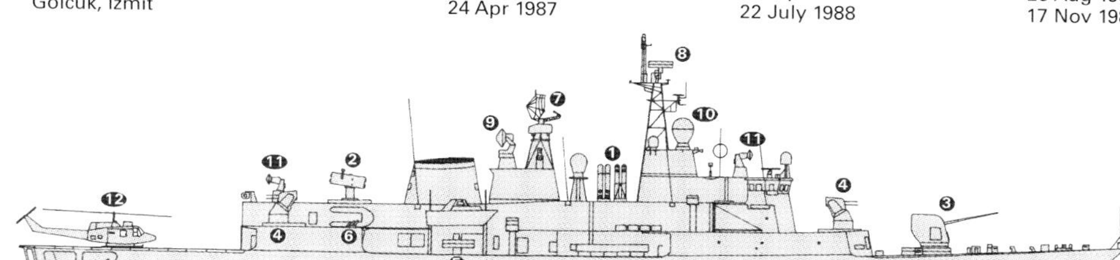

YAVUZ *(Scale 1 : 900), Ian Sturton* / 1153493

TURGUTREIS *7/2008*, C D Yaylali* / 1353405

Sonars: Raytheon SQS-56 (DE 1160); hull-mounted; active search and attack; medium frequency.

Helicopters: 1 AB 212ASW ⓬.

Programmes: Ordered 29 December 1982 with builders and Thyssen Rheinstahl Technik of Dusseldorf. Meko 200 type similar to Portuguese frigates. *Turgutreis* was renamed on 14 February 1988.
Operational: Helicopter has Sea Skua anti-ship missiles.

FATIH *8/2008*, C D Yaylali* / 1353406

YAVUZ *5/2007, Selim San* / 1167881

8 + (2) GAZIANTEP (OLIVER HAZARD PERRY) CLASS (FFGHM)

Name	*No*	*Builders*	*Laid down*	*Launched*	*Commissioned*	*Recommissioned*
GAZIANTEP (ex-*Clifton Sprague*)	F 490 (ex-FFG 16)	Bath Iron Works	30 Sep 1979	16 Feb 1980	21 Mar 1981	24 July 1998
GIRESUN (ex-*Antrim*)	F 491 (ex-FFG 20)	Todd Shipyards, Seattle	21 June 1978	27 Mar 1979	26 Sep 1981	24 July 1998
GEMLIK (ex-*Flatley*)	F 492 (ex-FFG 21)	Bath Iron Works	13 Nov 1979	15 May 1980	20 June 1981	24 July 1998
GELIBOLU (ex-*Reid*)	F 493 (ex-FFG 30)	Todd Shipyards, San Pedro	8 Oct 1980	27 June 1981	19 Feb 1983	22 July 1999
GÖKÇEADA (ex-*Mahlon S Tisdale*)	F 494 (ex-FFG 27)	Todd Shipyards, San Pedro	19 Mar 1980	7 Feb 1981	27 Nov 1982	8 June 2000
GEDİZ (ex-*John A Moore*)	F 495 (ex-FFG 19)	Todd Shipyards, San Pedro	19 Dec 1978	20 Oct 1979	14 Nov 1981	25 July 2000
GOKOVA (ex-*Samuel Eliot Morison*)	F 496 (ex-FFG 13)	Bath Iron Works	4 Aug 1978	14 July 1979	11 Oct 1980	11 Apr 2002
GÖKSU (ex-*Estocin*)	F 497 (ex-FFG 15)	Bath Iron Works	2 Apr 1979	3 Nov 1979	10 Jan 1981	4 Apr 2003

Displacement, tons: 2,750 light, 3,638 full load
Dimensions, feet (metres): 453 × 45 × 14.8; 24.5 (sonar) *(138.1 × 13.7 × 4.5; 7.5)*
Main machinery: 2 GE LM 2500 gas turbines; 41,000 hp *(30.59 MW)* sustained; 1 shaft; cp prop
2 auxiliary retractable props; 650 hp *(484 kW)*
Speed, knots: 29
Range, n miles: 4,500 at 20 kt
Complement: 206 (13 officers) including 19 aircrew

Missiles: SSM: 4 McDonnell Douglas Harpoon Block 1B; active radar homing to 92 km *(50 n miles)* at 0.9 Mach; warhead 227 kg.
SAM: 36 Raytheon Standard SM-1MR Block VIB; command guidance; semi-active radar homing to 38 km *(20.5 n miles)* at 2 Mach.
1 Mk 13 Mod 4 launcher for both SSM and SAM missiles ❶.
Guns: 1 OTO Melara 3 in *(76 mm)*/62 Mk 75 ❷; 85 rds/min to 16 km *(8.7 n miles)* anti-surface; 12 km *(6.6 n miles)* anti-aircraft; weight of shell 6 kg.
1 General Electric/General Dynamics 20 mm/76 6-barrelled Mk 15 Vulcan Phalanx ❸; 3,000 rds/min combined to 1.5 km.
4—12.7 mm MGs.
Torpedoes: 6—324 mm Mk 32 (2 triple) tubes ❹. 24 Honeywell Mk 46 Mod 5; anti-submarine; active/passive homing to 11 km *(5.9 n miles)* at 40 kt; warhead 44 kg.
Countermeasures: Decoys: 2 Loral Hycor SRBOC 6-barrelled fixed Mk 36 ❺; IR flares and chaff to 4 km *(2.2 n miles)*.
T-Mk-6 Fanfare/SLQ-25 Nixie; torpedo decoy.
ESM/ECM: SLQ-32(V)2 ❻; radar warning. Sidekick modification adds jammer and deception system.

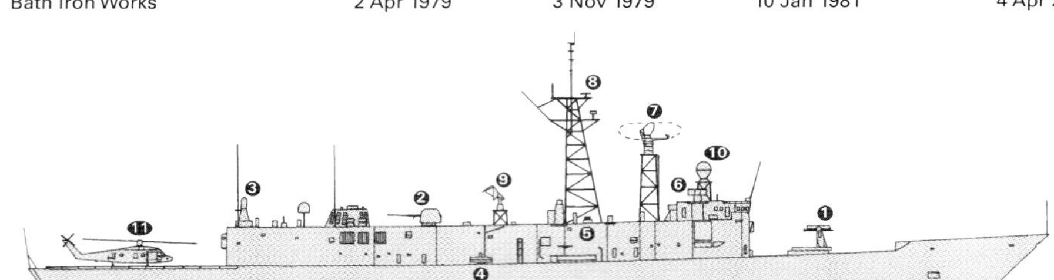

GÖKÇEADA *(Scale 1 : 1,200), Ian Sturton* / 0587565

Combat data systems: NTDS with Link 11 and 14. SATCOM.
Weapons control: SWG-1 Harpoon LCS. Mk 92 Mod 4 WCS with CAS (Combined Antenna System). The Mk 92 is the US version of the Signaal WM28 system. Mk 13 weapon direction system. 2 Mk 24 optical directors.
Radars: Air search: Raytheon SPS-49(V)4 ❼; C/D-band.
Surface search: ISC Cardion SPS-55 ❽; I-band.
Fire control: Lockheed STIR (modified SPG-60) ❾; I/J-band.
Sperry Mk 92 (Signaal WM28) ❿; I/J-band.
Navigation: Furuno; I-band.
Tacan: URN 25.
Sonars: Raytheon SQS-56; hull-mounted; active search and attack; medium frequency.

Helicopters: 1 S-70B Seahawk ⓫.

Programmes: Three approved for transfer by grant aid. Transfer delayed by Greek objections, and Turkish sailors were sent home from the US in mid-1996. Congress authorised the go-ahead again on 27 August 1997. Two more approved for transfer by sale 30 September 1998, one in February 2000, one in April 2002 and one in April 2003. At least one other *Duncan* FFG 10 for spares. The transfer of two further ships *George Philip* FFG 12 and *Sides* FFG 14 is under consideration.
Modernisation: The combat data system is being upgraded under the 'Genesis' programme. F 492 was the first to be modernised and returned to service on 18 May 2007. The other ships are to follow. MilSoft awarded a contract in August 2006 to develop a Link 11/16 datalink system. Mk 41 VLS launchers are to be installed in four ships. The arrangement is likely to be similar to the Australian FFG upgrade programme.
Structure: A flight deck extension programme, to enable S-70 helicopters has been completed. The work involved angling the transom as in later USN ships of the class.
Operational: Sonar towed arrays were not transferred.

GELIBOLU *11/2007, Selim San* / 1353408

GOKOVA *8/2007, Lisette Von Oss* / 1353407

1 TEPE (KNOX) CLASS (FFGH)

Name	*No*	*Builders*	*Laid down*	*Launched*	*Commissioned*	*Recommissioned*
ZAFER (ex-*Thomas C Hart*)	F 253 (ex-1092)	Avondale Shipyards	8 Oct 1971	12 Aug 1972	28 July 1973	30 Aug 1993

Displacement, tons: 3,011 standard; 4,260 full load
Dimensions, feet (metres): 439.6 × 46.8 × 15; 24.8 (sonar) *(134 × 14.3 × 4.6; 7.8)*
Main machinery: 2 Combustion Engineering/Babcock & Wilcox boilers; 1,200 psi *(84.4 kg/cm²)*; 950°F *(510°C)*; 1 Westinghouse turbine; 35,000 hp *(26 MW)*; 1 shaft
Speed, knots: 27. **Range, n miles:** 4,000 at 22 kt on 1 boiler
Complement: 288 (20 officers)

Missiles: SSM: 8 McDonnell Douglas Harpoon; active radar homing to 130 km *(70 n miles)* at 0.9 Mach; warhead 227 kg.
A/S: Honeywell ASROC Mk 16 octuple launcher with reload system (has 2 cells modified to fire Harpoon) ❶; inertial guidance to 1.6-10 km *(1-5.4 n miles)*; payload Mk 46 Mod 5 Neartip.
Guns: 1 FMC 5 in *(127 mm)*/54 Mk 42 Mod 9 ❷; 20-40 rds/min to 24 km *(13 n miles)* anti-surface; 14 km *(7.7 n miles)* anti-aircraft; weight of shell 32 kg.
1 General Electric/General Dynamics 20 mm/76 6-barrelled Mk 15 Vulcan Phalanx ❸; 3,000 rds/min combined to 1.5 km.
Torpedoes: 4—324 mm Mk 32 (2 twin) fixed tubes ❹. 22 Honeywell Mk 46 Mod 5; anti-submarine; active/passive homing to 11 km *(5.9 n miles)* at 40 kt; warhead 44 kg.
Countermeasures: Decoys: 2 Loral Hycor SRBOC 6-barrelled fixed Mk 36 ❺; IR flares and chaff to 4 km *(2.2 n miles)*.
T Mk-6 Fanfare/SLQ-25 Nixie; torpedo decoy. Prairie Masker hull and blade rate noise suppression.
ESM: SLQ-32(V)2 ❻; intercept.
Combat data systems: Signaal Sigma K5 with Link 11.
Weapons control: SWG-1A Harpoon LCS. Mk 68 Mod 3 GFCS. Mk 114 Mod 6 ASW FCS. Mk 1 target designation system. MMS target acquisition sight (for mines, small craft and low-flying aircraft).
Radars: Air search: Lockheed SPS-40B ❼; B-band.
Surface search: Raytheon SPS-10 or Norden SPS-67 ❽; G-band.
Navigation: Marconi LN66; I-band.
Fire control: Western Electric SPG-53D/F ❾; I/J-band.
Tacan: SRN 15.
Sonars: EDO/General Electric SQS-26CX; bow-mounted; active search and attack; medium frequency.

Helicopters: 1 AB 212ASW ❿.

Programmes: In late 1992 the US offered Turkey four of the class. A proposal was put to Congress in June 1993 and four approved for transfer on a five year lease, plus one more, *Elmer Montgomery* for spares, on a grant basis under the Foreign Assistance Act. The latter replaced the former destroyer *Muavenet* which was scrapped after being hit by a Sea Sparrow missile. A second batch of four transferred in 1994. All eight purchased outright in 1999. F 251 decommissioned in 2000, F 257 in 2001, F 252 in 2002, F 254 in 2003, F 256 in 2005, F 255 in 2006 and F 250 in 2007.
Modernisation: Hangar and flight deck enlarged. In 1979 a programme was initiated to fit 3.5 ft bow bulwarks and spray strakes adding 9.1 tons to a displacement. Sea Sparrow SAM replaced by Phalanx 1982–88. Link 11 fitted after transfer. Project 'Kalyon-5' integrated new multipurpose consoles into the combat data system.
Structure: Improved ASROC torpedo reloading capability (note slanting face of bridge structure immediately behind ASROC). Four Mk 32 torpedo tubes are fixed in the midships structure, two to a side, angled out at 45°. The arrangement provides improved loading capability over exposed triple Mk 32 torpedo tubes. A 4,000 lb lightweight anchor is fitted on the port side and an 8,000 lb anchor fits into the after section of the sonar dome.

ZAFER *(Scale 1 : 1,200), Ian Sturton* / 0506334

ZAFER *1/2002, M Declerck* / 0533245

CORVETTES

0 + 2 (10) MILGEM CLASS (FSG)

Name	*No*	*Builders*	*Laid down*	*Launched*	*Commissioned*
HEYBELIADA	F 511	Istanbul Naval Shipyard	26 July 2005	27 Sep 2008	2011
BÜYÜKADA	–	Istanbul Naval Shipyard	27 Sep 2008	2011	2014

Displacement, tons: 1,500 standard; 2,000 full load
Dimensions, feet (metres): 324.8 × 47.2 × 11.8 *(99.0 × 14.4 × 3.6)*
Main machinery: CODAG; 2 MTU 16V 595 TE 90 diesels; 11,750 hp *(8.76 MW)*; 1 GE LM 2500 gas turbine; 20,500 hp *(15.3 MW)*; 2 shafts; cp props
Speed, knots: 29. **Range, n miles:** 3,500 at 15 kt
Complement: 93

Missiles: SSM: 8 McDonnell Douglas Harpoon (2 quadruple); active radar homing to 130 km *(70 n miles)* at 0.9 Mach; warhead 227 kg.
SAM: 1 RIM-116 RAM 21-cell Mk 49 launcher.
Guns: 1—3 in *(76 mm)*. 2—12.7 mm MGs.
Torpedoes: 4—324 mm (2 twin) tubes.
Countermeasures: Decoys: To be announced.
ESM/ECM: To be announced.
Torpedo decoy system: Ultra Sea Sentor.
Combat data systems: 'Genesis' derivative.
Electro-optic systems: Thales Sting optronic director.
Radars: Air/surface search: Thales SMART-S Mk 2 3D; E/F-band.
Fire control: Thales Sting; I/K-band.
Navigation: To be announced.
Sonars: To be announced.

Helicopters: S-70B Seahawk.

HEYBELIADA (model) *8/2005, C D Yaylali* / 1133234

Programmes: The MILGEM project was launched in 1996 for the in-country design and construction of up to 12 anti-submarine warfare and offshore patrol vessels. The first two ships are under construction in Istanbul and construction of follow-on ships is likely to be shared between several shipyards.

6 BURAK (TYPE A 69) CLASS (FFGM)

Name	*No*	*Builders*	*Laid down*	*Launched*	*Commissioned*	*Recommissioned*
BOZCAADA (ex-*Commandant de Pimodan*)	F 500 (ex-F 787)	Lorient Naval Dockyard	15 July 1975	7 Aug 1976	20 May 1978	22 June 2001
BODRUM (ex-*Drogou*)	F 501 (ex-F 783)	Lorient Naval Dockyard	16 Oct 1973	30 Nov 1974	1 Oct 1976	18 Oct 2001
BANDIRMA (ex-*Quartier Maitre Anquetil*)	F 502 (ex-F 786)	Lorient Naval Dockyard	1 Aug 1975	7 Aug 1976	4 Feb 1978	15 Oct 2001
BEYKOZ (ex-*d'Estienne d'Orves*)	F 503 (ex-F 781)	Lorient Naval Dockyard	1 Sep 1972	1 June 1973	10 Sep 1976	18 Mar 2002
BARTIN (ex-*Amyot d'Inville*)	F 504 (ex-F 782)	Lorient Naval Dockyard	2 July 1973	30 Nov 1974	13 Oct 1976	3 June 2002
BAFRA (ex-*Second Maitre Le Bihan*)	F 505 (ex-F 788)	Lorient Naval Dockyard	1 Nov 1976	13 Aug 1977	7 July 1979	26 June 2002

Displacement, tons: 1,175 standard; 1,250 (1,330 later ships) full load
Dimensions, feet (metres): 264.1 × 33.8 × 18 (sonar) *(80.5 × 10.3 × 5.5)*
Main machinery: 2 SEMT-Pielstick 12 PC2 V 400 diesels; 12,000 hp(m) *(8.82 MW)*; 2 shafts; LIPS cp props
Speed, knots: 23. **Range, n miles**: 4,500 at 15 kt
Complement: 104 (10 officers)

Missiles: SSM: 2 Aerospatiale MM 38 Exocet ❶; inertial cruise; active radar homing to 70 km *(40 n miles)* or 42 km *(23 n miles)* at 0.9 Mach; warhead 165 kg; sea-skimmer.
SAM: Matra Simbad twin launcher for Mistral ❷; IR homing to 4 km *(2.2 n miles)*; warhead 3 kg. This may be replaced by Stinger.
Guns: 1 DCN/Creusot-Loire 3.9 in *(100 mm)*/55 Mod 68 CADAM automatic ❸; 80 rds/min to 17 km *(9 n miles)* anti-surface; 8 km *(4.4 n miles)* anti-aircraft; weight of shell 13.5 kg.
2 Giat 20 mm ❹; 720 rds/min to 10 km *(5.5 n miles)*.
4—12.7 mm MGs.
Torpedoes: 4 fixed tubes ❺. ECAN L5; dual purpose; active/passive homing to 9.5 km *(5.1 n miles)* at 35 kt; warhead 150 kg; depth to 550 m *(1,800 ft)*.

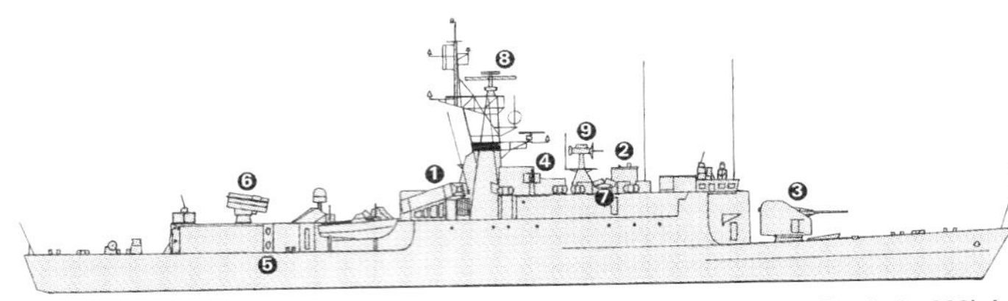

BOZCAADA *(Scale 1 : 900), Ian Sturton* / 0114803

A/S mortars: 1 Creusot-Loire 375 mm Mk 54 6-tubed trainable launcher ❻; range 1,600 m; warhead 107 kg.
Countermeasures: Decoys: 2 CSEE Dagaie 10-barrelled trainable launchers ❼; chaff and IR flares; H- to J-band. Nixie torpedo decoy.
ESM: ARBR 16; radar warning.
Weapons control: Thomson-CSF Vega system; CSEE Panda optical secondary director.
Radars: Air/surface search: Thomson-CSF DRBV 51A ❽; G-band.
Navigation: Racal Decca 1226; I-band.

Fire control: Thomson-CSF DRBC 32E ❾; I-band.
Sonars: Thomson Sintra DUBA 25; hull-mounted; search and attack; medium frequency.

Comment: Six Type A 69 class bought second-hand from France in October 2000. All, except *Bafra*, refitted at Brest. Work done on propulsion and weapons systems. Exocet MM 38 SSMs procured under separate contract. Operational use is coastal patrol duties, for which they were designed, in order to release more capable ships for front-line service.

BOZCAADA *4/2008*, Selim San* / 1353409

SHIPBORNE AIRCRAFT

Numbers/Type: 14 Agusta AB 212.
Operational speed: 106 kt *(196 km/h)*.
Service ceiling: 14,200 ft *(4,330 m)*.
Range: 230 n miles *(426 km)*.
Role/Weapon systems: Multirole helicopter. Sensors: L3 AQS-18 dipping sonar (in seven aircraft); BAe Ferranti Sea Spray Mk 3 radar, ECM/ESM. Weapons: ASW; two Mk 46 or 244/S torpedoes. ASuW; two Sea Skua missiles.

AB 212 *1/2002, M Declerck* / 0533250

Numbers/Type: 7 Sikorsky S-70B Seahawk.
Operational speed: 135 kt *(250 km/h)*.
Service ceiling: 10,000 ft *(3,050 m)*.
Range: 600 n miles *(1,110 km)*.
Role/Weapon systems: Contracts placed 3 June 1998 for first four. Second contract for four further aircraft on 31 December 1998. First three delivered 26 April 2002 and second four on 24 July 2003. One aircraft lost in accident. An order for a further 17 aircraft was placed on 24 June 2005. Deliveries to be made from 2009. Helras ASW weapon systems ordered. Sensors: APS-124 search radar; Helras dipping sonar. Weapons: ASW: 2 Mk 46 torpedoes; AGM-114B Hellfire II ASM.

SEAHAWK S-70B *6/2002, Selçuk Emre* / 0533251

LAND-BASED MARITIME AIRCRAFT

Numbers/Type: 6 CASA CN-235 D/K MPA.
Operational speed: 240 kt *(445 km/h)*.
Service ceiling: 26,600 ft *(8,110 m)*.
Range: 669 n miles *(1,240 km)*.
Role/Weapon systems: Initial batch of two delivered in 2001 and a further four in 2002. First flight with mission systems took place on 18 June 2007. Thales AMACOS mission control system. Long-range maritime patrol for surface surveillance and ASW. Sensors: Ocean Master radar (SAR, ISAR, MTI and air-to-air modes); FLIR; AAR-60 missile warning; DR 3000 A ESM; MAD; Link 11. Weapons: 2 Mk-46 torpedoes.

CN-235 *6/2006, Turkish Navy* / 1158698

Numbers/Type: 10 Alenia ATR-72 ASW.
Operational speed: 255 kt *(472 km/h)*.
Service ceiling: 22,000 ft *(6,705 m)*.
Range: 1,200 n miles *(2,200 km)*.
Role/Weapon systems: Project Meltem-3. Contract signed on 20 July 2005 for ten maritime patrol aircraft which are to receive a modified Thales Airborne Systems Amascos mission and sensor suite. Alenia will conduct platform modifications and perform systems integration on the first aircraft with the assistance of Turkish companies. First flight planned for 2009 and deliveries to take place 2010–2012. Full details of weapons and sensors to be announced. The ATR72-ASW is based on the ATR72-500 which is a stretched version of the ATR42.

ATR-72 (model) *9/2005, C D Yaylali* / 1133582

PATROL FORCES

7 + 2 KILIÇ CLASS (FAST ATTACK CRAFT—MISSILE) (PGGF)

Name	*No*	*Builders*	*Launched*	*Commissioned*
KILIÇ	P 330	Lürssen, Vegesack	15 July 1997	17 Mar 1998
KALKAN	P 331	Taşkizak, Istanbul	22 Sep 1998	22 July 1999
MIZRAK	P 332	Taşkizak, Istanbul	5 Apr 1999	8 June 2000
TUFAN	P 333	Lürssen, Vegesack	3 Feb 2003	26 July 2005
MELTEM	P 334	Istanbul Naval Shipyard	1 Sep 2004	26 July 2005
IMBAT	P 335	Istanbul Naval Shipyard	26 July 2005	7 July 2006
ZIPKIN	P 336	Istanbul Naval Shipyard	27 Sep 2006	17 Sep 2008
ATAK	P 337	Gölcük Naval Shipyard	4 Jan 2008	2009
BORA	P 338	Gölcük Naval Shipyard	2009	2010

Displacement, tons: 550 full load
Dimensions, feet (metres): 204.6 × 27.2 × 8.5 *(62.4 × 8.3 × 2.6)*
Main machinery: 4 MTU 16V 956 TB91 diesels; 15,120 hp(m) *(11.1 MW)* sustained; 4 shafts
Speed, knots: 38. **Range, n miles:** 1,050 at 30 kt
Complement: 46 (12 officers)

Missiles: SSM: 8 McDonnell Douglas Harpoon (2 quad) launchers; active radar homing to 130 km *(70 n miles)* at 0.9 Mach; warhead 227 kg.
Guns: 1 Otobreda 3 in *(76 mm)*/62 compact; 85 rds/min to 16 km *(8.7 n miles)* anti-surface; 12 km *(6.6 n miles)* anti-aircraft; weight of shell 6 kg.
2 Otobreda 40 mm/70 (twin); 300 rds/min to 12 km *(6.6 n miles)*; weight of shell 0.96 kg.
Countermeasures: Decoys: 2 Mk 36 SRBOC chaff launchers.
ESM: Racal Cutlass; intercept.
Combat data systems: Signaal/Thomson-CSF STACOS.
Weapons control: LIROD Mk 2 optronic director; Vesta helo datalink/transponder.
Radars: Surface search: Signaal MW08; G-band.
Fire control: Signaal STING; I/J-band.
Navigation: KH 1007; I-band.

Programmes: Contract for first three signed in May 1993 but there was a delay in confirming it. Further four ordered 19 June 2000 and a further two thereafter.
Structure: A development of the Yildiz class but with reduced radar cross-section mast and a redesigned bow to improve sea-keeping. The after gun and radars are also different to *Yildiz*. *Tufan* fitted with stealthy gun turret.
Operational: First of class arrived in Turkey in April 1998.

TUFAN *6/2005*, ***Michael Nitz*** / 1127054

KILIC *9/2008**, ***C D Yaylali*** / 1353410

2 YILDIZ CLASS (FAST ATTACK CRAFT—MISSILE) (PGGF)

Name	*No*	*Builders*	*Commissioned*
YILDIZ	P 348	Taşkizak Yard, Istanbul	3 June 1996
KARAYEL	P 349	Taşkizak Yard, Istanbul	19 Sep 1996

Displacement, tons: 433 full load
Dimensions, feet (metres): 189.6 oa; 178.5 wl × 25 × 8.8 *(57.8; 54.4 × 7.6 × 2.7)*
Main machinery: 4 MTU 16V 956 TB91 diesels; 15,120 hp(m) *(11.1 MW)* sustained; 4 shafts
Speed, knots: 38. **Range, n miles:** 1,050 at 30 kt
Complement: 45 (6 officers)

Missiles: SSM: 8 McDonnell Douglas Harpoon (2 quad) launchers; active radar homing to 130 km *(70 n miles)* at 0.9 Mach; warhead 227 kg.
Guns: 1 OTO Melara 3 in *(76 mm)*/62 compact; 85 rds/min to 16 km *(8.7 n miles)* anti-surface; 12 km *(6.6 n miles)* anti-aircraft; weight of shell 6 kg.
2 Oerlikon 35 mm/90 (twin); 550 rds/min to 6 km *(3.3 n miles)*; weight of shell 1.55 kg.
Countermeasures: Decoys: 2 Mk 36 SRBOC chaff launchers.
ESM: Racal Cutlass; intercept.
Combat data systems: Signaal/Thomson-CSF TACTICOS.
Weapons control: LIOD Mk 2 optronic director; Vesta helo datalink/transponder.
Radars: Surface search: Siemens/Plessey AW 6 Dolphin; G-band.
Fire control: Oerlikon/Contraves TMX; I/J-band.
Navigation: Racal Decca TM 1226; I-band.

Programmes: Ordered in June 1991. *Karayel* launched 20 June 1995.
Structure: Doğan class hull with much improved weapon systems.

YILDIZ *9/2008**, ***C D Yaylali*** / 1353411

8 DOĞAN CLASS (FAST ATTACK CRAFT—MISSILE) (PGGF)

Name	*No*	*Builders*	*Commissioned*
DOĞAN	P 340	Lürssen, Vegesack	23 Dec 1977
MARTI	P 341	Taşkizak Yard, Istanbul	1 Aug 1978
TAYFUN	P 342	Taşkizak Yard, Istanbul	9 Aug 1979
VOLKAN	P 343	Taşkizak Yard, Istanbul	25 July 1980
RÜZGAR	P 344	Taşkizak Yard, Istanbul	24 May 1985
POYRAZ	P 345	Taşkizak Yard, Istanbul	28 Aug 1986
GURBET	P 346	Taşkizak Yard, Istanbul	24 July 1988
FIRTINA	P 347	Taşkizak Yard, Istanbul	14 Oct 1988

Displacement, tons: 436 full load
Dimensions, feet (metres): 190.6 × 25 × 8.8 *(58.1 × 7.6 × 2.7)*
Main machinery: 4 MTU 16V 956 TB92 diesels; 17,700 hp(m) *(13 MW)* sustained; 4 shafts
Speed, knots: 38
Range, n miles: 1,050 at 30 kt
Complement: 40 (5 officers)

Missiles: SSM: 8 McDonnell Douglas Harpoon (2 quad) launchers; active radar homing to 130 km *(70 n miles)* at 0.9 Mach; warhead 227 kg.
Guns: 1 OTO Melara 3 in *(76 mm)*/62 compact; 85 rds/min to 16 km *(8.7 n miles)* anti-surface; 12 km *(6.6 n miles)* anti-aircraft; weight of shell 6 kg.
2 Oerlikon 35 mm/90 (twin); 550 rds/min to 6 km *(3.3 n miles)*; weight of shell 1.55 kg.
Countermeasures: Decoys: 2 Mk 36 SRBOC chaff launchers.
ESM: MEL Susie (344-347); intercept.
Combat data systems: Signaal mini TACTICOS (344-347).
Weapons control: LIOD Mk 2 optronic director.
Radars: Surface search: Racal Decca 1226; I-band.
Fire control: Signaal WM28/41; I/J-band.

Programmes: First ordered 3 August 1973 to a Lürssen FPB 57 design.
Modernisation: A mid-life programme includes upgrade to the combat data system, communications and ESM. Work on the first four was completed in 2002. Work on the second four has not been confirmed.
Structure: Aluminium superstructure; steel hulls. The last pair were built with optronic directors which are being retrofitted in all, together with an improved Signaal combat data system.

DOĞAN *7/2005*, ***C D Yaylali*** / 1133580

VOLKAN *11/2005*, ***Manuel Declerck*** / 1153503

8 KARTAL CLASS (FAST ATTACK CRAFT—MISSILE) (PTGF)

Name	*No*	*Builders*	*Commissioned*
DENIZKUŞU	P 321 (ex-*P 336*)	Lürssen, Vegesack	9 Mar 1967
ATMACA	P 322 (ex-*P 335*)	Lürssen, Vegesack	9 Mar 1967
ŞAHIN	P 323 (ex-*P 334*)	Lürssen, Vegesack	3 Nov 1966
KARTAL	P 324 (ex-*P 333*)	Lürssen, Vegesack	3 Nov 1966
PELIKAN	P 326	Lürssen, Vegesack	11 Feb 1970
ALBATROS	P 327 (ex-*P 325*)	Lürssen, Vegesack	18 Mar 1970
ŞIMŞEK	P 328 (ex-*P 332*)	Lürssen, Vegesack	6 Nov 1969
KASIRGA	P 329 (ex-*P 338*)	Lürssen, Vegesack	25 Nov 1967

Displacement, tons: 160 standard; 190 full load
Dimensions, feet (metres): 139.4 × 23 × 7.9 *(42.5 × 7 × 2.4)*
Main machinery: 4 MTU MD 16V 538 TB90 diesels; 12,000 hp(m) *(8.82 MW)* sustained; 4 shafts
Speed, knots: 42
Range, n miles: 500 at 40 kt
Complement: 39 (4 officers)

Missiles: SSM: 2 or 4 Kongsberg Penguin Mk 2; IR homing to 27 km *(14.6 n miles)* at 0.8 Mach; warhead 120 kg.
Guns: 2 Bofors 40 mm/70; 300 rds/min to 12 km *(6.6 n miles)*; weight of shell 0.96 kg.
Torpedoes: 2—21 in *(533 mm)* tubes; anti-surface.
Mines: Can carry 4.
Radars: Surface search: Racal Decca 1226; I-band.

Operational: *Meltem* sunk in collision with Soviet naval training ship *Khasan* in Bosphorus in 1985. Subsequently salvaged but beyond repair. Although these craft are getting old, there are no plans to decommission them in the short term.

ŞIMŞEK *4/2004*, ***Marco Ghiglino*** / 1133592

1 HISAR (PC 1638) CLASS (LARGE PATROL CRAFT) (PBO)

Name	*No*	*Builders*	*Commissioned*
AKHISAR (ex-*PC 1641*)	P 114	Gunderson, Portland	Dec 1964

Displacement, tons: 325 standard; 477 full load
Dimensions, feet (metres): 173.7 × 23 × 10.2 *(53 × 7 × 3.1)*
Main machinery: 2 Fairbanks-Morse diesels; 2,800 hp *(2.09 MW)*; 2 shafts
Speed, knots: 19. **Range, n miles**: 6,000 at 10 kt
Complement: 31 (3 officers)
Guns: 2 Bofors 40 mm/60.
Depth charges: 4 projectors; 1 rack (9).
Radars: Surface search: Decca 707; I-band.

Comment: Transferred from the US on build. ASW equipment removed. Three paid off in 2000, one in 2002 and one in 2005. P 114 likely to be decommissioned in 2009 and converted into a museum.

HISAR CLASS *6/2002, C D Yaylali* / 0533253

1 TRABZON CLASS (LARGE PATROL CRAFT) (PBO/AGI)

TERME (ex-*Trinity*) P 531 (ex-M 531)

Displacement, tons: 370 standard; 470 full load
Dimensions, feet (metres): 164 × 30.2 × 9.2 *(50 × 9.2 × 2.8)*
Main machinery: 2 GM 12-278A diesels; 2,200 hp *(1.64 MW)*; 2 shafts
Speed, knots: 15. **Range, n miles**: 4,500 at 11 kt
Complement: 35 (4 officers)
Guns: 1 Bofors 40 mm/60. 2—12.7 mm MGs.
Radars: Surface search: Racal Decca 1226; I-band.

Comment: Transferred from Canada and recommissioned 31 March 1958. Built by Davie SB Co 1951–53. Of similar type to British Ton class. Pennant number changed in 1991 reflecting use as patrol ship with all minesweeping gear removed.

TRABZON CLASS *6/1999, Selim San* / 0080879

6 VEGESACK CLASS (PBO/AGS)

Name	*No*	*Builders*	*Commissioned*
KARAMÜRSEL (ex-*Worms*)	P 307 (ex-M 520, M 1253)	Amiot, Cherbourg	30 Apr 1960
KEREMPE (ex-*Detmold*)	P 308 (ex-M 521, ex-M 1252)	Amiot, Cherbourg	20 Feb 1960
KILIMLI (ex-*Siegen*)	P 309 (ex-M 522, ex-M 1254)	Amiot, Cherbourg	9 July 1960
KOZLU (ex-*Hameln*)	P 301 (ex-M 523, ex-M 1251)	Amiot, Cherbourg	15 Oct 1959
KUŞADASI (ex-*Vegesack*)	P 302 (ex-M 524, ex-M 1250)	Amiot, Cherbourg	19 Sep 1959
KEMER (ex-*Passau*)	A 582 (ex-M 525, ex-M 1255)	Amiot, Cherbourg	15 Oct 1960

Displacement, tons: 362 standard; 378 full load
Dimensions, feet (metres): 155.1 × 28.2 × 9.5 *(47.3 × 8.6 × 2.9)*
Main machinery: 2 MTU MB diesels; 1,500 hp(m) *(1.1 MW)*; 2 shafts; cp props
Speed, knots: 15
Complement: 33 (2 officers)
Guns: 2 Oerlikon 20 mm (twin).
Radars: Navigation: Decca 707; I-band.
Sonars: Simrad; active mine detection; high frequency.

Comment: Transferred by West Germany and recommissioned in the mid-1970s. Sonars were fitted from 1989. *Kemer* paid off in 1998 but returned as a survey ship in 1999. *Kozlu* and *Kuşadasi* refitted as patrol ships in 1999 and *Karamürsel, Kerempe* and *Kilimli* in 2006.

KEMER *4/2005, Selim San* / 1133591

6 TURK CLASS (LARGE PATROL CRAFT) (PC)

Name	*No*	*Builders*	*Commissioned*
AB 27	P 127 (ex-P 1227)	Haliç Shipyard	27 June 1969
AB 28	P 128 (ex-P 1228)	Haliç Shipyard	Apr 1969
AB 29	P 129 (ex-P 1229)	Haliç Shipyard	21 Feb 1969
AB 31	P 131 (ex-P 1231)	Haliç Shipyard	17 Nov 1971
AB 35	P 135 (ex-P 1235)	Taşkizak Shipyard	13 Apr 1976
AB 36	P 136 (ex-P 1236)	Taşkizak Shipyard	13 Apr 1976

Displacement, tons: 170 full load
Dimensions, feet (metres): 132 × 21 × 5.5 *(40.2 × 6.4 × 1.7)*
Main machinery: 4 SACM-AGO V16CSHR diesels; 9,600 hp(m) *(7.06 MW)*
2 cruise diesels; 300 hp(m) *(220 kW)*; 2 shafts
Speed, knots: 22
Complement: 31 (3 officers)
Guns: 1 or 2 Bofors 40 mm/70.
1 Oerlikon 20 mm (in those with 1—40 mm). 2—12.7 mm MGs
A/S mortars: 1 Mk 20 Mousetrap 4 rocket launcher; range 200 m; warhead 50 kg.
Depth charges: 1 rack.
Radars: Surface search: Racal Decca; I-band.
Sonars: Plessey PMS 26; hull-mounted; active search and attack; high frequency.

Comment: Pennant numbers changed in 1991. Similar to *SG 21* Coast Guard class. One to Georgia *(AB 30)* in December 1998, one to Azerbaijan *(AB 34)* in July 2000 and one to Kazakhstan *(AB 26)* in July 2001. *AB 33* decommissioned in 2005.

AB 28 *5/2008*, C D Yaylali* / 1353412

4 PGM 71 CLASS (LARGE PATROL CRAFT) (PC)

AB 21–24 (ex-*PGM 104–107*) P121–124 (ex-P1221–1224)

Displacement, tons: 130 standard; 147 full load
Dimensions, feet (metres): 101 × 21 × 7 *(30.8 × 6.4 × 2.1)*
Main machinery: 8 GM diesels 2,040 hp *(1.52 MW)*; 2 shafts
Speed, knots: 18.5. **Range, n miles**: 1,500 at 10 kt
Complement: 31 (3 officers)
Guns: 1 Bofors 40 mm/60. 4 Oerlikon 20 mm (2 twin). 1—7.62 mm MG.
A/S mortars: 2 Mk 22 Mousetrap 8 rocket launchers; range 200 m; warhead 50 kg.
Depth charges: 2 racks (4).
Radars: Surface search: Raytheon 1500B; I-band.
Sonars: EDO SQS-17A; hull-mounted; active attack; high frequency.

Comment: Built by Peterson, Sturgeon Bay and commissioned 1967–68. Transferred from US almost immediately after completion. Pennant numbers changed in 1991.

AB 24 *11/2005, Manuel Declerck* / 1153506

0 + 1 (5) DEARSAN PATROL CRAFT (PC)

Name	*No*	*Builders*	*Laid down*	*Launched*	*Commissioned*
–	–	Dearsan Shipyard, Istanbul	3 May 2008	2010	2011

Displacement, tons: 400 full load
Dimensions, feet (metres): 182.9 × 29.0 × 8.2 *(55.75 × 8.85 × 2.5)*
Main machinery: 2 MTU 16V 4000 M 90 diesels; 7,300 hp *(5.44 MW)*; 2 shafts; cp props
Speed, knots: 25. **Range, n miles**: 2,000 at 12 kt
Complement: 34
Guns: 2—40 mm/70 (1 twin). 2—12.7 mm stabilised MGs.
A/S mortars: 2 Aselsan 6-barrelled launchers.
Countermeasures: To be announced.
Combat data systems: To be announced.
Weapons control: Aselflir 300.
Radars: Surface search/navigation: I-band.
Sonars: Simrad SP92; hull-mounted; high frequency; 20-30 kHz.

Comment: Contract signed with Dearsan Shipyard, Istanbul, on 23 August 2007 for the construction of 16 anti-submarine patrol craft to be built in four batches of four. The origin of the design has not been announced but may have been developed with foreign assistance. Steel hull and superstructure. The craft are to be employed on patrol duties in the vicinity of ports and bases.

DEARSAN PATROL CRAFT (model) *5/2007, C D Yaylali* / 1167962

2 KAAN 15 CLASS (FAST INTERVENTION CRAFT) (HSIC)

Displacement, tons: 19 full load
Dimensions, feet (metres): 54.8 × 13.2 × 3.9 *(16.7 × 4.04 × 1.2)*
Main machinery: 2 MTU 12V 183 TE93 diesels; 2,588 hp(m) *(1.93 MW)*; 2 Arneson ASD 12 B1L surface drives
Speed, knots: 65
Range, n miles: 350 at 35 kt
Complement: 2 plus 10 mission crew

Comment: Onuk MRTP 15 advanced composites design. Two delivered in 2002 for Turkish Special Forces.

KAAN 15 CLASS ***10/2000*** / 0106641

AMPHIBIOUS FORCES

Notes: (1) The prefix 'Ç' for smaller amphibious vessels stands for 'Çikarma Gemisi' (landing vessel) and indicates that the craft are earmarked for national rather than NATO control.
(2) A Request for Information for a new landing platform dock was issued on 6 April 2007. Capable of both military and humanitarian operations, the ship is expected to be of the order of 12-15,000 tons and to be capable of carrying 600 troops. Entry into service was planned to be 2012 although this may be delayed by funding constraints.
(3) Plans to acquire two Landing Ship Tank (LST) were announced on 19 January 2007.

1 OSMAN GAZI CLASS (LSTH/ML)

Name	*No*	*Builders*	*Launched*	*Commissioned*
OSMAN GAZI	NL 125	Taşkizak Yard, Istanbul	20 July 1990	27 July 1994

Displacement, tons: 3,773 full load
Dimensions, feet (metres): 344.5 × 52.8 × 15.7 *(105 × 16.1 × 4.8)*
Main machinery: 2 MTU 12V 1163 TB73 diesels; 8,800 hp(m) *(6.47 MW)*; 2 shafts
Speed, knots: 17
Range, n miles: 4,000 at 15 kt
Military lift: 900 troops; 15 tanks; 4 LCVPs
Guns: 2 Oerlikon 35 mm/90 (twin). 4 Bofors 40 mm/70 (2 twin). 2 Oerlikon 20 mm.
Radars: Navigation: Racal Decca; I-band.
Helicopters: Platform for 1 large.

Comment: Laid down 7 July 1989. Full NBCD protection. Equipped with a support weapons co-ordination centre to control amphibious operations. The ship has about a 50 per cent increase in military lift capacity compared with the Sarucabey class. Secondary role as minelayer. Second of class cancelled in 1991 and *Osman Gazi* took a long time to complete. Marisat fitted.

OSMAN GAZI ***5/2007, Selim San*** / 1167875

OSMAN GAZI ***6/2004, Camil Busquets i Vilanova*** / 1133590

2 ERTUĞRUL (TERREBONNE PARISH) CLASS (LSTH/ML)

Name	*No*	*Builders*	*Commissioned*
ERTUĞRUL (ex-*Windham County* LST 1170)	L 401	Christy Corporation	15 Dec 1954
SERDAR (ex-*Westchester County* LST 1167)	L 402	Christy Corporation	10 Mar 1954

Displacement, tons: 2,590 light; 5,800 full load
Dimensions, feet (metres): 384 × 55 × 17 *(117.1 × 16.8 × 5.2)*
Main machinery: 4 GM 16-278A diesels; 6,000 hp *(4.48 MW)*; 2 shafts; cp props
Speed, knots: 15
Complement: 163 (14 officers)
Military lift: 395 troops; 2,200 tons cargo; 4 LCVPs
Guns: 6 USN 3 in *(76 mm)*/50 (3 twin).
Weapons control: 2 Mk 63 GFCS.
Radars: Surface search: Racal Decca 1226; I-band.
Fire control: 2 Western Electric Mk 34; I/J-band.

Comment: Transferred by US and recommissioned 3 October 1973 and 24 February 1975 respectively. Purchased outright 6 August 1987. Marisat fitted.

SERDAR ***1/2008*, Guy Toremans*** / 1353413

2 SARUCABEY CLASS (LSTH/ML)

Name	*No*	*Builders*	*Launched*	*Commissioned*
SARUCABEY	NL 123	Taşkizak Naval Yard	30 July 1981	17 July 1984
KARAMÜRSELBEY	NL 124	Taşkizak Naval Yard	26 July 1984	19 June 1987

Displacement, tons: 2,600 full load
Dimensions, feet (metres): 301.8 × 45.9 × 7.5 *(92 × 14 × 2.3)*
Main machinery: 3 diesels; 4,320 hp *(3.2 MW)*; 3 shafts
Speed, knots: 14
Military lift: 600 troops; 11 tanks; 12 jeeps; 2 LCVPs
Guns: 4 Bofors 40 mm/70. 4 Oerlikon 20 mm (2 twin).
Mines: 150 in lieu of amphibious lift.
Radars: Navigation: Racal Decca 1226; I-band.
Helicopters: Platform only.

Comment: *Sarucabey* is an enlarged Çakabey design more suitable for naval requirements. Dual-purpose minelayers. NL 124 has superstructure one deck lower.

KARAMÜRSELBEY ***9/2007, C D Yaylali*** / 1353401

1 EDIC TYPE (LCT)

Ç 120

Displacement, tons: 580 full load
Dimensions, feet (metres): 186.9 × 39.4 × 4.6 *(57 × 12 × 1.4)*
Main machinery: 3 GM 6-71 diesels; 522 hp *(390 kW)* sustained; 3 shafts
Speed, knots: 8.5
Range, n miles: 600 at 10 kt
Complement: 15
Military lift: 100 troops; up to 5 tanks
Guns: 2 Oerlikon 20 mm. 2—12.7 mm MGs.
Radars: Navigation: Racal Decca; I-band.

Comment: Vessel built at Gölcük Naval Shipyard in 1973. French EDIC type.

EDIC TYPE ***2/1996, C D Yaylali*** / 0080888

23 LCT

Ç 123 **Ç 125–128** **Ç 132–135** **Ç 137–150**

Displacement, tons: 600 standard
Dimensions, feet (metres): 195.5 × 38 × 10.5 *(59.6 × 11.6 × 3.2)*
Main machinery: 3 GM 6-71 diesels; 522 hp *(390 kW)* sustained; 3 shafts *(119-138)* or 3 MTU diesels; 900 hp(m) *(662 kW)*; 3 shafts *(139-150)*
Speed, knots: 8.5. **Range, n miles:** 600 at 8 kt
Complement: 17 (1 officer)
Military lift: 100 troops; 5 tanks
Guns: 2 Oerlikon 20 mm. 2—12.7 mm MGs.
Radars: Navigation: Racal Decca; I-band.

Comment: Follow-on to the *Ç 107* type started building in 1977. *Ç 130* and *Ç 131* transferred to Libya January 1980 and *Ç 136* sunk in 1985. The delivery rate was about two per year from the Taşkizak and Gölcük yards until 1987. Then two launched in July 1987 and commissioned in 1991. Last three completed in 1992. Dimensions given are for *Ç 139* onwards, earlier craft are 3.6 m shorter and have less freeboard.

Ç 126 *7/2006, **Marco Ghiglino*** / 1158709

16 LCM 8 TYPE

Ç 305 **Ç 308** **Ç 312** **Ç 314** **Ç 316** **Ç 319** **Ç 321–327** **Ç 329–331**

Displacement, tons: 58 light; 113 full load
Dimensions, feet (metres): 72 × 20.5 × 4.8 *(22 × 6.3 × 1.4)*
Main machinery: 4 GM 6-71 diesels; 696 hp *(520 kW)* sustained; 2 shafts
Speed, knots: 9.5
Complement: 9
Military lift: 60 tons or 140 troops
Guns: 2—12.7 mm MGs.

Comment: Up to *Ç 319* built by Taşkizak and Haliç in 1965-66. *Ç 321-331* built by Taşkizak and Naldöken in 1987–89.

Ç 308 ***6/2003, Turkish Navy*** / 0567540

MINE WARFARE FORCES

Notes: (1) Minelayers: see *Sarucabey*, *Karamürselbey* and *Osmangazi* under Amphibious Forces.
(2) In 2006, approval for the transfer of two ex-US Navy Osprey-class minehunters (*Black Hawk* and *Shrike*) was given by the US Congress. There have been no further developments.

4 COVE CLASS (MINESWEEPERS—INSHORE) (MSI)

Name	No	Builders	Commissioned
FOÇA (ex-*MSI 15*)	M 500	Peterson, WI	19 Apr 1968
FETHIYE (ex-*MSI 16*)	M 501	Peterson, WI	24 Apr 1968
FATSA (ex-*MSI 17*)	M 502	Peterson, WI	21 Mar 1968
FINIKE (ex-*MSI 18*)	M 503	Peterson, WI	26 Apr 1968

Displacement, tons: 180 standard; 235 full load
Dimensions, feet (metres): 111.9 × 23.5 × 7.9 *(34 × 7.1 × 2.4)*
Main machinery: 4 GM 6-71 diesels; 696 hp *(520 kW)* sustained; 2 shafts
Speed, knots: 13. **Range, n miles:** 900 at 11 kt
Complement: 25 (3 officers)
Guns: 1—12.7 mm MG.
Radars: Navigation: I-band.

Comment: Built in US and transferred under MAP at Boston, Massachusetts, August-December 1967.

FINIKE ***6/2007, Maritime Photographic*** / 1167872

4 + 2 AYDIN CLASS (TYPE MHV 54-014) (MHSC)

Name	No	Builders	Launched	Commissioned
ALANYA	M 265	Abeking & Rasmussen	21 Mar 2003	26 July 2005
AMASRA	M 266	Istanbul Naval Shipyard	10 May 2004	26 July 2005
AYVALIK	M 267	Istanbul Naval Shipyard	26 July 2005	22 June 2007
AKÇAKOCA	M 268	Istanbul Naval Shipyard	27 Sep 2006	24 Jan 2008
ANAMUR	M 269	Istanbul Naval Shipyard	17 Sep 2007	2009
AKÇAY	M 270	Istanbul Naval Shipyard	27 Oct 2008	2010

Displacement, tons: 715 full load
Dimensions, feet (metres): 178.8 × 31.8 × 8.5 *(54.5 × 9.7 × 2.6)*
Main machinery: 2 MTU 8V 396 TB84 diesels; 2 Voith-Schneider props; 2 Schottel bow thrusters
Speed, knots: 14
Complement: 53 (6 officers)
Guns: 1 Otobreda 30 mm. 2—12.7 mm MGs.
Countermeasures: 2 ECA PAP 104 Mk 5. 1 Oropesa mechanical sweep.
Combat data systems: Alenia Marconi Nautis-M.
Radars: KH 1007; I-band.
Sonars: Thomson Marconi Type 2093; VDS; active high frequency.

Comment: Ordered from Abeking & Rasmussen and Lürssen on 30 July 1999. First one built in Bremen, remainder in Turkey. The design is based on the German Type 332 but with different propulsion and mine countermeasures equipment. Non-magnetic steel hull. First of class laid down 20 November 2000, second on 25 July 2001, third on 25 July 2002 and fourth on 24 July 2003, the fifth on 1 September 2004 and sixth on 26 July 2005.

ALANYA ***2/2007, Adolfo Ortigueira Gil*** / 1167874

AMASRA ***6/2007, Maritime Photographic*** / 1167873

5 EDINCIK (CIRCÉ) CLASS (MINEHUNTERS) (MHC)

Name	No	Builders	Commissioned	Recommissioned
EDINCIK (ex-*Cybèle*)	M 260 (ex-M 712)	CMN, Cherbourg	28 Sep 1972	24 July 1998
EDREMIT (ex-*Calliope*)	M 261 (ex-M 713)	CMN, Cherbourg	28 Sep 1972	28 Aug 1998
ENEZ (ex-*Cérès*)	M 262 (ex-M 716)	CMN, Cherbourg	7 Mar 1973	30 Oct 1998
ERDEK (ex-*Circé*)	M 263 (ex-M 715)	CMN, Cherbourg	18 May 1972	4 Dec 1998
ERDEMLI (ex-*Clio*)	M 264 (ex-M 714)	CMN, Cherbourg	18 May 1972	15 Jan 1999

Displacement, tons: 460 standard; 495 normal; 510 full load
Dimensions, feet (metres): 167 × 29.2 × 11.2 *(50.9 × 8.9 × 3.4)*
Main machinery: 1 MTU diesel; 1,800 hp(m) *(1.32 MW)*; 2 active rudders; 1 shaft
Speed, knots: 15. **Range, n miles:** 3,000 at 12 kt
Complement: 48 (5 officers)
Guns: 1 Oerlikon 20 mm.
Countermeasures: MCM: DCN Mintac minehunting system with PAP Plus ROV.
Radars: Navigation: Racal Decca 1229; I-band.
Sonars: Thomson Sintra DUBM 20B; hull-mounted; active search; high frequency.

Comment: Acquired from France on 24 September 1997. Full refits included installation of Mintac system before being handed over.

EDREMIT ***6/2007, Maritime Photographic*** / 1167871

5 MSC 289 CLASS (MINESWEEPERS—COASTAL) (MSC)

SILIFKE (ex-*MSC 304*) M 514
SAROS (ex-*MSC 305*) M 515
SIGACIK (ex-*MSC 311*) M 516
SAPANCA (ex-*MSC 312*) M 517
SARIYER (ex-*MSC 315*) M 518

Displacement, tons: 320 standard; 370 full load
Dimensions, feet (metres): 141 × 26 × 8.3 *(43 × 8 × 2.6)*
Main machinery: 4 GM 6-71 diesels; 696 hp *(519 kW)* sustained; 2 shafts (M 510-M 513) 2 Waukesha L 1616 diesels; 1,200 hp *(895 kW)*; 2 shafts (M 514-M 518)
Speed, knots: 14
Range, n miles: 2,500 at 10 kt
Complement: 35 (2 officers)
Guns: 2 Oerlikon 20 mm (twin).
Radars: Navigation: Racal Decca 1226; I-band.
Sonars: UQS-1D; hull-mounted mine search; high frequency.

Comment: Built 1965–67. Transferred from US. Commissioning dates in the Turkish Navy were respectively: 21 March 1966, 25 October 1966, 20 December 1965, 20 December 1965 and 7 December 1967.

SAPANCA *10/2003, C D Yaylali* / 0567556

SILIFKE *7/2006, Marco Ghiglino* / 1158710

8 MINEHUNTING TENDERS (YAG/YDT)

MTB 2 P 312
MTB 3 P 313
MTB 4 P 314
MTB 5 P 315
MTB 6 P 316
MTB 7 P 317
MTB 8 P 318
MTB 9 P 319

Displacement, tons: 70 standard
Dimensions, feet (metres): 71.5 × 13.8 × 8.5 *(21.8 × 4.2 × 2.6)*
Main machinery: 2 diesels; 2,000 hp(m) *(1.47 MW)*; 2 shafts
Speed, knots: 20
Guns: 1 Oerlikon 20 mm or 1—12.7 mm MG (aft) (in some).

Comment: All launched in 1942. Now employed as minehunting base ships.

MTB 6 *7/1995, van Ginderen Collection* / 0080886

SURVEY SHIPS

Notes: *Kemer* A 582 (ex-M 525) is listed under Vegesack class in Patrol Forces.

2 SILAS BENT CLASS (AGS)

Name	*No*	*Builders*	*Commissioned*
ÇESME (ex-*Silas Bent*)	A 599 (ex-TAGS 26)	American SB Co, Lorain	23 July 1965
ÇANDARLI (ex-*Kane*)	A 588 (ex-TAGS 27)	Christy Corp, Sturgeon Bay	19 May 1967

Displacement, tons: 2,843 full load
Dimensions, feet (metres): 285.3 × 48 × 15.1 *(87 × 14.6 × 4.6)*
Main machinery: Diesel-electric; 2 Alco diesel generators; 1 Westinghouse/GE motor; 3,600 hp *(2.69 MW)*; 1 shaft; cp prop; bow thruster 350 hp *(261 kW)*
Speed, knots: 15
Range, n miles: 12,000 at 14 kt
Complement: 31 plus 28 spare
Radars: Navigation: RM 1650/9X; I-band.

Comment: Çesme transferred from US on 28 October 1999 and *Çanadarli* on 14 March 2001.

ÇANDARLI *11/2005, Manuel Declerck* / 1153505

1 SURVEY SHIP (AGS)

Name	*No*	*Builders*	*Launched*	*Commissioned*
ÇUBUKLU (ex-*Y 1251*)	A 594	Gölcük	17 Nov 1983	24 June 1987

Displacement, tons: 680 full load
Dimensions, feet (metres): 132.8 × 31.5 × 10.5 *(40.5 × 9.6 × 3.2)*
Main machinery: 1 MWM diesel; 820 hp(m) *(603 kW)*; 1 shaft; cp prop
Speed, knots: 11
Complement: 37 (6 officers)
Guns: 2 Oerlikon 20 mm.
Radars: Navigation: Racal Decca; I-band.

Comment: Qubit advanced integrated navigation and data processing system fitted in 1991.

ÇUBUKLU *7/2008*, Selim San* / 1353414

2 SURVEY CRAFT (AGSC)

MESAHA 1 Y 35
MESAHA 2 Y 36

Displacement, tons: 38 full load
Dimensions, feet (metres): 52.2 × 14.8 × 4.3 *(15.9 × 4.5 × 1.3)*
Main machinery: 2 GM 6-71 diesels; 348 hp *(260 kW)* sustained; 2 shafts
Speed, knots: 10. **Range, n miles:** 600 at 10 kt
Complement: 9

Comment: Completed in 1994 and took the names and pennant numbers of their deleted predecessors.

MESAHA 2 *9/1994, C D Yaylali* / 0080890

TRAINING SHIPS

2 RHEIN CLASS (AG/AX)

Name	*No*	*Builders*	*Commissioned*
CEZAYIRLI GAZI HASAN PAŞA (ex-*Elbe*)	A 579	Schliekerwerft, Hamburg	17 Apr 1962
SOKULLU MEHMET PAŞA (ex-*Donau*)	A 577	Schlichting, Travemünde	23 May 1964

Displacement, tons: 2,370 standard; 2,940 full load
Dimensions, feet (metres): 322.1 × 38.8 × 14.4 *(98.2 × 11.8 × 4.4)*
Main machinery: Diesel-electric; 6 MTU MD diesels; 14,400 hp(m) *(10.58 MW)*; 2 Siemens motors; 11,400 hp(m) *(8.38 MW)*; 2 shafts
Speed, knots: 20.5. **Range, n miles:** 1,625 at 15 kt
Complement: 188 (15 officers)
Guns: 2 Creusot-Loire 3.9 in *(100 mm)*/55. 4 Bofors 40 mm/60. 2—12.7 mm MGs.
Radars: Surface search: Signaal DA02; E/F-band.
Fire control: 2 Signaal M 45; I/J-band.

Comment: *Elbe* transferred from Germany on 15 March 1993, taking over the same name and pennant number as the former *Ruhr*. *Donau* transferred 13 March 1995 taking the same name and pennant number as the deleted *Isar*.

SOKULLU MEHMET PAŞA *2/2007, Adolfo Ortigueira Gil* / 1167870

8 TRAINING CRAFT (AXL)

Name	*No*	*Builders*	*Commissioned*
E 1	A 1531	Bora-Duzgit	22 July 1999
E 2	A 1532	Bora-Duzgit	22 July 1999
E 3	A 1533	Bora-Duzgit	8 June 2000
E 4	A 1534	Bora-Duzgit	8 June 2000
E 5	A 1535	Bora-Duzgit	8 June 2000
E 6	A 1536	Bora-Duzgit	8 June 2000
E 7	A 1537	Bora-Duzgit	8 June 2000
E 8	A 1538	Bora-Duzgit	8 June 2000

Displacement, tons: 94 full load
Dimensions, feet (metres): 94.5 × 19.7 × 6.2 *(28.8 × 6 × 1.9)*
Main machinery: 1 MTU diesel; 1 shaft
Speed, knots: 12. **Range, n miles:** 240 at 12 kt
Complement: 15

Comment: Naval Academy training craft ordered in 1998.

E 1 *7/1999, Selçuk Emre* / 0080892

AUXILIARIES

Notes: (1) The tendering process for the procurement of a Submarine Rescue Mother Ship and for two tenders was initiated by the issue of a Request for Information on 25 July 2006. The broad requirement is for a national rescue system which would be interoperable with NATO assets.
(2) A Request for Information for two Rescue and Towing ships was released on 25 July 2006.

1 TRANSPORT SHIP (AK)

Name	*No*	*Builders*	*Commissioned*	*Recommissioned*
ISKENDERUN	A 1600	Camialti Shipyard, Istanbul	1991	25 July 2002

Measurement, tons: 10,583 gross; 3,872 net
Dimensions, feet (metres): 418.4 × 64.0 × 17.7 *(127.5 × 19.5 × 5.4)*
Main machinery: 4 Skoda and Sulzer diesels; 16,800 hp *(12.52 MW)*; 2 shafts
Speed, knots: 15.5
Complement: 129 (11 officers)

Comment: Car ferry (214 cars and passengers) built to Polish design. Commissioned in Turkish Navy on 25 July 2002.

ISKENDERUN *3/2004, Selim San* / 0587559

2 FLEET SUPPORT SHIPS (AORH)

Name	*No*	*Builders*	*Laid down*	*Launched*	*Commissioned*
AKAR	A 580	Gölcük Naval Dockyard	5 Aug 1982	17 Nov 1983	9 Sep 1987
YARBAY KUDRET GÜNGÖR	A 595	Sedef Shipyard, Istanbul	5 Nov 1993	15 Nov 1994	24 Oct 1995

Displacement, tons: 19,350 full load
Dimensions, feet (metres): 475.9 × 74.8 × 27.6 *(145.1 × 22.8 × 8.4)*
Main machinery: 1 diesel; 6,500 hp(m) *(4.78 MW)*; 1 shaft
Speed, knots: 16
Range, n miles: 6,000 at 14 kt
Complement: 203 (14 officers)
Cargo capacity: 16,000 tons oil fuel (A 580); 9,980 tons oil fuel (A 595); 2,700 tons water (A 595); 80 tons lub oil (A 595); 500 m³ stores (A 595)
Guns: 2—3 in *(76 mm)*/50 (twin) Mk 34 (A 580). 1—20 mm/76 Mk 15 Vulcan Phalanx (A 595). 2 Bofors 40 mm/70.
Weapons control: Mk 63 GFCS (A 580).
Radars: Fire control: SPG-34; I-band (A 580).
Navigation: Racal Decca 1226; I-band.
Helicopters: Platform for 1 medium.

Comment: Helicopter flight deck aft. *Akar* is primarily a tanker whereas the second ship of the same type is classified as logistic support vessel. *Güngör* was the first naval ship to be built at a civilian yard in Turkey.

YARBAY KUDRET GÜNGÖR *5/2007, Selim San* / 1167869

1 SUPPORT TANKER (AOTL)

Name	*No*	*Builders*	*Launched*	*Commissioned*
TAŞKIZAK	A 570	Taşkizak Naval DY, Istanbul	28 July 1983	14 Aug 1985

Displacement, tons: 1,440 full load
Dimensions, feet (metres): 211.9 × 30.8 × 11.5 *(64.6 × 9.4 × 3.5)*
Main machinery: 1 diesel; 1,400 hp(m) *(1.03 MW)*; 1 shaft
Speed, knots: 13
Complement: 57
Cargo capacity: 800 tons
Guns: 1 Bofors 40 mm/60. 2 Oerlikon 20 mm.
Radars: Navigation: Racal Decca 1226; I-band.

Comment: Laid down 20 July 1983.

TAŞKIZAK (Doğan class in background) *5/1990, A Sheldon Duplaix* / 0080893

2 SUPPORT TANKERS (AOT)

Name	*No*	*Builders*	*Commissioned*
ALBAY HAKKI BURAK	A 571	RMK Marine, Tuzla, Istanbul	21 Nov 1999
YUZBASI IHSAN TOLUNAY	A 572	RMK Marine, Tuzla, Istanbul	8 June 2000

Displacement, tons: 3,300 full load
Measurement, tons: 6,750 dwt
Dimensions, feet (metres): 359.2 × 56.4 × 23.0 *(109.5 × 17.2 × 7.0)*
Main machinery: 2 Caterpillar 3606TA diesels; 5,522 hp(m) *(4.06 MW)*; 2 shafts
Speed, knots: 13
Complement: 50
Cargo capacity: 2,355 m³ dieso

Comment: Ordered in 1998.

ALBAY HAKKI BURAK *6/2002, Selçuk Emre* / 0533258

1 SUPPORT TANKER (AORL)

Name	*No*	*Builders*	*Commissioned*
BINBAŞI SADETTIN GÜRCAN	A 573	Taşkizak Naval DY, Istanbul	4 Sep 1970

Displacement, tons: 1,505 standard; 4,460 full load
Dimensions, feet (metres): 294.2 × 38.7 × 17.7 *(89.7 × 11.8 × 5.4)*
Main machinery: Diesel-electric; 4 GM 16-567A diesels; 5,600 hp *(4.12 MW)*; 4 generators; 2 motors; 4,400 hp *(3.28 MW)*; 2 shafts
Speed, knots: 16
Complement: 63
Guns: 2 Oerlikon 20 mm.
Radars: E/F-band.

Comment: Main armament removed. Can be used for replenishment at sea.

BINBAŞI SADETTIN GÜRCAN *6/1995, Turkish Navy* / 0080895

3 WATER TANKERS (AWT)

SÖGÜT (ex-*FW 2*) A 598 (ex-Y 1217) **KAVAK** (ex-*FW 4*) A 600 **ÇINAR** (ex-*FW 1*) A 581

Displacement, tons: 626 full load
Dimensions, feet (metres): 144.4 × 25.6 × 8.2 *(44.1 × 7.8 × 2.5)*
Main machinery: 1 MWM diesel; 230 hp(m) *(169 kW)*; 1 shaft
Speed, knots: 9.5
Range, n miles: 2,150 at 9 kt
Complement: 12
Cargo capacity: 340 tons

Comment: *Sögüt* acquired from West Germany and commissioned 12 March 1976. Pennant number changed in 1991. *Kavak* transferred from Germany 12 April 1991 and *Çinar* in early 1996.

KAVAK *5/2007, Selim San* / 1167867

2 WATER TANKERS (AWT)

Name	*No*	*Builders*	*Commissioned*
VAN	A 597 (ex-*Y 1208*)	Camialti Shipyard	12 Aug 1968
ULUBAT	A 596 (ex-*Y 1209*)	Camialti Shipyard	3 July 1969

Displacement, tons: 1,250 full load
Dimensions, feet (metres): 174.2 × 29.5 × 9.8 *(53.1 × 9 × 3)*
Main machinery: 1 diesel; 650 hp(m) *(478 kW)*; 1 shaft
Speed, knots: 14
Complement: 39 (3 officers)
Cargo capacity: 700 tons
Guns: 1 Oerlikon 20 mm.
Radars: Racal Decca 707; I-band.

Comment: Pennant numbers changed in 1991.

VAN *6/2003, Turkish Navy* / 0567542

4 WATER TANKERS (YW)

PINAR 2 Y 112 (ex-Y 1212) **PINAR 4** Y 114 (ex-Y 1214)
PINAR 3 Y 113 (ex-Y 1213) **PINAR 6** Y 116 (ex-Y 1216)

Displacement, tons: 300 full load
Dimensions, feet (metres): 110.2 × 27.9 × 5.9 *(33.6 × 8.5 × 1.8)*
Main machinery: 1 GM diesel; 225 hp *(168 kW)*; 1 shaft
Speed, knots: 11
Complement: 12
Cargo capacity: 150 tons

Comment: Built by Taşkizak Naval Yard. Details given for *Pinar 3, 4* and *6*, sisters to harbour tankers H 500-502. *Pinar 2* built in 1958 of 1,300 tons full load, 167.3 × 27.9 ft *(51 × 8.5 m)*.

PINAR 3 *4/2007, C D Yaylali* / 1167951

3 HARBOUR TANKERS (YW)

H 500–502 Y 140–142 (ex-Y 1231–1233)

Displacement, tons: 300 full load
Dimensions, feet (metres): 110.2 × 27.9 × 5.9 *(33.6 × 8.5 × 1.8)*
Main machinery: 1 GM diesel; 225 hp(m) *(165 kW)*; 1 shaft
Speed, knots: 11
Complement: 12
Cargo capacity: 150 tons

Comment: Sisters of water tankers of Pinar series. Built at Taşkizak in early 1970s.

H 501 *5/2007, Selim San* / 1167868

1 HARBOUR TANKER (YO)

GÖLCÜK Y 50

Displacement, tons: 310 full load
Dimensions, feet (metres): 108.8 × 19.2 × 9.2 *(33.2 × 5.8 × 2.8)*
Main machinery: 1 diesel; 550 hp(m) *(404 kW)*; 1 shaft
Speed, knots: 12
Complement: 12

GÖLCÜK *7/1992, Selçuk Emre* / 0080898

1 DIVER CLASS (SALVAGE SHIP) (ARS)

Name	*No*	*Builders*	*Launched*	*Commissioned*
IŞIN (ex-*Safeguard* ARS 25)	A 589	Basalt Rock, Napa	20 Nov 1943	31 Oct 1944

Displacement, tons: 1,530 standard; 1,970 full load
Dimensions, feet (metres): 213.5 × 41 × 13 *(65.1 × 12.5 × 4)*
Main machinery: Diesel-electric; 4 Cooper-Bessemer GSB-8 diesels; 3,420 hp *(2.55 MW)*; 4 generators; 2 motors; 2 shafts
Speed, knots: 14.8
Complement: 110
Guns: 2 Oerlikon 20 mm.

Comment: Transferred from US 28 September 1979 and purchased outright 6 August 1987.

IŞIN *4/2005, C D Yaylali* / 1133575

1 CHANTICLEER CLASS (SUBMARINE RESCUE SHIP) (ASR)

Name	*No*	*Builders*	*Launched*	*Commissioned*
AKIN (ex-*Greenlet* ASR 10)	A 585	Moore SB & DD Co	12 July 1942	29 May 1943

Displacement, tons: 1,653 standard; 2,321 full load
Dimensions, feet (metres): 251.5 × 44 × 16 *(76.7 × 13.4 × 4.9)*
Main machinery: Diesel-electric; 4 Alco 539 diesels; 3,532 hp *(2.63 MW)*; 4 generators; 1 motor; 1 shaft
Speed, knots: 15
Complement: 111 (9 officers)
Guns: 1 Bofors 40 mm/60. 4 Oerlikon 20 mm (2 twin).
Radars: Navigation: Racal Decca 1226; I-band.

Comment: Transferred from US, recommissioned 23 December 1970 and purchased 15 February 1973. Carries a Diving Bell.

AKIN *9/2008*, Arda Mevlutoglu* / 1353415

1 TRANSPORT (AKS/AWT)

Name	*No*	*Builders*	*Commissioned*
KARADENIZ EREĞLI	A 592 (ex-Y 1157)	Erdem	30 Aug 1982

Displacement, tons: 820 full load
Dimensions, feet (metres): 166.3 × 26.2 × 9.2 *(50.7 × 8 × 2.8)*
Main machinery: 1 diesel; 1,440 hp *(1.06 MW)*; 1 shaft
Speed, knots: 10
Complement: 23 (3 officers)
Cargo capacity: 300 tons
Guns: 1 Oerlikon 20 mm.

Comment: Funnel-aft coaster type. Pennant number changed in 1991. Used as a stores ship.

2 BARRACK SHIPS (YPB)

YÜZBAŞI NAŞIT ÖNGÖREN (ex-US *APL 47*) Y 38 (ex-Y 1204)
BINBAŞI METIN SÜLÜŞ (ex-US *APL 53*) Y 39 (ex-Y 1205)

Comment: Ex-US barrack ships transferred on lease: Y 1204 in October 1972 and Y 1205 on 6 December 1974. Y 1204 based at Ereğli and Y 1205 at Gölcük. Purchased outright June 1987. Pennant numbers changed in 1991.

12 SMALL TRANSPORTS (YFB/YE)

ŞALOPA 11–12 **ŞALOPA 18** **ŞALOPA 22–24** **ŞALOPA 27** **ŞALOPA 30–33** **YAKIT** Y 139

Comment: Of varying size and appearance. Pennant numbers changed in 1991.

1 BOOM DEFENCE VESSEL (ABU)

Name	*No*	*Builders*	*Commissioned*
AG 6 (ex-*AN 93*, ex-Netherlands *Cerberus* A 895)	P 306	Bethlehem Steel Corporation, Staten Island, NY	10 Nov 1952

Displacement, tons: 780 standard; 855 full load
Dimensions, feet (metres): 165 × 33 × 10 *(50.3 × 10.1 × 3)*
Main machinery: Diesel-electric; 2 GM 8-268A diesels; 880 hp *(656 kW)*; 2 generators; 1 motor; 1 shaft
Speed, knots: 12.8
Range, n miles: 5,200 at 12 kt
Complement: 32 (3 officers)
Guns: 1 USN 3 in *(76 mm)*/50. 4 Oerlikon 20 mm.
Radars: Navigation: Racal Decca 1226; I-band.

Comment: Netlayer. Transferred from US to Netherlands in December 1952. Used first as a boom defence vessel and latterly as salvage and diving tender since 1961 but retained her netlaying capacity. Handed back to US Navy on 17 September 1970 but immediately turned over to the Turkish Navy under grant aid.

AG 6 *7/1995, Frank Behling* / 0080906

1 BOOM DEFENCE VESSEL (ABU)

Name	*No*	*Builders*	*Commissioned*
AG 5 (ex-*AN 104*)	P 305	Kröger, Rendsburg	25 Feb 1962

Displacement, tons: 960 full load
Dimensions, feet (metres): 173.8 × 35 × 13.5 *(53 × 10.7 × 4.1)*
Main machinery: Diesel-electric; 1 MAN G7V40/60 diesel generator; 1 motor; 1,470 hp(m) *(1.08 MW)*; 1 shaft
Speed, knots: 12
Range, n miles: 6,500 at 11 kt
Complement: 32 (3 officers)
Guns: 1 Bofors 40 mm/60. 3 Oerlikon 20 mm.
Radars: Navigation: Racal Decca 1226; I-band.

Comment: Netlayer P 305 built in US offshore programme for Turkey.

AG 5 *8/2008*, C D Yaylali* / 1353416

3 TORPEDO RETRIEVERS (YPT)

TORPIDO TENDERI Y 95 (ex-Y 1051) **TAKIP 1** Y 98 (ex-Y 1052) **TAKIP 2** Y 99

Comment: Of different types.

TORPEDO RETRIEVER *9/1998, C D Yaylali* / 0050297

2 OFFICERS' YACHTS (YAC)

GÜL **NEVCIVAN**

Comment: Pennant numbers not displayed.

GÜL *6/2003, Turkish Navy* / 0567541

NEVCIVAN *10/2003, C D Yaylali* / 0567559

13 FLOATING DOCKS/CRANES (YAC)

Name	Lift	Name	Lift
LEVENT Y 59 (ex-Y 1022)	–	**HAVUZ 5** Y 125 (ex-Y 1085)	400 tons
ALGARNA 1 Y 58		**HAVUZ 8** Y 128 (ex-Y-1088)	700 tons
ALGARNA 3 Y 60; (ex-Y 1021)	–	**HAVUZ 9** Y 129 (ex-Y-1089)	4,500 tons
HAVUZ 1 Y 121 (ex-Y 1081)	16,000 tons	**HAVUZ 10** Y 130 (ex-Y-1090)	3,500 tons
HAVUZ 2 Y 122 (ex-Y 1082)	12,000 tons	**HAVUZ 11** Y 134	14,500 tons
HAVUZ 3 Y 123 (ex-Y 1083); (ex-US AFDL)	2,500 tons	**HAVUZ 13** Y 136	7,500 tons
HAVUZ 4 Y 124 (ex-Y 1084)	4,500 tons		

Comment: Algarna and *Levent* are ex-US floating cranes.

HAVUZ 10 *8/2008*, C D Yaylali* / 1353417

1 POWHATAN CLASS (FLEET OCEAN TUGS) (ATF)

Name	No	Laid down	Commissioned
INEBOLU (ex-*Powhatan*)	A 590 (ex-T-ATF 166)	30 Sep 1976	15 June 1979

Displacement, tons: 2,260 full load
Dimensions, feet (metres): 226.0 × 42 × 15 *(68.9 × 12.8 × 4.6)*
Main machinery: 2 GM EMD 20-645F7B diesels; 7,250 hp(m) *(5.41 MW)* sustained; 2 shafts; Kort nozzles; cp props; bow thruster; 300 hp *(224 kW)*
Speed, knots: 14.5. **Range, n miles**: 10,000 at 13 kt
Complement: 16 civilians plus 4 naval
Guns: Space provided to fit 2—20 mm and 2—12.7 mm MGs.
Radars: Navigation: E/F/I-band.

Comment: Built at Marinette Marine Corp, Wisconsin patterned after commercial offshore supply ship design. Following de-activation from US MSC in 1999, operated on commercial lease to Don John Commercial Co until 25 February 2008. Following a refit at Detyens Shipyard, Charleston, commissioned in Turkish Navy on 15 March 2008. Equipped with 10-ton crane, two fire pumps and capable of supporting salvage operations. Bollard pull 54 tons.

POWHATAN CLASS *5/2006, M Declerck* / 1167637

TUGS

1 CHEROKEE CLASS (ATF)

GAZAL (ex-*Sioux* ATF 75) A 587

Displacement, tons: 1,235 standard; 1,675 full load
Dimensions, feet (metres): 205 × 38.5 × 17 *(62.5 × 11.7 × 5.2)*
Main machinery: Diesel-electric; 4 GM 12-278 diesels; 4,400 hp *(3.28 MW)*; 4 generators; 1 motor; 3,000 hp *(2.24 MW)*; 1 shaft
Speed, knots: 16. **Range, n miles**: 15,000 at 8 kt
Complement: 85
Guns: 1 USN 3 in *(76 mm)*/50. 2 Oerlikon 20 mm.
Radars: Navigation: Racal Decca; I-band.

Comment: Originally completed on 6 December 1942. Transferred from US and commissioned 9 March 1973. Purchased 15 August 1973. Can be used for salvage. 3 in gun removed in 1987 but has since been restored.

GAZAL *6/2008*, Selim San* / 1353418

1 TENACE CLASS (ATA)

Name	No	Builders	Commissioned
DEĞIRMENDERE (ex-*Centaure*)	A 576 (ex-A 674)	Chantiers de la Rochelle	14 May 1974

Displacement, tons: 1,454 full load
Dimensions, feet (metres): 167.3 × 37.8 × 18.6 *(51 × 11.5 × 5.7)*
Main machinery: 2 SACM AGO 240 V12 diesels; 4,600 hp(m) *(3.38 MW)*; 1 shaft; Kort nozzle
Speed, knots: 13
Range, n miles: 9,500 at 13 kt
Complement: 37 (3 officers)
Radars: Racal Decca RM 1226 and Racal Decca 060; I-band.

Comment: Transferred from French Navy 16 March 1999. Recommissioned after refit 22 July 1999. Bollard pull 60 tons.

DEĞIRMENDERE *1/2008*, Selim San* / 1353419

17 COASTAL/HARBOUR TUGS (YTB/YTM/YTL)

Name	No	Commissioned	Displacement, tons/ Speed, knots
AKBAŞ	A 586	1978	1660/14
SÖNDÜREN 2	A 1542	1999/2000	385/12
SÖNDÜREN 3	A 1543	1954	128/12
SÖNDÜREN 4	A 1544	1954	128/12
SÖNDÜREN 1	Y 51 (ex-Y 1117)	1954	128/12
KUVVET	Y 53 (ex-Y 1122)	1962	390/10
DOĞANARSLAN	Y 52 (ex-Y 1123)	1985	500/12
ATIL	Y 55 (ex-Y 1132)	1962	300/10
PENDIK	Y 56	2000	238/10
ERSEV BAYRAK	Y 64 (ex-Y 1134)	1946	30/9
AKSAZ (ex-*Koos*)	Y 57 (ex-Y 1651, ex-A 08)	1962	320/11
DENEY	Y 90	1970	400/14
ÖNDER	Y 160	1998	230/12
ÖNCÜ	Y 161	1998	230/12
ÖZGEN	Y 162	1999	230/12
ÖDEV	Y 163	1999	230/12
ÖZGÜR	Y 164	2000	230/12

Comment: In addition there are 47 Katir pusher berthing tugs. *Koos* was transferred from Germany on 7 October 1996.

ÖZGEN *5/2005, C D Yaylali* / 1133574

SÖNDÜREN 2 *4/2005, Selim San* / 1133588

1 OCEAN TUG (ATR)

DARICA A 578 (ex-Y 1125)

Displacement, tons: 750 full load
Dimensions, feet (metres): 134.2 × 32.2 × 12.8 *(40.9 × 9.8 × 3.9)*
Main machinery: 2 ABC diesels; 4,000 hp *(2.94 MW)*; 2 shafts
Speed, knots: 14
Range, n miles: 2,500 at 14 kt

Comment: Built at Taşkizak Naval Yard and commissioned 13 June 1991. Equipped for firefighting and as a torpedo tender. Pennant number changed in 1991.

DARICA *11/1994, van Ginderen Collection* / 0080910

COAST GUARD (SAHIL GÜVENLIK)

Notes: (1) A Request for Information for the procurement of up to 16 patrol craft has been issued. The broad requirement is for craft of about 50 m and 400 tons capable of speeds of over 25 kt.
(2) Patrol craft based in north Cyprus include KKTCSG 101 *(Raif Denktas)*, two 40 m craft (KKTCSG 01-02), two Kaan 15 class (KKTCSG 11, KKTCSG 12), two 14 m craft (KKTCSG 102-103) and a converted cabin cruiser KKTCSG 104.
(3) Four Vigilante class Boston Whalers were acquired by the Police in September 1999.

KKTCSG 104 *6/2004, Selçuk Emre* / 1133570

0 + 4 OFFSHORE PATROL VESSELS (PSOH)

Name	*No*	*Builders*	*Laid down*	*Launched*	*Commissioned*
DOST	–	RMK Marine, Tuzla	3 May 2008	2010	2011
UMUT	–	RMK Marine, Tuzla	2009	2010	2012
YASAM	–	RMK Marine, Tuzla	2009	2011	2012
GÜVEN	–	RMK Marine, Tuzla	2009	2011	2012

Displacement, tons: 1,520 full load
Dimensions, feet (metres): 290.0 × 40.0 × 15.1 *(88.4 × 12.2 × 4.6)*
Main machinery: 2 diesels; cp props; bow thruster
Speed, knots: 22. **Range, n miles:** 3,500 at 14 kt
Complement: 60 (5 officers)
Guns: 1—76 mm. 2—25 mm.
Weapons control: To be announced.
Radars: Surface search: To be announced.
Fire control: To be announced.
Navigation: To be announced.
Helicopters: 1 AB 412.

Comment: Contract signed with RMK Marine on 16 January 2007 for the construction of four offshore patrol vessels to carry out SAR and EEZ patrol duties. The design, based on the Italian Sirio class, includes a telescopic hangar, two high-speed RIBs, two firefighting monitors and anti-pollution equipment.

OPV *10/2007, Turkish Navy* / 1167863

14 LARGE PATROL CRAFT (WPB)

SG 80–91 **KKTCSG 01–02**

Displacement, tons: 195 full load
Dimensions, feet (metres): 133.5 × 23.3 × 7.2 *(40.7 × 7.1 × 2.2)*
Main machinery: 2 diesels; 5,700 hp(m) *(4.19 MW)*; 2 shafts
Speed, knots: 27
Complement: 25
Guns: 1 Breda 40 mm/70. 2—12.7 mm MGs.
Radars: Surface search: Racal Decca; I-band.

Comment: All built at Taşkizak Shipyard except SG 89 which was built at Istanbul Shipyard. SG 80-82 commissioned in 1996, 83-84 in 1997, 85 in 1998, 86-87 in 2000, 89-90 in 2001, 88 in 2002 and 91 in 2004. Two based in northern Cyprus with pennant numbers KKTCSG 01-02.

SG 90 *8/2008*, C D Yaylali* / 1353420

KKTCSG 02 *6/2004, Selçuk Emre* / 1044200

14 LARGE PATROL CRAFT (WPB)

SG 121–134

Displacement, tons: 180 full load
Dimensions, feet (metres): 132 × 21 × 5.5 *(40.2 × 6.4 × 1.7)*
131.2 × 21.3 × 4.9 *(40 × 6.5 × 1.5) (SG 130-134)*
Main machinery: 2 SACM AGO 195 V16 CSHR diesels; 4,800 hp(m) *(3.53 MW)* sustained
2 cruise diesels; 300 hp(m) *(220 kW)*; 2 shafts
Speed, knots: 22
Complement: 25
Guns: 1 or 2 Bofors 40 mm/60. 2—12.7 mm MGs.
Radars: Surface search: Racal Decca 1226; I-band.

Comment: *SG 121* and *122* built by Gölcük Naval Yard, remainder by Tas¸kizak Naval Yard. *SG 134* commissioned in 1977, remainder 1968–71. *SG 130-134* have minor modifications-knuckle at bow, radar stirrup on bridge and MG on superstructure sponsons. These are similar craft to the Turk class listed under *Patrol Forces* for the Navy.

SG 131 *6/2007, C D Yaylali* / 1167953

10 SAR 33 TYPE (LARGE PATROL CRAFT) (WPB)

SG 61–70

Displacement, tons: 180 full load
Dimensions, feet (metres): 113.5 × 28.3 × 9.7 *(34.6 × 8.6 × 3)*
Main machinery: 3 SACM AGO 195 V16 CSHR diesels; 7,200 hp(m) *(5.29 MW)* sustained; 3 shafts; cp props
Speed, knots: 33. **Range, n miles:** 450 at 24 kt; 550 at 18 kt
Complement: 24
Guns: 1 Bofors 40 mm/60. 2—12.7 mm MGs.
Radars: Surface search: Racal Decca; I-band.

Comment: Prototype Serter design ordered from Abeking & Rasmussen, Lemwerder in May 1976. The remainder were built at Taşkizak Naval Yard, Istanbul between 1979 and 1981. Fourteen of this class were to have been transferred to Libya but the order was cancelled. Two delivered to Saudi Arabia. The engines have been governed back and the top speed correspondingly reduced from the original 12,000 hp and 40 kt.

SG 67 *5/2004, Martin Mokrus* / 0589828

4 SAR 35 TYPE (LARGE PATROL CRAFT) (WPB)

SG 71–74

Displacement, tons: 210 full load
Dimensions, feet (metres): 120 × 28.3 × 6.2 *(36.6 × 8.6 × 1.9)*
Main machinery: 3 SACM AGO 195 V16 CSHR diesels; 7,200 hp(m) *(5.29 MW)* sustained; 3 shafts; cp props
Speed, knots: 33
Range, n miles: 450 at 24 kt; 550 at 18 kt
Complement: 24
Guns: 1 Bofors 40 mm/60. 2—12.7 mm MGs.
Radars: Surface search: Racal Decca 1226; I-band.

Comment: A slightly enlarged version of the Serter designed SAR 33 Type built by Taşkizak Shipyard between 1985 and 1987. A contract was signed on 21 May 2007 with Istanbul Denizcilik Gemi Inşaa Shipyard for the modernisation of the main machinery.

SG 71 *8/2000, C D Yaylali* / 0106645

9 KAAN 29 CLASS (LARGE PATROL CRAFT) (WPBF)

SG 101–109

Displacement, tons: 98 full load
Dimensions, feet (metres): 104.0 × 22.0 × 4.6 *(31.7 × 6.7 × 1.4)*
Main machinery: 2 MTU 16V 400 M90 diesels; 7,398 hp(m) *(5.44 MW)*; 2 MJP 753DD waterjets
Speed, knots: 49
Range, n miles: 750 at 20 kt
Complement: 13 (2 officers)
Guns: 4—12.7 mm MGs.
Radars: Surface search/navigation: Raytheon; I-band.

Comment: All built at Yonca Shipyard. Onuk MRTP 29 design. Advanced composites structure. *TCSG 101-103* commissioned 25 July 2001, *TCSG 104-105* on 25 July 2002, *TCSG 106-108* in 2003 and *TCSG 109* in February 2004. A stabilised machine gun is under development for installation in the Kaan 29 and 33 classes.

SG 107 *6/2007, Turkish Coast Guard* / 1353421

13 + 9 KAAN 33 CLASS (LARGE PATROL CRAFT) (WPBF)

SG 301–313

Displacement, tons: 115 full load
Dimensions, feet (metres): 116.8 × 22.0 × 4.7 *(35.6 × 6.7 × 1.4)*
Main machinery: 2 MTU 16V 4000 M90 diesels; 7,396 hp(m) *(5.44 MW)*; 2 MJP 753DD waterjets
Speed, knots: 47
Range, n miles: 650 at 20 kt
Complement: 18 (2 officers)
Guns: 4—12.7 mm MGs.
Radars: Navigation: Raytheon; I-band.

Comment: All built at Yonca Shipyard. Onuk MRTP 33 design. Advanced composites structure. TCSG 301 commissioned in July 2004, TCSG 302 in July 2005, TCSG 303 in September 2005, TCSG 304-306 in September 2006, TCSG 307 in December 2006, TCSG 308 (April 2007), TCSG 309 (July 2007), TCSG 310 (April 2008), TCSG 311 (July 2008), TCSG 312 (October 2008) and TCSG 313 (January 2009). A further nine craft have been ordered. ASELSAN stabilised gun (STAMP) fitted in some Kaan 33 and 29 craft.

SG 307 (with STAMP mounting) *6/2008*, Yonca-Onuk* / 1353422

4 KW 15 CLASS (LARGE PATROL CRAFT) (WPB)

SG 113–114 **SG 118–119**

Displacement, tons: 70 full load
Dimensions, feet (metres): 94.8 × 15.4 × 4.6 *(28.9 × 4.7 × 1.4)*
Main machinery: 2 MTU diesels; 2,700 hp(m) *(1.98 MW)*; 2 shafts
Speed, knots: 20. **Range, n miles:** 550 at 16 kt
Complement: 16
Guns: 1 Bofors 40 mm/60. 2 Oerlikon 20 mm.
Radars: Surface search: Racal Decca; I-band.

Comment: Built by Schweers, Bardenfleth. Commissioned 1961–62.

SG 119 *9/2002, Selim San* / 0533264

18 KAAN 15 CLASS (FAST INTERVENTION CRAFT) (WPBF)

SG 1–18

Displacement, tons: 20 full load
Dimensions, feet (metres): 54.8 × 13.2 × 3.9 *(16.7 × 4.04 × 1.2)*
Main machinery: 2 MTU 12V 183TE93 diesels; 2,300 hp(m) *(1.69 MW)*; 2 Arneson ASD 12 B1L surface drives
Speed, knots: 54. **Range, n miles:** 350 at 35 kt
Complement: 4 plus 8 mission crew
Guns: 2—12.7 mm MGs.
Radars: Surface search: Raytheon; I-band.

Comment: Contract for first six with Yonca Technical Investment signed in May 1997, second order for six more in February 1999, and third for 6 more in August 2000. All built at Tuzla-Istanbul shipyard. Three delivered in 1998, seven in 1999, two in April 2000, four in July 2001 and two in July 2002. Onuk MRTP 15 design. Advanced composites structure. Two based in northern Cyprus with pennant numbers KKTCSG 11-12.

SG 1 *6/2007, Turkish Coast Guard* / 1353423

SG 11 *6/2007, Maritime Photographic* / 1167866

3 KAAN 19 CLASS (FAST INTERVENTION CRAFT) (WPBF)

SG 19–21

Displacement, tons: 38 full load
Dimensions, feet (metres): 74.0 × 15.6 × 4.3 *(22.55 × 4.76 × 1.3)*
Main machinery: 2 MTU 12V 2000 M 92 diesels; 3,600 hp(m) *(2.7 MW)*; 2 MJP waterjets
Speed, knots: 60
Range, n miles: 350 at 35 kt
Complement: 5
Guns: 2—12.7 mm MGs.

Comment: Yonuk MRTP 20 (enlarged MRTP 15) design built at Yonca shipyard. Prototype completed in 2006. An order for two further craft was made on 2 March 2007.

SG 19 *6/2008*, Yonca-Onuk* / 1353424

11 COASTAL PATROL CRAFT (WPB)

SG 50–58 KKTCSG 102–103

Displacement, tons: 29 full load
Dimensions, feet (metres): 47.9 × 13.7 × 3.6 *(14.6 × 4.2 × 1.1)*
Main machinery: 2 diesels; 700 hp(m) *(514 kW)*; 2 shafts
Speed, knots: 15
Complement: 7
Guns: 1 — 12.7 mm MG or 1 Oerlikon 20 mm *(SG 102-103)*.
Radars: Surface search: Raytheon; I-band.

Comment: *KKTCSG 102-103* were built for North Cyprus and have been based there since August 1990 and July 1991 respectively. Both these craft were given a heavier gun in 1992. Second batch of three completed by Taşkizak in October 1992, three more in June 1993, three more in December 1993.

SG 58 *6/2007, Maritime Photographic* / 1167865

1 INSHORE PATROL CRAFT (WPBI)

RAIF DENKTAŞ 101 (ex-74)

Displacement, tons: 10 full load
Dimensions, feet (metres): 38 × 11.5 × 2.4 *(11.6 × 3.5 × 0.7)*
Main machinery: 2 Volvo Aquamatic AQ200F petrol engines; 400 hp(m) *(294 kW)*; 2 shafts
Speed, knots: 28
Range, n miles: 250 at 25 kt
Complement: 6
Guns: 1 — 12.7 mm MG.
Radars: Surface search: Raytheon; I-band.

Comment: Built by Protekson, Istanbul. Transferred to North Cyprus 23 September 1988. Can be equipped with a rocket launcher.

RAIF DENKTAŞ *6/2004, Selçuk Emre* / 1044201

1 HARBOUR PATROL CRAFT (WPBI)

SG 41

Displacement, tons: 35
Dimensions, feet (metres): 55.8 × 16.4 × 3.3 *(17 × 5 × 1)*
Main machinery: 2 diesels; 1,050 hp(m) *(771 kW)*
Speed, knots: 20
Complement: 7
Radars: Surface search: I-band.

Comment: Used for anti-smuggling duties. Probably confiscated drug smuggling craft.

SG 41 *5/2006, C D Yaylali* / 1158735

10 SECURITY AND SAFETY CRAFT (PBR)

Displacement, tons: To be announced
Dimensions, feet (metres): 25.4 × 9.5 × 1.6 *(7.75 × 2.9 × 0.5)*
Main machinery: 2 outboard motors; 180 hp *(135 kW)*
Speed, knots: 35
Complement: 3

Comment: Rigid-inflatable hull with fibre cabin.

SECURITY CRAFT *9/2008*, C D Yaylali* / 1353425

20 SECURITY AND SAFETY CRAFT (PBR)

Displacement, tons: To be announced
Dimensions, feet (metres): 31.1 × 9.8 × 1.6 *(9.5 × 3.0 × 0.5)*
Main machinery: 2 outboard motors; 350 hp *(260 kW)*
Speed, knots: 40
Complement: 3

Comment: Rigid-inflatable hull with fibre cabin.

SECURITY CRAFT *6/2007, Turkish Coast Guard* / 1170048

10 SAFETY CRAFT (PBR)

Displacement, tons: To be announced
Dimensions, feet (metres): 19.0 × 7.2 × 2.6 *(5.8 × 2.2 × 0.8)*
Main machinery: 2 outboard motors; 140 hp *(105 kW)*
Speed, knots: 30
Complement: 7

Comment: Inflatable hull craft.

SAFETY CRAFT *6/2007, Turkish Coast Guard* / 1170046

45 CONTROL CRAFT (PBR)

Displacement, tons: To be announced
Dimensions, feet (metres): 19.0 × 7.2 × 2.6 *(5.8 × 2.2 × 0.8)*
Main machinery: 2 outboard motors; 100 hp *(75 kW)*
Speed, knots: 35
Complement: 3

Comment: Inflatable hull craft.

CONTROL CRAFT *6/2007, Turkish Coast Guard* / 1170047

LAND-BASED MARITIME AIRCRAFT

Numbers/Type: 8 Agusta AB 412 EP.
Operational speed: 122 kt *(226 km/h)*.
Service ceiling: 17,000 ft *(5,180 m)*.
Range: 374 n miles *(656 km)*.
Role/Weapon systems: Nine aircraft ordered 15 April 1999. One lost on 30 July 2005. A further six ordered in early 2005. Operated by Coast Guard/Frontier Force for patrol SAR. Sensors: Radar and FLIR. Weapons: Unarmed.

AB 412 *6/2007, Turkish Coast Guard* / 1353427

Numbers/Type: 3 Casa CN-235.
Operational speed: 240 kt *(445 km/h)*.
Service ceiling: 26,600 ft *(8,110 m)*.
Range: 669 n miles *(1,240 km)*.
Role/Weapon systems: Three delivered in July 2002. Long range maritime patrol for surveillance.

CN-235 *6/2007, Turkish Coast Guard* / 1353426

Turkmenistan

Country Overview

Formerly part of the USSR, the Republic of Turkmenistan declared its independence in 1991. Situated in Central Asia, it has an area of 188,460 square miles and is bordered to the north by Kazakhstan, to the east by Uzbekistan and Afghanistan and to the south by Iran. It has a 954 n mile coastline with the Caspian Sea. Türkmenbashi, the principal port, is linked by rail to Ashgabat, the capital and largest city. Maritime claims in the Caspian Sea are yet to be resolved.The Navy acts under the operational control of the Border Guard but is the weakest component of the Turkmen armed forces.

Personnel

2009: 700

Base

Türkmenbashi (formerly Krasnovodsk)

PATROL FORCES

Notes: One 40 m Stenka class patrol craft has been reported operational.

1 POINT CLASS (WPB)

Name	*No*	*Builders*	*Commissioned*
MERJEN (ex-*Point Jackson*)	PB-129 (ex-82378)	USCG Yard Curtis Bay	3 Aug 1970

Displacement, tons: 66; 69 full load
Dimensions, feet (metres): 83 × 17.2 × 5.8 *(25.3 × 5.2 × 1.8)*
Main machinery: 2 Caterpillar 3412 diesels; 1,600 hp *(1.19 MW)*; 2 shafts
Speed, knots: 23.5
Range, n miles: 1,200 at 8 kt
Complement: 10 (1 officer)
Guns: 2 — 12.7 mm MGs.
Radars: Surface search: Hughes/Furuno SPS-73; I-band.

Comment: Steel hulled craft with aluminium superstructure. Transferred from United States on 30 May 2000.

MERJEN (inboard ship) *11/2000, Selim San* / 0104495

4 KALKAN (PROJECT 50030) M CLASS (INSHORE PATROL CRAFT) (PBI)

Displacement, tons: 8.5 full load
Dimensions, feet (metres): 38.1 × 10.8 × 2.0 *(11.6 × 3.3 × 0.6)*
Main machinery: 1 Type 475K diesel; 496 hp *(370 kW)*; 1 waterjet
Speed, knots: 34
Complement: 2
Guns: 1 — 12.7 mm MG.

Comment: Four craft delivered during 2002. Further craft were expected but reportedly not delivered. Built by Morye Feodosiya (Ukraine) and constructed with aluminium hulls and GRP superstructure. Can be armed with 7.62 mm or 12.7 mm MGs.

KALKAN *6/2003, Morye* / 0573698

5 GRIF-T CLASS (PB)

Displacement, tons: 39 full load
Dimensions, feet (metres): 80.05 × 17.1 × 5.1 *(24.4 × 5.2 × 1.57)*
Main machinery: 2 MTU 12V 2000 M 90 diesels; 2,700 hp *(2 MW)*; 2 shafts
Speed, knots: 40. **Range, n miles:** 500 at 15 kt
Complement: 13 (1 officer)
Guns: 1 — 20 mm. 1 — 12.7 mm MG.
Radars: Surface search: I-band.

Comment: Built by Morye Shipyard, Feodosia, Ukraine and delivered in about 2005. Modified versions of Zhuk class. Aluminium construction.

Tuvalu

Country Overview

Tuvalu, formerly the Ellice Islands, is a south Pacific island group which gained independence in 1978; the other part of the former British colony, the Gilbert Islands, became independent as Kiribati the following year. Situated some 1,600 n miles east of Papua New Guinea, the country comprises nine atolls of which Funafuti is the location of the capital, Fongafale, and home to more than 30 per cent of the population. An archipelagic state, territorial seas (12 n miles) are claimed. An Exclusive Economic Zone (EEZ) (200 n miles) is also claimed but limits have not been fully defined by boundary agreements.

Headquarters Appointments

Commander Maritime Wing:
Inspector Motulu Pedro

Bases

Funafuti

PATROL FORCES

1 PACIFIC CLASS (LARGE PATROL CRAFT) (PB)

Name	*No*	*Builders*	*Commissioned*
TE MATAILI	801	Transfield Shipbuilding, WA	8 Oct 1994

Displacement, tons: 165 full load
Dimensions, feet (metres): 103.3 × 26.6 × 6.9 *(31.5 × 8.1 × 2.1)*
Main machinery: 2 Caterpillar 3516TA diesels; 4,400 hp *(3.28 MW)* sustained; 2 shafts
Speed, knots: 18. **Range, n miles:** 2,500 at 12 kt
Complement: 18 (3 officers)
Guns: Can carry 1 — 12.7 mm MG but is unarmed.
Radars: Navigation: Furuno 1011; I-band.

Comment: This is the 18th of the class to be built by the Australian Government for Exclusive Economic Zone (EEZ) patrols in the Pacific islands. The programme originally terminated at 15 but was re-opened on 19 February 1993 to include construction of five more craft for Fiji, Kiribati and Tuvalu. Training and support assistance is given by the Australian Navy. Half-life refit completed at Gladstone in 2001. Following the decision by the Australian government to extend the Pacific Patrol Boat programme, *Te Mataili* will require a life-extension refit in 2011 in order to achieve a 30-year ship life.

TE MATAILI
2000, RAN
0106647

Ukraine

Country Overview

Formerly part of the USSR, Ukraine declared its independence in 1991. Situated in eastern Europe, it has an area of 233,090 square miles and is bordered to the north by Belarus, to the east by Russia, to the south-west by Romania and Moldova and to the west by Hungary, Slovakia and Poland. It has a 1,501 n mile coastline with the Black Sea and the Sea of Azov. Kiev is the capital and largest city while Sevastopol, Odessa, Kerch, and Mariupol are the principal ports. Territorial Seas (12 n miles) have been claimed. An EEZ (200 n miles) has been claimed but the limits have not been defined.

Division of the former Soviet Black Sea Fleet between Russia and Ukraine had been achieved on 28 May 1997. The agreement allows for the leasing of port facilities to the Russian Navy until 2017.

Headquarters Appointments

Commander of the Navy:
Vice Admiral Igor Tenukh
First Deputy Commander of the Navy and Chief of Staff:
Rear Admiral Mykola Kostrov
Commander Western Naval District:
Rear Admiral Dmytro Ukrainets
Commander Southern Naval District:
Rear Admiral Borys Rekuts

Bases

Sevastopol (HQ), Donuzlav (Southern Region), Odessa (Western Region), Mikolaiv, Feodosiya, Izmail, Balaklava, Kerch

Personnel

2009: 13,000 navy

Border Guard

The Maritime Border Guard is an independent subdivision of the State Committee for Border Guards, and is not part of the Navy. It has three cutter brigades, based in Kerch, Odessa and Balaklava, to patrol the 827 mile coastline and two river brigades, which include a gunship squadron, a minesweeping squadron, an auxiliary ship group and a training division. Pennant numbers changed in July 1999.

PENNANT LIST

Frigates

U 130 Hetman Sagaidachny
U 205 Lutsk
U 206 Vinnitsa
U 209 Ternopil

Patrol Forces

U 120 Skadovsk
U 153 Priluki
U 154 Kahovka
U 155 Nikopol
U 156 Kremenchuk
U 207 Uzhgorod
U 208 Khmelnitsky

Mine Warfare Forces

U 310 Zhovti Vody
U 311 Cherkasy
U 330 Melitopol
U 331 Mariupol
U 360 Genichesk

Amphibious Forces

U 410 Kirovograd
U 402 Konstantin Olshansky
U 420 Donetsk
U 862 Korosten
U 904 Bilyaïvka

Auxiliaries

U 240 Feodisiya
U 510 Slavutich
U 540 Chigirin
U 541 Smila
U 542 Darnicha
U 635 Skvyra
U 700 Netisin
U 705 Kremenets
U 706 Izyaslav
U 722 Borshev
U 728 Evpatoriya
U 733 Tokmak
U 753 Kriviy Rig
U 756 Sudak
U 757 Makivka
U 759 Bahmach
U 760 Fastiv
U 782 Sokal
U 783 Illichivsk
U 803 Krasnodon
U 811 Balta
U 830 Korets
U 831 Kovel
U 852 Shostka
U 860 Kamyankha
U 891 Kherson
U 947 Krasnoperekovsk
U 953 Dubno

Survey Ships

U 511 Simferopol
U 512 Pereyaslav
U 601 Alchevsk
U 754 Dzhankoi

SUBMARINES

Notes: The Foxtrot-class submarine *Zaporizya* was expected to return to operational service in 2004 but repairs were not completed and, in 2007, the Defence Minister stated that the boat was to be sold. Meanwhile, the submarine remains at Balaklava. Although plans for repairs were announced in early 2009, the future of the submarine is uncertain.

FRIGATES

1 KRIVAK III (NEREY) CLASS (PROJECT 1135.1) (FFHM)

Name	*No*	*Builders*	*Laid down*	*Launched*	*Commissioned*
HETMAN SAGAIDACHNY (ex-*Kirov*)	U 130 (ex-201)	Kamysh-Burun, Kerch	5 Oct 1990	29 Mar 1992	5 July 1993

Displacement, tons: 3,100 standard; 3,650 full load
Dimensions, feet (metres): 405.2 × 46.9 × 16.4 *(123.5 × 14.3 × 5)*
Main machinery: COGAG; 2 gas turbines; 55,500 hp(m) *(40.8 MW)*; 2 gas turbines; 13,600 hp(m) *(10 MW)*; 2 shafts
Speed, knots: 32
Range, n miles: 4,600 at 20 kt; 1,600 at 30 kt
Complement: 180 (18 officers)

Missiles: SAM: 1 SA-N-4 Gecko twin launcher ❶; semi-active radar homing to 15 km *(8.1 n miles)* at 2.5 Mach; warhead 50 kg; altitude 9.1-3,048 m *(30-10,000 ft)*; 20 missiles. The launcher retracts into the mounting for stowage and protection, rising to fire and retracting to reload. The two mountings are forward of the bridge and abaft the funnel.
Guns: 1—3.9 in *(100 mm)*/70 AK 100 ❷; 60 rds/min to 21.5 km *(11.5 n miles)*; weight of shell 15.6kg.
2—30 mm/65 ❸; 6 barrels per mounting; 3,000 rds/min combined to 2 km.
Torpedoes: 8—21 in *(533 mm)* (2 quad) tubes ❹. Combination of Russian 53 cm torpedoes.
A/S mortars: 2 RBU 6000 12-tubed trainable ❺; range 6,000 m; warhead 31 kg.
Countermeasures: Decoys: 4 PK 16 chaff launchers. Towed torpedo decoy.

HETMAN SAGAIDACHNY

(Scale 1 : 1,200), Ian Sturton / 0506208

ESM: 2 Bell Shroud; intercept.
ECM: 2 Bell Squat; jammers.
Radars: Air search: Top Plate ❻; 3D; D/E-band.
Surface search: Spin Trough ❼; I-band. Peel Cone ❽; E-band.
Fire control: Pop Group ❾; F/H/I-band (for SA-N-4). Kite Screech ❿; H/I/K-band. Bass Tilt (Krivak III) ⓫; H/I-band.
Navigation: Kivach; I-band.
IFF: Salt Pot (Krivak III).
Sonars: Bull Nose (MGK 335MS); hull-mounted; active search and attack; medium frequency.

Helicopters: 1 Ka-27 Helix ⓬.

Programmes: This is the last of the 'Krivak IIIs' originally designed for the USSR Border Guard. The seven others are based in the Russian Pacific Fleet. A ninth of class was not completed.
Operational: *Sagaidachny* has so far not been sighted with a helicopter embarked. Deployed to the Mediterranean in 1994 and late 1995, to the Indian Ocean in early 1995 and to the US in late 1996. Three further Krivak class have been decommissioned: 'Krivak II' *Sevastopol* (U 132) is probably being used for spares while 'Krivak I' *Mikolaiv* is to be scrapped. *Dnipropetrovsk* is reported to have sunk in the Black Sea in 2005.

HETMAN SAGAIDACHNY

7/2000 / 0106650

HETMAN SAGAIDACHNY

6/2003, Ships of the World / 0572651

3 GRISHA CLASS (PROJECT 1124EM/P) (FFLM)

Name	*No*	*Builders*	*Laid down*	*Launched*	*Commissioned*
LUTSK	U 205	Leninskaya Kuznitsa, Kiev	–	12 May 1993	12 Feb 1994
VINNITSA (ex-*Dnepr*)	U 206	Zrelenodolsk	23 Dec 1975	12 Sep 1976	31 Dec 1976
TERNOPIL	U 209	Leninskaya Kuznitsa, Kiev	–	20 Mar 2002	16 Feb 2006

Displacement, tons: 950 standard; 1,150 full load
Dimensions, feet (metres): 233.6 × 32.2 × 12.1 *(71.2 × 9.8 × 3.7)*
Main machinery: CODAG; 1 gas turbine; 15,000 hp(m) *(11 MW)*; 2 diesels; 16,000 hp(m) *(11.8 MW)*; 3 shafts
Speed, knots: 30
Range, n miles: 2,500 at 14 kt; 1,750 at 20 kt diesels; 950 at 27 kt
Complement: 70 (5 officers)

Missiles: SAM: SA-N-4 Gecko twin launcher ❶ (*Lutsk*); semi-active radar homing to 15 km *(8 n miles)* at 2.5 Mach; warhead 50 kg; altitude 9.1-3,048 m *(30-10,000 ft)*; 20 missiles.
Guns: 1—3 in *(76 mm)*/59 AK 176 ❷; (*Lutsk* and *Ternopil*); 120 rds/min to 15 km *(8 n miles)*; weight of shell 5.9 kg.
4—57 mm/75 AK 725 (twin) *(Vinnitsa)*; 120 rds/min to 12.7 km *(6.8 n miles)*; weight of shell 2.8 kg.
1—30 mm/65 ❸; (*Lutsk* and *Ternopil*); 6 barrels; 3,000 rds/min combined to 2 km.
Torpedoes: 4—21 in *(533 mm)* (2 twin) tubes ❹. SAET-60; passive homing to 15 km *(8.1 n miles)* at 40 kt; warhead 400 kg.
A/S mortars: 1 or 2 RBU 6000 12-tubed trainable ❺; range 6,000 m; warhead 31 kg.

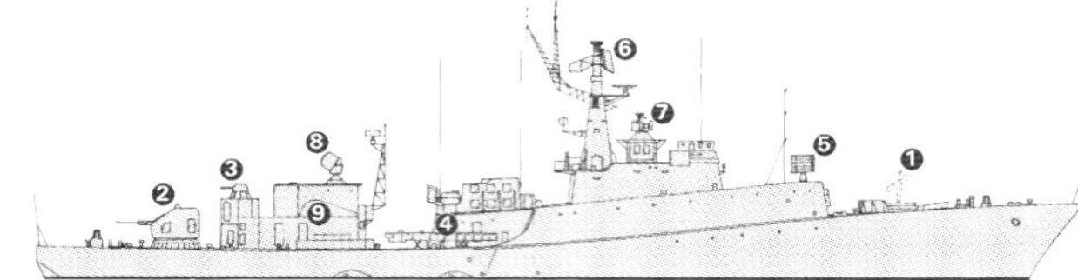

LUTSK *(Scale 1 : 900), Ian Sturton* / 0506209

Depth charges: 2 racks (12).
Mines: Capacity for 18 in lieu of depth charges.
Countermeasures: ESM: 2 Watch Dog. 2 PK 16 chaff launchers.
Radars: Air/surface search: Half Plate B ❻; (*Lutsk* and *Ternopil*); E/F-band.
Strut Curve *(Vinnitsa)*; F-band.
Navigation: Don 2; I-band.
Fire control: Pop Group ❼; (*Lutsk* and *Ternopil*); F/H/I-band (for SA-N-4). Bass Tilt ❽; (*Lutsk* and *Ternopil*); H/I-band (for 76 mm and 30 mm).
Muff Cobb *(Vinnitsa)*; G/H-band.
IFF: High Pole A or B. Square Head. Salt Pot.

Sonars: Bull Nose (MGK 335MS); hull-mounted; active search and attack; high/medium frequency.
Elk Tail VDS ❾; active search; high frequency.

Programmes: *Lutsk* is a 'Grisha V' (Type 1124EM) launched 12 May 1993 and completed 27 November 1993. *Ternopil* is also a Grisha V and was the first new ship to join the fleet since 1992 when it commissioned in 2006. *Vinnitsa* is a 'Grisha II' (Type1124P) ex-Russian Border Guard ship transferred in 1996. Two 'Grisha I' were also transferred but have been deleted.
Operational: All three are active. *Vinnitsa* damaged in storm on 11 November 2007.

VINNITSA *7/2000, Hartmut Ehlers* / 0106652

TERNOPIL *12/2005, Lemachko Collection* / 0581616

LAND-BASED MARITIME AIRCRAFT

Notes: The Naval Aviation Force is based at Sevastopol. It comprises 17 Ka-25 Hormone ASW helicopters, 2 Ka-27 Helix A ASW helicopter, 30 Mi-14 Haze, 5 An-12 Cub, 5 An-26 Curl and 11 Be-12 Mail. The Air Force inventory includes 100 Su-24 Fencer and 170 MiG-29 Fulcrum.

PATROL FORCES

Notes: A new corvette class is reported to be under development.

2 PAUK I (MOLNYA) (PROJECT 1241P) CLASS (PCM)

KHMELNITSKY (ex-MPK 116) U 208 **UZHGOROD** (ex-MPK 93) U 207

Displacement, tons: 440 full load
Dimensions, feet (metres): 189 × 33.5 × 10.8 *(57.6 × 10.2 × 3.3)*
Main machinery: 2 Type M 521 diesels; 16,184 hp(m) *(11.9 MW)* sustained; 2 shafts
Speed, knots: 32. **Range, n miles:** 2,400 at 14 kt
Complement: 32

Missiles: SAM: SA-N-5 Grail quad launcher; manual aiming; IR homing to 6 km *(3.2 n miles)* at 1.5 Mach; altitude to 2,500 m *(8,000 ft)*; warhead 1.5 kg; 8 missiles.
Guns: 1 – 3 in *(76 mm)*/59 AK 176; 120 rds/min to 15 km *(8 n miles)*; weight of shell 5.9 kg. 1 – 30 mm/65 AK 630; 6 barrels; 3,000 rds/min combined to 2 km.
Torpedoes: 4 – 16 in *(406 mm)*.
A/S mortars: 2 RBU 1200 5-tubed fixed; range 1,200 m; warhead 34 kg.
Depth charges: 2 racks (12).
Countermeasures: Decoys: 2 PK 16 or 4 PK 10 chaff launchers.
ESM: 3 Brick Plug and 2 Half Hat; radar warning.
Weapons control: Hood Wink optronic director.
Radars: Air/surface search: Peel Cone; E/F-band.
Surface search: Kivach or Pechora; I-band.
Fire control: Bass Tilt; H/I-band.
Sonars: Foal Tail; VDS (mounted on transom); active attack; high frequency.

Programmes: Built at Yaroslavl in 1985. Transferred from Black Sea Fleet Border Guard in 1996. Others of this class are in the Ukraine Border Guard.
Structure: ASW version of the Russian Tarantul class.
Operational: Second of class *Uzhgorod* was reportedly back in service in 2006 but operational status has not been confirmed.

KHMELNITSKY *7/2000, Hartmut Ehlers* / 0106653

1 ZHUK (GRIF) CLASS (PROJECT 1400M) (PB)

SKADOVSK (ex-*AK 327*) U 120

Displacement, tons: 39 full load
Dimensions, feet (metres): 78.7 × 16.4 × 3.9 *(24 × 5 × 1.2)*
Main machinery: 2 Type M 401B diesels; 2,200 hp(m) *(1.6 MW)* sustained; 2 shafts
Speed, knots: 30
Range, n miles: 1,100 at 15 kt
Complement: 13
Guns: 2 – 14.5 mm (twin). 1 – 12.7 mm MG
Radars: Surface search: Spin Trough; I-band

Comment: Transferred from Russia in 1997 and became operational in 2000. Others of the class are in service with the Border Guard.

SKADOVSK *7/2000, Hartmut Ehlers* / 0106655

2 TARANTUL II (MOLNYA) (PROJECT 1241.1/2) CLASS (FSGM)

PRIDNEPROVYE (ex-*Nikopol*, ex-*R-54*) U 155 **KREMENCHUK** (ex-R 63) U 156

Displacement, tons: 385 standard; 455 full load
Dimensions, feet (metres): 184.1 × 37.7 × 8.2 *(56.1 × 11.5 × 2.5)*
Main machinery: COGAG: 2 Nikolayev Type DR 77 gas turbines; 16,016 hp(m) *(11.77 MW)*; 2 Nikolayev DR 76 gas turbines with reversible gearboxes; 4,993 hp(m) *(3.67 MW)* sustained 2 shafts; cp props
Speed, knots: 36
Range, n miles: 1,650 at 14 kt
Complement: 34 (5 officers)

Missiles: SSM: 4 Raduga SS-N-2D Styx (2 twin); active radar or IR homing to 83 km *(45 n miles)* at 0.9 Mach; warhead 513 kg; sea skimmer at end of run
SAM: 1 SA-N-5 Grail quad launcher; manual aiming; IR homing to 6 km *(3.2 n miles)* at 1.5 Mach; warhead 1.5 kg.
Guns: 1 – 3 in *(76 mm)*/59 AK 176; 120 rds/min to 15 km *(8 n miles)*; weight of shell 5.9 kg. 2 – 30 mm/65 AK-630; 6 barrels per mounting; 3,000 rds/min to 2 km.
Countermeasures: Decoys: 4 PK 16 chaff launchers.
Weapons control: Hood Wink optronic director. Light bulb datalink. Band Stand; I-band (datalink).
Radars: Plank Shave; I-band.
Fire control: Bass Tilt; H/I-band (for guns).
Band Stand (Mineral ME); D-band (for SS-N-2D).
Navigation: Kivach III; I-band.
IFF: High Pole B.

Programmes: Built at Kolpino. U 155 originally commissioned in 1983 and U 156 in 1985. Both transferred in 1997 and recommissioned in 2002.

PRIDNEPROVYE *3/2002, Hartmut Ehlers* / 0529997

2 MATKA (VEKHR) CLASS (PROJECT 206MP) (FAST ATTACK CRAFT—MISSILE HYDROFOIL) (PGGK)

PRILUKI (ex-R-262) U 153 **KAHOVKA** (ex-R-265) U 154

Displacement, tons: 225 standard; 260 full load
Dimensions, feet (metres): 129.9 × 24.9 (41 over foils) × 6.9 (13.1 over foils) *(39.6 × 7.6; 12.5 × 2.1; 4)*
Main machinery: 3 Type M 504 diesels; 10,800 hp(m) *(7.94 MW)* sustained; 3 shafts
Speed, knots: 40
Range, n miles: 600 at 35 kt foilborne; 1,500 at 14 kt hullborne
Complement: 33

Missiles: SSM: 2 SS-N-2C/D Styx; active radar or IR homing to 83 km *(45 n miles)* at 0.9 Mach; warhead 513 kg; sea-skimmer at end of run.
Guns: 1 – 3 in *(76 mm)*/59 AK 176; 120 rds/min to 15 km *(8 n miles)*; weight of shell 5.9 kg. 1 – 30 mm/65 AK 630; 6 barrels per mounting; 3,000 rds/min to 2 km.
Countermeasures: Decoys: 2 PK 16 chaff launchers.
ESM: Clay Brick; intercept.
Weapons control: Hood Wink optronic directors.
Radars: Air/surface search: Plank Shave; E-band.
Navigation: SRN-207; I-band.
Fire control: Bass Tilt; H/I-band.
IFF: High Pole B or Salt Pot B and Square Head.

Comment: Five Russian Black Sea Fleet units transferred in 1996. Built between 1978 and 1983 with similar hulls to the Osa class. One was transferred to Georgia in 1999 and two others (*Uman* and *Tsurupinsk*) have been cannibalised for spares.

PRILUKI *6/2006, Lemachko Collection* / 1305219

AMPHIBIOUS FORCES

Notes: Two Vydra class LCUs, *Korosten* U 862 and *Bilyaïvka* U 904, are used as trials and transport craft. There are also two non-operational Ondatra class LCM, *Svatove* U 430 and *Vil* U 537 and a T-4LCM *Tarpan* U 538 which are laid up.

1 ROPUCHA I (PROJECT 775) CLASS (LST)

KONSTANTIN OLSHANSKY (ex-BDK 56) U 402

Displacement, tons: 4,400 full load
Dimensions, feet (metres): 370.7 × 47.6 × 11.5 *(113 × 14.5 × 3.6)*
Main machinery: 2 Zgoda-Sulzer 16ZVB40/48 diesels; 19,230 hp(m) *(14.14 MW)* sustained; 2 shafts
Speed, knots: 17.5. **Range, n miles:** 3,500 at 16 kt
Complement: 95 (7 officers)
Military lift: 10 MBT plus 190 troops or 24 AFVs plus 170 troops
Missiles: SAM: 4 SA-N-5 Grail quad launchers.
Guns: 4—57 mm/75 AK 725 (2 twin); 120 rds/min to 12.7 km *(6.8 n miles)*; weight of shell 2.8 kg.
Weapons control: 2 Squeeze Box optronic directors.
Radars: Strut Curve; F-band.
Navigation: Don 2; I-band.
Fire control: Muff Cob; G/H-band.
IFF: High Pole B.

Comment: Built at Gdansk, Poland in 1978 and transferred from Russia in 1996. Can be used to carry mines. Ro-Ro design with 540 m² of parking space between the stern gate and the bow doors.

KONSTANTIN OLSHANSKY *10/2008*, Laursen/Jarnasen* / 1353556

1 POLNOCHNY C (PROJECT 773 I) CLASS (LSM)

KIROVOGRAD (ex-SDK 123) U 401

Displacement, tons: 1,120 standard; 1,150 full load
Dimensions, feet (metres): 266.7 × 31.8 × 7.9 *(81.3 × 9.7 × 2.4)*
Main machinery: 2 Kolomna Type 40-D diesels; 4,400 hp(m) *(3.2 MW)* sustained; 2 shafts
Speed, knots: 18. **Range, n miles:** 2,000 at 12 kt
Complement: 40-42
Military lift: 350 tons including 6 tanks; 180 troops
Missiles: 4 SA-N-5 Grail quad launchers; manual aiming; IR homing to 6 km *(3.2 n miles)* at 1.5 Mach; warhead 1.5 kg; 32 missiles.
Guns: 4—30 mm/65 (2 twin); 2—140 mm 18-tubed rocket launchers.
Radars: Surface search: Spin Trough; I-band.
Fire control: Drum Tilt; H/I-band (for 30 mm guns).

Comment: Built in 1970s and transferred from Russian Fleet in 1994. Reported operational again in 2001 following refit.

KIROVOGRAD *6/2003, Ships of the World* / 0572650

1 POMORNIK (ZUBR) (PROJECT 1232.2) CLASS (ACV/LCUJM)

DONETSK U 420

Displacement, tons: 550 full load
Dimensions, feet (metres): 189 × 70.5 *(57.6 × 21.5)*
Main machinery: 5 Type NK-12MV gas turbines; 2 for lift, 23,672 hp(m) *(17.4 MW)* nominal; 3 for drive, 35,508 hp(m) *(26.1 MW)* nominal
Speed, knots: 60. **Range, n miles:** 300 at 55 kt
Complement: 31 (4 officers)
Military lift: 3 MBT or 10 APC plus 230 troops (total 170 tons)
Missiles: SAM: 2 SA-N-5 Grail quad launchers; manual aiming; IR homing to 6 km *(3.2 n miles)* at 1.5 Mach; altitude to 2,500 m *(8,000 ft)*; warhead 1.5 kg.
Guns: 2—30 mm/65 AK 630; 6 barrels per mounting; 3,000 rds/min combined to 2 km. 2 retractable 122 mm rocket launchers.
Mines: 80.
Countermeasures: Decoys: TSP 41 chaff.
ESM: Tool Box; intercept.
Weapons control: Quad Look (modified Squeeze Box) (DWU 3) optronic director.
Radars: Air/surface search: Cross Dome (Ekran); I-band.
Fire control: Bass Tilt MR 123; H/I-band.
IFF: Salt Pot A/B. Square Head.

Comment: *Donetsk* was completed by Morye, Feodosiya on 20 July 1993. Sister *U 421* was incomplete in 1999 when procured by Greece, delivery being made in 2001. Three further craft were transferred from Russia in 1996. Of these, *U 423* (ex-*MDK 123*) was also sold to Greece, *U 422* (ex-*MDK 57*) and *U 424* (ex-*MDK 93*) have been decommissioned.

DONETSK *8/2000, Lemachko Collection* / 0131164

MINE WARFARE FORCES

2 NATYA I CLASS (PROJECT 266M) (MSO)

CHERNIGIV (ex-*Zhovti Vody*, ex-*Zenitchik*) U 310 **CHERKASY** (ex-*Razvedchik*) U 311

Displacement, tons: 804 full load
Dimensions, feet (metres): 200.1 × 33.5 × 9.8 *(61 × 10.2 × 3)*
Main machinery: 2 Type M 504 diesels; 5,000 hp(m) *(3.67 MW)* sustained; 2 shafts; cp props
Speed, knots: 16. **Range, n miles:** 3,000 at 12 kt
Complement: 67 (8 officers)
Guns: 4—30 mm/65 (2 twin) AK 306 or 2—30 mm/65 AK 630; 4—25 mm/80 (2 twin).
A/S mortars: 2 RBU 1200 5-tubed fixed.
Depth charges: 62.
Mines: 10.
Countermeasures: MCM: 1 or 2 GKT-2 contact sweeps; 1 AT-2 acoustic sweep. 1 TEM-3 magnetic sweep
Radars: Surface search: Long Trough; E-band.
Fire control: Drum Tilt; H/I-band.
IFF: 2 Square Head. High Pole B.
Sonars: MG 79/89; hull-mounted; active minehunting; high frequency.

Comment: Built in the mid-1970s. Transferred from Russia in 1996. Both are operational.

ZHOVTI VODY *9/2002, C D Yaylali* / 0530030

2 SONYA (YAKHONT) (PROJECT 1265) CLASS (MHSC)

MELITOPOL (ex-BT 79) U 330 **MARIUPOL** (ex-BT 126) U 331

Displacement, tons: 460 full load
Dimensions, feet (metres): 157.4 × 28.9 × 6.6 *(48 × 8.8 × 2)*
Main machinery: 2 Kolomna diesels; 2,000 hp(m) *(1.47 MW)* sustained; 2 shafts
Speed, knots: 15. **Range, n miles:** 3,000 at 10 kt
Complement: 43
Guns: 2—30 mm/65 (twin). 2—25 mm/80 (twin).
Mines: 8.
Radars: Surface search: Don 2; I-band.
IFF: Two Square Head.
Sonars: MG 69/79; hull-mounted; active; high frequency.

Comment: Built in 1978. Transferred from Russia in 1996. Wooden hull.

MELITOPOL *10/2008*, Laursen/Jarnasen* / 1353555

1 YEVGENYA (KOROND) (PROJECT 1258) CLASS (MHC)

GENICHESK (ex-RT 214) U 360

Displacement, tons: 77 standard; 90 full load
Dimensions, feet (metres): 80.7 × 18 × 4.9 *(24.6 × 5.5 × 1.5)*
Main machinery: 2 Type 3-D-12 diesels; 600 hp(m) *(440 kW)* sustained; 2 shafts
Speed, knots: 11. **Range, n miles:** 300 at 10 kt
Complement: 10
Guns: 2—14.5 mm (twin) MGs.
Mines: 8 racks.
Radars: Surface search: Spin Trough or Mius; I-band.
IFF: Salt Pot.
Sonars: A small MG-7 sonar is lifted over stern on crane; a TV system may also be used.

Comment: Transferred from Russia in 1996. Reported as being operational.

GENICHESK *6/2003, Ships of the World* / 0572652

SURVEY SHIPS

Notes: (1) Also transferred in 1997 were two Muna class AGIs, *Pereyaslav* U 512 and *Dzhankoi* U 754. Both are used as transports, mostly for commercial goods.
(2) Ten former Russian civilian research ships were transferred in 1996/97. All are now in commercial service.
(3) There is an Onega class, *Severodonetsk* U 812.

1 MOMA (PROJECT 861M) CLASS (AGS)

SIMFEROPOL (ex-*Jupiter*) U 511

Displacement, tons: 1,600 full load
Dimensions, feet (metres): 240.5 × 36.8 × 12.8 *(73.3 × 11.2 × 3.9)*
Main machinery: 2 Zgoda-Sulzer diesels; 3,300 hp(m) *(2.43 MW)* sustained; 2 shafts; cp props
Speed, knots: 17. **Range, n miles:** 9,000 at 11 kt
Complement: 56
Radars: Navigation: Don 2; I-band.

Comment: U 511 transferred from Russia in February 1996 and is active. A second of class *U 602* has been decommissioned.

SIMFEROPOL *7/2000, Hartmut Ehlers* / 0106669

1 BIYA (PROJECT 870) CLASS (AGS)

ALCHEVSK U 601 (ex-*GS 212*)

Displacement, tons: 766 full load
Dimensions, feet (metres): 180.4 × 32.1 × 8.5 *(55 × 9.8 × 2.6)*
Main machinery: 2 diesels; 1,200 hp(m) *(882 kW)*; 2 shafts; cp props
Speed, knots: 13. **Range, n miles:** 4,700 at 11 kt
Complement: 25
Radars: Navigation: Don 2; I-band.

Comment: Built at Northern Shipyard, Gdansk 1972–76. Transferred from Russia in 1997. Laboratory and one survey launch, and a 5 ton crane.

ALCHEVSK *6/2005, Lemachko Collection* / 1305218

TRAINING SHIPS

Note: In addition there is one Bryza class training cutter *U 544*.

3 PETRUSHKA (UK-3) CLASS (AXL)

CHIGIRIN U 540 **SMILA** U 541 **NOVA KAHOVKA** (ex-*Darnicha*) U 542

Displacement, tons: 335 full load
Dimensions, feet (metres): 129.3 × 27.6 × 7.2 *(39.4 × 8.4 × 2.2)*
Main machinery: 2 Wola H12 diesels; 756 hp(m) *(556 kW)*; 2 shafts
Speed, knots: 11. **Range, n miles:** 1,000 at 11 kt
Complement: 13 plus 30 cadets

Comment: Training vessels built at Wisla Shiyard, Poland in 1989. Transferred from Russia in 1997. Used for seamanship and navigation training.

CHIGIRIN *10/2008*, Laursen/Jarnasen* / 1353564

AUXILIARIES

Notes: Other ships transferred from Russia in 1997, and possibly still in limited service, are a Keyla II class tanker, *Kriviy Rig* U 753, two Toplivo class tankers, *Fastiv* U 760 and *Bahmach* U 759 and a Shalanda class trials craft *Kamyankha* U 860.

FASTIV *10/2008*, Laursen/Jarnasen* / 1353563

1 AMUR (PROJECT 304) CLASS SUPPORT SHIP (AGF/AR)

DONBAS (ex-*Krasnodon*) U 500 (ex-U 803)

Displacement, tons: 5,500 full load
Dimensions, feet (metres): 400.3 × 55.8 × 16.7 *(122 × 17 × 5.1)*
Main machinery: 1 Zgoda 8TAD-48 diesel; 3,000 hp(m) *(2.2 MW)*; 1 shaft
Speed, knots: 12
Range, n miles: 13,000 at 8 kt
Complement: 145
Radars: Navigation: Don 2; I-band.

Comment: Transferred in 1977. Completed refit in 2001 to serve as command ship and support ships for surface ships and submarines based at Sevastopol. Has two 3-ton cranes and one 1.5-ton crane.

DONBAS *10/2008*, Laursen/Jarnasen* / 1353559

1 VODA (PROJECT 561) CLASS (WATER TANKER) (AWT)

SUDAK (ex-*Sura*) U 756

Displacement, tons: 982 standard; 2,250 full load
Dimensions, feet (metres): 266.8 × 37.4 × 11.3 *(81.3 × 11.4 × 3.44)*
Main machinery: 2 diesels; 2 shafts
Speed, knots: 12
Range, n miles: 2,900 at 10 kt
Complement: 22
Radars: Navigation: Don 2; I-band.

Comment: Transferred in 1977. Has a 3 ton derrick.

SUDAK *10/2008*, Laursen/Jarnasen* / 1353561

1 BEREZA CLASS (PROJECT 18061) (ADG)

BALTA U 811 (ex-SR 568)

Displacement, tons: 1,850 standard; 2,051 full load
Dimensions, feet (metres): 228 × 45.3 × 13.1 *(69.5 × 13.8 × 4)*
Main machinery: 2 Zgoda-Sulzer 8AL25/30 diesels; 2,938 hp(m) *(2.16 MW)* sustained; 2 shafts
Speed, knots: 14
Range, n miles: 1,000 at 14 kt
Complement: 88
Radars: Navigation: Kivach; I-band.

Comment: Built at Northern Shipyard, Gdansk in 1987. Transferred from Russia in 1997. Degaussing vessel with an NBC citadel and three laboratories.

BALTA *10/2008*, Laursen/Jarnasen* / 1353562

1 BAMBUK (PROJECT 12884) CLASS (AGFHM)

Name	*No*	*Builders*	*Launched*	*Commissioned*
SLAVUTICH	U 510 (ex-800, ex-SSV 189)	Nikolayev	12 Oct 1990	28 July 1992

Displacement, tons: 5,403 full load
Dimensions, feet (metres): 350.1 × 52.5 × 19.7 *(106.7 × 16 × 6)*
Main machinery: 2 Skoda 6L2511 diesels; 6,100 hp(m) *(4.5 MW)*; 2 shafts
Speed, knots: 16
Range, n miles: 8,000 at 12 kt
Complement: 178
Missiles: SAM: 2 SA-N-5/8 Grail quad launchers; manual aiming; IR homing to 6 km *(3.2 n miles)* at 1.5 Mach; altitude to 2,500 m *(8,000 ft)*; warhead 1.5 kg.
Guns: 2—30 mm/65 AK 630; 6 barrels per mounting.
Countermeasures: Decoys: 2 PK 16 chaff launchers.
Radars: Navigation: 3 Palm Frond; I-band.
CCA: Fly Screen; I-band.
Tacan: 2 Round House.

Comment: Laid down on 20 March 1988. Second of a class built for acoustic research but taken over before completion and used as a command ship by the Ukrainian Navy. The ship is not capable of helicopter operations as previously reported.

SLAVUTICH *10/2008*, Laursen/Jarnasen* / 1353560

1 SURA (PROJECT 145) CLASS (ABU)

SHOSTKA (ex-Kil 33) U 852

Displacement, tons: 2,370 standard; 3,150 full load
Dimensions, feet (metres): 285.4 × 48.6 × 16.4 *(87 × 14.8 × 5)*
Main machinery: Diesel-electric; 4 diesel generators; 2 motors; 2,240 hp(m) *(1.65 MW)*; 2 shafts
Speed, knots: 12
Range, n miles: 2,000 at 11 kt
Complement: 40
Cargo capacity: 900 tons cargo; 300 tons fuel for transfer
Radars: Navigation: 2 Don 2; I-band.

Comment: Transferred from Russia in 1997. Heavy lift ship built at Rostock in 1973. Lifting capacity includes one 65 ton derrick and one 65 ton stern cage. Can carry a 12 m DSRV, although this has not been seen in Ukrainian service.

SHOSTKA *10/2008*, Laursen/Jarnasen* / 1353558

1 YELVA (PROJECT 535M) CLASS (DIVING TENDER) (YDT)

NETISIN (ex-*VM 114*) U 700

Displacement, tons: 295 full load
Dimensions, feet (metres): 134.2 × 26.2 × 6.6 *(40.9 × 8 × 2)*
Main machinery: 2 Type 3-D-12A diesels; 630 hp(m) *(463 kW)* sustained; 2 shafts
Speed, knots: 12.5
Range, n miles: 1,870 at 12 kt
Complement: 30
Radars: Navigation: Spin Trough; I-band.

Comment: Diving tender built in mid-1970s. Transferred from Russia in 1997. Carries a 1 ton crane and diving bell. Operational.

YELVA CLASS (to left) *6/1998, van Ginderen Collection* / 0050315

12 HARBOUR CRAFT (YDT/YFL/YPT)

FEODOSIYA U 240
U 241
U 631–634
SKVYRA U 635
U 732
ILLICHIVSK U 783
SHULYAVKA U 853
KHERSON (ex-*Monastirishze*) U 891
U 926

Displacement, tons: 42 full load
Dimensions, feet (metres): 72.8 × 12.8 × 4.6 *(22.2 × 3.9 × 1.4)*
Main machinery: 1 diesel; 300 hp(m) *(220 kW)* sustained; 1 shaft
Speed, knots: 12
Complement: 8

Comment: Details given are for the Flamingo class harbour patrol craft of which there are four (U 240, U 241, U 634, U 732). There are also four 'Nyryat1' diving tenders and inshore survey craft (U 631, U 632, U 633, U 635) and one PO 2 class tender (U 926). There is also one Shelon class YPT (U 891), an ambulance craft (U 783) and a flag officers' yacht (U 853).

ILLICHIVSK *7/2003, Lemachko Collection* / 1043554

KHERSON *9/2004, Hartmut Ehlers* / 1043553

1 SK 620 CLASS (DRAKON) (YH/TFL)

SOKAL U 782

Displacement, tons: 236 full load
Dimensions, feet (metres): 108.3 × 24.3 × 6.9 *(33 × 7.4 × 2.1)*
Main machinery: 2 56ANM30-H12 diesels; 620 hp(m) *(456 kW)* sustained; 2 shafts
Speed, knots: 12
Range, n miles: 1,000 at 12 kt
Complement: 14 plus 3 spare

Comment: Built at Wisla Shipyard, Poland as a smaller version of the Petrushka class training ship. Transferred from Russia in 1997. Used as a general purpose craft. The status of two other craft, *Akar* and *Suvar* is not known.

2 POZHARNY (PROJECT 364) CLASS (FIREFIGHTING CRAFT) (YTR)

BORSZIV U 722 **EVPATORIYA** U 728

Displacement, tons: 180 full load
Dimensions, feet (metres): 114.5 × 20 × 6 *(34.9 × 6.1 × 1.8)*
Main machinery: 2 Type M 50 diesels; 2,200 hp(m) *(1.6 MW)* sustained; 2 shafts
Speed, knots: 12. **Range, n miles:** 250 at 12 kt
Complement: 26

Comment: A total of 84 built from mid-1950s to mid-1960s. Two craft transferred to Ukraine in 1996 and another 27 remain in Russian naval service.

BORSZIV *6/2006, Lemachko Collection* / 1159410

TUGS

6 TUGS (ATA/YTM)

KREMENETS U 705 **IZYASLAV** U 706 **KORETS** U 830 **KOVEL** U 831 **KRASNOPEREKOPSK** U 947 **DUBNO** U 953

Comment: All transferred from Russia in 1997. *U 706* and *U 831* are Okhtensky class coastal tugs built in 1958. *U 705* is a Goryn class ocean going tug with a bollard pull of 45 tons, *U 830* is a Sorum class and *U947* a Prometey class large tug. *U 953* is a Sidehole II class harbour tug.

KORETS *10/2008*, Laursen/Jarnasen* / 1353557

BORDER GUARD (MORSKA OKHORONA)

Notes: (1) There are plans to build new patrol cutters of the 'Kordon' (47 m) and 'Afalina' (44 m) classes, and new patrol boats of the 'Scif' (26 m) class. These new designs are also on offer for export by the Feodosiya Shipbuilding Association Morye. A 67 m OPV design, by Nikolayev 61 Kommuna shipyard, is also in the export market.
(2) The river brigades also include four minesweeping boats, and 16 training craft. Not all of these are operational.
(3) Border Guard vessels are painted dark grey with a thick yellow and thin blue diagonal line on the hull. From July 1999, pennant numbers were changed and are preceded by the letters BG.
(4) BG 01 *Krym* is a 45 m craft used for VIP duties.

1 SSV-10 CLASS (SUPPORT SHIP) (AGF)

DUNAI BG 80 (ex-500)

Displacement, tons: 340 full load
Dimensions, feet (metres): 129.3 × 23 × 3.9 *(39.4 × 7 × 1.2)*
Main machinery: 2 diesels; 2 shafts
Speed, knots: 12
Complement: 20 (4 officers)

Comment: Headquarters ship built in 1940. Taken over from the Russian Danube Flotilla and now acts as the command ship for the river brigades. Based at Odessa.

DUNAI (old number) *4/1998, Ukraine Coast Guard* / 0050322

3 PAUK I (MOLNYA) CLASS (PROJECT 1241) (PC)

GRIGORY KUROPIATNIKOV BG 50 (ex-PSKR 817)
GRIGORY GNATENKO BG 52 (ex-PSKR 815)
POLTAVA BG 51 (ex-PSKR 813)

Displacement, tons: 475 full load
Dimensions, feet (metres): 189 × 33.5 × 10.8 *(57.6 × 10.2 × 3.3)*
Main machinery: 2 Type M 521 diesels; 16,184 hp(m) *(11.9 MW)* sustained; 2 shafts
Speed, knots: 32
Range, n miles: 1,260 at 14 kt
Complement: 44 (7 officers)

Guns: 1 — 3 in *(76 mm)*/60; 120 rds/min to 15 km *(8 n miles)*; weight of shell 7 kg.
1 — 30 mm/65 AK 630; 6 barrels; 3,000 rds/min combined to 2 km.
Torpedoes: 4 — 16 in *(406 mm)* tubes. SAET-40; anti-submarine; active/passive homing to 10 km *(5.4 n miles)* at 30 kt; warhead 100 kg.
A/S mortars: 2 RBU 1200 5-tubed fixed; range 1,200 m; warhead 34 kg.
Depth charges: 2 racks (12).
Countermeasures: Decoys: 2 PK 16 or 4 PK 10.
ESM: Brick Plug and Half Hat; radar warning.
Weapons control: Hood Wink optronic director.
Radars: Air/surface search: Peel Cone; E/F-band.
Surface search: Kivach or Pechora or SRN 207; I-band
Fire control: Bass Tilt; H/I-band.
Sonars: Foal Tail; VDS (mounted on transom); active attack; high frequency.

Comment: Built at Yaroslavl in the early 1980s and transferred from Russian Black Sea Fleet. Pennant numbers changed from July 1999. All are based at Balaklava.

POLTAVA *9/2004, Hartmut Ehlers* / 1043548

GRIGORY GNATENKO *6/2003, B Lemachko* / 0576460

6 STENKA (TARANTUL) CLASS (PROJECT 205P) (PCF)

DONBAS BG 32 (ex-PSKR 705)
MIKOLAIV BG 57 (ex-PSKR 722)
ODESSA BG 61 (ex-033, ex-PSKR 652)
BUKOVINA BG 31 (ex-034, ex-PSKR 702)
PODILLIYA BG 62 (ex-036, ex-PSKR 709)
PAVEL DERZHAVIN BG 63 (ex-037, ex-PSKR 720)

Displacement, tons: 253 full load
Dimensions, feet (metres): 129.3 × 25.9 × 8.2 *(39.4 × 7.9 × 2.5)*
Main machinery: 3 Type M 517 or M 583 diesels; 14,100 hp(m) *(10.36 MW)*; 3 shafts
Speed, knots: 37
Range, n miles: 500 at 35 kt; 1,540 at 14 kt
Complement: 30 (5 officers)
Guns: 4 — 30 mm/65 (2 twin) AK 230.
Torpedoes: 4 — 16 in *(406 mm)* tubes.
Depth charges: 2 racks (12).
Radars: Surface search: Pot Drum or Peel Cone; H/I- or E-band.
Fire control: Drum Tilt; H/I-band.
Navigation: Palm Frond; I-band.
IFF: High Pole. 2 Square Head.
Sonars: Stag Ear or Foal Tail; VDS; high frequency; Hormone type dipping sonar.

Comment: Similar hull to the Osa class. Built in the 1970s and 1980s. Transferred from Russia. Others have been cannibalised for spares. Based at Kerch, Odessa and Balaklava.

ODESSA *6/2001, B Lemachko* / 0131160

1 MURAVEY (ANTARES) CLASS (PROJECT 133) (PCK)

GALICHINA BG 55 (ex-PSKR 115)

Displacement, tons: 212 full load
Dimensions, feet (metres): 126.6 × 24.9 × 6.2; 14.4 (foils) *(38.6 × 7.6 × 1.9; 4.4)*
Main machinery: 2 gas turbines; 22,600 hp(m) *(16.6 MW)*; 2 shafts
Speed, knots: 60
Range, n miles: 410 at 12 kt
Complement: 30 (5 officers)

Guns: 1—3 in *(76 mm)*/60; 120 rds/min to 15 km *(8 n miles)*; weight of shell 7 kg. 1—30 mm/65 AK 630; 6 barrels; 3,000 rds/min combined to 2 km.
Torpedoes: 2—16 in *(406 mm)* tubes; SAET-40; anti-submarine; active/passive homing to 10 km *(5.4 n miles)* at 30 kt; warhead 100 kg.
Depth charges: 6.
Weapons control: Hood Wink optronic director.
Radars: Surface search: Peel Cone; E-band.
Fire control: Bass Tilt; H/I-band.
Sonars: Rat Tail; VDS; active attack; high frequency; dipping sonar.

Comment: Built at Feodosiya in the mid-1980s for the USSR Border Guard. High speed hydrofoil craft. Based at Balaklava.

MURAVEY CLASS *3/1998, Ukraine Coast Guard* / 0050319

15 ZHUK (GRIF) CLASS (PROJECT 1400M) (PB)

SIVAS BG 100
BG 101
OBOLON BG 102
DARNITSYA BG 103
BG 104–105
BG 107
BG 109
LJUBOMIR BG 110
BG 111
BG 115–116
BATUTINETS BG 117
ARABAT BG 118
BG 119

Displacement, tons: 39 full load
Dimensions, feet (metres): 78.7 × 16.4 × 3.9 *(24 × 5 × 1.2)*
Main machinery: 2 Type M 401B diesels; 2,200 hp(m) *(1.6 MW)* sustained; 2 shafts
Speed, knots: 30
Range, n miles: 1,100 at 15 kt
Complement: 13 (1 officer)
Guns: 2—14.5 mm (twin, fwd) MGs. 1—12.7 mm (aft) MG.
Radars: Surface search: Spin Trough; I-band.

Comment: Russian Border Guard vessels built in the 1980s and transferred in 1996. Pennant numbers changed from the 600 series in mid-1999.

BG 119 *9/2004, Hartmut Ehlers* / 1043547

4 SHMEL CLASS (PROJECT 1204) (PGR)

LUBNY BG 81 (ex-171) **KANIV** BG 82 (ex-173) **NIZYN** BG 83 (ex-172) **IZMAYL** BG 84 (ex-174)

Displacement, tons: 77 full load
Dimensions, feet (metres): 90.9 × 14.1 × 3.9 *(27.7 × 4.3 × 1.2)*
Main machinery: 2 Type M 50 diesels; 2,200 hp(m) *(1.6 MW)* sustained; 2 shafts
Speed, knots: 25
Range, n miles: 600 at 12 kt
Complement: 12 (4 officers)
Guns: 1—3 in *(76 mm)*/48 (tank turret). 2—14.5 mm (twin) MGs. 5—7.62 mm MGs. 1 BP 6 rocket launcher; 18 barrels.
Mines: Can lay 9.
Radars: Surface search: Spint Trough; I-band.

Comment: Built at Kerch from 1967–74. Now part of the river brigade having been transferred from the Russian Danube flotilla. New pennant numbers are unconfirmed and there is doubt about the operational status of this class.

LUBNY (old number) *4/1998, Ukraine Coast Guard* / 0050323

12 KALKAN (PROJECT 50030) M CLASS (INSHORE PATROL CRAFT) (PBR)

BG 07–08 **BG 310** **BG 333** **BG 604** **BG 808**
BG 303–304 **BG 320** **BG 503–504** **MATROS MIKOLA MUSHNIROV** BG 807

Displacement, tons: 8.5 full load
Dimensions, feet (metres): 38.1 × 10.8 × 2.0 *(11.6 × 3.3 × 0.6)*
Main machinery: 1 Type 475K diesel; 496 hp *(370 kW)*; 1 waterjet
Speed, knots: 34
Complement: 2

Comment: Built by Morye Feodosiya and entered service from 1996. Aluminium hulls and GRP superstructure. Can be armed with 7.62 mm or 12.7 mm MGs and 'Strela' shoulder launched missile.

BG 08 *7/2007, Bob Fildes* / 1170242

6 PROJECT 1398B (AIST) CLASS (INSHORE PATROL CRAFT) (PBR)

BG 316 **BG 318** **BG 329** **BG 349** **BG 812** **BG 814**

Displacement, tons: 5 full load
Dimensions, feet (metres): To be announced
Main machinery: To be announced
Speed, knots: To be announced
Complement: To be announced

Comment: Inshore patrol craft originally designed in the 1960s by the Redan boat building yard in St Petersburg.

United Arab Emirates

Country Overview

The United Arab Emirates was formed on 2 December 1971 by the federation of seven states (formerly the Trucial States) lying along the east-coast of the Arabian Peninsula. With an area of 30,000 square miles, the country includes Abu Dhabi, Ajman, Dubai, al-Fujairah, Ras al Khaimah, Sharjah and Umm al-Qaiwain. It is bordered to the north by Qatar and to the south by Saudi Arabia. To the east lies Oman which is separated from its small exclave on the Musandam peninsula. There is a coastline of 713 n miles with the Gulf and with the Gulf of Oman. The city of Abu Dhabi is the capital and largest city while Dubai is the principal port and commercial centre. Territorial Seas (12 n miles) are claimed. An EEZ (200 n miles) has also been claimed but its limits have not been defined.

Following a decision of the UAE Supreme Defence Council on 6 May 1976 the armed forces of the member states were unified and the organisation of the UAE armed forces was furthered by decisions taken on 1 February 1978.

Headquarters Appointments

Commander, Naval Forces:
Rear Admiral Ahmedj Al Sabab Al Tenaiji
Deputy Commander, Naval Forces:
Brigadier Mohammed Mahmoud Al Madini

Personnel

(a) 2009: 2,400 (200 officers) Navy. 1,200 (110 officers) Coast Guard
(b) Voluntary service

Bases

Abu Dhabi (main base).
Mina Rashid and Mina Jebel Ali (Dubai),
Mina Saqr (Ras al Khaimah), Mina Sultan (Sharjah),
Khor Fakkan (Sharjah-East Coast).

SUBMARINES

Notes: Submarine training has been conducted in the past but acquisition of submarines is understood to be a long-term aspiration.

10 SWIMMER DELIVERY VEHICLES (SDV)

Comment: Two classes of indigenously built Long Range Submersible Carriers (LRSC) have been developed by Emirates Marine Technologies. The 7.35 × 0.95 m Class 4 variant, of which approximately ten are believed to have been in service with UAE Special Forces since 1998, is capable of deploying a 200 kg payload. These are likely to be augmented by the larger 9.1 × 1.15 m Class 5 variant which can deliver 450 kg. Constructed of glass and carbon fibres, both variants are manned by two people, have a top speed of 7 kt, a range of 60 n miles at 6 kt and an operational depth of 30 m. They are equipped with depth-sounder, sonar and built-in breathing system.

CLASS 5 LRSC
2001, Emirates Marine Technologies
0095256

FRIGATES

1 ABU DHABI (KORTENAER) CLASS (FFGHM)

Name	*No*	*Builders*	*Laid down*	*Launched*	*Commissioned*
ABU DHABI (ex-*Abraham Crijnssen*)	F 01 (ex-F 816)	Koninklijke Maatschappij De Schelde, Flushing	25 Oct 1978	16 May 1981	27 Jan 1983

Displacement, tons: 3,050 standard; 3,630 full load
Dimensions, feet (metres): 428 × 47.9 × 14.1; 20.3 (screws) *(130.5 × 14.6 × 4.3; 6.2)*
Main machinery: GOGOG; 2 RR Olympus TM3B gas turbines; 50,880 hp *(37.9 MW)* sustained
2 RR Tyne RM1C gas turbines; 9,900 hp *(7.4 MW)* sustained; 2 shafts; cp props
Speed, knots: 30
Range, n miles: 4,700 at 16 kt on Tynes
Complement: 176 (18 officers) plus 24 spare berths

Missiles: SSM: 8 McDonnell Douglas Harpoon (2 quad) launchers ❶; active radar homing to 130 km *(70 n miles)* at 0.9 Mach; warhead 227 kg.
SAM: Raytheon Sea Sparrow RIM-7P Mk 29 octuple launcher ❷; semi-active radar homing to 16 km *(8.5 n miles)* at 2.5 Mach; warhead 38 kg; 24 missiles.
Guns: 1 OTO Melara 3 in *(76 mm)*/62 compact ❸; 85 rds/min to 16 km *(8.6 n miles)* anti-surface; 12 km *(6.5 n miles)* anti-aircraft; weight of shell 6 kg.
1 Signaal SGE-30 Goalkeeper with General Electric 30 mm ❹; 7-barrelled; 4,200 rds/min combined to 2 km.
2 Oerlikon 20 mm.
Torpedoes: 4—324 mm US Mk 32 (2 twin) tubes ❺. Honeywell Mk 46 or Whitehead A-244S Mod 1.

ABU DHABI
(Scale 1 : 1,200), Ian Sturton / 0121417

Countermeasures: Decoys: 2 Loral Hycor SRBOC Mk 36 6-tubed launchers ❻; chaff distraction or centroid modes.
ESM/ECM: Ramses ❼; intercept and jammer.
Combat data systems: Signaal SEWACO II action data automation; Link 11.
Radars: Air search: Signaal LW08 ❽; D-band; range 264 km *(145 n miles)* for 2 m² target.
Surface search: Signaal Scout ❾; I-band.
Fire control: Signaal STIR ❿; I/J-band; range 140 km *(76 n miles)* for 1 m² target.
Signaal WM25 ⓫; I/J-band; range 46 km *(25 n miles)*.
Sonars: Westinghouse SQS-505; bow-mounted; active search and attack; medium frequency.

Helicopters: 2 Eurocopter AS 565 Panther ⓬.

Programmes: Contract signed on 2 April 1996 to transfer two Netherlands frigates, after refits by Royal Schelde. First one recommissioned in December 1997, second one in May 1998. Further transfers are unlikely.
Structure: Harpoon SSM and Goalkeeper CIWS has been purchased separately, as have the Scout radars. Additional air conditioning has been fitted.
Operational: Based at Jebel Ali. *Al Emirat* was sold in late 2007 for conversion into a luxury yacht and it is likely that *Abu Dhabi* is also to be decommissioned.

ABU DHABI
7/2007, M Declerck / 1170240

CORVETTES

Notes: Plans to procure a new anti-submarine corvette were announced in March 2009. The ship, to be built by Fincantieri, is to be based on the Comandante class in service in the Italian Navy. The ship is to be delivered in 2011 and there is reported to be an option for a second ship. This order has probably superseded Project Yas.

2 MURAY JIB (MGB 62) CLASS (FSGHM)

Name	*No*	*Builders*	*Commissioned*	*Recommissioned*
MURAY JIB	P 161 (ex-CM 01, ex-P 6501)	Lürssen, Bremen	Mar 1989	Nov 1990
DAS	P 162 (ex-CM 02, ex-P 6502)	Lürssen, Bremen	May 1989	Jan 1991

Displacement, tons: 630 full load
Dimensions, feet (metres): 206.7 × 30.5 × 8.2 *(63 × 9.3 × 2.5)*
Main machinery: 4 MTU 16V 538 TB92 diesels; 13,640 hp(m) *(10 MW)* sustained; 4 shafts
Speed, knots: 32
Range, n miles: 4,000 at 16 kt
Complement: 43

Missiles: SSM: 8 Aerospatiale MM 40 Exocet (Block II) ❶; inertial cruise; active radar homing to 70 km *(40 n miles)* at 0.9 Mach; warhead 165 kg; sea-skimmer.
SAM: Thomson-CSF modified Crotale Navale octuple launcher ❷; radar guidance; IR homing to 13 km *(7 n miles)* at 2.4 Mach; warhead 14 kg.
Guns: 1 OTO Melara 3 in *(76 mm)*/62 Super Rapid ❸; 120 rds/min to 16 km *(8.7 n miles)*; weight of shell 6 kg.
1 Signaal Goalkeeper with GE 30 mm 7-barrelled ❹; 4,200 rds/min combined to 2 km.
2—12.7 mm MGs.
Countermeasures: Decoys: 2 Dagaie launchers ❺; IR flares and chaff.
ESM/ECM: Racal Cutlass/Cygnus ❻; intercept/jammer.
Weapons control: CSSE Najir optronic director ❼.
Radars: Air/surface search: Bofors Ericsson Sea Giraffe 50HC ❽; G-band.
Navigation: Racal Decca 1226; I-band.
Fire control: Bofors Electronic 9LV 223 ❾; J-band (for gun and SSM).
Thomson-CSF DRBV 51C ❿; J-band (for Crotale).

Helicopters: 1 Aerospatiale Alouette SA 316 ⓫.

Programmes: Ordered in late 1986. Similar vessels to Bahrain craft. Delivery in October 1991.
Structure: Lürssen design adapted for the particular conditions of the Gulf. This class has good air defence and a considerable anti-ship capability. The helicopter hangar is reached by flight deck lift.
Operational: Pennant numbers changed in 2002.

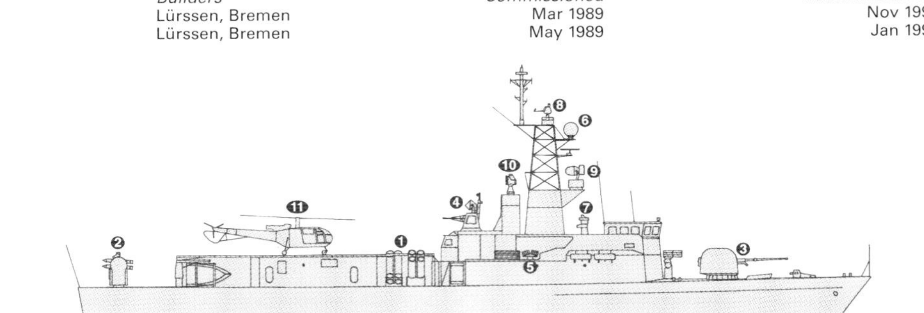

MURAY JIB *(Scale 1 : 600), Ian Sturton* / 0080921

MURAY JIB *5/2003, A Sharma* / 0567564

MURAY JIB *3/2005, Ships of the World* / 1127284

0 + 6 BAYNUNAH CLASS (FAST ATTACK CRAFT—MISSILE) (PGGMH)

Name	*No*	*Builders*	*Laid down*	*Launched*	*Commissioned*
–	–	CMN, Cherbourg	8 Sep 2005	2009	2010
–	–	Abu Dhabi Shipbuilding	6 July 2006	2010	2011
–	–	Abu Dhabi Shipbuilding	21 June 2007	2010	2011
–	–	Abu Dhabi Shipbuilding	5 Dec 2007	2010	2012
–	–	Abu Dhabi Shipbuilding	26 Oct 2008	2011	2013
–	–	Abu Dhabi Shipbuilding	2009	2012	2014

Displacement, tons: 630 full load
Dimensions, feet (metres): 229.6 × 36.1 × 9.2 *(70.0 × 11.0 × 2.8)*
Main machinery: 4 MTU 12V 595 TE 90 diesels; 22,500 hp *(16.8 MW)*; 3 (2-112 SII; 1-125 BII) Kamewa waterjets
Speed, knots: 32
Range, n miles: 2,400 at 15 kt
Complement: 37 (accommodation for 45)

Missiles: SSM: 8 MBDA MM 40 Block III ❶; inertial cruise; active radar homing to 70 km *(40 n miles)* at 0.9 Mach; warhead 165 kg.
SAM: Raytheon Evolved Sea Sparrow RIM-162 Mk 56 8-cell VLS ❷; semi-active homing to 18 km *(9.7 n miles)* at 3.6 Mach; warhead 38 kg.
1 GMLS Mk 49 RAM RIM-116B 21-cell launcher ❸; passive IR/anti-radiation homing to 9.6 km *(5.2 n miles)* at 2.5 Mach; warhead 9.1 kg. 21 rounds.
Guns: 1 OTO Melara 3 in *(76 mm)*/62 Super Rapid ❹; 120 rds/min to 16 km *(8.7 n miles)* weight of shell 6 kg.
2 Rheinmetall MLG 27 mm ❺.
Countermeasures: Decoys: 2 Rheinmetall MASS-2L launchers ❻.
RESM: Elettronica.
Combat data systems: Alenia Marconi Systems IPN-S. Link 11 and Link Y Mk 2.
Weapons control: Sagem-EOMS optronic director.
Radars: Air/surface search: Ericsson Sea Giraffe ❼; G/H-band.

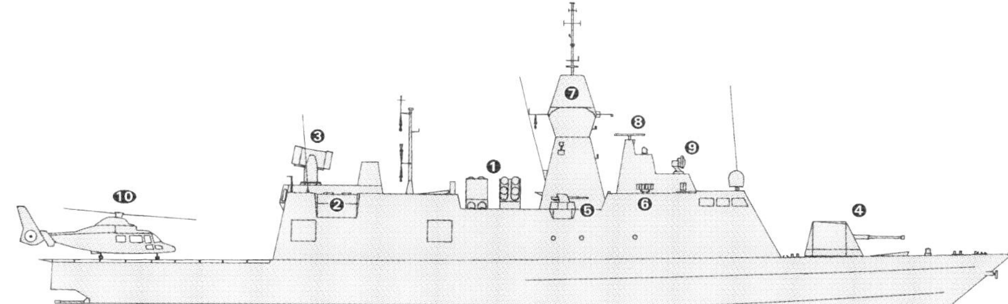

BAYNUNAH CLASS *(Scale 1 : 600), Ian Sturton* / 1305263

Surface search: Terma Scanter 2001 ❽; I-band.
Fire control: 1 Alenia Marconi NA-25/XM ❾; I-band.
Sonars: L-3 ELAC Nautik NDS 3070 mine avoidance sonar.

Helicopters: 1 Eurocopter AS 565 Panther ❿.

Comment: Project Baynunah succeeded Project LEWA 1 for the procurement of patrol boats and is a joint venture between Abu Dhabi Shipbuilding (ADSB) (Prime Contractor) and CMN of France. Systems integration is being undertaken by Abu Dhabi Systems Integration, a joint venture between ADSB and Selex Sistemi Integrati. Contract signed 28 December 2003 for four ships and option for a further two exercised in 2005. Based on a CMN BR67 design, it has a steel hull and aluminium superstructure. The first of class is under construction at Cherbourg while CMN is providing materials for follow-on vessels to be built by ADSB.

SHIPBORNE AIRCRAFT

Numbers/Type: 4 Aerospatiale SA 316/319S Alouette.
Operational speed: 113 kt *(210 km/h)*.
Service ceiling: 10,500 ft *(3,200 m)*.
Range: 290 n miles *(540 km)*.
Role/Weapon systems: Reconnaissance and general purpose helicopters. Sensors: radar. Weapons: Unarmed.

Numbers/Type: 7 Eurocopter AS 565SB Panther.
Operational speed: 165 kt *(305 km/h)*.
Service ceiling: 16,700 ft *(5,100 m)*.
Range: 483 n miles *(895 km)*.
Role/Weapon systems: Ordered in March 1995 and delivered from 2001. Sensors: Thomson-CSF Agrion radar. Weapons: ASV; Aerospatiale AS 15TT ASM.

AS 565SB *10/2002, Eurocopter/Patrick Penna* / 0526393

COUGAR *6/1994* / 0080927

LAND-BASED MARITIME AIRCRAFT

Notes: (1) Procurement of an AEW capability is under consideration. Contenders include the Northrop Grumman E-2D and the Boeing 737.
(2) Acquisition of four maritime patrol aircraft is under consideration. The EADS-CASA C-295M was selected in March 2001 but the contract was not finalised. Another possibility is the Alenia Aeronautica ATR-72.

Numbers/Type: 2 Pilatus Britten-Norman Maritime Defender.
Operational speed: 150 kt *(280 km/h)*.
Service ceiling: 18,900 ft *(5,760 m)*.
Range: 1,500 n miles *(2,775 km)*.
Role/Weapon systems: Coastal patrol and surveillance aircraft although seldom used in this role. Sensors: Nose-mounted search radar, underwing searchlight. Weapons: Underwing rocket and gun pods.

Numbers/Type: 5 Aerospatiale AS 332B/Super Puma.
Operational speed: 150 kt *(280 km/h)*.
Service ceiling: 15,090 ft *(4,600 m)*.
Range: 335 n miles *(620 km)*.
Role/Weapon systems: Former transport helicopters. Five updated from 1995 with ASW equipment. Two others used as VIP transports. Sensors: Omera ORB 30 radar; Thomson Marconi HS 312 dipping sonar. Weapons: ASV; one AM 39 Exocet ASM. ASW; A 244S torpedoes and mines.

PATROL FORCES

Notes: Three Fast Intercept Craft are reported to be in service.

6 ARDHANA CLASS (LARGE PATROL CRAFT) (PB)

Name	*No*	*Builders*	*Commissioned*
ARDHANA	P 3301 (ex-P 1101)	Vosper Thornycroft	24 June 1975
ZURARA	P 3302 (ex-P 1102)	Vosper Thornycroft	14 Aug 1975
MURBAN	P 3303 (ex-P 1103)	Vosper Thornycroft	16 Sep 1975
AL GHULLAN	P 3304 (ex-P 1104)	Vosper Thornycroft	16 Sep 1975
RADOOM	P 3305 (ex-P 1105)	Vosper Thornycroft	1 July 1976
GHANADHAH	P 3306 (ex-P 1106)	Vosper Thornycroft	1 July 1976

Displacement, tons: 110 standard; 175 full load
Dimensions, feet (metres): 110 × 21 × 6.6 *(33.5 × 6.4 × 2)*
Main machinery: 2 Paxman 12CM diesels; 5,000 hp *(3.73 MW)* sustained; 2 shafts
Speed, knots: 30
Range, n miles: 1,800 at 14 kt
Complement: 26
Guns: 2 Oerlikon/BMARC 30 mm/75 A32 (twin); 650 rds/min to 10 km *(5.5 n miles)*; weight of shell 1 kg or 0.36 kg.
1 Oerlikon/BMARC 20 mm/80 A41A; 800 rds/min to 2 km.
2—51 mm projectors for illuminants.
Radars: Surface search: Racal Decca TM 1626; I-band.

Comment: A class of round bilge steel hull craft. Originally operated by Abu Dhabi. New pennant numbers in 1996. To be replaced by the Project Baynunah craft from approximately 2009.

AL GHULLAN *2/1997, A Sharma* / 0567566

2 MUBARRAZ CLASS
(FAST ATTACK CRAFT—MISSILE) (PGGFM)

Name	*No*	*Builders*	*Commissioned*
MUBARRAZ	P 141 (ex-P 4401)	Lürssen, Bremen	Aug 1990
MAKASIB	P 142 (ex-P 4402)	Lürssen, Bremen	Aug 1990

Displacement, tons: 260 full load
Dimensions, feet (metres): 147.3 × 23 × 7.2 *(44.9 × 7 × 2.2)*
Main machinery: 2 MTU 20V 538TB93 diesels; 9,370 hp(m) *(6.9 MW)* sustained; 2 shafts
Speed, knots: 40. **Range, n miles:** 500 at 38 kt
Complement: 40 (5 officers)

Missiles: SSM: 4 Aerospatiale MM 40 Exocet; inertial cruise; active radar homing to 70 km *(40 n miles)* at 0.9 Mach; warhead 165 kg; sea-skimmer.
SAM: 1 Matra Sadral sextuple launcher; Mistral; IR homing to 4 km *(2.2 n miles)*; warhead 3 kg.
Guns: 1 OTO Melara 3 in *(76 mm)*/62 Super Rapid; 120 rds/min to 16 km *(8.7 n miles)*; weight of shell 6 kg.
2 Rheinmetall 20 mm.
Countermeasures: Decoys: 2 Dagaie launchers; IR flares and chaff.
ESM/ECM: Racal Cutlass/Cygnus; intercept/jammer.
Weapons control: CSEE Najir optronic director (for SAM).
Radars: Air/surface search: Bofors Ericsson Sea Giraffe 50HC; G-band.
Navigation: Racal Decca 1226; I-band.
Fire control: Bofors Electronic 9LV 223; J-band (for gun and SSM).

Programmes: Ordered in late 1986 from Lürssen Werft at the same time as the two Type 62 vessels. Delivered in February 1991.
Modernisation: Mid-life refits for both vessels to be undertaken by Abu Dhabi Shipbuilding from 2004.
Structure: This is a modified TNC 38 design, with the first export version of Matra Sadral. The radome houses the jammer. The 20 mm guns are mounted on the bridge deck aft of the mast.

MAKASIB *2/2002, A Sharma* / 0534063

MUBARRAZ *9/2000* / 0121415

6 BAN YAS (TNC 45) CLASS
(FAST ATTACK CRAFT—MISSILE) (PGGF)

Name	*No*	*Builders*	*Commissioned*
BAN YAS	P 151 (ex-P 4501)	Lürssen Vegesack	Nov 1980
MARBAN	P 152 (ex-P 4502)	Lürssen Vegesack	Nov 1980
RODQM	P 153 (ex-P 4503)	Lürssen Vegesack	July 1981
SHAHEEN	P 154 (ex-P 4504)	Lürssen Vegesack	July 1981
SAGAR	P 155 (ex-P 4505)	Lürssen Vegesack	Sep 1981
TARIF	P 156 (ex-P 4506)	Lürssen Vegesack	Sep 1981

Displacement, tons: 260 full load
Dimensions, feet (metres): 147.3 × 23 × 8.2 *(44.9 × 7 × 2.5)*
Main machinery: 4 MTU 16V 538TB92 diesels; 13,640 hp(m) *(10 MW)* sustained; 4 shafts
Speed, knots: 40
Range, n miles: 500 at 38 kt
Complement: 40 (5 officers)

Missiles: SSM: 4 Aerospatiale MM 40 Exocet Block III; inertial cruise; active radar homing to 70 km *(40 n miles)* at 0.9 Mach; warhead 165 kg; sea-skimmer.
Guns: 1 OTO Melara 3 in *(76 mm)*/62; 60 rds/min to 16 km *(8.7 n miles)*; weight of shell 6 kg.
2 Breda 40 mm/70 (twin); 300 rds/min to 12.5 km *(6.8 n miles)*; weight of shell 0.96 kg.
2—7.62 mm MGs.
Countermeasures: Decoys: 1 CSEE trainable Dagaie; IR flares and chaff.
ESM: Thales DR 3000; intercept.
Combat data systems: Saab Systems 9LV Mk 3E CETRIS.
Weapons control: Sagem EOMS optronic tracker.
Radars: Surface search: Bofors Ericsson Sea Giraffe 50HC; G-band.
Navigation: Signaal Scout; I-band.
Fire control: Philips 9LV 200 Mk 2/3; J-band.

Programmes: Ordered in late 1977. First two shipped in September 1980 and four more in Summer 1981. This class was the first to be fitted with MM 40.
Modernisation: Upgrade contract for ship and propulsion systems given to Newport News. Work done by Abu Dhabi Shipbuilding Company. First pair completed in late 1998, second pair in mid-1999 and the third pair in mid-2000. Further modernisation is being undertaken at ADSB under Project Tarif-45. The upgrade includes replacement of the combat data system with the Saab Systems 9LV Mk 3E, upgrade of the 9LV 200 radar with TV, IR and laser range-finder modules and modification of the Sea Giraffe surveillance radar. Exocet is being upgraded to Block III. The programme began in February 2004 and the first ship, *Ban Yas*, was completed in 2006.

TARIF *3/2008*, Guy Toremans* / 1353501

20 RAIDING CRAFT (PBF)

Displacement, tons: 4 full load
Dimensions, feet (metres): 27.9 × 9.7 × 2 *(8.5 × 3 × 0.6)*
Main machinery: 2 outboards; 450 hp *(336 kW)*
Speed, knots: 38
Complement: 1 plus 11 troops

Comment: There are eight Arctic 28 RIBs ordered from Halmatic, Southampton in June 1992 and delivered in mid-1993. GRP hulls. Speed given is fully laden. Used by Special Forces. There are also 12 Al-Shaali type ordered in1994 and built in Dubai.

ARCTIC *3/1995, H M Steele* / 0080926

MINE WARFARE FORCES

2 FRANKENTHAL CLASS (TYPE 332)
(MINEHUNTERS—COASTAL) (MHC)

Name	*No*	*Builders*	*Launched*	*Commissioned*
AL MURJAN (ex-*Frankenthal*)	M 02 (ex-M 1066)	Lürssenwerft	6 Feb 1992	16 Dec 1992
AL HASBAH (ex-*Weiden*)	M 01 (ex-M 1060)	Abeking & Rasmussen	14 May 1992	30 Mar 1993

Displacement, tons: 650 full load
Dimensions, feet (metres): 178.8 × 30.2 × 8.5 *(54.5 × 9.2 × 2.6)*
Main machinery: 2 MTU 16V 396TB84 diesels; 5,550 hp(m) *(4.08 MW)* sustained; 2 shafts; cp props; 1 motor (minehunting)
Speed, knots: 18
Complement: 37 (5 officers)

Missiles: SAM: 2 Stinger quad launchers.
Guns: 1 Bofors 40 mm/70; being replaced by Mauser 27 mm.
Combat data systems: STN MWS 80-4.
Radars: Navigation: Raytheon SPS-64; I-band.
Sonars: Atlas Elektronik DSQS-11M; hull-mounted; high frequency.

Programmes: Originally ordered for the German Navy in September 1988 with STN Systemtechnik Nord as main contractor. *Al Murjan* laid down at Lürssen 6 December 1989. Agreement for the purchase of both ships to UAE concluded in early 2006. Following decommissioning from the German Navy and recommissioning in the UAE Navy on 28 June 2006, both ships undertook refit work at the Neue Jadewerft shipyard in Wilhelmshaven before being transported to Abu Dhabi. *Al Hasbah* arrived in August 2006 and *Al Murjan* in Autumn 2006. A training programme for the crews was conducted prior to transfer.
Structure: Built of amagnetic steel with same hull, similar superstructure and high standardisation as Type 333 and 352 in service with the German Navy. Equipped with two STN Systemtechnik Nord Pinguin-B3 drones with sonar, TV cameras and two countermining charges.
Operational: Weapons and sensors are as for the ships in German service and may be different.

AL MURJAN *9/2006, Frank Findler* / 1167451

AMPHIBIOUS FORCES

Notes: There are also four civilian LCM ships, *El Nasirah 2, Baava 1, Makasib* and *Ghagha II.* Two Serna class LCUs are also civilian owned.

4 LCT

L 61–L 64 (ex-6401–6404)

Displacement, tons: 850 approx
Dimensions, feet (metres): 210 × 39.4 × 8.7 *(64.0 × 12.0 × 2.7)*
Main machinery: 2 Caterpillar diesels; 3,620 hp *(2.7 MW)*; 2 shafts
Speed, knots: 12
Guns: 2—12.7 mm MGs.

Comment: Built at Abu Dhabi Naval Base and completed in 1996–99. Details are incomplete. Pennant numbers changed in 2001.

L 62 ***3/2006, Ships of the World*** / 1127292

3 LANDING CRAFT (LCT)

L 65–67

Displacement, tons: 850 approx
Dimensions, feet (metres): 210 × 39.4 × 8.7 *(64.0 × 12.0 × 2.7)*
Main machinery: 2 Caterpillar 3508 diesels; 3,620 hp *(2.7 MW)*; 2 shafts
Speed, knots: 11
Complement: 19 (plus 56 troops)
Military lift: military vehicles

Comment: Fully designed in the UAE, the vessels were ordered from ADSB in November 2001 and laid down in early 2002 and delivery reportedly started in 2004. Details are speculative and based on the L 61 class. Weapons are expected to include medium calibre machine guns.

L 67 ***3/2008*, Guy Toremans*** / 1353500

12 + 12 TRANSPORTBÅT 2000 (LCP)

P 201–212

Displacement, tons: 43 full load
Dimensions, feet (metres): 79.4 × 16.7 × 3.6 *(24.2 × 5.1 × 1.1)*
Main machinery: 2 MTU 12V 2000 diesels; 2,660 hp *(2.0 MW)*; 2 Rolls Royce FF 550 waterjets
Speed, knots: 35
Complement: 3
Military lift: 42 troops or 10 tons
Guns: 2—12.7 mm MGs.
Radars: Navigation: Terma; I-band.

Comment: Project 'Ghannatha' was for 12 amphibious transport craft based on the Transportbåt 2000 craft in service with the Royal Swedish Navy. Three craft were constructed at the Djupviks yard in Sweden while ADSB built the other nine. Details of the aluminium craft are based on those in Swedish service. Delivery was completed in 2004. An order for a further 12 missile-armed craft was made in March 2009. These are to be stretched (26.5 m) variants equipped with MBDA Marte Mk 2 missiles. The original 12 craft are to be converted into two variants. Six are to be converted to a mortar-firing role and six to a gunboat role.

P 210 ***3/2008*, Michael Nitz*** / 1353499

3 AL FEYI CLASS (LCU)

AL FEYI L 51 (ex-5401) **DAYYINAH** L 52 (ex-5402) **JANANAH** L 53 (ex-5403)

Displacement, tons: 650 full load
Dimensions, feet (metres): 164 × 36.1 × 9.2 *(50 × 11 × 2.8)*
Main machinery: 2 diesels; 1,248 hp *(931 kW)*; 2 shafts
Speed, knots: 11
Range, n miles: 1,800 at 11 kt
Complement: 10
Military lift: 4 vehicles
Guns: 2—12.7 mm MGs.

Comment: *Al Feyi* built by Siong Huat, Singapore; completed 4 August 1987. The other pair built by Argos Shipyard, Singapore to a similar design and completed in December 1988. Used mostly as transport ships. Pennant numbers changed in 2001.

DAYYINAH (old number) ***6/1996*** / 0080929

2 LANDING CRAFT (LCU)

L 41 **UMM AL NARR** L 42

Measurement, tons: 380 dwt
Dimensions, feet (metres): 145.5 × 32.8 × 7.2 *(44.4 × 10.0 × 2.2)*
Main machinery: 2 Caterpillar CAT 3406TA diesels; 730 hp *(544 kW)*; 2 shafts
Speed, knots: 10
Range, n miles: 1,000 at 8.5 kt
Complement: 11 (3 officers) plus 40 troops
Military lift: Military vehicles

Comment: Fully designed in the UAE, these multimission landing craft were constructed by Abu Dhabi Shipbuilding in marine grade steel. The craft are equipped with three hydraulic deck cranes. The first ship was delivered to the navy in mid-2004 and the second to UAE Special Forces Command on 22 June 2006.

UMM AL NARR ***6/2006, Abu Dhabi Shipbuilding*** / 1159231

4 FAST SUPPLY VESSELS (LCP)

L 22–25

Displacement, tons: 53 standard; 73 full load
Dimensions, feet (metres): 85.3 × 17.7 × 4.3 *(26.0 × 5.4 × 1.3)*
Main machinery: 2 MTU 16V 2000 M70 diesels; 2,775 hp *(2.1 MW)*; 2 Rolls Royce FF 550 waterjets
Speed, knots: 32
Complement: 3
Military lift: 2—3 m containers plus 18 troops
Guns: 2—12.7 mm MGs.

Comment: A contract for the construction of four fast supply vessels was made with Abu Dhabi Shipbuilding on 27 June 2004. The aluminium craft were built to a SwedeShip Marine design, developed in conjunction with the Swedish Defence Material Administration. The principal design features include a hydraulically operated bow door and space for storage of two fully loaded 3 m containers or a vehicle. An NBC citadel includes the wheelhouse and medical quarters. The latter can accommodate four stretcher cases or 18 fully equipped troops. All four vessels had been delivered by March 2007.

L 22 *2/2007, Patrick Allen/Jane's* / 1311306

AUXILIARIES

1 DIVING TENDER (YDT)

AL GAFFA D 1051

Displacement, tons: 100 full load
Dimensions, feet (metres): 103 × 22.6 × 3.6 *(31.4 × 6.9 × 1.1)*
Main machinery: 2 MTU 12V 396 TB93 diesels; 3,260 hp(m) *(2.4 MW)* sustained; 2 waterjets
Speed, knots: 26
Range, n miles: 390 at 24 kt
Complement: 6

Comment: Ordered from Crestitalia in December 1985 for Abu Dhabi and delivered in July 1987. GRP hull. Used primarily for mine clearance but also for diving training, salvage and SAR. Fitted with a decompression chamber and diving bell. Lengthened version of Italian *Alcide Pedretti*.

AL GAFFA *3/1997* / 0019363

1 COASTAL TUG (YTB)

ANNAD A 3501

Displacement, tons: 795 full load
Dimensions, feet (metres): 114.8 × 32.2 × 13.8 *(35 × 9.8 × 4.2)*
Main machinery: 2 Caterpillar 3606TA diesels; 4,180 hp *(3.12 MW)* sustained; 2 shafts; cp props; bow thruster; 362 hp *(266 kW)*
Speed, knots: 14
Range, n miles: 2,500 at 14 kt
Complement: 14 (3 officers)
Radars: Navigation: Racal Decca 2070; I-band.

Comment: Built by Dunston, Hessle, and completed in April 1989. Bollard pull, 55 tons. Equipped for SAR and is also used for logistic support.

ANNAD *6/1994* / 0080930

2 HARBOUR TUGS (YTM)

TEMSAH A 51 **UGAAB** A 52

Displacement, tons: 90 full load
Dimensions, feet (metres): 54.1 × 16.4 × 5.9 *(16.5 × 5.0 × 1.8)*
Main machinery: 2 Volvo Penta TAMD-122A diesels; 760 hp *(560 kW)*; 2 shafts

Comment: Ordered from Damen shipyard, Gorinchem in 1996 and entered service in 1998. Main role to attend Kortenaer class frigates. Equipped with fire-fighting platform abaft the mainmast.

TEMSAH *7/2007, M Declerck* / 1170241

COAST GUARD

Notes: (1) Under control of Minister of Interior. In addition to the vessels listed below there is a number of Customs and Police launches including Barracuda craft, three Swedish Boghammar 13 m craft of the same type used by Iran and delivered in 1985, two Baglietto police launches acquired in 1988, about 10 elderly Dhafeer and Spear class of 12 and 9 m respectively, and two Halmatic Arun class Pilot craft delivered in 1990–91; some of these launches carry light machine guns.
(2) Plans to procure a fleet of 34 fast intercept craft for the UAE Critical National Infrastructure Authority were announced in March 2009. Capable of 50 kt, the craft are to be based on the Yonca-Onuk MRTP 16 design, which are extended versions of the Kaan 15 craft in service with the Turkish Coast Guard. The first 12 craft are to be built by Yonca-Onuk at Tuzla, Turkey, and the remaining 22 by Abu Dhabi Shipbuilding. Delivery of the first craft is expected in 2010.

POLICE BARRACUDA *1/2002, A Sharma* / 0534111

2 PROTECTOR CLASS (WPB)

101 (ex-1101) **102** (ex-1102)

Displacement, tons: 180 full load
Dimensions, feet (metres): 108.3 × 22 × 6.9 *(33 × 6.7 × 2.1)*
Main machinery: 2 MTU 16V 396TE94 diesels; 5,911 hp(m) *(4.35 MW)* sustained; 2 shafts; LIPS props
Speed, knots: 33
Complement: 14
Guns: 1 Mauser 20 mm. 2—12.7 mm MGs.
Weapons control: 1 SAGEM optronic director.
Radars: Surface search: I-band.

Comment: Ordered from FBM Marine, Cowes in 1998. Aluminium hulls. First one laid down 15 June 1998. Both delivered in late 1999. More may be built by Abu Dhabi Shipbuilders. Similar to Bahamas and Chilean naval craft.

PROTECTOR 101 (old number) *11/1999, UAE Coast Guard* / 0106675

5 CAMCRAFT 77 ft (COASTAL PATROL CRAFT) (WPB)

753–757

Displacement, tons: 70 full load
Dimensions, feet (metres): 76.8 × 18 × 4.9 *(23.4 × 5.5 × 1.5)*
Main machinery: 2 GM 12V-71TA diesels; 840 hp *(627 kW)* sustained; 2 shafts
Speed, knots: 25
Complement: 8
Guns: 2 Lawrence Scott 20 mm (not always embarked).
Radars: Surface search: Racal Decca; I-band.

Comment: Completed 1975 by Camcraft, New Orleans. Not always armed.

CAMCRAFT 755 *6/1997* / 0019364

16 CAMCRAFT 65 ft (COASTAL PATROL CRAFT) (WPB)

650–665

Displacement, tons: 50 full load
Dimensions, feet (metres): 65 × 18 × 5 *(19.8 × 5.5 × 1.5)*
Main machinery: 2 MTU 6V 396 TB93 diesels; 1,630 hp(m) *(1.2 MW)* sustained; 2 shafts (in 14)
2 Detroit 8V-92TA diesels; 700 hp *(522 kW)* sustained; 2 shafts (in 2)
Speed, knots: 25
Complement: 8
Guns: 1 Oerlikon 20 mm GAM-BO1.
Radars: Surface search: Racal Decca; I-band.

Comment: Built by Camcraft, New Orleans and delivered by September 1978.

CAMCRAFT 655 *12/2001, A Sharma* / 0534118

6 BAGLIETTO GC 23 TYPE (COASTAL PATROL CRAFT) (WPBF)

758–763

Displacement, tons: 50.7 full load
Dimensions, feet (metres): 78.7 × 18 × 3 *(24 × 5.5 × 0.9)*
Main machinery: 2 MTU 12V 396TB93 diesels; 3,260 hp(m) *(2.4 MW)* sustained; 2 Kamewa water-jets
Speed, knots: 43
Range, n miles: 700 at 20 kt
Complement: 9
Guns: 1 Oerlikon 20 mm. 2—7.62 mm MGs.
Radars: Surface search: I-band.

Comment: Built by Baglietto, Varazze. First two completed in March and May 1986, second pair in July 1987 and two more in 1988. All were delivered to UAE Coast Guard in Dubai.

BAGLIETTO 758 *1987, UAE Coast Guard* / 0080934

3 BAGLIETTO 59 ft (COASTAL PATROL CRAFT) (WPBF)

501–503

Displacement, tons: 22 full load
Dimensions, feet (metres): 59.4 × 13.9 × 2.3 *(18.1 × 4.3 × 0.7)*
Main machinery: 2 MTU 12V 183TE92 diesels; 2 shafts
Speed, knots: 40
Complement: 6
Guns: 2—7.62 mm MGs.
Radars: Surface search: Racal Decca; I-band.

Comment: Ordered in 1992 and delivered in late 1993.

BAGLIETTO 503 *10/1993, UAE Coast Guard* / 0080935

6 WATERCRAFT 45 ft (COASTAL PATROL CRAFT) (PB)

Displacement, tons: 25 full load
Dimensions, feet (metres): 45 × 14.1 × 4.6 *(13.7 × 4.3 × 1.4)*
Main machinery: 2 MAN D2542 diesels; 1,300 hp(m) *(956 kW)*; 2 shafts
Speed, knots: 26
Range, n miles: 380 at 18 kt
Complement: 5
Guns: Mounts for 2—7.62 mm MGs.
Radars: Surface search: Racal Decca; I-band.

Comment: Ordered from Watercraft, UK in February 1982. Delivery in early 1983. Four deleted. Two similar craft built by Halmatic were delivered to the Dubai Port Authority in October 1997.

WATERCRAFT 45 ft *1984, UAE Coast Guard* / 0506115

35 HARBOUR PATROL CRAFT (PB/YDT)

Comment: The latest are 11 Shark 33 built by Shaali Marine, Dubai and delivered in 1993–94. The remainder are a mixture of Barracuda 30 ft and FPB 22 ft classes. All are powered by twin outboard engines and most carry a 7.62 mm MG and have a Norden radar. There are also two Rotork craft used as diving tenders. Customs boats are operated separately by each of the UAE states. Some have been built for Kuwait.

BARRACUDA 271 *12/2001, A Sharma* / 0534117

0 + 12 AL SABER CLASS (PATROL BOATS) (PB)

Displacement, tons: 100
Dimensions, feet (metres): 111.5 × 23.0 × 5.2 *(34.0 × 7.0 × 1.6)*
Main machinery: 2 MTU diesels; 2 shafts
Speed, knots: 25
Range, n miles: 440 at 12 kt
Complement: 7
Guns: 1—25 mm. 1—12.7 mm MG.
Electro-optic systems: To be announced.
Radars: Surface search/navigation: I-band.
Navigation: I-band.

Comment: The contract for the construction of 12 patrol craft was announced on 6 March 2008. The vessels, to be constructed in composite materials, are to be built by Abu Dhabi Shipbuilding. The design features a stern-ramp to enable the accommodation of a fast intercept craft in a mother-daughter arrangement. The vessels are to be delivered from 2009.

AL SABER CLASS *6/2008*, ADSB* / 1353498

54 SEASPRAY ASSAULT BOATS (PB)

Displacement, tons: To be announced
Dimensions, feet (metres): 31.2 × 10.2 × 1.6 *(9.5 × 3.1 × 0.5)*
Main machinery: 2 outboards; 500 hp *(375 kW)*
Speed, knots: 50
Range, n miles: 450 at 17 kt
Complement: 5
Radars: Navigation: I-band.

Comment: Initial batch of 24 craft delivered in September 2003. A further thirty were ordered in early 2004. Designed by Sea Spray Aluminium Boats.

SEASPRAY *2/2004, ADSB* / 0563487

1 + 11 HALMATIC WORK BOATS (PB)

Displacement, tons: 13.3
Dimensions, feet (metres): 52.5 × 13.1 × 2.3 *(16.0 × 4.0 × 0.7)*
Main machinery: 2 diesels; 2 waterjets
Speed, knots: 24
Complement: 5
Radars: Navigation: I-band.

Comment: Construction of 12 craft started at Abu Dhabi Shipbuilding Composites in mid-2006. The first of class was completed by March 2007 but the delivery schedule for the remainder has not been confirmed. Based on the VT Halmatic Sea Keeper design with an asymmetric catamaran hull, the craft are highly manoeuvrable and are capable of carrying a 10 tonne payload.

WORK BOAT *2/2007, Patrick Allen/Jane's* / 1321982

United Kingdom

Country Overview

The United Kingdom of Great Britain and Northern Ireland is situated in north-western Europe. It has a coastline of 6,700 n miles with the English Channel, the North Sea, the Irish Sea and the Atlantic Ocean. With an area of 93,341 square miles, it comprises the island of Great Britain (England, Scotland and Wales) and the six counties of Ulster that remained a constituent part of UK after Irish independence in 1922. It also includes the Isle of Wight, Anglesey, the Scilly, Orkney, Shetland, and Hebridean archipelagos and numerous smaller islands. The Isle of Man and the Channel Islands are direct dependencies but are not part of the UK. Other dependent territories are: Anguilla; Bermuda; British Antarctic Territory; British Indian Ocean Territory (BIOT); British Virgin Islands; Cayman Islands; Cyprus Sovereign Base Areas; Falkland Islands; Gibraltar; Montserrat; Ducie, Henderson and Oeno; St Helena and Dependencies (Ascension and Tristan da Cunha); South Georgia and South Sandwich Islands and the Turks and Caicos Islands. London is the capital, largest city and a major port. Major oil ports are at Forth, Sullom Voe and Milford Haven and non-oil ports at Tees and Hartlepool, Grimsby and Immingham, Southampton, Liverpool, Felixstowe, Medway, and Dover. Territorial seas of 12 n miles are claimed around the UK mainland and many dependencies. An EEZ (200 n miles) is claimed for Bermuda, South Georgia and South Sandwich Islands and Pitcairn. A Fishery Zone (200 n miles) is claimed for the mainland and some dependencies.

Headquarters Appointments

Chief of the Naval Staff and First Sea Lord:
Admiral Sir Mark Stanhope, KCB, OBE
Commander-in-Chief, Fleet:
Admiral Sir Trevor Soar, KCB
Chief of Naval Personnel and Commander-in-Chief, Naval Home Command:
Vice Admiral A M Massey, CBE
Chief of Materiel (Fleet):
Vice Admiral A D H Matthews, CB
Controller of the Navy:
Rear Admiral A M Hussain
Assistant Chief of the Naval Staff:
Rear Admiral R G Cooling

Flag Officers, Operational and National Commanders

Chief of Joint Operations:
Lieutenant General Sir Nick Houghton, KCB, CBE
Deputy Commander-in-Chief, Fleet:
Vice Admiral R J Ibbotson, DSC
Chief of Staff (Capability) (Commandant General Royal Marines):
Major General A Salmon, OBE
Commander, Operations (Rear Admiral Submarines):
Rear Admiral M Anderson
Commander, UK Maritime Forces:
Rear Admiral P A Jones
Flag Officer, Sea Training:
Rear Admiral C A Snow
Flag Officer, Scotland, Northern England and Northern Ireland:
Rear Admiral M B Alabaster
Commander, British Forces Cyprus:
Air Vice-Marshal R Lacey, CBE
Commander United Kingdom Task Group:
Commodore D L Potts
Commander, UK Maritime Component, Bahrain:
Commodore T M Lowe
Commander Amphibious Task Group:
Commodore P D Hudson, CBE
Commander, 3 Commando Brigade:
Brigadier G K Messenger
Commander, British Forces Gibraltar:
Commodore M J Parr

Flag Officers, Operational and National Commanders—*continued*

Commander, British Forces South Atlantic Islands:
Air Commodore G Moulds, MBE
Commodore Royal Fleet Auxiliary:
Commodore W M Walworth
Commodore Portsmouth Flotilla:
Commodore M P Mansergh
Commodore Devonport Flotilla:
Commodore J S Westbrook, MBE
Captain Faslane Flotilla:
Captain S W Garrett, OBE
Hydrographer of the Navy:
Captain R G Stewart

Diplomatic Representation

Defence Attaché in Ankara:
Colonel C O Hodges MBE
Defence Attaché in Athens:
Colonel P Lodge
Defence Attaché in Bahrain:
Commander W Scarth
Deputy Attaché in Beijing:
Captain A J Tate
Naval Attaché in Berlin:
Group Captain F Simpson
Defence Attaché in Brasilia:
Group Captain W G S Dobson
Defence Adviser in Bridgetown:
Captain P T Morgan
Defence Adviser in Brunei:
Captain A E Rycroft
Defence Attaché in Buenos Aires:
Colonel A Thomson
Defence Attaché in Cairo:
Colonel N F W Hile
Defence Adviser/Naval Adviser in Canberra:
Brigadier J Robbins RM
Defence Attaché in Copenhagen:
Wing Commander R MacCormac
Defence Attaché in The Hague:
Colonel J Heal
Naval Adviser in Islamabad:
Group Captain F Harbottle
Defence Attaché in Jakarta:
Colonel N D J Rowe
Defence Attaché in Kiev:
Captain J L R Foreman
Defence Adviser in Kuala Lumpur:
Colonel P Edwards
Defence Attaché in Lisbon (based in London):
Commander D Fields
Naval Attaché in Madrid:
Captain D E Wolfe
Defence Attaché in Moscow:
Captain G Newton
Naval Attaché in Muscat:
Commander P Moss
Naval Advisor in New Delhi:
Captain A C Ashcroft
Naval Adviser in Ottawa:
Captain P Steel
Deputy Attaché in Paris:
Captain P F A Stonor
Naval Adviser in Pretoria:
Wing Commander R Whitworth
Naval Attaché in Riyadh:
Commander K Broadley
Naval Attaché in Rome:
Commander S Steeds
Defence Attaché in Santiago:
Colonel R Carrow
Defence Attaché in Seoul:
Brigadier M O'Hanlon
Defence Adviser in Singapore:
Group Captain T P Brewer OBE
Defence Attaché in Stockholm:
Commander B H G Falk

Diplomatic Representation—*continued*

Defence Attaché in Tokyo:
Captain G G J Derrick
Defence Attaché in Warsaw:
Lieutenant Colonel A Nowak
Naval Attaché in Washington:
Captain S C Ramm

Royal Marines Operational Units

HQ 3 Commando Brigade RM; 40 Commando RM; 42 Commando RM; 45 Commando RM; Commando Logistic Regiment RM (RN/RM/Army); 3 Commando Brigade Command Support Group, EW Troop RM, Tactical Air Command Posts RM (3 regular, 1 reserve); 539 Assault Squadron RM (hovercraft, landing craft and raiding craft); Brigade Patrol Troop (reconnaissance); Special Boat Service RM; Fleet Royal Marines Protection Group (FRMPG); T Company RMR; 29 Commando Regiment RA (Army); 59 Independent Commando Squadron RE (Army); 20 Commando Battery RA; 131 Independent Squadron RE (Volunteers).

Bases

Northwood: C-in-C Fleet; CJO; Commander Operations
Portsmouth: C-in-C Navhome; DC-in-C Fleet; COS Warfare; COS Support; COMUKMARFOR; COMUKAMPHIBFOR; Com Portsmouth Flotilla; COMUKTG
Devonport: FOST; Com Devonport Flotilla; COMATG
Faslane: FOSNNI; Captain Faslane Flotilla

Prefix to Ships' Names

HMS (Her Majesty's Ship)

Personnel

2009:
(a) Regulars: RN 27,490 (5,720 officers)
RM 6,600 (660 officers)
(b) Reserves: RN 2,200 (830 officers)
RM 980 (90 officers)

Fleet Disposition

Portsmouth: 2 CV; 8 Type 42 DDG, 6 Type 23 FFG; 2nd MCM Squadron; Fishery Protection Squadron; Antarctic Patrol Ship; 1st Patrol Boat Squadron; Fleet Diving Squadron; Gibraltar and Cyprus Squadrons; Falkland Islands Patrol Vessel
Devonport: 1 LPH; 2 LPD; 4 Type 22 FFG; 7 Type 23 FFG; 7 Trafalgar Class SSN; Surveying Squadron
Faslane: 4 SSBN; 1 Swiftsure class SSN; 1st MCM Squadron

Strength of the Fleet

Type	*Active (Reserve)*	*Building (Projected)*
SSBNs	4	–
Submarines—Attack	8	4 (3)
Aircraft Carriers	2 (1)	2
Destroyers	7	5
Frigates	17	–
Assault Ships (LPD)	2	–
Helicopter Carriers (LPH)	1	–
LSD (RFA)	4	–
Offshore Patrol Vessels	4	–
Patrol Craft	18	–
Minehunters	16	–
Repair/Maintenance Ships (RFA)	1	–
Survey Ships	5	–
Antarctic Patrol Ships	1	–
Large Fleet Tankers (RFA)	2	–
Support Tankers (RFA)	2	–
Small Fleet Tankers (RFA)	2	–
Casualty Receiving Ship (RFA)	1	–
Fleet Replenishment Ships (RFA)	4	–
Transport Ro-Ro (RFR)	6	–

Principal Fleet Air Arm Squadrons (see *Shipborne Aircraft* section) on 1 January 2009
HMA = Helicopter Maritime Attack.

F/W	*Aircraft*	*Role*	*Deployment*	*Squadron no*
12	Harrier	GR 7A/GR 9A	RAF Cottesmore	800/801
13	Jetstream	Aircrew Training	Culdrose, *Seahawk*	750
5	Grob	Aircrew Training	Yeovilton, *Heron*	727

Helicopters		*Role*	*Deployment*	*Squadron no*
2	Merlin HM Mk 1	OEU	Culdrose, *Seahawk*	700M
6	Merlin HM Mk 1	ASW/ASUW	Culdrose, *Seahawk*	814
4	Merlin HM Mk 1	ASW/ASUW	Culdrose, *Seahawk*	820
8	Merlin HM Mk 1	ASW/ASUW	Culdrose, *Seahawk*	824
8	Merlin HM Mk 1	ASW/ASUW	Culdrose, *Seahawk*	829
13	Sea King ASAC Mk 7	AEW	Culdrose, *Seahawk*	849/854/857
2	Sea King HU Mk 5	SAR	Prestwick, *Gannet*	SAR Flight
8	Sea King HU Mk 5	SAR/Training	Culdrose, *Seahawk*	771
10	Sea King HC 4	Commando Assault	Yeovilton, *Heron*	845
10	Sea King HC 4	Commando Assault	Yeovilton, *Heron*	846
10	Sea King HC 4	Commando Assault	Yeovilton, *Heron*	848
13	Lynx Mk 3/8	ASUW/ASW	Yeovilton, *Heron*	815
35	Lynx Mk 3/8	ASUW/ASW Aircrew training	Yeovilton, *Heron*	702
6	Lynx Mk 7	Commando Support	Yeovilton, *Heron*	847

Notes:
(1) Joint Force Harrier (JFH) formed on 1 April 2000. Operating Harrier GR.9 aircraft and complemented by RN and RAF pilots, it comprises four squadrons: No 1(F) Sqn RAF, No4 (AC) Sqn RAF and 800 and 801 Squadrons Naval Strike Wing (NSW).
(2) The Joint Helicopter Command (JHC) became operational on 1 April 2000 and brought all battlefield helicopters from all three services under one command at HQ Land, Wilton. Total helicopter assets number some 450. The command includes the Commando Helicopter Force (CHF), a group of four RN/RM squadrons, based at Yeovilton, which specialises in amphibious warfare and whose prime task is to support 3 Cdo Brigade.
(3) Mirach 100/5 subsonic drones are operated by 792 Squadron at Culdrose.
(4) The Royal Navy SAR force comprises 771 Squadron (Culdrose) and the Gannet SAR flight (Prestwick). 771 Squadron covers the SW approaches and the Gannet SAR flight the NW approaches and northern Irish Sea. In the future a Joint Search and Rescue Service is to be provided for the UK SAR region under a single contract. The service is to be manned by military and civilian aircrew and is to be managed jointly by the MoD and Maritime Coast Guard Agency.

DELETIONS

Submarines

2006 *Spartan, Sovereign*
2008 *Superb*

Destroyers

2009 *Southampton, Exeter*

Frigates

2006 *Grafton* (to Chile)

Patrol Forces

2007 *Dumbarton Castle*

Auxiliaries

2006 *Grey Rover, Sir Tristram, Sir Galahad*
2007 *Oakleaf, Brambleleaf*
2008 *Sir Bedivere*

PENNANT LIST

Notes: Numbers are not displayed on Submarines.

Submarines

Ballistic Missile Submarines

S 28 Vanguard
S 29 Victorious
S 30 Vigilant
S 31 Vengeance

Attack Submarines

S 20 Astute (bldg)
S 21 Artful (bldg)
S 22 Ambush (bldg)
S 23 Audacious (bldg)
S 87 Turbulent
S 88 Tireless
S 90 Torbay
S 91 Trenchant
S 92 Talent
S 93 Triumph
S 104 Sceptre
S 107 Trafalgar

Aircraft Carriers

R 06 Illustrious
R 07 Ark Royal

Destroyers

D 32 Daring
D 33 Dauntless (bldg)
D 34 Diamond (bldg)
D 35 Dragon (bldg)
D 36 Defender (bldg)
D 37 Duncan (bldg)
D 91 Nottingham
D 92 Liverpool
D 95 Manchester
D 96 Gloucester
D 97 Edinburgh
D 98 York

Frigates

F 78 Kent
F 79 Portland
F 81 Sutherland
F 82 Somerset
F 83 St Albans
F 85 Cumberland
F 86 Campbeltown
F 87 Chatham
F 99 Cornwall
F 229 Lancaster
F 231 Argyll
F 234 Iron Duke
F 235 Monmouth
F 236 Montrose
F 237 Westminster
F 238 Northumberland
F 239 Richmond

Amphibious Warfare Forces

L 12 Ocean
L 14 Albion
L 15 Bulwark
L 105 Arromanches
L 107 Andalsnes
L 109 Akyab
L 110 Aachen
L 111 Arezzo
L 113 Audemer
L 3006 Largs Bay
L 3007 Lyme Bay
L 3008 Mounts Bay
L 3009 Cardigan Bay

Mine Warfare Forces

M 30 Ledbury
M 31 Cattistock
M 33 Brocklesby
M 34 Middleton
M 37 Chiddingfold
M 38 Atherstone
M 39 Hurworth
M 41 Quorn
M 104 Walney
M 106 Penzance
M 107 Pembroke
M 108 Grimsby
M 109 Bangor
M 110 Ramsey
M 111 Blyth
M 112 Shoreham

Patrol Forces

P 163 Express
P 164 Explorer
P 165 Example
P 167 Exploit
P 257 Clyde
P 264 Archer
P 270 Biter
P 272 Smiter
P 273 Pursuer
P 274 Tracker
P 275 Raider
P 279 Blazer
P 280 Dasher
P 281 Tyne
P 282 Severn
P 283 Mersey
P 284 Scimitar
P 285 Sabre
P 291 Puncher
P 292 Charger
P 293 Ranger
P 294 Trumpeter

Survey Ships

H 86 Gleaner
H 87 Echo
H 88 Enterprise
H 130 Roebuck
H 131 Scott

Auxiliaries

A 109 Bayleaf
A 110 Orangeleaf
A 132 Diligence
A 135 Argus
A 171 Endurance
A 271 Gold Rover
A 273 Black Rover
A 385 Fort Rosalie
A 386 Fort Austin
A 387 Fort Victoria
A 388 Fort George
A 389 Wave Knight
A 390 Wave Ruler

SUBMARINES

Notes: Three 6.7 m US-made Mk VIII Mod 1 Swimmer Delivery Vehicles were acquired in 1999. Battery-powered, they can transport six combat swimmers and have a radius of 67 km *(36 n miles)*.

SDV Mk VIII ***1/2002, M Declerck*** / 0132551

Attack Submarines (SSN)

Notes: Future submarine requirements are being taken forward in a twin-track approach. In the short-term, technology advances to an extended Astute class are under consideration. Conceptual studies are also investigating requirements for a 'Maritime Underwater Future Capability' (MUFC) post 2020. Options are likely to include a development of the Astute class and linkage to future SSBN concept work is also a possibility.

0 + 4 (3) ASTUTE CLASS (SSN)

Name	*No*	*Builders*	*Laid down*	*Launched*	*Commissioned*
ASTUTE	S 20	BAE Systems, Barrow	31 Jan 2001	8 June 2007	2009
AMBUSH	S 21	BAE Systems, Barrow	22 Oct 2003	Dec 2009	2010
ARTFUL	S 22	BAE Systems, Barrow	11 Mar 2005	Apr 2011	2012
AUDACIOUS	S 23	BAE Systems, Barrow	24 Mar 2009	2013	2015
–	–	BAE Systems, Barrow	2010	2015	2017

Displacement, tons: 6,500 surfaced; 7,400 dived
Dimensions, feet (metres): 318.2 × 37.0 × 32.8 *(97 × 11.27 × 10)*
Main machinery: Nuclear; 1 RR PWR 2; 2 Alsthom turbines; 27,500 hp (20.5 MW); 1 shaft; pump jet propulsor; 2 turbo generators; 2 diesel alternators; 2 motors for emergency drive; 1 auxiliary retractable prop
Speed, knots: 29 dived
Complement: 140 (12 officers)

Missiles: SLCM: Raytheon Tomahawk Block IV; TERCOM and GPS aided navigation with DSMAC to 1,600+ km *(865+ n miles)* at 0.7 Mach; warhead (WDU 36B) 454 kg.
Torpedoes: 6—21 in *(533 mm)* tubes for Tomahawk, Sub Harpoon and Spearfish torpedoes. Total of 38 weapons.
Mines: In lieu of torpedoes.
Countermeasures: Decoys. ESM: Racal UAP 4; intercept.
Combat data systems: BAE Systems ACMS tactical data handling system. Links 11/16.
Radars: Navigation: I-band.
Sonars: Thomson Marconi 2076 integrated suite (bow, flank, fin and towed arrays).

ASTUTE *6/2007, Richard Scott / 1167735*

Programmes: Invitations to tender issued on 14 July 1994 to build three of the class with an option for two more. GEC-Marconi selected as prime contractor in December 1995. Contract to start building the first three placed on 17 March 1997. First steel cut late 1999 but although formal keel-laying took place in 2001, design, engineering and programme management difficulties led to a three-year delay to the first of class. This was extended to four years by a range of emergent first of class issues. There were similar delays to the second and third of class. Approval for construction of the fourth of class was given on 21 May 2007. A contract funded initial manufacture work and a follow-on contract is expected in mid-2009 to cover the balance of construction. A further three boats are expected to be built to a 22-month production 'drumbeat'.
Structure: An evolution of the Trafalgar design with increased weapon load and reduced radiated noise but with overall performance similar to Trafalgar after full modernisation. The fin is slightly longer and there are two Thales Optronics CM010 non-hull-penetrating optronic masts. A more advanced variant is to be fitted to *Audacious* and subsequent boats. The boats are to have a dry dock hangar capability (Project Chalfont). A fully reelable towed-array handling system is incorporated. A 'Thin Flank' array is to be fitted in *Audacious* and a lighter bow array in Boat 5.
Operational: Fitted with Core H, nuclear refuelling will not be necessary in the lifetime of the submarine. To be based at Faslane. Sea trials of *Astute* are to begin in mid-2009.

1 SWIFTSURE CLASS (SSN)

Name	*No*	*Builders*	*Laid down*	*Launched*	*Commissioned*
SCEPTRE	S 104	Vickers Shipbuilding & Engineering, Barrow-in-Furness	19 Feb 1974	20 Nov 1976	14 Feb 1978

Displacement, tons: 4,000 light; 4,400 standard; 4,900 dived
Dimensions, feet (metres): 272 × 32.3 × 28 *(82.9 × 9.8 × 8.5)*
Main machinery: Nuclear; 1 RR PWR 1; 2 GEC turbines; 15,000 hp *(11.2 MW)*; 1 shaft; pump jet propulsor; 2 WH Allen turbo generators; 3.6 MW; 1 Paxman diesel alternator; 1,900 hp *(1.42 MW)*; 1 motor for emergency drive; 1 auxiliary retractable prop
Speed, knots: 30+ dived
Complement: 116 (13 officers)

Missiles: SLCM: Hughes Tomahawk Block III; TERCOM aided inertial navigation system with GPS back-up to 1,600+ km *(865+ n miles)* at 0.7 Mach; warhead (WDU 36B) 454 kg. Fitted in S 104 only.
Torpedoes: 5—21 in *(533 mm)* bow tubes. Marconi Spearfish; wire-guided; active/passive homing to 26 km *(14 n miles)* at 65 kt; or 31.5 km *(17 n miles)* at 50 kt; attack speed 55 kt; warhead 300 kg directed charge; 20 reloads.
Mines: Can be carried in lieu of torpedoes.
Countermeasures: Decoys: SAWCS from 2002. 2 SSE Mk 6 launchers. Type 2066 torpedo decoys.
ESM: Racal UAP; passive intercept.
Combat data systems: Dowty Sema SMCS tactical data handling system. Link 11 can be fitted.
Radars: Navigation: Kelvin Hughes Type 1007; I-band.
Sonars: TUSL Type 2074 LRE; hull-mounted; active/passive search and attack; low frequency.
TUSL Type 2046; towed array; passive search; very low frequency.
Ultra Electronics 2082; active intercept and ranging.
Marconi Type 2077; ice navigation; active; high frequency.

SWIFTSURE CLASS *9/2001, Lockheed Martin / 0131248*

SWIFTSURE CLASS *1/2002, Ships of the World / 0131254*

Programmes: *Sceptre* ordered 1 November 1971.
Modernisation: Fitted with a PWR 1 Core Z during major refits to give a 8 to 10 year refit cycle (12 year life). *Sceptre* completed major refits in 1987 and 2001. Other improvements included acoustic elastomeric tiles, sonar processing equipment and improved decoys. Equipped with Tomahawk Block III in 2006.
Structure: The pressure hull in the Swiftsure class maintains its diameter for much greater length than earlier classes. Control gear by MacTaggart, Scott & Co Ltd for: attack and search periscopes, snort induction and exhaust, radar and ESM masts. The forward hydroplanes house within the casing. Fitted with Pilkington Optronics CK 33 search and CH 83 attack electro-optic periscopes.
Operational: Based at Faslane. *Swiftsure* paid off in 1992, *Splendid* in 2003, *Spartan* in early 2006, *Sovereign* on 26 September 2006 and *Superb* on 26 September 2008. *Sceptre* is to decommission in 2010.

SWIFTSURE CLASS *5/2003, B Prézelin / 0572689*

7 TRAFALGAR CLASS (SSN)

Name	*No*	*Builders*	*Laid down*	*Launched*	*Commissioned*
TRAFALGAR	S 107	Vickers Shipbuilding & Engineering, Barrow-in-Furness	25 Apr 1979	1 July 1981	27 May 1983
TURBULENT	S 87	Vickers Shipbuilding & Engineering, Barrow-in-Furness	8 May 1980	1 Dec 1982	28 Apr 1984
TIRELESS	S 88	Vickers Shipbuilding & Engineering, Barrow-in-Furness	6 June 1981	17 Mar 1984	5 Oct 1985
TORBAY	S 90	Vickers Shipbuilding & Engineering, Barrow-in-Furness	3 Dec 1982	8 Mar 1985	7 Feb 1987
TRENCHANT	S 91	Vickers Shipbuilding & Engineering, Barrow-in-Furness	28 Oct 1985	3 Nov 1986	14 Jan 1989
TALENT	S 92	Vickers Shipbuilding & Engineering, Barrow-in-Furness	13 May 1986	15 Apr 1988	12 May 1990
TRIUMPH	S 93	Vickers Shipbuilding & Engineering, Barrow-in-Furness	2 Feb 1987	16 Feb 1991	12 Oct 1991

Displacement, tons: 4,740 surfaced; 5,208 dived
Dimensions, feet (metres): 280.1 × 32.1 × 31.2 *(85.4 × 9.8 × 9.5)*
Main machinery: Nuclear; 1 RR PWR 1; 2 GEC turbines; 15,000 hp *(11.2 MW)*; 1 shaft; pump jet propulsor; 2 WH Allen turbo generators; 3.2 MW; 2 Paxman diesel alternators; 2,800 hp *(2.09 MW)*; 1 motor for emergency drive; 1 auxiliary retractable prop
Speed, knots: 32 dived
Complement: 130 (18 officers)

Missiles: SLCM: Raytheon Tomahawk Block IV; TERCOM and GPS aided inertial navigation system with DSMAC to 1,600+ km *(865+ n miles)* at 0.7 Mach; warhead (WDU 36B) 454 kg. Being fitted to all from 2008.
Torpedoes: 5—21 in *(533 mm)* bow tubes. Marconi Spearfish; wire-guided; active/passive homing to 26 km *(14 n miles)* at 65 kt; or 31.5 km *(17 n miles)* at 50 kt; attack speed 55 kt; warhead 300 kg directed charge; 20 reloads.
Mines: Can be carried in lieu of torpedoes.
Countermeasures: Decoys: SAWCS from 2002. 2 SSE Mk 8 launchers. Type 2066 torpedo decoys.
RESM: Racal UAP 1; passive intercept.
CESM: Eddystone.
Combat data systems: BAE Systems SMCS tactical data handling system.
Weapons control: BAE Systems SMCS.
Radars: Navigation: Kelvin Hughes Type 1007; I-band.
Sonars: TUSL 2074 LRE; hull-mounted; passive/active, search and attack; low frequency. TUSL 2046; towed array, passive search, very low frequency. Ultra Electonics 2082; active intercept and ranging.
TUSL 2076 (S90-93) integrated sonar suite comprising flank array, towed array, conformal bow array, mine avoidance array.
TUSL 2077; ice navigation.

Programmes: *Trafalgar* ordered 7 April 1977; *Turbulent* 28 July 1978; *Tireless* 5 July 1979; *Torbay* 26 June 1981; *Trenchant* 22 March 1983; *Talent* 10 September 1984; *Triumph* 3 January 1986.
Modernisation: *Trafalgar* completed refuel in December 1995 and was fitted with SMCS and Spearfish torpedoes. *Turbulent* refuelled by mid-1997 and was refitted with sonar 2074, SMCS and Spearfish. *Tireless* completed similar modernisation and refuelling in January 1999. Refuel periods for the last four boats are being undertaken in parallel with a major tactical modernisation programme, the main feature of which is installation of the sonar 2076 integrated sonar suite to replace the 2074 bow array and 2046 towed array. Other upgrades include enhancements to SMCS, a new command console and improved signature reduction measures. *Torbay* and *Trenchant* were the first and second boats to complete a 2076 refit and refuel in 2003 and 2004 respectively. *Talent* completed her three-year refit in January 2007 and *Triumph* is expected to complete her refit in 2009. Meanwhile, an ongoing programme of software replacement will continue to realise capability improvements in the last four boats. As a parallel programme, SMCS is being upgraded to SMCS NG and Tomahawk cruise missiles are being fitted to the whole class. *Triumph* and *Trafalgar* were completed by mid-2001, *Turbulent* in 2002 and *Trenchant* in 2004. *Tireless* and *Talent* were completed in 2006 and *Torbay* in 2007. Tomahawk Block IV missiles started to replace Block III missiles in March 2008. Following a joint UK/US feasibility study, a Torpedo-Tube Launched (TTL) variant of the missile was developed for UK use. A series of developmental tests began in 2005, culminating in the successful completion of a 650 n mile flight of a TTL missile, fired from *Trenchant*, on 21 June 2007. In parallel, the Tactical Tomahawk Weapons Control (TTWC) and Tomahawk Strike Network (TSN), first installed in *Trafalgar* in 2004, has been fitted in six of the class. *Triumph* is bneing upgraded during refit. Replacement of the CESM system was initiated in 2002 and upgrade of the RESM system UAP 1, was initiated in 2006.
Structure: The pressure hull and outer surfaces are covered with conformal anechoic noise reduction coatings. Retractable forward hydroplanes and strengthened fins for under ice operations. Diving depth in excess of 300 m *(985 ft)*. Fitted with Pilkington Optronics CK 34 search and CH 84 attack periscopes.
Operational: Trials of a high-frequency active sonar (AN/BQS-15/A derivative) conducted in *Trenchant* in 2008. All of the class based at Devonport. The class is planned to pay off as follows: *Trafalgar* 2009; *Turbulent* 2011; *Tireless* 2013 and the remainder of the class by 2022.

TRAFALGAR *6/2005, Per Körnefeldt* / 1153922

TORBAY *9/2008*, B Sullivan* / 1353553

TRAFALGAR *8/2006, Derek Fox* / 1167727

TRENCHANT *7/2008*, Ian Harris* / 1353552

TIRELESS *5/2008*, B Sullivan* / 1353554

Strategic Missile Submarines (SSBN)

Notes: It was announced on 4 December 2006 that the UK nuclear deterrent is to be maintained beyond the life of the Vanguard-class submarines. Detailed concept work on a next-generation nuclear-powered ballistic submarine (SSBN) began in 2007 with a view to a contract for their detailed design being let in 2012–14. Work on a common UK/US missile compartment was initiated in January 2009. Replacement of the current fleet of SSBNs, assuming a life extension of five years, is required from 2024. The future SSBN force is to be comprised of three or four boats. In parallel, UK is to participate in the US Navy's Trident D5 life-extension programme that is to prolong missile life to about 2042. Decisions on whether to acquire a successor to the life-extended D5 missile, and what form it is to take, are required in the 2020s. Policy to deploy up to 48 warheads on a single submarine is to continue and it was announced that the current inventory of operationally available warheads is to be reduced from 'fewer than 200' to 'fewer than 160'. Current warheads are expected to remain in service until the 2020s and a decision as to whether they are to be refurbished or replaced is expected by 2014.

4 VANGUARD CLASS (SSBN)

Name	*No*	*Builders*	*Laid down*	*Launched*	*Commissioned*
VANGUARD	S 28	Vickers Shipbuilding & Engineering, Barrow-in-Furness	3 Sep 1986	4 Mar 1992	14 Aug 1993
VICTORIOUS	S 29	Vickers Shipbuilding & Engineering, Barrow-in-Furness	3 Dec 1987	29 Sep 1993	7 Jan 1995
VIGILANT	S 30	Vickers Shipbuilding & Engineering, Barrow-in-Furness	16 Feb 1991	15 Oct 1995	2 Nov 1996
VENGEANCE	S 31	Vickers Shipbuilding & Engineering, Barrow-in-Furness	1 Feb 1993	19 Sep 1998	27 Nov 1999

Displacement, tons: 15,980 dived
Dimensions, feet (metres): 491.8 × 42 × 39.4 *(149.9 × 12.8 × 12)*
Main machinery: Nuclear; 1 RR PWR 2; 2 GEC turbines; 27,500 hp *(20.5 MW)*; 1 shaft; pump jet propulsor; 2 auxiliary retractable propulsion motors; 2 WH Allen turbo generators; 6 MW; 2 Paxman diesel alternators; 2,700 hp *(2 MW)*
Speed, knots: 25 dived
Complement: 135 (14 officers)

Missiles: SLBM: 16 Lockheed Trident 2 (D5) 3-stage solid fuel rocket; inertial guidance with stellar update to 12,000 km *(6,500 n miles)*; cep 90 m. Each missile can carry up to 12 warheads of (reported) selected yield up to 100 kT although, following a 1990 government decision, a maximum of 48 warheads is carried in UK SSBNs. The precise number deployed depends on prevailing circumstances.
Torpedoes: 4–21 in *(533 mm)* tubes. Marconi Spearfish; dual purpose; wire-guided; active/passive homing to 26 km *(14 n miles)* at 65 kt; or 31.5 km *(17 n miles)* at 50 kt; attack speed 55 kt; warhead 300 kg directed charge.
Countermeasures: Decoys: 3 SSE Mk 10 launchers Type 2066 and 2071 decoys.
ESM: Racal UAP 3; intercept.
Combat data systems: Alenia Marconi Systems SMCS NG.
Weapons control: Ultra Electronics Outfit DCM 4.
Radars: Navigation: Kelvin Hughes Type 1007; I-band.
Sonars: TMSL Type 2054 composite multifunctioned sonar suite includes towed array, hull-mounted active/passive search and passive intercept and ranging. Type 2081 Environmental Sensor System.

Programmes: On 15 July 1980 the decision was made to buy the US Trident I (C4) weapon system. On 11 March 1982 it was announced that the government had opted for the improved Trident II weapon system, with the D5 missile, to be deployed in a force of four submarines. *Vanguard* ordered 30 April 1986; *Victorious* 6 October 1987; *Vigilant* 13 November 1990 and *Vengeance* 7 July 1992.
Modernisation: *Vanguard* underwent LOP(R) at Devonport February 2002 to June 2005. *Victorious* started LOP(R) in April 2005 and completed in May 2008. *Vigilant* LOP(R) started in October 2008 and is to be completed in 2011. A contract for the upgrade of the inboard signal, data and display processing systems of sonar Type 2054 was let to Lockheed Martin in September 2006. The upgrade is to include open architecture processing based on the ARCI model in service in the US Navy. The first full system is to be in service in 2009. There are no plans to deploy conventional warheads on Trident or to modify launch tubes to accommodate cruise missiles. Upgrade of UAP 3 RESM is planned. Invitations to tender for the SMART programme, which is to modernise the inboard portion of the equipment, were issued in June 2006.
Structure: A new reactor core, Core H, has been fitted to *Vanguard* and *Victorious* and is to be installed in the other two boats at their LOP(R). No further reactor fuelling will be required during their service lives. The outer surface of the submarine is covered with conformal anechoic noise reduction coatings. Fitted with Pilkington Optronics CK 51 search and CH 91 attack periscopes.
Operational: Three successful submerged launched firings of the D5 missile from USS *Tennessee* in December 1989 and the US missile was first deployed operationally in March 1990. *Vanguard* started sea trials in October 1992; the first UK missile firing was on 26 May 1994 and the first operational patrol in early 1995. The eighth successful UK firing of a D5 missile was made by *Vanguard* on 10 October 2005. At least one SSBN has been at immediate readiness to fire ballistic missiles since 1969, but as a result of the Strategic Defence Review in 1998, readiness to fire has been relaxed 'to days rather than minutes'. There are no plans to phase out the two crew system. Submarines on patrol can be given secondary tasks without compromising security. Based at Faslane.

VENGEANCE ***6/2000*** / 0106676

VIGILANT ***7/2005, H M Steele*** / 1153921

VENGEANCE

6/2000 / 0106677

VENGEANCE

9/2007, B Moultrie / 1305171

AIRCRAFT CARRIERS

2 INVINCIBLE CLASS (CV)

Name	*No*	*Builders*	*Laid down*	*Launched*	*Commissioned*
ILLUSTRIOUS	R 06	Swan Hunter Shipbuilders, Wallsend	7 Oct 1976	1 Dec 1978	20 June 1982
ARK ROYAL	R 07	Swan Hunter Shipbuilders, Wallsend	14 Dec 1978	2 June 1981	1 Nov 1985

Displacement, tons: 20,600 full load
Dimensions, feet (metres): 685.8 oa; 632 wl × 118 oa; 90 wl × 26 (screws) *(209.1; 192.6 × 36; 27.5 × 8)*
Flight deck, feet (metres): 550 × 44.3 *(167.8 × 13.5)*
Main machinery: COGAG; 4 RR Olympus TM3B gas turbines; 97,200 hp *(72.5 MW)* sustained; 2 shafts
Speed, knots: 28
Range, n miles: 7,000 at 19 kt
Complement: 685 (60 officers) plus 366 (80 officers) aircrew plus up to 600 marines

Guns: 3 Signaal/General Electric 30 mm 7-barrelled Gatling Goalkeeper (R 06); 4,200 rds/min to 1.5 km.
3 General Dynamics 20 mm Phalanx Mk 15 (R 07) ❶; 6 barrels/launcher; 4,500 rds/min to 1.5 km.
2 Oerlikon/BMARC 20 mm GAM-BO1 ❷.
4 M 323 Mk 44 7.62 mm Miniguns.
Countermeasures: Decoys: Outfit DLH; 8 Sea Gnat 6-barrelled 130 mm/102 mm dispensers ❸.
ESM: Racal UAT Mod 1 ❹; intercept.
Torpedo defence: Prairie Masker noise suppression system. Type 2170 (SLQ-25A).
Combat data systems: ADAWS 20 Ed 3; Link 11 and Siemens Plessey JTIDS Link 16. JMCIS. SCOT 5 SATCOM ❺. WECDIS. AIS. CSS. BOWMAN.
Weapons control: Rademec optronic director.
Radars: Air search: Marconi/Signaal Type 1022 ❻; D-band.
Air/surface search: AMS Type 996 ❼; E/F-band.
Navigation: 2 Kelvin Hughes Type 1007 ❽; I-band.
1 Racal Decca 1008; E/F-band.
CCA: Finmeccanica SPN 720 (V)5; I/J-band
Tacan: TRN 26(M)

Fixed-wing aircraft: Tailored air group of up to 24 aircraft including: BAE Harrier GR 9A ❾.
Helicopters: Westland Merlin HM.Mk 1 ❿; Westland Sea King ASAC Mk 7. Chinook HC2. Apache AH1.

Programmes: The first of class (decommissioned in 2005), the result of many compromises, was ordered from Vickers on 17 April 1973. The order for the second ship was placed on 14 May 1976, the third in December 1978.

ARK ROYAL — *8/2008*, Maritime Photographic* / 1353550

Modernisation: In February 1994, R 06 completed modernisation which included a 12° ski ramp, space and support facilities for at least 21 aircraft, three Goalkeeper systems, Sea Gnat decoys, 996 radar, Flag and Command facilities and accommodation for an additional 120 aircrew and Flag Staff. Ski ramp was increased to 13°. Modifications to operate Harrier GR.7 were completed in both ships (R 06 – 1998 and R 07 – 2001). This included the removal of Sea Dart, increasing the flight deck area by 7 per cent (23 × 18 m) and fitting GR.7 support facilities. Both *Illustrious* (2004) and *Ark Royal* (2006) converted to undertake secondary role as LPH including the installation of additional accommodation, rework of magazines, improvement of amphibious command and control systems, including BOWMAN, and installation of the MARINARC mass escape system. TACAN and SPN 720(X) precision approach radar also fitted. Air planning spaces have also been refitted to undertake maritime strike role. Planned conversion of *Ark Royal* to replace Phalanx with Goalkeeper was cancelled.

Structure: The forward end of the flight deck (ski ramp) allows STOVL aircraft of greater all-up weight to operate more efficiently. *Illustrious* fitted with a composite third mast at the after end of the island structure to provide mountings for additional communications. She has also had substantial internal changes to accommodate troops in the LPH role. *Ark Royal* received an advanced technology mast in 2006 to house precision approach radar, 1007 radar and NEST.
Operational: The primary role of this class is to operate STOVL aircraft and helicopters. Sea Harriers were phased out in 2006 and the embarked fixed-wing air-group has migrated to an all Harrier GR. Mk 9A ground-attack force. Following a restorative docking in 2006, *Ark Royal* returned to service in 2007. *Invincible* decommissioned in 2005 and to be maintained at extended (18 months) readiness until 2010. Decommissioning dates of the other two ships are likely to be 2013 *(Ark Royal)* and 2015 *(Illustrious)*.

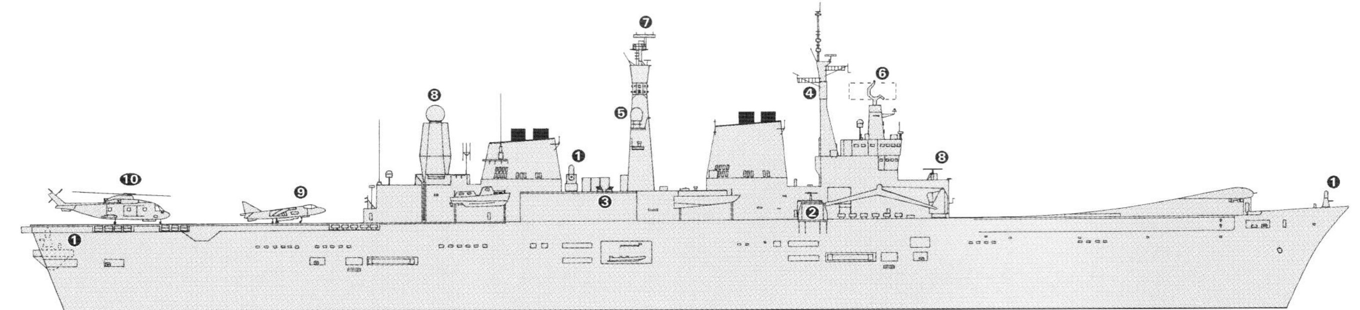

ARK ROYAL — *(Scale 1 : 1,200), Ian Sturton* / 1305265

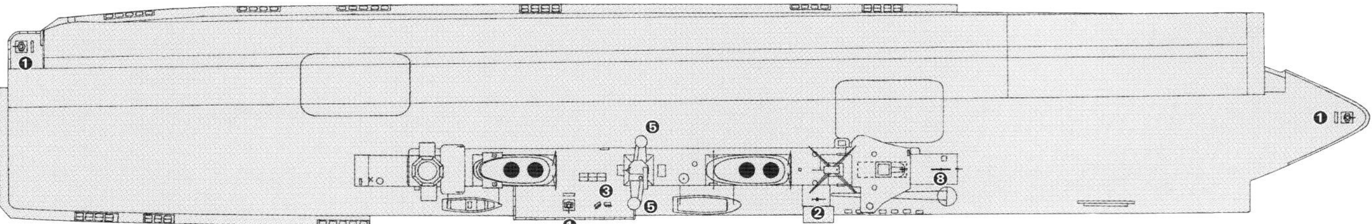

ARK ROYAL — *(Scale 1 : 1,200), Ian Sturton* / 1305264

ILLUSTRIOUS — *9/2008*, B Sullivan* / 1353549

ARK ROYAL

1/2007, B Sullivan / 1167469

ILLUSTRIOUS

9/2008*, B Sullivan / 1353548

0 + 2 QUEEN ELIZABETH CLASS (CV)

Name	*No*	*Builders*	*Laid down*	*Launched*	*Commissioned*
QUEEN ELIZABETH	–	BVT Surface Fleet Ltd/Babcock International	2009	2013	2015
PRINCE OF WALES	–	BVT Surface Fleet Ltd/Babcock International	2011	2015	2018

Displacement, tons: 66,600 full load
Dimensions, feet (metres): 931.7 × 127.9 × 32.5 *(284.0 × 39.0 × 9.9)*
Flight deck, feet (metres): 908.8 × 239.5 *(277.0 × 73.0)*
Main machinery: Integrated Full Electric Propulsion; 2 Rolls-Royce MT 30 gas turbine alternators; 93,870 hp *(70 MW)*; 4 Wärtsilä diesel generators; 53,064 hp *(39.6 MW)*; 2 induction motors; 53,640 hp *(40 MW)*; 2 shafts
Speed, knots: 26+. **Range, n miles:** To be announced
Complement: 672 (ship) + 610 (air group) + 95 (staff)

Guns: 3 General Dynamics 20 mm Phalanx ❶. 4—30 mm ❷. Miniguns.
Countermeasures: Torpedo defence: Type 2170 (SLQ-25A).
Combat data systems: BAE CMS-1. Link 16.
Weapons control: To be announced.
Radars: Air search: Thales Type 1046 (S 1850M) ❸; D-band.
Air/surface search: BAE Insyte ARTISAN ❹; 3D; E/F-band.
Navigation: To be announced ❺.
CCA: Finmeccanica SPN 720(V)5; I-band.
Tacan: To be announced.

Fixed-wing aircraft: Approximately 40: typically a mix of 30 F-35B combat aircraft, six Merlin anti-submarine aircraft and four Maritime Airborne Surveillance & Control aircraft.

Programmes: Following completion of the Demonstration Phase in 2007, it was announced on 25 July 2007 that approval (Main Gate) for the procurement of two aircraft carriers had been given. Approval for the Manufacturing Phase was announced on 20 May 2008 and, following the formation of BVT Surface Fleet Ltd (BAE Systems and VT Group joint venture) contracts for construction were signed on 3 July 2008. Construction of the ships is to be undertaken by the Aircraft Carrier Alliance (ACA) formed of BVT Surface Fleet Ltd, Thales UK, BAE Systems (Marine and Insyte), Babcock Marine and UK MoD as both client and participant. An Alliance Management Board, chaired by the UK MoD, leads and collectively manages the project; BVT Surface Fleet Ltd, is to be responsible for the integration of design, build, commissioning and acceptance of the ships; BAE Insyte has responsibility for mission systems design; Thales leads the management of the Stage 1 design of platform, power and propulsion and takes responsibility for the aviation interface. Construction and assembly of the ships is to be as follows: Blocks 3 and 4 (aft section) at BVTSF Govan; Block 2 (forward midships section) and the two superstructure islands at BVTSF Portsmouth; Block 1 (bow section) and final assembly at Babcock, Rosyth. The remaining 40 per cent of the ship (superstructure) is to be open to competition. Following a delay of up to two years to the construction programme announced on 11 December 2008, it is expected that *Queen Elizabeth* will be formally laid down in 2009. First steel was cut in December 2008.
Structure: The systems and structural design is to Lloyds Naval Ships Rules with some specific naval standards for certain equipments. Of steel construction, the principal design features include a two-island arrangement, with flight control from the after island, two deck-edge aircraft lifts and a ski-jump to operate Short Take-Off and Vertical Landing (STOVL) aircraft. Planning assumptions are that CVF is to operate the F-35B STOVL variant of the Joint Strike Fighter, the preferred choice to meet the UK Joint Combat Aircraft requirement; UK signed the MoU for the PFSD phase on 12 December 2006. The flight-deck has a single runway and ramp; five landing spots are positioned on the runway and there is a sixth spot to starboard for helicopter landings only. The design is adaptable in that it allows for the retrofit of catapults and arrestor gear at a later date if required. Other features include eight internal decks, 19 watertight sections each of which contains vertical access trunks for fire-fighting, and an integrated waste management system which is fully MARPOL compliant. Key spaces, such as the Operations Room, have been designed with reconfigurability in mind. All major machinery is controlled and monitored by an Integrated Platform Management System. Air weapons are supplied from two automated deep stores by a Highly Mechanised Weapon Handling System which uses commercial warehousing techniques. Blown Fibre Optic technology is used to connect over 850 compartments via 112 km of fibre.
Operational: To be based at Portsmouth.

CVF *7/2008*, Thales* / 1353551

CVF *9/2007, Thales* / 1167814

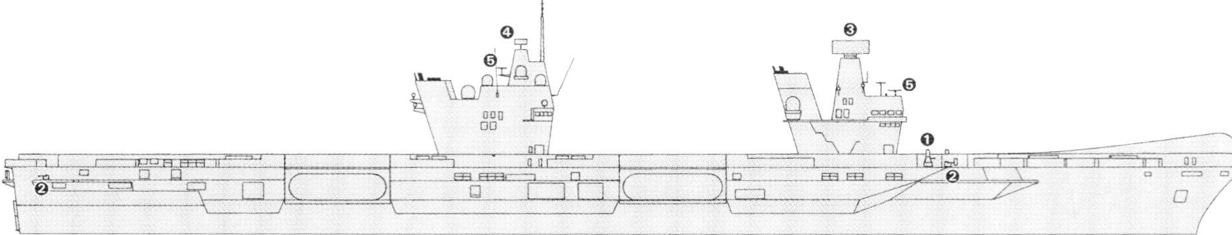
CVF *(Scale 1 : 1,800), Ian Sturton* / 1353510

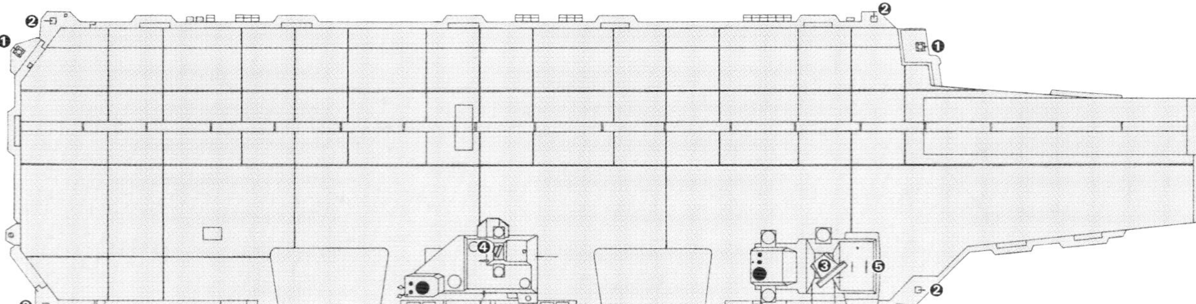
CVF *(Scale 1 : 1,800), Ian Sturton* / 1353509

DESTROYERS

Notes: *Bristol* (D 23) is an immobile tender used for training in Portsmouth Harbour.

2 TYPE 42 CLASS (BATCH 2) (DDGH)

Name	*No*	*Builders*	*Laid down*	*Launched*	*Commissioned*
NOTTINGHAM	D 91	Vosper Thornycroft, Woolston	6 Feb 1978	18 Feb 1980	14 Apr 1983
LIVERPOOL	D 92	Cammell Laird, Birkenhead	5 July 1978	25 Sep 1980	1 July 1982

Displacement, tons: 4,500 standard; 4,800 full load
Dimensions, feet (metres): 412 oa; 392 wl × 47 × 19 (screws) *(125; 119.5 × 14.3 × 5.8)*
Main machinery: COGOG; 2 RR Olympus TM3B gas turbines; 50,000 hp *(37.3 MW)* sustained; 2 RR Tyne RM1C gas turbines (cruising); 9,900 hp *(7.4 MW)* sustained; 2 shafts; cp props
Speed, knots: 29
Range, n miles: 4,000 at 18 kt
Complement: 287 (24 officers) (accommodation for 312)

Missiles: SAM: BAE Systems Sea Dart twin launcher ❶; semi-active radar guidance to 40 km *(21.5 n miles)* at 2 Mach; height envelope 100-18,300 m *(328-60,042 ft)*; 22 missiles; limited anti-ship capability.
Guns: 1 Vickers 4.5 in *(114 mm)*/55 Mk 8 ❷; 25 rds/min to 22 km *(11.9 n miles)* anti-surface; weight of shell 21 kg.
2 BMARC 20 mm GAM-BO1 ❸ or ❹; 1,000 rds/min to 2 km.
2 General Dynamics 20 mm Phalanx Mk 15 Mod 1b ❺; 6 barrels per launcher; 4,500 rds/min combined to 1.5 km.
2 M 323 Mk 44 7.62 mm Miniguns. 4 – 7.62 mm MGs.
Countermeasures: Decoys: Outfit DLH; 4 Sea Gnat 130 mm/102 mm 6-barrelled launchers ❻. Irvin DLF 3 offboard decoys.
ESM: Racal UAT Mod 1; intercept.
Torpedo defence: Type 2170 (SLQ-25A).
Combat data systems: ADAWS 20 Ed 3.1. 2 SCOT 1C (to be replaced by SCOT 1A and SCOT 5 (D 91 only) SATCOMs ❼; Link 11. JTIDS. Link 16. WECDIS. AIS. CSS. BOWMAN.
Weapons control: GWS 30 Mod 2; GSA 1 secondary system.
2 Radamec 2100 series optronic surveillance directors.
Radars: Air search: Marconi/Signaal Type 1022 ❽; D-band.
Air/surface search: AMS Type 996 ❾; E/F-band.
Navigation: Kelvin Hughes Type 1007 ❿; I-band and Racal Decca Type 1008 ⓫; E/F-band.
Fire control: 2 Marconi Type 909 ⓬; I/J-band.
Sonars: Ferranti/Thomson Type 2050 or Plessey Type 2016; hull-mounted; active search and attack; medium frequency.

TYPE 42 BATCH 2 CLASS *(Scale 1 : 1,200), Ian Sturton* / 0572736

NOTTINGHAM *7/2007, John Brodie* / 1305236

Helicopters: 1 Westland Lynx HAS 3/8 ⓭.

Programmes: Batch 1 ships decommissioned. All remaining ships Batch 2.
Modernisation: Phalanx replaced 30 mm guns in 1987–89. Batch 2 have had a command system update JTIDS (Link 16) improved ammunition.

Structure: Torpedo tubes removed.
Operational: *Birmingham* paid off in 1999, *Newcastle* and *Glasgow* in January 2005, *Cardiff* in August 2005 and *Southampton* on 12 February 2009. Decommissioning plans: *Exeter* 2009; *Nottingham* 2010; *Liverpool* 2012. Sonars not operational.

NOTTINGHAM *9/2005, Derek Fox* / 1153956

LIVERPOOL *9/2007, Shaun Jones* / 1305167

4 TYPE 42 CLASS (BATCH 3) (DDGH)

Name	*No*	*Builders*	*Laid down*	*Launched*	*Commissioned*
MANCHESTER	D 95	Vickers Shipbuilding & Engineering, Barrow-in-Furness	19 May 1978	24 Nov 1980	16 Dec 1982
GLOUCESTER	D 96	Vosper Thornycroft, Woolston	29 Oct 1979	2 Nov 1982	11 Sep 1985
EDINBURGH	D 97	Cammell Laird, Birkenhead	8 Sep 1980	14 Apr 1983	17 Dec 1985
YORK	D 98	Swan Hunter Shipbuilders, Wallsend-on-Tyne	18 Jan 1980	21 June 1982	9 Aug 1985

Displacement, tons: 4,500 standard; 5,200 full load
Dimensions, feet (metres): 462.8 oa; 434 wl × 49.9 × 19 (screws) *(141.1; 132.3 × 15.2 × 5.8)*
Main machinery: COGOG; 2 RR Olympus TM3B gas turbines; 50,000 hp *(37.3 MW)* sustained; 2 RR Tyne RM1C gas turbines (cruising); 10,680 hp *(8 MW)* sustained; 2 shafts; cp props
Speed, knots: 30+. **Range, n miles:** 4,000 at 18 kt
Complement: 287 (26 officers)

Missiles: SAM: BAE Systems Sea Dart twin launcher ❶; semi-active radar guidance to 40 km *(21 n miles)*; warhead HE; 22 missiles; limited anti-ship capability.
Guns: 1 Vickers 4.5 in *(114 mm)*/55 Mk 8 Mod 1 ❷; 25 rds/min to 27 km *(14.6 n miles)* anti-surface; weight of shell 21 kg. Mod 1 (range 33.5 km *(18.1 n miles)*) in D 97 and D 98.
2 BMARC 20 mm GAM-BO1 ❸; 1,000 rds/min to 2 km.
2 General Dynamics 20 mm Phalanx Mk 15 Mod 1b ❹; 6 barrels per launcher; 4,500 rds/min combined to 1.5 km.
2 M 323 Mk 44 7.62 mm Miniguns 4—7.62 mm MGs.
Countermeasures: Decoys: Outfit DLH; 4 Sea Gnat 130 mm/102 mm 6-barrelled launchers ❺. DLF-3 offboard decoys.
ESM: Racal UAT Mod 1; intercept.
Torpedo defence: Type 2170 (SLQ-25A).
Combat data systems: ADAWS 20 Ed 3.1 action data automation. SCOT 5 SATCOM ❻; Link 11. JTIDS. Link 16. WECDIS. AIS. CSS. BOWMAN.

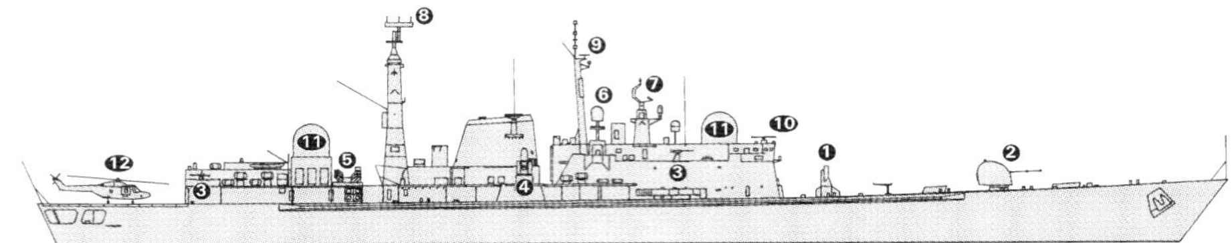

MANCHESTER *(Scale 1 : 1,200), **Ian Sturton*** / 0572735

Weapons control: GWS 30 Mod 2 (for SAM); GSA 1 secondary system. 2 Radamec 2100 series optronic surveillance directors.
Radars: Air search: Marconi/Signaal Type 1022 ❼; D-band.
Air/surface search: AMS Type 996 ❽; E/F-band.
Navigation: Kelvin Hughes Type 1007 ❾; I-band and Racal Decca Type 1008 ❿; E/F-band.
Fire control: 2 Marconi Type 909 Mod 1 ⓫; I/J-band.
Sonars: Ferranti/Thomson Type 2050 or Plessey Type 2016; hull-mounted; active search and attack.

Helicopters: 1 Westland Lynx HAS.Mk 3/8 ⓬.

Programmes: The completion of the last three ships was delayed to allow for some modifications resulting from experience in the Falklands' campaign (1982).

Modernisation: Vulcan Phalanx replaced 30 mm guns 1987–89. D 97 had a partial conversion in 1990 with the Phalanx moved forward and a protective visor fitted around the bow of the ship but reverted to the standard armament in 1994. All have had a command system update. Sea Gnat decoy launchers can fire a variety of devices. Mk 8 Mod 1 gun is being progressively fitted.
Structure: A strengthening beam has been fitted on each side which increased displacement by 50 tons and beam by 2 ft. Torpedo tubes removed. Transom flaps, to improve fuel efficiency, fitted in D 95 in 2006.
Operational: The helicopter carries the Sea Skua air-to-surface weapon for use against lightly defended surface ship targets. Sonars not operational. Decommissioning plans: *Manchester* 2011; *Gloucester* 2011; *York* 2012; *Edinburgh* 2013. Based at Portsmouth.

YORK ***11/2006, Michael Nitz*** / 1167546

EDINBURGH ***6/2006, Per Körnefeldt*** / 1167458

MANCHESTER ***5/2008*, Camil Busquets i Vilanova*** / 1353547

1 + 5 (0) DARING CLASS (TYPE 45) (DDGHM)

Name	*No*	*Builders*	*Laid down*	*Launched*	*Commissioned*
DARING	D 32	BAE Systems Marine/Vosper Thornycroft	28 Mar 2003	1 Feb 2006	Dec 2009
DAUNTLESS	D 33	BAE Systems Marine/Vosper Thornycroft	26 Aug 2004	23 Jan 2007	2010
DIAMOND	D 34	BAE Systems Marine/Vosper Thornycroft	25 Feb 2005	27 Nov 2007	2011
DRAGON	D 35	BAE Systems Marine/Vosper Thornycroft	19 Dec 2005	17 Nov 2008	2011
DEFENDER	D 36	BAE Systems Marine/Vosper Thornycroft	31 July 2006	2009	2012
DUNCAN	D 37	BAE Systems Marine/Vosper Thornycroft	26 Jan 2007	2010	2013

Displacement, tons: 5,800 standard; 7,450 full load
Dimensions, feet (metres): 500.1 oa; 462.9 wl × 69.6 × 17.4 *(152.4; 141.1 × 21.2 × 5.3)*
Main machinery: Integrated Electric Propulsion; 2 RR WR-21 gas turbine alternators; 42 MW; 2 Wärtsilä diesel generators; 4 MW; 2 motors; 40 MW; 2 shafts; fixed props
Speed, knots: 31
Range, n miles: 7,000 at 18 kt
Complement: 191 plus 41 spare

Missiles: SSM: Space for 8 Harpoon (2 quad) ❶.
SAM: 6 DCN Sylver A 50 48 cell VLS ❷ Sea Viper (GWS 45); typical mix of 32 Aster 30; active pulse doppler radar homing to 80 km *(43.2 n miles)* at 4.0 Mach; warhead 15 kg and 16 Aster 15; active pulse doppler radar homing to 30 km *(16 n miles)* at 3.0 Mach.
Guns: 1 Vickers 4.5 in *(114 mm)*/55 Mk 8 Mod 1 ❸. 25 rds/min to 27 km (14.6 n miles); weight of shell 21 kg.
2—20 mm Vulcan Phalanx Mk 15 Mod 1b (fitted for both not with) ❹. 2 REMSIG MSI DS 30A 30 mm/75; 650 rds/min to 10 km *(5.4 n miles)*; weight of shell 0.36 kg ❺.
Countermeasures: Decoys: 4 DLH (chaff, IR); DLF offboard decoys; ❻. Type 2170 torpedo defence system.
ECM: to be decided.
RESM: Thales Type UAT (mod) ❼; intercept.
CESM: to be decided.
Combat data systems: CMS-1 (based on DNA SSCS with additional AAW functions); Links 11, 16 STDL and 22. SATCOM ❽.
Weapons control: GSA 9 with 2 EOSP sensor heads (EOGCS) (based on Radamec 2500).
Radars: Air/surface search: Signaal/Marconi Type 1046 (S 1850M) ❾; D-band.
Surveillance/fire control: BAE Systems Type 1045 (Sampson) ❿; E/F-band; multifunction.
Surface search: Raytheon Type 1048 ⓫. E/F-band.
Navigation: 2 Raytheon Type 1047 ⓬; I-band.
Sonars: EDO/ULTRA MFS-7000; bow mounted; medium frequency.

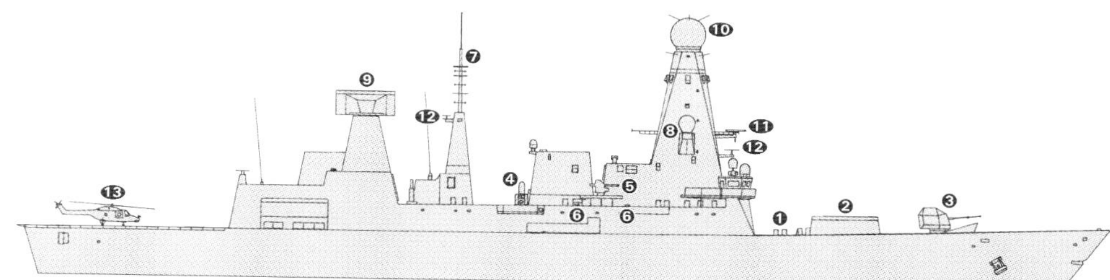

DARING

(Scale 1 : 1,200), **Ian Sturton** / 1353511

Helicopters: Lynx Mk HMA 8 (first batch) or Merlin HM.Mk 1 ⓭.

Programmes: This project has gone through many stages, the result of which has been a delay in the provision of a replacement anti-air warfare capability until 2010 and the concomitant extension of the ship-lives of the ageing Type 42s. Starting life as NFR 90 in the 1980s, it was taken forward via the Anglo-French Future Frigate, the tri-nation Common New Generation Frigate (Horizon) and finally, when UK withdrew from the collaborative ship programme on 25 April 1999, a national Type 45 ship project. The contract for the design and build of the first three ships (Batch 1) was placed with the prime contractor, BAE Systems, on 20 December 2000. This was amended in late 2001 to reflect a new procurement strategy in which commitment was made to the first six ships. The second three ships comprise Batch 2. Vosper Thornycroft is building and outfitting Blocks E/F, the forward section of each ship together with the masts and funnel. The remaining Blocks A-D are being built by BAES Surface Fleet Solutions. Final assembly of D 32 was at Scotstoun and assembly of follow-on ships is at Govan. It was announced on 19 June 2008 that plans to build two Batch 3 ships had been cancelled. Procurement of the missile system was pursued separately and a contract for full development and initial production of PAAMS (Sea Viper) was placed with the tri-national consortium, EUROPAAMS, in August 1999. Test firings are being conducted from the trials barge *Longbow* from 2008–09. System qualification is expected by the end of 2009 and the first ship-launched firing is planned from *Dauntless* in 2010.

Structure: Built to Lloyd's Naval Ship Rules. Provision for future installation of CEC, 155 mm gun or a 16-cell VLS silo, SSM, CIWS and magazine-launched torpedoes. An integrated technology mast is another potential modification. The ships are designed to support and deploy at least 30 troops. OTC facilities are to be included. The suitability of the Type 45 as a BMD platform is being studied.

Operational: Stage 1 sea trials of *Daring* were completed in September 2008 and the ship was accepted off contract on 10 December 2008. Stage 2 trials are to be conducted during 2009. *Dauntless* began sea trials in November 2008. In-service dates are likely to be about a year after commissioning dates.

DARING

7/2007, **BAE Systems** / 1167805

DARING

*5/2008**, **B Moultrie** / 1353546

FRIGATES

Notes: The Sustained Surface Combatant Capability (S2C2) study, started in 2006 by a joint MoD/industry team as a MoD 'Pathfinder' initiative, was completed in March 2007. The aim of the study was to balance the future capability and structure of the surface fleet while safeguarding the UKs long-term complex warship shipbuilding capacity. The conclusions of the study included the plan to procure a new family of ships (collectively known as the Future Surface Combatant (FSC)) to replace the Type 22 Batch 3 and Type 23 frigates and a range of minor war vessels. Reduction of whole-life costs is to be achieved by the use of common systems and equipment and open architecture technologies. Modular capabilities, particularly mine warfare, embarked military forces and unmanned vehicles will also be important features.The family is likely to include a high-capability multimission ASW and land-attack capable combatant (C1), a lower capability stabilisation combatant (C2) and an ocean-capable patrol vessel (C3). C1 and C2 would replace the Type 22 and 23 classes and may use the same generic 6,000 ton hull. C3 is likely to be of the order of 2,000 tons. The Assessment Phase (Initial Gate) is to be launched in 2009, the Demonstration and Manufacture Phase (Main Gate) in 2011 and the first of class is to enter service in 2019.

13 DUKE CLASS (TYPE 23) (FFGHM)

Name	*No*	*Builders*	*Laid down*	*Launched*	*Commissioned*
ARGYLL	F 231	Yarrow Shipbuilders, Glasgow	20 Mar 1987	8 Apr 1989	31 May 1991
LANCASTER	F 229 (ex-F 232)	Yarrow Shipbuilders, Glasgow	18 Dec 1987	24 May 1990	1 May 1992
IRON DUKE	F 234	Yarrow Shipbuilders, Glasgow	12 Dec 1988	2 Mar 1991	20 May 1993
MONMOUTH	F 235	Yarrow Shipbuilders, Glasgow	1 June 1989	23 Nov 1991	24 Sep 1993
MONTROSE	F 236	Yarrow Shipbuilders, Glasgow	1 Nov 1989	31 July 1992	2 June 1994
WESTMINSTER	F 237	Swan Hunter Shipbuilders, Wallsend-on-Tyne	18 Jan 1991	4 Feb 1992	13 May 1994
NORTHUMBERLAND	F 238	Swan Hunter Shipbuilders, Wallsend-on-Tyne	4 Apr 1991	4 Apr 1992	29 Nov 1994
RICHMOND	F 239	Swan Hunter Shipbuilders, Wallsend-on-Tyne	16 Feb 1992	6 Apr 1993	22 June 1995
SOMERSET	F 82	Yarrow Shipbuilders, Glasgow	12 Oct 1992	25 June 1994	20 Sep 1996
SUTHERLAND	F 81	Yarrow Shipbuilders, Glasgow	14 Oct 1993	9 Mar 1996	4 July 1997
KENT	F 78	Yarrow Shipbuilders, Glasgow	16 Apr 1997	27 May 1998	8 June 2000
PORTLAND	F 79	Yarrow Shipbuilders, Glasgow	14 Jan 1998	15 May 1999	3 May 2001
ST ALBANS	F 83	Yarrow Shipbuilders, Glasgow	18 Apr 1999	6 May 2000	6 June 2002

Displacement, tons: 3,500 standard; 4,200 full load
Dimensions, feet (metres): 436.2 × 52.8 × 18 (screws); 24 (sonar) *(133 × 16.1 × 5.5; 7.3)*
Main machinery: CODLAG; 2 RR Spey SM1A (F 229-F 236) or SM1C (F 237 onwards) gas turbines (see *Structure*); 31,100 hp *(23.2 MW)* sustained; 4 Paxman 12CM diesels; 8,100 hp *(6 MW)*; 2 GEC motors; 4,000 hp *(3 MW)*; 2 shafts
Speed, knots: 28; 15 on diesel-electric
Range, n miles: 7,800 miles at 15 kt
Complement: 181 (13 officers)

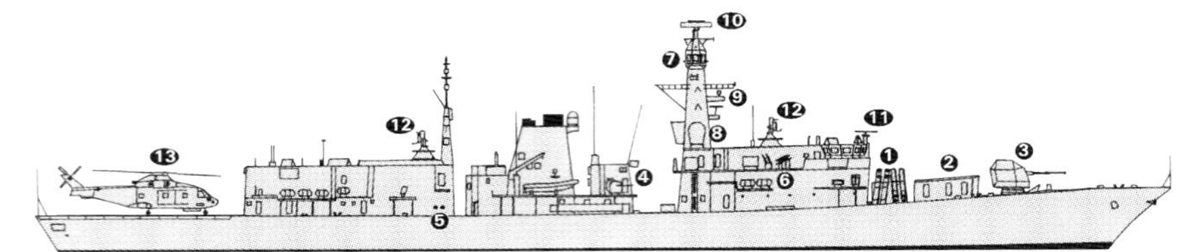

IRON DUKE *(Scale 1 : 1,200), Ian Sturton* / 0530055

PORTLAND *9/2008*, John Brodie* / 1353506

Missiles: SSM: 8 McDonnell Douglas Harpoon (2 quad) launchers ❶; active radar homing to 92 km *(50 n miles)* at 0.9 Mach; warhead 227 kg (84C). 4 normally carried.
SAM: British Aerospace Seawolf GWS 26 Mod 1 VLS ❷; command line of sight (CLOS) radar/TV tracking to 6 km *(3.3 n miles)* at 2.5 Mach; warhead 14 kg; 32 canisters.
Guns: 1 Vickers 4.5 in *(114 mm)*/55 Mk 8 ❸; 25 rds/min to 22 km *(11.9 n miles)*; 27.5 km *(14.8 n miles)* Mod 1 anti-surface; weight of shell 21 kg. Mk 8 Mod 1 being progressively fitted.
2 DES/MSI DS 30B 30 mm/75 (being replaced by 30 mm ASCG) ❹; 650 rds/min to 10 km *(5.4 n miles)* anti-surface; 3 km *(1.6 n miles)* anti-aircraft; weight of shell 0.36 kg.
2 M 323 Mk 44 7.62 mm Miniguns. 4—7.62 mm MGs.
Torpedoes: 4 Cray Marine 324 mm fixed (2 twin) tubes ❺. Marconi Stingray; active/passive homing to 11 km *(5.9 n miles)* at 45 kt; warhead 35 kg (shaped charge); depth to 750 m *(2,460 ft)*. Reload in 9 minutes.
Countermeasures: Decoys: Outfit DLH; 4 Sea Gnat 6-barrelled 130 mm/102 mm launchers ❻. DLF 2/3 offboard decoys.
Type 2170 torpedo defence system.
ESM: Racal UAT ❼; intercept.
Combat data systems: Insyte Surface Ship Command System (DNA); Link 11. 2 Matra Marconi SCOT 5 SATCOMs ❽. BOWMAN. RNCSS. WECDIS.
Weapons control: BAe GSA 8B/GPEOD optronic director ❾. GWS 60 (for SSM). GWS 26 (for SAM).
Radars: Air/surface search: Plessey Type 996(I) ❿; 3D; E/F-band.
Surface search: Racal Decca Type 1008 ⓫; E/F-band.
Navigation: Kelvin Hughes Type 1007; I-band.
Fire control: 2 Marconi Type 911 ⓬; I/Ku-band.
IFF: 1010/1011 or 1018/1019.
Sonars: Ferranti/Thomson Sintra Type 2050; bow-mounted; active search and attack.
Dowty Type 2031Z (F 229, 231, 234-236); towed array; passive search; very low frequency.
Thales Type 2087 (F 237, 238, 239, 82, 83, 81); active low-frequency (500 Hz) towed body with passive array (100 Hz).

Helicopters: 1 Westland Lynx HMA 3/8 or 1 Merlin HM 1 (Sonar 2087 fitted ships) ⓭.

Programmes: The first of this class was ordered from Yarrows on 29 October 1984. Further batches of three ordered in September 1986, July 1988, December 1989, January 1992 and February 1996. Further orders are unlikely. F 229 pennant number changed, because 232 was considered unlucky, as it is the RN report form number for collisions and groundings.
Modernisation: Major improvement programmes are in progress. The Command System has been upgraded to Phase 5 and DNA(2) is to be progressively installed from 2009 (F 236 first ship).The Mk 8 Mod 1 gun is to be installed in the whole class by 2009. Modifications to improve the performance of Type 966 radar are being made and 996 radar is to be replaced by BAE Insyte ARTISAN 3D radar 2010–14. The Seawolf system is being upgraded from 2008–2014; F 81 is the first ship to be upgraded, enhancements include improved I-band radar, an additional optronic tracker to improve low level performance and improved software. In a separate contract the Mk 4 SWELL (Seawolf Enhanced Low Level) fuze is being incorporated into existing rounds and in Block 2 missiles. Surface Ship Torpedo Defence, a development of Sonar 2070, is being fitted. Low Frequency Active Sonar (Type 2087) is replacing Type 2031 in eight ships. F 237, F 238, F 239, F82, F 83 and F 81 have been fitted. F 78 and F 79 are to follow in 2010. Trial launch and recovery of a Scan Eagle UAV were conducted in March 2006. The 30 mm gun is being replaced by the MSI Automated Small Calibre Gun (ASCG) from 2008 (F 82 first to be fitted).
Structure: Incorporates stealth technology to minimise acoustic, magnetic, radar and IR signatures. The design includes a 7° slope to all vertical surfaces, rounded edges, reduction of IR emissions and a hull bubble system to reduce radiated noise. The combined diesel electric and GT propulsion system provides quiet motive power during towed sonar operations. The SM1C engines although capable of 41 MW of power combined are constrained by output into the gearbox. MacTaggart Scott Helios helo landing system. PRISM enhanced helicopter landing and handling system being fitted to all except F 231.
Operational: F 78, F 83, F 229, F 234, F 237 and F 239 are based at Portsmouth and the remainder, at Devonport. *Norfolk* and *Marlborough* decommissioned in 2005 and *Grafton* in March 2006. All three ships have been sold to Chile. Further decommissionings are not planned to start until 2023, thereby extending ship-life to up to 35 years. ASW trials to test and prove Sonar 2087 and the Merlin helicopter were conducted in the Indian Ocean during 2008.

KENT *8/2008*, Junichi Hayashi* / 1353507

SOMERSET *6/2008*, Giorgio Ghiglione* / 1353508

LANCASTER *11/2008*, Guy Toremans* / 1353543

IRON DUKE *3/2008*, B Sullivan* / 1353542

4 BROADSWORD CLASS (TYPE 22 BATCH 3) (FFGHM)

Name	*No*	*Builders*	*Laid down*	*Launched*	*Commissioned*
CORNWALL	F 99	Yarrow Shipbuilders, Glasgow	14 Dec 1983	14 Oct 1985	23 Apr 1988
CUMBERLAND	F 85	Yarrow Shipbuilders, Glasgow	12 Oct 1984	21 June 1986	10 June 1989
CAMPBELTOWN	F 86	Cammell Laird, Birkenhead	4 Dec 1985	7 Oct 1987	27 May 1989
CHATHAM	F 87	Swan Hunter Shipbuilders, Wallsend-on-Tyne	12 May 1986	20 Jan 1988	4 May 1990

Displacement, tons: 4,200 standard; 4,900 full load
Dimensions, feet (metres): 485.9 × 48.5 × 21 (*148.1 × 14.8 × 6.4*)
Main machinery: COGAG; 2 RR Spey SM1A gas turbines; 29,500 hp (*22 MW*) sustained; 2 RR Tyne RM3C gas turbines; 10,680 hp (*8 MW*) sustained; 2 shafts; LIPS cp props
Speed, knots: 30; 18 on Tynes
Range, n miles: 4,500 at 18 kt on Tynes
Complement: 250 (31 officers) (accommodation for 301)

Missiles: SSM: 8 McDonnell Douglas Harpoon Block 1C (2 quad) launchers ❶; preprogrammed; active radar homing to 92 km (*50 n miles*) at 0.9 Mach; warhead 227 kg.
SAM: 2 British Aerospace Seawolf GWS 25 Mod 3 ❷; command line of sight (CLOS) with 2 channel radar tracking to 5 km (*2.7 n miles*) at 2+ Mach; warhead 14 kg.
Guns: 1 Vickers 4.5 in (*114 mm*)/55 Mk 8 ❸; 25 rds/min to 22 km (*11.9 n miles*); 27 km (*14.6 n miles*) Mod 1 anti-surface; weight of shell 21 kg.
1 Signaal/General Electric 30 mm 7-barrelled Goalkeeper ❹; 4,200 rds/min combined to 1.5 km.
2 GAM-BO1-1 20 mm ❺; 700-900 rds/min to 1 km.
2 M 323 Mk 44 7.62 mm Miniguns. 4—7.62 mm MGs.
Countermeasures: Decoys: Outfit DLH; 4 Sea Gnat 6-barrelled 130 mm/102 mm fixed launchers ❻. DLF offboard decoys.
Type 2170 torpedo defence system.
RESM: Racal UAT; intercept.
CESM: CoBLU; intercept.

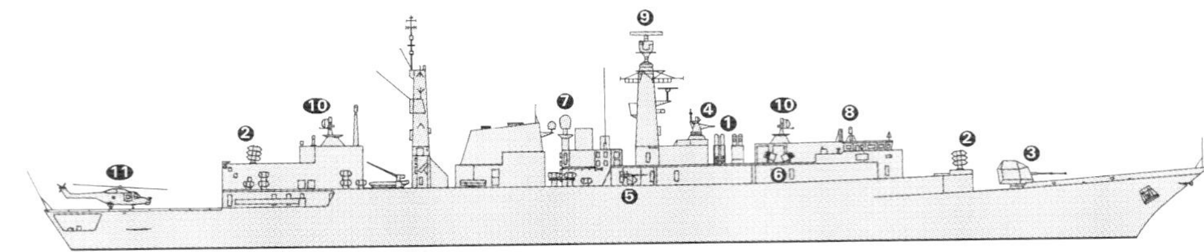

CORNWALL (*Scale 1 : 1,200*), *Ian Sturton* / 0572734

Combat data systems: CACS 5 action data automation; Link 11. 2 Matra Marconi SCOT 5 SATCOMs ❼. ICS-3 integrated comms. INMARSAT. BOWMAN. RNCSS. WECDIS.
Weapons control: 2 BAe GSA 8B GPEOD Sea Archer optronic directors with TV and IR imaging and laser rangefinders ❽. GWS 25 Mod 3 (for SAM). GWS 60.
Radars: Air/surface search: Marconi Type 967/968 ❾; D/E-band.
Navigation: Kelvin Hughes Type 1007; I-band.
Fire control: 2 Marconi Type 911 ❿; I/Ku-band (for Seawolf).
Sonars: Ferranti/Thomson Sintra Type 2050; hull-mounted; active search and attack.

Helicopters: 2 Westland Lynx HMA. Mk 3/8 ⓫.

Modernisation: A major upgrade to the Seawolf system is being implemented; starting with F 86 in 2009, a rolling installation programme is planned to be completed by 2012. Enhancements include an improved I-band radar, an additional optronic tracker to improve low level performance and improved software. In a separate contract, the Mk 4 SWELL (Seawolf Enhanced Low Level) fuze is being incorporated into existing rounds and in Block 2 missiles. Mk 8 Mod 1 gun is being progressively fitted to the class. Replacement of the CESM system (Project Shaman) is under consideration.
Structure: Batch 3 are stretched versions of original Batch 1. Flight decks enlarged to operate Sea King helicopters.
Operational: This class is primarily designed for ASW operations and is capable of acting as OTC. All have facilities for Flag and staff. One Lynx normally embarked. All are based at Devonport. Decommissioning plans: *Cornwall* 2019; *Campbeltown* 2020; *Cumberland* 2021; *Chatham* 2022.
Sales: All Batch 1 to Brazil. Batch 2 ships *London* and *Coventry* to Romania and *Sheffield* to Chile.

CHATHAM *3/2008*, B Sullivan* / 1353545

CAMBELTOWN *3/2008*, Michael Nitz* / 1353544

CORNWALL *4/2008*, John Brodie* / 1353505

SHIPBORNE AIRCRAFT

Notes: (1) The F-35B STOVL (Short Take-Off and Vertical Landing) variant of the Lockheed Martin Lightning II Joint Strike Fighter selected on 30 September 2002 to fulfil the Joint Combat Aircraft (JCA) requirement. The aircraft is to replace the RAF/RN aircraft operated by the Joint Force Harrier for operation both from the future carriers and from landbases. There are 138 aircraft planned, first delivery of which is expected to meet an in-service date of 2017. UK signed an MoU to begin full cooperation in the Production, Sustainment and Follow-on Development (PFSD) phase on 12 December 2006. The maiden flight of the F-35B took place on 11 June 2008 and the first full STOVL test is expected in 2009.
(2) Following the withdrawal from service of Sea Harrier, the Harrier force has migrated to an all GR force. 65 GR.7 and GR.7A and nine T.10 aircraft to receive an avionics and weapons upgrade to GR.9/GR.9A/T.12 standard by late 2009.
(3) A programme to replace the current organic airborne early-warning capability in 2012 is in progress. Initial Gate for The Maritime Airborne Surveillance and Control (MASC) programme was passed in July 2005 with Main Gate decisions to follow in 2009. Potential solutions are likely to be based on rotary-wing platforms and UAVs. The V-22 Osprey is a futher option.
(4) AgustaWestland Future Lynx selected on 27 March 2005 as preferred option to meet the requirement for the Maritime (Surface) Attack Helicopter. Entry into service is expected in 2015. Overall naval numbers are expected to be of the order of 28.
(5) Dauphin 2 helicopters with Royal Naval markings are leased by FOST for staff transfers.
(6) Proposals for a maritime version of the Chinook medium-lift helicopter were formalised in September 2004 with the launch of a three-year assessment phase.

DAUPHIN 2 *9/2008*, Ian Harris* / 1353541

Numbers/Type: 40 British Aerospace Harrier GR.7A/9A.
Operational speed: 575 kt *(1,065 km/h).*
Service ceiling: 45,000 ft *(13,716 m).*
Range: 594 n miles *(1,101 km).*
Role/Weapon systems: RAF all weather single-seat close support, battlefield interdiction night attack and reconnaissance aircraft, first operated from HMS *Illustrious* in 1994. All GR.7A (with upgraded engines) are being upgraded to GR.9A standard by late 2009. Sensors: FLIR, TIALD, Joint Recce pod, SNIPER Advanced Targeting Pod, ESM, ECM, chaff dispensers and BOL IR. Weapons: AAM; 2 or 4 AIM-9L Sidewinder ASRAAM CRV7. Ground attack: 'iron' bombs, Paveway II LGB, Paveway III LGB, Paveway IV Precision guided bomb, Maverick IR and TV, Brimstone advanced anti-armour weapon system.

HARRIER GR. 7A *6/2004, Royal Navy* / 1043610

Numbers/Type: 42 Westland/Agusta Merlin HM Mk 1.
Operational speed: 150 kt *(277 km/h).*
Service ceiling: 10,000 ft *(3,048 m).*
Range: 550 n miles *(1,019 km).*
Role/Weapon systems: Primary anti-submarine role with secondary anti-surface and troop-carrying capabilities. Contract for 44 signed 9 October 1991. In service with 814, 820, 824 and 829 Squadrons. A contract for a Capability Sustainment Programme (CSP) was awarded to Lockheed Martin UK on 21 December 2005. There are to be 30 (with an option for a further eight) aircraft upgraded from 2010 with the first modernised aircraft to enter service in 2013. CSP features include: upgrades to the sonar, radar, aircraft and tactical management systems and other key avionics systems. Sensors: GEC-Marconi Blue Kestrel 5000 radar, Thales Flash AQS 950 dipping sonar, GEC-Marconi sonobuoy acoustic processor AQS-903A, Thales Orange Reaper ESM, ECM. Link 11. Weapons: ASW; four Stingray torpedoes or Mk 11 Mod 3 depth bombs. ASV; OTHT for ship-launched SSM.

MERLIN HM MK 1 *1/2008*, Shaun Jones* / 1305161

Numbers/Type: 22/6 Westland/Agusta Merlin HC Mk 3/Merlin HC Mk 3A.
Operational speed: 150 kt *(277 km/h).*
Service ceiling: 13,125 ft *(4,000 m).*
Range: 550 n miles *(1,019 km).*
Role/Weapon systems: Operated by RAF. Roles include cargo and troop transport and combat SAR. Military lift is 24 troops and up to four tonnes underslung. Sensors: integrated defensive aids including Raytheon laser detection, BAE Systems Sky Guardian 2000 RWR, Doppler-based MAWS, Northrop Grumman AN/AAQ-24 Nemesis DIRCM and BAE Systems North America AN/ALE-47 chaff/flare dispensers. Weapons: machine guns.

MERLIN Mk 3 *6/2003, Paul Jackson* / 0572697

Numbers/Type: 15 Westland Sea King HU Mk 5.
Operational speed: 112 kt *(207 km/h).*
Service ceiling: 10,000 ft *(3,050 m).*
Range: 400 n miles *(740 km).*
Role/Weapon systems: Sea King HU Mk 5 is primary SAR platform and utilises night vision goggles for overland and oversea operations. Sensors: Sea Searcher radar, Orange Crop ESM (Mk 6 only). Weapons: The Mk 5 can be fitted with 7.62 mm MGs.

SEA KING HU MK 5 *8/2007, B Sullivan* / 1305160

Numbers/Type: 34/34 Westland Lynx HAS 3/Lynx HMA 8.
Operational speed: 120 kt *(222 km/h).*
Service ceiling: 10,000 ft *(3,048 m).*
Range: 320 n miles *(593 km).*
Role/Weapon systems: Primary role anti-surface warfare with capability to carry a variety of weapons. Embarked in a number of RN and RFA ships. All HMA Mk 8 variants to be upgraded with Saturn-capable radios by mid-2010. Sensors: Ferranti Sea Spray Radar, Orange Crop ESM, Sea Owl PID (Mk 8 only), Missile Approach Warner (Mk 8 only), IR Jammer (Mk 8 only) and flare dispenser (Mk 8 only). Weapons: Up to four Sea Skua missiles, two Stingray torpedoes, Mk 11 depth charge, M3M 0.5 in CL Cabin mounted Heavy Machine Gun.

LYNX HMA 8 *7/2008*, B Sullivan* / 1353540

LYNX HAS 3 *4/2007, Maritime Photographic* / 1305159

Numbers/Type: 13 Westland Sea King ASAC Mk 7.
Operational speed: 90 kt *(167 km/h)*.
Service ceiling: 10,000 ft *(3,050 m)*.
Range: 400 n miles *(740 km)*.
Role/Weapon systems: Primary role Airborne Surveillance and Control (ASaC) for maritime strike, littoral manoeuvre and force protection operations. Conversion contract awarded in October 1996 to upgrade AEW Mk 2 Fleet to ASAC Mk 7. Programme completed mid-2004. Two aircraft lost in Iraq conflict have been replaced by conversion of two ex-Mk 6 aircraft. Sensors: Thales Searchwater 2000, Racal MIR-2 'Orange Crop' ESM, IFF Mk XII, Litton 100 g navigation system and JTIDS/Link 16. Weapons: None.

SEA KING ASAC MK 7 *7/2008*, B Sullivan* / 1353539

Numbers/Type: 37 Westland Sea King HC Mk 4.
Operational speed: 112 kt *(208 km/h)*.
Service ceiling: 10,000 ft *(3,050 m)*.
Range: 664 n miles *(1,230 km)*.
Role/Weapon systems: Commando support helicopters capable of carrying most Commando Force equipment either internally or underslung. Current out of service date 2012. A Mk 4 Life Extension Programme, due for approval in 2009, would extend this date to 2018. Engines have been upgraded since 2003 to improve hot weather performance. In addition to Mk 4 aircraft, six HAS 6 ASW aircraft were converted to Mk 6C Commando configuration to provide temporary backfill during the HUMS modification programme. Sensors: AAR-47 ESM; IR jammer, chaff and IR flares ECM. Weapons: Can fit 7.62 mm GPMG or similar.

SEA KING HC MK 4 *8/2004, B Sullivan* / 1043561

Numbers/Type: 67 Westland/Boeing WAH-64D AH Mk 1.
Operational speed: 150 kt *(278 km/h)*.
Service ceiling: 21,000 ft *(6,400 m)*.
Range: 260 n miles *(480 km)*.
Role/Weapon systems: Agusta Westland selected on 13 July 1995 to build UK AH Mk 1 based on AH-64D Longbow Boeing Apache. All-weather attack helicopter with day and night capability. One squadron of 6 earmarked for amphibious operations. Operable from surface ships (CVS/LPH/LPD/LSL). Initial operational capability achieved in late 2005. Sensors: Lockheed Martin/Northrop Grumman AN/APG-78 Longbow radar, Lockheed Martin Target Acquisition and Designation Sight (TV and direct view) and Pilot's Night Vision FLIR sensor (TADS/PNVS) (being upgraded to M-TADS/MPNVS 2008–10), Selex SAS HIDAS helicopter integrated defensive aids system, including Sky Guardian 2000 RWR, Type 1223 Laser warning receiver, Thales (Vinten) Vicon 78 Srs 455 chaff/flare dispenser, BAE Systems AN/AAR-57(V) common missile warning system (CMWS) and Lockheed Martin AN/APR-48A radar frequency interferometer. Weapons: 16 Hellfire missiles or 76 CRV-7 70 mm rockets. 1—30 mm chain gun.

APACHE AH MK 1 *3/2004, Royal Navy* / 1153998

Numbers/Type: 6 Westland Lynx AH Mk 7.
Operational speed: 140 kt *(259 km/h)*.
Service ceiling: 10,600 ft *(3,230 m)*.
Range: 340 n miles *(630 km)*.
Role/Weapon systems: Military general purpose with 847 Squadron. Weapons: Heavy and light machine guns.

LYNX AH MK 7 *7/2005, Maritime Photographic* / 1153996

Numbers/Type: 34/6/8 Boeing Chinook HC Mk 2/Chinook HC Mk 2A/Chinook HC Mk 3.
Operational speed: 140 kt *(259 km/h)*.
Service ceiling: 10,140 ft *(3,090 m)*.
Range: 651 n miles *(1,207 km)*.
Role/Weapon systems: All-weather heavy-lift helicopter equivalent to CH-47D and operated by RAF. Operable from surface ships (CVS/LPH/LPD/LSL). Mk 2/2A capable of carrying 44 fully equipped troops or 54 light fighting order troops and up to 10 tonnes cargo. The Mk 3 was to be a Special Forces version but is now to enter service in 2009 in a support helicopter role. Sensors: defensive aids suite including missile approach warning, IR jammers and chaff/flare dispensers. Weapons: machine guns.

CHINOOK *6/2004, Royal Navy* / 1043609

LAND-BASED MARITIME AIRCRAFT (FRONT LINE)

Notes: Training and Liaison aircraft not listed include four Jetstream, Falcon 20 (under contract) and 16 Hawk (FRADU).

FALCON 20 *6/2005, Paul Jackson* / 1153997

Numbers/Type: 15 Hawker Siddeley Nimrod MR 2P/4.
Operational speed: 400 kt *(741 km/h)*.
Service ceiling: 42,000 ft *(12,800 m)*.
Range: 5,000 n miles *(9,265 km)*.
Role/Weapon systems: Maritime patrol aircraft with focus on ASW, ASUW and SAR; Nimrod can also support OTHT and C^3I at long range from shore bases. Following years of development and the first flight of MRA 4 prototype in 2004, the contract for production of 9 MRA 4 (with option to complete three development aircraft to production standard) was awarded to BAE Systems on 18 July 2006. To enter service from 2010. MRA 4 equipment includes Thales Searchwater 2000MR radar, Elta EL-8300 ESM. Ultra/GDC AQS 970 acoustics, CAE MAD, Ultra Sonobuoys and Northrop-Grumman Night Hunter EO turret. MR 2 equipment comprises Thales Searchwater radar, ECM, Yellowgate ESM, cameras, CAE MAD, Ultra sonobuoys, Ultra/GDC AQS 971 acoustics suite, WESCAM EO system, cameras. MR 2 weapons: ASW; 6.1 tons of Stingray torpedoes. Self-defence; four AIM-9L Sidewinder. MRA 4 has additional wing hard-points and Mil-Std wiring to carry greater range of external stores.

NIMROD MR 2 *6/2005, Michael Winter* / 1153949

NIMROD MRA 4 *8/2004, BAE Systems* / 0577851

Numbers/Type: 7 Boeing E-3D Sentry AEW Mk 1.
Operational speed: 460 kt *(853 km/h).*
Service ceiling: 36,000 ft *(10,973 m).*
Range: 870 n miles *(1,610 km).*
Role/Weapon systems: Airborne warning and control system aircraft with secondary role to provide coastal AEW for the Fleet; 6 hours endurance at the range given above. Sensors: Westinghouse APY-2 surveillance radar, Bendix weather radar, Mk XII IFF, Yellow Gate, ESM, ECM. Weapons: Unarmed.

E-3D ***10/2001, Ships of the World*** / 0131206

PATROL FORCES

Notes: It is planned to replace the 16 Archer class training craft (two are based in Cyprus for patrol duties) and two Halmatic M 160 craft, based at Gibraltar, with a single class of patrol craft capable of undertaking patrol, force-protection and training roles.

1 ANTARCTIC PATROL SHIP (AGOBH)

Name	*No*	*Builders*	*Commissioned*
ENDURANCE (ex-*Polar Circle*)	A 171 (ex-A 176)	Ulstein Hatlo, Norway	21 Nov 1991

Displacement, tons: 6,500 full load
Dimensions, feet (metres): 298.6 × 57.4 × 27.9 *(91 × 17.9 × 8.5)*
Main machinery: 2 Bergen BRM8 diesels, 8,160 hp(m) *(6 MW)* sustained; 1 shaft; cp prop; bow and stern thrusters
Speed, knots: 16
Range, n miles: 6,500 at 12 kt
Complement: 112 (15 officers) plus 14 Royal Marines
Radars: Surface search: Raytheon R 84 and M 34 ARG; E/F- and I-bands
Navigation: Kelvin Hughes Type 1007; I-band.
IFF: Type 1011.
Helicopters: 2 Westland Lynx HAS.Mk 3.

Comment: Leased initially in late 1991 and then bought outright in early 1992 as support ship and guard vessel for the British Antarctic Survey. Hull is painted red. Inmarsat fitted. Main machinery is resiliently mounted. Ice-strengthened hull capable of breaking 1 m thick ice at 3 kt. Helicopter hangar is reached by lift from the flight deck. Equipped with Simrad EM 710 multibeam echo-sounder, Simrad EA 600 single-beam echo-sounder and Furuno CH 250 forward looking echo-sounder. Carries two Survey Motor Boats (*James Caird* and *Nimrod*). Based at Portsmouth.

ENDURANCE ***11/2007, Ian Harris*** / 1170277

2 SCIMITAR CLASS (PATROL CRAFT) (PB)

SCIMITAR (ex-Grey Fox) P 284 **SABRE** (ex-Grey Wolf) P 285

Displacement, tons: 26 full load
Dimensions, feet (metres): 52.5 × 14.43 × 3.9 *(16 × 4.4 × 1.2)*
Main machinery: 2 MAN V10 diesels; 740 hp *(603 kW)*; 2 shafts
Speed, knots: 32. **Range, n miles:** 260 at 19 kt
Complement: 5
Guns: 2—7.62 mm MGs.
Radars: Racal Decca Bridgemaster 360; I-band.

Comment: Halmatic M160 craft operated in Northern Ireland from 1988 but transferred to Gibraltar in September 2002 to augment the Gibraltar squadron. Both vessels renamed and commissioned on 31 January 2003. After mid-life refit and design modifications, the vessels replaced *Trumpeter* and *Ranger* as Gibraltar guard ships in 2004.

SABRE ***2/2008*, Maritime Photographic*** / 1353538

16 ARCHER CLASS (PATROL CRAFT) (PB/AXL)

EXPRESS P 163 (ex-A 163)
EXPLORER P 164 (ex-A 154)
EXAMPLE P 165 (ex-A 153)
EXPLOIT P 167 (ex-A 167)
ARCHER P 264
BITER P 270
SMITER P 272
PURSUER P 273
TRACKER P 274
RAIDER P 275
BLAZER P 279
DASHER P 280
PUNCHER P 291
CHARGER P 292
RANGER P 293
TRUMPETER P 294

Displacement, tons: 54 full load
Dimensions, feet (metres): 68.2 × 19 × 5.9 *(20.8 × 5.8 × 1.8)*
Main machinery: 2 RR CV 12 M800T diesels; 1,590 hp *(1.19 MW)*; or 2 MTU diesels; 2,000 hp(m) *(1.47 MW)* (P 274-275); 2 shafts
Speed, knots: 22 or 25 (P 274-275)
Range, n miles: 550 at 15 kt
Complement: 5 (1 officer) plus 12 trainees
Guns: 2—7.62 mm MGs.
Radars: Navigation: Racal Decca 1216; I-band.

Comment: First 14 ordered from Watercraft Ltd, Shoreham. Commissioning dates: *Archer*, August 1985; *Example*, September 1985; *Explorer*, January 1986; *Biter* and *Smiter*, February 1986. The remaining nine were incomplete when Watercraft went into liquidation in 1986 and were towed to Portsmouth for completion in 1988 by Vosper Thornycroft. Initially allocated for RNR training but underused in that role and now employed as part of First Patrol Boat Squadron as training vessels for the University Royal Naval Units (URNU)- *Ranger* (Sussex), *Trumpeter* (Bristol), *Puncher* (London), *Blazer* (Southampton), *Smiter* (Glasgow), *Charger* (Liverpool), *Archer* (Aberdeen), *Biter* (Manchester and Salford), *Exploit* (Birmingham), *Express* (Wales), *Example* (Northumbria) and *Explorer* (Yorkshire). Two more ordered from BMT in early 1997 to a modified design and built at Ailsa, Troon. *Tracker* and *Raider* commissioned January 1998 for Oxford and Cambridge University respectively. *Dasher* and *Pursuer* are based at Cyprus.

RANGER ***5/2008*, Maritime Photographic*** / 1353523

EXAMPLE ***6/2008*, J Marechal*** / 1353522

3 RIVER CLASS (OFFSHORE PATROL VESSELS) (PSO)

Name	*No*	*Builders*	*Commissioned*
TYNE	P 281	Vosper Thornycroft, Woolston	4 July 2003
SEVERN	P 282	Vosper Thornycroft, Woolston	31 July 2003
MERSEY	P 283	Vosper Thornycroft, Woolston	26 Mar 2004

Displacement, tons: 1,700 full load
Dimensions, feet (metres): 261.7 × 44.6 × 12.5 *(79.75 × 13.6 × 3.8)*
Main machinery: 2 MAN 12RK 270 diesels; 11,063 hp *(8.25 MW)*; 2 shafts; bow thruster; 375 hp *(280 kW)*
Speed, knots: 20
Range, n miles: 5,500 at 15 kt
Complement: 30 (plus 18 boarding party)
Guns: 1—20 mm Oerlikon/BMARC. 2—7.62 mm MGs.
Radars: Surface search: Kelvin Hughes Nucleus; E/F-band.
Navigation: Kelvin Hughes Nucleus; I-band.
Helicopters: Vertrep only.

Programmes: In the first agreement of its kind, Vosper Thornycroft contracted on 8 May 2001 for the construction, lease and support of three vessels over initial five-year period to replace five ships of Island class. The lease was extended by a further five years in December 2006.
Structure: Based on Vosper Thornycroft EEZ Management Vessel concept design. The ships are capable of operating two RIBs. Fitted with a 3 tonne crane.
Operational: Part of Fishery Protection Squadron based at Portsmouth.

MERSEY ***2/2008*, Maritime Photographic*** / 1353537

1 MODIFIED RIVER CLASS (OFFSHORE PATROL VESSEL) (PSOH)

Name	*No*	*Builders*	*Launched*	*Commissioned*
CLYDE	P 257	VT Shipbuilding, Portsmouth	12 June 2006	30 Jan 2007

Displacement, tons: 1,847 full load
Dimensions, feet (metres): 267.4 × 44.6 × 12.5 *(81.5 × 13.6 × 3.8)*
Main machinery: 2 MAN 12RK diesels; 11,063 hp *(8.25 MW)*; 2 shafts; bow thruster; 375 hp *(280 kW)*; stern thruster; 248 hp *(185 kW)*
Speed, knots: 20
Range, n miles: 7,800 at 12 kt
Complement: 38 (plus 18 boarding party). Accommodation for 59
Guns: 1 DES/MSI DS 30B 30 mm; 650 rds/min to 10 km *(5.4 n miles)*; weight of shell 0.36 kg.
2 M323 Mk 44 7.62 mm Miniguns.
4—12.7 mm MGs.
Combat data systems: BAE Insyte CMS-1.
Radars: Surface search and navigation: Terma Scanter 4100; E/F/I-bands.
Helicopters: Platform for one Merlin-sized.

Comment: Contract let with VT Shipbuilding on the 28 February 2005 to build a modified River class to undertake Falkland Islands patrol duties. The ship is leased to the MoD with a Contractor Logistic Support (CLS) arrangement until 2012. The ship has been built to commercial standards with some military features. Following acceptance in January 2007, the ship assumed its role as Falkland Islands Guardship on 20 September 2007.

CLYDE *9/2007, Mario R V Carneiro* / 1353502

AMPHIBIOUS FORCES

Notes: (1) Further amphibious ships and craft covered in Auxiliaries and Army sections. These include a Helicopter Support Ship, four LSD, and six LCLs.
(2) QinetiQ awarded a contract in November 2006 to design, build, test and evaluate the Partial Air Cushion Supported Catamaran (PACSCAT) for littoral manoeuvre operations. The craft is a contender to fulfil the requirement for a Fast Landing Craft to enter service from about 2014. Such a craft, interoperable with amphibious ships, would be capable of carrying a payload of 55 tonnes at 25 kt. A class of up to six vessels is required.

1 HELICOPTER CARRIER (LPH)

Name	*No*	*Builders*	*Laid down*	*Launched*	*Commissioned*
OCEAN	L 12	Vickers Shipbuilding/Kvaerner Govan	30 May 1994	11 Oct 1995	30 Sep 1998

Displacement, tons: 21,758 full load
Dimensions, feet (metres): 667.3 oa; 652.2 pp × 112.9 × 21.3 *(203.4; 198.8 × 34.4 × 6.6)*
Flight deck, feet (metres): 557.7 × 104 *(170 × 31.7)*
Main machinery: 2 Crossley Pielstick 12 PC2.6 V 400 diesels; 18,360 hp(m) *(13.5 MW)* sustained; 2 shafts; Kamewa fp props; bow thruster; 612 hp *(450 kW)*
Speed, knots: 19
Range, n miles: 8,000 at 15 kt
Complement: 285 plus 206 aircrew plus up to 830 Marines
Military lift: 4 LCVP Mk 5 (on davits); 2 Griffon hovercraft; 40 vehicles and equipment for most of a marine commando unit

Guns: 8 BMARC 20 mm GAM-B03 (4 twin) ❶. 650 rds/min to 10 km *(5.4 n miles)* anti-surface; 3 km *(1.6 n miles)* anti-aircraft; weight of shell 0.36 kg.
3 General Dynamics 20 mm Phalanx Mk 15 ❷. 6 barrels per launcher; 4,500 rds/min combined to 1.5 km. 4 M323 Mk 44 7.62 mm Miniguns. 4—7.62 mm MGs.
Countermeasures: Decoys: Outfit DLH; 8 Sea Gnat 130 mm/102 mm launchers ❸.
ESM: Racal UAT Mod 1; intercept.
Torpedo defence: Type 2170 (SLQ-25A).
Combat data systems: Ferranti ADAWS 20 Ed 3.1; Link 11, Link 16; Marconi Matra SCOT 5 SATCOM ❹. BOWMAN.
Radars: Air/surface search: AMS Type 996 ❺; E/F-band.
Surface search: Racal Decca 1008 ❻; E/F-band.
Surface search/aircraft control: 2 Kelvin Hughes Type 1007 ❼; I-band.
IFF: Type 1016/1017.

Helicopters: 12 Sea King HC.Mk 4/Merlin plus 6 Lynx (or WAH-64 Apache by 2005).

Programmes: Initial invitations to tender were issued in 1987. Tenders submitted in July 1989 were allowed to lapse and it was not until 11 May 1993 that a contract was placed. The hull was built on the Clyde by Kvaerner Govan and sailed under its own power to Vickers at Barrow in November 1996 for the installation of military equipment.
Modernisation: Command and control facilities upgraded in 2002 to facilitate UKMCC role. Attack helicopter infrastructure fitted 2004–05. The davits had been replaced by 2007 and BOWMAN installed to support amphibious warfare staffs. Replacement of the combat data system is expected in 2015 and MIDAS EW system in due course. BAE Insyte ARTISAN radar is to replace 996 radar. Further improvements to attack helicopter facilities, troop accommodation and storage areas made in refit 2007–08. Larger sponsons for Phalanx also installed. Phalanx 1B to be fitted in due course.
Structure: The hull form is based on the Invincible class with a modified superstructure. The deck is strong enough to take Chinook helicopters. Six landing and six parking spots for the aircraft. Accommodation for 972 plus 303 bunk overload. A garage is situated at the after end of the hangar. This is accessible from the after aircraft lift and via ramps through the ship's stern. Hull 'blisters' were fitted at waterline level port and starboard during 2002 to improve deployment and recovery of LCVPs.
Operational: The LPH provides a helicopter lift and assault capability. The prime role of the vessel is embarking, supporting and operating a squadron of helicopters and carrying a Royal Marine Commando including vehicles, arms and ammunition. Up to 20 Sea Harriers can be carried but not supported. Operational sea trials started in June 1998 and completed in February 1999. Twin 20 mm guns are not always carried and may be replaced by single 20 mm. Based at Devonport.

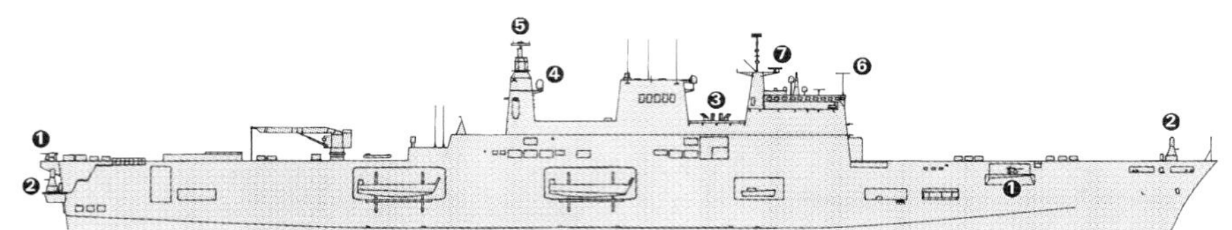

OCEAN *(Scale 1 : 1,800), Ian Sturton* / 1043485

OCEAN *11/2008*, B Sullivan* / 1353536

OCEAN *6/2005, Michael Nitz* / 1153993

OCEAN *6/2005, Maritime Photographic* / 1153992

2 ALBION CLASS (ASSAULT SHIPS) (LPD)

Name	*No*	*Builders*	*Laid down*	*Launched*	*Commissioned*
ALBION	L 14	BAE Systems, Barrow	22 May 1998	9 Mar 2001	19 June 2003
BULWARK	L 15	BAE Systems, Barrow	27 Jan 2000	15 Nov 2001	28 Apr 2005

Displacement, tons: 14,600 standard; 18,500 full load
Dimensions, feet (metres): 577.4 × 94.8 × 23.3 *(176 × 28.9 × 7.1)*
Main machinery: Diesel-electric; 2 Wärtsilä Vasa 16V 32E diesel generators; 17,000 hp(m) *(12.5 MW)*; 2 Wärtsilä Vasa 4R 32LNE diesel generators; 4,216 hp(m) *(3.1 MW)*; 2 motors; 2 shafts; LIPS props; 1 bow thruster; 1,176 hp(m) *(865 kW)*
Speed, knots: 18
Range, n miles: 8,000 at 15 kt
Complement: 325
Military lift: 305 troops; 710 troops (including overload); 67 support vehicles; 4 LCU Mk 10 or 2 LCAC (dock); 4 LCVP Mk 5 (davits)

Guns: 2—20 mm ❶. 2 Signaal/General Dynamics 30 mm 7-barrelled Goalkeeper; 4,200 rds/min to 1.5 km ❷. 4 M323 Mk 44 7.62 mm Miniguns. 4—7.62 mm MGs.
Countermeasures: Decoys: Outfit DLJ; 8 Sea Gnat launchers ❸ and DLH offboard decoys.
ESM/ECM: Racal Thorn UAT 1/4.
Torpedo defence: Type 2170 (SLQ-25A).
Combat data systems: ADAWS 20 Ed 3.1. Thomson-CSF/Redifon/BAeSEMA/CS comms system. Marconi Matra SCOT 5 SATCOM ❹. BOWMAN.
Weapons control: 2 Ultra UECCS EOSS optronic directors (L 15).
Radars: Air/surface search: Siemens Plessey Type 996 ❺; E/F-band.
Surface search: Racal Decca 1008; E/F-band.
Navigation/aircraft control: 2 Racal Marine Type 1007 ❻; I-band.
IFF: Type 1016/1017.

Helicopters: Platform for 3 Sea King Mk 4 ❼. Chinook capable.

Programmes: A decision was taken in mid-1991 to replace the then existing LPDs. Project definition studies by YARD completed in February 1994. Invitations to tender for design and build of two ships were issued to VSEL and Yarrow on 18 August 1994 with an additional tender package to Vosper Thornycroft in November 1994. In March 1995 it was announced that only VSEL would bid, conforming to the rules governing non-competitive tenders. The contract to build the ships was awarded on 18 July 1996. First steel cut 17 November 1997.
Modernisation: Davits have been replaced in both ships. BOWMAN installed to support amphibious warfare staffs. Replacement of the combat data system is expected in 2015 and MIDAS EW System in due course. BAE Insyte ARTISAN radar is to replace 996 radar.
Structure: The design includes a floodable well dock, garage (with capacity for six Challenger tanks), stern gate and side ramp access. The Flight Deck has two helicopter landing spots. A large joint operations room contains substantial command and control facilities. The ships are built to military damage control standards.
Operational: Based at Devonport.

ALBION *(Scale 1 : 1,500), Ian Sturton* / 0572733

ALBION *6/2007, Michael Nitz* / 1170273

BULWARK *3/2008*, Michael Nitz* / 1353535

BULWARK *10/2007, John Brodie* / 1305231

10 LCU MK 10

L 1001–1010

Displacement, tons: 170 light; 240 full load
Dimensions, feet (metres): 97.8 × 24.3 × 5.6 *(29.8 × 7.4 × 1.7)*
Main machinery: 2 MAN diesels; 2 Schottel propulsors; bow thruster
Speed, knots: 10. **Range, n miles:** 600 at 12 kt
Complement: 7
Military lift: 1 MBT or 4 vehicles or 120 troops
Radars: Navigation: I-band.

Comment: Ordered in 1998 from Ailsa Troon Yard. First pair delivered in November 1999 and, following extensive trials, modifications made to ballast tanks to improve beach landing capabilities. This work carried out by BAE Systems Marine, Govan, from whom a further eight craft were ordered for delivery by mid-2003. Fitted with interlocking bow and stern ramps, they operate from the Albion class LPDs.

LCU MK 10 *6/2008*, Michael Nitz* / 1353534

3 LCU MK 9S

L 705 L 709 L 711

Displacement, tons: 115 light; 175 full load
Dimensions, feet (metres): 90.2 × 21.5 × 5 *(27.5 × 6.8 × 1.6)*
Main machinery: 2 Paxman or Dorman diesels; 474 hp *(354 kW)* sustained; Kort nozzles or Schottel propulsors
Speed, knots: 10. **Range, n miles:** 300 at 9 kt
Complement: 7
Military lift: 1 MBT or 60 tons of vehicles/stores or 90 troops
Radars: Navigation: Raytheon; I-band.

Comment: Last remaining craft of class of 14. Built in the mid-1960s and originally designated Mk 9M. Upgraded with Schottel propulsors in the 1990s and redesignated Mk 9S.

LCU Mk 9 *3/2003, A Sharma* / 0572671

4 GRIFFON 2000 TDX(M) (LCAC(L))

C 21–24

Displacement, tons: 6.8 full load
Dimensions, feet (metres): 36.1 × 15.1 *(11 × 4.6)*
Main machinery: 1 Deutz BF8L513 diesel; 320 hp *(239 kW)* sustained
Speed, knots: 33. **Range, n miles:** 300 at 25 kt
Complement: 2
Military lift: 16 troops plus equipment or 2 tons
Guns: 1 — 7.62 mm MG.
Radars: Navigation: Raytheon; I-band.

Comment: Ordered 26 April 1993. Design based on 2000 TDX(M) hovercraft. Aluminium hulls. Speed indicated is at Sea State 3 with a full load.

C 23 *6/2005, Maritime Photographic* / 1153990

11 LCVP MK 4

8401–8402 8407 8409 8411–8413 8619–8622

Displacement, tons: 10.5 light; 16 full load
Dimensions, feet (metres): 43.8 × 10.9 × 2.8 *(13.4 × 3.3 × 0.8)*
Main machinery: 2 Perkins T6.3544 diesels; 290 hp *(216 kW)*; 2 shafts
Speed, knots: 15
Range, n miles: 150 at 14 kt
Complement: 3
Military lift: 20 Arctic equipped troops or 5.5 tons

Comment: Built by Souters and McTays. Introduced into service in 1986. Fitted with removable arctic canopies across well-deck. Some Royal Marines' craft replaced by LCVP Mk 5. Six craft operated by Royal Logistics Corps. These serve in rotation between the Falklands and UK.

LCVP MK 4 *7/2008*, A A de Kruijf* / 1353532

23 LCVP MK 5

LCVP 9473 9673–9692 9707–9708

Displacement, tons: 25 full load
Dimensions, feet (metres): 50.9 × 13.8 × 3 *(15.5 × 4.2 × 0.9)*
Main machinery: 2 Volvo Penta TAMD 72 WJ diesels; 2 PP 170 water-jets
Speed, knots: 25
Range, n miles: 210 at 18 kt
Complement: 3
Military lift: 35 troops plus 2 tons equipment or 8 tons vehicles and stores
Radars: Navigation: Raytheon 40; I-band.

Comment: Contract placed with Vosper Thornycroft on 31 January 1995 for one craft which was handed over on 17 January 1996. Four more ordered on 23 October 1996 for *Ocean* were delivered 6 December 1997; and two more for RM Poole in October 1998. Sixteen more ordered from FBM Babcock Marine in August 2001. Can beach fully laden on a 1 : 120 gradient. Speed 18 kt at full load.

LCVP MK 5 *10/2008*, Maritime Photographic* / 1353533

FAST INTERCEPT CRAFT (HSIC)

Comment: A new class of up to four 18 m high-speed insertion craft, reported to have been built by VT Halmatic, began to enter service in 2006. They are to replace the 16 m Very Slender Vessel craft which have been in service since the 1990s and also the two 15 m FB design FB 50 which entered service in 1996. The new craft feature a stepped planing hull and are powered by two MAN diesels driving twin Arneson drives. Top speed is likely to be in the region of 60 kt. Capable of operating in extreme climatic conditions, they are transportable by C 130.

FAST INTERCEPT CRAFT *7/2008*, A A de Kruijf* / 1353531

RRC AND RIB

Comment: (1) 36 RRC Mk 3: 2.6 tons and 7.4 m *(24.2 ft)* powered by single Yamaha 220 hp *(162 kW)* diesel; 36 kt fully laden (40 light); carry 8 troops. Some used by the Army. In service 1996–98.
(2) RIBs: Halmatic Arctic 22/Pacific 22/Arctic 28/Pacific 28. Rolling contract for all four types. Capable of carrying 10 to 15 fully laden troops at speeds of 26 to 35 kt.
(3) Offshore Raiding Craft: 9 m aluminium RIB hull with removable armour plating. Diesel powered and capable of up to 40 kt. Up to 46 craft to replace the RRC Mk 3.

ORC *7/2008*, A A de Kruijf* / 1353530

RRC *4/2005, Per Körnefeldt* / 1153943

MINE WARFARE FORCES

Notes: (1) The long-term future of the current mine-countermeasures (MCM) force is under consideration. The future capability is likely to be based on the requirement to conduct MCM in support of joint expeditionary operations in littoral waters. Speed of deployment is an important consideration. Future capability is likely to be delivered by a combination of:
(a) a portable, modular, self-contained system that could be delivered rapidly into theatre
(b) an organic mine reconnaissance capability, deployed from future classes of surface combatants
(c) a dedicated capability involving unmanned underwater vehicles deployed from auxiliary surface craft.
(2) Replacement of the Combined Influence Sweep (CIS), removed from the Hunt class, is under consideration. Plans to replace CIS with a new Remote Influence Minesweeping System (RIMS) were cancelled in 2002. The Shallow Water Influence Minesweeping System (SWIMS), brought into service during operations in Iraq during 2003, has not been maintained. Future options under examination include an influence sweep system deployable from an Unmanned Surface Vehicle (USV). A two-year technology readiness programme, known as FAST, was initiated in 2007.
(3) The Remote Control Mine Disposal Systems Mk 1 (PAP Mk 3) and 2 (PAP Mk 5) are to be replaced by the Atlas Electronik Seafox C expendable mine destructor. Stowage for 24 warshots and four surveillance vehicles is to be provided on each MCM platform.
(4) Mine reconnaissance in very shallow waters (less than 30 m) is to be met by the Hydroid Remus 100 Unmanned Underwater Vehicle (UUV). GPS-enabled, it is equipped with a high-frequency (900/1,800 kHz) side-scan sonar. Ten systems entered service in 2006.
(5) Mine reconnaissance in waters of 30–200 m is to be undertaken by the Hydroid Remus 600 UUV. Two vehicles are to be delivered by 2009. The vehicles are also capable of undertaking hydrographic survey and environmental monitoring. Secondary roles include support of search and salvage operations.
(6) The capability to conduct Rapid Environmental Assessment (REA) using a UUV in water depths up to 200 m is under investigation. This may be filled by commercially available vehicles. Introduction into service is planned during 2009.

8 HUNT CLASS (MINESWEEPERS/MINEHUNTERS—COASTAL) (MHSC/PP)

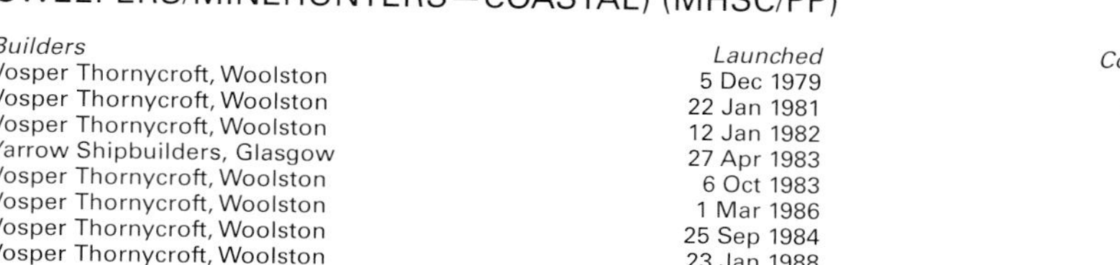

Name	*No*	*Builders*	*Launched*	*Commissioned*
LEDBURY	M 30	Vosper Thornycroft, Woolston	5 Dec 1979	11 June 1981
CATTISTOCK	M 31	Vosper Thornycroft, Woolston	22 Jan 1981	16 June 1982
BROCKLESBY	M 33	Vosper Thornycroft, Woolston	12 Jan 1982	3 Feb 1983
MIDDLETON	M 34	Yarrow Shipbuilders, Glasgow	27 Apr 1983	15 Aug 1984
CHIDDINGFOLD	M 37	Vosper Thornycroft, Woolston	6 Oct 1983	10 Aug 1984
ATHERSTONE	M 38	Vosper Thornycroft, Woolston	1 Mar 1986	30 Jan 1987
HURWORTH	M 39	Vosper Thornycroft, Woolston	25 Sep 1984	2 July 1985
QUORN	M 41	Vosper Thornycroft, Woolston	23 Jan 1988	21 Apr 1989

Displacement, tons: 633 light; 740 full load
Dimensions, feet (metres): 187 wl; 197 oa × 32.8 × 9.5 (keel); 11.2 (screws)
(57; 60 × 10 × 2.9; 3.4)
Main machinery: 2 Ruston-Paxman 9-59K Deltic diesels; 1,900 hp *(1.42 MW)*; 1 Deltic Type 9-55B diesel for pulse generator and auxiliary drive; 780 hp *(582 kW)*; 2 shafts; bow thruster
Speed, knots: 15 diesels; 8 hydraulic drive
Range, n miles: 1,500 at 12 kt
Complement: 45 (5 officers)

Guns: 1 DES/MSI DS 30B 30 mm/75; 650 rds/min to 10 km *(5.4 n miles)* anti-surface; 3 km *(1.6 n miles)* anti-aircraft; weight of shell 0.36 kg.
Dillon Aero M 134 7.62 mm Minigun; 6 barrels; 3,000 rds/min
Countermeasures: MCM: 2 PAP 104 Mk 3/105 (RCMDS 1) remotely controlled submersibles, (being replaced by Seafox C expendable mine-disposal system).
Combat data systems: BAE Insyte Nautis 3.
Radars: Navigation: Kelvin Hughes Type 1007; I-band.
Sonars: Thales 2193; hull-mounted; minehunting; 100/300 kHz. Hull-mounted; active; high frequency.

MIDDLETON *4/2008*, B Sullivan* / 1353529

Programmes: A class of MCM Vessels combining both hunting and sweeping (at 30 days notice) capabilities.
Modernisation: RCMDS is being replaced by Seafox C. 30 mm gun has replaced the Bofors 40 mm. Drumgrange Precise Fixing System fitted 2003–04. A new minehunting sonar (Sonar 2193) and NAUTIS III command system have been fitted in all eight ships 2004–05. M 134 Minigun CIWS fitted in 2007. The influence sweeping system has been removed and is at 30 days notice.
Structure: GRP hull. Combines conventional propellers with bow thrusters. Fitted with an improved two-man decompression chamber by 2005.
Operational: For operational deployments fitted with enhanced weapons systems. *Brecon*, *Cottesmore* and *Dulverton* were decommissioned in 2005. All eight ships based at Portsmouth.
Sales: *Bicester* and *Berkeley* to Greece in July 2000 and February 2001 respectively.

HURWORTH *5/2008*, Michael Nitz* / 1353528

CHIDDINGFORD *2/2008*, Maritime Photographic* / 1353527

8 SANDOWN CLASS (MINEHUNTERS) (MHC/SRMH)

Name	*No*	*Builders*	*Launched*	*Commissioned*
WALNEY	M 104	Vosper Thornycroft, Woolston	25 Nov 1991	20 Feb 1993
PENZANCE	M 106	Vosper Thornycroft, Woolston	11 Mar 1997	14 May 1998
PEMBROKE	M 107	Vosper Thornycroft, Woolston	15 Dec 1997	6 Oct 1998
GRIMSBY	M 108	Vosper Thornycroft, Woolston	10 Aug 1998	25 Sep 1999
BANGOR	M 109	Vosper Thornycroft, Woolston	16 Apr 1999	26 July 2000
RAMSEY	M 110	Vosper Thornycroft, Woolston	25 Nov 1999	22 June 2001
BLYTH	M 111	Vosper Thornycroft, Woolston	4 July 2000	20 July 2001
SHOREHAM	M 112	Vosper Thornycroft, Woolston	9 Apr 2001	2 Sep 2002

Displacement, tons: 537 standard; 409 full load
Dimensions, feet (metres): 172.2 × 34.4 × 7.5 *(52.5 × 10.5 × 2.3)*
Main machinery: 2 Paxman Valenta 6RP200E/M diesels; 1,523 hp *(1.14 MW)* sustained; Voith-Schneider propulsion; 2 Schottel bow thrusters
Speed, knots: 13 diesels; 6.5 electric drive. **Range, n miles**: 2,500 at 12 kt
Complement: 34 (5 officers) plus 6 spare berths

Guns: 1 DES/MSI DS 30B 30 mm/75; 650 rds/min to 10 km *(5.4 n miles)* anti-surface; 3 km *(1.6 n miles)* anti-aircraft; weight of shell 0.36 kg.
Dillon Aero M 134 7.62 mm Minigun; 6 barrels; 3,000 rds/min.
Countermeasures: MCM: ECA mine disposal system, 2 PAP 104 Mk 5 (RCMDS 2) (being replaced by Seafox C). These craft can carry 2 mine wire cutters, a charge of 100 kg and a manipulator with TV/projector. Control cables are 2,000 m. To be replaced by Seafox C expendable mine-disposal system.
Combat data systems: BAE Insyte Nautis 3.
Radars: Navigation: Kelvin Hughes Type 1007; I-band.
Sonars: Marconi Type 2093; VDS; VLF-VHF multifunction with 5 arrays; mine search and classification.

Programmes: A class designed for hunting and destroying mines and for operating in deep and exposed waters. Single role minehunter (SRMH) complements the Hunt class. On 9 January 1984 the Vosper Thornycroft design for this class was approved. First one ordered August 1985, four more on 23 July 1987. A contract was to have been placed for a second batch in 1990 but this was deferred twice, until an order for seven more (M 106-112) was placed in July 1994.
Modernisation: RCMDS 2 being replaced by Seafox C. Drumgrange Precise Fixing System fitted in 2004. Nautis M combat system replaced by Nautis 3. M 134 Minigun CIWS fitted in 2006.
Structure: GRP hull. Combines vectored thrust units with bow thrusters and Remote-Control Mine Disposal System (RCMDS). The sonar is deployed from a well in the hull. Batch 2 have larger diameter (1.8 m) Voith-Schneider props and an improved two-man decompression chamber.
Operational: All based at Faslane from mid-2006.
Sales: Three to Saudi Arabia. *Bridport*, *Sandown* and *Inverness* to Estonia 2007–08.

SHOREHAM *6/2007*, ***Maritime Photographic*** / 1170269

WALNEY *8/2007*, ***B Sullivan*** / 1170268

SURVEY SHIPS

1 GLEANER CLASS (YGS)

Name	*No*	*Builders*	*Launched*	*Commissioned*
GLEANER	H 86	Emsworth Shipyard	18 Oct 1983	5 Dec 1983

Displacement, tons: 26 full load
Dimensions, feet (metres): 51.2 × 15.4 × 5.2 *(15.6 × 4.7 × 1.6)*
Main machinery: 2 Volvo Penta TMD 112; 524 hp(m) *(391 kW)*; 2 shafts
Speed, knots: 19.5
Complement: 8 (2 officers)
Radars: Navigation: Raymarine Pathfinder; I-band.

Comment: This craft is prefixed HMSML-HM Survey Motor Launch. Primary task is conduct of high-resolution survey operations around UK ports and harbours. Fitted with integrated survey suite with C-Nav WADGPS positioning and Simrad EM 3002 MBES, EA 400 SBES, 2094 SSS and magnetometer towed sensors.

GLEANER *6/2005*, ***Camil Busquets i Vilanova*** / 1153981

1 SCOTT CLASS (AGSH)

Name	*No*	*Builders*	*Launched*	*Commissioned*
SCOTT	H 131	Appledore Shipbuilders, Bideford	13 Oct 1996	30 June 1997

Displacement, tons: 13,500 full load
Dimensions, feet (metres): 430.1 × 70.5 × 29.5 *(131.1 × 21.5 × 9)*
Main machinery: 2 Krupp MaK 9M32 9-cyl diesels; 10,800 hp(m) *(7.94 MW)*; 1 shaft; LIPS cp prop; retractable bow thruster
Speed, knots: 17.5
Complement: 62 (12 officers) (see *Comment*)
Radars: Navigation: Kelvin Hughes ARPA 1626; I-band.
Helicopters: Platform for 1 light.

Comment: Designed by BAeSEMA/YARD and ordered 20 January 1995 to replace *Hecla*. Ice-strengthened bow. Foredeck strengthened for helicopter operations. The centre of the OSV surveying operations consists of an integrated navigation suite, the Sonar Array Sounding System (SASS) and data processing equipment. Additional sensors include gravimeters, a towed proton magnetometer a Moving Vessel Profiler (MVP) 800 and the Sonar 2090 ocean environment sensor. The SASS IV multibeam depth-sounder is capable of gathering 121 individual depth samples concurrently over a 120° swathe, producing a three-dimensional image of the seabed. 8,000 tons of seawater ballast can be used to achieve a sonar trim. The ship is at sea for 300 days a year with a crew of 42 embarked, rotating with the other 20 ashore. *Scott* undertook a survey of the Indian Ocean tsunami epicentre in early 2005. Based at Devonport.

SCOTT *8/2008**, ***Maritime Photographic*** / 1353526

2 ECHO CLASS (AGSH)

Name	*No*	*Builders*	*Launched*	*Commissioned*
ECHO	H 87	Appledore, Bideford	4 Mar 2002	7 Mar 2003
ENTERPRISE	H 88	Appledore, Bideford	2 May 2002	17 Oct 2003

Displacement, tons: 3,470 full load
Dimensions, feet (metres): 295.3 × 55.1 × 18 *(90 × 16.8 × 5.5)*
Main machinery: Diesel electric; 4.8 MW; 2 azimuth thrusters; 1 bow thruster
Speed, knots: 15
Range, n miles: 9,000 at 12 kt
Complement: 72
Guns: 2—20 mm. 4—7.62 mm MGs.
Radars: Navigation: 2 sets; I-band.
Helicopters: Platform for VERTREP only.

Comment: The order for two multirole Hydrographic and Oceanographic Survey Vessels was placed with the prime contractor, Vosper Thornycroft Ltd, on 19 June 2000. The ships were built by Appledore Shipbuilders in Devon. The contract covers the design, build and through-life support of the ships over their 25 year service. In addition to specialist surveying tasks, the ships' operational roles include Rapid Environmental Assessment, Amphibious Warfare surveys and Mine Countermeasures Tasking Support. The survey suite consists of EM 1002 hull mounted multibeam sonar, EA 600 single beam echo-sounder, towed side scan sonar, towed undulating sensors, an adaptive survey planning system. Survey Motor Launches *Pathfinder* and *Pioneer* are embarked in *Echo* and *Enterprise* respectively. Both based at Devonport.

ENTERPRISE *7/2007*, ***Guy Toremans*** / 1170266

1 ROEBUCK CLASS (AGS)

Name	*No*	*Builders*	*Launched*	*Commissioned*
ROEBUCK	H 130	Brooke Marine, Lowestoft	14 Nov 1985	3 Oct 1986

Displacement, tons: 1,477 full load
Dimensions, feet (metres): 210 × 42.6 × 13
(63.9 × 13 × 4)
Main machinery: 4 Mirrlees Blackstone ESL8 Mk 1 diesels; 3,040 hp *(2.27 MW)*; 2 shafts; cp props
Speed, knots: 14
Range, n miles: 4,000 at 10 kt
Complement: 46 (6 officers)
Guns: 1—20 mm.
2 M323 Mk 44 7.62 mm Miniguns (fitted for).

Radars: Navigation: Kelvin Hughes Nucleus 2-6000; I-band.

Comment: Designed for hydrographic surveys to full modern standards on UK continental shelf. Air conditioned. Carries Survey Motor Launch *Nesbitt* (fitted with EM 3002 MBES, EA 400 SBES and 2094 SSS) and one 4.5 m RIB. The decision to decommission in 2003 was cancelled and a Ship Life Extension Programme started in September 2004 and was completed in mid-2005. The upgrade included refurbishment and renewal of engineering systems and habitability improvements. A 20 mm gun system has been installed. Roles include Rapid Environmental Assessment and Amphibious Warfare survey. The new survey suite consists of EM 1002 hull-mounted multibeam sonar, EA 600 SBES and 2094 towed side-scan sonar and adaptive planning system, Moving Vessel Profiler (MVP) 200 and WECDIS.

ROEBUCK ***5/2008*, Michael Nitz*** / 1353525

6 NESBITT CLASS (YGS)

NESBITT 9423
PAT BARTON 9424
COOK 9425
OWEN 9426
PIONEER
PATHFINDER

Displacement, tons: 11 full load
Dimensions, feet (metres): 34.8 × 9.4 × 3.3 *(10.6 × 2.9 × 1)*
Main machinery: 2 Perkins Sabre 185C diesels; 430 hp(m) *(316 kW)* sustained; 2 shafts
Speed, knots: 15
Range, n miles: 300 at 8 kt
Complement: 2 plus 10 spare

Comment: *Nesbitt, Pat Barton, Cook* and *Owen* delivered by Halmatic, Southampton by September 1996. *Pioneer* and *Pathfinder* built by Halmatic and delivered in 2003 as part of the contract to build *Echo* and *Enterprise*. *Nesbitt* embarked in *Roebuck, Pathfinder* in *Echo, Pioneer* in *Enterprise* and the other three based at the Hydrographic School, Devonport. Fitted with C-Nav WADGPS positioning system, EM 3000 MBES *(Pathfinder, Pioneer, Pat Barton)*, EM 3002 MBES *(Nesbitt, Cook, Owen)*, EA 400 SBES and 2094 SSS.

NESBITT ***11/1998, John Brodie*** / 0053244

RESCUE VEHICLES

0 + 1 NATO SUBMARINE RESCUE SYSTEM (DSRV)

Displacement, tons: 30 full load
Dimensions, feet (metres): 28.5 × 11.1 × 11.5
(8.7 × 3.4 × 3.5)
Main machinery: 2 external ZEBRA rechargeable sodium nickel chloride battery pods
Speed, knots: 3.8
Complement: 3

Comment: The three participant nations for NSRS are UK, Norway and France with the UK Defence Procurement Agency acting as contracting authority and host nation for project management and in-service phases. Following Invitations to Tender, a 10-year contract for the design and manufacture phase was awarded in June 2004 to a team led by Rolls-Royce Naval Marine. The core of the service is a new free-swimming Submarine Rescue Vehicle (SRV), built by Perry Slingsby, capable of accommodating 15 rescued personnel from a submarine at depths down to 600 m and at an angle of up to 60°. The SRV may be launched and recovered from suitable commercial or from military 'motherships', primarily offshore support vessels, capable of fitting the NSRS Portable Launch-And-Recovery (PLARS) installation. Battery endurance allows up to five rescue cycles without recharge but trickle charging during rescuee transfer will enable almost continuous operation. The NSRS includes an unmanned Intervention Remotely-Operated Vehicle (IROV), the Perry Slingsby Super Spartan, which can operate down to depths of 1,000 m and may be used to locate a stricken submarine, to conduct survey and rescue preparations and to resupply Emergency Life Support Stores in pressure tight pods whilst awaiting rescue. Other assets include a Transfer under Pressure system with decompression chambers for up to 72 personnel; medical treatment facilities and support equipment. The system entered service in November 2008 and is expected to remain in service unitl 2033. It is permanently maintained at HM Naval Base Clyde, Scotland, at 12 hours notice to move worldwide.

NSRS SRV
6/2008*, Richard Scott
1353524

AUXILIARIES

General

The Royal Fleet Auxiliary Service is a civilian-manned fleet under the command of the Commander in Chief Fleet from 1 April 1993. Its main task is to supply warships at sea with fuel, food, stores and ammunition. It also provides aviation platforms, amphibious support for the Navy and Marines and sea transport for Army units. All ships take part in operational sea training. An order in council on 30 November 1989 changed the status of the RFA service to government-owned vessels on non-commercial service.

New Construction

(1) The Maritime Role 3 Medical Capability was formerly known as the Joint Casualty Treatment Ship (JCTS). The requirement for such a vessel was identified in the 1998 Strategic Defence Review. The aviation support ship *Argus* was configured as a PCRF during the 1990–91 Gulf War and the 2003 Iraq War. The contract for the Assessment Phase was awarded to BMT Ltd in February 2002 since when the key drivers have been identified as a need for eight operating tables and a 150-200 bed hospital. A two-spot flight deck and the ability to embark personnel by sea or land are also required. Development of the Systems Requirement Document (SRD) by Atkins Aviation and Defence Systems has been completed and potential solutions range from a bespoke vessel to conversion/modification of an existing military or merchant hull. The ship will be manned by RFA personnel but is unlikely to enter service before 2020. The requirement for a second ship at 12 months notice is to be met by chartering a commercial hull.

(2) The future afloat support capability is being taken forward through the Military Afloat Reach and Sustainability programme (MARS). The Concept Phase formally ended at Initial Gate in mid-2005 when the Assessment phase began. The competition to select a lead project integrator was abandoned in 2007. Under a revised procurement strategy, BVT, Fincantieri, Hyundai and Navantia were shortlisted in 2008 to build up to six tankers but a contract, expected to be in 2009, has been delayed by up to three years funding difficulties. Overall the requirement for six fleet tankers; two fleet support ships and three joint sea-based logistic vessels remains.

Personnel

1 January 2009: 2,295 (825 officers)

2 WAVE CLASS (LARGE FLEET TANKERS) (AORH)

Name	*No*	*Builders*	*Laid down*	*Launched*	*Commissioned*
WAVE KNIGHT	A 389	BAE Systems, Barrow	22 Oct 1998	29 Sep 2000	8 Apr 2003
WAVE RULER	A 390	BAE Systems, Govan	10 Feb 2000	9 Feb 2001	27 Apr 2003

Displacement, tons: 31,500 full load
Measurement, tons: 23,294 grt
Dimensions, feet (metres): 644.0 × 90.9 × 43.0 *(196.3 × 27.7 × 13.1)*
Main machinery: Diesel-electric: 4 Wärtsilä 12V 32E/GECLM diesel generators; 25,514 hp(m) *(18.76 MW)*; 2 GECLM motors; 19,040 hp(m) *(14 MW)*; 1 shaft; Kamewa bow and stern thrusters
Speed, knots: 18
Range, n miles: 10,000 at 15 kt
Complement: 80 plus 22 aircrew
Cargo capacity: 16,000 m^3 total liquids including 3,000 m^3 aviation fuel; 8–20 ft refrigerated containers plus 500 m^3 solids

Guns: 2 Vulcan Phalanx CIWS; fitted for but not with. 2–30 mm. 5–7.62 mm MGs. 2 Mk 44 7.62 mm Miniguns.
Countermeasures: Decoys: Outfit DLJ(2).
Radars: Navigation: KH 1007; E/F/I-band.
IFF: Type 1017.
Helicopters: 1 Merlin HM.Mk 1.

Comment: Feasibility studies by BAeSEMA/YARD completed in early 1995. Draft invitation to tender issued 10 October 1995 followed by full tender on 26 June 1996. Contracts to build placed with VSEL (BAE Systems) on 12 March 1997. One spot flight deck with full hangar facilities for one Merlin. Enclosed bridge including bridge wings. Double hull construction. Inclined RAS gear with three rigs and two cranes.

WAVE KNIGHT *9/2008**, **Shaun Jones** / 1353521

2 APPLELEAF CLASS (SUPPORT TANKERS) (AOT)

Name	*No*	*Builders*	*Launched*	*Commissioned*
BAYLEAF	A 109	Cammell Laird, Birkenhead	27 Oct 1981	26 Mar 1982
ORANGELEAF (ex-*Balder London*, ex-*Hudson Progress*)	A 110	Cammell Laird, Birkenhead	1975	2 May 1984

Displacement, tons: 37,747 full load
Measurement, tons: 18,854 gross; 9,043 net
Dimensions, feet (metres): 560 × 85 × 36.1 *(170.7 × 25.9 × 11)*
Main machinery: 2 Pielstick 14 PC2.2 V 400 diesels; 14,000 hp(m) *(10.29 MW)* sustained; 1 shaft
Speed, knots: 15.5; 16.3 (A 109)
Complement: 56 (19 officers)
Cargo capacity: 22,000 m^3 dieso; 3,800 m^3 Avcat
Guns: 2 BMARC GAM-BO1 20 mm. 6–7.62 mm MGs. 2 Mk 44 7.62 mm Miniguns.
Radars: Navigation: Racal Decca 1226 and 1229; I-band.

Comment: Part of a four-ship order cancelled by Hudson Fuel and Shipping Co, but completed by the shipbuilders, being the only mercantile order then in hand. *Bayleaf* built under commercial contract to be chartered by MoD and purchased in 2006. *Orangeleaf* major refit September 1985 to fit full RAS capability and extra accommodation. Single-hull construction. To be replaced from about 2015.

BAYLEAF *1/2008**, **Shaun Jones** / 1170262

2 ROVER CLASS (SMALL FLEET TANKERS) (AORLH)

Name	*No*	*Builders*	*Launched*	*Commissioned*
GOLD ROVER	A 271	Swan Hunter Shipbuilders, Wallsend-on-Tyne	7 Mar 1973	22 Mar 1974
BLACK ROVER	A 273	Swan Hunter Shipbuilders, Wallsend-on-Tyne	30 Oct 1973	23 Aug 1974

Displacement, tons: 4,700 light; 11,522 full load
Measurement, tons: 7,892 gross; 2,367 net
Dimensions, feet (metres): 461 × 63.3 × 24 *(140.6 × 19.3 × 7.3)*
Main machinery: 2 SEMT-Pielstick 16 PA4 185 diesels; 15,360 hp(m) *(11.46 MW)*; 1 shaft; Kamewa cp prop; bow thruster
Speed, knots: 19
Range, n miles: 15,000 at 15 kt
Complement: 48 (17 officers) (A 269); 55 (18 officers) (A 271, 273)
Cargo capacity: 3,000 m^3 fuel
Guns: 2 BMARC GAM-BO1 20 mm. 4—7.62 mm MGs. 2 Mk 44 7.62 mm Miniguns.
Radars: Navigation: Racal Decca 52690 ARPA; Racal Decca 1690; I-band.
Helicopters: Platform for Westland Sea King HAS. Mk 5 or HC.Mk 4.

Comment: Single-hull construction. Small fleet tankers designed to replenish HM ships at sea with fuel, fresh water, limited dry cargo and refrigerated stores under all conditions while under way. No hangar but helicopter landing platform is served by a stores lift, to enable stores to be transferred at sea by 'vertical lift'. Capable of HIFR. Siting of SATCOM aerial varies. *Green Rover* sold in September 1992 to Indonesia. *Blue Rover* to Portugal in March 1993. *Grey Rover* decommissioned in 2006. To be replaced from about 2015.

GOLD ROVER *5/2008*, B Sullivan* / 1353520

2 FORT VICTORIA CLASS (FLEET REPLENISHMENT SHIPS) (AORH)

Name	*No*	*Builders*	*Laid down*	*Launched*	*Commissioned*
FORT VICTORIA	A 387	Harland & Wolff/Cammell Laird	4 Apr 1988	12 June 1990	24 June 1994
FORT GEORGE	A 388	Swan Hunter Shipbuilders, Wallsend-on-Tyne	9 Mar 1989	1 Mar 1991	16 July 1993

Displacement, tons: 36,580 full load
Measurements, tons: 28,821 grt; 8,646 net
Dimensions, feet (metres): 667.7 oa; 607 wl × 99.7 × 32 *(203.5; 185 × 30.4 × 9.8)*
Main machinery: 2 Crossley SEMT-Pielstick 16 PC2.6 V 400 diesels; 23,904 hp(m) *(17.57 MW)* sustained; 2 shafts
Speed, knots: 20
Complement: 134 (95 RFA plus 15 RN plus 24 civilian stores staff) plus 154 (28 officers) aircrew
Cargo capacity: 12,505 m^3 liquids; 3,000 m^3 solids

Guns: 2—20 mm GAM-BO.
2 Vulcan Phalanx 20 mm Mk 15. 2 Mk 44 7.62 mm Miniguns.
Countermeasures: Decoys: DLH.
ESM: Marconi Racal Thorn UAT; intercept.
Combat data systems: SCOT 5 SATCOM.
Radars: Navigation: Kelvin Hughes Type 1007; I-band.
Aircraft control: Kelvin Hughes NUCLEUS; E/F-band.

Helicopters: 5 Westland Sea King/Merlin helicopters.

Programmes: The requirement for these ships is to provide fuel and stores support to the Fleet at sea. *Fort Victoria* ordered 23 April 1986 and *Fort George* on 18 December 1987. *Fort Victoria* delayed by damage during building and entered Cammell Laird Shipyard for post sea trials completion in July 1992. The original plan for six of this class was progressively eroded and no more of this type will be built.
Structure: Single-hull construction. Four dual-purpose abeam replenishment rigs for simultaneous transfer of liquids and solids. Stern refuelling. Repair facilities for Merlin helicopters. The plan to fit Seawolf GWS 26 VLS was abandoned in favour of Phalanx CIWS fitted in 1998/99 to both ships.
Operational: Two helicopter spots. There is a requirement to provide an emergency landing facility for Harriers. To remain in service until 2019.

FORT VICTORIA *10/2006, B Sullivan* / 1167568

2 FORT GRANGE CLASS (FLEET REPLENISHMENT SHIPS) (AFSH)

Name	*No*	*Builders*	*Laid down*	*Launched*	*Commissioned*
FORT ROSALIE (ex-*Fort Grange*)	A 385	Scott-Lithgow, Greenock	9 Nov 1973	9 Dec 1976	6 Apr 1978
FORT AUSTIN	A 386	Scott-Lithgow, Greenock	9 Dec 1975	9 Mar 1978	11 May 1979

Displacement, tons: 23,384 full load
Measurement, tons: 20,043 grt
Dimensions, feet (metres): 607.4 × 79 × 28.2 *(185.1 × 24.1 × 8.6)*
Main machinery: 1 Sulzer RND90 diesel; 23,200 hp(m) *(17.05 MW)*; 1 shaft; 2 bow thrusters
Speed, knots: 22
Range, n miles: 10,000 at 20 kt
Complement: 114 (31 officers) plus 36 RNSTS (civilian supply staff) plus 45 RN aircrew
Cargo capacity: 3,500 tons armament, naval and victualling stores in 4 holds of 12,800 m^3
Guns: 2 BMARC GAM-BO1 20 mm. 4—7.62 mm MGs. 2 Mk 44 7.62 mm Miniguns.
Radars: Navigation: Kelvin Hughes Type 1007; I-band.
Helicopters: 4 Westland Sea King.

Comment: Ordered in November 1971. Fitted for SCOT SATCOMs but carry Marisat. Normally only one helicopter is embarked. ASW stores for helicopters carried on board. Emergency flight deck on the hangar roof. There are six cranes, three of 10 tons lift and three of 5 tons. Decommissioning dates: *Fort Rosalie* 2016, *Fort Austin* 2017.

FORT ROSALIE *9/2007, Shaun Jones* / 1170258

1 STENA TYPE (FORWARD REPAIR SHIP) (ARH)

Name	*No*	*Builders*	*Commissioned*	*Recommissioned*
DILIGENCE (ex-*Stena Inspector*)	A 132	Oresundsvarvet AB, Landskrona, Sweden	1981	12 Mar 1984

Displacement, tons: 10,765 full load
Measurement, tons: 8,048 grt
Dimensions, feet (metres): 367.5 × 67.3 × 22.3 *(112 × 20.5 × 6.8)*
Flight deck, feet (metres): 83 × 83 *(25.4 × 25.4)*
Main machinery: Diesel-electric; 5 V16 Nohab-Polar diesel generators; 2,650 kW; 4 NEBB motors; 6,000 hp(m) *(4.41 MW)*; 1 shaft; Kamewa cp prop; 2 Kamewa bow tunnel thrusters; 3,000 hp(m) *(2.2 MW)*; 2 azimuth thrusters (aft); 3,000 hp(m) *(2.2 MW)*
Speed, knots: 12
Range, n miles: 5,000 at 12 kt
Complement: 38 (15 officers) plus accommodation for 147 plus 55 temporary
Cargo capacity: Long-jib crane SWL 5 tons; maximum lift, 40 tons
Guns: 2 BMARC GAM-BO1 20 mm. 4—7.62 mm MGs. 2 Mk 44 7.62 mm Miniguns.

Helicopters: Facilities for up to Boeing Chinook HC. Mk 1 (medium lift) size.

Programmes: *Stena Inspector* was designed originally as a Multipurpose Support Vessel for North Sea oil operations, and completed in January 1981. Chartered on 25 May 1982 for use as a fleet repair ship during the Falklands War. Purchased from Stena (UK) Line in October 1983, and converted for use as Forward Repair Ship in the South Atlantic (Falkland Islands). Conversion by Clyde Dock Engineering Ltd, Govan from 12 November 1983 to 29 February 1984.

DILIGENCE ***11/2007, Shaun Jones*** / 1170257

Modernisation: Following items added during conversion: large workshop for hull and machinery repairs (in well-deck); accommodation for naval Junior Rates (new accommodation block); accommodation for crew of conventional submarine (in place of Saturation Diving System); extensive craneage facilities; overside supply of electrical power, water, fuel, steam, air, to ships alongside; large naval store (in place of cement tanks); armament and magazines; Naval Communications System; decompression chamber. Major refit conducted in Singapore 2005. Work included replacement/update of dynamic positioning system.

Structure: Four 5 ton anchors for four-point mooring system. Strengthened for operations in ice (Ice Class 1A). Kongsberg Albatross Positioning System has been retained in full. Uses bow and stern thrusters and main propeller to maintain a selected position to within a few metres, up to Beaufort Force 9. Controlled by Kongsberg KS 500 computers.
Operational: Principal role is operational maintenance and repair with Engineering Support Naval Party embarked. Has also been used as MCMV support ship in the Gulf and is capable of SSN support. To remain in service until 2014.

1 PRIMARY CASUALTY RECEIVING SHIP (APCR)

Name	*No*	*Builders*	*Commissioned*	*Recommissioned*
ARGUS (ex-*Contender Bezant*)	A 135	CNR Breda, Venice	1981	1 June 1988

Displacement, tons: 18,280 standard; 26,421 full load
Measurement, tons: 9,965 dwt
Dimensions, feet (metres): 574.5 × 99.7 × 27 *(175.1 × 30.4 × 8.2)*
Main machinery: 2 Lindholmen SEMT-Pielstick 18 PC2.5 V 400 diesels; 23,400 hp(m) *(17.2 MW)* sustained; 2 shafts
Speed, knots: 18
Range, n miles: 20,000 at 19 kt
Complement: 80 (22 officers) plus 35 permanent RN plus 137 RN aircrew
Military lift: 3,300 tons dieso; 1,100 tons aviation fuel; 138 4 ton vehicles in lieu of aircraft

Guns: 2—20 mm GAM-BO. 6—7.62 mm MGs. 2 Mk 44 7.62 mm Miniguns.
Countermeasures: Decoys: DLJ.
ESM: THORN EMI Guardian; radar warning.
Combat data systems: Racal CANE DEB-1 data automation. Inmarsat SATCOM communications. Marisat.
Radars: Air search: Type 994 MTI; E/F-band.
Air/surface search: Kelvin Hughes Type 1006; I-band.
Navigation: Racal Decca Type 994; I-band.

Fixed-wing aircraft: Provision to transport 12 Harriers.
Helicopters: 6 Westland Sea King HAS.Mk 5/6 or similar.

Programmes: Ro-Ro container ship whose conversion to aviation training ship was begun by Harland and Wolff in March 1984 and completed on 3 March 1988. Work to convert her to PCRF role completed in 2001 and upgraded in 2007.

ARGUS ***11/2007, B Sullivan*** / 1170259

Structure: Uses former Ro-Ro deck as hangar with four sliding WT doors able to operate at a speed of 10 m/min. Can replenish other ships underway. One lift abaft funnel. Domestic facilities are very limited if she is to be used in the Command support role. Flight deck is 372.4 ft *(113.5 m)* long and has a 5 ft thick concrete layer on its lower side. First RFA to be fitted with a command system. PCRF conversion work included modification of three decks into permanent 100-bed hospital with three operating theatres. Improvements to safety and evacuation facilities for casualties and staff, along with upgraded medical equipment, are to be installed in 2009. The forward lift is to be adapted for evacuation and only the aft lift remains available for aircraft.
Operational: Based at Falmouth. Operational life extended to 2020. Can conduct subsidiary role as aviation training ship.

6 TRANSPORT SHIPS (AKR)

Name	*No*	*Builders*	*Commissioned*
HURST POINT	–	Flensburger Schiffbau	16 Aug 2002
HARTLAND POINT	–	Harland & Wolff, Belfast	11 Dec 2002
EDDYSTONE	–	Flensburger Schiffbau	28 Nov 2002
ANVIL POINT	–	Harland & Wolff, Belfast	17 Jan 2003
LONGSTONE	–	Flensburger Schiffbau	24 Apr 2003
BEACHY HEAD	–	Flensburger Schiffbau	17 Apr 2003

Displacement, tons: 20,000 full load
Measurement, tons: 14,200 dwt
Dimensions, feet (metres): 633.4 × 85.3 × 24.3 *(193.0 × 26.0 × 7.4)*
Main machinery: 2 MaK 9M43 diesels; 21,700 hp *(16.2 MW)*; 2 cp props; bow thruster
Speed, knots: 21.5
Range, n miles: 9,200 at 21.5 kt

Complement: 18
Military lift: 2,650 linear metres of space for vehicles equating to 130 armoured vehicles plus 60 trucks and ammunition
Radars: Navigation: I-band.

Comment: On 26 October 2000, it was announced that AWSR Ltd had been awarded the contract to provide a strategic sealift service in support of the Joint Rapid Reaction Force (JRRF) until late 2024. A key feature of the contract is that four Ro-Ro are in constant MoD use while the remaining ships are available for use by AWSR for the generation of commercial revenue. These can be called upon to support major operations and exercises.

HURST POINT ***4/2008*, Maritime Photographic*** / 1353519

4 BAY CLASS LANDING SHIPS DOCK (AUXILIARY) (LSD)

Name	*No*	*Builders*	*Laid down*	*Launched*	*Commissioned*
LARGS BAY	L 3006	Swan Hunter (Tyneside) Ltd	28 Jan 2002	18 July 2003	28 Nov 2006
LYME BAY	L 3007	Swan Hunter (Tyneside) Ltd	22 Nov 2002	3 Sep 2005	26 Nov 2007
MOUNTS BAY	L 3008	BAE Systems Govan	25 Aug 2002	9 Apr 2004	13 July 2006
CARDIGAN BAY	L 3009	BAE Systems Govan	13 Oct 2003	8 Apr 2005	18 Dec 2006

Displacement, tons: 16,160 full load
Dimensions, feet (metres): 579.4 × 86.6 × 19 *(176.6 × 26.4 × 5.8)*
Main machinery: Diesel-electric; 2 Wärtsilä 8L26 generators; 6,000 hp *(4.5 MW)*; 2 Wärtsilä 12V26 generators; 9,000 hp *(6.7 MW)*; 2 steerable propulsors; bow thruster
Speed, knots: 18. **Range, n miles:** 10,000 at 15 kt
Complement: 69 plus up to 52 military augmentees (plus 356 troops or 600 in overload conditions)
Military lift: 1,130 linear metres of space for vehicles equating to 24 Challenger MBTs or 150 light trucks plus 200 tons ammunition or 24 × 24 TEU containers

Guns: 2—30 mm. 2 Mk 44 7.62 Miniguns. 6—7.62 mm MGs.
Radars: Navigation: E/F/I-bands.
Helicopters: Platform capable of operating Chinook.

Programmes: Two ships ordered from Swan Hunter on 18 December 2000. Contract for two further ships of the class, placed on 19 November 2001 with BAE Systems (Marine) at Govan. The programme was badly affected by escalating costs and delays and the whole project was passed to BAE Systems on 13 July 2006.

Structure: Based on the Royal Schelde Enforcer design, the LSD(A)s are designed to transport troops, vehicles, ammunition and stores in support of amphibious operations. Offload is enabled by a flight deck capable of operating heavy helicopters, an amphibious dock capable of operating one LCU Mk 10 and mexeflotes which can be hung on the ships' sides. There is no beaching capability. Davit-launched infantry landing craft (LCVPs) are not fitted but two can be carried in the dock or on deck. There are two 30 t cranes.

LARGS BAY *9/2007, Shaun Jones* / 1170261

CARDIGAN BAY *6/2007, Selim San* / 1170260

MARINE SERVICES AND GOVERNMENT AGENCY SERVICES

Notes: (1) A contract was awarded to SERCo. Denholm Marine Services Ltd in January 2008 for the provision of support to naval bases, mooring maintenance and support to military training and exercises. The contract expires in 2022.
(2) *Longbow* is a 12,000 ton trials barge whose conversion 2003–04 by FSL Portsmouth includes a mast, missile silo and firing system to facilitate PAAMS development trials.

LONGBOW *7/2007, Derek Fox* / 1305224

1 SUPPORT SHIP (AG)

Name	*No*	*Builders*	*Commissioned*
SD NEWTON	–	Scott-Lithgow, Greenock	17 June 1976

Displacement, tons: 3,140 light; 4,652 full load
Dimensions, feet (metres): 323.5 × 53 × 27.9 *(98.6 × 16 × 8.5)*
Main machinery: Diesel-electric; 3 Ruston 8 RK-215 diesels; 5,520 hp *(4.06 MW)*; 1 GEC motor; 2,650 hp *(1.97 MW)*; Kort nozzle; bow thruster
Speed, knots: 14. **Range, n miles:** 5,000 at 14 kt
Complement: 14
Radars: Navigation: Kelvin Hughes 1006; I-band.

Comment: Primarily used in support of RN training exercises. Limited support provided to trials. Mid-life refit and re-engining in 2001. To be decommissioned in August 2010 when she is replaced by *Victoria*.

NEWTON *3/2007, Maritime Photographic* / 1170255

1 SAL CLASS (MOORING SHIP) (ARSD)

Name	*No*	*Builders*	*Commissioned*
SD SALMAID	–	Hall Russell, Aberdeen	28 Oct 1986

Displacement, tons: 1,605 light; 2,225 full load
Dimensions, feet (metres): 253 × 48.9 × 21.6 *(77 × 14.9 × 6.6)*
Main machinery: 2 Ruston 8RKCZ diesels; 4,000 hp *(2.98 MW)*; 1 shaft; cp prop
Speed, knots: 15
Range, n miles: 5,000 at 14 kt
Complement: 15 (6 officers) plus 27 spare billets
Radars: Navigation: Racal Decca; I-band.

Comment: Ordered on 23 January 1984. *Salmaid* based at Devonport. Lift, 400 tons; 200 tons on horns. Can carry submersibles including NSRS. To be decommissioned in March 2011.

SAL CLASS *3/2005, Derek Fox* / 1153936

2 MOORHEN CLASS (MOORING SHIPS) (ARS)

Name	*No*	*Builders*	*Commissioned*
SD MOORHEN	–	McTay, Bromborough	26 Apr 1989
SD MOORFOWL	–	McTay, Bromborough	30 June 1989

Displacement, tons: 530 full load
Dimensions, feet (metres): 106 × 37.7 × 12.5 *(32.3 × 11.5 × 3.8)*
Main machinery: 2 Cummins KT19-M diesels; 796 hp *(594 kW)*; 2 Aquamasters; bow thruster
Speed, knots: 8
Complement: 12 (2 officers)

Comment: Classified as powered mooring lighters. The whole ship can be worked from a 'flying bridge' which is constructed over a through deck. Day mess for five divers. *Moorhen* at Portsmouth, *Moorfowl* at Devonport. To remain in service until 2022.

MOORHEN *7/2008*, A A de Kruijf* / 1335220

1 RESEARCH SHIP (AGOR)

Name	*No*	*Builders*	*Commissioned*
SD COLONEL TEMPLER (ex-*Criscilla*)	–	Hall Russell, Aberdeen	1966

Displacement, tons: 1,300 full load
Dimensions, feet (metres): 185.4 × 36 × 23.0 *(56.5 × 11 × 7.0)*
Main machinery: Diesel-electric; 2 Cummins KTA-38G3M diesels; 2,557 hp(m) *(1.88 MW)*; 2 Newage HC M734E1 generators; 1 Ansaldo DH 560S motor; 1,775 hp(m) *(1.3 MW)*; 1 Aquamaster azimuth thruster with contra rotating props
Speed, knots: 13.5
Range, n miles: 9,000 at 10 kt
Complement: 12 plus 12 scientists
Radars: Navigation: Racal Decca 2690 ARPA; I-band.

Comment: Built as a stern trawler. Converted in 1980 for use at RAE Farnborough as an acoustic research ship. Major rebuild in 1992. Re-engined in early 1997 with a raft mounted diesel-electric plant to reduce noise and vibration. Carries a 9 m workboat *Quest* Q 26. Well equipped laboratories. Capable of deploying and recovering up to 5 tons of equipment from deck winches and a 5 ton hydraulic A frame. The ship is also used to support diving operations. Based on the Clyde. To be decommissioned in June 2009.

COLONEL TEMPLER *7/2008*, Ian Harris* / 1335222

2 TORNADO CLASS (TORPEDO RECOVERY VESSELS) (YDT/YPT)

Name	*No*	*Builders*	*Commissioned*
SD TORNADO	–	Hall Russell, Aberdeen	15 Nov 1979
SD TORMENTOR	–	Hall Russell, Aberdeen	29 Apr 1980

Displacement, tons: 698 full load
Dimensions, feet (metres): 154.5 × 29.8 × 16.1 *(47.1 × 9.1 × 4.9)*
Main machinery: 2 Mirrlees-Blackstone ESL8 MGR diesels; 2,170 hp *(1.62 MW)*; 2 shafts
Speed, knots: 14. **Range, n miles:** 3,000 at 14 kt
Complement: 10
Radars: Navigation: Kelvin Hughes 1006; I-band.

Comment: Ordered on 1 July 1977. Both ships converted to support diving operations and mine laying/recovery trials. Based on the Clyde. *Tormentor* to be replaced by *Tremendous* and decommissioned in December 2009 and *Tornado* to be replaced by *Triumphant* and decommissioned in February 2010.

TORNADO *12/1999, W Sartori* / 0075841

1 WATERMAN CLASS (COASTAL TANKER) (AWT)

Name	*No*	*Builders*	*Launched*
SD WATERMAN	–	Dunston, Hessle	1978

Displacement, tons: 220 standard; 470 full load
Dimensions, feet (metres): 131.2 × 23.9 × 11.1 *(40.0 × 7.3 × 3.4)*
Main machinery: 1 Mirrlees Blackstone ERS8 diesel; 650 hp *(485 kW)*; 1 shaft
Speed, knots: 11. **Range, n miles:** 1,500 at 10 kt
Complement: 4
Cargo capacity: 250 tons fresh water

Comment: Based on the Clyde. To be decommissioned in 2011.

WATERMAN *6/2005, John Mortimer* / 1153976

1 RANGE SAFETY CRAFT (YFRT)

SIR WILLIAM ROE 8127

Displacement, tons: 20.2 full load
Dimensions, feet (metres): 48.2 × 11.5 × 4.3 *(14.7 × 3.5 × 1.3)*
Main machinery: 2 Volvo Penta TAMD-122D diesels; 820 hp *(612 kW)*; 2 shafts
Speed, knots: 22. **Range, n miles:** 300 at 20 kt
Complement: 3
Radars: Navigation: Furuno; I-band.

Comment: Built in the 1980s. Based in Cyprus and operated by the Royal Logistic Corps. New engines fitted since 1993.

RSC craft *10/2003, Maritime Photographic* / 0572713

9 ADEPT CLASS (COASTAL TUGS) (YTB)

SD FORCEFUL **SD POWERFUL** **SD BUSTLER** **SD CAREFUL** **SD DEXTEROUS**
SD NIMBLE **SD ADEPT** **SD CAPABLE** **SD FAITHFUL**

Displacement, tons: 441 standard; 540 full load
Dimensions, feet (metres): 127.3 × 29.9 × 13.1 *(38.8 × 9.1 × 4.0)*
Main machinery: 2 Ruston 6RKC diesels; 2,575 hp *(1.92 MW)*; 2 Voith-Schneider props
Speed, knots: 12. **Range, n miles:** 1,500 at 10 kt
Complement: 5

Comment: 'Twin unit tractor tugs' (TUTT). First four ordered from Richard Dunston (Hessle) on 22 February 1979 and next five on 8 February 1984. Primarily for harbour work with coastal towing capability. Nominal bollard pull, 27.5 tons. *Adept* accepted 28 October 1980, *Bustler* 15 April 1981, *Capable* 11 September 1981, *Careful* 12 March 1982, *Forceful* 18 March 1985, *Nimble* 25 June 1985, *Powerful* 30 October 1985, *Faithful* 21 December 1985, *Dexterous* 23 April 1986. *Powerful* and *Bustler* at Portsmouth, *Forceful, Faithful, Adept* and *Careful* at Devonport, *Nimble* and *Dexterous* on the Clyde. *Capable* is operated by Commander British Forces Gibraltar. *Nimble, Bustler, Dexterous* and *Powerful* to be decommissioned in 2010 when replaced by *Dependable, Bountiful, Resourceful* and *Reliable* respectively.

BUSTLER ***8/2008*, Maritime Photographic*** / 1298812

1 ATLAS CLASS (YTM)

SD ATLAS

Measurement, tons: 88 grt
Dimensions, feet (metres): 72.2 × 25.7 × 10.8 *(22.0 × 7.82 × 3.3)*
Main machinery: 2 Caterpillar diesels; 2,100 hp *(1.6 MW)*; 2 shafts
Speed, knots: To be announced
Complement: 3 plus 12 passengers

Comment: Brought into service by SERCo in 2005. Built in Istanbul in 1999 and on charter from a Turkish company. It is British registered. Based at Portsmouth. To remain in service until 2022.

ATLAS ***5/2007, Derek Fox*** / 1305225

3 DOG CLASS (YTM)

SD HUSKY **SD SPANIEL** **SD SHEEPDOG**

Displacement, tons: 248 full load
Dimensions, feet (metres): 94 × 23.9 × 12 *(28.7 × 7.3 × 3.7)*
Main machinery: 2 Lister-Blackstone ERS8 MGR diesels; 1,320 hp *(985 kW)*; 2 shafts
Speed, knots: 10. **Range, n miles:** 2,236 at 10 kt
Complement: 5

Comment: Harbour berthing tugs. Nominal bollard pull, 17.5 tons. Completed 1962–72. Serving at Portsmouth, Devonport and on the Clyde. Appearance varies considerably, some with mast, some with curved upper-bridge work, some with flat monkey-island. Decommissioning dates: *Spaniel* and *Husky* 2009; *Sheepdog* 2010. To be replaced by *Mars, Jupiter* and *Independent* respectively.

SHEEPDOG ***8/2008*, Maritime Photographic*** / 1298803

2 TRITON CLASS (YTL)

SD KITTY **SD LESLEY**

Displacement, tons: 107.5 standard
Dimensions, feet (metres): 57.7 × 18 × 9.2 *(17.6 × 5.5 × 2.8)*
Main machinery: 1 Lister Blackstone ARS4M diesel; 330 hp *(264 kW)*; 1 shaft
Speed, knots: 7.5
Complement: 2

Comment: Both completed by August 1974 by Dunstons. 'Water-tractors' with small wheelhouse and adjoining funnel. Voith-Schneider vertical axis propellers. Nominal bollard pull, 3 tons. Both to be decommissioned in 2009.

TRITON CLASS ***6/2001, A Sharma*** / 0131181

4 FELICITY CLASS (YTL)

SD FRANCES **SD FLORENCE** **SD GENEVIEVE** **SD HELEN**

Displacement, tons: 144 full load
Dimensions, feet (metres): 70 × 21 × 8.5 *(21.5 × 6.4 × 2.6)*
Main machinery: 1 Mirrlees-Blackstone ESM8 diesel; 615 hp *(459 kW)*; 1 Voith-Schneider cp prop
Speed, knots: 10
Range, n miles: 925 at 9 kt
Complement: 4
Radars: Navigation: Raytheon; I-band.

Comment: *Frances, Florence* and *Genevieve* ordered early 1979 from Richard Dunston (Thorne) and completed by end 1980. Nominal bollard pull, 5.7 tons. Based at Devonport and Portsmouth. Decommissioning dates: *Florence* and *Helen* 2010; *Genevieve* and *Frances* 2011. To be replaced by *Eileen, Suzanne, Christina* and *Deborah* respectively.

GENEVIEVE ***11/2008*, Maritime Photographic*** / 1353518

1 RANGE SUPPORT VESSEL (YFRT)

SD WARDEN

Displacement, tons: 900 full load
Dimensions, feet (metres): 159.4 × 34.4 × 16.4 *(48.6 × 10.5 × 5.0)*
Main machinery: 2 Ruston 8RKCZ diesels; 4,000 hp *(2.98 MW)*; 2 shafts; cp props
Speed, knots: 15
Range, n miles: 2,000 at 10 kt
Complement: 7
Radars: Navigation: Racal Decca RM 1250; I-band.
Sonars: Dowty 2053; high frequency.

Comment: Built by Richards, Lowestoft and completed 20 November 1989. Reverted in 1998 to being an RMAS ship at Kyle of Lochalsh in support of BUTEC. Modified in 1998 to act, at BUTEC, as a ROV host ship and weapons launch and recovery platform. To remain in service until 2022.

WARDEN ***5/2008*, Alistair MacDonald*** / 1335221

2 SUBMARINE BERTHING TUGS (YTL)

Name	*No*	*Builders*	*Commissioned*
SD IMPULSE	–	Dunston, Hessle	11 Mar 1993
SD IMPETUS	–	Dunston, Hessle	28 May 1993

Displacement, tons: 530 full load
Dimensions, feet (metres): 106.7 × 32.8 × 17.1 *(32.5 × 10.0 × 5.2)*
Main machinery: 2 WH Allen 8S12 diesels; 3,400 hp *(2.54 MW)* sustained; 2 Aquamaster Azimuth thrusters; 1 Jastrom bow thruster
Speed, knots: 12
Complement: 5

Comment: Ordered 28 January 1992 for submarine berthing duties. There are two 10 ton hydraulic winches forward and aft with break capacities of 110 tons. Bollard pull 38.6 tons ahead, 36 tons astern. Fitted with firefighting and oil pollution equipment. Designed for one-man control from the bridge with all round vision and a comprehensive Navaids fit. *Impulse* launched 10 December 1992; *Impetus* 9 February 1993. Based on the Clyde. To remain in service until 2022.

IMPETUS *10/2004, Maritime Photographic* / 1043618

9 RANGE SAFETY CRAFT (YFRT)

SMIT STOUR **SMIT ROTHER** **SMIT ROMNEY** **SMIT CERNE** **SMIT WEY**
SMIT FROME **SMIT MERRION** **SMIT PENALLY** **SMIT NEYLAND**

Displacement, tons: 6.1 full load
Dimensions, feet (metres): 37.1 × 11.2 × 3.9 *(11.3 × 3.4 × 1.2)*
Main machinery: 2 Volvo Penta KAD 42P diesels; 680 hp *(507 kW)*; 2 × Hamilton waterjets
Speed, knots: 35
Range, n miles: 160 at 21 kt
Complement: 2

Comment: MP-1111 class of vessels designed (based on a fast rescue boat) and built at Maritime Partners Ltd (Norway). Aluminium alloy hull and GRP superstructure. The order for the craft followed a contract awarded to Smit International (Scotland) Ltd for the provision of Range Clearance and Safety duties in and around the various sea danger areas of UK military ranges. Three based at Dover, Portland and Pembroke Dock.

SMIT STOUR *6/2004, Smit International* / 1043617

8 AIRCREW TRAINING CRAFT (YXT)

SMIT DEE **SMIT YARE** **SMIT SPEY** **SMIT TAMAR**
SMIT DON **SMIT TOWY** **SMIT DART** **SMIT CYMYRAN**

Displacement, tons: 55 full load
Dimensions, feet (metres): 90.5 × 21.6 × 4.9 *(27.6 × 6.6 × 1.5)*
Main machinery: 2 Cummins KTA 19M4 diesels; 1,400 hp *(1.04 MW)*; 2 shafts 1 Ultrajet 305 centreline waterjet; 305 hp *(227 kW)*
Speed, knots: 21
Range, n miles: 650 at 21 kt
Complement: 6
Radars: Furuno FR-2115 EPA; I-band.

Comment: Vessels built at Babcock Engineering Services, Rosyth, and FBMA Babcock Marine, Cebu, Philippines *(Yare, Towy* and *Spey)*. All delivered by 11 July 2003. Of aluminium alloy construction, the design is an adaptation of FBM Babcock Marine's Protector class patrol vessel. The order for the craft followed a contract awarded to MoD and to Smit International for provision of marine support to aircrew training, high speed marine target towing and recovery of air-sea rescue apparatus. The craft have an after docking well for a daughter craft. Based at Buckie *(Dee)*, Blyth *(Don)*, Great Yarmouth *(Yare)*, Pembroke Dock *(Towy)* and Plymouth *(Spey* and *Dart)*. *Smit Dart* is employed as a passenger craft. *Tamar* (Plymouth) and *Cymyran* (Holyhead) are similar second-hand craft used for passengers.

SMIT DART *6/2005, Per Körnefeldt* / 1153932

1 SUBMARINE TENDER (YFB)

Name	*No*	*Builders*	*Commissioned*
SD ADAMANT	–	FBM, Cowes	18 Jan 1993

Displacement, tons: 170 full load
Dimensions, feet (metres): 101 × 25.6 × 9.8 *(30.8 × 7.8 × 3.0)*
Main machinery: 2 Cummins KTA-19M2 diesels; 1,360 hp *(1 MW)*; 2 water-jets
Speed, knots: 23
Range, n miles: 250 at 22 kt
Complement: 4 plus 36 passengers plus 1 ton stores

Comment: Twin-hulled support ship ordered in 1991 and launched 8 October 1992. Used for personnel and stores transfers in the Firth of Clyde. In addition to the passengers, half a ton of cargo can be carried. Capable of top speed up to Sea State 3 and able to transit safely up to Sea State 6. To be withdrawn from service in late 2009 when replaced by *Eva*.

ADAMANT *10/1998, M Verschaeve* / 0053268

2 STORM CLASS (YFB)

Name	*No*	*Builders*	*Commissioned*
SD CAWSAND	–	FBM Marine, Cowes	July 1997
SD BOVISAND	–	FBM Marine, Cowes	Sep 1997

Displacement, tons: 97
Dimensions, feet (metres): 78.4 × 36.4 × 16.2 *(23.9 × 11.1 × 4.95)*
Main machinery: 2 Caterpillar 3408TA diesels; 1,224 hp(m) *(900 kW)*; 2 shafts
Speed, knots: 15
Range, n miles: 450 at 14 kt
Complement: 5 plus 75 passengers

Comment: Both based at Devonport. Swath design with hydraulically operated telescopic gangways. To remain in service until 2022.

CAWSAND *5/2008*, Peter Ford* / 1353503

3 OBAN CLASS (YFL)

SD OBAN **SD ORONSAY** **SD OMAGH**

Displacement, tons: 297 full load
Dimensions, feet (metres): 90.9 × 24 × 12.3 *(27.7 × 7.3 × 3.8)*
Main machinery: 2 Cummins N14M diesels; 1,050 hp(m) *(785 kW)*; 2 Kort-Nozzles
Speed, knots: 10
Range, n miles: 1,700 at 10 kt
Complement: 4

Comment: Built by McTay Marine and completed January to July 2000. Capable of carrying 60 passengers. *Oban* based at Devonport and the other two on the Clyde. To remain in service until 2022.

OBAN *5/2008*, A A de Kruijf* / 1335217

4 PADSTOW AND NEWHAVEN CLASSES (YFL)

SD PADSTOW **SD NEWHAVEN** **SD NUTBOURNE** **SD NETLEY**

Displacement, tons: 57 standard; 125 full load
Dimensions, feet (metres): 60 × 21.3 × 8.9 *(18.3 × 6.5 × 2.7)*
Main machinery: 2 Cummins 6 CTA diesels; 710 hp(m) *(522 kW)*; 2 shafts
Speed, knots: 10
Range, n miles: 230 at 10 kt
Complement: 3

Comment: Built by Aluminium Shipbuilders at Fishbourne, Isle of Wight and completed May to November 2000. Capable of carrying 60 passengers and based at Devonport *(Padstow)* and Portsmouth. Catamaran hulls. To remain in service until 2022.

PADSTOW *3/2008*, B Sullivan* / 1335216

3 MANLY CLASS (YAG)

SD MELTON **SD MENAI** **SD MEON**

Displacement, tons: 143 full load
Dimensions, feet (metres): 80 × 21 × 9.8 *(24.4 × 6.4 × 3.0)*
Main machinery: 1 Lister-Blackstone ESR4 MGR diesel; 320 hp *(239 kW)*; 1 shaft
Speed, knots: 10
Range, n miles: 700 at 10 kt
Complement: 6 (2 officers)

Comment: All built by Richard Dunston, Thorne. All completed by early 1983. *Melton* is at Kyle of Lochalsh, the other two are at Devonport. To remain in service until 2022.

MEON *8/2008*, Marco Ghiglino* / 1353517

1 FBM CATAMARAN CLASS (YFL)

SD NORTON

Displacement, tons: 21 full load
Dimensions, feet (metres): 51.8 × 18 × 4.9 *(15.8 × 5.5 × 1.5)*
Main machinery: 2 Mermaid Turbo 4 diesels; 280 hp *(209 kW)*; 2 shafts
Speed, knots: 10
Range, n miles: 400 at 10 kt
Complement: 2

Comment: Built by FBM Marine in 1989. Catamaran design. Can carry 30 passengers or 2 tons stores. Based at Portsmouth.

NORTON *7/2008*, A A de Kruijf* / 1335218

0 + 1 SUPPORT SHIP (AG)

Name	*No*	*Builders*	*Commissioned*
SD VICTORIA	–	Damen Shipyard, Galatz	May 2010

Displacement, tons: 2,500 full load
Measurement, tons: 850 dwt
Dimensions, feet (metres): 272.3 × 52.5 × 13.9 *(83.0 × 16.0 × 4.25)*
Main machinery: 2 Caterpillar 3526B diesels; 4,000 hp *(3.0 MW)*; 2 shafts; cp props; 1 bow thruster; 805 hp *(600 kW)*
Speed, knots: 14
Complement: 16 plus additional accommodation for 72
Radars: Surface search/navigation: E/F-band.
Navigation: I-band.

Comment: Damen Support Ship 8316 design. The ship, to replace *Newton*, is to be capable of worldwide operations including military training, transport of personnel and equipment and conduct of diving support operations. Facilities include classrooms, briefing and operations rooms, workshops, extensive storage areas, a helicopter winching deck, and provision to carry and operate Rigid Inflatable Boats (RIBs). To be delivered on 28 May 2010.

SUPPORT SHIP *6/2008*, Serco Denholm* / 1298813

0 + 4 BERTHING TUGS (YTM)

SD RELIABLE **SD BOUNTIFUL** **SD RESOURCEFUL** **SD DEPENDABLE**

Displacement, tons: 370
Dimensions, feet (metres): 95.5 × 32.8 × 15.7 *(29.1 × 10.0 × 4.8)*
Main machinery: 2 Caterpillar 3512 diesels; 4,025 hp *(3.0 MW)*; 2 Rolls Royce US 175 thrusters
Speed, knots: 12
Complement: To be announced
Radars: Navigation: 2 JRC 5210; I-band.

Comment: Damen Azimuth Tractor Drive (ATD) Tug 2909 design. *Reliable* (based on the Clyde) to be delivered on 27 November 2009, *Bountiful* (Clyde) on 2 April 2010, *Resourceful* (Portsmouth) on 28 May 2010 and *Dependable* (Portsmouth) on 23 July 2010.

ATD 2909 *6/2008*, Serco Denholm* / 1298811

0 + 2 SUPPORT VESSELS (AG)

Name	*No*	*Builders*	*Commissioned*
SD TREMENDOUS	–	ADYard, Abu Dhabi	2009
SD TRIUMPHANT	–	ADYard, Abu Dhabi	2009

Displacement, tons: 1,700
Dimensions, feet (metres): 164.4 × 42.6 × 13.9 *(50.1 × 13.0 × 4.25)*
Main machinery: 2 Caterpillar 3512 diesels; 3,800 hp *(2.85 MW)*; 2 shafts; 1 bow thruster; 500 kW; 1 stern thruster; 335 kW
Speed, knots: 12
Complement: 12 (6 officers)
Radars: Surface search/navigation: E/F-band.
Navigation: I-band.

Comment: Henderson design. Shallow draft, anchor handler design incorporating a large clear after deck, winches and deck crane. *Tremendous* (to replace *Tormentor*) to be delivered on 31 October 2009 and *Triumphant* (to replace *Tornado*) on 31 December 2009.

0 + 2 BERTHING TUGS (YTM)

SD INDEPENDENT **SD INDULGENT**

Displacement, tons: 345
Dimensions, feet (metres): 85.6 × 31.0 × 14.1 *(26.09 × 9.44 × 4.3)*
Main machinery: 2 Caterpillar 3512B diesels; 3,500 hp *(2.6 MW)*; 2 Rolls Royce US 155 thrusters; 1 bow thruster
Speed, knots: 13
Complement: 8
Radars: Navigation: JRC 5210; I-band.

Comment: Damen Azimuth Stern Drive Tug 2509 design. *Independent* to be delivered on 16 October 2009 and *Indulgent* on 31 December 2009. Both based at Portsmouth.

ASD 2509 *6/2008*, Serco Denholm* / 1298810

3 LARGE WORKBOATS (YTM)

SD HERCULES **SD MARS** **SD JUPITER**

Displacement, tons: 270
Dimensions, feet (metres): 87.3 × 27.7 × 10.2 *(26.61 × 8.44 × 3.12)*
Main machinery: 2 Caterpillar 3508B diesels; 2,200 hp *(1.6 MW)*; 2 shafts; 2 Van de Giessen nozzles
Speed, knots: 12
Complement: 9
Radars: Navigation: 2 JRC 5210; I-band.

Comment: Damen Stan Tug 2608 design. *Hercules* (based at Devonport) delivered on 9 January 2009, *Mars* (Clyde) on 27 March 2009 and *Jupiter* (Clyde) on 26 June 2009.

STAN TUG 2608 *6/2008*, Serco Denholm* / 1298809

0 + 1 TRANSPORT VESSEL (YFB)

SD EVA

Displacement, tons: 120
Dimensions, feet (metres): 108.9 × 24.3 × 6.4 *(33.2 × 7.4 × 1.95)*
Main machinery: 2 Caterpillar C32-C diesels; 2,800 hp *(2.1 MW)*; 2 shafts
Speed, knots: 22
Complement: 4 plus 34 passengers
Radars: JRC 5210; I-band.

Comment: Damen FCS 3307 design. A crew transport vessel embodying a 'Sea Axe' bow. Aluminium construction. To be delivered on 21 August 2009 and to be based on the Clyde. To replace *Adamant*.

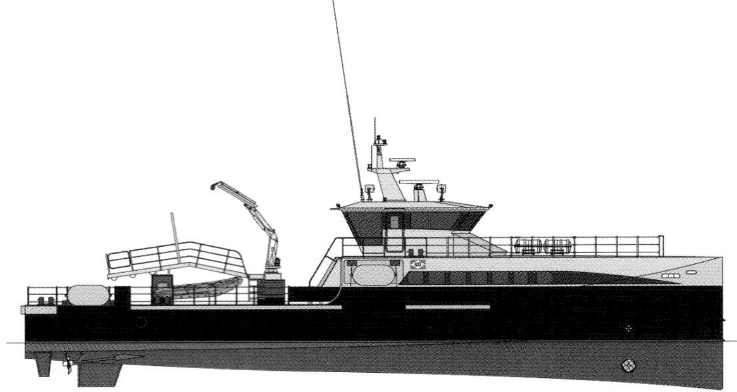

FCS 3307 *6/2008*, Serco Denholm* / 1298807

0 + 4 BERTHING TUGS (YTM)

SD EILEEN **SD SUZANNE** **SD CHRISTINA** **SD DEBORAH**

Displacement, tons: 245
Dimensions, feet (metres): 69.5 × 30.8 × 11.8 *(21.2 × 9.4 × 3.6)*
Main machinery: 2 Caterpillar 3508 diesels; 2,000 hp *(1.5 MW)*; 2 Rolls Royce US 155 thrusters
Speed, knots: 11
Complement: To be announced
Radars: Navigation: 2 JRC 5210; I-band.

Comment: Damen Azimuth Stern Drive Tug 2009 design. *Eileen* (based at Devonport) to be delivered on 21 May 2010, *Suzanne* (Portsmouth) on 30 July 2010, *Christina* (Portsmouth) on 8 October 2010 and *Deborah* (Devonport) on 17 December 2010.

ASD 2009 *6/2008*, Serco Denholm* / 1298808

3 PERSONNEL TENDERS (YFL)

SD CLYDE SPIRIT **SD SOLENT SPIRIT** **SD TAMAR SPIRIT**

Measurement, tons: 100 grt
Dimensions, feet (metres): 62.8 × 17.4 × 5.4 *(19.15 × 5.3 × 1.65)*
Main machinery: 2 Caterpillar C 32 diesels; 2,200 hp *(1.64 MW)*; 2 shafts
Speed, knots: 20
Complement: 3 plus 12 passengers
Radars: Navigation: JRC 5210; I-band.

Comment: Damen Stan Tender 1905 design. Steel hull with aluminium superstructure. Transport craft used for transfer of pilots, VIPs and personnel. *Clyde Spirit* (based on the Clyde) delivered on 27 June 2008, *Solent Spirit* (based at Portsmouth) on 25 July 2008 and *Tamar Spirit* (based at Devonport) on 17 October 2008.

SOLENT SPIRIT *8/2008*, Maritime Photographic* / 1298802

0 + 2 MULTIPURPOSE VESSELS (YAG)

SD NAVIGATOR **SD RAASAY**

Displacement, tons: 310
Dimensions, feet (metres): 86.3 × 34.9 × 8.4 *(26.3 × 10.64 × 2.55)*
Main machinery: 2 Caterpillar C18 diesels; 957 hp *(713 kW)*; 2 shafts; 1 Veth-jet bow thruster
Speed, knots: 8
Complement: 3 plus 12 passengers
Radars: JRC JMA 5210; I-band.

Comment: Damen Multi Cat 2510 design. *Navigator* is to be used for buoy handling and mooring; equipped with a single crane capable of lifting up to 9 tonnes, the ship is to be capable of support diving operations. She is to be delivered on 17 July 2009. *Raasay*, is to be equipped with two cranes to carryout torpedo recovery, towed sonar array deployment and recovery, diving training and other trials duties. To be based at Kyle of Lochalsh, she is to be delivered on 8 January 2010.

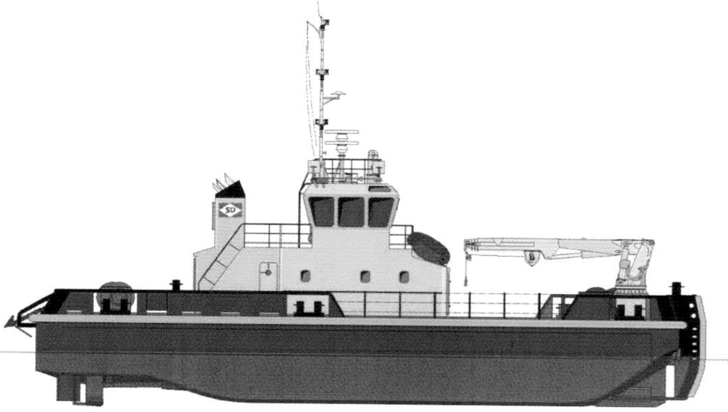

MULTI CAT 2510 (Buoy Handler) *6/2008*, Serco Denholm* / 1298806

3 PERSONNEL TENDERS (YFL)

SD CLYDE RACER **SD SOLENT RACER** **SD TAMAR RACER**

Measurement, tons: 100 grt
Dimensions, feet (metres): 52.5 × 15.9 × 4.1 *(16.0 × 4.85 × 1.25)*
Main machinery: 2 Caterpillar 3406 diesels; 1,100 hp *(820 kW)*; 2 shafts
Speed, knots: 20
Complement: 3 plus 10 passengers
Radars: Navigation: JRC 5210; I-band.

Comment: Damen Stan Tender 1505 design. Transport craft used for transfer of pilots, VIPs and personnel. *Clyde Racer* (based on the Clyde) delivered on 20 June 2008, *Solent Racer* (based at Portsmouth) on 19 September 2008 and *Tamar Racer* (based at Devonport) on 10 October 2008. Aluminium construction.

SOLENT RACER *8/2008*, Maritime Photographic* / 1304060

1 HARBOUR WORKBOAT (YTL)

SD TILLY

Displacement, tons: 45
Dimensions, feet (metres): 47.7 × 16.3 × 5.9 *(14.55 × 4.98 × 1.8)*
Main machinery: 2 Caterpillar 3406C diesels; 600 hp *(447 kW)*; 2 shafts; 2 Van de Giessen nozzles
Speed, knots: 9
Complement: To be announced
Radars: Navigation: JRC JAMA-5210; I-band.

Comment: Damen Stan Tug 1405 design. General purpose inshore waters and harbour workboat delivered on 9 January 2009. Based at Devonport.

STAN TUG 1405 *6/2008*, Serco Denholm* / 1298805

1 PENRYN CLASS (YTL)

SD PENRYN

Measurement, tons: 32 grt
Dimensions, feet (metres): 61.7 × 23.6 × 2.6 *(18.8 × 7.2 × 0.8)*
Main machinery: 2 Detroit 8082 diesels; 1,300 hp *(970 kW)*; 2 shafts
Speed, knots: 18
Complement: 3 plus 75 passengers

Comment: Built by Chantier Metalnox, France in 1990. Based at Devonport.

PENRYN *3/2008*, B Sullivan* / 1335215

2 HARBOUR WORKBOATS (YTL)

SD CATHERINE **SD EMILY**

Displacement, tons: 29.4
Dimensions, feet (metres): 40.3 × 13.5 × 5.1 *(12.3 × 4.13 × 1.55)*
Main machinery: 1 Caterpillar 3056 diesel; 165 hp *(123 kW)*; 1 shaft
Speed, knots: 8
Complement: To be announced
Radars: JRC JMA-5104; I-band.

Comment: Inshore waters and harbour workboats. Damen Pushy Cat 1204 design. Steel construction. *Catherine* (based at Portsmouth) delivered on 4 January 2008 and *Emily* (based on the Clyde) on 8 March 2008.

CATHERINE *2/2009*, Maritime Photographic* / 1353723

ARMY (ROYAL LOGISTIC CORPS)

Notes: (1) Six Mk 4 LCVPs are listed in the RN section. One is based in the Falklands.
(2) One Range Safety Craft is listed in RMAS section.
(3) 32 Combat Support Boats delivered by 2002. These are 8.2 m craft, road transportable and with a top speed of 30 kt.
(4) Four new 14 m Army workboats were delivered in 2008. They are to be capable of fire fighting, pollution control, mexeflote operations, towed flexible barge duties, diving operations and general tug duties.
(5) 17 Port and Maritime Regt, RLC is based at Marchwood, Southampton.

COMBAT SUPPORT BOAT *1/2004* / 1167573

WORKBOAT WB 41 *7/2008*, Derek Fox* / 1353504

6 RAMPED CRAFT, LOGISTIC (RCL)

Name	*No*	*Builders*	*Commissioned*
ANDALSNES	L 107	James and Stone, Brightlingsea	22 May 1984
AKYAB	L 109	James and Stone, Brightlingsea	15 Dec 1984
AACHEN	L 110	James and Stone, Brightlingsea	12 Feb 1987
AREZZO	L 111	James and Stone, Brightlingsea	26 Mar 1987
ARROMANCHES (ex-*Agheila*)	L 105 (ex-L 112)	James and Stone, Brightlingsea	12 June 1987
AUDEMER	L 113	James and Stone, Brightlingsea	21 Aug 1987

Displacement, tons: 295 full load
Dimensions, feet (metres): 109.2 × 28.2 × 4.9 *(33.3 × 8.6 × 1.5)*
Main machinery: 2 Dorman 8JTCWM diesels; 504 hp *(376 kW)* sustained; 2 shafts
Speed, knots: 10. **Range, n miles:** 900 at 10 kt
Complement: 6 (2 NCOs)
Military lift: 96 tons
Radars: Navigation: Racal Decca; I-band.

Comment: *Andalsnes* and *Akyab* based in Cyprus, remainder at Southampton.

ARROMANCHES *8/2007, Maritime Photographic* / 1170253

AUDEMER *7/2006, Frank Findler* / 1167453

SCOTTISH FISHERIES PROTECTION AGENCY

Notes: (1) The Agency is responsible for the enforcement of sea fisheries regulations around the Scottish coast to a distance of 200 n miles. It has a complement of 275.
(2) There are two Cessna F-406 Caravan II aircraft with Bendix 1500 radars.

2 JURA CLASS (PSO)

JURA **HIRTA**

Measurement, tons: 2,182 grt
Dimensions, feet (metres): 275.6 × 42.6 × 14.7 *(84.0 × 13.0 × 4.5)*
Main machinery: Diesel-electric; 3 Wärtsilä Gensets; 6,500 hp *(4.8 MW)*; 1 shaft; cp prop; 1 Brunvoll bow thruster *(Hirta)*; 1 Brunvoll stern thruster *(Hirta)*
Speed, knots: 18
Complement: 16 (7 officers)
Radars: Surface search/navigation: Sperry Marine Bridgemaster; E/F/I-bands.

Comment: *Jura* built by Ferguson Shipbuilders, Port Glasgow. Launched on 28 April 2005 and entered service in early 2006 to replace *Sulisker*. *Hirta* built by Stocznia Polnocna, Gdansk, launched on 17 August 2007 and entered service in late 2007. A third ship is no longer planned.

JURA *1/2006, SFPA* / 1159412

1 SULISKER CLASS (PSO)

NORNA

Displacement, tons: 1,586 full load
Dimensions, feet (metres): 234.3 × 38 × 17.6 *(71.4 × 11.6 × 5.4)*
Main machinery: 2 Ruston 6AT350 diesels; 6,000 hp *(4.48 MW)* sustained; 2 shafts; cp props; bow thruster; 450 hp *(336 kW)*
Speed, knots: 18
Range, n miles: 7,000 at 13 kt
Complement: 16 (7 officers) plus 6 spare bunks
Radars: Navigation: 2 Racal Decca Bridgemaster; I-band.

Comment: Built by Richards, Lowestoft and completed in June 1988. *Sulisker* was decommissioned in early 2006 and *Vigilant* in 2008.

NORNA *6/2005, Maritime Photographic* / 1153974

1 MINNA CLASS (PBO)

MINNA

Displacement, tons: 855 full load
Dimensions, feet (metres): 156.5 × 32.8 × 14.8 *(47.7 × 10.0 × 4.5)*
Main machinery: 2 Wärtsilä Gensets; 2,896 hp *(2.16 MW)*; 2 Indar propulsion motors; 2,145 hp *(1.6 MW)*; 2 shafts; 1 Kamewa transverse thruster *(150 kW)*
Speed, knots: 14
Complement: 15 (6 officers)

Comment: Built by Ferguson Shipbuilders, Port Glasgow. Launched in February 2003 and accepted by SFPA on 31 July 2003 as replacement for *Westra*. Procurement of a second similar ship was cancelled following a review in 2006.

MINNA *6/2003, SFPA* / 0561556

CUSTOMS

Notes: HM Revenue and Customs Maritime Branch operates five offshore patrol vessels. The fleet comprises four Damen 42 m craft *(Seeker, Searcher, Vigilant, Valiant)*, one Vosper Thornycroft 36 m craft *(Sentinel)*.

VALIANT *1/2009*, Maritime Photographic* / 1353516

SENTINEL *5/2001, A Sharma* / 0131218

TRINITY HOUSE

Notes: The Corporation of Trinity House, with its HQ in London, has three responsibilities. It is the General Lighthouse Authority (GLA) for England, Wales and the Channel Islands; a Deep Sea Pilotage Authority for UK; and a major maritime charity, funded by its endowments, which supports the education, welfare and training of mariners and the promotion of safety at sea. In its GLA role, Trinity House provides nearly 600 aids to navigation including lighthouses, lightvessels, buoys, beacons, a differential global positioning service and an experimental radio-navigation service e-LORAN. Funding for these operations is by light dues levied on commercial shipping calling at UK ports. Operations are controlled from its Harwich centre while a depot at Swansea serves the west coast.

PATRICIA

Displacement, tons: 3,139 full load
Dimensions, feet (metres): 284.0 × 46.0 × 14.0 *(86.3 × 13.8 × 4.3)*
Main machinery: 4 Ruston Oil diesels; 4,285 bhp (*3.2 MW*); connected via 4 generators to 2 motors; 3,452 hp *(2.54 MW)*; 2 shafts
Speed, knots: 14
Range, n miles: 10,000 at 12 kt
Complement: 25 (8 officers)

Comment: Built by Henry Robb Ltd, Leith. Commissioned in May 1982.

PATRICIA *7/2008*, Maritime Photographic* / 1353515

GALATEA

Displacement, tons: 3,960 full load
Dimensions, feet (metres): 275.5 × 54.1 × 14.8 *(84.0 × 16.5 × 4.25)*
Main machinery: 3 Wärtsilä 8L20 diesels; 2 shafts
Speed, knots: 13
Range, n miles: 5,250 at 12 kt
Complement: 18

Comment: New multifunction tender built by Stocznia Remontowa SA shipbuilders at Gdansk, Poland. Launched on 26 July 2006, she was named by The Queen on 17 October 2007. Design features include a large working deck area and a forward helicopter flight deck. She is equipped with a dynamic positioning system.

GALATEA *12/2008*, Maritime Photographic* / 1353514

ALERT

Displacement, tons: 325 full load
Dimensions, feet (metres): 128.9 × 26.2 × 7.8 *(39.3 × 8.0 × 2.4)*
Main machinery: 2 Caterpillar 3512 diesels; 4,023 hp *(3 MW)*; 2 shafts; cp props; bow thruster
Speed, knots: 16
Range, n miles: 400 at 12 kt
Complement: 5

Comment: Rapid intervention vessel built by Stocznia Remontowa SA shipbuilders at Gdansk, Poland. Launched on 11 October 2005, she was delivered in 2006. In addition to maintaining aids to navigation, the vessel providesa fast response capability and the means to carry out emergency wreck marking and hydrographic survey services. Her primary areas of operation are the Dover Strait, English Channel and Southern North Sea. The ship is equipped with a dynamic positioning system.

ALERT *5/2006, Mark Rayner* / 1167574

NORTHERN LIGHTHOUSE BOARD

Notes: The Northern Lighthouse Board (NLB) is the General Lighthouse Authority for Scotland and the Isle of Man. The Board provides Aids to Navigation (AtoN) including lighthouses, buoys and beacons and radio navigation aids. NLB is funded from the General Lighthouse Fund, which draws most of its income from the levy of light dues on commercial and fishing vessels calling at UK and Republic of Ireland ports. Operations are directed from its headquarters in Edinburgh.

PHAROS

Measurement, tons: 3,672 grt
Dimensions, feet (metres): 276.2 × 54.1 × 13.9 *(84.2 × 16.5 × 4.25)*
Main machinery: Diesel-electric; 2 azimuth props; 2 bow thrusters
Speed, knots: 13.5
Complement: 18 (7 officers) plus accommodation for 12

Comment: The contract for the construction of a new multifunction tender was signed with Remontowa Shipyard, Gdansk, Poland on 11 November 2004. The ship was launched on 3 February 2006 and delivered in March 2007. *Pharos* the tenth NLB vessel to carry the name has replaced the former vessel now used as a fishery patrol vessel by the government of South Georgia. The new ship is fitted with dynamic positioning, a large aft working deck area, buoy and chain handling, towing, integrated bridge management system, full hydrographic survey suite and moon pool, helicopter deck and a 30-tonne crane.

PHAROS *4/2007, NLB* / 1170250

POLE STAR

Displacement, tons: 1,373 full load
Dimensions, feet (metres): 169.0 × 39.4 × 11.5 *(51.5 × 12.0 × 3.5)*
Main machinery: Diesel-electric; 3 Cummins Wärtsilä generators; 3,700 hp *(2.8 MW)*; 2 motors; 2,680 hp *(2 MW)*; 2 azimuth props; 2 bow thrusters
Speed, knots: 12
Complement: 15 (6 officers)
Radars: Sperry Marine; E/F/I-bands.

Comment: Built by Ferguson Shipbuilders, Port Glasgow. Laid down on 28 July 1999 and delivered on 15 September 2000. Principal roles are hydrographic survey and buoy handling. Equipped with dynamic positioning and an 18-tonne crane.

POLE STAR *11/2007, NLB* / 1170249

MARITIME & COASTGUARD AGENCY

Notes: The Maritime & Coastguard Agency is responsible for the development, promotion and enforcement of high standards of marine safety, response to maritime emergencies 24 hours a day, reduction of the risk of pollution of the marine environment from ships and, where pollution occurs, minimisation of its impact on the United Kingdom.

Response to maritime emergencies within the UK SAR region is undertaken by HM Coastguard, the MCA's Counter-pollution Response Branch and firefighting teams from the Maritime Incident Response Group. SAR and counter pollution is co-ordinated through a network of 18 Maritime Rescue Co-ordination Centres (MRCCs). Each MRCC provides continuous emergency telephone, radio and satellite communications distress watch plus safety information and radio medical advice services. The counter-pollution branch provides response to marine pollution and provides scientific and technical advice on shoreline clean up.

The MCA provides four civilian SAR helicopters (Sikorsky S-92 and AgustaWestland 139) under contract from CHC Scotia. They are based at Sumburgh, Stornoway, Lee-on-Solent and Portland. Fixed-wing aircraft include a BN Islander which conducts surveillance patrols over the Dover Strait and forms part of the Channel Navigation Information Service while, for counter-pollution, a Cessna 404 and Cessna 406 are operated by the RVL Group of Coventry. Fitted with radar, IR and UV detection equipment. Additionally a Cessna 406 and two Lockheed Electra aircraft are available for dispersant spraying. Four emergency towing vessels for SAR, counter-pollution and salvage are under contract from Klyne Tugs Ltd: *Anglian Prince* (1,598 tons gwt), *Anglian Princess* and *Anglian Sovereign* (2,270 tons gwt) and *Anglian Monarch* (1,480 tons gwt). These are stationed in the Fair Isle, Minches, SW Approaches and Dover Strait areas.

HM Coastguard has its own corps of 3,500 volunteer Auxiliary Coastguards divided into 380 Coastguard Rescue Teams around the coast of UK. HM Coastguard also make significant use of Royal National Lifeboat Institution all-weather and inshore lifeboats and military SAR helicopters.

The MCA is also responsible for inspections and surveys of UK vessels, port state control inspections of non UK ships, the enforcement of merchant shipping legislation, the setting of ship and seafarer standards and maritime security.

ANGLIAN PRINCESS *3/2008*, B Sullivan* / 1353513

ANGLIAN PRINCE *10/2004, Maritime Photographic* / 1043623

AB-139 *7/2007, MCA* / 1353512

S-92 *7/2007, MCA* / 1170247

United States

Country Overview

The United States of America is a federal republic which comprises 48 contiguous states (bounded to the north by Canada and to the south by Mexico) and the states of Alaska and Hawaii. External territories include Puerto Rico, American Samoa, Guam and the US Virgin Islands. With an area of 3,717,800 square miles, it occupies much of North America and has a coastline of 10,762 n miles with the Atlantic and Pacific Oceans and with the Gulf of Mexico. Washington, DC is the capital while New York, New York, is the largest city and a leading seaport. Other principal ports include New Orleans, Louisiana; Houston, Texas; Valdez, Alaska; Baton Rouge, Louisiana; Corpus Christi, Texas; Long Beach, California; Norfolk, Virginia; Tampa, Florida; Los Angeles, California; St Louis, Missouri; and Duluth, Wisconsin. There is an extensive inland waterway network, the three main components of which are the Mississippi river system (13,000 n miles long), the Great Lakes (ocean-going vessels can sail between the Great Lakes and the Atlantic Ocean via the St Lawrence Seaway (opened 1959)) and coastal waterways. Territorial seas (12 n miles) are claimed. A 200 n mile EEZ has been claimed but the limits have only been partly defined by boundary agreements.

Unified Combatant Commanders

Commander, US Strategic Command:
General Kevin P Chilton
Commander, US Pacific Command:
Admiral Timothy J Keating
Commander, US Joint Forces Command:
General James N Mattis
Commander, US European Command:
General Bantz J Craddock
Commander, US Northern Command:
General Gene Renuart
Commander, US Southern Command:
Admiral James G Stavridis
Commander, US Central Command:
General David H Petraeus
Commander, US Africa Command:
General William E Ward
Commander, US Special Operations Command:
Admiral Eric T Olson

Headquarters Appointments

Chief of Naval Operations:
Admiral Gary Roughead
Vice Chief of Naval Operations:
Admiral Patrick M Walsh
Director, Naval Nuclear Propulsion:
Admiral Kirkland H Donald
Chief of Naval Personnel:
Vice Admiral Mark E Ferguson III

Headquarters Appointments—*continued*

Commander, Naval Sea Systems Command:
Vice Admiral Kevin M McCoy
Commander, Naval Air Systems Command:
Vice Admiral David J Venlet
Commander, Space and Naval Warfare Systems Command:
Rear Admiral Michael C Bachman

Fleet Commanders

Commander, US Fleet Forces Command:
Admiral Jonathan W Greenert
Commander, US Pacific Fleet:
Admiral Robert F Willard
Commander, Allied Joint Forces Command, Naples, and US Naval Forces Europe:
Admiral Mark Fitzgerald
Commander, Military Sealift Command:
Rear Admiral Robert D Reilly, Jr

Flag Officers (Atlantic Area)

Commander, Second Fleet:
Vice Admiral Mel Williams Jr
Commander, Naval Surface Force, Atlantic Fleet:
Rear Admiral Kevin M Quinn
Commander, Sixth Fleet, Allied Joint Command Lisbon and Striking and Support Forces NATO:
Vice Admiral James A Winnefeld
Commander, Submarine Force Atlantic and Allied Submarine Command:
Vice Admiral John J Donnelly
Commander, Naval Air Force, Atlantic Fleet:
Rear Admiral Richard J O'Hanlon
Commander, Navy Region Europe and Maritime Air, Naples:
Rear Admiral David J Mercer
Commander, Naval Forces Southern Command and Fourth Fleet:
Rear Admiral Joseph D Kernan

Flag Officers (Pacific Area)

Commander, Seventh Fleet:
Vice Admiral John M Bird
Commander, Naval Surface Force, Pacific Fleet:
Vice Admiral Derwood C Curtis
Commander, Third Fleet:
Vice Admiral Samuel J Locklear III
Commander, Naval Air Forces and Naval Air Force, Pacific Fleet:
Vice Admiral Thomas J Kilcline
Commander, US Naval Forces, Japan:
Rear Admiral James D Kelly

Flag Officers (Pacific Area)—*continued*

Commander, Submarine Force, Pacific Fleet:
Rear Admiral Douglas J McAneny
Commander, US Naval Forces, Korea:
Rear Admiral Thomas S Rowden
Commander, US Naval Forces, Marianas:
Rear Admiral William D French
Commander, Naval Mine and Anti-Submarine Warfare Command:
Rear Admiral Robert P Girrier

Flag Officer (Central Area)

Commander, US Naval Forces, Central Command, and Fifth Fleet:
Vice Admiral William E Gortney

Marine Corps

Commandant:
General James T Conway
Assistant Commandant:
General James F Amos
Commander, US Marine Corps Forces Command:
Lieutenant General Richard F Natonski
Commander, US Marine Corps Forces Pacific:
Lieutenant General Keith J Stalder
Commander, Marine Forces Reserve and Commander Marine Forces North:
Lieutenant General Jack W Bergman
Commanding General I MEF and Commander US Marine Corps Forces Central Command:
Lieutenant General Samuel T Helland
Commanding General II MEF:
Lieutenant General Dennis Hejlik
Commanding General III MEF and Commander, Marine Corps Bases, Japan:
Lieutenant General Richard C Zilmer

Prefix to Ships' Names

USS (United States Ship) Warships
USNS (United States Naval Ship) Military Sealift Command

Personnel

	1 Jan 2007	*1 Jan 2008*	*1 Jan 2009*
Navy			
Officers	51,880	49,709	49,735
Warrants	1,579	1,628	1,653
Enlisted	290,823	278,738	275,667
Marine Corps			
Officers	17,266	17,794	18,508
Warrants	1,826	1,829	1,849
Enlisted	159,385	166,103	179,994

Strength of the Fleet (1 January 2009)

Type	*Active (NRF) (Reserve)*	*Building (Projected) + Conversion/SLEP*
SHIPS OF THE FLEET		
Strategic Missile Submarines		
SSBN (Ballistic Missile Submarines) (nuclear-powered)	14	–
Cruise Missile Submarines (SSGN) (nuclear-powered)	4	–
Attack Submarines		
SSN Submarines (nuclear-powered)	53	13
Aircraft Carriers		
CVN Multipurpose Aircraft Carriers (nuclear-powered)	11	1 (1)
Cruisers		
CG Guided Missile Cruisers	22	–
Destroyers		
DDG 1000	–	2 (1)
DDG Guided Missile Destroyers	54	8 (8)
Frigates		
FFH Frigates	21 (9)	–
LCS Littoral Combat Ships	1	1
Patrol Forces		
PC Coastal Defense Ships	8	–
Command Ships		
LCC Command Ships	2	–
Amphibious Warfare Forces		
LHA Amphibious Assault Ships (general purpose)	2	1
LHD Amphibious Assault Ships (multipurpose)	7	1
LPD Amphibious Transport Docks	9	5 (1)
LSD Dock Landing Ships	12	–
LSV Logistic Support Vessels	8	–
Mine Warfare Forces		
MCM Mine Countermeasures Ships	14	–
Research		
AGE Research	2	1
HSV High Speed Vessels	2	1 (9)
AGOR Oceanographic	6	–
MILITARY SEALIFT COMMAND INVENTORY		
Naval Fleet Auxiliary Force		
T-AOE Fast Combat Support	4	–
T-AKE Auxiliary Cargo and Ammunition	6	4 (4)
T-AE Ammunition	4	–
T-AFS Combat Stores	3	–
T-AH Hospital	2	–
T-AO Oilers	14	–
T-ARS Salvage	4	–
T-ATF Fleet Ocean Tugs	4	–
Special Mission Ships		
AS Submarine Tenders	2	–
T-AG/T-AGM Miscellaneous	2	1
T-AGOS Surveillance/Patrol	5	–
T-AGS Surveying	8	–
T-ARC Cable Repair	1	–
Strategic Sealift Force		
T-AKR Fast Sealift	11	–
T-AOT Tankers	4	–
Prepositioning Programme		
T-AK	17	–
T-AKR Large, Medium-Speed, Ro-Ro	9	–
T-AG	1	–
T-AVB Aviation Logistic	2	–
Ready Reserve Force		
T-ACS Crane Ships	6	–
T-AK Break Bulk	6	–
T-AKR Ro-ro	35	–
T-AOT/T-AOG Product Tankers	1	–

Special Notes

To provide similar information to that included in other major navies' Deployment Tables the fleet assignment (abbreviated 'F/S') status of each ship in the US Navy has been included. The assignment appears in a column immediately to the right of the commissioning date. In the case of the Floating Dry Dock section this system is not used. The following abbreviations are used to indicate fleet assignments:

AA	active Atlantic Fleet
Active	active under charter with MSC
AR	in reserve Out of Commission, Atlantic Fleet
ASA	active In Service, Atlantic Fleet
ASR	in reserve Out of Service, Atlantic Fleet
Bldg	Building
CONV	ship undergoing conversion
LOAN	ship or craft loaned to another government, or non-government agency, but US Navy retains title and the ship or craft is on the NVR
MAR	in reserve Out of Commission, Atlantic Fleet and laid up in the temporary custody of the Maritime Administration
MPR	same as 'MAR', but applies to the Pacific Fleet
NRF	assigned to the Naval Reserve Force (ships so assigned are listed in a special table for major warships and amphibious ships)
Ord	the contract for the construction of the ship has been let, but actual construction has not yet begun
PA	active Pacific Fleet
PR	in reserve Out of Commission, Pacific Fleet
Proj	the ship is scheduled for construction at some time in the immediate future
PSA	active In Service, Pacific Fleet
PSR	in reserve Out of Service, Pacific Fleet
ROS	reduced Operating Status
TAA	active Military Sealift Command, Atlantic Fleet
TAR	in Ready Reserve, Military Sealift Command, Atlantic Fleet
TPA	active Military Sealift Command, Pacific Fleet
TPR	in Ready Reserve, Military Sealift Command, Pacific Fleet
TWWR	active Military Sealift Command, Worldwide Routes

Ship Status Definitions

In Commission: as a rule any ship, except a Service Craft, that is active, is in commission. The ship has a Commanding Officer and flies a commissioning pennant. 'Commissioning date' as used in this section means the date of being 'in commission' rather than 'completion' or 'acceptance into service' as used in some other navies.

In Service: all service craft (dry docks and with classifications that start with 'Y'), with the exception of *Constitution*, that are active, are 'in service'. The ship has an Officer-in-Charge and does not fly a commissioning pennant.

Ships 'in reserve, out of commission' or 'in reserve, out of service' are put in a state of preservation for future service. Depending on the size of the ship or craft, a ship in 'mothballs' usually takes from 30 days to nearly a year to restore to full operational service.

The above status definitions do not apply to the Military Sealift Command.

Approved Fiscal Year 2008 Programme

	Appropriations (US dollars millions)
CVN 21 (CVN 78)	3,021
CVN 21 (R&D, Advance procurement)	124
Virginia class (SSN 784)	1,893
1 DDG 1000 destroyer	2,757
DDG 1000 (Advance Procurement)	150
LPD 17	1,457
2 T-AKE	721

Approved Fiscal Year 2009 Programme

	Appropriations (US dollars millions)
CVN 21 (CVN 78)	2,685
CVN 21 (R&D, Advance procurement)	1,211
Virginia class (SSN 785)	2,101
1 DDG 1000	1,504
2 Littoral Combat Ships	1,017

Naval Aviation

Naval Aviation had an active inventory of 3,745 aircraft as of 1 January 2009, with approximately 33 per cent of those being operated by the US Marine Corps. The principal aviation organisations are 10 active carrier air wings and one reserve Tactical Support Wing,12 active and two reserve maritime patrol squadrons and three active and one reserve Marine aircraft wings. Reserve squadrons fly and maintain their own aircraft. Fleet Replacement Squadrons (FRS) train winged aviators in the aircraft they will fly in fleet.

Fighter Attack: 15 Navy active squadrons, two Navy reserve and one Navy FRS with F/A-18 Hornets. 12 Marine active squadrons, one reserve and one FRS with F/A-18 Hornets. 20 Navy actives quadrons and two Navy FRS with F/A-18 Super Hornets. Two Navy reserve squadrons of F-5 Tiger.
Attack: Seven Marine squadrons with AV-8B Harriers, one FRS.
Airborne Command and Control: 10 Navy active squadrons, one reserve and one FRS with E-2C Hawkeyes (FRS shared with C-2A Greyhounds)
Fleet Logistics Support: Two Navy active squadrons, and one FRS with C-2A Greyhounds (FRS shared with E-2C Hawkeyes); four Navy reserve squadrons with C-9; three Navy reserve squadrons with C-40; five Navy reserve squadrons with C-130; three Navy reserve squadrons with C-20 (one of which also has C-37)
Electronic Attack: 12 Navy active, one reserve, 1 FRS with EA-6B and EA-18G and four Marine squadrons with EA-6B. One Navy active with EA-18G.
Airborne Command Post: Two Navy active and one FRS squadron of E-6B Mercury. FRS squadron has no aircraft assigned.
Maritime Patrol: 12 active, two reserve and one FRS squadrons with P-3C Orion.
Signals Intelligence Reconnaissance: Two Navy active squadrons, with EP-3E (Aries II).
Helicopter Anti-Submarine: Nine Navy active squadrons and one FRS squadron with SH-60F and HH-60H Seahawks.
Helicopter Anti-Submarine Light: 10 Navy active, one reserve and one FRS squadron with SH-60B Seahawks.
Helicopter Mine Countermeasures: Two Navy squadrons with MH-53E Sea Dragons. Active and reserve in both squadrons, FRS in one.
Helicopter Sea Combat: Nine Navy active squadrons, two FRS and one reserve of MH-60S Knighthawks.
Helicopter Combat Support/Gunship: Six Marine squadrons with AH-1W Super Cobras and UH-1N Hueys, three reserve and one FRS. Two Marine squadrons with AH-1W and UH-1Y.
Helicopter Transport: 10 Marine squadrons of CH-46E Sea Knights, two reserve and one FRS; three with CH-53D Sea Stallions and seven with CH-53E Super Stallions, one reserve and one FRS.
Helicopter Maritime Strike: Three Navy active and one FRS squadron of MH-60R Seahawks.
In-Flight Refueling: Three Marine Squadrons with KC-130J and two reserve with KC-130T.
Tilt Rotor: Six Marine Squadrons with MV-22B and one FRS.

Aircraft Procurement Plan FY2008-2009

	08	*09*
Joint Strike Fighter	6	7
F/A-18E/F Super Hornet	37	23
EA-18G Growler	21	22
MV-22B Osprey	23	30
AH-1Z/UH-1Y Super Cobra/Huey	15	18
MH-60S Seahawk	20	18
MH-60R Seahawk	28	31
E-2D Advanced Hawkeye	–	2
C-40A Clipper	–	2
P-8A MMA	–	–
T-6A JPATS	44	44
KC-130J Tanker	13	2
VH-71 (VXX) Kestrel	–	–
MQ-8B VTUAV	3	3

Naval Special Warfare (NSW)

The Naval Special Warfare Command was commissioned 16 April 1987.

SEAL (Sea Air Land) teams are manned at a nominal six platoons per team, with 24 platoons on each coast based at Coronado, California (NSW Group One) and Little Creek, Virginia (NSW Group Two). There are three Special Boat Teams within NSW Group Four. These are located at Coronado, Little Creek and Stennis, Mississippi. There is one SEAL Delivery Vehicle (SDV) Team within NSW Group Three. It is located at Pearl City, Hawaii. NSW Teams are allocated to theatre commanders during operational deployments. The naval special warfare community is comprised of approximately 2,400 SEALs, 600 Special Warfare Combatant-craft Crewmen (SWCC) operators and 2,700 civilian, active duty and reserve personnel who support the NSW war fighters and their mission.

Bases

Naval Air Stations and Air Facilities

Naval Air Weapons Station (NAWS) China Lake, CA; Naval Air Facility (NAF) El Centro, CA; Naval Air Station (NAS) Lemoore, CA; NAF Washington, DC; NAS Jacksonville, FL; NAS Key West, FL; NAS Whiting Field (Milton), FL; NAS Pensacola, FL; NAS Atlanta (Marietta), GA; PMRF Barking Sands, HI; NAS Joint Reserve Base, New Orleans, LA; NAS Brunswick, ME; NAS Patuxent River, MD; NAS Meridian, MS; NAS Fallon, NV; Naval Air Engineering Station (NAES) Lakehurst, NJ; NAS Joint Reserve Base, Willow Grove, PA; NAS, Corpus Christi, TX; NAS Joint Reserve Base Fort Worth, TX; NAS Kingsville, TX; NAS Oceana, VA; NAS Whidbey Island (Oak Harbor), WA; NAS Sigonella, Italy; NAF Atsugi, Japan; NAF Misawa, Japan; NAF Mildenhall, UK.

Naval Stations and Naval Bases

Naval Station San Diego, CA; NB Coronado, CA; NB Ventura County, CA; NB Point Loma (San Diego), CA; NS Mayport, FL; Naval Station (NS) Pearl Harbor, HI; NS Great Lakes, ILL; NSA Annapolis, MD; NS Ingleside, TX; NS Newport, RI; Naval Amphibious Base (NAB) (Amphibious) Little Creek, VA; NS Norfolk, VA; NB Kitsap, WA; NS Everett, WA; NS Guantanamo Bay, Cuba; Commander Fleet Activities (CFA) Okinawa, Japan; CFA Sasebo, Japan; CFA Chinhae, Korea; CFA Yokosuka, Japan; NS Rota, Spain; CBC Gulfport.

Naval Support Facilities

Naval Post Graduate School Monterey, CA; NSA Washington, DC; NSA New Orleans, LA; NSA Mechanicsburg, PA; NSA Mid-South (Millington), TN; NSA Norfolk, VA.

NSF Diego Garcia, BIOT; NB Guam; NSA Souda Bay, Greece; NSA Naples, Italy; NSA Bahrain; Area Co-ordinator Singapore; NCTAMS EASTPAC (Hawaii); NSGA Kunia; NUWC Keyport (WA); NAVMAG Indian Island (WA); NAVWPNSTA Seal Beach (CA); NSA Crane (IN); NAVWPNSTA Earle (NJ); NSU Saratoga Springs (NY); NAVWPNSTA Yorktown; NSWC Philadelphia; NSGA Sugar Grove; NAVWPNSTA Charleston; NSA Panama City; NAVSCSCOL Athens (GA); NSA Orlando; NUWC Bahamas (Andros Is).

Submarine Bases

SUBASE Kings Bay, GA (East Coast); SUBASE New London, CT (East Coast).

Naval Shipyards

NSY/IMF Pearl Harbor, HI; Puget Sound NSY/IMF, Bremerton, WA; NSY Norfolk, VA; NSY Portsmouth, NH (located in Kittery, ME).

Marine Corps Air Stations and Helicopter Facilities

MCAS: Beaufort, SC; Yuma, AZ; Camp Pendleton, CA; Kaneohe Bay, Oahu, HI; Quantico, VA; Cherry Point, NC; Iwakuni, Honshu, Japan; New River (Jacksonville), NC. Futema, Okinawa, Miramar (San Diego), CA.

Marine Corps Bases

Camp Pendleton, CA; Twentynine Palms, CA; Marine Corps Logistic Base, Bastow, CA; Camp H M Smith (Oahu), HI; Camp Lejeune, NC; Marine Corps Logistic Base, Albany, NY; Marine Corps Base, Quantico, VA; Camp Smedley D Butler (Kawasaki), Okinawa, Japan.

Command and Control of US Naval Forces

Strategic and Operational Command

All US Military Forces operate under Title 10 of US Code and subsidiary Joint Force Doctrine publications. The President of the United States is the Commander-in-Chief of all US forces and exercises authority for the application of military force through the Secretary of Defense who is

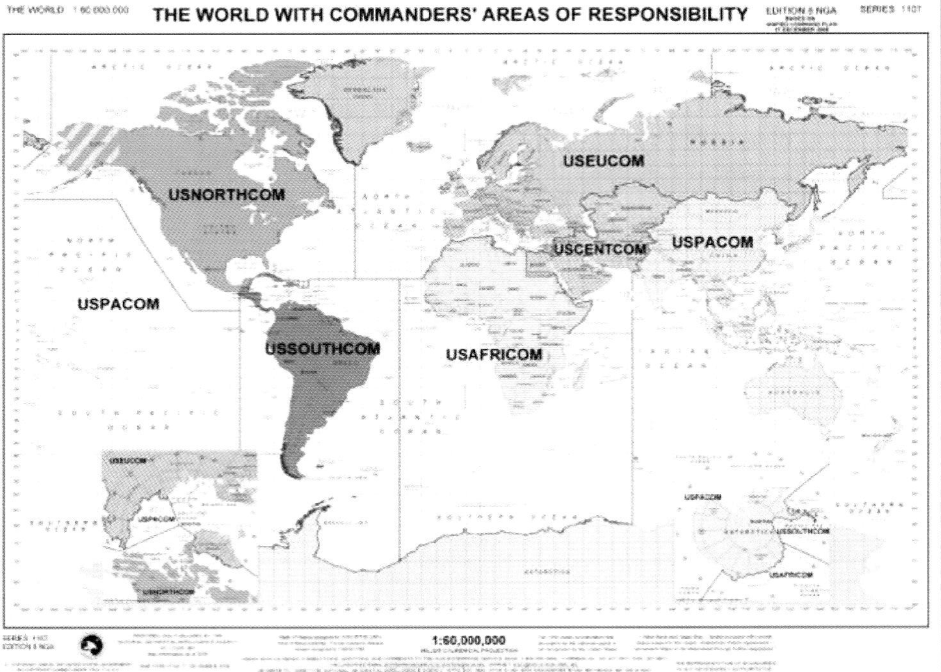

AREAS OF RESPONSIBILITY *12/2008*, US DOD* / 1353649

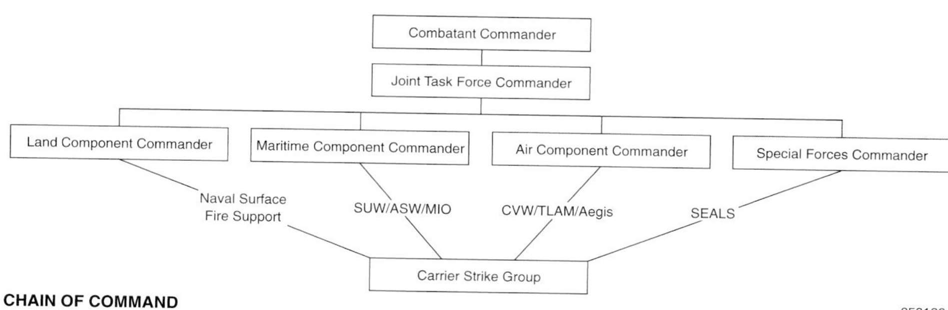

CHAIN OF COMMAND

0531964

advised by the Chairman of the Joint Chiefs of Staff. The Unified Combatant Commanders are four-star officers who have broad geographic area of functional responsibilities. Exercising Combatant Command (COCOM), they have authority to employ forces as necessary to accomplish assigned military missions and are as follows:

Commander US European Command (Stuttgart-Vaihingen, Germany)
Commander US Africa Command (Stuttgart, Germany)
Commander US Northern Command (Peterson AFB, Colorado)
Commander US Pacific Command (Honolulu, Hawaii)
Commander US Southern Command (Miami, Florida)
Commander US Central Command (MacDill AFB, Florida)
Commander US Joint Forces Command (Norfolk, Virginia)
Commander US Special Operations Command (MacDill AFB, Florida)
Commander US Transportation Command (Scott AFB, Illinois)
Commander US Strategic Command (Offutt AFB, Nebraska)

The Unified Combatant Commanders may decide to exercise Operational (OPCON) command of naval forces directly. Alternatively, they may delegate such powers to another officer who might be a subordinate Unified Commander (for example Commander, US Forces Korea), a service component commander (Army, Navy, Air Force, Marine Corps and so on), a functional component commander (air, maritime, land, special forces), a joint task force commander or a single service force commander.

Africa Command (AFRICOM) was established in October 2007 as a sub-unified command subordinated to US European Command for a transition period of one year. It became a stand-alone unified command on 1 October 2008, with the commander reporting to the Secretary of Defense like other unified commanders. AFRICOM Headquarters is at Kelley Barracks in Stuttgart, Germany. Future arrangements will be considered in co-operation with partner nations and the African Union. Unlike traditional unified commands, AFRICOM focuses on war prevention rather than war-fighting. The aim is to work with African nations and organisations to build regional security and crisis-response capacity. AFRICOM has assumed control over existing US government programmes in Africa that had been administered by US Central, European and Pacific Commands. The US force presence in Africa includes 1,700 personnel at Camp Lemonier in Djibouti. Military advisers assigned to US embassies and diplomatic missions help to co-ordinate peacekeeping training and other Defense Department programs in support of US foreign policy.

Navy force commanders have a dual chain of command. They report to the Chief of Naval Operations for administrative matters such as training and equipping of forces and are also responsible to the combatant commanders for providing forces to accomplish missions. They include the following:

Commander US Fleet Forces Command
Commander US Pacific Fleet
Commander US Naval Forces Europe
Commander US Naval Forces Central Command
Commander Navy Reserve Force
Commander Military Sealift Command

Once deployed in theatre, naval forces are operationally assigned to three-star numbered fleet commanders:

Commander US Second Fleet (Atlantic)
Commander US Third Fleet (Eastern Pacific)
Commander US Fourth Fleet (Caribbean, Central and South America)
Commander US Fifth Fleet (Arabian Gulf and Indian Ocean)
Commander US Sixth Fleet (Mediterranean)
Commander US Seventh Fleet (Western Pacific)

These arrangements are intended to provide a framework that provides a clear chain of command while retaining the flexibility to be adapted to the operational circumstances. For example, it is feasible for a multimission naval task group, such as a carrier strike group (CSG) (baseline composition: 1 CVN/CV, 2 CG/DDG, 1 DD/FFG, 1 SSN and 1 logistic support ship) or an expeditionary strike group (ESG) (baseline composition: 3 amphibious ships (LHD/LHA, LPD and LSD), 2 CG/DDG, 1 DD/FFG and 1 SSN) to support service, component, and other superior commanders simultaneously.

Tactical Command and Composite Warfare Commander

US naval task groups and forces operate under Composite Warfare Commander (CWC) doctrine. The officer in tactical command (OTC) is responsible for accomplishing the missions of his assigned forces. The CWC directs the force and controls warfare functions. The OTC may designate a subordinate commander as CWC but, in general practice, the roles are combined. The OTC/CWC is supported by Principal Warfare Commanders (PWC), Functional Warfare Commanders (FWC) and Coordinators.

PWCs include the Air Defense Commander (ADC), Strike Warfare Commander (STWC), Information Warfare Commander (IWC), Anti-submarine Warfare Commander (ASWC), and Surface Warfare Commander (SUWC). ASW and SUW areas can be combined under a Sea Combat Commander (SCC). PWCs collect and distribute information pertinent to their warfare areas and can be delegated authority to respond to threats with assigned assets.

FWCs perform duties of a scope or duration more limited than that of a PWCs. Typical FWCs include Maritime Interception Operations Commander (MIOC), Mine Warfare Commander (MIWC), Operational Deception Group Commander, Screen Commander (SC) and Underway Replenishment Group (URG) Commander.

Coordinators are responsible to the OTC/CWC for managing assets and resources. Among assigned Coordinators are the Air Resource Element Coordinator (AREC), Air Control Authority (ACA), Cryptologic Resource Coordinator (CRC), Force Over-the-horizon Track Coordinator (FOTC), Force Track Coordinator (FTC), Helicopter Element Coordinator (HEC), Submarine Operations Coordinating Authority (SOCA), TLAM Launch Area Coordinator (LAC) and TLAM Strike Coordinator (TSC).

The OTC/CWC may activate any or all of these warfare commanders and coordinators as necessary. The guiding principle of CWC doctrine is flexibility to meet operational requirements.

Multinational Operations

US naval forces regularly participate in peacetime and wartime multinational operations. Although the President always retains command authority over US forces, he may place them under control of a foreign commander as required to achieve specific military objectives. Multinational operations may be conducted under the structure of a formal alliance (such as NATO) or of an ad hoc coalition (Operation Desert Shield/Desert Storm).

Complex Naval Task Forces

Complex Task Forces usually consist of multiple CSGs and/or ESGs and may also include naval assets of allied nations. Such forces may operate together under three generic command and control structures.

In Situation A, the forces integrate, the senior officer present becomes the overall OTC/CWC and a new single CWC organisation is established.

In Situation B, task groups do not integrate. The senior OTC/CWC coordinates the tactical operations of all naval forces and delegates responsibilities and TACON of specific forces to junior commanders as appropriate. The senior OTC/CWC may also designate junior commanders as sector OTC/CWCs.

In Situation C, each group retains its own OTC/CWC and its own set of warfare commanders and coordinators. The OTC/CWC of the supported force (or a common superior) draws on the assets of the entire force to achieve joint and combined force objectives.

Amphibious Operations

'Commander Amphibious Task Force' (CATF) and 'Commander Landing Force' (CLF) are historic naval command terms whose functional responsibilities are recognised by Joint Doctrine. The common superior establishes command relationships between CATF and CLF who are considered coequal in planning. CATF is responsible for operations at sea while CLF dictates landing force objectives and landing and drop zones.

US Marine Corps Organisation

Marine Corps Structure

Title 10 directs that the Marine Corps is to consist of three divisions and three air wings with their necessary logistics support and that there is to be a similar organisation in the reserves consisting of one division, one air wing, and their respective logistical support groups. MEFs I (Camp Pendleton, CA), II (Camp Lejeune, NC) and III (Okinawa, Japan) are the three standing Marine Expeditionary Forces (MEFs).

The MEF is the USMC's principal war-fighting organisation. Commanded by a lieutenant general, it consists of 50–60,000 personnel and includes, typically, a division, air wing, Marine Logistics Group (MLG) and headquarters group. MEFs can conduct a broad scope of missions in any environment for 60 days and are supported by amphibious shipping and/or Maritime Prepositioning Squadrons (MPS). Because of its size, the MEF is normally committed sequentially, building on a smaller operational unit such as a Marine Expeditionary Brigade (MEB) or Marine Expeditionary Unit (MEU).

The MEB is designed as the lead element for a MEF or for small-scale contingencies. Command by a major general or brigadier, it consists of 14–18,000 Marine and Navy personnel and has thirty days sustainability. The ground combat element consists of an infantry regiment reinforced by artillery, some armour, light armoured vehicles, assault amphibian vehicles, and combat engineers. These assets can be divided into four battalion-size manoeuvre elements, supported by three to six fixed- and rotary-wing aircraft squadrons.

MEUs routinely forward deploy on Expeditionary Strike Groups (ESG). Commanded by a colonel, MEUs contain approximately 2,200 Marine and Navy personnel and can sustain operations for fifteen days. MEUs normally consist of a reinforced infantry Battalion Landing Team (BLT), a composite helicopter squadron (with air command and control and six Harriers), and a MEU Combat Logistics Battalion (CLB). Typically, such a force can act as the lead element for a larger force and/or provide shaping/engagement activities, deterrence, and limited power projection. It has the capability to conduct company to battalion-sized raids to the range limits of assigned helicopters, roughly 70–100 miles from the ESG. An ESG typically consists of 1 LHD/LHA, 1 LPD and 1 LSD.

Marine Corps Operations

Operations are conducted by Marine Air Ground Task Forces (MAGTFs) whose size and composition will be dictated by operational circumstances. A MAGTF can be established by drawing ground, aviation, and combat service support assets from divisions, air wings, and their support groups. At the lower end of the scale, MEUs are available as immediately responsive, sea-based MAGTFs while, on a much greater scale, a full MEF might be required. This might be based on one of the standing MEFs or, as in Operation Desert Shield/Desert Storm, drawn from all three standing MEFs. A MAGTF always consists of a Command Element (CE), Ground Combat Element (GCE), Aviation Combat Element (ACE) and a Combat Service Support Element (CSSE).

Composite Warfare Commander Structure

OTC/CWC

Principal Warfare Commanders

Air Defense Commander (ADC)
Antisubmarine Warfare Commander (ASWC)
Information Warfare Commander (IWC)
Sea Combat Commander (SCC)
Strike Warfare Commander (STWC)
Surface Warfare Commander (SUWC)

Functional Warfare Commanders

Maritime Interception Operations Commander (MIOC)
Mine Warfare Commander (MIWC)
Operational Deception Group Commander
Screen Commander (SC)
Underway Replenishment Group (URG) Commander

Coordinators

Air Resource Element Coordinator (AREC)
Cryptologic Resources Coordinator (CRC)
Force Track Coordinator (FTC)
Helicopter Element Coordinator (HEC)
Launch Area Coordinator (LAC)
Airspace Control Authority (ACA)
Force Over-the-Horizon Coordinator (FOTC)
Submarine Operations Coordinating Authority (SOCA)
TLAM Strike Coordinator (TSC)

CWC STRUCTURE

0531963

Embarked MEU

Marine Corps amphibious forces embarked on ESGs come under the OPCON of the naval or maritime component commander. They remain under the naval or maritime component commander throughout an amphibious operation if they will re-embark. If they transition to sustained operations ashore, they chop to either the Marine component commander or the land component commander. A Marine Corps component commander may be designated as the joint force maritime, land, or air component commander.

Communications and Data Systems

Advanced Combat Direction System (ACDS)

ACDS is a centralised, automated command and control system. An upgrade from the Naval Tactical Data System (NTDS) for aircraft carriers and large-deck amphibious ships, it provides the capability to identify and classify targets, prioritise and conduct engagements, and exchange targeting information and engagement orders within the battle group and among different service components in the joint theatre of operations. ACDS is a core Sea Shield component of non-Aegis/non-SSDS combat systems.

ACDS consists of two variants. The ACDS Block 0 system replaces obsolete NTDS computers and display consoles and incorporates new software. ACDS Block 0 is deployed on five aircraft carriers, five Wasp (LHD-1) class amphibious assault ships, and all five Tarawa (LHA-1) class amphibious assault ships. ACDS Block 1 is installed in one ship: *Wasp*. Following the OPEVAL failure of ACDS Block 1, it is to be replaced by the Ship Self Defense System (SSDS).

AEGIS Combat System

The AEGIS system is designed as a total weapon system, from detection to kill in the air, surface and sub-surface domains.

The SPY-1 radar system is the primary air and surface radar for the Aegis Combat System installed in the *Ticonderoga* (CG-47) and Arleigh Burke (DDG-51) class warships. It is a multifunction, phased-array radar capable of search, automatic detection, transition to track, tracking of air and surface targets, and missile engagement support. The third variant of this radar, SPY-1D(V), the Littoral Warfare Radar, improves the radar's capability against low-altitude, reduced radar cross-section targets in heavy clutter environments, and in the presence of intense electronic countermeasures. The SPY-1 Series radars also demonstrated the capability to detect and track theatre ballistic missiles. AEGIS equipped platforms include Spanish F-100 and Japanese DDG ship classes.

Automated Digital Network System (ADNS)

The Automated Digital Network System is responsible for the transport of all Wide Area Network (WAN) Internet Protocol (IP) services which connect afloat units to various global shore sites. It provides ship and shore IP connectivity and promotes efficient use of available satellite and line of sight communications bandwidth. ADNS converges all voice, video, and data communications between ship and shore to an IP medium and takes advantage of all shipborne RF to transmit data efficiently. Specifically, it automates routing and switching of tactical and strategic C4I data via Transmission Control Protocol/Internet Protocol (TCP/IP) networks linking deployed battle group units with each other and with the Defense Information Systems Network (DISN) ashore. ADNS uses Commercial Off-the-Shelf (COTS) and Non-Developmental Item (NDI) Joint Tactical Architecture (JTA) - compliant hardware (routers, processors and switches), and commercial-compliant software in a standardised, scalable, shock-qualified rack design.

Challenge Athena (WSC-8)

Challenge Athena is part of the Navy commercial wideband satellite program (CWSP). It is a full-duplex, high data-rate communications link that operates in the C-band spectrum up to 2.048 Mbps. The Challenge Athena terminal (AN/WSC-8(V)1,2) with modifications by the developer/manufacturer is also capable of operating in the Ku-band spectrum. Because of open ocean limitations, there are currently no plans to enhance Navy's commercial satelliteterminal to include Ku coverage. CWSP provides access to voice, video, data and imagery circuit requirements. It supports fleet commander flagships (LCC/AGF), aircraft carriers (CV/CVN), amphibious ships (LHA/LHD/LPD) and other selected ships, including hospital ships (T-AH) and submarine tenders (AS). Terminals are also installed at training locations in San Diego, California, and Norfolk, Virginia. Examples of communications circuits that are provided include: Joint Service Imagery Processing System-Navy/Concentrator Architecture (JSIPS-N/JCA), Naval and Joint Fires Network (NFN), Video Tele-Conferencing (VTC), Video Information Exchange system (VIXS), Video Tele-Medicine (VTM), Video Tele-Training (VTT), Afloat Personal Telephone Service (APTS), Automated Digital Network System (ADNS), Integrated Digital Switching Network (IDSN) for voice/telephone, Secret/Unclassified Internet Protocol Router Networks (SIPRNET/NIPRNET), and Joint Worldwide Intelligence Communications System (JWICS). The CWSP terminal uses commercial satellite connectivity and COTS/NDI Equipment. In recent years, it has become an integral part of Navy's SATCOM architecture because of the overburdened military satellite communications systems.

Co-operative Engagement Capability (CEC)

Co-operative Engagement Capability (CEC) improves battle force air-defense capabilities by integrating the sensor data of each co-operating ship and aircraft into a single, real-time, fire-control-quality composite track picture. CEC also interfaces the weapons capabilities of each CEC-equipped ship in the battle group to integrate engagement capability. By simultaneously distributing sensor data on airborne threats to each ship within a battle group, CEC extends the range at which a ship can engage hostile missiles to well beyond the radar horizon, thereby improving area, local, and self-defense capabilities. Operating under the direction of a designated commander, CEC enables a strike group or joint task force to act as a single, geographically dispersed combat system to confront the evolving threat of anti-ship cruise missiles and theatre ballistic missiles. As of 2008, CEC is installed on seven aircraft carriers, *Nimitz, Eisenhower, John C Stennis, George Washington, Ronald Reagan, Carl Vinson* and *George H W Bush*; nine Aegis cruisers; 26 new construction destroyers; 10 amphibious ships and 21 E-2C Hawkeyes. CEC is planned for installation in CVN 68, CVN 21, CG 47, DDG 51, LHA 6 and DDG 1000 class ships, all E-2D Advanced Hawkeye aircraft, the US Army's Joint Land Attack Cruise Missile Defense Elevated Netted Sensor System (JLENS), and the US Marine Corps' Composite Tracking Network (CTN).

Distributed Common Ground System-Navy (DCGS-N)

DCGS-N Increment One is the Navy component of the Department of Defense (DoD) DCGS family of systems. DCGS-N provides integration of intelligence, surveillance, reconnaissance, and targeting (ISR&T) capabilities. Increment One will include: the Global Command and Control System-Joint Integrated Imagery and Intelligence (GCCS-I3) for intelligence analysis and processing tools and capabilities; GALE Lite (Generic Area Limitation Environment) for SIGINT analysis; Common Geopositioning Services (CGS) for imagery processing and exploitation, as well as aim-point mensuration in support of precision guided and coordinate seeking weapons; implementation of the DCGS Integration Backbone (DIB) for sharing intelligence within the DCGS family of systems; use of Net Centric Enterprise Services (NCES) standards to enhance interoperability and expose ISR data to the wider DoD audience; and exchange of ISR&T and Command and Control (C^2) track information with the fielded GCCS family of systems. DCGS-N will migrate to a Common Computing Environment (CCE) construct in alignment with the Integrated Shipboard Network System (ISNS)/SCI Networks/Consolidated Afloat Networks and Enterprise Services (CANES) concept starting in FY14 with DCGS-N Increment Two. DCGS-N Increment One (Block One) will undergo an afloat operational evaluation (OPEVAL) in late 2009, with Initial Operational Capability (IOC) in 2010. DCGS-N Increment One will replace the JSIPS-N systems and will be fielded to all aircraft carriers, amphibious assault ships (LHA/LHD), fleet command ships (LCC), and to select shore ISR&T reach back sites.

Global Broadcast Service (GBS)

The Global Broadcast Service augments and interfaces with other systems to provide virtual two-way Internet Protocol (IP) networked communications to deliver a continuous, high-speed, one-way flow of high-volume information broadcast to support: routine operations, training and military exercises, special activities, crisis, situational awareness, weapons targeting, intelligence, and the transition to and conduct of operations short of nuclear war. Homeland defensive operations are supported by a requirement for continental US coverage, which also provides exercise support, training and work-ups for deployment. GBS also supports military operations with US allies or coalition forces. GBS is an information technologies, mission-essential, national security system providing network-centric warfare communications, but does not incorporate nuclear survivability and hardening features. GBS provides a limited anti-jam capability and this may become a required capability in future. GBS will provide the capability to disseminate quickly large information products to various joint and small user platforms. With increased capacity, faster delivery of data, and near real-time receipt of imagery and data to the warfighter, it will reduced reliance on current MILSATCOM systems.

Global Command and Control System (GCCS)

GCCS is a comprehensive, worldwide network-centric system which provides the National Command Authority (NCA), Joint Chiefs of Staff, combatant and functional unified commands, Services, Defense Agencies, Joint Task Forces and their Service components, and others with information processing and dissemination capabilities necessary to conduct Command and Control (C^2) of forces. GCCS is a means to implement the Command, Control, Communications, Computers, and Intelligence for the Warrior (C^4 IFTW) concept. GCCS provides the operational commanders with a near-realtime Common Operational Picture, intelligence information, collaborative joint operational planning and execution tools, and other information necessary for the execution of joint operations.

Global Command and Control System (Maritime) (GCCS-M) (ex-JMCIS)

GCCS-Maritime (GCCS-M) (formerly the Joint Maritime Command Information System (JMCIS)) is the designated command and control (C^2) migration system for the Navy and is the naval implementation of the Global Command and Control System (GCCS). The evolutionary integration of previous C^2 and intelligence systems, GCCS-M supports multiple warfighting and intelligence missions for commanders at every echelon, in all afloat, ashore, and tactical naval environments, and for joint, coalition, and allied forces. GCCS-M meets the joint and service requirements for a single, integrated, scalable Command and Control (C^2) system that receives, displays, correlates, fuses, and maintains geo-locational track information on friendly, hostile, and neutral land, sea, and air forces and integrates it with available intelligence and environmental information. GCCS-M supports evolving concepts for Network-Centric Operations by receiving, displaying, correlating, fusing, and integrating all available track, intelligence and imagery information for the warfighter. More than 56 joint and Naval systems are interfaced with GCCS-M to exchange data and support warfighter capabilities in 14 mission areas. Key capabilities include:

- Multisource information management
- Display and dissemination through extensive communications interfaces
- Multisource data fusion and analysis/decision making tools
- Force co-ordination.

GCCS-M is implemented afloat (capabilities formerly met by the Navy Tactical Command System-Afloat (NTCS-A) and Joint Maritime Command Information System (JMCIS) Afloat), at ashore fixed command centers (capabilities formerly met by the Operational Support System (OSS) and JMCIS Ashore), and as the command and control (C^2) portion of mobile command centers (known as Tactical Support Center (TSC) and Tactical-Mobile).

GCCS-M Version 4.1 will begin fielding in 2010. By using GCCS-Joint as its baseline, it will bring enhanced levels of interoperability with other GCCS-Joint based applications such as the Distributed Common Ground System family of systems. In addition to various other new capabilities, GCCS-M 4.1 will increase track capacity to 100,000 and Ballistic Missile Defense planning.

Integrated Broadcast Service/Joint Tactical Terminal (IBS/JTT)

The Integrated Broadcast Service (IBS) is a system-of-systems that will migrate the Tactical Receive Equipment and Related Applications Data Dissemination System (TDDS), Tactical Information Broadcast Service (TIBS), Tactical Reconnaissance Intelligence Exchange System (TRIXS), and Near Real-Time Dissemination (NRTD) system into an integrated service with a common format. The IBS will send data via communications paths, such as UHF, SHF, EHF, GBS, and via networks. This program supports Indications Warning (I&W), surveillance, and targeting data requirements of tactical and operational commanders and targeting staffs across all warfare areas. It comprises broadcast-generation and transceiver equipment that provides intelligence data to tactical users. The Joint Tactical Terminal (JTT) will receive, decrypt, process, format, distribute, and transmit tactical data according to preset user-defined criteria across open-architecture equipment. JTT will be modular and will have the capability to receive all current tactical intelligence broadcasts (TDDS, TADIXS-B, TIBS, and TRIXS). JTT will also be interoperable with the follow-on IBS UHF broadcasts. However, the current JTT form factor does not meet space and weight constraints for a majority of the Navy and Air Force airborne platforms. Therefore, to ensure joint interoperability, the Navy and Air Force are pursuing a Special Operations Command-designed Embedded National Tactical Receiver (ENTR) for airborne platforms.

Integrated Radar Optical Surveillance and Sighting System (IROS3)

IROS3 is the Situational Awareness component of the Shipboard Protection System (SPS) Increment one. It employs COTS-based/Open Architecture products, and its key components include SPS-73 or equivalent surface search radar, electro-optical/infra-red devices, an integrated surveillance system, spotlights, long range acoustic devices, and remotely operated stabilised small arms mounts. SPS Increment I is designed to detect, classify and engage real-time asymmetric threats at close-range to ships in port, at anchor and while transiting choke points or operating in restricted waters. The system provides 360° Situational Awareness (SA) and employs COTS integration to support incremental modifications as needed to tailor the system to the mission. The system has undergone extensive testing in the laboratory and a prototype is being tested at sea in *Ramage*. The system is scheduled to be installed in most ship classes, including surface combatants, patrol boats, amphibious and auxiliary ships, and Coast Guard cutters.

Joint Service Imagery Processing System (JSIPS-N)

JSIPS-N provides a digital imagery processing and management system, with the capability to task, process, exploit, and disseminate imagery, imagery-derived products, and imagery intelligence (IMINT) based on National, theatre, and tactical sensors. As a primary mission, JSIPS-N assists strike planners, tactical aviators, and USMC amphibious planners in the delivery of precision ordnance. JSIPS-N is installed on aircraft carriers (CVN), amphibious assault ships (LHA/LHD), Fleet command ships (LCC), and at selected shore sites. A Service Life Extension Program (SLEP) is underway (JSIPS-N 6.0). The JSIPS-N SLEP is comprised of four subsystems: Common Geopositioning Services (CGS); Image Product Library (IPL); Imagery Exploitation Support System (IESS) Client; and the VANTAGE Shared Airborne Reconnaissance Pod (SHARP) processing and exploitation capability. The JSIPS-N system will be replaced on a one-for-one basis by the Distributed Common Ground System-Navy (DCGS-N), Increment One, Block One starting in FY09.

Joint Surveillance Target Attack Radar System (JSTARS)

JSTARS is described as a 'bulletproof anti-jam datalink', utilising omnidirectional broadcast on UHF SATCOM. It receives and transmits real time MTI/FTI/SAR data via a secure uplink and downlink. It is used to demonstrate 'sensor to shooter' technology.

Joint Tactical Information Distribution System (JTIDS)

A joint program directed by the Office of the Secretary of Defense, JTIDS is a digital information-distribution system which provides rapid, crypto-secure, jam-resistant (frequency-hopping), and low-probability-of-exploitation tactical data and voice communication at a high data rate to Navy tactical aircraft and ships and Marine Corps units. JTIDS also provides capabilities for common-grid navigation and automatic communications relay. It has been integrated into numerous platforms and systems, including US Navy aircraft carriers, cruisers, destroyers, amphibious assault ships, E-2C Hawkeye aircraft and EP-3 Aries aircraft; US Air Force Airborne Warning and Command System (AWACS) aircraft; and US Marine Corps Tactical Air Operations Centers (TAOCs) and Tactical Air Command Centers (TACCs). Foreign country participants include Australia, Canada, France, Germany, Japan, NATO, Saudi Arabia and the United Kingdom. Additionally, JTIDS has been identified as the preferred communications link for Theatre Ballistic Missile Defense programs. JTIDS is the first implementation of the Link-16 Joint Message Standard (J - series) and provides the single, near real-time, joint datalink network for information exchange among joint and combined forces for command and control of tactical operations.

Land Attack Warfare System (LAWS)

This prototype system networks all shooters (tactical air, shore artillery and seaborne fire support) into a Battle Local Area Network (Battle LAN) known as the 'Ring of Fire'. This automatically assigns fire missions to the most capable unit in the Battle LAN. LAWS controls preplanned missions, including Tomahawk, as well as time critical calls for fire from land forces. Fleet Battle Experiment ALFA was the initial test of this system.

Mark XIIA Identification Friend or Foe (IFF) Mode 5

IFF provides positive friendly identification to improve mission effectiveness, increase situational awareness, and minimise likelihood of fratricide. It supports Common Operational and Tactical Pictures. The Mark XIIA system adds Mode 5 to the existing modes included in the Mark XII system. Mode 5 is an ACAT II program that achieved Milestone 'C' in July 2006. It is being fielded as an Engineering Change Proposal to existing IFF digital interrogators and transponders aboard selected Navy USMC and Coast Guard aircraft, surface, and subsurface units. Other Services and some NATO nations are also fielding IFF Mode 5 capability.

Miniature Demand Assigned Multiple Access (Mini-DAMA)

Mini-DAMA is a communications system that supports the exchange of secure and non-secure Battle Group coordination data, tactical data and voice between base band processing equipment over UHF SATCOM, 25/5 kHz DAMA, 25/5 kHz Non-DAMA, and UHF LOS. The Navy has completed installations for submarines and Arleigh Burke destroyers AV(2), mine warfare ships V(2) and aircraft V(3). Aircraft installations V(3) continue. These Mini-DAMA radio installation sprovide the channel utilisation efficiencies by employing Time Division Multiple Access (TDMA) methods that have been achieved for surface warfare ships and shore stations equipped with the larger version TD-1271 DAMA multiplexer.

Mission Data System (MDS)

This system allows planners to view Tomahawk Land Attack Missile information. MDS receives via TADIXS A or OTCIXS I digital Mission Data Updates (MDUs) from the Cruise Missile Support Activity (CMSA) and stores preplanned TLAM strike plans. Initial TLAM mission data fill is distributed via magnetic tape media provided by the CMSA.

Multifunctional Information Distribution - Low Volume Terminal (MIDS-LVT)

MIDS-LVT is a multinational co-operative development program to design, develop, and produce a tactical information distribution system equivalent in capability to Joint Tactical Information Distribution System (JTIDS), but in a low-volume, lightweight, compact terminal designed for fighter aircraft with applications in helicopters, ships, and ground sites. The United States is the MIDS-LVT program leader with France, Germany, Italy and Spain entering into a European partnership, called EUROMIDS. US Navy procurement is targeted for F/A-18 Hornet aircraft as the lead aviation platform and surface craft. MIDS-LVT is a pre-programmed product improvement (P3I) for JTIDS Class 2 Terminal and provides identical capabilities at a reduced size and weight. MIDS-LVT employs the Link-16 (TADIL-J) message standard of US Navy/NATO publications. MIDS-LVT is fully interoperable with JTIDS and was designed in response to current aircraft, surface ship, submarine, and ground-host volume and weight constraints. The solution variants-MIDS-LVT (1), MIDS-LVT (2), and MIDS-LVT (3) - support US Navy, US Marine Corps, and US Air Force aircraft; US Navy ships; US Army Patriot, THAAD, MEADS and ground-based defense systems; USAF and USMC ground-based Command and Control platforms; and potentially other tactical aircraft and ground-based systems. The MIDS-LVT (1) variant will be used in the MIDS on Ship (MOS) program providing the Link-16 capability to new-construction surface warships.

NATO Improved Link Eleven (NILE) Program

This program, known as either NILE or Link 22, fulfils a North Atlantic Treaty Organization (NATO) Operational Staff Requirement to develop a digital datalink with the aim of increasing the timeliness of the tactical information transfer even in a dense and hostile communications threat environment. The system is capable of using both fixed frequency and frequency hopping waveforms in both the Ultra High Frequency (UHF) and High Frequency (HF) bands. While designed toreplace Link 11 on these media, and to provide a more robust Tactical Beyond Line of Sight capability, the Link 22 message set is designed to be more aligned with and to compliment Link 16, easing multilink operations, Modern automated Network Management capabilities minimise the pre-planning requirements associated with Link 16 Networks. Link 22 has been developed to fulfil the operational requirement to exchange tactical data between tactical data systems (including operators) and to exchange necessary network management data. Link 22 incorporates F-series and FJ-series message standards (formats and protocols), a Time Division Multiple Access (TDMA) architecture, specific communications media and protocols, and specific procedures.

Ship Self-Defense System (SSDS) Mk 1 and 2

SSDS provides the integrated combat system for aircraft carriers and amphibious ships, enabling them to keep pace with the Anti-Ship Cruise Missile (ASCM) threat. Moving toward an open-architecture distributed-processing system, SSDS integrates the detection and engagement elements of the combat system. With automated weapons control doctrine, Cooperative Engagement Capability (CEC), and enhanced battlespace awareness, SSDS provides these ships with a robust self-defense capability in support of Sea Shield.

SSDS Mk 1 provides doctrine-based, Quick Reaction Combat Capability (QRCC), plus automated detect through multithreat engagement capability. It enhances capabilities for Force Protection using own-ship and remote data in support of AAW capstone requirements.

SSDS Mk 2 integrates with Co-operative Engagement Capability (CEC) and provides the QRCC of SSDS Mk 1 and selected features of the Advanced Combat Direction System (ACDS) to support multiwarfare area capability, improve joint interoperability and provide an integrated, coherent real-time command and control system for CVN, LPD and LHD class ships. SSDS Mk 1 has been installed in 12 LSDs; and SSDS Mk 2 in seven CVNs (CVN 68, 69, 70, 73, 74, 76, 77) and 10 LPDs (LPD 17, 18, 19, 20, 21, 22, 23, 24, 25, 26) and two LHDs (LHD 7, 8). An open-architecture version of Mk 2, similar to DDG 1000 OA, was installed on CVN 68.

Theatre Battle Management Core System (TBMCS)

TBMCS replaces the Contingency Theatre Automated Planning System (CTAPS) as the only command and control system authorised to produce the Air Tasking Order (ATO). TBMCS has the capability to plan and execute air operations in any theatre of operations and is considered the core system for the Air Force's Air Operation Center (AOC). All services use TBMCS and, within the USN, it is installed in carriers, command ships and large-deck amphibious ships (LHA/LHD) and the Maritime Operations Centers.

Trusted Information Systems (TIS)

The Multi-Level Security (MLS) capabilities of the Navy's Ocean Surveillance Information System (OSIS) and Radiant Mercury are complementary systems which have been combined into a single TIS programme. The aim is to facilitate development and expansion of a Commander's capability automatically to exchange critical intelligence and operational information with all forces whether US, allied, or coalition.

The OSIS Evolutionary Development (OED) system is DoD's only PL-4 accredited C4I processing and dissemination system. It serves as the backbone automated information system supporting the Common Operational Picture (COP) at US and allied Joint Intelligence Centers (JICs). OED receives, processes, and disseminates timely all-source surveillance information on fixed and mobile targets of interest, both afloat and ashore, within an MLS environment. OED permits operators to collaborate in multiple domains, monitor, analyse, and support multiple views of the battle space corresponding to multiple security classification levels. Its robust correlation and communications subsystems ensure extremely rapid delivery of both record message traffic and intelligence broadcasts in support of the Unified Combatant Commanders, Joint Task Force commanders, individual units, and allies. The MLS capabilities in OED are certified and accredited to support compartmented multilevel networks at the SCI level and are envisioned to serve as the core technology upon which future Navy networks and databases running at multiple classification levels can be effectively combined to allow appropriately cleared operators access to information from a single workstation.

Radiant Mercury (RM) provides the accredited capability to automatically sanitise, transliterate, and downgrade classified, formatted information to users at lower classification levels. RM helps ensure critical Indications and Warning intelligence is provided quickly to operational decision makers at various security and releasability levels. RM is currently fielded on Force Level ships bridging data transfer between SCI GCCS-M and GENSER GCCS-M. RM also serves as a sanitiser within OED. Radiant Mercury Imagery Guard (RMIG) combines a digital signature process with RM allowing the networked transfer of imagery between security domains.

Major commercial shipyards

Shipbuilders

Austal USA, Mobile, Alabama
General Dynamics Corporation, Bath Iron Works, Bath, Maine
General Dynamics Corporation, Electric Boat, Groton, Connecticut
General Dynamics Corporation, National Steel and Shipbuilding Company, San Diego, California
Marinette Marine Corporation, Marinette, Wisconsin
Northrop Grumman Shipbuilding, New Orleans, Louisiana
Northrop Grumman Shipbuilding, Pascagoula, Mississippi
Northrop Grumman Shipbuilding, Newport News, Virginia.

Ship Repairers

Al Larson Boat Shop, Terminal Island, California
Newport Shipyard. Newport, Rhode Island
Atlantic Dry Dock Corp., Jacksonville, Florida
Atlantic Marine, Inc, Jacksonville, Florida
Atlantic Marine, Inc, Mobile, Alabama
BAE Systems San Francisco Ship Repair, San Francisco, California
BAE Systems Norfolk Ship Repair, Norfolk, Virginia
BAE Systems San Diego Ship Repair, San Diego, California
BAE Systems Hawaii Shipyards, Inc., Honolulu, Hawaii
Bay Ship & Yacht Co., Alameda, California
Bender Shipbuilding & Repair Co., Inc, Mobile, Alabama
Cascade General Inc, Portland, Oregon
Colonna's Shipyard, Inc, Norfolk, Virginia
Detyens Shipyards, Inc, Charleston, South Carolina
Earl Industries, LLC, Portsmouth, Virginia
Intermarine USA, Savannah, Georgia
Lake Union Drydock Co., Seattle, Washington
Marine Hydraulics International Inc, Norfolk, Virginia
Metal Trades, Inc, Hollywood, South Carolina
Metro Machine Corp., Norfolk, Virginia
North Florida Shipyards, Inc, Jacksonville, Florida
Northrop Grumman Continental Maritime of San Diego, Inc., California
Pacific Ship Repair & Fabrication, San Diego, California.
Tampa Ship, LLC, Tampa, Florida
Tecnico Corporation, Chesapeake, Virginia
Todd Pacific Shipyards Corp., Seattle, Washington
VT Halter Marine Inc, Gulfport, Mississippi.

Notes: All the yards mentioned have been involved in naval shipbuilding, overhaul, or modernisation. General Dynamics/Electric Boat yard is engaged only in submarine work and Newport News is the only US shipyard capable of building nuclear-powered aircraft carriers.

Major Warships Taken Out of Service 2006 to mid-2009

Submarines

2006 *Honolulu*
2007 *Hyman G Rickover, Minneapolis-Saint Paul*
2008 *Augusta*

Aircraft Carriers

2007 *John F Kennedy*
2009 *Kitty Hawk*

Command Ships

2006 *Coronado*

Amphibious Forces

2006 *Austin, Trenton* (to India)
2007 *Saipan, Shreveport, Ogden*
2008 *Tarawa, Juneau*

Mine Warfare Ships

2006 *Osprey, Robin, Oriole* (to Taiwan), *Falcon* (to Taiwan)
2007 *Heron* and *Pelican* (to Greece), *Cardinal* and *Raven* (to Egypt), *Cormorant, Black Hawk, Shrike, Kingfisher*

Auxiliaries

2006 *Camden*
2008 *Kilauea, Niagara Falls, Spica*

Special Mission Ships

2008 *Hayes*

HULL NUMBERS

Notes: Ships in reserve not included.

SUBMARINES

Ballistic Missile Submarines

Ohio class

SSBN 730	Henry M Jackson
SSBN 731	Alabama
SSBN 732	Alaska
SSBN 733	Nevada
SSBN 734	Tennessee
SSBN 735	Pennsylvania
SSBN 736	West Virginia
SSBN 737	Kentucky
SSBN 738	Maryland
SSBN 739	Nebraska
SSBN 740	Rhode Island
SSBN 741	Maine
SSBN 742	Wyoming
SSBN 743	Louisiana

Cruise Missile Submarines

Ohio class

SSGN 726	Ohio
SSGN 727	Michigan
SSGN 728	Florida
SSGN 729	Georgia

Attack Submarines

Seawolf class

SSN 21	Seawolf
SSN 22	Connecticut
SSN 23	Jimmy Carter

Los Angeles class

SSN 688	Los Angeles
SSN 690	Philadelphia
SSN 691	Memphis
SSN 698	Bremerton
SSN 699	Jacksonville
SSN 700	Dallas
SSN 701	La Jolla
SSN 705	City of Corpus Christi
SSN 706	Albuquerque
SSN 711	San Francisco
SSN 713	Houston
SSN 714	Norfolk
SSN 715	Buffalo
SSN 717	Olympia
SSN 719	Providence
SSN 720	Pittsburgh
SSN 721	Chicago
SSN 722	Key West
SSN 723	Oklahoma City
SSN 724	Louisville
SSN 725	Helena
SSN 750	Newport News
SSN 751	San Juan
SSN 752	Pasadena
SSN 753	Albany
SSN 754	Topeka
SSN 755	Miami
SSN 756	Scranton
SSN 757	Alexandria
SSN 758	Asheville
SSN 759	Jefferson City
SSN 760	Annapolis
SSN 761	Springfield
SSN 762	Columbus
SSN 763	Santa Fe
SSN 764	Boise
SSN 765	Montpelier
SSN 766	Charlotte
SSN 767	Hampton
SSN 768	Hartford
SSN 769	Toledo
SSN 770	Tucson
SSN 771	Columbia
SSN 772	Greeneville
SSN 773	Cheyenne

Virginia class

SSN 774	Virginia
SSN 775	Texas
SSN 776	Hawaii
SSN 777	North Carolina
SSN 778	New Hampshire
SSN 779	New Mexico (bldg)
SSN 780	Missouri (bldg)
SSN 781	California (bldg)
SSN 782	Mississippi (bldg)
SSN 783	Minnesota (bldg)
SSN 784	North Dakota (bldg)
SSN 785	Jack Warner (bldg)

SURFACE COMBATANTS

Aircraft Carriers

Enterprise class

CVN 65	Enterprise

Nimitz class

CVN 68	Nimitz
CVN 69	Dwight D Eisenhower
CVN 70	Carl Vinson
CVN 71	Theodore Roosevelt
CVN 72	Abraham Lincoln
CVN 73	George Washington
CVN 74	John C Stennis
CVN 75	Harry S Truman
CVN 76	Ronald Reagan
CVN 77	George H W Bush

Gerald R Ford class

CVN 78	Gerald R Ford (bldg)

Cruisers

Ticonderoga class

CG 52	Bunker Hill
CG 53	Mobile Bay
CG 54	Antietam
CG 55	Leyte Gulf
CG 56	San Jacinto
CG 57	Lake Champlain
CG 58	Philippine Sea
CG 59	Princeton
CG 60	Normandy
CG 61	Monterey
CG 62	Chancellorsville
CG 63	Cowpens
CG 64	Gettysburg
CG 65	Chosin
CG 66	Hue City
CG 67	Shiloh
CG 68	Anzio
CG 69	Vicksburg
CG 70	Lake Erie
CG 71	Cape St George
CG 72	Vella Gulf
CG 73	Port Royal

Destroyers

Zumwalt class

DDG 1000	Zumwalt (bldg)
DDG 1001	Michael Mansoor (bldg)

Arleigh Burke class

DDG 51	Arleigh Burke
DDG 52	Barry
DDG 53	John Paul Jones
DDG 54	Curtis Wilbur
DDG 55	Stout
DDG 56	John S McCain
DDG 57	Mitscher
DDG 58	Laboon
DDG 59	Russell
DDG 60	Paul Hamilton
DDG 61	Ramage
DDG 62	Fitzgerald
DDG 63	Stethem
DDG 64	Carney
DDG 65	Benfold
DDG 66	Gonzalez
DDG 67	Cole
DDG 68	The Sullivans
DDG 69	Milius
DDG 70	Hopper
DDG 71	Ross
DDG 72	Mahan
DDG 73	Decatur
DDG 74	McFaul
DDG 75	Donald Cook
DDG 76	Higgins
DDG 77	O'Kane
DDG 78	Porter
DDG 79	Oscar Austin
DDG 80	Roosevelt
DDG 81	Winston S Churchill
DDG 82	Lassen
DDG 83	Howard
DDG 84	Bulkeley
DDG 85	McCampbell
DDG 86	Shoup
DDG 87	Mason
DDG 88	Preble
DDG 89	Mustin
DDG 90	Chaffee
DDG 91	Pinckney
DDG 92	Momsen
DDG 93	Chung-Hoon
DDG 94	Nitze
DDG 95	James E Williams
DDG 96	Bainbridge
DDG 97	Halsey
DDG 98	Forrest Sherman
DDG 99	Farragut
DDG 100	Kidd
DDG 101	Gridley
DDG 102	Sampson
DDG 103	Truxtun
DDG 104	Sterett
DDG 105	Dewey
DDG 106	Stockdale
DDG 107	Gravely (bldg)
DDG 108	Wayne E Meyer (bldg)
DDG 109	Jason Dunham (bldg)
DDG 110	William P Lawrence (bldg)
DDG 111	Spruance (bldg)
DDG 112	Michael Murphy (bldg)

Frigates

Oliver Hazard Perry class

FFG 8	McInerney
FFG 28	Boone (NRF)
FFG 29	Stephen W Groves (NRF)
FFG 32	John L Hall
FFG 33	Jarrett
FFG 36	Underwood
FFG 37	Crommelin (NRF)
FFG 38	Curts (NRF)
FFG 39	Doyle (NRF)
FFG 40	Halyburton
FFG 41	McClusky (NRF)
FFG 42	Klakring (NRF)
FFG 43	Thach
FFG 45	De Wert
FFG 46	Rentz
FFG 47	Nicholas
FFG 48	Vandegrift
FFG 49	Robert G Bradley
FFG 50	Taylor
FFG 51	Gary
FFG 52	Carr
FFG 53	Hawes
FFG 54	Ford
FFG 55	Elrod
FFG 56	Simpson (NRF)
FFG 57	Reuben James
FFG 58	Samuel B Roberts
FFG 59	Kauffman
FFG 60	Rodney M Davis (NRF)
FFG 61	Ingraham

Littoral Combat Ships

LCS 1	Freedom
LCS 2	Independence (bldg)
LCS 3	Fort Worth (bldg)
LCS 4	Coronado (bldg)

Coastal Patrol Craft

Cyclone class

PC 3	Hurricane
PC 5	Typhoon
PC 6	Sirocco
PC 7	Squall
PC 9	Chinook
PC 10	Firebolt
PC 11	Whirlwind
PC 12	Thunderbolt

COMMAND SHIPS

Blue Ridge class

LCC 19	Blue Ridge
LCC 20	Mount Whitney

AMPHIBIOUS FORCES

Amphibious Assault Ships

Wasp class

LHD 1	Wasp
LHD 2	Essex
LHD 3	Kearsarge
LHD 4	Boxer
LHD 5	Bataan
LHD 6	Bonhomme Richard
LHD 7	Iwo Jima
LHD 8	Makin Island (bldg)

Tarawa class

LHA 4	Nassau
LHA 5	Peleliu

America class

LHA 6	America

Amphibious Transport Docks

Austin class

LPD 7	Cleveland
LPD 8	Dubuque
LPD 9	Denver
LPD 13	Nashville
LPD 15	Ponce

San Antonio class

LPD 17	San Antonio
LPD 18	New Orleans
LPD 19	Mesa Verde
LPD 20	Green Bay
LPD 21	New York (bldg)
LPD 22	San Diego (bldg)
LPD 23	Anchorage (bldg)
LPD 24	Arlington (bldg)
LPD 25	Somerset (ord)

Amphibious Cargo Ships

Whidbey Island class

LSD 41	Whidbey Island
LSD 42	Germantown
LSD 43	Fort McHenry
LSD 44	Gunston Hall
LSD 45	Comstock
LSD 46	Tortuga
LSD 47	Rushmore
LSD 48	Ashland

Harpers Ferry class

LSD 49	Harpers Ferry
LSD 50	Carter Hall
LSD 51	Oak Hill
LSD 52	Pearl Harbor

MINE WARFARE FORCES

Mine Countermeasures Ships

Avenger class

MCM 1	Avenger
MCM 2	Defender (NRF)
MCM 3	Sentry (NRF)
MCM 4	Champion (NRF)
MCM 5	Guardian
MCM 6	Devastator
MCM 7	Patriot
MCM 8	Scout
MCM 9	Pioneer
MCM 10	Warrior
MCM 11	Gladiator (NRF)
MCM 12	Ardent
MCM 13	Dextrous
MCM 14	Chief

MATERIAL SUPPORT SHIPS

Submarine Tenders

Emory S Land class

AS 39	Emory S Land
AS 40	Frank Cable

MISCELLANEOUS

High Speed Vessels

HSV-2	Swift
HSV-4676	Westpac Express
FSF-1	Sea Fighter

Oceanographic Research Ships

AGOR 14	Melville
AGOR 15	Knorr
AGOR 23	Thomas G Thompson
AGOR 24	Roger Revelle
AGOR 25	Atlantis
AGOR 26	Kilo Moana

MILITARY SEALIFT COMMAND

NAVAL FLEET AUXILIARY FORCE

Fast Combat Support Ships

T-AOE 6	Supply
T-AOE 7	Rainier
T-AOE 8	Arctic
T-AOE 10	Bridge

Ammunition Ships

T-AE 32	Flint
T-AE 33	Shasta
T-AE 34	Mount Baker
T-AE 35	Kiska

Cargo and Ammunition Ships

T-AKE 1	Lewis and Clark
T-AKE 2	Sacagawea
T-AKE 3	Alan Shepard
T-AKE 4	Richard E Byrd
T-AKE 5	Robert E Peary
T-AKE 6	Amelia Earhart
T-AKE 7	Carl M Brashear (bldg)
T-AKE 8	Wally Schirra (bldg)
T-AKE 9	Matthew Perry (bldg)
T-AKE 10	Charles Drew (bldg)
T-AKE 11	Washington Chambers (bldg)
T-AKE 12	William McLean (bldg)

Combat Stores Ships

T-AFS 5	Concord
T-AFS 7	San Jose
T-AFS 10	Saturn

Hospital Ships

T-AH 19	Mercy
T-AH 20	Comfort

Oilers

Henry J Kaiser class

T-AO 187	Henry J Kaiser (PREPO)
T-AO 189	John Lenthall
T-AO 193	Walter S Diehl
T-AO 194	John Ericsson
T-AO 195	Leroy Grumman
T-AO 196	Kanawha
T-AO 197	Pecos
T-AO 198	Big Horn
T-AO 199	Tippecanoe
T-AO 200	Guadalupe
T-AO 201	Patuxent
T-AO 202	Yukon
T-AO 203	Laramie
T-AO 204	Rappahannock

Salvage Ships

T-ARS 50	Safeguard
T-ARS 51	Grasp
T-ARS 52	Salvor
T-ARS 53	Grapple

Fleet Ocean Tugs

Powhatan class

T-ATF 168	Catawba
T-ATF 169	Navajo
T-ATF 171	Sioux
T-ATF 172	Apache

SPECIAL MISSION SHIPS

Cable Repair Ship

T-ARC 7	Zeus

Aviation Logistic Ship

T-AG 5001	VADM K R Wheeler

Missile Range Instrumentation Ships

T-AGM 23	Observation Island
T-AGM 24	Invincible
T-AGM 25	Howard O Lorenzen (bldg)

Navigation Test/Launch Area Support Ship

T-AG 45	Waters

Surveying Ships/Oceanographic Ships

T-AGS 51	John McDonnell
T-AGS 60	Pathfinder
T-AGS 61	Sumner
T-AGS 62	Bowditch
T-AGS 63	Henson
T-AGS 64	Bruce C Heezen
T-AGS 65	Mary Sears

Ocean/Air Surveillance Ships

T-AGOS 19	Victorious
T-AGOS 20	Able
T-AGOS 21	Effective
T-AGOS 22	Loyal
T-AGOS 23	Impeccable

STRATEGIC SEALIFT FORCE

Fast Sealift Ships

T-AKR 287	Algol
T-AKR 288	Bellatrix
T-AKR 289	Denebola
T-AKR 290	Pollux
T-AKR 291	Altair
T-AKR 292	Regulus
T-AKR 293	Capella
T-AKR 294	Antares

Large, Medium-speed Ro-Ro

T-AKR 295	Shughart
T-AKR 296	Gordon
T-AKR 297	Yano
T-AKR 298	Gilliland
T-AKR 300	Bob Hope
T-AKR 301	Fisher
T-AKR 302	Seay
T-AKR 303	Mendonca
T-AKR 304	Pililaau
T-AKR 305	Brittin
T-AKR 306	Benavidez

Tankers

T-AOT 1122	Paul Buck
T-AOT 1123	Samuel L Cobb
T-AOT 1124	Richard G Matthiesen
T-AOT 1125	Lawrence H Gianella

PREPOSITIONING PROGRAMME

Container Ships

T-AK 4296	Capt Steven L Bennett
T-AK 4396	Maj Bernard F Fisher
T-AK 4543	Lt Col John U D Page
T-AK 4544	SSGT Edward A Carter Jr

Large, Medium-Speed, Ro-Ro

T-AKR 310	Watson
T-AKR 311	Sisler
T-AKR 312	Dahl
T-AKR 313	Red Cloud
T-AKR 314	Charlton
T-AKR 315	Watkins
T-AKR 316	Pomeroy
T-AKR 317	Soderman

Aviation Logistic Ships

T-AVB 3	Wright
T-AVB 4	Curtiss

Maritime Prepositioning Ships

T-AK 3000	CPL Louis J Hauge, Jr
T-AK 3002	PFC James Anderson, Jr
T-AK 3003	1st Lt Alex Bonnyman
T-AK 3005	SGT Matej Kocak
T-AK 3006	PFC Eugene A Obregon
T-AK 3007	MAJ Stephen W Pless
T-AK 3008	2nd Lt John P Bobo
T-AK 3009	PFC Dewayne T Williams
T-AK 3010	1st Lt Baldomero Lopez
T-AK 3011	1st Lt Jack Lummus
T-AK 3012	SGT William R Button
T-AK 3015	1st Lt Harry L Martin
T-AK 3016	L/Cpl Roy M Wheat
T-AK 3017	GYSGT Fred W Stockham

READY RESERVE FORCE

(see pages 961–962)

SUBMARINES

Notes: (1) **Deep submergence vehicles:** The Deep Submergence Vehicles (DSV) are listed following the 'Research Ships' section.
(2) **Seal Delivery Vehicles (SDVs):** There are 10 Mk VIII Mod 1 six-man mini wet submersibles in service for naval commando units. These SDVs can be carried by suitably modified SSNs and SSGN. Range 35 n miles at up to 150 ft. All have undergone SLEP from 1995 to improve performance. Attempts to introduce a more capable design, ASDS, were abandoned in 2008 and a Request for Information for a new class of submarine-launched Joint Multi-Mission Submarine (JMMS) was issued on 30 December 2008. A class of three units is to enter service from 2016.

SDV Mk VIII *10/1997, A McKaskle, USN* / 0053312

(3) **Unmanned Undersea Vehicles (UUVs):** Torpedo-sized and larger unmanned undersea vehicles are under development. Potential applications include underwater surveillance, mine-countermeasures and anti-submarine warfare. Early experience was gained with the Mine Search System (MSS), operational testing of which was completed in 1993. The 35 ft long vehicle had a titanium hull and demonstrated the performance of mine detection sonars and the ability of a UUV to survey designated areas with precise navigation. Further proof-of-concept experience was gained with the Long-Term Mine Reconnaissance System (LMRS) which was designed to be launched from the 21 in torpedo tubes of an SSN. An engineering development system was delivered in 2002 but the programme was discontinued in favour of development of a modular UUV in which payloads can be swapped. This concept is to be demonstrated in the experimental Advanced Development UUV (ADUUV). In late 2008, the Navy cancelled phase 1 of the Mission-Reconfigurable UUV (MRUUV) due to "technical and engineering limitations". The vehicle had been scheduled to enter service in 2016. Development of a large diameter UUV continued. In October 2007, the first successful end-to-end submerged operation of two UUVs was demonstrated in SSN 768 *Hartford*. Further ahead, MRUUVs of larger size and longer endurance might be developed for launch from submarines and surface ships. Surface ship near-term programmes include the Battlespace Preparation Autonomous Underwater Vehicle, to be deployed in the Littoral Combat Ship, and the Surface Mine Countermeasures UUV.

Strategic Missile Submarines (SSBN)

Notes: The Trident missile fitted SSBN force provides the principal US strategic deterrent under the control of US Strategic Command at Offutt Air Force Base, Nebraska. The Strategic Arms Reduction Treaty (START), implemented in December 2001, limits the combined number of SLBM and ICBM re-entry bodies (RBs) to 4,900. Although there may be further bi-lateral agreements with Russia to update verification regimes, the Bush administration has decided to pursue long-term strategic nuclear force reductions without further detailed arms control negotiations. The START II treaty has thus been overtaken. As part of the reduction, the first four Ohio class submarines are no longer required for strategic service. These boats have been converted into conventionally-armed guided missile SSGNs, capable also of deploying Special Forces. Although the missile tubes on SSGNs will not contain SLBMs, they will continue to count against START treaty limits.

14 OHIO CLASS (SSBN)

Name	*No*	*Builders*	*Launched*	*Commissioned*	*F/S*
HENRY M JACKSON	SSBN 730	General Dynamics (Electric Boat Div)	15 Oct 1983	6 Oct 1984	PA
ALABAMA	SSBN 731	General Dynamics (Electric Boat Div)	19 May 1984	25 May 1985	PA
ALASKA	SSBN 732	General Dynamics (Electric Boat Div)	12 Jan 1985	25 Jan 1986	AA
NEVADA	SSBN 733	General Dynamics (Electric Boat Div)	14 Sep 1985	16 Aug 1986	PA
TENNESSEE	SSBN 734	General Dynamics (Electric Boat Div)	13 Dec 1986	17 Dec 1988	AA
PENNSYLVANIA	SSBN 735	General Dynamics (Electric Boat Div)	23 Apr 1988	9 Sep 1989	PA
WEST VIRGINIA	SSBN 736	General Dynamics (Electric Boat Div)	14 Oct 1989	20 Oct 1990	AA
KENTUCKY	SSBN 737	General Dynamics (Electric Boat Div)	11 Aug 1990	13 July 1991	PA
MARYLAND	SSBN 738	General Dynamics (Electric Boat Div)	10 Aug 1991	13 June 1992	AA
NEBRASKA	SSBN 739	General Dynamics (Electric Boat Div)	15 Aug 1992	10 July 1993	PA
RHODE ISLAND	SSBN 740	General Dynamics (Electric Boat Div)	17 July 1993	9 July 1994	AA
MAINE	SSBN 741	General Dynamics (Electric Boat Div)	16 July 1994	29 July 1995	PA
WYOMING	SSBN 742	General Dynamics (Electric Boat Div)	15 July 1995	13 July 1996	AA
LOUISIANA	SSBN 743	General Dynamics (Electric Boat Div)	27 July 1996	6 Sep 1997	PA

Displacement, tons: 16,764 surfaced; 18,750 dived
Dimensions, feet (metres): 560 × 42 × 36.4 *(170.7 × 12.8 × 11.1)*
Main machinery: Nuclear; 1 GE PWR S8G; 2 turbines; 60,000 hp *(44.8 MW)*; 1 shaft; 1 Magnetek auxiliary prop motor; 325 hp *(242 kW)*
Speed, knots: 24 dived
Complement: 155 (15 officers)

Missiles: SLBM: 24 Lockheed Trident II; stellar inertial guidance to 12,000 km *(6,500 n miles)*; thermonuclear warheads of up to 12 MIRVs of either Mk 4 with W76 of 100 kT each, or Mk 5 with W88 of 300-475 kT each; CEP 90 m. A limit of 8 RVs was set in 1991 under the START counting rules.
Torpedoes: 4—21 in *(533 mm)* Mk 68 bow tubes. Raytheon Mk 48 ADCAP Mod 5/6/7; wire-guided (option); active/passive homing to 50 km *(27 n miles)*/38 km *(21 n miles)* at 40/55 kt; warhead 267 kg; depth to 800 m *(2,950 ft)*.
Countermeasures: Decoys: External and internal (reloadable) anti-torpedo decoy.
ESM: WLR-8(V)5; intercept. WLR-10; radar warning.

Combat data systems: DWS-118 and CCS Mk 2 Mod 3 with UYK 43/UYK 44 computers.
Weapons control: Mk 98 fire-control system.
Radars: Surface search/navigation/fire control: AN/BPS-15J and AN/BPS-16(V)2; I/J-band.
Sonars: IBM BQQ-6; passive search.
Raytheon BQS-13; spherical array for BQQ-6.
Ametek BQS-15; active/passive for close contacts; high frequency.
Western Electric BQR-15 (with BQQ-9 signal processor); TB-16 passive towed array. TB-23 thin line array.
Raytheon BQR-19; active for navigation; high frequency.

Programmes: The size of the SSBN forces has been reduced to 14 hulls. *Ohio* completed conversion to SSGN in 2005, *Florida* and *Michigan* in 2006 and *Georgia* in 2007.
Modernisation: All Ohio class SSBNs have been converted to deploy Trident II missiles. Ohio class SSBNs are being upgraded with ARCI (Acoustic Rapid COTS Insertion) sonar and CCS Mk 2 Block 1C fire-control systems. Installation in *Alaska*, *Nevada*, *Pennsylvania*, *West Virginia*, *Maryland*, *Kentucky*, *Alabama*, *Rhode Island*, *Henry M Jackson* and *Nebraska* is complete and is scheduled to be completed in *Tennessee* and *Maine* in 2009.
Structure: The size of the Trident submarine is dictated primarily by the 24 vertically launched Trident missiles and the reactor plant to drive the ship. The reactor has a nuclear core life of about 20 years between refuellings. Diving depth is 244 m *(800 ft)*. Kollmorgen Type 152 and Type 82 periscopes. Mk 19 Air Turbine Pump for torpedo discharge.
Operational: The eight Pacific Fleet units are based at Bangor, Washington, while the six Atlantic Fleet units are based at King's Bay, Georgia. SSBNs 741 and 743 transferred to Bangor on 1 October 2005. In the current state of worldwide tensions, a modified alert status has been implemented. Single crews were considered but rejected. Hull life of the class has been extended.

ALABAMA *4/2004, Ships of the World* / 1043704

PENNSYLVANIA *12/2005, Ships of the World* / 1154028

Cruise Missile Submarines (SSGN)

4 OHIO CLASS (SSGN)

Name	*No*	*Builders*	*Launched*	*Commissioned*	*F/S*
OHIO	SSGN 726 (ex-SSBN 726)	General Dynamics (Electric Boat Div)	7 Apr 1979	11 Nov 1981	PA
MICHIGAN	SSGN 727 (ex-SSBN 727)	General Dynamics (Electric Boat Div)	26 Apr 1980	11 Sep 1982	PA
FLORIDA	SSGN 728 (ex-SSBN 728)	General Dynamics (Electric Boat Div)	14 Nov 1981	18 June 1983	AA
GEORGIA	SSGN 729 (ex-SSBN 729)	General Dynamics (Electric Boat Div)	6 Nov 1982	11 Feb 1984	AA

Displacement, tons: 16,764 surfaced; 18,750 dived
Dimensions, feet (metres): 560 × 42 × 36.4 *(170.7 × 12.8 × 11.1)*
Main machinery: Nuclear; 1 GE PWR S8G; 2 turbines; 60,000 hp *(44.8 MW)*; 1 shaft; 1 Magnetek auxiliary prop motor; 325 hp *(242 kW)*
Speed, knots: 25+
Complement: 155 (15 officers)

Missiles: SLCM: Up to 154 Raytheon Tomahawk Block III and Block IV; TERCOM and GPS aided inertial navigation system with DSMAC to 1,600+ km *(865+ n miles)* at 0.7 Mach; warhead (WDU 36B) 454 kg.
Torpedoes: 4—21 in *(533 mm)* Mk 68 bow tubes. Raytheon Mk 48 ADCAP Mod 5/6/7; wire-guided (option); active/passive homing to 50 km *(27 n miles)*/38 km *(21 n miles)* at 40/55 kt; warhead 267 kg; depth to 800 m *(2,950 ft)*.
Countermeasures: Decoys: 8 launchers for Countermeasures Set Acoustic (CSA) and internal (reloadable) anti-torpedo decoy system.
ESM: BLQ-10; radar and comms intercept and analysis.
Combat data systems: AN/BYG-1 Combat Control System.
Weapons control: AN/BYG-1.
Radars: Surface search/navigation/fire control: AN/BPS 15J; I/J-band.

Sonars: Lockheed Martin AN/BQQ-10 suite.
AN/BQQ-6; passive search (spherical array).
TB-23; passive towed array (thin line).
TB-16; passive towed array (fat line).

Programmes: The 1994 nuclear posture review recommended a 14- SSBN force and that the remaining four Ohio class be converted to SSGN role. The SSGN would include land attack, special forces insertion and support and ISR roles. Conversion contract with General Dynamics Electric Boat in October 2002. *Ohio* started mid-life refuelling on15 November 2002 and conversion work (at Puget Sound Naval Shipyard) on 19 November 2003. She completed conversion in December 2005. *Florida* started mid-life refuelling in August 2003 and conversion work (at Norfolk Naval Shipyard) in April 2004. She completed conversion in April 2006. *Michigan* started refuelling in March 2004 and conversion work (at Puget Sound) in January 2005. She completed conversion in November 2006. *Georgia* started refuelling in March 2005 and started conversion (at Norfolk) in October 2005. She completed conversion in November 2007.
Modernisation: Conversion work allows SSGN to carry up to 154 Tomahawk or Tactical Tomahawk missiles by enabling seven cruise missiles to be fired from each of 22 of the current 24 Trident missile tubes. Eight of these tubes are interchangeable with Special Forces stowage canisters. The remaining two tubes are permanently configured for wet/dry launch of up to 66 special operations forces. The combat system is also to be upgraded and future payloads are being developed to augment the baseline configuration. SSGNs have been upgraded with Acoustic Rapid COTS Insertion (ARCI) sonar system.
Structure: The size of the submarine was dictated primarily by the 24 missile tubes and the reactor plant to drive the ship. The reactor has a nuclear core life of about 20 years between refuellings. Diving depth is 244 m *(800 ft)*. Type 8J periscope and Integrated Submarine Imaging System (ISIS). Mk 19 Air Turbine Pump for torpedo discharge.
Operational: *Georgia* played the part of an SSGN during Exercise 'Silent Hammer' in 2004. This tested procedures for strikes against time-critical targets and use of special operations forces. An onboard battle-centre tested communications and networking required to support them. All boats returned to the fleet by 2007. *Ohio* and *Michigan* are based at Bangor, WA, and *Florida* and *Georgia* are based at King's Bay, GA. During her year-long maiden deployment, which began in October 2007, *Ohio* swapped crew several times. *Ohio* based at Guam when forward deployed.

FLORIDA *4/2006*, **US Navy** / 1167577

OHIO *10/2006*, **US Navy** / 1167576

OHIO *11/2008**, **US Navy** / 1353648

Attack Submarines (SSN)

5 + 13 VIRGINIA CLASS (SSN)

Name	*No*	*Builders*	*Start date*	*Launched*	*Commissioned*	*F/S*
VIRGINIA	SSN 774	General Dynamics (Electric Boat)	5 Aug 1997	7 Aug 2003	23 Oct 2004	AA
TEXAS	SSN 775	Northrop Grumman, Newport News Shipbuilding	1 Aug 1998	9 Apr 2005	9 Sep 2006	PA
HAWAII	SSN 776	General Dynamics (Electric Boat)	6 Oct 1999	28 Apr 2006	5 May 2007	PA
NORTH CAROLINA	SSN 777	Northrop Grumman, Newport News Shipbuilding	1 Apr 2001	5 May 2007	3 May 2008	PA
NEW HAMPSHIRE	SSN 778	General Dynamics (Electric Boat)	1 Oct 2002	21 Feb 2008	25 Oct 2008	AA
NEW MEXICO	SSN 779	Northrop Grumman, Newport News Shipbuilding	1 Mar 2004	22 Jan 2009	2009	Bldg
MISSOURI	SSN 780	General Dynamics (Electric Boat)	1 Feb 2005	2010	2010	Bldg
CALIFORNIA	SSN 781	Northrop Grumman, Newport News Shipbuilding	1 Feb 2006	2011	2011	Bldg
MISSISSIPPI	SSN 782	General Dynamics (Electric Boat)	19 Feb 2007	2012	2012	Bldg
MINNESOTA	SSN 783	Northrop Grumman, Newport News Shipbuilding	1 Feb 2008	2013	2013	Bldg
NORTH DAKOTA	SSN 784	General Dynamics (Electric Boat)	2009	2014	2014	Bldg
JACK WARNER	SSN 785	Northrop Grumman, Newport News Shipbuilding	2010	2015	2015	Bldg

Displacement, tons: 7,800 dived
Dimensions, feet (metres): 377 × 34 × 30.5 *(114.9 × 10.4 × 9.3)*
Main machinery: Nuclear; 1 GE PWR S9G; 2 turbines; 40,000 hp *(29.84 MW)*; 1 shaft; pump jet propulsor; 1 secondary propulsion submerged motor
Speed, knots: 34 dived
Complement: 134 (14 officers)

Missiles: SLCM: Raytheon Tomahawk Block IV; land attack; TERCOM and GPS aided inertial navigation system with DSMAC to 1,600+ km *(865+ n miles)* at 0.7 Mach; warhead (WDU-36B) 454 kg. 12 VLS tubes (SSN 774-783) external to the pressure hull.
Torpedoes: 4—21 in *(533 mm)* bow tubes. Raytheon Mk 48 ADCAP Mod 5/6/7; wire-guided (option); active/passive homing to 50 km *(27 n miles)*/38 km *(21 n miles)* at 40/55 kt; warhead 267 kg; depth to 800 m *(2,950 ft)*. Air turbine pump discharge. Total of 38 including SLCM and torpedoes.
Mines: Can lay Mk 67 Mobile and Mk 60 Captor mines (until new mines are available).
Countermeasures: Decoys: External and internal (reloadable); anti-torpedo decoy.
ESM: AN/BLQ-10; radar and comms intercept and analysis.
Combat data systems: AN/BYG-1.
Radars: Surface search/navigation/fire control: AN/BPS 16(V)4; I/J-band.
Sonars: Lockheed Martin BQQ-10 sonar suite including bow spherical active/passive array; BQG-5A wide aperture flank passive arrays; high-frequency active keel and fin arrays; TB-16 and TB-29(A) towed arrays; WLY-1 acoustic intercept.

VIRGINIA ***7/2004, US Navy*** / 1043661

Programmes: In February 1997, a teaming agreement was reached between Electric Boat Division of General Dynamics Corporation and Newport News Shipbuilding (now Northrop Grumman Newport News) jointly to build and deliver the Virginia class. Electric Boat is the lead design yard and prime contractor and delivers the even numbered hulls. Newport News delivers the odd numbered hulls. Construction of sub-assemblies is undertaken at the Electric Boat facilities in Groton, CT, at Quonset Point RI and at Northrop Grumman Newport News. Components are then shipped either to the Groton shipyard or to Newport News for final assembly and delivery. This division of construction responsibility takes advantage of modular design and construction and provides the most affordable approach to submarine construction at the two shipyards. Advanced funding for first of class in FY96. Second of class funding in FY96, third in FY98 and fourth in FY00. The SSN 774-777 constitute Block I. A follow-on block buy procurement contract, signed in August 2003 for six submarines, maintained the Electric Boat and Northrop Grumman Newport News Teaming arrangement. This contract was modified in January 2004 to a multi-year procurement contract. This modification includes provisions to provide early funding, allowing the bulk purchase of materials for more than one submarine at a significant overall cost saving. SSN 778-783 constitute Block II. Another multi-year contract for the procurement of eight Block III (SSN 784-791) was signed on 22 December 2008. It calls for one boat per year in FY09 and FY10 and two per year in FY11, 12 and 13. A program of 30 hulls is planned.
Structure: Seawolf level quietening. Reactor core will last the life of the ship. Automated steering and diving control, using fly-by-wire technology, and automated hovering system. Host ship for Advanced SEAL Delivery System (ASDS) mini-submarine or Dry Deck Shelter (DDS). Integral lockout trunk and reconfigurable torpedo room to accommodate approximately 40 Special Operations Forces and equipment. Block III boats are to be built with a modified bow to incorporate a new sonar design and two large-diameter payload tubes to replace 12 VLS tubes in Blocks I and II. Fibre-optic photonics masts replace conventional periscopes for imaging. High frequency sonar for mine and obstacle detection. Twelve Vertical Launch System (VLS) tubes. Test depth 488 m *(1,600 ft)*.
Operational: Optimised for coastal operations without sacrificing traditional deep-water capabilities. Designed for flexibility to change missions and perform a variety of mission areas: anti-submarine warfare, anti-surface warfare, covert intelligence/surveillance and reconnaissance, clandestine mine warfare, battle group support, covert support of Special Operations Forces, and power projection/strike. SSN 775-777 to be homeported at Pearl Harbor from 2009.

VIRGINIA ***7/2004, US Navy*** / 1043660

3 SEAWOLF CLASS (SSN)

Name	*No*	*Builders*	*Start date*	*Launched*	*Commissioned*	*F/S*
SEAWOLF	SSN 21	General Dynamics (Electric Boat)	25 Oct 1989	24 June 1995	19 July 1997	PA
CONNECTICUT	SSN 22	General Dynamics (Electric Boat)	14 Sep 1992	1 Sep 1997	11 Dec 1998	PA
JIMMY CARTER	SSN 23	General Dynamics (Electric Boat)	12 Dec 1995	5 June 2004	19 Feb 2005	PA

Displacement, tons: 8,060 surfaced; 9,138; 12,158 (SSN 23) dived
Dimensions, feet (metres): 353; 453.2 (SSN 23) × 42.3 × 35.8 *(107.6; 138.1 × 12.9 × 10.9)* (see *Modernisation*)
Main machinery: Nuclear; 1 Westinghouse PWR S6W; 2 turbines; 45,000 hp *(33.57 MW)*; 1 shaft; pumpjet propulsor; 1 (4 in SSN 23) Westinghouse secondary propulsion submerged motor(s)
Speed, knots: 39 dived
Complement: 140 (14 officers)

Missiles: SLCM: Raytheon Tomahawk Block III and Block IV; TERCOM and GPS aided navigation with DSMAC to 1,600+ km *(865+ n miles)* at 0.7 Mach; warhead (WDU 36B) 454 kg.
Torpedoes: 8—26 in *(660 mm)* tubes (external measurement is 30 in *(762 mm)*); Raytheon Mk 48 ADCAP Mod 5/6/7; wire-guided (option); active/passive homing to 50 km *(27 n miles)*/38 km *(21 n miles)* at 40/55 kt; warhead 267 kg; depth to 800 m *(2,950 ft)*. Air turbine discharge. Total of 50 tube-launched missiles and torpedoes.
Mines: 100 in lieu of torpedoes.
Countermeasures: Decoys: External and internal (reloadable) anti-torpedo decoy.
ESM: BLD-1. AM/BLQ-10 radar and comms intercept.
Combat data systems: General Electric BSY-2 system. USC-38 EHF. JMCIS.
Weapons control: Raytheon Mk 2 FCS.
Radars: Navigation: AN/BPS-16(V)3; I/J-band.
Sonars: BSY-2 suite with bow spherical active/passive array and wide aperture passive flank arrays; TB-16 and TB-29(A) surveillance and tactical towed arrays. WLY-1 system.

Programmes: First of class ordered on 9 January 1989; second of class on 3 May 1991 and third on 30 April 1996. Design changes to *Carter* contracted in late 1999 delayed the launch by four years.
Modernisation: The hull of SSN 23 is about 30 m longer to accommodate an hour-glass shaped Ocean Interface section with larger payload apertures to the sea. Modular architecture allows configuration for specific missions. Payloads could include standoff vehicles, distributed sensors and leave-behind weapons that would be activated after the submarine has left the area. It also supports Special Operations Forces including Dry Deck Shelter (DDS) and the Advanced SEAL Delivery System (ASDS). *Carter* retains all of the Seawolf class's original war-fighting capability. All three boats have or are converting to a common open architecture and COTS Submarine Warfare Federated Tactical System (SWFTS) to establish a common submarine baseline that can be easily upgraded.
Structure: The modular design has more weapons, a higher tactical speed, better sonar and an ASW mission effectiveness 'three times better than the improved Los Angeles class' according to the Navy. It is estimated that over a billion dollars was allocated for research and development including the S6W reactor system. Panels around wide aperture sonar array and torpedo tube doors were redesigned and refitted following sea-trials of SSN 21. Mk 21 Air turbine torpedo discharge pump. There are no external weapons. Emphasis has been put on sub-ice capabilities including retractable bow planes. Test depth 1,950 ft *(594 m)*.
Operational: A quoted 'silent' speed of 20 kt. Other operational advantages include greater manoeuvrability and space for subsequent weapon systems development. All three boats transferred to new home port at Bremerton, WA, in 2007.
Opinion: This submarine was intended to restore the level of acoustic advantage (in the one to one nuclear submarine engagement against the Russians) which the USN had enjoyed for three decades. At the same time the larger capacity of the magazine enhances overall effectiveness in a number of other roles. The decision to discontinue building this very expensive design was the result of falling defence budgets at the end of the Cold War and changing submarine mission requirements.

SEAWOLF — ***4/2004, Ships of the World*** / 1043702

CONNECTICUT — ***11/2007, US Navy*** / 1353645

JIMMY CARTER — ***2/2005, Ships of the World*** / 1127057

45 LOS ANGELES CLASS (SSN)

Name	*No*	*Builders*	*Laid down*	*Launched*	*Commissioned*	*F/S*
LOS ANGELES	SSN 688	Newport News Shipbuilding	8 Jan 1972	6 Apr 1974	13 Nov 1976	PA
PHILADELPHIA	SSN 690	General Dynamics (Electric Boat Div)	12 Aug 1972	19 Oct 1974	25 June 1977	AA
MEMPHIS	SSN 691	Newport News Shipbuilding	23 June 1973	3 Apr 1976	17 Dec 1977	AA
BREMERTON	SSN 698	General Dynamics (Electric Boat Div)	8 May 1976	22 July 1978	28 Mar 1981	PA
JACKSONVILLE	SSN 699	General Dynamics (Electric Boat Div)	21 Feb 1976	18 Nov 1978	16 May 1981	PA
DALLAS	SSN 700	General Dynamics (Electric Boat Div)	9 Oct 1976	28 Apr 1979	18 July 1981	AA
LA JOLLA	SSN 701	General Dynamics (Electric Boat Div)	16 Oct 1976	11 Aug 1979	24 Oct 1981	PA
CITY OF CORPUS CHRISTI	SSN 705	General Dynamics (Electric Boat Div)	4 Sep 1979	25 Apr 1981	8 Jan 1983	PA
ALBUQUERQUE	SSN 706	General Dynamics (Electric Boat Div)	27 Dec 1979	13 Mar 1982	21 May 1983	AA
SAN FRANCISCO	SSN 711	Newport News Shipbuilding	26 May 1977	27 Oct 1979	24 Apr 1981	PA
HOUSTON	SSN 713	Newport News Shipbuilding	29 Jan 1979	21 Mar 1981	25 Sep 1982	PA
NORFOLK	SSN 714	Newport News Shipbuilding	1 Aug 1979	31 Oct 1981	21 May 1983	AA
BUFFALO	SSN 715	Newport News Shipbuilding	25 Jan 1980	8 May 1982	5 Nov 1983	PA
OLYMPIA	SSN 717	Newport News Shipbuilding	31 Mar 1981	30 Apr 1983	17 Nov 1984	PA
PROVIDENCE	SSN 719	General Dynamics (Electric Boat Div)	14 Oct 1982	4 Aug 1984	27 July 1985	AA
PITTSBURGH	SSN 720	General Dynamics (Electric Boat Div)	15 Apr 1983	8 Dec 1984	23 Nov 1985	AA
CHICAGO	SSN 721	Newport News Shipbuilding	5 Jan 1983	13 Oct 1984	27 Sep 1986	PA
KEY WEST	SSN 722	Newport News Shipbuilding	6 July 1983	20 July 1985	12 Sep 1987	PA
OKLAHOMA CITY	SSN 723	Newport News Shipbuilding	4 Jan 1984	2 Nov 1985	9 July 1988	AA
LOUISVILLE	SSN 724	General Dynamics (Electric Boat Div)	16 Sep 1984	14 Dec 1985	8 Nov 1986	PA
HELENA	SSN 725	General Dynamics (Electric Boat Div)	28 Mar 1985	28 June 1986	11 July 1987	PA
NEWPORT NEWS	SSN 750	Newport News Shipbuilding	3 Mar 1984	15 Mar 1986	3 June 1989	AA
SAN JUAN	SSN 751	General Dynamics (Electric Boat Div)	16 Aug 1985	6 Dec 1986	6 Aug 1988	AA
PASADENA	SSN 752	General Dynamics (Electric Boat Div)	20 Dec 1985	12 Sep 1987	11 Feb 1989	PA
ALBANY	SSN 753	Newport News Shipbuilding	22 Apr 1985	13 June 1987	7 Apr 1990	AA
TOPEKA	SSN 754	General Dynamics (Electric Boat Div)	13 May 1986	23 Jan 1988	21 Oct 1989	PA
MIAMI	SSN 755	General Dynamics (Electric Boat Div)	24 Oct 1986	12 Nov 1988	30 June 1990	AA
SCRANTON	SSN 756	Newport News Shipbuilding	29 June 1986	3 July 1989	26 Jan 1991	AA
ALEXANDRIA	SSN 757	General Dynamics (Electric Boat Div)	19 June 1987	23 June 1990	29 June 1991	AA
ASHEVILLE	SSN 758	Newport News Shipbuilding	1 Jan 1987	28 Oct 1989	28 Sep 1991	PA
JEFFERSON CITY	SSN 759	Newport News Shipbuilding	21 Sep 1987	24 Mar 1990	29 Feb 1992	PA
ANNAPOLIS	SSN 760	General Dynamics (Electric Boat Div)	15 June 1988	18 May 1991	11 Apr 1992	AA
SPRINGFIELD	SSN 761	General Dynamics (Electric Boat Div)	29 Jan 1990	4 Jan 1992	9 Jan 1993	AA
COLUMBUS	SSN 762	General Dynamics (Electric Boat Div)	7 Jan 1991	1 Aug 1992	24 July 1993	PA
SANTA FE	SSN 763	General Dynamics (Electric Boat Div)	9 July 1991	12 Dec 1992	8 Jan 1994	PA
BOISE	SSN 764	Newport News Shipbuilding	25 Aug 1988	20 Oct 1990	7 Nov 1992	AA
MONTPELIER	SSN 765	Newport News Shipbuilding	19 May 1989	6 Apr 1991	13 Mar 1993	AA
CHARLOTTE	SSN 766	Newport News Shipbuilding	17 Aug 1990	3 Oct 1992	16 Sep 1994	PA
HAMPTON	SSN 767	Newport News Shipbuilding	2 Mar 1990	28 Sep 1991	6 Nov 1993	PA
HARTFORD	SSN 768	General Dynamics (Electric Boat Div)	27 Apr 1992	4 Dec 1993	10 Dec 1994	AA
TOLEDO	SSN 769	Newport News Shipbuilding	6 May 1991	28 Aug 1993	24 Feb 1995	AA
TUCSON	SSN 770	Newport News Shipbuilding	15 Aug 1991	19 Mar 1994	9 Sep 1995	PA
COLUMBIA	SSN 771	General Dynamics (Electric Boat Div)	24 Apr 1993	24 Sep 1994	9 Oct 1995	PA
GREENEVILLE	SSN 772	Newport News Shipbuilding	28 Feb 1992	17 Sep 1994	16 Feb 1996	PA
CHEYENNE	SSN 773	Newport News Shipbuilding	6 July 1992	4 Apr 1995	13 Sep 1996	PA

Displacement, tons: 6,900 standard; 7,011 dived
Dimensions, feet (metres): 360.0 × 33 × 32.3 *(109.7 × 10.1 × 9.9)*
Main machinery: Nuclear; 1 GE PWR S6G; 2 turbines; 35,000 hp *(26 MW)*; 1 shaft; 1 Magnetek auxiliary prop motor; 325 hp *(242 kW)*
Speed, knots: 33 dived
Complement: 134 (13 officers)

Missiles: SLCM: Raytheon Tomahawk Block III and Block IV; TERCOM and GPS aided navigation with DSMAC to 1,600+ km *(865+ n miles)* at 0.7 Mach; warhead (WDU 36B) 454 kg.
SSN 719-722 and 751 onwards are equipped with the Vertical Launch System, which places 12 launch tubes external to the pressure hull behind the spherical array forward.
Torpedoes: 4—21 in *(533 mm)* bow tubes. Raytheon Mk 48 ADCAP Mod 5/6/7; wire-guided (option); active/passive homing to 50 km *(27 n miles)*/38 km *(21 n miles)* at 40/55 kt; warhead 267 kg; depth to 900 m *(2,950 ft)*.
Total of 26 weapons can be tube-launched, for example-12 Tomahawk, 14 torpedoes.
Mines: Can lay Mk 67 Mobile and Mk 60 Captor mines.
Countermeasures: Decoys: External and internal (reloadable) anti-torpedo decoy.
ESM: BRD-7/BLD-1; direction finding. WLR-1H (in 771-773). WLR-8(V)2/6; intercept. WSQ-5 (periscope) and WLR-10; radar warning. BLQ-10 radar and comms intercept.
Combat data systems: CCS Mk 2 (688-750) with UYK 7 computers; BSY-1 (751-773) with UYK 43/UYK 44 computers. JOTS, BGIXS and TADIX-A can be fitted. USC-38 EHF. Link 11; Link 16 being fitted. AN/BYG-1 fire control being fitted.
Radars: Surface search/navigation/fire control: AN/BPS-15H; I/J-band.
Sonars: Lockheed Martin AN/BQQ-10; passive/active search and attack; low frequency. BSY-1 (SSN 751 onwards).
TB-23/29(A) thin line array and TB-16; passive towed array.
BQS-15; active close range including ice detection; high frequency.
MIDAS (mine and ice detection avoidance system) (SSN 751 onwards); active high frequency.

Programmes: Various major improvement programmes and updating design changes caused programme delays in the late 1980s. From SSN 751 onwards the class is prefixed by an 'I' for 'improved'. Programme concluded at 62 hulls. Eleven paid off by mid-1999 and a further six by late 2008.
Modernisation: Mk 117 TFCS backfitted in earlier submarines of the class. EHF communications and Link 16 are being fitted. HDR antenna fitted on the majority of the class. BQQ-10 and TB-29 fitted in most. An ARCI (Acoustic Rapid COTS Insertion) AN/BQQ-10 programme from 1997 to 2006 to backfit BQQ-5 sonars with open system architecture. Five of the class (SSN 688, 690, 700, 701 and 715) are capable of operating with DDS. Two others (SSN 772, 766) are fitted to operate ASDS.
Structure: Every effort has been made to improve sound quieting and from SSN 751 onwards the class has acoustic tile cladding to augment the 'mammalian' skin which up to then had been the standard USN outer casing coating. Also from SSN 751 onwards the forward hydro planes are fitted forward instead of on the fin. The forward hydro planes are retractable mainly for surfacing through ice. The S6G reactor is a modified version of the D2G type. The towed sonar array is stowed in a blister on the side of the casing. Diving depth is 450 m *(1,475 ft)*. Various staged design improvements have added some 220 tons to the class displacement between 688 and 773.
Operational: The Los Angeles class is the mainstay of the attack submarine force. The land-attack mission has been a notable feature of operations in Iraq, Kosovo and Afghanistan. Under-ice operations are still a priority and several (SSN 751, 767) have surfaced at the North Pole. Special forces and intelligence gathering missions are also conducted. Normally additional Tomahawk missiles are carried internally (in addition to those stored externally). Weapon types/numbers vary according to mission. Neither TASM nor Harpoon are now deployed. Nuclear weapons disembarked but still available. ASDS trials in SSN 772 during 2002. SSN 711 seriously damaged in collision with an undersea mountain south of Guam on 8 January 2005. SSN 711 was fitted with the bow section of SSN 718. SSN 767 changed home port to San Diego in 2007 and SSN 699 to Pearl Harbour in 2008.

BOISE *7/2008*, B Prézelin* / 1353576

DALLAS (with DDS) *9/2006, US Navy* / 1167579

HELENA

10/2007, Michael Nitz / 1353647

TOPEKA

10/2007, Michael Nitz / 1353646

ASHEVILLE

2/2006, US Navy / 1167581

TOLEDO

1/2006, US Navy / 1167582

AIRCRAFT CARRIERS

1 ENTERPRISE CLASS (CVNM)

Name	*No*	*Builders*	*Laid down*	*Launched*	*Commissioned*	*F/S*
ENTERPRISE	CVN 65	Newport News Shipbuilding	4 Feb 1958	24 Sep 1960	25 Nov 1961	AA

Displacement, tons: 73,502 light; 75,700 standard; 89,600 full load
Dimensions, feet (metres): 1,123 × 133 × 39 *(342.3 × 40.5 × 11.9)*
Flight deck, feet (metres): 1,088 × 252 *(331.6 × 76.8)*
Main machinery: Nuclear; 8 Westinghouse PWR A2W; 4 Westinghouse turbines; 280,000 hp *(209 MW)*; 4 emergency diesels; 10,720 hp *(8 MW)*; 4 shafts
Speed, knots: 33
Complement: 3,350 (171 officers); 2,480 aircrew (225 officers); Flag staff 70 (25 officers)

Missiles: SAM: 2 Raytheon GMLS Mk 29 octuple launchers ❶; NATO Sea Sparrow RIM-7P; semi-active radar homing to 16 km *(8.6 n miles)* at 2.5 Mach; warhead 38 kg.
2 GMLS Mk 49 RAM RIM-116 ❷; 21 rds/launcher; passive IR/anti-radiation homing to 9.6 km *(5.2 n miles)* at 2.5 Mach; warhead 9.1 kg.
Guns: 2 General Electric/General Dynamics 20 mm Vulcan Phalanx 6-barrelled Mk 15 ❸; 3,000 rds/min (or 4,500 in Block 1) combined to 1.5 km.
Countermeasures: Decoys: SLQ-25 Torpedo Countermeasures Transmitting Set (Nixie).
ESM/ECM: SLQ-32(V)4; intercept and jammers.
Combat data systems: ACDS Block 0 naval tactical and advanced combat direction systems; Links 4A, 11, 14, 16 and Satellite Tadil J. GCCS(M) SATCOMS; SSR-1, WSC-3 (UHF DAMA), WSC-6 (SHF), WSC-8 (SHF), USC-38 (EHF), SSR-2A (GBS) (see Data Systems at front of section).
Weapons control: 2 Mk 91 Mod 1 MFCS directors (part of NSSMS Mk 57 SAM system).
Radars: Air search: ITT SPS-48E ❹; 3D; E/F-band.
Raytheon SPS-49(V)5 ❺; C/D-band.
Hughes Mk 23 TAS ❻; D-band. SPQ-9B in due course.
Surface search: Norden SPS-67; G-band.
CCA: SPN-41, SPN-43C; 2 SPN-46; J/F/K-band.
Navigation: Raytheon SPS-64(V)9; Furuno 900; I/J-band.
Fire control: 4 Mk 95; I/J-band (for SAM).
Tacan: URN 25.

Fixed-wing aircraft: Composition of air-wing depends on mission and typically includes: 44 F/A-18A/C/E/F Hornet; 4 EA-6B Prowler; 4 E-2C Hawkeye.
Helicopters: 4 SH-60F, 2 HH-60H Seahawk. Up to 9 SH-60B Seahawk are dispersed among carrier strike group.

Programmes: Authorised in FY58. Underwent a refit/overhaul at Puget Sound Naval SY, Bremerton, Washington from January 1979 to March 1982. Latest complex overhaul including refuelling started at Newport News in early 1991 and completed 27 September 1994. Minor refit in 1997 and again in 2002.
Modernisation: Mk 25 Sea Sparrow was installed in late 1967 and this has been replaced by two Mk 29 and supplemented with three 20 mm Mk 15 CIWS. A reshaping of the island took place in her 1979–82 refit. This included a replacement mast similar to the Nimitz class with SPS-48C and 49 radars. Improvements during latest overhaul included SPS-48E and Mk 23 TAS air search radars, SPN-46 precision approach and landing radar and C[3] and EW systems. RAM was fitted in 2004.
Structure: Built to a modified Forrestal class design. *Enterprise* was the world's second nuclear-powered surface warship (the cruiser *Long Beach* was completed a few months earlier). Aviation facilities include four deck edge lifts, two forward and one each side abaft the island. There are four 295 ft C 13 Mod 1 catapults. Hangars cover 216,000 sq ft with 25 ft deck head. Aviation fuel, 8,500 tons.
Operational: 12 days' aviation fuel for intensive flying. Scheduled to be decommissioned in 2013 after 52 years service. She will be replaced in the force structure by CVN 78. Based at Norfolk, VA.

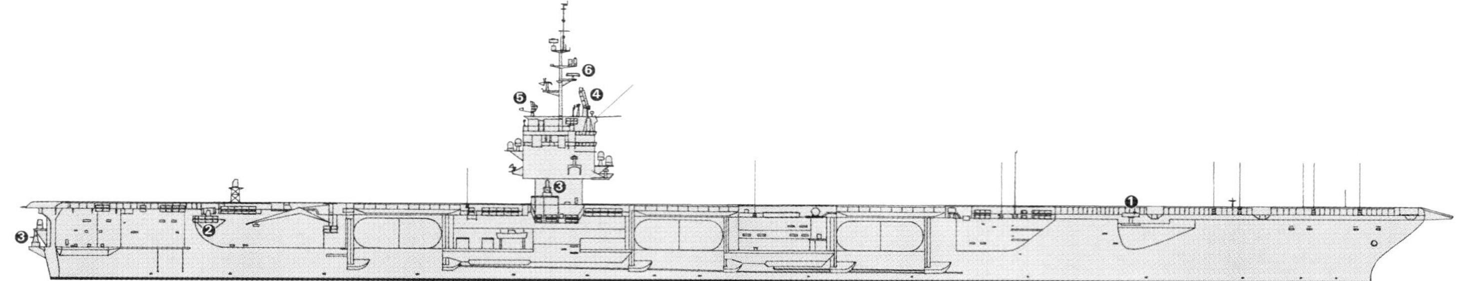

ENTERPRISE *(Scale 1 : 1,800), Ian Sturton* / 0573702

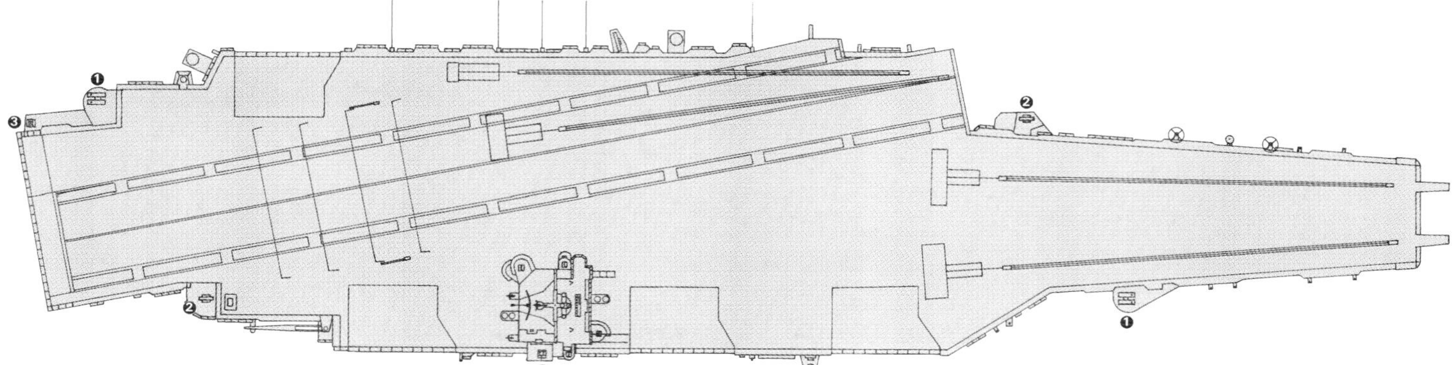

ENTERPRISE *(Scale 1 : 1,800), Ian Sturton* / 0573703

ENTERPRISE *7/2006, US Navy* / 1167592

10 NIMITZ CLASS (CVNM)

Name	*No*	*Builders*	*Laid down*	*Launched*	*Commissioned*	*F/S*
NIMITZ	CVN 68	Newport News Shipbuilding	22 June 1968	13 May 1972	3 May 1975	PA
DWIGHT D EISENHOWER	CVN 69	Newport News Shipbuilding	15 Aug 1970	11 Oct 1975	18 Oct 1977	AA
CARL VINSON	CVN 70	Newport News Shipbuilding	11 Oct 1975	15 Mar 1980	13 Mar 1982	PA
THEODORE ROOSEVELT	CVN 71	Newport News Shipbuilding	13 Oct 1981	27 Oct 1984	25 Oct 1986	AA
ABRAHAM LINCOLN	CVN 72	Newport News Shipbuilding	3 Nov 1984	13 Feb 1988	11 Nov 1989	PA
GEORGE WASHINGTON	CVN 73	Newport News Shipbuilding	25 Aug 1986	21 July 1990	4 July 1992	PA
JOHN C STENNIS	CVN 74	Newport News Shipbuilding	13 Mar 1991	13 Nov 1993	9 Dec 1995	PA
HARRY S TRUMAN	CVN 75	Newport News Shipbuilding	29 Nov 1993	13 Sep 1996	25 July 1998	AA
RONALD REAGAN	CVN 76	Newport News Shipbuilding	12 Feb 1998	4 Mar 2001	12 July 2003	PA
GEORGE H W BUSH	CVN 77	Newport News Shipbuilding	6 Sep 2003	9 Oct 2006	10 Jan 2009	AA

Displacement, tons: 72,916 (CVN 68-70), 73,973 (CVN 71) standard; 91,487 (CVN 68-70), 96,386 (CVN 71), 102,000 (CVN 72-77) full load
Dimensions, feet (metres): 1,040 pp; 1,092 oa × 134 wl × 37 (CVN 68-70); 38.7 (CVN 71); 39 (CVN 72-76); 39.8 (CVN 77) *(317; 332.9 × 40.8 × 11.3; 11.8; 11.9; 12.1)*
Flight deck, feet (metres): 1,092; 779.8 (angled) × 252 *(332.9; 237.7 × 76.8)*
Main machinery: Nuclear; 2 Westinghouse/GE PWR A4W/A1G reactors; 4 turbines; 280,000 hp *(209 MW)*; 4 emergency diesels; 10,720 hp *(8 MW)*; 4 shafts
Speed, knots: 30+
Complement: 3,200 (160 officers); 2,480 aircrew (320 officers); Flag 70 (25 officers)

Missiles: SAM: 2 (CVN 68, 69, 70, 73, 74, 76, 77) or 3 (CVN 71, 72, 75) Raytheon GMLS Mk 29 octuple launchers ❶; NATO Sea Sparrow RIM-7P; semi-active radar homing to 16 km *(8.5 n miles)* at 2.5 Mach; warhead 38 kg. ESSM in due course.
2 GMLS Mk 49 RAM RIM-116 launchers ❷; 21 rds/launcher; passive IR/anti-radiation homing to 9.6 km *(5.2 n miles)* at 2.5 Mach; warhead 9.1 kg.
Guns: 2 (CVN 70, 71, 73) or 3 (CVN 72, 74, 75) General Electric/General Dynamics 20 mm Vulcan Phalanx 6-barrelled Mk 15; 4,500 rds/min combined to 1.5 km.
Countermeasures: Decoys: SLQ 25 Torpedo Countermeasures Transmitting Set (Nixie).
ESM/ECM: SLQ-32(V)4 intercept and jammers.
Combat data systems: ACDS Block 0 (CVN 71-72, 75) naval tactical and advanced combat direction systems; Links 4A, 11, 16 and Satellite Tadil J. GCCS (M) SATCOMS; SSR-1, WCS-3A (UHF DAMA), WSC-6 (SHF), WSC-8 (SHF), USC-38 (EHF), SSR-2A (GBS) (see Data Systems at front of section). SSDS Mk 2 (CVN 68, 69, 70, 73, 74, 76, 77). To be back-fitted in all as part of the CAPSTONE combat system upgrade.
Weapons control: 3 Mk 91 Mod 1 MFCS directors (part of the NSSMS Mk 57 SAM system).
Radars: Air search: ITT SPS-48E ❸; 3D; E/F-band.
Raytheon SPS-49(V)5 (CVN 71, 72, 75) or SPS-49A(V)1 (CVN 68, 69, 70, 73, 74, 76, 77) ❹; C/D-band.
Hughes Mk 23 TAS (CVN 71, 72, 75) ❺; D-band or SPQ-9B (CVN 68-70, 73, 74, 76, 77).
Surface search: Norden SPS-67(V)1; G-band.
CCA: SPN-41, SPN-43C, 2 SPN-46; J/F/J/K-band.
TPX-42A Direct Altitude and Identity Readout (DAIR).
Navigation: Raytheon SPS-64(V)9 (CVN 71, 72, 75) or SPS-73(V)12 (CVN 68, 70, 73, 74) or SPS-73(V)17 (CVN 69, 76, 77); Furuno 900; I/J-band.
Fire control: 4 Mk 95; I/J-band (2 per GMLS Mk 29 launcher).
Tacan: URN 25.

Fixed-wing aircraft: Composition of air-wing depends on mission and typically includes: 44 F/A-18A/C/E/F Hornet; 4 EA-6B Prowler; 4 E-2C Hawkeye.
Helicopters: 4 SH-60F and 2 HH-60H Seahawk and up to 9 SH-60B Seahawk.

Programmes: *Nimitz* was authorised in FY67, *Dwight D Eisenhower* in FY70, *Carl Vinson* in FY74, *Theodore Roosevelt* in FY80 and *Abraham Lincoln* and *George Washington* in FY83. Construction contracts for *John C Stennis* and *Harry S Truman* were awarded in June 1988 and for *Ronald Reagan* in December 1994. Authorised in FY99, construction contract for *George H W Bush* awarded in January 2001.
Modernisation: CVN 68 completed a three-year Refuelling and Complex Overhaul (RCOH) in 2001. RCOH of CVN 69 started in 2001 and completed in January 2005. RCOH of CVN 70 started in November 2005 and is scheduled to be completed in March 2009. RCOH of CVN 71 is to start in 2009. SSDS Mk 2 Mod 0 originally installed in CVN 68 (upgraded to Mk 2 Mod 1 in 2006). This includes fitting two RAM systems and SPQ-9B radar vice Mk 23 TAS. SSDS Mk 2 Mod 1 fitted to CVN 68, 69, 76 and 77. RAM systems replace one Mk 29 and all Phalanx launchers on CVN 68 and 69. CVN 74 similarly refitted during 2005 docking but retains upgraded CIWS (Phalanx) mounts as well. CVN 73 was similarly upgraded in 2007.
The SSDS upgrade package in CVN 73 and 74 is known as the CAPSTONE combat system upgrade. CAPSTONE is being installed in CVN 70 during RCOH and will be scheduled for CVN 71, 72 and 75 indue course.
Structure: Damage control measures include sides with system of full and empty compartments (full compartments can contain aviation fuel), approximately 2.5 in Kevlar plating over certain areas of side shell, box protection over magazine and machinery spaces. Aviation facilities include four lifts, two at the forward end of the flight deck, one to starboard abaft the island and one to port at the stern. There are four steam catapults (C13-1 (CVN 68-71), C13-2 (CVN 72-77)) and four (or three on CVN 76 and 77) Mk 7 Mod 3 arrester wires. Launch rate is one every 20 seconds. The hangar can hold less than half the full aircraft complement, deckhead is 25.6 ft. Aviation fuel, 8,500 tons. Tactical Flag Command Centre for Flagship role. During RCOH, CVN 68 and 69 fitted with reshaped island (the mainmast has three yardarms to support more antennas). Major structural differences in CVN 76 and 77 include: a three-wire arresting system (to replace the four-wire system), an enlarged island structure which incorporates a bigger bridge, a three yardarm mainmast and the after mast (separate in previous ships) and an internal ordnance elevator. Other changes include a bulbous bow to reduce drag and a modified flight deck (angled deck increased by 0.1°) to allow the use of two catapults while aircraft land.
Operational: Multimission role of 'strike/ASW'. From CVN 70 onwards ships have an A/S control centre and A/S facilities; CVN 68 and 69 are backfitted. Endurance of 16 days for aviation fuel (steady flying) with greater than 1 million miles before nuclear reactor refuelling is required. Only one refuelling is required in the life of the ship. Ships' complements and air wing scan be changed depending on the operational task. CVNs 69, 75 and 77 based at Norfolk, VA. CVNs 68, 70 and 76 based at San Diego, CA, CVN 74 at Bremerton, WA, and CVN 72 at Everett, WA. CVN 73 replaced CV 63 at Yokosuka in late 2008. CVN 77 began initial sea trials on 13 February 2009.

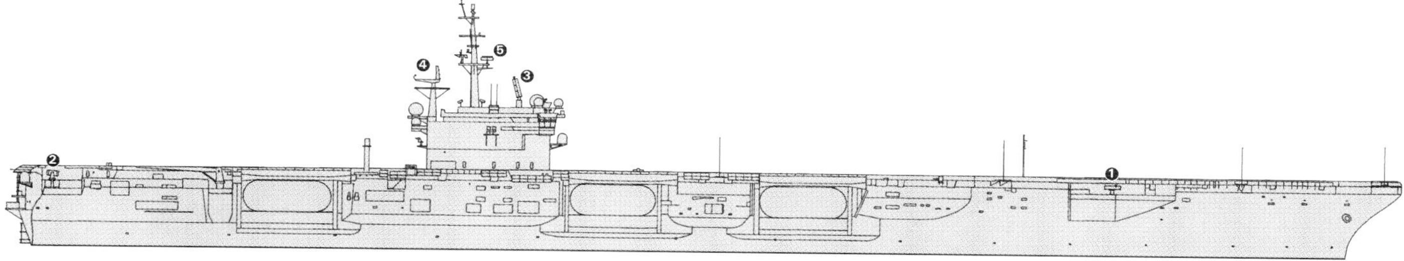

RONALD REAGAN

(Scale 1 : 1,800), Ian Sturton / 1043489

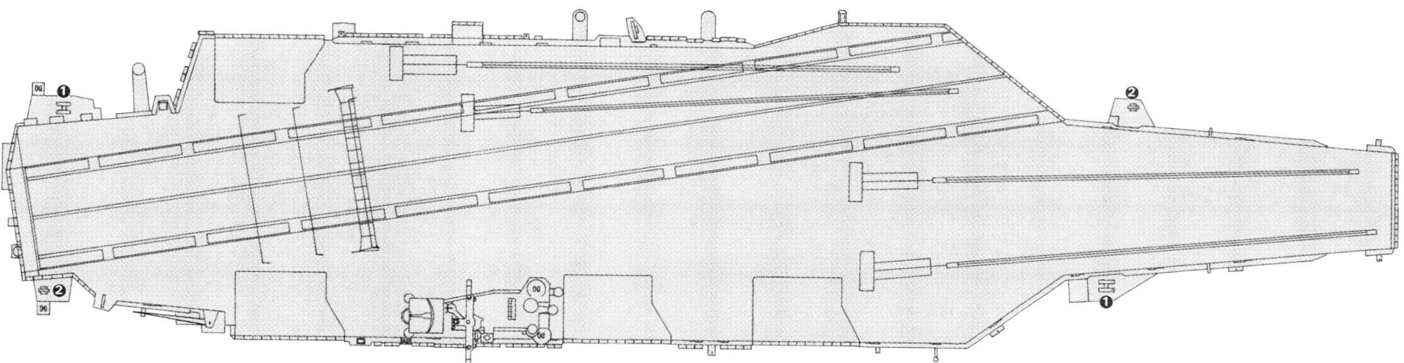

RONALD REAGAN

(Scale 1 : 1,800), Ian Sturton / 1043490

NIMITZ

2/2008*, Hachiro Nakai / 1353577

HARRY S TRUMAN *6/2004, Ships of the World* / 1043700

GEORGE WASHINGTON *8/2008*, US Navy* / 1353644

ABRAHAM LINCOLN *4/2008*, US Navy* / 1353620

DWIGHT D EISENHOWER *12/2006, Tom Philpott* / 1167588

GEORGE WASHINGTON *10/2008*, Michael Nitz* / 1353619

0 + 1 (2) GERALD R FORD CLASS (CVN)

Name	*No*	*Builders*	*Laid down*	*Launched*	*Commissioned*
GERALD R FORD	CVN 78	Northrop Grumman Newport News	2009	2013	2015
–	CVN 79	Northrop Grumman Newport News	2013	2017	2019
–	CVN 80	Northrop Grumman Newport News	2017	2021	2023

Displacement, tons: 100,000 approx
Dimensions, feet (metres): 1,091.8 × 134.0 × 40.8 *(332.8 × 40.8 × 12.4)*
Flight deck, feet (metres): 109.8 × 256 *(332.8 × 78.0)*
Main machinery: Nuclear; 2 reactors; 4 shafts
Speed, knots: 30+
Complement: 4,660 ship and aircrew

Missiles: SAM: 2 Raytheon GMLS Mk 29 launchers for Raytheon Evolved Sea Sparrow RIM-7.
2 GMLS Mk 49 RAM RIM-116.
Guns: 3 General Electric/General Dynamics 20 mm Vulcan Phalanx Mk 15 6-barrelled.
Countermeasures: ESM/ECM: SEWIP Block 2/3.
Torpedo defence: SLQ-25C.
Combat data systems: CEC; USG-2A; Links 4, 11, 16.
Weapons control: SSDS Mk II.
Radars: Air search: Dual Band Radar (DBR); Raytheon SPY-3; 3D; I-band and Lockheed Martin Volume Search Radar (VSR); 3D; E/F-band.
Navigation: SPS-73V(18).
Fire control: 4 Mk 95; I/J-band (2 per GMLS 29 launchers).
Tacan: URN-25.

Fixed-wing aircraft: Composition will depend on mission but will comprise 75+ aircraft (JSF, F/A-18E/F, EA-18G, E-2D, MH-60R/S, J-UCAS).

Programmes: Northrop Grumman Newport News awarded a construction preparation contract in May 2004 for detailed design, component development, long-lead procurement and advanced construction of the lead ship CVN 78. First steel cut on 11 August 2005.
Structure: The Ford class flight deck and below deck have been optimised to increase sortie rates and improve weapons movement. This is to be accomplished with a new design and relocation of the island, three aircraft lifts and an advanced weapons elevators (AWE). Other features include four Electromagnetic Aircraft Launching Systems (EMALS), Advanced Arresting Gear (AAG) system, new SSDS open architecture combat system, fully integrated warfare system, a new nuclear power plant, and a flexible ship architecture to support the rapid insertion of future warfighting technologies. Significant habitability improvements are to be incorporated.
Operational: CVN 78 class ships will require 500–900 fewer personnel than the Nimitz class complement. Increased sortie rates (by 25 per cent) and reduced depot maintenance requirements will increase operational availability. New command centre to combine force networking with flexible, open system architecture to support simultaneous multiple missions, including integrated strike planning, joint/coalition operations and special warfare missions. Planned service life 50 years.

CVN 78 (artist's impression) *4/2006, US Navy* / 1159240

CRUISERS

Notes: (1) **Integrated Ship Controls.** Formerly known as Smart Ship, Integrated Ship Controls (ISC) began as Naval Research Advisory Committee recommendation in 1996 to reduce manning through technology. *Yorktown* (CG 48) was selected as first Smart Ship with implementation of 47 workload-reduction initiatives tested and evaluated during a five-month deployment completed in June 1997. Fourteen more initiatives were installed in July 1997. Core systems included: Integrated Bridge System (IBS), Integrated Condition Assessment System (ICAS), Machinery Control System (MCS), Damaged Control System (DCS), Fuel Control System (FCS), fibre optic Local Area Network (LAN) and Wireless Internal Communication System (WICS). *Yorktown's* experience validated these technologies, combined with changes in policies, procedures and new watch routines, to generate substantial reductions in workload. *Monterey* (CG 61) was fitted in 2000; *Valley Forge* (CG 50) and *Mobile Bay* (CG 53) in 2001; *Antietam* (CG 54) in 2002; *Hue City* (CG 66) in 2003; *Cape St George* (CG71) in 2004; *San Jacinto* (CG 56) in 2006; *Leyte Gulf* (CG 55), *Philippine Sea* (CG 58) and *Chancellorsville* (CG 62) in 2007. *Bunker Hill* (CG 52) and *Lake Champlain* (CG 57) in 2008. Remaining ships of class are to receive ISC either as a stand-alone upgrade or during the Cruiser Modernisation Programme.
(2) CG(X) is the proposed replacement for the Ticonderoga (CG 47) class cruisers. It is expected to be a follow-on variant of the DDG 1000, incorporating an integrated power system and using a similar hull-form, but with enhanced missile-defence and air warfare capability. Results of the CG(X) Analysis of Alternatives were beingstaffed in early 2009.

GETTYSBURG *6/2008*, Michael Nitz* / 1353774

22 TICONDEROGA CLASS (CGHM)

Name	*No*	*Builder/Programme*	*Laid down*	*Launched*	*Commissioned*	*F/S*
BUNKER HILL	CG 52	Ingalls Shipbuilding	11 Jan 1984	11 Mar 1985	20 Sep 1986	PA
MOBILE BAY	CG 53	Ingalls Shipbuilding	6 June 1984	22 Aug 1985	21 Feb 1987	PA
ANTIETAM	CG 54	Ingalls Shipbuilding	15 Nov 1984	14 Feb 1986	6 June 1987	PA
LEYTE GULF	CG 55	Ingalls Shipbuilding	18 Mar 1985	20 June 1986	26 Sep 1987	AA
SAN JACINTO	CG 56	Ingalls Shipbuilding	24 July 1985	14 Nov 1986	23 Jan 1988	AA
LAKE CHAMPLAIN	CG 57	Ingalls Shipbuilding	3 Mar 1986	3 Apr 1987	12 Aug 1988	PA
PHILIPPINE SEA	CG 58	Bath Iron Works	8 May 1986	12 July 1987	18 Mar 1989	AA
PRINCETON	CG 59	Ingalls Shipbuilding	15 Oct 1986	2 Oct 1987	11 Feb 1989	PA
NORMANDY	CG 60	Bath Iron Works	7 Apr 1987	19 Mar 1988	9 Dec 1989	AA
MONTEREY	CG 61	Bath Iron Works	19 Aug 1987	23 Oct 1988	16 June 1990	AA
CHANCELLORSVILLE	CG 62	Ingalls Shipbuilding	24 June 1987	15 July 1988	4 Nov 1989	PA
COWPENS	CG 63	Bath Iron Works	23 Dec 1987	11 Mar 1989	9 Mar 1991	PA
GETTYSBURG	CG 64	Bath Iron Works	17 Aug 1988	22 July 1989	22 June 1991	AA
CHOSIN	CG 65	Ingalls Shipbuilding	22 July 1988	1 Sep 1989	12 Jan 1991	PA
HUE CITY	CG 66	Ingalls Shipbuilding	20 Feb 1989	1 June 1990	14 Sep 1991	AA
SHILOH	CG 67	Bath Iron Works	1 Aug 1989	8 Sep 1990	2 July 1992	PA
ANZIO	CG 68	Ingalls Shipbuilding	21 Aug 1989	2 Nov 1990	2 May 1992	AA
VICKSBURG	CG 69	Ingalls Shipbuilding	30 May 1990	2 Aug 1991	14 Nov 1992	AA
LAKE ERIE	CG 70	Bath Iron Works	6 Mar 1990	13 July 1991	24 July 1993	PA
CAPE ST GEORGE	CG 71	Ingalls Shipbuilding	19 Nov 1990	10 Jan 1992	12 June 1993	AA
VELLA GULF	CG 72	Ingalls Shipbuilding	22 Apr 1991	13 June 1992	18 Sep 1993	AA
PORT ROYAL	CG 73	Ingalls Shipbuilding	18 Oct 1991	20 Nov 1992	9 July 1994	PA

Displacement, tons: 9,957 full load
Dimensions, feet (metres): 567 × 55 × 31 (sonar) *(172.8 × 16.8 × 9.5)*
Main machinery: 4 GE LM 2500 gas turbines; 86,000 hp *(64.16 MW)* sustained; 2 shafts; cp props
Speed, knots: 30+
Range, n miles: 6,000 at 20 kt
Complement: 358 (24 officers); accommodation for 405 total

Missiles: SLCM: Raytheon Tomahawk Block III and Block IV; TERCOM and GPS aided navigation with DSMAC to 1,600+ km *(865+ n miles)* at 0.7 Mach; warhead (WDU 36B) 454 kg.
SSM: 8 McDonnell Douglas Harpoon (2 quad) ❶; active radar homing to 240 km *(130 n miles)* at 0.9 Mach; warhead 227 kg. Extended range SLAM can be fired from modified Harpoon canisters.
SAM: 122 Raytheon Standard SM-2 Block III and IVA; command/inertial guidance; semi-active radar and IR homing to 167 km *(90 n miles)* at 2.5 Mach. SAM and ASROC missiles are fired from 2 Mk 41 Mod 0 vertical launchers ❷ (61 missiles per launcher). Standard SM-3 Block 1A (in designated ships); command/inertial/GPS guidance and IR homing to 650 n miles *(1,200 km)* at 3 Mach.
A/S: Loral ASROC VLA which has a range of 16.6 km *(9 n miles)*; inertial guidance of 1.6-10 km *(1-5.4 n miles)*; payload Mk 46 Mod 5 Neartip or Mk 50.
Guns: 2 FMC 5 in *(127 mm)*/54 Mk 45 Mod 1 ❸; 20 rds/min to 23 km *(12.6 n miles)* anti-surface; weight of shell 32 kg.
2 General Electric/General Dynamics 20 mm/76 Vulcan Phalanx 6-barrelled Mk 15 Mod 2 ❹; 3,000 rds/min (4,500 in Block 1) combined to 1.5 km. To be fitted with high-definition thermal imagers (HDTI) for tracking small craft.
2 McDonnell Douglas 25 mm. 4—12.7 mm MGs.
Torpedoes: 6—324 mm Mk 32 (2 triple) Mod 14 tubes (fitted in the ship's side aft) ❺. 36 Honeywell Mk 46 Mod 5; anti-submarine; active/passive homing to 11 km *(5.9 n miles)* at 40 kt; warhead 44 kg or Alliant/Westinghouse Mk 50; active/passive homing to 15 km *(8.1 n miles)* at 50 kt; warhead 45 kg shaped charge.
Countermeasures: Decoys: Up to 8 Loral Hycor SRBOC 6-barrelled fixed Mk 36 Mod 2 ❻; IR flares and chaff. Nulka being acquired. SLQ-25 Nixie; towed torpedo decoy.
ESM/ECM: Raytheon SLQ-32V(3)/SLY-2 ❼; intercept, jammers.
Combat data systems: CEC being fitted 1996–2007 starting with CG 66 and 69. NTDS with Links 4A, 11, 14. GCCS (M) and Link 16 being fitted. Link 22 in due course. SATCOM WRN-5, WSC-3 (UHF), USC-38 (EHF). UYK-7 computers (CG 52-58); UYK 43/44 (CG 59 onwards); SQQ-28 for LAMPS sonobuoy datalink ❽ (see Data Systems at front of section).
Weapons control: SWG-3 Tomahawk WCS. SWG-1A Harpoon LCS. Aegis Mk 7 Mod 4 multitarget tracking with Mk 99 MFCS (includes 4 Mk 80 illuminator directors); has at least 12 channels of fire. Singer Librascope Mk 116 Mod 6 (53B) or Mod 7 (53C) FCS for ASW. Lockheed Mk 86 Mod 9 GFCS (to be replaced by Mk-160 Mod 11 from 2008).
Radars: Air search/fire control: RCA SPY-1A phased arrays ❾; 3D; E/F-band (CG 52-58).
Raytheon SPY-1B phased arrays; 3D; E/F-band (CG 59 on).

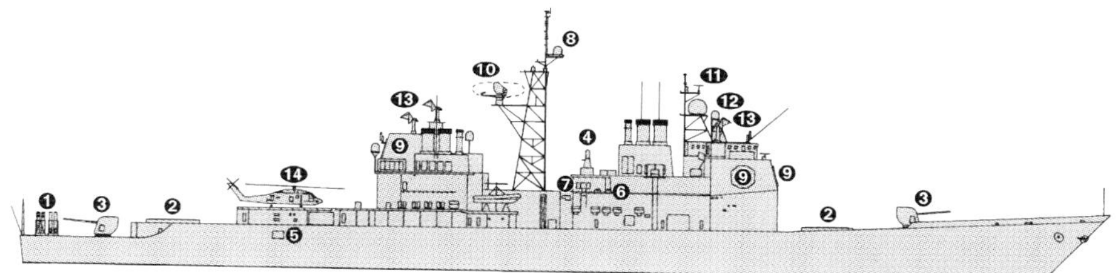

BUNKER HILL ***(Scale 1 : 1,500), Ian Sturton*** / 0581793

Air search: Raytheon SPS-49(V)7 or 8 ❿; C/D-band; range 457 km *(250 n miles)*.
Surface search: ISC Cardion SPS-55 ⓫; I/J-band.
Navigation: Raytheon SPS-64(V)9; I-band.
Fire control: Lockheed SPQ-9A/B ⓬; I/J-band.
Four Raytheon SPG-62 ⓭; I/J-band.
Tacan: URN 25. IFF Mk XII AIMS UPX-29.
Sonars: Gould/Raytheon SQQ-89(V)3 (CG 52 onwards); combines hull-mounted active SQS-53B (CG 52-67) or SQS-53C (CG 68-73) and passive towed array SQR-19.

Helicopters: 2 SH-60B Seahawk LAMPS III ⓮. UAV in due course.

Modernisation: The Cruiser Modernisation (CG Mod) Programme is an extensive capability enhancement and service-life extension that is to be applied to all 22 ships. The principal feature of the programme is to be installation of Aegis Open Architecture (AOA) to upgrade the Aegis Weapon System (AWS), ACB 08/ACB 12 Computer Programme and associated displays and computing infrastructure. The new computer programme is to replace several existing computer programme baselines and provide improved tactical performance and functionality. The AOA upgrade is to provide capacity for future combat system growth over the life of the class as well as mission expansion, such as Ballistic Missile Defense (BMD). The Mk 34 Mod 4 Gun Weapon System upgrade includes the Mk 45 Mod 2 5 in/62 caliber guns, associated Mk 160 Mod 11 fire-control system and optical sights for improved land-attack capability. Additionally, several upgraded command, control, communications, computers and intelligence (C4I) systems and enhanced force-protection capabilities are to be installed. Layered defence is improved through installation of the Vulcan Phalanx Block 1B, modification of the Mk 41 VLS launchers to fire ESSM, installation of the Mk 53 Mod 5 Decoy Launch System (Nulka) and replacement of SPQ-9A with SPQ-9B radar to increase detection and engagement of surface and air threats. Modernised Baseline 3 (CG 59-64) and 4 (CG 65-73) cruisers will rejoin the fleet equipped with improved anti-submarine warfare capability through installation of the SQQ-89A(V)15 upgrade and the Multi-Function Towed Array. Baseline 2 (CG 52-58) are to retain SQQ-89(V)3. The programme will also include a significant Hull, Mechanical and Electrical (HM&E) package that features alterations in weight and movement correction, hull and deckhouse structural improvements, corrosion-control enhancements, hangar deck strengthening, distributive system enhancements and many quality-of-service upgrades. The modernisation will install the Integrated Ship Controls (ISC), or Smartship, and all-electric modifications on ships that have not yet received the alterations. Cruisers with ISC previously installed will receive system upgrades.

Complete modernisation is to be accomplished in two primary phases. The first phase involves HM&E Centric Modernisation availabilities to include ISC and all-electric modifications, in addition to stand-alone combat systems ship changes. Duration of this phase is projected to be less than six months and is to occur in ship's homeport. The initial HM&E Centric Modernisation availability for *San Jacinto* began in July 2006 and was completed in January 2007. Three more cruisers completed their HM&E upgrades in 2007 and two more in 2008. The second phase involves the full Combat Systems Modernisation refits which include a fully integrated combat system upgrade and those HM&E ship changes not previously completed. *Bunker Hill* (CG 52) is the first ship to undergo the full upgrade and is scheduled to rejoin the fleet in 2009. She is to be followed by *Mobile Bay* and *Philippine Sea*. Modernisation for all ships is to be completed by 2017. CGs having previously received the HM&E upgrades will have integrated combat system upgrades installed during homeport upkeep periods.

Structure: The Ticonderoga class design is a modification of the Spruance class. The same basic hull is used, with the same gas-turbine propulsion plant although the overall length is slightly increased. The design includes Kevlar armour to protect vital spaces. No stabilisers. Later ships have a lighter tripod mainmast vice the square quadruped of the first two.

Operational: The sea-based element of the Ballistic Missile Defense Programme is known as Aegis BMD. *Lake Erie* has acted as the principal trials platform. Since the first intercept test in January 2002, a total of 20 tests had been conducted by late 2008. Of these, 16 have been successful. Tests involved both the Standard SM-3 (in the target's exo-atmospheric ballistic phase) and Standard SM-2 Block IV in the terminal phase. As of the end of 2006, three cruisers (*Lake Erie*, *Shiloh* and *Port Royal*) were capable of launching Standard Missile-3s (SM-3s) to intercept ballistic missiles. *Shiloh* was forward-deployed to Japan in 2006 to bolster missile defence in the region.

ANZIO ***4/2008*, B Moultrie*** / 1353614

MONTEREY *3/2008*, US Navy* / 1353617

COWPENS *10/2008*, Michael Nitz* / 1353615

LAKE ERIE *8/2008*, Michael Nitz* / 1353613

CAPE ST GEORGE

*8/2008**, *Shaun Jones* / 1353618

LEYTE GULF

*3/2008**, *US Navy* / 1353616

GETTYSBURG

*6/2008**, *Michael Nitz* / 1353612

DESTROYERS

28 ARLEIGH BURKE (FLIGHTS I AND II) CLASS (AEGIS) (DDGHM)

Name	*No*	*Builders*	*Laid down*	*Launched*	*Commissioned*	*F/S*
ARLEIGH BURKE	DDG 51	Bath Iron Works	6 Dec 1988	16 Sep 1989	4 July 1991	AA
BARRY (ex-*John Barry*)	DDG 52	Ingalls Shipbuilding	26 Feb 1990	10 May 1991	12 Dec 1992	AA
JOHN PAUL JONES	DDG 53	Bath Iron Works	8 Aug 1990	26 Oct 1991	18 Dec 1993	PA
CURTIS WILBUR	DDG 54	Bath Iron Works	12 Mar 1992	16 May 1991	4 Apr 1994	PA
STOUT	DDG 55	Ingalls Shipbuilding	8 Aug 1991	16 Oct 1992	13 Aug 1994	AA
JOHN S McCAIN	DDG 56	Bath Iron Works	3 Sep 1991	26 Sep 1992	2 July 1994	PA
MITSCHER	DDG 57	Ingalls Shipbuilding	12 Feb 1992	7 May 1993	10 Dec 1994	AA
LABOON	DDG 58	Bath Iron Works	23 Mar 1992	20 Feb 1993	18 Mar 1995	AA
RUSSELL	DDG 59	Ingalls Shipbuilding	24 July 1992	20 Oct 1993	20 May 1995	PA
PAUL HAMILTON	DDG 60	Bath Iron Works	24 Aug 1992	24 July 1993	27 May 1995	PA
RAMAGE	DDG 61	Ingalls Shipbuilding	4 Jan 1993	11 Feb 1994	22 July 1995	AA
FITZGERALD	DDG 62	Bath Iron Works	9 Feb 1993	29 Jan 1994	14 Oct 1995	PA
STETHEM	DDG 63	Ingalls Shipbuilding	11 May 1993	17 June 1994	21 Oct 1995	PA
CARNEY	DDG 64	Bath Iron Works	3 Aug 1993	23 July 1994	13 Apr 1996	AA
BENFOLD	DDG 65	Ingalls Shipbuilding	27 Sep 1993	9 Nov 1994	30 Mar 1996	PA
GONZALEZ	DDG 66	Bath Iron Works	3 Feb 1994	18 Feb 1995	12 Oct 1996	AA
COLE	DDG 67	Ingalls Shipbuilding	28 Feb 1994	10 Feb 1995	8 June 1996	AA
THE SULLIVANS	DDG 68	Bath Iron Works	27 July 1994	12 Aug 1995	19 Apr 1997	AA
MILIUS	DDG 69	Ingalls Shipbuilding	8 Aug 1994	1 Aug 1995	23 Nov 1996	PA
HOPPER	DDG 70	Bath Iron Works	23 Feb 1995	6 Jan 1996	6 Sep 1997	PA
ROSS	DDG 71	Ingalls Shipbuilding	10 Apr 1995	23 Mar 1996	28 June 1997	AA
MAHAN	DDG 72	Bath Iron Works	17 Aug 1995	29 June 1996	14 Feb 1998	AA
DECATUR	DDG 73	Bath Iron Works	11 Jan 1996	10 Nov 1996	29 Aug 1998	PA
McFAUL	DDG 74	Ingalls Shipbuilding	26 Jan 1996	18 Jan 1997	25 Apr 1998	AA
DONALD COOK	DDG 75	Bath Iron Works	9 July 1996	3 May 1997	4 Dec 1998	AA
HIGGINS	DDG 76	Bath Iron Works	14 Nov 1996	4 Oct 1997	24 Apr 1999	PA
O'KANE	DDG 77	Bath Iron Works	5 May 1997	28 Mar 1998	23 Oct 1999	PA
PORTER	DDG 78	Ingalls Shipbuilding	2 Dec 1996	12 Nov 1997	20 Mar 1999	AA

Displacement, tons: 8,950 (DDG 51-71); 8,946 (DDG 72-78)
Dimensions, feet (metres): 504.5 oa; 466 wl × 66.6 × 22.0; 32.1 (sonar)
(153.8; 142 × 20.3 × 6.7; 9.8)
Main machinery: 4 GE LM 2500 gas turbines; 105,000 hp *(78.33 MW)* sustained; 2 shafts; cp props
Speed, knots: 32
Range, n miles: 4,400 at 20 kt
Complement: 346 (DDG 51-71); 352 (DDG 72-78) (22 officers)

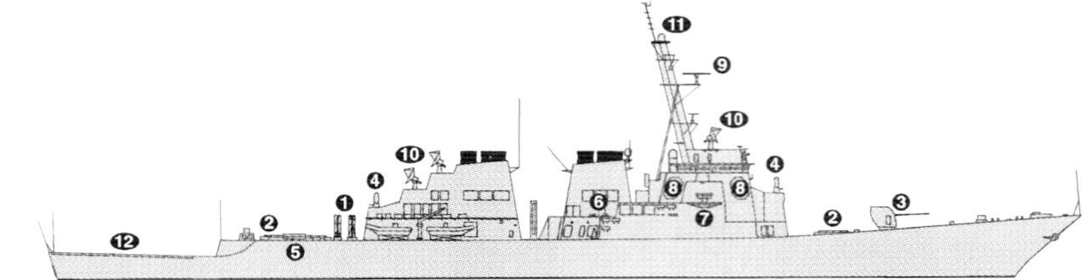
ARLEIGH BURKE ***(Scale 1 : 1,500), Ian Sturton*** / 0053331

Missiles: SLCM: 56 Raytheon Tomahawk Block III and IV; TERCOM and GPS aided navigation with DSMAC to 1,600+ km *(865+ n miles)* at 0.7 Mach; warhead (WDU 36B) 454 kg.
SSM: 8 McDonnell Douglas Harpoon (2 quad) ❶; active radar homing to 240 km *(130 n miles)* at 0.9 Mach; warhead 227 kg.
SAM: Raytheon Standard SM-2 Block III and IVA; command/inertial guidance; semi-active radar and IR homing to 167 km *(90 n miles)* at 2.5 Mach. Standard SM-3 Block 1A (in designated ships); command/inertial/GPS guidance and IR homing to 650 n miles *(1,200 km)* at 3 Mach. 2 Martin Marietta Mk 41 (Mod 0 forward, Mod 1 aft) Vertical Launch Systems (VLS) for Tomahawk, Standard and ASROC VLA ❷; 2 magazines; 29 missiles forward, 61 aft. Mod 2 from DDG 59 onwards.
A/S: Loral ASROC VLA; inertial guidance to 1.6-16.6 km *(1-9 n miles)*; payload Mk 46 Mod 5 Neartip.
Guns: 1 FMC/UDLP 5 in *(127 mm)*/54 Mk 45 Mod 1 or 2 ❸; 20 rds/min to 23 km *(12.6 n miles)*; weight of shell 32 kg. 2 General Electric/General Dynamics 20 mm Vulcan Phalanx 6-barrelled Mk 15 ❹; 3,000 rds/min (4,500 in Block 1) combined to 1.5 km. Being fitted with IR detectors for tracking small craft.
Torpedoes: 6—324 mm Mk 32 Mod 14 (2 triple) tubes ❺. Alliant Mk 46 Mod 5; anti-submarine; active/passive homing to 11 km *(5.9 n miles)* at 40 kt; warhead 44 kg or Alliant/Westinghouse Mk 50; active/passive homing to 15 km *(8.1 n miles)* at 50 kt; warhead 45 kg shaped charge.
Countermeasures: Decoys: 2 Loral Hycor SRBOC 6-barrelled fixed Mk 36 Mod 12 ❻; IR flares and chaff to 4 km *(2.2 n miles)*. SLQ-25 Nixie; torpedo decoy. NATO Sea Gnat. SLQ-95 AEB. SLQ-39 chaff buoy. Nulka being acquired.
ESM/ECM: Raytheon SLQ-32A(V)2 (DDG 51-67) ❼ or SLQ-32A(V)3/SLY-2 (DDG 68-78); radar warning. Sidekick modification adds jammer and deception system to (V)2. SRS-1 DF (from DDG 72).
CESM: AN/SRS-1A(V) Combat Direction Finding System (CDF).
Combat data systems: CEC being fitted. NTDS Mod 5 with Links 4A, 11, 14 and 16 (from DDG 72) and being back fitted. SATCOM SRR-1, WSC-3 (UHF), USC-38 (EHF). SQQ-28 for LAMPS processor datalink. TADIX B Tactical Information Exchange System (from DDG 72). Link 22 in due course (see Data Systems at front of section). Naval Fires Combat System (NFCS).
Weapons control: SWG-4 or SWG-5 Tomahawk WCS. SWG-1A Harpoon LCS. Aegis multitarget tracking with Mk 99 Mod 3 MFCS and three Mk 80 illuminators. Mk 34 GWS (includes Mk 160 computing system and Kollmorgen Mk 46 Mod 0/1 optronic sight). Singer Librascope Mk 116 Mod 7 FCS for ASW.
Radars: Air search/fire control: RCA SPY-1D phased arrays ❽; 3D; E/F-band.
Surface search: Norden/DRS SPS-67(V)3 ❾; G-band.
Navigation: Raytheon SPS-64(V)9; I-band.
Fire control: Three Raytheon/RCA SPG-62 ❿; I/J-band.
Tacan: URN 25 ⓫. IFF Mk XII AIMS UPX-29.
Sonars: Gould/Raytheon/GE SQQ-89(V)4 (DDG 51), SQQ-89(V)6 (DDG 52-78); combines SQS-53C; bow-mounted; active search and attack with SQR-19B passive towed array (TACTAS) low frequency.

Helicopters: Platform and facilities to fuel and rearm LAMPS III SH-60B/F helicopters ⓬. UAV in due course.

Programmes: First ship authorised in FY85, last pair in FY94. The first 21 are Flight I and the next seven are Flight II.
Modernisation: A mid-life modernisation program is planned. The scope of the upgrade is to be included initially during the construction of Flight IIA DDGs 111 and 112 and then retrofitted into DDG Flight I and II ships during two separate overhaul periods: the first for engineering control system upgrades and the second for combat system upgrades. Fifteen ships are modified toundertake the BMD mission. Aegis has been upgraded to BMD Version 3.6 in DDG 63. This is a tactical version which adds BMD capability to the other multimission capabilities of the Aegis system. DDGs 53, 54, 55, 56, 59, 60, 61, 62, 65, 69, 70, 73, 76 and 77 are currently equipped with Version 3.0 which is to be upgraded to Version 3.6 by 2009. Designated ships are equipped with Standard SM-3 Block 1A. This is to be upgraded to Block 1B from 2010. Following the identification of structural defects to the entire DDG 51 class, a bow-strengthening programme has been initiated. Repairs are to be carried out during planned docking periods.
Structure: The ship, except for the aluminium mast, is constructed of steel. 70 tons of armour provided to protect vital spaces. This is the first class of US Navy warship designed with a 'collective protection system for defense against the fallout associated with NBC warfare'. The ship's crew are protected by double air-locked hatches, fewer accesses to the weatherdecks and positive pressurisation of the interior of the ship to keep out contaminants. All incoming air is filtered and more reliance placed on recirculating air inside the ship. All accommodation compartments have sprinkler systems. Stealth technology includes angled surfaces and rounded edges to reduce radar signature and IR signature suppression plus Prairie Masker hull/blade rate suppression. The CIC room is below the waterline and electronics are EMP hardened. The original upright mast design has been changed to increase separation between electronic systems and the forward funnel. Differences in Flight II starting with DDG 72 include Link 16, SLQ-32(V)3 EW suite, extended-range SAM missiles and improved tactical information exchange systems. The topmast is vertical to take the SRS-1. There is also an increase in displacement caused by using more space to carry fuel.
Operational: Two of the class are based at Yokosuka in Japan. Repairs to *Cole*, damaged by a terrorist attack at Aden on 12 October 2000, began in January 2001 at Ingalls and completed on 19 April 2002 when she returned to the fleet. *Curtis Wilbur* began missile-defence patrols in the Sea of Japan in October 2004. *Milius* successfully fired a Tomahawk Block IV missile on 6 December 2006.

McFAUL ***9/2008*, C D Yaylali*** / 1353611

DONALD COOK

4/2008*, B Moultrie / 1353610

JOHN S McCAIN

10/2008*, Michael Nitz / 1353608

RAMAGE

11/2008*, Guy Toremans / 1353609

27 + 7 (8) ARLEIGH BURKE (FLIGHT IIA) CLASS

Name	*No*	*Builders*	*Laid down*	*Launched*	*Commissioned*	*F/S*
OSCAR AUSTIN	DDG 79	Bath Iron Works	9 Oct 1997	7 Nov 1998	19 Aug 2000	AA
ROOSEVELT	DDG 80	Ingalls Shipbuilding	15 Dec 1997	10 Jan 1999	14 Oct 2000	AA
WINSTON S CHURCHILL	DDG 81	Bath Iron Works	7 May 1998	17 Apr 1999	10 Mar 2001	AA
LASSEN	DDG 82	Ingalls Shipbuilding	24 Aug 1998	16 Oct 1999	21 Apr 2001	PA
HOWARD	DDG 83	Bath Iron Works	9 Dec 1998	20 Nov 1999	20 Oct 2001	PA
BULKELEY	DDG 84	Ingalls Shipbuilding	10 May 1999	21 June 2000	8 Dec 2001	AA
McCAMPBELL	DDG 85	Bath Iron Works	15 July 1999	2 July 2000	17 Aug 2002	PA
SHOUP	DDG 86	Ingalls Shipbuilding	13 Dec 1999	22 Nov 2000	22 June 2002	PA
MASON	DDG 87	Bath Iron Works	20 Jan 2000	23 June 2001	12 Apr 2003	AA
PREBLE	DDG 88	Ingalls Shipbuilding	22 June 2000	1 June 2001	9 Nov 2002	PA
MUSTIN	DDG 89	Ingalls Shipbuilding	15 Jan 2001	12 Dec 2001	26 July 2003	PA
CHAFFEE	DDG 90	Bath Iron Works	12 Apr 2001	2 Nov 2002	18 Oct 2003	PA
PINCKNEY	DDG 91	Ingalls Shipbuilding	16 July 2001	26 June 2002	29 May 2004	PA
MOMSEN	DDG 92	Bath Iron Works	16 Nov 2001	19 July 2003	28 Aug 2004	PA
CHUNG-HOON	DDG 93	Ingalls, Shipbuilding	14 Jan 2002	15 Dec 2002	18 Sep 2004	PA
NITZE	DDG 94	Bath Iron Works	17 Sep 2002	3 Apr 2004	5 Mar 2005	AA
JAMES E WILLIAMS	DDG 95	Ingalls Shipbuilding	15 July 2002	25 June 2003	11 Dec 2004	AA
BAINBRIDGE	DDG 96	Bath Iron Works	7 May 2003	30 Oct 2004	12 Nov 2005	AA
HALSEY	DDG 97	Ingalls Shipbuilding	5 Feb 2003	9 Jan 2004	30 July 2005	PA
FORREST SHERMAN	DDG 98	Ingalls Shipbuilding	12 Aug 2003	30 June 2004	28 Jan 2006	AA
FARRAGUT	DDG 99	Bath Iron Works	7 Jan 2004	9 July 2005	10 June 2006	AA
KIDD	DDG 100	Ingalls Shipbuilding	1 Mar 2004	15 Dec 2004	9 June 2007	PA
GRIDLEY	DDG 101	Bath Iron Works	30 July 2004	28 Dec 2005	10 Feb 2007	PA
SAMPSON	DDG 102	Bath Iron Works	14 Mar 2005	17 Sep 2006	3 Nov 2007	PA
TRUXTUN	DDG 103	Northrop Grumman Ship Systems	11 Apr 2005	2 June 2007	25 Apr 2009	AA
STERETT	DDG 104	Bath Iron Works	17 Nov 2005	20 May 2007	9 Aug 2008	PA
DEWEY	DDG 105	Northrop Grumman Ship Systems	3 Oct 2006	26 Jan 2008	Nov 2009	Bldg/PA
STOCKDALE	DDG 106	Bath Iron Works	10 Aug 2006	10 May 2008	18 Apr 2009	PA
GRAVELY	DDG 107	Northrop Grumman Ship Systems	26 Nov 2007	16 May 2009	Aug 2010	Bldg/AA
WAYNE E MEYER	DDG 108	Bath Iron Works	18 May 2007	18 Oct 2008	Oct 2009	Bldg/PA
JASON DUNHAM	DDG 109	Bath Iron Works	11 Apr 2008	July 2009	July 2010	Bldg/PA
WILLIAM P LAWRENCE	DDG 110	Northrop Grumman Ship Systems	8 Sep 2008	Feb 2010	Mar 2011	Bldg/PA
SPRUANCE	DDG 111	Bath Iron Works	12 Apr 2009	Jan 2010	Feb 2011	Bldg/PA
MICHAEL MURPHY	DDG 112	Bath Iron Works	28 June 2009	Sep 2010	Oct 2011	Bldg/PA

Displacement, tons: 9,155 full load
Dimensions, feet (metres): 509.5 oa; 471 wl × 66.6 × 22.0; 32.1 (sonar)
(155.3; 143.6 × 20.3 × 6.7; 9.8)
Main machinery: 4 GE LM 2500-30 gas turbines; 100,000 hp *(74.6 MW)* sustained; 2 shafts; cp props
Speed, knots: 31
Range, n miles: 4,300 at 20 kt
Complement: 278 (24 officers) (DDG 79-84); 276 (24 officers) (DDG 85-102)

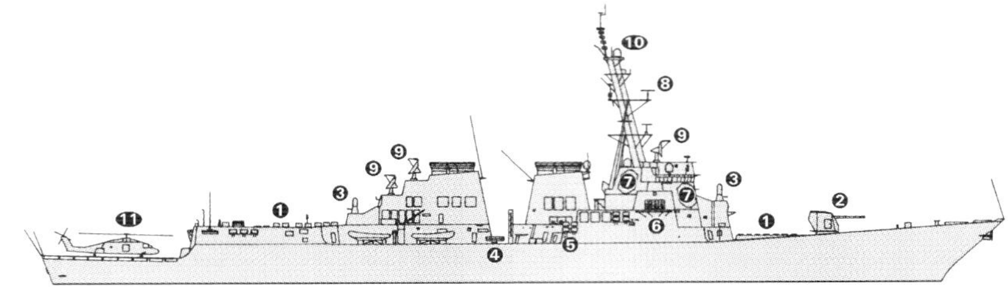

ROOSEVELT ***(Scale 1 : 1,500), Ian Sturton*** / 1167438

Missiles: SLCM: Raytheon Tomahawk Block III and Block IV; TERCOM and GPS aided navigation with DSMAC to 1,600+ km *(865+ n miles)* at 0.7 Mach; warhead (WDU 36B) 454 kg.
SAM: Raytheon Standard SM-2 Block III and IVA; command/inertial guidance; semi-active radar and IR homing to 167 km *(90 n miles)* at 2 Mach. 2 Lockheed Martin Mk 41 Vertical Launch Systems (VLS) for Tomahawk, Standard and ASROC VLS ❶; 2 magazines; 32 missile tubes forward, 64 aft. 32 Raytheon RIM-162 ESSM (4 quad forward, 4 quad aft); semi-active radar homing to 18.5 km *(10 n miles)* at 3.6 Mach; warhead 38 kg.
A/S: Loral ASROC VLA; inertial guidance to 1.6-16.6 km *(1-9 n miles)*; payload Mk 46 Mod 5 Neartip.
Guns: 1 BAE Systems 5 in *(127 mm)*/54 Mk 45 Mod 2 (DDG 79-80) ❷; 20 rds/min to 23 km *(12.6 n miles)*; weight of shell 32 kg.
BAE Systems 5 in *(127 mm)*/62 (DDG 81 onwards); 20 or 10 rds/min; GPS guidance to 116.7 km *(63 n miles)*; warhead 72 bomblets; cep 10 m.
2 General Electric/General Dynamics 20 mm/76 Vulcan Phalanx Mk 15 6-barrelled ❸; 4,500 rds/min combined to 1.5 km (DDG 79-84; to be fitted in all other units).
Torpedoes: 6—324 mm Mk 32 Mod 14 (2 triple) tubes ❹. Alliant Mk 46 Mod 5; anti-submarine; active/passive homing to 11 km *(5.9 n miles)* at 40 kt; warhead 44 kg or Alliant/Westinghouse Mk 50; active/passive homing to 15 km *(8.1 n miles)* at 50 kt; warhead 45 kg shaped charge.
Countermeasures: Decoys: 2 Loral Hycor SRBOC 6-barrelled fixed Mk 36 Mod 12 ❺; Nulka decoy (DDG 91 onwards); IR flares and chaff to 4 km *(2.2 n miles)*. SLQ-25A Nixie; torpedo decoy. NATO Sea Gnat. SLQ-95 AEB. SLQ-39 chaff buoy.
ESM/ECM: Raytheon SLQ-32(V)3/SLY-2 ❻; intercept and jammer.
CESM: AN/SRS-1A(V) CDF (DDG 79-95); COBLU (DDG 96-104); SSEE Increment E (DDG 105).
Combat data systems: TADIX-B and TADIL-J. CEC. Links 4A, 11 and 16. (See Data Systems at front of section.) Link 22 in due course. Command and Decision (upgrade for DDG 91 and following ships).
Weapons control: SWG-4 or SWG-5 Tomahawk WCS. Aegis multitarget tracking with Mk 99 Mod 3 MFCS and three Mk 80 illuminators. Mk 34 GWS (consisting of Mk 160 computing system and Kollmorgen Mk 46 optronic sight). AWCS Mk 116 Mod 7 NFCS.
Radars: Air search/fire control: Lockheed Martin SPY-1D (SPY-1D(V) DDG 91 onwards) phased arrays ❼; 3D; E/F-band.
Surface search: DRS SPS-67(V)3 (DDG 79-102), SPS-67(V)5 (DDG 103) ❽; G-band.
Navigation: Raytheon SPS-64(V)9 (DDG 79-86, 88); Sperry-Marine BME 740 (DDG 87, 89-112); I-band.
Fire control: Three Raytheon AN/SPG-62 ❾; I/J-band.
Tacan: AN/URN 25 ❿. IFF AIMS Mk XII with AN/UPX-29.
Sonars: Lockheed Martin SQQ-89(V)10 (DDG 79-84); SQQ-89(V)14 (DDG 85-90); SQQ-89(V)15 (DDG 91 and following); underwater combat system with SQS-53C; bow-mounted; active search and attack.
Remote Minehunting System (DDG 91-96).

Helicopters: 2 LAMPS III SH-60R helicopters ⓫.

Programmes: DDG 79 was authorised in the FY94 budget. Funding for DDG 80-82 provided in FY95 and DDG 83-84 in FY96 plus partial funding for a third. Balance for DDG 85 plus DDG 86-88 in FY97 and DDG 89-101 in FY98. On 6 March 1998, multi-year contract for six ships and one option (DDG 89) awarded to Ingalls Shipbuilding and contract for six ships awarded to Bath Iron Works. On 1 August 2002, contract awarded to Bath Iron Works for the construction of DDG 102 and on 13 September 2002 a fixed-price multi-year contract awarded to Bath Iron Works (DDGs 104, 106, 108, 109, 111 and 112) and Northrop Grumman Ship Systems (DDGs 103, 105, 107, 110) for the construction of ten ships. Following the curtailment of the DDG 1000 programme on 23 July 2008, an order for a further eight DDGs is under consideration.
Modernisation: A mid-life upgrade program is planned. The scope of the upgrade is to be included during the construction of DDGs 111 and 112 and then retrofitted into other DDG Flight IIA ships during two separate overhaul periods: the first for engineering control system and the second for combat system upgrades.
Structure: The upgrade from Flight II includes two hangars for embarked helicopters and an extended transom to increase the size of a dual RAST fitted flight deck at the expense of SQR-19 TACTAS. Vertical launchers are increased at each end by three cells. Other changes include the Kingfisher minehunting sonar, a reconfiguration of the SPY-1D arrays and the inclusion of a Track Initiation Processor in the Aegis radar system. Use of fibre optic technology should reduce weight and improve reliability.
Operational: The helicopter carries Penguin and Hellfire missiles. ESSM fired from DDG 86 on 24 July 2002, the first to be fired from a USN ship.

McCAMPBELL ***10/2008*, Michael Nitz*** / 1353607

SHOUP *9/2008*, Chris Sattler* / 1353605

HALSEY *10/2008*, Chris Sattler* / 1353606

BULKELEY *2/2008*, US Navy* / 1353604

0 + 2 (1) ZUMWALT (DDG 1000) CLASS (DDGH)

Name	*No*	*Builders*	*Laid down*	*Launched*	*Commissioned*
ZUMWALT	DDG 1000	General Dynamics Bath Iron Works	Nov 2010	May 2012	Mar 2014
MICHAEL MANSOOR	DDG 1001	Northrop Grumman Ship Systems	Nov 2011	May 2013	Apr 2015
–	DDG 1002	–	Apr 2012	2013	2015

Displacement, tons: 14,564
Dimensions, feet (metres): 600.0 × 80.7 × 27.5 *(182.8 × 24.6 × 8.4)*
Main machinery: Integrated Power System (IPS); 2 Main Turbine Generators (MTG); 2 Auxiliary Turbine Generators (ATG); 2 propulsion motors; 104,000 hp *(77.5 MW)*; 2 shafts
Speed, knots: 30
Range, n miles: To be announced
Complement: 142

Missiles: 80 peripheral VLS cells ❶.
SLCM: Raytheon Tomahawk Block IV; land attack; TERCOM and GPS aided inertial navigation system with DSMAC to 1,600+ km *(865+ n miles)* at 0.7 Mach; warhead (WDU-36B) 454 kg.
SAM: Standard SM-2 and Evolved Sea Sparrow.
A/S: Vertical launched ASROC.
Guns: 2—155 mm ❷ advanced gun systems capable of firing Long Range Land Attack Projectiles (LRLAP) at ranges over 66 n miles. 2—57 mm ❸ close-in guns.
Torpedoes: To be announced.
Countermeasures: ESM. ECM. Torpedo decoys.
Combat data systems: To be announced.
Weapons control: To be announced.
Radars: Air/surface search: Dual Band Radar (DBR) ❹; Raytheon SPY-3; 3D; I-band; Lockheed Volume Search Radar (VSR); 3D; E/F-band.
Navigation: To be announced.
Sonars: Bow-mounted active search and attack. Passive towed array. In Stride Mine Avoidance Sonar (ISMA).

Helicopters: 2 MH-60R ❺ or 1 MH-60R and 3 UAVs.

Programmes: The DDG 1000 (formerly DD(X)) programme was initiated in November 2001. Principal roles are sustained operations in the littorals and land-attack. Ten Engineering Development Models (EDMs) have passed Critical Design Review (CDR). Ship design completed CDR in September 2005 and received approval to proceed with Milestone B on 23 November 2005. This authorised commencement of detailed design and construction of the DDG 1000 class. Under the Dual Lead Ships acquisition strategy, detailed design contracts were awarded in August 2006 to Northrop Grumman Ship Systems and General Dynamics Bath Iron Works. Raytheon is the Mission Systems Integrator and BAE Systems provides the gun systems. Construction contracts were awarded to the shipyards on 14 February 2008. It was announced on 23 July 2008 that the DDG1000 programme was to be curtailed and confirmed on 18 August 2008 that only three ships are to be built.

Structure: Features of the ship include a wave-piercing 'tumblehome' hull, optimised for stealth. Hull structure and missile cells spread impacts outward to increase survivability and reduce risk of single-hit ship loss. Integrated deckhouse and composite superstructure encloses masts, sensors and antennas, bridge and exhaust silos. There are two shielded 155 mm Advanced Gun Systems (AGS) and an 80-cell peripheral (port and starboard) Vertical Launch System for both land attack and air defense missiles. An Integrated Power System (IPS), enables power to be distributed to any system as the tactical situation demands. IPS is designed to create sufficient reserve energy to power energy weapons in the future.

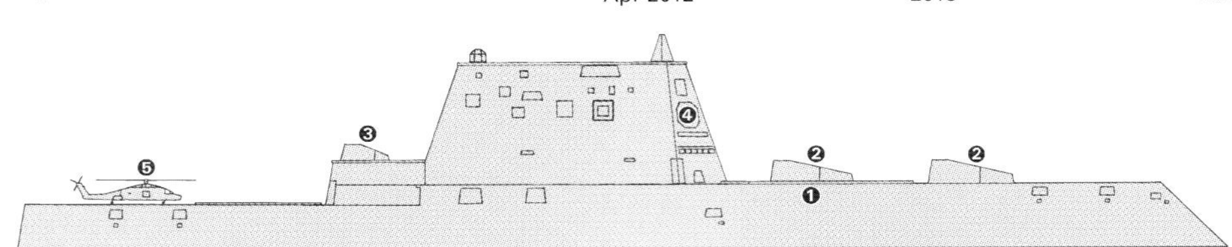

ZUMWALT *(Scale 1 : 1,500), Ian Sturton* / 1353579

ZUMWALT *12/2005, US Navy* / 1154036

FRIGATES

1 + 1 FREEDOM CLASS LITTORAL COMBAT SHIP FLIGHT 0

Name	*No*	*Builders*	*Laid down*	*Launched*	*Commissioned*	*F/S*
FREEDOM	LCS 1	Marinette Marine, Wisconsin	2 June 2005	23 Sep 2006	8 Nov 2008	PA
FORT WORTH	LCS 3	–	2009	2012	2013	

Displacement, tons: 3,089 full load
Dimensions, feet (metres): 378.2 × 43.0 × 12.8 *(115.3 × 13.1 × 3.9)*
Main machinery: CODAG: 2 Rolls Royce MT-30 gas turbines; 96,550 hp *(72 MW)*; 2 Fairbanks Morse Colt-Pielstick 16PA6B diesels; 17,160 hp *(12.8 MW)*; 4 Rolls Royce Kamewa 153SII waterjets
Speed, knots: 45. **Range, n miles:** 3,500 at 18 kt
Complement: 50

Missiles: 1 Raytheon RAM RIM-116 21-cell Mk 99 launcher ❶; passive IR/anti-radiation homing to 9.6 km *(5.2 n miles)* at 2.5 Mach; warhead 9.1 kg.
Guns: 1 BAE Systems 57 mm/70 Mk 2 ❷; 220 rds/min to 17 km (9 n miles); weight of shell 2.4 kg. 4—12.7 mm MGs.
Countermeasures: 2 SKWS/SRBOC decoy launching systems. ESM/ECM.
Combat data systems: COMBATSS-21.
Weapons control: FABA DORNA TV/IR tracker and laser range-finder ❸.
Radars: Air/surface search: EADS TRS-3D ❹; C-band.
Navigation: I-band.
Fire control: FABA DORNA; I-band.
Sonars: To be announced.

Helicopters: 2 MH-60 R/S helicopters ❺ or 1 MH-60 R/S and 3 Firescout VTUAVs.

Programmes: Two industry teams, one led by Lockheed Martin and the other by General Dynamics, were contracted in 2004 to develop designs for a fast, agile and networked surface combatant. In the original procurement programme, it was planned to build a number of each design and left open the option that both designs could proceed into series production. The keys to this approach were a fast building time of two years per ship and a relatively inexpensive cost. A total of 55 ships was proposed. In April 2007, the Navy cancelled its contract with Lockheed Martin for the construction of LCS 3 after negotiations to control cost overruns failed. The second General Dynamics ship (LCS 4) was also cancelled, in November 2007, after similar coast overruns. The funding of three further ships has also been cancelled or re-allocated. In March 2009, the decision to proceed with the construction of one of each LCS variant, re-using previous hull numbers, was announced. Seven mission modules (three mine warfare; two ASW and two ASUW) are being designed/fabricated to be interchangeable on LCS ships.

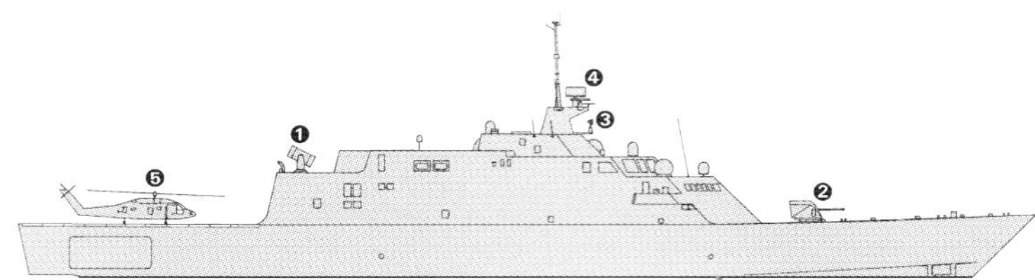

FREEDOM *(Scale 1 : 1,200), Ian Sturton* / 1353578

FREEDOM *7/2008*, Lockheed Martin* / 1335209

Structure: Semi-planing steel monohull design. Steel hull and aluminium superstructure. The design incorporates a large reconfigurable seaframe to allow rapidly interchangeable mission modules, a flight deck with integrated helicopter launch, recovery and handling system and the capability to launch and recover boats (manned and unmanned) from both the stern and side.

Operational: Concept of operations for LCS includes deployment of two or three-ship team to operate near shore in support of surface strike groups. Role in homeland defense also likely. Principal capabilities to include shallow-water ASW, mine countermeasures and defence against attacking small boats. LCS ships are to be networked to share tactical information with other units. *Freedom* began sea trials on 28 July 2008. The trials of ship systems and weapons are to be conducted from Little Creek, VA, during 2009 before deploying to its homeport of San Diego in 2010.

FREEDOM *7/2008*, Lockheed Martin* / 1335207

FREEDOM *7/2008*, Lockheed Martin* / 1335208

30 OLIVER HAZARD PERRY CLASS (FFH)

Name	No	Builders	Laid down	Launched	Commissioned	F/S
McINERNEY	FFG 8	Bath Iron Works	7 Nov 1977	4 Nov 1978	15 Dec 1979	AA
BOONE	FFG 28	Todd Shipyards, Seattle	27 Mar 1979	16 Jan 1980	15 May 1982	NRF
STEPHEN W GROVES	FFG 29	Bath Iron Works	16 Sep 1980	4 Apr 1981	17 Apr 1982	NRF
JOHN L HALL	FFG 32	Bath Iron Works	5 Jan 1981	24 July 1981	26 June 1982	AA
JARRETT	FFG 33	Todd Shipyards, San Pedro	11 Feb 1981	17 Oct 1981	2 July 1983	PA
UNDERWOOD	FFG 36	Bath Iron Works	3 Aug 1981	6 Feb 1982	29 Jan 1983	AA
CROMMELIN	FFG 37	Todd Shipyards, Seattle	30 May 1980	1 July 1981	18 June 1983	NRF
CURTS	FFG 38	Todd Shipyards, San Pedro	1 July 1981	6 Mar 1982	8 Oct 1983	NRF
DOYLE	FFG 39	Bath Iron Works	16 Nov 1981	22 May 1982	21 May 1983	NRF
HALYBURTON	FFG 40	Todd Shipyards, Seattle	26 Sep 1980	15 Oct 1981	7 Jan 1984	AA
McCLUSKY	FFG 41	Todd Shipyards, San Pedro	21 Oct 1981	18 Sep 1982	10 Dec 1983	NRF
KLAKRING	FFG 42	Bath Iron Works	19 Feb 1982	18 Sep 1982	20 Aug 1983	NRF
THACH	FFG 43	Todd Shipyards, San Pedro	10 Mar 1982	18 Dec 1982	17 Mar 1984	PA
De WERT	FFG 45	Bath Iron Works	14 June 1982	18 Dec 1982	19 Nov 1983	AA
RENTZ	FFG 46	Todd Shipyards, San Pedro	18 Sep 1982	16 July 1983	30 June 1984	PA
NICHOLAS	FFG 47	Bath Iron Works	27 Sep 1982	23 Apr 1983	10 Mar 1984	AA
VANDEGRIFT	FFG 48	Todd Shipyards, Seattle	13 Oct 1981	15 Oct 1982	24 Nov 1984	PA
ROBERT G BRADLEY	FFG 49	Bath Iron Works	28 Dec 1982	13 Aug 1983	11 Aug 1984	AA
TAYLOR	FFG 50	Bath Iron Works	5 May 1983	5 Nov 1983	1 Dec 1984	AA
GARY	FFG 51	Todd Shipyards, San Pedro	18 Dec 1982	19 Nov 1983	17 Nov 1984	PA
CARR	FFG 52	Todd Shipyards, Seattle	26 Mar 1982	26 Feb 1983	27 July 1985	AA
HAWES	FFG 53	Bath Iron Works	22 Aug 1983	18 Feb 1984	9 Feb 1985	AA
FORD	FFG 54	Todd Shipyards, San Pedro	16 July 1983	23 June 1984	29 June 1985	PA
ELROD	FFG 55	Bath Iron Works	21 Nov 1983	12 May 1984	6 June 1985	AA
SIMPSON	FFG 56	Bath Iron Works	27 Feb 1984	21 Aug 1984	9 Nov 1985	NRF
REUBEN JAMES	FFG 57	Todd Shipyards, San Pedro	19 Nov 1983	8 Feb 1985	22 Mar 1986	PA
SAMUEL B ROBERTS	FFG 58	Bath Iron Works	21 May 1984	8 Dec 1984	12 Apr 1986	AA
KAUFFMAN	FFG 59	Bath Iron Works	8 Apr 1985	29 Mar 1986	21 Feb 1987	AA
RODNEY M DAVIS	FFG 60	Todd Shipyards, San Pedro	8 Feb 1985	11 Jan 1986	9 May 1987	NRF
INGRAHAM	FFG 61	Todd Shipyards, San Pedro	30 Mar 1987	25 June 1988	5 Aug 1989	PA

Displacement, tons: 2,750 light; 3,638 (FFG 33); 4,100 full load
Dimensions, feet (metres): 445 (FFG 33); 453 × 45 × 14.8; 24.5 (sonar)
(135.6; 138.1 × 13.7 × 4.5; 7.5)
Main machinery: 2 GE LM 2500 gas turbines; 41,000 hp *(30.59 MW)* sustained; 1 shaft; cp prop
2 auxiliary retractable props; 650 hp *(484 kW)*
Speed, knots: 29. **Range, n miles**: 4,500 at 20 kt
Complement: 200 (15 officers) including 19 aircrew

Guns: 1 OTO Melara 3 in *(76 mm)*/62 Mk 75 ❶; 85 rds/min to 16 km *(8.7 n miles)* anti-surface; 12 km *(6.6 n miles)* anti-aircraft; weight of shell 6 kg.
1 General Electric/General Dynamics 20 mm/76 6-barrelled Mk 15 Block 1B Vulcan Phalanx ❷; 4,500 rds/min combined to 1.5 km.
2 Boeing 25 mm Mk 38 guns can be fitted amidships.
4—12.7 mm MGs.
Torpedoes: 6—324 mm Mk 32 (2 triple) tubes ❸. 24 Honeywell Mk 46 Mod 5; anti-submarine; active/passive homing to 11 km *(5.9 n miles)* at 40 kt; warhead 44 kg or Alliant/Westinghouse Mk 50; active/passive homing to 15 km *(8.1 n miles)* at 50 kt; warhead 45 kg shaped charge.
Countermeasures: Decoys: 2 Loral Hycor SRBOC 6-barrelled fixed Mk 36 ❹; IR flares and chaff to 4 km *(2.2 n miles)*. Mk 34 launcher for Mk 53 Nulka decoys.
T-Mk 6 Fanfare/SLQ-25 Nixie; torpedo decoy.
ESM/ECM: SLQ-32(V)2 ❺; radar warning. Sidekick modification adds jammer and deception system.
Combat data systems: NTDS with Link 11 and 14. Link 14 only (NRF ships). SATCOM ❻ SRR-1, WSC-3 (UHF). SQQ-28 for LAMPS III datalink.
Weapons control: Mk 92 (Mod 4 or Mod 6 (FFG 61 and during modernisation in 11 others of the class)), WCS with CAS (Combined Antenna System). The Mk 92 is the US version of the Signaal WM28 system. SYS 2(V)2 IADT (FFG 61 and in 11 others of the class - see *Modernisation*). SRQ-4 for LAMPS III.
Radars: Air search: Raytheon SPS-49(V)4 or 5 (FFG 61 and during modernisation of others) ❼; C/D-band; range 457 km *(250 n miles)*.

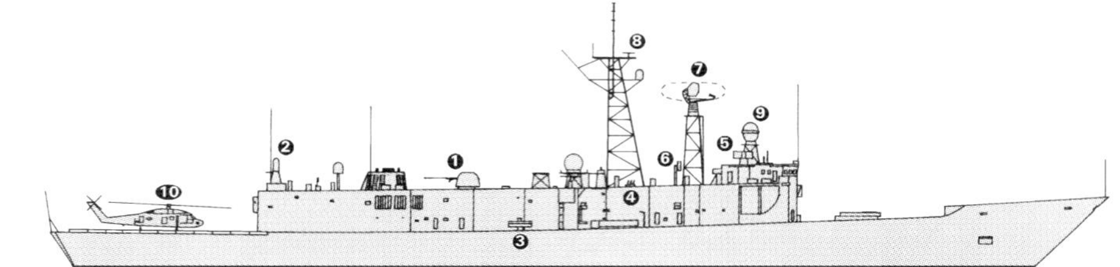

RENTZ *(Scale 1 : 1,200), Ian Sturton* / 0572737

Surface search: ISC Cardion SPS-55 ❽; I-band.
Fire control: Sperry Mk 92 (Signaal WM28) ❾; I/J-band.
Navigation: Furuno; I-band.
Tacan: URN 25. IFF Mk XII AIMS UPX-29.
Sonars: SQQ 89(V)2 (Raytheon SQS 56 and Gould SQR 19); hull-mounted active search and attack; medium frequency and passive towed array; very low frequency.

Helicopters: 2 SH-60B LAMPS III ❿ in Flight III/IV and certified ships.

Programmes: The lead ship was authorised in FY73.
Modernisation: To accommodate the helicopter landing system (RAST), the overall length of the ship was increased by 8 ft *(2.4 m)* by increasing the angle of the ship's transom, between the waterline and the fantail, from virtually straight up to a 45° angle outwards. LAMPS III support facilities and RAST were fitted in all ships authorised from FFG 36 onwards, during construction and have been backfitted to all. FFG 61 has much improved Combat Data and Fire-Control equipment which has been retrofitted in FFG 36, 47, 48, 50-55, 57 and 59. SQS-56 is modified for mine detection. Block 1B Phalanx fitted first in FFG 36 in October 1999. Engineering and platform improvements programme initiated in 2003. Upgrades include new diesel generators, the addition of reverse osmosis plants, COTS slewing arm davits, and self-contained breathing apparatus. Mk 13 launchers for Standard SM-1 and Harpoon missiles have been removed. Combat system improvements include the installation of Mk 53 Nulka decoys and Mk 15 Block 1B gun with surface mode capability.
Structure: The original single hangar has been changed to two adjacent hangars. Provided with 19 mm Kevlar armour protection over vital spaces. 25 mm guns can be fitted for some operational deployments.
Operational: Ships of this class were the first Navy experience in implementing a design-to-cost acquisition concept. On 14 April 1988, *Samuel B Roberts* (FFG 58), was mined in the Gulf but was subsequently repaired. One of the class is based at Yokosuka. Nine ships are assigned to the Combatant Naval Reserve Force. FFGs 28, 29 and 38 are commanded by full-time reserve officers. SAM and SSM systems removed by the end of FY04.
Sales: Australia bought four (FFG 17, 18, 35 and 44) of the class and has built two more. Spain has six and Taiwan eight. Transfers include eight to Turkey plus one for spares, four to Egypt, one to Bahrain and two to Poland.

RODNEY M DAVIS *8/2008*, Michael Nitz* / 1353603

CURTS

8/2008, Shaun Jones* / 1353602

NICHOLAS

5/2008, Derek Fox* / 1353565

THACH

10/2007, Michael Nitz / 1353601

0 + 2 INDEPENDENCE CLASS LITTORAL COMBAT SHIP FLIGHT 0

Name	*No*	*Builders*	*Laid down*	*Launched*	*Commissioned*	*F/S*
INDEPENDENCE	LCS 2	Austal USA, Mobile, Alabama	19 Jan 2006	4 Oct 2008	2009	Bldg/PA
CORONADO	LCS 4	–	2009	2012	2013	

Displacement, tons: 2,790 full load
Dimensions, feet (metres): 417.3 × 103.6 × 14.8 *(127.2 × 31.6 × 4.5)*
Main machinery: CODAG: 2 gas turbines, 2 diesels; 4 steerable waterjets; 1 steerable thruster
Speed, knots: 40
Range, n miles: 3,500 at 18 kt
Complement: 40

Missiles: 1 Raytheon RAM RIM-116 21-cell Mk 49 launcher; passive IR/anti-radiation homing to 9.6 km *(5.2 n miles)* at 2.5 Mach; warhead 9.1 kg.
Guns: 1 BAE Systems 57 mm/70 Mk 2; 220 rds/min to 17 km *(9 n miles)*; weight of shell 2.4 kg. 4—12.7mm MGs.
Countermeasures: Decoys: 4 Loral/Hycor SRBOC 6-barrelled fixed launchers. ESM/ECM.
Combat data systems: Northrop Grumman Electronic Systems Integrated Combat Management System (ICMS).
Weapons control: Seastar Safire III optronic director.
Radars: Air/surface search: Ericson Sea Giraffe; G/H-band.
Navigation: Sperry Bridgemaster; I-band.
Fire control: To be announced.
Sonars: To be announced.

Helicopters: 1 MH-60R/S and 3 VTUAV.

Programmes: Two industry teams, one led by Lockheed Martin and the other by General Dynamics, were contracted in 2004 to develop designs for a fast, agile and networked surface combatant. In the original procurement programme, it was planned to build a number of each design and left open the option that both designs could proceed into series production. The keys to this approach were a fast building time of two years per ship and a relatively inexpensive cost. A total of 55 ships was proposed. In April 2007, the Navy cancelled its contract with Lockheed Martin for the construction of LCS 3 after negotiations to control cost overruns failed. The second General Dynamics ship (LCS 4) was also cancelled, in November 2007, after similar cost overruns. The funding of three further ships has been cancelled or re-allocated. In March 2009, the decision to proceed with the construction of one of each LCS variant, re-using previous hull numbers, was announced. Seven mission modules (three mine warfare; two ASW and two ASUW) are being designed/fabricated to be interchangeable on LCS ships.

Structure: Trimaran hullform based on fast commercial ferry design for Fred Olsen Line. Aluminium construction. Large flight deck capable of operating heavy-lift helicopter. Stern launch of boats (manned and unmanned). Side-ramp Ro-Ro capability. Reconfigurable seaframe to allow rapidly interchangeable mission modules.

Operational: Concept of operations for LCS includes deployment of two or three-ship team to operate near shore in support of surface strike groups. Role in homeland defense also likely. Principal capabilities to include shallow-water ASW, mine countermeasures and defence against attacking small boats. To be based in San Diego.

LCS 2 *(Scale 1 : 1,200)*, **Ian Sturton** / 1153881

INDEPENDENCE *10/2008**, **Austal Ships** / 1294740

SHIPBORNE AIRCRAFT

Notes: (1) Numbers given are for 1 January 2009.
(2) **Joint Strike Fighter:** The JSF F-35 Lightning II is a family of next-generation strike aircraft combining stealth and enhanced sensors. The F-35C Carrier Variant (CV) will replace F/A-18A/C and complement the F/A-18E/F fleet. Marine Corps F-35B Short Take Off and Vertical Landing (STOVL) variant are to replace USMC AV-8B and F/A-18A/C/D. F-35 variants will share a high level of commonality. Mission systems avionics suite designed for interoperability with coalition partners. The contract for the Systems Development and Demonstration (SDD) phase was awarded on 26 October 2001 to the industry team of Lockheed Martin, Northrop Grumman and BAE Systems. International participants in the SDD phase were Australia, Canada, Denmark, Italy, Netherlands, Norway, Turkey and the UK. All of these had, by early 2007, signed MOUs for the subsequent Production, Sustainment, and Follow-on Development (PSFD) phase. Security Cooperation Partnership MOUs have been established with Israel and Singapore. Engine development is being undertaken by Pratt and Whitney and General Electric/Rolls Royce.
(3) **Tacair Integration:** Navy/Marine Corps Tactical Aviation Integration (TAI) plan was approved in 2002 to optimize combat capability and efficiencies by relying on fewer but more capable aircraft. As part of the TAI, the Navy/Marine Corps began integrating Marine Corps squadrons into carrier air wings and Navy squadrons into the Marine Corps' Unit Deployment Plan (UDP).
(4) **Capabilities Based Scheduling (CBS):** This scheduling mechanism is designed to source tactical aviation (TACAIR) requirements while promoting goals of TAI. Under CBS, all Department of the Navy (DON) TACAIR squadrons are available to fill land or sea-based requirements. Objective is to fill all operational and training requirements with the most appropriate unit while balancing operational tempo across force. CBS furthers integration to a fully interdependent DON TACAIR force in which VMFA and VFA squadrons routinely deploy as part of carrier wings and land-based expeditionary operations. CBS flexes TACAIR response to global sourcing requirements.
(5) **Global Force Management (GFM):** This scheduling management process is designed to fill tactical aviation (TACAIR) operational and training requirements with the most appropriate unit while balancing unit operational tempo across the force. This process furthers TACAIR integration, leading to a fully independent DON TACAIR force in which VMFA and VFA Squadrons routinely deploy as part of CVW and land-based expeditionary operations.
(6) **CH-53K:** A contract for the System Development and Demonstration of the CH-53K helicopter was awarded to Sikorsky on 3 January 2006. The aircraft is to replace the CH-53E helicopter, currently in service, and the USMC expects to buy 200 aircraft. The first test aircraft is scheduled to be delivered in 2012 with a view to achieving an initial operating capability in 2016.

Numbers/Type: 103/26/363/135 McDonnell Douglas F/A-18A/F/A-18B/F/A-18C/F/A-18D Hornet.
Operational speed: 1,032 kt *(1,910 km/h)*.
Service ceiling: 50,000 ft *(15,240 m)*.
Range: 1,000 n miles *(1,850 km)*.
Role/Weapon systems: Single-seat (F/A-18A/C) and two-seat (F/A-18B/D) strike interdictor (VFA) for USN/USMC air groups. Some are used for EW support with ALQ-167 jammers. Sensors: ESM: Litton ALR 67(V)2, ALQ 165 ASPJ jammer (18C/D), ALQ-126B jammer, APG-65 or APG-73 radar, AAS-38 FLIR, ASQ-228 ATFLIR, AN/AAQ-28 Litening FLIR (USMC only), AAR-50 Nav FLIR, ASQ-173 tracker. Weapons: ASV; four Harpoon or SLAM (ER) or AGM-88 HARM missiles. AGM-65 Maverick. Strike; up to 7.7 tons of bombs (or LGM). AD; one 20 mm Vulcan cannon, nine AIM-120/AIM-7/AIM-9 missiles. Typical ASV load might include 20 mm gun, 7.7 ton bombs including AGM 154A JSOW, two AIM-9 missiles. Typical AAW load might include 20 mm gun, four AIM-7 or AIM-120, two AIM-9 missiles.

F/A-18C *11/2008*, US Navy* / 1353600

Numbers/Type: 159/196 Boeing F/A-18E/F/A-18F Super Hornet.
Operational speed: 930 kt *(1,721 km/h)*.
Service ceiling: 50,000 ft *(15,240 m)*.
Range: 1,320 n miles *(2,376 km)*.
Role/Weapon systems: Single-seat (F/A-18E) and two-seat (F/A-18F) strike interdictor for USN. First one rolled out in September 1995. First 12 production aircraft ordered in FY97. First sea trials January 1997. Entered operational service November 1999. Initial deployment to CVN 72 in July 2002. 200th aircraft delivered in August 2004. The balance of 506 aircraft to be delivered by 2014. Sensors: APG-73 radar, APG-79 AESA radar, ALR-67(V)3 RWR. ECM: ALQ-165 ASPJ, ALQ-214 RFCM, towed decoys. Weapons: 11 wing stations for 8,680 kg of weapons (same armament as C/D) plus 20 mm guns.

F/A-18F *10/2007, Michael Nitz* / 1353599

Numbers/Type: 41/89/16 Boeing/British Aerospace AV-8B Harrier II/AV-8B II Plus Harrier II/TAV-8B Harrier II.
Operational speed: 585 kt *(1,083 km/h)*.
Service ceiling: 50,000 ft *(15,240 m)*.
Range: 800 n miles *(1,480 km)*.
Role/Weapon systems: Attack and destroy surface and air targets in support of USMC. Operational since 1985, a total of 91 AV-8B II Plus conversions completed in 2003. Sensors: Litening II targeting pod, Navigation FLIR, moving map, AN/AVS-9 night vision goggles, laser spot tracker and ECM; Litton ALR-67 ESM; APG-65 radar (AV-8B II Plus). Weapons: Strike; 500 and 1,000 lb general purpose bombs, Paveway II LGB, Joint Direct Attack Munition, Dual Mode Guide Bomb, AGM-65 Maverick, Cluster Bomb Units, 300—25 mm rounds, 2.75 in and 5.00 in rockets. Self-defence: one GAU-12/U 25 mm cannon and four AIM-9M Sidewinder.

AV-8B *4/2005, US Navy* / 1154041

Numbers/Type: 92 Grumman EA-6B Prowler.
Operational speed: 566 kt *(1,048 km/h)*.
Service ceiling: 41,200 ft *(12,550 m)*.
Range: 955 n miles *(1,769 km)*.
Role/Weapon systems: EW and jamming aircraft (VAQ) to provide electronic attack in support of strikes and armed reconnaissance. Block 89A avionics/computer upgrades first delivered 2001. ICAP III receiver system upgrade first delivered in 2005. Sensors: APS-130 radar; ALQ-99, ALQ-218 (ICAP III), USQ-113 communication jammer. Weapons: AGM-88 HARM anti-radiation missile capable.

EA-6B *12/2008*, US Navy* / 1353598

Numbers/Type: 66 Grumman E-2C Hawkeye.
Operational speed: 323 kt *(598 km/h)*.
Service ceiling: 37,000 ft *(11,278 m)*.
Range: 1,540 n miles *(2,852 km)*.
Role/Weapon systems: Carrier-borne multimission aircraft with primary AEW role and additional strike control, area surveillance, SAR and battle-management roles. Current configurations include 14 Group II aircraft, 23 Group II NAV upgrades, five Group II MCS/ACIS and 24 HE2000. All variants have APS-145 radar and Link 16. Sensors: ESM: ALR-73 or ALQ-217 PDS; Airborne tactical data system with Links 4A, 11 or 16; CEC from 2000. APS-145 radar; Mk XII IFF. Weapons: Unarmed.

E-2C *9/2008*, Hachiro Nakai* / 1353566

Numbers/Type: 84/9 Boeing MV-22/CV-22 Osprey.
Operational speed: 255 kt *(472 km/h).*
Service ceiling: 25,000 ft *(7,620 m).*
Range: 400 n miles *(740 km).*
Role/Weapon systems: Replacement for legacy assault/support helicopter (CH-46E) for Marines (MV), projected rescue and resupply for the Navy (Navy MV), and special operations for USAF SOCOM (CV). Three active MV-22 squadrons: VMM-263, 162 and 266. In addition, one squadron is used for testing and evaluation: VMX-22 and one FRS: VMMT-204. Final operational evaluation led to full rate production decision in September 2005. There were 16 aircraft procured in FY07. Annual production expected to increase to 36. MV-22 I0C was in July 2007. CV-22 I0C in 2009. Full fleet of 360 MV, 50 CV and 48 Navy MV projected. Sensors: AAR-47 ESM; AN/ALQ-211 Suite of Integrated RF CounterMeasures (SIRFC) (CV-22 only), AN/AAQ-24(V) Nemesis Directional Infra-Red CounterMeasures (DIRCM) (CV-22 only); AN/AAQ-27 FLIR; APR 39A(V)2 (MV-22 only). Weapons: M-240D 7.62 mm machine gun.

MV-22B *10/2006, US Navy* / 1167611

Numbers/Type: 147 Sikorsky SH-60B Seahawk (LAMPS Mk III).
Operational speed: 145 kt *(268 km/h).*
Service ceiling: 10,000 ft *(3,050 m).*
Range: 450 n miles *(833 km).*
Role/Weapon systems: LAMPS Mk III is airborne platform for ASW and ASUW: operated from cruisers, destroyers and frigates. First deployed in 1984. To be replaced by MH-60R. Sensors: APS-124 search radar, AAS-44 FLIR with laser designator, ASQ-81(V) MAD, 25 sonobuoys, ALQ-142 ESM, AAR-47 MWR, ALQ-144 IRCM suppressor and ALE-39 CMDS. UYS-1 Acoustic processor. Weapons: ASW; three Mk 46 or Mk 50 torpedoes. ASUW; one 7.62 mm MG or 12.7 mm MG, four AGM-114B/K Hellfire missile.

SH-60B *9/2008*, US Navy* / 1353596

Numbers/Type: 23 Sikorsky MH-60R Seahawk.
Operational speed: 145 kt *(268 km/h).*
Service ceiling: 10,000 ft *(3,050 m).*
Range: 450 n miles *(833 km).*
Role/Weapon systems: The plan is to replace the SH-60B/F fleet with the MH-60R which is to be the future tactical helicopter operated from carriers, cruisers, destroyers and frigates. The first production aircraft was flown on 28 July 2005 and the MH-60R entered front-line service in 2006. Sensors: APS-147 long-range search radar with ISAR, ALQ-210 ESM, AQS-22 dipping sonar, acoustic processor, Raytheon AAS-44 FLIR with laser designator, Hawklink sensor datalink, AAR-47 MWR, ALE-47 CMDS, and ALQ-144 IRCM. Weapons: ASW: three Mk 46/50 torpedoes. ASUW: four AGM-114B/K Hellfire missiles, one 7.62 mm MG or 12.7 mm MG. Pre-planned Product Improvements which are scheduled to be fielded incrementally from 2006 to 2009, will upgrade the aircraft with the AAS-44 3rd Gen multi-spectral FLIR, including Low Light Camera,CDL-N Ku-band sensor datalink, Link 16, fourth weapons station for eight AGM-114s or four torpedoes and ability to fire Mk 54 torpedoes.

MH-60R *10/2007, Michael Nitz* / 1353595

Numbers/Type: 70 Sikorsky SH-60F Seahawk (CV).
Operational speed: 145 kt *(268 km/h).*
Service ceiling: 10,000 ft *(3,050 m).*
Range: 600 n miles *(1,111 km).*
Role/Weapon systems: Derivation of SH-60B that replaced SH-3H Sea King to provide close-in ASW protection to Carrier Battle Groups. First deployed in *Nimitz* 1991. To be replaced by MH-60R. Sonar: AQS-13F dipping sonar; ASQ-81 (V) MAD; UYS-2 acoustic processor; 14 sonobuoys. Weapons: ASW: three Mk 46/54 torpedoes. ASUW: One GAU 16 12.7 mm MG or one M 240 7.62 mm MG.

SH-60F *10/2006, Michael Nitz* / 1305199

Numbers/Type: 36 Sikorsky HH-60H Seahawk.
Operational speed: 147 kt *(272 km/h).*
Service ceiling: 10,000 ft *(3,050 m).*
Range: 500 n miles *(926 km).*
Role/Weapon systems: Strike, special warfare support and SAR derivative (HCS) of the SH-60F. To be replaced by MH-60S. Sensors: AAS-44 FLIR with laser designator, APR-39A RWR, AVR-2 LWR and AAR 47 MWR, ALE-47 CMDS, ALQ-144 IRCM. Weapons: ASV; Hellfire AGM-114B/K; one GAU-16 12.7 mm MG or one M-240 7.62 mm MG. Can deploy eight SEAL to a range of 200 n miles.

HH-60H *7/2007, Mick Prendergast* / 1305245

Numbers/Type: 123 Sikorsky MH-60S Seahawk.
Operational speed: 154 kt *(284 km/h).*
Service ceiling: 10,000 ft *(3,050 m).*
Range: 420 n miles *(777 km).*
Role/Weapon systems: The MH-60S replaced the CH-46D in the Combat Support (HC) mission. Mission areas include vertical replenishment, vertical onboard delivery, day/night amphibious search and rescue, and special warfare support. Sensors: AAS-44 FLIR with laser designator, AAR-47 MWR, APR-39 RWR, ALE-47 CMDS, and ALQ-144 IRCM. Weapons: eight AGM-114B/K Hellfire missiles, two 7.62 mm or two 12.7 mm MGs. Organic Airborne Mine Countermeasures capabilities are scheduled for introduction by September 2010. Sensors: AN/AQS-20A Sonar Mine Detection Set, AN/AES-1 Airborne Laser Mine Detection System. Mine Neutralization Systems: Airborne Mine Neutralization System, AN/ALQ-220 Organic & Surface Influence Sweep, and AN/AWS-2 Rapid Airborne Mine Clearance System.

MH-60S *10/2007, Michael Nitz* / 1353594

Numbers/Type: 200 Boeing CH-46E Sea Knight.
Operational speed: 137 kt *(254 km/h).*
Service ceiling: 8,500 ft *(2,590 m).*
Range: 180 n miles *(338 km).*
Role/Weapon systems: Support/assault (HMM) for 18 Marines. To be replaced by V-22 in due course. Can lift 1.3 or 4.5 tons in a cargo net or sling. Sensors: None. Weapons: Unarmed.

CH-46E *10/2008*, US Navy* / 1353593

Numbers/Type: 34 Sikorsky CH-53D Sea Stallion.
Operational speed: 130 kt *(240 km/h).*
Service ceiling: 12,540 ft *(3,822 m).*
Range: 578 n miles *(1,070 km).*
Role/Weapon systems: Assault, support and transport helicopter; can carry 32 Marines, 24 litters or 8,000 lb *(3,570 kg).* Sensors: None. Weapons: Up to three 12.7 mm machine guns.

CH-53D *8/2008*, Michael Nitz* / 1353592

Numbers/Type: 152 Sikorsky CH-53E Super Stallion.
Operational speed: 150 kt *(278 km/h).*
Service ceiling: 18,500 ft *(5,638 m).*
Range: 480 n miles *(888 km).*
Role/Weapon systems: Upgraded, three-engined version of Sea Stallion for USMC heavy lift mission. Carries up to 32 Marines, 24 litters or 36,000 lb *(16,329 kg).* Sensors: AN/AAQ-29A FLIR. Weapons: Up to three 12.7 mm machine guns.

CH-53E *11/2008*, US Navy* / 1353591

Numbers/Type: 28 Sikorsky MH-53E Sea Dragon.
Operational speed: 150 kt *(278 km/h).*
Service ceiling: 10,000 ft *(3,048 m).*
Range: 1,000 n miles *(1,850 km).*
Role/Weapon systems: Three-engined AMCM helicopter (HM) similar to Super Stallion; tows ALQ-166 Mod 4 MCM sweep equipment; self-deployed if necessary. Sensors: Northrop Grumman 24A side-scan sonar. Weapons: Two 12.7 mm guns for self-defence.

MH-53E *5/2006, Guy Toremans* / 1167614

Numbers/Type: 163/6 Bell AH-1W/AH-1Z Super Cobra.
Operational speed: 135 kt *(250 km/h).*
Service ceiling: 10,000 ft *(3,048 m).*
Range: 260 n miles (AH-1W); 360 n miles (AH-1Z) *(481; 666 km).*
Role/Weapon systems: Close air support helicopter (HMLA) with own air-to-air capability. AH-1Z is four-bladed rotor upgrade to improve speed, range and lift. Remanufacture of AH-1W features glass cockpit, composite blades, new engines and gearboxes. To enter service in 2011. Sensors: Target Sight System (laser and FLIR targeting sensor). Weapons: Strike/assault; one triple 20 mm cannon, 16 Hellfire missiles and gun. AAW; two AIM-9M Sidewinder missiles.

AH-1W *8/2005, US Navy* / 1154053

Numbers/Type: 12/86/15 Bell HH-1N/UH-1N/UH-1Y Huey.
Operational speed: 107 kt (1N); 153 kt (1Y) *(198; 283 km/h).*
Service ceiling: 10,000 ft *(3,048 m).*
Range: 150 n miles (1N); 306 n miles (1Y) *(278; 567 km).*
Role/Weapon systems: HH-1N is SAR, training, support and logistics helicopter for USN/USMC operations ashore. Can carry eight Marines. UH-1N is USMC Light Utility platform for all-weather assault, transport, airborne command and control, armed reconnaissance and SAR. Can carry eight marines. Four-bladed upgrade being fitted from 2004 to improve speed, range and lift. UH-1Y features glass cockpit, composite blades and new engines gearboxes. Initial operating capability achieved in August 2008. Sensors: BRITE Star FLIR. Weapons: Can be armed with 12.7 mm or 7.62 mm machine guns and 2.75 in rockets.

UH-1N *5/1999, A Sharma* / 0084120

Numbers/Type: 16 EA-18G Growler.
Operational speed: 930 kt *(1,721 km/h).*
Service ceiling: 50,000 ft *(15,240 m).*
Range: 1,320 n miles *(2,376 km).*
Role/Weapon systems: Electronic Attack (EA) and Suppression of Enemy Air Defences (SEAD) aircraft to start replacing the EA-6B Prowler from 2009. First production aircraft based on F/A-18E/F handed over on 24 September 2007. All 10 EA-6B Prowler squadrons to be converted to EA-18G by 2013. Sensors: APG-79 AESA radar; ALQ-99 jamming pods; ALQ-218 receivers; ALQ-227 communication countermeasures. Weapons: AGM-88 HARM; AIM-120C AMRAAM.

EA-18G *10/2008*, US Navy* / 1353597

Numbers/Type: 2 Northrop Grumman E-2D Advanced Hawkeye.
Operational speed: 323 kt *(598 km/h).*
Service ceiling: 37,000 ft *(11,278 m).*
Range: 1,540 n miles *(2,852 km).*
Role/Weapon systems: Advanced Hawkeye uses E-2C 2000 configuration as a baseline but features a new radar and upgraded systems. Key objectives are to improve battle space target detection and situational awareness, support of Theatre Air and Missile Defense (TAMD) operations, and improved operational availability. Pilot production began in 2008 and low-rate initial production in 2009. Production deliveries are to begin in 2010 and a total of 75 aircraft is planned by 2022. Sensors: ADS-18 ESA radar. ESM: ALQ-217 PDS; airborne tactical data system with Links 11 and 16 and CEC, IFF Mark XII. Weapons: unarmed.

E-2D *8/2007, Northrop Grumman* / 1336041

Numbers/Type: 35 Northrop Grumman C-2A Greyhound.
Operational speed: 300 kt *(555 km/h).*
Service ceiling: 31,000 ft *(988 m).*
Range: 1,400 n miles *(2,592 km).*
Role/Weapon systems: Twin turbo-prop COD (Carrier Onboard Delivery) transport for high-priority cargo and passengers to and from aircraft carriers. Mission includes airlift and airdrop of special operating forces and airdrops for search and rescue. Maximum weight for payload and route support equipment is 10,000 lb and 26 passengers. First of C-2A follow-on aircraft planned to be delivered in 2020 and the fleet to be replaced by 2030. Weapons: unarmed.

C-2A *9/2008*, Hachiro Nakai* / 1353567

LAND-BASED MARITIME AIRCRAFT

Notes: (1) There are also 32/12 Lockheed KC-130F/R Hercules tankers.
(2) Replacement of the EP-3 Aries fleet is under consideration. The EPX programme is for a replacement capability to enter service in about 2019. Contract refinement contracts were awarded to Boeing, Lockheed Martin and Northrop Grumman on 6 February 2008. A contractor for the Development and Demonstration phase is expected to be selected in 2012.

Numbers/Type: 12 Lockheed EP-3E Aries.
Operational speed: 411 kt *(761 km/h).*
Service ceiling: 28,300 ft *(8,625 m).*
Range: 2,380 n miles *(4,407 km).*
Role/Weapon systems: Multi-intelligence, electronic warfare and signals intelligence gathering aircraft (VQ). A package of airframe and sensor upgrades is to be implemented from 2010 to extend life to about 2020. Sensors: EW equipment including AN/ALR-60, AN/ALQ-76, AN/ALQ-78, AN/ALQ-108, AN/ASQ-114 and AN/AAS-52. Weapons: Unarmed.

EP-3E *10/2003, Paul Jackson* / 0110197

Numbers/Type: 161 Lockheed P-3C Orion.
Operational speed: 411 kt *(761 km/h).*
Service ceiling: 28,300 ft *(8,625 m).*
Range: 2,380 n miles *(4,407 km).*
Role/Weapon systems: Of 161 total aircraft, 39 grounded in 2007 due to structural fatigue problems. Repairs likely to take 2 years. Twelve active squadrons. Other variants include NP-3C and NP-3D research and development aircraft. Primary ASW/ASUW; mission aircraft include Update III, Block Mod Upgrade (BMUP) and ASuW Improvement Program (AIP) configurations. Sensors (Update III/BMUP): APS-115 radar, ASQ-81 MAD, USQ-78/USQ-78B acoustic suite, 84 sonobuoys, AAS-36 FLIR and ALR-66B ESM. ASUW Improvement Program (AIP) aircraft employ the APS-137D(V)5 ISAR/SAR radar, ASQ-81 MAD, ASX-4 Electro-Optics, ALR-95 ESM, USQ-78/78A/78B acoustic suite, OASIS III/ OTCIXS communications suite, SATCOM and AAR 47 and ALE 47 chaff/IR dispenser. Weapons: ASW; Mk 46/50 torpedoes or depth bombs. ASUW; AGM-84C Harpoon, AGM-65F Maverick, AGM-84E SLAM-ER, Mk 52/56/62/63/65 mines, Mk 82 series bombs, and Mk 20 Rockeye. Counter-Drug Upgrade (CDU) aircraft employ APG-66 air-to-air radar and AVX-1 Electro-Optics.

P-3C *10/2007, Michael Nitz* / 1353590

Numbers/Type: Boeing P-8A Poseidon.
Operational speed: 490 kt *(907 km/h).*
Service ceiling: 41,000 ft *(12,500 m).*
Range: 1,380 n miles *(2,555 km).*
Role/Weapon systems: Contract for MMA System Development and Demonstration (SDD) awarded 14 June 2004. To replace fleet of P-3C aircraft. Design based on Boeing 737-800ERX. Crew of nine. First delivery in April 2009. To enter operational service in 2013. A total of 117 aircraft is planned. Sensors: To be equipped with modern ASW, ASUW and intelligence, surveillance and reconnaissance (ISR) sensors. Weapons: To be announced.

BOEING P-8A Poseidon *6/2004, US Navy* / 1043653

Numbers/Type: 16 Boeing E-6B Mercury.
Operational speed: 455 kt *(842 km/h).*
Service ceiling: 42,000 ft *(12,800 m).*
Range: 6,350 n miles *(11,760 km/h).*
Role/Weapon systems: Derived from Boeing's 707 aircraft, the E-6B provides Commander, US Strategic Command with the command, control and communications capability to direct and employ strategic forces. Designed to support a flexible nuclear deterrent posture with VLF emergency communications and Airborne National Command Post (ABNCP) missions. Sensors: Radar Bendix APS-133; ALR-68(V)4 ESM; supports Trident Fleet radio communications with up to 28,000 ft of VLF trailing wire antenna. Weapons: Unarmed.

E-6B *6/2005, Paul Jackson* / 1154051

UNMANNED AIR VEHICLES

Notes: (1) The US Navy continues to refine its path to the full integration of UAV systems into its concepts of operations and warfighting philosophy. The aim is to develop and employ a family of systems which includes both small, longer range tactical systems and large, high-altitude long-endurance systems. Interoperability, affordability and commonality are to be key parameters of all systems. Other important technology areas include miniaturised and low-cost payloads, vehicle survivability, shipboard operations, jam resistant links, reduced data redundancy, and autonomous and collaborative technologies.
(2) The UAV strategy was given increased impetus following Operation Desert Storm and operations in Afghanistan in 2001. The family of UAVs are seen meeting three principal capability requirements:
(a) Tactical Surveillance and Targeting: The USMC is transferring to the Shadow 200 UAV system. Pioneer has been retired. Fire Scout is to provide an organic UAV capability for the Littoral Combat Ship (LCS) in 2008. The US Navy also operates a Reaper system for US Joint Forces Command's Joint Operational Test Bed System (JOTBS) to examine UAV interoperability and to test war fighting concepts.
(b) Long Dwell/Stand-off Intelligence Surveillance and Reconnaissance (ISR): A Broad Area Maritime Surveillance (BAMS) UAV is sought for worldwide access and persistent maritime ISR. It is planned to achieve Initial Operational Capability of one base unit with sufficient assets, technical data, training systems, and enough spares and support equipment to operationally support one persistent ISR orbit by FY14. Full operational capability is to be achieved with up to five simultaneous orbits worldwide. For maritime demonstration, the Navy completed source selection in April 2008 and chose the RQ-4N Global Hawk (navy variant).
(c) Penetrating Surveillance/Suppression of Enemy Air Defences: Navy Unmanned Combat Air Systems (UCAS) program is intended to develop and mature technologies for carrier operation. Northrop Grumman X-47B selected on 1 August 2007 as potential carrier-launched unmanned system. Two prototype aircraft are to be built, test flights are to begin in 2009 and carrier-deck landing in 2011. The demonstrator aircraft are a precursor to a complement ofunmanned carrier-deployed aircraft planned for about 2020.

X-47B *8/2007, Northrop Grumman* / 1169081

Numbers/Type: 2 Northrop Grumman RQ-4A Global Hawk.
Operational speed: 343 kt *(635 km/h).*
Service ceiling: 65,000 ft *(19,810 m).*
Range: 12,000 n miles *(22,224 km).*
Role/Weapon systems: Two RQ-4A acquired for evaluation in 2005. Early flights were made from Edwards AFB, California. One took part in Exercise Trident Warrior in 2005 and later deployed to NAS Patuxent River for operation by US Navy test squadron VX-20 for participation in the Joint Expeditionary Force Experiment 2006 and also to develop ISR tactics and operational techniques. An aircraft also took part in Exercise RIMPAC 2006. The aircraft is being used to develop tactics, techniques and procedures and to refine CONOPS for the BAMS programme.

RQ-4A *6/2005, Northrop Grumman* / 1122583

Numbers/Type: 5 Northrop Grumman MQ-8B Fire Scout UAV.
Operational speed: 110 kt *(203 km/h)*.
Service ceiling: 20,000 ft *(6,094 m)*.
Range: 110 n miles *(205 km)*.
Role/Weapon systems: Vertical Take Off and Landing Tactical Unmanned Air Vehicle (VTUAV). Design based on the Schweizer Aircraft model 330 helicopter. No systems currently operational. Five RQ-8A versions were first procured; before evaluation to multifunction role with MQ-8B in mid-2005. Improvements included increased power, fuel and payload capacity to achieve more than double mission radius and time on station than in previous version. MQ variant completed first flight in December 2006. EMD completion and low-rate initial production began in 2007 with five MQ-8Bs delivered by May 2008. Operational evaluation to start in early 2009 with fleet introduction later that year. It is planned to acquire 131 VTUAV aircraft to meet LCS requirements. A VTUAV system is composed of three air vehicles, three mission sensor package payloads, two Ground Control Stations, Tactical Common Data Link, one UAV Common Automatic Recovery System for automatic take-off and landing, and shipboard grid and harpoon capture. When operational, Fire Scout will provide critical situational awareness, intelligence, surveillance, reconnaissance, and targeting data to forward deployed war fighters. Arming of MQ-8B with an air-to-surface missile system is under consideration.

MQ-8B *7/2005, US Navy* / 1167616

Numbers/Type: 16 AAI RQ-7 Shadow.
Operational speed: 110 kt *(195 km/h)*.
Service ceiling: 14,000 ft *(4,267 m)*.
Range: 67 n miles *(124 km)*.
Role/Weapon systems: The Shadow UAV system provides Reconnaissance, Surveillance and Target Acquisition (RSTA) as well as Battle Management and Battle Damage Assessment (BDA) capabilities. Three squadrons use the system. Each system is comprised on two Ground Control Stations and four Air Vehicles. Sensors: electro-optic/FLIR/infra-red imaging sensor.

SHADOW 200 *10/2006, US Army* / 1122581

Numbers/Type: 5 Northrop Grumman MQ-9 Reaper.
Operational speed: 260 kt *(481 km/h)*.
Service ceiling: 50,000 ft *(15,240 m)*.
Range: 400 n miles *(740 km)*.
Role/Weapon systems: The MQ-9 Reaper is a medium-to-high altitude, long-endurance unmanned aircraft system. These UAVs support a Navy requirement for test-bed sensor-suite integration, test and concept development for expeditionary ISR. Four Reapers were acquired 2005–07 and a fifth by 2008. A further three airframes have been ordered after which no further procurement of MQ-9 is planned.

MQ-9 *11/2006, Empics* / 1165386

PATROL FORCES

Notes: 'Spartan' is a technology demonstrator programme to prove utility of unmanned surface craft. It is envisaged that such craft will be capable of conducting mine warfare, force protection (including surveillance and reconnaissance) and anti-surface warfare. A prototype, a 7 m RHIB installed with navigation, communications and remote control equipment, underwent sea trials in 2003 which included embarkation in USS *Gettysburg* as part of the *Enterprise* carrier strike group.

8 CYCLONE CLASS
(PATROL COASTAL SHIPS) (PBFM)

Name	*No*	*Builders*	*Commissioned*	*F/S*
HURRICANE	PC 3	Bollinger, Lockport	15 Oct 1993	PA
TYPHOON	PC 5	Bollinger, Lockport	12 Feb 1994	AA
SIROCCO	PC 6	Bollinger, Lockport	11 June 1994	AA
SQUALL	PC 7	Bollinger, Lockport	4 July 1994	PA
CHINOOK	PC 9	Bollinger, Lockport	28 Jan 1995	AA
FIREBOLT	PC 10	Bollinger, Lockport	10 June 1995	AA
WHIRLWIND	PC 11	Bollinger, Lockport	1 July 1995	AA
THUNDERBOLT	PC 12	Bollinger, Lockport	7 Oct 1995	AA

Displacement, tons: 354 full load
Dimensions, feet (metres): 170.3 × 25.9 × 7.9 *(51.9 × 7.9 × 2.4)*
Main machinery: 4 Paxman Valenta 16RP200CM diesels; 13,400 hp *(10 MW)* sustained; 4 shafts
Speed, knots: 35
Range, n miles: 2,500 at 12 kt
Complement: 39 (4 officers) plus 9 SEALs or law enforcement detachment
Missiles: SAM: 1 Stinger MANPAD system (6 missiles).
Guns: 1 Bushmaster 25 mm Mk 38. 1 Bushmaster 25 mm Mk 96 (aft). 8—12.7 mm MGs (4 twin). 2—7.62 mm MGs. 2—40 mm Mk 19 grenade launchers (MGs and grenade launchers are interchangeable).
Countermeasures: Decoys: 2 Mk 52 sextuple.
ESM: Privateer APR-39; radar warning. Sensytech Bobcat.
Weapons control: FLIR systems AN/KAX-1 Marflir.
Radars: Surface search: 2 Sperry RASCAR; E/F/I/J-band.
Sonars: Wesmar; hull-mounted; active scanning sonar; high frequency.

Programmes: Contract awarded for eight in August 1990, five in July 1991 and one in August 1997.
Structure: Design based on Vosper Thornycroft Ramadan class modified for USN requirements including ballistic plating to protect electronics, communications and the pilot house. The craft have a slow speed loiter capability. Swimmers can be launched from a platform at the stern.
Modernisation: The ships have been modernised to incorporate advanced ESM, an integrated bridge system, a Mk 96 stabilised weapon platform and improved communications.
Operational: The ships perform maritime interdiction, homeland security, law enforcement and SAR missions. Can be operated in pairs with a maintenance team in two vans ashore. Operational control transferred from Special Operations Command to the Atlantic and Pacific Fleets on 1 October 2002. Five stern-ramp fitted ships (PC 2, PC 4, PC 8, PC 13 and PC 14) were transferred tothe USCG 2004–05. Of the PCs on loan, two (PC 2, PC 4) are to return to the Navy in FY09 and the other three in FY12. Remaining ships are to be upgraded at one ship per year from FY09. Modernisation work includes communication and radar upgrades and the installation of new diesel generators and air-conditioning units.
Sales: PC1 *(Cyclone)* transferred to the Philippines Navy for counter-terrorism duties.

CHINOOK *9/2008*, Shaun Jones* / 1353589

SQUALL *10/2002, M Mazumdar* / 0529973

20 MK V CLASS (HSIC)

Displacement, tons: 54 full load
Dimensions, feet (metres): 81.2 × 17.5 × 4.3 *(24.7 × 5.3 × 1.3)*
Main machinery: 2 MTU 12V 396 TE94 diesels; 4,506 hp *(3.36 MW)* sustained; 2 Kamewa water-jets
Speed, knots: 45
Range, n miles: 515 at 35 kt
Complement: 5
Military lift: 16 fully equipped troops
Guns: 5 Mk 46 Mod 4 mountings for twin 12.7 mm or 7.6 mm MGs, 1 Mk 19 40 mm grenade launcher.
Countermeasures: ESM: Sensytech Bobcat; radar intercept.
Radars: Navigation: Furuno; I-band.
IFF: APX-100(V).

Comment: This was the winning design of a competition held in 1994 to find a high-speed craft to insert and extract Navy SEAL teams and other special operations forces personnel. Fourteen delivered by mid-1998 and six more by mid-1999. All built at the Halter Marine Equitable Shipyard in New Orleans. The craft has an aluminium hull and is transportable by C-5 aircraft. Stinger missiles may be carried and gun armaments can be varied. A variant with three engines is in service with the Mexican Navy.

MK V *3/2007, **Paul Daly*** / 1305198

20 SPECIAL OPERATIONS CRAFT RIVERINE (SOCR)

Displacement, tons: 9.1 full load
Dimensions, feet (metres): 33.0 × 9.0 × 2.0 *(10.1 × 2.7 × 0.6)*
Main machinery: 2 Yanmar 6LY2M-STE diesels; 440 hp *(328 kW)*; 2 Hamilton HJ292 waterjets
Speed, knots: 40+
Range, n miles: 195
Complement: 4
Military lift: 8 fully equipped troops
Guns: Combination of Mk 19 40 mm, 12.7 mm MG, 7.62 mm/M60, M240, GAU17 at 5 stations.

Comment: Built by United States Marine, Inc. Aluminium hull.

SOCR *2/2005, **US Navy*** / 1043672

72 NSW 11 METRE RIB (RIGID INFLATABLE BOATS) (PBF)

Displacement, tons: 9 full load
Dimensions, feet (metres): 36.1 × 10.5 × 3 *(11 × 3.2 × 0.9)*
Main machinery: 2 Caterpillar 3126 diesels; 940 hp *(700 kW)*; 2 Kamewa FF 280 water-jets
Speed, knots: 35
Range, n miles: 200 at 33 kt
Complement: 4 plus 9 SEALs
Guns: 1—12.7 mm MG, 1—7.62 mm MG or Mk 19 Mod 3 grenade launcher.

Comment: Naval Special Warfare (NSW) RIB capable of carrying nine SEALS at 35 kt. Built by USMI, New Orleans. Entered service from 1998 to 2002.

NSW RIB *1/2002, **M Declerck*** / 0529972

NSW RIB *1/1998, **US Navy*** / 0016492

116 LIGHT PATROL BOATS (PBF)

Displacement, tons: 1.2 full load
Dimensions, feet (metres): 22.3 × 8.6 × 1.5 *(6.8 × 2.6 × 0.5)*
Main machinery: 2 OMC outboards; 300 hp *(224 kW)*
Speed, knots: 35
Complement: 3
Guns: 3—12.7 mm MGs. 1—7.62 mm MG.
Radars: Surface search: Furuno 1731; I-band

Comment: Built by Boston Whaler in 1988 for US Special Operations Command. Air transportable. Glass fibre hulls. Replacement began in 2001.

PBL-CD *1996, **Boston Whaler*** / 0084150

89 SEA ARK PATROL CRAFT (PBF)

400 series

Displacement, tons: 9.3 full load
Dimensions, feet (metres): 34.0 × 12.0 × 2.7 *(10.36 × 3.66 × 0.8)*
Main machinery: 2 Cummins QSB5.9-420 GS diesels; 740 hp *(550 kW)*; 2 Konrad 520 drives
Speed, knots: 36
Complement: 6
Guns: 4—12.7 mm MGs.
Radars: Navigation: Furuno; I-band.

Comment: SeaArk Marine Dauntless RAM design delivered from 2008. Aluminium construction transportable by aircraft. Employed on harbour and offshore installation protection tasks. First deployed with Naval Coastal Warfare Squadron-Five near San Diego.

CUTTER 429 *9/2008*, **Shaun Jones*** / 1353588

COMMAND SHIPS

Notes: Options for replacement of the two in-service command ships remain under consideration. They include new construction ships, service-life extensions of current ships and/or a mix of sea and land-based facilities.

2 BLUE RIDGE CLASS (COMMAND SHIPS) (LCCH/AGFH)

Name	*No*	*Builders*	*Laid down*	*Launched*	*Commissioned*	*F/S*
BLUE RIDGE	LCC 19	Philadelphia Naval Shipyard	27 Feb 1967	4 Jan 1969	14 Nov 1970	PA
MOUNT WHITNEY	LCC 20	Newport News Shipbuilding	8 Jan 1969	8 Jan 1970	16 Jan 1971	AA

Displacement, tons: 13,077 light; 19,648 full load *(Blue Ridge)* 12,435 light; 17,485 full load *(Mount Whitney)*
Dimensions, feet (metres): 634.0 × 107.9 × 24.8 *(193.2 × 32.9 × 7.6)*
Main machinery: 2 Foster-Wheeler boilers; 600 psi *(42.3 kg/cm²)*; 870°F *(467°C)*; 1 GE turbine; 22,000 hp *(16.4 MW)*; 1 shaft
Speed, knots: 23
Range, n miles: 13,000 at 16 kt
Complement: 786: 637 Flag staff (LCC 19). 303 (157 military, 146 civilian): 562 Flag staff (LCC 20)
Military lift: 700 troops; 3 LCPs; 2 LCVPs; 2—7 m RHIBs

Guns: 2 General Electric/General Dynamics 20 mm/76 6-barrelled Vulcan Phalanx Mk 15; 3,000 rds/min (4,500 in Block 1) combined to 1.5 km.
2—25 mm Mk 38.
2—12.7 mm MGs.
Countermeasures: Decoys: 4 Loral Hycor SRBOC 6-barrelled fixed Mk 36; IR flares and chaff to 4 km *(2.2 n miles)*. SLQ-25 Nixie; torpedo decoy.
ESM/ECM: SLQ-32(V)3; combined radar intercept, jammer and deception system.

Combat data systems: GCCS (M) Link 4A, Link 11, Link 14 and JTIDS. Theatre Battle Management Core Systems (TBMCS). Wide band commercial SATCOM, USC-38 SATCOM, WSC-3 EHF SATCOM, WSC-6(V)1 and 5, and WSC-6A(V)4 SHF SATCOM. High Frequency Radio Group (HFRG). Mission Display System (MDS). Demand Assigned Multiple Access (DAMA QUAD). Area Air Defense Commander, Naval Fires Network, Joint Service Imagery Processing System (JSIPS-N), Common High Bandwidth Data Link, Shipboard Terminal (CHBDL-ST), Ring Laser Gyro Network (RLGN), NITES 2000, Joint Tactical Information Distribution System (JTIDS), Navigational Sensor System Interface (NAVSSI). (See Data Systems at front of section.)
Radars: Air search: Lockheed SPS-40E; B-band.
Surface search: Lockheed SPS-10B; G-band.
Navigation: Marconi LN66; Raytheon SPS-64(V)9; I-band.
Tacan: URN 25. IFF: Mk XII AIMS UPX-29.

Helicopters: Platform for 1 Sikorsky SH-3H Sea King.

Programmes: Authorised in FY65 and 1966. Originally designated Amphibious Force Flagships (AGC); redesignated Command Ships (LCC) on 1 January 1969.
Modernisation: Modernisation completed FY87. 3 in guns removed in 1996/97 and Sea Sparrow missile launchers have been disembarked. Mk 23 TAS and RAM are not now to be fitted.
Structure: General hull design and machinery arrangement are similar to the Iwo Jima class assault ships. Accommodation for 250 officers and 1,300 enlisted men.
Operational: These are large force command ships of post-Second World War design. They can provide integrated command and control facilities for sea, air and land commanders in all types of operations. *Blue Ridge* is the Seventh Fleet flagship, based at Yokosuka, Japan. *Mount Whitney* served since January 1981 as flagship Second Fleet, based at Norfolk, Virginia except during the period June to November 1999 when she served as Sixth Fleet flagship. In March 2005, *Mount Whitney* became part of MSC Special Mission programme and replaced *La Salle* as flagship Sixth Fleet, based at Gaeta, Italy. *Mount Whitney* retains US Navy status but with a 'hybrid' military/civilian crew.

MOUNT WHITNEY *8/2006, Guy Toremans* / 1167618

BLUE RIDGE *5/2008*, US Navy* / 1353587

AMPHIBIOUS FORCES

Notes: (1) Additional capacity is provided by the maritime pre-positioning ships (see listing under *Military Sealift Command* (MSC) section) which are either new construction or conversions of commercial ships. One squadron is maintained on station in the Mediterranean, a second at Guam, and a third at Diego Garcia. Each squadron carries equipment to support a Marine Expeditionary Brigade.
(2) **Minesweeping**: Several of the larger amphibious ships have been used as operating bases for minesweeping helicopters.
(3) Five decommissioned LKAs and four LSTs are kept in Amphibious Lift Enhancement Program (ALEP) status. These are *Fresno* (LST 1182), *Tuscaloosa* (LST 1187), *Boulder* (LST 1190), *Racine* (LST 1191), *Charleston* (LKA113), *Durham* (LKA 114), *Mobile* (LKA 115), *St Louis* (LKA 116) and *El Paso* (LKA 117).

7 + 1 WASP CLASS (AMPHIBIOUS ASSAULT SHIPS) (LHDM)

Name	*No*	*Builders*	*Laid down*	*Launched*	*Commissioned*	*F/S*
WASP	LHD 1	Ingalls Shipbuilding	30 May 1985	4 Aug 1987	29 July 1989	AA
ESSEX	LHD 2	Ingalls Shipbuilding	16 Feb 1989	4 Jan 1991	17 Oct 1992	PA
KEARSARGE	LHD 3	Ingalls Shipbuilding	6 Feb 1990	26 Mar 1992	16 Oct 1993	AA
BOXER	LHD 4	Ingalls Shipbuilding	26 Mar 1991	13 Aug 1993	11 Feb 1995	PA
BATAAN	LHD 5	Ingalls Shipbuilding	16 Mar 1994	15 Mar 1996	20 Sep 1997	AA
BONHOMME RICHARD	LHD 6	Ingalls Shipbuilding	29 Mar 1995	14 Mar 1997	15 Aug 1998	PA
IWO JIMA	LHD 7	Ingalls Shipbuilding	12 Dec 1997	4 Feb 2000	30 June 2001	AA
MAKIN ISLAND	LHD 8	Northrop Grumman Ship Systems (Ingalls)	14 Feb 2004	22 Sep 2006	Oct 2009	Bldg/PA

Displacement, tons: 40,650 (LHD 1-4); 40,358 (LHD 5-7); 41,661 (LHD 8) full load
Dimensions, feet (metres): 847 oa; 788 wl × 140.1 oa; 106 wl × 26.6 *(258.2; 240.2 × 42.7; 32.3 × 8.1)*
Flight deck, feet (metres): 819 × 118 *(249.6 × 36.0)*
Main machinery: 2 Combustion Engineering boilers; 600 psi *(42.3 kg/cm²)*; 900°F *(482°C)*; 2 Westinghouse turbines; 70,000 hp *(52.2 MW)*; 2 shafts (LHD 1-7)
2 GE LM 2500+ gas turbines; 70,000 hp *(52.2 MW)*; 2 Alstom variable speed electric motors; 10,000 hp *(7.5 MW)* (LHD 8)
Speed, knots: 22
Range, n miles: 9,500 at 20 kt
Complement: 1,123 (65 officers)
Military lift: 1,687 (plus 184 surge) troops; 12 LCM 6s or 3 LCACs; 1,232 tons aviation fuel (LHD 1-4); 1,960 tons (LHD 5-8)

Missiles: SAM: 2 Raytheon GMLS Mk 29 octuple launchers ❶; 16 Sea Sparrow RIM-7P; semi-active radar homing to 16 km *(8.5 n miles)* at 2.5 Mach; warhead 38kg. ESSM in due course.
2 GDC Mk 49 RAM RIM-116 launchers; 21 rounds per launcher ❷; passive IR/anti-radiation homing to 9.6 km *(5.2 n miles)* at 2.5 Mach; warhead 9.1 kg.
Guns: 2 General Electric/General Dynamics 20 mm 6-barrelled Vulcan Phalanx Mk 15 ❸; 3,000 rds/min (4,500 in Batch 1) combined to 1.5 km.
3 Boeing Bushmaster 25 mm Mk 38. 4—12.7 mm MGs.
Countermeasures: Decoys: 4 or 6 Loral Hycor SRBOC 6-barrelled fixed Mk 36; IR flares and chaff to 4 km *(2.2 n miles)*.
SLQ-25 Nixie; acoustic torpedo decoy system. NATO Sea Gnat. SLQ-49 chaff buoys. AEB SSQ-95.
ESM/ECM: SLQ-32(V)3/SLY-2; intercept and jammers. Raytheon ULQ-20.
Combat data systems: ACDS Block 1 level 2 (LHD 1 and 7) and Block 0 (LHD 2-6). SSDS Mk 2 (LHD 8 on build and LHD 7 in 2007). Marine Tactical Amphibious C² System (MTACCS). Links 4A, 11 (modified), 14 and 16. SATCOMS ❹ SSR-1, WSC-3 (UHF), USC-38 (EHF). SMQ-11 Metsat (see Data Systems at front of section). Advanced Field Artillery TDS (LHD 6-8).
Weapons control: 2 Mk 91 MFCS (LHD 1-6). 2 Mk 9 MFCS (LHD 7-8).
Radars: Air search: ITT SPS-48E ❺; 3D; E/F-band.
Raytheon SPS-49(V)9 ❻; C/D-band.
Hughes Mk 23 TAS ❼; D-band. SPQ-9B (LHD 8 on build and LHD 7 in 2007).
Surface search: Norden SPS-67 ❽; G-band.
Navigation: SPS-73; I-band.
CCA: SPN-35B (LHD 1-7), SPN-35C (LHD 8) and SPN-43C.
Fire control: 2 Mk 95; I/J-band. SPQ-9B to be fitted.
Tacan: URN 25. IFF: CIS Mk XV UPX-29.

Fixed-wing aircraft: 6-8 AV-8B Harriers or up to 20 in secondary role. MV-22 Osprey and Joint Strike Fighter in due course.
Helicopters: Capacity for 42 CH-46E Sea Knight but has the capability to support: AH-1W Super Cobra, CH-53E Super Stallion, CH-53D Sea Stallion, UH-1N Twin Huey, AH-1T Sea Cobra, and SH-60B Seahawk helicopters. UAV in due course.

Programmes: The Wasp class was a follow-on to the Tarawa clas and shares the same basic hull and engineering plant. Contract awarded to Ingalls Shipbuilding in February 1984 to build the lead ship. The same shipyard was subsequently contracted to build the other ships of the class.

Modernisation: RAM launchers retrofitted in all. All ships to be modified to accommodate MV-22 Osprey and F-35B operations.
Structure: Two aircraft elevators, one to starboard and aft of the 'island' and one to port amidships. The well-deck is 267 × 50 ftand can accommodate up to three LCACs. The flight deck has nine helicopter landing spots. Cargo capacity is 125,000 cu ft total with an additional 20,000 sq ft to accommodate vehicles. Vehicle storage is available for five M1 tanks, 25 LAVs, eight M 198 guns, 68 trucks, 10 logistic vehicles and several service vehicles. The bridge is two decks lower than that of an LHA, command, control and communication spaces having been moved inside the hull to avoid 'cheap kill' damage. Fitted with a 64 bed capacity hospital and six operating rooms. Three 32 ft monorail trains each carrying 6,000 lbs, deliver material to the well-deck at 6.8 mph. *Iwo Jima* is likely to be the last oil-fired steam turbine ship in the USN. LHD 8 is fitted with gas turbine propulsion, electric drive, watermist fire suppression system, fibre-optic machinery control system, SPQ-9B radar and CEC. LHD-3 upgraded in 2006 to accommodate/operate MV-22 Osprey.
Operational: A typical complement of aircraft is a mix of 25 helicopters and six to eight Harriers (AV-8B). In the secondary role as a sea control ship the most likely mix is 20 AV-8B Harriers and four to six SH-60B Seahawk helicopters. LHD 3 modified to provide interim Mine Countermeasures Command (MCS) capability following decommissioning of *Inchon* in June 2002. LHD 6 first amphibious ship to deploy with MH-60S helicopter. LHDs 1, 3, 5 and 7 based at Norfolk, Virginia, and LHDs 4 and 6 at San Diego, California where LHD 8 is also to be based. LHD 2 is based at Sasebo, Japan. LHD 8 completed the second round of builders trials on 7 February 2009.

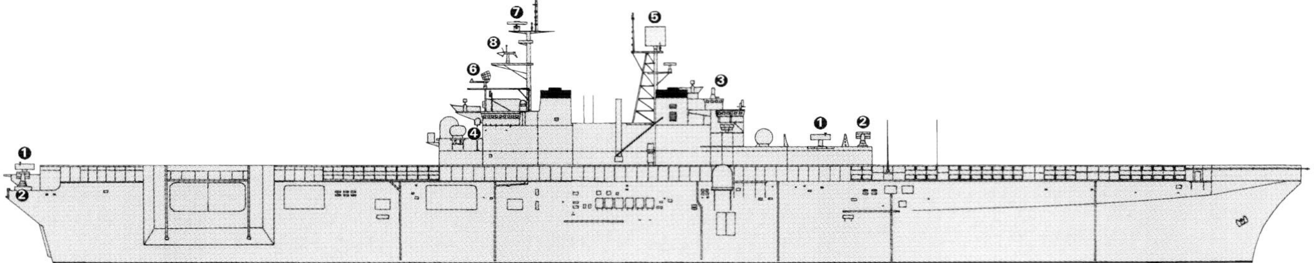

BONHOMME RICHARD *(Scale 1 : 1,500), Ian Sturton* / 0131367

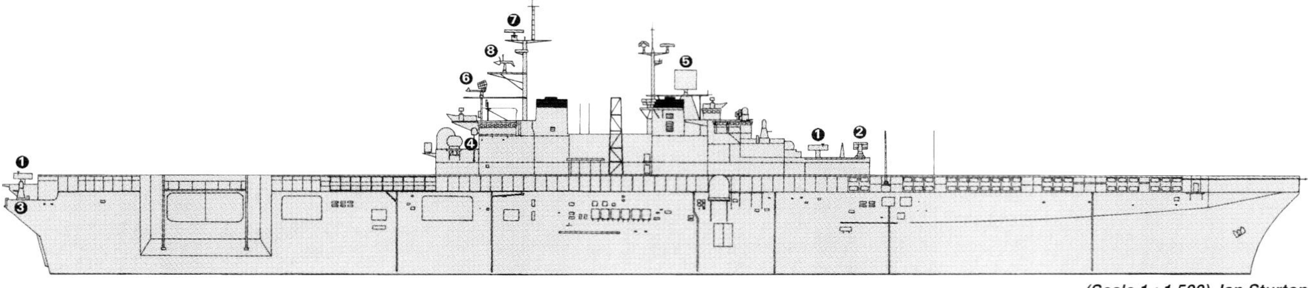

ESSEX *(Scale 1 : 1,500), Ian Sturton* / 0131368

BATAAN *5/2006, M Declerck* / 1167621

BONHOMME RICHARD *10/2006, Michael Nitz* / 1305195

IWO JIMA *10/2008*, US Navy* / 1353585

BOXER *5/2005, Hachiro Nakai* / 1154020

4 + 5 (1) SAN ANTONIO CLASS (AMPHIBIOUS TRANSPORT DOCKS) (LPDM)

Name	*No*	*Builders*	*Laid down*	*Launched*	*Commissioned*	*F/S*
SAN ANTONIO	LPD 17	Northrop Grumman Ship Systems (Avondale)	9 Dec 2000	19 July 2003	14 Jan 2006	AA
NEW ORLEANS	LPD 18	Northrop Grumman Ship Systems (Avondale)	14 Oct 2002	20 Dec 2004	10 Mar 2007	PA
MESA VERDE	LPD 19	Northrop Grumman Ship Systems (Ingalls)	25 Feb 2003	20 Nov 2005	15 Dec 2007	AA
GREEN BAY	LPD 20	Northrop Grumman Ship Systems (Avondale)	7 Aug 2003	11 Aug 2006	24 Jan 2009	PA
NEW YORK	LPD 21	Northrop Grumman Ship Systems (Avondale)	30 Aug 2004	1 Mar 2008	Nov 2009	Bldg/AA
SAN DIEGO	LPD 22	Northrop Grumman Ship Systems (Avondale)	23 May 2007	May 2009	Nov 2010	Bldg/PA
ANCHORAGE	LPD 23	Northrop Grumman Ship Systems (Avondale)	24 Sep 2007	Oct 2009	May 2011	Bldg/PA
ARLINGTON	LPD 24	Northrop Grumman Ship Systems (Avondale)	18 Dec 2008	May 2010	Nov 2011	Bldg/PA
SOMERSET	LPD 25	Northrop Grumman Ship Systems (Avondale)	2009	Sep 2010	May 2012	Ord

Displacement, tons: 25,885 full load
Dimensions, feet (metres): 683.7 × 104.7 × 23 *(208.4 × 31.9 × 7)*
Main machinery: 4 Colt Pielstick PC 2.5 diesels; 40,000 hp *(29.84 MW)*; 2 shafts; cp props
Speed, knots: 22
Complement: 360 (28 officers) plus 34 spare
Military lift: 720 troops; 2 LCACs, 14 EFVs

Missiles: SAM: 2 Raytheon RAM RIM-116 21-cell Mk 49 launchers; passive IR/anti-radiation homing to 9.6 km *(5.2 n miles)* at 2.5 Mach; warhead 9.1 kg ❶.
Guns: 2—30 mm Mk 46 ❷. 4—12.7 mm MGs.
Countermeasures: Decoys: 6 Mk 53 Mod 4 Nulka and chaff launcher ❸. SLQ-25A Nixie towed torpedo decoy.
ESM/ECM: SLQ-32A(V)2 ❹; intercept and jammer.
Combat data systems: SSDS Mk 2; GCCS (M), CEC, JTIDS (Link 16), AADS (see Data Systems at front of section).
Radars: Air search: ITT SPS-48E ❺; 3D; E/F-band.
Surface search/navigation: Raytheon SPS-73(V)13 ❻; I-band.
Fire control: Lockheed SPQ-9B ❼; I-band.

Helicopters: 1 CH-53E Sea Stallion or 2 CH-46E Sea Knight or 1 MV-22 Osprey.

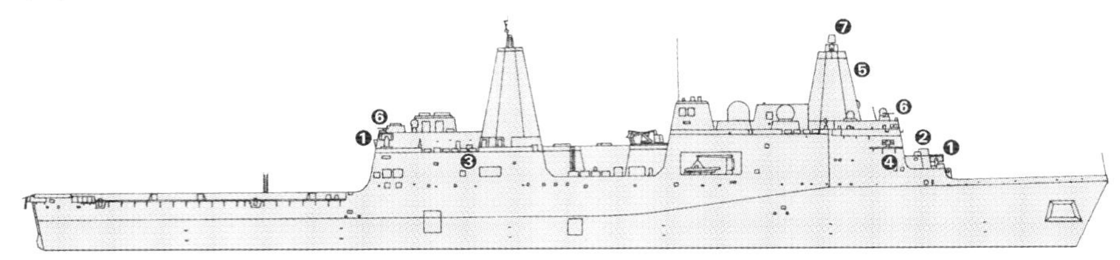

SAN ANTONIO *(Scale 1 : 1,800), Ian Sturton* / 1167439

Programmes: The LPD 17 (ex-LX) programme was first approved by the Defense Acquisition Board on 11 January 1993. It will replace four classes of amphibious ships: LPD 4s, LSTs, LKAs and LSD 36s. Contract for first ship, with an option on two more, awarded to Avondale on 17 December 1996. A protest about the award delayed the effective contract date to April 1997. The lead ship contract options for FY99 and FY00 on LPD 18 and LPD 19 were exercised in December 1998 and February 2000 respectively. A negotiated modification added the second FY00 ship, LPD 20, to the lead ship contract in May 2000. Contract awarded for LPD 21 in November 2003 and for LPD 22 and 23 on 1 June 2006. Contract for long lead items for LPD 24 and 25 awarded on 6 November 2006. Under agreement reached in June 2002, NGSS is to build all ships. Difficulties in design phase led to two-year delay to delivery date of lead ship. Launch and commissioning dates for LPD 18-20 delayed due to shipyard damage caused by Hurricane Katrina in 2005. Delivery of ninth ship is planned for 2012. Procurement of a tenth ship is under consideration.

Structure: Panama Canal-capable ships able to control and support landing forces disembarking either via surface craft such as LCACs or by VTOL aircraft, principally helicopters. The design supports a lift capability of 24,000 sq ft of deck space for vehicles, 34,000 cu ft of cargo below decks and 720 embarked Marines with surge lift capacity to 800 troops. The well-deck and stern gate arrangements are similar to those of the Wasp class; the well-deck can carry two LCACs or one LCU, or 14 Expeditionary Fighting Vehicles. The Flight deck can land/launch four CH-46s or two CH-53s or two MV-22s. The hangar will accommodate two CH-46s or one CH-53 or one MV-22. There is a 24-bed medical facility. Although with similar capabilities as the classes they are to replace, the ships are not equipped with the flag facilities of some Austin class LPDs, the heavy over-the-side lift capability of LKAs or the ability of LSTs to beach. There is a crane for support of boat operations and an Advanced Enclosed Mast System, trialled in DD 968, is being fitted in all. On 9 September 2003, salvaged steel from the World Trade Centre was cast into the bow section of USS *New York*.

Operational: The first two ships have experienced a variety of problems. The first of class, LPD 17, was late in starting its maiden deployment in August 2008 and subsequently required to undergo repairs in November 2008. LPD 18 was assessed 'degraded' in its InSurv report in August 2008. LPD 18 started her maiden deployment in January 2009.

SAN ANTONIO *10/2008*, US Navy* / 1353586

NEW ORLEANS *5/2007, US Navy* / 1305196

2 TARAWA CLASS (AMPHIBIOUS ASSAULT SHIPS) (LHAM)

Name	*No*	*Builders*	*Laid down*	*Launched*	*Commissioned*	*F/S*
NASSAU	LHA 4	Ingalls Shipbuilding	13 Aug 1973	21 Jan 1978	28 July 1979	AA
PELELIU (ex-*Da Nang*)	LHA 5	Ingalls Shipbuilding	12 Nov 1976	25 Nov 1978	3 May 1980	PA

Displacement, tons: 39,967 full load
Dimensions, feet (metres): 834 × 131.9 × 25.9 *(254.2 × 40.2 × 7.9)*
Flight deck, feet (metres): 820 × 118.1 *(250 × 36)*
Main machinery: 2 Combustion Engineering boilers; 600 psi *(42.3 kg/cm²)*; 900°F *(482°C)*; 2 Westinghouse turbines; 70,000 hp *(52.2 MW)*; 2 shafts; bow thruster; 900 hp *(670 kW)*
Speed, knots: 24. **Range, n miles**: 10,000 at 20 kt
Complement: 964 (56 officers)
Military lift: 1,703 troops; 4 LCU 1610 type or 2 LCU and 2 LCM 8 or 17 LCM 6 or 45 Assault Amphibian Vehicles; 1,200 tons aviation fuel. 1 LCAC may be embarked. 4 LCPL (replacement by RHIBs in progress)

Missiles: SAM: 2 GDC Mk 49 RAM RIM-116 ❶; 21 rounds per launcher; passive IR/anti-radiation homing to 9.6 km *(5.2 n miles)* at 2.5 Mach; warhead 9.1 kg.
Guns: 2 General Electric/General Dynamics 20 mm/76 6-barrelled Vulcan Phalanx Mk 15 ❷; 3,000 rds/min (4,500 in Block 1) combined to 1.5 km.
6 Mk 242 25 mm automatic cannons. 8—12.7 mm MGs.
Countermeasures: Decoys: 4 Loral Hycor SRBOC 6-barrelled fixed Mk 36; IR flares and chaff to 4 km *(2.2 n miles)*.
SLQ-25 Nixie; acoustic torpedo decoy system. NATO Sea Gnat. SLQ-49 chaff buoys. AEB SSQ-95.
ESM/ECM: SLQ-32(V)3; intercept and jammers.
Combat data systems: ACDS Block 0. Advanced Combat Direction System to provide computerised support in control of helicopters and aircraft, shipboard weapons and sensors, navigation, landing craft control and electronic warfare. Links 4A, 11 and 16. SATCOM SRR-1, WSC-3 (UHF), USC-38 (EHF). SMQ-11 Metsat (see Data Systems at front of section).
Radars: Air search: ITT SPS-48E ❸; E/F-band.
Lockheed SPS-40E ❹; B-band.
Hughes Mk 23 TAS ❺; D-band.
Surface search: Raytheon SPS-67(V)3 ❻; G-band.
Navigation: Raytheon SPS-73; I-band.
CCA: SPN-35A; SPN-43B.
Tacan: URN 25. IFF: CIS Mk XV/UPX-36.

Fixed-wing aircraft: Harrier AV-8B VSTOL aircraft in place of some helicopters as required. MV-22 Osprey in due course.

PELELIU *11/2008*, Chris Sattler* / 1333725

Helicopters: 19 CH-53D Sea Stallion or 26 CH-46D/E Sea Knight UAV in due course.

Programmes: Originally intended to be a class of nine ships. LHA 4 and LHA 5 were authorised in FY71.
Modernisation: Two Vulcan Phalanx CIWS replaced the GMLS Mk 25 Sea Sparrow launchers. Programme completed in early 1991. RAM launchers fitted to all of the class 1993–95. One launcher is above the bridge offset to port, and the other on the starboard side at the after end of the flight deck. Mk 23 TAS target acquisition radar fitted in LHA 5 in 1992 and LHA 4 in 1993. SPS-48E started replacing SPS-52D in 1994 to improve low altitude detection of missiles and aircraft. ACDS Block 0 in 1996. 5 in guns removed in 1997/98. Plans to fit SSDS have been shelved. Modifications to accommodate MV-22 Osprey operations and Collective Protection Systems upgrade in progress. Fuel oil compensation system has been installed to improve damaged stability.
Structure: There are two lifts, one on the port side aft and one at the stern. Beneath the after elevator is a floodable docking well measuring 268 ft in length and 78 ft in width which is capable of accommodating four LCU 1610 type landing craft. Also included is a large garage for trucks and AFVs and troop berthing for a reinforced battalion. 33,730 sq ft available for vehicles and 116,900 cu ft for palletted stores. Extensive medical facilities including operating rooms, X-ray room, hospital ward, isolation ward, laboratories, pharmacy, dental operating room and medical store rooms.
Operational: The flight deck can operate a maximum of nine CH-53D Sea Stallion or 12 CH-46D/E Sea Knight helicopters or a mix of these and other helicopters at any one time. With some additional modifications, ships of this class can effectively operate AV-8B aircraft. The normal mix of aircraft allows for six AV-8Bs. The optimum aircraft configuration is dependent upon assigned missions. Unmanned Reconnaissance Vehicles (URVs) can be operated. LHA 3 decommissioned 28 October 2005 and LHA 2 in 2007. LHA 1 decommissioned in December 2008.

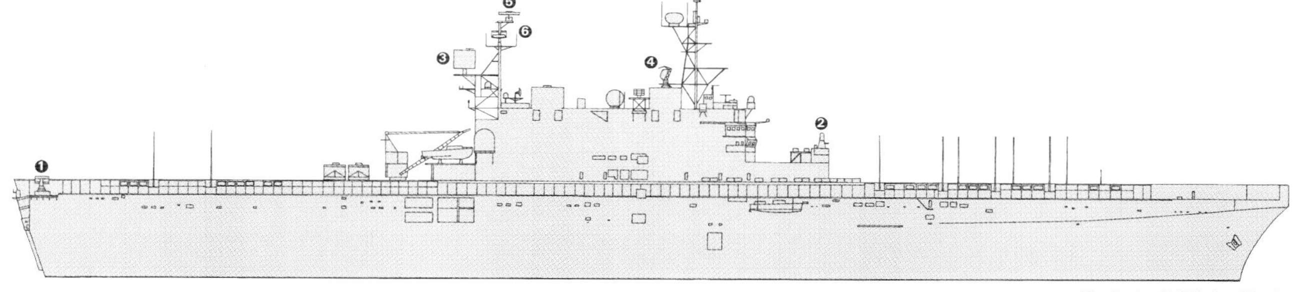

PELELIU *(Scale 1 : 1,500), Ian Sturton* / 0131369

PELELIU *11/2008*, US Navy* / 1353583

5 AUSTIN CLASS (AMPHIBIOUS TRANSPORT DOCKS) (LPD)

Name	*No*	*Builders*	*Laid down*	*Launched*	*Commissioned*	*F/S*
CLEVELAND	LPD 7	Ingalls Shipbuilding	30 Nov 1964	7 May 1966	21 Apr 1967	PA
DUBUQUE	LPD 8	Ingalls Shipbuilding	25 Jan 1965	6 Aug 1966	1 Sep 1967	PA
DENVER	LPD 9	Lockheed SB & Construction Co	7 Feb 1964	23 Jan 1965	26 Oct 1968	PA
NASHVILLE	LPD 13	Lockheed SB & Construction Co	14 Mar 1966	7 Oct 1967	14 Feb 1970	AA
PONCE	LPD 15	Lockheed SB & Construction Co	31 Oct 1966	20 May 1970	10 July 1971	AA

Displacement, tons: 9,130 light; 16,500–17,244 full load
Dimensions, feet (metres): 570 × 100 (84 hull) × 23 *(173.8 × 30.5; 25.6 × 7)*
Main machinery: 2 Foster-Wheeler boilers; 600 psi *(42.3 kg/cm²)*; 870°F *(467°C)*; 2 De Laval (General Electric in LPD 9 and LPD 10) turbines; 24,000 hp *(18 MW)*; 2 shafts
Speed, knots: 21. **Range, n miles:** 7,700 at 20 kt
Complement: 420 (24 officers); Flag 90 (in LPD 7-13)
Military lift: 930 troops (840 only in LPD 7-13); 9 LCM 6s or 4 LCM 8s or 2 LCAC or 20 LVTs. 4 LCPL/LCVP

Guns: 2 General Electric/General Dynamics 20 mm/76 6-barrelled Vulcan Phalanx Mk 15 ❶; 3,000 rds/min (4,500 in Block 1) combined to 1.5 km.
2—25 mm Mk 38. 8—12.7 mm MGs.
Countermeasures: Decoys: 4 Loral Hycor SRBOC 6-barrelled Mk 36; IR flares and chaff to 4 km *(2.2 n miles)*.
ESM: SLQ-32(V)1; intercept.
Combat data systems: SATCOM ❷, WSC-3 (UHF), WSC-6 (SHF) (see Data Systems at front of section).
Radars: Air search: Lockheed SPS-40E ❸; B-band.
Surface search: Norden SPS-67 ❹; G-band.
Navigation: Raytheon SPS-73(V)12; I-band.
Tacan: URN 25. IFF: Mk XII UPX-36.

Helicopters: Up to 6 CH-46D/E Sea Knight can be carried. Hangar for only 1 light.

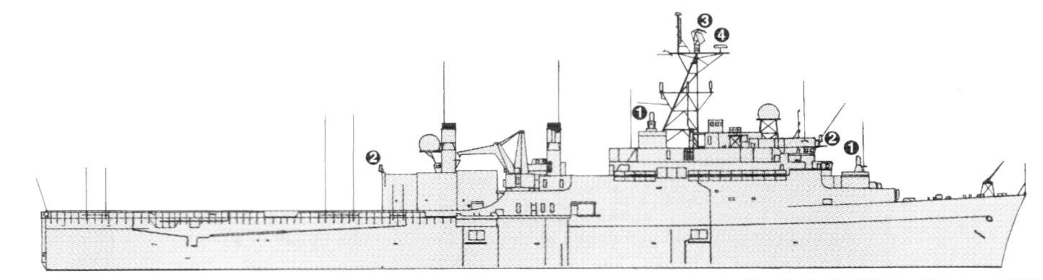
DENVER *(Scale 1 : 1,500), Ian Sturton* / 0016471

Programmes: LPD 7-10 authorised in FY63, LPD 13 in FY64, LPD 15 in FY65.
Modernisation: Modernisation carried out in normal maintenance periods from FY87. This included fitting two Phalanx, SPS-67 radar replacing SPS-10 and updating EW capability. 3 in guns have been removed. LPD 15 was the last LPD to receive machinery, electrical and habitability upgrades to extend life.
Structure: LPD 7-13 have an additional bridge and are fitted as flagships. One small telescopic hangar. There are structural variations in the positions of guns and electronic equipment in different ships of the class. Flight deck is 168 ft *(51.2 m)* in length. Well-deck 394 × 50 ft *(120.1 × 15.2 m)*. Communications domes are not uniformly fitted.
Operational: A typical operational load might include one Seahawk, two Sea Knight, two Twin Huey, four Sea Cobra helicopters and one Cyclone patrol craft. LPDs 7-9 based at San Diego and LPDs 13 and 15 at Norfolk. LPD 6 decommissioned in 2005, LPD 4 in 2006, LPDs 5 and 12 in 2007 and LPD 10 in 2008. LPD 14 transferred to the Indian Navy in January 2007. LPDs 9 and 13 to be decommissioned in 2009 and LPD 8 in 2010.

DENVER *7/2007, Guy Toremans* / 1305194

CLEVELAND *8/2005, John Mortimer* / 1154055

12 WHIDBEY ISLAND CLASS (DOCK LANDING SHIPS) (LSD)

Name	*No*	*Builders*	*Laid down*	*Launched*	*Commissioned*	*F/S*
WHIDBEY ISLAND	LSD 41	Lockheed SB & Construction Co	4 Aug 1981	10 June 1983	9 Feb 1985	AA
GERMANTOWN	LSD 42	Lockheed SB & Construction Co	5 Aug 1982	29 June 1984	8 Feb 1986	PA
FORT McHENRY	LSD 43	Lockheed SB & Construction Co	10 June 1983	1 Feb 1986	8 Aug 1987	PA
GUNSTON HALL	LSD 44	Avondale Industries	26 May 1986	27 June 1987	22 Apr 1989	AA
COMSTOCK	LSD 45	Avondale Industries	27 Oct 1986	16 Jan 1988	3 Feb 1990	PA
TORTUGA	LSD 46	Avondale Industries	23 Mar 1987	15 Sep 1988	17 Nov 1990	AA
RUSHMORE	LSD 47	Avondale Industries	9 Nov 1987	6 May 1989	1 June 1991	PA
ASHLAND	LSD 48	Avondale Industries	4 Apr 1988	11 Nov 1989	9 May 1992	AA
HARPERS FERRY	LSD 49	Avondale Industries	15 Apr 1991	16 Jan 1993	7 Jan 1995	PA
CARTER HALL	LSD 50	Avondale Industries	11 Nov 1991	2 Oct 1993	30 Sep 1995	AA
OAK HILL	LSD 51	Avondale Industries	21 Sep 1992	11 June 1994	8 June 1996	AA
PEARL HARBOR	LSD 52	Avondale Industries	27 Jan 1995	24 Feb 1996	30 May 1998	PA

Displacement, tons: 11,125 light; 15,939 (LSD 41-48), 16,740 (LSD 49 onwards) full load
Dimensions, feet (metres): 609.5 × 84 × 20.5 (*185.8 × 25.6 × 6.3*)
Main machinery: 4 Colt SEMT-Pielstick 16 PC2.5 V 400 diesels; 33,000 hp(m) (*24.6 MW*) sustained; 2 shafts; cp props
Speed, knots: 22
Range, n miles: 8,000 at 18 kt
Complement: 413 (21 officers)
Military lift: 402 (+102 surge) troops; 2 (CV) or 4 LCACs, or 9 (CV) or 21 LCM 6, or 1 (CV) or 3 LCUs, or 64 LVTs. 2 LCPL
Cargo capacity: 5,000 cu ft for marine cargo, 12,500 sq ft for vehicles (including four preloaded LCACs in the well-deck). The cargo version' has 67,600 cu ft for marine cargo, 20,200 sq ft for vehicles but only two LCACs. Aviation fuel, 90 tons.

Missiles: 1 GDC/Hughes Mk 49 RAM RIM-116 21-cell launcher ❶; passive IR/anti-radiation homing to 9.6 km (*5.2 n miles*) at 2.5 Mach; warhead 9.1 kg. Being fitted in all.
Guns: 2 General Electric/General Dynamics 20 mm/76 6-barrelled Vulcan Phalanx Mk 15 ❷; 3,000 rds/min (4,500 in Block 1) combined to 1.5 km.
2—25 mm Mk 38. 6—12.7 mm MGs.
Countermeasures: Decoys: 4 Loral Hycor SRBOC 6-barrelled Mk 36 and Mk 50; IR flares and chaff. SLQ-25 Nixie.
ESM: SLQ-32(V)1; intercept. SLQ-49.
Combat data systems: SATCOM SRR-1, WSC-3 (UHF) (see Data Systems at front of section). SSDS Mk 1.
Radars: Air search: Raytheon SPS-49(V)1 ❸; C-band.
Surface search: Norden SPS-67V ❹; G-band.
Navigation: Raytheon SPS-64(V)9 or SPS-73(V)12; I/J-band.
Tacan: URN 25. IFF: Mk XII UPX-29/UPX-36.

Helicopters: Platform only for 2 CH-53 Sea Stallion.

Programmes: Originally it was planned to construct six ships of this class as replacements for the Thomaston class LSDs. Eventually, the level of Whidbey Island class ships was established at eight, with four additional cargo-carrying variants to provide extra cargo capability. LSD 49-52 are also known as the Harper's Ferry class.
Modernisation: A Quick Reaction Combat Capability (QRCC)/Ship Self-Defense System (SSDS) was installed and successfully demonstrated in LSD 41 in 1993. During the QRCC demonstrations, the ship's SPS-49, SLQ-32, RAM and Phalanx were successfully integrated via SSDS. All ships of the class fitted with SSDS Mk 1. A mid-life upgrade package, to extend service life to 40 years, is planned for all LSD 41/49 class starting with LSD 44 in FY08.
Structure: Based on the earlier Anchorage class. One 60 and one 20 ton crane. Well-deck measures 440 × 50 ft (*134.1 × 15.2 m*) in the LSD but is shorter in the Cargo Variant (CV). The cargo version is a minimum modification to the LSD 41 design. Changes in that design include additional troop magazines, air conditioning, piping and hull structure; the forward Phalanx is forward of the bridge, RAM is on the bridge roof, and there is only one crane. There is approximately 90 per cent commonality between the two classes.
Operational: LSDs 41, 43, 44, 48, 49, 50 and 51 are based at Little Creek, VA. LSDs 42, 45, 47 and 52 are based at San Diego, CA. LSDs 46 and 49 are based at Sasebo, Japan.

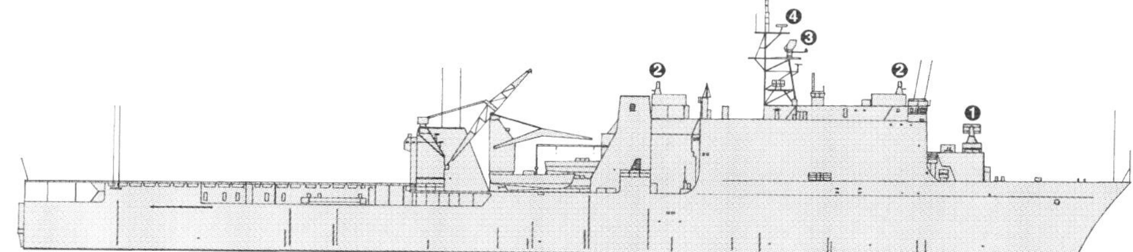

ASHLAND *(Scale 1 : 1,500)*, **Ian Sturton** / 0053362

CARTER HALL *11/2008*, Guy Toremans* / 1353581

GERMANTOWN *10/2007*, **Michael Nitz** / 1353580

COMSTOCK *7/2008*, US Navy* / 1353582

0 + 1 AMERICA CLASS (AMPHIBIOUS ASSAULT SHIP) (LHA)

Name	*No*	*Builders*	*Laid down*	*Launched*	*Commissioned*
AMERICA	LHA 6	Northrop Grumman Ship Systems, Pascagoula, MS	Apr 2009	2011	2012

Displacement, tons: 44,850 full load
Dimensions, feet (metres): 844 oa; 778 wl × 194 oa; 106 wl × 28.7 *(257.3; 237.1 × 59.1; 32.3 × 8.7)*
Flight deck, feet (metres): 819 × 118 *(249.6 × 36.0)*
Main machinery: COGES: 2 GE LM 2500+ gas turbines; 70,000 hp *(52.2 MW)*; 2 auxiliary propulsion motors; 10,000 hp *(7.46 MW)*; 2 shafts
Speed, knots: 22
Range, n miles: 9,000 at 12 kt
Complement: 1,059 (65 officers)
Military lift: 1,687 troops (plus 184 surge)

Missiles: SAM: 2 Raytheon GMLS Mk 29 octuple launchers; 16 Evolved Sea Sparrow RIM-162D; semi-active radar homing to 18 km *(9.7 n miles)* at 3.6 Mach; warhead 38 kg. 2 Raytheon RAM RIM-116 Mk 49 launchers; passive IR/anti-radiation homing to 9.6 km *(5.2 n miles)* at 2.5 Mach; warhead 9.1 kg.
Guns: 2 General Electric/General Dynamics 20 mm 6-barrelled Vulcan Phalanx Mk 15.
Countermeasures: Mk 53 Mod 3 NULKA DLS; SLQ-25 Nixie; acoustic torpedo decoy system.
ESM/ECM: SLQ-32B(V)2.
Combat data systems: SSDS Mk 2 Mod 4B, CEC USG-2A, Links 4A, 11 (modified), 16 and 22. SATCOMS: SSR-1, SRC-XX (UHF), USC-38 (EHF), URC-131(H)(HF), URC-139 (VHF) and 2 WSC-6C(V)9 (SHF). SMQ-11 Metsa. Advanced Field Artillery TDS.
Weapons control: NSSMS Mk 57 Mod 12 with 2 Mk 9 MFCS.
Radars: Air search: ITT SPS-48E(V)10; 3D; E/F-band; Raytheon SPS-49A(V)1; SPQ-9B.
Surface search/Navigation: 2 SPS-73; I-band.
CCA: SPN-35C and SPN-43C.
Tacan: URN 25. IFF: CIS UPX-29.

Fixed-wing aircraft: Similar to Wasp class with improved facilities to operate and support MV-22 Osprey and up to 23 F-35B Joint Strike Fighter (JSF).

Programmes: It was announced on 6 April 2004 that the LHA Replacement design was to be a modified version of the LHD 8 design. The detailed design phase started in January 2006 following ship design approval to proceed with Milestone B. A contract for the detailed design and construction of the first of class was let on 1 June 2007.
Structure: LHA Replacement is optimised for aviation operations and is to have additional cargo/magazine capacity in lieu of a traditional well deck. The flight deck has nine helicopter landing spots and is to be equipped with two aircraft elevators, one to starboard and aft of the island and one to port amidships; the folding capability has been removed. Cargo capacity is 160,000 cu ft total with an additional 12,000 sq ft to accommodate vehicle stowage. The ship is to be fitted with a 24 bed capacity hospital and two operating rooms. The bridge is two decks lower than that of an LHA 1; the command, control and communications spaces having been moved inside the hull. The ship has gas turbine propulsion and all electric auxiliaries.
Operational: Homeport is yet to be announced.

LHA(R) *6/2005, Northrop Grumman* / 1154062

80 LANDING CRAFT AIR CUSHION (LCAC)

Displacement, tons: 87.2 light; 170-182 full load
Dimensions, feet (metres): 88 oa (on-cushion) (81 between hard structures) × 47 beam (on-cushion) (43 beam hard structure) × 2.9 draught (off-cushion) *(26.8 (24.7) × 14.3 (13.1) × 0.9)*
Main machinery: 4 Allied-Signal TF40B marine gas turbines for propulsion and lift; 16,000 hp *(11.9 MW)* sustained; 2 shrouded reversible-pitch airscrews (propulsion); 4 double-entry fans, centrifugal or mixed-flow (lift). SLEP configuration, 4 Vericor Power Systems ETF40B marine gas turbines with Full Authority Digital Engine Control (FADEC) for propulsion and lift; 19,000 hp *(1.41 MW)* sustained; 2 shrouded reversible-pitch airscrews (propulsion); 4 double-entry fans, centrifugal or mixed-flow (lift)
Speed, knots: 40 (loaded)
Range, n miles: 300 at 35 kt; 200 at 40 kt
Complement: 5
Military lift: 23 troops; 1 Main Battle Tank or 60-75 tons
Radars: Navigation: Marconi LN66 or Decca Bridgemaster E; I-band.

LCAC 86 *6/2005, J Ciślak* / 1154056

Programmes: Built by Textron Marine and Land Systems and Avondale Gulfport. A total of 90 craft delivered 1984–1997. The final craft LCAC 91 delivered in 2001 in SLEP configuration.
Modernisation: 72 in-service craft to receive Service Life Extension Programme (SLEP) from 2002–2016. The programme includes the installation of more powerful engines to provide greater lift capacity, an improved deep skirt for better handling in heavier sea states and an integrated navigation suite for precise navigation, and advanced Multimode Integrated Communications System in either normal, secure modes. Four craft were upgraded in FY04, five in FY05, five in FY06 and the remainder planned for subsequent years.
Structure: Incorporates the best attributes of the JEFF(A) and JEFF(B) learned from over five years of testing the two prototypes. Bow ramp 28.8 ft, stern ramp 15 ft. Cargo space capacity is 1,809 sq ft. Noise and dust levels are high and if disabled the craft is not easy to tow. 30 mm Gatling guns can be fitted.
Operational: Ship classes capable of carrying the LCAC are Wasp (three), Tarawa (one), Austin (one), Whidbey Island (four), Harpers Ferry (two) and San Antonio (two). A portable transport module can be carried on the cargo deck to transport up to 180 troops. Some limitations in very rough seas. Shore bases on each coast at Little Creek, VA and Camp Pendleton, CA. Of 80 craft, 66 are operational and 14 undergoing SLEP.
Sales: Six to Japan. One of a similar type built by South Korea.

LCAC 81 *4/2008*, Hachiro Nakai* / 1353568

8 FRANK S BESSON CLASS
(LOGISTIC SUPPORT VESSELS) (LSV-ARMY)

Name	*No*	*Builders*	*Commissioned*
GEN FRANK S BESSON JR	LSV 1	Moss Point Marine, MS	18 Dec 1987
CW 3 HAROLD C CLINGER	LSV 2	Moss Point Marine, MS	20 Feb 1988
GEN BREHON B SOMERVELL	LSV 3	Moss Point Marine, MS	2 Apr 1988
LTG WILLIAM B BUNKER	LSV 4	Moss Point Marine, MS	18 May 1988
MG CHARLES P GROSS	LSV 5	Moss Point Marine, MS	30 Apr 1991
SP/4 JAMES A LOUX	LSV 6	Moss Point Marine, MS	16 Dec 1994
SSGT ROBERT T KURODA	LSV 7	VT Halter Marine	26 Aug 2006
MG ROBERT SMALLS	LSV 8	VT Halter Marine	15 Sep 2007

Displacement, tons: 4,265 full load
Dimensions, feet (metres): 272.8 × 60 × 12 *(83.1 × 18.3 × 3.7)*
314 (LSV 7) × 60.0 × 12.0 *(95.7 × 18.3 × 36.6)*
Main machinery: 2 GM EMD 16-645E2 diesels; 3,900 hp *(2.9 MW)* sustained; 2 shafts; Schottel bow thruster; 650 hp *(485 kW)*
Speed, knots: 11.6. **Range, n miles:** 8,300 at 11 kt
Complement: 31 (8 officers)
Military lift: 2,280 tons of vehicles including 26 M-1 tanks, containers or general cargo
Radars: Navigation: 2 Raytheon; E/F-band; I-band.

Comment: First one approved in FY85, second in FY87, remainder from Army reserve funds. Army owned ro-ro design with 10,500 sq ft of deck space for cargo. Capable of beaching with 4 ft over the ramp on a 1:30 offshore gradient. Payload is 2,000 tons of cargo. LSV 1 is based at Fort Eustis, Virginia, LSVs 2, 5 and 7 are based at Pearl Harbour, HI. LSV 3 is with the Army Reserve and based at Tacoma, WA. LSVs 4 and 6 are based in Kuwait. LSV 8 is based at Baltimore, MD. Two modified ships of the class built for the Philippines Navy in 1993–94.

CW 3 HAROLD C CLINGER *7/2002, **Chris Sattler*** / 0529979

39 MECHANISED LANDING CRAFT (LCM 6 TYPE)

Displacement, tons: 64 full load
Dimensions, feet (metres): 56.2 × 14 × 3.9 *(17.1 × 4.3 × 1.2)*
Main machinery: 2 Detroit 6V-71 diesels; 348 hp *(260 kW)* sustained or 2 Detroit 8V-71 diesels; 460 hp *(344 kW)* sustained; 2 shafts
Speed, knots: 9. **Range, n miles:** 130 at 9 kt
Complement: 5
Military lift: 34 tons or 80 troops

Comment: Welded steel construction. All used for various utility tasks, none as landing craft.

LCM 6 *6/1997, **J W Currie*** / 0016482

35 MECHANISED LANDING CRAFT: LCM 8 TYPE

Displacement, tons: 65.6 light; 127 full load
Dimensions, feet (metres): 73.7 × 21 × 5.2 *(22.5 × 6.4 × 1.6)*
Main machinery: 2 Detroit 12V-71 diesels; 400 hp *(298 kW)* sustained; 2 shafts; Kort nozzles
Speed, knots: 12. **Range, n miles:** 190 at 9 kt full load
Complement: 4
Military lift: 67.5 tons or 1 M48/1 M60 tank or 110 fully equipped troops or 200 non-combat troops

Comment: Eleven craft are for use in amphibious ships. There are 24 similar craft used by the Army.

LCM 8 *5/2003, **A Sharma*** / 0572786

35 LCU 2000 CLASS (UTILITY LANDING CRAFT) (LCU-ARMY)

RUNNYMEDE LCU 2001
KENNESAW MOUNTAIN LCU 2002
MACON LCU 2003
ALDIE LCU 2004
BRANDY STATION LCU 2005
BRISTOE STATION LCU 2006
BROAD RUN LCU 2007
BUENA VISTA LCU 2008
CALABOZA LCU 2009
CEDAR RUN LCU 2010
CHICKAHOMINY LCU 2011
CHICKASAW BAYOU LCU 2012
CHURUBUSCO LCU 2013
COAMO LCU 2014
CONTRERAS LCU 2015
CORINTH LCU 2016
EL CANEY LCU 2017
FIVE FORKS LCU 2018
FORT DONELSON LCU 2019
FORT MCHENRY LCU 2020
GREAT BRIDGE LCU 2021
HARPERS FERRY LCU 2022
HOBKIRK LCU 2023
HOMIGUEROS LCU 2024
MALVERN HILL LCU 2025
MATAMOROS LCU 2026
MECHANICSVILLE LCU 2027
MISSIONARY BRIDGE LCU 2028
MOLINO DEL RAY LCU 2029
MONTERREY LCU 2030
NEW ORLEANS LCU 2031
PALO ALTO LCU 2032
PAULUS HOOK LCU 2033
PERRYVILLE LCU 2034
PORT HUDSON LCU 2035

Displacement, tons: 1,102 full load
Dimensions, feet (metres): 173.8 × 42 × 8.5 *(53 × 12.8 × 2.6)*
Main machinery: 2 Cummins KTA50-M diesels; 2,500 hp *(1.87 MW)* sustained; 2 shafts; bow thruster
Speed, knots: 11.5
Range, n miles: 4,500 at 11.5 kt
Complement: 13 (2 officers)
Military lift: 350 tons
Radars: Navigation: 2 Raytheon; E/F-band; I-band.

Comment: Order placed with Lockheed by US Army 11 June 1986. First one completed 21 February 1990 by Moss Point Marine. The 2000 series have names, some of which duplicate naval ships. These are the first LCUs built to an Army specification. Seven are active, seven in reserve, 20 prepositioned and one used for training.

HOMIGUEROS *7/2003, **A Sharma*** / 0572813

MOLINO DEL RAY *6/2003, **A Sharma*** / 0572815

10 LANDING CRAFT (MPF TYPE)

Displacement, tons: 12.3
Dimensions, feet (metres): 44.1 ×14.5 × ? *(13.4 × 4.4 × ?)*
Main machinery: 2 Cummins QSM11 diesels; 660 hp *(492 kW)*; 2 Hamilton 364 waterjets
Speed, knots: 30 (light); 25 (full load)
Complement: 4
Guns: 2—12.7 mm MGs.
Radars: Navigation: Furuno 1834; I-band.

Comment: Contract for the construction of 10 MPF utility craft awarded to Kvichak Marine Industries, Seattle, WA, in August 2005. First craft delivered in February 2006. The craft are to replace the LCM-8 craft as part of the lighterage system in support of prepositioned Marine amphibious assault missions. Aluminium construction with an articulated bow-door for beach deployment. Two are stationed at San Diego, CA, two at Norfolk, VA, and six onboard prepositioned MSC ships. Each craft can transport 30 troops and equipment.

MPF CRAFT *6/2007, **Kvichak Marine*** / 1305174

75 LANDING CRAFT PERSONNEL (LCPL)

Displacement, tons: 11 full load
Dimensions, feet (metres): 36 × 12.1 × 3.8 *(11 × 3.7 × 1.2)*
Main machinery: 1 GM 8V-71TI diesel; 425 hp *(317 kW)* sustained; 1 shaft
Speed, knots: 20. **Range, n miles:** 150 at 20 kt
Complement: 3
Military lift: 17 troops
Radars: Navigation: Marconi LN66; I-band.

Comment: There are four variants of this craft: Mk 11, Mk 12, Mk 13 and 11 m LCPLs. Details given are for Mk 12 and 13. For use as control craft and carried aboard LHA, LPD and LSD classes.

LCPL Mk 13 *4/1991, Bollinger* / 0084143

34 LCU 1600 CLASS
(UTILITY LANDING CRAFT) (LCU-ARMY (2) AND NAVY (32))

Displacement, tons: 200 light; 375 full load
Dimensions, feet (metres): 134.9 × 29 × 6.1 *(41.1 × 8.8 × 1.9)*
Main machinery: 2 Detroit 12V-71 diesels; 400 hp *(298 kW)* sustained; 2 shafts; Kort nozzles
Speed, knots: 11. **Range, n miles:** 1,200 at 8 kt
Complement: 14 (2 officers)
Military lift: 134 tons; 3 M103 (64 tons), 2 M1A1 tanks or 350 troops
Guns: 4—12.7 mm MGs.
Radars: Navigation: Furuno; I-band.

Comment: Steel hulled construction. Versatile craft used for a variety of tasks. Most were built between the mid-1960s and mid-1980s. There are no plans for more of this type and a replacement craft is under consideration. Three converted to Diver Support Craft (ASDV). LCU 1667 and 1675 operated by the US Army. Two USN craft are in reserve. It is planned to reduce US Navy inventory to 28.

LCU 1600 class (Army) *2/2001, M Declerck* / 0529975

LCU 1632 *11/2008*, US Navy* / 1353636

MINE WARFARE FORCES

Notes: (1) There are no surface minelayers. Mining is done by carrier-based aircraft, land-based aircraft and submarines. The mine inventory includes Mk 56 moored influence mines, the Mk 67 submarine launched mobile mine (SLMM) and the Quickstrike series of bottom mines. Mk 56 is being phased out.
(2) NRF ships are manned by active and reserve crews.
(3) MH-53E Sea Stallion helicopters can be deployed in LHDs or transported by C-5 aircraft for mine countermeasures.
(4) The Long-term Mine Reconnaissance System (LMRS) (AN/BLQ-11), developed by Boeing, is being used as a risk reduction vehicle for the US Navy's 21 in Mission Reconfigurable Unmanned Undersea Vehicle System (MRUUV). This programme is to develop and procure a modular UUV capable of supporting multiple payloads, reconfigurable for mine countermeasures; intelligence, surveillance and reconnaissance; and other missions. The first submerged operation of two UUVs conducted from SSN 768 in October 2007. The UUVs form part of LMRS.
(5) Marine Mammal Systems (MMS) uses trained dolphins and sea lions for mine detection, detection of unauthorised swimmers, protection of fleet assets in port and critical infrastructure, and recovery of exercise mines and torpedoes. The dolphins can be transported by C-5 aircraft or amphibious ships. MMS is the only operational method of detecting and neutralising buried mines.
(6) The AN/WLD1 Remote Minehunting System (RMS) is an off-board minehunting system that will reside with a forward deployed battle group. Approved for low-rate production, RMS is comprised of a 14,500 lb diesel-powered semi-submersible (the Remote Minehunting Vehicle) combined with the towed AN/AQS-20A Sonar Mine Detecting Set. The vehicle tows variable depth sensor to detect, localise and classify bottom mines and moored mines. System includes line-of-sight and over-the horizon real-time data links, shipboard launch and recovery subsystem, and a software segment that integrates AN/WLD-1(V)1 into the ship's AN/SQQ-89(V)15 Undersea Warfare Combat System. RMS can conduct real-time detection and processing when using line-of sight communications. RMS will be deployed on Flight IIA Arleigh Burke-class DDGs as well as from the new Littoral Combat Ship (LCS) seaframes (where RMS forms part of the LCS Mine Warfare Mission Package) which was rolled out in September 2008. Installation of first system completed January 2007 aboard *Bainbridge* DDG 96.
(7) Rapid Airborne Mine Clearance System (RAMICS) is under development. RAMICS is to be operated from a MH-60S helicopter and consists of an electro-optic detection and ranging system and a 30 mm gun system to destroy near-surface and floating moored mines.
(8) Organic Airborne and Surface Influence Sweep (OASIS) is being developed for deployment from MH-60S helicopters, and selected surface craft. OASIS will provide organic, high-speed magnetic and acoustic influence minesweeping capability.

14 AVENGER CLASS (MINESWEEPERS/MINEHUNTERS) (MCM/MHSO)

Name	*No*	*Builders*	*Laid down*	*Launched*	*Commissioned*	*F/S*
AVENGER	MCM 1	Peterson Builders Inc	3 June 1983	15 June 1985	12 Sep 1987	NRF
DEFENDER	MCM 2	Marinette Marine Corp	1 Dec 1983	4 Apr 1987	30 Sep 1989	NRF
SENTRY	MCM 3	Peterson Builders Inc	8 Oct 1984	20 Sep 1986	2 Sep 1989	NRF
CHAMPION	MCM 4	Marinette Marine Corp	28 June 1984	15 Apr 1989	27 July 1991	NRF
GUARDIAN	MCM 5	Peterson Builders Inc	8 May 1985	20 June 1987	16 Dec 1989	PA
DEVASTATOR	MCM 6	Peterson Builders Inc	9 Feb 1987	11 June 1988	6 Oct 1990	AA
PATRIOT	MCM 7	Marinette Marine Corp	31 Mar 1987	15 May 1990	18 Oct 1991	PA
SCOUT	MCM 8	Peterson Builders Inc	8 June 1987	20 May 1989	15 Dec 1990	PA
PIONEER	MCM 9	Peterson Builders Inc	5 June 1989	25 Aug 1990	7 Dec 1992	AA
WARRIOR	MCM 10	Peterson Builders Inc	25 Sep 1989	8 Dec 1990	3 Apr 1993	AA
GLADIATOR	MCM 11	Peterson Builders Inc	7 July 1990	29 June 1991	18 Sep 1993	NRF
ARDENT	MCM 12	Peterson Builders Inc	22 Oct 1990	16 Nov 1991	18 Feb 1994	AE
DEXTROUS	MCM 13	Peterson Builders Inc	11 Mar 1991	20 June 1992	9 July 1994	AE
CHIEF	MCM 14	Peterson Builders Inc	19 Aug 1991	12 June 1993	5 Nov 1994	AA

Displacement, tons: 1,379 full load
Dimensions, feet (metres): 224.3 × 38.9 × 12.2 *(68.4 × 11.9 × 3.7)*
Main machinery: 4 Waukesha L-1616 diesels (MCM 1-2); 2,600 hp(m) *(1.91 MW)* or 4 Isotta Fraschini ID 36 SS 6V AM diesels (MCM 3 onwards); 2,280 hp(m) *(1.68 MW)* sustained; 2 Hansome Electric motors; 400 hp(m) *(294 kW)* for hovering; 2 shafts; cp props; 1 Omnithruster hydrojet; 350 hp *(257 kW)*
Speed, knots: 13.5. **Range, n miles:** 2,500 at 10 kt
Complement: 84 (8 officers)

Guns: 2—12.7 mm MGs.
Countermeasures: MCM: 2 SLQ-48; includes Honeywell/Hughes ROV mine neutralisation system, capable of 6 kt (1,500 m cable with cutter (MP1), and countermining charge) (MP 2). SLQ-37(V)3; magnetic/acoustic influence sweep equipment. Oropesa SLQ-38 Type 0 Size 1; mechanical sweep.
Combat data systems: SATCOM SRR-1; WSC-3 (UHF). GEC/Marconi Nautis M in last two ships includes SSN 2 PINS command system and control. USQ-119E(V), UHF Dama and OTCIXS provide JMCIS connectivity.
Radars: Surface search: ISC Cardion SPS-55; I/J-band.
Navigation: ARPA 2525 or LN66; I-band. Both to be replaced by SPS-73.
Sonars: Raytheon/Thomson Sintra SQQ-32(V)3; VDS; active minehunting; high frequency.

Programmes: The contract for the prototype MCM was awarded in June 1982. The last three were funded in FY90.

SCOUT *10/2008*, Shaun Jones* / 1353635

Modernisation: Integrated Ship Control System (ISCS) installed in all hulls.
Structure: The hull is constructed of oak, Douglas fir and Alaskan cedar, with a thin coating of fibreglass on the outside, to permit taking advantage of wood's low magnetic signature. A problem of engine rotation on the Waukesha diesels in MCM 1-2 was resolved; however, those engines have been replaced in the rest of the class by low magnetic engines manufactured by Isotta-Fraschini of Milan, Italy. Fitted with SSN2(V) Precise Integrated Navigation System (PINS).
Operational: *Avenger* fitted with the SQQ-32 for Gulf operations in 1991 and all of the class have been retrofitted. Two transferred to NRF in 1995, two more in 1996 and a fifth in October 2000. *Scout* and *Dextrous* permanently stationed in Bahrain, and *Guardian* and *Patriot* are at Sasebo, Japan. The remainder are based at Ingleside, Texas. Ingleside-based ships are to be homeported at San Diego by 2009.

RESEARCH SHIPS

Notes: (1) There are many naval associated research vessels which are civilian manned and not carried on the US Naval Vessel Register. In addition civilian ships are leased for short periods to support a particular research project or trial. Some of those employed include *RSB-1* (missile booster recovery), *Acoustic Pioneer* and *Acoustic Explorer* (acoustic research).
(2) The stealth ship prototype *Sea Shadow* was de-activated in 2006 and may be converted into a museum.

ACOUSTIC EXPLORER *10/2007, Michael Nitz* / 1353634

1 EXPERIMENTAL CATAMARAN (X-CRAFT) (AGE)

SEA FIGHTER FSF-1

Displacement, tons: 1,025 standard; 1,400 full load
Dimensions, feet (metres): 269 × 72.2 × 11.5 *(82.0 × 22.0 × 3.5)*
Main machinery: CODOG; 2 GE LM 2500 gas turbines; 60,000 hp *(44.7 MW)*; 2 MTU 16V595 diesels; 11,585 hp *(8.6 MW)*; four Rolls-Royce Kamewa 125 SII waterjets
Speed, knots: 50. **Range, n miles:** 4,000 at 20 kt
Complement: 17
Radars: Navigation: I-band.
Helicopters: Platform for 1 SH-60R.

Comment: In September 2002, the Office of Naval Research selected Titan Corporation of San Diego, California and Nigel Gee and Associates LTD of Southampton, UK to design an experimental vessel known as X-CRAFT. A contract for development and build of the vessel was awarded in February 2003. The keel was laid in June 2003 and the vessel was launched in February 2005 at Nichols Brothers Boat Builders in Whidbey Island, Washington. The vessel, an aluminium-hulled, wave-piercing catamaran, was delivered to the Navy in May 2005. Multipurpose stern ramp, with direct access to the mission bay, allows launch and recover of manned and unmanned surface and sub-surface vehicles. Flight deck has dual landing spots for two MH-60 helicopters or UAV. Between May 2005 and September 2006 the vessel was stationed in San Diego and manned by a combined Navy/Coast Guard crew to evaluate experimental manning an operational concepts. In October 2006 a civilian crew assumed operations and maintenance of the vessel. In March 2006 the homeport was changed from San Diego to Panama City, Florida where it is used as a test platform for at-sea science and technology experimentation and advanced concept demonstrations. Modifications to reduce ship signature as well as improvements to hull, mechanical and electrical capabilities were to be completed in April 2009.

SEAFIGHTER *10/2005, US Navy* / 1123764

1 EXPERIMENTAL SWATH (AGE)

STILETTO

Displacement, tons: 60 full load
Dimensions, feet (metres): 87.9 × 40.0 × 2.5 *(26.8 × 12.2 × 0.76)*
Main machinery: 4 Caterpillar diesels; 6,600 hp *(4.9 MW)*; 4 surface piercing propellers
Speed, knots: 50
Complement: 35
Radars: Navigation: To be announced.
Helicopters: Platform for 2 SH-60R.

Programmes: Developed by the Office of Force Transformation to act as a testbed for new technologies and to evaluate the potential uses of innovative hullforms. The ship was designed by M Ship Company of San Diego, California and constructed in 15 months by Knight & Carver Yacht Center, National City, CA. The ship was delivered in 2006 and trials (including mine warfare and special operations) are expected to last several years.
Structure: Small Water Area Twin Hull (SWATH) design of lightweight all-carbon composite construction. Multiple hulls reduce drag and generate hydrodynamic lift. The ship is capable of launching/recovering an 11 m RIB via a stern ramp and can also act as a platform for UAVs. In addition, the craft includes an 'electronic keel' which enables mission planning modules to be installed and networked.
Operational: The craft took part in Exercise Trident Warrior in August 2006. The craft was shipped to Norfolk, VA, in late 2006 where it is now based.

STILETTO *5/2006, US Navy* /1167633

0 + 1 EXPERIMENTAL CATAMARAN (AGE)

SUSITNA

Displacement, tons: 987 full load
Dimensions, feet (metres): 195.0 × 60.0 × 12.1 (SWATH); 4.8 (barge) *(59.7 × 18.3 × 3.7; 1.5)*
Main machinery: 4 MTU 12V 4000 diesels; 4 Wärtsilä waterjets
Speed, knots: 22. **Range, n miles:** 200 at 20 kt

Programmes: Originally developed by Lockheed Martin as the Varicraft concept, it attracted Congressional interest as a transformational technology and later became known as Expeditionary Craft (E-Craft). Sponsored jointly by the Office of Naval Research and Alaska's Matunuska Susitna Borough, the keel was laid at Alaska Ship and Drydock Inc at Ketchikan, AK, on 24 August 2006. When completed in 2010, the E-craft is to be operated as a ferry between Anchorage and Port Mackenzie while also serving as a three-year technology demonstrator to support expeditionary logistic-support concepts.
Structure: The ship has a reconfigurable hull form that has three modes of operation. A catamaran mode is for high-speeds, a Small-Water-Area Twin Hull (SWATH) mode is for stability in high sea states and a shallow draft landing-craft (barge) mode is for manoeuvring in shallow water. In addition the ship is claimed to be the world's first ice-breaking twin-hulled vessel. The ship's centre deck can be raised and lowered hydraulically while the buoyancy of the catamaran hulls can be adjusted while underway. The ship is designed as half scale of a potential future military vessel and is to be capable of carrying up to 150 passengers and 20 cars.

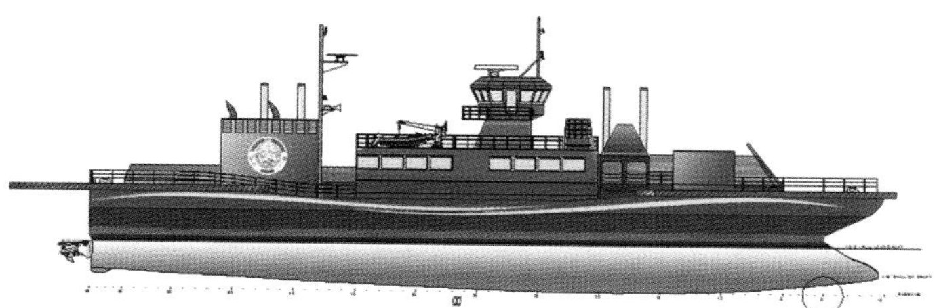

SUSITNA *2/2007, US Navy* / 1185948

1 ELECTRIC SHIP DEMONSTRATOR

SEA JET

Displacement, tons: 120 full load
Dimensions, feet (metres): 133 × ? × ? *(40.5 × ? × ?)*
Main machinery: 720-cell lead-acid battery bank; 2,690 hp *(2 MW)*; 2 motors; 2 AWJ-21 waterjets; 1 Caterpillar C9 diesel generator; 335 hp *(250 kW)*
Speed, knots: 16
Range, n miles: 200 at 8 kt
Complement: 3
Radars: Navigation: Furuno 1933C; I-band.

Comment: An Advanced Electric Ship Demonstrator (AESD) designed to test and develop electric ship and propulsor technologies. Funded by the Office of Naval Research, the craft is an approximately quarter-scale version of a destroyer-sized surface ship with tumblehome hullform. Its first task wasto test Rolls Royce Naval Marine's AWJ-21 waterjet technology. Testing of the General Dynamics RIMJET podded propulsor began in March 2008. Other technologies, such as low signature superstructure, are also to be trialled. The vessel was built by Dakota Creek Industries, Anacortes, WA, and is located at the Naval Surface Warfare Center Carderock Division, Acoustic Research Detachment in Bayview, Idaho. The vessel started trials on Lake Pend Oreille on 30 November 2005.

SEA JET *6/2005, US Navy* / 1116518

2 ASHEVILLE CLASS (YFRT)

ATHENA (ex-*Chehalis*) **ATHENA II** (ex-*Grand Rapids*)

Displacement, tons: 235 full load
Dimensions, feet (metres): 164.5 × 23.8 × 9.5 *(50.1 × 7.3 × 2.9)*
Main machinery: CODOG; 1 GE LM 1500 gas-turbine; 12,500 hp *(9.3 MW)*; 2 Cummins VT12-875 diesels; 1,450 hp *(1.07 MW)*; 2 shafts; cp props
Speed, knots: 16. **Range, n miles:** 1,700 at 16 kt
Complement: 22

Comment: Both built 1969–71. Work for the Naval Surface Warfare Center, at Panama City, Florida. Disarmed. *Lauren* was decommissioned in 2007 and is to be sunk as a target.

ATHENA II *6/1993, Giorgio Arra* / 0506179

RESEARCH OCEANOGRAPHIC SHIPS

2 MELVILLE CLASS (AGOR)

Name	*No*	*Builders*	*Commissioned*	*F/S*
MELVILLE	AGOR 14	Defoe SB Co, Bay City, MI	27 Aug 1969	Loan
KNORR	AGOR 15	Defoe SB Co, Bay City, MI	14 Jan 1970	Loan

Displacement, tons: 2,944 full load
Dimensions, feet (metres): 278.9 × 46.3 × 16.5 *(85 × 14.1 × 5.0)*
Main machinery: Diesel-electric; 3 Caterpillar 3516 diesel generators; 1 Caterpillar 3508 diesel generator; 2 motor-driven Z-drive azimuth thrusters; 3,000 hp *(2.2 MW)*; 1 bow thruster; 900 hp *(670 kW)*
Speed, knots: 14. **Range, n miles:** 10,060 at 11.7 kt
Complement: 23 (9 officers) plus 38 scientists
Sonars: Deep-water multibeam; sub-bottom profiler; Acoustic Doppler Current Profiler.

Comment: *Melville* operated by Scripps Institution of Oceanography and *Knorr* by Woods Hole Oceanography Institution for the Office of Naval Research, under technical control of the Oceanographer of the Navy. Fitted with internal wells for lowering equipment and observation ports. Problems with the propulsion system led to major modifications including electric drive (vice the original mechanical) and the insertion of a 34 ft central section increasing the displacement from the original 1,915 tons and allowing better accommodation and improved laboratory spaces. The forward propeller is retractable. These ships are highly manoeuvrable for precise position keeping.

MELVILLE *3/2003*, ***Robert Pabst*** / 0572738

1 AGOR-26 CLASS (AGOR)

Name	*No*	*Builders*	*Commissioned*
KILO MOANA	AGOR 26	Atlantic Marine, Jacksonville	3 Sep 2002

Displacement, tons: 2,542 full load
Dimensions, feet (metres): 186 × 88 × 25 *(56.7 × 26.8 × 7.6)*
Main machinery: Diesel-electric; 4 Caterpillar 3508B diesel generators; 2 Westinghouse motors; 4,025 hp *(3 MW)*; 1 bow thruster 1,100 hp *(820 kW)*
Speed, knots: 15. **Range, n miles:** 10,000 at 11 kt
Complement: 48 (31 scientists)

Comment: Replacement for R/V *Moana Wave*. Designed to commercial standards and constructed by Atlantic Marine, Jacksonville. Launched on 17 November 2001. The ship is a small waterplane area, twin hull (SWATH) oceanographic vessel capable of performing general purpose oceanographic research in coastal and deep ocean areas. The University of Hawaii School of Ocean and Earth Science and Technology operates the ship under a charter agreement for the Office of Naval Research (ONR). The survey suite consists of a Kongsberg EM 120 multibeam echosounder (12 kHz), a Kongsberg EM 1002 shallow water echo sounder (95 kHz), a Workhorse Mariner 300 kHz current profiler and an Ocean Surveyor 38 kHz current profiler.

KILO MOANA *6/2004*, ***University of Hawaii Marine Center*** / 1043633

3 THOMAS G THOMPSON CLASS (AGOR)

Name	*No*	*Builders*	*Launched*	*Commissioned*	*F/S*
THOMAS G THOMPSON	AGOR-23	Halter Marine	27 July 1990	8 July 1991	Loan
ROGER REVELLE	AGOR-24	Halter Marine	20 Apr 1995	11 June 1996	Loan
ATLANTIS	AGOR-25	Halter Marine	1 Feb 1996	3 Mar 1997	Loan

Displacement, tons: 3,400 full load
Dimensions, feet (metres): 274 oa; 246.8 wl × 52.5 × 19 *(83.5; 75.2 × 16 × 5.6)*
Main machinery: Diesel-electric; 6 Caterpillar diesel generators; 6.65 MW (3-1.5 MW and 3-715 kW); 2 motors; 6,000 hp *(4.48 MW)*; 2 Z-drives; bow thruster; 1,140 hp *(850 kW)*
Speed, knots: 15. **Range, n miles:** 15,000 at 12 kt
Complement: 22 plus 37 scientists
Sonars: Various multibeam seafloor mapping sonars and sub-bottome and Acoustic Doppler Current Profiling systems.

Comment: *Thomas G Thompson* was the first of a class of oceanographic research vessels capable of operating worldwide in all seasons and suitable for use by navy laboratories, contractors and academic institutions. Dynamic positioning system enables precise station-keeping. 4,000 sq ft of laboratories. AGORs 23, 24 and 25 are operated by academic institutions for the Office of Naval Research through charter party agreements (AGOR 23-University of Washington; AGOR 24-Scripps Institution of Oceanography; AGOR 25-Woods Hole Oceanographic Institution). Ships in this series are able to meet changing oceanographic requirements for general-purpose, year-round, worldwide research. This includes launching, towing and recovering a variety of equipment. The ships are also involved in hydrographic data collection. *Atlantis* is the support vessel for human-occupied research submersibles operated by the National Deep Submergence Facility.

THOMAS G THOMPSON *6/2004*, ***Mitsuhiro Kadota*** / 1043632

HIGH SPEED VESSELS

Notes: The T-Craft (Transformation Craft) program was launched by the Office of Naval Research in 2008 with the award of contracts to three shipbuilders: Umoe Mandal, Alion Science and Technology, and Textron Marine and Land. The requirement is to design and build prototype vessels that combine surface-effect and hovercraft capabilities. The T-Craft would be an upgrade to US Navy's current inventory of air-cushioned LCACs which have limited range, relatively small cargo capacity and are not designed for open ocean deployment. The vessel is to be high-speed (up to 40 kt), wave-skimming vessel able to cross oceans, ferry supplies from ship to shore, and transform into hovercraft with capability to slide ashore. The vessel, up to about 85 m long, would have a range of 2,500 n miles at 20 kt in transit mode. Prototypes are to be ready for testing in 2010 and the competition winner may receive a contract to build the first of class.

1 HIGH SPEED VESSEL (HSV/MCS)

SWIFT HSV-2

Displacement, tons: 1,800
Dimensions, feet (metres): 318.9 × 88.6 × 11.3 *(97.2 × 27.0 × 3.4)*
Main machinery: 4 Caterpillar 3618 diesels; 38,620 hp *(28.8 MW)*; 4 LIPS 150D waterjets
Speed, knots: 42 (light); 38 (full load)
Range, n miles: 2,400 at 35 kt
Complement: 17 civilian, 20 military
Military lift: 500 tons cargo and 325 personnel
Helicopters: Platform for AH-1, MH/SH-60, UH-1 or CH-46.

Comment: Built as *Incat 61* (Incat Evolution 10B) of aluminium construction. HSV-2 was under bareboat charter before being placed under long-term charter for up to five years from November 2008 to Military Sealift Command. The role of the ship is to conduct specialised missions worldwide. These have included deployment to the Horn of Africa, the Persian Gulf and Southeast Asia. *Swift* support relief operations in the US Gulf Coast region following hurricane Katrina. In 2007, the vessel served as the platform for an experiment for the Global Fleet Station concept, deploying to the Caribbean and South America.

SWIFT *2/2004*, ***US Navy*** / 1043637

1 HIGH SPEED VESSEL (HSV)

WESTPAC EXPRESS HSV 4676

Displacement, tons: 1,464
Dimensions, feet (metres): 331.4 × 87.4 × 13.8 *(101.0 × 26.65 × 4.2)*
Main machinery: 4 Caterpillar 3618 diesels; 38,620 hp *(28.8 MW)*; 4 Kamewa waterjets
Speed, knots: 40
Range, n miles: 1,100 at 35 kt
Military lift: 550 tonnes of equipment and 970 personnel

Comment: Following trials which started in July 2001, chartered by Military Sealift Command from Austal Ships, West Australia. The current charter was extended in February 2007 for up to 59 months. Aluminium construction. Employed by US Marine Corps Third Expeditionary Force (III MEF) to transport equipment and troops from Okinawa for training exercises in Yokohama, Guam and other regional destinations. The benefits include reduced dependence on and cost of airlift. The vessel will retain commercial livery and markings. Based at Okinawa.

WESTPAC EXPRESS *8/2001*, ***Mitsuhiro Kadota*** / 0131282

0 + 1 (9) JOINT HIGH SPEED VESSELS (TSV)

Displacement, tons: To be announced
Dimensions, feet (metres): 337.9 × 93.5 × 12.6 *(103.0 × 28.5 × 3.83)*
Main machinery: 4 MTU 20V8000 M71L diesels; 48,800 hp *(36.4 MW)*; 4 Wärtsilä WLD 1400 SR waterjets
Speed, knots: 43
Range, n miles: 1,200 at 35 kt
Military lift: 150 toops + 312 troops (seated) + 635 tonnes of equipment
Helicopters: Platform for one CH-53E.

Comment: The Joint High Speed Vessel (JHSV) Program is for 10 high-speed intra-theatre connector vessels. This program was initiated following signature of a Memorandum of Agreement (MOA) with the US Army which married the Army's Theater Support Vessel (TSV) program with the Navy's High Speed Connector (HSC) program. Acquisition for JHSV is under the auspices of the Navy's Program Executive Office, Ships, but each service is to fund procurement and life-cycle costs of its own ships. Contracts for the preliminary design of JHSV were awarded to Austal USA, Bath Iron Works and Bollinger Shipyards (teamed with Incat) on 31 January 2008. On 13 November 2008, the Navy awarded Austal USA a fixed-price incentive contract for detailed design and construction of one vessel. The contract includes priced options for the construction of up to nine additional ships and associated shore-based spares. The semi-SWATH catamaran design ship is of aluminium construction and has an articulated slewing stern ramp. The first vessel, for the Army, is to be delivered in 2011.

JHSV (artist's impression) *11/2008**, ***Austal Ships*** / 1353633

DEEP SUBMERGENCE VEHICLES

(Included in US Naval Vessel Register)
Notes: (1) Deep submergence vehicles and other craft and support ships are operated by Submarine Development Squadron Five (CSDS-5) Deep Submergence Unit (DSU) in San Diego, California. The Squadron is a Major Command that includes advanced diving equipment, divers trained in 'saturation' techniques. DSV-2 is in an inactive lay-up condition. Two unmanned vessels CURV (Cable Controlled Underwater Remote Vehicle) Super Scorpios made test dives to 5,000 ft *(1,524 m)*.
(2) The Supervisor of Salvage and Diving operates four additional Navy ROVs. They are all air-transportable and can be operated from a variety of warships and commercial vessels.

1 CUTTHROAT CLASS (DSV)

Name	*No*	*Builders*	*Commissioned*
CUTTHROAT	LSV-2	Newport News Shipbuilding and General Dynamics Electric Boat Division	Apr 2001

Displacement, tons: 205
Dimensions, feet (metres): 111 × 10 × 9 *(33.8 × 3.1 × 2.7)*
Main machinery: Permanent Magnet electric motor; 3,000 hp(m) *(2.23 MW)*
Speed, knots: 34 dived

Comment: The contract was placed with Newport News and Electric Boat in January 1999 to build *Cutthroat* LSV-2. The largest autonomous unmanned submarine in the world, it is a 1:3.4 scaled-down model of the Virginia-class submarine used to test advanced submarine technologies, including hydro-acoustics, hydrodynamics and manoeuvring. Its diving depth matches that of the Virginia class. The forward compartment contains 1,680 lead acid batteries and the after compartment contains the propulsion and auxiliary systems together with data recording and control systems. All appendages, including control surfaces and simulated sonar fairing, can be removed or relocated. LSV-2 is operated by the Acoustic Research Detachment at the instrumented range at Lake Pend Oreille in Bayview, Idaho. It is named after a species of trout indigenous to the lake.

CUTTHROAT *2000*, ***Newport News*** / 0105821

1 DEEP SUBMERGENCE VEHICLE: ALVIN TYPE (DSV)

Name	*No*	*Builders*	*F/S*
– (ex-*Alvin*)	DSV 2	General Mills Inc, Minneapolis	PSA

Displacement, tons: 18 full load
Dimensions, feet (metres): 26.5 × 8.5 *(8.1 × 2.6)*
Main machinery: 6 brushless DC motors; 6 thrusters; 2 vertical-motion thrusters (located near the centre of gravity); 2 horizontally (near stern) (1 directed athwartships, 1 directed longitudinally); 2 on rotatable shaft near stern for vertical or longitudinal motion
Speed, knots: 2
Range, n miles: 3 at 0.5 kt
Complement: 3 (1 pilot, 2 observers)

Comment: Ex-*Alvin* was built for operation by the Woods Hole Oceanographic Institution for the Office of Naval Research. Named for Allyn C Vine of Woods Hole Oceanographic Institution, the original configuration had an operating depth of 6,000 ft. Ex-*Alvin* accidentally sank in 5,051 ft of water on 16 October 1968, was subsequently raised in August 1969 and refurbished in 1970–71 to its original configuration. Placed in Naval service on 1 June 1971, she was subsequently refitted with a titanium pressure sphere to provide increased depth capability. Ex-*Alvin* has an operating depth of 4,500 m *(14,764 ft)* and is powered by two banks of lead-acid batteries providing a 120 V DC system with 47 kW/h of capacity. In October 2005, after conducting dive number 4,162, ex-*Alvin* was overhauled and provided with upgraded equipment. The National Science Foundation is funding a replacement, capable of depths of 6,500 m which is expected to become operational in 2010. Two other DSVs were placed out of service in 1997/98, one transferred to the Woods Hole Institute.

DSV 2 *10/2003*, ***Rod Catanach, Woods Hole Oceanographic Institution*** / 0009310

1 PRESSURIZED RESCUE MODULE

Displacement, tons: To be announced
Dimensions, feet (metres): To be announced
Main machinery: To be announced
Speed, knots: To be announced
Complement: To be announced

Comment: The Submarine Rescue, Diving and Recompression System (SRDRS) replaced DSRV on 1 October 2008. It consists of three principal components: a Pressurized Rescue Module (PRM), Submarine Decompression System (SDS) and an Atmospheric Diving Suit (ADS). The PRM is a tethered, remotely operated submersible launched and controlled from a vessel of opportunity in up to Sea State 4. It has a cylindrical hull on which navigation, video, propulsion, and life support systems are mounted externally. The vehicle is designed for submerged transit to a depth of 2,000 ft *(610 m)* of sea water, for docking and mating (up to a 45° angle) to a disabled submarine (DISSUB) and for evacuation and transfer of up to 16 rescued personnel directly to the Submarine Decompression Chambers (SDCs) into which rescued personnel can be transferred under pressure and safely decompressed to atmospheric pressure. ADS is a military adapted commercial diving suit that has been successfully tested to a depth of 2,000 ft *(610 m)*. The system is designed to be transportable worldwide in a standard shipping container. Overall, the system is capable of rescuing up to 155 personnel from a pressurized DISSUB.

SDRS *6/2008*, Richard Scott* / 1353632

AUXILIARIES

Notes: As of January 2009, the US Navy had about 440 active and 10 inactive service craft, primarily small craft, on the US Naval Vessel Register. A majority of these vessels provide services to the fleet in various harbours and ports. Others are ocean-going ships that provide services to the fleet for research purposes. Most of the service craft are rated as 'active, in service', while others are rated as 'in commission' and some are accommodation ships.

2 CAPE FLATTERY CLASS (TORPEDO TRIALS CRAFT) (YTT)

BATTLE POINT YTT 10 **DISCOVERY BAY** YTT 11

Displacement, tons: 1,168 full load
Dimensions, feet (metres): 186.5 × 40 × 10.5 *(56.9 × 12.2 × 3.2)*
Main machinery: 1 Cummins KTA50-M diesel; 1,250 hp *(932 kW)* sustained; 1 shaft; 1 bow thruster; 400 hp *(298 kW)*; 2 stern thrusters; 600 hp *(448 kW)*
Speed, knots: 11
Range, n miles: 1,000 at 10 kt
Complement: 31 plus 9 spare berths

Comment: Built by McDermott Shipyard, Morgan City, and delivered in 1991–92. Fitted with two 21 in Mk 59 and three (one triple) 12.75 in Mk 32 Mod 5 torpedo tubes. Used for torpedo trials and development at Keyport, Washington. A battery is fitted for limited duration operations with the diesel shutdown. Both based at Naval Underwater Warfare Centre, Keyport, WA.

YTT *9/1999, van Ginderen Collection* / 0084162

2 DIVING TENDERS (YDT)

YDT 17–18

Displacement, tons: 275 full load
Dimensions, feet (metres): 132 × 27 × 6.0 *(40.2 × 8.2 × 1.8)*
Main machinery: 2 Caterpillar diesels; 2,600 hp *(1.91 MW)*; 2 Hamilton waterjets
Speed, knots: 20
Complement: 8 plus 7 divers

Comment: Tenders used to support shallow-water diving operations and are based at Panama City, FL. Ordered from Swiftships in July 1997 and delivered in April 1999.

YDT 17 *8/1999, US Navy* / 0084159

23 PATROL CRAFT (YP)

YP 663 **YP 665** **YP 680–692** **YP 694–698** **YP 700–702**

Displacement, tons: 167 full load
Dimensions, feet (metres): 108 × 24 × 8 *(32.9 × 7.3 × 2.4)*
Main machinery: 2 Detroit 12V-71 diesels; 680 hp *(507 kW)* sustained; 2 shafts
Speed, knots: 13.3
Range, n miles: 1,500 at 12 kt
Complement: 6 (2 officers) plus 24 midshipmen
Radars: Navigation: I-band.

Comment: Built in the 1980s by Peterson Builders and Marinette Marine, both in Wisconsin. Twenty-one are based at the Naval Academy, Annapolis and two at Naval Underwater Warfare Centre, Keyport, WA.

YP 694 *5/2006, James E Mathwick* / 1167634

14 TORPEDO WEAPONS RETRIEVERS (YPT)

Comment: Four different types spread around the Fleet bases and at AUTEC. There are 2 TRs × 65 ft (aluminium), 1 TRB × 72 ft (wood), 4 TWRs × 85 ft (aluminium), and 5 TWRs × 120 ft (steel).

TR 6 *7/2000, Sattler/Steele* / 0106813

FLOATING DRY DOCKS

Notes: The US Navy operates a limited number of floating dry docks to supplement dry dock facilities at major naval activities. The larger floating dry docks are made sectional to facilitate movement and to render them self-docking. Some of the ARD-type docks have the forward end of their docking well closed by a structure resembling the bow of a ship to facilitate towing. Berthing facilities, repair shops and machinery are housed in sides of larger docks. None is self-propelled.

SMALL AUXILIARY FLOATING DRY DOCKS (AFDL)

Name/No	*Completed*	*Capacity (tons)*	*Construction*	*Status*
DYNAMIC (AFDL 6)	1944	950	Steel	Active, Norfolk, VA
ADEPT (AFDL 23)	1944	1,770	Steel	Commercial lease, Ingleside, TX
RELIANCE (AFDL 47)	1946	7,000	Steel	Commercial lease, Charleston, SC

Sales: AFDL 1 to Dominican Republic; 4, Brazil; 5, Taiwan; 11, Kampuchea; 20, Philippines; 22, Vietnam; 24, Philippines; 26, Paraguay; 28, Mexico; 33, Peru; 34 and 36, Taiwan; 39, Brazil; 40 and 44, Philippines. AFDL 23 to be sold to the current lessee.

DYNAMIC *11/2006, US Navy* / 1305191

AUXILIARY REPAIR DRY DOCKS AND MEDIUM AUXILIARY REPAIR DRY DOCKS (ARDM)

Name/No	*Commissioned*	*Capacity (tons)*	*Construction*	*Status*
SHIPPINGPORT (ARDM 4)	1979	7,800	Steel	Active, New London, CT
ARCO (ARDM 5)	1986	7,800	Steel	Active, San Diego, CA

Sales: ARD 2 to Mexico; 5, Chile; 6, Pakistan; 8, Peru; 9, Taiwan; 11, Mexico; 12, Turkey; 13, Venezuela; 14, Brazil; 15, Mexico; 17, Ecuador; 22 *(Windsor)*, Taiwan; 23, Argentina; 24, Ecuador; 25, Chile; 28, Colombia; 29, Iran; 32, Chile. ARDM 1 (ex-ARD 19) awaiting disposal decision.

ARCO *9/2008*, Julio Montes* / 1353631

UNCLASSIFIED MISCELLANEOUS (IX)

Notes: (1) In addition to the vessels listed below, one of the ex-Forrest Sherman class, *Decatur*, completed conversion on 21 October 1994 as a Self-Defence testing-ship, including high-energy laser trials. Tests with HFSWR (high-frequency surface wave radar) started mid-1997.
(2) *Mercer* APL 39 (ex-IX 502) and *Nueces* APL 40 (ex-IX 503) are barrack ships of mid-1940s vintage.
(3) IX 516 is a decommissioned SSBN used for propulsion plant training.
(4) IX 517 is a submarine sea trials escort vessel *(Gosport)*.
(5) IX 523 is used for security training, both at Norfolk, VA.
(6) IX 310 is an accommodation barge at Naval Undersea Warfare Center, Dresden, NJ.
(7) IX 521, IX 522 and IX 525 are individual drydock sections.
(8) IX 527 and IX 528 are submarine test platforms, IX 529 is a surface ship test platform and IX 531 a test platform for HM&E.
(9) IX 530 (ex-YFND 5) is a berthing barge.

IX 517 *7/2003, Declerck/Steeghers* / 1043688

1 CONSTITUTION CLASS (AXS)

Name	*Builders*	*Launched*	*Under Way*	*F/S*
CONSTITUTION	Edmund Hartt's Shipyard, Boston	21 Oct 1797	22 July 1798	AA

Displacement, tons: 2,250
Dimensions, feet (metres): 204 oa; 175 wl × 43.5 × 22.5 *(62.2; 53.3 × 13.2 × 6.8)*
Speed, knots: 13 under sail
Complement: 75 (4 officers)

Comment: The oldest ship remaining on the Navy List. One of six frigates authorised 27 March 1794. Best remembered for her service in the war of 1812, in which she earned the nickname 'Old Ironsides'. Following extensive restoration (1927–30), went on a three year goodwill tour around the United States (1931–34), travelling over 22,000 miles and receiving over 4 million visitors. Open to the public in her homeport of Boston, the ship receives over 400,000 visitors a year. The most recent overhaul was conducted at the Charlestown Navy Yard, Boston from 1992–96. Under fighting sails (jibs, topsails and spanker) *Constitution* sailed for the first time in 116 years on 21 July 1997 as part of her bicentennial celebration. Armament is 32 × 24 pounder guns, 20 × 32 pounder carronades and 2-24 pounder bow-chasers. Sail area 42,710 sq ft *(13,018 m²)*.

CONSTITUTION *7/1997, Todd Stevens, US Navy* / 0016501

1 TRAINING SHIP (AXT)

Name	*Builders*	*Commissioned*
IX 514 (ex-*YFU 79*)	Pacific Coast Eng, Alameda	1968

Displacement, tons: 380 full load
Dimensions, feet (metres): 125 × 36 × 8.0 *(38.1 × 10.9 × 2.4)*
Main machinery: 4 GM 6-71 diesels; 696 hp *(519 kW)* sustained; 2 shafts
Speed, knots: 8
Radars: Navigation: Racal Decca; I-band.

Comment: Harbour utility craft converted in 1986 with a flight deck covering two thirds of the vessel and a new bridge and flight control position at the forward end. Used for basic helicopter flight training at Pensacola, Florida. Similar craft *IX 501* deleted.

IX 514 *12/1994, van Ginderen Collection* / 0506212

1 RESEARCH SHIP (AGE)

SLICE

Displacement, tons: 180 full load
Dimensions, feet (metres): 105 × 55.5 × 14 *(32 × 16.9 × 4.3)*
Main machinery: 2 MTU 16V 396TB94 diesels; 13,700 hp(m) *(10.07 MW)*; 2 shafts; LIPS cp props
Speed, knots: 30
Complement: 12

Comment: Technology demonstrator built by Pacific Marine and owned by Lockheed Martin. Participated as a littoral warfare combatant in Fleet Battle Experiment Juliet (FBE-J) (part of Millennium Challenge 2002). Modular capability packages, carried to simulate Littoral Combat Ship (LCS), included Mine Countermeasures (MCM), Antisubmarine Warfare (ASW), Force Protection and Time Critical Targeting. Weapons tested during FBE-J included the Lockheed Martin/Oerlikon Contraves 35 mm Millennium Gun and the NetFires System and launcher.

SLICE *10/2002, US Navy* / 0572739

TUGS

16 LARGE HARBOUR TUGS (YTB)

MUSKEGON YTB 763	**NEODESHA** YTB 815
KEOKUK YTB 771	**WANAMASSA** YTB 820
MANISTEE YTB 782	**CANONCHET** YTB 823
KITTANNING YTB 787	**SANTAQUIN** YTB 824
OPELIKA YTB 798	**CATAHECASSA** YTB 828
MASSAPEQUA YTB 807	**DEKANAWIDA** YTB 831
WENATCHEE YTB 808	**SKENANDOA** YTB 835
ACCONAC YTB 812	**POKAGON** YTB 836

Displacement, tons: 356 full load
Dimensions, feet (metres): 109 × 30 × 13.8 *(33.2 × 9.1 × 4.2)*
Main machinery: 1 Fairbanks-Morse 38D8-1/8 diesel; 2,000 hp *(1.49 MW)* sustained; 1 shaft
Speed, knots: 12
Range, n miles: 2,000 at 12 kt
Complement: 10-12
Radars: Navigation: Marconi LN66; I-band.

Comment: Built between 1959 and 1975. Two transferred to Saudi Arabia in 1975. Being withdrawn from service and tugs are being provided by MSC charter.

MASSAPEQUA *5/2008*, Hachiro Nakai* / 1353569

MILITARY SEALIFT COMMAND (MSC)

Notes: (1) The Military Sealift Command (MSC) operates in four mission areas: Naval Fleet Auxiliary Force, Special Mission, Strategic Sealift and Prepositioning.
(2) Headquarters are in the Washington Navy Yard, Washington DC. The organisation is commanded by a US Navy Rear Admiral and operates six subordinate commands worldwide. The Military Sealift Fleet Support Command (MSFSC) in Norfolk, VA, crews, trains, equips and maintains MSC's government-owned, government-operated ships across the globe. MSFSC is commanded by a civilian member of the US Senior Executive Service. In addition, MSC has five operational commands called Sealift Logistic Commands (SEALOGs) which operate in the Atlantic, Pacific, Europe, Central and Far East areas of operation. Each SEALOG is commanded by a US Navy Captain.
(3) MSC ships are assigned standard hull designations with the added prefix 'T'. MSC ships carry no weapons systems. They are crewed by civilians who are either employed by the US federal government or private companies under contract to MSC. Many ships' funnels have black, grey, blue and gold horizontal bands.

NAVAL FLEET AUXILIARY FORCE

4 SUPPLY CLASS (FAST COMBAT SUPPORT SHIPS) (AOEH)

Name	*No*	*Builders*	*Laid down*	*Launched*	*Commissioned*	*F/S*
SUPPLY	T-AOE 6	National Steel & Shipbuilding Co	24 Feb 1989	6 Oct 1990	26 Feb 1994	AA
RAINIER	T-AOE 7	National Steel & Shipbuilding Co	31 May 1990	28 Sep 1991	21 Jan 1995	PA
ARCTIC	T-AOE 8	National Steel & Shipbuilding Co	2 Dec 1991	30 Oct 1993	16 Sep 1995	AA
BRIDGE	T-AOE 10	National Steel & Shipbuilding Co	16 Sep 1993	25 Aug 1996	5 Aug 1998	PA

Displacement, tons: 19,700 light; 48,500 full load
Dimensions, feet (metres): 753.7 × 107 × 38 *(229.7 × 32.6 × 11.6)*
Main machinery: 4 GE LM 2500 gas turbines; 105,000 hp *(78.33 MW)* sustained; 2 shafts
Speed, knots: 30
Range, n miles: 6,000 at 22 kt
Complement: 160 civilian; 28 naval
Cargo capacity: 156,000 barrels of fuel; 1,800 tons ammunition; 400 tons refrigerated cargo; 250 tons general cargo; 20,000 gallons water
Helicopters: 2 MH-60

Comment: Construction started in June 1988. *Supply* decommissioned and transferred to MSC in July 2001, *Arctic* in June 2002, *Rainier* in August 2003 and *Bridge* in June 2004.

RAINIER *8/2008*, Shaun Jones* / 1353630

7 + 5 (2) LEWIS AND CLARK CLASS (DRY CARGO/AMMUNITION SHIPS) (AKEH)

Name	*No*	*Builders*	*Launched*	*Commissioned*
LEWIS AND CLARK	T-AKE 1	National Steel & Shipbuilding Co	21 May 2005	20 June 2006
SACAGAWEA	T-AKE 2	National Steel & Shipbuilding Co	24 June 2006	27 Feb 2007
ALAN SHEPARD	T-AKE 3	National Steel & Shipbuilding Co	6 Dec 2006	26 June 2007
RICHARD E BYRD	T-AKE 4	National Steel & Shipbuilding Co	15 May 2007	8 Jan 2008
ROBERT E PEARY	T-AKE 5	National Steel & Shipbuilding Co	27 Oct 2007	5 June 2008
AMELIA EARHART	T-AKE 6	National Steel & Shipbuilding Co	6 Apr 2008	30 Oct 2008
CARL M BRASHEAR	T-AKE 7	National Steel & Shipbuilding Co	18 Sep 2008	4 Mar 2009
WALLY SCHIRRA	T-AKE 8	National Steel & Shipbuilding Co	8 Mar 2009	2009
MATTHEW PERRY	T-AKE 9	National Steel & Shipbuilding Co	2009	2010
CHARLES DREW	T-AKE 10	National Steel & Shipbuilding Co	2010	2011
WASHINGTON CHAMBERS	T-AKE 11	National Steel & Shipbuilding Co	2011	2012
WILLIAM McLEAN	T-AKE 12	National Steel & Shipbuilding Co	2011	2012

Displacement, tons: 24,833 light; 42,000 full load
Dimensions, feet (metres): 689.0 × 105.6 × 29.9 *(210.0 × 32.2 × 9.1)*
Main machinery: Integrated electric propulsion; 4 FM/MAN B&W 9L and 8L 48/60 diesel generators (35.7 MW); 2 Alstom motors; 1 shaft; fixed pitch prop; bow thruster
Speed, knots: 20
Range, n miles: 14,000 at 20 kt
Complement: 124 (11 naval)
Cargo capacity: 3,442 tons fuel; 200 tons potable water; 6,675 dry cargo; 1,716 tons refrigerated stores
Countermeasures: AN/SLQ-25 towed torpedo decoy.
Radars: Decca BridgeMaster; I-band.
Helicopters: 2 UH-46D/MH-60.

Comment: Design and construction contract placed on 18 October 2001 for delivery of first and second vessels. Contract for construction of the third of class in July 2002 and for the fourth in July 2003. A further two were ordered in January 2004 and two more on 11 January 2005. A ninth ship was ordered on 30 January 2006 and a tenth on 1 February 2008. T-AKE 11 and 12 were ordered on 16 December 2008. The contract includes long-lead items for T-AKE 13 and 14 which are to be ordered in 2010. The ships are being built to commercial standards to replace existing AE and AFS. Three RAS stations are to be fitted each side.

LEWIS AND CLARK *11/2008*, Guy Toremans* / 1353628

2 MARS CLASS (COMBAT STORES SHIPS) (AFSH)

Name	*No*	*Builders*	*Commissioned*	*F/S*
CONCORD	T-AFS 5	National Steel & Shipbuilding Co	27 Nov 1968	TPA
SAN JOSE	T-AFS 7	National Steel & Shipbuilding Co	23 Oct 1970	TPA

Displacement, tons: 9,200 light; 15,900–18,663 full load
Dimensions, feet (metres): 581 × 79 × 26 *(177.1 × 24.1 × 7.9)*
Main machinery: 3 Babcock & Wilcox boilers; 580 psi *(40.8 kg/cm²)*; 825°F *(440°C)*; 1 De Laval turbine (Westinghouse in AFS 6); 22,000 hp *(16.4 MW)*; 1 shaft
Speed, knots: 20
Range, n miles: 10,000 at 18 kt
Complement: 127 civilians plus 22 naval
Cargo capacity: 2,625 tons dry stores; 1,300 tons refrigerated stores (varies with specific loadings)
Radars: Navigation: 2 Raytheon; I-band.
Tacan: URN 25.
Helicopters: 2 MH-60.

Comment: *Concord* transferred to MSC on 15 October 1992 after disarming and conversion to a civilian crew. *San Jose* followed on 2 November 1993 and *Niagara Falls* on 23 September 1994. All have accommodation improvements and stores lifts installed. These ships carry comprehensive inventories of aviation spare parts as well as the cargo listed above. Two others of the class de-activated in 1997. *Niagara Falls* deactivated in 2008 and *Concord* and *San Jose* to follow in 2009.

SAN JOSE *9/2008*, Shaun Jones* / 1353629

4 KILAUEA CLASS (AMMUNITION SHIPS) (AEH)

Name	No	Builders	Commissioned	F/S
FLINT	T-AE 32	Ingalls Shipbuilding	20 Nov 1971	TPA
SHASTA	T-AE 33	Ingalls Shipbuilding	26 Feb 1972	TPA
MOUNT BAKER	T-AE 34	Ingalls Shipbuilding	22 July 1972	TAA
KISKA	T-AE 35	Ingalls Shipbuilding	16 Dec 1972	TPA

Displacement, tons: 9,340 light; 19,940 full load
Dimensions, feet (metres): 564 × 81 × 28 *(171.9 × 24.7 × 8.5)*
Main machinery: 3 Foster-Wheeler boilers; 600 psi *(42.3 kg/cm²)*; 870°F *(467°C)*; 1 GE turbine; 22,000 hp *(16.4 MW)*; 1 shaft
Speed, knots: 20. **Range, n miles:** 10,000 at 18 kt
Complement: 133 civilians plus 4 naval plus 35 (helo aircrew)
Radars: Navigation: 2 Raytheon; I-band.
Tacan: URN 25.
Helicopters: 2 CH-46E Sea Knight (cargo normally embarked).

Comment: *Kilauea* transferred to MSC 1 October 1980, *Flint* in August 1995, *Kiska* in August 1996, *Mount Baker* in December 1996, *Shasta* in October 1997 and *Santa Barbara* in September 1998. An eighth of class was to have transferred in 1999, but has been decommissioned. *Butte* decommissioned in 2002 and *Santa Barbara* in 2005. Ships underwent a civilian modification overhaul during which accommodation was improved. Main armament taken out. Seven UNREP stations operational: four port, three starboard. *Kilauea* was deactivated in 2008.

SHASTA *4/2008*, Hachiro Nakai* / 1353570

1 SIRIUS (LYNESS) CLASS (COMBAT STORES SHIP) (AFSH)

Name	No	Builders	Commissioned	F/S
SATURN (ex-*Stromness*)	T-AFS 10	Swan Hunter & Wigham Richardson Ltd, Wallsend-on-Tyne	10 Aug 1967	TAA

Displacement, tons: 9,010 light; 16,792 full load
Measurement, tons: 7,782 dwt; 12,359 gross; 4,744 net
Dimensions, feet (metres): 524 × 72 × 22 *(159.7 × 22 × 6.7)*
Main machinery: 1 Wallsend-Sulzer 8RD76 diesel; 11,520 hp *(8.59 MW)*; 1 shaft
Speed, knots: 18. **Range, n miles:** 12,000 at 16 kt
Complement: 118-127 civilians plus 24 naval
Cargo capacity: 8,313 m³ dry; 3,921 m³ frozen
Radars: Navigation: 2 Raytheon; I-band.
Tacan: URN 25.
Helicopters: 2 MH-60.

Comment: Purchased from the UK on 1 October 1983. Refitted from August 1992–96 to improve communications, RAS facilities and cargo handling equipment. *Sirius* deactivated in 2005. *Spica* in 2008 and *Saturn* to follow in 2009.

SATURN *5/2006, Marco Ghiglino* / 1167636

2 MERCY CLASS (HOSPITAL SHIPS) (AHH)

Name	No	Builders	Commissioned	F/S
MERCY (ex-SS *Worth*)	T-AH 19	National Steel & Shipbuilding Co	1976	ROS/TPA
COMFORT (ex-SS *Rose City*)	T-AH 20	National Steel & Shipbuilding Co	1976	ROS/TAA

Displacement, tons: 69,360 full load
Measurement, tons: 54,367 gross; 35,958 net
Dimensions, feet (metres): 894 × 105.6 × 32.8 *(272.6 × 32.2 × 10)*
Main machinery: 2 boilers; 2 GE turbines; 24,500 hp *(18.3 MW)*; 1 shaft
Speed, knots: 17. **Range, n miles:** 13,420 at 17 kt
Complement: 61 civilian crew; 820 military medical staff; 387 military support staff
Radars: Navigation: E/F/I-band.
Tacan: URN 25.
Helicopters: Platform only.

Comment: Converted San Clemente class tankers. *Mercy* was commissioned 19 December 1986; *Comfort* on 30 November 1987. Each ship has 1,000 beds and 12 operating theatres. Normally, the ships are kept in a reduced operating status in Baltimore, MD, and San Diego, CA, by a small crew of civilian mariners and active duty Navy medical and support personnel. Each ship can be fully activated and crewed within five days. *Mercy* deployed to Southeast Asia after tsunami of 26 December 2004. She spent two months off the Indonesian province of Banda Aceh. In 2006, *Mercy* conducted a four-month humanitarian assistance mission and treated over 60,000 patients in the Philippines, Bangladesh, Indonesia and East Timor. A similar mission was conducted by *Comfort* in South America and the Caribbean during 2007 and again by *Mercy* in Southeast Asia and the Pacific in mid-2008.

MERCY *8/2008*, Chris Sattler* / 1353626

14 HENRY J KAISER CLASS (OILERS) (AOH)

Name	No	Builders	Laid down	Commissioned	F/S
HENRY J KAISER	T-AO 187	Avondale	22 Aug 1984	19 Dec 1986	TPA/ROS
JOHN LENTHALL	T-AO 189	Avondale	15 July 1985	2 June 1987	TAA
WALTER S DIEHL	T-AO 193	Avondale	8 July 1986	13 Sep 1988	TPA
JOHN ERICSSON	T-AO 194	Avondale	15 Mar 1989	18 Mar 1991	TPA
LEROY GRUMMAN	T-AO 195	Avondale	7 June 1987	2 Aug 1989	TAA
KANAWHA	T-AO 196	Avondale	13 July 1989	6 Dec 1991	TAA
PECOS	T-AO 197	Avondale	17 Feb 1988	6 July 1990	TPA
BIG HORN	T-AO 198	Avondale	9 Oct 1989	31 July 1992	TAA
TIPPECANOE	T-AO 199	Avondale	19 Nov 1990	26 Mar 1993	TPA
GUADALUPE	T-AO 200	Avondale	9 July 1990	26 Oct 1992	TPA
PATUXENT	T-AO 201	Avondale	16 Oct 1991	21 June 1995	TAA
YUKON	T-AO 202	Avondale	13 May 1991	11 Dec 1993	TPA
LARAMIE	T-AO 203	Avondale	1 Oct 1994	24 May 1996	TAA
RAPPAHANNOCK	T-AO 204	Avondale	29 June 1992	7 Nov 1995	TPA

Displacement, tons: 40,900; 41,225 (T-AO 201, 203-204) full load
Dimensions, feet (metres): 677.5 × 97.5 × 36 *(206.5 × 29.7 × 10.9)*
Main machinery: 2 Colt-Pielstick 10 PC4.2 V 570 diesels; 34,422 hp(m) *(24.3 MW)* sustained; 2 shafts; cp props
Speed, knots: 20. **Range, n miles:** 6,000 at 18 kt
Complement: 74-89 civilian plus 5 naval
Cargo capacity: 180,000; 159,500 (T-AO 201, 203-204) barrels of fuel oil or aviation fuel
Countermeasures: Decoys: SLQ-25 Nixie; towed torpedo decoy
Radars: Navigation: 2 Raytheon; I-band.
Helicopters: Platform only.

Comment: Construction was delayed initially by design difficulties, by excessive vibration at high speeds and other problems encountered in the first ship of the class. There are stations on both sides for underway replenishment of fuel and solids. Fitted with integrated electrical auxiliary propulsion. T-AOs 201, 203 and 204 were delayed by the decision to fit double hulls to meet the requirements of the Oil Pollution Act of 1990. This modification increased construction time from 32 to 42 months and reduced cargo capacity by 17 per cent although this can be restored in an emergency. Hull separation is 1.83 m at the sides and 1.98 m on the bottom. T-AOs 191 and 192 were transferred from Penn Ship (when the yard became bankrupt) to Tampa. Tampa's contract was also cancelled on 25 August 1993. Neither ship was completed. T-AO 187 is kept in reduced operating status on the west coast. T-AO 188 and 190 were laid up in mid-1996 and T-AO 189 in September 1997, but returned to service in January 1999. T-AO 188 returned to reduced operating status in April 2005 but was transferred to the inactive fleet in October 2006.

BIG HORN *3/2006, M Declerck* / 1167635

HENRY KAISER *10/2007, Michael Nitz* / 1353627

4 SAFEGUARD CLASS (SALVAGE SHIPS) (ARS)

Name	No	Builders	Commissioned	F/S
SAFEGUARD	T-ARS 50 (ex-ARS 50)	Peterson Builders	16 Aug 1985	PA
GRASP	T-ARS 51 (ex-ARS 51)	Peterson Builders	14 Dec 1985	AA
SALVOR	T-ARS 52 (ex-ARS 52)	Peterson Builders	14 June 1986	PA
GRAPPLE	T-ARS 53 (ex-ARS 53)	Peterson Builders	15 Nov 1986	AA

Displacement, tons: 3,283 full load
Dimensions, feet (metres): 255 × 51 × 17 *(77.7 × 15.5 × 5.2)*
Main machinery: 4 Caterpillar diesels; 4,200 hp *(3.13 MW)*; 2 shafts; cp Kort nozzle props; bow thruster; 500 hp *(373 kW)*
Speed, knots: 14. **Range, n miles:** 8,000 at 12 kt
Complement: 26 civilians plus 4 naval comms plus up to 34 naval divers
Radars: Navigation: E/F/I-band.

Comment: Prototype approved in FY81, two in FY82 and one in FY83. The procurement of the fifth ARS was dropped on instructions from Congress. The design follows conventional commercial and Navy criteria. Can support surface-supplied diving operations to a depth of 58 m. Equipped with recompression chamber. Bollard pull, 65.6 tons. Using beach extraction equipment the pull increases to 360 tons. 150 ton deadlift. *Grasp* transferred from the US Navy on 19 January 2006 and *Grapple* on 13 July 2006. *Salvor* and *Safeguard* followed on 12 January 2007 and 26 September 2007 respectively.

GRAPPLE *9/2007, Michael Winter* / 1305243

4 POWHATAN CLASS (FLEET OCEAN TUGS) (ATF)

Name	*No*	*Laid down*	*Commissioned*	*F/S*
CATAWBA	T-ATF 168	14 Dec 1977	28 May 1980	TPA
NAVAJO	T-ATF 169	14 Dec 1977	13 June 1980	TPA
SIOUX	T-ATF 171	22 Mar 1979	1 May 1981	TPA
APACHE	T-ATF 172	22 Mar 1979	30 July 1981	TAA

Displacement, tons: 2,260 full load
Dimensions, feet (metres): 226.0 × 42 × 15 *(68.9 × 12.8 × 4.6)*
Main machinery: 2 GM EMD 20-645F7B diesels; 7,250 hp(m) *(5.41 MW)* sustained; 2 shafts; Kort nozzles; cp props; bow thruster; 300 hp *(224 kW)*
Speed, knots: 14.5. **Range, n miles:** 10,000 at 13 kt
Complement: 16 civilians plus 4 naval
Radars: Navigation: E/F/I-band.

Comment: Built at Marinette Marine Corp, Wisconsin patterned after commercial offshore supply ship design. Originally intended as successors to the Cherokee and Abnaki class ATFs. All transferred to MSC upon completion. 10 ton capacity crane and a bollard pull of at least 54 tons. A 'deck grid' is fitted aft which contains 1 in bolt receptacles spaced 24 in apart. This allows for the bolting down of a wide variety of portable equipment in support of salvage and training evolutions worldwide. There are two fire pumps supplying three fire monitors with up to 2,200 gallons of foam per minute. A deep module can be embarked to support naval salvage teams. Two of the class deactivated for commercial lease in 1999 and one other in 2005.

APACHE *6/2008*, Richard Scott* / 1353625

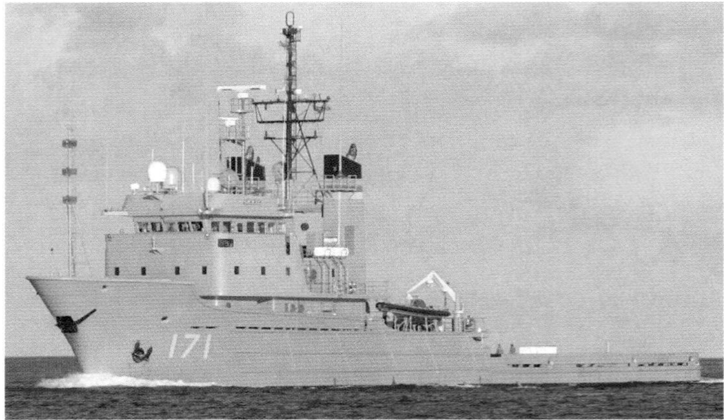

SIOUX *7/2004, Michael Nitz* / 1043636

SPECIAL MISSION SHIPS

Notes: (1) Most special missions ships are operated by civilian mariners who work for private companies under contract to MSC. USNS *Zeus* is crewed by civil service mariners (CIVMARs) working for MSC. USS *Mount Whitney* and USS *Emory S Land* have hybrid crews of navy sailors and CIVMARs. Technical work and communication support conducted by embarked military personnel as well as civilian technicians from other commands and agencies.
(2) There is also a number of chartered vessels: *Dolores Chouest, C-Commando* and *C-Champion* support the Naval SpecialWarfare Command and are owned and operated by Edison Chouest. MV *Greystone*, MV *Bluewater*, MV *Silverstar* and MV *Gemstone* provide submarine support and are owned and operated by Hornbeck Offshore Services.
(3) The Command Ship *Mount Whitney* LCC 20 transferred to MSC in 2004 and deployed to the Mediterranean Sea as the 6th Fleet command ship. *Mount Whitney* is one of the first ships to be operated jointly by uniformed personnel and CIVMARs from MSC.
(4) Submarine tender USS *Emory S Land* transferred to MSC in 2008 and its sister ship USS *Frank Cable* is scheduled to transfer to MSC in 2010. Sub tenders, like command ships, are unusual in that they have both uniformed Navy personnel and civil service mariners serving under the leadership of a US Navy Captain, which allows the ships to retain their commissioned status.

1 ZEUS CLASS (CABLE REPAIRING SHIP) (ARC)

Name	*No*	*Builders*	*Commissioned*	*F/S*
ZEUS	T-ARC 7	National Steel & Shipbuilding Co	19 Mar 1984	TAA

Displacement, tons: 8,370 light; 14,934 full load
Dimensions, feet (metres): 513 × 73 × 25 *(156.4 × 22.3 × 7.6)*
Main machinery: Diesel-electric; 5 GM EMD 20-645F7B diesel generators; 14.32 MW sustained; 2 motors; 10,200 hp *(7.51 MW)*; 2 shafts; bow thrusters (forward and aft)
Speed, knots: 15.8. **Range, n miles:** 10,000 at 15 kt
Complement: 55 civilians plus 10 scientists

Comment: Ordered 7 August 1979. Remotely manned engineering room controlled from the bridge. The only active cable laying/repair ship in the US Navy, she can lay up to 1,000 miles of cable in depths of 9,000 ft. The ship is also equipped for bottom mapping surveys to support cable operations.

ZEUS *8/2006, Hachiro Nakai* / 1167498

1 CONVERTED COMPASS ISLAND CLASS (MISSILE RANGE INSTRUMENTATION SHIP) (AGM)

Name	*No*	*Builders*	*Commissioned*	*F/S*
OBSERVATION ISLAND (ex-*Empire State Mariner*)	T-AGM 23 (ex-AG 154, ex-YAG 57)	New York Shipbuilding	5 Dec 1958	TPA

Displacement, tons: 13,060 light; 17,015 full load
Dimensions, feet (metres): 564 × 76 × 25 *(171.6 × 23.2 × 7.6)*
Main machinery: 2 Foster-Wheeler boilers; 600 psi *(42.3 kg/cm²)*; 875°F *(467°C)*; 1 GE turbine; 19,250 hp *(14.36 MW)*; 1 shaft
Speed, knots: 20
Range, n miles: 17,000 at 15 kt
Complement: 66 civilians plus 59 scientists
Radars: Raytheon 1650/9X and 1660/12S; I-band.
Tacan: URN 25.

Comment: Built as a Mariner class merchant ship (C4-S-A1 type); launched on 15 August 1953; acquired by the Navy on 10 September 1956 for use as a Fleet Ballistic Missile (FBM) test ship. Converted at Norfolk Naval Shipyard. In reserve from September 1972. On 18 August 1977, *Observation Island* was reacquired by the US Navy from the Maritime Administration and transferred to the Military Sealift Command. Reclassified AGM 23 on 1 May 1979. Converted to Missile Range Instrumentation Ship from July 1979-April 1981 at Maryland SB and DD Co to carry an Air Force shipborne phased-array radar system for collection of data on foreign and domestic ballistic missile tests. Operated by the Navy in the North Pacific for the US Air Force.

OBSERVATION ISLAND *4/2008*, Hachiro Nakai* / 1353571

1 IMPECCABLE CLASS (OCEAN SURVEILLANCE SHIP) (AGOS)

Name	*No*	*Builders*	*Commissioned*	*F/S*
IMPECCABLE	T-AGOS 23	Tampa Shipyard/Halter Marine	22 Mar 2001	TAA

Displacement, tons: 5,370 full load
Dimensions, feet (metres): 281.5 × 95.8 × 26 *(85.8 × 29.2 × 7.9)*
Main machinery: Diesel-electric; 3 GM EMD 12-645F7B diesel generators; 5.48 MW *(60 Hz)* sustained; 2 Westinghouse motors; 5,000 hp *(3.73 MW)*; 2 shafts; 2 omni-thruster hydrojets; 1,800 hp *(1.34 MW)*
Speed, knots: 12; 3 when towing
Range, n miles: 3,000 at 12 kt
Complement: 21 civilian crew plus 5 sponsor agency civilians plus 16 military
Radars: Raytheon; I-band.
Sonars: SURTASS; LFA and passive surveillance towed array.

Comment: Hull form based on that of *Victorious*. Acoustic systems include an active low frequency towed array (LFA), which has a series of modules each of which houses two high-powered active transducers. These can be used with either mono or bistatic receivers. The payload is lowered through a centre well. Laid down 2 February 1993. Ship was 60 per cent complete when shipyard encountered difficulties that led to termination in October 1993 of the contract for completion of two Kaiser class oilers. Work stopped on *Impeccable*, and the construction contract was also cancelled. The contract was assigned to Halter Marine on 20 April 1995 to complete the ship. Launched 25 April 1998. WSC-3(V)3 and WSC-6 communications fitted.

IMPECCABLE *5/2006, Hachiro Nakai* / 1167500

1 CONVERTED STALWART CLASS (MISSILE RANGE INSTRUMENTATION) (T-AGM)

Name	No	Laid down	Commissioned	F/S
INVINCIBLE	T-AGM 24	8 Nov 1985	3 Feb 1987	TPA

Displacement, tons: 2,285 full load
Dimensions, feet (metres): 224 × 43 × 14.9 *(68.3 × 13.1 × 4.5)*
Main machinery: Diesel-electric; 4 Caterpillar D 398B diesel generators; 3,200 hp *(2.39 MW)*; 2 motors; 1,600 hp *(1.2 MW)*; 2 shafts; bow thruster; 550 hp *(410 kW)*
Speed, knots: 11
Range, n miles: 4,000 at 11 kt
Complement: 38 (18 civilian mariners, 11 sponsor personnel)
Radars: US Air Force Cobra Gemini; dual-band; E/F/I-bands.
Navigation: Furuno; E/F/I-bands.

Comment: Converted to a Missile Range Instrumentation ship (T-AGM) in early 1999 and provides a seaborne radar platform for US Air Force data collection requirements on theatre ballistic missiles.

INVINCIBLE *6/1999, Ships of the World* / 0084177

1 WATERS CLASS (NAVIGATION TEST SUPPORT SHIP) (AGS)

Name	No	Builders	Commissioned	F/S
WATERS	T-AG 45	Avondale Industries	26 May 1993	TAA

Displacement, tons: 12,208 full load
Dimensions, feet (metres): 455 × 68.9 × 21 *(138.7 × 21 × 6.4)*
Main machinery: Diesel-electric; 5 GM EMD diesels; 7,400 hp *(5.45 MW)*; 2 Westinghouse motors; 6,800 hp *(15.07 MW)*; 2 shafts; 4 thrusters
Speed, knots: 12
Range, n miles: 6,500 at 12 kt
Complement: 66 civilians plus 59 scientists
Radars: 2 Raytheon; E/F- and I-bands.

Comment: Ordered 4 April 1990. Laid down 16 May 1991 and launched 6 June 1992. Carried out oceanographic and acoustic surveys in support of the Integrated Underwater Surveillance System. Converted in 1998 to support submarine navigation system testing and missile tracking. In 1999 has replaced *Vanguard* and *Range Sentinel*, both of which have been deactivated.

WATERS *4/1994, Giorgio Arra* / 0506213

4 VICTORIOUS CLASS (OCEAN SURVEILLANCE SHIPS) (AGOS)

Name	No	Builders	Commissioned	F/S
VICTORIOUS	T-AGOS 19	McDermott Marine	5 Sep 1991	TPA
ABLE	T-AGOS 20	McDermott Marine	22 July 1992	TAA
EFFECTIVE	T-AGOS 21	McDermott Marine	27 Jan 1993	TPA
LOYAL	T-AGOS 22	McDermott Marine	1 July 1993	TAA

Displacement, tons: 3,396 full load
Dimensions, feet (metres): 234.5 × 93.6 × 24.8 *(71.5 × 28.5 × 7.6)*
Main machinery: Diesel-electric; 4 Caterpillar 3512TA diesels; 5,440 hp *(4 MW)* sustained; 2 GE motors; 3,200 hp *(2.39 MW)*; 2 shafts; 2 bow thrusters; 2,400 hp *(1.79 MW)*
Speed, knots: 16; 3 when towing
Complement: 19 civilian plus 5 sponsor personnel and 7 military
Radars: Navigation: 2 Raytheon; I-band.
Sonars: SURTASS and LFA; towed array; passive/active surveillance.

Comment: All of SWATH design because of its greater stability at slow speeds in high latitudes under adverse weather conditions. A contract for the first SWATH ship, T-AGOS 19, was awarded in November 1986, and options for a further three were exercised in October 1988. T-AGOS 20 deactivated in July 2003 and re-activated in 2007 and reconfigured to accommodate LFA.

ABLE *8/2008** / 1353624

1 JOHN McDONNELL CLASS (SURVEYING SHIP) (AGS)

Name	No	Builders	Commissioned	F/S
JOHN McDONNELL	T-AGS 51	Halter Marine	16 Dec 1991	TPA

Displacement, tons: 2,054 full load
Dimensions, feet (metres): 208 × 45 × 14 *(63.4 × 13.7 × 4.3)*
Main machinery: 1 GM EMD 12-645E6 diesel; 2,550 hp *(1.9 MW)* sustained; 1 auxiliary diesel; 230 hp *(172 kW)*; 1 shaft
Speed, knots: 12
Range, n miles: 13,800 at 12 kt
Complement: 22 civilians plus 11 scientists

Comment: Laid down on 3 August 1989 and launched on 15 August 1990. Carries 34 ft survey launches for data collection in coastal regions with depths between 10 and 600 m and in deep water to 4,000 m. A small diesel is used for propulsion at towing speeds of up to 6 kt. Simrad high-frequency active hull-mounted and side scan sonars are carried. *Littlehales* was deactivated in March 2003 and transferred to NOAA.

JOHN McDONNELL *8/2004, Hachiro Nakai* / 1043695

6 PATHFINDER CLASS (SURVEYING SHIPS) (AGS)

Name	No	Builders	Launched	Commissioned	F/S
PATHFINDER	T-AGS 60	Halter Marine	7 Oct 1993	5 Dec 1994	TAA
SUMNER	T-AGS 61	Halter Marine	19 May 1994	30 May 1995	TPA
BOWDITCH	T-AGS 62	Halter Marine	15 Oct 1994	30 Dec 1995	TPA
HENSON	T-AGS 63	Halter Marine	21 Oct 1996	20 Feb 1998	TAA
BRUCE C HEEZEN	T-AGS 64	Halter Marine	17 Dec 1998	13 Jan 2000	TAA
MARY SEARS	T-AGS 65	Halter Marine	19 Oct 2000	17 Dec 2001	TAA

Displacement, tons: 4,762 full load
Dimensions, feet (metres): 328.5 × 58 × 19 *(100.1 × 17.7 × 5.8)*
Main machinery: Diesel-electric; 4 EMD/Baylor diesel generators; 11,425 hp *(8.52 MW)*; 2 GE CDF 1944 motors; 8,000 hp *(5.97 MW)* sustained; 6,000 hp *(4.48 MW)*; 2 LIPS Z drives; bow thruster; 1,500 hp *(1.19 MW)*
Speed, knots: 16
Range, n miles: 12,000 at 12 kt
Complement: 24 civilians plus 27 oceanographers

Comment: Contract awarded in January 1991 for two ships with an option for a third which was taken up on 29 May 1992. A fourth ship was ordered in October 1994 with an option for two more. Fifth ordered 15 January 1997 and sixth on 6 January 1999. There are three multipurpose cranes and five winches plus a variety of oceanographic equipment including multibeam echo-sounders, towed sonars and expendable sensors. ROVs may be carried. The aft deck and dry laboratory spaces are reconfigurable to support a variety of missions.

BOWDITCH *8/2006, Hachiro Nakai* / 1167501

HENSON *6/2007, L-G Nilsson* / 1305188

2 EMORY S LAND CLASS (SUBMARINE TENDERS) (ASH)

Name	*No*	*Builders*	*Laid down*	*Launched*	*Commissioned*	*F/S*
EMORY S LAND	AS 39	Lockheed SB & Construction Co, Seattle	2 Mar 1976	4 May 1977	7 July 1979	PA
FRANK CABLE	AS 40	Lockheed SB & Construction Co, Seattle	2 Mar 1976	14 Jan 1978	29 Oct 1979	PA

Displacement, tons: 13,911 standard; 22,978 full load
Dimensions, feet (metres): 643.8 × 85 × 28.5 *(196.2 × 25.9 × 8.7)*
Main machinery: 2 Combustion Engineering boilers; 620 psi *(43.6 kg/cm²)*; 860°F *(462°C)*; 1 De Laval turbine; 20,000 hp *(14.9 MW)*; 1 shaft
Speed, knots: 20. **Range, n miles**: 10,000 at 12 kt
Complement: AS 39: 1,268 (83 officers); AS 40: 1,270 (81 officers)

Guns: 4 Oerlikon 20 mm Mk 67
Radars: Navigation: ISC Cardion SPS-55; I/J-band
Helicopters: Platform only

Comment: The first US submarine tenders designed specifically for servicing nuclear-propelled attack submarines. Each ship can simultaneously provide services to four submarines moored alongside. Equipped with one 30 ton crane and two 5 ton mobile cranes. There is a 23-bed sick bay. *Frank Cable* is based at Guam and *Emory S Land* changed homeport to Bremerton, WA, in October 2007. *Emory S Land* transferred to Miliary Sealift Command in February 2008 and *Frank Cable* is scheduled to transfer in 2010 but, while operated by a hybrid crew of naval and civilian personnel, both ships remain under naval command and in commissioned status.

EMORY S LAND *4/1999, Jürg Kürsener* / 0084155

0 + 1 MISSILE RANGE INSTRUMENTATION SHIP (AGM)

Name	*No*	*Builders*	*Laid down*	*Launched*	*Commissioned*
HOWARD O LORENZEN	T-AGM 25	VT Halter Marine	13 Aug 2008	2009	2010

Displacement, tons: 12,575 standard
Dimensions, feet (metres): 534.1 × 88.6 × 21.3 *(162.8 × 27.0 × 6.51)*
Main machinery: Diesel-electric; 4 diesel generators; 2 motors; 20,115 hp *(15 MW)*; 2 shafts
Speed, knots: 20
Range, n miles: 12,000 at 12 kt
Complement: 30 + 46 technicians + 12 spare
Radars: Navigation: To be announced.

Comment: The Cobra Judy Replacement programme is for the replacement of the current missile range instrumentation ship *Observation Island* by 2012 and the development of a successor mission equipment system to conduct worldwide technical data collection against ballistic missiles in flight. Raytheon was awarded the contract in December 2003 for an integrated, computer-driver surveillance and data collection radar system that comprises a dual-band radar suite. This consists of I-band and E/F-band active phased array sensors and other related mission equipment.

STRATEGIC SEALIFT FORCE

Notes: These ships provide ocean transportation for Defense and other government agencies. As well as those listed below, MSC also contracts additional tankers and dry cargo ships as needed. As a result these numbers vary with the operational requirement.

2 SHUGHART CLASS (LARGE, MEDIUM-SPEED, RO-RO (LMSR) SHIPS) (AKR)

Name	*No*	*Commissioned*	*F/S*
SHUGHART (ex-*Laura Maersk*)	T-AKR 295	7 May 1996	TWWR
YANO (ex-*Leise Maersk*)	T-AKR 297	8 Feb 1997	TWWR

Measurement, tons: 54,298 grt
Dimensions, feet (metres): 906.8 × 105.5 × 34.4 *(276.4 × 32.2 × 10.5)*
Main machinery: 1 Burmeister & Wain 12L90 GFCA diesel; 46,653 hp(m) *(34.29 MW)*; 1 shaft; bow and stern thrusters
Speed, knots: 24
Range, n miles: 12,000 at 24 kt
Complement: 21-44 civilian; up to 50 military
Cargo capacity: 255,064 sq ft plus 47,023 sq ft deck cargo
Radars: Navigation: 2 Sperry ARPA; I-band.

Comment: Both were container ships built in Denmark in 1981 and lengthened by Hyundai in 1987. Conversion contract awarded to National Steel and Shipbuilding in July 1993. Both fitted with a stern slewing ramp, side accesses and cranes for both roll-on/roll-off and lift-on/lift-off capabilities. Two twin 57 ton cranes. Conversion for *Shughart* started in June 1994; *Yano* in May 1995; *Soderman* underwent conversion to maritime prepositioning ship and renamed *Stockham*.

YANO *12/2006, Adolfo Ortigueira Gil* / 1167638

2 GORDON CLASS (LARGE, MEDIUM-SPEED, RO-RO (LMSR) SHIPS) (AKR)

Name	*No*	*Commissioned*	*F/S*
GORDON (ex-*Selandia*)	T-AKR 296	23 Aug 1996	TWWR
GILLILAND (ex-*Jutlandia*)	T-AKR 298	24 May 1997	TWWR

Measurement, tons: 55,422 grt
Dimensions, feet (metres): 956 × 105.8 × 36.3 *(291.4 × 32.2 × 11.9)*
Main machinery: 1 Burmeister & Wain 12K84EF diesel; 26,000 hp(m) *(19.11 MW)*; 2 Burmeister & Wain 9K84EF diesels; 39,000 hp(m) *(28.66 MW)*; 3 shafts (centre cp prop); bow thruster
Speed, knots: 24. **Range, n miles**: 12,000 at 24 kt
Complement: 21-49 civilian; 50 military
Cargo capacity: 276,109 sq ft plus 45,722 sq ft deck cargo
Radars: Navigation: 2 Sperry ARPA; I-band.

Comment: Built in Denmark in 1972 and lengthened by Hyundai in 1984. Conversion contract given to Newport News Shipbuilding on 30 July 1993. Both fitted with a stern slewing ramp, side accesses and improved craneage. Conversion started for both ships on 15 October 1993.

GILLILAND *2/2000, A Sharma* / 0085304

7 BOB HOPE CLASS (LARGE, MEDIUM-SPEED, RO-RO (LMSR) SHIPS) (AKR)

Name	*No*	*Builders*	*Launched*	*Commissioned*	*F/S*
BOB HOPE	T-AKR 300	Avondale	27 Mar 1997	18 Nov 1998	TWWR
FISHER	T-AKR 301	Avondale	21 Oct 1997	4 Aug 1999	TWWR
SEAY	T-AKR 302	Avondale	25 June 1998	30 Mar 2000	TWWR
MENDONCA	T-AKR 303	Avondale	25 May 1999	30 Jan 2001	TWWR
PILILAAU	T-AKR 304	Avondale	18 Jan 2000	24 July 2001	TWWR
BRITTIN	T-AKR 305	Avondale	21 Oct 2000	11 July 2002	TWWR
BENAVIDEZ	T-AKR 306	Avondale	11 Aug 2001	10 Sep 2003	TWWR

Displacement, tons: 61,680 full load
Dimensions, feet (metres): 948.9 × 106 × 35 *(289.1 × 32.3 × 11)*
Main machinery: 4 Colt Pielstick 10 PC4.2 V diesels; 65,160 hp(m) *(47.89 MW)*; 2 shafts; cp props
Speed, knots: 24. **Range, n miles**: 12,000 at 24 kt
Complement: 26-45 civilian; up to 50 military
Cargo capacity: 317,510 sq ft plus 70,152 sq ft deck cargo

Comment: Contract awarded in 1993; options for additional ships exercised in 1994, 1995, 1996 and 1997. All fitted with a stern slewing ramp, side accesses and cranes for both roll-on/roll-off and lift-on/lift-off capabilities. Ramps extend to 130 ft *(40 m)*, and two twin 55 ton cranes are installed.

PILILAAU *1/2008*, Shaun Jones* / 1305187

4 CHAMPION CLASS (TANKERS) (AOT)

Name	*No*	*Builders*	*Commissioned*
PAUL BUCK	T-AOT 1122	American SB Co, Tampa, FL	7 June 1985
SAMUEL L COBB	T-AOT 1123	American SB Co, Tampa, FL	15 Nov 1985
RICHARD G MATTHIESEN	T-AOT 1124	American SB Co, Tampa, FL	18 Feb 1986
LAWRENCE H GIANELLA	T-AOT 1125	American SB Co, Tampa, FL	22 Apr 1986

Displacement, tons: 39,624 full load
Dimensions, feet (metres): 615 × 90 × 36 *(187.5 × 27.4 × 10.8)*
Main machinery: 1 Sulzer 5RTA76 diesel; 18,400 hp(m) *(13.52 MW)* sustained; 1 shaft
Speed, knots: 16. **Range, n miles:** 12,000 at 16 kt
Complement: 23 (9 officers)
Cargo capacity: 238,400 barrels of oil fuel

Comment: Built for Ocean Carriers Inc, Houston, Texas specifically for long-term time charter to the Military Sealift Command (20 years) as Point-to-Point fuel tankers. Purchased by the US Navy in 2003 and designated USNS. The last two are equipped with a modular fuel delivery system to allow them to rig underway replenishment gear.

LAWRENCE H GIANELLA ***1/2002, A Sharma*** / 0530036

PREPOSITIONING FORCE

Notes: (1) Military Sealift Command's Afloat Prepositioning Force (APF) improves US capabilities to deploy forces rapidly to any area of conflict. The force includes long-term chartered commercial vessels, activated Ready Reserve Force ships and government ships and includes vehicle/cargo carriers, container ships, aviation logistics ships and Large, Medium-Speed, Roll-on/roll-off (LMSR) ships. Together these ships preposition equipment and supplies for the Marine Corps, Navy, Army, Air Force and the Defense Logistics Agency. The APF comprises: the Maritime Prepositioning Force (MPF), Navy, Defense Logistics Agency and Air Force ships (NDAF) and Army Prepositioned Stocks-3 ships (APS-3).
(2) The MPF operates in forward-deployed Maritime Prepositioning Squadrons (MPSRONs): MPSRON One is located in the Eastern Atlantic Ocean and Mediterranean Sea; MPSRON Two at Diego Garcia in the Indian Ocean and MPSRON Three in the western Pacific Ocean. There are 15 ships loaded with equipment and supplies for the US Marine Corps.
(3) Three NDAF ships are loaded with US Air Force and Navy ammunition. One ship serves as an at-sea pumping station to transfer fuel to shore from a tanker as far as 8 miles from the coast. Two T-AVB ships serve as USMC intermediate maintenance facilities for rotary wing aircraft. Two high-speed vessels are also part of NDAF – one transports marines and their cargo in the Far East and the other conducts specialised missions worldwide.
(4) Nine APS-3 ships support requirements for US Army brigade and combat support/combat service support elements. In 2007, some of the LMSRs were put in reduced operating status. In 2008, one LMSR was assigned to the Maritime Prepositioning Force.
(5) Maritime Prepositioning Force (Future): the US Navy's Seabasing initiative, in which manoeuvre forces are supported by logistics and combat fire support in staging bases in or near the theatre of operations, is under development. This is likely to require a variety of platforms that can assemble offshore and either redeploy quickly or support continuing operations ashore. It is envisaged that a seabase would comprise an Expeditionary Strike Group (ESG), a Carrier Strike Group (CSG), and a Maritime Prepositioning Group (MPG) supported by a Combat Logistics Force. Various classes of Maritime Prepositioning Force (Future) ships are to be capable of selectively offloading standardised loads and other equipment. Large deck areas suitable for flight operations and ship-to-ship interface points supporting movement of cargo to smaller tactical watercraft are also necessary. MPF(F) might additionally assume some of the roles planned for the JCC(X) future command and control ship. Other potential applications of the MPF(F) include acting as intra-theatre shuttles, afloat medical care and mine-countermeasures support. Some 14 vessels are required and construction of the firstship is to begin in FY11.
(6) An integral vessel of the Maritime Prepositioning Force (Future) will be the Mobile Landing Platform (MLP) based on a Float On-Float Off (FLO-FLO) design. It is being developed primarily to provide a surface interface between other ships and connectors within a seabase. The MLP mission requirements and major functions include: projecting a Marine combat unit and its equipment via LCACs or EFVs; transporting six LCACs; accommodating a Marine combat unit of 728 personnel with ability to interface with MPF(F) LMSR, JHSV and other displacement type surface assault crafts to facilitate equipment, cargo and personnel transfer in sea base. The MLP will support the critical mission requirement to launch and recover surface assault craft loaded with vehicles, cargo and combat personnel by providing two LCAC stowage lanes (two craft interface points), RO/RO cargo holds of sufficient size to accommodate one-third of the Marine Expeditionary Brigade (MEB), Surface Battalion Landing Team (BLT) vehicles and accommodations for the combat troops being transferred ashore on the assault craft. The MLP will be a US flagged new construction ship. Plans are to buy 'pier in the ocean' MLP starting in FY10 with initial operational capability by FY17.
(7) Army Strategic Flotillas (ASF): The US Army prepositioning plan calls for the deployment of four ASFs. Two ASFs would be composed of LMSRs, one carrying an intermediate brigade combat team, and the other carrying an intermediate brigade combat team. The other two ASFs would each contain LMSRs carrying sustainment supplies plus an ammunition ship and a warehouse ship. ASFs will be based around Guam and Saipan inthe Pacific Ocean and Diego Garcia in the Indian Ocean.

1 OFFSHORE PETROLEUM DISTRIBUTION SHIP (AG)

Name	*No*	*Builders*	*Commissioned*	*F/S*
VADM K R WHEELER	T-AG 5001	Edison Chouest Offshore, Louisiana	20 Sep 2007	Sqn 3

Displacement, tons: 10,404
Measurement, tons: 5,565 grt
Dimensions, feet (metres): 348.5 × 70.0 × 22.7 *(106.22 × 21.33 × 6.9)*
Main machinery: 2 MAK V12M32C diesels; 16,314 hp *(12.1 MW)*; 2 shafts
Speed, knots: 15. **Range, n miles:** 20,220 at 13 kt
Complement: 24 civilians

Comment: An offshore petroleum distribution system that works as an at-sea pumping system to transfer fuel ashore from commercial and military tankers from up to 8 miles off the coast. The delivery rate is 1.7 million gallons per 20 h day. Steel construction.

VADM K R WHEELER ***9/2007, US Navy*** / 1305180

8 WATSON CLASS (LARGE, MEDIUM-SPEED, RO-RO (LMSR) SHIPS) (AKR)

Name	*No*	*Builders*	*Launched*	*Commissioned*	*F/S*
WATSON	T-AKR 310	NASSCO	26 July 1997	23 June 1998	PREPO
SISLER	T-AKR 311	NASSCO	28 Feb 1998	1 Dec 1998	PREPO
DAHL	T-AKR 312	NASSCO	2 Oct 1998	13 July 1999	PREPO
RED CLOUD	T-AKR 313	NASSCO	7 Aug 1999	18 Jan 2000	PREPO
CHARLTON	T-AKR 314	NASSCO	11 Dec 1999	23 May 2000	PREPO
WATKINS	T-AKR 315	NASSCO	28 July 2000	5 Dec 2000	PREPO
POMEROY	T-AKR 316	NASSCO	10 Mar 2001	14 Aug 2001	PREPO
SODERMAN	T-AKR 317	NASSCO	26 Apr 2002	25 Sep 2002	PREPO

Displacement, tons: 62,968 full load
Dimensions, feet (metres): 951.4 × 106 × 35 *(290 × 32.3 × 11)*
Main machinery: 2 GE Marine LM gas turbines; 64,000 hp *(47.7 MW)*; 2 shafts; cp props
Speed, knots: 24
Range, n miles: 12,000 at 24 kt
Complement: 26-45 civilian; up to 50 military
Cargo capacity: 394,673 sq ft. 13,000 tons

Comment: Contract awarded in 1993; options for additional ships exercised at one a year to 2002. All are fitted with a stern slewing ramp, side accesses and cranes for both roll-on/roll-off and lift-on/lift-off capabilities. Ramps extend to 130 ft *(40 m)*, and two twin 55 ton cranes are installed. All but *Sisler* serve as APS-3 ships *Sisler* is a Maritime Prepositioning Ship.

POMEROY ***3/2008*, Hachiro Nakai*** / 1353572

1 CONTAINER SHIP (AK)

Name	*No*	*Builders*	*Commissioned*	*F/S*
MAJ BERNARD F FISHER (ex-*Sea Fox*)	T-AK 4396	Odense	1985	PREPO

Displacement, tons: 48,012 full load
Dimensions, feet (metres): 652.2 × 105.6 × 36.1 *(198.1 × 32.2 × 11)*
Main machinery: 1 BMW diesel; 1 shaft
Speed, knots: 19
Complement: 19
Cargo capacity: 993TEU (on deck); 1,102 TEU (under deck)

Comment: Owned and operated by Sealift, Inc. under charter to MSC. When fully loaded the ship can carry 2,095 20 ft containers although current load of aviation munitions is less. Aviation munitions are to re-supply forward-deployed fighter and attack squadrons. The ship is fitted with an extensive cocoon system enabling it to store deck-loaded munitions in an environmentally controlled atmosphere. *Fisher* is an NDAF ship chartered in 2004.

MAJ BERNARD F FISHER ***6/1999, US Navy*** / 0084185

3 CPL LOUIS J HAUGE, JR CLASS (VEHICLE CARGO SHIPS) (AKRH)

Name	*No*	*Builders*	*Commissioned*	*F/S*
CPL LOUIS J HAUGE, JR (ex-MV *Estelle Maersk*)	T-AK 3000	Odense Staalskibsvaerft A/S, Lindo	Oct 1979	Sqn 3
PFC JAMES ANDERSON, JR (ex-MV *Emma Maersk*)	T-AK 3002	Odense Staalskibsvaerft A/S, Lindo	July 1979	Sqn 3
1st LT ALEX BONNYMAN (ex-MV *Emilie Maersk*)	T-AK 3003	Odense Staalskibsvaerft A/S, Lindo	Jan 1980	Sqn 3

Displacement, tons: 46,552 full load
Dimensions, feet (metres): 755 × 90 × 37.1 *(230 × 27.4 × 11.3)*
Main machinery: 1 Sulzer 7RND76M diesel; 16,800 hp(m) *(12.35 MW)*; 1 shaft; bow thruster
Speed, knots: 16.4
Range, n miles: 10,800 at 16 kt
Complement: 27 plus 10 technicians
Cargo capacity: Containers, 383; Ro-Ro, 121,595 sq ft; JP-5 bbls, 17,128; DF-2 bbls, 10,642; Mogas bbls, 3,865; stable water, 2,022; cranes, 3 twin 30 ton; 92,831 cu ft breakbulk
Helicopters: Platform only.

Comment: Converted from Maersk Line ships by Bethlehem Steel, Sparrow Point, MD. Conversion work included the addition of 157 ft *(47.9 m)* amidships. All operated by Maersk Line Ltd.

CPL LOUIS J HAUGE JR — *3/1998, A Sharma* / 0053410

1 RO-RO CONTAINER: CARGO SHIP (AKR)

Name	*No*	*Builders*	*Commissioned*	*F/S*
GYSGT FRED W STOCKHAM (ex-*Soderman*)	T-AK 3017	National Steel and Shipbuilding	July 2001	Sqn 2

Displacement, tons: 55,123 full load
Dimensions, feet (metres): 907 × 106 × 36 *(276.4 × 32.2 × 10.9)*
Main machinery: 1 Burmeister & Wain 12L90 GFCA diesel; 46,653 hp(m) *(34.29 MW)*; 1 shaft; bow and stern thrusters
Speed, knots: 24
Range, n miles: 12,000 at 24 kt
Complement: 28 crew, 12 cargo maintenance, 83 opp
Cargo capacity: 94,337 sq ft. 1,126 TEU

Comment: Ex-USNS *Soderman* joined the Maritime Prepositioning Force in July 2001 and is assigned to MPSRON Two. Carries USMC expeditionary airfield, fleet hospital package and construction equipment.

GYSGT FRED W STOCKHAM — *8/2001, van Ginderen Collection* / 0131276

2 CONTAINER SHIPS (AK)

Name	*No*	*Builders*	*Commissioned*	*F/S*
LTC JOHN U D PAGE (ex-*Newark Bay*)	T-AK 4543	Daewoo Shipbuilding	1985	PREPO
SSGT EDWARD A CARTER (ex-*OOCL Innovation*)	T-AK 4544	Daewoo Shipbuilding	1984	PREPO

Displacement, tons: 81,284 full load
Dimensions, feet (metres): 950 × 106 × 38 *(289.5 × 32.3 × 11.6)*
Main machinery: 1 Sulzer RLB 90 diesel; 1 shaft
Speed, knots: 18
Complement: 20
Cargo capacity: 2,500 TEU

Comment: *LTC John U D Page* delivered to MSC in February 2001 and *SSGT Edward A Carter* in June 2001. Both operated by Maersk Lines Limited and are APS-3 ships for army prepositioning in the Indian Ocean. Both ships re-chartered in December 2005.

SSGT EDWARD A CARTER — *7/2007, Nipper McDonnell* / 1305185

1 CONTAINER SHIP (AK)

Name	*No*	*Builders*	*Commissioned*	*F/S*
CAPT STEVEN L BENNETT (ex-*Sea Pride*)	T-AK 4296	Samsung Shipbuilding	1984	PREPO

Displacement, tons: 52,878 full load
Dimensions, feet (metres): 686.0 × 99.7 × 38.1 *(209.0 × 30.4 × 11.6)*
Main machinery: 1 diesel; 1 shaft
Speed, knots: 16
Complement: 19 civilian
Cargo capacity: 520 TEU (on deck); 1,006 TEU (under deck)

Comment: The ship is owned and operated by Sealift Inc, under charter to Military Sealift Command. When fully loaded, *Bennett* carries over 916 20 ft containers of various aviation munitions intended to resupply forward-deployed fighter and attack squadrons. The ship is fitted with an extensive cocoon system enabling it to store deck-loaded munitions in an environmentally controlled atmosphere. *Bennett* is an NDAF ship and was re-chartered in 2007.

CAPT STEVEN L BENNETT — *7/2007, Nipper McDonnell* / 1305184

1 RO-RO CONTAINER (CARGO SHIP) (AK)

Name	*No*	*Builders*	*Commissioned*	*F/S*
1st LT HARRY L MARTIN (ex-*Tarago*)	T-AK 3015	Bremer Vulkan, Vegesack	20 Apr 2000	Sqn 3

Displacement, tons: 47,777 full load
Dimensions, feet (metres): 754.3 × 106 × 36.1 *(229.9 × 32.3 × 11)*
Main machinery: 1 MAN K7-SZ-90/160 diesel; 25,690 hp(m) *(18.88 MW)*; 1 shaft
Speed, knots: 18
Range, n miles: 17,000 at 17 kt
Complement: 23 plus 100 military
Cargo capacity: 168,547 sq ft. 735 TEU

Comment: Completed in 1979. Acquired in February 1997 for conversion at Atlantic Drydock, Jacksonville. Carries USMC expeditionary airfield, fleet hospital package and construction equipment.

1st LT HARRY L MARTIN — *10/2008*, Hachiro Nakai* / 1353574

1 RO-RO CONTAINER (CARGO SHIP) (AK)

Name	*No*	*Builders*	*Commissioned*	*F/S*
L/CPL ROY M WHEAT (ex-*Bazaliya*)	T-AK 3016	Detyens Shipyards, Charleston, SC	Oct 2001	Sqn 1

Displacement, tons: 50,101 full load
Dimensions, feet (metres): 863.8 × 98.4 × 34.8 *(263.3 × 30 × 10.6)*
Main machinery: 2 gas turbines; 47,020 hp(m) *(34.56 MW)*; 2 shafts
Speed, knots: 20
Range, n miles: 12,000 at 20 kt
Complement: 30 plus 100 marines
Cargo capacity: 109,170 sq ft. 846 TEU

Comment: Acquired in March 1997 for conversion for Maritime Prepositioning Force by Bender Shipbuilding, Mobile. The ship has been lengthened by 117 ft. Carries USMC expeditionary airfield, fleet hospital package and construction equipment.

L/CPL ROY M WHEAT — *6/2007, M Declerck* / 1305183

3 SGT MATEJ KOCAK CLASS (VEHICLE CARGO SHIPS) (AKH)

Name	*No*	*Builders*	*Commissioned*	*F/S*
SGT MATEJ KOCAK (ex-SS *John B Waterman*)	T-AK 3005	Pennsylvania SB Co, Chester, PA	14 Mar 1981	Sqn 2
PFC EUGENE A OBREGON (ex-SS *Thomas Heywood*)	T-AK 3006	Pennsylvania SB Co, Chester, PA	1 Nov 1982	Sqn 1
MAJ STEPHEN W PLESS (ex-SS *Charles Carroll*)	T-AK 3007	General Dynamics Corp, Quincy, MA	14 Mar 1983	Sqn 3

Displacement, tons: 48,754 full load
Dimensions, feet (metres): 821 × 105.6 × 32.3 *(250.2 × 32.2 × 9.8)*
Main machinery: 2 boilers; 2 GE turbines; 30,000 hp *(22.4 MW)*; 1 shaft
Speed, knots: 20
Range, n miles: 13,000 at 20 kt
Complement: 29 plus 10 technicians
Cargo capacity: Containers, 562; Ro-Ro, 152,236 sq ft; JP-5 bbls, 20,290; DF-2 bbls, 12,355; Mogas bbls, 3,717; stable water, 2,189; cranes, 2 twin 50 ton and 1—30 ton gantry
Helicopters: Platform only.

Comment: Converted from three Waterman Line ships by National Steel and Shipbuilding, San Diego. Delivery dates T-AK 3005, 1 October 1984; T-AK 3006, 16 January 1985; T-AK 3007, 15 May 1985. Conversion work included the addition of 157 ft *(47.9 m)* amidships. All operated by Waterman SS Corp.

EUGENE A OBREGON *7/2007, Nipper McDonnell* / 1305182

5 2nd LT JOHN P BOBO CLASS (VEHICLE CARGO SHIPS) (AKRH)

Name	*No*	*Builders*	*Commissioned*	*F/S*
2nd LT JOHN P BOBO	T-AK 3008	General Dynamics, Quincy	14 Feb 1985	Sqn 1
PFC DEWAYNE T WILLIAMS	T-AK 3009	General Dynamics, Quincy	6 June 1985	Sqn 1
1st LT BALDOMERO LOPEZ	T-AK 3010	General Dynamics, Quincy	20 Nov 1985	Sqn 2
1st LT JACK LUMMUS	T-AK 3011	General Dynamics, Quincy	6 Mar 1986	Sqn 3
SGT WILLIAM R BUTTON	T-AK 3012	General Dynamics, Quincy	27 May 1986	Sqn 2

Displacement, tons: 44,330 full load
Dimensions, feet (metres): 675.2 × 105.5 × 29.6 *(205.8 × 32.2 × 9)*
Main machinery: 2 Stork-Wärtsilä Werkspoor 16TM410 diesels; 27,000 hp(m) *(19.84 MW)* sustained; 1 shaft; bow thruster; 1,000 hp *(746 kW)*
Speed, knots: 17.7
Range, n miles: 12,840 at 18 kt
Complement: 30 plus 10 technicians
Cargo capacity: Containers, 578; Ro-Ro, 156,153 sq ft; JP-5 bbls, 20,776; DF-2 bbls, 13,334; Mogas bbls, 4,880; stable water, 2,357; cranes, 1 single and 2 twin 39 ton
Helicopters: Platform only.

Comment: Built for MPS operations. T-AK 3008, 3009, 3010 and 3011 are government owned (purchased in 2006/07) and are operated by American Overseas Marine. T-AK 3012 is owned and operated by American Overseas Marine.

SGT WILLIAM R BUTTON *7/2007, Nipper McDonnell* / 1305181

2 AVIATION LOGISTICS SHIPS (AVB)

Name	*No*	*Builders*	*Commissioned*
WRIGHT (ex-SS *Young America*)	T-AVB 3	Ingalls Shipbuilding	1970
CURTISS (ex-SS *Great Republic*)	T-AVB 4	Ingalls Shipbuilding	1969

Comment: To reinforce the capabilities of the Maritime Prepositioning Ship programme, conversion of two ro-ro ships into maintenance aviation support ships was approved in FY85 and FY86. *Wright* was completed 14 May 1986, *Curtiss* 18 August 1987. Both conversions took place at Todd Shipyards, Galveston, Texas. Each ship has side ports and three decks aft of the bridge superstructure and has the capability to load the vans and equipment of a Marine Aviation Intermediate Maintenance Activity. The ships' mission is to service aircraft from an afloat platform. They can then revert to a standard sealift role if required. Maritime Administration hull design is C5-S-78a. These NDAF ships are operated by American Overseas Marine and maintained in a reduced operating status although they remain permanently available to the Prepositioning Force.

CURTISS *10/2007, Michael Nitz* / 1353623

READY RESERVE FORCE (RRF)

Notes: (1) The Ready Reserve Force was created in 1976, to support deployment and sustainment requirements and to respond to national emergencies. The RRF is designed to be made available quickly for military sealift operations. Its functions have been widened to include humanitarian and domestic security issues.
(2) On 1 January 2009 the RRF consisted of 48 ships, including Ro-Ro, breakbulk, auxiliary crane, heavy lift barge carriers, special mission tankers and aviation logistic support ships. These are maintained in various stages of readiness and able to get underway in five, 10 or 20 days. They are located in various ports along the US East, West and Gulf Coasts.
(3) The Department of Transportation's Maritime Administration (MARAD) is responsible for the maintenance and administration of the ships at all times. Military Sealift Command assumes operational control only once the ships are activated for military missions.
(4) RRF ships have red, white and blue funnel stripes.
(5) Eight Algol class Fast Sealift Ships transferred to MARAD control in October 2008.

1 PRODUCT TANKER (AOT)

PETERSBURG T-AOT 9109

Comment: *Petersburg* completed APS service in December 2007.

6 AUXILIARY CRANE SHIPS (AK)

Name	*No*	*Builders*	*Conversion*
KEYSTONE STATE (ex-SS *President Harrison*)	T-ACS 1	Defoe SB Co, Bay City	1984
GEM STATE (ex-SS *President Monroe*)	T-ACS 2	Defoe SB Co, Bay City	1985
GRAND CANYON STATE (ex-SS *President Polk*)	T-ACS 3	Dillingham SR, Portland	1986
GOPHER STATE (ex-*Export Leader*)	T-ACS 4	Norshipco, Norfolk	Oct 1987
FLICKERTAIL STATE (ex-*Export Lightning*)	T-ACS 5	Norshipco, Norfolk	Dec 1987
CORNHUSKER STATE (ex-*Staghound*)	T-ACS 6	Norshipco, Norfolk	Mar 1988

Comment: Auxiliary crane ships are container ships to which have been added up to three twin boom pedestal cranes which will lift containerised or other cargo from itself or adjacent vessels and deposit it on a pier or into lighterage.

GOPHER STATE *7/2003, W Sartori* / 0572766

2 BREAK BULK SHIPS (AK/AKR/AE)

CAPE JACOB T-AK 5029 **CAPE GIBSON** T-AK 5051

Comment: *Cape Jacob* is operational as an APS ship.

BREAK BULK SHIP *8/2002, Royal Australian Navy* / 0572796

27 RO-RO SHIPS (AKR)

CAPE ISLAND (ex-*Mercury*) T-AKR 10
CAPE INTREPID (ex-*Lyra*) T-AKR 11
CAPE TEXAS T-AKR 112
CAPE TAYLOR (ex-*Cygnus*) T-AKR 113
ADM WM H CALLAGHAN T-AKR 1001
CAPE ORLANDO (ex-*American Eagle*) T-AKR 2044
CAPE DUCATO T-AKR 5051
CAPE DOUGLAS T-AKR 5052
CAPE DOMINGO T-AKR 5053
CAPE DECISION T-AKR 5054
CAPE DIAMOND T-AKR 5055
CAPE ISABEL T-AKR 5062
CAPE HUDSON T-AKR 5066
CAPE HENRY T-AKR 5067
CAPE HORN T-AKR 5068
CAPE EDMONT T-AKR 5069
CAPE INSCRIPTION T-AKR 5076
CAPE KNOX T-AKR 5082
CAPE KENNEDY T-AKR 5083
CAPE VINCENT (ex-*Taabo Italia*) T-AKR 9666
CAPE RISE (ex-*Saudi Riyadh*) T-AKR 9678
CAPE RAY (ex-*Saudi Makkah*) T-AKR 9679
CAPE VICTORY (ex-*Merzario Britania*) T-AKR 9701
CAPE TRINITY (ex-*Santos*) T-AKR 9711
CAPE RACE (ex-*G&C Admiral*) T-AKR 9960
CAPE WASHINGTON (ex-*Hual Transporter*) T-AKR 9961
CAPE WRATH (ex-*Hual Trader*) T-AKR 9962

CAPE WASHINGTON *9/2007, Michael Winter* / 1305261

4 MISCELLANEOUS HEAVY LIFT SHIPS (AK/AKR)

Lash ships	Heavy lift ships
CAPE FLATTERY T-AK 5070	**CAPE MAY** T-AKR 5063
CAPE FAREWELL T-AK 5073	**CAPE MOHICAN** T-AKR 5065

CAPE MOHICAN ***3/1999, van Ginderen Collection*** / 0084193

8 ALGOL CLASS (FAST SEALIFT SHIPS) (AKRH)

Name	*No*	*Builders*	*Delivered*
ALGOL (ex-SS *Sea-Land Exchange*)	T-AKR 287	Rotterdamsche DD Mij NV, Rotterdam	7 May 1973
BELLATRIX (ex-SS *Sea-Land Trade*)	T-AKR 288	Rheinstahl Nordseewerke, Emden, West Germany	6 Apr 1973
DENEBOLA (ex-SS *Sea-Land Resource*)	T-AKR 289	Rotterdamsche DD Mij NV, Rotterdam	4 Dec 1973
POLLUX (ex-SS *Sea-Land Market*)	T-AKR 290	A G Weser, Bremen, West Germany	20 Sep 1973
ALTAIR (ex-SS *Sea-Land Finance*)	T-AKR 291	Rheinstahl Nordseewerke, Emden, West Germany	17 Sep 1973
REGULUS (ex-SS *Sea-Land Commerce*)	T-AKR 292	A G Weser, Bremen, West Germany	30 Mar 1973
CAPELLA (ex-SS *Sea-Land McLean*)	T-AKR 293	Rotterdamsche DD Mij NV, Rotterdam	4 Oct 1972
ANTARES (ex-SS *Sea-Land Galloway*)	T-AKR 294	A G Weser, Bremen, West Germany	27 Sep 1972

Displacement, tons: 55,355 full load
Measurement, tons: 25,389 net; 27,051-28,095 dwt
Dimensions, feet (metres): 946.2 × 105.6 × 36.8 *(288.4 × 32.2 × 11.2)*
Main machinery: 2 Foster-Wheeler boilers; 875 psi *(61.6 kg/cm²)*; 950°F *(510°C)*; 2 GE MST-19 steam turbines; 120,000 hp *(89.5 MW)*; 2 shafts
Speed, knots: 33. **Range, n miles:** 12,200 at 27 kt
Complement: 43 (as merchant ship); 29 (minimum); 15 (ROS)
Helicopters: Platform only.

Comment: All were originally built as container ships for Sea-Land Services, Port Elizabeth, NJ, but used too much fuel to be cost-effective as merchant ships. Six ships of this class were approved for acquisition in FY81 and the remaining two in FY82. The purchase price included 4,000 containers and 800 container chassis for use in container ship configuration. All eight were converted to Fast Sealift Ships, which are vehicle cargo ships. Conversion included the addition of roll-on/roll-off features. The area between the forward and after superstructures allows for a helicopter flight deck. Capacities are as follows: (sq ft) 150,016 to 166,843 ro-ro; 43,407 lift-on/lift-off; and either 44 or 46 20 ft containers. In addition to one ro-ro ramp port and starboard, twin 35 ton pedestal cranes are installed between the deckhouses and twin 50 ton cranes are installed aft. Ninety-three per cent of a US Army mechanised division can be lifted using all eight ships. Seven of the class moved nearly 11 per cent of all the cargo transported between the US and Saudi Arabia during and after the Gulf War. Six were activated for the Somalian operation in December 1992 and all have been used in various operations and exercises since then. All based in Atlantic and Gulf of Mexico ports. All transferred to US Maritime Administration (MARAD) on 1 October 2008 and maintained in the Ready Reserve Force.

DENEBOLA ***2/2005, Robert Pabst*** / 1154010

COAST GUARD

Headquarters Appointments

Commandant:
Admiral Thad W Allen
Vice Commandant:
Vice Admiral Vivien Crea
Commander, Atlantic Area:
Vice Admiral Robert J Papp
Commander, Pacific Area:
Vice Admiral David P Pekoske

Establishment

The United States Coast Guard was established by an Act of Congress approved 28 January 1915, which consolidated the Revenue Cutter Service (founded in 1790) and the Life Saving Service (founded in 1848). The act of establishment stated the Coast Guard 'shall be a military service and a branch of the armed forces of the USA at all times. The Coast Guard shall be a service in the Treasury Department except when operating as a service in the Navy'.

Congress further legislated that in time of national emergency or when the President so directs, the Coast Guard operates as a part of the Navy. The Coast Guard did operate as a part of the Navy during the First and Second World Wars.

The Lighthouse Service (founded in 1789) was transferred to the Coast Guard on 1 July 1939 and the Bureau of Navigation and Steamboat Inspection on 28 February 1942.

The Coast Guard was transferred from the Department of Transportation to the Department of Homeland Security on 1 March 2003.

Missions

The Coast Guard has five strategic aims:
Safety: Prevent deaths, injuries, and property damage associated with maritime transportation, fishing and recreational boating
National Defense: Defend the nation as one of the five US Armed Services. Enhance regional stability in support of the National Security Strategy specifically maritime homeland security
Maritime Security: Protect maritime borders from all intrusions by (a) halting the flow of illegal drugs, aliens, and contraband into the United States through maritime routes; (b) preventing illegal fishing; and (c) suppressing violations of federal law in the maritime arena
Mobility: Facilitate maritime commerce and eliminate interruptions and impediments to the economical movement of goods and people, while maximizing recreational access and enjoyment of the water
Protection of Natural Resources: Prevent environmental damage and natural resource degradation associated with maritime transportation, fishing, and recreational boating

Organisation

Headquarters: Buzzards Point, Washington DC
Atlantic area: Portsmouth, VA
1st District: Boston, MA
5th District: Portsmouth, VA
7th District: Miami, FL
8th District: New Orleans, LA
9th District: Cleveland, OH
Pacific area: Alameda, CA
11th District: Alameda, CA
13th District: Seattle, WA
14th District: Honolulu, HI
17th District: Juneau, AK
Each district: is further sub-divided into sectors.

Personnel

2009: 6,487 officers, 1,551 warrant officers, 32,274 enlisted, 7,640 reserves

Integrated Deepwater System (IDS)

IDS is a progressive 25-year programme to modernise, convert and replace USCG ships and aircraft and to improve command and control and logistics systems. The first contract for the programme, was awarded in June 2002 to Integrated Coast Guard Systems (ICGS), a partnership of Lockheed Martin and Northrop Grumman. Northrop Grumman Ship Systems will conduct the design and build three classes of new cutters and associated small boats. Up to 91 vessels are planned. Lockheed Martin is responsible for the C4ISR and system integration aspects of the programme and for aircraft procurement. Following a 2005 assessment of post-11 September 2001 (9/11) operational requirements, the Deepwater programme has been revised to incorporate more robust capabilities.

Cutter Strength

All Coast Guard vessels over 65 ft in length and that have adequate crew accommodation are referred to as 'cutters'. All names are preceded by USCG. The first two digits of the hull number for all Coast Guard vessels under 100 ft in length indicates the approximate length overall.

Approximately 2,000 standard and non-standard boats are in service ranging in size from 11 ft skiffs to 55 ft aids-to-navigation craft.

Category/Classification		*Active*	*Building (Projected)*
Cutters			
WHEC	High Endurance Cutters	12	–
WMEC	Medium Endurance Cutters	29	–
WMSL	National Security Cutters	1	1 (7)
WMSM	Offshore Patrol Cutters	–	(25)
Icebreakers			
WAGB	Icebreakers	3	–
WLBB	Icebreaker	1	–
WTGB	Icebreaking Tugs	9	–
Patrol Forces			
WPC	Patrol Coastal	3	(58)
WPB	Patrol Craft	106	8
Training Cutters			
WIX	Training Cutters	1	–
Buoy Tenders			
WLB	Buoy Tenders, Seagoing	16	–
WLM	Buoy Tenders, Coastal	14	–
WLI	Buoy Tenders, Inland	4	–
WLR	Buoy Tenders, River	18	–
Construction Tenders			
WLIC	Construction Tenders, Inland	13	–
Harbour Tugs			
WYTL	Harbour Tugs, Small	11	–

DELETIONS

Cutters

2007 *Storis*

Patrol Forces

2008 *Tempest, Monsoon* (both returned to US Navy)

Tenders and Tugs

2006 *Gentian*
2008 *Blackberry*

Icebreakers

2006 *Mackinaw*

HIGH ENDURANCE CUTTERS

1 + 2 (5) LEGEND CLASS (NATIONAL SECURITY CUTTERS) (PSOH/WMSL)

Name	*No*	*Builders*	*Laid down*	*Launched*	*Commissioned*	*Homeport*
BERTHOLF	WMSL 750	Northrop Grumman Ingalls Shipbuilding	29 Mar 2005	11 Nov 2006	4 Aug 2008	Alameda, CA
WAESCHE	WMSL 751	Northrop Grumman Ingalls Shipbuilding	11 Sep 2006	12 July 2008	2010	Alameda, CA
STRATTON	WMSL 752	Northrop Grumman Ingalls Shipbuilding	2009	2010	2011	Alameda, CA
–	WMSL 753	Northrop Grumman Ingalls Shipbuilding	2010	2011	2012	–

Displacement, tons: 3,206 standard; 4,112 full load
Dimensions, feet (metres): 418 × 54.0 × 21.0 *(127.4 × 16.5 × 6.4)*
Main machinery: CODAG; 1 GE LM2500 gas turbine; 29,500 hp *(22.0 MW)*; 2 MTU20V 1163 diesels; 19,310 hp *(14.4 MW)*; bow thruster; 2 shafts; cp props
Speed, knots: 28
Range, n miles: 12,000 at 9 kt
Complement: 108 (14 officers)

Guns: 1 Bofors 57 mm/70 Mk 3; 220 rds/min to 17 km *(9.3 n miles)*; weight of shell 2.4 kg.
1 General Dynamics 20 mm Phalanx Mk 15. 4—12.7 mm MGs.
Countermeasures: Decoys: Mk 53 Mod 6 Decoy System with Nulka and SRBOC.
ESM/ECM: SLQ 32.
Electro-optic systems: Kollmorgen Mk 46 optronic sight.
Radars: Surface search: TRS 3D/16; E/F-band.
Navigation: Hughes-Furuno SPS 73; I-band.
Fire control: SPQ-9B; I/J-band.
Tacan: AN/URN 25.
Helicopters: 1 HH-65C and two VUAV or 2 HH-65C.

Programmes: Contracts awarded to Northrop Grumman Ship Systems on 2 April 2003 for the design and long lead material procurement of the first of a class of eight Maritime (formerly National) Security Cutters to replace High Endurance Cutters. Lockheed Martin providing command/control/communications and intelligence integration and hardware. Contract for production and delivery of first ship on 28 June 2004 and for second on 18 January 2005.
Structure: Can carry up to 11 m interceptor craft; stern ramps for rapid launch and recovery. Two helicopter hangars. The hull of the third of class is being redesigned to reflect concerns about structural fatigue in the first two vessels. Modifications are to be made to the first two ships early in their lives.
Operational: Designed to deploy 230 days per year, crew deployments will continue to be 185 days away from homeport per year through a crew rotation concept.

BERTHOLF *2/2008*, Northrop Grumman* / 1305173

BERTHOLF
10/2008, Frank Findler*
1353573

12 HAMILTON AND HERO CLASSES (PSOH/WHEC)

Name	*No*	*Builders*	*Laid down*	*Launched*	*Commissioned*	*F/S*	*Home Port*
HAMILTON	WHEC 715	Avondale Shipyards	Jan 1965	18 Dec 1965	20 Feb 1967	PA	San Diego, CA
DALLAS	WHEC 716	Avondale Shipyards	7 Feb 1966	1 Oct 1966	1 Oct 1967	AA	Charleston, SC
MELLON	WHEC 717	Avondale Shipyards	25 July 1966	11 Feb 1967	22 Dec 1967	PA	Seattle, WA
CHASE	WHEC 718	Avondale Shipyards	27 Oct 1966	20 May 1967	1 Mar 1968	PA	San Diego, CA
BOUTWELL	WHEC 719	Avondale Shipyards	5 Dec 1966	17 June 1967	14 June 1968	PA	Alameda, CA
SHERMAN	WHEC 720	Avondale Shipyards	23 Jan 1967	23 Sep 1967	23 Aug 1968	PA	Alameda, CA
GALLATIN	WHEC 721	Avondale Shipyards	27 Feb 1967	18 Nov 1967	20 Dec 1968	AA	Charleston, SC
MORGENTHAU	WHEC 722	Avondale Shipyards	17 July 1967	10 Feb 1968	14 Feb 1969	PA	Alameda, CA
RUSH	WHEC 723	Avondale Shipyards	23 Oct 1967	16 Nov 1968	3 July 1969	PA	Honolulu, HI
MUNRO	WHEC 724	Avondale Shipyards	18 Feb 1970	5 Dec 1970	10 Sep 1971	PA	Kodiak, AK
JARVIS	WHEC 725	Avondale Shipyards	9 Sep 1970	24 Apr 1971	30 Dec 1971	PA	Honolulu, HI
MIDGETT	WHEC 726	Avondale Shipyards	5 Apr 1971	4 Sep 1971	17 Mar 1972	PA	Seattle, WA

Displacement, tons: 3,300 full load
Dimensions, feet (metres): 378 × 42.8 × 20 *(115.2 × 13.1 × 6.1)*
Flight deck, feet (metres): 88 × 40 *(26.8 × 12.2)*
Main machinery: CODOG; 2 Pratt & Whitney FT4A-6 gas turbines; 36,000 hp *(26.86 MW)*; 2 Fairbanks-Morse 38TD8-1/8-12 diesels; 7,000 hp *(5.22 MW)* sustained; 2 shafts; cp props; retractable bow propulsor; 350 hp *(261 kW)*
Speed, knots: 29
Range, n miles: 9,600 at 15 kt
Complement: 162 (19 officers)

Guns: 1 OTO Melara 3 in *(76 mm)*/62 Mk 75 Compact; 85 rds/min to 16 km *(8.7 n miles)* anti-surface; 12 km *(6.6 n miles)* anti-aircraft; weight of shell 6 kg.
2 Boeing 25 mm/87 Mk 38 Bushmaster.
1 GE/GD 20 mm Vulcan Phalanx 6-barrelled Mk 15; 3,000 rds/min combined to 1.5 km. 4—12.7 mm MGs.
Countermeasures: Decoys: 2 Loral Hycor SRBOC 6-barrelled fixed Mk 36; IR flares and chaff.
ESM: WLR-1C, WLR-3; intercept.
Combat data systems: SCCS 378 includes OTCIXS satellite link.
Weapons control: Mk 92 Mod 1 GFCS.
Radars: Air search: Lockheed SPS-40B; B-band.
Surface search: Hughes/Furuno SPS-73; E/F- and I-bands.
Fire control: Sperry Mk 92; I/J-band.
Tacan: URN 25.

Helicopters: 1 HH-65A or 1 HH-60J.

Programmes: Twelve built of a total of 36 originally planned.
Modernisation: FRAM programme for all 12 ships in this class from October 1985 to October 1992. Work included standardising the engineering plants, improving the clutching systems, replacing SPS-29 air search radar with SPS-40 radar and replacing the Mk 56 fire-control system and 5 in/38 gun mount with the Mk 92 system and a single 76 mm OTO Melara Compact gun. In addition Harpoon and Phalanx CIWS fitted to five of the class by 1992 and CIWS to all by late 1993. The flight deck and other aircraft facilities upgraded to handle a Jay Hawk helicopter including a telescopic hangar. URN 25 Tacan added along with the SQR-4 and SQR-17 sonobuoy receiving set and passive acoustic analysis systems. SRBOC chaff launchers were also fitted but not improved ESM which has been shelved. All missiles, torpedo tubes, sonar and ASW equipment removed in 1993–94. 25 mm Mk 38 guns replaced the 20 mm Mk 67. Shipboard Command and Control System (SCCS) fitted to all of the class by 1996. Surface search radar replaced 1997–99. First phase of C4ISR upgrades, including access to SIPRNET and classified networks, completed in 2004.
Structure: These ships have clipper bows, twin funnels enclosing a helicopter hangar, helicopter platform aft. All are fitted with elaborate communications equipment. Superstructure is largely of aluminium construction. Bridge control of manoeuvring is by aircraft-type joystick rather than wheel.
Operational: Ten of the class are based in the Pacific, leaving only two on the East Coast. The removal of SSMs and all ASW equipment refocuses on Coast Guard roles. *Munro* changed homeport to Kodiak, AK, in 2007. Decommissioning of the class is expected to begin in 2011.

DALLAS *9/2008*, C D Yaylali* / 1353622

MEDIUM ENDURANCE CUTTERS

Notes: The Offshore Patrol Cutter programme is for a class of approximately 25 ships to replace the Famour Cutter and Reliance classes. The broad requirement is for a 100 m ship, armed with a medium calibre gun and capable of operating a helicopter and/or UAVs. Although a contract for an accelerated design was signed with Northrop Grumman Ship Systems on 10 June 2004, construction of the first of class, which was expected to start in 2007, has been cancelled. The programme is to start anew with the concept design phase likely to begin in 2009 and construction of the ships, likely to follow the Legend class, projected to begin in about 2015.

13 FAMOUS CUTTER CLASS (PSOH/WMEC)

Name	*No*	*Builders*	*Laid down*	*Launched*	*Commissioned*	*F/S*	*Home Port*
BEAR	WMEC 901	Tacoma Boatbuilding Co	23 Aug 1979	25 Sep 1980	4 Feb 1983	AA	Portsmouth, VA
TAMPA	WMEC 902	Tacoma Boatbuilding Co	3 Apr 1980	19 Mar 1981	16 Mar 1984	AA	Portsmouth, VA
HARRIET LANE	WMEC 903	Tacoma Boatbuilding Co	15 Oct 1980	6 Feb 1982	20 Sep 1984	AA	Portsmouth, VA
NORTHLAND	WMEC 904	Tacoma Boatbuilding Co	9 Apr 1981	7 May 1982	17 Dec 1984	AA	Portsmouth, VA
SPENCER	WMEC 905	Robert E Derecktor Corp	26 June 1982	17 Apr 1984	28 June 1986	AA	Boston, MA
SENECA	WMEC 906	Robert E Derecktor Corp	16 Sep 1982	17 Apr 1984	4 May 1987	AA	Boston, MA
ESCANABA	WMEC 907	Robert E Derecktor Corp	1 Apr 1983	6 Feb 1985	27 Aug 1987	AA	Boston, MA
TAHOMA	WMEC 908	Robert E Derecktor Corp	28 June 1983	6 Feb 1985	6 Apr 1988	AA	Kittery, ME
CAMPBELL	WMEC 909	Robert E Derecktor Corp	10 Aug 1984	29 Apr 1986	19 Aug 1988	AA	Kittery, ME
THETIS	WMEC 910	Robert E Derecktor Corp	24 Aug 1984	29 Apr 1986	30 June 1989	AA	Key West, FL
FORWARD	WMEC 911	Robert E Derecktor Corp	11 July 1986	22 Aug 1987	4 Aug 1990	AA	Portsmouth, VA
LEGARE	WMEC 912	Robert E Derecktor Corp	11 July 1986	22 Aug 1987	4 Aug 1990	AA	Portsmouth, VA
MOHAWK	WMEC 913	Robert E Derecktor Corp	15 Mar 1987	5 May 1988	20 Mar 1991	AA	Key West, FL

Displacement, tons: 1,820 full load
Dimensions, feet (metres): 270 × 38 × 13.9 *(82.3 × 11.6 × 4.2)*
Main machinery: 2 Alco 18V-251 diesels; 7,290 hp *(5.44 MW)* sustained; 2 shafts; cp props
Speed, knots: 19.5
Range, n miles: 9,900 at 12 kt
Complement: 100 (14 officers) plus 5 aircrew

Guns: 1 OTO Melara 3 in *(76 mm)*/62 Mk 75; 85 rds/min to 16 km *(8.7 n miles)* anti-surface; 12 km *(6.6 n miles)* anti-aircraft; weight of shell 6 kg.
2—12.7 mm MGs or 2—40 mm Mk 19 grenade launchers.
Countermeasures: Decoys: 2 Loral Hycor SRBOC 6-barrelled fixed Mk 36; IR flares and chaff.
ESM/ECM: SLQ-32(V)2; radar intercept.
Combat data systems: SCCS-270; OTCIXS satellite link.
Radars: Surface search: Hughes/Furuno SPS-73; I-band.
Fire control: Sperry Mk 92 Mod 1; I/J-band.
Tacan: URN 25.

Helicopters: 1 HH-65A or HH-60J or MH-68A or SH-60B.

Programmes: The contract for construction of WMEC 905-913 was originally awarded to Tacoma Boatbuilding Co on 29 August 1980. However, under lawsuit from the Robert E Derecktor Corp, Middletown, Rhode Island, the contract to Tacoma was determined by a US District Court to be invalid and was awarded to Robert E Derecktor Corp on 15 January 1981.
Modernisation: OTCIXS satellite link fitted from 1992. C4ISR upgrades completed in 2004. *Tampa* refitted 2005–06 as part of the Mission Effectiveness Project to extend service lives. The work includes engineering and habitability measures. All of the class are to be similarly refitted.

NORTHLAND *5/2006, A A de Kruijf* / 1167496

Structure: They are the only medium endurance cutters with a helicopter hangar (which is telescopic) and the first cutters with automated command and control centre. Fin stabilisers fitted. Plans to fit SSM and/or CIWS have been abandoned as has towed array sonar and sonobuoy datalinks. New radars fitted 1997–99.
Operational: Very lively in heavy seas because the length to beam ratio is unusually small for ships required to operate in Atlantic conditions.

14 RELIANCE CLASS (PSOH/WMEC)

Name	*No*	*Builders*	*Commissioned*	*F/S*	*Home Port*
RELIANCE	WMEC 615	Todd Shipyards	20 June 1964	AA	Kittery, ME
DILIGENCE	WMEC 616	Todd Shipyards	26 Aug 1964	AA	Wilmington, NC
VIGILANT	WMEC 617	Todd Shipyards	3 Oct 1964	AA	Cape Canaveral, FL
ACTIVE	WMEC 618	Christy Corp	17 Sep 1966	PA	Port Angeles, WA
CONFIDENCE	WMEC 619	Coast Guard Yard, Baltimore	19 Feb 1966	AA	Cape Canaveral, FL
RESOLUTE	WMEC 620	Coast Guard Yard, Baltimore	8 Dec 1966	AA	St Petersburg, FL
VALIANT	WMEC 621	American Shipbuilding Co	28 Oct 1967	AA	Miami, FL
STEADFAST	WMEC 623	American Shipbuilding Co	25 Sep 1968	AA	Warrenton, OR
DAUNTLESS	WMEC 624	American Shipbuilding Co	10 June 1968	AA	Galveston, TX
VENTUROUS	WMEC 625	American Shipbuilding Co	16 Aug 1968	AA	St Petersburg, FL
DEPENDABLE	WMEC 626	American Shipbuilding Co	22 Nov 1968	AA	Cape May, NJ
VIGOROUS	WMEC 627	American Shipbuilding Co	2 May 1969	AA	Cape May, NJ
DECISIVE	WMEC 629	Coast Guard Yard, Baltimore	23 Aug 1968	AA	Pascagoula, MS
ALERT	WMEC 630	Coast Guard Yard, Baltimore	4 Aug 1969	PA	Warrenton, OR

Displacement, tons: 1,129 full load (WMEC 620-630)
1,110 full load (WMEC 618, 619)
Dimensions, feet (metres): 210.5 × 34 × 10.5 *(64.2 × 10.4 × 3.2)*
Main machinery: 2 Alco 16V-251 diesels; 6,480 hp *(4.83 MW)* sustained; 2 shafts; LIPS cp props
Speed, knots: 18. **Range, n miles**: 6,100 at 14 kt; 2,700 at 18 kt
Complement: 75 (12 officers)

Guns: 1 Boeing 25 mm/87 Mk 38 Bushmaster; 200 rds/min to 6.8 km *(3.4 n miles)*. 2—12.7 mm MGs.
Combat data systems: SCCS-210.
Radars: Surface search: Hughes/Furuno SPS-73; I-band.
Helicopters: 1 HH-65A or MH-68A embarked as required.

Modernisation: All 14 cutters underwent a Major Maintenance Availability (MMA) from 1987–94. The exhausts for main engines, ship service generators and boilers were run in a new vertical funnel which reduces flight deck size. 76 mm guns were replaced by 25 mm Mk 38. A Mission Effectiveness Project was initiated in 2005. Work, to extend service lives, includes engineering and habitability measures. *Dependable* is the first to be refitted and all of the class are to be similarly upgraded.
Structure: Designed for search and rescue duties. Design features include 360° visibility from bridge; helicopter flight deck (no hangar); and engine exhaust vent at stern which has been replaced by a funnel during MMA. Capable of towing ships up to 10,000 tons. Air conditioned throughout except engine room; high degree of habitability.
Operational: Normally operate within 500 miles of the coast. Primary roles are SAR, law enforcement homeland security and defence operations.
Sales: *Courageous* sold to Sri Lanka in 2004.

VENTUROUS *11/2008*, Marco Ghiglino* / 1353621

1 EDENTON CLASS (PSOH/WMEC)

Name	*No*	*Builders*	*Commissioned*	*F/S*	*Home Port*
ALEX HALEY (ex-*Edenton*)	WMEC 39 (ex-ATS 1)	Brooke Marine, Lowestoft	23 Jan 1971	PA	Kodiak, AK

Displacement, tons: 3,000 full load
Dimensions, feet (metres): 282.6 × 50 × 15.1 *(86.1 × 15.2 × 4.6)*
Main machinery: 4 Caterpillar 3516 DITAWJ diesels; 6,000 hp(m) *(4.41 MW)*; 2 shafts; cp props; bow thruster
Speed, knots: 18. **Range, n miles:** 10,000 at 13 kt
Complement: 99 (9 officers)
Guns: 2 McDonnell Douglas 25 mm/87 Mk 38; 200 rds/min to 6.8 km *(3.4 n miles)*. 2—12.7 mm MGs.
Radars: Surface search: Hughes/Furuno SPS-73; I-band.
Combat data systems: SCCS-282.
Helicopters: Platform for 1 HH-65A or 1 HH-60J.

Comment: Former Navy salvage ship paid off in 1996 and taken on by the Coast Guard in November 1997 for conversion. All diving and salvage gear removed, flight deck installed, and upgraded navigation and communications. Armed with 25 mm guns. Used in the Bering Sea, Gulf of Alaska and North Pacific as a multimission cutter from 16 December 1999.

ALEX HALEY *12/1999, USCG / 0084198*

1 DIVER CLASS (PSO/WMEC)

Name	*No*	*Builders*	*USN Comm*	*F/S*	*Home Port*
ACUSHNET (ex-*Shackle*)	WMEC 167 (ex-WAGO 167, ex-WAT 167, ex-ARS 9)	Basalt Rock Co, Napa, CA	5 Feb 1944	PA	Ketchikan, AK

Displacement, tons: 1,557 standard; 1,745 full load
Dimensions, feet (metres): 213 × 41 × 15 *(64.9 × 12.5 × 4.6)*
Main machinery: 4 Fairbanks-Morse diesels; 3,000 hp *(2.24 MW)* sustained; 2 shafts
Speed, knots: 15.5. **Range, n miles:** 9,000 at 8 kt
Complement: 75 (9 officers)
Guns: 2—12.7 mm MGs.
Radars: Navigation: 2 Raytheon SPS-73; I-band.

Comment: Large, steel-hulled salvage ship transferred from the Navy to the Coast Guard and employed in tug and oceanographic duties. Modified for handling environmental data buoys and reclassified WAGO in 1968 and reclassified WMEC in 1980. Major renovation work completed in 1983 and now used for SAR homeland security and law enforcement operations.

ACUSHNET *9/2006, Globke Collection / 1167494*

SHIPBORNE AIRCRAFT

Numbers/Type: 73/24 EADS HH-65C/MH-65C Dolphin.
Operational speed: 175 kt *(324 km/h)*.
Service ceiling: 10,000 ft *(3,048 m)*.
Range: 290 n miles *(537 km)*.
Role/Weapon systems: Short-range rescue and recovery (SRR) helicopter. All A and B models converted to C configuration, with Turbomeca Arriel 2C2 engines by 2007. Conversion included extended heat shields, reconfigured cockpit and improved avionics to facilitate multimission cutter operations. MH version has airborne use-of-force upgrade, interoperable with homeland security and local response agencies. Also configured to allow installation and removal of special AUF mission weapons. Sensors: Bendix RDR 1300 radar and Collins mission management system. Equipped with CDU-900G control displays and MFD-255 multifunctional displays. Weapons: 1—7.62 mm MG.

MH-65C *12/2008*, US Navy / 1353643*

Numbers/Type: 40/2 Sikorsky HH-60J/MH-60T Jayhawk.
Operational speed: 180 kt *(333 km/h)*.
Service ceiling: 13,000 ft *(3,961 m)*.
Range: 300 n miles *(555 km)*.
Role/Weapon systems: Coast Guard version of Seahawk, first flew in 1988. A life-extension programme began in 2005 and is to upgrade the entire fleet by 2013 to MH-60T configuration. Sensors: Bendix RDR-1300C (or Primus 701 in MH-607) weather/search radar. AAQ-15 FLIR. Weapons: 1—7.62 mm MG.

HH-60J *5/2006, Takatoshi Okano / 1167495*

LAND-BASED MARITIME AIRCRAFT

Notes: (1) A High Altitude Endurance Unmanned Air Vehicle (HAE-UAV) is planned to enter service from 2016 although this date may be brought forward. Equipped with high-resolution sensors (EO/FLIR, SAR, ISAR, GMT), the HAE-UAV is to provide long-range surveillance over large areas for extended periods of time. With a loiter altitude of up to 65,000 ft, they are to be capable of transmitting data and EO/IR imagery to shore-based command and control centres to contribute to the Common Operational Picture (COP). The programme is likely to be informed by the USN's BAMS (Broad Area Maritime Surveillance) programme, contenders for which include the Northrop Grumman RQ-4A Global Hawk. Four aircraft are planned.
(2) Four P-3B Orions are used for AEW by US Customs.

Numbers/Type: 8 EADS/CASA HC-144A (CN-235) 200 Ocean Sentry.
Operational speed: 236 kt *(437 km/h)*.
Service ceiling: 25,000 ft *(7,620 m)*.
Range: 1,565 n miles *(2,519 km)*.
Role/Weapon systems: First two aircraft ordered on 18 February 2004 and delivered in 2007. Roles include SAR, law enforcement, ice patrol and environmental protection. Airframe manufactured by EADS/CASA while Lockheed Martin completed integration and developmental testing of aircraft and C4ISR mission pallet. Aircraft made its first flight with the mission system pallet onboard in May 2007. Three of initial five HC-144A aircraft based at Coast Guard Aviation Training Center in Mobile, AL. Up to 36 aircraft may be acquired by 2020. Sensors: Surface search/weather radar; electro-optical/infra-red sensors; advanced 406 MHz DF; C4ISR/SIPRNET/DOD COP interoperable.

CN-235 *11/2008*, EADS/CASA / 1353642*

Numbers/Type: 1 Gulfstream VC-37A.
Operational speed: 459 kt *(850 km/h)*.
Service ceiling: 51,000 ft *(15,540 m)*.
Range: 5,600 n miles *(10,370 km)*.
Role/Weapon: Military version of Gulfstream V which replaced a C-20B Gulfstream III in May 2002. Based at Air Station Washington DC. Serves as a long-range command and control aircraft for Department of Homeland Security and Coast Guard officials.

GULFSTREAM G 550 *6/2003*, ***Paul Jackson*** / 0568402

Numbers/Type: 4/7/6 AMD-BA HU-25 A/HU-25 C/HU-25 D Guardian Falcon.
Operational speed: 420 kt *(774 km/h)*.
Service ceiling: 42,000 ft *(12,800 m)*.
Range: 1,500 n miles *(2,777 km)*.
Role/Weapon systems: Medium-range maritime surveillance role. 17 are operational; 21 are in storage or support aircraft. Sensors: APS-127 weather/search radar. APG-66 air search radar; APS-143B surface search radar. Weapons: unarmed.

HU-25 FALCON *6/2001*, ***Adolfo Ortigueira Gil*** / 0529903

Numbers/Type: 27/6 Lockheed HC-130H/C-130J.
Operational speed: 325 kt *(602 km/h)*.
Service ceiling: 33,000 ft *(10,060 m)*.
Range: 4,100 n miles *(7,592 km)*; 5,500 n miles *(1,018 km)* (HC-130J).
Role/Weapon systems: Long-range maritime reconnaissance role. Sixteen HC-130Hs undergoing upgrade to deliver Deepwater requirement for Long Range Search (LRS) capability and provision of heavy air transport for Maritime Safety & Security Teams (MSSTs), Port Security Units (PSUs), and National Strike Force (NSF). When modernisation is complete, there will be 22 aircraft: 16 HC-130H with upgraded radar and avionics, and six HC-130J. Delivery of first of new C-130J started in 2003. All six were operational by late 2008. Three C-130Js have been equipped with EDO EL/M 2022A(V)3 maritime surface search radar, mounted beneath the plane's fuselage, a nose-mounted APN-241 weather radar, electro-optical/infrared-FLIR Systems Star Safire III, DF-430 UHF/VHF Direction Finder System, and SAAB Transponder Tech AB R4A Airborne Automatic Identification System (AIS). C-130Js will have 90 per cent C4ISR commonality with CASA CN235-300M. Sensors (HC-130H): APS-137 or APS-125 weather/search radar. Wescam MX-20 EO/IR. Weapons: unarmed.

C-130J *3/2008**, ***USCG*** / 1295179

Numbers/Type: 1 Bombardier Challenger 604 C-143A.
Operational speed: 459 kt *(850 km/h)*.
Service ceiling: 41,000 ft *(12,496 m)*.
Range: 3,400 n miles *(6,296 km)*.
Role/Weapon systems: Military version of Challenger 604 replaced a VC-4 Gulfstream I in December 2005. Based at Air Station Washington DC., it serves as a medium-range command and control aircraf for Department of Homeland Security and Coast Guard officials.

PATROL FORCES

41 ISLAND CLASS (WPB)

Name	*No*	*Commissioned*	*Home Port*
FARALLON	WPB 1301	21 Feb 1986	Miami, FL
MAUI	WPB 1304	9 May 1986	Miami, FL
OCRACOKE	WPB 1307	4 Aug 1986	St Petersburg, FL
AQUIDNECK	WPB 1309	26 Sep 1986	Atlantic Beach, NC
MUSTANG	WPB 1310	3 Dec 1986	Seward, AK
NAUSHON	WPB 1311	5 Dec 1986	Ketchikan, AK
SANIBEL	WPB 1312	28 May 1987	Woods Hole, MA
EDISTO	WPB 1313	27 Mar 1987	San Diego, CA
SAPELO	WPB 1314	14 May 1987	San Juan, PR
MATINICUS	WPB 1315	19 June 1987	San Juan, PR
NANTUCKET	WPB 1316	10 Aug 1987	St Petersburg, FL
BARANOF	WPB 1318	25 May 1988	Miami, FL
CHANDELEUR	WPB 1319	8 June 1988	Miami, FL
CHINCOTEAGUE	WPB 1320	8 Aug 1988	San Juan, PR
CUSHING	WPB 1321	8 Aug 1988	San Juan, PR
CUTTYHUNK	WPB 1322	5 Oct 1988	Port Angeles, WA
DRUMMOND	WPB 1323	19 Oct 1988	Miami, FL
KEY LARGO	WPB 1324	24 Dec 1988	San Juan, PR
MONOMOY	WPB 1326	19 May 1989	Woods Hole, MA
ORCAS	WPB 1327	14 Apr 1989	Coos Bay, OR
SITKINAK	WPB 1329	31 May 1989	Miami, FL
TYBEE	WPB 1330	4 Aug 1989	Woods Hole, MA
WASHINGTON	WPB 1331	6 Oct 1989	Arpa Harbor, Guam
WRANGELL	WPB 1332	15 Sep 1989	South Portland, ME
ADAK	WPB 1333	17 Nov 1989	Sandy Hook, NJ
LIBERTY	WPB 1334	22 Sep 1989	Auke Bay, AK
ANACAPA	WPB 1335	13 Jan 1990	Petersburg, AK
KISKA	WPB 1336	21 Apr 1990	Hilo, HI
ASSATEAGUE	WPB 1337	15 June 1990	Arpa Harbor, Guam
GRAND ISLE	WPB 1338	19 Apr 1991	Gloucester, MA
KEY BISCAYNE	WPB 1339	23 Apr 1991	Key West, FL
JEFFERSON ISLAND	WPB 1340	16 Aug 1991	South Portland, ME
KODIAK ISLAND	WPB 1341	21 June 1991	Key West, FL
LONG ISLAND	WPB 1342	27 Aug 1991	Valdez, AK
BAINBRIDGE ISLAND	WPB 1343	20 Sep 1991	Sandy Hook, NJ
BLOCK ISLAND	WPB 1344	22 Nov 1991	Atlantic Beach, NC
STATEN ISLAND	WPB 1345	22 Nov 1991	Atlantic Beach, NC
ROANOKE ISLAND	WPB 1346	8 Feb 1992	Homer, AK
PEA ISLAND	WPB 1347	29 Feb 1992	Key West, FL
KNIGHT ISLAND	WPB 1348	22 Apr 1992	Key West, FL
GALVESTON ISLAND	WPB 1349	5 June 1992	Honolulu, HI

Displacement, tons: 168 (A series); 154 (B series); 134 (C series) full load
Dimensions, feet (metres): 110 × 21 × 7.3 *(33.5 × 6.4 × 2.2)*
Main machinery: 2 Paxman Valenta 16RP 200M diesels (A and B series); 6,246 hp *(4.62 MW)*, sustained; 2 Caterpillar 3516 DITA diesels (C series); 5,596 hp *(4.17 MW)* sustained; 2 shafts
Speed, knots: 29
Range, n miles: 3,928 at 10 kt
Complement: 16 (2 officers)
Guns: 1 McDonnell Douglas 25 mm/87 Mk 38. 2—12.7 mm M60 MGs.
Combat data systems: SCCS-Lite.
Radars: Navigation: Hughes/Furuno SPS-73; I-band.

Comment: All built by the Bollinger Machine Shop and Shipyard at Lockport, Louisiana. The design is based upon the 110 ft patrol craft built by Vosper Thornycroft, UK, in service in Venezuela, UAE and UK Customs, but modified to meet Coast Guard needs. Vosper Thornycroft supplied design support, stabilisers, propellers, and steering gear. Batches: A 1301-1316, B 1317-1337, C 1338-1349. Radars replaced by 1999. As part of the Deepwater programme, eight hulls were modified to include stretching of the hull to 123 ft by insertion of a 13 ft plug to enable installation of upgraded C4ISR systems, a stern launch and recovery system and various platform improvements. WPB 1303 was first to undergo conversion at Bollinger Shipyard in February 2004. She was followed by WPBs 1317, 1325 and 1328 in 2004 and 1302, 1305, 1306 and 1308 by 2007. However, following experience of significant deck cracking, hull deformation and shaft alignment problems, the conversion planned was terminated in December 2006 and all eight vessels were taken out of operational service. The remaining 110 ft cutters are to continue in service until replaced by the Fast Response Cutter and/or a stop-gap solution can be found. Six cutters operate from Bahrain.

MAUI *9/2008**, ***Shaun Jones*** / 1353641

70 + 3 MARINE PROTECTOR CLASS (WPB)

Name	*No*	*Commissioned*	*Home Port*
BARRACUDA	87301	24 Feb 1998	Eureka, CA
HAMMERHEAD	87302	17 May 1998	Woods Hole, MA
MAKO	87303	28 June 1998	Cape May, NJ
MARLIN	87304	2 Dec 1998	Fort Meyers, FL
STINGRAY	87305	13 Jan 1999	Mobile, AL
DORADO	87306	24 Feb 1999	Crescent City, CA
OSPREY	87307	7 Apr 1999	Port Townsend, WA
CHINOOK	87308	19 May 1999	New London, CT
ALBACORE	87309	30 June 1999	Little Creek, VA
TARPON	87310	11 Aug 1999	Tybee Island, GA
COBIA	87311	8 Sep 1999	Mobile, AL
HAWKSBILL	87312	6 Oct 1999	Monterey, CA
CORMORANT	87313	3 Nov 1999	Fort Pierce, FL
FINBACK	87314	1 Dec 1999	Cape May, NJ
AMBERJACK	87315	29 Dec 1999	Port Isabel, TX
KITTIWAKE	87316	26 Jan 2000	Lihue, HI
BLACKFIN	87317	23 Feb 2000	Santa Barbara, CA
BLUEFIN	87318	22 Mar 2000	Fort Pierce, FL
YELLOWFIN	87319	19 Apr 2000	Charleston, SC
MANTA	87320	17 May 2000	Freeport, TX
COHO	87321	14 June 2000	Pamana City, FL
KINGFISHER	87322	12 July 2000	Mayport, FL
SEAHAWK	87323	9 Aug 2000	Carrabelle, FL
STEELHEAD	87324	6 Sep 2000	Port Aransas, TX
BELUGA	87325	4 Oct 2000	Little Creek, VA
BLACKTIP	87326	1 Nov 2000	Oxnard, CA
PELICAN	87327	29 Nov 2000	Abbeville, LA
RIDLEY	87328	27 Dec 2000	Montauk, NY
COCHITO	87329	24 Jan 2001	Little Creek, VA
MANOWAR	87330	21 Feb 2001	Galveston, TX
MORAY	87331	21 Mar 2001	Jonesport, ME
RAZORBILL	87332	18 Apr 2001	Gulfport, MS
ADELIE	87333	16 May 2001	Port Angeles, WA
GANNET	87334	13 June 2001	Fort Lauderdale, FL
NARWHAL	87335	11 July 2001	Corona del Mar, CA
STURGEON	87336	8 Aug 2001	Grand Isle, LA
SOCKEYE	87337	5 Sep 2001	Bodega Bay, CA
IBIS	87338	3 Oct 2001	Cape May, NJ
POMPANO	87339	1 Nov 2001	Gulfport, MS
HALIBUT	87340	28 Nov 2001	Marina del Ray, CA
BONITO	87341	26 Dec 2001	Pensacola, FL
SHRIKE	87342	23 Jan 2002	Cape Canaveral, FL
TERN	87343	20 Feb 2002	San Francisco, CA
HERON	87344	20 Mar 2002	Sabine, TX
WAHOO	87345	17 Apr 2002	Port Angeles, WA
FLYINGFISH	87346	15 May 2002	Boston, MA
HADDOCK	87347	12 June 2002	San Diego, CA
BRANT	87348	10 July 2002	Corpus Christi, TX
SHEARWATER	87349	7 Aug 2002	Portsmouth, VA
PETREL	87350	4 Sep 2002	San Diego, CA
SEA LION	87352	19 Nov 2003	Bellingham, WA
SKIPJACK	87353	17 Dec 2003	Galveston, TX
DOLPHIN	87354	14 Jan 2004	Miami, FL
HAWK	87355	11 Feb 2004	St Petersburg, FL
SAILFISH	87356	10 Mar 2004	Sandy Hook, NJ
SAWFISH	87357	7 Apr 2004	Key West, FL
SWORDFISH	87358	9 Mar 2005	Port Angeles, WA
TIGER SHARK	87359	6 Apr 2005	Newport, RI
BLUE SHARK	87360	4 May 2005	Everett, WA
SEA HORSE	87361	1 June 2005	Portsmouth, VA
SEA OTTER	87362	29 June 2005	San Diego, CA
MANATEE	87363	27 July 2005	Corpus Christi, TX
AHI	87364	15 Feb 2006	Honolulu, HI
PIKE	87365	15 Jan 2006	San Francisco, CA
TERRAPIN	87366	1 Feb 2006	Bellingham, WA
SEA DRAGON	87367	14 Jan 2008	Kings Bay, GA
SEA DEVIL	87368	20 June 2008	Bangor, WA
CROCODILE	87369	5 Dec 2008	St Petersburg, FL
DIAMONDBACK	87370	17 Jan 2009	Miami, FL
REEF SHARK	87371	24 Mar 2009	San Juan, PR
ALLIGATOR	87372	2009	St Petersburg, FL
SEA DOG	87373	2009	Kings Bay, GA
SEA FOX	87374	2009	Bangor, WA

Displacement, tons: 91 full load
Dimensions, feet (metres): 86.9 × 19 × 5.2 *(26.5 × 5.8 × 1.6)*
Main machinery: 2 MTU 8V 396TE94 diesels; 2,680 hp(m) *(1.97 MW)* sustained; 2 shafts
Speed, knots: 25
Range, n miles: 900 at 8 kt
Complement: 10 (1 officer)
Guns: 2—12.7 mm MGs.
Radars: Navigation: I-band.

Comment: Designed by David M Cannell based on the hull of the Damen Stan Patrol 2600 which is in service with the Hong Kong police. Steel hull built by Bollinger with GRP superstructure by Halmatic. A stern ramp is used for launching a 5.5 m RIB. Following delivery of 65 vessels to the USCG and a further two to the Maltese Armed Forces, an order for a further eight was made by the USCG on 25 June 2007. Four (87367, 87368, 87373, 87374) of these latter craft were funded by the US Navy but are operated by the Coast Guard.

COCHITO *9/2007, Michael Winter* / 1305259

MORAY *10/2008*, Marco Ghiglino* / 1353640

3 CYCLONE CLASS (PATROL COASTAL SHIPS) (WPC/PB)

Name	*No*	*Builders*	*Commissioned*	*Home Port*
ZEPHYR	WPB 8 (ex-PC 8)	Bollinger, Lockport	15 Oct 1994	Pascagoula, MS
SHAMAL	WPC 13 (ex-PC 13)	Bollinger, Lockport	27 Jan 1996	Pascagoula, MS
TORNADO	WPC 14 (ex-PC 14)	Bollinger, Lockport	15 May 2000	Pascagoula, MS

Displacement, tons: 386 full load
Dimensions, feet (metres): 179 × 25.9 × 7.9 *(54.6 × 7.9 × 2.4)*
Main machinery: 4 Paxman Valenta 16RP 200M diesels; 14,400 hp *(10.7 MW)* sustained; 4 shafts
Speed, knots: 35
Range, n miles: 2,500 at 12 kt
Complement: 27 (2 officers)
Guns: 2 McDonnell Douglas 25 mm/87 Mk 38. 4—12.7 mm M60 MGs.
Combat data systems: SCCS-Lite.
Radars: Navigation: Hughes/Furuno SPS-73; I-band.

Comment: Contract awarded by USN for eight in August 1990 and five more in July 1991. Design based on Vosper Thornycroft Ramadan class modified for USN requirements including 1 in armour on superstructure. The craft have a slow speed loiter capability. These five vessels were modified to incorporate a semi-dry well, boat ramp and stern gate to facilitate deployment and recoveryof a fully loaded RIB while the ship is making way. Transferred to the USCG 2004–05. These are to fill a gap in Coast Guard resources. *Tempest* and *Monsoon* are to return to the Navy in 2008; the other three are to be transferred in FY12. Eight unconverted (without stern-ramps) vessels remain in USN service.

SHAMAL *11/2004, USCG* / 1167650

460 GUARDIAN CLASS (TPSB/YP)

Displacement, tons: 3 full load
Dimensions, feet (metres): 24.6 × 8.2 × 0.4 *(7.5 × 2.5 × 0.4)*
Main machinery: 2 Evinrude outboards; 350 hp *(261 kW)*
Speed, knots: 40
Complement: 4
Guns: 1—12.7 mm MG. 2—7.62 mm MGs.
Radars: Navigation: Raytheon; I-band.

Comment: Transportable Port Security Boats (TPSB) which serve with the six Port Security Units and a Training Detachment. Can be transported by aircraft.

GUARDIAN *7/2000, Hachiro Nakai* / 0105727

0 + 34 SENTINEL CLASS (PBO/WPC)

Displacement, tons: 353 full load
Dimensions, feet (metres): 153.4 × 25.4 × 8.4 *(46.7 × 7.7 × 2.6)*
Main machinery: 2 diesels; 5,760 hp *(4.3 MW)*; 2 shafts
Speed, knots: 28+
Range, n miles: To be announced
Complement: 22
Guns: 1 — 25 mm. 4 — 12.7 mm MGs.
Radars: Surface search: To be announced.
Navigation: To be announced.

Comment: The Fast-Response Cutter is part of the Integrated Deepwater modernisation programme for the Coast Guard to replace the Island class patrol boats. Its principal roles include fishery protection, barrier patrols, interdiction, SAR and disaster relief. Following evaluation of bids, a contract was awarded to Bollinger Shipyards of Lockport, LA, on 26 September 2008; there are options for 34 craft, the first of which is to be delivered in 2010 and based at Miami. Ultimately, a class of 58 is sought. The design is based on the Damen Stan Patrol 4708, modified to achieve 28+ kt; a stern-launch capability is incorporated; steel hull, aluminium superstructure. The first craft is to be based at Miami, FL.

SENTINEL CLASS *9/2008*, Bollinger Shipyards* / 1333755

ICEBREAKERS

Notes: Replacement of *Polar Star* and *Polar Sea* is under consideration in view of their age and of increasing economic, political and scientific interest in the polar regions.

1 ICEBREAKER (WLBB)

Name	*No*	*Builders*	*Commissioned*	*Home Port*
MACKINAW	WLBB 30	Manitowoc Marine, Wisconsin	10 June 2006	Cheboygan, MI

Displacement, tons: 3,500 full load
Dimensions, feet (metres): 240 × 58 × 16 *(73.1 × 17.7 × 4.8)*
Main machinery: Diesel-electric; 3 diesel generators; 12,600 hp *(9.4 MW)*; 2 podded propulsors; 6,700 hp *(5 MW)*
Speed, knots: 15
Complement: 55 (8 officers)
Radars: Surface search: Kongsberg Data Bridge 10.
Navigation: Kongsberg Integrated Bridge System.

Comment: Contract to build new icebreaker/buoy tender awarded 15 October 2001. Keel laid 10 February 2004. Launched in April 2005 and delivered in November 2005. Icebreaker replaced WAGB 83 and assumed the same name. In addition to breaking ice (up to 32 in thick at 3 kt ahead, 2 kt astern) for the primary shipping lanes on the Great Lakes, the new ship will service aids to navigation, as well as performing search and rescue, pollution control, homeland security, and law enforcement duties from its homeport of Cheboygan, Michigan. Principal feature is 'podded' or protected propellers that can rotate 360° for greater manoeuvrability. Other features include fully integrated bridge system, robust communications suite and 3,200 sq ft of buoy deck space. A crane of 60 ft can recover buoys weighing up to 20 tons.

MACKINAW *3/2006, Manitowoc Marine* / 1154627

1 HEALY CLASS (WAGBH)

Name	*No*	*Builders*	*Commissioned*	*F/S*	*Home Port*
HEALY	WAGB 20	Avondale, New Orleans	29 Oct 1999	PA	Seattle, WA

Displacement, tons: 16,400 full load
Dimensions, feet (metres): 420 oa; 397.8 wl × 82 × 29 *(128; 121.2 × 25 × 8.9)*
Main machinery: Diesel-electric; 4 Westinghouse/Sulzer 12ZA 40S diesels; 42,400 hp *(31.16 MW)*; 4 Westinghouse alternators; 2 motors; 30,000 hp *(22.38 MW)*; 2 shafts; bow thruster; 2,200 hp *(1.64 MW)*
Speed, knots: 17
Range, n miles: 16,000 at 12.5 kt
Complement: 75 (12 officers) plus 45 scientists
Helicopters: 2 HH-65A or 1 HH-60J.

Comment: In response to the 1984 Interagency Polar Icebreaker Requirements Study and Congressional mandate, approval was given for the construction of a new icebreaker as a replacement for two Wind class which were then decommissioned in 1988. However, no action was taken to provide funds for the new ship until Congress included it in the Navy's FY91 ship construction budget and after further delays the ship was ordered 15 July 1993. Icebreaking capability of 4 ft at 3 kt. Reached North Pole in September 2005, the third by a US surface ship. In a six-month Arctic expedition, the ship embarked 47 scientists from nine countries to study climate change.

HEALY *1/2003, Bob Fildes* / 0572759

2 POLAR CLASS (WAGBH)

Name	*No*	*Builders*	*Launched*	*Commissioned*	*F/S*	*Home Port*
POLAR STAR	WAGB 10	Lockheed SB	17 Nov 1973	19 Jan 1976	PA	Seattle, WA
POLAR SEA	WAGB 11	Lockheed SB	24 June 1975	23 Feb 1978	PA	Seattle, WA

Displacement, tons: 13,190 full load
Dimensions, feet (metres): 399 × 84 × 32 *(121.6 × 25.6 × 9.8)*
Main machinery: CODOG; diesel-electric (AC/DC); 6 Alco 16V-251F/Westinghouse AC diesel generators; 21,000 hp *(15.66 MW)* sustained; 3 Westinghouse DC motors; 18,000 hp *(13.42 MW)* sustained; 3 Pratt & Whitney FT4A-12 gas turbines; 60,000 hp *(44.76 MW)* sustained; 3 Philadelphia 75 VMGS gears; 60,000 hp *(44.76 MW)* sustained; 3 shafts; cp props
Speed, knots: 20
Range, n miles: 28,275 at 13 kt
Complement: 134 (15 officers) plus 33 scientists and 12 aircrew
Guns: 2 — 7.62 mm MGs.
Radars: Navigation: 2 Raytheon SPS-64; I-band.
Tacan: SRN 15.
Helicopters: 2 HH-65A or 1 HH-60J.

Comment: At a continuous speed of 3 kt, they can break ice 6 ft *(1.8 m)* thick, and by ramming can break 21 ft *(6.4 m)* pack. Conventional icebreaker hull form with 'White' cutaway bow configuration and well-rounded body sections to prevent being trapped in ice. The ice belt is 1.75 in *(44.45 mm)* thick supported by framing at 16 in *(0.4 m)* centres. Three heeling systems assist icebreaking and ship extraction. Two 15 ton capacity cranes fitted aft; one 3 ton capacity crane fitted forward. Two over-the-side oceanographic winches, one over-the-stern trawl/core winch. Deck fixtures for scientific research vans, and research laboratories provided for arctic and oceanographic research. Between 1986–92, science facilities were upgraded including habitability, lab spaces and winch capabilities. *Polar Sea* went to the North Pole in August 1994. *Polar Star* was placed in a 'special' status in 2006. The vessel is to undergo extensive upgrade and is to be reactivated in FY12.

POLAR STAR *2/2006, Chris Sattler* / 1167646

9 BAY CLASS (TUGS—WTGB)

Name	No	Launched	Commissioned	F/S	Home Port
KATMAI BAY	WTGB 101	7 Nov 1977	8 Jan 1979	GLA	Sault Sainte Marie, MI
BRISTOL BAY	WTGB 102	13 Feb 1978	5 Apr 1979	GLA	Detroit, MI
MOBILE BAY	WTGB 103	13 Feb 1978	2 Sep 1979	GLA	Sturgeon Bay, WI
BISCAYNE BAY	WTGB 104	29 Aug 1978	8 Dec 1979	GLA	St Ignace, MI
NEAH BAY	WTGB 105	6 Aug 1979	18 Aug 1980	GLA	Cleveland, OH
MORRO BAY	WTGB 106	6 Aug 1979	25 Jan 1981	AA	New London, CT
PENOBSCOT BAY	WTGB 107	24 July 1983	4 Sep 1984	AA	Bayonne, NJ
THUNDER BAY	WTGB 108	20 July 1984	29 Dec 1985	AA	Rockland, ME
STURGEON BAY	WTGB 109	9 July 1986	20 Aug 1988	AA	Bayonne, NJ

Displacement, tons: 662 full load
Dimensions, feet (metres): 140 × 37.6 × 12.5 *(42.7 × 11.4 × 3.8)*
Main machinery: Diesel-electric; 2 Fairbanks-Morse 38D8-1/8-10 diesel generators; 2.4 MW sustained; Westinghouse electric drive; 2,500 hp *(1.87 MW)*; 1 shaft
Speed, knots: 14.7. **Range, n miles:** 4,000 at 12 kt
Complement: 17 (3 officers)
Radars: Navigation: Raytheon SPS-64(V)1; I-band.

Comment: The size, manoeuvrability and other operational characteristics of these vessels are tailored for operations in harbours and other restricted waters and for fulfilling present and anticipated multimission requirements. All units are ice strengthened for operation on the Great Lakes, coastal waters and in rivers and can break 20 in of ice continuously and up to 8 ft by ramming. A self-contained portable bubbler van and system reduces hull friction. First six built at Tacoma Boatbuilding, Tacoma. WTGB 107-109 built in Tacoma by Bay City Marine, San Diego. *Bristol Bay* and *Mobile Bay* have had their bows reinforced to push the two aids-to-navigation barges on the Great Lakes. WTGB 106 was decommissioned in 1998 and re-activated on 4 February 2002.

THUNDER BAY *7/2000, Hachiro Nakai* / 0105725

PENOBSCOT BAY *5/2002, van Ginderen Collection* / 0144052

SEAGOING TENDERS

16 JUNIPER CLASS (BUOY TENDERS—WLB/ABU)

Name	No	Builders	Commissioned	Home Port
JUNIPER	WLB 201	Marinette Marine	12 Jan 1996	Newport, RI
WILLOW	WLB 202	Marinette Marine	27 Nov 1996	Newport, RI
KUKUI	WLB 203	Marinette Marine	9 Oct 1997	Honolulu, HI
ELM	WLB 204	Marinette Marine	29 June 1998	Atlantic Beach, NC
WALNUT	WLB 205	Marinette Marine	22 Feb 1999	Honolulu, HI
SPAR	WLB 206	Marinette Marine	9 Mar 2001	Kodiak, AK
MAPLE	WLB 207	Marinette Marine	21 June 2001	Sitka, AK
ASPEN	WLB 208	Marinette Marine	28 Sep 2001	San Francisco, CA
SYCAMORE	WLB 209	Marinette Marine	1 Mar 2002	Cordova, AK
CYPRESS	WLB 210	Marinette Marine	24 June 2002	Mobile, AL
OAK	WLB 211	Marinette Marine	17 Oct 2002	Charleston, SC
HICKORY	WLB 212	Marinette Marine	6 Mar 2003	Homer, AK
FIR	WLB 213	Marinette Marine	27 June 2003	Astoria, OR
HOLLYHOCK	WLB 214	Marinette Marine	15 Oct 2003	Port Huron, MI
SEQUOIA	WLB 215	Marinette Marine	21 Apr 2004	Apra Harbour, Guam
ALDER	WLB 216	Marinette Marine	2 Sep 2004	Duluth, MN

Displacement, tons: 2,064 full load
Dimensions, feet (metres): 225 × 46 × 13 *(68.6 × 14 × 4)*
Main machinery: 2 Caterpillar 3608 diesels; 6,200 hp *(4.6 MW)* sustained; 1 shaft; cp prop; bow; 460 hp *(343 kW)* and stern; 550 hp *(410 kW)* thrusters
Speed, knots: 15
Range, n miles: 6,000 at 12 kt
Complement: 40 (6 officers)
Guns: 2—12.7 mm MGs. 2—7.62 mm MGs.
Radars: Navigation: 2 Sperry/Litton BridgeMaster E340; I-band.

Comment: On 18 February 1993, the Coast Guard awarded Marinette Marine of Marinette, WI, a contract to construct the first of a new class of seagoing buoy tenders. Capable of breaking 14 in of ice at 3 kt or a minimum of 3 ft by ramming. Main hoist can lift 20 tons, secondary 5 tons. A dynamic positioning system can maintain the ship within a 10 m circle in up to 30 kt wind. The class is named after the first *Juniper*, which was built in 1940 and decommissioned in 1975.

ASPEN *10/2006, Michael Nitz* / 1305177

COASTAL TENDERS

14 KEEPER CLASS (BUOY TENDERS—WLM/ABU)

Name	No	Builders	Commissioned	Home Port
IDA LEWIS	WLM 551	Marinette Marine	1 Nov 1996	Newport, RI
KATHERINE WALKER	WLM 552	Marinette Marine	27 June 1997	Bayonne, NJ
ABIGAIL BURGESS	WLM 553	Marinette Marine	19 Sep 1997	Rockland, ME
MARCUS HANNA	WLM 554	Marinette Marine	26 Nov 1997	South Portland, ME
JAMES RANKIN	WLM 555	Marinette Marine	26 Aug 1998	Baltimore, MD
JOSHUA APPLEBY	WLM 556	Marinette Marine	20 Nov 1998	St Petersburg, FL
FRANK DREW	WLM 557	Marinette Marine	17 June 1999	Portsmouth, VA
ANTHONY PETIT	WLM 558	Marinette Marine	1 July 1999	Ketchikan, AK
BARBARA MABRITY	WLM 559	Marinette Marine	29 July 1999	Mobile, AL
WILLIAM TATE	WLM 560	Marinette Marine	16 Sep 1999	Philadelphia, PA
HARRY CLAIBORNE	WLM 561	Marinette Marine	28 Oct 1999	Galveston, TX
MARIA BRAY	WLM 562	Marinette Marine	6 Apr 2000	Mayport, FL
HENRY BLAKE	WLM 563	Marinette Marine	18 May 2000	Everett, WA
GEORGE COBB	WLM 564	Marinette Marine	22 June 2000	San Pedro, CA

Displacement, tons: 840 full load
Dimensions, feet (metres): 175 × 36 × 7.9 *(53.3 × 11 × 2.4)*
Main machinery: 2 Caterpillar 3508TA diesels; 1,920 hp *(1.43 MW)* sustained; 2 Ulstein Z-drives; bow thruster; 460 hp *(343 kW)*
Speed, knots: 12. **Range, n miles:** 2,000 at 10 kt
Complement: 18 (1 officer)
Radars: Navigation: Raytheon SPS-64; I-band.

Comment: Contract awarded 22 June 1993 for first of class with an option for 13 more. Capable of breaking 9 in of ice at 3 kt or 18 in by ramming. Named after Lighthouse Keepers for the Lighthouse Service, one of the predecessors of the modern Coast Guard. The ship is a scaled down model of the Juniper class for coastal service. Main hoist to lift 10 tons, secondary 3.75 tons. Able to skim and recover surface oil pollution using a vessel of opportunity skimming system.

GEORGE COBB *10/2007, Michael Nitz* / 1353639

BUOY TENDERS (INLAND-WLI)

2 BUOY TENDERS (WLI/ABU)

Name	No	Builders	Launched	Home port
BLUEBELL	WLI 313	Birchfield Shipyard, Tacoma	28 Sep 1944	Portland, OR
BUCKTHORN	WLI 642	Mobile Ship Repair, Mobile	18 Aug 1963	Sault Sainte Marie, MI

Displacement, tons: 226 (174 *Bluebell*) full load
Dimensions, feet (metres): 100 × 24 × 5 *(30.5 × 7.3 × 1.5)* (*Buckthorn* draught 4 *(1.2)*)
Main machinery: 2 Caterpillar diesels; 600 hp *(448 kW)*; 2 shafts
Speed, knots: 11.9; 10.5 *(Bluebell)*. **Range, n miles:** 2,700 at 10 kt
Complement: 15 (1 officer)

Comment: Different vintage but similar in design.

BUCKTHORN *3/2000, US Coast Guard* / 0084213

2 BUOY TENDERS (WLI/ABU)

Name	No	Builders	Home port
BAYBERRY	WLI 65400	Reliable Shipyard, Olympia	Oak Island, NC
ELDERBERRY	WLI 65401	Reliable Shipyard, Olympia	Petersburg, AK

Displacement, tons: 70 full load
Dimensions, feet (metres): 65 × 17 × 4 *(19.8 × 5.2 × 1.2)*
Main machinery: 2 GM diesels; 1 or 2 shafts
Speed, knots: 10
Complement: 8

Comment: Both completed in June 1954. *Blackberry* decommissioned in 2008.

BAYBERRY *5/1999, Hartmut Ehlers* / 0084211

BUOY TENDERS (RIVER) (WLR)

Notes: (1) All are based on rivers of USA especially the Mississippi, Missouri, Tennessee, Cumberland and their tributaries.
(2) Two ATON (aids to navigation) barges completed in 1991–92 by Marinette Marine. For use on the Great Lakes in conjunction with icebreaker tugs *Bristol Bay* and *Mobile Bay*.

6 RIVER TENDERS (WLR)

SANGAMON WLR 65506 **SCIOTO** WLR 65504 **OSAGE** WLR 65505
OUACHITA WLR 65501 **CIMARRON** WLR 65502 **OBION** WLR 65503

Displacement, tons: 146 full load
Dimensions, feet (metres): 65 × 21 × 4.5 *(19.8 × 6.4 × 0.4)*
Main machinery: 2 diesels; 750 hp *(560 kW)*; 2 shafts
Speed, knots: 10. **Range, n miles:** 3,500 at 8 kt
Complement: 13

Comment: All commissioned 1960–62. WLR 65501 and 65502 built by Platzer Shipyard, Houston, TX; 65503-65506 by Gibbs Shipyard, Jacksonville, FL. WLR push crane-equipped barges to deploy aids-to-navigation buoys on the inland river system. Some of the class have 'jetting' devices used to set and anchor buoys in sandy or muddy river beds.

SANGAMON *8/2005, USCG* / 1353711

12 RIVER TENDERS (WLR)

WEDGE WLR 75307 **CHIPPEWA** WLR 75404 **PATOKA** WLR 75408
GASCONADE WLR 75401 **CHEYENNE** WLR 75405 **CHENA** WLR 75409
MUSKINGUM WLR 75402 **KICKAPOO** WLR 75406 **KANKAKEE** WLR 75500
WYACONDA WLR 75403 **KANAWHA** WLR 75407 **GREENBRIER** WLR 75501

Displacement, tons: 150 full load
Dimensions, feet (metres) : 75 × 22 × 4 *(22.9 × 6.7 × 1.2)*
Main machinery: 2 Caterpillar diesels; 660 hp *(492 kW)*; 2 shafts
Speed, knots: 9. **Range, n miles:** 3,100 at 8 kt
Complement: 13

Comment: WLR 75401-75409 built 1964–70 by four different companies. WLR 75500 and 75501 were completed in early 1990. Details given are for the WLR 75401 series, but all are much the same size.

GASCONADE *2/2005, USCG* / 1043673

TRAINING CUTTERS

1 EAGLE CLASS (WIX/AXS)

Name	No	Builders	Commissioned	Home Port
EAGLE (ex-*Horst Wessel*)	WIX 327	Blohm + Voss, Hamburg	15 May 1946	New London, CT

Displacement, tons: 1,816 full load
Dimensions, feet (metres): 231 wl; 293.6 oa × 39.4 × 16.1 *(70.4; 89.5 × 12 × 4.9)*
Main machinery: 1 Caterpillar D 399 auxiliary diesel; 1,125 hp *(839 kW)* sustained; 1 shaft
Speed, knots: 10.5; 18 sail
Range, n miles: 5,450 at 7.5 kt diesel only
Complement: 185 (19 officers, 150 cadets)
Radars: Navigation: SPS-73; I-band.

Comment: Former German training ship. Launched on 13 June 1936. Taken by the US as part of reparations after the Second World War for employment in US Coast Guard Practice Squadron. Taken over at Bremerhaven in January 1946; arrived at home port of New London, Connecticut, in July 1946. (Sister ship *Albert Leo Schlageter* was also taken by the USA in 1945 but was sold to Brazil in 1948 and re-sold to Portugal in 1962. Another ship of similar design, *Gorch Fock*, transferred to the USSR in 1946 and survives as *Tovarisch*.) *Eagle* was extensively overhauled 1981–82. When the Coast Guard added the orange-and-blue marking stripes to cutters in the 1960s *Eagle* was exempted because of their effect on her graceful lines; however, in early 1976 the stripes and words 'Coast Guard' were added in time for the July 1976 Operation Sail in New York harbour. During the Coast Guard's year long bicentennial celebration, which ended 4 August 1990, *Eagle* visited each of the 10 ports where the original revenue cutters were homeported: Baltimore, Maryland; New London, Connecticut; Washington, North Carolina; Savannah, Georgia; Philadelphia, Pennsylvania; Newburyport, Maryland; Portsmouth, New Hampshire; Charleston, South Carolina; New York, New York; and Hampton, Virginia. The cutter currently serves as a training ship for cadets and officer candidates. During 2005, *Eagle* visited Bremerhaven for the first time since leaving its original homeport in 1945.
Fore and main masts 150.3 ft *(45.8 m)*; mizzen 132 ft *(40.2m)*; sail area, 25,351 sq ft.

EAGLE *6/2005, Martin Mokrus* / 1154016

CONSTRUCTION TENDERS (INLAND) (WLIC)

Notes: Although all operate on inland waters, they are administered by the Atlantic Area.

4 PAMLICO CLASS (WLIC)

PAMLICO WLIC 800 **HUDSON** WLIC 801 **KENNEBEC** WLIC 802 **SAGINAW** WLIC 803

Displacement, tons: 459 full load
Dimensions, feet (metres): 160.9 × 30 × 4 *(49 × 9.1 × 1.2)*
Main machinery: 2 Caterpillar diesels; 1,000 hp *(746 kW)*; 2 shafts
Speed, knots: 11
Complement: 14 (1 officer)
Radars: Navigation: Raytheon SPS-69; I-band.

Comment: Completed in 1976 at the Coast Guard Yard, Curtis Bay, Maryland. These ships maintain structures and buoys in bay areas along the Atlantic and Gulf coasts.

HUDSON *12/1989, Giorgio Arra* / 0506121

1 COSMOS CLASS (WLIC)

SMILAX WLIC 315

Displacement, tons: 218 full load
Dimensions, feet (metres): 100 × 24 × 5 *(30.5 × 7.3 × 1.5)*
Main machinery: 2 Caterpillar D 353 diesels; 660 hp *(492 kW)* sustained; 2 shafts
Speed, knots: 10.5
Complement: 14 (1 officer)
Radars: Navigation: Raytheon SPS-69; I-band.

Comment: Completed in 1944. Primary areas of operation are intercoastal waters from Virginia to Georgia. Pushes a 70 ft construction barge equipped with a crane and other aids-to-navigation equipment. Based at Atlantic Beach, NC.

COSMOS CLASS *7/1990, van Ginderen Collection* / 0506122

8 ANVIL/CLAMP CLASSES (WLIC)

ANVIL WLIC 75301
HAMMER WLIC 75302
SLEDGE WLIC 75303
MALLET WLIC 75304
VISE WLIC 75305
CLAMP WLIC 75306
HATCHET WLIC 75309
AXE WLIC 75310

Displacement, tons: 140 full load
Dimensions, feet (metres): 75 (76-WLIC 75306-75310) × 22 × 4 *(22.9 (23.2) × 6.7 × 1.2)*
Main machinery: 2 Caterpillar diesels; 750 hp *(559 kW)*; 2 shafts
Speed, knots: 10
Complement: 13 (1 officer in *Mallet, Sledge* and *Vise*)

Comment: Completed 1962–65. Primary areas of operation are intercoastal waters from Texas to New Jersey. Push 68 ftand 84 ft construction barges equipped with cranes and other aids-to-navigation equipment.

HATCHET *10/2008*, USCG* / 1353709

HARBOUR TUGS

11 65 ft CLASS (WYTL)

Name	*No*	*Home port*
CAPSTAN	WYTL 65601	Philadelphia, PA
CHOCK	WYTL 65602	Portsmouth, VA
TACKLE	WYTL 65604	Rockland, ME
BRIDLE	WYTL 65607	Southwest Harbor, ME
PENDANT	WYTL 65608	Boston, MA
SHACKLE	WYTL 65609	South Portland, ME
HAWSER	WYTL 65610	Bayonne, NJ
LINE	WYTL 65611	Bayonne, NJ
WIRE	WYTL 65612	Saugerties, NY
BOLLARD	WYTL 65614	New Haven, CT
CLEAT	WYTL 65615	Philadelphia, PA

Displacement, tons: 72 full load
Dimensions, feet (metres): 65 × 19 × 7 *(19.8 × 5.8 × 2.1)*
Main machinery: 1 Caterpillar 3412TA diesel; 400 hp *(298 kW)* sustained; 1 shaft
Speed, knots: 10. **Range, n miles:** 2,700 at 10 kt
Complement: 6
Radars: Navigation: Raytheon SPS-69; I-band.

Comment: Built between 1961 and 1967. The multimission tugs provide icebreaking, homeland security and aids-to-navigation services to several east coast areas. Re-engined 1993–96.

HAWSER *7/2000, Hachiro Nakai* / 0105731

RESCUE AND UTILITY CRAFT

Notes: Craft of several different types. All carry five or six figure numbers of which the first two figures reflect the craft's length in feet.

132 UTILITY BOATS (YAG/UTB)

Displacement, tons: 13.4 full load
Dimensions, feet (metres): 41.3 × 14.1 × 4.1 *(12.6 × 4.3 × 1.3)*
Main machinery: 2 diesels; 680 hp *(507 kW)* sustained; 2 shafts
Speed, knots: 26. **Range, n miles:** 300 miles at 18 kt
Complement: 3

Comment: 205 built by Coast Guard Yard, Baltimore 1973–83. Aluminium hull with a towing capacity of 100 tons. Used for fast multimission response in weather conditions up to moderate.

41416 *9/2008*, Marco Ghiglino* / 1353638

117 MOTOR LIFEBOATS (MLB/SAR)

Displacement, tons: 20 full load
Dimensions, feet (metres): 47.9 × 14.5 × 4.5 *(14.6 × 4.4 × 1.4)*
Main machinery: 2 Detroit diesels; 850 hp *(634 kW)* sustained; 2 shafts
Speed, knots: 25. **Range, n miles:** 220 at 25 kt
Complement: 4

Comment: Built by Textron Marine, New Orleans. The prototype completed trials in mid-1991. Five production boats delivered in 1994. The final hull was delivered in June 2003. Replaced the fleet of 44 ft lifeboats. Aluminium hulls, self-righting with a 9,000 lb bollard pull and a towing capability of 150 tons. Primarily a lifeboat but it has a multimission capability.

MLB 47245 *10/2008*, Frank Findler* / 1353575

503 + 35 DEFENDER CLASS (RESPONSE BOATS) (PBF)

Displacement, tons: 2.7 full load
Dimensions, feet (metres): 25.0 × 8.5 × 8.8 *(7.6 × 2.6 × 2.7)*
Main machinery: 2 Honda outboard motors; 450 hp *(335 kW)*
Speed, knots: 46. **Range, n miles:** 175 at 35 kt
Complement: 4
Guns: 2 — 7.62 mm MGs.
Radars: Furuno; I-band.

Comment: High-speed inshore patrol craft of aluminium construction and foam collar built by SAFE Boats International, Port Orchard, Washington. First delivery in July 2003 to replace nearly 300 non-standard shore based boats and provide a standardised platform for the USCG's new Maritime Safety and Security Teams (MSST), established as a result of the 11 September 2001 terrorist attacks. Transportable in a C-130.

DEFENDER 25579 *10/2006, Michael Nitz* / 1305175

1 + 0 (32) LONG RANGE INTERCEPTOR CRAFT (LRI)

Displacement, tons: 10.9
Dimensions, feet (metres): 30.0 × 10.5 × 3.0 *(9.1 × 3.2 × 0.9)*
Main machinery: 2 Cummins diesels; 2 Hamilton waterjets
Speed, knots: 45
Complement: 2 crew and 12 passengers

Comment: Built by Willard Marine. Aluminium construction. The first was delivered in October 2008. Interoperability trials successfully undertaken with *Bertholf* in early 2008. Launch and recovery is by a stern launch and recovery system.

LRI — *10/2004, Jeff Murphy, USCG* / 1121008

44 + 46 SPECIAL PURPOSE CRAFT (PBF)

Displacement, tons: 6.9 full load
Dimensions, feet (metres): 33.3 × 10.0 × 2.5 *(10.1 × 3.0 × 0.7)*
Main machinery: 3 Mercury outboard motors; 825 hp *(615 kW)*
Speed, knots: 50
Range, n miles: 250 at 30 kt
Complement: 4
Guns: 2—7.62 mm MGs.
Radars: Furuno; I-band.

Comment: Larger versions of the SAFE Boats International Defender class. Aluminium construction with foam collar. High-speed coastal craft procured for port security and law enforcement tasks, particularly the interception of suspicious vessels entering US territorial waters. First craft delivered in January 2006. A further 46 to be delivered by 2010.

SPECIAL PURPOSE CRAFT — *10/2008*, Marco Ghiglino* / 1353712

4 + 8 RESPONSE BOAT MEDIUM (YAG/UTB)

Displacement, tons: 16.3 full load
Dimensions, feet (metres): 44.9 × 14.6 × 3.3 *(13.7 × 4.45 × 1.0)*
Main machinery: 2 diesels; 2 waterjets
Speed, knots: 42
Range, n miles: 250 at 30 kt
Complement: 4
Guns: 2—7.62 mm MGs.
Radars: Furuno; I-band.

Comment: Multimission self-righting response craft to replace 41 ft utility boat in inland waterways and offshore up to 50 n miles. Capable of towing 100 tons. First boat delivered April 2008. Built by Marinette Marine Corp., Manitowac, Wisconsin, with Kvichak Marine Industries, Seattle. Up to 180 are planned to be procured by 2013.

RESPONSE BOAT — *1/2009*, USCG* / 1353710

NATIONAL OCEANIC AND ATMOSPHERIC ADMINISTRATION (NOAA)

HENRY B BIGELOW — *7/2007, Ships of the World* / 1305256

Headquarters Appointments

Under Secretary of Commerce for Oceans and Atmosphere:
Jane Lubchenco
Director, Office of Marine and Aviation Operations and NOAA Commissioned Officer Corps:
Rear Admiral Jonathan W Bailey
Director, Marine and Aviation Operations Centers:
Rear Admiral Philip M Kenul

Establishment and Missions

NOAA is the largest bureau of the US Department of Commerce, with a diverse set of responsibilities in environmental sciences. NOAA components include the Office of Marine and Aviation Operations; National Ocean Service; National Weather Service; National Marine Fisheries Service; National Environmental Satellite, Data and Information Service; and the Office of Oceanic and Atmospheric Research. NOAA's research vessels conduct operations in hydrography, bathymetry, oceanography, atmospheric research, fisheries assessments and research, and related programmes in marine resources. Larger research vessels operate in international waters, and smaller ones primarily in Atlantic and Pacific coastal waters, and the Gulfs of Mexico and Alaska. NOAA conducts diving operations. It also operates fixed-wing aircraft for hurricane research and reconnaissance; oceanographic and atmospheric research; marine mammal observations; hydrologic forecasts; and aerial mapping and remote sensing.

NOAA's active fleet numbers 18 ships, and now includes eight former Navy ships. The T-AGOS ship *Capable*, renamed *Okeanos Explorer*, was converted to conduct ocean exploration and commissioned in 2008. It is the first USfederal ship dedicated to ocean exploration. Of the remaining ex-naval ships, five areT-AGOS vessels: one has been converted for oceanographic research *(Ka'imimoana)*, two for fisheries research *(Gordon Gunter, Oscar Elton Sette)*, and two for coastal oceanographic research *(McArthur II* and *Hi'ialakai)*. *Oscar Elton Sette* replaced *Townsend Cromwell* and *McArthur II* replaced *McArthur* in 2003. *Hi'ialakai* (formerly *Vindicator*), homeported in Hawaii, was commissioned in 2004. The former naval T-AGS hydrographic survey ship *Littlehales* was transferred to NOAA in 2003 and recommissioned *Thomas Jefferson*, replacing *Whiting*. A former naval Yard Torpedo Test (YTT) vessel was converted for coastal research and became operational in 2003 as *Nancy Foster*, replacing *Ferrel*. A newly constructed oceanographic research ship, *Ronald H Brown* (AGOR 26), was commissioned in 1997. The hydrographic survey ship *Fairweather* was decommissioned in 1988, refurbished, and reactivated in 2004. A new class of Fisheries Survey Vessels (FSV) has been designed to NOAA specifications and standards set by the International Council for the Exploration of the Sea. *Oscar Dyson*, the first of four FSVs of the same design, was commissioned in May 2005 and operates in Alaskan waters. The second FSV, *Henry B Bigelow*, was commissioned in July 2007 and operates primarilyin the northeast United States. FSV 3, *Pisces*, will be delivered in early 2009. FSV 4, *Bell M Shimada*, is expected to be delivered in late 2009. The FSVs were built by VT Halter Marine, Moss Point, MS. A newly designed Small Waterplane Area Twin Hull (SWATH) coastal mapping vessel, *Ferdinand R Hassler*, is also under construction at VT Halter Marine. NOAA decommissioned three ships in 2008: *Rude*, a 41-year-old hydrographic survey vessel; *John N Cobb*, a 58-year-old fisheries research vessel, and *Albatross IV*, a 45-year-old fisheries research vessel.

Ships

The following ships may be met at sea.
Oceanographic Research Ships: *Ronald H Brown, Ka'imimoana, Okeanos Explorer.*
Multipurpose Oceanographic/Coastal Research Ships: *McArthur II, Nancy Foster, Hi'ialakai*
Hydrographic Survey Ships: *Rainier, Thomas Jefferson, Fairweather.*
Fisheries Research Ships: *Miller Freeman, Oregon II, Delaware II, David Starr Jordan, Gordon Gunter, Oscar Elton Sette, Oscar Dyson, Henry B Bigelow, Pisces.*

Personnel

2009: 300 officers plus 12,000 civilians

Bases

Major: Norfolk, VA and Seattle, WA.
Minor: Woods Hole, MA; Pascagoula, MS; Honolulu, HI; Charleston, SC; San Diego, CA; Ketchikan, AK, Kodiak, AK.

OSCAR ELTON SETTE ***8/2008*, Michael Nitz*** / 1353637

HI'IALAKAI ***6/2007, Ships of the World*** / 1305254

Uruguay

Country Overview

The Oriental Republic of Uruguay is situated in south-eastern South America. With an area of 68,037 square miles it has borders to the north with Brazil and to the west with Argentina. It has a coastline of 356 n miles with the south Atlantic Ocean and River Plate. There are some 675 n miles of navigable internal waterways. The capital, largest city and principal port is Montevideo. Territorial Seas (12 n miles) and an EEZ (200 n miles) are claimed.

Headquarters Appointments

Commander-in-Chief of the Navy:
Vice Admiral Juan Heber Fernández Maggio
Fleet Commander:
Rear Admiral Hugo Viglietti di Mattía
Commander Coast Guard:
Rear Admiral Oscar P Debali de Palleja

Diplomatic Representation

Naval Attaché in London:
Captain Fernando Franzini

Personnel

(a) 2009: 5,491 (730 officers) (including 450 naval infantry, 300 naval air and 1,950 Coast Guard)
(b) Voluntary service

Prefectura Nacional Naval (PNN)

Established in 1934 primarily for harbour security and coastline guard duties. In 1991 it was integrated with the Navy, although patrol craft retain Prefectura markings. There are three regions: Atlantic, Rio de la Plata, and Rio Uruguay.

Bases

Montevideo: Main naval base *(Lt Carlos Machitelli)* with two dry docks (A new naval base is under construction at Punta Lobos and will replace the current harbour facilities.)
La Paloma: Naval station *(Lt Cdr Ernesto Motto)*
Laguna del Sauce: Naval air station *(Lt Cdr Carlos Curbelo)*
Fray Bentos: River base *(Lt Luis Muselti)*

Marines

Cuerpo de Fusileros Navales consisting of 450 men in three rifleman companies and one combat support company plus a command company of 100.

Prefix to Ships' Names

ROU

DELETIONS

Frigates

2005 *General Artigas*
2007 *Uruguay*
2008 *Montevideo*

Patrol Forces

2008 *Comodoro Coé*

FRIGATES

Notes: Following the acquisition of two João Belo-class frigates from Portugal in early 2008, there is a programme to replace both these ships in about 2015. Options include Bremen-class frigates from Germany.

2 COMMANDANT RIVIÈRE CLASS (FF)

Name	*No*	*Builders*	*Launched*	*Commissioned*	*Recommissioned*
URUGUAY (ex-*João Belo*)	1 (ex-F 480)	ACB Nantes	6 Sep 1965	22 Mar 1966	1 July 1967
PEDRO CAMPBELL (ex-*Sacadura Cabral*)	2 (ex-F 483)	ACB Nantes	18 Aug 1967	15 Mar 1968	25 July 1969

Displacement, tons: 1,750 standard; 2,250 full load
Dimensions, feet (metres): 336.9 × 38.4 × 14.1 *(102.7 × 11.7 × 4.3)*
Main machinery: 4 SEMT-Pielstick 12 PC series diesels; 16,000 hp(m) *(11.8 MW)*; 2 shafts
Speed, knots: 25. **Range, n miles:** 7,500 at 15 kt
Complement: 159 (9 officers)

Guns: 2 DCN 3.9 in *(100 mm)*/55 Mod 1953 automatic ❶; dual purpose; 60 rds/min to 17 km *(9 n miles)* anti-surface; 8 km *(4.4 n miles)* anti-aircraft; weight of shell 13.5 kg.
2 Bofors 40 mm/60 ❷; 30 rds/min to 12 km *(6.6 n miles)*; weight of shell 0.89 kg.
Torpedoes: 6—324 mm Mk 32 Mod 5 (2 triple) tubes ❸; Honeywell Mk 46 Mod 5; active/passive homing to 11 km *(5.9 n miles)* at 40 kt; warhead 44 kg.
Countermeasures: Decoys: 2 Loral Hycor SRBOC 6-barrelled chaff launchers.
TCM: SLQ-25 Nixie.
ESM: AR-700 (V2); intercept.
Weapons control: C T Analogique. Sagem DMAA optical director.
Radars: Air search: Thomson-CSF DRBV 22A ❹; D-band.
Surface search: Thomson-CSF DRBV-50 ❺; G-band.
Navigation: Kelvin Hughes KH 1007; I-band.
Fire control: Thomson CSF DRBC 31D ❻; I-band.
Sonars: Thomson Sintra DUBA 3; active attack; high frequency.

Comment: *Uruguay* and *Pedro Campbell* procured from Portugal on 8 April 2008. It is reported that SQS 510 sonar was removed before transfer. Based at Montevideo.

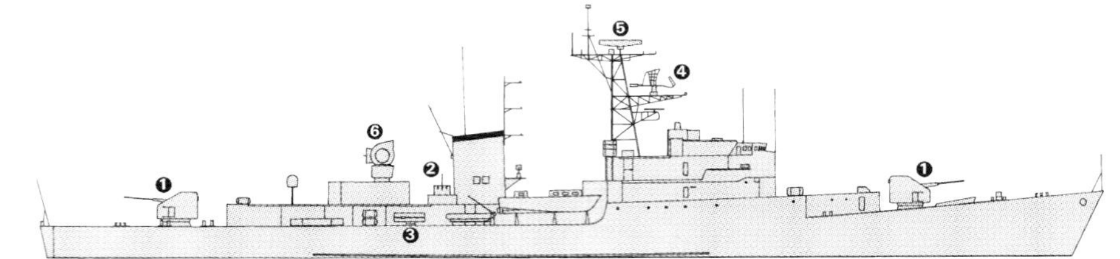

URUGUAY ***(Scale 1 : 900), Ian Sturton*** / 0121391

URUGUAY ***5/2008*, M Declerck*** / 1335314

PEDRO CAMPBELL ***5/2008*, Guy Toremans*** / 1335313

LAND-BASED MARITIME AIRCRAFT

Notes: (1) Fixed-wing: There are five further aircraft: one Beech B 200T maritime patrol aircraft (fitted with APS 128 radar), two Beech T-34C and two Jetstream T2.
(2) Helicopters: There are 10 helicopters: Two Westland Wessex HC Mk 2, one Bell 47G, one UH-13 AS 355 Esquilo (acquired from Brazil in October 2006 for operation from *General Artigas*) and six Bolkow BO-105 (acquired from Germany in August 2007).

JET STREAM T2 *2/2008*, A E Galarce* / 1335307

T-34C *6/2008*, Uruguay Navy* / 1335312

AS 355 *2/2008*, A E Galarce* / 1335309

Numbers/Type: 1 Grumman S-2G Tracker.
Operational speed: 140 kt *(260 km/h)*.
Service ceiling: 25,000 ft *(7,620 m)*.
Range: 1,350 n miles *(2,500 km)*.
Role/Weapon systems: Ex-Israeli aircraft. ASW and surface search with improved systems. Sensors: Search radar, MAD, sonobuoys. Weapons: ASW; torpedoes, depth bombs or mines. ASV; rockets underwing.

S-2G *2/2008*, A E Galarce* / 1335306

PATROL FORCES

Notes: There is a plan to acquire one offshore patrol vessel, possibly to be built in Chile.

1 WANGEROOGE CLASS (PBO/AG)

Name	*No*	*Builders*	*Commissioned*
MALDONADO (ex-*Norderney*)	23 (ex-A1455)	Schichau, Bremerhaven	15 Oct 1970

Displacement, tons: 854 standard; 1,024 full load
Dimensions, feet (metres): 170.6 × 39.4 × 12.8 *(52 × 12.1 × 3.9)*
Main machinery: Diesel-electric; 4 MWM 16-cyl diesel generators; 2 motors; 2,400 hp(m) *(1.76 MW)*; 2 shafts
Speed, knots: 14
Range, n miles: 5,000 at 10 kt
Complement: 24
Guns: 1 Bofors 40 mm/60.

Comment: Built as a salvage tug with ice-strengthened hull. Transferred from the German Navy on 21 November 2002. Employed as a support ship and for offshore patrol duties.

MALDONADO *11/2007, A E Galarce* / 1335308

2 VIGILANTE CLASS (LARGE PATROL CRAFT) (PBO)

Name	*No*	*Builders*	*Commissioned*
15 de NOVIEMBRE	5	CMN, Cherbourg	25 Mar 1981
25 de AGOSTO	6	CMN, Cherbourg	25 Mar 1981

Displacement, tons: 190 full load
Dimensions, feet (metres): 137 × 22.4 × 8.2 *(41.8 × 6.8 × 2.4)*
Main machinery: 2 MTU 12V 538 TB91 diesels; 4,600 hp(m) *(3.4 MW)* sustained; 2 shafts
Speed, knots: 28
Range, n miles: 2,400 at 15 kt
Complement: 28 (5 officers)
Guns: 1 Bofors 40 mm/70.
Weapons control: CSEE Naja optronic director.
Radars: Surface search: Racal Decca TM 1226C; I-band.

Comment: Ordered in 1979. Steel hull. First launched 16 October 1980 and second 11 December 1980. Based at La Paloma. *Comodoro Coé* decommissioned in 2008.

15 DE NOVIEMBRE *7/2001, A E Galarce* / 0534052

2 CAPE CLASS (LARGE PATROL CRAFT) (PB)

Name	*No*	*Builders*	*Commissioned*
COLONIA (ex-*Cape Higgon*)	10	Coast Guard Yard, Curtis Bay	14 Oct 1953
RIO NEGRO (ex-*Cape Horn*)	11	Coast Guard Yard, Curtis Bay	3 Sep 1958

Displacement, tons: 98 standard; 148 full load
Dimensions, feet (metres): 95 × 20.2 × 6.6 *(28.9 × 6.2 × 2)*
Main machinery: 2 GM 16V-149TI diesels; 2,322 hp *(1.73 MW)* sustained; 2 shafts
Speed, knots: 20. **Range, n miles:** 2,500 at 10 kt
Complement: 14 (1 officer)
Guns: 2 – 12.7 mm MGs.
Radars: Surface search: Raytheon SPS-64; I-band.

Comment: Designed for port security and search and rescue. Steel hulled. During modernisation in 1974 received new engines, electronics and deck equipment. Superstructure modified or replaced, and habitability improved. Transferred from the US Coast Guard 25 January 1990. Both based at Fray Bentos.

COLONIA *1/2007, A E Galarce* / 1167929

1 COASTAL PATROL CRAFT (PB)

Name	*No*	*Builders*	*Commissioned*
PAYSANDU	12 (ex-PR 12)	Sewart, USA	Nov 1968

Displacement, tons: 98 standard; 148 full load
Dimensions, feet (metres): 94.8 × 20.3 × 6.6 *(28.9 × 6.2 × 2.0)*
Main machinery: 2 GM 16V-71 diesels; 811 hp *(605 kW)* sustained; 2 shafts
Speed, knots: 20
Range, n miles: 2,500 at 10 kt
Complement: 8
Guns: 2—12.7 mm MGs.
Radars: Surface search: Raytheon SPS-34; I-band.

Comment: Based at Montevideo.

PAYSANDU ***2/2004, A E Galarce*** / 1044206

2 COAST GUARD PATROL CRAFT (WPB)

70 72

Displacement, tons: 90 full load
Dimensions, feet (metres): 72.2 × 16.4 × 5.9 *(22 × 5 × 1.8)*
Main machinery: 2 GM diesels; 400 hp *(298 kW)*; 2 shafts
Speed, knots: 12
Complement: 8

Comment: Built in 1957 at Montevideo.

PREFECTURA 70 ***11/2007, A E Galarce*** / 1335305

4 RIVER PATROL CRAFT (PBR)

URUGUAY 1–4

Displacement, tons: 5 full load
Dimensions, feet (metres): 37.1 × 10.7 × 2.6 *(11.3 × 3.25 × 0.8)*
Main machinery: 3 Volvo AD41P 220MOP diesels
Speed, knots: 32
Range, n miles: 1,500 at 24 kt
Complement: 6
Guns: 3—7.62 mm MGs.

Comment: Built by Nuevos Ayres yacht builders. Deployed to Congo as part of UN force during 2001.

URUGUAY 1 ***2001, Uruguay Navy*** / 0121420

16 RIVER PATROL CRAFT (PBR)

URUGUAY 5–20

Displacement, tons: 4 full load
Dimensions, feet (metres): 26.6 × 10.0 × 1.7 *(8.1 × 3.04 × 0.53)*
Main machinery: 2 Mercury outboards; 450 hp *(335 kW)*
Speed, knots: 50
Complement: 3
Guns: 1—7.62 mm MG.

Comment: Boston Whaler craft ordered in May 2008 for deployment to Haiti as part of MINUSTAH. To be used as patrol craft on Uruguay River and lakes on return.

9 TYPE 44 CLASS (WPB)

441–449

Displacement, tons: 18 full load
Dimensions, feet (metres): 44 × 12.8 × 3.6 *(13.5 × 3.9 × 1.1)*
Main machinery: 2 Detroit 6V-38 diesels; 185 hp *(136 kW)*; 2 shafts
Speed, knots: 14. **Range, n miles:** 215 at 10 kt
Complement: 3

Comment: Acquired from the US in 1999 and operated by the Coast Guard primarily as SAR craft.

PREFECTURA 442 ***11/2007, A E Galarce*** / 1335304

MINE WARFARE FORCES

3 KONDOR II CLASS (MINESWEEPERS—COASTAL) (MSC)

Name	*No*	*Builders*	*Launched*	*Recommissioned*
TEMERARIO (ex-*Riesa*)	31	Peenewerft, Wolgast	2 Oct 1972	11 Oct 1991
FORTUNA (ex-*Bernau*)	33	Peenewerft, Wolgast	3 Aug 1972	11 Oct 1991
AUDAZ (ex-*Eisleben*)	34	Peenewerft, Wolgast	2 Jan 1973	11 Oct 1991

Displacement, tons: 310 full load
Dimensions, feet (metres): 186 × 24.6 × 7.9 *(56.7 × 7.5 × 2.4)*
Main machinery: 2 Russki/Kolomna Type 40-DM diesels; 4,408 hp(m) *(3.24 MW)* sustained; 2 shafts; cp props
Speed, knots: 17. **Range, n miles:** 2,000 at 15 kt
Complement: 31 (6 officers)
Guns: 1 Bofors 40 mm/70.
Mines: 2 rails.
Radars: Surface search: TSR 333 or Raytheon 1900; I-band.

Comment: Belonged to the former GDR Navy. Transferred without armament. Minesweeping gear retained including MSG-3 variable depth sweep device. A fourth of class sunk after a collision with a merchant ship on 5 August 2000.

AUDAZ ***2/2004, A E Galarce*** / 1044205

SURVEY AND RESEARCH SHIPS

1 HELGOLAND (TYPE 720B) CLASS (AGS)

Name	*No*	*Builders*	*Commissioned*
OYARVIDE (ex-*Helgoland*)	22 (ex-A 1457)	Unterweser, Bremerhaven	8 Mar 1966

Displacement, tons: 1,310 standard; 1,643 full load
Dimensions, feet (metres): 223.1 × 41.7 × 14.4 *(68 × 12.7 × 4.4)*
Main machinery: Diesel-electric; 4 MWM 12-cyl diesel generators; 2 motors; 3,300 hp(m) *(2.43 MW)*; 2 shafts
Speed, knots: 17. **Range, n miles:** 6,400 at 16 kt
Complement: 34
Radars: Navigation: Raytheon; I-band.
Sonars: High definition, hull-mounted for wreck search.

Comment: Former German ocean-going tug launched on 25 November 1965. Paid off in 1997 and recommissioned on 21 September 1998 after being fitted out as a survey ship. Oceanographic equipment reported to have been fitted in 2002. Ice strengthened hull. Fitted for twin 40 mm guns.

OYARVIDE ***6/2002, A E Galarce*** / 0529549

1 INSHORE SURVEY CRAFT (AGSC)

TRIESTE

Displacement, tons: 12 full load
Dimensions, feet (metres): 39.7 × 11.8 × 3.3 *(12.1 × 3.6 × 1)*
Main machinery: 2 Kamewa waterjets
Speed, knots: 16. **Range, n miles:** 500 at 16 kt
Complement: 4
Sonars: Elac Compact Mk II; 180 kHz. Elac LAZ 4721; 200 kHz.

Comment: Formerly owned by the Academia Maritime Internacional de Trieste. Donated by Italian government in 2000.

TRIESTE *2001, Uruguay Navy* / 0121418

TRAINING SHIPS

Notes: *Bonanza* is a 13 ton sloop used as a sail training ship. The 15 m vessel was built in UK in 1984 and commissioned in July 1997.

1 SAIL TRAINING SHIP (AXS)

Name	*No*	*Builders*	*Commissioned*
CAPITÁN MIRANDA	20 (ex-GS 10)	SECN Matagorda, Cádiz	1930

Displacement, tons: 839 full load
Dimensions, feet (metres): 209.9 × 26.3 × 12.4 *(64 × 8 × 3.8)*
Main machinery: 1 GM diesel; 750 hp *(552 kW)*; 1 shaft
Speed, knots: 10
Complement: 49
Radars: Navigation: Racal Decca TM 1226C; I-band.

Comment: Originally a diesel-driven survey ship with pronounced clipper bow. Converted for service as a three-masted schooner, commissioning as cadet training ship in 1978. Major refit by Bazán, Cadiz from June 1993 to March 1994, including a new diesel engine and a 5 m extension to the superstructure. Now has 853.4 m² of sail.

CAPITÁN MIRANDA *7/2007, Adolfo Ortigueira Gil* / 1167887

AUXILIARIES

Notes: (1) *Comar II* is a motor yacht used by the Commander-in-Chief.
(2) A small buoy tender is to be built at Astilleros y Talleres Navales de la Armada at Montevideo. The new vessel is to be operated on the Uruguay River.

COMAR II *2/2007, A E Galarce* / 1167932

2 LCVPs

LD 45–46

Displacement, tons: 15 full load
Dimensions, feet (metres): 46.5 × 11.6 × 2.7 *(14.1 × 3.5 × 0.8)*
Main machinery: 1 GM 4-71 diesel; 115 hp *(86 kW)* sustained; 1 shaft
Speed, knots: 9
Range, n miles: 580 at 9 kt
Military lift: 10 tons

Comment: Built at Naval Shipyard, Montevideo and completed 1980.

LD 46 *6/2007, Uruguay Navy* / 1167849

1 PIAST CLASS (PROJECT 570) (SALVAGE SHIP) (ARS)

Name	*No*	*Builders*	*Commissioned*
VANGUARDIA (ex-*Otto Von Guericke*)	26 (ex-A 441)	Northern Shipyard, Gdansk	29 Dec 1976

Displacement, tons: 1,732 full load
Dimensions, feet (metres): 240 × 39.4 × 13.1 *(73.2 × 12 × 4)*
Main machinery: 2 Zgoda diesels; 3,800 hp(m) *(2.79 MW)*; 2 shafts; cp props
Speed, knots: 16
Range, n miles: 3,000 at 12 kt
Complement: 61
Radars: Navigation: 2 TSR 333; I-band.

Comment: Acquired from Germany in October 1991 and sailed from Rostock in January 1992 after a refit at Neptun-Warnow Werft. Carries extensive towing and firefighting equipment plus a diving bell forward of the bridge. Armed with four 25 mm twin guns when in service with the former GDR Navy.

VANGUARDIA *9/2007, Mario R V Carneiro* / 1335310

1 BUOY TENDER (ABU)

SIRIUS 21

Displacement, tons: 290 full load
Dimensions, feet (metres): 115.1 × 32.8 × 5.9 *(35.1 × 10 × 1.8)*
Main machinery: 2 Detroit 12V-71TA diesels; 840 hp *(626 kW)* sustained; 2 shafts
Speed, knots: 11
Complement: 15

Comment: Buoy tender built at Montevideo Naval Yard and completed on 5 February 1988. Endurance, five days.

SIRIUS *6/2007, Uruguay Navy* / 1167848

2 LCM CLASS (ABU)

LD 41–42

Displacement, tons: 24 light; 57 full load
Dimensions, feet (metres): 56.1 × 14.1 × 3.9 *(17.1 × 4.3 × 1.2)*
Main machinery: 2 Gray Marine 64 HN9 diesels; 330 hp *(264 kW)*; 2 shafts
Speed, knots: 9
Range, n miles: 130 at 9 kt
Complement: 5
Military lift: 30 tons

Comment: First one transferred on lease from USA October 1972. Lease extended in October 1986. Second built in Uruguay.

LD 42 *6/2007, Uruguay Navy* / 1335311

1 LÜNEBURG CLASS (SUPPORT SHIP) (ARL)

Name	*No*	*Builders*	*Commissioned*
GENERAL ARTIGAS (ex-*Freiburg*)	4 (ex-A 1413)	Blohm + Voss	27 May 1968

Displacement, tons: 3,900 full load
Dimensions, feet (metres): 388.1 × 43.3 × 13.8 *(118.3 × 13.2 × 4.2)*
Main machinery: 2 MTU MD 16V 538 TB90 diesels; 6,000 hp(m) *(4.1 MW)* sustained; 2 shafts; cp props; bow thruster
Speed, knots: 17
Range, n miles: 6,000 at 14 kt
Complement: 95 (15 officers)
Cargo capacity: 1,100 tons
Guns: 4 Bofors 40 mm/70 (2 twin).
Countermeasures: Decoys: 2 Breda 105 mm SCLAR launchers.
Radars: Navigation: Decca 1226/9; I-band.
Helicopters: AS 355 Esquilo.

Comment: Former auxiliary transferred to Uruguay on 12 April 2005. Used as a support ship for the Bremen class in German service, she was lengthened by 14.3 m in 1984 to accommodate a flight deck and a port-side crane. Her replenishment-at-sea capability will provide a much needed enhancement to Uruguayan operational capability. Other details are as for the shipin German service.

GENERAL ARTIGAS *10/2005, Mario R V Carneiro* / 1133599

TUGS

1 COASTAL TUG (YTB)

Name	*No*	*Builders*	*Commissioned*
BANCO ORTIZ (ex-*Zingst*, ex-*Elbe*)	27 (ex-7, ex-Y 1655)	Peenewerft, Wolgast	10 Sep 1959

Displacement, tons: 261 full load
Dimensions, feet (metres): 100 × 26.6 × 10.8 *(30.5 × 8.1 × 3.3)*
Main machinery: 1 R6 DV 148 diesel; 550 hp(m) *(404 kW)*; 1 shaft
Speed, knots: 10
Complement: 12
Guns: 1—12.7 mm MG.

Comment: Ex-GDR Type 270 tug acquired in October 1991. 10 ton bollard pull.

BANCO ORTIZ *10/2000, A E Galarce* / 0105807

Vanuatu

Country Overview

The Republic of Vanuatu, formerly the New Hebrides, was jointly administered by Britain and France until it gained independence in 1980. Situated in the southwestern Pacific Ocean, some 1,100 n miles southeast of Papua New Guinea, the country comprises a group of about 80 islands, of which 67 are inhabited, which run generally north-south. The four main islands are Espíritu Santo (the largest), Malekula, Efate and Tanna. Others include Epi, Pentecost, Aoba, Maewo, Erromanga and Ambrym. The capital, largest town and principal port is Port-Vila on Efate. An archipelagic state, territorial seas (12 n miles) are claimed. An Exclusive Economic Zone (EEZ) (200 n miles) is also claimed but limits have not been fully defined by boundary agreements. Disputed sovereignty of Matthew and Hunter Islands, both uninhabited, is one complication.

Headquarters Appointments

Commander, Maritime Wing:
Superintendent Tari Tamata

Bases

Port Vila, Efate Island

POLICE

1 PACIFIC CLASS (LARGE PATROL CRAFT) (PB)

Name	*No*	*Builders*	*Commissioned*
TUKORO	02	Australian Shipbuilding Industries	13 June 1987

Displacement, tons: 165 full load
Dimensions, feet (metres): 103.3 × 26.6 × 6.9 *(31.5 × 8.1 × 2.1)*
Main machinery: 2 Caterpillar 3516TA diesels; 4,400 hp *(3.28 MW)* sustained; 2 shafts
Speed, knots: 18
Range, n miles: 2,500 at 12 kt
Complement: 18 (3 officers)
Guns: 1—12.7 mm MG. 1—7.62 mm MG.
Radars: Navigation: Furuno 1011; I-band.

Comment: Under the Defence Co-operation Programme Australia has provided one Patrol Craft to the Vanuatu government. Training and operational and technical assistance is also given by the Royal Australian Navy. Ordered 13 September 1985 and launched 20 May 1987. A half-life refit was carried out in 1995 and, following extension of the Pacific Patrol Boat programme by the Australian government, a life-extension refit was carried out at Townsville in 2004. The ship is employed on Exclusive Economic Zone (EEZ) fishery patrol and surveillance, including customs duties.

TUKORO *8/2005, Chris Sattler* / 1129574

Venezuela

ARMADA DE VENEZUELA

Country Overview

The Republic of Venezuela is situated in northern South America. With an area of 352,144 square miles, it has borders to the east with Guyana, to the south with Brazil and to the west with Colombia. It has a 1,512 n mile coastline with the Caribbean Sea and Atlantic Ocean. Margarita is the principal offshore island, of which there are 70. The capital and largest city is Caracas which is served by the port of La Guaira. Other ports include Puerto Cabello, and Maracaibo. The chief port on the Orinoco River is Puerto Ordaz. Territorial Seas (12 n miles) are claimed. An EEZ (200 n miles) has also been claimed but the limits have not been fully defined by boundary agreements.

Headquarters Appointments

Commander General of the Navy:
Vice Admiral Zahim Ali Quintana Castro
Chief of Naval Staff and Inspector General:
Vice Admiral Pedro José González Diaz
Commander Operations:
Vice Admiral Luís Alberto Morales Márquez
Commander Naval Personnel:
Vice Admiral Jaime Enrique Toro Calderón
Commander Naval Logistics:
Vice Admiral Arístides Yibirin Peluffo

Diplomatic Representation

Defence Attaché in London:
Rear Admiral Gerardo Casanas

Personnel

(a) 2009: 15,800
(b) 2 years' national service

Fleet Organisation

The fleet is split into 'Type' squadrons – frigates (except GC 11 and 12), submarines, light and amphibious forces.

Fleet Organisation — *continued*

Service Craft Squadron composed of RA 33, BO 11 and BE 11. The Fast Attack Squadron of the Constitución class is subordinate to the Fleet Command.

Marines

Following restructuring, the Marines are formed into a division, *General Simón Bolívar*, which consists of two amphibious brigades. The 1st Amphibious Brigade comprises four infantry battalions: *Rafael Urdaneta* (Puerto Cabello), *Francisco de Miranda* (Punto Fijo), *Renato Beluche* (Maracaibo) and *Manuel Ponce Lugo* (Puerto Cabello). The 2nd Amphibious Brigade comprises three battalions: *General Simón Bolívar* (Maiquetía), *Mariscal Antonio José de Sucre* (Cumaná) and *General José Francisco Bermúdez* (Carúpano). Additionally, there is an Engineer Brigade with three construction battalions; a Fluvial Brigade with the Fluvial Frontier Command at Puerto Ayacucho (Amazonas State) and several posts on border rivers.

Coast Guard

Formed in August 1982. It is part of the Navy. Its Headquarters are at La Guaira (Vargas State) and further bases at Maracaibo, Punta Fijo, Puerto Cabello, Guanta, Pampatar and Güiria. Its primary task is the surveillance of the 200 mile Exclusive Economic Zone and other jurisdictional areas of Venezuelan waters. Coast Guard Squadron includes the frigates GC 11 and GC 12 and several patrol craft.

Naval Aviation

Headquarters are at Puerto Cabello (Carabobo State). Under the command of a Rear Admiral, there are five Squadrons: Training, ASW, Surveillance, Patrol and Transport.

Naval Bases

Caracas: Navy Headquarters and *La Carlota* Naval Aviation Facility.
Vargas State: Division de Infantería HQ and Naval Academy at Mamo; OCHINA (Hydrography) and OCAMAR (Marines Support) HQ. *Simón Bolívár* International Airport Naval Aviation Facility and Naval Police Training Centre at Maiquetía.
Puerto Cabello (Carabobo State): Fleet Command HQ. Two battalions of 1st Amphibious Brigade at *Contralmirante Agustín Armario* Naval Base and Naval Aviation Command at *General Salom* Airport, Naval Schools and Dockyard.
Punto Fijo (Falcón State): Western Naval Zone HQ, Patrol Ships Squadron and Infantry Battalion 'Francisco de Miranda' at *Mariscal Juán Crisóstomo Falcón* Naval Base.
Carúpano (Sucre State): Eastern Naval Zone HQ. Two battalions of the 2nd Amphibious Brigade and Marines Training Centre.
Ciudad Bolívar (Bolívar): Fluvial Brigade HQ at *Capitán de Fragata Tomás Machado* Naval Base, with several Naval Posts along the Orinoco River.
Turiamo (Aragua State): *Generalísimo Francisco de Miranda* Marines Special Operation Command at the *Capitán de Fragata Tomás Vega* Naval Station.
Puerto Ayacucho (Amazonas State): Fluvial Frontier Command *General de Brigada Franz Rízquez Iribarren* with several Naval Posts along Orinoco, Atabapo, Negro and Meta rivers.
El Amparo (Apure State): Fluvial Frontier Command HQ *Teniente de Navío Jacinto Muñoz*, with several Naval Posts along Arauca and Barinas rivers.
Puerto de Nutrias (Barinas State): River Post.
San José de Macuro (Delta Amacuro State): Atlantic naval post.
La Orchila (Caribbean Sea): Minor Naval Base and Naval Aviation Station.
Puerto Hierro (Sucre State): Minor Naval Base.
Maracaibo (Zulia State), Güiria (Sucre State), Guanta (Anzoátegui State) and Margarita Island (Nueva Esparta State): Main Coast Guard Stations.
Los Monjes (Gulf of Venezuela), Los Testigos, Aves de Sotavento, La Tortuga and La Blanquilla Island (Caribbean Sea): Secondary Coast Guard Stations.

Prefix to Ships' Names

ARV (Armada de la República de Venezuela)

SUBMARINES

Notes: Acquisition of up to three new submarines, to replace the current force, is under negotiation. A contract for the procurement of three Project 636 Kilo-class submarines is expected in 2009. Two boats would be built at Admiralty Yard, St Petersburg, and the third in another Russian Shipyard. Deliveries are expected from 2014. The contract would also include a training package.

2 SÁBALO (TYPE 209/1300) CLASS (TYPE 1300) (SSK)

Name	*No*	*Builders*	*Laid down*	*Launched*	*Commissioned*
SÁBALO	S 31 (ex-S 21)	Howaldtswerke, Kiel	2 May 1973	1 July 1975	6 Aug 1976
CARIBE	S 32 (ex-S 22)	Howaldtswerke, Kiel	1 Aug 1973	6 Nov 1975	11 Mar 1977

Displacement, tons: 1,285 surfaced; 1,600 dived
Dimensions, feet (metres): 200.1 × 20.3 × 18 *(61.2 × 6.2 × 5.5)*
Main machinery: Diesel-electric; 4 MTU 12V992 TB 90 diesels; 2,400 hp(m) *(1.76 MW)* sustained; 4 alternators; 1.7 MW; 1 Siemens motor; 4,600 hp(m) *(3.38 MW)* sustained; 1 shaft
Speed, knots: 10 surfaced; 22 dived
Range, n miles: 7,500 at 10 kt surfaced
Complement: 33 (5 officers)

Torpedoes: 8—21 in *(533 mm)* bow tubes. AEG SST 4; anti-surface; wire-guided; active/passive homing to 12 km *(6.6 n miles)* at 35 kt or 28 km *(15.3 n miles)* at 23 kt; warhead 260 kg. 14 torpedoes carried. Swim-out discharge.

Countermeasures: ESM: Thomson-CSF DR 2000; intercept.
Weapons control: Atlas Elektronik ISUS TFCS.
Radars: Navigation: Terma Scanter Mil; I-band.
Sonars: Atlas Elektronik CSU 3-32; hull-mounted; passive/active search and attack; medium frequency.
Thomson Sintra DUUX 2; passive ranging.

Programmes: Type 209, IK81 designed by Ingenieurkontor Lübeck for construction by Howaldtswerke, Kiel and sale by Ferrostaal, Essen, all acting as a consortium. Both refitted at Kiel in 1981 and 1984 respectively.
Modernisation: Carried out by HDW at Kiel. *Sábalo* started in April 1990 and left in November 1992 without fully completing the refit. *Caribe* docked in Kiel throughout 1993 but was back in the water in mid-1994, and completed in 1995. The hull was slightly lengthened and new engines, fire control, sonar and attack periscopes fitted. Refit of both boats at Dianca Shipyard began in December 2004 *(Caribe)* and March 2005 *(Sábalo)*. The upgrade includes new batteries and weapon control systems and is expected to be completed in 2009.
Structure: A single-hull design with two main ballast tanks and forward and after trim tanks. The additional length is due to the new sonar dome similar to German Type 206 system. Fitted with snort and remote machinery control. Slow revving single screw. Very high-capacity batteries with GRP lead-acid cells and battery-cooling. Diving depth 250 m *(820 ft)*.
Operational: Endurance, 50 days patrol. Based at Puerto Cabello.

CARIBE *6/1999* / 0084231

FRIGATES

6 MODIFIED LUPO CLASS (FFGHM)

Name	No	Builders	Laid down	Launched	Commissioned
MARISCAL SUCRE	F 21	Fincantieri, Riva Trigoso	19 Nov 1976	28 Sep 1978	10 May 1980
ALMIRANTE BRIÓN	F 22	Fincantieri, Riva Trigoso	June 1977	22 Feb 1979	7 Mar 1981
GENERAL URDANETA	F 23	Fincantieri, Riva Trigoso	23 Jan 1978	23 Mar 1979	8 Aug 1981
GENERAL SOUBLETTE	F 24	Fincantieri, Riva Trigoso	26 Aug 1978	4 Jan 1980	5 Dec 1981
GENERAL SALOM	F 25	Fincantieri, Riva Trigoso	7 Nov 1978	13 Jan 1980	3 Apr 1982
ALMIRANTE GARCIA (ex-*José Felix Ribas*)	F 26	Fincantieri, Riva Trigoso	21 Aug 1979	4 Oct 1980	30 July 1982

Displacement, tons: 2,208 standard; 2,520 full load
Dimensions, feet (metres): 371.3 × 37.1 × 12.1 (*113.2 × 11.3 × 3.7*)
Main machinery: CODOG; 2 Fiat/GE LM 2500 gas turbines; 50,000 hp (*37.3 MW*) sustained; 2 GMT A230.20M or 2 MTU 20V 1163 (F 21 and F 22) diesels; 8,000 hp(m) (*5.97 MW*) sustained; 2 shafts; LIPS cp props
Speed, knots: 35; 21 on diesels
Range, n miles: 5,000 at 15 kt
Complement: 185

Missiles: SSM: 8 Otomat Teseo Mk 2 TG1 ❶; active radar homing to 80 km (*43.2 n miles*) at 0.9 Mach; warhead 210 kg; sea-skimmer for last 4 km (*2.2 n miles*).
SAM: Selenia Elsag Albatros octuple launcher ❷; 8 Aspide; semi-active radar homing to 13 km (*7 n miles*) at 2.5 Mach; height envelope 15-5,000 m (*49.2-16,405 ft*); warhead 30 kg.
Guns: 1 OTO Melara 5 in (*127 mm*)/54 ❸; 45 rds/min to 16 km (*8.7 n miles*); weight of shell 32 kg.
4 Otobreda 40 mm/70 (2 twin) ❹; 300 rds/min to 12.5 km (*6.8 n miles*); weight of shell 0.96 kg.
2—12.7 mm MGs.
Torpedoes: 6—324 mm ILAS 3 (2 triple) tubes ❺. Whitehead A244S; anti-submarine; active/passive homing to 7 km (*3.8 n miles*) at 33 kt; warhead 34 kg (shaped charge).
Countermeasures: Decoys: 2 Breda 105 mm SCLAR 20-barrelled trainable ❻; chaff to 5 km (*2.7 n miles*); illuminants to 12 km (*6.6 n miles*). Can be used for HE bombardment.
ESM: Elisra NS 9003/9005; intercept.
Combat data systems: Selenia IPN 10. Elbit ENTCS 2000 (F 21 and F 22).
Weapons control: 2 Elsag NA 10 MFCS. 2 Dardo GFCS for 40 mm.
Radars: Air search: Selenia RAN 10S or Elta 2238 (F 21 and 22) ❼; E/F-band.
Air/surface search: Selenia RAN 11X; I-band.
Fire control: 2 Selenia Orion 10XP ❽; I/J-band.
2 Selenia RTN 20X ❾; I/J-band.
Navigation: SMA 3RM20; I-band.
Tacan: SRN 15A.
Sonars: EDO SQS-29 (Mod 610E) or Northrop Grumman 21 HS-7 (F 21 and F 22); hull-mounted; active search and attack; medium frequency.

Helicopters: 1 AB 212ASW ❿.

Programmes: All ordered on 24 October 1975. Similar to ships in the Italian and Peruvian navies.
Modernisation: F 21 and F 22 were scheduled to start a refit by Ingalls Shipyard in September 1992 but contractural problems delayed start until January 1998. Refits included upgrading the gas turbines, replacing the diesels, improving the combat data system, updating sonar and ESM, and overhauling all weapon systems. The ships were redelivered in mid-2002 but further work was later required to re-install the Elta radar on a mast above the bridge. F 23 and F 24 have been upgraded by Dianca, Puerto Caballo, and returned to service in December and October 2003 respectively. Work included modernisation of the main machinery, air-conditioning and weapon systems. F 25 and F 26 began similar refits at Dianca in 2004 but these had not been completed by early 2009.
Structure: Fixed hangar means no space for Aspide reloads. Fully stabilised.
Operational: Based at Puerto Cabello.

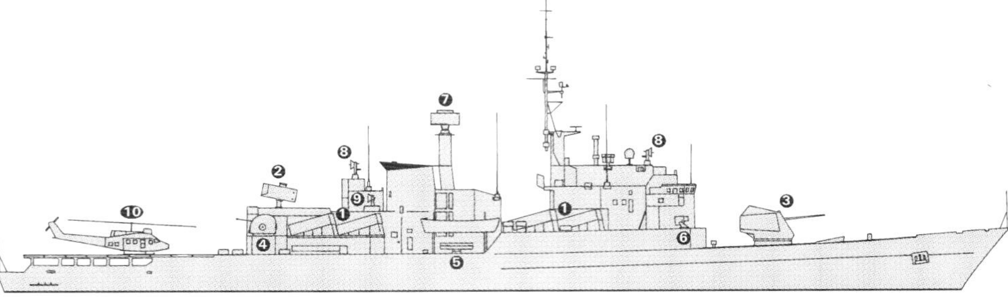

GENERAL URDANETA *(Scale 1 : 900), Ian Sturton* / 0529541

ALMIRANTE BRIÓN *6/2001, Northrop Grumman Ingalls* / 0096360

ALMIRANTE BRIÓN *9/2007, Mario R V Carneiro* / 1353650

SHIPBORNE AIRCRAFT

Notes: There are seven operational Bell 412EP helicopters, equipped with radar and FLIR. Four acquired in 1999 and three more delivered in 2003 of which one has been lost. This has been replaced by an Agusta Bell 412EP. There is also one Bell 206B which is used for training. Six Mi-17 were acquired from Russia in 2007 for use by the Marines.

Numbers/Type: 8 Agusta AB 212ASW.
Operational speed: 106 kt *(196 km/h).*
Service ceiling: 14,200 ft *(4,330 m).*
Range: 230 n miles *(426 km).*
Role/Weapon systems: ASW helicopter with secondary ASV role. All eight have been upgraded in Italy. Sensors: APS-705 search radar, Bendix AQS-18A dipping sonar. Weapons: ASW; two Mk 46 or A244/S torpedoes or depth bombs. ASV; mid-course guidance to Teseo Mk 2 missiles.

AB 212 *6/2005, Massimo Annati* / 1167652

LAND-BASED MARITIME AIRCRAFT (FRONT LINE)

Notes: (1) There are also two Beech King Air and three Cessnas used for training and transport.
(2) Two CASA CN-235 maritime patrol aircraft were ordered in April 2005. The contract was signed on 29 November 2005 but cancelled in October 2006.
(3) The contract for 24 Su-30 Mk 2 Flankers was signed with the Russian government on 21 July 2006. All had been delivered by mid-2008. The aircraft are capable of carrying a variety of air-to-surface weapons.

Numbers/Type: 3/2/3 CASA C-212 S 43/C-212 S 200/C-212 S 400 Aviocar.
Operational speed: 190 kt *(353 km/h).*
Service ceiling: 24,000 ft *(7,315 m).*
Range: 1,650 n miles *(3,055 km).*
Role/Weapon systems: Medium-range MR and coastal protection aircraft; limited armed action. Acquired in 1981–82 and 1985–86. Three modernised and augmented in 1998 by S 400 type. Previous numbers have reduced. Sensors: APS-128 radar. Weapons: ASW; depth bombs. ASV; gun and rocket pods.

C-212 *6/2002, CASA/EADS* / 0529548

PATROL FORCES

6 CONSTITUCIÓN CLASS (FAST ATTACK CRAFT—MISSILE AND GUN) (PBG/PG)

Name	*No*	*Builders*	*Laid down*	*Launched*	*Commissioned*
CONSTITUCIÓN	PC 11	Vosper Thornycroft	Jan 1973	1 June 1973	16 Aug 1974
FEDERACIÓN	PC 12	Vosper Thornycroft	Aug 1973	26 Feb 1974	25 Mar 1975
INDEPENDENCIA	PC 13	Vosper Thornycroft	Feb 1973	24 July 1973	20 Sep 1974
LIBERTAD	PC 14	Vosper Thornycroft	Sep 1973	5 Mar 1974	12 June 1975
PATRIA	PC 15	Vosper Thornycroft	Mar 1973	27 Sep 1973	9 Jan 1975
VICTORIA	PC 16	Vosper Thornycroft	Mar 1974	3 Sep 1974	22 Sep 1975

Displacement, tons: 170 full load
Dimensions, feet (metres): 121 × 23.3 × 6 *(36.9 × 7.1 × 1.8)*
Main machinery: 2 MTU MD 16V 538 TB90 diesels; 6,000 hp(m) *(4.4 MW)* sustained; 2 shafts
Speed, knots: 31
Range, n miles: 1,350 at 16 kt
Complement: 20 (4 officers)

Missiles: SSM: 2 OTO Melara/Matra Teseo Mk 2 TG1 *(Federación, Libertad* and *Victoria)*; active radar homing to 80 km *(43.2 n miles)* at 0.9 Mach; sea-skimmer for last 4 km *(2.2 n miles)*; warhead 210 kg.
Guns: 1 OTO Melara 3 in *(76 mm)*/62 compact *(Constitución, Independencia* and *Patria)*; 85 rds/min to 16 km *(8.7 n miles)*; weight of shell 6 kg.
1 Breda 30 mm/70 *(Federación, Libertad* and *Victoria)*; 800 rds/min; weight of shell 0.37 kg.
2—12.7 mm MGs.
Weapons control: Elsag NA 10 Mod 1 GFCS *(Constitución, Independencia* and *Patria)*. Alenia Elsag Medusa optronic director *(Federación, Libertad* and *Victoria)*.
Radars: Surface search: SMA SPQ-2D; I-band.
Fire control: Selenia RTN 10X (in 76 mm ships); I/J-band.
Navigation: Racal; I-band.

Programmes: Transferred from the Navy in 1983 to the Coast Guard but now back again with Fleet Command.
Modernisation: Single Breda 30 mm guns replaced the 40 mm guns in the missile craft in 1989. All were refitted at Puerto Cabello 1992–1995.
Operational: It is planned to replace these ships with new offshore patrol vessels. Meanwhile it is reported that their propulsion systems have been refitted. Based at Punta Fijo.

VICTORIA (missile craft) *7/1999, Venezuelan Navy* / 0084235

0 + 4 OFFSHORE PATROL VESSELS (PSOH)

Name	*No*	*Builders*	*Laid down*	*Launched*	*Commissioned*
GUAICAIPURO	F 30	Navantia, Puerto Real	11 Sep 2008	2009	May 2010
–	F 31	Navantia, Puerto Real	Mar 2009	2010	Sep 2010
–	F 32	Navantia, Puerto Real	Sep 2009	2010	Feb 2011
–	F 33	Navantia, Puerto Real	Mar 2010	2011	July 2011

Displacement, tons: 2,419 full load
Dimensions, feet (metres): 324.5 × 44.6 × 12.5 *(98.9 × 13.6 × 3.8)*
Main machinery: 4 MTU 12V 1163 TB93 diesels; 23,600 hp *(17.6 MW)*; 2 shafts; cp props
Speed, knots: 24. **Range, n miles:** 3,500 at 12 kt
Complement: 60 plus accommodation for 32
Guns: 1—76 mm. 1—35 mm.
Combat data systems: Thales Tacticos.
Electro-optic systems: Thales Sting optronic director. Thales Mirador: TEOOS.
Radars: Thales SMART-S; 3D; E/F-band.
Navigation: To be announced.
Fire control: Thales Sting; I/J-band.
Helicopters: To be announced.

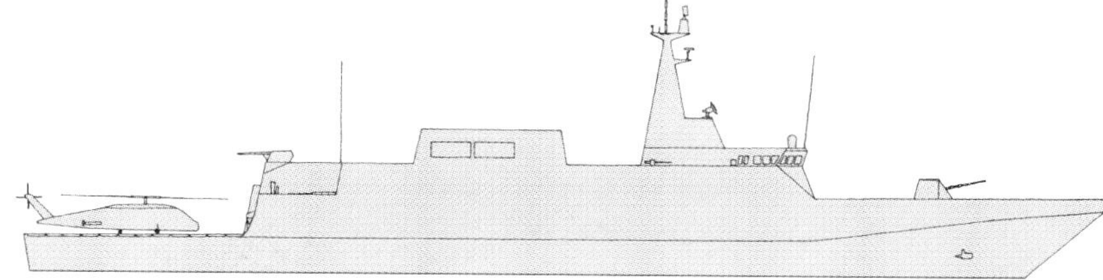

OFFSHORE PATROL VESSEL *(Scale 1 : 900), Ian Sturton* / 1167442

Programmes: Following agreement between the Spanish and Venezuelan governments signed on 28 November 2005, a contract for the construction of four offshore patrol vessels (POVZEE) was signed with Navantia on 26 May 2006. The ships are being constructed at the Puerto Real Shipyard at Cadiz and the programme is to be completed by 2012.

Operational: The vessels are to be employed on EEZ protection duties.

0 + 4 GUAICAMACUTO CLASS (PATROL VESSELS) (PSOH)

Name	*No*	*Builders*	*Laid down*	*Launched*	*Commissioned*
GUAICAMACUTO	GC 21	Navantia, San Fernando	17 Dec 2006	16 Oct 2008	Sep 2009
YAVIRE	GC 22	Navantia, San Fernando	2007	11 Mar 2009	2010
NAIGUATA	GC 23	Navantia, San Fernando	28 Nov 2007	2010	2011
TAMANACO	GC 24	Dianca, Puerto Cabello	2008	2011	2012

Displacement, tons: 1,500 full load
Dimensions, feet (metres): 262.1 × 37.7 × 12.1 *(79.9 × 11.5 × 3.7)*
Main machinery: To be announced
Speed, knots: 22
Range, n miles: 4,000 at 12 kt
Complement: 34 plus accommodation for 30
Guns: 1—76 mm. 1 Oerlikon Contraves 35 mm.
Combat data systems: To be announced.
Weapons control: To be announced.
Radars: Surface search: To be announced.
Navigation: To be announced.
Fire control: To be announced.
Helicopters: Platform for one medium.

Programmes: Following agreement between the Spanish and Venezuelan governments signed on 28 November 2005, a contract for the construction of four patrol vessels (BVL) was signed with Navantia on 26 May 2006. Three ships are to be constructed at the San Fernando Shipyard at Cadiz and the programme is to be completed by 2012 and the fourth at Puerto Cabello (to be confirmed).
Operational: The vessels are to be employed on coastal patrol duties.

GUAICAMACUTO *10/2008*, Carlos Pardo González* / 1353654

AMPHIBIOUS FORCES

Notes: (1) It is reported that 39 Griffon 2000TD hovercraft are being assembled at Dianca. The first was delivered on 29 May 2007 and the remainder are to be built by 2013.
(2) Procurement of one or more amphibious assault ships (LPD) is under consideration. The requirement is for a design to transport and deliver up to 750 troops with their equipment and vehicles in addition to civilian support and disaster relief roles.

2 AJEERA CLASS (LCU)

Name	*No*	*Builders*	*Commissioned*
MARGARITA	T 71	Swiftships Inc, Morgan City	20 Jan 1984
LA ORCHILA	T 72	Swiftships Inc, Morgan City	11 May 1984

Displacement, tons: 428 full load
Dimensions, feet (metres): 129.9 × 36.1 × 5.9 *(39.6 × 11 × 1.8)*
Main machinery: 2 Detroit 16V-149 diesels; 1,800 hp *(1.34 MW)* sustained; 2 shafts
Speed, knots: 13. **Range, n miles:** 1,500 at 10 kt
Complement: 26 (4 officers)
Military lift: 150 tons cargo; 100 tons fuel
Guns: 3—12.7 mm MGs.
Radars: Navigation: Raytheon 6410; I-band.

Comment: Both serve in Fluvial Command. Have a 15 ton crane.

MARGARITA *6/1999, Venezuelan Navy* / 0084238

4 CAPANA (ALLIGATOR) CLASS (LSTH)

Name	*No*	*Builders*	*Commissioned*
CAPANA	T 61	Korea Tacoma Marine	24 July 1984
ESEQUIBO	T 62	Korea Tacoma Marine	24 July 1984
GOAJIRA	T 63	Korea Tacoma Marine	20 Nov 1984
LOS LLANOS	T 64	Korea Tacoma Marine	20 Nov 1984

Displacement, tons: 4,070 full load
Dimensions, feet (metres): 343.8 × 50.5 × 9.8 *(104.8 × 15.4 × 3)*
Main machinery: 2 SEMT-Pielstick 16 PA6 V 280 diesels; 12,800 hp(m) *(9.41 MW)*; 2 shafts
Speed, knots: 14. **Range, n miles:** 5,600 at 11 kt
Complement: 117 (13 officers)
Military lift: 202 troops; 1,600 tons cargo; 4 LCVPs
Guns: 2 Breda 40 mm/70 (twin). 2 Oerlikon 20 mm GAM-BO1.
Weapons control: Selenia NA 18/V; optronic director.
Helicopters: Platform only.

Comment: Ordered in August 1982. Version III of Korea Tacoma Alligator type. Each has a 50 ton tank turntable and a lift between decks. *Goajira* was out of service from June 1987 to May 1993 after a serious fire. T 62 and T 63 reported to have been refitted in 2003 and T 61 2007–08. T 62 is likely to be similarly upgraded.

CAPANA *6/1998, Venezuelan Navy* / 0084236

ESEQUIBO *3/1999* / 0084237

SURVEY AND RESEARCH SHIPS

Notes: The contract for the construction of five survey ships was signed with Astillero Vulcano, Vigo, on 5 August 2008. There are to be four vessels of 90 m and a fifth Antarctic survey ship of 113 m. The latter ship is to have a reinforced hull and to be equipped with a flight deck for helicopter operations. Some of these ships may be for civilian use.

1 SURVEY AND RESEARCH SHIP (AGOR)

Name	*No*	*Builders*	*Launched*	*Commissioned*
PUNTA BRAVA	BO 11	Bazán, La Carraca	9 Mar 1990	14 Mar 1991

Displacement, tons: 1,170 full load
Dimensions, feet (metres): 202.4 × 39 × 12.1 *(61.7 × 11.9 × 3.7)*
Main machinery: 2 Bazán-MAN 7L20/27 diesels; 2,500 hp(m) *(1.84 MW)*; 2 shafts; bow thruster
Speed, knots: 13. **Range, n miles:** 8,000 at 13 kt
Complement: 49 (6 officers) plus 6 scientists
Radars: Navigation: ARPA; I-band.

Comment: Ordered in September 1988. Developed from the Spanish Malaspina class. A multipurpose ship for oceanography, marine resource evaluation, geophysical and biological research. Equipped with Qubit hydrographic system. Carries two survey launches. EW equipment is fitted. Assigned to the OCHINA (Hydrographic department).

PUNTA BRAVA *11/2008*, A A de Kruijf* / 1353653

2 SURVEY CRAFT (AGSC)

Name	*No*	*Builders*	*Commissioned*
GABRIELA (ex-*Peninsula de Araya*)	LH 11	Abeking & Rasmussen	5 Feb 1974
LELY (ex-*Peninsula de Paraguana*)	LH 12	Abeking & Rasmussen	7 Feb 1974

Displacement, tons: 90 full load
Dimensions, feet (metres): 88.6 × 18.4 × 4.9 *(27 × 5.6 × 1.5)*
Main machinery: 2 MTU diesels; 2,300 hp(m) *(1.69 MW)*; 2 shafts
Speed, knots: 20
Complement: 9 (1 officer)

Comment: LH 12 laid down 28 May 1973, launched 12 December 1973 and LH 11 laid down 10 March 1973, launched 29 November 1973. Acquired in September 1986 from the Instituto de Canalizaciones. Both assigned to the Fluvial Command.

GABRIELA (alongside *Alcatraz* PG 32) *1/1994, Maritime Photographic* / 0506180

TRAINING SHIPS

1 SAIL TRAINING SHIP (AXS)

Name	*No*	*Builders*	*Launched*	*Commissioned*
SIMÓN BOLÍVAR	BE 11	AT Celaya, Bilbao	21 Nov 1979	6 Aug 1980

Displacement, tons: 1,260 full load
Measurement, tons: 934 gross
Dimensions, feet (metres): 270.6 × 34.8 × 14.4 *(82.5 × 10.6 × 4.4)*
Main machinery: 1 Detroit 12V-149T diesel; 875 hp *(652 kW)* sustained; 1 shaft
Speed, knots: 10
Complement: 93 (17 officers) plus 102 trainees

Comment: Ordered in 1978. Three-masted barque; similar to *Guayas* (Ecuador), *Cuauhtemoc* (Mexico) and *Gloria* (Colombia). Sail area (23 sails), 1,650 m². Highest mast, 131.2 ft *(40 m)*. Has won several international sail competitions including Cutty Sark '96. A refit is reported to have been completed in 2008.

SIMÓN BOLÍVAR *6/2001, A Campanera i Rovira* / 0534070

AUXILIARIES

Notes: There is one navigational aids tender *Macuro* BB-11.

1 LOGISTIC SUPPORT SHIP (AORH)

Name	*No*	*Builders*	*Commissioned*
CIUDAD BOLÍVAR	T 81	Hyundai, Ulsan	2001

Displacement, tons: 9,750 full load
Dimensions, feet (metres): 451.8 × 59 × 21.7 *(137.7 × 18 × 6.6)*
Main machinery: 2 Caterpillar 3616 diesels; 2 shafts; LIPS cp props
Speed, knots: 18. **Range, n miles:** 4,500 at 15 kt
Complement: 104
Guns: 2 Bofors 40 mm/70. 2—12.7 mm MGs.

Comment: Ordered from Hyundai, South Korea, in February 1999. Delivered in October 2001. Capable of carrying 4,400 tons of fuel and 900 tons of cargo. Two replenishment stations on each beam. Hangar and deck for medium size helicopter. Replenishment operations reported conducted with both French and Netherlands units. Armament is not yet fitted.

1 + (1) OCEAN TUG (ATA)

Name	*No*	*Builders*	*Laid down*	*Launched*	*Commissioned*
GENERAL FRANCISCO DE MIRANDA (ex-*Almirante Bruzuar*)	RA 11	Damen, Gorinchem and DIANCA, Puerto Caballo, Venezuela	Apr 2004	2005	Mar 2007

Displacement, tons: 700 full load
Dimensions, feet (metres): 213.2 × 39.3 × 19.7 *(65.0 × 12.0 × 6.0)*
Main machinery: 2 CAT 3606TA diesels; 5,400 hp *(4 MW)*; 2 shafts
Speed, knots: 16. **Range, n miles:** 7,000 at 10 kt
Complement: To be announced
Radars: Navigation: I-band.

Comment: DIANCA, a shipyard owned and operated by the Venezuelan Navy, contracted in early 2004 to build an ocean-going tug with technical assistance from Damen Shipyards. Built of aluminium and steel, the ship is used for a variety of tasks including counter-drug, counter-piracy and counter-pollution operations as well as general sea-safety duties. It has a cargo capacity of 150 tons and was completed in 2006. A second ship is expected.

COAST GUARD

7 RIVER PATROL CRAFT (PBR)

MANAURE PF 21
MARA PF 22
GUAICAIPURO PF 23
TAMANACO PF 24
TEREPAIMA PF 31
YARACUY PF 33
SOROCAIMA PF 34

Displacement, tons: 15 full load
Dimensions, feet (metres): 54.1 × 14.1 × 4.3 *(16.5 × 4.3 × 1.3)*
Main machinery: 2 diesels; 2 shafts
Speed, knots: 10
Complement: 8
Guns: 1—12.7 mm MG.
Radars: Surface search: Raytheon 6410; I-band.

Comment: River craft used by the Marines. Details given are for four Manaure class. There are also three Terepaima class which are 10 m long and capable of 45 kt.

MANAURE *6/1998, Venezuelan Navy* / 0050737

4 PETREL (POINT) CLASS (WPB)

Name	*No*	*Builders*	*Commissioned*
PETREL (ex-*Point Knoll*)	PG 31	US Coast Guard Yard, Curtis Bay	26 June 1967
ALCATRAZ (ex-*Point Judith*)	PG 32	US Coast Guard Yard, Curtis Bay	26 July 1966
ALBATROS (ex-*Point Franklin*)	PG 33	US Coast Guard Yard, Curtis Bay	14 Nov 1966
PELÍCANO (ex-*Point Ledge*)	PG 34	US Coast Guard Yard, Curtis Bay	18 July 1962

Displacement, tons: 68 full load
Dimensions, feet (metres): 83 × 17.2 × 5.8 *(25.3 × 5.2 × 1.8)*
Main machinery: 2 Caterpillar diesels; 1,600 hp *(1.19 MW)*; 2 shafts
Speed, knots: 23.5
Range, n miles: 1,500 at 8 kt
Complement: 10 (1 officer)
Guns: 2—12.7 mm MGs.
Radars: Surface search: Raytheon SPS-64; I-band.

Comment: *Petrel* transferred from USCG on 18 November 1991 and *Alcatraz* on 15 January 1992, *Albatros* on 23 June 1998 and *Pelícano* on 3 August 1998. The transfer of four further craft is unlikely. Most of the class are believed to be operational.

ALCATRAZ *4/1999* / 0084242

1 ALMIRANTE CLEMENTE CLASS (WFS)

Name	*No*	*Builders*	*Laid down*	*Launched*	*Commissioned*
GENERAL JOSÉ TRINIDAD MORAN	GC 12	Ansaldo, Livorno	5 May 1954	12 Dec 1954	9 May 1956

Displacement, tons: 1,300 standard; 1,500 full load
Dimensions, feet (metres): 325.1 × 35.5 × 12.2 *(99.1 × 10.8 × 3.7)*
Main machinery: 2 GMT 16-645E7C diesels; 6,080 hp(m) *(4.47 MW)* sustained; 2 shafts
Speed, knots: 22
Range, n miles: 3,500 at 15 kt
Complement: 142 (12 officers)

Guns: 2 Otobreda 3 in *(76 mm)*/62 compact ❶; 85 rds/min to 16 km *(8.7 n miles)*; weight of shell 6 kg.
2 Breda 40 mm/70 (twin) ❷; 300 rds/min to 12.5 km *(6.8 n miles)*; weight of shell 0.96 kg.
Torpedoes: 6—324 mm ILAS 3 (2 triple) tubes ❸. Whitehead A 244S; anti-submarine; active/passive homing to 7 km *(3.8 n miles)* at 33 kt; warhead 34 kg (shaped charge).
Depth charges: 2 throwers.
Weapons control: Elsag NA 10 Mod 1 GFCS.
Radars: Air search: Plessey AWS 4 ❹; E/F-band.
Surface search: Racal Decca 1226 ❺; I-band.
Fire control: Selenia RTN 10X ❻; I/J-band.
Sonars: Plessey PMS 26; hull-mounted; active search and attack; 10 kHz.

Programmes: Survivor of a class of six ordered in 1953.
Modernisation: Refitted by Cammell Laird/Plessey group in April 1968. 4 in guns replaced by 76 mm. Both refitted again in Italy in 1984–85, prior to transfer to Coast Guard duties in 1986.
Structure: Fitted with Denny-Brown fin stabilisers and air conditioned throughout the living and command spaces.
Operational: *Almirante Clemente* decommissioned in 2008 and being used as spares.

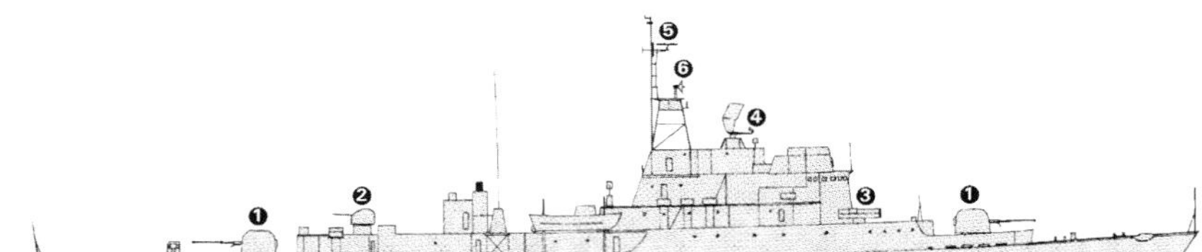
ALMIRANTE CLEMENTE CLASS *(Scale 1 : 900), Ian Sturton* / 0506215

GENERAL JOSÉ TRINIDAD MORAN *10/1998, E & M Laursen* / 0050734

ALMIRANTE CLEMENTE CLASS *4/2001* / 0114820

12 GAVION CLASS (WPB)

GAVION PG 401	**CHAMAN** PG 404	**FARDELA** PG 407	**PIGARGO** PG 410
ALCA PG 402	**CORMORAN** PG 405	**FUMAREL** PG 408	**PAGAZA** PG 411
BERNACLA PG 403	**COLIMBO** PG 406	**NEGRON** PG 409	**SERRETA** PG 412

Displacement, tons: 45 full load
Dimensions, feet (metres): 80 × 17 × 4.8 *(24.4 × 5.2 × 1.5)*
Main machinery: 2 Detroit 12V-92TA diesels; 2,160 hp *(1.61 MW)* sustained; 2 shafts
Speed, knots: 25
Range, n miles: 1,000 at 12 kt
Complement: 10
Guns: 2—12.7 mm MGs. 2—7.62 mm MGs. 1—40 mm Mk 19 grenade launcher.
Radars: Surface search: Raytheon R1210; I-band.

Comment: Ordered from Halter Marine 24 April 1998 and delivered from late 1999 to early 2000. Aluminium construction. Four craft refitted in 2003 and all believed to be operational.

GAVION *11/2008*, Marco Ghiglino* / 1353652

2 UTILITY CRAFT (YAG)

LOS TAQUES LG 11 **LOS CAYOS** LG 12

Displacement, tons: 350 full load
Dimensions, feet (metres): 87.3 × 23.3 × 4.9 *(26.6 × 7.1 × 1.5)*
Main machinery: 1 diesel; 850 hp(m) *(625 kW)*; 1 shaft
Speed, knots: 8
Complement: 10
Guns: 1—12.7 mm MG.

Comment: Former trawlers. Commissioned 15 May 1981 and 17 July 1984 respectively. Used for salvage and SAR tasks.

LOS CAYOS *11/2008*, A A de Kruijf* / 1353651

7 POLARIS CLASS (PBF)

POLARIS LG 21	**RIGEL** LG 23	**ANTARES** LG 25	**ALTAIR** LG 27
SIRIUS LG 22	**ALDEBARAN** LG 24	**CANOPUS** LG 26	

Displacement, tons: 5 full load
Dimensions, feet (metres): 26 wl × 8.5 × 2.6 *(7.9 × 2.6 × 0.8)*
Main machinery: 1 diesel outdrive; 400 hp(m) *(294 kW)*
Speed, knots: 50
Complement: 4
Guns: 1—12.7 mm MG.
Radars: Surface search: Raytheon; I-band.

Comment: Built by Cougar Marine and delivered in 1987. Used by the Coast Guard for drug interdiction. Two more reported operational.

ALDEBARAN *4/1999, Venezuelan Navy* / 0084247

1 + (14) DIANCA PATROL CRAFT (PB)

Displacement, tons: To be announced
Dimensions, feet (metres): 75.5 × 16.4 × ? *(23.0 × 5.0 × ?)*
Main machinery: To be announced
Speed, knots: 32
Complement: 10
Guns: To be announced.
Radars: To be announced.

Comment: Dianca Project P 698. First of class entered service in 2004 and a class of 15 is projected. Aluminium construction.

18 INSHORE PATROL BOATS (PBR)

CONSTANCIA LRG 001
PERSEVERANCIA LRG 002
HONESTIDAD LRG 003
TENACIDAD LRG 004
INTEGRIDAD LRG 005
LEALTAD LRG 006
+**12**

Displacement, tons: 11 full load
Dimensions, feet (metres): 39.4 × 9.2 × 5.6 *(12 × 2.8 × 1.7)*
Main machinery: 2 diesels; 640 hp(m) *(470 kW)*; 2 shafts
Speed, knots: 38
Complement: 4
Guns: 2—7.62 mm MGs.
Radars: Surface search: I-band.

Comment: First three speed boat type with GRP hulls delivered from a local shipyard in December 1991. Fourth completed in August 1993. Details given are for *Integridad* which is the first of two built at Guatire, and delivered in 1997/98. GRP construction. The twelve un-named craft are Boston Whaler Guardian class capable of 25 kt, mounting 2—12.7 mm and 2—6.72 mm MGs, and with Raytheon radars. These were donated by the US. All of these craft are used by Marines.

GUARDIAN INSHORE PATROL CRAFT *4/1999, Venezuelan Navy* / 0084245

8 PUNTA MACOLLA CLASS (PB)

PUNTA MACOLLA LSM 001
FARALLÓN CENTINELA LSM 002
CHARAGATO LSM 003
BAJO BRITO LSM 004
BAJO ARAYA LSM 005
CARECARE LSM 006
VELA DE COBO LSM 007
CAYO MACEREO LSM 008

Displacement, tons: 5 full load
Dimensions, feet (metres): 41.7 × 9.2 × 6.6 *(12.7 × 2.8 × 2)*
Main machinery: 2 diesels; 2 shafts
Speed, knots: 30
Complement: 4
Guns: 1—12.7 mm MG.
Radars: Surface search: Raytheon; I-band.

Comment: Built in Venezuela by Intermarine. Used by OCHINA (Hydrographic department) and for SAR. First six delivered by 1997 and last two in 2000.

BAJO ARAYA *3/1999, Venezuelan Navy* / 0084246

1 SUPPORT SHIP (AKSL)

Name	*No*	*Builders*	*Commissioned*
FERNANDO GOMEZ (ex-*José Felix Ribas*, ex-*Oswegatchie*)	RP 21 (ex-R 13)	Commercial Iron Works, Portland	14 Dec 1945

Displacement, tons: 245 full load
Dimensions, feet (metres): 100.1 × 25.9 × 9.5 *(30.5 × 7.9 × 2.9)*
Main machinery: 2 diesels; 1,270 hp *(947 kW)*; 1 shaft
Speed, knots: 10
Complement: 12
Guns: 2—12.7 mm MGs.
Radars: Navigation: Raytheon; I-band.

Comment: Former tug, originally acquired from the US in 1965. Out of service for some years but now employed as a logistic support ship and for occasional patrol and SAR.

FERNANDO GOMEZ *6/1998, Venezuelan Navy* / 0050738

PROTECTOR 3612 CLASS (PB)

CHICHIRIVICHE LG 31
CARUANTA LG 32

Displacement, tons: 11 full load
Dimensions, feet (metres): 36.1 × 13.1 × 1.6 *(11.1 × 4.0 × 0.5)*

Comment: Built by SeaArk Marine, Monticello, and delivered in 1994.

2 RIVER TRANSPORT CRAFT (LCM)

CURIAPO LC 21
YOPITO LC 01

Displacement, tons: 115 full load
Dimensions, feet (metres): 73.7 × 21 × 5.2 *(22.5 × 6.4 × 1.6)*
Main machinery: 2 Detroit diesels; 850 hp *(625 kW)*; 2 shafts
Speed, knots: 9
Complement: 5
Cargo capacity: 60 tons or 200 Marines
Guns: 2—12.7 mm MGs.

Comment: Details given are for *Curiapo* which is a former LCM. *Yopito* is a former LCU of 18 m. Both are used by the Marines. There are also 12 11 m LCVPs.

YOPITO *7/1999, Venezuelan Navy* / 0084248

1 + 3 DAMEN STAN PATROL 2606 (PB)

Displacement, tons: To be announced
Dimensions, feet (metres): 38.9 × 21.1 × ? *(26.5 × 5.9 × ?)*
Main machinery: 2 diesels; 2 cp props
Speed, knots: 25
Complement: To be announced
Guns: 3—12.7 mm MGs.

Comment: Contract signed with Damen Shipyards for construction at UCOCAR, Puerto Cabello, of one Damen Stan Patrol 2606 patrol craft. Aluminium construction. Launched on 14 August 2008. Three further craft to be built by 2010.

STAN PATROL 2606 *6/2008*, Damen Shipyards* / 1353713

NATIONAL GUARD (GUARDIA NACIONAL)

Notes: (1) There are also a large number of US and Canadian built river craft of between 6 and 9 m length, which are armed with MGs.
(2) Four intercept launches were delivered in 2003; two in July 2003 and two in October 2003.
(3) Some 60 Pirana class river patrol craft have been ordered. The first 15 were delivered in August 2003.
(4) It is reported that 66 patrol craft were ordered from Rodman in July 2007. The order includes 30 m Rodman 101, 20 m R 66 and 16 m Rodman 55. The deliveries are likely to be split between the Navy and the Coast Guard.

10 RIO ORINOCO II CLASS (PBF)

B 9801 series

Displacement, tons: 30 full load
Dimensions, feet (metres): 54 × 14 × 4.6 *(16.5 × 4.3 × 1.4)*
Main machinery: 2 MTU 12V 183TE93 diesels; 2,268 hp(m) *(1.67 MW)* sustained; 2 shafts
Speed, knots: 36
Range, n miles: 500 at 25 kt
Complement: 5
Guns: 2—12.7 mm MGs. 2—7.62 mm MGs.
Radars: Surface search: Raytheon R1210; I-band.

Comment: Ordered from Halter Marine 24 April 1998. All delivered by late 1999. Aluminium construction. Some of the similar sized Orinoco I craft built in the 1970s are still in limited use.

ORINOCO II *1/1999, Halter Marine* / 0050739

12 PROTECTOR CLASS (PB)

RIO ARAUCA II B 8421
RIO CATATUMBO II B 8422
RIO APURE II B 8423
RIO NEGRO II B 8424
RIO META II B 8425
RIO PORTUGUESA II B 8426
RIO SARARE B 8427
RIO URIBANTE B 8428
RIO SINARUCO B 8429
RIO ICABARU B 8430
RIO GUARICO II B 8431
RIO YARACUY B 8432

Displacement, tons: 15 full load
Dimensions, feet (metres): 43.6 × 14.8 × 3.9 *(13.3 × 4.5 × 1.2)*
Main machinery: 2 GM diesels; 1,100 hp *(810 kW)*; 2 shafts
Speed, knots: 28. **Range, n miles:** 390 at 25 kt
Complement: 4
Guns: 2—12.7 mm MGs.
Radars: Navigation: Raytheon; I-band.

Comment: Built by SeaArk Marine and completed in 1984.

RIO SARARE *2/1996, van Ginderen Collection* / 0084249

12 PUNTA CLASS (PB)

PUNTA BARIMA A 8201
PUNTA MOSQUITO A 8202
PUNTA MULATOS A 8203
PUNTA PERRET A 8204
PUNTA CARDON A 8205
PUNTA PLAYA A 8206
PUNTA MACOYA A 8307
PUNTA MORON A 8308
PUNTA UNARE A 8309
PUNTA BALLENA A 8310
PUNTA MACURO A 8311
PUNTA MARIUSA A 8312

Displacement, tons: 15 full load
Dimensions, feet (metres): 43.0 × 13.4 × 3.9 *(13.1 × 4.1 × 1.2)*
Main machinery: 2 MTU series 183 diesels; 1,500 hp *(1.1 MW)*; 2 shafts
Speed, knots: 34. **Range, n miles:** 390 at 25 kt
Complement: 4
Guns: 2—12.7 mm MGs.
Radars: Navigation: Raytheon; I-band.

Comment: Built by Robert E Derecktor, Mamaroneck, NY. Delivered July-December 1984.

Vietnam

Country Overview

The Socialist Republic of Vietnam was established in 1976 when the Democratic Republic of Vietnam in the north and the Republic of Vietnam in the south became one nation. The country had been divided at the 17th parallel from the end of French colonial rule in 1954 and during the ensuing Vietnam War. Located on the east coast of the Indochina peninsula, it has an area of 127,844 square miles and is bordered to the north by China and to the west by Cambodia and Laos. It has a 1,858 n mile coastline with the South China Sea. Hanoi is the capital while Ho Chi Minh City (formerly Saigon) is the largest city and a major port. There are further ports at Haiphong and Da Nang. Territorial seas (12 n miles) are claimed. An EEZ (200 n miles) has also been claimed but the limits have not been defined.

Headquarters Appointments

Chief of Naval Forces:
Vice Admiral Nguyen Van Hien
Deputy Chief of Naval Forces:
Captain Tran Quang Khue

Personnel

(a) 2009: 13,000 regulars
(b) Additional conscripts on three to four year term (about 3,000)
(c) 27,000 naval infantry

Organisation and Bases

The Vietnamese Navy is part of the People's Army of Vietnam (PAVN) and is formally known as the PAVN Navy.

The fleet is organised into four regions based on, from north to south, Haiphong (HQ), Da Nang, Nha Trang and Cân Tho. There are other bases at Cam Ranh Bay, Hue and Ha Tou.

Coast Guard

A Coast Guard was formed on 1 September 1998. It is subordinate to the Navy and may take on Customs duties.

SUBMARINES

2 YUGO CLASS (MIDGET SUBMARINES) (SSW)

Displacement, tons: 90 surfaced; 110 dived
Dimensions, feet (metres): 65.6 × 10.2 × 15.1 *(20 × 3.1 × 4.6)*
Main machinery: 2 diesels; 320 hp(m) *(236 kW)*; 1 shaft
Speed, knots: 12 surfaced; 8 dived
Range, n miles: 550 at 10 kt surfaced; 50 at 4 kt dived
Complement: 4 plus 6/7 divers

Comment: Transferred from North Korea in 1997. May be fitted with two short torpedo tubes and a snort mast, but used primarily for diver related operations. The conning tower acts as a wet/dry diver compartment. Operational status is doubtful.

YUGO (North Korean colours)
6/1998, Ships of the World
0052525

FRIGATES

Notes: The Barnegat class frigate (ex-seaplane tender) *Pham Ngu Lao* HQ 01 has probably been decommissioned.

0 + 2 (2) GEPARD (PROJECT 11661) CLASS (FFGM)

Name	*No*	*Builders*	*Laid down*	*Launched*	*Commissioned*
–	–	Zelenodolsk Shipyard	10 July 2007	2009	2010
–	–	Zelenodolsk Shipyard	28 Nov 2007	2010	2011

Displacement, tons: 1,560 standard; 2,100 full load
Dimensions, feet (metres): 335.3 × 43.0 × 17.4 *(102.2 × 13.1 × 5.3)*
Main machinery: CODOG; 2 gas turbines; 30,850 hp(m) *(23.0 MW)*; 1 Type 61D diesel; 7,375 hp(m) *(5.5 MW)*; 2 shafts; cp props
Speed, knots: 26 (18 on diesels)
Range, n miles: 5,000 at 10 kt
Complement: 103 (accommodation for 131)

Missiles: SSM: 8 Zvezda SS-N-25 (KH 35 Uran) (2 quad); IR or radar homing to 130 km *(70.2 n miles)* at 0.9 Mach; warhead 145 kg; sea-skimmer.
SAM: 1 SA-N-4 Gecko twin launcher; semi-active radar homing to 15 km *(8 n miles)* at 2.5 Mach; warhead 50 kg. 20 weapons.
Guns: 1—3 in *(76 mm)*/59 AK-176; 120 rds/min to 15 km *(8 n miles)*; weight of shell 5.9 kg.
2—30 mm/65 AK-630; 6 barrels per mounting; 3,000 rds/min combined to 2 km.
Torpedoes: 4—21 in *(533 mm)* (2 twin) tubes.
A/S mortars: 1 RBU 6000 12-tubed trainable.
Mines: 2 rails. 48 mines.
Countermeasures: Decoys: 4 PK 16 chaff launchers.
ESM/ECM: 2 Bell Shroud. 2 Bell Squat. Intercept and jammers.
Weapons control: 2 Light Bulb datalink. Hood Wink and Odd Box optronic systems. Band Stand datalink.
Radars: Air/surface search: Cross Dome; E/F-band.
Fire control: Bass Tilt; H/I-band (for guns). Pop Group; F/H/I-band (for SAM). Garpun-B (for SSM); I/J-band.
Band Stand (Mineral ME); D-band (for SS-N-25).
Navigation: Nayada; I-band.
IFF: 2 Square Head. 1 Salt Pot B.
Sonars: Ox Yoke; hull-mounted; active search and attack; medium frequency.
Ox Tail; VDS; active search and attack; medium frequency.

GEPARD CLASS ***7/2002, Military Parade*** / 0528304

Programmes: Contract signed with Rosoboronexport in late 2005 for the procurement of two Gepard-class frigates. The contract for construction was signed with Zelenodolsk Shipyard on 22 December 2006. Delivery is expected in 2010. Components may be supplied for the construction of two further ships at Ho Chi Minh City.
Operational: Details of weapons and sensors are speculative and based on those originally designated for the ships in Russian naval service.

5 PETYA (PROJECT 159A/AE) CLASS (FFL)

HQ 09 (ex-SKR-82) **HQ 11** (ex-SKR-96) **HQ 13** (ex-SKR-141) **HQ 15** (ex-SKR-130) **HQ 17** (ex-SKR-135)

Displacement, tons: 950 standard; 1,180 full load
Dimensions, feet (metres): 268.3 × 29.9 × 9.5 *(81.8 × 9.1 × 2.9)*
Main machinery: CODAG; 2 gas turbines; 30,000 hp(m) *(22 MW)*; 1 Type 61V-3 diesel; 5,400 hp(m) *(3.97 MW)* sustained; centre shaft; 3 shafts
Speed, knots: 32
Range, n miles: 4,870 at 10 kt; 450 at 29 kt
Complement: 98 (8 officers)

Guns: 4 USSR 3 in *(76 mm)*/59 AK 726 (2 twin); 90 rds/min to 15 km *(8 n miles)*; weight of shell 5.9 kg.
4—37 mm (2 twin) (HQ 11). 4—23 mm (2 twin) (HQ 11, 15).
Torpedoes: 3—21 in *(533 mm)* (triple) tubes (Petya III). SAET-60; passive homing to 15 km *(8.1 n miles)* at 40 kt; warhead 400 kg.
5—16 in *(406 mm)* (1 quin) tubes (Petya II). SAET-40; active/passive homing to 10 km *(5.5 n miles)* at 30 kt; warhead 100 kg.
A/S mortars: 4 RBU 6000 12-tubed trainable (HQ 09, 13, 17); range 6,000 m; warhead 31 kg.
4 RBU 2500 16-tubed trainable (HQ 11); range 2,500 m; warhead 21 kg.
Depth charges: 2 racks.
Mines: Can carry 22.
Countermeasures: ESM: 2 Watch Dog; radar warning.
Radars: Air/surface search: Strut Curve; F-band.
Navigation: Don 2; I-band.
Fire control: Hawk Screech; I-band.
IFF: High Pole B. 2 Square Head.

HQ 09 ***9/1995, G Toremans*** / 0506261

Sonars: Vychada MG 311; hull-mounted; active attack; high frequency.

Programmes: All built at Khabarovsk. Two Petya III (HQ 09, 11) (export version) transferred from USSR in December 1978 and three Petya IIs, (HQ 13, 15, 17); HQ 13 transferred in December 1983; HQ 15 in May 1984 and HQ 17 in December 1984.

Modernisation: Refitted and updated 1994 to 1999. The RBUs replaced by 25 mm guns and the torpedo tubes by 37 mm guns in some of the class. *HQ 17* completed major overhaul at Ba Son Shipyard in 2001.
Structure: The Petya IIIs have the same hulls as the Petya IIs but different armament.
Operational: Reported active between the coast and the Spratly Islands.

HQ 17 (PETYA II) ***11/2001*** / 0131341

CORVETTES

Notes: Ex-US Admirable class *HQ 07* is an alongside training hulk.

2 BPS 500 (PROJECT 12418) CLASS (FSGM)

HQ 381–382

Displacement, tons: 517 full load
Dimensions, feet (metres): 203.4 × 36.1 × 8.2 *(62 × 11 × 2.5)*
Main machinery: 2 MTU diesels; 19,600 hp(m) *(14.41 MW)*; 2 Kamewa waterjets
Speed, knots: 32. **Range, n miles:** 2,200 at 14 kt
Complement: 28

Missiles: SSM: 8 Zvezda SS-N-25 (KH-35 Uran) (2 quad) ❶; active radar homing to 130 km *(70.1 n miles)* at 0.9 Mach; warhead 145 kg.
SAM: SA-N-10. 24 missiles.
Guns: 1—3 in *(76 mm)*/59 AK 176 ❷; 120 rds/min to 15 km *(8 n miles)*; weight of shell 5.9 kg.
1—30 mm/65 AK 630 ❸; 6 barrelled; 3,000 rds/min combined to 2 km.
2—12.7 mm MGs.
Mines: Rails fitted.
Countermeasures: Decoys: 2 chaff launchers ❹.
Weapons control: Optronic director ❺.
Radars: Air/surface search: Cross Dome ❻; E/F-band.
Navigatio:n I-band.
Fire control: Bass Tilt ❼; H/I-band.

Comment: Severnoye design (improved Pauk) ordered in 1996 and two ships subsequently delivered in kit form to Ba Son Shipyard, Ho Chi Minh City. First unit launched in June 1998 and became operational in late 2001. The second unit is reported to have been completed.

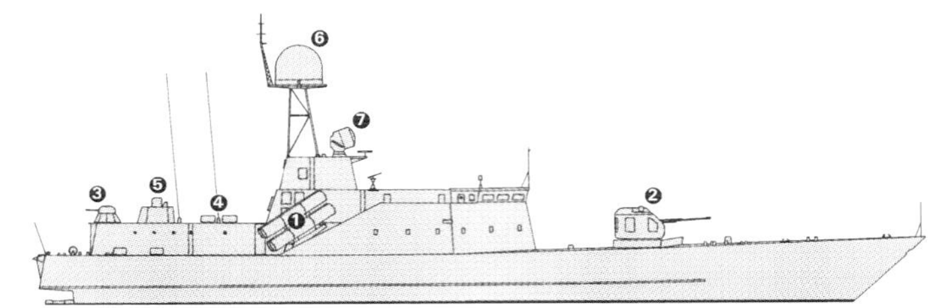

BPS 500 *(not to scale), Ian Sturton* / 0530054

HQ 381 *6/2008** 1353656

4 TARANTUL CLASS (PROJECT 1241RE) (FSGM)

HQ 371 HQ 372 HQ 374 HQ 378

Displacement, tons: 385 standard; 450 full load
Dimensions, feet (metres): 184.1 × 37.7 × 8.2 *(56.1 × 11.5 × 2.5)*
Main machinery: 2 Nikolayev Type DR 77 gas turbines; 16,016 hp(m) *(11.77 MW)* sustained; 2 Nikolayev Type DR 76 gas turbines with reversible gearboxes; 4,993 hp(m) *(3.67 MW)* sustained; 2 shafts
Speed, knots: 36
Range, n miles: 2,000 at 20 kt; 400 at 36 kt
Complement: 41 (5 officers)

Missiles: SSM: 4 SS-N-2D Styx; IR homing to 83 km *(45 n miles)* at 0.9 Mach; warhead 513 kg; sea-skimmer at end of run.
SAM: SA-N-5 Grail quad launcher; manual aiming; IR homing to 6 km *(3.2 n miles)* at 1.5 Mach; warhead 1.5 kg.
Guns: 1—3 in *(76 mm)*/59 AK 176; 120 rds/min to 15 km *(8 n miles)*; weight of shell 5.9 kg.
2—30 mm/65 AK 630; 6 barrels per mounting; 3,000 rds/min combined to 2 km.
Countermeasures: Decoys: 2 PK 16 chaff launchers.
Weapons control: Hood Wink optronic director.
Radars: Air/surface search: Plank Shave; E-band.
Navigation: Pechora; I-band.
Fire control: Bass Tilt: H/I-band.
IFF: Salt Pot, Square Head A.
Sonars: Foal Tail; active; high frequency.

Programmes: First pair ordered in October 1994. These were new hulls exported at a favourable price and completed by 1996. Some delay in delivery because of late payments, but both were in service by April 1996. Two further vessels were reported to have been ordered in 1999 for delivery in 2000. Imagery of HQ 374 suggests that the contract has been completed although this may be the result of a change in pennant numbers. Current numbers of vessels are thus uncertain.
Operational: Based at Da Nang.

HQ 371 *6/2007, Mazumdar Collection* / 1353655

HQ 378 *6/2007, Mazumdar Collection* / 1170244

2 + 8 TARANTUL V CLASS (PROJECT 1241.8) (FSGM)

HQ 375–376

Displacement, tons: 385 standard; 450 full load
Dimensions, feet (metres): 196.5 × 37.7 × 8.2 *(59.9 × 11.5 × 2.5)*
Main machinery: 2 Nikolayev Type DR 77 gas turbines; 16,016 hp(m) *(11.77 MW)* sustained; 2 Nikolayev Type DR 76 gas turbines with reversible gearboxes; 4,993 hp(m) *(3.67 MW)* sustained; 2 shafts
Speed, knots: 36. **Range, n miles:** 2,000 at 20 kt; 400 at 36 kt
Complement: 41 (5 officers)

Missiles: SSM: 16 (4 quad) SS-N-25 (Kh 35 Uran); active radar homing to 130 km *(70.2 n miles)* at 0.9 Mach; warhead 145 kg; sea-skimmer.
SAM: SA-N-5 Grail quad launcher; manual aiming; IR homing to 6 km *(3.2 n miles)* at 1.5 Mach; warhead 1.5 kg.
Guns: 1—3 in *(76 mm)*/59 AK 176; 120 rds/min to 15 km *(8 n miles)*; weight of shell 5.9 kg.
2—30 mm/65 AK 630; 6 barrels per mounting; 3,000 rds/min combined to 2 km.
Countermeasures: Decoys: 2 PK 16 chaff launchers.
Weapons control: Hood Wink optronic director.
Radars: Air/surface search: Strut Curve (Pozitiv-ME); I-band.
Surface search: Plank Shave; E/F-band (SS-N-25).
Fire control: Bass Tilt; H/I-band.
Navigation: Pechora; I-band.

Comment: A contract was signed in March 2004 for the supply of 10 further modified Tarantul V, armed with SS-N-25 (Kh 35 Uran). Two of these, built at Vympel Shipyard, Rybinsk, were delivered in late 2007. The remaining eight are to be constructed in Vietnam. Details are as for those in Russian service and may differ.

TARANTUL V (under construction) *9/2006, Lemachko Collection* / 1167503

LAND-BASED MARITIME AIRCRAFT

Notes: There are six Air Force Su-27 Flankers and 20 Su-22 Fitter-H that can be used for maritime surveillance.

Numbers/Type: 2 PZL Mielec M-28 B1R Bryza.
Operational speed: 181 kt *(335 km/h).*
Service ceiling: 13,770 ft *(4,200 m).*
Range: 736 n miles *(1,365 km).*
Role/Weapon systems: Polish-built aircraft originally based on the USSR Cash light transport. Contract in October 2003 for the procurement of up to ten aircraft configured for maritime surveillance. First two delivered in 2005 by late 2004. Sensors: MSC-400 mission system, ARS-400 radar (with SAR/ISAR) modes). Weapons: to be announced.

M-28 (Polish colours) *6/2003, J Ciślak* / 0567493

PATROL FORCES

Notes: (1) At least one Shanghai II class PC may still be operational.
(2) Some of the craft listed may be transferred to the Coast Guard and Maritime Police.

4 + (6) SVETLYAK (PROJECT 1041.2) CLASS (PGM)

HQ 261–264

Displacement, tons: 365 full load
Dimensions, feet (metres): 162.4 × 30.2 × 7.9 *(49.5 × 9.2 × 2.4)*
Main machinery: 3 diesels; 15,900 hp(m) *(11.85 MW)* sustained; 3 shafts; cp props
Speed, knots: 30
Range, n miles: 2,200 at 13 kt
Complement: 28 (4 officers)
Missiles: SAM: SA-N-10; shoulder launched and (manual aiming); IR homing to 5 km *(2.7 n miles)* at 1.7 Mach; warhead 1.5 kg.
Guns: 1—3 in *(76 mm)* /59 AK 176; 120 rds/min to 15 km *(8 n miles)*; weight of shell 5.9 kg.
1—30 mm/65 AK 630; 6 barrels; 3,000 rds/min combined to 2 km.
Countermeasures: Decoys: 2 chaff launchers.
Weapons control: Hood Wink optronic director.
Radars: Air/surface search: Peel Cone; E-band.
Fire control: Bass Tilt; H/I-band.
Navigation: Palm Frond B; I-band.

Comment: Contract for two craft signed with Almaz, St Petersburg in November 2001. First vessel launched on 17 July 2002 and second on 30 July 2002. Following acceptance on 17 October 2002, both vessels were shipped from St Petersburg on 14 December 2002. Two more are reported to have been delivered in 2007 and it is understood there is an option for a further six vessels.

SVETLYAK *9/2002, Almaz* / 0530061

8 OSA II (PROJECT 205) CLASS (FAST ATTACK CRAFT—MISSILE) (PTFG)

HQ 354 **HQ 357–360** **HQ 384–386**

Displacement, tons: 245 full load
Dimensions, feet (metres): 126.6 × 24.9 × 8.8 *(38.6 × 7.6 × 2.7)*
Main machinery: 3 Type M 504 diesels; 10,800 hp(m) *(7.94 MW)* sustained; 3 shafts
Speed, knots: 37. **Range, n miles:** 500 at 35 kt
Complement: 30
Missiles: SSM: 4 SS-N-2B Styx; active radar or IR homing to 46 km *(25 n miles)* at 0.9 Mach; warhead 513 kg.
Guns: 4 USSR 30 mm/65 (2 twin); 500 rds/min to 5 km *(2.7 n miles)*; weight of shell 0.54 kg.
Radars: Surface search: Square Tie; I-band.
Fire control: Drum Tilt; H/I-band.
IFF: High Pole. 2 Square Head.

Comment: Transferred from USSR: two in October 1979, two in September 1980, two in November 1980 and two in February 1981. All based at Da Nang. Operational status doubtful.

OSA II 354 *5/2000, Bob Fildes* / 0105740

5 TURYA (PROJECT 206M) CLASS (FAST ATTACK CRAFT—HYDROFOIL) (PCK)

HQ 321 **HQ 331–332** **HQ 334–335**

Displacement, tons: 190 standard; 250 full load
Dimensions, feet (metres): 129.9 × 29.9 (41 over foils) × 5.9 (13.1 over foils) *(39.6 × 7.6 (12.5) × 1.8 (4)*
Main machinery: 3 Type M 504 diesels; 10,800 hp(m) *(7.94 MW)* sustained; 3 shafts
Speed, knots: 40
Range, n miles: 600 at 35 kt foilborne; 1,450 at 14 kt hullborne
Complement: 30
Guns: 2 USSR 57 mm/75 AK 725 (twin, aft); 120 rds/min to 12.7 km *(6.8 n miles)*; weight of shell 2.8 kg.
2 USSR 25 mm/80 (twin, fwd); 270 rds/min to 3 km *(1.6 n miles)*; weight of shell 0.34 kg.
Torpedoes: 4—21 in *(533 mm)* tubes (not in all).
Depth charges: 2 racks.
Radars: Surface search: Pot Drum; H/I-band.
Fire control: Muff Cob; G/H-band.
IFF: High Pole B. Square Head.
Sonars: Foal Tail (not in all); VDS; high frequency.

Comment: Transferred from USSR: two in mid-1984, one in late 1984, two in January 1986. Two more acquired from Russia. Two of the five do not have torpedo tubes or sonar. Two scrapped so far, the remainder are probably non-operational.

TURYA 331 *5/2000, Bob Fildes* / 0105741

3 SHERSHEN (PROJECT 206T) CLASS (FAST ATTACK CRAFT) (PTFM)

HQ 301 series

Displacement, tons: 145 standard; 170 full load
Dimensions, feet (metres): 113.8 × 22 × 4.9 *(34.7 × 6.7 × 1.5)*
Main machinery: 3 Type 503A diesels; 8,025 hp(m) *(5.9 MW)* sustained; 3 shafts
Speed, knots: 45
Range, n miles: 850 at 30 kt; 460 at 42 kt
Complement: 23
Missiles: SAM: 1 SA-N-5 Grail quad launcher; manual aiming; IR homing to 6 km *(3.2 n miles)* at 1.5 Mach; altitude to 2,500 m *(8,000 ft)*; warhead 1.5 kg.
Guns: 4 USSR 30 mm/65 (2 twin); 500 rds/min to 5 km *(2.7 n miles)*; weight of shell 0.54 kg.
Torpedoes: 4—21 in *(533 mm)* tubes (not in all).
Depth charges: 2 racks (12).
Mines: Can carry 6.
Radars: Surface search: Pot Drum; H/I-band.
Fire control: Drum Tilt; H/I-band.
IFF: High Pole A. Square Head.

Comment: A total of 16 transferred from USSR: two in 1973, two in April 1979 (without torpedo tubes), two in September 1979, two in August 1980, two in October 1980, two in January 1983 and four in June 1983. Most have been cannibalised for spares.

SHERSHEN (refitting in Haiphong) *8/2000, P Marsan* / 0105742

14 ZHUK (PROJECT 1400M) CLASS (PB)

T 864 **T 874** **T 880** **T 881** **+10**

Displacement, tons: 39 full load
Dimensions, feet (metres): 78.7 × 16.4 × 3.9 *(24 × 5 × 1.2)*
Main machinery: 2 Type M 401B diesels; 2,200 hp(m) *(1.6 MW)* sustained; 2 shafts
Speed, knots: 30
Range, n miles: 1,100 at 15 kt
Complement: 11 (3 officers)
Guns: 4—14.5 mm (2 twin) MGs.
Radars: Surface search: Spin Trough; I-band.

Comment: Transferred: three in 1978, three in November 1979, one in November 1981, one in May 1985, three in February 1986, two in December 1989, two in January 1990, three in January 1996, two in January 1998 and two in April 1998. So far seven have been deleted but operational numbers are uncertain. Some are allocated to the Coast Guard.

4 + (12) STOLKRAFT CLASS (PBR)

HQ 56–59

Displacement, tons: 44 full load
Dimensions, feet (metres): 73.5 × 24.6 × 3.9 *(22.4 × 7.5 × 1.2)*
Main machinery: 2 MTU 12V 183TE93 diesels; 2,301 hp(m) *(1.69 MW)* sustained; 2 Doen waterjets
1 Volvo Penta diesel; 360 hp(m) *(265 kW)*; 1 shaft
Speed, knots: 30
Complement: 7
Guns: 1 Oerlikon 20 mm.

Comment: Four built by Oceanfast Marine, Western Australia and delivered in early 1997. Trimaran construction forward, transforming into a catamaran at the stern. Shallow draft needed for inshore and river operations. The centreline single shaft is used for loitering. The craft show the colours of the Customs department. Up to 12 more may have been built in Vietnam but this has not been confirmed.

STOLCRAFT *8/2005, Kuvel/Marsan* / 1154063

4 MODIFIED ZHUK CLASS (PB)

HQ 37 **HQ 55** **BP-29-01-01** **BP-29-98-01**

Displacement, tons: 38 full load
Dimensions, feet (metres): 95.1 × ? × ? *(29.0 × ? × ?)*
Main machinery: 2 Saab Scania diesels; 2,500 hp(m) *(18.64 MW)* sustained; 2 shafts
Speed, knots: 30
Complement: 11 (3 officers)
Guns: 2 — 12.7 mm MGs (2 twin).
Radars: Navigation: I-band.

Comment: Built in Vietnam to design based on Zhuk class.

HQ 55 (under construction) *8/2000, P Marsan* / 0105744

3 BP-29-12-01 PATROL CRAFT (PB)

BP-29-12-01 **BP-33-11-01** **BP-33-12-01**

Displacement, tons: To be announced
Dimensions, feet (metres): To be announced
Main machinery: 2 diesels; 2 shafts
Speed, knots: To be announced
Guns: 2 — 12.7 mm MGs.
Radars: Navigation: I-band.

Comment: Indigenously-built patrol craft of an unknown type.

PATROL CRAFT *11/2004, Marcel/Marsan* / 1154064

2 POLUCHAT (PROJECT 368) CLASS (COASTAL PATROL CRAFT) (PB/YPT)

Displacement, tons: 100 full load
Dimensions, feet (metres): 97.1 × 19 × 4.8 *(29.6 × 5.8 × 1.5)*
Main machinery: 2 Type M 50 diesels; 2,200 hp(m) *(1.6 MW)* sustained; 2 shafts
Speed, knots: 20. **Range, n miles:** 1,500 at 10 kt
Complement: 15
Guns: 2 — 12.7 mm MGs.
Radars: Navigation: Spin Trough; I-band.

Comment: Both transferred from USSR in January 1990. Can be used as torpedo recovery vessels.

POLUCHAT (Russian colours) *7/1993, Hartmut Ehlers* / 0506181

RIVER PATROL CRAFT

Comment: There are large numbers of river patrol boats, mostly armed with MGs. A 14.5 m craft ordered from Singapore TSE in 1994. More are being built locally with Volvo Penta engines.

RIVER PATROL BOAT *8/2000, P Marsan* / 0105743

AMPHIBIOUS FORCES

Notes: There is a landing ship HQ 521 of approximately 72 m.

3 POLNOCHNY (PROJECT 771) CLASS (LCM)

HQ 511 (ex-SDK-71) **HQ 512** (ex-SDK-112) **HQ 513** (ex-SDK-74)

Displacement, tons: 760 standard; 834 full load
Dimensions, feet (metres): 246.1 × 31.5 × 7.5 *(75 × 9.6 × 2.3)*
Main machinery: 2 Kolomna Type 40-D diesels; 4,400 hp(m) *(3.2 MW)* sustained; 2 shafts
Speed, knots: 19
Complement: 40
Guns: 2 or 4 USSR 30 mm/65 (1 or 2 twin). 2 — 140 mm rocket launchers.
Radars: Surface search: Spin Trough; I-band.
Fire control: Drum Tilt; H/I-band.

Comment: Transfers from USSR: one in May 1979 (B), one in November 1979 (A) and one in February 1980 (B). Details are for Polnochny B class. All are reported to be in poor condition.

HQ 512 and 513 *6/1995, Giorgio Arra* / 0084254

3 TANK LANDING SHIPS (LST)

TRAN KHANH DU (ex-Da Nang, ex-*Maricopa County* LST 938) HQ 501
VUNG TAU (ex-*Cochino County* LST 603) HQ 502
QUI NONH (ex-*Bulloch County* LST 509) HQ 503

Displacement, tons: 2,366 beaching; 4,080 full load
Dimensions, feet (metres): 328 × 50 × 14 *(100 × 15.2 × 4.3)*
Main machinery: 2 GM 12-567A diesels; 1,800 hp *(1.34 MW)*; 2 shafts
Speed, knots: 11. **Range, n miles:** 6,000 at 10 kt
Complement: 110
Guns: 8 Bofors 40 mm/60 (2 twin, 4 single). 4 Oerlikon 20 mm.

Comment: HQ 501 is LST 1-510 class and HQ 502 and 503 are LST 512-1152 class. All built in 1943–44. Transferred from US to South Vietnam in mid-1960s. Seldom seen at sea.

TRAN KHANH DU *8/2000* / 0105745

30 LANDING CRAFT (LCM AND LCU)

Comment: About five LCUs, 12 LCM 8 and LCM 6, and three LCVPs remain of the 180 minor landing craft left behind by the USA in 1975. In addition there are about 10 T4 LCUs acquired from the USSR in 1979.

LCU *6/2001* / 0131363

MINE WARFARE FORCES

2 YURKA (RUBIN) (PROJECT 266) CLASS (MINESWEEPERS—OCEAN) (MSO)

HQ 851 **HQ 885**

Displacement, tons: 540 full load
Dimensions, feet (metres): 171.9 × 30.8 × 8.5 *(52.4 × 9.4 × 2.6)*
Main machinery: 2 Type M 503 diesels; 5,350 hp(m) *(3.91 MW)* sustained; 2 shafts
Speed, knots: 17. **Range, n miles:** 1,500 at 12 kt
Complement: 45
Guns: 4 USSR 30 mm/65 (2 twin); 500 rds/min to 5 km *(2.7 n miles)*; weight of shell 0.54 kg.
Mines: 10.
Radars: Surface search: Don 2; I-band.
Fire control: Drum Tilt; H/I-band.
Sonars: Stag Ear; hull-mounted; active minehunting; high frequency.

Comment: Transferred from USSR December 1979. Steel-hulled, built in early 1970s.

YURKA (Egyptian colours) *10/1998, F Sadek* / 0017818

4 SONYA (YAKHONT) (PROJECT 1265) CLASS (MINESWEEPERS/HUNTER—COASTAL) (MHSC)

HQ 861 **HQ 862** (ex-BT-228) **HQ 863** (ex-BT-296) **HQ 864** (ex-BT-212)

Displacement, tons: 450 full load
Dimensions, feet (metres): 157.4 × 28.9 × 6.6 *(48 × 8.8 × 2)*
Main machinery: 2 Kolomna 9-D-8 diesels; 2,000 hp(m) *(1.47 MW)* sustained; 2 shafts
Speed, knots: 15. **Range, n miles:** 3,000 at 10 kt
Complement: 43
Guns: 2 USSR 30 mm/65 AK 630. 2—25 mm/80 (twin).
Mines: 8.
Radars: Surface search: Nayada; I-band.
Sonars: MG 69/79; active; high frequency.

Comment: First one transferred from USSR 16 February 1987, second in February 1988, third in July 1989, fourth in March 1990. Two based at Da Nang.

SONYA 862 *5/2000, R Fildes* / 0105746

2 YEVGENYA (KOROND) (PROJECT 1258) CLASS (MINEHUNTERS—INSHORE) (MHI)

HQ 782 **HQ 871**

Displacement, tons: 90 full load
Dimensions, feet (metres): 80.7 × 18 × 4.9 *(24.6 × 5.5 × 1.5)*
Main machinery: 2 Type 3-D-12 diesels; 600 hp(m) *(440 kW)* sustained; 2 shafts
Speed, knots: 11. **Range, n miles:** 300 at 10 kt
Complement: 10
Guns: 2 USSR 25 mm/80 (twin).
Mines: 8.
Radars: Surface search: Spin Trough; I-band.
Sonars: MG 7; active; high frequency.

Comment: First transferred from USSR in October 1979; two in December 1986. One deleted in 1990.

YEVGENYA (Ukraine colours) *6/2003, Ships of the world* / 0572652

5 K 8 (PROJECT 361T) CLASS (MINESWEEPING BOATS) (PBR)

Displacement, tons: 26 full load
Dimensions, feet (metres): 55.4 × 10.5 × 2.6 *(16.9 × 3.2 × 0.8)*
Main machinery: 2 Type 3-D-6 diesels; 300 hp(m) *(220 kW)* sustained; 2 shafts
Speed, knots: 18
Complement: 6
Guns: 2—14.5 mm (twin) MGs.

Comment: Transferred from USSR in October 1980. Probably used as river patrol craft.

SURVEY AND RESEARCH SHIPS

1 KAMENKA (PROJECT 870) CLASS (AGS)

Displacement, tons: 760 full load
Dimensions, feet (metres): 175.5 × 29.8 × 8.5 *(53.5 × 9.1 × 2.6)*
Main machinery: 2 Sulzer diesels; 1,800 hp(m) *(1.32 MW)*; 2 shafts; cp props
Speed, knots: 14. **Range, n miles:** 4,000 at 10 kt
Complement: 25
Radars: Navigation: Don 2; I-band.

Comment: Transferred from USSR December 1979. Built at Northern Shipyard, Gdansk in the late 1960s. May be civilian manned.

KAMENKA (Russian colours) *1984* / 0506127

0 + 1 SURVEY SHIP (AGSH)

Name	*No*	*Builders*	*Laid down*	*Launched*	*Commissioned*
–	–	Song Thu, Danang	26 July 2008	2010	2011

Displacement, tons: To be announced
Dimensions, feet (metres): 217.5 × 50.2 × 10.2 *(66.3 × 13.2 × 3.1)*
Main machinery: Diesel-electric; 3 diesel generators; 2,652 hp(m) *(1.95 MW)*; 1 motor; 1,073 hp(m) *(800 kW)*; 2 azimuth thrusters; 1 bow thruster
Speed, knots: 12. **Range, n miles:** 3,000 at 12 kt
Complement: 13 (accommodation for 71)
Radars: Navigation: E/F- and I-band.
Sonars: Multi and single beam; high frequency; active.

Comment: Damen 6613 design multipurpose hydrographic and oceanographic survey, training and mine countermeasures vessel. The ship is to be a derivative of the Snellius-class vessels built for the RNLN and is similar to the ship that entered Thai service in 2008. This ship is being built by Song Thu Company in Danang, Vietnam from a design- and material package supplied by Damen Shipyards, Gorinchem. The hydrographical survey equipment is to be supplied by Atlas.

DAMEN 6613 ***12/2005, Damen Shipyards*** / 1159224

AUXILIARIES

Notes: In addition to the vessels listed below there are two YOG 5 fuel lighters, two floating cranes, two ex-USSR unarmed Nyryat 2 diving tenders and approximately 10 harbour tugs.

1 VODA (PROJECT 561) CLASS (WATER TANKER) (AWT)

BO 82 (ex-MVT 19)

Displacement, tons: 2,115 full load
Dimensions, feet (metres): 267.4 × 37.7 × 14.1 *(81.5 × 11.5 × 4.3)*
Main machinery: 2 diesels; 1,600 hp *(1.2 MW)*; 2 shafts
Speed, knots: 12
Range, n miles: 3,000 at 10 kt
Complement: 38
Radars: Navigation: Don 2; I-band.

Comment: Built by Yantar, Kaliningrad, in the 1950s. Probably an ex-Russian Pacific Fleet unit transferred in about 1996. Carries about 1,000 tons of water.

20 OFFSHORE SUPPLY VESSELS (AKL)

TRUONG HQ 966	**HQ 601**	**HQ 618–619**	**HQ 651**	**HQ 673**
BD 621–622	**HQ 608**	**HQ 627**	**HQ 661**	**HQ 996**
BD 630–632	**HQ 614**	**HQ 643**	**HQ 669–671**	

Measurement, tons: 1,000 dwt
Dimensions, feet (metres): 231.6 × 38.7 × 13.1 *(70.6 × 11.8 × 4)*
Main machinery: 1 diesel; 1 shaft
Speed, knots: 12
Complement: 30

Comment: Details are for HQ 966 launched at Halong Shipyard in June 1994. This is one of a group of 20 freighters reported as used by the Navy for coastal transport, and to service the Spratleys garrison. BD pennant numbers have been assigned to Spratly Islands service. The ships are of various sizes and include fishing vessels adapted for supply tasks. All are likely to be armed with machine guns.

BD 621 (old number) ***3/1997*** / 0050742

1 SORUM (PROJECT 745) CLASS (ATA)

BD 105

Displacement, tons: 1,660 full load
Dimensions, feet (metres): 190.2 × 41.3 × 15.1 *(58.0 × 12.6 × 4.6)*
Main machinery: Diesel-electric; 2 Type 2-DW2 diesel generators; 2,900 hp *(2.13 MW)*; 1 motor; 2,000 hp *(1.47 MW)*; 1 shaft
Speed, knots: 14
Range, n miles: 3,500 at 13 kt
Complement: 35
Radars: Navigation: I-band.

Comment: Ocean tug built at Yaroslavl. Transferred from Russia in 1995.

2 FLOATING DOCKS

Comment: One has a lift capacity of 8,500 tons. Transferred from USSR August 1983. Second one *(Khersson)* has a lift capacity of 4,500 tons and was supplied in 1988.

Virgin Islands (UK)

Country Overview

A British dependency, the British Virgin Islands are situated in the eastern Caribbean Sea at the northern end of the Leeward Islands in the Lesser Antilles chain. Puerto Rico lies some 52 n miles to the west. Comprising a group of 36 islands, 16 of them inhabited, and more than 20 islets and cays there are four main islands: Tortola (21 square miles); Anegada (15 square miles); Virgin Gorda (8 square miles); and Jost Van Dyke (3.5 square miles). Other inhabited islands include Peter Island, Cooper Island, Beef Island, Salt Island, and Norman Island. The capital, only town and principal port is Road Town, Tortola. Territorial seas (3 n miles) and a Fishery Zone (200 n miles) are claimed. The remainder of the Virgin Islands form a separate external territory of the US.

Headquarters Appointments

Commissioner of Royal Virgin Islands Police Force:
Reynell Frazer

Bases

Road Town, Tortola

POLICE

Notes: (1) There is also a 12 m Scarab, fitted with three 225 hp outboard motors, and a 10 m Mako with two 150 hp outboards.
(2) Two Dauntless class 12 m patrol boats are operated by the US Virgin Islands whose waters are also patrolled by USCG craft.

1 DAUNTLESS CLASS (PATROL CRAFT) (PB)

ST URSULA

Displacement, tons: 17.4 full load
Dimensions, feet (metres): 55.0 × 16.0 × 5.0 *(16.8 × 4.9 × 1.5)*
Main machinery: 2 Caterpillar C-15 diesels; 1,600 hp *(1.2 MW)*; 2 shafts
Speed, knots: 32
Range, n miles: 300 at 28 kt
Complement: 4
Radars: Navigation: Furuno; I-band.

Comment: Dauntless design craft constructed by SeaArk Marine, Monticello, AR, and delivered on 1 December 2006 to replace previous vessel of same name decommissioned in 2003. Aluminium construction. The craft is employed on drug interdiction, combatting illegal immigration, search and rescue and border control duties.

ST URSULA ***12/2006, SeaArk Marine*** / 1167666

Yemen

Country Overview

The Republic of Yemen was formed in 1990 through the union of the People's Democratic Republic of Yemen and the Yemen Arab Republic. The country includes the islands of Socotra, Kamaran and Perim. With an area of 207,285 square miles, it is situated on the south-west coast of the Arabian Peninsula and is bordered to the north by Saudi Arabia and to the east by Oman. It has a 1,030 n mile coastline with the Red Sea and the Gulf of Aden, which are linked by a strategic strait, the Bab el Mandeb.

The capital and largest city is Sanaa while the principal ports are Aden and Al Hudaydah. Territorial seas (12 n miles) are claimed. A 200 n mile EEZ has been claimed but the limits have only been partly defined by boundary agreements.

Personnel

2009: 1,700 naval plus 500 marines

Bases

Main: Aden, Hodeida
Secondary: Mukalla, Perim, Socotra, Al Katib
Coast Defence regions: Al Ghaydah, Aden and Cameron Island

Coast Defence

Two mobile SS-C-3 Styx batteries. Some 100 mm guns installed in tank turrets at Perim Island.

PATROL FORCES

Notes: (1) In addition there are two 'Osa IIs', 122 and 124. One is in a poor state of repair and may have been decommissioned. The other was sighted in a floating dock in mid-2002 and may be seaworthy, although the SSM system is probably not operational.
(2) Three 32 m Halter Marine Broadsword patrol craft have been reported: *26th of September* (141); *Sanaa* (200); *Ghamdan* (300).
(3) There are 13 11 m Sea Spirit patrol craft.

1 TARANTUL I CLASS (PROJECT 1241) (FSGM)

124 (ex-971)

Displacement, tons: 385 standard; 580 full load
Dimensions, feet (metres): 184.1 × 37.7 × 8.2 *(56.1 × 11.5 × 2.5)*
Main machinery: 2 Nikolayev Type DR 77 gas turbines; 16,016 hp(m) *(11.77 MW)* sustained; 2 Nikolayev Type DR 76 gas turbines with reversible gearboxes; 4,993 hp(m) *(3.67 MW)* sustained; 2 shafts
Speed, knots: 36
Range, n miles: 400 at 36 kt; 2,000 at 20 kt
Complement: 50

Missiles: SSM: 4 SS-N-2C Styx (2 twin) launchers; active radar or IR homing to 83 km *(45 n miles)* at 0.9 Mach; warhead 513 kg; sea-skimmer at end of run.
SAM: SA-N-5 Grail quad launcher; manual aiming; IR homing to 10 km *(5.4 n miles)* at 1.5 Mach; altitude to 2,500 m *(8,000 ft)*; warhead 1.1 kg.
Guns: 1—3 in *(76 mm)*/59 AK 176; 120 rds/min to 5.9 km *(3.8 n miles)*; weight of shell 7 kg.
2—30 mm/65 AK 630; 6 barrels per mounting; 3,000 rds/min to 2 km.
Countermeasures: Decoys: 2 PK 16 chaff launchers.
Weapons control: Hood Wink optronic director.
Radars: Air/surface search: Plank Shave (also for missile control); E-band.
Navigation: Spin Trough; I-band.
Fire control: Bass Tilt; H/I-band.
IFF: Square Head. High Pole.

Programmes: Two export versions of the ship originally delivered from the USSR. First one on 7 December 1990, second on 15 January 1991. One decommissioned by 2001.
Operational: Facilities for servicing missiles in Aden were destroyed in mid-1994. This remaining ship is still in a reasonable state of repair although probably without missiles.

TARANTUL 124 *10/1995* / 0016612

3 HOUNAN (TYPE 021) CLASS (FAST ATTACK CRAFT—MISSILE) (PTG)

126–128

Displacement, tons: 171 standard; 205 full load
Dimensions, feet (metres): 126.6 × 24.9 × 8.9 *(38.6 × 7.6 × 2.7)*
Main machinery: 3 Type 42-160 diesels; 12,000 hp(m) *(8.8 MW)* sustained; 3 shafts
Speed, knots: 34
Range, n miles: 800 at 30 kt
Complement: 28
Missiles: SSM: 4 YJ-1 (Eagle Strike) (C-801); inertial cruise; active radar homing to 40 km *(22 n miles)* at 0.9 Mach; warhead 165 kg; sea-skimmer.
Guns: 4 30 mm/(2 twin AK 230); 500 rds/min to 5 km *(2.7 n miles)*.
Radars: Surface search: Square Tie; I-band.
Fire control: Rice Lamp; H/I-band.
IFF: 2 Square Head. High Pole A.

Comment: A variation of the Chinese Huangfen (Osa 1 type) class design. Delivered on 6 June 1995 at Aden having been built by the China Shipbuilding Corporation and completed in 1993. Payment was delayed by the Yemeni civil war. Based at Al Katib. *128* ran aground in September 1997 but was salvaged and may be operational again. *126* is in a reasonable state of repair but is not armed with missiles.

HOUNAN 126 *5/1995* / 0506339

6 BAKLAN (CMN 15-60) CLASS (HSIC)

BAKLAN 1201
SIYAN 1202
ZUHRAB 1203
AKISSAN 1204
HUNAISH 1205
ZAKR 1206

Displacement, tons: 12 full load
Dimensions, feet (metres): 50.9 × 9.8 × 2.6 *(15.5 × 3 × 0.8)*
Main machinery: 2 diesels; 2 surface drives
Speed, knots: 55
Range, n miles: 400 at 30 kt
Complement: 4
Guns: 2—12.7 mm MGs.
Radars: Surface search: Furuno; I-band.

Comment: Ordered from CMN Cherbourg on 3 March 1996. First five were delivered 1 August 1996 and the last one in mid-1997. Top speed in Sea States up to 3. Composite hull construction.

BAKLAN CLASS *8/1996, C M N Cherbourg* / 0084259

10 AUSTAL PATROL SHIPS (PB)

P 1022–1031

Displacement, tons: 90 full load
Dimensions, feet (metres): 123.0 × 23.6 × 7.2 *(37.5 × 7.2 × 2.2)*
Main machinery: 2 Caterpillar 3512 diesels; 3,500 hp *(2.61 MW)*; 2 shafts
Speed, knots: 29
Range, n miles: 1,000 at 25 kt
Complement: 19 (3 officers)
Guns: 2—14.5 mm (twin). 2—12.7 mm MGs.

Comment: Contract with Austal Ships on 9 June 2003 for a total of 10 patrol craft. All were shipped to Yemen in February 2005. Of aluminium construction, the design is based on the Bay class Australian Customs vessels. The contract included engineering and practical training for 60 Yemeni crew.

P 1022 *3/2007* / 1170245

AMPHIBIOUS FORCES

Notes: Ropucha 139 is an alongside hulk.

1 NS-722 CLASS (LSMM)

BILQIS

Displacement, tons: 1,383 full load
Dimensions, feet (metres): 295.4 × 31.8 × 7.9 *(90 × 9.7 × 2.4)*
Main machinery: 2 Caterpillar diesels; 5,670 hp *(4.2 MW)*; 2 shafts
Speed, knots: 18
Complement: 49
Military lift: 5 T-72 tanks and 111 marines
Missiles: SAM: SA-16 or ZM Mesko.
Guns: 4 ZSU-23-2MR Wrobel 23 mm (2 twin).

Comment: Ordered in late 1999 for delivery in 2002, development of the Polnochny class built by Naval Shipyard Gdynia, Poland. Shipped from Poland to Yemen on 24 May 2002. Roles include disaster relief and cadet training as well as amphibious warfare.

BILQIS *10/2001, J Ciślak* / 0131343

3 DEBA CLASS (PROJECT NS-717) (LCU)

HIMYER (ex-*Dhaffar*) **SAMBA** **ABDULKORI** (ex-*Thamoud*)

Displacement, tons: 221 full load
Dimensions, feet (metres): 134.5 × 23.3 × 5.6 *(41 × 7.1 × 1.7)*
Main machinery: 2 Cummins diesels; 2 shafts
Speed, knots: 15. **Range, n miles:** 500 at 14.5 kt
Complement: 10
Military lift: 16 tons and 50 troops
Guns: 2 ZU-23-2MR Wrobel 23 mm/87 (1 twin).
2—12.7 mm MGs.
Radars: Navigation: I-band.

Comment: Ordered from Poland in October 1999 and delivered in mid-2001. AK-630 CIWS may also be fitted at a later date.

ABDULKORI (on transport ship) *5/2001, J Ciślak* / 0131342

MINE WARFARE FORCES

1 NATYA CLASS (PROJECT 266ME) (MINESWEEPER—OCEAN) (MSO)

201

Displacement, tons: 804 full load
Dimensions, feet (metres): 200.1 × 33.5 × 10.8 *(61 × 10.2 × 3)*
Main machinery: 2 Type M 504 diesels; 5,000 hp(m) *(3.67 MW)* sustained; 2 shafts; cp props
Speed, knots: 16. **Range, n miles:** 3,000 at 12 kt
Complement: 67
Guns: 4—30 mm/65 (2 twin); 500 rds/min to 5 km *(2.7 n miles)*; weight of shell 0.54 kg.
4—25 mm/80 (2 twin); 270 rds/min to 3 km *(1.6 n miles)*; weight of shell 0.34 kg.
A/S mortars: 2 RBU 1200 five-tubed fixed launchers; range 1,200 m; warhead 34 kg.
Mines: 10
Countermeasures: MCM: Carries contact, acoustic and magnetic sweeps.
Radars: Surface search: Don 2; I-band.
Sonars: MG 69/79; hull-mounted; active minehunting; high frequency.

Comment: Transferred from USSR in February 1991. Operational status doubtful. A second of class was delivered to Ethiopia in October 1991 but sheltered in Aden for a time in 1992.

NATYA 201 *6/2002, Rahn/Globke* / 0530089

5 YEVGENYA (PROJECT 1258) CLASS (MINEHUNTERS) (MHC)

11–12 **15** **20** +1

Displacement, tons: 90 full load
Dimensions, feet (metres): 80.7 × 18 × 4.9 *(24.6 × 5.5 × 1.5)*
Main machinery: 2 Type 3-D-12 diesels; 600 hp(m) *(440 kW)* sustained; 2 shafts
Speed, knots: 11
Range, n miles: 300 at 10 kt
Complement: 10
Guns: 2—25 mm/80 (twin).
Radars: Navigation: Spin Trough; I-band.
Sonars: MG 7 small transducer lifted over stern on crane.

Comment: GRP hulls. Two transferred from USSR in May 1982, third in November 1987 and three more in March 1990. One deleted in 1994. Two based at Aden and three at Al Katib. Operational status doubtful.

YEVGENYA 20 *2/1997* / 0016615

AUXILIARIES

Notes: (1) A 4,500 ton Floating Dock acquired from the USSR.
(2) A 14 m Hydrographic craft acquired from Cougar Marine in 1988.
(3) An oil-pollution control craft acquired in 1999.
(4) Two Toplivo class tankers, *135* and *140*, are reported to have been decommissioned.

COAST GUARD

Notes: (1) The Yemeni Coast Guard was established in 2002 and began operating in 2003. Its tasks include counter-smuggling and immigration control duties, SAR, fishery protections, environmental protection and pollution control. Its headquarters are at Sana'a with regional headquarters at Aden (Gulf of Aden), Hodeidah (Red Sea) and Mukalla (Arabian Sea). There are plans to establish a coastal radar system with Italian assistance.
(2) In addition to the craft listed, there are reported to be a Fairey Marine Tracker II (1034), four Plascoa 15 m fast patrol craft (1501-1504) and three Geraldton 23 m patrol craft (2201-2203).

P 2202 *3/2007* / 1170246

16 PATROL CRAFT (PC)

1301–1316

Displacement, tons: 17.7 full load
Dimensions, feet (metres): 44.0 × 12.5 × 3.9 *(13.4 × 3.8 × 1.2)*
Main machinery: 2 General Motors Detroit 6V53 diesels; 2 shafts
Speed, knots: 13
Range, n miles: 200 at 11 kt
Complement: 4

Comment: Former US Coast Guard lifeboats constructed in the 1960s. First eight transferred on 16 February 2004 and the remainder in 2006.

2 ARCHANGEL CLASS (RESPONSE BOATS) (PBF)

Displacement, tons: To be announced
Dimensions, feet (metres): 42.0 × 13.0 × 2.5 *(12.8 × 4.0 × 0.8)*
Main machinery: 2 Caterpillar diesels; 2 Hamilton 322 waterjets
Speed, knots: 40
Range, n miles: 300 at 25 kt
Complement: 4
Guns: 1 — 12.7 mm MG.
Radars: To be announced.

Comment: High-speed inshore patrol craft of aluminium construction and foam collar built by SAFE Boats International, Port Orchard, Washington. Donated by the US government in October 2005.

ARCHANGEL CLASS *6/2006, SAFE BOATS* / 1167667

4 DEFENDER CLASS (RESPONSE BOATS) (PBF)

0801–0804

Displacement, tons: 2.7 full load
Dimensions, feet (metres): 25.0 × 8.5 × 8.8 *(7.6 × 2.6 × 2.7)*
Main machinery: 2 Honda outboard motors; 450 hp *(335 kW)*
Speed, knots: 46. **Range, n miles:** 175 at 35 kt
Complement: 4
Guns: 1 — 12.7 mm MG.
Radars: To be announced.

Comment: High-speed inshore patrol craft of aluminium construction and foam collar built by SAFE Boats International, Port Orchard, Washington. Donated by the US government in October 2005.

DEFENDER 0804 *6/2006, SAFE BOATS* / 1167668

Zimbabwe

Country Overview

The Republic of Zimbabwe gained independence on 17 April 1980. Formerly the British colony of Southern Rhodesia and, between 1953 and 1963, part of the Federation of Rhodesia and Nyasaland (now Malawi), a unilateral declaration of independence on 11 November 1965 precipitated a turbulent period of guerilla war. This eventually led to a peace settlement in 1979 and elections in 1980. A landlocked country with an area of 150,873 square miles, it is situated in central southern Africa and is bordered to the north by Zambia, to the east by Mozambique, to the south by South Africa and to the west by Botswana and Namibia. It has a shoreline of approximately 350 n miles with Lake Kariba, artificially formed by the Kariba Dam, from which the country gets much of its electric power. The capital, largest city and commercial centre is Harare (formerly Salisbury). The railway system is linked to the port of Beira in Mozambique.

Bases

Kariba, Binga.

PATROL FORCES

2 RODMAN 46HJ CLASS (PB)

Displacement, tons: 12.5 full load
Dimensions, feet (metres): 45.9 × 12.5 × 2.0 *(14.0 × 3.8 × 0.6)*
Main machinery: 2 Caterpillar 3280 diesels; 850 hp *(633 kW)*
Speed, knots: 30
Range, n miles: 350 at 18 kt
Complement: 4

Comment: GRP hull. Built in 1999 by Rodman, Vigo. Operated by Zimbabwe Police.

RODMAN 46 *6/1999, Rodman* / 0570998

3 RODMAN 38 CLASS (PB)

Displacement, tons: 10 full load
Dimensions, feet (metres): 36.1 × 12.8 × 2.3 *(11.0 × 3.9 × 0.7)*
Main machinery: 2 diesels; 2 waterjets
Speed, knots: 28
Range, n miles: 300 at 15 kt
Complement: 4

Comment: GRP hull. Built in 1999 by Rodman, Vigo. Operated by Zimbabwe Police.

RODMAN 38 *6/1999, Rodman* / 0571000

5 RODMAN 790 CLASS (PB)

Displacement, tons: 2.4 full load
Dimensions, feet (metres): 26.6 × 8.9 × 2.3 *(8.1 × 2.72 × 0.7)*
Main machinery: 2 Volvo Penta TAMD diesels
Speed, knots: 30
Complement: 2

Comment: GRP hull. Built in 1999 by Rodman, Vigo. Operated by Zimbabwe Police.

RODMAN 790 *6/1999, Rodman* / 0570999

INDEXES

Indexes

Country abbreviations

Alb	Albania
Alg	Algeria
Ana	Anguilla
Ang	Angola
Ant	Antigua and Barbuda
Arg	Argentina
Aust	Australia
Az	Azerbaijan
Ban	Bangladesh
Bar	Barbados
Bel	Belgium
Ben	Benin
Bhm	Bahamas
Bhr	Bahrain
BIOT	British Indian Ocean Territory
Blz	Belize
Bmd	Bermuda
Bol	Bolivia
Bru	Brunei
Brz	Brazil
Bul	Bulgaria
Cam	Cameroon
Can	Canada
Cay	Cayman Islands
Chi	Chile
CI	Cook Islands
Cmb	Cambodia
Col	Colombia
Com	Comoros
ConD	Congo, Democratic Republic
CPR	China, People's Republic
CpV	Cape Verde
CR	Costa Rica
Cro	Croatia
CtI	Côte d'Ivoire
Cub	Cuba
Cypr	Cyprus (Republic)
Den	Denmark
Dji	Djibouti
Dom	Dominica
DPRK	Korea, Democratic People's Republic (North)
DR	Dominican Republic
Ecu	Ecuador
Egy	Egypt
ElS	El Salvador
EqG	Equatorial Guinea
Eri	Eritrea
Est	Estonia
ETim	East Timor
Fae	Faroe Islands
FI	Falkland Islands
Fij	Fiji
Fin	Finland
Fra	France
Gab	Gabon
Gam	Gambia
GB	Guinea-Bissau
Geo	Georgia
Ger	Germany
Gha	Ghana
Gn	Guinea
Gra	Grenada
Gre	Greece
Gua	Guatemala
Guy	Guyana
HK	Hong Kong
Hon	Honduras
Hun	Hungary
Ice	Iceland
Ind	India
Indo	Indonesia
Iran	Iran
Iraq	Iraq
Ire	Ireland
Isr	Israel
Ita	Italy
Jam	Jamaica
Jor	Jordan
Jpn	Japan
Kaz	Kazakhstan
Ken	Kenya
Kir	Kiribati
Kwt	Kuwait
Lat	Latvia
Lby	Libya
Leb	Lebanon
Lit	Lithuania
Mac	Macedonia, Former Yugoslav Republic of
Mad	Madagascar
Mex	Mexico
MI	Marshall Islands
Mic	Micronesia, Federated States of
Mld	Maldives
Mlt	Malta
Mlw	Malawi
Mly	Malaysia
Mon	Montenegro
Mor	Morocco
Moz	Mozambique
Mtn	Mauritania
Mrt	Mauritius
Myn	Myanmar
Nam	Namibia
NATO	NATO
Nic	Nicaragua
Nig	Nigeria
Nld	Netherlands
Nor	Norway
NZ	New Zealand
Omn	Oman
Pak	Pakistan
Pal	Palau
Pan	Panama
Par	Paraguay
Per	Peru
Plp	Philippines
PNG	Papua New Guinea
Pol	Poland
Por	Portugal
Qat	Qatar
RoK	Korea, Republic of (South)
Rom	Romania
Rus	Russian Federation
SA	South Africa
Sam	Samoa
SAr	Saudi Arabia
Sen	Senegal
Ser	Serbia
Sey	Seychelles
Sin	Singapore
SL	Sierra Leone
Slo	Slovenia
Sol	Solomon Islands
Spn	Spain
Sri	Sri Lanka
StK	St Kitts and Nevis
StL	St Lucia
StV	St Vincent and the Grenadines
Sud	Sudan
Sur	Suriname
Swe	Sweden
Swi	Switzerland
Syr	Syria
Tan	Tanzania
Tkm	Turkmenistan
Tld	Thailand
Tog	Togo
Ton	Tonga
TT	Trinidad and Tobago
Tun	Tunisia
Tur	Turkey
Tuv	Tuvalu
Twn	Taiwan
UAE	United Arab Emirates
UK	United Kingdom
Ukr	Ukraine
Uru	Uruguay
US	United States
Van	Vanuatu
Ven	Venezuela
VI	Virgin Islands, UK
Vtn	Vietnam
Yem	Yemen
Zim	Zimbabwe

Named ships

1st Lt Alex Bonnyman (US) 960
1st Lt Baldomero Lopez (US) 961
1st Lt Harry L Martin (US) 960
1st Lt Jack Lummus (US) 961
1. Inönü (Tur) 828
2nd Lt John P Bobo (US) 961
3 de Febrero (Par) 598
3 de Noviembre (Pan) 593
4 de Noviembre (Pan) 593
5 de Noviembre (Pan) 593
6 of October (Egy) 217
10 de Noviembre (Pan) 593
15 de Noviembre (Uru) 975
18 Mart (Tur) 828
18 of June (Egy) 217
21 of October (Egy) 217
23 of July (Egy) 217
25 de Agosto (Uru) 975
25 of April (Egy) 217
28 de Noviembre (Pan) 593
101 series (Swe) 775

A

A 33-35 (Lby) 486
A 72 (Ind) 349
A 120, 212 (Alb) 2
A 223 (Alb) 3
A 521 (Sri) 766
A 530 (Sri) 766
A 542 (Sri) 766
A 543 (Sri) 766
A 545 (Sri) 766
A 641 (Alg) 7
A 671 (Az) 44
A 702-705, 751, 753-756 (Swe) 780
Aachen (UK) 900
Aamchit (Leb) 482
AB 21-24, 27-29, 31, 35-36 (Tur) 836
AB 1050-1051, 1053, 1056, 1058-1067 (Aust) 40
AB 2000-2005 (Aust) 39
Abad (Iran) 380
Abadejo (Arg) 23
Abalone (Can) 105
Abanto (Spn) 760
Abay (Kaz) 449
Abdul Aziz (SAr) 714, 716
Abdul Halim Perdanakusuma (Indo) 354
Abdul Rahman Al Fadel (Bhr) 49
Abdulkori (Yem) 994
Abeetha II (Sri) 762
Abeille Bourbon (Fra) 274
Abeille Flandre (Fra) 274
Abeille Languedoc (Fra) 274
Abeille Liberté (Fra) 274
Aber-Wrach (Fra) 276
Abha (SAr) 712
Abhay (Ind) 341
Abigail Burgess (US) 969
Able (US) 957
Abou Abdallah El Ayachi (Mor) 536
Abdoubekr Ben Amer (Mtn) 510
Abraham Lincoln (US) 917
Abrolhos (Brz) 82
Absalon (Den) 197
Abu Al Barakat Al Barbari (Mor) 536
Abu Bakr (Ban) 55
Abu Dhabi (UAE) 857
Abu El Ghoson (Egy) 221
Abu Obaidah (SAr) 714
Abu Qir (Egy) 215
Abukuma (Jpn) 426, 441
Aby (CtI) 180
Acamar (DR) 202
Acamar (Mex) 520
Acanthe (Fra) 270
Acconac (US) 954
Acevedo (Spn) 749
Acharné (Fra) 273
Achéron (Fra) 266
Achernar (Mex) 520
Achimota (Gha) 299
Aconcagua (Chi) 126
Aconit (Fra) 256
Acrux (Mex) 520
Active (US) 964
Acuario (Mex) 522
Acushnet (US) 965
Adak (US) 966
Adamastos (Gre) 311
Adang (Tld) 813
Addriyah (SAr) 715
Adelaide (Aust) 35
Adelie (US) 967
Adept (US) 953
ADF 104, 106-107 (Per) 605
Adhara (Mex) 520
Adhara II (Arg) 24
Adi 01-04 (Mex) 526
Adil (Mly) 504
Aditya (Ind) 348
Adm W M H Callaghan (US) 961
Admiral Branimir Ormanov (Bul) 94
Admiral Chabanenko (Rus) 668
Admiral Cowan (Est) 229
Admiral Gorshkov (Rus) 675
Admiral Horia Macelariu (Rom) 643
Admiral Kharlamov (Rus) 669
Admiral Kuznetsov (Rus) 664
Admiral Levchenko (Rus) 669
Admiral Panteleyev (Rus) 669
Admiral Petre Barbuneanu (Rom) 643
Admiral Pitka (Est) 228
Admiral Tributs (Rus) 669
Admiral Ushakov (Rus) 670
Admiral Vinogradov (Rus) 669
Admiral Vladimirskiy (Rus) 685
Admiral Yuri Ivanov (Rus) 688
Adour (Fra) 276
ADRI XXXII-LVIII (Indo) 368
Adrias (Gre) 303
Adventure (NZ) 561
Aegeon (Gre) 303
Aegeus (Gre) 311
Aegir (Ice) 323
Afif (SAr) 715
Afonso Cerqueira (Por) 632
AG 5-6 (Tur) 842
Al Agami (Egy) 223
Agathos (Cypr) 187
Agios Efstathios (Gre) 312
Ägir (Swe) 779
Agradoot (Ban) 59
Agray (Ind) 341
AGS 5106 (Jpn) 432
Agu (Nig) 565
Aguacero (Pan) 594
Aguascalientes (Mex) 526
Aguaytia (Per) 607
Aguia (Por) 634
Aguila (Mex) 522
Águila (Spn) 760
Aguirre (Per) 600
Agusan (Plp) 615
Ahalya Bai (Ind) 351
Åhav (Nor) 574
Ahi (US) 967
Ahmad El Fateh (Bhr) 49
Ahmad Yani (Indo) 354
Ahmadi (Kwt) 477
Al-Ahamadi (Kwt) 476
Ahmed ES Sakali (Mor) 536
Ahn Jung-Geun (RoK) 460
Ahti (Est) 229
Al Ahweirif (Lby) 486
Aias (Gre) 311
Aidon (Gre) 308
El Aigh (Mor) 536
Aigle (Fra) 266
Ailette (Fra) 275
Ain Zaghouan (Tun) 825
Aina Vao Vao (Mad) 491
Air Cushion-Tei (1-6) Gou (Jpn) 430
Airavat (Ind) 345
Aisberg (Rus) 701
Aishima (Jpn) 431
Aisling (Ire) 382
Ait Baâmrane (Mor) 537
Aittitos (Gre) 306
Aiyar Lulin (Myn) 542
Aiyar Mai (Myn) 543
Aiyar Maung (Myn) 543
Aiyar Minthamee (Myn) 543
Aiyar Minthar (Myn) 543
Ajak (Indo) 359
Ajay (Ind) 341
Ajeera (Bhr) 50
Ajonc (Fra) 270
Ajral (Ind) 349
AK 1, 2, 6 (Ger) 294, 295
Akademik Isanin (Rus) 686
Akademik Seminikhin (Rus) 686
Akademik Vladimir Kotelnikov (Rus) 695
Akagi (Jpn) 442
Akaishi (Jpn) 438
Akamas (Cypr) 187
Akar (Tur) 840
Akbaş (Tur) 843
Akçakoca (Tur) 838
Akçay (Tur) 838
Akdu (Egy) 222
Akebono (Jpn) 422
Akhisar (Tur) 836
Akhmeta (Geo) 279
El Akid (Mor) 534
Akigumo (Jpn) 443
Akin (Bul) 95
Akin (Tur) 842
Akissan (Yem) 993
Akka Devi (Ind) 351
Aksaz (Tur) 843
Akshay (Ind) 341
Aktau (Kaz) 449
Akwayafe (Cam) 97
Akyab (UK) 900
Al Agami (Egy) 223
Al-Ahamadi (Kwt) 476
Al Ahweirif (Lby) 486
Al Amane (Mor) 537
Al Antar (Egy) 223
Al Assad (Syr) 785
Al Aziziah (SAr) 716

Al Bahr (Egy) 224
Al Bat'nah (Omn) 577
Al Bushra (Omn) 577
Al Dammam (SAr) 710
Al Deebel (Qat) 638
Al Dekheila (Egy) 223
Al Doghas (Omn) 578
Al Dorrar (Kwt) 476
Al Farouk (Egy) 220
Al Farouq (SAr) 714
Al Feyi (UAE) 861
Al Fikah (Lby) 485
Al Forat (SAr) 717
Al Furat (Egy) 222
Al Gabbar (Egy) 219
Al Gaffa (UAE) 862
Al Ghariyah (Qat) 639
Al Ghullan (UAE) 859
Al Hadi (Egy) 219
Al Hakim (Egy) 219
Al Hani (Lby) 484
Al Hasbah (UAE) 860
Al Hassan (Jor) 448
Al Hirasa (Syr) 783
Al Hunain (Lby) 483
Al Hussein (Jor) 448
Al Iskandarani (Egy) 223
Al Jabiri (Bhr) 49
Al Jala (Tun) 824
Al Jarim (Bhr) 49
Al Jasrah (Bhr) 49
Al Jawf (SAr) 715
Al Jouf (SAr) 716
Al Jubatel (SAr) 717
Al Keriat (Lby) 486
Al Kharj (SAr) 715
Al Khyber (Lby) 483
Al Kirch (Alg) 5
Al Leeth (SAr) 716
Al Mabrukah (Omn) 575
Al Maks (Egy) 223
Al Manama (Bhr) 48
Al Manoud (Lby) 486
Al Mansoor (Omn) 577
Al Mathur (Lby) 485
Al Mua'zzar (Omn) 576
Al Muharraq (Bhr) 48, 50
Al Munassir (Omn) 578
Al Munjed (Lby) 486
Al Murjan (UAE) 860
Al Najah (Omn) 577
Al Neemran (Omn) 578
Al Nil (Egy) 222
Al Nil (SAr) 717
Al Nour (Egy) 219
Al Qatar (Egy) 219
Al Qiaq (SAr) 715
Al Qirdabiyah (Lby) 484
Al Quonfetha (SAr) 716
Al Quysumah (SAr) 715
Al Rafa (Egy) 219
Al Riffa (Bhr) 49
Al Riyadh (SAr) 710, 716
Al Ruha (Lby) 485
Al Said (Omn) 579
Al Salam (Egy) 219
Al Sanbouk (Kwt) 475
Al Shaheed (Kwt) 477
Al Sharqiyah (Omn) 577
Al Siddiq (Egy) 220
Al Siddiq (SAr) 714
Al Soumood (Kwt) 478
Al Sulayel (SAr) 715
Al Sultana (Omn) 579
Al Tabkah (Lby) 486
Al Tahaddy (Kwt) 478
Al Taweelah (Bhr) 49
Al Temsah (Omn) 578
Al Udeid (Qat) 638
Al Ula (SAr) 715
Al Wadeeah (SAr) 715
Al Wakil (Egy) 219
Al Whada (Mor) 537
Al Yamama (SAr) 716
Al Yarmook (SAr) 713
Al-Yarmouk (Kwt) 476
Al Zuara (Lby) 485
Al Zubara (Bhr) 50
Alabama (US) 910
Alacalufe (Chi) 125
Alacran (Mex) 523
Alagez (Rus) 693
Alan Shepard (US) 954
Alanya (Tur) 838
Alaska (US) 910
Albacore (US) 967
Alban (Iran) 380
Albany (Aust) 35
Albany (US) 914
Albardão (Brz) 82
Albatros (Bel) 65
Albatros (Fra) 262
Albatros (Rus) 703
Albatros (Spn) 760
Albatros (Tur) 835
Albatros (Ven) 983
Albatros II-III (Spn) 760
Albay Hakki Burak (Tur) 840
Alberti (Ita) 410
Alberto Navaret (Plp) 611
Albion (UK) 885
Alboran (Spn) 749
Alborz (Iran) 371
Albuquerque (US) 914
Alca (Ven) 984
Alca I (Spn) 760
Alca III (Spn) 760
Alcanada (Spn) 749
Alcatraz (Ven) 983
Alcaudon II (Spn) 760
Alcavarán I-V (Spn) 760
Alchevsk (Ukr) 853
Alcide Pedretti (Ita) 401
Alcotán (Spn) 760
Alcyon (Fra) 275
Aldebaran (Den) 195
Aldebarán (DR) 202
Aldébaran (Fra) 265
Aldebaran (Ven) 984
Alder (US) 969
Aldhahran (SAr) 716
Aldie (US) 947
Alejandro De Humboldt (Mex) 524
Aleksandrovets (Rus) 674
Aleksey Lebedev (Rus) 684
Aleksin (Rus) 675
Alert (US) 964
Alerta (Spn) 753
Ålesund (Nor) 573
Alex Haley (US) 965
Alexander Nevsky (Rus) 653
Alexander Otrakovskiy (Rus) 681
Alexander Shabalin (Rus) 681
Alexandr Pushkin (Rus) 693
Alexandria (US) 914
Alfahaheel (Kwt) 476
Alferez Sobral (Arg) 17
Alfonso De Albuquerque (Por) 634
Alfonso Pena (Brz) 86
Alfonso Vargas (Col) 174
Alfred Needler (Can) 112
Alfredo Peckson (Plp) 611
Algarna 1, 3 (Tur) 843
Alghero (Ita) 403
Algol (Mex) 522
Algol (US) 962
Algonquin (Can) 102
Alholm (Den) 194
Ali Haider (Ban) 55
Aliakmon (Gre) 310
Alidade (Alg) 7
Alioth (Mex) 520
Aliseo (Ita) 396
Alizé (Fra) 269
Alkahrj (SAr) 716
Alkaid (Mex) 520
Alkura (Indo) 360
Alkyon (Gre) 308
Alleppey (Ind) 346
Alliance (NATO) 546
Alligator (US) 967
Almaty (Kaz) 449
Almaz (Rus) 703
Almejas (Mex) 525
Almirante Blanco Encalada (Chi) 118
Almirante Brión (Ven) 980
Almirante Brown (Arg) 12
Almirante Carrero Blanco (Spn) 744
Almirante Cochrane (Chi) 118
Almirante Condell (Chi) 118
Almirante Diaz Pimienta (Spn) 758
Almirante Didiez Burgos (DR) 201
Almirante Don Juan De Borbón (Spn) 744
Almirante Gago Coutinho (Por) 635
Almirante Garcia (Ven) 980
Almirante Gastão Motta (Brz) 86
Almirante Graça Aranha (Brz) 83
Almirante Grau (Bol) 68
Almirante Grau (Per) 600
Almirante Guilhem (Brz) 86
Almirante Guillobel (Brz) 86
Almirante Irizar (Arg) 21
Almirante Jeronimo Gonçalves (Brz) 86
Almirante Juan Alexandro Acosta (DR) 201
Almirante Latorre (Chi) 117
Almirante Lynch (Chi) 118
Almirante Maximiano (Brz) 82
Almirante Padilla (Col) 170
Almirante Riveros (Chi) 118
Almirante Saboía (Brz) 82
Almirante Schieck (Brz) 86
Almirante Williams (Chi) 119
Alnilán (Mex) 520
Alphecca (Mex) 520
Alpheratz (Mex) 520
Alphonse Faye (Sen) 718
Alphonse Reynolds (StL) 708
Alrosa (Rus) 661
Alsace (Fra) 259
Alskär (Fin) 239
Alsin (Den) 199
Alster (Ger) 293
Alta (Nor) 572
Altair (DR) 202
Altaïr (Fra) 265
Altair (Mex) 523
Altair (Swe) 778
Altair (US) 962
Altair (Ven) 984
Altar (Ecu) 209
Altay (Rus) 697
Altmark (Ger) 294, 297
Alu-Alu (Mly) 504
Alugara (Indo) 367
Alumine (Arg) 23
Alvand (Iran) 371
Alvares Cabral (Por) 631
Alvaro de Bazán (Spn) 744
AM 7, 8 (Ger) 295
AM 237-244, 428 (Aust) 40
Amagiri (Jpn) 423
Amakusa (Jpn) 436
Amami (Jpn) 441
Aman (Kwt) 477
Amanah (Mly) 504
Al Amane (Mor) 537
Amapá (Brz) 79
Amasra (Tur) 838
Amatola (SA) 735
Amazonas (Per) 603
Ambe (Nig) 565
Amberjack (US) 967
Ambuda (Ind) 348
Ambush (UK) 867
Amelia Earhart (US) 954
America (US) 946
Amerigo Vespucci (Ita) 404
Améthyste (Fra) 244
Amir (Iran) 378
Ammersee (Ger) 294
Ammiraglio Magnaghi (Ita) 404
Amorim Do Valle (Brz) 83
Amougna (CtI) 180
Amphitrite (Gre) 300
Amrit Kaur (Ind) 351
Amsterdam (Nld) 555
Amundsen (Can) 106
Amur (Rus) 701
AMUR I-II (Rus) 690
Amyr (SAr) 714
An Dong (RoK) 466
An Hai (Twn) 792
An Heol (Fra) 272
An Yang (RoK) 467
Anacapa (US) 966
Anadyr (Rus) 700, 701
Anafartalar (Tur) 828
Anaga (Spn) 750
Anakonda (Indo) 360
Anamur (Tur) 838
Anand (Ind) 349
Anastacio Cacayorin (Plp) 611
Anatoly Korolev (Rus) 703
Anatoly Shilinsky (Rus) 706
Anawrahta (Myn) 539
Anchorage (US) 942
Ancón (Per) 606
Andagoya (Col) 177
Andalsnes (UK) 900
Andamans (Ind) 348
Andenes (Nor) 574
PFC James Anderson, Jr (US) 960
Andrea Doria (Ita) 394
Andrey Rozhkov (Rus) 704
Andrija Mohorovičič (Cro) 183
Andromache (Sey) 722
Andromeda (Den) 195
Andromède (Fra) 266
Andromeda (Gre) 305
Andromeda (Por) 635
Andromeda (Rus) 685
Anegagada De Adentro (Mex) 523
Ang Pangulo (Plp) 613
Angamos (Chi) 121
Angamos (Per) 599
Angelini (Ita) 410
Angostura (Par) 598
Anhatomirim (Brz) 82
Anirban (Ban) 56
Ankaa (Mex) 520
Ankaran (Slo) 732
Ann Harvey (Can) 107
Anna Kakurukaze Mungunda (Nam) 545
Annad (UAE) 862
Annapolis (US) 914
Annie Besant (Ind) 351
Anqing (CPR) 142
Anshun (CPR) 144
Al Antar (Egy) 223
Antares (Brz) 83
Antares (Bul) 93
Antares (Den) 195
Antares (DR) 202
Antarès (Fra) 265
Antares (Mex) 523
Antares (Rus) 685
Antares (Spn) 753
Antares (Swe) 778
Antares (Swi) 783
Antares (US) 962
Antares (Ven) 984
Antarktyda (Rus) 685
Ante Banina (Che) 528
Anteo (Ita) 407
Anthony Petit (US) 969
Anthypoploiarchos Laskos (Gre) 305
Anthypoploiarchos Pezopoulos (Gre) 305
Anthypoploiarchos Ritsos (Gre) 304
Antias (Rus) 701
Antietam (US) 921
Antioquia (Col) 170
Antofagasta (Bol) 68
Antofagasta (Chi) 125
Antofagasta (Per) 599
Antonio Enes (Por) 632
Antonio Luna (Plp) 611
Antonio Peluso (Ita) 412
Anvil (US) 971
Anvil Point (UK) 892
Anzac (Aust) 28
Anzio (US) 921
Anzone (Gha) 299
Aoife (Ire) 382
Aoshima (Jpn) 431
Apache (US) 956
Apolinario Mabini (Plp) 609
Apollo (Den) 195
Apollo Tiano (Plp) 612
Apruzzi (Ita) 410
Apsheron (Rus) 690
Aquarius (Swi) 783
Aquidneck (US) 966
Aquiles (Chi) 123
Aquitaine (Fra) 259
Aquitaine Explorer (Fra) 275
Arabat (Ukr) 856
Araçatuba (Brz) 82
Arachthos (Gre) 311
Aradu (Nig) 564
Arago (Fra) 261
Aramis (Fra) 270
SSCIM Senen Alberto Arango (Col) 172
Arao (Spn) 760
Arar (SAr) 716
Ararat (Aust) 35
Aras (Iran) 380
Arase (Jpn) 442
Arashio (Jpn) 416
Aratu (Brz) 82
Arauca (Col) 172
Araucano (Chi) 124
Arauco (Chi) 125
Araz (Az) 42
Archangelsk (Rus) 706
Archer (UK) 883
Arco (US) 953
Arctic (US) 954
Arctowski (Pol) 623
Arcturus (DR) 202
Arcturus (Mex) 520
Arcturus (Swe) 778
Arda Dedali (Indo) 367
Ardent (StK) 707
Ardent (US) 948
Ardhana (UAE) 859
Aretusa (Ita) 404
Arezzo (UK) 900
Argal (Rus) 701
Argens (Fra) 276
Argo (Swe) 778
Argonaute (Fra) 274
Argos (Por) 634
Arguin (Mtn) 510
Argus (Nld) 557
Argus (UK) 892
Argyll (UK) 878
Arholma (Swe) 776
Ariake (Jpn) 422
Ariarí (Col) 177
Arica (Chi) 125
Arica (Per) 599
Aries (Den) 195
Aries (DR) 202
Aries (Mex) 522
Aries (Sey) 721
Ark Royal (UK) 872
Arkhangelsk (Rus) 650
Arleigh Burke (US) 924
Ärlig (Swe) 774
Arlington (US) 942
Armada I (Col) 176
Armatolos (Gre) 306
Armen (Fra) 273
Armidale (Aust) 35
Arnhem Bay (Aust) 41
Arnomendi (Spn) 749
Arosa (Spn) 754
Arpão (Por) 630
Arromanches (UK) 900
Arrow Post (Can) 108
Artemio Ricarte (Plp) 609
Artful (UK) 867
Artigliere (Ita) 397
Arturus (Col) 176
Arun (Indo) 365
Aruna Asaf Ali (Ind) 351
Arung Samudera (Indo) 364
Arunta (Aust) 28
Arvak (Den) 199
Arvand (Iran) 380
Ary Parreiras (Brz) 85
Ary Rongel (Brz) 82
AS 13, 15, 21-26, 28, 30, 33-37 (Rus) 662, 663, 689
Asagiri (Jpn) 434, 443
Asama (Jpn) 442
Asashio (Jpn) 416
Asayuki (Jpn) 424
Aschau (Ger) 294
Ashdod (Isr) 387
Asheville (US) 914
Ashigara (Jpn) 418
Ashitaki (Jpn) 442
Ashland (US) 945
Ashmore Guardian (Aust) 41
Askeri (Fin) 239
Askø (Den) 194
Aslam (Iran) 380
Aso (Jpn) 439
Asogiri (Jpn) 445
Asoyuki (Jpn) 444
Aspen (US) 969
Aspirante Nascimento (Brz) 84
Assa (Mor) 538
El Assad (Alg) 8
Al Assad (Syr) 785
Assad Bin Fourat (Tun) 826
Assateague (US) 966
Assir (SAr) 716
Assiyut (Egy) 221
Aster (Bel) 64
Astice (Ita) 405
Astra (Lat) 481
Astrakhan (Rus) 680
Astrea (Swe) 778
Astrolabio (Spn) 754
Astute (UK) 867
Asuka (Jpn) 433
Asuncion (Mex) 525
Aswan (Egy) 220
Atabarah (Egy) 222
Atago (Jpn) 418
Atahualpa (Ecu) 209
Atak (Tur) 835
Atalaia (Brz) 82
Atalaya (Per) 607
Atalaya (Spn) 748
Atauro (ETim) 204
Athabaskan (Can) 102
Athena (US) 949
Athena II (US) 949
Atherstone (UK) 887
Athos (Fra) 270
Atil (Tur) 843
Atilay (Tur) 829
Atiya (Bul) 95
Atlanta (Por) 635
Atlantis (US) 950
Atlin Post (Can) 110
Atmaca (Tur) 835
Atrak (Iran) 380
Atrefs (Gre) 311
Atria (DR) 203
Atromitos (Gre) 311
Atsmout (Isr) 386

Attock (Pak) 589
Atyrau (Kaz) 449
Audacious (UK) 867
Audaz (Uru) 976
Audemer (UK) 900
Auerbach (Ger) 291
Augsburg (Ger) 286
Auki (Sol) 733
Aukštaitis (Lit) 487
Auriga (Mex) 522
Auriga (Por) 635
Aurith (Ger) 297
Ausma (Lat) 481
Auté (Fra) 271
Auvergne (Fra) 259
Avallone (Ita) 410
Avangard (Rus) 684
Avel Aber (Fra) 271
Avel Mor (Fra) 271
Avenger (US) 948
Aviere (Ita) 397
Avior (Mex) 520
Avra (Gre) 308
Avvaiyyar (Ind) 351
Awagiri (Jpn) 443
Awanami (Jpn) 444
Awashima (Jpn) 432
Axe (US) 971
Axel Von Fersen (Fin) 238
Axios (Gre) 310
Ayabane (Jpn) 447
Ayam (Nig) 565
Ayanami (Jpn) 444
Ayanka (Rus) 698
Ayeda 3, 4 (Egy) 222
Ayety (Geo) 280
Ayidawaya (Myn) 543
Aysberg (Rus) 678
Aysén (Chi) 125
Ayvalik (Tur) 838
Al Aziziah (SAr) 716
Azopardo (Arg) 22
El Azoum (Alg) 6
Azov (Rus) 681
Azumanche (Gua) 315

B

B 3, 7, 11 (Pol) 626
B 11, 33-34, 83 (Ger) 295
B 187, 394, 439, 445, 806 (Rus) 661
B 9801 series (Ven) 986
Babitonga (Brz) 80
Babur (Pak) 584
Bacamarte (Por) 635
El Bachir (Mor) 534
Bacolod City (Plp) 612
Bad Bevensen (Ger) 291
Bad Bramstedt (Ger) 296
Bad Düben (Ger) 297
Bad Rappenau (Ger) 291
Baden-Württemberg (Ger) 288
Badik (Indo) 358
Badr (Egy) 218
Badr (Pak) 584
Badr (SAr) 713
Bafra (Tur) 834
Bagong Lakas (Plp) 611
Bagong Silang (Plp) 611
Bahadur (Ind) 349
Bahamas (Bhm) 45
Bahía Cupica (Col) 175
Bahía Honda (Col) 175
Bahía Malaga (Col) 175
Bahía Portete (Col) 175
Bahia San Blas (Arg) 20
Bahía Santa Catalina (Col) 176
Bahía Solano (Col) 175
Bahía Utria (Col) 175
Bahía Zapzurro (Col) 175
Bahia Blanca (Arg) 22
Al Bahr (Egy) 224
Bahram (Iran) 374
Bahregan (Iran) 379
Bainbridge (US) 926
Bainbridge Island (US) 966
Baixa-Mar (Por) 637
Baja (Hun) 323
Baja California (Mex) 519
Bajarang (Ind) 349
Bajo Araya (Ven) 985
Bajo Brito (Ven) 985
Bakassi (Cam) 97
Bakinets (Az) 42
Baklan (Yem) 993
Baladewa (Indo) 368
Balaguier (Fra) 273
Balchik (Bul) 92
Baldur (Ice) 323
Balgzand (Nld) 557
Balikpapan (Aust) 34
Balikpapan (Indo) 365
Ballali (Ita) 410
Ballarat (Aust) 28
Balram (Ind) 349
Balshil (Ind) 349
Balta (Ukr) 854
Baltrum (Ger) 296
Baltyk (Pol) 625
Ban Yas (UAE) 860
Banco Ortiz (Uru) 978
Bandar Abbas (Iran) 379
Banderas (Mex) 525
Bandicoot (Aust) 35
Bandirma (Tur) 834
Bang Rachan (Tld) 814
Bangaram (Ind) 344
Banggi (Mly) 503
Bangkeo (Tld) 814
Bangor (UK) 888
Bangpakong (Tld) 803
Baptista De Andrade (Por) 632
Bar (Mon) 530
Baradero (Arg) 18
Barakuda (Indo) 359
Barama (Nig) 566
Baranof (US) 966
Baratang (Ind) 344
Barbara Mabrity (US) 969
Barbariso (Ita) 410
Barbaros (Tur) 830
Barceló (Spn) 749
Barcolet Point (TT) 821
Barentshav (Nor) 574
Barkat (Ban) 57
Barkat (Pak) 590
Barletta (Ita) 410
Barracuda (Guy) 317
Barracuda (Por) 629
Barracuda (US) 967
Barranca (Per) 606
Barranqueras (Arg) 18
Barroso (Brz) 76
Barry (US) 924
Bars (Rus) 701
Bartin (Tur) 834
Bartlett (Can) 107
Bartolomeu Dias (Por) 630
Baruna Jaya I-IV, VIII (Indo) 363
Barzan (Qat) 638
Basking Shark (Sin) 730
Bat Galim (Isr) 387
Bat Yam (Isr) 387
Bataan (US) 940
Batangas (Plp) 614
Bathurst (Aust) 35
Batiray (Tur) 829
Al Bat'nah (Omn) 577
Batroun (Leb) 482
Batti Malv (Ind) 344
Battle Point (US) 952
Batutinets (Ukr) 856
Baumholder (Ger) 295
Baunen (Den) 195
Baung (Mly) 499
Baxianshan (CPR) 153
Bayan (Kwt) 477
Bayandor (Iran) 372
Bayberry (US) 970
Baye Sogui (Sen) 718
Bayern (Ger) 284
Bayintnaung (Myn) 539
Baykal (Rus) 701
Bayleaf (UK) 890
Bayreuth (Ger) 296
Bayóvar (Per) 605
Bayu (Mly) 506
BC 1601-1610, 2001-2007, 3001-3007, 4001-4006, 5001-5006, 6001-6006, 7001-7006, 8001-8006, 9001-9006, 10001-10002, 20001-20003 (Indo) 366
BC Dutt (Ind) 349
BD 02, 04-05 (EIS) 226
BD 105 (Vtn) 992
BD 621-622, 630-632 (Vtn) 992
BDK-98 (Rus) 681
Beachy Head (UK) 892
Bear (US) 964
Beas (Ind) 336
Beautemps-Beaupré (Fra) 266
Beaver (Mex) 522
Bedi (Ind) 346
Bedok (Sin) 730
Begonia (Fra) 272
Behr Paima (Pak) 589
Beidiao (CPR) 157
Beihai (CPR) 144
Beirut (Leb) 482
Belankas (Mly) 502
Belati (Indo) 367
Belgica (Bel) 64
Bélier (Fra) 272
Bell Salter (Col) 176
Bellatrix (DR) 202
Bellatrix (Mex) 520
Bellatrix (Por) 636
Bellatrix (US) 962
Bellis (Bel) 64
Belomore (Rus) 688
Belos III (Swe) 779
Beluga (US) 967
Benalla (Aust) 36
Benavidez (US) 958
Bendahara Sakam (Bru) 88
Bendeharu (Bru) 89
Benevente (Brz) 80
Benfold (US) 924
Capt Steven L Bennett (US) 960
Benvenuti (Ita) 411
Berani (Mly) 504
Bergantín (Spn) 750
Bergen (Nor) 574
Berkut (Kaz) 449
Berkut (Rus) 702
Berlin (Ger) 293
Bernacla (Ven) 984
Bérrio (Por) 636
Bersagliere (Ita) 397
Bertholf (US) 963
Bertoldi (Ita) 411
Besique (Per) 606
Bespokoiny (Rus) 670
Bessang Pass (Plp) 615
Gen Frank S Besson Jr (US) 947
Betano (Aust) 34
Betelgeuse (Mex) 520
Betwa (Ind) 336
Beykoz (Tur) 834
Bezboyaznennyy (Rus) 670
BG 07-08, 101, 104-105, 107, 109, 111, 115-116, 119, 303-304, 310, 316, 318, 320, 329, 333, 349, 503-504, 604, 808, 812, 814 (Ukr) 856
BGK series (Rus) 686
Bhavnagar (Ind) 346
Bhikaji Cama (Ind) 351
Bhim (Ind) 349
Bholu (Pak) 590
Bi Sheng (CPR) 157
Bianco (Ita) 411
Bicentenario (Mex) 519
Bickerton (Can) 111
Bidong (Mly) 503
Bielik (Pol) 617
Bienvenido Salting (Plp) 611
Big Horn (US) 955
Bigliani (Ita) 410
Bigua (Arg) 23
Bihoro (Jpn) 441
Bijak (Mly) 504
Bilgola (Aust) 40
Billfish (Sin) 731
Bilqis (Yem) 994
Binbaşi Metin Sülüş (Tur) 842
Binbaşi Sadettin Gürcan (Tur) 841
Biriusa (Rus) 693
Birkholm (Den) 194
Biro Bong (RoK) 468
Biscayne Bay (US) 969
Bishkhali (Ban) 58
Bisma (Indo) 368
Bison (Fra) 272
Bistari (Mly) 504
Biter (UK) 883
Bitol (Gua) 315
Bitra (Ind) 344
Bizan (Jpn) 442
Bizerte (Tun) 824
Black Marlin (Sin) 731
Black Rover (UK) 891
Blackfin (US) 967
Blacktip (US) 967
Blacktip Shark (Sin) 730
Blagoveshchensk (Rus) 705
Blas De Lezo (Spn) 744
Blåtunga (Swe) 775
Blazer (UK) 883
Block Island (US) 966
Blue Marlin (Sin) 731
Blue Ridge (US) 939
Blue Shark (Sin) 730
Blue Shark (US) 967
Bluebell (US) 969
Bluefin (US) 967
Blyth (UK) 888
BO 82 (Vtn) 992
Boa (Indo) 360
Bob Hope (US) 958
Bocachica (Col) 176
Bocaina (Brz) 80
Bocas Del Toro (Pan) 593
Bodri (Bul) 91
Bodrum (Tur) 834
Boga (Arg) 23
Bogra (Ban) 58
Boiga (Indo) 360
Boiky (Rus) 673
Boise (US) 914
Bolados (Chi) 121
Bollard (US) 971
Bolognesi (Per) 600
Bolong Kanta (Gam) 278
Bonhomme Richard (US) 940
Bonite (Fra) 273
Bonito (US) 967
Bonny Serrano (Plp) 611
Bonsu (Gha) 299
Boone (US) 930
Bopa (Den) 194
Bora (Rus) 676
Bora (Tur) 835
Boraida (SAr) 715
Borby (Ger) 294
Borda (Fra) 267
Börde (Ger) 297
Boris Butoma (Rus) 691
Bormida (Ita) 407
Borodino (Rus) 670
Boronia (Aust) 39
Borovsk (Rus) 680
Borsziv (Ukr) 855
Bosisio (Brz) 74
Botany Bay (Aust) 41
Bottsand (Ger) 295
Bouboulina (Gre) 303
Boutwell (US) 963
Bovienzo (Ita) 410
Bowditch (US) 957
Boxer (US) 940
Bozcaada (Tur) 834
BP 401, 421-431, 433-443, 445-446, 462-471, 451-461 (Col) 174
BP-29-01-01, 29-12-01, 29-98-01, 33-11-01, 33-12-01 (Vtn) 990
BPC 2201, 2203, 2206-2209, 3201-3202, 3207-3209 3214-3215, 3220, 3222-3223, 3225 (Pan) 593
Bracui (Brz) 80
Brahmaputra (Ind) 336
Brandenburg (Ger) 284
Brandon (Can) 103
Brandy Station (US) 947
Brant (US) 967
Brasil (Brz) 84
I C Bratianu (Rom) 644
Braunschweig (Ger) 288
Brave (Sin) 727
Bravo (Chi) 121
Bredstedt (Ger) 296
Breezand (Nld) 557
Breitgrund (Ger) 292
Bremen (Ger) 286
Bremerton (US) 914
Brendan Simbwaye (Nam) 544
Brest (Rus) 674, 701
Bretagne (Fra) 259
Brettingen (Nor) 571
Briansk (Rus) 651
Bridge (US) 954
Bridle (US) 971
Brigaden (Den) 194
Brigadier Abraham Campo (Plp) 611
Brigadier José Mariá de la Vega (Mex) 518
Brimil (Fae) 233
Brisbane (Aust) 27
Bristoe Station (US) 947
Bristol Bay (US) 969
Brittin (US) 958
Briz (Bul) 93
Briz (Rus) 703
Broad Run (US) 947
Brocklesby (UK) 887
Bromo (Indo) 365
Bronzewing (Aust) 39
Broome (Aust) 35
Bruce C Heezen (US) 957
Bruinvis (Nld) 547
Brunei (Aust) 34
Brutus (Aust) 40
BSK 1-12 (Rus) 703
BT 44, 48, 100, 114-115, 215, 230, 256, 232 (Rus) 684
Bu Chon (RoK) 466
Buckthorn (US) 969
Budenovsk (Rus) 680
Budiman (Mly) 504
Budstikken (Den) 195
Buena Vista (US) 947
Buenaventura (Col) 176
Buenos Aires (Arg) 22, 23
Buevlyanin (Rus) 684
Buffalo (US) 914
Buffle (Fra) 272
Bug (Rus) 701
BUK 600 (Rus) 699
Buk Han (RoK) 468
Bukhansan (RoK) 473
Bukovina (Ukr) 855
Bukowo (Pol) 622
Bulkeley (US) 926
Bullarijia (Tun) 826
Bulta (Lat) 479
Bulwark (UK) 885
Bums (Ger) 293
Buna (PNG) 595
Bundaberg (Aust) 35
Bundeena (Aust) 40
Bungo (Jpn) 430
LTG William B Bunker (US) 947
Bunker Hill (US) 921
Buonocore (Ita) 410
Buque Escuela Naval Militar (Bol) 69
Burakreis (Tur) 828
Buran (Rus) 697
Buratti (Ita) 411
Burespadoongkit (Tld) 818
Burevi (Mld) 507
Burgas (Bul) 93
Burny (Rus) 670
Burq (Pak) 591
Burujulasad (Indo) 364
Burullus (Egy) 221
Burya (Bul) 92
Bushehr (Iran) 379
Al Bushra (Omn) 577
Butrinti (Alb) 3
SGT William R Button (US) 961
Büyükada (Tur) 833
Byblos (Leb) 482
Bystry (Rus) 670

C

C 21-24 (UK) 886
C 63, 109-116 (Ind) 351
C 131-138, 140-142 (Ind) 352
Ç 120, 123, 125-128, 132-135, 137-150, 305, 308, 312, 314, 316, 319, 321-327, 329-331 (Tur) 837, 838
Cabezo (Mex) 523
Cabo Blanco (CR) 179
Cabo Blanco (Per) 606
Cabo Catoche (Mex) 521
Cabo Corrientes (Arg) 22
Cabo Corrientes (Col) 172
Cabo Corrientes (Mex) 521
Cabo Corzo (Mex) 521
Cabo De Hornos (Arg) 20

Cabo De La Vella (Col)............ 172
Cabo Fradera (Spn)................... 750
Cabo Manglares (Col)............... 172
Cabo Tiburon (Col).................. 172
Caboclo (Brz).............................. 79
Cabrales (Chi)........................... 121
Cacheu (GB).............................. 316
Cacine (GB)............................... 316
Cacine (Por).............................. 633
Cacique Nome (Pan)................. 593
Cadete Virgilio Uribe (Mex)..... 520
Caio Duilio (Ita)........................ 394
Cakra (Indo).............................. 353
Calaboza (US)........................... 947
Calabrese (Ita)........................... 410
Calamar (Arg)............................. 23
Calamar (Pan)........................... 593
Calanus II (Can)........................ 112
Calchaqui (Arg)........................... 21
Caldas (Col).............................. 170
Caldera (Chi)............................. 125
Calgary (Can)............................ 100
Calicuchima (Ecu).................... 209
California (US).......................... 912
Calima (Col).............................. 176
Adm W M H Callaghan (US)... 961
Callao (Per)............................... 603
Calmaria (Por)........................... 637
Caloyeras (Per).......................... 604
Calypso (Gre)............................ 308
Camana (Per)............................. 606
Camaron (Arg)............................ 23
Camboriú (Brz)............................ 81
El Camino Español (Spn).......... 755
Campbell (US)........................... 964
Campbeltown (UK).................... 880
Campo (Cam)............................... 97
Canal Beagle (Arg)..................... 20
Canal Bocayna (Spn)................ 759
Canal Costanero (Arg)................ 24
Canal de Beagle (Arg)................. 22
Canal Emilio Mitre (Arg)............ 24
Çanakkale (Tur)......................... 828
Canarias (Spn)........................... 745
Canberra (Aust)............................ 35
Cancer (Mex)............................. 522
Çandarli (Tur)............................ 839
Cándido Pérez (Spn)................. 749
El Caney (US)............................ 947
Cangzhou (CPR)........................ 146
Cannanore (Ind)......................... 346
Canonchet (US).......................... 954
Canopus (DR)............................. 202
Canopus (Mex)........................... 520
Canopus (Por)............................ 636
Canopus (Ven)............................ 984
Cantabria (Spn).......................... 755
Canterbury (NZ)......................... 562
Cap Aux Meules (Can).............. 111
Cap Breton (Can)....................... 111
Cap De Rabast (Can)................. 111
Cap D'espoir (Can).................... 111
Cap Nord (Can).......................... 111
Cap Percé (Can)......................... 111
Cap Rozier (Can)....................... 111
Cap Tourmente (Can)................ 111
Capana (Ven).............................. 982
Capayán (Arg)............................. 21
Cape Ann (Can).......................... 111
Cape Bojeador (Plp).................. 614
Cape Calvert (Can).................... 111
Cape Caution (Can).................... 111
Cape Chaillon (Can).................. 111
Cape Cockburn (Can)................ 111
Cape Commodore (Can)............ 111
Cape Decision (US)................... 961
Cape Diamond (US).................. 961
Cape Discovery (Can)................ 111
Cape Domingo (US).................. 961
Cape Douglas (US).................... 961
Cape Ducato (US)...................... 961
Cape Dundas (Can).................... 111
Cape Edensaw (Can).................. 111
Cape Edmont (US)..................... 961
Cape Farewell (Can).................. 111
Cape Farewell (US)................... 962
Cape Flattery (US).................... 962
Cape Fox (Can).......................... 111
Cape Gibson (US)...................... 961
Cape Hearne (Can)..................... 111
Cape Henry (US)........................ 961
Cape Horn (US)......................... 961
Cape Hudson (US)..................... 961
Cape Hurd (Can)........................ 110
Cape Inscription (US)................ 961
Cape Intrepid (US).................... 961
Cape Isabel (US)........................ 961
Cape Island (US)........................ 961
Cape Jacob (US)......................... 961
Cape Kennedy (US)................... 961
Cape Knox (US)......................... 961
Cape Kuper (Can)...................... 111
Cape Lambton (Can)................. 111
Cape May (US).......................... 962
Cape Mckay (Can)..................... 111
Cape Mercy (Can)..................... 111
Cape Mohican (US)................... 962
Cape Mudge (Can).................... 111
Cape Norman (Can)................... 111
Cape Orlando (US).................... 961
Cape Providence (Can)............. 111
Cape Race (US)......................... 961
Cape Ray (US)........................... 961
Cape Rise (US).......................... 961
Cape Roger (Can)...................... 108
Cape Spry (Can)........................ 111
Cape St George (US)................. 921
Cape St James (Can)................. 111
Cape Storm (Can)..................... 111
Cape Sutil (Can)........................ 111
Cape Taylor (US)...................... 961
Cape Texas (US)........................ 961
Cape Trinity (US)...................... 961
Cape Victory (US)..................... 961
Cape Vincent (US)..................... 961
Cape Washington (US).............. 961
Cape Wrath (US)....................... 961
Capella (DR).............................. 202
Capella (Mex)............................ 520
Capella (US).............................. 962
Caph (Mex)................................ 522
Capitaine Moulié (Fra).............. 276
Capitán Bretel (Bol)..................... 68
Capitán Cabral (Par).................. 596
Capitán Castro (Col)................. 177
Capitán de Fragata Pedro Sáinz de Baranda (Mex)....................... 520
Capitán De Navio Blas Godinez (Mex)...................................... 518
Capitán De Navio Sebastian José Holzinger (Mex)..................... 518
Capitán Jaime Rook (Col)......... 174
Capitán Jorge Enrique Marquez Duran (Col)............................ 171
Capitán Miranda (Uru).............. 977
Capitán Ortiz (Par).................... 597
Capitán Pablo Jos De Porto (Col).. 171
Capitán Palomeque (Bol)............ 68
Capitán Prat (Chi)..................... 117
Capitan Rigoberto Giraldo (Col).. 177
Capotillo (DR)........................... 201
Cappelletti (Ita)......................... 410
Caprera (Ita).............................. 407
Capri (Ita).................................. 407
Capricia (Ita).............................. 405
Capricorne (Fra)........................ 266
Capricorno (Mex)...................... 522
Capstan (US).............................. 971
Capt Steven L Bennett (US)...... 960
Captain Mulzac (StV)................ 709
Car Nicobar (Ind)....................... 345
Carangue (Fra)........................... 275
Cardiel (Arg)................................ 23
Cardigan Bay (UK).................... 893
Carecare (Ven)........................... 985
Caribe (Ven).............................. 979
Caribou (Can)............................ 104
Caribou Isle (Can)..................... 110
Carina (Den).............................. 195
Carl M Brashear (US)................ 954
Carl Vinson (US)....................... 917
Carlo Bergamini (Ita)................ 397
Carlo Margottini (Ita)................ 397
Carlos Albert (Plp).................... 611
Carlos Chagas (Brz).................... 85
Carlos Galindo (Col)................. 174
Carlos Manuel De Cespedes (Cub)...................................... 186
Carlskrona (Swe)....................... 778
Carney (US)............................... 924
Caroly (Ita)................................ 405
Caroni (TT)............................... 821
Carr (US)................................... 930
Carrasco (Per)........................... 604
Carreca (Ita).............................. 410
Carrera (Chi)............................. 116
Carrillo (Per).............................. 604
Cartagena De Indias (Col)........ 176
SSGT Edward A Carter (US).... 960
Carter Hall (US)........................ 945
Carthage (Tun)........................... 823
Caruanta (Ven)........................... 985
Carvajal (Per)............................. 601
Casabianca (Fra)........................ 244
Cascadura (TT).......................... 821
Casma (Chi)............................... 121
Casotti (Ita)................................ 411
Cassard (Fra).............................. 252
Cassiopée (Fra).......................... 266
Cassiopea (Ita)........................... 401
Cassiopeia (Por)......................... 634
Castilla (Spn)............................. 751
Castor (DR)................................ 203
Castor (Swi)............................... 783
Casuarina (Aust).......................... 36
Catahecassa (US)....................... 954
Catanduanes (Plp)...................... 615
Catawba (US)............................. 956
Cattistock (UK).......................... 887
Cau-Cau (Chi)............................ 126
Cavaglia (Ita).............................. 410
Cavatorto (Ita)............................ 410
Cavour (Ita)................................ 391
Cavtat (Cro)............................... 181
Cayman Defender (Cay)............ 114
Cayman Guardian (Cay)............ 114
Cayman Protector (Cay)............ 114
Cayo Cochinas (Hon)................. 318
Cayo Macereo (Ven).................. 985
Cazadora (Spn)........................... 747
Ceará (Brz)................................... 81
Cebu (Plp).................................. 610
Cedar Run (US).......................... 947
Cekal (Mly)................................ 504
Celurit (Indo)............................. 367
Cenepa (Ecu).............................. 209
Centauro (Mex).......................... 522
Centauro (Por)............................ 634
Centinela (Spn)........................... 748
Centurion (Sin)........................... 724
Céphée (Fra)............................... 266
Cerberus (Nld)............................ 557
Çesme (Tur)............................... 839
Cetina (Cro)................................ 182
Cezayirli Gazi Hasan Paşa (Tur).. 840
CG 001-002, 004-006, 012-018, 055-057 (TT).......... 822
CG 119 (Can)............................. 111
CG 121-124, 131-137 (Jam)............................... 412, 413
CGC 103, 110, 115, 128-130, 132-136 (Plp)......................... 616
Chacabuco (Chi)........................ 122
Chacachacare (TT).................... 822
Chacagua (Mex)......................... 525
Chacal (Fra)............................... 268
Chacao (Chi).............................. 125
Chaffee (US).............................. 926
Chairel (Mex)............................. 525
Chakra (Ind)............................... 325
Chakri Naruebet (Tld)............... 801
Chala (Per)................................. 606
Challenger (Sin)......................... 724
Chaman (Ven)............................ 984
Chamela (Mex)........................... 525
Chamelecon (Hon)..................... 318
Champion (US).......................... 948
Chan Chiang (Twn).................... 791
Chancay (Per)............................. 606
Chancellorsville (US)................ 921
Chand Bibi (Ind)........................ 351
Chandeleur (US)........................ 966
Chang (Tld)................................ 812
Chang Bogo (RoK).................... 459
Chang Chien (Twn).................... 788
Changsha (CPR)......................... 139
Changxingdao (CPR)................. 161
Changzhi (CPR)......................... 144
Chanthara (Tld).......................... 815
Chantij-Mansisk (Rus)............... 706
Chao Phraya (Tld)...................... 803
Chaohu (CPR)............................ 141
Charagato (Ven)......................... 985
Charak (Iran).............................. 379
Charente (Fra)............................ 276
Charger (UK)............................. 883
Charles De Gaulle (Fra)............ 248
Charles Drew (US)..................... 954
Charlotte (US)............................ 914
Charlotte Maxeke (SA).............. 734
Charlottetown (Can).................. 100
Charlton (US)............................. 959
Chasanyabadee (Tld)................. 817
Chase (US)................................. 963
Chatham (UK)............................ 880
Chawengsak Songkram (Tld).... 818
Che Ju (RoK).............................. 464
Cheboksary (Rus)....................... 702
Cheetah (Ind).............................. 345
Cheikh Oumar Fall (Sen)........... 719
Cheleken (Rus)........................... 685
Cheliabinsk (Rus)....................... 654
Chen Te (Twn)........................... 789
Chena (US)................................. 970
Cheng Ho (Twn)......................... 788
Cheng Kung (Twn)..................... 788
Cheong Hae Jin (RoK)..................................... 471
Cheriyam (Ind)........................... 345
Cherkasy (Ukr)........................... 852
Chernigiv (Ukr).......................... 852
Chetlat (Ind)............................... 345
Chevalier Paul (Fra).................. 251
Chevreuil (Fra).......................... 269
Cheyenne (US)................... 914, 970
Chi Kuang (Twn)....................... 788
Chicago (US).............................. 914
Chicama (Per)............................ 606
Chichiriviche (Ven)................... 985
Chickahominy (US)................... 947
Chickasaw Bayou (US)............. 947
Chicoutimi (Can).......................... 98
Chiddingfold (UK).................... 887
Chief (US).................................. 948
Chieftain (Sin)........................... 724
Chigirin (Ukr)............................ 853
El Chihab (Alg)............................. 5
Chihaya (Jpn)............................ 435
Chik (Tld).................................. 816
Chikoko I (Mlw)........................ 491
Chikugo (Jpn)............................ 441
Chikuma (Jpn)........................... 426
Chikuzen (Jpn)........................... 438
Childers (Aust)............................. 35
Chiloé (Chi)............................... 125
Chilreu (Spn).............................. 749
Chimborazo (Ecu)..................... 209
Chimère (Fra)............................ 268
Chimera (Ita).............................. 398
Chin Hsing (Twn)...................... 796
Chin Yang (Twn)....................... 790
Chincoteague (US).................... 966
Chinook (US).................... 937, 967
Chioggia (Ita)............................. 403
Chios (Gre)................................ 307
Chipana (Chi)............................. 121
Chipana (Per)............................. 599
Chippewa (US)........................... 970
Chiquilyán (Arg).......................... 21
Chiriqui (Pan)............................ 593
Chiroo (Iran).............................. 379
Chita (Rus)................................ 661
Chitose (Jpn).............................. 441
Chitra (Ban)................................. 56
Chiyoda (Jpn)............................. 435
Chock (US)................................. 971
Choi Muson (RoK)..................... 459
Choi Young (RoK)..................... 461
Cholmsk (Rus)........................... 703
Choluteca (Hon)......................... 318
Chon An (RoK).......................... 466
Chon Buri (Tld).......................... 810
Chon Nam (RoK)....................... 464
Chongmingdao (CPR)................ 161
Chongqing (CPR)....................... 139
Chorrillos (Per).......................... 606
Chosin (US)............................... 921
Choukai (Jpn)............................. 419
Christina (Lit)............................. 490
Chu Chiang (Twn)..................... 791
Chuang (Tld).............................. 816
Chukotka (Rus).......................... 701
Chula (Tld)................................. 816
Chulmasan (RoK)...................... 473
Chulupi (Arg)............................... 21
Chun Jee (RoK).......................... 472
Chung Cheng (Twn)................... 792
Chung Chi (Twn)........................ 793
Chung Chien (Twn).................... 793
Chung Chih (Twn)..................... 793
Chung Chuan (Twn)................... 793
Chung Hai (Twn)....................... 793
Chung Ho (Twn)........................ 792
Chung Ju (RoK)................ 464, 466
Chung Kuang (Twn).................. 793
Chung Ming (Twn)..................... 793
Chung Nam (RoK).................................... 464
Chung Pang (Twn)..................... 793
Chung Ping (Twn)...................... 792
Chung Shun (Twn)..................... 793
Chung Suo (Twn)....................... 793
Chung Yeh (Twn)....................... 793
Chung-hoon (US)....................... 926
Chungmugong Yi Sun-shin (RoK).................................... 461
Ch'ungnam (RoK)...................... 471
Churubusco (US)........................ 947
Ciara (Ire)................................... 382
Ciclope (Ita)............................... 408
Cidade De Natal (Brz)................. 86
Cienaga De San Juan (Col).. 177
Cimarron (US)............................ 970
Çinar (Tur)................................. 841
Cinque (Ind)............................... 345
Cinuli (Ita).................................. 410
Ciorlieri (Ita).............................. 410
Cirro (Por).................................. 637
Cisne (Arg)................................... 23
Cisne (Por).................................. 634
Cisne Branco (Brz)...................... 84
Citlaltepl (Mex).......................... 526
City Of Corpus Christi (US).. 914
Ciudad Bolívar (Ven)................ 983
Ciudad de Rosario (Arg).............. 21
Ciudad de Zarate (Arg)................ 21
CL 01-09, 11-158, 214, 233, 238-239, 241-242, 244-249, 251, 253-254, 256-257, 259, 261, 264 (Jpn)......................... 444
Clamp (US)................................ 971
Clark's Harbour (Can)............... 111
Cleat (US).................................. 971
Cleveland (US)........................... 944
CW 3 Harold C Clinger (US).... 947
Clorinda (Arg).............................. 18
Clyde (UK)................................. 884
Coamo (US)............................... 947
Coati (Bol).................................... 68
Cobia (US)................................. 967
Cobija (Bol).................................. 68
Cochimie (Mex)......................... 521
Cochin (Ind)............................... 348
Cochito (US).............................. 967
Coho (US).................................. 967
Coishco (Per).............................. 606
Colán (Per)................................. 606
Cole (US)................................... 924
Colhue (Arg)................................ 23
Colhue Huapi (Arg)..................... 23
Colima (Mex)............................. 521
Colimbo (Ven)............................ 984
Colimbo II-IV (Spn).................. 760
Collins (Aust)............................... 26
Colonel Djoue-dabany (Gab).... 277
Colonia (Uru)............................. 975
Columbia (US)........................... 914
Columbus (US)........................... 914
Comandante Arandia (Bol)......... 68
Comandante Bettica (Ita).......... 400
Comandante Borsini (Ita).......... 400
Comandante Cigala Fulgosi (Ita)... 400
Comandante Foscari (Ita).......... 400
Comandante General Irigoyen (Arg)... 17
Comandante Manhães (Brz)....... 83
Comandante Toro (Chi)............ 125
Comandante Varella (Brz)........... 83
Comfort (US)............................. 955
Commandant Azouggarh (Mor)...................................... 534
Commandant Birot (Fra)........... 257
Commandant Blaison (Fra)....... 257
Commandant Bouan (Fra)......... 257
Commandant Boutouba (Mor)...................................... 534
Commandant Ducuing (Fra)..... 257
Commandant El Harty (Mor).... 534
Commandant El Khattabi (Mor)...................................... 534
Commandant l'Herminier (Fra)....................................... 257
Commander Apayi Joe (Nig).... 566
Commander Georgiu (Cypr)..... 187
Commander Tsomakis (Cypr)... 187
Comodoro Carlos Castillo Bretón (Mex)...................................... 520
Comodoro Manuel Azueta (Mex)...................................... 525
Comodoro Rivadavia (Arg)......... 19
Comstock (US)........................... 945
Concepción Del Uruguay (Arg)... 18
Conceptión (Chi)........................ 125
Concord (US)............................. 954
Conder (Aust)............................... 36
Condestable Zaragoza (Spn)..... 756
Conejera (Spn)........................... 749
Confidence (US)......................... 964
Congrio (Arg)............................... 23
Connecticut (US)....................... 913
Conqueror (Sin)......................... 724
Conrado Yap (Plp)..................... 612
Constancia (Ven)........................ 985
Constanta (Rom)........................ 646
Constitución (Ven)..................... 981
Constituição (Brz)....................... 75
Constitution (US)....................... 953
Contamana (Per)......................... 607
Contralmirante Angel Ortiz Monasterio (Mex)................... 520
Contramaestre Antero (Spn)..... 754
Contramaestre Casado (Spn)..... 755
Contramaestre Lamadrid (Spn)....................................... 754
Contramaestre Navarrete (Spn)....................................... 754
Contramaestre Sánchez Fernández (Spn)....................................... 754
Contre Admiral Eustatiu Sebastian (Rom)...................................... 643
Contre-almirante Oscar Viel Toro (Chi)... 122
Contreras (US)........................... 947
Conversano (Ita)........................ 410

Cook (UK) 889
Copiapó (Chi) 126
Coquimbo (Chi) 125
Cora (Mex) 526
Coral (Por) 635
Coral Snake (Aust) 40
Coralline (Fra) 271
Corinth (US) 947
Corio Bay (Aust) 41
Cormoran (Arg) 19, 23
Cormoran (Fra) 262
Cormoran (Ven) 984
Cormorán (Spn) 760
Cormorant (US) 967
Corner Brook (Can) 98
Cornhusker State (US) 961
Cornwall (Jam) 412
Cornwall (UK) 880
Coronado (US) 932
Corozal Point (TT) 821
Corral (Chi) 125
Corregidor (Plp) 616
Corrias (Ita) 411
Corsaro II (Ita) 405
Corte Real (Por) 631
Cortile (Ita) 411
Corvina (Arg) 23
Corvo Marino (Spn) 759
Cosme Acosta (Plp) 612
Cotopaxi (Ecu) 209
Cotuhe (Col) 177
Cougar (Can) 104
Courbet (Fra) 256
Courtenay Bay (Can) 111
Cove Isle (Can) 110
Cowpens (US) 921
Coyuca (Mex) 525
CPCIM Guillermo Londoño Vargas (Col) 172
CPL Louis J Hauge, Jr (US) 960
Creoula (Por) 635
Crocodile (US) 967
Crocus (Bel) 64
Croix Du Sud (Fra) 266
Crommelin (US) 930
Crotone (Ita) 403
Crown Point (TT) 821
Cruzeiro Do Sul (Brz) 84
CTCIM Jorge Moreno Salazar (Col) 172
CTM (Sen) 719
CTM 17-31 (Fra) 265
Cuauhtémoc (Mex) 525
Çubuklu (Tur) 839
Cucut (Indo) 360
Cuddalore (Ind) 346
Cuenca (Ecu) 208
Cultrona (Ita) 411
Cumberland (UK) 880
Cumella (Can) 110
Cundrik (Indo) 367
Curaumila (Chi) 125
Curiapo (Ven) 985
Currawong (Aust) 39
Curtis Wilbur (US) 924
Curtiss (US) 961
Curts (US) 930
Cushing (US) 966
Cut Nyak Dien (Indo) 356
Cutthroat (US) 951
Cuttyhunk (US) 966
CVN 79-80 (US) 920
CW 3 Harold C Clinger (US) 947
Cygnus (Can) 108
Cypress (US) 969
Czajka (Pol) 622

D

D 431-433, 436-437 (Az) 43
D. Carlos I (Por) 635
D. Francisco Da Almeida (Por) 630
Dabie (Pol) 622
Dachs (Ger) 290
Dae Chon (RoK) 466
Dae Chung (RoK) 472
Daejoyoung (RoK) 461
Dagestan (Rus) 673
Dague (Fra) 265
Dagupan City (Plp) 612
Dahl (US) 959
Daisen (Jpn) 438
Daiyunshan (CPR) 153
Dajlah (SAr) 717
Dakhla (Mor) 536
Dalian (CPR) 140
Dallas (US) 914, 963
Al Dammam (SAr) 710
D'Amato (Ita) 410
Dame Roma Mitchell (Aust) 41
Damisa (Nig) 565
Damour (Leb) 483
Damrong Rachanuphap (Tld) 817
Damsah (Qat) 639
Damuan (Bru) 89
Damyat (Egy) 215
Dana (Den) 196
Danaide (Ita) 398
Danbjørn (Den) 199
Dandong (CPR) 144
Danga (Mly) 504
Danil Moskovskiy (Rus) 659
Dannebrog (Den) 198
Danxiashan (CPR) 153
Daoud Ben Aicha (Mor) 536
Daqhiliya (Egy) 221
Daqingshan (CPR) 153
Dareen (SAr) 716
Darica (Tur) 844
Daring (Sin) 727
Daring (UK) 877
Darnitsya (Ukr) 856
Darshak (Ban) 60
Darshak (Ind) 346
Darwin (Aust) 30
Daryavand II (Iran) 380
Das (UAE) 858
Dasher (UK) 883
Dasman (Kwt) 477
Dastoor (Kwt) 477
Dat Assawari (Egy) 221
Datteln (Ger) 291
Datu Marikudo (Plp) 610
Daugava (Rus) 690
Dauntless (Sin) 727
Dauntless (UK) 877
Dauntless (US) 964
Dauriya (Rus) 690
Davao Del Norte (Plp) 614
David Hansen (Gha) 299
Daylam (Iran) 379
Dayyinah (UAE) 861
DB 411, 413, 417, 419, 422, 426, 429, 431-432, 435 (Plp) 615
DBM 241 (Mon) 529
DDG 1002 (US) 928
DDH 182 (Jpn) 417
De Falco (Ita) 410
De Grasse (Fra) 243, 255
De Ianni (Ita) 411
De Los Heros (Per) 602
De Mist (SA) 738
De Rosa (Ita) 410
De Ruyter (Nld) 548
De Santis (Ita) 411
De Wert (US) 930
De Zeven Provincien (Nld) 548
Debundsha (Cam) 97
Decatur (US) 924
Dechaineux (Aust) 26
Décimo Aniversario (Spn) 760
Decisive (US) 964
Al Deebel (Qat) 638
Defender (StL) 708
Defender (UK) 877
Defender (US) 948
Defensora (Brz) 75
Değirmendere (Tur) 843
Dehloran (Iran) 380
Dejima (Jpn) 438
Dekanawida (US) 954
Al Dekheila (Egy) 223
Delair (Pak) 590
Delfin (Arg) 22
Delfin (Rus) 702
Delhi (Ind) 332
Delvar (Iran) 379
Démocrata (Mex) 521
Denden (Eri) 228
Deneb (DR) 202
Deneb (Mex) 520
Denebola (Mex) 520
Denebola (US) 962
Deney (Tur) 843
Denizkuşu (Tur) 835
Denti (Fra) 268
Denver (US) 944
Dependable (US) 964
Dera'a 2, 4-5, 6-8, 11-14(Bhr) 51, 52
Derafsh (Iran) 373
Derbent (Rus) 703
Derna (Lby) 486
Des Groseilliers (Can) 106
Descubierta (Spn) 747
Devastator (US) 948
Dewa (Jpn) 439
Dewa Kembar (Indo) 363
Dewaruci (Indo) 364
Dewey (US) 926
Dextrous (US) 948
DF 300-303, 305, 307-313, 321-323, 325-332, 334, 347 (Plp) 615, 616
Dhansiri (Ban) 56
Dharuba (Fra) 271
Dheba (SAr) 716
Dheeb Al Bahar 1, 2-3 (Omn) 580, 581
Dhofar (Omn) 577
Di Bartolo (Ita) 410
Di Hua (Twn) 789
Diamantina (Aust) 35
Diamond (UK) 877
Diamondback (US) 967
Diana (Den) 194
Diana (Rus) 701
Diana (Spn) 747
Diaz (Chi) 121
Dili (Indo) 361
Diligence (UK) 892
Diligence (US) 964
Diligente (Col) 174
Dillingen (Ger) 291
Dimitrovgrad (Rus) 677
Dinder (Sud) 767
Diomidis (Gre) 311
Dione (Fra) 270
Dionysos (Cypr) 187
Diopos Antoniou (Gre) 306
Dioscoro Papa (Plp) 611
Diphda (Mex) 520
Diponegoro (Indo) 357
Discovery Bay (US) 952
El Djari (Alg) 6
Djärv (Swe) 774
El Djasur (Alg) 6
DJB 103-104, 107 (Cro) 183
DJC 106 (Cro) 183
DJC 411-415, 614-616, 618, 627-628 (Mon) 529
Djebel Chenoua (Alg) 5
Djerdap (Ser) 720
Djukas (Lit) 488
DK-143, 259, 453, 323, 285, 458, 447 (Rus) 707
DKA 67, 70, 144, 148, 164, 325, 464, 704 (Rus) 682
Dmitriy Donskoy (Rus) 650
Dobrotich (Bul) 94
Dock A (Ger) 295
Doğan (Tur) 835
Doğanarslan (Tur) 843
Doğanay (Tur) 829
Al Doghas (Omn) 578
Doirani (Gre) 310
Dokdo (RoK) 469
Dolfijn (Nld) 547
Dolphin (Ana) 9
Dolphin (Iran) 380
Dolphin (Isr) 383
Dolphin (US) 967
Dolphin Mira (Nig) 566
Dolphin Rima (Nig) 566
Dolunay (Tur) 829
Don Vizo (Col) 177
Donald Cook (US) 924
Donau (Ger) 293
Donbas (Ukr) 853, 855
Donchedi (Tld) 814
Donets (Rus) 692
Donetsk (Ukr) 852
Dong Hae (RoK) 467
Dongdiao (CPR) 157
Dongguan (CPR) 144
Dongtingshan (CPR) 153
Donuzlav (Rus) 685
Dorado (Arg) 23
Dorado (US) 967
Dorado I-III (Pan) 594
Dordanda (Ban) 56
Dore (Indo) 361
Al Dorrar (Kwt) 476
Dost (Tur) 844
Doutor Montenegro (Brz) 85
Doxa (Gre) 307
Doyle (US) 930
Dozornyy (Rus) 699
Dr Bernardo Houssay (Arg) 24
Dr Soeharso (Indo) 360
Dragão (Por) 634
Dragon (UK) 877
Dragonera (Spn) 749
Drakensberg (SA) 738
Dranske (Ger) 296
Drazki (Bul) 90
Dreger (PNG) 595
Driade (Ita) 398
Dristig (Swe) 774
Druckdock (Dock C) (Ger) 295
Drummond (Arg) 14
Drummond (US) 966
Druzno (Pol) 622
DSRV II (RoK) 471
DSV 2 (US) 951
Dubhe (Den) 195
Dubhe (Mex) 520
Dubna (Rus) 691
Dubno (Ukr) 855
Dubrovnik (Cro) 182
Dubuque (US) 944
Duero (Spn) 753
Dugay Trouin (Fra) 243
Dugong (Aust) 39
Dumbea (Fra) 276
Dumit (Can) 109
Dumont d'Urville (Fra) 265
Dunafoldvar (Hun) 322
Dunagiri (Ind) 337
Dunai (Ukr) 855
Dunaújváros (Hun) 322
Dunay (Rus) 691
Duncan (UK) 877
Dungeness (Can) 105
Dungun (Mly) 505
Dupetit Thouars (Fra) 243
Dupleix (Fra) 253
Dupuy De Lôme (Fra) 267
Duquesne (Fra) 243
Durango (Mex) 519
Duranta (Ban) 56
Durbar (Ban) 56
Durdam (Ban) 56
Durdanta (Ban) 56
Durdharsha (Ban) 56
Durgabai Deshmukh (Ind) 351
Durvedya (Ban) 56
Duwa (Myn) 540
Duyfken (Aust) 36
Dvina (Rus) 706
Dwight D Eisenhower (US) 917
Dynamic (US) 953
Dzata (Gha) 299
Dzerzhinsky (Rus) 700

E

E 1-8 (Tur) 840
E P Le Québécois (Can) 111
Eagle (US) 970
Eagle Ray (Sin) 730
Earl Grey (Can) 107
Echigo (Jpn) 438
Echizen (Jpn) 442
Echo (UK) 888
Eckaloo (Can) 109
Eddystone (UK) 892
Edinburgh (UK) 876
Edincik (Tur) 838
Edisto (US) 966
Edithara II (Sri) 762
Edmonton (Can) 103
Edremit (Tur) 838
EDSA II (Plp) 614
EDVP 30-37 (Arg) 19
Edward Cornwallis (Can) 107
Effective (US) 957
Eglantine (Fra) 268
Eilat (Isr) 384
Eisk (Rus) 674
Eithne (Ire) 381
Ejnar Mikkelsen (Den) 193
Ekaterinburg (Rus) 651
Ekpe (Nig) 565
Ekun (Nig) 565
Ekvator (Rus) 688
El Aigh (Mor) 536
El Akid (Mor) 534
El Assad (Alg) 8
El Azoum (Alg) 6
El Bachir (Mor) 534
El Camino Español (Spn) 755
El Caney (US) 947
El Chihab (Alg) 5
El Djari (Alg) 6
El Djasur (Alg) 6
El Essahir (Mor) 535
El Fateh (Egy) 221
El Hadj Slimane (Alg) 4
El Hahiq (Mor) 534
El Hamil (Alg) 8
El Hamis (Alg) 6
El Hamiss (Mor) 534
El Haris (Mor) 535
El Horriya (Egy) 221
El Idrissi (Alg) 7
El Jail (Mor) 535
El Kaced (Mor) 537
El Kadessaya (Egy) 218
El Kanass (Alg) 6
El Karib (Mor) 534
El Kechef (Alg) 6
El Khafir (Mor) 535
El Maher (Mor) 534
El Mahir (Alg) 6
El Majid (Mor) 534
El Mikdam (Mor) 535
El Mouderrib I-VII (Alg) 8
El Moukadem (Alg) 6
El Mounkid I-IV (Alg) 8
El Mourafek (Alg) 7
El Mourakeb (Alg) 6
El Moutarid (Alg) 6
El Nasr (Mtn) 510
El Nasser (Egy) 216
El Oro (Ecu) 206
El Rassed (Alg) 6
El Saher (Alg) 6
El Suez (Egy) 215
El Tawfiq (Mor) 534
El Temsah (Lby) 486
El Tinai (Alg) 6
El Wacil (Mor) 535
El Yadekh (Alg) 6
El Yarmouk (Egy) 218
Élan (Fra) 269
Elbe (Ger) 293
Elderberry (US) 970
Electronica (Rom) 646
Eleftheria (Gre) 307
Elettra (Ita) 404
Elicura (Chi) 122
Elli (Gre) 303
Elm (US) 969
Elnath (Mex) 520
Élorn (Fra) 276
Elouera (Aust) 40
Elrod (US) 930
Eltanin (Mex) 520
Emden (Ger) 286
Emeishan (CPR) 153
Emer (Ire) 382
Émeraude (Fra) 244
Emil Racovita (Rom) 645
Emilio Aguinaldo (Plp) 611
Emilio Jacinto (Plp) 609
Emory S Land (US) 958
Endeavor (DR) 203
Endeavour (NZ) 561
Endeavour (Sin) 729
Endurance (Sin) 729
Endurance (UK) 883
Enez (Tur) 838
Enif (Mex) 520
Enø (Den) 194
Enrique Jurado (Plp) 611
Enriquillo (DR) 203
Ensdorf (Ger) 291
Enseigne De Vaisseau Jacoubet (Fra) 257
Enshuu (Jpn) 436
Enterprise (Bar) 61
Enterprise (UK) 888
Enterprise (US) 916
Enymiri (Nig) 564
Epron (Rus) 697
Ercsi (Hun) 323
Erdek (Tur) 838
Erdemli (Tur) 838
Erfurt (Ger) 288
Éridan (Fra) 266
Erimo (Jpn) 438
Erraced (Mor) 537
Errachiq (Mor) 534
Erraid (Mor) 537
Ersev Bayrak (Tur) 843
Ertholm (Den) 194
Ertuğrul (Tur) 837
Esan (Jpn) 439
Esbern Snare (Den) 197
Escanaba (US) 964
Escandallo (Spn) 754
Escaut (Fra) 276
Eschwege (Ger) 296
Escorpião (Por) 634
Escudo De Veraguas (Pan) 592
Esequibo (Ven) 982
Esmeralda (Chi) 123
Esmeraldas (Ecu) 206
Espadarte (CpV) 113
Espalmador (Spn) 749
Espartana (Col) 172
Esperanza (Par) 598
Esperanza (Arg) 24
Espero (Ita) 396
Esploratore (Ita) 401
Espora (Arg) 15
El Essahir (Mor) 535
Essaid (Mor) 537
Essequibo (Guy) 317
Essex (US) 940
Esterel (Fra) 272
Estéron (Fra) 276
Estrellemar (Arg) 23
Etair (Alg) 8

Eten (Per) 603
Ethel Joy (Aust) 40
Etna (Ita) 406
Etomo (Jpn) 439
Euljimundok (RoK) 463
Euro (Ita) 396
Europa 1-3 (Ger) 296
Evagoras (Cypr) 188
Eversand (Ger) 295
Evertsen (Nld) 548
Evgeny Khorov (Rus) 698
Evniki (Gre) 308
Evpatoriya (Ukr) 855
Evropi (Gre) 308
Evros (Gre) 310
Evrotas (Gre) 311
Evstati Vinarov (Bul) 94
Example (UK) 883
Excellence (Bar) 61
Exploit (UK) 883
Explorer (UK) 883
Express (UK) 883

F

F 1-F 24 (Iraq) 381
F 31-33 (Ven) 981
FABG 7-12, 14-21, 23-30, 32-39, 41-45, 47-57, 59 (Twn) 791
Fabian Wrede (Fin) 238
FACG 60 (Twn) 792
Faenø (Den) 194
Fagnano (Arg) 23
Failaka (Kwt) 476
Fais (Ita) 410
Faisal (Jor) 448
Faisal (SAr) 714
Faisal 1-4 (Jor) 448
Fajar Samudera (Mly) 501
Falakhon (Iran) 373
Falemé II (Sen) 719
Falken (Swe) 778
Falkner (Arg) 23
Fantasma Azul (Pan) 594
Fantome (Aust) 36
Farallon (US) 966
Farallón Centinela (Ven) 985
Fardela (Ven) 984
Farfadet (Fra) 268
Farm (Nor) 575
Farncomb (Aust) 26
Faroleiro Mário Seixas (Brz) 84
Fårösund (Swe) 779
Al Farouk (Egy) 220
Al Farouq (SAr) 714
Farragut (US) 926
Farrallon (Mex) 525
Farsi (Iran) 378
Fatahillah (Indo) 355
El Fateh (Egy) 221
Fatih (Tur) 831
Fatimah I (Gam) 278
Fatsa (Tur) 838
Faust Vrančič (Cro) 184
Favignana (Ita) 406
Faysal (Jor) 448
FB 31-42 (Sin) 728
Fearless (Sin) 727
Federación (Ven) 981
Federico Martir (Plp) 611
Fehmarn (Ger) 295
Feliciani (Ita) 410
Felinto Perry (Brz) 85
Felix Apolinario (Plp) 611
Feng Chiang (Twn) 791
Feng Yang (Twn) 790
Fengcang (CPR) 160
Fenice (Ita) 398
Fenix (Spn) 760
Feodor Golovin (Rus) 688
Feodosiya (Ukr) 854
Fernando Gomez (Ven) 985
Fernando Nuara Engonda (EqG) 227
Fethiye (Tur) 838
Al Feyi (UAE) 861
Figueira Da Foz (Por) 633
Fijab (Sud) 767
Al Fikah (Lby) 485
Filigonio Hichamón (Col) 177
Filipino Flojo (Plp) 611
Finback (US) 967
Finike (Tur) 838
Fir (US) 969
Firebird (Can) 105
Firebolt (US) 937
Firebrand (Can) 105
Firtina (Tur) 835
Fisalia (Por) 635
Fisher (US) 958
Maj Bernard F Fisher (US) 959
Fitzgerald (US) 924
Five Forks (US) 947
Fjell (Nor) 571
Flamant (Fra) 262
Flamenco (Pan) 594
Flaming (Pol) 622
Flickertail State (US) 961
Flint (US) 955
Floréal (Fra) 258
Florenca Nuno (Plp) 611
Florida (US) 911
Flyingfish (US) 967
Fo Wu 5-7 (Twn) 795
Foça (Tur) 838
Foca (Arg) 23
Folegandros (Gre) 308
Fomalhaut (Mex) 520
Fong Yang (Twn) 790
Fontana (Arg) 23
Al Forat (SAr) 717
Forbin (Fra) 251
Ford (US) 930
Formentor (Spn) 749
Formidable (Sin) 725
Forrest Sherman (US) 926
Fort Austin (UK) 891
Fort Donelson (US) 947
Fort George (UK) 891
Fort Mchenry (US) 945, 947
Fort Rosalie (UK) 891
Fort Victoria (UK) 891
Fort Worth (US) 928
Fortuna (Ita) 410
Fortuna (Uru) 976
Fortune (Can) 105
Fortune (Sey) 721
Forur (Iran) 378
Forward (US) 964
Foshan (CPR) 144
Fotiy Krylov (Rus) 697
Foudre (Fra) 264
Fouque (Iran) 378
Fournoi (Gre) 312
Fouta (Sen) 718
Francesco Mimbelli (Ita) 395
Francis Garnier (Fra) 265
Francisco De Gurruchaga (Arg) 17
Francisco I Madero (Mex) 521
Francisco J Mugica (Mex) 521
Francisco Javier Mina (Mex) 514
Frank Cable (US) 958
Frank Drew (US) 969
Frankfurt Am Main (Ger) 293
Frankfurt/oder (Ger) 297
Frans Kaisiepo (Indo) 357
Frederick G Creed (Can) 112
Fredericton (Can) 100
Freedom (US) 928
Freedom (Sin) 727
Fréhel (Fra) 273
Freja (Den) 194
Frettchen (Ger) 290
Fridtjof Nansen (Nor) 568
Friesland (Nld) 551
Fritz Hagale (Col) 174
Frontin (Brz) 76
Fu Hsing (Twn) 796
Fuchsia (Fra) 272
Fuji (Jpn) 442
Fukue (Jpn) 442
Fulda (Ger) 291
Fulk Al Salamah (Omn) 579
Fulmar (Fra) 276
Fulmar (Spn) 760
Fumarel (Ven) 984
Al Furat (Egy) 222
Furusund (Swe) 779
Fusco (Ita) 410
Futalaufquen (Arg) 23
Futami (Jpn) 432
Fuxian Hu (CPR) 163
Fuyushio (Jpn) 416
Fuzhou (CPR) 135
Fyrholm (Den) 194

G

G 01-36 (Mex) 522
G 26, 40, 44, 46-47, 49-52, 56-58, 60-61, 64-65 (Ita) 410
G 100 series (Fin) 240
Al Gabbar (Egy) 219
Gabes (Tun) 826
Gabriela (Ven) 983
Gaeta (Ita) 403
Al Gaffa (UAE) 862
Gagah (Mly) 504
Gaisma (Lat) 481
Gaj (Ind) 349
Galana (Ken) 451
Galapagos (Ecu) 209
Galatea (Ita) 404
Galeota (TT) 821
Galera Point (TT) 821
Galerna (Spn) 741
Galeshewe (SA) 736
Galiano (Ita) 410
Galichina (Ukr) 856
Galicia (Spn) 751
Gallant (Sin) 727
Gallatin (US) 963
Galvarino (Chi) 124
Galveston Island (US) 966
Gama (Pak) 590
Ganas (Mly) 499
Gang Gam Chan (RoK) 461
Ganga (Ind) 335
Ganga Devi (Ind) 351
Gannet (US) 967
Ganyang (Mly) 499
Gapeau (Fra) 270
Garcia d'Ávila (Brz) 81
Gardénia (Fra) 270
Gardno (Pol) 622
Gardouneh (Iran) 373
Garnata (Lby) 486
Garnier Sampaio (Brz) 83
Garoh (Kwt) 476
Garsøy (Nor) 574
Garulli (Ita) 411
Gary (US) 930
Garyounis (Lby) 486
Garzoni (Ita) 410
Gasconade (US) 970
Gascoyne (Aust) 35
Gaspar Obiang Esono (EqG) 227
Gasper Grande (TT) 822
Gauden (Per) 604
Gavatar (Iran) 379
Gavilán II-IV (Spn) 760
Gavion (Ven) 984
Gaviota (Arg) 23
Gävle (Swe) 772
Gazal (Tur) 843
Gazelle (Fra) 269
Gaziantep (Tur) 832
GC 102-114, 152-184 (Arg) 23
GC 201-202, 205 (Nic) 563
GC 231-236 (TT) 823
GC 271-276 (Gua) 316
Gediz (Tur) 832
Gelibolu (Tur) 832
Gem State (US) 961
Gemini (Den) 195
Geminis (Mex) 522
Gemlik (Tur) 832
Gempita (Mly) 498
Gen Brehon B Somervell (US) 947
Gen Frank S Besson Jr (US) 947
Genaveh (Iran) 379
Gendarme Perez (Fra) 272
Genêt (Fra) 270
Generał Kazimierz Pułaski (Pol) 619
Generał Tadeusz Kościuszko (Pol) 619
General Artigas (Uru) 978
General Banzer (Bol) 68
General Bejar (Bol) 68
Général d'Armée Ba-Oumar (Gab) 277
General Delfosse (Fra) 272
General Felipe B Berriozábal (Mex) 518
General Francisco De Miranda (Ven) 983
General José Trinidad Moran (Ven) 984
General Mariano Alvares (Plp) 609
General Matrosov (Rus) 701
General Mazniashvili (Geo) 280
Général Nazaire Boulingui (Gab) 278
General Paraschiv Vasilescu (Rom) 644
General Pereira d'Eça (Por) 632
General Ryabikov (Rus) 696
General Salom (Ven) 980
General Soublette (Ven) 980
General Urdaneta (Ven) 980
Genichesk (Ukr) 852
Genkai (Jpn) 436
Genrich Gasanov (Rus) 691
Gentiane (Fra) 272
Genun (Jpn) 447
Geofjord (Nor) 572
Geographe (Aust) 36
W G George (Can) 111
George Cobb (US) 969
George H W Bush (US) 917
George R Pearkes (Can) 107
George Slight Marshall (Chi) 123
George Washington (US) 917
Georges Leygues (Fra) 253
Georgia (US) 911
Georgiy Pobedonosets (Rus) 681
Georgy Kozmin (Rus) 693
Georgy Titov (Rus) 693
Gepard (Ger) 290
Gepard (Rus) 656
Gerald R Ford (US) 920
Géranium (Fra) 275
Gerifalte I (Spn) 760
German Busch (Bol) 68
German Ugryumov (Rus) 684
Germantown (US) 945
Germinal (Fra) 258
Gettysburg (US) 921
Geyzer (Rus) 678
GGS 1012-1014 (Ita) 407
Ghanadhah (UAE) 859
Ghardia (Lby) 486
Gharial (Ind) 345
Al Ghariyah (Qat) 639
Ghat (Lby) 486
Ghazee (Mld) 507
Al Ghullan (UAE) 859
Gianfranco Gazzana Priaroggia (Ita) 390
Gidrolog (Rus) 685
Giens (Fra) 273
Gigante (Ita) 408
Gigas (Gre) 311
Gigrometer (Rus) 685
Gilliland (US) 958
Ginga (Jpn) 446
Giorgio Cini (Ita) 409
Giovanni Denaro (Ita) 410
Giralda (Spn) 754
Giresun (Tur) 832
Giroflée (Fra) 270
Giscon (Tun) 824
Giuliano Prini (Ita) 390
Giuseppe Garibaldi (Ita) 392
Giza (Egy) 220
Glace Bay (Can) 103
Gladan (Swe) 778
Gladiator (US) 948
Glaive (Fra) 275
Glavkos (Gre) 300
Gleaner (UK) 888
Glenbrook (Can) 105
Glendale (Can) 105
Glendyne (Can) 105
Glenelg (Aust) 35
Glenevis (Can) 105
Glenside (Can) 105
Glenten (Den) 193
Glimt (Nor) 570
Gloria (Col) 176
Gloucester (UK) 876
Glycine (Fra) 268
Gniezno (Pol) 622
Gnist (Nor) 570
Goajira (Ven) 982
Goascoran (Hon) 318
Goblin Shark (Sin) 730
Godavari (Ind) 335
Godetia (Bel) 65
Goiana (Brz) 78
Gökçeada (Tur) 832
Gokova (Tur) 832
Göksu (Tur) 832
Gölcük (Tur) 841
Gold Rover (UK) 891
Golfo San Matias (Arg) 22
Golok (Indo) 367
Gomati (Ban) 55
Gomati (Ind) 335
Gomez Roca (Arg) 15
Gonzalez (US) 924
Goose Bay (Can) 103
Gopher State (US) 961
Goplo (Pol) 622
Gorch Fock (Ger) 293
Gordi (Bul) 90
Gordon (US) 958
Gordon Reid (Can) 109
Gorgona (Col) 176
Gorgona (Ita) 407
Gorizont (Rus) 685
Gorz (Iran) 373
Gotland (Swe) 770
Gottardi (Ita) 411
Gouwe (Nld) 557
GP 401-404 (Nic) 563
Graúna (Brz) 78
Grajaú (Brz) 78
Gramorgu (Sur) 767
Granatiere (Ita) 397
Granby (Can) 105
Grand Canyon State (US) 961
Grand Isle (US) 966
Granville (Arg) 14
Granville (Can) 105
Grapple (US) 955
Grasp (US) 955
Gravataí (Brz) 78
Gravely (US) 926
Gravona (Fra) 276
Great Bridge (US) 947
Grébe (Fra) 262
Grecale (Ita) 396
Greco (Ita) 410
Green Bay (US) 942
Greenbrier (US) 970
Greeneville (US) 914
Greenhalgh (Brz) 74
Gregos (Gre) 309
Gremyashchiy (Rus) 670
Gribben (Den) 193
Gridley (US) 926
Griep (Ger) 295
Grif (Rus) 702
Griffon (Can) 107
Grigore Antipa (Rom) 645
Grigory Gnatenko (Ukr) 855
Grigory Kuropiatnikov (Ukr) 855
Grimsby (UK) 888
Grinda (Rus) 701
Grizzly (Can) 104
Grom (Pol) 620
Grömitz (Ger) 291
Groningen (Nld) 551
Grosa (Spn) 750
MG Charles P Gross (US) 947
Groza (Rus) 706
Grozavu (Rom) 647
GRS/G 1010-1012 (Ita) 407
GRS/J 1013 (Ita) 407
Grum (Bul) 92
Grumete Perez (Chi) 124
Grundsund (Swe) 779
GS 01-02 (Jpn) 444
GS 44, 47, 66, 78, 84, 86, 87, 113 ,118, 193, 198, 199, 200, 202, 204, 207, 208, 210, 211, 214, 260, 269, 270, 271, 272, 278, 296, 297, 301, 392, 397, 399, 400, 403, 402, 404, 405, (Rus) 686
GS 525-526 (Rus) 687
Guadaloupe Victoria (Mex) 514
Guadalupe (US) 955
Guaiba (Brz) 78
Guaicaipuro (Ven) 981, 983
Guaicamacuto (Ven) 982
Guaiteca (Chi) 125
Guajará (Brz) 78
Guama (Cub) 186
Guanabara (Brz) 78
Guanaja (Hon) 318
Guanajuato (Mex) 519
Guangzhou (CPR) 136
Guaporé (Brz) 78
Guaqui (Bol) 68
Guarani (Par) 597
Guarapari (Brz) 81
Guaratuba (Brz) 78
Guarda Marinha Brito (Brz) 84
Guarda Marinha Jansen (Brz) 84
Guardiamarina Barrutia (Spn) 754
Guardiamarina Chereguini (Spn) 754
Guardiamarina Rull (Spn) 754
Guardiamarina Salas (Spn) 754
Guardian (Bmd) 67
Guardian (Mrt) 511
Guardian (US) 948
Guardian Rios (Per) 605
Guarionex (DR) 203
Guaroa (DR) 203
Guarocuya (DR) 203
Guarujá (Brz) 78
Guayaquil (Ecu) 208
Guayas (Ecu) 208
Guaymuras (Hon) 317
Gucumaz (Gua) 315
Guépard (Fra) 268
Guépratte (Fra) 256
Guerrico (Arg) 14
Guia (Por) 636
Guilin (CPR) 139
Guillermo Prieto (Mex) 518
Gül (Tur) 842
Guldar (Ind) 345
Gür (Tur) 828
Gull Isle (Can) 110
Gunnar Seidenfaden (Den) 198
Gunnar Thorson (Den) 198
Guns (Pak) 591
Gunston Hall (US) 945

Gurbet (Tur) 835
Guria (Geo) 279
Gurupá (Brz) 78
Gurupi (Brz) 78
Güven (Tur) 844
Gwadar (Pak) 589
GYSGT Fred W Stockham (US) 960

H

H 4-10 (Pol) 626
H 22 (Lit) 489
H 181-186 (Ind) 352
H 500-502 (Tur) 841
H K Tannis (StV) 709
Haamoon (Iran) 380
Haarlem (Nld) 554
Habbah Khatun (Ind) 351
Hachijyo (Jpn) 431
Hadar (Mex) 520
Haddock (US) 967
Al Hadi (Egy) 219
El Hadj Slimane (Alg) 4
CPL Louis J Hauge, Jr (US) 960
El Hahiq (Mor) 534
Hae Nam (RoK) 471
Hae Yang (Twn) 790
HAI 521 (CPR) 158
Hai Bao (Twn) 787
Hai Cheng (Twn) 798
Hai Ching (Twn) 798
Hai En (Twn) 798
Hai Hu (Twn) 786
Hai Ko (Twn) 799
Hai Liang (Twn) 798
Hai Lung (Twn) 786
Hai Shih (Twn) 787
Hai Ta (Twn) 799
Hai Tung (Twn) 799
Hai Ying (Twn) 799
Haijing 1001-1003 (CPR) 166
Haikou (CPR) 137
Hail (SAr) 716
Hairoun (StV) 709
Haixun 21, 31 (CPR) 167
Haiyang 20 (CPR) 158
Haiyangshan (CPR) 153
Hakata (Jpn) 439
Al Hakim (Egy) 219
Hakuni (Fin) 238
Hakusan (Jpn) 439
Halaib (Egy) 222
Halcón II (Spn) 760
Halibut (US) 967
Halifax (Can) 100
Halland (Swe) 770
Hallebarde (Fra) 265
Hallef (Chi) 125
Halli (Fin) 240
Halote (Sud) 767
Halsey (US) 926
Halten (Nor) 571
Halyburton (US) 930
Hamagiri (Jpn) 423
Hamagumo (Jpn) 444
Hamal (DR) 202
Hamal (Mex) 520
Hamana (Jpn) 435
Hamanami (Jpn) 444
Hamashio (Jpn) 446
Hamayuki (Jpn) 424, 443
Hamazuki (Jpn) 443
Hamburg (Ger) 287
Hameln (Ger) 291
Hämeenmaa (Fin) 236
El Hamil (Alg) 8
Hamilcar (Tun) 824
Hamilton (US) 963
Hamina (Fin) 235
El Hamis (Alg) 6
El Hamiss (Mor) 534
Hammer (US) 971
Hammerhead (US) 967
Hammerhead Shark (Sin) 730
Hampton (US) 914
Hamza (Pak) 583
Hamzah (Iran) 379
Han Jih (Twn) 795
Han Kang (RoK) 472
Hancza (Pol) 622
Handalan (Mly) 498
Händig (Swe) 774
Hang Tuah (Mly) 501
Hangam (Iran) 380
Hangzhou (CPR) 135
Hanhak Sattru (Tld) 809
Al Hani (Lby) 484
Hanit (Isr) 384
Hanko (Fin) 235
Hankoniemi (Fin) 238
Hanna (Lby) 486
Hannibal (Tun) 824
Hannon (Tun) 824
Hansaya (Sri) 766
Haouz (Mor) 538
Haras 1-5 (Omn) 581
Haras 21-34 (Omn) 580
Haras 6-10 (Omn) 580
Harbin (CPR) 138
Hårek (Nor) 571
Harima (Jpn) 432
Hari-Rud (Iran) 380
El Haris (Mor) 535
Härnösand (Swe) 771
Harp (Can) 109
Harpers Ferry (US) 945, 947
Harriet Lane (US) 964
Harry Claiborne (US) 969
Harry S Truman (US) 917
Harstad (Nor) 574
Hartford (US) 914
Hartland Point (UK) 892
Haruna (Fin) 239
Harunami (Jpn) 444
Harusame (Jpn) 422
Harushio (Jpn) 416
Haruyuki (Jpn) 424
Hasan Basri (Indo) 356
Al Hasbah (UAE) 860
Hasdrubal (Tun) 824
Hashidate (Jpn) 436
Hashim (Jor) 448
Hashmat (Pak) 582
Al Hassan (Jor) 448
Hassan (Jor) 448
Hassan II (Mor) 531
Hästö (Fin) 239
Hatagumo (Jpn) 443
Hatakaze (Jpn) 420
Hatchet (US) 971
Hateruma (Jpn) 439
Hatsuyuki (Jpn) 424
Hauki (Fin) 238
Haukipää (Fin) 240
Havfruen (Den) 194
Havkatten (Den) 193
Havørnen (Den) 198
Havouri (Fin) 238
Havuz 1-5, 8-11, 13 (Tur) 843
Hawaii (US) 912
Hawar (Bhr) 49
Hawar 1-2 (Bhr) 51
Hawea (NZ) 560
Hawes (US) 930
Hawk (US) 967
Hawkesbury (Aust) 35
Hawksbill (US) 967
Hawser (US) 971
Hay Tan (Twn) 795
Hayabusa (Jpn) 428
Hayagiri (Jpn) 444
Hayagumo (Jpn) 443
Hayanami (Jpn) 444
Hayashio (Jpn) 416, 446
Hayato (Jpn) 438
HDB 01-16 (Mrt) 512
Healy (US) 968
Hefei (CPR) 139
Heimdal (Nor) 575
Hejaz (Iran) 378
Hekkingen (Nor) 571
Helanshan (CPR) 153
Helena (US) 914
Helge Ingstad (Nor) 568
Hellen (Nor) 571
Hellevoetsluis (Nld) 554
Helmsand (Ger) 292
Helsingborg (Swe) 771
Hendijan (Iran) 379
Hengam (Iran) 377
Hengshan (CPR) 154
Henry Blake (US) 969
Henry J Kaiser (US) 955
Henry Larsen (Can) 106
Henry M Jackson (US) 910
Henson (US) 957
Hera (Swe) 780
Heracleo Alano (Plp) 611
Heraklis (Gre) 311
Hérault (Fra) 276
Herceg Novi (Mon) 530
Hercules (Arg) 19
Hercules (Den) 195
Hercules (Rom) 647
Herev (Isr) 385
Heriberto Jara Corona (Mex) 521
Herluf Bidstrup (Rus) 701
Hermelin (Ger) 290
Hermenegildo Galeana (Mex) 515
Hernán Cortés (Spn) 750
SSIM Julio Correa Hernández (Col) 177
Heroina (Arg) 12
Heron (US) 967
Heron I-IV (Bmd) 67
Heros (Swe) 780
Herrera (Per) 602
Herten (Ger) 291
Hervey Bay (Aust) 41
Hespérides (Spn) 753
Hess (Arg) 23
Hessa (Nor) 572
Hessen (Ger) 287
Hetman Sagaidachny (Ukr) 849
Hettein (Egy) 218
Hetz (Isr) 385
Heweliusz (Pol) 623
Heybeliada (Tur) 833
Hibiki (Jpn) 432
Hibueras (Hon) 317
Hickory (US) 969
Hida (Jpn) 438
Hidra (Por) 634
Hiei (Jpn) 426
Hiev (Ger) 295
Higgins (US) 924
Higgit (Can) 113
Hijau (Mly) 506
Hila (Fin) 239
Hilario Ruiz (Plp) 611
Himilcon (Tun) 824
Himyer (Yem) 994
Hinnøy (Nor) 572
Hipocampo (Arg) 23
Hipolito Micha (EqG) 227
Al Hirasa (Syr) 783
Hirashima (Jpn) 431
Hirmand (Iran) 380
Hirsala (Fin) 238
Hirsholm (Den) 194
Hirta (UK) 900
Hiryu (Jpn) 445
Hitachi (Jpn) 441
Hitra (Nor) 573
Hitteen (SAr) 713
Hiu (Indo) 358
Hiuchi (Jpn) 436
HJ I (Spn) 760
HJ III-X (Spn) 760
HJA (Spn) 760
Hjortø (Den) 194
HK 21 (Lit) 488
Ho Chao (Twn) 793
Ho Chi (Twn) 793
Ho Chie (Twn) 793
Ho Chuan (Twn) 793
Ho Chun (Twn) 793
Ho Chung (Twn) 793
Ho Fong (Twn) 793
Ho Hsing (Twn) 796
Ho Hu (Twn) 793
Ho Huei (Twn) 793
Ho Meng (Twn) 793
Ho Mou (Twn) 793
Ho Seng (Twn) 793
Ho Shan (Twn) 793
Ho Shou (Twn) 793
Ho Shun (Twn) 793
Ho Ten (Twn) 793
Ho Yao (Twn) 793
Ho Yung (Twn) 793
Hobart (Aust) 27
Hobkirk (US) 947
Hofouf (SAr) 712
Högsåra (Fin) 239
Hokuto (Jpn) 446
Holdfast Bay (Aust) 41
Holger Danske (Den) 195
Holland (Nld) 551
Hollyhock (US) 969
Homburg (Ger) 291
Homigueros (US) 947
Honduras (Hon) 317
Honestidad (Ven) 985
Hongzhu (CPR) 160
Hopper (US) 924
Horacio Ugarteche (Bol) 69
Hormuz (Iran) 378
Hormuz (Omn) 579
Horobetsu (Jpn) 441
Horria (Tun) 824
El Horriya (Egy) 221
Hortensia (Fra) 276
Hotaka (Jpn) 442
Houou (Jpn) 442
Houston (US) 914
Houtskär (Fin) 238
Houun (Jpn) 447
Howard (US) 926
Howard O Lorenzen (US) 958
HP 1-2, 4 (Mld) 507
HQ 09, 11, 13, 15, 17 (Vtn) 987
HQ 261-264, 301, 321, 331-332, 334-335, 354, 357-360, 384-386 (Vtn) 989
HQ 301 series (Vtn) 989
HQ 37, 55-59 (Vtn) 990
HQ 371-372, 374-376, 378, 381-382 (Vtn) 988
HQ 511-513 (Vtn) 990
HQ 601, 608, 614, 618-619, 627, 643, 651, 661, 669-671, 673, 996 (Vtn) 992
HQ 782, 851, 861-864, 871, 885 (Vtn) 991
Hrvatska Kostajnica (Cro) 181
Hsad Dan (Myn) 543
Hsian Chiang (Twn) 791
Hsin Chiang (Twn) 791
Hsin Kang (Twn) 795
Hua Hin (Tld) 809
Hua Luogeng (CPR) 157
Huadingshan (CPR) 153
Huaibei (CPR) 142
Huaihua (CPR) 142
Huainan (CPR) 142
Huala (Arg) 23
Hualien (Twn) 797
Huancavilca (Ecu) 205
Huanchaco (Per) 606
Huanggangshan (CPR) 153
Huangshan (CPR) 141
Huangshi (CPR) 146
Huashan (CPR) 154
Huasteco (Mex) 526
Huaura (Per) 607
Huayin (CPR) 144
Hudson (Can) 112
Hudson (Chi) 121
Hudson (US) 970
Hue City (US) 921
Humberto Cortez (Col) 174
Al Hunain (Lby) 483
Hunaish (Yem) 993
Hunze (Nld) 557
Huon (Aust) 35
Huoqiu (CPR) 156
Huracan (Mex) 517
Hurawee (Mld) 507
Hurmat (Pak) 582
Hurricane (US) 937
Hurst Point (UK) 892
Hurtig (Swe) 774
Hurworth (UK) 887
Al Hussein (Jor) 448
Hussein (Jor) 448
Huveaune (Fra) 276
Huvudskär (Swe) 774
Huwar (Qat) 638
Hvasser (Nor) 571
Hvidbjørnen (Den) 189
Hvidsten (Den) 194
Hwa Chun (RoK) 472
Hwai Yang (Twn) 790
Hyäne (Ger) 290
Hyangro Bong (RoK) 468
Hydra (Gre) 302
Hydra (Nld) 557
Hydrograf (Pol) 624
Hylje (Fin) 240
Hymara (Guy) 317
Hyperion (Gre) 310
Hysnes (Nor) 571
Hyuga (Jpn) 417

I

I Karavoyiannos Theophilopoulos (Gre) 311
Ibis (US) 967
Ibn Haritha (Lby) 485
Ibn Ouf (Lby) 485
Ida Lewis (US) 969
Idabato (Cam) 97
El Idrissi (Alg) 7
Ieshima (Jpn) 432
Igaraparaná (Col) 177
Ignacio Allende (Mex) 514
Ignacio L Vallarta (Mex) 520
Ignacio López Rayón (Mex) 521
Ignacio Mariscal (Mex) 521
Ignacio Ramirez (Mex) 521
Igor Belousov (Rus) 696
Ikaria (Gre) 307
Ikazuchi (Jpn) 422
Ikhlas (Mly) 504
Ikigumo (Jpn) 443
Ilam (Iran) 380
Ilarion (Cypr) 187
Ile Saint-Ours (Can) 110
Ilga (Rus) 697
Ilim (Rus) 691
Iliniza (Ecu) 209
Iliria (Alb) 3
Illichivsk (Ukr) 854
Illustrious (UK) 872
Ilocos Norte (Plp) 614
Iloilo (Plp) 610
Ilya Muromets (Rus) 697
Iman (Rus) 691
Iman Bonjol (Indo) 356
Iman Gazzali (Ban) 59
Imanta (Lat) 480
Imbat (Tur) 835
IMP I-II (Spn) 760
Impeccable (US) 956
Imperial Marinheiro (Brz) 79
Inagua (Bhm) 46
Inasa (Jpn) 442
Inazuma (Jpn) 422
Indaw (Myn) 540
Independência (Brz) 75
Independence (Mic) 527
Independence (Sin) 727
Independence (US) 932
Independencia (Bol) 68
Independencia (Mex) 519
Independencia (Pan) 592
Independencia (Per) 606
Independencia (Ven) 981
Independiente (Col) 170
Indiga (Rus) 692
Indlovu (SA) 738
Indomable (Col) 169
Indomita (Arg) 18
Inebolu (Tur) 843
Inej (Rus) 678
Infanta Cristina (Spn) 747
Infanta Elena (Spn) 747
Ingeniero Gumucio (Bol) 68
Ingeniero Julio Krause (Arg) 20
Ingeniero Mery (Chi) 123
Ingeniero White (Arg) 22
Ingraham (US) 930
Inguri (Rus) 692
Inhaúma (Brz) 76
Inirida (Col) 177
Inkster (Can) 113
Integridad (Ven) 985
Intrépido (Col) 169
Intrepid (Sin) 725
Intrepida (Arg) 18
Inttisar (Kwt) 477
Investigator (Ind) 346
Invincible (US) 957
Inya (Myn) 540
Inzerilli (Ita) 410
Inzucchi (Ita) 410
Ios (Gre) 308
IPP I (Spn) 760
IPP III (Spn) 760
Iquique (Chi) 125
Irakleia (Gre) 308
Iron Duke (UK) 878
Iroquois (Can) 102
Irtysh (Rus) 692
Isaac Dyobha (SA) 736
Isandlwana (SA) 735
Isaza (Chi) 121
Isazu (Jpn) 441
Isbjørn (Den) 199
Iseshio (Jpn) 446
Iseyuki (Jpn) 443
Ishikari (Jpn) 441
Işin (Tur) 841
Al Iskandarani (Egy) 223
Iskandhar (Mld) 507
Iskar (Bul) 94
Iskenderun (Tur) 840
Iskra (Pol) 624
Isku (Fin) 239
Isla Burica (CR) 179
Isla Coronado (Mex) 521
Isla Cozumel (Mex) 521
Isla De La Plata (Ecu) 210
Isla Del Coco (CR) 179
Isla Española (Ecu) 210
Isla Fernandina (Ecu) 210
Isla Guadalupe (Mex) 521
Isla Isabela (Ecu) 211
Isla Lobos (Mex) 521
Isla Paridas (Pan) 594
Isla Puná (Ecu) 210
Isla San Cristóbal (Ecu) 211
Isla San Salvador (Ecu) 210
Isla Santa Clara (Ecu) 210
Isla Santa Cruz (Ecu) 211
Isla Santa Rosa (Ecu) 210
Isla Seymour (Ecu) 210
Islay (Per) 599
Isle Rouge (Can) 110
Isluga (Chi) 126
Ismael Lomibao (Plp) 611
Isonami (Jpn) 443
Isongo (Cam) 97

Isoshi (Jpn) 446
Isoshio (Jpn) 415
Isoyuki (Jpn) 424
Isozuki (Jpn) 443
Istiklal (Tun) 824
Istiqlal (Kwt) 476
Isuzu (Jpn) 441, 442
Itaf Deme (Sen) 719
Itaipú (Par) 596
Italia (Ita) 405
Ithaki (Gre) 307
Ivan Bubnov (Rus) 691
Ivan Golubets (Rus) 683
Ivan Gren (Rus) 680
Ivan Lednev (Rus) 706
Ivan Yevteyev (Rus) 706
Ivanovets (Rus) 677
Ivar Huitfeldt (Den) 192
Iveria (Geo) 279
Iwami (Jpn) 439
Iwo Jima (US) 940
IX 514 (US) 953
Iximche (Gua) 315
Iyonami (Jpn) 444
Izaro (Spn) 750
Izhora (Rus) 691
Izmayl (Ukr) 856
Iztaccihuatl (Mex) 526
Izu (Jpn) 437
Izunami (Jpn) 443
Izushima (Jpn) 431
Izyaslav (Ukr) 855

J

Jabanne (Cam) 97
Jaberi (Kwt) 477
Al Jabiri (Bhr) 49
Jaceguai (Brz) 76
Jacinto Candido (Por) 632
Jack Warner (US) 912
W Jackman (Can) 111
Jackpot (Sol) 733
Jacksonville (US) 914
Jacob Hägg (Swe) 782
Jacques Cartier (Fra) 265
Jadayat (Indo) 367
Jadran (Mon) 529
Jae Chon (RoK) 466
Jaemin I (RoK) 473
Jaemin II-III (RoK) 474
Jaemin VII-VIII (RoK) 475
Jägaren (Swe) 775
Jagatha (Sri) 762
Jaguar (Fra) 268
Jaguar (Nld) 558
El Jail (Mor) 535
Jaime Gómez Castro (Col) 173
Al Jala (Tun) 824
Jalalat (Pak) 587
Jalanidhi (Indo) 364
Jalashwa (Ind) 346
Jamaran (Iran) 371
James E Williams (US) 926
James Rankin (US) 969
Jamno (Pol) 622
Jamuna (Ban) 57
Jamuna (Ind) 346
Jananah (UAE) 861
Janbaz (Pak) 590
Jarabakka (Sur) 767
Jaradah (Bhr) 50
Jarak (Mly) 503
Al Jarim (Bhr) 49
Jaroslavl (Rus) 661
Jarrett (US) 930
Jarvis (US) 963
Jasiri (Ken) 451
Jasmin (Fra) 275
Al Jasrah (Bhr) 49
Jason (Gre) 311
Jason Dunham (US) 926
Al Jawf (SAr) 715
Jayasagara (Sri) 761
Jean Bart (Fra) 252
Jean De Vienne (Fra) 253
Jeanne d'Arc (Fra) 250
Jebat (Mly) 494
Jebel Antar (Alg) 8
Jebel Hando (Alg) 8
Jefferson City (US) 914
Jefferson Island (US) 966
Jeongji (RoK) 460
Jerai (Mly) 500
Jerambak (Bru) 88
Jerba (Tun) 823, 826
Jernih (Mly) 501
Jerong (Mly) 499
Jesus Gonzalez Ortega (Mex) 520
Jian (CPR) 144
Jiangmen (CPR) 144
Jiaxin (CPR) 142
Jija Bai (Ind) 351
Jimmy Carter (US) 913
Jin Chiang (Twn) 791
Jin Hae (RoK) 466
Jin Ju (RoK) 466
Jing Chiang (Twn) 791
Jinhua (CPR) 144
Jintsu (Jpn) 426
Jishou (CPR) 144
Jiuhuashan (CPR) 153
Jiujiang (CPR) 144
João Coutinho (Por) 632
João Roby (Por) 632
Johan De Witt (Nld) 553
John C Stennis (US) 917
John Ericsson (US) 955
John Gowlland (Aust) 36
John L Hall (US) 930
John Lenthall (US) 955
John Mcdonnell (US) 957
John P Tully (Can) 112
John Paul Jones (US) 924
John S McCain (US) 924
Jonquille (Fra) 275
Jordan Nikolov Orce (Mon) 528
Jorge Villarroel (Bol) 68
José Andrada (Plp) 611
José Artiaga Jr (Plp) 612
Jose Joaquin Fernandez De Lizardi (Mex) 521
José Loor Sr (Plp) 611
Jose Manuel Pando (Bol) 69
Jose Maria Del Castillo Velazco (Mex) 521
José Maria Garcia Y Toledo (Col) 173
José Maria Palas (Col) 173
Jose Natividad Macias (Mex) 521
Josefa Ortiz De Dominguez (Mex) 521
Joshan (Iran) 373
Joshila (Pak) 590
Joshua Appleby (US) 969
Josué Alvarez (Col) 177
Jotvingis (Lit) 489
Al Jouf (SAr) 716
Joumhouria (Tun) 824
Jounieh (Leb) 482
Joves Fiallo (Col) 177
Juan Antonio De La Fuente (Mex) 521
Juan de la Barrera (Mex) 520
Juan Lucio (Col) 174
Juan Magluyan (Plp) 611
Juan N Alvares (Mex) 520
Juan Nepomuceno Eslava (Col) 173
Juan Nepomuceno Peña (Col) 173
Juan Rafael Mora (CR) 179
Juan Ricardo Oyola Vera (Col) 172
Juan Sebastián de Elcano (Spn) 754
Juanchaco (Col) 176
Juang (Mly) 506
Al Jubatel (SAr) 717
Juist (Ger) 296
Jujur (Mly) 504
Juli (Per) 607
Julian Apaza (Bol) 69
Julio De Noronha (Brz) 76
Julio Olmos (Bol) 69
Jumping Marlin (Sin) 731
Jung Woon (RoK) 459
Juniper (US) 969
Junon (Sey) 721
Jupiter (Den) 195
Jura (UK) 900
Jurga (Rus) 706
Jurrat (Pak) 587
Justice (Sin) 727
Justo Sierra Mendez (Mex) 518
Jymy (Fin) 239
Jyoti (Ind) 347

K

K 4, 10 (Pol) 623
K 8 (Pol) 625
K 35, 39, 41-42 (Mly) 506
KA 10-11 (Lat) 481
Kaani (Mld) 507
El Kaced (Mor) 537
El Kadessaya (Egy) 218
Kadmos (Gre) 311
Kagayuki (Jpn) 445
Kagitingan (Plp) 611
Kahovka (Ukr) 851
Kahu (NZ) 561
Kaibil Balan (Gua) 315
Kaifeng (CPR) 140
Kaimon (Jpn) 442
Kairi (TT) 822
Kairyu (Jpn) 445
Kaiyo (Jpn) 446
Kajava (Fin) 237
Kakap (Indo) 359
Kakinada (Ind) 346
Kala 4, 6 (Fin) 238
Kala Hitam (Indo) 362
Kalaat Beni Hammad (Alg) 6
Kalaat Beni Rached (Alg) 6
Kalakae (Indo) 360
Kalar (Rus) 697
Kalat (Iran) 379
Kalinga (Plp) 614
Kalinga Apayao (Plp) 612
Kaliningrad (Rus) 681, 702
Kalkan (Tur) 835
Kallang (Sin) 730
Kallanpää (Fin) 240
Kalliroe (Gre) 310
Kallisto (Gre) 308
Kalmat (Pak) 589
Kalmykia (Rus) 675
Kaluga (Rus) 661
Kaman (Iran) 373
Kamchatka (Rus) 701
Kamla Devi (Ind) 351
Kampela 1-3 (Fin) 238
Kamui (Jpn) 442
Kanak Lata Baura (Ind) 351
Kanaris (Gre) 303
El Kanass (Alg) 6
Kanawha (US) 955, 970
Kang Ding (Twn) 789
Kang Jin (RoK) 470
Kang Kyeong (RoK) 470
Kang Reung (RoK) 467
Kangan (Iran) 378
Kangwon (RoK) 471
Kanimbla (Aust) 32
Kanin (Rus) 706
Kaning'A (Mlw) 491
Kaniv (Ukr) 856
Kankakee (US) 970
Kano (Jpn) 441
Kantang (Tld) 810
Kao Chiang (Twn) 791
Kao Hsiung (Twn) 793
Kaoh Chhlam (Cmb) 96
Kaoh Rong (Cmb) 96
Kapak (Indo) 367
Kapatakhaya (Ban) 55
Kapitan 1st Rank Dimitri Dobrev (Bul) 95
Kapitan Patimura (Indo) 356
Kara (Tog) 820
Karabala (Iran) 378
Karabane (Sen) 719
Karachejevo-Cherkessia (Rus) 680
Karadeniz Ereğli (Tur) 842
Karamürsel (Tur) 836
Karamürselbey (Tur) 837
Karang Banteng (Indo) 361
Karang Galang (Indo) 361
Karang Pilang (Indo) 361
Karang Tekok (Indo) 361
Karang Unarang (Indo) 361
Karatoa (Ban) 55
Karayel (Tur) 835
Karel Satsuitubun (Indo) 354
Karelia (Rus) 651, 701
El Karib (Mor) 534
Kariba (Jpn) 442
Karkheh (Iran) 380
Karlsøy (Nor) 573
Karlsruhe (Ger) 286
Karlstad (Swe) 771
Karmøy (Nor) 572
Karmukh (Ind) 338
Karnaphuli (Ban) 57
Karpasia (Cypr) 187
Karpaty (Rus) 696
Karrar (Pak) 588
Kartal (Tur) 835
Karthala (Com) 177
Karwar (Ind) 346
Kashalot (Rus) 656
Kashima (Jpn) 433
Kasimov (Rus) 674
Kasirga (Tur) 835
Kasos (Gre) 306
Kassir (Kwt) 477
Kasturba Gandhi (Ind) 351
Kasturi (Mly) 495
Kasungu (Mlw) 491
Kaszub (Pol) 620
Katherine Walker (US) 969
Katmai Bay (US) 969
Katon (Indo) 360
Katong (Sin) 730
Katori (Jpn) 439
Katsonis (Gre) 301
Katsura (Jpn) 441
Katsuragi (Jpn) 442
Katsuren (Jpn) 447
Kauffman (US) 930
Kavak (Tur) 841
Kavarna (Bul) 93
Kawagiri (Jpn) 443
Kayvan (Iran) 374
Kazanets (Rus) 675
KB 59, 71 (Mly) 506
KBV 001-003, 103-105 (Swe) 780
KBV 004-005, 010, 020, 044-051, 401-408 (Swe) 782
KBV 181, 201-202, 281-283, 285-290, 301-311, 591-593 (Swe) 781
KD 11-13 (Pol) 622
Kearsarge (US) 940
El Kechef (Alg) 6
Kedah (Mly) 496
Kedrov (Rus) 700
Keelung (Twn) 787, 797
Kefallinia (Gre) 307
Kekrops (Gre) 311
Kelabang (Indo) 362
Kelantan (Mly) 496
Kelefstis Stamou (Gre) 306
Kelibia (Tun) 826
Kem (Rus) 693
Kemaindera (Bru) 89
Kemalreis (Tur) 830
Kemer (Tur) 836
Kennebec (US) 970
Kennesaw Mountain (US) 947
Kent (UK) 878
Kentucky (US) 910
Keokuk (US) 954
Kepah (Mly) 502
Kerapu (Indo) 359
Kerch (Rus) 667
Kerempe (Tur) 836
Kéréon (Fra) 273
Al Keriat (Lby) 486
Keris (Indo) 358
Kerkini (Gre) 310
Kerkira (Gre) 307
Kermeur (Fra) 271
Kernaleguen (Fra) 271
Kesari (Ind) 345
Keshet (Isr) 385
Ketam (Mly) 502
Key Biscayne (US) 966
Key Largo (US) 966
Key West (US) 914
Keystone State (US) 961
Khabarovsk (Rus) 706
Khadang (Iran) 373
Khadem (Ban) 60
El Khafir (Mor) 535
Khaibar (Pak) 584
Khaireddine (Tun) 825
Khalid (Pak) 583
Khalid (SAr) 714
Khalid Bin Walid (Ban) 53
Khamronsin (Tld) 806
Khan Jahan Ali (Ban) 59
Khandag (Iran) 380
Khanjar (Ind) 339
Khanjar (Iran) 373
Kharg (Iran) 379
Al Kharj (SAr) 715
Khassab (Omn) 578
Kherson (Ukr) 854
Khirirat (Tld) 807
Khmelnitsky (Ukr) 851
Khukri (Ind) 339
Al Khyber (Lby) 483
Khyber (Egy) 218
Ki Hajar Dewantara (Indo) 364
Kibua (Tan) 800
Kichli (Gre) 308
Kickapoo (US) 970
Kidd (US) 926
Kidon (Isr) 385
Kihu (Lit) 489
Kii (Jpn) 439
Kiiski 1-7 (Fin) 237
Kiisla (Fin) 234
Kikau (Fij) 233
Kikuchi (Jpn) 442
KIL 22, 27, 29, 31, 143, 158, 164, 168, 498, 927 (Rus) 693
Kildin (Rus) 688
Kiliç (Tur) 835
Kilimli (Tur) 836
Kilo Moana (US) 950
Kim Chon (RoK) 466
Kim Men (Twn) 795
Kim Po (RoK) 470
Kimanis (Mly) 504
Kinabalu (Mly) 500
King (Arg) 20
King Abdullah (Jor) 448
Kingfisher (US) 967
Kingston (Can) 103
Kinmen (Twn) 796
Kino (Mex) 525
Kinugasa (Jor) 447
Al Kirch (Alg) 5
Kirch (Ind) 338
Kirisame (Jpn) 422
Kirishima (Jpn) 419, 442
Kiro (Fij) 233
Kirovograd (Ukr) 852
Kirpan (Ind) 339
Kiska (US) 955, 966
Kiso (Jpn) 438
Kissa (Gre) 308
Kitagumo (Jpn) 443
Kitakami (Jpn) 441
Kitimat II (Can) 110
Kittanning (US) 954
Kittiwake (US) 967
Kittur Chennamma (Ind) 351
Kiyotaki (Jpn) 445
Kiyozuki (Jpn) 444
Kizljar (Rus) 703
Kjøkøy (Nor) 571
Kjeøy (Nor) 573
KKTCSG 01-02 (Tur) 844
KKTCSG 102-103 (Tur) 846
Klaeng (Tld) 809
Klakring (US) 930
Kled Keo (Tld) 816
Klints (Lat) 481
Klongyai (Tld) 810
Klueng Badaan (Tld) 817
Knechtsand (Ger) 296
Knight Island (US) 966
Knorr (US) 950
Knud Rasmussen (Den) 193
Knurrhahn (Ger) 294
Ko Chang (RoK) 470
Ko Ryeong (RoK) 470
Kobchik (Rus) 702
Kobra (Indo) 360
Kochab (Mex) 520
Kodiak Island (US) 966
Kojima (Jpn) 438
Kojoon Bong (RoK) 468
Kola (Rus) 691
Kolam (Tld) 813
Kolkata (Ind) 330
Kolomna (Rus) 684
Köln (Ger) 286
Komandor (Rus) 701
Komayuki (Jpn) 443
Kombo A Janea (Cam) 97
Komendor (Rus) 683
Kommuna (Rus) 695
Konarak (Iran) 379
Kondopoga (Rus) 681
Kondor (Pol) 617
Kong Ju (RoK) 466
Kongou (Jpn) 419, 442
Konkan (Ind) 346
Konstantin Olshansky (Ukr) 852
Kontradmiral Vlasov (Rus) 683
Kontradmiral X Czernicki (Pol) 624
Kopås (Nor) 571
Kora (Ind) 338
Koramshahr (Iran) 379
Korcula (Cro) 183
Korets (Rus) 674
Korets (Ukr) 855
Korolev (Rus) 681
Korsakov (Rus) 703
Korshun (Rus) 702
Koshiki (Jpn) 439
Koster (Swe) 777
Kostroma (Rus) 657
Kotelnich (Rus) 684
Kotobiki (Jpn) 443
Kou (Est) 230
Koun (Jpn) 447
Kountouriotis (Gre) 303
Kourion (Cypr) 187
Kouya (Jpn) 442
Kovel (Ukr) 855
Kovrovets (Rus) 683
Koyda (Rus) 691
Kozara (Ser) 720
Kozhikode (Ind) 346
Kozlu (Tur) 836
Kråkenes (Nor) 571
Kraburi (Tld) 803
Krait (Indo) 360

Krakow (Pol) ... 622
Kralj Dmitar Zvonimir (Cro) ... 182
Kralj Petar Kresimir Iv (Cro) ... 182
Krasnokamensk (Rus) ... 661
Krasnoperekopsk (Ukr) ... 855
Krasnoyarsk (Rus) ... 654
Krateos (Gre) ... 306
Krechet (Rus) ... 702
Kremenchuk (Ukr) ... 851
Kremenets (Ukr) ... 855
Krilon (Rus) ... 685
Krishna (Ind) ... 347
Kristaps (Lat) ... 481
Krka (Cro) ... 182
Kronshtadt (Rus) ... 660
Kronsort (Ger) ... 292
Kuban (Rus) ... 702
Kudaka (Jpn) ... 438
Kuha 21-26 (Fin) ... 236
Kujang (Indo) ... 367
Kukui (US) ... 969
Kukulkán (Gua) ... 315
Kukup (Mly) ... 503
Kula (Fij) ... 233
Kulish (Ind) ... 338
Kullen (Swe) ... 777
Kulmbach (Ger) ... 291
Kum Wha (RoK) ... 470
Kumano (Jpn) ... 441
Kumataka (Jpn) ... 428
Kumbhir (Ind) ... 345
Kumejima (Jpn) ... 432
Kun Ming (Twn) ... 789
Kun San (RoK) ... 466
Kunashiri (Jpn) ... 441
Kunigami (Jpn) ... 439
Kunisaki (Jpn) ... 429, 439
Kunlunshan (CPR) ... 152
Kupang (Indo) ... 361
Kupang (Mly) ... 502
Kurama (Jpn) ... 425
Kuraman (Mly) ... 503
Kureren (Den) ... 195
Kuriat (Tun) ... 823
Kurihama (Jpn) ... 433
Kurikoma (Jpn) ... 438
Kurily (Rus) ... 688
Kurinami (Jpn) ... 444
Kurki (Fin) ... 234
Kurmuk (Sud) ... 767
Kurobe (Jpn) ... 434
SGT Matej Kocak (US) ... 961
SSGT Robert T Kuroda (US) ... 947
Kurokami (Jpn) ... 441
Kuroshima (Jpn) ... 431
Kuroshio (Jpn) ... 415
Kurs (Rus) ... 701
Kuršis (Lit) ... 488
Kurushima (Jpn) ... 446
Kuşadasi (Tur) ... 836
Kusiyara (Ban) ... 56
Kustrin-Kiez (Ger) ... 297
Kuthar (Ind) ... 339
Kuvvet (Tur) ... 843
Kuwano (Jpn) ... 441
Kuzbass (Rus) ... 656
Kvitsøy (Nor) ... 571
Kwan Myong (RoK) ... 466
Kwang Yang (RoK) ... 471
Kwanggaeto Daewang (RoK) ... 463
Kyanwa (Nig) ... 565
Kyknos (Gre) ... 305
Kyong Buk (RoK) ... 464
Kyong Ju (RoK) ... 466
Kyrenia (Cypr) ... 187

L

L-01-01-L-01-20 (ElS) ... 226
L 02, 04-11 (Spn) ... 759
L 011-013 (Ban) ... 60
L 22-25 (UAE) ... 862
L 32-39 (Ind) ... 345
L 41, 61-67 (UAE) ... 861
L 404 (Kwt) ... 478
L 601-614 (Spn) ... 752
L 705, 709, 711, 1001-1010 (UK) ... 886
L 820-821 (Sri) ... 766
L 4540-L 4546 (Nor) ... 571
L 9525-9529, 9536-9541 (Nld) ... 551
L 9530-9535, 9565-9576 (Nld) ... 554
L/CPL Roy M Wheat (US) ... 960
La Argentina (Arg) ... 12
La Belle Poule (Fra) ... 268
La Boudeuse (Fra) ... 262
La Capricieuse (Fra) ... 262
La Cruz (Per) ... 606
La Divette (Fra) ... 271
La Fayette (Fra) ... 256
La Fougueuse (Fra) ... 262
La Galité (Tun) ... 823
La Glorieuse (Fra) ... 262
La Gracieuse (Fra) ... 262
La Graciosa (Spn) ... 754
La Graña (Spn) ... 757
La Grand Hermine (Fra) ... 268
La Grandire (Fra) ... 265
La Grazietta (Lby) ... 486
La Houssaye (Fra) ... 273
La Jolla (US) ... 914
La Loude (Fra) ... 271
La Malfa (Ita) ... 410
La Moqueuse (Fra) ... 262
La Motte-Picquet (Fra) ... 254
La Orchila (Ven) ... 982
La Piccirella (Ita) ... 411
La Plata (Arg) ... 22
La Punta (Per) ... 606
La Railleuse (Fra) ... 262
La Rieuse (Fra) ... 262
La Sota (Ben) ... 66
La Spina (Ita) ... 410
La Tapageuse (Fra) ... 262
Labas (Mly) ... 503
Laboe (Ger) ... 291
Laboon (US) ... 924
Labuan (Aust) ... 34
Lacar (Arg) ... 23
Lachs (Ger) ... 291
Ladny (Rus) ... 671
Ladoga (Rus) ... 701
Ladse (Slo) ... 732
Laganà (Ita) ... 410
Laguna (Plp) ... 612
Lahav (Isr) ... 384
Laheeb (Lby) ... 485
Lake Buhi (Plp) ... 613
Lake Bulusan (Plp) ... 613
Lake Champlain (US) ... 921
Lake Erie (US) ... 921
Lake Paoay (Plp) ... 613
Lake Taal (Plp) ... 613
Laksamana Hang Nadim (Mly) ... 497
Laksamana Muhammad Amin (Mly) ... 497
Laksamana Tan Pusmah (Mly) ... 497
Laksamana Tun Abdul Jamil (Mly) ... 497
Lakshmi Bai (Ind) ... 351
Lambung Mangkurat (Indo) ... 356
Lampo Batang (Indo) ... 365
Lan Yang (Twn) ... 790
Lana (Nig) ... 566
Lanao Del Norte (Plp) ... 612
Lancaster (UK) ... 878
Lancha Ambulancia (Col) ... 176
Landsort (Swe) ... 776
Lang (Mly) ... 503
Lang Siput (Mly) ... 501
Lang Tiram (Mly) ... 501
Langeness (Ger) ... 296
Langeoog (Ger) ... 296
Langkawi (Mly) ... 503
Languedoc (Fra) ... 259
Lanta (Tld) ... 812
Lanzhou (CPR) ... 137
Laotieshan (CPR) ... 153
Lapérouse (Fra) ... 267
Laplace (Fra) ... 267
Lapwing (Ana) ... 9
Larak (Iran) ... 377
Laramie (US) ... 955
Lardier (Fra) ... 273
Largs Bay (UK) ... 893
Larkana (Pak) ... 588
Larrakia (Aust) ... 35
Larrea (Per) ... 602
Las Palmas (Spn) ... 753
Lascar Catargiu (Rom) ... 644
Lassen (US) ... 926
Lastunul (Rom) ... 645
Lat Ya (Tld) ... 814
Lata (Sol) ... 733
Late (Ton) ... 820
Latouche-Tréville (Fra) ... 254
Lauca (Chi) ... 126
L'Audacieuse (Fra) ... 262
L'Audacieux (Cam) ... 96
Launceston (Aust) ... 35
Lautaro (Chi) ... 124
Lautoka (Fij) ... 234
Lavan (Iran) ... 377
Lavande (Fra) ... 272
Lawrence H Gianella (US) ... 959
Lawrenceville (Can) ... 105
Laxen (Den) ... 193
Laya (Spn) ... 749
Layang (Indo) ... 358
LC 01-02 (NZ) ... 561
LC 1 (Mld) ... 507
LCM 701-710 (Myn) ... 542
LCP 1-4 (Den) ... 195
LCT 101-102, 104 (Ban) ... 60
LCVP 9473 (UK) ... 886
LD 41-42 (Uru) ... 978
LD 45-46 (Uru) ... 977
Le Four (Fra) ... 273
Le Malin (Fra) ... 270
Le Téméraire (Fra) ... 246
Le Terrible (Fra) ... 246
Le Triomphant (Fra) ... 246
Le Vigilant (Fra) ... 246
L'etoile De Mer (Fra) ... 271
Lealtad (Ven) ... 985
Lech (Pol) ... 625
Ledang (Mly) ... 500
Ledbury (UK) ... 887
Lee Eokgi (RoK) ... 459
Lee Jongmu (RoK) ... 459
Lee Sunsin (RoK) ... 459
Al Leeth (SAr) ... 716
Leeuwin (Aust) ... 36
Legare (US) ... 964
Leikvin (Nor) ... 573
Lekir (Mly) ... 495
Lekiu (Mly) ... 494
Lely (Ven) ... 983
Lemadang (Indo) ... 358
Lena (Rus) ... 691
Lenguado (Arg) ... 23
Leon Guzman (Mex) ... 521
Leon Tadina (Plp) ... 612
Leona Vicario (Mex) ... 521
Leonard C Banfield (Bar) ... 61
Leonard J Cowley (Can) ... 108
Leonardo (NATO) ... 546
Leonid Demin (Rus) ... 685
Léopard (Fra) ... 268
Leopard (Rus) ... 656
Leopold 1 (Bel) ... 62
Leopoldo Regis (Plp) ... 612
Leovigildo Gantioque (Plp) ... 611
Lerici (Ita) ... 403
Lerøy (Nor) ... 571
Leroy Grumman (US) ... 955
Lesbos (Gre) ... 307
Leticia (Col) ... 172
Letizia (Ita) ... 410
L'étoile (Fra) ... 268
Leuser (Indo) ... 366
Levanzo (Ita) ... 407
Levent (Tur) ... 843
Levera (Gra) ... 314
Leviathan (Isr) ... 383
Levuka (Fij) ... 234
Lewis and Clark (US) ... 954
Leyte Gulf (US) ... 921
Leytenant Ilin (Rus) ... 684
LG 63-64 (Ecu) ... 212
LG 131-134, 151-153, 191-192 (Ecu) ... 211
Lianjiang (CPR) ... 150
Lianyungang (CPR) ... 142
Liaoyang (CPR) ... 155
Libeccio (Ita) ... 396
Liberal (Brz) ... 75
Liberation (Bel) ... 64
Liberato Picar (Plp) ... 611
Liberta (Ant) ... 10
Libertad (Arg) ... 20
Libertad (Ven) ... 981
Libertador (Bol) ... 68
Liberty (US) ... 966
Libra (Ita) ... 401
Libra (Sey) ... 721
Lienchiang (Twn) ... 796
Lieutenant Colonel Errhamani (Mor) ... 532
Lieutenant de Vaisseau Lavallée (Fra) ... 257
Lieutenant de Vaisseau Le Hénaff (Fra) ... 257
Lieutenant Dimitrie Nicolescu (Rom) ... 645
Lieutenant General Dimo Hamaambo (Nam) ... 544
Lieutenant Lupu Dunescu (Rom) ... 645
Lieutenant Remus Lepri (Rom) ... 645
Ligia Elena (Pan) ... 592
Ligitan (Mly) ... 503
Lilas (Fra) ... 272
Lilian (Lit) ... 489
Limam El Hadrami (Mtn) ... 510
Liman (Rus) ... 688
Limasawa (Plp) ... 614
Limnos (Can) ... 112
Limnos (Gre) ... 303
Lindsay (Can) ... 113
Line (US) ... 971
Linfen (CPR) ... 144
Linga (Lat) ... 479
Linge (Nld) ... 557
Lingyanshan (CPR) ... 153
Linosa (Ita) ... 406
L'intrépide (CtI) ... 180
Lion (Fra) ... 268
Lipari (Ita) ... 407
Lipetsk (Rus) ... 661
Lippi (Ita) ... 410
Liseron (Fra) ... 270
Lissus (Alb) ... 3
Listerville (Can) ... 105
Liupanshan (CPR) ... 153
Liven (Rus) ... 678
Liverpool (UK) ... 875
Ljubomir (Ukr) ... 856
Lobelia (Bel) ... 64
Lode (Lat) ... 479
Lohi (Fin) ... 239
Lohm (Fin) ... 239
Loja (Ecu) ... 206
Loke (Swe) ... 780
Løkhaug (Nor) ... 571
Lokki (Fin) ... 237
Loksa (Rus) ... 698
Lokys (Lit) ... 489
Lombardi (Ita) ... 410
Lomor (MI) ... 509
Long Island (US) ... 966
Longlom (Tld) ... 806
Longstone (UK) ... 892
Lopburi Rames (Tld) ... 817
Loreto (Per) ... 603
Loreto Danipog (Plp) ... 612
Lorraine (Fra) ... 259
Los Angeles (US) ... 914
Los Cayos (Ven) ... 984
Los Galapágos (Ecu) ... 206
Los Llanos (Ven) ... 982
Los Rios (Ecu) ... 206
Los Taques (Ven) ... 984
Louis M Lauzier (Can) ... 108
Louis S St Laurent (Can) ... 106
Louisbourg (Can) ... 108
Louise-Marie (Bel) ... 62
Louisiana (US) ... 910
Louisville (US) ... 914
Loutre (Fra) ... 273
Sp/4 James A Loux (US) ... 947
Lovat (Rus) ... 692
Loyal (US) ... 957
LP 01, 07, 09-11, 101-102, 104 (Par) ... 597
LP 01-42 (Bol) ... 68
LPM 4201 (Chi) ... 126
LR 7 (CPR) ... 159
LS 010, 015, 020, 025, 030, 035, 040, 050, 114-119, 121-123, 125-128, 133-136 (Gre) ... 312
LS 137-172 (Gre) ... 314
LS 169-170, 194-195, 201, 216-223 (Jpn) ... 447
LS 51-52, 55, 65, 84-88, 95, 97, 101, 103, 106-107, 109-110, 112, 129-132, 155-157, 401, 413-415, 601-615 (Gre) ... 313
LTC John U D Page (US) ... 960
LTG William B Bunker (US) ... 947
Lübeck (Ger) ... 286
Lubéron (Fra) ... 272
Lubin (Mon) ... 530
Lublin (Pol) ... 622
Lubny (Ukr) ... 856
Ludwigshafen (Ger) ... 288
Luigi Dattilo (Ita) ... 412
Luigi Durand De La Penne (Ita) ... 395
Luna (Den) ... 195
Lung Chiang (Twn) ... 791
Luoxiaoshan (CPR) ... 153
Luoyang (CPR) ... 142
Lushan (CPR) ... 154
Lütje Hörn (Ger) ... 296
Lutsk (Ukr) ... 850
Luymes (Nld) ... 554
L V Rabhi (Mor) ... 534
Lyme Bay (UK) ... 893
Lynch (Arg) ... 22
Lynx (Fra) ... 268
Lyø (Den) ... 194
Lyra (Den) ... 195
Lyre (Fra) ... 266

M

M 1, 12, 21-22 (Pol) ... 626
M 02-M 14 series (Spn) ... 758
M 35, 38-40 (Pol) ... 623
M 111 (Alb) ... 2
M 325-326 (Az) ... 44
M 327-328 (Az) ... 43
MA 1-3 (Ger) ... 294
Maanshan (CPR) ... 140
Maassluis (Nld) ... 554
Al Mabrukah (Omn) ... 575
Macareu (Por) ... 637
Macchi (Ita) ... 410
Macha (Per) ... 603
Machado (Chi) ... 121
Macham (Iran) ... 379
Machaon (Fra) ... 271
Machitis (Gre) ... 306
Mackinaw (US) ... 968
Macko (Pol) ... 625
Macon (US) ... 947
Mactan (Plp) ... 613
Madan Singh (Ind) ... 349
Madeleine (Lit) ... 489
Madhumati (Ban) ... 55
Madina (SAr) ... 712
Madryn (Arg) ... 22
Maejima (Jpn) ... 432
Maestrale (Ita) ... 396
Maga (Myn) ... 540
Magadan (Rus) ... 656
Magadnets (Rus) ... 701
Magamed Gadgiev (Rus) ... 684
Magar (Ind) ... 345
Magat Salamat (Plp) ... 610
Magdalena (Mex) ... 525
Magdeburg (Ger) ... 288
Magnetica (Rom) ... 646
Magneto-Gorsk (Rus) ... 661
Magnolia (Fra) ... 270
Magua (DR) ... 203
Mahón (Spn) ... 757
Mahamiru (Mly) ... 500
Mahan (Iran) ... 374
Mahan (US) ... 924
Maharajalela (Bru) ... 89
Mahawangsa (Mly) ... 500
El Maher (Mor) ... 534
El Mahir (Alg) ... 6
Mahish (Ind) ... 345
Mahnavi-Hamraz (Iran) ... 377
Mahnavi-Taheri (Iran) ... 377
Mahnavi-Vahedi (Iran) ... 377
Mahroos (Kwt) ... 477
Mahsuri (Mly) ... 502
Mahury (Fra) ... 276
Maimon (Kwt) ... 477
Main (Ger) ... 293
Maine (US) ... 910
Maistros (Gre) ... 309
Maitland (Aust) ... 35
Maïto (Fra) ... 273
Maj Bernard F Fisher (US) ... 959
El Majid (Mor) ... 534
Maj Stephen W Pless (US) ... 961
MAK 160 (Rus) ... 677
Makasib (UAE) ... 860
Makassar (Indo) ... 360
Makhachkala (Rus) ... 680
Makigumo (Jpn) ... 443
Makin Island (US) ... 940
Makinami (Jpn) ... 421
Makishima (Jpn) ... 432
Makishio (Jpn) ... 415
Makkah (SAr) ... 710
Makkum (Nld) ... 554
Mako (US) ... 967
Mako Shark (Sin) ... 730
Makrelen (Den) ... 193
Al Maks (Egy) ... 223
Makung (Twn) ... 787
Makut Rajakumarn (Tld) ... 804
Malabar (Fra) ... 272
Malahayati (Indo) ... 355
Malan (Pak) ... 591
Malaspina (Spn) ... 754
Malawali (Mly) ... 504
Maldonado (Col) ... 177
Maldonado (Uru) ... 975
Mallard (Can) ... 111
Mallet (US) ... 971
Malmö (Swe) ... 773
Malmøya (Nor) ... 571
Måløy (Nor) ... 572
Malpelo (Col) ... 175
Malu Baizam (Aust) ... 39
Malvern Hill (US) ... 947
Malzwin (Nld) ... 557
Mamba (Ken) ... 450
Mamba (Tan) ... 799
Mamry (Pol) ... 623
Man Klang (Tld) ... 812
Man Nai (Tld) ... 812
Man Nok (Tld) ... 812
Manabi (Ecu) ... 206
Manacacías (Col) ... 177
Al Manama (Bhr) ... 48

Manatee (US) 967
Manaure (Ven) 983
Manawanui (NZ) 562
Manchester (UK) 876
Manchzhur (Rus) 701
Máncora (Per) 607
Mandau (Indo) 358
Mandubi (Arg) 22
Manduruyu (Arg) 23
Mangyan (Plp) 614
Manini (Fra) 273
Manistee (US) 954
Manjung (Mly) 504
Manø (Den) 194
Manoora (Aust) 32
Al Manoud (Lby) 486
Manowar (US) 967
Al Mansoor (Omn) 577
Manta (US) 967
Manta Ray (Sin) 730
Manthatisi (SA) 734
Mantilla (Arg) 22
Manuel Clavero (Per) 603
Manuel Doblado (Mex) 520
Manuel Gomez (Plp) 611
Manuel Gutierrez Zamora (Mex) 520
Manuel José Arce (ElS) 226
Manuel Trujillo (Par) 597
Manuela Saenz (Col) 174
Manych (Rus) 692
Manzanillo (Mex) 522
Maoming (CPR) 144
Maple (US) 969
Mar Caribe (Spn) 756
Mar Del Plata (Arg) 22
Mara (Ven) 983
Marajo (Brz) 86
Marañon (Per) 602
Marasesti (Rom) 642
Marban (UAE) 860
Marcus Hanna (US) 969
Margarita (Ven) 982
Maria Bray (US) 969
Maria L Pendo (Arg) 23
Mariano Abasolo (Mex) 514
Mariano Escobedo (Mex) 520
Mariano Matamoros (Mex) 520
Mariategui (Per) 601
Marie Miljø (Den) 199
Marinero Jarano (Spn) 756
Mario Marino (Ita) 401
Mario Villegas (Col) 172
Mariscal de Zapita (Bol) 68
Mariscal Sucre (Ven) 980
Mariupol (Ukr) 852
Marjata (Nor) 572
Markab (Mex) 520
Markhad (Alg) 8
Marlim (Brz) 78
Marlin (Mly) 505
Marlin (US) 967
Marn Vichai (Tld) 817
Marne (Fra) 269
Maroa (Fra) 273
Marola (Spn) 750
Maroub (Sud) 767
Marqués de la Ensenada (Spn) 756
Marra (Ita) 411
Mars (Rus) 685
Mars (Swi) 783
Marshal Gelovani (Rus) 685
Marshal Krylov (Rus) 687
Marshal Shaposhnikov (Rus) 669
Marshal Ustinov (Rus) 666
Marsopa (Arg) 23
Marsouin (Alg) 8
Martadinata (Indo) 353
Marte (Per) 605
Martha L Black (Can) 107
Marti (Tur) 835
Martin Garcia (Arg) 22
Martín Posadillo (Spn) 755
Maru (Est) 230
Marudu (Mly) 504
Mary Sears (US) 957
Maryborough (Aust) 35
Maryland (US) 910
Maryut (Egy) 222
Marzoug (Kwt) 477
Masan (RoK) 464
Mascardi (Arg) 23
Mash'Noor (Kwt) 477
Mashtan (Bhr) 50
Mashuk (Rus) 697
Mashuu (Jpn) 434
Maskan (Kwt) 476
Mason (US) 926
Massapequa (US) 954
Mataco (Arg) 21
Matacora (Indo) 360
Matamoros (US) 947
Matanga (Ind) 349
Mataphon (Tld) 813
Matarani (Per) 606
Matelot (TT) 822
Matelot Alioune Samb (Sen) 718
Matelot Brice Kpomasse (Ben) 66
Matelot Oumar Ndoye (Sen) 718
Al Mathur (Lby) 485
Matias De Cordova (Mex) 521
Matias Romero (Mex) 518
Matinicus (US) 966
Matlalcueye (Mex) 526
Matros Mikola Mushnirov (Ukr) 856
Matrozos (Gre) 301
Matsilo (Mad) 490
Matsunami (Jpn) 443
Matsuura (Jpn) 441
Matsuyuki (Jpn) 424
Matthew (Can) 112
Matthew Perry (US) 954
Mattoso Maia (Brz) 80
Maui (US) 966
Maule (Chi) 126
Maullín (Chi) 126
Maury (Fra) 276
Max Paredes (Bol) 69
Maya (Mex) 525
Mayom (Sud) 767
Mayor Jaime Arias Arango (Col) 177
Mazzarella (Ita) 410
Mazzei (Ita) 410
MB 4, 15, 19, 21, 23, 28, 37, 38, 56, 58, 61, 76, 99, 100, 105, 110, 119, 148, 162, 166, 172, 174, 304 (Rus) 698
McCampbell (US) 926
McClusky (US) 930
McFaul (US) 924
McInerney (US) 930
MDK 18, 88 (Rus) 682
MDLC Jacques (Fra) 276
MDLC Richard (Fra) 276
MDN 94-104, 108-109, 114-117 (Ita) 402
Mechanicsville (US) 947
Mecklenburg-Vorpommern (Ger) 284
Meda (Aust) 36
Medardo Monzon Coronado (Col) 173
Medas (Spn) 750
Medusa (Arg) 23
Meduza (Pol) 625
Meen (Ind) 347
Meera Behan (Ind) 351
Meerkatze (Ger) 297
Meghna (Ban) 57
Megrez (Mex) 520
Meiyo (Jpn) 446
Melbourne (Aust) 30
Meleban (Mly) 501
Melia (Fra) 276
Melita I-II (Mlt) 508
Melitopol (Ukr) 852
Mellon (US) 963
Melo (Per) 604
Meltem (Tur) 835
Melva (Arg) 23
Melville (Aust) 36
Melville (Dom) 200
Melville (US) 950
Memet Sastrawiria (Indo) 356
Memphis (US) 914
MEN 212, 215-216 (Ita) 408
MEN 217-222, 227-228, 551 (Ita) 401
Menab (Iran) 380
Mendez Nuñez (Spn) 744
Mendi (SA) 735
Mendonca (US) 958
Mengam (Fra) 273
Menkar (Mex) 520
Menzhinsky (Rus) 700
Merak (Mex) 522
Mercuur (Nld) 555
Mercy (US) 955
Merikarhu (Fin) 241
Merino (Chi) 124
Merjen (Tkm) 847
Mermaid (Aust) 36
Mero (Arg) 23
Merrickville (Can) 105
Mersey (UK) 883
Mersuji (Mly) 504
Mesa Verde (US) 942
Mesaha 1-2 (Tur) 839
Mestia (Geo) 279
Metel (Rus) 674
Meteoro (Spn) 750
Mette Miljø (Den) 199
Meuse (Fra) 269
Mewa (Pol) 622
MG Charles P Gross (US) 947
MG Robert Smalls (US) 947
MGB 102, 110 (Myn) 542
Miami (US) 914
Mianyang (CPR) 142
Miaplacidus (Mex) 522
Micalvi (Chi) 121
Miccoli (Ita) 410
Michael Mansoor (US) 928
Michael Murphy (US) 926
Michele Fiorillo (Ita) 412
Michigan (US) 911
Michishio (Jpn) 415
Micronesia (Mic) 527
Middelburg (Nld) 554
Middlesex (Jam) 412
Middleton (UK) 887
Midgett (US) 963
Midhili (Mld) 507
Midia (Rom) 646
Mielno (Pol) 622
Mier (Bel) 65
Miguel Ela Edjodjomo (EqG) 227
Miguel Malvar (Plp) 610
Miguel Silva (Col) 177
Miguel Sotoa (Par) 597
El Mikdam (Mor) 535
Mikhail Kogalniceanu (Rom) 644
Mikhail Konovalov (Rus) 706
Mikhail Rudnitsky (Rus) 693
Mikolaiv (Ukr) 855
Milano II (Spn) 760
Milazzo (Ita) 403
Milius (US) 924
Miljø 101-102 (Den) 198
Mimosa (Fra) 276
Minabe (Jpn) 441
Mineralny Vodi (Rus) 684
Minerva (Ita) 398
Mineyuki (Jpn) 424
Minna (UK) 900
Minnesota (US) 912
Minoo (Jpn) 445
Minos (Gre) 311
Minsk (Rus) 681, 702
Mirach (Mex) 522
Mirazh (Rus) 678
Mircea (Rom) 646
Mirfak (Mex) 520
Misairutei-San-Gou (Jpn) 428
Misasa (Jpn) 441
Missionary Bridge (US) 947
Mississippi (US) 912
Missouri (US) 912
Mistral (Fra) 263
Mistral (Spn) 741
Mitilo (Ita) 405
Mitscher (US) 924
Mittelgrund (Ger) 292
Miura (Jpn) 438
Miyajima (Jpn) 431
Mizar (Mex) 520
Mizrak (Tur) 835
Mizuho (Jpn) 437
Mizuki (Jpn) 442
Mizunami (Jpn) 444
Mjølner (Nor) 573
MK 391, 1277, 1303, 1407-1411, 1556 (Rus) 689
MK 391, 1303, 1407-1409 (Rus) 694
MK 405 (Rus) 689
MLM 6-10 (Tld) 814
Moawin (Pak) 589
Mobark (Kwt) 477
Mobile Bay (US) 921, 969
Mochishio (Jpn) 415
Mocovi (Arg) 21
Moctezuma II (Mex) 524
Modig (Swe) 774
Mogochey (Rus) 661
Mohammed Brahim Rejeb (Tun) 826
Mohammed V (Mor) 531
Mohawk (US) 964
Moho (Per) 607
Mok Po (RoK) 466
Molino Del Ray (US) 947
Mollendo (Per) 604
Mollymawk (Aust) 39
Momsen (US) 926
Monastir (Tun) 824
Moncão (Por) 637
Monchegorsk (Rus) 674
Moncton (Can) 103
Mondolkiri (Cmb) 96
Monge (Fra) 267
Monmouth (UK) 878
Mono (Tog) 820
Monomoy (US) 966
Monsekela (CtI) 180
Mont Arreh (Dji) 200
Montcalm (Fra) 253
Monterey (US) 921
Montero (Per) 601
Monterrey (US) 947
Montpelier (US) 914
Montreal (Can) 100
Montrose (UK) 878
Mooam (Iran) 379
Moonmu Daewang (RoK) 461
Moose (Can) 104
Moran Valverde (Ecu) 206
Moray (US) 967
Morcoyán (Arg) 21
Mordoviya (Rus) 681
Moresby (PNG) 595
Morgenthau (US) 963
Moriah (TT) 822
Morona (Per) 605
Moroz (Rus) 678
Morro Bay (US) 969
Morrosquillo (Col) 175
Morse (Fra) 273
Morshansk (Rus) 677
Moruga (TT) 821
Mørvika (Nor) 571
Mosel (Ger) 293
Moshchny (Rus) 698
Moskva (Rus) 666
Motajica (Ser) 720
Motobu (Jpn) 439
Motorist (Rus) 683
Motoura (Jpn) 441
Mou Hsing (Twn) 796
Mouanco (Cam) 97
El Mouderrib I-VII (Alg) 8
El Moukadem (Alg) 6
El Mounkid I-IV (Alg) 8
El Mourafek (Alg) 7
El Mourakeb (Alg) 6
Mount Baker (US) 955
Mount Whitney (US) 939
Mounts Bay (UK) 893
Mourad Rais (Alg) 4
Mouro (Spn) 750
El Moutarid (Alg) 6
Móvik (Nor) 571
Móvil I-II (Col) 176
SSIM Manuel A Moyar (Col) 177
MPK 17, 82, 107, 113, 139, 178, 191, 197 (Rus) 674
MPK 105, 192, 227 (Rus) 675
MRD 1-6 (Den) 196
MSB 11-17 (Tld) 814
MSD 02-04 (Aust) 36
MSF 1-4 (Den) 195
MT 264-265 (Rus) 683
MTB 2-9 (Tur) 839
Al Mua'Zzar (Omn) 576
Mubarak (Egy) 214
Mubarraz (UAE) 860
Muhafiz (Pak) 588
Muhammed (Jor) 448
Al Muharraq (Bhr) 48, 50
Mujahid (Pak) 588
Mulia (Mly) 504
Mulnaya (Bul) 91
Multatuli (Indo) 365
Mumbai (Ind) 332
Al Munassir (Omn) 578
Al Munjed (Lby) 486
Munro (US) 963
Munsif (Pak) 588
Munster (Ger) 295
Munter (Swe) 774
Murakumo (Jpn) 443
Murasame (Jpn) 422
Murature (Arg) 20
Muray Jib (UAE) 858
Murban (UAE) 859
Murene (Alg) 8
Al Murjan (UAE) 860
Murmansk (Rus) 701
Muromets (Rus) 674
Muroto (Jpn) 435
Murozuki (Jpn) 445
Murray (Can) 113
Mursu (Fin) 238
Muskegon (US) 954
Muskingum (US) 970
Mussandam (Omn) 577
Mustang (US) 966
Musters (Arg) 23
Mustin (US) 926
Mutiara (Mly) 500
Mutilla (Chi) 123
Mutin (Fra) 269
Myosotis (Fra) 270
Myoukou (Jpn) 419
Mysore (Ind) 332
Mzia (Tan) 799
Mzizi (Tan) 799

N

Naantali (Fin) 235
Nacaome (Hon) 318
Nachi (Jpn) 443
Na Daeyong (RoK) 459
Nadezhnyy (Rus) 699
Nadon (Can) 113
Nafanua (Sam) 710
Naftilos (Gre) 309
Nagashima (Jpn) 432
Naghdi (Iran) 372
Nagozuki (Jpn) 443
Nahid (Iran) 374
Nahidik (Can) 109
Nahuel Huapi (Arg) 23
Naif (Kwt) 477
Naiguata (Ven) 982
Naiki Devi (Ind) 351
Najaden (Den) 194
Al Najah (Omn) 577
Najim Al Zaffer (Egy) 216
Najran (SAr) 716
Nakat (Rus) 678
Nakhoda Ragam (Bru) 88
Nakhodka (Rus) 702
Naklo (Pol) 622
Nakul (Ind) 349
Nala (Indo) 355
Nam Won (RoK) 466
Nanaimo (Can) 103
Nanawa (Par) 596
Nanchang (CPR) 139
Nandimithra (Sri) 761
Nanggala (Indo) 353
Nanhai (CPR) 150
Nanjing (CPR) 139
Nanning (CPR) 139
Nanping (CPR) 144
Nanryu (Jpn) 445
Nantong (CPR) 144
Nantou (Twn) 797
Nantucket (US) 966
Naos (Pan) 592
Naoshima (Jpn) 431
Naquora (Leb) 482
Narathiwat (Tld) 805
Narcis (Bel) 64
Naresuan (Tld) 802
Narushio (Jpn) 415
Narwhal (US) 967
Naryan-Mar (Rus) 674
Nashak (Ind) 340
Nashville (US) 944
El Nasr (Mtn) 510
Nasr (Pak) 589
El Nasser (Egy) 216
Nasr Al Bahr (Omn) 578
Nassau (Bhm) 45
Nassau (US) 943
Nastoychivy (Rus) 670
Nathanael Maxwilili (Nam) 545
Natsugiri (Jpn) 444
Natsugumo (Jpn) 443
Natsui (Jpn) 441
Natsushio (Jpn) 416
Natsuzuki (Jpn) 443
Naushon (US) 966
Nautilus (Nld) 557
Navajo (US) 956
Navarin (Egy) 221
Navarinon (Gre) 303
Navarra (Spn) 745
Navmachos (Gre) 306
Nawigator (Pol) 624
Naxos (Gre) 308
Nayband (Iran) 379
Nazim (Pak) 590
Neah Bay (US) 969
Nebraska (US) 910
Necko (Pol) 622
Al Neemran (Omn) 578
Negron (Ven) 984
Negros Occidental (Plp) 610
Neiafu (Ton) 820
Nelson (TT) 821
Neocaligus (Can) 112
Neodesha (US) 954
Neon Antonov (Rus) 706
Nepryadava (Rus) 693
Neptun (Rus) 703
Neptuno (Spn) 756
Nereus (Gre) 300

Nerpa (Rus) ... 656
Nerz (Ger) ... 290
Nesbitt (UK) ... 889
Nesebar (Bul) ... 92
Nestor (Gre) ... 311
Nestor Reinoso (Plp) ... 611
Nestos (Gre) ... 311
Netisin (Ukr) ... 854
Netzahualcoyotl (Mex) ... 513
Neukrotimy (Rus) ... 671
Neustrashimy (Rus) ... 672
Neustrelitz (Ger) ... 297
Neva (Rus) ... 701
Nevada (US) ... 910
Nevcivan (Tur) ... 842
Nevelsk (Rus) ... 703
New Hampshire (US) ... 912
New Mexico (US) ... 912
New Orleans (US) ... 942, 947
New York (US) ... 942
Newcastle (Aust) ... 30
Newport News (US) ... 914
Neyba (DR) ... 203
Neyzeh (Iran) ... 373
Ngunguri (Tan) ... 799
Niamh (Ire) ... 382
Nicanor Jimenez (Plp) ... 612
Nichinan (Jpn) ... 432
Nicholas (US) ... 930
Nicobar (Ind) ... 348
Nicolas Bravo (Mex) ... 515
Nicolas Mahusay (Plp) ... 611
Nicolas Suarez (Bol) ... 69
Nicolay Chiker (Rus) ... 697
Niedersachsen (Ger) ... 286
Niels Juel (Den) ... 190, 192
Nieuwediep (Nld) ... 557
Nijigumo (Jpn) ... 443
Niki (Gre) ... 307
Nikiforos (Gre) ... 306
Nikiforos Fokas (Gre) ... 303
Nikolay Filchenkov (Rus) ... 681
Nikolay Kaplunov (Rus) ... 702
Nikolay Matusevich (Rus) ... 685
Nikolay Sipyagin (Rus) ... 706
Nikolay Starshinov (Rus) ... 706
Nikolay Vilkov (Rus) ... 681
Al Nil (Egy) ... 222
Al Nil (SAr) ... 717
Nils Strömcrona (Swe) ... 782
Nimitz (US) ... 917
Nimr (Egy) ... 224
Ning Hai (Twn) ... 792
Ning Yang (Twn) ... 790
Ningbo (CPR) ... 135
Nioi (Ita) ... 410
Nipat (Ind) ... 340
Nirbhik (Ind) ... 340
Nirbhoy (Ban) ... 56
Nirdeshak (Ind) ... 346
Nireekshak (Ind) ... 348
Nirghat (Ind) ... 340
Nirolhu (Mld) ... 507
Nirupak (Ind) ... 346
Nishank (Ind) ... 340
Nisr (Egy) ... 224
Niterói (Brz) ... 75
Nitze (US) ... 926
Nitzhon (Isr) ... 386
Nividic (Fra) ... 273
Nivôse (Fra) ... 258
Nizhny Novgorod (Rus) ... 658
Nizyn (Ukr) ... 856
Njambuur (Sen) ... 718
Njord (Nor) ... 575
N N O Salammbo (Tun) ... 825
Noakhali (Ban) ... 58
Nobaru (Jpn) ... 442
Noguera (Per) ... 604
Nombre de Dios (Pan) ... 594
Nongsarai (Tld) ... 814
Noor (Iran) ... 369
Nordkapp (Nor) ... 574
Nordrhein-Westfalen (Ger) ... 288
Nordsøen (Den) ... 198
Nordstrand (Ger) ... 296
Norfolk (US) ... 914
Norge (Nor) ... 573
Norikura (Jpn) ... 442
Norman (Aust) ... 35
Normandie (Fra) ... 259
Normandy (US) ... 921
Norna (UK) ... 900
Nornen (Nor) ... 575
North Carolina (US) ... 912
North Dakota (US) ... 912
Northland (US) ... 964
Northumberland (UK) ... 878
Noto (Jpn) ... 430, 439
Notojima (Jpn) ... 431
Nottingham (UK) ... 875
Al Nour (Egy) ... 219
Nova Kahovka (Ukr) ... 853
Novi Sad (Mon) ... 528
Novi Sad (Ser) ... 720
Novigrad (Cro) ... 181
Novomoskovsk (Rus) ... 651
Novorossiysk (Rus) ... 702
Novosibirsk (Rus) ... 661
Ntringui (Com) ... 177
Nueva Reqena (Per) ... 607
Nueva Vizcaya (Plp) ... 614
Nuku (Indo) ... 356
Numana (Ita) ... 403
Numancia (Spn) ... 745
Nunki (Mex) ... 520
Nunobiki (Jpn) ... 443
Nur (Egy) ... 224
Nusa (Mly) ... 504
Nusa Utara (Indo) ... 361
Nusrat (Pak) ... 590
Nwamba (Nig) ... 565
Nyayo (Ken) ... 450
Nyireh (Mly) ... 503
Nyköping (Swe) ... 771
Nymphea (Fra) ... 272

O

Oak (US) ... 969
Oak Hill (US) ... 945
Oaxaca (Mex) ... 519
OB 93 (Cro) ... 181
Obion (US) ... 970
Obninsk (Rus) ... 659
Obolon (Ukr) ... 856
PFC Eugene A Obregon (US) ... 961
Observation Island (US) ... 956
Observer (Dom) ... 201
Observer (Mrt) ... 511
Óbuda (Hun) ... 322
Obula (Nig) ... 565
Ocean (UK) ... 884
Oceanic Viking (Aust) ... 41
Ocracoke (US) ... 966
Oddane (Nor) ... 571
Oderbruch (Ger) ... 297
Odessa (Ukr) ... 855
Odet (Fra) ... 276
Ödev (Tur) ... 843
Odinn (Ice) ... 323
Odisseus (Gre) ... 311
Odysseus (Cypr) ... 188
Oecussi (ETim) ... 204
Ogishima (Jpn) ... 431
O'Higgins (Chi) ... 116
Ohio (US) ... 911
Ohue (Nig) ... 566
Oirase (Jpn) ... 442
O'Kane (US) ... 924
Okba (Mor) ... 533
Okeanos (Gre) ... 300
Oker (Ger) ... 293
Oki (Jpn) ... 438
Okinami (Jpn) ... 444
Okishio (Jpn) ... 446
Okitsu (Jpn) ... 441
Oklahoma City (US) ... 914
Oldenburg (Ger) ... 288
Olekma (Rus) ... 691
Olenegorskiy Gorniak (Rus) ... 681
Olev (Est) ... 229
Olfert Fischer (Den) ... 190
Oljevern 01-04 (Nor) ... 572
Ologbo (Nig) ... 565
Oltramonti (Ita) ... 410
Olympia (US) ... 914
Olympias (Gre) ... 309
Omsk (Rus) ... 654
Ona (Arg) ... 21
Ona (Chi) ... 125
Öncü (Tur) ... 843
Önder (Tur) ... 843
Onega (Rus) ... 674
Ongjin (RoK) ... 471
Onisilos (Cypr) ... 187
Onjuku (Mex) ... 524
Oonami (Jpn) ... 421
Oosumi (Jpn) ... 429, 438
Ootaka (Jpn) ... 428
Ooyodo (Jpn) ... 426
Opanez (Rom) ... 644
Opelika (US) ... 954
Opilio (Can) ... 112
Oqbah (SAr) ... 714
Orädd (Swe) ... 774
Orangeleaf (UK) ... 890
Orazio Corsi (Ita) ... 412
Orca (Arg) ... 23
Orca (Can) ... 104
Orcas (US) ... 966
Ordóñez (Spn) ... 749
Orel (Rus) ... 654, 700
Orella (Chi) ... 121
Organabo (Fra) ... 276
Orienburg (Rus) ... 663
Orik (Alb) ... 3
Oriole (Can) ... 104
Orion (Col) ... 176
Orion (DR) ... 202
Orion (Ecu) ... 208
Orion (Fra) ... 266
Orion (Gre) ... 310
Orion (Por) ... 634
Orion (Swe) ... 777
Orion (Swi) ... 783
Orione (Ita) ... 400
Orkan (Pol) ... 620
Orla (Ire) ... 382
Orlan (Rus) ... 702
Ormi (Gre) ... 306
El Oro (Ecu) ... 206
Orompello (Chi) ... 122
Orsa Maggiore (Ita) ... 405
Orsha (Rus) ... 692
Orsk (Rus) ... 681
Ortiz (Chi) ... 121
Orucreis (Tur) ... 830
Oryx (Nam) ... 545
Orzeł (Pol) ... 618
Osage (US) ... 970
Oscar Austin (US) ... 926
Oslyabya (Rus) ... 681
Osman (Ban) ... 54
Osman Gazi (Tur) ... 837
Osprey (Can) ... 111
Osprey (US) ... 967
Oste (Ger) ... 293
Östergötland (Swe) ... 769
Östhammar (Swe) ... 774
Osternes (Nor) ... 571
Ostria (Gre) ... 309
Oswald Siahaan (Indo) ... 354
Oswaldo Cruz (Brz) ... 85
Otago (NZ) ... 560
Otarie (Fra) ... 273
Otomi (Mex) ... 526
Otra (Nor) ... 572
Ottawa (Can) ... 100
Otto Sverdrup (Nor) ... 568
Ottonelli (Ita) ... 410
Ouachita (US) ... 970
Ouha (Kwt) ... 476
Oumi (Jpn) ... 434
Ouranos (Gre) ... 310
Owen (UK) ... 889
Oyarvide (Uru) ... 976
Oyashio (Jpn) ... 415
Ozelot (Ger) ... 290
Özgen (Tur) ... 843
Özgür (Tur) ... 843

P

P 001-002 (Egy) ... 222
P 01 (Mlt) ... 509
P 01-02 (Pak) ... 588
P 03, 05-07 (StL) ... 708
P 04 (Bar) ... 61
P 04-08 (Sur) ... 768
P 6, 13-24, 26-38 (Fra) ... 274
P 010-021 (Sri) ... 765
P 13, 16-17 (Dji) ... 200
P 23-24, 32-33, 51-52, 61 (Mlt) ... 508
P 41 (Bhm) ... 45
P 42-43, 48-49, 110-113 (Bhm) ... 46
P 43-44 (Tan) ... 799
P 63, 084-088, 151-153 (Eri) ... 228
P 101-104 (Eri) ... 227
P 101-104 (Fra) ... 273
P 101-105, 701-702, 203-206 (Iraq) ... 380
P 102-104, 106, 203-207, 209 (Geo) ... 280
P 106-107, 115-118, 119, 120-138, 140-156, 201, 211, 215, 221-224, 250, 252-253, 480-481, 483-485 (Sri) ... 764
P 107 (Par) ... 597
P 107-116 (Mor) ... 535
P 110-113 (Sri) ... 765
P 111, 114 (Spn) ... 749
P 115 (Alb) ... 2
P 201-212 (UAE) ... 861
P 213-215 (Az) ... 42
P 222 (Az) ... 45
P 281-282 (RoK) ... 473
P 313-327 (Nig) ... 565
P 401-406, 440-443, 460, 462, 464-465, 470-475 (Sri) ... 763
P 410-415, 417, 419-424, 430, 432-437, 439, 450-451, 490-492, 494, 497 (Sri) ... 762
P 1022-1031 (Yem) ... 993
PA 01-02 (ElS) ... 226
Pabna (Ban) ... 58
Pacasmayo (Per) ... 606
Pacific Marlin (BIOT) ... 87
Pacu (Arg) ... 23
Padma (Ban) ... 57
Pagaza (Ven) ... 984
LTC John U D Page (US) ... 960
Pahang (Mly) ... 496
Paiño (Spn) ... 760
Paitá (Per) ... 603
Palacios (Per) ... 600
Palan (Ind) ... 348
Palangrin (Fra) ... 271
Palawan (Plp) ... 615
Palikir (Mic) ... 527
Palinuro (Ita) ... 405
Paliya (Rus) ... 701
Palmaria (Ita) ... 407
Palmetto (Ant) ... 10
Palo Alto (US) ... 947
Paluma (Aust) ... 36
Pamir (Rus) ... 697
Pamlico (US) ... 970
Pampanga (Plp) ... 614
Pampeiro (Brz) ... 80
Pan Chao (Twn) ... 788
Panagos (Cypr) ... 187
Panama (Pan) ... 593
Panan (Indo) ... 367
Panana (Indo) ... 360
Panarea (Ita) ... 406
Pancha Carrasco (CR) ... 179
Pandalus III (Can) ... 112
Pandora (Gre) ... 310
Pandrong (Indo) ... 359
Pandrosos (Gre) ... 310
Pangai (Ton) ... 820
Pangan (Tld) ... 812
Pangasinan (Plp) ... 610
Panquiaco (Pan) ... 592
Pansio (Fin) ... 236
Pantelleria (Ita) ... 407
Panter (Nld) ... 558
Pantera (Rus) ... 656
Panthère (Fra) ... 268
Panyu (CPR) ... 150
Paolini (Ita) ... 410
Papanikolis (Gre) ... 301
Pará (Brz) ... 84
Paracas (Per) ... 606
Paradoks (Rus) ... 698
Paraguassú (Brz) ... 85
Paraguay (Par) ... 596
Parang (Indo) ... 367
Parati (Brz) ... 80
Parella (Rus) ... 701
Pari (Mly) ... 499
Park Wi (RoK) ... 459
Parker (Arg) ... 15
Parksville (Can) ... 105
Parnaiba (Brz) ... 79
Paros (Gre) ... 308
Parramatta (Aust) ... 28
Partipilo (Ita) ... 410
Partisan (Den) ... 195
Parvin (Iran) ... 374
Pasadena (US) ... 914
Passat (Rus) ... 678
Passau (Ger) ... 291
PAT 01-15 (Indo) ... 367
Pat Barton (UK) ... 889
Patagonia (Arg) ... 20
Pathfinder (UK) ... 889
Pathfinder (US) ... 957
Pati Unus (Indo) ... 356
Patiño (Spn) ... 755
Patoka (US) ... 970
Patola (Indo) ... 360
Patonga (Aust) ... 40
Patria (Nld) ... 556
Patria (Ven) ... 981
Patriot (US) ... 948
Patrioten (Den) ... 195
Pattani (Tld) ... 805
Patuakhali (Ban) ... 58
Patuca (Hon) ... 318
Patuxent (US) ... 955
Paul Bogle (Jam) ... 413
Paul Buck (US) ... 959
Paul Hamilton (US) ... 924
Paulus Hook (US) ... 947
Paus (Mly) ... 499
Pavel Derzhavin (Ukr) ... 855
Paysandu (Uru) ... 976
Paz Zamora (Bol) ... 68
PB 1-4 (HK) ... 319
PB 211-215 (Ken) ... 450
PC 01-09 (ElS) ... 226
PC 111, 211-216, 302 (Ser) ... 720
PC 114-116 (Jpn) ... 443
PC 201-232 (Sin) ... 732
PC 351-354 (Plp) ... 612
PC 501-503, 505-507 (RoK) ... 474
PC 1001-1003 (RoK) ... 472
PCL 3, 5-9 (Twn) ... 792
PDB 11-15, 63, 68 (Bru) ... 89
Pea Island (US) ... 966
Peacock (Mex) ... 520
Pearl Harbor (US) ... 945
Pechenga (Rus) ... 691
Pecos (US) ... 955
Pedang (Indo) ... 367
Pedro Campbell (Uru) ... 974
Pedro David Salas (Col) ... 176
Pedro Teixeira (Brz) ... 79
Pegas (Rus) ... 685
Pégase (Fra) ... 266
Pégaso (Por) ... 634
Pegasso (Col) ... 176
Pegnitz (Ger) ... 291
Pejerrey (Arg) ... 23
Pejuang (Bru) ... 88
Pelícano (Ven) ... 983
Peleliu (US) ... 943
Pelias (Gre) ... 311
Pelican (US) ... 967
Pelikaan (Nld) ... 556
Pelikan (Tur) ... 835
Pelikanen (Swe) ... 779
Pelluhue (Chi) ... 125
Pemanggil (Mly) ... 503
Pembroke (UK) ... 888
Pemburu (Bru) ... 89
Penac (Can) ... 112
Pendant (US) ... 971
Pendekar (Mly) ... 498
Pendik (Tur) ... 843
Penedo (Brz) ... 80
Penfeld (Fra) ... 276
Pengawal 1-8, 11-12 (Mly) ... 505
Penggalang 1-2 (Mly) ... 504
Penhu (Twn) ... 797
Peninjau (Mly) ... 504
Pennsylvania (US) ... 910
Penobscot Bay (US) ... 969
Penyelamat 1-4 (Mly) ... 504
Penyerang (Bru) ... 89
Penzance (UK) ... 888
Perak (Mly) ... 496, 506
Perantau (Mly) ... 501
Perca (Arg) ... 23
Perdana (Mly) ... 499
Peregrina (Spn) ... 754
Perekop (Rus) ... 689
Peresvet (Rus) ... 681, 697
Perissinotto (Ita) ... 411
Perkasa (Mly) ... 498
Perkons (Lat) ... 480
Perle (Fra) ... 244
Perryville (US) ... 947
Persée (Fra) ... 266
Perseus (Gre) ... 311
Perseus (Swi) ... 783
Perseverancia (Ven) ... 985
Persey (Rus) ... 685
Persistence (Sin) ... 729
Perth (Aust) ... 28
Perwira (Bru) ... 89
Pescarusul (Rom) ... 645
Peter Tordenskiold (Den) ... 190
Peter Willemoes (Den) ... 192
Petersburg (US) ... 961
Petr Gradov (Rus) ... 686
Petrel (Arg) ... 23
Petrel (US) ... 967
Petrel (Ven) ... 983
Petrel I (Spn) ... 760
Petropavlosk Kamchatsky (Rus) ... 652
Peykan (Iran) ... 373
PF 01-06 (ElS) ... 226
PF 305-313 (Col) ... 174
PFC Dewayne T Williams (US) ... 961
PFC Eugene A Obregon (US) ... 961
PFC James Anderson, Jr (US) ... 960
PFR 1-8 (ElS) ... 226
PGM 401-406, 421-423 (Myn) ... 542
PGM 412-415 (Myn) ... 541
Phaéton (Fra) ... 271
Pharuehatsabodi (Tld) ... 814
Phekda (Mex) ... 520
Phetra (Tld) ... 813
Philadelphia (US) ... 914
Philippine Sea (US) ... 921
Phoque (Fra) ... 273
Phosamton (Tld) ... 815
Phraongkamrop (Tld) ... 818
Phromyothee (Tld) ... 817

Phuket (Tld) 810
Phuttha Loetla Naphalai (Tld) 804
Phuttha Yotfa Chulalok (Tld) 804
Piast (Pol) 625
Piccinni Leopardi (Ita) 411
Picharnpholakit (Tld) 818
Pico Del Teide (Spn) 759
Pierre Radisson (Can) 106
Pigargo (Ven) 984
Pigasos (Gre) 305
Pijao (Col) 169
Pike (US) 967
Pikkala (Fin) 240
Pikker (Est) 230
Pilefs (Gre) 311
Pililaau (US) 958
Piloto Pardo (Chi) 125
Pin Klao (Tld) 815
Pinar 2-6 (Tur) 841
Pinckney (US) 926
Pinguino (Arg) 23
Pintar (Mly) 504
Pioneer (UK) 889
Pioneer (US) 948
Piorun (Pol) 620
Pipinos (Gre) 301
Pirai (Guy) 317
Piraim (Brz) 85
Pirajá (Brz) 80
Piratini (Brz) 80
Pirie (Aust) 35
Pisagua (Chi) 124
Pisagua (Per) 599
Pisces (Sey) 721
Pisco (Per) 603
Piton (Indo) 360
Pittsburgh (US) 914
Pivoine (Fra) 272
Pizarro (Spn) 750
PKM 212-375 series (RoK) 468
PL 3 (HK) 319
PL 5-10, 20-21, 40-45, 90-96, (HK) 321
PL 11-17, 22-32, 46-49, 51-56, 60-65, 70-73, 75, 77, 79-80, 82-83, 85-89 (HK) 320
PL 66-69 (Jpn) 439
Planet (Ger) 292
Playa Blanca (Col) 176
Pleias (Gre) 308
Maj Stephen W Pless (US) 961
Plotarchis Blessas (Gre) 305
Plotarchis Maridakis (Gre) 305
Plotarchis Sakipis (Gre) 305
Plotarchis Vlahavas (Gre) 305
Pluton (Fra) 266
Pluton (Rus) 685
Pluvier (Fra) 262
Plymouth (TT) 821
PM 6-8, 10-12 (ElS) 225
PM 10, 15, 30, 56, 59, 63, 64, 69, 82, 86, 97, 138, 140, 156 (Rus) 690
PM 30-36 (Jpn) 442
PM 2031-2045, 2050, 2052-2054 (Chi) 126
Po Chiang (Twn) 791
Po Hang (RoK) 466
Pochetnyy (Rus) 698
Podilliya (Ukr) 855
Podolsk (Rus) 652, 703
Podor (Sen) 718
Poema (Nld) 558
Pohjanmaa (Fin) 236
Point Henry (Can) 110
Point Race (Can) 110
Pokagon (US) 954
Polar (Por) 636
Polar Sea (US) 968
Polar Star (US) 968
Polaris (Mex) 520
Polaris (Ven) 984
Polemistis (Gre) 306
Polifemo (Ita) 408
Pollux (DR) 203
Pollux (Mex) 520
Pollux (Swi) 783
Pollux (US) 962
Poltava (Ukr) 855
Polyarny (Rus) 684
Pomeroy (US) 959
Pompano (US) 967
Ponce (US) 944
Pono (Tan) 800
Ponta Delgada (Por) 633
Pontos (Gre) 300
Ponza (Ita) 407
Popocateptl (Mex) 526
Poponguine (Sen) 718
Pori (Fin) 235
Porkkala (Fin) 236
Porpora (Ita) 405
Port Cros (Fra) 273
Port Hudson (US) 947
Port Royal (US) 921
Porte Grande (Ban) 58
Porter (US) 924
Portete (Col) 177
Portland (UK) 878
Porto Conte (Ita) 409
Porto Corsini (Ita) 409
Porto Empedocle (Ita) 409
Porto Ferraio (Ita) 409
Porto Fossone (Ita) 409
Porto Pisano (Ita) 409
Porto Salvo (Ita) 409
Porto Torres (Ita) 409
Porto Venere (Ita) 409
Portobelo (Pan) 594
Porvoo (Fin) 235
Posada (Rom) 644
Poseidon (Cypr) 188
Poseidon (Gre) 300
Poshak (Ind) 348
Potengi (Brz) 86
Poti (Brz) 80
Pourquoi Pas? (Fra) 267
Povorino (Rus) 674
Poyeni (Per) 607
Poyraz (Tur) 835
Poznan (Pol) 622
PP 2001, 2003, 2005-2010, 2012-2019, 2021-2023, 2025-2033, 2035-2038, 2050-2053, 2055-2056, 2058-2063, 2065-2067, 3002-3003, 3005-3009, 3011-3012, 3015-3019, 3516-3522, 3525, 3527, 3530-3531, 3535-3539, 5033, 5035, 5037-5039, 5050-5053, 6001-6003 (Twn) 798
PP 10001, 10003, 10025-10029 (Twn) 797
PR 001, 005 (Cam) 97
Prab (Tld) 812
Prabal (Ind) 340
Prabparapak (Tld) 809
Pradhayak (Ind) 348
Prairial (Fra) 258
Pralaya (Ind) 340
Príncipe de Asturias (Spn) 742
Prata (Ita) 411
Prathong (Tld) 812
Prathpa (Sri) 762
Preble (US) 926
Predanyy (Rus) 699
Prefecto Derbes (Arg) 22
Prefecto Fique (Arg) 22
Preia-Mar (Por) 637
Premier Maître L'her (Fra) 257
Preserver (Can) 104
President El Hadj Omar Bongo (Gab) 278
President H I Remeliik (Pal) 591
Presidente Eloy Alfaro (Ecu) 206
Prespa (Gre) 310
Preveze (Tur) 828
PRF 301-304, 314-319 (Col) 174
PRF 320-322 (Col) 173
Priazove (Rus) 688
Pribaltika (Rus) 688
Priboy (Bul) 93
Priboy (Rus) 678
Pridneprovye (Ukr) 851
Prignitz (Ger) 297
Priluki (Ukr) 851
Primauguet (Fra) 254
Primera Dama (CR) 179
Primo Longobardo (Ita) 390
Primorye (Rus) 701
Primula (Bel) 64
Prince of Wales (UK) 874
Princeton (US) 921
Priyadarshini (Ind) 351
PRM 01-04 (ElS) 225
Procida (Ita) 407
Procion (DR) 202
Procyón (Mex) 520
Proet (Tld) 816
Prometeo (Ita) 408
Prometheus (Gre) 309
Prong (Tld) 816
Protea (SA) 737
Protecteur (Can) 104
Protector (StL) 708
Protegat (FI) 232
Proteo (Bul) 95
Proteus (Gre) 300
Provence (Fra) 259
Providence (US) 914
Providencia (Col) 175
Provo Wallis (Can) 107
Prut (Rus) 691
Psara (Gre) 302
PSK 382, 405, 673, 1411, 1518 (Rus) 694
PSKA series (Rus) 704
Pskov (Rus) 658, 700
PSKR 52-59 (Rus) 705
PSKR series (Rus) 705
PSKR-631, 641, 657, 659, 660, 665, 690, 700, 714, 715, 717, 718, 723, 725 (Rus) 703
PT 1-19, 21-29, 31-39, 61-67 (Sin) 731
PT 71 (Cro) 184
Pter. Almaz (Rus) 703
Pucusana (Per) 607
Pudeto (Chi) 126
Puebla (Mex) 521
Puelo (Arg) 23
Puerto Buenos Aires (Arg) 24
Puerto Deseado (Arg) 19
Puerto Inca (Per) 607
Puerto Montt (Chi) 125
Puerto Natales (Chi) 125
Puerto Quepos (CR) 179
Pukaki (NZ) 560
Pulai (Mly) 506
Pulau Raas (Indo) 362
Pulau Rangsang (Indo) 362
Pulau Rempang (Indo) 362
Pulau Rengat (Indo) 363
Pulau Rimau (Indo) 362
Pulau Romang (Indo) 362
Pulau Rote (Indo) 362
Pulau Rupat (Indo) 363
Pulau Rusa (Indo) 362
Puleo (Ita) 410
Puma (Ger) 290
Puncher (UK) 883
Punggol (Sin) 730
Puni (Bru) 89
Puno (Per) 605
Punta Alta (Arg) 21
Punta Arenas (Chi) 125
Punta Arenas (Per) 606
Punta Ballena (Ven) 986
Punta Barima (Ven) 986
Punta Brava (Ven) 982
Punta Cardon (Ven) 986
Punta Caxinas (Hon) 319
Punta Macolla (Ven) 985
Punta Macoya (Ven) 986
Punta Macuro (Ven) 986
Punta Malpelo (Per) 603
Punta Mariusa (Ven) 986
Punta Mastun (Mex) 521
Punta Mero (Per) 603
Punta Mogotes (Arg) 18
Punta Moron (Ven) 986
Punta Morro (Mex) 521
Punta Mosquito (Ven) 986
Punta Mulatos (Ven) 986
Punta Perret (Ven) 986
Punta Playa (Ven) 986
Punta Sal (Per) 603
Punta Unare (Ven) 986
Purak (Ind) 348
Puran (Ind) 348
Pursuer (UK) 883
Pusan (RoK) 464, 471
Pushpa (Ind) 348
Puteri Mahsuri (Mly) 501
Putian (CPR) 142
Putlos (Ger) 295
Putsaari (Fin) 240
Putumayo (Per) 603
Putuoshan (CPR) 153
PV 5-10, 30-37 (HK) 321
PVH 1 (Est) 231
PVK 001-003, 006, 008, 010-013, 016-017, 020-021, 025 (Est) 231
Pyhäranta (Fin) 236
Pyi Daw Aye (Myn) 544
Pylky (Rus) 671
Pyong Taek (RoK) 471
Pyotr Velikiy (Rus) 665
Pytheas (Gre) 309
Pytlivy (Rus) 671
PZHK 3, 5, 17, 30-32, 36-37, 41-47, 49, 53-55, 59, 63, 66, 68, 79, 82, 84, 86, 415, 417, 900, 1296, 1378, 1514-1515, 1544-1547, 1560, 1680, 1859, 2055 (Rus) 695
PZHS 64, 92, 96, 98, 123, 273, 282, 309, 551 (Rus) 698

Q

Q 31-36 series (Qat) 639
Qahir Al Amwaj (Omn) 576
Al Qatar (Egy) 219
Qaysan (Sud) 767
Qeshm (Iran) 378
Qiandao Hu (CPR) 160
Al Qiaq (SAr) 715
Qina (Egy) 220
Qingchengshan (CPR) 153
Qingdao (CPR) 138
Qinghai Hu (CPR) 160
Al Qirdabiyah (Lby) 484
Quanza (Por) 633
Quartier Maître Alfred Motto (Cam) 97
Queen Elizabeth (UK) 874
Queen Modjadji I (SA) 734
Queitao (Chi) 125
Querandi (Arg) 21
Quest (Can) 104
Quezon (Plp) 610
Qui Nonh (Vtn) 991
Quilca (Per) 607
Quillen (Arg) 23
Quilotoa (Ecu) 209
Quindio (Col) 176
Quiñónes (Per) 600
Quintero (Chi) 125
Quisquis (Ecu) 209
Quitasueño (Col) 173
Quito (Ecu) 208
Quokka (Aust) 39
Al Quonfetha (SAr) 716
Quorn (UK) 887
Quwwat (Pak) 587
Al Quysumah (SAr) 715

R

R 2, 5, 11, 14, 18, 19, 20, 24, 29, 47, 60, 71, 79, 109, 125, 187, 239, 257, 297, 298 (Rus) 677
R 117-118, 122-128, 215-217, 224-228 (Alb) 3
Raahe (Fin) 235
Rabaul (PNG) 595
Rad (Lby) 485
Rademaker (Brz) 74
Radhwa 1-6, 12, 14-17 (SAr) 716
Radoom (UAE) 859
Raet (Tld) 817
Al Rafa (Egy) 219
Rafael Del Castillo Y Rada (Col) 173
Rafael Pargas (Plp) 611
Rafaqat (Pak) 590
Raffaele Rossetti (Ita) 404
Rahma (Lby) 486
Rahova (Rom) 644
Raider (Bol) 68
Raider (UK) 883
Raif Denktaş (Tur) 846
Rainier (US) 954
Raïs Al Mounastiri (Mor) 534
Rais Ali (Alg) 5
Raïs Bargach (Mor) 534
Raïs Britel (Mor) 534
Raïs Charkaoui (Mor) 534
Rais Hadj Mubarek (Alg) 4
Rais Hamidou (Alg) 5
Rais Kellich (Alg) 4
Rais Korfou (Alg) 4
Raïs Maaninou (Mor) 534
Raizan (Jpn) 442
Rajah Humabon (Plp) 608
Rajaji (Ind) 349
Rajkamal (Ind) 351
Rajkiran (Ind) 351
Rajput (Ind) 331
Rajshahi (Pak) 587
Raju (Fin) 239
Ramadan (Egy) 218
Ramadevi (Ind) 351
Ramage (US) 924
Raminthra (Tld) 818
Ramon Aguirre (Plp) 611
Ramsey (UK) 888
Ramunia (Mly) 504
Rana (Ind) 331
Ranadeera (Sri) 762
Ranagaja (Sri) 765
Ranajaya (Sri) 762
Ranarisi (Sri) 762
Ranavijaya (Sri) 765
Ranawickrama (Sri) 762
Rancagua (Chi) 122
Rang (Tld) 817
Rangamati (Ban) 58
Ranger (UK) 883
Ranger I (StK) 707
Rani Jindan (Ind) 351
Ranjit (Ind) 331
Rankin (Aust) 26
Ranvijay (Ind) 331
Ranvir (Ind) 331
Rapel (Chi) 126
Rapière (Fra) 265
Raposo Tavares (Brz) 79
Rapp (Swe) 774
Rappahannock (US) 955
Ras Ajdir (Tun) 826
Ras Al Fulaijah (Lby) 485
Ras Al Hani (Lby) 485
Ras Al Massad (Lby) 485
Ras Al Qula (Lby) 485
Ras Bougaroni (Alg) 8
Ras Djenad (Alg) 8
Ras El Blais (Tun) 826
Ras El Edrak (Tun) 826
Ras El Hilal (Lby) 486
Ras El Manoura (Tun) 826
Ras Enghela (Tun) 826
Ras Ifrikia (Tun) 826
Ras Nouh (Alg) 8
Ras Oullis (Alg) 8
Ras Sisli (Alg) 8
Ras Tamentfoust (Alg) 8
Ras Tara (Alg) 7
Ras Tekkouch (Alg) 8
Ras Tenes (Alg) 8
Rasalhague (Mex) 520
Rascas (Fra) 273
Rasheed (Egy) 215
El Rassed (Alg) 6
Rassvet (Rus) 678
Ratanakiri (Cmb) 96
Ratcharit (Tld) 809
Ratnagiri (Ind) 346
Rattanakosin (Tld) 806
Rauma (Fin) 235
Rauma (Nor) 572
Raven (Can) 104
Ravnen (Den) 193
Rawi (Tld) 813
Rayo (Spn) 750
Rayyan (Kwt) 477
Razia Sultana (Ind) 351
Razliv (Rus) 678
Razorbill (US) 967
RB 01-03 (Twn) 798
RB 1, 7, 57, 98, 158, 173, 179, 201-202, 217, 239, 262, 265, 296, 314, 327, 360, 362 (Rus) 698
RB 2, 5, 17, 20, 22, 23, 25, 26, 29, 40, 43, 44, 46, 49, 51, 52, 108-109, 136, 167-168, 192, 193, 194, 197, 198, 199, 212, 232, 233, 237, 240, 244, 246, 247, 248, 249, 250, 255, 256, 280,310, 311, 325-326 (Rus) 699
Rbigah (Qat) 639
RCP 2-3, 6, 8-9 (Mly) 500
Rebun (Jpn) 439
Recalada (Arg) 24
Red Cloud (US) 959
Red Viper (Aust) 40
Reef Shark (US) 967
Reform (TT) 823
Regele Ferdinand (Rom) 641
Regge (Nld) 557
Regina (Can) 100
Regina Maria (Rom) 641
Régulus (Mex) 520
Regulus (US) 962
Rehmat (Pak) 590
Reina Sofía (Spn) 745
Reiun (Jpn) 447
Relámpago (Spn) 750
Reliance (Aust) 40
Reliance (US) 953, 964
Remada (Tun) 824
Remora (Arg) 23
Remora (Aust) 37
Renard (Can) 104
Rencong (Indo) 358
Rentap (Mly) 504
Rentz (US) 930
Requin (Alg) 8
Rescue I-II (Bmd) 67
Rescuer (Dom) 201
Rescuer (Mrt) 511
Réséda (Fra) 276
Reshitelni (Bul) 91
Resilience (Sin) 727
Resko (Pol) 622
Resolute (Can) 105
Resolute (US) 964
Resolution (NZ) 561
Resolution (Sin) 729
Retriever (Mrt) 511
Reuben James (US) 930
Revi (Fra) 270
Rey Juan Carlos I (Spn) 752

RG 91-94 (Qat) 639
Rhein (Ger) 293
Rheinland-Pfalz (Ger) 286
Rhode Island (US) 910
Rhoen (Ger) 297
Rhön (Ger) 294, 297
Rhu (Mly) 504
Richard E Byrd (US) 954
Richard G Matthiesen (US) 959
Richmond (UK) 878
W E Ricker (Can) 112
Ridley (US) 967
Al Riffa (Bhr) 49
Rigel (Ecu) 208
Rigel (Mex) 520
Rigel (Spn) 753
Rigel (Ven) 984
Rimini (Ita) 403
Rin (Tld) 817
Rindunica (Rom) 646
Ringen (Den) 194
Rio Adaja (Spn) 758
Rio Alfambra (Spn) 758
Rio Almanzora (Spn) 758
Rio Andarax (Spn) 758
Rio Apure II (Ven) 986
Rio Ara (Spn) 758
Rio Arauca II (Ven) 986
Rio Arba (Spn) 758
Rio Babahoyo (Ecu) 211
Rio Bulu Bulu (Ecu) 212
Rio Bernesga (Spn) 758
Rio Cabriel (Spn) 758
Rio Cañar (Ecu) 212
Río Cañete (Per) 607
Rio Catamayo (Ecu) 212
Rio Catatumbo II (Ven) 986
Rio Caudal (Spn) 758
Rio Cedenta (Spn) 758
Rio Cervantes (Spn) 758
Rio Cervera (Spn) 758
Rio Chambira (Per) 607
Rio Chira (Per) 606
Rio Chone (Ecu) 211
Rio Coangos (Ecu) 212
Rio Coco (Hon) 318
Rio Daule (Ecu) 211
Rio de Janeiro (Brz) 81
Rio de La Plata (Arg) 22
Rio Deseado (Arg) 22
Rio Duero (Spn) 758
Rio Esmeraldas (Ecu) 210
Rio Francoli (Spn) 758
Rio Gallo (Spn) 758
Rio Guadalaviar (Spn) 758
Rio Guadalentin (Spn) 759
Rio Guadalobon (Spn) 758
Rio Guadalope (Spn) 758
Rio Guadalquivir (Spn) 759
Rio Guadiana (Spn) 758
Rio Guadiaro (Spn) 758
Rio Guaporé (Bol) 68
Rio Guarico II (Ven) 986
Rio Hondo (Mex) 524
Río Huallaga (Per) 607
Rio Huarmey (Per) 606
Rio Icabaru (Ven) 986
Rio Ilave (Per) 607
Rio Itaya (Per) 607
Rio Jiloca (Spn) 758
Rio Jubones (Ecu) 212
Rio Jucar (Spn) 758
Rio Ladra (Spn) 758
Rio Lujan (Arg) 22
Río Lurin (Per) 607
Rio Macara (Ecu) 212
Río Majes (Per) 607
Rio Manta (Ecu) 212
Rio Martin (Spn) 758
Rio Matador (Per) 607
Rio Mataje (Ecu) 211
Rio Meta II (Ven) 986
Rio Minho (Por) 634
Rio Miño (Spn) 759
Rio Muisne (Ecu) 212
Rio Nalon (Spn) 758
Río Nanay (Per) 607
Rio Napo (Ecu) 209
Rio Napo (Per) 607
Rio Negro (Uru) 975
Rio Negro II (Ven) 986
Rio Nepeña (Per) 606
Rio Nervion (Spn) 758
Rio Ocoña (Per) 606
Rio Palma (Spn) 758
Rio Palora (Ecu) 212
Rio Papaloapan (Mex) 523
Rio Paraguay (Arg) 22
Rio Parana (Arg) 22
Rio Pas (Spn) 759
Rio Patayacu (Per) 607
Rio Pisuerga (Spn) 758
Rio Piura (Per) 606
Rio Portoviejo (Ecu) 212
Rio Portuguesa II (Ven) 986
Río Putumayo (Per) 607
Rio Puyango (Ecu) 211
Rio Puyo (Ecu) 212
Rio Quequen (Arg) 22
Rio Quinindé (Ecu) 212
Rio Ramis (Per) 607
Rio San Miguel (Ecu) 212
Río Santa (Per) 607
Rio Santa Eulalia (Spn) 758
Rio Santiago (Arg) 18
Rio Santiago (Ecu) 210
Río Santiago (Per) 607
Rio Sarare (Ven) 986
Rio Sinaruco (Ven) 986
Rio Suchiate (Mex) 523
Rio Tambo (Per) 606
Rio Tambopata (Per) 607
Rio Tangare (Ecu) 212
Rio Tena (Ecu) 212
Rio Tordera (Spn) 759
Rio Tuxpan (Mex) 524
Rio Ulla (Spn) 758
Rio Uribante (Ven) 986
Rio Uruguay (Arg) 22
Rio Verde (Ecu) 212
Río Viru (Per) 607
Rio Yaguachi (Ecu) 212
Rio Yaracuy (Ven) 986
Rio Yavari (Per) 607
Rio Zamora (Ecu) 212
Rio Zaña (Per) 606
Rio Zapote (Per) 607
Rio Zarumilla (Ecu) 211
Riohacha (Col) 172
Riquelme (Chi) 121
Al Riyadh (SAr) 710, 716
Rizal (Plp) 610
Rizo (Mex) 523
Ro (Gre) 312
Roald Amundsen (Nor) 568
Roanoke Island (US) 966
Roatan (Hon) 318
Robaldo (Arg) 23
Robert E Peary (US) 954
Robert G Bradley (US) 930
Robinson (Arg) 15
Robinson Crusoe (Chi) 126
Roca (Arg) 23
Rocca (Ita) 411
Rodney M Davis (US) 930
Rodos (Gre) 307
Rodqm (UAE) 860
Roebuck (UK) 889
Roebuck Bay (Aust) 41
Roger De Lauria (Spn) 744
Roger Revelle (US) 950
Roisin (Ire) 382
Romaleos (Gre) 311
Romat (Isr) 385
Romblon (Plp) 614, 615
Romzuald Muklevitch (Rus) 685
Ronald Reagan (US) 917
Rondônia (Brz) 79
Roosevelt (US) 926
Roraima (Brz) 79
Rosales (Arg) 15
Rosati (Ita) 410
Ross (US) 924
Rossi (Ita) 411
Rostani (Iran) 379
Rotoiti (NZ) 560
Rotte (Nld) 557
Rotterdam (Nld) 552
Rottweil (Ger) 292
Rouget (Fra) 273
Rover I (StK) 708
Rover II (StK) 708
Rovine (Rom) 644
RP 101-106, 108-116, 118-134 (Ita) 409
RPC 11-19 (Myn) 542
RPL 60-63 (Sin) 728
RT 57, 210, 231, 233, 248, 249, 252, 273, 341 (Rus) 684
Rubis (Fra) 244
Rubodh (Bhr) 50
Rudyard Lewis (Bar) 61
Al Ruha (Lby) 485
Rumbek (Sud) 767
Rumbia (Mly) 503
Runnymede (US) 947
Ruposhi Bangla (Ban) 57
Rupsha (Ban) 60
Rush (US) 963
Rushmore (US) 945
Rūsiņš (Lat) 480
Russell (US) 924
Rüzgar (Tur) 835
RV-37, 113, 150 (Fin) 241
RV 50 (Nld) 557
RVK Series (Rus) 694
Ryazan (Rus) 652
Ryba (Rus) 702
Ryukyu (Jpn) 438
Ryusei (Jpn) 445

S

S 005-006, 11-12, 703 (Az) 44
S 008 (Az) 45
S 14 (Az) 45
S 81-84 (Spn) 740
S A Agulhas (SA) 737
Saad (Kwt) 477
Saad (Pak) 583
Sab Sahel (Iran) 378
Saba Al Bahr (Omn) 578
Sabac (Ser) 721
Sabahan (Mly) 505
Sabalan (Iran) 371
Sabalo (Arg) 23
Sábalo (Ven) 979
Saban (Myn) 544
Sabha (Bhr) 47
Sabhur 7 (Omn) 581
Sabik (Mex) 520
Sabotøren (Den) 195
Sabre (Fra) 265
Sabre (UK) 883
Sacagawea (US) 954
Sachsen (Ger) 287
Sacre (Spn) 760
Sadaqat (Pak) 590
Sadd (Pak) 591
Sadh (Omn) 578
Sadko (Rus) 697
Saettia (Ita) 412
Safaga (Egy) 221
Safeguard (US) 955
Saffar (Kwt) 478
Safra 2-3 (Bhr) 51
Safwa (SAr) 715
São Paulo (Brz) 72
Sagar (Ban) 58
Sagar (Ind) 350
Sagar (UAE) 860
Sagara (Sri) 765
Sagardhwani (Ind) 346
Saginaw (US) 970
Sagitario (Por) 634
Sagittaire (Fra) 266
Sagres (Por) 635
Sagu (Myn) 541
Saham 1-3 (Bhr) 52
El Saher (Alg) 6
Şahin (Tur) 835
Sahyadri (Ind) 335
Saiburi (Tld) 803
Al Said (Omn) 579
Saif (Pak) 586, 591
Saif 1-10 (Bhr) 51
Saikai (Jor) 447
Saikat (Ban) 58
Sailfish (Sin) 731
Sailfish (US) 967
Saint Petersburg (Rus) 660
Saire (Fra) 273
Saittra (Myn) 540
Sakala (Est) 229
Sakarya (Tur) 828
Sakhalin (Rus) 701
Saku (Fij) 233
Sakushima (Jpn) 431
Salah Rais (Alg) 5
Salak (Sud) 767
Salam (Ban) 57
Al Salam (Egy) 219
Salamaua (PNG) 595
Salamis (Cypr) 187
Salamis (Gre) 302
CTCIM Jorge Moreno Salazar (Col) 172
Saldiray (Tur) 829
Salema (Spn) 758
Salerno (Ita) 411
Salihreis (Tur) 830
Salina (Ita) 406
Salinas (Chi) 121
Salinas (Per) 606
Salmon (Arg) 23
Salone (Ita) 410
Şalopa 11-12, 18, 22-24, 27, 30-33 (Tur) 842
Salta (Arg) 12
Saltholm (Den) 194
Salthorse (Aust) 37
Salvador Abcede (Plp) 611
Salvatore Pelosi (Ita) 390
Salvatore Todaro (Ita) 389
Salvor (US) 955
Sálvora (Spn) 754
Salwa (SAr) 717
SAM 01-02, 04, 06-07 (Swe) 776
SAM 01-06 (Jpn) 431
Sama (Per) 606
Samaesan (Tld) 817
Samanco (Per) 606
Samar (Ind) 350
Samara (Rus) 656
Samba (Yem) 994
Sambongho (RoK) 474
Sambro (Can) 111
Sambu (Indo) 365
Samed (Tld) 816
Samidare (Jpn) 422
Samos (Gre) 307
Sampson (US) 926
Samrat (Ind) 350
Samudra Paharedar (Ind) 350
Samudra Pavak (Ind) 350
Samudra Prahari (Ind) 350
Samudura (Sri) 761
Samuel B Roberts (US) 930
Samuel L Cobb (US) 959
Samuel Risley (Can) 107
Samui (Tld) 816
Samum (Rus) 676
San Alejandro (Per) 607
San Andres (Col) 172
San Andres (Mex) 525
San Antonio (Chi) 125
San Antonio (US) 942
San Diego (US) 942
San Francisco (US) 914
San Giorgio (Ita) 402
San Giusto (Ita) 402
San Ignacio (Mex) 525
San Jacinto (US) 921
San Jose (US) 954
San Juan (Arg) 11
San Juan (Plp) 614
San Juan (US) 914
San Lorenzo (Per) 604
San Marco (Ita) 402
San Martin (Arg) 23
San Nicolas (Per) 606
Sanbe (Jpn) 442
Al Sanbouk (Kwt) 475
Sanca (Indo) 360
Sanchez Carrión (Per) 602
Sandbar Shark (Sin) 730
Sandhayak (Ind) 346
Sangamon (US) 970
Sangay (Ecu) 209
Sanges (Ita) 411
Sangitan (Mly) 505
Sangram (Ind) 350
Sangu (Ban) 55
Sanibel (US) 966
Sankalp (Ind) 350
Sanket (Ban) 59
Sanming (CPR) 142
Sanna (Ita) 410
Santa Cruz (Arg) 11
Santa Cruz De La Sierra (Bol) 68
Santa Fe (US) 914
Santa María (Spn) 745
Santa Rosa (Per) 606
Santamaria (CR) 179
Santaquin (US) 954
Santillana (Per) 602
Santos Degollado (Mex) 520
SAP 1-11 (Gre) 307
Sapanca (Tur) 839
Sapelo (US) 966
Saphir (Fra) 244
Sapri (Ita) 403
Saqa (Fij) 233
SAR 1-2 (Den) 195
SAR 12-14, 17-19, 511, 515-516, 520 (Gre) 313
Sarafand (Leb) 482
Sarandi (Arg) 12
Sarang (Ind) 350
Saratov (Rus) 681
Sarbsko (Pol) 622
Sardasht (Iran) 378
Sariyer (Tur) 839
Sarojini Naidu (Ind) 351
Saroma (Jpn) 442
Saros (Tur) 839
Sarov (Rus) 662
Sarucabey (Tur) 837
Sarvekshak (Ind) 346
Sarych (Rus) 702
Saskatoon (Can) 103
Satakut (Tld) 812
Satang (Mly) 503
Satauma (Jpn) 438
Satpura (Ind) 335
Sattahip (Tld) 810
Saturn (Rus) 698
Saturn (Swi) 783
Saturn (US) 955
Saturno (Ita) 408
Saule (Lat) 481
Save (Por) 633
Savea (Ton) 820
Savitri (Ind) 344
Savitri Bai Phule (Ind) 351
Sawagiri (Jpn) 423
Sawahil (Kwt) 479
Sawakaze (Jpn) 425
Sawayuki (Jpn) 424
Sawfish (US) 967
Sayany (Rus) 693
Sayura (Sri) 761
Sazanami (Jpn) 421
SB 5 (Rus) 698
SB 36 (Rus) 698
SB 406 (Rus) 698
SB 521-523 (Rus) 698
SB 931 (Rus) 698
Sbeitla (Tun) 826
Scarpe (Fra) 276
Sceptre (UK) 867
Schambyl (Kaz) 449
Scharhörn (Ger) 296
Schedar (Mex) 520
Schelde (Nld) 557
Schiedam (Nld) 554
Schlei (Ger) 291
Schleswig-Holstein (Ger) 284
School Shark (Sin) 730
Schultz Xavier (Por) 636
Schwedeneck (Ger) 292
Schwedt (Ger) 297
Schwimmdock 3 (Ger) 295
Scimitar (UK) 883
Scioto (US) 970
Sciré (Ita) 389
Scirocco (Ita) 396
Scott (UK) 888
Scout (US) 948
Scranton (US) 914
Sculpin (Can) 105
SD 13 (Pol) 625
SD Adamant (UK) 896
SD Adept (UK) 895
SD Atlas (UK) 895
SD Bountiful (UK) 897
SD Bovisand (UK) 896
SD Bustler (UK) 895
SD Capable (UK) 895
SD Careful (UK) 895
SD Catherine (UK) 899
SD Cawsand (UK) 896
SD Christina (UK) 898
SD Clyde Racer (UK) 899
SD Clyde Spirit (UK) 898
SD Colonel Templer (UK) 894
SD Deborah (UK) 898
SD Dependable (UK) 897
SD Dexterous (UK) 895
SD Eileen (UK) 898
SD Emily (UK) 899
SD Eva (UK) 898
SD Faithful (UK) 895
SD Florence (UK) 895
SD Forceful (UK) 895
SD Frances (UK) 895
SD Genevieve (UK) 895
SD Helen (UK) 895
SD Hercules (UK) 898
SD Husky (UK) 895
SD Impetus (UK) 896
SD Impulse (UK) 896
SD Independent (UK) 898
SD Indulgent (UK) 898
SD Jupiter (UK) 898
SD Kitty (UK) 895
SD Lesley (UK) 895
SD Mars (UK) 898
SD Melton (UK) 897
SD Menai (UK) 897
SD Meon (UK) 897
SD Moorfowl (UK) 894
SD Moorhen (UK) 894
SD Navigator (UK) 899
SD Netley (UK) 897
SD Newhaven (UK) 897
SD Newton (UK) 893
SD Nimble (UK) 895
SD Norton (UK) 897
SD Nutbourne (UK) 897
SD Oban (UK) 897
SD Omagh (UK) 897
SD Oronsay (UK) 897
SD Padstow (UK) 897
SD Penryn (UK) 899
SD Powerful (UK) 895
SD Raasay (UK) 899
SD Reliable (UK) 897
SD Resourceful (UK) 897

SD Salmaid (UK) 894
SD Sheepdog (UK) 895
SD Solent Racer (UK) 899
SD Solent Spirit (UK) 898
SD Spaniel (UK) 895
SD Suzanne (UK) 898
SD Tamar Racer (UK) 899
SD Tamar Spirit (UK) 898
SD Tilly (UK) 899
SD Tormentor (UK) 894
SD Tornado (UK) 894
SD Tremendous (UK) 898
SD Triumphant (UK) 898
SD Victoria (UK) 897
SD Warden (UK) 895
SD Waterman (UK) 894
Sea Devil (US) 967
Sea Dog (US) 967
Sea Dragon (Aust) 40
Sea Dragon (US) 967
Sea Fighter (US) 949
Sea Fox (US) 967
Sea Horse (US) 967
Sea Jet (US) 949
Sea Lion (US) 967
Sea Otter (US) 967
Sea Witch (Aust) 40
Seadler (Ger) 297
Seahawk (US) 967
Seahorse Chuditch (Aust) 39
Seahorse Horizon (Aust) 38
Seahorse Mercator (Aust) 37
Seahorse Quenda (Aust) 39
Seahorse Spirit (Aust) 38
Seahorse Standard (Aust) 38
Seal (Aust) 39
Seawolf (US) 913
Seay (US) 958
Sebak (Ban) 60
Sebo (Gha) 299
Sebou (Mor) 537
Sechelt (Can) 105
Seeadler (PNG) 595
Seeb (Omn) 578
Seefalke (Ger) 297
Seehund 1-18 (Ger) 292
Sefid-Rud (Iran) 380
Segama (Mly) 505
Segantang (Mly) 503
Segei Osipov (Rus) 691
Segura (Spn) 753
Seinda (Myn) 541
Seiun (Jpn) 447
Sejeri (Col) 177
Sejong Daewang (RoK) 461
Sekiun (Jpn) 447
Selangor (Mly) 496
Seleuta (Tun) 826
Selis (Lit) 488
Sella (Spn) 753
Sembilang (Mly) 504
Sempadi (Mly) 503
Sendai (Jpn) 426, 441
Seneca (US) 964
Sénégal II (Sen) 718
Senezh (Rus) 685
Senja (Nor) 574
Sentinella (Ita) 401
Sentry (US) 948
Seongin Bong (RoK) 468
Seoul (RoK) 464
Sęp (Pol) 617
Sequoia (US) 969
Serang (Mly) 499
Serasa (Bru) 89
Serasan (Mly) 504
Serdar (Tur) 837
Serdity (Rus) 698
Sergei Kolbassev (Rus) 684
Sergey Sudetsky (Rus) 706
Seri (Mex) 526
Serifos (Gre) 308
Serrano (Chi) 121
Serreta (Ven) 984
Serviola (Spn) 748
Seteria (Bru) 88
Sethya (Myn) 544
Setia (Mly) 504
Setia Sekal (Mly) 502
Setogiri (Jpn) 423, 444
Setoshio (Jpn) 415
Setoyuki (Jpn) 424
Settsu (Jpn) 438
Setun (Rus) 693
Setyahat (Myn) 544
Sevastopol (Rus) 660
Sever (Rus) 685
Severn (UK) 883
Severodvinsk (Rus) 653
Severomorsk (Rus) 669
Severstal (Rus) 650
Sévre (Fra) 276
Sfinge (Ita) 398
SFP 173, 240, 286, 295, 542, 562 (Rus) 686
SG 1-21, 71-74, 101-109, 113-114, 118-119, 301-311 (Tur) 845
SG 036, 213-216 (Pol) 627
SG 41, 50-58 (Tur) 846
SG 061-066, 411-412 (Pol) 628
SG 80-91, 121-134, 61-70 (Tur) 844
SG-002-008, 142, 144-146, 150, 152, 211-212 (Pol) 627
SG-311-312 (Pol) 626
SGT Matej Kocak (US) 961
SGT William R Button (US) 961
Shabab Oman (Omn) 578
Shabhaz (Pak) 591
Shackle (US) 971
Shafak (Lby) 485
Shah Amanat (Ban) 60
Shah Makhdum (Ban) 60
Shah Poran (Ban) 60
Shahayak (Ban) 59
Al Shaheed (Kwt) 477
Shaheed Aktheruddin (Ban) 56
Shaheed Daulat (Ban) 56
Shaheed Farid (Ban) 56
Shaheed Mohibullah (Ban) 56
Shaheed Ruhul Amin (Ban) 55
Shaheen (UAE) 860
Shahid Absalan (Iran) 373
Shahid Dara (Iran) 373
Shahid Golzam (Iran) 373
Shahid Hejat Zadeh (Iran) 373
Shahid Kord (Iran) 373
Shahid Marjani (Iran) 378
Shahid Mehdavi (Iran) 373
Shahid Rahisi Raisi (Iran) 373
Shahid Sahrabi (Iran) 373
Shahid Shafihi (Iran) 373
Shahid Towsali (Iran) 373
Shahjahan (Pak) 584
Shahjalal (Ban) 59
Shaibal (Ban) 58
Shakhter (Rus) 698
Shakthi (Sri) 765
Shaladein (Egy) 222
Shalki (Ind) 327
Shamal (US) 967
Shambu Singh (Ind) 349
Shamook (Can) 112
Shamsheer (Pak) 586
Shamshir (Iran) 373
Shankul (Ind) 327
Shankush (Ind) 327
Shantou (CPR) 144
Shaoguan (CPR) 144
Shapla (Ban) 58
Shaqra (SAr) 715
Sharabh (Ind) 345
Sharada (Ind) 344
Shardul (Ind) 345
Shark (Aust) 39
Sharm El Sheikh (Egy) 214
Al Sharqiyah (Omn) 577
Shasta (US) 955
Shaula (DR) 203
Shaula (Mex) 520
Shawinigan (Can) 103
Shearwater (US) 967
Sheean (Aust) 26
Shehab (Lby) 485
Shengshan (CPR) 154
Shenyang (CPR) 134
Shenzhen (CPR) 137
Shepparton (Aust) 36
Sherman (US) 963
Shetgang (Ban) 58
Shi Lang (CPR) 134
Shibsha (Ban) 60
Shichang (CPR) 159
Shijiazhuang (CPR) 134
Shikinami (Jpn) 444
Shikine (Jpn) 439
Shikishima (Jpn) 437
Shiloh (US) 921
Shimagiri (Jpn) 444
Shimakaze (Jpn) 420
Shimanami (Jpn) 443
Shimayuki (Jpn) 433
Shimokita (Jpn) 429, 439
Shinas (Omn) 578, 579
Shinonome (Jpn) 444
Shinzan (Jpn) 442
Shippingport (US) 953
Shiraito (Jpn) 445
Shirakami (Jpn) 441
Shirane (Jpn) 425
Shirase (Jpn) 436
Shirataka (Jpn) 428
Shirayuki (Jpn) 424
Shiretoko (Jpn) 439
Shishijima (Jpn) 431
Shishumar (Ind) 327
Shiu Hai (Twn) 792
Shivalik (Ind) 335
Shizuki (Jpn) 442
Shkiper Gyek (Rus) 701
Shkval (Bul) 93
Shkval (Rus) 705, 706
Shoalhaven (Aust) 40
Shoreham (UK) 888
Shoryu (Jpn) 445
Shostka (Ukr) 854
Shouaiai (Lby) 485
Shoula (Lby) 485
Shoup (US) 926
Shoyo (Jpn) 445
Shrike (US) 967
Shtorm (Bul) 93
Shtyl (Rus) 678
Shughart (US) 958
Shujaa (Ken) 450
Shujaat (Pak) 587
Shulyavka (Ukr) 854
Shun Hu 1 (Twn) 796
Shun Hu 2 (Twn) 796
Shun Hu 3 (Twn) 796
Shun Hu 5 (Twn) 797
Shun Hu 6 (Twn) 797
Shunde (CPR) 150
Shupavu (Ken) 450
Shwepazun (Myn) 544
Shwethida (Myn) 541
Shyri (Ecu) 205
Si Ning (Twn) 789
Si Racha (Tld) 809
Siada (Indo) 359
Siakap (Mly) 504
Siamil (Mly) 503
Siangin (Mly) 504
Sibarau (Indo) 359
Sibbald (Chi) 121
Šibenik (Cro) 181
Sibilla (Ita) 398
Sibiriyakov (Rus) 685
Sichang (Tld) 812
Sicié (Fra) 273
Al Siddiq (Egy) 220
Al Siddiq (SAr) 714
Sidi Bou Said (Tun) 825
Sidi Daoud (Tun) 825
Sidi Mohammed Ben Abdallah (Mor) 535
Sidon (Leb) 482
Siegburg (Ger) 291
Sigacik (Tur) 839
Sigalu (Indo) 359
Sigurot (Indo) 359
Sikanni (Can) 105
Siktivkar (Rus) 703
Sikuda (Indo) 359
Silas Papare (Indo) 356
Silea (Indo) 359
Silifke (Tur) 839
Siliman (Indo) 359
Silver Marlin (Sin) 731
Simón Bolívar (Ven) 983
Simeoforos Kavaloudis (Gre) 305
Simeoforos Simitzopoulos (Gre) 305
Simeoforos Starakis (Gre) 305
Simeoforos Xenos (Gre) 305
Simeon Castro (Plp) 611
Simferopol (Ukr) 853
Similan (Tld) 815
Simpson (Chi) 117
Simpson (US) 930
Şimşek (Tur) 835
Sin Hung (RoK) 466
Sinai (Egy) 221
Sindhudhvaj (Ind) 326
Sindhughosh (Ind) 326
Sindhukesari (Ind) 326
Sindhukirti (Ind) 326
Sindhuraj (Ind) 326
Sindhurakshak (Ind) 326
Sindhuratna (Ind) 326
Sindhushastra (Ind) 326
Sindhuvijay (Ind) 326
Sindhuvir (Ind) 326
Sines (Por) 633
Singa (Indo) 359
Sinmin (Myn) 541
Sioux (US) 956
Sipa (Mon) 530
Sipadan (Mly) 503
Siping (CPR) 147
Sipu Muin (Can) 112
Siput (Mly) 502
Sir Milton (SL) 722
Sir Wilfred Grenfell (Can) 108
Sir Wilfrid Laurier (Can) 107
Sir William Alexander (Can) 107
Sir William Roe (UK) 894
Siri (Nig) 565
Siribua (Indo) 359
Sirik (Iran) 379
Sirio (Ita) 400
Sirius (Aust) 38
Sirius (Brz) 83
Sirius (Bul) 93
Sirius (Col) 176
Sirius (DR) 202
Sirius (Mex) 520
Sirius (Swi) 783
Sirius (Uru) 977
Sirius (Ven) 984
Sirjan (Iran) 379
Sirocco (US) 937
Siroco (Fra) 264
Siroco (Spn) 741
Sisargas (Spn) 754
Sisler (US) 959
Sisola (Rus) 692
Sitkinak (US) 966
Sivas (Ukr) 856
Siyan (Yem) 993
Siyay (Can) 112
SKA 12-14, 16 (Den) 196
Skaden (Den) 193
Skadovsk (Ukr) 851
Skaftö (Swe) 777
Skalvis (Lit) 488
Skenandoa (US) 954
Skipjack (US) 967
Skjold (Nor) 570
Skrolsvik (Nor) 571
Skua (Can) 111
Skudd (Nor) 570
Skvyra (Ukr) 854
Slamet Riyadi (Indo) 354
Slavutich (Ukr) 854
Sledge (US) 971
Sleipner (Den) 198
Sleipner (Nor) 573
Sleipner (Swe) 778
Slice (US) 953
Slotterøy (Nor) 571
MG Robert Smalls (US) 947
Smalto (Ita) 410
Smardan (Rom) 644
Smeli (Bul) 90
Smelyy (Rus) 699
Smerch (Bul) 92
Smerch (Rus) 678
Smetlivy (Rus) 667
Smila (Ukr) 853
Smilax (US) 971
Smit Cerne (UK) 896
Smit Cymyran (UK) 896
Smit Dart (UK) 896
Smit Dee (UK) 896
Smit Don (UK) 896
Smit Frome (UK) 896
Smit Merrion (UK) 896
Smit Neyland (UK) 896
Smit Penally (UK) 896
Smit Romney (UK) 896
Smit Rother (UK) 896
Smit Spey (UK) 896
Smit Stour (UK) 896
Smit Tamar (UK) 896
Smit Towy (UK) 896
Smit Wey (UK) 896
Smit Yare (UK) 896
Smiter (UK) 883
F C G Smith (Can) 112
Smolensk (Rus) 654
Smolny (Rus) 689
SN 109, 126, 128, 401, 1318, 1520 (Rus) 694
Snellius (Nld) 554
Snezhnogorsk (Rus) 659
Sneznogorsk (Rus) 674
Sniardwy (Pol) 623
Sobat (Sud) 767
Sochi (Rus) 703
Sockeye (US) 967
Soderman (US) 959
Södermanland (Swe) 769
Sögüt (Tur) 841
Sohag (Egy) 220
Sohn Won-Il (RoK) 460
Sok Cho (RoK) 466
Sokal (Ukr) 854
Sökaren (Swe) 777
Sokhumi (Geo) 279
Sokól (Pol) 617
Sokol (Rus) 702, 703
Sokullu Mehmet Paşa (Tur) 840
Søløven (Den) 193
Šolta (Cro) 181
Somerset (UK) 878
Somerset (US) 942
Gen Brehon B Somervell (US) 947
Somme (Fra) 269
Söndüren 1-4 (Tur) 843
Song Nam (RoK) 466
Songkhla (Tld) 810
Songshan (CPR) 154
Sonora (Mex) 519
Soobrazitelny (Rus) 673
Sooke (Can) 105
Sooke Post (Can) 110
Soputan (Indo) 366
Sorachi (Jpn) 441
Sorocaima (Ven) 983
Sorokos (Gre) 309
Sorong (Indo) 365
Soroo (Iran) 379
Sortland (Nor) 574
Sosha (Rus) 692
Sotong (Mly) 502
Sottile (Ita) 410
Soummam (Alg) 7
Al Soumood (Kwt) 478
Sour (Leb) 483
Souryu (Jpn) 415
South Cotabato (Plp) 612
Sovereignty (Sin) 727
Sovershenny (Rus) 673
Sovetskaya Gavani (Rus) 674
Sovetskiy Pogranichnik (Rus) 706
Søviknes (Nor) 571
Soya (Jpn) 438
Sozopol (Bul) 92
Sp/4 James A Loux (US) 947
Spar (US) 969
Spari (Sur) 767
Spårö (Swe) 777
Spearfish (Sin) 731
Speditøren (Den) 194
Spencer (US) 964
Spessart (Ger) 294
Spetsai (Gre) 302
Spica (Ita) 401
Spica (Mex) 520
Spiekeroog (Ger) 296
Spiggen II (Swe) 768
Spikefish (Sin) 731
Spindrift (Can) 111
Spioenkop (SA) 735
Spiro (Arg) 15
Spray (Can) 111
Spreewald (Ger) 297
Springfield (US) 914
Spruance (US) 926
Sprut (Rus) 701
Sputnik (Rus) 698
Squall (US) 937
Squitieri (Ita) 410
SR 26, 111, 179-180, 188, 203, 233, 267, 280, 334, 370, 455 (Rus) 695
SR 28, 74, 120, 137, 216, 245, 478, 479, 541, 548, 569, 570, 936, 938, 939 (Rus) 696
Sri Gaya (Mly) 500
Sri Indera Sakti (Mly) 500
Sri Inderapura (Mly) 499
Sri Johor (Mly) 499
Sri Perlis (Mly) 499
Sri Tiga (Mly) 500
Srinakarin (Tld) 817
Sriyanont (Tld) 818
SRV 300 (Ita) 406
SS 51-77 (Jpn) 444
SS 503-505 (Jpn) 415
SS 750 (Rus) 693
SSCIM Senen Alberto Arango (Col) 172
SSGT Edward A Carter (US) 960
SSGT Robert T Kuroda (US) 947
SSIM Julio Correa Hernández (Col) 177
SSIM Manuel A Moyar (Col) 177
St Albans (UK) 878
St John's (Can) 100
St Lykoudis (Gre) 311
St Ursula (VI) 992
Stålbas (Nor) 573
Staffetta (Ita) 401
Stalwart (StK) 707
Stalwart (Sin) 725
Stangnes (Nor) 571
Stanisci (Ita) 410
Stapa (Mly) 504
Starace (Ita) 411
Staten Island (US) 966
Stavropol (Rus) 703
Steadfast (Sin) 725
Steadfast (US) 964
Steelhead (US) 967
Steil (Nor) 570

Stella Polare (Ita) 405
Stelyak (Rus) 674
Stephen W Groves (US) 930
Sterden (Fra) 272
Steregushchiy (Rus) 673
Sterett (US) 926
Stern (Bel) 65
Sterne (Can) 111
Sterne (Fra) 261
Stethem (US) 924
Stiglich (Per) 604
Stikine (Can) 105
Stiletto (US) 949
Stimfalia (Gre) 310
Stingray (US) 967
Stockdale (US) 926
GYSGT Fred W Stockham (US) 960
Stockholm (Swe) 773
Stoiky (Rus) 673
Stollergrund (Ger) 292
Stolt (Swe) 774
Støren (Den) 193
Storm (Nor) 570
Storm (Rus) 706
Storm Bay (Aust) 41
Storochevik (Rus) 703
Stout (US) 924
Strabon (Gre) 309
Stratton (US) 963
Strelets (Rus) 685
Striped Marlin (Sin) 731
Stromboli (Ita) 406
Stuart (Aust) 28
Stupinets (Rus) 677
Sturgeon (US) 967
Sturgeon Bay (US) 969
Sturkö (Swe) 777
Stvor (Rus) 685
Styrsö (Swe) 777
Styx (Fra) 266
Su Won (RoK) 467
Su Yong (RoK) 468
Suão (Por) 637
Suao (Twn) 787
Suarez Arana (Bol) 68
Sub Lieutenant Alexandru Axente (Rom) 645
Subahi (Kwt) 477
Subhadra (Ind) 344
Subhadra Kumari Chauhan (Ind) 351
Suboficial Castillo (Arg) 17
Suboficial Rogelio Lesme (Par) 597
Subqat (Pak) 590
Subteniente Osorio Saravia (Gua) 315
Success (Aust) 38
Sucheta Kripalani (Ind) 351
Sudak (Ukr) 853
Sūduvis (Lit) 488
El Suez (Egy) 215
Sufa (Isr) 385
Suffren (Fra) 243
Suganami (Jpn) 444
Sugashima (Jpn) 431
Suhail (Mex) 520
Sui Chiang (Twn) 791
Suiryu (Jpn) 445
Sujata (Ind) 344
Suk (Tld) 815
Sukanya (Ind) 344
Sukhothai (Tld) 806
Al Sulayel (SAr) 715
Sulayman Jun-Kung (Gam) 278
Sulpicio Fernandez (Plp) 612
Al Sultana (Omn) 579
Sultan Hasanuddin (Indo) 357
Sultan Iskandar Muda (Indo) 357
Sultan Kudarat (Plp) 610
Sultan Thaha Syaifuddin (Indo) 356
Suluh Pari (Indo) 360
Sulzbach-Rosenberg (Ger) 291
Suma (Jpn) 432
Sumjinkang (RoK) 474
Summerside (Can) 103
Sumner (US) 957
Sun Chon (RoK) 466
Sundsvall (Swe) 772
Sunjin (RoK) 472
Suou (Jpn) 436
Suphairin (Tld) 809
Supply (US) 954
Supreme (Sin) 725
Sur (Pak) 591
Sura (Indo) 359
Surabaya (Indo) 360
Suranimala (Sri) 761
Surcouf (Fra) 256
Surel (Arg) 23
Surin (Tld) 812
Suriya (Tld) 816
Surma (Ban) 57
Surovi (Ban) 58
Surrey (Jam) 412
Surubi (Arg) 23
Suruga (Jpn) 439
Susitna (US) 949
Sutanto (Indo) 356
Sutedi Senoputra (Indo) 356
Sutherland (UK) 878
Sutlej (Ind) 346
Suvarna (Ind) 344
Suwad (Bhr) 50
Suzdalets (Rus) 674
Suzuka (Jpn) 439
Suzunami (Jpn) 421
Svalbard (Nor) 574
SVG 03, 06, 07 (StV) 709
Svir (Rus) 692
Svyataya Kseniya (Rus) 704
Swaraj Deep (Ind) 348
Sweepers (Nor) 572
Swift (US) 950
Swordfish (Sin) 731
Swordfish (US) 967
Sycamore (US) 969
Sydney (Aust) 27, 30
Syöksy (Fin) 239
Syvatoy Giorgiy Pobedonosets (Rus) 652
Syzran (Rus) 688

T

T 4-7 (Aust) 34
T 11-19, 81-83, 91-99, 110 (Tld) 810
T 21-29, 210-212, 213-214, 216-226, 991-993 (Tld) 811
T 55-59 (Ind) 344
T 80-86 (Ind) 343
T 710 (Az) 43
T 864, 874, 880-881 (Vtn) 989
Ta Fung (Twn) 795
Ta Han (Twn) 795
Ta Hu (Twn) 795
Ta Kang (Twn) 795
Ta Kuan (Twn) 794
Ta Tai (Twn) 795
Ta Wan (Twn) 795
Taape (Fra) 269
Taba (Egy) 214
Tabah (Mly) 504
Tabar (Ind) 334
Tabarca (Spn) 750
Tabarja (Leb) 483
Tabark (Tun) 826
Tabarka (Tun) 825
Tabarzin (Iran) 373
Tabasco (Mex) 521
Tabbouk (SAr) 717
Al Tabkah (Lby) 486
Taboga (Pan) 592
Tabuk (SAr) 713
Tackle (US) 971
Tae Pung Yang I (RoK) 473
Tae Pung Yang II, VI-VIII (RoK) 475
Tagil (Rus) 692
Tagomago (Spn) 750
Taguermess (Tun) 825
Al Tahaddy (Kwt) 478
Taheri (Iran) 378
Tahoma (US) 964
Taichung (Twn) 797
Taif (SAr) 712
Taillat (Fra) 273
Tailor (Aust) 38
Taimuang (Tld) 810
Taina (Fra) 271
Tainha (CpV) 114
Taipei (Twn) 797
Taishan (CPR) 154
Taizhou (CPR) 135, 144
Tajo (Spn) 753
Takachiho (Jpn) 442
Takanami (Jpn) 421
Takashima (Jpn) 431
Takashio (Jpn) 415
Takatori (Jpn) 441
Takatsuki (Jpn) 442
Takbai (Tld) 810
Takip 1-2 (Tur) 842
Taksin (Tld) 802
Takuyo (Jpn) 446
Talcahuano (Chi) 123, 125
Talent (UK) 868
Talibong (Tld) 813
Talita II (Arg) 24
Talivaldis (Lat) 480
Taliwangsa (Indo) 360
Tallashi (Ban) 60
Talwar (Ind) 334
Tamanaco (Ven) 982, 983
Tamanami (Jpn) 443
Tamaulipas (Mex) 521
Tambaú (Brz) 81
Tambora (Indo) 365
Tambov (Rus) 659
Tambre (Spn) 753
Tamjeed (Ban) 56
Tammar (Aust) 39
Tamoio (Brz) 71
Tampa (US) 964
Tan Chiang (Twn) 791
Tana (Ken) 451
Tangen (Nor) 571
Tanjung Fatagar (Indo) 360
Tanjung Kambani (Indo) 362
Tanjung Nusanive (Indo) 360
Tanu (Can) 108
Tanveer (Ban) 56
Tapajó (Brz) 71
Tapi (Tld) 807
Tapper (Swe) 774
Tara Bai (Ind) 351
Tarafdaar (Ind) 349
Taragiri (Ind) 337
Tarakan (Aust) 34
Tarangini (Ind) 347
Tarasa (Ind) 344
Tarasco (Mex) 525
Tareq (Iran) 369
Tarif (UAE) 860
Tarifa (Spn) 749
Tarihu (Indo) 360
Tarik (Mor) 538
Tariq (Pak) 584
Tariq (SAr) 714
Tariq Ibn Ziyad (Lby) 484
Tarpon (US) 967
Tarshish (Isr) 385
Taşkizak (Tur) 840
Tasuja (Est) 229
Tatarstan (Rus) 673
Tatsugumo (Jpn) 443
Taunoa (Fra) 273
Taupo (NZ) 560
Taurus (Brz) 83
Taurus (Ecu) 209
Taurus (Sey) 721
Tavi (Fin) 241
Tavolara (Ita) 407
Tavriya (Rus) 688
Al Taweelah (Bhr) 49
El Tawfiq (Mor) 534
Tawfiq (Ban) 56
Tawheed (Ban) 56
Tayfun (Tur) 835
Taylor (US) 930
Tayrona (Col) 169
TB 1-4 (Ban) 58
TB 35-38 (Ban) 56
Tchusovoy (Rus) 687
Te Kaha (NZ) 559
Te Kukupa (CI) 178
Te Mana (NZ) 559
Te Mataili (Tuv) 848
Teanoai (Kir) 451
Tebicuary (Par) 597
Tebrau (Mly) 504
Tech (Fra) 276
TECIM Jaime E Cárdenas Gomez (Col) 173
Teculapa (Mex) 525
Tecun Uman (Gua) 315
Tedong Naga (Indo) 360
Tedorico Dominado Jr (Plp) 612
Tedung Selar (Indo) 360
Tegas (Mly) 504
Tegernsee (Ger) 294
Tegucigalpa (Hon) 318
Teh Hsing (Twn) 796
Tehuelche (Arg) 21
Tekuma (Isr) 383
Tekwane (SA) 737
Telenn Mor (Fra) 270
Teleost (Can) 112
Telkkä (Fin) 241
Tellez (Chi) 121
Telopea (Aust) 39
Teluk Amboina (Indo) 361
Teluk Banten (Indo) 361
Teluk Bayur (Indo) 361
Teluk Berau (Indo) 362
Teluk Bone (Indo) 361
Teluk Celukan Bawang (Indo) 362
Teluk Cendrawasih (Indo) 362
Teluk Cirebon (Indo) 365
Teluk Ende (Indo) 361
Teluk Gilimanuk (Indo) 362
Teluk Hading (Indo) 362
Teluk Jakarta (Indo) 362
Teluk Kau (Indo) 361
Teluk Lampung (Indo) 362
Teluk Langsa (Indo) 361
Teluk Manado (Indo) 362
Teluk Mandar (Indo) 361
Teluk Parigi (Indo) 362
Teluk Peleng (Indo) 362
Teluk Penyu (Indo) 361
Teluk Ratai (Indo) 361
Teluk Sabang (Indo) 365
Teluk Saleh (Indo) 361
Teluk Sampit (Indo) 361
Teluk Sangkuring (Indo) 362
Teluk Semangka (Indo) 361
Teluk Sibolga (Indo) 362
Teluk Tomini (Indo) 361
Tembah (Can) 109
Temerario (Uru) 976
Tempur 1, 11-14, 21-24, 31-34, 41-44 (Mly) 498
Temryuk (Rus) 685
Al Temsah (Omn) 578
El Temsah (Lby) 486
Temsah (UAE) 862
Tenace (Fra) 272
Tenace (Ita) 408
Tenacidad (Ven) 985
Tenacious (Sin) 725
Tenente Boanerges (Brz) 83
Tenente Castelo (Brz) 83
Teniente Alejandro Baldomero Salgado (Col) 177
Teniente Farina (Par) 596
Teniente Herreros (Par) 598
Teniente José Azueta (Mex) 520
Teniente Luis Bernal (Col) 177
Teniente Olivieri (Arg) 17
Teniente Robles (Par) 597
Teniente Soliz (Bol) 68
Tennessee (US) 910
Tenryu (Jpn) 434
Tenyo (Jpn) 446
Tepoca (Mex) 525
Teraban (Bru) 89
Terek (Rus) 691
Terengganu (Mly) 496
Terepaima (Ven) 983
Teritup (Mly) 502
Terme (Tur) 836
Terminos (Mex) 525
Termoli (Ita) 403
Tern (SA) 737
Tern (US) 967
Ternopil (Ukr) 850
Terrapin (US) 967
Terry Fox (Can) 106
Teshio (Jpn) 441
Testimo Figuracion (Plp) 611
Teuku Umar (Indo) 356
Texas (US) 912
Tha Din Daeng (Tld) 814
Thach (US) 930
Thafir (Kwt) 477
Thalang (Tld) 813
Thames Crespo (Bol) 69
Thar (Egy) 224
Thayanchon (Tld) 806
The Sullivans (US) 924
Themistocles (Gre) 303
Theodore Roosevelt (US) 917
Thepha (Tld) 810
Theseus (Gre) 311
Thétis (Fra) 267
Thetis (Den) 189
Thetis (Gre) 310
Thetis (US) 964
Thexas (Cypr) 187
Thihayarzar I-II (Myn) 541
Thomas G Thompson (US) 950
Thompson (Arg) 22
Thomson (Chi) 117
Thong Kaeo (Tld) 813
Thong Lang (Tld) 813
Thorbjørn (Den) 199
Thor Heyerdahl (Nor) 568
Thorsteinson (Nor) 574
Thresher Shark (Sin) 730
Thunder Bay (US) 969
Thunder Cape (Can) 111
Thunderbolt (US) 937
Tiagha (CtI) 180
Tiantaishan (CPR) 153
Tianzhushan (CPR) 153
Tiaré (Fra) 271
Tiburon (Arg) 23
Ticino (Ita) 407
Tien Tan (Twn) 788
Tierra Bomba (Col) 176
Tiger Shark (Sin) 730
Tiger Shark (US) 967
Tighatlib (Bhr) 49
Tigr (Rus) 656
Tigre (Fra) 268
Tiira (Fin) 241
Tiira (Lat) 480
Tikuna (Brz) 70
Tillicum (Can) 105
Timbira (Brz) 71
Tineycheide (Spn) 758
El Tinai (Alg) 6
Tioman (Mly) 505
Tippecanoe (US) 955
Tippu Sultan (Pak) 584
Tir (Ind) 347
Tirad Pass (Plp) 615
Tiran (Iran) 374
Tirapuka (Guy) 317
Tireless (UK) 868
Tirso (Ita) 407
Tista (Ban) 57
Titano (Ita) 408
Titas (Ban) 56
Titran (Nor) 574
Tjaldrid (Fae) 233
Tjiptadi (Indo) 356
TL and KRKH series (Rus) 694
TL series (Rus) 694
Tlaloc (Mex) 526
Tlaxcala (Mex) 526
Toba (Arg) 21
Tobias Hainyeko (Nam) 545
Tobie (SA) 737
Tobishima (Jpn) 432
Tobruk (Aust) 34
Todak (Indo) 358
Todak (Mly) 499
Todendorf (Ger) 295
Todo Santos (Mex) 525
Tofiño (Spn) 754
Tokachi (Jpn) 441
Tokara (Jpn) 442
Tokerau (Chi) 125
Tokinami (Jpn) 444
Tokiwa (Jpn) 435
Toledo (US) 914
Toletela (Lby) 486
Toll (Arg) 22
Tolmi (Gre) 306
Tolyatti (Rus) 702
Tom Thumb (Aust) 36
Tomas Batilo (Plp) 611
Tomsk (Rus) 654
Tonb (Iran) 377
Tone (Jpn) 426
Tongkol (Indo) 359
Tongling (CPR) 142
Tonina (Arg) 22
Tonnerre (Can) 105
Tonnerre (Fra) 263
Tony Pastrana Contreras (Col) 172
Toowoomba (Aust) 28
Topaz (Sey) 722
Topeka (US) 914
Tor (Nor) 575
Toralla (Spn) 749
Torås (Nor) 571
Torbay (UK) 868
Torm (Est) 231
Tormenta (Mex) 517
Torna (Spn) 750
Tornado (US) 967
Tornio (Fin) 235
Toronto (Can) 100
Torpen (Nor) 573
Torpido Tenderi (Tur) 842
Torsö (Fin) 239
Tortuga (US) 945
Tortuguero (DR) 201
Torun (Pol) 622
Tosa (Jpn) 438
Tosagiri (Jpn) 443
Tourville (Fra) 243, 255
Toushka (Egy) 214
Towada (Jpn) 435
Toxotis (Gre) 305
Toyoshima (Jpn) 431
Tracker (UK) 883
Tracy (Can) 107
Trafalgar (UK) 868
Traful (Arg) 23
Tramontana (Spn) 741
Tran Khanh Du (Vtn) 991
Träskö (Fin) 239
Tremiti (Ita) 407
Trenchant (UK) 868
Trevally (Aust) 38
Trezza (Ita) 410
Trichonis (Gre) 310
Trident (Bar) 61
Tridente (Brz) 86

Tridente (Por) 630
Trieste (Uru) 977
Trieux (Fra) 276
Triki (Mor) 533
Trinidad (Bol) 68
Trinkat (Ind) 344
Tripoli (Leb) 482
Trishul (Ind) 334
Tritão (Brz) 86
Triton (Aust) 41
Triton (Den) 189
Triton (Gre) 300
Triumph (UK) 868
Triunfo (Brz) 86
Triunfo (Par) 598
Tromp (Nld) 548
Troncoso (Chi) 121
Trondenes (Nor) 571
Trossö (Swe) 778
Trumpeter (UK) 883
Truong (Vtn) 992
Truxtun (US) 926
Trygg (Swe) 774
Tsekoa II (Can) 110
Tseng Chiang (Twn) 791
Tsesar Kunikov (Rus) 681
Tshukudu (SA) 738
Tsi Chiang (Twn) 791
Tsibar (Bul) 93
Tsotne Dadiani (Geo) 280
Tsoying (Twn) 787
Tsugaru (Jpn) 438
Tsukishima (Jpn) 432
Tsukuba (Jpn) 442
Tsunoshima (Jpn) 431
Tsuruugi (Jpn) 442
Tsushima (Jpn) 431, 446
Tuapse (Rus) 702
Tucson (US) 914
Tufan (Tur) 835
Tukoro (Van) 978
Tula (Rus) 651
Tulcea (Rom) 647
Tulugaq (Den) 194
Tumpat (Mly) 505
Tun Razak (Mly) 492
Tuna (Aust) 38
Tunas Samudera (Mly) 501
Tunda Satu 1-3 (Mly) 502
Tunis (Tun) 823
Tunku Abdul Rahman (Mly) 492
Tupi (Brz) 71
Turag (Ban) 55
Turaif (SAr) 716
Turbinist (Rus) 683
Turbulent (UK) 868
Turgutreis (Tur) 831
Turia (Spn) 753
Tursas (Fin) 241
Tuwaig (SAr) 716
Tver (Rus) 701
Tybee (US) 966
Tyne (UK) 883
Typhoon (US) 937
Tyr (Ice) 323
Tyr (Nor) 573
Tyrrel Bay (Gra) 314
Tzacol (Gua) 315
Tzu-i (Twn) 788

U

U 15-18, 23-24 (Ger) 283
U 31-36 (Ger) 282
U 201-211, 301-312 (Fin) 239
U 241, 631-634, 732, 926 (Ukr) 854
U 400 series (Fin) 239
U 601-636 (Fin) 240
UAM 101-102, 122, 203, 304, 601-602, 605, 610, 612, 618-619, 623-624, 626, 629, 631, 634, 636, 639, 640-641, 650-651, 659, 662, 667, 669, 673, 675, 684-696, 810-812, 830, 840, 852, 901, 907-908, 913, 918 (Por) 637
Ubaldo Diciotti (Ita) 412
Überherrn (Ger) 291
Ucayali (Per) 602
Uckermark (Ger) 297
Udara (Sri) 762
Al Udeid (Qat) 638
Udomdet (Tld) 809
Uerkouane (Tun) 826
Ugaab (UAE) 862
Ugandi (Est) 229
Uisko (Fin) 241
Ukale (Dom) 200
Ukushima (Jpn) 431
Al Ula (SAr) 715
Ula (Nor) 567
Ulsan (RoK) 464
Ulua (Hon) 318
Ulubat (Tur) 841
Ulvön (Swe) 777
Um Almaradim (Kwt) 476
Umalusi (SA) 738
Umar Farooq (Ban) 54
Umhloti (SA) 737
Umigiri (Jpn) 423, 443
Umitaka (Jpn) 428
Umkomaas (SA) 737
Umlus (SAr) 716
Umm Al Narr (UAE) 861
Umoja (Ken) 450
Umut (Tur) 844
Umzimkulu (SA) 737
Underwood (US) 930
União (Brz) 75
Unity (Sin) 727
Unryu (Jpn) 415
Untung Suropati (Indo) 356
Uppland (Swe) 770
Uraga (Jpn) 430
Uragon (Bul) 92
Ural (Rus) 701
Uranami (Jpn) 444
Urania (Ita) 398
Urania (Nld) 555
Uranus (Swi) 783
Urayuki (Jpn) 443
Ureca (EqG) 227
Uredd (Nor) 567
Urengoy (Rus) 706
Urf (Swe) 777
Uribe (Chi) 121
Urk (Nld) 554
Urso (Ita) 410
Uruguay (Uru) 974
Uruguay 1-20 (Uru) 976
Ushuaia (Arg) 22
Ust-Bolsheretsk (Rus) 661
Ust-Kamshats (Rus) 661
Usumacinta (Mex) 523
Utatlan (Gua) 315
Uthaug (Nor) 567
Utila (Hon) 318
Utique (Tun) 823, 826
Utsira (Nor) 567
Utstein (Nor) 567
Uttal (Ban) 56
Utvaer (Nor) 567
Uusimaa (Fin) 236
Uwajima (Jpn) 432
Uzhgorod (Ukr) 851
Uzushio (Jpn) 415, 446

V

V 3-8, 10-20 (Ger) 295
V 101-106 (Tun) 824
V 601-635, 2000-2033, 5000-5020, 5100, 6003-6012 (Ita) 411
V Adm Vorontsov (Rus) 685
V Gumanenko (Rus) 683
VA II-V (Spn) 760
Vaarlahti (Fin) 238
Vaccaro (Ita) 410
VADM K R Wheeler (US) 959
Vaedderen (Den) 189
Vagli (Ind) 325
Vahakari (Fin) 238
Vaindlo (Est) 229
Vajra (Ind) 350
Vakta (Can) 110
Valas (Fin) 238
Valcke (Bel) 65
Valdivia (Chi) 122
Valentin Chujkin (Rus) 704
Valentin Gomez Farias (Mex) 520
Valentin Pikul (Rus) 683
Valiant (Sin) 726
Valiant (US) 964
Valkyrien (Nor) 573
Valle Del Cauca (Col) 171
Valour (Sin) 726
Valparaíso (Chi) 125
Valpas (Lat) 481
Valvas (Est) 230
Van (Tur) 841
Van Amstel (Nld) 550
Van Kinsbergen (Nld) 555
Van Speijk (Nld) 550
Vancouver (Can) 100
Vandegrift (US) 930
Vanguard (UK) 870
Vanguardia (Uru) 977
Vänö (Fin) 238
Vapper (Est) 231
Vaqar (Pak) 591
Var (Fra) 269
Varad (Ind) 350
CPCIM Guillermo Londoño Vargas (Col) 172
Varna (Bul) 93
Varonis (Lat) 480
Varuna (Ind) 347, 350
Varyag (Rus) 666
Vasco Da Gama (Por) 631
Vasiliy Suntzov (Rus) 706
Vasily Ilyashenko (Rus) 704
Vassily Tatischev (Rus) 688
Vaygach (Rus) 687
Vector (Can) 112
Vedetta (Ita) 401
Veer (Ind) 340
Veera (Ind) 350
Vega (DR) 202
Vega (Ita) 401
Vega (Mex) 520
Vehdat (Pak) 590
Vela (Ind) 325
Vela De Cobo (Ven) 985
Velarde (Per) 602
Vella Gulf (US) 921
Ven (Swe) 777
Vencedora (Spn) 747
Vendémiaire (Fra) 258
Vendaval (Por) 637
Vengadora (Col) 174
Vengeance (Sin) 726
Vengeance (UK) 870
Ventôse (Fra) 258
Venturous (US) 964
Venus (Swi) 783
Vepr (Rus) 656
Veracruz (Mex) 519
Veraguas (Pan) 593
Verchoture (Rus) 651
Verdecchia (Ita) 411
Verdon (Fra) 276
Verni (Bul) 90
Verseau (Fra) 266
Vertonne (Fra) 276
Vestkysten (Den) 198
Vésubie (Fra) 276
Vesuvio (Ita) 406
Vetluga (Rus) 690
Viana Do Castelo (Por) 633
Viareggio (Ita) 403
Viben (Den) 193, 198
Vibhuti (Ind) 340
Vice Admiral Constantin Balescu (Rom) 645
Vice Admiral Eugeniu Rosca (Rom) 643
Vicealmirante Othón P Blanco (Mex) 520
Vicksburg (US) 921
Victor Kingisepp (Rus) 701
Victor Subbotin (Rus) 686
Victoria (Can) 98
Victoria (Spn) 745
Victoria (Ven) 981
Victorious (UK) 870
Victorious (US) 957
Victory (Sin) 726
Vidal Gormaz (Chi) 123
Videla (Chi) 121
Vidyut (Ind) 340
Viedna (Arg) 23
Vieste (Ita) 403
Viesturs (Lat) 480
Vigía (Spn) 748
Vigilance (Dom) 201
Vigilance (Sin) 726
Vigilant (Mrt) 511
Vigilant (UK) 870
Vigilant (US) 964
Vigilante (CpV) 113
Vigorous (US) 964
Vigour (Sin) 726
Vigra (Nor) 572
Vigraha (Ind) 350
Vijaya (Ind) 350
Viken (Nor) 573
Vikram (Ind) 350
Vikramaditya (Ind) 328
Vikrant (Ind) 330
Viktor Leonov (Rus) 688
Villavisencio (Per) 601
Ville De Québec (Can) 100
Vilyachinsk (Rus) 654
Vinash (Ind) 340
Vincenzo Martellotta (Ita) 404
Vindhyagiri (Ind) 337
Vinga (Swe) 777
Vinha (Fin) 239
Vinnitsa (Ukr) 850
Violette (Fra) 275
Viper (Indo) 360
Vipul (Ind) 340
Viraat (Ind) 329
Virginia (US) 912
Virgo (Sey) 721
Virsaitis (Lat) 480
Visborg (Swe) 778
Visby (Swe) 771
Vise (US) 971
Vishera (Rus) 691
Vishwast (Ind) 350
Visvaldis (Lat) 480
Vitali (Ita) 410
Vitse Admiral Kulakov (Rus) 669
Vitse-Admiral Zakharin (Rus) 683
Vitseadmiral Zhukov (Rus) 683
Vivek (Ind) 350
Vizir (Rus) 685
Vlaardingen (Nld) 554
Vladikavkaz (Rus) 661
Vladimir Kolechitsky (Rus) 691
Vladimir Monomach (Rus) 653
Vladimir Valek (Col) 177
Vladimirets (Rus) 680
VM 20, 72, 146, 153, 154, 250, 263, 268, 270, 277, 409, 413-416, 420, 425, 429, 725, 807, 809, 907-910, 915, 916, 919, 596 (Rus) 695
Vogelsand (Ger) 296
Vogtland (Ger) 297
Volga (Rus) 701
Volgocherensk (Rus) 680
Volgodonsk (Rus) 680
Volk (Rus) 656
Volkan (Tur) 835
Vologda (Rus) 661
Voron (Rus) 702
Voronezh (Rus) 654
V Adm Vorontsov (Rus) 685
Vorovsky (Rus) 700
Voum-Legleita (Mtn) 510
VTN series (Rus) 692
VTR 94 (Rus) 696
VTR 140 (Rus) 682
VTS 3-4 (Den) 194
Vučedol (Ser) 720
Vukovar (Cro) 182
Vulcain (Fra) 266
Vung Tau (Vtn) 991
Vyacheslav Denisov (Rus) 706
Vyazma (Rus) 692
Vyborg (Rus) 661, 703

W

Waban-Aki (Can) 112
El Wacil (Mor) 535
Wadah (Kwt) 477
Al Wadeeah (SAr) 715
Waesche (US) 963
Wagio (Indo) 365
Wahag (Lby) 485
Wahoo (US) 967
Wakagumo (Jpn) 445
Wakasa (Jpn) 432, 439
Wakashio (Jpn) 416
Wakataka (Jpn) 428
Al Wakil (Egy) 219
Wallaby (Aust) 39
Wallaroo (Aust) 35
Waller (Aust) 26
Wally Schirra (US) 954
Walney (UK) 888
Walnut (US) 969
Walrus (Nld) 547
Walter S Diehl (US) 955
Wanamassa (US) 954
Wang Geon (RoK) 461
Wang Nai (Tld) 813
Wang Nok (Tld) 813
Wangerooge (Ger) 296
Wanyang-Shan (CPR) 153
Warakas (Indo) 360
Warnow (Ger) 295
Warramunga (Aust) 28
Warrigal (Aust) 39
Warrior (US) 948
Washington (US) 966
Washington Chambers (US) 954
Wasp (US) 940
Waspada (Bru) 88
Waters (US) 957
Watkins (US) 959
Watson (US) 959
Wattle (Aust) 39
Wave Knight (UK) 890
Wave Ruler (UK) 890
Wayne E Meyer (US) 926
Wdzydze (Pol) 623
Wedge (US) 970
Weeraya (Sri) 762
Wei Hsung (Twn) 796
Weilheim (Ger) 291
Weishan Hu (CPR) 160
Welang (Indo) 360
Weling (Indo) 360
Wellington (NZ) 560
Wenatchee (US) 954
Wenzhou (CPR) 140
Werra (Ger) 293
Wesp (Bel) 65
West Virginia (US) 910
Westerwald (Ger) 294
Westminster (UK) 878
Westpac Express (US) 951
Westport (Can) 111
Westwal (Nld) 557
Wewak (Aust) 34
L/CPL Roy M Wheat (US) 960
VADM K R Wheeler (US) 959
Al Whada (Mor) 537
Whidbey Island (US) 945
Whirlwind (US) 937
White Marlin (Sin) 731
White Shark (Sin) 730
Whitehorse (Can) 103
Whitetip Shark (Sin) 730
Wicko (Pol) 622
Wickrama II (Sri) 762
Wierbalg (Nld) 557
Wiesel (Ger) 290
Wigry (Pol) 623
Wilfred Templeman (Can) 112
Wilhelm Carpelan (Fin) 238
Wilhelm Pullwer (Ger) 292
Willemstad (Nld) 554
William Mclean (US) 954
William P Lawrence (US) 926
William Tate (US) 969
PFC Dewayne T Williams (US) 961
Willow (US) 969
Windsor (Can) 98
Winnipeg (Can) 100
Winston S Churchill (US) 926
Wiratno (Indo) 356
Wire (US) 971
Wische (Ger) 294
Witthayakhom (Tld) 809
WMSL 753 (US) 963
Wodnik (Pol) 624
Wolf (Can) 104
Wollongong (Aust) 35
Wombat (Aust) 39
Won Ju (RoK) 466
Won San (RoK) 470
Wrangell (US) 966
Wright (US) 961
Wrona (Pol) 625
Wu Chang (Twn) 789
Wu Kang (Twn) 795
Wu Yi (Twn) 795
Wudangshan (CPR) 151
Wufengshan (CPR) 153
Wuhan (CPR) 136
Wuhu (CPR) 146
Wustrow (Ger) 296
Wuxi (CPR) 144
Wyaconda (US) 970
Wyatt Earp (Aust) 36
Wyoming (US) 910
Wyulda (Aust) 39

X

X 01-03 (Pak) 583
Xavier Pinto Telleria (Bol) 69
Xia (CPR) 128
Xiamen (CPR) 144
Xiangfan (CPR) 142
Xinantecatl (Mex) 526
Xinhui (CPR) 150
Xining (CPR) 139
Xuefengshan (CPR) 153
Xueshan (CPR) 154
Xuzhou (CPR) 141

Y

Y 07, 30 (Moz) 538
Y 116, 118, 121-126, 137-142, 144-145, 147-148, 172-183 (Spn) 757
Y 231, 251-255 (Spn) 755
Y 301-310 (Myn) 542
Y 311 (Myn) 541
Y 502-511, 521-531, 534-535, 539-540, 545, 548-549, 554-558, 579-582, 584, 586-589 (Spn) 756

Y 675-679 (Fra) 272
Y 830-835 (CPR) 160
Y 1500 series (SA) 737
Yacoub Ould Rajel (Mtn) 511
Yadanabon (Myn) 544
El Yadekh (Alg) 6
Yadryn (Rus) 684
Yaeshio (Jpn) 415
Yaeyama (Jpn) 431
Yaezuki (Jpn) 443
Yaffo (Isr) 385
Yagan (Chi) 125
Yahiko (Jpn) 438
Yakal (Plp) 613
Yakit (Tur) 842
Yakushima (Jpn) 431
Yamagiri (Jpn) 434
Yamagumo (Jpn) 443
Yamakuni (Jpn) 441, 442
Yamal (Rus) 681
Al Yamama (SAr) 716
Yamayuki (Jpn) 424
Yan Aye Aung (Myn) 541
Yan Khwin Aung (Myn) 541
Yan Min Aung (Myn) 541
Yan Myat Aung (Myn) 541
Yan Nyein Aung (Myn) 541
Yan Paing Aung (Myn) 541
Yan Win Aung (Myn) 541
Yan Ye Aung (Myn) 541
Yan Zwe Aung (Myn) 541
Yana (Rus) 692
Yandanshang (CPR) 153
Yang Yang (RoK) 471
Yangjiang (CPR) 150
Yangmanchun (RoK) 463
Yano (US) 958
Yaqui (Mex) 526
Yaracuy (Ven) 983
Yarbay Kudret Güngör (Tur) 840
Al Yarmook (SAr) 713
Al-Yarmouk (Kwt) 476
El Yarmouk (Egy) 218
Yaroslav Mudryy (Rus) 672
Yaroslavl (Rus) 702
Yarra (Aust) 35
Yasam (Tur) 844
Yashima (Jpn) 437
Yastreb (Rus) 702
Yavaros (Mex) 525
Yavire (Ven) 982
Yavuz (Tur) 831
Yay Bo (Myn) 543
YD 200, 204-205 (Plp) 614
YDT 01-06 (Jpn) 435
YDT 11 (Can) 105
YDT 17-18 (US) 952
Yee Ree (RoK) 466
Yegorlik (Rus) 691
Yehuin (Arg) 23
Yellow Elder (Bhm) 46
Yellowfin (US) 967
Yellowknife (Can) 103
Yelnya (Rus) 684, 691
Yenisei (Rus) 692
Yevgeniy Kocheshkov (Rus) 681
YF 2121, 2124-25, 2127-29, 2132, 2135, 2138, 2141, 2150-51 (Jpn) 430
Yhaguy (Par) 597
Yi Chon (RoK) 459
Yi I (RoK) 462
Yi Yang (Twn) 790
Yibin (CPR) 144
Yichang (CPR) 142
Yildiray (Tur) 829
Yildirim (Tur) 831
Yildiz (Tur) 835
Yinchuan (CPR) 139
YL 9-15 (Jpn) 436
Yo Su (RoK) 466
Yodo (Jpn) 443
Yogaga (Gha) 299
Yonakuni (Jpn) 439
Yong Ju (RoK) 466
Yongxingdao (CPR) 161
Yoon Young-Ha (RoK) 467
Yopito (Ven) 985
York (UK) 876
Yos Sudarso (Indo) 354
Yoshino (Jpn) 442
Young Endeavour (Aust) 37
YP 663, 665, 680-692, 694-698, 700-702 (US) 952
Ypoploiarchos Daniolos (Gre) 304
Ypoploiarchos Degiannis (Gre) 305
Ypoploiarchos Grigoropoulos (Gre) 304
Ypoploiarchos Kristallidis (Gre) 304
Ypoploiarchos Mikonios (Gre) 305
Ypoploiarchos Roussen (Gre) 304
Ypoploiarchos Tournas (Gre) 305
Ypoploiarchos Troupakis (Gre) 305
Ypoploiarchos Votsis (Gre) 305
YR 01-02 (Jpn) 435
Yser (Fra) 276
YT 58-94 (Jpn) 436
YTB 45-49, 150-157 (Twn) 795
YTE 13 (Jpn) 434
YTL 16-17, 27-30, 32-39, 41-43 (Twn) 795
Yu (Mly) 499
Yuan Wang 1-2 (CPR) 157
Yuan Wang 3-6 (CPR) 158
Yubari (Jpn) 441
Yucatan (Mex) 521
Yueh Fei (Twn) 788
Yuen Feng (Twn) 795
Yugeshima (Jpn) 432
Yukigumo (Jpn) 443
Yukon (US) 955
Yulin (CPR) 142
Yun Hsing (Twn) 799
Yunbou (SAr) 715
Yunes (Iran) 369
Yung Chia (Twn) 794
Yung Chuan (Twn) 794
Yung Feng (Twn) 794
Yung Fu (Twn) 794
Yung Ku (Twn) 794
Yung Ren (Twn) 794
Yung Shun (Twn) 794
Yung Sui (Twn) 794
Yung Teh (Twn) 794
Yung Ting (Twn) 794
Yung Tzu (Twn) 794
Yung Yang (Twn) 794
Yunga (Rus) 674
Yuntaishan (CPR) 153
Yunwashan (CPR) 153
Yura (Jpn) 430
Yuri Dolgoruky (Rus) 653
Yushan (CPR) 154
Yusoutei-ichi-gou (Jpn) 430
Yusoutei-ni-gou (Jpn) 430
Yusup Akaev (Rus) 684
Yuubari (Jpn) 427
Yuubetsu (Jpn) 427
Yuudachi (Jpn) 422
Yuugiri (Jpn) 423
Yuzbasi Ihsan Tolunay (Tur) 840
Yüzbaşi Naşit Öngören (Tur) 842
Yuzhno-Sakhalinsk (Rus) 703
Yuzuki (Jpn) 443

Z

Z 101-203 (Sri) 765
Zabaykalye (Rus) 701
Zaccola (Ita) 410
Zafer (Tur) 833
Zahra 14-15, 17-18, 21 (Omn) 581
Zaire (Por) 633
Zakr (Yem) 993
Zakynthos (Gre) 307
Zamboanga Del Sur (Plp) 612
Zannotti (Ita) 410
Zao (Jpn) 438
Zapolarye (Rus) 701
Zapoteco (Mex) 526
Zarrar (Pak) 588
Zborul (Rom) 645
Zbyszko (Pol) 625
Zeeland (Nld) 551
Zeeleeuw (Nld) 547
Zeemeeuw (Bel) 65
Zeffiro (Ita) 396
Zefiros (Gre) 309
Zelenodolsk (Rus) 675
Zelenograd (Rus) 652
Žemaitis (Lit) 488
Zenobe Gramme (Bel) 64
Zephyr (US) 967
Zeus (Gre) 310
Zeus (US) 956
Zeyda (Myn) 540
Zhanjiang (CPR) 140
Zhaotong (CPR) 144
A Zheleznyakov (Rus) 683
Zhenghe (CPR) 159
Zhenjiang (CPR) 144
Zhigulevsk (Rus) 688
Zhoushan (CPR) 141
Zhuhai (CPR) 140
Zibar (Bul) 94
Zibens (Lat) 479
Zierikzee (Nld) 554
Zigong (CPR) 144
Zijinshan (CPR) 153
Zinat Al Bihaar (Omn) 579
Zipkin (Tur) 835
Zobel (Ger) 290
Zorkiy (Rus) 699
Zorrillos (Per) 607
Zorritos (Per) 605, 606
Zoubin (Iran) 373
Al Zuara (Lby) 485
Al Zubara (Bhr) 50
Zuhrab (Yem) 993
Zuiderkruis (Nld) 556
Zuidwal (Nld) 557
Zuiun (Jpn) 447
Zulfiquar (Pak) 586
Zulurab (SAr) 716
Zumwalt (US) 928
Zunyi (CPR) 139
Zurara (UAE) 859
Zvezdochka (Rus) 687
Zyb (Rus) 678

Named classes

2nd Lt John P Bobo (US)..........961
10 De Agosto (Ecu)..........211
19DD (Jpn)..........420
65 ft (US)..........971
300 ton (Jpn)..........435
430 ton (RoK)..........473

A

A-125 (Rus)..........704
Abamin (Myn)..........543
Abdullah (Dauntless) (Jor)..........448
Abhay (Project 1241 PE) (Pauk II) (Ind)..........341
Abnaki (Mex)..........526
Absalon (Den)..........197
Abu Dhabi (Kortenaer) (UAE)..........857
Abukuma (Jpn)..........426
Achelous (Plp)..........613
Actif (Fra)..........273
Acuario (Mex)..........522
Addriyah (MSC 322) (SAr)..........715
Adelaide (Oliver Hazard Perry) (Aust)..........30
Adept (UK)..........895
Aditya (Ind)..........348
Adjutant and MSC 268 (Twn)..........794
Admiral Gorshkov (Project 22350) (Rus)..........675
Aegir (Ice)..........323
Agdlek (Den)..........194
Aggressive (Twn)..........794
Agor-26 (US)..........950
Agosta (S 70) (Spn)..........741
Agosta 70 (Pak)..........582
Aguascalientes (Mex)..........526
Águila (Mex)..........518
Aguinaldo (Plp)..........611
Aguirre (Lupo) (Per)..........600
Ahmad El Fateh (TNC 45) (Bhr)..........49
Ahmad Yani (Van Speijk) (Indo)..........354
Aist (Dzheyran) (Project 1232.1) (Rus)..........682
Ajeera (Bhr, Ven)..........50, 982
Akademik Krylov (Project 852/856) (Rus)..........685
Akagi (Jpn)..........442
Akizuki (Jpn)..........443
Akshay (Ban)..........57
Akula (Rus)..........650
Akula (Schuka-B) (Ind, Rus)..........325, 656
Akula (Project 1176) (Rus)..........682
Akvamaren (Project 266M) (Rus)..........683
Al Bushra (Omn)..........577
Al Feyi (UAE)..........861
Al Hussein (Hawk) (Jor)..........448
Al Jarim (FPB 20) (Bhr)..........49
Al Jawf (Sandown) (SAr)..........715
Al Jouf (SAr)..........716
Al Jubatel (SAr)..........717
Al Manama (MGB 62) (Bhr)..........48
Al Riffa (FPB 38) (Bhr)..........49
Al Riyadh (Modified La Fayette) (SAr)..........710
Al Saber (UAE)..........864
Al Shaheed (Kwt)..........477
Al Siddiq (SAr)..........714
Al Tahaddy (Kwt)..........478
Alamosa (Plp)..........613
Albacora (Daphné) (Por)..........629
Albatros (Ecu, Lit, Tun)..........212, 487, 824
Albatros 630 (Ecu)..........212
Albatros 730 (Ecu)..........212
Albatros 830 (Ecu)..........212
Albatros 1100 (Ecu)..........212
Albatros (Project 1124/1124M/1124K/1124EM) (Rus)..........674
Albatros (Project 1124P/1124M/1124MP/1124MU) (Rus)..........699
Albatroz (ETim, Por)..........204, 634
Albion (UK)..........885
Alboran (Spn)..........749
Algerine (Tld)..........815
Algol (US)..........962
Alize (Fra)..........269
Alkmaar (Tripartite) (Lat, Nld)..........480, 554
Alkyon (MSC 294) (Gre)..........308
Allende (Knox) (Mex)..........514
Alliance (Twn)..........794
Alligator (RoK, Ven)..........468, 982
Alligator (Tapir) (Project 1171) (Rus)..........681
Almirante Brown (Meko 360 H2) (Arg)..........12
Almirante Clemente (Ven)..........984
Almirante Guilhem (Brz)..........86
Almirante Padilla (Col)..........170
Alpinist (Project 503) (Rus)..........701
Alpinist (Project 503M/R) (Rus)..........688
Al-Shaali type (Kwt)..........478
Altair (Swe)..........778
Alucat 850 (Arg)..........23
Alucat 1050 (Arg)..........23
Alusafe 1290 (Nor)..........571
Alvand (Vosper Mk 5) (Iran)..........371
Alvaro De Bazán (Spn)..........744
Älvsborg (Chi, Swe)..........124, 778
Amami (Jpn)..........441
Amazon (Pak)..........584
Ambassador III (Egy)..........218
America (US)..........946
Amga (Project 1791) (Rus)..........690
Amorim do valle (River) (Brz)..........83
Amsterdam (Nld)..........555
Amur (Project 304) (Ukr)..........853
Amur (Project 304/304M) (Rus)..........690
AN-2 (Hun)..........323
Anaga (Spn)..........750
Anawrahta (Myn)..........539
Anchorage (Twn)..........792
Andrea Doria (Horizon) (Ita)..........394
Andrómeda (Col)..........174
Andromeda (Por)..........635
Angamos/Islay (Type 209/1200) (Per)..........599
Antarès (BRS) (Fra)..........265
Antares (Mlw, Ukr)..........491, 856
Antonio Zara (Ita)..........410
Antoniou (Gre)..........306
Antyey (Project 949B) (Rus)..........654
Anvil/Clamp (US)..........971
Anwei (Type 920) (CPR)..........162
Anzac (MEKO 200) (Aust, NZ)..........28, 559
Appleleaf (UK)..........890
Aquarius (Swi)..........783
Aquitaine (Fra)..........259
Aquitaine Explorer (Fra)..........275
Aragosta (Ham) (Ita)..........405
Aratu (Schütze) (Brz)..........82
Arauca (Col)..........172
Archangel (Chi, Ken, Yem)..........126, 450, 995
Archer (UK)..........883
Arcor 46 (Mor)..........537
Arcor 53 (Mor)..........538
Arctic (Nor)..........574
ARD 12 (Ecu)..........209
Ardhana (UAE)..........859
Argos (Por)..........634
Arguin (Mtn)..........510
Arkösund (Swe)..........779
Arleigh Burke (Flights I and II) (US)..........924
Arleigh Burke (Flight IIA) (US)..........926
Armatolos (Osprey 55) (Gre)..........306
Armidale (Aust)..........35
Arrecife (ex-Olmeca II) (Mex)..........523
Arrow Post (Can)..........108
Artigliere (Lupo) (Ita)..........397
Arun 60 (Gre)..........313
Arvak (Den)..........199
Asagiri (Jpn)..........423, 434
Ashdod (Eri, Isr)..........228, 387
Asheville (Col, Gre, US)..........173, 306, 949
Ashoora I (Sud)..........767
Ashoora I (MIG-G-0800) (Iran)..........376
Aso (Jpn)..........439
Asogiri (Jpn)..........445
Assad (Mly)..........497
Assault boats (Tld)..........812
Astute (UK)..........867
Asuka (Jpn)..........433
Atago (Jpn)..........418
Atilay (209) (Tur)..........829
Atlas (UK)..........895
Atlant (Rus)..........666
Attack (Indo)..........359
Auk (Mex, Plp)..........520, 610
Austin (Ind, US)..........346, 944
Avenger (US)..........948
Axios (Lüneburg) (Type 701) (Gre)..........310
Aydin (Tur)..........838
Azteca (Mex)..........521

B

Bacolod City (Frank S Besson) (Plp)..........612
Bad Bramstedt (Ger)..........296
Baden-Württemberg (Type 125) (Ger)..........288
Badr (SAr)..........713
Baglietto Mangusta (Alg)..........8
Baglietto Type 20 (Alg)..........8
Bahamas (Bhm)..........45
Bahtera (Mly)..........504
Bakassi (Type P 48S) (Cam)..........97
Baklan (CMN 15-60) (Yem)..........993
Baklazhan (Project 5757) (Rus)..........697
Baldur (Ice)..........323
Balsam (Col, DR, EIS, Est, Gha, Nig, Pan, Plp)..........172, 201, 226, 230, 299, 565, 592, 614
Baltyk (Pol)..........625
Balzam (Asia) (Project 1826) (Rus)..........688
Bambuk (Project 12884) (Ukr)..........854
Ban Yas (TNC 45) (UAE)..........860
Bang Rachan (Tld)..........814
Bangaram (Ind)..........344
Baptista de Andrade (Por)..........632
Baradero (Dabur) (Arg)..........18
Barbaros (Tur)..........830
Barceló (Spn)..........749
Barentshav (VS 794) (Nor)..........574
Barkat (Pak)..........590
Barracuda (Fra, Rus)..........243, 657
Barroso (Brz)..........76
Barroso Pereira (Brz)..........85
Barzan (Vita) (Qat)..........638
Baskunchak (Rus)..........706
Batral (Chi, Mor)..........122, 536
Batral type (Fra)..........265
Bay (Aust, UK, US)..........41, 893, 969
Bayandor (PF 103) (Iran)..........372
Bayóvar (Per)..........605
Baynunah (UAE)..........859
Beautemps-Beaupré (Fra)..........266
Bedok (Landsort) (Sin)..........730
Bélier (Fra)..........272
Bellatrix (DR)..........202
Bendeharu (Bru)..........89
Bereza (Ukr)..........854
Bereza (Project 130) (Bul, Rus)..........95, 696
Bergamini (Ita)..........397
Berkot-B (Rus)..........667
Berlin (Ger)..........293
Bester (Rus)..........689
Bigliani (Ita)..........410
Bihoro (Jpn)..........441
Bin Hai (CPR)..........158
Biya (Project 870) (Ukr)..........853
Biya (Project 870/871) (Rus)..........686
Biya (Project 871) (Cub)..........186
Bizerte (Tun)..........824
Bizerte (Type PR 48) (Cam)..........96
Blanco Encalada (Karel Doorman) (Chi)..........118
Blue Ridge (US)..........939
Bluebird (Tld)..........814
Bob Hope (US)..........958
Bolva (Project 688/688A) (Rus)..........690
Bombarda (Por)..........635
Bonite (Type RP 380) (Fra)..........273
Boraida (Mod Durance) (SAr)..........715
Borey (Rus)..........653
Boris Chilikin (Project 1559V) (Rus)..........691
Bormida (Ita)..........407
Botica (Mac, Ser)..........490, 720
Bouchard (Par)..........596
BPS 500 (Project 12418) (Vtn)..........988
Bracui (River) (Brz)..........80
Brahmaputra (Ind)..........336
Brandenburg (Ger)..........284
Braunschweig (K130) (Ger)..........288
Bravo (Bronstein) (Mex)..........515
Bredstedt (Ger)..........296
Bremen (Ger)..........286
Bremse (Mlt, Tun)..........508, 826
Briz (Sonya) (Project 12650) (Bul)..........93
Broadsword (Brz, Chi, Gua, Rom, UK)..........74, 119, 315, 641, 880
Bronstein (Mex)..........515
Brooke Marine 29 metre (Mly)..........505
Brunei (Bru)..........88
Brutar II (Rom)..........644
Bukhansan (RoK)..........473
Burak (Type A 69) (Tur)..........834
Buratti (Ita)..........411
Burespadoongkit (Tld)..........818
Al Bushra (Omn)..........577
Burya (Alg)..........5
Buyan (Project 21630) (Rus)..........680

C

C 14 (Iran)..........376
Cabildo (Twn)..........792
Cacine (Por)..........633
Cakra Type 209/1300 (Indo)..........353
Calmaria (Por)..........637
Canberra (Aust)..........35
Cannon (Plp, Tld)..........608, 815
Canopus (Swiftships 110 ft) (DR)..........202
Canterbury (NZ)..........562
Capana (Alligator) (Ven)..........982
Cape (Iran, Uru)..........374, 975
Cape Flattery (US)..........952
Cape (PGM 71) (Mex)..........521
Cape Roger (Can)..........108
Car Nicobar (Ind)..........345
Carlskrona (Swe)..........778
Carpentaria (Indo, Myn)..........368, 541
Carvajal (Modified Lupo) (Per)..........601
Casma (Saar 4) (Chi)..........121
Cassard (Fra)..........252
Cassiopea (Ita)..........401
Castor (Spn)..........753
Cavour (Ita)..........391
CDIC (Fra)..........265
Ceará (Thomaston) (Brz)..........81
Centauro (Por)..........634
Cetina (Silba) (Cro)..........182
CGC type (Myn)..........542
Chaho (DPRK)..........456
Chakri Naruebet (Tld)..........801
Challenger (Bhm)..........45
Challenger (Sjöormen) (Sin)..........724
Chamo (Eri)..........228
Chamois (Fra, Mad)..........269, 490
Champion (US)..........959
Chang Bogo (Type 209/1200) (RoK)..........459
Chanticleer (Tur)..........842
Chao Phraya (Tld)..........803
Charles de Gaulle (Fra)..........248
Cheng Kung (Twn)..........788
Cheong Hae Jin (RoK)..........471
Cheoy Lee (HK)..........321
Cherokee (Arg, Ecu, Mld, Per, Sri, Tur, Twn)..........17, 209, 507, 605, 764, 795, 843
Chicama (Dauntless) (Per)..........606
Chihaya (Jpn)..........435
Chimere (Fra)..........268
Chinese 27 metre (Ben, CpV)..........66, 114
Chios (Jason) (Gre)..........307
Chiyoda (Jpn)..........435
Chon Buri (Tld)..........810
Chong-Jin (DPRK)..........456
Chong-Ju (DPRK)..........456
Christina (Griffon 2000 TD) (Lit)..........490
Chui-E (Alg)..........8
Chun Jee (RoK)..........472
Circé (Tur)..........838
Claud Jones (Indo)..........353
Clemenceau (Brz)..........72
Cochrane (Chi)..........118
Collins (Aust)..........26
Colombo MK I/II/III/IV (Sri)..........762
Comandante (Ita)..........400
Combatboat 90N (Nor)..........571
Combattante I (Kwt)..........476
Combattante II (Iran)..........373
Combattante II G (Lby)..........485
Combattante III M (Qat, Tun)..........639, 823
Combattante IIIB (Nig)..........565
Commandant Rivière (Uru)..........974
Commander (Jor)..........448
Conafi 55 (Por)..........637
Conejera (Spn)..........749
Conjera (Mtn)..........510
Conrado Yap (Sea Hawk/Killer) (Plp)..........612
Constitución (Ven)..........981
Constitution (US)..........953
Converted Compass Island (US)..........956
Converted Stalwart (US)..........957
Cormoran (Col, Mor)..........172, 534
Corregidor (Plp)..........616
Corrubia (Ita)..........410
Corsar (Rom)..........645
Cosmos (US)..........971
Costa Sur (Arg)..........20
Cougar Enforcer 40 (Kwt)..........478
County (Damen Stan Patrol 4207) (Jam)..........412
Cove (Tur)..........838
Cove Island (Can)..........110
CPL Louis J Hauge, Jr (US)..........960
Crestitalia MV-45 (Qat)..........639
Crestitalia MV 55 (Pak)..........591
Crestitalia MV 70 (Egy)..........223
Croitor (Rom)..........646
Cumella (Can)..........110
Cutlass (Gua, Tld)..........315, 818
Cutthroat (US)..........951
Cyclone (Plp, US)..........609, 937, 967
Czilim (Project 20910) (Rus)..........706

D

Dabur (Arg, Chi, Fij, Isr, Nic)........18, 121, 233, 386, 563
Dachou (CPR)........164
Dadie (CPR)........157
Dadong (Type 946) (CPR)........160
Daewoo Type (RoK)........474
Dagger (Indo)........358
Dahua (CPR)........157
Dajiang (Type 925) (CPR)........161
Dakhla (Mor)........536
Dalang (Type 922 II/III) (CPR)........161
Damen Mk III (HK)........320
Damen Polycat 1450 (Qat)........639
Damen Stan Patrol 4207 (Jam)........412
Damsah (Combattante III M) (Qat)........639
Danbjørn (Den)........199
Dandao (CPR)........162
Danlin (CPR)........161
Danyao (CPR)........163
Daozha (CPR)........164
Daphne (EqG)........227
Daphné (Por)........629
Daring (UK)........877
Darss (Spn)........753
Dauntless (Ant, Bhm, Cay, Dom, Geo, Gra, Gua, Jam, Jor, Kaz, Per, StK, StL, StV, VI)........10, 46, 114, 200, 280, 314-315, 413, 448-449, 606, 707-709, 992
Daxin (Alg, CPR)........7, 159
Dayun (Type 904) (CPR)........161
Dazhou (Type 946) (CPR)........161
De Havilland (Plp)........616
De La Penne (ex-Animoso) (Ita)........395
De Ruyter (Per)........600
De Zeven Provincien (Nld)........548
Deba (Pol, Yem)........622, 994
Defender (Chi, Iraq, Isr, Ken, Mex, Nig, US, Yem)........126, 381, 387, 450, 522, 565, 971, 995
Delfin (Col, Rus)........174, 651
Delhi (Ind)........332
Delta III (Kalmar) (Rus)........652
Delta III Stretch (Project 667 BDR) (Rus)........663
Delta IV (Delfin) (Rus)........651
Delvar (Iran)........379
Démocrata (Mex)........521
Depoli (Ita)........407
Dergach (Sivuch) (Project 1239) (Rus)........676
Descubierta (Egy, Spn)........215, 747
D'Estienne d'Orves (Type A 69) (Fra)........257
Dhofar (Province) (Omn)........577
Diana (SF MK II) (Den)........194
Diciotti (Iraq, Mlt)........380, 508
Dilos (Cypr, Geo, Gre)........187, 279, 312
Diver (Tur, US)........841, 965
Djebel Chenoua (C 58) (Alg)........5
Dobrynya Nikitich (Project 97) (Rus)........697
Dog (UK)........895
Doğan (Tur)........835
Dokkum (Per)........604
Dolphin (Type 800) (Isr)........383
Dong Hae (RoK)........467
Drina (Mon)........530
Drummond (Type A 69) (Arg)........14
Dubna (Rus)........691
Duke (UK)........878
Dumit (Can)........109
Durance (Arg, Aust, Fra)........20, 38, 269
Durango (Mex)........519
Durbar (Hegu) (Ban)........56
Durdharsha (Huangfen) (Ban)........56
Durjoy (Hainan) (Ban)........56
Dvora (Sri)........763
Dzheyran (Project 1232.1) (Rus)........682

E

Eagle (US)........970
Echo (UK)........888
Eckaloo (Can)........109
Edenton (RoK, US)........471, 965
Edic (Mad, Sen)........491, 719
Edic 700 (Fra, Sen)........265, 719
Edincik (Circé) (Tur)........838
Edsall (Mex)........525
EDVM 25 (Brz)........81
Eilat (Saar 5) (Isr)........384
Eithne (Ire)........381
Ekpe (Lürssen 57) (Nig)........565
El Mouderrib (Chui-E) (Alg)........8
El Mounkid (Alg)........8
El Wacil (P 32) (Mor)........535
Elbe (Ger)........293
Elbrus (Osimol) (Project 537) (Rus)........693
Eleuthera (Keith Nelson) (Bhm)........46
Elicura (Chi)........122
Elli (Kortenaer) (Gre)........303
Emba (Project 1172/1175) (Rus)........693
Emory S Land (US)........958
Endurance (Sin, Tld)........729, 812
Enforcer II (Rus)........705
Ensdorf (Ger)........291
Enterprise (US)........916
Éridan (Pak)........588
Éridan (Tripartite) (Fra)........266
Erraid (P 32) (Mor)........537
Ertuğrul (Terrebonne Parish) (Tur)........837
Esmeraldas (Ecu)........206
Espada (Ecu)........210
Espadarte (CpV)........113
Esploratore (Ita)........401
Espora (Meko 140 A16) (Arg)........15
Esterel (Type RPC 50) (Fra)........272
Etna (Gre, Ita)........309, 406
Europa (Ger)........296
Evniki (Osprey) (Gre)........308
Evropi (Hunt) (Gre)........308
Express Shark Cat (Aust)........40

F

Fabian Wrede (Fin)........238
Fairey Marine Spear (StK)........707
Fairey Sword (Bhr)........51
Faisal (Commander) (Jor)........448
Famous cutter (US)........964
Fatahillah (Indo)........355
Faysal (Jor)........448
FB 55SC (HK)........321
FB RIB 42SC (HK)........321
Fearless (Sin)........727
Felicity (UK)........895
Al Feyi (UAE)........861
Finik (Project 872) (Rus)........686
Fish (Aust)........38
Flamant (OPV 54) (Fra)........262
Flamingo (Tanya) (Project 1415) (Rus)........694
Floréal (Fra)........258
Floreal (Mor)........531
Flower (Bel)........64
Flower (Tripartite) (Bul)........93
Flyvefisken (Den, Lit)........193, 488
Forbin (Horizon) (Fra)........251
Formidable (Project Delta) (Sin)........725
Fort Grange (UK)........891
Fort Victoria (UK)........891
Foudre (Fra)........264
Foxtrot (Lby)........483
Foxtrot (Project 641) (Ind)........325
FPB 57 type (Kwt)........476
Frank S Besson (Plp, US)........612, 947
Frankenthal (Ger, UAE)........291, 860
Frauenlob (Type 394) (Est)........229
Freedom (US)........928
Fregat (Rus)........669
Fregat II (Rus)........668
Fréhel (Fra)........273
Fremm (Mor)........533
French Edic (Leb)........483
Fridtjof Nansen (Nor)........568
Frosch I (Indo)........362
Frosch II (Indo)........365
Fuchi (CPR)........160
Fulin (CPR)........162
Fulmar (Fra)........276
Fuqing (CPR, Pak)........160, 589
Furusund (Swe)........779
Futami (Jpn)........432
Futi (CPR)........156
Future Aircraft Carrier (Fra)........247
Future Frigates (FFX) (RoK)........466
Fuzhou (CPR)........163

G

Gabes (Tun)........826
Gaeta (Aust, Tld)........35, 814
Gagah (Mly)........504
Gahjae (Iran)........375
Galana (Ken)........451
Galerna (Agosta) (S 70) (Spn)........741
Galicia (Spn)........751
Ganzhu (CPR)........158
Garibaldi (Ita)........392
Gavion (Ven)........984
Gaziantep (Oliver Hazard Perry) (Tur)........832
Gearing (Fram 1) (Pak)........590
Georges Leygues (Fra)........253
Gepard (Ger)........290
Gepard (Project 11661) (Rus, Vtn)........673, 987
Gerald R Ford (US)........920
Geranium (Fra)........275
Ghaem (MIG-S-1800) (Iran)........374
Ghazee (Mld)........507
Glavkos (Gre)........300
Gleaner (UK)........888
Glycine (Fra)........268
Godavari (Ind)........335
Golf (CPR)........129
Goliat (Lat)........480
Golok (Indo)........367
Goplo (Notec) (Pol)........622
Gordon (US)........958
Gordon Reid (Can)........109
Gorya (Type 12660) (Rus)........683
Goryn (Project 714) (Rus)........698
Gotland (A 19) (Swe)........770
Gowind 200 (Bul)........91
GPB-480 (Project 1896) (Rus)........686
Göteborg (Swe)........772
Grajaú (Brz, Nam)........78, 544
Granby (Can)........105
Grèbe (Fra)........262
Griffon (Can)........107
Griffon 2000 TD (Lit)........490
Griffon 2000 TDX (Pol, Swe)........628, 781
Griffon 8000 TD(M) (Ind)........352
Griffon 8000 TD(M) (SAr)........717
Griffon 8100TD (Type 392) (Swe)........776
Grif-T (Tkm)........847
Grisha (Ukr)........850
Grisha (Albatros) (Project 1124/1124M/1124K/1124EM) (Rus)........674
Grisha (Albatros) (Project 1124P/1124M/1124MP/1124MU) (Rus)........699
Grisha III (Albatros) (Lit)........487
Grom (Rus)........670
Gromovoy (CPR)........165
Grumete Diaz (Dabur) (Chi)........121
Guaicamacuto (Ven)........982
Guangzhou (CPR)........163
Guardian (Gra, Hon, US)........314, 318, 967
Gulf (Can)........106
Gumdoksuri (RoK)........467
Guns (Pak)........591
Guppy II (Twn)........787
Gus (Skat) (Project 1205) (Rus)........682
Gyda (Nor)........571

H

H 960 (Pol)........626
Hai Cheng (Twn)........798
Hai Lung (Twn)........786
Hai Ou (Twn)........791
Hai Ying (Twn)........799
Haijiu (Type 037/1) (CPR)........149
Hainan (Ban, Egy, DPRK)........56, 219, 455
Hainan (Type 037) (China, Myn)........150, 541
Haiqing (Type 037/1S) (CPR)........150
Haixun 21 (CPR)........167
Haixun 31 (CPR)........167
Haizhui (Type 062/1) (Ban)........57
Haizhui (Type 062/1G) (Sri)........762
Haizhui/Shanghai III (Type 062/1) (CPR)........151
Halcon (Type B 119) (Arg)........22
Halifax (Can)........100
Halmatic 20 metre (Bhr)........51
Halmatic 160 (Bhr)........51
Halmatic M 160 (Ana, Qat)........9, 640
Hamashio (Jpn)........446
Hämeenmaa (Fin)........236
Hamilton and Hero (US)........963
Hamina (Fin)........235
Han (CPR)........130
Han Kang (RoK)........472
Hanchon (DPRK)........457
Handalan (Spica-M) (Mly)........498
Hang Tuah (Type 41/61) (Mly)........501
Hantae (DPRK)........457
Hårek (Alusafe 1300) (Nor)........571
Haruna (Jpn)........426
Harushio (Jpn)........416
Hashidate (Jpn)........436
Hashim (Rotork) (Jor)........448
Hashmat (Agosta 70) (Pak)........582
Hatakaze (Jpn)........420
Hateruma (Jpn)........439
Hatsushima/Uwajima (Jpn)........432
Hatsuyuki (Jpn)........424
Hainan (Ban)........56
Hauki (Fin)........238
Hawar (Bhr)........51
Hawk (Jor)........448
Hayabusa (Jpn)........428
Hayagumo (Jpn)........443
Hayanami (Jpn)........444
Healy (US)........968
Hecla (Indo, SA)........363, 737
Hegu (Egy)........219
Helgoland (Ger)........295
Helgoland (Type 720B) (Uru)........976
Hellenic 56 (Gre)........306
Helsinki (Cro)........182
Hendijan (Iran)........379
Hengam (Iran)........377
Henry J Kaiser (US)........955
Hercules (Type 42) (Arg)........19
Hermes (Ind)........329
Hero (Jam)........413
Hetz (Saar 4.5) (Isr)........385
Hibiki (Jpn)........432
Hida (Jpn)........438
Hila (Fin)........239
Hirashima (Jpn)........431
Hiryu (Jpn)........445
Hisar (PC 1638) (Tur)........836
Hiuchi (Jpn)........436
Ho Hsing (Twn)........796
Hobart (Aust)........27
Hokuto (Jpn)........446
Holland (Nld)........551
Holm (Den)........194
Holzinger (Águila) (Mex)........518
Hongqi (CPR)........162
Horizon (Ita)........394
Houbei (Type 022) (CPR)........149
Houdong (Iran)........373
Houjian (or Huang) (Type 037/2) (CPR)........150
Hounan (Type 021) (Yem)........993
Houxin (Type 037/1G) (CPR, Myn)........149, 540
Hua Hin (Tld)........809
Huangfen (Ban, Pak)........56, 590
Huangpu (Mtn)........510
Huasteco (Mex)........526
Huchuan (Ban, Tan)........56, 799
Hudong (Tld)........815
Hujiu (Ban, CPR)........60, 164
Huludao (CPR)........165
Humboldt (Mex)........524
Hungnam (DPRK)........457
Hunt (Gre, Lit, UK)........308, 488, 887
Huon (Gaeta) (Aust)........35
Huracan (Saar 4.5) (Mex)........517
Al Hussein (Hawk) (Jor)........448
Huxin (CPR)........166
Hydra (Gre)........302
Hyuga (Jpn)........417

I

Igor Belousov (Project 23100) (Rus)........696
Ilocos Norte (Plp)........614
Impeccable (US)........956
Imperial Marinheiro (Brz, Nam)........79, 544
Improved Hirashima (Jpn)........431
Improved Osprey 55 (Sen)........718
Improved Romeo (Egy)........213
Improved Sauro (Ita)........390
Improved Tetal (Rom)........643
Improved Tursas (Fin)........241
Improved Y 301 (Myn)........541
Independence (US)........932
Indigenous Aircraft Carrier (Ind)........330
Ingul (Project 1453) (Rus)........697
Inhaúma (Brz)........76
Interceptor (Sen)........718
Intrepida (Arg)........18
Inttisar (OPV 310) (Kwt)........477
Invincible (UK)........872
Iran (Iran)........378
Iran Hormuz 21 (Iran)........378
Iran Hormuz 24 (Iran)........378
Iroquois (Can)........102
Iscar (Vanya) (Project 257D) (Bul)........94
Ishikari/Yuubari (Jpn)........427
Iskra (Pol)........624
Isla (Mex)........521
Isla Fernandina (Vigilante) (Ecu)........210
Island (Ban, TT, US)........55, 821, 966
Itaipú (Par)........596
Ivan Susanin (Project 97P) (Rus)........701
Ivar Huitfeldt (Den)........192
Izar IVP-22 (Spn)........758
Izu (Jpn)........437

J

Jacinto (Peacock) (Plp)........609
Jägaren (Swe)........775
Jaime Gómez (MK III PB) (Col)........173
Jalalat (Pak)........587
Al Jarim (FPB 20) (Bhr)........49
Jastreb (Rus)........672
Al Jawf (Sandown) (SAr)........715
Jayasagara (Sri)........761
Jeanne d'Arc (Fra)........250
Jebel Antar (Alg)........8

Jerong (Mly) 499
Jianghu (CPR) 166
Jianghu I (Egy) 216
Jianghu I/II/V (Type 053H/053H1/053H1G) (CPR) 144
Jianghu III (Type 053 H2) (CPR) 146
Jianghu IV (Type 053HTH) (CPR) 147
Jiangkai I (Type 054) (CPR) 140
Jiangkai II (Type 054A) (CPR) 141
Jiangwei I (Type 053 H2G) (CPR) 142
Jiangwei II (Type 053H3) (CPR) 142
Jija Bai Mod 1 (Ind) 351
Jin (CPR) 128
Jin Chiang (Twn) 791
Jingsah II (CPR) 155
Jinyou (CPR) 163
João Coutinho (Por) 632
Johan de Witt (Nld) 553
John McDonnell (US) 957
José Andrada (Plp) 611
José Maria Palas (Swift 110) (Col) 173
Al Jouf (SAr) 716
Al Jubatel (SAr) 717
Juniper (US) 969
Jura (UK) 900
Jurmo (Fin) 240
Jurrat (Pak) 587
Jyoti (Ind) 347

K

K 8 (Project 361T) (Vtn) 991
Kaan 15 (Tur) 837, 845
Kaan 19 (Tur) 845
Kaan 29 (Tur) 845
Kaan 33 (Tur) 845
Kachalot (Rus) 663
Kagitingan (Plp) 611
Kajami (Iran) 375
Kakap (PB 57) (Indo) 359
Kal Kangean (Indo) 367
Kal-40 (Indo) 360
Kala (Fin) 238
Kaliningradneft (Rus) 692
Kalkan (Project 50030) M (EqG, Tkm, Ukr) 227, 847, 856
Kalmar (Rus) 652
Kalmar (Project 1206) (Rus) 682
Kaman (Combattante II) (Iran) 373
Kamenka (Project 870) (Vtn) 991
Kamenka (Project 870/871) (Rus) 686
Kampela (Fin) 238
Kan (CPR) 157
Kang Ding (La Fayette) (Twn) 789
Kangan (Iran) 378
Kanimbla (Newport) (Aust) 32
Kanin (Rus) 706
Kaoh (Cmb) 96
Kaper (Pol) 626
Kapitan Patimura (Parchim I) (Indo) 356
Kara (Berkot-B) (Rus) 667
Karbala (MIG-S-3700) (Iran) 378
Karel Doorman (Bel, Chi, Nld, Por) 62, 118, 550, 630
Karnaphuli (Kraljevica) (Ban) 57
Kartal (Tur) 835
Kashdom II (Iran) 376
Kashima (Jpn) 433
Kashin II (Ind) 331
Kashin (Project 61) (Rus) 667
Kashtan (Project 141) (Rus) 693
Kasos (Hellenic 56) (Gre) 306
Kasturi (Type FS 1500) (Mly) 495
Kaszub (Pol) 620
Katun (Rus) 698
Kayvan (Cape) (Iran) 374
KBV 001 (Swe) 780
KBV 041 (Lit) 489
KBV 101 (Lit, Swe) 489, 780
KBV 181 (Swe) 781
KBV 201 (Swe) 781
KBV 236 (Est, Lat) 231, 481
KBV 281 (Swe) 781
KBV 288 (Swe) 781
KBV 301 (Swe) 781
KBV 591 (Griffon 2000 TDX) (Swe) 781
KDX-2 (RoK) 461
Kebir (Alg, Bar) 6, 61
Kedah (Meko 100 RMN) (Mly) 496
Keelung (Kidd) (Twn) 787
Keeper (US) 969
Kefallinia (Zubr) (Gre) 307
Keith Nelson (Bhm) 46
Keka (HK) 320
Khalid (Agosta 90B) (Pak) 583
Khamronsin (Tld) 806
Khobi (Indo, Rus) 365, 692
Khukri (Ind) 339
Ki Hajar Dewantara (Indo) 364
Kidd (Twn) 787
Kiiski (Fin) 237
Kiisla (Fin) 234
Kilauea (US) 955
Kiliç (Tur) 835
Kilo (Alg, CPR, Iran, Pol, Rus) 4, 132, 369, 618, 661
King (Arg) 20
Kingston (Can) 103
Kirov (Orlan) (Rus) 665
Klasma (Project 1274) (Rus) 692
Knox (Egy, Mex, Tld, Tur, Twn) 215, 514, 804, 833, 790
Knud Rasmussen (Den) 193
Knurrhahn (Ger) 294
Kobben (Type 207) (Pol) 617
Kogalniceanu (Rom) 644
Kojima (Jpn) 438
Kolkata (Project 15A) (Ind) 330
Komandor (Rus) 701
Komar (DPRK) 455
Končar (Mon) 528
Končar (Type R-02) (Cro) 181
Kondor (Rus) 658
Kondor I (CpV, Tun) 113, 826
Kondor II (Uru) 976
Kondor II (Type 89) (Indo) 362
Kongbang (DPRK) 457
Kongou (Jpn) 419
Koni (Alg, Bul) 4, 90
Koni (Project 1159) (Lby) 484
Kora (Ind) 338
Kormoran (Pol) 625
Korond (Project 1258) (Ukr, Vtn) 852, 991
Kortenaer (Gre, UAE) 303, 857
Koster (Swe) 777
Kotor (Mon) 528
Kowan (DPRK) 457
Kozara (Ser) 720
Krab (Project 535M) (Rus) 695
Kralj (Type R-03) (Cro) 182
Kraljevica (Ban) 57
Krivak (Project 1135/1135M/1135MP) (Rus) 671
Krivak III (Nerey) (Ukr) 849
Krivak III (Nerey) (Project 1135MP) (Rus) 700
Krogulec (Pol) 622
KSS-2 (Type 214) (RoK) 460
Ku Song, Sin Hung and Mod Sin Hung (DPRK) 456
Kuha (Fin) 236
Kujang (Indo) 367
Kulik (Project 1415PV) (Rus) 705
Kulmbach (Ger) 291
Kurihama (Jpn) 433
Kurmuk (Type 15) (Sud) 767
Kurobe (Jpn) 434
Kutter (Lit) 489
Kuznetsov (Orel) (Rus) 664
Kuznetsov (Orel) (Project 1143.5/6) (CPR) 134
KW 15 (Tur) 845
KW 15 (Type 369) (Kaz) 449
Kwang Hua 6 (Twn) 792
Kwanggaeto Daewang (KDX-1) (RoK) 463

L

La Belle Poule (Fra) 268
La Combattante II (Mly) 499
La Combattante IIA (Gre) 305
La Combattante III (Gre) 305
La Cruz (Per) 606
La Fayette (Fra, Twn) 256, 789
Lada (Rus) 660
Lake (NZ) 560
Laksamana (Assad) (Mly) 497
Lama (Type 323/323B) (Rus) 696
Landing ships (Alg) 6
Landsort (Sin, Swe) 730, 776
Langkawi (Mly) 503
Lapérouse (Fra) 261, 267
Lapérouse (BH2) (Fra) 267
Larkana (Pak) 588
Laskos (La Combattante III) (Gre) 305
Lat Ya (Gaeta) (Tld) 814
Latorre (Chi) 117
Lazaga (Col, Mor) 171, 534
LCM (Uru) 978
LCM 6 (SAr, Twn) 716, 793
LCM 8 (Aust, EIS, RoK) 40, 226, 468
LCP (Den) 195
LCT 3 (Alb) 3
LCU 501 (Twn) 793
LCU 1466 (Bhr, Twn) 50, 793
LCU 1512 (Ban) 60
LCU 1600 (DR, US) 203, 948
LCU 1610 (Brz, SAr) 81, 715
LCU 2000 (US) 947
LCU Mk IX (Nld) 551
LCVP (Ban) 60
LCVP MK 2 (Nld) 554
LCVP MK III (Nld) 551
LCVP MK V (Nld) 554
LCVPs (Arg) 19
Le Malin (Fra) 270
Le Triomphant (Fra) 246
Leander (Ecu, Ind) 206, 337
Leander (Batch 3A) (Ind) 347
Lebed (Kalmar) (Project 1206) (Rus) 682
Leeuwin (Aust) 36
Legend (US) 963
Leizhou (CPR) 162
Lekiu (Mly) 494
Leonard J Cowley (Can) 108
Leopard (Ban) 55
Léopard (Fra) 268
Lerici (Mly, Nig) 500, 566
Lerici/Gaeta (Ita) 403
Lewis and Clark (US) 954
LHT-130 (Spn) 754
Lida (Sapfir) (Project 10750) (Rus) 684
Lima (SA) 738
Lindau (Type 331) (Geo, Lit) 280, 488
Lindormen (Est) 229
Lohi (Fin) 239
Lokki (Fin, Lat, Lit) 237, 480, 489
Loreto (Per) 603
Los Angeles (US) 914
Louisbourg (Can) 108
LPR-40 (Col) 172
LS 51 (Gre) 313
LSIL 351 (Tld) 812
LST 1-510 and 512-1152 (Twn) 793
LST 1-511 and 512-1152 (Indo) 361
LST 512-1152 (Plp, RoK, Tld, Twn) 468, 612, 793, 812
Lubin (Mon) 530
Lublin (Pol) 622
Luda (Type 051DT/051G/051G II) (CPR) 140
Luda (Types 051/051D/051Z) (CPR) 139
Luga (Az) 43
Luhai (CPR) 137
Luhu (Type 052) (CPR) 138
Luneburg (Col) 176
Lüneburg (Egy, Uru) 222, 978
Lüneburg (Type 701) (Gre) 310
Lung Chiang (Twn) 791
Lung-Teh (HK) 321
Lupo (Ita, Per) 397, 600
Lushun (Type 062/1G) (Sri) 762
Lürssen FPB 45 (Gha) 299
Lürssen PB 57 (Gha) 299
Lürssen VSV 15 (Indo) 366
Luyang I (Type 052B) (CPR) 136
Luyang II (Type 052C) (CPR) 137
Luzhou (CPR) 134
Lynch (Arg) 22
Lyness (US) 955

M

M 10 (Sri) 766
Maagen (Est) 229
Machitis (Gre) 306
Madhumati (Sea Dragon) (Ban) 55
Madina (Type F 2000s) (SAr) 712
Maestrale (Ita) 396
Magar (Ind) 345
Mahamiru (Lerici) (Mly) 500
Maipo (Batral) (Chi) 122
Maïto (Fra) 273
Makar (Ind) 347
Malakhit (Project 1259) (Rus) 684
Malaspina (Spn) 754
Malawali (Mly) 504
Malina (Project 2020) (Rus) 690
Mamba (Ken) 450
Mamry (Notec II) (Pol) 623
Man Nok (Tld) 812
Al Manama (MGB 62) (Bhr) 48
Máncora (Per) 607
Mandovi (Mtn) 510
Mangust (Project 12150) (Rus) 704
Manly (UK) 897
Manta (Ecu, Kwt) 210, 478
Manuel Azueta (Edsall) (Mex) 525
Manuel Clavero (Per) 603
Manych (Project 1549) (Rus) 692
Mar del Plata (Z-28) (Arg) 22
Marañon (Per) 602
Marasesti (Rom) 642
Marine Protector (Mlt, US) 508, 967
Marlim (Meatini) (Brz) 78
Marlin (Mly) 505
Mars (US) 954
Marshal Nedelin (Project 1914) (Rus) 687
Marte (Per) 605
Martha L Black (Can) 107
Mashuu (Jpn) 434
Mataphon (Tld) 813
Matka (Vekhr) (Rus, Ukr) 680, 851
Matsunami (Jpn) 443
Mazinger (RoK) 472
Mazzei (Ita) 410
MCC 1101 (Ita) 406
MCMV 2010 (Fin) 235
Meatini (Brz, Ita) 78, 410
Meghna (Ban) 57
Meiyo (Jpn) 446
Meko 200 PN (Por) 631
Meko Type 360 H1 (Nig) 564
Melville (US) 950
Men 212 (Ita) 408
Men 215 (Ita) 408
Mercy (US) 955
Meriuisko (Fin) 239
Mesar (Bul) 95
MHV 90 (Den) 195
MHV 800 (Den) 195
MHV 900 (Den) 194
Micalvi (Chi) 121
Michao (Myn) 542
Mihashi and Raizan (Jpn) 442
Mikhail Rudnitsky (Project 05360/1) (Rus) 693
MIL 40 (Iran) 377
MIL 55 (Iran) 377
Milgem (Tur) 833
Minerva (Ita) 398
Ming (CPR) 133
Minna (UK) 900
Mirazh (Project 14310) (Rus) 704
Mirna (Mon) 530
Mirna (Type 140) (Cro) 181
Missile Range Instrumentation Ship (US) 958
Mistral (Fra) 263
Miura (Jpn) 438
Mizuho (Jpn) 437
Mk V (Kwt, US) 476, 938
Moa (NZ) 561
Mod Altay (Rus) 691
Mod Durance (SAr) 715
Mod Haizhui (Lushun) (Type 062/1G) (Sri) 762
Mod Shanghai II (Sri) 762
Mod Sorum (Project 1454) (Rus) 687
Mod Yanha (CPR) 164
Modified Alligator (Project 11711E) (Rus) 680
Modified Descubierta (Mor) 532
Modified Finik 2 (Pol) 623
Modified Georges Leygues (Fra) 254
Modified Hai Ou (Par) 597
Modified Haizhui (Tun) 823
Modified Hiryu (Jpn) 445
Modified Hvidbjørnen (Est) 228
Modified Kiev (Ind) 328
Modified La Fayette (SAr) 710
Modified Lupo (Per, Ven) 601, 980
Modified Moma (Pol) 624
Modified MTM 217 (Ita) 402
Modified Niterói (Brz) 84
Modified Patra (Cypr) 187
Modified Poolster (Nld) 556
Modified R (Can) 106
Modified River (UK) 884
Modified Sportis (Pol) 628
Modified Stenka (Cmb) 96
Modified Ulsan (Ban) 53
Modified Zhuk (Vtn) 990
Mollendo (Per) 604
Molnya (Ukr) 855
Molnya (Project 12412) (Rus) 702
Molnya (Project 1241P) (Ukr) 851
Moma (Project 861) (Bul, Cro, Rus) 94, 183, 685
Moma (Project 861M) (Rus, Ukr) 688, 853
Moorhen (UK) 894
Morkov (Project 1461.3) (Rus) 695
Morona (Per) 605
Morrosquillo (LCU 1466A) (Col) 175
Moskit (Pol) 625
Moskit (Project 1248) (Rus) 706
El Mouderrib (Chui-E) (Alg) 8
El Mounkid (Alg) 8
Mourad Rais (Koni) (Alg) 4
MPMB (Cro) 183
Mrowka (Pol) 625
MSB 5 (Pan) 594
MSC 289 (Tur) 839
MSF (Den) 195
MSF Mk 1 (Swe) 777
MTC 1011 (Ita) 407
MTM 217 (Ita) 401
MTP 96 (Ita) 402
Mubarraz (UAE) 860

Mukha (Sokol) (Project 1145) (Rus) 680
Muna (Type 1823) (Rus) 696
Munsif (Éridan) (Pak) 588
Murakumo (Jpn) 443
Murasame (Jpn) 422
Muravey (Antares) (Ukr) 856
Muravey (Antares) (Project 133) (Rus) 702
Muray Jib (MGB 62) (UAE) 858
Murce (MIG-G-0900) (Iran) 376
Muroto (Jpn) 435
Musca (Rom) 645
Mustang (Project 18623) (Rus) 702
Myanmar (Myn) 540

N

Nahang (Iran) 370
Nahidik (Can) 109
Najin (DPRK) 454
Namacurra (Ang, Mlw, Moz, Nam, SA) 9, 491, 538, 545, 737
Nampo (DPRK) 457
Nanuchka (Rus) 678
Nanuchka II (Burya) (Alg) 5
Nanuchka II (Project 1234) (Lby) 484
Nanyun (CPR) 160
Napo (Ecu) 211
Naresuan (Tld) 802
Nascimento (Brz) 84
Nasty (Gre) 305
Natsugiri (Jpn) 444
Natya (Yem) 994
Natya (Project 266M) (Syr) 785
Natya (Project 266ME) (Lby) 485
Natya I (Ind, Ukr) 346, 852
Natya I (Akvamaren) (Project 266M) (Rus) 683
Neftegaz (Project B-92) (Rus) 697
Negrita (Pan) 593
Neon Antonov (Project 1595) (Rus) 706
Nepa (Project 530) (Rus) 696
Nesbitt (UK) 889
Nestin (Hun, Ser) 322, 720
Neustadt (Bul, Rom) 92, 644
Neustrashimy (Jastreb) (Rus) 672
Newport (Aust, Brz, Chi, Mex, Mly, Mor, Spn, Twn) 32, 80, 122, 523, 499, 535, 750, 792
NFI (Indo) 366
Nichinan (Jpn) 432
Nicobar (Ind) 348
Niels Juel (Den) 190
Niijima (Jpn) 431
Niki (Thetis) (Type 420) (Gre) 307
Nilgiri (Leander) (Ind) 337
Nimitz (US) 917
Ning Hai (Twn) 792
Nisr (Egy) 224
Niterói (Brz) 75
Nojima (Jpn) 438
Noosacat 930 Workboats (Aust) 40
Nordkapp (Nor) 574
Nordriza (Col) 172
Normed (Tld) 812
Nornen (Nor) 575
Notec (Pol) 622
Notec II (Pol) 623
NS-722 (Yem) 994
Nunobiki (Jpn) 445
Nusa (Mly) 504
Nyayo (Ken) 450
Nyryat 2 (Project 522) (Rus) 694
Nyryat I (Project 1896) (Rus) 694
Nyryat I (Project 522) (Egy) 222

O

Oaxaca (Mex) 519
Ob (Project 320) (Rus) 692
Oban (UK) 897
Ocea FPB 98 (Alg) 8
October (Egy) 219
Odinn (Ice) 323
Ogonek (Project 12130) (Rus) 705
Ohio (US) 910-911
Ohre (Ger) 294
Ojika (Jpn) 438
Okba (PR 72) (Mor) 533
Okhtensky (Egy) 223
Okhtensky (Project 733/733S) (Rus) 698
Oksøy/Alta (Nor) 572
OL 44 (Gre) 313
Olekma (Rus) 691
Oliver Hazard Perry (Aust, Bhr, Egy, Pol, Tur, US) 30, 47, 214, 619, 832, 930
Olivieri (Arg) 17
Olya (Malakhit) (Project 1259) (Rus) 684
Olya (Project 1259) (Bul) 94
Ondatra (Akula) (Project 1176) (Rus) 682
Onega (Project 1806) (Rus) 686
Onjuku (Mex) 524
Oosumi (Jpn) 429
OPV 54 (Mtn) 510
Orca (Can) 104
Orel (Rus) 664
Orkan (Sassnitz) (Pol) 620
Orlan (Rus) 665
Osa (DPRK) 455
Osa (Project 205) (Bul, Syr) 92, 784
Osa I (Project 205) (Egy) 218
Osa II (Alg, Cub) 6, 185
Osa II (Project 20S) (Az) 45
Osa II (Project 205) (Lby, Vtn) 485, 989
Oscar II (Antyey) (Project 949B) (Rus) 654
Osimol (Rus) 693
Osman (Jianghu I) (Ban) 54
Osman Gazi (Tur) 837
Osprey (Egy, Gre, Myn, Twn) 220, 308, 540, 794
Osprey 55 (Gre) 306
Osprey FV 710 (Nam) 545
Osprey Mk II (Mor) 534
Oste (Ger) 293
Ouranos (Gre) 310
Outrage (Hon) 318
Oyashio (Jpn) 415

P

P 21 (Ire) 382
P 41 Peacock (Ire) 382
P 101 (Spn) 749
P 400 (Fra, Gab) 262, 277
P-2000 (Mrt) 511
Pabna (Ban) 58
Pacific (CI, Fij, Kir, Mic, Ml, Pal, PNG, Sam, Sol, Ton, Tuv, Van) 178, 233, 451, 527, 509, 591, 595, 710, 733, 820, 848, 978
Padstow and Newhaven (UK) 897
Paita (Terrebonne Parish) (Per) 603
Paltus/X-ray (Project 1851) (Rus) 662
Paluma (Aust) 36
Pamlico (US) 970
Pansio (Fin) 236
Panuco (Mex) 522
Pao Hsing (Twn) 796
Papanikolis (Type 214) (Gre) 301
Pará (Brz) 84
Parchim I (Indo) 356
Parchim II (Rus) 675
Parnaiba (Brz) 79
Parvin (PGM-71) (Iran) 374
Pashe (MIG-G-1900) (Iran) 374
Pathfinder (US) 957
Patiño (Spn) 755
Patra (Ctl, Fra, Gab, Mtn) 180, 275, 278, 510
Pattani (Tld) 805
Pauk I (Molnya) (Ukr) 855
Pauk I (Molnya) (Project 12412) (Rus) 702
Pauk I (Molnya) (Project 1241P) (Ukr) 851
Pauk II (Cub) 185
Pauk II (Project 1241 PE) (Rus) 702
PB 90 (Myn) 540
PCE 827 (Plp) 610
PCF 46 (Plp) 615
PCF 50 (Swift Mk 1 and Mk 2) (Plp) 615
PCF 65 (Swift Mk 3) (Plp) 612, 615
Peacock (Plp) 609
Pedretti (Ita) 401
Pedro Teixeira (Brz) 79
Pegasus (SAr) 716
Pelym (Project 1799) (Cub, Rus) .. 186, 695
Pembanteras (Mly) 506
Pengawal (Mly) 505
Penggalang (Mly) 504
Peninjau (Mly) 504
Penryn (UK) 899
Penyelamat (Mly) 504
Perdana (La Combattante II) (Mly) 499
Perwira (Bru) 89
Pescalonso (Spn) 749
Peterson MK 4 (Gam, Sen) 278, 718
Petrel (Point) (Ven) 983
Petrushka (UK-3) (Az, Rus, Ukr) 42, 689, 853
Petya (Project 159A/AE) (Vtn) 987
Petya II (Project 159A) (Az) 42
Petya III (Project 159A) (Syr) 783
Peykaap I (IPS 16) (Iran) 375
Peykaap II (IPS 16 Mod) (Iran) 375
PG 01 (Sparviero) (Jpn) 428
PGM-39 (Plp) 615
PGM-71 (Ecu) 211
PGM 71 (Per, Tld, Tur) 606, 810, 836
Phaéton (Fra) 271
Piast (Pol, Uru) 625, 977
Pijao (Type 209/1200) (Col) 169
Pikker (Est) 230
Piraña (Ecu) 211
Piranha (ElS) 226
Piratini (Brz) 80
Piyavka (Project 1249) (Rus) 705
Plascoa (Dji) 200
PO 2 (Project 501) (Alb, Bul) 2, 94
PO Hang (RoK) 466
Point (Arg, Az, Col, CR, DR, Ecu, EIS, Geo, Mex, Pan, Plp, StL, TT, Tkm, Ven) 18, 45, 172, 179, 202, 210, 225, 280, 521, 593, 611, 708, 821, 847, 983
Poisk-2 (Project 1832) (Rus) 689
Polar (US) 968
Polaris (Mex, Ven) 520, 984
Polaris II (Mex) 522
Polnochny (Project 771) (Vtn) 990
Polnochny A (Project 770) (Az, Bul, Egy) 43, 93, 220
Polnochny B (Alg, Az, Rus, Syr) 7, 43, 682, 784
Polnochny C (Project 773 I) (Ukr) 852
Polnochny C (Project 773 I) and D (Ind) 345
Poluchat (Project 368) (Vtn) 990
Poluchat 1 (Alg, Egy, Geo) 7, 222, 279
Poluchat I, II and III (Project 364) (Rus) 694
Pomornik (Zubr) (Project 1232.2) (Rus, Ukr) 681, 852
Pondicherry (Natya I) (Ind) 346
Ponza (Ita) 407
Poolster (Pak) 589
Poseidon (Cypr) 188
Post (Can) 110
Pourquoi Pas? (Fra) 267
Powhatan (Tur, US) 843, 956
Pozharny (Project 364) (Rus, Ukr) 855
PR 48 (Sen) 718
PR 72M (Sen) 718
Prabparapak (Tld) 809
Predator (Iraq) 380
Preveze (Type 209/1400) (Tur) 828
Prignitz (Ger) 297
Principe De Asturias (Spn) 742
Priyadarshini (Ind) 351
Priz (Project 1855) (Rus) 689
Project 621 Gawron II (Meko A 100) (Pol) 618
Project 890 (Pol) 624
Project 1398B (Aist) (Ukr) 856
Project 11980 (Rus) 695
Project 18280 (Rus) 688
Project 19910 (Rus) 687
Project 20120 Experimental Submarine (Rus) 662
Project 22460 (Rus) 704
Prometey (Project 498/04983/04985) (Rus) 698
Prometheus (Etna) (Gre) 309
Protecteur (Can) 104
Protector (Bhm, Chi, EIS, NZ, Tan, UAE, Ven) 46, 125, 226, 560, 799, 863, 986
Protector 3612 (Ven) 985
Protector (ASI 315) (HK) 320
Providencia (Col) 175
Province (Omn) 577
Provo Wallis (Can) 107
Prut (Project 527M) (Rus) 697
PS 700 (Lby) 485
Pulau Rengat (Tripartite) (Indo) 363
Punta (Ven) 986
Punta Macolla (Ven) 985
Punta Malpelo (Per) 603

Q

Qahir (Omn) 576
Qiongsha (CPR) 160
Québécois (Can) 111
Queen Elizabeth (UK) 874
Quetzalcoatl (Gearing Fram I) (Mex) 513
Quito (Lürssen 45) (Ecu) 208

R

R (Can) 106
R-2 Mala (Cro, Mon) 181, 527
Rafael Del Castillo Y Rada (Swift 105) (Col) 173
Raidco RPB 18 (Mtn) 511
Raïs Bargach (Mor) 534
Rajput (Kashin II) (Ind) 331
Ramadan (Egy) 218
Ramunia (Bahtera) (Mly) 504
Ratcharit (Tld) 809
Rattanakosin (Tld) 806
Rauma (Fin) 235
Red (Arg) 21
Reliance (Col, Sri, US) 171, 761, 964
Replenishment Tanker (Ind) 348
Reshef (Saar 4) (Isr) 386
Reshitelni (Pauk I) (Project 1241P) (Bul) 91
Rhein (Tur) 840
Rhu (Mly) 504
Al Riffa (FPB 38) (Bhr) 49
Rinker (Ecu) 211
Rio (Col) 174
Río Cañete (Per) 607
Rio Minho (Por) 634
Rio Nepeña (Per) 606
Rio Orinoco II (Ven) 986
Rio Puyango (Ecu) 211
Río Santa (Per) 607
Río Viru (Per) 607
Riquelme (Tiger) (Chi) 121
River (Ban, Brz, Guy, SA, UK) 58, 83, 317, 737, 883
Al Riyadh (Modified La Fayette) (SAr) 710
Robert D Conrad (Chi, Mex, Mor, Tun) 123, 523, 536, 825
Rodman 20 m (Bhr) 52
Rodman 38 (Por, Tun, Zim) 637, 826, 995
Rodman 46 (Cam) 97
Rodman 46HJ (Zim) 995
Rodman 55 Canarias (Spn) 758
Rodman 55HJ (Cypr, Spn) 187, 758
Rodman 55M (Spn, Sur) 758, 768
Rodman 58 (Omn, Spn) 580, 759
Rodman 66 (Spn) 754, 759
Rodman 82 (Spn) 758
Rodman 101 (Nic, Spn, Sur) 563, 758, 767
Rodman 790 (Zim) 995
Rodman 800 (Chi) 126
Roebuck (UK) 889
Roisin (Ire) 382
Romeo (Project 033) (DPRK) 453
Ropucha (Project 775/775M) (Rus) 681
Ropucha I (Project 775) (Ukr) 852
Roraima (Brz) 79
Roslavl (CPR) 165
Rotork (Jor, Mlw) 448, 491
Rotterdam (Nld) 552
Roussen (Super Vita) (Gre) 304
Rover (Indo, Por, UK) 365, 636, 891
Rubin (Project 266) (Vtn) 991
Rubis Améthyste (Fra) 244
Ruposhi Bangla (Ban) 57
Rus (Project 16810) (Rus) 689

S

S 80A (Spn) 740
Saar 4 (Chi, Gre, Isr, Sri) 121, 312, 386, 761
Saar 4.5 (Isr) 385
Sabac (Ser) 721
Sábalo (Type 209/1300) (Ven) 979
Al Saber (UAE) 864
Sachsen (Ger) 287
Saeta-12 (Spn) 759
Saettia (Ita) 412
Safeguard (US) 955
Sagar (T 43) (Ban) 58
Sagardhwani (Ind) 346
Sal (UK) 894
Salisbury (Ban) 54
Salta (Type 209/1200) (Arg) 12
Salvage Lifting Ship (Rus) 695
Sam (Jpn, Swe) 431, 776
Samadikun (Claud Jones) (Indo) 353
Samaesan (Tld) 817
Samar (Ind) 350
Samara (Project 860) (Rus) 685
Sambongho (RoK) 474
Samudra (UT 517) (Ind) 350
Samuel Risley (Can) 107
San Antonio (US) 942
San Giorgio (Ita) 402
San Juan (Plp) 614
Sandhayak (Ind) 346
Sandown (Est, SAr, UK) 229, 715, 888
Sang-O (DPRK) 453
Sankalp (Ind) 350
Santa Cruz (Bol) 68
Santa Cruz (TR 1700) (Arg) 11
Santa María (Spn) 745
Sariwon (DPRK) 454
Sarojini Naidu (Ind) 351
Sapfir (Rus) 684

Sarych (Rus) 670
Sarucabey (Tur) 837
Sassnitz (Ger, Pol) 297, 620
Sattahip (PSMM Mk 5) (Tld) 810
Sav (Den) 196
Sawahil (Kwt) 476, 479
Saygak (Project 1408) (Kaz) 449
Saygak (Project 14081/14081M) (Rus) 706
Schuka (Rus) 659
Schütze (Brz) 82
Schwedeneck (Ger) 292
Schwedt (Ger) 297
Scimitar (UK) 883
Scorpene (Chi, Ind, Mly) 116, 327, 492
Scott (UK) 888
SDB MK 2 Raj (Ind) 351
SDB MK 3 (Ind, Mrt) 344, 511
SDB MK 5 (Bangaram) (Ind) 344
SDB MK 5 (Mld, Sey) 507, 722
Sea Ark 49 ft Cutters (Bhm) 46
Sea Dolphin (Ban, Plp) 56, 611
Sea Dolphin/Wildcat (RoK) 468
Sea Dragon (Ban) 55
Sea Dragon/Whale (RoK) 474
Sea Guard (SAr) 716
Sea Hawk/Killer (Plp) 612
Sea Spectre MK III (Tld) 811
Sea Spectre PB MK III (Egy) 224
Sea Stalker 1500 (HK) 320
Sea Wolf/Shark (RoK) 473
Seaspray (HK) 320
Seawolf (US) 913
Sechelt (Can) 105
Seeb (Vosper 25) (Omn) 578
Segura (Spn) 753
Sejong Daewang (KDX-3) (RoK) 462
Sembilang (Mly) 504
Sentinel (US) 968
Serna (Rus) 682
Serviola (Spn) 748
Sewart (Gua, Iran, Sud) 315, 377, 767
SGT Matej Kocak (US) 961
Al Shaheed (Kwt) 477
Shaheed (Shanghai II) (Type 062) (Ban) 56
Shaldag (Cypr, Isr, Sri) 188, 387, 763
Shang (CPR) 129
Shanghai II (Alb, DPRK, Egy, ETim, Pak, Tan) 2, 204, 219, 455, 590, 799
Shanghai II (Type 062) (Ban, CPR, ConD, Sri) 56, 151, 178, 762
Shanghai III (Type 062/1) (SL) 722
Shapla (River) (Ban) 58
Shark (Sin) 730
Shark Cat 800 (Aust) 40
Shelon I/II (Project 1388/1388M) (Rus) 694
Shengli (CPR) 162
Shershen (Egy) 219
Shershen (Project 206T) (Vtn) 989
Shichang (CPR) 159
Shikinami (Jpn) 444
Shikishima (Jpn) 437
Shimagiri (Jpn) 444
Shimayuki (Jpn) 433
Shirane (Jpn) 425
Shiretoko (Jpn) 439
Shishumar (Type 209/1500) (Ind) 327
Shivalik (Project 17) (Ind) 335
Shmel (Ukr) 856
Shmel (Project 1204) (Rus) 705
Shoyo (Jpn) 445
Shughart (US) 958
Shuguang (CPR) 157
Shupavu (Ken) 450
Shyri (Type 209/1300) (Ecu) 205
Sibarau (Attack) (Indo) 359
Sibiriyakov (Project 865) (Rus) 685
Al Siddiq (SAr) 714
Sidehole I and II (Project 737 K/M) (Rus) 699
Sierra (Mex) 518
Sierra I (Barracuda) (Rus) 657
Sierra II (Kondor) (Rus) 658
Sigma (Indo, Mor) 357, 533
Silas Bent (Tur) 839
Silba (Cro, Mon) 182, 529
Silmä (Est) 230
Silver Ships 48 ft (Az) 44
Simeto (Ita, Tun) 407, 825
Similan (Hudong) (Tld) 815
Simonneau (Sri) 764
Sindhughosh (Kilo) (Project 877EM/8773) (Ind) 326
Singa (PB 57) (Indo) 359
Sinpo (DPRK) 456
Sipadan (Mly) 503
Sir Bedivere (Brz) 82
Sir Galahad (Brz) 81
Sir Wilfred Grenfell (Can) 108
Sirius (Aust, Brz) 38, 83
Sirius (Lyness) (US) 955
Sivuch (Project 1239) (Rus) 676
Sjöormen (Sin) 724
SK 620 (Rus, Ukr) 694, 854
Skat (Rus) 682
Skjold (Nor) 570
Slava (Atlant) (Rus) 666
Slepen (Project 1208) (Rus) 705
Slingsby SAH 2200 (Lby) 485
Sliva (Project 712) (Rus) 698
Smolny (Project 887) (Rus) 689
Snellius (Nld) 554
SO 1 (DPRK) 455
Sobol (Project 12200) (Rus) 703
Socomena (Tun) 826
Södermanland (A 17) (Swe) 769
Soho (DPRK) 453
Soju (DPRK) 455
Sokol (Project 1145) (Rus) 680
Sokól (Kobben) (Type 207) (Pol) 617
Sokzhoi (Rus) 703
Song (CPR) 131
Sonya (Cub) 185
Sonya (Briz) (Bul) 93
Sonya (Yakhont) (Project 1265) (Ukr, Vtn) 852, 991
Sonya (Yakhont) (Project 12650) (Az, Syr) 44, 784
Sonya (Yakhont) (Project 12650/1265M) (Rus) 684
Sorum (Project 745) (Rus, Vtn) 698, 992
Sorum (Project 745P) (Rus) 701
Sotoyomo (Arg, DR) 17, 203
Souryu (Jpn) 415
Souter Wasp 17 metre (TT) 821
South Korean Killer (Sri) 763
Sovremenny (CPR) 135
Sovremenny (Sarych) (Rus) 670
Soya (Jpn) 438
Sparviero (Jpn) 428
Spasilac (Cro, Lby) 184, 486
Spica-M (Mly) 498
Sportis (Pol) 627
Sprut (Project 6457S) (Rus) 701
SSV-10 (Ukr) 855
Stalwart (NZ, Por) 561, 635
STAN patrol 1500 (Mly) 505
Steber (Aust) 40
Stenka (Project 205P) (Az) 44
Stenka (Tarantul) (Cub, Ukr) 186, 855
Stenka (Tarantul) (Project 205P) (Rus) 703
Steregushchiy (Rus) 673
Sterne (Fra) 261
Stingray Interceptor (Isr) 387
Stividor (Project 192) (Rus) 699
Stockholm (Swe) 773
Stolkraft (Vtn) 990
Stollergrund (Ger, Isr) 292, 387
Storm (Est, Lat, Lit, UK) 231, 479, 488, 896
Straznik (Pol) 627
Stromboli (Ita) 406
Styrsö (Swe) 777
Subahi (Kwt) 477
Suffren (Barracuda) (Fra) 243
Sugashima (Jpn) 431
Sukanya (Ind, Sri) 344, 761
Sulisker (UK) 900
Suma (Jpn) 432
Super Dvora (Eri) 227
Super Dvora Mk I (Sri) 763
Super Dvora Mk I and Mk II (Isr) 386
Super Dvora Mk II (Ind, Sri) 343, 763
Super Dvora Mk III (Isr) 385
Super Vita (Gre) 304
Supervittoria 800 (Mlt) 508
Supply (US) 954
Support ship (Alg) 7
Sura (Project 145) (Rus, Ukr) 693, 854
Svetlyak (Project 1041.2) (Vtn) 989
Svetlyak (Project 1041Z) (Rus, Slo) 703, 732
Swallow (RoK) 470, 591
Swallow 65 (Ind) 351
Swari (Dji) 200
Swift (Mlt, Tld) 508, 811
Swift 36 ft (CR) 179
Swift 42 ft (CR) 179
Swift 65 ft (Ant, CR, Dom, Hon, StL) 10, 179, 200, 318, 708
Swift 85 ft (Hon) 318
Swift 105 ft (CR, Hon) 179, 317
Swift 110 (Col) 173
Swift PBR (Cam) 97
Swift type PGM (Myn) 542
Swiftships (Col, Ecu) 173, 210
Swiftships 35m (DR) 202
Swiftships 65 ft (ElS) 225
Swiftships 77 ft (ElS) 225
Swiftships 93 ft (Egy) 223
Swiftships 105 ft (Eri) 228
Swiftships 110 ft (StK) 707
Swiftships 120 ft (StV) 709
Swiftships Protector (Egy) 224
Swiftsure (UK) 867
Sword (TT) 822
Sword (F22P) (Pak) 586

T

T-4 (Project 1785) (Az) 43
T 43 (CPR, Egy) 156, 221
T 43 (Project 254) (Alb) 2
T 81 (Tld) 810
T 91 (Tld) 810
T 213 (Tld) 811
T 227 (Tld) 811
T 991 (Tld) 811
Tachikaze (Jpn) 425
Taechong (DPRK) 456
Al Tahaddy (Kwt) 478
Takanami (Jpn) 421
Takatori (Jpn) 441
Takatsuki (Jpn) 442
Takuyo (Jpn) 446
Talwar (Project 1135.6) (Ind) 334
Tanu (Can) 108
Tapi (PF 103) (Tld) 807
Tapper (Swe) 774
Tara Bai (Ind) 351
Tarantul (Cub, Ukr, Vtn) 186, 855, 988
Tarantul (Project 205P) (Rus) 703
Tarantul (Molnya) (Project 1241.1/1241.1 M/1241.1MP/1242.1) (Rus) 677
Tarantul I (Ind, Rom, Yem) ... 340, 645, 993
Tarantul II (Bul) 91
Tarantul II (Molnya) (Project 1241.1/2) (Ukr) 851
Tarantul V (Vtn) 988
Tarawa (US) 943
Tariq (Amazon) (Pak) 584
Tarlan (Iran) 375
TB 11PA and TB 40A (DPRK) 457
Telkkä (Fin) 241
Tembah (Can) 109
Tenace (Tur) 843
Tenerife (Col) 174
Tenryu (Jpn) 434
Tenyo (Jpn) 446
Tepe (Knox) (Tur) 833
Teraban (Bru) 89
Terrebonne Parish (Per, Tur) 603, 837
Terrier (Project 14170) (Rus) 702
Terry Fox (Can) 106
Teshio (Jpn) 441
Tetal (Rom) 643
Thetis (Den) 189
Thetis (Type 420) (Gre) 307
Thomas G Thompson (US) 950
Thomaston (Brz) 81
Thomson (Type 209/1300) (Chi) 117
Thondor (Houdong) (Iran) 373
Thong Kaeo (Tld) 813
Thorbjørn (Den) 199
Ticonderoga (US) 921
Tiger (Chi, Egy) 121, 217
Tikuna (Brz) 70
Timsah (Egy) 223
Tir (Ind) 347
Tir (IPS 18) (Iran) 375
Tir II (IPS 18) (Syr) 784
Tisza (Indo) 365
Todak (PB 57) (Indo) 358
Todaro (Type 212A) (Ita) 389
Tokara (Jpn) 442
Toledo (Col) 173
Tolmi (Asheville) (Gre) 306
Tolya (Project 696) (Rus) 684
Tomas Batilo (Sea Dolphin) (Plp) 611
Toplivo (Rus) 692
Toplivo 2 (Egy) 222
Toralla (Spn) 749
Tornado (UK) 894
Tourville (Fra) 255
Towada (Jpn) 435
Town (Pak) 587
Trabzon (Tur) 836
Tracker II (Mld, Nam) 507, 545
Tracker Mk 2 (Leb) 482
Tracy (Can) 107
Trafalgar (UK) 868
Tral (DPRK) 454
Trinity Marine (Sri) 764
Tripartite (Bul, Fra, Indo, Lat, Nld) 93, 266, 363, 480, 554
Tritão (Brz) 86
Triton (UK) 895
Trossö (Swe) 778
Tsaplya (Murena E) (Project 12061) (RoK) 470
Tsaplya (Murena) (Project 12061) (Rus) 707
Tsuruugi (Jpn) 442
Tupi (Brz) 71
Turk (Tur) 836
Turk (AB 25) (Az, Kaz) 42, 449
Tursas (Fin) 241
Turya (Project 206M) (Vtn) 989
Tuzhong (CPR) 164
Type 20 Biscaya (Ser) 720
Type 21 (Mon) 529
Type 22 (Mon) 529
Type 42 (UK) 875, 876
Type 44 (Chi, ElS, Guy, Hon, Uru) 125, 225, 317, 318, 976
Type 83 (Egy) 223
Type 123K (Chinese P4) (Ban) 58
Type 206A (Ger) 283
Type 209/1400 MOD (SA) (SA) 734
Type 209PN (Por) 630
Type 212A (Ger) 282
Type 214 (Tur) 829
Type 215 (Bul) 95
Type 246 (Alb) 3
Type 520 (Ger) 291
Type 701 (Par) 597
Type 751 (Ger) 292
Type 1200 (Chi) 122
Type 1496 (Rus) 704
Typhoon (Akula) (Rus) 650
Tzira (Defender) (Isr) 387

U

Uda (Rus) 691
Udaloy (Fregat) (Rus) 669
Udaloy II (Fregat) (Rus) 668
Ula (Nor) 567
Ulsan (RoK) 464
Ulstein UT 507 (Fra) 274
Ulstein UT 512 (Nor) 574
Ulstein UT 512L (Ice) 323
Ulstein UT 515 (Fra) 274
Ulstein UT 704 (Fra) 275
Ulstein UT 710 (Fra) 274
Ulstein UT 711 (Fra) 275
Um Almaradim (Combattante I) (Kwt) 476
Uniform (Kachalot) (Rus) 663
Upholder (Can) 98
Uraga (Jpn) 430
Uribe (Mex) 520
US Mk II (Iran) 375
US Mk III (Iran) 374

V

V 600 Falco (Ita) 411
V 2000 (Ita) 411
V 5000/6000 (Ita) 411
Vai (Dabur) (Fij) 233
Vakta (Can) 110
Valas (Fin) 238
Valle (Auk) (Mex) 520

Valour (SA)....735
Valpas (Lat)....481
Van Speijk (Indo)....354
Van Straelen (Per)....604
Vanguard (UK)....870
Vanya (Project 257D) (Bul)....94
Vapper (Est)....231
Vasco Da Gama (Meko 200 PN) (Por)....631
Västergötland (A 17) (Sin)....723
VCSM (Mor, Sen)....535, 718
VD 141 (Rom)....644
Veer (Tarantul I) (Ind)....340
Vegesack (Tur)....836
Vekhr (Rus, Ukr)....680, 851
Veritas (Chi)....124
Verlarde (PR-72P) (Per)....602
Viana Do Castelo (NPO 2000) (Por)....633
Victor III (Schuka) (Rus)....659
Victoria (Upholder) (Can)....98
Victorious (US)....957
Victory (Sin)....726
Victory Team P 46 (Kwt)....477
Vidar (Lat, Lit)....480, 489
Vigilant (Mrt)....511
Vigilante (Ecu, Gua, Uru)....210, 316, 975
Vigilante (Napa 500) (Brz)....79
Vihuri (Fin)....239
Viima (Est)....230
Vikhr (IVA) (Project B-99) (Az)....44
Vikram (Ind, Sri)....350, 765
Vinograd (Rus)....687
Virginia (US)....912
Visby (Swe)....771
Vishnya (Project 864) (Rus)....688
Vita (Qat)....638
Vittoria (Cypr)....187
Voda (Project 561) (Ukr, Vtn)....853, 992
Vosh (Moskit) (Project 1248) (Rus)....706
Vosper 25 (Omn)....578
Vosper Europatrol 250 Mk 1 (Gre)....312
Vosper Thornycroft 75 ft type (Tan)....800
Votsis (La Combattante IIA) (Type 148) (Gre)....305
VSC 14 (Fra)....276
VTP (Fra)....271
VTS (Den)....194
Vydra (Az, Egy)....43, 220
Vydra (Project 106K) (Bul, Geo)....93, 279
Vytegrales II (Project 596P) (Rus)....690

W

El Wacil (P 32) (Mor)....535
Walchensee (Ger)....294
Walrus (Nld)....547
Wangerooge (Ger, Uru)....296, 975
Warrior (ex-Minister) (SA)....736
Wasp (US)....940
Wasp 11 Metre (Bhr)....52
Wasp 20 Metre (Bhr, TT)....51, 822
Wasp 30 Metre (Bhr)....50
Waspada (Bru)....88
Water (Ecu)....209
Waterman (UK)....894
Waters (US)....957
Watson (US)....959
Wattle (Aust)....39
Wave (UK)....890
Wellington (BH.7) (Iran)....378
Westerwald (Egy, Ger)....222, 294
Whidbey Island (US)....945
White Sumac (DR, Tun)....201, 825
Wielingen (Bul)....90
Wilkes (Tun)....825
Wisloka (Pol)....627
Wochi (CPR)....155
Wodnik (Pol)....624
Wolei (CPR)....155
Won San (RoK)....470
Wosao (Type 082) (CPR)....155
Wozang (CPR)....156
Wu Kang (Twn)....795

X

Xia (CPR)....128

Y

Y 301 (Myn)....542
Yaeyama (Jpn)....431
Yakhont (Project 1265) (Ukr, Vtn)....852, 991
Yamayuri (Com)....177
Yanbing (Mod Yanha) (CPR)....164
Yang Yang (RoK)....471
Yanha (CPR)....164
Yannan (CPR)....163
Yantai (CPR)....161
Yarrow type (Tld)....804
Yasen (Rus)....653
Yavuz (Tur)....831
Yaz (Slepen) (Project 1208) (Rus)....705
Yelva (Krab) (Project 535M) (Rus)....695
Yelva (Project 535M) (Lby, Ukr)....486, 854
Yen Pai (CPR)....163
Yenlai (CPR)....158
Yevgenya (Az, Cub)....43, 186
Yevgenya (Korond) (Project 1258) (Ukr, Vtn)....852, 991
Yevgenya (Project 1258) (Bul, Syr, Yem)....94, 785, 994
YF 2150 (Jpn)....430
Yildiz (Tur)....835
Yodo (Jpn)....443
Yono (IS 120) (Iran)....370
YTL 422 (Tld)....817
Yuan (CPR)....130
Yubei (Type 074A) (CPR)....154
Yuch'in (Ban)....60
Yuch'in (Type 068/069) (CPR)....154
Yuch'in (Type 069) (Tan)....800
Yudao (CPR)....154
Yudeng (Type 073) (CPR)....151
Yug (Project 862) (Rus)....685
Yugo (Vtn)....986
Yugo and P-4 (DPRK)....452
Yuhai (Type 074) (Wuhu-A) (CPR)....154
Yuhai (Wuhu-A) (Type 074) (Sri)....765
Yukan (Type 072) (CPR)....153
Yukto (DPRK)....457
Yuliang (Type 079) (CPR)....153
Yun Hsing (Twn)....799
Yung Feng (MWV 50) (Twn)....794
Yunnan (Cam, CPR, Sri)....97, 154, 766
Yunshu (CPR)....154
Yura (Jpn)....430
Yurka (Egy)....220
Yurka (Rubin) (Project 266) (Vtn)....991
Yusoutei (Jpn)....430
Yuting I (Type 072 II) (CPR)....153
Yuting II (Type 072 III) (CPR)....153
Yuyi (CPR)....155
Yuzhao (Type 071) (CPR)....152
YW (Ecu)....209

Z

Z (Egy)....221
Zborul (Tarantul I) (Rom)....645
Zbyszko (Pol)....625
Zeus (US)....956
Zhuk (Geo)....280
Zhuk (Grif) (Az, Cub, EqG, Ukr)....45, 186, 227, 851, 856
Zhuk (Grif) (Project 1400/1400M) (Rus)....704
Zhuk (Grif) (Project 1400M) (Syr)....784
Zhuk (Project 1400) (Kaz)....449
Zhuk (Project 1400M) (Bul, Sey, Vtn)....92, 721, 989
Zhuk (Type 1400M) (Mrt)....511
Zorritos (Per)....606
Zubr (Gre)....307
Zumwalt (DDG 1000) (US)....928
Zvezdochka (Project 20180) (Rus)....687

Aircraft by countries

Algeria....6
Argentina....16, 24
Australia....31-32
Bahrain....48
Belgium....63
Bolivia....68
Brazil....77-78
Brunei....89
Bulgaria....92
Canada....103
Chile....120
China....147-148
Colombia....171
Croatia....181
Cyprus....186
Denmark....192
Dominican Republic....203
Ecuador....207-208
Egypt....217
Finland....237
France....259-261
Gabon....278
Georgia....279
Germany....290
Greece....304
Hong Kong....322
India....341-343
Indonesia....358
Iran....372
Ireland....382
Israel....385
Italy....399-400
Japan....427-428, 439-440
Korea, South....467
Latvia....481
Libya....484
Malaysia....498
Malta....509
Mauritania....511
Mexico....516-517
Morocco....533
Netherlands....551
New Zealand....560
Norway....570
Oman....577
Pakistan....586-587
Panama....594
Paraguay....597
Peru....602
Philippines....610
Poland....621
Portugal....633
Romania....644
Russian Federation....679-680
Saudi Arabia....713
Senegal....719
Seychelles....721
Singapore....727
South Africa....736
Spain....746-747
Sweden....774
Syria....784
Taiwan....790-791
Thailand....807-808
Turkey....834, 847
Ukraine....851
United Arab Emirates....859
United Kingdom....881-883
United States....933-936, 965-966
Uruguay....975
Venezuela....981
Vietnam....989

Offshore Patrol Vessels
Visby Class Corvettes
K130 Corvettes
MEKO® A-200 SAN Frigates
Class 124 Frigates
Class 209/1400 Submarines
Class 212A Submarines
Class 214 Submarines
Class 125 Frigate
MHD Multirole Helicopter Dockship
MEKO® CSL Corvette

Naval Solutions

ThyssenKrupp Marine Systems' European naval yards in Germany, Greece and Sweden arguably embody the world's most innovative shipbuilding group. Proven vessels ranging from brown water OPVs to state-of-the-art corvettes and blue water MEKO® frigates, from the phenomenally stealthy VISBY to futuristic twin hulled SWATHs are in current operation world wide. Below the sea, ThyssenKrupp Marine Systems' family of low signature, air independent submarines are an impressive demonstration of maritime technological leadership today. Looking ahead, the newly developed Class 125 frigate, the MEKO® CSL and the MHD 150 Multirole Helicopter Dockship are the realistic solutions for forthcoming naval and humanitarian assignments.

www.thyssenkrupp-marinesy

ThyssenKrupp